International
WHO'S WHO in

Classical
MUSIC

2016

International WHO'S WHO in Classical MUSIC

2016

32nd Edition

Routledge
Taylor & Francis Group

LONDON AND NEW YORK

Thirty-second edition published 2016
by Routledge
2 Park Square, Milton Park, Abingdon, Oxon., OX14 4RN, United Kingdom

and by Routledge
711 Third Avenue, New York, NY 10017, USA

www.routledge.com

Routledge is an imprint of the Taylor & Francis Group, an informa business

First published 1935

ISBN: 978-1-85743-816-1
ISSN: 1740-0155

Typeset in Frome by Data Standards Limited

Senior Editor: Robert J. Elster
Editorial Researchers: Shubha Banerjee (Deputy Team Leader), Herina Gangmei (Editorial Researcher), Meer Hussain (Editorial Researcher), Puja Kumari (Editorial Researcher)
Consulting Editors: Gerard Delaney, Annabella Gabb, Sue Leckey, Justin Lewis
Editorial Assistant: Eleanor Simmons
Editorial Director: Paul Kelly

Printed and bound in Great Britain by
TJ International Ltd, Padstow, Cornwall

FOREWORD

The 32nd edition of the INTERNATIONAL WHO'S WHO IN CLASSICAL MUSIC provides biographical information on more than 8,000 prominent people in the fields of classical and light classical music, including composers, instrumentalists, conductors, singers, arrangers, writers and managers. The biographies include information on career, education, repertoire, compositions, recordings, publications and, where available, personal and contact details.

For each edition, entrants are given the opportunity to make necessary amendments and additions to their biographies. Supplementary research is done by the editorial department in order to ensure that the book is as up to date as possible on publication.

In addition to the biographical information, the directory section provides appendices of orchestras, opera companies, festivals, music organizations, and competitions and awards. The names of entrants whose death has been reported over the past year are included in the obituary.

Readers are referred to the book's companion title in The Europa Biographical Reference Series, the INTERNATIONAL WHO'S WHO IN POPULAR MUSIC, for a comprehensive collection of information on the most famous and influential people in the popular music industry.

The biographical information contained in this edition, as well as information on past entrants, deceased entrants and entrants from the wide range of other Europa biographical sources, is provided online in WORLD WHO'S WHO. Using the product's sophisticated search functions, researchers can easily and quickly access the rich biographical data in the comprehensive Europa biographical database. As well, online users can take advantage of the quarterly updating cycle that ensures the data is as current as possible. Details of this resource are available at www.worldwhoswho.com

The assistance of the individuals and organizations included in this publication in providing up-to-date material is invaluable, and the editors would like to take this opportunity to express their appreciation.

March 2016

ALPHABETIZATION AND THE TRANSCRIPTION OF NAMES

The list of names is alphabetical, with the entrants listed under their family name. If part of an entrant's family name is in parentheses, indicating that this part is not usually used, this will be ignored for the purposes of the alphabetical listing.

If an entrant's name is spelt in a variety of ways, a cross-reference is provided. An entrant who is known by a pseudonym or by an abbreviation of their name is either listed under this name or a cross-reference is provided. Multiple pseudonyms are cross-referenced where considered necessary.

Titles as part of a pseudonym, such as DJ, are ignored for the purposes of the alphabetical listing. Pseudonyms that include numbers as part of the name are listed alphabetically under the spelling of that number.

All names beginning Mc and Mac are listed as if they began Mac, e.g. McDevitt before MacDonald.

In the case of surnames beginning De, Des, Du, van or von the entries are normally found under the prefix. Names beginning St are listed as if they began Saint, e.g. St Germain before Salamun.

It should be noted that in some countries (including The People's Republic of China, The Republic of Korea, The Democratic People's Republic of Korea, Cambodia and Viet Nam) the family name is given first, followed by the given name; however, this does not affect alphabetization.

In Indonesia some people have only one name, under which their entries are alphabetized. In Thailand people often have two names, but these do not always equate to Western usage. We alphabetize the entries under the better-known name, providing the full name in the entry and cross-references where considered necessary.

Arabic names have been transliterated from the written form, rather than from pronunciation (which can vary from place to place). However, in Arabic pronunciation, when the word to which the definite article, al, is attached begins with one of certain letters called 'Sun-letters', the l of the article changes to the initial letter in question, e.g. al-shamsu (the sun) is pronounced ash-shamsu. Accordingly, where the article is attached to a name beginning with a Sun-letter, it has been rendered phonetically. Names beginning with 'Moon-letters', however, retain the l of the definite article. Names with Arabic prefixes are alphabetized after the prefix, unless requested otherwise by the entrant.

In a few cases consistency of transliteration has been sacrificed in order to avoid replacing a familiar and accepted form of a name by another which, although more accurate, would be unrecognizable.

CONTENTS

ABBREVIATIONS

AA	Associate in Arts
AAA	Agricultural Adjustment Administration
AAAS	American Association for the Advancement of Science
AAF	Army Air Force
AASA	Associate of the Australian Society of Accountants
AB	Aktiebolag
AB	Alberta
AB	Bachelor of Arts
ABA	American Bar Association
ABC	American Broadcasting Company
ABC	Australian Broadcasting Corporation
ABRSM	Associated Board for the Royal Schools of Music
AC	Companion of the Order of Australia
ACA	American Composers' Alliance
ACA	Associate of the Institute of Chartered Accountants
Acad.	Académie, Academy
Acad.	Académie
Acad.	Academy
ACCA	Associate of the Association of Certified Accountants
Accad.	Accademia
accred	accredited
ACIS	Associate of the Chartered Institute of Secretaries
ACLS	American Council of Learned Societies
ACM	Academy of Country Music
ACP	American College of Physicians
ACS	American Chemical Society
ACT	Australian Capital Territory
ADB	African Development Bank
ADC	Aide-de-camp
Adm.	Admiral
Admin.	Administration, Administrative, Administrator
Admin	Administration
Admin.	Administrative
Admin.	Administrator
AE	Air Efficiency Award
AERE	Atomic Energy Research Establishment
AF	Air Force
AFC	Air Force Cross
affil.	affiliated
AFL	American Federation of Labor
AFM	Air Force Medal
AFofM	American Federation of Musicians
AFTRA	American Federation of Television and Radio Artists
AG	Aktiengesellschaft (Joint Stock Company)
AGMA	American Guild of Musical Artists
Agric.	Agriculture
a.i.	ad interim
AIA	American Institute of Architects, Associate of the Institute of Actuaries
AIA	American Institute of Architects
AIA	Associate of the Institute of Actuaries
AIAA	American Institute of Aeronautics and Astronautics
AIB	Associate of the Institute of Bankers
AICC	All-India Congress Committee
AICE	Associate of the Institute of Civil Engineers
AIChE	American Institute of Chemical Engineers
AIDS	Acquired Immune Deficiency Syndrome
AIEE	American Institute of Electrical Engineers
AIME	American Institute of Mining Engineers, Associate of the Institution of Mining Engineers
AIME	American Institute of Mining Engineers
AIME	Associate of the Institution of Mining Engineers
AIMechE	Associate of the Institution of Mechanical Engineers
AIR	All-India Radio
AK	Alaska
AK	Knight of the Order of Australia
aka	also known as
Akad.	Akademie
AL	Alabama
Ala	Alabama
ALCS	Authors' Lending and Copyright Society
ALS	Associate of the Linnaean Society
Alt.	Alternate
AM	Albert Medal, Alpes Maritimes, Master of Arts, Member of the Order of Australia
AM	Albert Medal
AM	Alpes Maritimes

AM	amplitude modulation
AM	Master of Arts
AM	Member of the Order of Australia
Amb.	Ambassador
AMICE	Associate Member of the Institution of Civil Engineers
AMIEE	Associate Member of the Institution of Electrical Engineers
AMIMechE	Associate Member of the Institution of Mechanical Engineers
ANC	African National Congress
ANU	Australian National University
AO	Officer of the Order of Australia
AP	Andhra Pradesh (India)
Apdo	Apartado (Post Box)
APEC	Asia and Pacific Economic Co-operation
approx.	approximately
appt	appointment
apptd	appointed
APRA	Australian Performing Rights Association
apt	apartment
apto	apartamento
A&R	Artists and Repertoire
AR	Arkansas
ARA	Associate of the Royal Academy
ARAM	Associate of the Royal Academy of Music
ARAS	Associate of the Royal Astronomical Society
ARC	Agriculture Research Council
ARCA	Associate of the Royal College of Art
ARCM	Associate of the Royal College of Music
ARCO	Associate of the Royal College of Organists
ARCS	Associate of the Royal College of Science
ARIBA	Associate of the Royal Institute of British Architects
Ariz.	Arizona
Ark.	Arkansas
ARSA	Associate of the Royal Scottish Academy, Associate of the Royal Society of Arts
ARSA	Associate of the Royal Scottish Academy
ARSA	Associate of the Royal Society of Arts
ASCAP	American Society of Composers, Authors and Publishers
ASEAN	Association of South-East Asian Nations
ASLIB	Association of Special Libraries and Information Bureaux
ASME	American Society of Mechanical Engineers
Asoc.	Asociación
Ass.	Assembly
Asscn	Association
Assoc.	Associate
ASSR	Autonomous Soviet Socialist Republic
Asst	Assistant
ATD	Art Teacher's Diploma
ATV	Associated Television
Aug.	August
autobiog.	autobiography
Avda	Avenida (Avenue)
AZ	Arizona
b.	born
BA	Bachelor of Arts, British Airways
BA	Bachelor of Arts
BA	British Airways
BAAS	British Association for the Advancement of Science
BAC&S	British Academy of Composers and Songwriters
BAFTA	British Academy of Film and Television Arts
BAgr	Bachelor of Agriculture
BAgrSc	Bachelor of Agricultural Science
BAO	Bachelor of Obstetrics
BAOR	British Army of the Rhine
BArch	Bachelor of Architecture
Bart	Baronet
BAS	Bachelor in Agricultural Science
BASc	Bachelor of Applied Science
BASCA	British Association of Songwriters, Composers and Authors (now BAC&S)
BBA	Bachelor of Business Administration
BBC	British Broadcasting Corporation
BC	British Columbia
BCC	British Council of Churches
BCE	Bachelor of Civil Engineering
BChir	Bachelor of Surgery
BCL	Bachelor of Canon Law, Bachelor of Civil Law

ABBREVIATIONS

BCL	Bachelor of Canon Law		CBS	Columbia Broadcasting System
BCL	Bachelor of Civil Law		CBSO	City of Birmingham Symphony Orchestra
BCom	Bachelor of Commerce		CC	Companion of the Order of Canada
BComm	Bachelor of Commerce		CChem	Chartered Chemist
BCS	Bachelor of Commercial Sciences		CCMA	Canadian Country Music Association
BD	Bachelor of Divinity		CCMI	Companion of the Chartered Management Institute
Bd	Board			(formerly CIMgt)
BDS	Bachelor of Dental Surgery		CCP	Chinese Communist Party
Bdwy	Broadway		CD	Canadian Forces Decoration, Commander Order of
BE	Bachelor of Education, Bachelor of Engineering			Distinction
BE	Bachelor of Education		CD	Canadian Forces Decoration
BE	Bachelor of Engineering		CD	Commander Order of Distinction
BEA	British European Airways		CD	compact disc
BEcons	Bachelor of Economics		Cdre	Commodore
BEd	Bachelor of Education		CD-ROM	compact disc read-only memory
Beds.	Bedfordshire		CDU	Christlich-Demokratische Union
BEE	Bachelor of Electrical Engineering		CE	Chartered Engineer, Civil Engineer
BEM	British Empire Medal		CE	Chartered Engineer
BEng	Bachelor of Engineering		CE	Civil Engineer
Berks.	Berkshire		CEAO	Communauté Economique de l'Afrique de l'Ouest
BET	Black Entertainment Television		Cen.	Central
BFA	Bachelor of Fine Arts		CEng	Chartered Engineer
BFI	British Film Institute		CENTO	Central Treaty Organization
BIM	British Institute of Management		CEO	Chief Executive Officer
biog.	biography		CERN	Conseil (now Organisation) Européen(ne) pour la Recherche
BIS	Bank for International Settlements			Nucléaire
BJ	Bachelor of Journalism		CFR	Commander of the Federal Republic of Nigeria
BL	Bachelor of Laws		CGM	Conspicuous Gallantry Medal
BLA	Bachelor of Landscape Architecture		CGT	Confédération Général du Travail
Bldg	Building		CH	Companion of Honour
BLit	Bachelor of Letters		Chair.	Chairman, Chairwoman, Chairperson
BLit	Bachelor of Literature		Chair.	Chairman
BLit(t)	Bachelor of Letters		Chair.	Chairperson
BLitt	Bachelor of Letters		Chair.	Chairwoman
BLitt	Bachelor of Literature		ChB	Bachelor of Surgery
BLL	Bachelor of Laws		CHB	Companion of Honour of Barbados
BLS	Bachelor in Library Science		Chem.	Chemistry
blvd	boulevard		ChM	Master of Surgery
BM	Bachelor of Medicine		CI	Channel Islands
BM	Bachelor of Music		CIA	Central Intelligence Agency
BMA	British Medical Association		Cia	Compagnia, Companhia (Company)
BME	Bachelor of Music Education		Cía	Compañía (Company)
BMEd	Bachelor of Music Education		CID	Criminal Investigation Department
BMI	Broadcast Music Incorporated		Cie	Compagnie (Company)
BMus	Bachelor of Music		CIE	Companion of (the Order of) the Indian Empire
Bn	Battalion		CIEE	Companion of the Institution of Electrical Engineers
BNOC	British National Oil Corporation		CIMgt	Companion of the Institute of Management (now CCMI)
BOAC	British Overseas Airways Corporation		C-in-C	Commander-in-Chief
BP	Boîte Postale (Post Box)		CIO	Congress of Industrial Organizations
BPA	Bachelor of Public Administration		CIOMS	Council of International Organizations of Medical Science
BPharm	Bachelor of Pharmacy		circ.	circulation
BPhil	Bachelor of Philosophy		CIS	Commonwealth of Independent States
Br.	Branch		CLD	Doctor of Civil Law (USA)
Brig.	Brigadier		CLit	Companion of Literature
BS	Bachelor of Science, Bachelor of Surgery		CM	Canada Medal, Master of Surgery
BS	Bachelor of Science		CM	Canada Medal
BS	Bachelor of Surgery		CM	Master of Surgery
BSA	Bachelor of Scientific Agriculture		CMA	Country Music Association
BSc	Bachelor of Science		CMEA	Council for Mutual Economic Assistance
BSE	Bachelor of Science in Engineering (USA)		CMG	Companion of (the Order of) St Michael and St George
BSFA	British Science Fiction Association		CNAA	Council for National Academic Awards
Bt	Baronet		CNRS	Centre National de la Recherche Scientifique
BTh	Bachelor of Theology		CO	Chamber Orchestra
BTI	British Theatre Institute		CO	Colorado
Bucks.	Buckinghamshire		CO	Commanding Officer
			Co.	Company, County
c.	circa		Co.	Company
c.	child(ren)		Co.	County
c/o	care of		COI	Central Office of Information
CA	California		Col	Colonel
CA	Chartered Accountant		Col.	Colonia, Colima (hill)
Calif.	California		Coll.	College
Cambs.	Cambridgeshire		Colo	Colorado
CAMI	Columbia Artists Management International		COMECON	Council for Mutual Economic Assistance
Cand.	Candidate, Candidature		COMESA	Common Market for Eastern and Southern Asia
Cand.	Candidate		Comm.	Commission
Cand.	Candidature		Commdg	Commanding
Cantab.	of Cambridge University		Commdr	Commander, Commandeur
Capt.	Captain		Commdr	Commander
Cards.	Cardiganshire		Commdr	Commandeur
CB	Companion of (the Order of) the Bath		Commdt	Commandant
CBC	Canadian Broadcasting Corporation		Commr	Commissioner
CBE	Commander of (the Order of) the British Empire		CON	Commander of Order of Nigeria
CBI	Confederation of British Industry		Conf.	Conference
CBIM	Companion of the British Institute of Management		Confed.	Confederation
CBiol	Chartered Biologist		Conn.	Connecticut

ABBREVIATIONS

Contrib.	contribution, Contributor
Contrib.	contribution
Contrib.	Contributor
COO	Chief Operating Officer
Corp.	Corporate
Corpn	Corporation
Corresp.	Correspondent, Corresponding
Corresp.	Correspondent
Corresp.	Corresponding
CP	Caixa Postal (Post Box), Communist Party
CP	Caixa Postal, Case Postale, Casella Postale (Post Box)
CP	Communist Party
CPA	Certified Public Accountant
CPA	Commonwealth Parliamentary Association
CPhys	Chartered Physicist
CPP	Convention People's Party (Ghana)
CPPCC	Chinese People's Political Consultative Conference
CPSU	Communist Party of the Soviet Union
cr.	created
CRNCM	Companion of the Royal Northern College of Music
CSc	Candidate of Sciences
CSCE	Conference on Security and Co-operation in Europe
CSI	Companion of (the Order of) the Star of India
CSIRO	Commonwealth Scientific and Industrial Research Organization
CSSR	Czechoslovak Socialist Republic
CStJ	Commander of (the Order of) St John of Jerusalem
CT	Connecticut
Cttee	Committee
CUNY	City University of New York
CV	Commanditaire Vennootschap
CVO	Commander of the Royal Victorian Order
CWA	(British) Crime Writers' Association
d.	daughter(s)
DArch	Doctor of Architecture
DB	Bachelor of Divinity
DBA	Doctor of Business Administration
DBE	Dame Commander of (the Order of) the British Empire
DC	District of Columbia
DC	Distrito Central
DCE	Doctor of Civil Engineering
DCL	Doctor of Canon Law, Doctor of Civil Law
DCL	Doctor of Canon Law
DCL	Doctor of Civil Law
DCM	Distinguished Conduct Medal
DCMG	Dame Commander of (the Order of) St Michael and St George
DCnL	Doctor of Canon Law
DComm	Doctor of Commerce
DCS	Doctor of Commercial Sciences
DCT	Doctor of Christian Theology
DCVO	Dame Commander of the Royal Victorian Order
DD	Doctor of Divinity
Dd'ES	Diplôme d'études supérieures
DDR	Deutsche Demokratische Republik (German Democratic Republic)
DDS	Doctor of Dental Surgery
DE	Delaware
Dec.	December
DEcon	Doctor of Economics
DEd	Doctor of Education
DEFRA	Department for Environment, Food and Rural Affairs
Del.	Delaware, Delegate, Delegation
Del.	Delaware
Del.	Delegate
Del.	Delegation
Denbighs.	Denbighshire
DenD	Docteur en Droit
DEng	Doctor of Engineering
DenM	Docteur en Medicine
Dep.	Deputy
Dept	Department
DES	Department of Education and Science
Desig.	Designate
DèsL	Docteur ès Lettres
DèsSc	Docteur ès Sciences
Devt	Development
DF	Distrito Federal
DFA	Diploma of Fine Arts, Doctor of Fine Arts
DFA	Diploma of Fine Arts
DFA	Doctor of Fine Arts
DFC	Distinguished Flying Cross
DFM	Distinguished Flying Medal
DH	Doctor of Humanities
DHist	Doctor of History
DHL	Doctor of Hebrew Literature

DHSS	Department of Health and Social Security
DHumLitt	Doctor of Humane Letters
DIC	Diploma of Imperial College
DipAD	Diploma in Art and Design
DipAgr	Diploma in Agriculture
DipArch	Diploma in Architecture
DipEd	Diploma in Education
DipEng	Diploma in Engineering
DipMus	Diploma in Music
DipScEconSc	Diploma of Social and Economic Science
DipTh	Diploma in Theology
Dir	Director
Dist	District
DIur	Doctor of Law
DIurUtr	Doctor of both Civil and Canon Law
Div.	Division, Divisional
Div.	Division
Div.	Divisional
DJ	disc jockey
DJur	Doctor of Law
DK	Most Esteemed Family (Malaysia)
DL	Deputy Lieutenant
DLit	Doctor of Letters
DLit	Doctor of Literature
DLit(t)	Doctor of Letters, Doctor of Literature
DLitt	Doctor of Letters
DLitt	Doctor of Literature
DLS	Doctor of Library Science
DM	Doctor of Medicine (Oxford)
DM	Doctor of Music
DMA	Doctor of Musical Arts
DMD	Doctor of Dental Medicine
DME	Doctor of Musical Education
DMEd	Doctor of Musical Education
DMedSc	Doctor of Medical Science
DMilSc	Doctor of Military Science
DMinSci	Doctor of Municipal Science
DMS	Director of Medical Services
DMus	Doctor of Music
DMusEd	Doctor of Music Education
DMV	Doctor of Veterinary Medicine
DN	Distrito Nacional
DO	Doctor of Ophthalmology
DPH	Diploma in Public Health
DPhil	Doctor of Philosophy
DPM	Diploma in Psychological Medicine
DPS	Doctor of Public Service
dpto	departamento
Dr	Doctor
Dr(a)	Doctor(a)
Dr rer. nat	Doctor of Natural Sciences
Dr rer. pol	Doctor of Political Science
DrAgr	Doctor of Agriculture
DrIng	Doctor of Engineering
DrIur	Doctor of Laws
DrMed	Doctor of Medicine
DrOecPol	Doctor of Political Economy
DrOecPubl	Doctor of (Public) Economy
DrPhilNat	Doctor of Natural Philosophy
DrSc	Doctor of Sciences
DrSci	Doctor of Sciences
DrScNat	Doctor of Natural Sciences
DS	Doctor of Science
DSC	Distinguished Service Cross.
DSc	Doctor of Science
DSci	Doctor of Sciences
DScS	Doctor of Social Science
DSM	Distinguished Service Medal
DSO	Companion of the Distinguished Service Order
DSocSc	Doctor of Social Science
DSocSci	Doctor of Social Science
DST	Doctor of Sacred Theology
DTech	Doctor of Technology
DTechSc	Doctor of Technical Sciences
DTechSci	Doctor of Technical Sciences
DTh	Doctor of Theology
DTheol	Doctor of Theology
DTM	Diploma in Tropical Medicine
DTM&H	Diploma in Tropical Medicine and Hygiene
DUniv	Doctor of the University
DUP	Diploma of the University of Paris
DVD	digital versatile disc
E	East, Eastern
EBRD	European Bank for Reconstruction and Development
EC	European Commission, European Community

ABBREVIATIONS

EC	European Commission	FCA	Fellow of the Institute of Chartered Accountants
EC	European Community	FCAE	Fellow of the Canadian Academy of Engineering
ECA	Economic Commission for Africa, Economic Co-operation Administration	FCGI	Fellow of the City and Guilds of London Institute
ECA	Economic Commission for Africa	FCIA	Fellow of the Chartered Institute of Arbitrators
ECA	Economic Co-operation Administration	FCIB	Fellow of the Chartered Institute of Bankers
ECAFE	Economic Commission for Asia and the Far East	FCIC	Fellow of the Chemical Institute of Canada
ECE	Economic Commission for Europe	FCIM	Fellow of the Chartered Institute of Management
ECLA	Economic Commission for Latin America	FCIS	Fellow of the Chartered Institute of Secretaries
ECLAC	Economic Commission for Latin America and the Caribbean	FCMA	Fellow of the Chartered Institute of Management Accountants
ECO	Economic Co-operation Organization	FCO	Foreign and Commonwealth Office
Econ.	Economic	FCSD	Fellow of the Chartered Society of Designers
Econ(s)	Economic(s)	FCT	Federal Capital Territory
Econs	Economics	FCWA	Fellow of the Institute of Cost and Works Accountants (now FCMA)
ECOSOC	Economic and Social Council		
ECSC	European Coal and Steel Community	FDGB	Freier Deutscher Gewerkschaftsbund
ECWA	Economic Commission for Western Asia	FDP	Freier Demokratische Partei
ED	Doctor of Engineering (USA), Efficiency Decoration	Feb.	February
ED	Doctor of Engineering (USA)	Fed.	Federal, Federation
ED	Efficiency Decoration	Fed.	Federal
ed	educated	Fed.	Federation
ed.	edited, editor	FEng	Fellow(ship) of Engineering
ed	edited	FFCM	Fellow of the Faculty of Community Medicine
Ed.	Editor	FFPHM	Fellow of the Faculty of Public Health Medicine
ed.	editor	FGCM	Fellow of the Guild of Church Musicians
EdD	Doctor of Education	FGS	Fellow of the Geological Society
Edif.	Edificio (Building)	FGSM	Fellow of the Guildhall School of Music and Drama
Edin.	Edinburgh	FIA	Fellow of the Institute of Actuaries
EdM	Master of Education	FIAL	Fellow of the International Institute of Arts and Letters
Edn	Edition	FIAM	Fellow of the International Academy of Management
edn	edition	FIAMS	Fellow of the Indian Academy of Medical Sciences
Educ.	Education	FIAP	Fellow of the Institution of Analysts and Programmers
EEC	European Economic Community	FIArb	Fellow of the Institute of Arbitrators
EFTA	European Free Trade Association	FIB	Fellow of the Institute of Bankers
e.g.	exempli gratia (for example)	FIBA	Fellow of the Institute of Banking Associations
eh	Ehrenhalben (Honorary)	FIBiol	Fellow of the Institute of Biologists
EIB	European Investment Bank	FICE	Fellow of the Institution of Civil Engineers
EM	Edward Medal, Master of Engineering (USA)	FIChemE	Fellow of the Institute of Chemical Engineers
EM	Edward Medal	FID	Fellow of the Institute of Directors
EM	Master of Engineering (USA)	FIE	Fellow of the Institute of Engineers
Emer.	Emerita, Emeritus	FIEE	Fellow of the Institution of Electrical Engineers
EMI	Electrical and Musical Industries	FIEEE	Fellow of the Institute of Electrical and Electronics Engineers
Eng	Engineering	FIFA	Fédération Internationale de Football Association
EngD	Doctor of Engineering	FIJ	Fellow of the Institute of Journalists
ENO	English National Opera	FilLic	Licentiate in Philosophy
EP	extended-play (record)	FIM	Fellow of the Institute of Metallurgists
EPLF	Eritrean People's Liberation Front	FIME	Fellow of the Institute of Mining Engineers
ESA	European Space Agency	FIMechE	Fellow of the Institute of Mechanical Engineers
ESCAP	Economic and Social Commission for Asia and the Pacific	FIMI	Fellow of the Institute of the Motor Industry
ESCWA	Economic and Social Commission for Western Asia	FInstF	Fellow of the Institute of Fuel
esq.	esquina (corner)	FInstM	Fellow of the Institute of Marketing
est.	established	FInstP	Fellow of the Institute of Physics
etc.	et cetera	FInstPet	Fellow of the Institute of Petroleum
ETH	Eidgenössische Technische Hochschule (Swiss Federal Institute of Technology)	FIPM	Fellow of the Institute of Personnel Management
		FIRE	Fellow of the Institution of Radio Engineers
Ets	Etablissements	FITD	Fellow of the Institute of Training and Development
EU	European Union	FL	Florida
EURATOM	European Atomic Energy Community	FLA	Fellow of the Library Association
eV	eingetragener Verein	Fla	Florida
Exec.	Executive	FLN	Front de Libération Nationale
Exhbn	Exhibition	FLS	Fellow of the Linnaean Society
Ext.	Extension	FM	frequency modulation
		FMA	Florida Music Association
f.	founded	FMedSci	Fellow of the Academy of Medical Sciences
FAA	Fellow of the Australian Academy of Science	fmr	former
FAAS	Fellow of the American Association for the Advancement of Science	fmrly	formerly
		FNI	Fellow of the National Institute of Sciences of India
FAATS	Fellow of the Australian Academy of Technological Sciences	FNZIA	Fellow of the New Zealand Institute of Architects
FACC	Fellow of the American College of Cardiology	FRACP	Fellow of the Royal Australasian College of Physicians
FACCA	Fellow of the Association of Certified and Corporate Accountants	FRACS	Fellow of the Royal Australasian College of Surgeons
		FRAeS	Fellow of the Royal Aeronautical Society
FACE	Fellow of the Australian College of Education	FRAI	Fellow of the Royal Anthropological Institute
FACP	Fellow of the American College of Physicians	FRAIA	Fellow of the Royal Australian Institute of Architects
FACS	Fellow of the American College of Surgeons	FRAIC	Fellow of the Royal Architectural Institute of Canada
FAHA	Fellow of the Australian Academy of the Humanities	FRAM	Fellow of the Royal Academy of Music
FAIA	Fellow of the American Institute of Architects	FRAS	Fellow of the Royal Asiatic Society, Fellow of the Royal Astronomical Society
FAIAS	Fellow of the Australian Institute of Agricultural Science		
FAIM	Fellow of the Australian Institute of Management	FRAS	Fellow of the Royal Asiatic Society
FAO	Food and Agriculture Organization	FRAS	Fellow of the Royal Astronomical Society
FAS	Fellow of the Antiquarian Society	FRBS	Fellow of the Royal Society of British Sculptors
FASE	Fellow of the Antiquarian Society of Edinburgh	FRCA	Fellow of the Royal College of Anaesthetists
FASSA	Fellow of the Academy of Social Sciences of Australia	FRCM	Fellow of the Royal College of Music
FBA	Fellow of the British Academy	FRCO	Fellow of the Royal College of Organists
FBI	Federal Bureau of Investigation	FRCOG	Fellow of the Royal College of Obstetricians and Gynaecologists
FBIM	Fellow of the British Institute of Management		
FBIP	Fellow of the British Institute of Physics	FRCP	Fellow of the Royal College of Physicians (UK)

ABBREVIATIONS

FRCPath	Fellow of the Royal College of Pathologists		HE	His (or Her) Excellency
FRCP(E)	Fellow of the Royal College of Physicians (Edinburgh)		Herefords.	Herefordshire
FRCPE	Fellow of the Royal College of Physicians, Edinburgh		Herts.	Hertfordshire
FRCPGlas	Fellow of the Royal College of Physicians (Glasgow)		HH	His (or Her) Highness
FRCPI	Fellow of the Royal College of Physicians of Ireland		HHD	Doctor of Humanities
FRCR	Fellow of the Royal College of Radiology		HI	Hawaii
FRCS	Fellow of the Royal College of Surgeons		HIV	human immunodeficiency virus
FRCS(E)	Fellow of the Royal College of Surgeons (Edinburgh)		HLD	Doctor of Humane Letters
FRCSE	Fellow of the Royal College of Surgeons, Edinburgh		HM	His (or Her) Majesty
FRCVS	Fellow of the Royal College of Veterinary Surgeons		HMS	His (or Her) Majesty's Ship
FREconS	Fellow of the Royal Economic Society		Hon.	Honorary, Honourable
FREng	Fellow of the Royal Academy of Engineering		Hon.	Honorary
FRES	Fellow of the Royal Entomological Society		Hon.	Honourable
FRFPS	Fellow of the Royal Faculty of Physicians and Surgeons		Hons	Honours
FRG	Federal Republic of Germany		Hosp.	Hospital
FRGS	Fellow of the Royal Geographical Society		HQ	Headquarters
FRHistS	Fellow of the Royal Historical Society		HRH	His (or Her) Royal Highness
FRHortS	Fellow of the Royal Horticultural Society		HS	Heraldry Society
FRIBA	Fellow of the Royal Institute of British Architects		HSH	His (or Her) Serene Highness
FRIC	Fellow of the Royal Institute of Chemists		HSP	Hungarian Socialist Party
FRICS	Fellow of the Royal Institute of Chartered Surveyors		HSWP	Hungarian Socialist Workers' Party
FRMetS	Fellow of the Royal Meteorological Society		Hunts.	Huntingdonshire
FRNCM	Fellow of the Royal Northern College of Music			
FRPS	Fellow of the Royal Photographic Society		IA	Iowa
FRS	Fellow of the Royal Society		Ia	Iowa
FRSA	Fellow of the Royal Society of Arts		IAAF	International Association of Athletics Federations
FRSAMD	Fellow of the Royal Scottish Academy of Music and Drama		IAEA	International Atomic Energy Agency
FRSC	Fellow of the Royal Society of Canada, Fellow of the Royal Society of Chemistry		IATA	International Air Transport Association
			IBA	Independent Broadcasting Authority
FRSC	Fellow of the Royal Society of Canada		IBRD	International Bank for Reconstruction and Development (World Bank)
FRSC	Fellow of the Royal Society of Chemistry			
FRSE	Fellow of the Royal Society of Edinburgh		ICAO	International Civil Aviation Organization
FRSL	Fellow of the Royal Society of Literature		ICC	International Chamber of Commerce
FRSM	Fellow of the Royal Society of Medicine		ICE	Institution of Civil Engineers
FRSNZ	Fellow of the Royal Society of New Zealand		ICEM	Intergovernmental Committee for European Migration
FRSS	Fellow of the Royal Statistical Society		ICFTU	International Confederation of Free Trade Unions
FRSSA	Fellow of the Royal Society of South Africa		ICI	Imperial Chemical Industries
FRTS	Fellow of the Royal Television Society		ICOM	International Council of Museums
FSA	Fellow of the Society of Antiquaries		ICRC	International Committee for the Red Cross
FSIAD	Fellow of the Society of Industrial Artists and Designers		ICS	Indian Civil Service
FTCL	Fellow of Trinity College London		ICSID	International Centre for Settlement of Investment Disputes
FTI	Fellow of the Textile Institute		ICSU	International Council of Scientific Unions
FTS	Fellow of Technological Sciences		ID	Idaho
FWAAS	Fellow of the World Academy of Arts and Sciences		Ida	Idaho
FZS	Fellow of the Zoological Society		IDA	International Development Association
			IDB	Inter-American Development Bank
GA	Georgia		i.e.	id est (that is to say)
Ga	Georgia		IEA	International Energy Agency
GATT	General Agreement on Tariffs and Trade		IEE	Institution of Electrical Engineers
GB	Great Britain		IEEE	Institution of Electrical and Electronic Engineers
GBE	Knight (or Dame) Grand Cross of (the Order of) the British Empire		IFAD	International Fund for Agricultural Development
			IFC	International Finance Corporation
GC	George Cross		IGAD	Intergovernmental Authority on Development
GCB	Knight Grand Cross of (the Order of) the Bath		IISS	International Institute for Strategic Studies
GCIE	Knight Grand Commander of (the Order of) the Indian Empire		IL	Illinois
			Ill.	Illinois
GCMG	Knight (or Dame) Grand Cross of (the Order of) St Michael and St George		ILO	International Labour Organization
			IMC	International Music Council
GCSI	Knight Grand Commander of (the Order of) the Star of India		IMCO	Inter-Governmental Maritime Consultative Organization
GCVO	Knight (or Dame) Grand Cross of the Royal Victorian Order		IMechE	Institution of Mechanical Engineers
GDR	German Democratic Republic		IMF	International Monetary Fund
Gen.	General		IMMIE	Indian Music Excellence (award)
GHQ	General Headquarters		IMO	International Maritime Organization
GLA	Greater London Authority		IN	Indiana
Glam.	Glamorganshire		Inc.	Incorporated
GLC	Greater London Council		incl.	including
Glos.	Gloucestershire		Ind.	Independent, Indiana
GM	George Medal		Ind.	Independent
GmbH	Gesellschaft mit beschränkter Haftung (Limited Liability Company)		Ind.	Indiana
			Insp.	Inspector
GMT	Greenwich Mean Time		Inst.	Institute, Institution
GOC	General Officer Commanding		Inst.	Institute
GOC-in-C	General Officer Commanding-in-Chief		Inst.	Institution
Gov.	Governor		Int.	International
Govt	Government		INTERPOL	International Criminal Police Organization
GP	General Practitioner		INTUC	Indian National Trades Union Congress
GPO	General Post Office		IOC	International Olympic Committee
Grad.	Graduate		IPC	Institute of Professional Critics
GRSM	Graduate of the Royal School of Music		IPU	Inter-Parliamentary Union
GSMD	Guildhall School of Music and Drama, London		IRCAM	Institut de Recherche et Coordination Acoustique/Musique
GSO	General Staff Officer		ISCM	International Society for Contemporary Music
			ISM	Incorporated Society of Musicians
Hants.	Hampshire		ISO	Companion of the Imperial Service Order
hc	honoris causa		ITA	Independent Television Authority
HE	His Eminence, His (or Her) Excellency		ITN	Independent Television News
HE	His Eminence		ITU	International Telecommunications Union

ABBREVIATIONS

ITV	Independent Television		Ltd(a)	Limited, Limitada
IUPAC	International Union of Pure and Applied Chemistry		Ltda	Limitada
IUPAP	International Union of Pure and Applied Physics		LTh	Licentiate in Theology
			LVO	Lieutenant, Royal Victorian Order
Jan.	January		LW	long wave
JCB	Bachelor of Canon Law		LWT	London Weekend Television
JCD	Doctor of Canon Law			
JD	Doctor of Jurisprudence			
JMK	Johan Mangku Negara (Malaysia)		m.	marriage, married, metre(s)
JP	Justice of the Peace		m.	marriage
Jr	Junior		m.	married
JSD	Doctor of Juristic Science		m.	metre(s)
Jt	Joint		MA	Massachusetts
Jtly	Jointly		MA	Master of Arts
JuD	Doctor of Law		MAgr	Master of Agriculture (USA)
JUD	Juris utriusque Doctor (Doctor of both Civil and Canon Law)		Maj.	Major
JUDr	Juris utriusque Doctor (Doctor of both Civil and Canon Law), Doctor of Law		MALD	Master of Arts in Law and Diplomacy
			Man.	Management, Manager, Managing, Manitoba
			Man.	Management
Kan.	Kansas		Man.	Manager
KBE	Knight Commander of (the Order of) the British Empire		Man.	Managing
KC	King's Counsel		Man.	Manitoba
KCB	Knight Commander of (the Order of) the Bath		MArch	Master of Architecture
KCIE	Knight Commander of (the Order of) the Indian Empire		Mass	Massachusetts
KCMG	Knight Commander of (the Order of) St Michael and St George		MAT	Master of Arts and Teaching
			Math.	Mathematical, Mathematics
KCSI	Knight Commander of (the Order of) the Star of India		Math.	Mathematical
KCVO	Knight Commander of the Royal Victorian Order		Math.	Mathematics
KG	Royal Knight of the Most Noble Order of the Garter		MB	Bachelor of Medicine
KGB	Committee of State Security (USSR)		MB	Manitoba
KK	Kaien Kaisha		MBA	Master of Business Administration
KLM	Koninklijke Luchtvaart Maatschappij (Royal Dutch Airlines)		MBE	Member of (the Order of) the British Empire
km	kilometre(s)		MBS	Master of Business Studies
KNZM	Knight of the New Zealand Order of Merit		MC	master of ceremonies
KP	Knight of (the Order of) St Patrick		MC	Military Cross
KS	Kansas		MCC	Marylebone Cricket Club
KStJ	Knight of (the Order of) St John of Jerusalem		MCE	Master of Civil Engineering
Kt	Knight		MCh	Master of Surgery
KT	Knight of (the Order of) the Thistle		MChD	Master of Dental Surgery
KY	Kentucky		MCL	Master of Civil Law
Ky	Kentucky		MCom	Master of Commerce
			MComm	Master of Commerce
LA	Los Angeles		MCP	Master of City Planning
LA	Louisiana		MD	Doctor of Medicine
La.	Louisiana		MD	Maryland
Lab.	Laboratory		Md	Maryland
LAMDA	London Academy of Music and Dramatic Art		MD	Music Director
Lancs.	Lancashire		MDiv	Master of Divinity
LDP	Liberal Democratic Party		MDS	Master of Dental Surgery
LDS	Licentiate in Dental Surgery		Me	Maine
LEA	Local Education Authority		ME	Maine
Legis.	Legislative		ME	Myalgic Encephalomyehtis
Leics.	Leicestershire		MEconSc	Master of Economic Sciences
LenD	Licencié en Droit		MEd	Master of Education
LèsL	Licencié ès Lettres		mem.	member
LèsSc	Licencié ès Sciences		MEng	Master of Engineering (Dublin)
LG	Lady of (the Order of) the Garter		MEngSc	Master of Engineering
LHD	Doctor of Humane Letters		MEP	Member of European Parliament
LI	Long Island		Met	Metropolitan Opera House, New York
LicenDer	Licenciado en Derecho		MFA	Master of Fine Arts
LicenFil	Licenciado en Filosofia		Mfg	Manufacturing
LicenLet	Licenciado en Letras		Mfrs	Manufacturers
LicMed	Licentiate in Medicine		Mgr	Monseigneur, Monsignor
Lincs.	Lincolnshire		Mgr	Monseigneur
LittD	Doctor of Letters		Mgr	Monsignor
LLB	Bachelor of Laws		MHRA	Modern Humanities Research Association
LLC	Limited Liability Company		MHz	megahertz (megacycles)
LLD	Doctor of Laws		MI	Marshall Islands
LLL	Licentiate of Laws		MI	Michigan
LLM	Master of Laws		MIA	Master of International Affairs
LLP	Limited Liability Partnership		MICE	Member of the Institution of Civil Engineers
LM	Licentiate of Medicine, Licentiate of Midwifery		Mich.	Michigan
LM	Licentiate of Medicine		MIChemE	Member of the Institution of Chemical Engineers
LM	Licentiate of Midwifery		Middx	Middlesex
LN	League of Nations		MIDI	Musical Instrument Digital Interface
LP	long-playing (record)		MIEE	Member of the Institution of Electrical Engineers
LPh	Licentiate of Philosophy		Mil.	Military
LPO	London Philharmonic Orchestra		MIMarE	Member of the Institute of Marine Engineers
LRAM	Licentiate of the Royal Academy of Music		MIMechE	Member of the Institution of Mechanical Engineers
LRCP	Licentiate of the Royal College of Physicians		MIMinE	Member of the Institution of Mining Engineers
LRSM	Licentiate of the Royal Schools of Music		Minn.	Minnesota
LSE	London School of Economics and Political Science		MInstT	Member of the Institute of Transport
LSO	London Symphony Orchestra		Miss.	Mississippi
Lt	Lieutenant		MIStructE	Member of the Institution of Structural Engineers
LTCL	Licentiate of Trinity College of Music, London		MIT	Massachusetts Institute of Technology
Ltd	Limited		MJ	Master of Jurisprudence

MLA	Master of Landscape Architecture, Member of the Legislative Assembly	NE	North East
		NEA	National Endowment for the Arts
MLA	Master of Landscape Architecture	Neb.	Nebraska
MLA	Member of the Legislative Assembly	NEDC	National Economic Development Council
MLA	Modern Language Association	NEH	National Endowment for the Humanities
MLC	Member of the Legislative Council	NERC	Natural Environment Research Council
MLitt	Master of Letters	Nev.	Nevada
MLitt	Master of Literature	NF	Newfoundland
MLS	Master of Library Science	NFSPS	National Federation of State Poetry Societies
MM	Master of Music	NGO	non-governmental organization
MM	Military Medal	NH	New Hampshire
MME	Master of Music Education	NHK	Nippon Hoso Kyokai (Japanese broadcasting system)
MMEd	Master of Music Education	NHS	National Health Service
MMus	Master of Music	NI	Northern Ireland
MN	Minnesota	NIH	National Institutes of Health
MNOC	Movement of Non-Aligned Countries	NJ	New Jersey
MO	Missouri	NL	Newfoundland and Labrador
Mo.	Missouri	NM	New Mexico
MOBO	Music of Black Origin	NME	New Musical Express
MOH	Medical Officer of Health	no.	number
Mon.	Monmouthshire	Northants.	Northamptonshire
Mont.	Montana	Notts.	Nottinghamshire
Movt	Movement	Nov.	November
MP	Madhya Pradesh (India), Member of Parliament	NPC	National People's Congress
MP	Madhya Pradesh (India)	nr	near
MP	Member of Parliament	NRC	Nuclear Research Council
MP3	MPEG-1 Audio Layer-3 (audio compression format)	NRK	Norsk Rikskringkasting (Norwegian broadcasting system)
MPA	Master of Public Administration (Harvard)	NS	Nova Scotia
MPEG	Moving Picture Experts Group	NSAI	Nashville Songwriters' Association International
MPh	Master of Philosophy (USA)	NSF	National Science Foundation
MPhil	Master of Philosophy	NSW	New South Wales
MPolSci	Master of Political Science	NT	Northern Territory
MPP	Member of Provincial Parliament (Canada)	NT	Northwest Territories
MRAS	Member of the Royal Asiatic Society	NU	Nunavut Territory
MRC	Medical Research Council	NUJ	National Union of Journalists
MRCP	Member of the Royal College of Physicians	NV	Naamloze Vennootschap
MRCP(E)	Member of the Royal College of Physicians (Edinburgh)	NV	Nevada
MRCPE	Member of the Royal College of Physicians, Edinburgh	NW	North West
MRCS	Member of the Royal College of Surgeons of England	NWT	North West Territories
MRCSE	Member of the Royal College of Surgeons, Edinburgh	NY	New York (State)
MRCVS	Member of the Royal College of Veterinary Surgeons	NYPO	New York Philharmonic Orchestra
MRI	Member of the Royal Institution	NYSO	New York Symphony Orchestra
MRIA	Member of the Royal Irish Academy	NZ	New Zealand
MRIC	Member of the Royal Institute of Chemistry	NZIC	New Zealand Institute of Chemistry
MRP	Mouvement Républicain Populaire	NZSA	New Zealand Society of Authors
MS	manuscript		
MS	Master of Science, Master of Surgery	O	Ohio
MS	Master of Science	OAPEC	Organization of Arab Petroleum Exporting Countries
MS	Master of Surgery	OAS	Organization of American States
MS	Mississippi	OAU	Organization of African Unity
MSA	Memphis Songwriters' Association	OBE	Officer of (the Order of) the British Empire
MSc	Master of Science	OC	Officer of the Order of Canada
MScS	Master of Social Science	Oct.	October
MSO	Melbourne Symphony Orchestra	OE	Order of Excellence (Guyana)
MSP	Member Scottish Parliament	OECD	Organisation for Economic Co-operation and Development
MT	Montana	OEEC	Organization for European Economic Co-operation
MTh	Master of Theology	Of.	Oficina (Office)
MTS	Master of Theological Studies	OFS	Orange Free State
MTV	Music Television	OH	Ohio
MUDr	Doctor of Medicine	OHCHR	Office of the United Nations High Commissioner for Human Rights
MusB	Bachelor of Music		
MusBac	Bachelor of Music	OIC	Organization of the Islamic Conference
MusD	Doctor of Music	OJ	Order of Jamaica
MusDoc	Doctor of Music	OK	Oklahoma
MusM	Master of Music (Cambridge)	Okla	Oklahoma
MVD	Master of Veterinary Medicine	OM	Member of the Order of Merit
MVO	Member of the Royal Victorian Order	ON	Ontario
MW	Master of Wine	ON	Order of Nigeria
MW	medium wave	Ont.	Ontario
MWA	Mystery Writers of America	ONZ	Order of New Zealand
		ONZM	Officer of the New Zealand Order of Merit
N	North, Northern	OP	Ordo Praedicatorum (Dominicans)
NABOB	National Association of Black-Owned Broadcasters	OPCW	Organization for the Prohibition of Chemical Weapons
NARAS	National Academy of Recording Arts and Sciences	OPEC	Organization of the Petroleum Exporting Countries
NAS	National Academy of Sciences (USA)	OPM	Office of Production Management
NAS	National Academy of Songwriters	OQ	Officer National Order of Québec
NASA	National Aeronautics and Space Administration	OR	Oregon
Nat.	National	Ore.	Oregon
NATO	North Atlantic Treaty Organization	Org.	Organization
Naz.	Nazionale	ORTF	Office de Radiodiffusion-Télévision Française
NB	New Brunswick	OSB	Order of St Benedict
NBC	National Broadcasting Company	OSCE	Organization for Security and Co-operation in Europe
NC	North Carolina	OST	original soundtrack
ND	North Dakota	Oxon.	of Oxford University, Oxfordshire
NDD	National Diploma in Design	Oxon.	of Oxford University
NE	Nebraska	Oxon.	Oxfordshire

PA	Pennsylvania		q.v.	quod vide (to which refer)
Pa	Pennsylvania			
Parl.	Parliament, Parliamentary		RA	Royal Academician, Royal Academy, Royal Artillery
Parl.	Parliament		RA	Royal Academician
Parl.	Parliamentary		RA	Royal Academy
PBS	Public Broadcasting Service		RA	Royal Artillery
PC	Privy Councillor		RAAF	Royal Australian Air Force
PCC	Provincial Congress Committee		RAC	Royal Armoured Corps
PdB	Bachelor of Pedagogy		RACP	Royal Australasian College of Physicians
PdD	Doctor of Pedagogy		RADA	Royal Academy of Dramatic Art
PdM	Master of Pedagogy		RAF	Royal Air Force
PDS	Partei des Demokratischen Sozialismus		RAFVR	Royal Air Force Volunteer Reserve
PE	Prince Edward Island		RAH	Royal Albert Hall, London
PEI	Prince Edward Island		RAI	Radio Audizioni Italiane
Pembs.	Pembrokeshire		RAM	Royal Academy of Music
PEN	Poets, Playwrights, Essayists, Editors and Novelists (Club)		RAMC	Royal Army Medical Corps
Perm.	Permanent		RAOC	Royal Army Ordnance Corps
PETA	People for the Ethical Treatment of Animals		R&B	Rhythm and Blues
PF	Postfach (Post Box)		RC	Roman Catholic
PGCE	Postgraduate Certificate of Education		RCA	Radio Corporation of America, Royal Canadian Academy, Royal College of Art
PharmD	Docteur en Pharmacie		RCA	Radio Corporation of America
PhB	Bachelor of Philosophy		RCA	Royal Canadian Academy
PhD	Doctor of Philosophy		RCA	Royal College of Art
PhDr	Doctor of Philosophy		RCAF	Royal Canadian Air Force
Phila	Philadelphia		RCM	Royal College of Music
PhL	Licentiate of Philosophy		RCO	Royal College of Organists
PLA	People's Liberation Army, Port of London Authority		RCP	Romanian Communist Party
PLA	People's Liberation Army		RCP	Royal College of Physicians
PLA	Port of London Authority		RCPI	Royal College of Physicians of Ireland
PLC	Public Limited Company		Regt	Regiment
PLO	Palestine Liberation Organization		REME	Royal Electric and Mechanical Engineers
PMB	Private Mail Bag		Rep.	Representative, Represented
pnr	partner		Rep.	Representative
PO	Philharmonia Orchestra		Rep.	Represented
PO	Post Office		Repub.	Republic
PO Box	Post Office Box		resgnd	resigned
POB	Post Office Box		retd	retired
POW	Prisoner of War		Rev.	Reverend
PPR	Polish Workers' Party		rev. edn	revised edition
PPRA	Past President of the Royal Academy		RFH	Royal Festival Hall, London
PPRNCM	Professsional Performer of the Royal Northern College of Music		RGS	Royal Geographical Society
PQ	Province of Québec		RI	Rhode Island
PR	Puerto Rico		RIAS	Radio im Amerikanischen Sektor
PR(O)	Public Relations (Officer)		RIBA	Royal Institute of British Architects
PRA	President of the Royal Academy		RLPO	Royal Liverpool Philharmonic Orchestra
Pref.	Prefecture		RMA	Royal Military Academy
Prep.	Preparatory		RMA	Royal Musical Association
Pres.	President		RN	Royal Navy
PRI	President of the Royal Institute (of Painters in Water Colours)		RNCM	Royal Northern College of Music (formerly Royal Manchester College of Music)
PRIBA	President of the Royal Institute of British Architects		RNLI	Royal National Life-boat Institution
Prin.	Principal		RNR	Royal Naval Reserve
Priv Doz	Privat Dozent (recognized teacher not on the regular staff)		RNVR	Royal Naval Volunteer Reserve
PRO	Public Relations Officer		RNZAF	Royal New Zealand Air Force
Proc.	Proceedings		RO	Radio Orchestra
Prod.	Producer		ROC	Rock Out Censorship
Prof.	Professor		ROH	Royal Opera House, London
promo	promotional		RP	Member Royal Society of Portrait Painters
Propr	Proprietor		rpm	revolutions per minute
Prov.	Province, Provincial		RPO	Royal Philharmonic Orchestra
Prov.	Province		RPR	Rassemblement pour la République
Prov.	Provincial		RSA	Royal Scottish Academy, Royal Society of Arts
PRS	Performing Right Society		RSA	Royal Scottish Academy
PRS	President of the Royal Society		RSA	Royal Society of Arts
PRSA	President of the Royal Scottish Academy		RSAMD	Royal Scottish Academy of Music and Drama
PSM	Panglima Setia Mahkota (Malaysia)		RSC	Royal Shakespeare Company, Royal Society of Canada
pt	part		RSC	Royal Shakespeare Company
Pty	Proprietary		RSC	Royal Society of Canada
Publ.	Publication		RSDr	Doctor of Social Sciences
publ.	publication		RSFSR	Russian Soviet Federative Socialist Republic
Publr	Publisher		RSL	Royal Society of Literature
Publ(s)	Publication(s)		RSNO	Royal Scottish National Orchestra (formerly SNO)
Publs	Publications		RSO	Radio Symphony Orchestra
publs	publications		RSPB	Royal Society for Protection of Birds
Pvt.	Private		Rt Hon.	Right Honourable
PZPR	Polish United Workers' Party		Rt Rev.	Right Reverend
			RTÉ	Radio Telefís Éireann
QC	Province of Québec		RTF	Radiodiffusion-Télévision Française
QC	Queen's Counsel		RTS	Royal Television Society
QEH	Queen Elizabeth Hall, London		RVO	Royal Victorian Order
QGM	Queen's Gallantry Medal		RWS	Royal Society of Painters in Water Colours
Qld	Queensland			
QPM	Queen's Police Medal		S	South, Southern
QSO	Queen's Service Order		S.	San
QSO	Queensland Symphony Orchestra		s.	son(s)

ABBREVIATIONS

SA	Sociedad Anónima, Société Anonyme, South Africa	ThB	Bachelor of Theology
SA	Sociedad Anónima (Limited Company)	ThD	Doctor of Theology
SA	Société Anonyme (Limited Company)	THDr	Doctor of Theology
SA	South Africa	ThM	Master of Theology
SA	South Australia	TLS	Times Literary Supplement
SAARC	South Asian Association for Regional Co-operation	TN	Tennessee
SACEM	Société d'Auteurs, Compositeurs et Editeurs de Musique	trans.	translated
SADC	South African Development Community	Trans.	Translation, translator
SAE	Society of Aeronautical Engineers	Trans.	Translation
SAG	Screen Actors' Guild	Trans.	translator
Salop.	Shropshire	Treas.	Treasurer
SALT	Strategic Arms Limitation Treaty	TU(C)	Trades Union (Congress)
Sask.	Saskatchewan	TV	television
SATB	soprano, alto, tenor, bass	TX	Texas
SB	Bachelor of Science (USA)		
SC	Senior Counsel	u.	utca (street)
SC	South Carolina	UAE	United Arab Emirates
SCAP	Supreme Command Allied Powers	UAR	United Arab Republic
ScB	Bachelor of Science	UCLA	University of California at Los Angeles
ScD	Doctor of Science	UDEAC	L'Union Douanière et Economique de l'Afrique Centrale
SD	South Dakota	UDR	Union des Démocrates pour la République
SDak	South Dakota	UED	University Education Diploma
SDLP	Social and Democratic Liberal Party	UHF	ultra-high frequency
SDP	Social Democratic Party	UK	United Kingdom (of Great Britain and Northern Ireland)
SE	South East	UKAEA	United Kingdom Atomic Energy Authority
SEATO	South East Asia Treaty Organization	ul.	ulitsa (street)
SEC	Securities and Exchange Commission	UMIST	University of Manchester Institute of Science and Technology
Sec.	Secretary	UMNO	United Malays National Organization
Secr.	Secretariat	UN(O)	United Nations (Organization)
SED	Sozialistische Einheitspartei Deutschlands (Socialist Unity Party of the German Democratic Republic)	UNA	United Nations Association
		UNCED	United Nations Council for Education and Development
Sept.	September	UNCHS	United Nations Centre for Human Settlements (Habitat)
S-et-O	Seine-et-Oise	UNCTAD	United Nations Conference on Trade and Development
SFWA	Science Fiction and Fantasy Writers of America	UNDCP	United Nations International Drug Control Programme
SGA	Songwriters' Guild of America	UNDP	United Nations Development Programme
SHAEF	Supreme Headquarters Allied Expeditionary Force	UNDRO	United Nations Disaster Relief Office
SHAPE	Supreme Headquarters Allied Powers in Europe	UNEF	United Nations Emergency Force
SJ	Society of Jesus (Jesuits)	UNEP	United Nations Environment Programme
SJD	Doctor of Juristic Science	UNESCO	United Nations Educational, Scientific and Cultural Organization
SK	Saskatchewan		
SL	Sociedad Limitada	UNFPA	United Nations Population Fund
SLD	Social and Liberal Democrats	UNHCR	United Nations High Commissioner for Refugees
SM	Master of Science	UNICEF	United Nations International Children's Emergency Fund
SO	Symphony Orchestra	UNIDO	United Nations Industrial Development Organization
SOAS	School of Oriental and African Studies	UNIFEM	United Nations Development Fund for Women
Soc.	Société, Society	UNITAR	United Nations Institute for Training and Research
Soc.	Société	Univ.	University
Soc.	Society	UNKRA	United Nations Korean Relief Administration
SOCAN	Society of Composers, Authors and Music Publishers of Canada	UNRRA	United Nations Relief and Rehabilitation Administration
		UNRWA	United Nations Relief and Works Agency
SOSA	State Opera of South Australia	UNU	United Nations University
SpA	Società per Azioni	UP	United Provinces, Uttar Pradesh (India)
SPD	Sozialdemokratische Partei Deutschlands	UP	United Provinces
SPNM	Society for the Promotion of New Music	UP	Uttar Pradesh (India)
Sr	Senior	UPU	Universal Postal Union
SRC	Science Research Council	Urb.	Urbanización (urban district)
Srl	Società a responsabilità	US	United States
SSM	Seria Seta Mahkota (Malaysia)	USA	United States of America
SSR	Soviet Socialist Republic	USAAF	United States Army Air Force
St	Saint	USAF	United States Air Force
Sta	Santa	USAID	United States Agency for International Development
Staffs.	Staffordshire	USN	United States Navy
STB	Bachelor of Sacred Theology	USNR	United States Navy Reserve
STD	Doctor of Sacred Theology	USPHS	United States Public Health Service
Ste	Sainte	USS	United States Ship
STL	Licentiate of Sacred Theology	USSR	Union of Soviet Socialist Republics
STM	Master of Sacred Theology	UT	Utah
str.	strasse	UWI	University of the West Indies
SUNY	State University of New York		
Supt	Superintendent	VA	Virginia
SVSA	South West Virginia Songwriters' Association	Va	Virginia
SW	short wave	VC	Victoria Cross
SW	South West	VHF	very high frequency
SWAPO	South West Africa People's Organization	VI	(US) Virgin Islands
		Vic.	Victoria
TA	Territorial Army	Vol.	Volume
TCL	Trinity College of Music, London	vol.	volume
TD	Teachta Dála (mem. of the Dáil), Territorial Decoration	Vol(s)	Volume(s)
TD	Teachta Dála (mem. of the Dáil)	Vols	Volumes
TD	Territorial Decoration	vols	volumes
Tech.	Technical, Technology	VSO	Victoria State Opera
Tech.	Technical	VSO	Voluntary Service Overseas
Tech.	Technology	VT	Vermont
Temp.	Temporary	Vt	Vermont
Tenn.	Tennessee		
Tex.	Texas	W	West, Western

xvi

ABBREVIATIONS

INTERNATIONAL TELEPHONE CODES

To make international calls to telephone and fax numbers listed in the book, dial the international code of the country from which you are calling, followed by the appropriate country code for the organization you wish to call (listed below), followed by the area code (if applicable) and telephone or fax number listed in the entry.

	Country code	+ or – GMT*
Abkhazia	7	+4
Afghanistan	93	+4½
Åland Islands	358	+2
Albania	355	+1
Algeria	213	+1
American Samoa	1 684	−11
Andorra	376	+1
Angola	244	+1
Anguilla	1 264	−4
Antigua and Barbuda	1 268	−4
Argentina	54	−3
Armenia	374	+4
Aruba	297	−4
Ascension Island	247	0
Australia	61	+8 to +10
Austria	43	+1
Azerbaijan	994	+5
Bahamas	1 242	−5
Bahrain	973	+3
Bangladesh	880	+6
Barbados	1 246	−4
Belarus	375	+2
Belgium	32	+1
Belize	501	−6
Benin	229	+1
Bermuda	1 441	−4
Bhutan	975	+6
Bolivia	591	−4
Bonaire	599	−4
Bosnia and Herzegovina	387	+1
Botswana	267	+2
Brazil	55	−3 to −4
British Indian Ocean Territory (Diego Garcia)	246	+5
British Virgin Islands	1 284	−4
Brunei	673	+8
Bulgaria	359	+2
Burkina Faso	226	0
Burundi	257	+2
Cabo Verde	238	−1
Cambodia	855	+7
Cameroon	237	+1
Canada	1	−3 to −8
Cayman Islands	1 345	−5
Central African Republic	236	+1
Ceuta	34	+1
Chad	235	+1
Chile	56	−4
China, People's Republic	86	+8
Christmas Island	61	+7
Cocos (Keeling) Islands	61	+6½
Colombia	57	−5
Comoros	269	+3
Congo, Democratic Republic	243	+1
Congo, Republic	242	+1
Cook Islands	682	−10
Costa Rica	506	−6
Côte d'Ivoire	225	0
Croatia	385	+1
Cuba	53	−5
Curaçao	599	−4
Cyprus	357	+2
Czech Republic	420	+1
Denmark	45	+1
Djibouti	253	+3
Dominica	1 767	−4

	Country code	+ or – GMT*
Dominican Republic	1 809	−4
Ecuador	593	−5
Egypt	20	+2
El Salvador	503	−6
Equatorial Guinea	240	+1
Eritrea	291	+3
Estonia	372	+2
Ethiopia	251	+3
Falkland Islands	500	−4
Faroe Islands	298	0
Fiji	679	+12
Finland	358	+2
France	33	+1
French Guiana	594	−3
French Polynesia	689	−9 to −10
Gabon	241	+1
Gambia	220	0
Georgia	995	+4
Germany	49	+1
Ghana	233	0
Gibraltar	350	+1
Greece	30	+2
Greenland	299	−1 to −4
Grenada	1 473	−4
Guadeloupe	590	−4
Guam	1 671	+10
Guatemala	502	−6
Guernsey	44	0
Guinea	224	0
Guinea-Bissau	245	0
Guyana	592	−4
Haiti	509	−5
Honduras	504	−6
Hong Kong	852	+8
Hungary	36	+1
Iceland	354	0
India	91	+5½
Indonesia	62	+7 to +9
Iran	98	+3½
Iraq	964	+3
Ireland	353	0
Isle of Man	44	0
Israel	972	+2
Italy	39	+1
Jamaica	1 876	−5
Japan	81	+9
Jersey	44	0
Jordan	962	+2
Kazakhstan	7	+6
Kenya	254	+3
Kiribati	686	+12 to +13
Korea, Democratic People's Republic (North Korea)	850	+9
Korea, Republic (South Korea)	82	+9
Kosovo	381†	+3
Kuwait	965	+3
Kyrgyzstan	996	+5
Laos	856	+7
Latvia	371	+2
Lebanon	961	+2
Lesotho	266	+2
Liberia	231	0
Libya	218	+1
Liechtenstein	423	+1
Lithuania	370	+2
Luxembourg	352	+1

	Country code	+ or – GMT*
Macao	853	+8
Macedonia, former Yugoslav republic	389	+1
Madagascar	261	+3
Malawi	265	+2
Malaysia	60	+8
Maldives	960	+5
Mali	223	0
Malta	356	+1
Marshall Islands	692	+12
Martinique	596	–4
Mauritania	222	0
Mauritius	230	+4
Mayotte	262	+3
Melilla	34	+1
Mexico	52	–6 to –7
Micronesia, Federated States	691	+10 to +11
Moldova	373	+2
Monaco	377	+1
Mongolia	976	+7 to +9
Montenegro	382	+1
Montserrat	1 664	–4
Morocco	212	0
Mozambique	258	+2
Myanmar	95	$+6\frac{1}{2}$
Nagornyi Karabakh	374	+4
Namibia	264	+2
Nauru	674	+12
Nepal	977	$+5\frac{3}{4}$
Netherlands	31	+1
New Caledonia	687	+11
New Zealand	64	+12
Nicaragua	505	–6
Niger	227	+1
Nigeria	234	+1
Niue	683	–11
Norfolk Island	672	$+11\frac{1}{2}$
Northern Mariana Islands	1 670	+10
Norway	47	+1
Oman	968	+4
Pakistan	92	+5
Palau	680	+9
Palestinian Territories	970 or 972	+2
Panama	507	–5
Papua New Guinea	675	+10
Paraguay	595	–4
Peru	51	–5
Philippines	63	+8
Pitcairn Islands	872	–8
Poland	48	+1
Portugal	351	0
Puerto Rico	1 787	–4
Qatar	974	+3
Réunion	262	+4
Romania	40	+2
Russian Federation	7	+3 to +12
Rwanda	250	+2
Saba	599	–4
Saint-Barthélemy	590	–4
Saint Christopher and Nevis	1 869	–4
Saint Helena	290	0
Saint Lucia	1 758	–4
Saint-Martin	590	–4
Saint Pierre and Miquelon	508	–3
Saint Vincent and the Grenadines	1 784	–4
Samoa	685	+13
San Marino	378	+1
São Tomé and Príncipe	239	0
Saudi Arabia	966	+3
Senegal	221	0
Serbia	381	+1

	Country code	+ or – GMT*
Seychelles	248	+4
Sierra Leone	232	0
Singapore	65	+8
Sint Eustatius	1721	–4
Sint Maarten	1721	–4
Slovakia	421	+1
Slovenia	386	+1
Solomon Islands	677	+11
Somalia	252	+3
South Africa	27	+2
South Ossetia	7	+4
South Sudan	211	+2
Spain	34	+1
Sri Lanka	94	$+5\frac{1}{2}$
Sudan	249	+2
Suriname	597	–3
Svalbard	47	+1
Swaziland	268	+2
Sweden	46	+1
Switzerland	41	+1
Syria	963	+2
Taiwan	886	+8
Tajikistan	992	+5
Tanzania	255	+3
Thailand	66	+7
Timor-Leste	670	+9
Togo	228	0
Tokelau	690	+15
Tonga	676	+13
Transnistria	373	+2
Trinidad and Tobago	1 868	–4
Tristan da Cunha	290	0
Tunisia	216	+1
Turkey	90	+2
'Turkish Republic of Northern Cyprus'	90 392	+2
Turkmenistan	993	+5
Turks and Caicos Islands	1 649	–5
Tuvalu	688	+12
Uganda	256	+3
Ukraine‡	380	+2
United Arab Emirates	971	+4
United Kingdom	44	0
United States of America	1	–5 to –10
United States Virgin Islands	1 340	–4
Uruguay	598	–3
Uzbekistan	998	+5
Vanuatu	678	+11
Vatican City	39	+1
Venezuela	58	$-4\frac{1}{2}$
Viet Nam	84	+7
Wallis and Futuna Islands	681	+12
Yemen	967	+3
Zambia	260	+2
Zimbabwe	263	+2

* The times listed compare the standard (winter) times in the various countries. Some countries adopt Summer (Daylight Saving) Time—i.e. +1 hour—for part of the year.

† Mobile telephone numbers for Kosovo use either the country code for Monaco (377) or the country code for Slovenia (386).

‡ The Republic of Crimea and the city of Sevastopol were placed in the time zone GMT+4 following their annexation by Russia in 2014.

Note: Telephone and fax numbers using the Inmarsat ocean region code 870 are listed in full. No country or area code is required, but it is necessary to precede the number with the international access code of the country from which the call is made.

OBITUARY

Arp, Klaus	4 January 2016	Masur, Kurt	19 December 2015
Barová, Anna	23 September 2015	Messiereur, Petr	16 December 2015
Bielawa, Herbert	23 December 2015	Milnes, Rodney	5 December 2015
Body, Jack	10 May 2015	Minde, Stefan P.	21 May 2015
Boulez, Pierre	5 January 2016	Négyesy, János	20 December 2013
Braunfels, Michael	15 May 2015	Nejceva, Liljana	7 January 2015
Campbell, Margaret	7 August 2015	Neighbour, Oliver Wray	20 January 2015
Carson, Clarice	2 May 2015	Nentwig, Franz Ferdinand	14 July 2015
Castel, Nicola	31 May 2015	Nguyen-Thien, Dao	20 November 2015
Cleve, George	27 August 2015	Nicolet, Aurèle	29 January 2016
Collot, Sergey	11 August 2015	Nystedt, Knut	8 December 2014
Cowan, Richard	16 November 2015	Ogdon, Wilbur L	6 October 2013
Craft, Robert Lawson	10 November 2015	Paita, Carlos	19 December 2015
Cropper, Peter	29 May 2015	Parsch, Arnost	19 September 2013
Curtis, Alan	15 July 2015	Porter, Andrew Brian	3 April 2015
Darlow, Denys	24 February 2015	Rattay, Evzen	25 December 2015
Dobbs, Mattiwilda	8 December 2015	Ronconi, Luca	21 February 2015
Doufexis, Stella	15 December 2015	Rössler, Almut	13 February 2015
Duval, Denise	25 January 2016	Schneider-Siemssen, Günther	2 June 2015
Dvoráková, Ludmila	30 July 2015	Schuller, Gunther	21 June 2015
Eaton, John C.	2 December 2015	Scott, John Gavin	12 August 2015
Eshpai, Andrey Yakoulevitch	8 November 2015	Senator, Ronald	30 April 2015
Ewington, John	15 August 2015	Sereni, Mario	24 July 2015
Fricke, Heinz	7 December 2015	Silverstein, Joseph	21 November 2015
Goennenwein, Wolfgang	26 July 2015	Smalley, Roger	18 August 2015
Greenfield, Edward Henry	7 July 2015	Smith, Daniel W.	19 December 2015
Guy, (Ruth) Maureen	14 February 2015	Smith, Lawrence Leighton	25 October 2013
Hopferwieser, Josef	10 July 2015	Smolka, Jaroslav	19 August 2011
Johnson, Camellia	26 August 2015	Sondeckis, Saulius	3 February 2016
Kaipainen, Jouni Ilari	23 November 2015	Stevenson, Ronald	28 March 2015
Kastu, Matti	3 March 2015	Stucky, Steven	14 February 2016
Katin, Peter Roy	19 March 2015	Suss, Reiner	29 January 2015
Kern, Patricia	19 October 2015	Tomaszewski, Rolf	22 December 2015
Kos, Bozidar	29 March 2015	Van Oortmerssen, Jacques	21 November 2015
Laderman, Ezra	28 February 2015	Vickers, Jon	10 July 2015
Lehnhoff, Nikolaus	22 August 2015	Ward-Steiman, David	14 April 2015
Lipkin, Seymour	16 November 2015	Weller, Walter	14 June 2015
Maier, Franz-Josef	16 October 2014	Willcocks, David Valentine	17 September 2015
Martin, Adrian	9 December 2014	Xiao, Wenyan	19 September 2013
Martinoty, Jean-Louis	27 January 2016	Yordanov, Luben	4 September 2011

Biographies

A

AADLAND, Eivind; Norwegian conductor; b. 19 Sept. 1956, Bergen. *Education:* Norwegian State Music Acad., Oslo with Camilla Wicks, Int. Menuhin Music Acad., Switzerland with Alberto Lysy and Yehudi Menuhin, masterclasses with Sándor Végh. *Career:* has appeared in major halls and festivals world-wide, including Musikverein, Vienna, Concertgebouw, Amsterdam, Salle Pleyel, Paris and Gewandhaus, Leipzig; fmr Concertmaster, Bergen Philharmonic Orchestra; Music Dir European Community Chamber Orchestra 1988–97; Chief Conductor and Music Dir Trondheim Symphony Orchestra 2003–11. *Recordings:* 12 albums. *Current Management:* c/o Maestro Arts, Milliners House, Riverside Quarter, Eastfields Avenue, London, SW18 1LP, England. *Telephone:* (20) 3637-2789. *E-mail:* jordi@maestroarts.com; christian@maestroarts.com. *Website:* www.maestroarts.com.

AAQUIST, Svend; Danish composer, conductor and computer programmer; *CEO, Ajour Data & Musik;* b. (Svend Aaquist Johansen), 7 Dec. 1948, Lyngby, Copenhagen; s. of Tove and Frede Johansen; m. Anne Turner; one d. *Education:* Univ. of Copenhagen, Royal Danish Acad. of Music, Copenhagen; teachers include pianist Elisabeth Klein, conductors Arne Hammelboe and Michel Tabachnik. *Career:* debut 1969; conductor for numerous choirs, chamber ensembles and orchestras 1969–; high school teacher 1969–75; Teacher of Conducting, Royal Danish Acad. of Music and State Acad. of Music at Esbjerg; teacher at numerous postgraduate workshops and seminars and courses for musicians and conductors; Chief Conductor and Artistic Dir Esbjerg Symphony Orchestra 1984–89; Artistic Adviser, Esbjerg Ensemble 1984–89; Founder and first Dir Danish Chamber Players (Storstrøms Kammerensemble) 1990–96; numerous concerts, festivals, radio and TV recordings, in Denmark and abroad; concerts given with many orchestras, including Odense Symphony Orchestra, Danish State Radio Orchestra, Copenhagen Philharmonic Orchestra; concert tours with West German Chamber Orchestra, Ensemble Modern 1981, 1982, 1984; opera and theatre conductor, Royal Danish Theatre 1988–95; Co-founder and mem. LUT and LYT; CEO Ajour Data & Musik 1986–; mem. Danish State Music Council 1972–77, Nordic Composers' Council (Pres. 1973–74), Soc. for Publ. of Danish Music (Bd mem. 1974–84), Danish Composers' Soc. (Bd mem. 1972–84, 1996–, Chair. 1973–74), DUT Danish ISCM (Chair. 1980–84), Danish Royal Library (consultant 2011–). *Compositions include:* Pentagram 1969, Salut-Salut 1970, Ke-Tjak 1973, Unite 1974, Floes 1974, 'for two pianos' 1974, Sinfonia Sisyphus 1976, The Lilac Shall Bloom In May, It Shall! for cello solo 1976, Concert Oratorie Sisyphus Sings 1979, Sun 1983, Malinche 1984, Hymn With Dances 1985, Tai Yang 1988, High Voltage Rag 1991, Le Malade Imaginaire 1994, Babylon 1997, Frida Floss Four 2005, Vandspejl 2006, Abandoned City and Blue Bird with Golden Globe 2010. *Honours:* Hon. Award, Danish Composers' Soc. 2001, Hon. Award, Danish Conductors' League 2008. *Address:* Bruserup Strand 9, 4873 Væggerløse, Denmark (home). *Telephone:* 54-16-70-00 (office). *E-mail:* aa@ajourdata.dk (office).

ABBADO, Marcello, DipMus; Italian composer and pianist; b. 7 Oct. 1926, Milan; s. of Michelangelo Abbado and Maria Carmela Savagnone; m. Costanza Tessarolo; two s. *Education:* Milan Conservatory. *Career:* soloist and conductor in Europe, America, Africa, Asia, Australia 1944–; performed all Debussy and all piano concertos of Mozart; Prof. of Piano at Conservatories of Cagliari, Venice and Milan, and of Composition at Parma and Bologna 1950; Dir Liceo Musicale, Piacenza 1958, Rossini Conservatory, Pesaro 1966, Verdi Conservatory, Milan 1972–96; founder Symphony Orchestra Verdi, Milan 1993; jury mem., int. competitions of chamber music, composition, conducting, piano, violin, voice and others worldwide; mem. Admin. Council, Teatro alla Scala 1973–96; mem. Fondazione Curci (Naples), Fondazione Puccini (Lucca). *Compositions include:* ballet: Scena Senza Storia, Hawaii 2000, Suite Concertante from the Ballet Hawaii 2000; orchestral: Concerto for Orchestra, Hommage à Debussy, Costruzioni... E Ricostruzioni for Orchestra, Variazioni sopra un tema di Mozart, Risonanze for two pianos and chamber orchestra, La strage degli innocenti for vocal soloists, choir and orchestra, seven Ricercari and six Intermezzi for violin and orchestra, Quadruplo Concerto for piano, violin, viola, cello and orchestra 1970, Double Concerto for violin, piano and double chamber orchestra, L'Idea fissa for violin 'scordato' and percussion orchestra 1994, Ostinato on a Rhythmic Motif from the Overture to Il Signor Bruschino by Rossini, for piano, string orchestra and percussions 1994, Ottavo Ricercare for violin and orchestra 1997, Concerto for flute and orchestra 2002, Ten Songs of Sicily for voice, violin and orchestra, Musica Celeste for violin and orchestra, Asif Saleem Nasreen No. 1 and No. 2 for violin, alto, cello and string orchestra 2002, Harmonic Variations on Mozart's Marche Funèbre del Signor Maestro Contrapunto, KV 453a 2000, Costruzione for 12 cellos 2001, Risonanza magnetica for piano and percussion orchestra 2003, Concerto for harp and strings orchestra 2003, Concerto for carillon and orchestra 2005, Fantasia Russa for violin and strings orchestra 2005, Concerto for two pianos and orchestra 2007, Concerto for four violins and string orchestra 2008, Van Cliburn Concerto for four pianos and orchestra 2008, Gloria to Gloria for voice, choir and orchestra 2009, For two orchestras 2009, Alicante for 16 horns, 16 trumpets, 16 trombonists 2010, Dream for orchestra 2010; other: Velicianie Aleksandr Nevsky for violin and choir, The Bells of Moscow for violin and percussion 1998, Lento e Rondo for violin and percussions, 15 Poesie T'ang for voice and four instruments, Ciapo for voice

and nine instruments, Three Quatuor, Duo for violin and cello, Fantasia No. 1 for 12 instruments, Fantasia No. 2 for four instruments and 31 percussions, Capriccio su un tema di Paganini for violin and piano, Chaconne for solo violin, Riverberazioni for wind instruments and piano, Divertimento for four winds and piano, Concertante for piano and instrument, Sonata for flute, Incastri No. 1 and No. 2 for winds, Lamento for the Mother's Death for clavichord, Variazioni sopra un minuetto di Bach for piano, Aus dem Klavier for piano, Responsorio for choir and organ, Sarà Sara for guitar, Duo for harp and cello 1998, Nuova Costruzione for Wind Octet 2002, Australia for violin, didgeridoo and percussions 2002, Six Ninne Nanne for solo voice, Desprez, Entre Paris et la France, Fijetto dei corni for choir 1999, Music for Jean Cocteau's La voix humaine 2003, Il buio negli occhi (scenic action) 2003, Tankstream for string quartet 2005, Carillon on Joyce Yang for piano and percussion 2006, Bali for violin and Indonesian gamelan 2006, Kazakh Fantasy for violin and Kazakh orchestra 2006, Arrivals Symphony 2006, Four Viola Fantasy for oboe, trumpet, piano, vibraphone 2006, Mondrian Trio for violin, cello and piano 2007, Requiem per Michelangelo for double choir of eight singers 2007, Für Gloria und Andrea for piano and violin 2008, Carillon on Min-on for piano 2008, Java for percussion 2008, Dialogue for Two, for piano left hand 2009, Per due orchestre 2009, Asia for percussions, registration of Asiatic voices and instruments 2010, Sogno for Orchestra 2010, Marlaena Kessick for flute orchestra 2011, Dialogue for harp and trumpet 2011, Sitkovetsky Wu for violin and piano 2011, Fantasy for cello 2011, Trio for piano, voice and dance 2012, Ungarn Fantasy for flute 2012, Trio for violin, cello and double bass 2012, Ashes for piano 2012, Ashes for strings 2012, Alhambra for orchestra 2012, Vocalize on Ma Se Mi Toccano from Il Barbiere di Siviglia by Rossini 2013, Vocalize on Sharon Zhai, Cosi Non Fan Tutte (ballet) 2013, Free elaboration of Principal Theme, Symphony No. 7, Op 60 by Dimitri Shostakovich (Leningrad) for violin and piano 2014, Vocalize on Lilia Ianeva 2014, Vocalize on Katarzyna Medlarska 2014, Vocalize on Daniela Bertozzi 2014, Carillon on Andreea Bratu for piano 2014, Preludio, Cadenza, Finale for violin and string orchestra 2014, Vocalize on Tahirih Scarpa 2015. *Recordings:* works recorded by Curci, Carisch, Ricordi, Suvini Zerboni in Milan. *Address:* Viale Monza 9, 20125 Milan, Italy (home). *Telephone:* (03) 402371167 (home). *Fax:* (02) 700505157 (office).

ABBADO, Roberto; Italian conductor; *Music Director, Palau de les Arts Reina Sofía;* b. 30 Dec. 1954, Milan. *Education:* Pesaro and Milan Conservatories, studied with Franco Ferrara in Rome and at Teatro La Fenice, Venice. *Career:* debut with Orchestra of Accademia Santa Cecilia 1977; operatic debut with a new production of Simon Boccanegra at Macerata 1978; festival appearances at Edinburgh 1982, Israel 1984, Lille and Munich 1989; Chief Conductor, Munich Radio Orchestra 1991–98; engagements with Staatskapelle Dresden, Bamberg Symphony, Royal Concertgebouw, Orchestre National de France, RAI Turin, The Orchestra of St Luke's in New York, Maggio Musicale Fiorentino Orchestra; opera engagements at La Scala with world premieres of Flavio Testi's Il Sosia, Riccardo III and Don Pasquale; Vienna State Opera with production of La Cenerentola; Bayerische Staatsoper, Munich, with production of La Traviata 1993, and Adriana Lecouvreur, Manon Lescaut, Don Pasquale; conducted La Forza del Destino at San Francisco 1993; appeared at Rome, Florence, Bologna, Venice, Berlin Deutsche Oper, Zürich, Barcelona and Tokyo with Teatro Comunale Bologna 1993; conducted Adriana Lecouvreur at the Metropolitan, New York 1994; Opéra Bastille debut in Lucia di Lammermoor 1995; Houston Grand Opera debut in Norma 1996; Aida at the 1997 Munich Festival; Le Comte Ory at Florence 1998; guest conductor with Los Angeles Philharmonic Orchestra, Philadelphia, San Francisco, St Louis, Baltimore and Atlanta Symphony Orchestras; Artistic Partner, St Paul Chamber Orchestra 2005–; currently Music Dir Palau de les Arts Reina Sofía, Valencia. *Recordings include:* Bellini's I Capuleti e i Montecchi 1998. *Honours:* Deutsche Phono Akademi Echo Klassic Deutscher Schallplattenpreis (for recording of Rossini's Tancredi) 1997, Franco Abbiati Award, Nat. Asscn of Italian Music Critics 2008, 2012, Best Performance and Production, Rossini Opera Festival 2012. *Current Management:* IMG Artists, 00-232 Warsaw, Ul. Ciasna 6, Poland. *E-mail:* gmacheda@imgartists.com. *Website:* imgartists.com/artist/roberto_abbado. www.thespco.org; www.lesarts.com/Palau/Home.

ABBASSI, Nader; Egyptian conductor, singer, bassoonist and composer; *Artistic and Musical Director, KATARA Culture Foundation;* b. 1963, Cairo. *Education:* Acad. of Arts, Cairo, Geneva Conservatory. *Career:* began musical studies aged five; as bassoonist (soloist) played several seasons with Cairo Symphony Orchestra and Geneva Chamber Orchestra); performed as a baritone for 10 years at Grand Théâtre de Genève; also composed ballet The Nile Bride 2001; conducted various int. orchestras, including Sinfonieorchester Basel, Staatsphilharmonie Rheinland-Pfalz, Philharmonisches Orchester Heidelberg, Orchester des Richard Strauss Konservatoriums München, Orchestre Philharmonique de Marseille, Orchestre Nat. des Pays de la Loire, Orchestre de la Suisse Romande, Orchestre de Chambre de Genève, Chaliapin and Nuriev Festival with the Bashkir Opera Orchestra, Orquesta Sinfonica de Guanajuato, Norrköping Philharmonic Orchestra, Euro Orchestra da camera di Bari, Lisbon Philharmonic Orchestra; US debut conducting the Sacramento Philharmonic Orchestra 2008, 2010; Perm. mem. Jury, Int. Stenhammar Singing Competition; mem. Chambre Syndicale des Agents pour la Musique

Classique; Full mem. Int. Artist Managers' Asscn; Artistic Dir and Prin. Conductor Cairo Opera Orchestra 2002–; Artistic Dir Orchestre pour la Paix, Paris 2003–; Musical Dir and Prin. Conductor, Qatar Philharmonic Orchestra 2009–11; Artistic and Musical Dir KATARA Culture Foundation, Doha 2011–. *Operas conducted include:* Hamlet, Un Ballo in Maschera, La Belle Hélène, Aida, La Traviata, Madama Butterfly, Tosca, Cavalleria Rusticana, Pagliacci, The Magic Flute, The Merry Widow, Oedipus Rex, Nutcracker, Romeo and Juliet, Zorba, Carmina Burana, Le Sacre du Printemps. *Honours:* Citation of Excellence and Outstanding Music Award 1980, 1982, Winner of Egyptian Ministry of Culture Award for bassoon and composition 1986, 1995, 1996, Mozart Chamber Music Competition 1992. *Current Management:* c/o Philippe Kahn-Salmon, International Music Talents, 59 Quai de Valmy, 75010 Paris, France. *Telephone:* 1-40-40-94-75. *Fax:* 1-40-40-94-84. *E-mail:* pks@imt-agency.com. *Website:* www.imt-agency.com; naderabbassi.multiply.com.

ABBOTT, Jocelyn, ARCT, BMus, LRAM, DipRAM, ARAM; Canadian pianist; b. 15 Sept. 1954, Toronto. *Education:* Victoria Conservatory of Music, Victoria, BC, Royal Conservatory of Music, Toronto, Univ. of Victoria and Royal Acad. of Music, London. *Career:* concerts and recordings as soloist and accompanist, part of ensemble The Abbott O'Gorman Piano Duo with Laura O'Gorman, including commissioning transcriptions and arranging orchestral repertoire 1992–; mem. Incorporated Soc. of Musicians. *Recordings include:* Ravel à quatre mains 1994, Classical Jazz à quatre mains 1999. *Publications include:* contribs to Pianist Magazine. *Honours:* Steinway Artist 1996. *Current Management:* Cubitt Music Management, 40 Cubitt Terrace, London, SW4 6AR, England. *Telephone:* (7771) 725002. *Fax:* (20) 7720–8660. *E-mail:* enquiries@cubittmusic.co.uk. *Website:* www.cubittmusic.co.uk.

ABDRAZAKOV, Askar; Russian singer (bass); b. 1960, Ufa, Bashkortostan. *Education:* Ufa Conservatoire and with Irina Arkipova in Moscow. *Career:* soloist with the Bashkirian Opera 1990–; repertoire includes Sobakin in The Tsar's Bride, Konchak in Prince Igor, Gremin in Eugene Onegin, Boris in Boris Godunov, Ruslan in Ruslan and Lyudmila, Ramphis in Aida, Zaccaria in Nabuco, Kotchubej in Mazepa, Attila in Attila, Count Walter in Luisa Miller, Grand Inquisitor in Don Carlos, Raimondo in Lucia di Lammermoor; sang in world premiere of Slinimsky's Visions of Ioann Grozny; concerts include the Verdi Requiem, Puccini Messa di Gloria; Russian and French songs and lieder; has performed with Opera di Trieste, Teatro Comunale di Firenze, San Carlos Nat. Opera, Lisbon, Berlin Deutsche Oper, Opera di Genova, La Scala, Milan; Minister of Culture, Bashkortostan 2010–11. *Honours:* prizewinner, Glinka Competition 1991, winner, Int. Singing Competition, Pretoria 1994, winner, Chaliapin Bass Competition, Kazan 1994, Grand Prix Maria Callas Competition, Athens 1995, winner, Int. Rakhmaninov Competition 1998, People's Artist of the Repub. of Bashkortostan. *Current Management:* APA Artists Management, Alexandra Mercer Studio 1, 79 Bedford Gardens, London, W8 7EG, England. *E-mail:* alexandra@mercer.uk.com. *Website:* www.apaartistsmanagement.com/askarabdrazakov.html. *E-mail:* askar.abdrazakov@tiscali.fr (office). *Website:* askar.abdrazakov.chez-alice.fr.

ABDRAZAKOV, Ildar; Russian singer (bass); b. 1976, Ufa, Bashkortostan. *Education:* State Inst. of Arts. *Career:* has appeared with most major opera co. in USA and Europe; also sung on stages of Barcelona's Teatre Liceu, Barcelona, Madrid's Teatro Real, Opéra Bastille, Paris, Metropolitan Opera, San Francisco Opera, Washington Nat. Opera, Los Angeles Opera; has given concert recitals in Russia, Italy, Japan and USA, and performed with orchestras including Chicago Symphony, Vienna Philharmonic, Leipzig Gewandhaus Orchestra, Bayerische Rundfunk, Rotterdam Philharmonic, Orchestre Nat. de France, Orchestra Filarmonica della Scala, Accad. Nazionale di Santa Cecilia; has collaborated with conductors including Riccardo Muti, Valery Gergiev, James Levine, Gianandrea Noseda, Bernard de Billy, Riccardo Frizza, Riccardo Chailly and Antonio Pappano; Amb. for Zegna & Music project 2007–. *Repertoire includes:* Father Frost (The Snow Maiden), Rodolfo (La sonnambula), Raimondo Bide-the-Bent (Lucia di Lammermoor), Attila (Attila), Banco (Macbeth), Guardiano, Marchese di Calatrava (La forza del destino), Don Giovanni, Leporello (Don Giovanni), Guglielmo (Così fan tutte), Dosifei (Khovanshchina), Viking Guest (Sadko), Assur (Semiramide), Oroveso (Norma), Basilio (Il barbiere di Siviglia), Mustafa (L'italiana in Algeri), Selim (Il turco in Italia), Moses (Mosè in Egitto), Mahomet II (Le siège de Corinthe), Don de Silva (Ernani), Oberto (Conte di San Bonifacio), Monterone (Rigoletto), Ferrando (Il trovatore), Pharaoh and Ramfis (Aida), Mephistopheles (Mefistofele, Faust and La Damnation de Faust), Escamillo (Carmen), Figaro (Le nozze di Figaro). *Recordings include:* unpublished arias by Rossini (conducted by Riccardo Muti), Masses by Cherubini (Bayerische Rundfunk Orchestra under Riccardo Muti), Shostakovich's Sonnets of Michelangelo as well as Rossini's opera Moïse et Pharaon (orchestra of the Teatro alla Scala under Riccardo Muti), Verdi Requiem/Chicago Symphony/Muti (Grammy Awards for Best Classical Album and for Best Choral Performance) 2011, Attila, Ivan the Terrible 2014, Verdi Requiem, conducted by Philippe Jordan 2014, Power Player: Russian Arias for Bass 2014. *Honours:* First Prize, 17th Int. Glinka Competition, Moscow 1997, Grand Prix, Third Int. Rimsky-Korsakov Competition 1998, Grand Prix, Int. Elena Obraztsova Competition 1999, Grand Prix, Fifth Int. Maria Callas Competition 2000, Honoured Artist of the Repub. of Bashkortostan. *Current Management:* c/o Centre Stage Artist Management, Stralauer Allee 1, Berlin 10245, Germany. *Telephone:* (30) 520071761. *E-mail:* Judith.Neuhoff@centrestagemanagement.com. *Website:* www.centrestagemanagement.com; ildarabdrazakov.com.

ABDULLAH, Kazem; American conductor; b. 1979, Indiana. *Education:* Cincinnati Conservatory of Music, Univ. of Southern California, Peabody Inst., John Hopkins Univ. *Career:* began career as clarinettist; Asst and Cover Conductor Metropolitan Opera 2006–09; debuts with Metropolitan Opera with Gluck's Orfeo ed Euridice, Mexico City Philharmonic, Oregon Symphony, Indianapolis Symphony with world premiere of Gabriela Frank's Peregrinos 2008–09, Chicago Sinfonietta, Huntsville Symphony, Dayton Philharmonic and the Staatskapelle Weimar 2009–10; also conducted New World Symphony, Charles Ives Festival 2009, Orquestra de São Paulo, US coast-to-coast tour 2009–10; other projects include Scott Joplin's Treemonisha at Théâtre du Châtelet, Paris, and appearances with Nat. Arts Center Orchestra of Ottawa, Chautauqua Music School Festival Orchestra, Berliner Kammerphilharmonie, Finnish Radio Orchestra, Helsinki Philharmonic, Tanglewood Music Center Orchestra. *Honours:* Solti Foundation US Career Assistance Award 2010. *Current Management:* Columbia Artists Management Inc., 1790 Broadway, New York, NY 10019-1412, USA. *Telephone:* (212) 841-9500. *Fax:* (212) 841-9744. *E-mail:* info@cami.com. *Website:* www.cami.com; www.kazemabdullah.com.

ABDURAIMOV, Behzod; Uzbekistani pianist; b. 11 Sept. 1990, Tashkent. *Education:* Uspensky State Central Lyceum, Tashkent, Int. Center for Music, Park Univ., USA; studied with Tamara Popovich and Stanislav Ioudenitch. *Career:* began playing the piano aged five; performed first solo recital aged eight with Nat. Symphony Orchestra of Uzbekistan; annual performances at Spivakov Int. Charity Foundation, Moscow 2004–, Int. Keyboard Inst. and Festival, New York 2005–; performed at Int. Summer Piano Academy, Como, Italy 2006; performed with Sydney Symphony Orchestra under Vladimir Ashkenazy on tour of China and Kuala Lumpur 2009–10, Musikfest Bremen, Germany 2010; Artist-in-Residence, Park Univ. 2014–15. *Recordings include:* debut recital CD 2012 which won Choc de Classica and Diapason Découverte, first concerto CD featuring Prokofiev Piano Concerto No. 3 and Tchaikovsky Concerto No. 1 with Orchestra Sinfonica Nazionale della Rai under Juraj Valčuha 2014. *Honours:* Republican Competition First Prize 1999, Diploma, Int. Tchaikovsky Competition for Young Musicians 2002, first prize and Grand Prix, Le Muse Int. Piano Competition, Italy 2003, winner, Lennox Young Artist Competition 2008, winner, Corpus Christi Int. Competition 2008, winner, London Int. Piano Competition 2009. *Current Management:* Harrison/Parrott Artist Management, 5–6 Albion Court, Albion Place, London, W6 0QT, England. *Telephone:* (20) 7229-9166. *E-mail:* info@harrisonparrott.co.uk. *Website:* www.harrisonparrott.com; www.behzodabduraimov.com.

ABE, Keiko Kimura; Japanese marimba player and composer; b. 18 April 1937, Tokyo. *Education:* studied xylophone with Eiichi Asabuki, Tokyo Gakugei Univ. with Shosuke Ariga and Toshio Kashiwagi, studied percussion with Masao Imamura and Yusuke Oyake. *Career:* began professional career as xylophone soloist for NHK Radio 1952; freelance marimbist in Tokyo and in recording, TV and radio studios and as an extra with orchestras from 1957; formed Tokyo Marimba Group 1962, Tokyo Quintet 1973; presented first solo recital of serious classical music for the marimba: Keiko Abe Evening of Marimba 1968; has performed all compositions written for the marimba including four world premieres; soloist with numerous orchestras including Tokyo Symphony Orchestra under Yuzo Toyama 1968, Tokyo Philharmonic Orchestra under Toshiharu Araya 1970, Japan Philharmonic Orchestra under Hiroshi Kumagai 1970, Japan Shinsei Symphony Orchestra under Kazuo Yamada 1979, Tokyo Philharmony Orchestra under Tadaaki Odaka 1980, Sapporo Symphony Orchestra under Yasushi Akutagawa 1980, Kyoto Symphony Orchestra under Kazuo Yamada 1981, Tokyo Symphony Orchestra under Michiyoshi Inoue 1983, Amsterdam Percussion Ensemble 1983, Amsterdam Royal Concertgebouw Orchestra 1984, New Japan Philharmonic under Yasushi Akutagawa 1984, Michigan Wind Symphonic Orchestra under Robert Reynolds 1986, Kroumata Percussion Ensemble at Scandinavia Music Today, Tokyo 1987, Sweden Symphony Band under Loguin Anders 1987, Osaka Municipal Symphonic Band under Yoshihiro Kimura, Strasbourg Percussion Ensemble, Tokyo, Tokyo Metropolitan Symphony Orchestra under Hiroyuki Iwaki 1990, Pro Musica Nipponia, Japan Shinsei Symphony Orchestra under Kazuo Yamada 1989, Guatemala Nat. Symphony Orchestra 1990, Tokyo Symphony Orchestra under Naoto Otomo 1991, Sapporo Symphony Orchestra under Hiroshi Ishimaru, New Japan Philharmonic under Noriyuki Tezuka 1992, Kyushu Symphony Orchestra under Hiroshi Ishimaru, New Symphony Orchestra, Berlin Philharmonic Hall under Moki Ishii 1993, Umeå Symphony Orchestra under A. Volmer 1996, Korean Symphony Orchestra, Seoul under Duck Ki Kim 1997, Seoul Philharmonic Orchestra under M. Ermler 2001, Orquesta Sinfonica de RTVE at Mallorca Int. Percussion Event under T. Renaud 2001, Nat. Taiwan Symphony Orchestra under Wen-Pin 2002, North Texas Wind Symphony under E. M. Corporon 2003, New Japan Philharmonic under Michiyoshi Inoue 2005, Japan Philharmonic Orchestra at Suntory Renewal Anniversary Special Concert under Michiyoshi Inoue 2007, Suisse Romande Orchestra 2009, Japan Philharmonic Orchestra under Michiyoshi Inoue 2010; visited USA at invitation of Int. Percussion Arts Soc. 1977; has conducted master classes at more than 110 music schools world-wide, including Eastman School of Music, Univ. of Michigan, Conservatoire Nat. Supérieur de Musique et de Danse de Paris; concert tour of Europe and USA 1981, premiered Lauda Concertata at New York Carnegie Hall, joint performance with New York Philharmonic at New York Percussion Day 1981; summer concert by invitation of Vienna City; Strasbourg Int. Percussion Festival, France 1983, Seven Oaks Summer

Festival, UK, Freiburg Int. Festival 1983; recital and joint performance with Stuttgart Percussion Ensemble at Ludwigsburg Festival 1985; solo concert in Berlin and joint concert with members of Berlin Philharmonic and Deutsche Oper Berlin at Berlin Percussion Festival 1985; premiered Marimba Concerto by Marta Ptaszynska in USA 1986; guest artist at the Banff Fine Arts Centre, Canada 1986, 1988; concert tours in the Netherlands, Sweden, Denmark, Germany and UK 1987; special master class for Japan's present marimba works at Hochschule für Musik und Darstellende Kunst, Stuttgart; joint performance with Nexus Percussion Ensemble at New Music Concert, Toronto; performance at Int. Music Festival, Taipei; soloist at Latin America Festival Symphonic Concert under Jorge Sarmientos; concert tours and festival in Spain and East Germany, with Pohronea Percussion Group in Peru, Bolivia, Costa Rica, Guatemala, with Dave Samuels in Japan, in the Netherlands, Germany, Finland, France and Spain and at Holland Int. Percussion Festival; concert tours with Kroumata Percussion Ensemble in Japan 1992, in Sweden and Germany 1992; Budapest Spring Festival, Seventh Kurashiki Music Festival 1993; concert tour at Kaiser-Friedrich Hall, Germany, with Michigan Chamber Ensemble; Mostly Percussion Festival, Zürich, Mexico Music Japan Festival, Mexico; soloist at World Asscn for Symphonic Bands and Ensemble under T. Raynish 1995; concert tour with Kroumata Percussion Ensemble in Japan, joint performance with Yuriko Kuronuma, violinist in Tokyo; concert tour with Michigan Chamber Ensemble; concert tour with Tambuco, Mexican Percussion Ensemble in Japan, with Michigan Chamber Ensemble in Japan; guest performance, concert and master class at Int. Percussion Forum in France; concert and master class at Stockholm Int. Percussion Festival, Sweden 1999; played at Nagasaki Dejima Music Festival in preparation for 400th anniversary of Japan/Holland exchange project 1999; concerts and master classes in Belgium, England, Switzerland, Germany, Austria, the Netherlands 2000; two concerts at 400th anniversary of Japan/Holland exchange in the Netherlands Festival, concert and master class at the Hamamatsu Int. Wind Acad. 2000; concert at Percussion Festival, UK 2002; First Vienna Int. Percussion Festival Concert and master class in Vienna 2002; concert and master class in Kiel and Bad Sobernheim 2005, master-class in Villecroze, France, concert in Seoul; joint concert with Marimba Ensemble Japan at Marimba World of Keiko Abe 2010; concert with Taipei Chinese Orchestra, Taipei 2013, Symphony of Japan Self-Defense Forces 2013, New Symphony Orchestra 2014, Japan Philharmonic Symphony Orchestra 2014; performed Marimba – The World of Keiko Abe at Blossom Hall, Ginza 2010; Artistic Dir First Latin America Marimba Competition 2011; concert and master class at Jianli Percussion Festival, Shanxi, Taiyuan, China 2011; Lecturer, Tōhō Gakuen Coll. of Music 1970–91, Assoc. Prof. 1991–93, Prof. 1993–2008, Guest Prof., Music Dept 2008, Prof. Emer. 2009–; Guest Prof., Utrecht Univ. 1985–87, Nagoya Coll. of Music 2002, Shanghai Conservatory of Music 2006–08, Sichuan Conservatory of Music 2011, Kurashiki Sakuyo Univ. 2015; Visiting Prof., Staatliche Hochschule für Musik und Darstellende Kunst, Stuttgart 1989–2004; taught at Keiko Abe Int. Marimba Acad., Belgium 2007, Keiko Abe Int. Marimba Acad., Hamamatsu 2007, Fourth Keiko Abe Int. Marimba Acad., Tokyo 2007, Fifth Keiko Abe Int. Marimba Acad., Tokyo 2010, Keiko Abe Int. Marimba Seminar, Korea 2010, Sixth Keiko Abe Int. Marimba Acad., Tokyo 2011, Tenth Keiko Abe Int. Marimba Acad., Tokyo 2015; Abe Keiko Int. Marimba Camp, Korea 2011, Keiko Abe Lausanne Int. Marimba Acad. 2011, Second Keiko Abe Marimba Acad., SUNY Fredonia, USA 2013, Second Keiko Abe Lausanne Int. Marimba Acad. 2013, Third Keiko Abe Lausanne Int. Marimba Acad. 2015; Artistic/Gen. Dir World Marimba Festival, Osaka 1998, Percussion Festival of Japan Week at Seoul, Korea 1999; Chair. Jury, Second World Marimba Competition, Okaya 1999, mem. Special Jury, First World Marimba Competition, Stuttgart 1996, Special Jury, Third World Marimba Competition, Stuttgart 2002, Special Jury, Int. Marimba Competition, Paris 2003, Artistic Dir and mem. Jury, Fourth World Marimba Competition, Shanghai 2005, Hon. Jury mem. Int. Marimba Concerto Competition, Ljubljana, Slovenia 2005, Hon. Jury mem. Marimba Competition Belgium 2007, mem. Jury, 56th ARD Int. Music Competition, Munich 2007, Hon. Jury mem. Fifth World Marimba Competition, Stuttgart 2008, Jury mem. Geneva Int. Music Competition 2009; Cultural Consultant, Shanghai Percussion Asscn 2010; Fellow, Royal Northern Coll. of Music 2014; mem. Bd of Dirs Yamaha Music Foundation. *Compositions include:* Frog, Michi, Variations on Japanese Children's Songs, Dream of the Cherry Blossoms, Sea of Galilee for Six Mallets, Wind in the Bamboo Grove, Ancient Vase, Memories of the Seashore, Prism for solo marimba, Little Windows, Memories of the Seashore II for two marimbas, Conversation in the Forest I for solo marimba and three percussionists, In Praise of Nature for marimba and tape, Sylvan Stanzas, Mountain Stanzas, From the Far Side of Earth for marimba and tape, Prism for two marimbas, Voice of Matsuri Drums, Wind across Mountains for six mallets, Wind across Mountains for solo marimba, Conversation in the Forest II for marimba, oboe and two percussionists, Itsuki Fantasy for six mallets, Tambourin Paraphrase for two marimbas, Prism Rhapsody for solo marimba and wind ensemble, Prism Rhapsody Piano Reduction for solo marimba and orchestra or wind ensemble (Marimba Concerto), Prism Rhapsody for solo marimba and orchestra, Memories of the Seashore for marimba ensemble, Conversation in the Forest for two marimbas, Wind across Mountains for two marimbas, Wind Sketch III for solo marimba and percussion players, Tambourin Paraphrase for marimba ensemble, Michi II, Wind Sketch II for two marimbas, Conversation in the Forest III for two marimbas and three percussionists, Ancient Letter, Marimba Concertino 'The Wave' for solo marimba and four percussionists, Wind Sketch IV for two marimbas and two percussionists, Prism Rhapsody (second edn) for solo marimba and orchestra, Prism Rhapsody (second edn) for solo marimba and wind ensemble, Prism Rhapsody II for two marimbas and orchestra, Song of the Seashore for solo marimba, Kazak Lullaby for solo marimba, Piacer d'amor for solo marimba, Prism Rhapsody II for two marimbas and wind ensemble, Prism Rhapsody II Piano Reduction for two marimbas and orchestra or wind ensemble (Marimba Concerto), Reflections on Japanese Children's Songs III for two marimbas and percussionist, Reflections on Japanese Children's Songs II for two marimbas, Alone for marimba, Wind Across Mountains for marimba ensemble, Wind in the Bamboo Grove II for two marimbas, Tambourin Paraphrase III for two marimbas and percussionist, Reflections on Japanese Children's Songs III for marimba ensemble and two percussionists, The Wave Impressions for marimba ensemble and gamelan jegog, Prism Rhapsody II for two marimbas and six percussionists, Prism Variations for marimba ensemble and four percussionists, Michi III for marimba and voice, Memories of the Seashore III for marimba, percussion and voice, Variations on Dowland's Lachrimae Pavana for solo marimba, Conversation in the Forest V for marimba ensemble and two percussionists, Kodama for solo marimba, The Breath of the Tree II for two marimbas, Michi Paraphrase for solo marimba, Prism II (revised edn) for two marimbas, Conversation in the Forest IV for marimba quartet, Prism Variations for marimba ensemble and four percussionists, She Dies, My Water Lily Tonneke, Torrent, Sylvan Stroll, Early Spring, Autumn in Nara, Sunday Afternoon, Dream, Labyrinth, Aqua-Harmonia based on Memories of the Seashore. *Television includes:* concert in Vienna by invitation of Int. Music Center (IMZ) 1982, appearance on ORF TV (Austria) 1982, North German Broadcast Asscn (NDR) 1982, as a soloist with Yomiuri Nippon Symphony Orchestra under Yoshikazu Tanaka 1990, CD/DVD recording of concert, 'Letters from Nature' with the Galaxy Percussion in Japan 2003. *Recordings include:* Nobara-ni-yosete 1959, Keiko Abe Evening of Marimba (Fine Arts Festival Excellence Award) 1968, Art of Keiko Abe: Marimba Fantasy (Fine Arts Festival Excellence Award for recording, also for recital 1971) 1969, World of the Tokyo Quintet (Fine Arts Festival Award) 1974, Quintessence of Keiko Abe's Marimba (Fine Arts Festival Excellence Award) 1976, Marimba Spiritual – Keiko Abe and World's Percussionists (Fine Arts Festival Excellence Award) 1989. *Honours:* elected to Percussive Arts Soc. Hall of Fame (USA) 1993, Academy Award, Academic Soc. of Japan for Wind and Band 1997. *Address:* c/o Tōhō Gakuen College of Music, 1-41-1 Wakaba-chô, Chôfu-shi, 182-0003 Tokyo, Japan. *Website:* www.keiko-abe.com.

ABEL, Yves; French-Canadian conductor; *Chief Conductor, Nordwestdeutsche Philharmonie*; b. 1963, Canada. *Education:* Univ. of Toronto, Royal Conservatory, Mannes Coll. of Music, Tanglewood Music Center with Leonard Bernstein, Seiji Ozawa, Gunther Herbig and Roger Norrington. *Career:* Prin. Guest Conductor, Deutsche Oper Berlin 2005–10; Chief Conductor, Nordwestdeutsche Philharmonie 2015–; has conducted La Traviata at New York City Opera, televised on Live from Lincoln Center series; La Cenerentola with Seattle Opera and the Pesaro Festival; La Belle Hélène, with Opera Theatre of St Louis; Roméo et Juliette with Florida Grand Opera; Herold's Zampa at 1993 Wexford Festival and Wagner's Das Liebesverbot at 1994 Festival, also conducting Brahms' Ein Deutsches Requiem; Rigoletto with Opera Lyra Ottawa; Massenet's Werther at Skylight Opera; Dido and Aeneas at Canada's Elora Festival, broadcast nationwide on CBC Radio; Madama Butterfly with Opera Theater of Connecticut; Music Dir, L'Opéra Français de New York, with performances at Lincoln Center and Alice Tully Hall, conducting Offenbach's Barbe-Bleue, Médée by Cherubini and Le Comte Ory by Rossini; recently acclaimed debuts include Don Carlos with Opera North, Le Comte Ory with Glyndebourne Festival Opera, Hamlet with San Francisco Opera, L'elisir d'amore with Royal Danish Opera, Rossini Opera Festival and performances of Faust with Paris Opera; debut at Lyric Opera of Chicago with L'elisir d'amore, Seattle Opera for Forza del Destino, Netherlands Opera for Barbiere and a revival of Les Dialogues des Carmélites, Royal Danish Opera for Verdi, Welsh Nat. Opera for Leonore 2000, Bilbao Opera for Barbiere di Siviglia; third season at Metropolitan Opera with Carmen, with Domingo and Denyce Graves; Lyric Opera in Chicago for Barbiere 2001; season 2002–03 with Metropolitan Opera (Carmen) and Netherlands Opera, as well as new productions with Santa Fe Opera (Così fan tutte), Dallas Opera (Ermione), Deutsche Oper Berlin (Don Pasquale) and Teatro Comunale di Bologna (Iphigénie en Tauride); debut at La Scala with La Fille du Régiment 2007, Théâtre du Capitole (Les Contes d'Hoffmann) 2008; performed with Rotterdam Philharmonic, Orchestre du Capitole de Toulouse, Stavanger Symphony Orchestra 2009–10, Vienna State Opera (Madama Butterfly, Simon Boccanegra, L'italiana in Algeri, Un ballo in maschera, L'elisir d'amore, Il barbiere di Siviglia) 2008–10, Bilbao Opera (La Fille du Régiment, Norma) 2009, Seattle Opera (Il trovatore) 2009–10, Gran Teatro del Liceu (La Fille du Régiment, Roberto Devereux, Madama Butterfly) 2010, Metropolitan Opera and Covent Garden (La Traviata) 2010, 2016; conducted La Fille du Régiment and Madama Butterfly for the Met, La Fille du Régiment for Royal Opera, Covent Garden 2012; has conducted numerous symphonic concerts with San Francisco Symphony, Symphonies in Toronto, Montreal, Edmonton, Orchestra of St Luke's in New York, Rotterdam Philharmonic, Liverpool Philharmonic, theatre orchestras in Bologna, Naples, Genoa, Palermo and, in Spain, orchestras in Oviedo and Granada; has also conducted Copenhagen Philharmonic for the Tivoli Festival; 2013 season included Barber of Seville, Met, two Ravel operas, Teatro Massimo, Palermo, L'elisir d'amore for Vienna Staatsoper, I Capuleti ed i Montecchi for Staatsoper, Munich, Così fan tutte, New Nat. Theatre of Tokyo, debut at San Diego Opera with La Fille du

Régiment 2013; 2015 included Les Contes de Hoffman at the Met and Madama Butterfly for Deutsche Oper; La Traviata, Covent Garden 2016, Madama Butterly, San Diego 2016. *Recordings include:* Thaïs with Renée Fleming and Thomas Hampson, recording of French music with Susan Graham and Patricia Petibon, Arias with Elina Garanča 2012. *Honours:* Chevalier des Arts et des Lettres 2009. *Current Management:* c/o Atelier Musicale S.r.L., via Caselle 76, 40068 San Lazzaro di Savena, Bologna, Italy. *Telephone:* (051) 19984444. *Fax:* (051) 19984420. *E-mail:* info@ateliermusicale.it. *Website:* www.ateliermusicale.com; www.yvesabel.com.

ABELL, David Charles, BA, MA; American/British conductor; b. 1958, N Carolina, USA; s. of David Robert Abell and Elizabeth Phelps Abell; partner Seann Alderking. *Education:* Yale Univ., Juilliard School, New York, Conservatoire Américain, Fontainebleau, France, studied with Leonard Bernstein, John Mauceri, Jorge Mester, Sixten Erhling and Nadia Boulanger. *Career:* many appearances in USA and Europe with leading orchestras; London resident from 1996; has conducted London Symphony, BBC Symphony, London Philharmonic, Royal Philharmonic, City of Birmingham Symphony, Royal Liverpool Philharmonic, Hallé Orchestra, Bournemouth Symphony, BBC Nat. Orchestra of Wales, Royal Scottish Nat. Orchestra, Ulster Orchestra, Wiener Symphoniker, Wiener Akademie, Orchestre Pasdeloup, Iceland Symphony, Hong Kong Philharmonic, BBC Concert Orchestra (including three appearances at Proms); Rossini's La Gazza Ladra with Opera North, Madama Butterfly and Carmen at Royal Albert Hall, Menotti's Maria Golovin at Spoleto Festival (Italy), Rigoletto and Manon Lescaut at Lugio Musicale Trapanese, Il Barbiere di Siviglia with New York City Opera, Porgy and Bess with Cape Town Opera and Cincinnati Opera; engagements with New York City Opera, Washington and Michigan Operas, Seattle and Alabama Symphonies, Opera Pacific, Michigan Opera Theater; Carnegie Hall debut with New York Pops 2007; musicals conducted include Show Boat, Kiss Me, Kate, West Side Story, Candide, On the Town, Les Misérables, Miss Saigon, Martin Guerre, Napoleon, Love Never Dies, Sweeney Todd (Châtelet), Pacific Overtures (Yokohama). *Recordings include:* Tobias and the Angel, The Little Prince, Puccini excerpts, Les Misérables, Miss Saigon, Man of La Mancha, Diana Damrau. *Television:* Strauss: The Waltz King, A Night in Vienna, Rodgers Centenary, Candide, Japan, Les Misérables Tenth and 25th Anniversary concerts, BBC Proms, Cymry for the World, Sondheim 80th Birthday Concert (UK). *Honours:* Pegasus Prize, Spoleto Festival, Italy 2007. *Current Management:* c/o Mark Kendall, Mark Kendall Artists Management, 56 St Anselm's Road, Worthing, West Sussex, BN14 7EN, England; c/o John Miller, Pinnacle Arts Management, 889 Ninth Avenue, 2nd Floor, New York, NY 10019, USA. *Telephone:* (1903) 223229 (Kendall); (212) 397-7911 (Pinnacle); 7525-916598 (mobile, Kendall); 7793-559507 (mobile, Kendall). *E-mail:* markkendallartists@me.com; jmiller@pinnaclearts.com. *Website:* www.markkendallartists.com; www.pinnaclearts.com; www.davidcharlesabell.com.

ABLINGER-SPERRHACKE, Wolfgang; Austrian singer (character tenor); b. 1967, Zell am See. *Education:* Musikhochschule, Vienna. *Career:* first engagements in Linz, Basel and Gärtnerplatz, Munich; debut at Opéra Nat. de Paris 1997, subsequently sang there: Goro, Monostatos, 1st Armed Man, Capito/Mathis der Maler, Mime in Ring, world premiere of Philippe Manoury's K; other engagements have included Vašek/Bartered Bride, Reverend/Peter Grimes, Arnalta/L'Incoronazione di Poppea, Witch/Hänsel und Gretel, Tanzmeister/Ariadne auf Naxos and Podestà/Finta giardiniera at Glyndebourne Festival (more than 130 performances there to date), Valzacchi/Rosenkavalier (La Monnaie, Baden-Baden, MET), Dr Cajus/Falstaff (Aix, Madrid, Champs-Elysées), Mime/Das Rheingold (Dresden, Paris, La Scala, Berlin, Montreal, Amsterdam, Tokyo), Mime in Siegfried (Toulouse, Madrid, Paris, La Fenice, Bayerische Staatsoper, Stuttgart, Amsterdam), Pedrillo in Die Entführung aus dem Serail (La Coruña, Madrid, Naples), world premiere of Battistelli's Divorzio all'italiana (Nancy), Hauptmann in Wozzeck (Nancy, Scala, Bayerische Staatsoper, Opernhaus Zürich), Loge (Strasbourg, Lucerne Festival, Opera North), Aegisth in Elektra (Strasbourg), Piet in Grand Macabre (ENO), Witch (Lyon, Bayerische Staatsoper), Herodes in Salome (Volksoper, Staatsoper Wien, Opernhaus Zürich), Pirzel in Soldaten (Salzburg, La Scala), Prinz/Kammerdiener/Marquis (Bayerische Staatsoper, Staatsoper Berlin); world premiere of scenic production of Gurrelieder/Klaus Narr in Amsterdam; has worked with numerous conductors, including Petrenko, Barenboim, Thielemann, Conlon, Nagano, Jordan, Haim, Metzmacher, Gatti, Pappano, Haenchen, Ticciati, Luisi, Marc Albrecht and Tate; has appeared widely in concert, including BBC Proms at Royal Albert Hall (Arnalta and Witch semi-staged with Glyndebourne), Concertgebouw, São Paulo (Mahler's Das Lied von der Erde), Melbourne (Schönberg's Gurrelieder), Bergen Festival, Philharmonie Berlin (Grand Macabre); future engagements include Siegfried-Mime in Toronto, Loge of Opera North, Rheingold-Mime at Staatsoper Berlin, Gurrelieder in Göteborg, Hanover and Hamburg, Pollux/Liebe der Danae at Salzburg Festival, Valzacchi and Iwan/Nase at Covent Garden. *Recordings on DVD:* Falstaff, Die Fledermaus, Haensel und Gretel, L'Incoronazione di Poppea, Rosenkavalier, Rheingold, Lulu, Zauberflöte, Soldaten, Ariadne auf Naxos, Ring, Gurrelieder, Wozzeck. *Current Management:* c/o Bernd Schmickl, Artists Management Vienna, Höfergasse 1A/Top 3, 1090 Vienna, Austria. *Telephone:* (1) 5816271. *E-mail:* bschmickl@hotmail.com. *Website:* www.ablinger-sperrhacke.com.

ABRAHAMSEN, Hans; Danish composer; b. 23 Dec. 1952, Copenhagen. *Education:* Royal Danish Conservatory, Copenhagen, Jutland Acad. of Music,

Århus with Pelle Gudmundsen-Holmgreen, Per Nørgård and György Ligeti. *Career:* co-cr. Århus Sinfonietta 1990; Asst Prof. in Composition and Instrumentation, Royal Danish Conservatory of Music, Copenhagen 1995–; Four Pieces for Orchestra premiered at BBC Proms (BBC Scottish Symphony Orchestra conducted by Ilan Volkov) 2005; works performed by Nat. Symphony Orchestra, Washington, DC. *Compositions:* orchestral: Foam 1970, Symphony in C 1972, Symphony No. 1 1974, Stratifications 1973–75, Nach und Trompeten 1981, Marchenbilder for 14 players 1984, Cello Concerto 1987, Concerto for piano and orchestra 2000, Four Pieces for Orchestra 2004; chamber: Fantasy Pieces After Hans Jorgen Nielsen for flute, horn, cello and piano 1969, revised 1976, October for piano left hand 1969, revised 1976, Round and In Between for brass quintet 1972, two Woodwind Quintets: No. 1 Landscapes 1972, No. 2 Walden 1978, Nocturnes for flute and piano 1972, Flowersongs for three flutes 1973, Scraps for cello and piano 1973, Universe Birds for 10 sopranos 1973, two String Quartets: No. 1 1973, No. 2 1991, 10 Preludes 1973, No. 2 1981, Flush for saxophone 1974, revised 1979, Double for flute and guitar 1975, Songs of Denmark for soprano and five instruments 1974, revised 1976, Herbst for tenor, flute, guitar and cello 1970–72, revised 1977, Canzone for accordion 1978, Winternacht for seven instruments 1976–79, Aria for soprano and four instruments 1979, Geduldspiel for 10 instruments 1980, Six Pieces for violin, horn and piano 1984, 10 Studies for piano 1983–87, Autumn Song for soprano and ensemble 1992, Schnee for chamber ensemble 2008, Wald (BBC Radio 3 commission) 2009. *Honours:* Carl Nielsen Prize 1989, Wilhelm Hansen Prize 1998. *Address:* c/o Edition Wilhelm Hansen, Bornholmsgade 1A, 1266 Copenhagen K, Denmark (office). *Website:* www.musicsalesclassical.com.

ABRAMSKY, Dame Jennifer (Jenny) Gita, DBE, CBE, BA; British radio producer, editor and broadcasting industry executive; *Chair, Governing Body, Royal Academy of Music;* b. 7 Oct. 1946, d. of the late Chimen Abramsky and Miriam Abramsky (née Nirenstein); m. Alasdair D. MacDuff Liddell 1976 (died 2012); one s. one d. *Education:* Holland Park School and Univ. of East Anglia. *Career:* joined BBC Radio as Programme Operations Asst 1969, Producer, The World at One 1973, Ed. PM 1978–81, Producer Radio Four Budget Programmes 1979–86, The World at One 1981–86, Ed. Today programme 1986–87, News and Current Affairs Radio 1987–93, est. Radio Four News FM 1991, Controller BBC Radio Five Live 1993–96, Dir Continuous News Services, BBC (including Radio Five Live, BBC News 24, BBC World Service, BBC News Online, Ceefax) 1996–98, Dir BBC Radio 1998–2000, BBC Radio and Music 2000–06, Head, Audio and Music Group 2006–08, also in charge of BBC Radio Drama and Popular Music TV 2007–08, mem. Exec. Bd; Chair., Heritage Lottery Fund and Nat. Heritage Memorial Fund 2008–14; Chair., Governing Body, Royal Acad. of Music 2014–; Chair. Univ. of London 2008–; News Int. Visiting Prof. of Broadcast Media, Exeter Coll., Oxford 2002; mem. Econ. and Social Research Council 1992–96, Editorial Bd British Journalism Review 1993–; Vice-Chair. Digital Radio Devt Bureau 2002–08, RAM; mem. Bd of Dirs Hampstead Theatre 2003–, Chair. 2005–; mem. Bd of Govs BFI 2000–06; Gov. Royal Ballet; Trustee, Shakespeare Schools Festival, Central School of Ballet; Radio Acad. Fellowship 1998; Fellow, Central School of Speech and Drama. *Honours:* Hon. Prof., Thames Valley Univ. 1994, Hon. RAM 2002; Hon. MA (Salford) 1997, Dr hc (Westminster), (East Anglia), Hon. DCL (Kent) 2011; Woman of Distinction, Jewish Care 1990, Sony Radio Acad. Award 1995. *Address:* Royal Academy of Music, Marylebone Road, London, NW1 5HT, England (office). *Telephone:* (20) 7873-7373 (office). *Website:* www.ram.ac.uk (office).

ABREU, José Antonio, PhD; Venezuelan pianist, economist and orchestra director; b. 7 May 1939, Valera. *Education:* studied with Doralisa Jiménez de Medina, Barquisimeto, Caracas Musical Acad., Univ. Católica Andrés Bello, Univ. of Michigan, USA. *Career:* fmr Del. Asamblea Nacional; fmr Prof., Univ. Católica Andrés Bello, Univ. Simón Bolívar; f. Symphony Orchestra Simón Bolívar and Nat. Symphony Youth Orchestra 1975–; led to the establishment of youth orchestras in other Venezuelan states and foundation of Nat. System of Children's and Youth Orchestras of Venezuela (FESNOJIV, El Sistema) 1994, Foundation Dir 1994–; Minister of Culture 1983–88; Special Rep. and Nat. Co-ordinator, UNESCO World Movt of Youth Orchestras and Choirs Project; UNESCO Goodwill Amb. 1998–. *Honours:* Order of the Rising Sun, Grand Cordon (Japan) 2007, Officier, Légion d'honneur (France) 2009; Hon. mem. Royal Philharmonic Soc. 2008; Dr hc (Metropolitana Univ., Caracas) 2010, (Inst. of Education, Univ. of London) 2012; Symphonic Music Nat. Prize 1967, UNESCO Int. Music Prize 1993, Right Livelihood Award 2001, World Culture Open Creative Arts Award 2004, Prince of Asturias Arts Award 2008, Glenn Gould Prize, Canada 2008, B'nai B'rith Human Rights Award 2008, Polar Music Prize, Royal Swedish Acad. of Music 2009, Crystal Award, World Economic Forum 2009, Erasmus Prize 2010. *Address:* FESNOJIV, Parque Central, Torre Oeste, Piso 18, Caracas 1010, Venezuela (office). *Telephone:* (212) 576-55-11 (office). *E-mail:* contacto@fesnojiv.gob.ve (home). *Website:* www.fesnojiv.gob.ve (office).

ACHIM, Erzsébet; Hungarian organist; b. 6 Nov. 1954, Gyula; m. Miklós Thaisz 1978; two s. *Education:* Bartók Béla Konzervatórium, Ferenc Liszt Acad of Music. *Career:* played piece by Bartók for Hungarian Radio aged five; performs at organ concerts and concerts with orchestra, also as soloist and with choirs; teaches church music; several interviews and concerts broadcast by Hungarian radio and television; appeared at Int. Kodaly Festival 2007; Artistic Dir concert series TonArt Brother Klaus; mem. Hungarian Church Music Soc. *Recordings include:* several of chamber music 1990–96, Handel:

Six Organ Concertos op 4 1994, Glocken und Orgeln in Selm 1999. *Publications:* contrib. articles in Magyar Nemzet, Hungarian dailies, Uj Magyarország, Der Landbote, Switzerland, Südwest Presse, Germany, BBC Music Magazine. *Honours:* Ferenc Liszt Int. Musical Competition Prize for Interpretation of Hungarian Composers 1978. *Address:* Apor Vilmos tér 3, 1124 Budapest, Hungary. *E-mail:* elisabetha9@gmail.com.

ACHÚCARRO, Joaquín; Spanish pianist; b. 1 Nov. 1936, Bilbao. *Education:* Accademia Chigiana, studied with Walter Gieseking. *Career:* numerous solo and concert performances worldwide from 1959, including appearances with Berlin, New York, London and Los Angeles Philharmonic Orchestras, London, Chicago and Dallas Symphony Orchestras, Philharmonia, City of Birmingham, Royal Scottish, Orchestre National de France, RTE Dublin, Yomiuri of Tokyo, Western Australia, RIAS Berlin, Hamburg, Stuttgart, Dusseldorf, Santa Cecilia Rome, La Scala Milan, La Fenice Venice, Orquesta Nacional de España and Warsaw Nat. Orchestra; venues include Avery Fisher Hall, Carnegie Hall, Concertgebouw, Kennedy Center, Musikverein, Royal Albert Hall, Salle Gaveau, Salle Pleyel, Teatro alla Scala, Suntory Hall, Sydney Opera House, Teatro Colón and Barbican; worked with 349 conductors such as Claudio Abbado, Sir Adrian Boult, Riccardo Chailly, Sir Colin Davis, Zubin Mehta, Sir Yehudi Menuhin, Seiji Ozawa and Sir Simon Rattle; soloist-conductor with chamber orchestras in UK, Italy, Germany and Spain; Joel Estes Tate Chair, Southern Methodist Univ., Dallas 1989–; Prof., Int. Summer Courses, Accademia Musicale Chigiana, Siena, Italy; BBC recitals on tour 1997; played at inauguration of Bilbao Guggenheim Museum 1997, with audience of 25,000, broadcast live in over 100 countries. *Recordings include:* albums of Granados, Falla, Schubert, Ravel, Debussy, Mussorgsky, Rodrigo and Brahms, including Rodrigo's Piano Concerto 1997, Schumann's Kreisleriana op.16 and Fantasie op.17 2005. *Honours:* mem. Real Academia de Bellas Artes de San Fernando, Académico Honorario de la Real Academia de Bellas Artes de Granada 2011; Comendador, Order of Isabel la Católica, Great Cross of Civil Merit 2003; winner, Liverpool Int. Competition 1959, Premio Nacional de Música 1992, Gold Medal of Fine Arts 1996, Premio Larios for Musical Excellence 1997, UNESCO Artist for Peace award for extraordinary artistic achievement 2000, Great Cross of Civil Merit 2003. *Current Management:* c/o Conciertos Augusto, Calle Viento nº 15, 2ºB, 28220 Majadahonda, Madrid, Spain. *Telephone:* 916340205. *Fax:* 916340250. *E-mail:* info@conciertosaugusto.com. *Website:* www.conciertosaugusto.com; www.achucarro.com.

ACKERT, Stephen, DMus; American musician and arts administrator; *Head, Music Department, National Gallery of Art, Washington, DC*; b. 13 May 1944, Crookston, Minn.; m. Golnoush Khaleghi. *Education:* Oberlin Coll., Ohio, Univ. of Wisconsin, Madison Northwestern Univ., Evanston, Ill. *Career:* resident keyboard artist and Music Dir of resident orchestra, Nat. Iranian Radio and TV Network, Tehran 1974–78; Dir of Music St Margaret's Episcopal Church, Washington, DC 1979–86; music program specialist, Nat. Gallery of Art, Washington, DC 1986–2004, Head of Music Dept 2004–; concert organist; teacher of applied organ; host of weekly classical music broadcasts on WOBC, Oberlin, OH and the Nat. Iranian Radio and TV Network, Tehran; organ recitals in USA and Europe; mem. Bd of Advisors, Amalfi Coast Music and Art Festival. *Publications:* articles in The American Organist, concert programme notes for Nat. Gallery of Art. *Honours:* Fulbright Scholarship, Robert F. Smith Research Fellowship, Nat. Fed. of Music Clubs Award, Alumnus of the Year Award, Oberlin Coll. 2002. *Address:* National Gallery of Art, Washington, DC 20565, USA (office). *Telephone:* (202) 842-6075 (office). *Fax:* (202) 712-7489 (office). *E-mail:* s-ackert@nga.gov (office). *Website:* www.nga.gov (office).

ACOSTA, Adolovni Punsalan, BM, MM, MS; Philippine/American pianist, music teacher and music director; b. 3 Feb. 1946, Manila. *Education:* Wesleyan Univ., Conn., Univ. of the Philippines, Juilliard School, New York, New York Univ. *Career:* New York debut, Carnegie Recital Hall 1971; solo recitals in Europe, the Middle East, N and S America, Asia and the Pacific, Australia, NZ and at venues including Carnegie Hall, Alice Tully Hall in Lincoln Center, Merkin Concert Hall, Steinway Hall, New York, Wigmore Hall and Purcell Room, London, Salle Cortot, Paris, Hallwylska Museet, Stockholm, Odd Fellow Palaet, Copenhagen, Der Beethovensaal at La Redoute, Bonn, Yamaha Concert Hall, Vienna, Centrepointe Theatre, Ottawa, Centro Cultural Recoleta, Buenos Aires, Sala Carlos Chavez, Mexico City, Teatro Nacional, Brasilia, Cultural Center of the Philippines, Manila, Sunderland and Wolverhampton Art Galleries, UK, and in Hamburg and Berlin at JFK Int. School, and at univs in USA, Australia and NZ; selected by Jack Kahn Pianos to give a solo recital at Bösendorfer Piano in Concert at the Center for Inter-American Relations, New York City along with Paul Badura-Skoda and Aldo Ciccolini; masterclasses and recitals at Ho Chi Minh City Conservatory of Music, Saigon, Univ. of Canterbury School of Music, Christchurch, NZ, Monash Univ. School of Music-Conservatorium, Clayton, Melbourne, Univ. of the Philippines Coll. of Music, Univ. of Santo Tomas Conservatory of Music, Manila, Calcutta School of Music, India, and in Malaysia and Brunei; performances featured on Swedish Radio, Argentine TV Acercando Oriente and Radio Belgrano, Vietnam TV, Brunei TV, Manila Radio and TV stations, Voice of America, Nat. Public Radio Network (USA) and New York City radio stations; participated in a concert at The White House for Rosalyn Carter and wives of the diplomatic corps 1980; Full Assistantship, Wesleyan Univ. 1968–69; Visiting Prof., Mahasarakham Univ. Coll. of Music, Thailand. *Recordings:* Andalucia and Danzas Afro Cubanas of Ernesto Lecuona, Piano Music of Carl Nielsen, Malagueña: Piano Music from Cuba and the Philippines 2008. *Honours:* John D. Rockefeller III scholarship from The Juilliard School 1969–71, named one of the "Ten Outstanding Young Women of America" 1982, included as one of the "100 Young Women of Promise" by Good Housekeeping magazine in its 100th anniversary issue 1985, elected to Nat. Music Honor Soc. of Phi Kappa Lambda, New York Univ. chapter 1982, included as a performer in Chronology of Western Classical Music 1751–2000 by Charles J. Hall, Philippine Presidential Award 2006. *Address:* 310 Riverside Drive, Apt 313, New York, NY 10025, USA (home). *E-mail:* adolovniacosta2@alum.juilliard.edu (office).

ACS, Janos, DipMus; Italian (b. Hungarian) conductor; b. 23 March 1952; m. (divorced); one s. two d. *Education:* Bela Bartók Inst., F. Liszt Acad., Budapest, Verdi Conservatorio, Milan. *Career:* debut, Fidelio at Teatro Carlo Felice, Genoa 1979; Idomeneo at Opera di Roma, Tancredi at La Fenice, Falstaff, I Capuleti, Amico Fritz at Arena di Verona, Offenbach at Comunale di Firenze, La Bohème at Frankfurt, Symphonic Programmes in Tokyo, Manon, Pagliacci, La Traviata, and Otello in Denver, Carmen, Il Trovatore, and Tristan und Isolde in Pretoria, Faust in Hong Kong, and Luciano Pavarotti in Mexico, Venezuela, Finland, Valencia, Brasilia, Hannover, Budapest, Bilbao, Lyon; also with Chicago Symphony and audience of 60,000 in 2000, Beijing and Hong Kong 2001, at four Football World Championships (three tenors), and in Bath, UK and Columbus, USA 2003; also Turandot at Stade de France in Paris, Olympic Stadiums at Schalke Arena, Gelsenkirchen, and in Munich 2005; Principal Conductor, Pact Theater, Pretoria 1983–88; Principal Conductor, Opera Colorado, Denver, USA 1985–91; one of Pavarotti's conductors from 1991; Artistic Dir, Municipal Theatre of Salerno, Italy 1994–99; Conductor, Orchestra of the Three Tenors 1999–2003; Artistic Dir, Fondazione Pitti, Budapest; Co-Dir, Franz Liszt Soc. of Germany; masterclasses. *Recordings:* Bellini Overtures, Donizetti Overtures, I Puritani, Carmen (video of Pact Theater in Pretoria), Respighi's Gli Uccelli, Trittico Botticelliano, Járdányi: Violin Concertino 2001, Bottesini: Works for Double Bass, Vol. 4 2003, Vol. 5 2005. *Honours:* Respighi Memorial Concert and Prize 1985. *Current Management:* Arepo Music & Artists Promotion. *E-mail:* info@arepo.it. *Address:* c/o Via Carducci 38, 2100 Milan, Italy. *E-mail:* janosacs@janosacs.com. *Website:* www.janosacs.com.

ADAM, Theo; German singer (bass-baritone); b. 1 Aug. 1926, Dresden; s. of Johannes Adam and Lisbeth Adam (née Dernstorf); m. Eleonore Matthes 1949; one s. one d. *Education:* Gymnasium and Conservatory. *Career:* engagements with Dresden State Opera 1949, Bayreuth Festival 1952–80, Salzburg Festival 1969, 1970, 1980–89, 1992, 1995; mem. Deutsche Staatsoper, Berlin 1953–; has appeared with Vienna and Munich State Operas since 1967; Pres. of Curatorium Oper, Dresden 1985–; sang at Semper Opera House, Dresden 1985; staged Graun's Cesare e Cleopatra, Berlin State Opera 1992; performed at Royal Festival Hall, London 1994, Berlin Staatsoper 1997; retd from stage 2006; numerous recordings; Österreichischer Kammersänger, Bayerischer Kammersänger. *Publications:* Seht, hier ist Tinte, Feder, Papier 1980, Die 100 Rolle, Wie schön ist doch die Musik 1996. *Honours:* Nat. Prize (First Class) of GDR . *Address:* Schillerstrasse 14, 01326 Dresden, Germany (home). *Telephone:* (351) 2683997 (home).

ADAMIS, Mihalis (Michael); Greek composer and choral director; b. 19 May 1929, Piraeus; m. Pany Carella 1973; two s. *Education:* Athens University, Piraeus Conservatory, Hellenicon Conservatory, Brandeis University, Boston, USA. *Career:* founder and Dir, Hellenic Royal Palace Boys Choir 1950–67 and Athens Chamber Chorus 1958–61; taught Byzantine Music, directed choir, Greek Orthodox Coll. of Theology, Boston, USA 1961–63; f. first electronic music studio in Athens, Greece 1968; Head of Music Dept, Choir Dir, Pierce Coll., Athens 1968–; f. Music Dept, Ionian Univ., Corfu 1992; many festival commissions including Hellenic Weeks of Contemporary Music 1967–72, English Bach Festival 1971, 1973; world-wide performances of works include ONCE Festival, USA 1962, Barcelona 1973, Leicester 1976, Greek Month in London 1975, 1989, Art Weeks throughout Europe, Middle and Far East; many int. radio and television broadcasts; toured Europe and the Americas with ballet piece, Genesis 1973; Pres., Supreme Council for Music, Ministry of Culture 1993. *Compositions include:* Anikylesis for flute, oboe, celesta, viola and cello 1964, Byzantine Passion 1967, Apokalypsis 1967, Kratima 1971, Tetelestai oratorio 1971, Photonymon for psaltis, choir and percussion 1973, Evolutiones for orchestra 1980, Melisma for tenor and flute 1981, Rodanon for psaltis, Byzantine chorus and instrumental ensemble 1983, Epallelon for orchestra 1985, Kalophonikon for saxophone quartet 1988, Hirmos for voices, Vision of God for mixed chorus and orchestra 1997, Who is as Great as God? for women's chorus 1999, Melos for alto saxophone 2000. *Recordings:* Genesis; Apocalypsis; Minyrismos; Metallic Sculptures; Byzantine Passion; Psalmic Ode. *Address:* Gravias 43, 15342 Ayia Paraskevi, Athens, Greece.

ADAMO, Mark, BMus; American opera composer, librettist and stage director; b. 1962, Philadelphia; pnr John Corigliano. *Education:* New York Univ., Catholic Univ. of America. *Career:* first opera Little Women premiered Houston Grand Opera 1998, over 60 int. engagements including performances by New York City Opera, Minnesota Opera, Calgary Opera, State Opera South Australia, Tokyo City Opera; second opera Lysistrata, or, The Nude Goddess premiered Houston Grand Opera 2005; composer-in-residence New York City Opera 2001–06; Master Artist Atlantic Center for the Performing Arts 2003; debut as stage dir, Lyric Opera Cleveland (Little Women) 2004; currently Professor of Music Composition, Steinhardt School of Culture, Education and Human Devt, New York Univ. *Compositions:* opera: Little Women 1998, Avow (miniature chamber opera) 1999, Lysistrata, or, The Nude

Goddess 2005, The Gospel of Mary Magdalene; orchestral: Late Victorians for singer, speaker, soloists and orchestra 1995, Alcott Music (Suite from Little Women) for strings and percussion 1999, Four Angels (Concerto for harp and orchestra) 2007, August Music (Concerto for two flutes and strings) 2008; choral: No.10/Supreme Virtue for double SATB choir a capella 1999, Cantate Domino for solo soprano, double SATB choir and piano 1999–2000, The Poet Speaks of Praising for SATB or TTBB choir a capella 2000, Pied Beauty for unaccompanied SATB chorus 2000, Garland for SSAA choir and piano or chamber ensemble 2006, Matewan Music for soprano and unaccompanied SATB chorus 2009, God's Grandeur for SATB chorus and piano 2010. *Publications:* John Corigliano: A Monograph 2000; has annotated programmes for Stagebill, the Freer Gallery of Art, BMG Classics; criticism and interviews in publs, including The Washington Post, Stagebill, Opera News, The Star-Ledger, The New Grove Dictionary of Music and Musicians. *Honours:* Paulette Goddard Remarque Scholarship for outstanding undergraduate achievement in playwriting, Theodore Pressler Prize for outstanding undergraduate achievement in composing. *Current Management:* c/o G. Schirmer Music Publishers, 257 Park Avenue S, 20th Floor, New York, NY 10010, USA. *Telephone:* (212) 254-2100. *Fax:* (212) 254-2013. *E-mail:* schirmer@schirmer.com. *Website:* www.schirmer.com. *Address:* Department of Music and Performing Arts Professions, Steinhardt School of Culture, Education and Human Development, 35 W. 4th Street, Suite 777, New York, NY 10012, USA (office). *Telephone:* (212) 998-5424 (office). *Website:* steinhardt .nyu.edu/music/composition/faculty/adamo (office); www.markadamo.com.

ADAMONYTE, Jurgita, MMus; Lithuanian singer (mezzo-soprano); b. 1979, Vilnius. *Education:* Lithuanian Acad. of Music under Vladimiras Prudnikovas, Royal Acad. of Music, London with Anne Howells and Audrey Hyland. *Career:* debut as Zerlina in Don Giovanni with Lithuanian Nat. Opera and Ballet Theatre 2002; sang Maddalena in Rigoletto at Nat. Moravian-Silesian A. Dvorak Opera Theatre, Ostrava (Czech Repub.) 2003, Ursula in Béatrice and Bénédict, Chicago Opera Theater 2007. *Honours:* Opera Rara Bel Canto Prize, RAM 2006. *Current Management:* Parnassus Arts Productions, Erzherzog Wilhelm-Ring 13/4, 2500 Baden, Austria. *Telephone:* (2252) 82-777. *Fax:* (2252) 25-93-08. *E-mail:* parnassus@kabsi.at.

ADAMS, Byron, DMA; American composer, conductor, writer and teacher; b. 9 March 1955, Atlanta, Georgia. *Education:* Jacksonville Univ., Univ. of Southern California, Cornell Univ. *Career:* compositions performed in USA by West Virginia Symphony, Syracuse Symphony, Cantori New York, Chamber Music Palisades, Pacific Serenades, new music ensemble Xtet, and in Europe; Composer-in-Residence, Music Center, Univ. of the South 1979–84; Guest Composer, 26th Warsaw Autumn Festival 1983, and San Francisco Conservatory 1986; Lecturer, Cornell Univ., New York City 1985–87; Asst Prof., Assoc. Prof., Univ. of California at Riverside, now Prof. of Musicology; scholar-in-residence, Bard Music Festival Elgar and His World 2007. *Compositions:* Nightingales for soprano, clarinet, cello and piano 1979, Quintet for piano and strings 1979, Concerto for trumpet and string orchestra 1983, Sonata for trumpet and piano 1983, Concerto for violin and orchestra 1984, Go Lovely Rose for male chorus 1984, Missa brevis 1988, Three Epitaphs 1987, Magnificat for chorus, trumpet and organ 1988, Quatre Illuminations for soprano and chamber ensemble 1991, To Cecilia, Singing and Dancing for soprano solo, chorus, organ and orchestra (text by Ursula Vaughan Williams) 1994, Music for Duke Orsino's Table for flute, viola and harp 1996, Trois Illuminations for chamber chorus and harp 1999, Concerto for violoncello and orchestra 2001, Four Old American Hymns for baritone and harp 2001, The Vision of Dame Julian of Norwich for soprano, harp and string quartet 2002, Praises of Jerusalem (Psalm 122) for chorus and organ 2003, Bright Portals of the Sky for chorus and organ 2003, Variationis achemisticae for flute, viola, cello and piano 2005, Le Jardin Provençal for flute, oboe, harpsichord and cello 2006, Ashes of Soldiers for a cappella mixed chorus 2007. *Recordings:* Nightingales 1979; Serenata aestiva 1986. *Publications:* Vaughan Williams Essays (co-Ed.), Edward Elgar and His World (Ed.) 2007; contrib. to The Instrumentalist, Musical Quarterly, Notes, Grove Dictionary of Music & Musicians. *Honours:* Ralph Vaughan Williams Research Fellowship 1985, American Musicological Society Philip Brett Award for his scholarly work on the intersections of gender and nationalism in British music 2000. *Address:* Department of Music, University of California at Riverside, Riverside, CA 92521, USA (office). *Telephone:* (951) 827-5727 (office). *E-mail:* byron.adams@ ucr.edu (office).

ADAMS, David, BA; Australian composer, conductor and librettist; b. 19 April 1949, Box Hill, Victoria. *Education:* Canberra School of Music. *Career:* Lecturer in Music (History and Composition), Preston Technical College 1977; Lowther Hall Anglican Girls Grammar School 1977–81; Scotch Coll. 1978–83; his ballet Strangers performed at Sydney Opera House by Sydney Dance Company with the composer as conductor 1982; Melbourne Coll. of Advanced Education 1985–87; Conductor, Monash Univ. Orchestra 1988–; commissions from Sydney Dance Company, Australian Musicians Guild, British Musical Soc. 1987. *Compositions include:* Memories of the Future for guitar and 1979; Strangers, ballet for string quartet, oboe, horn and percussion 1981, being divinely for soprano, percussion and strings 1983, Variations for oboe and guitar 1983, In Memoriam, for soprano and ensemble 1984, Fan Fare for chorus, orchestra, soprano and viola 1985, Time Locked in his Tower, music theatre for flutes, guitar and percussion 1987, In My Craft of Sullen Art for soprano and viola 1994, Lunar aspects, song cycle for soprano and guitar 1996. *Honours:* Winner, Australian Composition Sections at Geelong Eisteddfod,

also Bandigo Eisteddfod 1981–83. *Address:* c/o APRA, 16 Mountain Street, Ultimo, NSW 2007, Australia.

ADAMS, H. Leslie, MusM, PhD; American composer; b. 30 Dec. 1932, Cleveland, OH. *Education:* Glenville High School, Oberlin Coll. Conservatory of Music, OH, California State Univ., Long Beach, Ohio State Univ., Univ. of Kansas, Cleveland Inst. of Music. *Career:* piano accompanist for ballet and dance companies in New York, numerous performances of his compositions 1957–62; Assoc. Musical Dir Karamu House, Cleveland, OH 1964–65, Composer-in-Residence 1979–80; Musical Dir Kaleidoscope Players, Raton, NM 1967–68; Composer-in-Residence, Cuyahoga Community Coll., Cleveland 1980, Cleveland Music School Settlement 1981–82; Founder and Pres. Accord Assocs. Inc. 1980–86, Exec. Vice-Pres. and Composer-in-Residence 1986–92; Exec. Vice-Pres. and Composer-in-Residence, Creative Arts Inc. 1997–; teacher, Soehl Jr High School, Linden, NJ 1962–63, secondary schools in Raton, NM 1966–67; Asst Prof. of Music, Florida A&M Univ., Tallahassee 1968; Assoc. Prof. of Music, Dir of the Univ. Choir and Dir of Choral Clinics, Univ. of Kansas, Lawrence 1970–78; mem. Advisory Council, Musical Arts Asscn (Cleveland Orchestra) 1982; mem. American Choral Dirs Asscn, American Guild of Organists. *Compositions:* Hark, to the Shouting Wind! 1951, I Hear A Voice 1951, Night 1951, The Constant Lover 1951, Break, Break, Break 1951, Teach Me, O Lord (from Psalm 119) 1951, Turn Away Mine Eyes 1951, Four Pieces for piano 1951, Pastorale for violin and piano 1952, Asperges Me for chorus 1952, Two Vachel Lindsay Songs 1952–53, Of Man's First Disobedience (from Paradise Lost) 1953, On the Sea 1953, Seven Amen Chorale Responses 1953, Intermezzo for violin and piano 1953, Theme and Variations in A-flat Major (or Variations on a Serious Theme) 1953, A Kiss in Xanadu (ballet) 1954, The Congo 1955, Romance for orchestra 1960, Five Songs on Texts by Edna St Vincent Millay (or Five Millay Songs) 1960, Six Songs (on Texts by African-American Poets) 1961, A White Road 1961, Sonata for violin and piano 1961, Three Preludes for piano 1961, Sonata for horn and piano 1961, Contrasts for piano 1961, Concerto for piano and orchestra (or CitiScape) 1964, All the Way Home 1965, Madrigal for chorus 1969, Love Song for chorus 1969, Hosanna to the Son of David for chorus 1969, Psalm 121 for chorus 1969, Under the Greenwood Tree for chorus 1969, Psalm 23 for chorus 1970, There Was an Old Man for chorus 1970, Vocalise for chorus 1973, Man's Presence: A Song of Ecology for chorus 1975, Trombone Quartet 1975, Sonata for cello and piano 1975, Etude in G Minor 1977, Prelude and Fugue for organ 1979, Ode to Life for orchestra 1979, Dunbar Songs (or Three Songs on Texts of Paul Laurence Dunbar) 1981, Christmas Lullaby 1983, Night Song for flute and harp 1983, Symphony No. 1 1983, The Righteous Man: A Cantata to the Memory of Dr Martin Luther King Jr (or Cantata No. 1) 1985, Blake (opera) 1986, The Wider View 1988, Hymn to Freedom 1989, Love Expressions 1990, Love Memory 1990, What Love Brings 1991, A Christmas Wish for chorus 1991, Offering of Love for organ 1991, Amazing Grace 1992, Song of the Innkeeper's Children 1992, Song to Baby Jesus 1992, Christmas Lullaby for orchestra with chorus 1993, Song of Thanks 1993, Love Request 1993, Lullaby Eternal 1993, Anniversary Song 1993, Flying 1993, Midas, Poor Midas 1994, From a Hotel Room 1994, Daybirth 1994, Western Adventure for orchestra 1994, Hymn to All Nations for chorus 1997, Slaves (a drama with music) 2005. *Publications:* contrib. articles The Mahlerian Mystique 1969, The Problems of Composing Choral Music for High School Use 1973. *Honours:* Nat. Asscn of Negro Women Inc. Composition Competition, New York 1963, Nat. Educ. Defense Act Fellowship 1969–70, Christian Arts Inc. Nat. Award for Original Composition for Choral Ensemble, New York 1974, Nat. Endowment for the Arts Award 1979, Rockefeller Foundation Study and Conference Center, Bellagio Italy 1979, Yaddo Artists Colony, Saratoga Springs NY 1980, 1984, Cleveland Foundation Fellow 1980, Jennings Foundation Fellow 1981, 'Meet The Artist' Cleveland Ohio Public Schools, Nat. Opera Asscn Legacy Award 2006, Distinguished Alumnus Award, California State Univ., Long Beach 2006, Gems of Cleveland Award 2007. *Current Management:* Creative Arts Inc., 9409 Kempton Avenue, Cleveland, OH 44108; Avava Artists Management, 229 West 134th Street, New York, NY 10030, USA. *E-mail:* CreativeArtsInc@webtv.net; avidw@avavaartists.com. *Telephone:* (212) 502-0306 (office). *E-mail:* HLeslieAdams@webtv.net (home). *Website:* www .hleslieadams.com.

ADAMS, John Coolidge; American composer and conductor; b. 15 Feb. 1947, Worcester, Mass. *Education:* Harvard Univ. *Career:* appearances as clarinettist and conductor; Head, Composition Dept, San Francisco Conservatory of Music 1971–81; advisor on new music, San Francisco Symphony Orchestra 1978–82, Composer-in-Residence 1982–85; Creative Advisor, St Paul Chamber Orchestra 1988–89; Creative Chair, Los Angeles Philharmonic Orchestra 2009–; Guggenheim Fellowship 1982, Fellow, BAC&S 2005. *Film:* as composer: Io sono l'amore 2009. *Compositions include:* opera and stage works: Nixon in China 1987, The Death of Klinghoffer 1991, I Was Looking at the Ceiling and Then I Saw the Sky 1995, El Niño 1999, Doctor Atomic 2004, A Flowering Tree, 2006, The Gospel According to the Other Mary 2012; orchestral works: Shaker Loops 1978, Common Tones in Simple Time 1979, Harmonium 1980, Grand Pianola Music 1981–82, Harmonielehre 1984–85, The Chairman Dances 1985, Short Ride in a Fast Machine 1986, Tromba Lontana 1986, Fearful Symmetries 1988, The Wound-Dresser 1989, Eros Piano 1989, El Dorado 1991, Violin Concerto (Grawemeyer Award for Music Composition) 1993, Gnarly Buttons 1996, A Flowering Tree 2008; chamber and ensemble works: Christian Zeal and Activity 1973, China Gates 1977, Phrygian Gates 1977, Chamber Symphony 1992, John's Book of Alleged Dances 1994, Road Movies 1995, Naïve and Sentimental Music 1998, El Niño

2000, Guide to Strange Places 2001, On the Transmigration of Souls (Pulitzer Prize for Music 2003, Grammy Awards for Best Classical Album, Best Orchestral Performance, Best Classical Contemporary Composition 2005, Classical BRIT Award for Contemporary Music 2005) 2002, Doctor Atomic Symphony (British Composer Award for Best Int. Composition 2009) 2005, The Dharma at Big Sur 2003, My Father Knew Charles Ives (Classical BRIT Award for Contemporary Composer 2007) 2003, City Noir 2009, Son of Chamber Symphony 2007, Absolute Jest 2012. *Publications:* Hallelujah Junction (memoir) (Northern California Book Award for Creative Nonfiction) 2008; contribs to New York Times Book Review, New Yorker. *Honours:* Dr hc (Yale Univ.), (Harvard Univ.), (Univ. of Cambridge), (Northwestern Univ.), (Juilliard School); Opera News Award 2008, Nat. Endowment for the Arts Opera Award 2009. *Current Management:* IMG Artists, 7 West 54th Street, New York, NY 10019, USA. *E-mail:* artistsny@imgartists.com. *Website:* imgartists.com; www.earbox.com.

ADAMS, John Luther; American composer; b. 23 Jan. 1953, Meridian, Miss. *Education:* California Inst. of the Arts. *Career:* moved to Alaska in 1978; timpanist and prin. percussionist, Fairbanks Symphony Orchestra and Arctic Chamber Orchestra 1982–89; composition methods have included percussion ensembles, Alaska Native voices, orchestral residencies, sound and light installations; music performed by Bang on a Can, the California E.A.R. Unit, Percussion Group Cincinnati, American Composers Orchestra, Chicago Symphony Orchestra. *Compositions include:* for orchestra: A Northern Suite 1979–80, The Far Country of Sleep 1988, Dream in White On White 1992, Sauyatugvik: The Time of Drumming 1995, Clouds of Forgetting, Clouds of Unknowing 1991–95, In the White Silence 1998, The Light That Fills the World 1999–2000, for Lou Harrison 2003, Dark Waves 2007, The Light Within 2010, Become Ocean (Pulitzer Prize for Music 2014) 2013; for solo/small ensemble: songbirdsongs (for two piccolos and three percussion) 1974–80, Five Yup'ik Dances (for harp) 1991–94, Make Prayers to the Raven (for flute, violin, harp (or piano), cello, percussion) 1996/98, In a Treeless Place, Only Snow (for celesta, harp (or piano), 2 vibraphones, string quartet) 1999, Among Red Mountains (for solo piano) 2001, The Immeasurable Space of Tones (for violin, vibraphone, piano, sustaining keyboard, contrabass instrument) 1998–2001, After the Light (for alto flute, vibraphone, harp) 2001, Dark Wind (for bass clarinet, vibraphone, marimba, piano) 2001, Red Arc/Blue Veil (for piano, mallet percussion and processed sounds) 2002, The Light Within (for alto flute, bass clarinet, vibraphone/crotales, piano, violin, cello and electronic sounds) 2007, Across the Distance (for French Horn) 2015; for percussion: Strange and Sacred Noise (six pieces for percussion quartet) 1991–97, Three Drum Quartets from Earth and the Great Weather 1993, The Mathematics of Resonant Bodies (for solo percussion and processed sounds) 2002, Always Very Soft (for percussion trio) 2007, Inuksuit 2009, Four Thousand Holes (for piano, percussion and electronic sounds) 2010; electronic: The Place Where You Go to Listen (continuous light and sound environment at Univ. of Alaska, Fairbanks Museum of the North) 2004–06, Veils (three soundscapes) 2005, the place we began (four electro-acoustic soundscapes) 2008; vocal & choral: Night Peace (for antiphonal choirs, solo soprano, harp, percussions) 1976, Little Cosmic Dust Poem (for voice & piano) 2007, Sky with Four Suns and Sky with Four Moons (for four choirs) 2008, I L I M A Q 2012, Sila: The Breath of the World 2014. *Recordings include:* The Far Country, Dark Wind, The Light that Fills the World, In the White Silence, Strange & Sacred Noise 2005, The Mathematics of Resonant Bodies 2006, The Place We Began 2009, The Wind In High Places 2015, Ilimaq 2015. *Publications include:* Winter Music: A Composer's Journal 1998–99, The Place Where You Go To Listen 2009. *Honours:* US Artists Fellow, awards and fellowships from Nat. Endowment for the Arts, Rockefeller Foundation, Rasmuson Foundation, Foundation for Contemporary Arts, Michael Ludwig Nemmers Prize in Music Composition 2010, Heinz Award 2012, Columbia Univ. William Schuman Award 2015. *E-mail:* johnlutheradams.info@gmail.com; jla@alaska.net. *Website:* www .johnlutheradams.net.

ADAMS, Piers; British recorder player; b. 21 Dec. 1963. *Career:* has given recitals in most major UK festivals and concert halls and in most European countries, as well as visits to USA, Canada, Russia and the Far East; has performed concertos with numerous orchestras, including BBC Symphony and Concert orchestras, the Philharmonia, Academy of Ancient Music, English Sinfonia, City of London Sinfonia, London Musici, Singapore Symphony Orchestra; also performs with baroque quartet Red Priest; repertoire includes: Vivaldi Four Seasons, Vivaldi Concertos, Sammartini Concerto for Descant Recorder, Telemann Concertos in F and C for Treble Recorder, Telemann Suite in A minor, Babell Concerti in D major and E minor for Sixth Flute, David Bedford Recorder Concertos, works by Malcolm Arnold, Vladislav Shoot, Christopher Gander, Gerald Plain, David Pugsley and John Mayer. *Recordings:* albums: solo: Shine & Shade, Recorder Bravura, Vivaldi Concertos, David Bedford Recorder Concerto, Handel Recorder Sonatas, Vision of Delight, English Nightingale, Dances with Gods, Wild Men of the Seicento; with Red Priest: Johann I'm Only Dancing, Pirates of the Baroque, Vivaldi The Four Seasons, Nightmare in Venice, Priest on the Run, Handel in the Wind. *Honours:* First Prize, Moeck Int. Recorder Competition 1985. *Current Management:* c/o Upbeat Classical Management, 170 Thirlmere Gardens, Northwood, HA6 2RU, England. *Telephone:* (1923) 836220. *E-mail:* admin@upbeatclassical.co.uk. *Website:* www.upbeatclassical.co.uk. *E-mail:* piers@redpriest.com (home). *Website:* www.piersadams.com.

ADAMS-BARBARO, Jennifer, AGSM; British singer (soprano); b. 22 March 1953, London. *Education:* Guildhall School of Music and Drama. *Career:* opera debut aged 15, Juliet in Gounod's Romeo and Juliet; operatic roles, Gretel, Galatea, Euridice, Dido, Micaela, Naiad and Turandot; star singer on Friday Night is Music Night 1985; Glyndebourne Festival Opera; Mozart Requiem, Swansea Festival, Jane Glover 1991. *Recordings:* numerous BBC solo recordings, including Rossini Petite Messe, Verdi Four Sacred Pieces with BBC Symphony Orchestra; Promenade concert; Bartók Five Village Scenes with Pierre Boulez, Concertgebouw, Amsterdam (video). *Honours:* world finalist Luciano Pavarotti Prize 1985. *Address:* 68 Bellingham Road, Catford, London, SE6 2PT, England.

ADÈS, Thomas Joseph Edmund, MA, MPhil; British composer, pianist and conductor; b. 1 March 1971, London; s. of Timothy Adès and Dawn Adès. *Education:* Univ. Coll. School, Guildhall School of Music, King's Coll., Cambridge, St John's Coll., Cambridge. *Career:* solo recitalist with Composers Ensemble 1992; PLG Young Concert Artists Platform concert at Purcell Room 1993; Composer-in-Assocn, Hallé Orchestra 1993–95; Lecturer, Univ. of Manchester 1993–94; Fellow Commoner in Creative Arts, Trinity Coll., Cambridge 1995–97; Benjamin Britten Prof. of Music, RAM 1997–99; Musical Dir Birmingham Contemporary Music Group 1998–2000; Artistic Dir Aldeburgh Festival 1999–2008; R. and B. Debs Composer Chair., Carnegie Hall, New York 2007–08; conducted the BBC Symphony Orchestra at BBC Proms. *Compositions include:* Five Eliot Landscapes 1990, Chamber Symphony 1990, Catch 1991, Darkness Visible 1992, Under Hamelin Hill 1992, Fool's Rhymes 1992, Still Sorrowing 1993, Life Story 1993, Living Toys 1993, … but all shall be well 1993, Sonata da Caccia 1994, The Origin of the Harp 1994, Arcadiana (Ernst von Siemens Prize) 1994, Powder Her Face 1995, Traced Overhead 1995–96, These Premises are Alarmed 1996, Asyla (Royal Philharmonic Soc. Award for Large-scale Composition 1997, Grawemeyer Prize 1999) 1997, Concerto Conciso 1997–98, America (A Prophecy) 1999, January Writ 1999, Piano Quintet 2000, Brahms 2001, The Tempest (Olivier Award for outstanding achievement in opera 2005, Royal Philharmonic Soc. award for large-scale composition 2005) 2004, Three Studies from Couperin 2006, Tevot (Royal Philharmonic Soc. Award for large-scale composition) 2007, The Four Quarters (British Composer Award for Best Chamber Music 2012) 2011, Totentanz (for mezzo-soprano, baritone and orchestra 2013. *Television includes:* Music for the 21st Century: Thomas Adès (Channel 4), Powder her Face (Channel 4). *Honours:* Lutine Prize, GSM 1986, winner Paris Rostrum, for best piece by composer under 30 1994, Royal Philharmonic Prize 1997, Elise L. Stoeger Prize 1996, Royal Philharmonic Soc. Award for Large-scale Composition 2005, Salzburg Easter Festival Prize 1999, Hindemith Prize 2001, ISCM Young Composers Award 2002, Musical America Award for Composer of the Year 2011. *Current Management:* IMG Artists, LLC, Carnegie Hall Tower, 152 West 57th Street, 5th Floor, New York, NY 10019-3433, USA. *E-mail:* aelsesser@imgartists.com. *Website:* thomasades .com.

ADEY, Christopher, FRAM, FRCM, FRWCMD; British conductor; b. 19 Feb. 1943, London; m. Catherine Cave 1965 (divorced 1985); one s. *Education:* Royal Acad. of Music. *Career:* violinist with Hallé Orchestra 1963–65, London Philharmonic Orchestra 1967–71; Assoc. Conductor, BBC Scottish Symphony Orchestra 1973–76; Ulster Orchestra 1981–83; Conductor and Prof., Royal Coll. of Music (RCM) 1979–92, Dir of Orchestral Studies, RCM Jr Dept 1973–84; Principal Conductor, Nat. Youth Orchestra of Wales 1996–2002; Chief Conductor and Artistic Dir Royal Oman Symphony Orchestra 2000–04; Conductor-in-Residence, Wells Cathedral School 2001–; also currently Prin. Guest Conductor, Orchestra of the Music Makers, Singapore. *Publication:* Orchestral Performance: A Guide for Conductors and Players 1998. *Honours:* Hon. Vice-Pres. Welsh Music Guild; Commemorative Medal of Czechoslovakian Govt 1986. *Current Management:* Performing Arts, 6 Windmill Street, London, W1T 2IB, England. *E-mail:* info@performing-arts.co.uk. *Address:* 137 Anson Road, Willesden Green, London, NW2 4AH, England (home).

ADLER, Samuel Hans, BM, MA; American composer, conductor and writer; *Composition Faculty Member, Juilliard School of Music;* b. 4 March 1928, Mannheim, Germany; s. of Hugo Adler and Selma Adler; m. 1st Carol Ellen Stalker (divorced 1991); two d.; m. 2nd Emily Freeman Brown 1991. *Education:* Boston Univ., Harvard Univ., studied composition with Herbert Fromm, Hugo Norden, Walter Piston, Randall Thompson, Paul Hindemith and Aaron Copland, musicology with Karl Geiringer, conducting with Serge Koussevitzky at Berkshire Music Centre, Tanglewood. *Career:* Founder and first Conductor, 7th Army Symphony Orchestra 1952; Dir of Music, Temple Emanu-El, Dallas, Tex. 1953–66; Conductor, Dallas Lyric Theatre 1955–57; Prof. of Composition, North Texas State Univ., Denton 1957–66; Prof. of Composition, Eastman School of Music, Rochester, NY 1966–95, Prof. Emer. 1966–95, Chair. Composition Dept 1973–95; guest conductor, symphony orchestras and opera cos world-wide; guest lecturer in USA and other countries; teacher of composition, Juilliard School of Music, New York, Composition Faculty mem. 1997–; mem. American Acad. of Arts and Letters 2001–. *Compositions include:* operas: The Outcasts of Poker Flat 1959, The Wrestler 1970, The Lodge of Shadows 1973; orchestral works include: six symphonies 1953–85, Rhapsody for violin and orchestra 1961, Elegy for string orchestra 1962, Requiescat in Pace in memory of President John F. Kennedy 1963, Concerto for orchestra 1971, Sinfonietta 1971, Flute Concerto 1977, Piano Concerto No. 1 1983, Time in Tempest Everywhere for orchestra 1993, Guitar Concerto 1994, Cello Concerto 1995, Piano Concerto No. 2 1996, Piano

Concerto No. 3 2000, Horn Concerto 2002; chamber music includes: nine string quartets 1945, 1950, 1953, revised 1964, 1963, 1969, 1975, 1981, 1990, 2007, organ pieces. *Publications include:* Anthology for the Teaching of Choral Conducting 1971, Sight Singing 1979, The Study of Orchestration 1982; contrib. to numerous journals. *Honours:* Special Citation from US Army; four hon. doctorates; Music Award, American Acad. and Inst. of Arts and Letters, Aaron Copland Award for Lifetime Achievement, American Soc. of Composers, Authors and Publrs 2003. *Address:* 9412 Sheffield Road, Perrysburg, OH 43551, USA (home). *Telephone:* (419) 666-9519 (home). *Fax:* (419) 666-6417 (home). *E-mail:* sadlercomp@yahoo.com (home). *Website:* www.samueladler .com.

ADNI, Daniel; Israeli/British pianist; b. 6 Dec. 1951, Haifa; m. Tessa Katzenellenbogen 1999. *Education:* high schools in Haifa and Tel-Aviv, Conservatoire of Music, France. *Career:* first recital in Haifa 1963; professional debut, London 1970; New York debut 1976; has played at musical centres in UK, Germany, Israel, USA, Japan, South Africa, Switzerland, Norway, Netherlands, Romania, Australia, New Zealand, Finland, Austria; has taught master-classes including at Dartington Summer School, UK. *Honours:* First Prize, Paris Conservatoire, First Prize, Young Concert Artists' Auditions, New York. *Address:* c/o 64A Menelik Road, London, NW2 3RH, England (home). *Telephone:* (20) 7794-4076 (home). *Fax:* (20) 7794-4076 (home). *E-mail:* danieladni@waitrose.com.

ADOLPHE, Bruce, BS, MMus; American composer, lecturer and author; *Director of Family Concerts and Resident Lecturer, Chamber Music Society of Lincoln Center;* b. 31 May 1955, New York; s. of Jules Adolphe and Anita Lituchy; m. Marija Stroke; one d. *Education:* Juilliard School, New York. *Career:* taught at Tisch School, New York Univ. 1983–93, Yale Univ. 1984–85; Composer-in-Residence, 92nd Street Y School Concert Series 1988–90, Santa Fe Chamber Music Festival 1989, La Jolla SummerFest 1998–2001, 2003, 2005, Music from Angel Fire 1984, 1985, Chamber Music Northwest 1989, 1990, 1992; Distinguished Composer-in-Residence, Mannes Coll. of Music 2004, Music@Menlo 2008; Artistic Advisor and Educ. Advisor, Chamber Music Soc. of Lincoln Center, New York 1992–98, currently Dir of Family Concerts and Resident Lecturer; currently also Composer-in-Residence, The Brain and Creativity Inst., Univ. of Southern California; Artistic Dir Off the Hook Arts Festival, Colo; Creative Dir, The Learning Maestros; composer-in-residence at festivals throughout USA; compositions have been performed in Boston, Florence, Los Angeles, New York, Washington, Zurich and more by artists including Yo-Yo Ma, Joshua Bell, Eugene Drucker, Carlo Grante; commissions from Orpheus Chamber Orchestra, Chamber Music Soc. of Lincoln Center, Itzhak Perlman, Beaux Arts Trio, Chamber Orchestra of Philadelphia, Brentano String Quartet, Metropolitan Opera Guild, Chicago Chamber Musicians, Chicago Humanities Festival; operas produced by Washington Nat. Opera, Washington Performing Arts Soc., American Chamber Opera, Jewish Opera; mem. Faculty, Julliard School; Lecturer, Tisch School of Arts, New York Univ.; Fellow, Ezra Stiles Coll., Yale. *Compositions include:* The Tell-Tale Heart (one-act opera after Edgar Allan Poe) 1982, Mikhoels The Wise (opera in two acts) 1982, The False Messiah (opera in two acts) 1983, Out of the Whirlwind (oratorio on Holocaust texts and melodies) 1984, Whispers of Mortality: String Quartet No. 4 1992, And All is Always Now (for violin and piano) 1992, The Amazing Adventure of Alvin Allegretto (one-act comic children's opera) 1994, Tyrannosaurus Sue: A Cretaceous Concerto 2000, Red Dogs and Pink Skies: A Musical Celebration of Paul Gauguin 2003, Time Flies (for chamber orchestra) 2004, The Tiger's Ear: Listening to Abstract Expressionist Paintings (for flute, oboe, violin, viola, cello and piano) 2004, Three Secret Stories (for violin and piano) 2005, What Dreams May Come? (for chamber orchestra) 2005, Violin Concerto 2005, Memories of a Possible Future (for piano and string quartet) 2005, Songs of Life and Love: to Poems by Persian, Arab, Israeli, and American Women (for mezzo-soprano and piano) 2005, Let Freedom Sing: The Story of Marian Anderson (opera in one act with libretto by Carolivia Herron) 2009, Self Comes to Mind (for cello and two percussionists, with a text by Antonio Damasio and visual images based on brain scans by Hanna Damasio) 2009, Reach Out, Raise Hope, Change Society (cantata for chorus SATB, wind quintet, 3 percussionists, with texts about social justice, civil rights and freedom) 2011, Obedient Choir of Emotion for SATB and piano (text by Antonio Damasio) 2012, Coyote Scatters the Stars for violin and piano 2012, Fra(nz)g-mentation based on a Schubert fragment for the Brentano String Quartet, Piano Concerto composed for Jon Kimura Parker 2012, Einstein Light (for violin and piano) 2015, Chopin Dreams (solo piano) 2015, Seven Thoughts Considered as Music (solo piano) 2015, Suite for Pete (for guitar) 2016. *Film score:* for film about the history of Anti-Semitism for the Holocaust Museum of Washington, DC,. *Radio:* composer and pianist, Piano Puzzlers (American Public Media) 2002–. *Television:* host and commentator, Live From Lincoln Center for The Chamber Music Soc. of Lincoln Center. *Publications:* The Mind's Ear 1990 (revised edn 2013), What To Listen For In The World 1996, Of Mozart, Parrots, and Cherry Blossoms in the Wind: A Composer Explores Mysteries of the Musical Mind 1999. *E-mail:* julian .fifer@gmail.com. *Website:* www.laurenkeisermusic.com. *Address:* Chamber Music Society of Lincoln Center, 70 Lincoln Center Plaza, 10th Floor, New York, NY 10024, USA (office). *Telephone:* (212) 875-5775 (office). *E-mail:* bruce .adolphe@gmail.com (office). *Website:* www.chambermusicsociety.org (office); www.thelearningmaestros.com (office).

ADORJÁN, András; Danish (b. Hungarian) flautist; b. 26 Sept. 1944, Budapest, Hungary. *Education:* studied in Copenhagen (dentistry), music with Jean-Pierre Rampal and Aurèle Nicolet. *Career:* Prin. with Orchestra of the Royal Opera, Stockholm 1970–72, Gürzenich Orchestra, Cologne 1972–73, Südwestfunk Baden-Baden 1973–74, Bavarian Radio Symphony Orchestra 1974–88; teacher, Nice Summer Acad. 1971–85; Prof., Hochschule für Musik, Cologne, Germany 1987–96, Hochschule für Musik, Munich 1996–; gave dedicated pieces: 'Ground', Concerto for flute and orchestra by Sven-Erik Werner 1981; 'Aria', Concerto for flute and orchestra by Gunnar Berg 1984, Concerto No. 2 for flute and orchestra, Opus 147 by Vagn Holmboe 1985, 'Moz-Art à la Mozart' by Alfred Schnittke 1990, 'Badinerie' by Jörg Widmann 1993, Concerto for flute and harp by Edison Denisov 1995, 'Burlesk'alla Ongarese' by Krzysztof Meyer 2008. *Recordings include:* first complete recording of all 14 flute concertos by François Devienne. *Publication:* Lexikon der Flöte. *Honours:* Jacob Gade Prize 1968, Concours Int. de Flûte, Montreux 1968, Premier Grand Prix, Concours Int. de Flûte de Paris 1971. *Address:* Hochschule für Musik München, Arcisstraße 12, 80333 Munich, Germany (office). *Website:* www.musikhochschule-muenchen.mhn.de (office).

AFANASSIEV, Valery; Russian pianist; b. 1947, Moscow. *Education:* Moscow Conservatory with Emil Gilels. *Career:* debut in Moscow 1962; performances throughout Eastern Europe after winning 1969 Bach Competition at Leipzig; settled in Brussels 1974, Versailles thereafter; chamber musician with violinist Gidon Kremer; concerts throughout Europe, Japan and USA; performs in own plays as actor and pianist, has performed these one-man shows in several countries and in four languages. *Recordings:* Bach, Beethoven, Brahms, Mozart and Schubert, including Das Wohltemperierte Klavier Complete Vols I and II, by J. S. Bach 1997, Sonatas D 958, D 959, D960 by Schubert 1997, Diabelli Variations and Chopin's Nocturnes. *Publications:* four novels (in French), two plays inspired by Mussorgsky's Pictures at an Exhibition and Schumann's Kreisleriana. *Honours:* winner Queen Elisabeth of the Belgians Competition, Brussels 1972. *Address:* 1 place de Furstenberg, 78150 Le Chesnay, France (home).

AFANASYEVA, Veronika; Russian violinist; b. 1960, Moscow. *Education:* Central Music School, Moscow. *Career:* co-founder, Quartet Veronique 1989; many concerts in Russia, notably in the Russian Chamber Music Series and 150th birthday celebrations for Tchaikovsky 1990; masterclasses at Aldeburgh Festival 1991; concert tour of the UK 1992–93; repertoire includes works by Beethoven, Brahms, Tchaikovsky, Bartók, Shostakovich and Schnittke. *Recordings include:* Schnittke's 3rd Quartet. *Honours:* with Quartet Veronique: winner All-Union String Quartet Competition at St Petersburg 1990–91, third place Int. Shostakovich Competition at St Petersburg 1991.

AFKHAM, David; German conductor; b. 1983, Freiburg. *Education:* Musikhochschule Freiburg, Liszt School, Weimar. *Career:* began piano and violin lessons aged six; has taken part in masterclasses with George Albrecht, T Koutnik, Miguel Angel Pérez Garrido, Salvador Mas Conde and Bernard Haitink; conductor, Loh-Orchester Sondershausen, Vogtland Philharmonie Greiz/Reichenbach, Westböhmischen Symphonieorchester Marienbad, Nordböhmischen Philharmonie Teplice, Jenaer Philharmonie; Chief Conductor, KHG Symphony Orchestra, Freiburg 2006; Asst Guest Conductor, Baden-Württemburg Youth Orchestra 2007; Asst to Bernard Haitink with Concertgebouw Orkest Amsterdam 2008; Asst Conductor London Symphony Orchestra 2008–. *Honours:* winner, Jugend Musiziert Piano Competition 2002, Bernard Haitink Award for Young Talent 2008, Donatella Flick Conducting Competition 2008, Nestlé and Salzburg Festival Young Conductors Award 2010. *Address:* c/o London Symphony Orchestra, 6th Floor, Barbican Centre, Silk Street, London, EC2Y 8DS, England (office). *Website:* www.lso.co.uk/conductors (office).

AGACHE, Alexandru; Romanian singer (baritone); b. 16 Aug. 1955, Cluj-Napoca. *Education:* Cluj Conservatory. *Career:* made debut as Silvano in Un Ballo in Maschera, Cluj 1979; sang with Opera di Livorno 1983–87; tour of Japan with Berlin Staatsoper 1985; made debut at Covent Garden 1988; debut with Metropolitan Opera 1999; repertoire includes Capitan Spavento in Le Maschere, Conte Almaviva in Le Nozze di Figaro, Sharpless in Madama Butterfly, Enrico Ashton in Lucia di Lammermoor, Belcore in L'Elisir d'amore, Marquis di Posa in Don Carlo, Marcello in La Bohème, Amonasro in Aida, Luna in Il Trovatore, Germont in La Traviata, Malatesta in Don Pasquale, also in Don Giovanni, Simon Boccanegra, Rigoletto, Nabucco, Otello, La Gioconda, Il Barbiere di Siviglia, La Fanciulla del West. *Recordings include:* Golem The Rebel by Nicolas Bretan, video of Covent Garden performance of Simon Boccanegra under Solti. *Honours:* winner, Concorso Voci Puccianiane 1983. *Current Management:* Stage Door, Via San Giorgio 4, 40121 Bologna, Italy. *Telephone:* (051) 262126. *Fax:* (051) 271452. *E-mail:* info@stagedoor.it. *Website:* www.stagedoor.it.

AGAZHANOV, Artyomovich; Russian composer and pianist; b. 3 Feb. 1958, Moscow. *Education:* Moscow Central Music School, Moscow State Tchaikovsky Conservatoire. *Career:* teacher, Moscow Central Music School 1983–; concert appearances as composer and pianist in Russia, Bulgaria, Italy, Germany, including festivals Moscow autumne 1986, 1987, 1989, 1994, Moscow Stars 1989, and Int. Music Festival 1988; mem. Union of Russian Composers. *Compositions include:* Pax in terra for orchestra 1983, On Beauty, Sorrow, Laughter and Grieving (cantata no. 2) for high soprano and large orchestra (texts by Issa Kobayashi, Matsuo Basho, Ihara Saikaku) 1983, Gloria (cantata no. 3) for soprano, mezzo-soprano, tenor, baritone, mixed chorus, large orchestra, tape ad libitum 1984, Way of the Poet (cantata no. 4) for tenor, mixed chorus, large orchestra (text by Mikhail Lermontov) 1989, Kolobrod (music for film) 1990, Incite the City to Rebellion (music for film) 1992, Confessing Sinner (cantata no. 5) for mezzo-soprano, tenor, tenor/baritone, bass, large orchestra, tape ad libitum 2000, Farewell in June (music for film) 2003. *Recordings include:* Vision for violin and piano 1988, Sonata for violoncello and piano 1989, Gust Overture for orchestra 1989, From 3 till 6 for piano 1989, Variations on a Theme by Chopin for piano 1992, Six Japanese Hokku for soprano and piano 1993, Way of the Poet (cantata no. 4) vocal symphony poem for tenor, mixed choir and full orchestra 1994, Without Trace vocal cycle for contralto and piano 1999. *Publication:* Without Colouring the Truth 1993. *Honours:* winner All Union Competition of Young Composers 1981. *Address:* Brusov 8–10 Apt 55, Moscow 103009, Russia. *E-mail:* aaartem@mtu-net.ru.

AGHOVA, Livia; Slovak singer (soprano); b. 1961. *Education:* studied in Bratislava. *Career:* sang in opera at Bratislava 1983–88; Mozart's Susanna, Donna Elvira and Pamina, Mimi, Micaela and Marguerite in Faust; National Theatre, Prague 1988–; Marenka Marzellina and Martinů's Julietta; Berlin Staatsoper as Antonia in Hoffmann; Munich Staatsoper as Xenia in Dvořák's Dimitri; as Donna Elvira, Savonlinna Festival 1991; Liu in Turandot, Houston 1994; Puccini's Lauretta, Prague 1996; other roles include Jenůfa, Strauss's Sophie, Gounod's Juliette and Nedda in Pagliacci; concerts include Beethoven's Ninth and Dvořák's St Ludmilla and The Spectre's Bride; sang Janáček's Vixen at Venice 1999. *Recordings:* Dimitri, Supraphon; Janáček's Osud, Orfeo; Glagolitic Mass. *Address:* c/o Music International, 13 Ardilaun Road, London, N5 2QR, England.

AGLER, David; American/Canadian conductor; *Artistic Director, Wexford Opera Festival;* b. 12 April 1947, South Bend, Indiana. *Education:* Westminster Choir Coll., Princeton, NJ. *Career:* fmr Prin. Conductor Australian Opera; fmr Resident Conductor San Francisco Opera; fmr Prin. Guest Conductor Oper der Stadt Köln; fmr Music Dir Syracuse Opera, Vancouver Opera; fmr Artistic Dir Opera Festival of New Jersey; Artistic Dir Wexford Opera Festival 2005–; also Chief Opera Conductor, Banff Centre, Canada; fmr admin. Spoleto Festival; has conducted operas with Wexford Opera, Santa Fe Opera, Seattle Opera, Pittsburgh Opera, Opera Co. of Philadelphia, Opera Theater of St Louis, Edmonton Opera, New York City Opera, Calgary Opera, Manitoba Opera, Opera de Montréal, Opera Pacific, Banff Festival Orchestra, Western Australia Opera, Netherlands Opera, Teatro Comunale Rossini, Lugo; has conducted concerts with San Francisco Symphony, Minnesota Orchestra, Sydney Symphony Orchestra, Winnipeg Symphony, Warsaw Philharmonic, Nat. Arts Center Orchestra Ottawa, CBC Vancouver, Netherlands Radio Symphony, Netherlands Chamber Orchestra, Charlotte Symphony Orchestra, San Francisco Chamber Symphony, Kitchener-Waterloo Symphony; Visiting Lecturer, Banff Centre 2004. *Current Management:* Pinnacle Arts Management, 889 Ninth Avenue, Second Floor, New York, NY 10019, USA. *Telephone:* (212) 397-7915. *Fax:* (212) 397-7920. *Website:* www.pinnaclearts.com. *Address:* Wexford Festival Opera, Wexford Opera House, High Street, Wexford, Ireland (office). *Telephone:* (53) 9122400 (office). *Fax:* (53) 9122144 (office). *E-mail:* david@wexfordopera.com (office). *Website:* www.wexfordopera.com (office).

AGNEW, Paul; British singer (tenor) and conductor; b. 1964, Glasgow, Scotland. *Education:* chorister at St Chad's Cathedral, Birmingham, lay clerkships at Birmingham and Lichfield Cathedrals, choral scholar at Magdalen Coll., Oxford. *Career:* interpreter of baroque and pre-classical repertoire; tours with the Consort of Musicke to Germany, Switzerland, Netherlands, Italy, Spain, Austria, Sweden and Australia; Handel songs in the Nat. Gallery, London with the Parley of Instruments; Promenade Concerts debut in 1989 in The Judgement of Paris; has sung the Evangelist in the St Matthew Passion for the London Handel Orchestra; South Bank debut at the Purcell Room celebrating the centenary of Ivor Gurney's birth; St John Passion with the Schola Cantorum of Basel and for Les Noces in Zürich; tour of the USA with the Festival of Voices, directed by Paul Hillier; sang in Monteverdi Madrigals with the Consort of Musicke at the Proms, London 1993; Palais Garnier, Paris 1996, as Rameau's Hippolyte; sang with New London Consort at the Purcell Room, London 1997; season 1999 with Charpentier's Extremum Dei Judicum and Lalande's Dies Irae at the Proms, London, sang in Rameau's Platée at the Palais Garnier; season 2000 in Rameau's La Guirlande at Cologne and Acis and Galatea at the Salzburg Easter Festival; season 2008–09 includes Renaud in Armide, Théâtre des Champs Elysées, The Turn of the Screw, Opéra de Bordeaux, Acis and Galatea, Covent Garden; as conductor, Messiah for Le Concert d'Astrée and Royal Liverpool Philharmonic Orchestra 2011 and Handel's La Resurrezione at the Atelier of Opéra Nat. de Paris 2012; debuts with Royal Scottish Nat. Orchestra (Messiah) and Norwegian Chamber Orchestra 2012; opera conducting debut with Mozart's Der Schauspieldirektor at Opéra de Rennes 2011; Assoc. Conductor, Les Arts Florissants 2007–, tours to Austria, France and China, London debut, Barbican 2009, also conducting complete cycle of Monteverdi Madrigals in nearly 100 concerts 2011–(15); Music Dir, Orchestre Français des Jeunes Baroque 2009–; Co-Dir, acad. for young singers Le Jardin des Voix. *Recordings include:* over 100 recordings including Monteverdi Madrigals, Rameau's Dardanus 2007, Purcell: The Food of Love 2009, Lamentazione – works by Scarlatti and Caldara, with Les Arts Florissants 2011. *Current Management:* Harrison Parrott, 5–6 Albion Court, London, W6 0QT, England. *Telephone:* (20) 7229-9166. *Fax:* (20) 7221-5042. *E-mail:* ian.stones@harrisonparrott.co.uk. *Website:* www.harrisonparrott.com.

AGOPOV, Vladimir; Armenian composer; *Lecturer, Sibelius Academy;* b. 23 Nov. 1953, Luhansk, Ukrainian SSR, USSR; m. 1977; two s. one d. *Education:* Moscow Conservatory, studied with Aram Khachaturian, Edison Denisov; Sibelius Acad., Finland, studied with Paavo Heininen. *Career:* debut in diploma concert, Moscow 1977; moved to Finland 1978; Lecturer in Music Theory, Sibelius Acad. 1988–; mem. Soc. of Finnish Composers. *Music for the theatre:* The Cherry Orchard (Chekhov). *Compositions include:* String Quartet No. 1 1982, String Quartet No. 2 1988, Music for Chamber Orchestra 1982, Concerto for cello and orchestra 'Tres viae' 1987, Ergo for violin and piano 1985, Four Songs to Words by Alice Meynell for soprano, flute and accordion 1986, Offrets timme to Words by Edith Södergran for baritone and piano 1987, Decimetto 1997, 2013, Settembre per orchestra grande 2004, Two pieces for the Big Band, La noche & Nordic Song 2009, Motetus for chamber choir, organ, harp and percussion 2011, Concerto for orchestra 2013, Solveig's song for harp solo 2013, Pater Noster for mix choir 2014, Folia for oboe solo 2015; arrangements: Engelbert Humperdinck's opera Hans und Gretel for chamber orchestra 1996, 2014, Mussorgsky-Agopov Pictures at an Exhibition for concert band 2010, Paganini Caprice 24 for 24 violins 2011. *Music for radio:* Tre kvinnor och en stad (Three Women and One City) 2000. *Recordings:* Sonata for clarinet and piano 1991, Concerto for cello and orchestra 1992, Siciliana 1992. *Honours:* Competition in Kouvola, Finland 1982, Sibelius Violin Competition for Composers 1985, 17th Edvard Grieg Competition. *Address:* Sibelius Academy, PO Box 86, 00251 Helsinki, Finland (office). *Telephone:* 500-504847 (mobile). *E-mail:* vagopov@siba.fi (office); vladimir.agopov@uniarts.fi. *Website:* www.fimic.fi (office).

AGUERA, Luc-Marie; French violinist; b. 1960. *Education:* Paris Conservatoire with Jean-Claude Pennetier and with members of the Amadeus and Alban Berg Quartets. *Career:* f. mem. Ysaÿe String Quartet 1985–; many concert performances on all continents; festival engagements at Salzburg, Tivoli, Bergen, Lockenhaus, Barcelona and Stresa; many appearances in Italy, notably playing the Haydn Quartets of Mozart; tours of Japan and USA 1990, 1992; performed all 69 quartets of Joseph Haydn at Besançon festival 2006, Beethoven's complete Quartet Cycle at the Musée d'Orsay, Paris 2008; many premieres of new works including Friedrich Cerha's clarinet quintet at Konzerthaus Vienna with Paul Meyer 2006; co-f. Ysaÿe Records 2003–. *Recordings:* quartets of Ravel, Debussy, Mendelssohn, Beethoven, Mozart, Haydn and Fauré/Magnard. *Honours:* Grand Prix, Evian Int. String Quartet Competition 1988, Special Prizes for Best Performances of a Mozart Quartet, the Debussy Quartet and a contemporary work, Grand Prix de l'Académie Charles Cros for recording of complete quartets by André Boucourechliev, Prix Georges Enesco, SACEM 2004. *Address:* c/o Olga Kriloff, Ysaÿe Records, 24 rue Molière, 13200 Arles, France (office). *Telephone:* 4-90-96-84-00 (office). *E-mail:* olga.kriloff@ysayerecords.com (office).

AHLIN, Sven Åke; Swedish composer and teacher; b. 6 April 1951, Sundsvall; m. Emma Rosendal 1989; two s. one d. *Education:* Royal Coll. of Music, Stockholm, Indiana Univ., USA. *Career:* debut, Stockholm 1977; numerous performances of his choir music and chamber music in Sweden, including trombone concerto with Christian Lindberg as soloist in Jönköping; broadcasts include four first performances by the Swedish Radio Choir, and piano concerto with Mats Widlund as soloist; performances abroad in Norway, Iceland, Russia, France, Spain, Hungary and the Netherlands; mem. Soc. of Swedish Composers. *Compositions:* Al Fresco, piano concerto; Narratives, trombone concerto; Across for orchestra; Ritual for Huitzilopochtli; Choral music including Dream of Elysium; Clashing Worlds; I have a dream; Concertos: Al fresco (piano); Narratives (trombone); Turning Points (String Quartet No. 2) 1997; Concerto for vihuela and string orchestra 1998; Skuggan av ett regn (The shadow of a rain) for mezzo-soprano and chamber ensemble, Med pukor och klarinett 2001, Missa 2001, Adorazione for violin 2003, Feverish for symphonic band 2005, Castle in the air in ruins for violin and piano 2006, Sketches and Drawings for tenor sax solo and winds, piano, el-bas, percussion; numerous pieces of chamber music. *Address:* Ålstorp, Mossehus, 312 94 Laholm, Sweden. *Telephone:* (430) 61027. *E-mail:* sven.ahlin@laholm.com.

AHLSTEDT, Douglas; American singer (tenor); *Associate Professor of Voice, Carnegie Mellon University;* b. 16 March 1945, Jamestown, NY. *Education:* State Univ. of New York at Fredonia, Eastman School of Music. *Career:* debut as Ramiro in La Cenerentola, Western Opera Theater, San Francisco 1971; sang at Metropolitan Opera from season 1974–75, with debut as Italian Singer in Rosenkavalier, then as Fenton in Falstaff; mem. Deutsche Oper Düsseldorf 1975–84, and guest appearances in Vienna, Hamburg, Zürich and Karlsruhe; returned to New York 1983 and sang Iopas in Les Troyens, Almaviva in Barbiere di Siviglia and Debussy's Pelléas 1988; Salzburg Festival as Alfinoma in the Henze-Monteverdi Il Ritorno d'Ulisse 1985; Teatro San Carlo in Naples as Orestes in Ermione by Rossini 1988; other engagements in Dallas, Philadelphia and Santiago as Don Ottavio, Genoa, Avignon and Rome as Idreno in Semiramide 1982; other roles include Tamino, Jacquino in Fidelio, Narcisio in Turco in Italia, the Fox in Cunning Little Vixen and Peter Quint in The Turn of the Screw, Dorvil in La Scala di Setat, Flamand in Capriccio, Pelleas in Pelleas et Melisande, Miles in The Turn of the Screw; Assoc. Prof. of Voice, Carnegie Mellon Univ. *Recordings include:* Il Bellerofonte, Elijah, Soliloquia Sancti Aurelii Augustini, James Levine 25th Anniversary Collection. *Address:* Carnegie Mellon School of Music, 5000 Forbes Avenue, Pittsburgh, PA 15123-3815, USA (office). *Telephone:* (412)

268-2372 (office). *E-mail:* ahlstedt@andrew.cmu.edu (office). *Website:* music.web.cmu.edu (office); www.douglasahlstedt.com.

AHN, Ah Ruem; South Korean pianist; b. 1984, Suwon. *Education:* Yonsei Univ., Hochschule für Musik, Germany, studied with Elena Margolina and Bob Versteegh; masterclasses with Andras Schiff, Menahem Pressler, Bernd Goetzke, Ralf Gothoni, Arnulf von Arnim. *Career:* moved to Detmold, Germany to study; has performed with orchestras including Orquesta Sinfónica de Madrid, Real Filharmonía de Galicia, Dortmunder Philharmoniker, NWD Philharmonie, Orchestre Philharmonique du Maroc. *Honours:* several awards including First Prize in Paul Hindemith Competition 2009, Smetana Competition 2010, Stefano Marizza Piano Competition 2010. *E-mail:* ahruemahn@hotmail.com. *Website:* www.ahruemahn.com.

AHNSJÖ, Claes H.; Swedish singer (tenor); b. 1 Aug. 1942, Stockholm; m. Helena Jungwirth. *Education:* studied in Stockholm with Erik Saeden, Aksel Schiotz and Max Lorenz. *Career:* debut at Royal Opera Stockholm in 1969 as Tamino; sang in Stockholm until 1973, then with the Munich Opera notably in operas by Mozart and Rossini; Drottningholm Opera from 1969; Bayreuth Festival, 1973; Kennedy Music Center, NY, 1974 in Die Jahreszeiten by Haydn; guest appearances in Frankfurt, Cologne, Tokyo, Hamburg, Stuttgart and Nancy; Concert tours of Italy and Spain; Sang at Munich in 1985 as the Painter in Lulu, and in the premiere of Le Roi Bérenger by Sutermeister; Sang at Berlin in 1987 as Ramiro in La Cenerentola by Rossini; Sang Wolfgang Capito in Mathis der Maler and the Abbé in Adriana Lecouvreur, 1989; Munich Festival in premiere of Penderecki's Ubu Rex in 1991; Season 1997–98 in Monteverdi's Poppea and as Melot in Tristan und Isolde; Director of the Stockholm Royal Opera 1999–2003. *Recordings:* Bastien und Bastienne; Orlando Paladino, La Vera Costanza and L'Infedeltà Delusa by Haydn; Betulia Liberata by Mozart; Die Lustigen Weiber von Windsor; Bruckner's Te Deum. *Address:* Richard Wagner Str 68, 82152 Munich, Germany (home). *E-mail:* ahnsjoe@t-online.de (home).

AHO, Kalevi; Finnish composer, teacher and writer on music; b. 9 March 1949, Forssa. *Education:* Sibelius Acad., Helsinki, Staatliche Hochschule für Musik und Darstellende Kunst, Berlin with Einojuhani Rautavaara, Boris Blacher. *Career:* Lecturer on Music, Univ. of Helsinki 1974–88; Prof. of Composition, Sibelius Acad. 1988–93; Composer-in-Residence, Sinfonia Lahti 1992–2011; freelance artist in Helsinki 1993–. *Compositions include:* works for the stage: Avain (The Key, dramatic monologue) for baritone and chamber orchestra 1977–78, Hyönteiselämää (Insect Life, comic opera) 1985–87, Ennen kuin me kaikki olemme hukkuneet (Before We Are All Drowned, opera) 1995–99, Salaisuuksien kirja (The Book of Secrets, opera) for soloists, choir and orchestra 1998, Frida y Diego (opera) 2012–13; orchestral works: Symphonies, No. 1 1969, No. 2 1970/95, No. 3 for violin and orchestra 1971–73, No. 4 1971–73, No. 5 1975–76, No. 6 1979–80, No. 7 Insect Symphony 1988, No. 8 for organ and orchestra 1993, No. 9 for trombone and orchestra 1993–94, No. 10 1996, No. 11 for 6 percussionists and orchestra 1997–98, No. 12 Luosto 2002–03, No. 13 Symphonic Characterizations 2003, No. 14 Rituals 2007, No. 15 2009–10, Symphonic Dances 2001, Chamber Symphonies Nos 1–3 for strings 1976, 1992, 1996, Pergamon for four instrumental groups, voices and organ 1990, Hiljaisuus for orchestra 1982, Rejoicing of Deep Waters for orchestra 1995, Tristia, fantasy for wind orchestra 1999, Louhi for orchestra 2003, Minea for orchestra 2008, Gejia – Chinese Images for orchestra 2012; concertos: Violin Concerto 1981, Cello Concerto 1984, Piano Concerto No. 1 1988–89, Tuba Concerto 2000–01, Concerto No. 2 for piano and string orchestra 2001–02, Flute Concerto 2002, Concerto for two violoncelli and orchestra 2003, Bassoon Concerto 2004, Contrabassoon Concerto 2004–05, Double Bass Concerto 2005, Clarinet Concerto 2005, Viola Concerto 2006, Oboe Concerto 2007, The Bells – Concerto for Saxophone Quartet and Orchestra 2008, Trombone Concerto 2010, Sieidi – Concerto for Percussion and Orchestra 2010, Trumpet Concerto 2011, Horn Concerto 2011, Eight Seasons – Concerto for Theremin and Chamber Orchestra 2011; chamber music, quintets and quartets include 3 string quartets 1967–71, Quintet for oboe and string quartet 1973, Quintet for flute, oboe, violin, viola and cello 1977, Quintet for bassoon and string quartet 1977, Quintet for alto saxophone, bassoon, viola, cello and double bass 1994, Quintet for clarinet and string quartet 1998, Three Tangos for violin, accordion, guitar, double bass and piano 1999, Quintet for flute, violin, two violas and cello 2000, Wind Quintet 2006, Trio for clarinet, viola and piano 2006, HAHE for 4 cellos 2008, String Quintet Hommage à Schubert 2009, ARS for 4 cellos 2012; sonatas: Sonata for oboe and piano 1985, Sonata for two accordions 1989, Sonatine for two pianos 1997, Ballade for flute, bassoon, cello and piano 1999, Quasi una fantasia for horn and organ 2011; solo instruments: Sonata for violin 1973, Ludus solemnis for organ 1978, In memoriam for organ 1980, Piano Sonata 1980, Sonata No. 1 for accordion 1989, Sonata No. 2 for accordion Mustat linnut (Black Birds) 1990, Three Interludes for organ 1993, Solo I for violin 1975, Solo II for piano 1985, Solo III for flute 1991–92, Solo IV for cello 1997, Solo V for bassoon 1999, Solo VI for double bass 1999, Solo VII for trumpet 2000, Solo VIII for baritone horn 2003, Solo IX for oboe 2010, Solo X for horn 2010, Alles Vergängliche – Symphony for organ 2007, In memoriam Pehr Henrik Nordgren for violin 2009; vocal works: Lasimaalaus (Stained Glass) for female choir 1975, Kolme laulua elämästä (Three Songs about Life) for tenor and piano 1977, Mysteerio for female choir 1994, Ilo ja epäsymmetria (Joy and Asymmetry), suite for mixed choir 1997, Kiinalaisia lauluja (Chinese Songs) for soprano and orchestra 1997, Kolme Bertrandin monologia (Three Monologues of Bertrand) for baritone and orchestra 1999, Kysymysten kirja (Book of Questions) for mezzo-soprano and chamber orchestra 2006, Kolme Mawlana Rumin runoa (Three Poems by Mawlana Rumi) for mixed choir 2010; orchestrations and arrangements: Modest Mussorgsky: Songs and Dances of Death 1984, Uuno Klami: Whirls (instrumentation of the first act of the ballet) 1988, Erik Tulindberg: 6 string quartets (completion) 1995, Sibelius: Karelia (reconstruction) 1997, Sibelius: Promootiokantaatti 1897 (Cantata for the University Graduation Ceremonies 1897), reconstruction and completion 2010, Bach: Contrapunctus XIV from Die Kunst der Fuge, completion for organ or string orchestra 2011. *Recordings:* all works apart from the operas recorded. *Publications include:* Finnish Music and the Kalevala 1985, Taiteilijan tehtävät postmodernissa yhteiskunnassa (The Tasks of the Artist in Postmodern Society) 1992, Finnish Music (co-author) 1996, Art and Reality 1997. *Honours:* Léonie Sonning Prize, Copenhagen 1974, Award of City of Hamburg 1982, Henrik Steffens Prize 1990, Flisaka '96 Prize, Toruń, Poland 1996, Stiftung Kulturfonds Award, Berlin 1998, Pro Finlandia 1999. *Current Management:* Fennica Gehrman, PO Box 158, 00121 Helsinki, Finland. *E-mail:* info@fennicagehrman.fi. *Address:* Taivaskalliontie 15, 00600 Helsinki, Finland. *E-mail:* ahokalevi@hotmail.com (office).

AHRENS, Hans-Georg; German singer (bass-baritone); b. 4 July 1944, Hitzacker an der Elbe. *Education:* Berlin Hochschule für Musik, with G. Wilhelms. *Career:* sang at Städtischen Bühnen Mainz Opera, 1973–75, Augsburg, Kassel; mem. Kiel Opera 1978–; teacher of voice, Univ. of Kiel 1994–2002, Univ. of Flensburg 2002–; roles include Leporello and Figaro, Gauguin in Vincent, Don Alfonso, the Doctor in Wozzeck, Hagen in Götterdämmerung, Wagner's King Henry, Marke and Gurnemanz, Gianni Schicchi, Dulcamara and Schigolch in Lulu; concerts in music by Bach. *Recordings:* Don Giovanni, Così fan tutte. *Address:* Oper Kiel, Theater Kiel, 24015 Kiel, Germany (office). *Website:* www.theater-kiel.de/oper (office).

AÏELLO, Evelyne Josette Nicole; French conductor; b. 23 July 1958, Casablanca, Morocco; d. of Joseph Aïello and Germaine Aïello (née Gragnani); four d. *Education:* Lycée Jeanne d'Arc, Clermont-Ferrand, École Normale de Musique de Paris, Conservatoire Nat. Supérieur de Musique de Paris, Acad. Chigiana, Siena, Italy and Mozarteum, Salzburg, Austria. *Career:* conductor in France and abroad; Conductor Orchestre de la Garde Républicaine 1983, Ballets de l'Opéra de Paris 1985, Orchestre Nat. d'Ile-de-France 1989, Mozart Concert, Salle Pleyel 1989, Sofia Orchestra, Hungarian Radio Orchestra, Budapest, New Boston Orchestra, USA, Raanana, Israel 1995 etc.; Artistic Dir and Conductor Festival Lyrique de Gattières 1997–99, Orchestre Philarmonique de Qatar, Orchestre Symphonique, USA 2009; Guest Conductor with orchestras including Opéra de Nantes and Opéra Nat. de Lorraine playing ballet music, contemporary music, opera etc. *Recording:* album tribute to Marcel Landowski 1995. *Honours:* Médaille Maurice Ravel, Ministry of Culture 1976, Médaille d'honneur de la Ville de Clermont-Ferrand 1976, 1984, First Prize for Conducting, Conservatoire Nat. Supérieur de Musique 1983, Laureate Fondation Menuhin 1983, Int. Conducting Prize, Salzburg 1984, Laureate, first Concours des jeunes chefs d'orchestre, Ministry of Culture 1986, Médaille d'honneur de la Ville de Saint-Paul de Vence 1997, 1998. *Address:* CRR, 22 rue de la Belle Feuille, 92100 Boulogne-Billancourt, France.

AIKIN, Laura; American singer (soprano); b. 1965, Buffalo. *Education:* Buffalo Univ., Indiana Univ., Hochschule für Musik, Munich, Germany, studied with Reri Grist. *Career:* began career as mem. Deutsche Staatsoper Berlin, over 300 performances, roles including Lulu in Lulu, Queen of Night in Die Zauberflöte, Zerbinetta in Ariadne auf Naxos, Amenaide in Tancredi, Sophie in Der Rosenkavalier, Adele in Die Fledermaus and Zaide in Zaide; Strauss's Zerbinetta at the Vienna Staatsoper and a Jonathan Miller production of Ariadne auf Naxos at Florence 1997; other roles include Marzelline in Fidelio, Lucia in Lucia di Lammermoor, Konstanze in Die Entführung aus dem Serail; Il trionfo del Tempo by Handel at the Styriate Festival with Nicolas Harnoncourt and Concentus Musicus 1997; further concerts include Schoenberg's oratorio Die Jakobsleiter under Michael Gielen, Beethoven's Christus am Ölberg with Daniel Barenboim in Jerusalem and Chicago, and Pierre Boulez 70th birthday celebrations at Carnegie Hall; Met debut as the Queen of Night; Madeleine in Le Postillon de Lonjumeau at the Berlin Staatsoper 1998; numerous appearances with The Ensemble Intercontemporain including Salzburg, Edinburgh and Schleswig Holstein festivals; Handel's Alcina at the Beaune Festival with Les Arts Florissants and William Christie; Ariadne at the Chicago Lyric; Suite from Prometeo by Luigi Nono with Claudio Abbado and the Berlin Philharmonic at Carnegie Hall 1999; also performed at Vienna State Opera, La Scala, Metropolitan Opera, Lyric Opera Chicago, Opéra de Lyon, Semperoper Dresden, San Francisco Opera, Bavarian State Opera, Salzburg Festival and Glyndebourne Festival Opera, Opernhaus Zürich, La Bastille, Paris, Liceu, Barcelona, Glyndebourne and major orchestras in Europe and USA and with conductors including Daniel Barenboim, Pierre Boulez, Lorin Maazel, Riccardo Muti, and Claudio Abbado. *Recordings include:* Beethoven's Christus am Ölberg with Daniel Barenboim, Songs and Cycles by Ned Rorem for Orfeo with pianist Donald Sulzen, Schoenberg's Die Jakobsleiter with the Sudwestfunk Symphony Orchestra, Respighi's La Campana Sommersa with the Montpellier Opera, Strauss songs with Donald Sulzen. *Honours:* winner, Lake Constance Int. Competition. *Current Management:* Ingpen & Williams Ltd, 7 St George's Court, 131 Putney Bridge Road, London, SW15 2PA, England. *Telephone:* (20) 8874-3222. *Fax:* (20) 8877-3113. *E-mail:* info@ingpen.co.uk. *Website:* www.ingpen.co.uk. *E-mail:* lala@lauraaikin.com (home). *Website:* www.lauraaikin.com.

AIMARD, Pierre-Laurent; French pianist; *Artistic Director, Aldeburgh Festival*; b. 1957, Lyon; m. Irina Kataeva; two c. *Education:* Paris Conservatory, studied with Yvonne Loriod and Maria Curcio in Paris. *Career:* winner of the Olivier Messiaen Int. Competition 1973; invited by Pierre Boulez to be a founding mem. of Ensemble Intercontemporain 1977; has performed worldwide under conductors, including Boulez, Seiji Ozawa, Zubin Metha, Charles Dutoit, André Previn, Andrew Davis, Sir Simon Rattle, David Robertson, Esa-Pekka Salonen, Edo de Waart; US debut with Chicago Symphony Orchestra 1977; Carnegie Hall debut 2001; has performed with orchestras, including Boston SO, San Francisco Symphony, Toronto Symphony, London Philharmonia, Royal Concertgebouw, Orchestre de Paris, Orchestre Nat. de France; has featured at festivals, including Tanglewood, Salzburg, Berlin, Vienna, Edin., Köln Triennale, Holland, Paris Autumn; regular collaborations with composers, including Ligeti, Boulez and Stockhausen; Artistic Dir, Aldeburgh Festival 2009–; contrib. to TV series on 20th-century composers (Arte TV). *Recordings:* György Ligeti Edition 3, Works for Piano 1997, György Ligeti, Project Vol. One (Melodien for Orchestra, Chamber Concerto, Piano Concerto, Mysteries of the Macabre), Boulez Conducts Ligeti (Piano Concerto), Olivier Messiaen, Vingt Regards sur l'Enfant-Jésus 2000, Olivier Messiaen, Turangalîla Symphony, Pierre-Laurent Aimard at Carnegie Hall 2002, Beethoven, Piano Concertos Nos 1–5 2003, Debussy, Images-Études 2003, Dvořák, The Golden Spinning Wheel 2004, Beethoven, Triple Concerto, Rondo in B flat, Choral Fantasy 2004, Ravel, Gaspard de la nuit/Carter, Night Fantasies 2005, Charles Ives, Three Quarter-Tone Pieces, Bach, The Art of Fugue 2008, Messiaen, Piano Works 2008, Ravel, The Piano Concertos; Miroirs 2010. *Honours:* Royal Philharmonic Soc. Award for Best Instrumentalist 2005. *Current Management:* c/o Lydia Connolly, Harrison Parrott Ltd, 5–6 Albion Court, London, W6 0QT, England. *Telephone:* (20) 7229-9166. *Fax:* (20) 7221-5042. *E-mail:* lydia.connolly@harrisonparrott.co.uk. *Website:* www.harrisonparrott.co.uk.

AINSLEY, John Mark; British singer (tenor); b. 9 July 1953, Crewe, Cheshire; s. of John Alwyn Ainsley and Dorothy Sylvia Ainsley (née Anderson); partner William Whitehead. *Education:* Royal Grammar School, Worcester, Madgalen Coll., Oxford. *Career:* debut in Stravinsky's Mass, Royal Festival Hall 1984; many concert performances from 1985 with Taverner Consort, New London Consort and London Baroque; appearances in Mozart Masses at The Vienna Konzerthaus with Heinz Holliger, Handel's Saul at Göttingen with John Eliot Gardiner, Mozart Requiem under Yehudi Menuhin at Gstaad and Pulcinella at the Barbican under Jeffrey Tate; other concerts with Ulster Orchestra and Bournemouth Sinfonietta; debut in USA at Lincoln Center in Bach's B Minor Mass with Christopher Hogwood 1990; opera debut at the Innsbruck Festival in Scarlatti's Gli Equivoci nel Sembiante, at ENO in the Return of Ulysses 1989; title role in Méhul's Joseph for Dutch Radio, Handel's Acis in Stuttgart and Solomon for Radio France under Leopold Hager; has sung Mozart's Tamino for Opera Northern Ireland and Ferrando for Glyndebourne Touring Opera; sang Ferrando at Glyndebourne 1992, Don Ottavio 1994, Haydn's The Seasons with the London Classical Players; BBC Proms Concerts, London 1993, Stravinsky concert under Andrew Davis at Royal Festival Hall 1997, Monteverdi's Orfeo for Munich Opera Festival 1999, Jupiter in Semele for ENO 1999, Bach's St Matthew Passion at BBC Proms 2002, Skuratov in From the House of the Dead for Amsterdam, Vienna and Aix en Provence Festivals, 2007, Captain Vere in Billy Budd for Frankfurt Opera 2007, Emilio in Partenope for ENO 2008, title role in Idomeneo and Bazajet in Tamerlano for Munich Opera Festival 2008. *Recordings include:* Purcell, Odes (with Trevor Pinnock) 1988, Handel's Nisi Dominus (under Simon Preston) 1989, Handel, Saul 1991, Handel, Acis and Galatea 1993, Blow, Fairest Work of Happy Nature 1993, Great Baroque Arias (with the King's Consort) 1994, Handel, Jephtha 1994, Zelenka, Lamentations of Jeremiah 1994, Finzi, Dies Natalis and Intimations 1996, Warlock, Curlew Capriol Serenade Songs 1997, Mozart, Requiem 1998, Mozart, Songs 1998, Ireland, Songs 1999, Mozart's C Minor Mass (with Christopher Hogwood) 1999, Quilter, Songs 2000, Vaughan Williams, Songs 2000, L'invitation au voyage 2006, Finzi, Intimations of Immortality 2009, Grainger, Jungle Book and Other Choral Works 2011, Britten: War Requiem (BBC Music Magazine Choral Award 2014). *Honours:* Grammy Award for Best Opera Recording 1995, Munich Festival Prize 1999, Royal Philharmonic Soc. Singer Award 2007. *Current Management:* c/o Askonas Holt Limited, Lincoln House, 300 High Holborn, London, WC1V 7JH, England. *Telephone:* (20) 7400-1700. *Fax:* (20) 7400-1799. *E-mail:* jane.balmer@askonasholt.co.uk; kate.baylis@askonasholt.co.uk. *Website:* www.askonasholt.co.uk.

AINSLIE, Christopher; South African and German singer (counter-tenor); b. 5 July 1978, Cape Town. *Education:* Univ. of Cape Town, Royal Coll. of Music, private study with Mark Tucker, Paul Farrington and Audrey Hyland. *Career:* started singing career as chorister, St George's Cathedral, Cape Town; opera performances include The Spirit in Dido and Aeneas, Cape Town Opera 2003, Arsamenes in Xerxes, Edinburgh Symphony Baroque 2006, Alessandro in Tolomeo, London Handel Festival 2006, Handel's Poro, London Handel Festival 2007, Medoro in Orlando, Wigmore Hall 2008, Handel's Rinaldo, Summer Festival, Sigulda, Latvia 2008, Arsace in Partenope, Les Azuriales Opera Festival, France 2008, Fourth Innocent in The Minotaur, Royal Opera, Covent Garden 2008, title role in Artaxerxes, Covent Garden 2009, Ottone in L'incoronazione di Poppea, Glyndebourne 2010, Eustazio in Rinaldo, Glyndebourne 2011, counter-tenor in Venus and Adonis, Versailles 2012; oratorio performances include Vivaldi's Gloria, Winchester Cathedral 2007, Cyrus in Belshazzar, Dresden Frauenkirche 2007, Handel's Messiah,

Philadelphia Orchestra, Philadelphia 2007, Bach's Mattäus-Passion, London Handel Festival 2008. *Honours:* Michael Oliver Handel Singing Prize 2007, Richard Tauber Prize 2008, Gianni Bergamo Prize 2011. *Current Management:* Rayfield Allied, Southbank House, Black Prince Road, London, SE1 7SJ, England. *Telephone:* (20) 7138-3593. *E-mail:* ben@rayfieldartists.com. *Website:* www.rayfieldartists.com. *Telephone:* (7985) 981800 (office). *E-mail:* cdainslie@yahoo.com (office). *Website:* www.christopherainslie.com.

AITKEN, Robert Morris, OC, MMus; Canadian flautist, conductor, teacher and composer; b. 28 Aug. 1939, Kentville, NS; m. Marion I. Ross. *Education:* Royal Conservatory of Music, Toronto with Nicholas Fiore, Univ. of British Columbia with Barbara Pentland, Univ. of Toronto, also studied with John Weinzweig, Myron Schaeffer. *Career:* Princ. Flute, Vancouver Symphony Orchestra 1958–59, Stratford Festival Orchestra, Ontario 1962–64; co-Prin. Flute, Toronto Symphony Orchestra 1965–70; soloist with orchestras and chamber music player in concerts worldwide 1970–; some 50 works written for him by composers including John Cage, Henry Brant, George Crumb, Elliott Carter, Toru Takemitsu and Arne Nordheim; Artistic Dir, Music Today, Shaw Festival, Niagara-on-the-Lake 1970–72, and New Music Concerts, Toronto 1971–; advanced studies in music programme 1985–89; Prof. of Flute, Staatliche Hochschule für Musik, Freiburg im Breisgau 1988–2004; masterclasses worldwide including Germany, Thailand, Luxembourg, Italy 2012. *Compositions include:* Rhapsody for orchestra 1961, Music for flute and electronic tape 1963, Concerto for 12 solo instruments 1964, Kebyar for flute, clarinet, two double basses, percussion and tape 1971, Shadows III, Nira for solo violin, flute, oboe, viola, double bass, piano and harpsichord 1974–88, Icicle for flute 1977, Folia for woodwind quintet 1980, Berceuse for flute and orchestra 1992, My Song for two flutes 1994, A Little Ground for Max 1997, Shadows V: concerto for flute and string orchestra 1999. *Recordings:* over 40 albums as composer, soloist or chamber music artist. *Honours:* Chevalier, Ordre des Arts et des Lettres; Lifetime Achievement Award, Nat. Flute Asscn (USA), Canada Council's Walter Carsen Prize for Excellence in the Arts 2009. *Address:* 14 Maxwell Avenue, Toronto, ON M5P 2B5, Canada (home). *E-mail:* nmc@interlog.com (home). *Website:* www.bobaitken.ca.

AKIMOV, Yevgeny; Russian singer (tenor); b. 1967, St Petersburg. *Education:* St Petersburg Conservatory. *Career:* soloist, Zazerkalye Children's Music Theatre 1991–96, with Kirov Opera at the Mariinsky Theatre 1996–; roles have included Bayan in Ruslan and Lyudmila, Prince Vladimir in Prince Igor, God's Fool in Boris Gudunov, Andrei Khovansky in Khovanshchina, Indian Merchant in Sadko, Ivan Lykov in The Tsar's Bride, Tsar Berendey in The Snow Maiden, Lensky in Eugene Onegin, Andrei in Mazepa, Prince Sinodal in The Demon, Dante in Francesca di Rimini, Fisherman in Le Rossignol, Mikola in Semyon Kotko, Don Antonio in Betrothal in a Monastery, Zinovy Borisovich in Lady Macbeth of Mtsensk, Edgardo in Lucia di Lammermoor, Almaviva in Il Barbiere di Siviglia, Duke of Mantua in Rigoletto, Alfredo in La Traviata, Cassio in Otello, Rodolfo in La Bohème, B.F. Pinkerton in Madama Butterfly, Rinuccio in Gianni Schicchi, Don Ottavio in Don Giovanni, Froh in Das Rheingold, Narraboth in Salome; also performed at Metropolitan Opera, New York, La Scala, Milan, Covent Garden, London, Opéra de Paris, Teatro Regio, Turin, Nat. Grand Theatre of China, Beijing, Accademia Santa Cecilia, Rome and San Francisco Opera; regularly works with Nat. Opera of Moldova; concert performances include Mozart's Requiem, Beethoven's Ninth Symphony, Mahler's Eighth Symphony, Rachmaninoff's Bells; has worked with conductors including Lorin Maazel (Avery Fisher Hall 2002), Mstislav Rostropovich (Accademia Nazionale di Santa Cecilia 2002), Esa-Pekka Salonen (Hollywood Bowl 2007), Jukka-Pekka Saraste (in Finland, Norway and Sweden 2009), Gianandrea Noseda (Teatro Regio, Turin) and Semyon Bychkov (in Florence 2006, and Cologne 2008). *Recordings:* Betrothal in a Monastery (with Anna Netrebko), Semyon Kotko, Stars of the Mariinsky Opera Sing Rossini, Bellini, Donizetti & Mozart. *Honours:* prizewinner, Int. Pechkovsky Singing Competition 1994, Golden Mask Theatre Prize 1997, 2003, Golden Sofit Prize 2001, 2004, two Sergei Rachmaninoff Foundation medals for performance (in Francesca da Rimini and Bells) 2009. *Current Management:* c/o James Fox Artist Management, One Riverplace Drive, Suite 420, La Crosse, WI 54601, USA. *E-mail:* peter@jfartists.com. *Address:* Kirov Opera, Mariinsky Theatre, 190000 St Petersburg, Teatralnaya pl. 1, Russia (office). *Telephone:* (812) 326-41-41 (office). *Fax:* (812) 314-17-44 (office). *E-mail:* post@mariinsky.ru (office). *Website:* www.mariinsky.ru/en/opera/soloist/akimov (office); www.akimov.spb.ru.

AKIYAMA, Kazuyoshi; Japanese conductor; b. 2 Jan. 1941, Tokyo. *Education:* Toho School of Music, Tokyo with Hideo Saito. *Career:* debut with Tokyo Symphony Orchestra 1964; Music Dir Tokyo Symphony Orchestra 1964; conductor with numerous Japanese orchestras; Music Dir American Symphony Orchestra, New York 1973–78; Resident Conductor and Music Dir Vancouver Symphony Orchestra, BC 1972–85; Music Dir Syracuse Symphony Orchestra, NY 1985–93, Conductor Emer. 1993–; Prin. Conductor and Music Adviser, Hiroshima Symphony Orchestra 1998–; Prin. Guest Conductor, Edmonton Symphony Orchestra 2004–05; currently Prin. Conductor, Kyushu Symphony Orchestra. *Honours:* Emperor's Purple Ribbon Medal 2001, Suntory Music Award, Kyoto Music Award, Mainichi Arts Award, Arts Encouragement Prize of the Minister of Educ. *Current Management:* Columbia Artists Management, 1790 Broadway, New York, NY 10019-1412, USA. *Telephone:* (212) 841-9500. *Fax:* (212) 841-9744. *E-mail:* info@cami.com. *Website:* www.cami.com.

AKOKA, Gérard; French conductor; b. 2 Nov. 1949, Paris. *Education:* Paris Conservatoire, Accademia di Santa Cecilia, studied with Jean Martinon, Igor Markevitch, Sergiu Celibidache and Franco Ferrara. *Career:* fmr Asst to Daniel Barenboim and Leonard Bernstein; Asst to Pierre Boulez, Orchestre de Paris 1977; Musical Dir, Lorraine Philharmonic 1983–84; Artistic advisor and Principal Conductor, Nat. Symphony Orchestra of Taiwan 1986–90; engagements as guest conductor with Orchestra Sinfonica di Milano, BBC Symphony Orchestra, Nouvel Orchestre Philharmonique, Orchestre Nat. de Radio France, Teatro la Fenice, Venice, RAI Milan, Pomerrigi Musicali, Milan, Teatro Regio de l'Opera de Turin, Korean Broadcasting Nat. Symphony Orchestra, Seoul, Istanbul Devlet Symphony Orchestra, Ankara Belkin Symphony Orchestra, Orchestra of Cairo Opera; masterclasses; mem. jury numerous conducting competitions. *E-mail:* gerard.akoka@gmail.com.

ALAGNA, Roberto; French singer (tenor); b. 7 June 1963, Clichy-sous-Bois; m. 2nd Angela Gheorghiu 1996. *Education:* studied in Paris, France and Italy. *Career:* debut as Alfredo in La Traviata, Glyndebourne Touring Opera at Plymouth 1988; Met, New York debut as Rodolfo 1996; appearances worldwide at Covent Garden, London, Monte Carlo, Vienna Staatsoper, Théâtre du Châtelet, Paris, La Scala, Milan, Chicago and at the New York Met; repertoire includes Rodolfo (La Bohème), Edgard (Lucia di Lammermoor), Rigoletto, L'Elisir d'amore, Roméo, Don Carlos, Roberto Devereux, Duke of Mantua, Don Carlos, Alfredo, L'Amico Fritz, La Rondine, Faust. *Recordings include:* Duets and Arias (with Angela Gheorghiu), La Bohème 1996, Don Carlos 1996, La Rondine 1997, My Life is an Opera 2014. *Honours:* Chevalier, Ordre des Arts et des Lettres 1996, Officier, Ordre des Arts et des Lettres 2002, Officier, National Order of Merit 2003; winner, Pavarotti Competition 1988, Personalité Musicale de l'Année 1994, Laurence Olivier Award for Outstanding Achievement in Opera 1995, Lyric Artist of the Year, Victoires de la Musique Awards 1997, 2004, Vermeil Medal of the City of Paris 2001. *Current Management:* Theateragentur Dr Germinal Hilbert, Maximilianstrasse 22, 80539 Munich, Germany. *Telephone:* (89) 2907470. *Fax:* (89) 29074790. *E-mail:* agentur@hilbert.de. *Website:* www.hilbert.de; www.robertoalagna.net/en.

ALAIMO, Simone; Italian singer (bass-baritone); b. 3 Feb. 1950, Villabate, Palermo; m. Vittorio Mazzoni, 1988; one s. one d. *Education:* Univ. of Palermo, Scuola di Perfezionamento, Teatro alla Scala, Milan with Giovani Lirici. *Career:* debut in Don Pasquale at Pavia 1977; appearances at La Scala, Teatro dell'Opera, Rome, Teatro Comunale, Florence, Teatro San Carlo, Naples, Chicago, San Francisco, Dallas, Vienna, Monaco, Paris, Madrid, Barcelona, Lisbon and Marseilles; radio and television broadcasts in Luisa Miller, Cavalleria Rusticana and Zaira; sang Mustafà in L'Italiana in Algeri at San Francisco 1992, followed by Dulcamara, Rossini's Don Basilio at Genoa 1992; Faraone in Mosè in Egitto at Covent Garden 1994; New York Met from 1995, as Mozart's Figaro and Rossini's Basilio; Rossini's Basilio at Genoa 1998; first modern production of Donizetti's Alahor in Granata, Seville 1998; appeared in film of Il Barbiere di Siviglia; Mustafà for New Israeli Opera 2000; Rossini's Don Magnifico at Covent Garden 2003; season 2008 Dr Dulcamara in L'Elisir d'Amore at Metropolitan Opera and Covent Garden, Count Rodolfo in La Sonnambula in Cagliari, Don Basilio in Il Barbiere di Siviglia in Liège, and Selim in Il Turco in Italia in Genoa. *Recordings:* La Cenerentola, Don Giovanni, Il Turco in Italia, Maria Stuarda, I Masnadieri, L'Ebreo, Torquato Tasso, L'Esule di Roma, Convenienze Teatrali, Barbiere di Siviglia. *Honours:* Lions Prize 1977, Voce Verdiane di Busseto Int. Competition 1978, Beniamino Gigli di Macerata Int. Competition 1978, Maria Callas Int. Competition 1980. *Current Management:* c/o Columbia Artists Management, 1790 Broadway, New York, NY 10019-1412, USA. *Telephone:* (212) 841-9500. *Fax:* (212) 841-9744. *E-mail:* info@cami.com. *Website:* www.cami.com.

ALBERGA, Eleanor, LRSM, ARAM; British composer; b. 30 Sept. 1949, Kingston, Jamaica. *Education:* Royal Acad. of Music, London. *Career:* numerous solo and orchestral works commissioned and performed by Lontano, London Philharmonic Orchestra, Royal Philharmonic Orchestra, Scottish Chamber Orchestra, Music Theatre Wales, Royal Opera House, BBC Symphony Orchestra and others. *Compositions:* Jamaican Medley (for piano) 1983, Clouds (for piano quintet) 1984, Suite (for two pianos, four hands) 1986, Fizz (for piano) 1988, Sun Warrior (for orchestra) 1990, Three-Day Mix (for piano duet) 1990, Dancing with the Shadow (for ensemble) 1991, Jupiter's Fairground (for orchestra) 1991, Snow White and the Seven Dwarfs (for narrators and orchestra) 1994, Three String Quartets 1993, 1994, 2000, The Wild Blue Yonder for piano and violin 1995, If the Silver Bird Could Speak (for piano) 1996, Only a Wish Away (for piano) 1997, No-Man's Land Lullaby (for violin and piano) 1997, On a Bat's Back I do Fly (for ensemble) 2000, Violin Concerto 2001, Tiger Dream in Forest Green (for four players) 2003, Piano Quintet 2004, Langvad (for ten players) 2006, Succubus Moon (for oboe and string quartet) 2007, My Heart Danceth (for SATB choir) 2007, Letters of a Love Betrayed (opera) 2009, Shining Gate of Morpheus (horn and string quartet) 2012, Arise, Athena! (symphony orchestra, chorus and organ) 2015. *Honours:* ABRSM Scholarship 1970, NESTA Fellowship 2002. *Telephone:* 7516-076447 (mobile) (office). *E-mail:* info@eleanoralberga.com (office). *Website:* www.eleanoralberga.com.

ALBERMAN, David, MA, LRAM; British violinist; b. 1959, London. *Education:* Merton Coll., Oxford; studied with Mary Long, Emanuel Hurwitz, Sheila Nelson, Vera Kantrovich, Igor Ozim in Cologne. *Career:* Leader, Nat. Youth Orchestra of Great Britain 1977; performed with London Mozart Players, Royal Philharmonic Orchestra, London Symphony (Assoc. mem. 1983–85),

and Acad. of St Martin-in-the-Fields; fmr Leader, Chamber Orchestra of Europe; performed music by Lutosławski, Penderecki, Osborne and Bainbridge with such groups as the Ballet Rambert and Divertimenti; mem., Arditti Quartet 1986–94; many performances at festivals across Europe and North America; resident string tutor, Darmstadt Ferienkurse for New Music 1986; Music in camera programme for BBC television 1987; Cycle of Schoenberg's Quartets, Purcell Room, London, November 1988; recital in the Russian Spring Series, South Bank, May 1991; performed in all the quartets of Berg, Webern and Schoenberg at Antwerp, Cologne, Frankfurt, London and Paris 1991–93; took part in premieres of quartets by Bose, No. 3 1989, Bussotti 1988, John Cage, Music for 4 1988, 1989, Ferneyhough, Nos 3 and 4; Gubaidulina, No. 3 1987; Harvey, No. 2; Kagel, No. 3 1987; Nancarrow, No. 3 1988, Pousseur, No. 2 1989, Rihm, Nos 6 and 8, Xenakis, Akea, Piano Quintet 1986, Tetora 1991, Isang Yun, Flute Quintet 1987, Lachenmann's Second String Quartet; premiere of Nono's Hay que caminar soñando for violin duo, with Irvine Arditti, violin 1989; duo with pianist Rolf Hind 1995–, has played recitals in Vienna, Darmstadt, London, Stockholm, Oslo, Stuttgart and Brussels; Guest Professor of New String Music, Guildhall School of Music and Drama, London 1996–; Principal, London Symphony Orchestra 1999–, has played as guest concertmaster in London Symphony Orchestra, BBC Symphony Orchestra, Ensemble Recherche Freiburg, Sinfonia 21 and London Sinfonietta; appeared as chamber musician with London Sinfonietta, Nash and Razumovsky ensembles, as soloist with Orchestre de Lille, BBC Nat. Orchestra of Wales and ORF Radio Symphony Orchestra, Vienna. *Recordings include:* Elliott Carter's Quartets; Quartets by Ferneyhough. *Address:* 14 Fairmead Road, London, N19 4DF, England.

ALBERT, Donnie Ray; American singer (bass-baritone); b. 1950, Louisiana. *Career:* sang Gershwin's Porgy at Houston 1976, and sang there regularly until 1990; guest appearances at the New York City Opera (Scarpia 1978), Washington Opera (Amonasro 1990), Boston, San Francisco and elsewhere in the USA; appearances in Berlin and Florence as Porgy; other roles include Carlos in Ernani, Monterone, Nabucco, Iago, Jack Rance, Jochanaan, Escamillo, Varlaam, and the title role in Gruenberg's Emperor Jones; season 1996 as Wagner's Dutchman at Cologne and Hidraot in Gluck's Armide at La Scala; Villains in Hoffmann at Cologne 1998; season 1999–2000 as Macbeth at Cologne, Amonasro at Cincinnati and Gershwin's Porgy at Munich; concert engagements in New York, Los Angeles and Chicago. *Current Management:* Pinnacle Arts: Miller Division, 889 Ninth Avenue, Second Floor, New York 10019, USA. *Telephone:* (212) 397-7911. *Fax:* (212) 397-7920. *E-mail:* jmiller@pinnaclearts.com. *Website:* www.pinnaclearts.com; www.donnierayalbert.com.

ALBERT, Marian; Polish singer (tenor); b. 1961, Poznań. *Education:* studied at Lubin, Poznań and the Salzburg Mozarteum. *Career:* choir and orchestra director in Poland, 1982–87; Sang Fenton, Vladimir in Price Igor, Lensky, Tamino, Narciso in Il Turco in Italia and Amenofi in Rossini's Mosè, Poznan Opera, 1988–; Guest at Brussels as Tamino and Wagner's Froh; Antwerp as Cavaradossi and Berne as Belmonte; Belmonte, Strauss's Brighella and Giannetto in La Gazza Ladra, Theater am Gärtnerplatz, Munich, 1992; Cadi in Der Barbier von Bagdad by Cornelius, Frankfurt, 1994; appearances at Salzburg Mozartwochen and Prague Spring Festivals. *Address:* Theater am Gärtnerplatz 3, 8000 Munich 5, Germany.

ALBERT, Thomas; German conductor and director; b. 1950. *Career:* violinist with La Petite Bande and Musicalisches Compagney; f. Fiori Musicale 1978, for performances of Baroque music; f. Forum Alte Musik 1982, Bremen Acad. of Early Music 1986; Teacher, Hamburg Acad. of Music and Strasbourg Conservatoire; Prof. of Baroque Violin, Bremen Acad. of Music 1989–; Artistic Dir, Bremen Music Festival 1989–. *Recordings:* Bach Cantatas 56 and 82; Keiser's Masagniello Furioso; Lubeck Cantatas. *Address:* c/o Musikfest Bremen, Postfach 10 30 63, 28030 Bremen (office); c/o Musikhochschule Bremen, Dechanatstrasse 13, 28195 Bremen, Germany (office). *E-mail:* t.albert@hfk-bremen.de (office). *Website:* www.musikfest-bremen.de.

ALBERT, Werner Andreas; German conductor; b. 1935, Weinheim. *Education:* Mannheim Hochschule für Musik, Heidelberg Univ.; studied conducting with Herbert von Karajan and Hans Rosbaud. *Career:* debut, Heidelberg Chamber Orchestra 1961; fmr Chief Conductor, North West German Philharmonic, Gulbenkian Orchestra, Lisbon, Nuremberg Symphony Orchestra, Queensland Symphony Orchestra, Queensland Philharmonic Orchestra, Australian and Bavarian Youth Orchestra; Prin. Guest Conductor, Southern Sinfonia Orchestra, New Zealand 2007–; Sr Lecturer, Meistersinger Conservatorium, Nuremberg; Adjunct Prof., Queensland Univ.; Pres., Siegfried Wagner Soc. *Recordings:* over 600 recordings including Oboe Concertos by Leclair, Haydn and Dittersdorf, Beethoven's 9th Symphony, Rossini's Petite Messe Solennelle, Cello Concertos by Sutermeister, Mozart's Clarinet Concerto and Horn Concerto K447, Puccini's Messa di Gloria. *Honours:* mem. Erste Klasse, Bundesverdienstkreuz, Bayerischer Verdienstorden; Dr hc (Queensland, Australia) 2010; First Prize, German Recording Industry 1994, American Menza Award 1994, Music Prize, Bavarian Acad. of Fine Arts 1998. *Current Management:* Maxima Artist Management Ltd, 10 Corinth Street, Remuera, Auckland, New Zealand. *Telephone:* (9) 522-1620. *Fax:* (9) 520-0562. *E-mail:* albert@maximaltd.com. *Website:* maximaltd.com/wernerandreasalbert. *Address:* Rankestrasse 19, 90461 Nürnberg, Germany (home).

ALBERY, Tim; British theatre and opera director; b. 20 May 1952. *Career:* began career in theatre and turned to opera in 1980s; numerous productions for Royal Opera House, ENO, Opera North, Scottish Opera, others. *Plays directed include:* War Crimes 1981, Secret Gardens 1983, Venice Preserv'd 1983, Hedda Gabler 1984, The Princess of Cleves 1985, Mary Stuart 1988, As You Like It 1989, Berenice 1990, Wallenstein 1993, Macbeth 1996, Attempts on Her Life 1997, Nathan the Wise 2004. *Operas directed include:* (for ENO) Billy Budd 1988, Beatrice and Benedict 1990, Peter Grimes 1991, Lohengrin 1993, From the House of the Dead 1997, La Bohème 2000, War and Peace 2001, Boris Godunov 2008; (for Opera North) The Midsummer Marriage 1985, The Trojans 1986, La Finta Giardiniera 1989, Don Giovanni 1991, Don Carlos 1992, Luisa Miller 1995 Così fan tutte 1997, Katya Kabanova 1999, Così fan tutte 2004, One Touch of Venus 2004, 2005, Croesus 2007, Macbeth 2008; (for Welsh Nat. Opera) The Trojans 1987, Nabucco 1995; (for Scottish Opera) The Midsummer Marriage 1988, The Trojans 1990, Fidelio 1994, The Ring Cycle 2003, Don Giovanni 2006; (for Australian Opera) The Marriage of Figaro 1992; (for Netherlands Opera) Benvenuto Cellini 1991, La Wally 1993, Beatrice and Benedict 2001; (for Bayerische Staatsoper) Peter Grimes 1993, Simon Boccanegra 1995, Ariadne Auf Naxos 1996; (for Batignano Festival, Italy) The Turn of the Screw 1983; (for Bregenz Festival, Austria) La Wally 1990; (for Royal Opera House) Cherubin 1994, The Flying Dutchman 2009, Tannhäuser 2010; (for Metropolitan Opera, New York) Midsummer Night's Dream 1996, The Merry Widow 2000; (for Minnesota Opera) Passion 2004; (for Canadian Opera Company, Toronto) Rodelinda 2005, Gotterdammerung 2006, War and Peace 2008; (for Reisopera, Netherlands) Nabucco 2008; (for Luminato Festival, Toronto) The Children's Crusade 2009, Prima Donna 2010; (for Dallas Opera) Otello 2009; (for Sadler's Wells, London) Prima Donna 2010; (for Santa Fe Opera) The Magic Flute 2010. *Current Management:* c/o Harriet Cruickshank, Cruickshank Cazenove, 97 Old South Lambeth Road, London, SW8 1XU, England. *Telephone:* (20) 7735-2933. *Fax:* (20) 7582-6405. *E-mail:* office@cruickshankcazenove.com.

ALBRECHT, Georg-Alexander; German conductor; b. 15 Feb. 1935, Bremen. *Education:* studied violin, piano and composition. *Career:* debut as conductor 1949; Chief Conductor, Bremen Opera 1958–61; Gen. Music Dir, Hannover Opera 1965–93; Guest Conductor, Semperoper Dresden 1990–95, also with Staatskapelle Dresden, Berlin, Munich and Warsaw Philharmonics, Orchestre Philharmonique de Paris, Opernhaus Zürich, Wiener Staatsoper, NHK-Orchester Tokyo, and others; Gen. Music Dir, Deutschen Nationaltheaters Weimar and the Staatskapelle Weimar 1996–2002; Prof. Hannover Conservatory. *Recordings:* works by Liszt, Wagner, Strauss, Humperdinck and Furtwängler with Staatskapelle Weimar. *Publications:* Die Symphonien Gustav Mahlers. *Honours:* Hon. Prof., Hochschule für Musik Franz Liszt, Weimar, Conductor Laureate, Staatskapelle Weimar 2002; Bundesverdienstkreuz 1998; Prix d'excellence, Accademia Chigiana, Siena 1954, Gustav Mahler Gold Medal 1985, Australian Critics Award for Conducting (Opera) 2005. *Current Management:* artesystem GmbH, Kurfürstendamm 157, D-10709 Berlin, Germany. *E-mail:* bernds@artesystem.com. *Address:* c/o Hochschule für Musik Weimar, Postfach 25 52, 99406 Weimar, Germany (office).

ALBRECHT, Hansjörg; German conductor, organist and harpsichordist; *Artistic Director, Munich Bach Choir;* b. Freiberg. *Education:* studied conducting and organ in Hamburg, Lyon and Köln. *Career:* fmrly Asst Organist, St Michaelis Church, Hamburg; Artistic Dir, Munich Bach Choir & Bach Orchestra 2005–; regular conductor, Munich Symphony, Bach Collegium Munich and C.P.E. Bach Choir Hamburg and guest conductor at European festivals and music venues; as conductor, worked across Europe with ensembles including Orchestra Sinfonica Nazionale della RAI Turin, Orchestra del Teatro di San Carlo Naples, Orchestra Sinfonica Siciliana, Prague Philharmonia, Bavarian State Orchestra, Münchner Rundfunkorchester, Hamburg Symphony and Baroque Orchestra Moscow; as organist, soloist and chamber musician, performed in concert halls and cathedrals in Europe and Russia with orchestras including Israel Philharmonic Orchestra, Los Angeles Opera Orchestra, St Luke's Chamber Orchestra New York, Orchestre de la Suisse Romande, Orchestra Sinfonica di Santa Cecilia Rome, Camerata Salzburg, Czech Philharmonic Orhcestra, Kremerata Baltica and Symphonieorchester des Bayerischen Rundfunks. *Recordings include:* The Art of Organ Transcription (series) and works by Bach, Brahms, Mahler, Braunfels and Poulenc. *Current Management:* Matthias Müller, Wichernstrasse 18, 01445 Dresden-Radebeul, Germany. *Telephone:* (351) 65616444. *E-mail:* info@mueller-concert.com. *Website:* www.mueller-concert.com. *E-mail:* hansjoergalbrecht@yahoo.de (office). *Website:* www.hansjoerg-albrecht.com (office).

ALBRECHT, Marc; German conductor; *Chief Conductor, Netherlands Opera and Netherlands Philharmonic Orchestra;* b. 15 March 1964, Hanover. *Career:* fmrly personal asst to Claudio Abbado at the Gustav Mahler Youth Orchestra, Vienna; Music Dir, Staatstheater Darmstadt 1995–2001; Prin. Guest Conductor, Deutsche Oper, Berlin 2001–04; Artistic Dir and Chief Conductor, Orchestre Philharmonique de Strasbourg 2006–11; Chief Conductor, Netherlands Philharmonic and Chamber Orchestras and Netherlands Opera 2011–; has appeared with Berlin Philharmonic Orchestra, Royal Concertgebouw Orchestra, City of Birmingham Symphony Orchestra, Accademia di Santa Cecilia, Rome, Chamber Orchestra of Europe, Staatskapelle Dresden, Munich Philharmonic, Oslo Philharmonic, Royal Stockholm Philharmonic, Orchestre National de France, Vienna Symphony, Orchestre Nat. de Lyon, Hallé Orchestra, Cleveland Orchestra, Dallas Symphony, St Louis Symphony, Gothenberg Symphony, Sinfonieorchester Stuttgart; BBC Proms debut, London with BBC Scottish Symphony Orchestra 2006; opera performances include Der fliegende Holländer, Bayreuth Festival 2003–06, Wellesz' Die Bacchantinnen, Salzburg Festival 2003, Janacek's From the House of the Dead, Opéra Nat. de Paris 2005, Berlioz' La Damnation de Faust and Strauss's Die Frau ohne Schatten, Semperoper Dresden 2007, Henze's Die Bassariden, Munich State Opera 2008, Beethoven's Fidelio, Strasbourg Opera 2008, Elektra, Dresden 2009, Carmen, Netherlands Opera 2009; debut, Royal Opera House, Covent Garden with Der Fliegende Holländer 2009, Berg's Lulu at Salzburg Festival (Vienna Philharmonic). *Current Management:* IMG Artists Europe, The Light Box, 111 Power Road, London, W4 5PY, England. *Telephone:* (20) 7957-5800. *Fax:* (20) 7957-5801. *E-mail:* nmathias@imgartists.com. *Website:* www.imgartists.com.

ALBRECHT, Theodore John, BME, MM, MLS, PhD; American conductor, musicologist and academic; b. 24 Sept. 1945, Jamestown, New York; m. Carol Padgham 1976. *Education:* St Mary's Univ., North Texas State Univ. *Career:* Asst Prof., Appalachian State Univ. 1975–76; Conductor, German Orchestra of Cleveland 1977–80; Music Dir, Northland Symphony Orchestra, Kansas City, Mo. 1980–87; Prof., Park Coll. 1980–92; Music Dir, Philharmonia of Greater Kansas City 1987–92; Prof., Kent State Univ. 1992–; notable performances include US premieres of Bruckner Dialog by Gottfried von Einem 1982, Symphony in C, Op. 46 by Hans Pfitzner 1983, Ludi Leopoldini by Gottfried von Einem 1984; first American conductor to conduct all nine Dvořák symphonies; world premiere of Song of the Prairie by Timothy Corrao 1987. *Publications include:* Dika Newlin, Friend and Mentor: A Birthday Anthology (ed.) 1973; translation of Felix Weingartner's On the Performance of the Symphonies of Mozart 1985, translations of Felix Weingartner's Schubert and Schumann 1986, Thayer, Salieri, Rival of Mozart (ed.) 1989, Letters to Beethoven and Other Correspondence (three vols) 1996, Beethoven im Gespräch 2002; more than 60 journal articles. *Honours:* ASCAP Deems Taylor Award 1997, Distinguished Alumnus Award, Univ. of North Texas 1999, Distinguished Scholar Award and Grad. Teaching Award, Kent State Univ. 2011. *Address:* 1635 Chadwick Drive, Kent, OH 44240, USA (home). *E-mail:* talbrech@kent.edu (office).

ALCANTARA, Theo; American conductor; b. 16 April 1941, Cuenca, Spain; m. Susan Alcantara. *Education:* Madrid Conservatory and Salzburg Mozarteum. *Career:* Conductor, Frankfurt am Main 1964–66; Dir of Orchestras, Univ. of Michigan at Ann Arbor 1968–73; Music Dir, Grand Rapids Symphony Orchestra, MI 1973–78, Phoenix Symphony Orchestra 1978–89; Artistic Dir, Music Acad. of the West, Santa Barbara, CA 1981–84; Principal Conductor, Pittsburgh Opera 1987–2006; Artistic Dir and Prin. Conductor, Bilbao Symphony Orchestra –1999; also Conductor, Symphony Silicon Valley Orchestra; has appeared as Guest Conductor with Philadelphia Orchestra, Detroit Symphony, Pittsburgh Symphony, Dallas Symphony, Baltimore Symphony, San Diego Symphony, Rochester Philharmonic, Utah Symphony, Florida Philharmonic, New Orleans Symphony, Vancouver Symphony, Oregon Symphony and Seattle Symphony, and with major orchestras in Canada, Europe and South America. *Honours:* silver medal, Mitropoulos Competition 1966. *Address:* 14908 North 114th Place, Scottsdale, AZ 85255-1684 (home); c/o Symphony Silicon Valley Orchestra, PO Box 790, San Jose, CA 95106-0790, USA (office).

ALDEN, Christopher; American opera director. *Career:* has directed operas, including Der Fliegende Holländer (Canadian Opera 1996, Pittsburgh), Virgil Thomson's The Mother of Us All (Glimmerglass 1998, San Francisco 2003), Rigoletto (Chicago 2000), The Rape of Lucretia (Glimmerglass 2001, New York City Opera 2003), Bluebeard (Glimmerglass 2003), Arianna in Creta (Gotham Chamber Opera 2005), Imeneo (Glimmerglass, New York City Opera), Harvey Milk (world premiere), Henze's Das Verratene Meer (US premiere), Les Contes d'Hoffmann and L'Incoronazione di Poppea (all San Francisco Opera), La Vida Breve, L'Occasione fa il Ladro, Pagliacci and Djamileh (all Opera North), Cavalleria Rusticana and Pagliacci (Cologne), Madama Butterfly (Bilbao 2006), The Makropulos Case (ENO 2006); in 2009/10, produced Don Giovanni (New York City Opera), Tosca and Handel's Partenope (Opera Australia), Der fliegende Holländer (Canadian Opera Company), Les Contes d'Hoffmann (Santa Fe Opera); in 2010/11 Bernstein's A Quiet Place (New York City Opera), Lully's Phaeton (Staatstheater Saarbrücken), Turandot (Portland Opera and Welsh National Opera) and Britten's A Midsummer Night's Dream (ENO); has also worked with Basel Opera, New Israeli Opera, Scottish Opera, Opéra Comique, Paris, Dallas Opera, Houston Grand Opera, Prague Nat. Theatre and Deutsche Oper, Berlin. *Honours:* New York City Opera Prize for Excellence for The Mother of Us All, Olivier Award for Best UK opera production of 2008/09 for Partenope at ENO. *Current Management:* c/o Angela Blasi, Columbia Artists Management Inc., 1790 Broadway, New York, NY 10019-1412, USA. *Telephone:* (212) 841-9500. *Fax:* (212) 841-9744. *E-mail:* amblasi@cami.com.

ALDEN, David; American stage director; b. 16 Sept. 1949, New York, NY. *Education:* Univ. of Pennsylvania. *Career:* stage director of operas, working with cos worldwide; also directed an int. concert tour for the Pet Shop Boys. *Productions include:* (for Bavarian State Opera) Il ritorno d'Ulisse in patria, L'incoronazione di Poppea, Rinaldo, Rodelinda, Ariodante, Tannhäuser, Pique Dame, Lulu, La Calisto, La forza del destino, Der Ring des Nibelungen, Die Walküre, Siegfried, Gotterdammerung, Orlando; (for Scottish Opera) Wozzeck, Rigoletto, Mahagonny; (for WNO) Poppea, Elektra, Giulio Cesare, Il ritorno d'Ulisse in patria; (for ENO) Mazeppa, Simon Boccanegra, Un ballo in maschera, Ariodante, La Damnation de Faust, Tristan und Isolde, Jenůfa, Oedipus Rex, Duke Bluebeard's Castle, Peter Grimes, Lucia de Lammermoor, Katya Kabanova, Radamisto; (for Aldeburgh Festival) Powder her Face; (for Vienna Volksoper) Faust, Der Zigeunerbaron; (for Netherlands Opera) Il prigioniero, Der Zwerg, The Rake's Progress; (for Komische Oper Berlin) Tamerlano, Alcina; (in Cologne) Don Giovanni; (in Frankfurt) Der Schatzgräber; (for Vlaamse Opera, Antwerp) Ariodante, Peter Grimes; (in Graz) Parsifal; (for New Israeli Opera) Les Contes d'Hoffmann, Idomeneo, La Bohème, Faust, Sweeney Todd, Kat'a Kabanová, L'incoronazione di Poppea, Alpha and Omega, The Sorrows of Job; (for San Francisco Opera) Rodelinda, Ariodante, The Duchess of Malfi, Wolf Trap, Washington Square, Don Perlimpin; (for Chicago Lyric Opera) Wozzeck, Věc Makropoulos, Aufstieg und Fall der Stadt Mahagonny, Macbeth; (for Metropolitan Opera) Wozzeck, Fidelio; (for Houston Grand Opera) Macbeth, Ariodante, Kat'a Kabanová, Jenůfa; (for Dallas Opera) Kat'a Kabanová; (for Santa Fe Opera) Věc Makropoulos, The Turn of the Screw, Judith; (for Long Beach Opera) Les Contes d'Hoffmann, King Roger; (for Washington Opera) Jenůfa; (at Spoleto) Transformations, Giasone; (for Royal Danish Opera, Copenhagen) Il ritorno d'Ulisse in patria; (for Lithuanian Opera) Salome; (for Gran Teatre del Liceu, Barcelona) L'incoronazione di Poppea; (for Theatre St Gallen) Medea in Corinto; (for Oviedo Opera House, Spain) Ariodante; (for Royal Opera House, Covent Garden) La Calisto; (for Netherlands Opera) Ercole Amante; (for Grange Park Opera) The Cunning Little Vixen. *Television:* documentary on Verdi. *Honours:* Bavarian Theatre Prize for Individual Artistic Achievement 2006, South Bank Show Award (for Peter Grimes) 2009. *Current Management:* Intermusica Artists Management Ltd, 36 Graham Street, Crystal Wharf, London, N1 8GJ, England. *Telephone:* (20) 7608-9900. *Fax:* (20) 7490-3263. *E-mail:* mail@intermusica.co.uk. *Website:* www.intermusica.co.uk.

ALDRIDGE, Robert Livingston, BA, MMA, PhD; American composer and academic; *Professor and Director of Music, Mason Gross School of the Arts, Rutgers University;* b. 1954, Richmond, Va; m. Paula Stark; one d. *Education:* Univ. of Wisconsin, New England Conservatory of Music, Yale School of Music. *Career:* Prof. of Composition, Montclair State Univ. 2000–12, Chair. Music Dept 2005–11, Dir John J. Cali School of Music 2006–09; Prof. and Dir of Music, Mason Gross School of the Arts, Rutgers Univ. 2012–; Fellow, MacDowell Colony five times 1987–; fmrly Composer-in-Residence, American Orchestral League/Music Alive, American Dance Festival, Univ. of Minnesota and Univ. of Colorado; Composer-in-Residence, Brevard Music Festival 2006–; commissions from New Jersey Symphony Orchestra, Orpheus Chamber Orchestra, LA Chamber Orchestra, Topeka Symphony, Keith Lockhart and Brevard Center Orchestra, Boston Classic Orchestra, Nashville Symphony and others; f. Composers in Red Sneakers consortium, Boston. *Compositions:* over 80 works including: for orchestra: Ecstatic Overture 1996, Leda and the Swan for full orchestra 2004, Brand New Day 2004, Janus Overture 2008, Tango for Gabriela; for voice: Love Songs (song-cycle for tenor and piano) 2004, Bless This House for a cappella chorus 2004, Elmer Gantry (opera) 2007, Parables (oratorio) 2010, Keillor Songs (five songs for mezzo-soprano and piano) 2012, Sister Carrie (opera) 2012–; instrumental: Short and Suite for solo piano 1982, Combo Platter for violin, alto sax and marimba 1983, Quartet for an Outdoor Festival for soprano saxophone, violin, violoncello and piano 1989, Three Folksongs for B flat clarinet and string quartet 1992, Carolinian Dances for violin and piano 1999, Clarinet Concerto 2004, Three Waltzes for solo piano 2011; music-theatre: Larger Than Life 1997, The Third Person 1998–2001, Murietta 2006–10. *Recordings include:* Copland/Aldridge Clarinet Concertos 2009, Elmer Gantry (Opera News Best Opera Recording of the Year, Grammy Award for Best Contemporary Classical Composition 2012) 2011. *Honours:* Fellowships from Nat. Acad. of Recording Arts and Sciences, Guggenheim Foundation, American Acad. of Arts and Letters, Nat. Endowment for the Arts, NY Foundation for the Arts, Pennsylvania Council on the Arts, Massachusetts Artist's Foundation, Lila Wallace Reader's Digest Fund, Meet the Composer, American Symphony Orchestra League, New Jersey Council on the Arts and Geraldine R. Dodge Foundation. *Address:* Music Department, Mason Gross School of the Arts, Rutgers University, 81 George Street, New Brunswick, NJ 08903-0270, USA (office). *Telephone:* (732) 932-8860 (office). *E-mail:* bob@robertaldridge.com (office). *Website:* www .robertaldridge.com (office).

ALEKSASHKIN, Sergei; Russian singer (bass); b. 1954, Saratov. *Education:* Saratov Conservatory, studied at La Scala. *Career:* mem., Kirov Opera from 1984, including tours; roles include Don Giovanni, Mephistopheles, Sarastro, Sobakin in The Tsar's Bride, Ivan Susanin, Glinka's Ruslan and Farlaf, Kutuzov in War and Peace, Rimsky's Ivan the Terrible, Gremin in Eugene Onegin, Boris Godunov, Prince Igor, The Damnation of Faust, Philip II in Don Carlos, Rossini's Basilio, King Henry in Lohengrin, Rachmaninov's Miserly Knight, Balducci in Benvenuto Cellini, the General in The Gambler by Prokofiev, Mendoza in Betrothal in a Monastery 2006, King Dodon in The Golden Cockerel 2006, Prince Gremin in Eugene Onegin 2008, The General in The Gambler 2009, Enchanted Wonderland 2010; concerts include Shostakovich's 13th Symphony with the Chicago Symphony Orchestra 1995, Mussorgsky's Songs and Dances of Death (UK debut with the BBC Philharmonic Orchestra) 1996, Shostakovich's 14th Symphony at the Vienna Konzerthaus, Bach's B Minor Mass, Mozart's Requiem, Beethoven's Choral Symphony and the Verdi Requiem. *Current Management:* Robert Slotover, Allied Artists, Southbank House, Black Prince Road, London, SE1 7SJ,

England. *Telephone:* (20) 7589-6243. *Fax:* (20) 7581-5269. *E-mail:* Robert@ alliedartists.co.uk. *Website:* www.alliedartists.co.uk.

ALER, David; Swedish singer (baritone); b. 26 April 1959, Stockholm. *Education:* studied in Gothenburg with Jacqueline Delman, further studies with Geoffrey Parsons, Janet Baker, Kim Borg and Galina Vishnevskaya. *Career:* sang at Landestheater Coburg and in Sweden 1988–, as Don Giovanni, Guglielmo and Tarquinius in The Rape of Lucretia; appeared in Vadstena and Reykjavík 1988–89 in the premiere production of Someone I Have Seen by Karolina Eriksdottir; Stora Theater in Gothenburg as Schaunard in La Bohème 1989; Drottningholm Festival 1996, as Allworthy in Tom Jones by Philidor; Salzburg Festival 1998, as Frère Massée in St François d'Assise; concert engagements in Stockholm with Drottningholm Baroque Ensemble and Chapelle Royale de Versailles.

ALER, John, BMus, MMus; American singer (tenor); b. 4 Oct. 1949, Baltimore, MD. *Education:* School of Music, Catholic Univ. of America, Juilliard School of Music, American Opera Center and Opera Training Department, studied with Oren Brown and Martin Isepp. *Career:* has sung in opera, oratorio and recitals in USA, Canada, the UK and most of Europe; many appearances including Tanglewood, Glyndebourne, Cincinnati May, Ravinia, Aspen, Salzburg and Aix-en-Provence Festivals, La Scala and London Proms; Vienna Staatsoper debut 1982; toured Japan with Royal Opera, Covent Garden 1986; toured Taiwan with Ludwigsburg Festival Chorus and Orchestra 1987; sang Eumolpus in Stravinsky's Persephone at BBC Proms, London 1993; Britten's War Requiem under James Conlon with Moscow Philharmonic 2006 and Munich Philharmonic 2008, Mendelssohn's Elijah with Dallas Symphony under Claus Peter Flor, Britten's Saint Nicholas with Indianapolis Symphony under Raymond Leppard, Bach's St Matthew Passion and Mozart's Mass in C minor under James Conlon at Cincinnati May Festival 2009, Britten's Canticle II, Abraham and Isaac at Kennedy Center 2010, Bernstein's Candide under John Axelrod, and Mozart's Nozze di Figaro with the Chicago Symphony under James Conlon at Ravinia Festival 2010. *Recordings include:* Berlioz Requiem (Grammy Award for Best Classical Vocal Soloist) 1985, Handel's Messiah 1986, Bizet's Les Pêcheurs des Perles 1989, Songs and Duos of Saint-Saëns (with John Ostendorf and John van Buskirk) 1989, Enesco's Oedipe, Semele (with Kathleen Battle) 1990, title role in Gazzaniga's Don Giovanni, Orfeo 1990, Stravinsky works with London Sinfonietta 1990, Rossini's Songs of My Old Age 1991, Handel's Joshua 1991, Gounod's Mors et Vita with Orchestre du Capitole de Toulouse under Michel Plasson 1992, Dvořák's Stabat Mater with New Jersey Symphony 1994, Merry Widow, Glyndebourne company in concert 1994, Handel – Semele (Grammy Award for Best Opera Recording) 1994, Songs We Forgot to Remember 1996, Bartók – Cantata Profana (Grammy Award for Best Classical Album). *Current Management:* c/o Donald E. Osborne, California Artists Management, 564 Market Street, Suite 420, San Francisco, CA 94104-5412, USA. *Telephone:* (415) 362-2787. *Fax:* (415) 362-2838. *E-mail:* don@calartists.com. *Website:* www.calartists.com.

ALESSANDRINI, Rinaldo; Italian conductor and harpsichordist; b. Rome. *Career:* leading interpreter of Italian early music; founder and Music Dir Concerto Italiano ensemble; numerous worldwide performances with Concerto Italiano, including London, Edin., Vienna, Barcelona, Paris, Köln, Milan, Buenos Aires, Rio de Janeiro, New York, Tokyo, Pergolesi's Missa Romana in Rome, Handel's Theodora in Spain, St Olav Festival, Trondheim, and int. tours of Monteverdi's Il Combattimento di Tancredi e Clorinda, Handel's Il Trionfo del Tempo e del Disinganno; has conducted Teatro del Maggio Musicale Fiorentino, Orchestre Nat. Bordeaux Aquitaine, Orchestra Regionale Toscana, Scottish Chamber Orchestra, Northern Sinfonia, Detroit Symphony, Orchestra of the Age of Enlightenment, Freiburger Barockorchester; has conducted operas, including Handel's Semele at Spoleto Festival, Jommelli's L'isla Disabitata for Rome Opera, Monteverdi's L'Incoronazione di Poppea, Mozart's Le Nozze di Figaro and The Abduction from the Seraglio for WNO, Handel's Amadigi at Teatro di San Carlo di Napoli, Handel's Alcina for Liceu Barcelona, Handel's Giulio Cesare for Oslo Opera. *Recordings include:* with Concerto Italiano: Vivaldi's Vespri per l'Assunzione di Mari Vergine, L'Olympiade, Le Quattro Stagioni, Concerti Ripieni, La Senna Festeggiante, Concerti per Archi, Monteverdi's Musica Sacra/Le Passioni dell' Anima, Vespro della Beata Vergine, Secondo libro de' Madrigali, Quinto libro de' Madrigali, Domenico Scarlatti, Stabat mater a dieci voci, Marenzio, Madrigali, libro II, Pergolesi/Scarlatti, Stabat Mater, Bach, The Art of Fugue, Harpsichord Concertos, Vivaldi Gloria 2009, Melani: Mottetti 2010, Monteverdi Vespri solenni per la festa di San Marco (Gramophone Award for Best Baroque Vocal Recording 2015) 2014; other: Dietrich Buxtehude, Harpsichord Pieces, Bach, A la Maniera Italiana, Georg Boehm, Suites and Partitas, Bernardo Pasquini, Sonate per Gravicembalo, Bach Brandenburg Concertos (Gramophone Award for Best Baroque Instrumental Recording 2006) 2005. *Honours:* Chevalier, Ordre des Arts et des Lettres 2003; Preis der deutschen Schallplattenkritik, Gramophone Award 1994, Prix de la Nouvelle Académie du disque, Cini Foundation Premio internationale del disco Antonio Vivaldi, Prix de l'Académie Charles Cros, Premio Abbiati. *Current Management:* c/o Handel and Haydn Society, 300 Massachusetts Avenue, Boston, MA 02115, USA.

ALEXANDER, Roberta; American singer (soprano); b. 3 March 1949, Lynchburg, VA. *Education:* University of Michigan, Royal Conservatory, The Hague with Herman Woltman. *Career:* European debut as Rossini's Fanny, La Cambiale di Matrimonio, Netherlands Opera in 1975; sang Pamina at

Houston in 1980 and Strauss's Daphne at Santa Fe in 1981; Covent Garden debut as Mimi in La Bohème; Metropolitan debut in 1983 as Zerlina and returned to New York as Jenůfa, Mimi, Vitellia, Countess and Gershwin's Bess; sang at Netherlands Opera as Vitellia, Fiordigili and Violetta, Vienna State Opera as Donna Elvira, Jenůfa, and Hamburg State Opera as Elettra in Idomeneo, Donna Elvira and Countess; Glyndebourne debut in 1989 as Jenůfa; sang Mozart's Vitellia at Zürich in 1989 and Elettra, Idomeneo, at the Hamburg Staatsoper in 1990; Sang Vitellia at Glyndebourne 1995; Donna Elvira at Fort Lauderdale, 1997; concert appearances include Strauss Four Last Songs with Los Angeles Philharmonic under Previn, and San Francisco Symphony, Mahler No. 4 with Boston Symphony under Ozawa, Concertgebouw under Haitink, Cleveland under Ashkenazy, and Mahler No. 8 at the Salzburg Festival under Maazel; Concerts with Concentus Musicus Wien under Harnoncourt; engaged for premiere of Angels in America, by Peter Eötvös, Paris Châtelet, 2004. *Recordings:* Mahler No. 4; Porgy and Bess excerpts; St John Passion; Giulio Cesare excerpts; Don Giovanni; Telemann Cantatas; Songs by Ives, Strauss, Mozart, Bernstein, Barber and Puccini; Goldschmidt's Beatrice Cenci and Der gewaltige Hahnrei. *Current Management:* Alferink Artists Management Amsterdam BV, Herengracht 340, 1016 CG Amsterdam, Netherlands. *Telephone:* (20) 6643151. *Fax:* (20) 6752426. *E-mail:* info@alferink.org. *Website:* www.alferink.org.

ALEXEEV, Dmitri Konstantinovich; Russian pianist; *Professor of Advanced Piano, Royal College of Music*; b. 10 Aug. 1947, Moscow; s. of Konstantin Alekseyev and Gertrude Bolotina; m. Tatiana Sarkisova 1970; one d. *Education:* Moscow Conservatoire. *Career:* studied under Dmitri Bashkirov; performs regularly in Russia, in UK and throughout Europe and USA and has toured Japan, Australia etc.; has performed with orchestras including Berlin Philharmonic, Chicago Symphony Orchestra, Philadelphia Orchestra, Royal Concertgebouw Orchestra of Amsterdam, London Symphony Orchestra, London Philharmonic Orchestra, Philharmonia Orchestra, Royal Philharmonic, BBC Symphony Orchestra, Orchestre de Paris, Israel Philharmonic and the Munich Bavarian Radio Orchestra; worked with Ashkenazy, Boulez, Dorati, Gatti, Gergiev, Giulini, Jansons, Muti, Pappano, Rozhdestvensky, Salonen, Svetlanov, Temirkanov, Rostropovich, Lynn Harrell, Yuri Bashmet, Joshua Bell, Nicolai Gedda, Elisabeth Soderstrom and Barbara Hendricks; world premiere of Penderecki's Piano Sextet, Vienna Musikverein 2000, premiere of Penderecki's Piano Concerto under the baton of the composer, Beijing Festival 2002; Artistic Dir Leeds Int. Recital Series 2008–09; Prof. of Piano, Royal Coll. of Music, London 2005–. *Recordings:* works by Bach, Brahms, Chopin, Grieg, Liszt, Medtner, Prokofiev, Rachmaninov, Schumann, Shostakovich, Scriabin, Glazunov, Gershwin and Hindemith. *Honours:* prizewinner Int. Marguerite Long Competition, Paris 1969, Int. George Enescu Competition, Bucharest 1970, Int. Tchaikovsky Competition, Moscow 1974, 5th Leeds Int. Piano Competition 1975 and other int. competitions; Edison Award (Netherlands) for his recording of the complete Rachmaninov Preludes. *Current Management:* c/o IMG Artists, The Light Box, 111 Power Road, London, W4 5PY, England. *Telephone:* (20) 7957-5800. *Fax:* (20) 7957-5801. *E-mail:* artistseurope@imgartists.com. *Website:* www.imgartists.com.

ALEXEYEV, Anya; Russian pianist; *Associate Professor of Piano, Wilfrid Laurier University*; b. 21 March 1972, Moscow; m.; two c. *Education:* Moscow Conservatory with Dmitri Bashkirov, Royal Coll. of Music with Irina Zaritskaya. *Career:* frequent appearances in Europe, North America, South America and Asia; past engagements have included performances with orchestras including the Royal Philharmonic, BBC Philharmonic, Moscow State Symphony, Vienna Chamber, The Philharmonia, Royal Scottish National, Deutschland Radio, City of Birmingham Symphony, Bournemouth Symphony and Sinfonietta, St. Petersburg Philharmonic, London Mozart Players, BBC National Orchestra of Wales, English Chamber, Malaysian Philharmonic, Belgian National Symphony, Quebec Symphony and St Petersburg Philharmonic; currently Assoc. Prof. of Piano, Wilfrid Laurier Univ., Canada. *Honours:* winner Newport Int. Piano Competition 1991, Anna Instone Memorial Award 1993, Queen Mother's Award, Royal Coll. of Music 1994, John Hopkinson Gold Medal, Royal Coll. of Music 1994, Merit Award, Wilfrid Laurier Univ. 2006, 2009. *Address:* Faculty of Music, Office A416, Wilfrid Laurier University, 75 University Avenue West, Waterloo, Ontario, N2L 3CS, Canada (office). *Telephone:* (519) 884-0710 (office). *Fax:* (519) 747-9129 (office). *E-mail:* anya_alex@yahoo.ca (office). *Website:* www.wlu.ca (office).

ALEXEYEV, Valery; Russian singer (baritone); b. 1954, Novosibirsk, Siberia. *Education:* studied in Novosibirsk and Milan. *Career:* sang with the Kirov Opera, St Petersburg, 1984 in Prokofiev's War and Peace, The Enchantress by Tchaikovsky and the baritone leads in Prince Igor, Eugene Onegin and Boris Godunov; as Tomsky in The Queen of Spades, Vienna Staatsoper, 1996; as Ruprecht in Prokofiev's Fiery Angel, Covent Garden, 1992; Iago in Otello, Barcelona, 1992; Boris in Lady Macbeth, Frankfurt, 1993; sang Nabucco, Bregenz Festival, 1993 and Rangoni in Boris Godunov, Salzburg, 1994; sang Escamillo at Verona, 1995; Eugene Onegin, Zürich, 1996; season 2000–01 as Giancotto in Francesca da Rimini at Buenos Aires, Iago for the Berlin Staatsoper and Count Luna at the New York Met; Tonio in I pagliacci at the Mariinsky Theatre 2006, Shaklovity in Khovanshchina with Bayerische Staatsoper 2007; other roles include Scarpia, Verdi's Miller, Santiago; Don Giovanni, Rigoletto, Mazeppa, Posa in Don Carlos and Valentin in Faust. *Recordings:* Otello. *Current Management:* Pinnacle Arts: Dietsch Division, Thierschstrasse 11/5 OG, 80802 Munich, Germany. *Telephone:* (89) 34086300. *Fax:* (89) 34086310. *E-mail:* jdietsch@pinnaclearts.com. *Website:* www.pinnaclearts.com. *Address:* c/o Kirov Opera, 1 Theatre Square, St Petersburg, Russia.

ALGIERI, Stefano, (Stephen Algie), BMus, MMus; American singer (tenor) and voice professor; *Professor of Voice, Schulich School of Music, McGill University*; b. 1951, Hoboken, New Jersey; m. Mariana Paunova 1980 (died 2002); one s. one d. *Education:* Manhattan School of Music, New York. *Career:* recital debut, Carnegie Hall 1974; concert opera debut in Refice's Cecilia, Avery Fischer Hall, Lincoln Center, New York 1976; stage debut in Pique Dame, 1st Spoleto USA Festival, Charleston, S Carolina 1977; European debut as Rodolfo in Luisa Miller, Bielefeld Opera 1984; other roles include Gustav III in Un Ballo in Maschera, Essen 1986, Turiddu in Cavalleria Rusticana, New York City Opera 1987; Boris in Katya Kabanova, Amsterdam, Paris and Berlin, Radames in Aida, Miami Opera 1988, Don Carlos in Don Carlos, Toronto Opera 1989, Don Jose in Carmen, Andrea Chenier in Andrea Chenier, Strasbourg, Don Alvaro in La Forza del Destino, Scottish Opera 1989, Pollone in Norma 1993, Laca in Jenufa, Bonn 1994, Hans Schweib in Mathis der Maler, Barcelona 1996, Tristan und Isolde, Saarbrücken 2001, Otello in Otello, Dusseldorf 2001, Un Ballo in Maschera, Quebec 2004; Prof. of Voice, Schulich School of Music, McGill Univ. 2003–. *Recordings include:* La Forza del Destino, Aida, Norma, Don Carlo. *Honours:* Gold Medal, Liriche Voci del Nuovo Mundo, winner, Montréal Voice Competition 1977. *Address:* McGill University Schulich School of Music, 555 Sherbrooke Street West, Montréal, PQ H3A 1E3, Canada (office). *Telephone:* (514) 398-4535 (office). *E-mail:* stefano.algieri@mcgill.ca (office); smalgieri@aol.com (home). *Website:* people.mcgill.ca/stephen.algie (office).

ALI-ZADEH, Franghiz; Azerbaijani composer and pianist; b. 29 May 1947, Baku. *Education:* Baku Conservatory. *Career:* teacher at the Baku Conservatory 1977–90, Prof. of Contemporary Music and History of Orchestral Styles 1990–; championed works of Messiaen, Schoenberg, Cage and Crumb including premieres in Azerbaijan; own works performed at festivals including Pesaro Festival, Swedish Spring Festival, Stockholm 1982, Warsaw Autumn festival 1983, Berlin Festival Weeks 1986, Almeida Festival, London 1987, Int. Festival for New Music, Heidelberg 1989, Holland Festival, Amsterdam 1989, Frankfurt Festival 1989, Hamburg Women's Festival 1990, Prokofiev Festival, Duisburg 1991, Schleswig-Holstein Music Festival 1993; has lived in Germany since 1999; British premiere of Ask havası for solo violin by Aexander Ivashkin at Royal Festival Hall, London 2003; commissioned to write orchestral work to mark re-opening of Baku Philharmonie (conducted by Mstislav Rostropovich) 2004; toured in USA as soloist and with Kronos Quartet 2005, commissions from ensembles including Calouste Gulbenkian Foundation, 12 cellists of Berlin Philharmonic, Cho-Liang Lin, Celli Monighetti, Camerata Bern, Altenberg Trio Vienna, Evelyn Glennie, Yo Yo Ma, Kronos Quartet and others; Chair, Composers Union of Azerbaijan 2007–. *Compositions include:* Piano concerto 1972, 2 piano sonatas 1970, 1990, String Quartet 1974, Symphony 1976, Songs about the Motherland, oratorio 1978, Ode for chorus and orchestra 1980, The Legend about White Horseman, rock opera 1985, Concerto for chamber orchestra 1986, Crossings for chamber ensemble 1992, Songs, Empty Cradle, ballet 1993, String Quartets Nos 3 and 4 1995, 1998, Journey to the Immortal for baritone, chorus and ensemble 1995–99, Dervish 2000, Habil-Sayagy (In Habil's Style) for cello and piano, Concerto for Violoncello and Orchestra, Concerto for Marimba and String Orchestra, Nagillar for large orchestra 2002, Shyshtar (Metamorphoses for 12 Violoncelli) 2002, Oasis for string quartet and tape, Apsheron Quintet, Music for Piano, Mugam Sayagi, Concerto for Violoncello and Orchestra, Crossing II, Journey to Immortality, Sabah for violin, violoncello, pipa and prepared piano, Counteractions (Yanar Dag) 2003, Hommage for orchestra 2004. *Recordings include:* La Strimpellata Bern: Crossings: Music by Frangiz Ali-Zade 1997, Kronos Quartet: Mugam Sayagi: Music of Franghiz Ali-Zadeh 2005. *Honours:* Azerbaijani Composers' Union Prize 1980, Meritorious Artist of the Azerbaijani Soviet Socialist Repub. 1990, People's Artist of the Repub. of Azerbaijan 2000, UNESCO Artist for Peace 2008. *Website:* www.ali-sade.tk.

ALIBERTI, Lucia; Italian singer (soprano), musician (piano, guitar, accordion, violin, mandolin) and composer; b. Messina, Sicily. *Education:* Messina Conservatory, studies in Rome with Luigi Ricci, further studies with Alfredo Kraus. *Career:* won Spoleto and ENAL competitions; began operatic career as Amina in Bellini's La Sonnambula in Spoleto at Festival dei Due Mondi under Giancarlo Menotti and Raffaello de Banfield; has sung at world's major theatres, including Metropolitan Opera, New York, Washington Opera, Royal Opera House, Covent Garden, London, La Scala, Milan, Deutsche Oper, Berlin, Bayerische Staatsoper, Munich, Hamburg Staatsoper, Staatstheater, Stuttgart, Vienna State Opera, Opera House, Zurich, Bolshoi Theatre, Moscow, Royal Opera, Stockholm, Opera Rome, Teatro San Carlo, Naples, Teatro Bellini, Catania, Teatro Real, Madrid, Nederlandse Opera, Amsterdam, Théâtre de la Monnaie, Brussels and Teatro Colon, Buenos Aires; has given concerts in major concert halls, including Grosses Festspielhaus, Salzburg, KKL, Lucerne, Concertgebouw, Amsterdam, Queen Elizabeth Hall, London, Théâtre des Champs-Elysées, Paris, Auditorium Milano, Alte Oper, Frankfurt, Philharmonie, Berlin, Gewandhaus, Leipzig, Herkulessaal, Munich, Suntory Hall, Tokyo and Seoul Arts Centre; specializes in repertoire of Bellini (Norma, La Sonnambula, Il Pirata, I Puritani, I Capuleti e I Montecchi, Beatrice di Tenda, La Straniera); other important composers in her repertoire include Donizetti (Lucia di Lammermoor, Anna Bolena,

Lucrezia Borgia, L'elisir d'amore, Don Pasquale, Linda di Chamounix), Rossini (Semiramide, Tancredi, Stabat Mater), Verdi (La Traviata, Rigoletto, Luisa Miller); has composed numerous pieces for piano, clarinet, flute and voice. *Recordings include:* Lucia Aliberti – Verdissimo, Lucia Aliberti – Live at Semperoper Dresden (DVD), Lucia Aliberti – Viva! Belcanto, Lucia Aliberti – A Portrait. *Honours:* Goldene Feder Award, Hamburg 2006, Premio Callas, Milan 2006. *Current Management:* c/o Stefan Schmerbeck Artists Management, Knöbelstr. 10B, 80538 Munich, Germany. *Telephone:* (89) 21329994. *Fax:* (89) 21024727. *E-mail:* stefan@stefanschmerbeck.de. *Website:* www.stefanschmerbeck.de; www.lucia-aliberti.com.

ALIEV, Eldar; Russian singer (bass); b. 1968, Baku. *Education:* Baku Conservatory, studied with Anatoly Eusev. *Career:* debut as Sarastro in Die Zauberflöte, conducted by Peter Maag, Treviso 1994; appearances at the Wexford Festival, in Giordano's Siberia, in Verdi's Attila at Genoa, as Sparafucile in Rigoletto at Lausanne, and Debussy's Arkel at Bologna; Commendatore in Don Giovanni at the Berlin State Opera, and Opéra Bastille, Paris; further roles include Puccini's Colline, Ferrando in Il trovatore, Philip II in Don Carlo, Baldassare in La Favorita, Oroveso in Norma, Capiello in I Capuleti e i Montecchi, Banquo in Macbeth, Timur in Turandot; concert repertoire includes Beethoven's 9th and Shostakovich's 13th Symphonies, Verdi and Mozart Requiems.

ALLEN, Giselle; Northern Irish singer (soprano); b. 1970, Belfast; m. Lawrence Zazzo; one d. *Education:* Univ. of Wales, Guildhall School, RAM. *Career:* roles include Britten's Helena, Suor Angelica, Parassia in Sorochintsky Fair, Cressida in Troilus and Cressida, Tatyana in Eugene Onegin, Svatava in Sarka, Iris in Iris and the Countess, Helena in Midsummer Night's Dream, Geraldine in A Hand of Bridge, Giulietta in Les Contes d'Hoffman, Wellgunde in Das Rheingold, Gutrune in Götterdämmerung, Salomé in Herodiade, Vitellia in La Clemenza, Musetta in La Bohème, Ellen Orford in Peter Grimes, Gerhilde in Walküre, the Fox in Cunning Little Vixen, Marenka in The Bartered Bride, Donna Elvira in Don Giovanni, Marie in Wozzeck, Donna Eleonora in Prima la Musica poi le Parole, Ellen in Peter Grimes for Opera North 2006, Katya Kabanova 2007, Rusalka 2010, Jenůfa for Glyndebourne on Tour 2009, Tosca for Northern Ireland Opera 2011; concerts include Messiah, Albert Hall with David Willcocks, The Vaughan Williams Serenade with Simon Rattle and recitals in Northern Ireland. *Honours:* Guildhall and Ricordi Singing Prizes, Lady Nixon Prize, Countess of Munster scholarship, Sybil Tutton Award, BBC Music Magazine Opera Award (for Britten: Peter Grimes) 2014. *Current Management:* c/o Sue Nicholls, Hazard Chase, 25 City Road, Cambridge, CB1 1DP, England. *Telephone:* (1223) 312400. *Fax:* (1223) 460827. *E-mail:* sue.nicholls@hazardchase.co.uk. *Website:* www.hazardchase.co.uk.

ALLEN, Paschal; Northern Irish singer (bass); b. 1932, Armagh; m. Sheila McGrow; one s. *Education:* studied in Belfast and at Guildhall School, London, with Norman Walker. *Career:* appearances at the Wexford and Glyndebourne Festivals, with English Nat. Opera and for Dublin Grand Opera; repertoire includes Leporello, Bartolo, Colline in La Bohème, Kecal in The Bartered Bride, Figaro and Sarastro; frequent tours with the English Opera Group; concerts at Edinburgh and Aldeburgh Festivals; broadcasts for BBC and Radio Telefis Eireann; engagements for Royal Opera, Covent Garden, include English stage premiere of Hindemith's Mathis der Maler, directed by Peter Sellars 1995. *Address:* 13 Earlsfield Road, London, SW18 3DB, England (home). *Telephone:* (20) 8874-2341 (home).

ALLEN, Sir Thomas Boaz, Kt, CBE, MA, FRCM, FRAM; British singer (baritone); *Chancellor, Durham University*; b. 10 Sept. 1944, Seaham Harbour, Co. Durham; s. of Thomas Boaz Allen and Florence Allen; m. 1st Margaret Holley 1968 (divorced 1986); one s.; m. 2nd Jeannie Gordon Lascelles 1988; one step-s. one step-d. *Education:* Robert Richardson Grammar School, Ryhope, Royal Coll. of Music, London, Univs of Newcastle, Birmingham and Durham. *Career:* Prin. Baritone, Welsh Nat. Opera 1969–72, Royal Opera House, Covent Garden 1972–78; freelance opera singer 1978–, singing at Glyndebourne Opera 1973, ENO, London Coliseum 1986, La Scala 1987, Chicago Lyric Opera 1990, Royal Albert Hall 2000, London Proms 2002, Royal Opera House, Covent Garden 2003, Metropolitan Opera, New York 2005; Prince Consort Prof., Royal Coll. of Music 1994; Hambro Visiting Prof. of Opera, Univ. of Oxford 2000–01; Pres. British Youth Opera 2000–; Patron Samling Foundation, Music in Hosps, Oxford Lieder Festival, Kathleen Ferrier Awards; Chancellor, Durham Univ. 2011–; performances include: Die Zauberflöte 1973, Le Nozze di Figaro 1974, Così fan tutte 1975, 2010, 2012, Don Giovanni 1977, The Cunning Little Vixen 1977, Simon Boccanegra, Billy Budd, La Bohème, L'Elisir d'Amore, Faust, Albert Herring, Die Fledermaus, La Traviata, A Midsummer Night's Dream, Gianni Schicchi 2008, Der Rosenkavalier 2009–10, Die Meistersinger von Nürnberg 2010, Hänsel und Gretel 2010–11, Il turco in Italia 2011, Il barbiere di Siviglia 2011; Albert Herring (as producer) 2002; Dir Così fan tutte, Samling Opera, The Sage, Gateshead 2005, Le nozze di Figaro 2006, Il barbiere di Siviglia 2007, Der Rosenkavalier 2009, Il turco in Italia 2009, Gianni Schicchi 2010. *Recordings:* numerous including: Duruflé, Requiem and Four Motets 1987, Duparc, Songs 1989, Duruflé and Fauré, Requiems 1998, Songs My Father Taught Me 2002, More Songs My Father Taught Me 2003. *Art Exhibitions:* Chelsea Festival 2001, Salisbury Playhouse 2001. *Film:* Mrs Henderson Presents 2005, The Real Don Giovanni 2009. *Publication:* Foreign Parts: A Singer's Journal 1993. *Honours:* Hon. Fellow, Univ. of Sunderland, Jesus Coll., Oxford; Hon. mem. RAM; Hon. MA (Newcastle) 1984, Hon. DMus (Durham) 1988, (Birmingham) 2004; Queen's Prize 1967, Gulbenkian Fellow 1968, Royal Philharmonic Soc. BBC Radio 3 Listeners' Award 2004, Bayerischer Kammersänger, Bavarian State Opera, Queen's Medal for Music 2013.

ALLIK, Kristi, MusBac, MFA, PhD; Canadian composer and academic; *Professor Emerita of Theory and Composition, School of Music, Queen's University*; b. 6 Feb. 1952, Toronto, Ont. *Education:* Univ. of Toronto, Princeton Univ. and Univ. of Southern California, USA. *Career:* Assoc. Prof. of Theory and Composition, Queen's Univ., Kingston, Ont., co-founder of electronic music studio, now Prof. Emer. *Compositions include:* Loom Sword River, opera 1982, Of all the People for voices and ensemble 1983, Skyharp, sound sculpture 1991; Multi-media works with electronics Electronic Zen Garden 1983, Rondeau 1985, Comatose 1986, Rhythm and Culture 1986, Till Rust do us Part 1988, Vitamin B-52 1989; Piano trio 1979; Lend me your Harp for chorus and chamber orchestra,1981, Zone Two for ensemble 1984, Rohan for cello and chamber orchestra 1988, Trio for clarinet, piano and low voice 1989, Three Textures for strings 1992, Illustrated Earth for orchestra 1993, Nel mezzo del camina for soprano, guitar and tape 1995, Ecotonal Landscapes 1998, The~infoweaver 2001. *Address:* Queen's University, School of Music, Harrison-LeCaine Hall, Room 204, 39 Bader Lane, Kingston, ON K7L 3N6, Canada (office). *E-mail:* allikk@queensu.ca (office). *Website:* www.queensu.ca/music (office).

ALLIOT-LUGAZ, Colette; French singer (soprano); b. 20 July 1947, Notre-Dame-de-Bellecombe. *Education:* studied at Bonneville with Magda Fonay-Besson in Geneva and at the Opera Studio Paris with Rene Koster and Vera Rozsa; further study at the Lyon Conservatoire. *Career:* has sung widely in France and elsewhere as Mozart's Pamina, Cherubino and Zerlina; engagements as Messager's Véronique, Rosina and Weber's Aennchen and in operas by Monteverdi, Haydn and Rameau; often appeared as Debussy's Mélisande notably at Lyon Opéra 1980; festival performances at Aix and Glyndebourne, at Paris Opéra and Théâtre de la Monnaie, Brussels; modern repertory includes La Passion de Gilles by Boesmans, creation 1983, and Berio's Opera; sang Ascanius in Les Troyens at the opening of Opéra Bastille, Paris 1990; appeared as Lully's Alceste at Théâtre des Champs-Elysées 1992; season 1992–93 as Gluck's Alceste at Montpellier and Siebel in Faust at Paris Opéra; sang in Les Troyens by Berlioz with Toulouse Orchestra under Michel Plasson at Toulouse and Athens 1994; during 1995 gave many concerts with Orchestre des Pays de Savoie; sang a concert version of Pulcinella by Stravinsky at Salle Pleyel 1996, and Brahms Requiem at Lyon 1997; season 1997–98 sang with the Cantate des Alpes in many concerts of traditional alpine songs throughout Rhône-Alpes region. *Recordings include:* Pelléas et Mélisande, conducted by Charles Dutoit; Fragoletto in Les Brigands by Offenbach; Campra's Tancrède; Video of Pelléas et Mélisande, from Lyon (Arthaus), Ravel, L'Enfant et les sortilèges 2009. *Honours:* Nadia and Lili Boulanger Prize, Académie des Beaux-Arts, Paris 1993. *Address:* Les Frasses, 73590 Notre Dame de Bellecombe, France.

ALLISON, John, BMus, PhD, ARCO; British editor and critic; *Editor, Opera*; b. 20 May 1965, Cape Town, South Africa; s. of David Allison and Adele Allison; m. Nicole Galgut. *Education:* Univ. of Cape Town. *Career:* fmr organist at Cape Town Cathedral; music critic for The Times; Ed. Opera magazine 2000–; Judge, Opera Awards 2015. *Publications include:* Edward Elgar: Sacred Music 1994, Mitchell Beazley Pocket Guide to Opera 1998, A Way of Seeing: Perception, Imagination, and Poetry 2003, The English Historical Constitution: Continuity, Change and European Effects 2007, Dropped Stitches in Tennessee History 2010; contrib. to Opera News, BBC Music Magazine, Classic FM Magazine, Financial Times, London Evening Standard, The Observer, The Australian, New Grove Dictionary of Music and Musicians, The New Penguin Opera Guide, Music and Words – Essays in Honour of Andrew Porter. *Address:* Opera Magazine, 36 Black Lion Lane, London, W6 9BE, England (office). *Telephone:* (20) 8563-8893 (office). *Fax:* (20) 8563-8635 (office). *E-mail:* editor@opera.co.uk (office). *Website:* www.opera.co.uk (office).

ALLWOOD, Ralph, BA, MBE; British teacher, conductor and choral director; *Music Director, Old Royal Naval College, Greenwich*; b. 30 April 1950, Walton-on-Thames. *Education:* Tiffin School, Durham Univ., Univ. of Cambridge. *Career:* Precentor and Dir of Music, Eton Coll. 1985–2011; Music Dir, Old Royal Naval Coll., Greenwich 2012–; f. and directs the seven annual Eton Choral Courses; Co-founder Junior Choral Courses, three in UK and two in Shanghai; Founder and Dir Rodolfus Choir; Dir Windsor and Eton Choral Soc.; adjudicator for Llangollen Int. Eisteddfod; regular visitor to several Welsh choirs, including Nat. Youth Choir of Wales; choral adviser for Novello & Co. Ltd, Voices Foundation, Nat. Youth Choir of GB; now freelance choral trainer and conductor; teaches at Trinity Laban Conservatoire and Tiffin Boys School; Founder Inner Voices (choir for young people from 10 Inner London state schools); has led choral courses and workshops world-wide; Fellow Commoner advising in Music at Queens' Coll., Cambridge. *Recordings:* Music from Eton 1986, I Will Lift up Mine Eyes 1986, A Sequence for the Ascension 1992, Mater Ora Filium 1993, Music from Eton Choirbook 1994, Grier: Twelve Anthems 1995, Among the Leaves So Green 1996, Choral Evensong from Eton College 1997, Welsh Songs, Hymns and Anthems 1997, Parry: Songs of Farwell 1998, Eberlin: Sacred Choral Music 1999, Christmas Music from Eton College 2000, By Special Arrangement 2002, A Christmas Collection 2003, Musica Etonensis 2004, Abendlied 2004, Thomas Tallis: Latin Motets and Anthems 2005, A Celebration of Christmas 2005, A Bach Christmas 2005, Choral Arrangements by Clytus Gottwald 2007, Monteverdi Vespers 2007, Hear my Words 2007, Herbert Howells 2010, French Choral Music 2010, Bach

Mass in B Minor 2010. *Publications:* German Romantic Motets, Vol. 1, By Special Arrangement, By Popular Request, German Romantic Motets Vol. 2, Russian Choral Masterpieces, Choral Music of Pearsall. *Honours:* Hon. FRSCM 2002; Hon. ARAM 2003; Hon. Fellow, Univ. Coll., Durham. *Telephone:* (20) 7233-9455 (office). *E-mail:* pa@ralphallwood.com (office). *Website:* www.etonchoralcourses.co.uk; www.ralphallwood.com.

ALMERARES, Paula; Argentine singer (soprano); b. 1970. *Education:* studied in Buenos Aires with Mirtha Garbarini from Teatro Colón, and Janine Reiss in France. *Career:* debut as soloist in Mahler's 4th Symphony, La Plata 1990; stage debut as Musetta at Teatro Argentino, La Plata 1990; early roles were Micaela and Donizetti's Norina; sang Offenbach's Antonia with Alfredo Kraus at Teatro Colón, Buenos Aires 1993, also in Roméo et Juliette, Don Pasquale, La Bohème and Falstaff; premiere of Mario Peruso's Guayaquil 1993; Zarzuelas with Plácido Domingo, Teatro Avenida, Buenos Aires 1994; Gluck's Euridice, Venice 1995; sang Adina in L'Elisir d'amore at Teatro Verdi di Trieste 1996, Adina in L'Elisir d'amore at Teatro Verdi di Trieste 1996, Adina in Il viaggio a Reims at the Teatro Argentina, La Plata, Pamina at Auditorio Nacional del Sodre de Montevideo, Lucia di Lammermoor for the Teatro El Círculo de Rosario, Argentina 2010; concert appearances include Debussy Le Martire de Saint-Sebastien with London Symphony Orchestra under Michel Tilson Thomas, Mozart and Brahms Requiems, Rossini and Pergolesi Stabat Mater, Bach Magnificat, Cantata 147 and Oratorio de Pascua, and Mozart Exsultate Jubilate; tours of Europe with Claudio Scimone; worked with conductors including Julius Rudel, Lorin Maazel, Daniel Oren, Sir Neville Marriner, Romano Gandolfi, Giuliano Carella, Maurizio Arena, Stanislaw Skrowaczewski, Donato Renzetti and Pedro I. Calderon. *Recordings:* Giulietta e Romeo (N. Vaccai). *Honours:* Best Soprano, Belvedere Competition, Vienna 1993, winner, Traviata 2000 Competition, Pittsburgh 1994, Konex Prize for Best Female Singer 1999. *Current Management:* c/o Steven Swales Artist Management, 46 Twinwood Road, Clapham, Bedford, MK41 6HL, England. *Telephone:* (1234) 353239. *Fax:* (7742) 882167. *E-mail:* mail@ssartists.co.uk. *Website:* www.ssartists.co.uk; www.paulaalmerares.com (home).

ALONSO-CRESPO, Eduardo, MFA; Argentine composer and conductor; *Composer in Residence and Principal Guest Conductor, Orquesta Sinfónica de Salta;* b. 18 March 1956, Tucumán, Argentina. *Education:* Universidad Nacional de Tucumán, Carnegie Mellon University, USA. *Career:* Prof. of Piano, School of Musical Arts, Universidad Nacional de Tucumán; debut conducting: Carnegie Mellon Philharmonic in Ginastera, USA 1987; Asst Conductor, Pittsburgh Civic Orchestra 1988–90; Assoc. Conductor, Carnegie Mellon Philharmonic 1989–91; Music Dir, Tucumán Symphony Orchestra and Carnegie Mellon Contemporary Ensemble 1989–2001; Conductor-in-Residence, Carnegie Mellon Univ. 1991–92, currently Visiting Lecturer; currently Composer in Residence and Prin. Guest Conductor, Orquesta Sinfónica de Salta; guest conducting, Argentina, USA; debut at Teatro Colón in Buenos Aires, conducting Mahler's Fourth Symphony 1998; works performed throughout Argentina, and in USA, Netherlands, Germany, Finland, Italy, Spain, Taiwan, Venezuela, Chile, Peru. *Compositions include:* opera: Gorbachev, Juana, La Loca 1991, Putzi, Yubarta; other: Medea, ballet, for chorus and orchestra 1985, incidental music for Macbeth (Iris Marga Award for best original score for drama 1994, Piano Concerto 1–3, Concertos for bassoon, clarinet, viola, Commentaries on Three Waltzes by Alberdi, Epic Dances for Wind Ensemble, Two Stories of Birds for Orchestra, Sinfonietta for String Orchestra, String Quartets 1 & 2, Symphonies 1–4. *Recordings:* Macbeth. *Honours:* numerous awards including Premio Alejandro Shaw, Academia Nacional de Bellas Artes, Cristóbal Colón Int. Prize for Symphonic Music 1986, Nat. Endowment for the Arts of Argentina Symphonic Commission Award 1987. *Address:* Orquesta Sinfónica de Salta, Casa de la Cultura, Caseros 460, CP4400 Salta, Argentina (office). *Telephone:* (38) 7421-5763 (office). *Fax:* (38) 7421-5763 (office). *E-mail:* info@ossalta.com (office); eac@tucbbs.com.ar. *Website:* www.ossalta.com (office); www.angelfire.com/music3/eduardoalonsocrespo.

ALPERIN, Yoram; Romanian cellist; b. 1945. *Education:* Rubin Acad. of Music, Tel-Aviv with Uzi Wiezel. *Career:* mem. and solo appearances with Israel Philharmonic 1971–; co-founder, Jerusalem String Trio 1977–, giving many chamber concerts in Israel and abroad; repertoire includes String Trios by Beethoven, Dohnányi, Mozart, Reger, Schubert and Taneyev, piano quartets by Beethoven, Brahms, Dvořák, Mozart and Schumann; concerts with Radu Lupu and Daniel Adni; founder mem., Dafna String Quartet 2000–. *E-mail:* alperin@netvision.net.il.

ALSOP, Marin, MusM; American violinist and conductor; b. 16 Oct. 1956, New York City; d. of Keith LaMar Alsop and Ruth Alsop (née Condell); m. Kristin Jurkscheit Auden; one s. *Education:* began piano studies aged two, violin studies aged five; Juilliard Pre-Coll., Yale Univ. and Juilliard School of Music. *Career:* freelance violinist with New York Symphony Orchestra, Mostly Mozart, New York Chamber Symphony, American Composers Orchestra, several Broadway shows 1976–79; began conducting studies with Carl Bamberger 1979, Harold Farberman 1985; f. String Fever (14-piece swing band) 1981; Founder and Dir Concordia Orchestra 1984–; debut with London Symphony Orchestra 1988; Assoc. Conductor Richmond Symphony 1988; studied with Leonard Bernstein, Seiji Ozawa and Gustav Meier, Tanglewood

Music Center 1989; Music Dir Eugene Symphony, Ore. 1989–96, Conductor Laureate 1996–; Music Dir Long Island Philharmonic 1990–96; debut with Philadelphia Orchestra and Los Angeles Philharmonic 1990; Artistic Dir Cabrillo Festival of Contemporary Music 1992–2016; Music Dir Colorado Symphony, Denver 1993–2005; debut Schleswig Holstein Music Festival 1993; Creative Conductor Chair. St Louis Symphony Orchestra 1996–98; Prin. Guest Conductor, Royal Scottish Nat. Symphony 1999–; Prin. Guest Conductor, City of London Sinfonia 1999–; Prin. Conductor Bournemouth Symphony Orchestra (first woman to head UK symphony orchestra) 2001–07; guest teacher/artist, Nat. Orchestral Inst. 1991–2001, Oberlin 1998, Interlochen Center for the Arts 1998, Curtis Inst. 1998; Music Dir Baltimore Symphony Orchestra 2007–; Music Dir, São Paulo Symphony Orchestra 2012–; Dir of Graduate Conducting, Peabody Inst., Johns Hopkins Univ. 2015–; Fellow, American Acad. of Arts and Sciences. *Achievements include:* first woman to conduct the orchestra at La Scala, Concertgebouw Orchestra 2007; est. Orchkids after-school programme in inner city Baltimore 2008; first woman to conduct Last Night of the BBC Promenade Concerts, London 2013. *Recordings include:* Fever Pitch, Fanfares for the Uncommon Woman, Saint-Saens, Blue Monday, Victory Stride, Fiddle Concerto for Violin and Orchestra, Gorgon, Music of Edward Collins, Too Hot to Handel, Barber Vols I–IV, Passion Wheels, Tchaikovsky Symphony No. 4, Bernstein Chichester Psalms, Brahms cycle with London Philharmonic, Barber cycle with Royal Scottish Nat. Orchestra, John Adams' Nixon in China, Bernstein's Mass. *Honours:* Hon. RAM 2012, Hon. mem. Royal Philharmonic Soc. 2014; Hon. DLitt (Gonzaga Univ.) 1995, (Univ. of Minnesota) 2009; Leonard Bernstein Conducting Fellow, Tanglewood Music Festival 1988, 1989, Stokowski Conducting Competition 1988, Koussevitzky Conducting Prize 1989, ASCAP Award for Adventuresome Programming of Contemporary Music 1991, Univ. of Colorado Distinguished Service Award 1997, State of Colorado Gov.'s Award for Excellence in the Arts 1998, Royal Philharmonic Soc. Conducting Award 2003, Gramophone Artist of the Year 2003, Classical BRIT Award for Female Artist of the Year 2005, MacArthur Fellow and Grant 2005, MacArthur Genius Award 2005, Royal Philharmonic Soc. BBC Radio 3 Listeners' Award 2006, Musical America Award for Conductor of the Year 2009. *Current Management:* c/o David V. Foster, Opus 3 Artists, 470 Park Avenue South, 9th Floor North, New York, NY 10016, USA; c/o Intermusica Artists Management Ltd, Crystal Wharf, 36 Graham Street, London, N1 8GJ, England. *Telephone:* (212) 584-7568 (Opus 3). *E-mail:* rachel@rachelbowron.com; dfoster@opus3artists.com. *Website:* www.opus3artists.com; www.intermusica.co.uk. *E-mail:* marinalsop@aol.com. *Website:* www.marinalsop.com.

ALSPAUGH, Blanton, MM; American sound engineer, record producer and conductor; *Senior Producer, Soundmirror.* *Education:* Tennessee Technological Univ., Shepherd School of Music, Rice Univ. *Career:* joined classical music recording and production company Soundmirror 1991–, now sr producer of recordings ranging from large operatic and symphonic productions to solo piano for all major classical labels. *Honours:* Grammy Award for Classical Producer of the Year and Best Choral Performance 2012. *Address:* Soundmirror, 76 Green Street, Boston, MA 02130-2271, USA (office). *Telephone:* (617) 522-1412 (office). *Fax:* (617) 524-8377 (office). *Website:* www.soundmirror.com (office).

ALSTED, Birgitte; Danish composer and violinist; b. 15 June 1942, Odense. *Education:* Royal Danish Academy of Music, Music Academy, Warsaw, Poland, composition seminars with Per Norgard, Copenhagen, Det Jyske Musikkonservatorium – RAMA Aarhus. *Career:* performer of new music in Det unge Tonekunstnerselskab; Kvinder i Musik; Danmarks Radio, Television Acting Musician, Experimental Theatre; Teacher, Compositions performed in DUT, Radio, Television, KIM, Paris, Rome, New York, Mexico City, Berlin, Stockholm, London; Commissions, Contemporary Dance Theatre, London, Nordiske Forum 88, Danmarks Radio; mem, Dansk Komponistforening; Kvinder i Musik; Det Unge Tonekunstnerselskab. *Compositions include:* Klumpe, 1972; Stykke 2, 1973; 12 toner i Zoo, 1973; Smedierne i Granada, 1976; Strygekvartet i CD, 1977; Konkurrence, 1979; Haiku-Sange, 1979; Solen og jeg, 1981; Gentagne Gange, 1980; Solen på Moddingen, 1982; Phasing Moon Facing Changing, 1983; Antigone, 1983; Kaere Allesammen, 1984; På Afstand af Bolgen, 1984–85; Om Natten, 1985; Skiftetid, 1985; Kindleins Schlaflied, 1986; Frokost i det Gronne, 1985; Nostalgisk Extranummer, 1985; Extra Nostalgisk no. 2, 1986; Espressione Emotionale, 1987; Fatsy, 1987; Dromme-spil, 1988; Opbrud, 1988; Vakst, 1989; Lyst, 1990; 2 sange til Doden, 1990; Episoder til Thomas, 1991; Havet ved Forår, 1991; Karen's Å, 1992; Unoder, 1992; Natterdag, 1992; Berceuse Neptunoise, 1993; Spring I, 1994; Stelle, 1995; Sorgsang, 1995; Hojsang 1995, Sorgsang II (Lament for baritone and piano) 1995, Sorgsang V 1996, She Cinderella, opera 1996, Church Bells for orchestra 1996, Very Sure, electro-acoustic 1997, Zweigeigen 2001, Zu versuchen, die Fragen 2002, Odysseus on a Minicruise 2002, Dance with Bells 2006. *Recordings:* Antigone; Frokost i det Gronne; Vakst; Natterdag; To Sange til Doden; Planetarium Music – Electroacoustic Music From DIEM II (with Michael Nyvang) 1997, Zweigeigen (with Duo Gelland) 2001. *Honours:* Komponistforeningens Jubilaeumslegat, 1985; Gustav Enna's Mindelegat, 1988; Several grants, Art Foundation of Danish State, including 3 years, 1980–83. *Address:* Dansk Komponistforening, Grabrodretorv 16, 1154 Copenhagen K, Denmark.

ALTENBURGER, Christian; Austrian violinist; b. 5 Sept. 1957, Heidelberg, Germany. *Education:* Vienna Academy of Music, Juilliard School, New York, studied violin with father and Dorothy DeLay. *Career:* debut in 1964; formal debut in recital, Musikverein, Vienna 1976; soloist with various major orchestras in Europe and the USA; with Bruno Canino played the Sonata by Strauss, Schoenberg's Fantasy and Bartók's 2nd Sonata, Salzburg Festival 1990; Artistic Dir, Mondseetage Festival 1999–2005, Chamber Music Festival Schwäbischer Frühling 2003–06, Loisiartee Festival 2006–; Prof. of Music, Hannover Univ. 1990–2001, Universität für Musik und darstellende Kunst, Vienna 2001–; gives masterclasses, mem. competition juries. *Current Management:* c/o Christiane Gonzalez Mayoral, Krummgasse 14/8, 1030 Vienna, Austria. *Telephone:* 681 10542699. *E-mail:* office@mayoral-artists.com. *E-mail:* CAltenburger@aol.com (home). *Website:* www.christian-altenburger.at.

ALTINOGLU, Alain; French conductor and musician (piano); b. 9 Oct. 1975, Paris; m. Nora Gubisch. *Education:* Conservatoire Nat. Supérieur de Musique, Paris. *Career:* guest conductor at Metropolitan Opera, New York, Lyric Opera of Chicago, Teatro Colón, Buenos Aires, Berlin State Opera, Deutsche Oper Berlin, Bavarian State Opera, Vienna State Opera, Paris Opéra, Théâtre du Châtelet, Opéra-Comique, Théâtre des Champs-Elysées and festivals in Salzburg, Aix-en-Provence and Orange; has conducted Don Giovanni (Paris Opéra and Vienna State Opera), Le nozze di Figaro, Simon Boccanegra, Don Carlos (Wiener Staatsoper), Rabaud's Marouf, savetier du Caïre, Manon Lescaut (Bayerische Staatsoper) and Salome; has conducted orchestras including Berlin Staatskapelle, Konzerthausorchester Berlin, Staatskapelle Dresden, City of Birmingham Symphony Orchestra, Orchestra della Fenice, Venice, Orchestre Nat. de France, Orchestre de Paris, Orchestre Philharmonique de Radio France, Orchestre Nat. de Lyon, Tonhalle Orchester Zürich, Gulbenkian Orchestra, Lisbon and Ensemble Intercontemporain; Royal Opera House, Covent Garden debut (Don Giovanni) 2015; also performs as pianist, particularly as accompanist in the Lied repertory; taught vocal ensemble class for 10 years at Conservatoire Nat. Supérieur de Musique, Paris. *Recordings include:* Dusapin/Perelà 2005, Alexandre Tansmann: Le Serment, Eric Tanguy: Concertos pour violoncelle 2008, Henri Duparc: Mélodies 2011, Bernard Hermann: Les Hauts de Hurlevent (Wuthering Heights) 2011, Lalo: Fiesque 2013. *Website:* www.alainaltinoglu.com.

ALTMEYER, Jeannine; American singer (soprano); b. 2 May 1948, La Habra, CA. *Education:* studied with Martial Singher and Lotte Lehmann in Santa Barbara, California; attended the Salzburg Mozarteum. *Career:* operatic debut as the Heavenly Voice in Don Carlos, Metropolitan Opera, New York, 25 Sept. 1971; appeared with the Chicago Lyric Opera, 1972, in Salzburg, 1973 and at Bayreuth, 1979; member of the Wurttemberg State Theatre, Stuttgart, 1975–79; then sang throughout Europe, achieving success as a Wagnerian; roles: Elsa, Eva, Sieglinde, Isolde, Elisabeth, Gutrune and Brünnhilde; sang Isolde at Bayreuth, 1986; Paris Opéra and Los Angeles, 1987 as Chrysothemis, Isolde; Brünnhilde in Götterdämmerung at the Zürich Opera, 1989; sang Leonore at La Scala, 1990; Turin 1991, as Goldmark's Queen of Sheba; sang Brünnhilde in Götterdämmerung for Netherlands Opera, 1998; Elektra at Aachen, 1999. *Recordings:* sang Brünnhilde in The Ring under Janowski; Video and DVD of Die Walküre, in production from Bayreuth. *Current Management:* Hilbert Artists Management, Maximilianstrasse 22, 80539 Munich, Germany. *Telephone:* (89) 2907470. *Fax:* (89) 29074790. *E-mail:* agentur@hilbert.de. *Website:* www.hilbert.de.

ALVA, Luigi; Peruvian singer (tenor); b. 10 April 1927, Lima. *Education:* studied with Rosa Morales in Lima and with Emilio Ghiradini and Ettore Campogalliani in Milan. *Career:* debut singing at Lima in the Zarzuela Luisa Fernanda, 1949; Beppe in Pagliacci, 1950; Sang Paolino in Cimarosa's Il matrimonio segreto at La Scala, 1955; Salzburg Festival, 1957–58, as Fenton in Falstaff and Ferrando in Così fan tutte; Sang Rossini's Almaviva more than 300 times, starting with La Scala, 1956; Returned to Milan in 1958 for the local premiere of Janáček's The Cunning Little Vixen and world premieres of Una domanda di matrimonio by Luciano Chailly and Malipiero's La donna e mobile; appeared in Holland Festival in 1959 in Il mondo della luna by Haydn and made his Covent Garden debut in 1960; Glyndebourne Festival, 1961–62, as Nemorino in L'Elisir d'amore; Aix-en-Provence from 1960, Vienna Staatsoper from 1961; Metropolitan Opera, 1964–76 as Ernesto in Don Pasquale, Almaviva, Lindoro in L'Italiana in Algeri and Mozart's Tamino; Other appearances in Hamburg, Berlin, Moscow, Edinburgh, Stockholm, Lisbon, Venice, Florence and Mexico City; Artistic Director of Prolirica in Lima from 1982; Retired as singer, 1989; sponsors Luigi Alva Prize for young singers, gives masterclasses, teaches singing at La Scuola di Canto, La Scala Milan. *Recordings include:* Il Barbiere di Siviglia, Il matrimonio segreto and Falstaff (Columbia); La Cenerentola (Deutsche Grammophon); Handel's Alcina, L'Italiana in Algeri and Mozart's Il re pastore (Decca); Haydn's L'Isola disabitata (Philips); Alfonso und Estrella by Schubert (Melodram). *Address:* c/o La Scuola di Canto La Scala, Via Santa Marta 18, 20123 Milan, Italy.

ALVARES, Eduardo; Brazilian singer (tenor); b. 10 June 1947, Rio de Janeiro. *Career:* started career in Europe, (debut as Don José) Linz, Frankfurt, Vienna and Stuttgart, returned to Brazil and then sang Des Grieux (Manon Lescaut) at Metropolitan, and Netherlands Opera (also Dick Johnson in Fanciulla del West), Manrico in Il Trovatore for Opera North and Calaf in Turandot for Scottish Opera; English National Opera as Radames in Aida, 1985 and Cavaradossi, 1987; Teatro Municipal Rio de Janeiro, 1987–88, as Don José and Bacchus; Other roles include Alfredo, Gabriele Adorno, Don Carlos, Faust, Werther and Alva in Lulu; Wexford Festival, 1983–84, in Hans Heiling and The Kiss.

ALVAREZ, Carlos; Spanish singer (baritone); b. 1963, Málaga. *Education:* Málaga Conservatory. *Career:* sang Morales in Carmen with Luis Lima and gave concert with him at the Teatro Arriaga in Bilbao; further appearances at the Teatro La Zarzuela, Madrid, Teatro Colón Buenos Aires, Vienna Staatsoper, La Scala Milan and Royal Opera, Covent Garden; operas have included Eugene Onegin (at Madrid), La Bohème, Il Barbiere di Siviglia (Zürich), La Traviata and Fedora (London), Don Carlos (Mannheim) and Madama Butterfly (Milan); frequent appearances with Plácido Domingo, including Il Guarany by Gomes at Bonn and concerts in Tokyo, Berlin, Madrid and Seville; Les Troyens with the London Symphony at the Barbican Hall under Colin Davis 1993; guest engagements in New York, Geneva and Washington; Posa in Don Carlos at Salzburg 1998; Don Giovanni at the Vienna Theater an der Wien 1999; season 2000–01 as Germont at Zürich, Don Carlo in Ernani at Madrid and Posa in Don Carlos at the Vienna Staatsoper; Rigoletto at Covent Garden 2002; Don Carlo di Vargas in La forza del destino, Simon Boccanegra, and Graf René Ankarström in Un ballo in maschera at Vienna State Opera 2009, Ford in Falstaff at Rome Opera 2010, Rigoletto, and Ezio in Attila at Metropolitan Opera, New York 2010, Simon Boccanegra at Opera Real, Madrid 2010. *Honours:* Opera Actual magazine Award for best baritone 2005. *Current Management:* c/o Alfonso G. Leoz Lyric Art, Salamanca 26, Las Matas, 28290 Madrid, Spain. *Telephone:* (91) 6309059. *Fax:* (91) 6301395. *E-mail:* alfonsoleoz@telefonica.net. *Website:* www.alfonsoleoz.com.

ÁLVAREZ, Marcelo; Argentine singer (tenor); b. 1963, Cordóba. *Career:* debut in Bellini's La Sonnambula at Teatro la Fenice, Venice 1995; operatic roles include: The Duke in Rigoletto, Trieste, London 1996, Toulouse 1997, Verona 1997, Buenos Aires 1997, Brussels 1998, Metropolitan Opera New York 1999, Tokyo 2000, London 2001, Paris 2001, Macerata 2002, Barcelona 2004; Alfredo in La Traviata, Hamburg, Genoa, Venice, Vienna, Paris, The Met 1998, Royal Albert Hall, London 1998, Berlin 1999–2000, Fiorentino 1999–2000, Bavaria 2002; title role in Massenet's Werther Genoa, Toulouse 1999–2000, Trieste 2002, London 2004, Vienna 2005; The Italian Tenor in Der Rosenkavalier at The Met 2000–01; Tonio in La Fille du Régiment, Bilbao 1997; Arturo in I Puritani, Bologna 1997; Fenton in Falstaff, Berlin 1998; Edgardo in Lucia di Lammermoor, Toulouse 1997–98, Naples 2001–02, Paris 2002, Japan 2002–03, Chicago 2004; Des Grieux in Massenet's Manon, Genoa 1997–98, Paris 2000–01, Naples 2001–02; title role in Gounod's Faust, Munich 1999–2000; title role in Tales of Hoffman, Covent Garden, London 2000–01; Gennaro in Lucrezia Borga, Teatro alla Scala, Milan 2002–03; Rodolfo in La Bohème at La Scala 2002–03, Paris 2003, Verona 2005; Rodolfo in Luisa Miller, London 2003; Riccardo in Un Ballo di Maschera at Covent Garden 2005, Zürich 2005. *Recordings:* Bel Canto 1998, Marcelo Alvarez sings Gardel 2000, French Tenor Arias 2002, Duetto (with Salvatore Licitra) 2003, Jules Massenet's Manon 2003, The Tenor's Passion 2004. *Honours:* Echo Klassik Singer of the Year Award, Germany 2002, L'Opera magazine Tenor of the Year Award, Italy 2003, Premios Líricos Teatro Campoamor Award for Best Male Opera Singer 2008. *Current Management:* Zemsky/Green Artists Management, 730 Fifth Avenue, Suite 1802, New York, NY 10019, USA. *Telephone:* (212) 300-8003. *Fax:* (212) 300-8001. *E-mail:* zgartists@aol.com. *Website:* www.zemskygreen.com; www.marceloalvarez.com.

ALVES DA SILVA, Luiz; Brazilian singer (countertenor); *Director, Ensemble Turicum*; b. 1964, Videira, Santa Catarina. *Education:* studied with Roberto da Regina, Schola Cantorum Basiliensis, Basel and Int. Opera Studio, Zurich, Switzerland. *Career:* sang with various European vocal groups, including the Clemencic Consort, Vienna, Hesperion XX, Instituzioni Harmoniche of Bologne, Capella Real of Barcelona; baroque and contemporary works on stage and the concert platform; f. mem. and Dir Ensemble Turicum, Zurich, Switzerland; Prof. of Vocal Music Interpretation, Zurich Conservatory. *Recordings:* GG Brunetti's Stabat Mater. *Honours:* winner young soloists competition, Orquestra Sinfônica de São Paulo 1982, Ernst Göhner Foundation Award. *Address:* Ensemble Turicum, Mühlebachstrasse 148, 8008 Zurich, Switzerland (office). *Telephone:* 3832421 (office). *E-mail:* contact@ensembleturicum.ch (office). *Website:* www.ensembleturicum.ch (office).

ALWARD, Peter Andrew Ulrich; British classical music consultant; b. 20 Nov. 1950, London, England; s. of the late Herbert Andrew Alward and Marion Evelyne Schreiber. *Education:* Bryanston School, Guildhall School of Music and Drama. *Career:* worked for Simrock Music Publrs 1968–70; EMI Records UK 1970–74, European Co-ordinator EMI Classical Div. (Munich) 1975–83, Exec. Producer for all EMI recordings with Herbert von Karajan 1976–89, Man. (UK) Artists and Repertoire 1983, Int. Dir A&R 1985, Vice-Pres. 1989, Sr Vice-Pres. 1997, Pres. EMI Classics 2002–04; mem. Royal Opera House Covent Garden Opera Advisory Bd 1998–99; mem. Bd Trustees Young Concert Artists Trust 1999–2004; mem. Artistic Cttee, Herbert von Karajan Stiftung 2003–10; mem. European Advisory Bd, The Cleveland Orchestra 2009–11; Trustee, Masterclass Media Foundation 2006–15; mem. Editorial Advisory Bd, BBC Music 2006–16; Dir (non-exec.) Royal Opera House Enterprises 2007–16, Opera Rara 2009–11; mem. Kuratorium Salzburg Int. Stiftung Mozarteum 2008–13; consultant, Bavarian Radio Symphony Orchestra record label 2008–; Jury Pres. ARD Piano Competition Munich 2011; Jury Vice-Pres. Santander Piano Competition 2012; Jury mem. Salzburg Festival/Nestlé Young Conductors Award 2010–; Intendant and Man. Dir Osterfestspiele Salzburg (Salzburg Easter Festival) 2010–15. *Honours:* Ring of the City of Salzburg; Gramophone Special Achievement Award 2004. *Address:* 24 Midway, Walton-on-Thames, Surrey, KT12 3HZ, England (home). *Telephone:* (1932) 226741 (home). *E-mail:* peter@wotan844

.fsnet.co.uk (home); pa@ofs-sbg.at (office). *Website:* www.osterfestspiele-salzburg.at (office).

ALWYN, Kenneth, FRAM, ARAM, GRSM, LRAM; British conductor, composer and writer; *Musical Director, Philomusica*; b. 28 July 1925, Croydon, Surrey (now South London); m. Mary Law; two d. *Education:* Royal Schools of Music, London. *Career:* Conductor, Royal Choral Union, New Zealand, Sadler's Wells Theatre Ballet, Royal Ballet, Royal Opera House, Covent Garden; BBC Staff Conductor; Prin. Conductor, Yomiuri Nippon Symphony Orchestra, Tokyo; currently Musical Dir Philomusica; radio and TV presenter; mem. Inc. Soc. of Musicians, BBC Central Music Advisory Cttee. *Compositions:* various concert, radio and TV commissions. *Recordings:* numerous recordings with leading orchestras; conductor of first stereophonic recordings by Decca with London Symphony Orchestra 1958, Tchaikovsky's 1812 Overture (Gold Disc); complete recording, Hiawatha, with Bryn Terfel and Welsh Nat. Opera 1991. *Publication:* Is Anyone Watching?! (autobiography). *Honours:* Mann's Prize for Conducting 1951, Gramophone Award for Best Film Music 1998. *Address:* Horelands, West Chiltington Lane, Broadford Bridge, Billingshurst, West Sussex, RH14 9EA, England (home). *E-mail:* filomusicuk@aol.com (office). *Website:* www.Kenneth-Alwyn.co.uk (home); www.impulse-music.co.uk/kenneth-alwyn.htm (office).

ÅM, Magnar; Norwegian composer and academic; *Professor, Volda University College*; b. 9 April 1952, Trondheim; s. of Olav Åm and Eldgjørg Åm. *Education:* Bergen Conservatory, studied with Lidholm, Stockholm. *Career:* Prof., Volda Univ. Coll. *Compositions include:* Prayer for soprano, chorus and string orchestra 1972, Song for brass and percussion 1974, Dance for harp, guitar and harpsichord 1977, Octet 1977, Point Zero for soprano, alto, chorus, children's chorus and amateur orchestra 1979, two alternative versions, Ajar double-bass concerto 1981, A Cage-bird's Dream (multimedia piece) 1981, Inconceivable Father for child soprano, children's chorus, bass clarinet, timpani, double bass and organ 1982, My Planet, My Soul symphony 1982, piano pieces, Like a Leaf on the River for guitar 1983, Omen for violin, horn, piano 1983, Conqilia for violin, horn, piano, recitor 1984, Right Through All This for orchestra 1985, Freetonal Conversations for violin, cello and piano 1986, Hovering depths for double bass 1986, A Miracle and a Tear for mixed chorus 1987, If We Lift As One for orchestra 1988, Tonebath experience room 1989, And Let the Boat Slip Quietly Out for orchestra 1989, ...And Life (oratorio) 1990, Quiet Ruby for choir 1992, Glimpses of an Embrace for trumpet, horn and mountain echoes 1994, Among Mirrors for violin, cello and piano 1995, Be Quiet, My Heart for orchestra 1995, The Silver Cord for string quartet 1996, On the Wings of the Ka-bird for choir 1996, The Wondering and the Wonder for orchestra and dolphins 1996, You Are Loved for soprano, choir (SSA), two horns and harp 1997, But in the Middle of the Whirl for Hardanger-fiddle, cello and piano 1998, Wandering Heaven for alto voice and string sextet 1998, 5 Paradoxes for organ 1999, Tree of Tenderness (oratorio) 1999, Aching Hard, Aching Soft for solo violin 2000, Here in the Resurrection for string quartet and reciter 2001, Lonely/Embraced for bassoon and orchestra 2003, You Behind You for symphonic band 2004, Stalagmite Time for violin and orchestra 2004, Be the Purpose for harp and string sextet 2005, This Our Virgin Now for harp and girls' choir 2005, 'Tisn't the Snow Falling, It's Us Leaving the Ground for orchestra (European Composers' Award for Best Composition at young.euro.classics, Berlin 2006) 2006, God's I's (oratorium/opera) 2007, Countercurrent 2007. *Recordings:* Hovering Depths, Study on a Norwegian Hymn, Point Zero, Like a Leaf on the River, The Silver Cord, Gratia, The Light in your Chest, You Are Loved, Wandering Heaven, Va Bene, Octet – in nude, Aching Hard, Aching Soft, Zusammengefugt, SONaR. *Honours:* Der Europäische Komponistenpreis, Berlin 2006, Arne Nordheims Komponistpris, Oslo 2009. *Address:* Vevendelvegen 46, 6100 Volda, Norway (home). *Telephone:* 70-07-75-26 (home); 91-38-59-53 (mobile). *E-mail:* magnar.am@online.no (home). *Website:* www.magnaram.com.

AMADUCCI, Bruno; Italian conductor; b. 5 Jan. 1925, Viganello-Lugano, Switzerland. *Education:* Conservatorio Giuseppe Verdi, Milan, Italy; Ecole normale de Musique, Paris, France. *Career:* first concert, Mozart Requiem, Swiss Radio Monteceneri 1951; first public concert with Alfred Cortot and Orchestra, Pomeriggi Musicali, Milan 1951; fmr Conductor, Metropolitan Opera, Vienna State Opera, Vienna Symphony Orchestra, Paris Opera, Deutsche Oper, Berlin; jury mem., Concorso Voci Verdiane, Busseto, Italy and Concours Internationale, Geneva. *Publications:* L'Amfiparnaso de Orazio Vecchi par rapport au développement de l'expression du langage musicale 1951, La Musica nella Svizzera Italiana e La Presenzadella Radio-Orchestra 1973, The Puccini Dynasty 1973. *Address:* Via Privata Maraini 21, 6942 Savosa, Switzerland (home). *Telephone:* 919664020 (home).

AMARA, Lucine; American singer (soprano); *Artistic Director, New Jersey Association of Verismo Opera*; b. 1 March 1925, Hartford, Conn.; d. of George Armaganian and Adrine Armaganian (née Kazanjian). *Career:* debut at Hollywood Bowl, LA 1948; soloist, San Francisco Symphony 1949–50; performances with Metropolitan Opera, New York, New Orleans Opera, Hartford Opera, Conn. Pittsburgh Opera, St Louis Opera, St Petersburg Opera, Fla, Stockholm Opera, Venezuela Philharmonic Orchestra and Glyndebourne and Edinburgh Festivals, UK; opera and concert tours of fmr USSR 1965, Philippines 1968, France 1966, Mexico 1966, Hong Kong and People's Repub. of China 1983, Yugoslavia 1988; currently Artistic Dir New Jersey Assen of Verismo Opera. *Operas include:* Aida, Turandot, Tosca, Un Ballo in Maschera. *Recordings include:* Beethoven's Symphony No. 9, I Pagliacci, La Bohème, Verdi's Requiem. *Honours:* First Prize, Atwater-Ken Radio Auditions 1948; mem. Acad. of Vocal Arts Hall of Fame. *Address:* c/o New Jersey Association of Verismo Opera, PO Box 3024, Fort Lee, NJ 07024-9024, USA (office). *Telephone:* (201) 342-1970 (office). *Fax:* (201) 224-6911 (office). *E-mail:* comments@njavo.org (office). *Website:* www.njavo.org (office).

AMARTUVSHIN, Enkhbat; Mongolian singer (baritone); b. 23 March 1986, Sukhbatar. *Education:* State Univ. of Culture and Arts, Ulan Bator. *Career:* performed in Romania, China, Italy, South Korea and Russia; soloist, State Academic Opera and Ballet Theatre of Mongolia 2008–. *Honours:* Honoured Artist of Mongolia, 1st Prize, Int. Opera Competition, Baikal 2011, Silver Medal and Audience Prize for Best Male Singer, Int. Tchaikovsky Competition 2010, 1st Prize (jtly) Plácido Domingo's Operalia Competition 2012. *Current Management:* c/o Sergei Molchanov, Smolart Concert Agency, 127254 Moscow, Rustaveli st. 12/7-B-6, Russia. *Telephone:* (926) 211-1387. *Fax:* (495) 619-6092. *E-mail:* molchanov@smolart.com. *Website:* www.smolart.com.

AMBACHE, Diana Bella, BA, ARAM, LRAM, CELTA; British pianist, orchestra director, musicologist and academic, broadcaster, lecturer and teacher; b. 18 June 1948, Kent; d. of Dr Nachman and Dr Stella Ambache; m. Jeremy Polmear 1982. *Education:* Royal Acad. of Music, Univ. of Sheffield, St Giles International. *Career:* debut, Purcell Room 1979; Founder and Musical Dir Mozart Chamber Orchestra 1977–83; Founder and Musical Dir Ambache Chamber Orchestra 1984–2008; int. touring to 33 countries on five continents 1977–; first performances of Complete Version in Modern Times of Mozart, Rondo in D, K386 1980; Dussek Piano Concerto in G Minor Opus 49 1981; Fantasy for Piano by Francis Shaw 1982; 45 premieres of works by female composers of the last 250 years, including Germaine Tailleferre, Clara Schumann, Fanny Mendelssohn, Kozeluch, Benda, Amy Beach, Helen Hopekirk, Luise Le Beau, Marion Bauer, Louise Talma and others; Lecturer for Martin Randall Travel; Artistic Dir Women of Note 1995–97, Old Masters, New Mistresses; recorded 17 new CDs; teacher of English as a foreign language 2013; Founder, Ambache Charitable Trust; f. www.womenofnote.co.uk 2015. *Radio:* broadcasts for BBC World Service, BBC Radio 4, BBC Radio 3, Classic FM. *Recordings include:* 18 recordings of Mozart's piano concertos and chamber music by Mozart, Beethoven, Louise Farrenc, Amy Beach, Louise Talma, Marion Bauer and Ottorino Respighi, Sweet Melancholy: 20th Century English oboe and piano works, Old Masters, New Mistresses (concert series) 2002–04, Musical Meze, Très Français, Seven Sisters, Liberté, Egalité, Sororité. *Publications include:* Marie Grandval, Deux Pieces (ed.) 2001, Hélène Liebmann, Grand Trio in A, Op 11 (ed.) 2002, Dorothy Howell, Air, Variations and Finale (ed.) 2009. *Honours:* Gold Medal, Associated Bd 1966, Royal Acad. of Music Scholarship 1967; exhibition from Univ. of Sheffield 1970. *Address:* 9 Beversbrook Road, London, N19 4QG, England (office). *Telephone:* (20) 7263-4027 (office). *E-mail:* diana@ambache.co.uk (office). *Website:* www.ambache.co.uk (home); www.ambachecharitabletrust.org (home); www.womenofnote.co.uk (home).

AMIRKHANIAN, Charles Benjamin, BA, MA, MFA; American composer, percussionist and radio producer; *Executive and Artistic Director, Other Minds, San Francisco*; b. 19 Jan. 1945, Fresno, Calif.; s. of Benjamin Vresh Amirkhanian and Eleanor Kaprielian Amirkhanian; m. Carol L. Law 1968. *Education:* California State Univ., Fresno, San Francisco State Univ., Mills Coll., Oakland, California; studied electronic music and sound recording techniques with David Behrman, Robert Ashley and Paul de Marinis. *Career:* Composer-in-Residence, Ann Halprin's Dancers Workshop Co. 1968–69; Music Dir, KPFA Radio, Berkeley, Calif. 1969–92; Exec. Dir, Djerassi Resident Artists Program, Woodside, Calif. 1993–97; Artistic Dir, Composer-to-Composer Festival, Telluride, Colo 1988–91; Artistic Dir, Other Minds Festival 1992–98; Exec. and Artistic Dir, Other Minds, San Francisco 1998–. *Compositions:* Symphony I 1965, Ode to Gravity 1967, Serenade II Janice Wentworth (composed with Ted Greer) 1967–68, Words 1969, Oratora Konkurso Rezulto: Autoro de la Jaro 1970, Radii 1970, If In Is 1971, Just 1972, Heavy Aspirations 1973, Seatbelt Seatbelt 1973, Mugic 1973, Muchrooms 1974, Mahogany Ballpark 1976, Dutiful Ducks 1977, Dreams Freud Dreamed 1979, Egusquiza to Falsetto 1979, Spoilt Music 1979, Church Car 1980, Hypothetical Moments [in the Intellectual Life of Southern California] 1981, Dot Bunch 1981, History of Collage 1981, Andas 1982, Dog of Stravinsky 1982, Gold and Spirit 1984, Metropolis San Francisco 1985–86, Dumbek Bookache 1986, Walking Tune 1986–87, Pas de voix 1987, Politics as Usual 1988, Im Fruhling 1990, Loudspeakers 1990, A Berkelium Canon 1991, Chu Lu Lu 1992, Son of Metropolis San Francisco 1997, Ka Himena Hehena 1997, Miatsoom 1997, Octet for Ratchets 1998, Pianola [Pas de mains] 1997–2000, Musical Lou 2003, Rippling the Lamp for violin and tape 2006–07, Quince Quinoa 2007. *Recordings include:* Lexical Music 1979, Walking Tune 1998. *Publications:* The Guests Go in to Supper (sound poetry texts) (ed. Sumner) 1987; articles in music magazines. *Honours:* American Music Center Letter of Distinction 1984, 2005, ASCAP-Deems Taylor Broadcast Award 1989, Ella Holbrook Walker Fellowship, Bellagio Study and Conf. Center, Rockefeller Foundation, Italy 1999–2000, Chamber Music America/ASCAP Award for Adventurous Programming of Contemporary Music (with Other Minds) 2009. *Address:* Other Minds, 333 Valencia Street, Suite 303, San Francisco, CA 94103-3552, USA (office). *Telephone:* (415) 934-8134 (office). *Fax:* (415) 934-8136 (office). *E-mail:* charles@otherminds.org (office). *Website:* www.otherminds.org (office); www.radiOM.org.

AMORETTI, Ruben; Spanish singer (tenor); b. 1968, Burgos. *Education:* studied in Berne, Bloomington, Indiana, USA. *Career:* repertoire includes Mephisto in La Damnation de Faust, Escamillo in Carmen Mefistofele in

Mefistofele, Il Conte in Il Matrimonio Segreto, Dulcamara in L'Elisir d'Amore, Raimondo in Lucia di Lammermoor, Mephisto in Faust, Alfio in Cavalleria Rusticana, Leporello in Don Giovanni, Figaro in Le Nozze di Figaro, Sarastro in Die Zauberflote, Uberto in La Serva Padrona, Scarpia in Tosca, Colline in La Bohème, Simpson in La Tabernera del Puerto, Basilio in Il Barbiere di Siviglia, Ramfis in Aida, Zaccaria in Nabucco, Sparafucile in Rigoletto, Filippo in Don Carlo, Gil in Il Segreto du Susanna, Lautrec in Lautrec; has performed in Prague, Zurich, Rome, Florence, Geneva, Madrid, Palm Beach, Moscow, Mexico. *Recordings:* songs by Falla, Verdi, Bellini and Respighi, Gallo. *Current Management:* Beate I. Mennicken Artist Communication, Heinrich-zillestrasse 19, 15711 Zeesen, Germany. *Telephone:* (3375) 5249877. *Fax:* (3375) 5249879. *E-mail:* info@mennicken-pr.com. *Website:* www.mennicken-pr.com.

AMOYAL, Pierre Alain Wilfred; French violinist; b. 22 June 1949, Paris; s. of Dr Wilfred Amoyal and Vera Amoyal (née Popravka); m. 2nd Leslie Chabot 1988. *Education:* Cours d'Etat, Vanves, Conservatoire Nat. Supérieur de Musique, Univ. of Southern California, USA; studied with Jascha Heifetz. *Career:* invited by Sir Georg Solti to perform Berg's violin concerto with Orchestre de Paris 1971 and by Pierre Boulez to perform Schoenberg's Concerto with Orchestre de Paris 1977; recital debut at Carnegie Hall 1985; numerous performances worldwide with orchestras including Berlin Philharmonic, Vienna Symphony Orchestra, Filarmonica della Scala, Milan, Royal Philharmonic, New Philharmonia, Orchestre Nat. de France, Residentie-Orkest, The Hague; Prof. of Violin, Conservatoire Nat. Supérieur de Musique, Paris 1977–88, Lausanne Conservatory 1987–, Univ. Mozarteum, Salzburg; Co-founder (with Alexis Weissenberg) and Artistic Dir Lausanne Summer Music Acad. 1991–; f. Camerata of Lausanne 2002, ensemble orchestra of young musicians; mem. Jury, Singapore Int. Violin Competition 2015. *Recordings include:* Symphonie espagnole (Lalo), Violin Concerto (Mendelssohn), Concertos No. 1 and 2 and Two Sonatas (Prokofiev), Tartini's concertos, Third Concerto, Havanaise and Rondo Capriccioso (Saint-Saëns), Concerto No. 1 (Bruch), Concerto (Glazunov), Sonatas (Fauré), Horn Trio (Brahms), Concertos (Mozart), Concerto (Sibelius), Concerto (Tchaikovsky), Sonatas (Brahms), Concerto (Schoenberg), works of Albert Huybrechts 2009. *Honours:* Chevalier, Ordre des Arts et des Lettres 1985, Chevalier, Ordre Nat. du Mérite 1995; First Prize, Conservatoire de Versailles 1960, Conservatoire Nat. Supérieur de Musique, Paris 1962, for chamber music, Conservatoire Nat. Supérieur de Musique, Prix Ginette Neveu, Prix Paganini, Prix Enesco 1970, Grand Prix du Disque 1974, 1977, Prix du Rayonnement de la Fondation Vaudoise pour la Promotion et la Création artistique 2002, Prix de Lausanne 2006. *Address:* University Mozarteum, Mirabellplatz 1, 5020 Salzburg, Austria (office). *E-mail:* pierre@amoyal.com. *Website:* www.amoyal.com.

AMRAM, David Werner, BA, MusD, LLD; American composer, conductor, musician and academic; b. 17 Nov. 1930, Philadelphia, Pa; one s. two d. *Education:* Oberlin Conservatory of Music, Manhattan School of Music, George Washington Univ., Moravian Coll., , Muhlenberg Coll., Univ. of Hartford, St Lawrence Univ. *Career:* pioneer of French horn in jazz and Latin music during late 1940s, played French horn with Nat. Symphony Orchestra 1951–52; world tours as a jazz player, multi-instrumentalist, folklorist, composer and conductor; Dir of Music, New York Shakespeare Festival 1956–67, Lincoln Center Theater 1963–65; Composer-in-Residence, New York Philharmonic Orchestra 1966–67; Dir of Music for Young People's Concerts and Parks Concerts, Brooklyn Philharmonic 1971–98; Composer-in-Residence, Democratic Nat. Convention, Denver 2008; fmr Leo Block Chair of Arts and Humanities, Univ. of Denver; work commissioned to celebrate opening of Jefferson Wing of Library of Congress 1995; guest conductor with more than 75 symphony orchestras around the world; composer of 110 orchestral compositions for symphony orchestras and chamber music groups; collaborated with Jack Kerouac 1956–69, Leonard Bernstein, Arthur Miller, Lionel Hampton, Elia Kazan, Bob Dylan, Dizzy Gillespie, Archibald MacLeish, Pete Seeger, Charles Mingus, Eugene Ormandy, Jacques d'Amboise, Titi Puente, Joseph Papp, Odetta, Alan Ginsberg, Paquito d'Rivera, John Frankenheimer, Betty Carter, Lawrence Ferlinghetti; mem. BMI. *Compositions include:* Ode to Lof Buckley for orchestra, The Final Ingredient (opera), 12th Night (opera), A Little Rebellion: Thomas Jefferson for narrator and orchestra, American Dance Suite, Trombone Alone 1996, Kokopelli: A Symphony in Three Movements 1997, Giants of the Night (flute concerto for James Galway) 2000, This Land: Symphonic Variations on a Song by Woody Guthrie 2007, Greenwich Village Portraits 2014. *Compositions for film and television:* Pull My Daisy 1958, The Turn of the Screw (TV series episode 'Startime') 1959, Cry Vengeance! (TV film) 1961, The Young Savages 1961, Splendor in the Grass 1961, The Manchurian Candidate 1962, The Arrangement 1969, Medea (TV film) 1983, Pigeon Feathers (TV film) 1987, The Beat Generation: An American Dream 1987, Frog Crossing 1996, The Source 1999, Boys of Winter (documentary) 2001, The Frontier Gandhi: Badsha Khan (documentary) 2009, 333 (documentary) 2012, Isn't it Delicious 2013. *Dance:* composed music for many Jacques d'Amboise choreographed pieces. *Plays include:* JB, After the Fall, The Passion l of Joseph D, Tartuffe. *Recordings include:* Triple Concerto 1970, No More Walls 1971, An American Original 1993, Hava New York 1995, Three Concertos 1995, The Final Ingredient 1996, At Home/Around the World 1996, Visions of Cody 1996, Southern Stories 2000, Back to My Roots (with Lil Greenwood) 2007, Songs of the Soul 2007. *Publications include:* Vibrations: The Musical Times of David Amram 1968, Offbeat: Collaborating with Kerouac 2002, Upbeat: Nine Lives of a Musical Cat 2007. *Honours:* six hon. degrees; Obie Award, Jay McShann Lifetime Achievement Award 2011, Bruce Ricter Lifetime Film Achievement Award 2012, Pete and Toshi Seeger Power of Song Award 2012. *Current Management:* c/o Douglas Yeager, 300 West 55th Street, Suite 15E, New York, NY 10019, USA. *Telephone:* (212) 245-0240. *Fax:* (212) 245-6576. *E-mail:* yeagerprod@aol.com. *E-mail:* amramdavid@aol.com. *Website:* www.davidamram.com.

AMSELLEM, Norah; French singer (soprano); b. 1970, Paris, France. *Education:* studied in New York; participant in Met's Young Artist Development Program. *Career:* debut as Micaela at the Metropolitan Opera, 1995; concert debut at Alice Tully Hall, New York; opera appearances as Micaela at the Opéra Bastille, Paris, and Lyon; Liu at the Met and Mozart's Countess at the 1997 Glyndebourne Festival; season 1997–98 as Micaela at the Met, under James Levine and with Placido Domingo, Liu in debut at the San Francisco Opera; Norina (Don Pasquale) and Gounod's Juliette at the Grand Théâtre, Bordeaux; Manon of Massenet at La Scala, Milan, and in Toulouse and Bordeaux; Micaela in Monte Carlo and Japan. *Current Management:* Columbia Artists Management, 1790 Broadway, New York, NY 10019-1412, USA. *Telephone:* (212) 841-9500. *Fax:* (212) 841-9744. *E-mail:* info@cami.com. *Website:* www.cami.com. *Address:* c/o Metropolitan Opera, Lincoln Center, New York, NY 10023, USA.

AMY, Gilbert; French conductor, music educator and composer; b. 29 Aug. 1936, Paris. *Education:* studied piano with Loriod and composition with Milhaud and Messiaen at the Paris Conservatory, attended Boulez's courses in new music at Darmstadt. *Career:* commenced conducting 1962; Dir, Domaine Musical, Paris 1967–73; founder-Conductor, Nouvel Orchestre Philharmonique de Radio France, Paris 1976–81; taught analysis and composition, Yale Univ. 1982; Dir, Conservatoire National Superieur de Musique, Lyon 1984–2000; works performed at major contemporary music venues including Darmstadt, Venice, Royan, Berlin, Warsaw. *Compositions include:* orchestral: Mouvements 1958, Diaphonies 1962, Antiphonies for two orchestras 1964, Triade 1965, Chant 1968–69, revised 1980, Refrains 1972, Orchestrale 1985, Trois Scènes for orchestra 1995, Concerto for cello and orchestra 2000, Concerto for piano and orchestra 2005, L'espace du souffle, for orchestra 2007, Après...Ein 'Es praeludium' for string orchestra and 2 horns 2008; chamber: Piano Sonata 1957–60, Epigrammes for piano 1961, Inventions for ensemble 1959–61, Alpha-Beta for wind sextet 1963–64, Cycle for percussion sextet, seven Bagatelles for organ 1975, Quasi scherzando for cello 1981, two String Quartets 1992, 1995, Le Temps du souffle I, for 2 clarinets (2 basset horns) 1996, Le Temps du souffle II, for violin, saxophone (alto and tenor) and trombone 1993, Symphonies pour cinq cuivres, for brass quintet 1992, String Quartet No.3 2009; vocal: Cantata breve for soprano and three instruments 1957, Strophe for soprano and orchestra 1966, D'un Espace déployé for soprano, two pianos and two orchestral groups 1973, Une saison en enfer for soprano, piano, percussion and tape 1980, Missa cum jubilo (Prix de la Critique dramatique et musicale 1988) 1983, Ecrits sur toiles for reciter and small ensemble 1983, Posaunen for four trombones 1986, Choros for soloists, chorus and orchestra 1989, Le Premier Cercle, opera in four acts (premiered Lyon) 1999. *Honours:* Grand Prix Nat. de la Musique 1979, Grand Prix de la SACEM 1983, Grand Prix Musical de la Ville de Paris 1986, Prix du disque de l' Acad. Charles Cros 1987, Prix Cino del Duca for his entire oeuvre 2004. *Current Management:* c/o Annie de Valmalète, Bureau de Concerts de Valmalète, 7 rue Hoche, 92300 Levallois-Perret, France. *E-mail:* herve.corre@valmalete.com. *Website:* www.valmalete.com.

AN, Chengbi-seungpil, BA; Chinese composer; b. 25 July 1967. *Education:* CNSM Paris, Shanghai Conservatory of Music. *Career:* debut as pianist aged seven; with Yanbian Korean Arts Troupe of Jilin, Beijing Chinese Arts Troupe 1984–86; teaching asst, Department of Composition, Shanghai Conservatory of Music 1991–93, Lecturer 1993–94; has lived in Paris, France since 1994; founder, Prof. of Composition and Artistic Dir, Electro-Acoustic Music Centre, Shanghai Conservatory of Music 2002–; Artist-in-Residence DAAD, Berlin, Germany 2007–08; Visiting Prof., Nanchang Univ., China 2009–; commissions and performances include Ensemble Intercontemporain for Radio France at Centre Pompidou, Paris, and at new music festivals in Salzburg and Berlin by Berlin Radio Symphony Orchestra and the Austrian Ensemble for New Music, also elsewhere in Europe, SE Asia and N America; Radio France commission Gyul premiered by Philharmonic Orchestra Radio France under Myung-Whung Chung in Shanghai during 2010 Universal World Expo. *Compositions include:* orchestral: Symphony Overture for orchestra 1990, Ressac, for orchestra of 30 musicians 1997, Ouverture & Aria of Sanhong, for soprano and orchestra 2001, Constellation, for solo violin and orchestra 2005, Gyol, for orchestra 2007, Dun.Wu, Double concerto for accordion, piano and orchestra 2009; chamber: Sanjo, for violin and piano 1987, Ming-Wu (Awakening), for six musicians (winner, Olympia Int. Composition Competition, Athena, Greece) 1988, Loushiming, for flute, piano, cello 1990, Lu, for seven Chinese fiddles (erhu) 1992, Ru, for Chinese flutes (dizi) and percussion 1993, Nong-Mou (Dense Fog), for six musicians 1995, Scintillations, for chamber orchestra 1996, Soo-Ho, for string quartet 2000, Constellation, for violin and piano 2003, Jinghuashuiyue, Ensemble pour trois instruments traditionnels chinois (dizi, sheng, zheng) 2006, Huanri (Parhelion), for solo percussion 2008, Anliu (Undercurrent), for two pianos and two percussions 2011; electronic: New Millennium Sunrise 1999, Aurore 2004, Aurore II 2004, The Combination of Cells 2007, The Combination of Cells II, for electroacoustic music 2011; mixed: Shin.Woon (Mystical Movement), for clarinet and fixed sounds 2001, Moo-Nui (Moirés), for viola solo and electronic disposal 2002, Saek-Gong (Space of colours), for flute, string quartet and fixed sounds 2002, Gediao, for piano solo and electronic disposal 2006. *Honours:* winner, 15th IRINO Int. Composition Competition, 8th Gino Contilli Int. Composition Competition, Messina, Italy; 8th Alfredo Casella Int. Composition Competition, Siena, Italy; 7th Int. Electronic Music Competition, Int. Center of New Musical Sources, Turin, Italy, selected as one of Six Top Young Composers of Forum 96 by the Int. Music Council of UNESCO. *Address:* Appt S1-121, Hall Pascal, 32 Avenue Corentin Cariou, 75019 Paris, France (home). *Telephone:* 1-40-35-89-71 (home). *E-mail:* info@anchengbi.com (office). *Website:* www.anchengbi.com (office).

ANANIASHVILI, Nina Gedevanovna; Georgian/Russian ballet dancer; *Artistic Director, State Ballet of Georgia*; b. 28 March 1963, Tbilisi; d. of Gedevan Ananiashvili and Lia Gogolashvili; m. Gregory Vashadze 1988; one s. one d. *Education:* State Choreographic Schools of Georgia and Bolshoi Theatre, Russia. *Career:* Prima Ballerina, Bolshoi Ballet, Moscow 1981–, Prin., American Ballet Theater 1993–2009; has performed on tour world-wide with New York City Ballet, Royal Ballet, Royal Danish Ballet, Kirov Ballet, Royal Swedish Ballet, Ballet de Monte Carlo, The Munich Ballet, La Scala Ballet, Houston Ballet, Boston Ballet, Tokyo Ballet and others; Prima Ballerina and Artistic Dir, State Ballet of Georgia 2004–, ballets staged include classical works and ballets by Balanchine, Ashton, Bournonville and Kylián; tours to USA 2007, 2008, 2010, Edinburgh Int. Festival 2008 and Japan 2012. *Dance:* over 100 roles including Giselle, Odette/Odile (Swan Lake), Aurora (Sleeping Beauty), Raimonda, Juliet (Romeo and Juliet), Nikya (La Bayadère), Kitri (Don Quixote). *Honours:* Order for Outstanding Service to Fatherland (Russia) 2000, Order of Honour (Georgia) 2003, Presidential Order of Light (Georgia) 2010, Order of the Star of Italian Solidarity 2011; numerous awards include Grand Prix Int. Ballet Competition, Jackson 1986, People's Artist of Repub. of Georgia and of USSR, State Prize of Russia 1992, State Prize of Georgia 1993, Dance Magazine Award for Outstanding Achievements, USA 2002. *Address:* Tbilisi Opera and Ballet Theatre, 0108 Tbilisi, Rustaveli Ave. 25, Georgia (office); 119270 Moscow, Frunzenskaya nab. 46, Apt. 79, Russia. *E-mail:* ballet@comtv.ru (office). *Website:* www.opera.ge (office).

ANASTASSOV, Orlin; Bulgarian singer (bass); b. 1976, Rousse. *Education:* studied in Sofia. *Career:* debut singing Ramfis in Aida on tour to Germany with Ruse Opera; has sung Il Barbiere di Siviglia and Aida at La Scala, Milan, La Battaglia di Legnano, Simon Boccanegra and Faust at Covent Garden, London, Don Carlo in Valencia, Faust in Munich, La Bohème and Aida at Orange Festival; concerts with Colin Davis and the London Symphony Orchestra; has sung Verdi's Requiem in Paris, Monte Carlo, Milan and Amsterdam; has sung Verdi's Simon Boccanegra in Valencia and at the Royal Opera House, Covent Garden. *Current Management:* Ernesto Palacio Artists Management, Via Donizetti 11, 24050 Lurano (BG), Italy. *Telephone:* (35) 800623. *Fax:* (35) 4877812. *E-mail:* ernestopalacio@tiscali.it. *Website:* www.ernestopalacio.com.

ANDERSEN, Bo; Danish composer, organist and musicologist; b. 10 Nov. 1963. *Education:* University of Copenhagen, studied with Ib Nørholm, Yngve Trede and Erik Norby, Royal Danish Academy of Music, Copenhagen, Royal Academy, Copenhagen. *Career:* numerous performances of most of his works, many commissions from ensembles and soloists; mem, Danish Composer's Association; Society for Publication of Danish Music. *Compositions:* Main Works: Vier Stücke im alten Stil, (String Quartet, No. 1), 1989 (revised 2001); Pezzo Concertante, 4 accordions and 2 percussionists, 1991, Pensieri notturni No. 1 for 3 woodwinds (former Serenade), flute, clarinet and bassoon, 1991 (revised, 1998); Moments Musicaux for 2 accordions, 1999 (revised 2001); Three Flowersongs for soprano and piano, 2000–01, texts by Kirsten Ahlemann; A Fantasia for the Viol for solo cello, 1999; Invocation for solo flute, 1993 (revised 2001); Dream Calls for trumpet, percussion and orchestra; Concerto for trombone and orchestra. *Honours:* Astrid and Aksel Agerby Memorial Grant, 1993; several grants from the Danish State Arts Foundation. *Address:* c/o S E Mielche, Frederiksberg Allé 78 1.mf, 1820 Frederiksberg C, Denmark.

ANDERSEN, Stig Fogh; Danish singer (tenor) and stage director; b. 24 Feb. 1950, Hørsholm. *Education:* Music High School of Århus, Royal Acad. of Music, Copenhagen. *Career:* sang at Århus from 1978 and made debut at Royal Opera Copenhagen 1980, as Macduff in Macbeth; mem. Royal Opera Ensemble 1980–; many appearances in Copenhagen and elsewhere as guest, singing Tamino 1985, Sergei in Shostakovich's Lady Macbeth 1990, Don José 1992, Leander in Maskarade, Don Carlos, Lensky, Otello and Florestan; sang Siegfried at Århus 1994; Cardinal Albrecht in Mathis der Maler at Covent Garden 1995; Siegfried in The Ring at the Royal Albert Hall and in Birmingham for the Royal Opera 1998; Meistersinger and Tannhäuser, Munich 1999; Siegfried in The Ring, Metropolitan Opera House, New York 2000; Tristan, Houston 2000; Parsifal, Covent Garden 2001; season 2000–01 as Herman in The Queen of Spades at Copenhagen, Siegfried at Mannheim and Geneva, and Tannhäuser at the Deutsche Oper Berlin; Siegfried, Munich 2002; Siegfried and Die Walküre 2005, Siegfried in Lyon, Oslo, Esbjerg 2007, Salome, Munich 2008, Die Meistersinger, Berlin 2008, Siegfried and Götterdämmerung, Seattle 2009, Tristan, Copenhagen 2009 and 2010, Herodes in Salome in Salzburg and Paris 2011, Parsifal in Copenhagen 2012, Loge in Das Rheingold at Royal Opera House, London 2012, Tannhauser in Tokyo and Copenhagen 2013; concert performances and lied recitals include Haydn Die Jahreszeiten, Brahms Rinaldo, Mahler 8th Symphony and Das Lied von der Erde, Schmidt Das Buch mit sieben Siegeln and Schönberg Gurrelieder. *Productions as stage director:* for Royal Opera House: Kain og Abel 2006, Tristan und Isolde 2009; Götterdämmerung at Den Ny Opera, Esbjerg 2008. *Recordings include:* Franz Schmidt's Das Buch mit sieben Siegeln, Mussorgsky's Boris Godunov (conducted by Dimitri Kitajenko), Weyse's The Sleep Potion, Nørgård's Siddharta, Rinaldo by Brahms, Siegfried and Götterdämmerung with De Nederlandse Opera. *Honours:* Ridder af Dannebrog, 1 Grad 2000, awarded title of Kammersänger by Royal Theatre, Copenhagen. *Current Management:* Caecilia Lyric Department, Rennweg 15, 8001 Zürich, Switzerland. *Telephone:* (44) 2213388 (office). *Fax:* (44) 2117182 (office). *E-mail:* caecilia@caecilia-lyric.ch (office). *Website:* www.caecilia.ch (office). *Address:* c/o Det Kongelige Teater, Ekvipagemestervej 10, 1438 Copenhagen K, Denmark (office). *E-mail:* info@stigandersen.com (office). *Website:* www.kgl-teater.dk (office); www.stigandersen.com (office).

ANDERSEN, Terje; Norwegian singer (tenor); b. 1970, Oslo. *Education:* Guildhall School of Music & Drama and National Opera Studio, London; Milan with Franco Corelli. *Career:* at Guildhall School of Music & Drama roles included Male Chorus (The Rape of Lucretia, Le Chevalier (Les Dialogues des Carmélites), Don Eusebio (L'Occasione fa il Ladro) and Le Terrier (L'Enfant et les Sortilèges); concert work includes the World Mass for Peace, written and performed for the Nobel Peace Prize, with Oslo Philharmonic Orchestra conducted by Vladimir Ashkenazy, Verdi Requiem, Gounod Mors et Vita, Mendelssohn's Elias, Bach Weihnachts Oratorium, Mozart, Dvořák and Lloyd Webber Requiems and Rossini Stabat Mater; operatic engagements include debuts at Norwegian State Opera in the role of Tamino (Die Zauberflöte), Staatstheater Stuttgart as Macduff (Macbeth), English National Opera as Nemorino (L'elisir d'amore) and a prestigious debut at Glyndebourne Festival Opera as Gabriele Adorno in a new production of Simon Boccanegra under Mark Elder; as mem. of Städtische Bühnen Münster, sang Tamino Froh (Das Rheingold), Camille de Rossillon (Die lustige Witwe) and Ein Piemonteser (Der Friedenstag); debut as Alfredo (La Traviata) on tour with Welsh Nat. Opera; made his debut at Royal Opera Stockholm, as Cavaradossi in gala concert in memory of Jussi Bjoerling; sang Pinkerton at both Stadttheater Klagenfurt and Theater der Stadt Koblenz; latest engagements include Cavaradossi (Tosca) at the Festungsspiele Ehrenbreitstein, Macduff (Macbeth) for Singapore Lyric Opera, Rodolfo (La Bohème) and Pinkerton (Madama Butterfly) for Royal Swedish Opera Stockholm, Lyonel (Martha) for the Anna Livia Int. Opera Festival and Rinuccio (Gianni Schicchi) at Theater Lübeck, Duca (Rigoletto) and Sou Chong (Land des lächelns) at Stadttheater Koblenz.

ANDERSON, Avril, MPhil, GRSM, LTCL; British composer; *Teacher of Composition and Musicianship, Royal Northern College of Music Junior Department*; b. 10 June 1953, Southsea, Hants.; m. David Sutton-Anderson. *Education:* Royal Coll. of Music with Humphrey Searle and John Lambert, New England Conservatory, studied with David del Tredici in New York and with Jonathan Harvey at Univ. of Sussex. *Career:* Co-Artistic Dir of contemporary music group Sounds Positive 1987; Composer-in-Residence, The Young Place, London Contemporary Dance School 1990–; PRS Composer in Education 1996–97; Adjunct Prof., Univ. of Notre Dame, London Programme; Teacher of Composition and Musicianship, Royal Coll. of Music Jr Dept. *Compositions:* Mono-staus for 3 clarinets 1975, Où allons nous? for soprano and orchestra 1976, Edward II, opera in 1 act 1978, Black Eyes in an Orange Sky for soprano and piano 1979, Private Energy for soprano and ensemble 1983, Dynamics of Matter for piano 1989, Winds of Change 1989, Beating the System 1993, Repetitive Strain for organ 1995, Deadwood 1996, Sephardic Songs 1996, Dead on Time for ensemble 1998, Nature's Voice, dance score 1998, Rest Assured 1999, Three Farewells 2005, Friday night in the city 2005, For Lenny 2006, Monody 2006. *Recordings:* Deadwood, Sephardic Songs, Rest Assured. *Honours:* Cobbett Prize, Sullivan and Farrar Prize. *Address:* 28 Cavendish Avenue, London, N3 3QN, England (home).

ANDERSON, Barry; Australian/Italian singer (baritone) and singing teacher; b. 25 Dec. 1959, Australia; m. Rosanna Pessot. *Education:* Musikhochschule, Vienna, singing lessons in Milan. *Career:* appearances in Naples as Verdi's Renato; in Catania as Rigoletto; in Cagliari as Count Luna; as Puccini's Sharpless and as Michonnet in Adriana Lecouvreur, Trieste 1989; with Bergamo Opera as Warney in Donizetti's Elisabetta al Castello di Kenilworth; with Dresden Staatsoper as Macbeth and Munich Opera as Sharpless; as Macbeth, Simon Boccanegra and Rigoletto, Cologne Opera 1991–94; Mascagni's Gianni Rantzau, Livorno 1992; Ezio in Verdi's Attila in Buenos Aires; Jago in Otello, Melbourne 1993; other repertory includes Verdi's Il Corsaro, Nîmes; Valentin in Gounod's Faust, Cagliari 1996; Don Carlo in Verdi's Ernani, Montpellier 1999; sang Germont, Jesi 2000; Michele in Il Tabarro by Puccini, Sydney Opera House 2001; Gérard in Andrea Chénier, Brisbane 2002; Gianni Schicchi by Puccini, Nantes 2002; Nabucco, Adelaide 2006, Un Ballo in Maschera, Cairo 2008; Scarpia in Tosca, Livorno 2009; Amonasro in Aida, Dublin and Belfast 2009; performances of Rigoletto on tour in Italy 2010; sang Germont in Italy and Conte di Luna and Rigoletto in Greece 2011; participated in orchestral concerts of sacred music in Italy 2012. *Recordings include:* Elisabetta al Castello di Kenilworth (Donizetti), I Rantzau (Mascagni), L'Arlesiana (Cilea), Zazà (Leoncavallo). *Telephone:* (0438) 415869 (office); 345-8426646 (mobile). *Fax:* (0438) 415869 (office). *E-mail:* barrytone@alice.it (office). *Website:* www.barryanderson.it.

ANDERSON, Beth, BA, MA, MFA; American composer and musician (piano); b. 3 Jan. 1950, Lexington, KY; m. Elliotte Rusty Harold. *Education:* Univ. of California at Davis with Larry Austin and John Cage, Mills Coll., Oakland with Terry Riley and Robert Ashley. *Career:* founder Ear Magazine, New York 1975; solo performer as vocalist and piano accompanist at dance studios; producer Women's Work series, Greenwich House Arts, New York; mem. New York Women Composers, Int. Alliance of Women in Music, Poets and Writers. *Compositions include:* April Swale for viola and harpsichord, August Swale for woodwind quintet, Belgian Tango, Brass Swale for brass quintet, Elizabeth Rex: Or The Well Bred Mother Goes To Camp (musical), Flute Swale for harpsichord, German Swale for tape, Guitar Swale for guitar duet, January Swale for string quartet, Joan (oratorio), March Swale for string quartet, May Swale for viola solo, Minnesota Swale for orchestra, Mourning Dove Swale for string orchestra, Net Work, New Mexico Swale for chamber ensemble, Nirvana Manor (musical), Pennyroyal Swale for string quartet, Queen Christina (opera), Revel for orchestra, Rhode Island Swale for harpsichord, Riot Rot (text-sound piece), Rosemary Swale for string quartet, Saturday/ Sunday Swale for brass quintet, September Swale for mandolin and guitar, Soap Tuning (musical), The Fat Opera (musical), Three Swales for string orchestra, Trio: Dream In 'D'. *Recordings include:* Peachy Keen-O 2003, Swales and Angels 2004, Quilt Music 2005. *Publications:* Beauty is Revolution, The Internet for Women in Music. *Honours:* Nat. Endowment for the Arts Grant, Nat. Public Radio Satellite Program Development Fund Grant. *Current Management:* Jeffrey James Arts Consulting, 45 Grant Avenue, Farmingdale, NY 11735, USA. *Telephone:* (516) 586-3433. *Fax:* (516) 586-3433. *E-mail:* jamesarts@worldnet.att.net. *Website:* www.jamesarts.com. *E-mail:* beth@beand.com (office). *Website:* www.beand.com.

ANDERSON, David Maxwell; British singer (tenor); *Professor of Vocal Studies, Royal Northern College of Music;* b. 1964, Scotland. *Education:* Glasgow Acad., Queen's Coll., Cambridge, Royal Coll. of Music, Nat. Opera Studio. *Career:* debut as Rinuccio in Gianni Schicchi for Opera North 1990; has sung Rinuccio for ENO, Rodolfo in La Bohème for Scottish Opera and Glyndebourne Touring Opera, Pinkerton in Madama Butterfly for Opera North, the Duke of Mantua in Rigoletto for Opera North and the Teatro di Pisa, Alfredo in La Traviata for the Teatro di Pisa and Opera North, Pinkerton in Madam Butterfly for Opera North, Števa in Jenůfa for ENO, Oronte in I Lombardi for Opera North, Enzo, Pollione, Cavaradossi, Riccardo, Duke of Mantua, Elemer, Lensky, Stiffelio, Ismaele and Anatole in Samuel Barber's Vanessa at Monte Carlo 2001, and at Royal Opera House, Covent Garden; concert engagements include the Verdi Requiem (David Willcocks), Vaughan Williams Serenade to Music (Vernon Handley), Bruckner Te Deum (Alexander Gibson and John Eliot Gardiner), and the Rossini Stabat Mater (Rafael Frühbeck de Burgos), with orchestras including Washington Symphony Orchestra, BBC Philharmonic, the BBC Symphony Orchestra, Bournemouth Symphony Orchestra, BBC Wales Symphony Orchestra, London Philharmonic Orchestra, Royal Philharmonic Orchestra, RTE Orchestra and NDR-Sinfonieorchester; Professor of Vocal Studies, RAM 2001, also at Royal Coll. of Music and Royal Northern Coll. of Music. *Address:* Royal Northern College of Music, 124 Oxford Road, Manchester, M13 9RD, England (office). *Website:* www.davidmaxwellanderson.com.

ANDERSON, (Evelyn) Ruth; American composer and flautist; b. 21 March 1928, Kalispell, Montana. *Education:* Univ. of Washington, Columbia and Princeton Univs with Earl Kim and Ussachevsky; further studies with Nadia Boulanger, Darius Milhaud and Jean-Pierre Rampal. *Career:* flautist with the Totenberg Instrumental Ensemble, the Portland and Seattle Symphony Orchestras and the Boston Pops Orchestra during 1950s; orchestrator for NBC television 1960–66, and Broadway shows; turned to electronic music during the 1960s at Vladimir Ussachevsky's Columbia-Princeton Electronic Music Center; teacher of composition and electronic music, Hunter Coll., New York 1966–89. *Compositions include:* The Pregnant Dream 1968, DUMP (collage) 1970, Three Studies 1970, State of the Union Message (collage) 1973, Conversations 1974, Dress Rehearsal 1976, I Come Out of your Sleep 1979, Mixed Media: Centering (dance for four performers and live electronics) 1979, Sound Sculptures: Sound Environment 1975, Time and Tempo 1984. *Recordings include:* 1750 Arch 1977, Opus One 1981, CRI 1997, 1998, XI 1998. *Honours:* five MacDowell Colony Fellowships 1957–73, Fulbright Scholarships 1958, 1959, Martha Baird Rockefeller Fund, Alice M. Ditson Fund. *Address:* c/o ASCAP, ASCAP Building, 1 Lincoln Plaza, New York, NY 10023, USA.

ANDERSON, Julian, BMus; British composer; *Professor of Composition and Composer-in-Residence, Guildhall School of Music and Drama;* b. 1967, London. *Education:* Royal Coll. of Music, London, studied with Tristan Murail in Paris, Alexander Goehr at Cambridge and with Oliver Knussen; attended Dartington Int. Summer School, Britten-Pears School, Tanglewood. *Career:* freelance composer, with performances at the 1996 Int. Rostrum of Composers (Paris), at the Brighton, Huddersfield Contemporary Music and Cambridge Elgar Festivals; further performances at the 1995 Ars Musica Festival, Brussels, London Proms, Tanglewood and 1996 Warsaw Festival; Composer-in-Residence, Sinfonia 21 1996–2001; Prof. of Composition, RCM 1996–2004, Head of Composition 1999–2004; Composer with City of Birmingham Symphony Orchestra 2000–05; Composer-in-Focus, London Philharmonic Orchestra 2002–03, Artistic Dir of their Music of Today series 2002–; Fanny Mason Prof. of Music, Harvard Univ., USA 2004–07; Cleveland Orchestra Daniel Lewis Young Composer Fellow 2005–07; Prof. of Composition and Composer-in-Residence, Guildhall School of Music and Drama 2007–; Composer-in-Residence, London Philharmonic Orchestra 2010–11, Wigmore Hall 2013–. *Compositions include:* Diptych two movements for orchestra 1991–95,

Khorovod for 15 players 1994, The Bearded Lady for oboe, clarinet and piano 1994, The Colour of Pomegranates for alto flute and piano 1994, Scherzo with Trains for four clarinets 1989–93, Tiramisu for ten players 1994–95, I'm Nobody Who Are You for tenor, violin and piano 1995, Three Parts off the Ground for 13 players 1995, Piano Etudes Nos 1 and 2 1995–96, The Crazed Moon for orchestra 1995–96, Past Hymns for 15 solo strings 1996, Poetry Nearing Silence divertimento for seven instruments 1997, The Stations of the Sun 1998, Towards Poetry (extended ballet version of Poetry Nearing Silence) 1998, Alhambra Fantasy for 16 players (Gramophone Award for Best Contemporary Recording 2007) 2000, The Bird Sings with its Feathers, ballet for chamber orchestra 2001, Shir Hashirim for soprano and chamber orchestra 2001, Imagin'd Corners for orchestra 2002, Symphony (British Composer Award, Orchestra category) 2004, Eden 2005, Book of Hours for ensemble and electronics (Royal Philharmonic Soc. Award for Large-scale Composition 2006) 2005, Heaven is Shy of Earth 2006, Alleluia 2007, Fantasias (British Composer Award, Orchestra category) 2011, Bell Mass (British Composer Award, Liturgical category) 2011, The Discovery of Heaven for orchestra, (South Bank Show Award 2013) 2011. *Honours:* Royal Philharmonic Soc. Award for Young Composer 1992. *Current Management:* Faber Music Ltd, 74–77 Great Russell Street, London, WC1B 3DA, England. *Telephone:* (20) 7908-5310. *Fax:* (20) 7908-5339. *E-mail:* information@fabermusic.com. *Website:* www.fabermusic.com. *Address:* Department of Composition, Guildhall School of Music and Drama, Silk Street, Barbican, London, EC2Y 8DT, England (office). *Telephone:* (20) 7628-2571 (office). *Fax:* (20) 7256-9438 (office). *Website:* www.gsmd.ac.uk (office).

ANDERSON, June, BA; American singer (soprano); b. 30 Dec. 1952, Boston, Mass. *Education:* Yale Univ. *Career:* debut with New York City Opera in the Magic Flute 1978, European debut as Semiramide at Rome Opera; performances at most major opera houses in USA and Europe, for companies including Metropolitan Opera, New York, Milwaukee Florentine Opera, San Diego Opera, Seattle Opera, Chicago Lyric Opera, Royal Opera, London, La Scala, Milan, Opéra de Paris, Teatro Colon, Buenos Aires, Gran Teatre del Liceu, Barcelona, Wiener Staatsoper, La Fenice, Venice; has worked with conductors including Leonard Bernstein, James Conlon, Charles Dutoit, Daniele Gatti, James Levine, Zubin Mehta, Riccardo Muti, Seiji Ozawa. *Roles include:* Queen of the Night in The Magic Flute, New York City Opera 1978, title role in Lucia di Lammermoor, Milwaukee Florentine Opera 1982 and Chicago 1990, Gulnara in Il Corsaro, San Diego Opera Verdi Festival 1982, I Puritani, Edmonton Opera 1982–83, title role in Semiramide, Rome Opera 1982–83 and Metropolitan Opera 1990, Rosina in The Barber of Seville, Seattle Opera and Teatro Massimo 1982–83, Cunégonde in Candide 1989, Metropolitan Opera debut as Gilda in Rigoletto 1989, title role in Luisa Miller, La Fenice, Venice 2006; Dialogues des Carmélites at Opéra de Nice and Salome at Opéra Royal de Wallonie 2011, Adams' Nixon in China at Théâtre du Châtelet, Paris 2012; concert and oratorio vocalist: Chicago Pops Orchestra, Handel Festival Kennedy Center, Denver Symphony, St Louis Symphony, Cincinnati Symphony, Maracaibo (Venezuela) Symphony; first Messa di Requiem by Verdi in Paris 2007; concerts/recitals/festivals in Canada, France, Palestine and Israel 2012. *Honours:* Commdr, Ordre des Arts et des Lettres; Bellini d'Oro Prize, Grammy Award for Best Classical Album (for Bernstein: Candide) 1991. *Current Management:* Bettina Brentano, 44, rue Barbet de Jouy, 75007 Paris, France. *E-mail:* contact@oia-brentano.com. *Website:* www.oia-brentano.com; www.june-anderson.com.

ANDERSON, Laurie P., MFA; American performance artist, musician (keyboards, violin) and writer; b. 5 June 1947, Wayne, Ill.; d. of Arthur T. Anderson and Mary Louise Anderson (née Rowland); m. Lou Reed 2008 (died 2013). *Education:* Columbia Univ., Barnard Coll. *Career:* instructor in Art History, City Coll., CUNY 1973–75; freelance critic, Art News, Art Forum; composer and performer in multi-media exhbns; Artist-in-Residence, ZBS Media 1974, NASA 2002–04; Distinguished Artist-In-Residence, Experimental Media and Performing Arts Center, Rensselaer Polytechnic Inst. 2012–; fmr Artist-In-Residence High Performance Rodeo, Calgary, Alberta, UCLA Center for the Art of Performance; residencies at Yaddo (retreat for writers and artists) 2011, 2012, 2014, American Acad. in Rome; Guest Dir Brighton Festival, UK 2016; Guggenheim Fellow 1983. *Exhibitions include:* solo shows: Barnard Coll. 1970, Harold Rivkin Gallery, Washington 1973, Artists' Space, New York 1974, Holly Solomon Gallery, New York 1977, 1980–81, Museum of Modern Art 1978, Queen's Museum, New York 1984, Barbican, London 2002, Vito Schnabel Gallery, New York 2012; numerous group exhbns 1972–. *Other projects:* New York Social Life, Voices From The Beyond, Talk Normal, Natural History, Songs and Stories for Moby Dick 1999, Happiness 2002, The End of the Moon (performance piece) 2004, Homeland (performance piece) 2006, Delusion (performance piece) 2010. *Film performances:* Carmen, Personal Service Announcements, Beautiful Red Dress, Talk Normal, Alive From Off Center, What You Mean We?, Language Is A Virus, This Is The Picture, Sharkey's Day, Dear Reader, Home of the Brave (writer, dir, performer) 1986, Puppet Motel (CD-ROM) 1995, Heart of a Dog 2015. *Recordings include:* O Superman 1981, Big Science 1982, United States 1983, Mister Heartbreak 1984, Strange Angels 1989, Bright Red 1994, The Ugly One With The Jewels And Other Stories 1995, Life on a String 2001, Live At Town Hall, New York City 2002, Homeland 2010; film scores: Home Of The Brave 1986, Swimming To Cambodia, Monster In A Box. *Publications include:* The Package 1971, October 1972, Transportation, Transportation 1973, The Rose and the Stone 1974, Notebook 1976, Artifacts at the End of a Decade 1981, Typisch Frac 1981, United States 1984, Empty Places: A Performance

1989, Laurie Anderson's Postcard Book 1990, Stories from the Nerve Bible 1993, Night Life 2007. *Honours:* Dr hc (Art Inst. of Chicago), (Philadelphia Coll. of the Arts); Gish Prize 2007, Pratt Inst. Honorary Legends Award 2011, Yaddo Artist Medal 2015. *Current Management:* Curtis R. Priem Experimental Media and Performing Arts Center, Rensselaer Polytechnic Institute, 110 8th Street, Troy, NY 12180, USA. *Telephone:* (518) 276-3921 (office). *E-mail:* studio@difficultmusic.com. *Website:* empac.rpi.edu (office); www .laurieanderson.com.

ANDERSON, Lorna; British singer (soprano); b. 1962, Glasgow, Scotland. *Education:* Royal Scottish Acad. of Music with Patricia MacMahon, Royal Coll. of Music, London. *Career:* concerts with Bach Choir, English Concert under Trevor Pinnock, and Scottish Chamber Orchestra; tour of Spain and Poland and appearances at Kings Lynn, City of London, Brighton, Edinburgh and Aldeburgh Festivals; sang with London Baroque under Charles Medlam, with the London Mozart Players under Andrew Parrott and the Bournemouth Sinfonietta under Roger Norrington 1988; Promenade Concert debut 1988; further concerts with London Classical Players, Orchestra of the Age of Enlightenment, Scottish Nat. Orchestra, Florilegium, The King's Consort, BBC Scottish Symphony Orchestra; sang Innocenza in first modern revival of Marazzoli's La Vita Humana, Scottish Early Music Consort, Glasgow 1990; The Fairy Queen with the Sixteen, Queen Elizabeth Hall 1990; Les Noces with Pierre Boulez and Ensemble Intercontemporain 1990, 1992; Morgana in Alcina, Halle Handel Festival and Innsbruck Festival 1992; Mozart Mass in C minor with Scottish Chamber Orchestra under Charles Mackerras 1992; sang in Bach's St John Passion, Royal Festival Hall, London 1997; opera: Clorinda in Il Combattimento di Tancredi e Clorinda, Netherlands Opera 1991, 1993, Pulcheria in Handel's Riccardo Primo, Göttingen 1996; title role in Theodora, Glyndebourne Touring Opera 1997. *Recordings include:* The Fairy Queen with Harry Christophers/The Sixteen, Linley Shakespeare Ode with The Parley of Instruments; Complete Schubert; Complete Britten Folksongs; Complete Scottish Folksong arrangements by Joseph Haydn with Haydn Trio Eisenstadt; Hyperion: L'Allegro (Handel), The King's Consort; Semper Amor with Apollo Chamber Players; Messiah with David Willcocks and Mormon Tabernacle Choir. *Honours:* First Prize in Peter Pears and Royal Overseas League Competition 1984, Purcell-Britten Prize for Concert Singers, Aldeburgh 1986. *Address:* Dormer Cottage, 98 Trull Road, Taunton, TA1 4QW, England.

ANDERSON, (Leonard) Mark, BMus, MA, LRAM, PPRNCM; American pianist, teacher and business executive; *Assistant Professor of Piano and Chamber Music, University of British Columbia;* b. 8 Oct. 1963, Eureka, Calif.; s. of Leonard A. Anderson and Alyce M. Anderson; one d. *Education:* San Jose State Univ., Royal Northern Coll. of Music, Manchester and Royal Acad. of Music, UK, Cal-State East Bay. *Career:* debut in New York 1988, San Francisco 1988, Tokyo 1992, Toronto 1993, London 1994, Zürich 1994; played in Alice Tully Hall, New York 1994; performances with leading orchestras and conductors at major venues world-wide; currently Exec. Dir New World Music Acad., Pleasanton, Asst Prof. of Piano and Chamber Music, Univ. of British Columbia. *Recordings include:* various solo piano works of Liszt, Brahms and Schumann 1994, Brahms First Piano Concerto with the Hungarian State Symphony Orchestra, Adam Fischer conducting 1995, Liszt Recital 1996; Brahms Variations, op 118 and 119 1997; live solo concert of works by Copland and Gershwin 1999; two-piano CD works by Stravinsky and Mussorgsky with pianist Tamriko Siprashvili 2004, two recordings of the piano music of Hans von Bülow 2011, 2013. *Publications:* contrib. to Piano Quarterly, Keyboard Stylist. *Honours:* winner, Leeds Pianoforte Competition 1993, First Prize, William Kapell Int. Piano Competition, Washington, DC 1994. *Address:* New World Music Academy, 4430 Willow Road, Suite M, Pleasanton, CA 94588, USA (office); 3515 Wesbrook Mall #204, Vancouver, BC V6T 1Z4, Canada (home). *Telephone:* (604) 827-2532 (Vancouver) (office); (925) 462-5400 (Pleasanton) (office). *Fax:* (925) 462-5402 (Pleasanton) (office). *E-mail:* markand0180@gmail.com; mark.anderson@ubc.ca (office); mark@ newworldmusicacademy.com (office). *Website:* www.markandersonpianist .com (office).

ANDERSON, Nicholas Maurice William, MA; British musician, writer and producer; b. 29 March 1941, Exeter, Devon, England; m.; one d. *Education:* Westminster School, London, New Coll., Oxford, Univ. Coll., Durham. *Career:* Editorial Man., Decca Record Co. Ltd 1968–71; music producer, BBC Radio 3 1971–91; music consultant to Warner Music 1991–97, 2002–10; freelance record producer with Harmonia Mundi, Virgin Classics, Chandos Record Co.; Dir Collegium Musicum 90. *Recordings as producer:* more than 50 albums for Collegium Musicum 90. *Publications include:* Baroque Music from Monteverdi to Handel 1994; contribs to A Companion to the Concerto 1988, Cambridge Guide to the Arts in Britain 1991, Oxford Composer Companions: J. S. Bach 2000, New Grove Dictionary of Music and Musicians, Collins Classical Music Encyclopedia 2000. *Address:* The Old Bank House, Nether Stowey, Somerset, TA5 1NG, England. *Telephone:* (1278) 733747. *E-mail:* nicholas.anderson@btinternet.com.

ANDERSON, Robert David, MA, FSA; British conductor, writer and editor; b. 20 Aug. 1927, Shillong, Assam, India; s. of Robert David Anderson and Gladys Anderson (née Clayton). *Education:* Gonville and Caius Coll., Cambridge. *Career:* Asst Ed. Record News 1954–56; Asst Master and Dir of Music Gordonstoun School 1956–62; Conductor Moray Choral Union; Asst Conductor Spoleto Festival 1962; Conductor St Bartholomew's Hosp. Choral Soc. 1965–90; Extra-Mural Lecturer, Univ. of London 1966–77; Assoc. Ed. The

Musical Times 1967–85; critic, The Times 1967–72; Visiting Lecturer, City Univ. 1983–92; Co-ordinating Ed. Elgar Complete Edition 1983–2003; mem. Egypt Exploration Soc. (Hon. Sec. 1971–82), Royal Musical Asscn. *Publications include:* Egyptian Antiquities in the British Museum III: Musical Instruments 1976, Wagner 1980, Egypt in 1800 (co-ed.) 1988, Wagner, in Heritage of Music III 1989, Elgar in Manuscript 1990, Elgar 1993, Music and Dance in Pharaonic Egypt in Civilisations of the Ancient Near East IV 1995, Elgar and Chivalry 2002, Baalbek 2006, Men That Strove with Gods 2010, St Shenoute of the White Monastery 2012, A Traveller in an Antique Lane 2013. *Honours:* Hon. Prof. of History, State Univ. of Rostov-on-Don 2002; Hon. DMus (City Univ.) 1985, Hon. DHist (Russian State Univ. for Humanities, Moscow) 2000; Liveryman Worshipful Co. of Musicians 1977. *Address:* 54 Hornton Street, London, W8 4NT, England (home). *Telephone:* (20) 7937-5146 (home).

ANDERSON, Sylvia; American singer (mezzo-soprano) and dramatic soprano; b. 1938, Denver, Colorado; m. Matthias Kuntzsch. *Education:* Eastman School with Anna Kaskas, Cologne Musikhochschule with Ellen Bosenius, Maestro Luigi Toffolo, Trieste Italia. *Career:* debut in Cologne 1962, as Fyodor in Boris Godunov; sang at the Hamburg Staatsoper 1965–69, notably as Ophelia in the 1968 premiere of Searle's Hamlet; Bayreuth Festival 1970–71; Salzburg Festival 1973, in the premiere of De Temporum fine Comoedia by Orff; sang 20 Wagnerian roles at Bayreuth; US engagements at the Metropolitan and New York City Operas, and in San Francisco (17 roles), Washington and Santa Fe; has sung Salome, Octavian, The Marschallin, Tosca and Carmen over 100 times; has sung 80 opera roles in Italy, Austria, Spain, Switzerland, Portugal, Belgium, France, Netherlands, Poland, fmr USSR, Iran, Argentina, Mexico, Brazil, USA and Germany; repertoire included operas by Gluck, Purcell, Rossini, Verdi, Wagner and modern composers; many concert appearances including contemporary works of Elinor Armer, Günter Bialas, John Cage, John Duke, Humphrey Searle, Robert Moran, Gloria Coates, Jack Beeson, Neely Bruce, David Conte and David Garner; joined voice faculty, San Francisco Conservatory of Music 1990–; f., Artistic Dir and Pres. Bd, Bay Area Summer Opera Theater Inst. (BASOTI) 1992–2013. *Recordings:* Stockhausen's Drei Lieder, Schubert Masses, De Temporum fine Comoedia. *Address:* San Francisco Conservatory of Music, 50 Oak Street, San Francisco, CA 94102-6011, USA (office). *Telephone:* (415) 457-5255 (home). *E-mail:* operaprof@aol.com (home). *Website:* www.sylviaanderson.org.

ANDERSON, Thomas Jefferson, Jr, BMus, MEd, PhD; American composer and academic; b. 17 Aug. 1928, Coatesville, Pa; m.; three c. *Education:* West Virginia State Coll., Pennsylvania State Univ., Cincinnati Conservatory of Music with Scott Huston, Univ. of Iowa, studied with Philip Bezanson and Richard Hervig, Aspen School of Music with Darius Milhaud. *Career:* teacher of instrumental music, High Point, North Carolina Public Schools 1951–54; Instructor, West Virginia State Coll., Inst., West Virginia 1955–56; Prof. of Music and Chair of Music Dept, Langston Univ., Okla 1958–63; Prof. of Music, Tennessee State Univ., Nashville 1963–69; orchestrated first complete performance of Treemonisha by Scott Joplin 1972; Composer-in-Residence, Atlanta, Georgia 1971–72; Prof. of Music and Chair of Music Dept 1972–80, Tufts Univ. Chair and Austin Fletcher Prof. of Music 1976–90, Prof. Emer. 1990–; Scholar-in-Residence, The Rockefeller Foundation, Study and Conference Centre, Bellagio, Italy 1984, 1994; Fellowship, John Simon Guggenheim Foundation 1988; Fellow, Nat. Humanities Centre, Research Triangle Park, NC 1996–97; mem. American Acad. of Arts and Letters 2005–. *Compositions include:* stage: Spirituals for orchestra, jazz quartet, chorus, children's choir, tenor and narrator 1979, Soldier Boy, Soldier (opera) 1982, Walker (chamber opera with words by Derek Walcott) 1992; orchestral: Introduction and Allegro 1959, Classical Symphony 1961, Six Pieces for clarinet and chamber orchestra 1962, Symphony in Three Movements 1964, Songs of Illumination (song cycle) 1990, Whatever Happened to the Big Bands 1991, Bahia, Bahia for chamber orchestra 1991, Spirit Songs (commissioned by Yo-Yo Ma, for cello and piano) 1993, Here in the Flesh (hymn) 1993, Seven Cabaret Songs for jazz singer 1994, Flute, viola, cello and piano, Broke Baroque for violin and piano 1996, Shouts 1997, Huh? What did you say? for solo clarinet, string trio and solo violin 1998, Boogie Woogie Fantasy for solo piano 1999, Slip Knot, an opera in two acts 2000, Game Play for flute, viola, cello, harp 2002, Slavery Documents for chorus, orchestra, soloists 2002, Boogie Woogie Concertante for improvised piano, wind instruments and percussion 2003, Gospel Ghost for flute and piano 2003, Ragged Edge for chamber orchestra 2005, Fragments (a J.S. Bach/T.J. Monk Fantasy) for improvised piano and orchestra 2006. *Recordings:* Chamber Symphony: London Philharmonic Orchestra, James Dixon conductor; Variations on a Theme by M. B. Tolson; Contemporary Chamber Ensemble, Arthur Weisberg conductor; Squares: Baltimore Symphony Orchestra, Paul Freeman conductor; Intermezzi, Videmus, Vivian Taylor, Artistic Director. *Honours:* Hon. DMus (Bridgewater State Coll.) 1991, (Northwestern Univ.) 2002, (Tufts Univ.) 2007; Hon. DMA (Coll. of the Holy Cross) 1983, (St Augustine's Coll.) 1996, (Bates Coll.) 2005; Hon. DM (West Virginia State Coll.) 1984. *Address:* 3750 Peachtree Road NE #860, Atlanta, GA 30319-1322, USA (home). *Telephone:* (404) 231-7860 (home). *E-mail:* tj@ aol.com (home). *Website:* www.tjandersonmusic.com.

ANDERSON, Valdine, BMus; Canadian singer (soprano) and voice teacher; b. 4 July 1960, Winnipeg; d. of Barry and Helga Anderson; m. Ian Baragar; four c. *Career:* European operatic debut as Maid in Thomas Adès' Powder Her Face, Cheltenham Festival 1995, role reprised for Opéra de Nantes 2001–02,

Mariinsky Theatre, St Petersburg 2007; US tour of Dutilleux's Correspondances with the Berlin Philharmonic Orchestra under Sir Simon Rattle 2003; ENO debut in Gavin Bryar's Dr Ox's Experiment 1998; performances of Elliott Carter's What Next?, Concertgebouw, Amsterdam and Queen Elizabeth Hall, London 2000; Elizabeth Zimmer in Henze's Elegy for Young Lovers with the Orchestre Philharmonique de Radio France 2004–05; regular performances in UK include Boulez' Pli selon pli and Mahler Symphony No. 4 with BBC Scottish Symphony Orchestra; BBC Proms début with BBC Symphony Orchestra and Mark Elder 1998, subsequent Proms performances of Nielsen Symphony No. 3 with the BBC Symphony Orchestra under Jukka-Pekka Saraste and Knussen Higglety Pigglety Pop! with the London Sinfonietta; roles for Edmonton Opera, Manitoba Opera and Vancouver Opera include Blonde (Die Entführung aus dem Serail), Micaela (Carmen) and Papagena (The Magic Flute), Gretel (Hansel and Gretel) for Edmonton Opera, Susannah (Susannah) for Calgary Opera, concert performance of The Scarlet Princess for Canadian Opera Co.; performances with Montreal Symphony, New York Philharmonic, Orchestre Nat. de France, Orchestre Philharmonique de Radio France, Chamber Orchestra of Europe, Stockholm Philharmonic Orchestra, Boston Symphony Orchestra, Chicago Symphony Orchestra, City of Birmingham Symphony and Orchestre de Paris; appearances with Nash Ensemble, Gavin Bryar's Ensemble, Hilliard Ensemble, Asko Ensemble, Netherlands Chamber Orchestra, Ensemble Modern and Ensemble Intercontemporain; collaborations with composers George Benjamin, Sir Harrison Birtwistle, Pierre Boulez, Gavin Bryars, Gérard Grisey; has worked with conductors including Daniel Barenboim, Pierre Boulez, Philippe Herreweghe, Edo de Waart and David Zinman; Voice Instructor, Univ. of Manitoba 2004–. *Recordings include:* Maxwell-Davies' Job, Freedman's Spirit Song, Adès' Five Eliot Landscapes, Lutosławski's Chantefleurs et Chantefables, Bryars' Adnan's Songbook, Torke's Book of Proverbs, Songs of a Fairy Princess, Adès' Powder Her Face, Carter's What Next?. *Honours:* Prairie Music Award 2001. *Current Management:* Ingpen & Williams Ltd, 7 St George's Court, 131 Putney Bridge Road, London, SW15 2PA, England. *Telephone:* (20) 8874-3222 (office). *Fax:* (20) 8877-3113 (office). *E-mail:* info@ingpen.co.uk (office). *Address:* Marcel A. Desautels Faculty of Music, University of Manitoba, 65 Dafoe Road, Winnipeg, MB R3T 2N3, Canada (office). *E-mail:* music@umanitoba.ca (office); valdinea@shaw.ca (office).

ANDERSSON, Anders; Swedish singer (tenor); b. 1954. *Education:* Stockholm Music High School and Ave Opera Studio of the Royal Opera. *Career:* debut as Erland in Singoalla by de Frumerie, also at Savonlinna, Stockholm 1989; has also sung Gunnar in Den Fredlose by Inger Wikstrom at Ulriksdal, Gudmund in Stenhammar's Gildet pa Solhaug, title role in a revival of J. G. Naumann's Gustaf Wasa, Samson, the Emperor in Turandot; concert appearances and teaching engagements. *Recording:* Gustaf Wasa.

ANDERSSON, B(engt) Tommy; Swedish conductor, composer and academic; *Professor of Orchestral Conducting, Royal College of Music, Stockholm;* b. 26 July 1964, Borås. *Education:* studied conducting at Royal Coll. of Music, Stockholm with Jorma Panula, Kjell Ingebretsen, Eric Ericson, Gennady Rozhdestvensky, Brian Priestman, Sergiu Comissiona; further conducting studies with Peter Eötvös, Mark Foster, Jiří Bělóhlavek, Peter Lücker, Milos Alexander Machek, Georg Tintner, Kirk Trevor, composition studies with Sven-Eric Johanson, Hans Eklund and Sven-David Sandström. *Career:* debut in Le nozze di Figaro, Södra Teatern, Stockholm, 1992; recurrent engagements with opera houses in Stockholm, Göteborg, Malmö, Umeå, Vadstena and Karlstad, including Die Geisterinsel (Reichardt) 1992, Fidelio (Beethoven) 1997, Il Prigioniero (Dallapiccola) 1997, Un ballo in maschera (Verdi) 1998, Wozzeck (Berg) 1999, Orlando (Handel) 2000, The Cunning Little Vixen (Janáček) 2000, Macbeth (Sandström) 2001, Lulu (Berg) 2002, William (B. Tommy Andersson) 2006; recurrent concert engagements with all major orchestras and most chamber orchestras in Sweden; guest conducting in Germany, UK, Switzerland, Netherlands, Finland, Denmark, Norway, Iceland, Uruguay, Czech Repub., Romania, Lithuania and Hungary; premiered more than 151 works, including 13 operas; Royal Stockholm Philharmonic Orchestra presented a four-day festival of his music April 2009; Artistic Dir KammarensembleN, an ensemble for contemporary music 1994–99; Prin. Conductor Stockholm Symphonic Wind Ensemble 1997–2005; Artistic Leader and Prin. Conductor Swedish Nat. Orchestra Acad., Gothenburg 2003–09; Prof. of Orchestral Studies, Gothenburg Univ. School of Music 2003–09; Prof. of Orchestral Conducting, Royal Coll. of Music, Stockholm; Composer in asscn with BBC National Orchestra of Wales 2014–15; mem. Swedish Composers' Asscn, Swedish Section of ISCM, Soc. of Swedish Conductors, Royal Swedish Acad. of Music. *Compositions include:* Concerto for piano, winds and percussion 1984, Stabat Mater 1985, Te Deum 1987, Impromptu, for clarinet and vibraphone 1987, Sonata for Percussion and Piano 1987, Conflicts, for percussion ensemble 1988, Intrada for winds and percussion 1989, Notturno, for cello and organ 1989, Epitaffio, for string orchestra 1989, A Bed of Roses, for percussion ensemble 1989, Concerto for Horn and Orchestra 1993, Dark Shadows, for recorder and marimba 1990, Apollo, Concerto for percussion solo and orchestra 1995, Antique (Rimbaud), for male voice and piano 1999, Satyricon, for large orchestra 2000, Sonnet XVIII (Shakespeare), for mixed chorus a cappella 2002, Games for Giton, for wind quintet 2002, Reflections, Concerto for soprano saxophone and orchestra 2003, Kyssar vill jag dricka (Song of Songs), for mixed chorus a cappella 2004, A Song of Joys (Whitman), for solo voice, male chorus and one percussionist 2005, William, chamber opera in two acts 2006, Pieces for Pontus, for piano solo 2007, Bohèmiana, for orchestra (after Giacomo Puccini) 2007, Passacaglia, for large orchestra 1988/2008, Processional, for organ 2008, Prelude, for organ 1983/2008, Nocturne, for organ 1990/2008, The Garden of Delights, for orchestra 2009, Fanfare, for organ 2009, Adagio mesto, for organ 1982/2009, Elegy for an Angel, for organ 2009, A Christmas Gloria, for chorus, large organ and orchestra 2009, The Secrets of Eros, for ensemble 2010, Warriors, for orchestra 2010, Toccata, Aria & Chaconne, for string orchestra 2011, Awakening of the Beauteous Faun, for 8 violoncellos 2012, The Tyger (Blake), for mixed chorus and organ 2012, Death in Venice (Richard Wagner in memoriam) for orchestra 2013, From March 1979 (Tranströmer) for mixed chorus and organ 2013, Albertus Pictor, Concerto for organ and strings 2014, Pan, for large orchestra with large organ 2015. *Recordings include:* own works: Impromptu 1987, Intrada 1989, Apollo 1995, Satyricon, Concerto for Horn and Orchestra, Reflections, Pieces for Pontus, Sonnet XVIII; Kyssar vill jag dricka 2009, The Garden of Delights, Warriors 2011; music by Atterberg, Hallén, Hallström, Norman, Nyström, Wiklund and Auber, several recordings of Swedish contemporary music with a.o. Swedish Radio Symphony Orchestra, Royal Stockholm Philharmonic Orchestra and KammarensembleN. *Honours:* Swedish Royal Acad. Scholarship 1990, 1993, Crusell Award for Young Conductors 1993, Sten Frykberg Award 1994, Crystal Prize for Interpretation of Contemporary Music 1995, Swedish Composers' Asscn Interpreters Prize 1998, Scholarship for Composers, Musikföreningen i Stockholm 2014. *Current Management:* c/o Maria Dalayman, Good Company AB, Karlbergsvägen 64, 113 35 Stockholm, Sweden. *Telephone:* (8) 54580554; 73-5048207 (mobile). *Fax:* (8) 344354. *E-mail:* maria@goodcompany.se. *Website:* www.goodcompany.se/en/artists/conductors/b-tommy-andersson. *Address:* Sankt Eriksgatan 82, 113 62 Stockholm, Sweden (home). *E-mail:* bta@comhem.se. *Website:* btommyandersson.com.

ANDERSSON, Laila; Swedish singer (soprano); b. 30 March 1941, Losen, Blekinge; m. Ulf Palme 1984. *Education:* studied with Sylvia Mang-Borenberg, Ragnar Hultén, and Hjördis Schymberg in Stockholm. *Career:* with Royal Opera Stockholm 1964–, has sung 100 roles, including Susanna, Leonore in Il Trovatore, Mathilde in Guillaume Tell, Madama Butterfly, Jenůfa, Sophie, in Il Pastore Fidelo, Tosca, Macbeth; sang in the premieres of Herr von Hancken by Blomdahl 1965 and Granskibbutzen by Karkoff 1975; sang the title role in Berg's Lulu 1977; frequent visits to the Drottningholm Festival from 1967 (Gustaf Adolf och Ebba Brahe by the Abbé Vogler 1973); guest engagements at the Edinburgh Festival 1974, Copenhagen, Wiesbaden, Helsinki and Oslo; sang Tosca at Stockholm, Grenoble and Bonn 1977, Salome at the Metropolitan (debut 1981), Gelsenkirchen, Vienna, Rio de Janeiro, Berlin and Montréal 1985; sang Brünnhilde at Århus, Denmark 1987; Fidelio at Washington and Montreal 1988; sang Tiresias in the premiere of Backanterna by Daniel Börtz 1992; as Elektra, Stockholm Opera 1993; premiere of Schederin's Lolita, Stockholm 1994; mem. Nya Bjorling Vocal Quartet; Chair., Theatre Order, 105 Sisters; mem. Royal Swedish Acad. of Music. *Honours:* Singer of the Royal Court 1985, Litteris et Artibus 1992. *Address:* Köpmantorget 10, 111 31 Stockholm, Sweden (home). *Telephone:* (8) 10-74-74 (home). *Fax:* (8) 10-74-74 (home).

ANDERSZEWSKI, Piotr; Polish pianist; b. 4 April 1969, Warsaw. *Education:* Conservatoires of Lyon and Strasbourg, Univ. of Southern California, USA, Chopin Acad., Warsaw. *Career:* recitals in Poland, USA and France; Wigmore Hall, London debut 1991; further British engagements include the Harrogate Festival 1991 and concerts with the Royal Liverpool Philharmonic and Hallé Orchestras; Festival Hall debut with the London Philharmonic conducted by Franz Welser-Möst; recordings for Polish radio and television; European recital tour 1992; regular duo pnr with violinist Viktoria Mullova 1992–93 season; Edinburgh Festival debut in recital 1994; concert performances with City of Birmingham Symphony Orchestra 1994, Ulster Orchestra 1995, Lahti Symphony 1994, Nat. Symphony Orchestra of Ireland 1995; recitals with the Berlin Philharmonic, Théâtre des Champs-Élysées, QEH, Zankel Hall, Carnegie Hall, New York, Concertgebouw, Amsterdam, LSO, appearances with the symphony orchestras of Chicago, Boston, Atlanta, Berlin and Houston, SWR Sinfonieorchester, Chamber Orchestra of Europe; European tour with Frank Peter Zimmermann 2011. *Recordings include:* Prokofiev Sonata for Violin and Piano No. 1 Op. 80 (recital with Viktoria Mullova), Debussy Sonata for Violin and Piano, Janáček Sonata for Violin and Piano, Brahms Sonatas for Piano and Violin, Bach, Beethoven and Webern solo works, Bach keyboard works, Beethoven's Diabelli Variations (Diapason d'or, Choc du Monde de la Musique, France) 2000, Mozart piano concerti, Bach's Partitas 1, 3 and 6, Szymanowski Piano Works (Gramophone Award for Best Instrumental Recording 2006) 2005, Beethoven Bagatelles 2008, Unquiet Traveller 2009, Schumann, Humoreske (BBC Music Magazine Instrumental Award and Recording of the Year Award 2012) 2010, Bach English Suites Nos 1, 3 & 5 (Gramophone Award for Best Instrumental Recording 2015) 2014. *Films:* Piotr Anderszewski Plays the Diabelli Variations 2001, Unquiet Traveller 2008. *Honours:* Int. Piano Foundation Scholarship to IPF on Lake Como, Italy 1994–95; Szymanowski Prize 1999, Royal Philharmonic Soc. Best Instrumentalist Award 2001, Gilmore Artist 2002–06. *Address:* c/o EMI Classics, 27 Wrights Lane, London, W8 5SW, England (office). *Telephone:* (20) 7795-7000 (office). *Fax:* (20) 7495-1307 (office). *Website:* www.emiclassics.com (office); www.anderszewski.net.

ANDONIAN, Andrea; American singer (mezzo-soprano); b. 1950, Colorado. *Education:* Florida and Ohio Univs, Operastudio in Cologne. *Career:* sang at Cologne Offenbach Theatre 1977–78; engaged at Krefeld-Monchengladbach 1978–85; has sung with Cologne Opera 1985–, Deutsche Oper Berlin 1986–;

guest appearances in Germany and elsewhere, in repertory including Cherubino, Dorabella, Ramiro in Mozart's Finta Giardiniera, Idamante in Idomeneo and Annio in La Clemenza di Tito, Humperdinck's Hansel, Siebel in Faust, the Prince in Massenet's Cendrillon, and Britten's Lucretia and Hermia; sang Urbain in Les Huguenots with Deutsche Oper 1987, and at Covent Garden 1991, at Paris Opéra-Comique 1992, in Rossini's L'Occasione fa il Ladro, La Scala di Seta, La Cambiale di Matrimonio and Il Signor Bruschino; sang Auntie in Peter Grimes at Cologne 1994; season 1999–2000 at Cologne as Annina in La Traviata, Wellgunde in Götterdämmerung, Larina in Eugene Onegin and Sycorax in Spohr's Faust; in Cavalleria Rusticana, Les Contes d'Hoffmann, Hansel & Gretel, Le Nozze di Figaro and Jenůfa 2007; sang Annina in La Traviata, Frau Förstein/Owl in Cunning Little Vixen, Siegrune in Die Walküre 2010; sang Margret in Wozzeck 2011. *Recordings include:* Schumann's Requiem. *Address:* c/o Oper Köln, Offenbachplatz, 50667, Köln, Germany.

ANDRADE, Levine; British violist and conductor; b. 1954, Bombay (now Mumbai), India; m. four c. *Education:* Yehudi Menuhin School with Robert Masters, studied with Menuhin, Nadia Boulanger, Patrick Ireland, Royal Acad. of Music with Frederick Grinke, Max Gilbert, Sidney Griller and Colin Hampton. *Career:* Co-founder, Arditti String Quartet 1974–89; frequent concerts with London Symphony Orchestra, Royal Philharmonic, Acad. of St Martin-in-the-Fields, London Sinfonietta and London Mozart Players; Guest Prof., Royal Acad. of Music; many concerts with the Arditti Quartet in Europe and North America; festival engagements at Aldeburgh, Bath, BBC Proms, Berlin, Budapest, Paris, Venice Biennale, Vienna and Warsaw; Music in Camera programme, BBC television, 1987; series of seven recitals for Radio 3, 1987; played in all Schoenberg's quartets in a single recital, Queen Elizabeth Hall, London 1988; took part in the premieres of quartets by Georges Aperghis 1985, Berio Divertimento for Trio 1987, Bose No. 3 1989, Britten Quartettino 1983, Gavin Bryars 1985, Bussotti 1988, John Cage Music for 4 1988, Davies 1983, Ferneyhough Nos 2 and 3, Gubaidulina No. 3 1987, Harvey Nos 1 and 2, Hindemith Quartet 1915 1986, Kagel 1987, Nancarrow No. 3 1988, Ohana No. 2 1982, Pousseur No. 2 1989, premiered quartets by Michael Finnissy, Michael Nyman and Tim Souster; also performed numerous film scores; f. Telefilmonic Orchestra (for film and commercial recordings). *Recordings include:* Henze's Five String Quartets (Deutsche Schallplattenpreis 1987). *Honours:* with Arditti String Quartet: Grand Prix du Disque, Ernst von Siemens Music Foundation Prize. *Address:* 80 Whellock Road, London, W4 1DJ, England (office). *Telephone:* (1483) 570105 (office). *Fax:* (7092) 045955 (office). *E-mail:* telefilmonic@gmail.com (office). *Website:* www.telefilmonic.co.uk (office).

ANDRADE, Rosario; Mexican singer (soprano); b. 6 April 1951, Veracruz. *Education:* studied in Veracruz and Accademia di Santa Cecilia, Rome. *Career:* debut as Madama Butterfly, Mexico City, 1974; sang at Glyndebourne Festival as Donna Elvira in Don Giovanni, 1977–78; Many guest appearances in Europe and North America, Brussels, 1978, Lyon (in Cavalli's La Calisto), 1979, Warsaw, 1981–82, Connecticut, 1987, Pittsburgh and Mississippi Opera Company, 1988; Metropolitan Opera debut, 1982, as Antonia in Les Contes d'Hoffmann, returning as Manon, 1986; Other roles include Mimi, Micaela, Marguerite, Donna Anna, Aida and Maddalena in Andrea Chénier; Concert repertory includes Marguerite in La Damnation de Faust. *Address:* c/o Metropolitan Opera, Lincoln Center, New York, NY 10023, USA.

ANDRÉ, Martin; British conductor; b. 10 Dec. 1960, West Wickham. *Education:* Yehudi Menuhin School, Royal Coll. of Music and Univ. of Cambridge. *Career:* played with the Nat. Youth Orchestra as percussionist from 1970; founded the Mozart Chamber Ensemble at Cambridge and was apptd conductor of the Univ. Orchestra and Chorus, and the Univ. Chamber Orchestra; conducted his edition of Purcell's King Arthur at Cambridge and the Minack Theatre, Cornwall 1982; worked with the WNO from 1982, leading Aida, Jenůfa, Ernani, Rigoletto, Madama Butterfly, Un Ballo in Maschera, Eugene Onegin and Il Barbiere di Siviglia; Vancouver Opera from season 1986–87 with Janáček's From the House of the Dead and Cunning Little Vixen, Ariadne auf Naxos, La Traviata and La Bohème; Seattle Opera 1987, Carmen; London concert debut January 1987, with the English Chamber Orchestra at the Barbican; further concerts with the Scottish Chamber Orchestra and the Northern Sinfonia; Scottish Opera from 1989, The Merry Widow and La Clemenza di Tito; conducted The Love of Three Oranges at the ENO 1990, and at Teatro São-Carlos, Lisbon 1991; Madama Butterfly for Opera North; world premiere, The Bacchae by John Buller for ENO, 1992; Music Dir, English Touring Opera 1993; recent notable debuts include Verdi's Un Ballo in Maschera at the Royal Opera House, Covent Garden; conducted the UK premiere of Matthus' Cornet Christoph Rilke's Song of Love and Death for Glyndebourne Touring Opera; The Makropulos Case for GTO in 1997; engagements with the New Israeli Opera include conducting Don Pasquale and Love for Three Oranges; The Magic Flute for Opera Northern Ireland, 1998; cr. The Independent Youth Orchestra of Portugal/Momentum Perpetuum 2006, numerous concerts; premiere of Offenbach's Blaubart at Bregenz Festival, Austria 2006 and at St Pölten Festival 2007, Martinů's Mirandolina, and Janáček's The Excursions of Mr Brouček for Opera North and Scottish Opera 2009, Offenbach's Orpheus in the Underworld, Central City Opera, Colorado, USA 2010; concerts in 2011 with Opera North Orchestra, Collegium Musicum Bergen, Norway, and Orquestra Nacional do Porto to celebrate Portugal's centenary. *Current Management:* c/o Thomas Hull, Ingpen & Williams, 7 St George's Court, 131 Putney Bridge Road, London, SW15 2PA, England. *Telephone:* (20) 8874-3222. *Fax:* (20) 8877-3113. *E-mail:* th@ ingpen.co.uk. *Website:* www.ingpen.co.uk. *E-mail:* laza@martinandre.com. *Website:* www.martinandre.com.

ANDREAE, Marc Edouard; Swiss conductor; b. 8 Nov. 1939, Zürich. *Education:* Zurich Conservatory, Univ. of Zurich, studied with Nadia Boulanger in Paris, with Franco Ferrara in Rome. *Career:* Musical Dir Swiss-Italian Radio/TV Symphony Orchestra 1969–91; Permanent Conductor, Sinfonia Concert Series, Engadine Symphony Orchestra 1989–; Music and Artistic Dir Angelicum Orchestra, Milan, Italy 1990–93; Conductor-in-Residence, Symphony Orchestra Göttingen 1999–2000; f. Orchestra dell'Insubria 2001–; regular guest conductor with numerous European, Mexican and Japanese symphony orchestras and at festivals in Paris, Berlin, Lucerne, Vienna, Salzburg, Ascona, Brescia, Vlaanderen, Milan, Florence, Zurich and Lugano; numerous concerts and operas for TV, including Eurovision; mem. Swiss Music Edition (past Pres.). *Recordings include:* more than 50 albums with NDR Hamburg, Hamburg Philharmonic Orchestra, Munich Philharmonic, Cologne Radio Symphony Orchestra, Bamberg Symphony, National Orchestra of France, NHK Symphony Orchestra, Tokyo. *Honours:* Officer, Order of St Agate (San Marino) 2005; First Prize, Swiss Nat. Competition 1966, two Grand Prix, Italian Record Critics 1974, LP Techno Distinction, Tokyo 1975, UBS Cultural Award 2000. *Current Management:* c/o Stricker Cultural Management GmbH, Niederfeldstraße 42, 68199 Mannheim, Germany. *Telephone:* (621) 4398222. *Fax:* (621) 4398223. *E-mail:* info@ strickerm.de. *Website:* www.strickerm.de. *Address:* Via Moretto 6, 6924 Sorengo, Switzerland. *E-mail:* marc.andreae@bluewin.ch. *Website:* www .marcandreae.ch.

ANDREESCU, Horia; Romanian conductor and academic; *Main Conductor, George Enescu Philharmonic Orchestra;* b. 18 Oct. 1946, Brasov. *Education:* Brasov School of Music, Bucharest Conservatoire, studied with Hans Swarowsky in Vienna and Sergiu Celibidache in Munich. *Career:* Chief Conductor, Ploiesti Philharmonic 1974–87; Perm. Guest Conductor, Mecklenburgische Staatskapelle Schwerin 1979–90, Radio Symphony Orchestra, Berlin 1981–91, Dresden Philharmonia 1983–91; Main Conductor, George Enescu Philharmonic Orchestra, Bucharest 1987–; Prof., Acad. of Music 1988–90; Conductor Virtuosi of Bucharest Chamber Orchestra, Bucharest George Enescu Philharmonic Orchestra; Chief Conductor and Gen. Music Dir Bucharest Nat. Radio Orchestra 1992–2010; guest engagements with Gewandhaus Leipzig, Staatskapelle Berlin, Berlin Symphony (now Konzerthaus Orchestra), Komische Oper Berlin, WDR Symphony Orchestra Cologne, MDR Radio Symphony Leipzig, Stuttgart Philharmonic, Vienna Symphony, Radio Symphony Vienna, Royal Philharmonic, London Symphony, Spanish Radio Symphony, Danish Radio Symphony, BBC Scottish, Dutch Radio Philharmonic, Dutch Radio Chamber Orchestra, Dutch Radio Symphony, Netherlands Chamber Orchestra, Torino Philharmonic, Orchestra dell'Arena di Verona. *Recordings include:* first complete orchestral work of George Enescu; recordings for Radio Bucharest, Radio East Berlin (Haydn, Brahms, Wagner, Stravinsky, Hindemith, Prokofiev), Radio Leipzig (Bartók), BBC (Haydn, Mozart, Beethoven, Tchaikovsky), Radio Madrid, Radio Copenhagen and Radio Suisse Romande. *Honours:* prizewinner, Geneva and Copenhagen Competitions. *Current Management:* c/o Konzertdirektion Martin Müller, Uhrs Knäppken 8, 59320 Ennigerloh-Ostenfelde, Germany. *Telephone:* (2524) 263480. *Fax:* (2524) 263481. *E-mail:* info@kdmueller.de. *Website:* www.kdmueller.de.

ANDREEV, Andrei; Russian violinist; b. 1950, Crimea. *Career:* co-founder, Rachmaninov Quartet under auspices of Sochi State Philharmonic Society, Crimea 1974; many concerts in former Soviet Union; from season 1975–76 tours to Switzerland, Austria, Bulgaria, Norway and Germany; participation in Shostakovich Chamber Music Festival, Vilnius 1976 and festivals in Moscow and St Petersburg; repertoire includes works by Haydn, Mozart, Beethoven, Bartók, Brahms, Schnittke, Shostakovich, Boris Tchaikovsky, Chalayev and Meyerovich. *Honours:* prizewinner All-Union Borodin String Quartet Competition (with Rachmaninov Quartet) 1987.

ANDRETTA, Giancarlo; Italian conductor; *Chief Conductor, Aarhus Symfoniorkester.* *Education:* Hochschule für Musik, Vienna. *Career:* Asst Conductor, Vienna State Opera and Salzburg Sommerfestspiele 1988–93; Prin. Guest Conductor and Consultant, Graz Opera House 1994–97; Chief Conductor, Orchestra Filarmonia Veneta 1996–2003; Artistic Dir, Teatro Olimpico, Vicenza 1996–2003; Chief Conductor, Aarhus Symfoniorkester 2003–(12); First Guest Conductor, Göteborg Opera 2010–; Guest Prof. of Piano, Hochschule für Musik, Vienna 1990–94, Guest Prof. of Conducting, Royal Acad. of Music, Copenhagen 2005. *Recordings:* Lalo: Symphony in G Minor 1996, Campagnoli: Concertos 1999. *Honours:* winner, Italian Competition for Professorship in Conducting. *Address:* Aarhus Symfoniorkester, Musikhuset Aarhus, Skovgaardsgade 2 C, 8000 Aarhus C, Denmark (office). *Telephone:* 89-40-90-90 (office). *E-mail:* symfoni@aarhus.dk (office). *Website:* www.aarhussymfoni.dk (office).

ANDREW, Jon; New Zealand singer (tenor); b. 1936. *Education:* studied in Auckland. *Career:* debut as Don José in Carmen, Auckland, 1962; sang with Sadler's Wells Opera, 1963–68, as Ricardo, Radames, Don José, and Agrippa in the British premiere of The Fiery Angel (New Opera Company); sang in Germany, 1969–80, notably in Karlsruhe, Mannheim and Düsseldorf in Wagner roles including Siegmund in Die Walküre; Glyndebourne Festival as the Italian singer in Rosenkavalier, 1965; Covent Garden, 1967 and 1974, as Froh in Das Rheingold and Dimitri in Boris Godunov; further appearances with WNO, Handel Opera Society, 1967, and at San Diego as Siegmund and Otello, 1975–76; also sang Siegmund at Madrid, Berlin Staatsoper, and with ENO 1975; Wexford Festival as Pedro in Tiefland, 1978; further engagements at La Scala, Milan, and Nice and Santiago, 1981; other roles have included Turiddu, Erik in Fliegende Holländer, Max in Der Freischütz, Laca in Jenůfa, and Bob Boles in Peter Grimes; soloist in Gounod's St Cecilia Mass in Bordeaux 2004; vocal coach 1997–. *E-mail:* royaltoria@ntlworld.com. *Website:* .

ANDREW, Kerry, PhD; British composer and singer; b. 1978, High Wycombe, Bucks. *Education:* Univ. of York. *Career:* works heard in Westminster Cathedral, Wigmore Hall, York Minster, LSO St Luke's and Southbank Centre and at Edinburgh Fringe Festival; one of 20 composers chosen to compose for London 2012 Cultural Olympiad; commissioned by Wigmore Hall to write community chamber opera for Britten centenary celebrations 2013; has written large-scale works for City Chorus, Nat. Youth Choir and Youth Music Voices, performed at London 2012 Festival; works performed in Europe, USA, Australia and Japan by ensembles including Hilliard Ensemble, The Ebor Singers, Halcyon (Australia), Alamire, Psappha and Joyful Company of Singers and by soprano Jane Manning and countertenor Nicholas Clapton; broadcast on BBC Radio 3 and Classic FM and internationally; as performer, mem. vocal trio juice, also DOLLYman and Metamorphic, and as soloist You Are Wolf; festivals as performer include SXSW Festival, Austin, USA and Tampere Festival, Finland; teacher, Junior Trinity Coll. of Music. *Compositions include:* choral: Out of the Orient Crystal Skies, Adam and the Mother, The Cherry Tree Carol, Drop, Drop Slow Tears, o lux beata trinitas, maranatha, O nata lux, York Mass 2008, Magnificat 2010, Fall 2010, Winning By Daylight 2011, A Still Roar 2011; vocal: Peace song 2000, Luna-cy for 3 female voices 2001, Lullaby for the Witching Hour, Sundial Songs 2005, The Song of Doves 2006, Goodnight Irene 2012; chamber: Shifting Sands for oboe, horn, bassoon, viola and double bass 2005, Wine, Whisky and Songs for mezzo, baritone, clarinet in A and piano 2008, Dawnsong for alto/piano, baritone/crotales 2009; also electronica, orchestral, music theatre and education works. *Recordings include:* Fall (Making Music Award, British Composer Awards 2010); with juice: Songspin (Ind. Music Award 2012). *Honours:* Tampere Int. Festival Prize, PRS Music Foundation Make Music Award 2011. *Address:* c/o Music Department, OUP, Great Clarendon Street, Oxford, OX2 6DP, England (office). *E-mail:* kj_funk@hotmail.com (office). *Website:* kerryandrew.net (office).

ANDREW, Ludmilla, BA; Canadian singer (soprano); b. Vancouver. *Career:* operatic debut in Vancouver as Donna Elvira in Don Giovanni; British debut as Madam Butterfly with Sadler's Wells Opera; noted for Russian song repertoire; has given many broadcasts of French, German and Russian song repertoire with Geoffrey Parsons; many recital tours; now appears regularly at world's leading opera houses and at major int. music festivals; Vocal and Language Coach (Song/Russian), Royal Acad. of Music; mem. Bd of Dirs and Asst Artistic Adviser, Opera Rara. *Roles include:* Aida, Anna Bolena, Leonore, Norma, Senta, Sieglinde, Turandot, Der Fliegende Holländer, Die Walküre, Fidelio. *Honours:* Hon. ARAM. *Address:* Opera Rara, 134–146 Curtain Road, London, EC2A 3AR (office); Royal Academy of Music, Marylebone Road, London, NW1 5HT, England. *Telephone:* (20) 7613-2858 (Opera Rara) (office). *Fax:* (20) 7613-2261 (Opera Rara) (office). *E-mail:* info@opera-rara.com (office). *Website:* www.opera-rara.com (office).

ANDREW, Sarah; British bassoonist and academic; b. 1975. *Education:* Royal Coll. of Music with Martin Gatt, studied in Vienna. *Career:* co-founded Aurora Ensemble 1997; Co-Principal Bassoonist, Hong Kong Philarmonic Orchestra 1998–2000; Principal Bassoonist, Hong Kong Chamber Orchestra 1998–2000; Asst Principal Bassoonist, BBC Scottish Symphony Orchestra 2002–11; currently teacher, Royal Coll. of Music Junior Dept, London; also performed with Hallé Orchestra, BBC Scottish Symphony Orchestra, Britten Sinfonia; venues include ORF studios, Vienna, Purcell Room (London), Cheltenham and English Music Festivals, South Bank Centre Rimsky-Korsakov Festival and International Akademia Prag-Wien-Budapest; mem. BBC Radio 3 Young Artists' Forum Series, fmr mem. Haffner Wind Ensemble; 2nd bassoon, BBC Scottish Symphony Orchestra. *Honours:* prizewinner, Music d'Ensemble Competition, Paris 2001. *Address:* Royal College of Music, Prince Consort Road, London, SW7 2BS, England (office). *Telephone:* (20) 7591-4334 (office). *E-mail:* jd@rcm.ac.uk (office). *Website:* www.rcm.ac.uk/junior (office).

ANDREYEV, Kostyantyn; Ukrainian singer (tenor); b. 1971, Odessa. *Career:* performed at Ten Tenors Gala, Royal Festival Hall, London 2004; opera roles include Manek in Foerester's Eva, Wexford Festival 2004, title role in Jules Massenet's Werther, Turin 2005, Giosta Berling in I cavalieri di Ekebu, Catania 2006, Puccini's La Bohème, Jerez 2006, Luisa Miller, Leipzig 2006, Carmen, Bari 2006; recitals, London 2005; concerts include with Orchestre Nat. de France at Théâtre des Champs Elysées 2010. *Recordings:* Josef Bohuslav Foerester, Eva 2005. *Current Management:* Atelier Musicale, Via Caselle 76, San Lazzaro di Savena, 40068, Italy. *Telephone:* (51) 19-98-44-44. *Fax:* (51) 19-98-44-20. *E-mail:* info@ateliermusicale.com. *Website:* www.ateliermusicale.com.

ANDRIESSEN, Louis; Dutch composer; b. 6 June 1939, Utrecht; s. of Hendrik Andriessen. *Education:* studied with his father, Royal Conservatory of Music, The Hague with Kees van Baaren, with Luciano Berio in Milan. *Career:* Trilogy of the Last Day received the UK premiere at the 1999 London Prom concerts; Passion – The Music of Louis Andriessen, concert series at South Bank Centre, London 2002; Richard and Barbara Debs Composer's Chair, Carnegie Hall, New York 2009–10. *Compositions include:* stage: Reconstructie (opera, in collaboration with four colleagues) 1968–69, Matthew Passion 1976, Orpheus 1977, George Sand 1980, De Materie 1985–88, ROSA The Death of a Composer 1993–94, Odysseus' Women (ballet) 1995, Writing to Vermeer (music theatre) 1997–98, La Commedia 2008; instrumental and orchestral: Flute Sonata 1956, Percosse for flute, trumpet, bassoon and percussion 1958, Nocturnen for soprano and chamber orchestra 1959, Aanloop en sprongen 1961, A Flower Song I for violin 1963, II for oboe 1963, III for cello 1964, Double for clarinet and piano 1965, Ittrospezione II 1963, Ittrospezione III 1964, Souvenirs d'enfance for piano and tape 1966, Anachronie I 1966–67, Contra tempus 1968, Hoe het is for live electronic improvisers and 52 strings 1969, Uproar for 16 winds, six percussionists and electronic instruments 1970, The Nine Symphonies of Beethoven for promenade orchestra and ice cream bell 1970, Spektakel 1970, Volkslied 1971, The Persistence for piano and winds 1972, De Staat for four women's voices and 27 instruments 1972–76, On Jimmy Yancey 1973, Hymne to the Memory of Darius Milhaud 1974, Il Principe for two choirs, winds, piano and bass guitar 1974, Workers Union 1975, Hoketus 1977, Symphony for open strings 1978, Felicitatie for three trumpets 1979, Mausoleum for two baritones and chamber ensemble 1979, revised 1981, Time for choir and orchestra 1981, Disco for violin and piano 1982, Overture to Orpheus for harpsichord 1982, Velocity 1982–83, Madrigal Concerto for choir 1984, De Stijl 1984–85, De Materie 1985–88, Dubbelspoor 1986, Hadewijch 1988, Facing Death 1990, Hout 1991, Dances 1991–92, Zilver 1994, Trilogy of the Last Day for orchestra 1996–97, Three Dancing on the Bones for children's voices and ensemble 1997, Die Herauten 1997, Inanna's Descent 2000, Bells for Haarlem 2002, Fanfare, to start with 2002, Garden of Eros 2002, Pupazzetti 2002–03, Inanna 2003, Ruttmann 2003, Vermeer Pictures for orchestra 2005, De Opening 2005, ...miserere... 2006–07, The Hague Hacking 2008, Christiaan Andriessen's uitzicht op de Amstel 2009, La Commedia (opera) (Grawemeyer Award for Music Composition 2011). *Honours:* Musical America Award for Composer of the Year 2010. *Address:* c/o Boosey & Hawkes Music Publishers Ltd, Aldwych House, 71–91 Aldwych, London, WC2B 4HN, England (office). *Telephone:* (20) 7054-7200 (office). *E-mail:* composers@boosey.com (office). *Website:* www.boosey.com (office).

ANDSNES, Leif Ove; Norwegian pianist; b. 7 April 1970, Stavanger; m.; three c. *Education:* Bergen Music Conservatory, studied with Jirí Hlinka. *Career:* debut, Oslo 1987; British debut with Oslo Philharmonic, Edinburgh Festival 1989; US debut with Cleveland Orchestra under Neeme Järvi 1990; recitals in London, Berlin, Vienna, Amsterdam, New York (Carnegie Hall); performed with Orchestre Nat. de France, Berlin Philharmonic, Chicago Symphony, BBC Symphony, London Symphony, LA Philharmonic, Japan Philharmonic, New York Philharmonic; soloist, Last Night of the Proms 2002; Co-Artistic Dir Risør Music Festival. *Recordings include:* Rachmaninov Piano Concertos 1 and 2 (Classical BRIT Award for Instrumentalist of the Year 2006, Gramophone Award for Best Concerto Recording 2006) 2005, Horizons (Classical BRIT Award for Instrumentalist of the Year 2007) 2006, Rachmaninov Piano Concertos 3 and 4 2010, Schumann Complete Works for Piano Trio (Gramophone Award for Best Chamber Recording 2012) 2011, The Beethoven Journey Volume 1 (Spellemannpris 2013, Prix Caecilia 2013), also works of Brahms, Chopin, Grieg, Janácek, Liszt, Schumann. *Honours:* Commdr, Royal Norwegian Order of St Olav 2002; first prize, Hindemith Competition, Frankfurt am Main, prizewinner at other int. competitions, Levin Prize (Bergen) 1988, Norwegian Music Critics' Prize 1988, Grieg Prize (Bergen) 1990, Dorothy B. Chandler Performing Arts Award, Los Angeles 1992, Rolf H. Gammeleng Prize 1993, Bragdprisen 1994, Gilmore Prize 1997, Lindeman Prize 1997, Anders Jahres Kulturpris 1999, Royal Philharmonic Soc. Instrumentalist Award 2000, Gramophone Award for Best Concerto Recording 2000, for Best Instrumental Recording 2002, Sibelius Prize 2005, Peer Gynt Prize 2007. *Current Management:* c/o Kathryn Enticott, Enticott Music Management, IMG Artists, The Light Box, 111 Power Road, London, W4 5PY, England. *Telephone:* (20) 7957-5800. *Fax:* (20) 7957-5801. *E-mail:* kathryn@enticottmusicmanagement.com. *Website:* www.andsnes.com.

ANGEL, Marie; Australian singer (soprano); b. 30 July 1953, Pinnaroo, SA; m. David Freeman. *Career:* has sung with Opera Factory London and Opera Factory Zürich in Così fan tutte (Fiordiligi, also televised); The Knot Garden (Denise); Birtwistle's Punch and Judy (Pretty Polly); Aventures by Ligeti; Mahagonny Songspiel; Gluck's Iphigenia operas (title role); Donna Anna and Mozart's Countess Fiordiligi 1991 (all televised); other roles include Euridice in Monteverdi's Orfeo and Hecate and the Oracle of the Dead in the premiere of The Mask of Orpheus 1986 for ENO; Mozart's Queen of Night for WNO; Musetta for Opera North; sang Berio's Recital at South Bank and Jo-Ann for Glyndebourne Touring Opera in Tippett's New Year; created the role of Morgan le Fay in the premiere of Birtwistle's Gawain at Covent Garden 1991; sang Monteverdi's Poppea in a new production by Opera Factory 1992; has also sung Donna Anna for Victoria State Opera and appeared with Houston Grand Opera and at the New York City Opera; created the role of Esmerelda in Rosa, the opera by Peter Greenaway and Louis Andriessen at the Music Theatre, Amsterdam 1994; sang Hecate in The Mask of Orpheus at the Festival Hall, London 1996 (recorded); ENO 1996, as Countess de la Roche in Zimmermann's Die Soldaten, and at Basle 1998–99; Kagel's Aus Deutschland, Dichterin and Kammersängerin, Basle and Holland Festivals 1997; In Satyricon by Maderna, sang Fortunata for Basle and toured to Venice 1998; sang title role in Die Lustige Witwe at Basle Theatre 1999, Michael Nyman's

Facing Goya in Spain 2000, Cixi in Willem Jeth's Hotel de Peking at Nat. Reisopera, Netherlands 2008, Peter Greenaway's Rosa The Death of a Composer, Copenhagen 2010. *Recordings:* Gawain 1994, Andriessen's Rosa (recorded and filmed) 1998, Prospero's Books (P. Greenaway, recorded and filmed) 1989, Hannover, Europera 5 (John Cage) 2001/02, Nyman's Facing Goya (Spanish tour) 2002. *Current Management:* Allied Artists Agency, 42 Montpelier Square, London, SW7 1JZ, England. *Telephone:* (20) 7589-6243. *Fax:* (20) 7581-5269. *E-mail:* info@alliedartists.co.uk. *Website:* www.alliedartists.co.uk.

ANGEL, Ryland; British singer (countertenor and tenor); b. 22 Nov. 1969, Bristol; s. of Rev. Gervais and Evelyn Angel. *Education:* vocal studies with David Mason in London and Gerald Lesne. *Career:* chorister at Bristol Cathedral; appearances in Handel's Amadigi at the Karlsruhe Festival 1996–97, Purcell's Dido and Aeneas, Blow's Venus and Adonis with René Jacobs at De Vlaamse Opera; Peri's Euridice with Opéra Normandie, Play of Daniel in New York, Caldara's oratorio La Santissima Annunziata with Le Parlement de Musique at the Louvre, Paris; settings of Orfeo by Monteverdi and Gluck with ENO and English Touring Opera, Purcell Fairy Queen with the English Bach Festival and for ENO 1998, also with Boston Baroque; further concerts with La Chapelle Royale, Le Concert Spirituel and Les Jeunes Solistes; festival appearances at Lucerne, BBC Proms, Athens, Lufthansa Baroque Festival (London), Boston Early Music Festival and Venice Int. Contemporary Music Festival; sang Zephyrus in Mozart's Apollo et Hyacinthus, Britten Theatre, London 1998, Venus and Adonis conducted by Christophe Rousset at Opéra de Nancy; further engagements include: Bertarido in Handel's Rodelinda with Il Combattimento in Amsterdam, concert tour with La Fenice; season 1999–2000 title role in Handel's Radamisto at St Louis Festival and Non Erat Bonus by Brixi with Musiktheater Transparant; Adrasto in Sant'Alessio, Paris, Nancy, Caen, Luxembourg 2007–08; sang Messiah at Carnegie Hall, New York with Musica Sacra, also Charpentier's The Prodigal Son at Avery Fisher Hall, Lincoln Center 2013; has performed with William Christie, René Jacobs, Ivor Bolton, Roy Goodman, Christophe Rousset, Philippe Herreweghe, Hervé Niquet, Christophe Coin, Gabriel Garrido, Cantus Köln, Le Concert Spirituel, Le Parlement de Musique, Ensemble of Early Music of New York and Ensemble La Fenice. *Recordings include:* Charpentier Messe des Morts, A Bohemian Christmas, Venus and Adonis, O magnum Mysterium, In Sure and Certain Hope, Charpentier Te Deum, The New Voice of Christmas 2007, Ryland Angel 2011, Freud und Lust (Buxtehude and Bach) 2013. *Current Management:* Robert Gilder & Co., N102 Westminster Business Square, 1–45 Durham Street, London, SE11 5JH, England. *Telephone:* (20) 7580-7758 (office). *Fax:* (20) 7580-7739 (office). *E-mail:* rgilder@robert-gilder.com (office). *Website:* (office). *Address:* 39 rue de Rivoli, 75004 Paris, France (home). *Website:* www.rylandangel.com (home).

ANGELICH, Nicholas; American pianist; b. 1970, Cincinnati, OH. *Education:* Conservatoire Nat. Supérieur de Musique, Paris, France with Aldo Ciccolini, Yvonne Loriod and Michel Beroff, numerous masterclasses. *Career:* resident pianist of the Fondazione Internazionale per il Pianoforte, Cadennabia, Italy 1996; performed at the Fourth Annual Miami Int. Piano Festival of Discovery 2001, Mostly Mozart Festival at Lincoln Center, New York 2009; recital debut in Metropolitan Museum of Art's Concert and Lecture series, and Los Angeles Philharmonic debut under Stéphane Denève 2010; many performances of works by Rachmaninov, Prokofiev, Shostakovich, Bartók, Ravel, Messiaen, Stockhausen, Boulez, Tanguy and Pierre Henry. *Recordings:* Rachmaninov: Etudes–Tableaux, Brahms: Sonates pour alto et piano, Ravel: Miroirs, Gaspard de la nuit, La Valse, Liszt: Les Années de pélerinage, Brahms: Piano Trios, Brahms: Violin Sonatas 2005, Brahms trios (Preis der deutschen Schallplattenkritik), Sonatas for violin and piano, Brahms: Piano Concerto No. 1, Fauré: Complete Chamber Music for Strings and Piano (ECHO Klassik Award for Chamber Music Recording of the Year 2012) 2011. *Honours:* Second Prize R. Casadesus Int. Competition, Cleveland 1989, Fifth Prize Tokyo Int. Competition, First Prize Gina Bachauer Int. Competition 1994, Second Prize Umberto Micheli Competition 1997, Instrumental Soloist of the Year, Les Victoires 2013. *Address:* c/o Jacques Thelen, 15 ave Montaigne, 75008 Paris, France.

ANGELO, Mariana; Bulgarian singer (soprano); b. 1954, Sofia. *Education:* Conservatoire of Sofia. *Career:* sang at the Komische Oper Berlin, 1978–84; Berne Opera, 1984–86; has appeared at the Nationaltheater Mannheim, 1987–, and has sung as guest at Dresden, Karlsruhe, Sofia, Graz, Nancy, Paris, Ghent and Antwerp; Lausanne Opera, 1989, as Liu in Turandot; other roles include Verdi's Leonora (Il Trovatore and La Forza del Destino), Amelia Grimaldi, Aida, Violetta and Desdemona; Puccini's Mimi, Manon Lescaut and Madama Butterfly; Nedda, Tatiana and Mathilde in Guillaume Tell; sang Aida at the Berlin Staatsoper, 1991. *Address:* c/o Music International, 13 Ardilaun Road, London N5 2QR, England.

ANGERER, Paul; Austrian conductor, composer and instrumentalist; b. 16 May 1927, Vienna; s. of Otto Angerer and Elisabeth Angerer; m. Anita Rosser 1952; two s. two d. *Education:* Hochschule für Musik und darstellende Kunst, Vienna. *Career:* viola player, Vienna Symphony Orchestra 1947, leading solo viola player 1953–57; viola player, Tonhalle Zürich 1948, Suisse Romande Orchestra, Geneva 1949; Dir and Chief Conductor, Chamber Orch. of Wiener Konzerthausgesellschaft 1956–63; composer and conductor, Burgtheater, Vienna and Salzburg and Bregenz festivals 1960–; Perm. Guest Conductor, Orchestra Sinfonica di Bolzano e Trento 'Haydn' 1964–90; First Conductor, Bonn City Theatre 1964–66; Music Dir Ulm Theatre 1966–68; Chief of Opera, Salzburger Landestheater 1967–72; Dir SW German Chamber Orch., Pforzheim 1971–82; Prof. Hochschule, Vienna 1983–92; Moderator ORF 1984–2001, Radio Stephansdom 2001; Leader of Concilium Musicum Vienna. *Works include:* orchestral pieces, chamber works, viola and piano concertos, a dramatic cantata, television opera, works for organ, harp, viola, harpsichord, etc.; numerous recordings both as soloist and conductor. *Publications:* Und s'ist alles nicht wahr! Briefe eines Eipeldauers, Mozart auf Reisen: Reisebriefe Leopold Mozarts aus Wien 1762–63, 1767–69, 1773, aus Paris und London 1763, aus Italien 1771–73. *Honours:* Austrian Order of Honour for Sciences and Arts First Class 2001; several prizes including Austrian State Prize for Music 1956, Theodor Körner Prize 1958, Vienna Cultural Prize 1983, Cultural Prize of Lower Austria 1987; Nestroy-Ring, City of Vienna 1998. *Address:* Esteplatz 3/26, 1030 Vienna, Austria. *Telephone:* (676) 84036244 (mobile). *E-mail:* paulangerer@concilium.at (home).

ANGERMÜLLER, Rudolph Kurt, MA, PhD; German/Austrian music editor and music librarian; *General Secretary, International Mozarteum Foundation*; b. 2 Sept. 1940, Bielefeld, Germany; m. Hannelore Johannböke; one s. one d. *Education:* Försterling Conservatory of Music, Bielefeld. *Career:* Asst, Musicology Inst., Univ. of Salzburg; Chief Ed., New Mozart Edition, and Librarian, Int. Mozarteum Foundation 1972–; Chief of Research Dept, Int. Mozarteum Foundation 1981–, Gen. Sec. 1988, Prof. 1993; mem. Int. Musicological Soc., Soc. for Music Research, Austrian Musicological Soc. *Publications:* Untersuchungen zur Geschichte des Carmen-Stoffes 1967, Antonio Salieri, Sein Leben und seine weltichen Werke unter besonderer Berücksichtigung seiner grossen Opern, 3 Vols 1971, 1972, 1974, W. A. Mozarts Musikalische Umwelt in Paris 1778, Eine Dokumentation 1982, Mozart's Operas 1988, Ich johannes chrisostomus Amadeus Wolfgangus Sigismundus Mozart 1991, Mozarts Reisen in Italien 1994, Franz Xaver Wolfgang Mozart, Reisetagebuch 1819–1821 1994, Mozart auf der Reise nach Prag, Dresden, Leipzig und Berlin 1995, Geistliche Werke von Antonio Salieri in der Hofkapelle in Wien 1996, Francesco Benucci: Mozarts erster Figaro und Guglielmo 1998, Pariser Don Juan: Rezensionen 1805–1806 1998, Antonio Salieri: Dokumente seines Lebens 2000, Angewandte Systemforschung 2002, Angetörnt 2004, Florilegium Pratense. Mozart, seine Zeit, seine Nachwelt 2005, Biographie W. A. Mozarts (Ed.) 2010; contrib. to Bulletin of the International Mozarteum Foundation, Mozart-Jahrbuch, Haydn-Jahrbuch, Die Musikforschung, Österreichische Musikzeitschrift, Wiener Figaro, Musical Times, Deutsches Jahrbuch für Musikwissenschaft, numerous other professional journals and books. *Honours:* Socio Accademia degli Agiati Rovereto 1995, Socio d'onore R. Accademia Filarmonica di Bologna 1997, Stella d'oro al valor mozartiano 2001. *Address:* 92A Moosstrasse, 5020 Salzburg, Austria. *Telephone:* 826735 (office).

ANGERVO-KARTTUNEN, Heljä, BA; Finnish singer (mezzo-soprano); b. 3 June 1940, Helsinki; d. of Prof. Kyösti Angervo and Piippa Angervo; m. Antero Karttunen 1963; one s. *Education:* Sibelius Acad., Helsinki and Helsinki Univ. *Career:* debut 1964, with Finnish Nat. Opera as Dorabella in Così fan tutte; performances with Finnish Nat. Opera 1965–94, Asst Dir 1992–, Artistic Co-ordinator 1994–2001; performances with Hamburg State Opera 1974–75; guest appearances with Berlin Philharmonic Orchestra, BBC Symphony Orchestra and numerous other orchestras and at Bayreuth Festival 1974, Salzburg Festival 1972–77; mem. jury of several int. competitions; numerous recordings. *Honours:* Pro Finlandia Prize 1986. *Address:* Laajalahdentie 19A, Helsinki 00330, Finland. *E-mail:* helja.angervo@welho.com.

ANGUS, David Anthony, BMus; British conductor; *Music Director, Glimmerglass Opera*; b. 2 Feb. 1955, Reading, England; m.; one d. *Education:* Surrey Univ., Leeds Univ., Royal Northern Coll. of Music. *Career:* debut as chorister at King's College, Cambridge; Chorus Master and Staff Conductor, Glyndebourne 1989–95; fmr Principal Conductor, Symphony Orchestra of Flanders, currently Hon. Conductor; conducted most major orchestras in the UK, including London Philharmonic Orchestra, Scottish Chamber Orchestra, BBC Philharmonic, Scottish Symphony, and London Mozart Players; many performances at Glyndebourne, Opera North and Aldeburgh Festival; appears regularly in Italy; broadcasts with BBC Orchestra and BBC Singers; appeared in Denmark, Norway, Finland, Austria, Belgium and France; USA debut with Glimmerglass Opera 2006; Music Dir Glimmerglass Opera 2008–; Music Dir Boston Lyric Opera 2010–; specialises in Mozart, romantic and 20th Century opera. *Recordings:* Richard Rodney Bennett's Piano Concerto with Nat. Symphony Orchestra of Ireland, Dvorak's Symphony No.8 with Symphony Orchestra of Flanders, The World Quintet with London Mozart Players and Herbert Grönemeyer, Aurora with London Mozart Players, Britten's Curlew River, modern British choral and orchestral works with London Philharmonic Orchestra. *Honours:* three Ricordi prizes for opera conducting 1985–87. *Current Management:* Patrick Garvey Management, 40 North Parade, York, YO30 7AB, England. *Telephone:* (1904) 621222. *Fax:* (1723) 514678. *E-mail:* patrick@patrickgarvey.com. *Website:* www.patrickgarvey.com. *E-mail:* david@david-angus.com (office). *Website:* www.david-angus.com.

ANIEVAS, Agustin; American pianist and fmr teacher; b. 11 June 1934, New York. *Education:* Juilliard School of Music, New York with Steuermann, Samaroff and Marcus. *Career:* formal debut as soloist with the Little Orchestra Soc., New York 1952; later toured North and South America, Europe, Australia and the Far East; performances in SE Asia, including appearances and master classes at Beijing Piano Festival 2012; Prof. of Piano, City Univ. of New York Brooklyn Coll. Conservatory 1974–99. *Recordings:* For

Angel-EMI and Seraphim, notably of music by Bartók, Prokofiev, Rachmaninov, Chopin and Liszt, Schumann Fantasie in C and Chopin Etudes 2011. *Honours:* Concert Artists Guild Award 1959, first prize, Dimitri Mitropoulos Competition 1961. *Current Management:* Parker Artists, 382 Central Park West, New York, NY 10025, USA. *Telephone:* (212) 864-7928. *Website:* www .parkerartists.com. *E-mail:* gusncarol@gmail.com (office). *Website:* www .agustinanievas.com.

ANISIMOV, Alexander; Russian singer (bass); b. 1960, Fergana. *Education:* studied with Yuri Barsov in Tashkent. *Career:* debut as soloist with the Bolshoi Opera, Moscow 1990; sang major roles in Tchaikovsky's Iolanta and Glinka's A Life for the Tzar 1990; int. debut as the Old Convict in Shostakovich's Lady Macbeth of Mtsensk at the Paris Opera in a production that also travelled to La Scala, conducted by Myung-Whun Chung 1992; debut with La Scala, Milan as The Grand Inquisitore in new production by Franco Zefferelli of Verdi's Don Carlo with Luciano Pavarotti, conducted by Riccardo Muti, also performed at La Scala as Commendatore in Mozart's Don Giovanni with Muti; sang Prince Gremin in Tchaikovsky's Eugene Oneguin at Chatelet Theater in Paris, conducted by Semyon Bychkov; Metropolitan Opera debut as the Old Convict in Shostakovich's Lady Macbeth of Mtsensk under the baton of James Conlon 1994, regular guest at the Met, appeared as Lodovico in opening night production of Verdi's Otello with Placido Domingo and Renee Fleming, conducted by James Levine; operatic engagements include Fiesco (Simon Boccanegra) with L'Opera de Nancy Zaccaria (Nabucco) and Il Padre Guardiano (La Forza del Destino) at New Jersey State Opera, Banco (Macbeth) and Raimondo (Lucia di Lammermoor) in Tenerife, Ramfis (Aida) at the Met, Aspen Festival, Dallas Opera, Timur (Turandot) for Metropolitan Opera, Lyric Opera of Chicago, Oroveso (Norma) with Canadian Opera Co., Sarastro (Zauberflöte) in Baltimore, Basilio (Barbiere di Siviglia) in Bogota and Las Palmas, Sparafucile (Rigoletto) at the Met, Berlin State Opera, Vigevano Festival, Canadian Opera Co. and Israel Philharmonic Orchestra, King Dodon in Rimsky-Korsakov's The Golden Cockerel at Nice Opera, Lodovico (Otello) with Minnesota Orchestra and the Met, Boris Godunov (Boris Godunov) with Milwaukee Symphony Orchestra and Seattle Opera, Pimen (Boris Godunov) in Frankfurt Opera and in Geneva, King Rene (Iolanta) with Canadian Opera Co., Gremin (Eugen Onegin) in Paris, Chatelet, St Gallen and Seattle Opera, Inquisitore, Frate, Filippo (Don Carlo) in Palm Beach, Barcelona, La Scala, the Met, Old Convict (Lady Macbeth of Mtsensk) in Geneva, Cologne, La Scala, the Met, Paris Opera, Dresden, Commendatore (Don Giovanni) in Frankfurt Opera, La Scala, Bavarian State Opera, Konchak (Prince Igor), Ruslan (Ruslan and Ludmila), Mefistofele (Mefistofele), Father (Aleko), Demon (The Demon), Kochubey (Mazeppa), Silva (Ernani), Pistol (Falstaff), Prochida (I Vespri Siciliani); also appeared in The Gambler at the Met, Attila in Florence, Un Ballo in Maschera at San Diego Opera, Madam Butterfly at Bastille Opera, Ivan el Terrible (Prokofiev) with Orquestra Sinfonica de Tenerife; concert performances include Verdi's Requiem with Jerusalem Symphony Orchestra, Connecticut Orchestra, Vlaamse Opera, Orquestra Sinfonica de Tenerife and Madrid Philharmonic, Janacek's Glagolitic Mass with London Philharmonic Orchestra, BBC Symphony Orchestra, conducted by Andrew Davis, along with scenes from Boris Godunov, at Festival de Saint-Denis in Paris with Charles Dutoit and Orchestre Nat. de France; has sung in concerts with Cleveland Symphony Orchestra conducted by Christoph von Dohnanyi and BBC Proms with Mark Elder, in Gala concerts in Montreal and Deutsche Oper Berlin AIDS Benefit Gala, as well as in recitals in Colmar and Rheingau Festivals, in Jahrhunderthalle, Frankfurt; other concert performances include Oroveso in Bellini's Norma at Carnegie Hall and gala concerts in Germany, Spain, Russia, Canada, US, SA and Japan; sang recitals in Alte Oper Frankfurt and Gremin (Eugen Onegin) with Seattle Opera, where he debuted in title role of Boris Godunov (Performer of the Season Award) 2000; sang Pimen (Boris Godunov) in Geneva, Gremin (Eugene Onegin) with J. Kout in St Gallen and King Dodon (The Golden Cockerel) in Toulouse where he returned as Pimen in Boris Godunov 2005 under baton of Bernhard Kontarsky, Timur (Turandot) in Stadium in Paris, Munich and Gelsenkirschen; season 2005–06, sang the Devil (Cherevichki/Tchaikovsky) in La Scala, Angelotti (Tosca) and Old Cardinal in world premier of Galilee by Michael Jarrell in Geneva; season 2006–07, appeared in concerts of Shostakovich's Symphony No. 13 (Baby Yar) with Bochumer Symphoniker, as Ramfis (Aida) in Liège, Janácek's Glagolitic Mass in Alte Oper Frankfurt. *Recordings include:* Opera Gala with Young Artists, Berlin Radio Symphony Orchestra, conductor Jun Märkl; Don Carlo, Aria, Act IV: Elle giammai m'amo; La Boheme, Finale, Act I; Koch-Schwann 1993; Tchaikovsky – Eugene Onegin, conductor Semyon Bychkov; Arkhipova, Focile, Borodina, Walker, Hvorostovsky, Shicoff, Anisimov (Prince Gremin) 1994; Orthodox Church Chants Bewahr' uns, Herr, die Glaubenskraft... with Academy of Choral Arts, Moscow, conductor Victor Popov 2000; Verdi – Don Carlo (recorded live), Orchestra e coro del Teatro alla Scala, conductor Riccardo Muti; Ramey, Pavarotti, Dessi, Coni, d'Intino, Anisimov (Grand Inquisitore) 1994, (DVD) 2004; Verdi – Otello (recorded live), Metropolitan Opera, conductor James Levine; Domingo, Fleming, Morris, Croft, Anisimov (Lodovico) (DVD) 2004; Puccini Turandot (recorded live), Stade de France, conductor János Acs; Gordei, Martinucci, Hong, La Guardia, Anisimov (Timur) (DVD) 2005. *Honours:* winner Glinka Competition 1987, Tchaikovsky Competition 1990.

ANISIMOVA, Tanya; American (b. Russian) cellist and composer; b. (Tatiana Mikhailovna Anisimova), 15 Feb. 1966, Grozny; d. of Mikhail Anisimova and Zoia Anisimova; m. Alexander Anufriev. *Education:* Central

Music School, Moscow, 1975–84; studied cello with Natalia Shakhovskaya, Igor Gavrysh, Galina Kozolupov; Assistantship, Cello, String Quartet, Graduate School, Moscow Conservatory 1989–90; studied with George Neikrug, Artist's Diploma, Boston Univ. 1990–92; graduate studies with Aldo Parisot, Yale Univ. School of Music 1992–. *Career:* solo recitals, Russia, Massachusetts, Virginia, Washington DC, and soloist with orchestras, Young Performers Series, Moscow, Minsk, Gorky, Ulianovsk, Lugansk and local Philharmonic Orchestras, Russia, and Central Massachusetts Symphony, USA 1985–91; moved to USA 1990; performances with Glazunov String Quartet in Russia, Poland, Greece, Japan, Germany; Artist-in-Residence, Banff Music Festival 1993; appearances in 2009 at Wintergreen Summer Music Festival, Middlebury Summer Festival in Vermont, Morelia Int. Music Festival in Mexico, as well as concerts in Beijing and Tianjin, China; works performed by Russian Chamber Orchestra, St Petersburg String Quartet, Prokofiev Quartet, cellists Paul Katz and Igor Gavrysh, and others; radio broadcasts in Europe, Asia, North America, and Australia. *Compositions:* Seasons cello concerto (premiered at The Sandler Center for the Performing Arts, Virginia Beach by Anisimova and Symphonicity Orchestra 2008), Appalachi for Violin, Cello & Piano (premiered at Wintergreen Music Festival 2009), Trio for clarinet, piano and cello (premiered by Ilya Itin, Julian Milkis and Anisimova in Chamber Concerts at Sugden Theatre, Naples, Florida 2010). *Recordings:* Bach Complete Sonatas and Partitas for Solo Violin 2001, Bach Six Cello Suites 2004, Sufi Soul – Tanya Performs Tanya 2006, Mystical Strings – The Enchanted Cello, Brahms Complete Sonatas for Cello and Piano and Violin and Piano. *Publications:* contrib. to magazines, reviews, journals. *Honours:* 1st Prize, Concertino Praha Int. Competition, Prague 1981; 1st Prize, All-Union String Quartet Competition, Voronezh, Russia 1987. *E-mail:* tanya@tanyaanisimova.com (home). *Website:* www.tanyaanisimova.com (home).

ANISSIMOV, Alexander; Russian conductor; *Principal Conductor, National Symphony Orchestra of Belarus;* b. (Alexander Mikhailovich Anissimov), 1947. *Education:* St Petersburg Conservatory and Moscow Conservatory. *Career:* Prin. Conductor Bolshoi Theatre, Belarus 1980; Founder and Conductor Nat. Youth Orchestra of Belarus; Prin. Guest Conductor, Radio Telefís Éireann (RTÉ) Nat. Symphony Orchestra, Dublin 1995–98, Prin. Conductor 1998–2001, Conductor Emer. 2001–11; currently Prin. Conductor Nat. Symphony Orchestra of Belarus; Prin. Conductor and Music Dir Rostov State Musical Theatre 2003–; Prin. Conductor Busan Philharmonic 2005–; regular Guest Conductor with Nat. Youth Orchestra of Ireland; Prin. Conductor Belorussian State Philharmonic 1996, Nat. Philharmonic Orchestra of Belarus 2001, Opera Rostov-on-the-Don, Russia 2003; has conducted world-wide, including Bolshoi Theatre (Moscow), Kirov Opera (St Petersburg), Opéra Bastille (Paris), Staatsoper Hamburg, Komische Oper Berlin, State Opera of South Australia, Norske Opera (Oslo), North Holland Sinfonia, Concertgebouw (Amsterdam), Opera Ireland, Teatro del Liceo (Barcelona), Teatro Colón (Buenos Aires), San Francisco Opera, Houston Grand Opera, La Fenice (Venice), Florence Opera. *Recordings include:* Beethoven Symphony No. 9 in D minor, Alexander Konstantinovich Glazunov Orchestral Works Vol. 1 (Raymonda, Op. 57), Vol. 5 (Symphonies Nos 2 & 7 'Pastoral'), Vol. 7 (Symphonies Nos 1 'Slavyanskaya' & 4), Vol. 8 (The Seasons, Op. 67, Op. 52, Op. 81), Vol. 12 (Symphonies Nos 3 & 9), Vol. 13 (Symphony No. 6, Op. 58 Symphonic Poem 'The Forest', Op. 19), Vol. 15 (Symphonies Nos 5 & 8), Rachmaninov Symphony Vol. 1 and Op. 13 Caprice Bohémien and Op. 12, Rachmaninov Symphony No. 2, Rachmaninov Symphony No. 3 and Op. 44 Mélodie in E Polichinelle, Rachmaninov The Bells Op. 35, Mahler Symphony No. 2 'The Resurrection', Anton Rubinstein The Demon, Tchaikovsky Symphony No. 5 and Concerto No. 1, Classical Favourites Vols 1 and 2, Vivat Opera Live 1999. *Honours:* Hon. Pres. Wagner Soc. of Ireland 2002–; Hon. DMus (Nat. Univ. of Ireland) 2001. *Website:* www.askonasholt.co.uk/artists/conductors/alexander-anissimov.

ANNEAR, Gwynneth; Australian singer (soprano, mezzo-soprano); b. 1939, Tailenbend. *Education:* University of Adelaide, Royal College of Music, London. *Career:* debut, sang in Amahl and the Night Visitors while at the Royal College of Music, 1964; Sang the title role in Anna Bolena by Donizetti at the 1965 Glyndebourne Festival; Tour of Italy with Italian Company, 1968, in Fidelio and Così fan tutte; Has sung at the Camden Festival and with opera companies in Australia; Frequent broadcasts and concert engagements; Glyndebourne Festival 1970 and 1973, First Lady in Die Zauberflöte.

ANRAKU, Mariko, BM, MM; Japanese harpist; *Associate Principal Harpist, Metropolitan Opera Orchestra;* b. 7 March 1970. *Education:* Juilliard School, New York, Royal Conservatory of Music, Toronto, Canada. *Career:* debut as soloist with Toronto Symphony led by Sir Andrew Davis; recitals at Weill Recital Hall at Carnegie Hall and Merkin Concert Hall, New York, Jordan Hall, Boston, Bing Theater at Los Angeles Co. Museum, Opéra Comique de Paris, Palazzo dell'Esposizione, Rome and Casals, Kioi and Oji Halls, Tokyo etc; soloist with numerous orchestras including Vienna Chamber Orchestra, New Japan Philharmonic Orchestra, Yomiuri Symphony Orchestra, Tokyo Symphony, Israel Philharmonic Orchestra and Concert Soloists of Philadelphia; performances at festivals including Donaueschinger Musiktage, Tubingen and Köln in Germany, Spoleto in Italy, Festival of Sound and Banff in Canada, Karuizawa and Takefu in Japan, Newport, Tanglewood and Bridgehampton Festivals in USA, and Wien Modern in Austria; performed premieres of works by Toshio Hosokawa and Jean-Michel Damase's Concerto Ballade with Cincinnati Chamber Orchestra at the American Harp Soc. Conf.; Assoc.

Prin. Harpist, Metropolitan Opera Orchestra 1995–. *Recordings:* Mariko Anraku harp recital I and II 1997, 1998, Eternal Story 2002, Beau Soir (French and Japanese melodies, with Emmanuel Pahud, flute) 2003. *Honours:* First Prize, First Int. Harp Competition, Japan 1989, Third Prize and the Pearl Chertok Prize, Int. Harp Contest, Israel 1992, Pro Musicis Int. Award 1993, First Prize, Channel Classics Recording Prize and Corpn Prize, Concert Artists Guild Competition, NY 1995. *Current Management:* Columbia Artists Management, 1790 Broadway, New York, 10019, USA. *Telephone:* (212) 841-9568 (office). *Website:* www.cami.com (home). *Address:* c/o The Metropolitan Opera Orchestra, Lincoln Center, New York, NY 10023, USA (office).

ANSELL, Gillian, MNZM; New Zealand violist; b. 1968, Auckland. *Education:* Royal Coll. of Music, London, Musikhochschule Cologne with Igor Ozim and the Amadeus Quartet. *Career:* played with Kent Opera Orchestra, Chamber Orchestra of Europe and Philharmonia 1984; co-founder, New Zealand String Quartet, under auspices of Music Federation of New Zealand 1987–; debut concert, Wellington 1988; concerts at Tanglewood School, USA, Banff Int. Competition, Canada; premiered over 40 works for string quartet; performances with Lindsay Quartet at Int. Festival of the Arts, Wellington 1990; soloist with New Zealand Symphony Orchestra; Artist-in-Residence, Victoria Univ., Wellington; tour to Australia for Musica Viva Australia 1990; New Zealand tours 1992; concerts in New York 1993; co-Artistic Dir, Adam New Zealand Festival of Chamber Music 2001–; played at State Funeral for Sir Edmund Hillary. *Recordings include:* with New Zealand String Quartet: Debussy & Ravel String Quartets 1999, Beethoven Rasumovsky Quartets 2002, Székely Quartet and Dvořák Quartet in Eb major 2003, Berg/Wolf 2007, Mendelssohn: String Quartets Vols 1, 2 & 3 2008, Bartók: The Complete String Quartets 2009, Notes from a Journey 2010. *Current Management:* Sarah Bruce, Lomonaco Artists, 11 Wotton Court, 6 Jamestown Way, London, E14 2DB, England. *Telephone:* (20) 7538 2203. *E-mail:* info@lomonaco-artists.com. *Website:* www.lomonaco-artists.com. *Telephone:* (4) 463-5866 (office). *E-mail:* ga@nzsq.co.nz (office). *Website:* www.nzsq.co.nz.

ANSYARI, Juhad; Indonesian oboist and conductor; *Chief Conductor Jakarta Symphony Orchestra*; b. Yogyakarta. *Education:* High School of Music, Yogyakarta, Institut Seni Indonesia, Rotterdam Conservatory, Netherlands. *Career:* represented Indonesia in ASEAN Music Workshop 1991; fmrly Prin. Oboist, ASEAN Youth Orchestra; oboist in several orchestras including Jakarta Symphony Orchestra, Twilite Orchestras, Nusantara Symphony Orchestra, Amadeus Orchestra; fmr guest performer, Singapore Symphony Orchestra; Chief Conductor, Jakarta Symphony Orchestra 2003–. *Address:* Jakarta Symphony Orchestra, Komplek Jatipadang Baru, Blok F No 1, Jakarta 12540, Indonesia (office). *Telephone:* (217) 804910 (office). *Fax:* (217) 8842848 (office). *E-mail:* info@thejakartasymphony.com (office). *Website:* www.thejakartasymphony.com (office).

ANTHONY, Susan B.; American singer (soprano); b. 1959, Kalamazoo, Michigan. *Education:* Western Michigan Univ., Zürich Opera Studio. *Career:* appearances in opera throughout Europe from 1985; Berlin Staatsoper from 1991 as the Trovatore Leonora, Ines in L'Africaine; Elena in Vespri Siciliani and Eva in Die Meistersinger, 1994; sang Strauss's Daphne, 1991, and Leonore in Fidelio, 1996, Rome Opera; Bregenz, 1995; season 1995–96 as Tatiana at Cologne and Elsa in Lohengrin at the Vienna Staatsoper; Geneviève in Chausson's Roi Arthus at Bregenz and Cologne and Freia in Das Rheingold at La Scala and Hamburg; season 1997 in Fidelio at Buenos Aires; season 1998 as Leonore in Paris, Marie in Wozzeck at Montpellier; sang Maria in Strauss's Friedenstag at Dresden; Senta in Tokyo and Fidelio in Vienna; season 1999 as Elsa in Paris and Vienna; Ariadne and Empress in Frau ohne Schatten in Dresden; Liebe der Danaë in Munich and Marie in Wozzeck in Cologne; season 2000 with Salome in Bologna, Ariadne at La Scala and Frau ohne Schatten in Dresden and at Vienna Staatsoper, Barcelona; world premiere of 'K' by Phillipe Manouri, Bastille Opéra; Brünnhilde (Siegfried) at Grand Théâtre, Geneva; Elektra at Santa Fe Opera; season 2002–04 in Paris as the Empress in Strauss's Frau and also in Vienna and Dresden and new productions in the Deutsche Oper, Berlin, Washington, Rome, Barcelona and two in Tokyo; Senta in Madrid, with Barenboim 2003, and at Unter den Linden and Richard Wagner Festival Wels 2006, Gran Teatro del Liceu, Barcelona 2007; Leonora in Fidelio in Hamburg 2004; Marietta in Barcelona and Madrid 2006, Salome at Concertgebouw, Amsterdam 2007, Ghita in Der Zwerg at Los Angeles Opera 2008; performances in 2009 included Fidelio in Seoul, Cassandra at Deutsche Oper Berlin and Elektra at Semperoper Dresden; in concert, Verdi Requiem in Picayune, Miss. 2005 and Mostly Mozart in Kalamazoo 2008. *Recordings:* Ernest Chausson's Le Roi Artus, Zemlinsky's Der Traumgörge, Arte Nova Voices (with Slovak Radio Symphony Orchestra, Bratislava), Portrait 2004. *Honours:* Opernwelt Singer of the Year 1995–96, 1997–98. *Current Management:* Laifer Artists Management, 410 W 24th Street, Suite 2i, New York, NY 10011-1369, USA. *Telephone:* (212) 929-7429. *Fax:* (212) 633-2628. *E-mail:* laiferart@aol.com. *Website:* www.laiferart.com; www.susan-anthony.com.

ANTINORI, Nazzareno; Italian singer (tenor); b. 2 July 1950, Anzio. *Education:* Accademia di Santa Cecilia, Rome. *Career:* debuted as Pinkerton in Madam Butterfly, Teatro dell'Opera, Rome 1979, repeated at Verona Arena 1983; appearances at Naples, Trieste, Macerata and Palermo; sang Forresto in Atilla, La Scala, Milan 1991; other roles have included Verdi's Ismaele, Alfredo, Malcolm, Don Carlos, Cavaradossi, Maurizio in Adriana Lecouvreur, Števa in Jenůfa, Cavaradossi, Ismaele; also teacher of singing, Conservatorio di Musica G.B. Pergolesi, Fermo, and Artistic Dir of Lyric Theatre, Scuola Civica Beniamino Gigli, Recanati and Istituto del Melodramma Mario del Monaco; masterclasses in Anzio, Ischia, Tokyo and New York 2008–10. *Recordings:* Tosca and Madama Butterfly. *Honours:* winner, ENAL, Palermo, Mario de Monaco competition, Maria Callas Competition 1980. *Address:* Via del Velini 131, 62100 Macerata, Italy (home). *E-mail:* info@nazzarenoantinori.com (home). *Website:* nazzarenoantinori.com (home).

ANTOINE, Bernadette; French singer (soprano); b. 8 March 1940, Nancy. *Education:* Conservatories of Nancy and Paris. *Career:* debut at Theatre Region Parisienne 1967, as Musetta; has sung at the Grand Opéra and the Opéra-Comique, Paris and in Lyon, Marseille, Toulouse, Rouen, Hamburg, Brussels, Lisbon and Geneva; ORTF, Radio France, in the 1972 premiere of Don Juan ou l'amour de la geometrie by Semenov; Strasbourg 1974, in the premiere of Les Liaisons Dangereuses by Prey; Repertoire includes works by Gluck, Mozart, Puccini, Berlioz, Debussy, Poulenc, Britten and Prokofiev; Many concert appearances; Member of the Saarbrücken Opera, 1985–86. *Recordings include:* Honegger: Les Aventures Du Roi Pausole 1995, Lehár: Le Pays du Sourire 2005, Gounod's Mireille 2007.

ANTOKOLETZ, Elliott Maxim, BA, MA, PhD; American musicologist, academic and writer; *Professor of Musicology, University of Texas, Austin*; b. 3 Aug. 1942, Jersey City, NJ; s. of Jack Antokoletz and Esther Antokoletz; m. Juana Canabal 1972; one s. *Education:* Juilliard School of Music, Hunter Coll., Graduate School and Univ. Center, City Univ. of New York. *Career:* Lecturer and mem. of faculty string quartet, Queens Coll., CUNY 1973–76; Prof. of Musicology, Univ. of Texas, Austin 1976–, Head of Musicology Div. 1992–94, Tacquard Endowed Centennial Chair. 1983–84, E.W. Doty Prof. in Fine Arts 1994–95; Co-ed. International Journal of Musicology 1992–; mem. American Musicological Soc. *Publications include:* The Music of Béla Bartók: A Study of Tonality and Progression in Twentieth-Century Music 1984, Béla Bartók: A Guide to Research 1988, Twentieth-Century Music 1992, Bartók Perspectives (co-ed. with V. Fischer and B. Suchoff) 2000, Musical Symbolism in the Operas of Debussy and Bartók 2004; contrib. three chapters to The Bartók Companion, one chapter to Sibelius Studies, one chapter to Copland and his World; contrib. to scholarly books and professional journals. *Honours:* Nat. Endowment for the Humanities Grants 1980, 1982, Béla Bartók Memorial Plaque and Diploma 1981, Teaching Excellence Award 1981, PhD Alumni Award, CUNY 1987. *Address:* School of Music, University of Texas, 1 University Station, E3100, Austin, TX 78712, USA (office). *Telephone:* (512) 471-7764 (office). *Fax:* (512) 441-7520 (office). *E-mail:* antokoletz@mail.utexas.edu (office). *Website:* www.music.utexas.edu (office).

ANTONACCI, Anna Caterina; Italian singer (soprano); b. 5 April 1961, Ferrara. *Education:* Bologna Conservatory. *Career:* initial experience in Bologna Comunale Theatre Chorus; debut as Rosina, Arezzo 1986; subsequent roles include Flora in La Traviata, Bologna, Dorliska in Torvaldo and Dorliska, Savona 1988, Elcia in Mosè in Egitto, Rome 1988 and London 1994, Horatia in Gli Orazi ed i Curiazi, Cimarosa, Rome 1989 and Lisbon, Elizabeth in Maria Stuarda, Bari 1989, Ninetta in La gazza ladra, Philadelphia 1989, and Zelmira, Rome 1989; sang Fiordiligi at Venice and Macerata, Adalgisa at Catania, Polyxena in Manfroce's Ecuba and the title role of Paisiello's Elfrida at Savona 1990; Anaide in Mosè, Bologna 1991, Semiramide Catania 1991, Elisabetta, regina d'Inghilterra, Naples 1991, title role of Ermione, Rome 1991, London 1992 (also Buenos Aires, San Francisco concert performance and Glyndebourne for two seasons), Elena in La donna del lago, Amsterdam 1992; other roles at this time include Mayr's La rosa bianca e la rosa rossa at Bergamo, Polissena in Manfroce's Ecuba; sang Donna Elvira in Ferrara, Gluck's Alceste in Vienna and Berlin and Gluck's Armide at La Scala; an Adalgisa in Catania 1990, which she later sang at San Francisco and in Naples 1995; sang Monteverdi's Poppea in Bologna, Milan and Buenos Aires, the title role in Gluck's Armide at La Scala 1996, and Angelina in La Cenerentola, Toronto 1996; season 1999 included Fiordiligi at Naples, Rodelinda at Glyndebourne, Donna Elvira at Vienna and Ravenna, and Gluck's Armide and Paisiello's Nina at La Scala; season 2001–02, sang Dido at Florence, Marchesa del Poggia in Un giorno di regno at Bologna, and Elisabetta in a concert performance of Maria Stuarda in Edinburgh; recent roles include Agrippina at the Barbican 2003, Cassandra in Les Troyens at the Chatelet Theatre 2003, Carmen for Glyndebourne 2004 and Covent Garden 2006, Cherubini's Medea at the Chatelet in 2005, Alceste in Salzburg Festival 2005, Nerone in L' incoronazione di Poppea in Cremona, Como, Ferrara, Pavia, Ravenna 2005–06, Poppea in L' incoronazione di Poppea, Munich 2006, Vitellia in La Clemenza di Tito, Geneva 2006, Carmen at Covent Garden 2006; concerts/recitals Luxembourg and Wigmore Hall, London 2006. *Recordings include:* Paisiello's Elfrida, Mayr's La Rosa Bianca e La Rosa Rossa, Polissena in Manfroce's Ecuba, Fiordiligi in Così fan tutte, Ermione, Puccini's Messa di Gloria, Stravinsky's Pulcinella, Pergolesi's Stabat Mater, Era la notte 2006, Berlioz, Cléopatre 2011. *Honours:* Chevalier, Légion d'Honneur 2009; won Verdi Competition, Busseto 1987, Pavarotti Competition, Philadelphia 1988, Maria Callas Competition 1988. *Address:* c/o Naïve Records, 9 rue Victor Masse, 75009 Paris, France (office); c/o BIS Records, Stationsvägen 20, 184 50 Åkersberga, Sweden. *Telephone:* (1) 56-02-20-00 (office); (8) 544-102-30 (office). *Fax:* (1) 56-02-20-20 (office); (8) 544-102-40 (office). *E-mail:* contact@naive.fr (office); info@bis.se (office). *Website:* en.naive.fr (office); www.bis.se (office).

ANTONINI, Giovanni; Italian conductor and musician (recorder, baroque transverse flute); *Artistic Director, Wratislava Cantans Festival*; b. Milan. *Education:* Civica Scuola di Musica, Milan, Centre de Musique Ancienne,

Switzerland. *Career:* Founder-mem. Baroque ensemble Il Giardino Armonico 1985–, leader 1989–, appeared with Il Giardino Armonico as conductor and soloist on the recorder and Baroque transverse flute in Europe, USA, Canada, South America, Australia, Japan and Malaysia; has collaborated with artists including Cecilia Bartoli, Isabel Faust, Viktoria Mullova, Giuliano Carmignola, Giovanni Sollima, Sol Gabetta, Katia and Marielle Labèque and Kristian Bezuidenhout; guest conductor with numerous orchestras including Berliner Philharmoniker, Concertgebouworkest, Tonhalle Orchester, Mozarteum Orchester, Orquesta Nacional de España, Leipzig Gewandhausorchester; opera productions have included Le Nozze di Figaro and Handel's Alcina at Teatro alla Scala in Milano and Alcina at Zurich Opera 2013, Handel's Giulio Cesare (2012) and Bellini's Norma (2013) at Salzburg Festival; Artistic Dir Wratislava Cantans Festival, Poland 2013–. *Recordings include:* with il Giardino Armonico: instrumental works by Vivaldi and other 17th and 18th-century Italian composers, J.S. Bach, Biber and Locke, also Vivaldi's Ottone in Villa 2010; with Kammerorchester Basel: complete Beethoven symphonies; other: Bellini's Norma (Echo Klassik Award for Opera Recording of the Year – 19th century 2014) 2013. *Honours:* Gramophone Award for Best Baroque Instrumental Recording 1996, Grammy Award (The Vivaldi Album) 2000, Diapason d'or (Vivaldi Violin Concertos) 2005. *Website:* www.askonasholt.co .uk. *Address:* c/o Il Giardino Armonico, Via Edolo 27, 20125 Milan, Italy (office). *Telephone:* (02) 67077538 (office). *Fax:* (02) 67077538 (office). *E-mail:* info@ilgiardinoarmonico.com (office). *Website:* www.ilgiardinoarmonico.com (office).

ANTONIOU, Theodore; Greek composer, conductor and teacher; *Professor of Music Composition and Theory Emeritus, Boston University*; b. 10 Feb. 1935, Athens. *Education:* Nat. Conservatory, Athens, studied composition with Yannis Papaioannou, Hellenic Conservatory, composition and conducting with Gunter Bialas, Munich Hochschule für Musik, Int. Music Centre, Darmstadt. *Career:* active as a conductor with various contemporary music groups; Teacher of Composition and Orchestration, Stanford Univ. 1969–70, Univ. of Utah 1970, Philadelphia Music Acad. 1970–75, Univ. of Pennsylvania 1978; Prof. of Music Composition and Theory, Boston Univ. 1978–2008, Emer. 2008–; Asst Dir of Contemporary Activities, Tanglewood 1974–85; Dir, Music Dept, Hellenic American Univ., Athens; Dir, Experimental Stage, Nat. Opera of Greece 2004–11; founder several contemporary music ensembles including ALEA II, ALEA III, Philadelphia New Music Group, Hellenic Group of Contemporary Music. *Compositions include:* Stage Periander, opera 1977–79, Bacchae, ballet 1980, The Magic World, ballet 1984, The Imaginary Cosmos, ballet 1984, Bacchae, opera 1992, Monodrama for actor and ensemble 1992, Oedipus at Colonus, opera 1998, orchestral: Concerto for clarinet, trumpet, violin and orchestra 1959, Antithese 1962, Piano Concertino 1962, Jeux for cello and strings 1963, Micrographies 1964, Violin Concerto 1965, Kinesis ABCD for two string orchestras 1966, Threnos for wind ensemble, piano, percussion and double bass 1972, Double Concerto for percussion and orchestra 1977, The GBYSO Music 1982, Ode for soprano and ensemble 1992, First Symphony 2002, Moirologhia 2004, Second Symphony 2010, Third Symphony 2012, Just Drumming (concerto for snare drum and orchestra) 2012; various choral works, solo vocal pieces and chamber music; also mixed media scores, incidental music to various dramas, film scores. *Recordings:* as conductor of his own works and of works by other contemporary composers. *Honours:* Commdr, Order of Honour (Hellenic Repub,) 2007; many commissions and awards, including Music Award, Greek Acad. of Arts and Letters 1997, Richard Strauss Prize, Metcalf Award for Excellence in Teaching (Boston Univ.) 1991, Herder Prize 2004, Harvard Univ. 'Honoring Greek Culture' Award 2011, Nat. Opera of Greece Apollo Award 2013. *Address:* c/o School of Music, Boston University, 855 Commonwealth Avenue, Boston, MA 02215, USA (office). *E-mail:* antoniou@bu.edu (office). *Website:* www.bu.edu/cfa/music/faculty/antoniou (office).

ANTONIOZZI, Alfonso; Italian singer (bass-baritone); b. 29 Aug. 1964. *Education:* studied with Sesto Bruscantini. *Career:* appeared widely in Italy in Turandot (as Ping), Rossini's L'occasione fa il ladro, Adina and Don Bartolo in Il Barbiere di Siviglia from 1986; San Francisco 1992, as Taddeo in L'Italiana in Algeri; other roles have included Falstaff, Bizet's Don Procopio, Schaunard in La Bohème, Patroclus in Paer's Achille, Carmina Burana, Aeneas, Il Conte in Figaro, Don Inigo in L'Heure Espagnole, Don Bartolo in Il Barbiere di Siviglia, Il Poeta and Don Geronio in Il Turco in Italia; season 1995–96 as Mustafà in Rossini's Adina at Rome and Don Magnifico at Monte Carlo, San Francisco and Dallas 1996, as Leporello; Glyndebourne debut as Don Alfonso in Così Fan Tutte 2007, at Royal Opera House Covent Garden in Matilde di Shabran; Contes d'Hoffmann in Turin and Don Pasquale at Zurich Opernhaus; debut as Scarpia in Trento and Pisa and Michonnet in Turin 2009; in 2010 sang Gennaro Iovine in Rota/De Filippo's Napoli Milionaria at the Festival di Martina Franca, and Elisir d'amore at Staatsoper Berlin and Opernhaus Zurich; contemporary opera has included Bernstein's Candide at Accad. di Santa Cecilia with Jeffrey Tate, Britten's Death in Venice at Genoa and Florence with Bruno Bartoletti, and Il Cappello di Paglia di Firenze at La Scala and in Turin with Bruno Campanella; has also worked with Riccardo Chailly, Valery Gergiev, Riccardo Muti and Claudio Scimone; teaches at Scuola dell'Opera Italiana, Turin and Bologna. *Recordings include:* Don Procopio and Cimarosa's I traci amanti (Bongiovanni). *Current Management:* Atelier Musicale, Via Caselle 76, San Lazzaro di Savena 40068, Italy. *E-mail:* info@ateliermusicale.com. *Website:* www.ateliermusicale.com. *E-mail:* alfonso@alfonsoantoniozzi.com (office). *Website:* www.alfonsoantoniozzi.com.

ANTONSEN, Ole Edvard, DipMus; Norwegian musician (trumpet); b. 25 April 1962, Ringsaker. *Education:* Norwegian State Acad. of Music with Harry Kvaebek. *Career:* played with the Oslo Philharmonic 1982–90; solo career from 1990; concerto appearances with Atlanta Symphony, Dresdner Philharmonie, Stuttgart Chamber Orchestra, I Fiamminghi Chamber Orchestra, Wurtembergisches Kammerorchester, Swedish Radio Symphony Orchestra, Oslo and Bergen Philharmonic Orchestras in Sweden, Kioi Sinfonietta, Tokyo, Israel Chamber Orchestra, Orchestre de la Suisse Romande, Leipzig Radio Orchestra, Prague Symphony, London Festival Orchestra, Royal Swedish Chamber Orchestra and Cantilena (Scotland); tour of 15 different countries 1989, including Russia and Brazil; season 1990 with Paris debut (Oslo Philharmonic) and engagements in Spain, USA (New York and Washington recitals), West Germany and Switzerland; plays jazz and contemporary music as well as the standard classics; season 1995–96 included a recital debut with Wayne Marshall at the Royal Festival Hall, London; appearances for the Istanbul International, City of London and Bermuda Festivals, concerts in Germany, Switzerland, Scandinavia and Austria and a 6th tour of Japan; 1997 included a return to the Schleswig-Holstein Festival, a tour with Dmitri Sitkovetsky and the New European String Orchestra and engagements in Europe, North America and the Far East; recital with the Norwegian Chamber Orchestra, conducted by Iona Brown; with Wayne Marshall and the ECO 1992; Berlin Philharmonic Orchestra with M. Jansons and M. Rudy for EMI. *Recordings include:* The Virtuoso Trumpet 1989, Tour de Force 1992, Trumpet Concertos 1993, Popular Pieces for Trumpet & Organ 1994, Shostakovich Concerto for Piano and Trumpet 1995, Trumpet and piano recital with Wolfgang Sawallisch 1996, Read My Lips 1997, Twentieth Century Trumpet 1998, New Sound of Baroque 2000, Ars Nova 2002, Willem Breuker Kollektief 2002, Jan van der Roost In Flanders' Fields Vol. 39 2003, ABSOLUTE 2004, Frelsesarmeens Juleplate 2004, The Golden Age of the Cornet 2007, Landscapes 2008. *Honours:* First Prize, CIEM-Competition, Geneva 1987, Laureat UNESCO Competition, Bratislava 1989, Norwegian Grammy, Arets, Spillemann (for Tour de Force) 1992. *Address:* Svensk Konsertdirection AB, v/Gunilla Lodding Ruijsenaars, Danska Vägen 25 B, 412 74 Göteborg, Sweden. *E-mail:* agent@oleedvardantonsen.com. *Website:* www .oleedvardantonsen.com.

ANTUNES, Jorge, PhD; Brazilian academic, composer, conductor, violinist and poet; *Professor of Music Composition, University of Brasilia*; b. 23 April 1942, Rio de Janeiro; s. of Carlos Antunes and Olinda de Freitas Antunes; m. Mariuga Lisboa Antunes 1969; three s. *Education:* Univ. of Brazil, Instituto Torcuato di Tella, Buenos Aires, Sonology Inst., Univ. of Utrecht, Netherlands, Sorbonne, Univ. of Paris, France. *Career:* Prof. of Composition, Univ. of Brasilia, also Dir of Electronic Music Lab., Co-ordinator of Composition and Conducting, Gen. Co-ordinator of Nucleus for Studies and Research in Sonology; numerous radio and TV appearances; mem. Academia Brasileira de Música, Brazilian Soc. for Electroacoustic Music (Pres. 2004–). *Compositions include:* Cromorfonetica 1969, Tartinia MCMLXX 1970, Para Nascer Aqui 1970–71, Macroformobiles 1 1972–73, Catastrophe Ultra-Violette 1974, Plumbea Spes 1976, Congadasein 1978, Elégie Violette pour Monseigneur Romero 1980, Qorpo-Santo, opera 1983, Sinfonia das Diretas 1984, Dramatic Polimaniquexixe 1985, Modinha para Mindinha 1986, Serie Meninos, for young violinist and tape 1986–87, Amerika 500 1992, Olga, opera 1993, Rimbaudiannisia MCMXCV, for children's choir, lights, masks and orchestra 1994, Ballade Dure, electro-acoustic music 1995, La beauté indiscrète d'une note violette 1995, Cantata dos Dez Povos 1999, Sinfonia em cinco movimentos 2000, Eloquens 2003, Toccata Irisée 2004, Voyage au fond de l'océan cérébral 2005, Concert Chiasmatique pour sax baryton et orchestre de flûtes 2007, Frevinho da Sonia 2008, O Massapê Vivo 2009, Historia Naturalis Brasilae 2009, Variações 50 Brasília 2009–10, O Massapê Vivo (symphonic poem) 2010, Quê que a gente Faz? Concertino for guitar, string orchestra and pre-recorded sounds 2012, A Cartomante, opera 2014, Apoteose de Rousseau (symphonic poem) 2014, Columbine Lunaire, quintet 2014. *Recordings include:* Musica Eletronica 1975, 1978, No Se Mata La Justicia! 1982, Musica Eletronica 70s, Vol. I 1994, Musica Eletronica 70s, Vol. II 1995, Musica Eletronica 90s Vol.III 1997, Savage Songs, early Brazilian electronic music by Jorge Antunes, Pogus, NY 2001, Cantata dos Dez Povos 2005, Poeticus 2009, Coloratus 2011, In Defense of the Machine 2013. *Publications include:* Sobre a correspondencia entre os sons e as cores 1982, Notaçao na musica contemporânea 1989, Uma Poetica Musical brasileira e revolucionaria 2002, Sons Novos para o piano, a harpa e o violao 2004, Sons Novos para as cordas e os sopros 2005, Sons novos para a voz 2007, Sons Novos para a Percussão 2009. *Honours:* Chevalier des Arts et des Lettres 2002, Comenda da Liberdade e da Cidadania 2011; Premio Città di Trieste 1970, Premio Angelicum di Milano 1971, Premio Vitae, Brazil 1991, Premio APAC 1992, Prix Musica Criativa 1994, Cidadão Honorário de Brasília 2002, Premio Funarte 2009, Resident-Composer Ibermusicas 2013, ARSC Prize 2014. *Current Management:* c/o Sistrum Music Productions, SHIN QI 5, Conjunto 3, lote 23, 71505-730, Brasilia, DF, Brazil. *Telephone:* (61) 3368-1794. *Fax:* (61) 3368-1797. *E-mail:* sistrum@sistrum.com .br. *Website:* www.sbme.com.br. *Address:* Universidade de Brasilia, Departamento de Música, 70910-970 Brasilia, DF, Brazil (office). *Fax:* (61) 3368-1797 (office). *E-mail:* antunes@unb.br (office). *Website:* www.americasnet.com.br/antunes.

ANTUNES DE OLIVEIRA, Glacy, MMus, PhD; Brazilian pianist and academic; b. 15 Oct. 1943, Goiania, Goias. *Education:* Conservatory of Music at the Federal Univ. of Goias, Nat. School of Music at the Federal Univ. of Rio de Janeiro, Inst. of Arts at the Federal Univ. of Goias, postgraduate work in

Rio de Janeiro and USA. *Career:* fmr Dir School of Music and Performing Arts, Universidade Federal de Goiás (UFG), Prof., School of Music and Performing Arts, mem. Univ. Council; Prof., School of Music and Performing Arts, Univ. of Missouri, USA 1972–; mem. Advisory Bd Gina Bachauer International Piano Competition, USA, Sydney International Piano Competition, Australia; has worked under Prof. José Kliass, São Paulo, and at Brigham Young Univ., Utah; Founder and Dir Musika Centro de Estudos, Goiania; Pres. Brazilian Music Asscn 2005–; Co-ordinator of postgraduate diploma course in music, Inst. of Arts, Federal Univ. *Recordings:* three as soloist with Orquestra de Camara de Blumenau. *Address:* Rua 19 No. 32 South Oeste, Goiania, Goias 740001-970, Brazil.

ANZAGHI, Davide; Italian composer and teacher; *President, Società Italiana Musica Contemporanea*; b. 29 Nov. 1936, Milan; s. of Luigi Oreste Anzaghi and Margherita Colombo; one s. *Education:* Milan Conservatory, studied composition with E. Pozzoli, A. Maggioni, G. Ghedini and F. Donatoni. *Career:* Prof., Istituto Musicale Donizetti, Bergamo, Conservatory of Brescia; Prof. of Composition, Milan Conservatory, mem. Bd 1997–2003; f. Novurgia (Associazione Italiana per l'Arte, lo Spettacolo, la Cultura, Oggi); Pres. Società Italiana Musica Contemporanea. *Compositions include:* orchestral: Limbale, for chamber orchestra 1973, Ausa, for great orchestra 1973, Egophonie, for chamber orchestra 1974, Aur'ore, for mixed chorus and great orchestra 1975–76, Ermosonio, for great orchestra 1978, Anco for chamber orchestra 1987, First Piano Concert, for piano and orchestra 1987–88, Flügelkonzert, for piano and great orchestra 1988, Second Piano Concert, for piano and orchestra 1990–91, Concerto Breve, for clarinet and strings 1990–91, Concerto, for violin and orchestra 1992, Third Piano Concert, for piano and orchestra 1993, Archindò, for violin and strings 1998, Le Streghe Di Benevento, for flute and strings 1998, Albóre, for violin and orchestra 2003, Concerto Dell'Ali, for piano and orchestra 2003, Concerto Dell'Ali, version for piano and 14 instruments 2003, Flügelsymphonie, for concerting piano and orchestra 2003; chamber music: Limine, for violin, viola and cellos 1971, In-Chiostro, for 2 violins and viola 1975 (revised 1982), Alena, for 10 wind instruments 1976, Remota, for 7 players 1977, Alia, for bass clarinet and piano 1980, Oiseau Triste, for piccolo and piano 1980, Soavodia, for clarinet and piano 1980, Eco, for cello and piano 1980, Onirama, for soprano and piano 1980, Tornelli, for oboe and piano 1981, Labia, for string quartet 1982, Ricrìo, for brass octet 1982, Soliludio, for flute, clarinet, violin, cello and piano 1982, Mitofania, for flute, clarinet, violin, cello, piano and percussion 1982, For Four, for string quartet 1983, Elan, for 9 instruments 1984, Pri-ter, for string quartet 1985, Queen That, for wind quintet 1985, Apogeo, for 5 instruments 1987, Tremes, for viola and piano 1988, Viol-Once-All, 3 Pieces for solo cello 1988, Settimino, for clarinet, horn, bassoon, piano, violin, viola and cello 1992, Elea, for violin and piano 1994, Riturgia, for two recitant voices, chorus and orchestra 1994, Chitattro and Repetita for 4 guitars 1995, Phantasus, for cello and piano 1995, Ludus I, for ensemble 1995, Declinava Un'Estate Inquieta, for recitant, piano and percussion 1996, In nomine Filii, oratorio for recitant, chorus, soprano and ensemble 1997, Disklaviermusic, for piano and disklavier 2001, Chifla, for flute and guitar 1998 (revised 2002), Il Labirinto Di Sangue, for recitant, 2 pianos and 2 percussion 1998, Spettri, for violin and piano 2002, Musica Per Tre, for violin, cello and piano 1995 (revised 1998), Musica Percussiva, for piano and 5 percussionists 2003, Rondò D'Aura for oboe (or sax soprano) and harp 2003, Selon Moi, for piano and 14 instruments 2003, Ariette Dolenti (I–IV) for soprano and piano 2003–04, Rondò, for oboe (or sax soprano) and piano (or harpsichord) 2004, Brin, for flute and piano 2007, Hommage for bajan and percussion 2007, Hommage, for accordion and percussion, 2007, Tenebrae, for 4 double basses, 2008, Elogio Della Luna, for flute, clarinet, vibraphone and percussion (only one interpreter), piano, violin and cello 2009, Rondello, for sax soprano and piano 2009, Clartronic, for bass clarinet in B flat, percussion or tape 2009–10, Ecco Mormorar L'Onde, for bass clarinet in B flat and piano 2010, A Las Cinco De La Tarde, for baritone and piano 2010, Cavour Trio (Klaviertrio), for violin, cello and piano 2010, Sachikarama, for soprano and piano 2011, Spleen Music, for violin, viola and cello 2011, Introitus (I and II), for flute, accordion and cello 2012, Ludus II, for flute, clarinet, percussion, piano, violin and cello 2012–13, D'Anza, for dancers and ensemble 2012–13; piano (solo, 2 pianos, 4 hands piano): Sonata 1957, Jazz suite (I–X) 1957, Segni 1968–70, Ritografia 1971, Revenants 1981, Segni e Suoni 1983, Due Intermezzi 1983, Rapsodia (Rhapsody), for 2 pianos 1984, Due Improvvisi 1985, Sèpalo, for 4 hands piano 1985, Variazioni Su Un Tema Esoterico (Variations On An Esoteric Theme) 1990–91, Schumann Suite 2006, Marcia Funebre con Variazioni 1997, Notturni D'Averno 1999, Variazione Su Un Tema Di Diabelli 2000, Tre Notturni 2001, Notturno D'Imeon 2001, Klaviermusicduo for two pianos 2001–02, Klaviermusicsolo 2001–03, Variazione Senza Tema (Variation Without Theme), for 2 pianos 2002, Change 2002, Serial Children 2002, Canto Popolare, piano version of History Of A Poplar 2003, Novelletta 2004, Piano D'Antan (I–IV) 2003–05, Valzer Da Concerto (from Valzer Da Concerto di E. Pozzoli for accordion) 2007, Children's Corner (Berceuse (I–III), 3 little and tonal lullabies 1999, 2001, 2010, Albertinum 2012, Vertigo, for 4 hands piano 2013; solo instrumental: Airy, for clarinet in B flat 1983, D'Ance, for accordion 1996, Variazioni Per Percussion, for vibraphone and percussion (only one interpreter) 2005, Scatole Cinesi, for vibraphone and percussion (only one interpreter) (revision of Variazioni 2005), Elegia, for solo cello 2008–09, Rondò Per Pia, for sax soprano 1999, Aforismi (I–IV), for cello 2002–07, Melodie, for clarinet 2003, Phisarama (I–III), for accordion 2008–09, Imagines (I–V), for vibraphone and percussion (only one interpreter) 2008–10, Sololos, for solo violin 2009, Super Flumina, for organ 2012, Arpadia, for harp 2013, Juvenilia, for harp 2013; guitar (solo, duo, quartet): Invenzione, Schizzo, Variazioni 1994, Repetita, for 4 guitars 1995, Guitare D'Antan (I–VI), 6 tonal pieces 2009–12, Chitarama (I–XII) 2010, Segoviana 2010, Chitattro, for 4 guitars 1995 (revised 2010), Microchit (I–III) 2011, Rossiniana 2012, Guitarduo, for 2 guitars 2011, Kit, for 2 guitars 2010 (revised 2012), Storia Di Un Pioppo (History Of A Poplar) 2012, Suite Serotina 2013; solo flute: Halpith 1984, Flaodia (I–V) 2007–10, Flauti, flutti e flotti 2012; opera: Il Luogo Della Mente I (The Place Of Mind I) opera in one act, for soprano and piano 1977, Il Luogo della Mente II (The Place Of Mind II) opera in one act, for soprano and orchestra 1977–2013. *Honours:* Winner, Int. Composers' Competition Olivier Messiaen 1974. *Address:* via Domenichino 12, 20149 Milan, Italy (home). *Telephone:* 345-0505525 (mobile) (office). *E-mail:* davide.anzaghi@fastwebnet.it (home); simc@fastwebnet.it (office); info@novurgia.it (office). *Website:* www.simc-italia.it (office); www.novurgia.it (office); www.davideanzaghi.com; www.davideanzaghi.it.

ANZELLOTTI, Teodoro; Italian musician (accordion); b. 1959, Apulia. *Education:* Hochschulen in Karlsruhe and Trossingen. *Career:* regular guest at major festivals and with leading orchestras since 1980s; more than 300 new works have been written for him by composers including George Aperghis, Brice Pauset, Heinz Holliger, Toshio Hosokawa, Mauricio Kagel, Michael Jarrell, Isabel Mundry, Gerard Pesson, Matthias Pintscher, Wolfgang Rihm, Salvatore Sciarrino, Marco Stroppa, Jörg Widmann, Hans Zender; teaches at Hochschule der Künste Bern 1987–, Musikhochschule Freiburg im Breisgau 2002–; worked with Ensemble InterContemporaine Paris, Schönberg Ensemble Amsterdam, Ensemble Modern Frankfurt, Ensemble recherche Freiburg. *Recordings include:* Berio Sequenza I – XIII, Musik für Akkordeon, The Contemporary Accordion, Erik Satie, Domenico Scarlatti, Push-pull, Kagel, John Cage, Matthias Pintscher, Beiseit, Strike the Ear, Thomas Demenga, Gegenwelten, Gerhard Stäbler, Wolfgang Rihm, Dokumentations-CD 75 Jahre Donaueschinger Musiktage, Hugo Herrmann Wettbewerb 85, Klingen im Gegenwind, Johannes Schöllhorn, SurPlus live auf Solitude, Stiebler, Isabel Mundry, Wittener Tage für neue Kammermusik 1997 – Dokumentationen, Wittener Tage für neue Kammermusik 1998 – Dokumentationen, Rebecca Saunders, Donaueschinger Musiktage, Musik in Deutschland 1950–2000, Wittener Tage für neue Kammermusik 2004 – Dokumentationen, Jörg Birkenkötter, Heavenly Blue, Donaueschinger Musiktage 2004, Nadir Vassena. *Honours:* Int. Hugo Herrmann Competition 1985, Instrumentalist of the Year (Accordion), ECHO Klassik 2011. *Address:* Hochschule der Künste Bern, Department of Music, Papiermühlestrasse 13A, 3014 Bern, Switzerland (office); Bayernstr. 18, 79100 Freiburg im Breisgau, Germany. *Telephone:* (31) 8483999 (office); (761) 1377333 (mobile). *Fax:* (31) 8483998 (office). *E-mail:* teodoro.anzelotti@hkb.bfh.ch (office); teodoro@anzellotti.de. *Website:* www.hkb.bfh.ch (office); www.anzellotti.de.

APERGHIS, Georges; Greek composer; b. 23 Dec. 1945, Athens; m. Édith Scob. *Career:* instrumental and vocal compositions, chamber and orchestral music, musical theatre and opera; Founder music theatre workshop Atelier Théâtre et Musique (ATEM) 1976–; commissions, works performed by Ensemble Intercontemporain, Ictus Ensemble, Neue Vocalsolisten, SWR Vokalensemble, Klangforum Wien ensemble, London Sinfonietta, Musikfabrik, remix ensemble Porto, Westdeutschen Rundfunks, Symphonieorchester des Bayerischen Rundfunk; also at Opera de Lille and festivals including Avignon, Festival Agora/Opera de Paris, Eclats de Stuttgart Festival, Salzburg, Witten, Donaueschingen, Parma, Tallin, Strasbourg, Warsaw, São Paulo; Composer in residence, Strasbourg 1997–2000. *Compositions include:* La tragique histoire du nécromancien Hieronimo et de son miroir, for two women's voices, lute and cello 1971, Vesper 1972, Pandaemonium (opera) 1973, Histoire de loups (opera) 1976, La bouteille à la mer 1976, Récitations 1978, Conversations 1985, Tourbillons for solo voice 1989, Enumerations 1988, Jojo 1990, H, litanie musicale et égalitaire 1992, Sextuor 1993, Commentaires 1996, Die Hamletmaschine-Oratorio 2000, Machinations (Grand Prix, Société des auteurs, compositeurs et éditeurs de musique) 2000, Dark Side (Prix Salabert), Avis de tempête (opera) (Grand Prix de la Critique 2005) 2004, Wölfli Kantata 2006, Contretemps 2006, Zeugen (musical spectacle for voice, puppeteer/narrator, bass clarinet, alto saxophone, accordion, cimbalom, piano and live video) 2006, Happy End (animation-film-concert for instrumental ensemble, electronics with film 2007, Teeter-Totter 2008, Shot in the Dark 2011, Etudes pour orchestre 2012, 2013, Le soldat inconnu 2013. *Recordings:* Avis de Tempête, Musique de Chambre, Machinations, Alles Theater!, Simulacres, Sextuor, Récitations. *Publications include:* Zig Bang 2004, Machinations 2001, Voix Croisées 2004, Avis de tempête 2007, Tempête sous un crâne. *Honours:* Commdr, Ordre des Arts et Lettres; Prix SACEM 1974, Prix Paul Gilson 1978, Grand Prix, Ville de Paris 1988, Grand Prix Nat. de la Musique 1998, winner, Prince Pierre of Monaco Prize for Composition 2007, Maurizio Kagel Prize 2011, Golden Lion for Lifetime Achievement, Venice Biennale Musica 2015. *Current Management:* Emilie Morin, 228 boulevard Voltaire, 75011 Paris, France. *E-mail:* emilie.m9@gmail.com (office). *Address:* c/o Durand-Salabert-Eschig, Universal Music Publishing Group, 16 rue des Fossés Saint-Jacques, 75005 Paris, France (office). *Telephone:* 1-44-41-50-90 (office). *Fax:* 1-44-41-50-91 (office). *E-mail:* georges.aperghis@wanadoo.fr (office). *Website:* www.salabert.fr (office); www.aperghis.com.

APKALNA, Iveta; Latvian organist; b. 1976, Rezekne (Lettland). *Education:* Vitols Latvian Acad. of Music, London Guildhall School for Music and Drama (scholarship), Conservatory of Stuttgart. *Career:* official organist during the visit of Pope John Paul II to Latvia 1993; regular organ and piano performances with Latvian Chamber Orchestra and Rezekne Symphony Orchestra; concerts and recitals at major halls and festivals and toured extensively in Europe; Berlin Philharmonic debut in Hector Berlioz' Te Deum under Claudio Abbado 2007. *Recordings:* Orgel 2003, Touchdown in Riga, Himmel und Hoelle (Heaven and Hell) (ECHO Klassik Instrumentalist of the Year Award, Germany 2005) 2004, Plays the Organ of Parish Church St Martin in Wangen, Prima Volta: Schumann, Mozart, Weiner, Bach, Hakim, Jongen and Prokofiev 2006, Trumpet and Organ: Works of Messaien, Shostakovich, Eben and Takemitsu 2008, L'Amour et la Mort: Works of Widor, Saint-Saëns, Bizet and Fauré 2011. *Honours:* third prize Lahti Int. Organ Competition, Finland 1997, first prize N London Piano School Competition 1998, third prize Int. M.K. Ciurlionis Organ Competition, Lithuania 1999, Royal Bank Calgary Int. Organ Festival and Competition Bach Ancillary Prize 2002, Int. M. Tariverdiev Organ Competition, Kaliningrad 2003, Great Music Award for special accomplishments in music 2003. *E-mail:* info@boleroartists.com. *Website:* www.boleroartists.com/ia_b.htm. *E-mail:* lpollack@gmx.net.

APONTE-LEDÉE, Rafael, DipMus; Puerto Rican composer and teacher; b. 15 Oct. 1938, Guayama. *Education:* Madrid Conservatory with Cristobal Halffter, Latin American Inst. of Higher Musical Studies with Alberto Ginastera, Di Tella Inst., Buenos Aires. *Career:* teacher of theory and composition, Univ. of Puerto Rico 1968–73, and Puerto Rico Conservatory of Music 1968–; Dir, Festival de las Artes de Puerto Rico 2006–; Pres., Latin American Foundation for Contemporary Music. *Compositions include:* Orchestral: Elejia 1965, revised 1967, Impulsos, in memoriam Julia de Burgos 1967, Dos Cuentos Para Orquesta 1987, Canción de Albada for orchestra 1991, Cuentos de Daniel Santos for orchestra 1995; Orchestra and Soloist: Cantata 1988; Chamber Orchestra: A Flor De Piel with 2 singers; Chamber Opera: El Paseo de Buster Keaton; Solo Instruments: Tres Bagatelas for Guitar, Tema Y Seis Diferencias for Piano, Azaleas for clarinet 1988; Chamber: Dialogantes for Flute and Viola 1965, El otro cielo for flute, English horn, clarinet, French horn, trombone, percussion and piano 1996, Canciones para voz y piano, Aphorismos 2007; many other works for various instruments, tape. *Recordings:* Música de Cámara 1976, La Canción De Arte Puertorriquena with Margarita Castro 1989, La Música De Rafael Aponte Ledée. *Publications:* Tema y seis diferencias, Sombras, Zona de Carga y Descarga, La Ventana Abierta. *Honours:* ASCAP 1989, 1990, 1991. *Address:* c/o Conservatorio de Música de Puerto Rico, 350 Calle Rafael Lamar, San Juan, 00918 Puerto Rico.

APPEL, Andrew, DMA; American harpsichordist; *Director, The Four Nations Ensemble*; b. 8 June 1951, New York. *Education:* Duke Univ., Juilliard School, Royal Flemish Conservatory, Antwerp, Belgium. *Career:* debut at Carnegie Recital Hall 1977; solo recitals in Europe and USA; festival participation at Spoleto, Aston Magna, Mostly Mozart; teacher, Temple Univ., Juilliard, Princeton Univ.; currently Musical Dir The Four Nations Ensemble; Performing Arts Man., Wave Hill, New York; mem. Chamber Music America (fmr Trustee), Early Music America. *Recordings:* Bach, Works for Harpsichord 1983, Couperin, Works for Harpsichord 1989, JB Bach-Bridge 1987, Couperin 1991. *Publications:* Gaspard Le Roux – Complete Works 1989. *Honours:* First prize, Erwin Bodkey Competition 1977. *Address:* The Four Nations Ensemble, PO Box 1112, Hudson, NY 12534, USA (office). *Telephone:* (212) 928-5708 (office). *E-mail:* FourNationsInc@aol.com (office). *Website:* www.fournations.org (office).

APPELGREN, Curt; Swedish singer (bass-baritone); b. 1945. *Career:* began as a violinist and later made his debut as a singer at Drottningholm Court Theatre as Dulcamara in L'Elisir d'amore; mem. Royal Theatre Stockholm 1976–78, 1983–97; sang Pogner in Götz Friedrich's production of Die Meistersinger at the Royal Opera, Stockholm; other Swedish roles include Cimarosa's Maestro di Capella, Jokanaan in Salome and Leporello in Don Giovanni; sang Oxenstierna in premiere of Christina by Hans Gefors 1986; Perugia Festival in Spontini's La Vestale; sang at Glyndebourne as Rocco and Bottom, and in Peter Hall's productions of Fidelio and A Midsummer Night's Dream; sang Bottom at Hong Kong Festival and Rossini's Basilio at Glyndebourne; appearances with London Choral Soc. and London Philharmonic Orchestra at Royal Festival Hall, London; sang Johann in a revival of Vogler's Gustaf Adolf och Ebba Braha at Drottningholm 1990; King Mark in Tristan und Isolde at Royal Festival Hall, London 1993; san Publio in La Clemenza di Tito at Glyndebourne 1995; Oroveso in Norma at Stockholm 1997. *Address:* c/o Stiftelsen Kungliga Teaterns Solister, PO Box 16 253, 10324 Stockholm, Sweden. *E-mail:* info@operasolisterna.se.

ARAD, Atar; Israeli violist; b. 1943, Tel-Aviv. *Career:* mem., Cleveland Quartet 1980–87; regular tours of USA, Canada, Europe, Japan, South America and Israel; concerts in Paris, Lyon, London, Bonn, Prague, Brussels and Houston; appeared at Salzburg, Edinburgh, Aspen, Berlin, Mostly Mozart and Lucerne festivals; guest performances as soloist with major orchestras and with ensembles including the Guarneri, Emerson, Tokyo, Mendelssohn, American, Chillingrian, Vermeer, New Zealand and Orion string quartets; in addition to standard repertory, performs works by John Harbison, Samuel Adler, Christopher Rouse, Toru Takemitsu; also composer, works commissioned and performed in Chicago, London's Wigmore Hall, Bloomington, Brussels, Stockholm and Berlin; taught at Eastman School of Music, Aspen School and Festival, Shepherd School of Music at Rice Univ., currently Prof. of Music (viola), Jacobs School of Music, Indiana Univ., Bloomington. *Compositions include:* Solo Sonata for viola 1992, String Quartet 1998 premiered by Corigliano Quartet 1999, Six Caprices for Viola 2003, Viola Concerto 2005, Toccatina Alla Turk for two violins, Esther for violin and viola, Tikvah for solo viola 2008, Listen (three poems by W. S. Merwin) for tenor, clarinet, viola, cello and bass 2009. *Recordings include:* with Cleveland Quartet: Brahms Piano Quintet in F Minor (with Emanuel Ax), Schubert: Quintet D 956 (with Yo-Yo Ma), Atar Arad: Sonata for Viola Solo and String Quartet 2002. *Publications:* contribs essays in The Strad, American String Teacher and Strings. *Honours:* City of London Prize, Carl Flesch Competition for violin and viola 1972, First Prize, Int. Viola Competition, Geneva 1972. *E-mail:* aarad@indiana.edu. *Website:* www.riax.com/host/atararad.

ARAGALL GARRIGA, Giacomo Jaime; Spanish singer (tenor); b. 6 June 1939, Barcelona; s. of Ramon Aragall and Paola Garriga; m. Luisa Aragall 1964; three s. *Career:* has sung in several opera productions at Verona 1965, Covent Garden 1968, Metropolitan Opera 1968, San Francisco 1973, Budapest, Venice, Genoa, Palermo, Parma, Modena, Naples, Rome and Turin; Founder-Pres. Concurso Internacional de Canto Jaume Aragall 1994–. *Operas include:* Gerusalemme 1963, L'amico Fritz, Esclarmonde 1974, Joan Sutherland 1975, Donizetti's Caterina Cornaro, Lucia di Lammermoor, Madama Butterfly, La Favorita, La Traviata, Werther, Faust, Tosca, Manon, Don Carlo, Adriana Lecouvreur, Un Ballo in Maschera and Simon Boccanegra. *Honours:* winner, Voci Verdian, Busseto, Peseta de Oro and Medalla de Plata for appearing at 1992 Barcelona Olympics, Medalla de Oro de Bellas Artes 1992. *Address:* Concurso Internacional de Canto Jaume Aragall, Sra. Silvia Gasset, C/ Rocafort, 39-1st 2nd, 08015 Barcelona, Spain (office). *Telephone:* (60) 9423896 (office). *Fax:* (93) 2893871 (office). *Website:* www.concursaragall.com (office).

ARAIZA ANDRADE, José Francisco; Mexican singer (tenor) and teacher; *Professor, Staatliche Hochschule für Musik Stuttgart*; b. 4 Oct. 1950, Mexico City; s. of José Araiza and Guadalupe Andrade; m. 1st Vivian Jaffray (divorced); one s. one d.; m. 2nd Ethery Inasaridse; one s. one d. *Education:* Univ. of Mexico City and Nat. School of Music and Munich Acads of Music. *Career:* first engagement as lyric tenor in Karlsruhe, Germany 1974; debut as Ferrando in Così fan Tutte 1975; debut at Zurich Opera House with Almaviva 1976, perm. mem. 1978–; has performed at major opera houses in London, Paris, Munich, Berlin, Madrid, Barcelona, Milan, Parma, New York, Chicago, San Francisco, Tokyo as well as in concerts or recitals; named Kammersänger by Vienna State Opera 1988; has participated in festivals of Salzburg (debut under von Karajan 1980), Hohenems, Bayreuth, Edinburgh, Pesaro, Verona, Macerata, Aix-en-Provence, Orange, Garmisch; Prof., Staatliche Hochschule für Musik Stuttgart 2003–, Int. Opernstudio IOS, Zurich 2005–; Dir Int. Hugo Wolf Akad. 2007–09; Bertelsmann Neue Stimmen (Jury and Master-classes) 1998–; Artist-in-Residence, Boston Univ. Coll. of Fine Arts 2013. *Films include:* videos: Manon, Faust, La Cenerentola (two), Falstaff, Die Entführung aus dem Serail, Don Giovanni, Die Schöpfung, Recital Tokio, Die Zauberflöte (two), Così fan tutte, Mozart Gala Verona 1 & 2, Bach Magnificat, Francisco Araiza – I am a Romantic, Fast ein Gentleman (TV film), Schumann's Dichterliebe, Schubert's Winterreise. *Television includes:* Melodien zum Muttertag 2000, Gala der Europahilfe 2000, Kein Schöner Land 2000, Zauber der Musik mit André Rieu 2002, Sternstunden der Musik 2003. *Recordings include:* The Magic Flute, Faust, Das Lied von der Erde, Die schöne Müllerin, Der Freischütz, Maria Stuarda, Don Pasquale, Die Schöpfung, Mozart Requiem, Don Giovanni, Idomeneo, Rossini's Messa di Gloria, 200 Jahre La Fenice, Die Winterreise, La Bohème, Berlioz' Requiem, Verdi, No Limits from Mozart to Wagner 2013. *Honours:* Deutscher Schallplattenpreis, Orphée d'Or, Mozart Medal, Univ. of Mexico City, Otello d'Oro, Goldener Merkur, Best Performer Award, Munich 1996, Dr A. Ortiz Tirado Medal (Sonora, Mexico) 2008, Gold Medal, Instituto Nacional de Bellas Artes y Literatura y la Compañia Nacional de Opera Mexico City for Lifetime Achievement 2011. *Current Management:* c/o Opern-Agentur und Artists' Mgt, Tal 15, 80331 Munich, Germany. *Telephone:* (89) 29161662 (home). *Fax:* (89) 29161667 (home). *E-mail:* tschaidse@opern-agentur.com (home). *Website:* www.opern-agentur.de (home). *E-mail:* faraiza@aol.com. *Website:* www.franciscoaraiza.com.

ARASON, Jon Runar; Icelandic singer (tenor); b. 29 March 1962. *Education:* studied in Iceland with Magnus Johnnson, in Sweden with Harald Ek. *Career:* debut as Rodolfo, La Bohème, at Århus, Denmark 1995; sang roles of Pinkerton in Madama Butterfly and First Jew in Salome, Gothenburg Opera 1996–97; Duke in Rigoletto, Oslo Opera 1996–97; Pinkerton 1997–98; Rodolfo, La Bohème; worked at operas in both Reykjavík and Gothenburg as chorus mem.; Mozart's Magic Flute; Roderigo in Otello; Borsa, Rigoletto; Bardolfo, Falstaff; Beppe, Donizetti's Rita; Swan, Orff's Carmina Burana; Tenor, Rossini's Stabat Mater. *Address:* c/o Oslo Arts Management AS, Den Gamle Logen, Grev Wedels Plass 2, 0151 Oslo 1, Norway.

ARAYA, Graciela; Chilean singer (mezzo-soprano); b. 16 May 1958, Santiago. *Education:* studied in Santiago and São Paulo. *Career:* debut, as Maddalena in Rigoletto, Santiago, 1981; sang in South America until 1985; sang in Germany in Weise von Liebe und Tod by Matthus, Deutsche Oper Berlin, 1985; as Cherubino, Hansel, Cenerentola, Britten's Lucretia and Sesto in Handel's Giulio Cesare, 1989, Deutsche Oper am Rhein from 1986; guest appearances as Massenet's Charlotte, Stuttgart; as Octavian and Rosina, Aachen; as Carmen, Bremen; Season 1994–95: as Enriquetta in I Puritani, Vienna Staatsoper in premiere of Schnittke's Gesualdo; US debut as Carmen, Costa Mesa, 1995; Mignon by Thomas at the Vienna Volksoper, 1996; Season 1998 as Maddalena at Antwerp and Amastre in Serse, Geneva; Charlotte,

Venice; Season 2000–01 as Countess Geschwitz in Lulu at Vienna, Clairon in Capriccio at Amsterdam, and Maddalena in Rigoletto at Antwerp; has sung at La Monnaie, Brussels, Venice, Rome, Genoa, Turin, La Bastille, Paris 1995/96, Metropolitan Opera, New York 1999, Covent Garden, London 2001, 2002 and 2006, Seattle, Los Angeles and Tokyo. *E-mail:* graciela.fanmail@gmail.com (office). *Website:* www.gracielaaraya.com.

ARCHER, Neill; British singer (tenor); b. 31 Aug. 1961, Northampton. *Education:* Univ. of East Anglia, Brevard Music Centre, NC, USA. *Career:* concert engagements with the London Philharmonic, BBC Symphony, English Baroque Soloists and the Junge Deutsche Philharmonie; Promenade Concerts debut in 1983 with Babylon The Great is Fallen, by Alexander Goehr; Festival Hall debut in Mozart's Requiem followed by Schoenberg's Moses und Aron under John Pritchard; Sang in Bach's St John Passion at the Accademia di Santa Cecilia in Rome, the St Matthew Passion in Stavanger and Schumann's Das Paradies und die Peri at Paris Opéra; Season 1987–88 with Tamino for Kent Opera, Ferrando for Scottish Opera and Don Ottavio with Welsh National Opera; Teatro Regio Turin in 1988 in Testi's Riccardo III; Returned to Italy as Andres in Wozzeck at Parma; Buxton Festival in 1988 as Ubaldo in Haydn's Armida followed by Carmina Burana at the Edinburgh Festival; Sang Ferrando in Così fan tutte for Opera Factory, also televised; Season 1989–90 included Almaviva in Oslo and for Opera North; Sang at English National Opera and Covent Garden in 1991 as Tamino and Jacquino; Sang Pylade in Iphigénie en Tauride at Basle in 1991; Season 1991–92 included Don Ottavio in New Zealand and Pelléas with WNO in a Pierre Boulez/Peter Stein presentation of Debussy's opera; Sang the Steersman in a new production of Der fliegende Holländer at Covent Garden in 1992; Season 1994 as Tamino for ENO and Almaviva at Garsington; Opera North 1996, as Achille in Gluck's Iphigenie en Aulide and 1998 as Jenik; retired from stage 1999 and became Anglican priest.

ARCHIBALD, Ann; British singer (soprano); b. 1967, Scotland. *Education:* Royal Scottish Acad. of Music and Drama with Elizabeth Izatt. *Career:* concert debut with the City of Glasgow Philharmonic at Glasgow Royal Concert Hall; concert repertory includes Carmina Burana, Handel and Bach Cantatas (Göttingen Festival), Beethoven's Ninth (with the Royal Scottish Nat. Orchestra) and Mahler's 4th Symphony; opera debut 1992, as Papagena with Scottish Opera; further appearances as Second Niece in Peter Grimes, Mozart's Barbarina and Mrs Honor in Tom Jones by Philidor (Drottningholm Festival 1995); season 1995–96 as Musetta and the Sandman in Hansel and Gretel for Scottish Opera, and in Monteverdi's Orfeo for ENO; sang the role of Fish in Broken Strings in a Param Vir double bill for Scottish Opera 1998, and Exsultate Jubilate with the Scottish Chamber Orchestra. *Recordings:* Carmina Burana with the Royal Philharmonic Orchestra. *Honours:* numerous prizes with the Royal Scottish Acad.

ARCHIBALD, Paul, FRAM; British musician (trumpet); *Principal Trumpet, Britten Sinfonia. Career:* Co-Prin. Trumpet, Royal Opera House –1980; f. English Brass Ensemble 1974–; fmr mem. Philip Jones Brass Ensemble and London Sinfonietta; chamber concerts worldwide; Principal Trumpet, Britten Sinfonia 1992–; Prin. Trumpet, BBC Nat. Orchestra of Wales 1995–; performs regularly as soloist with numerous UK orchestras including London Philharmonic, Bournemouth Symphony Orchestra, Brandenburg Sinfonia, London Concert Orchestra and Chamber Orchestra of Europe, as chamber musician with Trio D'Art, English Brass and the Fibonacci Sequence and in duo recitals with Helen Reid; orchestral music as prin. of Orchestra of St John's, Britten Sinfonia and London Mozart Players; Prof., Royal Coll. of Music and RAM; co-f. recording label Brass Classics 2005; Artistic Dir English Brass Acad.; annual masterclasses at Dartington Int. Summer School; Musical Dir Regent Brass section band (London & Southern Counties Champions). *Recordings include:* Joie de Vivre 2005, Divertissement 2006, Peter Maxwell Davies' Trumpet Sonata; as conductor: Proclamation (with International Celebrity Trumpet Ensemble), Hodie Gloriosa (with London Mozart Players Brass Ensemble); other: Shostakovich Concerto for trumpet, piano and strings with Alain Lefèvre, Mathias Bamert and the London Mozart Players (Juno Award for Best Classical Album 2010) 2009. *Honours:* prize winner, Toulon Prix de Concours 1984. *Address:* c/o Brass Classics, Flat 1, 3 Rodway Road, London, SW15 5DN, England (office). *E-mail:* pa@paularchibald.co.uk (office). *Website:* www.brittensinfonia.com/about-us/player/paul-archibald (office).

ARDAM, Elzbieta; Polish singer (mezzo-soprano); b. 22 Sept. 1959, Kielczewo, Poland; m. Udo Gefe 1991; one s. *Education:* Conservatory of Poznań. *Career:* mem. Teatr Wielki, Poznań 1982–87; debut, Santuzza 1983; Reigen, world premiere at Brussels 1983; at La Scala di Milan, Orfeo under Riccardo Muti, Emelia in Otello with Luciano Pavarotti under Sir Georg Solti; Chicago Symphony and New York Carnegie Hall; mem. Théâtre Royal de la Monnaie, Brussels 1987–91, as Gluck's Orpheus, Ottone in Poppea, Anna in Les Troyens and Donna Elvira; mem., Frankfurt Opera 1999–2008, Amme in Eugene Onegin, Suzuki in Madama Butterfly, Kabanicha in Katja Kabanová, Mary in Der fliegende Holländer, Marthe in Gounod's Faust, Klytämnestra in Elektra, Countess in Pique Dame, La Nourrice in Ariane et Barbe-bleue, Rosalia in Tiefland and Kedruta in The excursions of Mr Broucek; soloist in world premiere of Lea Auerbachs Russian Requiem at music festivals of Bremen and Cuenca; Mrs Quickly in Falstaff at Vlaamse Opera 2009 and Hannover State Opera 2010, Burja in Jenůfa at Opéra de Rouen 2011. *Recordings:* Janáček Diary; Boesmans Reigen. *Honours:* Silver Medal, Geneva, 1981; Tchaikovsky Bronze Medal, Moscow, 1982; R Vinas Bronze Medal, Barcelona, 1984. *Current Management:* c/o Peter Seyfferth, Seyfferth Artist Management, 385 Avenue de la Concorde, 06190 Roquebrune Cap Martin, France. *Telephone:* (4) 93-35-01-05. *Fax:* (4) 93-35-02-17. *E-mail:* peter@seyfferth.de. *Website:* www.seyfferth.de. *Address:* Gartenstrasse 38, 60596 Frankfurt, Germany.

ARDEN-GRIFFITH, Paul, GRSM, GRNCM, ARMCM; British singer (tenor); *Associate Director and Musical Director, Make It So*; b. 18 Jan. 1952, Stockport, Greater Manchester, England; s. of Jack Griffith and Alma Griffith (née Arden); partner Ken Spencer. *Education:* Royal Manchester Coll. of Music, Royal Northern Coll. of Music, Cantica Voice Studio, London. *Career:* debut as Puck in Benjamin Britten's Midsummer Night's Dream, Sadler's Wells Theatre, London 1973; other performances include Franz Lehar's The Merry Widow, Henze's We Come to the River, Britten's Paul Bunyan, Carlisle Floyd's Of Mice and Men, Carl Orff's Carmina Burana, Prokofiev's The Duenna, Count Almaviva in Rossini's Barber of Seville, Puccini's Il Tabarro, Rossini's The Count Ory, Verdi's La Traviata, Mozart's Die Zauberflöte, Lloyd Webber's Phantom of the Opera, The Legendary Lanza, Babes in the Wood, Lloyd Webber's Sunset Boulevard, That Old Minstrel Magic; concerts and cabarets include London Dorchester Hotel, Hyde Park Intercontinental, Piccadilly Theatre, The Belfry Club, Savoy Hotel, Tramshed, Theatre Royal Drury Lane, The Limelight Club, Royal Artillery House; worldwide concert tours, festival appearances, master-classes and lecture tours of UK, Netherlands, Hong Kong, USA music colls and arts faculties; founder-mem. Arts Council's Opera 80 Touring Co.; Pres. Barezzi Theatre School; Assoc. Dir and Musical Dir, Make It So; performances include Strauss' Die Fledermaus with White Horse Opera 2001, Puccini's La Bohème with Somerset Opera 2003, Sondheim's Sweeney Todd, Covent Garden 2003–04, Strauss' Die Fledermaus with Opera Holland Park, London 2004, The Pocket Orchestra (The Unlikely Lives of the Great Composers) at Trafalgar Studio 2, West End, London 2006, City Varieties, Leeds 2006, 42nd Street, West Side Story, Honk!, Stagedoor Manor Performing Arts Center, New York 2007, Guys and Dolls, The Music Man, Phantom, Stagedoor, New York 2008, A Little Night Music, Me and My Girl, The Mikado, Stagedoor, New York 2009, The Great American Songbook, UK tour 2009, Eric Wetherell's A Foreign Field, Redgrave Theatre, Bristol 2010, Aladdin, Assembly Rooms, Derby 2010, The Mystery of Edwin Drood, Woman in White, Annie, Stagedoor, New York 2011, Aladdin, Playhouse Theatre, Weston-Super-Mare 2011, Gala Concert, Lincoln Cathedral 2012, Aladdin, Plaza Theatre, Stockport 2012, Dick Whittington, Plaza Theatre, Stockport 2013, Cinderella, Plaza Theatre, Stockport 2014; Intimate Opera (MD), London 2015, Cinderella, Middlesbrough Theatre 2015. *Recordings include:* The Song Is You 1986, Phantom Of The Opera (original cast recording) 1987, An Evening With Alan Jay Lerner 1987, Minstrel Magic (cast soundtrack) 1993, A Minstrel On Broadway 1994, Encore! 1995, The Classic Collection 1995, Accolade! 1996. *Publications include:* contrib. to Phantom of the Opera: The First Year Backstage by Marcus Tyler. *Honours:* Gwilym Gwalchmai Jones Scholarship for Singing 1974. *Current Management:* c/o MBA, Concorde House, 18 Margaret Street, Brighton, BN2 1TS, England. *Telephone:* (1273) 685970. *Fax:* (1273) 685971. *E-mail:* info@mbagency.co.uk. *Website:* www.mbagency.co.uk. *Address:* Make It So, 18 Margaret Street, Brighton, BN2 1TS, England (office). *Telephone:* 7800-810349 (mobile) (office). *E-mail:* pag@makeitso.gb.com (office). *Website:* www.makeitso.gb.com (office).

ARDITTI, Irvine; British violinist; b. 8 Feb. 1953, London, England; m. Jenny Whitelegg, three s. *Education:* Royal Acad. of Music with Clarence Myerscough and Manoug Parikian. *Career:* co-founder and Leader, Arditti String Quartet, with many performances worldwide 1974–; joined London Symphony Orchestra 1976, co-leader 1978–80; engagements at major festivals in cities throughout Europe, including Aldeburgh, Bath, BBC Proms, Berlin, Budapest, Edinburgh, Paris, Venice Biennale, Vienna, Warsaw, and in the USA; resident String Tutor, Darmstadt Ferienkurse for New Music 1982–; BBC television Music in Camera, Radio 3 series of seven recitals 1987; all Schoenberg's quartets in single recital, QEH, London 1988; solo appearances in Turin, Brussels, Berlin, Belgian and Turin Radio Symphony Orchestras, London Sinfonietta, Spectrum and Ensemble Cologne; world premiere of solo works by various composers, including Xenakis' Dox Orkh and Hosokawa's Landscape III, both for violin and orchestra, and Ferneyhough's Terrain, Francesconi's Riti Neurali and Body Electric, Dillon's Vernal Showers, Harvey's Scena, Pauset's Vita Nova, Reynolds Aspiration and Sciarrino's Le Stagioni Artificiali, all for violin and ensemble; with Arditti Quartet has given complete quartets of Berg, Webern and Schoenberg and numerous other composers; Berio's Corale in Madrid and Valencia 2009. *Recordings:* solo: Nono's La Lontananza, solo violin works by Carter, Estrada, Ferneyhough and Donatoni, complete Cage violin music series, Violin concertos by Berio, Xenakis and Mira; over 170 CDs with Arditti Quartet. *Honours:* gold medal Worshipful Soc. of Musicians 1994, RPS Chamber Music Award. *E-mail:* info@ardittiquartet.com (office).

ARDOVA, Asya Lazar, DipPed; Russian pianist, publisher, musicologist, translator and music teacher; b. 11 Oct. 1972, St Petersburg. *Education:* Music Coll. at St Petersburg Conservatoire, St Petersburg Pedagogical Univ. *Career:* debut with Shostakovich Preludes and Fugues, St Petersburg 1996; concerts in St Petersburg and elsewhere in Russia; festivals include Musical Spring, St Petersburg 1998–2000, Congress of Composers 2000, Int. Children's Festival, St Petersburg 2001, Spring Festival of Contemporary Music, St Petersburg 2009; Sec., Asscn of Modern Music (AMM) 1996–2001; mem. editorial bd and Man., Compozitor Publishing House, St Petersburg 1999–; concert master, St Petersburg Pedagogical Univ.; music school teacher.

Publications include: monographs on Arkhidimandritov, Firtich, Boethius; translation from Russian into English and publication of: Vivaldi The Seasons (poems), J. S. Bach Six Flute Sonatas (preface and commentaries); S. Slonimsky The Visions of Ioann Grozny (libretto and commentaries; B. Tischenko Letters of D. D. Shostakovich to B. Tischenko 2000. *Address:* Belgradskaya St. 44-1-44, St Petersburg, Russia. *E-mail:* ardova@compozitor .spb.ru. *Website:* ardisonata.net.

AREÁN, José; Mexican/Spanish conductor; b. 1966, Mexico City; m. Irene Strachan. *Education:* Escuela Nacional de Música, Vienna Conservatory, Austria. *Career:* Asst Dir and Artistic Co-ordinator, Orquestra del Teatro de Bellas Artes 1997–2001; Musical Dir, Onix Ensemble 1998–; Dir Gen., Festival de México en el Centro Histórico 2002–07; Assoc. Dir, Orquestra Sinfónica de Minería 2005–; Dir Gen., Ópera de Bellas Artes 2007–09; Music Dir Mexico City Philharmonic 2009–15; conducted Carlos Chávez's The Visitors 1999, Mexican premiere of Judith Weir's The Consolations of Scholarship 2003, world premiere of Marcela Rodríguez's Séneca 2004, Gualtiero Dazzi's En Murmullos los Muertos 2005, Unicamente la Verdad, The Visitors; has worked with Plácido Domingo, Francisco Araiza, Maria Katazarava, Ramón Vargas, Rolando Villazón, Fernando de la Mora, Ainhoa Arteta, Genaro Sulvarán, Alfredo Daza, Lourdes Ambríz, Encarnación Vázquez, Irasema Terrazas, Janice Baird, Sarah Chang, Giora Feidman, Philippe Quint. *Films include:* conducted soundtracks of Las Paredes Hablan, Bajo California, La virgén de la Lujuria. *Television includes:* host of Escenarios on Channel 22, Mexico (more than 300 episodes), Academic Dir Opera Prima (Mexico's first opera singing competition and reality show). *Recordings include:* Romeo and Juliet 1998, The Visitors (Best Record, Mexico Critics Guild) 2000, L'Elisir d'Amore 2000, Macbeth 2001, La virgén de la Lujuria 2002, El Tiempo 2003, The Consolations of Scholarship 2003, Séneca 2005, Laberintos 2007, Unicamente la Verdad 2014. *Honours:* Pantalla de Cristal for Best Original Music, Mexican Critics' Guild Award for Best Album, chosen by Lideres Mexicanos magazine as one of Mexico's 300 most influential leaders 2005, 2006. *Current Management:* c/o ArtCor Artists Agency, Meissnergasse 5/1/1, 1220 Vienna, Austria. *Telephone:* (1) 901-09-95. *Fax:* (1) 958-79-40. *E-mail:* office@artcor.org (home). *Website:* www.artcor.org (home). *Address:* Sinfónica de Minería, Carrillo Puerto 78, Col Coyoacan, Mexico City, DF 04000, Mexico (office). *Telephone:* (55) 5554-4560 (office). *Fax:* (55) 5521-8878 (office). *E-mail:* info@josearean.com (home). *Website:* www .sinfonicademineria.org (office); www.josearean.com (home).

ARENS, Rolf-Dieter; German pianist; *President, Kulturstiftung, Leipzig*; b. 16 Feb. 1945, Zinnwald. *Education:* Leipzig Musikhochschule. *Career:* many appearances in Germany and elsewhere in Europe as soloist and chamber musician; soloist with the Berlin Symphony Orchestra 1986–; teacher, Leipzig Hochschule 1970–, Hochschule für Musik Franz Liszt, Weimar 1976–, Rector 2001–10; Chair. The Liszt Foundation 2007–; Pres. Culture Foundation (Kulturstiftung), Leipzig 2011–; masterclasses and concerts, Japan, S Korea; radio and TV appearances; several recordings. *Honours:* prizewinner Bach Int., Leipzig 1968, Long-Thibaud Competition, Paris 1971. *Address:* Hochschule für Musik Franz Liszt, Platz der Demokratie 2–3, 99423 Weimar (office); Haupstrasse 31, 04463 Großpösna, Germany (home). *Telephone:* (341) 2118518 (office); (342) 9716040 (home). *E-mail:* a.rd45@gmx.de (office).

ARESKOUG, Nils-Göran, BA, MFA, MBA, MD, PhD; Swedish academic, composer, conductor, pianist and writer and physician; *Director, Are Akademi*; b. 18 May 1951, Växjö. *Education:* Stockholm Univ., Stockholm School of Music, Univ. de Lausanne, Uppsala Univ., Finland, Lund Univ., Norwegian School of Management, Mozarteum Salzburg with Hans Leygraf, studied in Växjö with Ladis Müller, Nils Andersson, Boiana Müller, Janis Ozolins, Sylvia Mang Borenberg, Ture Olsson. *Career:* Lecturer in Music Theory and Interpretation, Stockholm State Coll. of Music, Edsberg Coll. of Music, Sollentuna 1975–85; Lecturer in Music History, Stockholm Univ. 1976; music critic, Svenska Dagbladet 1977–81; Exec. Music Chief, Kronoberg Music Foundation, Växjö 1987–; currently Dir, Are Akademi (Nordic Values for Europe); currently Dir, Collegium Europaeum, Stockholm; mem. STIM, Sveriges Författaförbund, New York Acad. of Sciences, Int. Musicological Soc. *Compositions:* numerous for piano, chamber music, voice, choir and orchestra, including Symphony for Peace for orchestra and choir with poems by Dag Hammarskjöld (commissioned for The Great Peace Journey), Invitazione: Emmanuel Swedenborg in Memoriam 1988, Concerto St George for piano and orchestra 1990, Violin Concerto 1994, Symphony for Europe 1995, The Arreskow Saga (opera) 2006–. *Publications include:* Musical Interpretation in Performance 1983, Bilder Ur Musikens Historia 1984, Musical Interpretation Research 1984, MIR vols I–II 1984, Aesthetic Criteria of Musical Interpretation in Contemporary Performance 1994; contrib. to Symposium on Systems Research in the Arts 2001, Aesthetic Experience and Organizational Change: A Musical Model for Managerial Cognition (Innovative Man. Research) 2002; also about 300 articles and reviews in numerous publications, including Nutida Musik, Bonniers Musiklexikon, Sohlmans Musiklexikon, Svenska Dagbladet, Smålandsposten. *Address:* c/o Ulrike Kolb, Kröneinstrasse 10, 8044 Zurich, Switzerland (office). *E-mail:* nilsare@gmail.com (home).

ARÉVALO, Octavio; Mexican singer (tenor); b. 1963, Mexico City. *Education:* Verdi Conservatoire, Milan, Hochschule für Musik, Munich. *Career:* concert appearances in Switzerland, in Bach's Christmas Oratorio and Mozart's C Minor Mass; stage debut as Paolino in Il Matrimonio Segreto at the Gärtnerplatz Theatre, Munich 1989; sang Tamino at Mexico City 1990; ensemble mem. Stadttheater Lucerne, roles include as Mozart's Belmonte, Tamino and Don Ottavio, Nemorino, Rodolfo and Pinkerton 1991–; debut with Vienna Staatsoper as Nemorino 1992; season 1994–95 as Rinuccio in Gianni Schicchi at the Komische Oper Berlin, Ferrando (Così fan tutte) at Mexico City, Verdi's Fenton in Madrid and Polyceute in Donizetti's Les Martyrs at Nancy; season 1996–97 in Le Roi Arthus by Chausson at the Bregenz Festival, Orombello in Beatrice di Tenda at the Deutsche Oper Berlin and Leicester in Maria Stuarda at the Herkulessahl, Munich; further concert repertory includes Dvořák's Stabat Mater (in Zürich), the Verdi Requiem (Moscow) and Bruckner's Te Deum (Madrid 1997). *Recordings include:* Il Signor Bruschino, Semiramide, Adelia, Maria Stuarda, Maria di Rohan, Bel Canto (with Sumi Jo), Le Roi Arthus, La Vida Breve,. *Current Management:* c/o Marcus Carl, Musica Management GmbH, Neubauerstrasse 4, 65193 Wiesbaden, Germany. *Telephone:* (611) 2386811. *Fax:* (611) 2386810. *E-mail:* marcus.carl@opernagent.de. *Website:* www.opernagent.de; octavioarevalo.site11.com.

ARGENTA, Nancy; Canadian singer (soprano); b. (Nancy Maureen Herbison), 17 Jan. 1957, Nelson, BC. *Education:* Univ. of Western Ont., studied singing in Germany and with Peter Pears, Gerard Souzay, Vera Rozsa. *Career:* appearances at the Vienna and Schwetzingen Festivals with London Baroque; sang in Scarlatti's La Giuditta in Italy, Mozart Mass in C minor with the English Chamber Orchestra, Handel's Messiah and Giulio Cesare in Canada; concerts with the Songmakers' Almanac; opera engagements as Susanna with WNO, Haydn's L'Infedeltà Delusa in Paris, Brussels and Cologne, Astreia in Handel's Tamerlano at the Opéra de Lyon, La Chasseuresse in Rameau's Hippolyte et Aricie and Purcell's King Arthur at Aix-en-Provence; sang the title role in L'Incoronazione di Poppea, on South Bank, London; Purcell's Dido in Utrecht, Paris, Beaune and Saintes; further concerts in the Schoenberg Reluctant Revolutionary series on South Bank and Cupid in Venus and Adonis by Blow at the 1989 Promenade Concerts; sang Vespina in Haydn's L'Infedeltà Delusa, Antwerp 1990; Rossanne in the N American premiere of Floridante, Toronto 1990; sang Clärchen's songs in Beethoven's Egmont at the Festival Hall 1991; Mozart's Requiem at the 1991 Proms, conducted by Roger Norrington; debut in 1996 at the Salzburg, Flanders and Budapest Festivals, singing Euridice in Gluck's Orfeo ed Euridice with Ivan Fischer and the Budapest Festival Orchestra; also performed with Tafelmusik in Toronto, the Nat. Arts Centre Ottawa, the Scottish Chamber Orchestra, Ensemble Baroque de Limoges, the Orchestra of the Age of Enlightenment, Acad. of Ancient Music and at the Ansbach, Halle and Spitalfields Festivals; Mahler's 2nd Symphony at the Festival Hall 1997; Mozart's Exultate Jubilate and Haydn's Nelson Mass at the 1999 London Proms. *Recordings include:* Handel's Solomon and the Magnificat by Bach, Bach B Minor Mass, St John Passion and Christmas Oratorio, Monteverdi's Orfeo, Handel's Tamerlano, Barbarina in Le nozze di Figaro, Mozart's Requiem and Don Giovanni, Bach Solo Cantatas, Handel's Saul. *Honours:* Virginia Parker Prize 1990. *Address:* c/o Arts Music e.K., Hauptstrasse 6, 85462 Reisen, Germany (office). *Telephone:* (81) 22972721 (office). *Fax:* (81) 22972740 (office). *E-mail:* info@artsmusic.de (office). *Website:* www.arts-music .de (office).

ARGENTO, Dominick, BA, PhD; American composer and teacher; b. 27 Oct. 1927, York, PA. *Education:* Peabody Conservatory of Music, Baltimore with Nicolas Nabokov and Hugo Weisgall, Florence Conservatory with Pietro Scarpini and Luigi Dallapiccola, Eastman School of Music with Bernard Rogers, Howard Hanson and Alan Hovhaness. *Career:* Music Dir, Hilltop Opera, Baltimore; teacher of theory and composition, Univ. of Minnesota 1958–97, Regents Prof. 1979–97, now Prof.; works performed throughout USA and in Europe; premiere of Evensong: Of Love and Angels by Cathedral Choral Soc. at Washington Nat. Cathedral 2008; numerous commissions; endowed professorship at Eastman School of Music, Univ. of Rochester 2012; mem. Acad. of Arts and Letters 1979. *Compositions include:* operas: The Boor 1957, Christopher Sly 1962–63, The Shoemaker's Holiday 1967, Postcard from Morocco 1971, The Voyage of Edgar Allan Poe 1975–76, Miss Havisham's Fire 1979 (revised 2000), Casanova's Homecoming 1980–84, The Aspern Papers 1988, The Dream of Valentino 1993; monodramas: A Water Bird Talk 1974; ballets: The Resurrection of Don Juan 1955, incidental music to plays; orchestral: Ode to the West Wind Concerto for soprano and orchestra 1956, Bravo Mozart! 1969, In Praise of Music 1977, Le Tombeau d'Edgar Poe 1985; chamber: Divertimento for piano and strings 1954, Songs About Spring for soprano and piano or chamber orchestra 1954; song cycles: Letters from Composers for tenor and guitar 1968, To Be Sung Upon the Water for high voice, clarinet and piano 1972, From the Diary of Virginia Woolf for mezzo-soprano and piano 1974, I Hate and I Love for chorus and percussion 1981, Andrée Expedition 1983, Casa Guidi 1983, Miss Manners on Music for mezzo-soprano and piano 1998; other voice: The Revelation of St John the Divine for tenor, men's voices, brass and percussion 1966, Te Deum for chorus and orchestra 1987, Spirituals and Swedish Chorales 1994, Walden Pond for chorus, three cellos and harp 1996, A Few Words About Chekhov for mezzo-soprano, baritone and piano 1996, The Bell-Man anthem for mixed chorus and bells 1998, Brother Sun, Sister Moon for SATB chorus and organ 2004, Dover Beach Revisited for SATB chorus and piano 2004, Apollo in Cambridge for men's chorus and piano 2005, Evensong: Of Love and Angels for solo treble voice, solo soprano, reader, mixed chorus and orchestra 2007, Cenotaph for chorus and orchestra 2008, The Choir Invisible rhapsody for mixed chorus a cappella 2009, The Choirmaster's Burial for mixed chorus a cappella 2009. *Honours:* Composer Laureate, Minnesota Orchestra; hon. doctorates; Fulbright Fellowship 1951–52, Guggenheim Fellowships 1957, 1964, Pulitzer

Prize in Music 1975. *Address:* c/o Boosey & Hawkes Music Publishers Ltd, Aldwych House, 71–91 Aldwych, London, WC2B 4HN, England (office). *Website:* www.boosey.com.

ARGERICH, Martha; Argentine pianist; b. 5 June 1941, Buenos Aires. *Education:* studied with V. Scaramuzzo, Friedrich Gulda, Nikita Magaloff, Madeleine Lipatti and Arturo Benedetti Michelangeli. *Career:* debut Buenos Aires 1949; London debut 1964; soloist with leading orchestras and conductors worldwide; debut at BBC London Proms (Schumann Concerto) 2000; as chamber musician, has toured Europe, USA and Japan with Gidon Kremer and Mischa Maisky; numerous recordings including most of repertoire for four hands and for two pianos with Nelson Freire, Stephen Bishop-Kovacevich, Nicolas Economou and Alexandre Rabinovitch; performances at Lockenhaus, Munich Piano Summer, Lucerne and Salzburg Festivals; Artistic Dir, Beppu Festival, Japan 1998–; Founder and Jury Pres. Int. Martha Argerich Piano Competition 1999–; f. Progetto Martha Argerich, Lugano 2002; f. Martha Argerich Presents Project, to bring together young players and renowned artists to play rarely performed compositions and masterpieces of the repertoire. *Recordings include:* works by Brahms, Rachmaninov, Ravel and Schubert (with Nelson Freire) 2009, Argerich plays Chopin 2010, Argerich Lugano Concertos 2002–2010 (four CDs) 2012, Brahms & Schumann (with Bashmet Maisky) 2012. *Honours:* Accademica di Santa Cecilia di Roma 1997, Officier, Ordre des Arts et Lettres 1996, Commdr, Ordre des Arts et des Lettres 2004, Order of the Rising Sun, Gold Rays with Rosette (Japan) 2005; First Prize, Busoni Contest and Geneva Int. Music Competition 1957, Int. Chopin Competition, Warsaw 1965, Prix Caecilia 1991, Diapason d'Or 1992, Edison Award 1993, Tokyo Record Academy Award 1995, CD Compact Award 1997, Musical America Musician of the Year 2001, Praemium Imperiale Award (Japan) 2005, Gramophone Awards Artist of the Year, three Grammy Awards. *Current Management:* Agence Artistique Jacques Thelen, 15 Avenue Montaigne, 75008 Paris, France. *Telephone:* 1-56-89-32-00. *Fax:* 1-56-89-32-01. *E-mail:* jthelen@wanadoo.fr. *Website:* jacquesthelen.com.

ARHO, Anneli; Finnish composer; b. 12 April 1951, Helsinki. *Education:* Sibelius Academy, Helsinki, studied with Klaus Huber and Brian Ferneyhough at Freiburg. *Career:* teacher at the Sibelius Academy 1979–. *Compositions:* Minos for harpsichord 1978, Answer for mezzo, horn and string quartet 1978, Once upon a Time for wind quintet 1979, Par comparison for 3 cellos 1981, Les temps emboîtés for 3 cellos 1987 Aikaika for three cellos 1987, Atmosphere 1997, In sordina, five short pieces for string quartet 2006. *Address:* c/o Sibelius Academy of Music, Töölönkatu 28, 00260 Helsinki, Finland.

ARISTO, Giorgio, MMus; American singer (tenor); b. 28 Dec. 1950, New York, NY. *Education:* New York State Univ., Manhattan School of Music, studied in Milan and Zürich. *Career:* has performed across Europe and USA; repertoire includes Don Jose in Carmen, Werther, Chénier in Andrea Chénier, Alfredo in La Traviata, Carlos in Don Carlos, Manrico in Il Trovatore, Radames in Aida, Alvaro in La Forza del Destino, Ismaele in Nabucco, Carlo in Joan of Arc, Adorno in Simon Boccanegra, Pollione in Norma, Foresto in Attila, Cassio in Otello, Turridu in Cavalleria Rusticana, Rodolfo in La Bohème, Cavaradossi in Tosca, Dick Johnson in Girl of the Golden West, Calaf in Turandot, Lenski in Eugene Onegin, Hans in The Bartered Bride, Singer in Der Rosenkavalier; oratorio repertoire includes Beethoven's Ninth Symphony, Missa Solemnis, Berlioz's Requiem, Bizet's Te Deum, Dvořák's Requiem, Liszt's Missa Solemnis and 13th Psalm, Rossini's Stabat Mater, Verdi's Requiem and Hymn to the Nations; f. Aristo Vocal Performance Studio. *E-mail:* melodyaristo@gmail.com (office). *Website:* www .giorgioandmelody.com (home).

ARKADIEV, Mikhail; Russian conductor and pianist; b. 1958, Moscow. *Education:* Tchaikovsky Conservatoire, Moscow, Gnessin Inst. *Career:* solo piano debut in Berlin 1990; performances throughout Russia and recital accompanist to baritone Dmitri Hvorostovsky from 1990; festivals and tours to Europe, America and East Asia; as conductor, symphony and opera performances with orchestras throughout Russia 2000–; Chief Conductor and Music Dir, Volgograd Opera Theater 2002–; Chief Conductor and Artistic Dir, Pacific Symphony Orchestra, Vladivostok 2007–; Prof. of Piano, Acad. of Choral Art, Moscow 1992–2000; Prof. of Piano, Gnessin Acad. of Music, Moscow 2000–. *Compositions include:* Missa brevis for choir and organ (also recording), vocal and chamber works. *Recordings include:* solo: Mussorgsky, Skrjabin, Arkadiev; with Dmitri Hvorostovsky: My Restless Soul, Russia cast Adrift: Romances by Sviridov and Rachmaninov. *Publications include:* The Temporal Structures of New European Music; An Essay in Phenomenological Study 1992. *E-mail:* m@ arkadiev.ru (home). *Website:* www.arkadiev.ru (home).

ARMENGAUD, Jean-Pierre; French pianist; b. 17 June 1943, Clermont-Ferrand. *Education:* Ecole Normale, Sorbonne, Univ. of Paris, and studied with Jacques Février. *Career:* has performed throughout France and elsewhere in Europe in a wide repertory, including 20th century music; founded the Sainte-Baume music festival and co-founded a trio with clarinet and piano 1970; French cultural ambassador to Sweden 1982–85, and to Greece 1985–88; Prof., Univ. of Evry Val d'Essonne, f. Laboratoire RASM; Dir, Univ. of Évry Festival "Les Friches musicales". *Recordings include:* Debussy Complete Piano Works, Vols 1–4, Complete Piano Works by Edison Denisov, Scriabin: Oeuvres Mystiques Pour Piano, La Musique Russe Des Avant-gardes, Satie Complete Piano Works. *Publications include:* History of Music

from Beethoven to the Present Day, and works on Satie, Dubuffet, Dutilleux and Edison Denisov.

ARMILIATO, Fabio Carlo; Italian singer (tenor); b. 17 Aug. 1961, Genoa; m Daniela Dessì; two d. *Education:* Niccolò Paganini Conservatory, Genoa, Accad. Virgiliana, Mantua. *Career:* debut at Teatro Pergolesi di Jesi as Licinio in Spontini's La Vestale 1986; debut at Metropolitan Opera, New York in Verdi's Il Trovatore 1993, appeared there successively in Aida, Cavalleria Rusticana, Simon Boccanegra, Fedora, Tosca and Madama Butterfly; debut at Teatro alla Scala, Milan as Faust in Boito's Mefistofele under the direction of Riccardo Muti 1995, then at Teatro Colon of Buenos Aires with Adriana Leucouvreur and Tosca; debut at Paris Opera with Manon Lescaut 1996, at San Francisco Opera with Aida and Il Trovatore, at Wiener Staatsoper with Un ballo in maschera 1998; Season 1999–2000 sang with Andrea Chénier at Nice, in Madama Butterfly at Teatro alla Scala, Milan; Season 2001–02 sang in Tosca at Arena of Verona, with Andrea Chénier at Turin and Venice 2003; artistic association with his wife, Daniela Dessì, in Manon Lescaut at Seville, Adriana Lecouvreur at Naples and Aida at the Liceu Theatre at Barcelona, Tosca at Teatro Real in Madrid, Simon Boccanegra as premiere of Verdi Festival in Parma 2004 and Francesca da Rimini by Riccardo Zandonai at Teatro dell'Opera di Roma nel 2003 and at Teatro dello Sferisterio in Macerata 2004; took part in celebrations for 100th anniversary of Madama Butterfly at Puccini Festival in Torre del Lago, conducted by Zubin Mehta at Staatsoper, Munich and Maggio Musicale 2004; performed in five-act version of Don Carlo 2004; sang Andrea Chènier at Teatro Comunale di Bologna, Teatro Massimo di Palermo, A.B.A.O. in Bilbao and at Staatsoper in Vienna 2005; Season 2005–06 sang in Aida at Verdi Festival in Parma, in Fanciulla del West at Torre del Lago, as Don Carlo al Theatre du Capitol in Toulouse and with Manon Lescaut in Parma and at Deutsche Oper Berlin and with Tosca at Wiener Staatsoper; Season 2006–07 highlights included comeback at La Scala with Tosca conducted by Lorin Maazel, another Tosca at Covent Garden conducted by A. Pappano, Madama Butterfly at Arena di Verona and the Opera di Roma tour in Korea and Japan with the original Tosca production of 1900. *Recordings:* DVDs: Tosca (BBC), Aida (BBC), Madama Butterfly; CDs: Love Duets, Manon Lescaut, A Tribute to Verdi, Toselli, Le romanze ritrovate. *Honours:* Winner Tito Schipa Competition 1986, Winner Int. Pavia Lirica Competition 1987, Gigli d'Oro Prize, Recanati 2000, Regione Liguria Prize, Genoa 2001, A. Petile Prize, Asti 2002, F. Cliea Prize, Regione Calabria 2003, Mascagni d'Oro Prize 2006. *Current Management:* Atelier Musicale, Via Caselle 76, San Lazzaro di Savena 40068, Italy; Opéra et Concert, 7 rue de Clichy, 75009 Paris, France. *Telephone:* (051) 19984444 (Italy); 1-42-96-18-18 (France). *E-mail:* info@ateliermusicale.com; agence@opera-concert.com. *Website:* www.ateliermusicale.com; www.opera-concert.com. *Address:* Via Mirabella 7, 25064 Gussago (BS), Italy (office). *Telephone:* (030) 2521689 (office). *E-mail:* fabio@fabioarmiliato.com (office). *Website:* www .fabioarmiliato.com.

ARMING, Christian; Austrian conductor; *Music Director, New Japan Philharmonic Orchestra;* b. 1971, Vienna; m. Katharina Arming; two c. *Education:* Hochschule für Musik, Vienna. *Career:* Chief Conductor, Janáček Philharmonic Orchestra 1995–2002; Chief Conductor, Lucerne Symphony Orchestra 2001–04, Music Dir, Lucerne Theatre 2001–04; Music Dir, New Japan Philharmonic Orchestra 2003–; collaborations with Seiji Ozawa and Boston Symphony Orchestra, Tanglewood, Frankfurt Opera, Accademia Santa Cecilia; guest conductor with over fifty orchestras worldwide; has conducted many operas including: for Frankfurt Opera: Wagner, Der Fliegender Holländer 2004, Mozart, Don Giovanni 2006, Janáček, Jenůfa 2007, Offenbach, Les Contes d'Hoffmann 2011; with New Japan Philharmonic Orchestra: Poulenc, Les Mamelles de Tirésias 1997, Debussy, Pelléas et Mélisande 1998, Beethoven, Leonore 2005, Wagner, Lohengrin 2006. *Recordings:* albums: as conductor: Janáček, Taras Bulba 2000, Brahms, Symphony No. 1/Mahler, Symphony No. 3 2004, MacDowell, Piano Concerto No. 2 2006, Mahler, Symphony No. 5 2006, Beethoven, Symphony No. 9 2007, Schmidt, Das Buch Mit Sieben Siegeln 2010. *Current Management:* PRIMUSIC, Thomas Wolfram Artists Management, Herrengasse 6–8/2/22, 1010 Vienna, Austria. *Telephone:* (1) 532-71-24. *Fax:* (1) 532-71-40. *E-mail:* office@primusic .at. *Website:* www.primusic.at. *Current Management:* Sullivan Sweetland, 1 Hillgate Place, Balham Hill, London, SW12 9ER, England. *Telephone:* (20) 8772-3470. *Fax:* (20) 8673-8959. *E-mail:* info@sullivansweetland.co.uk. *Website:* www.sullivansweetland.co.uk.

ARMITSTEAD, Melanie; British singer (soprano); b. 1957, England. *Education:* Guildhall School of Music, Nat. Opera Studio. *Career:* debut as Frasquita and Micaela in Carmen for Scottish Opera; appearances with Kent Opera 1987–, as Venus in Rameau's Pygmalion, First Lady in The Magic Flute, and Minerva in The Return of Ulysses; Scottish Opera debut as Titania in Eugene Onegin 1988, returning as Fiordiligi; ENO and Opera North debuts 1990 as Nicoletta in The Love for Three Oranges and Mélisande in Ariane et Barbe-Bleue; returned to Leeds as Xenia in Boris Godunov 1992; created the Niece in Fenelon's Le Chevalier Imaginaire, Théâtre du Châtelet, Paris 1992, also appeared as Arbate in Mitridate; concert performances with Liverpool Philharmonic, the Halle and Royal Philharmonic; season 1989–90 included Vivaldi's Gloria with English Chamber Orchestra, Messiah with Tokyo Philharmonic, St John Passion in The Netherlands, and Bach's Magnificat at the Barbican Hall; recitalist at the Wigmore Hall (debut 1987), Purcell Room and QEH; appearances with the pianist Julian Drake and oboist Nicholas

Daniel; adjudicator at competitions and festivals; Sr Singing Teacher, Sherborne Girls' School, Dorset.

ARMOUR, Julian, BMus; Canadian cellist and arts administrator; *Artistic Director, Chamber Players of Canada*; b. 29 Sept. 1960, Missoula, Mont. USA; s. of Leslie Armour; m. Guylaine Lemaire. *Education:* Univ. of Ottawa, McGill Univ., studied with Walter Joachim, János Starker, Ralph Kirshbaum, Aldo Parisot and Leonard Rose. *Career:* Prin. Cellist, Montreal Chamber Orchestra 1982–86; Conductor, Purcell Chamber Orchestra 1984–85; cellist, Nat. Arts Centre Orchestra 1986–98; performed with Manfred Trio 1986–89 and Ottawa String Quartet 1989–94; mem. Thirteen Strings 1986–, Prin. Cellist 1990–; performed and recorded with Chamber Players of Canada 1991–, now Artistic Dir; f. Ottawa Chamber Music Soc.; f. Ottawa Int. Chamber Music Festival, Artistic and Exec. Dir 1994–2007; Pres. Ottawa Festival Network 2003–09; Chamber Music Programmer, Galaxie; Artistic and Exec. Dir, Music and Beyond Festival 2010–; teacher, Univ. of Ottawa; premiered over 200 new works; numerous radio broadcasts. *Recordings include:* over 30 CDs of chamber music. *Honours:* Chevalier, Ordre des Arts et des Lettres 2002, Gov.-Gen.'s Meritorious Service Medal 2003; Victor Tolgesy Arts Award, Canada Council for the Arts 2000, Ottawa Sun's Arts Newsmaker of the Year 2005, Friends of Canadian Music Award, Canadian League of Composers/Canadian Music Centre 2011. *Address:* Chamber Players of Canada, Box 20443, RPO Rideau East, Ottawa, ON K1N 1A3, Canada (office). *E-mail:* info@chamberplayers.ca (office). *Website:* www.chamberplayers.ca (office).

ARMSTRONG, Craig, OBE; British composer; b. 1959, Shettleston, Scotland. *Education:* Royal Acad. of Music. *Career:* resident student composer, London Contemporary Dance Theatre 1980; music and dance specialist, Strathclyde Council 1982; founder of performance music, theatre and dance group 1988; fmr mem., Hipsway, The Big Dish, The Kindness of Strangers, Texas; worked with Björk, Evan Dando, Massive Attack, Madonna, McAlmont, Luciano Pavarotti, Tina Turner, U2; f. Winona (with Scott Fraser) 2007–. *Recordings include:* albums: Hope 1993, The Space Between Us 1998, As If To Nothing 2002, Piano Works 2004, Memory Takes My Hand 2008; with Winona: Rosebud 2008. *Compositions for films include:* Daddy's Gone 1994, Close 1995, Fridge 1995, A Good Day for the Bad Guys 1995, Romeo and Juliet (Ivor Novello Award, Anthony Asquith Award, BAFTA Award) 1996, Orphans 1997, Best Laid Plans 1998, Plunkett & Macleane 1998, One Day in September (documentary) 1999, The Bone Collector (ASCAP Award) 1999, Moulin Rouge! (Golden Globe for Best Original Music 2001, IF Award 2001) 2000, Kiss of the Dragon 2001, The Quiet American 2002, Love Actually 2003, The Clearing 2004, Ray 2004, Fever Pitch 2005, Must Love Dogs 2005, Ray (Grammy Award for Best Score Soundtrack Album for Motion Picture, Television or Other Visual Media 2006) 2005, The Incredible Hulk 2008, Wall Street: Money Never Sleeps 2010, In Time 2011, The Great Gatsby 2013; contrib. music to Mission Impossible, Goldeneye, Batman Forever, Spider-Man 2 (Escape). *Compositions for television include:* Encounters (BBC2) 1991, Tartan Shorts (STV) 1994, London Bridge (Carlton) 1995. *Other compositions:* 7 Stations 1985, String Quartet 1988, Crow 1988, Losing Alec 1988 score to Macbeth (Tron Theatre) 1993, score to The Broken Heart (RSC, Barbican) 1994, If Time Must Pass 1999, When Morning Turns To Light 2000, My Grandmother's Love Letters 2000, Visconti 2001, Northern Sounds...Islands 2002, One Minute 2005, Immer (violin concerto) 2007, The Lady from the Sea (opera) 2012. *Honours:* GLAA Young Jazz Musician of the Year 1980, World Soundtrack Award for Discovery of the Year 2001, American Film Inst. Award for Composer of the Year 2001, Grammy Award for Best Score Soundtrack Album for Motion Picture, Television or Other Visual Media 2005. *Current Management:* IE Music Ltd., 111 Frithville Gardens, London W12 7JQ, England. *Telephone:* (20) 8600-3400. *Fax:* (20) 8600-3401. *E-mail:* info@iemusic.co.uk. *Website:* www.iemusic.co.uk. *E-mail:* contact@craigarmstrongonline.com (office). *Website:* www.craigarmstrong.com.

ARMSTRONG, Karan; American singer (soprano); b. 14 Dec. 1941, Horne, Mont.; m. Götz Friedrich (died 2000). *Education:* studied in Minnesota with Thelma Halverson, in California with Lotte Lehmann and Fritz Zweig. *Career:* debut at Metropolitan Opera 1969 in Hansel and Gretel; appearances with opera companies in Houston, Seattle, Cincinnati and Portland; roles include Donizetti's Norina, Puccini's Butterfly, Verdi's Alice Ford and Wagner's Eva; sang at New York City Opera 1975–78 as Minnie, Tosca, Concepcion and the Queen of Shemakha; European debut at Strasbourg 1976 as Salomé; guest appearances in Munich, Frankfurt, Geneva, Oslo and Vienna; Bayreuth debut 1979 as Elsa; world premiere performances in Von Einem's Jesu Hochzeit, Vienna 1980, Sinopoli's Lou Salomé at Munich 1981 and Berio's Un Re in Ascolto at Salzburg 1984; Covent Garden 1981 as Lulu in the first British performance of the three-act version of Berg's opera; other roles include Berg's Marie and the Woman in Schoenberg's Erwartung; sang Katerina Izmailova at Berlin 1988 and Emilia Marty and Regina in Mathis der Maler 1990; Wiesbaden Festival 1989 as Katya Kabanova, Alice Ford at Los Angeles 1990, followed by Leonore; sang Wagner's Sieglinde and Gutrune at Covent Garden 1991, Janáček's Emilia Marty at Los Angeles 1992, and Megara in the premiere of Desdemona und Ihre Schwestern by Siegfried Matthus at Schwetzingen Festival 1992; concert appearances in the Four Last Songs of Strauss, Zemlinsky's Lyric Symphony and the Bruchstücke from Wozzeck; sang Schoenberg's Woman at the Deutsche Oper Berlin 1994; Jocasta in Enescu's Oedipe at Berlin 1996; Floyd's Susannah 1997; sang Brünnhilde in Götterdämmerung at Helsinki 1998; season 2000–01 as the Marschallin and Wagner's Venus at the Deutsche Oper Berlin, Weill's Begbick at Genoa. *Recordings include:* Elsa in Lohengrin from Bayreuth. *Current Management:* Boris Orlob Management, Jägerstrasse 70, 10117 Berlin, Germany. *Telephone:* (30) 20450839. *Fax:* (30) 20450849. *E-mail:* info@orlob.net. *Website:* www.orlob.net. *Current Management:* Aria's di Novella Partacini & Alexandra Plaickner, Via Josef Weingartner 4, 39022 Lagundo, Italy. *Telephone:* (0473) 200200. *Fax:* (0473) 222424. *E-mail:* info@arias.it. *Website:* www.arias.it.

ARMSTRONG, Sir Richard, Kt, CBE; British conductor; b. 1 July 1943, Leicester, England. *Education:* Univ. of Cambridge. *Career:* mem. of music staff, Royal Opera, Covent Garden 1966–68; Music Dir, WNO 1973–86; Covent Garden debut in 1982 with Billy Budd, returning for Andrea Chénier, Un Ballo in Maschera and Don Carlos 1989; conducted Elektra, Die Frau ohne Schatten, Wozzeck, operas by Janáček, The Midsummer Marriage and Peter Grimes; led the WNO in The Ring at Covent Garden 1986; guest engagements with Netherlands Opera in Elektra, Komische Oper Berlin in Peter Grimes, Frankfurt in Der fliegende Holländer, with new productions of Elektra and Ariadne auf Naxos and at Geneva in Don Carlos; conducted the premiere of John Metcalf's Tornrak for WNO 1990, followed by Otello and House of the Dead; Music Dir, Scottish Opera 1993–2005 (adviser 2005–07); conducted Moses und Aron and La Voix Humaine at the 1992 Edinburgh Festival, Werther at Toulouse 1997; British stage premiere of Magic Fountain by Delius, Scottish Opera 1999; new production of Parsifal 2000; Wagner's Ring Cycle 2003; has conducted regularly at Royal Opera House, Covent Garden, ENO and at Edinburgh Festival, and in Frankfurt, Geneva, Paris, Munich, Berlin, Amsterdam, Rome, Brussels, Los Angeles, Toronto, Tokyo and Sydney; appearances at BBC Proms and Vienna Festival; has worked with orchestras including London Philharmonic, Philharmonia, BBC Symphony, BBC Nat. Orchestra of Wales, Hallé, Bournemouth Symphony, Scottish Chamber Orchestra, Royal Liverpool Philharmonic, City of Birmingham Symphony Japan Philharmonic, Berlin Symphony, Melbourne Symphony and Orquesta Sinfônica de São Paulo; many recordings with artists including Thomas Hampson, Roberto Alagna, Deborah Voigt and Angela Gheorghiu. *Honours:* Janáček Medal 1978, Royal Philharmonic Soc. Conductor of the Year 2004. *Current Management:* Ingpen & Williams Ltd, 7 St George's Court, 131 Putney Bridge Road, London, SW15 2PA, England. *Telephone:* (20) 8874-3222. *Fax:* (20) 8877-3113. *E-mail:* jg@ingpen.co.uk. *Website:* www.ingpen.co.uk.

ARMSTRONG, Sheila Ann, FRAM; British singer (soprano); b. 13 Aug. 1942, Ashington, Northumberland; d. of William R. Armstrong and Janet Armstrong; m. David E. Cooper 1980 (divorced 1999). *Education:* Hirst Park Girls' School, Ashington and Royal Acad. of Music. *Career:* sang Despina in Così fan tutte at Sadler's Wells 1965, Belinda in Dido and Aeneas, Glyndebourne 1966, Mozart's Pamina and Zerlina and Fiorella in Rossini's Il Turco in Italia, Glyndebourne; sang in the premiere of John McCabe's Notturni ed Alba at Three Choirs Festival 1970; New York debut with New York Philharmonic 1971; sang with Los Angeles Philharmonic under Mehta; Covent Garden debut as Marzelline in Fidelio 1973; sang Donizetti's Norina and Mozart's Donna Elvira for Scottish Nat. Opera; concert engagements included Messiah at the Concertgebouw, tour of the Far East with the Bach Choir; numerous recordings; fmr Pres. Kathleen Ferrier Soc.; fmr Trustee, Kathleen Ferrier Award; Fellow, Hatfield Coll., Durham Univ. 1992; mem. Royal Philharmonic Soc. *Recordings include:* Samson, Dido and Aeneas, Mozart's Requiem, Carmina Burana, Elgar's Apostles, The Pilgrim's Progress, Cantatas by Bach, Haydn's Stabat Mater, Beethoven's Ninth Symphony, Mahler's 2nd and 4th, Spring Symphony, Child of Our Time, Semele, Fauré Requiem, Rachmaninov's The Bells, Grieg's Peer Gynt Suite, Schubert's Lazarus, Holst's The Mystic Trumpeter, Messiah Highlights, Don Giovanni Highlights, Britten's Spring Symphony, Strauss' Four Last Songs with Royal Philharmonic, Elgar's Oratorios, Vaughan Williams' Sea Symphony and Hugh the Drover, Mozart Arias (with Barry Tuckwell). *Honours:* Hon. MA (Newcastle); Hon. DMus (Durham) 1991; Mozart Prize 1965, Kathleen Ferrier Memorial Award 1965.

ARNET, Marie; Swedish singer (soprano); b. 1970, Solna. *Education:* Royal Academies, Stockholm and London, and Nat. Opera Studio with Alison Pearce. *Career:* Anne Trulove, in The Rake's Progress and Mozart's Sandrina and Barbarina for RAM; Adelaide in Handel's Lotario for the London Handel Soc.; Susanna for Clonter Opera, Rossini's Berta for British Youth Opera, and in Burning Mirrors for ENO Studio; recitals and oratorios in Sweden, Qatar, Brussels, Aix-en-Provence and Sicily; concert repertoire includes Bach's St John Passion, Mahler's Symphony no. 2 and 4, Brahms, Fauré and Mozart Requiems, Rossini's Petite Messe Solonelle, Pergolesi's Stabat Mater, Haydn's Nelson Mass and The Creation, and Bruckner's Te Deum; television appearances in Madrid in performances of A Child of Our Time and Stravinsky's Les Noces; Berlioz's L'enfance du Christ at the Three Choirs Festival and Mozart's Requiem with Paul McCreesh and the Gabrieli Consort; Handel's Solomon for the NDR with René Jacobs and the Orchestra of the Age of Enlightenment, Bach's Christmas Oratorio on tour with William Christie and Les Arts Florissants, and Brahms German Requiem at the BBC Proms with James Conlon; opera appearances include Barbarina in Le Nozze di Figaro and Diana in Iphigénie en Aulide at Glyndebourne, Sophie in Der Rosenkavalier at Opera North (debut) and Pamina in Die Zauberflöte for Scottish Opera; debut as Ilia in Idomeneo at the Glyndebourne Festival under Sir Simon Rattle, Drusilla in Poppea in 2008; Giulietta in I Capuleti e I Montechi for Opera North 2008, Pamina in The Magic Flute for Los Angeles Opera under James Conlon 2009, Alceste in Handel's Admeto with Nicholas McGegan and

Göttingen Festival 2009; Malkovich: The Infernal Comedy at Deutsches Schauspielhaus Hamburg 2010; Eurydice in Orphée et Eurydice at the Royal Opera in Stockholm and Oslo 2011. *Current Management:* c/o Lucie Davienne, Hazard Chase, 25 City Road, Cambridge, CB1 1DP; c/o Martin Gregor Lütje, Lütje Artist Management, Winterfeldtstr.77, 10777 Berlin, Germany. *Telephone:* (1223) 312400 (Hazard Chase). *Fax:* (1223) 460827 (Hazard Chase). *E-mail:* lucie.davienne@hazardchase.co.uk; martin.gregor@luetjeartist.com. *Website:* www.luetjeartist.com.

ARNOLD, David Charles; American singer (baritone); *Artist-in-Residence, Temple University*; b. 30 Dec. 1949, Atlanta, Ga. *Education:* Indiana Univ., New England Conservatory. *Career:* debut, Metropolitan Opera as Enrico in Lucia; ENO as Escamillo in Carmen; New York City Opera as Zurga in Les Pêcheurs de Perles; Escamillo in Carmen, Komische Oper Berlin; performances of many world premieres, including John Harbison's Full Moon in March and his Winter's Tale, David Diamond's Ninth Symphony for Baritone and Orchestra, Leonard Bernstein conducting at Carnegie Hall, Charles Fussell's Specimen Days, James Grant's Such Was the War, Andrea Clearfield's Fire and Ice; two guest appearances at the White House singing Berlioz's L'Enfance du Christ and performance of American song repertoire; performances of Amonasro in Aida with Opera Co. of Boston, L'Opéra de Montréal and Opera Omaha and Le nozze di Figaro with L'Opéra de Québec; performances with most leading orchestras, including The Boston Symphony for six seasons, St Louis Symphony, Atlanta Symphony, American Symphony Orchestra, San Francisco Symphony, Chicago Symphony, Buffalo Philharmonic, Singapore Symphony Orchestra, The Spoleto Festivals, Philadelphia Orchestra and the Israel Philharmonic; Artist-in-Residence, Temple Univ., Phila 2003–. *Recordings include:* Schoenberg's Gurrelieder, Boston Symphony; Harbison's Full Moon in March; Judith Lang's Zaimont's Magic World; Mendelssohn's Walpurgisnacht; Beethoven's 9th Symphony; Mozart's Requiem; Haydn's Lord Nelson Mass; Cherubini's Médée; Elijah; Bach's St Matthew Passion; Scott McLean's Scripture Songs; Moravec's Songs of Love and War. *Honours:* Nat. Opera Inst. Career Grant, New York City Opera Gold Debut Award. *Current Management:* c/o William Knight, Grant House, 309 Wood Street, Burlington, NJ 08016, USA. *Telephone:* (609) 386-3933.

ARONICA, Roberto; Italian singer (tenor); b. 1968. *Education:* studied with Carlo Bergonzi. *Career:* appearances as Rodolfo, Turin 1992; as Donizetti's Edgardo at Macerata as Alfredo, at Treviso 1995; guest engagements as the Duke of Mantua, Santiago 1992; as Alfredo, WNO; as Rodolfo and Alfredo, San Francisco 1993, 1995; further appearances as Rodolfo at La Scala 1996; as Rodolfo, Opéra Bastille, Paris and Tel-Aviv 1998; season 2000–01 as Alfredo at the New York Met and the Duke of Mantua at Chicago; debut in Faust at Teatro Regio in Parma 2006; other performances have included Pinkerton in Madama Butterfly in Rome, Madrid, Berlin and Dresden, Duke of Mantua in Rigoletto at Metropolitan Opera, New York, Lisbon and Bologna, La Traviata in Berlin, Rodolfo in La Bohème in Munich, New York and Chicago, Macbeth in New York; season 2009/10 Les Contes d'Hoffmann in Turin, Simon Boccanegra in Madrid, Don Carlos in Bilbao, Faust in Barcelona. *Current Management:* Iberkonzert, C/ Rodríguez Arias 23 - 6º - Dt.10, 48011 Bilbao, Spain. *Telephone:* (94) 4104746. *Fax:* (94) 4218582. *E-mail:* agencia@iberkonzert.com. *Website:* www.iberkonzert.com.

ARONOFF, Josef, MBC, AGSM, LRAM; Polish violinist, violist and conductor; b. 13 June 1932, Budapest, Hungary; m. Astrid Gray; three s. one d. *Education:* Franz Liszt Academy of Music, Budapest, Guildhall School of Music, London. *Career:* radio and television broadcasts, Hungary, Austria, UK, Portugal, France, Germany, USA, Hong Kong, Australia; Prof., Royal Manchester Coll. of Music, England 1965–70; Head of String Dept, Queensland Conservatorium of Music, Australia 1970–75; Musical Dir, Conservatorium Chamber Orchestra 1970–75; Musical Dir, Artemon Ensemble and Orchestra 1971–, also with Philomela and Concertante Ensembles; Concertmaster, Dir of Instrumental Studies, Darling Downs Inst. of Advanced Educ. 1975–77; Conductor, Allegri Players 1975–77; Sr Lecturer, Adelaide Coll. of Arts 1977–79; Musical Dir, South-Western Symphony Orchestra 1977–79; Prof., Guildhall School of Music and Drama, England 1979–88; Prof., Birmingham School of Music 1979–88; Sr Examiner, Australian Guild Music Examination Bd 1988–; master-classes. *Recordings:* Viola Concerto 1989 by C Reichard-Gross; Memories of Sunny Days for Violin and Orchestra by C Reichard-Gross, with Hungarian Northern Symphony Orchestra, soloist Josef Aronoff (viola/violin), conductor Laszlo Kovacs. *Address:* 40 Isabella Street, Tarragindi, Brisbane, Queensland 4121, Australia.

ARREY, Javier; Chilean singer (baritone); b. 1982, Valdivia. *Education:* studied singing with Hanns Stein at Universidad de Chile, Santiago, and choir conducting at Teatro Municipal. *Career:* took part in Neue Stimmen masterclass with Katia Ricciarelli, Francisco Araiza, Siegfried Jerusalem and Gustav Kuhn; has also interpreted baroque music, mainly Bach, with Hans-Joachim Rotzsch in Leipzig; has performed under numerous conductors including Daniel Montané, Roberto Rizzi Brignoli, Gustav Kuhn, Jan Latham-König, Hans-Joachim Rotzsch, Andreas Mitisek; semi-finalist at Operalia 2007; finalist in Competizione dell'Opera, SemperOper, Dresden 2008; represented Chile in the BBC Cardiff Singer of the World Competition BBC, finishing as a finalist for the Song Prize 2009; selected by Dolora Zajick to join her programme at Inst. for Young Dramatic Voices, Orem, Utah, USA 2009; with Domingo-Cafritz Young Artist Program, Washington Nat. Opera 2010–12, appeared as Yamadori in Madama Butterfly and as A Scythian in Iphigénie en Tauride 2011; debut at Palau de les Arts Reina Sofia, Valencia, Spain in Menotti's Amelia al ballo and The Telephone; numerous concerts and recitals. *Repertoire includes* Conte (Le nozze di Figaro), Masetto (Don Giovanni), Guglielmo and Alfonso (Così fan tutte), Enrico (Lucia di Lammermoor) and Figaro (Il barbiere di Siviglia), baritone solo parts in Handel's Messiah, Brahms' Requiem, Fauré's Requiem, Beethoven's Ninth Symphony and Bach's Christmas Oratorio and St John Passion; lieder repertoire includes Schumann's Dichterliebe, Dvorák's Biblical Songs and Mahler's Lieder eines fahrenden Gesellen. *Honours:* The Culturarte Prize, OPERALIA – The World Opera Competition 2011. *Address:* c/o Washington National Opera, The John F. Kennedy Center for the Performing Arts, 2700 F Street, NW, Washington, DC 20566, USA. *Telephone:* (202) 467-4600. *E-mail:* info@kennedy-center.org. *Website:* www.kennedy-center.org.

ARROYO, Martina, BA; American singer (soprano) and academic; *Distinguished Professor Emerita, School of Music, Indiana University*; b. 2 Feb. 1937, New York; d. of Demetrio Arroyo and Lucille Arroyo (née Washington); m. 1st Emilio Poggioni (divorced); m. 2nd Michel Maurel (deceased). *Education:* City Univ. of New York, Hunter Coll. and Metropolitan Opera, New York. *Career:* Visiting Prof., Louisiana State Univ., Baton Rouge; debut Carnegie Hall (New York) 1958; Leading Soprano, Metropolitan Opera, New York; appearances at all major US opera houses and La Scala, Milan, Italy, Munich Staatsoper and Berlin Deutsche Oper, Germany, Rome Opera, Vienna State Opera, Royal Opera House, Covent Garden, London, Teatro Colon, Argentina and Edinburgh, Tanglewood, Vienna, Berlin and Helsinki Festivals; fmr Distinguished Prof. of Voice, Indiana Univ. School of Music, now Distinguished Prof. Emer.; f. Martina Arroyo Foundation 2003; fmr mem. Nat. Endowment for the Arts, Washington, DC; Fellow, American Acad. of Arts and Sciences 2002–; Trustee Carnegie Hall, New York. *Recordings:* more than 50 recordings. *Honours:* Dr hc (Hunter Coll.); Outstanding Alumna, Hunter Coll., Amici di Verdi Medal 2002, Nat. Endowment of the Arts Opera Honor 2010, Kennedy Center Honors 2013. *Address:* Martina Arroyo Foundation, Inc., 57 West 57th Street, 4th Floor, New York, NY 10019, USA. *Telephone:* (212) 315-9190. *Fax:* (212) 397-7257. *E-mail:* martinaarroyo@aol.com; info@martinaarroyofdn.org. *Website:* www.martinaarroyofoundation.org; www.martinaarroyo.com.

ARTAUD, Pierre-Yves; French flautist and academic; *Professor of Flute, Conservatoire National Supérieur de Musique et de Danse de Paris*; b. 13 July 1946, Paris; s. of Maurice Artaud and Huguette Artaud; m. Daniel Chantal (divorced); three d.; civil partner Carine Dupré; four d. *Education:* Conservatoire Nat. Supérieur de Musique et de Danse de Paris. *Career:* played the piccolo in Orchestre Philharmonique, Île-de-France 1964–68, and flute with Orchestra Laetitia Musica 1971; directed contemporary flute studies at Sainte-Baume 1973–80; Visiting Prof., Pecs and Csongrad, Hungary 1978; responsible for instrumental research at Institut de Recherche et Coordination Acoustique/Musique, Paris, Electronic Music Studio 1981; Prof., Darmstadt 1982; performer in recital groups including Arcadie (quartet of flutes) 1964, Da Camera (wind quintet) 1970–72, Albert Roussel Quintet 1973–74; collaboration with harpist Sylvie Beltrando and harpsichordist Pierre Bouyer; f. French Flute Orchestra 1985; has premiered works by Brian Ferneyhough, Betsy Jolas, Tristan Murail, Franco Donatoni, Maurice Ohana and André Boucourechliev; Prof. of Chamber Music, Paris Conservatoire 1985–, also of Flute 1987–; teacher, Ecole Normale de Musique Alfred Cortot, Paris 1996; Founder Pres. Orchestre français de flûtes 1985–; Pres. La Traversière 2011. *Publications include:* La Flûte 1987, Méthode élémentaire pour la flûte 1970, Flûtes au présent 1980, A propos de pédagogie 1991; numerous articles in various publs. *Honours:* Chevalier des Arts et des Lettres; Dr hc (Bucharest) 2000; First Prize, Paris Conservatoire 1969, 1970, Medal of Arts, Sciences and Letters 1978, Grand Prix of French Contemporary Music Interpretation 1982, Prix Acad. du Disque Français 1984, Prix Charles Cros 1985. *Address:* Conservatoire National Supérieur de Musique et de Danse de Paris, 209 avenue Jean Jaurès, 75019 Paris, France (office). *Telephone:* 1-40-40-45-45 (office). *E-mail:* pyartaud@aol.com. *Website:* www.cnsmdp.fr (office); www.pyartaud.com.

ARTETA, Ainhoa; Spanish singer (soprano); b. 1966, Tolosa. *Career:* appearances at N American opera houses from 1990; debut as Mimi in La Bohème at Metropolitan Opera; other Met roles have included Musetta, Violetta in La Traviata, Gilda and Liu in Turandot; sang Micaela in Carmen for Scottish Opera 1992; as Olga in Fedora, and Mimi; Leila in Les Pêcheurs de perles, Seattle 1994; Magda in La Rondine, Bonn; Mimi for Netherlands Opera; Zarzuela performances with Plácido Domingo, Hamburg 1996; season 1998 as Magda at Washington, Violetta at Cincinnati; sang Musetta in La Bohème at the New York Met 2000; has sung in concert at the White House and at Carnegie Hall with Michael Tilson Thomas and the New World Symphony, also Palau de la Musica in Barcelona; performed with Plácido Domingo in Berlin, Hamburg, Istanbul, Leipzig, Madrid, Paris, Munich, Valencia, Brazil and London (debut at Royal Opera House, Covent Garden); debut in Manon and as Blanche in Dialogues des Carmélites in Bilbao, premiere of Dulcinea by Lorenzo Palomo at the Konzerthaus in Berlin, a tour with Sir Neville Marriner and the Orchestra of Cadaqués, debut at Musikverein in Vienna with pianist Roger Vignoles, Beethoven's Ninth Symphony with the Tenerife Symphony Orchestra under the direction of Victor Pablo Pérez, La Bohème at Metropolitan Opera under Carlo Rizzi; centenary recital with Jose Carreras at Lyric Gala, and several recitals with pianist Malcolm Martineau; has worked with conductors including Sir Neville Marriner, Vasily Petrenko, Pablo Gonzalez, Friedrich Haider and Pier Giorgio

Morandi; recent engagements include La Bohème, Eugene Onegin, Manon Lescaut, Turandot, Otello, Simon Boccanegra and Cyrano de Bergerac (with Plácido Domingo), at venues including the Metropolitan Opera, Liceu in Barcelona, ABAO, Las Palmas, Teatro alla Scala in Milan and in San Francisco; further engagements include performances with Orquesta Nacional de España, Orquesta Sinfónica de Galicia, Orquesta Sinfónica de Euskadi, Orquesta Sinfónica de Tenerife and Orquesta de Cadaqués, with conductors including Sir Neville Marriner, Gianandrea Noseda, Christopher Hogwood, Vasily Petrenko, Pablo González, Adrian Leaper, Víctor Pablo Pérez, Friedrich Haider, Pier Giorgio Morandi and Miguel Ángel Gómez Martínez; Academician, Royal Acad. of Fine Arts of Cádiz. *Recordings:* solo: Recital, Entrañable, Zarazuela, La Vida 2008; other: Dona Francisquita, Romeo y Julieta 2002, Turandot 2002, Fedora 2004, La Bohème 2007, La Rondine, Don't Give Up 2010, Mayi 2015. *Honours:* 'Universal Basque', Basque Govt; Metropolitan Auditions and Plácido Domingo Competition 1993, Prize of the Hispanic Society of America for Contribution to the Arts; Best Classical Music Artist; Federico Romero Prize of the Fundación Autor for int. career, Gold Medal, Palau de la Música de Valencia, Gold Microphone, Fed. of Radio and Television of Spain, Enric Granados Prize and Gold Medal, Asscn of Opera's Friends in Lleida, Award of Arts and Letters, City of Alcalá. *Current Management:* c/o Iberkonzert, Rodríguez Arias 23 - 2º Dpto 2, 48011 Bilbao, Spain; c/o Zemsky/Green Artists Management, 104 West 73rd Street, Suite 1, New York, NY 10023, USA. *Telephone:* (94) 4104746 (Spain); (212) 579-6700 (USA). *Fax:* (94) 4218582 (Spain); (212) 679-4723 (USA). *E-mail:* agencia@iberkonzert.com; bzemsky@zemskygreen.com. *Website:* www.iberkonzert.com; www.zemskygreen.com.

ARTYOMOV, Vyacheslav; Russian composer; b. 29 June 1940, Moscow; m. Valeriya Lyubetskaya. *Education:* Moscow Conservatory, studied with A. Pirumov and N. Sidelnikov. *Career:* mem. Russian Acad. of Natural Sciences. *Compositions include:* orchestral: Concert of the 13 for piano and 12 musicians 1967, In Memoriam (symphony with violin solo) 1968–84, Tempo Costante (concerto for 2 actors and chamber orchestra) 1970, 1980, A Symphony of Elegies for two violins and chamber orchestra 1977, A Garland of Recitations for woodwind solos and chamber orchestra 1981, Tristia I for piano solo and orchestra 1983, Way To Olympus (symphony for orchestra) 1984, Lamentations for chamber orchestra or choir 1985, Gurian Hymn for 3 violins and chamber orchestra 1986, Sola Fide (By Faith Alone), ballet-requiem 1987–2015, Requiem for soloists, 2 choirs and orchestra 1988, On the Threshold of a Bright World (symphony for orchestra) 1990, 2002 (revised 2013), Gentle Emanation (symphony) 1991, 2008, Maltian Hymn Ave, Crux Alba for choir and orchestra 1994, 2012, In Spe (symphony with violin and cello solos) 1995–2014, Pieta for cello and chamber orchestra 1996, Ave Atque Vale for percussion player and orchestra 1997–98, Tristia II for piano solo, romantic actor and orchestra 1998 (revised 2011), Latin Hymns for soprano, choir and chamber orchestra 2003, In the Kingdom of Nix (Concerto infernale) for piano and orchestra 2008–16; chamber music: Northern Songs for mezzo-soprano, percussion and piano 1966, 0 Clarinet Sonatas 1966, Confession for Clarinet 1971, Variations: Nestling Antsali for flute and piano 1974, Capriccio For the '75 New Year's Eve for soprano saxophone, baritone saxophone and vibraphone 1975, Totem for percussion group 1976, Awakening for 2 violins 1978, Scenes for 5 players 1971, Sonata of Meditations for Percussion Group 1978, Incantations for soprano and percussion group 1981, Star Wind for 6 players 1981, Moonlight Dreams, a cantata for soprano/mezzo-soprano, alto flute, cello and piano 1982, Hymns of Sudden Wafts for soprano and tenor saxophones, piano and harpsichord 1983, Litanies for different ensembles, Recitations for woodwind solos, Sola Fide (Only by Faith), Libretto (with Valeriya Lyubetskaya) 1997–2015, Gentle Emanation 2010, On the Threshold of a Bright World 2013; various works for different instruments. *Honours:* Order of Friendship 2010. *Address:* Moscow 119034, Pomerantsev per. 9–19, Russia (home). *Telephone:* (499) 766-40-56 (home). *Fax:* (499) 245-06-18 (home). *E-mail:* slart241@gmail.com. *Website:* fonspic.net.

ARTZT, Alice Josephine, BA; American classical guitarist, writer and teacher; b. 16 March 1943, Philadelphia, Pa; d. of Maurice Gustav Artzt and Harriett Green Artzt; m. Bruce B. Lawton, Jr. *Education:* Columbia Univ. and studied composition with Darius Milhaud and guitar with Julian Bream, Ida Presti and Alexandre Lagoya. *Career:* taught guitar at Mannes Coll. of Music, New York 1966–69, Trenton State Univ. 1977–80; worldwide tours as soloist 1969–94; f. Alice Artzt Guitar Trio (with M. Rutscho and R. Burley) 1989; toured in duo with R. Burley; fmr mem. Bd of Dirs Guitar Foundation of America (Chair. 1986–89). *Recordings include:* Baroque Recital, Guitar Music by Fernando Sor, Guitar Music by Francisco Tarrega, 20th Century Guitar Music, English Guitar Music, The Music of Manuel Ponce, The Glory of the Guitar, Virtuoso Romantic Guitar, Musical Tributes, Variations, Passacaglias and Chaconnes, American Music of the Stage and Screen, Alice Artzt Classic Guitar, Alice Artzt Plays Original Works. *Publications include:* The Art of Practicing, The International GFA Guitarists' Cookbook (ed.), Rhythmic Mastery 1997; numerous articles in guitar and music periodicals. *Honours:* several Critics' Choice Awards. *Address:* 51 Hawthorne Avenue, Princeton, NJ 08540, USA (home). *Telephone:* (609) 921-6629 (home). *E-mail:* guitartzt@aol.com. *Website:* guitartzt.com.

ARUHN, Britt Marie; Swedish singer (soprano); b. 11 Nov. 1943, Motala. *Education:* Stockholm Acad. of Music. *Career:* debut, Stockholm in Les Contes d'Hoffmann 1974; has sung at Stockholm and the Drottningholm Festival as Norina, Zerbinetta, Gilda, Violetta, Mélisande, Susanna, Rosina, Musetta, Mimi, Micaela, Marguerite, Nedda, Sophie, Gepopo and Adina; Staatsoper Dresden as Gilda and Sophie 1976, Covent Garden as Zerbinetta 1978, Wiener Staatsoper as Gilda 1978, Sophie 1980, Paris as Gepopo in Der Grosse Makaber and Zdenka 1981, Hamburg Staatsoper as Olympia 1981, Musetta 1982, Brussels as La Fée in Cendrillon, La Comtesse in Le Conte d'Ory and Musetta 1983, Mélisande and Susanna 1984, Adèle 1985, Sandrina in La Finta Giardiniera (and at Drottningholm) 1987, La Scala as Lucio Cinna in Lucio Silla 1984, Drottningholm as Sandrina 1987, and in Luigi Rossi's Orfeo 1997, Helsinki as Violetta 1988, Oslo as Violetta 1991, Marshchallin in Stockholm 1995, Madama Butterfly 1996, Countess in Powder her Face in Umeå 2005, Amelia in Un Ballo in Maschera, Norway 2007. *Recordings include:* Brahms' Ein Deutsches Requiem; Strauss' Vier Letzte Lieder. *Film:* First Lady in The Magic Flute 1974. *Honours:* Litteris et Artibus 2010, Royal Court Singer 1998. *Address:* Kungliga Operan, PO Box 16094, 10322 Stockholm, Sweden (office). *E-mail:* brittmarie@aruhn.se.

ARVIDSSON, Bjorn; Swedish singer (tenor); b. 1965, Stockholm; m. Jennifer Bird. *Education:* Sundsgarden, Malmo, Guildhall School of Music and Drama, England with Laura Sarti. *Career:* soloist, Landestheater Coburg 2000–03, Theater Dortmund 2004–06; guest appearances as Nemorino in L'Elisir d'amore at Bernini Opera, Robinson Crusoe with British Youth Opera, several roles for Opera Holland Park and Travelling Opera, Rodolfo for Kent Opera, as Tamino on tour with Pavilion Opera, Rene and Armand in Der Graf von Luxemburg for D'Oyly Carte Opera, four roles in Poppea for WNO; appeared in Antwerp, Netherlands; tour of Ireland with Co-Opera, also at Théâtres de Caen and Rouen, France; festivals include Aix en Provence and Academie Europèene de Musique; toured France, Italy and Switzerland; Don Jose in Carmen at Landestheater Coburg 2006; regular appearances in concert and oratorio including arias and duets by Mozart, Smetana, Verdi and Bizet at Landestheater Coburg 2010 and Verdi Requiem with Sacramento Choral Society & Orchestra 2011. *Current Management:* c/o Theateragentur Heidi Schäfer, Postfach 18 03 80, 60084 Frankfurt am Main, Germany. *Telephone:* 1712884544 (mobile). *E-mail:* hs@santuzza.de.

ASAWA, Brian; American singer (countertenor); b. 1966. *Education:* studied in New York. *Career:* season 1995 as Britten's Oberon with the London Symphony Orchestra, Endimione in La Calisto at Brussels, Arsamenes in Handel's Xerxes at the Cologne Opera and a Wigmore Hall recital with Melvyn Tan; season 1996–97 in Handel's Semele at the Berlin Staatsoper, Monteverdi's Orfeo in Amsterdam and Lyon; Seattle and Göttingen debuts as Arsamenes, Opéra Bastille and Covent Garden debuts as Tolomeo in Giulio Cesare; season 1997–98 in Mozart's Mitridate for Lyon Opéra and Monteverdi's Nero for Australian Opera, and Dallas Opera debut in Handel's Ariodante; Handel's Admeto in Australia and at Montpellier 1998; recitals at Lincoln Center, Geneva Opera, Sydney Festival and on tour to Japan; season 2000–01 as Farnace in Mozart's Mitridate at the Paris Châtelet, Handel's Tolomeo in Sydney, Baba the Turk in The Rake's Progress for San Francisco Opera; has sung Tolomeo in Handel's Giulio Cesare for Seattle Opera, Metropolitan Opera, Bordeaux Opera, Opera Australia, Royal Opera House, Covent Garden, Paris Opera at Palais Garnier, Madrid's Teatro Real, Barcelona's Gran Teatre del Liceu, New Israeli Opera, and Hamburg Staatsoper; Prince Orlofsky in Johann Strauss' Die Fledermaus for San Francisco Opera and San Diego Opera; Arsamene in Handel's Xerxes for Los Angeles, Cologne, and Santa Fe Operas, and Grand Théâtre de Genève; Farnace in Mozart's Mitridate for Theatre de la Monnaie, Brussels; Belize in Peter Eotvos's Angels in America; Mascha in Eotvos's Tri Sestri and Ottone in Monteverdi's L'Incoronazione di Poppea for Hamburg; Ottone in Poppea for Glimmerglass Opera and Nero in Poppea for Opera Australia; Endimione in Cavalli's La Calisto in Brussels; Fyodor in Mussorgsky's Boris Godunov for Netherlands Opera and Teatre del Liceu in Barcelona; Orfeo in Gluck's Orfeo ed Euridice for Nederlandse Opera; David in Handel's Saul for Bayerische Staatsoper, Munich; Oberon in Britten's A Midsummer Night's Dream for San Francisco and Houston Grand Operas and Teatro di San Carlo in Naples. *Recordings include:* A Midsummer Night's Dream, Arsamene in Xerxes, Farnace in Mitridate, Arcadian Duets 2002, Il Ritorno d'Ulisse in Patria 2005, Messiah 2005, Boris Godunov 2006: solo: The Dark is My Delight and Other Lute Songs 1997, Vocalise 1999, More Than a Day: Music of Ned Rorem 2000, Scarlatti Cantatas Vol. 3 2000. *Honours:* winner Metropolitan Opera Auditions 1991, Richard Tucker Foundation grant 1993, prizewinner Placido Domingo Operalia Competition 1994, Adler Fellow for San Francisco Opera, Seattle Opera Artist of the Year Award for his portrayal of Arsamene in Handel's Xerxes. *E-mail:* contact@brianasawa.com. *Website:* www.brianasawa.com.

ASBURY, Stefan; British conductor; b. 2 July 1965, Dudley, West Midlands; one s. *Education:* Christ Church Coll., Oxford, Royal Coll. of Music, London, Tanglewood Music Centre. *Career:* regular guest of many of the leading orchestras worldwide encompassing the US, Europe, Asia and Australia; engagements with SWR Stuttgart, SWR Sinfonieorchester Baden-Baden & Freiburg, WDR Cologne, NDR Hamburg, NDR Hannover, Deutschland Radio, RIAS Kammerchor, Århus Symphony, Norwegian Radio Orchestra, Royal Scottish Nat. Orchestra and contemporary ensembles, including Ensemble Modern, musikFabrik, Asko Ensemble, London Sinfonietta, Klangforum Wien, Ensemble Intercontemporain; festival appearances include Berlin Festival, Wien Modern, Ultima Festival, Venice Biennale; opera includes premiere of Rob Zuidam's Freeze at Munich Biennale, Birtwistle's Punch & Judy and Chagas Rosa's Melodias Estranhas with Remix Ensemble, Judith

Weir's The Blond Eckbert with NDR Hamburg, premieres of Staud's Berenice at Munich Biennale and Berlin Festival 2004, van Vlijmen's Thyeste at La Monnaie, Britten's Midsummer Night's Dream at Tanglewood 2004; world premiere of Jan Van Vlijmen's Thyeste with La Monnaie in Brussels and Dutch Touring Opera; Season 2004–05 included performances of Alfred Schnittke's accompaniment to The Last Days of St Petersburg in Amsterdam and Lincoln Center, New York, a Steve Reich project with Ensemble Modern at the Barbican Centre, London and Alte Oper, Frankfurt, profile of Jorg Widmann with NDR Hamburg, concert with Tapiola Sinfonietta at Musica Nova Festival, Helsinki, performance and subsequent recording of works by Enno Poppe at Berlin Festival with Klangforum Wien, Venice Biennale with Orchestra della Toscana and concerts with Residentie Orchestra, WDR Cologne, NDR Hamburg, New World Symphony and Munich Chamber Orchestra; Salzburg Festival debut with Klangforum Wien 2005; conducted Shanghai Philharmonic Orchestra in first ever musical event focusing on the music of Benjamin Britten as part of the Shanghai Spring Festival 2006; master classes at instns such as the Hochschule der Kunste (Zurich), Venice Conservatoire, and Tokyo Wonder Site; Music Dir, Remix Ensemble, Casa da Musica Porto for four years; mem. Faculty, Tanglewood Music Center 1995–, Assoc. Dir, New Music Activities 1999–2002, Sana H. Sabbagh Master Teacher Chair on the Conducting Faculty 2005–; Music Dir Remix Ensemble Casa da Musica Porto 2001–05; Artist in Residence, Tapiola Sinfonietta 2008–. *Recordings include:* Harvey, One Evening with Ensemble Intercontemporain (Monde de la Musique CHOC Award), Grisey 'Les Espaces Acoustiques' with orchestra of WDR Cologne and Asko Ensemble (Preis der deutschen Schallplattenkritik, Diapason d'Or, France), works by Unsuk Chin with Ensemble Intercontemporain, music by Isang Yun with Deutsches Symphonie Orchester, Berlin, works by Elliott Carter with Ensemble Sospeso, portrait discs of Philip Cashian with Birmingham Contemporary Music Group and Rebecca Saunders with musikFabrik. *Honours:* Leonard Bernstein Fellowship, Tanglewood 1990, Conducting Prize, Munich Biennale 1994. *Current Management:* Harrison Parrott, 5–6 Albion Court, London, W6 0QT, England. *Telephone:* (20) 7229-9166. *Fax:* (20) 7221-5042. *E-mail:* info@harrisonparrott.co.uk. *Website:* www.harrisonparrott.com.

ASCHENBACH, Hans; American singer (tenor); b. 1965, Idaho. *Education:* studied in Idaho and with Neville Marriner. *Career:* engagements at the New Orleans Opera, Lyric Opera of Queensland, New York Metropolitan, ENO and Connecticut Opera; sang Schoenberg's Aron with the Leipzig Opera and in concert with the Philharmonic Orchestra at the Royal Festival Hall, London 1996; other roles include Alwa in Lulu, Nuremberg Opera 1996; season 2000–01 as Lohengrin at Weimar and Tannhäuser at Schwerin; concerts at Carnegie Hall and throughout Europe. *Current Management:* Agentur Sigrid Rostock, Eugen-Schönhaar-Strasse 1, 10407 Berlin, Germany. *Telephone:* (30) 4257514. *Fax:* (30) 4239136. *E-mail:* sigridrostock@web.de. *Website:* hansaschenbach.com.

ASGEIRSSON, Jón Gunnar; Icelandic composer and music educator (retd); b. 11 Oct. 1928, Isafjördur; m. Elisabet Thorgeirsdottir; two s. one d. *Education:* Reykjavík School of Music, Royal Scottish Acad. of Music, Glasgow and Guildhall School of Music, London, UK. *Career:* music teacher at elementary school, Hafnarfjördur 1958–62; music teacher, Coll. of Educ., Univ. of Iceland 1962–81, Lecturer 1981–94, Prof. 1994–98; music critic for Morgunbladid 1970–2002; mem. Soc. de Compositeurs d'Islande, Tónskáldafélag Islands. *Compositions include:* orchestral: Folklore Rhapsody, Lilja, symphonic poem, A Poem of Seven Strings, Blindisleikur, ballet suite, Ancient Dances Suite; concertos: Cello and Orchestra, Horn and Orchestra, Clarinet and Orchestra, Flute and Orchestra, Trumpet and Orchestra, Piano and Orchestra; chamber music: Woodwinds Octet, 2 Woodwind Quintets, Folkloric Quintet for Piano and String Quartet, Four Movements for Solo Guitar, String Quartet 2000, Ten Icelandic Folk Songs for solo guitar 2000, Choral works and songs; operas: Thrymskvida, based on mythological poem, Galdra-Loftur, based on a play by Johann Sigurjónsson, Möttulssaga based on ancient sagas; numerous arrangements of Icelandic folksongs and dances. *Recordings include:* For Icelandic Broadcasting Service; Ten Icelandic Folk Songs, 1999; Galdra-Loftur (opera); Svarfálfa dans (Dance of the Black Elves), Sjöstrengjaljóð, Complete Works for Voice and Piano by Jón Asgeirsson. *Honours:* Reykjavík City Artist 1996; Fálkaordan (Islandiae sigillum ordinis Falconis) from Pres. of Iceland 2001; Dr hc (Univ. of Iceland) 2000; First Prize in Opera Competition, Icelandic Nat. Theatre 1974, DV cultural awards for music 1997. *Current Management:* c/o Gudrún Jóhanna Jónsdóttir, Gulathing 7, 203 Kópavogur, Iceland. *Telephone:* 8950291. *E-mail:* gunnaogstig@simnet.is. *Address:* Fródengi 7, 112 Reykjavík, Iceland (home). *Telephone:* 5522158 (office).

ASHE, Rosemary (Rosie) Elizabeth, LRAM, ARAM; British singer (soprano) and actress; b. 28 March 1953, Lowestoft; d. of Philip Stephen Ashe and Dorothy May Ashe; . *Education:* Royal Acad., London Opera Centre. *Career:* sang in the premiere of Tavener's Thérèse at Covent Garden 1979; for ENO has sung Papagena, Esmeralda in Bartered Bride, Fiakermilli in Arabella, Venus in Orpheus in the Underworld and ZouZou in La Belle Vivette; other roles include the Queen of Night and Julie Laverne in Showboat for Opera North, Despina in Così fan Tutte and Lucy Lockitt in The Beggar's Opera on BBC television, Frasquita at Earl's Court and Japan, Josephine in HMS Pinafore at City Center New York, Musetta for Opera Northern Ireland, Offenbach's Hélène at Sadler's Wells and Clorinda in La Cenerentola at Garsington, Dinah in Trouble in Tahiti for Musiktheater Transparant in Antwerp; season 1994–95 as Shakespeare's Hermia at Barbados and in Brand's Maschinist Hopkins in Amsterdam; Ruth in The Pirates of Penzance for Carl Rosa; performed in Coward's After the Ball at the Covent Garden Festival 1999; many appearances in musicals; created role of Carlotta in Andrew Lloyd Webber's The Phantom of the Opera; created role of Felicia Gabriel in The Witches of Eastwick at the Theatre Royal, Drury Lane, London 2000–01 and also at the Princess Theatre, Melbourne 2002; Madame Thenardier in Les Misérables 2002–03; Suzanne in Robinson Crusoe, Iford Festival, Bath 2004; Miss Andrew in Mary Poppins, Prince Edward Theatre, London 2004–06; Ruth in The Pirates of Penzance, Carl Rosa Opera Co., American tour 2007, The Beggar Woman in Sweeney Todd, London 2007, Mrs Lovett in Sweeney Todd, Gothenburg Opera 2008, Mrs Fraser in Stepping Out 2009, Dotty Otley in Noises Off, Wolsey Theatre 2010, Lottie Grady in When We Are Married, The Garrick Theatre 2010, Mona Kent in Dames At Sea, The Union Theatre 2011, On The Sunny Side of the Street, Jermyn Street Theatre, Call Me Merman, Yvonne Arnaud Theatre, Guildford, Little Buttercup in HMS Pinafore 2012, There's No Place Like A Home, The Mill at Sonning 2013–14, The Witches of Eastwick, The Watermill, Newbury 2014, Jack and The Beanstalk, Newcastle Theatre Royal 2014, The Secret Diary of Adrian Mole, Leicester Curve 2015, Crush (musical, touring) 2015. *Recordings:* original cast recordings of The Phantom of the Opera, The Boyfriend, Bitter Sweet, Kismet, Oliver!, The Student Prince, The Witches of Eastwick, Mary Poppins, The Killer Soprano, Serious Cabaret. *Current Management:* c/o Cole Kitchenn, 212 Strand, London, WC2R 1AP, England. *Telephone:* (20) 7427-5680. *Fax:* (20) 7353-9639. *E-mail:* info@colekitchenn.com. *Website:* www.colekitchenn.com. *E-mail:* rosieashe@yahoo.co.uk (office). *Website:* www.rosemaryashe.com; www.rosemaryashemasterclass.com.

ASHER, Nadine; American singer (contralto); b. 24 Dec. 1957, Chicago. *Education:* Indiana Univ. and Juilliard School, New York. *Career:* sang at first in concert, then opera engagement at Kiel from 1984; Guest appearances at Heidelberg, Munster and Lucerne, as Bostania in Cornelius's Barbier von Bagdad; Zürich Opera from 1987, as Wagner's Flosshilde and Grimgerde, Edwige in Guillaume Tell and Ulrica in Un Ballo in Maschera; Zürich 1996 in the premiere of Schlafes Bruder by H Willi; Arnalta in The Coronation of Poppea; Voice Prof., Oakland Univ. *E-mail:* washiong@oakland.edu (office).

ASHKENASI, Shmuel; American/Israeli violinist; *Professor of Violin and Chamber Music, Curtis Institute of Music;* b. 11 Jan. 1941, Tel-Aviv, Israel; m. Mihaela Ionescu Ashkenasi; two s. *Education:* Musical Acad. of Tel-Aviv, Curtis studied with Efrem Zimbalist at Inst. of Music. *Career:* concert violinist since 1962; First Violinist, Vermeer String Quartet; Prof. of Music and Artist-in-Residence, Univ. of Northern Illinois 1969–2007; also taught at Roosevelt Univ., Chicago and Musikhochshcule Lübeck, Germany; mem. Performance Faculty, Curtis Inst. of Music 2007–, Prof. of Violin and Chamber Music 2007–; also teaches at Bard Coll.; has collaborated with Rudolf Serkin, Thomas Hampson, Murray Perahia, Peter Serkin, Menahem Pressler. *Honours:* First Prize, Merriweather Post Contest, Washington, DC 1958, Finalist, Queen Elizabeth Competition, Brussels 1959, Second Prize, Tchaikovsky Competition, Moscow 1962. *Address:* Curtis Institute of Music, 1726 Locust Street, Philadelphia, PA 19103 (office); 3800 North Lakeshore Drive, Chicago, IL 60613, USA (home). *Telephone:* (215) 893-5252 (office); (773) 348-5087 (home). *Fax:* (215) 893-9065 (office). *E-mail:* sdashkenasi@gmail.com (home). *Website:* www.curtis.edu (office).

ASHKENAZY, Dimitri; Icelandic clarinettist; b. 8 Oct. 1969, New York; s. of Vladimir Davidovich Ashkenazy and Thórunn Sofia Jóhannsdóttir; brother of Vovka Ashkenazy. *Education:* Lucerne Conservatory with Giambattista Sisini. *Career:* concerts 1992–93 at the Hollywood Bowl and with the Royal Philharmonic in London (Mozart's Concerto); first tour of Japan 1993, followed by Maxwell Davies's Strathclyde Concerto No. 4 with the composer conducting; 1994 premiere of Marco Tutino's concerto at La Scala; collaborations with Barbara Bonney 1995, 1997, 1998, 2003 and Krzysztof Penderecki 1997, 1998, 1999; season 1996–97 with the premiere of Filippo del Corno's Concerto and concerts in Japan with the European Soloists Ensemble; tours with Sinfonia Varsovia in Spain and Poland playing Penderecki's concerto with the composer conducting 1998–99, and collaboration with Edita Gruberova 1999; appearance at Casals Festival, Puerto Rico 2000; tours of Japan 2000, 2002, including duo recitals with Vovka Ashkenazy and appearance with Gary Bertini at Suntory Hall, Tokyo; appearances in S Africa with KwaZulu-Natal Philharmonic 2002–03, 2006, 2008, with Brodsky Quartet 1999–2004, Amsterdam debut 2005; duo recitals with Vladimir Ashkenazy in Germany and Austria 2003; world premiere of Maxwell Davies's Clarinet Quintet, Hymn to Artemis Locheia with The Brodsky Quartet at the Lucerne Festival 2004; Berlin debut with the Rundfunk-Sinfonie-Orch. Berlin, Konzerthaus 2004; tours to Australia 2007–08; appearances with Benrd Glemser 2007–08, with Andrey Boreyko 2008; masterclasses in Australia, Spain, Iceland, Switzerland and the USA. *Recordings include:* Rossini Variations in C, Richard Strauss Duet-Concertino, Stravinsky Ebony Concerto, Stravinsky Chamber Music, Françaix Clarinet Concerto, Finzi, Copland, Bozza Clarinet Concertos, Blacher Clarinet Concerto. *Current Management:* c/o Ives Quartet, PO Box 60464, Palo Alto, CA 94306, USA. *E-mail:* info@ivesquartet.org. *Website:* www.ivesquartet.org.

ASHKENAZY, Vladimir Davidovich; Icelandic/Swiss (b. Russian) pianist and conductor; b. 6 July 1937, Gorky, USSR; s. of David Ashkenazy and Evstolia Ashkenazy (née Plotnova); m. Thórunn Sofia Jóhannsdóttir 1961; two s. three d. *Education:* Cen. Music School, Moscow and Moscow Conservatoire.

Career: Prin. Guest Conductor, Philharmonia Orchestra 1982–83, Conductor Laureate 2000–; Music Dir Royal Philharmonic Orchestra 1987–94, Deutsches Symphonie-Orchester Berlin (fmrly Berlin Radio Symphony) 1989–99; Chief Conductor Czech Philharmonic Orchestra 1998–2003; Music Dir EUYO (European Union Youth Orchestra) 2002–; Music Dir NHK Symphony, Tokyo 2004–07; Prin. Conductor and Artistic Adviser, Sydney Symphony Orchestra 2009–13; Dir Accademia Pianistica Internazionale di Imola 2013–; Conductor Laureate, Iceland Symphony Orchestra; fmr Prin. Guest Conductor, Cleveland Orchestra; apptd Artist Laureate, Royal Liverpool Philharmonic Orchestra during Liverpool's tenure as European City of Culture 2008. *Recordings include:* numerous recordings including Ashkenazy: 50 Years on Decca 2013. *Publication:* Beyond Frontiers (with Jasper Parrott) 1985. *Honours:* Hon. RAM; Order of the Falcon (Iceland); Hon. DMus (Nottingham) 1995; Second Prize, Int. Chopin Competition, Warsaw 1955, Gold Medal, Queen Elizabeth Int. Piano Competition, Brussels 1956, Jt Winner (with John Ogdon) Int. Tchaikovsky Piano Competition, Moscow 1962, Grammy Award for Best Instrumental Soloist Performance (with orchestra) for Prokofiev's Piano Concertos Nos 2 and 3 2010, Sergei Rachmaninov Int. Award 2014. *Current Management:* Harrison Parrott, 5–6 Albion Court, London, W6 0QT, England. *Telephone:* (20) 7229-9166 (office). *Fax:* (20) 7221-5042 (office). *E-mail:* info@harrisonparrott.co.uk (office). *Website:* www.harrisonparrott.com/artist/profile/vladimir-ashkenazy (office); www.vladimirashkenazy.com.

ASHKENAZY, Vovka; Russian pianist; b. 1961, Moscow; s. of Vladimir Davidovich Ashkenazy and Thórunn Sofia Jóhannsdóttir; brother of Dimitri Ashkenazy; m. Ariane Haering. *Education:* early piano studies in Iceland with Rögnvaldur Sigurjonsson, Royal Northern College of Music. *Career:* debut, Barbican Hall, London 1983 in Tchaikovsky 1st Piano Concerto with London Symphony Orchestra; appearances with most London orchestras in concertos by Brahms, Schumann, Grieg, Tchaikovsky and Rachmaninov; US debut with Los Angeles Philharmonic, at Hollywood Bowl; also Berlin Symphony Orchestra and Australian Chamber Orchestras; recitalist and chamber musician; appearances in many countries including Austria, Australia, Belgium, Cambodia, Canada, Denmark, Finland, France, Greece, Guatemala, Germany, Iceland, Italy, Ireland, Israel, Japan, Malta, Netherlands, New Zealand, Norway, Philippines, Russia, Spain and Switzerland; worked with conductors including Semyon Bychkov, Martin Fischer-Dieskau and Stanislaw Skrowaczewski at venues including Sydney Opera House, Berlin Philharmonie and Royal Festival Hall, London; festivals include Marlboro, Edinburgh, Spoleto, Piano en Valois and Athens Megaron; duo tours with father Vladimir in Istanbul and China 2010, Japan and Korea 2011, Switzerland 2012; Prof. of Piano, Conservatoire Gabriel Fauré, Angoulême, France 1998–2007; mem. chamber music coaching staff, Pro Corda music acad. 2010–; master classes. *Recordings include:* with Vladimir Ashkenazy: Bartók Sonata for Two Pianos and Percussion 1989, Debussy and Ravel: Music for Two Pianos 2009, Russian Fantasy, Piano Duets by Rachmaninov and Borodin 2011; other: Piano and Wind (with Reykjavik Wind Quintet) 2007, Arensky and Tchaikovsky Piano Trios (with R. Stamper and C. Jackson) 2008. *Current Management:* c/o Harrison Parrott, 5–6 Albion Court, Albion Place, London, W6 0QT, England. *E-mail:* jasper.parrott@harrisonparrott.co.uk.

ASHMAN, Mike; British opera director and administrator; b. 16 April 1950, Hertford, Herts. *Education:* Magdalene Coll., Cambridge. *Career:* Staff Dir with WNO and Royal Opera House, Covent Garden 1979–86; Visiting Dir in Music Theatre Banff Centre Alberta, Canada 1988–90; Assoc. Prod. for Royal Coll. of Music Opera School, London 1988–98; Artistic Dir Opera Zuid, Maastrict, The Netherlands 2000–04; has directed for Scottish Opera Go-Round, Opera Holland Park, Opera Ireland; has made performing translations of The Bartered Bride and Weill's Der Jasager. *Productions include:* for Den Norske Opera: Der fliegende Hollander 1999, Der Ring des Nibelungen 1993–97; for Royal Danish Opera: L'Elisir d'Amore 1999; French premieres of Cox and Box and Trial by Jury, Musee d'Orsay, Paris 1999; for Opera Zuid: Dutch premiere of Death in Venice 2001, Un Ballo in Maschera 2003, Der fliegende Hollander 2004; for Cincinnati Opera: Le Nozze di Figaro 2002; La jolie fille de Perth for Buxton Festival, Pierrot Lunaire for Almeida Festival, Faust with New Zealand Opera and the Sound of Music in Waterford, Ireland. *Publications:* contrib. to journals, newspapers, CD booklets and opera programmes. *Current Management:* Musichall Ltd, Vicarage Way, Ringmer, East Sussex, BN8 5LA, England. *Telephone:* (1273) 814240. *Fax:* (1273) 813637. *E-mail:* info@musichall.uk.com. *Website:* www.musichall.uk.com.

ASHWORTH, Valerie Grace, ARCM, LLRAM; British pianist, teacher and accompanist; b. 12 Sept. 1956, Sale, Cheshire, England; m. Vincent Pirillo, two d. *Education:* Chetham's School of Music, Manchester, Royal Coll. of Music, London with Kendall Taylor, Hochschule für Musik, Vienna with William Glock, Albert Ferber, Rudolf Firkusny. *Career:* radio debut, Young Artists 1969; soloist, chamber musician and accompanist in England, France, Switzerland, Italy, Denmark, Germany, Japan, Hungary and Austria; television debut on John Amis Music On Two 1972, Austrian television debut 1982; American debut at Carnegie Hall 1989; official accompanist, including Jacqueline du Pré masterclasses, England 1979, Summer Acad., Nice, France 1980, Irwin Gage in Zürich 1984–86, Carinthia Summer 1984 and Summer Acad. at Salzburg 1991; teacher in String Dept 1982–87, Vocal Dept 1987–89, Hochschule für Musik, Vienna; taught piano at Univ. of Osnabruck 1989–93; now teaches privately.

ASIKAINEN, Matti Tapio, DipMus, MA; Finnish pianist and composer; b. 25 June 1957, Hankasalmi. *Education:* Univ. of Jyväskylä, Sibelius Acad., Helsinki, Moniuszko Acad. of Music, Gdańsk, Poland. *Career:* debut in the concert hall of Sibelius Acad., Helsinki, 1974; recordings for Finnish Broadcasting Co. 1971–; appearances on Finnish, Lithuanian and Polish television; solo recitals also in Russia and Italy, including Incontri di Serra Maiori Festival; participant, Probaltica Festival of Chamber Music, Poland; soloist, Symphony Orchestras of Polish Philharmonia; Lecturer in Music Education, Univ. of Jyväskylä; mem. Int. Rachmaninoff Soc., England, Chopin Soc. of Finland, Asscn of Finnish Piano Teachers. *Publications:* contributions to music magazines and reviews. *Honours:* Vienna Musikseminar Int. Piano Competition, 1985; Knight Cross of Merit, Order of Merit (Polish President's award), 2002. *Address:* Department of Music, University of Jyväskylä, PO Box 35 (M), 40014 University (office); Pyynpolku 5, 40900 Säynätsalo, Finland (home). *Telephone:* (14) 378-2827 (home). *Fax:* (14) 260-1331 (home).

ASKER, Björn; Swedish singer (baritone); b. 23 Sept. 1941, Stockholm. *Education:* Royal Music Acad., Stockholm, studied with Tito Gobbi in Rome. *Career:* many appearances at Royal Opera, Stockholm from 1969, including the premiere of Werle's Tintomara 1973 and as Don Giovanni, Macbeth, Rossini's Figaro, Telramund, Wotan, Kurwenal, Alberich and Simon Boccanegra; guest appearances at Helsinki, Tel-Aviv and the Drottningholm Festival; sang Renato in Un Ballo in Maschera at Stockholm 1986; Lionel in Tchaikovsky's Maid of Orleans, Rigoletto and Wagner's Dutchman; Amfortas in Mexico and USA; many concert and recital dates; Swedish Court Singer 1983. *Address:* Stiftelsen Kungliga Teaterns Solister, PO Box 16253, 10324 Stockholm, Sweden (office). *E-mail:* info@operasolisterna.se (office). *Website:* www.operasolisterna.se/cv/bjorn_asker.

ASSAD, Sérgio; Brazilian composer, guitarist and arranger; *Professor of Guitar, San Francisco Conservatory of Music*; b. 26 Dec. 1952, Mococa, São Paulo. *Education:* Escola Nacional de Música, Rio de Janeiro. *Career:* formed guitar duo with brother Odair; studied classical guitar under Monina Tavora; studied composition with Esther Scliar; has arranged compositions for Gidon Kremer, Dawn Upshaw, Yo Yo Ma, Nadja Salerno-Sonnenberg, Iwao Furusawa; currently Prof. of Guitar, San Francisco Conservatory of Music. *Compositions:* numerous including: Três Cenas Brasileiras for two guitars 1984, Suite Brasileira for two guitars 1986, Aquarelle for solo guitar 1986, Children's Cradle for solo guitar 1992, Saga dos Migrantes for two guitars 1992, Giomatta a Nettuno for guitar ensemble 1993, Fantasia Carioca for solo guitar 1994, Summer Garden, suite for two guitars 1994, The Chase for two guitars 1996, Pieces for violin and two guitars 1996, Winter Impressions for flute, viola and guitar 1996, Campusca for two guitars 1996, Eterna for two guitars 1996, Circulo Mágico for flute and guitar 1997, Uarekena for guitar quartet 1997, Fantasia Carioca bis for two guitars and chamber orchestra 1998, Pieces for Clarinet and Guitar 1998, Sonata for solo guitar 1999, Mikis (Concerto Fantasia) for solo guitar and string orchestra 1999, Three Greek Letters for solo guitar 2000, Menino for cello and two guitars 2003. *Recordings:* albums: Complete Villa-Lobos Works for Solo Guitar 1978, Os Choros de Camera 1980, Musica Nova do Brasil 1981, Marlos Nobre Yanomani 1983, Gnattali, Rodrigo, Piazzolla 1984, Latin American Music for Two Guitars 1985, Alma Brasileira 1988, Two Concertos for Two Guitars 1991, Play Rameau/Scarlatti/Couperin/Bach 1993, Natsu no Niwa Suite 1994, White Moon: Songs to Morpheus 1995, Saga Dos Migrantes 1996, El Tango 1997, Soul of the Tango 1997, Sérgio and Odair Assad Play Piazzolla 2001, Sérgio and Odair Assad and Their Family: A Brazilian Songbook 2005, Jardim Abandonado 2008, Origins 2009. *Honours:* Dr hc (Univ. of Arizona, Tucson); Latin Grammy for best classical composition 2008. *Current Management:* c/o Neil Benson, Opus 3 Artists, 470 Park Avenue South, 9th Floor North, New York, NY 10016, USA. *Telephone:* (212) 584-7512. *Fax:* (646) 300-8212. *E-mail:* nbenson@opus3artists.com. *Website:* www.opus3artists.com. *Address:* c/o GHA Records, rue Alexandre Markelbach 101, 1030 Brussels, Belgium (office). *Telephone:* (2) 242-59-21 (office). *Fax:* (2) 241-38-85 (office). *E-mail:* info@gha.be (office). *Website:* www.gharecords.com (office); www.assadbrothers.com.

ASTI, Eugene, BMus, MA, FHEA; American/Italian pianist and music teacher; *Professor of Piano Accompaniment and Vocal Coach, Guildhall School of Music and Drama*; b. 30 May 1962, New York, NY; s. of Eugene Jofré Asti and Hilda Edna Carlson; partner Simon Kent. *Education:* Mannes Coll. of Music with with Jeannette Haien, Fontainebleau, France, Guildhall School of Music and Drama, UK. *Career:* appearances at Aldeburgh, Brighton, Buxton and Cheltenham Festivals; accompanist for Dame Margaret Price throughout Europe and recitals with Dame Felicity Lott; Wigmore Hall debut with Elizabeth Connell; further recitals with, Sir Willard White, Sir Thomas Allen, Bryn Terfel, Sarah Connolly, Angelika Kirchschlager, Sophie Karthäuser, Susan Gritton, Sophie Daneman, Rebecca Evans, Kate Royal, Nancy Argenta, Alison Buchanan, Susanna Andersson, Helene Wold, Andrew Kennedy, Mark Padmore, Stephan Loges, James Rutherford, Adrian Thompson, Richard Edgar-Wilson, Neil Davies and Stephen Varcoe; Brahms and Mendelssohn recital series in London and Bristol 1997; Strauss/Poulenc recital series, London 1999; Schumann series, London 2003; Mendelssohn series, London 2009; recitals at Lincoln Center and Weill Recital Hall, New York, Musikverein, Vienna, Concertgebouw, Amsterdam, Kölner Philharmonie, Palais des Beaux Arts, Brussels, Barbican Hall, London; currently Prof. of Piano Accompaniment and Vocal Coach, Guildhall School of Music and Drama; also Vocal Accompaniment Coordinator, Trinity Laban Conservatoire of Music and Dance, London; master-classes in UK and internationally. *Radio:* numerous broadcasts for BBC Radio 3. *Recordings:* various recordings of songs by Felix and Fanny Mendelssohn, Clara Schumann, Robert Schumann, Mozart, Eric Coates and others. *Publication:* edited edn of rare Lieder by Felix Mendelssohn 2008. *Honours:* Ferdinand Rauter Award (Richard Tauber Competition) for piano accompaniment; Megan Foster Award (Maggie Teyte Competition) for piano accompaniment. *Current Management:* c/o Harlequin Artist Agency, 203 Fidlas Road, Llanishen, Cardiff, CF14 5NA, Wales. *Telephone:* (29) 2075-0821. *Fax:* (29) 2075-5971. *E-mail:* peter@harlequin-agency.co.uk; sioned@harlequin-agency.co.uk. *Website:* www.harlequin-agency.co.uk. *Address:* Guildhall School of Music and Drama, Silk Street, London, EC2Y 8DT (office); Trinity Laban Conservatoire of Music and Dance, Faculty of Music, King Charles Court, Old Royal Naval College, Greenwich, London, SE10 9JF, England (office). *Telephone:* (20) 8305-4444 (Trinity Laban) (office). *E-mail:* e.asti@trinitylaban.ac.uk (office). *Website:* www.gsmd.ac.uk/music (office); www.trinitylaban.ac.uk/study/music (office).

ATANASIU, George; Romanian cellist and conductor; *Professor of Cello, Rowan University*; b. 15 Nov. 1958, Galati; two s. *Education:* Bucharest Acad. of Music with Serafim Antropov, Petre Lefterescu, Uzi Wiesel and Laszlo Meszo, Bayreuth Youth Festival, Weimar Int. Music Seminar, Hitzaker Chamber Music Acad. *Career:* debut as soloist with Galati Youth Orchestra, Golterman cello concerto, aged 13; Cello Prof., Rowan Univ.; Conductor, PYPO Orchestra and Enescu Piano Trio 1988–; appeared as soloist or in recitals on radio and television in Romania, USA, Germany, Italy, Spain, Switzerland, Hungary, Austria, UK and Venezuela; performed at Bayreuth Youth Festival, Weimar Int. Music Seminar, Hitzacker Chamber Music Acad., Carmel Bach Festival, Calif. and George Enescu Int. Festival, Bucharest; Principal cellist of the Garden State Philharmonic 1988–90, South Jersey Symphony Orchestra 1990–94; mem. American String Teacher Asscn. *Recordings:* George Enescu Trio in A minor no. 2. *Honours:* winner of Romania Nat. Competition, cello 1975, 1983; Chamber music 1979; Bronze medal at Int. Chamber Music Competition, Florence 1983. *Address:* College of Fine and Performing Arts, Rowan University, 201 Mullica Hill, Gassboro, NJ 08027-1701, USA (office). *Telephone:* (856) 256-4555 (office). *Fax:* (856) 256-4644 (office). *E-mail:* atanasiu@rowan.edu (office). *Website:* www.rowan.edu/music (office).

ATHERTON, David, OBE, MA, LRAM, LTCL, LGSM; English conductor; *Conductor Laureate, Hong Kong Philharmonic Orchestra*; b. 3 Jan. 1944, Blackpool, Lancs.; s. of Robert Atherton and Lavinia Atherton; m. 1st Ann Gianetta Drake 1970; one s. two d.; m. 2nd Eleanor Ann Roth 2012. *Education:* Univ. of Cambridge. *Career:* Répétiteur, Royal Opera House 1967–68, Resident Conductor 1968–79; Co-founder and Artistic Dir London Sinfonietta 1968–73, 1989–91; youngest-ever conductor at Royal Opera House and Henry Wood Promenade Concerts, London 1968; debut, Royal Festival Hall, London 1969, La Scala, Milan 1976, San Francisco Opera 1978, Metropolitan Opera, New York 1984; has conducted performances in Europe, Middle East, Far East, Australasia, N America 1970–; Artistic Dir and Conductor, London Stravinsky Festival 1979–82, Ravel/Varèse Festival 1983–84; Prin. Conductor and Artistic Adviser, Royal Liverpool Philharmonic Orchestra 1980–83, Prin. Guest Conductor 1983–86; Music Dir and Prin. Conductor, San Diego Symphony Orchestra 1980–87; Prin. Guest Conductor, BBC Symphony Orchestra 1985–89; Music Dir and Prin. Conductor, Hong Kong Philharmonic Orchestra 1989–2000, Conductor Laureate 2000–; Founder and Artistic Dir Mainly Mozart Festival, Southern Calif. and Northern Mexico 1989–2013; Prin. Guest Conductor, BBC Nat. Orchestra of Wales 1994–97; Co-founder, Pres. and Artistic Dir Global Music Network 1998–2002. *Publications include:* The Complete Instrumental and Chamber Music of Arnold Schoenberg and Roberto Gerhard (ed.) 1973, Pandora and Don Quixote Suites by Roberto Gerhard (ed.) 1973; contrib. to The Musical Companion 1978, The New Grove Dictionary 1981. *Honours:* Conductor of the Year Award, Composers' Guild of GB 1971, Edison Award 1973, Grand Prix du Disque 1977, Koussevitzky Award 1981, Int. Record Critics' Award 1982, Prix Caecilia 1982. *Website:* www.askonasholt.co.uk.

ATHERTON, Diane; British singer (soprano); b. 1970, Yorkshire; m. Michael McCarthy. *Education:* Guildhall School, London. *Career:* appearances in Mendelssohn's Midsummer Night's Dream, as Eva in Joseph Tal's The Garden and Carmina Burana by Orff, all at the Queen Elizabeth Hall, London; Britten's Aminta in Mozart's Il Re Pastore at Aldeburgh; Opera Holland Park as Musetta, and as Mozart's Zerlina, Pamina and Susanna; British tour in Strauss Gala, conducted by Christopher Warren-Green; Handel's Messiah for HTV, Wales; sang Pythia in the British premiere of Oresteia by Xenakis, for the English Bach Festival, Linbury Studio, Covent Garden 2000, also Gilda in Rigoletto 2009; Belinda in Dido & Aeneas and solos from Carmina Burana at Alba Music Festival, Italy 2009; concert performances have included Bach's Christmas Oratorio with Bournemouth Sinfonietta, Handel's Samson, Mahler's Eighth Symphony, Vaughan-Williams' Serenade to Music, Bach Cantatas and Masses by Haydn, Mozart, Schubert, Rossini, Gounod, Poulenc and Tippett; Italian debut singing Rhapsodia by Aldo Clementi under Gabriele Ferro at Teatro di San Carlo, Naples; sang Adele in Die Fledermaus in France, Eve (The Garden) at Queen Elizabeth Hall, London, Tytania at Hampton Court Festival, Aminta in Il Re Pastore at Aldeburgh, and 1st priestess in Gluck's Iphigenie en Tauride at Royal Opera House and in Athens under Marc Minkowski; performances of Musetta (Opera East), Pamina (Travelling Opera, Opera East), Zerlina (British Youth Opera, Travelling Opera, Opera à La Carte), Leila and Susanna (Opera Holland Park and Linbury Studio); Micaela and Frasquita (First Act Opera and Opera East); sang Schutz's Requiem Mass with Choral Arts Soc., then Bruckner's Te Deum at Kennedy Center and US premiere of Kleiburg's Requiem at the Washington Nat. Cathedral 2010. *Recordings include:* Purcell's Faerie Queen, The Diary of One Who Vanished with Ian Bostridge. *E-mail:* diane@dianeatherton.com (office). *Website:* www.dianeatherton.com.

ATHERTON, Joan, GRSM, ARCM; British violinist; b. 6 April 1948, Blackpool, Lancs., England; d. of Robert Atherton and Lavinia Atherton; one d. *Education:* Royal Coll. of Music. *Career:* freelance violinist, solo, chamber and orchestral player; Prin., London Sinfonietta 1970–; mem. Inc. Soc. of Musicians, Musicians' Union. *Honours:* Tagore Gold Medal 1970. *Address:* 12 Addison Way, London, NW11 6AJ, England (office). *E-mail:* joanatherton@hotmail.co.uk (office).

ATHERTON, Michael, MA; Australian composer, musician, author and academic; *Emeritus Professor, University of Western Sydney*; b. 17 Feb. 1950, Liverpool, England; s. of John F. Jones and Gisela Oppermann; m. Catherine Kagan. *Education:* Univ. of New South Wales, Univ. of Sydney, Univ. of New England, Australia. *Career:* family migrated to Australia 1965; with Renaissance Players 1974–80; music therapist, Rivendell 1978–80; founding mem. Sirocco (world music group) 1980–86, founding mem. Southern Crossings 1987–93, co-founder (with Garth Paine) Sync 2005–, performed at Ircam/NIME Paris 2006, Ircam/Electronic Arts Festival, New York 2007; Artist-in-Residence, Australian Museum 1993; Foundation Chair. of Music, Univ. of Western Sydney (UWS) 1993–, Chair of Contemporary Arts 2000–02, Dir of Research, then Assoc. Dean of Research, Coll. of Arts 2003–, now Emer. Prof., Dean's Unit, School of Humanities & Communication Arts; est. UWS Golden Stave Music Therapy Centre; Fleischmann Fellow in Anthropology (Australian Museum) 1998; performer of classical, early music, folk and Asia Pacific instruments in various groups internationally; mem. electroacoustic duo, SynC; festivals included Electronic Arts Festival, New York 2007, Aurora Festival 2008, New Interfaces for Musical Expression in New York 2011 and Paris 2012; serves on State and Commonwealth Ministerial Cttees for the Arts; Fellow, Royal Soc. of Arts, Manufacturers and Culture. *Compositions include:* The Mahogany Ship for children's choir 1993, Namatjira for choir 1995, Exhortation 1996, Songs for Imberombera for choir, strings and percussion 1997, Kalliopeia Sopha 2001, Kamawarah for orchestra and indigenous performers 2001, Jiriyai 2006, Runsten 2008, Songs of Stone and Silence 2008, Takatin 2008, Utility Horn Groove 2008, Patina 2009, Woman Dreaming, music theatre, The Greedy Octopus for voice and piano 2012. *Recordings:* Ankh: the sound of ancient Egypt 1998, Abundance 2003, Aurora 2003, Sea and Mountain 2003, Melismos 2004, A Pocketful of Songs 2004, Parallel Lines 2006, Surface Texture Line 2008, Nine-Elemental Songs 2008. *Radio:* Darwin's Wings ABC radio score 2005. *Film:* Dogwatch 2000. *Television:* theme music and variations for TVS Sydney 2006. *Publications:* Australian Made, Australian Played 1991, The ABC Book of Musical Instruments 1992, Music of the Spirit: Asian-Pacific Musical Identity (co-ed.) 2008, Musical Instruments and Sound-Producing Objects of Oceania 2010. *Honours:* Centenary Medal for Services to Society (Music) 2003. *Address:* c/o Dean's Unit, School of Humanities & Communication Arts, University of Western Sydney, Penrith, NSW 1797, Australia (office). *Telephone:* (2) 9772-6306 (office). *Fax:* (2) 9772-6737 (office). *E-mail:* mjatherton@optusnet.com.au (office). *Website:* www.myspace.com/mjatherton (office).

ATKINSON, Ann, BEd, LRAM; Welsh conductor and singer (mezzo-soprano); b. 24 Aug. 1965, Corwen, Clwyd; m. Kevin John Sharp. *Education:* Univ. of Wales, Royal Acad. of Music with Kenneth Bowen, studied with Ryland Davies. *Career:* performed with Britain's leading opera cos, including Scottish Opera, Glyndebourne Festival and Touring Opera, Wexford Festival Opera; operatic roles include Carmen for Garden Opera, Azucena and Ines (Il Trovatore) for Scottish Opera, Niklausse (Tales of Hoffmann), Larina and Filipyevna (Eugene Onegin), Annina (La Traviata) for Glyndebourne, Maddalena (Rigoletto), Marcellina (Le Nozze di Figaro); also sang Mamma Lucia (Cavalleria Rusticana) in Ho Chi Minh City; created roles of Mrs Baines in Andrew Gant's The Basement Room and Ann Clwyd, MP in world premiere of Alun Hoddinott's opera Tower for Opera Box; numerous concert performances include Verdi's Requiem, Beethoven's 9th Symphony, Brahms' Alto Rhapsody, Mozart's Requiem, Mendelssohn's Elijah (QEH), Handel's Messiah; performed at Sydney Opera House as guest soloist on tour with Lion's Male Voice Choir 2009; Musical Dir, male voice choirs, Cor Meibion Bro Glyndwr 1998–, and Cor Meibion Froncysyllte 2002–09; Artistic Dir, North Wales Int. Music Festival and St Asaph City of Music Initiative. *Honours:* winner Nat. Eisteddfod of Wales, Llangollen Int. Eisteddfod. *Address:* Glaslwyn, Mill Street, Corwen, Denbighshire, LL21 0AU, Wales (home). *Telephone:* (1490) 412735 (home). *E-mail:* info@annatkinson.co.uk (office); annatkinson@ntlworld.com (home). *Website:* www.annatkinson.co.uk.

ATKINSON, Lynton; British singer (tenor); b. 11 Oct. 1962, London, England. *Education:* studied in Cambridge with George Guest, and London with David Mason and Gita Denise. *Career:* concert appearances in festivals at Innsbruck, Utrecht, Malta, Brighton and Edinburgh; sang at cathedrals of Canterbury, Wells, Durham and Birmingham, at King's College Cambridge and the Sheldonian Theatre in Oxford; has sung in Bach's St John Passion on tour to Spain, the St Matthew Passion in Bad Homburg and L'Incoronazione di Poppea at the Spitalfields Festival; Vienna in 1989 with Handel's Susanna under Martin Haselbrock; sang Alfredo in a production of La Traviata in Mauritius; Handel's Belshazzar with Concerto Köln in Germany and Italy; sang at Edinburgh Festival and in Poland with the City of London Sinfonia under Richard Hickox; Covent Garden 1990–91 as First Prisoner in Fidelio and Ywain in the world premiere of Birtwistle's Gawain; sang at Buxton Festival and Spitalfields in 1991 in Il Sogno di Scipione by Mozart and Acis and Galatea; season 1992 as Nathaniel in Hoffmann and Zefirino in Il Viaggio a Reims at Covent Garden; has sung principal roles in L'Elisir d'Amore, La Traviata, Pearl Fishers, Don Giovanni, Zauberflöte, Entführung, and The Merry Widow, in UK and Europe, including Strasbourg, Amsterdam, Berlin, Turin, Trieste, Boston, Dublin and Maastricht; concerts included Haydn's The Seasons at Stresa Festival with the Freiburg Bach Orchestra, Christmas Oratorio in Oslo for Norwegian Radio, Bach's St Matthew Passion in Stockholm and Frankfurt, Britten's St Nicholas in Berlin's Konzerthaus, and Verdi's Requiem with the Brighton Festival Chorus and Harrogate Choral Soc.; debut with the Bach Choir in Royal Festival Hall, Bach's B Minor Mass and Mozart's Requiem with Israel Camerata; performs regularly in USA, notably Monteverdi's Orfeo and Il Ritorno d'Ulisse with Boston Baroque; debuts at Tanglewood and Ravinia festivals 2004; voice teacher, Winchester Coll.; also private vocal tutor. *Recordings include:* L'Incoronazione di Poppea, Fidelio as First Prisoner, Covent Garden (video), Die Entführung with Sir Charles Mackerras. *Honours:* winner, Richard Tauber Competition 1988, Prizewinner, Alfredo Kraus Int. Singing Competition, Las Palmas 1990. *Address:* 84 Lowther Road, Bournemouth, BH8 8NS, England (home). *Telephone:* (1202) 293145 (home). *Fax:* (1202) 255643 (home). *E-mail:* ljatkin@attglobal.net (home). *Website:* homepage.ntlworld.com/ljatkinson1000.

ATLANTOV, Vladimir Andreevich; Russian singer (tenor); b. 19 Feb. 1933, Leningrad. *Education:* Leningrad Conservatory (pupil of Natalya Bolotina). *Career:* mem. CPSU 1966–88; joined Leningrad Kirov 1963; further study at La Scala, Milan 1963–65; won Tchaikovsky Competition 1966 and Int. Contest for Young Singers, Sofia 1967; soloist with Moscow Bolshoi Theatre 1968–88, with Vienna State Opera 1987–; Kammersänger 1987; major roles include German in The Queen of Spades, José in Carmen, Otello, Cavaradossi in Tosca. *Honours:* RSFSR People's Artist 1972, USSR People's Artist 1976.

ATLAS, Allan Warren, BA, MA, PhD; American musicologist; b. 19 Feb. 1943, New York. *Education:* Hunter Coll. of the CUNY, New York Univ. *Career:* faculty mem., Brooklyn Coll., CUNY 1971–, Exec. Officer, PhD and DMA Programs in Music and Dir, Center for the Study of Free-Reed Instruments, Graduate School, CUNY, now Distinguished Prof. of Music; Visiting Prof., New York Univ. 1971, 1984, 1986. *Publications:* The Cappella Giulia Chansonnier: Rome, Biblioteca Apostolica Vaticana (CG XIII. 27, two vols) 1975–76, Music at the Aragonese Court of Naples 1985, The Wheatstone English Concertina in Victorian England 1996, Renaissance Music 1998, Anthology of Renaissance Music 1998, Contemplating the Concertina: An Historically-Informed Tutor for the English Concertina 2003, Jean Japart: The Collected Works; contrib. articles in the New Grove Dictionary of Music and Musicians and in various journals. *Address:* CUNY Graduate Center, 365 Fifth Avenue, New York, NY 10016, USA (office). *Telephone:* (212) 817-8590 (office). *Fax:* (212) 817-8590 (office). *E-mail:* aatlas@gc.cuny.edu (office).

ATTROT, Ingrid; Canadian singer (soprano); b. 1961. *Education:* Univ. of Toronto Opera School, Britten-Pears School at Aldeburgh, Nat. Opera Studio, UK. *Career:* has appeared as Mozart's Countess and Donna Anna and Meg Page in Sir John In Love by Vaughan Williams, Ibert's Angélique and Respighi's Maria Egiziaca; sang Madeline in Debussy's Fall of the House of Usher at QEH 1989; Wigmore Hall and Purcell Room recitals 1989; Handel's Ode to St Cecilia with Charles Dutoit and the Montréal Symphony; Bach's B minor Mass in Montréal; Vivaldi's Gloria in Ottawa and New York under Trevor Pinnock; Mendelssohn's Midsummer Night's Dream under Neville Marriner at the Festival Hall; season 1989–90 with Carmina Burana and the Petite Messe Solennelle; Szymanowski recital at the Purcell Room; Handel's Floridante in Canada and California; Stravinsky's Les Noces in Antwerp and Elgar's The Kingdom; tour of Russia with ENO productions of Macbeth and The Turn of The Screw; season 1992 as Mathilde in Guillaume Tell for Haddo House Opera and the Governess in The Turn of the Screw for Pimlico Opera; sang Donna Anna at Belfast 1994; performed with Richard Hickox in Britten's War Requiem, Peter Grimes (Ellen Orford) and Beethoven's Fidelio (Leonora); has appeared with London Symphony Orchestra, City of Birmingham, Montreal and Los Angeles Symphony Orchestras; festivals include Salzburg, Warsaw Autumn, Holland Festival in Amsterdam and BBC Proms; recitals at Concertgebouw Amsterdam, Le Monnaie in Brussels, Royal Opera House and Wigmore Hall, London; Artistic Dir, Summer Music on the Shannon Youth Opera Theatre, Univ. of Limerick, Ireland 2003–07; Music Dir, Out of the Box Productions 2004–06; co-Artistic Dir, Nelson Courses for Singers; Head of Voice Dept, Victoria Conservatory of Music. *Recordings include:* Respighi's Deità Silvane and Stanford's Stabat Mater, with BBC Philharmonic, Vaughan Williams' Riders to the Sea, Holst's The Wandering Scholar with the Northern Sinfonia (Hickox), Vivaldi's Gloria with The English Consort (Pinnock), and Handel's Floridante with Tafelmusik (Curtis). *Honours:* winner Eckhardt-Gramatte Competition for Contemporary Music, Canada, awards from Canada Council, Univ. of Toronto, Canadian Aldeburgh Foundation, Friends of Covent Garden. *Address:* Victoria Conservatory of Music, 900 Johnson Street, Victoria, British Columbia, V8V 3N4, Canada (office). *E-mail:* attrot@vcm.bc.ca (office).

ATZMON, Moshe; Israeli conductor; b. (Miklos Groszberger), 30 July 1931, Budapest, Hungary; m. 1954; two d. *Education:* Tel-Aviv Acad. of Music, Jerusalem Acad. of Music, Guildhall School of Music, UK. *Career:* left Hungary for Israel 1944; played the horn professionally in various orchestras for several years; has conducted in Israel, England, Australia, Germany, Sweden, Norway, Switzerland, Spain, Finland, Italy, Austria, Turkey and USA; Chief Conductor, Sydney Symphony Orchestra 1969–71; Chief Conductor, North German Radio Symphony Orchestra 1972–74; Musical Dir Basel Symphony Orchestra 1972–86; Chief Conductor Tokyo Metropolitan Orchestra 1979–83, Nagoya Philharmonic Orchestra 1987–92, Conductor Laureate 1992–; Musical Dir Dortmund Opera House and Philharmonic Orchestra 1991–93. *Honours:* second prize Dimitri Mitropoulos Competition for Conductors, New York 1963, Leonard Bernstein Prize 1963, First Prize, Int. Conductors Competition, Liverpool, England 1964. *Current Management:* Artists Management Company srl unipersonale, Piazza R. Simoni, 1E, 37122 Verona, Italy; Patrick Garvey Management, 40 North Parade, York, YO30 7AB, England. *E-mail:* panozzo@amcmusic.com; patrick@patrickgarvey.com. *Website:* www.amcmusic.com/en/artists/biography/moshe-atzmon; www.patrickgarvey.com.

AUBERT, Patrick Marie; French chorus director and conductor; b. Aix-en-Provence. *Education:* Conservatoire d'Aix-en-Provence. *Career:* mem. (trumpet), La Lyre aixoise, marching band of city of Aix-en-Provence 1971–77, Dir 1977–79; Conductor, symphony orchestra of Conservatoire d'Aix-en-Provence 1979–81; choral singing tutor, Conservatoire Léo Delibes de Clichy, Hauts-de-Seine, apptd Dir 1991; Music Dir Divertimento orchestra 1992–2003; Founding Dir Vox Hominis 1996; Asst Dir of Music, French Army (rank of Lt in Nat. Gendarmerie) 1981–82, various singing and conducting posts in Choir of the French Army 1982–90, Deputy Chorus Dir 1991–95, Dir 1996–2000, performing at nat. events including ceremonies at the Panthéon, Bastille Day celebrations, Football World Cup, promoted to Squadron Leader 1997, retd from Army 2003; Chorus Dir Opéra de Nantes 2001–03, then Chorus Dir Capitole de Toulouse 2003–09; Chorus Dir Opéra Nat. de Paris 2009–14; worked with conductors including Maurizio Arena, Serge Baudo, Maurizio Benini, Roberto Benzi, Jean-Claude Casadesus, Christoph Eschenbach, Claus Peter Flor, Eliahu Inbal, Jiri Kout, Günter Neuhold, Marc Minkowski, Gianandrea Noseda, Jean-Yves Ossonce, Evelino Pidò, Michel Plasson, Georges Prêtre, Roberto Rizzi Brignoli, Yutaka Sado, Pinchas Steinberg and Jeffrey Tate; mem. jury, 1st Paris Int. Opera Awards 2012. *Honours:* Chevalier, Légion d'honneur; Officier, Ordre nat. du Mérite; Commdr, Ordre des Arts et des Lettres. *E-mail:* patrickmarieaubert@orange.fr. *Website:* www.patrickmarieaubert.com.

AUBIER, Eric; French trumpeter; b. 1960, Paris. *Education:* Conservatoire Nat. Supérieur de Musique, Paris. *Career:* apptd solo trumpet, Orchestre de l'Opéra de Paris, at age 19; int. soloist 1995–; regular performances at Salle Pleyel, Salle Gaveau, Lincoln Center and at festivals including Comminges, Auvers-sur-Oise, Monte Carlo, Vézère, Lieksa (Finland), Hamamatsu (Japan) and Taipei (Taiwan); new works dedicated to him by composers including Nicolas Bacri, Thierry Escaich, Betsy Jolas, Carlos Grätzer, Martin Matalon and Charles Chaynes; broadcasts on Radio-France; teacher, Conservatoire Nat. Régional of Reuil-Malmaison; Visiting Prof. of Trumpet, RAM. *Recordings include:* over 100 works including La Trompette Française (Diapason d'Or), Thierry Escaich: Tanz Fantaisie (Grand Prix des Lycéens, Lettre du Musicien/Musique Nouvelle en Liberté), Skaalkottas: Concertino, Matalon: Trame V, Concerto for trumpet 2004, Classical Trumpet Concertos, Les Grands Concertos Français pour Trompette 2006. *Current Management:* c/o Barbara Scales, Latitude 45 Arts Promotions, 109 boulevard St-Joseph Ouest, Montréal, PQ H2T 2P7, Canada. *Telephone:* (514) 277-1072. *Fax:* (514) 905-4143. *E-mail:* bscales@latitude45arts.com. *Website:* www.latitude45arts.com. *Address:* c/o Royal Academy of Music, Marylebone Road, London, NW1 5HT (office). *E-mail:* ea@ericaubier.com (office). *Website:* www.ericaubier.com (office).

AUDI, Pierre; French stage director; *Artistic Director, Netherlands Opera;* b. 1957, Beirut, Lebanon. *Education:* Exeter Coll., Oxford. *Career:* founder, Almeida Theatre, London 1979, Dir of theatre and annual contemporary music festival 1979–89; directed stage works by Wolfgang Rihm, Michael Finnissy (The Undivine Comedy) and John Casken (Golem) for Almeida Theatre; Artistic Dir, Netherlands Opera 1988–, productions include Schoenberg's Die Glückliche Hand, Monteverdi's Il Ritorno d'Ulisse, Wagner's Ring, Tamerlano and Alcina, Berlioz's Les Troyens and Puccini's La Bohème, also world premieres of contemporary music theatre works including Theo Loevendie's Gassir, Guus Janssen's Noach and Hier, Jonathan Harvey's Wagner Dream, Tan Dun's Tea, Param Vir's Snatched by the Gods and Broken Strings, Kaija Saariaho's Je sens un deuxième coeur and Wolfgang Rihm's Dionysos; produced Birtwistle's Punch and Judy, Feldman's Neither and Messiaen's Saint François d'Assise; British stage premiere of Verdi's Jerusalem, Opera North 1990, premiere of Henze's Venus and Adonis, Bavarian State Opera at Munich 1997, Rameau's Zoroastre at Drottningholms Slottsteater, Stockholm 2005, 2006, Die Zauberflöte at Salzburg Festival 2006, L'incoronazione di Poppea at Los Angeles Opera 2006, Jonathan Harvey's Wagner Dream in Luxembourg and Amsterdam 2006, Castor et Pollux in Amsterdam 2007, Cimarosa's Il matrimonio segreto and Vivaldi's Orlando Furioso at Théâtre des Champs-Elysées, Handel's Partenope at Theater an der Wien, Pelléas et Mélisande at Rome Opera House, Verdi's Attila for Metropolitan Opera, New York 2010; Artistic Dir, Holland

Festival 2004–. *Honours:* Order of the Dutch Lion, Chevalier de la Légion d'honneur; Lesley Boosey Award 1990, Johannes Vermeer Award for Artistic Achievement 2009. *Current Management:* Maestro Arts, Milliners House, Riverside Quarter, Eastfields Avenue, London, SW18 1LP, England. *Telephone:* (20) 3553-4652. *E-mail:* info@maestroarts.com. *Website:* www .maestroarts.com. *Address:* De Nederlandse Opera, Waterlooplein 22, 1011 PG Amsterdam, The Netherlands (office). *E-mail:* directie@dno.nl (office). *Website:* www.dno.nl (office).

AUGUIN, Philippe; French conductor; *Music Director, Orchestre Philharmonique de Nice*; b. 1962. *Education:* studied in Vienna and Florence. *Career:* musical asst to Herbert von Karajan 1986; associated with Georg Solti at the Salzburg Festival; La Scala Milan, with Don Giovanni, La Damnation de Faust, Die Zauberflöte and Figaro; Covent Garden with La Traviata and Un Ballo in Maschera; Music Dir, Braunschweig Opera, leading Tristan und Isolde, Parsifal, Salome, Pelléas et Mélisande and Wozzeck; Mahler and Schoenberg cycles with Czech and Royal Philharmonics, Dresden State Orchestra and Orchestre Nat. de France, Vienna Philharmonic, Wiener Staatsoper; fmrly Prin. Conductor, Staatstheater Stuttgart, with Tannhäuser, Elektra, Lohengrin, Rosenkavalier and Ariadne; Otello at the Hamburg Staatsoper, Der fliegende Holländer at Leipzig and La Sonnambula at Cologne; Salzburg Festival; with Fidelio; Figaro at La Scala, Tannhäuser for Australian Opera, Le Roi Arthus in Cologne and concerts with the Royal Scottish Nat.; Gen. Music Dir, Nuremberg State Theatre 1998–2005; Music Dir, Orchestre Philharmonique de Nice 2010–; Music Dir, Washington Nat. Opera 2010–. *Current Management:* c/o Mag. Kurt-Walther Schober, Opera4u.com GmbH, Hermanngasse 3, 1070, Vienna, Austria. *Telephone:* (1)-5137592. *Fax:* (1)-5129351. *E-mail:* schober@opera4u.com. *Website:* www .opera4u.com; www.philippeauguin.com.

AUSTBØ, Håkon; Norwegian pianist; b. 22 Oct. 1948, Kongsberg. *Education:* studied in Norway and at the Paris Conservatoire and Ecole Normale de Musique, France, Juilliard School, New York, USA and Staatliche Hochschule für Musik, Munich, Germany, and in London. *Career:* played with Bergen Philharmonic Orchestra 1963; first Oslo recital 1964; concert and solo engagements throughout Scandinavia and Europe; piano duo with Marina Horak, and chamber concerts with Trio du Nord until 1985; solo appearances throughout Europe, America and Asia; numerous radio and television performances; Prof., Univ. of Utrecht 1979–2007; Prof. of Piano, Univ. of Stavanger 2007–. *Recordings include:* Messiaen's Catalogue d'Oiseaux (excerpts), 10 Skryabin sonatas (Norwegian Grammy Award 1990), Messiaen's Vingt Regards sur l'Enfant-Jésus (Norwegian Grammy Award 1995), complete Catalogue d'Oiseaux with Petites Esquisses d'Oiseaux (Edison Prize for best solo recording 1998), Schumann, Norse melodrama EddaDa, works by Satie, Janacek and Brahms, complete songs by Messiaen, complete solo works of Debussy and Grieg, and Messiaen's Oiseaux Exotiques. *Honours:* winner, Messiaen Competition for Contemporary Music, Royan 1971, prizewinner, Scriabin Competition, Oslo 1972, Ravel Competition, Paris 1975, Norwegian Music Critics Prize 1989, Performer of the Year 1992, Grieg Prize 2003. *Current Management:* c/o Pro Arte, Vardesvingen 92f, 5141 Fyllingsdalen, Norway. *Telephone:* 55319435. *Fax:* 55960765. *E-mail:* proarte@online.no. *Address:* Hans C. Gjefles vei 5e, 1182 Oslo, Norway (home). *Telephone:* 21695271 (home). *Website:* www.austbo.info.

AUSTIN, Larry Don, BME, MM; American composer and music educator; b. 12 Sept. 1930, Duncan, Okla; m. Edna Navarro 1953; two s. three d. *Education:* Univ. of North Texas, Denton, Mills Coll., Oakland, Calif. with Darius Milhaud, Univ. of California, Berkeley with Seymour Shifrin and Andrew Imbrie, Stanford Univ. and Massachusetts Inst. of Tech. *Career:* works performed by New York Philharmonic, Boston Symphony, Nat. Symphony Orchestras, Cincinnati Philharmonia and Nat. Philharmonic of Warsaw; residencies in Rome and Bellagio, Italy, Birmingham and York, UK, Tokyo and MacDowell Colony; many commissions; Prof., Univ. of California, Davis 1958–72, Dir of Univ. bands 1958–72, Co-Dir New Music Ensemble 1963–68; Publr and journal owner, Source: Music of the Avant Garde and Composer/Performer Edn 1966–74; teacher, Univ. of South Florida, Tampa 1972–78, Univ. of North Texas 1978–96; Founder and Pres. CDCM: Consortium to Distribute Computer Music, producer of CDCM Computer Music Series on Centaur Records 1986–2000; mem. Bd, Int. Computer Music Asscn 1984–88, 1994–98 (Pres. 1990–94). *Compositions include:* Woodwind Quintet 1949, Mass for chorus and orchestra 1955–58, Quartet Three for electronic music on tape 1971, Quadrants 1–11, Catalogo Sonoro-Narcisso for viola and tape 1978, Protoforms hybrid music for three sopranos and computer 1980, Euphonia: A Tale of the Future (opera) 1982, Sonata Concertante for pianist and computer 1983–84, Violet's Invention for piano 1988, A Universe of Symphony: The Earth, Life Pulse and Heavens 1974–93, Accidents Two: Sound Projections for piano with computer music 1992, Variations... Beyond Pierrot (electro-acoustic) 1995, Shin-Edo: CityscapeSet (electro-acoustic) 1996, BluesAx (Magistère de Bourges Prize) 1996, Djuro's Tree 1997, Tárogató 1998, Singing! for baritone and tape 1998, Tableaux: Convolutions on a Theme for alto saxophone, video, and octophonic computer music 2003, Adagio: Convolutions on a Theme by Mozart for clarinet and computer 2005, Les Flûtes de Pan: Hommage à Debussy for flute (piccolo) and octophonic computer music 2005–06, John explains, octophonic computer music 2007, Redux 2007, ReduxTwo for piano and octophonic computer music 2008. *Recordings include:* Rompido! 1993, BluesAx, Ottuplo! Larry Austin: The Eighth Decade 2007, Octo Mixes. *Publications:* Learning to Compose: Modes,

Materials and Models of Musical Invention (with Thomas Clark) 1988; contrib. of articles to various publs. *Honours:* numerous grants, commissions and awards, including Int. Electroacoustic Music Competition, Bourges, France 1996, SEAMUS Lifetime Achievement Award 2009. *Address:* 10205 Murray S. Johnson Street, Denton, TX 76207, USA (home). *E-mail:* larryaustin@grandecom.net (home). *Website:* cemi.music.unt.edu/ larry_austin (office).

AUSTIN-PHILIPS, Eric, BMus; Australian composer and conductor; b. 12 Oct. 1947, Melbourne. *Education:* Univ. of Melbourne, studied composition with John McCabe and conducting with Roger Norrington. *Career:* Faculty mem., The University High School 1972–85; conductor, music critic; commissions from the British Music Soc. 1972, Melbourne Mandolin Orchestra and The Melbourne Chronicle 1982; first conductor, Melbourne Youth Orchestra; mem. Bd, Melbourne Youth Music. *Compositions include:* Portraits of my Friends and Others, for flute, oboe, clarinet, bassoon and piano 1973; Nirthanjali for mandolin and orchestra 1973; Into the Air for piano 1976; Macavity: The Mystery Cat, for choir 1981; Comfits and Joys for soprano, choir and strings 1982; The Black Swan, for choir 1984; Sinfonietta No. 2 for plectra ensemble 1986. *Honours:* Dorian Le Gallienne Prize 1972. *Address:* c/o Melbourne Youth Music, PO Box 963, Melbourne 3205, Australia (office). *Website:* www.mym.org.au (office).

AUVINEN, Ritva; Finnish singer (soprano); b. 1945. *Education:* Sibelius Academy, Helsinki, studied with Gina Cigna in Rome and Peter Klein in Vienna. *Career:* debut: Helsinki concert 1965; many appearances with Finnish Nat. Opera from 1965, notably as Riita in the premiere of Kokkonen's The Last Temptations 1975, also at the New York Met 1983; other roles include Renata in Prokofiev's The Fiery Angel 1985, Strauss's Ariadne 1986, Janáček's Emilia Marty 1988, Lady Macbeth at the Savonlinna Festival 1993; guest engagements at St Petersburg, Zürich and Stockholm, with concerts and recitals in New York, London, Vienna and Salzburg; sang Ms Lovett in Sondheim's Sweeney Todd at Helsinki 1997–98; premiere of Tapio Tuomela's Mother and Daughter at Helsinki (concert) 1999; vocal coach; mem. jury Toivo Kuula singing competition 2012. *Honours:* Pro Finlandia Medal 1979. *Address:* c/o Toivo Kuula -laulukilpailun projektipäällikkö, Alavuden Kaupunki, Kuulantie 6, 63300 Alavus, Finland.

AVDEEVA, Yulianna; Russian pianist; b. 3 July 1985, Moscow. *Education:* Gnessin School of Music, Moscow, Hochschule für Musik, Zürich, Int. Piano Academy, Lake Como, Italy; studied with Elena Ivanova, Konstantin Scherbakov and Vladimir Tropp. *Career:* asst to Konstantin Scherbakov 2006–09; has performed in over 25 countries including UK, Austria, Italy, Switzerland, Japan and Poland. *Recordings include:* Chopin Piano Concerto in E minor, Sonata in B flat minor, Mazurkas 2010, Chopin Piano Concertos 1&2 2013, Chopin, Schubert & Prokofiev 2014. *Honours:* winner, Int. Carl Czerny Young Pianists Competition 1997, winner, AMA Calabria Int. Piano Competition 2002, First Prize, Arthur Rubinstein Competition 2003, winner, Bremer Klavierwettbewerb Competition 2003, winner, Concorso Citta di Cantú 2005, First Prize, Int. Fryderyk Chopin Piano Competition 2010. *Current Management:* c/o Sabine Frank, Harrison/Parrott Ltd, Johannisplatz 3a, 81667 Munich, W6 0QT, Germany. *Telephone:* (89) 679710455. *E-mail:* sabine.frank@harrisonparrott.de. *Website:* www.harrisonparrott.com; www .avdeevapiano.com.

AVITAL, Avi; Israeli musician (mandolin); b. 1978, Be'er Sheva. *Education:* Jerusalem Acad. of Music, Cesare Pollini Conservatory Padua, Italy, student of Ugo Orlandi. *Career:* began learning the mandolin age eight; first mandolin player ever to win Israel's Aviv competition for soloists 2007; performances at numerous venues including Carnegie Hall and Lincoln Center, New York, Wigmore Hall, London, Berlin Philharmonie, Vienna Konzerthaus, Lucerne's KKL, Forbidden City Concert Hall, Beijing, as well as Tanglewood, Spoleto and Ravenna festivals; has collaborated with numerous artists including clarinettist Giora Feidman, soprano Dawn Upshaw, trumpeter-composer Frank London; toured Australia in 2014 with Australian Brandenburg Orchestra; concerts with Venice Baroque Orchestra and in Berlin, Paris and Poland; further concerts in Germany with I Musici di Roma, in China with Cologne Acad., Hamburger Symphoniker, Israel Camerata, Mahler, Lithuanian and Amadeus chamber orchestras, Freiburg Baroque Orchestra and Danish String Quartet; collaborations with Mahan Esfahani, Andreas Scholl and Richard Galliano; recitals throughout Europe and N America, including at Verbier, Salisbury, Torgau and Bristol Proms festivals; Between Worlds recitals in Taiwan, UK, Ireland, Germany, Switzerland, Italy, Brazil. *Recordings include:* David Orlowsky Trio's Noema (Echo Without Boundaries Award 2008), Avner Dorman's Mandolin Concerto 2010, Bach concertos for harpsichord and violin arranged for mandolin and orchestra (own transcriptions); Between Worlds 2014, Vivaldi (Echo Klassik Award for Concerto Recording of the Year) 2015. *Current Management:* c/o Angela Sulivan, Sulivan Sweetland, 1a Hillgate Place, Balham Hill, London, SW12 9ER, England. *Telephone:* (20) 8772 3470. *E-mail:* as@sulivansweetland.co.uk. *Website:* www.sulivansweetland.co.uk. *E-mail:* avi@aviavital.com. *Website:* www.aviavital.com.

AVNI, Tzvi Jacob; Israeli composer and academic; *Professor Emeritus of Music Theory and Composition, Jerusalem Academy for Music and Dance*; b. (Herman Steinke), 2 Sept. 1927, Saarbrucken, Germany; s. of Samuel Steinke and Regina Steinke; m. Hanna Avni 1979; one s. one d. *Education:* Israel Music Acad., Tel-Aviv, studied in USA, individual studies with Aaron Copland

and Lukas Foss, Vladimir Ussachevsky. *Career:* resident in Israel since 1935; Dir AMLI Cen. Music Library, Tel-Aviv 1961–75; Prof. of Music Theory and Composition, Jerusalem Acad. for Music and Dance 1976–, currently Prof. Emer., also Dir Electronic Music Studio 1971–95; North East Univ., Boston, 1993–94; Queens Coll., New York 1994–95; Jury Chair., Arthur Rubinstein Int. Piano Competition 1989, 1992; mem. Israel Composers League, Chair. 1978–80; Chair. Israel Nat. Music Cttee 1984–88, Israel Jeunesses Musicales 1995–. *Compositions include:* two piano sonatas, three string quartets, wind quintet, five Pantomimes for 8 Players; works for choir, various electronic pieces, piano music, works for ballet, art films and radio plays; Meditations on a Drama for chamber orchestra 1965, Vitrage for Harp Solo 1990, Desert Scenes, symphony in three movements 1990, Three Lyric Songs on P. Celan Poems for Mezzo Soprano, English Horn and Harp 1990, Fagotti Fugati for 2 Bassoons 1991, Variations on a Sephardic Tune for Recorder Ensemble 1992, Hallelujah for Mixed Choir 1993, Triptych for Piano 1994, The Three Legged Monster, musical legend, for Narrator, Piano and Small Orchestra with text by Hanna Avni 1994, Anthropomorphic Landscapes, No. 1 Flute Solo, No. 2 Oboe Solo, No. 3 Clarinet Solo, Songs and Melodies, for mixed choir, in memory of Itzhak Rabin 1996–97, Pray for the Peace of Jerusalem for symphony orchestra 1997, Se Questo é un Uomo, five songs for soprano and orchestra on poems by Primo Levi 1998, The Ship of Hours, four orchestral sketches on paintings by M. Ardon 1999, Apropos Klee, four pieces for choir and instruments on Paul Klee Paintings 2000, Bassoon Concerto 2001, Phoenix for viola solo 2001, Pas de Deux for violin and piano 2006, Saxophone Quartet 2007, Credo for string trio 2007, Psalm 23 for choir 2007, Piano Concerto 2009, Fantasy for Harp 2010, Kol for violin solo 2011, Five Preludes for flute, cello, harp and narrator, on poems by Rose Ausländer 2012. *Recordings include:* Love Under a Different Sun, Chamber-Vocal Works, Program Music 1980 with Israel Philharmonic and Mehta, Piano Sonata No. 1, String Quartet No. 1 (Summer Strings), Israeli String Quartet, 5 Variations for Mr 'K', for percussion, Epitaph (sonata No. 2) for Piano 1998, There is a Time for Everything for mixed choir 2009, Clarinet Quintet 2011. *Publications include:* An Orchestra is Born, Gittit, Israel (ed.) 1966–80; contribs to Dictionary of 20th-Century Music, Music in Israel, Personal Rhythm: A Life in Music 2012. *Honours:* Hon. Citizen of Tel-Aviv and of Saarbrücken, Germany; Acum Prize 1965, Israel Prime-Minister's Prize for Life Achievements 1998, Saarland (Germany) State Prize for lifetime achievement 1998, Israel State Prize in Music 2001. *Address:* 54 Bourla Street, Tel-Aviv 69364 (home); Israel Music Institute, 55 Begin Blvd, Tel-Aviv (office); Jerusalem Academy for Music and Dance, Giv'at Ram, Jerusalem, Israel (office). *Telephone:* (3) 6991105 (Tel-Aviv) (home); (2) 6759911 (Jerusalem) (office); (3) 6247095 (Tel-Aviv) (office). *Fax:* (3) 6993937 (Tel-Aviv) (home); (2) 6527713 (Jerusalem) (office); (3) 5612826 (Tel-Aviv) (office). *E-mail:* avniador@netvision.net.il (home). *Website:* www.imi.org.il (office); www.tzvi-avni.com.

AWAD, Emil, BM, PhD; Mexican composer, conductor and educator; *Professor of Composition and Theory, Universidad Veracruzana*; b. 2 Aug. 1963. *Education:* Juilliard School, Manhattan School of Music, Harvard Univ. *Career:* Artistic Dir Dudley Orchestra, Harvard 1989–93, Ensemble de las Rosas 1994–96, Camerata 21, Universidad Veraruzana 1998–; Guest Conductor, Manhattan Contemporary Ensemble, Harvard Contemporary Ensemble, Orquesta de Cámara de Bellas Artes; Artistic Dir of hundreds of premieres in Mexico 1994–, including works by Babbitt, Carter, Davidovsky, Kim, Martino and Nichols; Chair. Composition Dept, Conservatorio de las Rosas 1994–98; Fellow and Composer-in-Residence, Universidad Veracruzana 1998–99, Prof. of Composition and Theory and Dir of Grad. Studies 1999–; Artistic Dir, new music festival Camerata 21 1998–; Composer-in-Residence, CENCREM Querétaro, Mexico 2003, 2005, Univ. of Victoria, Canada 2007, Univ. of Nuevo Leon 2008, 2009, Univ. of Zacatecas 2009, City Univ. of New York 2010, Univ. of Houston 2011; works performed by orchestras including Juilliard Orchestra, Harvard Contemporary Ensemble, Manhattan Contemporary Ensemble, Manhattan Symphony, and members of the New York Philharmonic and Boston Symphony. *Compositions include:* Cuatro Danzas para Clarinete, Paisaje for soprano, Concerto for English Horn and Strings, Duo for Violin and Piano, Cuatro Elementos for guitar quartet, Woodwind Trio Macondito, Paskat for women's chorus, harp and string orchestra, Zazil for orchestra, Piedras Sueltas (text by Octavio Paz) for flute, clarinet, cello, piano and soprano. *Recordings:* Artificios, Cuarteto Manuel M. Ponce 2002, Camerata 21, Vol. 1 2010. *Publications:* compositions published by American Composers Editions Inc., New York. *Honours:* composition grants: State of Veracruz Inst. of Culture 1999, 2005, Nat. Endowment for Culture and the Arts of Mexico 2001, 2002, 2012–14, Nat. Inst. of Arts of Mexico 2000, 2005, Harvard Grant, Secr. of Education, Mexico 2001–10, Juilliard School of Music Composition Prize. *Current Management:* c/o American Composers Alliance, 802 West 190th Street, Suite 1B, New York, NY 10040, USA. *Telephone:* (212) 925-0458 (office). *Fax:* (212) 925-6798 (office). *Website:* composers.com/emil-awad. *Address:* Facultad de Música, Universidad Veracruzana, Barragán No. 32, Xalapa, Veracruz CP 91000, Mexico (office). *E-mail:* eawad@uv.mx (office). *Website:* www.uv.mx (office).

AX, Emanuel, BA; American pianist; b. 8 June 1949, Lvov, Poland; m. Yoko Nozaki 1974; one s. one d. *Education:* Columbia Univ., Juilliard School of Music. *Career:* concert pianist, 1974–; appearances in USA and abroad; performances with major orchestras including the New York Philharmonic, Philadelphia Orchestra, Chicago Symphony Orchestra, Los Angeles Philharmonic Orchestra, Cleveland Orchestra, Concertgebouw Orchestra, NHK Symphony and London Philharmonic; played Beethoven's 2nd Concerto with London Philharmonic, Festival Hall 1991, and Brahms' 1st Concerto at Promenade Concerts in 1991; Mozart's D minor Concerto 1994 Proms; world premieres of concertos by John Adams with the Cleveland Orchestra 1997, Christopher Rouse (New York Philharmonic) 1999, Bright Sheng (Boston Symphony) 2000; all-Beethoven concerto cycles with New York Philharmonic at Lincoln Center Festival 1999, Cleveland Orchestra 2001; Mozart K482 at London Proms 2000; Schoenberg concerto at Salzburg Festival 2000; Beethoven's Concerto No. 4 in G Major, London Proms 2002; Mary and James G. Wallach Artist-in-Residence, New York Philharmonic 2012–13; mem, Advisory Board, Palm Beach Festival; mem. Chopin Soc. *Recordings include:* with Philadelphia Orchestra, Chicago Symphony, Cleveland Quartet and Guarneri Quartet; Brahms Concerto (Boston Symphony/Haitink); Adams Concerto (Cleveland Orchestra); chamber music with Yo-Yo Ma, Isaac Stern, Jaime Laredo; duos with Yo-Yo Ma; trios with Yo-Yo Ma and Itzhak Perlman. *Honours:* 1st Prize, Arthur Rubenstein Int. Piano Master Competition 1974; Record of the Year Award, Stereo Review, 1977; one of five Best Records of the Year Award, Time Magazine, 1977; Avery Fisher Award 1979, Grammy Award for Best Chamber Music Performance 1986, 1987, 1992, 1993, 1996, Grammy Award for Best Instrumental Soloist Performance 1995, 2004. *Current Management:* Opus 3 Artists, 470 Park Avenue South, 9th Floor North, New York, NY 10016, USA. *Telephone:* (212) 584-7500. *Fax:* (646) 300-8200. *E-mail:* info@opus3artists.com. *Website:* www.opus3artists.com; www.emanuelax.com (home).

AXELROD, John, BMus; American conductor; *Principal Conductor, Giuseppe Verdi Symphony Orchestra*; b. 28 March 1966, Houston, Tex.; pnr Annette Gerlach; one d. *Education:* Harvard Univ.; studied at St Petersburg Conservatory with Ilya Musin. *Career:* studied with American Symphony Orchestra League conductors' programme; Founder, Artistic Dir and Conductor Orchestra X, Houston 1996; Music Dir 'Hollywood in Vienna' Film Music Gala Concert, Österreichischer Rundfunk Radio Symphony Orchestra, Vienna 2009; Music Dir and Chief Conductor Lucerne Symphony Orchestra 2004–09; Music Dir Desig. Orchestre Nat. des Pays de la Loire, Nantes/Angers 2009–10, Music Dir 2010–11; Prin. Conductor, Giuseppe Verdi Symphony Orchestra, Milan 2011–; Prin. Guest Conductor Sinfonietta Cracovia 2000–; has conducted over 130 orchestras since 2000; opera includes premiere performances of Bernstein's Candide at Théâtre du Châtelet, Paris and Teatro alla Scala, Milan, Wagner's Tristan and Isolde for Angers/Nantes Opera 2009, Krenek's Kehraus um St Stephan at the Bregenz Festspiele. *Recordings:* recordings including music by Schreker, Krenek and Burger, Bernstein, Schoenberg and Weill, Dvorák's Ninth with the Würtemberg Philharmonic, works by Wladislaw Szpilman with the Berlin RSO and Rolf Wallin's percussion concerto Das war schön! with Martin Grubinger and the Oslo Philharmonic. *Address:* Fondazione Orchestra Sinfonica e Coro Sinfonico di Milano Giuseppe Verdi, corso San Gottardo 39, 20136 Milan, Italy (office). *Telephone:* (02) 83389-302 (office). *Fax:* (02) 83389-303 (office). *Website:* www.laverdi.org (office); www.johnaxelrod.com.

AYDIN, Özgür; Turkish pianist; b. 4 June 1972, Boulder, CO, USA. *Education:* Ankara Conservatory, Royal Coll. of Music, London, Hannover Musikhochschule. *Career:* appeared at the 1994 Salzburg Festival and the 1995 Schleswig-Holstein Music Festival; concerts broadcast by Classic FM, London 1993, ABC Sydney 1996, North German Radio 1997; played Brahms' D minor piano concerto with the Bavarian Radio Symphony Orchestra, Munich, broadcast live by Bavarian Radio and television 1997; appeared at the Int. Istanbul Music Festival and the Rheingau Music Festival in 1998; concerts broadcast by Deutschland Radio Berlin and North German Radio 1998; appeared as soloist with orchestras in Germany and Turkey, and with BBC Concert Orchestra, London, Simon Bolivar Youth Orchestra, Venezuela and Canada's Calgary Philharmonic; chamber music concerts and recitals, in the Auditorium du Louvre, Herkulessaal and Gasteig in Munich, Hamburg's Musikhalle, Queen Elizabeth Hall in London, L'Auditori in Barcelona, Tokyo's Suntory Hall and Opera City Recital Hall, the 92nd Street Y in New York, Cleveland's Severance Hall, and Kennedy Center in Washington, DC; founding mem., Aurata Quintet; lives in Berlin. *Honours:* winner, Int. Music Competition of the ARD, Munich 1997, Nippon Music Award, Tokyo 1997, Prizewinner, Esther Honens Calgary Int. Piano Competition, Canada 2000, Prizewinner and Mozart Prize, Cleveland Int. Piano Competition, USA 2001. *Address:* Florastr. 67 Hinterhaus, 13187 Berlin, Germany (office). *E-mail:* ozgur@ozguraydin.com (office). *Website:* www.ozguraydin.com.

AYKAL, Gürer, PhD; Turkish/American music director and conductor; *General Music Director and Principal Conductor, Borusan Istanbul Philarmonic Orchestra*; b. 22 May 1942, Eskişehir; m. (deceased); three s. *Education:* Ankara State Conservatory, Guildhall School of Music, London, Accademia Santa Cecilia, Pontifical Inst. of Sacred Music with Dominico Bartolucci, studied with André Previn and George Hurst in London. *Career:* Resident Conductor under direction of Franco Ferrera, Accademia Santa Cecilia 1973; apptd Perm. Conductor of Presidential Symphony Orchestra, Turkey 1975; Founder, Ankara Chamber Orchestra; toured Russia as conductor of Moscow State Symphony Orchestra 1984; toured South America and Caribbean Islands as conductor of English Chamber Orchestra; Music Dir and Conductor, Lubbock Symphony Orchestra, Tex. 1987–93; conducted Istanbul Symphony Orchestra 1989; Prin. Guest Conductor of Amsterdam Concertgebouw Chamber Orchestra 1989; Music Dir and Conductor, El Paso Symphony Orchestra, Tex. 1991–2003; currently Gen. Music Dir and Prin. Conductor, Borusan Istanbul Philarmonic Orchestra. *Recordings:* works with London

Philharmonic Orchestra. *Honours:* Conductor's Medal, Accademia Chigiana 1972, Turkish Govt State Artist 1981. *Address:* Borusan Istanbul Philarmonic Orchestra, Istiklal Caddesi 213, 34433 Beyoglu, Istanbul, Turkey (office). *Telephone:* (212) 3363280 (office). *Fax:* (212) 2524591 (office). *E-mail:* info@borusansanat.com (office); keremg@borusansanat.com (office). *Website:* www.borusansanat.com (office).

AYRTON, Norman Walter; British fmr theatre and opera director; b. 25 Sept. 1924, London, England. *Education:* Old Vic Theatre School, London with Michael Saint Denis. *Career:* war service, RNVR 1939–45; mem. Old Vic Co. 1949, Festival Season 1951; repertory at Farnham and Oxford 1949–50; staff mem. Old Vic Theatre School 1949–52; opened own teaching studio 1952; began dramatic coaching for Royal Opera House, Covent Garden 1953; Asst Prin. 1954–66, Prin. 1966–72, London Acad. of Music and Dramatic Art; taught at Shakespeare Festival, Stratford, Ont., Canada and Royal Shakespeare Theatre, England 1959–62; Dir Artaxerxes for Handel Opera Soc., Camden Festival 1963, La Traviata at Covent Garden 1963, Manon at Covent Garden 1964, Sutherland-Williamson Grand Opera Season, Australia 1965; Britten's Midsummer Night's Dream, Sydney 1973, Lakmé for Australian Opera 1976, Der Rosenkavalier for Australian Opera 1983; guest dir for many int. productions 1973–84; Faculty, Juilliard School of Music, New York 1974–85; Stage Dir American Opera Center 1979–85, Vancouver Opera 1975–83, Melbourne Theatre Co. 1974–, Hartford Stage Co. and American Stage Festival 1978–, Spoleto Festival, USA 1984, Vassar Coll., New York 1990–, Utah Shakespeare Festival 1994, Cornell Univ., New York 1995, 1998, Sarah Lawrence Coll., New York 1994, 1997, 2001, British American Dramatic Acad. (BADA) Midsummer Conservatory Programme, Oxford 2006–; Dir of Opera, RAM 1986–90; Dean, BADA 1986–98, Florida State Univ., Sarasota 1997–2003. *Television:* The Reluctant Prima Donna with Joan Sutherland 2006. *Honours:* Hon. RAM 1989, Hon. FLAMDA 2009. *Address:* c/o British American Drama Academy, 14 Gloucester Gate, London, NW1 4HG, England (office); 40A Birchington Road, London, NW6 4LJ, England (home). *Telephone:* (20) 7487-0730 (office); (20) 7328-6056 (home). *Fax:* (20) 7487-0731 (office).

AZARMI, Nassrin; Iranian singer (soprano); b. 5 Jan. 1949, Brujderd. *Education:* studied in Tehran and Cologne. *Career:* debut as Mozart's Despina, Tehran 1967; sang at the Vienna Volksoper, 1968–69; Linz, 1969–71; Deutsche Oper am Rhein, Düsseldorf from 1971 as Mozart's Queen of Night, Pamina, Susanna and Constanze, Adina in L'Elisir d'amore, Offenbach's Olympia, Rossini's Elvira; Guest appearances include Berg's Lulu at Antwerp, 1982; In Die Zauberflöte at Salzburg, 1990; Sang Musetta at Düsseldorf, 1993; Further roles have included Nicolai's Frau Fluth, Gilda, Micaela, Strauss's Aminta and Nannetta in Falstaff; concert and oratorio engagements.

AZEVEDO, (António) Sérgio (Arede Torrado Marques), DMus; Portuguese composer, academic and writer; *Teacher of Composition, Escola Superior de Música de Lisboa;* b. 23 Aug. 1968, Coimbra; s. of Octávio Sérgio de Matos Azevedo and Isabel da Conceição Torrado Marques Azevedo. *Education:* Academia de Amadores de Música and Escola Superior de Música de Lisboa, Inst. de Estudos da Criança, Univ. do Minho, Braga. *Career:*

teacher of orchestration and theory, Orquestra Metropolitana de Lisboa 1987–95; teacher of composition, orchestration and theory, Escola Superior de Música de Lisboa 1993–; Vice-Pres., Academia de Amadores de Música 1994–95; ed. for Portuguese Nat. Radio 1993–2007. *Compositions include:* Aspetto for wind quintet 1996, Atlas' Journey for 15 players 1998, Keep Going for orchestra 1998, Concerto for two pianos and orchestra 1999–2003, Concertino for solo piano and 14 players 2001, Sequenza Ultima for solo oboe and 10 players 2001, Sinfonietta Semplice for orchestra 2003, Ariane dans son Labyrinthe for wind quintet and piano 2004, La Vera Storia d'Ulisse in mare for orchestra 2005, Berliner Trio for clarinet, violoncello and piano 2006, História de uma gaivota e do gato que a ensinou a voar for speaker and 18 players 2008, Bernardino for speaker and 16 players, Erasing Mahler 2013, Clarinet Concerto 2014. *Publications include:* 1958–1998: Forty Years of Contemporary Music in Portugal, World New Music Magazine 1998, A Invenção dos Sons 1998; Olga Prats: Um Piano Singular 2007. *Honours:* 1st Prize Joly Braga-Santos Competition 1991, 1994, 1st Prize Juventude Musical Portuguesa 1992, United Nations Prize 1994, 1st Prize Fernando Lopes-Graça 1997, 1998, Portuguese Soc. of Authors Prize 2010. *Address:* R. João de Barros 134 – 1° esq, Alapraia, São João do Estoril 2765-099, Portugal (home). *Telephone:* (9) 6339-7727 (mobile) (home). *E-mail:* sergio.aze@sapo.pt. *Website:* www.editions-ava.com (office).

AZMAIPARASHVILI, Zaza; Georgian conductor; b. 16 June 1962, Tbilisi; s. of Givi Azmaiparashvili and Liana Gomelauri; m. Valentina Azmaiparashvili; one s. *Education:* Tbilisi State Conservatoire, St Petersburg N. A. Rimsky-Korsakov State Conservatoire. *Career:* has conducted Tchaikovsky Symphony Orchestra, Moscow, St Petersburg Academic Philharmonic Orchestra, Russian State Symphony Orchestra, Moscow, E. Mikeladze State Symphony Orchestra, Tbilisi, Georgian Radio and TV Symphony Orchestra, Tbilisi; Artistic Principal Conductor, Tbilisi Z. Paliashvili Opera and Ballet State Theatre 2004–09; Assoc. Prof., opera theatre dept, Tbilisi State Conservatoire 1991–. *Honours:* second prize Int. Prokoviev Conducting Competition 1996. *Address:* c/o Tbilisi Zakharia Paliashvili Opera and Ballet State Theatre, 25 Rustaveli Avenue, Tbilisi, Georgia (office). *E-mail:* info@opera.ge (office). *Website:* www.opera.ge/eng/administration (office).

AZZOLINI, Sergio; Italian bassoonist; b. 15 Jan. 1967, Bolzano. *Education:* Claudio Monteverdi Conservatory of Music, Bolzano with Romano Santi and Hanover Musikhochschule with Klaus Thunemann. *Career:* principal solo bassoon, European Community Youth Orchestra; Prof., Stuttgart Musikhochschule 1989–98; Prof., Basle State Acad. of Music 1998–; as soloist, collaborated with Sonatori de la Gioiosa Marca and La Stravaganza Köln; directs his own ensemble, Il Proteo; mem. Ma'alot Quintett, Sabine Meyer Bläserensemble and Maurice Bourgue Trio; collaborates with early music ensembles Parnassi Musici and L'Ensemble Baroque de Limoges; Artistic Dir Philarmonic Chamber Orchestra, Potsdam, Germany 2002–07. *Honours:* first prizes in int. competitions at Ancona, Prague, Belgrade, Martigny, Bonn, first prize C.M. von Weber competition, Munich. *Current Management:* Cesare Venturi Music Management, Via Scrimiari 5, 37129 Verona, Italy. *Telephone:* (045) 8009284. *Fax:* (045) 8009284. *E-mail:* ceventu@tin.it. *Website:* www.cesareventuri.it (office).

B

BABINGTON, Amanda-Louise, BMus, MusM; British musician and musicologist; b. 12 Oct. 1979, Oxford. *Education:* Univ. of Manchester. *Career:* freelance Baroque violinist and recorder player 2003–; violinist with Les Talens Lyrique (Christophe Rousset) 2003–06, Welsh Baroque 2005–09, Manchester Baroque (Leader) 2005–09, Eighteenth Century Concert Orchestra 2006–09, Dunedin Consort 2007–09, Gabrieli Consort 2009, also worked with Acad. D'Ambronay (Paul McCreesh), Leeds Baroque Orchestra (Peter Holman), Britten Pears Baroque Orchestra (Richard Egarr, Emmanuelle Haim, Paul McCreesh), Northern Baroque; Graduate Teaching Asst, Univ. of Manchester 2003–; Recorder Teacher, Univ. of Liverpool 2005–; Dir Manchester Univ. Baroque Orchestra 2006–; mem. Musicians' Union. *Recordings:* Wagner Prelude to Die MeisterSinger, Ravel Daphnis et Chloé, National Youth Orchestra of Scotland, Takho Yuasa 1999, Tragédiennes 2005, Aristeo 2006, Il Tutore Burlato 2006. *Publications:* Handel's Solo Sonatas, Early Music Performer Issue II March 2003. *Honours:* Scottish Arts Trust 2003, 2002, 2001, SRP Walter Bergmann Memorial Fund 2001, The Robert Nicol Trust 2001, Proctor Gregg Travel Award 1999, 2001, 2000. *Address:* 9 Patterson Avenue, Chorlton, Manchester, M21 9NB, England (home). *Telephone:* (161) 881-1672 (home). *E-mail:* ababington@hotmail.com (home).

BABYKIN, Anatoly; Russian singer (bass); b. 29 Sept. 1944, Tscheljabinsk. *Education:* Astrakhan Conservatory. *Career:* member of the Bolshoi Opera at Moscow from 1976; Roles have included King René (Iolanthe), Gremin (Eugene Onegin), Leporello in The Stone Guest by Dargomyzhsky and Don Alfonso (Così fan tutte); Sang with the Bolshoi at the Edinburgh Festival in 1991, operas by Tchaikovsky and Rimsky-Korsakov.

BACCHETTI, Andrea; Italian musician (piano); b. 1977. *Education:* Int. Piano Acad. Incontri con il Maestro, Imola, studied with Franco Scala. *Career:* debut aged 11 with I Solisti Veneti, conducted by Claudio Scimone; regular appearances at int. festivals across Italy and at Lucerne, Salisbury, Belgrade, Santander, Toulouse (Piano aux Jacobins), Paris (La Serre d'Auteil), Bad Wörishofen, Husum and Pacific Music Festival in Sapporo 2012; tours in S America and Japan; regular performer in Italy at theatres such as Teatro alla Scala, Milan, Teatro Carlo Felice, Genoa and Teatro La Fenice, Venice; has played with more than 50 conductors and orchestras including Lucerne Festival Strings, Camerata Salzburg, RTVE Madrid, ONBA Bordeaux, MDR Sinfonieorchester Lipsia, Sinfónica de Tenerife, Sinfónica dell'Estado de Mexico, Philharmonique de Nice and Philharmonique de Cannes, Prague Chamber Orchestra, Cappella Istropolitana of Bratislava, Sinfónica de Castilla y León, European Union Chamber Orchestra, Philharmonie der Nationen, SWKO Pforzheim, Enesco Philharmonic of Bucarest, Orquesta Sinfónica del Principado de Asturias (Oviedo), Simfonicni Orkester RTV Slovenia; as chamber musician, collaborates with Rocco Filippini, Domenico Nordio, Uto Ugh and with ensembles including Prazak, Ysaÿe, Cremona and Teatro della Scala quartets; debut in New York at Frick Museum 2014; concerts broadcast by BBC Radio 3, ORF Austria, Radio France (at La Roque d'Anthéron), RAI Radio Tre, Italy, New Zealand Radio, RNE Spain, MDR Leipzig, CBC Radio 3 Canada, Poiskm Russia. *Recordings include:* Bach: English Suites, Berio Piano Works, Bach: Goldberg Variations, Cherubini: 6 Sonatas, Sonatas by Galuppi and Marcello, Inventions and Symphonies, Toccatas, Andrea Bacchetti plays Bach, Bach: French Suites (Supersonic Award, Pizzicato, Belgium, one of Musical Opinion magazine's best CDs for 2012). *E-mail:* andreabacchetti@libero.it. *Website:* www.andreabacchetti.net.

BACELLI, Monica; Italian singer (mezzo-soprano); b. 1960. *Career:* debut as Mozart's Dorabella, Spoleto Festival, 1987; sang Zerlina at Rome, 1990; Cecilio in Mozart's Lucio Silla, San Francisco, 1991; Appearances as Cherubino, Salzburg Festival, 1992; Covent Garden Vienna State Opera and Rossini Festival, Pesaro; Roles include Rosina, Nicklausse, Ravel's Child and Mozart's Idamante, Idomeneo; Season 1998 with Cherubino, Rome; Sang Ascanio in Benvenuto Cellini in concert, at the Barbican, London, 1999; Season 1999–2000: Premiere of Berio's Cronaca del Luogo, Salzburg; Rossini's Isabella for Netherlands Opera; Ottavia in Poppea at Florence and Bellini's Romeo at Catania; Berio's Outis at La Scala and the Châtelet, Paris; Season 2001 in Handel's Tamerlano at Halle; debut as Donna Elvira in Don Giovanni with Antonio Pappano and Accad. di S. Cecilia Rome 2006, also at La Scala Milan; Cecilio in Lucio Silla at Teatro La Fenice and Salzburg Festival, Berio's Altra Voce in Milan and the Wiener Konzerthaus with Maurizio Pollini, Le Martyre de S. Sebastien by Debussy with Berlin Philharmonic and Sir Simon Rattle, La Clemenza di Tito at the Teatro Regio, Turin with Roberto Abbado, Pelléas et Melisande in Rome, and Sesto in La Clemenza di Tito in Naples with Jeffrey Tate; appeared in La Calisto at Bavarian State Opera 2007 and Royal Opera House, Covent Garden 2008, Giulietta in Les Contes d'Hoffman at Teatro Regio, Turin 2009; numerous concerts and recitals. *Recordings:* La Finta giardiniera 2006; Le nozze di Figaro, Mozart's Lucio Silla, Handel's Tamerlano conducted by Trevor Pinnock, Luciano Berio's Folksongs, Handel's Tamerlano with Placido Domingo (DVD) 2008. *Honours:* Abbiati Award 1997. *Address:* c/o Netherlands Opera, Waterlooplein 22, 1011 Amsterdam, Netherlands.

BACH, Andreas; German pianist; b. 29 July 1968, Dennbach. *Education:* studied with Prof. Karl-Heinz Kammerlung, Hannover. *Career:* debut with Alte Oper, Frankfurt in 1984; appearance in Eurovision Competition, 1984; first tour to USA with debuts at New York, San Francisco and Washington DC 1987 and to Japan 1988; several further tours to USA and appearances in France, Germany, England, Switzerland, Italy and Portugal; Marlboro Music Festival 1999; debut in S America at Teatro Municipal, Santiago 1999, returning for solo recitals and a programme for two pianos (with Alfredo Perl); performances in China 2005 and 2008; solo recital at Klavierfestival Ruhr 2007. *Recordings:* Schumann Op 6, Op 7 1989; Beethoven Op 7, Op 31 No. 2, Op 126 1990, also works by Brahms and Bartok. *Honours:* winner, several Youth Competitions 1975–84, Bernhard Sprengel Prize for Music 1985, Bruno Leonardo Gelber Prize 1987, Kulturpreis von Rheinland-Pfalz 1990. *Address:* Xantener Str. 3a, 50733 Cologne, Germany (home). *Telephone:* (64) 02382 (home). *Fax:* (64) 02386 (home). *E-mail:* info@andreas-bach.com (home). *Website:* www.andreas-bach.com (home).

BACH, Jan Morris, BMus, MMus, DMA; American composer and educator (retd); *Distinguished Research Professor Emeritus, Northern Illinois University;* b. 11 Dec. 1937, Forrest, IL; m. Dalia Zakaras 1971; two d. *Education:* Univ. of Illinois, Urbana-Champaign. *Career:* Asst First Horn, US Army Band 1962–65; Instructor in Music, Univ. of Tampa, FL 1965–66; Prof. of Music, Northern Illinois Univ., Dekalb 1966–98; Presidential Research Prof., Northern Illinois Univ. 1982–86, Distinguished Research Prof. Emer. 1986–; Guest Composer, Wheaton Coll., Univ. of South Florida, Wesleyan Univ., Green Mountain Coll.; mem. American Soc. of Composers, Authors and Publishers, BMI. *Compositions include:* Four Two-Bit Contraptions 1967, Skizzen 1967, Burgundy Variations 1968, Woodwork 1970, Eisteddfod 1972, The System 1973, Piano Concerto 1975, The Eve of St Agnes, for antiphonal wind ensemble 1976, Praetorius Suite 1977, Canon and Caccia, for five French horns 1977, Happy Prince 1978, Quintet for Tuba and Strings 1978, Gala Fanfare 1979, The Student from Salamanca 1979, Rounds and Dances 1980, Sprint 1982, French Suite, for unaccompanied horn 1982, Horn Concerto 1983, Dompes and Jompes 1986, Harp Concerto 1986, Concerto for Trumpet and Wind Ensemble 1987, Concerto, for Euphonium and Orchestra 1990, Anachronisms, for string quartet 1991, People of Note 1993, Concerto for Steel Pan and Orchestra 1994, The Last Flower 1995, Foliations 1995, Concertino for Bassoon and Strings 1996, Pilgrimage 1997, Variations on a theme of Brahms 1997, Choral: Hair Today 1977, Dear God 1998, In the Hands of the Tongue 1999, The Duel 2000, Songs of the Streetwise 2000, Tuba Concerto 2003, Oompah Suite 2005. *Recordings include:* Laudes for Brass Quintet, Skizzen for Woodwind Quintet, Four Two-Bit Contraptions, Eisteddfod 1972, My Very First Solo 1973, Praetorius Suite 1976, Concert Variations, for Euphonium and Piano 1977, Fanfare and Fugue for Five Trumpets 1979, Rounds and Dances 1980, Triptych, for Brass Quintet 1989, Steel Pan Concerto 1994, The Duel 2000, Oompah Suite 2005, Horn Concerto 2006, Gala Fanfare 2006, French Suite 2006, Helix 2006. *Publications:* selected compositions published by Galaxy-Highgate 1980–85, many other choral and chamber works published by other publrs. *Honours:* First Prize, Broadcast Music Student Composers Contest 1957, Koussevitsky Composition Award, Tanglewood 1961, Winner, Mannes Coll. Opera Contest 1973, Award for Excellence in Undergraduate Educ., Northern Illinois Univ. 1978, Winner, New York City Opera Contest 1980, Honouree, Fox Valley (Ill.) Arts Hall of Fame 2004. *Address:* PO Box 403, Wasco, IL 60183, USA (home). *Telephone:* (630) 531-7166 (office). *E-mail:* janbach@janbach.com (office). *Website:* www.janbach.com.

BACH, Mechthild; German singer (soprano); b. 1970, Limburg an der Lehn. *Education:* Frankfurt Musikhochschule with Elsa Calveti; Hartmut Holl and Michael Schneider, Studio for Early Music; Vera Rozsa and Laura Sarti in London. *Career:* Darmstadt Staatstheater and the opera studio of the Deutsche Oper am Rhein, Düsseldorf, Heidelberg Opera 1991–96, also in Munich and Hamburg; stage and concert appearances with conductors Frieder Bernius, Reinhard Goebel, Michael Schneider, Helmuth Rilling and Sigiswald Kuijken; performed at Dresden Days of Music, Stuttgart Bach Academy, Berlin and Cologne Philharmonies, and Amsterdam Concertgebouw; Antigone in Admetus at Händel-Festspiele in Halle an der Saale 2006, Mahler's 4th Symphony at Mahler-Festwochen in Toblach 2006, Alice Ford in Falstaff in Lucerne 2007; singing teacher, Trossingen Conservatory. *Recordings:* Flavio in Jommelli's Il Vologeso, Jommelli's Didone Abbandonata as Selene, Orfeo, Gristostomo in Telemann's Don Quichotte, Durante's Lamentations, Monteverdi's Vespers, Mendelssohn's Lobesgesang, Handel's Acis and Galatea and Ode for St Cecilia's Day, Mozart Masses, Zelenka's Missa Dei Patris (German Record Critics Prize 2002), Haydn: Missa in honorem Sanctae Ursulae/Mozart: Ave verum corpus 2009. *Address:* c/o Staatliche Hochschule für Musik Trossingen, Schultheiss-Koch-Platz 3, 78647 Trossingen, Germany (office). *E-mail:* Mechthild.Bach@gmx.de (home).

BACHLER, Nikolaus (Klaus); Austrian artistic director; *Intendant, Bayerische Staatsoper;* b. 1951. *Education:* Max Reinhardt Seminar, Vienna. *Career:* trained as an actor in Vienna; made acting debut at Landestheater Salzburg, spent several years acting in theatres in Germany; apptd Artistic Dir State Drama Theatre, Berlin 1987; Artistic Dir of Operations, Schiller Theater, Berlin 1978–90; Producer, Taller Europe Festival, Paris 1990; Dir Vienna Festival 1991–96; Dir Volksoper, Vienna 1996–99; Dir Burgtheater, Vienna 1999–2008; Intendant (Dir), Bayerische Staatsoper, Munich 2008–.

Address: Bayerische Staatsoper, Max-Joseph-Platz 2, 80539 Munich, Germany (office). *Telephone:* (89) 21851001 (office). *Fax:* (89) 21851133 (office). *Website:* www.bayerische.staatsoper.de (office).

BACHLUND, Gary; American singer (tenor) and composer; b. 1958, New York. *Education:* studied voice in New York, composition at UCLA. *Career:* sang Parsifal at Carnegie Hall and appeared in operas by Mussorgsky, Wagner (Das Rheingold) and Gounod (Roméo et Juliette) at the Metropolitan Opera; sang Strauss's Bacchus with Minnesota Opera; Florestan for Boston Opera and Don José for Scottish Opera at Glasgow (European debut 1986); other roles include Agrippa in The Fiery Angel, Jimmy in Mahagonny and Aegisthus in Elektra (all at Los Angeles); Ennée in Les Troyens at the Opéra Bastille, Paris 1990 and Wagner's Erik at Cologne 1992; sang Tristan at Florentine Opera, Milwaukee 1993, 2004 (also at Brunswick 1996); Don José in Santiago 1993; Tannhäuser at Kaiserslautern 1995, and Palm Beach Opera 2002; season 2000 as Tristan at Honolulu and Dmitri in Boris Godunov at Kassel; composer-in-residence, All Saints Church, Pasadena 1992–; compositions commissioned and performed by artists and organisations in USA and Europe. *Compositions include:* one-act chamber operas based on Hans Christian Andersen's fables: Prelude to a Fable, The Emperor's New Clothes, The Little Match Girl, A Love Charm; Concerto grosso in B major for harpsichord, organ and chamber orchestra (American Guild of Organists commission) 1997, Requiem for the Victims of AIDS 2001, The Jerusalem Windows organ symphony 2003, Alice (two-act opera) 2001–04, An Echo from the Shore for soprano, oboe, violin, violoncello and harpsichord (Pacific Serenades commission); choral works and over 1,000 songs in many languages; settings of poems of e.e.cummings. *Current Management:* Peter Seyfferth Artists Management, Avenue de la Concorde 385, 06190 Roquebrune Cap Martin, France. *Telephone:* 4-93-35-01-05. *Fax:* 4-93-35-02-17. *E-mail:* peter@seyfferth.de. *Website:* www.seyfferth.de. *E-mail:* bachlund@bachlund.org (office). *Website:* www.bachlund.org (home).

BACHMANN, Rhonda; American singer (soprano); b. 24 Oct. 1952, Chicago; d. of Dr C. Charles Bachmann and Mary Lee Bachmann; m. Arthur Hammond 1986 (died 1991). *Education:* Conservatoire Nat. Superieur de Musique de Paris, Northwestern Univ. *Career:* with Chicago Opera Theatre 1979–80, Opéra de Lyon 1981, Opéra de Wallonie, Belgium 1982, Opéra du Rhin, Strasbourg 1981–84, Théâtre du Palais Royal, Paris 1981; concerts include, Radio France 1980, 1989–1993 Marie Antoinette Bicentennial, Naantali Festival, Finland 1981, Salle Gaveau, Paris 1981, Royal Opera House, Friends of Covent Garden Christmas Gala 1985, Institut Français London 1986, Pavillon Dauphine, Paris 1986; many recitals and chamber music concerts in Paris, Germany, Italy, including the music of Vivaldi, Bach, Handel, Mozart, Schubert, Spohr, Brahms, Schoenberg, Ravel and Dowland; TV appearances in New York, Paris, Marseilles; acted in 3 films 1974–76; leading role Harriet Smithson, The Life of Berlioz, 1981; toured extensively with recital in 18th-century costume as Queen Marie Antoinette, Songs for the Queen, Songs for the Revolution, seven programmes, 550 performances of which 282 in Grand Trianon, Versailles, 1988–2010; tours to USA, UK, Ireland, Bulgaria, Austria, Italy with Peter Gellhorn, piano, 100 performances 1992–2003; 13 recital programmes, Malibran and Viardot (bel canto repertoire), The Romantic Nightingale (Lieder) and From Times of War (20th century up to 1948), tours to Italy, France, Austria and UK, Covent Garden Festival; Molière Festival, Versailles 2004–10; Owner, La Reine Artiste; Dir Carl Rosa Trust 1992–2004. *Plays:* Jean de la Fontaine, Rose Marie. *Recordings:* Cassettine: Quand tu étais petit, Lieder in French translation by Mozart, Schubert and Brahms with Noel Lee, piano; Video: Queen Marie Antoinette and the Kindling Fire, with Peter Gellhorn, piano, 2000, Jenny Lind: Queen Victoria's Songbird, Jenny Lind: The Nightingale at Song, Songs from Napoleon's Empire, Berlioz in Britain, Freemasonry in Victorian Museum and Drama, with Peter Gellhorn 2002–03, In Memory of Dresden, with Juan Biava (organ) 2005, Aloysia in Exile, Mozart's Muse, with Julie Koontz (piano) 2006. *Honours:* First Prize, Master Singers Contest, Paris 1973, Cramer Award for Excellence in Opera 1977. *Address:* 7 Norfolk House, Courtlands, Sheen Road, Richmond, Surrey, TW10 5AT, England (office). *Telephone:* (20) 8940-3613 (office). *E-mail:* lareineartiste@yahoo.com (office). *Website:* www.rhondabachmann.com (office).

BACHMANN-ARNOLD, Ulrike; German musician (piano) and music teacher; b. 14 June 1961. *Education:* Musikhochschule, Lübeck. *Career:* piano duettist with Silvia Zenker (q.v.) 1984–89; has given concerts in Germany and abroad, and performances on radio and TV; numerous recordings of works for piano (duets). *Honours:* First Prize in Music, Possehlstiftung Lübeck 1984; Hansekulturpreis, Stadt Lübeck 1987; First Prize Int. Piano Duet Competition, Italy 1988. *Address:* Zaunkönigsweg 1, 55765 Birkenfeld, Germany.

BACK, Andrée; British singer (soprano); b. 1950. *Education:* Royal Coll. of Music. *Career:* has sung in oratorios, recitals and symphony concerts with appearances in most major European and American cities; frequent engagements in Switzerland, Norway, Austria, Belgium and the Netherlands (Radio Symphony Orchestra, Rotterdam); has sung in Carmina Burana at Liège, Siegen and Edinburgh, Berlioz's La Mort de Cléopâtre with Berlin Symphony Orchestra, Mozart's Requiem and Coronation Mass in Marienstatt with the Bonn Bach Choir, and Mozart Concert Arias with the Schwabische Symphony Orchestra; sang in Mahler's 4th Symphony at Cheltenham Festival and in A Child of Our Time at Bury St Edmunds, Telemann Cantatas in Hamburg and Haydn's Berenice and Strauss's Four Last Songs with the Billings Symphony Orchestra 1989; other concert repertoire includes Bach's Mass in B minor, Magnificat, Passions and Christmas Oratorio, Beethoven's Missa Solemnis, Mass in C and Choral Symphony, Requiems by Brahms, Fauré, Britten and Verdi, Handel's Messiah, Judas Maccabaeus, Jephtha, Joshua, Acis and Galatea, Hercules, Israel in Egypt, Samson, Saul and Chandos Anthems, Janáček's Glagolitic Mass, Mahler's 2nd and 8th Symphonies, Rückert Lieder, Schubert's Salve Regina, Masses, Vivaldi's Gloria and Magnificat, Wagner's Wesendonck Lieder. *Address:* Mancroft Towers, Oulton Broad, Lowestoft, Suffolk NR32 3PS, England.

BACQUIER, Gabriel; French singer (baritone); b. 17 May 1924, Béziers; s. of Augustin Bacquier and Fernande Severac; m. 1st Simone Teisseire 1943; one s.; m. 2nd Mauricette Bénard 1958; one s. *Education:* Paris Conservatoire. *Career:* debut at Théâtre Royal de la Monnaie, Brussels 1953; joined Opéra de Paris 1956; debut at Carnegie Hall 1960, Metropolitan Opera, New York 1961; has appeared at the Vienna State Opera, Covent Garden, La Scala, Opéra de Paris and most leading opera houses; repertoire includes Otello, Don Giovanni, Pelléas et Mélisande, Damnation de Faust, Tosca, Falstaff; retired from stage in 1994; taught at Paris Conservatoire and Acad. de Musique de Monaco; several recordings. *Films include:* La Grande Récré, Falstaff. *Honours:* Chevalier, Légion d'honneur, Officier, Ordre nat. du Mérite, Commdr des Arts et des Lettres; Prix nat. du disque français 1964, Médaille de Vermeil, City of Paris, Victoires de la Musique 1985. *Address:* c/o OIA, 16 avenue Franklin D. Roosevelt, 75008 Paris, France.

BACRI, Nicolas; French composer; b. 23 Nov. 1961, Paris. *Education:* Conservatoire National Supérieur de Musique, Paris, studied with Serge Nigg, Michel Philippot, also with Louis Saguer, Elliott Carter, Jean Catoire, Claude Ballif, Marius Constant, Brian Ferneyhough. *Career:* Composer Laureate, French Acad. in Rome, Villa Medici 1983–85; Head of Chamber Music Dept, Radio France 1987–91; Composer Laureate, Casa de Velasquez, Spain 1991–93, Fondation d'entreprise du Crédit National (Natixis Banque) 1994–96; Composer-in-Residence, Orchestre Symphonique Français 1995–96, Orchestre de Picardie 1996–98, CNR and Orchestre de Bayonne 2001, Festival des forêts (Compiègne) 2010–12; Assoc. Composer, Ensemble Orchestral de Paris 2008–11; commissions from groups including Radio France, City of Paris for Orchestre Philharmonique de Radio France, Ensemble Orchestrale de Paris, Festspielhaus Berlin, Alte Oper Frankfurt; works performed in Europe, Asia and USA in halls including Théâtre du Châtelet, Royal Festival, Barbican and Wigmore Halls, Salle Pleyel, Musikverein Wien and Théâtre des Champs-Elysées by orchestras including London Symphony Orchestra, BBC Singers, Symphony Orchestra WDR Köln, Shanghaï Symphony Orchestra and Nat. Orchestras of France and Spain under conductors including Leonard Slatkin, Daniel Harding, Semyon Bychkov and Pascal Rophé; teacher of orchestration, Geneva Conservatory 2005–11. *Compositions include:* for stage: Fleur et le miroir magique (songs for children) 1996–7; orchestral: six symphonies (op. 11 1983-4, op. 22 Sinfonia dolorosa 1986–90, op. 33 Sinfonia da requiem, with Mez and chorus 1988–94, op. 49 Classical Symphony Sturm und Drang 1995–96, op. 55 Concerto for Orchestra 1996–7, op. 60 1998), A Short Overture 1978, 2002–03, Musica per archi for string orchestra 1991–92, Sinfonietta for string orchestra 2001, Elegy in memoriam D.S.C.H. for string orchestra 2003, Partita concertante for oboe, clarinet or bassoon 2004, Via Crucis 2008; three violin concertos (op. 7 1982–83, op.29 3 canti e finale 1987–89, op. 83 1999–2000/2003), Une Prière 1995–97, two clarinet concertos (op. 20 Capriccio notturno 1986–87, op. 61 Concerto da camera 1998); two trumpet concertos (op. 39 1992, op. 65, Im Angedenken J. S. Bachs 2000); Cello concerto, op.17 1985–87, Requiem 1987-8, Folia 1990, Symphonie concertante 1995–96/rev. 2006, Flute concerto 1999, Divertimento 1999–2000, Notturno 2001, Concerto nostalgico op. 80 n° 1 L'automne 2000–02, Concerto amoroso op. 80 n° 2 Le printemps 2004–05, Partita concertante 2004 and other pieces; vocal: Notturni 1985–86, six cantatas including Fils d'Abraham 1988–94; n°4, op. 44 Sonnet 66 by W. Shakespeare 1994–95, Isiltasunaren ortzadarra 2001–02; n° 6 op. 87 Cantata vivaldiana sur le Nisi Dominus 2004, Lamento, op. 81 Ach das ich Wassers genug hätte (after Jeremy) 2002, Three Love Songs (Rûmi), op. 9 2005, Melodias de la melancolia, op. 119 2010; choral: Sinfonia da requiem, three Alleluia 1994; four Alleluia 1994, five Motets de souffrance et de consolation 1998, Nisi Dominus (6th Motet op. 62) 1998, Benedicat Israel Domino (Trittico mistico op. 64) 2000, O Lux Beatissima (7th Motet op. 71) 2001, Beatus Vir (8th Motet op. 78) 2002, Lamento (9th Motet op. 81b) 2002, Stabat Mater 2003, Miserere (10th Motet op. 93) 2004; chamber music: without piano: Seven String Quartets (op.1 Fantaisie 1980, op.5 Five Pieces 1982, op. 18 Esquisses pour un Tombeau 1985–89, op. 42 Omaggio a Beethoven 1989–94, op. 57 1997, op. 97 2005–06, op. 101 Variations sérieuses 2006–07), Duo, op. 25 1987–92, Sonata in memoriam Bela Bartók 2005, Two String Trios (op. 8 6 Sonatas 1982–83, op. 37 Divertimento 1991–92), String sextet op. 36 1991–92, Concerto da camera, op. 61 1998, Divertimento, op. 37b 1991–92, Im Volkston, op.43 1994, Night Music, op. 73 2001, Partita da camera 2004, Méditation d'après un thème de Beethoven 2005, with piano: Four Piano Trios (op. 34 Toccata sinfonica 1987–93, op. 47 Les contrastes 1995, op. 54 Sonata notturna 1996–97, op. 99 Sonata seria 2006), Sonata op. 32 1990–94, Sonata op. 40 1993–94, Sonata da camera 1977/97–2000, Sonata no. 2 op. 75 2002, 3 Impromptus, op. 115 2009, 4 Elégies 2012, Sonata no. 2, op. 128 2012, and other pieces; for solo instruments: for piano: Two Sonatas (op. 68 Sonata corta 1978–79, rev. 2003, op. 106 2007), Nine Preludes (op. 24 1988, op. 28 1989, op. 33 n°3b 1991, op. 46 1994–95), L'enfance de l'art op. 69, Prelude & fugue op. 91 2004, Second Prelude & fugue Arioso barocco e fuga monodica a due voci op. 100 2006, Suite baroque op. 104 2007, Nocturne pour la main gauche op. 105 2007, Diletto classico, 3 Cahiers de piano en hommage aux maîtres baroques et classiques, op. 100 2007, Saison (4 Intermezzi), op. 123 2010–12, and other pieces; for other instruments: Six Suites for Cello (op. 31 n°1, 2 & 3 in memoriam B. Britten 1987–93, op. 50 1994/96, op. 70b 2000-01/03, op. 88 2004), Three Sonatas for violin (op. 45 Sonata breve (Sonatina in omaggio a Mozart) 1994, op. 53 1996, op. 76 Kol Nidrei sonata 2002), Sonata variata op. 70 2000–01, Mondorf sonatina op. 58 n°2 1997, 12 Monologues pascaliens op. 92 2004, and other pieces. *Recordings include:* Musique de Chambre 1997, Concerto pour violoncelle/ Folia/Requiem/Tre canti e finale 2001, Cantates 2003, Une Prière 2002, Musique pour clarinette 2005, String Quartets 2007, Sturm und Drang 2009, Piano Music (performed by Eliane Reyes) 2011. *Honours:* Prix Stéphane Chapelier, SACEM 1987, Prix André Caplet 1989, Prix Pineau-Chaillou, Nantes 1991, Prix Hervé Dugardin, SACEM 1992, Grand Prix Académie du Disque 1993, Prix Georges Wildenstein 1993, Lauréat de la Fondation d'entreprise Natixis 1993–96; Prix Pierre Cardin 1994, Lauréat du 5° Concours Jeunes artistes européens: Jeunes compositeurs, Leipzig, Prix Claude Arrieu, SACEM 1995. *Address:* c/o Peer Musikverlag, Muhlenkamp 45, 22303 Hamburg, Germany (office). *E-mail:* bacrinicolas@hotmail.fr (office). *Website:* www.peermusic-classical .de (office); www.nicolasbacri.net.

BÁCS, Ludovic; Romanian composer and conductor; *Professor, Bucharest Conservatory;* b. 19 Jan. 1930, Petrila; s. of Ludovic Bács and Iuliana Bács (née Venczel); m. Ercse Gyöngyver, 1952; two s. *Education:* Dima Gh. Conservatory, Cluj-Napoca Tchaikovski Conservatory, Moscow, Cluj-Napoca Coll. of Philosophy 1948–49. *Career:* began career as conductor Symphonic Orchestra of Romanian Radio, also Artistic Dir 1964–; Prof., Bucharest Conservatory 1960–66, 1990–; Assoc. Prof., Transilvania Univ. of Braşov; Conductor Romanian Radio Chamber Orchestra 1990–; f. Musica Rediviva 1966, first group of performers to render ancient Romanian music; has conducted concerts in USSR, Poland, Czechoslovakia, Hungary, Bulgaria, Germany, Holland, Argentina, Switzerland, Spain, France; mem. Romanian Composers' Union. *Works include:* orchestration of Bach's Art of the Fugue (on record), numerous adaptations from 15th–18th century music: Bach, Monteverdi, Backfarg, from Codex Caioni a.o.; Suitá de Musicá Veche 17th–18th century, Variations Sinfoniques e Double Fugue sur une Thème Populaire Hongroise, Trois Madrigales pour Choeur, Variations et Fugue sur une Colinde Roumaine, Potpourri sur des Colindes. *Honours:* Cultural Merit Award, Medal of Labour, Prize of the Theatre and Music Asscn . *Address:* 31 D. Golescu, Sc III, Et V ap. 87, Bucharest 1, Romania (home).

BACULEWSKI, Krzysztof Jan, MA, PhD; Polish composer and academic; *Professor, Fryderyk Chopin University of Music;* b. 26 Dec. 1950, Warsaw; m. Agnieszka Dmowska 1979. *Education:* Acad. of Music, Warsaw, Conservatoire Nat. Supérieur de Musique, Paris, Warsaw Univ. *Career:* debut in Warsaw 1975; numerous compositions performed at Warsaw Autumn Int. Festival of Contemporary Music and abroad, including USA, France, Germany, Finland, Hungary, S America; Prof., F. Chopin Univ. of Music, Warsaw 1982–; Guest Prof., Johannes-Gutenberg Univ., Mainz, Germany; has lectured at numerous Polish music acads and abroad in Bulgaria, Finland and Germany; mem. Polish Composers Union, ISCM, Soc. of Authors ZAiKS. *Compositions include:* Epitaphium for Orchestra 1973, Vivace e Cantilena for Chamber Ensemble 1975, Ground for Orchestra 1981, Concerto for Orchestra 1983, four string quartets 1984, 1985, 1986, 2014, Concerto Armonico for Strings 1987, Antitheton I, for Piano Trio 1989, A Walking Shadow for Orchestra 1990, Rilke-Lieder for two choirs 1995, Antitheton II for Baroque instruments 1996, Gloria for alto and mixed choir 1996, Sonata Canonica for two violins 1998, Miserere for mixed choir a cappella 1999, Les Adieux, a cantata 2001, Etudes for piano 2006, Prelude, Psalms and Meditation, for mixed choir and organ 2007, Antitheton III, for baroque instruments 2013, Piano quintet 2015, Refrain, for mixed choir and ensemble 2015. *Recordings:* Sonata for Percussion, Rilke-Lieder for Choir a Cappella, Nox Ultima, Motet for Choir a Cappella, The Profane Anthem to Anne, text by John Donne, a Cantata, Sonata Canonica for two violins 1998, Chansons Romanesques et Frivoles for voices and baroque instruments 2000, Works for Orchestra 2009, Choral Works 2010. *Publications:* Polish Musical Output, 1945–1984 1987, The History of Music in Poland. The Contemporary Era, Part 1: 1939–1974 (ed 2006), The History of Music in Poland. The Contemporary Era, Part 2: 1975–2000 (ed 2012). *Honours:* numerous prizes at Polish competitions, Gloria Artis Silver Medal 2007. *Address:* Fryderyk Chopin University of Music, ul. Okólnik, 00-368 Warsaw, Poland (office). *E-mail:* kbacul@chopin.edu.pl (office). *Website:* www.chopin.edu.pl (office); www.polmic.pl (office).

BADER, Hans-Dieter; German singer (tenor); b. 16 Feb. 1938, Stuttgart. *Education:* studied with Rudolf Gehrung and in Stuttgart. *Career:* debut at Stuttgart Staatsoper in 1960 as Arturo in Lucia di Lammermoor; sang at Brunswick, Karlsruhe, Essen, Kassel and Mannheim; mem. Niedersächsischen Staatsoper in Hanover 1965–84; also appeared at Nuremberg, Hamburg, Düsseldorf, Strasbourg and Vienna Volksoper; repertoire of 90 roles includes Rodolfo in La Bohème, Faust, Ferrando in Così fan tutte and the Duke of Mantua; season 1995–96, as Herod in Salome and Tiresias in Orff's Antigonae at Hannover; Strauss's Emperor at Kiel; season 2000–01 as Shuisky in Boris Godunov and Aegisthus in Elektra, at Hanover; concert tours to South Africa, Jordan, Lesotho, Chile, Brazil, France, Paraguay, the Netherlands and in Asia. *Recordings include:* Reger's Requiem; Sly by Wolf-Ferrari; Strauss's Feuersnot. *Honours:* Bundesverdienstkreuz am Bande 1996. *Address:* Staatstheater Hannover, Opernhaus, Opernplatz 1, 30159 Hannover, Germany.

BADIAN, Maya, BMus, MMus, DMus; Canadian/Romanian composer, musicologist and academic; *Professor and Senior Examiner, Royal Conservatory of Music Examinations;* b. 18 April 1945, Bucharest, Romania; d. of Hugo Badian and Suzana Badian; m. Lucian Munteanu Badian; one s. (died 1989). *Education:* Nat. Univ. of Music, Bucharest, Univ. of Montréal , Canada. *Career:* debut with Symphonic Movement, Romania 1968; Musical Dir Romanian Radio-TV Corpn (RTV), Bucharest 1968–72; Prof. of Composition and Keyboard, Bucharest 1972–87; settled in Montreal, Canada since 1987; teacher, Univ. of Montreal 1990–; currently Prof. and Sr Examiner, Royal Conservatory of Music Examinations; lecturer at int. contemporary music festivals and congresses in Europe and Canada; concerts in Europe, USA and Canada; mem. various int. juries. *Compositions include:* over 80 compositions including Symphonic: Holocaust–In Memoriam, symphony; concertante music: Concertos for Piano, for Violin, for Guitar, for Cello, for Marimba and Vibraphone for Clarinet and Saxophone for Four Timpani (To Mircea Badian), Children's World for orchestra 1997; vocal-orchestral works: Canada 125–Cantata Profana, Towards The Pinnacle, poem for Soprano; chamber music: Concerto for horn and percussion, solos, duos, trios and other chamber ensembles. *Recordings:* Maya Badian, Romania 1977, Towards The Pinnacle, Canada 1994, Fate, Life, Death: Symphonies by Badian and Tchaikovsky 1997, Maya Badian: Orchestral Works 1998, Reflets Laurentiens 2000, Multimusic Canada: Compositions by Maya Badian 2001, Concert Music: Compositions by Maya Badian 2002, Compositions for Instrumental Ensembles 2003, By a Canadian Lady 2006, Canadian Compositions for Young Pianists. *Honours:* all archival documents and manuscripts are deposited at the Manuscript Collection, Music Division, National Library of Canada, Ottawa. *Current Management:* Lucian Badian Editions, 195 Clearview Avenue, Unit 2020, Ottawa, ON K1Z 6S1, Canada. *Telephone:* (613) 722-2822 (home). *E-mail:* badian@sympatico.ca (home). *Website:* www3.sympatico .ca/badian; www.rcmexaminations.org (office).

BADINSKI, Nikolai, DipMus; German/Bulgarian composer, violinist and educator; b. 19 Dec. 1937, Sofia, Bulgaria. *Education:* Acad. of Music, Sofia, master-class in composition, Acad. of Arts, Berlin, scholarships for master-classes, Accad. Musicale, Siena, Italy. *Career:* active as composer, univ. teacher in Berlin, Sofia, Halle; concert violinist soloist; concertmaster; special adviser for music educ., String Quartet; active in the Darmstadt Int. Courses for New Music 1974–78; Guest Prof., Stanford Univ., Univs of Stockholm and Copenhagen, Shanghai Conservatory; Asst to Max Deutsch, Sorbonne and Ecole Normale de Musique, Paris 1982; Scholar of the French Govt, Paris 1985–86; Composer-in-Residence, Djerassi Foundation and Fulbright Scholar, Calif. 1987; appearances at various festivals; numerous performances, radio and TV broadcasts; mem. European Acad. of Arts, Sciences and Humanities (Paris). *Compositions include:* Amekdil (Symphony), Vol. 1 1967, Bewegung 1969, Shanghai Impulses 1969, Triptych for violin, percussion and string orchestra: I Violin Concerto 1970–72, II Concerto for violin and orchestra 1970–72, III Concerto for violin and orchestra 1970–72, Col-legno Concerto for viola and orchestra 1975, Amekdil (Symphony), Vol. 2 1978, Homage to Stravinsky for strings 1978, Amekdil (Symphony), Vol. 3 1981, Connections for violin, piano and orchestra 1982, Garland Structures for trombone and string orchestra 1982, 2016, Reflections of the Wisdom for soloists, choir and orchestra 1983, The Intoxicated Bat for orchestra 1991, Enlightenment for violin and orchestra 1992, Requiem – Seven Memorial Stones in Memoriam of the Holocaust Victims 1993, Signals for 8 trumpets and orchestra 1993, Berlin Divertimento – A Bulgarian in Berlin for flute, clarinet, percussion and double bass 1968, Sono ancora qui, il sole gira... cantata for medium voice and instruments 1970, The Ruins under Sofia Octet 1972, Silenzio Disturbato for sextet 1976, Omaggio a Bach Concerto for harpsichord and instruments 1977, Meetings of Infinities for amplified instruments and CD 1982, Disegni Concerto for flute and instruments 1984, Fragilità e Vitalità Concerto for piano and instruments 2000, ...Ocean Colours and Moods... for string orchestra 2005–06, Leto's Dream Before the Birth of Apollo and Artemis for soprano and string quartet 2009, Lost in Chekhov's Universe... for cello and string orchestra 2009–10. *Address:* Froeaufstr 3, 12161 Berlin, Germany. *E-mail:* badinski@gmx.de. *Website:* www.n-badinski.com.

BADURA-SKODA, Eva, PhD; German musicologist; b. 15 Jan. 1929, Munich; m. Paul Badura-Skoda; two s. two d. *Education:* Univs of Heidelberg, Vienna and Innsbruck, Hochschule für Musik, Vienna. *Career:* freelance lecturer and writer –1962; summer school Lecturer, Mozarteum Salzburg; Prof., Univ. of Wisconsin 1964–74; Guest Prof., Univ. of Boston 1976, Queen's Univ., Kingston, Canada 1979, McGill Univ., Montréal, Canada 1981–82, Universitat Göttingen 1982–83; mem. Int. Musicological Soc., Haydn Inst., Cologne, Zentralinstitut für Mozart-Forschung des Mozarteums, Salzburg. *Publications:* Mozart Interpretation 1957, Interpreting Mozart on the Keyboard 1961, Mozart's C Minor Piano Concerto 1971, An Unknown Singspiel by Joseph Haydn 1972, Schubert Studies 1982, Internationaler Joseph Haydn Kongress Wien 1982 Congress Report 1985, Aspects of Performance Practice 1994; contrib. to Musical Journals, New Grove Dictionary of Music and Musicians 1980; more than 100 scholarly articles on history of Viennese classical music and history of the fortepiano. *Honours:* Hon. Cross Litteris et Artibus, Austria. *Address:* Zuckerkandlgasse 14, 1190 Vienna, Austria.

BADURA-SKODA, Paul; Austrian pianist; b. 6 Oct. 1927, Vienna; s. of Ludwig Badura and Margarete Badura (née Winter); m. Eva Badura-Skoda (née Halfar); two s. two d. *Education:* Realgymnasium courses in conducting and piano, Konservatorium der Stadt Wien and Edwin Fischer's masterclass in Lucerne. *Career:* regular concerts since 1948; tours world-wide as soloist and with leading orchestras; conductor of chamber orchestra 1960–; yearly master classes fmrly in Edin., Salzburg and Vienna Festival 1958–63; Artist in Residence, Univ. of Wisconsin, master classes in Madison, Wis. 1966–71; recorded more than 200 LP records and CDs, including complete Beethoven, Mozart and Schubert sonatas. *Compositions include:* Mass in D, Cadenzas to Piano, Flute and Violin Concertos by Mozart and Haydn, completion of five unfinished Piano Sonatas by Schubert 1976 and of unfinished Larghetto and Allegro for 2 Pianos by Mozart, Elégie pour Piano 1990, Sonatine Romantique for Violin and Piano 1994, Sonate romantique for Flute (or Violin) and Piano. *Publications:* Die Klaviersonaten von Beethoven (with Jörg Demus) 1970, Interpreting Bach at the Keyboard 1993, Interpreting Mozart on the Keyboard (with Eva Badura-Skoda) (second edn) 2008; Editions of Schubert, Mozart, Chopin; numerous articles. *Honours:* Austrian Cross of Honour for Science and Arts (First Order) 1976, Bösendorfer-Ring 1978, Chevalier, Légion d'honneur 1992, Commdr des Arts et des Lettres 1997, Grosses Silbernes Ehrenzeichen mit dem Stern der Republik Österreich 2007, Goldenes Ehrenzeichen für die Verdienste um das Land Wien 2007; Dr hc (Mannheim) 2006, (Pontificia Universidad Católica del Perú) 2010, (Kraków) 2013; First Prize, Austrian Music Competition 1947. *Address:* Hilda Woolf Arts Management, 12, rue Christiani, 75018 Paris, France. *Website:* www .badura-skoda.com.

BAEK, Kwang-hoon; South Korean singer (baritone) and choir conductor; b. 29 April 1954, Soon-chun City; m. Park Kyung-nyum 1987; one s. *Education:* Kyung-Hee Univ., Seoul; postgraduate studies of singing and choir conducting, Music Univ., Wuppertal, Germany. *Career:* debut as Scarpia in Tosca at Nat. Theatre, Seoul; freelance singer and choir conductor; Schubert's Winterreise, KBS Broadcasting Station 1989; has sung main parts in Tosca, La Traviata, Pagliacci, Le nozze di Figaro, Cavalleria Rusticana, Noye's Fludde, Madama Butterfly, Un Ballo in Maschera in Korea and Slovakia; mem. Schubert Asscn, Seoul, Opera Asscn, Seoul, Deutscher Liederverein, Germany. *Recordings:* Winterreise; Hymns Solo, Haydn's The Creation (conductor). *Address:* 101 Ho, 1428-7, Seocho-Dong, Seocho-Ku, Seoul, Republic of Korea.

BAERG, Theodore; Canadian singer (baritone) and teacher; b. 19 Dec. 1952, Toronto; m. Irena Welhasch Baerg. *Career:* debut with Canadian Opera Company 1978, as Monterone in Rigoletto; sang in the Canadian premiere of Tchaikovsky's The Maid of Orleans 1980, and in Lulu, The Merry Widow and Die Zauberflöte (Papageno); other roles include Mozart's Count at Hamilton Opera 1984, Rossini's Figaro in Vancouver and Ramiro in L'Heure Espagnole at Glyndebourne (European debut) 1988; guested as Marcello in La Bohème at San Diego 1990, and Papageno at Washington 1991; Toronto 1992, in the premiere of Mario and the Magician by Harry Somers; debut at Metropolitan Opera, New York, as Count Homonay in Strauss's Zigeunerbaron, conducted by Kurt Masur 1995; has appeared with opera companies throughout Canada and USA and with orchestras including New York Philharmonic, Dallas Symphony, Rochester Philharmonic, The National Symphony, Los Angeles Philharmonic and Houston Symphony; opera repertoire of over 75 roles includes Wozzeck, Ford in Falstaff, Rigoletto, Eugene Onegin, Don Giovanni, Figaro in Il Barbiere di Siviglia and Peter in Hänsel and Gretel; other roles include Sharpless in Madama Butterfly, Count Almaviva in Le Nozze di Figaro, Dandini in La Cenerentola, Lescaut in Manon Lescaut, Silvio in I Pagliacci, Valentin in Faust, George in Of Mice and Men, the Fabulist in Peter's The Golden Ass and many more; Assoc. Prof. of Voice, Opera and Music Theatre, Univ. of Western Ontario. *Recordings include:* Turandot (Ping), La Mystique d'Amour, Enchanted Evenings. *Current Management:* MIC Artists, 154 Chemin des Vingt, CP 1113, St-Basile-le-Grand, Quebec, J3N 1M5, Canada. *Telephone:* (519) 661-2111 ext. 85388. *Fax:* (450) 653-2833. *E-mail:* MICartists@aol.com. *Address:* c/o University of Western Ontario Faculty of Music, Talbot College, Room 210, London, Ontario, Canada (office). *E-mail:* tbaerg@uwo.ca. *Website:* www.baergarts.com (office).

BAEVA, Vera; Bulgarian composer and pianist; b. 18 March 1930, Burgas. *Education:* Sofia State Acad. *Career:* fmr Conductor, Radio Sofia chorus; as pianist, performed with several ensembles, with Bulgarian Nat. Radio Symphony Orchestra and at festivals; teacher of voice, Sofia State Acad. 1982–88; teacher of chamber music, Open Soc. Foundation 1993; composed over 200 vocal, instrumental and orchestral works. *Compositions include:* Pirin, cantata 1954, Five Impressions for piano 1973, Four Songs 1975, two Preludes for cello 1984, Nostalgichno for chamber ensemble 1986, Sonata for piano 4 hands 1988, My Homeland for choir and orchestra 1985, Butterfly for female voices and ensemble 1989, Tristezza for violin 1990, Tangra for male voices and ensemble 1991, Two Pieces for violin and piano 2002, Circus for reader, flute, violoncello, piano and percussion 2003, Three Songs for mezzo-soprano and piano 2003. *Address:* c/o Union of Bulgarian Composers, rue IV Vazov, 1000 Sofia, Bulgaria.

BAGHBOUDARIAN, Missak; Syrian/Armenian conductor; *Chief Conductor, Syrian National Symphony Orchestra;* b. Damascus. *Education:* State Music School of Damascus, Music Inst. of Damascus; studied conducting with Solhi Al Wadi. *Career:* made debut as conductor at Auditorium of the Congresses of Damascus 1994; Chair of Orchestration, Music Inst. of Damascus 1995–97, Asst Conductor, Music Inst. of Damascus Symphony Orchestra 1995–97; Founding mem. Cantiri Musicale di Toscana 1998–; Artistic Dir, Estate Regina Festival, Montecatini Terme, Italy 1998–2006;

Conductor, Amadeus Orchestra, Florence, Italy 2001–03; Chief Conductor, Syrian Nat. Symphony Orchestra 2003–; has also conducted the Bruno Maderna Symphony Orchestra, Forli, Hans Swarowsky Orchestra, Milan, Damascus Chamber Orchestra. *Honours:* Stella della Solidarietà, Italy 2010. *Address:* Syrian National Symphony Orchestra, PO Box 6645, Damascus, Syria (office). *Telephone:* (11) 2230447 (office). *Fax:* (11) 2245054 (office). *E-mail:* info@syriansymphony.org (office). *Website:* www.syriansymphony.org (office).

BAGINSKI, Zbigniew, MA; Polish composer and teacher; *Professor, Frederic Chopin University of Music;* b. 19 Jan. 1949, Szczecin; m. Alicja Baginski 1988; two d. *Education:* High School of Music, Warsaw. *Career:* many performances of compositions in Germany, UK, Denmark, Sweden, USA, USSR, Netherlands, Hungary, Cuba, Italy, Spain, Mexico; Asst Prof., Frederic Chopin Acad. of Music, Warsaw 1978–88, Assoc. Prof. 1988–96, Prof. 1996–, Vice-Dean, Dept of Composition, Conducting and Music Theory 1987–90, Head of Composition Faculty 2004–; mem. Polish Composers Union, Vice-Pres. Warsaw Br. 1985–89, Gen. Sec. 1989–99, Pres., Warsaw branch 2001–11. *Compositions include:* Expeditions on the Other Side 1973, Acho for Organ 1974, Refrain for 2 Pianos 1975, Trio with Coda 1983, Sinfonia Notturna 1984, Concerto for Harpsichord and Orchestra 1985, Oh, Sweet Baroque Suite for String Orchestra 1985, String Quartet No. 2 1986, Canons, Scherzos and Epigrams 1987, Symphony in Seven Scenes 1988, Nocturne-Berceusee 1989, String Quartet No. 3 1992, Mass for chorus 1995, Little Elegiac Symphony 1995, Piano Concerto 1995, Piano Quartet 1990, Violin Concerto 2001, Piano Quintet 2004, Danza Generale 2005, Piccolo quartetto 2005, Circulations 2006, Accor-dance 2007, Two Preludes for Piano 2009, Double Flutter 2010. *Address:* Frederic Chopin University of Music, ul. Okólnik, 00-368 Warsaw, Poland (office). *E-mail:* wkditm@chopin.edu.pl (office); baginskizb@poczta .onet.pl (home). *Website:* www.chopin.edu.pl (office); www.polmic.pl.

BAGLIONI, Bruna; Italian singer (mezzo-soprano) and teacher; b. 8 April 1947, Frascati; one d. *Education:* studied with Gina Maria Rebori and Walter Cataldi-Tassoni in Rome. *Career:* debut, Festival Dei Due Mondi, Spoleto in Boris Godunov 1970, soon afterwards sang La Favorita in Bologna with Luciano Pavarotti; has sung at major theatres including La Favorita, Norma, Un Ballo In Maschera, Cavalleria Rusticana at La Scala, Milan, La Fenice, Venice, San Carlo, Naples, Trieste, Rome, Bologna, Palermo, Torino; Arena of Verona for 21 years; Eboli in Don Carlos at Covent Garden, London, Metropolitan, New York, Tokyo, Berlin, Munich, Hamburg, Paris, Vienna; particularly identified with the role of Verdi's Amneris; major tours include Norma in Moscow with La Scala Milan, Dalila in Samson and Dalila with the Met, New York and with Covent Garden in Korea and Japan; repertoire includes Amneris in Verdi's Aida, Azucena in Il Trovatore, Ulrica in Un Ballo in Maschera, Eboli in Don Carlos, Preziosilla in La Forza del Destino, Fenena in Nabucco and Messa da Requiem, Laura in La Gioconda of Ponchielli, Charlotte in Massenet's Werther, Leonore in Donizetti's la Favorite, Fedora, Dalila in Samson et Dalila, Santuzza in Cavalleria Rusticana, Giovanna Seymour in Anna Bolena, Carmen, Principessa of Bouillon in Adrian Lecouvreur, Adalgisa in Norma. *Recordings include:* videos: Don Carlos at Covent Garden, Nabucco at Arena of Verona, Aida in Luxor; albums: Norma with La Scala in Moscow, Luisa Muiller at La Scala, Milan, La Favorita in Bern, Laura in La Gioconda at Metropolitan Opera. *Address:* Vicolo Manara 9, 00044 Frascati, Rome, Italy (home).

BAGRATUNI, Suren; Armenian cellist and academic; *Professor of Cello, Michigan State University;* b. 17 March 1963, Yerevan. *Education:* Yerevan State Komitas Conservatory and Central Music School, Yerevan, Moscow State Conservatory, New England Conservatory, Boston (USA). *Career:* concerto soloist aged 14, with Armenian State Radio Orchestra, Yerevan 1978; has performed with all major orchestras in fmr Soviet Union including Moscow Philharmonic under Valery Gergiev, also with Boston Pops, Orchestre Jeune Philharmonie Paris, Weimar Staatskapelle, Stuttgarter Kammerorchester, Orquestra Sinfônica de São Paulo, Symphony Orchestras of Chile, Guatemala, Dominican Repub.; solo recitals in Grand Hall, Moscow Conservatory, Carnegie Hall's Weill Recital Hall, New York, Jordan and Symphony Halls, Boston, Gasteig-München, Salle Gaveau, Paris, Alice Tully and Merkin Halls, New York, Tonhalle Zürich, and in St Gallen, Rome, Geneva, Leipzig, Dresden, Berlin, Munich, St Petersburg, Cairo, Cape Town, Johannesburg, Pretoria, Seoul, Taipei and Melbourne; also chamber music performances; mem. Nobilis Trio; frequent broadcasts; Prof. of Cello, Michigan State Univ.; fmr mem. Faculty, New England Conservatory and Univ. of Illinois. *Recordings include:* Solo Cello and Two Cellos 1995, Shostakovich, Prokofiev Sonatas 1997, Trios by Beethoven (Op 1, No. 3), Brahms (Op 8), Tchaikovsky, Rachmaninov 1997, Babajanian, Trio 1997, Short Pieces for cello and piano 1997, Shostakovich and Prokofiev Cello Sonatas (Great Russian Cello Sonatas) 1998, Rachmaninov, Debussy Sonatas, Stravinsky Suite Italienne 2001, Music for Cello and Piano 2004, Bach: Six Suites for cello solo 2005, Khudoyan/Crumb/Hindemith Cello Sonatas 2005, Beethoven Complete Cello Sonatas and Variations. *Honours:* Armenia Nat. Prize 1980, Transcaucasus Prize 1981, USSR Nat. Prize 1981, silver medal, Tchaikovsky Competition 1986, first prize, Vittorio Gui competition 1988. *Current Management:* c/o Susan Dearborn, Boston Concert Artists, 1208 Massachusetts Avenue, Suite 3, Cambridge, MA 02138, USA. *Telephone:* (617) 547-3090. *Fax:* (617) 354-4804. *E-mail:* BCArtists@aol.com. *Address:* College of Music, 217 Music Building, Michigan State University, East Lansing, MI

48864, USA (office). *Telephone:* (517) 432-9793 (office). *E-mail:* bagratun@msu.edu (office). *Website:* www.music.msu.edu (office); www.surenbagratuni.com.

BAHK, Jehi, MA; Austrian violinist; *Leader, Philharmonia Corea*; b. 26 June 1971, Vienna. *Education:* Univ. for Music and Performing Arts, Vienna. *Career:* debut, Konzerthaus, Vienna 1995; Founding mem. and Leader, Hugo Wolf Quartet 1993–2004; Salzburg Mozarteum, Schubertiade Feldkirch, Carinthian Summer 1996; Munich Herkules-Saal, Nurnberg Kaiserburg, Prague, Rudolfinum 1997; Edinburgh Festival, Carnegie Hall, New York 1998; Musikverein Vienna, Cité de la musique, Paris, Palais des Beaux-Arts Brussels, Philharmonie Cologne 1999; Wigmore Hall, London, Philharmonie, Berlin 2000; Tonhalle, Zürich 2003; Amsterdam Concertgebouw, Birmingham Symphony Hall, Megaron, Athens; Prof. of Violin, German School of Music, Weimar, Kangnam Univ., Repub. of Korea 2005–08; Assoc. Concertmaster, Seoul Philharmonic Orchestra 2005–08; Leader, Philharmonia Corea 2009–. *Publications:* Hugo Wolf, Italian Songbook (Vol. 2, arrangement for string quartet and voice) 2003. *Honours:* First Prize, Int. Competition for String Quartets, Cremona, Italy 1995. *Address:* Schützengasse 13/12, 1030 Vienna, Austria (office); Chungcheonnam-Do, Dangjin-Gun, Songak-Myeon, Gahak-Ri, Daerim, ePyeonhansaesang 104-Dong, Apt 305, Republic of Korea (office). *E-mail:* jehi.bahk@gmx.net (office).

BAILES, Anthony James; British lutenist; b. 18 June 1947, Bristol; m. Anne Van Royen. *Education:* Bulmershe Coll. of Further Education, studied with Michael Watson in Bristol, Diana Poulton in London, Gusta Goldschmidt in Amsterdam, Eugen M. Dombois (Schola Cantorum Basiliensis). *Career:* debut in Purcell Room 1971; solo concerts and tours throughout Europe and Scandinavia; many recordings both solo and in ensemble; Prof. of Lute; hon. mem. Lute Soc., Svenska Gitarr Och Luta Sallskapet. *Recordings include:* Pièces de Luth, Lauten Galanterie, A Musical Banquet, Airs de Cour, Lautenmusik der Habsburgische Lande, Apollon Orateur. *Publications:* An Introduction to 17th-Century Lute Music 1983, Lessons for the Lute (with A. Van Royen) 1983, 32 Easy Pieces for Baroque Lute 1984; contrib. articles to various journals and magazines. *Honours:* Edison Klassiek Award 1977. *Address:* Hollenweg 3A, 4144 Arlesheim, Switzerland (home).

BAILEY, Judith Margaret, BMus, ARAM, GRSM, LRAM, ARCM; British composer, conductor and clarinettist; b. 18 July 1941, Camborne, Cornwall. *Education:* Royal Acad. of Music. *Career:* conductor and composer 1971–; fmr Conductor (30 years), Southampton Concert Orchestra and Petersfield Orchestra; Conductor, Cornwall Chamber Orchestra 2002–, Penzance Orchestral Soc. 2003–; mem. BASCA, BASBWE, COMA, Cornish Music Guild, Portsmouth District Composers Alliance. *Compositions:* orchestral: Trencrom, symphonic poem 1978, 2 symphonies 1981, 1982, Seascape for women's chorus, woodwind trio and orchestra 1985, Penwith, overture 1986, Fiesta for orchestra 1988, Concerto for clarinet and strings 1988, Havas for orchestra 1991, Joplinesque for wind band; Festive Concert Piece for wind band, From Three Sea Paintings of Paul Nash, Concerto for Orchestra, Cliff Walk Symphony, Noel and Wassail (Christmas Fantasies), Double Bass Concerto in the style of Haydn; for strings: two string quartets, Corollow, Egloshayle Trio, Caledonia String Quintet, Sounds of Gosport, Platinum Wood, Deo Gratias for string orchestra, Worcester Source – four pieces for cello and double bass; for wind ensemble: Sinfonietta for 15 wind instruments, Chamber Concerto for 10 wind instruments, Music for four clarinets, Wind Quintet, Wind-willows for woodwind trio, Three Songs for a River for two clarinets, Mor Gwyns for clarinet choir, Stems from Cornwall, Windward, Theme and Variations for Wind Octet, Zigzag for saxophone quartet, Intrada for six wind instruments; for solo instruments (with piano): Mordryg for clarinet and piano, The Towers of San Gimignano for solo piano, Y-Gwynt for clarinet and piano, Aquamarine Waltz for cello and piano, Quicksilver for oboe and piano, Scherzo for John for bassoon and piano, Five Miniatures for Double Bass and Piano; music for symphonic wind and brass bands and mixed ensembles; choral, vocal and organ works. *Address:* c/o Recital Music, Vale Cottage, The Hamlet, Templecombe, Somerset, BA8 0HJ, England (office). *Telephone:* (1963) 370051 (office).

BAILEY, Norman Stanley, CBE, BMus; British singer (bass-baritone); b. 23 March 1933, Birmingham, England; s. of the late Stanley Ernest Bailey and Agnes Train Bailey (née Gale); m. 1st Doreen Evelyn Simpson 1957 (divorced 1983); two s. one d.; m. 2nd Kristine Ciesinski 1985. *Education:* East Barnet Grammar School, England, Boksburg High School, South Africa, Prince Edward School, Rhodesia, Rhodes Univ., South Africa, Akad. für Musik und Darstellende Kunst, Vienna. *Career:* engaged full time at Linz Landestheater, Austria 1960–63, Wuppertaler Bühnen 1963–64, Deutsche Oper am Rhein, Düsseldorf and Duisburg 1964–67; Prin. Baritone, English Nat. Opera, Sadler's Wells 1967–71; freelance 1971–; debut at La Scala, Milan 1967, Royal Opera House, Covent Garden 1969, Bayreuth Festival 1969, Paris Opera 1973, Vienna State Opera 1976, Metropolitan Opera, New York 1976; appearances Paris Opera, Edin. Festival, Hamburg State Opera, Munich State Opera; Prof. of Voice, Royal Coll. of Music, London 1990–. *Major recordings and TV films include:* Der fliegende Holländer, Die Meistersinger von Nürnberg, King Priam, Der Ring des Nibelungen, Macbeth, La Traviata, Falstaff. *Honours:* Hon. RAM 1981; Hon. DMus (Rhodes) 1986; Sir Charles Santley Memorial Prize 1977. *Address:* PO Box 655, Victor, ID 83455, USA. *E-mail:* nbnsbailey@aol.com (office).

BAILEY, Simon, RNCM; British singer (bass baritone); *House Soloist, Frankfurt Opera*; b. 1972, Lincoln; m. Anna Ryberg. *Education:* Royal Northern Coll. of Music, Clare Coll., Cambridge, Acad. of Teatra alla Scala, Milan. *Career:* appearances at La Scala in supporting roles in La Bohème, Carmélites, Wozzeck, Peter Grimes and Ariadne auf Naxos; season 2001–02 with Jeffrey Tate, James Conlon and Riccardo Muti; roles in Turandot and Verdi's Un giorno de regno; premieres of Tatiana by Corghi, and in Figaro at Rouen; season 2002–03 at Frankfurt Opera in Salome, Hercules by Handel, Der Schatzgräber by Schreker, Berio's Un re in ascolto, Manon and Verdi's Jérusalem; Papageno in Die Zauberflöte and Dulcamara in L'elisir d'amore; debut as Bartolo (Barber of Seville), La Scala, Milan 2005. *Recordings include:* Stainer Crucifixion (with Clare Coll. Choir). *Honours:* first prize Concorso Int. di Musica Sacra 2004. *Current Management:* Hazard Chase, 25 City Road, Cambridge, CB1 1DP, England. *Telephone:* (1223) 312400. *Fax:* (1223) 460827. *Website:* www.hazardchase.co.uk.

BAILLIE, Alexander; British cellist; b. 6 Jan. 1956, Stockport, Lancashire, England. *Education:* Royal Coll. of Music with Jacqueline du Pré, studied with André Navarra in Vienna. *Career:* many performances with leading British orchestras; concerts in Europe and North America include the first Canadian performance of Penderecki's 2nd Concerto; tour of the UK with the Budapest String Orchestra 1991, followed by tour of the Far East; Promenade concert appearances include the Concerto by Colin Matthews 1984, Henze's Sieben Liebeslieder, Takemitsu's Orion and Pleiades 1989, Schumann Concerto 1990 and the Delius Concerto 1993; has premiered works by Lutoslawski (Grave), Schnittke (Sonata for cello and piano), Gordon Crosse (Wave-Songs) and Takemitsu (Orion and Pleiades); principal guest artist with the East of England Orchestra; concerts with the Villiers Piano Quartet; recital debut at the Kennedy Center in Washington 1992; season 1993 with US concerto debut, Boston Philharmonic, and visits to the Edinburgh and Harrogate Festivals; recital of unaccompanied works at the Wigmore Hall, London 1997; Prof., Royal Acad. of Music. *Recordings include:* Tippett Triple Concerto with Ernst Kovacic and Gerard Causse; Concertos by Elgar, Colin Matthews and Bernard Stevens; Frank Bridge's Oration, the Britten Cello Suites and Sonata; Sonatas by Rachmaninov, Shostakovich, Prokofiev and Schnittke. *Honours:* prizewinner Competitions at Budapest (Casals) and Munich (ARD). *Current Management:* TransArt (UK) Ltd, Cedar House, 10 Rutland Street, Filey, North Yorkshire, YO14 9JB, England. *Telephone:* (1723) 515819. *Fax:* (1723) 514678. *E-mail:* transartuk@transartuk.com. *Website:* www.transartuk.com.

BAILLIE, Peter; New Zealand singer (tenor); b. 29 Nov. 1933, Hastings. *Education:* studied in Australia and New Zealand. *Career:* sang with New Zealand Opera and the Elizabethan Opera Trust at Sydney, from 1963; roles included Tamino, Ferrando, Jacquino (Fidelio) and Gounod's Faust; member of the Vienna Volksoper 1967–88, in such character roles as Mozart's Bartolo and Monostatos, Albert Herring and Nando in Tiefland; also appeared in The Bartered Bride, From the House of the Dead and Zemlinsky's Kleider machen Leute; Glyndebourne debut 1968, as Hervey in Anna Bolena, Mozart's Titus in Wexford 1968, and in first modern revival of Mozart's Mitridate in Salzburg 1971; other roles included Ernesto in Don Pasquale, Malcolm in Macbeth and Svatopluk Cech in The Excursions of Mr Brouček; sang Mozart's Basilio for Wellington City Opera, 1995; teacher, Victoria Univ. of Wellington. *Address:* c/o Keay Burridge, Victoria Community Continuing Education, Victoria University, PO Box 600, Wellington 6140, New Zealand (office).

BAINBRIDGE, Elizabeth; British singer (mezzo-soprano); b. 28 March 1936, Lancashire, England. *Education:* Guildhall School with Norman Walker. *Career:* debut, Glyndebourne 1963 in Die Zauberflöte; sang in British premiere of Rossini's La Pietra del Paragone, London 1963; mem. Covent Garden Opera from 1965, in Butterfly (Suzuki), The Midsummer Marriage, Götterdämmerung (Norn), Falstaff (Mistress Quickly), Les Troyens, Un Ballo in Maschera (Arvidson), Troilus and Cressida and Lulu, Erda, (Rheingold, Siegfried), Amelia, Otello, Jenůfa (Grandmother), Onegin (Nurse), Aida (Amneris); tours to La Scala, Milan 1976, Far East 1979, Los Angeles, Athens Festival; guest appearances with ENO, Scottish Opera, WNO; US debut, Chicago, 1977 in Peter Grimes; Buenos Aires debut 1979, Israel, Jenůfa 1993, 1995; Covent Garden, First Maid in Elektra, Innkeeper's Wife in The Cunning Little Vixen 1990; Peter Grimes, Dublin Grand Opera Soc.; Widow Sweeney in The Rising of the Moon, Wexford Festival; sang the Hostess in the Covent Garden premiere of Prokofiev's The Fiery Angel 1992; Grandmother Burjya in Jenůfa at Geneva 2001. *Recordings include:* Dido and Aeneas, Sir John in Love, The Rape of Lucretia, Peter Grimes, Cendrillon, Eugene Onegin, Troilus and Cressida, Midsummer Marriage. *Address:* 57 Sadlers Walk, Emsworth, PO10 8JR, England (home). *Telephone:* (1243) 372633 (home).

BAINBRIDGE, Simon Jeremy, FRCM; British composer and conductor; *Head of Composition, Royal Academy of Music*; b. 30 Aug. 1952, London; m. Lynda Richardson 1980; one d. *Education:* Central Tutorial School for Young Musicians (now Purcell School), Highgate School, Royal College of Music, studied composition with John Lambert at the Berkshire Music Center, Tanglewood, Massachusetts, USA with Gunther Schuller. *Career:* freelance composer 1972–; Head of Composition, Royal Acad. of Music 1999–; his music performed extensively in the United Kingdom, USA, Europe, Australia; has worked as conductor with BBC Symphony Orchestra, BBC Scottish Symphony Orchestra, Bournemouth Symphony Orchestra, London Sinfonietta, Northern Sinfonia, Nash Ensemble, Composers' Ensemble, Capricorn and Divertimenti; teaches composition at Royal College of Music and Guildhall School of Music and Drama; mem. exec. cttees, Society for the Promotion of New Music, International Society for Contemporary Music, Association of

Professional Composers. *Compositions include:* Wind Quintet, String Quartet, String Sextet, Clarinet Quintet, Works for small and large Chamber Ensembles, with and without voice, Choral Music, works for large orchestra, Dance Score for Rambert Dance Company, music for two Madame Tussaud exhibitions, London and Amsterdam, Double Concerto for oboe, clarinet and chamber orchestra 1990, Mobile for cor anglais and piano 1991, Toccata for orchestra 1992, Kinneret Pulses 1992, From an English Folk Song 1992, Clarinet Quintet 1993, Herbsttag 1993, For Miles for trumpet 1994, Mobile for viola and ensemble 1994, Henry's Mobile for viol consort 1995, Henry's Rondeau for orchestra 1995, Landscape and Memory for horn and ensemble 1995, 4 Primo Levi Settings for mezzo-soprano, clarinet, viola and piano 1996, 'Tis Time I Think for soprano and string quartet 1996, 60 Seconds for Elliott 1996, Eichá for mezzo-soprano, chorus and wind ensemble 1997, Chant for 12 amplified voices and ensemble 1998, Three Pieces for orchestra 1998, Guitar Concerto 1998, Towards the Bridge for large ensemble 1999, Dances for Moon Animals for guitar 1999, Elphegus in carcere 1999, Chant 1999, Scherzi for orchestra 2000, Paths and Labyrinths for ensemble 2001, Voices, for bassoon and 12 strings 2001, Voiles 2002, Cheltenham Fragments 2004, Three Duos 2005, Landscape on Canvas 2005, Music Space Reflection for ensemble 2006, Orpheus 2006, Diptych 2006. *Recordings:* Music of Simon Bainbridge: Fantasia for Double Orchestra with BBC Symphony Orchestra/Composer, Viola Concerto with London Sinfonietta, Michael Tilson Thomas and Walter Trampler (viola), Concertante in moto perpetuo with Composers' Ensemble and Nicholas Daniel (oboe). *Honours:* Hon. RAM; Margaret Lee Crofts Fellowship, USA 1973, Leonard Bernstein Fellowship, USA 1974, Forman Fellowship 1976, USA-UK Bicentennial Fellowship 1978. *Address:* Department of Composition, Royal Academy of Music, Marylebone Road, London, NW1 5HT, England (office). *Telephone:* (20) 7873-7479. *E-mail:* composition@ram.ac.uk. *Website:* www.ram.ac.uk.

BAIOCCHI, Regina Harris, BA, MM, PR Cert.; American composer and musician; b. 16 July 1956, Chicago, Ill.; d. of Egie Harris, Sr and Lanzie Harris (née Belmont); m. Gregory D. Baiocchi. *Education:* Richards Vocational High School, Chicago, Paul Laurence Dunbar Vocational High School, Roosevelt Univ., Illinois Inst. of Tech., Inst. of Design, Chicago, New York Univ., DePaul Univ. *Career:* began composing aged ten; Orchestral Suite performed at Detroit Symphony Orchestra/Unisys Corpn Symposium 1992; composer-in-residence, Mostly Music Inc. 1992; guest composer, Wayne State Univ., Detroit 1993–94; guest composer/public relations lecturer, Northeastern Ill. Univ., Chicago 1993–94; guest composer, Columbia Coll., Chicago 1995, Northwestern Univ., Evanston 1996; composer, Musical Dir, Steppenwolf Theatre, Chicago 1997; 'Miles Per Hour' performed by Chicago Symphony Orchestra 1989; 'Muse' performed by Detroit Symphony Orchestra 1997; commissioned by Evanston Township High School to write orchestral 'ETHS Fanfare' for 150th anniversary; premiered 'Congregational Mass', 'Caint see to caint see' (spiritual) and 'Doxology' for pipe organ at Rockefeller Chapel, Univ. of Chicago 2011. *Compositions:* Equipoise by Intersection for piano 1978, Realizations for strings 1978, Chasé 1979, Who Will Claim The Baby? for chorus 1984, Send Your Gifts for chorus 1984, Father We Thank You for chorus 1986, Zora Neale Hurston Songs 1989, Psalm 138 for chorus 1990, We Real Cool for jazz ensemble 1990, Miles Per Hour (Jazz Sonatina) for trumpet 1990, Autumn Night for flute 1991, Crystal Stair for vocal ensemble 1991, Foster Pet 1991, Langston Hughes Songs 1991, Orchestral Suite 1991–92, Sketches for piano trio 1992, Shadows 1992, A Few Black Voices 1992, Teddy Bear Suite for orchestra 1992, Legacy 1992, Bwana's Libation 1992, QFX 1993, Much in Common for vocal ensemble 1993, Nobody's Child for chorus 1993, Mason Room 1993, Three Pieces for Greg 1994, Deborah for percussion 1994, Liszten, My Husband is Not a Hat for piano 1994, After the Rain 1994, Friday Night 1995, Darryl's Rose 1995, Gbeldahoven: No One's Child (opera) 1996, African Hands for orchestra with soloists 1997, Skins for percussion 1997, Dreamhoppers 1997, Nikki Giovanni 1997, Muse for orchestra 1997, Message to My Muse 1997, Dream Weaver 1997, Déjà Vu, for solo piano 1999, Communion, for marimba and strings 1999, HB4A, for piano, bass, drums and saxophone 2000, Karibu, for B-flat clarinet 2007, Congregational Mass for SATB 2011, Caint see to caint see (SATB spiritual) 2011, Doxology for pipe organ 2011. *Publications:* books: Indigo Sound 2003, Urban Haiku and Other Selected Poems 2004, Blues Haiku and Other New Poems 2005; online Study Guides for Chicago Humanities Festival 2012. *Honours:* City of Chicago Dept of Cultural Affairs CAAP grant 1992–94, 1996, AT&T grant 1994, Nat. Endowment for the Arts/Randolph Street Gallery Regional Artist Program grant 1995, Chicago Music Assen Award 1995, ASCAP Special Awards grants 1996, 1997, Art Inst. of Chicago and the Lila Wallace/Reader's Digest Fund Award 1997, 3Arts Foundation Award 2011. *Address:* PO Box 450, Chicago, IL 60605, USA (office). *Telephone:* (312) 253-7453 (home). *Fax:* (312) 922-3978 (office). *E-mail:* Regina@ReginaHarrisBaiocchi.com. *Website:* www.reginaharrisbaiocchi.com.

BAIRD, Janice; American singer (soprano); b. New York. *Education:* studied with Astrid Varnay and Birgit Nilsson. *Career:* sang as mezzo-soprano; dramatic soprano roles in opera throughout Germany from 1991; made US debut as Isolde in Tristan and Isolde with Metropolitan Opera 2008; repertory includes the Dyer's Wife in Die Frau Ohne Schatten, Marie in Wozzeck, Brünnhilde in Der Ring des Nibelungen, Minnie in La Fanciulla del West, Lady Macbeth in Macbeth, Ariadne in Ariadne auf Naxos, Ortrud in Lohengrin, Senta in The Flying Dutchman, Abigaille in Nabucco, Amelia in Un Ballo in Maschera, title roles in Elektra, Salome, Turandot, Fidelio, Violanta; has performed with Vienna State Opera, Hamburgische Staatsoper, Opéra de Marseille, Staatsoper Stuttgart, Deutsche Oper Berlin, Semperoper Dresden, Berlin Staatsoper, Hannover Staatsoper, Oper Leipzig, Teatro dell'Opera Rome, Opéra Toulouse, Teatro Colón Buenos Aires, Opernhaus Zürich, Grand Théâtre de Genève, Teatro de la Maestranza Seville, Teatro La Fenice Venice, Teatro Bellini Catania. *Current Management:* Jennifer Bredtmeyer, Barbarossastrasse 5, 10781 Berlin, Germany. *Telephone:* (30) 21969181. *Fax:* (30) 2169770. *E-mail:* bredtmeyer@bokab.de. *Website:* www.janicebaird.com.

BAIRD, Julianne, MA, PhD; American singer (soprano); *Distinguished Professor of Music, Rutgers University at Camden*; b. 10 Dec. 1952, Stateville, NC. *Education:* Eastman School with Masako Ono Toribara, Stanford Univ., studied with Walter Berry and Nikolaus Harnoncourt, Salzburg Mozarteum. *Career:* Asst Prof. of Music, West Chester Univ. 1983–88; Asst Prof. of Music, Rutgers Univ. at Camden 1989–91, Assoc. Prof. 1992–97, Prof. (now Distinguished Prof.) 1997–; sang in New York with Waverly Consort and Concert Royal; stage debut in Handel's Il Pastor Fido; later appearances at Santa Fe, Washington DC, Philadelphia and Los Angeles in operas by Gluck, Mozart, Purcell, Charpentier and Gagliano; appeared as soloist with orchestras including Cleveland Orchestra, Brooklyn Philharmonic, New York Philharmonic and Philadelphia Orchestra; festivals have included Tanglewood and Int. Lufthansa Festival of Baroque Music, London; concert engagements in sacred music by Bach and French Baroque music; master classes throughout North America, lectures world-wide. *Recordings include:* Handel's Imeneo, Acis and Galatea, Joshua and Siroe; Cantatas by Bach, Telemann and Clérambault; Bach's Magnificat and B Minor Mass; J. C. Bach's Amadis de Gaule; La Serva Padrona by Pergolesi and Monteverdi's Orfeo; Handel's Faramondo 1996, Schubert's Winterreise 1997, Fanny Mendelssohn Lieder 1999, English Mad Songs and Ayres 2005, Italian Lute Song 2005, Celtic Caravans 2005. *Publications:* Introduction to the Art of Singing; contribs to journals such as Continuo and Early Music. *Honours:* Hon. DMus (Shenandoah Univ.) 1995; Astral Foundation Award 1987, 1988, 1990, 1991, Noah Greenburg Award, American Musicological Soc. 1991, Regents Award, Univ. of California ar Santa Cruz 1997, Presidential Award, Stanford Univ. 1997, Gramophone Award for Recording of the Year. *Address:* Department of Fine Arts, Rutgers University at Camden, 314 Linden Street, Camden, NJ 08102-11403, USA (office). *Telephone:* (856) 225-6210 (office). *Fax:* (856) 225-6330 (office). *E-mail:* jbaird@camden.rutgers.edu (office). *Website:* juliannebaird.camden.rutgers.edu (office).

BAKELS, Kees; Dutch conductor; b. 14 Jan. 1945, Amsterdam. *Education:* Amsterdam Conservatory, Accad. Chigiana, Siena with Franco Ferrara and Bruno Rigacci, studied with Kiril Kondrashin. *Career:* tours to England, Belgium, Spain and USA; has led all the major Dutch orchestras and has guested with Warsaw Philharmonic, BBC Philharmonic, BBC Nat. Orchestra of Wales, San Diego, Quebec and Oregon Symphony Orchestras, New Belgian Chamber Orchestra, Ulster Orchestra, Scottish Chamber, Bournemouth Sinfonietta, Royal Liverpool Philharmonic; appeared with Nat. Youth Orchestra at BBC Promenade Concerts 1985; Chief Guest Conductor, Bournemouth Symphony and Prin. Conductor, Netherlands Radio Symphony Orchestra; has worked with soloists including Yehudi Menuhin, Claudio Arrau, Pierre Fournier, Paul Tortelier, David Oistrakh and Ruggiero Ricci; appearances with Netherlands Opera in Nabucco, Ariadne auf Naxos, Carmen, Lucia di Lammermoor, Idomeneo and I Puritani; San Diego Opera, Oberto and Madama Butterfly; Vancouver Opera, Carmen, Così fan tutte, Le nozze di Figaro and Die Zauberflöte; conducted Lyon Opéra in Cinderella (also on tour to Poland); Welsh Nat. Opera with Die Zauberflöte, La Bohème and Carmen; at ENO has led Aida and Fidelio; conducted Carmen at San Diego 1992; Prin. Conductor and Artistic Adviser, Malaysian Philharmonic Orchestra 1997–2005, Conductor Laureate 2005–11; recent performances with Tapiola Sinfonietta, Quebec Symphony, Netherlands Symphony, Bern Symphony, Ensemble Orchestral de Paris, Netherlands Radio Chamber Orchestra, Bournemouth Symphony, Philharmonie Zuidnederland. *Recordings:* with the Bournemouth Symphony Orchestra: Vaughan Williams Symphonies, Complete Nielsen Concerti. *Current Management:* c/o IMG Artists, The Light Box, 111 Power Road, London, W4 5PY, England. *Telephone:* (20) 7957-5800. *Fax:* (20) 7957-5801. *E-mail:* njives@imgartists.com. *Website:* www.imgartists.com.

BAKER, Alice, BMus, MMus; American singer (mezzo-soprano); b. 27 March 1961, Detroit, Mich. *Education:* Oakland Univ., California State Univ., Los Angeles, apprenticeships with Lyric Opera of Chicago and San Diego Opera. *Career:* debut in USA in alternating productions of Otello with Plácido Domingo and Madama Butterfly with Leona Mitchell, Los Angeles 1986; European debut as Carmen opposite José Carreras at Teatro dell'Opera di Roma 1987; in Europe has appeared in Rome as Giulio Cesare 1998; Carmen 1987; Isabella 1987; L'Italiana in Algeri 1987; Siebel in Faust 1988; Suzuki in Madama Butterfly 1990; Stabat Mater 1989; in Turin as Elisabeth I in Maria Stuarda 1999; As the Old Lady, Candide 1997; in Venice, Leonora, La Favorita 1988; Concert in Debussy's La Damoiselle Elue 1989; in concert in smaller cities, Santa Margherita, Verdi Requiem 1998 and Beethoven's 9th Symphony 1997; Verona, in recital 1989; Rome, in recital 1996; Mantua, La Forza del Destino 1999; UK debut with Wexford Festival Opera 1988, as Carlotta in Elisa e Claudio; on tour to London at Queen Elizabeth Hall; in Germany as Rosina in Il Barbiere di Siviglia at Frankfurt Opera 1988, 1989, 1990; Brahms Alto Rhapsody 1992; in Spain in title role of La Cenerentola, Teatro Liceu, Barcelona 1992; in Norway in concert with Stavanger Symphony, Mozart

Grand Mass in C Minor 1989; in Slovenia at Int. Festival Ljubljana, Verdi Requiem 1998; Carmen 2000; in USA and Canada: return engagements in Los Angeles to sing the title role in Cenerentola 1988; revivals of Otello 1989; Hermia in A Midsummer Night's Dream 1988; The Mother Superior in The Fiery Angel 1989; Vancouver Opera debut, Suzuki in Madama Butterfly 1995; Edmonton Opera as Cornelia in Giulio Cesare 1994; Amneris in Aida for Greenville Opera 1988; Preziosilla in La Forza del Destino, Washington Opera, Kennedy Center, Washington DC 1989; Ruggero in Alcina, Opera Theatre of St Louis 1987; concert debuts in USA: Parsifal with Los Angeles Philharmonic at Hollywood Bowl 1985; Parsifal at Carnegie Hall, New York 1986; Lyric Opera of Chicago as Peep-Bo in Peter Sellers' The Mikado 1983; St Louis Symphony, Mahler Third 1988, return appearances for Otello 1989; Pittsburgh Symphony debut in Rossini's Stabat Mater 1989; Festival Internazionale Valentiniano, Rieti, Italy, Rossini's Stabat Mater with Moscow State Orchestra 2000; Verdi's Manzoni Requiem 2001; recital tour in USA of songs by American and British composers and by Bizet 2001. *E-mail:* info@cmi -arts.com. *Website:* www.cmi-arts.com.

BAKER, Claude, DMA; American composer and academic; *Chancellor's Professor, Jacobs School of Music, Indiana University;* b. 12 April 1948, Lenoir, N Carolina. *Education:* Eastman School, Rochester, New York. *Career:* Prof., Univ. of Louisville 1976–88; Chancellor's Prof., Jacobs School of Music, Indiana Univ., Bloomington 1988–; Composer-in-Residence, St Louis Symphony Orchestra 1991–99. *Compositions include:* Canzonet for solo tuba 1972, Elegy for Solo Violin 1979, Divertissement for clarinet, violin, cello and piano 1980, Omaggi e Fantasie for tuba and piano 1981, revised 1987, The Glass Bead Game for orchestra 1982, Omaggi e Fantasie for double bass and piano 1984, 4 Nachtszenen for harp 1985, revised 1990, Fantasy Variations for string quartet 1986, Tableaux Funèbres for piano and string quartet 1988, revised 2003, Three Pieces for 5 timpani, 5 roto-toms and wind ensemble 1990, Shadows for orchestra 1990, Awaking the Winds for orchestra 1993, for chamber orchestra 1994, Whispers and Echoes for orchestra 1995, Into the Sun, for mezzo-soprano and orchestra 1996, Flights of Passage for piano 1998, Sleepers Awake for mezzo-soprano, percussion and strings 1998, The Mystic Trumpeter for orchestra 1999, Symphony No. 1 2000, Aus Schwanengesang for orchestra 2001, Three Phantasy Pieces for viola and percussion 2003, revised 2005, Maerchenbilder for orchestra 2005, revised 2008, Lamentations for saxophones and orchestra 2006, String Quartet No. 2: Capriccio 2007, Burlesque for alto saxophone, violin, cello and piano 2008, Concerto for Piano and Orchestra: From Noon to Starry Night 2010, Canti guerrieri ed amorosi for orchestra 2013, Hor che'l ciel e la terra for 24-voice chorus and 4 percussionists 2014, Sept Hommages for Organ 2015. *Honours:* The American Soc. of Composers, Authors and Publrs Serious Music Awards, annually 1976–, Manuel de Falla Prize, Madrid 1976, Kennedy Center Friedheim Awards 1979, 1984, George Eastman Prize 1985, Eastman-Leonard Prize 1988, Acad. Award in Music, American Acad. of Arts and Letters 2002, Pogorzelski-Yankee Prize, American Guild of Organists 2015; fellowships: Rockefeller Foundation 1982, 1995, Nat. Endowment for the Arts 1991, John Simon Guggenheim Memorial Foundation 2001, Koussevitzky Music Foundation 2002, Bogliasco Foundation 2002, Fromm Foundation 2005, Barlow Endowment for Music Composition 2008, Paul Fromm Residency, American Acad. in Rome 2008, Meet the Composer (Commissioning Music/USA) 2011. *Address:* Jacobs School of Music, Indiana University, Bloomington, IN 47405, USA (office). *Telephone:* (812) 855-7423 (office). *Fax:* (812) 855-4936 (office). *E-mail:* bakerwc@indiana.edu (office). *Website:* mypage.iu.edu/~bakerwc (office).

BAKER, Gregg; American singer (baritone); b. 7 Dec. 1955, Chicago, IL. *Education:* Northwestern University, studied with Andrew Smith. *Career:* sang on Broadway in musicals; Metropolitan Opera debut, as Crown in Porgy and Bess 1985, appearing later as Escamillo, High Priest in Samson and Delilah, Silvo, di Luna, Belcore, Amonasro and Donner; has also sung Crown at Glyndebourne 1985, and in Helsinki and Tulsa; concert performance of Porgy and Bess at the QEH, London 1989; other roles include Ford in Falstaff, Count Almaviva and Marcello in La Bohème; Old Vic Theatre, London in Carmen Jones 1991; sang Crown in Porgy and Bess at Covent Garden, London and Savonlinna Festival, Finland 1992; Caesaerea 1993 as Amonasro; Jokanaan at Philadelphia and Detroit 1995–96; Jokanaan in Salome at Vancouver 1997; Italian debut as Escamillo, at the 1996 Verona Festival; season 2000 as Amonasro at Houston, Scarpia at Philadelphia, and Escamillo at Naples; title roles in Macbeth at Memphis Opera and Rigoletto at Berkshire Opera 2004; sang Robert Garner in premiere of Richard Danielpour's Margaret Garner with Michigan Opera 2008; has performed at Wiener Staatsoper, Arena di Verona, Glyndebourne Festival, Hamburg Opera, New Israeli Opera, Stuttgart Opera, Frankfurt Opera, Vancouver Opera, Baden-Baden Opera, Scottish Nat. Opera, Michigan Opera Theater, Opera Co. of Philadelphia, Houston Grand Opera, Greater Miami Opera and Berkshire Opera; appeared in concert and recorded with orchestras including Royal Philharmonic, London Philharmonic, London Symphony Orchestra, New York Philharmonic, Los Angeles Philharmonic, Pittsburgh Symphony, Boston Symphony, Danish Symphony and Radio Stuttgart Symphony, with conductors including James Levine, Sir Simon Rattle, Zubin Mehta, Lorin Maazel, Esa-Pekka Salonen, Sir Roger Norrington, Daniel Oren and Eric Kunzel. *Recordings include:* Porgy and Bess, Sweeney Todd 2013. *Current Management:* c/o Dietsch Artists International, 143 South Centre Street, South Orange, NJ 07079, USA. *Telephone:* (973) 763-8836. *Fax:* (973) 763-8837. *E-mail:* dietsch@dietschartists.com. *Website:* www.dietschartists.com.

BAKER, Dame Janet Abbott, CH, DBE, CBE, FRSA; British singer (mezzo-soprano); b. 21 Aug. 1933, Hatfield, Yorks.; d. of Robert Abbott Baker and May Baker (née Pollard); m. James Keith Shelley 1957. *Education:* York Coll. for Girls and Wintringham School, Grimsby. *Career:* Pres. London Sinfonia 1986–; Chancellor Univ. of York 1991–2004; Trustee, Foundation for Sport and the Arts 1991–; mem. Munster Trust. *Publication:* Full Circle (autobiog.) 1982. *Honours:* Hon. Fellow, St Anne's Coll., Oxford 1975, Downing Coll., Cambridge 1985; Hon. DMus (Birmingham) 1968, (Leicester) 1974, (London) 1974, (Hull) 1975, (Oxford) 1975, (Leeds) 1980, (Lancaster) 1983, (York) 1984, (Cambridge) 1984, Hon. LLD (Aberdeen) 1980, Hon. DLitt (Bradford) 1983; Commdr des Arts et des Lettres; Daily Mail Kathleen Ferrier Memorial Prize 1956, Queen's Prize, Royal Coll. of Music 1959, Hamburg Shakespeare Prize, Hamburg 1971, Grand Prix, French Nat. Acad. of Lyric Recordings 1975, Léonie Sonning Prize (Denmark) 1979, Gold Medal of Royal Philharmonic Soc. 1990, Inc. Soc. of Musicians' Distinguished Music Award 2008, Gramophone Award for Lifetime Achievement 2011. *Address:* Foundation for Sport and the Arts, Walton House, 55 Charnock Road, Walton, Liverpool, L67 1AA, England (office). *Telephone:* (15) 1259-5505 (office). *Fax:* (15) 1230-0664 (office). *E-mail:* contact@thefsa.net (office). *Website:* www.thefsa.net (office).

BAKER, Mark, BMus, MA; American singer (tenor); b. 1953, Tulsa, OK. *Education:* Indiana Univ. *Career:* Metropolitan Opera from 1986, as Paris in Roméo et Juliette (debut role), Narraboth in Salome, Froh in Das Rheingold and Melot in Tristan und Isolde; Glimmerglass Opera 1987, as Lensky in Eugene Onegin; Santa Fe 1988 (Erik in Fliegende Holländer); Glyndebourne Touring Opera 1990, as Florestan; sang Števa in Jenůfa and Ferrando in Così fan tutte at 1989 Glyndebourne Festival; Nantes 1991, as Monteverdi's Ulisse; Théâtre du Châtelet, Paris 1992; Met 1997, as the Drum Major in Wozzeck; season 1995–96 as Siegmund at Santiago and Vladimir in Prince Igor at San Francisco; Laca in Jenůfa at Santiago 1998; Samson in Samson et Dalila and Tom in The Great Gatsby at the Met (world premiere 1999–2000) and Siegmund in Die Walküre at San Francisco Opera; season 2000–01 as the Drum Major in Wozzeck at Dallas and Samson for Cleveland Opera. *Recordings include:* Jenůfa, from Glyndebourne. *Honours:* winner Metropolitan Opera Nat. 1986. *Current Management:* Munro Artists Management, 786 Dartmouth Street, South Dartmouth, MA 02748, USA. *Telephone:* (508) 993-9011. *Fax:* (508) 993-9044. *E-mail:* operamom@aol.com.

BAKER, Michael Conway, BMus, MA; Canadian composer and lecturer (retd); b. 13 March 1937, West Palm Beach, FL, USA; s. of Phil Baker and Peggy Cartwright; m. Penny Anne Baker. *Education:* Univ. of British Columbia, Western Washington State Coll. *Career:* film and concert composer; has taught and developed music programmes for children of all ages, adult education and univ. students; taught two courses at Univ. of British Columbia as well as one extension course at Simon Fraser Univ.; composer-in-residence for various groups; mem. ALCM; Assoc. Canadian Music Centre. *Compositions include:* Counterplay for viola and strings 1971, Concerto for flute and strings 1974, Sonata for piano 1974, Concerto for piano and orchestra 1976, Symphony No. 1, Highland 1977, Washington Square, 60-minute ballet for orchestra 1978, Evocations for flute, quartet and orchestra 1982, Seven Wonders: A Song Cycle for soprano and piano 1983, Chanson Joyeuse for orchestra 1987, Intermezzo for flute and harp 1988, Through the Lions' Gate: Tone Poems for orchestra 1989, Capriccio for clarinet and orchestra 1991, Cinderella – Frozen in Time, 90-minute ice ballet 1993, Century Symphony (No. 2) 1994, Summit Concerto for trumpet and orchestra 1995, Vancouver Variations 1996, His Fanfare to Expo '86 opened the proceedings in Vancouver, Siguiriya, harp concerto 2011. *Recordings:* 155 concert works and 200 film projects including Washington Square 1994, Hope's Journey 1995, Summit Concerto for trumpet & chamber orchestra 1995, Cinderella....-Frozen in Time 1996. *Honours:* Order of British Columbia 1997; Juno Award for Best Classical Composition 1991, Queen's Jubilee Medal 2003, three Genie Awards. *Address:* 2440 Treetop Lane, North Vancouver, BC V7H 2K5, Canada (home). *Telephone:* (604) 929-8732 (home). *E-mail:* mconwayb@shaw.ca (home). *Website:* www.michaelconwaybaker.com.

BAKER, Richard Douglas James, OBE, MA; British broadcaster and author; b. 15 June 1925, s. of Albert Baker and Jane I. Baker; m. Margaret C. Martin 1961; two s. *Education:* Kilburn Grammar School and Peterhouse, Cambridge. *Career:* served in RN 1943–46; actor 1948; teacher 1949; BBC Third Programme announcer 1950–53, BBC TV newsreader 1954–82, commentator for State Occasion Outside Broadcasts 1967–70, TV introductions to Promenade concerts 1960–95, panellist, Face the Music (BBC 2) 1966–79, presenter, Omnibus (BBC TV) 1983 presenter of various other shows on BBC Radio including Start the Week 1970–87, These You Have Loved 1972–77, Baker's Dozen 1978–87, Mainly for Pleasure 1986–92, Comparing Notes 1987–95; presenter, Classic Countdown for Classic FM radio 1995–97, Sound Stories Radio 3 1998–2000, Melodies for You 1999–2003, Your Hundred Best Tunes 2003–; mem. Broadcasting Standards Council 1988–93. *Publications:* Here is the News (broadcasts) 1966, The Terror of Tobermory 1972, The Magic of Music 1975, Dry Ginger 1977, Richard Baker's Music Guide 1979, Mozart 1982, London, A Theme with Variations 1989, Richard Baker's Companion to Music 1993, Franz Schubert 1997, The Classical Music Quiz Book (compilation) 2006. *Honours:* Hon. Fellow, London Coll. of Music; Hon. FRCM; Hon. mem. Royal Liverpool Philharmonic Soc.; Hon. LLD (Strathclyde) 1979, (Aberdeen) 1983; TV Newscaster of the Year (Radio Industries Club), 1972, 1974, 1979, BBC Radio Personality of the Year (Variety Club of GB) 1984, Sony Gold Award for Radio 1996. *Current Management:* c/o

Stephanie Williams Artists, 9 Central Chambers, Wood Street, Stratford upon Avon, CV37 6JQ, England.

BAKER, Simon; British singer (countertenor); b. 1973, Edinburgh, Scotland. *Education:* Edinburgh Acad., Christ's Hospital, Royal Coll. of Music with Ashley Stafford. *Career:* sang Handel's Ottone, and Claudio in the modern premiere of Silla at the 23rd London Handel Festival 2000; Arsamenes in Xerxes for British Youth Opera at the QEH, Messiah in Dublin and London and Canticles by Britten for the Spitalfields Winter Festival; season 2001 with Flavio for the London Handel Festival, St Matthew Passion at Wells Cathedral, St John Passion at Christ's Hospital and Fileno in Handel's Clori, Tirsi e Fileno for the Covent Garden Festival; other roles include Nero in Monteverdi's Poppea. *Recordings include:* Silla, by Handel (conducted by Denys Darlow).

BAKHCHIEV, Alexander, MA; Russian pianist; b. 27 July 1930, Moscow; m. Elena Sorokina 1962; one d. *Education:* Moscow Conservatory. *Career:* debut in solo programme, Liszt, Beethoven Hall, Bolshoi Theatre, Moscow 1954; state television and radio, over 35 years; solo, with orchestra, in chamber music ensembles, with singers; regular duo with wife; played with orchestras conducted by Rozhdestvensky, Svetlanov, Kondrashin, Chaikin, with V. Popov (bassoon), A. Korneyev (flute), others; performed in France 1954; chamber music concerts 1970s; many educational television and radio series; concerts all over USSR, including Moscow State Conservatory and with St Petersburg Philharmonic; duets, Soviet and British modern music, England 1989; int. festivals including Mozart Festival, Tokyo 1991; taught Chamber Ensemble, Moscow State Conservatory 1990–; eight programmes, all Schubert piano duets (with wife); piano duo festivals at Novosibirsk and Ekaterinburg 1993–95; piano duet lecture series for teachers and students, Russia; music dedicated to him and wife by Boyarsky, Lubovksy, Fried, Moore; Gubaidulina's concerto Introitus written for him. *Recordings include:* solo recordings include Haydn, Liszt, Bach, Handel, Rubinstein, Arensky/ Liadov/Stravinsky, Glazunov/Lyapunov, Mussorgsky, Borodin; with ensembles: all sonatas, flute, harpsichord, Bach, Handel; Vivaldi (with A Korneyev); with V. Popov: Masterpieces of Baroque; Czechoslovakian music, bassoon, piano; series: Early Mozart, solo, ensembles; duets with wife: The Golden Duet, Schubert Compositions for Piano Four Hands, Complete Mozart Piano Duets, Piano Duos by Rachmaninov, Russian Salon Piano Music, Music of France, Music of Old Vienna, J. S. Bach, his family and pupils, Czerni, Bach and Koželuh concertos. *Address:* 4-32 Koshkin str, Moscow 115409, Russia.

BAKKE, Ruth; Norwegian composer and organist; *Organist, Storetveit Church, Bergen*; b. 2 Aug. 1947, Bergen. *Education:* Bergen Music Conservatory, Univ. of Oslo, Texas Lutheran Coll., Univ. of Redlands, Washington State Univ., USA. *Career:* organist and choir conductor, Storetveit Church, Bergen 1972–; teacher of music theory, Bergen Teacher Training Coll. and Bergen Music Conservatory; works performed at festivals including Aspen, USA. *Compositions include:* orchestral: Chromocumuli for symphony orchestra 1972, Songs of the Sea, symphony for brass 1988, Illuminations, bassoon concerto 1994, Tubazzo, tuba concerto 1998, Lone Star Memories 2000, Songs of the Seasons, violin concerto 2008; electronic music: Dolorosa 1998, Body & Soul; chamber: Organ sonata 1970, Bönn for organ, soprano and guitar 1976, Rumus for chamber orchestra 1976, Des Kaisers neue Kleider for flute, clarinet, percussion, Hammond organ, viola & cello 1978, Into the Light for violin and organ 1982, Meditation for horn and organ 1986, Mysterious Mountains for piano 1986, Brumlebuff II for 5 flutes, 2 clarinets, timpani, percussion, 3 violins & 3 cellos 1986, Rock Bottom for timpani and tuba 1988, Bruddet (Broken) 1982/1995, Sphaerae 1992, Fra det dype (Kutoka Kwa Kina) 2011; vocal: De Profundis (Psalm 130) for choir, organ and cymbals 1971, Danse Psychotique: En dødsdans for 2 voices, flute, electric guitar, percussion & harp 1983, An expected end? for chorus, synthesizer, bass guitar & percussion 1985, (Fragments d')un homme moderne for baritone, percussion, synthesizers & tape 1985, A Vision Blurred for baritone & cello 1986, Nonsense 1–3 for solo voice 1990; brass band: Ragadòn 2007; Dies Irae for organ 2009; Tango del Corazón for violin, accordion, piano & contrabass 2011, Agnus Dei for voice, saxophone, electric guitar and keyboards 2015; organ improvisations. *Honours:* Fulbright Grant. *E-mail:* ruth.bakke@gmail.com.

BAKST, Lawrence; American singer (tenor); b. 1955, Washington, DC. *Education:* studied with Hans J. Heinz at Juilliard School, USA and in Europe. *Career:* sang Radames with Opera Delaware and Kentucky Opera, Macduff in New Jersey; European debut as Hagenbach in Catalani's La Wally at Wexford Festival; mem. Wuppertal Opera, sang Faust, Cavaradossi and Edgar (Lucia di Lammermoor) early 1990s; sang Verdi's Don Carlos at several Italian centres, Macduff in Barcelona and Marseilles, Gabriele Adorno, Riccardo, Manrico, Canio, Calaf and Faust in Mefistofeles; appearances at New York City Opera, Paris, Toulouse, Marseille, Barcelona, Madrid, Rome, Turin, London, Athens, Rio de Janeiro, Tokyo, Zagreb, Detmold and Opera Forum in Holland; specialised in Verdi and Puccini tenor roles including Il Trovatore, Aida, Don Carlos, Luisa Miller and Otello; other roles included Pylade in Iphigénie en Tauride, Herodes in Salome, Turandot, Tosca, Rodolfo in La Bohème, Madama Butterfly, Don Carlos, Un Ballo in Maschera, Meyerbeer's Le Prophète, Tannhauser and Siefgried at Nat. Theatre Weimar, in Magdeburg and Detmold 2009, Tristan in Aachen 2012; concert repertoire includes Beethoven 9th Symphony, Bruckner, Gounod and Puccini Masses, Dvořák and Verdi Requiems. *Honours:* Winner, Metropolitan Opera Nat. Council Auditions Competition, Premier Grand Prix and Best Tenor Award in the Viñas Competition, Barcelona, Concours Int. de Chant, Toulouse, 1st Prize, G. B. Viotti Competition, Vercelli. *Current Management:* c/o Antonia Klein, Hanselmannstrasse 11, 80809 Munich, Germany. *Telephone:* (89) 45579931. *E-mail:* aklein@agenturklein.de. *Website:* www.agenturklein.de. *Address:* Klausener Platz 18, 14059 Berlin, Germany (home). *E-mail:* larry .bakst@gmail.com (home). *Website:* larry.bakst.de (office).

BALADA, Leonardo; Spanish/American composer and academic; *University Professor of Composition, Carnegie Mellon University*; b. 22 Sept. 1933, Barcelona; m. 1st; one s.; m. 2nd Joan Winer 1979. *Education:* Liceu Conservatory, Barcelona, Juilliard School, studied with Copland, Tansman, Persichetti, Markevitch. *Career:* teacher, United Nations International School 1963–70; mem. faculty 1970–75 Carnegie-Mellon Univ., Prof. 1975–90, Univ. Prof. of Composition 1990–; works performed worldwide; commissions for Aspen Festival, the San Diego Opera, the Pittsburgh, Cincinnati and Hartford Symphony Orchestras, Nat. Endowment for the Arts, Benedum Center for the Performing Arts, the Lausanne Chamber Orchestra, The Millennium of Catalonia, Sociedad Estatal para el V Centenario, National Orchestra of Spain, Radio TV Orchestra of Madrid, Opera Teatro Real, Berlin Radio Symphony Orchestra, Barcelona Symphony Orchestra. *Compositions include:* operas: Hangman, Hangman! 1982, Christopher Columbus 1987, premiered in 1989, Barcelona Opera, with José Carreras and Monserrat Caballé singing leading roles, Death of Columbus 1996, The Town of Greed 1997, Faust-bal 2007; other: Concerto for Piano and Orchestra 1964, Guitar Concerto 1965, Guernica 1966, Sinfonia in Negro 1968, Maria Sabina 1969, Concerto for Bandoneon and Orchestra 1970, Las Moradas 1970, Steel Symphony 1972, Auroris 1973, Ponce de Leon for narrator and orchestra 1974, Concerto for Piano, Winds and Percussion 1974, Homage to Casals and Sarasate 1975, Concerto for Four Guitars and Orchestra 1976, Three Anecdotes 1977, Sardana 1979, Quasi un Pasodoble 1981, Zapata: Images for Orchestra 1987, Fantasias Sonoras 1987, Reflejos 1987, Alegrias for flute and string orchestra 1988, Columbus: Images for Orchestra 1991, Divertimentos 1991, Symphony No. 4 1992, Celebration 1992, Symphony No. 4 Lausanne 1992, Thunderous Scenes 1992, Music for oboe and orchestra 1993, Shadows 1995, Morning Music 1995, Line and Thunder 1996, Concierto Magico for guitar and orchestra 1997, No-Res 1997, Cantata 1997, Folk Dreams for orchestra 1998, Echoes 1998, Concerto for Piano and Orchestra No. 3 1999, Music for Flute and Orchestra 2000, Passacaglia 2000, Symphony No. 5 American 2003, Prague Sinfonietta 2003, Caprichos No. 1 2003, Caprichos No. 2 2004, Ebony Fantasies 2004, Caprichos No. 3 2005, Symphony No. 6 – Symphony of Sorrows 2005, Concerto for Three Cellos and Orchestra – A German Concerto 2006, A Little Night Music in Harlem for string orchestra 2006, Caprichos No. 4 2007, Caprichos No. 5 2008, Caprichos No. 6 2009, Caprichos No. 7 2009, Viola Concerto 2010. *Recordings include:* Steel Symphony with Pittsburgh Symphony Orchestra under Lorin Maazel; Torquemada, cantata; Concerto for Piano, Winds and Percussion; Music for Oboe and Orchestra; Maria Sabina, Cantata with Louisville Orchestra; Divertimentos for string orchestra. *Honours:* Nat. Composition Prize of Catalonia, Barcelona 1993, Premio Antara, Peru. *Current Management:* Music Associates of America, 224 King Street, Engelwood, NJ 07631, USA. *Telephone:* (201) 569-2898. *Fax:* (201) 569-7023. *E-mail:* maasturm@sprynet.com. *Address:* School of Music, Carnegie Mellon University, Pittsburgh, PA 15213, USA (office). *Telephone:* (412) 268-2372 (office). *E-mail:* balada@andrew.cmu.edu (office). *Website:* www.andrew .cmu.edu/user/balada (office).

BALASHOV, Oleg; Russian singer (tenor); b. 1968, Moscow. *Education:* Moscow Conservatoire. *Career:* sang with Moscow Municipal Theatre New Opera 1998–99; performed at Spoleto Festival 1999; soloist, Mariinsky Theatre, St Petersburg, 1999–, performed with them at Metropolitan Opera, New York, Royal Opera House, Covent Garden, La Scala, Milan, Teatro Real, Madrid and Théâtre du Châtelet, Paris, also toured to Berlin, Stockholm, Beijing, Tokyo, Los Angeles, Washington, Amsterdam and Rotterdam; roles with the Kirov Opera and elsewhere have included Andrei in Mazepa, Vaudémont in Iolanta, Kuragin in War and Peace, Alfredo in La Traviata, Bayan in Ruslan and Lyudmila, Andrei Kovansky in Khovanshchina, Chekalinsky in The Queen of Spades, Vsevolod in The Legend of the Invisible City of Kitezh and the Maiden Fevronia, Elisey Bomoly in The Tsar's Bride, Oedipus in Oedipus Rex, The Marquis in The Gambler, Sergei in Lady Macbeth of Mtsensk, Edgardo in Lucia di Lammermoor, Don Carlo in Don Carlo, Cassio in Otello, Rodolfo in La Bohème, B.F. Pinkerton in Madama Butterfly, Pong in Turandot, Nathaniel in Les Contes d'Hoffmann, Daland in Der Fliegende Holländer, Siegmund in Die Walküre, Parsifal, Narraboth in Salome, Aegisth in Elektra, Lensky in Eugene Onegin, Shuisky in Boris Godunov; US debut as Parsifal at Washington DC Opera with Valery Gergiev 2006; performed at Salzburg Festival 2005, also at Metropolitan Opera, Canadian Opera, Vancouver Opera, Israeli Opera and Teatro Municipal, Santiago. *Current Management:* c/o James Fox Artist Management. *Telephone:* (310) 531-0213. *E-mail:* peter@jfartists.com. *Address:* Kirov Opera, Mariinsky Theatre, 190000 St Petersburg, Teatralnaya pl. 1, Russia (office). *Telephone:* (812) 326-41-41 (office). *Fax:* (812) 314-17-44 (office). *E-mail:* post@ mariinsky.ru (office). *Website:* www.mariinsky.ru/en/opera/soloist/balashov (office).

BALASSA, Sándor, DLA; Hungarian composer; b. 20 Jan. 1935, Budapest; s. of János Balassa and Eszter Bora; m. Marianna Orosz; one s. one d. *Education:* Budapest Conservatory and Music Acad. of Budapest, studied composition under Endre Szervánszky. *Career:* began career as a mechanic; entered Budapest Conservatory at age 17; Music Dir, Hungarian Radio 1964–80; Asst

Prof., later Lecturer, Music Acad. of Budapest 1981–93, Univ. Prof. 1993–96. *Compositions include:* vocal: Eight Songs from Street Rottenbiller 1957, Two Songs to Poems by Dezső Kosztolányi 1957, Two Songs to Poems by Attila József 1958, Five Choruses (for children's choir) 1967, Legenda 1967, Antinomia 1968, Summer Night (for female choir) 1968, Requiem for Lajos Kassák 1969, Cantata Y 1970, Motetta 1973, Tresses 1979, Kyrie (for female choir) 1981, Madaras énekek (for children's choir) 1984, The Third Planet, opera-cantata 1986, Bánatomtól szabadulnék (for female choir) 1988, Oldott kéve (for mixed choir) 1992, Kelet népe (for children's choir) 1992, Damjanich's prayer (for mixed choir) 1993, Chant of Orphans (for mixed choir) 1995, Capriccio (for female choir) 1996, Spring Song, Autumn Song (for female choir) 1997, Woodcutter (for male choir) 1998, Moon-gesang and Sun-anthem (for male choir) 1998, Winter cantata (for children's chorus and string orchestra) 1999, Christmas (for female choir) 1999, Secrets of Heart (for solo tenor and string orchestra) 2002, Songs from Sümegvár Street 2003, A Gólyához (for mixed choir) 2003, Three songs to poems by Albert Wass 2003, Cry in December 2005; opera: Az ajtón kivül (The Man Outside) 1976, The Third Planet 1986, Karl and Anna 1992, Földindulás 2001, Erderschütterung; instrumental: Dimensioni 1966, Quartetto per percussioni 1969, Xenia 1970, Tabulae 1972, The Last Shepherd 1978, Quintet for Brass 1979, The Flowers of Hajta 1984, Divertimento for two cimbaloms 1992, Sonatina for harp 1993, Little Garland (trio for flute, viola and harp) 1994, Five Brothers (piano) 1994, Jánosnapi muzsika (solo violin) 1994, Vonósnégyes (string quartet) 1995, Bells of Nyirbátor (for twelve brass instruments) 1996, Sonatina for Piano 1996, Preludes and Fantasia for Organ 1996, Duets (for flute and harp) 1998, Pastoral and Rondo (for violin and horn) 1998, Eight Movements for two clarinets 2001, Sonatina II (for piano) 2003, Párosító Hegedüduók (Duet for violins) 2003, Xenia II (nonetto) 2004, Letters from a Reservation (for Cimbalom) 2004, Greeting to Viola (for solo viola) 2004, Three Movements for Cello 2005, Ha szól a Tárogató 2006, Eszterlánc Duets (for flute and violin 2006, Fantasia for Piano 2006, Four Pieces for Cimbalom 2006, Trio I for Strings 2006, Művész utca II/a 2007, Obne Doom-Doom 2007, Trio II for Strings 2008; orchestral: Violin Concerto 1965, Lupercalia 1971, Iris 1972, Chant of Glarus 1978, The Island of Everlasting Youth 1979, Calls and Cries 1980, A Daydreamer's Diary 1983, Three Phantasias 1984, Little Grape and Little Fish 1987, Tündér Ilona 1992, Prince Csaba (for string orchestra) 1993, Bölcske Concerto (for string orchestra) 1993, Dances of Mucsa 1994, Sons of the Sun 1995, Four Portraits 1996, Number 301 Parcel 1997, Pécs Concerto 1998, Hungarian Coronation Music 1998, Hun's Valley (Val d'Anniviers) 1999, Double Concerto (for oboe, horn and string orchestra) 2000, Fantasy (for harp and string orchestra) 2002, Flowers of October 2003, Gödöllö Concerto (for guitar orchestra) 2003, Excursion to the Sun Mountain (for string orchestra) 2003, Concerto (for trumpet) 2004, Szeged concerto (for string orchestra) 2005, Summer Music (for flute and string orchestra) 2005, Civisek Városa 2005, Journeys in Bihar 2005, Lovagi erények dícsérete 2007, Overture and Scenes (for string orchestra) 2007. *Recordings include:* Karl and Anna 2003, Pécs Concerto 2003, Violin Concerto No. 3 2006, The Third Planet 2006, The Man Outside 2007, Journeys in Bihar Country 2008, Works for String Orchestra 2010. *Honours:* Erkel Prize 1972, Critics' Prize, Hungarian Radio 1972, 1974, Listeners' Prize, Hungarian Radio 1976, Distinction for Best Work of the Year, Paris Int. Tribune of Composers 1972, Merited Artist of the Hungarian People's Repub. 1978, Kossuth Prize 1983, Bartók-Pásztory Prize 1988, 1999, Excellent Artist of the Hungarian People's Repub. 1989. *Address:* str. 18 Sümegvár, 1118 Budapest, Hungary (home). *Telephone:* (1) 319-7049 (home). *E-mail:* sandor@balassa.hu (home). *Website:* www.balassa.hu.

BALATSCH, Norbert; Austrian chorus master; b. 10 March 1928, Vienna. *Education:* Vienna Music Acad. *Career:* sang with the Vienna Boys' Choir as a child 1938–44, Artistic Dir 1998–2001; joined chorus, Vienna Staatsoper 1952, Chorus Master 1978–84; Dir, Vienna Men's Chorus 1953–83; Dir, Bayreuth Festival Chorus 1972–2000, Philharmonia Chorus, London 1974–79, Chorus of Accademia di Santa Cecilia, Rome 1984–99; has directed sacred works by Mozart, Haydn and others at the chapel of the Viennese Court; led the chorus in Der fliegende Holländer at Bayreuth 1990; Nikikai Chorus Group of Tokyo, Lohengrin 1997. *Honours:* Wilhelm Pitz Prize for outstanding services to opera (Germany) 1990, Grammy Award for Best Choral Performance 2001.

BALDWIN, Dalton, BM; American pianist; b. 19 Dec. 1931, Summit, NJ. *Education:* Juilliard School of Music, New York, Oberlin Coll. Conservatory of Music, studied with Nadia Boulanger and Madeleine Lipatti in Paris. *Career:* toured extensively as accompanist for artists including Gérard Souzay, Elly Ameling, Marilyn Horne, Theresa Berganza, Nicolai Gedda and Jessye Norman; permanent pianist of Souzay for over three decades, touring on five continents and making numerous recordings; took part with Souzay in the premiere of Rorem's War Scenes 1969; played for instrumentalists including Henryk Szeryng, Pierre Fournier and the Via Nova Quartet; Adjunct Prof., Westminster Conservatory of Music, Rider Univ. *Recordings include:* complete songs of Fauré, Debussy, Ravel and Poulenc. *Honours:* Chevalier de l'Ordre des Arts et des Lettres (France); Hon. DMus (Oberlin Coll.). *Address:* c/o Westminster Conservatory of Music, 101 Walnut Lane, Princeton, NJ 08540, USA (office). *E-mail:* dbaldwin@rider.edu (office).

BALKIND, Jonathan Paul Brenner; British impresario, civil servant and architectural conservationist; b. 6 July 1946, Los Angeles, Calif.; s. of the late Gabriel Balkind and of the late May Balkind (nee Covitz). *Education:* Univ. of Cambridge, Architectural Asscn, London. *Career:* historic buildings inspector, GLC/English Heritage with special responsibility for Spitalfields 1974–88; Co-founder, now Hon. Sec. and Trustee, Friends of Christ Church Spitalfields; bd mem. and adviser, Endymion Ensemble 1980–97; Gen. and Artistic Dir, Opera London 1988–; Grant Assessor, Arts Council England, Arts Councils of Scotland and Northern Ireland, Nat. Heritage Lottery Fund and Community Fund 1996–2000; Dir, Songbird Films (Music and Arts) –1992; Artistic Adviser, City of London Sinfonia 1988–91; Chair., Collegium Music 90 1991–98; Founder and Co-Dir (with Richard Hickox), Spitalfields Festival 1976–82; Festivals of Handel 1977, Early Music 1978, English Music 1979, Young Mozart 1980; produced Mozart Lucio Silla, last performances by Janet Baker of Dido and Aeneas and many other concerts, commissions and first performances; produced operas for stage in Spitalfields and other festivals, Barbican, South Bank and Sadler's Wells, including Gluck's Armide at Spitalfields 1982 (broadcast by BBC), Handel's Alcina (restaged in Los Angeles), Monteverdi's L'Incoronazione di Poppea, and Britten's A Midsummer Night's Dream (with James Bowman) (all recorded); produced extensive music theatre with Endymion Ensemble, including Birtwistle's Punch and Judy with Opera Factory; directed operas by Gluck, Mozart and Mussorgsky; Music Adviser on TV films including Janet Baker – Full Circle (BBC) 1982, Jessye Norman –Singer (BBC) 1986, dance documentaries (Channel 4), Beethoven in Love (BBC); Sr Administrator, UN Peacekeeping Dept; Dir of Planning, Mitrovica. *Publications include:* contrib. to various publications, notes for concerts by Endymion Ensemble and City of London Sinfonia; ed., festival and opera programmes. *Address:* 45 Chalcot Road, London, NW1 8LS, England (home).

BALL, Christopher, ARAM, LRAM, ARNCM; British composer, conductor and academic; b. 7 July 1936, Leeds. *Education:* Royal Acad. of Music, Royal Northern Coll. of Music, Guildhall School of Music. *Career:* debut as Dir, Praetorius Consort, Wigmore Hall 1971; conductor, BBC Philharmonic, BBC Scottish Symphony Orchestra, Ulster Orchestra, City of Birmingham Symphony Orchestra, Vancouver Symphony Orchestra, Royal Opera House Covent Garden Orchestra, Bavarian Opera Orchestra, Maggio Musicale Orchestra of Florence; mem Performing Right Soc., RAM Club, Composers' Guild. *Compositions:* Recorder Concerto, The Piper of Dreams, Oboe concerto, Flute concerto, Orchestral dances, Dance contrasts for full orchestra, Scenes from a comedy, Pagan Piper, Pan Overheard, On a Summer Day, Celtic Moods, Adderbury in Spring, The Coming of Summer, Autumn Landscape, Christmas at the Rookery. *Recordings:* Dances From Terpsichore, German And Polish Dances, The Dancing School Of Lambrangi, Orchésographie, music by Holborne; recordings by London Baroque Trio, The Praetorius Consort, Joyful Noyse. *Honours:* Gold Medal for Orchestral Playing, John Solomon Wind Prize, Ricordi Conducting Prize. *Address:* 122 Wigmore Street, London, W1U 3RX, England (home). *Telephone:* (20) 7935-1270 (home). *E-mail:* c.ball23@ntlworld.com (home). *Website:* www.christopherballcomposer.com.

BALL, Michael, DMus, ARCM; British composer; b. 10 Nov. 1946, Manchester. *Education:* Royal Coll. of Music, London. *Career:* compositions within most genres, including six commissions from the BBC; main publr, Novello; professional mem. British Acad. of Composers and Songwriters, Inc. Soc. of Musicians. *Compositions include:* Sainte Marye Virgine 1979, Resurrection Symphonies 1982, Frontier! 1984, A Hymne to God my God 1984, Omaggio 1986, Danses vitales: Danses macabres 1987, Nocturns 1990, Chaucer's Tunes 1993, Saxophone Concerto 1994, Whitsun Wakes 1997, Euphonium Concerto 2002, ...all the flowers of the mountain... 2004. *Honours:* RCM Octavia Travelling Scholarship. *Address:* 31 Sefton, Rochestown Avenue, Dun Laoghaire, Co. Dublin, Ireland (home). *E-mail:* michaelball@iol.ie (home). *Website:* www.cmc.ie/composers/composer.cfm?composerID=3; www.chesternovello.com/composer/70/main.html.

BALLESTRA, Jean-Luc; French singer (baritone); b. 1976, Nice. *Education:* Conservatoire Nat. de Région de Nice. *Career:* Centre Nat. d'Insertion Professionnelle d'Artistes Lyriques (CNIPAL) 2000–02; debut with Verdi recital, Orchestre Régional de Cannes 2001; opera roles include Obigny in La Traviata, Opéra de Nancy 2001, Mars in Orpheus in the Underworld, Mercutio in Romeo and Juliet, Opéra de Nancy 2002, Schaunard in La Bohème, Le Dancaïre in Carmen, Duparquet in Die Fledermaus, Opéra de Nice, Opéra de Marseille 2002, debut with Opéra Nat. de Paris in Les Dialogues des Carmélites 2004, Johann in Werther, Opéra de Monte Carlo 2005, Morales in Carmen, Opéra de Montpellier 2006, Pantalon in L'Amour des Trois Oranges and Steuermann in Tristan und Isolde at Opéra Nat. de Paris 2006, Silvano in Verdi's Un Ballo in Maschera at Opéra de Paris 2007, Haly in L'Italiana in Algeri at Opéra de Lille and touring through France 2007, Lescaut in Massenet's Manon at Opéra de Nice 2008, Grégorio in Roméo et Juliette at the Salzburg Festival 2008, Escamillo in Carmen, Glyndebourne on Tour 2008, Cyprien in Yvonne Princess de Bourgogne at the Opéra Nat. de Paris and at the Wiener Festwochen 2009, Lescaut in Puccini's Manon Lescaut at Opéra de Nice 2009 and Valvert et Carbon in Alfano's Cyrano de Bergerac at the Maestranza Theatre of Seville 2009, Escamillo in Carmen at Opéra de Lille and Hong-Kong 2010, Marcello in La Boheme at Nice 2011, Cecco le Vecchio in Rienzi at Rome 2012, Ramiro in L'heure espagnole at Rome, Masetto in Don Giovanni at La Monnaie 2014, Albert in Werther at Rome 2015. *Recordings:* Carmen (with Orchestre Nat. de France, conducted by Chung Myung-Whun) 2005. *Honours:* winner, Révélations Lyriques de l'ADAMI 2001, Révélation lyrique de l'Année 2007. *Current Management:* IMG Artists, 31–33 rue du Temple, 75004 Paris, France. *Telephone:* 1-44-31-44-38. *E-mail:* cfeazey@imgartists.com. *Website:* www.imgartists.com.

BALLEYS, Brigitte; Swiss singer (mezzo-soprano); b. 18 June 1959, Martigny, Wallis. *Education:* Bern Conservatory with Jakob Stämpfli, studied with Elisabeth Schwarzkopf. *Career:* sang in concert from 1982, notably sacred music by Bach, the Brahms Alto Rhapsody, Masses by Mozart, Haydn, Schubert, Bruckner, Dvořák and Rossini; Schumann and Mahler Lieder; appearances in Switzerland, Germany, Austria, Italy, France, Portugal, Spain, South America, USA, Czechoslovakia; festival engagements at Zürich, Lucerne, Florence and Siena; recitalist in songs by de Falla, Shostakovich, Schoeck and Wolf-Ferrari, as well as French chansons and German songs; sang in opera at Freiburg 1985, with guest appearances at Zürich, Geneva, Avignon, Schwetzingen, Lausanne, and Montpellier; Vienna Staatsoper 1987, as Cherubino conducted by Leinsdorf; sang Octavian in Bern, Montpellier, Toulouse 1990; season 1992 as Fragoletto in Offenbach's Les Brigands at Amsterdam and Ramiro in Jean-Claude Malgoire's Vivaldi pastiche Montezuma at Monte Carlo; sang Nerone in Monteverdi's Poppea at Amsterdam 1996; other roles include Jocasta in Oedipus Rex (at Palermo), Gluck's Orpheus, Ottavia in Coronation of Poppea, Charlotte in Werther by Massenet, Meg Page and Orlofsky, Mrs Montgomery in L'Héritière by Damasé (at Marseille); Geneviève in Debussy's Pelléas at the Paris Opéra-Comique 1998 and at La Scala, Milan 2004; season 1999 sang Sesto in Giulio Cesare by Handel at Montpellier and the title role in Didon by Henri Desmarest at Beaune, Versailles and Metz; sang Isadora in Le Foy by Marcel Landowski at Montpellier 2000; sang in Nerone at BAM Festival, Brooklyn, NY 2002; teacher at Lausanne Conservatoire 2001–; also teacher at Académie de Musique Tibor Varga. *Recordings include:* Debussy's La Demoiselle Elue and Janáček's Diary of One who Disappeared; Mendelssohn's St Paul and Die Zauberflöte, as Second Lady; Zelenka's Requiem; Leguerney's Melodies; Martucci's Canzone de Ricordi; Respighi, Il Tramonto; Berlioz's Les Nuits d'Été; Schumann's Lieder; Honegger's Judith; Frank Martin's In Terra Pax, Der Cornet; Ernest Bloch's 4 chants d'automne; Löffler's Melodies, Chants du Japon, Le Poème de l'Amour et de la Mer; Chabrier's Mélodies. *Honours:* first prize Benson and Hedges in London 1983, Special Prize for Lied. *Address:* Conservatoire de Lausanne, Département Classique HEM, rue de la Grotte 2, Case Postale 5700, 1002 Lausanne (office); Chemin des Planches 19, 1008 Prilly, Switzerland (home). *Telephone:* (21) 634-4877 (home). *E-mail:* brigitte .balleys@cdlhem.ch (office). *Website:* www.cdlhem.ch (office).

BALLISTA, Antonio; Italian pianist; b. 30 March 1936, Milan. *Education:* Milan Conservatory. *Career:* toured widely as a soloist; many duo recitals with the pianist Bruno Canino; took part in the premieres of Rapsodia 1984, by Davide Anzaghi, Concerto for two pieces by Berio 1973, Tableaux Vivants 1964, by Berio, Fogliod'album 1976, by Bussotti, Couplets 1979, by Castiglioni, B.A.C.H. 1970, and Piano Concerto 1976, by Aldo Clementi, Estratto 1969, by Donatoni and De La Nuit 1971, by Sciarrino; Prof., Giuseppe Verdi Conservatory from 1964.

BALOGH, Endre; American violinist and photographer; b. 1954, Los Angeles, CA. *Education:* Yehudi Menuhin School, England, studied with Joseph Piastro, Manuel Compinsky and Mehli Mehta. *Career:* debut at New York Town Hall 1971; played first concerto with orchestra aged six; recital in Los Angeles aged 15; first European tour including concerts in Berlin and London 1973; performed in Austria, The Netherlands and Italy; recital for BBC, London, and on-the-air, Amsterdam; appearances with various orchestras, including Los Angeles Philharmonic and Washington, Seattle, Honolulu and other Symphony Orchestras; numerous recitals in US cities; performed as soloist with Berlin Philharmonic, Rotterdam Philharmonic, Frankfurt Symphony, Tonhalle Orchestra of Zürich, Basel Symphony; numerous appearances with American Youth Symphony under Mehli Mehta; played benefit concerts for State of Israel, UN, Philosophical Research Soc. and others; as chamber musician, violinist with Pacific Trio, performed for nearly 30 years throughout USA, Canada and in Europe; played with musicians including Vladimir Horowitz and Leonard Pennario; played in duo with guitarist James Smith, and with violist Steven Gordon, also trios and quartets; curtailed concert schedule to develop his photography 2004–; commissioned by repertory theatre company A Noise Within to compose original music for its productions. *Compositions:* music for stage: The Winter's Tale, Desire Under the Elms, Sarah Gruel's Eurydice. *Recordings include:* Pacific Trio 1990, Brahms C major and Shostakovich E major trios. *Website:* www.endresphotos .com.

BALSACH, Llorenç; Spanish composer and music theorist; b. 16 April 1953, Sabadell; m. Sedes García-Cascon 1991. *Education:* Univ. of Barcelona, Conservatories of Music of Sabadell and Barcelona, studied with Josep Soler. *Career:* freelance composer 1976–; comms for Baden-Baden Südwestfunk Orchestra 1979, Associació Catalana de Compositors 1983, 1991, CDMC, Barcelona City Council 1991, Vallès Symphony Orchestra 1991, Spanish Ministry of Culture 1992, Radio Nacional de España 1993, 1994, film Entreacte 1985, and stage works; creator, pioneer music software in Gadin Co. 1983–87; Ed., La Ma de Guido Music Publishing House 1986–; Consultant, Phonos, Pompeu Fabra Univ. 1994–. *Compositions include:* orchestral: Gran Copa Especial 1979, Poema Promiscu 1981, Visions Grotesques 1992, Quatre dibuixos per a guitarra i cordes 1994; chamber: De Caldetes a Moià 1978, Suite Gàstrica 1979, Rondó 1983, Musica-Màgica 1992, Trio per a cordes 1992, Tres Converses for ten instruments 1997, Finestral for cobla 2007; vocal: Música groga 1980, Sis cançons Breus 1982, Tres Palíndroms per a cor 1990, Olis d'olimpia 1991, Paralàlia de paralaues for mezzo soprano and piano 1992, Circ for mezzo soprano and piano 1999, La meva estrella for choir 2009; for solo instrument: St estudis modals 2006, Nocturn for piano 2011, Breu des Concert 2013. *Recordings include:* Musicas per a cordes, veus i piano, Visions grotesques 2000, Musica Concreta 2008. *Publications include:* La Convergència Harmònica 1994, Application of Virtual Pitch Theory in Music Analysis (article) 1997, Fundamentos de las tensiones armónicas 2013. *Address:* Les Planes 37, 08201 Sabadell, Barcelona, Spain (home). *Fax:* (93) 7276327 (home). *E-mail:* balsach@lamadeguido.com. *Website:* www.lamadeguido.com/ balsach.html.

BALSADONNA, Renato; Italian conductor, chorus director and pianist; *Chorus Director, Royal Opera, Covent Garden;* b. 1966, Venice; one s. *Education:* Milan Conservatoire. *Career:* Chorus Dir, La Monnaie, Brussels 1997; Chorus Dir, Royal Opera, Covent Garden 2004–; Conductor, Royal Philharmonic Orchestra 2012, Grange Park Festival 2014, Frankfurt Oper 2016. *Honours:* Cavaliere, Ordine al Merito della Repubblica Italiana. *Current Management:* c/o International Classical Artists, 28 Queen Street, London, EC4R 1BB, England. *Telephone:* (20) 7902-0520. *Fax:* (20) 7681-2667. *E-mail:* aknight@icartists.co.uk. *Website:* www.icartists.co.uk/artists/renato -balsadonna. *Address:* Royal Opera House, Floral Street, Covent Garden, London, WC2E 9DD, England (office). *Telephone:* (20) 7240-1200 (office). *E-mail:* renato.balsadonna@roh.org.uk (office). *Website:* www.roh.org.uk (office).

BALSLEV, Lisbeth; Danish singer (soprano); b. 21 Feb. 1945, Åbenrå. *Education:* Vestjysk Conservatory in Esbjerg, and Royal Opera School, Copenhagen. *Career:* has performed at La Scala Milan, Wiener Staatsoper, Bolshoi in Moskow, Deutsche Oper Berlin, Staatsoper Munich and in Hong Kong, Tel Aviv and others; debut in Copenhagen 1976, as Jaroslavna in Prince Igor; sang Mozart's Fiordiligi, Leonora in Il Trovatore and Wagner's Senta in Copenhagen; Bern Opera 1977, as Electra in Idomeneo; Bayreuth from 1978, as Senta in Der fliegende Holländer; with Hamburg Opera 1979–83, debut 1979, as Elsa in Lohengrin; Munich Staatsoper 1979, in the title role of Iphigénie en Tauride by Gluck; guest appearances in Dresden, Amsterdam, Berlin, Stuttgart, Cologne and Frankfurt; La Scala, Milan 1987, as Salome; Lisbon and Berne 1987, Senta and Elisabeth; Turin and Florence 1988, as Wagner's Isolde; Leonore in Fidelio with Cologne Opera, Hong Kong 1989; Isolde in a concert performance of Tristan und Isolde with Jutland Opera, Edinburgh Festival 1990; Agave in The Bassarids at Düsseldorf 1991; Nice 1993 and Montpellier 1996, as Isolde; debut as Elektra in Århus, and at Royal Opera House, Copenhagen 1998. *Recordings include:* Senta in Der fliegende Holländer from Bayreuth. *Honours:* Dame, Order of the Dannebrog 1993; Tagea Brandt Rejselegat 1996, first recipient of the Reumert Prize 1999.

BALSOM, Alison; British musician (trumpet); b. 7 Oct. 1978, Herts. *Education:* Guildhall School of Music, London, Paris Conservatoire, studied with Håkan Hardenberger. *Career:* concerto finalist, BBC Young Musician competition 1998; performs wide range of recital and concerto repertoire, from Albinoni to Zimmermann, and performs on modern and baroque trumpets; performances include BBC Proms (including Last Night of the Proms 2009), Barbican Mostly Mozart Festival, Stuttgart Radio Symphony with Sir Roger Norrington, Los Angeles Philharmonic Orchestra, San Francisco Symphony Orchestra, Kammerphilharmonie Bremen, BBC Symphony, Japan Philharmonic Orchestra, San Francisco Symphony Orchestra, Orchestre de Paris, Orchestre Nat. de France, Orchestra Sinfonica di Milano Giuseppe Verdi, Philharmonia Orchestra, City of Birmingham Symphony Orchestra; US TV debut with Orchestra of St Luke's, The Late Show with David Letterman 2010; world premiere performance of James MacMillan's Seraph at Wigmore Hall 2011; season 2011–12: returns to China to perform with Lorin Maazel and Nat. Symphony Orchestra in televised New Year Gala event in Beijing; performances also with Toronto Symphony Orchestra, Nat. Symphony Orchestra of Washington, Wiener Symphoniker, Chamber Orchestra of Philadelphia, Royal Philharmonic Orchestra); major int. tours planned with I Musici di Roma, Scottish Ensemble, Kremerata Baltica, kammerorchester-basel, Concerto Köln; Joby Talbot's Trumpet Concerto commissioned for her by Munich Chamber Orchestra and Liverpool Philharmonic; currently Visiting Prof., Guildhall School of Music and Drama, London; mem. BBC Radio 3 New Generation Artists scheme; formed own ensemble. *Recordings:* Trumpet and Organ Recital 2002, Bach works for trumpet 2005, Caprice (Gramophone/Classic FM Listeners' Choice Award) 2006, Haydn and Hummel Concertos 2008, Alison Balsom plays Trumpet Concertos 2008, Italian Concertos 2010, Seraph Trumpet Concertos (ECHO Klassik Award for Instrumentalist of the Year/Trumpet) 2012, Sound the Trumpet 2012. *Honours:* Feeling Musique Prize for quality of sound, Fourth Maurice André Int. Trumpet Competition, Paris 2000, Classical BRIT Awards for Young British Classical Performer 2006, for Female Artist of the Year 2009, Gramophone Award for Listeners Choice 2006, ECHO Klassik Award for Best Young Artist 2007, Artist of the Year, Gramophone Classical Music Awards 2013. *Current Management:* c/o Maggie O'Herlihy, Harrison Parrott Ltd, 5–6 Albion Court, Albion Place, London, W6 0QT, England. *Telephone:* (20) 7313-3571. *Fax:* (20) 7221-5042 (office). *E-mail:* maggie.oherlihy@ harrisonparrott.co.uk. *Website:* www.harrisonparrott.co.uk; www .alisonbalsom.com.

BALTHROP, Carmen Arlen; American singer (soprano); b. 14 May 1948, Washington, DC. *Education:* Univ. of Maryland, Coll. Park and the Catholic Univ. of America. *Career:* debut in Washington, DC 1973, as Virtue in L'Incoronazione di Poppea, and as Minerva in the US premiere of Il Ritorno d'Ulisse 1974; sang the title role in Scott Joplin's Treemonisha at Houston

Opera 1975; sang in Cavalli's L'Egisto at Wolf Trap and made her Metropolitan debut as Pamina 1977; sang at New York City Opera 1978 as Roggiero in Rossini's Tancredi; Innsbruck Early Music Festival 1980 as Monteverdi's Poppea, in the edition by Alan Curtis; sang Poppea at Spoleto 1979 and Santa Fe 1986; sang in Venice as Gluck's Euridice and Poppea in Handel's Agrippina 1982–83; Michigan Opera Theater as Treemonisha and Pamina 1982–84; sang Gretel at Milwaukee 1995; created the title role in Vanqui by Leslie Burrs for Opera Columbus 1999. *Recordings include:* Treemonisha. *Honours:* winner Metropolitan Opera Auditions 1975. *Current Management:* Dorothy Cone Artist Representatives, 150 West 55th Street, New York, NY 10019, USA. *Telephone:* (212) 765-7412. *Fax:* (212) 765-7443. *E-mail:* dcone@ix.netcom .com. *Website:* www.dorothyconeartistrep.com. *Address:* c/o Santa Fe Opera, PO Box 2408, Santa Fe, NM 878504, USA.

BALTSA, Agnes; Greek singer (mezzo-soprano); b. Lefkas. *Education:* Acad. of Music, Athens and Maria Callas Scholarship, Munich. *Career:* opera debut as Cherubino, Frankfurt 1968; debut at Vienna State Opera as Octavian 1970, Salzburg Festival 1970, La Scala, Milan (Dorabella) 1976, Paris Opera and Covent Garden, London (Cherubino) 1976, Metropolitan Opera, New York (Octavian) 1980; mem. Deutsche Oper Berlin 1973–; performs at all maj. opera houses in world, and has given concerts in Europe, USA and Japan with Karajan, Böhm, Bernstein, Muti and others; sang Elektra at Opernhaus Zurich, Théâtre du Capitole, Toulouse, Deutsche Oper Berlin, Bayerische Staatsoper, Staatsoper Munich and Wiener Staatsoper 2009–12, also several lieder concerts. *Honours:* Österreichische Kammersängerin 1980, Deutscher Schallplattenpreis 1983, Prix Prestige Lyrique (French Ministry of Culture) 1984. *Address:* c/o Management Rita Schültz, Rütistr 52, 8044 Zurich-Gockhausen, Switzerland.

BALUN, Frantisek; Slovak singer (baritone); b. 13 Sept. 1948, Chminianska Nová Ves; m. Melánia Balúnová; three s. one d. *Education:* State Conservatory, Brno with Prof. Richard Novák. *Career:* debut at Jonás Záborsky Theatre, Presov 1968; Slovak Nat. Theatre, Bratislava 1972–77; State Theatre, Košice 1977–, sang Tchaikovsky's Iolanta and Ravel, The Spanish Hour; sang Nabucco in Paris 1994; sang in Germany, in Bettelstudent 1996, Carmen 1997; sang in Austria in Nabucco and Carmen 1997; in Czech Repub. in Il Trovatore, Madama Butterfly; opera and operetta arias, folk songs for Slovak radio; Artistic Dir, East Slovak Theatre of Košice 1999; mem. Ján Cikker Foundation. *Honours:* Musical Fund for Tosca (Scarpia) Prize (for Il Trovatore), Musical Fund and Ministry of Culture Prize (for the performance of Mr Scrooge by Ján Cikker). *Address:* c/o Štátne Divadlo Košice, Hlavná 58, 042 77 Košice (office); Dvorkinova 6, 040 22 Košice, Slovakia.

BALZANI, Vincenzo; Italian pianist; *Artistic Director, Valsesia Musica;* b. 10 Dec. 1951, Milan. *Education:* Giuseppe Verdi Conservatory, Milan with Alberto Mozzati. *Career:* has performed in public since age 14; Prof. of Piano, Giuseppe Verdi Conservatory, Milan 1973–; Italian engagements at La Scala, Milan, San Carlo, Naples, La Fenice, Venice, Comunale di Bologna, Teatro Verdi, Trieste, Teatro Petruzzelli, Bari, Accademia Filarmonica Romana; further appearances in France, Germany and Spain; fmr jury mem. numerous int. piano competitions; currently Artistic Dir Valsesia Musica, Monterosa, Città di Pavia and Città di Cantù competitions. *Recordings include:* music by Liszt, Mozart and Hummel; Chopin Etudes Op. 10. *Honours:* La Spezia Nat. Piano Competition 1965, Liszt Prize, Maria Canals Competition in Barcelona 1967, City of Treviso Prize 1970, G.B. Viotti Prize 1970. *Address:* Conservatorio di Musica Giuseppe Verdi, Via Conservatorio 12, 20122 Milan (office); Via Spalato 5, 20159 Milan, Italy (home). *Telephone:* (02) 7621101 (office). *E-mail:* vincebalzani@yahoo.it (office). *Website:* www.consmilano.it (office). www.vincenzobalzani.com.

BAMBERGER, David, BA; American opera director and producer; *Artistic Director, Cleveland Institute of Music Opera Theater;* b. 14 Oct. 1940, Albany, NY; m. Carola Beral; one s. *Education:* Yale Univ. School of Drama, Université de Paris, France, Swarthmore Coll. *Career:* stage director/producer: The Barber of Seville, The Magic Flute, Der Rosenkavalier, New York City Opera; Rigoletto, Lucia di Lammermoor, Nat. Opera, Santiago, Chile; Madama Butterfly, Don Pasquale, Cincinnati Opera; Don Pasquale, Pittsburgh Opera; The Flying Dutchman, Harford Opera Company; producer/director: Don Giovanni, Four Saints in Three Acts, Madama Butterfly, Così fan tutte, The Gondoliers, Die Fledermaus, Menotti's Tamu-Tamu (first production after world premiere), Oberlin Music Theatre, Ohio; Gen. Dir, Cleveland Opera 1976–2004, over 200 productions including La Traviata, La Bohème, Daughter of the Regiment, Tosca, Aida, Faust, Falstaff, The Medium, The Secret Marriage, The Merry Widow, Holy Blood and Crescent Moon (world premiere); Artistic Dir, Toledo (Ohio) Opera 1983–85, staged Faust, Don Pasquale, Aida, Barber of Seville; Artistic Dir, Cleveland Inst. of Music Opera Theater 2004–. *Address:* Cleveland Institute of Music, 11021 East Boulevard, Cleveland, OH 44106, USA (office). *Telephone:* (216) 791-5000 (office). *Fax:* (216) 791-3063 (office). *Website:* www.cim.edu (office).

BAMERT, Matthias; Swiss conductor and composer; b. 5 July 1942, Ersigen; m. Susan Exline 1969; one s. one d. *Education:* studied in Bern and Paris, studied composition with Jean Rivier and Pierre Boulez. *Career:* asst conductor to Leopold Stokowski 1970–71; Resident Conductor Cleveland Orchestra 1971–78; Music Dir Swiss Radio Orchestra, Basel 1977–83; Prin. Guest Conductor Scottish Nat. Orchestra 1985–90; Dir Musica Nova Festival, Glasgow 1985–90, Lucerne Festival 1992–98; Music Dir London Mozart Players 1993–2000; has appeared with Orchestre de Paris, Rotterdam Philharmonic, Cleveland Orchestra, Pittsburgh Symphony, Montreal Symphony, Royal Philharmonic Orchestra, London, London Philharmonic Orchestra, BBC Philharmonic, City of Birmingham Symphony Orchestra and at BBC Promenade Concerts, London; Prin. Conductor and Artistic Adviser, Malaysian Philharmonic Orchestra 2005–08. *Compositions include:* Concertino for English horn, string orchestra and piano 1966, Septuria Lunaris for orchestra 1970, Rheology for string orchestra 1970, Mantrajana for orchestra 1971, Once Upon an Orchestra for narrator, 12 dancers and orchestra 1975, Ol-Okun for string orchestra 1976, Keepsake for orchestra 1979, Circus Parade for narrator and orchestra 1979. *Honours:* George Szell Memorial Award 1971. *Current Management:* c/o Andrew Strange, International Classic Artists, Dunstan House, 14a St Cross Street, London, EC1N 8XA, England. *Website:* www.icartists.co.uk. *E-mail:* contact@matthias-bamert.com. *Website:* www.matthias-bamert.com.

BANDITELLI, Gloria; Italian singer (mezzo-soprano); b. 1954. *Career:* sang first in Sacchini's Fra Donato, for RAI, Naples; Siena 1980, in Cavalieri's La Rappresentazione; Teatro Vale Rome 1982, in Gagliano's Dafne, Innsbruck Festival 1983, as Cesti's Tito, followed by Handel's Rodrigo, Medea in Cavalli's Giasone, Teodata in Handel's Flavio and Amastris in Serse; Bologna 1984, 1991, in Gluck's Armide and as Maria in Mosè in Egitto; La Scala, Milan 1988, in Jommelli's Fetonte, Utrecht Festival 1988, in Giasone and Montpellier 1989, as Gluck's Orpheus; concerts include Mozart's Requiem in Vienna on 200th anniversary of his death; sang the Messenger in Monteverdi's Orfeo at Palermo 1996; Monteverdi's Penelope at Palermo 1998; season 2000–01 in Monteverdi's Orfeo and Poppea at Beaune, and in Dido and Aeneas at Florence; also appeared in Il turco in Italia, Gianni Schicchi, Manon Lescaut, Alceste, Eugene Onegin, La Cenerentola, Le nozze di Figaro, Il ritorno d'Ulisse in Patria and Giulio Cesare; sang in major venues in Italy and Europe including La Scala, La Fenice, Teatro Comunale di Bologna, Teatro dell'Opera di Roma, San Carlo de Napoli, Regio Turin, Maggio Musicale Florence, Wiener Staatsoper, Gran Teatre del Liceu in Barcelona, Théâtre des Champs-Elysées and Théâtre du Chatelet in Paris, Musikverein in Vienna and Concertgebouw in Amsterdam, under the direction of conductors including Riccardo Chailly, René Clemencic, Zubin Mehta, Riccardo Muti, Claudio Abbado and Lorin Maazel; concerts and master classes. *Recordings include:* Le Cinesi by Gluck, Pergolesi's Adriano in Siria, Penelope in Monteverdi's Ulisse. *Current Management:* c/o Atelier Musicale, Via Caselle 76, San Lazzaro di Savena 40068, Italy. *Telephone:* (51) 19984444. *Fax:* (51) 19984420. *E-mail:* info@ ateliermusicale.com. *Website:* www.ateliermusicale.com.

BANFIELD, Stephen David, BA, DPhil, FRCO; British academic and writer; *Professor Emeritus of Music, University of Bristol;* b. 15 July 1951, Dulwich, London. *Education:* Clare Coll., Cambridge, Harvard Univ., USA, St John's Coll., Oxford. *Career:* Lecturer, Univ. of Keele 1978–88, Sr Lecturer 1988–92; Elgar Prof. of Music, Univ. of Birmingham 1992–2003, Head, School of Performance Studies 1992–97, Head, Dept of Music 1996–98; Visiting Prof. of Musicology, Univ. of Minnesota, USA 1998; Stanley Hugh Badock Prof. of Music, Univ. of Bristol 2003–12, Prof. Emer. 2012–; Vice-Pres. British Music Soc.; mem. American Musicological Soc., Corresponding mem. 2015–; mem. Royal Musical Asscn, Kurt Weill Foundation. *Publications include:* Sensibility and English Song 1985, Sondheim's Broadway Musicals 1993, The Blackwell History of Music in Britain, Vol. VI: The Twentieth Century (ed.) 1995, Gerald Finzi 1997, Jerome Kern 2006, The Sounds of Stonehenge 2009, Music and the Wesleys 2010; contribs to scholarly books and journals. *Honours:* Hon. Prin. Fellow, Univ. of Melbourne 2007–; First Kurt Weill Prize, USA, Irving Lowens Award, USA 1995. *Address:* 43 Woodland Road, Clifton, Bristol, BS8 1UU; 21 Kingsgate House, 2-8 Kingsgate Place, London, NW6 4TA, England (home). *Telephone:* (20) 7625-1119 (home). *E-mail:* s.d.banfield@bristol.ac.uk (office).

BANFIELD, William (Bill) Cedric, BMus, MA, DMA; American composer, academic and musician (guitar); *Professor of Liberal Arts, Berklee College of Music;* b. 24 March 1961, Detroit, MI. *Education:* Cass Tech. High School, New England Conservatory of Music, Boston, Tufts Univ., Medford, Boston Univ., Univ. of Mich. at Ann Arbor. *Career:* mem. Detroit bands, including Cool Breeze and The Sapphire from age 12; f. Bill Banfield Quintet 1980; founder and operator, B Magic Operations, Boston 1984–88; guest guitar soloist with Detroit Metropolitan Orchestra 1984, 1989; conductor, La Chorale des Martyrs de L'Ouganda (Senegalese Choir and Orchestra) 1988; f. Undine Smith Moore Collection, Ind. Univ. 1993; teacher public schools, Boston 1980–86; Musical Dir, Days in the Arts Program, Tanglewood Music Festival, Tanglewood, MA 1984–88; Minister of Educ., Union United Church, Boston 1984–88; Program Co-ordinator, Boston Theological Inst. 1985–88; founder and Dir, Young Artists Devt Inc., Boston 1985–88, Boston Music Community Center 1986–88; guitar instructor, Univ. of Mich. at Ann Arbor 1988–89, jazz instructor 1988–90; private instructor in composition, arranging and guitar pedagogy 1988–92; instructor, Hartford Biblical Studies Inst., Detroit, MI 1989–92; Asst Prof., Dept of Afro-American Studies, Ind. Univ. at Bloomington 1992–97; Prof. of Music, Ind. Univ./Purdue Univ., Indianapolis 1992–97; Dir and composer-in-residence, Soul Revue/Black Popular Arts Ensemble, Afro-American Arts Inst., Ind. Univ. 1992–97; witness series, composer-in-residence, Plymouth Music Series, Minneapolis, MN 1993–95; visiting artist and scholar at numerous insts., including Univ. of Mich. at Ann Arbor 1994, Carleton Coll. 1995, St Augustine Coll. 1995, Tufts Univ. 1995, Univ. of Mass at Amherst 1995, Univ. of Minneapolis 1995, Butler Univ. 1996, Duke Univ. 1996, Univ. of Akron 1996; W. E. B. Dubois Fellow, Harvard Univ. 2001; Endowed Chair Humanities and Fine Arts, Univ. of St Thomas, St Paul

1997–2006, also Dir American Cultural Studies Program and Assoc. Prof.; Prof. of Liberal Arts, Berklee Coll. of Music 2006–; mem. American Guild of Organists, Nat. Advisory Council, ASCAP, Coll. Music Soc., Minn. Composers' Forum, Nat. Asscn of Negro Musicians. *Compositions include:* for solo instruments: Warmly Embraced for piano 1980, A Stroll in Lydian for piano 1981, Reversed Roles for piano 1981, One Segment Samba for piano 1981, Belshazzar for guitar 1981, Hanaha for guitar 1981, A Little Look At Me for piano 1982, I V bVIII 5b7 b7 for piano 1982, Karla for guitar 1982, Song for Earl for guitar 1983, Song for Mic for guitar 1983, Gibbit for oboe 1985, Fantasy for piano 1987, Mead 28 for piano 1989, Waggussyduke for piano 1989, Suite for Richard for trumpet 1990, Two Tall Tales for bassoon 1992; for small instrumental ensembles: Derwin E.: Six Minutes for String Quartet No. 1 1983, Susan: String Quartet No. 2 1985, El Dia de Derber: Wedding Suite for string quartet and piano 1985, Bobby's Theme 1985, Brass Belly 1988, Spirituals 1988, Zola 1988, Cone Tone: String Quartet No. 3 1989, Four Persons 1991, For Bass Wrapped in Pita Pocket with Ketchup, Mayo and a Dash of Hot Mustard 1991, Can We All Get Along? 1992, Dance Like The Wind for woodwind 1995; for jazz ensemble: The Dream Suite 1980, Carla 1983, Straightline 1983, A Friend's Advice 1984, Just A Note From Sam 1988, Her Embrace 1990, Last Night She Had a Really Good Dream 1992, Blues for Anne 1992, Lisa 1993, Magdalene 1993, Rachel 1993, Derry Alan 1993, Brooke 1993, And What Would You Like to Hear Little Lady? 1995, TIM (Time in Motion) 1995, She Made It Crystal Clear 1995, Song for George 1996, Three Late Night Discussions 1996, Bill's Blue 1996, Brookes Way 1997, A Prayer 1997; for concert band: Concerto for Wind Symphony 1995, The Seed: Fanfare for Wind Symphony 1998; for full orchestra: Fantasy for Orchestra on Themes from Shakespeare 1989, Symphony No. 1: Brevities of Experience 1990, Dreams Realized/Nightmare Resolved 1992, Symphony No. 5: Five Shades of a Woman in Black 1993, Four Songs for Five American Voices: Symphony No. 6 1993, Essay for orchestra 1995; for orchestra with soloists: Marsheila 1982, Baroque Suite for guitar and string orchestra 1987, Susej Moments for guitar and string orchestra 1987, Three Movements and Themes on Shakespeare 1988, Jenny Festival for guitar and orchestra 1989, Moods and Colors concerto for trombone and orchestra 1991, You Can Tell the World 1992, Delancey Street 1994, Symphony No. 7: Reveries, A Summer's Circle 1997; for orchestra with chorus: Guide Us Through the Years 1988, Visions: Symphonic Songs for orchestra and double chorus 1988, Job's Song: Symphony No. 3 1992, Life Suite 1995; vocal: Pleasing Thought 1979, I'm Won 1984, Are You Thinking About Me? 1984, Baby You 1984, All I Gotta Do 1984, Unmistakable You 1985, Steadfast Love: Psalm 118 for chorus 1986, Harp Song 1989, Summer Lies 1989, The Prophetess 1989, Steadfast Love: Psalm 138 for chorus 1989, I Love You My Life 1990, Momma Why?: Questions of a Young American (opera) 1991, Spiritual Songs 1991, Desire: Langston Living Amongst the Poets Unknown 1992, The Prophetess II 1992, Eyes (musical) 1995, Luyala (opera) 1997, Fisherman's Dock (opera) 1997. *Recordings:* albums: with Bill Banfield Band: Spring Forward 2009. *Publications:* Musical Landscapes in Color: Conversations with Black American Composers 2003, Black Notes: Essays of a Musician writing in a Post-Album Age 2004; contrib. numerous articles. *Honours:* Chrysler Corpn Scholarship, Youth of Understanding 1978, Boston Foundation Artist Award 1987, winner Savannah Symphony American Symphony Orchestra League nat. search for black talent 1994, McKnight Foundation Composers-in-Residence Fellowship from the American Composers Forum, Carleton Coll., Univ. of St Thomas 1995–96, Detroit Symphony/UNISYS Award 1995. *Address:* Department of Liberal Arts, Berklee College of Music, 1140 Boylston Street, Boston, MA 02215, USA (office). *Telephone:* (617) 747-2552 (office). *Website:* www.berklee.edu (office); www.billbanfield.com.

BANKS, Barry; British singer (tenor); b. 1960, Stoke-on-Trent, England. *Education:* Royal Northern Coll. of Music with Josef Ward. *Career:* Covent Garden debut as Beppe in Pagliacci 1989; other roles and appearances include Rossini's Almaviva, Fenton, the Novice in Billy Budd, Mozart's Basilio, Arturo in Lucia di Lammermoor, Iopas in Les Troyens, Griffiths/Mozart pastiche The Jewel Box, Pedrillo in Die Entführung, Il Signor Bruschino, Peri's Euridice, Tamino in Die Zauberflöte, Mozart's Mitridate, Gianetto in The Thieving Magpie, Tom Rakewell, Edgardo, Candide, Lucio Silla, Argirio in Tancredi, Britten's Flute, Nemorino in L'Elisir d'Amore, Belfiore in Il Viaggio a Reims, Don Ottavio in Don Giovanni, Brighella in Ariadne auf Naxos, Lindoro in L'Italiana in Algeri, Don Ramiro in La Cenerentola, Oreste in Ermione, Don Narciso in Il Turco in Italia, L'Astrologue in Le Coq D'Or, Uberto in La Donna del Lago. *Recordings include:* L'Elisir d'Amore, Don Pasquale, Don Giovanni, The Thieving Magpie, Die Zauberflöte, La Bohème, Un Ballo in Maschera, Trial by Jury, Barry Banks sings Bel Canto Arias 2004. *Honours:* Peter Moores Foundation Scholarship 1983. *Current Management:* Harrison Parrott, 5–6 Albion Court, London, W6 0QT, England. *Telephone:* (20) 7229-9166. *Fax:* (20) 7221-5042. *E-mail:* info@harrisonparrott.co.uk. *Website:* www.harrisonparrott.com.

BANNATYNE-SCOTT, Brian; British singer (bass); b. 4 Nov. 1955, Edinburgh, Scotland; m. Frances Stewart Leaf 1979; one s. one d. *Education:* St Andrew's Univ., Guildhall School of Music, studied with Norman Bailey. *Career:* debuts at La Fenice Venice 1981 and Rome Opera 1982; Scottish Opera from 1982, as Colline, Don Fernando in Fidelio, Nourabad in The Pearl Fishers, The Speaker in The Magic Flute; ENO from 1987 as Monterone in Rigoletto, Pogner and the Commendatore 1991; Varlaam in Boris Godunov, Opera North and BBC Proms 1992; Banquo, ENO 1993; sang Fafner and Hagen in the City of Birmingham Touring Opera version of The Ring; tour of Europe as Cold Genius in Purcell's King Arthur; Salzburg Festival debut 1991, as Polyphemus in Acis and Galatea; Bermuda Festival 1991, as Don Alfonso in Così fan tutte; concert engagements with leading British orchestras; sang Christus in the St John Passion settings of Bach and Arvo Pärt (in Italy, Germany and Japan); Stravinsky's Les Noces with London Sinfonietta and Simon Rattle 1993; Aldeburgh masterclasses with Galina Vishnevskaya (also televised) and recital at 1990 Prom concert; appearances include The Trojans, London Symphony Orchestra 1993, 1994, Swallow in Peter Grimes, Nantes, Bastille Opéra, Tosca, Gurrelieder, City of Birmingham Symphony Orchestra, Flanders Festival, Handel's Chandos Anthems, Liège, Der Kaiser von Atlantis; season 1995 as Bartolo in Figaro at the Bermuda Festival, Sarastro in Magic Flute at Nantes, Purcell's King Arthur in Europe and Buenos Aires; sang Araspe in Handel's Tolomeo at Halle 1996. *Recordings include:* King Arthur, Poppea, Dioclesian and Timon of Athens, The Wreckers, A Midsummer Night's Dream, Tolomeo. *Current Management:* c/o Robert Gilder and Co., N102, Westminster Business Square, 1–45 Durham Street, London, SE11 5JH, England. *Telephone:* (20) 7580-7758. *Fax:* (20) 7580-7739. *E-mail:* rgilder@robert-gilder.com; sam@robert-gilder.com. *Website:* www.robertgilder.com. *E-mail:* info@bannatynescott.co.uk. *Website:* www.bannatynescott.co.uk.

BANSE, Juliane; German singer (soprano); b. 10 July 1969, Tettnang, Baden-Württemberg; m. Christoph Poppen; three c. *Education:* trained as ballet dancer in Zürich, studied in Zürich and with Brigitte Fassbaender and Daphne Evangelatos in Munich. *Career:* debut as Pamina in Harry Kupfer's production of Die Zauberflöte at Komische Oper Berlin 1989; engagements at Komische Oper as Ilia and Susanna 1991–92; Pamina in Stuttgart and Brussels; Sophie in Rosenkavalier at Landestheater Salzburg and Zerlina at Glyndebourne 1994, 1995; Sophie, Susanna, Pamina and Zdenka; contract with Vienna State Opera 1993–; operatic repertoire includes Fiordiligi, Genoveva, Agathe, Elvira, Cunning Little Vixen, Ighino, Tatjana; concert repertoire includes all major oratorio repertoire; European concert performances with Orchestre de la Bastille, Paris, Mahler's 4th Symphony with Vienna Philharmonic Orchestra under Claudio Abbado; many lieder recitals throughout Europe; USA debut 1995 in St Louis and Indianapolis; sang in Henze's Raft of the Medusa at the Festival Hall, London 1997; season 1998 as Musetta at Cologne and Manon at the Deutsche Oper, Berlin; Mahler's 4th Symphony with Cleveland and Philadelphia Orchestra; Mahler's 2nd Symphony with the Vienna Philharmonic and Simon Rattle at the 1999 London Prom concerts; cr. the title role in Holliger's Schneewittchen, Zürich 1998; season 2000 as Pamina at the Vienna Staatsoper, and soloist in the premiere of Lukas Passion by Wolfgang Rihm (Stuttgart); Prof., Hochschule für Musik, Munich 2004–07. *Recordings include:* Lieder by Schoeck; Bach's Christmas Oratorio with the Windsbacher Knabenchor, Berg's Lulu Suite and Altenberg Lieder with Vienna Philharmonic Orchestra, Claudio Abbado, Mendelssohn's Paulus with H. Rilling; Don Giovanni, Glyndebourne (video) 1995, Piano Songs by Mozart and Debussy (with András Schiff) 2003, Kurtág's Kafka-Fragmente op. 24 (with András Keller) (Edison Classical Music Award for Contemporary Music 2007) 2005, Koechlin's vocal works with orchestra (Midem Classical Award for Vocal Recitals 2006), Opera Arias Per Amore, Tief in der Nacht. *Television:* Hunter's Bride (Der Freischütz). *Honours:* winner Kulturforum Competition, Munich 1989, Schubert Award, Vienna 1993, Münchener Merkur Theaterpreis 2003. *Current Management:* KünstlerSekretariat am Gasteig, Elisabeth Ehlers Lothar Schacke oHG, Rosenheimer Str. 52, 81669 Munich, Germany. *Telephone:* (89) 44488790. *Fax:* (89) 4489522. *E-mail:* team@ks-gasteig.de. *Website:* www.ks-gasteig.de. *Current Management:* Ulrike Wilckens, Ophelias PR, Lucile-Grahnstrasse, 81675 Munich, Germany. *Telephone:* (89) 45726153. *Fax:* (89) 45726171. *E-mail:* letter@ophelias-pr.com. *Website:* www.ophelias-pr.com; www.julianebanse.com.

BAPTISTE, Eric; French radio executive and music industry executive; *CEO, Society of Composers, Authors and Music Publishers of Canada (SOCAN).* *Education:* Institut d'études politiques, École nationale d'admin. *Career:* Gen. Man., Radio France International 1990–95; Exec. Pres. Musiques France Plus 1995–98; CEO Radio 95.2 Paris 1996–98; Pres. Radio Néo; Dir-Gen. Int. Confed. of Socs of Authors and Composers (CISAC) 1999–2010, Chair. 2014–; CEO Soc. of Composers, Authors and Music Publrs of Canada (SOCAN) 2010–; Chair. Vive la Radio asscn 1994–98; Chair. govt think-tank on digital convergence 2001–02. *Publications include:* Rapport sur les relations entre les diffuseurs télévisuels et les producteurs cinématographiques et audiovisuels 1989, L'infosphère: stratégies des médias et rôle de l'État 2000. *Honours:* Chevalier des Arts et des Lettres 2006. *Address:* Society of Composers, Authors and Music Publishers of Canada, 41 Valleybrook Drive, Toronto, ON M3B 2S6, Canada (office); CISAC Secretariat, 20–26 boulevard du Parc, 92200 Neuilly-sur-Seine, France. *Telephone:* (416) 442-3373 (Toronto) (office); 1-55-62-08-50 (Paris) (home). *Fax:* 1-55-62-08-60 (Paris) (home). *E-mail:* baptistee@socan.ca (office); eric@ericbaptiste.net. *Website:* www.socan.ca (office).

BÄR, Olaf; German singer (baritone) and academic; *Professor of Lieder Interpretation, Hochschule für Musik, Dresden*; b. 19 Dec. 1957, Dresden. *Education:* studied in Dresden. *Career:* sang in Dresden Kreuzchor 1967–76; prin. mem., Dresden State Opera–1991; British debut 1983, at Wigmore Hall; returned summer 1985; Covent Garden debut 1985, as Harlekin in Ariadne auf Naxos; Aix-en-Provence Festival 1986, in Ariadne; Die Zauberflöte at La Scala; Glyndebourne Festival 1987, as the Count in Capriccio; Aix 1988, as Guglielmo in Così fan tutte, conducted by Jeffrey Tate; concert performances in Europe and USA; US debut 1987, as Christus in the St Matthew Passion with the Chicago Symphony Orchestra conducted by Solti; tours of Australia 1989, 1993, Japan 1989, 1992; created roles in premieres of operas by Matthus 1985, and Mayer 1989; at Royal Opera Covent Garden sang Papageno 1991; Glyndebourne as Don Giovanni 1991; sang in Britten's War Requiem; Oliver in Capriccio, Opernhaus Zürich 1992; Marcello in La Bohème, Staatsoper Dresden 1992; Count in Le nozze di Figaro, Netherlands Opera Amsterdam 1993; US operatic debut Papageno, Chicago 1996; sang in Schubert's Alfonso und Estrella at the Vienna Festival 1997; Mozart's Count at Rome and Wolfram in Tannhäuser by Wagner at Dresden 1998; new production of Ariadne auf Naxos at Dresden 1999, Die Fledermaus at the Vienna Festival 1999; sang Froila in Schubert's Alfonso und Estrella at Zürich 2001; Die Fledermaus, Salzburg 2001; Spielman in Königskinder, Naples 2002, Der Ring des Nibelungen, Bayreuth 2002–04; Die Tote Stadt, Zürich 2003; Die Zauberflöte, Paris 2005; Euryanthe at Dresden 2006, From the House of the Death, Vienna, Amsterdam, Aix en Provence 2007, Capriccio, Paris 2007; currently Prof. of Lieder Interpretation, Hochschule für Musik, Dresden. *Films:* Hunter's Bride. *Recordings include:* Schumann Dichterliebe Op 48 and Liederkreis Op 39, Kerner-Lieder Op 35 and Liederkreis Op 24, Schubert Die schöne Müllerin, Winterreise and Schwanengesang, Wolf Mörike Lieder, Brahms Lieder, Beethoven Lieder, Mozart Arien, Bach Christmas Oratorio (with John Eliot Gardiner and the Monteverdi Choir), Christus in the St Matthew Passion, St John Passion, Fauré and Duruflé Requiems, Papageno in Mozart's Die Zauberflöte, Adam in Haydn's Creation and Harlekin in Strauss's Ariadne auf Naxos, Hugo Wolf: Italienisches Liederbuch (with Dawn Upshaw), Spanisches Liederbuch (with Ann-Sophie von Otter), Kurwenal in Tristan und Isolde. *Honours:* Robert-Schumann Preis der Stadt Zwickau 1998.

BARAN, Peter; Slovak cellist; b. 16 March 1950, Bratislava; m. Beata Baranova 1975, two s. *Education:* Music School, Bratislava, Conservatory, Bratislava, Hochschule für Musik und Darstellende Kunst, Vienna. *Career:* debut with Haydn's Cello Concerto in D major 1972; mem. Slovak Philharmonic Orchestra 1972–, Concertmaster and section leader 1989–; mem. Suchoň Quartet 1973–, Bratislava Chamber Harmony 1973–, Capella Istropolitana Chamber Orchestra 1982–, Bratislava String Trio 1985–; guest soloist, Kyoto Symphony Orchestra 1997–; guest mem. and soloist, Orchestra Ensemble Kanasawa, Japan 2004–; sometime mem. Kontrapunkte ensemble (20th-century music), Vienna; solo performances include Concerto for two celli (Handel) with Slovak Philharmonic Orchestra 1984, Symphonia Concertante (Haydn) with Slovak Chamber Orchestra 1985, Cello Concerto op 33 (Saint-Saëns) with Slovak Philharmonic Orchestra 1985, Concerto for string trio and orchestra (C. Stamitz) 1987, Quatuor pour la fin du temps (Messiaen) at BHS Festival 1987, Brahms Double Concerto and Sonata da Camera and Orchestra (Martinů) both with Slovak Philharmonic Orchestra 1993, Don Quixote with Slovak Philharmonic 1997; Slovak and Austrian radio broadcasts include 'Hunt' Quartet (Mozart), Cello Concerto in C major (Haydn), Concerto in C (Korngold) 2009; for television Sonata in F major (op 99, Brahms), String Trio Serenade (Dohnányi), Divertimento (Mozart), Trio in G major (Hummel), Little Trio (A. Moyzes), Ernest Bloch, Schelomo, Hebraic Rhapsody for violoncello and orchestra; regular chamber cycles at Salzburg Festival; mem. Slovak Music Union, Musicians' Union, Japan. *Recordings:* Vivaldi: Cello Concerto in A minor, Concerto in G minor for 2 celli; Beethoven: Septet, op 20; String Trio in G major by Hummel; Clarinet Quartet E flat, J. N. Hummel and Concerto for string trio and orchestra, C. Stamitz; Concerto No. 1 G Major by C. Stamitz, Vivaldi: Famous Concerti, Vivaldi: Favourite Concerti. *Address:* c/o Slovak Philharmonic Orchestra, Medená 3, 81601 Bratislava, Slovakia (office).

BARANOWSKI, Marcin; Polish violinist and academic; *Professor, Paderewski Academy of Music;* b. 30 Nov. 1961, Poznań; m. Monika Rosenkiewicz 2000. *Education:* Acad. of Music, Poznań. *Career:* debut with State Philharmonic Orchestra playing Szymanowski Violin Concerto, Poznań 1984; mem. Amadeus Chamber Orchestra 1981–2005, leader of second violins 1995; concerts in most of Europe and in USA, Canada, Mexico, Brazil, Japan, Kuwait and Taiwan; radio and TV appearances; mem. Collegium Musicorum Posnaniensium early music ensemble 2002–; Prof., Paderewski Acad. of Music, Poznań 1992–, also teaches at Nowowiejskiego Acad. of Music, Bydgoszcz; master classes in Poland, Germany and Austria. *Recordings:* more than 20 recordings; with Amadeus Chamber Orchestra 1989, 1993, with New Polish String Quartet 1994. *Honours:* Third Prize, Int. Chamber Music Competition, Łódź 1983, Award of Ministry of Culture 1992. *Address:* Ignacy Jan Paderewski Academy of Music, ul. Święty Marcin 87, 61-808 Poznań (office); Rysia 10, 61-066 Poznań, Poland (home). *Telephone:* 60-3137399 (mobile) (office). *E-mail:* marcin.baranowski1@neostrada.pl (home); *Website:* marcinbaranowski.com.pl.

BARANTSCHIK, Alexander; Russian violinist; *Concertmaster, San Francisco Symphony Orchestra;* b. 1953, Leningrad. *Education:* Leningrad Conservatory; studied with Prof. Waiman. *Career:* gave concerts in Russia, then emigrated 1979, becoming Leader of the Bamberg Symphony Orchestra; Leader, Radio Philharmonic Orchestra of The Netherlands 1982; solo engagements with leading orchestras in Germany, The Netherlands, UK and Hungary; appearances in Russia with Kazan Symphony and Leningrad Philharmonic; performed Sibelius Concerto with London Symphony Orchestra in Spain 1987, Prokofiev's 1st Violin Concerto in USA and London 1989–90; Leader, London Symphony Orchestra 1989–2001, played Tchaikovsky Violin Concerto with orchestra 1991, Bach on tour to USA 1991,

Brahms Double Concerto at the Barbican 1997; Concertmaster, San Francisco Symphony Orchestra 2001–; performed as soloist in Mendelssohn Violin Concerto, Bach Concerto No. 3 for Two Violins, Schnittke Violin Concerto No. 4, Mozart Violin Concerto No. 3, Brahms Double Concerto for Violin and Cello, Britten Double Concerto, Prokofiev's Violin Concerto No. 1 in D Major, Op. 19 and all the Bach Brandenburg concertos; premiered works by André Previn and Viktor Kissine; as a chamber musician, has performed with Mstislav Rostropovich, Maxim Vengerov and Yuri Bashmet; mem. collegiate faculty, San Francisco Conservatory of Music. *Honours:* Winner, Int. Violin Competition, Sion 1980. *Address:* San Francisco Symphony Orchestra, Davies Symphony Hall, San Francisco, CA 94102, USA (office). *Telephone:* (415) 503-6200 x6566 (office). *E-mail:* barantschik@comcast.net (office).

BARBACINI, Paolo; Italian singer (tenor) and artist manager; b. 20 Nov. 1946, Reggio Emilia. *Career:* has sung throughout Italy in operas by Mozart and Rossini, notably Don Giovanni, Il Re Pastore, Cenerentola, Il Turco in Italia, Adina and Aureliano in Palmira; La Scala Milan from 1980, in Falstaff and Figaro and on tour to Tokyo and Sofia; has sung in La Pietra del Paragone for the Israel Festival, Il Turco in Italia in Aix and Rossini's Elisabetta in Turin and on tour to the USA, Pang in Turandot at Macerata, Bardolph in Falstaff; modern repertoire includes Manzoni's Doctor Faustus (premiere, at La Scala, 1985), Wozzeck, Orff's Catulli Carmina and the premiere of Bussotti's L'Ispirazione, Doctor in Penderecki's Devils of Loudun; voice coach, Teatro Romolo Velli, Reggio Emilia 1998–2003; numerous recordings of opera and sacred music; founder, Paolo Barbacini Artist Management. *Address:* Paolo Barbacini Artist Management, Via Pansa 47, 42100 Reggio Emilia, Italy (office). *Telephone:* (348) 2657958 (office). *E-mail:* paolo@paolobarbacini.org (office). *Website:* www.paolobarbacini.org (office).

BARBAUX, Christine; French singer (soprano); b. 1955, Saint-Mande. *Education:* Paris Conservatoire. *Career:* debut at Strasbourg, as Despina, 1977; sang Barbarina in Le nozze di Figaro in Paris, 1978, Vienna and Salzburg under Karajan; further engagements in Geneva in The Love of Three Oranges, 1984; Théâtre de la Monnaie, Brussels, as Servilia in La Clemenza di Tito and Sophie in Rosenkavalier, 1982, 1986, Aix-en-Provence as Sophie, Amsterdam and Norina, 1988, Salzburg Festival as Servilia, 1988; other roles include Ophelia in Hamlet by Thomas, Gilda, and Blanche Force in Les Dialogues des Carmélites; sang Alice Ford in Falstaff at Bonn, 1991; sang Contesse Fedora in Donizetti's Gli Esiliati di Siberia at Montpellier, 1999. *Recordings include:* Werther and Pelléas et Mélisande; Fauré's Pénélope; Le nozze di Figaro.

BARBER, Graham David, BA, MMus, FRCO, ARNCM; British organist, harpsichordist, pianist and conductor; *Professor of Performance Studies, University of Leeds;* b. 30 Dec. 1948, London; m. Dianne Mackay 1990; one d. *Education:* University of East Anglia, Royal Northern College of Music. *Career:* debut, Royal Festival Hall, London 1978; int. concert organist; frequent BBC radio broadcasts as organist, mainly featuring German Baroque music and Max Reger; Lecturer in Music, Univ. of Leeds 1981–98, Prof. of Performance Studies 1998–; Chorus Master, Leeds Philharmonic Soc. 1983–92; Curator, Historic Schulze Organ, St Bartholomew's Church, Armley 1986–; Chorus Master, Sheffield Philharmonic Chorus 1987–97; Tutor in Organ Studies, Royal Northern Coll. of Music 1995–2000; Vice-Patron, Percy Whitlock Trust; Chair. of Trustees, Royal Coll. of Organists 2008–10; mem. Incorporated Soc. of Musicians, BIOS, ABC, Karg Elert Soc. (pres. 1998–), Incorporated Asscn of Organists. *Recordings include:* Johann Gottfried Walther Organ Works (Reid Concert Hall, Edinburgh), Franz Schmidt: Organ Works, English Romantic at Truro Cathedral, Bach Neumeister Chorales and Early Organ Works Vol. 1, Vol. 2, Organ Music from Salisbury Cathedral, The Sandtner Organ at Villingen Münster, The Klais Organ at Altenberg Dom, Complete Organ Works of Percy Whitlock (three vols). *Publications:* contrib. to Musical Times 1984, Cambridge Companion to the Organ 1998. *Honours:* Limpus and F. J. Reed Prizes, NESTA Fellowship 2006–09. *Telephone:* (7891) 699959 (home). *E-mail:* graham.barber1@btinternet.com (home); g.d.barber@leeds.ac.uk (office). *Website:* www.grahambarber.org.uk.

BARBER, Kimberly, BMus; Canadian singer (mezzo-soprano) and academic; *Associate Professor of Voice, Wilfrid Laurier University;* b. 21 Dec. 1959, Guelph, Ont.; d. of John Montgomery Barber and Carolyn Madeline Barber; m. Markus Philipp 1991; two d. *Education:* Univ. of Toronto (also Diploma in Operatic Performance). *Career:* professional debut singing Hansel in Hansel and Gretel for Calgary Opera 1985; performed with Frankfurt Opera 1989–94; has sung widely in Canada, USA and Europe in travesti roles by Mozart, Handel, Rossini and Strauss, including title role in Handel's Xerxes for Canadian Opera Co. and Ariodante for Paris Opera; other roles include Massenet's Charlotte in Werther, Nicklausse in Les Contes d'Hoffmann and Lazuli in L'Etoile, Strauss's Composer, Hermia, Ramiro in La Finta Giardiniera, Dorabella, Cherubino, Rosina, Pauline in The Gambler, Nerone in Agrippina, Annio in La Clemenza di Tito, Erika in Vanessa, Concepción in L'heure espagnole; created role of Jessica in John Estacio's Frobisher and Grandmother/Caroline in John Burge's The Auction; performed in Canadian premieres of Heggie's Dead Man Walking, Blitzstein's Regina and Adamo's Little Women; has appeared in concert with the Chicago, Toronto and Cincinnati Symphonies, London Symphony, Accademia di Santa Cecilia, Mostly Mozart Orchestra, Minnesota Orchestra, St Paul Chamber Orchestra; major companies performed with: Paris Opera, New York City Opera, Chicago Lyric Opera, Seattle Opera, ENO, Grand Théâtre de Genève, Frankfurt Opera, Deutsche Oper am Rhein (Düsseldorf), Canadian Opera Co.,

Vancouver, Montreal, Calgary and Edmonton Operas, Opera Zuid (Holland); Assoc. Prof. of Voice, Wilfrid Laurier Univ. (WLU) 2002–, Coordinator of Opera Programme; Founding mem. L'accordéoniste ensemble 2008–. *Radio includes:* multiple broadcasts on CBC Radio (Saturday Afternoon at the Opera, Two New Hours, numerous recital broadcasts), NPR Broadcasts (New York Festival of Song). *Recordings include:* Cincinnati Pops, The Sound of Music 1988, A Village Romeo and Juliet 1990, American (Day) Dreams 1995, Concepción in L'heure espagnole (with André Previn) 1999, Faustina Bordoni: Portrait of a Prima Donna 2005, title role in Handel's Rinaldo 2006, L'accordéoniste (with own ensemble) 2009, Florent Schmitt's Le petit elfe 2011. *Honours:* Career Devt Grant, Canada Council for the Arts 1988, Merit Award, WLU 2004, 2008, 2012, Strategic Initiatives Grant, WLU 2007, 2012, Centennial Grant, WLU 2010, Kitchener-Waterloo Arts Fund Grant 2009, CD recording grant, WLU 2009. *Current Management:* c/o Dean Artists Management, 204 St George Street, Toronto, ON M5R 2N5, Canada. *Telephone:* (416) 969-7300 (home). *Fax:* (416) 969-7969 (home). *E-mail:* info@deanartists.com. *Website:* www.deanartists.com. *E-mail:* kbarber@wlu.ca. *Website:* www.accordeoniste.ca; www.kimberlybarber.com.

BARBERA, René; American singer (tenor); b. (Erich Rene Barbera), 18 March 1984, Laredo, Tex.; s. of Miguel Barbera, Jr and Graciela Barbera; m. Anna Michelle Barbera (née Cypher). *Education:* North Carolina School of the Arts, American Inst. of Vocal Arts, Graz, Austria, Vocal Arts Symposium, Colorado Springs, Univ. of Texas, San Antonio, Merola Opera Program, Ryan Opera Center. *Career:* began singing aged 10 as boy soprano in San Antonio Boys' Choir; won Metropolitan Opera Nat. Council Auditions 2008; Young Artist with San Francisco Opera Merola Opera Program 2008, with Florida Grand Opera 2008–09, with Lyric Opera of Chicago Ryan Opera Center 2009–12; performances as a leading tenor at numerous opera houses worldwide, including Lyric Opera of Chicago, San Francisco Opera, Canadian Opera Company, Ravinia Festival, Paris Opera, Teatro San Carlo, Seattle Opera, Los Angeles Opera, Santa Fe Opera, Rome Opera, Rossini Opera Festival. *Roles include:* with Lyric Opera of Chicago: Edgardo in Lucia di Lammermoor 2011, Ernesto in Don Pasquale 2012; with Ravinia Festival: Tamino in Die Zauberflöte 2012; with Vancouver Opera: Count Almaviva in Il Barbiere di Siviglia 2012; with Canadian Opera Company: Rinuccio in Gianni Schicchi 2012; with Washington Concert Opera: Elvino in La Sonnambula 2012; with Michigan Opera Theater: Count Almaviva in Il Barbiere di Siviglia 2012; with Seattle Opera: Don Ramiro in La Cenerentola 2013; with Los Angeles Opera: Don Ramiro in La Cenerentola 2013; with Santa Fe Opera: Rodrigo di Dhu in La Donna del Lago 2013; with Melbourne Symphony Orchestra and Seattle Symphony: Tenor Soloist in Verdi's Messa da Requiem 2013; with Opera Nat. de Paris: Arturo in I Puritani 2013; with Teatro San Carlo: Count Almaviva in Il Barbiere di Siviglia 2013; with Opera Nat. de Paris: Almaviva in Il Barbiere di Siviglia 2014; with San Francisco Opera: La Cenerentola/ Les Troyens/ Il Barbiere di Siviglia 2014–15. *Honours:* First Place, Heafner/Williams Vocal Competition 2006, winner, Sullivan Foundation Award 2011, Placido Domingo Operalia World Opera Competition First Prize, Zarzuela Prize and Audience Prize 2011. *Website:* renebarbera.com.

BARBONI YANS, Geneviève, PhD; Italian stage designer, costume designer, musicologist, producer and singing teacher; *Teacher and Manager, Centro Canto Cesenatico;* b. 26 Dec. 1947, Montegnée, Belgium. *Education:* Univ. of Liège, Belgium, Univ. of Reims, France. *Career:* debut as opera producer, at Opera House, Liège, Belgium; broadcast: introductions to concerts, RTB, Liège 1969; staging (set, costumes): Walloon Gala, Li Voyèdje di Tchaudfontaine, opera by J.-N. Hamal, Liège 1970; Ravel, ballet gala, Grand Théâtre, Nancy 1975; staging for TV and radio: Evolution of the Opera in Emilia-Romagna, RAI Bologna 1982; Man. Centro Canto Cesenatico, specialised services for the education, re-education and improvement of the speaking and singing voice 1991–; transcriptions of operas: Cavalli's L'Hipermestra, Stradella's La Circe; mem. Voice Foundation, Philadelphia 1996–, Italian Soc. of Phonatricians and Logopedists 1995–2000. *Recordings include:* Li Voyèdje di Tchaudfontaine (video) 1970. *Publications include:* Un opéra de Francesco Cavalli, pour la cour de Florence: L'Hipermestra 1979, Contributo alla storia della gestione degli spettacoli nel Ducato Estense dal 1650 al 1790 1994; contribs to various Italian magazines and journals. *Address:* Via Viola 13, 47042 Cesenatico, Italy (office). *Telephone:* (0547) 672477 (office). *Fax:* (0547) 672477 (office). *E-mail:* info@centrocanto.com (office). *Website:* www.centrocanto.com (office).

BARCELLONA, Daniela; Italian singer (mezzo-soprano); b. 28 March 1969, Trieste; m. Alessandro Vitiello. *Education:* studied in Trieste. *Career:* early appearances at Spoleto, Florence, Bordeaux, Rome, Wexford Festival and Geneva; has sung at La Scala, Genoa, Naples, Rome Opera, Santa Cecilia, Pesaro, Turin, Trieste, Palermo, Florence, Ravenna Festival, Verona, Spoleto Festival, Parma; concerts include the Verdi Requiem in Dresden, Rome, Berlin and elsewhere, Roméo et Juliette by Berlioz at Barbican Hall, London 2000, Beethoven's Missa Solemnis at the Concertgebouw and Rossini's Stabat Mater; New York Met debut 2001, in a Verdi Gala, returning for Bellini's Norma; also sang at Paris Opéra, Munich, Wien Staatsoper, Dresden, Salzburg Festival, Madrid, Barcelona, Seville, Valencia, Amsterdam, Marseille, Montepellier, Las Palmas, Bilbao, San Sebastian, Tokyo. *Recordings include:* La Fedeltà Premiata by Haydn, Verdi Requiem, Tancredi, Biance e Falliero, Ginevra di Scozia. *Honours:* Opera Actual magazine Premio de la Mejor Mezzo-Soprano 2005, Rossini d'Oro. *Current Management:* Ernesto Palacio Artist Management, Via Donizetti 11, Lurano (BG), Italy. *Telephone:* (035) 800645. *Fax:* (035) 4877767. *E-mail:* ernestopalacio@ernestopalacio.com. *Website:* www.ernestopalacio.com; www.danielabarcellona.it (office).

BARCLAY, Yvonne, DipMusEd, DRSAMD; British singer (soprano); b. Ayrshire, Scotland. *Education:* Royal Scottish Acad., Glasgow and Nat. Opera Studio, London. *Career:* appearances with the Royal Opera, Covent Garden as Frasquita in Carmen, Mozart's Barbarina and Papagena, High Priestess in Aïda and Javotte in Manon; ENO as Lucia in The Rape of Lucretia, Echo in Ariadne auf Naxos, Sandman in Hansel and Gretel, Euridice in Monteverdi's Orfeo and Caroline in The Fairy Queen; Opera North as Eurydice in Orpheus in the Underworld; Glyndebourne Touring Opera as Blondchen in Die Entführung and Mélisande in Pelléas et Mélisande; Glyndebourne Festival Opera as Emmie in Albert Herring; for Scottish Opera, roles in Die Zauberflöte, Hansel and Gretel, L'Egisto by Cavalli and Death in Venice; English Bach Festival as Belinda in Dido and Aeneas; further roles include Blondchen and Gretel at Leipzig Opera and First Niece in Peter Grimes at Paris Châtelet, and in Lisbon and Bremen; frequent concert appearances and broadcasts. *Recordings:* HMS Pinafore (as Josephine, for D'Oyly Carte Opera), Peter Grimes (as First Niece) (Grammy Award). *Address:* c/o Royal Opera House, Bow Street, Covent Garden, London, WC2E 9DD, England (office). *Telephone:* (20) 7240-1200 (office). *Website:* www.roh.org.uk (office).

BARCZA, Peter; Canadian singer (baritone); b. 23 June 1949, Stockholm, Sweden. *Education:* Univ. of Toronto, L'École d'Art Lyrique, Paris. *Career:* began career with Canadian Opera Company, notably as Guglielmo in Così fan Tutte, Papageno in The Magic Flute, Enrico in Lucia di Lammermoor, Marcello and Germont; guest appearances at Memphis, New Orleans, Seattle and the New York City Opera; European appearances include Monteverdi's Ulisse at Bad Hersfeld; other roles include Rossini's Figaro, Malatesta in Don Pasquale, Luna, Ping in Turandot, Valentin in Faust, Rangoni in Boris Godunov, Marcello in La Bohème, Filippo in Beatrice di Tenda. *Current Management:* Ludwig Brunner Management, 165 West 66th Street, Suite 15L, New York, NY 10023, USA. *Telephone:* (212) 721-6541. *Fax:* (212) 721-6547. *E-mail:* lbmgmt@aol.com. *Website:* www.peterbarcza.com.

BARDEN, Mark; American composer; b. 1980, Cleveland, Ohio. *Education:* Oberlin Conservatory, Freiburg Hochschule für Musik, Germany, Goldsmiths Univ. of London, UK, studied composition with Lewis Nielsen, Mathias Spahlinger and Jörg Widmann; private studies with Rebecca Saunders in Berlin. *Career:* commissions from groups including Ensemble Intercontemporain, Ensemble Recherche, Freiburg Baroque Orchestra, Witten Festival for New Chamber Music, Donaueschinger Musiktage, Darmstadt New Music Courses, Akad. der Künste Berlin, Radio France, Klangforum Wien; music has been performed in Europe, North America and Israel by Collegium Novum Zürich, Ensemble Nikel, hand werk, Elison, Ensemble Mosaik, KNM Berlin, Wet Ink, ekmeles, Zafraan Ensemble, Mivos Quartet. *Compositions include:* Kairos incised, sextet 2007, Unterdruck, for solo prepared harp 2007, die Haut Anderer, for e.h., piano solo and optional video 2008, Gauze I, nonet 2009, Personæ, for bass flute and bass clarinet 2009, Gauze II, nonet 2010, Viscera, for viola, cello, double bass 2010, Anatomy, large orchestra and percussion solo 2010, Alam (Pain), concert installation for ensemble & electronics 2011, Machine, open instrumentation 2011, Two masks, open instrumentation 2011, Tenebrae, octet for modern and Baroque instruments 2011, — caul —, for ensemble 2011–12, Flesh | veil for octet 2012, Witness, for electric guitar, soprano sax, percussion, piano 2012, Puls, for solo percussion 2012, A tearing of vision, for large ensemble 2012, Nocturne, string quartet 2013, Harvest, quartet 2013–14, Five monoliths, for ensemble 2014, Viscosity, amplified string trio with volume pedals 2014, Gehören, for chamber orchestra 2015. *Honours:* Thomas J. Watson Fellowship, Oscar and Vera Ritter Foundation Fellowship, grants from Darmstadt New Music Courses and Akad. der Künste Berlin, First Prize, Concertare int. composition competition 2010, Ernst von Siemens Foundation Composer's Award 2015. *E-mail:* mark.j.barden@gmail.com. *Website:* www.mark-barden.com.

BARDON, Patricia; Irish singer (mezzo-soprano); b. 1964, Dublin; m. Nicholas Sears; one s. *Education:* Coll. of Music, Dublin, under Veronica Dunne. *Career:* operatic engagements include Tancredi, Arsace in Semiramide at La Fenice, Venice; Carmen, Hamburg Staatsoper, WNO, Scottish Opera; Penelope in Il Ritorno d'Ulisse at the Maggio Musicale Florence; Orlando in New York, Paris and Lyon; Smeaton in Anna Bolena at San Francisco; Amastris in Xerxes at the Munich Staatsoper; Juno in Sémele at Innsbruck; 3rd Lady in Die Zauberflöte at Verona; Azucena in Il Trovatore; and roles in Rigoletto, Mosè in Egitto, Guillaume Tell and Mefistofele for Royal Opera at Barbican Hall; concert engagements have taken her to USA, Canada, Japan and all major European Centres including La Scala, La Monnaie (Brussels), BBC Proms London, Edinburgh, Aix en Provence and Montreux Festivals, Concertgebouw, Amsterdam and Schauspielhaus, Berlin; season 2000–01 as Erda in The Rhinegold, for ENO, and Ursule in Béatrice et Bénédict for Netherlands Opera; Cornelia in Giulio Cesare at Glyndebourne 2005; Baba the Turk in The Rake's Progress at Covent Garden, Rosmira in Partenope and Maurya in Riders to the Sea for ENO 2008. *Recordings include:* Orlando, Elijah, Olga in Eugene Onegin and Giovanna in Rigoletto, Handel's Messiah. *Honours:* prizewinner Cardiff Singer of the World Competition 1983. *Current Management:* c/o Shirley Thomson, Harrison Parrott Ltd, 5-6 Albion Court, Albion Place, London, W6 0QT, England. *Telephone:* (20) 7313-3573. *Fax:* (20) 7221-5042. *E-mail:* shirley.thomson@harrisonparrott.co.uk. *Website:* www.harrisonparrott.com.

BARENBOIM, Daniel, FRCM; Israeli/Palestinian pianist and conductor; *Music Director, Teatro alla Scala, Milan*; b. 16 Nov. 1942, Buenos Aires, Argentina; s. of Enrique Barenboim and Aida Barenboim (née Schuster); m. 1st Jacqueline du Pré 1967 (died 1987); m. 2nd Elena Bashkirova 1988; two s. *Career:* studied piano with his father and other musical subjects with Nadia Boulanger, Edwin Fischer and Igor Markevitch; debut in Buenos Aires aged seven; played Bach D Minor Concerto with orchestra at Salzburg Mozarteum aged nine; has played in Europe regularly 1954–; yearly tours of USA 1957–; has toured Japan, Australia and S America; has played with or conducted London Philharmonic, Philharmonia Orchestra, London Symphony Orchestra, Royal Philharmonic, Chicago Symphony Orchestra, New York Philharmonic, Philadelphia Orchestra, Israel Philharmonic, Vienna Philharmonic, Berlin Philharmonic; frequently tours with English Chamber Orchestra and with them records for EMI (projects include complete Mozart Piano Concertos and late Symphonies); other recording projects include complete Beethoven Sonatas and Beethoven Concertos (with New Philharmonia Orchestra conducted by Klemperer); has appeared in a series of masterclasses on BBC TV; presented Festival of Summer Music on South Bank, London 1968, 1969; leading role in Brighton Festival 1967–69; appears regularly at Edinburgh Festival; conductor, Edinburgh Festival Opera 1973; Music Dir Orchestre de Paris 1975–89, Chicago Symphony Orchestra 1991–2006, Hon. Conductor for Life 2006–; Gen. Music Dir Deutsche Staatsoper, Berlin 1992– (Chief Conductor for Life Staatskapelle Berlin 2000–); projects with the late Edward Said, the West-Eastern Divan Workshop (Orchestra) 1999–; Music Dir and mem. Bd of Trustees, Barenboim-Said Foundation (which promotes music and co-operation through projects targeted at young Arabs and Israelis); Charles Eliot Norton Prof., Harvard Univ. 2006; Maestro Scaligero, La Scala, Milan 2006–11, Music Dir 2011–; debut with Metropolitan Opera 2008. *Publications include:* A Life in Music (jtly) 1991, Parallels and Paradoxes (with Edward W. Said) 2003, La Musica Sveglia il Tempo 2007, Everything is Connected 2008. *Honours:* Commdr, Légion d'honneur 2007, Grand Officer 2011, Hon. KBE 2011; Hon. DMus (Manchester) 1997, (Oxford) 2007; Beethoven Medal 1958, Paderewski Medal 1963, Beethoven Soc. Medal 1982, Prix de la Tolérance, Protestant Acad. of Tutzing 2002, Premio Príncipe de Asturias 2002, Grammy Award (for recording of Wagner's Tannhäuser) 2003, Wilhelm Furtwängler Prize (with Staatskapelle Berlin) 2003, Wolf Foundation Prize in Arts 2004, chosen to deliver Reith Lectures 2006, Zwickau Robert Schumann Prize 2006, Conductor of the Year, ECHO Klassik Awards 2006, Ernst von Siemens Prize 2006, Hessischer Peace Prize 2006, Goethe Medal 2007, Praemium Imperiale 2007, Royal Philharmonic Soc. Gold Medal 2008, Otto Hahn Peace Medal 2010, Edison Award for Lifetime Achievement 2011, ECHO Klassik Award for Lifetime Achievement 2012, BBC Music Magazine Award for Recording of the Year 2014 (for Elgar & Carter Concerti 2012). *Current Management:* c/o Opus 3 Artists, 470 Park Avenue South, 9th Floor North, New York, NY 10016, USA. *Telephone:* (212) 584-7500. *Fax:* (646) 300-8200. *E-mail:* info@opus3artists.com. *Website:* www.opus3artists.com. *Address:* Teatro alla Scala, Via Filodrammatici 2, 20121 Milan, Italy (office). *Telephone:* (02) 88791 (office). *E-mail:* danielbarenboim@hotmail.com. *Website:* www.teatroallascala.org (office); www.danielbarenboim.com.

BARGIELSKI, Zbigniew, PhD; Austrian (b. Polish) composer; *Professor and Head of Department of Composition and Theory of Music, Bydgoszcz Academy of Music*; b. 21 Jan. 1937, Lomza, Poland. *Education:* studies in piano at Lublin Conservatory, Warsaw Conservatory with Szeligowski, Music Acad., Katowice with Boleslaw Szabelski; composition studies with Nadia Boulanger in Paris and at Graz. *Career:* music critic and journalist; Pres. Young Polish Composers 1967–70; Sec. Polish Composers Asscn, Warsaw 1967–70; premiere of opera In a Small Country House (The Little Haunted Manor) at Warsaw Grand Theatre 1984; mem. Polish Composer's Asscn, Österreichischer Komponistenbund; Prof. and Head of Dept of Composition and Theory of Music, Bydgoszcz Acad. of Music, Poland 2002–; compositions have been performed throughout Europe, in USA, Australia and South America and at int. festivals for contemporary music including Warsaw-Autumn, Muzicki Biennale Zagreb, Festival de Paris, Steirischer Herbst, Graz, Austria, Leningrad Spring, Encontros Gulbenkian, Lisbon, Helsinki Festival, Tsumari Triennale, Festival de Strasbourg, World Music Festival, and others. *Compositions include:* Danton, or Some Scenes from the History of the Great French Revolution (opera) 1968–69, The Little Prince (musical tale) 1970, Alice in Wonderland (youth opera) 1972, Phantoms do not Lie (comic opera) 1981, Parades for orchestra 1965, Percussion Concerto 1975, Espace étrapé for orchestra 1973, Violin Concerto 1975, Ballads for wind and percussion 1976, String Quartet No. 1 1976, String Quarter No. 2 ('Primaverile') 1980, String Quartet No. 3 ('Still Life with a Scream') 1985, In Nobody's Land (oratorio) 1989, Requiem for orchestra 1991–92, Trigonalia for guitar, accordion, percussion and chamber orchestra 1994, String Quarter No. 4 ('Le temps ardent') 1994, Fountain of hope for alto saxophone and marimba 1995, Dance on the Verge of Light for chamber ensemble 1995, A la recherche du son perdu for flute 1996, Landscape of remembrance for violin, cello and piano 1996, A la espagnola for guitar 1996, Hierofania for five percussionists 1996, Forgotten – Regained for violin 1996, Slapstick for chamber orchestra 1997, Tango for chamber ensemble 1997, Shrine for an Anonymous Victim, (computer musiic) 1999, Light Cross (computer music) 2000, Towards Organic Geometry (computer music) 2001, String Quartet No 5 ('Le temps qui n'est plus) 2001, Music for Children for piano 2001–02, Le cristal flamboyant for harpsichord and tape 2002, Jeux à trois for three accordions 2003. *Recordings include:* works by Zbigniew Bargielski 1996. *Publications include:* Sacrum in der Musik 1996. *Honours:* Order 'Merit for Polish Culture' 1990; Officer's Cross, Order of Polonia Restituta 1995; First Prize, Young Polish Composers Competition (Warsaw) 1965, Arthur Malawski Composer's Competition Award, Kraków 1976, UNESCO Int. Composer's Rostrum Award, Paris 1981, 1995, Austrian Govt Grant of the German Academic Exchange Service 1985, First Prize, Int. Composers Competition 1986, Anton Benya Prize (Vienna) 2000, Polish Composers' Union Prize (Warsaw) 2001. *Address:* ul. Słowackiego 7, 85-008 Bydgoszcz, Poland (office). *Telephone:* (52) 3210582 (office). *Fax:* (52) 3210582. *Website:* www.amuz.bydgoszcz.pl.

BARKAUSKAS, Vytautas Pranas Marius; Lithuanian composer and academic; *Professor of Composition, Lithuanian Academy of Music and Theatre*; b. 25 March 1931, Kaunas; m. 1st Elena Tverijonaite 1954; m. 2nd Tiina Vabrit 1984; m. 3rd Svetlana Cherniavska 1991; one s. one d. *Education:* Vilnius Pedagogical Inst., Lithuanian State Conservatory, Vilnius. *Career:* accompanist, Vilnius Coll. of Music 1954–58; Instructor, House of the People's Creative Work of the Republic 1958–61; Prof. of Theory, Composition, Lithuanian State Acad. of Music, Vilnius 1961–; mem. Union of Composers, Lithuania. *Compositions include:* seven symphonies, 1962, 1971, 1979, 1984, 1986, 2001, 2011; Intimate Composition for oboe and 12 strings 1968, Three Aspects for symphony orchestra 1969, Contrast Music for flute, cello and percussion 1969, Gloria Urbi for organ 1972, Prelude and Fugue for chorus 1974, Legend About Love (opera) 1975, Salute Your Land oratorio-mystery 1976, Sonatas for violin and piano, No. 1 Sonata subita 1976, No. 2 Dialogue 1978, No. 3 1984, Open Window for mezzo-soprano and five instruments 1978, Rondo capriccioso 1981, Concerto for viola and chamber orchestra 1981, The Sun (symphonic picture) 1983, Duo Sonata for violin, viola 1984, Sonata for two pianos and three performers 1984, Sextet 1985, Cantus Amores (cantata) 1986, Sonata for double bass and piano 1987, Hope (oratorio) 1988, The Second Legend of Čiurlionis for piano 1988, Credo for organ 1989, Concerto for piano and orchestra 1992, Konzertstück für Orchester No. 1 1992, Concert Suite for cello, piano 1993, Reminiscence for harpsichord 1993, Intimate Music, op. 100 for flute, percussion 1993, Divertimento for piano six hands 1993, The Third Legend of Ciurlionis for piano 1993, Inspiration for organ 1994, Konzertstück No. 2 für Orchester 1994, Trio à deux for violin, viola, cello 1995, Allegro Brillante for two pianos 1996, Modus vivendi for violin, cello and piano 1996, Scherzo for violin and chamber orchestra 1996, Duo for guitar and piano 1997, Toccamento No. 2 for viola solo, violin, cello and piano 1998, Here and Now for symphonic orchestra 1998, Symphony No. 6 2001, Jeux, concerto for violin and symphony orchestra 2002–03, Agnus Dei for mixed choir and organ 2003, Summer 2004, Nido 2004, Duo concertante for violin and symphony orchestra 2004, Lune à l'Aube d'Été for coloratura soprano and eight cellos 2004, Silhouette for violin solo 2004, Opus 126 in E for string orchestra 2005, Echoes for percussion 2005, Contactus for clarinet, piano and string quartet 2006, Flashes for piano 2007, Impulses for flute, cello and piano 2007, Intermezzo Italiano for harp 2007, Trio Concertante for three pianos and symphony orchestra 2009, Symphony No. 7 (Competition Prize, Lithuanian Composers' Union 2011) 2010, Three Fragments for viola and violoncello 2011, Avanti for strings orchestra 2011, Seven Little Clouds (children's pieces for piano) 2012, Duettissimo for violin and cello 2013. *Recordings include:* Ars vivendi 1992, Cavalli 1993, Proud Sound 1995, Lithuanian New Music series 1997, Ondine 1997, Triton 2002, AVIE 2005, AVIE 2008. *Honours:* Médaille d'honneur de St-Nazaire, France 2002, Order of the Grand Duke of Lithuania Gediminas 2007; Lithuanian Theatre Festival Prize 1967, Lithuanian State Prize 1972, Sinfonia Baltica Int. Composers' Competition Prize 2001, Lithuanian Nat. Prize for Art 2003, Lithuanian Composers' Union Competition Prize for best chamber work 2005. *Current Management:* c/o A. Mickeviciaus Street 29, Vilnius 08117, Lithuania. *Telephone:* (5) 2123027. *E-mail:* linas@mic.lt. *Address:* Šaltiniu Street 11/15 b. 44, Vilnius 03214, Lithuania (home). *Telephone:* (5) 2162813 (home). *Fax:* (5) 2162813 (home). *E-mail:* svetvyt@takas.lt.

BARKER, Cheryl; Australian singer (soprano); b. 22 April 1960, Sydney; m. Peter Coleman-Wright; one s. *Education:* studied with Joan Hammond. *Career:* appearances as the Governess in The Turn of the Screw, Princess in Rusalka, Oksana in Rimsky's Christmas Eve, with ENO 1989–; sang Cherubino and Marzelline, Glyndebourne Touring Opera 1989; sang Mozart's Annio, Tatiana in Eugene Onegin and Adina, L'Elisir d'amore, Scottish Opera 1991–94; sang Tatiana at Sydney 1994; Violetta at Auckland 1995; season 1996 in The Midsummer Marriage at Covent Garden and as Suor Angelica at Antwerp; season 1997–98 as Madama Butterfly for Opera Australia, Falla's Salud at Brussels, Liu in Turandot and Butterfly for ENO; season 2000–01 as Madama Butterfly and Suor Angelica at ENO and Donna Elvira for Australian Opera; title role in Tosca for ENO 2002; premiere of Jake Heggie's The End of the Affair at Houston 2004; Salome for ENO 2005; Katya Kabanova in Geneva and with WNO; Jenůfa and Emilia Marty in Makropoulos Case for ENO 2006; tours with Musica Viva 2005, 2008; title role in Tosca for Opera Australia 2013. *Recordings include:* Puccini=Passion 2004, La Bohème, Katya Kabanova 2006, Pure Diva: A Tribute to Joan Hammond 2010. *Honours:* Hon. DMus (Victorian Coll. of the Arts). *Current Management:* c/o Melba Recordings, PO Box 415, Elwood, VIC 3184, Australia. *Telephone:* (3) 9534-5004 (office). *Website:* www.cherylbarker.be.

BARKER, Paul Alan, GGSM, MMus, PhD; British composer and academic; b. 1 July 1956, Cambridge, England; m. 1st Christine Susan Barker 1977 (divorced 1991); m. 2nd Maria Huesca 1992. *Education:* Guildhall School of Music, Durham Univ., Hertfordshire Univ. *Career:* boy chorister, Jesus Coll.,

Cambridge; Visiting Lecturer, City Univ. 1978–83; Musical Dir, Dancers Anonymous 1979–86; Assoc. Lecturer, Kingsway-Princeton Coll. 1984–90; Artistic Dir, Modern Music Theatre Troupe 1985–94; Composer-in-Residence, West Sussex 1990–94; Musical Dir, Proteus Theatre and Spirals Theatre 1993–98, European Youth Theatre 1994–98; Composer-in-Association, London Mozart Players 1994–96; founder and Artistic Dir, Optemus 2002–05; Resident Composer, Djerassi Resident Artist Program, San Francisco July 2005; Prof. of Music Theatre, Central School of Speech & Drama; numerous commissions worldwide; mem. exec. cttee APC; mem. PCS cttee ISM. *Compositions include:* operas: The Marriages Between Zones 3, 4 and 5 1985, Phantastes 1986, The Pillow Song 1988, La Malinche 1989, Albergo Empedocles 1990, Prologue 1992, The Sorceress' Tale 1995, Dirty Tricks 1997, Stone Angels 1999, The Mechanical Operation of the Spirit 2000, Songs Between Words 2004, Nye Tand, Eh? 2005, El Gallo 2009, Hello, Mr Darwin! 2010; orchestral works: Fantasy on Four Notes 1978, Harlequin Concerto 1988, Three Songs for Sylvia 1994, Concerto for violin and orchestra 1996; chamber music: Barbican Fanfare 1979, The Pied Piper of Hamelin 1980, Excalibur 1994, Concerto for Eight 1995, Clarinet Quintet: In Memoriam 2004, Death & Resurrection 2005, Interludes 2008, Kabara's Lullaby II 2012; other: ten contemporary dance scores for European companies; instrumental ensemble, vocal and choral and works; music for theatre, children's operas and educational music. *Recordings:* Entre Palabras 2005, Turquoise Swans 2008, El Gallo 2011. *Publications:* Devised and Collaborative Theatre 2002, Composing for Voice 2004. *Honours:* hon. assoc. mem. OMTF, Royal Philharmonia Soc. Prize for Composition 1978. *Address:* Central School of Speech & Drama, Eton Avenue, London, NW3 3HY (office). *Website:* www.paulalanbarker.net.

BARKIN, Elaine Radoff, BA, MFA, PhD; American composer, academic and writer on music; b. 15 Dec. 1932, New York, NY; d. of Victor Radoff and Edith Radoff; m. George J. Barkin 1957; three s. *Education:* Queens Coll., Brandeis Univ., Berlin Hochschule für Musik, studied with Karol Rathaus, Irving Fine, Boris Blacher, Arthur Berger and Harold Shapero. *Career:* Asst to Co-Ed., Perspectives of New Music 1963–85; Lecturer in Music, Queens Coll. 1964–70, Sarah Lawrence Coll. 1969–70; Asst, later Assoc. Prof. of Music Theory, Univ. of Michigan 1970–74; Visiting Asst Prof., Princeton Univ. 1974; Assoc. Prof. of Composition and Theory, UCLA 1974–77, Prof. 1977–97; Co-founder Open Space Music 1989; guest lecturer at various colls and univs. *Compositions:* String Quartet 1969, Sound Play for violin 1974, String Trio 1976, Plein Chant for alto flute 1977, Ebb Tide for two vibraphones 1977, Two Emily Dickinson Choruses 1977, ...The Supple Suitor... for soprano and five players 1978, many improvised group and duo sessions on tape 1980–, De Amore (chamber mini-opera) 1980, Impromptu for violin, cello and piano 1981, Media Speak (theatre piece) 1981, At the Piano for piano 1982, for string quartet 1982, Quilt Piece (graphic score) for seven instruments 1984, On the Way to Becoming for four-track tape collage 1985, Demeter and Persephone for violin, tape, marimba and dancers 1986, three Rhapsodies for flutes and clarinet 1986, Encore for Javanese gamelan ensemble 1988, Out of the Air for basset horn and tape 1988, To Whom It May Concern for four-track tape collage and reader 1989, Legong Dreams for oboe 1990, Gamélange for harp and mixed gamelan band 1992, Five Tape Collages 1993, For My Friends' Pleasure for soprano and harp 1993, Lagu Kapal Kuning for Balinese gamelan ensemble 1996, Touching All Bases for electric bass, percussion and Balinese gamelan 1998, music for soloists and small ensembles 1974–1993, Poem for winds and percussion 1999, Song for Sarah for violin 2001, Ballade for violoncello 2002, Tambellan Suite for mallet percussion 2004, instrumental and vocal music 1977–2004, Four Midi Pieces 2005, Four Little Machine Pieces 2006, Suite for piano 2007, Three Pieces for Violin Duet 2008, Violin Duo 2008, XTET: Last Dance for Milton 2011. *Publications:* An Anthology, music, text and graphics, 1997, Audible Traces: gender, identity, music (co-ed.) 2000. *Honours:* Fulbright Award 1957, Nat. Endowment for the Arts Award 1975, 1979, Rockefeller Foundation Award 1980, Meet the Composer Award 1994. *Address:* Department of Music, 405 Hilgard Avenue, University of California, Los Angeles, CA 90095, USA (office). *E-mail:* elainerb@ucla.edu (office).

BARKL, Michael Laurence Gordon, BMus, DipEd, MMus, PhD, DCA, FTCL, AMusTCL; Australian composer and academic; *Head Teacher of Music, Illawarra Institute*; b. 9 Aug. 1958, Sydney, New South Wales; m. Sharyn Lee 1986; one d. *Education:* Sydney Conservatorium of Music, Trinity Coll. of Music, Univ. of New England, Univ. of Sydney, Deakin Univ., Univ. of Wollongong. *Career:* tutor, Univ. of New England 1982; Head Teacher of Music, Illawarra Inst. 1987–; comms from Seymour Group, Synergy, Elision, Duo Contemporain, Manly Art Gallery and Orange City Council. *Compositions include:* The Time, The Time for choir 1981, Voce di Testa and Voce di Petto for orchestra 1981–82, Chroma for harpsichord 1981, Drumming for piano 1983, Psychonaut for chorus 1983, Iambus for wind quintet and strings 1983, Ballade for six instruments 1984, Cabaret for orchestra 1985, Expressive and Ferocious for string quartet 1985, Backyard Swing for concert band 1986, Blues for clarinet and marimba 1986, The Laird of Drumblair for seven instruments 1987, Rondo for chamber orchestra 1988, Disco for percussion quartet 1989, Smoky for harpsichord 1997, Here... for clarinet, cello and piano 2008; electronic works: The Paradox of Pythagoras 2007, Music of the Spheres 2007, Music of Grace 2008. *Honours:* Hon. DipMus (Australian International Conservatorium of Music); Segnalata, Valentino Bucchi competition for Composition, Italy 1981, Frank Hutchens Prize 1982. *Address:* PO Box 1223, Wollongong, NSW 2500, Australia (office). *Telephone:* (2) 4229-0058 (office). *E-mail:* michael.barkl@det.nsw.edu.au (office). *Website:* www.australianmusiccentre.com.au/artist/barkl-michael.

BARLEY, Matthew; British cellist; b. 1965; m. Viktoria Mullova. *Education:* Guildhall School, London and Moscow Conservatoire. *Career:* debut, Shostakovich First Concerto with London Symphony Orchestra at Barbican Hall; guest principal with the LSO, London Philharmonic Orchestra, Philharmonia, RPO, London Sinfonietta; solo and chamber music engagements in North America, Asia, Australasia and throughout Europe; concertos with London Sinfonietta, Orchestra Internazionale d'Italia, Royal Scottish National Orchestra, Brno Symphony Orchestra, Athens Camerata, Hong Kong Sinfonietta, New Zealand Symphony Orchestra; festival appearances at Taranaki, New Zealand, WOMAD, Lucerne, Prague Autumn, Dijon, Koshigaya, Harrogate, Norwich, Dartington, Chester, Salisbury, City of London, Cheltenham; premieres of works by John Woolrich, Carl Vine, Peter Wiegold, Fraser Trainer, Detlev Glanert, Dave Maric, Deirdre Gribben; non-classical collaborations with Viktoria Mullova, Amjad Ali Khan, Julian Joseph, Django Bates and others; founder and Artistic Dir of performance and education group, Between the Notes 1997–, appeared at Sydney Opera House, Royal Opera House and Int. Symposium of Contemporary Music, Hong Kong; On the Road tour, UK 2006; Guest Music Dir, Chamber Music Week, Australian Youth Orchestra 2007; Around Britten tour to over 50 locations in Britain to celebrate Britten's centenary 2013. *Recordings include:* Through the Looking Glass 2000, The Silver Swan 2003, Strings Attached 2003, Reminding 2005, The Dance of the Three Legged Elephants 2009, Constant Filter 2010, Around Britten 2013; with Between the Notes: Knots 2005, Extraordinary Improvisations 2007; with Victoria Mullova and the Matthew Barley Ensemble: The Peasant Girl 2011. *Television:* Music Dir, Classical Star (BBC 2) 2007. *Current Management:* Sarah Bruce, Lomonaco Artists. *Telephone:* (7538) 2203; (7803) 92366. *E-mail:* info@lomonaco-artists.com. *Website:* www.lomonaco-artists.com; www.matthewbarley.com; www.betweenthenotes.co.uk.

BARLOW, Stephen, MA, FRCO, FGSM; British conductor, composer and pianist; *Artistic Director, Buxton Festival*; b. 30 June 1954, Seven Kings, Essex, England; s. of George William Barlow and Irene Catherine Barlow (née Moretti); m. Joanna Lumley. *Education:* studied in Canterbury, at Trinity Coll. and Guildhall School of Music. *Career:* f. New London Chamber Group, based at the Riverside Studios, Hammersmith; guest conductor of opera at Guildhall School, notably Falstaff and Maw's The Rising of the Moon; Glyndebourne Festival and tour 1979–85, leading Die schweigsame Frau, Der Rosenkavalier, Arabella, Oliver Knussen double bill, Così fan tutte, Gluck's Orfeo, The Rake's Progress and Love for Three Oranges; for ENO conducted The Flying Dutchman, Carmen, Abduction from the Seraglio, The Damnation of Faust, La Cenerentola, L'Italiana in Algeri, Barber of Seville; Scottish Opera from 1983, with Hansel and Gretel, The Bartered Bride, Intermezzo; conducted Opera 80 from its inception, Musical Dir from 1987, leading Marriage of Figaro, A Masked Ball, The Rake's Progress, The Merry Widow 1989–90; Covent Garden debut 1989, with Turandot, returning for Die Zauberflöte 1991; San Francisco Opera 1990, Capriccio; has also worked for Opera North and Vancouver Opera; Australian debut, Melbourne, in Die Zauberflöte 1991; conducted Faust for Opera Northern Ireland 1992; conducted Capriccio in Catania, Marriage of Figaro at Garsington, Carmen in Adelaide, Madama Butterfly at Auckland 1994 and Belfast 1997; season 1998 with Falstaff at Garsington, Elektra and Gounod's Faust, Seville, The Cunning Little Vixen, Berlin, Capriccio and I Capuletti ed I Montecchi in Sicily, Rigoletto, Tirana, Il Barbiere di Siviglia, Riga, Madama Butterfly, Don Giovanni and Il Trovatore, Auckland, La Cenerentola and Turandot with Florida Grand Opera, Carmen, Melbourne, Turandot, Miami, Roméo et Juliette for State Opera of South Australia, La Bohème, Falstaff, Rusalka, Norma, Capriccio, Tristan und Isolde and Pique Dame, Carmelites and Peter Grimes for Grange Park Opera; Les Contes d'Hoffmann in Beijing, Barber of Baghdad, Cornelius, Intermezzo, The Jacobin, Rossini's Otello, Louise, Lucia di Lammermoor, Buxton Festival, Rape of Lucretia, IYO, Koanga, Wexford, Cenerentola, Stuttgart; concert engagements with English Chamber Orchestra, City of London Sinfonia, London Sinfonietta, City of Birmingham Symphony, Royal Liverpool Philharmonic, Scottish Chamber Orchestra, BBC Scottish, Bournemouth Sinfonietta and Belgrade Philharmonic; concerts in Spain, The Netherlands, Germany; BBC Nat. Orchestra of Wales, Radio Philharmonic Orchestra, Hilversum, Sinfonica Siciliana, Italy, New Zealand, Vancouver, Melbourne and Detroit Symphony Orchestras, BBC Philharmonic, Ulster Orchestra, Lausanne Sinfonietta, Sicilian Symphony Orchestra; Artistic Dir, Opera Northern Ireland 1996–98; Music Dir, Queensland Philharmonic Orchestra 1996–98; Artistic Dir Buxton Festival 2012–. *Compositions include:* King (opera) 2006, Nocturne for solo clarinet, strings and marimba 2010, The Rainbow Bear 2010. *Recordings include:* with baritone Mark Stone, Quilter Songbook, Complete Delius Songs, English Love; Graham Koehne Ballets with the Queensland Philharmonic Orchestra, Rainbow Bear with the English Northern Philharmonia. *Current Management:* c/o Musichall Ltd, Vicarage Way, Ringmer, East Sussex, BN8 5LA, England. *Telephone:* (1273) 814240. *Fax:* (1273) 813637. *E-mail:* info@musichall.uk.com. *Website:* www.musichall.uk.com. *Address:* Festival Office, 3 The Square, Buxton, Derbyshire, SK17 6AZ, England (office). *Telephone:* (1298) 70395 (office). *E-mail:* stephen@buxtonfestival.co.uk (office). *Website:* www.buxtonfestival.co.uk (office).

BARNA-SABADUS, Valer, (Valer Sabadus); Romanian singer (countertenor); b. 1986, Arad. *Education:* Hochschule für Musik Munich, studied with

Gabriele Fuchs. *Career:* moved to Germany aged five; debut Salzburg Whitsun Festival 2009; as opera singer, has performed at festivals including Salzburg, Ravenna, Aix-en-Provence, Handel Festival Halle, Rheingau and Schwetzingen Mozart Summer Festival, and at Opéra Nat. de Paris, Frankfurt Opera, Deutsche Oper Berlin, Opéra Royal de Versailles, Semperoper Dresden, Theater an der Wien, Théâtre des Champs Elysées and Deutsche Oper am Rhein Dusseldorf; has sung in concert with Concerto Köln, Les Talens Lyriques at Alte Oper Frankfurt and Utrecht Early Music Festival, with l'Arte del Mondo at Festival Palace Sanssouci Potsdam and Festival of Ancient Music Köln; solo concerts and recitals included Philharmonie Köln with Pera Ensemble and Schwetzingen Winter Festival, Festival d'Aix-en-Provence 2013. *Recordings include:* with Pera Ensemble: Kaffee für den König 2011, Baroque Oriental 2011, Café: Orient meets Occident 2012; solo: Hasse: Reloaded 2012, English Songs 2013, Mozart Castrato Arias 2015; other: Pergolesi: Stabat Mater 2012, Vinci: Artaserse 2013, Le belle immagini 2014. *Honours:* Int. Classical Music Awards Young Artist of the Year 2013. *Current Management:* c/o Frank Behrendt, Hilbert Artists Management, Maximilianstrasse 22, 80539 Munich, Germany. *Telephone:* (89) 2907470. *Fax:* (89) 29074790. *E-mail:* behrendt@hilbert.de. *Website:* www.hilbert.de; www.valer-barna-sabadus.com (office).

BARNARD, Keith, AMus; British composer, poet and teacher; b. 26 Oct. 1950, London. *Education:* Trinity Coll. of Music, London; studied composition with Arnold Cooke; Int. Writers' Asscn, Int. Poets' Acad., Madras, India. *Career:* teacher of piano, music theory and composition 1972–; numerous concerts and recitals of his own compositions; conductor, multicultural concert; mem. Performing Rights Asscn, Musicians' Union, New Age Music Asscn. *Compositions include:* Healing 1–4 for Piano, Colour Harmonies for Keyboard Synthesizer, Healing Rays of Emerald-Blue for 5 Flutes, The Golden Temple of Wisdom for 4 Flutes, Angelic Nocturne for Piano. *Publications:* Outer World Poems 1982, The Sacred Cup 1982, The Legend of Bran 1982, The Legend of Fonn 1983, The Adventures of Fionn Mac Chumail 1984, Heroes and Rituals 1984, Dreams of Wisdom 1986, Visions 1988, Perspectives 1989, Dream Soul 1990, Kingdoms 1991; contrib. to East-West Voices, Rising Stars, Samvedana-Creative Bulletin, Poet International, Souvenir Tribute to Professor Saidhana, Canopy, Indian Literary Journal. *E-mail:* eleven22001@yahoo.co.uk.

BARNARD, Trevor (John), ARAM, ARCM; British/Australian pianist and academic; b. 3 Jan. 1938, London, England; m. Helen Richmond 1974. *Education:* Royal Acad. of Music, Royal Coll. of Music, Inst. of Musical Instrument Tech.; studied with Herbert Fryer, Harold Craxton. *Career:* Pianist-in-Residence, Boston Univ. Radio 1967–71; Faculty, New England Conservatory, Boston, Mass 1968–72; piano tutor, Monash Univ., Australia 1972–74; Lecturer in Music, Melbourne Coll. of Advanced Educ. 1974–88; Lecturer in Piano, Univ. of Melbourne 1989–2003; Examiner, Australian Music Examinations Bd 1989–; many appearances as pianist, BBC and ABC; Music-in-the-Round, Chamber Music Festivals; many orchestras, music socs; mem. Australian Musicians' Guild (Hon. Sec. 1982–93), Camberwell Music Soc. (Pres. 1990–2000, Hon. Life mem. 2000). *Recordings include:* Bliss Piano Concerto, Schubert Die schöne Müllerin D. 795 for Voice and Piano (with Philip Langridge), J.S. Bach transcriptions and piano music from Australia, Busoni 24 Preludes and Bliss Sonata, Blue Wrens: piano music from Australia, A Piano Odyssey, William Lovelock Sonata for Saxophone and Piano (with Peter Clinch). *Recordings for television and film:* Schumann and Bliss Concerti, Mozart Concert Rondo, K382. *Publications include:* Pedalling and Other Reflections on Piano Teaching 1991, A Guide to the Study of Solo Piano Repertoire at Tertiary Level 1996, A Practical Guide to Solo Piano Music 2006, Neglected Areas of Piano Teaching 2008; contribs to Clavier and Clavier Companion (journals) 1998–2015, Australia Music Teacher International (magazine) 1992–2007, Australian Pianists Book 2010. *Honours:* Full Scholarship, Royal Coll. of Music 1955. *Address:* 10 Grosvenor Road, Glen Iris, Vic. 3146, Australia (home). *Telephone:* (3) 9822-3156 (home).

BARNEA, Sever Aurelian; Romanian singer (baritone), curator, academic and pianist; b. 1 July 1960, Bucharest; one s. *Education:* piano principal study, Lyceum of Art, singing principal study, Universitatea de Muzica, int. music classes, Weimar. *Career:* First Perm. Baritone, Romanian Nat. Opera Bucharest 1989; repertoire includes Papageno in Mozart's Magic Flute, Figaro in Le nozze di Figaro, title role in Don Giovanni, Don Alfonso in Così fan tutte; Dr Malatesta in Donizetti's Don Pasquale and Dulcamara in L'Elisir d'amore; Amonasro in Verdi's Aida, Iago in Otello, title role in Falstaff, Paolo in Simon Boccanegra; Mephisto in Gounod's Faust; Mustafa in Rossini's L'Italiana in Algeri, Bartolo and Basilio in Il Barbiere di Siviglia, Don Magnifico in La Cenerentola; The Grand Priest of Dagon in Saint-Saëns' Samson and Delilah; Barnaba in Ponchielli's Gioconda, C Gomes, Don Gil de Tarragona in Maria Tudor; Marcello in Puccini's La Bohème, Sharpless in Madama Butterfly, Scarpia in Tosca, Ping in Turandot; Escamillo in Bizet's Carmen; title role in Tchaikovsky's Eugene Onegin; Holländer in Wagner's Der fliegende Holländer; title role in Georges Enescu's Oedipe, Laertes in Pascal Bentoiu's Hamlet, title role in Nicolae Bretan's Golem; Bach, Haydn, Fauré, Carl Orff, Charpentier; participated in several festivals including Georges Enescu Int. Festival, Romania, Temps Musicaux, Ramatuelle Festival, Anvers sur Oise, France, Medway Arts Festival, Athens Festival; toured Austria, Belgium, France, Spain, Bulgaria, Germany, Greece, Switzerland, Netherlands, UK, Italy, Hungary, Poland, Japan, Albania, Moldova, Macedonia; recordings broadcast on Romanian nat. radio and TV, in Bulgaria and on BBC. *Honours:* Performanta in Spectacolul de Opera Award,

Actualitatea Musicala 2000, Meritul Cultural in Grad Cavaler Presidential Award 2004. *Address:* Bucharest, Bd. 1 Mai (Compozitorilor), Nr. 30 bis Bl. 12 Sc. 3, Apt 32, Sector VI, Cod, 061633, Romania (home). *Telephone:* (21) 7252429 (home); 743-775846 (mobile); 745-074023 (mobile). *E-mail:* barneasever@yahoo.com; barneaaurelian@yahoo.com.

BARNES, Gerald Linton, FRCO, GRSM, ARAM, ARCM, LTCL; British musician; b. 6 June 1935, Hampstead, London; s. of William Leslie Barnes and Constance Grace Linnington; m. Rachel Mary Townsend. *Education:* Kilburn Grammar School, Hertford Coll., Oxford, Royal Acad. of Music. *Career:* organist, Bloomsbury Central Church 1956–81, St Columba's, Pont Street 1988–; Prof., Examiner London Coll. of Music 1965–; Lecturer, City Literary Inst. 1971–2013; Conductor, Elysian Choir 1975–2013, Wembley Philharmonic Soc. 1981–2013, Thiman Orchestra of London 1985–; Festival Organist, Free Church Choir Union 1996–; appeared as organist on television, radio and at cathedrals, univs and major concert halls in England, Europe and USA; mem. Savage Club, Royal Soc. of Musicians. *Compositions:* hymn tunes and anthems. *Recordings:* various organ recordings. *Publications:* contrib. to Musical Times, Musical Opinion and choral and musical journals. *Honours:* Hon. FLCM 1985. *Address:* 13 Regency House, 269 Regents Park Road, London, N3 3JZ, England (home). *Telephone:* (20) 8346-6637 (home).

BARRELL, David, ARAM; British singer (baritone); b. 1962, England. *Education:* Univ. of London, Royal Acad. of Music, Juilliard School, New York. *Career:* sang Gounod's Ourrais in Mireille and Don Giovanni at Juilliard; repertoire includes Enée in Les Troyens, Peter Grimes, Hagenbach in La Wally, Boris in Katja Kabanova, Laca in Jenůfa, Canio in Pagliacci, Ruggero in La Rondine, Des Grieux in Manon Lescaut, Pinkerton in Madama Butterfly, Cavaradossi in Tosca, Luigi in Il Tabarro, Calaf in Turandot, Herman in Pique Dame, The Blackened Man, Tristan in Tristan und Isolde, Adolar in Euryanthe, Florestan in Fidelio; appearances with Welsh Nat. Opera, ENO, Scottish Opera, Metropolitan Opera, Teatro Regio Turin, Opera de Nice, Maggio Musicale Florence, Glyndebourne Festival, Spoleto Festival, also in Tokyo, Rio de Janeiro, Madrid; oratorio repertoire includes Bruckner's Te Deum, Elgar's Dream of Gerontius, The Kingdom, The Apostles, Mendelssohn's Elijah, Mozart's Requiem, C Minor Mass, Puccini's Messa di Gloria, Verdi's Requiem. *Honours:* winner, New York Oratorio Soc. Int. Soloist Competition, Carnegie Hall. *E-mail:* barrellissimo@o2.co.uk (office). *Website:* davidbarrelltenor.xbuild.com.

BARRERA, Giulia; American singer (soprano); b. 28 April 1942, Brooklyn, NY. *Education:* studied in New York with Dick Marzollo. *Career:* debut with New York City Opera 1963, as Aida; sang in Baltimore, New Orleans, Pittsburgh, Washington and Seattle; mem., New York City Opera, with roles including Verdi's Amelia and Leonora (Il Trovatore), Santuzza, Don Giovanni, Sieglinde in Die Walküre, Tosca, Manon Lescaut, Venus in Tannhäuser and Monteverdi's Euridice; guest appearances in Copenhagen, Rome, Parma, Cardiff, Montréal and Nuremberg. *Recordings include:* The Mother in Dallapiccola's Il Prigioniero.

BARRETT, Richard; British composer and performer; b. 7 Nov. 1959, Swansea, Wales. *Education:* studied with Peter Wiegold and in Darmstadt. *Career:* Co-Dir Ensemble Exposé 1984–93; formed electro-acoustic duo FURT (with Paul Obermayer) 1986; teacher of electronic music, Instituut voor Sonologie, Royal Conservatory, The Hague 1996–2001, 2009–; stipend, DAAD Berliner Künstlerprogramm 2001–02, Prof. of Music, Brunel Univ., London 2006–09. *Compositions:* principal works include: Ne Songe plus à fuir for amplified cello 1986, Negatives for ensemble 1983, Vanity for orchestra 1994, Tract for piano 1996, Opening of the Mouth for two female voices, instruments and electronics 1997, Stress for string quartet 1995–97; Unter Wasser, opera for mezzo-soprano and 13 instruments 1998, transmission for electric guitar and electronics 1999, Blattwerk for cello and electronics 2002, DARK MATTER for 20 performers and electronics 2003, NO for orchestra 2004, Flechtwerk for clarinet and piano 2006, Nacht und Träume for cello, piano and electronics 2008, Mesopotamia for ensemble 2009, IF for orchestra 2010, CONSTRUCTION for voices, ensemble and electronics 2011, life-form for cello and electronics 2012. *E-mail:* richard@furtlogic.com (home). *Website:* richardbarrettmusic.com (office).

BARRIÈRE, Jean-Baptiste Marie, LèsSc, DEA, PhD; French composer and director of music research; b. 2 Jan. 1958, Paris; m. Kaija Saariaho 1984. *Education:* University of Paris I, Panthéon Sorbonne. *Career:* mem., Synthesizer Ensemble of the Centre Européen pour la Recherche Musicale, Metz 1976–77; Researcher, Composer, Institut de Recherche et de Coordination Acoustique Musique, Paris 1981–84, Director of Musical Research 1984–97; mem, Collectif pour la Recherche en Information Musicale. *Compositions:* Pandémonium: Ville Ouverte 1975, Pandémonium: Non, Jamais l'Esperance 1976, Sophistic Variations 1980, Chreode I 1983, Collisions 1984, Epigénèse 1986, Hybris 1987, World Skin 1997, Cellitude 1998, Time Dusts 1998. *Recordings:* Pandémonium: Ville Ouverte 1977, Pandémonium: Non, Jamais l'Esperance 1978. *Publications:* Le Timbre: Métaphores pour la Composition 1987–88, Actes du Symposium Systèmes Personnels et Informatique Musicale 1987; contrib. to Chreode I: A Path to a New Music with the Computer, for Contemporary Music Review No. 1 1984; Mutations de l'Escriture, Mutations du Matériau, for Inharmoniques No. 1 1987. *Honours:* Digital Music Prize in the Electro-Acoustic Music Competition, Bourges, France 1983, Prix Ars Electronica, Linz 1998. *Address:* c/o Centre de

Documentation de la Musique Contemporaine, Cité de la Musique, 16 Place de la Fontaine aux Lions, 75019 Paris, France (office).

BARROSO, Sergio Fernández; Cuban/Canadian composer, synthesist and harpsichordist; b. 4 March 1946, Havana, Cuba. *Education:* Nat. Conservatory, Havana, Prague Superior Acad. of Music, Univ. of Havana, CCRMA, Stanford Univ., USA. *Career:* Prof. of Composition, Amadeo Roldán Conservatory, Havana 1968–80, Superior Inst. of Arts, Havana 1975–80; broadcaster, Cuban Nat. Radio and TV Inst. 1969–80, Vancouver Cooperative Radio 1985–90; Music Writer, Juventud Rebelde (daily) 1975–80; Head of Music Dept, Havana Nat. Library 1970–72, Univ. of Havana 1972–76, Ministry of Culture, Cuba 1976–80; moved to Canada 1980; has taught at Simon Fraser Univ., Univ. of Victoria, Carlos Chávez Conservatory, Mexico City; performances include Prague Symphony Orchestra FOK 1968, Varna Int. Ballet Festival, Bulgaria 1970, Monte Carlo Theatre 1972, Warsaw Autumn Festivals 1972, 1985, Havana Symphony Orchestra 1972, 1977, 1979, Havana Nat. Theatre 1972, 1975, Budapest Opera 1976, Teatro de la Zarzuela, Madrid 1976, MET-Lincoln Center, New York 1977–78, San Francisco Opera 1977, Bratislava Philharmonic Hall 1979, Int. Soc. for Contemporary Music (ISCM) Festival, Belgium 1980, IRCAM, Paris 1980, Array, Toronto 1981, Utrecht Conservatorium, The Netherlands 1982, Manuel de Falla Festival, Granada 1985, Music Gallery, Toronto 1986, 1996, 1999, ACREQ, Montréal 1987, Foro Festivals, Mexico City 1978, 1988, Nat. Arts Centre, Ottawa 1988, South Bank Centre, London 1989, Toronto New Music Concerts 1990, Oslo 1990, Sub-Tropics Festival, Miami 1991, LIEM, Centro Reina Sofia, Madrid 1991, ICSM, Montréal 1991, Seattle 1992, 2007, Brussels 1992, Pollack Hall, Montréal 1995, 2000, Buenos Aires 1996, São Paulo Philharmonic Hall 1999, Rio de Janeiro 1999, Santiago de Chile 2005, Sequitur Ensemble, New York City 2006. *Compositions include:* ballets: Plásmasis 1970, Dinamia 1972, La Casa de Bernarda Alba 1975; instrumental: Oboe Concerto 1968, Concerto for 2 pianos, percussion and audience 1969, Oda al Soldado Muerto for orchestra 1970, Yantra I for guitar and tape 1971, Yantra II for double wind ensemble 1972, Yantra III for guitar and tape 1973, Yantra IV for flute and tape 1975, Yantra V for solo guitar 1975, Yantra VI for piano and tape 1976, Yantra VII for orchestra 1977, Yantra VIII for piano 1978, Yantra IX for sop/alto saxophone 1979, Yantra X for bassoon and tape 1982, Las Barricadas Misteriosas, computer music 1982, Ireme for voice, percussion and tape 1985, En Febrero Mueren las Flores for violin and tape 1987, Canzona for tape 1988, Soledad for tape 1989, La Fiesta for synthesizers and tape 1989, La Fiesta Grande for synthesizers and orchestra 1990, Tablao for guitar and tape 1991, Crónicas de Ultrasueño for oboe and synthesizers 1992, Sonatada for solo synthesizers 1992, Charangas Delirantes for midi trio 1993, Jintajáfora for violin, orchestra and live electronics 1993, Viejas Voces for viola and tape 1993–95, Crónicas II for viola and synthesizers or tape 1995–96, Concerto for viola and orchestra 1996, Viola Desnuda for viola solo 1997, La Noche for viola, bass clarinet and tape 1997, Sandunga for viola or clarinet and tape 1998, Cuartetas for viola, bass clarinet, piano and tape 1999, Callejeos for bass clarinet and tape 1999, Pregones for cello and tape 2000, Rocambole for violin, cello and tape 2001, Hélice for sopano saxophone and tape 2005, Verdehalago for soprano, instrumental ensemble and tape 2006, Tuyuca for piano and tape 2007. *Radio:* Francis Poulenc Concerto for 2 pianos and Orchestra, ICRT Havana 1971, J.S. Bach Harpsichord Concerto in D minor Havana Symphony Orchestra, ICRT 1975, Yantra II Symphony Orchestra 1976, François Couperin Suites, ICRT Havana 1978, Yantra VII, Havana Symphony Orchestra 1978, Contemporary Music for Harpsichord, ICRT Havana 1979, Yantra IV 1985, Yantra VI 1986, La Fiesta Grande (CBC), Hamilton Philharmonic 1990, Music for digital keyboard by Canadian Composers, CBC Two New Hours 1988–2000, Concerto for Viola and Orchestra, Laura Wilcox, Esprit Orchestra (CBC) 1996 and São Paulo State Symphony Orchestra (Radio Cultura SP) 1999, Jitanjáfora, Adele Armin, Esprit Orchestra (CBC) 1993, 1994. *Recordings include:* Yantra I for guitar and tape 1971, Oda al Soldado Muerto 1972, Concerto for two pianos, percussion and audience 1978, Yantra III 1979, Yantra IV 1979, Yantra VI 1976, Yantra VIII 1978, Yantra IX 1979, Yantra X 1982, Music for Digital Keyboard 1988, (Canzona, Soledad) 1988, La Fiesta 1990, La Fiesta Grande 1990, Crónicas de Ultrasueño 1992, Charangas Delirantes (9 works for solo and electronics) 1998, Viola Desnuda 2000, 2002, Jitanjáfora 2006, Concerto for viola and orchestra 2006, Canción para Dormir en el Sillón for piano 2006, Unmeasured Preludes by Louis Couperin and Jean-Henry D'Anglebert (complete) on harpsichord 2007, Crónicas II for viola and synthesizers 2009, Tuyuca for piano and tape 2009. *Publications:* 67 music pieces for Juventud Rebelde Havana; trans., prologue and catalogue for Béla Bartók by Serge Moreux, ICL Havana 1976, trans. and prologue for Serial Composition by Reginald Smith Brindle, ICL Havana 1979. *Honours:* Nat. Chamber Music Award, Havana 1973, 1974, Nat. Electroacoustic Music Award, Havana 1979, ISCM TRIMALCA, Bogotá 1979, ISCM Rostrum of Composers, Paris 1980, 1994, ISCM Rostrum of Electroacoustic Music, Oslo 1990, Helsinki 1992, Cintas Composition Award, New York 1999, 2009, Lynch-Staunton Nat. Composition Award, Ottawa 2000. *Address:* 7938 122A Street, Surrey, BC V3W 3T3, Canada (home). *Telephone:* (604) 590-4198 (office); (321) 507-1080 (office). *E-mail:* ireme.ems@gmail.com (office).

BARRUECO, Manuel; American classical guitarist; b. 16 Dec. 1952, Santiago de Cuba, Cuba. *Education:* Ešteban Salas Conservatory, Santiago de Cuba and the Peabody Conservatory of Music, MD, USA. *Career:* debut, New York 1974; many concert appearances as soloist with leading orchestras in USA and world-wide; gave the US premiere of Takemitsu's guitar concerto

1985; tours to musical centres including Royal Albert Hall, London, Musikverein Vienna, Concertgebouw Amsterdam, Philharmonie Berlin, Teatro Real Madrid, Palau de la Musica in Barcelona; numerous tours to S America and Japan and repeated appearances in Korea, Taiwan, Singapore and Hong Kong; guest soloist with orchestras including Russian State Symphony, Helsinki Philharmonic, Royal Philharmonic, NHK Symphony, New Japan Philharmonic, Auckland Symphony and radio symphonies of Munich and Frankfurt; collaborated with composers including Steven Stucky, Michael Daugherty, Roberto Sierra, Arvo Pärt, Dmitri Yanov-Yanovsky and Toru Takemitsu; recitals worldwide; faculty mem., Peabody Conservatory; assisted in the creation of a faculty for guitar at the Manhattan School of Music; gives regular master classes at Puerto Rico Conservatory, San Juan, also residences and master classes in Europe and N America. *Recordings include:* Rodrigo (with Plácido Domingo), Bach Sonatas, Manuel Barrueco plays Lennon and McCartney, Manuel Barrueco plays Granadas and de Falla, Manuel Barrueco plays Albéniz and Turina, Manuel Barrueco plays Bach and de Visée, Manuel Barrueco plays de Falla, Ponce and Rodrigo, 300 Years of Guitar Masterpieces, Mozarts Duets for Flute and Guitar, Cantos y Danzas, !Cuba!, Nylon and Steel (with Al Di Meola, Steve Morde and Andy Summers), Concierto Barroco (with Orquesta Sinfónica de Galicia), Solo Piazzolla 2007, Tango Sensations (with Cuarteto Latinoamericano) 2008, Virtuoso Guitar Duos (with Franco Platino) 2009, Tárrega! 2010, Chaconne 2012. *Honours:* Concert Artists' Guild Award 1974, US Artists Fellowship for Artistic Excellence 2011. *Current Management:* M. B. General Management, PO Box 4466, Timonium, MD 21094, USA. *Website:* www.barrueco.com.

BARRY, Gerald; Irish composer; b. 28 April 1952, Clarecastle. *Education:* studied in Cologne with Stockhausen and Kagel, studied organ with Piet Kee in Amsterdam. *Career:* commissions from organisations including the BBC, Inst. for Contemporary Art, London, Channel 4 Television, Radio France, Birmingham Contemporary Music Group, London Southbank Centre, Musica Viva, Munich, London Sinfonietta and St Paul Chamber Orchestra; works premiered by orchestras including Mariinsky Orchestra, ENO and Bavarian Radio Symphony Orchestra, and at festivals including the Almeida, Aldeburgh and Festival Présences. *Compositions include:* Chevaux de frise for orchestra (performed at the Proms 1988), The Intelligence Park (opera, ICA commission, first performed at the 1990 Almeida Festival), The Triumph of Beauty and Deceit (Channel 4 TV commission 1992), The Conquest of Ireland (vocal and orchestral work, BBC Symphony Orchestra commission), String Quartet 1994, The Ring for chorus and orchestra 1995, Quintet 1995, Octet 1995, Piano Quintet No. 2 1996, The Road for orchestra 1997, The Bitter Tears of Petra Von Kant (based on the play and film by Rainer Werner Fassbinder, first performed at ENO) 2005, La Plus Forte 2007, Feldman's Sixpenny Editions for ensemble 2008/09, Le Vieux Sourd for piano 2008/10, Schott and Sons, Mainz for bass voice and choir 2009, The Importance of Being Earnest (opera, written for Los Angeles Philharmonic and the Barbican, London) 2009/10, First Sorrow string quartet (for Crash Ensemble), Beethoven for bass voice and ensemble, Long Time for SATB choir 2011, Piano Concerto 2012. *Recordings include:* The Intelligence Park 1990, Piano and Chamber music (with Noriko Kawai on piano and the Nua Nos ensemble) 1993, Orchestral Works 1998, Triumph of Beauty and Deceit 1999, The Bitter Tears of Petra Von Kant 2005. *Publications:* contrib. The Intelligence Park (in Contemporary Music Review) Vol. 5, Irish Wit (in The Musical Times) Sept. 1993, Bob's Your Uncle (in The Musical Times) April 1995. *Address:* c/o Oxford University Press, Great Clarendon Street, Oxford, OX2 6DP, England (office). *Website:* www.oup.co.uk/music/repprom/barry.

BARSTOW, Dame Josephine Clare, DBE, CBE, BA; British singer; b. 27 Sept. 1940, Sheffield, Yorks., England; d. of Harold Barstow and Clara Barstow; m. 1st Terry Hands 1964 (divorced 1968); m. 2nd Ande Anderson 1969 (died 1996). *Education:* Univ. of Birmingham. *Career:* taught English in London area for two years; debut in operatic profession with Opera for All 1964; for short time company mem. Welsh Nat. Opera, then ENO; now freelance singer in all nat. opera houses in UK and in Paris, Vienna, Salzburg, Zürich, Geneva, Turin, Florence, Cologne, Munich, Berlin, USSR, Chicago, San Francisco, New York, Houston and many other American opera houses. *Chief roles:* Violetta in La Traviata, Leonora in Forza del Destino, Elisabeth in Don Carlos, Lady Macbeth, Amelia in Ballo in Maschera, Attila, Leonore in Fidelio, Sieglinde, Senta, Arabella, Salome, Octavian, The Marschallin, Chrysothemis, Amelia, Tosca, Mimi, Minnie, Musetta, Manon Lescaut, Emilia Marty, Jenůfa, Katya Kabanova, Medea, Renata in The Fiery Angel, Katerina Ismailova, Kostelnicka in Jenůfa, Marie in Wozzeck, Gloriana, Lady Billows in Albert Herring; world premieres of Tippett, Henze and Penderecki. *Television films:* Macbeth 1972, Idomeneo 1974, Un ballo in maschera 1989, Gloriana 2000, Owen Wingrave 2001. *Recordings include:* Verdi Recital Record with ENO Orchestra and Mark Elder, Amelia with Herbert von Karajan, Anna Maurant in Street Scene, Kate in Kiss Me Kate, Four Finales, Gloriana, Albert Herring, Wozzeck, Carmelites. *Honours:* Hon. DMus (Birmingham, Kingston, Sheffield, Sheffield Hallam, Leeds, Hull); Fidelio Medal. *Current Management:* c/o Musichall Ltd, Oast House, Crouch's Farm, Hollow Lane, East Hoathly, BN8 6QX, England. *E-mail:* info@musichall.uk .com. *Website:* www.musichall.uk.com.

BÁRTA, Aleš; Czech organist; b. 30 Aug. 1960, Rychnov; m. 1984; one s. *Education:* Brno Conservatoire, Acad. of Music, Prague. *Career:* debut with Prague Symphony Orchestra, Prague Spring Festival 1984; tours of Denmark 1979, Austria 1983, Hungary 1984, 1985, Turkey 1985, Germany 1986, 1990,

France 1987, Russia 1988; US debut at concert of Czech music, New York 1990; also Japan, China, Hong Kong, Finland, Switzerland, Spain; festival appearances include recitals at Prague Spring Festival 1984, 1988 and 1991, Avignon Festival 1987, Istanbul Festival 1985, Leipzig Festival 1986; debut with Prague Radio Symphony Orchestra, Berlin Festival 1987, also Tokyo, Yokohama, Sapporo, Passau, Linz and Zürich festivals; concerts with Czech Philharmonic Orchestra and Czech Radio Symphony Orchestra; Czech Radio soloist 1995–. *Recordings:* Organ recital of Bach, Reger and Flosman 1986, Organ recital of Bach 1991, Organ recital live recording of Bach, Reger, Sokola 1992, Organ Works of Mozart, Complete Organ Works of J. S. Bach, Russian Organ Music, Organ Illusion, Reger Organ Works, The Best of German Organ Music, Liszt Organ Works, Gems of French Organ Music, Czech Organ Music across the Centuries. *Honours:* first prize Anton Bruckner Int. Organ Competition, Linz 1982, first prize Czech Organists Competition 1984, first prize Prague Spring Int. Organ Competition 1984, Supraphon Gold Disc (for Bach's Organ Works recording) 1993, Japanese Critics Prize 1995. *Current Management:* Arco Diva Management, Balbinova 14, 120 00 Prague 2, Czech Republic. *Telephone:* 224238673. *Fax:* 224238619. *E-mail:* arcodiva@arcodiva.cz. *Website:* www.arcodiva.cz/barta. *Address:* Nuselska 6, 140 00 Prague 4, Czech Republic (home). *Telephone:* 241741097 (home). *E-mail:* barta.ales@tiscali.cz (home).

BARTA, Michael (Mihály); Hungarian violinist and academic; *Professor of Violin and Chamber Music, Southern Illinois University*; b. 6 Feb. 1954, Budapest; m. Irene Barta 1980; one s. *Education:* Béla Bartók Conservatory, F. Liszt Acad., Budapest, studied with Arthur Grumiaux. *Career:* first violinist, Kodály String Quartet 1975–80, toured world-wide; soloist, Hungarian Nat. Philharmonic Orchestra 1975–80; granted asylum in USA 1980; Prof. of Violin, Central Michigan Univ. 1981–85; Concertmaster, Saginaw and Midland Symphonies 1981–85; apptd Assoc. Prof., Southern Illinois Univ. at Carbondale 1985, Prof. of Violin and Chamber Music 1986–; concerts across USA, in 23 European cities and in Japan at venues including Wigmore Hall, London, Alice Tully Hall and Carnegie Recital Hall, New York, Detroit Art Inst., AIMS Summer Festival, Spain; Asst Concertmaster, Illinois Symphony and Chamber Orchestra 1986–; radio and TV broadcasts worldwide; master-classes in USA, Bulgaria, Malta, Hungary, Spain and Latvia; co-f. Southern Illinois Chamber Music Soc. *Recordings:* Goldmark Suite for Violin and Piano, Prokofiev: Sonata for Two Violins, Szőllősy Solo Violin Sonata; numerous recordings for major labels and nat. and int. radio stations. *Honours:* Second Prize, Joseph Szigeti Int. Competition, Budapest 1973, Gold Medal, Belgian Eugene Ysaÿe Soc. 1973, Special Prize, Tchaikovsky Int. Competition, Moscow 1974. *Address:* Southern Illinois University at Carbondale School of Music, Mail Code 4302, Altgeld 021, Carbondale, IL 62901 (office); 45 Twin Creeks Lane, Murphysboro, IL 62966, USA (home). *E-mail:* misi1954@yahoo.com (office); barta@siu.edu (office). *Website:* music.siu.edu/facultystaff/barta.html (office).

BARTELINK, Bernard G. M., DipMus; Dutch organist and composer; b. 24 Nov. 1929, Enschede; m. Rina Stolwyk 1955, two s. *Education:* Amsterdam Conservatory. *Career:* recitals in major concert halls, cathedrals and churches in UK, Europe and USA, including Royal Festival Hall, London, St Paul's and Westminster Cathedrals, London, Notre Dame, Paris, Nat. Cathedral, Washington DC; tours in NZ and S America; radio broadcasts in many countries; Prof. of Organ, Sweelinck Conservatory, Amsterdam –1989; Organist, Cathedral of St Bavo, Haarlem 1971–99, Royal Concertgebouw Orchestra –1994; master classes; fmr chair. jury, Int. Improvisation Competition of the Festival of European Church Music, Schwäbisch Gmünd, Germany. *Compositions:* chamber and orchestral music, songs and works for choir on secular texts, masses, motets and songs on liturgical texts, and organ works; comms from Dutch Govt and City of Amsterdam. *Honours:* Kt, Papal Order of St Sylvester, Officer, Order of Oranje-Nassau; First Prize, Int. Organ Improvisation Contest, Haarlem 1961, Silver Medal of the Academic Soc., Arts, Sciences and Letters, Paris. *Address:* Waddenstraat 313, 2036 LH Haarlem, The Netherlands. *Telephone:* (23) 5327070.

BARTH, Ned; American singer (baritone); b. 1963, Syracuse, NY. *Education:* Princeton Univ. and Manhattan School of Music. *Career:* debut in Berne 1987, as Mozart's Count; sang Mandryka in Arabella, Wolfram in Tannhäuser, Donizetti's Enrico, Germont, Nabucco and Napoleon in Prokofiev's War and Peace, Karlsruhe Opera 1989–92; guest appearances as Verdi's Don Carlo, Marseille; Paolo, Dresden, Marcello 1994; Cologne, Iago 1996; as Wolfram, Flanders Opera at Antwerp; season 1998: as Scarpia at Cologne; season 1999 as Scarpia at Cologne, Posa for Komische Oper Berlin and Jokanaan in Salome for Glimmerglass Opera; season 2000, Don Carlo and Orest in Elektra in Berlin, Iago at Palm Beach Opera, Escamillo in Carmen and Amonasro in Aida at Liceu, Barcelona, Ben in Blitzstein's Regina at Florida Grand Opera in Miami; Tonio in I Pagliacci at Glimmerglass and Scarpia in Barcelona 2002; Jochanaan in Salome in Miami and Elektra at Opéra de Marseille 2003; in 2004, sang Don Giovanni at Florida Grand Opera in Miami, La Fanciulla del West in Baltimore and Kurwenal in Tristan und Isolde in Verona; season 2005–06: Elektra in Nantes and Rouen, Tristan in Frankfurt, A Midsummer Night's Dream in Barcelona, La Traviata in Baltimore and Wotan in concert; in 2006–07, sang Tristan in Turin, Genoveva in Palermo and Tosca for Opera Omaha; La Forza del Destino in Baltimore and Tosca for Florida Grand Opera 2008; other roles include Riccardo in I Puritani, Eugene Onegin, Verdi's Renato and Ford, Don Giovanni and Belcore; concerts include Schubert's Winterreise, Carmina Burana, Mahler's Wunderhorn Lieder, Cologne 1996, and works by Bach and Stravinsky; collaborated with conductors including James Conlon, Edo de Waart, Peter Maag, Stefan Soltesz ad Vladimir Jurowski. *Current Management:* Peter Seyfferth Artists Management, Avenue de la Concorde 385, 06190 Roquebrune Cap Martin, France. *Telephone:* 4-93-35-01-05. *Fax:* 4-93-35-02-17. *E-mail:* peter@seyfferth.de. *Website:* www.seyfferth.de.

BARTHA, Clarry; Swedish singer (soprano); b. 1958. *Education:* Santa Cecilia Conservatorium and Accademia di Santa Cecilia, Rome with Maria Teresa Pediconi and George Favaretto, studied with Vera Rozsa in London. *Career:* debut as Donna Anna at Drottningholm, Sweden 1981; has sung Donna Anna in Catania, at the Montepulciano Festival and at Brighton Festival with the Drottningholm Company; at Marseille has sung Lisa in The Queen of Spades, Fiordiligi and Margherita in Mefistofele; Basle Opera as Agathe, Tatiana in Eugene Onegin and Mozart's Countess; performances of Gluck's La Danza at Bologna season 1986–87; Frankfurt Opera 1987–94 as Iphigénie en Tauride, Desdemona, Rusalka and Fiordiligi; sang Mozart's Countess at Rome 1989; sang Katya Kabanova at Basle 1991; season 1995–96 as Katya at Düsseldorf and Leipzig, Chrysothemis at Nice; sang Tosca at Bonn 2000; since performed at European opera houses including Théâtre Royal de la Monnaie in Brussels, Palais Garnier and Opéra de la Bastille in Paris, Teatro dell'Opera in Rome, Royal Opera House, Covent Garden in London, Welsh Nat. Opera in Cardiff, La Scala in Milan, and in Marseille, Montpellier, Nancy, Catania, Stockholm, Bologna, Genoa, Linz, Innsbruck, Berlin, Leipzig, Nürnberg and Düsseldorf; concert commitments at the Prague Spring, Palermo and Ravello Festivals; has sung with the Italian Radio, RAI, in Rome, Naples and Milan; Accademia di Santa Cecilia in Rome and the Maggio Musicale in Florence; Mozart's Vespers and Mendelssohn's Elijah in Stockholm; tour of Israel with Gary Bertini. *Recordings include:* Les Danaïdes, Günter von Schwarzburg, Tchaikovsky's Women. *Honours:* first prize, Beniamino Gigli and Vincenzo Bellini singing competitions. *Current Management:* Haydn Rawstron Ltd, Constanze Koenemann, 29a High Street, West Wickham, Kent, BR4 0LP, England. *Address:* Am Seebuckel 1, 97944 Boxberg, Germany (home). *E-mail:* info@clarrybartha.com (office). *Website:* www.clarrybartha.com (office).

BARTKIEWICZ, Urszula, DMus; Polish harpsichordist and academic; b. 28 Jan. 1952, Bielsko-Biała; m. Jerzy Kozub 1987, one s. *Education:* Acad. of Music, Kraków, Conservatoire Nat. de Bobigny, Paris with Huguette Dreyfus, studied with Zuzana Ruzickova, Rafael Puyana and Kenneth Gilbert, Polish Acad. of Sciences. *Career:* numerous concerts in Poland, including int. festivals, Warsaw Autumn, Łańcut Vratislavia Cantans, Lancut Chamber Festival, early music festivals in Warsaw, Lublin, Gdansk, Radio Festival Szymanowski; concerts in France, Czech Repub., Germany, Netherlands, Russia, Spain, Switzerland, Belgium, Austria, Lithuania, Latvia, Slovakia, Switzerland, UK and USA; collaborations with the Polish Nat. Philharmony, Jerzy Maksymiuk Polish Chamber Orchestra; several television and radio broadcasts in Poland and USA; masterclasses, seminars, workshops and lectures in early music at institutions including Wayne State Univ., Detroit (USA) and Banska Bystrica Acad. of Arts (Slovakia); teacher of harpsichord, Feliks Nowowiejski Acad. of Music in Bydgoszcz 1998–, Head of Dept of Harpsichord, Organ and Early Music 2006–, Assoc. Prof. 2009–; teacher and Dept Head, Zespół Państwowych School of Music, Warsaw. *Recordings:* for Polish radio 1975–90; int. and Polish harpsichord music from XVI–XXth centuries, solo and chamber music; with Polish Nat. Philharmony and Jerzy Maksymiuk's Polish Chamber Orchestra, basso continuo, Wohltemperiertes Klavier by J. S. Bach (Frederick Prize) 2000, Polish Harpsichord Music Vols I and II 2009, Handel Trio Sonatas. *Address:* Dept of Harpsichord, Organ and Early Music, Nowowiejski Academy of Music, ul. Słowackiego 7, 85–008 Bydgoszcz, Poland (office). *Website:* www.amuz.bydgoszcz.pl.

BARTLETT, Clifford Alfred James; British musicologist and writer on music; b. 15 Aug. 1939, London; m. Elaine King 1975; one s. one d. *Education:* Dulwich Coll., Magdalene Coll., Cambridge. *Career:* Deputy Music Librarian, BBC 1970–82; Keyboard Player for Ars Nova 1969–75; Editor, Brio 1974–85; Freelance Writer and Publisher 1983–; Editor, chief writer and publisher of Early Music Review 1994–; Dir, Early Music Centre Festival 1987–88; Chair., Eastern Early Music Forum, Nat. Early Music Asscn. *Publications:* under his own imprint, King's Music, has published editions of a large quantity of music, especially opera, by Monteverdi, Purcell, Handel and other baroque composers; also edited Handel's Messiah, Coronation Anthems and other works for Oxford University Press; contrib. monthly surveys in Early Music News 1977–94; contrib. of numerous programme notes for major record companies and festivals. *Address:* Redcroft, Banks End, Wyton, Huntingdon, Cambridgeshire, PE28 2AA, England (home). *E-mail:* clifford.bartlett@btopenworld.com (home).

BARTO, Tzimon; American pianist and conductor; b. 1963, Florida. *Education:* Juilliard School. *Career:* composed first opera aged eight; began conducting at 14; performer, Spoleto Festival 1985; numerous performances in Europe, USA and Japan with orchestras including New York Phiharmonic, Cleveland and Philadelphia orchestras, Chicago, Houston, National and San Francisco symphonies, Mariinsky Orchestra, Berlin Philharmonic, Dresden Staatskapelle, Hamburg NDR Symphony Orchestra, Leipzig Gewandhaus Orchestra, Vienna Symphony Orchestra, London Philharmonic, Orchestre de Paris, ONE Madrid and NHK Symphony Orchestra Tokyo; regular guest at festivals including Salzburg Easter and Summer Festivals 1989, Ravinia Festival (USA) and White Nights Festival in St Petersburg; regular performer in Asia, especially China, appeared in Guangzhou and Shanghai 2012/13; created int. composition competition for piano solo, the Barto Prize 2006. *Recordings:* Prokofiev's Piano Concerto No.3; Ravel's Concerto in G Major; Chopin-Liszt-Schumann recital programme; Bartók's piano concerto No.2; Rachmaninov's Piano concerto No.3; Chopin piano concerto No. 2; Liszt piano concerto No. 2, Royal Philharmonic Orchestra, Chopin Preludes & Nocturnes, Rameau: A Basket of Wild Strawberries 2004, Ravel Orchestral Versions 2004, Haydn: Unexpected Encounters 2008, Schubert Album 2008, Schumann (with Christoph Eschenbach) 2009, Tchaikovsky Piano Concerto No.1 2010, Remembering JFK: Gershwin Piano Concerto in F 2011. *Current Management:* Opus 3 Artists, 470 Park Avenue South, 9th Floor North, New York, NY 10016, USA. *Telephone:* (212) 584-7500. *Fax:* (646) 300-8200. *E-mail:* info@opus3artists.com. *Website:* www.opus3artists.com; www.tzimonbarto.com.

BARTOLI, Cecilia; Italian singer (coloratura mezzo-soprano) and recitalist; b. 4 June 1966, Rome; d. of Pietro Angelo Bartoli and Silvana Bazzoni. *Education:* Accademia di Santa Cecilia. *Career:* professional career began with TV appearance aged 19; US debut in recital at Mostly Mozart Festival, New York 1990; Paris debut as Cherubino in The Marriage of Figaro, Opéra de Paris Bastille 1990–91; debut, La Scala, Milan in Rossini's Le Comte Ory 1990–91 season; appeared as Dorabella in Così fan tutte, Maggio Musicale, Florence 1991; debut with Montreal Symphony Orchestra and Philadelphia Orchestra 1990–91 season; recitals in collaboration with pianist András Schiff since 1990; appeared in Marriage of Figaro and Così fan tutte conducted by Daniel Barenboim in Chicago Feb. 1992; debut at Salzburg Festival 1992; appeared in recital at Rossini bicentenary celebration at Lincoln Center, New York 1992; has appeared with many leading conductors including Herbert von Karajan, Claudio Abbado, Riccardo Chailly, Myung-Whun Chung, William Christie, Charles Dutoit, Adam Fischer, Nikolaus Harnoncourt, Christhopher Hogwood, James Levine, Sir Neville Marriner, Zubin Mehta, Riccardo Muti, Giuseppe Sinopoli and Sir George Solti; particularly associated with the operas of Mozart and Rossini; Artistic Dir, Salzburg Whitsun Festival 2012–; Euroopean concert tour with Rolando Villazón 2015. *Recordings include:* albums: Rossini Arias, Rossini Songs, Mozart Arias, Rossini Heroines, Chants d'amour, If You Love Me 1992, Mozart Portraits 1995, An Italian Songbook 1997, Cecilia Bartoli – Live Vivaldi Album 1999, Cecilia & Bryn, Il Turco in Italia, Mitridate, Rinaldo, Armida in Italy, The Salieri Album, The Vivaldi Album, Gluck Italian Arias, Opera proibito 2005, Maria (Gramophone Award for Best Recital 2008) 2007, Sacrificium (Grammy Award for Best Classical Vocal Performance 2011) 2009, St Petersburg 2014. *Honours:* Hon. mem. RAM 2005, Royal Swedish Acad. of Music; Hon. mem. Advisory Bd Halle Handel House Foundation 2009; Chevalier, Ordre des Arts et des Lettres, Légion d'Honneur, Officier, Ordre du Mérite, Chevalier, Ordre du Mérite Culturel (Monaco) 2012; two Grammy Awards for Best Classical Vocal Album 1994, Deutsche Schallplatten Preis, La Stella d'Oro, Italy, Caecilia Award, Belgium, Diapason d'Or, France, Best Opera Recording of the Year for La Cenerentola, Japan, Classical BRIT Award for Female Artist of the Year 2004, Echo Klassik Award for Female Singer of the Year 2008, Sonning Music Prize 2010, Halle Handel Prize 2010, Herbert von Karajan Prize 2012, Swiss Award for Culture 2012, Bellini d'Oro, Medalla de Oro al Mérito en las Bellas Artes (Spain), Médaille Grand Vermeil de la Ville de Paris. *Website:* www.ceciliabartolionline.com.

BARTOLI, Sandro Ivo; Italian pianist; b. 10 Feb. 1970, Pisa. *Education:* Florence State Conservatory, RAM, London, studied with Shura Cherkassky in London. *Career:* debut with Mozart's Concerto K 271 at The Imperial Theatre, San Remo 1991; perfomed Respighi Toccata for piano and orchestra, BYCO (BBC recording debut); Bach Double Concertos with Alex Kelly at the Basilica di San Giovanni, Lucca 1993; Mozart Concertos K 413, 414, and 415 at St John's, Smith Square, London 1995; PBS live broadcast debut, Seeger Auditorium, Johnson City, TN, USA 1995; Beethoven Concerto No. 5 at St James's, Piccadilly, London (BBC live recording) 1996; recitalist at Centre Georges Pompidou, Paris 1996; performed Mozart concertos at Livorno Festival 1997; Rachmaninov's Paganini Rhapsody at the Bridgewater Hall, Manchester 1999; recitalist at Warwick and Leamington Festival 1999; Troldhallen, Bergen 2000; Nybrokayen Music Acad. 2000; Brighton Festival, England 2000; Aix-en-Provence (radio broadcast) 2000; Ogier and Le Masurier International Piano Festival, Jersey, Channel Islands 2000; Fairfield Hall, London 2001; performed Beethoven Concerto No. 5, Nordhausen, Germany 2001; Shostakovich Concerto No. 1, Stockholm 2001; performed at the Festival d'Avignon, France 2001; recitalist, Teatro Carignano, Turin, Italy 2002; Opera Holland Park, London 2002; performed Rachmaninov Concerto No. 3, London 2003; performed eight concertos 2010/11; Rachmaninov Concerto No. 2 in Dresden, Liszt Totentanz and Haydn's D Major piano concerto in Munich 2012; Puccini Festival, Torre del Lago, Lucca 2013; founded, directed and performed at Opera Etcetera, London 2002; Artistic Dir, Accademia de' Concerti music soc. *Recordings:* Malipiero: Piano Music 1995, Fugitives – works by Casella, Grainger and Pabst 1997, Casella: Piano Music 1998, Opera Etcetera 2003, Encores 2003, Fugitives 2005, Malipiero: Piano Concertos 2007, Chopin Brillante 2008, Liszt–Busoni Transcriptions 2011, Respighi works for piano and orchestra 2011, Ferruccio Busoni piano works 2011, The Frescobaldi Legacy 2012. *Honours:* Mary Elizabeth B'Stard Scholarship 1991–92, Royal Acad. Foundation Scholarship 1991–92, Lyric Club Renato Bruson Gina Rosso Prize for Outstanding Work in the Arts, Turin 2002. *Current Management:* The Agency, Excellent Entertainment, Suites 2–5, The Business Centre, 120 West Heath Road, London, NW3 7TU, England. *Telephone:* (20) 8458-4212. *E-mail:* theagency@excellententertainment.biz. *Website:* www.excellententertainment.biz. *E-mail:* info@sandroivobartoli.com (office). *Website:* www.sandroivobartoli.com (office).

BARTOLINI, Lando; Italian singer (tenor); b. 11 April 1937, Casale di Prato, Florence; m. Deanna Mungai 1966, two d. *Education:* Academy of Vocal Arts, Philadelphia, USA, studied with Nicola Moscona. *Career:* debut in Iris of Mascagni at the Gran Liceo of Barcelona, Oct 1973; USA debut in Cavalleria Rusticana, New York City Opera 1976; appeared at special events including Concert with Philadelphia Orchestra, new production of Ernani with Chicago Lyric, Manon Lescaut with Vienna State Opera in Tokyo, Simon Boccanegra at Festival d'Orange, new production of Turandot at Munich State Opera, Turandot with La Scala, Milan; in Seoul during Olympic Games; has sung in many other major venues around the world including La Scala, Arena di Verona, Opéra de Paris, Metropolitan Opera, Covent Garden, Vienna, Budapest, Buenos Aires, Santiago del Chile, South Africa, Canada, Lisbon, Boston and Cleveland with Metropolitan Opera; wide repertoire includes Aida, Tosca, La Bohème, Il Trovatore, Don Carlo, Macbeth, Forza del Destino, Il Tabarro, Mephistopheles and Rigoletto; sang Manrico in Il Trovatore at the Orange Festival 1992; Radames for Opera Pacific 1994; sang Des Grieux in Manon Lescaut at Torre del Lago 1996; season 1996 as Radames at the Vienna Staatsoper and Verdi's Alvaro at Antwerp, Andrea Chénier at Monte Carlo 1998; season 1999–2000 as Radames at Florence and Puccini's Des Grieux at Catania; sang Calaf in Turandot in new production at Maggio Musicale in Florence 1997, many tours with production; Otello at Hamburg State Opera 2002; regular guest at Torre del Lago. *Recordings:* I Cavalieri di Ekebu, with director Gianandrea Gavazzeni 1992, Respighi's La Semirama (first recording), Solo Tenor Arias 1991, Turandot Last Duet Alfano (first recording) 1990. *Publications:* La Follia Di New York, 1989; Orpheus Berlin, 1990; Das Opern Glas Germany, 1990; Opera News New York, 1991–93. *Current Management:* Sardos Artists Management, 180 West End Avenue, Suite 22B, New York, NY 10023, USA. *Address:* Via Bargo 12, 50047 Casale di Prato, Florence, Italy.

BÄRTSCHI, Werner; Swiss pianist, composer and conductor; *Artistic Director*, *Rezital*; b. 1 Jan. 1950, Zürich; m.; two c. *Education:* Volksschule and Gymnasium, Zurich; studied as pianist, composer and conductor in Zürich and Basel. *Career:* concerts in 40 countries on five continents; festival appearances include Yehudi Menuhin Festival, Gstaad, Lucerne Festival, Zürcher Festspiele, Festival int. de piano de la Roque d'Anthéron, Salzburger Festspiele, Antalya Piyano Festivali; f. Satie-Saison 1980–81 and Ives-Zyklus 1985–86, both in Zürich; premiered works by John Cage, Moritz Eggert, Klaus Huber, Wilhelm Killmayer, Terry Riley, Dieter Schnebel, Wladimir Vogel and others; has performed with musicians including Peter Lukas Graf, Aurèle Nicolet, Fabio di Casola, Ana Chumachenco, Patricia Kopatchinskaja, Yehudi Menuhin, Sol Gabetta, Wen-Sinn Yang, Vesselina Kasarova, Noëmi Nadelmann, Laszlo Polgar, Carmina Quartet, Tokio Quartet, Armin Jordan, Edwin Loehrer, Paul Sacher, Edmond de Stoutz, Mario Venzago; Pres. Music Cttee of City of Zurich 1990–92; Artistic Adviser to 1991 June Festival, Zurich; Artistic Dir Rezital, Musikkollegium Zürcher Oberland, Schaffhauser Meisterkonzerte, Schaffhauser Meisterkurse; performances of his own compositions in over 35 countries; several broadcasts and recordings; mem. Schweizerischer Tonkünstlerverein, Schweizerischer Musikpädagogischer Verband, Schweizerische Akad. für Musikpädagogik, Komponistensekretariat Zürich. *Compositions include:* over 50 works of orchestral music, chamber music, vocal music, piano music; several transcriptions: Rossini, Fauré, Schoeck, Schnebel. *Recordings:* over 40 recordings as pianist, including music of over 40 composers. *Publications include:* Die unvermeidliche Musik des John Cage 1969, Musik der Entfremdung – entfremdete Musik 1981–82, Ratio und Intuition in der Musik, Kunst und Wissenschaft 1984, Italian trans. 1989, Zu meinem Klavierstück in Trauer und Prunk 1989, Leistung und Plausch im Musikunterricht 1989, German edns of selected writings by Erik Satie 1980 and Charles Ives 1985, Music Editions of works by Zdenek Fibich 1988, and Wladimir Vogel 1989. *Honours:* Grand Prize, Acad. du disque française 1983. *Address:* zum Komet, 8200 Schaffhausen, Switzerland (home). *Fax:* (52) 6204647. *E-mail:* wernerbaertschi@bluewin.ch; baertschi.w@rezital.ch. *Website:* www.wernerbaertschi.ch.

BARTZ, (Anjara) Ingrid; German singer (mezzo-soprano); b. 20 March 1964, Aachen. *Education:* studied at Musikhochschule Koln with Juliette Bise-Delnon, Edith Mathis and Brigitte Fassbaender. *Career:* sang at Aachen Opera 1982, including Britten's Hermia; opera studio at Düsseldorf Opera, with Hänsel 1987–88; at Karlsruhe Opera, as Cherubino, Octavian, the Composer in Ariadne auf Naxos, Suzuki, Flora, Rosina, Mignon and Sesto in Handel's Giulio Cesare 1988–93; Bonn Opera 1993–; Bayerischen Staatsoper Munich 1999–; guest appearances include major roles at Düsseldorf, Liège, Luxembourg, Strasbourg, Zürich, Lucerne, Frankfurt, Mannheim, Wiesbaden, Essen, Cologne, Vienna and at halls in Italy; concert and recording engagements with most German radio and television stations and abroad; Bonn Opera, 1993–, including several premieres and debuts: Nicklausse, Zerlina, Orlofsky, Fenena; roles include Octavian, Komponist, Charlotte, Hänsel, Suzuki; since 1999, guest appearances at Bavarian State Opera, Munich include Rossweisse, Wellgunde in Götterdämmerung and Ludmilla in The Bartered Bride; 2007: stage appearances in Regensburg and Bonn as Rösslwirtin Josepha Vogelhuber in R. Benatzky's Im weissen Rössl, with I.D. Fürstin Mariae Gloria von Thurn und Taxis 2007; jury mem. singing competitions. *Recordings include:* Lieder by Mahler (Rückert and Wunderhorn Lieder), Brahms (Zigeunerlieder) and Wagner (Wesendoncklieder) 1997,

Liebessehnsucht/Yearning for Love by Franz Lehár (Frasquita) 2000, Stille Nacht 2000, Die Walküre, from Munich 2002, Pique Dame (Judith) 2009. *Current Management:* c/o NWB Apollon & Hermes, PR-Arts-Media Services Production, Im Flögerhof 12, 53819 Neunkirchen, Cologne, Germany. *Telephone:* 2247-912164 (office). *Fax:* 2247-912165 (office). *E-mail:* post@apollonhermes.com (office). *Website:* www.bartz-a-voce.de (home).

BARYLLI, Walter; Austrian violinist; b. 16 June 1921, Vienna. *Education:* Vienna Hochschule, studied with F. von Reuter, Munich. *Career:* debut in Munich 1936; concert tours throughout Europe and overseas; mem., Vienna State Opera Orchestra, Vienna Philharmonic 1938–, fmr leader of both orchestras; Leader, Barylli Quartet 1945–; Prof. of Violin, Vienna Conservatory 1969–. *Honours:* Kreisler Prize (twice).

BASHFORD, Christina, BA, MMus, PhD, CertTHE; British musicologist and academic; b. 20 Dec. 1961, Penryn, Cormwall; m. John Wagstaff. *Education:* King's Coll. London, Wadham Coll., Oxford. *Career:* Man. Ed., New Grove Dictionary of Opera 1988–92; Lecturer, then Sr Lecturer, Oxford Brookes Univ. 1994–; mem. Royal Musical Asscn, British Asscn of Victorian Studies. *Publications:* Music and British Culture 1785–1914: Essays in Honour of Cyril Ehrlich (ed. with Leanne Langley) 2000; contrib. to The New Grove Dictionary of Music and Musicians 2001. *Honours:* Jack Westrup Prize (Music and Letters) 1991. *Address:* Oxford Brookes University, Headington, Oxford, OX3 0BP, England (office). *Telephone:* (1865) 484985 (office). *E-mail:* cmbashford@brookes.ac.uk (office).

BASHKIROV, Dmitri Aleksandrovich; Russian pianist and academic; *Professor Titular, Escuela Superior de Música Reina Sofía*; b. 1 Nov. 1931, Tbilisi, Georgia; s. of Alexandr Bashkirov and Ester Ramendik; m. Natalya Bashkirova 1987; one s.; one s. from second marriage; one d. from a previous marriage. *Education:* Moscow P. I. Tchaikovsky State Conservatory. *Career:* studied in Tbilisi under A. Virsaladze, Moscow State Conservatory under A. Goldenweiser; concerts since 1955 in more than 30 countries; participated in Wiener Festwochen, Verbier, Switzerland, Helsinki, Granada, Ruhr Piano Fest, Germany and other festivals; repertoire includes works by Mozart, Schumann, Brahms, Debussy, Prokofiev; Moscow State Conservatory 1957, Prof. 1976–90; mem. jury numerous int. competitions; Prof. classes Acad. Mozarteum Salzburg, Sibelius Acad. Helsinki, Acad. of Music Jerusalem, Paris National Conservatory and others in London, Vienna, New York, Los Angeles, Lisbon, Stockholm; Prof. Internat. Acad. di Musica, Como, Italy 1992–; fmr Prof., Moscow Conservatory; Chair. Piano Dept Queen Sofía Higher School of Music, Madrid 1991–, now Titular Prof.; taught at Conservatory of The Hague 2008. *Music:* more than 30 recordings on various labels, including Melodia, RCD, EMI, Erato and Harmonia Mundi. *Honours:* Hon. Prof., Schanchaj Conservatorium; Grand Prix M. Long Int. Competition (Paris) 1955, People's Artist of Russia, Hon. R. Schumann Medal (Zwickau, Germany) 1970, Hon. Medal, Univ. Autónoma de Madrid, Hon. Prix Ruhr pianisten festivals. *Address:* San Antonio 17, Pozaelo, Madrid, Spain (home); Studencheskaja 31, app. 74, Moscow, Russia (home). *Telephone:* (91) 3511060 (office); (95) 2493741 (home). *Fax:* (91) 3570788 (office); (95) 2493741 (home). www.escuelasuperiordemusicareinasofia.es (office).

BASHMET, Yuri Abramovich; Russian violist and conductor; *Artistic Director and Principal Conductor, Symphony Orchestra of New Russia (Novaya Rossiya State Symphony Orchestra)*; b. 24 Jan. 1953, Rostov-on-Don; m. Natalia Bashmet; one d. *Education:* Moscow State Conservatory. *Career:* concerts since 1975; gave recitals and played with maj. orchestras of Europe, America and Asia; played in chamber ensembles with Sviatoslav Richter, Vladimir Spivakov, Victor Tretyakov and others; restored chamber repertoire for viola, commissioned and was first performer of music by contemporary composers, including concertos by Alfred Schnittke, Giya Kancheli, Aleksander Tchaikovsky; first viola player to give solo recitals at leading concert halls including Tchaikovsky Hall, Moscow, Concertgebouw, Amsterdam, La Scala, Milan, Suntory Hall, Tokyo; Founder and Artistic Dir Chamber Orchestra Soloists of Moscow 1989–; Founder and Artistic Dir Moscow Soloists 1992–; Artistic Dir and Prin. Conductor Symphony Orchestra of New Russia (Novaya Rossiya State Symphony Orchestra) 2002–; f. Yuri Bashmet Int. Competition for Young Viola Players 1994; Artistic Dir December Nights Festival, Moscow 1998–, Moscow Soloists; Founder and Artistic Dir Elba Music Festival 1998–; f. Yu. Bashmet Viola Competition, Moscow 1999–; f. Int. Foundation to award annual Shostakovich Prize. *Honours:* prize winner of int. competitions in Budapest 1975, Munich 1976; People's Artist of Russia 1986, State Prize of Russia 1993, Sonning Prize (Denmark) 1995, Russian Biographic Soc. Man of the Year 2000, Olympus Nat. Award 2003. *Current Management:* International Classical Artists, Dunstan House, 14a St Cross Street, London EC1N 8XA, England. *E-mail:* info@icartists.co.uk. *Address:* 103009 Moscow, Briyusov per. 7, Apt. 16, Russia (home). *Telephone:* (495) 561-66-96 (office); (495) 229-73-25 (home). *Website:* www.yuribashmet.com; www.nros.ru/nros/ru.

BASS, Alexandra, ARCM, GRSM, PGCE; British musician (flautist); b. 15 Dec. 1962, Funtington, W Sussex; m. Sebastian Toke-Nichols; one s. one d. *Education:* Royal Coll. of Music, Homerton Coll., Cambridge, Conservatoire Hector Berlioz and Ecole Normale, Paris, Guildhall School of Music and Drama, London. *Career:* led 1986 expedition to Peru and Bolivia to study the indigenous music of the Indians; orchestral player, BBC Symphony Orchestra, London Philharmonic Orchestra, Royal Philharmonic Orchestra, Liverpool Philharmonic Orchestra, Hallé Orchestra, Orchestra of the Royal Opera House, Covent Garden; soloist and chamber music player; Founder and Music Dir Alibas; mem. Inc. Soc. of Musicians, Musicians' Union. *Recordings include:* Humoreske (Alibas flute and guitar duo) 2005. *Honours:* Chamber Music Prize, Royal Coll. of Music 1980, Prix Supérieur, Hector Berlioz Conservatoire, Paris 1987.

BASYSTIUK, Olga, BA; Ukrainian singer (soprano); b. 18 Aug. 1951, Poliana; d. of the late Ivan Basystiuk and of Maria Basystiuk; m. Vladimir Gaptar 1986; one s. *Education:* State Lysenko Musical Conservatory. *Career:* soloist, Franko Opera and Ballet Theatre, Lvov 1974, State Organ Hall, Kiev 1981–; repertoire includes Baroque arias, Schubert lieder, Ukrainian and Russian folk songs, 20th century opera, and especially Italian lyric operas of Bellini, Donizetti and Verdi and Russian art songs. *Recordings include:* 7 Concurson Int. de Canto 1975, O. Basystiuk 1978. *Honours:* Hon. Artist of Ukraine 1976; Order of King Yaroslav the Wise 1995; Grand Prix Int. Singers' Competition, Rio de Janeiro, Brazil 1975, Gold Medal, 10th Int. Popova Singers' Festival, Pleven, Bulgaria 1975, Laureate, UNESCO Int. Record Competition, Bratislava, Czechosovakia 1978, People's Artist of Ukraine 1985, UN Peace Medal 1985, Laureate, State Taras Shevchenko Prize 1987, Gold Medal and Prize, Mikhailo Dem'yaniv Int. Foundation 1993, Winner, Buenos Aires Song Competition (lyric, Italian and Slavic Lieder). *Address:* ul Lysenko 4, kv 20, Kiev 252034, Ukraine. *Telephone:* (44) 2256791.

BATCHVAROVA, Vania Petrova; Bulgarian opera director; *Associate Professor and Opera Stage Director, State Conservatory, Cukurova University, Adana, Turkey*; b. 22 May 1950, Pleven; m. Rusko Russkov 1985. *Education:* studied Piano, Music High School, Russe, Bulgaria 1965–69; Music Theory and Pedagogy, Bulgarian Acad. of Music, Sofia 1970–72; Musicology, Martin Luther Univ., Halle/Saale, Germany 1972–73; Masters Degree, Opera and Stage Direction, Masters in Music (Piano), Hochschule für Musik 'Hanns Eisler', Berlin, Germany 1973–78; Teatro alla Scala di Milano, Italy 1986; St Petersburg, Russia, Simeon Ilitch Lapirov 1989; New Bulgarian Univ. 1992–97. *Career:* Stage Dir, Russe Opera House 1979–82; Assoc. Prof. of Opera Stage Directing and Opera Singing, Bulgarian Acad. of Music, Sofia 1982–97; Dean, Music and Performing Arts Dept, New Bulgarian Univ., Sofia, Assoc. Prof. of Opera Stage Directing and Opera Singing 1992–98; Prin. Stage Dir, Plovdiv Opera House 1996–97; Assoc. Prof., Cukurova Univ., State Conservatory, Turkey 1998–; directed works include Wagner's Götterdämmerung, Leipzig 1976, Mussorgsky's Boris Godunov, Russe 1979, Verdi's Falstaff, Sofia Opera House; productions and directed works include: Dvořák, Rusalka, Plauen, Germany 1978. Donizetti, L'Elisir d'amore, Stara Zagora 1983, Puccini, Madama Butterfly, Sliven 1986, Verdi, Nabucco, Burgas 1987, Otto Nicolai's Die Lustige Weiber, Bulgaria, Moldova, Russia 1989, Donizetti, Lucia di Lammermoor, Russe 1995, Mozart, Le nozze di Figaro, New Bulgarian Univ. 1995, Verdi, Il Trovatore, Rigoletto, Nabucco, Plovdiv, Bulgaria, Seville, Spain and Palma de Mallorca, Menorca, 1996, etc.; established Music Dept in NBU and first educ. programme for opera stage directors in Bulgaria; performances of children's musicals; performances for students in voice and opera education, Bulgaria (Acad. of Music, NBU), Turkey (Cukurova Univ.), guest in Vilnius, Lithuania and Moscow, Russian Fed.; mem. organizing cttee and jury of the following competitions in Bulgaria: Sv. Obretenov Nat. Competition for singers and players, Int. Competition for Young Talented Musicians, G.Zl. Cherkin Natsonal Competition for Singers; participated in Int. Festival for the Young 'Euroart2004' in Bulgaria; participated in and submitted papers to numerous symposia and int. confs in art, music educ. and semiotics; workshops; TV opera productions; piano and chamber concerts; numerous radio programmes about opera. *Publications:* Libretto, Bulgarian Roses, musical for children; The Golden Donkey by Apulej, opera; Books: Educating the Singing Actor 1995; A View of Mozart's Philosophy through His Operas, 1997; Requiem for Dried Up Rivers, essays, 1998; The Dramaturgy of Opera, 1999; Contributions: numerous articles in newspapers and magazines. *Address:* C.U. State Conservatory, 01330 Balcali/ Adana, Turkey (office). *Telephone:* (322) 3386264 (office); (532) 3011590 (office). *Fax:* (322) 3386265 (office). *E-mail:* ria7772001@yahoo.com (office). *Website:* www.cu.edu.tr (office).

BATE, Jennifer Lucy, OBE, BA, FRCO, FRSA, LRAM, ARCM; British organist; b. 11 Nov. 1944, London; d. of Horace Alfred Bate and Dorothy Marjorie Bate. *Education:* Univ. of Bristol. *Career:* Shaw Librarian, LSE 1966–69; full-time concert career 1969–; has performed world-wide; has organised several teaching programmes; collaboration with Olivier Messiaen 1975–92; designed portable pipe organ with N.P. Mander Ltd 1984 and a prototype computer organ 1987; gives masterclasses world-wide and lectures on a wide range of musical subjects; mem. Inc. Soc. of Musicians, British Music Soc. (Vice-Pres.), Royal Philharmonic Soc., Royal Soc. of Arts; North London Festival (Vice-Pres.). *Compositions include:* Toccata on a Theme of Martin Shaw, Introduction and Variations on an Old French Carol, Four Reflections, Homage to 1685: Four Studies, The Spinning Wheel, Lament, An English Canon, Variations on a Gregorian Theme, Suite on 'Veni Creator Spiritus'. *Recordings include:* Complete Works of Messiaen, Complete Works of Franck, An English Choice, Virtuoso French Organ Music, Panufnik: Metasinfonia, Vivaldi Double and Triple Concertos, Jennifer Bate and Friends, Jennifer Bate Plays Vierne, From Stanley to Wesley on period instruments, Reflections: The Organ Music of Jennifer Bate, Samuel Wesley Organ Music, The Wesleys and their Contemporaries, Complete Works of Felix Mendelssohn, Complete Organ Works of Peter Dickinson. *Television:* South Bank Show on Messiaen, La Nativité du Seigneur (Channel 4). *Publications include:* articles in Grove's

Dictionary of Music and Musicians, Organist's Review. *Honours:* hon. Italian citizenship for services to music 1996; Hon. DMus (Bristol) 2007; F.J. Read Prize, Royal Coll. of Organists, Young Musician 1972, voted Personnalité de l'Année, France 1989, one of the Women of the Year, UK 1990–97, Grand Prix du Disque (Messiaen), Diapason d'Or, Prix de Répertoire, France, Preis der deutschen Schallplattenkritik, Germany and MRA Award for 18th-century series From Stanley to Wesley. *Current Management:* c/o Andrew Roberts, 28 Oakenbrow, Sway, Lymington, Hampshire, SO41 6DY, England. *Telephone:* (1590) 682060. *E-mail:* andrewlroberts@btinternet.com. *Address:* 35 Collingwood Avenue, Muswell Hill, London, N10 3EH, England (office). *Telephone:* (20) 8883-3811 (office). *Fax:* (20) 8444-3695 (office). *E-mail:* jenniferbate@classical-artists.com (office). *Website:* www.classical-artists.com/jbate.

BATES, Lucy; British singer (soprano); b. 1973, Beverly, Yorkshire. *Education:* Royal Northern Coll. of Music with Sandra Dugdale, masterclasses with Evelyn Tubb, Nigel Douglas and Robin Bowman. *Career:* roles with RNCM included Mozart's Papagena and Blondchen, Ophelia, Catherine in La Jolie Fille de Perth, Barena in Jenůfa and Sandrina in La finta giardiniera, Yum-Yum in The Mikado and Frasquita for Phoenix Opera, Rossini's Elvira for the Accademia Rossiniana and Belinda in Dido and Aeneas; Glyndebourne Festival debut 2000, as Barbarina in Le nozze di Figaro. *Honours:* Peter Moores Foundation Scholar, finalist Frederic Cox Competition 2000.

BATES, Mason; American composer, producer and DJ; *Composer-in-Residence, Kennedy Center for the Performing Arts;* b. 23 Jan. 1977, Philadelphia, Pa. *Education:* Juilliard School, Univ. of California, Berkeley, studied with Edmund Campion. *Career:* apptd Margaret Lee Crofts Fellow in Composition, Tanglewood Music Festival aged 20; Composer-in-Residence, Young Concert Artists, Inc. 2000–02; Composer-in-Residence, Mobile Symphony 2005–06, Young American Composer-in-Residence, California Symphony 2007–10; Mead Composer-in-Residence, Chicago Symphony Orchestra 2010–15; Composer-in-Residence, Kennedy Center for the Performing Arts, Washington, DC 2015–, performances with Nat. Symphony, appearances with Jason Moran on Kennedy Center Jazz; works have been championed by Riccardo Muti, Michael Tilson Thomas and Leonard Slatkin; featured in San Francisco Symphony's Beethoven & Bates Festival; sessions as DJ in clubs and art spaces in San Francisco; Charles Ives Fellowship 2002, Guggenheim Fellowship 2008. *Music for film:* The Sea of Trees. *Compositions include:* numerous compositions, including Alternative Energy (premiered by Chicago Symphony 2011), Liquid Interface 2006–07, The B-Sides, Auditorium (premiered by San Francisco Symphony 2015), Anthology of Fantastic Zoology, acoustic work for orchestra. *Recordings include:* solo: Mothership 2015; other: Digital Loom 2009, Stereo is King 2014. *Honours:* Rome Prize, American Acad. in Rome, American Acad. in Berlin Prize, American Acad. of Arts and Letters Award in Music 2007, Van Cliburn American Composers Invitational (for White Lies for Lomax) 2009, Heinz Medal for the Humanities 2012, Composer of the Year, Pittsburgh Symphony Orchestra 2012–13. *Current Management:* c/o Opus 3 Artists, 5670 Wilshire Boulevard, Suite 1790, Los Angeles, CA 90036, USA. *Telephone:* (323) 954-1776. *E-mail:* info@opus3artists.com. *Website:* www.opus3artists.com. *Address:* John F. Kennedy Center for the Performing Arts, 2700 F Street, NW, Washington, DC 20566, USA (office). *Website:* www.kennedy-center.org (office); www.masonbates.com.

BATIASHVILI, Elisabeth (Lisa); Georgian violinist; b. 1979. *Education:* Munich Musikhochschule with Ana Chumachenco, studied with Mark Lubotsky in Hamburg. *Career:* appearances in Mozart's Sinfonia Concertante K364, with Colin Davis, at Ravinia with the Chicago SO, recitals at the Wigmore Hall and Châtelet, Paris, and with the Cleveland Orchestra at the Blossom Festival; London Proms debut 2000; further engagements with the City of Birmingham SO, Orchestre de Paris, Melbourne SO, NHK Symphony (Tokyo), Los Angeles PO, Philadelphia Orchestra and St Petersburg PO; played Prokofiev's First Concerto with the CBSO at the London Proms 2002; debut with the Berlin Philharmonic Orchestra 2004; with New York Philharmonic 2005; chamber musician with Pierre-Laurent Aimard, Till Fellner, Alban Gerhardt and Steven Osborne. *Recordings include:* Brahms, Schubert and Bach recital, Brahms Double Concerto with Alban Gerhardt. *Honours:* prizewinner Sibelius Competition, Helsinki 1995, Leonard Bernstein Award in Schleswig Holstein 2003. *Current Management:* Harrison Parrott, 5–6 Albion Court, London, W6 0QT, England. *Telephone:* (20) 7229-9166. *Fax:* (20) 7221-5042. *E-mail:* info@harrisonparrott.co.uk. *Website:* www.harrisonparrott.com.

BÁTIZ, Enrique; BA; Mexican pianist and conductor; *Music Director and Principal Conductor, Orquesta Sinfónica del Estado de México;* b. 4 May 1942, Mexico City; m. 1965 (divorced 1982); one s. one d. *Education:* Mexico Univ. Centre, Southern Methodist Univ., Dallas, USA, Juilliard School of Music, New York, studied with Adele Marcus, Jorge Mester, Warsaw Conservatory. *Career:* debut in Mexico City 1969; founder, Music Dir and Principal Conductor, Orquesta Sinfónica del Estado de México 1971–73, 1990–; Guest Conductor, Royal Philharmonic Orchestra, London 1984–; guest conductor with 150 orchestras worldwide; Conductor, Royal Philharmonic Orchestra tour in Mexico 1988; mem. IAPA, Club de Clubes, Club Cambridge (Mexico City). *Compositions:* Es Tiempo de Paz (symphonic poem) 1976. *Recordings:* with the Royal Philharmonic, with the Orquesta Sinfónica del Estado de México and with the Mexico City Philharmonic Orchestra. *Address:* Orquesta Sinfónica del Estado de México, Regina 52, segundo piso, Colonia Centro, 06080 México DF, Mexico (office). *Telephone:* (72) 2214-4684 (office). *Fax:* (72)

2214-5219 (office). *E-mail:* osem@edomex.gob.mx (office). *Website:* web.edomexico.gob.mx/OSEM (office).

BÁTIZ CAMPBELL, Enrique; Mexican conductor; *Director, Orquesta Sinfónica del Estado de México;* b. 4 May 1942, Mexico City; s. of José Luis Bátiz and María Elena Campbell; m. 1st Eva María Zuk 1965 (divorced 1983); one s. one d.; m. 2nd Elena Campbell Lombardo. *Education:* Centro Universitario México, Southern Methodist Univ. and Juilliard School, USA, Warsaw Conservatoire, Poland. *Career:* Founder and Prin. Conductor, Orquesta Sinfónica del Estado de México 1971–83, now Dir –; Artistic Dir Orquesta Filarmónica de la Ciudad de México 1983–90; Prin. Guest Conductor, Royal Philharmonic Orchestra, London 1984–; Chief Conductor, Symphonic Orchestra of Guanajuato 2005–; Guest Conductor with numerous orchestras. *Honours:* Order of Rio Branco (Brazil) 1986; Distinguished Artist of the Year, Mexican Union of Theatrical and Musical Broadcasters 1971, 1981, 1983, 1996, Mozart Medal, Domecq Cultural Inst. 1991, Sor Juana Ines de la Cruz Award for Arts and Letters 1994, State of Mexico Prize 1995. *Website:* www.edomexico.gob.mx.

BATJER, Margaret; American violinist; b. 17 Feb. 1959, San Angelo, TX; m. Joel McNeely 1985. *Education:* Interlochen Acad., Curtis Inst. of Music with Ivan Galamian and David Cerone. *Career:* debut solo appearance in Violin Concerto by Menotti with Chicago Symphony aged 15; appeared as soloist with Philadelphia Orchestra at Acad. of Music, with Dallas and Seattle Symphonies in Mendelssohn's Concerto at the St Louis Symphony; Chamber Orchestra of Europe; Prague Chamber Orchestra; Berlin Symphony Orchestra; New York String Orchestra at Carnegie Hall; Radio Telefis Dublin, with Prokofiev's 2nd Concerto; concerts at the Marlboro Music Festival, Vermont and US tour with Music of Marlboro Ensemble; tour of Germany 1984. *Recordings:* Bach Concerto for two violins with Salvatore Accardo and the Chamber Orchestra of Europe; Mozart Concertone with Salvatore Accardo and the Prague Chamber Orchestra; Verdi and Borodin String Quartets, Mozart Complete Viola Quintets. *Honours:* winner G. B. Dealey Competition, Dallas 1979. *Address:* 5971 Lubao Avenue, Woodland Hills, CA 91367, USA.

BATTEL, Giovanni Umberto, BMus; Italian pianist; b. 11 Dec. 1956, Portoguaro, Venice; m. Mariangela Zamper 1985. *Education:* Conservatory Tartini, Trieste, Nat. Music Acad. St Cecilia, Rome, Bologna Univ. *Career:* S. Remo Theatre 1980; RAI Radio 3 1981; Stresa Festival 1981; with symphony orchestra, Auditorium RAI Rome 1982; RAI 1 1982, 1983, 1984; Alghero Festival 1983; Mater Festival 1983; Trondheim Symphony Orchestra 1983; with Scarlatti Orchestra, Auditorium RAI Naples 1983; Trieste Theatre 1985; Auditorium Cagliari 1985; Musik Halle Hamburg 1986; Lubeck, Bonn 1986; Athens, Salonika, Greece 1986; San Francisco, Los Angeles (USA), Paris, Nantes, Lille (France) 1987; Todi Festival 1988; London 1988; Dir, Conservatory of Music 'Benedetto Marcello', Venice; artistic dir of piano competitions and of musical asscns. *Recordings:* Miroirs and Valses Nobles et Sentimentales, Ravel; Busoni's Piano Concerto; E. Wolf-Ferrari, Piano Trios Op. 5 and Op. 7. *Honours:* first prize in nat. competitions, including La Spezia 1975, Trieste 1978, Taranto 1979, Albenga 1979 and in int. competitions second prize Vercelli 1978, second prize Seregno 1979, fourth prize Bolzano 1980, first prize Enna 1982.

BATTERHAM, Andrew Bruce, BMus; Australian composer and musician; b. 22 July 1968, Melbourne; m.; one s. two d. *Education:* Univ. of Melbourne. *Career:* National Music Camp, Sydney 1987, 1988; Australian Composers' Orchestral Forum 1997; Queensland Philharmonic 1995; Perihelion 1997; Tasmanian Symphony 1997; Eliseon 1988; Melbourne Symphony 1999; Australian Chamber Orchestra 1999; Melbourne Symphony 2000, 2002; mem. Australian Performing Right Asscn, Musicians and Arrangers Guild of Australia, Melbourne Composers' League, Australian Music Centre, Sydney. *Compositions:* Thugine Legend, Cortege, Symphony No. 1: Off The Leash, Chiaroscuro, Organ Sonata, Maniacs and Broken Glass, Drum and Bass, The End of All Journeys 2000. *Honours:* Quantas Youth Award 1994, Corbould Composition Competition winner 1995. *Address:* 26 Rosslyn Street, Blackburn, Melbourne 3130, Australia.

BATTLE, Kathleen Deanna, MMus; American singer (soprano); b. 13 Aug. 1948, Portsmouth, Ohio; d. of Ollie Layne Battle and Grady Battle. *Education:* Coll. Conservatory of Music, Univ. of Cincinnati. *Career:* professional debut in Brahms Requiem, Cincinnati May Festival, then Spoleto Festival, Italy 1972; debut with Metropolitan Opera, New York as shepherd in Wagner's Tannhäuser 1977; regular guest with orchestras of New York, Chicago, Boston, Philadelphia, Cleveland, LA, San Francisco, Vienna, Paris and Berlin, at Salzburg, Tanglewood and other festivals and at major opera houses including Metropolitan, New York, Covent Garden, London, Paris and Vienna. *Recordings include:* Brahms Requiem and Songs, Mozart Requiem, Don Giovanni, Seraglio and concert arias, Verdi's Un Ballo in Maschera and Berg's Lulu Suite, New Year's Eve Gala, Vienna, Best of Kathleen Battle 2004. *Honours:* Dr hc (Univ. of Cincinnati), (Westminster Choir Coll.), (Ohio Univ.), (Xavier Univ., Cincinnati), (Amherst Coll.), (Seton Hall Univ.), (Wilberforce Univ.), (Manhattanville Coll.), (Shawnee State Univ.); five Grammy Awards, Emmy Award for Outstanding Individual Achievement in a Classical Program on Television 1991, inducted into NAACP Image Award Hall of Fame and Hollywood Bowl Hall of Fame, Ray Charles Award, Wilberforce Univ. *Current Management:* Columbia Artists Management Inc., 1790 Broadway, New York, NY 10019-1412, USA. *Telephone:* (212) 841-9500. *Fax:* (212) 841-9744. *E-mail:* info@cami.com. *Website:* www.cami.com.

BATURIN, Sergei; Russian violist; b. 1952, Moscow. *Education:* Moscow Conservatoire with Fjodor Druzhinin. *Career:* co-founder, Amistad Quartet 1973, changed named to Tchaikovsky Quartet 1994; many concerts in former Soviet Union and Russia, with repertoire including works by Haydn, Mozart, Beethoven, Schubert, Brahms, Tchaikovsky, Borodin, Prokofiev, Shostakovich, Bartók, Bucci, Golovin and Tikhomirov; concert tours to Mexico, Italy and Germany; series in commemoration of Tchaikovsky in Moscow; bd mem., Moscow Int. Chamber Music Festival Spring for Russia. *Honours:* Honoured Artist of Russia, prizewinner Béla Bartók Festival (with Amistad Quartet) 1976, Bucchi Competition, Rome (with Amistad Quartet) 1990.

BAUDO, Serge; French conductor; b. 16 July 1927, Marseille; s. of Etienne Baudo and Geneviève Tortelier; m. Madeleine Reties 1947; one s. one d. *Education:* Conservatoire nat. supérieur de musique, Paris. *Career:* Music Dir Radio Nice 1957–59; Conductor, Paris Opera Orchestra 1962–66; titular Conductor and Orchestral Dir a.i. Orchestre de Paris 1968–70; Music Dir Opéra de Lyon 1969–71, Orchestre Nat. de Lyon 1971–87; Prin. Conductor, Orchestra della Svizzera Italiana 1997–2000; Prin. Conductor, Orchestre Symphonique de Prague 2001–06; has conducted many of world's leading orchestras; Founder, Berlioz Festival, Lyon 1979–89. *Films:* music for Le Monde sans Soleil 1964. *Honours:* Officier, Légion d'honneur, Ordre des Arts et Lettres, Chevalier, Ordre nat. du Mérite; numerous prix du disque and other awards. *Address:* Les Hauts du Ferra, 2901 Chemin Charré, 13600 Ceyreste, France (home).

BAUER, Hartmut; German singer (bass); b. 1939, Kassel. *Education:* Frankfurt Musikhochschule. *Career:* sang at Augsburg Opera 1965–68, Coburg 1968–70, Wuppertal from 1970–90, notably as Creon in the 1972 German premiere of Milhaud's Médée; Bayreuth Festival 1973–75, as Fafner and Hans Schwarz; other appearances as Ariodeno in Cavalli's L'Ormindo, Mozart's Bartolo and Commendatore, Ramphis (Aida), Colline (La Bohème), Pimen, Schigolch (Lulu) and Cornelius' Abu Hassan; guest at Cologne, Frankfurt, Barcelona and Hannover; sang in the premiere of V. D. Kirchner's Erinys, Wuppertal 1990; Gurnemanz in Parsifal 1994; season 1999 as Rocco in Fidelio at Eutin, Sarastro and Baron Ochs at Gelsenkirchen.

BAUER, Thomas E.; German singer (baritone); b. 15 June 1970, Metten, Bavaria. *Education:* Regensburg Cathedral Choir, studied singing at Hochschule für Musik, Munich with Hanno Blaschke and Siegfried Mauser. *Career:* co-f. Singer Pur (vocal ensemble) 1990; debut at the Salzburg Festival in Salvatore Sciarrino's Quaderno di strada 2006; appears with ensembles including Boston Symphony Orchestra (Bernard Haitink), Nat. Symphony, Washington, DC (Iván Fischer), Concentus Musicus (Nikolaus Harnoncourt), Gürzenich-Orchester Köln (Markus Stenz), Netherlands Radio Chamber Philharmonic, Hilversum (Masaaki Suzuki), Orchester der Oper Zürich (Adam Fischer), NDR Sinfonieorchester (Thomas Hengelbrock), New Japan Philharmonic Orchestra (Naoto Otomo), Orquesta Sinfónica de RTVE, Madrid (Walter Weller), Tonhalle-Orchester, Zürich (Sir Roger Norrington), Anima Eterna (Jos van Immerseel), Tonkünstler-Orchester Niederösterreich (Paul Goodwin), Residentie Orkest (Jan Willem de Vriend), Concertgebouw Orkest, Amsterdam (Philippe Herreweghe), Gewandhausorchester, Leipzig (Riccardo Chailly), Monteverdi Choir (Sir John Eliot Gardiner), Chamber Orchestra of Europe (Nikolaus Harnoncourt); appears throughout Europe with the theatre ensemble La Fura dels Baus in a production of Orff's Carmina Burana; has sung in numerous world premieres; recitals with fortepiano specialist Jos van Immerseel; appeared in recital with Roger Vignoles 2011; invited to the Styriarte Graz for a Schumann recital 2013; sang at Salzburg Festspiele (with Manfred Honeck) 2014. *Film:* featured in Klaus Voswinckel's documentary film Winterreise – Schubert in Sibirien 2005. *Recordings include:* Elijah (ECHO Prize), Beethoven's Ninth Symphony, Bach Cantatas, Vier Toteninseln, Zelenka's Missa votiva, several Schumann lied recordings, Handel Apollo e Dafne (Gramophone Award for Baroque Vocal Disc, Stanley Sadie Handel Recording Prize) 2011, Schubert: Die Winterreise (Orphée d'Or and La Musica Korea) 2011. *Honours:* several prizes, including Bavarian Federal Govt and Ernst von Siemens Music Endowment Fund, Cité Internationale des Arts Paris, Schneider Schott Music Prize 2003. *Current Management:* c/o Daniela Spering, ORFEO Artist Management, Mönchsgüterweg 4, 50999 Cologne, Germany. *Telephone:* (2236) 381340. *Fax:* (2236) 381996. *E-mail:* ds@orfeo-artist-management.de. *Website:* www.orfeo-artist-management.de.

BAULD, Alison Margaret, BMus, DPhil; Australian composer; b. 7 May 1944, Sydney, NSW; m. Nicholas Evans 1978; one s. one d. *Education:* National Inst. of Dramatic Art, Sydney, Sydney Univ., York Univ., New South Wales Conservatorium with Sverjensky, studied with Elisabeth Lutyens and Hans Keller. *Career:* professional actress; Musical Dir, Laban Centre for Dance, Goldsmiths' Coll., London 1975–78; Composer-in-Residence, New South Wales Conservatory, Sydney 1978; teaches part time for Univ. of Delaware, Hollins Coll. and Pepperdine Univ., London; works performed and broadcast, London, Aldeburgh, York and Edinburgh Festivals, several European countries, Australia; mem. Asscn of Professional Composers, Musician's Union. *Compositions include:* On the Afternoon of the Pigsty for speaker and ensemble 1971, Humpty Dumpty for tenor, flute and guitar 1972, In a Dead Brown Land (music theatre) 1972, Mad Moll for solo soprano 1973, Dear Emily for soprano and harp 1973, One Pearl for soprano and string quartet 1973, Concert for piano and tape 1974, Exiles (music theatre) 1974, Van Diemen's Land for choir 1976, One Pearl II for soprano, flute and strings 1976, I Loved Miss Watson for soprano, piano and tape 1977, Banquo's Buried for soprano and piano 1982, Richard III for voice and string quartet 1985, Monody for solo

flute 1985, Copy Cats for violin and piano 1985, Once Upon a Time (music theatre) 1986, Nell (ballad opera) 1988, My Own Island for clarinet and piano 1989, Farewell Already for string quartet 1993, In Memoriam Uncle Ken for baritone and piano 1997, Death of Cleopatra 2002, Portia, Confess and Love 2003, Queen Margaret, She-Wolf of France 2003, No More of Love 2005. *Publications:* Play Your Way (piano and composition tutor) 1993, Mozart's Sister (novel) 2005. *Honours:* Gold Medal for Piano, New South Wales 1959, Paris Rostrum (composition) 1973, finalist Radcliffe Competition 1973. *Address:* c/o Chester Music and Novello & Co., 14–15 Berners Street, London W1T 3LJ, England (office). *E-mail:* promotion@musicsales.co.uk (office). *Website:* www.chesternovello.com (office); www.alisonbauld.com.

BAUMANN, Herbert Karl Wilhelm; German composer and conductor; b. 31 July 1925, Berlin; s. of Wilhelm Baumann and Elfriede Baumann (née Bade); m. Marianne Brose 1951; two s. *Education:* Berlin Classical High School, Schillergymnasium and Int. Music Inst. *Career:* Conductor, Tchaikovsky Symphony Orchestra 1947; Composer and Conductor, Deutsches Theater, Berlin 1947–53, Staatliche Berliner Bühnen: Schillertheater and Schlossparktheater 1953–70, Bayerisches Staatsschauspiel: Residenztheater, Munich 1971–79; freelance composer 1979–; mem. GEMA for 50 years. *Works include:* stage music for more than 500 plays, 40 TV plays and the ballets Alice in Wonderland and Rumpelstiltskin, music for radio, cinema and TV, orchestral, chamber and choir works, several suites for plucked instruments, music for strings, music for wind instruments, three concertos and works for organ. *Films include:* Das Jahrhundert des Kindes, Die Stadt von Morgen, Menschen in der Stadt, König Fußball, Timpi Tox und Ali Bum, Berlin Sketchbook. *Honours:* Mem. of Honour, BDZ 1990; Bundesverdienstkreuz 1998; Diploma of Honour Salsomaggiore (Italy) 1981; Silbernes Ehrenzeichen GDBA 1979. *Address:* Weitlstrasse 66, Apt 2049, 80935 Munich, Germany (home). *Telephone:* (89) 38582049 (home). *Fax:* (89) 38582049 (home). *E-mail:* hkwbau@augustinum.net. *Website:* www.komponisten.net/baumann.

BAUMANN, Ludwig; German singer (baritone); b. 9 Nov. 1950, Rosenheim. *Education:* studied in Munich, USA and Italy. *Career:* sang bass roles at the Munich State Opera 1970–72 including the premiere of Sim Tjong by Isang Yun; baritone at the Coburg Opera 1972–79 with many concerts elsewhere; Theater am Gärtnerplatz, Munich 1979–85; Cologne Opera from 1985 with guest appearances at Lausanne, Valentin in Faust 1986; Paris Châtelet, Gluck's Oreste 1988; Turin, Hamlet by Thomas; sang Kurwenal in Tristan, Marseilles 1992; Wolfram in Tannhäuser at Naples 1998; other roles include Rameau's Thesée, Opéra Comique, Paris; Rossini's Figaro at Nancy; Mozart's Papageno and Guglielmo. *Recordings:* La Bohème, Strauss's Daphne.

BAVOUZET, Jean-Efflam; French pianist; b. 1962. *Education:* Paris Conservatoire with Pierre Sancan, masterclasses with Paul Badura-Skoda, Nikita Magaloff, Menahem Pressler, György Sandor. *Career:* recitals in concert halls worldwide, including the Kennedy Center, Lincoln Center, Kaufmann Hall, New York and the Salle Gaveau, Paris; tours of Japan and USA; British engagements from 1987; engagements in Germany, The Netherlands, Japan, France and USA; Ravel's Left Hand Concerto with the Solingen Philharmonica and the Bournemouth Symphony 1991; has performed with many leading international orchestras, including Gurzenich Orchestra of Cologne, Bournemouth Symphony, Hallé Orchestra, Manchester, Weimar Staatskapelle, Hong Kong Philharmonic, Calgary Philharmonic, Utah Symphony, Hungarian National Philhamonic and Symphony Nat. de Belgique; debut with the Boston Symphony Orchestra under Ingo Metzmacher 2002; Berliner Sinfonie Orchester under Jean-Claude Casadesus and Orchestre de Paris under Pierre Boulez 2003; season 2004–05 appearances with London Symphony Orchestra; concerto repertoire includes all the concerti of Bartók, Beethoven and Prokofiev, complete solo piano works of Ravel and Schumann. *Recordings include:* Haydn's Four Sonatas and Fantaisie, Ravel's complete solo works for piano, MDG, Haydn and Schumann recitals, Debussy's Etudes, Complete Works for Piano (Gramophone Award for Best Instrumental Recording 2009), Haydn's Piano Sonatas Nos 31, 39, 47 and 49, Bartók's Piano Concertos, Debussy Fantaisie/Ravel Piano Concertos/Massenet Piano works (Gramophone Award for Best Concerto Recording 2011, BBC Music Magazine Orchestral Award 2012) 2011, Prokofiev Complete Piano Concertos (Gramophone Award for Best Concerto Recording) 2014. *Honours:* finalist Leeds International Competition 1987, prizewinner Young Concert Artists Competition, USA 1986, Tomassoni-Beethoven Cologne 1986, Special Jury Prize, Santander, Spain, Guilde Française des Artistes Solistes, Paris Conservatoire first prize for piano and chamber music, Chamber Music Prize 1989, 'Choc' Award from Le Monde de la musique (for Ravel complete solo works for piano and Haydn recordings), Diapason d'Or (for Ravel complete solo works for piano), Artist of the Year Award, Int. Classical Music Awards 2012. *Current Management:* Harrison Parrott, 5–6 Albion Court, Albion Place, London, W6 0QT, England. *Telephone:* (20) 7229-9166. *E-mail:* info@harrisonparrott.co.uk. *Website:* www.harrisonparrott.com.

BAWDEN, Rupert; British composer, conductor and violinist; b. 1958, London. *Education:* Univ. of Cambridge with Robin Holloway. *Career:* debut as conductor at the 1986 Aldeburgh Festival; plays violin and viola with various ensembles, including London Sinfonietta and the English Concert; performances of works by Birtwistle, Goehr, Harvey, Weir and Hoyland, including several world premieres; television recordings of works by Gruber, Holloway and Kagel; Michael Nyman's The Man who Mistook his Wife for a Hat for BBC radio; engagements with the Bath, King's Lynn and London Int. Opera Festivals; BBC Symphony and Scottish Chamber Orchestra; works have been performed in USA, Australia, Far East, the UK and France; 1989 performances by the London Sinfonietta and at the Promenade Concerts; ballet commission from Munich Biennale 1990. *Compositions:* Railings for flute and piano 1980, Three-part Motet for soprano, mezzo, baritone and orchestra 1980, Passamezzo di Battaglia for oboe, horn and harpsichord 1984, Sunless for ensemble 1984, Seven Songs from the House of Sand for brass quintet 1985, Le Livre de Fauvel for soprano, mezzo and ensemble 1986, The Angel and the Ship of Souls for 19 players 1983–87, Souvenirs de Fauvel for two pianos 1987, Dramatic Cantata on the Legend of Apollo and Daphne for violin, cello and 13 players 1989, Ultima Scena (commissioned by Henry Wood Promenade Concerts) 1989, Le Livre de Fauvel (ballet) 1990. *Address:* c/o Chester Music and Novello & Co., 14–15 Berners Street, London, W1T 3LJ, England. *Telephone:* (20) 7612-7400. *Fax:* (20) 7612-7545. *E-mail:* promotion@ musicsales.co.uk.

BAX, Alessio; Italian pianist; b. 1977, Bari; m. Lucille Chung. *Education:* Bari Conservatory, Chigiana Acad., Siena, Southern Methodist Univ., Dallas with Joaquin Achucarro. *Career:* recitals throughout Europe, USA and Asia; concerts with London Philharmonic, City of Birmingham Symphony, Royal Liverpool Philharmonic, Royal Scottish Symphony Orchestra, Dallas Symphony, Houston Symphony, NHK Symphony, Tokyo Symphony, New Japan Philharmonic; tours of Japan (Suntory and Kioi Hall), Italy, Germany, UK, USA, Israel, Spain; worked with Sir Simon Rattle, Vernon Handley, Petr Altrichter, Owain Arwel Hughes, Sergiu Commissiona, Dmitry Sitkovetsky, Ken-ichiro Kobayashi; festivals include London Int. Piano Series, Bath, Harrogate, Ruhr Klavier Festivals, Beethoven Fest Bonn, Mecklenburg and the Snape Maltings Proms in Aldeburgh. *Recordings include:* Baroque Reflections, Piano and Organ music by Marcel Dupré, Brahms D minor Concerto with New Japan Philharmonic, Ligeti Two piano and four hands music with Lucille Chung, Beethoven Third Concerto with Hamamatsu SO, Carnival of the Animals by Saint-Saëns with Lucille Chung and Fort Worth Symphony Orchestra. *Honours:* winner Hamamatsu Int. Piano Competition 1977, Leeds Int. Pianoforte Competition 2000. *Current Management:* c/o Stefan Bown, Warner Classics, Griffin House, 3rd Floor, 161 Hammersmith Road, London, W6 8BS, England. *Telephone:* (20) 8563-5100. *Fax:* (20) 8563-6226. *E-mail:* stefan.bown@warnermusic.com. *Website:* www.warnerclassics .com; www.alessiobax.com.

BAXTER, Paul, BMus; British record producer; *Managing Director, Delphian Records*; b. 26 Sept. 1978, Cromartyshire, Scotland. *Education:* Univ. of Edinburgh. *Career:* co-f. music label Delphian Records 2000 while still a student, with support from Prince's Scottish Youth Business Trust; special focus on chamber and instrumental music, particularly recording and promotion of new music; first part-orchestral record released in 2008 with Scottish Chamber Orchestra and conductor Garry Walker, following a grant from Scottish Government; artists on roster include Michael Bonaventure, Gordon Ferries, Mr McFall's Chamber, Robert Irvine, John Kitchen, Simon Smith, David Wilde, Choir of Gonville & Caius Coll., Cambridge/Geoffrey Webber, Nat. Youth Choir of Great Britain/Mike Brewer. *Honours:* Gramophone Award for Label of the Year 2014. *Address:* Delphian Records Ltd, 34 Wallace Avenue, The Meadows, Wallyford, East Lothian, EH21 8BZ, Scotland (office). *Telephone:* (845) 644-9308 (office). *Fax:* (7092) 165783 (office). *E-mail:* psb@delphianrecords.co.uk (office). *Website:* www.delphianrecords.com (office).

BAXTRESSER, Jeanne; American flautist, author, lecturer and teacher; *Vira I. Heinz Professor of Flute, Carnegie Mellon School of Music. Education:* Juilliard School. *Career:* fmr Prin. Flautist, Montreal Symphony Orchestra, Toronto Symphony Orchestra; soloist for 15 years New York Philharmonic; featured soloist with leading orchestras across N America and Europe; fmr mem. Faculty, Manhattan School of Music and Juilliard School; Vira I. Heinz Prof. of Flute, Carnegie Mellon Univ. School of Music, Pittsburgh 1998–, Univ. Prof. 2006–; Visiting Artist Lecturer, New England Conservatory of Music, Boston 2006–. *Recordings include:* Orchestral Excerpts for Flute, New York Legends – Jeanne Baxtresser, Chamber Music for Flute 2005, Jeanne Baxtresser – A Collection of My Favorites 2005. *Publications:* Orchestral Excerpts for Flute with Piano Accompaniment, Great Flute Duos from the Orchestral Repertoire (winner Flute Asscn Newly Published Music Competition 2004), Flower Duet from Lakmé. *Honours:* Lifetime Achievement Award, Nat. Flute Asscn 2006. *Address:* Carnegie Mellon School of Music, 5000 Forbes Avenue, Pittsburgh, PA 15213-3815, USA (office). *Telephone:* (908) 608-1325 (office). *E-mail:* cmufluteinquiries@hotmail.com (office). *Website:* music.web.cmu.edu (office); www.jeannebaxtresser.com.

BAYLEY, Clive; British singer (bass); b. 15 Nov. 1960, Manchester, England; m. Paula Bradley 1989. *Education:* Royal Northern Coll. of Music, Nat. Opera Studio. *Career:* debut with Opera North; sang in The Rape of Lucretia, Il Barbiere di Siviglia and as Claggart in Billy Budd, while at the RNCM; professional debut as Schwarz in Die Meistersinger for Opera North, followed by the King in Aida, Colline in La Bohème, Don Basilio, Banquo, Bartolo in Le nozze di Figaro and in British premiere of Verdi's Jerusalem; ENO debut 1987, as Pietro in Simon Boccanegra, followed by appearances in Billy Budd, Un ballo in Maschera, Don Giovanni, Doctor Faust and The Return of Ulysses; Netherlands Opera 1989, as Trufaldino in Ariadne auf Naxos; 1989 in a concert performance of Bernstein's Candide, conducted by the composer; sang in the premiere of Birtwistle's Gawain at Covent Garden 1991; concert repertory includes the Verdi Requiem, Elgar's Dream of Gerontius and Apostles, the Brahms Requiem, Handel's Messiah, Israel in Egypt, the Choral

Symphony, Rossini's Petite Messe Solennelle and Christus in the St Matthew Passion; roles at ROH with parts in Fidelio, The Fiery Angel, Die Meistersinger, Colline in La Bohème; further roles at Opera North include Sparafucile, The Monk in Don Carlos and Raleigh in Gloriana; sang Ferrando in Il Trovatore for Opera North 1994; Mozart's Figaro for Opera North 1996; season 1998 as Kecal in The Bartered Bride and Verdi's Grand Inquisitor for the Royal Opera; season 2000–01 as Debussy's Arkel for ENO, Alvise in La Gioconda for Opera North, Drago in Schumann's Genoveva at Garsington, and as Britten's Collatinus at Lausanne; Weber's Euryanthe at the London Proms 2002. *Recordings include:* Candide. *Honours:* Curtis Gold Medal for Singing, RNCM Robin Kay Memorial Prize for Opera. *Current Management:* c/o IMG Artists, The Light Box, 111 Power Road, London, W4 5PY, England. *Telephone:* (20) 7957-5800. *Fax:* (20) 7957-5801. *E-mail:* bsegal@imgartists .com. *Website:* www.imgartists.com.

BAYO, Maria; Spanish singer (soprano); b. 1964, Navarra. *Career:* appeared from 1998 at Lucerne (Lucia di Lammermoor) and St Gallen (Amina in La Sonnambula); sang Susanna at Madrid and Marseille (1990), Micaela at Monte Carlo (1991) and Musetta in La Bohème (debut role at La Scala, 1991); season 1991–92 as Susanna at the Opéra Bastille, Paris, Norina in Don Pasquale at Hamburg, Amenaide in Tancredi at Schwetzingen and Rosina at Strasbourg; season 1993–94 as Zerlina at Buenos Aires and Ensoleillad in Massenet's Chérubin at Covent Garden; Cavalli's Calisto at Brussels (1993); Berlin Staatsoper (1996) and Lyon Opéra (1999); Cherubino at Salzburg, 1998; sang Liu in Turandot at the reopening of the Liceu Theatre, Barcelona, 1999; season 2000–01 as Susanna at Salzburg, Manon at Madrid and Bizet's Leila for Marseilles Opera; concert repertory includes Rossini's Stabat Mater and Mahler's 2nd Symphony. *Honours:* prizewinner Francisco Vines and Maria Callas Competitions. *Current Management:* Hilbert Artists Management, Maximilianstrasse 22, 80539 Munich, Germany. *Telephone:* (89) 2907470. *Fax:* (89) 29074790. *E-mail:* agentur@hilbert.de. *Website:* www .hilbert.de; www.mariabayo.net.

BAYRAKDARIAN, Isabel, BEng; Canadian singer (soprano); b. Lebanon; m. Serouj Kradjian. *Education:* Univ. of Toronto. *Career:* opera performances include title roles in L'incoronazione di Poppea at Teatro del Liceu, and Kurt Weill's Marie Galante with Opéra Français de New York, Pamina in Die Zauberflöte at Metropolitan Opera, Zerlina in Don Giovanni at Salzburg Festival's celebration of Mozart's birthday and at Metropolitan Opera, Mélisande in Pélleas et Mélisande at Canadian Opera Company, title role in The Cunning Little Vixen at Saito Kinen Festival, Le nozze di Figaro at Covent Garden and Houston Grand Opera, Blanche in Poulenc's Dialogues of the Carmelites at Lyric Opera of Chicago; also in world premiere of Jake Heggie and Gene Sheer's opera To Hell and Back with San Francisco's Philharmonia Baroque Orchestra; tours with the Manitoba Chamber Orchestra 2008–09; recitals. *Film soundtracks:* as singer: Lord of the Rings: The Two Towers 2002, Ararat 2002. *Recordings include:* Millennium, Joyous Light, Azulão, Cleopatra, Mahler's Symphony No. 2, Mozart's Arie & Duetti (with Russell Braun and Michael Schade), Tango Noturno, Gomidas Songs. *Honours:* Metropolitan Opera Nat. Council Award 1997, first prize, Operalia Competition 2000, four Juno awards, the Queen Elizabeth II Golden Jubilee Medal, Virginia Parker Prize, Canada Council for the Arts 2005, Leonie Rysanek Award, George London Foundation. *Current Management:* c/o Stephanie Reiss, IMG Artists, Carnegie Hall Tower, 152 West 57th Street, 5th Floor, New York, NY 10019, USA. *Telephone:* (212) 994-3500. *Fax:* (212) 994-3500. *E-mail:* sreiss@imgartists.com. *Website:* imgartists.com/artist/ isabelbayrakdarian; www.bayrakdarian.com.

BAZOLA, François; French singer (bass); b. 1965, Paris. *Education:* Paris Conservatoire with William Christie. *Career:* has sung with Les Arts Florissants in Lully's Atys (in Paris and New York), Rameau's Les Indes Galantes and Castor et Pollux, Purcell's Fairy Queen (Aix-en-Provence) and Charpentier's Le malade imaginaire; Sang Arcas in Médée by Charpentier in Paris, Lisbon and New York (1993) and Pan in King Arthur by Purcell (Paris and London, 1995); Assistant to William Christie with the choir of Les Arts Florissants 1994–; Chorus Leader, Philidor Ensemble, Tours. *Honours:* Chevalier, Ordre des Artes et des Lettres 2006. *Address:* 55 rue Mirabeau, 37000 Tours, France (home). *Telephone:* 2-47-66-47-65 (home). *E-mail:* fbazola@aol.com (home).

BEACH, David Williams, BA, MMus, PhD; American academic and administrator; b. 5 Sept. 1938, Hartford, CT; m. Marcia Francesca Salemme 1964, one s. one d. *Education:* Brown Univ., Yale Univ. *Career:* Asst Prof., Yale Univ. 1964–71; Asst Prof., Brooklyn Coll., CUNY 1971–72, Assoc. Prof. 1974–85; Chair Theory Dept, Eastman School of Music 1981–90, 1995–96, Prof. 1985–; Univ. Dean of Graduate Studies, Univ. of Rochester 1991–95; Prof. and Dean Faculty of Music, Univ. of Toronto 1996–; mem. Soc. for Music Theory (exec. bd 1984–87); Chair., Publications Cttee 1979–84; mem. American Musicological Soc. *Publications:* The Art of Strict Musical Composition, by J. P. Kirnberger (co-trans. and notes) 1982, Aspects of Schenkerian Theory (ed.) 1983, Music Theory in Concept and Practice (co-ed.) 1997; contrib. to Acta Musicologia, Music Analysis, Journal of Music Theory, Music Theory Spectrum, Theory and Practice, Journal of Musicological Research, Integral, Journal of Music Theory Pedagogy. *Honours:* ASCAP Deems Taylor Award 1983.

BEALE, Matthew; British singer (tenor); b. 1975, England. *Education:* Choral Scholar, New Coll., Oxford, Royal Coll. of Music (RCM) with Margaret

Kingsley. *Career:* choral singing with the Tallis Scholars, The Sixteen and The Gabrieli Consort; Carmina Burana with the Liverpool Philharmonic Orchestra, Messiah at Worcester Cathedral and Bach's B Minor Mass at St John's Smith Square, 2000; opera roles include Mozart's Ferrando, Cimarosa's Paolino, Sir Philip and Narrator in Britten's Owen Wingrave and Sellem in The Rake's Progess; title role in the premiere of Francis Grier's St Francis of Assisi; Ugone in Flavio from the London Handel Festival, 2001; recitals in Japan, England and Wales; On Wenlock Edge by Vaughan Williams at St John's Smith Square, London, 2001; currently pursuing career in the wine trade. *Honours:* Sybil Tutton Award, RCM.

BEAMISH, Sally, DMus, GRNCM; British composer and violist; b. (Sarah Frances Beamish), 26 Aug. 1956, London; d. of Anthony Beamish and Ursula Snow-Beamish; one s. two d. *Education:* Royal Northern Coll. of Music, Staatliche Hochschule für Musik, Detmold, Germany. *Career:* viola player, Raphael Ensemble, Acad. of St Martin-in-the-Fields, London Sinfonietta, Lontano 1979–1990; Composer 1990–; Composer-in-Residence, Swedish Chamber Orchestra 1998–2002, Scottish Chamber Orchestra 1998–2002; performed premiere of her Viola Concerto at BBC Henry Wood Promenade Concert, London 1995; Reed Stanzas premiered at Proms 2011; comms from the City of Reykjavík, BBC TV, English Nat. Opera, Brighton Festival, others; one of 20 composers commissioned to write a piece of music for the 2012 Cultural Olympiad; Co-Dir, St Magnus Composers' Course, Equal Voices for LSO/RSNO 2014, The Tempest for Birmingham Royal Ballet 2016. *Compositions include:* orchestral/choral/instrumental genres, incuding Symphony 1992, Violin Concerto 1994, Viola Concerto 1995, Cello, Viola and Oboe Concertos, Soprano Saxophone Concerto, The Seafarer Trio, Piano Sonata 1996, Knotgrass Elegy (BBC Proms commission) 2001, Monster (opera) 2002, Flute Concerto (Callisto), Reed Stanzas (String Quartet No.3) (Royal Philharmonic Soc. Award for Chamber-Scale Composition 2011), Spinal Chords 2012, Saxophone Sonata 2012, Intoxicating Rose Garden (stage). *Recordings include:* River (Cello, Viola and Oboe Concertos), Imagined Sound of Sun on Stone (Concertos), The Seafarer, The Singing 2015. *Honours:* Dr hc (Glasgow) 2001; Paul Hamlyn Award for Outstanding Achievement in Composition 1993, Creative Scotland Award 2000, BBC Radio 3 Composer of the Week Feb. 2012. *Current Management:* c/o Katie Tearle, Peters Edition Ltd, 2-6 Baches Street, London, N1 6DN, England. *Telephone:* (20) 7553-4000. *E-mail:* katie.tearle@editionpeters.com. *Website:* www.sallybeamish.com.

BEARDSLEE, Bethany; American singer (soprano); b. 25 Dec. 1927, Lansing, MI; m. 1st Jacques-Louis Monod; m. 2nd Godfrey Winham 1956. *Education:* Michigan State Univ. and Juilliard School. *Career:* debut in New York 1949; concerts with Jacques-Louis Monod, giving the US premieres of works by Berg, Stravinsky, Webern, Krenek and Schoenberg; concerts of medieval and renaissance music with the New York Pro Musica 1957–60; commissioned and performed Babbitt's Philomel 1964; performed Schoenberg's Pierrot Lunaire with mems of the Cleveland Orchestra 1972; teacher, Westminster Choir Coll. from 1976; partnership with pianist Richard Goode 1981; Prof. of Singing, Univ. of Texas, Austin 1981–82, Brooklyn Coll., CUNY from 1983. *Recordings:* Pierrot Lunaire, works by Babbitt, George Perle, Mel Powell, Bach, Haydn and Pergolesi. *Honours:* Dr hc (Princeton Univ.) 1977; American Composers' Alliance Laurel Leaf 1962, Ford Foundation grant 1964.

BEARE, Charles, OBE; British musical instrument restorer; *Chairman, J. & A. Beare Ltd. Career:* currently Chair. and Dir musical instrument restorer, J. & A. Beare Ltd. *Publication:* Antonio Stradivari: The Cremona Exhibition of 1987 1994. *Address:* J. & A. Beare Ltd, 30 Queen Anne Street, London, W1G 8HX, England (office). *Telephone:* (20) 7307-9666 (office). *Fax:* (20) 7307-9651 (office). *E-mail:* violins@beares.com (office). *Website:* www.beares.com (office).

BEAT, Janet Eveline, BMus, MA; British composer and lecturer; b. 17 Dec. 1937, Streetly, Staffordshire. *Education:* Birmingham Univ. *Career:* freelance horn player 1962–65; Lecturer in Music, Madeley Coll. of Education 1965–67; Lecturer in Music, Worcester Coll. of Education 1967–71; Lecturer, Royal Scottish Acad. of Music and Drama 1972–96; part-time Lecturer Music Dept, Univ. of Glasgow 1996–2004; mem. BACS, MU. *Compositions include:* brass: Hunting Horns are Memories 1977, Fireworks in Steel 1987, Chard Fanfare 1992, Bold as Brass! 1996, Vision Nocturne 2003, Threnody: the warm sap seeps 2004, Harmony in Autumn 2005, Fanfare for Katja 2006, The Splendor Falls 2008; choral: Study of the Object No. 3 1970, Summer Poem No. V 1970, Sylvia Myrtea 1985, Aspara Music One 1994, Canite Tuba 2006; keyboard: Pentad 1969, Piangam 1978–79, Sonata No. 1 1985–87, Cross Currents and Reflections 1981–82, Alexa's Comet 1984, Capriccios Vol. 1 1999–2002, Fanfare for Haydn 2000, Dynamism 2000, Sunsets and Lakes 2003, At the Circus 2004, Palimpsest 2006, My Menagerie 2006, Geryon 2007; orchestra: Synchronism 1977; strings: Le Tombeau de Claude 1973, Circe 1974, After Reading 'Lessons of War' 1977, Vincent Sonata 1979–80, A Willow Swept by Rain 1982, Arabesque 1985, Cat's Cradle for the Nemuri Neko 1991, The Song of the Silkie 1991, Convergencies 1992, Scherzo Notturno 1992, Joie de Vivre 1994, Equinox Rituals 1996, Violin Sonata No. 2 1997, Concealed Imaginings 1998, String Quartet No. 1 1992–99, Violin Sonata No. 3 1999, Scenes from my Travels 1999, Mexican Night of the Dead 2001, Harmony of Opposites 2002, Encounter 2002, The Dream Magus 2002, Gedenkstück für Kaethe 2003, Nocturne: The Cry of the Peacocks 2006; vocal: The Fiery Sunflower 1972, The Leaves of My Brain 1974, Landscapes 1976–77, Premiers Désirs 1978, Mitylene Mosaics 1983–84, Nomoi Aulodiki 1984, Aztec Myth 1987, Puspawarna 1989–90, La Sera 2004, Lullaby for the Christ Child 2007; woodwind: Two Essays 1968, 1974, Apollo and Marysas 1972–73, Inventions for woodwind 1974, Seascape with Clouds 1978, Noctuary 1979, Mestra 1979, Pastore d'Aria 1979, Dreamscapes 1980, Rousseau's Snake Charmer 1986, Two Caprices 1998, Nomoi Aulodiki 1984, En Plein Air 2000–01; electronic: Aztec Myth 1987, A Springtime Pillow Book 1990, Beating Around the Bush 1990, Not Necessarily: As She Opened Her Eyes 1990, Lydian Mix 1990, Mandala 1990, Memories of Java 1990, The Song of the Silkie 1991, Fêtes Pour Claude 1992, Der Regenpalast 1993. *Honours:* Hon. Research Fellow (Glasgow Univ.) 1999; G. D. Cunningham Award 1963. *Current Management:* Furore Verlag, Naumburger Strasse 40, 34127 Kassel, Germany. *Telephone:* (561) 50049311. *Fax:* (561) 50049320. *E-mail:* info@furore-verlag.de. *Website:* www.furore-verlag.de. *Address:* c/o Scottish Music Centre, City Halls, Candleriggs, Glasgow, G1 1NQ, Scotland (office). *Telephone:* (141) 552-5222 (office). *E-mail:* info@scottishmusiccentre.com (office). *Website:* www .scottishmusiccentre.com/janet_beat.

BEATH, Betty, DipMus; Australian composer and pianist; *Partner and Artistic Director, Beath-Cox Art Enterprises*; b. (Elizabeth Margaret Eardley), 19 Nov. 1932, Bundaberg, Queensland; d. of Maurice Wilmot Eardley and Edith Mary Anderson; m. 1st John Helmsley Beath 1953; one s. one d.; m. 2nd David Dundas Cox 1976. *Education:* Queensland and New South Wales Conservatories, Australian Music Educ. Bd, Trinity Coll. of Music, London. *Career:* lecturer and accompanist, Queensland Conservatory 1967–98; many nat. and int. broadcasts, including interview and performance of works to mark her 80th birthday, Australian Broadcasting Corpn (ABC) Classic FM 1996; comms from Queensland Opera 1973, Philharmonic 1995 and ABC 1992, 1994, 1996, KEYS Nat. Festival for Australian Music 2003, Brisbane Writers Festival 2004, Queensland Conservatorium, Griffith Univ. 2007, 2013, Australian Mandolin Music Asscn 2008, Southern Cross Soloists 2008, Brisbane Mandolins 2010, Griffith Univ. Encounters 2013, Central Queensland String Orchestra 2013, Australian Piano Duo 2013; Co-State Adviser on Music, Nat. Council of Women of Queensland Inc.; currently Partner and Artistic Dir, Beath-Cox Art Enterprises; also currently Examiner, Australian Music Examinations Bd. *Compositions include:* Strange Adventures of Marco Polo, one-act opera 1972, Francis, one-act opera 1974, Songs from the Beasts' Choir for soprano and piano 1978, Poems from the Chinese for soprano, clarinet, cello and percussion 1979, Piccolo Victory 1982, Black on White for piano left hand 1983, Points in a Journey for soprano, flute and piano 1987, Abigail and the Mythical Beast, music theatre 1985, River Songs for soprano and piano 1992, Lagu Lagu Manis for cello and piano 1994, Asmaranda for orchestra 1994, Journeys: An Indonesian Triptych for chamber orchestra 1994, Indonesian Diptych 1994, Golden Hours for chamber orchestra 1995, Dreams and Visions 1996, From a Quiet Place 1997, Encounters for violin and cello 1999, Lament for Kosovo 1999, Heart Song for solo cello 2001, A Garland for St Francis for soprano, string quartet, flute, clarinet and percussion 2002, Key Connections for solo piano 2003, Towards the Psalms (song cycle) 2004, Merindu Bali . . .Bali Yearning 2003, Let's Dance for solo piano 2004, A Loving Embrace for solo piano 2005, The Sweet Perfume of Jasmine for solo piano 2005, Indonesian Triptych (song cycle) 2005, From a Bridge of Dreams for flute and piano 2005, Moon, Flowers, Man for voice, flute and piano 2005, Music for Gillian for alto flute and piano 2005, Nawang Wulan Guardian of the Earth and Rice for alto flute and piano 2005, Peace of the Running Waves for You for voice and piano 2005, Encounters with a Whirlwind for solo piano 2005, Genesis for solo voice and piano 2006, St Brigid's Blessing for voice and piano 2006, Gambar Gambar Jawa... Images of Java for voice and orchestra 2007, Sunda Song for flute, harp, cello, percussion 2007, Night Moods for flute and piano 2007, From a Lake of Honey for cello and piano 2007, Though I Travel Far. . . I do not forget, for mandolin and orchestra 2008, Snapshots for oboe, clarinet, horn, bassoon, percussion, voice and piano 2008, Woman's Song for solo piano 2008. *Recordings include:* on Music from Six Continents: Indonesian Diptych 1995, Lagu Lagu Manis 1996, Lament for Kosovo 2001; others: Dreams and Visions 1997, River Songs 1998, Woman's Song, From a Quiet Place 2003, Music of Betty Beath 2009. *Honours:* Perform/4MBS Award 2000, Pacific Opera Vocal Writing Prize 2008. *Address:* Beath-Cox Art Enterprises, 8 St James Street, Highgate Hill, Queensland 4101 (office); Wirripang, 18/106 Corrimal Street, Wollongong, NSW 2500, Australia (office). *Telephone:* (7) 3844-6798 (office); (2) 4228-9388 (home). *E-mail:* beathcox@ bigpond.com (office); keats@wirripang.com.au. *Website:* www.beathcox.com (office).

BEAUCHAMP, Michael John; British opera director, theatre director and teacher; b. 2 June 1949, London, England. *Education:* University College, Durham, Glyndebourne Opera. *Career:* staff producer, Sadler's Wells and English National Opera, 1973–75; resident producer, Australian Opera, 1975–80; freelance, 1980–; productions include: Happy End, Simon Boccanegra, HMS Pinafore, La Bohème for Australian Opera, La Bohème for National Opera of New Zealand and Glyndebourne Touring Opera; Rake's Progress in Brisbane and Sydney; Rigoletto in Perth, Western Australia and Melbourne; Lucia di Lammermoor, Tancredi in Wexford; The Happy Prince, Dunstan and The Devil, Morley Opera; Dir gala premieres for Australian Bicentennial, New South Wales Directorate; teaching posts in Australia and England. *Address:* 40A Regents Park Road, London NW1 7SX, England.

BEAUDRY, Jacques, BA; Canadian symphony and opera conductor; b. 10 Oct. 1924, Sorel, Quebec; m. Pauline Bonneville. *Education:* Univ. of Montréal, Royal Conservatory of Music, Belgium, studied with René Defossez, Paul Van Kempen, Willem Van Otterloo. *Career:* Prof. of Orchestral Conducting, Univ. of Montréal; toured Europe as conductor with Montréal

Symphony, Opéra Comique, Opéra de Paris and New York Metropolitan Opera; radio broadcasts in Canada, Belgium, Netherlands, Italy, Czechoslovakia, Norway, Luxembourg and France; concerts in Russia, Poland, Guatemala, Switzerland, Greece, Monaco and USA; TV appearances in Canada and France. *Honours:* Gold Medal of Quebec, Lt Gov.'s Award 1958. *Current Management:* c/o Beaudry Concerts, 235 Sherbrooke O P2, Montréal, QC H2X 1X8, Canada. *Telephone:* (514) 287-9435.

BEAUMONT, Adrian, MMus, DMus, ARCM; British composer and lecturer; b. 1 June 1937, Huddersfield, England; m. Janet Price 1963. *Education:* Univ. of Wales, Cardiff; composition with Nadia Boulanger in Fontainebleau. *Career:* appointed to staff of Music Dept, Univ. of Bristol 1961, subsequently Reader in Composition –2002; founder-conductor Bristol Bach Choir 1967–78. *Compositions include:* 3 Symphonies, Now Burns the Bright Redeeming Fire, Oboe Concerto, Summer Ecstasies, two string quartets, A Glimmer of Unshapen Dawn, Cello Sonata, three song cycles. *Publications:* Expectation and Interpretation in the Reception of New Music in Thomas (ed), Composition, Performance, Reception. *Address:* 73 Kings Drive, Bishopston, Bristol, BS7 8JQ, England (home). *Telephone:* (117) 9248456 (home).

BEAUMONT, Jo; Australian violinist and artistic director; *Artistic Director, Orchestra Victoria;* b. New Zealand. *Education:* studied in Melbourne with Nathan Gutman, Accademia Chigiana, Siena. *Career:* Assoc. Concertmaster, Orchestra of Teatro della Scala 1978–97; Prof., Conservatorio di Musica Giuseppe Verdi, Milan 1978–99; Sr mem., Orchestra Filarmonica della Scala 1979–99; Foundation mem., I Solisti della Scala 1979–99; Co-ordinator of String Studies, Australian Nat. Acad. of Music, Melbourne 1999–2000, Head of String Studies 2000–; Guest Concertmaster, Australian Opera and Ballet Orchestra 2000; Concertmaster, Orchestra Victoria 2000–09, currently Artistic Dir. *Address:* Orchestra Victoria, PO Box 836, South Melbourne, Vic. 3205, Australia (office). *Telephone:* (3) 9694-3600 (office). *Fax:* (3) 9694-3611 (office). *E-mail:* info@orchestravictoria.com.au (office). *Website:* www .orchestravictoria.com.au (office).

BEAUPRÉ, Odette; Canadian singer and stage director; b. 5 April 1952, Rivière-du-Loup, Quebec; d. of Maurice Beaupré and Eméline Beaupré (née Pelletier). *Education:* studied at Music Conservatory of Québec with Marguerite Pâquet, Rolande Dion and Janine Lachance, and with Marlena Malas and Bonne Hamilton. *Career:* mem. Canadian Opera Co. Ensemble 1983–86; performances with Opera of Québec, Montréal Opera, Edmonton Opera, Canadian Opera Co., Québec Symphony Orchestra, Montréal Symphony Orchestra, Les Jeunesses Musicales du Canada; founding mem. Opéra Mobile; European debut as Zerlina in Don Giovanni, Nice 1987; oratorio repertoire includes Bach's St Matthew Passion, Beethoven's Ninth Symphony, Mozart's Great Mass in C Minor, Requiem by both Verdi and Duruflé, Handel's Messiah, Dubois' Les sept paroles du Christ, Vivaldi's Gloria, Saint-Saëns' Oratorio de Noël, Brahms' Alto Rhapsody, de Falla's El Amor Brujo, Evangelista's Ramillete de canciones populares, Pergolesi's Stabat Mater, Poulenc's Trois Chansons de Mallarmé; recital repertoire includes works by Fauré, Debussy, Poulenc, Ravel, Weill, Strauss, Mahler, Brahms and Schumann, as well as jazz and Broadway; frequent performances on CBC radio; Prof., Université du Québec à Trois-Rivières 1995–2001; f. Voix Multiples/Odette Beaupré singing school, Trois-Rivières 2001; Asst Dir Opera Lyra Ottawa 2002. *Operas include:* Così fan tutte, Faust, Madam Butterfly, The Merry Widow, The Beggar's Opera, Carmen, Cavalleria Rusticana, Roméo et Juliette, Rigoletto, Otello, Dialogues des Carmélites, Les Contes d'Hoffmann, La Périchole, La rappresentatione di anima e di corpo, La Belle Hélène, Le Comte Ory, L'Incoronazione di Poppea, Werther, Mignon, La Fille du Régiment, Dido and Aeneas, Dalila, Die Fledermaus, Ariadne auf Naxos, Jeanne d'Arc, L'Enfant et les Sortilèges, L'Heure espagnole, Il Trovatore. *Recordings include:* Al-Hamra: Music of Montañés, Evangelista and De Falla with Ensemble contemporain de Montréal 1997, Ravel: L'Enfant et les Sortilèges with Orchestre symphonique de Montréal. *Honours:* Third Prize, Indiana Opera Theater MacAllister Award competition 1985, First Prize, Int. Festival of Toronto 1986, Scholarship, Floyd S. Chalmer's Foundation, Ontario Arts Council 1986, Prix du public, Le Conseil québécois de la musique 2000. *Address:* Voix Multiples/Odette Beaupré, 511 Rue Sainte Ursule, Trois-Rivières, PQ G9A 1N8, Canada (office). *Telephone:* (819) 374-8452 (office). *Website:* www.voixmultiples-odettebeaupre.com (office).

BECCARIA, Bruno; Italian singer (tenor); b. 4 July 1957, Rome. *Career:* debut at Bologna 1986, as Edgardo in Lucia di Lammermoor; sang at La Scala, Milan 1986–87, as Ismaele and Pinkerton; Philadelphia Opera 1986, 1988, Vienna Staatsoper from 1987, New York Metropolitan debut 1987, as Rodolfo; Verona Arena from 1988, as Enzo in La Gioconda, Radames and Turiddu; Teatro La Fenice Venice 1990, as Ernani; other roles include Gabriele Adorno (Catania 1992), Andrea Chénier (San Francisco Opera), Faust, Don Carlos, and Maurizio in Adriana Lecouvreur. *Recordings include:* Beethoven's Mass in C.

BECHLY, Daniela; German singer (soprano); b. 1960, Hamburg; m.; three c. *Education:* Hamburg Hochschule für Musik. *Career:* debut, Vienna Kammeroper 1984; Wexford Festival 1986, as Humperdinck's Goose Girl in Königskinder; sang at Brunswick Opera 1983; appeared with the Krefeld-Mönchengladbach co. 1985–87; soloist at the Deutsche Oper Berlin 1987–; sang Susanna, Zerlina, Aennchen, Pamina, Anna in Die Lustige Weiber von Windsor, Gretel, Sandrina in La Finta Giardiniera, Elvira in Don Giovanni, Bern 1991; Malwina in Der Vampyr by Marschner, Wexford 1992 and Haydn's

L'Incontro Improvviso; Rhinemaiden, Covent Garden 1997; Cherubino, Deutsche Oper am Rhein, Düsseldorf, and Agathe at the Opera Festival at Zwingenberg, Germany 1998; recital, Women and Music, Villa Musica, Germany 1999; collaboration with Trio Kairos on Shostakovich Op. 127 and Haydn-Beethoven Folksongs arrangements; Marguérite in Faust, Opera South 2005; concert repertoire includes all major Oratorio works and Lieder, Mozart concert arias, Strauss Four Last Songs, Mahler Lieder eines fahrendenGesellen, Rueckert Lieder, Wagner Wesendonck; engagements in Ireland, Denmark, Norway, France, Italy, Austria. *Recordings:* Blumenmädchen in Parsifal recording under Barenboim, Ronnefeld Song Cycles 2000, Haydn Beethoven Folksong arrangements with Trio Kairos Hamburg. *Honours:* first prize Hamburg Singing Contest 1980, finalist Vienna Belvedere Competition 1984, second prize Bordeaux Festival Int. de Jeunes Solistes. *Current Management:* Music International, 13 Ardilaun Road, London, N5 2QR, England. *Telephone:* (20) 7359-5183. *Fax:* (20) 7226-9792. *E-mail:* music@musicint.co.uk. *Website:* www.musicint.wd-uk.com. *Telephone:* (1206) 271291. *E-mail:* danielabechly@tiscali.co.uk.

BECK, Jeremy, DMA, BSc, MA; American composer; b. 15 Jan. 1960, Painesville, OH. *Education:* Yale Univ., Duke Univ., Mannes Coll. of Music, Dagbe Drumming Inst., Ghana. *Career:* debut at Carnegie Recital Hall 1987; Assoc. Prof., Univ. of Northern Iowa; guest Lecturer in American Music, St Petersburg Conservatory, Russia, Univ. of West Bohemia. *Compositions:* Toccata for piano solo 1988, Kopeyia for percussion ensemble 1995, Death of a Little Girl with Doves for soprano and orchestra 1998, Laughter in Jericho (chamber opera) 1997, Songs Without Words for flute and harp 1997, three Sonatas for cello and piano 1981, 1988, 1997, three String Quartets 1987, 1990, 1994. *Publication:* contrib. Elliott Carter's Tonal Practice in the Rose Family, to Essays in American Music Vol. II.

BECKER, Andreas; German singer (bass-baritone); b. 13 May 1940, Berlin. *Education:* Berlin Conservatory. *Career:* debut as Landgrave in Tannhäuser, Osnabruck 1966; repertoire of about 350 roles, opera, operetta and musicals; appearances throughout Germany from 1966, notably at Krefeld, Bielefeld and Essen; Dortmund Opera from 1972, with guest appearances at Munich and elsewhere; other roles have included Pizarro and Rocco in Fidelio, Wagner's Marke, Hunding and Fasolt, Verdi's Zaccaria and King Philip; Mozart's Osmin and Sarastro, Ochs (Rosenkavalier) and Alfonso, with further engagements at Munich, Hamburg, Paris, The Netherlands and the Far East; sang Mordred in Le Roi Arthus by Chausson at Dortmund 1996; Doolittle in My Fair Lady and also appeared in The Merry Widow; teacher, Dortmund Hochschule; season 2000–01 at Dortmund as Kecal in The Bartered Bride and in the premiere of Wallenberg by Erkki-Sven Tüür.

BECKER, Rolf; German singer (bass); b. 31 March 1935, Leipzig. *Career:* sang with Cologne Opera 1959–62, Hannover 1962–92; roles have included Mozart's Sarastro and Commendatore, Rocco, Daland, Fafner, Hunding, Gurnemanz, and Mephistopheles; has also sung such modern repertory as Wesener in Die Soldaten by Zimmermann and buffo roles, including Basilio, Osmin, Kecal and Bartolo; concert engagements in Spain, France and Italy.

BECKWITH, Daniel; American conductor; b. 1954, Chicago. *Education:* Westminster Choir Coll., Princeton. *Career:* engagements in Il Matrimonio Segreto, Falstaff, Die Entführung aus dem Serail and Il Barbiere di Siviglia at Wolf Trap, Così fan tutte for the Lyric Opera of Chicago, Grétry's Zemire et Azor at Houston; Giulio Cesare, The Rape of Lucretia and Turandot at Edmonton; The Coronation of Poppea and Mozart's Il Re Pastore for Canadian Opera; Lucia di Lammermoor in Cincinatti; other engagements include Don Giovanni at the Metropolitan 1995, 1997, Figaro at Vancouver and Il Barbiere di Siviglia in Florida; L'Italiana in Algeri for Cleveland Opera; season 1997 with Theodora at the Glyndebourne Festival, L'Elisir d'amore at Fort Worth, Handel's Xerxes in Seattle and Rinaldo for the Geneva Opera; The Crucible and The Magic Flute at Washington, DC; Il Barbiere di Siviglia at Opera North, England 1998; further performances of Orphée et Eurydice in Utah; Platée (Rameau) at New York City Opera; The Magic Flute, Seattle; Don Giovanni, San Francisco; Artistic Dir, Lake George Summer Opera Festival 1999.

BECKWITH, John, CM, BMus, MMus; Canadian composer, teacher, writer and pianist; b. 9 March 1927, Victoria, BC. *Education:* Univ. of Toronto, Royal Conservatory of Music, Toronto with Alberto Guerrero, studied composition with Nadia Boulanger in Paris. *Career:* Public Relations Dir Royal Conservatory of Music, Toronto 1948–50; staff writer for radio music continuity, CBC, Toronto 1953–55; freelance radio programmer and writer 1955–70; reviewer and columnist, Toronto Daily Star 1959–62, 1963–65; part-time special lecturer, Univ. of Toronto 1952–53, Lecturer 1954–60, Asst Prof. 1960–66, Assoc. Prof. 1966–70, Dean 1970–77, Prof. 1977–90; Dir Inst. for Canadian Music 1984–90; Gen. Ed. Canadian Composers Series 1975–91; Canadian Consultant, The New Grove, London 1980. *Compositions:* The Great Lakes Suite 1949, 4 songs to poems of e e cummings 1950, Fall Scene and Fair Dance 1956, Night Blooming Cereus 1958, Concerto Fantasy 1960, Flower Variations and Wheels 1962, Jonah 1963, The Trumpets of Summer 1964, Sharon Fragments 1966, Circle, with Tangents 1967, Canada Dash, Canada Dot 1967, Gas! 1969, Taking a Stand 1972, All the Bees and All the Keys 1973, Musical Chairs 1973, Quartet 1977, The Shivaree 1978, Keyboard Practice 1979, 3 Motets on Swan's China 1981, Sonatina in 2 movements 1981, A Little Organ Concert 1981, Mating Time 1981, 6 Songs to poems by e e cummings 1982, A Concert of Myths 1983, Études 1983, Arctic Dances 1984,

Harp of David 1985, Crazy to Kill 1988, Peregrine 1989, The Hector 1990, Round and Round 1992, Taptoo! 1994, Eureka 1996, Stacey 1997, Basic Music 1998, Lady Wisdom 2000, A New Pibroch 2002, Back to Bolivia 2006, Fractions 2006; restoration: Lucas et Cécile (J. Quesnel, c. 1809); orchestration: Orgelbuechlein (J.S. Bach). *Recordings:* Harp of David, Quartet, Keyboard Practice, Études, Arctic Dances, Sharon Fragments, Circle, with Tangents, 3 Motets on Swan's China, Stacey, Round and Round, A Concert of Myths, Synthetic Trios, The Trumpets of Summer, Taking a Stand. *Publications:* Music Papers 1997, In Search of Alberto Guerrero 2006; ed. or co-ed. The Modern Composer and his World 1961, Contemporary Canadian Composers 1975, The Canadian Musical Heritage, Vol. 5 1986, Vol. 18 1995, Musical Canada 1987, Weinzweig 2010. *Honours:* five hon. doctorates, including Hon. DMus, Hon. LLD. *Address:* 121 Howland Avenue, Toronto, ON M5R 3B4, Canada (home).

BECZALA, Piotr; Polish singer (tenor); b. 1968, Czechowice-Dziedzice. *Education:* Katowice Music Acad., master-classes with Sena Jurinac, coached by Dale Fundling. *Career:* co. mem., Linz Landestheater 1992–98; closely connected to Zürich Opera 1998–; also performed frequently in Vienna, Salzburg, Frankfurt, Hamburg, Berlin, Amsterdam, Brussels, Bilbao, Covent Garden, London and at San Francisco Opera; 2006 debuts with Teatro alla Scala, Milan, Munich State Opera and New York Metropolitan Opera; opera repertoire includes Mozart's Tamino, Don Ottavio, Belmonte, Italian Belcanto (Elvino, Orombello, Edgardo), Verdi's Duca di Mantova, Alfredo, French repertoire (Faust, Werther) and Slavic roles (Shepherd in Szymanowski's King Roger, Lenski and Vaudémont by Tchaikovsky); also performs a widely spread concert repertoire and works frequently with leading conductors; performances include Roméo in Roméo et Juliette, Covent Garden 2010 and Metropolitan Opera 2011, Rodolfo in La Bohème, Tokyo and Nagoya 2011, also La Scala and Salzburg 2012, Alfredo in La Traviata, Covent Garden 2011, Edgardo in Lucia di Lammermoor, Tokyo 2011, Vienna 2012, Chevalier des Grieux in Manon, Eugene Onegin; season 2013: Teatro alla Scala in Milan as Alfredo, Prince in Rusalka, Gustavo III in Un Ballo in Maschera (San Diego), debuts as Hoffmann in Les Contes d'Hoffmann (Vienna State Opera) 2014, Rusalka and Rigoletto (Vienna State Opera), Iolanta and Un Ballo in Maschera (Met Opera), title role in Gounod's Faust at Opéra Nat. de Paris, La Bohème (Royal Opera House Covent Garden); concerts in Baden-Baden, Amsterdam, Madrid, Katowice, Budapest, Oman, Verdi's Requiem (Vienna Musikverein). *Recordings include:* various CD and DVD releases of music by Mozart, Berlioz, Offenbach, Dvořák, Tchaikovsky, Szymanowski, Strauss, Lehár, Verdi, Borodin, Rimsky-Korsakov, Rachmaninoff, Moniuszko, Żeleński, Nowowiejski, Smetana, Tauber. *Current Management:* c/o Universal Music Group, Stralauer Allee 1, 10245 Berlin, Germany. *Telephone:* (30) 520071761. *Fax:* (30) 5200731761. *E-mail:* info@centrestagemanagement .com. *Website:* www.centrestagemanagement.com. *E-mail:* piotr@beczala .com (home). *Website:* www.beczala.com.

BEDFORD, Luke; British composer; *Composer-in-Residence, Wigmore Hall;* b. 25 April 1978, Wokingham. *Education:* St Crispin's School, Wokingham, Royal Coll. of Music, RAM. *Career:* Composer-in-Residence, Wigmore Hall, London 2008–; works have been performed by London Sinfonietta, Chicago Symphony Orchestra, Hallé Orchestra, Deutsches Symphonie-Orchester, London Symphony Orchestra, Tokyo Philharmonic, Brunel Ensemble, Gould Piano Trio, Endymion Ensemble, Continuum Ensemble and Chroma. *Compositions:* Five Abstracts (chamber work for 14 players) 2001, Catafalque (solo piano piece) 2002, Chiaroscuro (for piano trio) 2002, Man Shoots Strangers From Skyscraper (for chamber ensemble) 2002, Rode With Darkness (for large orchestra) 2003, Slow Music (for chamber ensemble) 2005, On Voit Tout En Aventure (song cycle for soprano and 16 players) 2006, Outblaze the Sky (for orchestra) 2007, Good Dream She Has (for soprano, mezzo-soprano, tenor and 14 players) 2007, Wreathe (for orchestra) 2007. *Honours:* Royal Philharmonic Soc. Award for Composition 2000, BBC Radio 3 Listeners' Award 2004, Paul Hamlyn Artists' Award 2007, Ernst von Siemens Music Foundation Composers Prize 2012. *Address:* Wigmore Hall, 36 Wigmore Street, London, W1U 2BP, England (office). *Telephone:* (20) 7258-8200 (office). *Fax:* (20) 7258-8201 (office). *E-mail:* info@wigmore-hall.org.uk (office). *Website:* www.wigmore-hall .org.uk (office).

BEDFORD, Steuart John Rudolf, OBE, BA, FRCO, FRAM; British conductor; b. 31 July 1939, London, England; s. of L. H. Bedford and Lesley Bedford (née Duff); m. 1st Norma Burrowes (q.v.) 1969 (divorced 1980); m. 2nd Celia Harding 1980; two d. *Education:* Lancing Coll., Sussex, Univ. of Oxford, Royal Acad. of Music. *Career:* operatic training as repetiteur, Asst Conductor, Glyndebourne Festival 1965–67; English Opera Group (later English Music Theatre), Aldeburgh and London 1967–73; Co-Artistic Dir, English Musical Theatre 1976–80, Artistic Dir English Sinfonia 1981–90, Artistic Dir (also Exec. Artistic Dir) Aldeburgh Festival 1987–98; freelance conductor, numerous performances with ENO, Welsh Nat. Opera, Metropolitan Opera, New York (operas include Death in Venice, The Marriage of Figaro), Royal Danish Opera; also at Royal Opera House, Covent Garden (operas include Owen Wingrave, Death in Venice, Così fan tutte) Santa Fe Opera, Teatro Colón, Buenos Aires, Opéra de Lyon, Garsington Opera, Opéra de Toulon, San Diego Opera, Boston Lyric Opera, Opera Theatre of St Louis etc.; conductor for Orchestre Philharmonique de Montpellier, Mahler Chamber Orchestra, Southern Sinfonia. *Recordings include:* Death in Venice, Phaedra, Beggar's Opera, Collins Britten series, Britten: Peter Grimes (BBC Music Magazine Opera Award 2014). *Film:* Peter Grimes. *Honours:* Medal of the Worshipful

Co. of Musicians. *Current Management:* c/o Harrison Parrott, 5–6 Albion Court, London, W6 0QT, England. *Telephone:* (20) 3725-9120. *E-mail:* linda .marks@harrisonparrott.co.uk; katie.cardell-oliver@harrisonparrott.co.uk. *Website:* www.harrisonparrott.com.

BEECROFT, Norma Marian; Canadian composer; b. 11 April 1934, Oshawa, Ont.; d. of Julian Beecroft and Eleanor Beecroft (née Norton). *Education:* Toronto Royal Conservatory of Music, Berkshire Music Centre, Acad. of St Cecilia, Italy, and in Germany and UK. *Career:* joined CBC 1954 as script asst for music programs, later music consultant, studied in Europe and returned to CBC as script assistant 1962–63, talent relations officer 1963–64, national program organizer for radio 1964–66, producer 1966–69 (resgnd); freelance career as producer and commentator on contemporary music 1969–; fmr host, weekly series Music of Today (CBC); produced numerous documentaries for CBC on major Canadian composers; Pres. Canadian Music Associates (Toronto concert cttee of Canadian League of Composers) 1956–57; Pres. Ten Centuries Concerts 1965–68; Co-founder (with Robert Aitken) New Music Concerts 1971, Pres. and Gen. Man. 1971–89; Dir of Workshops, York Univ., Ont. 1984–87; mem. Canadian League of Composers, Composers, Authors and Publishers Asscn of Canada; Assoc., Canadian Music Centre. *Compositions include:* Tre Pezzi Brevi 1961, From Dreams of Brass 1964, Elegy and Two Went to Sleep 1967, Undersea Fantasy 1967, The Living Flame of Love 1967, Three Impressions From Sweetgrass 1973, Piece for Bob 1975, Consequences for Five 1977, Quaprice 1980, Cantorum Vitae 1981, Troissants 1982, Macbeth (score) 1983, Midsummer Night's Dream (score) 1984, Jeu de Bach 1985, Images 1987, The Dissipation of Purely Sound 1988, Accordion Play 1988, Hemispherics 1990, Evocations: Images of Canada 1991, Amplified String Quartet 1991–92, Esprit Eternel 1994, Face à Face 1994. *Honours:* Hon. mem. Canadian Electro-acoustic Community 2002; Dr hc (York) 1996; Armstrong Award for Excellence in FM Broadcasting, Victor M Lynch–Staunton Award 1978–79, 1989–90.

BEER, Birgit; German singer (soprano); b. 1962, Lubeck. *Education:* Lubeck Musikhochschule. *Career:* debut as Tebaldo in Don Carlos at Augsburg; sang at Saarbrucken, 1984–85; Lucerne, 1985–87; Vienna Volksoper, 1987–90; further study with Renate Holm and Hanna Ludwig in Vienna; Theater am Gärtnerplatz, 1990–92 as Mozart's Blondchen, Offenbach's Olympia, Zerbinetta, and Adele in Die Fledermaus; guest appearances at the Vienna Staatsoper, in Verona and Berlin and as Papagena at La Scala, Milan; Deutsche Oper Berlin as Rosina and Salzburg, 1994, as Frasquita in Carmen; Bonn Opera from 1992, as Puccini's Lauretta and Lisetta; Season 1996 as Papagena at Bonn and Marzelline in Fidelio at Liège; sang Musetta at Essen, 1999. *Current Management:* Opera Vladarski, Döblinger Hauptstrasse 57/18, 1190 Vienna, Austria. *Telephone:* 1 368 69 60/61. *Fax:* 1 368 69 62. *E-mail:* opera.vladarski@utanet.at.

BEESLEY, Mark, MSc; British singer (bass); b. 1961, Harrogate, Yorks., England; m. Jan Beesley; one s. one d. *Education:* Univ. of Sussex, studied with Dennis Wicks and Laura Sarti. *Career:* Prin. Bass, Royal Opera 1989–95, roles included Colline in La Bohème, Timur in Turandot, Haly in L'Italiana in Algeri, Lodovico in Otello, Angelotti in Tosca, Dr Grenville in La Traviata, Walter Furst in Guillaume Tell, Hobson in Peter Grimes, Il Re in Aida, Sam in Un Ballo in Maschera, Der Sprecher in Die Zauberflöte, Giove in Arianna, Ceprano in Rigoletto; Prin. Bass, ENO 1998–, roles included Dalano in The Flying Dutchman, Basilio in Il Barbiere di Siviglia, Bartolo in Le nozze di Figaro; other roles include Raimondo in Lucia di Lammermoor, Aliprando in Matilde di Shabran, Foltz in Die Meistersinger, Fiesco in Simon Boccanegra, Doctor in Pelléas et Mélisande, Plunkett in Martha, Theseus in A Midsummer Night's Dream, Varlaam in Boris Godunov, McLean in Susannah, Pater Profundis in Faust, Zunga in Carmen, Swallow in Peter Grimes, Daland in Der Fliegende Holländer, Fotis in Greek Passion, Jeronimus in Maskerade; has also performed at Glyndebourne Festival, Aix en Provence Festival, Anna Livia Opera Festival, Dublin, Opera Holland Park; currently freelance artist. *Current Management:* c/o Athole Still Opera Ltd, Foresters Hall, 25–27 Westow Street, London, SE19 3RY, England. *Telephone:* (20) 8771-5271. *Fax:* (20) 8771-8172. *E-mail:* enquiries@atholestill.co.uk. *Website:* www.atholestill .com; www.markbeesley.com.

BEFFA, Karol; French composer, pianist and musicologist; b. 1973, Paris. *Education:* École Normale Supérieure, Paris, ENSAE, CNRS Paris, Univ. of Cambridge, UK. *Career:* child actor aged seven to 12; teacher, Université de Paris IV (Sorbonne) 1998–2003, École Polytechnique 2003–08; Composer-in-Residence, Orchestre Nat. du Capitole de Toulouse 2006–09; works performed in France (Salle Pleyel and Théâtre du Châtelet, Olivier Messiaen auditorium and Théâtre des Champs Elysées), Germany, Italy, UK, Russia, Japan and USA by ensembles including A Sei Voci, Cambridge Voices, Tapiloa Choir, Orchestre Philharmonique de Radio France, Orchestre de l'Opéra de Lyon, Bayerische Kammerphilharmonie, St Petersburg Philharmonia, London Symphony Orchestra and Orchestre Nat. d'Île de France; as pianist, solo performances at venues including Salle Cortot and Salle Gaveau in Paris, Radio France Festival Montpellier, Valois Festival, Périgord Noir Festival and Piano aux Jacobins Festival; Chair of Creative Arts, Collège de France 2012–13; Lecturer in Musicology, École Normale Supérieure, Paris. *Compositions include:* Masques for violin and cello 2004, Trumpet Concerto 2005, Marie-Madeleine, la robe de pourpre, oratorio-ballet 2005, Subway for trumpet and piano, Metropolis for viola and piano, Destroy for piano and string quartet 2007, Paradis artificiels 2007, Salve Regina for children's choir a cappella 2007, Violin Concerto 2008, Oblivion for string ensemble 2008,

Obsession for saxophone 2009, Les ruines circulaires for symphony orchestra 2009, Piano Concerto (commissioned by Boris Berezovsky) 2009, Trio for flute, alto and harp (for Philharmonie Berlin) and String Quartet (for Quatuor Capuçon) 2009, Prélude et Passacaille for organ 2009, Trois chorals dans le style de Bach, for piano 2010, Concerto for viola and string orchestra 2011, Corps et Âmes, ballet 2011, K ou le piste du château 2011–13, Babel for mixed choir and four voices a cappella 2012, L'oeil du loup 2012, Le Miroir des heures for guitar 2013, Le Pavillon d'or for ensemble 2013. *Recordings include:* solo albums: Masques 2009, Improvisations 2009. *Honours:* Chevalier, Ordre des Arts et des Lettres, Ordre Nat. du Mérite; award from Lili and Nadia Boulanger Foundation 2001, Charter Prize, Acad. des Beaux-Arts 2008, Young Composer of the Year, SACEM 2008, Composer of the Year, Victoires de la Musique Classique 2013; 15 film scores, two theatre scores. *Address:* Département Histoire & Théorie des Arts, École Normale Supérieure, 45 rue d'Ulm, 75230 Paris, France (office). *Telephone:* 1-44-32-35-79 (office). *E-mail:* karol.beffa@ens.fr (office).

BEGGS, Patricia K.; American opera administrator; *Harry Fath General Director & CEO, Cincinnati Opera. Career:* joined Cincinnati Opera as Dir of Marketing 1984–91, Asst Man. Dir 1991–97, Man. Dir 1997–2004, Gen. Dir and CEO 2004–15, Harry Fath Gen. Dir and CEO 2015–; bd mem. and treas. OPERA America; bd mem. Downtown Cincinnati Inc., Music Hall Working Group, Cincinnati Arts Asscn. *Address:* Cincinnati Opera, Music Hall, 1243 Elm Street, Cincinnati, OH 45202-7531, USA (office). *Telephone:* (513) 768-5500 (office). *Fax:* (513) 768-5552 (office). *E-mail:* info@cincinnatiopera.org (office). *Website:* www.cincinnatiopera.org (office).

BEGLARIAN, Eve, BA, MA; American composer and record producer; b. 22 July 1958, Ann Arbor, MI. *Education:* Princeton Univ., Columbia Univ. *Career:* music performed at Washington Ballet, Kennedy Center 1991, Anthony de Hare, Kennedy Center 1990, New York New Music Ensemble 1988; Dinosaur Annex, Boston 1989, 1990; Monday Evening Concerts, Los Angeles 1990, 1991; Weill Recital Hall 1987. *Compositions include:* Eloise for electric cello and tape, The Beginning of Terror for electronic tape, Making Sense of It for flute, cello, violin, violoncello, pianoforte, percussion and tape, Miranda's Kiss for piano solo, A Big Enough Umbrella for viola and tape, Elf Again for ensemble 1998, Father/Daughter Dance (electro-acoustic) 1998, Non-Jew for two speakers 1998, Spherical Music, The Garden of Cyrus, Born Dancin', The Marriage of Heaven and Hell, Landscaping for Privacy, My Feelings Now, Wolf Chaser, Flamingo, Play Nice, Not Worth, The Continuous Life, Do Not be Concerned, Until It Blazes, Fireside, Five Things, Nigh Psalm. *E-mail:* eve@evbvd.com (office). *Website:* www.evbvd.com.

BEGLEY, Kim; British singer (tenor); b. 23 June 1952, Wirral, Cheshire. *Education:* Guildhall School of Music, National Opera Studio. *Career:* Royal Opera House Covent Garden from 1983 as Andres in Wozzeck; Lysander in A Midsummer Night's Dream; The Prince in Zemlinsky's Florentine Tragedy; Achilles in King Priam and Froh in Das Rheingold; Other appearances include Boris in Katya Kabanova, Pellegrin in Tippett's New Year and Laca in Jenůfa for Glyndebourne Festival; Dancing Master in Ariadne and Male Chorus in Rape of Lucretia for ENO; Shuisky in Boris Godunov, Fritz in the British premiere of Der Ferne Klang, 1992, and Lohengrin and Alfred, Die Fledermaus in Frankfurt; Narraboth at the 1993 Salzburg Festival; Sang in Pfitzner's Palestrina at Covent Garden, Drum Major in Wozzeck at La Scala and Der Freischütz in Berlin, 1997; Sang Captain Vere in Billy Budd at the Opéra de La Bastille and Max in Der Freischütz at La Scala, 1998; Season 1999–2000 as Parsifal for ENO and Peter Grimes for Netherlands Opera; Wagner's Erik at Covent Garden, 2000; Season 2000–01 as Loge in Das Rheingold at Bayreuth and Florestan at Glyndebourne; Mendelssohn's Elijah at the London Proms, 2002; Drum Major in new production of Wozzeck at Covent Garden, 2003; Concert appearances include Die Fledermaus, Alfred, with André Previn at the Royal Philharmonic Orchestra; Elgar's Dream of Gerontius with the Philharmonia under Vernon Handley, Tippett's New Year with the London Philharmonic Orchestra and Janáček's From the House of the Dead with the BBC Symphony Orchestra. *Recordings include:* Florestan in Leonore with John Eliot Gardiner; Mephistopheles in Dr Faustus with Kent Nagano. *Current Management:* c/o Shirley Thomson, Harrison Parrott Ltd, 5-6 Albion Court, Albion Place, London, W6 0QT, England. *E-mail:* shirley.thomson@harrisonparrott.co.uk. *Website:* www.harrisonparrott.com.

BEHLE, Daniel; German singer (tenor); b. Hamburg. *Education:* Univ. of Music and Theatre, Hamburg. *Career:* opera engagements with Oldenburger Staatstheater, La Scala, Milan, Frankfurt Opera, Cologne Opera, Royal Opera in Stockholm, Opéra nat. de Lyon, State Operas of Vienna, Munich, Berlin and Hamburg and to Aix-en-Provence Festival and Salzburg's Mozart Week; concerts with WDR Radio Orchestra, Concertgebouw Orchestra, Amsterdam and Capella Augustina; debut with Staatskapelle Dresden under Christian Thielemann 2011; lives in Basel. *Recordings include:* Lieder (works by Schubert, Beethoven, Grieg, Britten and Trojahn, selected by the Metropolitan Opera Guild as one of the 15 best new releases of 2009) 2009, Mozart's (Die Zauberflöte) 2010, Die schöne Müllerin/Auf dem Strom 2010, Dichterliebe/Der Hirt auf dem Felsen 2011. *Honours:* Robert Stolz Competition 2004, Queen Sonja Int. Music Competition, Oslo 2005, BBC Music Magazine Awards 2011. *Current Management:* c/o Sabine Gießelmann, Konzertdirektion Schmid, Königstraße 36, 30175 Hannover, Germany. *Telephone:* (511) 3660780. *Fax:* (511) 3660781. *E-mail:* sabine.giesselmann@kdschmid.de. *E-mail:* info@danielbehle.de. *Website:* www.danielbehle.de.

BEHLE, Renate; Austrian singer (mezzo-soprano); *Professor, Hochschule für Musik und Theater, Hamburg;* b. Graz. *Education:* Univ. and Music Acad. of Graz. *Career:* sang as mezzo-soprano at Gelsenkirchen, 1979–82; Hanover State Opera, 1982–97, as Minnie, Mozart's Elettra, Leonore in Fidelio, Sieglinde, Tosca, the Marschallin and Ariadne; Other Strauss roles include the Dyer's Wife in Die Frau ohne Schatten, 1993–, and Chrysothemis (at Barcelona, 1997); Guest engagements at Hamburg, Cologne, La Scala Milan (as Salome) and Los Angeles (Isolde, 1997); 20th Century repertory includes Agave in Henze's Bassarids, Shostakovich's Katarina and Montezuma in Rihm's Die Eroberung von Mexico, all at Hamburg; Katya Kabanova; New productions of Fidelio and Die Walküre at Stuttgart; Tristan und Isolde in Houston; Sieglinde and Senta in Hamburg; Dyer's Wife, Salome, Leonore and Isolde in Dresden and all three Brünnhildes in Cologne. Concerts include the Dvořák Requiem, the Shostakovich 14th Symphony in Leipzig and Beethoven's Ninth in Granada, 1997; Zemlinsky's Lyrische Sinfonie in Amsterdam and Munich; Mahler's Symphony No. 8 on tour with Michael Gielen and the Südwestfunk-Sinfonieorchester; Guest Visit to Carnegie Hall, New York with Bernd Alois Zimmermann's Requiem for a Young Poet; Fidelio in Valencia; Siegfried with the Bamberg Symphony Orchestra and Schoenberg's Gurrelieder at the Ravinia Festival; Further engagements include Die Walküre in Austin, Texas, and Die Frau ohne Schatten in Essen; Sang the Götterdämmerung Brünnhilde at Bonn 2000; Ortrud, Klytemnästra in Hamburg and Dresden 2005; Schönberg's Erwartung in Montreal and Glasgow 2005; Herodias in Cologne 2005; Prof., Hochschule für Musik und Theater, Hamburg 2000–. *Recordings include:* Zemlinsky's Der Kreidekreis and Spohr's Jessonda, Die Eroberung von Mexico (W. Rihm), Penthesilea, Fidelio/Walküre, Stuttgart (DVD). *Honours:* Kammersängerin Staatsoper Hannover 1987. *Current Management:* c/o Haydn Rawstron Ltd, 29a High Street, First Floor, West Wickham, Kent, BR4 0LP, England. *Telephone:* (20) 8777-6070. *Fax:* (20) 8777-4073. *E-mail:* enquiries@haydn-rawstron.com. *Website:* www.haydn-rawstron.com; www.renatebehle.de.

BEHNKE, Anna-Katharina; Austrian singer (soprano); b. 1964, Wuppertal, Germany; d. of Georg Nowak; m.; one d. *Education:* Munich Musikhochschule. *Career:* debut, Vienna Kammeroper as Mozart's Susanna 1986; wide repertoire includes roles as Aida, Desdemona, Elisabeth in Tannhäuser, Chrysothemis, Lulu (Basle 1994, Karlsruhe 1995, debut at Opéra Bastille, Paris 1998), Shostakovich's Lady Macbeth (Karlsruhe 1996), Marschallin (Munich 1996), Bartók's Judith (Halle 1996–2000), Lucia di Lammermoor (Nat. Theatre, Prague 1998), Korngold's Violanta (Bergen 1998), Die Frau in Schoenberg's Erwartung (BBC Wales 1999), Gutrune and Senta (Trieste 2001), the Arabella (Paris 2002), Beethoven's Leonore (Kassel, Mainz, Graz, Wiesbaden and Antwerp 2002), Elsa in Lohengrin (Essen 2002) Marietta (Braunschweig 2003), Janáček's Fox in Cunning Little Vixen (La Scala, Milan 2003), Emila Marty in The Makropoulos Case (Braunschweig 2004), Salome (Bologna, Nuremberg, Hanover, Mannheim, Düsseldorf, La Scala, Milan debut 2002, Tokyo 2004), Senta (Moscow debut 2004, Rome debut 2004). *Current Management:* Aria's di Novella Partacini and Alexandra Plaickner, Rappresentanza Artisti, Via Josef Weingartner 4, 39022 Lagundo, Italy. *Telephone:* (0473) 200200. *Fax:* (0473) 222424. *E-mail:* info@arias.it. *Website:* www.arias.it.

BEHR, Randall; American conductor and pianist; b. 1958. *Career:* conducted Peter Hall's production of Salome at Los Angeles Music Center 1989; returned to Los Angeles for La Traviata, Tosca (with Maria Ewing and Placido Domingo) and Peter Hall's production of Die Zauberflöte 1993; other repertory includes the Oliver Knussen double bill, Orfeo ed Euridice, Nixon in China, Così fan tutte, Die Frau ohne Schatten, La Bohème and Vivaldi's Orlando Furioso; Music Dir, Long Beach Opera, CA; Peter Brook's La Tragédie de Carmen on Broadway; conducted La Traviata at the Liceu, Barcelona 1992; Die Walküre in Valencia and Tancredi at Bilbao, with Marilyn Horne; Vienna Staatsoper debut 1993–94, Madama Butterfly; Hansel and Gretel at Toronto 1998; appearance as pianist with Maria Ewing at Covent Garden and at the Teatro Comunale Florence, Théâtre du Châtelet Paris, the Vienna Konzerthaus and the Opéra de Lyon.

BEHRMAN, David; American composer; b. 16 Aug. 1937, Salzburg, Austria. *Education:* studied in New York with Wallingford Riegger, Princeton with Walter Piston, studied with Henri Pousseur and Karlheinz Stockhausen. *Career:* toured widely in the USA with the Sonic Arts Union, giving performances of electronic music 1966–76; associated with John Cage, David Tudor and Gordon Mumma at the Merce Cunningham Dance Co. 1970–76; fmr Artist-in-Residence, Mills Coll., Oakland, serving as Co-Dir of the Center for Contemporary Music 1975–80; mem. arts faculty, Bard Coll. 1998–. *Compositions include:* Players with Curtains 1966, Wave Train 1966, Runthrough 1967, For Nearly an Hour 1968, A New Team Takes Over 1969, Pools of Phase-locked Loops 1972, Cloud Music 1974–79, Figure in a Clearing 1977, On the Other Ocean 1977, Touch Tones 1979, Indoor Geyser 1979–81, Singing Stick 1981, She's Wild 1981, Sound Fountain 1982, 6-Circle 1984, Orchestral Construction Set 1984, Interspecies Smalltalk 1984, Installation for La Villette 1985, Leapday Night 1988, Useful Information 2004, My Dear Siegfried 2005, Long Throw 2007. *Honours:* John Cage Award 2004. *Address:* Milton Avery Graduate School of the Arts, Bard College, PO Box 5000, 30 Campus Road, Annandale-on-Hudson, NY 12504, USA (office). *Telephone:* (845) 758-7481 (office). *E-mail:* behrman@bard.edu (office). *Website:* www.bard.edu/mfa (office).

BEILMAN, Benjamin, BMus; American violinist; b. 25 Nov. 1989, Washington, DC. *Education:* studied at Music Inst. of Chicago with Almita and Roland Vamos, Curtis Inst. of Music with Ida Kavafian. *Career:* started playing violin around age five years; appeared on From the Top (broadcast series for young classical musicians) with Bay Chamber Trio at age 13, Rockport, Me; Philadelphia Orchestra debut with conductor Rossen Milanov, June 2009; appearances as soloist with Detroit, Kalamazoo and Toledo Symphony Orchestras, as well as RAI Nat. Symphony Orchestra, Turin; has appeared as chamber musician since the age of 17 at the Marlboro Festival, Vt. *Recordings:* Prokofiev: Complete Violin Sonatas 2011, Live From The Marlboro Music Festival: Debussy, Ravel Quartets 2011. *Honours:* Gold Medal, Stulberg Int. String Competition 2007, Presidential Scholar in the Arts 2007, First Prize, George and Peggy Schmidbauer Int. Young Artist Competition 2009, First Prize and Bach Special Prize, Corpus Christi Int. Competition for Piano and Strings 2009, Nat. Foundation for Advancement in the Arts Gold Award in Music, First Prize and People's Choice Award, Montréal Int. Musical Competition 2010, winner, Young Concert Artists Int. Auditions 2010, Bronze Medal, Indianapolis Int. Violin Competition 2010, Philadelphia Musical Fund Soc. Career Advancement Award 2010, Kronberg Acad. Prince of Hesse Prize 2011. *Current Management:* Young Concert Artists, Inc., General Management, 250 West 57th Street, Suite 1222, New York, NY 10107, USA. *Telephone:* (212) 307-6655 (office). *Website:* benjaminbeilman.instantencore.com.

BEILMAN, Douglas, MMus; American violinist; b. 1965, Kansas. *Education:* Juilliard School, New England Conservatory with Dorothy DeLay, San Francisco Conservatory of Music. *Career:* co-founder, Sierra Quartet; performed at the Olympic Music Festival; co-founder, New Zealand String Quartet 1989–, under the auspices of the Music Federation of New Zealand; concerts at the Tanglewood School, USA, Banff Int. Competition, Canada; soloist with New Zealand Symphony Orchestra; Artist-in-Residence, Victoria Univ., Wellington; co-founder and Artistic Dir, Adam New Zealand Festival of Chamber Music –2001. *Address:* School of Music, Room 212, PO Box 2332, Wellington, New Zealand (office). *Telephone:* (4) 463-5866 (office). *E-mail:* douglas.beilman@vuw.ac.nz (office). *Website:* www.nzsm.ac.nz (office).

BEKOVA, Alfia; Kazakhstani musician (cello); b. Karaganda. *Education:* Cen. Music School for Children, Moscow, studies at Moscow Conservatoire with Mstislav Rostropovich, and with Shafran and Jacqueline du Pré. *Career:* moved to UK 1989; London debut, with sisters Elvira Bekova (q.v.) and Eleonora Bekova (q.v.) with Nakipbekova Sisters Trio (Bekova Trio), Royal Festival Hall 1989; tours to Canada, Australia and Far East 1996; concert performances include Moscow, Russian Fed. 1995, Lebanon Festival, Lincoln Center, New York, USA and Queen Elizabeth Hall, London, UK 1996; recitals of solo cello works by J. S. Bach, Paganini, Gubaidullina, Vasks and Hesford; performed 'Bach Marathon' series in London, Oxford, Aldeburgh, Melbourne and Brussels; Co-founder Cellorhythmics. *Recordings include:* Brahms: Cello Sonatas 1996, Sergei Larin – Tchaikovsky Songs 1996, Shostakovich: Chamber and Vocal Works 1997, Martinů – Chamber Works (chosen by BBC Classical Music Magazine as one of best CDs of 1998), Music by Charles Ives and Rebecca Clarke (Gramophone Magazine Critics' Choice 2000), Spanish Piano Trios – Granados, Cassadó, Turina/Bekova Trio 2001. *Honours:* Special Prize for Outstanding Mastery of the Cello, Casals Competition, Budapest 1980. *Telephone:* (20) 7226-8412 (office). *Fax:* (20) 7226-8412 (office). *E-mail:* cellorhythmics@blueyonder.co.uk (office). *Website:* www.alfianakipbekova.com.

BEKOVA, Eleonora; Kazakhstani musician (piano); b. Karaganda; one s. *Education:* Music Conservatory, Moscow with Emil Gilels. *Career:* moved to UK 1989; London debut, with sisters Elvira Bekova (q.v.) and Alfia Bekova (q.v.) with Nakipbekova Sisters Trio (Bekova Trio), Royal Festival Hall 1989; tours to Canada, Australia and Far East 1996; concert performances include Moscow, Russian Fed. 1995, Lebanon Festival, Lincoln Center, New York, USA and Queen Elizabeth Hall, London, UK 1996; Artistic Dir Malta Int. Summer Festival 2004; Founder Kazakh Gala (charity foundation); f. Eleonora Bekova Music Acad. *Recordings include:* Rachmaninov/Shostakovich Cello Sonatas, Brahms Cello Sonatas, Songs by Rachmaninov (with Sergei Larin), Martinu Piano Sonata, Fantaisie and Toccata, Eight Preludes, Dream – Western Poets in Russian Music, Vol. 1 (with Sergei Larin), Romance – Western Poets in Russian Music, Vol. 2 (with Sergei Larin) 2001, Eternity – Western Poets in Russian Music, Vol. 3 (with Sergei Larin). *E-mail:* info@kazakhgala.co.uk. *Website:* www.kazakhgala.co.uk.

BEKOVA, Elvira; Kazakhstani musician (violin); *Artistic Director, Felcino Bianco*; b. (Elvira Nakipbekova), Karaganda; one d. *Education:* studies with Roman Mazanov and with Igor Bezrodny at Moscow Conservatoire. *Career:* invited to play Khatchaturian's Violin Concerto before composer himself at concert in Armenia aged 15; moved to UK 1989; London debut, with sisters Eleonora Bekova (q.v.) and Alfia Bekova (q.v.), Royal Festival Hall 1989; tours to Canada, Australia and the Far East 1996; concert performances include Moscow, Russian Fed. 1995, Lebanon Festival, Lincoln Center, New York, USA, and the Queen Elizabeth and Wigmore Halls, London, UK 1996; repertoire includes all major violin concertos by composers including Mozart, Beethoven, Bach, Brahms, Mendelssohn, Sibelius, Saint-Saëns, Tchaikovsky, Lalo, Bartók, Prokofiev, Paganini, Wienawsky, and contemporary works by Zhubanova, Khreunikov, Eshpai, Tshedrin, Denisov and Shostakovich; trio has performed with London Philharmonic, Moscow and Leningrad Philharmonic, Lithuanian Chamber Orchestra, Resident Orchestra, The Hague, State Orchestra, Ankara; concerts have been broadcast by major TV and radio stations in UK (BBC and ITV), Germany, Belgium, Finland, Ireland, France, Netherlands, USA, Canada, Turkey and Australia; trio has given world premieres as dedicatees of works by David Heath, Michael Finnesy, Steven Gerber, Timur Tleukan and Sergei Zhukov; also marathon cycle 'From Haydn to Schnittke'; gave premiere performance of new violin concerto written for her by Sergei Zhukov, Moscow 2004; Artistic Dir Felcino Bianco (runs summer schools and other courses for professional and gifted amateur musicians and students); mem. int. jury for inaugural strings competition, Almaty, Kazakhstan 2004. *Recordings include:* Shostakovich: Piano Trio No. 2/Seven Romances on Verses by A. Blok 1997, Franck: Piano Trio No. 1/Violin Sonata 2000, B. Martiny: Chamber Works, Tchaikovsky: Trio Seasons, Mussorgsky: Pictures from an Exhibition. *Publications:* The Bekova Sisters Piano Trio Collections 1, Piano Trio Collections 2. *Honours:* Honoured Artist of Kazakhstan. *Address:* Felcino Bianco, Le Ville 79, 52031 Anghiari (AR), Tuscany, Italy (office). *E-mail:* music@felcinobianco.com (office). *Website:* felcinobianco.com (office).

BELAMARIC, Miro; Croatian composer and conductor; b. 9 Feb. 1935, Sibenik, Dalmatia. *Education:* Zagreb Acad. of Music with Milan Horvat and Stjepan Sulek, studied with Lovro von Matacic in Salzburg, Sergiu Celibidache in Siena. *Career:* Asst to Herbert von Karajan at Salzburg Festival 1965–68, to Karl Böhm 1975–77; fmr Conductor, Symphony Orchestra of Zagreb Radio; fmr Chief Conductor, Komedija Theatre; Chief Conductor, Zagreb Opera 1978–90; has conducted orchestras in Europe, Japan, Mexico. *Compositions include:* opera: The Love of Don Perlimplin 1975, Don Juan – ein Rebell für alle Zeiten 1983, Tales from the Vienna Woods 1993; other: Aria for violin and piano 1953, Three Pieces for flute and piano 1954, Transfigurations for baritone and piano 1955, Carnival in Dalmatia 1956, Danze Antiche 1958, Croatian Love Poetry for choir 1959–81, Passacaglia and Fugue 1967, How to Kill Mozart for piano and orchestra 1968, Portraits for piano 1979, String Quartet 1982, 5 Poemas del Cante Jondo for soprano and piano 1983–84, Sanctum Antonium Laudamus 1983, Croatia for symphony orchestra 1993, Spectrum for symphony orchestra 1995, Poem for Death Lovers 1997, Solemn Euro 1998, Arise, Banus 1990, Croatian Marches 1998. *Honours:* winner Vienna State Opera Competition (for Don Juan) 1983. *Address:* Brunhildengasse 4/2/12, 1150 Vienna, Austria (home). *E-mail:* belamaric@gmx.at.

BELCHER, Daniel, MMus; American singer (baritone); b. St Joseph, Mo.; s. of Jim Belcher and Dorothy Belcher. *Education:* William Jewell Coll., Liberty, Mo., New England Conservatory, Juilliard School of Music. *Career:* mem. chorus, Central City Opera Young Artist Program 1993–95; Young Artist with Houston Grand Opera (HGO) Studio 1997–99; professional opera debut with HGO as Andy Warhol in world premiere of Michael Daugherty's Jackie O 1997; debut with San Francisco Opera as Harlequin in Ariadne auf Naxos 2002; Paris debut as Prior Walter in world premiere of Peter Eötvös's Angels in America, Théâtre du Châtelet; UK debut as Guglielmo in Così fan tutte at Garsington Festival and Barbican Mostly Mozart Festival, London; other opera appearances with Central City Opera, New York City Opera, Lyric Opera of Kansas City, Opera Co. of Philadelphia, Grand Théâtre de Genève, Santa Fe Opera, Utah Symphony & Opera, Portland Opera, De Nederlandse Oper, Opera Ireland. *Opera repertoire includes:* Rossini heroes including Dandini in La Cenerentola, Figaro in The Barber of Seville; John Brooke in Mark Adamo's Little Women, Harlequin in Ariadne auf Naxos, Papageno in The Magic Flute, Marcello in La bohème, Taddeo in L'italiana in Algeri, Ned Keene in Peter Grimes, Guglielmo in Così fan tutte. *Recordings:* L'Amour de Loin (Grammy Award for Best Opera Recording, Diapason d'Or Prize, France) 2011. *Honours:* several awards including Central City Opera Young Artist Award and Outstanding Studio Artist Award, William Jewell's Citation for Achievement Award 2010. *Current Management:* Mirshak Artists Management, 1173 Second Avenue, #313, New York, NY 10065, USA. *Telephone:* (917) 282-0687. *Fax:* (646) 395-1368. *E-mail:* robert@mirshakartists.com. *Website:* www.danielbelcherbaritone.com.

BELCOURT, Emile, BSc; Canadian singer (tenor); b. 27 June 1926, Laflèche, near Regina. *Education:* Univ. of Saskatchewan, Acad. of Music, Vienna, studied in Paris with Pierre Bernac and Germaine Lubin. *Career:* early opera appearances in Germany and France, including with Paris Opéra Comique as Pelléas; sang in Debussy's opera for Scottish Opera 1962; made English debut at Covent Garden as Gonzalez in L'Heure Espagnole 1963; joined Sadler's Wells/ENO 1963–90, singing Die Fledermaus, Orpheus in the Underworld, Bluebeard, The Violins of St Jacques, Patience, Salome and Lucky Peter's Journey, Loge in The Ring; made Canadian Opera Company debut as Bernard of Clairvaux in premiere of Charles Wilson's Heloise and Abelard 1973, also as Camille in The Merry Widow, Shuisky in Boris Godunov, Gonzalve, Dr Falke in Die Fledermaus, Macheath in The Beggar's Opera; sang in premieres of Bennett's A Penny for a Song 1967, Hamilton's The Royal Hunt of the Sun 1977, Blake's Toussaint l'ouverture 1977; lead in stage musicals Man of La Mancha and Kiss Me Kate; performed Ring Cycle, Seattle 1979.

BELKIN, Boris; Belgian violinist; b. 26 Jan. 1948, Sverdlovsk, USSR. *Education:* violin studies aged six, Central Music School, Moscow, Moscow Conservatory with Yankelevitz and Andrievsky. *Career:* public appearances from 1955; emigrated 1974; debut in the West with Zubin Mehta and the Israel Philharmonic 1974; has appeared with orchestras including Berlin Philharmonic, Concertgebouw, Israel Philharmonic, Los Angeles Philharmonic, Philadelphia, Cleveland; Season 1987–88, Pittsburgh, Royal Philharmonic and Tokyo Philharmonic Orchestras; conductors include Muti,

Bernstein, Maazel, Haitink, Mehta, Ashkenazy and Steinberg. *Recordings:* Paganini Concerto No. 1 with the Israel Philharmonic; Tchaikovsky and Sibelius Concertos with the Philharmonia Orchestra; Prokofiev's Concertos with the Zürich Tonhalle Orchestra; Brahms Concerto with the London Symphony; Glazunov and Shostakovich Concerto No. 1 with the Royal Philharmonic; Brahms Sonatas with Dalberto. *Honours:* Winner, Soviet Nat. Competition for Violinists 1972.

BELL, Christopher, BMus, MMus, MUniv; British conductor and artistic director; b. 1 May 1961, Belfast, Northern Ireland; s. of John Christopher Bell and Christina Carole Bell. *Education:* Univ. of Edinburgh, masterclasses in Dublin and Wiener Meisterkurse. *Career:* Assoc. Conductor, BBC Scottish Symphony Orchestra 1989–91; Chorusmaster, Royal Scottish Nat. Orchestra Chorus 1989–2002; Artistic Dir Edinburgh Royal Choral Union 1993–94; Prin. Guest Conductor, State Orchestra of Victoria, Australia 1997–99; Founder and Music Dir Ulster Youth Choir 1999–2004; Artistic Dir Children's Classic Concerts 2001–08; Chorusmaster, Belfast Philharmonic Choir 2005–11; Founder, Phil Kids, Conductor 2007–11; currently Chorus Dir Grant Park Music Festival, Chicago USA; currently Chorusmaster, RSNO Jr Chorus and Edinburgh Festival Chorus; currently Artistic Dir and Founder, Nat. Youth Choir of Scotland; currently Assoc. Conductor, Ulster Orchestra; conducted Royal Philharmonic, London Philharmonic, Ulster, Scottish Chamber, City of London Sinfonia, London Concert, RTE Nat. Symphony and Bournemouth Symphony Orchestras; overseas has worked with Duisburg Symphony Orchestra, Basel Symphony Orchestra, Dutch Radio Symphony, Brabants Orkest, Orquesta Filharmonica de Gran Canaria, Noord Nederlands Orkest, Philharmonie of Essen, New Zealand, Melbourne and Perth Symphony Orchestras. *Honours:* Scotsman of the Year Award for Creative Talent 2001, Charles Grove Prize for contrib. to cultural life in Scotland and rest of UK 2003, Margaret Hills Award for Choral Excellence, Chorus America (with Chorus of Grant Park Music Festival) 2006. *Current Management:* c/o Robert Gilder & Co., 91 Great Russell Street, London, WC1B 3PS, England. *Telephone:* (20) 7580-7758. *Fax:* (20) 7580-7739. *E-mail:* rgilder@robert -gilder.com. *Website:* www.robert-gilder.com. *Address:* National Youth Choir of Scotland, 201 North Street, Glasgow, G3 7DN, Scotland (office). *Telephone:* (141) 287-2856 (office). *Fax:* (141) 287-2858 (office). *E-mail:* admin@nycos.co .uk (office). *Website:* www.nycos.co.uk (office).

BELL, Donald Munro; Canadian academic and singer (baritone); b. 19 June 1934, Burnaby, BC. *Education:* Royal Coll. of Music, Stadtische Oper Studio, Berlin. *Career:* debut at Wigmore Hall 1958; Bayreuth 1958, The Night-watchman in Meistersinger 1959–1960; the Herald in Lohengrin, the Steersman in Tristan and Isolde; CBC, BBC, NOS Holland, WDR, Nord Deutsche Rundfunk, Germany; appeared at Luzern Festival with Thomas Beecham 1959, Glyndebourne 1963 as the Speaker in Die Zauberflöte; Grand Théâtre, Geneva, London Royal Festival Hall, Royal Albert Hall, by invitation at the opening of Lincoln Center, New York and Carnegie Hall with the Philadelphia Orchestra and many other venues; mem. Rotary Club, NATS. *Publications:* papers: Using Digital Technology in a Voice Lesson 1997, Acoustic Characteristics of Vibrato Onset in Singing (with Dr Michael Dobrovolsky) 1999. *Honours:* recipient of various honours and awards.

BELL, Donaldson; British singer (bass); b. 1958, Ayrshire, Scotland. *Education:* Royal Scottish Acad., Glasgow. *Career:* company principal, Royal Opera from 1978; appearances in operas, including Werther, La Fanciulla del West, Die Entführung, Der Rosenkavalier, Die Meistersinger (Night-Watchman), Die Zauberflöte, La Traviata, and Death in Venice; Royal Opera House education workshops; oratorio and recital engagements in UK and abroad.

BELL, Elizabeth, (Elizabeth Friou), BA, BS; American composer; b. (Elizabeth Buckner Bell), 1 Dec. 1928, Cincinnati, OH; d. of William Procter Bell and Sophie Buckner Bell; m. 1st Frank D. Drake 1953 (divorced 1977); m. 2nd Robert E. Friou 1983 (died 2009). *Education:* Wellesley Coll., Wellesley, Mass, Juilliard School of Music, New York, studied with Peter Mennin, Vittorio Giannini, Paul Alan Levi. *Career:* performances throughout USA, also Russia, Ukraine, Bulgaria, Armenia, France, Japan, Australia, Canada, South America; retrospective ('all-Bell') concerts in Ithaca, NY 1973, Cincinnati 1985, New York City 1991, 1998, 2003, Yerevan, Armenia 2004; music critic, Ithaca Journal 1971–75; mem., founder and officer, Dir New York Women Composers; mem. American Composers' Alliance (mem. Bd of Govs 2000–05); mem. Soc. of Composers Inc., NACUSA, Int. Alliance of Women in Music. *Compositions include:* Variations and Interludes for piano 1952, String Quartet 1957, Songs of Here and Forever 1970, Fantasy-Sonata for cello and piano 1971, Symphony No. 1 1971, 2nd Sonata for piano 1972, Soliloquy for solo cello 1980, Loss-Songs for soprano and piano 1983, Perne in a Gyre for clarinet, violin, cello and piano 1984, Duovarios for two pianos 1987, Millennium for soprano, clarinet and piano 1988, Spectra for 11 instruments 1989, Night Music for piano 1990, River Fantasy for flute and string trio 1991, Andromeda for piano, string orchestra and percussion 1993, Les Neiges d'Antan, sonata for violin and piano 1998. *Recordings include:* albums: The Music of Elizabeth Bell, Snows of Yesteryear, A Collection of Reflections. *Honours:* first prize, Utah Composers' Competition 1986, Grand Prize, Utah Composers' Competition 1996, Delius Prize 1994, awards from Meet the Composer and New York Council for the Arts. *Address:* 21 Beech Lane, Tarrytown, NY 10591-3001, USA (home). *Telephone:* (914) 631-4361 (home). *Fax:* (914) 631-6444 (home). *E-mail:* ebelfri@earthlink.net (home).

BELL, Emma; British singer (soprano); b. 1970, Leamington Spa; m. Finnur Bjarnason; one s. *Education:* Royal Acad., London with Joy Mammer. *Career:* sang Handel's Radamisto and Salustia (Alessandro Severo) and Lia in Debussy's L'Enfant Prodigue at the RAM; Handel's Rodelinda for the Glyndebourne Tour 1998, and at the Festival 1999; season 1999–2000 with Mozart's Exsultate Jubilate K165 at the QEH and Elvira in Don Giovanni for Opera North; sang Handel's Rodelinda at the Royal Festival Hall 2002; mem. of co., Komische Oper, Berlin 2002–05, singing Mimi in La Bohème, the Countess in Marriage of Figaro; sang Vitellia in La Clemenza di Tito for ENO 2005; Covent Garden debut as Leonore in Nielsen's Maskarade 2005; sang Violetta in La Traviata, London Coliseum 2006; recital of Strauss songs with Emanuel Ax at Wigmore Hall 2008; sang Electra in Idomeneo at Barbican Hall 2008, for ENO 2010; sang in Le Nozze di Figaro at Metropolitan Opera, New York 2009; Donna Elvira in Don Giovanni, La Scala 2010 and Met Opera 2012; Fox in The Cunning Little Vixen, Covent Garden 2010 and Glynde-bourne 2012; Elsa von Brabant in Lohengrin, Welsh Nat. Opera 2013. *Recordings:* Emma Bell 2004, Handel Arias (with Richard Egarr and the Scottish Chamber Orchestra) 2005, Handel: Saul and Messiah 2005, Britten: The Turn of the Screw 2007. *Honours:* Yamaha Music Foundation of Europe Scholarship, RAM Dove Prize, Kathleen Ferrier Award 1988, Borletti-Buitoni Trust grant 2003. *Current Management:* Robert Clarke, Hazard Chase, 25 City Road, Cambridge, CB1 1DP, England. *Telephone:* (1223) 312400. *Fax:* (1223) 460827. *E-mail:* robert.clarke@hazardchase.co.uk. *Website:* www .hazardchase.co.uk.

BELL, Joshua; American violinist; b. 9 Dec. 1967, Indiana. *Education:* Indiana Univ. *Career:* European tour with St Louis Symphony 1985; German tour with Indianapolis Symphony 1987; European tour with Dallas Symphony 1997; European tours with Nat. Symphony Orchestra 2002, Minnesota Orchestra 2003; guest soloist with numerous orchestras in USA, Canada, Europe; has also appeared in USA and Europe as a recitalist; played premiere of violin concerto by Nicholas Maw, written for him, with Philharmonia Orchestra 1993; Music Dir, Acad. of St Martin in the Fields 2011–; Artistic Partner, St Paul Chamber Orchestra; currently Sr Lecturer, Jacobs School of Music, Indiana Univ.; Visiting Prof., RAM, London; mem. Artist Cttee, Kennedy Center Honors; mem. Bd of Dirs New York Philharmonic. *Record-ings include:* Mendelssohn and Bruch concertos with the Academy of St Martin-in-the-Fields and Sir Neville Marriner, Tchaikovsky and Wieniawski concertos with the Cleveland Orchestra and Vladimir Ashkenazy, recital album of Brahms, Paganini, Sarasate and Wieniawski with Samuel Sanders, Lalo Symphonie Espagnole and Saint-Saëns Concerto with Montreal Sym-phony Orchestra and Charles Dutoit, Franck, Fauré and Debussy, Chausson Concerto for violin, piano and string quartet with Thibaudet and Isserlis, Poème with Royal Philharmonic Orchestra and Andrew Litton, Mozart Concertos Nos 3 and 5 with the English Chamber Orchestra and Peter Maag, Prokofiev violin concertos with Montréal Symphony Orchestra and Charles Dutoit, Barber and Walton concertos and Bloch Baal Shem with Baltimore Symphony Orchestra and David Zinman, recital disc with Olli Mustonen, Gershwin Fantasy with London Symphony Orchestra and John Williams, Short Trip Home with Edgar Meyer, The Red Violin film soundtrack with Philharmonia Orchestra, Sibelius Goldmark Concertos with Los Angeles Philharmonic Orchestra and Esa-Pekka Salonen, Maw Concerto for violin with London Philharmonic Orchestra and Roger Norrington, Bernstein Serenade and West Side Story Suite with Philharmonia Orchestra and David Zinman, Beethoven and Mendelssohn concertos with Camerata Salzburg and Sir Roger Norrington, Irish film soundtrack, Romance of the Violin 2003, Tchaikovsky Violin Concerto 2005, Voice of the Violin 2006, The Red Violin Concerto 2007, Vivaldi: The Four Seasons 2008, At Home with my Friends 2009, French Impressions with Jeremy Denk (ECHO Klassik Award for Chamber Music Recording of the Year/Strings – 19th Century) 2012. *Honours:* Gramophone Award for Best Concerto Recording 1998 (for Barber Concerto), Mercury Music Award 2000, Acad. Award for Best Soundtrack (for Red Violin), Grammy Award 2001, Avery Fisher Prize 2007, named Young Global Leader by World Econ. Forum 2007, Musical America Award for Instrumen-talist of the Year 2010, Paul Newman Award, Arts Horizons 2011, Huberman Award, Moment Magazine 2011. *Current Management:* Jane Covner, JAG Entertainment, 4265 Hazeltine Avenue, Sherman Oaks, CA 91423; c/o IMG Artists, Carnegie Hall Tower, 152 West 57th Street, 5th Floor, New York, NY 10019, USA. *E-mail:* jcovner@jagpr.com. *E-mail:* heidi@joshuabell.com; jb@ joshuabell.com. *Website:* www.joshuabell.com.

BELLING, Susan; American singer (soprano); b. 3 May 1943, Bronx, NY. *Education:* Chatham Square Music School, Kathryn Long School, Metropol-itan Opera Studio, Manhattan School of Music. *Career:* masterclasses and workshops at Stanford Univ., CA 1978, Univ. of Houston 1978, Manhattan School of Music 1984; faculty mem., New School of Social Research 1986–; over 100 American and world premieres; sang title role in Reimann's Melusine for Santa Fe Opera, and Kirchner's Lily with New York City Opera; performance of Arnold Schoenberg's Second Quartet with Erich Leinsdorf and the Boston Symphony; sang Belinda in Dido and Aeneas for Metropolitan Opera's premiere season of the Forum Opera, Lincoln Center; performed on numerous occasions with conductor James Levine in such roles as Zerlina in Don Giovanni at Hollywood Bowl, Papagena in Magic Flute with Cleveland Concert Associates, as soprano soloist in A Midsummer Night's Dream and the Mahler Fourth Symphony with the Chicago Symphony, and with Atlanta Symphony in The Marriage of Figaro; debut in Europe at Baroque Festival of Venetian Music, Castelfranco, Veneto and Teatro Olimpico, Italy 1977;

numerous other performances include Haydn's Lord Nelson Mass with Minnesota Orchestra, Neville Marriner conducting, and Pamina in The Magic Flute.

BELLO, Vincenzo; Italian singer (tenor); b. 1950, Mogliano, Treviso. *Career:* debut in Manrico in Il Trovatore, Treviso 1975; appearances throughout Italy from 1975 and at Barcelona and Munich; sang Manrico at Verona and the Metropolitan, New York 1978; festival engagements at Macerata, Orange, Florence; repertoire includes Alfredo, Verdi's Macduff, Ismaele in Nabucco, Donizetti's Edgardo, Rodolfo in La Bohème, Ruggero in La Rondine, Edgardo, Rodolfo in Luisa Miller, Arturo in Bellini's La Straniera, Verdi's Riccardo, Roberto Devereux. *Honours:* winner Toti dal Monte Competition 1975.

BELLU, Cristina, DipMus, MMus; Italian cellist; b. 7 Feb. 1968, Florence; m. James A. Holzwarth 1992. *Education:* Conservatorio State Luigi Cherubini, studied with Settimio Guadagni, Chicago Musical Coll. and Roosevelt Univ., USA. *Career:* mem. Civic Orchestra of Chicago; appearances with Orchestra da Camera Fiorentina, Orchestra Lirico-Sinfonica del Teatro del Giglio di Lucca, Univ. of Chicago Symphony Orchestra, Chicago Chamber Orchestra, Orchestra del Maggio Musicale Fiorentino; numerous performances worldwide; Co-founder Operacion Tango group; soloist, Livorno Philharmonic Orchestra 1992–2001; currently Prof. of Violoncello, Ecole Nationale a Rayonnement Departmental Mulhouse, HEMU Lausanne, Scuola Universitaria Lugano, Switzerland; research project 'Investigation of Cello and Motor Development' (ICE MODE), doctoral student in Educ. at Univ. of Geneva; Pres. ESTA-France (European String Teachers Asscn), represents ESTA International at the Council of Europe. *Recordings include:* Operacion Tango en Concert 1999, Waat mot Komme Ge Reinders Liedjes. Juin 2007, Concerti pour clavier de J. S. Bach 2007, Hardy Mertens Live at Roda Hall 2010, Le jouer de flute de Hamelin 2014. *Honours:* SNF grant for ICE MODE project 2010–12. *Address:* Conservatorio della Svizzera Italiana, via Soldino 9, 6900 Lugano, Switzerland (office). *E-mail:* info@conservatorio.ch (office). *Website:* www.conservatorio.ch (office).

BELLUCCI, Giacomo, DipMus; Italian composer; b. 20 Jan. 1928, Recanati. *Education:* Rossini Conservatory, Pesaro with Giorgi, S. Cecilia, Rome with Margola and Mortari, studied with Ferrara. *Career:* conductor of orchestra and choir (also in lyric stage and polyphony), performing in Italy and abroad (Europe and USA); founder and Dir, Recanati's Gigli Music Inst. 1977–82; Prof., Rossini Conservatory, Pesaro 1965–98; principal of various Italian conservatories 1982–90. *Compositions:* Coreographie (ballet), Il Punto (opera ballet), three symphonies, three overtures, three suites, 16 concertos for solo instrument and orchestra, 16 string quartets, seven trios, five oratorios, two psalms, many chamber works for various instruments, voice, organ and sacred music. *Publications:* contrib. many articles, texts and essays on music, critical notes to concertos for dailies and periodicals.

BĚLOHLÁVEK, Jiří; Czech musician and conductor; *Chief Conductor, Czech Philharmonic Orchestra;* b. 24 Feb. 1946, Prague; m. Anna Fejérová 1971; two d. *Education:* Acad. of Performing Arts, Prague with Sergiu Celibidache. *Career:* Conductor Orchestra Puellarum Pragensis (chamber orchestra), Prague 1967–72; Asst Conductor Czech Philharmonic Orchestra 1970–71, Conductor 1981–90, Prin. Conductor and Music Dir 1990–92, Music Dir and Chief Conductor 2012–; Conductor Brno State Philharmonic Orchestra 1971–77; Chief Conductor Prague Symphony Orchestra 1977–90; Conductor Int. Philharmonic Youth Orchestra, Prague 1987–89; Founder and Music Dir Prague Philharmonia 1994–2005; Prin. Guest Conductor BBC Symphony Orchestra 1995–2000, Chief Conductor 2006–12, Conductor Laureate 2012–; Prof., Acad. of Music, Prague 1995–; Prin. Guest Conductor Nat. Theatre Prague 1998; guest appearances with numerous orchestras, including USSR State Symphony Orchestra, BBC Philharmonic, BBC Nat. Orchestra of Wales, Scottish Nat. Orchestra, Royal Liverpool Philharmonic, City of Birmingham Symphony, Berlin Philharmonic, Vienna Symphony Orchestra, Leipzig Gewandhaus, Stockholm Philharmonic, Bavarian Radio Orchestra, Dresden Philharmonic, Deutsche Kammerphilharmonie, Tonhalle Orchestra Zürich, New York Philharmonic, Boston Symphony Orchestra, St Louis Orchestra, Washington Nat. Orchestra, Montreal Symphony Orchestra, NHK Philharmonic Tokyo. *Recordings include:* with BBC Symphony Orchestra: The Excursions of Mr Broucek (Gramophone Award for Best Opera Recording 2009) 2008, Martinů The 6 Symphonies (Gramophone Award for Best Orchestral Recording 2012) 2011, Josef Suk: Prague/A Summer's Tale (Gramophone Award for Best Orchestral Recording 2013) 2012. *Honours:* Hon. CBE 2012; Supraphon Prize 1977, Artist of Merit 1986, Supraphon Golden Disc 1986, 1987, 1994, 1999, Diapason d'Or 1992, Barclay Theatre Award 2000, Medal for Merit, Prague 2001. *Address:* Czech Philharmonic Orchestra, Alsovo nabrezi 12, 110 00, Prague 1, Czech Republic (office); c/o BBC Symphony Orchestra, BBC Maida Vale Studios, Delaware Road, London, W9 2LG, England (office). *Telephone:* 227059221 (Prague) (office); (20) 7765-2956 (London) (office). *Fax:* 227059246 (Prague) (office). *E-mail:* info@cfmail.cz (office). *Website:* www.ceskafilharmonie.cz/en; www.jiribelohlavek.com.

BELSKAYA, Nina; Russian violist; b. 1960, Moscow. *Education:* Moscow Conservatoire with Prof. Strakhovos. *Career:* mem., Prokofiev Quartet, founded at the Moscow Festival of World Youth and the International Quartet Competition at Budapest; many concerts in the former Soviet Union and on tour to Czechoslovakia, Germany, Austria, USA, Canada, Spain, Japan and Italy; repertoire includes works by Haydn, Mozart, Beethoven, Schubert, Debussy, Ravel, Tchaikovsky, Bartók and Shostakovich.

BELTON, Ian, BMus, GRNCM, PPRNCM; British violinist; b. 1959, England. *Education:* Royal Northern Coll. of Music, Manchester Univ. *Career:* founder mem., Brodsky String Quartet; resident at Univ. of Cambridge four years, later residencies at Dartington Int. Summer School, Devon; concert engagements include the Shostakovich Quartets at the QEH, London and performances at the Ludwigsburg and Schleswig-Holstein Festivals; New York debut at the Metropolitan Museum; tours of Italy, North America, Australia, Poland, Czechoslovakia, Turkey and Japan; complete quartets of Schoenberg for the BBC; French concerts include Théâtre du Châtelet, Paris; concert in Amsterdam and performances at Berlin Festival, Carnegie Hall; tour of Australia 1993. *Recordings include:* Quartets of Elgar and Delius; Schubert A minor and Beethoven Op 74; Complete Quartets of Shostakovich; Borodin Quartet No. 2; Tchaikovsky Quartet No. 3; Juliet Letters (collaboration with Elvis Costello).

BELTRAN, Tito; Swedish (b. Chilean) singer (tenor); b. 1 July 1965; m.; six c. *Education:* Gothenburg Acad. and with Vera Rosza and Robin Stapleton, London. *Career:* roles include Nemorino, Ernesto, Edgardo, Rodolfo, Ruggero in La Rondine, Pinkerton, Rinuccio, Cavaradossi, Italian Tenor in Der Rosenkavalier, Duca, Macduff, Riccardo in Un Ballo in Maschera, Ismaele, Alfredo, Tybalt, Tebaldo, Osaka (Iris by Mascagni); has sung at Covent Garden (debut as Rodolfo 1995), Opera North, Vienna (debut as Nemorino 1997), Hamburg, Ludwigshafen, Bayerische Staatsoper Munich, Deutsche Oper Berlin, Leipzig, Mannheim, Opera Bastille (debut in Der Rosenkavalier 2002), Toulouse, Bordeaux, La Scala (debut in Der Rosenkavalier 2003), Genoa, Teatro Regio Torino, Parma, Arena di Verona, Roma, Lucca, Cosenza, Fenno, Monte Carlo, Geneva, Zurich, Royal Opera Stockholm, Gothenburg, Copenhagen, Norske Opera Oslo, Iceland, Menorca, Santiago, Rio de Janeiro, Michigan (USA debut as Rodolfo 1996), San Francisco, Orlando, Pittsburgh, Portland, New Nat. Theatre, Tokyo; numerous worldwide concerts and TV appearances; lives in Sweden. *Recordings:* four solo CDs for Silva Screen Classics: Tito, Romantica, A Tenor At The Movies, Amazing Grace; Celemin in La Dolores by Tomas Bretón (with Placido Domingo) for Decca. *Television:* sang Tybalt in Iambic Productions film of Romeo et Juliette (with Roberto Alagna and Angela Gheorghiu) (Channel 4) 2004. *Honours:* finalist Cardiff Singer of the World Competition 1993, Opera Now Artist of the Year 1999. *Current Management:* c/o Giandomenico Bisi, Melodrama, Viale Augusto 119, 80125 Naples, Italy. *Telephone:* (081) 5932553. *Fax:* (081) 5933705. *E-mail:* gianbisi@tin.it. *Website:* www.titobeltran.com; www.titobeltrantenor.com.

BELYAEV, Yevegeni; Russian violinist; b. 1950, Crimea. *Career:* co-founder, Rachmaninov Quartet 1974, under auspices of the Sochi State Philharmonic Soc., Crimea; many concerts in the fmr Soviet Union and from 1975–76 tours to Switzerland, Austria, Bulgaria, Norway and Germany; participation in the 1976 Shostakovich Chamber Music Festival at Vilnius and in festivals in Moscow and St Petersburg; repertoire has included works by Haydn, Mozart, Beethoven, Bartók, Schnittke, Shostakovich, Boris Tchaikovsky, Chalayev and Meyerovich. *Honours:* prizewinner All-Union Borodin String Quartet Competition (with Rachmaninov Quartet) 1987.

BEN-OR, Nelly; British pianist and teacher; *Professor, Piano Department, Guildhall School of Music and Drama;* b. Warsaw, Poland. *Education:* Music High School, Poland, Music Acad., Israel, Alexander Foundation, London. *Career:* in Israel: solo recitals, chamber music broadcasts; soloist with Radio Orchestra; in England: recitals in London, including Queen Elizabeth Hall, Wigmore Hall, St John's, Smith Square, for BBC and throughout UK; recitals, broadcasts and master-classes world-wide; teacher of the Alexander Technique 1963–; specialist in application of the Alexander Technique to piano playing; Prof. in Piano Dept, Guildhall School of Music and Drama, London 1975–; mem. Inc. Soc. of Musicians, European Piano Teachers' Asscn (UK Founder Cttee mem.), Soc. of Teachers of the Alexander Technique. *Radio:* solo recitals on BBC Radio 3. *Recordings:* Piano Variations (various composers), Beethoven Complete Bagatelles, Beethoven Piano Quartet op 16 (with Jerusalem String Trio), Chopin Dances, Debussy (Complete Images), Schubert Impromptus D899 and D935, Dvořák/Fibich Piano Quartets (with Jerusalem String Trio), Bach Toccata in D, Chopin (Mazurkas), Kinghorn piano sonata, Mazurkas from Poland and Mexico (Chopin, Szymanowski and Ponce). *Publications:* contributed articles to various professional publs, including publs on the application of the Alexander Technique to piano playing. *Honours:* First Prize, Mozart Competition, Israel. *Address:* c/o Roger Clynes, 23 Rofant Road, Northwood, Middx, HA6 3BD, England. *Telephone:* (1923) 822268. *E-mail:* roger.clynes@virgin.net. *Website:* www.pianocourseswithalexandertechnique.com. *E-mail:* nelly.ben-or@virgin.net (office).

BEN-YOHANAN, Asher, MMus; Israeli composer and music educator; b. 22 May 1929, Kavala, Greece; m. Shoshana Zwibel; one s. one d. *Education:* studied oboe and piano; composition studies with Paul Ben-Haim, Israel, Aaron Copland, USA and Luigi Nono, Italy; studied with Gustave Reese and Jan La Rue, New York Univ.; Univ. of Michigan. *Career:* compositions performed in Israel, Europe, USA, South America and Hong Kong; Head of Music Dept and Teacher of Theory, Thelma Yellin Music and Arts School, Tel-Aviv, Israel 1966–87; Prof. of Music, Bar-Ilan Univ. 1973–96; mem. Israel Composers' League, Chair. 1989–92. *Compositions include:* Festive Overture, for orchestra 1957, Two Movements for Orchestra 1959, String Quartet 1962–64, Music for Orchestra 1967, Chamber Music for 6 1968, Quartetto Concertato 1969, Mosaic 1971, Concerto for String Orchestra 1973, Four Summer Songs 1974, Impressions for Piano 1976, Soliloquy for Violin 1977,

Desert Winds for Flute 1979, Three Songs without Titles 1983, Episode for Trombone 1984, Woodwind Quintet 1985, Divertimento for Brass Trio 1988–89, Hidden Feelings for Harp 1990, Meditations for chamber orchestra 1992, and other works; several prize-winning works and commissions. *Recordings include:* A Composer's Profile 2005. *Publications:* Music in Israel, A Short Survey 1975, Music Notation 1983. *Honours:* Morse Fellowship in Composition, Univ. of Cincinnati, USA 1971, Acum Prize for Lifetime Contrib. to Israeli music and culture 2009. *Address:* 4 Bloch Street, Tel-Aviv 64161, Israel (home).

BENACKOVA, Gabriela; Czech singer (soprano); b. 25 March 1944, Bratislava. *Education:* Bratislava Acad. with Janko Blaho and Tatiana Kiesakova. *Career:* debut at Prague National Theatre 1970 as Natasha in War and Peace; returned as Mimi, Marenka in The Bartered Bride, Jenůfa and Libuše in Smetana's opera 1983; appeared at Covent Garden 1979 as Tatiana in Eugene Onegin, Cologne Opera 1983 as Maddalena in Andrea Chénier, Vienna Staatsoper 1985 as Marguerite in a new production of Faust directed by Ken Russell, San Francisco 1986 as Jenůfa, Vienna Staatsoper 1987 as Rusalka; sang Desdemona at Stuttgart 1990, Leonore at 1990 Salzburg Festival, Katya Kabanova at the Metropolitan 1991; season 1992 as Fidelio at Covent Garden; sang Maddalena in Andrea Chénier at Zürich 1994; sang Wagner's Senta at Hamburg 1996; Jenůfa at Zürich 1998; sang Desdemona at the New York Met 1991, and Janáček's Emilia Marty at Brno 2001. *Recordings:* Janáček's Jenůfa and The Cunning Little Vixen, The Bartered Bride, Libuše, Rusalka, soloist in Janáček's Glagolitic Mass, Dvořák's Requiem. *Honours:* prizewinner Janáček Competition, Luhacovice 1962, winner Dvořák Competition, Karlovy Vary 1963, Czech Nat. Artist 1985.

BENARY, Barbara, BA, PhD; American composer and gamelan player; b. 7 April 1946, Bay Shore, NY. *Education:* Sarah Lawrence Coll., Wesleyan Univ. *Career:* has played the violin and has performed on various stringed instruments of India, China and Bulgaria; formed the Gamelan Son of Lion, an ensemble of Javanese instruments 1974; Asst Prof., Livingstone Coll., Rutgers Univ., NJ 1973–80. *Compositions include:* music theatre: Three Sisters Who are Not Sisters 1967, The Only Jealousy of Emer 1970, The Interior Castle 1973, The Gauntlet 1976, Sanguine 1976, The Tempest 1981; for gamelan: Convergence 1975, Braid 1975, No Friends in an Auction 1976, In Time Enough 1978, Sleeping Braid 1978, The Zen Story 1979, In Scroll of Leaves 1980, Moon Cat Chant 1980, Singing Braid 1980, Solkattu 1980, Sun Square 1980, Exchanges 1981, Hot-Rolled Steel 1984; dance scores: Night Thunks 1980, A New Pantheon 1981, Engineering 1981.

BENEDETTI, Nicola, MBE; Scottish violinist; b. 1987, West Kilbride. *Education:* Yehudi Menuhin School, studied with Natasha Boyarskaya, further studies with Maciej Rakowski in London, studied jazz with Wynton Marsalis and others, currently taking lessons from Pavel Vernikov in Vienna. *Career:* began violin lessons aged five; led Nat. Children's Orchestra of Scotland aged eight; has performed at venues including Royal Festival Hall, Queen Elizabeth Hall, St Martin-in-the-Fields, Wigmore Hall, Purcell Room, Glasgow Royal Concert Hall, Sage, Gateshead, Fazoli Concert Hall, Usher Hall, Glastonbury Classical Festival, Sacile (Italy), Lincoln Center, New York, Gardner Museum, Boston, Terrace Theater, Washington DC; performed with Scottish Symphony Orchestra at Scottish Proms, Glamis Castle 2004; invited to perform at opening of Scottish Parl. 2004; took part in special performances at Windsor Castle for HM the Queen, at G8 Summit, Gleneagles 2005, and for Comic Relief's Gala concert 'Classic Relief'; Carnegie Hall debut with Eos Orchestra of New York 2005; has performed with almost all of UK and Ireland's major symphony orchestras, including London Philharmonic, Philharmonia and City of Birmingham Symphony Orchestras; invited to work with int. orchestras, including Deutsche Symphony Orchestra in Berlin, Tonhalle Orchestra in Zürich, NDR Orchester in Llubljana, Het Brabants Orkest, Orchestre de Picardie, KBS Symphony and Japan Philharmonic; has performed in N America with Toronto, Vancouver, Colorado, Phoenix and Indianapolis Symphony Orchestras; season 2012–13 immediately preceded by a performance at BBC's Last Night of the Proms with the BBC Symphony Orchestra and Jiří Bělohlávek; other highlights include performances with the New Zealand Symphony Orchestra, MDR Leipzig Radio Symphony Orchestra, Netherlands Radio Philharmonic Orchestra, Danish Radio Orchestra, Royal Scottish Nat. Orchestra, Hong Kong Philharmonic and Singapore Symphony; appearances with the Dallas, Pittsburgh and Indianapolis symphony orchestras; performed in chamber music concerts throughout UK in her regular trio with cellist Leonard Elschenbroich and pianist Alexei Grynyuk; has visited schools throughout UK in conjunction with CLIC Sargent Practice-a-thon since 2005; became involved in Sistema Scotland's Big Noise project (music initiative partnered with Venezuela's El Sistema (Fundación Musical Simón Bolívar) 2010, makes regular visits to Raploch, Scotland to conduct masterclasses and work closely with the children; performed at Opening Ceremony of 2014 Commonwealth Games; World Premiere of a work by Mark-Anthony Turnage written for Benedetti and cellist Leonard Elschenbroich 2016; UNICEF Celebrity Supporter; plays the Gariel Stradivarius (1717), courtesy of Jonathan Moulds. *Recordings include:* debut album, Szymanowski, Violin Concerto No. 1 (with London Symphony Orchestra and Daniel Harding), Saint Saëns, Massenet and Brahms 2005, Mendelssohn's Violin Concerto and works by Mozart, Schubert and MacMillan with Acad. of St Martin-in-the-Fields 2006, Works by Tavener and Vaughan Williams' The Lark Ascending with London Philharmonic Orchestra 2007, Fantasie 2009, Works by Sarasate, Fauré, Rachmaninov, Pärt and Ravel 2009, Tchaikovsky and Bruch Violin Concertos 2010, Italia – Music of the Italian Baroque 2011, The Silver Violin (featuring the Korngold Violin Concerto) 2012, My First Decade 2013, Homecoming – A Scottish Fantasy 2014, Marsalis - Violin Concerto 2015. *Honours:* BBC Young Musician of the Year 2004, Classic BRIT Award for Young British Classical Performer 2008, Classic BRIT Award for Best Female Artist 2012. *Telephone:* 7867 430 630 (mobile). *E-mail:* elaine@emblemartists.com. *Website:* emblemartists.com; www.nicolabenedetti.co.uk.

BENEDICT, Roger; British violist; b. 1962, England. *Education:* Royal Northern Coll. of Music with Patrick Ireland and Eli Goren. *Career:* principal violist, Philharmonia Orchestra; soloist in Strauss's Don Quixote at the Edinburgh Festival and Festival Hall, London; Vaughan Williams Flos Campi with the New London Orchestra and premiere of Michael Berkeley's Concerto, with Philharmonia Orchestra 1994; also plays concerto works by Mozart, Bartók, Walton and Berlioz with Philharmonia, Royal Philharmonic, Ulster Orchestra; mem., Bell'Arte Ensemble with performances at Symphony Hall, Birmingham; performed with Wanderer Trio, Hagai Shaham and Noriko Ogawa at the Bastad Festival in Sweden; al-Bustan Festival, Beirut with flautist Patrick Gallois and harpist Fabrice Pierre 1998; on leaving the Philharmonia became regular principal of English Chamber Orchestra; Prof., Royal Northern Coll. of Music 1998; int. engagements include performances in South Africa, Scandinavia, the Middle East and Japan; moved to Australia 2002; principal viola in the Sydney Symphony Orchestra; Artistic Dir, James Fairfax Young Artists Programme; Sr Lecturer, Sydney Conservatorium; solo tours of Japan 2002; soloist with SSO and other Australian Orchestras. *Address:* 9 Alison Street, Roseville, NSW 2069, Australia. *Telephone:* (2) 9880-7005. *E-mail:* rogerbenedict@dodo.com.au.

BENELLI, Ugo; Italian singer (tenor); *Teacher, Montalto Opera Studio*; b. (Ugo Gino Fortunato), 20 Jan. 1935, Genoa; s. of Renato Benelli and Minerva Chiti; m. Angela Maria Patrone; one s. one d. *Education:* Scuola di Perfezionamento del Teatro alla Scala with Giulio Confalonieri. *Career:* debut, Piccola Scala 1960; opening of La Scala, Milan with L'Italiana in Algeri, conductor Claudio Abbado 1973; sang 16 roles at La Scala, toured with La Scala to Vienna Festival and Bolshoi Theatre, Moscow (La Cenerentola); festival appearances include Wexford, Glyndebourne, Salzburg, Vienna, Edinburgh, Aix-en-Provence, Wiesbaden and Rossini Opera Festival Pesaro; roles include Rossini's Almaviva, Lindoro, Don Ramiro, Bellini's Elvino, Donizetti's Nemorino, Ernesto and Tonio, Bizet's Nadir, Massenet's Des Grieux and Morfontaine, Weber/Mahler's Die drei Pintos, Conte Riccardo in I Quattro Rusteghi, Contino Belfiore and Don Anchise in La Finta Giardiniera, Basilio in Le Nozze di Figaro, Hauk in The Makropulos Case, Hans Styx in Orphée aux Enfers, Jack O'Brien in Mahagonny, Falsacappa in Offenbach's Les Brigands, Truffaldino in L'Amour des trois oranges, Ernesto in Don Pasquale etc.; teacher, Montalto Opera Studio; gives numerous master classes. *Recordings include:* Il Barbiere di Siviglia, La Cenerentola, Mozart's Requiem, I Pagliacci, Don Pasquale, La figlia del Reggimento, Il Cappello di Paglia di Firenze, L'Aio nell'imbarazzo, Elisabeth d'Inghilterra, Rossini's Messa di Gloria, La Spinalba, Le Nozze di Figaro, L'Italiana in Algeri, La Riconoscenza, Linda di Chamounix, La Buona Figliuola, Il Mondo della Luna, Il Dixit, Il Barone di Rocca Antica, La Finta Giardiniera, Il Giovedì Grasso, Il Crociato in Egitto, L'Innocenza Giustificata, La Rita, Il Campiello. *Honours:* La Cara Vella d'Oro, Genoa 1959, Ausgezeichnet mit der Tz-Rose, Munich 1972, Il Palco Scenico d'Oro 1979, Premio Regionale le Ligure 1983, La Margherita d'Oro, Santa Margherita Ligure 2001, Premio Melvin Jones Fellow 2001. *Address:* Viale Nazario Sauro, 6A Int. 4, 16145 Genoa, Italy (home). *Telephone:* (010) 311381 (home); 349-3933217 (mobile). *Fax:* (010) 311381 (home). *E-mail:* tenore@ugobenelli.com (home). *Website:* www.ugobenelli.com.

BENEŠ, Jiří, PhDr, Mgr; Czech violist and musicologist; *Dramaturg, Brno Philharmonic Orchestra*; b. 24 Sept. 1928, Komárno (now in Slovakia); m. 1st; one s.; m. 2nd Zdenka Bubeníčkova; one d. *Education:* Univ. of Brno, Conservatory of Brno, Janáček Acad. of Musical Arts. *Career:* debut as viola player, Brno 1952; State Philharmonic Orchestra, Brno 1951–69; Moravian Quartet 1965–92; Dramaturg (Programme Dir), Brno Philharmonic Orchestra 1993–, including Brno Int. Music Festival (Moravian Autumn) 1993–2008; radio and TV appearances with Moravian Quartet, in Czechoslovakia, Germany, Sweden, Italy; tours of most European countries; teacher, Janáček Acad. 1968–74, Conservatory of Brno 1969–82, Masaryk Univ. 2003–04; mem. Czech Musical (Janáček) Soc. *Publications:* contrib. to professional journals, radio programme notes, concert and record sleeve notes. *Honours:* Italian Quartet Prize 1965, Janáček Medal 1978, Prize of Novecento Musicale Europeo, Naples 1988, Czech Music Council Award 2002, City of Brno Award 2010. *Address:* Filharmonie Brno, Komenského nám. 8, 60200 Brno, Czech Republic (office). *Telephone:* (53) 9092825 (office). *E-mail:* jiri.benes@filharmonie-brno.cz (office). *Website:* www.filharmonie-brno.cz (office).

BENGL, Volker; German singer (tenor); b. 19 July 1960, Ludwigshafen. *Education:* Mannheim-Heidelberg Musikhochschule, Munich. *Career:* Staatstheater am Gartnerplatz, Munich; guest, Vienna, Berlin, Wiesbaden; sang at Saarbrucken from 1985; Dresden Semperoper; guest appearances in Essen, Brunswick, Karlsruhe and Heidelberg; sang Jenik in The Bartered Bride at Kaiserslautern 1990; other roles include Max in Der Freischütz, Tamino, Belfiore in La Finta Giardiniera, Don José, Pinkerton and parts in operetta; as concert singer appeared in New York 1989, Berlin (Bruckner F minor Mass and Te Deum) and elsewhere in Europe; other repertoire includes Bach Christmas Oratorio and Dvořák Requiem; sang Wilhelm Meister in

Mignon at the Munich Gärtnerplaztheater 2000. *Compositions:* Wiegenlied (words and music) 1997. *Recordings include:* Vorhang auf, Schön is die Welt.

BENGUEREL, Xavier; Spanish composer; b. 9 Feb. 1931, Barcelona. *Education:* studied in Santiago and Barcelona with Cristobal Taltabull. *Career:* represented Spain at ISCM Festival 1960. *Compositions include:* two violin sonatas 1953, 1959, String Quartet 1955, Concerto for piano and strings 1955, Cantata d'Amic i Amat 1959, Concerto for two flutes and strings 1961, Sinfonia Continua 1962, Successions for wind quartet 1960, Duo for clarinet and piano 1963, Nocturno for soprano, chorus and orchestra 1963, Violin Concerto 1965, Sinfonia per a un Festival 1966, Sinfonia for small orchestra 1967, Paraules de cada día for voice and chamber orchestra 1967, Musica for three percussionists 1967, Sinfonia for large orchestra 1969, Dialogue Orchestrale 1969, Musica Riservata for strings 1969, Crescendo for Organ 1970, Organ Concerto 1971, Arbor (cantata) 1972, Verses for guitar 1973, Destructio for orchestra 1973, Capriccio Stravagante for ensemble 1974, Thesis for chamber group, Concerto for percussion and orchestra 1976, Spleen (opera) 1984, Le Livre Vermeil de Montserrat 1988, 7 Faules de La Fontaine 1995, Dos Poemas de Charles Baudelaire for baritone and orchestra 1999, Dalí (opera) 1999, Concerto for piano and orchestra 2004. *Honours:* Composition Prize of the Barcelona Juventudes Musicales 1955, Luigi Dallapicola Award 1977. *Current Management:* c/o Sociedad General de Autores y Editores, Fernando VI 4, 2804 Madrid 4, Spain. *Telephone:* (91) 349 9742. *Website:* www .sgae.es.

BENHAM, Hugh Raymond, BA, PhD, ARCO, FGCM; British organist, examiner, writer and composer; b. 14 Dec. 1943, Westbury, Wilts., England; m.; one d. *Education:* Univ. of Southampton. *Career:* organist 1965–; teacher 1968–97; examiner 1980–92, 1996–; writer on English music and for educ. publs; mem. Royal Musical Assen, Incorporated Soc. of Musicians, Royal Coll. of Organists, Guild of Church Musicians (Fellowship Dir and Chair. of Academic Board), Ralph Vaughan Williams Soc., The Hymn Soc. of Great Britain and Ireland, The Hymn Soc. in the USA and Canada. *Compositions include:* A Triumph Song, Allegro scherzando for organ, Behold the Lamb of God, Love Came Down at Christmas, Blest are the Pure in Heart. *Recording:* A Triumph Song 2011, Piano Sonata 2015. *Publications:* Latin Church Music in England 1460–1575, John Taverner (complete edn, Early English Church Music), John Taverner: his Life and Music, Baroque Music in Focus; contrib. to Music & Letters, The Musical Times, The Music Review, Early Music, Plainsong and Medieval Music, Music Teacher, Classroom Music, RSCM Quarterly, New Grove Dictionary of Music and Musicians 2001, Oxford Dictionary of National Biography 2004, Die Musik in Geschichte und Gegenwart, Rhinegold Education, Allegro scherzando for organ 2014, Behold the Lamb of God 2014. *E-mail:* hugh.benham@talk21.com (home); H.Benham@soton.ac.uk (home).

BENINI, Maurizio; Italian conductor; b. 1968. *Education:* Bologna Conservatory. *Career:* opera debut with Rossini's Il Signor Bruschino, Teatro Comunale di Bologna; made debut at Teatro alla Scala with La Donna del Lago and Don Carlo 1992; Principal Conductor, Filarmonici del Teatro Comunale, Bologna 1984–91; Principal Conductor, Wexford Festival 1995–97; Principal Conductor, Teatro Municipal de Santiago de Chile 1997–2006; Principal Guest Conductor, Teatro San Carlo, Naples 2010–12; has also conducted at Opéra Bastille, Opéra de Paris, Palais Garnier, Paris, Metropolitan Opera, Wiener Staatsoper, Royal Opera House, Gran Teatre de Liceu, Barcelona, Teatro Real, Madrid, Lyric Opera of Chicago, Opéra in Montecarlo, Théâtre du Capitole de Toulouse, Teatro La Fenice, Venice, Glyndebourne Festival. *Recordings:* Elena da Feltre. *Current Management:* Stage Door, Via San Giorgio 4, 40121 Bologna, Italy. *Telephone:* (051) 262126. *Fax:* (051) 271452. *E-mail:* info@stagedoor.it. *Website:* www.stagedoor.it.

BENJAMIN, George William John, CBE; British composer, conductor, pianist and teacher; b. 31 Jan. 1960, London; s. of William Benjamin and Susan Benjamin (née Bendon); civil partner Michael Waldman. *Education:* Westminster School, Paris Conservatoire, King's Coll., Cambridge, Institut de recherche et coordination acoustique/musique, France. *Career:* first London orchestral performance, BBC Proms 1980; Prince Consort Prof. of Composition, Royal Coll. of Music, London 1984–2001; Henry Purcell Prof. of Composition, King's Coll. London 2001–; has conducted widely in GB, Europe, USA, Australia and Far East; Prin. Guest Artist, Hallé Orchestra 1993–96; operatic conducting debut: Pelléas et Mélisande, La Monnaie, Brussels 1999; Carte Blanche at Opéra Bastille, Paris 1992; Founding Artistic Dir Wet Ink Festival, San Francisco Symphony Orchestra 1992, Meltdown Festival, South Bank 1993; Featured Composer, 75th Salzburg Festival 1995, Tanglewood Festival 1999, 2000, 2003, Deutsches Symphonie Orchester 2004–05, Strasbourg Musica Festival 2005, Spanish Nat. Orchestra 2005, Festival d'Automne, Paris 2006, Lucerne Festival 2008, Project San Francisco 2010; London Symphony Orchestra Retrospective 'By George', Barbican, London 2002–03; Artistic Consultant, BBC Sounding the Century 1996–99; Music Dir Ojai Music Festival, Calif. 2010; mem. Bavarian Acad. of Fine Arts 2000. *Compositions include:* orchestral works: Ringed by the Flat Horizon 1980, A Mind of Winter 1981, At First Light 1982, Jubilation 1985, Antara 1987, Sudden Time 1993, Three Inventions for Chamber Orchestra 1995, Sometime Voices 1996, Palimpsests 2002, Dance Figures 2004, Duet for piano and orchestra 2008; chamber music: Piano Sonata 1978, Octet 1978, Flight 1979, Sortilèges 1981, Three Studies for Piano 1985, Upon Silence 1990, Viola, Viola 1997, Shadowlines for solo piano 2001, Three Miniatures for violin 2001, Olicantus 2002, Piano Figures 2004; stage works: Into the Little Hill (Royal Philharmonic Soc. Award for Best Large-Scale Composition 2009) 2006, Written on Skin 2012. *Honours:* Hon. RAM, Hon. RCM, Hon. GSMD, Hon. mem. Royal Philharmonic Soc.; Chevalier, Ordre des Arts et des Lettres 1996; Lili Boulanger Award, USA 1985, Koussevitzky Int. Record Award 1987, Grand Prix du Disque de l'Académie Charles Cros 1987, Gramophone Contemporary Award 1990, Edison Award 1998, Schönberg Prize, Deutsche Sinfonie Berlin 2002; Royal Philharmonic Soc. Award 2003, 2004. *Website:* www.askonasholt.co.uk/artists/conductors/george-benjamin. *Address:* c/o Faber Music, 74–77 Great Russell Street, London, WC1B 3DA, England (office). *Telephone:* (20) 7908-5310 (office). *Fax:* (20) 7908-5339 (office). *E-mail:* information@fabermusic.com (office). *Website:* www.fabermusic.com (office).

BENNETT, Elinor, OBE, LLB, DMus, FRAM; Welsh harpist; *Artistic Director, William Mathias Music Centre*; b. 17 April 1943, Llanidloes, Wales; m. Dafydd Wigley 1967; three s. (two deceased) one d. *Education:* University College of Wales, Royal Academy of Music, London. *Career:* debut, Wigmore Hall, London; freelance harpist with London Symphony Orchestra, Philharmonia, English Chamber Orchestra, 1967–71; soloist and recitalist, BBC Radio 3; HTV, A Day in the Life of Elinor Bennett; BBC, At Home (Richard Baker); chamber music player; dir of festivals; dedicatee of many new works by contemporary composers, including Alun Hoddinott, Malcolm Williamson and John Metcalf; Artistic Dir, William Mathias Music Centre 2002–. *Recordings:* Two Harps, With Harp and Voice, The Harp of Wales, Portrait of the Harp 1988, Nimbus: Images and Impressions, with Judith Hall (flute), Lorelt: Sea of Glass 1994, Nimbus: Mathias, Santa Fe Suite and other 20th century classics 1995, Sain: Harps and Songs, Portrait of the Harp, The Harp of Wales, Two Harps, Victorian Harp Music, John Thomas: 24 Welsh Melodies–The Complete Collection 1998, A Collection of Welsh, Irish and Scottish Airs. *Publications:* Living Harp, Living Harp II 1998, John Thomas' Harp Duets 2000. *Honours:* Hon. Fellow, Aberystwyth Univ., Cardiff Univ., Royal Welsh Coll. of Music and Drama. *Address:* Hen Efail, Bontnewydd, Caernarfon, Gwynedd LL54 7YH, Wales (home). *Telephone:* (1286) 830010 (home). *E-mail:* elinor@elinorbennett.com (home). *Website:* www.elinorbennett.com.

BENNETT, William, OBE; British flautist; b. 7 Feb. 1936, London. *Education:* Guildhall School London with Geoffrey Gilbert, studied in Paris with Jean-Pierre Rampal, and with Marcel Moyse. *Career:* former Principal Flautist with the London Symphony and Royal Philharmonic Orchestra, English Chamber Orchestra and Academy of St Martin-in-the-Fields; many appearances as soloist in Britain and abroad in concerto repertory, including works dedicated to him by William Matthias and Richard Rodney Bennett; contributed to worldwide development of flute manufacture tuned to William Bennett Scale; teacher, Royal Acad. of Music, London, and transcriber of various works for flute. *Recordings:* many albums in solo and chamber music repertory including works by Bach and Mozart. *Address:* c/o William Bennett Flute Summer School, 50 Lansdowne Gardens, Stockwell, London, SW8 2EF, England. *E-mail:* mmichie@msn.com. *Website:* www.williambennettflute.com.

BENOIT, Jean-Christophe; French singer (bass-baritone); b. 18 March 1925, Paris. *Education:* Paris Conservatoire. *Career:* sang in the French provinces, then at the Paris Opéra and Opéra-Comique; Guest appearances in Geneva for the premieres of Monsieur de Pourceaugnac by Martin, 1963; Milhaud's La Mère Coupable, 1966; Aix-en-Province Festival, 1954–57; Salzburg Festival, 1956; La Scala Milan, 1958; Further engagements at the Holland Festival, Monte Carlo and Brussels; Best known as Mozart's Guglielmo and Antonio; Rossini's Basilio; Raimbaud in Le Comte Ory; Somarone in Béatrice et Bénédict; Boniface in Le Jongleur de Notre Dame; Torquemada in L'Heure Espagnole; Brussels 1983, in the premiere of La Passion de Gilles by Philippe Boesmans; fmr Prof. of Singing, Paris Conservatoire. *Recordings:* Carmen; Platée; Lakmé; Les Contes d'Hoffmann and Il Barbiere di Siviglia; Les Indes Galantes; Paer's Le Maître de Chapelle.

BENSON, Joan, MMus; American clavichordist, fortepianist, academic and writer; b. 9 Oct. 1925, St Paul, Minnesota; d. of John Raymond Benson and Frances Ostergren Benson. *Education:* Pomona Coll., Univ. of Illinois, studied with Edwin Fischer in Switzerland, with Fritz Neumeyer in Germany, with Santiago Kastner in Portugal, studied in Vienna, Paris, Italy and Germany. *Career:* concerts, lectures, appearances in festivals; TV and radio appearances throughout USA, Europe, Near and Far East; Lecturer in Music, Stanford Univ. 1970–76; Asst Prof. of Music, Univ. of Oregon 1976–82, Adjunct Prof. 1982–87; mem. artist faculty, Aston Magna Acad. 1980s; clavichord masterclasses, Indiana Univ. 2007. *Recordings include:* Music for Clavichord 1962, C. P. E. Bach on Clavichord and Fortepiano 1972, Boston Museum of Fine Arts Clavichords 1982, Music by Kuhnau and C. P. E. Bach 1988, The Artistry of Joan Benson 2014, Haydn and Pasquini. *Publications include:* Haydn and the Clavichord 1982, The Clavichord in 20th Century America 1992, Bach and the Clavier 1996; contrib. articles: International Haydn Congress, Vienna, The Effect of Clavichord Technique on the Fortepiano 1986, Honoring Macario Santiago Kastner, Gulbenkian Society, Portugal, The Clavichord in 20th Century America 1989, American Liszt Society Journal, Edwin Fischer 1985, Clavier Magazine, Bach and the Clavier 1990, Qigong for Pianists, Piano and Keyboard 1998, Clavichord Technique in the Mid-Twentieth Century, De Clavicordio 1993, Clavichord Perspectives from Goethe to Pound, De Clavicordio 2003, Piano to Clavichord 1925–1962, Clavichord International 2006, The Harpsichord and Clavichord, An Encyclopedia 2007, Studying with Macario Kastner a Half-Century Ago, De Clavicordo 2008, The Interplay of Clavichord and Modern Piano, De Clavicordio 2014, Clavichord for Beginners (also DVD and CD) 2014. *Honours:* Performer's Award, Indiana Univ., Kate

Neal Kinley Award for Performance. *Address:* 2795 Central Blvd, Eugene, OR 97403, USA (home). *Telephone:* (541) 686-0729 (office). *E-mail:* joanb@uoregon .edu (office); joanb@darkwing.uoregon.edu (office). *Website:* darkwing.uoregon .edu/~joanb (office); www.joanbenson.com.

BENT, Ian David, BA, BMus, MA, PhD, ARCO; British academic; b. 1 Jan. 1938, Birmingham, England; m. Caroline Coverdale 1979; two s. one d. *Education:* St John's Coll., Cambridge. *Career:* Lecturer in Music, King's Coll. London 1965–75; Sr Consulting Ed., The New Grove Dictionary of Music 1970–80; Prof. of Music, Univ. of Nottingham 1975–87; Visiting Prof., Harvard Univ., USA 1982–83; Visiting Prof., Columbia Univ. 1986–87, Prof. 1987–2003, Emer. 2003–; Hon. Prof. in the History of Music Theory, Univ. of Cambridge 2003–; mem. American Musicological Soc., Royal Musical Asscn, Soc. for Music Theory, Int. Musicological Soc. *Publications:* The Early History of the English Chapel Royal 1066–1327 1969, Source Materials and the Interpretation of Music, A Memorial Volume to Thurston Dart 1981, Analysis 1987, Music Analysis in the Nineteenth Century (two vols) 1994, Music Theory in the Age of Romanticism (ed.) 1996, Cambridge Studies in Music Theory and Analysis (gen. ed.); contrib. to Journal of the American Musicological Society, Music Analysis, Musical Times, Music and Letters, Proceedings of the Royal Musical Association, Theoria. *Address:* c/o Faculty of Music, University of Cambridge, 11 West Road, Cambridge, CB3 9DP, England (office).

BENT, Margaret Hilda, CBE, PhD; British musicologist; b. 23 Dec. 1940, St Albans, England; m. Ian Bent. *Education:* Girton Coll., Cambridge. *Career:* taught at Cambridge, King's Coll. London 1965–75, Goldsmiths' Coll. 1972–75; teacher, Brandeis Univ. 1975–81, Princeton from 1981; researched Old Hall MS under Thurston Dart at Cambridge, published study with Andrew Hughes; Pres., American Musicological Soc. 1983. *Publications:* The Old Hall Manuscript in the Corpus Mensurabilis Musicae series, XLVI 1969–73, Dunstable, London 1981; contrib. articles on John Dunstable, Notation, Old Hall MS, Leonel Power and Square in the New Grove Dictionary of Music and Musicians 1980; Rossini's Il Turco in Italia (ed. for the Critical Edition) 1988, The Grammar of Early Music: Preconditions for Analysis (ed.) 1998. *Address:* All Souls College, Oxford, OX1 4AL, England (office). *E-mail:* margaret.bent@all-souls.oxford.ac.uk (office).

BENTLEY, Andrew, BA, DPhil; British composer and computer music researcher; b. 30 June 1952, Fleetwood, England; m. Anna-Kaarina Kiviniemi 1975, two s. *Education:* Univ. of York, England. *Career:* designer, Electronic Music Studio; Finnish Radio Experimental Studio 1976–84; teacher, Sibelius Acad., Helsinki 1981–82; Studio Dir, Helsinki Univ. 1982–84; Lecturer, Salford Coll. of Technology 1985–86; Dir Composers' Desktop Project, York 1986–; Leverhulme Computer Music Fellow, Univ. of Nottingham 1987–. *Compositions include:* Bowing 1979, Portrait 1979, Modulo 1979, Contact with Bronze 1979, Zoologic 1980, Winter Winters 1980, Aerial Views 1981, Time for Change 1981, Divertimento 1983, Small Print 1983. *Publications:* Electronic Music for Schools 1984; contrib. to professional journals. *Honours:* Bourges Int. EAM Competition 1979, Luigi Russolo Competition 1979.

BENZA, Georgina; Hungarian singer (soprano); b. 1959, Karpat, Ukraine. *Education:* studied in Kiev and Budapest and in Munich with Wilma Lipp. *Career:* has sung at the Munich Staatsoper from 1983, in such roles as Adina, Lauretta, Sophie, Pamina and Fiordiligi; more recent repertory includes Violetta, Tosca, Tatiana, Suor Angelica, Madama Butterfly, Marguerite and Aida; guest engagements in Berlin (Deutsche Oper and Staatsoper), Frankfurt, Copenhagen, Leipzig, Bonn, Dresden and Barcelona; Bielefeld Opera as Tosca and Amelia in Un Ballo in Maschera; sang Abigaille in Nabucco at Saarbrücken 1999. *Honours:* winner Mozart Prizes in Vienna and Salzburg. *Current Management:* Verena Keller Artists Management, Lohwisstrasse 52, 8123 Ebmatingen, Switzerland. *Telephone:* 4498011513. *Fax:* 449803686. *Website:* www.keller-artistsmanagement.ch. office@georginavonbenza.com. *Website:* www.georginavonbenza.com.

BENZI, Roberto; Italian/French conductor; b. 12 Dec. 1937, Marseille, France; s. of the late Giuseppe Benzi and the late Maria Pastorino; m. Jane Rhodes 1966 (died 2011). *Education:* Univ. of Paris (Sorbonne), studied conducting with Andre Cluytens. *Career:* debut as conductor, France 1948; tours in Europe and S America 1949–52; opera conducting debut 1954; conducted Carmen, Paris Opera 1959, Faust, Met 1971–72; guest conductor Europe, Japan, China, Israel, Mexico, Canada, USA, S Africa and main music festivals; Music Dir Bordeaux-Aquitaine Orchestra 1973–87, Arnhem Philharmonic 1989–98, Dutch Nat. Youth Orchestra 1991–96. *Publications:* orchestrations of Brahms op. 23 Schumann Variations 1970, Brahms op. 24 Variations and Fugue on a theme by Handel 1973, Rossini Prélude, Thème et Variations 1978, Erik Satie Je te veux, valse 1987. *Honours:* Chevalier, Légion d'honneur, Ordre Nat. du Mérite, Ordre des Palmes Académiques, Order of Orange-Nassau (Netherlands). *Address:* 12 Villa Ste-Foy, 92200 Neuilly-sur-Seine, France (home). *Telephone:* 1-46-24-27-85 (home). *Fax:* 1-46-24-55-73 (home). *E-mail:* roberto.benzi@free.fr. *Website:* www.robertobenzi.com.

BERBIÉ, Jane; French singer (mezzo-soprano); b. 6 May 1934, Villefranche-de-Lauragais, Toulouse. *Education:* Toulouse Conservatory. *Career:* after debut 1958, sang at La Scala 1960, in L'Enfant et les Sortilèges; Glyndebourne Festival 1969–71, 1983–84, as Despina in Così fan tutte; London Coliseum in the British premiere (concert) of Roussel's Padmavati, Aix-en-Provence 1969–70; Salzburg Festival 1974, as Marcellina in Le nozze di Figaro; Paris Opéra from 1975, as Zerlina and in Das Rheingold and Jenůfa; guest appearances in Tokyo, Munich, London, Cologne and Milan, Rosina in Il

Barbiere di Siviglia; other roles include Concepción in L'Heure Espagnole, Orsini in Lucrezia Borgia, Cherubino and Ascanio in Benvenuto Cellini; Salzburg Festival 1988 as Mozart's Marcellina; sang Annina in Der Rosenkavalier at the Théâtre des Champs Elysées, Paris 1989; Teatro San Carlos, Lisbon, as the Marquise in La Fille du Régiment 1989. *Recordings:* Benvenuto Cellini, conducted by Colin Davis; Così fan tutte; L'Enfant et les Sortilèges; Il Turco in Italia; Massenet's Cendrillon. *Honours:* Grand Prix Toulouse Conservatory.

BERCZELLY, Istvan; Hungarian singer (baritone); b. 9 Sept. 1939, Budapest. *Education:* studied in Budapest. *Career:* debut at Debrecen 1967, as Don Giovanni; sang at Debrecen until 1970; Budapest Nat. Theatre from 1970, notably as Verdi's Renato, Basilio in La Fiamma by Respighi, Valentin (Faust), Bellini's Capulet, Wagner's Gunther, and the title role in Samson by Szokolay; Budapest 1987, in the premiere of Szokolay's Ecce Homo; premiere of A Man from Venice by Ferenc Farkas 1991; sang Wagner's Hagen at Budapest 1998.

BERDULLAS DEL RÍO, Jorge; Spanish composer; b. 20 Aug. 1960, Villagarcia de Arosa, Pontevedra. *Education:* conservatories in La Coruña, Santiago and Madrid. *Career:* conducted choirs; became state music teacher/player 1985; f. contemporary music group Talea 1986; Founder-mem. Galician Asscn of Composers 1987. *Compositions include:* El Paso (Op. 15a and 15b) for six and twelve percussionists and two conductors 1989, Biomecánicas (Letania para el día de los derechos del hombre, Op. 17) for piano, performer and bass voice 1990, Proum (Homenaje a El Lissitzky) String Quartet No. 2 (Op. 19) 1991, Alogón (El dominio del caos, Op. 20) for string orchestra and four mixed voices amplified 1991, Aevum (Op. 21) for large orchestra and three conductors temporised by computer 1992, Axis Mundi o El séptimo rayo (Hacia una arquitectura del movimiento, Op. 22) for two large ensembles, large vocal ensemble and three conductors temporised by computer 1993–94, Las estructuras del caos (Methodology for a science of movement and simultaneous tempi in music, Op. 23) (scientific work in which more than 3,000 metronomic speeds are studied and analysed) 1995–96, Res Facta (Bajo el impulso de neoriel, Op. 24) for five orchestral groups (voice and instruments) situated in different places, and five conductors temporised by computer 1998–2000, El Apocalipsis según San Juan (Op. 25) for 12 orchestral groups (vocals and instruments) in different places, 12 speakers and 12 conductors 2001–05, Sunt Illiae, letras numerales que contienen los misterios del genio solar (Op. 26), work for 30 vocal and instrumental groups and 30 conductors temporised by computer, in ten movements and two interludes 2006–13, work's extension includes approx. 100,000 bars. *Address:* Calle Rua Agriña No. 16 bajo derecha, 15705 Santiago de Compostela, Spain (home). *Telephone:* (981) 557225 (home). *E-mail:* jorgeberdullasdelrio@gmail.com (office).

BERENS, Barbara; German singer (soprano); b. 25 April 1966, St Ingbert. *Education:* studied with Erika Köth and Josef Metternich, in London with Vera Rozsa. *Career:* sang with the Deutsche Oper am Rhein at Düsseldorf from 1988, notably as Susanna, Fiordigili, Pamina, Elvira in I Puritani, Liu and Hanna Glawari; guest engagements in Cologne (as Gretel), Saarbrucken (Mme Cortese in Il Viaggio a Reims) and elsewhere in Germany; also a recitalist.

BERESFORD, Hugh; British singer (baritone, tenor); b. 17 Dec. 1925, Birkenhead. *Education:* Royal Northern College of Music, Manchester, Vienna Music Academy; studied with Dino Borgioli and Alfred Piccaver. *Career:* debut, Linz, 1953, as Wolfram in Tannhäuser; Sang at Deutsche Oper am Rhein, Düsseldorf, from 1960; Sang in Graz, Augsburg and Wuppertal; Guest appearances at Covent Garden, Vienna, Munich, Stuttgart, Cologne, Brussels and Paris; Holland Festival, 1963, 1966; Venice, 1966, as Mandryka in Arabella; Sang further as Rigoletto, Posa in Don Carlos and Don Giovanni; Later career as tenor with Otello and Florestan at the Vienna Staatsoper, 1973; Tannhäuser at Bayreuth, 1972–73; Cologne Opera, 1981 as Florestan, and Erik in Der fliegende Holländer.

BEREZOVSKY, Boris Vadimovich; Russian pianist; *Artistic Director, Festival Pianoscope;* b. 4 Jan. 1969, Moscow; three s. *Education:* Moscow Conservatoire. *Career:* London début Wigmore Hall 1988; appeared with Soviet Festival Orchestra, London 1990; recitals in New York, Washington, London, Amsterdam, Salzburg, Moscow, Leningrad, Tokyo, Osaka, etc.; appearances with orchestras including Philharmonia, New York Philharmonic, Philadelphia Orchestra, NDR Hamburg and Danish Nat. Radio Symphony Orchestra; Artistic Dir Festival Pianoscope, Beauvais 2013–. *Recordings:* numerous recordings including Chopin Godowsky Etudes 2005, Saint-Saëns's Carnaval des Animaux (Choc de la Musique of the Year 2010) 2010. *Honours:* winner, Prize of Hope competition, City of Ufa 1985, Gold Medal, Int. Tchaikovsky Piano Competition, Moscow 1990. *Address:* Festival Pianoscope, Direction des Affaires Culturelles, Rue de Gesvres, 60000 Beauvais, France (office). *Website:* pianoscope.beauvais.fr (office).

BERG, Nathan; Canadian singer (baritone); b. 1968, Saskatchewan. *Education:* Augustana Univ., Alberta, Univ. of Western Ontario, Maitrise Nationale de Versailles, Guildhall School with Vera Rozsa. *Career:* debut recital at Wigmore Hall, London; sang Thésée in Rameau's Hippolyte, Peter Quince, Dr Falke and Eustachio in Donizetti's L'Assedio di Calais at the Guildhall School; has sung professionally as Guglielmo, Masetto, Leporello, Figaro (Mozart), Schuanard, Thésée; various recordings and appearances with Abbado, Dohnányi, Salinnen, Shaw, Tilson Thomas; Leppard and

William Christie among others; various oratorio and recital work; sang Abramane in Rameau's Zoroastre at Brooklyn Acad. and on tour to Europe 1998; season 2000–01 in Handel's Theodora at Salzburg Easter Festival, Masetto at Glyndebourne and Leporello for ENO. *Honours:* prizewinner, Peter Pears, Kathleen Ferrier, Walter Gruner and Royal Overseas League Competitions. *Current Management:* c/o IMG Artists, Carnegie Hall Tower, 152 West 57th Street, 5th Floor, New York, NY 10019, USA. *Telephone:* (410) 480-2095. *Fax:* (212) 994-3550. *E-mail:* againes@imgartists.com. *Website:* www.imgartists.com.

BERGAMIN, Peter; Canadian conductor; b. 1965. *Education:* Univ. of Toronto. *Career:* appearances with the Toronto Symphony, Israel Chamber Orchestra, Royal Liverpool Philharmonic Orchestra, Scottish Nat. Orchestra and Winnipeg Symphony; Music Dir, Vienna Taschenoper 1994–97, with Maxwell Davies' Resurrection in Vienna and at Glasgow Mayfest; further engagements with the Opéra National de Lyon, North Hungarian Symphony Orchestra and the King's Singers, London, Herziya Chamber Orchestra, Israel; repertoire includes Mozart, Mahler, Beethoven, Wagner, Strauss and contemporary music.

BERGANZA, Teresa; Spanish singer (mezzo-soprano); b. 16 March 1933, Madrid; d. of Guillermo Berganza and Ascensión Berganza; m. 1st Felix Lavilla 1957; one s. two d.; m. 2nd José Rifa 1986. *Career:* debut in Aix-en-Provence 1957, in UK at Glyndebourne 1958; has sung at La Scala, Milan, Opera Rome, Metropolitan, New York, Chicago Opera House, San Francisco Opera, Covent Garden, etc.; has appeared at festivals in Edinburgh, the Netherlands, Glyndebourne; concerts in France, Belgium, the Netherlands, Italy, Germany, Spain, Austria, Portugal, Scandinavia, Israel, Mexico, Buenos Aires, USA, Canada; sung Carmen, at opening ceremony of Expo 92, Seville, also at opening ceremonies of Barcelona Olympics 1992; mem. Real Academia de Bellas Artes de San Fernando, Spanish Royal Acad. of Arts 1994. *Films include:* The Barber of Seville 1972, Don Giovanni 1979, Werther 1980, Carmen 1980. *Publication:* Flor de Soledad y Silencio 1984. *Honours:* Grande Cruz, Isabel la Católica, Commdr, Ordre des Arts et des Lettres; Premio Lucrezia Arana, Premio Extraordinario del Conservatorio de Madrid, Harriet Cohen Award, Int. Critic Award 1988, Grand Prix du Disque (six times), Grand Prix Rossini. *Address:* c/o Javier Lavilla, Avenida Juan de Borbón y Battenberg, 16, 28200 San Lorenzo del Escorial, Madrid, Spain (office). *Telephone:* (67) 0237485 (office). *Fax:* (67) 0237489 (office). *E-mail:* info@ teresaberganza.com (office). *Website:* www.teresaberganza.com.

BERGASA, Carlos; Spanish singer (baritone); b. 1966, Madrid. *Education:* Escuela Superior de Canto. *Career:* made professional debut as Marcello in La Bohème, Sabadell 1990; many engagements at opera houses in Spain and elsewhere in Europe, notably as Schaunard in La Bohème, Lescaut in Manon Lescaut, Valentin in Faust, Belcore in L'Elisir D'Amore, Figaro in Il Barbiere di Siviglia, Silvio in Pagliacci, Sulpice in La Fille du Régiment, Albert in Werther, Sharpless in Madama Butterfly, Enrico in Lucia di Lammermoor, Guglielmo in Così fan Tutte, Lescaut in Massenet, Germano in La Scala di Seta. *Honours:* winner, Concurso Logroño 1987, Concurso Francisco Alonso 1993. *Current Management:* Operazigor Agencia Artística, Calle Muga 8, 31180 Zizur Mayor, Spain. *Telephone:* (948) 183589. *Fax:* (948) 183589. *E-mail:* info@operazigor.com. *Website:* www.operazigor.eu.

BERGEN, Beverly; New Zealand singer (mezzo-soprano); b. 1950. *Education:* London Opera Centre. *Career:* as soprano appeared as guest artist at the Deutsche Oper Berlin, also in Hamburg, Düsseldorf and elsewhere in Germany; sang in premiere of Maderna's Hyperion at Brussels; operatic roles include Constanze, Jenůfa, Strauss's Countess, Katherina in Lady Macbeth of Mtsensk, Senta, Luisa Miller, Violetta, Musetta and Lucia di Lammermoor; has performed throughout Australia in Messiah, Beethoven's Ninth and Das klagende Lied by Mahler; other repertoire includes Mozart's Requiem, The Trojans, Bruckner's Te Deum, with the Sydney Symphony Orchestra and Judas Maccabaeus with St Hedwig's Cathedral Choir, Berlin; changed to mezzo-soprano repertoire 1989, appeared as Amneris in Aida; engagements with Opera Factory, London. *Television:* presenter, Aria and Pasta (Sky Arts).

BERGER, Roman; Polish composer; b. 9 Aug. 1930, Cieszyn; m. Ruth Strbova 1968. *Education:* Acad. of Musical Arts, Katowice, Acad. of Musical Arts, Bratislava. *Career:* Prof. of Piano, Conservatoire, Bratislava 1955–66; Fellow, television sound laboratory 1966–67; Sec., Union of Slovak Composers 1967–69; Lecturer on Theory of Composition, Contemporary Music and Electronic Music, Acad. of Musical Arts, Bratislava 1969–71, 1983–85; faculty mem., Musicological Inst. of the Slovak Acad. of Sciences 1977–91. *Compositions include:* Fantazia quasi una sonata 1955, Inventions 1959–61, Romance 1960, Little Suite 1961, Lullaby 1962, Suite in Ancient Style for strings, percussion and keyboard 1963, Transformations (four symphonic pieces) 1965, Convergence I 1969, Convergence II 1970, Copernicus for electronics 1973, Memento for orchestra 1974, Epitaph to Convergence III 1975, De Profundis for bass, cello and electronics 1980, Exodus (four pieces for organ) 1982, Adagio for Jan Branny 1987, Soft November Music 1989, Semplice 2000, Korczak in memoriam 2000, Arch 2007. *Publications:* Music and Truth (essays) 1997–87, Theory Wrongly Present 1989, Velvet Revolution and Music 1990, Permanent Conflict Between Art and Power 1992, The Structure and Meaning of Heritage 1996.

BERGLUND, Ingela; Swedish singer (soprano); b. 1959. *Education:* Stockholm Coll. of Music, State Opera School, Stockholm with Kerstin Meyer and Elisabeth Söderström. *Career:* debut at Royal Opera Stockholm 1988, as

Donna Anna; mem., Royal Stockholm Philharmonic Orchestra 1979–84; sang Mozart's Countess and the Woman in La Voix Humaine at Stockholm 1988; Salzburg Landestheater 1989–92 as Donna Anna, Musetta, Tatiana, Fiordiligi and Hanna Glawari in Die Lustige Witwe; Beatrice in Boccaccio by Suppé at Royal Opera, Stockholm; guest appearances at Semper Opera, Dresden, and in Austria, USA, Spain and Japan. *Address:* Asogatan 67 VI, 118 29 Stockholm, Sweden.

BERKELEY OF KNIGHTON, Baron (Life Peer), cr. 2013, of Knighton in the County of Powys; **Michael Fitzhardinge Berkeley,** CBE, FRAM, FRWCMD; British composer and broadcaster; b. 29 May 1948, London, England; s. of the late Sir Lennox Berkeley and of Elizabeth Freda Berkeley (née Bernstein); m. Deborah Jane Coltman-Rogers 1979 (died 2014); one d. *Education:* Westminster Cathedral Choir School, The Oratory School, Royal Acad. of Music. *Career:* writer on music and arts for the Observer, Vogue and The Listener 1970–75; presenter, music programmes (including Proms) for BBC TV 1975–; BBC Radio 3 announcer 1974–79; apptd Assoc. Composer, Scottish Chamber Orchestra 1979; Dir Britten-Pears Foundation 1996–; mem. Exec. Cttee Asscn of Professional Composers 1982–84; Cen. Music Advisory Cttee, BBC 1986–90; Music Panel Adviser to Arts Council 1986–90; Visiting Prof. Huddersfield Univ. (fmrly Polytechnic) 1991–94; Artistic Dir Cheltenham Int. Festival 1995–2004; Co-Dir Spitalfields Festival 1994–97; Dir Royal Opera House, Covent Garden 1996–2000 (mem. 1994–98, Chair. Opera Bd 1998); Chair. Bd of Govs Royal Ballet 2003–; Composer-in-Asscn, BBC Nat. Orchestra of Wales 2000–09; Visiting Prof. in Composition, Royal Welsh Coll. of Music and Drama (RWCMD) 2002–, has also composed music for film, TV and radio; mem. (Crossbench), House of Lords 2013–; Trustee, Benjamin Britten Will Trust, Cambrian Music Trust. *Major works include:* Meditations for Strings, Oboe Concerto 1977, Fantasia Concertante, Gregorian Variations (orchestra), For The Savage Messiah (piano quintet), Or Shall We Die? (oratorio to text by Ian McEwan) 1982, 4 String Quartets, Piano Trio, Songs of Awakening Love, Entertaining Master Punch, Clarinet Concerto, Speaking Silence, Viola Concerto, Catch Me If You Can (chamber), Dark Sleep (keyboard), Tristessa (orchestra), Magnetic Field (string quartet), Winter Fragments, Odd Man Out, Abstract Mirror (string quartet), Gabriel's Lament for orchestra, Piano Quintet, Gethsemane (for tenor and ensemble) 1990, Twenty-One 1991, Baa Baa Black Sheep (opera, libretto by David Malouf based on the childhood of Rudyard Kipling) 1993, Secret Garden (orchestra) 1997, The Garden of Earthly Delights (orchestra) 1998, Jane Eyre (opera, libretto by David Malouf) 2000, For You (chamber opera, libretto by Ian McEwan) 2009, Collision (electro-acoustic and visual installation, collaboration with artist Kevin Laycock) 2009, Three Rilke Sonnets (written for the Nash Ensemble and soprano Claire Booth) 2011, Hollow Fires (song cycle for baritone and piano setting texts by Housman and Hardy) 2011, Atonement (opera, libretto by Craig Raine) 2013, Tango! 2015, The Tale of Andrew 2015. *Radio:* presenter, Private Passions (BBC Radio 3). *Publications:* The Music Pack 1994; numerous articles in newspapers and magazines. *Honours:* Guinness Prize for Composition 1977, Silver Medal, Worshipful Co. of Musicians 2003. *Address:* c/o Oxford University Press, Repertoire Promotion Department, Great Clarendon Street, Oxford, OX2 6DP, England (office). *E-mail:* repertoire.promotion.uk@oup.com (office). *Website:* ukcatalogue.oup .com/category/music/composers/berkeley.do (office); www.michaelberkeley.co .uk.

BERKES, Kálmán; Hungarian clarinettist; b. 1952, Budapest. *Education:* Béla Bartók Conservatory, Ferenc Liszt Acad. of Music. *Career:* principal clarinettist, Budapest State Opera Orchestra and Budapest Philharmonic 1972; Budapest Chamber Ensemble and Jeunesses Musicales Wind Quintet 1973; extensive guest performances throughout Europe, including Austria, France, Germany, The Netherlands, Italy and Switzerland; played trios by Beethoven, Brahms and Zemlinsky at St John's, London 1997. *Recordings include:* Bartók's Contrasts. *Honours:* silver medal Geneva Int. Musical Competition 1972.

BERKOWITZ, Paul, FGSM; Canadian pianist; *Professor of Music, University of California, Santa Barbara;* b. 1 Oct. 1948, Montréal. *Education:* McGill Univ., Curtis Inst., USA with Rudolf Serkin and Horszowski. *Career:* debut in London 1973 New York solo debut at Alice Tully Hall 1978; recitalist, Wigmore Hall and QEH, London; Tivoli, Copenhagen and throughout Europe and North America; soloist with orchestras in the UK and North America; festival engagements in Belgium, Denmark, England, France, Italy, Scotland and Spain; frequent solo radio broadcasts and recitals for BBC and CBC; Barcelona Festival with the Endellion Quartet and the Albion Ensemble; Beethoven duets with Richard Goode at the Wigmore Hall 1990–91; appearances with the BBC Scottish Symphony and English Sinfonia; Prof. of Music, Guildhall School of Music 1975–93, Univ. of California, Santa Barbara 1993–; master-classes at McGill Univ., Univ. of British Columbia, Queens Univ., Royal Conservatory of Music, Toronto, in Canada and Yehudi Menuhin School and elsewhere in the UK, France and Spain; repertoire includes sonatas and other major works by Schubert, Beethoven, Brahms, Mozart, Schumann, Chopin and Bartók. *Recordings include:* Complete Sonatas of Schubert (seven vols), Schumann's Kreisleriana and Davidsbündlertänze, Brahms Piano Pieces Opp 116-118. *Honours:* Canada Council grants 1989–91, BBC Record Review and BBC Magazine First Choice Award (for recording of Schumann's Kreisleriana) 1993. *Address:* Department of Music, University of California, Music Building, Room 305, Santa Barbara, CA 93106-6070, USA (office).

Telephone: (805) 893-2066 (office). *E-mail:* berkowit@music.ucsb.edu (office). *Website:* www.music.ucsb.edu (office).

BERL, Christine, BS, MA; American composer; b. 22 July 1943, New York, NY; two s. *Education:* Mannes Coll. of Music, Queens Coll. *Career:* performances by Emanuel Ax in Highland Park, Ravinia 1988; commissioned by Peter Serkin for 1989–90, The Chamber Music Soc. of Lincoln Center for their 20th-anniversary season 1989, Cornell Univ. Chorus 1989; concert devoted to Berl's works on Distinguished Artists Series of 92nd Street Y 1990; commissioned work for two pianos for Peter Serkin and Emmanuel Ax; world premiere by French violinist Pierre Amoyal and Jeremy Menuhin of Masmoudi, a violin sonata commissioned by Radio France; New York premiere of Masmoudi at Merkin Concert Hall 1994. *Compositions:* Elegy for piano solo 1974, Three Pieces for chamber ensemble 1975, Ab La Dolchor for soprano, female chorus and orchestra 1979, Sonata for piano 1986–87, Dark Summer for mezzo-soprano, piano and string trio, The Lord of the Dance (for Peter Serkin), The Violent Bear it Away for orchestra 1988, Cantilena for cello and piano (for Matt Haimovitz), Masmoudi for violin and piano 1991.

BERMAN, Boris, BA, MA; Russian pianist and academic; *Professor of Piano, Yale University;* b. 3 April 1948, Moscow; m. Zina Tabachnikova 1975; one s. one d. *Education:* Moscow Tchaikovsky Conservatory, studied with Lev Oborin. *Career:* debut in Moscow 1965; performances in more than 40 countries; has appeared with Concertgebouw, London Philharmonic Orchestra, BBC Philharmonic, Royal Scottish, Gewandhaus, Detroit, Minnesota, Houston, Atlanta, Toronto, Israel Philharmonic, Moscow Philharmonic, St Petersburg Philharmonic and many others; festivals include Bergen, Ravinia, Israel, Marlboro; numerous radio and TV appearances world-wide; fmr Prof. of Piano, Tel-Aviv Univ., Indiana Univ., Boston Univ.; currently Prof. of Piano, School of Music, Yale Univ.; Music Dir, Music Spectrum concert series, Tel-Aviv 1975–84; Music Dir, Yale Music Spectrum, USA 1984–97; Dir, Summer Piano Inst. at Yale 1990–92, Dir. Summer Piano Inst., Hong Kong 1995–97; juror at various nat., int. piano competitions. *Recordings:* all solo piano works by Prokofiev in 9 vols, Stravinsky Concerto with Orchestre de la Suisse Romande, N Järvi, Prokofiev Concertos 1, 4, 5 with Concertgebouw Orchestra, N Järvi, Shostakovich, Scriabin all Sonatas in 2 vols; recitals or works by Debussy, Stravinsky, Shostakovich, Schnittke, Cage; numerous chamber recordings. *Publication:* Notes from the Pianist's Bench 2000. *Honours:* Hon. Prof., Shanghai Conservatory, China; Edison Classic Award, Netherlands 1990. *Current Management:* c/o Pro Artist, 54 Beaconsfield Road, London, SE3 7LG, England. *Telephone:* (20) 8858-0785. *Fax:* (20) 8269-1722. *E-mail:* info@proartist.co.uk. *Website:* www.proartist.co.uk. *Address:* Yale University School of Music, PO Box 208246, New Haven, CT 06520, USA (office). *Website:* www.borisberman.com.

BERMEL, Derek, DMA; American composer, clarinettist, singer and songwriter; b. 1967. *Education:* Yale Univ., Univ. of Michigan; studied composition with William Albright, Louis Andriessen, William Bolcom, Henri Dutilleux, André Hajdu and Michael Tenzer, and clarinet with Ben Armato and Keith Wilson; also studied ethnomusicology and orchestration in Jerusalem with André Hajdu, Thracian folk style with Nikola Iliev in Bulgaria, caxixi with Julio Góes in Brazil, and Lobi xylophone with Ngmen Baaru in Ghana. *Career:* worked with numerous musicians including Wynton Marsalis, Midori, John Adams, Philip Glass, James Galway, Gustavo Dudamel and Stephen Sondheim; commissions from Pittsburgh, National, Boston, Saint Louis, New Jersey, Albany and Pacific Symphonies, Los Angeles and Westchester Philharmonics, New York Youth Symphony, Chamber Music Soc. of Lincoln Center, WNYC Radio, eighth blackbird, Guarneri String Quartet, Music from China, De Ereprijs (Netherlands), Jazz Xchange (UK), Figura (Denmark), electric guitarist Wiek Hijmans, cellist Fred Sherry, pianists Christopher Taylor and Andy Russo and from Lincoln Center Jazz Orchestra and ACO, and Koussevitzky and Fromm Foundations; appeared as soloist with BBC Symphony Orchestra, Los Angeles Philharmonic in Adams' Gnarly Buttons, performed own concerto Voices at Beijing Modern Music Festival, Copland Concerto and world premiere of Fang Man's clarinet concerto Resurrection, conducted by George Manahan, Bolcom's Concerto with the Lexington Philharmonic and Greensboro Symphony, and André Hajdu's klezmer concerto Jewish Rhapsody with Westchester Philharmonic, NY; residencies at Yaddo, Tanglewood, Aspen, Banff, Bellagio, Copland House, Sacatar, Civitella Ranieri and Inst. for Advanced Study; Creative Adviser, American Composers Orchestra at Carnegie Hall; mem. TONK ensemble and Peace by Piece band. *Compositions include:* Migration Series, A Shout, A Whisper, and a Trace, Mar de Setembro, The Good Life for chorus, soloists and orchestra, Golden Motors, music theatre. *Recordings include:* Soul Garden (chamber music) 2007, Voices (orchestral) 2009, Canzonas Americanas (large ensemble) 2012; with Peace by Piece: Peace by Piece, The Elements 2004. *Honours:* Alpert Award in the Arts, Rome Prize in Musical Composition, Guggenheim and Fulbright Fellowships, American Music Center Trailblazer Award, American Acad. of Arts and Letters Acad. Award. *Current Management:* c/o Todd Vunderink, Peermusic Classical, 250 West 57th Street, Suite 820, New York, NY 10107, USA. *Telephone:* (212) 265-3910. *E-mail:* peerclassical@peermusic.com. *Website:* www.derekbermel.com.

BERN, Jeni; British singer (soprano); b. 1973, Glasgow, Scotland. *Education:* Royal Scottish Academy, Royal College of Music, London. *Career:* debut at Covent Garden Company 1998 as Mozart's Barbarina; Mozart's Susanna for English Touring Opera; Deidamia, and Sigismondo in Arminio for the London Handel Festival; Atalanta in Serse for the Early Opera Company; Dalinda in Ariodante for the Covent Garden Festival and Donizetti's Adina at Cambridge; Cristina in The Makropulos Case for Scottish Opera Go Round, Purcell's Belinda for Israel Chamber Orchestra and Jano in Jenůfa at Glyndebourne, 2000; Other roles include Britten's Titania, Janáček's Vixen and Narcissa in Haydn's Philemon and Baucis; Concerts include Messiah in Switzerland, Bruckner's Te Deum, a British tour with Vivaldi by Candlelight and the premiere of Michael Torke's Book of Proverbs, Flowermaiden in Parsifal with the Royal Opera in concert. *Honours:* Countess of Munster Award. *Current Management:* Musicmakers International Artists Representation, Tailor House, 63–65 High Street, Whitwell, Hertfordshire, SG4 8AH, England. *Telephone:* (1438) 871708. *Fax:* (1438) 871777. *E-mail:* musicmakers@compuserve.com. *Website:* www.operauk.com.

BERNARD, André, DipMus; French conductor and soloist; b. 6 April 1946, Gap. *Education:* Conservatoire Nat. Supérieur de Paris, studied with Carlo Maria Giulini and with Bruno Bartoletti in Siena, Italy. *Career:* guest conductor for many int. orchestras, including London Philharmonic, London Symphony Orchestra, Royal Philharmonic Orchestra, Mozarteum Salzburg, Prague and Budapest Opera Orchestras; opera conducting in Strasbourg, Lille, Montreal, Siena etc.; TV appearances in France, Germany and Japan; radio broadcasts in USA, Canada, Japan, Germany, Italy and France; solo appearances include Salzburg Festival, Berlin Philharmonie, Carnegie Hall and Lincoln Center in New York, Paris, Tokyo, London, Rome, Prague, Mexico, Madrid, Venice, Washington; appearances with the world's leading orchestras; more than 30 concerts on tour conducting Philharmonia Hungarica, including Carnegie Hall and Los Angeles; concert series in London; Prin. Conductor New Symphony Orchestra of London and London Chamber Orchestra 1982–87; Prin. Guest Conductor Irish Chamber Orchestra, Orchestra Sinfonica Abruzzese, Janáček Philharmonic, Hungarian Symphony Orchestra. *Recordings include:* 30 CDs with Academy of St Martin-in-the-Fields, English Chamber Orchestra, I Virtuosi Italiani, New Symphony Orchestra of London, Janáček Philharmonic. *Honours:* Laureate Int. Trumpet Competition, Geneva, Switzerland 1968. *Telephone:* (934) 873833. *Fax:* (934) 877892. *E-mail:* sanz@sanzkonzert.es. *Website:* www.sanzkonzert.es. *Address:* 8 rue Christine, 75006 Paris (home); 11 avenue Amiral Ganteaume, 13260 Cassis, France (home). *Telephone:* 6-09-93-06-26 (mobile). *E-mail:* andrebernard1@orange.fr. *Website:* andre-bernard.com.

BERNARD, Claire Marie Anne; French violinist; b. 31 March 1947, Rouen; d. of Yvan Bernard and Marie Chouquet. *Education:* Conservatoire Régional de Musique, Rouen and Conservatoire Nat. Supérieur de Musique (CNSM). *Career:* began professional career as solo violinist 1965; mem. jury, Tchaikovsky Int. Competition, Moscow 1974; Prof. of Violin at state-run conservatoires and music schools in France; Asst at Conservatoire nat. supérieur de musique, Lyon 1990–; mem. contemporary music ensemble Les Temps Modernes 1993–; Prof., CNR, Conservatoire Nat. Supérieur de Musique (CNSM); recordings include works by Khatchaturian, Prokofiev, Barber, Milhaud, Mozart, Haydn, Sarasate, Leclair, Gaviniès, Telemann and Vivaldi. *Honours:* Chevalier, Ordre nat. du Mérite; First Prize George Enesco Int. Competition 1964 and other awards and prizes. *Address:* 53 rue Rabelais, 69003 Lyon, France (home). *Telephone:* 6-69-45-53-07 (mobile). *E-mail:* bernard-claire16@bbox.fr (home).

BERNARDINI, Alfredo, DipMus; Italian oboist; b. 30 Oct. 1961, Rome; two s. one d. *Education:* Royal Conservatory, The Hague, The Netherlands, Univ. of Oxford, England. *Career:* performs with European ensembles, such as Hesperion XX, Les Arts Florissants, La Petite Bande, Capella Coloniensis, Amsterdam Baroque Orchestra, Collegio Strumentale Italiano, La Grande Ecurie, Concerto Armonico Budapest and Concerto Italiano. *Publications:* contrib. articles to Il Flauto Dolce, Early Music, Journal of the American Musical Instruments Society.

BERNAS, Richard; American conductor, pianist and academic; b. 21 April 1950, New York; m. 1st Deirdre Busenberg (divorced); m. 2nd Beatrice Harper; two s. *Career:* debut, as pianist, Kent Univ. 1966; as conductor, London, England 1976; Warsaw Autumn Festival 1977, Vienna Festival 1984, Opéra de Lyon and Paris Opéra 1985, London Sinfonietta 1986, Edinburgh Festival 1986, The Royal Helsinki Philharmonic 1988, Royal Ballet, Covent Garden, BBC Symphony Orchestra 1989, Holland Festival 1989, Aldeburgh Festival Opera, Suffolk, England 1990, ENO 1990, Netherlands Opera, Amsterdam and The Hague 1991, Ars Musica Festival, Brussels 1991, Orchestre National de Belgique, Brussels 1993, Netherlands Radio Symphony Orchestra 1994, Opéra de Bastille 1995, Musique Oblique, Paris 1995, Théâtre du Capitole, Toulouse 2000, Royal Ballet 2000, 2005, 2006, 2007, Norwegian Nat. Ballet 2000, San Francisco Ballet 2001, 2004; Conductor, Saltarello Choir 1976–80; Founder, Music Projects/London 1978; Conductor-in-Residence, Sussex Univ. 1979–82; Lecturer, Leicester Polytechnic (now De Monfort Univ.) 1982–87; Guest Lecturer, City Univ. 1999–2005; Music Consultant, Tate Modern, London 2001–12; Assoc. Research Fellow, Inst. of Musical Research, School of Advanced Study, London Univ. 2011–14. *Current Management:* Robert Gilder & Co., Westminster Business Square, 1–45 Durham Street, London, N102, England. *E-mail:* rgilder@robert-gilder.com. *Website:* robertgilder.co/richard-bernas. *Address:* 11 Elmwood Avenue, London, W4 3DY, England (home).

BERNASCONI, Silvano; Swiss pianist and composer; b. 16 Oct. 1950, Chiasso; m. Irene Cairoli Alessandra 1984, one s. *Education:* Conservatoire de Lausanne, Conservatorio Santa Cecilia in Rome, studied with Francesto Zaza,

Andor Kovach, Rainer Bosch, Vieri Tosatti, Domenico Bartolucci, Ferdinando Germani, Franco Evangelisti. *Career:* debut in Rome 1974; pianist and composer 1980–85; executions of music commissioned by Musica Ticinensis 1982 and television; mem. Association of Swiss Musicians; mem. and co-founder European Composers' Union 1991–. *Compositions:* Sounds and Crystals for two vibraphones 1982, Psallite four lines for organ 1974, Tourbillon for violin and orchestra 1993. *Publications:* Didactics Compositions in the European Year of Music 1985; contrib. to Musica & Teatro magazine.

BERNASEK, Vaclav; Czech violoncellist; b. 29 Oct. 1944, Kladno, Czecho-slovakia; m. Milka Berskova1968; one d. *Education:* Acad. of Music, Prague. *Career:* Debut: Principal Cello, Prague Symphony Orchestra; Founder, Mem., Kocian Quartet, 1972–; Teacher, Docent, Chamber Music, Acad. of Music, Prague; mem., Czech Music Soc. *Recordings:* Bruckner, String Quartet in F major; Schubert, String Quintet in C major; Dvořák, String Quartets No. 10, 12, 13, 14; Mozart, String Quartets Nos 14–23; Brahms, String Sextets Op. 18 and Op. 36, with members of Smetana Quartet; Haydn, String Quartets op 20; Fibich, String Quartets; Tchaikovsky, Sextet; Schulhoff, Quartets and duo for Violin and Cello. *Honours:* Grand Prix du Disque; Académie Charles Cros; Diapason d'Or. *Address:* Kadnerova 312, 16400 Prague 6, Czech Republic (home). *Telephone:* (603) 802129 (home). *E-mail:* bernasek@h.amu.cz (office). *Website:* www.concerts-prague.cz/kocian.

BERNATHOVA, Eva, DipArt, Prof.'s Dip; British fmr pianist and academic; b. 4 Dec. 1922, Budapest, Hungary; m. Joseph Bernath 1947. *Education:* Gymnasium, Budapest, Franz Liszt Acad. of Music, Budapest. *Career:* debut in Prague 1948; has toured in Europe, USA, Canada, Far East, India, Japan, Australia and New Zealand; soloist with many world-famous orchestras, including Berlin Philharmonic, Czech Philharmonic, Orchestre de la Suisse Romande, Royal Philharmonic Orchestra, Gewandhaus Orchestra; fmrly Sr Lecturer, Trinity Coll. of Music, London. *Recordings include:* Solo works by J. H. Vorišek, Franz Liszt, M. Balakirev, J. Suk, Mozart; Janáček's Concertino for Piano and Chamber Orchestra, Martinů's Concertino for Piano and Orchestra; Franck's Symphonic Variations; Ravel's Concerto in G; Bartók's Concerto No. 3; Chamber Music: Dvořák's Piano Quintet in A, Brahms' Piano Quintet in F minor, Franck's Piano Quintet in F minor, Shostakovich's Piano Quintet in G minor, Martinů's Piano Quintet. *Honours:* Grand Prix du Disque Français, Paris (for Janáček piano solo works), Grand Prix du Disque Acad. Charles Cros, Paris (for Franck's Piano Quintet with the Janáček Quartet). *Address:* 8 Purley Avenue, London, NW2 1SJ, England (home). *Telephone:* (20) 8452-3936 (home).

BERNER, Christoph; Austrian pianist; b. Vienna. *Education:* studied at Universität für Musik und Darstellende Kunst, Vienna with Imola Joo, Hans Graf and Hans Petermandl and in Fiesole, Italy with Maria Tipo. *Career:* regular appearances at several major concert halls including Vienna Musikverein and Vienna Konzerthaus; has played at many well-known festivals including the Carinthian Summer, the Schubertiade Schwarzenberg, the Menuhin Festival Gstaad and Gidon Kremer's Lockenhaus Chamber Music Festival; concert tours to most European countries, as well as Morocco, Japan, Mexico and USA (Carnegie Hall, New York); has played as soloist with prestigious orchestras including Orchestre Nat. du Toulouse, Moscow Tchaikovsky Orchestra, Bremen and Dresden Philharmonic, Bergen Philharmonic and Goteborg Symphony Orchestras, Northern Sinfonia, Mahler Chamber Orchestra and Vienna Chamber Orchestra, with conductors including Neeme Järvi, Michel Plasson, Vladimir Fedosejev, Rafael Frühbeck de Burgos, Andrew Litton, Thomas Zehetmair, Walter Weller and Dennis Russell-Davies. *Recordings:* Mozart Späte Klavierwerke, Christoph Berner spielt Schumann 1999, Schubert Die Winterreise (BBC Music Magazine Award, Vocal Category 2011). *Current Management:* Cadenza Concert, Alja Bàtthyany-Vàgh, Franz Josef Kai 3, 5020 Salzburg, Austria. *Telephone:* (662) 84-05-05. *E-mail:* office@cadenza-concert.at. *Website:* www.christophberner.com.

BERNHARDSSON, Sibbi, BMus, MMus; Icelandic violinist. *Education:* Rejkjavik Coll. of Music; studied with Gudny Gudmundsdottir, Roland Vamos, Almita Vamos, Matias Tacke and Shmuel Ashkenasi; Oberlin Conservatory of Music, Northern Illinois Univ. *Career:* fmr mem. Icelandic String Octet; founder mem. Pacifica Quartet 1994–, Faculty Quartet-in-Residence, Univ. of Illinois at Champagn/Urbana 2003–, Quartet-in-Residence, Metropolitan Museum of Art 2009–; faculty mem., Univ. of Illinois at Champagn/Urbana 2003–, Univ. of Chicago; *Recordings:* with The Pacifica Quartet: String Quartets by Easley Blackwood 1999, Dvořák: String Quartet No. 13 in G Major and String Quintet in E-flat Major 2001, Mendelssohn: The Complete String Quartets 2005, Declarations: Music Between the Wars 2006, Elliott Carter: String Quartets Nos 1 and 5 (Grammy Award for Best Chamber Music Performance 2009) 2008. *Honours:* Lindar Award, Grand Prize, Coleman Chamber Music Competition 1996, Walter F. Naumburg Chamber Music Award 1998, Chamber Music America's Cleveland Quartet Award 2002, Avery Fisher Career Grant 2006, Musical America Award for Ensemble of the Year 2009. *Current Management:* Melvin Kaplan Inc., 115 College Street, Burlington, VT 05401, USA. *Telephone:* (802) 658-2592. *Fax:* (802) 658-6089. *E-mail:* music@melkap.com. *Website:* www.melkap.com. *E-mail:* pacificaquartet@yahoo.com (office); sibbisibbi@hotmail.com (home). *Website:* www.pacificaquartet.com.

BERNHEIMER, Martin, BMus, MA; American music critic; b. 28 Sept. 1936, Munich; m. 1st Lucinda Pearson 1961 (divorced 1989), one s. three d.; m. 2nd Linda Winer 1993. *Education:* Brown Univ., New York Univ. *Career:* teacher, New York Univ. 1959–62; contributing critic, New York Herald Tribune 1959–62; Contributing Ed., Musical Courier 1961–64; temporary music critic, New York Post 1961–65; Asst to Music Ed., Saturday Review 1962–65; Man. Ed., Philharmonic Hall Programme, New York 1962–65; New York corresp., Opera 1962–65, Los Angeles corresp. 1965–97; Music Ed. and Chief Music Critic, Los Angeles Times 1965–96; teacher, Univ. of Southern California 1966–71, UCLA 1969–75, California Inst. of the Arts 1975–82, California State Univ., Northridge 1978–81; New York Music Critic, Financial Times 1996–; guest critic, Newsday 1996; music critic, New York Sidewalk (Microsoft) 1997; Lecturer, Metropolitan Opera Guild 1997–; mem. Editorial Bd Opera Magazine; mem. Pulitzer Prize music jury 1984, 1986, 1989. *Publications:* contrib. articles to New Grove Dictionary of Music and Musicians, New Grove Dictionary of American Music, New Grove Dictionary of Opera; reviews in various journals, liner notes for recordings, panellist, moderator, essayist on Metropolitan Opera broadcasts. *Honours:* winner, Pulitzer Prize in Criticism 1981. *Address:* Financial Times, 330 Hudson Street, New York, NY 10013, USA.

BERNIUS, Frieder; German conductor; b. 1945, Ludwigshafen. *Education:* studied in Stuttgart and Tübingen. *Career:* Founder, Stuttgart Chamber Choir 1968; regular appearances with Stuttgart Baroque and Chamber Orchestras and German Chamber Philharmonic, Bremen; Suisse Romande Orchestra; Prague Philharmonic; Founder, International Festival of Early Music, Stuttgart 1987; Prof., Mannheim Musikhochschule; Conductor, Haydn's Orfeo, London; Jommelli's Il Vologeso, Stuttgart 1993; Demofoonte, Rome; Schwetzingen 1995; Dresden Semperoper, Hasse's Olimpiade and Artemisia; operas by Rameau, including Hippolyte et Aricie at Bad Urach. *Recordings include:* Il Vologeso. *Honours:* Order of Merit of the Federal Republic of Germany 1993; Edison Award 1990, Diapason d'Or 1990, Robert-Edler-Preis 2001, Bach-Medaille der Stadt Leipzig 2009. *Address:* Musik Podium Stuttgart e.V., Büchsenstr. 22, 70174 Stuttgart, Germany. *Website:* musikpodium.de.

BERNSTEIN, Lawrence F., BS, PhD; American musicologist and academic; b. 25 March 1939, New York, NY. *Education:* Hofstra Univ., New York Univ. *Career:* Instructor in Music and Humanities, Univ. of Chicago 1965–66, Asst Prof. 1966–70, Assoc. Prof. 1970–81, Chair Dept of Music 1972–73, 1974–77; Prof. of Music, Univ. of Pennsylvania 1981–; Visiting Lecturer, Columbia Univ. Graduate School of Arts and Sciences 1979; Visiting Assoc. Prof., Princeton Univ. 1980; Visiting Prof., Rutgers Univ. 1982–83; Supervising Ed., Masters and Monuments of the Renaissance 1970–; Ed.-in-Chief, Journal of the American Musicological Soc. 1975–77. *Publications:* Ihan Gero, Madrigali italiani et canzoni francese a due voci (with James Haar) 1980, La Couronne et fleur des chansons a troys 1984, The French Secular Chanson in the Sixteenth Century; contrib. articles in New Grove Dictionary of Music and Musicians 1980, articles and reviews in journals and other publications. *Address:* c/o Department of Music, University of Pennsylvania, 201 S 34th Street, Philadelphia, PA 19104-6313, USA.

BÉROFF, Michel; French pianist; b. 9 May 1950, Épinal. *Education:* Conservatories of Nancy and Paris with Yvonne Loriod. *Career:* debut in Paris 1966; has appeared on television and at festivals in Portugal and Iran 1967, also at Royal and Oxford Bach Festivals; has lectured and given recitals and concerts in various European and South American countries; appearances with the London Symphony Orchestra, Concerts Colonne, Orchestre de Paris, New York Philharmonic and BBC Symphony Orchestras; toured Japan and South Africa. *Recordings include:* Prokofiev's Visions Fugitives; Messiaen's Quatuor pour la fin du Temps and Vingt Regards sur L'Enfant Jésus; Debussy's Préludes, Estampes and Pour le Piano; music by Bartók, Stravinsky and Mozart. *Honours:* first prize Nancy Conservatory 1962, 1963, Paris Conservatory 1966, Olivier Messiaen Competition, Royan.

BERONESI, Debora; Italian singer (mezzo-soprano); b. 1965, Rome. *Education:* Accademia di Santa Cecilia, Rome. *Career:* debut at Spoleto 1988 as Eboli in Don Carlos; appearances at Macerata and Treviso as Dorabella, Rossini's Isabella at Trieste and Meg Page in Falstaff at Enschede; Isaura in Rossini's Tancredi at Bologna; Palermo 1993 in the premiere of Alice by Testoni; Salzburg Festival 1993–94 as the Messenger in Monteverdi's Orfeo; Nero in Monteverdi's Poppea at La Scala, Milan and Antwerp; Frankfurt Opera 1995 as Cecilio in Lucio Silla by Mozart and Idamante in Idomeneo; sang Purcell's Dido at the 2001 Maggio Musicale, Florence. *Honours:* winner A. Belli Competition, Spoleto 1988.

BERRY, John, CBE; British musician (clarinet) and opera director; *Artistic Director, English National Opera. Career:* fmr freelance clarinettist; spent several years as an artists' manager working both independently and with the London agency Harrison Parrott; developed the largest privately run music centres in UK 1985; f. Brereton Int. Music Symposium, working closely with Birgit Nilsson, Thomas Hampson, Renata Scotto and numerous world-renowned instrumentalists; est. music coll., Sounds Alive, for young musicians in northern England; Casting Dir, ENO 1995, Dir of Opera Programming 2003–, also Artistic Dir 2005–; has acted as artistic consultant to numerous orgs, including BBC, Channel 4, Hallé Orchestra and Royal Coll. of Music; has sat on guest competition panels, including Metropolitan Opera Guild, Young Concert Artists Trust. *Address:* English National Opera, London Coliseum, St Martin's Lane, Trafalgar Square, London, WC2N 4ES, England (office). *Telephone:* (20) 7836-0111 (home). *Website:* www.eno.org/about/eno-now/eno-people/senior-management/john-berry (office).

BERTELSMEIER, Birke J., MMus; German composer; b. 1981, Hilden. *Education:* Hochschule für Musik Köln, Hochschule für Musik Karlsruhe, studied under Pavel Gililov and Wolfgang Rihm. *Career:* musical theatre, film scores, orchestral works, chamber music and solo pieces; commissions from Festival Heidelberger Frühling, Munich Biennale, Beijing Int. Music Competition, Deutsche Oper Berlin, Darmstadt Summer School; works performed at Deutsche Oper Berlin 2014, Konzerthaus Berlin 2015 int. festivals and by performers including Arditti Quartet, Quatuor Diotima, Ensemble Modern and mems of Berlin Philharmonic; has taught composition at youth seminars of Beethovenhaus Bonn and North Rhine-Westphalia's Musikrat NRW, and at Hochschule für Musik Hannover. *Compositions include:* Studie for ensemble 2007, Pandämonium for harp and violin 2007, A Route of Evanescences for female singer, clarinet, flute, harp, viola and violoncello 2007, Dringlich for chamber orchestra 2007, Privatissimae for violin, violoncello and piano 2007, Per se for oboe and piano 2008, Trinklied for baritone and drums 2008, Quartettstück for string quartet 2008, Si tu l'dis for wind orchestra 2008, Kurz vor'm for ensemble 2009, Im Nu for orchestra 2009, Acanthes 2009, Sehnlich for female choir 2009, Papiersammlung for clarinet, trumpet, violoncello and piano (for film) 2010, Tit for Tat for horn, trombone and tuba 2010, ... reichen Hall for orchestra 2010, Stück for baroque orchestra 2010, Sonntag for saxophone, double bass, drum and piano (for film) 2010, Bagatelle sans atonalité for saxophone and piano 2010, Chimineau for string quartet 2010, ... von der anderen Seite for piano 2011, ... und andere Galanterien, verfertigt ...for trumpet und tenor saxophone 2011, Studie for piano 2011, Allerleirauh for female singer, clarinet and piano 2011, Giromaniaco for large ensemble 2013, verso di for piano quartet 2013, Trio for clarinet, accordion, viola and violoncello 2013, WhirliGique for solo flute 2012, nichtsdestotrotz for ensemble 2012, Der Mann, der sich ins Märchen trommelte for flute, clarinet, harp, piano, drum and cello; Text: Moritz Rinke 2012, Hineidunke for string quartet 2012, Folklich for flute, oboe clarinet, bassoon, horn, flügelhorn, drum, piano, violin, viola, violoncello and double bass 2012, Hertzlich for six drums 2013, Zu-neigend for trumpet 2014, Unstet for trumpet 2014, Amorette I und II for four pianists on two pianos 2014–15, ! for ensemble 2015, Am Rad drehen for violin 2015, Anhänglich for piano 2015, Zimzum for orchester 2015; musical theatre: Querelle 2014, Nachtigall 2013–14. *Recordings include:* Folklich 2015. *Honours:* grants from International Ensemble Modern Acad., Akad. Musiktheater heute, Herrenhaus Edenkoben and Villa Massimo in Rome 2013, Karlsruhe Composition Prize, Yvar Mikhashoff Trust for New Music Award Schneider-Schott Music Prize 2012, Ernst von Siemens Music Foundation Composer's Award 2015. *E-mail:* contact@birkebertelsmeier .com. *Website:* www.birkebertelsmeier.com.

BERTHOLD, Beatrice; German pianist; b. 11 Sept. 1964, Wiesbaden. *Education:* Acad. of Music, Vienna, Acad. of Music, Cologne and Acad. of Music, Detmold. *Career:* debut at Wiesbaden National Theatre 1978 (C. M. von Weber, konzertstück); television debut on ZDF/Eurovision (Liszt, piano concerto No. 2); solo recitals and concerts with renowned orchestras in Europe; Lucerne Music Festival, Berlin (Philharmonie), Hamburg (Musikhalle), Cologne (Philharmonie), London 1983–; US debut at the German American Piano Festival in Atlanta 1995; several concert tours to South America, including Porto Alegre (Teatro da Ospa), Caracas (Teatro Teresa Careno) 1996–; television and radio appearances with Beethoven Piano Concerto No. 5; Rachmaninov Piano Sonata No. 1 and 2; Granados, Goyescas; Brahms, Fantasias op 116; Rhapsodies op 78; Scriabin, Fantasia op 28; Villa-Lobos, Ciclo Brasiliero. *Recordings:* The Young Rachmaninov 1990, Tchaikovsky/Rachmaninov/Scriabin: Early Piano Works 1992, Granados: Goyescas + El Pelele 1992, Hommage au Piano 1994. *Address:* Grünstrasse 13, 58313 Herdecke, Germany.

BERTI, Marco; Italian singer (tenor); b. 1961, Turin. *Education:* Verdi Conservatory, Milan. *Career:* sang widely in Italy as Jim in Mahagonny by Weill; sang Pinkerton in Consenza 1990, and Don Ottavio at Macerata 1991; Frankfurt 1991, as Guevara in a concert performance of Franchetti's Cristoforo Colombo; Strasbourg 1992, as Alfredo; St Gallen 1993, as Roberto Devereux; season 1994–95 as Rodolfo and in Verdi's Stiffelio at La Scala; season 1999–2000 as Foresto in Attila at Karlsruhe, Ismaele in Nabucco at the Deutsche Oper Berlin and Macduff at the Vienna Staatsoper; Riccardo (Ballo in Maschera) at the Bregenz Festival and Don José at Copenhagen; sang Foresto at Montpellier, and made Covent Garden debut 2002, as Gabriele Adorno; Pinkerton 2003. *Recordings include:* Cristoforo Colombo, Don Giovanni, Manon Lescaut. *Current Management:* IMG Artists, 31–33 rue du Temple, 75004 Paris, France. *Telephone:* 1-44-31-00-10. *Fax:* 1-44-31-44-40. *E-mail:* pwiggins@imgartists.com. *Website:* www.imgartists.com; www.marco -berti.com.

BERTIN, Pascal; French singer (countertenor); b. 1970. *Education:* Paris Conservatoire with William Christie. *Career:* Children's Choir of Paris, from age 11, with tours throughout the world; founder, Indigo, vocal jazz group, 1995; many concert and opera appearances with conductors Marc Minkowski, Christophe Rousset, John Eliot Gardiner, Sigiswald Kuijken and Philippe Herreweghe. *Recordings:* Handel's Riccardo Primo (Oronte), Caldara's Conversione di Clovedeo, The Countertenors, Pathways of Baroque Music: Cathedrals and Chapels, Handel's Amadigi (Orlando). *Honours:* first prize, Baroque vocal music, Paris Conservatoire. *Current Management:* Sorek

Artists Management, Burgemeester Patijnlaan 450, 2585 BW, The Hague, Netherlands. *Website:* www.sorekartists.com.

BERTOLINO, (Ercole) Mario; Italian singer (bass-baritone); b. 10 Sept. 1934, Palermo. *Education:* studied in Palermo, with Mario Basiola in Milan, Giuseppe Danise in New York. *Career:* debut at Teatro Nuovo Milan 1955, as Marcello in La Bohème; sang at La Scala, in Rome, Palermo, Munich, Lyon and Mexico City; moved to Forest Hills, NY, sang widely in the US at Boston, Cincinnati, Pittsburgh, San Antonio, Washington and New York City Opera; roles have included Verdi's Amonasro, Renato, Macbeth, Iago, Germont and Luna; Donizetti's Dulcamara, Don Pasquale and Enrico; Gerard in Andrea Chénier; Puccini's Sharpless and Lescaut; Iago in Otello; Connecticut Opera 1987–88 as Don Pasquale and Dulcamara; Rome 1989, as Mozart's Bartolo; also sang in concert.

BERTOLO, Aldo; Italian singer (tenor); b. 22 Oct. 1949, Turin. *Career:* debut in Mozart's Ferrando at Susa 1978; many appearances in Italy; South America; Europe, in the lyric repertoire; roles include Donizetti's Edgardo, Tonie and Ernesto; Pylades in Piccinni's Iphigénie en Tauride; Rossini's Lindoro, Adalbert in Adelaide di Borgogna and Don Ottavio; season 1985 sang Arturo in I Puritani at Martina Franca; Ramiro in La Cenerentola, in Santiago; at Valle d'Itria 1986, sang Thoas in the first modern revival of Traetta's Ifigenia en Tauride; Elvino in La Sonnambula at Piacenza 1986; Teatro Carlo Felice, Genoa 1988, as Narciso in L'Italiana in Algeri; other roles include the Fisherman in Guillaume Tell, Lorenzo in Fra Diavolo and Verdi's Alfredo; season 1991, as Ernesto at Pisa and Narciso at Trieste.

BERTRAND, Emmanuelle; French cellist; b. 5 Nov. 1973, Firminy. *Education:* Conservatoire Nat. Supérieur de Musique, Lyon and Paris, studied with Jean Deplace and Philippe Muller. *Career:* regular soloist with Jerusalem Symphony Orchestra, Orchestre Métropolitain du Grand Montréal, Nat. Symphony Orchestra of Ukraine, BBC Nat. Orchestra of Wales, Wuhan Symphony Orchestra, Orchestre Symphonique du Québec, Ensemble Orchestral de Paris and Orchestre Nat. de Lille; has appeared in main concert halls in Paris and in festivals in Europe, Japan, China, Korea and N America; has premiered numerous contemporary works including Nicolas Bacri's Fourth Suite for solo cello, Japan 1997 and Luciano Berio's last solo cello work, Chanson pour Pierre Boulez 2000; duo partnership with pianist Pascal Amoyal 1999–; Artistic Dir, Beauvais Cello Festival. *Recordings include:* Dutilleux/Ligeti/Bacri/Crumb/Henze 2000, Alkan/Liszt 2001, Bloch: Suites pour violoncelle 2003, Olivier Greif: Sonate de Requiem 2006, Saint-Saëns: Sonate No. 1 & Suite Op. 16 2007, Charles-Valentin Alkan: Sonate de Concert op. 47 2008, Grieg: Cello Sonata Op. 36 2008, Le violoncelle parle (Diapason de l'or de l'année) 2011, Le Violoncelle Romantique 2011, Strauss/Reger: Sonates pour violoncelle et piano 2012, Dmitry Shostakovich: Cello Concerto No. 1 2013. *Honours:* Chevalier, Ordre des Arts et des Lettres 2004; First Prize, Japan Chamber Music Competition and Prix Acad. Int. Maurice Ravel, Young Artist of the Year, Victoires de la Musique Classique 2002, Grand Prix de la Critique Française 2002. *Current Management:* c/o Argine Jermann, Tandem Concerts, 2 rue des Écoles, 68700 Wattwiller, France. *Telephone:* 6-47-01-27-42. *E-mail:* tandemconcerts@orange.fr. *Website:* tandemconcerts.over-blog .com; www.emmanuelle-bertrand.com (office).

BESA, Alexander; Czech violist; b. 28 Feb. 1971; m.; two d. *Education:* Music School, Znojmo, Czech Republic, State Conservatory, Brno, Int. Menuhin Music Acad., Switzerland, Musik Akad., Basel. *Career:* debut, Mozart Sinfonia Concertante K364 with Moravian Chamber Orchestra, Brno 1990; has appeared throughout Europe, Hong Kong, Japan, N and S America with Berliner Festwochen, Concentus Moraviae, Euroart Festival Prague, Ittinger Pfingstkonzerte, Lucerne Festival, Menuhin Festival in Gstaad, Phillips Gallery, Washington, Prague Spring and Salzburger Festspiele; as soloist with Czech Philharmony, Camerata Bern, Kurphälzisches Kammerorchester, Mannheim, Camerata Lysy, Basel Symphony and Radio Orchestra, Janáček Philharmonic, Ostrava, B. Martinů Philharmonic, Zlin, Lucerne Symphony Orchestra, Prague Philharmonia, State Opera of Prague, Hong Kong Philharmonic Orchestra; as chamber musician: collaborations with Magdalena Koẑená, Ruth Ziesak, Ana Chumachenko, Alberto Lysy, Bohuslav Matoušek, Thomas Zehetmair, Nobuko Imai, Christoph Schiller, Tabea Zimmermann, Jiří Bárta, Patrick and Thomas Demenga, Jana Boušková, Heinz Holliger, Ludmila Peterková, Dimitri Ashkenazy and Michel Lethiec, Marie Louise Neunecker and Radovan Vlatkovich and ensembles including Aria Quartet, Basel Quartet, Stamitz Quartet, Wallinger Quartet, Wihan Quartet, Zehetmair Quartet, The Serenade String Trio, Merel Quartet, Swiss Nonet, Ensemble Kaleidoscope and Ensemble Paul Klee. *Recordings:* String Quintets by Brahms and Herzogenberg 1996, Octets by Mendelssohn and Gade 1998, Music for Viola and Piano, Clarinet Quintets by Francaix, Penderecki and Martinů 1999, M. Bruch: Double Concerto for clarinet, viola and orchestra, Alessandro Rolla: Sonatas for viola and bass 2002, Clarinet Quintets by Mozart and Weber 2005, B. Martinů: Chamber Music with Viola 2008. *Honours:* Winner, Beethoven Int. Viola Competition, Czech Repub. 1994, Winner, H. Schaeuble Viola Competition, Lausanne 1995, Morris Maddrell Prize, L. Tertis Viola Competition, Isle of Man, UK 1997. *Current Management:* c/o Central European Music Agency, Kapucínské nám. 308/14, 602 00 Brno, Czech Republic. *E-mail:* agency@cema-music.com. *Website:* www .cema-music.com.

BEST, Jonathan; British singer (bass); b. 1958, Kent, England. *Education:* Univ. of Cambridge and Guildhall School of Music. *Career:* debut as Sarastro with WNO 1983; many leading roles in the bass repertory, with WNO, Scottish Opera, Dublin Grand Opera, Kent Opera and Opera North; appearances at Covent Garden in Die Meistersinger, Otello, Don Carlos and King Arthur (as Grimbauld, with Les Arts Florissants 1995); season 1994–95 in The Rake's Progress at Salzburg, in The Queen of Spades at Glyndebourne and The Fairy Queen for ENO; other roles include Don Alfonso in Così fan tutte (Opera North 1997); sang Trulove in The Rake's Progress for WNO 1996; season 1998 with Cassandro in Mozart's Finta Semplice at Garsington and Garibaldo in Rodelinda for GTO at Glyndebourne; season 1999–2000 as Leporello and Britten's Bottom for Opera North; St Magnus Festival 2000 in the premiere of Mr Emmett takes a Walk, by Peter Maxwell Davies; Don Alfonso at Grange Park Opera; Doctor Wozzeck and Rocco Fidelio with BOCO. *Current Management:* Musichall Ltd, Oast House, Crouch's Farm, Hollow Lane, East Hoathly, BN8 6QX, England. *E-mail:* info@musichall.uk.com. *Website:* www.musichall.uk.com.

BEST, Matthew, MA (Hons); British singer (bass-baritone) and conductor; b. 6 Feb. 1957, Farnborough, Kent, England; s. of Peter Best and Isabel Best; m. Rosalind Mayes 1983; one s. one d. *Education:* King's Coll., Cambridge, Nat. Opera Studio, studied with Otakar Kraus, Robert Lloyd and Patrick McGuigan. *Career:* debut as Seneca in The Coronation of Poppea, Cambridge Univ. Opera Soc. 1978; Prin. Bass, Royal Opera 1980–86; guest artist with Welsh Nat. Opera (WNO), Opera North, Netherlands Opera, Scottish Opera, ENO, Royal Opera, Glyndebourne Festival Opera, Glyndebourne Touring Opera, Oper Frankfurt, Royal Swedish Opera, Oper Leipzig, Opéra de Lyon, Théâtre du Châtelet, Paris, Théâtre de la Monnaie, Brussels, Staatstheater Stuttgart, Santa Fe Opera; extensive concert career; Founder and Dir Corydon Singers 1973–, Corydon Orchestra 1991–; Prin. Conductor The Hanover Band 1998–99; has also worked frequently, as Guest Conductor, with English Chamber Orchestra, Northern Sinfonia, London Mozart Players, City of London Sinfonia, plus appearances with English Northern Philharmonia, Manchester Camerata, RTÉ Concert Orchestra, Royal Seville Symphony Orchestra, BBC Nat. Orchestra of Wales, Sonderjyllands Symfoniorkester; prin. opera roles include Wotan (complete Ring cycles, Edinburgh Int. Festival 2003), Amfortas (Parsifal), Kurwenal (Tristan und Isolde), Scarpia (Tosca), Pizarro (Fidelio), Commendatore (Don Giovanni), all for Scottish Opera; Pizarro (Leonore) at Salzburg Festival 1996, BBC Proms, Lincoln Center Festival, New York; The Flying Dutchman, Wotan (Das Rheingold), Jochanaan (Salome), King Mark (Tristan & Isolde), Kutuzov (War and Peace), Ramfis (Aïda), Swallow (Peter Grimes), Sparafucile (Rigoletto) and Commendatore for ENO; Swallow (Peter Grimes), Sprecher (Die Zauberflöte), Timur (Turandot) for Royal Opera; Wotan (Walküre), Der Wanderer (Siegfried) and Orest (Elektra) for Staatstheater Stuttgart, Der Wanderer for Opéra de Lyon, Kurwenal for Théâtre de la Monnaie and Opéra de Nancy; Scarpia for Florida Grand Opera, WNO, Scottish Opera and Opera North; Jochanaan for WNO and LSO; Peneios (Daphne) and Tsargo (Adriana Mater, US premiere) for Santa Fe Opera; Der Fliegende Holländer for Opéra de Rouen, King Mark (Tristan und Isolde) for Oper Leipzig, WNO, Opera Bilbao, CBSO and Philharmonia Orchestra, King Heinrich (Lohengrin) for Royal Swedish Opera, Cadmus (The Bassarids) for Théâtre du Châtelet, Paris and Opera Köln, Vairochana (Wagner Dream, world premiere) for Netherlands Opera; prin. engagements as conductor include extensive concert appearances at UK and European festivals, Royal Festival Hall, Queen Elizabeth Hall, Royal Albert Hall and BBC Promenade Concerts. *Composition:* Alice (opera), performed at Aldeburgh Festival 1979. *Recordings include:* as singer: Beethoven, Leonore; Elgar, The Dream of Gerontius; Britten, Peter Grimes; Billy Budd; Berlioz, L'Enfance du Christ; Verdi, Don Carlo (video); Vaughan Williams, Sir John in Love; as conductor: Bruckner, Te Deum and Masses; Berlioz L'Enfance du Christ; Beethoven Mass in C and Emperor Cantatas; Fauré Requiem; Duruflé Requiem; Vaughan Williams, Hugh the Drover; Rachmaninov Vespers; Works by Vaughan Williams, Britten, Finzi, Tchaikovsky, Mendelssohn, Simpson and others, all with Corydon Singers, Corydon Orchestra, English Chamber Orchestra, City of London Sinfonia. *Honours:* SE Arts Assen Bursary, Friends of Covent Garden Bursary 1980, Decca-Kathleen Ferrier Prize 1982. *Current Management:* c/o Intermusica Artists' Management, 36 Graham Street, Crystal Wharf, London, N1 8GJ, England. *Telephone:* (20) 7608-9900. *Fax:* (20) 7490-3263. *E-mail:* jmaynard@intermusica.co.uk. *Website:* www.intermusica.co.uk.

BESUTTI, Paola; Italian musicologist; b. 18 April 1960, Mantua; m. Roberto Giuliani 1992. *Education:* Parma University, Conservatory of Music in Mantua. *Career:* Prof. at Pesaro Conservatory of Music; mem. of editorial staff of Rivista Italiana di Musicologia; Prof., Researcher, Institute of Musicology of Parma University, 1990–; collaborated with Parrott, Vartolo, Savall; mem. American Musicological Society; International Musicological Society; Società Italiana di Educazione Musicale; Società Italiana di Musicologia. *Publications include:* La corte musicale di Ferdinando Carlo Gonzaga, Mantova Areari, 1989; Hildegard von Bingen, Ordo Virtutum, Sa musique et s. idée de théatre, in Actes de la Societé Internationale pour l'étude du théatre médiéval, Barcelona, Institut del Teatro, 1997; Ave maris stella: la tradizione mantovana nuovamente posta in musica da Monteverdi in Claudio Monteverdi, Studi e prospettive, Firenze, Olschki, 1997; Tasso contra Guarini: una Rappresentazione con intermedi degli Intrichi d'amore (1606) in Torquato Tasso e la cultura estense, Firenze, Olschki, 1997; La figura professionale del cantante d'opera: Quaderni storici, XXXII n 2 agosto, 1997; Giostre e tornei a Mantova Parma e Piacenza fra Cinque e Seicento in Musica e tornei nel Seicento Italiano, Lucca, LIM; contrib. to music reviews and publications including: Atlas Mondiale du Baroque, Dizionario degli Editori Musicali Italiani, The New Grove, The New Grove Dictionary of Opera. *Address:* Piazzale Vittorio Veneto 1, 46100 Mantova, Italy.

BEUDERT, Mark; American singer (tenor); b. 4 June 1961, New York. *Education:* Columbia Univ. and Michigan Univ. *Career:* sang at Santa Domingo Opera from 1983; Grand Rapids Opera 1985; at Philadelphia and the New York City Opera; Washington 1986, as Pedrillo in Die Entfuhrung; Queensland State Opera at Brisbane as Pinkerton and Faust 1987, 1991; season 1988–89 as Candide by Bernstein for Scottish Opera and the Old Vic Theatre, London; Sam Kaplan in Weill's Street Scene for ENO. *Honours:* winner Pavarotti Competition at Philadelphia 1985.

BEURON, Yann; French singer (tenor); b. 1970. *Education:* Paris Conservatoire with Anna Maria Bondi. *Career:* appearances as Belmonte, Strasbourg; Fernando at Bordeaux and in Rossini's Cenerentola at the Ascoli Festival; in Rameau's Hippolyte et Aricie, Paris Palais Garnier, Geneva, Opéra in Offenbach's Orphée 1997; concerts include the Evangelist in Bach's Passions; soloist, Berlioz te Deum. *Recordings:* Le Chevalier Danois, Gluck's Armide. *Current Management:* IMG Artists, 31–33 rue du Temple, 75004 Paris, France. *Telephone:* 1-44-31-00-10. *Fax:* 1-44-31-44-40. *E-mail:* pwiggins@imgartists.com. *Website:* www.imgartists.com.

BEYER, Amandine; French musician (violin); b. 1974, Aix-en-Provence. *Education:* Conservatoire Nat. Supérieur de Musique, Paris, Schola Cantorum Basiliensis (Switzerland), studied with Chiara Banchini. *Career:* fmr mem. medieval ensemble Mala Punica; soloist with orchestras including ensemble 415, Le Concert Français, Accademia Montis Regalis, Les Siècles; has worked with musicians including Pierre Hantaï, Giuliano Carmignola and Chiara Banchini; mem. Les Cornets Noirs; f. Gli Incogniti; performances broadcast on French, German and Italian radio; teaches an annual course in baroque music at Barbaste, France and in Early Music Dept at Escola Superior de Música, Artes e Espectáculo, Porto, Portugal 2004–, and at Schola Cantorum Basiliensis, Switzerland 2010–. *Recordings include:* with L'Assemblée des Honnestes Curieux: Rebel: Sonates pour Violons et Basse Continue 2006; with Gli Incogniti: Bach: Concerti a Violino Certato 2007, Vivaldi: Les quatre saisons & autres concertos 2008, Nicola Matteis: False Consonances of Melancholy Ayres 2009, Johan Rosenmüller: Beatus Vir? Motets & Sonates 2010, Nuova Stagione: Vivaldi Concerti 2012, Corelli: The Complete Concerti Grossi (Diapason d'Or de l'Année) 2013; solo: Bach Sonates and Partites (Diapason d'Or de l'Année, Choc de Classica de l'année) 2011; with Chiara Banchini: Italian Baroque: Sonatas & Concertos 2012. *Honours:* Juventus Foundation scholarship 2000, First Prize, Antonio Vivaldi Baroque Violin Competition 2001, Prix Charles Cros. *E-mail:* info@amandinebeyer.com (office). *Website:* www.amandinebeyer.com (office).

BEYNON, Emily, FRAM; British flautist; *Principal Flautist, Royal Concertgebouw Orchestra*; b. 1969, Swansea, South Wales. *Education:* Royal Coll. of Music (Jr Dept) with Margaret Ogonovsky, Royal Acad. of Music with William Bennett, and with Alain Marion in Paris. *Career:* BBC Proms debut, Royal Albert Hall, London 1999; fmr Prin. Flautist, BBC Nat. Orchestra of Wales and Glyndebourne Touring Opera; Prin. Flautist, Royal Concertgebouw Orchestra, Amsterdam 1995–; concerto soloist with Royal Concertgebouw Orchestra, Philharmonia Orchestra, BBC Orchestras, NHK Symphony, Vienna, Prague, Netherlands and English Chamber Orchestras, Acad. of St Martin-in-the-Fields; guest appearances as chamber musician with Nash Ensemble, Skampa Quartet, Steven Isserlis, Dame Felicity Lott, Jean-Yves Thibaudet, Kungsbacka Trio, Brodsky Quartet and others; many new works written for her by leading composers, including John Woolrich, Sally Beamish, Jonathan Dove, Errollyn Wallen and Roxanna Panufnik; taught at Royal Conservatoire, The Hague for 11 years, Conservatorium van Amsterdam for two years, Netherlands Flute Acad. (Neflac) which she co-f. (with Suzanne Wolff) 2009–; masterclasses world-wide. *Recordings include:* 11 solo recordings: Pastoral & Fantaisie, Mozart Concerto, Rutland Boughton, John McCabe's Flute Concerto & Les Six, Alwyn/Berkeley/Poulenc/Dove, Flute Mystery, Remote Galaxy. *Publications:* Universal 'Flute Project' and educational series for De Haske (Bel Canto, Köhler/Gariboldi studies and The Art of Baroque). *Address:* Royal Concertgebouw Orchestra, Jacob Obrechtstraat 51, 1071 KJ Amsterdam, Netherlands (office). *Telephone:* (20) 3051010 (office). *E-mail:* emilybeynon@planet.nl (home). *Website:* www.concertgebouworkest.nl (office); www.emilybeynon.com.

BEZALY, Sharon; Israeli/Swedish flautist. *Education:* Conservatoire Nat. Supérieur de Musique, Paris with Alain Marion, Raymond Guiot and Maurice Bourgue. *Career:* debut concert as soloist with Israel Philharmonic Orchestra under Zubin Mehta aged 14; prin. flautist in Sándor Végh's Camerata Academica Salzburg –1997; Artist-in-Residence, Residentie Orchestra, The Hague, Netherlands 2007–08; has performed with orchestras including Tokyo and Osaka Philharmonics, Gothenburg Symphony, Stockholm Philharmonic, BBC Wales and Royal Scottish Nat., Minnesota and São Paulo Symphony Orchestras, SWR and Belgian Nat. Orchestra, BBC Symphony Orchestra, in venues such as Vienna Musikverein, Cologne Philharmonie, Tokyo Suntory Hall, Rudolfinum, Prague, Palais des Beaux Arts, Brussels, Châtelet and Salle Gaveau, Paris, Sydney Opera House, BBC Proms; inspired several commissions by composers including Sofia Gubaidulina, Kalevi Aho and Sally Beamish, 20 flute concertos dedicated to her. *Recordings include:* Chamber Music 1997, The Israeli Connection 1998, Flutissimo 1999, Paul Kletzki 2004, Mozart Flute Concertos 2000, Solo Flute from A to Z, Vol. 1 2001, Café au Lait (with Roland Pöntinen) 2001, Antal Dorati (with Aalborg Symphony Orchestra) 2002, Apéritif 2002, Solo Flute from A to Z, Vol. 2 2003, Chamber Music for Flute, Viola and Piano (with Nobuko Imai and Ronald Brautigam) 2003, Solo Flute from A to Z, Vol. 3 2004, Nordic Spell 2005, Mozart Flute Concertos 2005, Masterworks for Flute and Piano (with Ronald Brautigam) 2006, Bridge Across the Pyrenees 2006, Gubaidulina: The Deceitful Face of Hope and Despair 2006, Seascapes 2007, French Delights 2007, Barocking Together 2008, Spellbound – Sharon Bezaly 2008, Remembrance 2009, Brett Dean – Water Music 2009, Beamish – Orchestral Works 2010, Across the Sea – Chinese-American Flute Concertos 2011, LigAlien – Music by Mari Takano 2011. *Honours:* Instrumentalist of the Year, Echo Klassik Awards (Germany) 2002, Young Artist of the Year Cannes Classical Awards 2003. *Current Management:* c/o Käst Artists & Promotion, Steintorweg 8, 20099 Hamburg, Germany. *Telephone:* (40) 25336793. *Fax:* (40) 25336796. *E-mail:* info@kaechartists.com. *Website:* www.kaechartists.com.

BEZDÜZ, Soner Bülent; Turkish singer (tenor); b. 9 May 1970, Ankara; m. Kamile Rayman Bezdüz; two c. *Education:* Music Acad. of Gazi Univ., Ankara and European Opera Centre, Manchester, UK. *Career:* made his European debut in title role of Mozart's Lucio Silla on tour in UK, Ireland and Denmark with European Opera Centre; regularly appears at both Mersin State Opera and Istanbul Opera; worked with many prestigious conductors and directors, including Sir Colin Davis, Riccardo Chailly, Vladimir Jurowski, David Parry, Richard Jones, Phyllida Lloyd, David Alden, Enrique Mazzola and Antonello Allemandi. *Recordings include:* Rossini's Ermione for Opera Rara. *Honours:* prizewinner, Concours Int. de Chant de Paris 1999, Andante Classical Music Award 2010, three Grammy Awards. *Current Management:* c/o Athole Still Opera Ltd, Foresters Hall, 25–27 Westow Street, London, SE19 3RY, England. *Telephone:* (20) 8771-5271. *Fax:* (20) 8771-8172. *E-mail:* enquiries@atholestill.co.uk. *Website:* www.atholestill.co.uk; www.bulentbezduz.com.

BEZNOSIUK, Lisa, GGSM; British flautist; *Principal Flute, Orchestra of the Age of Enlightenment and English Concert*; b. 20 Aug. 1956, Sheffield, Yorks.; m. Richard Tunnicliffe; one d. *Education:* Guildhall School of Music and Drama (GSMD), studied flute with Kathryn Lukas and Stephen Preston, harpsichord continuo with David Roblou. *Career:* solo debut in London 1983; Prin. Flute, English Concert, English Baroque Soloists, Acad. of Ancient Music, New London Consort, London Classical Players; Founder-mem. Orchestra of the Age of Enlightenment, currently Prin. Flute; recitals with harpsichordists Maggie Cole, Malcolm Proud, Paul Nicholson and Richard Egarr, lutenists Nigel North, Paula Chateauneuf and Elizabeth Kenny, Pavlo Beznosiuk (violin), Richard Tunnicliffe (cello) and Sarah Cunningham (viola da gamba); Prof. at RAM, Royal Coll. of Music (RCM), GSMD. *Recordings include:* Mozart Flute Concerto in G, Flute and Harp Concerto K299 (Acad. of Ancient Music/Christopher Hogwood) 1990, J.S. Bach Four Orchestral Suites (English Concert, English Baroque Soloists, Orchestra of the Age of Enlightenment, New London Consort), Bach Brandenburg Concertos (English Concert, Orchestra of the Age of Enlightenment, New London Consort), Concord of Sweet Sounds, with Nigel North lute/guitar, J.C. Bach 3 Quintets/Sextet (English Concert), Vivaldi Op. 10 Flute Concertos (English Concert) 1990, Vivaldi Concerti (Orchestra of the Age of Enlightenment) 2001, Handel Complete Flute Sonatas 2001, Bach Complete Flute Sonatas 2001, Mozart Flute Quartets/Beethoven Serenade, with Pavlo Beznosiuk, Tom Dunn and Richard Tunnicliffe 2006. *Honours:* Hon. RCM, RAM . *Address:* 133 Dunlace Road, London, E5 0NG, England (office). *E-mail:* lisabezno@yahoo.com (office). *Website:* www.oae.co.uk (office); www.ram.ac.uk (office).

BEZNOSIUK, Pavlo Roman; Irish/Ukrainian violinist; *Director, The Avison Ensemble*; b. 4 July 1960, London, England. *Education:* Guildhall School of Music and Drama. *Career:* Leader of Parley of Instruments 1984–87; founded Beethoven String Trio of London 1992; solo debut at Proms 1993; Prof. of Baroque Violin, Koninklijk Conservatorium, The Hague; soloist and concertmaster with period-instrument orchestras, including The Acad. of Ancient Music, Amsterdam Baroque Orchestra, Orchestra of the Age of Enlightenment and the Hanover Band; currently Dir The Avison Ensemble. *Recordings include:* Bach Brandenburg Concertos with the New London Consort, Vivaldi's Op. 6 Concertos with Academy of Ancient Music, Schubert Octet with Hausmusik, Biber's Rosary Sonatas. *Address:* The Avison Ensemble, 3 Bentinck Place, Newcastle-upon-Tyne, NE4 6XN, England (office). *Telephone:* (191) 226-0799 (office). *Website:* www.avisonensemble.com (office).

BEZUIDENHOUT, Kristian; South African pianist, fortepianist and harpsichordist; b. 1979. *Education:* studied at Eastman School of Music, Rochester, NY with Rebecca Penneys, Malcolm Bilson and Paul O'Dette. *Career:* moved with family from South Africa to Queensland, Australia 1988; gained int. recognition at age 21 after winning first prize and also audience prize, Bruges Fortepiano Competition 2001; frequent guest artist with several ensembles including Freiburg Baroque Orchestra, Orchestra of the 18th Century, Concerto Köln, Chamber Orchestra of Europe, Collegium Vocale Ghent, Handel and Haydn Soc.; has performed with artists such as Frans Brüggen, Pieter Wispelwey, Daniel Hope, Viktoria Mullova and Christopher Hogwood; regular Lied recitals with Carolyn Sampson, Mark Padmore and Jan Kobow; performs regularly with baroque violinist Petra Müllejans; appearances at early music festivals of Barcelona, Boston, Bruges, Innsbruck, St Petersburg, Venice and Utrecht, Saintes Festival, La Roque d'Anthéron, Chopin Festival Warsaw, Musikfest Bremen, Tanglewood Festival, Mostly Mozart Lincoln Center. *Recordings include:* Schubert Die schöne Müllerin 2005, Mozart: Sonatas for Fortepiano and Violin 2009, Mozart Complete Keyboard Music Vol. I (Diapason Découverte Award, Caecilia Prize) 2010, Vol. II 2011, Schumann Dichterliebe (with Mark Padmore) (Edison Award) 2010, Beethoven Violin Sonatas (with Viktoria Mullova) (Int. Classical Music Award for Best Chamber Music Recording 2011) 2010, Mozart Sturm und Drang 2011, Mozart: Keyboard Music, Vol. 7 2015. *Honours:* Erwin Bodky Prize 2007. *Current Management:* Interartists Management Klinkhamer van der Vliet, Willemsparkweg 114, 1071 HN Amsterdam, Netherlands. *Telephone:* (20) 6754061. *Fax:* (20) 6754771. *E-mail:* stephan.brekelmans@ky-artists.nl. *Website:* kristianbezuidenhout.com.

BEZUYEN, Arnold; Dutch singer (tenor); b. 1965. *Education:* Int. Opera Centrum Nederland, Alkmaar. *Career:* debut as Rodolfo in La Bohème, at Alkmaar; sang at Augsburg and Bremen as Turiddu, Pinkerton, Alfredo in La Traviata, Ismael in Nabucco and Aegisthus in Elektra; Bayreuth Festival as Loge, and in Parsifal and Lohengrin; La Scala Milan in Die Frau ohne Schatten, under Giuseppe Sinopoli; season 2001–02 as the Berlioz Faust at Bremen, Shuisky in Boris Godunov at Kassel, Wagner's Vogelgesang for Netherlands Opera and Beethoven's Florestan for Nationale Reisopera; other roles include Cassio in Otello, Idomeneo and Don José. *Recordings include:* Das Rheingold, conducted by Gustav Kuhn (Arte Nova). *Address:* Bel Canto Global Arts, 3808 Riverside Drive, NE, Cedar Rapids, IA 52411, USA. *Website:* www.arnoldbezuyen.com.

BEZZUBENKOV, Gennady; Russian singer (bass); b. 1955, St Petersburg. *Education:* St Petersburg Conservatoire. *Career:* appearances in opera throughout Russia; Kirov Opera from 1989; roles have included Glinka's Ivan Susannin, Khan Konchak in Prince Igor, Gremin in Eugene Onegin, Pimen, Varlaam and Ivan Khovansky; further engagements as Wagner's Gurnemanz and King Henry, Verdi's Grand Inquisitor and Mozart's Bartolo, and in London concert performances of The Legend of the Invisible City of Kitezh (Barbican Hall, 1994), Katerina Izmailova by Shostakovich and Parsifal (Royal Albert Hall, 1999); sang Kutuzov in War and Peace and Dosifei in Khovanshchina with the Kirov Opera at Covent Garden, 2000; Sang Banquo at St Petersburg and the premiere of Gubaidulina's St John Passion, at Stuttgart, 2000; St John Passion at the London Proms, 2002. *Recordings include:* War and Peace, The Gambler, The Maid of Pskov, Sadko and Ruslan and Lyudmilla.

BIANCONI, Lorenzo Gennaro, PhD; Swiss/Italian musicologist and academic; *Professor of Musical Dramaturgy, University of Bologna*; b. 14 Jan. 1946, Muralto, Switzerland; m. Giuseppina La Face 1979; two s. *Education:* Univ. of Heidelberg, Germany, studied music theory with Luciano Sgrizzi in Lugano, Switzerland. *Career:* collaborator, Répertoire International des Sources Musicales, Italy 1969–70; mem., German Inst., Venice 1974–76; Guest Asst, German Historical Inst., Rome 1976; Guest Prof., Princeton Univ., USA 1977; Prof. of Musical Dramaturgy, Univ. of Bologna, Italy 1977–; Prof. of the History of Music, Siena Univ., Arezzo, Italy 1980–83; Co-Ed., Rivista Italiana di Musicologia 1973–79; Ed., Acta Musicologica 1987–91; Head of Programme Cttee, 14th Int. Musicological Congress, Bologna 1987; Co-Ed., Musica e Storia 1993–; Co-Ed., Il Saggiatore Musicale 1994–; Ed., Historiae Musicae Cultores 1999–; Head of Music Dept, Bologna Univ., Italy 1998–2001; coordinated School of Specialization for Secondary education, music education classes 2006–09; Hon. mem. Accademia Filarmonica, Bologna 2001; corresponding mem., American Musicological Soc. 1995, Acad. of Sciences of Turin 2006. *Publications include:* B. Marcello, Sonates pour clavecin (ed. with Luciano Sgrizzi) 1971, P. M. Marsolo, Madrigali a 4 voci (1614) 1973, A Il Verso, Madrigali a tre e a cinque voci (1605–19) 1978, Il Seicento 1982, La Drammaturgia Musicale 1986, Storia dell'Opera Italiana 1987, I Libretti Italiani di G. F. Händel (with G. La Face) 1992, Il Teatro d'Opera in Italia 1993, G. Frescobaldi, Madrigali a cinque voci (with M. Privitera) 1996, Opera Production and Its Resources (co-ed.) 1998, Opera on Stage (co-ed.) 2002, Opera in Theory and Practice, Image and Myth (co-ed.) 2003, Guida al percorso museale (Museo della Musica, Bologna) 2004. *Honours:* Dent Medal of the Royal Musical Assen 1983, Premio Imola per la Critica 1994. *Address:* Dipartimento di Musica e Spettacolo, Università di Bologna, via Barberia 4/2, 40123, Bologna (office); via A. Frank 17, 40068 San Lazzaro di Savena, Bologna, Italy (home). *Telephone:* (20) 92000 (office). *E-mail:* lorenzo.bianconi@unibo.it (office). *Website:* www.unibo.it/docenti/lorenzo.bianconi (office).

BIANCONI, Philippe; French pianist; b. 1960. *Career:* numerous appearances world-wide in concerto repertory and recitals; Carnegie Hall debut recital 1987; engagements with orchestras of Cleveland, Chicago, Los Angeles, Baltimore, Pittsburgh, Atlanta and Montréal; BBC London Proms debut with Orchestre de Paris and Semyon Bychkov; other orchestras include Orchestre Nat. de France, Orchestre de l'Opéra de Paris, Rundfunk Sinfonieorchester Berlin, Orchestre de Monte Carlo, Orchestre du Capitole de Toulouse, Nederlands Philharmonic, Warsaw Philharmonic; conductors include Lorin Maazel, Georges Prêtre, Kurt Masur, Christoph von Dohnányi, James Conlon, Tugan Sokhiev, Edo de Waart; European recitals in London, Berlin, Paris, Vienna, Milan, Amsterdam and Hamburg; recitals in Japan, China, Australia; chamber concerts with Sine Nomine Quartet, Guarneri String Quartet, Janos Starker, Gary Hoffman, Tedi Papavrami, Xavier Phillips, Hermann Prey, Dame Felicity Lott; season 2010–11 with concerts in Australia, USA, Germany, France; recital debut in Théâtre des Champs-Elysées, Paris. *Recordings include:* Ravel, Schubert, Schumann and Debussy solo albums, Brahms Piano Quintet, Brahms Piano and Violin sonatas, Shostakovich and

Prokofiev Cello and Piano Sonatas, Chausson chamber music, Schubert song cycles with Hermann Prey. *Honours:* First Prize, Robert Casadesus Int. Competition, Cleveland, USA, Silver Medal, Van Cliburn Int. Competition. *Current Management:* c/o CAMI, 1790 Broadway, New York, NY 10019-1412, USA. *Telephone:* (212) 841-9568.

BIBBY, Gillian; New Zealand composer; b. 31 Aug. 1945, Lower Hutt. *Education:* Univ. of Otago, Victoria Univ. with Douglas Lilburn, studied in Berlin and Cologne with Aloys Kontarsky, Kagel and Stockhausen. *Career:* teacher in New Zealand; Ed., Canzona 1982–84. *Compositions include:* Lest You Be My Enemy (ballet) 1976, Synthesis for tape 1977, In Memoriam for eight voices, organ and percussion 1979, Marama Music (music theatre) 1978, 11 Characters in Search of a Composer for military band and percussion.

BICCIRÈ, Patrizia; Italian singer (soprano); b. 1973, Porto San Giorgio. *Education:* Conservatorio Rossini and Accademia Rossiniana in Pesaro. *Career:* debut at Rossini Festival at Pesaro 1992, as Protagonist in La Scala di Seta; many appearances throughout Italy in bel canto and Mozart repertory; Glyndebourne Festival debut 2000, as Elvira in Don Giovanni; season 2000–01 as Nannetta in Falstaff at La Monnaie, Brussels, and Susanna in Le nozze di Figaro at Glyndebourne; Il turco in Italia at Grand Théâtre, Geneva. *Current Management:* IMG Artists, 31–33 rue du Temple, 75004 Paris, France. *Telephone:* 1-44-31-00-10. *Fax:* 1-44-31-44-40. *E-mail:* pwiggins@imgartists.com. *Website:* www.imgartists.com.

BICKERSTAFF, Robert; Australian singer (baritone) and voice teacher; b. 26 July 1932, Sydney; m. Ann Howard. *Education:* New South Wales Conservatorium with Lyndon Jones, Melbourne Conservatorium with Henry Portnoj, Paris with Dominique Modesti. *Career:* debut, Marseilles 1962, as Thoas in Iphigénie en Tauride; sang in Nice, Bordeaux and Marseille; Principal Baritone Sadler's Wells and English National Opera, 1964–70; roles included: Amonasro, Escamillo, Macbeth, Boccanegra, Scarpia, Wotan, Mozart's Count and Eugene Onegin; guest appearances with Pittsburgh Opera, Welsh National Opera and at Covent Garden; over 60 roles in Opera; other roles included Wagner's Dutchman, Ezio in Attila, Luna, Renato in Un Ballo in Maschera, Enrico in Lucia di Lammermoor and Massenet's Hérode; Boris in Lady Macbeth of Mtsensk by Shostakovich, Adelaide Festival; Oratorio and recital performances; appearances on BBC radio and television; previously Professor of Singing at the Royal Academy of Music, London and Singing Tutor at King's College, Cambridge. *Recordings:* La Juive, Raritas; Private Collection; Society of Musicians, London. *Honours:* Hon. ARAM. *Address:* 8 William Street, North Sydney 2060, Australia.

BICKET, Harry; British conductor and harpsichordist; *Artistic Director, The English Concert*; b. 1961, Liverpool. *Education:* Royal Coll. of Music, London, Univ. of Oxford. *Career:* especially noted for interpretations of Baroque and classical repertoire; Glyndebourne Festival debut with Peter Sellars' Theodora 1996, returned in 1999 and 2003; began relationship with Metropolitan Opera in 2004 (Rodelinda), later Cesare 2006/07, Clemenza di Tito 2008; debuts with Lyric Opera of Chicago conducting Partenope 2003, Royal Opera House, Covent Garden conducting Handel's Orlando 2003; debut at Bayerische Staatsoper in 2000 (Rinaldo), later Ariodante, Serse, Orlando, Orfee, Barbiere, Entführung and Zauberflöte, Liceu (Giulio Cesare; Opera Critics Prize for Best Conductor), returned for Midsummer Night's Dream 2005, Ariodante 2006 and L'Arbore di Diana 2009; opera has included Santa Fe Opera (Platée, Radamisto), Minnesota Opera (Croesus), Theater an der Wien (Mitridate); other recent performances include Messiah and Missa Solemnis with Minnesota Orchestra, Messiah with the New York Philharmonic and debuts with the Israel Philharmonic, Boston Symphony Orchestra and Royal Stockholm Philharmonic; staged opera has included Opera Australia (Giulio Cesare), Scottish Opera (Gluck's Orfeo), New York City Opera (Figaro, Entführung, Clemenza, Rinaldo), Royal Danish Opera (Gluck's Orfeo), Glimmerglass (Partenope, Agrippina), New Israeli Opera (Poppea), Aldeburgh Festival (Purcell's Faerie Queen), Edinburgh Festival (Clemenza), Spoleto Festival (Giasone, Tamerlano, L'ile de Merlin), ENO (Orfeo, Ariodante, Semele, Xerxes, Combattimento), Welsh Nat. Opera (Clemenza di Tito), Opera North (Radamisto, Return of Ulysses, Magic Flute, Croesus), Los Angeles Opera (Cesare, Poppea), Canadian Opera (Rodelinda, Idomeneo); symphonic guest conducting has included San Francisco Symphony, Bayerische Rundfunk, Detroit Symphony, BBC Scottish Symphony Orchestra, Orchestre Philharmonique de Monte Carlo, Houston, Symphony, Seattle Symphony, St Paul Chamber Orchestra, NACO Ottawa, Scottish Chamber Orchestra and Indianapolis Symphony, Orchestra of the Age of Enlightenment and the Handel and Haydn Soc., festivals including Glimmerglass, Spoleto, Aspen, Tanglewood and Santa Fe; recent highlights include Los Angeles Philharmonic, Japanese debut with Tokyo Symphony Orchestra, productions for Liceu Barcelona (L'Arbore di Diana), Theater an der Wien (Iphigenie en Tauride), Atlanta Opera (Orfeo), Canadian Opera Co. (Idomeneo); concerts and tours with The English Concert (BBC Proms, Spain, Middle East, Austria, Germany, USA), returns to Royal Liverpool Philharmonic Orchestra (including world premiere of Ken Hesketh's oratorio Like the sea, like time), Rotterdam Philharmonic (St Matthew Passion), Royal Stockholm Philharmonic Orchestra and Los Angeles Chamber Orchestra; season 2010–11 included Chicago Symphony, Los Angeles and St Paul Chamber Orchestras and opera productions for Chicago Lyric (Hercules), Minnesota (Orfeo), Canadian Opera (Orfeo); Artistic Dir The English Concert 2007–. *Television includes:* My Night with Handel (Channel 4) 1996. *Recordings:* Susan Graham and Orchestra of the Age of Enlightenment (OAE), David Daniels and OAE, Ian Bostridge and OAE, Sarah Connolly and Rosemary Joshua and The English Concert. *Address:* The English Concert, 8 St George's Terrace, London, NW1 8XJ, England (office). *Telephone:* (20) 7911-0905 (office). *Fax:* (20) 7911-0904 (office). *E-mail:* ec@englishconcert.co.uk (office). *Website:* www.englishconcert.co.uk (office).

BICKLEY, Susan; British singer (mezzo-soprano); b. 27 May 1955, Liverpool, England. *Education:* City University, London and the Guildhall School of Music. *Career:* debut as Proserpina in Monteverdi's Orfeo, at Florence; opera roles include Baba the Turk and Ulrica for Opera 80, Mozart's Marcellina and Elvira, Janáček's Kabanicha and Kostelnicka for the Glyndebourne Tour, Britten's Florence Pike, Hippolyta and Mrs Sedley at the Glyndebourne Festival, Dorabella and Andromache in King Priam for English National Opera, Feodor in Boris Godunov at Covent Garden; further engagements as Kabanicha and a Flowermaiden at the Opéra Bastille, Octavian at the Hong Kong Festival and Herodias in Salome at San Francisco; Concerts include Ligeti's Requiem at the Salzburg Festival and the Missa Solemnis on tour with Les Arts Florissants to Vienna and in France, El Amor Brujo in Rome and Stravinsky's Faun and Shepherdess in Hong Kong; further concerts with the London Symphony, Philharmonia, London Philharmonic Orchestra, London Sinfonietta, London Classical Players and Allegri and Brodsky Quartets, Messiah with the Hallé Orchestra, Stravinsky with the BBC Symphony Orchestra and Das Lied von der Erde with the BBC National Orchestra of Wales; performed in UK premiere of Henze's The Prince of Homburg 1996; Handel's Admeto at Beaune, 1998; sang in the premiere of Louis Andriessen's Writing to Vermeer, Amsterdam 1999; performed the Ghost in the premiere production of Birtwistle's The Last Supper, Berlin Staatsoper and Glyndebourne Touring Opera and the premiere of David Sawer's From Morning to Midnight, for ENO; London Proms 2002. *Recordings include:* Socrate by Satie, Monteverdi's Il Ballo delle Ingrate, Dido and Aeneas, The Fairy Queen. *Honours:* Royal Philharmonic Soc. Singer Award 2011. *Current Management:* Intermusica Artists Management Ltd, 36 Graham Street, Crystal Wharf, London N1 8GJ, England. *Telephone:* (20) 7608-9900. *Fax:* (20) 7490-3263. *E-mail:* mail@intermusica.co.uk. *Website:* www.intermusica.co.uk.

BIDDINGTON, Eric Wilhelm, BA, BSc, BMus, MusB (Hons); New Zealand composer; b. 19 Oct. 1953, Timaru; m. Elizabeth Ann Biddington 1989. *Education:* Univ. of Canterbury, Christchurch. *Career:* debut, Christchurch Arts Centre, Christchurch; major recitals of chamber music, Christchurch 1985–97, Lower Hutt 1988, Hamilton 1989; premiere performance of Concerto for Two Violins and String Orchestra at Tempe, Arizona, USA 1989. *Compositions include:* mainly chamber music and some orchestral works, including Suite for Violin and Piano 1985, Three Pieces for Cello and Piano 1986, Scherzetto for Clarinet and Piano 1986, Autumn Music for Viola and Piano 1987, Flute Concerto 1987, Music for Friends for piano trio 1988, Suite for Oboe and Piano 1989, Two Dances for Alto Saxophone and Piano 1989, Four Piano Preludes 1990, Three Bagatelles for Flute and Piano 1990, Haere Ra, A Song for 2-part Treble Voices and Piano, Flute Concerto 1991, Introduction for Clarinet and Piano 1993, Concertos for Oboe, Alto Saxophone, Two Violins, Flute (2), Viola and Clarinet, Overtures, Suites for String Orchestra (3), Concerto Movements, Sonatinas for Violin and Pianoforte, Tenor Saxophone and Piano, Oboe and Piano, Clarinet and Piano, Treble Recorder and Piano, Flute and Piano, and Trumpet and Piano; Beauty and The Beast, ballet 1994, Divertimento for Orchestra 1996. *Recordings include:* 18 DVDs of music recorded, some also featuring spoken voice text, The Chamber Music of Eric Biddington, Music for Friends, Southern Melodies, Tunes and Airs, Flute Concerto and Chamber Music, Concerto Movements and Music for Strings, Concertos for Flute, Oboe, Clarinet and Viola. *Publications include:* 70 publs of chamber music, 10 with Nota Bene Music, 60 others, Pastorale for Clarinet and Piano 1994, Introduction and Allegro for Alto Saxophone and Piano 1994, Two Amourettes for Oboe and Piano 1995. *Honours:* Award, Composers Asscn of New Zealand Trust Fund 1989. *E-mail:* ebiddington@actrix.co.nz.

BIEITO, Calixto; Spanish opera and theatre director; b. 2 Nov. 1963, Miranda de Ebro, Burgos; m. Roser Camí; two s. *Career:* noted for his controversial interpretations of classic works; Artistic Dir Teatre Romea, Barcelona 1999–2011; with Companyia Teatre Romea: Life is a Dream, Barbican Centre, London 1999, Brooklyn Acad. of Music, New York 1999, Barbaric Comedies, Edinburgh 2000, La Vida es Sueño, Teatre Romea, Barcelona 2000, Teatro de la Comedia, Compañía Nacional de Teatro Clásico, Madrid, on tour in Spain, El Rei Lear, Teatre Romea – Festival d'Estiu de Barcelona Grec 2004, Macbeth, Int. Festival, Edinburgh 2001, La Ópera de Cuatro Cuartos, Barcelona 2002, Bobigny, Paris 2003, Le Maillon, Strasbourg, Ruhr Festspiele Recklinghausen, Germany 2004, Peer Gynt, Bergen Festival 2006, Festival Internacional de las Artes de Castilla y León, Salamanca, Festival Grec, Barcelona, Festival Ibsen, Oslo, Festival de Otoño, Madrid, Festival Temporada Alta, Girona, Atrium Viladecans, Barcelona 2006, Plataforma, Edinburgh 2006, Festival of Brescia, Festival of Helsinki 2007, Tirant lo Blanc, HAU, Berlin 2007, Festival Internacional Cervantino, Guanajuato, Mexico 2008, Don Carlos, Festival internacional de las Artes de Castilla y León, Salamanca, Nationaltheater, Mannheim, Estivales, Festival Perpignan, GREC '09 Festival of Barcelona, Centro Dramático Nacional, Madrid 2009; other works include Hamlet, Edinburgh 2003, Dublin Theatre Festival 2005, La Celestina, Edinburgh Int. Festival 2004, Brand, Festival Int. of Bergen, Nat. Theatre of Oslo, Festival Ibsen, Oslo 2008, Iceberg, Sinfonia Poètica Visual, EXPO, Zaragoza 2008, Lulu, Nationaltheater of

Mannheim 2009; opera productions directed include: La Verbena de la Paloma (Zarzuela), Edinburgh Festival 1997, Pierrot Lunaire, Barcelona 1998, Il Mondo Della Luna, Maastricht 1999, Carmen, Festival Peralada 1999, Così fan tutte, Welsh Nat. Opera 2000, Un Ballo in Maschera, Barcelona 2001, ENO 2002, Don Giovanni, ENO 2001, 2004, Die Fledermaus and La Bohème, Welsh Nat. Opera 2002, The Abduction from the Seraglio, Komische Oper, Berlin 2003, Il Trovatore, Staatsoper Hannover and Edin. Festival 2004, Carmen, Flemish Opera, Antwerp and Ghent 2004, Madame Butterfly, Berlin 2005, Wozzeck, Barcelona 2005, The Rake's Progress, Teatro Comunale, Bologna, Mozart Festival, A Coruña 2006, La forza del destino, ENO 2015; invited lectures and courses in schools and univs in UK, Germany and Spain; invited by RSC, with mems of Companyia Romea, to participate in 440th anniversary celebrations of Shakespeare's birth 2004; taught course in corporal dramaturgy at Universität der Künste, Berlin 2005, 2007; Guest Dir Norwegian Nat. Opera 2015; Dir Theater Basel. *Honours:* Premio Ercilla, Soc. of Spanish Stage Dirs (for Life is a Dream) 2000, Best Dir Award, Irish Times-ESB Theatre Awards (for Barbaric Comedies, Edinburgh Festival) 2000, Glasgow Herald Archangel Award to Best Artist of Edinburgh Festival (for Hamlet, performed by ensemble of Birmingham Repertory Theatre) 2003, Best Dir Award, Theatre Critics of Barcelona (for Plataforma) 2007, Butaca Award for Best Play and Best Dir 2007, included by Opernwelt magazine in list of most important artists 2007, Tendencies Award, El Mundo newspaper 2008, co-recipient (with Marc Rosich) Award for Best Stage Adaptation of the Theatre Critics in Barcelona (for dramaturgy of novel Tirant lo Blanc) 2009, European Culture Award, European Cultural Foundation Pro Europa 2009. *E-mail:* calixto@calixtobieito.com (office). *Website:* www.calixtobieito.com (office).

BIEL, Ann-Christin; Swedish singer (soprano); b. 1958. *Education:* Royal Music Academy, Stockholm with Birgit Sternberg, studied with Daniel Ferro in New York. *Career:* debut at Drottningholm 1981, as Cherubino; has appeared at the Summer festival at Drottningholm, Stockholm, as Pamina 1982, 1989; Fiordiligi, 1984–85; Ilia, 1986, 1991; Susanna 1987; Serpetta in La Finta Giardiniera, 1988, 1990; Royal Opera Stockholm 1985, L'arbore di Diana by Martín y Soler; 1986 as Oscar in Un Ballo in Maschera; Sang Konstanze in the Berne, 1986, world premiere of Armin Schibler's Mozart und der graue Bote, Mozart's last days; Toured as Micaela in the Peter Brook version of Carmen, Paris, Hamburg, New York and Tokyo, 1982–86; Théâtre des Champs-Elysées, Paris 1986, as Barbarina in Le nozze di Figaro; Sang Julie in the world premiere of Miss Julie at Stockholm 1990; (music by Margareta Hallin, the part of Julie written for Ms Biel); Sang Gluck's Orpheus at Drottningholm, 1992; Concert appearances in Stockholm, New York, Paris, Amsterdam, Parma, Verona, Milan and Copenhagen; repertoire includes Bach's Passions, Die Schöpfung, Mozart's Vespers and Requiem, Monteverdi's Vespers and Ein Deutsches Requiem. *Recordings:* videos of Mozart operas from Drottningholm, directed by Goran Järvefelt, conducted by Arnold Östman.

BIERHANZL, Petr; Czech classical guitarist; b. 27 July 1952, Prague, Czechoslovakia (now Czech Repub.); m. Jana Bierhanzlova 1977; one s. *Education:* Conservatory of Prague. *Career:* debut in Prague 1975; mem. guitar duo with Jana Bierhanzlova; performances in Czech Repub. 1975–97, Poland 1986, 1990, 1994, Germany 1995, 1997, 1998, Lithuania 1997, Lithuania 2001, Spain 2002; repertoire includes John Dowland's Lachrimae Pavan, Welcome Home, A Michna's Czech Lute, J. S. Bach's Preludes and Fugues, Scarlatti's Sonata K 380, Vivaldi's Concerto Op. 3 No. 6, Soler's Sonatas, Mozart's Divertimento KV 439b, F. Sor's L'Encouragement Op. 34, F. Carulli's Duo Op. 34 No. 2, E. Granados' Danzas Espanolas, I. Albeniz's Granada, Sevilla, Dvořák's Sonatina Op. 100; Prof., Jezek Conservatory of Prague 1980–. *Radio:* Poland 1990, Czech Repub. 1992, 1993, 1995, 1996, 1997. *Television:* German TV 1978, Czech TV 1992, 1993, 1994, 1996, 1997. *Recordings:* The European Guitar Duets (Czech Guitar Duo), Scarlatti, Carulli, Sor and Truhlar (the first Czech recording of a guitar duo) 1992, English Renaissance Music (Czech Guitar Duo), Dowland, Byrd, Johnson and Bull, Czech Guitar Duo Plays Flamenco 2001. *Address:* V Sareckem Udoli 2, 160 00 Prague 6, Czech Republic. *E-mail:* art-agency-sarka@quick.cz (office). *Website:* czech-guitar-duo.com (office).

BILGRAM, Hedwig; German organist and harpsichordist; b. 31 March 1933, Memmingen, Bavaria. *Education:* studied with Karl Richter and Friedrich Wührer. *Career:* apptd teacher, Munich Hochschule für Musik 1961, Prof. 1964–; mem. Berlin Haydn Ensemble 1990–; numerous performances under Karl Richter in Munich and elsewhere, in Baroque repertoire; has appeared with trumpeter Maurice André; premieres of works by André Jolivet, Henri Tomasi and Harald Genzmer. *Current Management:* c/o CCM Classic Concerts Management, Mühlenstrasse 22, 86842 Türkheim, Germany. *Telephone:* (8245) 960960. *Fax:* (8245) 960980. *E-mail:* info@ccm-international.de. *Website:* www.ccm-international.de.

BILIŃSKA, Jolanta, DipMus; Polish musicologist; b. 1 March 1951, Rzeszów. *Education:* Jagiellonian Univ., Kraków. *Career:* Sec., Warsaw Int. Festival of Contemporary Music 1979–95; Dir, Polish Radio Music Recording Dept. *Publications:* Opery Mozarta na scenach polskich w latach 1783–1830 (Mozart's Operas on Polish Stages from 1783–1830), Musikbibliothek und Musikleben am Hof der Fuerstin Izabella Lubomirska in Lancut 1791–1816, Musik des Ostens, Bd 11 1989, Recepcja dziel Mozarta w Polsce 1783–1830 (Reception of Mozart's Works in Poland 1783–1830) 1991; contrib. to Ruch Muzyczny (bi-weekly music magazine), Polish Music (quarterly).

BILLONE, Pierluigi; Italian composer; b. 1960. *Education:* studied composition with Salvatore Sciarrino and Helmut Lachenmann. *Career:* music has been performed by ensembles including Klangforum Wien, Ensemble Intercontemporain, Ensemble Modern, Ensemble Recherche, Instant Donné, Ensemble Contrechamps, Neue Vocalsolisten and bassoonist Lorelei Dowling, and at festivals including Donaueschinger Musiktage, Wien Modern, Wittener Tage für neue Kammermusik, Ars Musica Brussels and Festival d'Automne, Paris; commissions from Südwestrundfunk, Westdeutschen Rundfunk and other ensembles; regular broadcasts; Visiting Prof. of Composition, Musikhochschule Graz 2006–08, 2010–12 and Frankfurt 2009; lectured in composition at Darmstadt summer courses, Impuls Akad. Graz, Tzlil Meducan Israel, MCME Int. Acad., Russia, IEMA/Ensemble Modern Acad., Univ. of the Arts, Vienna, and Harvard and Columbia Univs, USA. *Compositions include:* APSU for voices and ensemble 1990, AN NA for ensemble 1992, Ke.an-Cerchio for low voice 1995, Scrittura Cammino for 36 voices and 5 instruments 1998, Mani Giacometti for violin, viola and cello 2000, Legno Inutile, study for ensemble 2002, Studi da concerto for bassoon 2003, Mani de Leonardis for 4 automobile springs and glass 2004, PA for oboe and 5 instruments 2005, TA for ensemble 2005, Mani Mono for spring drum 2007, Bocca Kosmoi for voice, trombone and orchestra 2007, Due Frammenti for voice and accordion 2009, Phonogliphi for voice, bassoon and orchestra 2011, Quattro alberi for voice, bassoon, accordion and percussion 2011. *Recordings include:* Mani Long 2003, Me A An – Iti Ke Mi 2005, 1+1=1 2006, Mani Percussion Solos 2010; works included on recordings of soloists and ensembles. *Honours:* Busoni Composition Prize, Berlin Acad. of the Arts 1996, Vienna Int. Composition Prize 2004, Ernst Krenek Prize, Vienna 2006, Ernst von Siemens Foundation Composers Award 2010. *E-mail:* pierluigibillone@libero.it (office). *Website:* www.pierluigibillone.com (office).

BILSON, Malcolm, BA, DMA; American pianist; b. 24 Oct. 1935, Los Angeles, CA; m. Elizabeth Jármay 1961; two d. *Education:* Bard Coll., Vienna State Acad., Reifezeugnis, Ecole Normale de Musique, Paris, Univ. of Illinois. *Career:* Asst Prof., Cornell Univ. 1968, Assoc. Prof. 1970, Prof. 1975, Frederick J. Whiton Prof. of Music 1990; specializes in repertoire of Viennese Classical School on period fortepianos; toured extensively in North America, Europe, the Far East and Oceania as soloist, chamber musician and soloist with orchestras, including the English Baroque Soloists, the Acad. of Ancient Music, Tafelmusik, Concerto Köln, Philharmonia Baroque and numerous modern-instrument orchestras; workshops and masterclasses worldwide, including the Sibelius Acad., Helsinki, Liszt Acad., Budapest, Kunitachi Coll., Tokyo, Griffith Conservatory, Brisbane, Jerusalem Music Centre, Scottish Acad. of Music and Dance, Glasgow, Royal Coll. of Music, London; Adjunct Prof., Eastman School of Music 1992–; mem. American Acad. of Arts and Sciences. *Recordings:* Complete Mozart Concertos for fortepiano and orchestra, with John Eliot Gardiner and the English Baroque Soloists; complete Mozart piano-violin sonatas with Sergui Luca; complete Mozart solo piano Sonatas; complete Beethoven piano sonatas (with other players), Claves; complete Beethoven cello-piano sonatas with Anner Bijlsma; complete Schubert piano sonatas (including unfinished works); Schubert 4-hand piano works with Robert Levin. *Honours:* Dr hc (Bard Coll.) 1991. *Current Management:* c/o Grant Rogers Musical Artists' Management, 8 Wren Crescent, Bushey Heath, Hertfordshire, WD23 1AN, England. *Telephone:* (20) 8950-2220. *Fax:* (20) 8950-3570. *E-mail:* info@ngrartists.com. *Website:* www.ngrartists.com. *Address:* c/o Department of Music, Lincoln Hall, Cornell University, Ithaca, NY 14853, USA.

BINGHAM, Judith, FRNCM, ARAM, FRSCM; British singer (contralto) and composer; b. 21 June 1952, Nottingham, England; m. Andrew Petrow 1985. *Education:* Royal Acad. of Music, London, studied with Hans Keller, Alan Bush and Eric Fenby. *Career:* mem. BBC Singers 1983–95, Assoc. Composer 2004–09; mem. Incorporated Soc. of Musicians. *Compositions:* Cocaine Lil for soprano and piano 1975, A Divine Image for harpsichord 1976, Chopin for piano 1979, A Falling Figure for baritone, clarinet, piano 1979, Mercutio for baritone, piano 1980, Iago for bass-baritone, piano 1980, Clouded Windows for mezzo, piano 1980, The Ruin 1981, A Midsummer Night's Dream for mezzo, piano 1981, Into the Wilderness for organ 1982, Pictured Within for piano 1982, Ferrara for tenor, piano 1982, A Hymn Before Sunrise in the Vale of Chamounix for 24 singers 1982, Cradle Song of the Blessed Virgin 1983, Mass Setting, Sterna Paradisaea for singers and organ 1984, A Winter Walk at Noon for 27 solo voices 1984, Just Before Dawn 1986, Chartres for orchestra 1987, Dove Cottage by Moonlight for two pianos 1989, The Ghost of Combermere Abbey for chorus 1993, Beyond Redemption for orchestra 1995, The Temple at Karnak for orchestra 1996, The Mysteries of Adad (children's theatre) 1996, The American Icons for wind band 1997, The Snow Descends for brass ensemble, Passaggio concerto for bassoon 1998, The Shooting Star concerto for trumpet 1999, Walzerspiele for orchestra 1999, Water Lilies for chorus 1999, Shelley Dreams for violin and piano 1999, The Christmas Truce (British Composer Award for choral work) 2004, Missa brevis: The Road to Emmaeus (British Composer Award for liturgical work) 2004, Down and Out 2004, Edington Canticles 2005, A Formal Order 2005, Ghost Towns of the American West 2005, The Shepheardes Calender 2006, Fanfare Ziggurat 2007, Shakespeare Requiem 2008, The Lost Works of Paganini 2005–08, Actaeon, his strange new face 2009, Annunciation II 2009, Distant Thunder 2010, The Life and Opinions of Tomkat Murr 2010, The Wells Service 2010, The Pilgrimes Travels 2010, A Bird is Singing 2010, Annunciation III 2010, Now the Magi Arrive 2010, Holy of Holies 2010, Corpus Christi Carol 2010, The Everlasting Crown 2010, Ave Virgo Sanctissima 2011, Eden 2011.

Honours: Prin.'s Prize for Composition 1971, BBC Young Composer 1976, British Composer Award 2004 (twice), 2006, 2008, Barlow Prize (USA) 2005. *Address:* c/o Peters Edition Ltd, 2–6 Baches Street, London, N1 6DN, England (office). *Telephone:* (20) 7553-4000 (office). *E-mail:* newmusic@editionpeters.com (office). *Website:* www.editionpeters.com (office).

BINI, Carlo; Italian singer (tenor); b. 1947, Naples. *Education:* Naples Conservatory. *Career:* debut at Teatro San Carlo, Naples 1969, as Pinkerton; sang in Italy and at the Deutsche Oper Berlin; State Opera Houses of Munich and Stuttgart; Hamburg Staatsoper 1974, as Alfredo in La Traviata and Rodolfo; sang in Brussels, Paris, Marseille, Rio de Janeiro and New York City Opera; Metropolitan Opera 1982, as Enzo in La Gioconda; La Scala 1984, in I Lombardi; sang Arrigo in I Vespri siciliani at Santiago 1990; Avito in Montemezzi's L'amore dei tre re at Palermo 1990; other roles include Rodolfo in Luisa Miller, Don Carlos, Gabriele Adorno, Don José, Laca in Jenůfa and Tchaikovsky's Vakula. *Recordings:* Verdi Requiem, Eine Nacht in Venedig, I Lombardi (video).

BINNS, Malcolm, ARCM; British pianist; b. 29 Jan. 1936, Nottingham; s. of Douglas Priestley Binns and May Walker. *Education:* Bradford Grammar School, Royal Coll. of Music. *Career:* soloist with numerous leading orchestras and conductors around the world (including Boulez, Boult, Dorati, Haitink and Rattle) 1960–; toured with Scottish Nat. Orchestra and Limbourg Orchestra 1987–88; regular performer at Wigmore Hall 1958–, the Promenade Concerts 1962–; concerts at Aldeburgh, Leeds, Three Choirs and Canterbury Festivals; solo and concerto performances broadcast regularly on BBC. *Recordings:* more than 30 recordings, including piano sonatas by Bax, Ireland and Bridge for the British Music Soc. 2007, Balakirev Piano Concerti 1 and 2, Rimsky-Korsakov Piano Concerto (English Northern Philharmonia) 1992. *Honours:* Chappell Medal 1956, Medal of Worshipful Co. of Musicians 1956. *Current Management:* c/o Michael Harrold Artist Management, 13 Clinton Road, Leatherhead, Surrey, KT22 8NU, England. *Telephone:* (1372) 375728. *E-mail:* management@angelus.co.uk. *Website:* www.angelus.co.uk. *Address:* 233 Court Road, Orpington, Kent, BR6 9BY, England (home). *Telephone:* (1689) 831056 (home).

BIONDI, Fabio; Italian violinist and conductor; b. 15 March 1961, Palermo. *Education:* studied with Salvatore Cicero and Mauro lo Guercio. *Career:* concerto debut with Italian Radio Symphony Orchestra aged 12; formed Stendhal Quartet 1981; worked with Hesperion XX, Les Musiciens du Louvre, Musica Antiqua of Vienna, the Camerata di Lugano and the orchestra of the Due Dimensioni festival, Parma; founder ensemble, Europa Galante 1990; works as soloist and guest conductor with orchestras including the Santa Cecilia in Rome, Rotterdam Chamber Orchestra, the Opera of Hallé, Zurich Chamber Orchestra, Norwegian Chamber Orchestra, Orchestre Nationale de Montpellier, Orquesta Ciudad de Granada; Conductor, New York Collegium; directed European Union Baroque Orchestra 2002, Ensemble Orchestral de Paris; Artistic Dir of Baroque Music, Stavanger Symphony Orchestra, Mozarteum Orchestra, Salzburg, Orchestre de Berne, The English Concert. *Recordings include:* Italian Violin Sonatas (Veracini, Locatelli, Mascitti, Geminiani, Tartini), J. S. Bach Arias and Cantatas with Ian Bostridge, Vivaldi's L'Estro armonico, String Quintets by Boccherini, Vivaldi's violin concertos, Il cimento dell'armonia e dell'inventione (including The Four Seasons), Vivaldi Stabat mater, Scarlatti Concerti and Sinfonie, Vivaldi Bajazet (Midem Classical Music Award for Opera 2006). *Honours:* (with Europa Galante) Académie Charles Cros, Diapason d'Or de l'Année, Prix RTL and Grand Prix du Discophile. *Current Management:* c/o Satirino, 59 rue Orfila, 75020 Paris, France. *Telephone:* 9-77-19-80-77. *Fax:* 1-53-01-33-46. *E-mail:* ianmalkin@satirino.fr. *Website:* www.satirino.fr.

BIRET, Idil; Turkish pianist; b. 1941, Ankara; d. of Münir Biret and Leman Biret; m. Sefik Büyükyüksel 1976. *Education:* Paris Conservatoire. *Career:* debut 1957; has given concerts throughout the world with major orchestras including Boston Symphony Orchestra, St Petersburg Philharmonic, Leipzig Gewandhaus, London Symphony, Tokyo Philharmonic, Sydney Symphony, Dresden Staatskapelle; has performed with major conductors and at int. festivals including Montréal, Athens, Berlin, Dubrovnik (Croatia), Istanbul (performance with Yehudi Menuhin), others; mem. jury, Queen Elisabeth Competition, Belgium, Van Cliburn Competition, USA, Busoni, Italy; Lily Boulanger Memorial Fund, Boston 1954, 1964. *Recordings include:* over 100 recordings including Beethoven, Liszt, Brahms, Chopin, Rachmaninov, Boulez, Ligeti and Stravinsky. *Honours:* Chevalier, Ordre Nat. du Mérite 1976, Distinguished Service Order/Cavalry Cross (Poland) 2007; Harriet Cohen/Dinu Lipatti Gold Medal, London 1959, State Artist of Turkey 1973, Polish Award for Artistic Merit 1974, Grand Prix du Disque Chopin, Poland 1995, Diapason d'Or, France 1995. *Current Management:* c/o Anthony Purkiss, 35 Fonthill Road, Hove, E Sussex, BN3 6HB, England. *Telephone:* (1273) 774730. *E-mail:* tonypurkiss@talktalk.net. *Address:* 526 avenue Louise, 1050 Brussels, Belgium (home); 255 Moda cad, Kadiköy, Istanbul, Turkey (home). *Fax:* (2) 648-40-17 (Belgium) (home). *E-mail:* Sefik.Buyukyuksel.dc.67@aya.yale.edu (home). *Website:* www.idilbiret.eu.

BIRKELAND, Oystein; Norwegian cellist; b. 1958. *Education:* Norwegian State Acad. of Music, studied in Basel with Heinrich Schiff, in London with William Pleeth and Ralph Kirshbaum. *Career:* has worked with Frans Helmersson, Arto Noras, Erling Blondal Bengtsson and Jacqueline du Pré; mem., Norwegian Chamber Orchestra 1982–, Principal Cellist 1985–; performances as soloist in Norway, UK, Germany, Switzerland, in concertos by Haydn, Boccherini, Vivaldi and others; has played with Oslo Philharmonic, Trondheim Symphony Orchestra and Norwegian Radio Orchestra; debut with Acad. of St Martin-in-the-Fields, playing the Haydn Concerto in C major in Oslo, Helsinki and Stockholm; festival appearances include Bergen Int. Music Festival, Contemporary Music Festivals Platform, London, and Schleswig Holstein Music Festival; plays a cello by Francesco Ruggiere (Cremona 1680).

BIRKS, Ronald; British violinist; b. 1945, England. *Education:* Royal Manchester Coll. of Music with Béla Katona, Walter Jorysz and Alexander Moskovsky. *Career:* mem., Lindsay String Quartet, later The Lindsays 1971–2005; regular tours of Europe, the UK, USA; quartet-in-residence Univ. of Sheffield 1972–78, Univ. of Manchester 1978; premiered the 4th Quartet of Tippett at the Bath Festival 1979, commissioned Tippett's 5th Quartet 1992; Chamber Music Festival established at Sheffield 1984; resident ensemble Music in the Round Festival, Sheffield –2005; plays Campo Selice Stradivarius of 1694. *Recordings:* Complete Cycles of Bartók, Tippett and Beethoven quartets, Mozart Quintets, Haydn Quartets Live from the Wigmore Hall, Second Series of Beethoven Quartets, All Haydn Quartets from Op. 20 onwards. *Honours:* Dr hc (Univs of Keele, Manchester, Leicester, Sheffield (two) and Sheffield Hallam); Gramophone Chamber Award for late Beethoven quartets 1984, Classic FM Gramophone Special Achievement Award 2005.

BIRTWISTLE, Sir Harrison, Kt, CH; British composer; b. 15 July 1934, Accrington, Lancs.; m. Sheila Birtwistle 1958; three s. *Education:* Royal Manchester Coll. of Music and Royal Acad. of Music. *Career:* Dir of Music, Cranborne Chase School 1962–65; Visiting Fellow, Princeton Univ. (Harkness Int. Fellowship) 1966; Cornell Visiting Prof. of Music, Swarthmore Coll. 1973–74; Slee Visiting Prof., State Univ. of New York , Buffalo 1975; Assoc. Dir Nat. Theatre 1975–88; Composer-in-Residence, London Philharmonic Orchestra 1993–98; Henry Purcell Prof. of Composition, King's Coll., London 1994–2001; Visiting Prof., Univ. of Alabama at Tuscaloosa 2001–02; Dir of Contemporary Music, RAM 1996–2001; works have been widely performed at major festivals in Europe including Venice Biennale, Int. Soc. of Contemporary Music Festivals in Vienna and Copenhagen, Warsaw Autumn Festival and at Aldeburgh, Cheltenham and Edinburgh; co-f. (with Sir Peter Maxwell Davies) The Pierrot Players. *Operatic and dramatic works:* The Mark of the Goat (cantata) 1965, Punch and Judy (one-act opera) 1966, The Visions of Francesco Petrarca (sonnets for baritone and orchestra) 1966, Monodrama for soprano, speaker, ensemble 1967, Down by the Greenwood Side (dramatic pastoral) 1969, The Mask of Orpheus 1973, Ballet, Frames, Pulses and Interruptions 1977, Bow Down 1977, Yan Tan Tethera 1983, Gawain 1988, The Second Mrs Kong 1992, The Last Supper 1999. *Orchestral works:* Chorales for Orchestra 1962, Three Movements with Fanfares 1964, Nomos 1968, An Imaginary Landscape 1971, The Triumph of Time 1970, Grimethorpe Aria for Brass Band 1973, Melencolia I 1976, Silbury Air for small orchestra 1977, Still Movement for 13 solo strings 1984, Earth Dances 1985, Endless Parade for trumpet, vibraphone, strings 1987, Ritual Fragment 1990, Antiphonies for piano and orchestra 1992, The Cry of Anubis for tuba and orchestra 1994, Panic 1995, Night's Black Bird (British Composer Award, British Acad. of Composers and Songwriters 2005), Concerto for Violin and Orchestra (British Composer Award, British Acad. of Composers and Songwriters 2012) 2011. *Choral works and narration:* Monody for Corpus Christi for soprano and ensemble 1959, A Description of the Passing Year for chorus 1963, Entr'actes and Sappho Fragments for soprano and ensemble 1964, Carmen Paschale for chorus and organ 1965, Ring a Dumb Clarion for soprano, clarinet, percussion 1965, Cantata for soprano and ensemble 1969, Nenia on the Death of Orpheus for soprano and ensemble 1970, The Fields of Sorrow for two sopranos, chorus, ensemble 1971, Meridian for mezzo, chorus, ensemble 1970, Epilogue: Full Fathom Five for baritone and ensemble 1972, arrangement for 16 solo voices and three instruments 1979, On the Sheer Threshold of the Night for four solo voices and 12-part chorus 1980, White and Light for soprano and ensemble 1989, Four Poems by Jaan Kaplinski for soprano and ensemble 1991, The Woman and the Hare, for soprano, reciter and ensemble 1999, Ring Dance of the Nazarene (British Composer Award, British Acad. of Composers and Songwriters 2005). *Instrumental works:* Refrains and Choruses for wind quintet 1957, The World is Discovered for ensemble 1960, Tragoedia for ensemble 1965, Three Lessons in a Frame 1967, Chorales from a Toyshop 1967, Verses for Ensembles 1969, Ut heremita solus, arrangement of Ockeghem 1969, Hoquetus David, arr of Machaut 1969, Medusa for ensemble 1970, Chronometer for 8-track tape 1971, For O For O the Hobby Horse is Forgot for six percussion 1976, Carmen Arcadiae Mechanicae Perpetuum for ensemble 1977, Pulse Sampler 1980, Clarinet Quintet 1980, Secret Theatre 1984, Words Overheard 1985, Fanfare for Will 1987, Salford Toccata for brass band and bass drum 1988, Nine Movements for string quartet 1991, An Uninterrupted Endless Melody for oboe and piano 1991, Five Distances for five instruments 1992, Tenebrae for soprano and ensemble 1992, Night for soprano and ensemble 1992, Movement for string quartet 1992, Slow Frieze for piano and 13 instruments 1996, Pulse, Shadows 1997, Harrison's Clocks for piano 1998, The Silk House Tattoo for two trumpets and percussion 1998, Three Niedecker Verses for soprano and cello 1998, Exody 1998, The Axe Manual 2000, The Shadow of Night 2001, Theseus Game 2002, The Io Passion 2004, Night's Black Bird 2004, Orpheus Elegies 2004, The Tree of Strings (Royal Philharmonic Soc. Award for Best Chamber-Scale Composition 2009) 2007, The Minotaur 2008, Tree of Strings 2008, The Corridor 2009, Angel Fighter 2010, Piano Trio 2011, Oboe Quartet 2011. *Theatre:* music for Hamlet, Nat. Theatre 1975, The Oresteia, Nat. Theatre

1986, The Bacchae, Nat. Theatre 2002. *Honours:* Hon. FRNCM 1990; Chevalier, Ordre des Arts et des Lettres; Siemens Prize 1995, Grawemeyer Award, Univ. of Louisville 1987, Ivor Novello Award for Classical Music 2006. *Current Management:* Rayfield Allied, Southbank House, Black Prince Road, London, SE1 7SJ, England. *E-mail:* info@rayfieldallied.com. *Website:* www.rayfieldallied.com.

BISATT, Susan; British singer (soprano); b. 1963, England. *Career:* frequent festival engagements, including Almeida Contemporary Opera (Isabelle Rimbaud in The Man Who Strides the Wind by Kevin Volans) and Edinburgh (Salome in the opera by Strauss); roles with Opera Restor'd in Britain and abroad, in Dido and Aeneas, The Death of Dido (Pepusch) and Pyramus and Thisbe (Lampe); other appearances with Opera North (as Papagena) and elsewhere as Violetta, Donna Elvira, Lucia di Lammermoor, Gilda, Norina and the soprano leads in Les Contes d'Hoffmann; Gluck's Eurydice, Mozart's Countess, and Rosina; tours of the UK, Ireland and Finland with Opera Circus; opera workshops with Opera North, Compact Opera, Théâtre de Complicité and the David Glass Ensemble. *Television includes:* The Singing Voice (for Channel 4). *Recordings include:* English Baroque Opera, scenes from operas by Charles Dibdin, Purcell Songs.

BISCARDI, Chester, BA, MA, MM, MMA, DMA; American composer and teacher; *Director of Music Program, Sarah Lawrence College*; b. 19 Oct. 1948, Kenosha, Wis.; s. of Chester Biscardi and Anne Rose Rizzo. *Education:* Univ. of Wisconsin, Madison, Università di Bologna, Conservatorio di Musica G. B. Martini, Bologna, Yale Univ. School of Music. *Career:* teacher, Univ. of Wisconsin 1970–74, Yale Univ. 1975–76; teacher in Music Faculty, Sarah Lawrence Coll., Bronxville, NY 1977–, currently Dir of Music Program, also 1st William Schuman Chair in Music 1994–2007, Margot C. Bogert Distinguished Service Chair 2007–10; Visiting Artist, American Acad. in Rome 1987, Visiting Prof., Univ. of Michigan in Florence at Villa Corsi-Salviati 1987, 1994. *Compositions include:* Tartini (for violin and piano) 1972, Indovinello (for 12 voices) 1974, Heabakes: Five Sapphic Lyrics (for mixed chorus, two sopranos, alto and percussion) 1974, Tenzone (for two flutes and piano) 1975, They Had Ceased to Talk (for violin and viola, horn in F and piano) 1975, Trusting Lightness (for soprano and piano) 1975, Music for The Duchess of Malfi (for nine instrumentalists and voices) 1975, Trio 1976, At the Still Point 1977, Eurydice (for women's chorus and 17 instruments) 1978, Mestiere (for piano) 1979, Trasumanar (for 12 percussionists and piano) 1980, Di Vivere (for clarinet in A and piano with flute, violin and violoncello) 1981, Good-bye My Fancy! (for mixed chorus a cappella and narrator) 1982, Music for Witch Dance (for two percussionists) 1983, Piano Concerto 1983, Chez Vous (for voice and piano) 1983, revised 2007, Incitation to Desire (Tango) for piano 1984/1993, for clarinet, horn (or viola), violin, violoncello, percussion and piano 1984/1993, for marimba 1984/2006, Tight-Rope (chamber opera) 1985, Piano Sonata 1986, Traverso (for flute and piano) 1987, Companion Piece for Morton Feldman (for contrabass and piano) 1981, (for piano) 1989/1991, No Feeling is the Same as Before (for soprano and saxophone) 1988, Netori (for violin, oboe, horn, clarinet, violoncello, piano) 1990, The Gift of Life (for soprano and piano) 1990–93, Music for an Occasion (for brass, piano and percussion) 1992, Nel giardinetto della villa (for piano four hands) 1994, Baby Song of the Four Winds (for voice and piano) 1994, Guru (for voice(s) and piano) 1995, Resisting Stillness (for two guitars) 1996, Modern Love Songs (for voice and piano) 1997–2002, What a Coincidence 1997, I Wouldn't Have Known About That 1997, Someone New 1999, Now You See It, Now You Don't 1998, At Any Given Moment 2002, Prayers of Steel (for baritone and piano) 1998, Music for NASDAQ MarketSiteTV (for flute, horn, violin, violoncello, percussion and piano) 1999, The Child Comes Every Winter (for voice and piano) 1999, (for SATB) 1999/2001, Recovering (for voice and piano) 2000, In Time's Unfolding (for piano) 2000, Piano Quintet (for piano, violin, viola and violoncello) 2004, The Viola Had Suddenly Become a Voice (for viola and piano) 2005, Recognition (for piano and violin with string orchestra) 2004–07, You've Been On My Mind (for voice and piano) 2007, Sailors & Dreamers (for voice and piano, or voice and chamber ensemble) 2007–10, Seven O'Clock at the Cedar (Ode to Kline/de Kooning) (for voice and piano) 2008, Play Me a Song (for voice and piano) 2008, It's Time to Feel Alright Now (for voice and piano) 2009, Do You Remember? 2010, I Dance the Tango 2010, Falling Fast 2010, Footfalls (after Beckett) (for flute, oboe, two guitars, tingsha, violin and violoncello, or flute, oboe, piano, violin and violoncello) 2012. *Recordings include:* Piano Sonata, Mestiere, Trasumanar, Traverso, The Gift of Life, Companion Piece, Incitation to Desire (tango), Tenzone, At the Still Point, Resisting Stillness, Nel giardinetto della villa, In Time's Unfolding, Baby Song of the Four Winds, Recovering, Guru, Tartini, Piano Quintet, Mestiere and Di Vivere, Companion Piece (for Morton Feldman), The Viola had Suddenly Become a Voice. *Honours:* American Acad. and Inst. of Arts and Letters Charles E. Ives Scholarship 1975–76, American Acad. in Rome Prize 1976–77, John Simon Guggenheim Memorial Foundation Fellowship in Music Composition 1979–80, Nat. Endowment for the Arts Composer/Librettist Fellowship grants 1977–78, 1980–81, MacDowell Colony Fellowships 1981, Norlin Foundation Fellowships in Honor of Aaron Copland 1984, 1992, 1993, 1994–95, Frances and William Schuman Fellowships 1998, 2000, 2004, Djerassi Foundation Music/Composition Fellowship (Ridge Vineyards) 1989, Japan Foundation Professional Fellowship 1989–90, New York Foundation for the Arts Fellowships in Music Composition 1990, 1998, Rockefeller Foundation Bellagio Study and Conference Center Fellowship, Villa Serbelloni, Lago di Como, Italy 1993, Univ. of Wisconsin Alumni Asscn Distinguished Alumni Award 1997, Bogliasco Foundation Liguria Study Center for the Arts and Humanities Fellowship, Villa Orbiana, Bogliasco, Italy 1999, 2005, Harvard Comm. Fromm Music Foundation 1999–2002, Copland House Aaron Copland Award 2001, Bank of New York Teaching Excellence Award, Sarah Lawrence Coll. 2006, Acad. Award in Music, American Acad. of Arts and Letters 2007, Koussevitsky Music Foundation Award, Library of Congress Comm. 2007–08, Alice M. Ditson Fund of Columbia Univ. Grant 2009, Yale Univ. Alumni Ventures Grant 2009–10. *Address:* Music Program, Sarah Lawrence College, One Meadway, Bronxville, NY 10708-5888 (office); 380 Riverside Drive, 4C, New York, NY 10025-1819, USA (home). *Telephone:* (914) 395-2334 (office); (212) 665-3349 (home). *Fax:* (914) 395-2507 (office). *E-mail:* biscardi@slc.edu (office). *Website:* www.chesterbiscardi.com.

BISCHOF, Rainer, PhD; Austrian composer; b. 20 June 1947, Vienna. *Education:* Univ. of Vienna, studied with Hans Apostel. *Compositions:* Sonatine for Clarinet, 1969; Sonatine for Horn, 1970; Duo for Flute and Clarinet, 1970; Theme and 7 variations for Oboe and Cello, 1970; Quartet for Flute, Oboe, Horn and Bassoon, 1971; Grave for Violin and Piano, 1970–71; Deduction for Strings, 1973–74; Characteristic Differences for Violin and Piano, 1974; In Memoriam Memoriae, song cycle for Mezzo-soprano, Speaker, Vibraphone, Celesta, Bass, Clarinet and Cello, 1975–77; Orchesterstücke, 1976–82; Flute Concerto, 1978–79; Studies from the Flute Concerto for solo flute, 1978; Concerto for Violin, Cello and Orchestra, 1979–80; Variations for Organ, 1981; Viola Tricolor, 32 variations for Viola, 1982; Music for 6 Recorders, 1982–83; String Sextet, 1990; Studie in PP, 1991; Das Donauergeschenk, chamber opera, 1991; Quasi una fuga for orchestra, 1995; Sinfonia, 1995; Gesänge zur Kunst for chorus, 1996; Auf der Suche nach... for piano, 1996; Totentanz for orchestra, 1999; Der narrische Uhu, concerto for violin, 2001; Requiem fur Errol, 2003. *Address:* AKM, 111 Baumstr 8–10, 1031 Vienna, Austria.

BISENGALIEV, Amir; Kazakhstani violinist. *Education:* Central Music School, Almaty, Purcell School, London and Royal Coll. of Music, London, studied with Itzhak Rashkovsky in London. *Career:* debut with Kazakh State Symphony Orchestra aged seven; moved to UK aged twelve; attended Keshet Eilon Violin Mastercourse, Israel; performed at Sir Adrian Boult Hall and Birmingham Symphony Hall (Birmingham), Royal Festival Hall, Hellenic Centre, Wigmore Hall (London), Bridgewater Hall (Manchester), Brangwyn Hall (Swansea), Tel-Aviv Opera House, Cairo Opera House; has performed with Philharmonia Orchestra, Leeds Sinfonia, Manchester Camerata, Cairo Symphony Orchestra. *Recording:* album 2000. *Honours:* Llangollen Int. Musical Eisteddfod Int. Instrumentalist of the Year 1999. *Telephone:* (115) 847-8719 (office). *E-mail:* dawn@foxroe.com (office). *Website:* www.foxroe.com (office). *E-mail:* info@amir.kz. *Website:* www.amir.kz.

BISENGALIEV, Marat; Kazakhstani violinist and music director; *Artistic Director, Symphony Orchestra of India*; b. 1962. *Education:* studied at Tchaikovsky Conservatoire, Moscow with Boris Belinki and Valery Klimov. *Career:* f. Kazakh Chamber Orchestra 1989; British debut with Royal Philharmonic Orchestra 1991; f. West Kazakhstan Philharmonic Orchestra 1993; f. Turan Alem Kazakhstan Philharmonic Orchestra 2006; Artistic Dir Symphony Orchestra of India, Mumbai 2006–; has given concerts in over 35 countries with numerous major orchestras; venues include Carnegie Hall, Royal Albert Hall, Barbican, Wigmore Hall, Bridgewater Hall, Manchester, Waterfront, Belfast, Sheffield City Hall. *Recordings include:* Wieniawski Violin Showpieces 1992, Brahms Hungarian Dances 1994, Mendelssohn Concertos 1996, Elgar: Rediscovered Works for Violin, Vols 1 and 2 1999, 2001, Brian Violin Concerto 2006, Tlep 2006 (Sony Gold Disc), Karl Jenkins Concertos 2008. *Honours:* Kazakhstan Govt Medal of Honour 2000; prizewinner Leipzig Int. Bach Competition, Germany 1988, Int. Nicanor Zabaleta Competition, Spain 1991, first Independent Platinum Tarlan Award 2000. *Current Management:* Tarlan Artists' Management. *E-mail:* tarlanartists@yahoo.com (office). *Address:* The Symphony Orchestra of India, National Centre for the Performing Arts, NCPA Marg, Nariman Point, Mumbai 400 021, India (office). *Telephone:* (22) 66223729 (office). *Fax:* (22) 22845350 (office). *E-mail:* info@soimumbai.in (office). *Website:* www.soimumbai.in (office); www.maratbisengaliev.com.

BISPO, Antonio Alexandre, PhD; Brazilian/German architect, musicologist, cultural scientist and academic; *Professor, University of Cologne*; b. 17 March 1949, São Paulo, Brazil; s. of Antonio Bispo and Ermelinda do Rego Bispo. *Education:* Conservatory Carlos Gomes, Univ. of São Paulo, Instituto Musical de São Paulo, Faculty for Music and Art Educ. of São Paulo, Univ. of Cologne, Germany. *Career:* Dir Soc. Nova Difusão 1968–; Dir Conservatorio J. America, São Paulo 1971–72; Researcher, Associação Brasileira de Folclore, Museu de Folclore, São Paulo 1972; Lecturer in Ethnomusicology and Aesthetics of Music, Fac. de Música e Educação Artística do Instituto Musical de São Paulo 1972–74; moved to Germany 1974; Researcher and Chair. Ethnomusicology Section, Institut für Hymnologische und Musikethnologische Studien Maria Laach 1979–2002; Councillor, Pontifical Asscn of Church Music 1979–85; Dir Musikschule der Stadt Leichlingen 1981–84; Dir Institut für Studien der Musikkultur des portugiesischen Sprachraumes e.V. 1989–; Lecturer, Musikwissenschaftliches Institut, Univ. of Cologne 1997–, Prof. 2005–; Lecturer, Musikwissenschaftliches Seminar, Univ. of Bonn 2002–04; Inst. of Hymn and Ethnomusicology Studies 1984–; Pres. Akad. Brasil-Europa für Kultur- und Wissenschaftswissenschaft 1991–; Dir Centro de Estudos Brasil-Europa 1997–; Ed. Revista Brasil-Europa 1989–. *Publications include:* Die katholische Kirchenmusik in der Provinz São Paulo 1979, Collectanea Musicae Sacrae Brasiliensis 1981, Grundlagen christlicher

Musikkultur in der aussereuropäischen Welt der Neuzeit 1989, Revista Brasil-Europa/Correspondência Euro-Brasileira (ed.) 1989–, Leben und Werk von Martin Braunwieser 1991–92, Christliche Volkstraditionen und Synkretismus in Brasilien 1989–90, Die Musikkulturen der Indianer Brasiliens 1994–2002 (I–IV), Christliche Musikanthropologie 1999, Brasil-Europa 500 Jahre: Musik und Visionen 2000, Poética da Urbanidade 2003, Musik Projekte und Perspektiven 2003. *Honours:* Nat. Order of Bandeirantes; Award of Univ. of Cologne, Award of Academia Paulistana de Historia, Honour, Brazil Asscn of Folklore, Medalha Pontificia, Award for the Int. Congress 500 Years Brazil-Europe. *Address:* Dieringhauser Str. 66, 51645 Gummersbach, Nordrhein-Westphalen, Germany. *E-mail:* bispo@netcologne.de.

BISS, Jonathan; American pianist; b. 18 Sept. 1980, Bloomington, Ind.; s. of Paul Biss and Miriam Fried. *Education:* Indiana Univ., studied with Evelyne Brancart, Curtis Inst. of Music, studied with Leon Fleischer. *Career:* New York Philharmonic debut 2000–01 season; has worked with various conductors, including Alsop, Barenboim, Conlon, Davies, Dutoit, Levine, Maazel, Marriner, Morlot, Pappano, Robertson, Slatkin, Tilson-Thomas, Zukerman and Zinman; has appeared with major US orchestras, including Los Angeles and New York Philharmonics, Boston, Cincinnati, Chicago, Pittsburgh and San Francisco Symphonies, Cleveland, Philadelphia and Metropolitan Opera Orchestras, and many orchestras in Europe, also recitals and chamber music. *Recordings:* Piano Works 2004, Schumann (Diapason d'Or award, young talent category) 2007, Beethoven Piano Sonatas (Edison Award for Best Solo Recital Recording 2008) 2007, Mozart Piano Concertos 21 & 22 2008, Schubert Piano Sonatas 2009, Beethoven, Piano Sonatas Vol. 1 – Nos. 5, 11, 12 and 26 2012, Beethoven: Piano Sonatas Vol.2 - Nos. No. 4, 14 'Moonlight', 24, Fantasy in G minor 2013. *Honours:* Wolf Trap's Shouse Debut Artist Award 1997, Avery Fisher Career Grant 1999, Lincoln Center's Martin E. Segal Award 2002, Gilmore Young Artist 2002, Andrew Wolf Memorial Chamber Music Award 2002, Borletti-Buitoni Trust Award 2003, BBC Radio 3's New Generation Artists programme 2002–04, Leonard Bernstein Award 2005. *Current Management:* c/o Jessica Ford, Intermusica Artists Management, 36 Graham Street, Crystal Wharf, London, N1 8GJ, England. *Telephone:* (20) 7608-9900. *Fax:* (20) 7490-3263. *E-mail:* jford@intermusica.co.uk. *Website:* www.intermusica.co.uk. *Address:* c/o Lisa Jaehnig, Shuman Associates, 120 West 58th Street, Suite 8D, New York, NY 10019, USA (office). *Telephone:* (212) 315-1300 (office). *E-mail:* ljaehnig@shumanassociates.net (office). *Website:* jonathanbiss.com.

BISSON, Yves; Algerian singer (baritone); b. 31 May 1936, Mostaganem. *Education:* Paris Conservatoire with Renée Gilly-Musy and Louis Noguera. *Career:* sang at Paris Opéra, and Opéra-Comique, notably in Manon, Faust, Platée, La Bohème, Werther, Roméo et Juliette, and Les Pêcheurs de Perles (all televised); festival engagements at Aix-en-Provence as Rodolphe in Les Fêtes Vénitiennes by Campra, Avignon, Carpentras and Orange; has sung in France, New York, Washington, Amsterdam, Brussels, Covent Garden London, Lisbon, Geneva, Zürich, Barcelona, Madrid, Vienna, Naples and Russia; other roles include Lescaut in Auber's Manon Lescaut, Escamillo, Nilakantha in Lakmé, Mercutio, Sander in Zémire et Azor by Grétry, Massenet's Lescaut, Albert and Caoudal in Sapho, Mozart's Figaro and Masetto, Rangoni in Boris Godunov, Puccini's Marcello, Schaunard, Sharpless and Lescaut, Rameau's Oromases in Zoroastre and Citheron in Platée, Verdi's Posa, Germont and Ford; sang François in Le Chemineau by Leroux at Marseille 1996.

BISWAS, Anup Kumar; Indian composer and cellist; b. 1957, West Bengal. *Education:* studied in India with Rev. T. Mathieson, Royal Coll. of Music, studied with Pierre Fournier in Geneva, Jacqueline du Pré in London. *Career:* concerts throughout the UK, including St James and Lambeth Palaces, QEH, Wigmore Hall, Grays Inn, Riverside Studios; festival engagements at Cleveland, Belfast, Greenwich, Hereford; masterclasses at the Dartington Summer School and concerts in Germany, Finland and Norway; J.S. Bach Tercentenary concerts in cathedrals and churches in the UK, featuring the suites for unaccompanied cello; Artistic Dir, Dante Alighieri Orchestra from 1989; Royal Albert Hall 1992, performing Celebration from his own ballet, Ten Guineas under the Banyan Tree; Purcell Room Concert 1993, playing Beethoven, Shostakovich, Walton and Brahms. *Compositions:* Music for Theatre Taliesin, Wales, production of Tristan and Yseult, featured by BBC Wales.

BITTOVÁ, Iva; Czech singer, musician (violin) and composer; b. 22 July 1958, Bruntál; d. of Koloman Bitto and Ludmila Bittová (née Masařová); two s. *Education:* State Conservatorium, Brno, music drama and violin with Rudolf Šťastný, Masaryk Univ. in Brno. *Career:* actress, singer and violinist 1976–; worked for more than ten years at avant-garde theatre co. Husa na provázku; roles in various TV and Brno Radio productions; moved to USA 2007; performances world-wide. *Films include:* Die Insel der Silberreiher (The Island of Silver Herons) (TV), The Diary of One Who Disappeared, Růové Sny (Rosy Dreams) 1976, Jak se budi princezny 1977, Balada pro banditu (Ballad for a Bandit) 1978, Unos moravanky 1983, Mikola a Mikolko 1988, Neha (Tenderness) 1991, Zelary 2003, Tajnosti (Best Actress Award, Slnko v sieti, Bratislava 2008, Best Actress Award, Syracuse Int. Film Festival, USA 2008) 2007. *Film music:* Mikola a Mikolko 1988, Step Across the Border 1990, Milenci bez siat (Lovers Without Clothes) 1996, Holocaust: A Music Memorial Film (TV) (song, Gypsy Lament) 2005, Women Refugees (documentary) 2011, Tři bratři (Three Brothers) 2014. *Recordings include:* Bittová–Fajt 1989, Bittová Iva 1991, River of Milk 1991, Ne nehledej 1994, Kolednice 1995, Divná

slečinka 1996, Pustit musíš 1996, Iva Bittová 1997, 44 Duets for Two Violins 1997, Bittová & Fajt 1997, Bílé Inferno 1997, Classic 1998, Iva Bittová – kniha 2000, Echoes 2001, Čikori 2001, Ples Upírů 2002, Jako host 2002, Step across the border 2003, The Man Who Cried 2003, Leoš Janáček: Moravská lidová poezie v písních 2004, Elida 2005, Mater 2006, Superchameleon 2006, Susumu Yokota 2006, Tajnosti 2007, Moravian Gems 2007, Funny Lady with NBE 2012, Zvon 2012, Iva Bittová Fragments 2013, Eviyan live 2013, Entwine 2014. *Honours:* numerous awards for films and recordings, including Top Ten awards as artist in Brno 2006–13. *Address:* Poňava 258/64, Lelekovice 66431, Czech Republic (home). *Telephone:* 604-208352 (mobile) (home). *E-mail:* iva@bittova.com. *Website:* www.bittova.com.

BJARNASON, Daniel; Icelandic composer; b. 26 Feb. 1979, Copenhagen, Denmark. *Education:* studied piano, composition and conducting in Reykjavik, then orchestra conducting at Freiburg Univ. of Music, Germany. *Career:* commissioned by and worked with numerous orchestras and ensembles including Los Angeles Philharmonic, New York Philharmonic, Toronto Symphony Orchestra, Cincinnati Symphony Orchestra, BBC Scottish Symphony Orchestra, Adelaide Symphony Orchestra, Britten Sinfonia, Ulster Orchestra, Sinfonietta Cracovia, So Percussion, Rambert Dance Co., Calder Quartet, Danish Nat. Opera, Decoda, Icleand Symphony Orchestra; performances of his compositions have been led by conductors such as Gustavo Dudamel, Louis Langrée, James Conlon, John Adams, Ilan Volkov, André de Ridder, Anna-Maria Helsing and Alexander Mickelthwate; collaborations with non-classical musicians including Sigur Rós, Hjaltalín, Efterklang, Ben Frost; currently Artist-in-Residence, Iceland Symphony Orchestra. *Film score:* The Deep (Best Film Score, Icelandic Film And Television Awards 2013) 2012. *Compositions include:* Five possibilities, for clarinet in Bb, violoncello, and piano 2014, Five Chinese Poems, score and instrumental parts, Collider, for large orchestra, Frames dance music, Stillshot, quartet 2015. *Recordings include:* solo: Processions (Best Composer category, Icelandic Music Awards) 2010, Over Light Earth 2013; other: Solaris (with Ben Frost); works included on CDs of other musicians including Kveikur (Sigur Rós) 2013. *Honours:* Int. Rostrum for Composers special commendations 2008 and 2011, Kraumur Music Award 2010, Best Composer, Icelandic Music Awards 2013, 2015. *Address:* c/o C.F. Peters Ltd & Co., Talstr.10, 04103 Leipzig, Germany. *Telephone:* (341) 9897920. *Fax:* (341) 98979254. *E-mail:* info.de@editionpeters.com; info@danielbjarnason.net; *Website:* danielbjarnason.net; danielbjarnason.bandcamp.com.

BJARNASON, Finnur; Icelandic singer (tenor); b. 1975, Reykjavík. *Education:* Guildhall School, National Opera Studio, London. *Career:* debut with Male Chorus in the Rape of Lucretia for Icelandic Opera; sang Don Ottavio for Glyndebourne Touring Opera, 2000; appearances in Messiah throughout Britain and Beethoven's Ninth with the Icelandic Symphony Orchestra; recitals at St George's, Bristol, for the BBC and Wigmore Hall with Graham Johnson; season 2001–02 with Tebaldo in I Capuleti e i Montecchi for Grange Park Opera, Tamino with Icelandic Opera, and Don Ottavio at the 2002 Glyndebourne Festival. *Current Management:* Hazard Chase, 25 City Road, Cambridge, CB1 1DP, England. *Telephone:* (1223) 312400. *Fax:* (1223) 460827. *E-mail:* info@hazardchase.co.uk. *Website:* www.hazardchase.co.uk.

BJERNO, Majken; Danish singer (soprano); b. 29 May 1963, Århus. *Education:* studied in Copenhagen. *Career:* debut at Opera Studio Copenhagen, 1989, as Pamina; Royal Opera Copenhagen from 1989 as Offenbach's Antonia, Mozart's Countess, Micaela, Mimi, Fiordiligi in Così fan tutte, Leonora in Nielsen's Maskarade and Mihail in Saul and David; guest appearances at the Jutland Opera, Århus as Gutrune in Götterdämmerung and Mimi; concert engagements in Bach's Passions; Beethoven's Ninth and Missa Solemnis; requiems by Fauré, Brahms and Dvořák; Handel's Saul and Messiah; masses by Mozart and Carmina Burana; also sang recitals. *Recordings include:* Mahler's 8th Symphony. *Address:* Tivoli Artists Management, 3 Vesterbrogade, POB 233, 1630 Copenhagen, Denmark. *Telephone:* 33-75-04-00. *Fax:* 33-75-03-75. *E-mail:* artistsmanagement@tivoli.dk. *Website:* www.tam.dk.

BJORNSSON, Sigurd; Icelandic singer (tenor); b. 19 March 1932, Hafnarfjordur. *Education:* studied with Gerhard Husch in Munich. *Career:* debut at Stuttgart 1962, as Arturo in Lucia di Lammermoor; sang at Stuttgart until 1968, Kassel 1968–72, Graz 1972–75, and Theater am Gärtnerplatz Munich until 1977; among roles were Mozart's Belmonte, Ferrando and Tamino, Lionel in Martha, Nicolai's Fenton, Wagner's Froh and Steuermann, Bellini's Riccardo and Rinuccio in Gianni Schicchi; guest appearances at the Deutsche Oper Berlin, Munich, Hamburg, the Vienna Volksoper and the Bregenz and Schwetzingen Festivals.

BLACK, James, (James Jeffries), MA, ARCM, RSA; British singer (counter-tenor) and music agent; b. (James R.H. Black), 18 Oct. 1964, Canterbury. *Education:* Magdalen Coll., Oxford, Peterhouse Coll., Cambridge, Royal Coll. of Music. *Career:* sang professionally, making debut in Handel's Israel in Egypt, St John's, Smith Square, London; concerts in oratorio and concert repertoire throughout the UK; as well as in Canada, France, Germany, Ireland and The Netherlands; operatic performances in the UK, as well as in Denmark, Greece, Germany, The Netherlands and Norway; retd from stage 2003; est. James Black Management (artist agency) 2004. *Roles include:* created role of Caspar in world premiere of Alexander Knaifel's Alice in Wonderland, Netherlands Opera 2002. *Address:* James Black Management, The Old Grammar School, High Street, Rye, East Sussex, TN31 7JF, England (office). *Telephone:* (1797) 224668 (office). *Fax:* (1797) 229891 (office). *E-mail:* james@jamesblackmanagement.com (office). *Website:* www .jamesblackmanagement.com (office).

BLACK, Jeffrey, BMus, PGCE; Australian singer (baritone) and teacher; b. 6 Sept. 1962, Brisbane; m. Janice Black; one s. one d. *Career:* European debut as Harlekin in Ariadne auf Naxos at Monte Carlo 1986; sang with Australian Opera from 1985 as Mercutio, Schaunard, Papageno, Dr Falke, Dandini, Rossini's Figaro and Ottone in Poppea; Glyndebourne Festival from 1986, as Sid in Albert Herring, Demetrius and the Count in Figaro and Capriccio; Covent Garden appearances as well as engagements at Los Angeles as Guglielmo and Marcello 1993, Opéra Bastille in Paris, Puccini's Lescaut, Opéra de Genève, Fieramosca in Benvenuto Cellini, San Francisco, Rossini's Figaro; Lyric Opera of Chicago and 1993 Salzburg Festival as Guglielmo, Teatro Colón, (Buenos Aires) as Dandini, Don Giovanni in Antwerp, Count (Le nozze di Figaro) in Washington, Figaro (Barbiere) at the Met, New York and in Munich, Valentin (Faust) in Geneva and Eugene Onegin at San Diego; returned to Australia to appear with Lyric Opera of Queensland and Victoria State Opera, Melbourne; sang Britten's Demetrius for New Israeli Opera 1994; Mozart's Count at the Metropolitan, and Onegin at Sydney, Australia 1997; Tannhäuser at Sydney and Posa in Don Carlos for Opera North 1998; Don Carlo in Australia 1999; concerts include tour of Australia with Geoffrey Parsons and the ABC Orchestras, Carmina Burana with the London Philharmonic and Christus in the St Matthew Passion under Franz Welser-Möst; Kiri Te Kanawa int. tour 1999; currently Headmaster, Putney Park Preparatory School. *Recordings include:* Carmina Burana, Songs of the Wayfarer (Mahler).

BLACK, Leo, MA, BMus; British writer, broadcaster, translator and pianist; b. 28 July 1932, London; s. of Charles Black and Phyllis Black; m. Felicity Vincent. *Education:* Univ. of Oxford. *Career:* music publisher, Universal Edition, Vienna, London 1956–60; music programmes, BBC radio 1960–88, Producer 1960–71, Chief Producer 1971–82, Exec. Producer 1982–88; concerts as a song-accompanist; lecture-recital on Schubert's Arpeggione Sonata, with cellist Felicity Vincent. *Radio:* numerous programmes of classical music (mostly chamber, Lieder, French and English song, thematic sequences). *Television:* Script for programmes on Schubert, Bruckner, Brahms. *Publications:* Franz Schubert: Music and Belief 2003, Edmund Rubbra: Symphonist 2008, BBC Music in the Glock Era and After 2010; translations include Willi Reich: Schönberg, A Critical Biography, Schönberg Style and Idea, Webern: The Path to New Music, Badura-Skoda Interpreting Mozart on the Keyboard; articles: Über die Aufnahme der Musik Franz Schmidts 1986, Franz Schmidt und das musikalische Hören 1992, The Music of Hugh Wood, A Few Pointers Before Hearing Hugh Wood's Violin Concerto, Heimito von Doderer, An English View 1996; five major bicentenary articles on Schubert 1997, Schubert's VDB 2001; articles in Musical Times, The Listener, Opera Quarterly, Books and Bookmen. *Address:* 112 Chetwynd Road, London, NW5 1DH, England (home). *Telephone:* (20) 7485-1211 (home). *Fax:* (20) 7485-1211 (office). *E-mail:* leo.black@btinternet.com (home).

BLACK, Lynton, DipRAM, ARAM, LRAM; British singer (bass-baritone); b. 1960, England. *Education:* Royal Acad. of Music. *Career:* debut as High Priest in Handel's Teseo, Covent Garden; appearances with English Touring Opera, English Bach Festival, Garsington Festival Opera and Grange Park Opera; principal bass, D'Oyly Carte Opera 1994–98; Salzburg Festival in Monteverdi's Orfeo 1993; Paris Opéra as Notar in Der Rosenkavalier 1996; Basle Opera as Achille in Handel's Giulio Cesare 1998; Aix-en-Provence Festival as Achilles in La Belle Hélène 1999; La Monnaie, Brussels as Lesbo in Handel's Agrippina 2000; Barcelona Opera as Achille in Giulio Cesare 2001; Glyndebourne as Bartolo in Le nozze di Figaro 2001; other roles include Commendatore in Don Giovanni, Budd in Albert Herring, Don Alfonso in Così fan tutte, Frank in Die Fledermaus, Dick Deadeye in HMS Pinafore, The Mikado, Sultan in Haydn's L'Incontro Improvviso, Antonio in Le nozze di Figaro (Salzburg 1995, 1996, 1998; Paris Opéra 1999), Sciarrone in Tosca (La Monnaie, Brussels 2000), Sagrestano in Tosca (Paris 2000), Hobson in Peter Grimes (Paris 2001); Munich Staatsoper as Father Trulove in The Rake's Progress 2002; other roles include Bass Israel in Egypt, Cadmus & Somnus in Handel's Semele; mem. Equity, Savage Club, Sketch Club, Loophole Club, Curzon Club, Pres. D'Oyly Carte Dining Club. *Recordings:* Die Fledermaus (Frank), Rose of Persia (Gaoler). *Address:* 3 Temple Fortune Lane, London, NW11 7UB, England. *E-mail:* lyntonbass@aol.com. *Website:* www .LyntonBlack.com.

BLACK, Neil, OBE, BA; British oboist; *Professor of Oboe, Guildhall School of Music and Drama.* *Education:* Univ. of Oxford. *Career:* fmr mem. Nat. Youth Orchestra of Great Britain; fmr prin. oboist LPO, Acad. of St Martin-in-the-Fields, English Chamber Orchestra; numerous int. tours and festivals; currently Prof. GSMD; Musical Dir Kirckman Concert Soc. *Recordings include:* with the Acad. of St Martin-in-the-Fields: Vivaldi: L'estro armonico 1994, Vivaldi: The Four Seasons 2000, Mozart: Clarinet and Oboe Concertos 2000; with the English Chamber Orchestra: Delius/Vaughan Williams/ Walton: Orchestral Works 1993, Haydn: The London Concert 2004; other: Baroque Concerto in England, with Thames Chamber Orchestra, Mozart/ Strauss/Weber, Wind Concertos with Philadelphia Orchestra. *Honours:* Hon. Fellow RAM . *Address:* Guildhall School of Music and Drama, Silk Street, Barbican, London, EC2Y 8DT, England (office). *E-mail:* music@gsmd.ac.uk (office). *Website:* www.gsmd.ac.uk (office).

BLACK, Virginia, DipRAM, FRAM; British harpsichordist; b. 1950, England; m. Howard Davis; two s. *Career:* London concerts in the Wigmore Hall, Purcell Room and QEH; appearances at major festivals in the UK and Europe including the Prague Spring Festival; recordings for the BBC and the Westdeutsche Rundfunk; television performance of Bach's 5th Brandenburg Concerto, with the English Chamber Orchestra; tours to Europe, the USA, Australia and New Zealand; concerts with Howard Davis, violin; other repertoire includes sonatas by Soler and Scarlatti, Bach's Chromatic Fantasy and Fugue, Concertos in E and C Minor, Fantasie and Fugue in A minor, Toccata in D and Partitas, Bach's Goldberg Variations, pieces by Rameau, Dandrieu, Duphly and Forqueray, Falla's Harpsichord Concerto; Prof. of Harpsichord, Royal Acad. of Music, Postgraduate Tutor since 1999, Chair of Postgraduate Diploma Studies from 2002. *Recordings:* 17 albums of harpsichord music, including The Essential Harpsichord.

BLACK, William David, BM, MM, DMA; American pianist; b. 23 Feb. 1952, Dallas, TX. *Education:* Oberlin Coll., Juilliard School. *Career:* debut in New York 1977; London, England 1979; solo and orchestral engagements across the USA, Canada, England, France, The Netherlands, Belgium, Germany, Iceland, Japan, People's Republic of China and Italy; television appearances in the USA and numerous US and European radio broadcasts, including worldwide broadcasts of the Voice of America; mem. Bohemians, New York Musicians Club, European Piano Teachers' Asscn. *Recordings:* works of David Diamond, world premiere recording of the original version of the 4th Piano Concerto of Sergei Rachmaninov; Hunter Johnson Piano Sonata; Gershwin, Rhapsody in Blue. *Honours:* Concert Artists Guild Award, Juilliard School Morris Loeb Award, NEA Solo Recitalist grant 1991.

BLACKBURN, Bonnie Jean, MA, PhD, FBA; American/British musicologist and editor; b. 15 July 1939, Albany, New York; d. of John Hall Blackburn and Ruth Blackburn; m. 1st Edward E. Lowinsky 1971 (died 1985); m. 2nd Leofranc Holford-Strevens 1990. *Education:* Wellesley Coll., Univ. of Chicago. *Career:* Research Asst, Dept of Music, Univ. of Chicago 1963–76, Visiting Assoc. Prof. 1986; Lecturer, School of Music, Northwestern Univ. 1987; Visiting Assoc. Prof., State Univ. of New York, Buffalo 1989–90; freelance ed. 1990–; Gen. Ed., Monuments of Renaissance Music 1993–; John Simon Guggenheim Memorial Foundation Fellowship 1988–89; mem. American Musicological Soc., Royal Musical Asscn, Int. Musicological Soc., Koninklijke Vereniging voor Nederlandse Muziekgeschiedenis, Plainsong and Mediaeval Music Soc., Renaissance Soc. of America, Soc. for Renaissance Studies, Società Italiana di Musicologia, Academia Europaea; Fellow, British Acad. *Publications include:* Josquin des Prez: Proceedings of The International Josquin Festival-Conference (co-ed.) 1976, Music for Treviso Cathedral in the Late Sixteenth Century: A Reconstruction of the Lost Manuscripts 29 and 30 1987, Johannis Lupi Opera omnia, three vols (ed) 1980–89, Music in the Culture of the Renaissance and Other Essays by Edward E. Lowinsky (ed) 1989, A Correspondence of Renaissance Musicians , (co-ed.) 1991, The Oxford Companion to the Year (with Leofranc Holford-Strevens) 1999, Composition, Printing and Performance: Studies in Renaissance Music 2000, Music as Concept and Practice in the Late Middle Ages (New Oxford History of Music, 3, second edn, Part 1) (co-ed.) 2001, New Josquin Edn, 21–22: Motets on Non-Biblical Texts De Domino Jesu Christo 1–2 (ed.) 2003–07, Canons and Canonic Techniques, 14–16th Centuries: Theory, Practice and Reception History, Proceedings of the Int. Analysis in Context Conference (co-ed.) 2005, Florentius de Faxolis, Liber de musica (co-ed.) 2010, Eroticism in Early Music (jtly) 2015; contrib. to Musical Quarterly, Journal of The American Musicological Society, Musica Disciplina, Early Music History, The New Grove Dictionary of Music and Musicians, Early Music, Studi Musicali, Journal of Musicology, Die Musik in Geschichte und Gegenwart, Journal of the Royal Musical Association, Oxford Dictionary of National Biography, Basler Jahrbuch für Historische Musikpraxis, Tijdschrift der Vereniging voor Muziekgeschiedenis, Journal of Alamire Foundation, Proceedings of the British Academy, The Lute. *Honours:* Emer. Fellow, Wolfson Coll. *Address:* 67 St Bernard's Road, Oxford, OX2 6EJ, England (home). *Telephone:* (1865) 552808 (office). *Fax:* (1865) 512237 (office). *E-mail:* bonnie.blackburn@wolfson .ox.ac.uk (office).

BLACKBURN, Olivia; British singer (soprano); b. 1960, London, England. *Education:* Trinity Coll., London and Pears-Britten School. *Career:* regular concert on South Bank, London, in Die Schöpfung by Haydn, Vivaldi's Magnificat and Handel's Jephtha; German Requiem by Brahms at the Barbican with the Philharmonia and the St Matthew Passion with the Steinitz Bach Players; European performances in the Bach B Minor Mass, Haydn's Paukenmesse (Missa in tempore belli), Messiah and the Mozart Requiem; opera debut in The Poisoned Kiss by Vaughan Williams at the Bloomsbury Theatre; Wexford Festival 1987; with Cologne Opera has sung Naiad in Ariadne auf Naxos, Siebel in Faust, Sandrina (La Finta Giardiniera), Helena in A Midsummer Night's Dream and Pamina; song recitals in Paris, Dublin, London and Cambridge; appearances with the Songmakers' Almanac in London and at the Nottingham and Buxton Festivals; season 1989–90 in Ode to the West Wind by Arnell, Aci in Handel's Aci, Galatea e Polifemo with London Baroque at the Beaune Festival and Mendelssohn's Lobgesang conducted by Richard Hickox; Mozart's C Minor Mass in Scotland and in France with Malgoire and Portugal with Brüggen conducting; Covent Garden debut 1992, as a Young Nun in The Fiery Angel; television recording of Handel's Roman Vespers in Vienna. *Recordings include:* Bach B Minor Mass.

BLACKHAM, Joyce; British singer (soprano); b. 1 Jan. 1934, Rotherham, Yorkshire, England; m. Peter Glossop (divorced). *Education:* Guildhall School of Music with Joseph Hislop. *Career:* debut at Sadler's Wells Opera 1955, as Olga in Eugene Onegin; Covent Garden debut as Esmeralda in The Bartered Bride; roles include Carmen, Dorabella, Mimi, Norina, Rosina and roles in operettas by Offenbach, Johann Strauss and Lehar; guest appearances Berlin, New York and New Zealand; with WNO sang Rosina, Amneris and Cherubino; sang Maddalena in Rigoletto at Covent Garden 1974.

BLACKWELL, Harolyn; American singer (soprano); b. 1955, Washington, DC. *Education:* Catholic Univ. of America, studied with Carlo Bergonzi and Renata Tebaldi in Italy. *Career:* has sung Jemmy in Guillaume Tell at the San Antonio Festival, Papagena in Cleveland, Oscar in Hamburg, Gilda with the Miami Opera, Sister Constance in Dialogues des Carmélites for Canadian Opera and Clara in Porgy and Bess at the Glyndebourne Festival 1986; symphonic engagements with the Nat. Symphony, St Louis Philharmonic, Cincinnati Symphony, Minnesota Orchestra and Buffalo Philharmonic; Carnegie Hall as Xanthe in Die Liebe der Danaë by Strauss; recitals in Buffalo, Denver, Dallas and New York (debut 1987); season 1986–87 with debuts at Chicago as Oscar (Un Ballo in Maschera) and at the Metropolitan as Pousette in Manon; Xenia in Boris Godunov, conducted by James Conlon; season 1987–88 with concert performance of Porgy and Bess under Simon Rattle, Nannetta in Falstaff at Nice and the Princess in L'Enfant et les Sortilèges at Glyndebourne; season 1988–89 included Schubert's A-flat Mass in Detroit, Barbarina and Sophie (Werther) at the Met, Olga in Giordano's Fedora at Carnegie Hall and Zdenka (Arabella) at Glyndebourne; season 1989–90 with Adele at the Met and Marie (La Fille du Régiment) in Seattle; Blondchen in Die Entführung at Aix-en-Provence; season 1990–91 highlights were Oscar at the Met, Mahler's 4th Symphony in Florida and Charleston, Bach and Handel with the New York Chamber Symphony, Mozart's Le nozze di Figaro (Susanna) in Toronto; Mozart's Zerlina at San Francisco 1991; La Fille du Regiment at the Met 1992–93; sang Lakmé and Lucia di Lammermoor at Seattle 2000; Norina in Don Pasquale with Seattle Opera 2003. *Recordings include:* Porgy and Bess, Blackwell sings Bernstein, Strange Hurt, Brahms: Ein deutsches Requiem, Candide, All Through the Night, Sondheim: A Celebration at Carnegie Hall. *Honours:* Hon. DHL (Siena Coll.), Hon. DMus (George Washington Univ.). *Current Management:* Columbia Artists Management, 1790 Broadway, New York, NY 10019-1412, USA. *Telephone:* (212) 841-9500. *Fax:* (212) 841-9744. *E-mail:* info@cami.com. *Website:* www.cami .com.

BLACKWOOD, Easley; American composer, pianist and music educator; b. 21 April 1933, Indianapolis, IN. *Education:* studied in Indianapolis, Berkshire Music Center, Tanglewood, MA, Indiana Univ. School of Music, Bloomington, Yale Univ., studied with Boulanger in Paris. *Career:* appeared as soloist with the Indianapolis Symphony Orchestra 1947; concerts throughout North American and Europe; faculty mem., Univ. of Chicago 1958–68, Prof. 1968–97 (retd). *Compositions:* orchestral: Symphony No. 1 1954–55, No. 2 1960, No. 3 1964, No. 4 1977, No. 5 1992, Chamber Symphony 1954, Clarinet Concerto 1964, Symphonic Fantasy 1965, Oboe Concerto 1965, Violin Concerto 1967, Flute Concerto 1968, Piano Concerto 1970; chamber: Viola Sonata 1953, two string quartets 1957, 1959, Concerto for five instruments 1959, two violin sonatas 1960, 1973, Fantasy for cello and piano 1960, Pastorale and Variations for wind quintet 1961, Sonata for flute and harpsichord 1962, Fantasy for flute, clarinet and piano 1965, Symphonic Episode for organ 1966, Piano Trio 1967, 12 Microtonal Etudes for synthesizer 1982, piano pieces; other: Un Voyage à Cythère for soprano and winds 1966, four Letter Scenes from Gulliver's Last Voyage for mezzo-soprano, baritone and tape 1972, Sonatina for piccolo, clarinet and piano 1994, Sonata for piano 1996, Two Nocturnes for piano 1996. *Recordings:* piano works of Casella, Szymanowski, Ives, Copland, Prokofiev, Stravinsky, Berg, Nielsen and Alain. *Publication:* The Structure of Recognizable Diatonic Tunings 1986. *Honours:* Fulbright Scholarship 1954–56, first prize Koussevitzky Music Foundation 1958, Brandeis Univ. Creative Arts Award 1968. *Address:* 5300 S Shore Drive, #44, Chicago, IL 60615, USA (home).

BLADIN, Christer; Swedish singer (tenor); b. 1947, Stockholm. *Education:* studied in Freiburg and Stockholm. *Career:* sang at the Freiburg Opera 1972–76, Berne 1976–78, Darmstadt 1978–84, and at the Bonn Opera from 1986; guest appearances at Perugia (Salieri's Les Danaides 1984, Haydn's Orfeo 1985) and Aix-en-Provence (Rossini's Armida 1988); other roles include Froh in Das Rheingold (Barcelona 1986), Mozart's Belmonte and Tamino, Admète in Lully's Alceste and Ernesto in Don Pasquale; has also appeared at La Scala, Milan, Nantes, Ghent and Marseille; Montpellier 1993–94, in operas by Philippe Hersant and René Koering.

BLÁHA, Ivo, MgA; Czech composer and teacher; b. 14 March 1936, Litomyšl, Czechoslovakia (now the Czech Repub.); s. of Václav Bláha and Eugenie Bláhová-Stuchlá; m. Lidmila Vrhelová 1961; two d. *Education:* Acad. of Performing Arts (AMU), Prague, with Jaroslav Řídký, Vladimír Sommer, Emil Hlobil, and with M. Kabeláč and E. Herzog at Experimental Sound Studio, Radio Plzeň. *Career:* Lecturer in Dept of Composition, Music Faculty, Acad. of Performing Arts (AMU), Prague 1964–72, Docent in the Film and TV Faculty of AMU 1967, Founder and Head of Dept of Sound Design, FAMU 1993–2011, Prof. 1999; mem. Asscn of Czech Composers. *Compositions include:* four string quartets: I 1957, II 1966, III 1983 (first place, Int. Rostrum of Composers, UNESCO 1991), IV (Curriculum vitae) 2000, Concerto for orchestra 1957, Three Movements (Sonata) for violin and piano 1961,

Spring Plays for wind quintet 1962, Concerto for percussion and orchestra 1964, Solitude – sonata for violin solo 1965, Music for wind quintet 1965, Three Toccata Studies for piano 1967, Duetto facile per violini 1970, Music to Pictures of a Friend for flute, oboe and clarinet 1971, Cello Sonata 1972, Two Inventions for solo flute 1974, Duo for bass clarinet and piano 1975, Cet amour for speaker, wood instruments and tape 1975, Rays for piano 1976, Sinfonia 'Per archi' 1977, Sonata transparenta for flute and piano 1981, Moravian Lullabies 1982, Something for Ear for children's choirs with piano 1983, Zoolessons for guitar 1984, 1987 (Annual Prize of CHF, Prague 1993), Vaults for organ 1986, Funny Things with Four Strings, Five Miniatures for two to three violins or violin ensemble 1986, Imaginations for violin and piano 1988, Sonata Introspecta for viola 1989, Joy to Everyone: Christmas cantata for children's choir and instrumental ensemble 1997, To Ancient Strings for children's choir a cappella 1998, Quasi Sonata for harpsichord 1998, Welcome Spring! 1998, Macrocosmos for piano 1998, Bergamasca (symphonic scherzo) 2000, Soliloquy with Marimba for marimba and player's voice 2001, Living Water, songs for choir of younger children and piano 2001, 1 Plus Minus 1: musical scene for female flautist and male violinist 2001, Hádes, ancient picture for contrabassoon and piano 2002, Ornaments for piano and orchestra 2003, Satyr's Circles for clarinet solo 2003, Missing Bow (Senza arco) for viola quartet 2004, Bear's Songs for children's choir and piano 2004, Quadrille, dance fantasy for viola foursome 2004, Alter ego for violin and viola 2005, Cyclorama for symphonic orchestra 2005, Piano trio No. 1 for violin, cello and piano 2006, Air Therapy, treatment by breath for wind and percussion 2008, Re- for three guitars 2009, Passacaglia on theme of J.S. Bach for cello and string orchestra 2009, Orbis Musicus for three guitars and chamber orchestra 2011, Homage to Horns for four French horns 2011, Piano trio No. 2 for violin, cello and piano 2013, Levitation for violin solo 2014. *Film:* Soliloquy with Marimba. *Publication:* Sound Dramaturgy of Audio-visual Work 2006. *E-mail:* ivoblaha@seznam.cz (home). *Website:* www.scoreexchange.com/ profiles/ivoblaha; ivo-blaha.webnode.cz.

BLAHOVA, Eva; Slovak academic and singer; b. 1 Dec. 1944, Skalica; m. (divorced); one s. one d. *Education:* Music Acad., Bratislava, Music Acad., Vienna, Austria, masterclasses with Prof. D. Ferro and Erik Werba. *Career:* debut with Slovak Philharmony 1965; sang in concert festivals and music festivals in Bratislava, Slovakia, Kraków, Easter Festival, Poland, The Prague Spring Festival, Czech Republic, Carinthian Summer Festival, Ossiach, Austria, Ottawa, Montréal, Canada, Parma, Trento, Italy, Chartres, France, Vienna, Austria, Washington, DC, New Jersey, USA, Hyundai Arts Center, Republic of Korea, Tokyo, Osaka, Japan; Prof. of Singing, Music Acad., Bratislava 1969–, European Music Foundation 1992–98; masterclasses in The Netherlands and Czech Republic. *Recordings:* Nine German Arias 1979, Haydn, Mozart, Beethoven Concert Arias 1983, Romantic Songs 1997.

BLAHUSIAKOVA, Magdalena; Czech singer (soprano); b. 1947. *Education:* studied in Sofia and Bratislava. *Career:* mem., Brno Opera 1969–82, notably as Santuzza, Aida, Donna Anna and Donna Elvira, Fiordiligi, Tatiana and Amelia (Simon Boccanegra and Un Ballo in Maschera); guest appearances in Barcelona 1980, Genoa (as Jenůfa), and Lausanne (Rusalka); sang Santuzza in Cuba 1987 and Yaroslavna in Prince Igor with the Slovak National Opera at Edinburgh 1991; concert engagements in The Spectre's Bride by Dvořák, Vienna 1984, the Requiems of Dvořák and Mozart and Beethoven's Ninth; concert tour of the USA 1985.

BLAIR, James; Scottish conductor; *Artistic Director and Principal Conductor, Young Musicians Symphony Orchestra*; b. 1950, Stirling. *Education:* Trinity Coll., London, studied with Adrian Boult and Franco Ferrara. *Career:* Artistic Dir and Principal Conductor, Young Musicians Symphony Orchestra 1971–; many performances of Mahler, Messiaen and Strauss; engagements with all leading British orchestras and works with Opera North, Dublin Grand Opera and Athens Opera; US debut 1984, with the Delaware Symphony; later conducted Colorado Springs and Kansas City Symphony Orchestras; many Young Musicians Symphony Orchestra concerts given on BBC, including Mahler's 8th Symphony. *Recordings include:* Late Romantic repertory. *Honours:* Hon. FTCL; Ricordi Conducting Prize, Italian Govt Scholarship to study in Siena and Venice. *Address:* Young Musicians Symphony Orchestra, Flat 4, 11 Gunnersbury Avenue, London, W5 3NJ, England (office). *Telephone:* (20) 8993-3939 (home). *E-mail:* admin@ymso.org .uk (office); jamesmblair@hotmail.com (home).

BLAKE, Christopher, BE, QSO; New Zealand composer, civil servant and arts administrator; *Chief Executive, New Zealand Symphony Orchestra*; b. 1949, Christchurch. *Education:* Univ. of Canterbury, Univ. of Southampton, UK. *Career:* fmr Chief Exec., Dept of Internal Affairs; fmr Gen. Man. Nat. Opera of New Zealand, Auckland Philharmonia Orchestra and Canterbury Orchestra; fmr Man. Concert FM, Radio New Zealand Concert; Foundation Chief Exec., Ministry for Culture and Heritage 1991–97; Chief Exec. and Nat. Librarian, Nat. Library of New Zealand 1997–2002; Chief Exec. of Internal Affairs (govt dept 2002–07, then Chief Exec. and Sec. for Labour, Dept of Labour; Chief Exec., New Zealand Symphony Orchestra 2012–; numerous comms for a wide range of performers and ensembles. *Works include:* Till Human Voices Wake Us 1986, The Coming of Tane Mahuta 1987, Clairmont Triptych 1988, Bitter Calm (opera) 1994, Symphony – The Islands' 1996, Concerto Aoraki 2006; Northland Panels (includes Angel at Ahipara 2000, Night Journey to Pawarenga 2005, Anthem on the Kaipara 2007). *Publications include:* Music in New Zealand Spring 1989. *Address:* New Zealand Symphony Orchestra, Level 8, Alcatel-Lucent House, 13-27 Manners Street,

Wellington 6011, New Zealand (office). *Telephone:* (4) 801-3890 (office). *Fax:* (4) 801-3891 (office). *E-mail:* info@nzso.co.nz (office). *Website:* www.nzso.co.nz (office).

BLAKE, David, BA, MA; British composer; b. 2 Sept. 1936, London, England; m. Rita Muir 1960; two s. one d. *Education:* Gonville and Caius Coll., Cambridge, Deutsche Akademie der Künste, Berlin, Germany. *Career:* Lecturer in Music 1964–71, Sr Lecturer 1971–76, Prof. of Music 1976–2001, Univ. of York, retd 2001. *Compositions include:* Variations for Piano, 1960; Three Choruses to Poems of Robert Frost, 1964; What is the Cause for Chorus; Fulke Greville, 1967; Nonet for Wind, 1971; Violin Concerto, BBC Proms, 1976; Toussaint, libretto Anthony Ward, premiere London Coliseum, 1977, opera in 3 acts, 1974–77; Clarinet Quintet, 1980; Scherzi ed Intermezzi for Orchestra, 1984; Seasonal Variants for 7 Players, 1985; Pastoral Paraphrase for Bassoon and Small Orchestra, 1988; The Plumber's Gift, libretto John Birtwhistle, premiere, London Coliseum, 1989; A Little More Night Music, for Saxophone Quartet, 1990; Mill Music for Brass Band, 1990; Cello Concerto, 1992; Three Ritsos Choruses, 1992; The Griffin's Tale for Baritone and Orchestra, text by John Birtwhistle, 1994; The Fabulous Adventures of Alexander the Great, for soloists, chorus and orchestra of young people, text by John Birtwhistle, 1996; Scoring a Century, an entertainment, text by Keith Warner, 1999; The Shades of Love for bass baritone and small orchestra, poems by C. P. Cavafy, 2000; String Quartet No. 4, 2003, Rings of Jade for medium voice and orchestra (text by Ho Chi Minh, trans. by Birtwhistle). *Recordings:* Violin Concerto In Praise of Krishna, Variations for Piano, The Almanack. *Publications:* Hanns Eisler: A Miscellany 1995. *Address:* Mill Gill, Askrigg, Nr Leyburn, North Yorkshire, DL8 3HR, England (home). *Telephone:* (1969) 650364 (home). *E-mail:* david.blake9@btopenworld.com (home).

BLAKE, Howard, OBE, FRAM; British composer, pianist and conductor; b. 28 Oct. 1938, London. *Education:* Royal Acad. of Music with Harold Craxton and Howard Ferguson. *Career:* freelance composer 1971–; choral work Benedictus (oratorio, 1980) performed at Manchester, Llandaff and St Albans Westminster, Worcester, Winchester and Salisbury Cathedrals, Perth and Three Choirs Festivals, by the Bach Choir in London 1988, and with the Philharmonia RFH 1989; Barbican concerts for children; Dir, PRS and Exec. 1978–87; Visiting Prof. of Composition Royal Acad. of Music 1992; Dir Highbridge Music Ltd, Howard Blake Entertainments Ltd; mem. MU, APC, Inc. Soc. of Musicians, Groucho Club. *Compositions:* The Station (comic opera) 1987; orchestral: Toccata 1976, The Annunciation (ballet), Concert Dances 1984, Clarinet Concerto 1984, Diversions for cello and orchestra 1985, Three Sussex Songs 1973, Two Songs of the Nativity 1976, The Song of St Francis 1976, A Toccata of Galuppi's for baritone and harpsichord 1978, Benedictus (dramatic oratorio) 1979, The Snowman for narrator, boy soprano and orchestra 1982, Festival Mass for double choir a capella 1987, Shakespeare Songs for tenor and string quartet 1987; instrumental: Piano Quartet 1974, The Up and Down Man (children's suite) 1974, Penillion for violin and harp 1975, Eight Character Pieces for piano 1976, Dances for two pianos 1976, Prelude for solo viola 1979, Sinfonietta for 10 brass 1981, Piano Concerto (Philharmonia commission to celebrate 30th birthday of HRH Princess of Wales) 1991, Violin Concerto, The Snowman (ballet) 1993, Charter for Peace (commissioned for UN 50th anniversary) 1995, A Midsummer Night's Dream (commissioned by RSC) 1996, Eva (ballet) 1996, The Bear 1998, Stabat Mater for soprano, narrators, chorus and orchestra 2001 (reworked as The Passion of Mary 2009), many scores for films, theatre, ballet. *Recordings include:* The Passion of Mary 2009, Chamber Music, Concertos for piano, Woodwind concertos 2013, The Snowman, Piano works, Ashkenazy 2014. *Address:* Highbridge Music Ltd, Studio 6, 18 Kensington Court Place, London, W8 5BJ, England (office). *Telephone:* (7711) 617718 (office). *Fax:* (20) 7938-1969 (office). *E-mail:* howardblake.obe@virgin.net (office). *Website:* www.howardblake.com.

BLAKE, Rockwell Robert; British singer (tenor); b. 10 Jan. 1951, Plattsburgh, NY; m. Deborah Jeanne Bourlier 1973. *Education:* studied with Renata Booth in high school, State Univ. of New York, Fredonia, Catholic Univ. of America, Washington, DC. *Career:* soloist with US Navy Band; Washington Opera 1976; Hamburg State Opera 1977–79; Vienna State Opera 1978; New York City Opera 1979–81; Metropolitan Opera, New York 1981–83, 1986, 1988, as Lindoro in L'Italiana in Algeri, Almaviva, Don Ottavio and Arturo in I Puritani; Chicago Lyric Opera 1983, 1987, Rossini Opera Festival, Pesaro 1983–85, 1987–88; San Francisco Opera 1984; Paris Opéra 1985; Naples San Carlo 1985–88; Opéra-Comique, Paris 1987; Bavarian State Opera, Munich 1987; Rome Opera 1988–89; sang James V in La Donna del Lago at Bonn 1990; Arturo in I Puritani at Barcelona 1990; Tonio (La Fille du Régiment) at Santiago; concert performance of Meyerbeer's Il Crociato in Egitto at the 1990 Montpellier Festival; Rossini cantatas at Martina Franca; title role in Il Pirata at Lausanne 1992; season 1992 as Rossini's Almaviva at Genoa, Selim in Rossini's Adina at Rome, James V in La Donna del Lago at La Scala, Mozart's Ferrando at Dallas; Almaviva at the 1992 Caracalla Festival; sang in Semiramide at the 1994 Pesaro Festival; Aix Festival 1996, as Jupiter in the French premiere of Handel's Semele; Ramiro in Cenerentola at Hamburg 1998; sang Oronte in Alcina at the Paris Palais Garnier and Lyric Opera of Chicago 1999; season 2000–01 as Libenskof in Il Viaggio a Reims at La Coruña, and as Idreno in Semiramide at Liège; various concert engagements. *Recordings:* The Rossini Tenor, The Mozart Tenor, Encore Rossini, Alina la Regina di Golconda, Il Barbiere di Siviglia, Rossini's Barber (video, from the Metropolitan). *Honours:* Richard Tucker Award 1978, Nat. Opera Inst. grant 1975, 1976, Hon. DMus (State Orchestra). *Current Management:* Thea Dispeker Inc., 59 East 54th Street, Suite 81, New York, NY 10022, USA. *Telephone:* (212) 421-7676. *Fax:* (212) 935-3279. *E-mail:* info@dispeker.com. *Website:* www.dispeker.com.

BLANCK, Kirsten; German singer (soprano); b. 1965, Neumünster, Holstein. *Education:* studied in Hamburg with Judith Beckmann and in Kiel and Lubeck. *Career:* debut at Saarbrucken, 1986; sang at the Lubeck and Kiel Operas from 1990, notably as Mozart's Queen of Night, and in Dresden, Berlin, Stuttgart and Frankfurt; other roles include Donna Anna (Kiel, 1991), Gilda (Hanover, 1993), Sophie in Der Rosenkavalier, Zerbinetta, and Lulu; season 1992–93 at Kiel as Violetta and Donna Clara in Zemlinsky's Der Zwerg; Aminta in Die schweigsame Frau at Dresden, 1998; season 2000–01 as Zerbinetta at La Scala, The Queen of Night at Dresden, Sophie in Der Rosenkavalier for San Francisco Opera and Constanze at Chemnitz; many concert appearances. *Current Management:* Aria's di Novella Partacini & Alexandra Plaickner, Via Josef Weingartner 4, 39022 Lagundo, Italy. *Telephone:* (0473) 200200. *Fax:* 0(473) 222424. *E-mail:* info@arias.it. *Website:* www.arias.it.

BLANCKE-BIGGS, Elizabeth, BMus; American singer (soprano); b. 12 Oct. 1966. *Education:* California State Univ. at Los Angeles. *Career:* appearances include Madama Butterfly and Liu in Turandot for Opera Grand Rapids, Nedda in Pagliacci for El Paso Opera and the Trovatore Leonora for Augusta Opera, Micaela for Opera Colorado, Mimi in La Bohème at Virginia Opera, Norma for the Di Capo Opera Theatre, Violetta in La Traviata and Ortlinde in Die Walküre for the Metropolitan Opera, Tosca and Ginevra in Un Racconto for New York City Opera, Minnie in La Fanciulla del West for Florida Grand Opera, Musetta for Baltimore Opera, Leonora in Il Trovatore for New Jersey Opera Theater, Desdemona in Otello for Utah Opera; European engagements as Donizetti's Maria Stuarda in Turin, Honegger's Le Roi David in Nice, Mary Stuart at Teatro Regio, Turin; concerts repertoire include Beethoven's Ninth Symphony and Die Walküre in New Zealand, Fauré's Requiem, Mozart's C Minor Mass, Beethoven's Mass in C, Verdi's Requiem, Brahms' Ein Deutsches Requiem; sang Mozart's Countess at the Aotea Centre, Auckland. *Current Management:* Robert Lombardo Associates, 61 W 62nd Street, Suite 6F, New York, NY 10023, USA. *Telephone:* (212) 586-4453. *Fax:* (212) 581-5771. *E-mail:* robert@robertlombardo.com. *Website:* www.rlombardo.com. *E-mail:* requests@elizabethblancke-biggs.com (office). *Website:* www.elizabethblancke-biggs.com.

BLANKENBURG, Heinz Horst; American singer (baritone) and stage director; b. 15 Oct. 1931, New York, NY; m. 1st; two s. one d.; m. 2nd Gayle Cameron-McComb 1986. *Education:* studied in Los Angeles. *Career:* debut with San Francisco Opera 1955; leading baritone, Glyndebourne Festival Opera 1957–70, roles there included Mozart's Papageno and Figaro, Rossini's Rimbaud and Busoni's Arlecchino; Hamburg State Opera 1959–73, San Francisco Opera 1955–66; as Beckmesser, Schaunard, Fra Melitone (Forza del Destino) and Paolo in Simon Boccanegra; sang with the Hamburg Staatsoper in the British premiere of Die Frau ohne Schatten, Sadler's Wells Theatre 1966; guest baritone with opera companies of Munich, Berlin, Vienna, Paris, Frankfurt, Metropolitan, Amsterdam, Rome, Brussels, Lausanne, Basle, Strasbourg, Naples, Venice, New Zealand, St Louis, Portland, Vancouver 1978, Seattle, Los Angeles; faculty mem., Univ. of California at Los Angeles and California State Univ., Los Angeles. *Honours:* Hon. DArts (California State Univ., Los Angeles) 1977, (Univ. of California at Los Angeles) 1986; Kammersänger, Hamburg State Opera 1966, Maori Welcome, New Zealand 1971.

BLANKENSHIP, Rebecca; American/Swiss singer (dramatic soprano), actress and author; *Artistic and Musical Consultant, Ex Machina*; b. 24 March 1954, New York, NY; d. of William Blankenship and Barbara Blankenship. *Education:* studied voice in New York with Judith Oas-Natalucci, acting at Herbert Berghoff School. *Career:* sang two seasons at Ulm as mezzo-soprano: Cherubino, Idamantes, Nicklaus, Prince Orlofsky; engaged as dramatic soprano, Basel 1986–88, roles included title role in Lady Macbeth of Mtsensk (also Wiener Volksoper) and Ariadne (also Staatsoper Berlin), Elettra in Idomeneo, Leonora in Il Trovatore, Female Chorus in The Rape of Lucretia; since 1988 regular appearances at Wiener Volksoper, including Martha in Tiefland, Agathe in Der Freischutz, title role in Merry Widow (also Japan tour); title role Fidelio in Stuttgart and the Netherlands, Elsa in Lohengrin in Liège and Senta in Der Fliegende Holländer at Bregenz Festival; Sieglinde in Die Walküre (San Francisco Opera and Wiener Staatsoper), Foreign Princess in Rusalka (Wiener Staatsoper), Grete in Der Ferne Klang (Wiener Staatsoper), Marie in Wozzeck (Wiener Staatsoper, La Fenice Venice, Tokyo), Katarina in Lady Macbeth of Mtsensk (Wiener Volksoper), Die Frau in Robert Lepage's Erwartung (Canadian Opera, Toronto, also at Edinburgh Festival, Melbourne, Geneva Opera, Hong Kong), Erwartung (Graz Opera), Kostelnicka in Jenůfa (Dortmund), Erwartung (Aldeburgh Festival 2009); works regularly as collaborator, author and performer in plays and films of Robert Lepage (including Seven Streams of the River Ota and LIPSYNCH theatre piece 2008–12); performer and artistic and musical consultant, Ex Machina; Asst to Robert Lepage as artistic and musical consultant on the Ring Cycle, Metropolitan Opera 2010–12 and Asst Dir The Tempest, Metropolitan Opera 2012–13; Artistic and Musical Consultant, Vienna State Opera for the Tempest 2015; Dir Don Giovanni, Mongolian Opera 2015; co-directed with sister Beverly Blankenship the opera 'Brundibar' Holocaust memorial, Austrian Parl. 2015; project with EntartOpera

'Baruch's Schweigen' 2016; also teaches privately. *Address:* Ex Machina, 109 rue Dalhousie, Quebec, PQ G1K 4B9, Canada (office).

BLANZAT, Anne-Marie Eliane; French singer (soprano); b. 24 Nov. 1944, Neuilly-sur-Seine; d. of Marius Blanzat and Paulette Blanzat (née Delaveau); m. Jacques Plas 1965; one s. *Education:* Maîtrise de Radio-France. *Career:* began singing career in child operatic roles aged 13; int. career performing at operas, concerts and festivals including Aix-en-Provence, Glyndebourne and Gulbenkian Festivals, Opéra de Bruxelles, Paris, Geneva, Lyon, Strasbourg, Naples, Palermo, Turin, Lisbon; Founder and Dir Acad. de Thil. *Operas include:* Pelléas et Mélisande, Carmen, Le Nozze di Figaro, Falstaff, Les dialogues des Carmélites, Les contes d'Hoffmann, Béatrice et Bénédicte, Les pêcheurs de perles, Les liaisons dangereuses, Manon, Le Consul, La dame de pique, La Voix Humaine. *Videos:* Pelléas et Mélisande 1982, Les dialogues des Carmélites 1982, Manon 1984. *Honours:* Officier des Arts et des Lettres 1998; Oscar for Best Lyric Singer in France 1974. *Address:* 8 bis boulevard Clémenceau, 21000 Dijon (home); 2 square Servan, 21390 Vic-sous-Thil, France. *Telephone:* (3) 80-64-41-97 (home); (3) 80-73-28-06. *E-mail:* jam.plasblanzat@neuf.fr.

BLASI, Angela Maria; American singer (soprano); b. 16 Aug. 1956, Brooklyn, NY. *Education:* Loyola Univ., Los Angeles. *Career:* ensemble mem., Hessen State Theater, Wiesbaden 1982–85; Bavarian State Opera, Munich 1985–88; debut as Pamina at Salzburg Festival, Covent Garden, La Scala Milan; guest appearances in European opera houses, including Hamburg, Berlin, Vienna, Zürich, Florence; appeared as Liu in Turandot in the Forbidden City, Beijing with Zubin Mehta 1998; Marguerite in Faust, Munich 2000; New York Met debut as Pamina 2000; Ellen Orford in Peter Grimes, Montpellier, France 2001; Conception in L'Heure Espagnole, Brussels, Belgium 2001; Nedda in Pagliacci, Brussels Monnaie 2002; La Bohème at the Met 2003; Agathe in Der Freischutz, Montpellier 2003. *Film:* Comencini's film of La Bohème (Musetta) 1987. *Recordings:* Mozart's Requiem and Mahler's 4th Symphony. *Honours:* Bavarian Kammersängerin 1994, Munich Merkur Prize, People's Choice Award for Interpretation of Marguerite in Faust at the Bavarian State Opera. *E-mail:* office@angelamariablasi.com (office). *Website:* www.angelamariablasi.com.

BLASIUS, Martin; German singer (bass); b. 5 June 1956, Schwelm, Westfalen. *Education:* Folkwang-Musikhochschule, Essen. *Career:* sang at first in concert, notably for Austrian and Italian radio, at the Bach-Woche Ansbach, the Göttingen Handel Festival and at the Frankfurt Festival; opera debut as Dulcamara, Gelsenkirchen 1983; moved to Hannover 1987 and Düsseldorf 1989; guest appearances in opera and concert throughout Germany; appeared in a new production of Henze's The Bassarids, Duisburg 1991 and sang the Grand Inquisitor in Don Carlos at Düsseldorf; Gärtnerplatztheater Munich 1992, as Mussorgsky's Ivan Khovansky; Bielefeld 1988, as Orth in Weill's Burgschaft; season 1999–2000 as Wagner's Hunding in Münster, and Fafner in Siegfried. *Recordings include:* Der Traumgörge by Zemlinsky; Saint-Saëns's Christmas Oratorio; Golgotha by Martin; Kreutzer's Das Nachtlager von Granada.

BLATNÝ, Pavel, Magister; Czech composer, conductor, musician (piano) and musicologist; b. 14 Sept. 1931, Brno; m. Danuse Spirková 1982; one s. one d. *Education:* Brno Conservatory, Univ. of Brno, Berklee Coll. of Music, Boston, USA. *Career:* more than 2,000 recitals of piano music, often in a third-stream mode, mixing jazz and classical techniques; conductor of many concerts in the fmr Czechoslovakia; Chief of the Music Div., Czech television 1971–92; Prof., Janáček Acad. of Musical Arts, Brno 1979–90; Pres. Club of Moravian Composers. *Compositions include:* Music for Piano and Orchestra 1955, Concerto for Orchestra 1956, Concerto for Jazz Orchestra 1962–64, Twelfth Night (based on Shakespeare's play) 1975, Forest Tales: The Well and Little House (television opera for children) 1975, The Willow Tree (cantata with orchestra) 1980, The Bells, symphonic movement 1981, Christmas Eve (cantata with orchestra) 1982, The Midday Witch (cantata with orchestra) 1982, Two Movements for Brasses 1982, Hommage à Gustav Mahler for orchestra 1982, Prologue for mixed choir and jazz orchestra 1984, Ring a Ring o' Roses, for solo piano 1984, Signals for Jazz Orchestra 1985, Confrontation (written with his son, Marek Blatný), for rock group and symphony orchestra 1995, Play Rock, Play New Music (written with his son, Marek Blatný) 1997, Meditation 1999, Symphony Erbenia'da 2003, An old song, antivariations for symphony orchestra on song of Thomas Aquin 2008; other music for wind instruments, for piano. *Recordings:* Pavel Blatný – Jazz in Modo Classico 1980, Jubileum 2006. *Honours:* winner, Composition Prize, Prague Jazz Festival 1966, 1967, Leoš Janáček Prize 1984, Anfiteatro d'Argento, Naples, Italy 1989, Lifetime Achievement Award, Brno 2000. *Address:* Absolonova 35, 62400 Brno, Czech Republic (home). *Telephone:* (5) 4122-3062 (home). *E-mail:* pblatny@atlas.cz.

BLATTERT, Susanne; German singer (mezzo-soprano); b. 1966, Freiburg. *Education:* studied in Hamburg with Judith Beckman. *Career:* sang at Gelsenkirchen Musiktheater, 1990–93; Essen Opera from 1993; further appearances at Hamburg, Cologne, the Bregenz Festival and in Budapest; roles have included Mozart's Zerlina, Cherubino and Dorabella, Rossini's Rosina, Tancredi and Cenerentola; Essen, 1996 as Sesto in La Clemenza di Tito; season 1997–98 as Wellgunde in Das Rheingold at Bonn; season 2000–01 at Bonn as Dorabella, Wellgunde, and Micha in a staged version of Handel's Saul. *Honours:* prizewinner Concours International de Chant, Toulouse 1992. *Current Management:* Alferink Artists Management, Herengracht 340, 1016 CG Amsterdam, The Netherlands. *Telephone:* (20) 6643151. *Fax:* (20) 6752426. *E-mail:* info@alferink.org. *Website:* www.alferink.org.

BLAUMANE, Kristina; Latvian musician (cello); *Principal Cello, London Philharmonic Orchestra*; b. Riga. *Education:* Latvian Acad. of Music, studied with Eleonora Testeleca, Guildhall School of Music and Drama, UK, with Stefan Popov. *Career:* fmrly lead cellist, Amsterdam Sinfonietta; Prin. Cello, London Philharmonic Orchestra 2007–; has performed as soloist with Amsterdam Sinfonietta, Chicago Civic Orchestra, Kremerata Baltica, Britten Sinfonia, Lithuanian Chamber Orchestra, Sofia Soloists, Netherlands Wind Ensemble and Dalarna Sinfonietta, and all primary orchestras in Latvia; performed as chamber musician, has worked with artists including Isaac Stern, Gidon Kremer, Yo Yo Ma, Yuri Bashmet, Leiv Ove Andsnes, Janine Jansen, Julian Rachlin, Dmitry Sitkovetsky, Bruno Giuranna, Misha Maisky, Nikolaj Znaider, Tatyana Grindenko, Oleg Maisenberg; festival performances include Lockenhaus, Gstaad, Salzburg, Verbier, Basel, Jerusalem, Utrecht, Spitalfields, Cheltenham, Aldeburgh, Homecoming, Crescendo; has given several world premieres and had works dedicated to her, among them cello concertos by Dobrinka Tabakova, Kristaps Petersons, Peteris Plakidis, Artem Vassiliev. *Recordings include:* chamber: Barber, Grieg & Martinu: Sonatas for Cello and Piano 2007, Brahms's chamber music works 1 & 2 2010/2011, Shostakovich: Piano Concertos & Piano Quintet (with London Philharmonic Orchestra) 2011, Beethoven 2012, Dobrinka Tabakova: String Paths 2013. *Honours:* Latvian Philharmonic Young Musician of the Year, Carmel Int. Competition, Musicians Benevolent Fund and Lord Mayor's Prize, Great Music Award 2005, 2007. *Current Management:* c/o Go Direct Artists Management, Gran Vía 6 - 4°, 28013 Madrid, Spain. *E-mail:* vmourelle@godirect-am.com. *Address:* London Philharmonic Orchestra, 89 Albert Embankment, London, SE1 7TP (office). *Telephone:* (20) 7840-4200 (office). *Website:* www.lpo.org.uk (office).

BLAUSTEIN, Susan Morton; American composer; b. 22 March 1953, Palo Alto, CA. *Education:* studied with Pousseur in Liège, at Yale with Jacob Druckman and Betsy Jolas. *Career:* fmr Jr Fellow, Harvard Univ.; Asst Prof., Columbia Univ., New York 1985–90; commissions from the Koussevitsky and Fromm Foundations. *Compositions include:* Commedia for eight players 1980, To Orpheus (four sonnets) 1982, String Quartet 1982, Sextet 1983, Concerto for cello and chamber orchestra 1984, Song of Songs for mezzo, tenor and orchestra 1985.

BLAZE, Robin, MA; British singer (countertenor) and academic; *Professor of Vocal Studies, Royal College of Music*; b. 1971, England; m.; one s. one d. *Education:* Magdalen Coll., Oxford, Royal Coll. of Music. *Career:* regular solo engagements in Europe, USA, S America and Asia with the King's Consort, the Acad. of Ancient Music, Bach Collegium Japan, Collegium Vocale, Gent, The English Concert, The Gabrieli Consort, Orchestra of the Age of Enlightenment, RIAS Kammerchor, Amsterdam Bach Orchestra, and The Sixteen; soloist with Nat. Symphony Orchestra Washington, St Paul Chamber Orchestra, BBC Philharmonic, BBC Nat. Orchestra of Wales, Hallé Orchestra, La Chapelle Royale, Scottish Chamber Orchestra, and Tafelmusik; appearances at festivals, including Edinburgh, BBC Proms, Bremen, Barossa, Boston, Schwetsingen, Istanbul, Potsdam, Leipzig, Flanders, Melbourne, Ambronay and Beaune; opera performances include Bertarido in Rodelinda (Glyndebourne Touring Opera and at the Göttingen Handel Festival), Anfinomo in Il Ritorno d'Ulisse in Patria (Teatro Sao Carlos, Lisbon), Arsamenes in Xerxes (ENO), Athamas in Semele (Royal Opera House, Covent Garden) 2003; chamber music concerts with Concordia, Fretwork, Sonnerie, Palladian Ensemble; recitals at the Wigmore Hall, BBC Radio 3, in Karlsruhe, Innsbruck, Göttingen, Halle and many UK festivals; Prof. of Vocal Studies, Royal Coll. of Music. *Recordings:* over 40 albums, including Bach Cantata Cycle with Bach Collegium Japan and recitals with lute player, Elizabeth Kenny, Handel: Great Oratorio Duets (with Carolyn Sampson) 2006. *Current Management:* c/o Rayfield Artists, 34 Handforth Road, London, SW9 0LP, England. *Telephone:* (20) 7582-2650; 7976-357636 (mobile). *Fax:* (870) 131-4959. *E-mail:* ben@rayfieldartists.com. *Website:* www.rayfieldartists.com.

BLECHACZ, Rafał; Polish pianist; b. 30 June 1985, Nakło nad Notecią. *Education:* Arthur Rubinstein Music School, Feliks Nowowiejski Music Acad., Bydgoszcz, studied with Katarzyna Popowa-Zydroń in Bydgoszcz. *Career:* performed at festivals in Ruhr, Verbier, La Roque d'Antheron 2006; concert appearances include Warsaw Philharmony Hall 2006, Łazienki Park, Warsaw 2006, Moscow Conservatory with the Mariinsky Orchestra under Valery Gergiev 2006, Tonhalle, Zürich 2006, Tokyo Opera City 2006, Concertgebouw, Amsterdam 2006, Herkules Saal, Munich 2007, Wigmore Hall, London 2007, 2009, Auditorio Nacional, Madrid 2007, Suntory Hall, Tokyo 2007, Palais des Beaux Arts, Brussels 2007, Royal Festival Hall, London 2008, Lincoln Center, New York 2008, Théâtre des Champs Elysées, Paris 2009. *Recordings:* Piano Recital 2005, Chopin Piano Competition 2005, Chopin: The Complete Preludes 2007, Sonatas: Haydn, Beethoven, Mozart 2008, Chopin Piano Concertos 2009, Debussy/Szymanowski (ECHO Klassik Award for Solo Recording of the Year – 20th/21st Century – Piano 2012) 2011. *Honours:* second prize Arthur Rubinstein Young Pianist Competition, Bydgoszcz 2002, second prize Int. Young Pianist Competition, Hamamatsu, Japan 2003, winner Int. Piano Competition, Morocco 2004, winner (and four other prizes) Int. Frédéric Chopin Piano Competition, Warsaw 2005. *Current Management:* Andrzej Haluch, Kazimierzowska 47/5, Warsaw 02-572, Poland. *Telephone:* (22) 6462829. *Fax:* (22) 8487666. *E-mail:* andrzejhaluch@wp.pl. *Website:* www.haluch.com.pl. *Current Management:* Opus 3 Artists, 470 Park Avenue

South, 9th Floor North, New York, NY 10016, USA. *Telephone:* (212) 584-7500. *Fax:* (646) 300-8214. *E-mail:* eblackburn@opus3artists.com. *Website:* www.opus3artists.com. *E-mail:* sekretariat@blechacz.net (office). *Website:* www.blechacz.net.

BLEGEN, Judith; American singer (soprano); b. Lexington, Ky; d. of Dr Halward Martin Blegen and Dorothy Mae (Anderson) Blegen; m. 1st Peter Singher 1967 (divorced 1975); one s.; m. 2nd Raymond Gniewek 1977. *Education:* Curtis Inst. of Music, Philadelphia, Pa, Music Acad. of the West, Santa Barbara, Calif. *Career:* leading soprano, Nuremberg Opera, FRG 1965–68, Staatsoper, Vienna, Austria 1968–70, Metropolitan Opera, New York 1970–84; Vienna roles include Zerbinetta in Ariadne auf Naxos, Rosina in The Barber of Seville, Aennchen in Der Freischütz, Norina in Don Pasquale; numerous performances at Metropolitan include Marzelline in Fidelio, Sophie in Werther, Mélisande in Pelléas et Mélisande, Sophie in Der Rosenkavalier, Adina in L'Elisir d'amore, Juliette in Roméo et Juliette, Susanna in The Marriage of Figaro; other appearances include title role in Manon, Tulsa Opera, Gilda in Rigoletto, Chicago, Despina in Così fan tutte, Covent Garden, Blondchen in The Abduction from the Seraglio, Salzburg Festival, Mélisande in Pélleas et Mélisande, Spoleto Festival, Susanna in The Marriage of Figaro, Edinburgh Festival, Sophie, Paris Opera; Fulbright Scholarship; Artistic Advisor, Opera Naples. *Recordings include:* La Bohème, Carmina Burana, Symphony No. 4, Harmoniemesse, The Marriage of Figaro, A Midsummer Night's Dream, Nelson Mass, Gloria, Peer Gynt Suite, Lieder recital (Richard Strauss and Hugo Wolf), baroque music recital. *Honours:* Grammy Awards. *Address:* c/o Opera Naples, 6017 Pine Ridge Road, PO Box 386, Naples, FL 34119, USA. *Website:* www.operanaples.com.

BLEICHER, Stefan Johannes; German organist and teacher; *Professor of Organ, Hochschule für Musik Trossingen;* b. 1962. *Education:* studied organ and organ improvisation with Lionel Rogg at Conservatoire Supérieur de Musique, Geneva (Soloist Diploma Prize for Virtuosity) and Ewald Kooiman at Amsterdam Coll. of the Arts, as well as historical performance practice with Nikolaus Harnoncourt at Mozarteum, Salzburg. *Career:* organist, Winterthur City Church; fmr Lecturer, State Music Acad., Ochsenhausen; Head of S German Organ Acad. on historical performance practice of the great Baroque organs in Baden-Württemberg 1991–; Prof. of Organ, Zürich Univ. of the Arts 2001–09; Prof. of Organ, Hochschule für Musik Trossingen 2009–; has performed at all major cathedrals and churches in Europe, including Westminster Abbey and St Paul's, London, Notre Dame, Paris, and the cathedrals in Oslo, Stockholm, Copenhagen, Antwerp, Budapest, Graz, Salzburg, Strasbourg, Brussels, Barcelona, Cremona, Trento, Bologna, St Pölten, Bremen, Freiburg, Bamberg, Münster, Berlin, Zürich, Basel, Lausanne and Dublin, St Thomas Church and Leipzig Gewandhaus, Schauspielhaus Berlin studio of the WDR Köln, Philharmonie St Petersburg, Summer Acad., Mozarteum Salzburg, and at major music centres in USA and Canada; guest classes for organ interpretation and improvisation at various music schools and univs at home and abroad. *Recordings:* more than 30 CD recordings including Barocke Orgelmusik aus Süddeutschland, Barocke Orgelmusik aus Frankreich, F. Mendelssohn Sämtliche Orgelwerke, Franz Liszt Sämtliche Orgelwerke, Camille Saint-Saëns Sämtliche Orgelwerke, Orgelduette mit Mario Hospach-Martini, Luigi Boccherini Sonaten, J. S. Bach Orgelwerke, Franz Liszt Die grossen Orgelwerke, Franz Xaver Schnizer Sonaten, Meditations für Horn und Orgel mit Ifor James, F. X. Brixi Sämtliche Konzerte, R. Schumann Missa Sacra, G. Ch. Wagenseil, Brahms/Rheinberger/Schumann/Reger, Rheinberger. *Honours:* 19th Century Recording of the Year (Organ), ECHO Klassik Awards 2011. *Address:* State Academy of Music Trossingen, Mayor Koch-Platz 3, 78647 Trossingen, Germany (office). *Telephone:* (425) 94910 (office). *Fax:* (425) 949148 (office). *E-mail:* rector@mh-trossingen.de (office); info@stefanjohannesbleicher.de (office). *Website:* www.stefanjohannesbleicher.de (office).

BLINKHOF, Jan; Dutch singer (tenor); b. 10 July 1940, Leiden. *Education:* studied in Amsterdam, with Joseph Metternich in Cologne and with Luigi Ricci in Rome. *Career:* debut with Netherlands Opera 1971, as Arturo in Lucia di Lammermoor; Holland Festival 1971, in premiere of Spinoza by Ton de Kruyf; Amsterdam 1974, in premiere of Dorian Gray by Kox; Geneva Opera 1985, as Tristan; Nice 1986, as Herman in The Queen of Spades; sang Laca in Jenůfa at Zürich Opera 1986; other roles include Ismaele in Nabucco; Boris in Katya Kabanova, and roles in Wozzeck, The Rape of Lucretia, The Gambler by Prokofiev and Henze's Der Junge Lord; sang Tristan at Nice 1986–87, Laca at Covent Garden 1988; Deutsche Oper Berlin 1988, as Sergei in Lady Macbeth of the Mtsensk District; sang Boris in Katya Kabanova at Geneva and Florence 1989; Albert Gregor in The Makropulos Case at Berlin 1990, followed by Sergei in Hamburg and Laca (Jenůfa) at Barcelona; season 1994 as Florestan at Lisbon and Sergei at Florence; season 1996 as Luca in From the House of the Dead at Nice and Florestan in Fidelio at Rome; Laca at Hamburg 1998; Calaf at Barcelona 1999; sang Drum Major in Wozzeck at Vienna Staatsoper 2000, Janáček's Laca and Shuisky in Boris Godunov at Hamburg.

BLISS, Julian; British clarinettist; b. Harpenden, Herts. *Education:* Ind. Univ., USA, Royal Acad. of Music, master-classes with Sabine Meyer in Lübeck. *Career:* has appeared with orchestras, including London Philharmonic Orchestra, BBC Symphony Orchestra, City of Birmingham Symphony Orchestra, Seattle Symphony, Zurich Chamber, Bergen Philharmonic, Munich Chamber, City of Birmingham Symphony, Swedish Radio Symphony, Orchestre National de France, Royal Philharmonic, Malaysian Philharmonic, Royal Liverpool Philharmonic, Munich Chamber, Tokyo Symphony and the

Academy of St Martin in the Fields, and performed chamber music with Joshua Bell, Hélène Grimaud, Steven Isserlis, Steven Kovacevich and other great interpreters; performances include Golden Jubilee celebrations, Buckingham Palace 2002, BBC Proms, Mostly Mozart, Barbican Hall, and at Verbier and Gstaad Festivals. *Recordings:* Music for Clarinet and Piano (with Julien Quentin), Krommer, Spohr (with Sabine Meyer). *Honours:* First Prize, Philadelphia's Concerto Soloists Young Artists Competition. *Current Management:* Music Productions Limited, Pinewood Studios, Pinewood Road, Iver Heath, Bucks., Aylesbury, SL0 0NH, England. *Telephone:* (20) 7957-5800. *Fax:* (20) 7957-5801. *E-mail:* nicola@musicprods.co.uk; claire@musicprods.co.uk. *Website:* www.musicprods.co.uk; www.musicprods.co.uk; www.julianbliss.com.

BLOCHWITZ, Hans Peter; German singer (tenor); b. 28 Sept. 1949, Garmisch-Partenkirchen. *Education:* studied in Darmstadt, Mainz and Frankfurt. *Career:* sang at first in concert, notably as the Evangelist in the St Matthew Passion and in Lieder recitals (Die schöne Müllerin by Schubert); Opera debut Frankfurt 1984, as Lensky; Sang in the Scala-staged version of the St Matthew Passion at San Marco, Milan, 1985; Théâtre de la Monnaie, Brussels, and Geneva 1986, as Don Ottavio and Lensky; Guest appearances in Hamburg, Amsterdam and London (Ferrando in Così fan tutte, 1989); Aix-en-Provence Festival 1987–89, as Belmonte and Ferrando; Sang Idamante in Idomeneo at San Francisco, 1989; Don Ottavio at the Metropolitan Opera, 1990; Sang in the Choral Symphony at the 1993 Prom Concerts, London; Wilhelm in Henze's Der Junge Lord, Munich, 1995; Flamand in Capriccio at Dresden, 1996; Title role in Il ritorno d'Ulisse in Patria, Athens, 1997; Mozart's Titus at Glyndebourne, 1999; Teaches at Musikhochschule, Bern. *Recordings include:* Bach St Matthew Passion; Bach Christmas Oratorio; Bach B-Minor Mass; Mozart Requiem; Mozart Die Zauberflöte; Mozart Don Giovanni; Mozart Così fan tutte; Mozart La Finta Semplice; Mozart C-Minor Mass; Mozart Coronation Mass; Beethoven Missa Solemnis; Beethoven Fidelio; Handel Theodora; Handel Messiah; Haydn Schöpfung; Mendelssohn Lobgesang Symphony; Mendelssohn St Paul; Schubert and Die schöne Magelone by Brahms.

BLOMSTEDT, Herbert Thorsson; Swedish conductor; b. 11 July 1927, Springfield, Mass, USA; s. of Adolphe Blomstedt and Alida Armintha Thorson; m. Waltraud Regina Peterson 1955 (died 2003); four d. *Education:* Royal Acad. of Music, Stockholm, Uppsala Univ., Mozarteum, Austria, Schola Cantorum, Switzerland, Juilliard School and Tanglewood, USA. *Career:* Music Dir, Norrköping Symphony Orchestra 1954–61; Prof. of Conducting, Swedish Royal Acad. of Music 1961–70; Perm. Conductor, Oslo Philharmonic 1962–68; Music Dir Danish Radio Symphony Orchestra 1967–77, Dresden Staatskapelle Orchestra 1975–85, Swedish Radio Symphony Orchestra 1977–82; Music Dir and Conductor, San Francisco Symphony Orchestra 1985–95, Conductor Laureate 1995–; Music Dir NDR Symphony Orchestra, Hamburg 1996–98, Leipzig Gewandhaus Orchestra 1998–2005; mem. Royal Acad. of Music, Stockholm 1965. *Publications:* Till Kennedomen om Johann Christian Bachs Symfonies 1951, Lars-Erik Larsson och Lars Convertinor (co-author) 1957, Berwald: Sinfonie Singulière 1965. *Honours:* Hon. Conductor NHK Symphony, Tokyo 1985, Bamberg Symphony Orchestra 2006, Danish Nat. Symphony Orchestra 2006, Swedish Radio Symphony Orchestra 2006, Gewandhausorchester, Leipzig; Kt Royal Order of the North Star, Kt Royal Order of Dannebrog (Denmark), Grosses Verdienstkreuz der Bundesrepublik Deutschland 2003; Hon. DMus (Andrews); Dr hc (Gothenburg) 1999, (Southwestern-Adventist Univ., Tex.) 1993; Jenny Lind Scholarship, Swedish Royal Acad. of Music, Litteris et Artibus, Gold Medal (Sweden), Deutscher Schallplattenpreis 1978, Golden Reward Prize, Tokyo 1984, Grand Prix du Disque 1989, Gramophone Award, London 1990, Record Acad. of Japan Award 1991, Ditson Award for Distinguished Services to American Music, Columbia Univ., New York 1992, Grammy Awards 1993, 1996, Schallplattenpreis der Deutschen Musikkritik 1994, Ehrenpräsident der Stiftung Musikforschung Zentralschweiz 2001, Anton-Bruckner-Preis der Betil-Östbo-Bruckner-Stiftung, Linz 2001, Haederpris, Carl Nielsen Soc., Denmark 2002, Julio Kilenyi Medal of Honor, Bruckner Soc. of America. *Address:* KünstlerSekretariat am Gasteig, Rosenheimer Strasse 52, 81669 Munich, Germany (office). *Telephone:* (89) 444-8879-0 (office). *Fax:* (89) 444-9522 (office).

BLOOMFIELD, Arthur John, BA; American music critic and food writer; b. 3 Jan. 1931, San Francisco, Calif.; m. Anne E. Buenger 1956; one s. two d. *Education:* Stanford Univ. *Career:* music critic, San Francisco Examiner 1965–79; San Francisco correspondent, Opera 1964–89; program notes writer, Music and Arts records 1996–; currently Resident Historian and columnist, Operawarhorses.com. *Publications include:* Fifty Years of the San Francisco Opera 1972, The San Francisco Opera 1922–78 1978, Arthur Bloomfield's Restaurant Book 1987, Sunday Evenings with Pierre Monteux 1997, The Gastronomical Tourist 2002, Gables and Fables (co-author) 2007, More than the Notes: The Conducting of Toscanini, Furtwaengler, Stokowski and Friends 2010. *Address:* 2229 Webster Street, San Francisco, CA 94115, USA (home). *E-mail:* chumbo@earthlink.net.

BLUMENTHAL, Daniel; American pianist; *Professor of Piano, Conservatoire Royal de Bruxelles;* b. 23 Sept. 1952, Landstuhl, Germany. *Education:* Univ. of Michigan, Juilliard School. *Career:* many performances in Europe and elsewhere in the solo and chamber repertoire, notably French and American music; with the Piano Trio of La Monnaie, Brussels, premiered the G minor Trio of Debussy, 1985; other partners include Pierre Amoyal, Barry Tuckwell and the Orlando Quartet; Prof. of Piano, Conservatoire Royal de

Bruxelles 1985–; also Artist Prof., Thy Masterclass Chamber Music Festival, Denmark. *Recordings include:* over 80 recordings. *Address:* Conservatoire Royal de Bruxelles, 30 rue de la Régence, 1000 Brussels, Belgium (office). *Telephone:* (2) 511-04-27 (office). *Fax:* (2) 512-69-79 (office). *E-mail:* pianodan@skynet.be (home). *Website:* www.conservatoire.be (office); www.danielblumenthal.com.

BLUNIER, Stefan; Swiss conductor; *Chief Musical Director, City of Bonn*; b. 1964, Bern. *Education:* Folkwang Coll., Essen, Germany. *Career:* Gen. Music Dir, Darmstadt Nat. Theatre 2001–08; Chief Musical Dir, City of Bonn 2009–; Chief Conductor, Beethoven Orchester Bonn and Oper Bonn 2009–; Prin. Guest Conductor, Orchestre Nat. de Belgique, Brussels 2011–; conducted premiere of Georg Friedrich Haas's Bluthaus at Schwetzingen Festival with SWR Radio Symphony Orchestra 2010; opera productions include Poulenc's Dialogues des Carmélites at Komische Oper Berlin 2011, Puccini's Manon Lescaut in Bonn 2011; has conducted orchestras including Gewandhausorchester Leipzig, Beethovenorchester Bonn, Staatsphilharmonie Ludwigshafen, Duisburger Sinfoniker and several orchestras in Denmark, Belgium, Korea, France and Switzerland; has conducted operas in Munich, Hamburg, Leipzig, Stuttgart, Berlin (Komische Oper and Deutsche Oper), Montpellier, Oslo and Bern; performed at Philharmonie Köln, Conzertgebouw Amsterdam, Schwetzingen Festival, Semperoper Dresden. *Honours:* Besançon 1990, Malko in Copenhagen 1992, ECHO Klassik Award for Opera Recording of the Year (20th/21st century) for Eugen d'Albert Der Golem with Beethoven Orchester Bonn/Chor Oper Bonn 2011. *Address:* Beethoven Orchester Bonn, Wachsbleiche 1, 53111 Bonn, Germany (office). *Telephone:* (228) 776614 (office). *Fax:* (228) 776625 (office). *E-mail:* brigitte.rudolph@bonn.de (office). *Website:* www.beethoven-orchester.de (office). *Current Management:* c/o Angela Sulivan, Sulivan Sweetland, 1 Hillgate Place, Balham Hill, London, SW12 9ER, England. *Telephone:* (20) 8772-3470. *Fax:* (20) 8673-8959. *E-mail:* as@sulivansweetland.co.uk. *Website:* www.sulivansweetland.co.uk.

BLUNT, Marcus, BMus; British composer; b. 31 Dec. 1947, Birmingham, England; m. Maureen Ann Marsh 1988. *Education:* Univ. Coll. of Wales, Aberystwyth. *Career:* compositions performed world-wide and on BBC Radio 3 and Classic FM; woodwind teacher 1976–2007; complete solo piano music recorded by Murray McLachlan 2006; mem. Performing Rights Soc. *Compositions:* 2 Symphonies, The Rings of Saturn for Orchestra, Piano Concerto, Once in a Western Island... for violin and orchestra, Concerto Pastorale for oboe and strings, Aspects of Saturn for strings, Scottish Song Suite and English Song Suite for concert band, Capricorn for 12 winds, Venice Suite for brass ensemble, Cerulean for wind quintet, two string quartets, A Celebration of Brahms and Joachim for piano trio, Sonatas for oboe/clarinet/viola/saxophone/bassoon and piano, three piano sonatas. *Address:* Craigs Cottage, Lochmaben, Lockerbie, Dumfriesshire, DG11 1RW, Scotland (home). *E-mail:* marcusblunt@argonet.co.uk (home). *Website:* www.scottishmusiccentre.com/marcus_blunt.

BLYTHE, Stephanie; American singer (mezzo-soprano); b. 1970, Mongaup Valley, NY. *Education:* Crane School of Music, Potsdam, NY. *Career:* Metropolitan Opera from 1994 in Parsifal, as Mistress Quickly in Falstaff, Baba the Turk in The Rake's Progress and Cornelia in Handel's Giulio Cesare 1999; Mascagni's Mama Lucia on tour to Japan 1997; Lincoln Center recital debut 1997; season 1999–2000 as Mistress Quickly at the Opéra Bastille, Paris, Fricka in The Ring for Seattle Opera, Carmen with Tulsa Opera and Rossini's Isabella at Philadelphia; concerts include Mahler 8 with the San Francisco Symphony Orchestra 1999; Beethoven 9 with the Boston Symphony Orchestra; Schumann's Scenes from Faust in Paris; Messiah with the Minnesota and Florida Orchestras 1999–2000; Covent Garden debut 2003, as Mistress Quickly in Falstaff, followed by Ino in Semele; Metropolitan Opera season 2011 in Rodelinda, Aida and the complete Ring Cycle. *Operatic repertoire includes:* title roles in Carmen, Samson et Delila, Orfeo ed Euridice, L'Italiana in Algeri, La Grande Duchesse, Tancredi, Mignon, and Guilio Cesare; Frugola, Principessa and Zita in Il Trittico, Fricka in both Das Rheingold and Die Walküre, Waltraute in Götterdämmerung, Azucena in Il Trovatore, Ulrica in Un Ballo in Maschera, Baba the Turk in The Rake's Progress, Jezibaba in Rusalka, Jocasta in Oedipus Rex, Mere Marie in Dialogues des Carmélites, Mistress Quickly in Falstaff, Ino/Juno in Semele, Orlofsky in Die Fledermaus. *Honours:* Richard Tucker Career Grants 1995–96, Musical America Award for Vocalist of the Year 2009. *Current Management:* Opus 3 Artists, 470 Park Avenue South, 9th Floor North, New York, NY 10016, USA. *Telephone:* (212) 584-7500. *Fax:* (646) 300-8200. *E-mail:* info@opus3artists.com. *Website:* www.opus3artists.com.

BO, Sonia; Italian composer; b. 27 March 1960, Lecco. *Education:* Milan Conservatory, studied with Donatoni in Rome. *Career:* teacher of composition, Piacenza Conservatory. *Compositions:* Concerto for chamber orchestra 1984, Come un'allegoria for soprano and ensemble 1986, D'Iride for ensemble 1988, Polittico five songs with ensemble 1992. *Honours:* winner Guido d'Arezzo International Competition 1985.

BOCELLI, Andrea; Italian singer (tenor); b. 22 Sept. 1958, Lajatico, Pisa; s. of the late Alessandro Bocelli and of Edi Bocelli; m. 1st Enrica Cenzatti 1992; two s.; m. 2nd Veronica Berti 2014; one d. *Education:* Univ. of Pisa. *Career:* began piano lessons aged six, later learned to play the flute, saxophone, trumpet, trombone, harp, guitar and drums; became blind following a football accident aged 12; won first song competition, Margherita d'Oro in Viareggio with O sole mio aged 14; earned money performing in piano bars; completed law school and spent one year as a court-appointed lawyer; won Newcomers section of Sanremo Music Festival 1994; has recorded 13 solo studio albums, of both pop and classical music, two greatest hits albums and nine complete operas; biggest-selling solo artist in history of classical music; duet with Celine Dion, The Prayer, for animated film The Quest for Camelot, won Golden Globe for Best Original Song 1999. *Recordings include:* albums: Bocelli 1995, Viaggio Italiano 1995, Romanza 1997, Aria 1998, Sacred Arias 1999, Sogno 1999, Verdi 2000, La Bohème 2000, Verdi Requiem 2001, Cieli di Toscana 2001, Sentimento (Classical BRIT Award for Best Album 2003) 2002, Tosca 2003, Aria: The Opera Album 2005, MW 2006, Vivere 2007, Incanto 2008, My Christmas 2009, Andrea Chénier 2010, Carmen: Duets & Arias 2010, Concerto: One Night in Central Park 2011, Notte Illuminata 2011, Opera 2012, Roméo et Juliette 2012. *Publications:* The Music of Silence: A Memoir (La musica del silenzio) (autobiog.) 2000 (reworked 2010). *Honours:* Grande Ufficiale, Ordine al merito della Repubblica Italiana 2006, Grand Officer, Orden al Mérito de Duarte, Sánchez y Mella (Dominican Repub.) 2009; named one of People Magazine's 50 Most Beautiful People 1998, honoured with a star on Hollywood Walk of Fame 2010, World Music Award for World's Best-selling Classical Artist 2010, America Award, Italy-USA Foundation 2012, Classic BRIT Award for Int. Artist of the Year in association with Raymond Weil 2012. *Current Management:* c/o Michele Torpedine, MT Opera and Blues Production and Management, via Mario Musolesi, 40138 Bologna, Italy. *Telephone:* (51) 251117. *Fax:* (51) 251123. *E-mail:* mtorped@tin.it. *Website:* www.mt-operaandblues.it; www.andreabocelli.org.

BOCHKOVA, Irina; Russian violinist; b. 2 Nov. 1938, Moscow. *Education:* studied in Kazan and at the Moscow Conservatoire. *Career:* many appearances in Russia and Europe from 1962, notably as chamber music partner with Vladimir Krainev (piano) and Natalia Gutman (cello); teacher at the Moscow Conservatory from 1978. *Honours:* Silver Medal, 1962 Tchaikovsky Competition, Moscow; winner Long-Thibaud Competition, Moscow 1963. *Address:* c/o Moscow Conservatory, ul Gertzena 13, 103009 Moscow, Russia.

BOCHMANN, Christopher, OBE, MA, DMus; British composer, conductor and teacher; *Head of Music Department and Professor of Music, University of Évora*; b. 8 Nov. 1950, Chipping Norton, Oxfordshire; m.; two d. *Education:* Oxford Univ., studied with David Lumsden, Kenneth Leighton, Robert Sherlaw Johnson, Richard Rodney Bennett, Nadia Boulanger. *Career:* cellist, Nat. Youth Orchestra 1966–67; taught composition, Escola de Música, Brasília 1978–80, Instituto Gregoriano, Lisbon 1980–91, Conservatório Nacional 1981–85; Conductor, Orquestra Sinfónica Juvenil, Lisbon 1984–; Prof. of Composition, Escola de Música, Lisbon 1986–2006, Head of Composition Dept 1990–2006, Dir 1995–2001; Head of Music Dept and Prof. of Music, Univ. of Évora 2006–. *Compositions include:* choral: Prayer of Mary Queen of Scots 1976, Chamber Étude No. 2 1977, Motets for Holy Week 1980–83, Gestures II 1982, Ego Sum Resurrectio et Vita 1985, Motets for Christmas 1987–89, Echoes 1991, Maria Matos Medley 1997, Magnificat 1998, My Monstrous Mountain'd Walke 1999, Morning 2000, Leipziger Motetten 2002, Laudate Dominum 2004; for ensemble: Snakes of Silver Throat 1976, Hymn 1979, Stars 1980, Mobiles for Alexandra 1985, Melodies and Mobiles 1990, Epigrams 1991, Songs for Elizabeth 1992, Sonnet 1993, Motet 1994, Metamorphoses 1995, Musette 1995, Memorial to Jorge Luís Borges 1999, Lacrimae 2001, Lament 2001, Lauda 2002, Seven Lessons 2003, Leituras de Liberdade 2003, Canzona I 2005, Canzona II 2008; orchestral: Accede ad ignem hunc 1970, Four Rhythmic Studies 1973, Eventail 1974, Tableaux Concertants 1976, Nimbus 1977, The Round Horizon 1982, Gestures I, III, IV 1982, Aleafonia Concertante 1984–86, Em Homenagem 1984, Plaint 1987, Epistle 1991, Epitaph 1991, Songs for Simeon 1992, Miserere Mei 1994, Metaphors 1996, Linus 2002, Lupercalia 2002, Symphony 2005, Cicero Dixit 2006; opera: Corpo e Alma 2008. *Honours:* Medal of Cultural Merit, Ministry of Culture, Portugal 2004; winner, Lili Boulanger Prize 1968, 1976, John Osgood Memorial Prize 1970, Trio Competition, Fontainebleau 1970, Stroud Festival Int. Competition 1974, Clements Memorial Prize 1978, Basque Choral Composition Competition 1988. *Address:* Rua 23, Casa 32, Bairro da Ercarnação, 1800-374 Lisbon, Portugal (home). *Telephone:* (21) 8511180 (home). *Fax:* (21) 8511180 (home). *E-mail:* bochmann@uevora.pt (office); bochmann@netcabo.pt (home).

BODE, Hannelore; German singer (soprano); b. 2 Aug. 1941, Berlin; m. Heinz Feldholf. *Education:* studied with Ria Schmitz-Gohr in Berlin, Salzburg Mozarteum, with Fred Husler in Lugano, Karl-Heinz Jarius in Frankfurt. *Career:* sang in Bonn from 1964; Basle, 1967–68; Deutsche Oper am Rhein, Düsseldorf, from 1968, notably as Weber's Agathe, Wagner's Elsa, Eva, Elisabeth and Sieglinde; Kammersängerin, Nationaltheater, Mannheim, 1971–; appearances in London, Buenos Aires, Washington, Vienna, Munich, Berlin; Bayreuth, 1969–80, as Elsa, Eva and in The Ring; sang at Mannheim 1996, in Hannas Traum by Harold Weiss and 1998 as Leocadia Begbick in Weill's Mahagonny. *Recordings:* Parsifal; Die Meistersinger conducted by Solti; Die Meistersinger, conducted by Varviso; Trionfo d'Afrodite by Orff.

BODER, Michael; German conductor; *Principal Conductor & Artistic Adviser, Royal Danish Opera*. *Education:* Hochschule für Musik, Hamburg. *Career:* asst to and student of Riccardo Muti and Zubin Mehta, Florence 1980–84; worked with Michael Gielen, Frankfurt Opera 1984–88; Music Dir and Chief Conductor, Basle Opera 1989–93; Music Dir, Gran Teatre del Liceu, Barcelona 2008–12; Principal Conductor and Artistic Adviser, Royal Danish Opera 2012–; conducts regularly at Vienna State Opera, Munich State Opera, Berlin State Opera, San Francisco Opera; world premieres include Penderecki's Ubu Rex in Munich, Reimann's Das Schloss in Berlin, Trojahn's Was Ihr Wollt in Munich, Peter Turrini and Friedrich Cerha's Der Reise vom Steinfeld in Vienna 2002, Reimann's Finite Infinity at Zürich Tonhalle; conducted Alban Berg's Wozzeck, Vienna 1995, San Francisco 1999, Berg's Lulu in Vienna 2000, 2005, Munich 2004, Schönberg's Die Jakobsleiter, Vienna 2000, Puccini's Gianni Schicchi, Vienna 2000, Richard Strauss's Elektra in Vienna 2001, Wagner's Ring Cycle, San Francisco 1999, Wagner's Der Fliegende Holländer, San Francisco 2003, Enescu's Oedipe, Vienna 2005, Bucharest 2005, Ligeti's Le Grand Macabre, San Francisco 2005, Richard Strauss's Die Frau ohne Schatten in Dresden 2005, Beethoven's Fidelio, Tokyo 2005, Isang Yun's Bara, Berlin 2005; has also conducted concerts with Hamburg Philharmonic, Vienna Radio SO, Leipzig Gewandhaus, Oslo Philharmonic, New Hong Kong SO, Tokyo PO. *Address:* c/o Royal Danish Opera, The Opera House, Ekvipagemestervej 10, 1010 Copenhagen K, Denmark (office). *Website:* www.kglteater.dk (office).

BODIN, Lars-Gunnar; Swedish composer; b. 15 July 1935, Stockholm; m. Margareta Bodin; two c. *Education:* studied with Lennart Wenstrom, visited Darmstadt. *Career:* Composer-in-Residence, Mills Coll., Oakland 1972, Dartmouth Coll. 1990; teacher, Stockholm Coll. of Music 1972–76; Dir Electronic Music Studio, Stockholm 1979–89; collaboration with Bengt Emil Johnson in text-sound compositions; mem. Royal Swedish Acad. of Music 1978–. *Compositions include:* Dance pieces, Place of Plays 1967, and... from one point to any other point 1968, Music for brass instruments 1960, Arioso for ensemble 1962, Semi-Kolon: Dag Knutson in Memoriam for horn and ensemble 1962, Calendar Music for piano 1964, My World in Your World for organ and tape 1966, Primary Structures for bassoon and tape 1976, Enbart for Kerstin for mezzo and tape 1979, Anima for soprano, flute and tape 1984, Diskus for wind quintet and tape 1987, Electronic: Winter Events 1967, Toccata 1969, Traces I and II 1970–71, Memoires d'un temps avant la destruction 1982, For Jon II Retrospective Episodes 1986, Wonder-Void 1990, Divertimento for Dalle 1991, Best Wishes from the Lilac Grove 1994, Bobb – The Life Manager 1997, Jenseits von Licht und Dunkel 2000, Lipton's Adventures 2002, Text-sound pieces. *Recordings:* En Face 1990, The Pioneers 1992, Clouds 2005. *Honours:* Rosenberg Prize 1984, The Stockholm City Award 1986, Atterberg Award 2004. *Address:* Helgalunden 17, 11858 Stockholm, Sweden. *Telephone:* (8) 642-52-44 (home). *E-mail:* bodin.l-g@swipnet.se (home).

BODLEY, Seoirse; Irish composer; b. 4 April 1933, Dublin. *Education:* Royal Irish Acad., studied in Stuttgart with Johann Nepomuk David. *Career:* Assoc. Prof. of Music, Univ. Coll., Dublin. *Compositions:* five symphonies 1959, 1980, 1981, 1990, 1991, two chamber symphonies 1964, 1982, Piano Concerto 1996, Sinfonietta 1998, Violin Sonata 1957, Scintillae for two harps 1968, two String Quartets 1969, 1992, choruses and incidental music, Pax Bellumque for soprano and ensemble 1997, News from Donabate for piano 1999.

BODOROVA, Sylvie; Czech composer; b. 31 Dec. 1954, České Budějovice; m. Jiri Stilec 1984; one s. *Education:* studied in Brno, Bratislava and Prague, with Franco Donatoni in Siena, with Ton de Leeuw in Amsterdam. *Career:* performances of works in the Czech Repub., UK, USA, Germany and others, also at the Prague Spring Festival, Smetana Festival, Litomyšl; teacher, CCM Cincinnati, OH 1995–96; Quattro, Prague. *Compositions include:* Passion Plays for viola and orchestra 1982, Pontem video for organ, percussion and strings 1983, Canzoni for guitar and strings 1985, Messaggio Violin concerto 1989, Magikon for oboe and strings 1990, Panamody for flute and strings 1992, vocal and instrumental music, including Ancora una volta prima vera (violin sonata) 1992, Dona Nobis Lucem 1995, Concerto dei Fiori 1996, Terezin Ghetto Requiem 1997, Concierto de Estío 1999, Saturnalia 1999, Shofarot String Quartet 2000, Juda Maccabeus, oratorio 2002, Mysterium druidum for harp and strings 2003, Bern Concerto for Camerata Bern 2006, Come D'accordo, Concerto for piano and orchestra 2007, Moses oratorio 2008, Carmina lucemburgiana for strings 2009, Kafkas Traüme 2010, Symphony No. 1 2010. *Recordings:* Prague Guitar Concertos, Pontem Video, Terezin Ghetto Requiem, Concierto de Estío, Juda Maccabeus, Ja la laj, Carmina Lucemburgiana. *Current Management:* ArcoDiva Agency, Balbínova 14, 120 00 Prague 2, Czech Republic. *E-mail:* jistilec@arcodiva.cz (office). *Website:* www.arcodiva.cz (office). *Address:* Lidická 990, 253 01 Hostivice, Czech Republic (home). *Website:* www.bodorova.cz.

BOE, Alfred (Alfie); British singer (tenor); b. 1974, Fleetwood, Lancashire. *Education:* Royal Coll. of Music and Nat. Opera Studio, London, Vilar Young Artists' Programme, Covent Garden. *Career:* performances with D'Oyly Carte Co. from 1994; concerts include Verdi Requiem, Rossini Petite Messe and Stabat Mater, Puccini Messa di Gloria and Elijah; season 1999–2000 as Ernesto for Scottish Opera-Go-Round and Rodolfo for Glyndebourne Touring Opera; season 2001–02 as Roderigo in Otello at La Monnaie, Brussels, Ferrando for Grange Park Opera, First Night of London Proms 2001, and Albert Herring at the 2002 Glyndebourne Festival. *Recordings include:* Alfie Boe 2006, Bring Him Home 2010, Alfie 2011. *Honours:* prizewinner Lyric Tenor of the World Competition, Munich, winner John McCormack Golden Voice, Athlone 1998. *Telephone:* (1451) 851100. *E-mail:* jill@brilpr.co.uk. *Website:* www.brilpr.co.uk; www.alfieboe.com.

BOESCH, Christian; Austrian singer (baritone); b. 27 July 1941, Vienna. *Education:* Vienna Hochschule für Musik. *Career:* debut in Berne 1966; sang in Saarbrucken, Lucerne and Kiel; joined Vienna Volksoper 1975; sang at Salzburg Festival 1978 as Papageno in Die Zauberflöte, Metropolitan Opera from 1979 as Papageno, Masetto and Wozzeck, and as Papageno at the Théatre des Champs Elysées, Paris 1987; often heard in modern repertoire; sang in Wolf-Ferrari's La Donne Curiose at the Cuvilliés Theatre in Munich 1989; sang Wozzeck at Buenos Aires 1989. *Recordings:* Die Zauberflöte; Il Prigioniero by Dallapiccola; Haydn's Die Feuersbrunst. *Honours:* Österreichisches Ehrenzeichen für Wissenschaft und Kunst 2006.

BOESE, Ursula; German singer (mezzo-soprano); b. 27 July 1928, Hamburg. *Education:* Musikhochschule, Hamburg. *Career:* began career as concert soloist; Bayreuth Festival 1958–65, in Parsifal and Der Ring des Nibelungen; Hamburg Opera from 1960, notably in Handel's Giulio Cesare 1969; San Francisco 1968, in Oedipus Rex; guest appearances in Milan, Rome, Buenos Aires, London, Paris and New York; opera roles have included Gluck's Orpheus, Handel's Cornelia, Dalila, Gaea in Daphne, Jocasta, Verdi's Ulrica and Azucena and Wagner's Fricka, Erda, Waltraute and Magdalene; Schwetzingen Festival 1982, in the premiere of Udo Zimmermann's Die wundersame Schustersfrau; often sang Bach in concert. *Recordings:* Christmas Oratorio by Bach; Der Evangelimann by Kienzi; Salome and Lulu; Parsifal and The Devils of Loudun. *Honours:* Kammersängerin 1969.

BOESMANS, Phillipe; Belgian composer; b. 17 May 1936, Tongeren. *Education:* Liège Conservatory with Froidebise and Pousseur. *Career:* Music Prod., Belgian radio from 1961; worked at Liège electronic music studios, Centre de Recherches Musicales de Wallonie from 1971; pianist with the Ensemble Musique Nouvelle. *Compositions include:* Etude I for piano 1963, Sonance for two pianos 1964, Sonance II for three pianos 1967, Impromptu for 23 instruments 1965, Correlations for clarinet and two instrumental groups 1967, Explosives for harp and 10 instrumentalists 1968, Verticles for orchestra 1969, Blocage for voice, chorus and chamber ensemble 1970, Upon La, Mi for voice, amplified horn and instrumental group 1970, Fanfare for two pianos 1971, Fanfare II for organ 1972, Intervalles I for orchestra 1972, Intervalles II for orchestra 1973, Intervalles III for voice and orchestra 1974, Sur MI for two pianos, electric organ, crotale and tam-tam 1974, Multiples for two pianos and orchestra 1974, Element-Extensions for piano and chamber orchestra 1976, Doublures for harp, piano, percussion and four instrumental groups 1976, Attitudes musical spectacle for voice, two pianos, synthesizer and percussion 1977, Piano Concerto 1978, Violin Concerto 1979, Concerto for violin and orchestra 1980, Conversions for orchestra 1980, La Passion de Gilles (opera) 1983, Ricercar for organ 1983, Extases II 1985, String Quartet I 1988, Surfing for alto solo and instrumental ensemble 1989, Daydreams for marimba 1991, Love and Dance Tunes for baritone and piano (after Shakespeare) 1993, Reigen (opera) 1993, Summer Dreams for string quartet 1994, Smiles for two percussions 1995, Ornamented Zone for alto clarinet, piano and cello 1996, Wintermärchen (opera after Shakespeare) 1999, Julie (opera) 2005, Yvonne, Princess of Burgundy (opera) 2009. *Honours:* Italia Prize 1971. *Address:* c/o Peters Edition Ltd., Hinrichsen House, 10–12 Baches Street, London, N1 6DN, England (office). *Telephone:* (20) 7553-4000 (office). *Fax:* (20) 7490-4921 (office). *Website:* www.editionpeters.com (office).

BOETTCHER, Wolfgang; German cellist; b. 1940, Berlin. *Education:* Hochschule der Kunste, Berlin. *Career:* soloist, Berlin Philharmonic until 1976; Co-founder Brandis String Quartet 1976, with chamber music appearances in Munich, Hamburg, Milan, Paris, London and Tokyo, including concerts with the Wiener Singverein and the Berlin Philharmonic; festival engagements at Salzburg, Lucerne, Vienna, Florence, Tours, Bergen and Edinburgh; co-premiered Helmut Eder's Clarinet Quintet 1984, the 3rd Quartet of Gottfried von Einem 1981, and the 3rd Quartet of Giselher Klebe 1983; Founder-mem. Philharmonische Solisten, Berlin; concerto appearances; Prof., Hochschule der Kunste, Berlin. *Recordings include:* albums in the standard repertoire from 1978, quartets by Beethoven, Weill, Schulhoff and Hindemith and the String Quintet by Schubert. *Honours:* prizewinner, Int. ARD Competition, Munich.

BOGACHEV, Vladimir; Russian singer (tenor); b. 1960, Moscow. *Career:* numerous appearances at Bolshoi, Moscow and in Europe as Radames, Cavaradossi, Don José, Dmitri in Boris Godunov and Otello; Lensky in Eugene Onegin and Herman in Queen of Spades, Montréal 1990; season 1993 with Otello at Orlando, Florida, Radames in Liège and Don Carlos in Portland; sang in Tchaikovsky's Iolanta at Dresden, staged by Peter Ustinov; sang Aeneas in Les Troyens with London Symphony Orchestra under Colin Davis at Barbican Hall, London 1993, repeated at La Scala 1996; season 1996 as Otello in Amsterdam, Calaf at Macerata Festival and in Khovanshchina at Brussels; numerous appearances on Russian broadcasting services; sang Otello for Royal Opera at Albert Hall and Calaf at Dallas 1997–98.

BOGACHEVA, Irina; Russian singer (mezzo-soprano); b. 1940. *Education:* Leningrad Conservatory. *Career:* appearances with the Kirov Opera, St Petersburg, from 1963 as Verdi's Amneris, Azucena, Ulrica and Eboli; Marina in Boris Godunov, Hélène in War and Peace, Konchakovna in Prince Igor, Lyubava in Sadko and Clarice in The Love for Three Oranges; further engagements as Carmen, Dalila, Charlotte in Werther, Naina in Ruslan and Lyudmilla, Grandmother in The Gambler and the Sorceress in The Fiery Angel; guest appearances at the Opéra Bastille, Paris, New York Met and La Scala, Milan; sang with the Kirov in Summer season at Covent Garden, 2000. *Honours:* Honoured Artist of Russia. *Address:* c/o Mariinsky Theatre, 1 Theatre Square, 190000 Saint Petersburg, Russia.

BOGDANOVIĆ, Maja; French/Serbian cellist; b. 1982, Belgrade. *Education:* Kosta Manojlovic Music School, Zemun, Conservatoire Nat. Supérieur de

Musique et de Danse, Paris, Universität der Künste, Berlin. *Career:* started playing cello at age six; debut tour at age 16 with Serbian Radio and TV Orchestra; moved to France aged 16; has played with Orchestre de la Garde Républicaine, Chamber Orchestra of St George, Dusan Skovran Chamber Orchestra, Orchestre des Lauréats du Conservatoire de Paris, Munchener Kammerorchester; played with Trio Estampe chamber ensemble for 2006 season; active as both soloist and chamber musician. *Honours:* winner, Trofeo Kawai, Italy 1995, Grand Prix de Normandie 2003, ESTA Competition, Paris 2003, Aldo Parisot Int. Cello Competition, Repub. of Korea 2007. *Current Management:* Hispania Clasica, Los Madrazo 16, 28014 Madrid, Spain. *Telephone:* (91) 4292625. *Fax:* (91) 4293530. *E-mail:* musica@hispaniaclasica.com. *Website:* www.hispaniaclasica.com. *E-mail:* majabogdanovic@gmail.com (office). *Website:* www.majabogdanovic.com.

BOGUSLAVSKI, Igor; Russian violist, viola d'amore player and academic; *Professor of Viola, Moscow Institute of Music*; b. 18 July 1940, Moscow; s. of Isaak Boguslavski and Nina Boguslavski; m. 2nd Inna Manolova Gurevich 2012; one d. from previous marriage (died 2003). *Education:* Gnesin Acad. of Music and Moscow Tchaikovsky Conservatory with V. Borissovski. *Career:* debut as viola soloist with Moscow Conservatory Symphony Orchestra, conducted by Y. Aranovich; appearances with BSO on Russian radio and TV playing concertos by Hindemith including viola d'amore chamber music, Bartók and Berlioz; Prin. Viola Soloist, Bolshoi Theatre Orchestra 1977–; Prof., Moscow Inst. of Music 1977–; only active soloist to give concerts on viola d'amore; played with numerous conductors including Rozhdestvensky, Blazhkov, Fedosseev, Lazarev and Simonov, Aranovich and Dudarova; repertory includes Bach, Purcell, Vivaldi, Mozart, Paganini, Brahms, Glinka, Schumann, Bartók, Tchaikovsky, Britten, Hindemith, Martinů, Milhaud, Shostakovich, Prokofiev, Schnittke, Denisov; several works specially composed for him; viola teacher, giving masterclasses and participating in festivals in France, Taiwan, USA and Japan; has given world premieres of concertos for viola and orchestra by A. Holminov, A. Baltin, S. Kallosc, J. Butzko, Y. Grinstein and V. Bibik; also premieres of Paganini's Sonata for viola and strings in C major (new version for orchestra), Martini's Plaisir d'amore for viola d'amore and strings, Shostakovich's Viola Sonata (version for viola and strings by P. Lando), Stravinsky's Russian Song for viola and strings, Grinstein's Concerto in Retro Style for viola and strings; performed in Tchaikovsky Conservatory Great Concert Hall and Russian Composers' Union Concert Hall, both in Moscow; mem. Viola d'Amore Soc. of America; jury mem., Tchaikovsky Competition, Moscow, competitions in Geneva, Munich, Markneukirchen; mem. UN Acad. of Information. *Recordings:* Hindemith, Kammermusik No. 5, Der Schwanendreher, for viola and orchestra; Strauss, Don Quixote; Brahms, Two Sonatas for Viola and Piano; J.C. Bach, Viola Concerto; Paganini, Sonata for Grand Viola and Strings; Graupner, Concerto for Viola d'Amore, viola and strings; Glinka, Sonata for Viola and Piano; Denisov, Variations on a Choral Theme by J.S. Bach; Three Pictures by Paul Klee, for viola and instrumental ensemble; Schnittke, Suite in the Old Style for viola d'amore, harpsichord and percussion; Igor Boguslavski plays the viola and viola d'amore with Bolshoi String Orchestra, conducted by Pavel Lando; Suslin Sonata for viola and cimbalo; J.S. Bach First Suite (arranged for viola), C.P.E. Bach Sonata for Viola and Piano, B. Britten Lacrimae, D. Shostakovich Sonata for Viola and Piano (DVD) 2005; Denisson Variations on a Theme by J.S. Bach, Paganini Sonata, Mozart Sinfonia Concertante (DVD) 2005; more than 60 recordings on discs, CD and from radio. *Publications:* Alfred Shnittke, Suite in the Old Style, Ed. of score for viola d'amore solo, cembalo, companelli, vibratono, campane and marimba 2004, Sir A. Bliss, Viola Sonata, N. Paganini, Viola Sonata (with cadenza by Boguslavski), B. Martini, Viola Sonata, K. M. Weber, Andanta, Rondo. *Honours:* Honoured Art Worker of Russia. *Address:* Studencheskaya Street, 30, b. 2, Apt 5, 121165 Moscow, Russia (home). *Telephone:* (499) 7761631 (home). *Fax:* (499) 7761631 (home). *E-mail:* igorbogus@gmail.com (home).

BOHAN, Edmund, MA; New Zealand singer (tenor) and writer; b. 5 Oct. 1935, Christchurch; m. Gillian Margaret Neason 1968; one s. one d. *Education:* Canterbury Univ., New Zealand; singing with Godfrey Stirling, Sydney, Eric Green and Gustave Sacher, London. *Career:* oratorio debut 1956, opera debut 1962; repertoire of more than 170 operas and major works, including oratorio; concerts in England, Europe, Australasia and Brazil; opera, English Opera Group, Dublin Grand Opera, London Chamber Opera, State Opera of South Australia, Canterbury Opera New Zealand, Nat. Opera of Wellington, New Zealand; Wexford Festival, New Zealand Int. Festival of the Arts, Aldeburgh Festival, Norwich Triennial, Adelaide Festival; TV includes Australian Broadcasting Corpn, BBC Proms and New Zealand Radio; film, Barber of Seville; venues include Royal Festival Hall, Queen Elizabeth Hall and other major halls with Royal Philharmonic Orchestra, London Concert, BBC Concert and Ulster Orchestras; oratorio soloist with British, Australian and New Zealand Choral Socs. *Recordings include:* A Gilbert and Sullivan Spectacular, When Song is Sweet, Sweet and Low, Gilbert and Sullivan with Band and Voice, The Olympians and Intaglio (Bliss). *Publications include:* The Writ of Green Wax 1970, The Buckler 1972, The ISM: The First Hundred Years 1982, Edward Stafford: New Zealand's First Statesman 1994, The Opawa Affair 1996, The Dancing Man 1997, The Story So Far: A Short Illustrated History of New Zealand 1997, Blest Madman: FitzGerald of Canterbury 1998, To Be A Hero: Sir George Grey 1998, The Matter of Parihaka 2000, The Irish Yankee 2001, A Present for the Czar 2003, Burdon: A Man of Our Time 2004, Climates of War: Conflict in New Zealand 1859–1869 2005, The House of Reed 1907–1983: Great Days in New Zealand Publishing 2005, Singing Historian: A Memoir 2012; contribs to The Theatre Royal Christchurch: An Illustrated History, Remembering Godley, The Irish in New Zealand: Historical Contexts and Perspectives, Ulster–New Zealand Migration and Cultural Transfers, Ireland and Irish Antipodes: One World or Worlds Apart?. *Address:* 4/84 Wildberry Street, Woolston/Opawa, Christchurch, New Zealand (home).

BÖHM, Ludwig; German music archivist, writer and editor; b. 5 July 1947, Munich; great-grandson of Theobald Böhm. *Education:* Univ. of Munich, Univ. of Würzburg. *Career:* secondary school teacher of English, French and Spanish, Munich 1981–83; Founder, Theobald Böhm Archives 1980, Theobald Böhm Soc. 1990; organiser of commemorative concerts 1981, 1994, 2006, 2011 and first and second Int. Theobald Böhm Competition for Flute and Alto Flute, Munich 2006, 2011. *Publications include:* Commemorative Publication on the Occasion of Böhm's 200th Birthday 1994, Letters to and Articles about Böhm concerning Flute Construction (ed.) 2006, Letters to and Articles about Böhm not concerning Flute Construction (ed.) 2006, Catalogue of the Concerts by and with Böhm 2006, Catalogue of the Musical Works of Böhm 2010, Catalogue of the Still Existing Flutes of Böhm 2010, Complete Letters and Articles by Böhm (ed.) 2010, Five Publications on Flute Construction by Böhm (ed.) 2010, Biographies of Böhm by Karl von Schafhäutl, Marie Böhm and Karl Böhm (ed.) 2010, Complete Musical Works for Flute by Theobald Böhm and works dedicated to him (ed.) 2010. *Address:* Asamstrasse 6, 82166 Gräfelfing, Germany (home). *Telephone:* (89) 875367 (home). *E-mail:* ludwig.boehm@t-online.de (home). *Website:* theobald-boehm-archiv-und-wettbewerb.de (office).

BOHMAN, Gunnel; Swedish singer (soprano); b. 4 March 1959, Stockholm. *Education:* Opera School, Stockholm. *Career:* engaged by Lorin Maazel for the Vienna Staatsoper; sang at the Mannheim Opera as Pamina, Fiordiligi and Marenka in The Bartered Bride; sang Pamina at the Bregenz Festival and appeared further in Vienna, Zürich, Houston and Hamburg as Mozart's Countess, Agathe, Micaela, Mimi and Lola; sang in the Jussi Björling Memorial Concert in Stockholm, 1985, with Birgit Nilsson, Elisabeth Söderström, Nicolai Gedda and Robert Merrill; Bregenz Festival, 1985–86, as Pamina, Vienna Volksoper from 1987 (as Fiordiligi), Staatsoper from 1988; Zürich and Parma, 1987, as Smetana's Marenka and Gluck's Euridice; Glyndebourne Festival, 1989, as the Countess in Figaro (also at the Albert Hall); Sang Elisabeth in Tannhäuser at the 1996 Savonlinna Festival; Luisa Miller and Hanna Glawari at Frankfurt, 1996; Weber's Agathe, 1998; Sang Jenůfa for Flanders Opera 1999; Season 2000–01 as Luisa Miller, and the Daughter in Hindemith's Cardillac, at Frankfurt; Concert repertoire includes Bach's Passions, B minor Mass and Christmas Oratorio; Ein Deutsches Requiem and Requiems of Mozart and Dvořák; Haydn Die Schöpfung and Die Jahreszeiten; Strauss Vier Letzte Lieder and Wagner Wesendonck Lieder. *Honours:* Jenny Lind Fellowship 1978. *Current Management:* Svenska Konsertbyrån AB, Jungfrugatan 45, 11444 Stockholm, Sweden. *Telephone:* (8) 665-8088. *Fax:* (8) 665-8066. *E-mail:* info@svenskakonsertbyran.se. *Website:* www.svenskakonsertbyran.se.

BOISSEAU, Adrien; French musician (viola); b. 1991. *Education:* studied with Marc Coppey and Jean Sulem at Conservatoire Nat. Supérieur de Musique in Paris, with Tabea Zimmermann at Musikhochschule Hanns Eisler in Berlin and with Nobuko Imai at Kronberg Acad.; masterclasses with Diemut Poppen, Barbara Westphal and the Juilliard String Quartet. *Career:* Resident Artist, Concertgebouw Amsterdam 2014–15; as soloist, appearances at int. festivals including Festival de Pâques and Août Musical Deauville, Festival des Arcs, Encuentro Santander, Escapades musicales du Bassin d'Arcachon, Festival de Cordes sur Ciel, Festival Messiaen La Grave, Festival de Pordic, Next Generation Festival Bad Ragaz, Menuhin Festival Gstaad, Festival Les Vacances de Monsieur Haydn La Roche Posay; performed Bruch's Double Concerto for Viola and Clarinet and Léo Smit's Concerto for Viola and Strings with Deutsches Symphonie-Orchester Berlin under Krzysztof Urbanski at the Berlin Philharmonie, broadcast on Deutschland Radio Kultur 2011; gave three recitals at Festival Radio France Montpellier, one broadcast on France Musique 2013, concerts at Bad Kissingen and La Baule 2014; has been invited to perform with orchestras including Orchestre Pasdeloup, Sinfonieorchester Liechtenstein, Zagreb Soloists, Les Siècles, Kammerakademie Potsdam, Trondheim Symphony Orchestra, Deutsches Symphonie-Orchester, Tokyo Metropolitan Symphony Orchestra, Théâtre des Champs-Elysées, Paris, and worked with conductors including Manfred Honeck, Pierre Boulez, Vladimir Ashkenazy, Kazushi Ono and Myun-Whun Chung; has performed as chamber musician with Renaud Capuçon, Christophe Coin, Adam Laloum, Jérome Pernoo, Alexandra Soumm, Julien Quentin, Alina Ibragimova, Jérome Ducros, Quatuor Ebène; mem. Quatuor Ebène 2015–; duo with pianist Gaspard Dehaene. *Honours:* First Prize and Audience Prize, Max Rostal Viola and Violin Competition, Berlin 2009, Audience Prize and Best interpretation of a Takemitsu work, Int. Viola Competition, Tokyo 2012, International Classical Music Awards Young Artist of the Year 2014, among others. *Current Management:* c/o Musica Prima, 16 rue Pierre Sémard, 94120 Fontenay sous Bois, France. *E-mail:* contact@musicaprima.fr. *Website:* www.classic360.fr.

BOISSEAU, Pierrick; French singer (baritone); b. 1970. *Education:* Conservatoire National de Région de Versailles, Royal College of Music with Ryland Davies. *Career:* sang with Paris Opéra Boys Choir as a child; Les Chantres de la Chapelle, Centre for Baroque Music at Versailles, under Jean-Claude Malgoire, Christophe Rousset and Ton Koopman; Oratorio soloist in

Paris, Athens, Morocco, USA and Malta; Handel's Julius Caesar and Alcindoro in La Bohème, with the Centre de Formation Lyrique de l'Opéra Bastille; Season 2000–2001 in the St John Passion at St John's Smith Square, under Peter Schreier, and Lotario in Flavio, with the London Handel Festival. *Honours:* Lavoisier Scholarship and Audrey Sacher RCM Scholarship. *Current Management:* Agence Artistique Internationale Véronique Valray, 19 rue du Couvent, 33520 Bruges, Belgium. *Telephone:* (5) 5628-3075; (6) 0807-4132 (mobile). *Fax:* (5) 5628-3075. *E-mail:* veroniquevalray@free.fr. *Website:* www.agenceartistiqueveroniquevalray.com.

BOISSY, Nathalie; French singer (soprano); b. 1963, Beaune, Côte d'Or. *Education:* studied at Colmar, Strasbourg, Paris and Oberlin Conservatory, USA. *Career:* sang at Linz Opera from 1988, as Frau Fluth (Nicolai), Marzelline, Countess in Roméo et Juliette, Mimi, Romilda in Xerxes, Micaela, Leila in Les Pêcheurs de Perles and Infantin in Der Zwerg by Zemlinsky; sang Micaela at Bregenz 1991 and in Mendelssohn's Elijah at Linz 1991; Donna Anna at Munich Gärtnerplatztheater 1999. *Address:* General-Eccher-Strasse 11, 6020 Innsbruck, Austria. *E-mail:* nathalieboissy@web.de.

BOKES, Vladimir, Mgr. Art.; Slovak composer; *Professor, Academy of Music, Bratislava;* b. 11 Jan. 1946, Bratislava; m. Klara Olejárová 1970; two s. one d. *Education:* Secondary Music School, Konzervatorium, Acad. of Music, Vysoka skola muzickych umeni, Bratislava. *Career:* teacher in Conservatory, Bratislava 1971–75; Asst. Acad. of Music, Bratislava 1975, Docent 1988, Prof. 1993–; mem. Union of Slovak Composers (Pres. 1995–99), Slovak section of Int. Soc. for Contemporary Music, Int. Festival of Contemporary Music Melos-Ethos Bratislava (Pres. 1993–97). *Compositions:* Symphony No. 1 1970, No. 2 1978, No. 3 1980, No. 4 1982, No. 5 1987, No. 6 2003, No. 7 2009; Piano Concerto No. 1 1976, No. 2 1984; String Quartet No. 1 1970, No. 2 1974, No. 3 1982; Wind Quintet No. 1 1971, No. 2 1975, No. 3 1982; Piano Sonata No. 1 1973, No. 2 1979, No. 3 1980, No. 4 1985, No. 5 2004; vocal cycles, Sposob ticha, The way of silence 1977, Na svoj sposob, In its own way 1978, Departures 2011; Music for organ and wind instruments 1986, Preludes and Fugues for piano 1989, Missa Posoniensis for four soli, choir, organ and orchestra 1991, Variations on a Theme from Jan Egry for eight wind instruments 1995, Commedia dell'arte, aria for tenor and piano 1995, Divertimento for chamber orchestra 2001. *Recordings:* Variations on a Theme from Haydn for piano 1975, Piano Concerto No. 1 1978, Symphony No. 3 1989, Sonata for viola and piano 1993, Cadenza II 2000, Music for piano (Preludes and Fugues, Sonata No. 2 and No. 4) 2001, Inquieto for clarinet and piano 2003, Capriccio for flute and piano 2007, Albrecht Suite for piano 2007, Sequenza per 9 Stromenti 2009, Sonata for violin and piano 2009, Coll Age for piano quintet 2009, Nur eine Weile... for violin, violoncello and accordion 2009, Musica stricta 2009, Sonata No. 5 for piano 2009, Postludium 2009, Comments on Departures 2011, Fugue for 7 instruments 2012, Concertino for violoncello and chamber ensemble 2012. *Publications:* contribs to Hudobny zivot, Bratislava: Biennale Zagreb 1977, Communicativity in Music 1988, Music of Defiance (interview) 1990, to Slovenska hudba, Bratislava: Cantate Domino Canticum Sacrum 1991, Interview with Vladimir Bokes 2001. *Honours:* J.L. Bella Prize 1991, Slovak Critics' Asscn Prize 2000. *Address:* Bjornsonova 11, 811 05 Bratislava, Slovakia (home). *E-mail:* vbokes@gmail.com (office). *Website:* www.vladimir.bokes.org.

BOLCOM, William Elden, BA, MA, DMusArt; American composer, pianist and academic; *Professor Emeritus of Composition, School of Music, Theatre and Dance, University of Michigan;* b. 26 May 1938, Seattle, Wash.; s. of the late Robert Samuel Bolcom and Virginia Bolcom (née Lauermann); m. 1st Fay Levine (divorced 1967); m. 2nd Katherine Agee Ling (divorced 1969); m. 3rd Joan Morris 1975. *Education:* Univ. of Washington, Mills Coll., Paris Conservatoire de Musique, Stanford Univ., studied with Berthe Poncy Jacobson (piano), John Verrall, Leland Smith, Darius Milhaud, George Rochberg (composition). *Career:* Acting Asst Prof. of Music, Univ. of Washington 1965–66; Lecturer, then Asst Prof. of Music, Queen's Coll., CUNY 1966–68; visiting critic in music theatre, Drama School of Yale Univ. 1968–69; Composer-in-Residence, New York Univ. School of the Arts 1969–71; Asst Prof., School of Music, Univ. of Michigan 1973–83, Prof. 1983–2008, Ross Lee Finney Distinguished Prof. of Composition 1993–2008, Prof. Emer. 2008–; mem. Bd American Music Center, Charles Ives Soc., American Composers' Alliance. *Films:* scores for Hester Street 1979, Illuminata 2000. *Ballet scores:* Murray Louis Troupe, Pacific Northwest Ballet, New York City Ballet and others have set dances to his music. *Compositions include:* four Violin Sonatas 1956–94, four Sonatas for violin and piano 1956–97, nine Symphonies 1957–2011, Concerto for piano 1975–76, for violin 1983, for clarinet 1990, for flute 1993, Concert Suite for alto saxophone and band 1998, two piano quintets 2000, 2011, 11 string quartets 1950–2007, 12 Etudes for Piano 1959–66, 12 New Etudes for piano 1977–86, Sonata for cello and piano 1989, Casino Paradise (musical) 1990, McTeague (opera) 1992, A View from the Bridge (opera) 1999, A Wedding (opera) 2003, Songs of Innocence and of Experience 1956–82, Cabaret Songs 1978–97, First Symphony for Band 2008, Prometheus for orchestra, piano and chorus 2010, Romanza for violin and strings 2010, numerous songs for voice and piano. *Publications:* Reminiscing with Sissle and Blake 1973; contribs to Grove Dictionary of Music, Annals of Scholarship and to music industry magazines. *Honours:* Dr hc (San Francisco Conservatory of Music), (Albion Coll.), (New England Conservatory of Music), (New School University, New York), (Baldwin-Wallace Coll.), (Univ. of Hartford); Second Prize, Paris Conservatoire, Kurt Weill Award for Composition 1963, Guggenheim Foundation Fellow, Rockefeller Foundation Awards,

Nat. Endowment for the Arts grants, Pulitzer Prize for Music 1988, American Acad. of Arts and Letters Award 1993, Henry Russel Lectureship, Univ. of Michigan 1997, three Grammy Awards 2006, Nat. Medal of Arts 2006, Detroit Music Award 2006, Musical America's Composer of the Year 2007, Eddie Medora King Award, Univ. of Texas, Austin 2010, American Music Center Letter of Distinction 2011. *Address:* 3080 Whitmore Lake Road, Ann Arbor, MI 48105, USA (home). *E-mail:* wbolcom@umich.edu (office). *Website:* www.williambolcom.com.

BOLDOCZKI, Gábor; Hungarian trumpeter; *Professor, Franz Liszt Academy of Music;* b. 1976, Szeged; m. *Education:* Leo Weiner Conservatory, Franz Liszt Conservatory, Budapest. *Career:* has performed with numerous orchestras, including Bavarian Radio Symphony Orchestra, Vienna Symphony Orchestra, Beethoven Orchestra, Bonn, Dresden Philharmonic, Beijing Symphony Orchestra, Sinfonia Varsovia, Berlin Symphony Orchestra, Gulbenkian Symphony Orchestra, Festival Orchestra Budapest, Hungarian Nat. Philharmonic Orchestra, Lucerne Symphony Orchestra, Strasbourg Philharmonic Orchestra, Prague Symphony Orchestra, Czech Philharmonic Orchestra, Orchestre Nat. de Belgique, also chamber orchestras including Franz Liszt Chamber Orchestra, Camerata Salzburg, Zurich Chamber Orchestra, Munich Bach Collegium, Salzburg Mozarteum, Prague Chamber Orchestra, Haydn Philharmonie, Moscow Soloists, Cappella Gabetta, Bach Orchestra of the Gewandhaus Leipzig; Concertgebouw Amsterdam debut with Netherlands Philharmonic Orchestra under Yakov Kreizberg 2010; performed trumpet concertos of Michael Haydn at Salzburg Festival 2010; gave world premiere of Krzysztof Penderecki's first trumpet concerto at Musikfestspiele Saar 2015; mem. Baroque Duet; Prof., Franz Liszt Acad. of Music, Budapest 2010–. *Recordings:* Glanz der Trompete 2002, Gábor plays Haydn, Mozart, Hummel 2004, Italian Concertos 2006, Händel, Telemann 2007, Gloria 2008, Bach 2010, Tromba Veneziana 2013. *Honours:* Grand Prix de la Ville de Paris, Third Int. Maurice André Competition, Paris 1997, Reemtsma Foundation's Prix Davidoff 1999, Young Artist of the Year 2002, ECHO Klassik Award for Best Newcomer 2003, German Phono Acad. Instrumentalist of the Year 2008, winner, Prague Spring Int. Music Competition 2009. *Current Management:* c/o Winfried Roch, Classic Concert Management GmbH, Mühlenstrasse 22, 86842 Türkheim, Germany. *Telephone:* (8245) 960960. *Fax:* (8245) 960980. *E-mail:* info@ccm-international.de. *Website:* www.ccm-international.de; www.gabor-in-concert.com.

BOLGAN, Marina; Italian singer (soprano); b. 20 March 1957, Mestre, Venice. *Education:* Conservatories in Venice, Siena and Rome. *Career:* sang Rosina in various Italian cities 1981; sang Nannetta in Falstaff at the Teatro della Zarzuela, Madrid 1982, and Gilda at Toulouse; Adina in L'Elisir d'amore, Venice 1984; Bellini's Elvira at the Bregenz Festival 1985; Paisiello's Nina at Catania; Annetta in Crispino e la comare by the brothers Ricci at Teatro La Fenice, Venice, and Théâtre des Champs Elysées, Paris; Elvira and Lucia, Zürich Opera 1987, 1989; at the Hamburg Staatsoper, sang Adina and elsewhere in Donizetti's La Romanziera and Betly; further appearances at Bologna, Verona and the Vienna Staatsoper (Lucia 1988); sang Selinda in Vivaldi's Farnace at the Valle d'Istria Festival, Martina Franca 1991; Gnese in Wolf-Ferrari's Il Campiello at Trieste 1991 and Mascagni's Lodoletta at Mantua 1994.

BOLKVADZE, Eliso; Georgian pianist; b. 2 Jan. 1967, Tbilisi. *Education:* Special School of Music, Tbilisi, Conservatoire Superieur in Tbilisi. *Career:* worked with Michel Sogny in Austria 1989–92; debut at Concert Hall, Tbilisi; Herkules Saal, Munich; Alt Opera, Frankfurt; Auditorium Louvre, Salles Pleyel and Gaveau, Paris; Pasadena Hall, Los Angeles; Concert Hall, Chicago; Teatro Mauzoni, Milan; Schubert Hall, Vienna. *Recordings:* four albums with orchestra in Tbilisi 1994–96, Saint Petersburg, two albums at Villa Schindler, Austria. *Honours:* first prize Lisbon Vianna de Motta Competition 1987, Van Cliburn Competition 1989, third prize Dublin Competition 1987. *Address:* Villa Schindler, Obermarktstrasse 45, 6410 Telfs, Tirol, Austria.

BOLLIGER, Phillip John; Australian composer and classical guitarist; b. 2 May 1963, Sydney, NSW; m.; one s. one d. *Education:* Vienna Hochschule, University of Sydney, studied in Siena and Basle, and with Peter Sculthorpe. *Career:* freelance guitarist and private teacher; composer of film music 1991–. *Compositions include:* Inventions for guitar 1986, The Birds of My Gully for flute 1988, Sailing Song for piano 1990, Four Greek Dances for two guitars 1990, Romance for flute and orchestra 1990, Three Preludes for guitar 1992, Benedictus Balaenarum for trombone and piano 1993, Requiem Chernobyl for choir and orchestra 1993, Zagorsk for string quartet and piano 1993, Monsoon for flute 1997. *Honours:* First Prize, City of Sydney Eisteddfod 1987, First Prize, Warringah Eisteddfod 1992. *E-mail:* pjbolli@yahoo.com.au (home).

BOLOGNESI, Mario; Italian singer (bass-baritone); b. 1957, Rome. *Career:* sang Apollo in Gagliano's Dafne, London 1981; season 1983–84 in Gli Orazi e i Curiazi by Cimarosa at Savona and in Gluck's Alceste at Bologna; further early repertory includes Albinoni's Il nascimento dell' Aurora, Venice 1984; Jommelli's La Schiava liberata, Naples; Agenore in Mozart's Il re Pastore, Rome 1989; season 1989 in the premiere of Manzoni's Doktor Faust at La Scala and Rossini's Basilio at Glyndebourne; season 1994–95 in Rossini's Maometo II at La Scala, Bardolph at Navarra and as Lucarno in Poppea by Monteverdi; season 1997–98 as Pasqua in Wolf-Ferrari's Il Campiello at Bologna and Spoletta in Tosca at the Verona Arena; season 2000–01 at La Scala and Palermo, in Adriana Lecouvreur and Tosca.

BOLTON, Ivor; British conductor; *Chief Conductor, Mozarteum Orchester, Salzburg;* b. 17 May 1958, Lancs. *Education:* Clare Coll., Royal Coll. of Music, Nat. Opera Studio. *Career:* Conductor Schola Cantorum of Oxford, Glyndebourne 1982–92; Conductor Gluck's Orfeo, Glyndebourne 1989; led Il Barbiere di Siviglia, Die Zauberflöte, The Rake's Progress and La Bohème for the Touring Co.; Music Dir Glyndebourne Touring Opera, La Clemenza di Tito 1993–94; f. St James Baroque Players 1984, and directs annual Lufthansa Festival of Baroque Music at St James, Piccadilly; Music Dir English Touring Opera 1990–93, leading Don Giovanni, Figaro, Lucia di Lammermoor, Così fan tutte, Die Zauberflöte, La Cenerentola and Carmen; Così fan tutte at Aldeburgh Festival; ENO debut with Xerxes 1992; La Gazza Ladra for Opera North and Monteverdi's Poppea in Bologna 1993; season 1997 with Giulio Cesare, Serse and Poppea at Munich Festival; Chief Conductor Scottish Chamber Orchestra 1994–, Mozarteum Orchester, Salzburg 2004–; regular concerts with London Mozart Players, English Chamber Orchestra, Scottish Symphony, Bournemouth Sinfonietta and BBC Symphony; Die Entführung at Geneva 2000; Handel's Saul and Rodelinda for the Bayerische Staatsoper 2003, La Calisto, Munich 2006, Peter Grimes, Semper Oper, Dresden 2007, Don Giovanni and Iphigénie en Tauride, Covent Garden 2007. *Recordings include:* Bach's concertos for Harpsichord, Purcell's Dido and Aeneas, Brahms and Mendelssohn Violin Concertos, Vivaldi's Stabat Mater, Handel's Ariodante 2000, Xerxes and Monteverdi's Poppea, all for Bayerische Staatsoper, Munich. *Honours:* Bayerische Theaterpreis 1998. *Current Management:* Ingpen & Williams Ltd, 7 St George's Court, 131 Putney Bridge Road, London, SW15 2PA, England. *Telephone:* (20) 8874-3222. *Fax:* (20) 8877-3113. *Website:* www.ingpen.co.uk.

BONAZZI, Elaine; American singer (mezzo-soprano); b. 1936, Endicott, NY. *Education:* Eastman School of Music, Rochester and Hunter Coll., New York. *Career:* Santa Fe Opera from 1959, notably as Meg Page in Falstaff and in the 1961 US premiere of Hindemith's Neues vom Tage; appearances in Cincinnati, Houston, Dallas, Pittsburgh, Mexico City, Vancouver and New York (City Opera); Caramoor Festival New York in Semele 1969; often heard in operas by Rossini and in contemporary music; sang the Marquise in La Fille du Régiment at St Louis 1990; sang Linfea in La Calisto for Glimmerglass Opera 1996; many engagements as concert singer; taught at Peabody Conservatory, Baltimore; mem. American Acad. of Teachers of Singing, Nat. Asscn of Teachers of Singing. *Recordings:* La Pietra del Paragone by Rossini, Le Rossignol by Stravinsky. *Honours:* Sullivan Foundation grant 1960, Concert Artists Guild Award 1960, Eastman Alumni Award 1972, Peabody Acad. Directors' Recognition Award 1989.

BONCOMPAGNI, Elio; Italian conductor; b. 8 May 1933, Arezzo. *Education:* studied in Florence, Padua, Perugia and Hilversum. *Career:* debut in Bologna 1962, Don Carlos; conductor at opera houses in Europe, including Théâtre de la Monnaie, Brussels from 1974; British debut 1983, Cherubini's Médée at the Barbican Hall, London; Un Ballo in Maschera for Opera Montréal 1990; conducted José Carreras concert at the Scottish Exhibition Centre, Glasgow 1991; Gen. Musical Dir, Aachen, Germany 1996–2002, including Musical Dir Theater Aachen and Artistic and Musical Dir Sinfonie Orchester Aachen. *Honours:* prizewinner, Italian Radio Int. Competition 1961, Mitropoulos Competition, New York 1967. *Website:* www.elioboncompagni.com.

BOND, Graham; British conductor; b. 20 March 1948, Blackburn, Lancs. *Education:* Royal Coll. of Music, London, Accademia Chigiana, Siena. *Career:* Repetiteur, London Opera Centre 1969–70; Conductor, London Festival Ballet 1970–1975; Principal Conductor, London Festival Ballet 1975–80, Music Dir 1980–94; many British, European and other world tours 1970–79; theatres and orchestras in France, Spain, Italy, Germany, China, Yugoslavia, Greece, Venezuela and Turkey; two extensive tours of Australia and two long seasons in Paris with Nureyev 1975 and 1977; guest performances Royal Theatre, Copenhagen1978–81, Stuttgart Ballet Co., Capetown Ballet Co., Conducting staff, Royal Coll. of Music, London 1984; Series of concerts, St John's Smith Square 1984–95, Monte Carlo Opera 1984, Tivoli Symphony Orchestra, Copenhagen 1985, Stanislavsky Theatre, Moscow 1987, Turin Opera, Granada Festival; Guest Conductor, Hong Kong Philharmonic Orchestra, Hong Kong Festival 1987, also Champs Elysées Theatre, Paris, and the Teatro Massimo, Sicily; Deutsche Oper, Berlin 1990; Guest Conductor, Bolshoi Ballet, during tour of England 1991; Guest engagement, Durban, South Africa 1992, Opera House, Budapest; Guest Conductor, Sofia Opera Orchestra, Athens Festival 1993, Palacio de Bellas Artes, Mexico City 1993; apptd Chief Ballet Conductor, Royal Danish Ballet, Royal Theatre, Copenhagen 1994–; Guest performances in 1994 in Prague, Bratislava, Sicily and Orange County, USA; Conductor, Peter Maxwell Davies's Caroline Mathilde ballet, Royal Opera House, London 1995, The Love of Three Oranges, Royal Theatre, Copenhagen and Bergen Festival 1996; Guest Conductor, Dutch Nat. and Netherlands Dance Companies 1996–97, Deutsche Oper, Berlin 1997–98; Conductor, Peter Grimes, Royal Theatre, Copenhagen 1997, Guest Conductor, London Royal Ballet 1998 and Far East tour 1999; Guest, Teatro Real, Madrid 1998, The Magic Flute and Madama Butterfly, Royal Danish Opera 1998; Guest Conductor, Royal Opera, London 2000–05 including tours to Bolshoi and Maryinsky Theatres; Guest Conductor, Royal Opera, Stockholm 2004–05. *Honours:* Worshipful Co. of Musicians Medal 1969. *Address:* 8 Calverley Park Crescent, Tunbridge Wells, TN1 2NB, England (home).

BOND, Timothy M., BMus, ARCM, FRCO; British organist and lecturer; b. 21 July 1948, Mullion, Cornwall, England. *Education:* Royal Coll. of Music, London. *Career:* debut at Westminster Cathedral 1974; British premiere, Schoenberg's Molto moderato (Sonata for organ) 1974; premieres at Henry Wood Proms of Ligeti – Two Studies 1976, Schoenberg Variations on a Recitative 1979, Messiaen L'Ascension 1981, Schmidt, Das Buch mit sieben Siegeln 2000, Britten, Voluntary on Tallis' Lamentation (world premiere) 2004; Schoenberg Festival, Royal Festival Hall 1989; other festival appearances include, Aldeburgh, Huddersfield, Southampton, City of London, Normandy; for television: Ceremonies and Rituals, directed by Barrie Gavin 1981 and many broadcasts of modern organ music, including: Schoenberg, Satie, Milhaud, Messiaen, Stockhausen, Berio, Pousseur, Goehr; British premiere of original version of Schoenberg's Variations on a Recitative 1974; comm. and premieres of works specially written including Uccelli by John Lambert 1992, Echo Toccata by John Lambert 1993, The Grass is Sleeping by Avril Anderson 1979, Concerto for organ and orchestra: Crossing the Great Water, by David Sutton-Anderson 1992; Lecturer, Royal Coll. of Music, London 1976–2004. *Recordings:* Messiaen: L'Ascension 1997, Britten (complete solo organ music), John Lambert, Tippett, Vaughan Williams, Howells 2004, Schoenberg: Variations on a Recitative, Molto moderato (Sonata for organ) 2008, John Lambert, Gary Carpenter, Avril Anderson, Richard Blackford, David Sutton-Anderson (world premiere recordings) 2008. *Publications:* contrib. to Musical Times 1978, 2004, Mirror of Perfection by Richard Blackford 1997 (version with organ accompaniment), Britten for Organ (Britten complete solo organ music) (ed with Colin Matthews) 2004, Roger Hilton Night Letters (ed.) 2009. *Honours:* SPNM Young Artists and Twentieth-Century Music 1975. *Address:* An der Spreekenhorst 14, 27321 Bahlum, Germany. *E-mail:* tmbond@t-online.de.

BOND, Victoria Ellen, DMus; American composer and conductor; b. 6 May 1945, Los Angeles, Calif.; d. of Philip Bond and Jane Courtland; m. Stephan Peskin 1974. *Education:* Univ. of Southern Calif., Juilliard School of Music. *Career:* Asst Conductor, Juilliard New Music Ensemble 1974–77; Asst Conductor, Aspen Music Festival Opera 1975–76; Asst Conductor, Cabrillo Music Festival 1975; Asst Conductor, White Mountains Music Festival 1976; Exxon/Arts Endowment Conductor, Pittsburgh Symphony 1978–80; Musical Dir, New Amsterdam Symphony Orchestra, New York 1978–80, Pittsburgh Youth Symphony Orchestra 1978–80, Bel Canto Opera, New York 1983–86, Roanoke Symphony Orchestra 1986–95, Empire State Youth Orchestra 1988–90; Artistic Dir Opera Roanoke 1989–95, Bel Canto Opera 1986–88, Harrisburg Opera, Pennsylvania 1997–2002; fmr Artistic Adviser Wuhan Symphony, China; currently Prin. Guest Conductor, Chamber Opera Chicago; guest conductor with numerous orchestras, including Anchorage Symphony and Anchorage Opera, Colorado Philharmonic, Houston Symphony, Buffalo Philharmonic, Pittsburgh Symphony, Hudson Valley Philharmonic, RTE Symphony, Dublin, Albany Symphony, Des Moines Symphony, Virginia Symphony, Shanghai Symphony; Pres. and Artistic Dir Welltone New Music, Inc. 2003–, Founder and Artistic Dir Cutting Edge Concerts New Music Festival; mem. Music Panel, New York State Council of Arts 1987; fmr mem. Bd of Dirs American Music Center, Conductors Guild; mem. American Soc. of Composers, Authors and Publishers, American Fed. of Musicians, American Symphony Orchestra League; pre-concert lecturer, New York Philharmonic 2008–, pre-opera lecturer, Metropolitan Opera HD Broadcasts 2012–. *Recordings include:* Live from Shanghai, Victoria Bond: Compositions, Yes, Peculiar Plants, American Piano Concertos Vols I and II. *Honours:* Dr hc (Hollins Coll.) 1995, (Roanoke Coll.) 1995; numerous awards from ASCAP, Victor Hubert Award 1977, named Exxon Arts Endowment Conductor 1978–90, Virginia Woman of the Year 1990, Walter Hinrichsen Award, American Acad. of Arts and Letters, Miriam Gideon Prize. *Address:* Welltone New Music, 20 Vesey Street, Floor 7, New York, NY 10007, USA (office). *E-mail:* info@welltonenewmusic.org (office). info@victoriabond.com. *Website:* cuttingedgeconcerts.org (office); www.victoriabond.com.

BONDARENKO, Andrei; Ukrainian singer (baritone); b. 1987, Kamianets-Podilskyi. *Education:* Nat. Tchaikovsky Acad. of Music, Kiev Conservatory. *Career:* fmr soloist, Ukraine Nat. Philharmonic Soc.; soloist, Mariinsky Acad. of Young Singers 2007–; currently performing with Orchester Wiener Akad.; toured with Larissa Gergieva in France, Switzerland and UK; worked intensively with Michael Schade at the Salzburg Festival Young Artists Programme 2009, took masterclasses with Christa Ludwig, Marjana Lipovšek and Thomas Quasthoff, invited to return to Salzburg Festival to take part in production of Gounod's Roméo et Juliette under Yannik Nézet-Seguin 2010 and Stravinsky's Le Rossignol with Ivor Bolton 2011; has performed at many musical festivals; debut with Glyndebourne Festival & Touring Opera 2012. *Repertoire includes:* Dr Malatesta, Don Pasquale (Donizetti), Belcore, L'elisir d'amore (Donizetti), Grégorio, Roméo et Juliette (Gounod), Silvio, I Pagliacci (Leoncavallo), Guglielmo, Così fan tutte (Mozart), Il conte, Le nozze di Figaro (Mozart), Papageno, Die Zauberflöte (Mozart), Marcello, La Bohème (Puccini), Aeneas, Dido and Aeneas (Purcell), title role, Eugene Onegin (Tchaikovsky), Robert, Iolanta (Tchaikovsky), Marullo, Rigoletto (Verdi). *Opera performance includes:* The Giacomo Variations 2011. *Honours:* First Prize, Int. Vocal Competition 'Art in the 21st Century', Vorzel, Ukraine, winner, Int. Rimsky-Korsakov Competition 2006, winner, Nadezhda Obuhova Young Vocalists' Festival 2008, Song Prize, BBC Cardiff Singer of the World 2011. *Address:* Mariinsky Theatre, St Petersburg 190 000, Theatre Square, Russia (office). *Telephone:* (812) 326-41-41 (office). *Website:* www.mariinsky.ru (office).

BONDE-HANSEN, Henriette; Danish singer (soprano); b. 3 Sept. 1963, Funen; m. Reinaldo Macias 2006. *Education:* Royal Acad. of Music and Opera Acad., Copenhagen. *Career:* operatic roles include Ilia in Idomeneo, Susanna in Le Nozze di Figaro, Zerlina in Don Giovanni, title role in Mozart's Zaïde, Celia in Lucio Silla, Aminta in Il re pastore, Aspasia in Mitridate, Fiordiligi in Così fan tutte, Pamina in Die Zauberflöte, Adina in L'Elisir d'Amore, Marzelline in Fidelio, Gilda in Rigoletto, Juliette in Romeo et Juliette, Nanetta in Falstaff, Valencienne in Die lustige Witwe, Marionette in La Vedova Scaltra, Sophie in Der Rosenkavalier, Najade in Ariadne auf Naxos, Zdenka in Arabella and Mélisande in Pelleas et Mélisande, Dircé in Médée, Rosaura in La Vedova Scaltra, Fiorilla in Turco in Italia, Angelica in Orlando, Aminta in La finta giardiniera, Marguerite in Les Huguenots; performances at the Concertgebouw Amsterdam, De Nederlandse Opera-Amsterdam, Flamish Opera-Antwerp, Det Kongelige Teater-Copenhagen, Den Jyske Opera-Aarhus, Staatstheater Stuttgart, Scottish Opera, Canadian Opera Company, Teatro Municipal in Santiago-Chile, Opéra Nat. La Monnaie-Brussels, Opéra Nat. du Rhin-Strasbourg, Opera de Bordeaux, Opera de Nice, Théâtre du Capitole-Toulouse, Opéra Nat. de Montpellier, Opéra de Nancy et de Lorraine, Théâtre du Châtelet-Paris and Opéra Nat. de Paris-Bastille; recitals include Bach's St Matthew Passion, St John Passion and B minor Mass, Haydn's Die Jahreszeiten and Die Schöpfung, Mozart's Concert Aria's, Great Mass in C minor, the Requiem and Exsultate Jubilate, Brahms' Ein Deutsches Requiem, Liszt's Christus, Fauré's Requiem, Mahler's 2nd, 4th and 8th Symphonies, Poulenc's Stabat Mater and Gloria, Nielsen's 3rd Symphony, Frederic Delius' Lieder and Schierbeck's Den Kinesiske Flojte, Dutilleux's Correspondances, Delius' Lieder, Handel's Israel, Haydn's Orlando Paladino, Beethoven's Missa Solemnis and Mass in C Major (Op. 86). Recordings include: Mahler's 8th Symphony, Bizet's Ivan IV, Mozart's Operas, Lucio Silla, Mitridate, Il re pastore, Idomeneo, Delius Danish songs, Delius Norwegian songs, Delius English Masterworks. Current Management: c/o Alferink Artists Management, Herengracht 340, 1016 CG Amsterdam, The Netherlands. Telephone: (20) 6643151. Fax: (20) 6752426. E-mail: info@ alferink.org. Website: www.alferink.org.

BONELL, Carlos Antonio; British musician, teacher, guitarist and composer; b. 23 July 1949, London; s. of Carlos Bonell and Ana Bravo; m. Pinuccia Rossetti 1975; two s. Education: William Ellis School, Highgate and Royal Coll. of Music, under John Williams. Career: debut as solo guitarist, Wigmore Hall, London 1971; concerto debut with Royal Philharmonic Orchestra 1975; American debut, Avery Fisher Hall, New York 1978; concert appearances with prin. British orchestras; appearances with John Williams, Teresa Berganza, Pinchas Zukerman 1975–; formed Carlos Bonell Ensemble 1983; Prof., Royal Coll. of Music 1972–, London Coll. of Music 1983–; Profesor Invitado, Univ. of Guanajuato, Mexico. Recordings include: Guitar Music of Spain 1975, Guitar Music of the Baroque 1976, Showpieces 1981, Rodrigo Concerto 1981, Paganini Trios and Quartets 1983, Twentieth Century Music for Guitar 1987, Once Upon a Time, with Xer-Wai (violin) 1992, Walton Bagatelles and Anon in Love 1993, Britten Folksongs (with Philip Langridge) 1994, The Sea in Spring 1997, The Private Collection 1998, Kinkachoo I Love You (Millennium Guitar, The First 1000 Years) 2000, Trinity Coll. Grade pieces 2003, Carlos Bonell plays Gordon Mizzi 2003, Guitar Classics 2004. Publications: 20 First Pieces 1982, Tarrega: Fantasia on "La Traviata", 3 Spanish Folk Songs, Purcell: Music from the Fairy Queen, Fantasy for 3 Guitars 1995, Technique Builder 1997, Millennium Guitar, The First 1000 Years 2000. Honours: Hon. ARCM . Current Management: Patrick Allen, Connaught Artists Management Ltd, Penhurst House, 352-356 Battersea Park Road, London, SW11 3BY, England. Telephone: (20) 7978-0144. E-mail: classicalmusic@ connaughtartists.com. E-mail: carlos@carlosbonell.com. Website: www .carlosbonell.com.

BONETTI, Antoni Robert, M.Mus, AMusA, DSCM, ARCM; Australian violinist, conductor and academic; b. 6 Nov. 1952, London, England; m. Ruth Back 1974; three s. Education: New South Wales Conservatorium. Career: Prin. Second Violin, Australian Youth Orchestra 1968–72; tour of Japan 1970, South East Asia 1974; freelance violinist, London 1975–76, appearing with Royal Philharmonic Orchestra, New Philharmonia Orchestra, London Mozart Players; Concertmaster, Norrlands Opera Orchestra, Sweden 1976–77, Stockholm Ensemble 1977–78; Conductor, Musik Sällskap, Umeå 1978; Baroque Violin with Gammerith Consort, Austria 1978; mem. Kurpfalzisches Kammerorchester 1979–81; Concertmaster, Queensland Theatre Orchestra 1981–84; Lecturer, Queensland Conservatorium of Music 1982–92; Head of Orchestral Studies, St Peter's Lutheran Coll. 1985–2009; Lecturer, Univ. of Queensland School of Music 2003–13; Conductor, Baroque Orchestra of Brisbane, Brisbane Christian Chamber Orchestra 1986–89, Concert Soc. Orchestra 1987–90; extensive tours with Divertimento Bonetti ensemble throughout Europe; various conducting engagements with Redcliffe City Choir, Cleveland Symphony Orchestra, Ipswich Youth Orchestra 1989; Founder and Dir Brisbane Symphony Orchestra 1990–, Noosa Orchestra 2010–; Co-founder ensemble Quartetto Bonetti; adjudicator, various Eisteddfods; currently Head of Strings, St Aidans Anglican Girls School and Sr String teacher, Good Shepherd Lutheran College, Noosa. Composition: Jacaranda for orchestra 1992. Honours: Australian Council for the Arts Fellowship 1974. Address: Warana Street, The Gap, Queensland 4061, Australia. Telephone: (4) 0778-2404 (office). E-mail: antoni@antonibonetti.com. Website: www .antonibonetti.com; musicabonetti.com.

BONFATTI, Gregory; Italian singer (tenor); b. 1964. Career: debut as Don Ramiro in La Cenerentola at Spoleto 1991; many appearances throughout Italy and elsewhere in Europe in the bel canto repertory; Ravenna Festival as Paolino in Cimarosa's Il Matrimonio Segreto, Tebaldo (I Capuleti e i

Montecchi) and Lindoro in L'Italiana in Algeri; Festival della Valle d'Itria, Macerata, as Don Rodrigo in Mercadante's Caritea, regina di Spagna; Pubblio in Pacini's L'Ultimo Giorno di Pompei 1996; Monte Carlo Opera 1996 in Pagliacci, with Leo Nucci and Placido Domingo. Recordings include: Caritea, regina di Spagna, and L'Ultimo Giorno di Pompei. Honours: winner Singing Competition of Teatro Belle, Spoleto 1991.

BONIG, Andrea; German singer (mezzo-soprano); b. 1959, Bamberg. Education: studied with Donald Grobe in Berlin, and in Basle and Frankfurt. Career: many concert engagements in Germany and elsewhere, including Liszt's Legend of St Elizabeth with the Bamberg Symphony Orchestra; Donizetti's Requiem with the Berlin Philharmonic; Teatro Liceo Barcelona, 1990 as Dryad in Ariadne auf Naxos; Rossweise in Die Walküre in Valencia and Bonn, 1991–92; Berlin Staatsoper from 1996, including Flosshilde in Das Rheingold; Season 1997–98 with Hippolyta in A Midsummer Night's Dream at the Vienna Volksoper; Further concert repertory includes Beethoven's Ninth and Saint-Saëns's Christmas Oratorio. Current Management: c/o Mag. Jana Mertová, Michael Lewin International Artists' Management, IAAC Kulturmanagement GmbH, Gluckgasse 1/1, 1010 Vienna, Austria. Telephone: (676) 375-19-63. E-mail: mertova@lewin-management.com. Website: www.andrea -boenig.de.

BÓNIS, Ferenc, DMus; Hungarian musicologist; b. 17 May 1932, Miskolc; s. of József Bónis and Ilona Kelemen; m. Terézia Csajbók. Education: Ferenc Liszt Acad. of Music, Budapest. Career: Music Producer, Hungarian Radio 1950–70; Scientific Collaborator, Musicological Inst. of Hungarian Acad. of Sciences 1961–73; Prof., Musicological Faculty, Ferenc Liszt Acad. of Music 1972–86; Ed. Magyar Zenetudomány (Hungarian Musicology) 1959–, Magyar Zenetörténeti Tanulmányok (Studies on History of Hungarian Music) 1968–, Complete Edition of B. Szabolcsi's Works 1977–; Leader Music Dept for Children and Youth, Hungarian Radio 1970–94; Leading Music Producer, Hungarian Radio 1994–96; Pres. Ferenc Erkel Soc. 1989–2012, Hungarian Kodály Soc. 1993–2007; honoured in book Details to the Whole 2012; mem. Musicological Cttee, Hungarian Acad. of Sciences 2010. Recordings: Early Hungarian Chamber Music (ed.); works by P. Wranitzky and L. Mozart; Béla Bartók – As We Saw Him (recollections); Zoltán Kodály – As We Saw Him (recollections). Publications include: Mosonyi Mihály 1960, G. Mahler und F. Erkel 1960, Béla Bartók, His Life in Pictures and Documents 1980, Zoltán Kodály, A Hungarian Master of Neoclassicism 1982, Tizenhárom találkozás Ferencsik Jánossal (Meeting J. Ferencsik) 1984, International Kodály Conference (with E. Szönyi and L. Vikár) 1986, Kodály Zoltán Psalmus Hungaricusa (commented facsimile edn) 1987, Harminchárom óra ifjabb Bartók Bélával (33 hours with B. Bartók Jr) 1991, Hódolat Bartóknak és Kodálynak (Devotion to Bartók and Kodály) 1992, Bartók-Lengyel, A csodálatos mandarin 1993, Himnusz (Hungarian Nat. Anthem, facsimile edn) 1994, Igy láttuk Kodályt (Kodály as We Saw Him; third enlarged edn) 1994, Igy láttuk Bartókot (Bartók as We Saw Him; second enlarged edn) 1995, A Himnusz születése és másfél százada (The Birth of the Hungarian Nat. Anthem and its 150 Years) 1995, Das leidende Volk und die unterdrückte Nation auf der ungarischen Opernbühne 1995, Ein städtisches Fest und die Idee der Vereinigung: Budapest 1923 1996, Brahms und die ungarische Musik 1996, Heldentum und Sehnsucht nach Freiheit. Zur Frage Beethoven und die ungarische Musik 1998, The Dance Suite of Béla Bartók (commented facsimile edn) 1998, Szabolcsi, Kodály and the Bach-theory of Reverend Werker 1999, From Mozart to Bartók 2000, Die Ungarn im Finale der Symphonie No. 4 von Brahms 2001, Üzenetek a XX. századból (Messages from the 20th Century) 2002, Mihály Mosonyi 2002, Bartók-Lengyel, The Miraculous Mandarin 2002, Gondolatok Bartók zenekari Concertójáról (On Bartók's Concerto for Orchestra) 2004, A Budapesti Filharmóniai Társaság százötven esztendeje (150 Years of the Budapest Philharmonic Society) 2005, Élet-képek: Bartók Béla (Life-pictures: Béla Bartók) 2006, Schumann und Mosonyi: Die Kinderszenen und die Ungarische Kinderwelt 2006, Hunyadi László von Ferenc Erkel und die Herausgestaltung des Opernrepertoires im Pester Nationaltheater 1837–1849 2009, Rákóczi March by Hector Berlioz (commented facsimile edn) 2010, Himnusz (Hungarian nat. anthem by Ferenc Kölcsey and Ferenc Erkel, second commented enlarged edn) 2010, Geh und sieh, doch frage nimmer: Béla Bartók's Oper Herzog Blauberts Burg 2010, Élet-pálya: Zoltán Kodály (A Way of Life: Zoltán Kodály) 2011, Béla Bartók/Paul Sacher, Briefwechsel 1936–1940 2013, Zoltán Kodály und die Universal Edition 1938–1966 2013, 1918–1929 2015. Honours: Hon. Freeman of F. Erkel's native town Gyula 1999; Officer's Cross, Order of the Hungarian Repub. 1992; Doctor of the Hungarian Acad. of Sciences 2003; Ferenc Erkel Prize 1973, Széchenyi Prize 2008. Address: Belgrád rakpart 27.I.5, Budapest 1056, Hungary (home). Telephone: (1) 337-9975 (home). Fax: (1) 337-9975 (home).

BONIZZONI, Fabio; Italian harpsichordist and organist; Music Director, La Risonanza; b. Milan. Education: studied under Ton Koopman. Career: specialist in early music, played with ensembles including Amsterdam Baroque, Le Concert des Nations and Europa Galante; Founding Music Dir vocal/orchestral ensemble La Risonanza 1995, evolved into period instrument baroque chamber orchestra; concerts at halls and festivals across Europe including Utrecht, San Sebastián, Cuenca, Rheingau, Teatro San Carlo Naples, Accademia di Santa Cecilia; as soloist and with La Risonanza, numerous radio broadcasts on BBC, WDR, Radio France, SWF, ORF and HR; Prof. of Harpsichord, Royal Conservatory of the Hague and Conservatory of Trapani, Italy; Founding Pres. Associazione Hendel; Dir Atelier départemental de musique ancienne, Aisne, France. Recordings include: as soloist: Claudio

Merulo Toccate, Ricercari, Canzoni d'Intavolatura d'Organo, Scarlatti Keyboard Sonatas, Goldberg Variations, J.S. Bach Art of the Fugue, Frescobaldi Toccatas & Partitas; with La Risonanza: six vols of Handel's Italian Cantatas including Le Cantate per il Cardinal Pamphili, Clori, Tirsi e Fileno and Apollo e Dafne (Stanley Sadie Handel Recording Prizes 2007, 2010 and 2012); many other recordings including works of Giovanni Salvatore, Giovanni Picchi (Deutscher Schallplattenpreis), Francesco Geminiani, Bernardo Storace, Domenico Scarlatti. *Address:* c/o Glossa Music, Timoteo Padrós 31, San Lorenzo de el Escorial 28200, Spain (office). *E-mail:* ceventu@alice.it (office).

BONNEMA, Albert; Dutch singer (tenor); b. 18 April 1953, Trummarum. *Education:* Sweelinck Conservatory, Amsterdam and studied with Nicolai Gedda. *Career:* sang in operettas by Lehar and Offenbach at Amsterdam and Enschede; Guest appearances in Berlin, Salzburg and Klagenfurt (Cassio in Otello, 1989); Lensky in Eugene Onegin at Berne; Giovanni in Mona Lisa by Schillings at Kiel and Walther in Die Meistersinger at Amsterdam, 1995; Števa in Jenůfa at Dresden, 1996; season 1997–98 as Lohengrin at Tokyo and Števa at Hamburg; Season 2000–01 at Dresden as Števa in Jenůfa, Wagner's Erik and Apollo in Strauss's Daphne; Florestan at the Komische Oper Berlin, the Götterdämmerung Siegfried at Stuttgart, and Dmitri in Boris Godunov at Hamburg;Modern repertory includes Goldschmidt's Der gewaltige Hahnrei and Judith by Siegfried Matthus, both at Berne; Frequent concert appearances. *Current Management:* Artists Management Zürich, Rütistrasse 52, 8044 Zürich-Gockhausen, Switzerland. *Telephone:* (44) 8218957. *Fax:* (44) 8210127. *E-mail:* schuetz@artistsman.com. *Website:* www.artistsman.com.

BONNER, Yvette, DipRAM, ARAM; British singer (soprano). *Education:* Arts Education School, London, Royal Acad. of Music. *Career:* debut as Yniold in Pelléas and Mélisande, for ENO; performances include Jennie Hildebrand in Street Scene with Houston Grand Opera 1994; Flora in Turn of the Screw for WNO 1995; Shepherd Boy in Tannhäuser for Opera North 1997; Semele in Die Liebe der Danaë 1999; First Maid in Die Agyptische Helena; debut for Royal Opera (in concert) as Hermione in Strauss's Die Agyptische Helena 1998; Esmeralda in The Bartered Bride 1999; Flora in The Turn of the Screw for WNO 2000; season 2001–02, premiere of Alice in Wonderland, title role, for Nederlandse Opera; Esmeralda in The Bartered Bride for Royal Opera, Covent Garden; Genevieve in Siruis on Earth for Almeida Opera; El Trujaman in El Retablo De Maese Pedro, London Proms 2002; Vixen in The Cunning Little Vixen, Aix en Provence Festival and tour 2002–03, Susanna and Barbarina in The Marriage of Figaro, Savoy Opera 2004, Esmeralda in The Bartered Bride, Royal Opera 2005, Gretel in Hansel and Gretel, Cork Opera 2005, Rusalka, Ilford Festival 2005, Sophie in Werther, Rome Opera 2006; concert work includes Les Illuminations, Acad. of St Martin-in-the-Fields, Carmina Burana, The Symphony Hall, Birmingham, Bach Magnificat and Vivaldi Gloria for the English Chamber Orchestra, Haydn's Nelson Mass at St John's, Smith Square. *Recordings:* Weill's Street Scene (Joan, with ENO) 1989, Emmie in Albert Herring 1996, Die Liebe der Danae, The Marriage of Figaro 2004, The Bartered Bride 2005. *Honours:* Blyth-Buesst Operatic Prize 1998, Emmy Destinn Award for Young Singers; for Czech opera and song 2000. *E-mail:* info@yvettebonner.co.uk. *Website:* www.yvettebonner.co.uk.

BONNEY, Barbara; American singer (soprano); b. 14 April 1956, Montclair, NJ; d. of Alfred Bonney III and Janet Gates; m. 1st Håkan Hagegård 1989; m. 2nd Maurice Whittaker. *Education:* Univ. of New Hampshire, Mozarteum, Austria. *Career:* chorus mem. Darmstadt City Opera 1979–83; with Frankfurt Opera 1983–84; maj. early appearances include Der Rosenkavalier, Covent Garden 1984, Metropolitan Opera, New York 1990, Die Zauberflöte, La Scala 1985, Falstaff, Metropolitan Opera 1990, The Marriage of Figaro, Covent Garden 1995, Zurich Opera, Metropolitan Opera 1998, 1999, Les Boréades, Salzburg Festival 1999, Idomeneo, San Francisco 1999; noted especially for Mozart and Strauss interpretations; appeared regularly as recitalist accompanied by Geoffrey Parsons; Founder Bonney Foundation; currently Prof., Mozarteum, Salzburg; Visiting Prof., RAM; mem. Swedish Acad. of Music. *Recordings include:* Le Nozze di Figaro, Don Giovanni, Die Zauberflöte, Die Fledermaus, Fidelio, Hansel und Gretel, The Merry Widow, Vocalise, Miss Sallie Chisum Remembers Billy The Kid, Emily Dickinson Songs, Samuel Barber's Hermit Songs, Six Elizabethan Songs, Frauenliebe und-leben, Les mamelles de Tirésias, Diamonds in the Snow (Gramophone Award for Best Solo Vocal Recording), While I Dream. *Honours:* Dr hc (New Hampshire), (Bowdoin Coll.), (Royal Acad. of Music). *Current Management:* Michael Storrs Music Ltd, 211 Piccadilly, London, W1J 9HF, England. *E-mail:* info@michaelstorrsmusic.co.uk. *Website:* www.michaelstorrsmusic.co.uk; www.barbarabonney.com; www.thebonneyfoundation.org.

BONYNGE, Richard, AO, CBE; Australian conductor; b. 29 Sept. 1930, Sydney, NSW; s. of C. A. Bonynge; m. Dame Joan Sutherland 1954 (died 2010); one s. *Education:* New South Wales Conservatorium of Music, Royal Coll. of Music,UK. *Career:* trained as a pianist; debut as conductor with Santa Cecilia Orchestra, Rome 1962; conducted first opera Faust, Vancouver 1963; Musical Dir Sutherland/Williamson Grand Opera Co., Australia 1965; Artistic Dir Vancouver Opera 1974–77; Musical Dir Australian Opera 1976–86; has conducted La Sonnambula, La Traviata, Faust, Eugene Onegin, L'Elisir d'amore, Orfeo, Semiramide, Giulio Cesare, Lucia di Lammermoor, Norma, The Tales of Hoffmann and numerous others; has revived many operas not in the repertoire, including Les Huguenots, La Fille du Régiment, Maria Stuarda, Lucrezia Borgia and Thérèse. *Videos include:* Les Huguenots, La Fille du Régiment, The Merry Widow, Norma, Die Fledermaus and The Magic Flute. *Recordings include:* opera: Alcina, La Sonnambula, Norma, Beatrice di

Tenda, I Puritani, Faust, Semiramide, Lakmé, La Fille du Régiment, Messiah, Don Giovanni, Les Huguenots, L'Elisir d'amore, Lucia di Lammermoor, Rigoletto, Les Contes d'Hoffmann, Thérèse, Le Toréador, The Land of Smiles and Giuditta, Lucrezia Borgia, Maria Stuarda, Giulio Cesare, Merry Widow, L'Oracolo, Esclarmonde, Le Roi de Lahore, Suor Angelica, Die Fledermaus, Hamlet, I Masnadieri, La Traviata, Il Trovatore; ballet: Le Diable à Quatre, Giselle, Marco Spada, La Péri, Les Sylphides, Coppélia, Sylvia, Le Carillon, La Cigale, Le Papillon, La Boutique Fantastique, Aschenbrödel, The Nutcracker, Sleeping Beauty, Swan Lake, La Sonnambula; recitals: Tchaikovsky and Grieg Piano Concertos, Kalman's Die Herzogin von Chicago, Die Czardasfurstin. *Recordings include:* recordings with Pavarotti, Tebaldi, Sumi Jo, Jerry Hadley, Deborah Riedel, Rosamund Illing, Yvonne Kenny, Cheryl Barker. *Publications:* The Joan Sutherland Album (with Dame Joan Sutherland) 1986, A Collector's Guide to Theatrical Postcards 1988. *Honours:* Hon. Assoc., Accademia Filarmonica di Bologna 2007; Commdr, Ordre Nat. des Arts et des Lettres 1989. *Current Management:* Colbert Artists Management, 307 Seventh Avenue, Suite 2006, New York, NY 10001, USA.

BOOGAARTS, Jan; Dutch university lecturer, choir director, organist and composer (retd); b. 10 May 1934, Helmond; m. Dorine Sniedt 1964; two s. one d. *Education:* Conservatory of Tilburg, Royal Conservatory, The Hague, Inst. of Musicology, Univ. of Utrecht. *Career:* radio recordings for numerous radio stations, TV channels; Docent Choir Direction, Royal Conservatory, The Hague; Lecturer, Univ. of Utrecht; visiting professorships throughout Europe and USA. *Recordings include:* 30 including Plainsong, Holy Week, Ordo Missae Instauratus Concilii Vaticani II, Vespers, Compline; Missa Ambrosiana, Famous Hymni and Sequentiae; Renaissance Music: Madrigals and Chansons with texts by Petrach and Ronsard; Works of R. White, Josquin, Lassus, Isaak, Senfl and others. *Publications include:* Inleiding tot het Gregoriaans 1985; contrib. of numerous articles to period Festschrift and small publs, magazines and journals. *Honours:* Commendatore, Ordinis Sancti Gregori Magni 2006, Kt, Order of the Netherlands Lion 2007. *Address:* Havezate Die Magerhorst, Ploenstraat 48, 6921 PN, Duiven The Netherlands (home). *Telephone:* (316) 261456 (home).

BOONE, Charles, BM, MA; American composer; b. 21 June 1939, Cleveland, OH. *Education:* Vienna Acad. of Music with Karl Schiske, Univ. of Southern California at Los Angeles, San Francisco State Coll., studied with Ernst Krenek and Adolph Weiss in Los Angeles. *Career:* Chair., San Francisco Composers' Forum; co-ordinator, Mills Coll. Performing Group and Tape Music Center; Composer-in-Residence, Berlin, under the sponsorship of the Deutscher Akademischer Austauchdienst 1975–77; writer and lecturer on contemporary music. *Compositions:* three Motets for chorus 1962–65, Oblique Formation for flute and piano 1965, Starfish for flute, clarinet, two percussions, two violins and piano 1966, A Cool Glow of Radiation for flute and tape 1966, The Edge of the Land for orchestra 1968, Not Now for clarinet 1969, Zephyrus for oboe and piano 1970, Vermilion for oboe 1970, Quartet for clarinet, violin, cello and piano 1970, Chinese Texts for soprano and orchestra 1971, First Landscape for orchestra 1971, Vocalise for soprano 1972, Second Landscape for chamber orchestra 1973, and for orchestra 1979, String Piece for string orchestra 1978, Streaming for flute 1979, Little Flute Pieces 1979, Springtime for oboe 1980, Winter's End for soprano, countertenor, viola da gamba and harpsichord 1980, Slant for percussion 1980, The Watts Tower for one percussion 1981, Trace for flute and ten instruments 1981–83, Solar One for flute and trumpet 1985, The Timberline and other pieces for carillon 1987, Morphosis for six percussion 1997. *Honours:* NEA grants 1968, 1975, 1983.

BOOTH, Claire, BA; British singer (soprano). *Education:* Trinity Coll., Oxford, ENO Studio Baylis Programme, Guildhall School of Music and Drama, Nat. Opera Studio, London and pvt study with Rudolf Piernay. *Career:* professional debut at Royal Festival Hall (RFH) singing Oliver Knussen's Océan de Terre for composer's 50th birthday celebrations concert; numerous appearances with Knussen, including with London Sinfonietta and BBC Symphony Orchestra as well as two BBC Proms performances: his Whitman Settings 2005, Requiem; Songs for Sue 2007; concert career has included appearances with City of Birmingham Symphony Orchestra (CBSO), Chicago Symphony Orchestra, BBC Scottish Symphony Orchestra, Netherlands Radio Orchestra, London Sinfonietta, Ensemble Intercontemporain and Mahler Chamber Orchestra, with conductors including Pierre Boulez, Ilan Volkov, Edward Gardner, Andris Nielsons and Sakari Oramo; operatic highlights in recent seasons include debut at ENO singing Nora in Riders to the Sea directed by Fiona Shaw, roles of Mrs Green (Birtwistle's Down by the Greenwood Side) and Soprano Narrator (Benjamin in Into the Little Hill) for Royal Opera Linbury Theatre, Mélisande in Pelleas et Mélisande for Opera Theatre Company, Anne Trulove in The Rake's Progress with CBSO, Zerlina in Don Giovanni and 1st Niece in Peter Grimes, both for Opera North, Despina in Così fan tutte for Opera Nantes-Angers, Miranda in Adès' The Tempest, Amsterdam Concertgebouw, Belinda in Dido and Aeneas and Anicia Eritea in Cavalli's Eliogabalo for Grange Park Opera, Max in Knussen's Where the Wild Things Are with BBC Symphony Orchestra, Agilea in Teseo for English Touring Opera and the creation of Prakriti in Harvey's Wagner Dream for Netherlands Opera; season 2010 included concerts at Muziekgebouw in Amsterdam, Caldara's oratorio Maddalena a piedi di Christo in Barcelona and Poland, Bach's Matthew Passion at RFH and a return to Aldeburgh Festival with EIC and Pierre Boulez; Lucia in The Rape of Lucretia, Aldeburgh 2011; Rosina for Scottish Opera 2012. *Honours:* Sybil Tutton Award 2003, 2004, Worshipful Co. of Musicians Silver Medal, Harold Rosenthal Award, Susan

Chilcott Scholarship 2006. *Current Management:* c/o Ingpen and Williams, 7 St George's Court, Putney, London, SW15 9PA, England. *Telephone:* (20) 8874-3222. *E-mail:* ds@ingpen.co.uk. *Website:* www.ingpen.co.uk.

BOOTH, Juliet; British singer (soprano); b. 1961, London, England; m. William Symington 1996. *Education:* Bristol Univ. and the Guildhall School of Music. *Career:* Opera North from 1987, Frasquita (debut role), Ninetta in The Love for Three Oranges, Xenia in Boris Godunov; Pusette in Manon, Arminda in La Finta Giardiniera, Norina in Don Pasquale and Lauretta; has also sung Mélisande at Aldeburgh, Virtu and Valletto in Opera London's L'Incoronazione di Poppea and Mozart's Countess for WNO; Aix-en-Provence 1991, as Helena in A Midsummer Night's Dream; concert appearances at the South Bank and the Barbican, in France, Belgium and Singapore; Handel's Solomon in Berlin and Carmina Burana at the Edinburgh Festival under Neeme Järvi; television appearances include Dennis O'Neill and Friends on BBC 2; season 1990–91 with The Kingdom (Elgar), Haydn's Nelson Mass and Creation, Salieri's Prima la Musica with the City of London Sinfonia; concert arias with the English Chamber Orchestra; Messiah; Gilda in Rigoletto, Opera North 1992; Countess in Figaro, Glyndebourne Touring Opera 1992; Morgana in Alcina, Covent Garden debut 1992; Musetta and Mimi in La Bohème, Opera North 1993; Alexina in Le Roi malgré Lui 1994. *Recordings include:* L'Incoronazione di Poppea conducted by Richard Hickox, Bruckner Mass in F 1992. *Honours:* gold medal for singers Schubert Prize for Lieder, Guildhall School Ricordi Opera Prize. *Address:* c/o Opera North, Grand Theatre, 46 New Briggate, Leeds, Yorkshire, LS1 6NU, England.

BOOTH, Philip; American singer (bass); b. 6 May 1942, Washington, DC. *Education:* sang with US Army Chorus, Eastman School of Music with Julius Huehn, studied with Todd Duncan in Washington. *Career:* Kennedy Center, Washington 1971, in Ariodante; many appearances as concert singer; engagements at the opera houses of San Diego, Houston and San Francisco; Metropolitan Opera from 1973, as Pimen in Boris Godunov, Ramphis, Fasolt and Fafner in Der Ring des Nibelungen, Basilio and Osmin; sang in the US premiere of Mascagni's Le Maschere, with Westchester Opera 1989.

BOOTH-JONES, Christopher, ARAM; British singer (baritone); b. 4 Oct. 1943, Somerset; s. of Lt Col C.E. Booth-Jones and Ann Booth-Jones; m. Leonora Booth-Jones; two s., one step-s., three step-d. *Education:* Dover Coll., Royal Acad. of Music, London. *Career:* toured with Welsh Nat. Opera (WNO) for All as Mozart's Figaro and Rossini's Bartolo 1972–73; with WNO, Figaro in Mozart's Marriage and Bohème; Glyndebourne Festival and Touring Opera; Phoenix Opera; English Music Theatre; London Musical Theatre Co. Narrator in Brecht's Caucasian Chalk Circle, Newcastle Festival; ENO from 1982 in Roméo et Juliette, Patience, Così fan tutte, Pagliacci, La Bohème, War and Peace, Osud, Akhnaten and Xerxes; sang Claudio in a new production of Beatrice and Benedict 1990; Mr Astley in a revival of The Gambler; English Music Theatre in Tom Jones, La Cenerentola and The Threepenny Opera; Die Zauberflöte; Opera North in Der Freischütz, A Midsummer Night's Dream, Beatrice and Benedict and Danilo in The Merry Widow; Kent Opera as Monostatos in Die Zauberflöte; season 1992 with ENO in the premiere of Bakxai by John Buller and as the Music Master in Ariadne auf Naxos; Demetrius in A Midsummer Night's Dream, Count in The Marriage of Figaro and Schaunard in La Bohème 1996; season 1998 as Ford in Falstaff and Puccini's Sharpless for ENO; Germont Père in La Traviata 1997, 1998, 1999; sang Melot in Tristan und Isolde, Carmen and Die Frau Ohne Schatten (Strauss) for the Royal Opera in London 2000. *Recordings:* Julius Caesar and Pacific Overtures; Tosca; Videos of The Gondoliers, Princess Ida, Rusalka, Xerxes, Billy Budd, Carmen, Great Things: 20th Century English Song, Bright is the Ring of Words (English song cycles) 2015. *Current Management:* Helen Sykes Artists Management, 100 Felsham Road, Putney, London SW15 1DQ, England. *E-mail:* helen@helensykesartists.co.uk.

BOOTHBY, Richard; British viola da gamba player and cellist; b. 1955, England. *Career:* mem. Purcell Quartet, debut concert at St John's Smith Square, London 1984; extensive tours and broadcasts in France, Belgium, Netherlands, Germany, Austria, Switzerland, Italy and Spain; tours of the USA and Japan, 1991–92; British appearances include Purcell concerts at the Wigmore Hall; repertoire includes music on the La Folia theme by Vivaldi, Corelli, C P E Bach, Marais, A Scarlatti, Vitali and Geminiani; instrumental works and songs by Purcell, music by Matthew Locke, John Blow and Fantasias and Airs by William Lawes, 17th century virtuoso Italian music by Marini, Buonamente, Gabrieli, Fontana, Stradella and Lonati, J. S. Bach and his forerunners: Biber, Scheidt, Schenk, Reinken and Buxtehude; mem. of Fretwork, debut concert at the Wigmore Hall 1986; appearances in the Renaissance and Baroque repertoire in Sweden, Austria, Belgium, Netherlands, France and Italy, Russia; other repertory includes In nomines and Fantasias by Tallis and Parsons, dance music by Holborne and Dowland (including Lachrimae), London Cries by Gibbons and Dering, Resurrection Story and Seven Last Words by Schütz. *Recordings include:* with the Purcell Quartet: On the La Folia theme; Purcell's Sonatas for two violins, viola da gamba and continuo, Sonatas by Vivaldi and Corelli; with Fretwork: Agricola's Chansons, The Cries of London, Bach's Alio modo, Im Maien, William Byrd's Consort Songs, Above the Stars, The Art of Fugue BWV 1080, The Hidden Face, Harmonice Musices Odhecaton, Celestiall Witchcraft, Sit Fast, The Mirrour and Wonder of his Age, Matthew Locke's Concord is conquer'd, Henry Purcell's The English Viol, The Complete Fantazias (Gramophone Award for Best Baroque Instrumental Recording 2009), William Byrd's A Play of Passion, For ye violls, John Dowland's Go nightly cares, Orlando Gibbons' Heart's Ease, In Nomine. *Address:* Fretwork, 12b Herndon Road, London, SW18 2DG, England (office). *Telephone:* (20) 8874-2571 (office). *E-mail:* forgueray1@mac.com (office). *Website:* www.fretwork.co.uk (office).

BOOZER, Brenda Lynn, BA; American singer (mezzo-soprano); b. 25 Jan. 1948, Atlanta, GA; m. Robert Martin Klein 1973. *Education:* Florida State Univ., Tallahassee, Juilliard School, New York. *Career:* Chicago Lyric Opera 1978; Festival of Two Worlds, Spoleto, Italy 1978, 1979; Greater Miami Opera 1979; Houston Grand Opera 1979; Metropolitan Opera, New York 1979–83, 1985, as Hansel, Meg Page, the Composer (Ariadne auf Naxos), Octavian and Orlofsky; Netherlands Opera, Amsterdam 1981; Paris Opéra 1982–83; Falstaff, at Covent Garden 1983; Spoleto Festival 1989, as Nicklausse in Les Contes d'Hoffmann; concerts and television appearances.

BORAC, Luiza; Romanian pianist; b. 1968. *Education:* Music Acad., Bucharest, Acad. of Music and Drama, Hanover, Germany with Karl-Heinz Kämmerling. *Career:* soloist Young Artists Int. Festival, Los Angeles and debut Carnegie Recital Hall, New York 1999; recitals include Concertgebouw, Amsterdam, Steinway Hall, New York, Radio Hall, Hamburg, Palais Palffy, Vienna, Cologne Philharmonie, Puccini Hall, Milan, Athenaeum, Bucharest; festivals include Grieg Festival, Oslo, Prokofiev Festival, Barbican Centre, London, Aldeburgh Festival, Chopin Festivals in Vienna and Milan, South Bohemian Music Festival, Braunschweiger Classix, Schleswig-Holstein Music Festival; has performed as soloist with many orchestras including Netherlands Philharmonic Orchestra, Utah Symphony Orchestra, Bucharest and Cologne Radio Orchestras, Philharmonic Orchestra of Nations; teaches piano, Acad. of Music and Drama, Hanover. *Recordings include:* George Enescu's Three Piano Suites 2003, Wanderer: music by Schubert and Liszt 2005, Enescu The Three Piano Suites 2003, George Enescu Piano Works (BBC Music Magazine Award for Best Instrumental CD 2007) 2005, George Enescu: The Two Piano Sonatas (BBC Award 2007) 2006, Chopin 24 Etudes and 6 Polish Songs 2009, Frühlingsglaube 2010, Dinu Lipatti 2012, Piano Music of Dinu Lipatti 2013, Chants nostalgiques 2014. *Honours:* winner, Enescu Int. Piano Festival 1991, Young Artist of the Year Romanian Critics Prize 1991, Silver Medal Gina Bachauer Int. Piano Competition, Salt Lake City 1998, East & West Int. Prize for a New York Debut 1999, first prizes at Viotti-Valsesia (Italy) and Mendelssohn-Germany Int. Piano Competitions, Mozarteum Salzburg Prize, Prix d'Oslo, Audience Prize and Special Prize for Best Grieg Interpretation, Concours Grieg Int. Piano Competition, Oslo 2002, Henry Havergal Memorial Prize in Glasgow, Richard Wagner Int. Award in Bayreuth, Music News Award. *Current Management:* mbm-management, Münsterstr. 46, 88662 Überlingen, Germany. *Address:* Klavierhaus Doell, Schmiedestrasse 8, 30159, Hanover, Germany. *E-mail:* info@luizaborac.com. *Website:* www.luizaborac.com.

BORCHERS, James, MMus; American composer, percussionist and teacher. *Education:* Univ. of Nebraska, Aaron Copland School of Music, Queens Coll., New York. *Career:* works performed by New York Youth Symphony, ICE ensemble, Sospiro Winds, Ebony Strings Quartet; has performed at Storm King Music Festival, Bang on a Can marathon, and with Ballet Hispanico, New York Youth Symphony at Carnegie Hall, New Amsterdam and Musica Bella orchestras; participated in American Opera Projects composers and the voice workshop 2005–06; has composed orchestral and chamber music, electronic music, and music for opera and theatre; currently teacher Rhapsody Music and Art Center mem. duo (with singer/songwriter Audrey Ryan). *Compositions include:* Ravens (string quartet), Old Song (opera) 2006, Christmas Day (opera) 2006. *Address:* Rhapsody Music and Art Center, 138 Hartford Avenue, Hopedale, MA 01747, USA (office). *Telephone:* (508) 634-3917 (office). *E-mail:* rmaac@comcast.net (office). *Website:* www.rhapsodymusicandartcenter.com (office).

BORDA, Deborah, BA; American orchestra executive; *President and CEO, David C. Bohnett Presidential Chair, Los Angeles Philharmonic Association*; b. 15 July 1949, New York; d. of William Borda and Helene Borda (née Malloy). *Education:* New England Conservatory of Music, Bennington Coll., Vt, and Royal Coll. of Music, London. *Career:* began studying the violin aged six, took up the viola aged 15; summer post at Marlboro Music Festival, Vt; Program Dir Mass Council of Arts and Humanities, Boston 1974–76; Man. Boston Musica Viva 1976–77; Dir Handel and Haydn Soc., Boston 1977–79; Artistic Admin., later Gen. Man. San Francisco Symphony 1979–86; Pres. and Man. Dir St Paul Chamber Orchestra 1986–88; Exec. Dir Detroit Symphony Orchestra 1989–90, New York Philharmonic Orchestra 1991–99; fmr Chair. Music Panel Nat. Endowment for the Arts; Pres. and CEO, David C. Bohnett Presidential Chair, Los Angeles Philharmonic Asscn 2000–; Hauser Leader-in-Residence, Harvard Kennedy School for Public Leadership 2015. *Address:* Los Angeles Philharmonic Association, 151 South Grand Avenue, Los Angeles, CA 90012, USA (office). *Telephone:* (323) 850-2000 (office); (213) 972-7291 (office). *Website:* www.laphil.org (office).

BORDAS, Ricard; Spanish singer (countertenor); b. 1965, Barcelona; m. Margaret Cook; one s. *Education:* Royal Acad. of Music, UK with Charles Brett. *Career:* Proms debut in the St Matthew Passion under Joshua Rifkin 1994; Carmina Burana at La Scala and Granada Festival and Bach's Magnificat at Barbican, London; London Handel Festival as Siroe and in Alexander's Feast; Ottone in Handel's Agrippina for Midsummer Opera and Scarlatti's Mitridate at Schwetzingen Festival 1996; Jonathan Miller's staged St Matthew Passion, tour of Dido and Aeneas in Mexico and Monteverdi's Poppea with Netherlands Opera; season 1996–97 as Selino in Cesti's L'Argia at Innsbruck, Monteverdi Vespers in Ripon Cathedral and Handel's Israel in Egypt at Bristol; sang Valentiniono in Handel's Ezio at Halle 1998; Music Dir Camerata Hispanica, London and Group Vocal Odarum, Barcelona; guest teacher at London colls; currently Choirmaster, First (Scots) Presbyterian Church, Charleston, South Carolina; also currently Asst Prof. of Music, Charleston Southern Univ.; Conductor Charleston Men's Chorus; writer for Revista Musical Catalana, Spanish journal of classical music. *Honours:* RAM Shinn Fellowship. *Address:* Lightsey Music Building 106, Charleston Southern University, 9200 University Boulevard, Charleston, SC 29406, USA (office). *E-mail:* rbordas@csuniv.edu (office). *Website:* www.csuniv.edu/music (office).

BORDEN, David, BM, MM, MA; American composer and musician (piano, synthesizer); *Composer and Director, Mother Mallard's Portable Masterpiece Company*; b. 25 Dec. 1938, Boston, Mass; s. of Raymond Borden and Natalie Mallard Borden; m. 2nd Rebecca Godin 1994; one s. *Education:* Eastman School of Music, Harvard Univ., Hochschule für Musik, Berlin, Germany. *Career:* fmr Dir, Digital Music Program, Cornell Univ.; performances at WBAI Free Music Store, The Kitchen, The Knitting Factory, Dance Theatre Workshop, Town Hall, Lincoln Center, Roulette, Issue Project Room (all New York), Gatherings (Philadelphia), Tivoli Konzert Halle (Copenhagen), Barbican Centre (London), Portsmouth Festival (England), New Music America (Montreal, Canada); Composer and Dir, Mother Mallard's Portable Masterpiece Co.; mem. Herbert F. Johnson Museum of Art, Ithaca, New York, Brown Univ., Providence, Duquesne, Pittsburgh, MOOG FEST, Asheville, New Music USA, Berlin Atonal, Germany 2015. *Film soundtrack:* The Exorcist (part) 1973. *Compositions:* for synthesizer ensemble: The Continuing Story of Counterpoint, Easter, Enfield in Winter, Cayuga Night Music, Variations on a Theme of Philip Glass, Angels, Heaven-kept Soul for piano and two laptop computers, Smart Hubris for electric violin and three laptop computers, K216.01 for electric violin and three laptop computers, Vienna for electric guitars and wind, Tribute to Ruth St Denis and Ted Shawn for four laptops and video projection, Viola Farber in seven movements, Earth Journeys for four laptops; for two pianos: Unjust Malaise, Double Portrait, The FOTH Variations, TCSOC Part 2, TCSOC Part 88.01, TCSOC Part 11, I Trill Tunes. *Recordings include:* The Continuing Story of Counterpoint, Place, Times and People, Mother Mallard's Portable Masterpiece, Like a Duck to Water, Cayuga Night Music, ... It's Gone (DVD), Variations on a Theme of Philip Glass 2014; recordings on Cuneiform, New World, , Arbiter, Spectrum Spools. *Publications include:* Dialogues for Trumpet and Trombone, Heaven-Kept Soul for solo piano and laptops. *Honours:* Foundation for Contemporary Arts Grant, Award for Innovative Teaching, Cornell Univ. *Address:* 227 Enfield Falls Road, New York, NY 14850, USA (office). *Telephone:* (607) 277-4155 (office). *E-mail:* drb4@cornell.edu (office); davidborden@mac.com. *Website:* www.mothermallard.com; www.davidborden.org.

BORETZ, Benjamin Aaron, BA, MFA, PhD; American composer, music theorist, teacher and writer on music; b. 3 Oct. 1934, New York, NY. *Education:* Brooklyn Coll., Manhattan School of Music, New York, Brandeis Univ., Aspen Music School, Univ. of California, Los Angeles, Princeton Univ., studied with Julius Rudel, Erwin Bodky, Irving Fine, Harold Shapero, Arthur Berger, Darius Milhaud, Lukas Foss, Roger Sessions. *Career:* consultant and writer, Fromm Music Foundation 1960–70; founding Co-Ed. 1961–64, Ed. 1964–84, 1993–95, Perspectives of New Music; music critic, The Nation 1962–70; teacher, New York Univ. 1964–69, Columbia Univ. 1969–72, Bard Coll. 1973–; Distinguished Visiting Prof., Univ. of California, Los Angeles 1991; Visiting Prof., Univ. of California, Santa Barbara 1991; invited, Interdisciplinary Conference, Calgary 1991; Co-Ed., The Open Space magazines 1998–. *Compositions include:* Concerto grosso for string orchestra 1956, Violin Concerto 1956, Divertimento for five instruments 1957, String Quartet 1958, Group Variations I for orchestra 1967, II for computer 1971, Liebeslied for piano 1974, ...my chart shines high where the blue milk's upset... for piano 1978, Passage for Roger Sessions for piano 1979, Language as a Music: Six Marginal Pretexts for Composition for speaker, piano and pre-recorded tape 1980, Soliloquy I for piano 1981, soundscore works, score for composing series 1991–93, Music/Consciousness/Gender (sound/video) 1995, Echoic/Anechoic for piano 1997, Black/Noise I, II, III for video and computer sound 1997–98, Camille (video piece) 1997, UN (-) for orchestra 1999. *Recordings include:* An Experiment in Reading 1981, One (exercise – eight piano solo sound sessions) Open Space 1992. *Publications include:* Perspectives on Schoenberg and Stravinsky (ed. with Edward T. Cone) 1968, Perspectives on American Composers (ed. with Edward T. Cone) 1971, Perspectives on Contemporary Music Theory (ed. with Edward T. Cone) 1972, Perspectives on Notation and Performance (ed. with Edward T. Cone) 1976, If I am a Musical Thinker 1981, Language as a Music 1985, Music Columns from the Nation 1962–1968 1989, Open Space 1991, Meta-variations: Studies on the Foundations of Musical Thought 1994; contrib. to professional magazines and journals.

BOREYKO, Andrey; German conductor; b. 22 July 1957, St Petersburg, Russia; m. Julia Volk 1990; one d. *Education:* conducting and composition with Elisabeta Kudriavzeva and Alexander Dimitriev, Rimski-Korsakov Conservatory. *Career:* debut as conductor, aged 20; founder, Dir, Res Facta early music group, Leningrad 1977, Barocco Consort, Leningrad 1984; Conductor, St Petersburg Theatre of Music 1985–86; Prin. Conductor, State Symphony Orchestra of Ulyanovsk, Russia, and Chamber Music Theatre 1987–89; Gen. Music Dir, Ural Philharmonic Orchestra, Yekaterinenburg 1990–92; Artistic Dir, Chief Conductor, Poznań Philharmonic Orchestra, Poland 1992–95; Prin. Assoc. Conductor, Russian Nat. Orchestra 1998–2001; Chief Conductor, Gen. Music Dir Jenaer Philharmonie 1998–2003, Prin. Guest Conductor, Vancouver Symphony, 1998–2003; Music Dir, Winnipeg Symphony Orchestra 2001–05; Chief Conductor, Hamburger Symphoniker 2004–07, Principal Guest Conductor, SWR Radio Symphony Orchestra, Stuttgart 2004–; Chief Conductor, Berner Symphonie-Orchester 2005–; Gen. Music Dir, Düsseldorfer Symphoniker 2009–; int. guest performances and concerts with Deutsches Symphonie-Orchester Berlin, Gewandhausorchester Leipzig, Württembergisches Staatsorchester Stuttgart, SWR Radio Symphony Orchestra Stuttgart, Bamberger Symphoniker, NDR Symphony Orchestra Hamburg, Hamburger Symphoniker, Radio Symphony Orchestra Berlin, Radio Symphony Orchestra Frankfurt, Nationaltheater Orchester Mannheim, Dresdner Philharmonie, Symphony Orchestra of the MDR Leipzig, Cologne Gürzenich Orchester, Beethoven Orchester Bonn, Orchestre de la Suisse Romande, Stockholm Royal Philharmonic, Malmö Symphony, Bergen Philharmonic, Trondheim Symphony Orchestra, Royal Flanders Philharmonic Orchestra, Belgian Nat. Orchestra, Philharmonia Orchestra, BBC Symphony Orchestra London, St Petersburg Symphony Orchestra, Prague Symphony Orchestra FOK, Orchestra del Maggio Musicale Fiorentino, Danish Nat. Orchestra, Oslo Philharmonic, Warsaw Philharmonic Orchestra, Polish Nat. Radio Orchestra, Symphony Orchestras of Montréal, Toronto, Detroit, San Diego, Sydney, Melbourne, Brisbane, Adelaide, Chamber Orchestra of the Kremerata Baltica, Amsterdam Sinfonietta, Royal Concertgebouw Orchestra Amsterdam, Berliner Philharmoniker, Chicago Symphony Orchestra, Münchner Philharmoniker, and others; guest at festivals in the Netherlands, Germany, Austria, Switzerland, Belgium, Italy, France and the USA. *Recordings:* Silvestrov, Monodia, Sinfonie No. 4, 1992; Silvestrov, Sinfonie No. 5, 1992; Ginastera, Ballettmusik, Philharmonie Poznań, 1993; Takemitsu, Nostalghia für Violine und Orchester, 1998, Liszt, Konzert für Klavier und Orchester, Berlioz Symphonie Fantastique op. 14, Bloch Sinfoine Es-Dur 2002, Beethoven Bearbeitung des Violinkonzertes für Klavier 2004, Schnittke Faust-Kantate, Pärt Lamentate (with SWR Stuttgart RSO) 2005. *Honours:* hon. conductor, Jenaer Philharmonie, best concert programme from Deutscher Musikverleger-Verband 1999–2000, 2001–02, 2002–03. *Current Management:* Harrison Parrott, 5–6 Albion Court, London, W6 0QT, England; c/o Monica Ott, Berliner Konzertagentur, Dramburger Strasse 46, 12683 Berlin, Germany. *Telephone:* (20) 7229-9166 (HP); (30) 5144858 (Berlin). *Fax:* (20) 7221-5042 (HP); (30) 5142659 (Berlin). *E-mail:* info@harrisonparrott.co.uk; BerlinKonzert.ott@t-online.de. *Website:* www.harrisonparrott.com; www.BerlinKonzert-ott.de.

BORG, Matti, DipMus; Danish composer and singer (baritone); b. 1956, Copenhagen; Gitta-Maria Sjoberg 1989; one s. *Education:* Univ. of Copenhagen, Royal Conservatory of Denmark. *Career:* debut at Copenhagen 1987; appeared as soloist in concerts in Scandinavia and on television and radio; opera debut in Sweden, Norrlandsoperan; works performed in Sweden, Norway, Denmark, Belgium, Spain and Canada; mem. Danish Composers' Soc. *Compositions:* choral works, chamber music and songs, music for theatre, musicals; Symboise for mixed choir and solo instruments 1979, Thirteen Ways of Looking at a Blackbird trio for soprano, flute and piano 1981, Recollection for string quartet 1983, What Are We Dreaming Of (musical) 1986, Irene and Her Men (musical) 1991, Fabliau for female voice and 12 celli 1995, Poems by Mörike for mixed choir 1997.

BORGSTEDE, Michael; German musician (harpsichord, fortepiano, organ), journalist and academic; *Professor, Musikhochschule Köln*; b. 27 Dec. 1976. *Education:* Royal Conservatory, The Hague, studied with Jacques Ogg, also studies with Ton Koopman, Lars Ulrik Mortensen and Gustav Leonhardt on harpsichord and Bernard Winsemius and Harald Vogel on organ. *Career:* plays on historical keyboard instruments; soloist and mem. chamber music ensemble Musica ad Rhenum, toured most of Europe, USA, Asia, S America and the Middle East and performed at major venues and festivals; regular master-classes and lectures on historical performance practice; Prof., Musikhochschule Köln 2014–; also regular journalism; Middle East correspondent for Frankfurter Allgemeine Sonntagszeitung. *Recordings include:* Couperin: 4 Livres de Pièces de Clavecin (11 CDs) 2006, Handel harpsichord suites (4 CDs) 2008, Forqueray: Works for Harpsichord (Diapason d'Or) 2009; with traverso player Jed Wentz: J. S. Bach: Complete Chamber Music for Flute (Diapason d'Or) 2013, C. P. E. Bach: Complete Solo Flute Sonatas 2013; with Wentz and Musica ad Rhenum: Telemann: Paris Quartets, Blavet: Flute Sonatas, Couperin: Les Nations, Couperin: Concerts Royaux, Couperin: Complete Chamber Music; several operas. *Publication:* Leben in Israel: Alltag im Ausnahmezustand 2008. *Address:* Hochschule für Musik und Tanz, Unter Krahnenbäumen 87, 50668 Cologne, Germany (office). *E-mail:* michael.borgstede@hfmt-koeln.de (office). *Website:* www.michaelborgstede.com.

BORISO-GLEBSKY, Nikita; Russian violinist; b. 1985, Volgodonsk. *Education:* Rostov Coll. of Arts, Moscow Tchaikovsky Conservatory, Chapelle Musicale Reine Elisabeth, Belgium. *Career:* first performance with Rostov Philharmonic Orchestra aged 10; has worked with orchestras including Mariinsky Theatre Symphony Orchestra, Svetlanov State Academic Symphony Orchestra, Orchestre Nat. de Belgique, NDR Symphony, New Haifa Symphony Orchestra, Royal Philharmonic Orchestra, Amadeus Chamber Orchestra (Poland); has worked with numerous conductors including Valery Gergiev, David Geringas, Yuri Simonov, Maxim Vengerov, Christoph Poppen, Paul Goodwin, Gilbert Varga; performed at Salzburg Festival, Rheingau Musik Festival, Sviatoslav Richter's December Evenings, Beethoven Festival

(Bonn), Dubrovnik Summer Festival, Stars of the White Nights and Arts Square, St Petersburg; collaborated with musicians including Rodion Shchedrin, Natalia Gutman, Alexander Kniazev, Augustin Dumay, David Geringas, Jian Wang. *Honours:* Winner, Yampolsky Competition 2000, Kloster-Schönthal (Germany) 2003, Joseph Joachim Int. Competition, Hannover 2006, David Oistrakh Int. Competition, Moscow 2007, Second Prize and Silver Medal, XIII Int. Tchaikovsky Competition, Moscow (five special prizes) 2007, Queen Elisabeth Competition, Brussels 2009, Violinist of the Year Award, Rodion Shchedrin Foundation 2009, Int. Jean Sibelius Violin Competition, Helsinki 2010, Int. Fritz Kreisler Violin Competition, Vienna 2010, Int. Montreal Music Competition 2010. *Current Management:* c/o Moscow State Philharmonic Society, 103050 Moscow, Tverskaya Ulitsa 31, Russia. *Telephone:* (495) 699-49-81. *Fax:* (495) 694-58-22. *E-mail:* info@philharmonia.ru. *Website:* www.meloman.ru.

BORK, Robert; American singer (baritone); b. 1959, Chicago, IL. *Education:* Wheaton College, Illinois and Cologne Opera Studio. *Career:* sang at Cologne from 1987, notably as Hummel in Reimann's Gespenstersonate, as Tarquinius in The Rape of Lucretia, Papageno, Belcore, Escamillo, Tsar Peter in Lortzing and Schaunard in La Bohème; Dörfling in Der Prinz von Homburg by Henze, Cologne 1992; sang Donner in Das Rheingold at Toulouse and Redburn in Billy Budd at the Vienna Staatsoper 2001; concerts include The Raft of the Medusa by Henze, Bach's B Minor Mass and St Matthew Passion, Ein Deutsches Requiem and Mahler's 8th. *Current Management:* Boris Orlob Management, Jägerstrasse 70, 10117 Berlin, Germany. *Telephone:* (30) 20450839. *Fax:* (30) 20450849. *E-mail:* info@orlob.net. *Website:* www.orlob.net.

BORKOWSKI, Marian, MA, MMusicol, PhD; Polish composer, musicologist, pianist and educator; *Professor Emeritus, Frederic Chopin Academy of Music;* b. 17 Aug. 1934, Pabianice; s. of Witold Borkowski and Bronistawa Cieniewska; m. Maria Borkowska (née Nowak); two s. *Education:* Acad. of Music, Warsaw with Kazimierz Sikorski, Jan Ekier and Natalia Hornowska, Warsaw Univ. with Jozef M. Chomiński, Paris Conservatory and American Conservatory in Fontainebleau with Nadia Boulanger and Olivier Messiaen, Ecole Pratique des Hautes Etudes, Paris with Iannis Xenakis, Paris Univ. (Sorbonne) with Jacques Chailley and Barry S. Brook, Sorbonne and Collège de France with Jean Hyppolite and Jules Vuillemin, Int. Courses of New Music at Darmstadt, Accad. Musicale Chigiana, Siena, Italy with Gyorgy Ligeti, Iannis Xenakis, Karlheinz Stockhausen and Franco Donatoni. *Career:* Asst Lecturer and Sr Asst Lecturer, Dept of Composition, Frederic Chopin Acad. of Music, Warsaw 1968–71, Asst Prof. of Composition 1971–76, Assoc. Prof. 1976–89, Prof. 1989–, now Emer., Dean, Faculty of Composition, Conducting and Music Theory 1996–99, Vice-Pres. Acad. 1978–81, 1987–90, Head, Chair of Music Theory 1993–99, Head, Chair of Composition 1999–2004; Visiting Prof. at numerous univs including Concordia Univ., Montréal, Conservatoire de Musique du Québec, Québec City, Univ. of Montréal, Canada, Nat. Conservatory of Music, Paris, Accad. Musicale Chigiana, Siena, San Francisco State Univ., Eastman School of Music, Rochester, Univ. of North Texas, Denton, Univ. of Charleston, Rice Univ., Houston, Baldwin-Wallace Conservatory, Berea, OH, Pontifica Universidad Católica, Valparaíso, Chile, Seoul Nat. Univ., Chonnam Nat. Univ., Hanyang Univ., Seoul, Seoul Conservatory of Music, Korean Nat. Univ. of Arts, Seoul, Univ. of Suwon 1989–; compositions have been performed at chamber and symphonic music concerts worldwide; pieces also performed at more than 100 music festivals; many compositions recorded for radio and TV in more than 25 countries; piano recitals in Poland, France, Italy, Canada, Republic of Korea, USA, Austria, Russia; jury mem. int. competitions in composition in Poland and abroad; Deputy Chair. Warsaw Br. Polish Composers Union 1971–77; founder and Artistic Dir Festival – Laboratory of Contemporary Music 1985–; Chair. Academic Council Polish Inst. of Music 1985–; Pres. Lab. of Contemporary Music Asscn 1995–; mem. The Author's Asscn ZAIKS (mem. Repartition Comm.), Int. Fed. of Jeunesses Musicales (mem. Cttee for Belgrade Music Competition 1985–90), Int. Soc. of Contemporary Music, Inamori Foundation, Kyoto, Int. Festival of Sacred Music in Czestochowa (mem. Artistic Council), Acad. of Phonography (mem. Council); Foreign mem. Soc. for Electro-Acoustic Music (USA). *Compositions include:* two Mazurkas for piano 1958, Toccata for piano 1960, Sfere for chamber orchestra 1961, Sonata for piano 1961, Lyrical Preludes for soprano and piano, to words by Konstanty I. Galczynski 1962, Visions I for solo cello 1962, Fragment! for piano 1962, Aria for soprano and seven instruments 1963, Epitaphium for female choir and instrumental ensemble 1968, Lullaby for mixed choir a cappella 1970, Images I for any solo voice 1973, Psalmus for organ 1975, Nonvidiana 75 for female voice and chamber ensemble 1975, Images II for any solo string instrument 1975, Variant for instrumental ensemble 1976, Speranza for flute and piano 1976, Dialoghi for two pianos 1977, Mont for orchestra 1978, Spectra for solo percussion 1980, Dynamics I for six percussionists 1981, Mater mea for mixed choir a cappella, to words by Krzysztof K. Baczynski 1982, Apasionante for two instruments (string and brass) 1983, Concerto for any solo string instrument and orchestra 1985–86, Pax in terra I for female voice, four guitar groups and tubular bells 1987, Pax in terra II for female voice, percussion and organ 1988, Adoramus for mixed choir a cappella 1991, Hosanna I for mixed choir and four instruments 1993, Regina caeli for mixed choir a cappella 1995, Kassándra for female voice, mixed choir and orchestra 1996–97, Metallica for brass quintet 1999, Ave Alleluia Amen for mixed choir a cappella 2000, Con-Son for string orchestra 2001, Dies irae for mixed choir and orchestra 2004, Hymnus for mixed choir and orchestra 2005, Libera me for mixed choir a cappella 2005, Sonus for instrumental ensemble 2006, Pax in terra II for mixed choir, strings and percussion 2007, Lux aeterna for mixed choir and symphony orchestra 2008–10, Sanctus for mixed choir a cappella 2009, Hosanna II for mixed choir and symphony orchestra 2009, Dynamics II for six percussionists 2010. *Recordings:* more than 50 albums. *Publications:* contrib. to more than 25 scholarly works on contemporary music; numerous critiques in magazines and newspapers. *Honours:* Hon. mem. Musica Sacra Asscn 2004, Karol Nieze Music Soc. 2006, Hon. Citizen of Pabianice 2005; Silver Cross of Merit (Poland) 1977, Kt's Cross of Order Polonia Restituta 1984, Commdr's Cross 2002; numerous prizes including Young Composers' Competition, Warsaw 1966, Int. Composers' Competition G.B. Viotti, Vercelli 1969, K. Szymanowski Competition for Composers in Warsaw 1974, Silver Medal Premio Vittorio Gui (Italy) 1979, Medal of Chopin Acad. of Music 1981, Medal, Seoul Nat. Univ. 1988, Int. New Music Composers Competition, New York 1990, Award of Minister of Culture and Art 1976, 1980, 1982, 2004, Badge of Merit in Culture 1985, Plaque of Honour, Chopin Acad. of Music 2004, Silver Olympic Laurel 2004, Hon. Award, Polish Composers' Union 2008, Silver Medal Gloria Artis 2008, Medal of Merit, Frédéric Chopin Acad. of Music 2010. *Address:* Frédéric Chopin Academy of Music, ul. Okólnik 2, 00-368 Warsaw (office); ul. Klaudyny 6 m. 83, 01-684 Warsaw, Poland (home). *Telephone:* (22) 827-7241 ext. 243, 285 (office); (22) 827-7141 ext. 243, 485 (office); (22) 833-6859 (home). *Fax:* (22) 827-8310 (office); (22) 827-8306 (office). *E-mail:* borkowski@chopin.edu.pl (office). *Website:* www.chopin.edu.pl (office); www.marianborkowski.pl.

BORNEMANN, Barbara; German singer (mezzo-soprano); b. 8 March 1955, Dingelstadt. *Education:* studied in Weimar and at the Hanns Eisler Musikhochschule Berlin with Hannelore Kuhse. *Career:* debut at Halberstadt, 1978, as Olga in Eugene Onegin; sang at Halberstadt until 1981, at Schwerin, 1981–86; mem. of the Berlin Staatsoper from 1986; Further appearances in Dresden, Leipzig Czechoslovakia, Poland and Japan; Bayreuth Festival, 1990 as Mary in Der fliegende Holländer; Geneviève in Pelléas et Mélisande in Berlin, 1991; Sang Gaea in Strauss's Daphne (concert performance) Rome, 1991; other roles include Mozart's Marcellina, Verdi's Ulrica and Mistress Quickly, Wagner's Magdalene and Fricka; Season 1994–95 as Cimarosa's Fidalma in Berlin and in Lulu at Salzburg; Housekeeper in Die schweigsame Frau at Dresden, 1998; Concert repertoire includes Bach's Christmas Oratorio and St John Passion, the Mozart and Verdi Requiems, Mendelssohn's Elijah and St Paul, Mahler's Kindertotenlieder. *Current Management:* Musiespaña, Calle José Marañón 10, 28010 Madrid, Spain. *Telephone:* (91) 5913290. *Fax:* (91) 5913291. *E-mail:* horan@musiespana.com.

BÖRNER, Klaus; German pianist, conductor, composer and academic; b. 22 June 1929, Senftenberg; m. Helga Kibat 1958; one s. one d. *Education:* Weimar Acad. of Music, Lausanne Conservatoire de Musique, masterclasses with Alfred Cortot, Edwin Fischer, Wilhelm Kempff. *Career:* debut, Weimar, Mozart Piano Concerto E flat major K482, conductor Carl Ferrand 1950; concerts as Pianist, 70 countries, soloist with orchestras, Berlin, Düsseldorf, Budapest, Lima, Guatemala, elsewhere; chamber music with Melos String Quartet, Michael Goldstein, others; festivals include Berlin, Madrid, Bad Hersfeld, New Zealand; numerous radio and TV appearances; teacher, Düsseldorf Conservatory 1956–69; founder, Acting Dir, Int. Music Summer Camp, Sylt 1959–89; Prof., Mainz Univ. 1969–97; Guest Prof., Hong Kong, Japan, Indonesia, New Zealand; juror, nat. and int. competitions. *Compositions:* Trio for horn, violin, piano 1961, three Lieder for soprano, piano 1990, Fantasie über eine Phantasie, Hommage à Mozart for piano four hands 1991, Quartet for four bassoons 1997. *Recordings:* Handel Chaconne G, J. S. Bach Partita E minor, Haydn Sonatas, C minor, C# minor, Beethoven Sonatas, A major op 2,2, G major op 31,1, Schumann Papillons op 2, Kreisleriana op 16. *Publications:* Klavierschulen für den Aufangsunterricht – Eine vergleichende Analyse 1978, Chance und Dilemma des Urtextes 1982, Handbuch der Klavierliteratur zu vier Händen 2005. *Honours:* Prize for Young soloists, Weimar 1950, scholarship of German Industry 1953, first prize Int. piano competitions in Barcelona 1956, Milan/Monza 1967, selected for Konzerte junger Künstler (German Art Council) 1959, hon. mem. Jeunesses Musicales, German section 1990. *Address:* Nibelungenstr 38, 41462 Neuss, Germany. *Telephone:* (2131) 542536 (home).

BORODINA, Olga Vladimirovna; Russian singer (mezzo-soprano); b. Leningrad (now St Petersburg); d. of Vladimir Nikolaevich and Galina Fedorovna Borodin; m. Ildar Abdrazakov; three s. *Education:* Leningrad Conservatory (student of Irina Bogacheva). *Career:* soloist of Kirov (now Mariinsky) Theatre of Opera and Ballet 1987–; debut as Delilah in Samson and Delilah at Royal Opera House, Covent Garden with Plácido Domingo 1992; leading roles in operas including Marfa in Khovanshchina, Konchakovna in Prince Igor, Poline in Queen of Spades, Lubava in Sadko, Marina Mnichek in Boris Godunov, Cinderella in La Cenerentola, Carmen, Amneris in Aïda, Eboli in Don Carlos, Isabella in The Italian Girl in Algiers, Laura in La Gioconda, Delilah in Samson and Delilah, La Principessa in Adriana Lecouvreur, Giulietta in Les Contes d'Hoffmann, Marguerite in La Damnation de Faust; regular performances in all major opera houses as well as recitals and concerts world-wide. *Recordings include:* Verdi Requiem, Chicago Symphony Orchestra, conductor Riccardo Muti (Grammy Award for Best Classical Album, first Russian to win a Grammy Award) 2011. *Honours:* winner of First Prizes: All-Union Glinka Competition 1987, Int. Rosa Poncell Competition, New York 1987, Int. Francisco Viñas Competition, Barcelona

1989, People's Artist of Russia 2002, State Prize of Russia 2007. *Current Management:* c/o NFBM Ltd, 3rd Floor, 24 Endell Street, London, WC2H 9HQ, England. *Telephone:* (20) 7359-4771. *Fax:* (20) 3292-1913. *E-mail:* nicola-fee@nfbm.com. *Website:* www.nfbm.com.

BORODINA, Tatiana; Russian singer; b. 1972, Perm. *Education:* Perm Musical Coll. and St Petersburg Conservatoire. *Career:* Young Singers' Acad. of the Mariinsky Theatre, St Petersburg, 1998; repertoire has included Tchaikovsky's Tatiana and Iolanta, Marguerite in Faust, Mimi, Maria in Mazeppa and Wagner's Elsa and Freia; sang Elsa at Baden-Baden, 1999, Maria and Kupara in Rimsky-Korsakov's The Snow Maiden with the Kirov Opera at Covent Garden, 2000. *Honours:* prizewinner, New Voices of the West Competition, Rome 1997; prizewinner, International Rimsky-Korsakov Competition, St Petersburg.

BOROWSKA, Joanna; Polish singer (soprano); b. 1956, Warsaw. *Education:* studied in Warsaw and at Opera Studio of Vienna Staatsoper. *Career:* debut as Romilda in Serse and Micaela in Carmen at Warsaw 1980; mem. Vienna Staatsoper from 1982, notably as Marenka in The Bartered Bride and as Mozart's Fiordiligi, Susanna and Marzelline, Gluck's Iphigénie en Aulide 1987, Mimi 1988, and Marguerite in Faust; further engagements at Klagenfurt (Countess in Figaro), Bregenz (in Zeller's Der Vogelhändler 1984), Barcelona and Covent Garden, London, Marenka at Bonn 1991. *Recordings include:* Emma in Khovanshchina, Vienna Staatsoper 1989, Maidservant in Elektra, conducted by Abbado.

BOROWSKI, Daniel; Polish singer (bass); b. 1968, Lodz. *Education:* Chopin Academy of Music, Warsaw with Teresa Zylis-Gara, also studied in London, UK. *Career:* began career at Polish Nat. Opera, Warsaw and Gret Theatre, Poznań; roles have included the King and Ramfis in Aida, Ferrando in Il Trovatore, Il Commendatore in Don Giovanni, the Monk in Don Carlos, Colline in La Bohème, Massimiliano in I Masnadieri, Fiesco in Simon Boccanegra, Vodnik in Rusalka, Bellinis Oroveso in Norma, Don Fernando in Fidelio, Raimondo in Lucia di Lammermoor, Dottore Bartolo in Le Nozze di Figaro, Sarastro in Die Zauberflöte, Timur in Turandot, Basilio in Il Barbiere di Siviglia, Un frate in Don Carlo, Banco in Macbeth, Sparafucile in Rigoletto, Daland in Der Fliegende Holländer, Archiereios in Krol Roger; has performed at major opera houses in Europe and USA and at Glyndebourne, Orange, Schwetzingen and Spoleto festivals; performed with Academy of St Martin in the Fields, BBC Philharmonic, Dresdner Philharmoniker, London Symphony, Nationale de Lyon, Turin Sinfonica Nazionale, San Francisco Symphony, Santa Cecilia Rome and Czech Philharmonic orchestras; concert pieces include Beethoven's Christ on the Mount of Olives and Symphony IX, Bellini's Mass in G Major, Berlioz's L'Enfance du Christ, Handel's Messiah, Haydn's The Creation and The Seasons, Janácek's Glagolitic Mass, Mendelssohn's First Walpurgisnacht, Mozart's Requiem and Coronation Mass, Mussorgsky's Songs and Dances of Death, Rossini's Stabat Mater, Shostakovich's Symphony No. 14, Verdi's Requiem. *Recordings include:* Stabat Mater, Symphony IX, Adhémar/Jérusaleme, Fidelio, Simon Boccanegra. *Honours:* winner, Int. Stanislaw Moniuszko Singing Competition, Warsaw 1995, Glyndebourne Festival Opera's John Christie Award 1998, Debut Artist of the Year Award, New York City Opera 2001. *Current Management:* Artistainternational, Kyffhäserstrasse 3, 10781 Berlin, Germany. *Telephone:* (172) 1907999. *Website:* www.artistainternational.com. *Current Management:* Zemsky/Green Artists Management, 730 Fifth Avenue, Suite 1802, New York, NY 10019, USA. *Telephone:* (212) 300-8003. *Fax:* (212) 300-8001. *E-mail:* zgartists@aol.com. *Website:* www.zemskygreen.com.

BORRIS, Kaja; Dutch singer (mezzo-soprano); b. 8 Jan. 1948, Den Haag. *Education:* studied in Cologne and Opera Studio of Deutsche Oper Berlin, Germany. *Career:* mem. Deutsche Oper Berlin from 1973, singing Verdi's Mistress Quickly and Ulrica, Annina in Rosenkavalier, Azucena and Emilia (Othello), Geneviève in Pelléas et Mélisande 1984, and Marthe in Faust 1988; appeared in premiere of Reimann's Gespenstersonate 1984; Salzburg Easter Festival 1982–83, as Mary in Fliegende Holländer; further engagements at Munich, Hamburg, Vienna and Schwetzingen and in concert hall; sang Sphinx in Enescu's Oedipe at Deutsche Oper 1996, and La Cieca in La Gioconda 1998; season 2000–01 in Strauss's Die Aegyptische Helena (concert) and Mistress Quickly in Falstaff. *Recordings include:* Der fliegende Holländer; Feuersnot by Strauss; Die Lustige Witwe; Der Corregidor by Wolf; Schmidt's Notre Dame and Midwife in Zemlinsky's Der Kreidekreis.

BORROFF, Edith, PhD; American composer and musicologist; b. 2 Aug. 1925, New York, NY. *Education:* Oberlin Conservatory, American Conservatory of Music in Chicago, Univ. of Michigan. *Career:* teacher, Milwaukee Downer Coll. 1950–54, Hillsdale Coll., MI 1958–62, Univ. of Wisconsin 1962–66, Eastern Michigan Univ. 1966–72, State Univ. of New York at Binghamton 1973–92. *Compositions include:* String Trio 1943, Passacaglia for organ 1946, Clarinet Quintet 1948, Sonata for cello and piano 1949, Spring Over Brooklyn (musical) 1954, Sonata for horn and piano 1954, IONS for flute and piano 1968, The Sun and the Wind (musical fable) 1976, Game Pieces for woodwind quintet 1980, Concerto for marimba and small orchestra 1981, The Elements sonata for violin and cello 1987, music for piano and organ, choral music and songs. *Recordings include:* Elisabeth Jacquet de la Guerre 1966, The Music of the Baroque 1970, Music in Europe and the USA: A History 1971, Music in Perspective 1976, Three American Composers 1987, Music Melting Round: A History of Music in the United States 1995.

BORST, Danielle; Swiss singer (soprano); b. 27 Jan. 1946, Geneva; m. Philippe Huttenlocher. *Education:* Geneva Conservatoire, studied with Juliette Bisse and Philippe Huttenlocher. *Career:* former mem., Ensemble Vocale de Lausanne, under Michel Corboz; opera appearances in Geneva, Lausanne, Biel-Solothurn, Aix-en-Provence, Montpellier and Vienna (Staatsoper); Paris Opéra, 1988, as Eurydice in Orphée aux Enfers; Mezières, 1988, as Gluck's Euridice; Sang Urbain in Les Huguenots at Montpellier, 1990; Hero in Béatrice et Bénédict at Toulouse, Pamina at Monte Carlo and Vitellia in Gluck's La Clemenza di Tito at Lausanne, 1991; Other roles include Mozart's Despina, Susanna, Sandrina and Illia, Gounod's Juliette, Dalinda (Ariodante), Rameau's Aricie, Micaela and Aennchen in Der Freischütz; Sang Mitrena in Vivaldi's Montezuma, at Monte Carlo, 1992; Gounod's Mireille at Lausanne, 1994; sang Rosalinde at Lyon, 1995–96; concerts include: Haydn's Schöpfung and Jahreszeiten, Berlioz L'Enfant du Christ, Honegger's Roi David, Passions and Oratorios by Bach, works by Monteverdi, Pergolesi, Handel and Mahler. *Recordings include:* Fauré's Pénélope, Armide by Lully, Monteverdi's Orfeo, Dido and Aeneas; Iphigénie en Tauride; title role in L'Incoronazione di Poppea, conducted by René Jacobs.

BORST, Martina; German singer (mezzo-soprano); b. 13 Jan. 1957, Aachen. *Education:* studied with Elsa Cavelti in Frankfurt, with Carla Castellani in Milan. *Career:* sang at Nat. Theater Mannheim from 1981, notably as Annius in La Clemenza di Tito, Cherubino, Dorabella, Rosina, Cenerentola, Orpheus and Composer in Ariadne auf Naxos; Ludwigsburg Festival 1982, 1984 as Annius and as Juno in Semele; Vienna Volksoper 1987, as Dorabella; Bregenz Festival 1988 as Nicklausse in Les Contes d'Hoffmann; Liège and Nantes 1989 as Bersi in Andrea Chénier; sang Octavian at Hanover 1990; Schwetzingen Festival 1995 as Timante in Demofoonte by Jommelli; sang Countess Geschwitz in Lulu at Mainz 1999; numerous concert hall appearances, including Mahler's Kindertotenlieder. *Recordings include:* Così fan tutte. *E-mail:* info@martinaborst.de. *Website:* www.martinaborst.de.

BÖRTZ, Daniel; Swedish composer; b. 8 Aug. 1943, Osby. *Education:* Univ. of Utrecht, Stockholm Music High School with Blomdahl and Lidholm, studied with Hilding Rosenberg. *Career:* debut with Voces for orchestra, Concert Hall, Stockholm 1968; freelance composer 1968–; opera Backanterna performed at the Royal Opera, Stockholm in production by Ingmar Bergman, 1991; mem. Royal Swedish Acad. of Music (Pres. 1998–2003). *Compositions include:* 2 string quartets, 1971, 1987; 10 Sinfonias, 1973–92; Concerto Grosso No. 2 for wind band, 1981; Violin Concerto, 1985; Oboe Concerto, 1986; 3 Cello concertos, 1981, 1985, 1996; Parodos for orchestra, 1987; Intermezzo for orchestra, 1989–90; Backanterna opera after Euripides, 1991; Songs about Death, for soprano and orchestra. 1992–94; Ballad for alto guitar, 1992–94; Strindberg Suite for orchestra, 1993–94; Variations and Intermezzi for strings, 1994; Sonata for piano, 1994; Songs and dances, trumpet concerto, 1994–95; Songs and Shadows, Violin concerto No. 2, 1995–96; Marie Antoinette, opera, 1996–97; Songs and Light, clarinet concerto, 1998; A Joker's Tales, recorder concerto, 1999–2000; Piano Trio, 2000; Songs, piano concerto, 2000–01; His Name was Orestes, oratorio, 2001–02. *Recordings include:* Parodos Symphonies Nos 1 and 7, Strindberg Suite with Stockholm Royal Philharmonic Orchestra and Gennady Rozhdestvensky; Symphony No. 6, chamber and choir works, with Stockholm Royal Philharmonic Orchestra, Hugh Wolff, Eric Ericson chamber choir; The Bacchae opera; Oboe Concerto; Marie Antoinette, opera; Songs and Dances, trumpet concerto; Sonata for Piano; A Joker's Tales; His Name was Orestes, oratorio. *Honours:* Christ Johnson Music Prize, Stockholm, 1987; Int. Rostrum of Composers, Paris, 1989; Litteris et Artibus, Stockholm, 1995.

BORYS, Roman; Canadian musician (cello) and producer; b. Toronto. *Education:* Indiana Univ., Yale Univ., studied with Janos Starker and Aldo Parisot. *Career:* Founder-mem. Gryphon Trio; regular tours across Canada and USA, and in Europe; producer of Gryphon Trio education and outreach initiatives including multi-media project Constantinople and Listen Up! workshop for schools; Artist-in-Residence (with Gryphon Trio) and mem. Faculty, Univ. of Toronto Faculty of Music; Artistic Dir, Ottawa Chamber Music Soc. and Chamberfest Ottawa 2008–; contrib. to film soundtracks. *Recordings with Gryphon Trio:* Haydn: Four Piano Trios 1996, Dvorak/Mendelssohn: Piano Trios 1998, Mendelssohn/Lalo: Piano Trios 2002, Beethoven: Piano Trios Op. 1 Nos 1 & 3 2003, Canadian Premieres (Juno Award for Classical Album of the Year 2004) 2003, Mozart: Complete Piano Trios 2006, Shostakovich: Complete Works for Piano Trios 2006, Christos Hatzis: Constantinople 2007, Schubert: Complete Piano Trios 2007, Tango Nuevo 2008, Beethoven: Piano Trios Op. 1 No. 2 and Op. 97 Archduke 2009, Beethoven: Piano Trios Op. 70 Nos 1 & 2 and Op. 11 (Juno Award for Classical Album of the Year 2011) 2010, Jeffrey Ryan: Fugitive Colours 2011, Broken Hearts & Madmen 2011, Great Piano Trios 2011, For the End of Time 2012. *Honours:* (with Gryphon Trio) Walter Carsen Prize for Excellence in the Arts, Canada Council 2013. *Current Management:* Melvin Kaplan, Inc., 115 College Street, Burlington, VT 05401, USA. *Telephone:* (802) 658-2592. *E-mail:* music@melkap.com. *Website:* www.melkap.com. *E-mail:* roman.borys@utoronto.ca (office). *Website:* www.gryphontrio.com (office).

BOSQUET, Thierry; Belgian stage designer and costume designer; b. 1932. *Education:* National School of Architecture, Art and Design, Brussels. *Career:* from 1959 designed more than 200 sets and 6000 costumes for over 75 operas and ballets at the Théâtre Royale de la Monnaie, Brussels; many other stagings in France, Italy, Switzerland, Germany, Canada, South America and Australia; Rigoletto and Otello in Liège, La Belle Hélène for Canadian Opera;

New York City Opera with Werther, Die Zauberflöte and La Traviata; San Francisco Opera from 1980, with costumes for Aida, Carmen, Fledermaus and Capriccio; Realisations of original designs and costumes for Ruslan and Lyudmila (1995), Der Rosenkavalier (original Alfred Roller designs) and Tosca (San Francisco premiere 1932), Pelléas et Mélisande at San Francisco 1997.

BOSTOCK, (Nigel) Douglas, BMus, MMus; British conductor; b. 11 June 1955, Northwich, Cheshire. *Education:* Northern School of Music, Manchester, Univ. of Sheffield, pvt. study with Adrian Boult, London, postgraduate study with Prof. Dr Francis Travis, Freiburg Hochschule für Musik, Germany, Higher Artistic Diploma (Conducting). *Career:* Music Dir and regular Guest Conductor, Southwest German Philharmonic, Konstanz, Germany 1979–93; Prin. Conductor and Music Dir Karlovy Vary Symphony Orchestra, Czech Repub. 1991–98; Prin. Guest Conductor Chamber Philharmonic of Bohemia 1991–2009; Perm. Guest Conductor Munich Symphony Orchestra 1997–2006; Prin. Conductor Tokyo Kosei Wind Orchestra 1999–2006, Prin. Guest Conductor 2006–; Prin. Conductor Aargau Symphony Orchestra, Switzerland 2001–; Guest Prof., Nat. Univ. of Arts, Tokyo and Senzoku Gakuen Coll. of Music, Japan; guest conducting appearances with major orchestras throughout Europe, America and Asia; conducted for radio and TV; guest artist at many int. music festivals. *Recordings:* more than 80 recordings, including Dvořák, Fibich, Smetana, Novák, Mozart, Brahms, Bellini, Beethoven, Schumann, and other composers; series of rare French music, three vols; albums in Czech Repub., UK with Royal Philharmonic, Germany, Japan, Baroque music in Italy, Germany, Japan; complete Nielsen orchestral works with Royal Liverpool Philharmonic etc, eight vols; British Symphonic Collection with various orchestras: Bax, Delius, Vaughan Williams, Elgar, Holst, Butterworth, Arnold Gregson, McCabe, Hoddinott etc, 16 vols. *Publication:* Hans Pfitzner: The Last Romantic 1979; various articles. *Honours:* Martinu Medal (Czech Repub.), Dvořák Plaque (Czech Repub.). *Current Management:* c/o Tivoli & Crescendi Artists, Læderstræde 9, 4, 1202 Copenhagen K, Denmark; c/o Ars/Koncert, Hybešova 29, 602 00 Brno, Czech Republic. *Telephone:* 86-51-86-28 (Copenhagen); (54) 3420951 (Brno). *Fax:* (54) 3420950 (Brno). *E-mail:* info@crescendi.org; ars@arskoncert.cz. *Website:* www.crescendi.org; www.arskoncert.cz. *Address:* Seestrasse 68, 78479 Reichenau, Germany (home). *E-mail:* info@douglasbostock.net (office). *Website:* www.douglasbostock.net (office).

BOSTRIDGE, Ian Charles, CBE, MA, DPhil; British singer (tenor); b. 1965, London; s. of the late Leslie John Bostridge and of Lilian Winifred (née Clark); m. Lucasta Miller 1992; two c. *Education:* Westminster School, Univs of Oxford and Cambridge. *Career:* debut recital performance in Wigmore Hall, London 1993; operatic debut in Edinburgh Festival 1994; has since performed at Carnegie Hall and Lincoln Center, New York, Salzburg Festival, Théâtre du Châtelet, Philharmonie, Berlin etc.; has appeared in concert with Berlin Philharmonic, Vienna Philharmonic, Royal Concertgebouw, Boston Symphony, London Symphony, New York Philharmonic, Los Angeles Philharmonic, Orchestra of the Metropolitan Opera; annual lieder recitals Munich Opera Festival; Humanitas Prof. of Classical Music, Univs of Oxford 2014–15. *Television:* Winterreise (Channel 4) 1997, Britten Serenade (BBC) 1999, The South Bank Show (ITV) 2000, Janacek documentary (BBC 4) 2004. *Opera:* A Midsummer Night's Dream, Edin. Festival 1994, The Magic Flute, ENO 1996, The Turn of the Screw, Royal Opera House 1997, 2002, The Bartered Bride, Sadler's Wells 1998, L'incoronazione di Poppea, Munich Festival 1998, The Diary of One Who Vanished, Munich and New York 1999, The Rake's Progress, Munich Festival 2002, Don Giovanni, Royal Opera House, Covent Garden 2003, Ades and The Tempest, Covent Garden 2004, The Rape of Lucretia, Munich 2004, Aldeburgh 2011. *Recordings include:* Britten 2005, Wolf: Lieder 2006, Schubert: Lieder and Sonata 2007, Great Handel 2007, Schubert: The Wanderer: Lieder and Fragments 2008, Schubert: Schwanengesang 2009, Three Baroque Tenors 2010. *Publications:* Witchcraft and its Transformations 1650–1750 1997, A Singer's Notebook 2011, Schubert's Winter Journey: Anatomy of an Obsession 2015. *Honours:* Hon. Fellow, Corpus Christi Coll., Oxford; Hon. DMus (St Andrews); awards include Gramophone Solo Vocal Awards 1996, 1998, Time Out Classical Music Award 1999, Edison Award 1999, 2002, Grammy Award (opera) 1999, Critics' Choice Classical Brit Award (for The English Songbook) 2000, Preis der Deutschen Schallplattenkritik 2001, Acad. Charles Cros, Grand Prix du Disque 2001. *Website:* www.askonasholt.co.uk/artists/singers/tenor/ian-bostridge (office).

BOTES, Christine; British singer (mezzo-soprano); b. 1964, Kingston upon Thames. *Education:* Durham Univ., Royal Northern College of Music with Frederic Cox and Nat. Opera Studio. *Career:* sang with Glyndebourne Chorus then with the RSC in The Tempest; appearances with Scottish Opera as Iolanthe and Second Lady in The Magic Flute; Opera Factory as Diana in La Calisto, Thea in Knot Garden and Dorabella, also televised; Mozart roles include Cherubino at Sadler's Wells, Donna Elvira in the Netherlands and Belgium; with English National Opera has sung as Hansel on tour to Russia in 1990 and as the Fox in The Cunning Little Vixen 1991; for ENO sang Cherubino in The Marriage of Figaro 1991; sang in the Mikado 1991, Proserpina in Orfeo 1992, Minerva in Return of Ulysses in 1992; concert engagements with the Royal Philharmonic in Elgar's Sea Pictures and the London Sinfonietta, City of London Sinfonia and The Hanover Band; Bach's B Minor Mass in France and Poland and Messiah with the Orchestre de Liège and the City of Birmingham Choir; concerts in Cologne and Lisbon with the Ensemble Modern of Frankfurt; Sang Herodias in Stradella's San Giovanni Battista, Batignano 1996. *Website:* www.christinebotes.co.uk.

BOTHA, Johan; South African singer (tenor); b. 1965, Rustenberg. *Education:* studied in Pretoria. *Career:* sang at Pretoria from 1988, in the premiere of Hofmeyer's The Fall of the House of Usher and other works; in Europe 1990–, roles include Gustavus in Un Ballo in Maschera, the Prince in The Love for Three Oranges, Max in Der Freischütz, Florestan, Pinkerton in Madama Butterfly, Cassio in Otello, Pedro in Tiefland, Theo in Rautavaara's Vincent, Rodolfo, Turiddu, Verdi's Arrigo, Radames, the Emperor in Die Frau ohne Schatten; sang at major opera and concert stages including Gran Teatre del Liceu, Barcelona, the State Operas of Berlin, Hamburg and Dresden, the Lyric Opera of Chicago, the Grand Théatre Geneva, the Royal Opera House, London, the Los Angeles Opera, La Scala, Milan, the Paris' Opera Bastille and the Chatelet, the Salzburg Festival, the Vienna Volksoper and Opera Australia, Sydney. *Honours:* Kammersänger 2003. *Current Management:* Opernagentur, Tal 15, 80331 Munich, Germany. *Telephone:* (29) 161661. *Fax:* (29) 161667. *E-mail:* johan.botha@opern-agentur.com. *Website:* opern-agentur.com; www.johan-botha.com.

BOTSTEIN, Leon; American conductor; *Music Director and Principal Conductor, Jerusalem Symphony Orchestra*; b. 14 Dec. 1946; m. Barbara Haskell. *Education:* Univ. of Chicago, Harvard Univ. *Career:* Co-Artistic Dir, Bard Music Festival 1990–; Music Dir and Prin. Conductor, American Symphony Orchestra 1993–; Music Dir, Jerusalem Symphony Orchestra 2003–; has also conducted BBC Symphony, London Symphony Orchestra, London Philharmonic, NDR Hamburg, NDR Hannover, Royal Scottish Nat. Orchestra, St Petersburg Philharmonic, Budapest Festival Orchestra, Bamberg Symphony, Teatro Real Madrid Orchestra, Bern Symphony, Düsseldorf Symphony, New Mexico Symphony; mem. Bd of Dirs After-School Corpn; mem. American Philosophical Soc. 2010–. *Recordings:* albums: as conductor: Joachim, Overtures/Violin Concerto in D 1992, Brahms, Serenade No. 1 1994, Kazuko Hayamin Plays Meyer Kupferman 1995, Schubert Orchestrated 1995, Von Dohnányi, Symphony No. 1 1998, Bruckner, Symphony No. 5 1998, Mendelssohn, Paulus 1998, Hartmann: Symphonies No. 1 and No. 6 1999, Bruch, Odysseus 1999, Bartók, Concerto for orchestra 2001, Reger and Romanticism 2002, Toch, Piano Concerto No. 1 2002, Liszt, Dante Symphony/Tasso 2003, Richard Strauss, Die Ägyptische Helena 2003, Gliere, Symphony No. 3 2003, Popov, Symphony No. 1/Shostakovich, Theme and Variations 2004, Wilson/Kupferman: 2 American Concertos 2005, Chausson, Le Roi Arthus 2005, Wilson/Starer/Wernick: 3 Concertos 2005, Dukas, Ariane et Barbe-Bleue 2007, Walter, Symphony in D minor 2009. *Publications include:* Jefferson's Children: Education and the Promise of American Culture 1997. *Honours:* Carnegie Academic Leadership Award 2009. *Current Management:* c/o Tim Fox, Columbia Artists Management Inc., 1790 Broadway, New York, NY 10019-1412, USA. *Telephone:* (212) 841-9500. *Fax:* (212) 841-9744. *E-mail:* info@cami.com. *Website:* www.cami.com. *Address:* American Symphony Orchestra, 333 West 39th Street, Suite 1101, New York, NY 10018, USA (office). *Telephone:* (212) 868-9276 (office). *Fax:* (212) 868-9277 (office). *E-mail:* musicdirector@americansymphony.org (office). *Website:* www.americansymphony.org (office).

BOTT, Catherine; British singer (soprano); b. 11 Sept. 1952, Leamington Spa. *Career:* many appearances with leading early music ensembles, notably the New London Consort; appearances at major concert halls in Europe, Latin America and USSR; British engagements include Early Music Network tours; festival concerts at Bath, Edinburgh and City of London; Mediaeval Christmas Extravaganza on the South Bank and concerts for the South Bank's 21st anniversary; season 1988–89 with visits to Israel, Spain, The Netherlands and Italy; French debut as Salome in Stradella's San Giovanni Battista at Versailles; solo recitals at Flanders and Utrecht Festivals, Sadler's Wells Theatre and the King's Singers Summer Festival at the Barbican; Promenade Concert, London 1990, with The Bonfire of the Vanities (Medici Wedding Celebration of 1539); season 1991 with concerts and recordings in France, recitals in The Netherlands and Belgium and tour of Japan; sang Mozart's Zaide at QEH 1991; Purcell's Dido at the Barbican 1992; sang in Michael Nyman concert on South Bank 1996; Oswald von Wolkenstein concert 1997. *Recordings include:* Monteverdi Vespers and Orfeo; Virtuoso Italian vocal music: de Rore, Rasi, Cavalieri, Luzzaschi, G and F Caccini, Gagliano, Marini, Rossi, Frescobaldi, Monteverdi, Barnardi and Carissimi (Il Lamento di Maria Stuarda); Cantigas de Amigo by Martin Codax and Cantigas di Santa Maria, anon (all with the New London Consort); Vaughan Williams Sinfonia Antarctica, with the London Symphony Orchestra; English canzonets and Scottish songs, with Melvyn Tan; English restoration theatre music: mad songs by Purcell and by Eccles and Weldon; Walton film music, with the Academy of St Martin-in-the-Fields.

BOTTI, Patrick; French conductor; b. 27 July 1954, Marseille; m. Catherine Fuller; two d. *Education:* Conservatoire National Supérieur de Musique, École Normale de Musique, Université de Paris (Sorbonne), New England Conservatory of Music, USA, Boston Univ., Conservatoire National de Marseille, Université de Droit et Sciences Politiques, Aix-en-Provence. *Career:* debut as a pianist, Palais des Festivals, Cannes, France 1967, as a conductor, Marseille 1974; conducted in France, England, Italy, Canada, USA; Music Dir Concilium Musicum of Paris 1977–82, now Prin. Conductor and Artistic Adviser; Music Dir and Conductor, French Symphony of Boston 1984; Artistic Dir and Conductor, New Hampshire Philharmonic Orchestra 1993–2000; Prin. Guest Conductor, Central Massachusetts Symphony Orchestra 1992–2003; Music Dir Waltham Philharmonic Orchestra May–Dec. 2007; Founder and Music Dir Waltham Symphony Orchestra; Guest Conductor,

Colorado Springs Symphony Orchestra, Boston Philharmonic. *Address:* 30 Fuller Road, Lexington, MA 02420, USA. *Telephone:* (781) 861-9925. *E-mail:* patrickbotti@patrickbotti.com. *Website:* patrickbotti.com; www.walthamsymphony.org.

BOTTONE, Bonaventura, FRAM; British singer (tenor); b. 19 Sept. 1950. *Education:* Royal Acad. of Music with Bruce Boyce. *Career:* debut at Covent Garden, as Italian Singer in Der Rosenkavalier, conducted by Haitink; returned in Capriccio by Strauss; US debut as Pedrillo in Die Entführung, at Houston Opera; has sung with ENO as David in Die Meistersinger, the Duke of Mantua, Beppe, Nanki Poo in Jonathan Miller's production of The Mikado, Sam Kaplan in Weill's Street Scene, Truffaldino in the Love for Three Oranges, 1989 and Alfredo in La Traviata 1990; Scottish Opera 1989, as Governor General in Candide and Loge in Das Rheingold; sang the Italian Tenor in Capriccio at Glyndebourne 1990; season 1992 as Verdi's Fenton for ENO and Conte di Libenskof in Il Viaggio a Reims at Covent Garden; sng the Berlioz Faust with ENO 1997; season 1998 as Doctor Ox in the premiere of Gavin Bryar's opera and Rodolfo in La Bohème for ENO, debut at Santiago, Chile as Alfred in Die Fledermaus, and Italian Singer in Capriccio at Glyndebourne and the Metropolitan Opera; frequent broadcaster in a wide range of BBC programmes; sang in the Berlioz Te Deum, Royal Festival Hall 2000; season 2001 in Caruso and Mario Lanza tributes in Manchester and Dublin, Verdi's Riccardo for Atlanta Opera, Pinkerton at Santiago and Beethoven's Ninth in Germany; season 2002–03 as Verdi's Duke in Milwaukee and roles with Chicago Lyric and Met Operas. *Recordings:* The Mikado; Orpheus in the Underworld. *Current Management:* Stafford Law, Candleway, Broad Street, Sutton Valence, Kent ME17 3AT, England. *Website:* www.stafford-law.com.

BOTTONE, Rebecca; British singer (soprano); b. Beds., England; d. of Bonaventura Bottone and Jennifer Dakin. *Education:* Royal Acad. of Music and Royal Coll. of Music, London. *Career:* inaugural Assoc. Artist, Classical Opera Co. 2006; worked with conductors including Sir Colin Davis, Sir Charles Mackerras, Richard Hickox, Marc Minkowski. *Opera performances include:* Blonde in Die Entführung aus dem Serail for the Aix-en-Provence Festival conducted by Minkowski, Casilda in The Gondoliers for ENO, Hansel and Gretel for Scottish Touring Opera, Paisiello's Il Barbiere di Siviglia for Bampton Classical Opera, Nanetta in Falstaff for English Touring Opera, Despina in Così fan tutte, Melia in Apollo and Hyacinthus and Elisa in El re pastore for Classical Opera Co., Adelaide di Borgogna with Scottish Chamber Orchestra, conducted by Giuliano Carella, Christ on the Mount of Olives with Royal Scottish Nat. Orchestra, conducted by David Robertson, Dialogues des Carmélites with Royal Scottish Nat. Orchestra, conducted by Stéphane Denève, Charmeuse in Thaïs at Théâtre du Châtelet, Paris conducted by Eschenbach; other performances include Beethoven's C Minor Mass with Royal Scottish Nat. Orchestra, conducted by David Robertson, Handel arias with the King's Consort at Wigmore Hall, London and St John Passion with Orchestra Sinfonica di Milano Giuseppe Verdi at Teatro degli Arcimboldi, Milan and Adès' Five Eliot Landscapes for Radio France; recent opera engagements include Cricket and Parrott in world premiere of Jonathan Dove's Pinocchio for Opera North, Blonde for Scottish Opera, Marie in Rufus Wainwright's Prima Donna for Manchester Festival, Tytania in A Midsummer Night's Dream for Garsington Opera and for Royal Opera House, Covent Garden, First Innocent in world premiere of Birtwistle's Minotaur and the Maid in Adès' Powder Her Face at Linbury Studio. *Honours:* Gramophone Award for Best Opera Recording 2011. *Current Management:* Askonas Holt, Lincoln House, 300 High Holborn, London, WC1V 7JH. *Telephone:* (20) 7400-1700. *Fax:* (20) 7400-1799. *E-mail:* info@askonasholt.co.uk. *Website:* www.askonasholt.co.uk/artists/singers/soprano/rebecca-bottone.

BOUCHARD, Antoine, BA, LTh; Canadian organist and academic; *Professor Emeritus, Faculty of Music, Laval University;* b. 22 March 1932, St Philippe-de-Neri, Québec. *Education:* Laval Univ., Québec. *Career:* concerts and festivals, Québec City, Montréal, Paris, France; concerts in Canada and USA; radio performances, CBC and ORTF; series of concerts on 20 European historical organs, Radio Canada; Organ Prof. and Dir School of Music, Laval Univ., Québec 1977–80, Prof. Emer. 1999–. *Compositions:* Prelude and In Paradisum, for organ, in Le Tombeau de Henri Gagnon. *Recordings:* Music by Dandrieu and Buxtehude, Noels français du 18e Siècle, Bach and Pachelbel, Anthologie de l'organiste, Vols I, II, III, The Early Pipe Organs of Quebec, Vols II, IV, VII, The 18 Chorals, by J. S. Bach, Oeuvres de Gaston Litaize, L'Orgue Français classique en Nouvelle-France, seven historical organs of northwestern Germany, Nicolas Lebègue, Complete Pachelbel organ works (world premiere, 11 CDs). *Publications:* L'Organiste (three vols) 1982, Quelques réflexions sur le jeu de l'orgue 2003; contrib. to The Organ Yearbook, Netherlands, L'Orgue, Paris, Musicanada, L'Encyclopédie de la musique au Canada: Bulletin des Amis de l'Orgue. *Address:* 908 rue du Belvédère, St-Nicolas-Est, Québec, G7A 3V3, Canada (home). *E-mail:* antoinebou@videotron.ca (home).

BOUÉ, Géori (Georgette); French singer (soprano); b. 16 Oct. 1918, Toulouse; m. Roger Bourdin (died 1973). *Education:* Toulouse Conservatory, studied in Paris with Henri Büsser and Reynaldo Hahn. *Career:* debut in Toulouse 1935, as Urbain in Les Huguenots; Mireille in the opera by Gounod; sang at Toulouse as Siebel in Faust, Hilda in Reyer's Sigurd, Mathilde in Guillaume Tell and Bizet's Micaela; Opéra-Comique Paris from 1938; Opéra de Paris from 1942, notably in Les Indes Galantes by Rameau 1953; guest appearances in Arles, Brussels, Nice, Barcelona, Germany, Mexico City and

Italy; La Scala Milan as Debussy's Mélisande; tour of Russia as Tatiana in Eugene Onegin and Madama Butterfly; Théâtre de la Monnaie Brussels 1960, in La Belle Hélène; Die Lustige Witwe; appeared as Malibran in the film by Sacha Guitry; f. Centre Lyrique Populaire de France, Paris 1966. *Recordings:* Thaïs, Urania; Faust conducted by Beecham; Les Contes d'Hoffmann; L'Aiglon.

BOUGHTON, William Paul, AGSM; British conductor; *Music Director and Principal Conductor, New Haven Symphony Orchestra;* b. 18 Dec. 1948, Birmingham, England; m. Susan Ann Cullis 1981. *Education:* Guildhall School of Music, London and Prague Acad. *Career:* Founder, Artistic Dir, Music Dir and Principal Conductor, English Symphony Orchestra; Artistic Dir, Malvern Festival 1983–88, 1996–2000; Artistic Dir and Music Dir, Jyvaskyla Sinfonia, Finland 1986–93; Artistic Dir, Nimbus Foundation, including the Wyastone Summer Series 2000–; Music Dir and Principal Conductor, New Haven Symphony Orchestra 2007–; guest conductor with Philharmonia, Royal Philharmonic Orchestra, London Philharmonic Orchestra and London Symphony Orchestra; mem. Royal Overseas League. *Recordings include:* first recordings of Finzi's Love's Labours Lost and Parry's 1st Symphony and Death to Life. *Honours:* Hon. Assoc., Janáček Acad.; Dr hc (Coventry Univ.) 1993; Jyvaskyla City Award. *Address:* New Haven Symphony Orchestra, PO Box 9718, New Haven, CT 06536, USA (office). *Telephone:* (203) 865-0831 (office). *Fax:* (203) 931-2999 (office). *E-mail:* mail@williamboughton.com (office). *Website:* www.newhavensymphony.com (office); www.williamboughton.com.

BOULEYN, Kathryn; American singer (soprano); b. 3 May 1947, Maga Vita, MD. *Education:* Indiana Univ. and the Curtis Inst. *Career:* debut at San Diego 1978, as Nannetta in Falstaff; Miami 1978, as Desdemona; New York City Opera from 1979; Spoleto Festival at Charleston in Haydn's La Vera Costanza, St Louis 1981, in the US premiere of Fennimore and Gerda by Delius (as Fennimore); European debut 1981, as Janáček's Fox (The Cunning Little Vixen) with Netherlands Opera; other appearances as Gutrune at San Francisco 1985, Mozart's Countess at San Diego 1986, Tatiana in Eugene Onegin for WNO 1988, Vitellia in La Clemenza di Tito (Scottish Opera), Donna Elvira, Elisabeth de Valois, Mimi, Manon Lescaut, Micaela and Venus in Tannhäuser; Seattle 1991 as Mozart's Countess.

BOULIN, Sophie; French singer (soprano) and composer; b. 1960. *Education:* Paris Conservatoire and Paris Opéra Studio. *Career:* contemporary music concerts with Vinko Globokar, Diego Masson and Claude Prey; baroque music with René Jacobs, Gustav Leonhardt, Jean-Claude Malgoire, Sigiswald Kuijken, William Christie and Philippe Herreweghe; Opera appearances in France and Germany, notably in productions by Herbert Wernicke of Monteverdi's Poppea, Gluck's Echo et Narcisse and Graun's Montezuma. *Compositions:* Le leçon de musique dans un parc, premiered under William Christie, 1982; Tou azimuts, given at Hamburg, Paris and Munich. *Recordings:* Echo in Echo et Narcisse; Rossane in Handel's Alessandro; Cantatas by Jacquet de la Guerre.

BOULTON, Timothy, FTCL; British violist; b. 14 July 1960; m.; four c. *Career:* mem. Domus Piano Quartet 1985–95, Raphael Ensemble 1991–98, Vellinger String Quartet 1998–2002; Prof. of Viola, Guildhall School of Music and Drama, London 1986–2006; Dir Cornwall Youth Orchestra, South West Music School; freelance music educator. *Recordings include:* many recordings with the aforementioned groups. *Honours:* Gramophone Chamber Music Award 1996. *Telephone:* (1736) 350887 (home). *E-mail:* tboulton@phonecoop.coop.

BOUMAN, Hendrik, DipMus; Dutch harpsichordist, fortepianist, conductor and academic; b. 29 Sept. 1951, Dordrecht; one s. *Education:* Sweelinck Conservatorium, Amsterdam. *Career:* debut conducting, Basilica of Notre Dame, Montréal, Canada, premiere of Tu me cherches by Alain Pierard; Mass for orchestra; several hundred Choristers; harpsichordist of Musica Antiqua Köln 1976–83; extensive tours throughout Europe; festivals in Berlin, London, Netherlands, Flanders, Besancon, Festival de Paris; world tours of South America 1980, North America 1981, Asia, including India and Japan 1982; regular radio recordings for all major European stations; Founder and Dir Ensemble Les Nations de Montréal 1986 and of other ensembles Haydn Heritage, Arcadia, Concerto Felice, Baroque SaMuse/The Baroque Muse; Prof., Univ. of Laval, Québec 1987, Concordia Univ. 1985; master-classes and lectures 1979–; mem. CAPAC. *Compositions:* several transcripts for harpsichord duo. *Publications:* Basso Continuo realisations for Marais; Sonnerie; Maresienne; Mancini; Recorder Concerto; Figured Bass and Harpsichord Improvisation. *Honours:* Diapason d'Or 1982 (for Giles), Diapason d'Or (for Monteverdi) 1982, Deutscher Schallplattenpreis 1982, Early Music Award 1982. *E-mail:* hbouman@hendrikbouman.com. *Website:* www.hendrikbouman.com.

BOURGEOIS, Derek, MA, DMus; British composer and director of music; b. 16 Oct. 1941, Kingston on Thames; m. Jean Berry 1965. *Education:* Magdalene Coll., Cambridge, Royal Coll. of Music. *Career:* Lecturer in Music, Bristol Univ. 1971–84; Dir of Music, Nat. Youth Orchestra of Great Britain, 1984–93; Founder, Nat. Youth Chamber Orchestra of Great Britain, 1989–93; Dir of Music, St Paul's Girls' School, London, 1994–2002; mem., Vice-Pres., Composers Guild of Great Britain (Chair. 1980–83). *Compositions include:* 240 works, including 28 symphonies; Concertos for double bass, clarinet, trombone (2), tuba, organ, euphonium, 3 trombones, percussion, trumpet and bass trombone, tenor horn, saxophone; 4 Concertos for Brass Band; 6

Symphonies for Wind Orchestra; Symphonic Fantasy: The Globe; 8 works for chorus and orchestra; 2 operas. *Recordings:* many original compositions. *Honours:* Balearic Composer of the Year 2006. *Address:* La Tramuntana, Calle Orquidea No. 24 - Betlem, 07579 Arta, Mallorca, Spain (home). *Telephone:* 971 589236 (home). *E-mail:* tramuntana@infoarta.com (home). *Website:* www .tramuntana.infoarta.com (home).

BOURGUE, Daniel; French horn player; b. 12 Jan. 1937, Avignon. *Education:* Avignon Conservatoire and Paris Conservatoire. *Career:* soloist and chamber musician; concerts with the Musica wind quintet, 1961–67; horn soloist, Garde Républicaine Orchestra, 1963; at Concerts Pasadeloup, 1964; Opéra-Comique, 1967; Orchestre National de France; The Ensemble Inter-contemporain; Ensemble Orchestral de Paris; Nouvel Orchestre Philharmonique; first horn soloist Paris Opéra Orchestra, 1964–89; mem., Paris Octet 1965–82; performed in Europe, Scandinavia, Africa, USA, Latin America, Canada, Japan; has premiered works by Messiaen, (Appel Interstellaire), Francaix (Divertimento); Xenakis (Anaktoria, 1965), Pousseur, Jolas, Ballif, Constant and Delerue (Concerto); teaches at Versailles Conservatoire; lectures, masterclasses in France, Belgium, Germany, Italy, Bulgaria, USA, Canada, Spain, Japan; organizes training sessions with the Spanish National Youth Orchestra three times a year 1987–; Dir, Editions Billaudot's Florilège Collection; Pres., Asscn Nat. des Cornistes Français. *Recordings:* music by Mozart, Handel, Rossini, Telemann, Haydn, Strauss, Saint-Saëns, Stamitz, Hoffmeister, Dukas, Chabrier, Corrette, Bréval, d'Indy, Gounod and others. *Publications:* five-volume teaching work Techni-cor (publr); Parlons du cor. *Current Management:* c/o Valmalète, 7 rue Hoche, 92300 Levallois Perret, Paris, France. *Address:* 12 rue Erik Satie, 94440 Santeny, France (home). *Telephone:* 1-43-86-04-61 (home). *E-mail:* danbourg@tele2.fr (home).

BOURGUE, Maurice; French oboist and conductor; b. 6 Nov. 1939, Avignon. *Education:* Paris Conservatoire. *Career:* principal oboist, Basle Orchestra 1964–67, Orchestre de Paris 1967–79; solo appearances with the Israel Chamber Orchestra, I Solisti Veneti, I Musici, Lucerne Festival Strings and all major French orchestras; made UK debut at the Wigmore Hall 1979; engagements with the English Chamber Orchestra, Chamber Orchestra of Europe, Royal Philharmonic, and the London Symphony Orchestra under Abbado; premieres include Chemins IV by Berio 1974, Les Citations by Dutilleux 1991, and Messiaen's Concert à Quatre 1994; founder, Ensemble à Vent Maurice Bourgue 1972; co-founder, Ensemble Continuum 2004; has conducted the Oslo Philharmonic Orchestra, Ensemble Orchestral de Paris, Israel Chamber Orchestra and orchestras in Lyon, Montpellier, Nancy and the Auvergne; Prof., Conservatoire Nat. Supérieur de Musique et de Danse de Paris, and Conservatoire de Musique de Geneve; mem. Int. Double Reed Soc. *Honours:* winner Competitions at Birmingham 1985, Prague 1968, Budapest 1970.

BOURIAKOV, Denis V., FRAM; Russian musician (flute); *Principal Flute, New York Metropolitan Opera;* b. 23 Oct. 1981, Crimea. *Education:* Moscow Central Special Music School, studied with Y.N. Dolzhikov, RAM, studied with William Bennett. *Career:* Prin. Flute, Tampere Philharmonic 2004–07; Prin. Flute, Barcelona Symphony under Eiji Oue 2008; Prin. Flute, New York Metropolitan Opera 2009–; has performed world-wide at major concert halls and festivals as recitalist and as soloist with numerous orchestras including Moscow Philharmonic, Prague Chamber Orchestra, Odense Symphony, Munich Chamber Orchestra, Hiroshima Symphony, Lithuanian Symphony and Tampere Philharmonic Orchestra; taught at Tampere Conservatory of Music; offers masterclasses worldwide. *Recordings include:* Bach/Sibelius/Saint-Saens 2009, Bach Concerto for 2 Violins in D minor with William Bennett and English Chamber Orchestra, Prokofiev/Copland/Debussy 2012. *Honours:* ARAM 2006; prizewinner, Jean-Pierre Rampal, Munich ARD, Prague Spring, Carl Nielsen and Kobe competitions. *Website:* www .bouriakov.com.

BOUŠKOVÁ, Jana, DocMgr; Czech harpist; *Principal Harpist, Czech Philharmonic Orchestra;* b. 27 Sept. 1970, Prague. *Education:* Prague Conservatory, Ostrava Univ., Indiana Univ., USA, studied with Libuse Vachalova, Susann McDonald. *Career:* concert harpist, solo, chamber; recital at Lincoln Center 1993; concerts at major concert halls of the world, including Berliner and Köln Philharmonies; int. music festivals; many recordings for TV and radio; concerts at World Harp Congresses; duos with Patrick Gallois, Mstislav Rostropovich, Sharon Kam, Maxim Vengerov, Christian Tetzlaff and others; teacher, Prague Conservatory 1993–2012, Royal Conservatory, Brussels 2005–, Acad. of Music, Prague 2006–; Prin. Harpist, Czech Philharmonic Orchestra 2005–; Artistic Chair. Seventh World Harp Congress, Prague 1999; mem. Artistic Cttees, Acad. of Music, Czech Philharmonic; guest teacher, Indiana Univ. 2004, Haute Ecole de Musique de Genève, Switzerland 2012. *Recordings include:* more than 20 solo albums, including Harp Recital (Scarlatti, Bach, Tournier, etc.), Harp Recital (J. L. Dussek), Harp Recital (J. F. Fischer), Harp Concertos (Handel, Krumpholz, Boieldieu), Harp Concertos (J. Ch. Bach), Harp Concertos (J. K. Krumpholz Nos 1–6), Harp Recital (Bach, Fischer), Harp-Violin (Kreutzer-Nocturnos), Harp-Flute (Spohr, Ravel), Jana Bouskova Plays Virtuoso Encores (Chopin, Liszt, Bach), Solos for Harp (Ravel and Debussy), Harp Concertos (Dittersdorf, Wagenseil, Albrechtsberger), Duos for flute and harp (Saint-Saëns, Fauré). *Honours:* first prize and gold medal, USA Int. Harp Competition 1992, second prize, Int. Harp Contest, Israel 1992, Talent of the Year Award 1996, first prize, Grand Prix Concours Int. de Musique de Chambre de Paris 1998, first prize, TIM Torneo Internazionale di Musica 1999, Harpa Award 1999, Czech Music Council

Award 2002, Lady Pro Award 2004, Prague. *Current Management:* c/o Stephan Popp, Klangkultur, Arnold-Schönberg-Straße 4, 40593 Düsseldorf, Germany. *Telephone:* (49) 17905872; (49) 7488610. *Fax:* (49) 17905871. *E-mail:* info@klangkultur-popp.de. *Website:* www.klangkultur-popp.de. *E-mail:* jana.bouskova@gmail.com. *Website:* www.musica.cz/bouskova; www .janabouskova.com.

BOVINO, Maria; British singer (soprano); b. 1960, England. *Education:* Sheffield Univ. and Guildhall School of Music and Drama. *Career:* debut at King's Coll. London, as Bella in Schubert's Die Verschworenen; sang Fiorella in Offenbach's Les Brigands with the Intermezzi Ensemble; Opera 80 from 1982 as Adele in Die Fledermaus, Despina in Così fan tutte and Elvira in L'Italiana in Algeri; season 1984–85 as Emmie in Albert Herring at Glyndebourne and Titania in A Midsummer Night's Dream for Glyndebourne tour; sang First Boy in The Magic Flute for ENO 1986, followed by the Queen of Night 1988; with Scottish Opera from 1987 as Blondchen in Die Entführung and Papagena; English Bach Festival in Gluck's Orfeo and Dido and Aeneas in London, Granada and Athens; Covent Garden debut 1989 in Albert Herring; performances with Travelling Opera in season 1990–91 as Mimi and Gilda; also Gilbert and Sullivan with the London Savoyards; sang Susanna with Crystal Clear Productions 1991; sang Gilda with English Touring Opera 1996; Queen of Night for Mid-Wales Opera 1998.

BOWATER, Helen; New Zealand composer; b. 16 Nov. 1952, Wellington. *Education:* studied with Gwyneth Brown and at Victoria Univ., Wellington. *Career:* resident composer, Nelson School of Music 1992; Mozart Fellow Univ. of Otago 1993. *Compositions include:* Black Rain for soprano and cello 1985, Songs of Mourning for baritone and string quartet 1989, Stay Awake Ananda for five percussionists 1990, The Bodhi Tree for string quartet 1991, Witch's Mine for tape 1991, Magma for orchestra 1992.

BOWEN, Geraint Robert Lewis, MA, MusB, FRCO; British conductor and organist; *Organist and Director of Music, Hereford Cathedral;* b. 11 Jan. 1963, London, England; m. Lucy Dennis 1987; two s. *Education:* Univ. of Cambridge, Trinity Coll., Dublin, studied with Christopher Herrick, John Scott and Stephen Cleobury. *Career:* Organ Scholar, Jesus Coll., Cambridge 1982–85; TV and radio broadcasts as organ accompanist and conductor 1984–; Asst Organist, Hampstead Parish Church, St Clement Danes Church 1985–86, St Patrick's Cathedral, Dublin 1986–89, Hereford Cathedral 1989–94; Festival Organist, Hereford Three Choirs Festival 1991, 1994; appearances as conductor and recitalist in the UK, Ireland, USA, South Africa and Australia; Organist and Master of the Choristers, St Davids Cathedral, Wales 1995–2001; Artistic Dir St Davids Cathedral Festival 1995–2001; Founder and Conductor St Davids Cathedral Festival Chorus 1996–2001; Dir of choral workshops in USA 1997–; Organist and Dir of Music, Hereford Cathedral 2001–; Conductor, Hereford Choral Soc. 2001–; Conductor, Three Choirs Festival 2002–; orchestras conducted include Bournemouth Symphony Orchestra, City of Birmingham Symphony Orchestra, Orchestra of the Age of Enlightenment, Philharmonia, Royal Philharmonic Orchestra. *Recordings include:* several recordings with the choir of Hereford Cathedral. *Honours:* Hon. Fellow, Guild of Church Musicians 2012. *Address:* 7 College Cloisters, The Close, Hereford, HR1 2NG, England (home). *Telephone:* (1432) 374238 (office). *E-mail:* organist@herefordcathedral.org (office). *Website:* www .herefordcathedral.org (office).

BOWEN, John; British singer (tenor); b. 1968, England. *Education:* Royal College of Music. *Career:* appearances with Bath and Wessex Opera, Garsington Festival, City of Birmingham Touring Opera and Opera Factory Zürich; roles include Ugone in Flavio and Pan in La Calisto; concerts with the English Chamber Orchestra, Royal Liverpool Philharmonic Orchestra, London Mozart Players, and The King's Consort in The Indian Queen and Judas Maccabaeus; sang in the premiere of Tavener's Apocalypse at the London Proms in 1994 and tour of Bach's B minor Mass with René Jacobs; sang Soliman in Mozart's Zaide at the 1996 Covent Garden Festival; currently pursuing a career in the legal profession. *Recordings include:* Rachmaninov's Vespers; Messiah; Monteverdi's Vespers.

BOWEN, Kenneth John, BA, BMus, MA; British singer (tenor), conductor and teacher; b. 3 Aug. 1932, Llanelli, Wales; m. Angela Mary Bowen 1959, two s. *Education:* Univ. of Wales, St John's Coll., Cambridge, Inst. of Education, Univ. of London. *Career:* debut as Tom Rakewell, New Opera Company, Sadler's Wells 1957; Flying Officer, Education Branch, RAF 1958–60; Prof. of Singing, RAM 1967–91; Head of Vocal Studies 1987–91; Conductor, London Welsh Chorale 1983–, London Welsh Festival Chorus; former concert and operatic tenor, retd 1988; appeared at Promenade Concerts, Aldeburgh, Bath, Swansea, Llandaff and Fishguard Festivals, throughout Europe, Israel, North America and the Far East; performed at Royal Opera House, ENO, WNO, Glyndebourne Touring Opera, English Opera Group, English Music Theatre, Kent Opera and Handel Opera Soc.; frequent broadcasts, numerous first performances and many recordings. *Honours:* first prize Geneva Competition, 's-Hertogenbosch Competition, Liverpool Competition, Munich Int. Competition, Queens Prize, Hon. RAM, GPWM John Edwards Memorial Award.

BOWERS, Evan; American singer (tenor); b. 1960, New York. *Career:* Sang Alfredo and Gounod's Tybalt for Texas Opera Theatre, Ernesto in San Francisco and for the Metropolitan Opera Guild; Ferrando and the Duke of Mantua for Israeli Vocal Arts Institute; European debut 1992, as Don Ottavio for the Wiener Kammeroper; Engagement with the Nuremberg Opera as Tamino, Oberon, Leopold in La Juive, Andres in Wozzeck and Rossini's

Almaviva; Guest as Fenton at Innsbruck and Nemorino at the Salzburg Landestheater; Leipzig Opera from 1994, as Rodolfo, Lensky and Don Ottavio; Graz Opera debut as Tamino; Season 1996–97 as Beethoven's Jacquino, Don Ottavio at the Schönbrunn Festival and Gratiano in The Merchant of Venice for Portland Opera; Concerts include: The Missa Solemnis, Haydn's Creation and Seasons, Requiems of Verdi and Mozart; Venues include: France, Germany and the USA.

BOWERS-BROADBENT, Christopher Joseph, FRAM; British organist and composer; *Organist and Choirmaster of Gray's Inn and Organist of the West London Synagogue*; b. 13 Jan. 1945, Hemel Hempstead, Herts.; s. of Henry W. Bowers-Broadbent and Doris E. Mizen; m. Deirdre Cape 1970; one s. one d. *Education:* Berkhamsted School, King's Coll., Cambridge and Royal Acad. of Music. *Career:* Organist and Choirmaster of St Pancras Parish Church 1965–88; Organist of West London Synagogue 1973–; Organist and Choirmaster of Gray's Inn 1983–; debut organ recital, Camden Festival 1966; Prof. of Organ, RAM, London 1976–92. *Recordings include:* Trivium, O Domina Nostra, Méditations sur le Mystère de la Sainte Trinité, Mattins Music, Duets and Canons. *Operas include:* The Pied Piper 1972, The Seacock Bane 1979, The Last Man 1983–2000, The Face 2012. *Honours:* Three Choirs Festival Composers' Competition Prize 1978. *Address:* 94 Colney Hatch Lane, Muswell Hill, London, N10 1EA, England. *Telephone:* (20) 8883-1933. *Fax:* (20) 8883-8434; (20) 8888-8434. *E-mail:* kitbb@btinternet.com. *Website:* www .christopherbowers-broadbent.com.

BOWLES, Edmund Addison, BA, PhD; American musicologist and timpanist; b. 24 March 1925, Cambridge, MA; m. Marianne von Recklinghausen; one s. one d. *Education:* Swarthmore Coll., Yale Univ., Berkshire Music Center, Tanglewood, MA. *Career:* instructor in humanities, MIT 1951–55; Publicity Staff, Bell Telephone Laboratories 1955–59; Sr Program Adminstrator, IBM Corpn 1959–88; Consultant, Music Div., Library of Congress 1955–; mem. American Musical Instrument Soc., American Musicological Soc., The Galpin Soc., Int. Musicological Soc., Medieval Acad. of America, Percussive Arts Soc. *Publications:* Computers in Humanistic Research: Readings and Perspectives 1967, Musikleben des 15. Jahrhunderts 1976, Musical Performance in The Late Middle Ages 1983, Musical Ensembles in Festival Books: An Iconographical and Documentary Survey 1989, The Timpani: A History in Pictures and Documents 2002, The Timpani: More Pictures and Documents 2009; contribs to various professional journals, Dictionary of the Middle Ages, Encyclopaedia Britannica, Garland Encyclopedia of Percussion, Several New Grove dictionaries, The New Harvard Dictionary of Music. *Honours:* American Council of Learned Socs Grant 1964, Nat. Endowment for the Humanities Grant 1971, Andrew W. Mellon Summer Fellowship 1980, Bessaraboff Prize 1991, Curt Sachs Award, American Musical Instrument Soc. 1997. *Address:* 3210 Valley Lane, Falls Church, VA 22044, USA (home).

BOWLES, Garrett H., BA, MA, MLS, PhD; American music librarian; b. 3 Feb. 1938, San Francisco, CA; one s. one d. *Education:* University of California at Davis, San Jose State University, University of California at Berkeley, Stanford University. *Career:* Head Music Cataloguer, Stanford University, 1965–79; Head Music Librarian, 1979–, Assistant Adjunct Professor of Music, 1980–, University of California, San Diego; Visiting Lecturer at University of Exeter, England, 1983. *Compositions include:* Festklang for Ernst Krenek, in Perspectives of New Music, 1985. *Recordings:* Handel's Messiah, 1984. *Publications:* Directory, Music Library Automation Projects, 1973, 1979; Ernst Krenek, Bio-bibliography, 1989; Editor, Ernst Krenek Newsletter, 1990–; contrib. to Journal of Association for Recorded Sound Collectors; Notes; Forte Artis Musicae. *Address:* Music Library 0175-Q, University of California at San Diego, 9500 Gilman Drive, La Jolla, CA 92093-0175, USA.

BOWMAN, James Thomas, CBE, DipEd, MA; British singer (countertenor); b. 6 Nov. 1941, Oxford. *Education:* Cathedral Choir School, Kings School, Ely, Cambridgeshire, New Coll., Oxford. *Career:* sang with English Opera Group 1967–, with debut as Britten's Oberon; sang with Early Music Consort 1967–76; operatic performances include Sadler's Wells Opera 1970–, Glyndebourne Festival Opera 1970–, Opéra Comique, Paris 1979–, Geneva 1983, Dallas and San Francisco Operas, USA; operatic roles include Endymion in La Calisto, The Priest in Taverner in the world premiere at Covent Garden 1972, Apollo in Death in Venice, Astron in The Ice Break 1977 premiere; title roles include Handel's Giulio Cesare, Tamerlano, Scipione; appearances include La Scala, Milan 1988 as Jommelli's Fetonte, ENO 1989 as Amphinomous in The Return of Ulysses, Promenade Concerts 1991 in Purcell's Ode for St Cecilia's Day; sang Britten's Oberon at Aix-en-Provence 1992, Barak in Handel's Deborah 1993 Prom Concerts, London; other roles include Goffredo in Rinaldo, Lidio in Cavalli's Egisto, Ruggiero in Vivaldi's Orlando; sang Herod in Fux's La Fede Sacrilega in Vienna and Monteverdi's Ottone in Poppea at the Spitalfields Festival, London; Bach's St John Passion at St John's, London 1997; Daniel in Handel's Belshazzar, Göttingen Festival 1996; sang Britten's Oberon at the Barbican 1998; title role in Handel's Silla, Royal Coll. of Music 2000. *Recordings:* oratorio, Mediaeval and Renaissance vocal music. *Honours:* Hon. DMus (Univ. of Newcastle upon Tyne) 1996;Hon. Fellow (New Coll., Oxford) 1998. *E-mail:* pattle@globalnet.co.uk (home). *Website:* www.users.globalnet.co.uk/~pattle/bowman.

BOWYER, Kevin John; British organist; *Organist, University of Glasgow*; b. 9 Jan. 1961, Essex, England; m. Ursula Steiner 1981; two s. two d. *Education:* Royal Acad. of Music with Douglas Hawkridge and Christopher Bowers-Broadbent, studied with David Sanger. *Career:* debut, Royal Festival Hall 1984; concerts throughout Europe and N America, specializing in unusual and contemporary repertoire; performances of Kaikhosru Sorabji's Organ Symphony in London 1987, Århus 1988, Linz 1992, Sorabji's Organ Symphony No. 2 (eight hours in length) in Glasgow and Amsterdam 2010; broadcasts for BBC Radio 3 include works by Ligeti, Hugh Wood, Malcolm Williamson, Berio, Henze, Brian Ferneyhough, Charles Camilleri, Niccolo Castiglioni; numerous broadcasts for other networks; Sr Lecturer in Organ, Royal Northern Coll. of Music, Manchester 1999–2008; Organist, Univ. of Glasgow 2005–; teaches in Glasgow for the St Giles Int. Organ School. *Recordings:* A Late Twentieth Century Edwardian Bach Recital, Alkan Organ Works, Brahms Complete Organ Works, Reubke's 94th Psalm Sonata, Schumann's 6 Fugues on Bach, Organ Works by Dupré, Langlais, Hindemith, Pepping, Arnold Schoenberg, Complete Organ Works of J. S. Bach, Messiaen Organ Works (two vols), Sorabji Organ Symphony No. 1, works by Busoni, Ronald Stevenson, Alistair Hinton. *Publications:* contrib. of articles on Sorabji to The Organ and Organists Review; occasional humorous articles, all organ related. *Honours:* Countess of Munster Musical Trust grant, First Prize, St Albans Int. . Organ Festival 1983, First Prize, int. organ festivals in Dublin, Paisley, Odense and Calgary 1990. *Address:* Chaplaincy, University of Glasgow, University Avenue, Glasgow, G12 8QQ, Scotland (office). *Telephone:* 7870-685974 (mobile). *E-mail:* kevinbowyer2@aol.com. *Website:* www.kevinbowyer.net.

BOYD, Anne Elizabeth, AM, BA (Hons), DPhil; Australian composer and professor of music; *Professor of Music and Associate Dean (Staff Development), Sydney Conservatorium, University of Sydney*; b. 10 April 1946, Sydney; d. of James David Boyd and Annie Freda Osborn; one d. *Education:* Univ. of Sydney, Univ. of York, NSW Conservatorium of Music, studied with Peter Sculthorpe, Wilfrid Mellers, Bernard Rands. *Career:* debut at Adelaide Festival of Arts 1966; festival performances include Adelaide 1966, 1968, 1976, Opening Season Festival of Sydney Opera House 1973; appearances at Edinburgh and Windsor Festivals 1974, Aldeburgh Festival 1980, Hong Kong Arts Festival 1985, ISCM Festival, Hong Kong 1986, 'Donne in Musica', Fiuggi, Italy 1999, Vale of Glamorgan Festival, Wales 2001; Lecturer in Music, Univ. of Sussex 1972–77; founding Head and Reader Dept of Music, Univ. of Hong Kong 1981–90; Prof. of Music and Chair. Arts Music Unit, Univ. of Sydney 1990–2007; Prof. of Music, Sydney Conservatorium of Music, Univ. of Sydney 2008–, Pro Dean (Academic) 2008–12, Assoc. Dean (Staff Devt) 2013–. *Compositions include:* Angklung meditations for solo piano 1974, Book of the Bells for piano 1980, String Quartets Nos 1 and 2, The Voice of the Phoenix for solo piano, guitar, harp, harpsichord and full orchestra, As It Leaves The Bell for piano, two harps and four percussion, Goldfish Through Summer Rain for flute and piano 1979, Red Sun, Chill Wind for flute and piano 1980, Cloudy Mountain for flute and piano 1981, Bali Moods No. 1 for flute and piano 1987, Black Sun for orchestra 1989, Grathwai for orchestra 1993, Uluru Mourns and Uluru Dances for cello 1996, ...at the rising of the sun... for orchestra 2001; choral: As I Crossed a Bridge of Dreams 1975, The Little Mermaid (children's opera) 1978, The Death of Captain Cook (oratorio) 1978, Coal River (choral symphony) 1979, The Beginning of the Day (children's opera) 1979, The Last of his Tribe 1980, Revelations of Divine Love 1995, Dreams for the Earth (youth cantata) 1998, A Vision: Jesus Reassures his Mother for vocal soloists 1999, Missa Pacifica 2008, Seraphim Canticles for piano trio 2008, Lament of the Pious Women of Jerusalem 2008, Cum Rex Gloriae 2009; song cycles for voice and chamber ensemble: My Name is Tian 1979, Cycle of Love 1981, Meditations on a Chinese Character 1996, Last Songs of the Kamikaze 1997, Opera Daisy Bates at Ooldea 2012, Kabarli meditation (Dawn) for solo piano 2011, String Quartet No 3 'Forever Peter' 2015. *Publications:* contribs to Music Now, Musical Times, Miscellanea Musicologica, Australian Journal of Music Education, Sounds Australia, Intercultural Music, The Soundscapes of Australia, Matters of the Musical Mind, Opera Indigine. *Honours:* Hon. DUniv (York) 2003; AMC-APRA Award for Distinguished Services to Australian Music 2005, Sir Bernard Heinz Award 2014. *Address:* Arts Music Unit, Conservatorium of Music, University of Sydney, Seymour Theatre Building JO9, Sydney, NSW 2006, Australia (office). *Telephone:* (2) 9351-6947 (office). *Fax:* (2) 9351-7340 (office). *E-mail:* anne.boyd@sydney.edu.au (office). *Website:* www.music.usyd.edu.au (office).

BOYD, Douglas, FRAM, ARAM, FRNCM; British conductor and fmr oboist; *Artistic Director, Garsington Opera*; b. 1 March 1959, Glasgow, Scotland; s. of Marcus Boyd and Agnes Boyd; m. 1st Gabrielle Lester 1987 (divorced 1990); one s.; m. 2nd Sally Pendlebury; one s. one d. *Education:* Royal Acad. with Janet Craxton, studied with Maurice Bourgue in Paris. *Career:* Co-founder and Prin. Oboist, Chamber Orchestra of Europe 1989–2002; performed as soloist with Claudio Abbado, Yehudi Menuhin, Sir Roger Norrington, Michael Tilson Thomas; performed at Edinburgh, Berlin, Salzburg Int. festivals; Visiting Conductor, Chamber Orchestra of Europe, BBC Symphony Orchestra, City of Birmingham Symphony Orchestra, Scottish Chamber Orchestra, Seattle, Baltimore, Indianapolis, Detroit and Dallas Symphony Orchestras; in Europe, Visiting Conductor with Tonhalle Orchestra, Zürich, Gurzenich Orchestra, Cologne, Budapest Festival Orchestra, Mozarteum Orchestra, Salzburg; Artistic Partner, St Paul Chamber Orchestra; Prin. Guest Conductor, City of London Sinfonia –2009, Colorado Symphony Orchestra 2008–10; Prin. Conductor, Manchester Camerata 2001–11, Musikkollegium Winterthur 2009–; opera: Magic Flute, Garsington Opera 2008, Fidelio 2009, La Grotto di Trofonio, Glyndebourne Touring Opera 2009, Zurich Opera 2009, Marriage of Figaro 2010 and Don Giovanni 2011 at Garsington Opera, La clemenza di Tito, Opera North 2013; performed complete Beethoven cycle with Melbourne Symphony Orchestra 2011; Artistic Dir Garsington Opera 2012–.

Recordings: as oboist: Strauss and Mozart Concerti, Bach Oboe Concerti, Ligeti Double Concerto; as conductor: Beethoven Symphonies cycle with Manchester Camerata, Mahler Symphony No. 4 with Manchester Camerata, Schubert Symphonies Nos 4 and 8 with St Paul Chamber Orchestra, Beethoven Symphonies cycle with Manchester Camerata 2011. *Current Management:* c/o Ingpen & Williams, 7 St George's Court, 131 Putney Bridge Road, London, SW15 2PA, England; c/o Frank Salomon Associates, 201 W 54th Street, Suite 1C, New York, NY 10019, USA. *Telephone:* (20) 8874-3222 (London). *Fax:* (20) 8877-3113 (London). *E-mail:* info@ingpen.co.uk. *Website:* www.ingpen.co.uk.

BOYD, James; British violist; b. 1960. *Education:* Yehudi Menuhin School, Guildhall School of Music, Menuhin Acad., Gstaad. *Career:* debut on South Bank, London, in premiere of Robert Simpson's 13th Quartet; BBC Radio 3 debut 1991; frequent tours with the Rafael Ensemble; Co-founder, Vellinger String Quartet 1990; formed London Haydn Quartet 2001; also plays in Ludwig String Trio with Peter Cropper and Paul Watkins; participated in master-classes with Borodin Quartet at Pears-Britten School 1991; concerts at Ferrara Music Festival, Italy; season 1992–93 concerts in London, Glasgow, Cambridge, Davos Festival, Switzerland and Crickdale Festival in Wiltshire; played at Wigmore Hall with works by Haydn, Gubaidulina and Beethoven, and at Purcell Room with Haydn's Seven Last Words; Co-founder Music-Works, chamber music course for young string players; teaches chamber music at Chamber Studio, Univ. of Cambridge. *Recordings include:* Elgar's Quartet and Quintet, with Piers Lane. *Honours:* jt winner, Bernard Shore Viola Prize 1988. *Website:* londonhaydnquartet.co.uk/biographies/james-boyd.

BOYD, Liona Maria, OC, CM, BMus, LLD; Canadian/American classical guitarist, composer and singer/songwriter; *Owner, Moston Productions, Moston Records and Mid-Continental Music*; b. 11 July 1950, London; d. of John Boyd and Eileen Boyd (née Hancock); m. John B. Simon 1992 (divorced 2004). *Education:* Kipling Collegiate, Univ. of Toronto, privately under Alexandre Lagoya in Paris. *Career:* composer and guitarist, performs and composes both classical and popular music; numerous pvt and command performances including royal families in UK and Spain, presidents in US and Mexico, prime ministers in Canada, France and UK; concerts in Tokyo, Hong Kong, Beijing, Bangkok, New Delhi, Edinburgh, Paris, Auckland, Frankfurt, Santiago, Rio, Bogotá, Havana, London, Copenhagen, Lisbon, Mexico City and all major US cities; first Canadian to perform in the Kremlin 1991; guest artist with orchestras including The Boston Pops; has recorded with Sir Andrew Davis and the English Chamber Orchestra, Yo Yo Ma, Georges Zamfir and Michael Kamen; toured with Gordon Lightfoot and Tracy Chapman and recorded with Chet Atkins, Eric Clapton, David Gilmour, and Roger Whittaker, Al di Meola, Strunz and Farah, Jesse Cooke, Steve Morse, Srdjan Givoje; numerous TV specials; Owner, Moston Productions, Moston Records, Mid-Continental Music; mem. American Fed. of Musicians. *Recordings include:* The Guitar Artistry of Liona Boyd 1976, Miniatures for Guitar 1977, The First Lady of the Guitar 1978, Spanish Fantasy 1980, A Guitar for Christmas 1981, Virtuoso 1983, Live in Tokyo 1984, The Romantic Guitar of Liona Boyd 1985, Persona 1986, Encore! 1989, Christmas Dreams 1989, Highlights 1989, Paddle-To-The-Sea 1990, Dancing on the Edge 1991, The Spanish Album 1999, Passport to Serenity 2000, Latin Cafe 2000, Baroque Favorites 2000, Camino Latino/Latin Journey 2004, Romanza 2006, 2009, The Return...To Canada with Love 2013, Songs of Love, Seven Journeys, Music for the Soul, Imagination. *Films include:* as performer: A Walk in the Clouds, A Dream of White Elephants, A Kid in King Arthur's Court. *Publications include:* Folk Songs From Around the World, Meet Liona on the Guitar, Favourite Songs, In My Own Key (autobiog.) 1999. *Honours:* Hon. Mayor of San Antonio, Tex., USA; Order of Ontario 1991; Hon. LLD (Lethbridge) 1982, (Brock) 1990, (Simon Fraser) 1991; Hon. DMus (Victoria), (Toronto); First Prize, Canadian Nat. Music Competition Vanier Award 1979, five Juno Awards for Instrumental Artist of the Year, four Gold and one Platinum recordings, winner (five times) Best Classical Guitarist, Guitar Player Magazine. *Address:* 3 Canterbury Road, Islington, ON M9A 5B2, Canada (home). *Telephone:* (416) 231-0670 (home). *Fax:* (310) 275-4111 (home). *E-mail:* liona@lionaboyd.com. *Website:* www.lionaboyd.com.

BOYD, Nathaniel; British cellist; b. 1983. *Education:* studied with Selma Gokcen and William Pleeth at Jr Guildhall School of Music, Royal Northern Coll. of Music. *Career:* started learning cello aged four; prin. cellist, Jr Guildhall School of Music Symphony Orchestra and String Ensemble; plays with Navarra String Quartet 2002–, also with The Volterra Trio; performed at St James' Piccadilly with London Pergolesi Sinfonietta 2002; has performed at numerous Chamber Music Festivals both in England and abroad at venues such as St Martin in the Fields, the Barbican. *Repertoire includes:* Beethoven Sonata No. 2 in G minor, Boccherini Cello Concerto in G major, Brahms Double Concerto, Brahms Sonata in F major, Shostakovich First Cello Concerto, Shostakovich Sonata in D minor, Saint-Saens Cello Concert No. 1, Schumann Concerto in A minor. *Honours:* Royal Northern Coll. of Music Leonard Rose Prize 2005. *Current Management:* c/o Sue Hudson and Rosemary Pickering, Young Concert Artists Trust, 23 Garrick Street, London WC2E 9BN, England. *Telephone:* (20) 7379-8477. *Fax:* (20) 7379-8467. *E-mail:* info@ycat.co.uk. *Website:* www.ycat.co.uk. *E-mail:* nb@navarra.co.uk (office). *Website:* www.navarra.co.uk.

BOYDE, Andreas; German pianist; b. 13 Nov. 1967, Oschatz, Saxony. *Education:* Spezialschule and Musikhochschule, Dresden, Guildhall School of Music and Drama, London, master-classes at Musikfestwochen Luzern. *Career:* debut with Berlin Symphony Orchestra 1989; concerts with Dresden Philharmonic Orchestra 1992, 1996; recital, Munich Philharmonic Hall, Gasteig 1992; Festival La Roque d'Anthéron, France 1993; concert, Zürich Tonhalle with Zürich Chamber Orchestra 1994; concerts with Freiburg Philharmonic Orchestra 1994, 1997, 1999; Dresden State Orchestra 1994, 1995; recitalist in Schumann Cycle, Düsseldorf 1995; South American debut, recital in Teatro Municipal Santiago, Chile 1996; concert, Munich Herkulessaal, with Munich Symphony 1997; concert tour with Northwest German Philharmonic Orchestra 1997; recital, Munich Prinzregenten Theatre 1997; concert tour with Odessa Philharmonic Orchestra, including Cologne Philharmonic Hall and Stuttgart Liederhalle 1997; recital, Dresdner Musikfestspiele 1998; gave European premiere of piano concerto, Four Parables by Schoenfield, with Dresdner Sinfoniker 1998; concerts with Hallé Philharmonic 1999, 2004; Schumann recital tour including own reconstruction of Schubert Variations in New York, Germany, London Wigmore Hall 2000; world premiere of piano concerto by John Pickard with Dresdner Sinfoniker 2000; concerts at Konzertsaal KKL Lucerne with Lucerne Symphony Orchestra 2000; concerts with Bamberger Symphoniker 2000, 2001; concert tour with Nat. Symphony Orchestra of Ukraine in UK 2001; concert with Bournemouth Symphony Orchestra 2001; recital tour in UK 2001; concerts with Israel Northern Symphony Orchestra 2001; Beethoven Fest, Bonn 2001; concert tour with Bolshoi Symphony Orchestra, UK 2001; recital, Wigmore Hall, London 2001; concerts with Bucharest Philharmonic Orchestra 2002, with Slovak Philharmonic Orchestra 2002, with London Philharmonic Orchestra 2002, with Hallé Orchestra, Manchester 2002, 2003, 2005; concert tour with Nat. Youth Orchestras of Scotland 2002; concert, Prague Autumn Festival 2003; Beethoven recital, Santiago, Chile 2003; concerts with Malaysian Philharmonic Orchestra 2003, with London Mozart Players 2004, Munich Prinzregenten Theater 2004, Cologne Philharmonic Hall with Weimar Staatskapelle 2005; concerts with Stuttgart Philharmonic Orchestra 2006, 2009, 2011; recitals, Schumann Fest Düsseldorf 2006; concerts with El Paso Symphony Orchestra, USA 2006; recitals, St Louis, USA 2006, 2009; concerts with Munich Symphony 2006, 2009; Brahms cycle with Westdeutscher Rundfunk 2007, 2008; concert with Spartanburg Philharmonic 2007, 2015; concert with Graz Philharmonic 2007, with Virtuosi Saxoniae, Cologne Philharmonic Hall 2009; recital, Munich 2009; concerts with Winnipeg Symphony Orchestra 2010; recitals, Dresden 2010; concerts with Auckland Philharmonia Orchestra 2010, 2012, Cyprus Symphony Orchestra 2011; film recordings for Opus You 2011, 2012; concert with Slovenian Philharmonic Orchestra 2012, Zagreb Philharmonic Orchestra 2012, Belgrade Philharmonic Orchestra 2012, 2015, Vietnam Nat. Symphony Orchestra 2012, Brandenburg Sinfonia London 2012; recital, Auckland 2012, London 2012, 2014; Cologne Philharmonic Hall with Dresdner Kapellsolisten 2012; concerts with Dresdner Philharmonie 2013, Miami Symphony Orchestra 2013; recital, Dresden 2013; concerts with Norrköping Symphony Orchestra 2014; frequent broadcasts with German radio stations and the BBC. *Recordings include:* works by Schumann, Tchaikovsky, Mussorgsky, Ravel, Dvořák, Schoenfield, Brahms, Scriabin and Rachmaninov. *Publications include:* Robert Schumann, Variationen über ein Thema von Schubert, reconstructed score by Andreas Boyde. *Honours:* Citizen of the Book of Honour, Oschatz. *Current Management:* Costa Peristianis, Ikon Arts Management, 114 Business Design Centre, 52 Upper Street, London, N1 0QH, England. *Telephone:* (20) 7354-9199. *E-mail:* costa@ikonarts.com. *Website:* www.ikonarts.com; www.andreasboyde.com.

BOYER, Peter, BA, DMus; American composer, conductor and academic; *Helen M. Smith Chair in Music, Claremont Graduate University*; b. 10 Feb. 1970, Providence, RI. *Education:* Rhode Island Coll., Hartt School, Univ. of Hartford, pvt. study with John Corigliano. *Career:* began composing at age 15; joined faculty Claremont Graduate Univ. 1996, Helen M. Smith Chair in Music 1999–; f. Propulsive Music 2003; orchestral works have been performed more than 200 times by more than 70 orchestras; best-known work, Ellis Island: The Dream of America, has received over 90 performances by 40 orchestras; has also scored works for film and TV. *Compositions include:* Titanic (tone poem) (BMI Award 1995) 1995, The Phoenix 1997, At the Crossings 1998, Three Olympians 2000, Ghosts of Troy 2000, New Beginnings 2000, Ellis Island: The Dream of America 2003, Silver Fanfare 2004, And the night shall be filled with music 2005, American Rhapsody 2007, Dreaming a World 2007. *Recordings:* The Music of Peter Boyer (with London Symphony Orchestra) 2001, Ellis Island: The Dream of America 2005. *Honours:* Hon DMus (Rhode Island Coll.) 2004; numerous awards including BMI Student Composer Awards 1994, 1996, First Music Carnegie Hall commission, Ithaca Coll. Heckscher Prize 2001. *Address:* Propulsive Music, 3736 N. Hollingsworth Road, Altadena, CA 91001, USA (office). *Telephone:* (626) 398-3377 (office). *Fax:* (626) 398-3373 (office). *E-mail:* info@propulsivemusic.com (office); peter.boyer@cgu.edu (office). *Website:* www.propulsivemusic.com (office).

BOYKAN, Martin, BA, MM; American composer, pianist, academic and writer; *Irving G. Fine Professor Emeritus of Music, Brandeis University*; b. 12 April 1931, New York; s. of Joseph Boykan and Matilda Caspe; m. Susan Schwalb 1983. *Education:* Harvard Univ., Yale Univ., Berkshire Music Center, Tanglewood, Univ. of Zürich, studied composition with Walter Piston, Aaron Copland and Paul Hindemith, piano with Eduard Steuermann. *Career:* pianist, Boston Symphony Orchestra 1964–65; performed concerts with Joseph Silverstein, Jan de Gaetani; Composer-in-Residence, Composers' Conf., Wellesley 1987, Warebrook Festival 1998, Abravanel Distinguished

Composer, Salt Lake City 2001; Visiting Prof. of Composition, Columbia Univ. 1988–89, New York Univ. 1993, 1999–2000, Bar-Ilan Univ., Israel 1994; also lectures at Harvard Univ., Yale Univ., Princeton Univ., American Acad. in Berlin; apptd Irving G. Fine Prof. of Music, Brandeis Univ., now Prof. Emer.; mem. American Acad. of Arts and Letters 2011. *Compositions include:* Psalm 126 1965, String Quartets No. 1 1967, No. 2 1972, No. 3 1988, Concerto for 13 Players 1971, Piano Trio 1976, Elegy for soprano and six instruments 1982, Epithalamion 1985, Shalom Rav 1987, Fantasy-Sonata for piano 1987, Symphony No. 1 1989, Piano sonata No. 2, Nocturne for cello, piano and percussion 1990, Eclogue for 5 instruments 1991, Echoes of Petrarch, for flute, clarinet and piano 1992, Voyages for soprano and piano 1992, Sonata for cello and piano 1992, Sea-Gardens for soprano and piano 1993, Impromptu for violin solo 1993, Three Psalms for soprano and piano 1993, Pastorale for piano 1993, Sonata for violin and piano 1994, Maariv Settings for chorus and organ 1995, City of Gold for flute solo 1996, String Quartet No. 4 1996, Three Shakespeare's Songs for Women's Chorus 1996, Piano Trio No. 2 1997, Psalm 121, for soprano and string quartet 1997, Usurpations for piano solo 1997, Sonata for violin solo 1998, Flume for clarinet and piano 1999, Romanza for flute and piano 1999, A Packet for Susan, five songs for voice and piano 2000, Motet–Al Mishkavi for mezzo-soprano and consort of viols 2001, version for clarinet, viola and cello 2005, Concerto for violin and orchestra 2003, Songlines for flute, clarinet, violin and cello 2004, Second Chances, songs for mezzo-soprano and piano 2005, Piano Trio No. 3 2006, Piano Sonata No. 3 2007, Towards the Horizon for piano solo 2007, Soliloquies for an Insomniac, songs for mezzo-soprano and piano 2008, Sonata No. 2 for Violin and Piano 2009, As once on a deserted street for violin, cello, clarinet, horn and piano 2011, Sonata for Viola and Piano 2012, Piano Trio No. 4 2014. *Publications include:* String Quartets Nos 1–4, Fantasy-Sonata for Piano, Piano Sonata No. 2, Usurpations for piano, Sonata for cello and piano, Echoes of Petrarch for flute, clarinet and piano, Impromptu for violin solo, Sonata for violin and piano, City of Gold for flute solo, Psalm 126, Piano Trio No. 1, Silence and Slow Time: Studies in Musical Narrative 2004, The Power of the Moment: Essays on Classical Music 2011. *Honours:* Fulbright Award 1953, 1994, Jeunesses Musicales Award 1967, Rockefeller Award 1974, Fromm Foundation Commission Award 1976, National Endowment for the Arts Grant 1983, winner Nat. Competition of Int. Soc. for Contemporary Music 1984, Guggenheim Fellowship 1984, Serge Koussevitzky Foundation Grant 1985, American Acad. and Nat. Inst. of Arts and Letters Awards 1986, 1988. *Address:* 10 Winsor Avenue, Watertown, MA 02472, USA (home). *Telephone:* (617) 926-0188 (home). *E-mail:* boykan@brandeis.edu (office). *Website:* www.martinboykan.com.

BOYLAN, Orla; Irish singer (lyric soprano); b. Sept. 1971, Dublin. *Education:* studied in Dublin and Milan, Italy, masterclasses with Leyla Gencer, Robert Kettleson and Renata Scotto. *Career:* concerts include Mozart's Requiem, Coronation Mass and Mass in C minor, Weill's Street Scenes, Orff's Carmina Burana, Messiah, Rossini's Petite Messe, premiere of Barry's Bitter Tears of Petra von Kant; RTE production of Mendelssohn's A Midsummer Night's Dream and Strauss's Four Last Songs with the Wexford Symphonia, Mahler Symphony No 2 with Estonian Nat. Symphony Orchestra, Verdi's Requiem with Royal Philharmonic Orchestra at St Paul's Cathedral, London; song recitals at the Salle Cortot, Paris, and throughout Ireland; season 1996–97 with Mozart's Fiordiligi in Milan, the C Minor Mass in Liverpool and Dublin and concerts with the RTE Concert Orchestra; season 1997–98, leading roles in Falstaff, Turn of the Screw, Nozze di Figaro, Eugene Onegin; sang Celia in Mozart's Lucio Silla, Opera for Europe 1998; appearances in The Rape of Lucretia and The Valkyrie; title role in Die Liebe der Danae, Jenufa and Kat'a Kabanova at Glyndebourne Opera; Arabella at Garsington Opera,The Governess (Turn of the Screw), Angers Nantes Opera, Tatyana (Eugene Onegin) for EU Opera; The Valkyrie (Act III) with ENO, Glastonbury, 2004; title role in Ariadne (WNO) 2010; Queen of Spades for Opera North 2011. *Honours:* winner Veronica Dunne Bursary 1995, prize winner European Operatic Singing Competition, La Scala 1996, Belvedere Int. Singing Competition Graz and Klagenfurt special prizes, Vienna 1996, Austrian Theatre Ibla Grand Prize. *Current Management:* Harrison Parrott, 5–6 Albion Court, London, W6 0QT, England. *Telephone:* (20) 7229-9166. *Fax:* (20) 7221-5042. *E-mail:* info@harrisonparrott.com. *Website:* www.harrisonparrott.com.

BOYLAN, Patricia; British singer (mezzo-soprano); b. 1945, London, England. *Education:* Trinity Coll. of Music, Nat. Opera School and London Opera Centre. *Career:* English Opera Group with tours in Britten's operas under the composer to Russia; appearances with Scottish Opera in Peter Grimes and Die Walküre, concerts and oratorios throughout the UK, including the Aldeburgh and Edinburgh Festivals; following career break, returned to the concert hall in such works as Beethoven's Ninth and Mass in C, Mozart's C minor Mass and Requiem, the Verdi Requiem and Mahler's Kindertotenlieder; sang in El Amor Brujo at the Manuel de Falla Festival in Seville; operatic appearances as Larina in Eugene Onegin in Lisbon, Azucena in Madrid, Orpheus, Carmen and Amneris at Malaga; sang Clytemnestra in Elektra for WNO 1992 and Auntie in Peter Grimes for Scottish Opera 1993; Witch in Hansel and Gretel at Belfast 1998.

BOZARTH, George S., MFA, PhD; American historical musicologist; *Ruth Water Endowed Professor of Music, University of Washington*; b. 28 Feb. 1947, Trenton, NJ. *Education:* Princeton University. *Career:* Ruth Water Endowed Prof. of Music, Univ. of Washington; Exec. Dir American Brahms Soc.; Dir of Brahms Archive, Seattle, WA; Dir Int. Brahms Conference, Washington DC 1983; Performer on historical pianos of late 18th through mid-19th centuries; Artistic Dir Gallery Concerts in Seattle, Musique du Jour Festival, Sanford, Maine; mem., The Classical Consort. *Publications:* editions: Johannes Brahms, Orgelwerke, The Organ Works, Munich, G Henle 1988, J. S. Bach, Cantata, Ach Gott vom Himmel sieh darein, BWV2, Neue Bach Ausgabe, 1/16 1981, 1984, The Brahms-Keller Correspondence 1996, On Brahms and his Circle: Essays and Studies by Karl Geiringer, Johannes Brahms and George Henschel: An Enduring Friendship 2008; facsimile editions of Brahms' manuscripts; Editor of Brahms Studies: Analytical and Historical Perspectives 1990; contrib. numerous articles on Brahms' Lieder and Duets, the genesis and chronology of Brahms' works, Brahms' piano sonatas and First Piano Concerto, editorial problems and questions of authenticity, Brahms' pianos and piano music; performance practice in Brahms' late chamber music, the life and work of Anglo-Irish piano inventor William Southwell. *Honours:* grants from American Philosophical Soc., American Council of Learned Societies, Nat. Endowment for the Humanities. *Address:* School of Music, Box 353450, University of Washington, Seattle, WA 98195-3450, USA (office). *E-mail:* brahms@u.washington.edu (office).

BOŽIČ, Darijan; Slovenian composer; b. 29 April 1933, Slavonski Brod, Croatia. *Education:* Ljubljana Academy of Music, studied in London and Paris. *Career:* Conductor and Director of Studies, Slovene Opera, 1968–70; Conductor and Artistic Director, Slovenia Philharmonic, 1970–74; Professor, University of Ljubljana, 1980–94, University of Maribor, 1988–95; Director of SNG Opera, Ljubljana, 1995. *Compositions include:* Stage Works: La Bohème, 57, Opera, 1958; La Putain Respecteuse, Opera after Sartre, 1960; Iago, Happening for 8 performers and tape after Shakespeare, 1968; Ares-Eros Musical Drama after Aristophanes, 1970; Lysistrata 75, Operatic Farce after Aristophanes; Kralj Lear, Music Drama after Shakespeare, 1985; Telmah, Music Drama after Shakespeare; Bolt's A Man for All Seasons, 1990; 2 Symphonies, 1965, 1994; Concerto for Two, 1994; Piece of Music for Gerry Mulligan, for 5 saxophones and computer, 1996.

BRABBINS, Martyn; British conductor; *Principal Guest Conductor, Royal Flemish Philharmonic Orchestra*; b. 1959, England. *Education:* Goldsmiths' Coll., London and Leningrad Conservatoire with Ilya Musin. *Career:* from 1988 appearances with most leading chamber and symphony orchestras in the UK, including all the BBC Orchestras (BBC Scottish at the 1997 Edinburgh Festival); further festival engagements at Lichfield (Philharmonia Orchestra), Windsor, Cheltenham, Bath, Aldeburgh, Three Choirs and St Magnus Proms, annually since 1993; guest with the St Petersburg Philharmonic Orchestra, North German Radio Symphony Orchestra and Orchestra of Gran Canaria; tour with Australia Youth Orchestra 1995; tour of Russia with Sinfonia 21 1996, Contemporary Music Network tour of the UK 1997; opera includes Don Giovanni at the Kirov, Magic Flute for ENO, Schreker's Der ferne klang for Opera North, From Morning to Midnight for ENO and Alice in Wonderland for Netherlands Opera; Assoc. Principal Conductor BBC Scottish Symphony Orchestra, Principal Conductor of Sinfonia 21 and Conducting Consultant at the Royal Scottish Acad.; premiere recording of Die Kathrin by Korngold with BBC Concert Orchestra 1997; season 1999 with Elgar's Enigma Variations at the London Prom concerts; conducted the BBC Symphony Chorus, the BBC Scottish Symphony Orchestra and Sinfonia 21 at the London Proms 2002; founder and Dir, Orkney Conducting Course (annual event) 2003–, coinciding with the St Magnus Festival; Artistic Dir, Cheltenham Int. Festival of Music 2005–07; Principal Guest Conductor, Royal Flemish Philharmonic Orchestra 2009–. *Honours:* winner Leeds Conductors' Competition 1988. *Current Management:* c/o Intermusica Artists Management Ltd, 36 Graham Street, Crystal Wharf, London, N1 8GJ, England. *Telephone:* (20) 7608-9900. *Fax:* (20) 7490-3263. *E-mail:* mail@intermusica.co.uk. *Website:* www.intermusica.co.uk.

BRABEC, Lubomir; Czech classical guitarist; b. 21 May 1953, Plzeň. *Education:* Conservatoire Plzeň, Conservatoire Prague, Royal Acad. of Music, Early Music Centre. *Career:* regular appearances with Prague Orchestras; has performed throughout Europe, Russia, North and Latin America; first musician to perform a concert in Antarctica 1997. *Recordings:* over 30 albums including interpretations of Sor, Tárrega, Paganini, Vivaldi, Villa-Lobos, Trojan and Granados; Bach, Handel, Weiss and Jelinek baroque music; Spanish works by Torroba, Falla, Albeniz; Turina, Rodrigo, Vivaldi—Guitar Concertos with Prague Chamber Orchestra (with violist L. Maly and guitarist M. Myslivecek); arrangements by Satie, Falla, Prokofiev; Transformation II—Bach, Janáček, Mussorgsky, Marcello; Lubomir Brabec Live at Prague Spring Festival—Dowland, Bach, Villa-Lobos; Viola and Guitar, Italian Music with V. Drapal; Complete works of H. Villa-Lobos (with Gabriela Benackova); Album of Songs (with Gabriela Benackova). *Honours:* Laureate of the Concours Int. de Guitare, Paris 1974, H. Villa-Lobos Medal 1987. *Current Management:* Iva Production Agency, Radlická 61, 150 00 Prague, Czech Republic. *Telephone:* 251119272. *E-mail:* agentura@ivaproduction.cz. *Website:* www.ivaproduction.cz; www.lubomirbrabec.cz.

BRACANIN, Philip Keith, MA, PhD; Australian composer; *Professor Emeritus, School of Music, University of Queensland*; b. 26 May 1942, Kalgoorlie, Western Australia; s. of Nikola Bracanin and Andriana Svicarevic. *Education:* Univ. of Western Australia. *Career:* mem. Faculty, Univ. of Queensland 1970–2008, Prof. and Head, School of Music 1997–2008, now Prof. Emer.; comms from Univ. of Queensland and Queensland Symphony Orchestra; mem. Bd of Dirs Queensland Symphony Orchestra. *Compositions include:* With and Without for small orchestra 1975, Trombone Concerto 1976,

Selections from the Omar Khayyam for choir and strings 1979, Heterophony for orchestra 1979, Rondellus for string orchestra 1980, Because We Have No Time, song cycle for low voice and orchestra 1981, Concertino for piano and strings 1983, Clarinet Concerto 1985, Concerto for Orchestra 1985, Throw Me a Heaven Around a Child, for baritone and chamber orchestra 1986, Concerto for Orchestra No. 2 1987, Cello Concerto 1989, Dance Poem for chamber orchestra 1990, Guitar Concerto 1991, Symphony No. 2 for soprano, SATB choir and symphony orchestra 1995, Symphony No. 3 1995, Eternal Images for soprano, clarinet, horn and piano 1998, Dance Gundah 1999, Windmills of Time for string orchestra 2000, Blackwood River Suite for guitar quintet 2001, Clocktower for orchestra 2002, Blackwood River Concerto for guitar and marimba/vibraphone 2002 and for orchestra, Shades of Autumn, concerto for oboe and chamber orchestra 2003, Shadows of Time double concerto for oboe and guitar 2005, Symphony No. 4 2006, Psalms of Thanksgiving and Praise for SATB choir, soprano solo and instrumental ensemble 2007, St Lucia Suite for string trio and string orchestra 2007, Travel Music for David for piano trio 2010, Centenary Overture 2010, Se baila como eres I and II tangos for clarinet and guitar 2013, Concerto for oboe and string orchestra 2014. *Recordings include:* Guitar Concerto, Clarinet Concerto, Violin Concerto, Symphony No. 2, Symphony No. 3, Dance Gundah Concerto for Didjeridu and Orchestra, Under Yaarandoo for Didjeridu, Guitar and Orchestra, Eternal Image. *Publications include:* Symphony No. 2 1998, Symphony No. 3 1998, Symphony No. 4 2010. *Honours:* Australasian Performing Right Asscn Award 1995. *Address:* 50/12 Bryce Street, St Lucia, Qld 4067 (home); PO Box 4303, St Lucia, Qld 4067, Australia (office). *Telephone:* (7) 3371-9889 (home). *E-mail:* p.bracanin@uq.edu.au (office). *Website:* www.uq.edu.au/music (office); www.bracanin.com.

BRACEFIELD, Hilary Maxwell, MA, DipMus, DipTchg, LTCL; New Zealand music lecturer and critic; b. 30 June 1938, Briggs, Dunedin. *Education:* Univ. of Otago. *Career:* teacher Bayfield High School, Dunedin; Lecturer Worcester Coll. of Education; Sr Lecturer and Head of Dept Univ. of Ulster; currently part-time lecturer Univ. of Ulster and Open Univ.; mem. Incorporated Soc. of Musicians, Royal Musical Asscn, Int. Fed. of Univ. Women. *Publications:* Contact Journal of Contemporary Music (part ed.), contrib. to Music and Musicians, Musical Times, Radio Times, BBC Radio; academic articles. *Honours:* Blair Trust Travelling Fellowship 1970–73; Hon. MUniv (Open Univ.) 1999. *Address:* 114 Monkstown Road, Newtownabbey, County Antrim, BT37 0LE, Northern Ireland (home). *Telephone:* (28) 9086-9044 (home). *Fax:* (28) 9086-9044 (home). *E-mail:* HM.Bracefield@btinternet.com (home).

BRACHT, Roland; German singer (bass); b. 1952, Munich. *Education:* Munich Musikhochschule, Munich Music College with Prof. Blaschke. *Career:* debut at the National Theatre in Verdi's Don Carlos; Sang at the Munich Opera Studio from 1971; Member of the Stuttgart Opera from 1973, notably as the Commendatore, in the production of Don Giovanni which reopened the Staatsoper, 1984; Ludwigsburg, 1978 as Masetto; Schwetzingen Festival, 1983, in the premiere of The English Cat by Henze; San Francisco, 1985 in Der Ring des Nibelungen; Debut in the War Memorial Opera House in San Francisco, June 1985; Debut at the Metropolitan Opera as King Heinrich, 1986; Sang Pogner in Die Meistersinger at the opening of the new Essen Opera, 1988; King Heinrich at Pretoria, 1989; sang Colline in La Bohème at Stuttgart, 1991 and Mustafà in L'Italiana in Algeri, 1996; season 1998 as Mozart's Osmin, and Rocco in Fidelio; season 2000–01 at Stuttgart as Wagner's Hagen and Philip II in Don Carlos. *Recordings:* Don Giovanni; Die Entführung; Das Rheingold; Die Zauberflöte; Oedipus Rex; Alceste by Gluck; Die Feen by Wagner; Video of Der Freischütz. *Current Management:* Opera Vladarski, Döblinger Hauptstraße 57/18, 1190 Vienna, Austria. *Telephone:* (1) 368-6960/61. *Fax:* (1) 368-6962. *E-mail:* opera.vladarski@utanet.at.

BRADBURY, Colin; British clarinettist; b. 1935, England. *Education:* Royal Coll. of Music with Frederick Thurston. *Career:* Principal Clarinettist, BBC Symphony 1968–93; performances of concertos by Mozart, Weber, and Nielsen at the London Prom Concerts and director of the RCM Wind Ensemble; duo partnership with pianist, Oliver Davies from 1978 with performances and recordings of Italian operatic fantasias, sonatas by Reger, Victorian music and The Art of The Clarinettist; tutor, National Youth Orchestra of Great Britain.

BRADLEY, Gwendolyn; American singer (soprano); b. 12 Dec. 1952, New York, NY. *Education:* North Carolina School of the Arts, Winston-Salem, NC, Curtis Inst. of Music, Philadelphia and Acad. of Vocal Arts, Philadelphia. *Career:* debut as Nannetta, Falstaff, Lake George Opera, New York 1976; Metropolitan Opera debut, Nightingale, L'Enfant et les Sortilèges 1981; appeared as Blondchen, Gilda and Offenbach's Olympia; European debut, Corfu Festival, Greece 1981; guest appearances with opera companies in Cleveland, Philadelphia, Central City, Amsterdam, Glyndebourne, Hamburg, Berlin, Monte Carlo, Nice; sang Rodelinda with Netherlands Opera 1983–84 (also Sophie in Der Rosenkavalier); Paris Opéra 1986, as Zerbinetta; appeared as the Fiakermilli in Arabella at the 1987 Glyndebourne Festival; Deutsche Oper Berlin 1989, as Musetta; sang Gilda at the Wiesbaden Festival 1990, with the company of the Deutsche Oper; sang the Heavenly Voice in Don Carlos at the Deutsche Oper 1992; Mozart's Blonde at Los Angeles 1995; season 1995–96 with Oscar and Nannetta at the Berlin Staatsoper; Pamina at Los Angeles 1998; Deutsche Oper Berlin 2000, as Verdi's Oscar and Gilda; many engagements as soloist with leading US orchestras; recitals.

BRADSHAW, Claire; British singer (mezzo-soprano); b. 1970, Hull, England; m. Craig Ogden. *Education:* Royal Northern Coll. of Music, studied with Barbara Robotham, David Pallard. *Career:* appearances 1994–, with Scottish Opera-Go-Round and Scottish Opera as Maddalena, Cherubino, Hansel and Dryad, and concert performances as Carmen for WNO; Spoleto Festival with Richard Hickox and in Vaughan Williams's The Poisoned Kiss with Hickox and the London Symphony Orchestra; concerts throughout the north of England at King's Coll., Cambridge (Messiah), with the Hallé Orchestra and in Western Australia and Provence; with Suzuki in concert (Royal Liverpool Philharmonic Orchestra) and recitals throughout the UK and Australia, 1997; sang Suzuki for WNO, 1998; Season 1999 included Lisetta in Il Mondo della Luna, 2nd Lady for WNO and a tour of South Africa with her husband, Australian classical guitarist Craig Ogden, in recital and appearing with major orchestras; sang St Matthew Passion with Aalborg Symphony Orchestra, Copenhagen; Mercédès with WNO, 2000; Varvara in Katya Kabanova with WNO, 2001. *Honours:* Webster Booth/ESSO Award; James Gulliver Prize, Scotland. *Current Management:* Harlequin Agency Limited, 203 Fidlas Road, Cardiff, CF14 5NA, England.

BRADSHAW, Murray Charles, MMus, PhD; American musicologist and academic; *Professor Emeritus of Musicology, UCLA Herb Alpert School of Music;* b. 25 Sept. 1930, Illinois; m.; two s. one d. *Education:* American Conservatory of Music, Univ. of Chicago. *Career:* Prof. of Musicology, Univ. of California at Los Angeles Herb Alpert School of Music, currently Prof. Emer.; mem. International and American Musicological Socs, American Guild of Organists. *Compositions:* several organ compositions in The Organists Companion. *Publications:* The Origin of the Toccata 1972, The Falsobordone 1978, Francesco Severi 1981, Girolamo Diruta Il Transilvano 1984, Giovanni Luca Conforti 1985, Gabriele Fattorini 1986, Emilio de'Cavalieri 1990, Giovanni Luca Conforti: Breve et facile 1999; contrib. to Journal of Musicology, Performance Practice Review, The Music Quarterly, The Music Review, Studi Musicali, Musica Antiqua, Musica Disciplina, Tijdschrift. *Honours:* American Philosophical Soc. award 1987. *Address:* Department of Musicology, UCLA Herb Alpert School of Music, 2539 Schoenberg Hall, Los Angeles, CA 90095-7234, USA (office). *Website:* www.schoolofmusic.ucla.edu.

BRAEM, Thuering L. M., DipMus, MA; Swiss conductor and composer; b. 10 April 1944, Basel; m. Dr Penny Boyes Braem; two d. *Education:* Basel Univ., Heidelberg Univ., Acad. of Music, Basel, Univ. of California, Berkeley, Curtis Inst. of Music, Philadelphia. *Career:* Music Dir, Regio-Choir, Basel 1976–2009; Dir, Music School, Basel 1973–87, Lucerne Conservatory 1987–2006; Founder and Conductor, Junge Philharmonie Zentralschweiz 1987–2006; Artistic Co-Dir The Lucerne Master Courses 1987–2002; Pres. Jeunesses Musicales, Switzerland 1984–90, Pres. of Jury, Concours de Festival de Musiques Sacrées, Fribourg 1985–; Swiss Rep., Bd of the Asscn of European Conservatories 2000–06; mem. Research Cttee, Swiss Science Foundation 2004–11. *Compositions include:* Lettres de Cézanne, Alleluja for Voice, Ara for Flute Ensemble, chamber music (including five string quartets), choral music, Ombra for violin, viola and string orchestra 1991, Torrenieri for horn and strings 1992, Concerto for piano trio and orchestra 1992, Luci e ombre oratorio 1996, Florestan und Eusebius for orchestra, Dirge, concerto for violin and brass 2000, Il Gong Magico 2002, Concerto for pipa and orchestra 2007, Transitions for pipa and choir 2008, Aloise: C'est beau le rouge, vous savez (chamber opera) 2009–10, La Cantatrice (chamber opera) 2014, Shapeshifting, 7 bagatelles for large orchestra 2014, Ogna (for horn quartet) 2015. *Recordings:* Children's Songs of the American Indians, Fauré's Requiem, Music for Cello and Orchestra by Martinů, Fauré, Dvořák and Tchaikovsky, Panton, Orchestral Music with Young Philharmonic of Central Switzerland. *Publications:* Musik und Raum 1986, Series, Information und Versuche 1975–90, 20 Issues, Bewahren and Oeffnen 1992, Research and Development in Future Institutions of Higher Learning in Music 1997, InterViews 2005, The Orchestra as Pedagogical Instrument 2007; contributed articles to newspapers and journals. *Honours:* Edwin Fischer Prize 1992, Culture and Art Prize, City of Lucerne 2005. *Address:* Lerchenstrasse 56, 4059 Basel, Switzerland (home). *Website:* www.braem-boyes.ch (home); www.arsbraemia.ch (home); www.aloiseopera.org (home).

BRAITHWAITE, Nicholas Paul Dallon, FRAM; British musician and conductor; b. 26 Aug. 1939, London, England; s. of Henry Warwick Braithwaite and Lorna Constance Braithwaite; m. Gillian Agnes Haggarty 1985; one s. one d. *Education:* Royal Acad. of Music, Festival masterclasses in Bayreuth and with Hans Swarowsky, Vienna. *Career:* Chief Conductor, Adelaide Symphony Orchestra 1987–91; Prin. Guest Conductor, Manchester Camerata 1977–84, Prin. Conductor 1984–91; Chief Conductor, Tasmanian Symphony Orchestra; Perm. Guest Conductor, Norwegian State Radio Orchestra; Assoc. Conductor to Constantin Silvestri with Bournemouth Symphony Orchestra; frequent Guest Conductor for all major orchestras in the UK; toured Japan and Korea as Assoc. Conductor to Georg Solti with London Philharmonic Orchestra; appearances with ORTF Orchestra, Paris, Oslo Philharmonic, Bergen Harmonien Symphony Orchestra, Odense Symphony Orchestra, New Zealand Symphony Orchestra, Melbourne Symphony Orchestra, Sydney Symphony Orchestra, Danish Radio Orchestra, Bergen Festival, Symphony Nova Scotia, Halifax, Opera Australia, Opera New Zealand, State Opera of South Australia; Musical Dir and Chief Conductor, Stora Teater Opera and Ballet Cos, Gothenberg 1981–84; Musical Dir, Glyndebourne Touring Opera 1976–80; Assoc. Prin. Conductor, ENO 1970–74; Dean of Music, Victorian Coll. of the Arts 1988–91; conducted Tosca at Elder Park, Adelaide 1990, Francesca da Rimini for Chelsea Opera Group 1994, Die Fledermaus for Scottish Opera 1997; mem. ISM, MU. *Address:*

Taringa Park, PO Box 401, 11 Storch Lane, Mount Barker Road, Hahndorf, SA 5245, Australia (home).

BRAMALL, Anthony; British conductor; b. 6 March 1957, London; m. Elisabeth Werres. *Education:* Guildhall School of Music and Drama, London. *Career:* Musical Dir, Southend Symphony Orchestra, Musical Dir, Southend Symphony Chorus 1979–81; Asst to the Music Dir, Municipal Opera Pforzheim, Germany 1981–85; House Conductor and Head of Music Staff, Municipal Opera Augsburg 1985–89; Guest Conductor, Southwest German Chamber Orchestra, Vienna Chamber Orchestra, State Opera Brunswick, State Opera Darmstadt; Conductor, RIAS Radio Symphony Orchestra, and debut in the Berlin Philharmonie 1988; Senior House Conductor, Coburg Opera 1989; Senior House Conductor, State Opera Hanover, and Guest Conductor with the NDR Radio Symphony Orchestra 1990–95; debut, Semper Opera, Dresden 1992; Music Dir, Opera Krefeld and Principal Conductor, Niederrhein Symphony 1995–2002; Music Dir Badisches Staatstheater, Karlsruhe 2002–07, Principal Conductor 2002–; recent productions: La Bohème, La Cenerentola, La Clemenza di Tito (Dresden), Elektra, Turandot, Der Rosenkavalier, Madama Butterfly, Parsifal, Falstaff, Flying Dutchman, Figaro, Otello, Tosca, Wozzeck; Prof. of Conducting, Hochschule für Musik Franz Liszt, Weimar. *Recordings:* with Slovak Philharmonic and the Slovak Radio Symphony Orchestra; radio broadcasts with RIAS Berlin, NDR Hanover, Badischen Staatskapelle, Deutsche Händel Solisten. *Honours:* International Hans Swarowsky Conducting Competition special prize for 20th-century music. *Telephone:* (163) 8643936 (office). *E-mail:* bramall.werres@t-online.de (office). *Website:* www.anthony-bramall.com.

BRANDIS, Thomas; German violinist; b. 1935, Hamburg. *Education:* Musikhochschule Hamburg with Eva Hauptmann, studied with Max Rostal in London. *Career:* Leader, Berlin Philharmonic Orchestra 1962–63; Co-founder, Brandis Quartet 1976; numerous chamber engagements in Europe and Tokyo, with Wiener Singverein and Berlin Philharmonic; festival appearances at Salzburg, Florence, Vienna, Edinburgh, Tours and Bergen; has co-premiered Clarinet Quintet by Helmut Eder 1984, and 3rd Quartets of Gottfried von Einem and Giselher Klebe 1981, 1983; solo concerto work under such conductors as Karajan, Böhm, Solti, Abbado, Schmidt-Isserstedt, Keilberth, Jochum, Tennstedt, and Albrecht; teacher at Staatliche Hochschule für Musikm 1968–76, Univ. of Arts, Berlin 1976; Prof. of Violin, Berlin Univ. 1983–2002; Visiting Prof., RAM 2002–, apptd Sidney Griller Chair 2008; led Orchester-Akademie von Claudio Abbado, Ferrara, Italy 2001–04. *Recordings include:* as soloist: albums with Karajan and Böhm; with the Brandis Quartet: complete quartets of Schubert and Beethoven and other repertoire. *Honours:* Hon. RAM 2005; prize, German Hochschulen Competition 1946, International ARD Competition, Munich 1947.

BRANDON, Sarah-Jane; South African singer (soprano); b. 1984, Johannesburg. *Education:* S African Coll. of Music, Univ. of Cape Town, Benjamin Britten Int. Opera School, Royal Coll. of Music. *Career:* performed frequently with Kwa-Zulu Natal Philharmonic Orchestra, and sang Pamina in Die Zauberflöte and Countess in Le Nozze di Figaro with Cape Town Opera, S Africa; appearances include Sandrina in La finta giardiniera, Royal Coll. of Music, Lisaura in Alessandro at London Handel Festival; engagements have included Maddalena in Handel's La Resurrezione, London Handel Festival with the Gabrieli Consort and Paul McCreesh, Vivaldi's Gloria at Bridgewater Hall with the Choir of King's College, Cambridge and Stephen Cleobury, Elijah with the London Philharmonic Orchestra and Kurt Masur; also tour of China with the Amadeus Orchestra and appearances at Wigmore Hall, London and in the Crush Bar of the Royal Opera House, Covent Garden; featured Young Artists, 2011 Salzburg Festival; season 2014–15 appeared as Contessa in Le nozze di Figaro, Dresden Semperoper and Savonlinna Opera Festival, Finland, as well as debut at Teatro Real, Madrid in Handel's L'Allegro, il Penseroso ed il Moderato; Assoc. Artist, Classical Opera Company. *Honours:* Maggie Teyte Prize and Miriam Licette Scholarship, Musicians Benevolent Fund, Overseas Trophy, Lorna Viol and Audrey Strange Prizes, Royal Over-Seas League Competition 2008, Cuthbert Smith Prize, RCM's Lies Askonas Competition, winner, Kathleen Ferrier Award 2009. *Address:* c/o The Classical Opera Company, Britannia House, 11 Glenthorne Road, London, W6 0LH, England (office). *Telephone:* (20) 8846-9744 (office). *E-mail:* info@classicalopera.co.uk (office). *Website:* www.classicalopera.co.uk (office).

BRANDSTETTER, John; American singer (baritone); b. 2 Oct. 1949, Wayne, Neb. *Education:* Univ. of Nebraska, studied with Richard Hughes in New York. *Career:* debut at Minnesota Opera 1976, as Ben in Conrad Susa's Black River; sang at Minneapolis in premiere of Argento's The Voyage of Edgar Allan Poe 1976; has also sung in premieres of Bernstein's A Quiet Place 1983, repeated in Vienna 1986, as Josuke in Miki's Joruri, St Louis 1985, and in The Balcony by Di Domenica, Boston 1990; season 1986–87 appeared as Enrico (Lucia di Lammermoor) at Seattle, Silvio (Pagliacci) in Detroit and as Beast in US premiere of Stephen Oliver's Beauty and the Beast, at St Louis; sang Egberto in Verdi's Stiffelio at Sarasota 1990, and High Priest in Alceste at Chicago Lyric Opera; other roles include Mozart's Almaviva and Papageno, Figaro, Germont and Falke; has also appeared at Düsseldorf, City Opera New York, Miami and Philadelphia.

BRANDT, Anthony, BA; American composer; b. 23 June 1961, New York, NY; m.; one s. one d. *Education:* Harvard Univ., California Inst. of the Arts. *Career:* Asst Prof. of Composition, Rice Univ. 1998–; Visiting Lecturership,

Harvard Univ. 1993–97, Tufts Univ. 1996, MIT 1997; Composer-in-Residence, Int. Music Festival of Morelia, Mexico 1996; Ed.-in-Chief, Soundout Digital Press. *Compositions:* Septet-à-tête for seven players 1993, String Quartet 1994, Hidden Motives for two pianos 1996, Octopiece for eight players 1996, Songs for soprano and string quartet 1997, Turbulent Tones for orchestra 1998, Breathing Room for soprano and string orchestra 1998, Piéce de Résistance for three trombones, piano and percussion 1998, Creeley Songs for soprano and piano 1999, Roman à Clef for cello and piano 2000, Crucible of the Millennium (documentary film score) 2001, Four Shadowings – String Quartet No.2 2001–02, Express for orchestra 2002, Handful for piano 2002. *Honours:* Fellow MacDowell Colony 1996, 1998, Fellow Tanglewood Music Center 1994, Fellow Wellesley Composers 1993.

BRAUCHLI, Bernard, DMus; Swiss clavichord, harpsichord, fortepiano and organ player; *Founder-President, Festival Musica Antica a Magnano;* b. 2 May 1944, Lausanne. *Education:* piano studies in Lausanne and Vienna, studied musicology at New England Conservatory with Julia Sutton, researched Iberian keyboard music in Lisbon with Macario Santiago Kastner. *Career:* devoted to performance, study and revival of early keyboard instruments, in particular the clavichord; has travelled extensively with his instruments in USA, Canada, Mexico, Australia and Europe, giving concerts, lectures and introducing audiences to early keyboard instruments and historical performance practices; taught in Boston, USA at series of early music courses at Museum of Fine Arts 1978–82, New England Conservatory of Music 1983–92; Music Dir Cambridge Soc. for Early Music, Cambridge, Mass (Pres. for many years), f. Chamber Music by Candlelight series; organized int. symposia on the Clavichord 1993, 1995 etc. with Christopher Hogwood, Int. Centre for Clavichord Studies 1996; mem. Artistic Cttee Festival Int. de l'Orgue Ancien de Valère (Switzerland); Founder and Pres. Festival Musica Antica a Magnano 1985–; Founder Swiss Clavichord Soc. 1995. *Recordings include:* The Renaissance Clavichord Titanic, The Renaissance Clavichord II, Keyboard Sonatas of Padre Antonio Soler, Keyboard Sonatas of Carlos Seixas, 18th-Century Basque Keyboard Music, 18th-Century Portuguese Keyboard Music, Antonio Soler – Six Concertos for Two Keyboard Instruments (with Esteban Elizondo), The Organ of Evora Cathedral, 18th-Century Music for Two Keyboard Instruments (with Esteban Elizondo), Keyboard Works of Carl Philip Emmanuel Bach, The 1794 Giovanni Bruna Organ of Magnano, Italy, Carlos Seixas, Keyboard Sonatas, Mozart, The Nannerl's Notebook, The Organ of the Temple of San Cayetano, La Valenciana, Guanajuato, Mexico, Música Portuguesa para Teclado dos Séculos XVI e XVII, L'organo italiano tra Settecento e Ottocento, Antonio de Cabezon and His Contemporaries. *Publications include:* The Clavichord (Nicholas Bessaraboff Prize, American Musical Instrument Soc. 2001, British Clavichord Soc. Award 2004) 1998 (second edn 2000); contribs to numerous academic and professional journals. *Honours:* Hon. Life mem. Midwestern Historical Keyboard Soc.; Hon. Citizen, Magnano (BI), Italy 2010; Julius Adams Stratton Prize for Cultural Achievement, Friends of Switzerland in Boston (USA) 1983. *Address:* Associazione Musica Antica a Magnano, via Roma 43, 13887 Magnano, Italy (office). *Telephone:* (015) 679260 (office); 345-9108561 (mobile) (office). *Fax:* (015) 2589082 (office). *E-mail:* bernard.brauchli@me.com (office); info@musicaanticamagnano.com (office). *Website:* www.musicaanticamagnano.com (office); www.bernard-brauchli.com.

BRAUN, Lioba; German singer (mezzo-soprano); b. 1963. *Education:* studied with Charlotte Lehmann. *Career:* appearances in opera at Karlsruhe 1987–89; Vienna Volksoper 1989–90; Vienna Staatsoper 1992–93, notably in The Ring, conducted by Dohnányi; Mannheim Opera from 1993, as Wagner's Fricka, Venus and Brangaene; Countess Geschwitz in Lulu, Dalila, Carmen and Azucena; Bayreuth Festival as Brangaene in Tristan and Isolde, conducted by Barenboim; further engagements at La Scala (The Ring from 1994), Dresden, Zürich, Rome (Waltraute in Götterdämmerung) and Tokyo (season 1999–2000); Kundry in Parsifal at Mannheim 2000, and Mahler's 8th Symphony in Berlin; other concerts at Leipzig, Amsterdam, Munich and Rome (Gurrelieder by Schoenberg); season 2001–02 in Das Rheingold at the Vienna State, the Brahms Alto Rhapsodie in Dresden, Mahler's 3rd in Munich and Waltraute at Bayreuth, Brangaene at Barcelona 2002; festival appearances include the Semperoper of Dresden, Opera Leipzig, the Opera House of Zurich, the State Theatre Stuttgart, in Genova, in Rome and La Scala, performing with the Munich Philharmonic, the Viennese and the Bamberg Symphony Orchestras, the Leipzig Gewandhaus Orchestra, the Concertgebouw Amsterdam and the conductors Blomstedt, Barenboim, Abbado, Maazel, Herreweghe, Levine, Muti, Sawallisch, Stein and Sinopoli. *Address:* c/o Theateragentur Dr G. Hilbert, Maximilianstr. 22, 80539 Munich, Germany. *E-mail:* schmidt@hilbert.de. *Website:* www.hilbert.de.

BRAUN, Russell; German singer (baritone); b. 1968, Frankfurt. *Education:* studied in Frankfurt and Toronto. *Career:* appearances with Canadian Opera as Mozart's Guglielmo and Papageno, Rossini's Figaro and in concert performances of Henri VIII by Saint-Saëns and Massenet's Cendrillon; New York City Opera 1992, as Morales in Carmen, Pacific Opera 1993 as Britten's Demetrius; concerts include Messiah in Montréal, Belshazzar's Feast with the Hartford Symphony Orchestra and at Salzburg in Mozart concert arias; season 1995–96 as Mozart's Count in Monte Carlo and at the Paris Opéra-Comique; sang Borilée in Rameau's Les Boréades at the 1999 London Prom concerts; season 2000–01 as Chorèbe in Les Troyens at Salzburg and Billy Budd in Toronto. *Current Management:* Moira Johnson Consulting, 180 Metcalfe Street, Suite 404, Ottawa, ON K2P 1P5, Canada. *Telephone:* (613)

565 0666. *Fax:* (613) 565 5467. *E-mail:* moira@moirajohnson.com. *E-mail:* andante@russellbraun.com. *Website:* www.russellbraun.com.

BRAUTIGAM, Ronald; Dutch pianist; b. 1 Oct. 1954, Haarlemmermeer; m. Mary Elizabeth Jane Cooper 1995. *Education:* Sweelinck Conservatory, Amsterdam, RAM, London and studied with Rudolf Serkin in the USA. *Career:* debut at Concertgebouw Amsterdam 1979; appearances with all major orchestras in The Netherlands; foreign engagements include Oslo Philharmonic Orchestra, Bavarian Radio Symphony Orchestra Munich, English Chamber Orchestra, Tafelmusik, Orchestra of the Age of Enlightenment, Freiburger Barockorchester, Concerto Copenhagen, Orchestre des Champs-Elysées; Salzburg Festival debut with the Concertgebouw Orchestra under Frans Brüggen 1992; mem. Ronald Stevenson Soc., Edinburgh, Frank Martin Soc. *Recordings:* over 30 albums including Shostakovich, Concerto No. 1, Hindemith, 2nd Kammermusik, Mendelssohn, piano concertos, Complete Piano Sonatas of W. A. Mozart and J. Haydn on fortepiano, complete Beethoven cycle. *Honours:* two Edison Awards, two Diapasons d'Or, Nederlandse Muziekprijs 1984, Cannes Classical Award 2004, Midem Classical Award 2010. *Current Management:* c/o Marianne Brinks, Brinks Artists Management, Herengracht 453, 10127 BS, Amsterdam, The Netherlands. *Telephone:* (20) 6432043. *Fax:* (20) 6403961. *E-mail:* mbrinks@xs4all.nl. *Website:* www.brinksartists.nl. *E-mail:* ronald@ronaldbrautigam.com (office). *Website:* www.ronaldbrautigam.com.

BRAY, Roger, MA, DPhil; British university teacher; *Professor Emeritus of Music, Lancaster University;* b. 29 March 1944, Sheffield, Yorks., England; m. Juliet Brown; one s. one d. *Education:* King's Coll. Choir School, Cambridge, King Edward's School, Birmingham, Magdalen Coll., Oxford. *Career:* Lecturer, Univ. of Victoria, Canada 1968–70, Asst Prof. 1970; Lecturer in Music, Univ. of Manchester 1970–79; Prof. of Music, Lancaster Univ. 1979–2006, Prof. Emer. 2006–; mem. Royal Musical Asscn. *Publications:* Blackwell History of Music in Britain II, The Sixteenth Century (ed.), Robert Fayrfax, Complete Works I, II and III (ed.), Early English Church Music 43, 45, 53 (ed.); contrib. to John Morehen (ed.), English Choral Practice 1400–1650 1995, James Haar (ed.), European Music 1520–1640 2006, Linda P. Austern (ed.), Psalms in the Early Modern World 2011, Music and Letters, Early Music, Musica Disciplina, Proceedings of the Royal Musical Association, RMA Research Chronicle, Journal of Plainsong and Medieval Music Society. *E-mail:* r.bray@lancaster.ac.uk (office).

BRAZDA, Josef; Czech horn player; b. 12 March 1939, Babice u Rosic, Brno; m. Vlasta Brázdová 1974; two d. *Education:* private artistic school, Brno, State Conservatoire, Brno, Janáček Acad. of Musical Arts, Brno. *Career:* debut: State Philharmonic Orchestra, Brno; Prague Academic Wind Quintet; Prague Chamber Orchestra; I Musici di Praga Chamber Orchestra; Haydn Sinfonietta Vienna; solo concertos and sonatas; horn instructor. *Compositions:* Instructive Compositions for 2, 3, 4 Horns. *Recordings:* Richard Strauss, Horn Concerto No. 2; Paul Hindemith, Horn Concerto; Franz Danzi, Horn Concerto in E Major; Paul Hindemith, both Sonatas; Joseph Haydn, Horn Concerto in D Major, Hob VII; Joseph Haydn, Divertimenti, Baritone Octets, with Haydn Sinfonietta Vienna. *Honours:* second prize IX Int. Musikwettbewerb, Munich 1960, first prize XV Int. Prague Spring Festival 1962. *Address:* Roklanska 1095, 25101 Ricany u, Prague, Czech Republic. *Fax:* 323631568 (home).

BREAM, Julian, CBE, FRCM, FRNCM; British classical guitarist and lutenist; b. 15 July 1933, London, England; s. of Henry G. Bream; m. 1st Margaret Williamson; one adopted s.; m. 2nd Isobel Sanchez 1980 (divorced). *Education:* Royal Coll. of Music. *Career:* began professional career at Cheltenham 1947, London debut, Wigmore Hall 1950; has made numerous transcriptions for guitar of Romantic and Baroque works; commissioned new works from Britten, Walton, Henze and Arnold; tours throughout the world, giving recitals as soloist and with the Julian Bream Consort (f. 1960); many recitals with Sir Peter Pears and Robert Tear, and as guitar duo with John Williams; 60th Birthday Concert, Wigmore Hall, London 1993. *Honours:* Hon. DUniv (Surrey) 1968; Hon. DMus (Leeds) 1984; Villa-Lobos Gold Medal 1976, Gramophone Award for Best DVD (for My Life in Music) 2007, Lifetime Achievement Award, Gramophone Classical Music Awards 2013; numerous recording awards. *Current Management:* c/o Hazard Chase Ltd, 25 City Road, Cambridge, CB1 1DP, England. *Telephone:* (1223) 312400. *Fax:* (1223) 460827. *E-mail:* info@hazardchase.co.uk. *Website:* www.hazardchase.co.uk.

BRECKNOCK, John; British singer (tenor); b. 29 Nov. 1937, Long Eaton, Derbyshire, England. *Education:* Birmingham Music School with Frederic Sharp and Dennis Dowling. *Career:* debut as Alfred in Die Fledermaus, Sadler's Wells, London 1967; later repertoire includes Rossini's Almaviva and Comte Ory, Mozart's Belmonte and Ottavio and Verdi's Duke of Mantua; with ENO at the London Coliseum sang in the British stage premieres of Prokofiev's War and Peace 1972, and Henze's The Bassarids 1974, and in the world premiere of Gordon Crosse's The Story of Vasco 1974; Covent Garden debut 1974, as Fenton in Falstaff; Glyndebourne debut 1971; has sung at the Metropolitan Opera and toured Canada 1973; at the Teatro Regio Parma 1985, sang Almaviva in Il Barbiere di Siviglia; season 1985–86 sang Rossini roles in Paris. *Recordings include:* Alfredo in an English-language Traviata.

BREEDT, Michelle; South African singer (mezzo-soprano); b. 1962, Johannesburg. *Education:* Cape Town Univ. *Career:* debut in Mozart's Cherubino in Cape Town; performances in Cologne, Brunswick and Oldenburg as Adalgisa in Norma, Zerlina in Don Giovanni, Meg Page in Falstaff;

Tchaikovsky's Pauline and Bellini's Romeo; other roles include Emilia in Otello by Rossini; Verdi's Flora; Hansel, and Lola in Cavalleria Rusticana; Idamante in Idomeneo for Pretoria Opera; season 1997–98 as Diana in Cavalli's Calisto for the Vienna Kammeroper and as Nicklausse in Les Contes d'Hoffmann at Cape Town; many concert engagements in South Africa; season 2000–01 as Magdalena at Bayreuth, Charlotte at Innsbruck and Nicklausse for the Vienna Staatsoper. *Current Management:* Hilbert Artists' Management, Maximilianstr. 22, 80539 Munich, Germany. *Telephone:* (89) 2907470. *Fax:* (89) 29074790. *E-mail:* agentur@hilbert.de. *Website:* www.hilbert.de; www.michellebreedt.com.

BRELL, Mario; German fmr singer (tenor); b. 1936, Hamburg. *Education:* studied at Hamburg. *Career:* sang operetta at Hof 1963–65, Lucerne 1965–67, Oldenburg 1967–71, Krefeld 1971–73, Gelsenkirchen 1973–82; sang such repertory as Lohengrin, Parsifal, Zemlinsky's Zwerg, Hoffmann in Les Contes d'Hoffmann; mem., Deutsche Oper am Rhein, Düsseldorf from 1982, singing Diomedes in Penthesilea by Schoeck 1986; guest appearances in Zürich, Frankfurt, Karlsruhe, Milan, Barcelona and Berlin (both Die Fledermaus), Cologne, Hamburg and Bilbao (all Lohengrin), Gothenburg (Hoffman's Erzählungen), Wiesbaden (premiere of Kirchner's Belshazar 1986), Antwerp (Ariadne auf Naxos), Barcelona (Fledermaus), Amsterdam (Busoni's Mephisto and in Alexander von Zemlinsky's Kreidekreis); Bielefeld as Bacchus in Ariadne auf Naxos 1990; other roles include the Count in Schreker's Irrelohe and Max in Der Freischütz; sang the major in Einem's Besuch der alten Dame, Gelsenkirchen 1991; Dortmund as Siegfried 1995; broadcasts include Dessau's Lukullus, Smetana's The Kiss, Nestroy's Tannhäuser-Parodie, Mahagonny. *Recordings include:* Der Zar lässt sich photographieren by Weill, Tannhäuser-Parodie by Nestroy. *Address:* Siegener Str. 29, 47533 Kleve, Germany (home).

BREM, Peter; German violinist; b. 1948, Munich. *Education:* Richard Strauss Conservatory, Munich. *Career:* with Berliner Philharmoniker 1970–, Co-Man. Dir Berliner Philharmoniker GbR 1992–2002, mem. Media Bd Stiftung Berliner Philharmoniker 2002–07; Co-founder, Brandis String Quartet 1976, with concerts in Tokyo, London, Hamburg, Munich, Paris and Milan and engagements with Wiener Singverein and Berlin Philharmonic; festival appearances at Salzburg, Edinburgh, Lucerne, Tours, Bergen, Florence and Vienna; has co-premiered 3rd Quartets of Gottfried von Einem and Giselher Klebe 1981, 1983, and Clarinet Quintet of Helmut Eder 1984; solo concerts with such orchestras as Radio-Sinfonieorchester Berlin; mem. Berlin Philharmonic Octet. *Recordings include:* albums in standard repertoire from 1978, Beethoven, Weill, Schulhoff and Hindemith and Schubert String Quintet. *Honours:* prizewinner, Deutsche Hochschulewettbewerb. *Address:* Berliner Philharmonie, Herbert-von-Karajan-Str. 1, 10785 Berlin, Germany. *Website:* www.berliner-philharmoniker.de.

BRENDEL, Alfred; Austrian pianist and writer; b. 5 Jan. 1931, Wiesenberg; s. of Ing. Albert Brendel and Ida Brendel (née Wieltschnig); m. 1st Iris Heymann-Gonzala 1960 (divorced 1972); one d.; m. 2nd Irene Semler 1975; one s. two d. *Education:* studied piano under Sofija Deželić, Zagreb, Ludovika v. Kaan, Graz, Edwin Fischer, Lucerne, Paul Baumgartner, Basel, Edward Steuermann, Salzburg; studied composition under A. Michl and harmony under Franjo Dugan. *Career:* first piano recital Musikverein Graz 1948; concert tours through Europe, Latin America, North America 1963–2008, Australia 1963, 1966, 1969, 1976; has appeared at numerous music festivals, including Salzburg 1960–2008, Vienna, Edinburgh, Aldeburgh, Athens, Granada, Lucerne, Puerto Rico, London Proms and has performed with most major orchestras of Europe and USA; mem. American Acad. of Arts and Sciences. *Recordings include:* extensive repertoire; Beethoven's Complete Piano Works, Beethoven Sonatas, three sets of Beethoven Concertos (with Vienna Philharmonic Orchestra and Simon Rattle) 1998. *Publications:* essays on music and musicians in Phono, Fono Forum, Österreichische Musikzeitschrift, Music and Musicians, Hi-Fi Stereophonie, New York Review of Books, Die Zeit, Frankfurter Allgemeine Zeitung, Musical Thoughts and Afterthoughts 1976, Nachdenken über Musik 1977, Music Sounded Out (essays) 1990, Musik beim Wort genommen 1992, Fingerzeig 1996, Störendes Lachen während des Jaworts 1997, One Finger Too Many 1998, Kleine Teufel 1999, Collected Essays on Music 2001, Augerechnet Ich (aka The Veil of Order: In Conversation with Martin Meyer) 2001, Spiegelbild und Schwarzer Spuk (poems) 2003, Cursing Bagels (poems) 2004, Alfred Brendel über Musik 2005, A bis Z eines Pianisten 2012. *Honours:* Hon. RAM; Hon. RCM; Hon. Fellow, Exeter Coll., Oxford 1987; Hon. KBE 1989,; Commdr, Ordre des Arts et des Lettres 1985, Ordre pour le Mérite (Germany) 1991; Hon. DMus (London) 1978, (Oxford) 1983, (Warwick) 1991, (Yale) 1992, (Exeter) 1998, (Southampton) 2002; Hon. DLitt (Sussex) 1981; Dr hc (Cologne) 1995, (RAM 1999, (Hochschule Franz Liszt Weimar) 2009, (New England Conservatory 2009), (McGill) 2011, (Juilliard School) 2011, (Cambridge) 2012; Premio Città di Bolzano, Concorso Busoni 1949, Grand Prix du Disque 1965, Edison Prize (five times 1973–87), Grand Prix des Disquaires de France 1975, Deutscher Schallplattenpreis (four times 1976–84, 1992), Wiener Flötenuhr (six times 1976–87), Gramophone Award (six times 1977–83), Japanese Record Acad. Award (five times 1977–84, with Scottish Symphony Orchestra/Sir Charles Mackerras 2002), Japanese Grand Prix 1978, Franz Liszt Prize (four times 1979–83), Frankfurt Music Prize 1984, Diapason D'Or Award 1992, Heidsieck Award for Writing on Music 1990, Hans von Bülow-Medaille, Kameradschaft der Berliner Philharmoniker eV, 1992, Cannes Classical Award 1998, Ehrenmitgliedschaft der Wiener Philharmoniker 1998, Léonie Sonnings

Musikpris, Denmark 2002, Ernst von Siemens Musikpreis 2004, Premio Artur Rubinstein 2007, Prix Venezia 2007, Praemium Imperiale 2008, Herbert von Karajan Prize 2008, Gramophone Lifetime Achievement Award 2010, Franz Liszt Ehrenpreis 2011, Juillard Medal 2011, Golden Mozart Medal, Salzburg Mozarteum 2014. *Address:* c/o Ingpen & Williams, 7 St George's Court, 131 Putney Bridge Road, London, SW15 2PA, England (office). *E-mail:* info@ingpen.co.uk (office). *Website:* www.alfredbrendel.com.

BRENDEL, Wolfgang; German singer (baritone); b. 20 Oct. 1947, Munich. *Education:* studied in Munich. *Career:* sang Don Giovanni in Kaiserslautern 1970, then became mem. of the Bayerische Staatsoper Munich; roles include Papageno, Germont and Pelléas; guest appearances in Hamburg, Düsseldorf, and Karlsruhe; Metropolitan Opera debut 1975, as Mozart's Count; sang Verdi's Miller with the Chicago Lyric Opera 1983; Bayreuth Festival 1985, as Wolfram in Tannhäuser; Covent Garden debut 1985, as Luna in Il Trovatore; Eugene Onegin and Donizetti's Enrico 1988; Metropolitan Opera and Bayreuth Festival 1989, as Germont and Wolfram; Teatro San Carlos, Lisbon 1989, as Amfortas; Chicago 1990, as Eugene Onegin; other roles include Puccini's Marcello and Strauss's Mandryka; season 1991–92 as Amfortas in Parsifal at La Scala and as Count Luna at Munich; sang Verdi's Renato 1994; Wagner's Dutchman at the Deutsche Oper Berlin 1997; sang the Count in Capriccio at the New York Met 1998; season 2000–01 as Amfortas and the Dutchman at the Deutsche Oper, Berlin, Strauss's Mandryka at Zürich and Munich, Barak in Die Frau ohne Schatten at Essen. *Recordings:* Die Lustigen Weiber von Windsor, Paer's Leonora, Der Freischütz, Die Zauberflöte, La Bohème, Zar und Zimmermann, Ein Deutsches Requiem, Die Meistersinger (DVD with Deutsche Oper) 1995.

BRENER, Uri; Russian/Israeli composer and pianist; b. 17 July 1974, Moscow; m. Ingrid Klüger 1995; one s. *Education:* Central Special Music School, Gnessin Coll. Robert Schumann Hochschule, Germany, Köln Hochschule, Sweelinck Conservatory, The Netherlands. *Career:* concerts in Russia, Germany and Israel; broadcasts by Israeli classical music radio channel 1998; performances by Israeli modern music performers, as well as soloists; Composer-in-Residence Israeli Sinfonietta Orchestra, Beer-Sheba 2007; mem. GEMA, Israel Composer's League. *Compositions:* Sacrifice for soprano, violin and piano 1990, Aquarelles 1990–97, String Quartet 1990, Wind Quintet 1991, Triptych for piano solo 1991, three vocal pieces 1993, Preludium, Fantasia und Fuga for nine players 1993, Form, Farbe und Licht 1995, Au debut et a la fin 1996, Three Ballet Scenes for six players 1996, String Quartet 1997, Aphorismes 1997, On the Other Side of Sound 1998, Quartet for oboe, horn, cello and piano 1998; pieces for solo clarinet, marimba, cello, tuba, clarinet and violin with piano. *Honours:* Special Cttee of Israeli Govt award for extraordinary talented composer 1998, Prime Minister Prize for composition 2006, ACUM Award 2008, 2010, Second Prize, Liberson Competition (for his third string quartet Four Homages) 2013, Boston Metro Opera Concert Award (Opera Special Award for Operatorio Shunamit) 2014. *Website:* uribrener.com.

BRENET, Thérèse; French fmr composer; b. 22 Oct. 1935, Paris; d. of Gen. François Brenet and Marguerite Warnier. *Education:* Paris Conservatoire. *Career:* Prof., Paris Conservatoire from 1970. *Compositions include:* Fantasio 1961, La nuit de Maldoror for female voice, piano and cello 1963, Aube morte 1964, Clamavit 1965, Six Pièces Brèves for orchestra 1966, Sept poèmes chinois 1966, Concerto pour un poème inconnu 1966, Hommage à Signorelli 1967, Fragor 1969, Inter Silentia 1969, Les Mains 1970, Sidérales 1970, Pantomime for flute 1974, Hapax 1977, Tétrapyle 1978, Lyre d'etoiles for string trio with recitative 1979, Caprice d;une chatte anglaise 1979, Ce que pensent les étoiles 1980, Accordance 1981, Anamnèse 1982, Cristaux for Celtic harp and mandolin 1982, Thrène 1983, Incandescence 1984, Vibration for Celtic harp and strings 1984, Les Chants du Sommeil et de la Mort 1984, Moires for six ondes martenots and strings 1985, Gémeaux I et II 1985, Plus Souple que l'Eau 1986, Oceanides for piano left hand 1986, Boustrophédon 1986, Vision Flamboyante 1987, Tout l'Azur pour émail 1988, Le chemin de Croix inachevé 1988, Des grains de sable d'or aux mains 1988, Le tambour des dunes 1989, Petite suite pour M. Ré Dièze et Mlle Mi Bémol 1989, Le Fascinateur 1989, Aeterno certamine 1990, Odi et Amo for violin and orchestra 1992, Odi et amo 1992, Chimeres for mandolin and orchestra 1993, Poème pour violon et orchestre 1994, Le Retour de Quetzalcoatl for cello and orchestra 1995, Anamnèse II 1996, Aréthuse 1997, Des grains de sable d'or aux mains II 1997, Au vent d'ouest for piano 2000, Seuls tes yeux demeurèrent 2000. *Honours:* Premier Grand Prix de Rome 1965, Hon. Prof. Conservatoire Nat. Superieur de Paris. *Address:* c/o SACEM, 225 avenue Charles de Gaulle, 92521 Neuilly sur Seine Cédex, France (office). *E-mail:* contact@theresebrenet.com (office). *Website:* theresebrenet.com/index2.html.

BRESNICK, Martin, BA, MA, DMA; American composer and academic; *Professor in the Practice of Composition, School of Music, Yale University*; b. 13 Nov. 1946, New York; m. Lisa Moore; one d. *Education:* Hartt School of Music, Univ. of Hartford, Stanford Univ., Akademie für Musik, Austria. *Career:* currently Prof. in the Practice of Composition and Coordinator of Composition Dept, Yale School of Music; taught at San Francisco Conservatory of Music 1971–72, Stanford Univ. 1972–75; Valentine Prof. of Music, Amherst Coll. 1993; Mary Duke Biddle Prof. of Music, Duke Univ. 1998; Composer-in Residence, American Acad. in Rome 1999; Cecil and Ida Green Visiting Prof. of Composition, Univ. of British Columbia 2000; Composer-in-Residence, Australian Youth Orchestra Nat. Music Camp 2001, 2004; Dir of Composition, International Bartok Seminar 2001; Visiting Prof. of Composition, Eastman School of Music 2002–03; Visiting Prof., New Coll., Oxford 2004; Housewright Eminent Scholar and Featured Guest Composer, Florida State Univ. 2005; Visiting Composer, RAM 2005; Visiting Composer, Harvard Univ. 2009; Visiting Composer, Yonsei Univ., South Korea 2009; Macgeorge Fellow, Melbourne Univ. 2010; Composer-in-Residence, Mannes Coll. of Music 2010–11; Master Artist, Atlantic Center for the Arts 2013; Composer-in-Residence, Univ. of Michigan 2014; Composer-in-Residence, Royal Conservatoire, Glasgow, Scotland 2014; Inst. of Advanced Studies Fellowship, Univ. of Western Australia 2014; mem. American Acad. of Arts and Letters 2006–. *Compositions include:* Trio for two trumpets and percussion 1966, Introit 1969, Ocean of Storms 1970, Intermezzi 1971, Musica 1972, B's Garlands 1973, Wir Weben, Wir Weben 1978, Conspiracies 1979, Der Signal 1982, High Art 1983, String Quartet No. 2 Bucephalus, One 1986, Lady Neil's Dumpe 1987, Trio 1988, Pontoosuc 1989, Musica Povera Nos 1–12 1991–1999, String Quartet No. 3 1992, Cadillac Desert 1996, GRACE concerto for two marimbas and orchestra 2000, Songs of the House People 1999, For the Sexes: The Gates of Paradise for solo piano and DVD 2001, My Twentieth Century (chamber music) 2002. *Recordings include:* B's Garlands, Conspiracies, three Intermezzi, String Quartet No. 2 Bucephalus, Wir Weben, Wir Weben, Lady Neil's Dumpe, Piano Trio, Just Time. *Publications:* How Music Works; contrib. to Mosaic, Yale Journal of Music Theory. *Honours:* Fulbright Fellowship 1969-70, Walter J. Gores Award for Excellence in Teaching, Stanford Univ. 1973, Rome Prize Fellowship 1975–76, MacDowell Colony Fellowship 1977, Morse Fellowship, Yale Univ. 1980–81, First Prize, Premio Ancona 1980, First Prize, Int. Sinfonia Musicale Competition 1982, Connecticut Comm. on the Arts Grant, with Chamber Music America 1983, First Prize, Composers Inc. Competition 1985, 1989; Elise L. Stoeger Prize for Chamber Music, Chamber Music Soc. of Lincoln Center 1996, Charles Ives Living Award, American Acad. of Arts and Letters 1998, Aaron Copland Prize for teaching, ASCAP Foundation 2000, Berlin Prize Fellow, American Acad. in Berlin 2001, Guggenheim Fellowship 2003. *Address:* Yale School of Music, 98 Wall Street, New Haven, CT 06520, USA (office). *E-mail:* martinbresnick@gmail.com (home). *Website:* www.martinbresnick.com; music.yale.edu (office).

BRETT, Charles, MA; British singer (countertenor); b. 27 Oct. 1941, Maidenhead, Berkshire, England; m. 1st Brigid Barstow 1973 (divorced); one s. one d.; m. 2nd Cecile Bourasset 1999. *Education:* King's Coll., Cambridge. *Career:* leading performer with early and Baroque music ensembles led by Munrow, Harnoncourt, Leonhardt, Hogwood, Gardiner, Herreweghe and Malgoire; engagements in USA, France, Switzerland, Germany, Spain and Norway; Handel's Theodora, in Oslo; Israel in Egypt in Geneva; Bach's Christmas Oratorio in Versailles; Bach's St John Passion in Cambridge and London; B Minor Mass with Collegium Vocale Gent at Lourdes, Paris and Lyon; many concerts with Le Grande Ecurie et la Chambre du Roy, conducted by Malgoire; opera debut 1984, in Angelica Vincitrice di Alcina by Fux, at Graz; Handel's Semele at Ludwigsburg; tour of France with La Clemenza di Tito by Gluck; Aachen Opera 1987, as Oberon; founder and Dir, Amaryllis Consort (vocal group specializing in Renaissance repertoire); Prof., Royal Acad. of Music; masterclass in Canada, Belgium, Germany, Spain, Mexico, France; as conductor, performances of works by various composers in France; Dido and Aeneas for Cervantino Festival, Mexico 1995; Visiting Prof., Toulouse Conservatoire; mem. ISM. *Recordings include:* Handel's Dixit Dominus, Rinaldo, Messiah, The Triumph of Time and Truth, Bach's B Minor Mass, Lambert's Leçons des Ténèbres, Mozart Masses, Bach's Cantatas, Burgon's Canciones de Alma, Italian and English madrigals with Amaryllis Consort, Vivaldi's Nisi Dominus and Stabat Mater, Blow's Ode on the Death of Mr Henry Purcell. *Honours:* Hon. RAM 1991.

BRETT, Kathleen; Canadian singer (soprano); b. 4 Sept. 1962, Campbell River, BC. *Career:* appearances with Canada Opera Ensemble and elsewhere in Canada as Susanna, Bizet's Leila (Manitoba Opera), Adina (Calgary Opera) and Pamina (Edmonton Opera); European debut as Dorinda in Handel's Orlando at Antwerp, followed by Mozart's Barbarina at Covent Garden, Susanna at Monte Carlo and Amor in Gluck's Orphée et Euridice with L'Opera Française in New York; other repertory includes Kristina in The Makropulos Case (San Francisco), Drusilla in Monteverdi's Poppea (Dallas Opera), Despina (Vancouver Opera), Zerlina, and Amarilli in Handel's Pastor Fido (at Toronto); concerts include Messiah at Montréal, Fauré Requiem with Vancouver Symphony Orchestra, and A Midsummer Night's Dream by Mendelssohn; long artistic collaboration with Canadian Opera Co.; Guest Artist, Vancouver Symphony Orchestra; mem. Faculty, Victoria Conservatory of Music. *Honours:* Int. Mozart Competition Best Canadian Singer 1991, Sullivan Award, Canadian Council Career Development Grant. *Address:* Victoria Conservatory of Music, 900 Johnson Street, Victoria, BC V8V 3N4, Canada. *E-mail:* info@vcm.bc.ca. *Website:* vcm.bc.ca/kathleen-brett.

BREVIG, Per Andreas, BA, BS, DMus, DMA; Norwegian/American conductor and fmr trombonist; *Music Director, East Texas Symphony Orchestra*; b. 7 Sept. 1936, Halden; s. of Aslaug B. Maarud and Knut Brevig; m. Berit Brevig 1959; two s. two d. *Education:* Juilliard School, USA, also studied in Bergen, Norway, Norrköping, Sweden, Hilversum, Netherlands, Leopold Stokowski Symposium for Young Conductors, USA. *Career:* Prin. Trombonist, Bergen Philharmonic Orchestra, Norway 1956–65, debut as soloist with Bergen Philharmonic Orchestra 1961; Prin. Trombonist, Detroit Symphony Orchestra 1966, American Symphony Orchestra, New York 1966–70, Metropolitan Opera Orchestra, New York 1968–94; Music Dir and Conductor, Empire State Opera Co., New York 1990–; Conductor, Island Lyric Opera, New York 1993–2000; Music Dir East Texas Symphony Orchestra 2002–; Faculty mem.

Juilliard School, Manhattan School of Music, Mannes Coll. of Music, New York, Aspen Music Festival, Colorado; guest conductor for opera and symphonies and with orchestras worldwide; Founder and Pres. Edvard Grieg Soc. Inc., New York; mem. Advisory Bd Medical Problems of Performing Artists, Musikphysiologie und Musik Medizin; mem. Bd Musicians Club of New York, mem. American Acad. for Arts and Letters. *Commissions and dedications include:* Roger Smith, Sonata for trombone and piano 1965, Alcides Lanza, Acufenos for trombone and four instruments 1966, Egil Hovland, Concerto for trombone and orchestra, Noel Da Costa, Four Preludes for trombone and piano 1973, Vincent Persichetti, Parable for solo trombone 1978, Robert Starer, Serenade for trombone, vibraphone and strings 1982, Paul Turok, Canzona Concertante No. 2 1982, Walter Ross, Trombone Concerto No. 2 for trombone and orchestra 1984, Melvyn Broiles, The Great Northern Posaune for trombone and brass ensemble 1989, Arne Nordheim, Return of the Snark and Hunting of the Snark for trombone and electronic tape 1989. *Publications include:* Avant Garde Techniques in solo Trombone Music: Problems of Notation and Execution 1974, Losing One's Lip and Other Problems of Embouchure 1990, Edvard Grieg and the Edvard Grieg Society 1993, Medical Problems of Musicians 1995. *Honours:* Hon. Texan 2011; Koussevitsky Fellowship, Henry B. Cabot Award, three Naumburg Fellowships, Neill Humfeld Award for excellence in teaching, Royal Medal of St Olav (presented by King Olav V of Norway in recognition of his efforts on behalf of Norwegian music and culture in the USA) 1990, ITA Award' for his distinguished career and his impact on the world of trombone performance' 2012.

BREVIK, Tor; Norwegian composer, conductor and music critic; b. 22 Jan. 1932, Oslo. *Education:* Oslo Conservatory, studied in Sweden. *Career:* founder, Youth Chamber Orchestra, Oslo 1958; mem. Soc. of Norwegian Composers. *Compositions:* Da kongen kom til Spilliputt (opera) 1973, Adagio and Fugue for strings 1958, Overture 1958, Serenade for strings 1959, Chaconne for orchestra 1960, Concertino for clarinet and strings 1961, Music for violin 1963, Canto Elegiaco for orchestra 1964, Contrasts (chamber ballet) 1964, Elegy for soprano, viola, double bass and percussion 1964, Divertimento for wind quintet 1964, Adagio Religioso for horn 1967, String Quartet 1967, Concertino for strings 1967, Music for four strings 1968, Intrada for orchestra 1969, Romance for violin and orchestra or piano 1972, Andante Cantabile for violin and strings 1975, Septet 1976, Fantasy for flute 1979, Light of Peace (Christmas play for children) 1980, Viola Concerto 1982, Sinfonietta 1989, Sinfonia Brevik 1991, The Singing Raft cantata for soprano, mixed chorus, children's chorus and strings 1992, Music for orchestra 1993, Serenade for ten winds 1994, On Request! for band 1994.

BREWER, Aline; British harpist; b. 14 Sept. 1963, Shropshire, England. *Education:* Royal Coll. of Music with Marisa Robles. *Career:* debut at Wigmore Hall 1990; Principal Harp, Royal Philharmonic Orchestra; fmr mem., European Community Orchestra and the Britten-Pears Orchestra; solo appearances with the London Mozart Players, Primavera and the Britten-Pears Orchestra; duo recitals with flautist Jennifer Stinton; mem., Britten-Pears Ensemble, with performances throughout the UK and USA. *Recordings include:* Romantic Music for Flute and Harp, Mozart's Concerto K299 (with Jennifer Stinton and the Philharmonia Orchestra). *Honours:* jt winner South East Arts Young Artists Platform.

BREWER, Bruce, MM; American singer (tenor) (retd); b. 12 Oct. 1941, San Antonio, TX; m. (divorced). *Education:* studied with Josephine Lucchese at Univ. of Texas, Austin, and with Richard Bonynge in New York and London; further study with Nadia Boulanger and Rosalyn Tureck. *Career:* sang first in concert, notably in Baroque and early music; opera debut as Don Ottavio in San Antonio 1970; Camden Festival, London, in Donizetti's Torquato Tasso, 1974; sang at opera houses in Boston, San Francisco, Berlin, Paris, Toulouse, Spoleto and London, Covent Garden 1979; Aix-en-Provence Festival in revival of music by Campra; La Scala Milan 1980, in L'Enfance du Christ by Berlioz; Rossini's Le Comte Ory 1991; sang Rossini's La Gazza Ladra, Teatro Rossini, Rossini Opera Festival, Pesaro 1981, Mozart, Teatro Reggio, Torino 1981, Rossini's Otello 1980 and Le Comte Ory 1981 at Teatro Massimo, Palermo; sang in Festival of Two Worlds, Teatro Nuovo, Spoleto; often heard in Bach and Mozart; sang Lord Puff in Henze's English Cat in Paris, and in premieres of Balliff's Dracula and Denisov's L'écume des jours; Paris Opéra 1988, in the premiere of La Célestine by Maurice Ohana; sang Fatty in Weill's Mahagonny at Maggio Musicale, Florence 1990; Truffaldino in Busoni's Turandot at Lyon 1992; teaches and prepares professional singers. *Recordings:* Les Indes Galantes by Rameau, Rameau's Platée and Les Paladins, Messiaen's St François d'Assise, Rameau's Zoroastre, Boulevard Solitude by Henze, Beethoven's 9th Symphony, Berlioz's works for Soloists and Chorus, Les Nuits d'été, Gretry's L'Amant Jaloux, Liszt's Complete Songs for Tenor, Lully's Alceste, Offenbach's Orphée aux Enfers. *Address:* 1 rue du Coufrier, 53250 Couptrain, France.

BREWER, Christine; American singer (soprano); b. 1960. *Education:* studied with Birgit Nilsson. *Career:* appearances with the Opera Theatre of St Louis as Ellen Orford in Peter Grimes, Ariadne, Donna Anna (also for Vancouver Opera, 1994); Sang Sifare in Mozart's Mitridate at the 1992 Mostly Mozart Festival in New York, Lady Billows in Albert Herring at San Diego and Vitellia in La Clemenza di Tito; concert engagements include Szymanowki's Stabat Mater in Cleveland, the Vaughan Williams Benedicte in Louisville and Poulenc's Stabat Mater with the Leipzig Gewandhaus Orchestra; Beethoven's Ninth Symphony at Columbus and the Missa Solemnis at

Washington, DC and San Diego; Mendelssohn's Elijah with the Houston and Honolulu Symphonies; engagements include the Mozart and Dvořák Requiems in Toronto, the Janáček Glagolitic Mass in Atlanta and at the Mann Music Center with the Philadelphia Orchestra under Charles Dutoit; Gretchen in Schumann's Faust at the Caramoor Festival; Donna Anna at Covent Garden, 1996; Strauss's Ariadne at Santa Fe, 1999; Schoenberg's Gurrelieder and Mahler's Symphony of a Thousand, at the London Proms, 2002; sang in Le Roi Arthus by Chausson at the 2002 Edinburgh Festival; sang Isolde in concert with the BBC SO, 2002–03. *Honours:* winner Metropolitan Opera National Council auditions 1989, Royal Philharmonic Soc./Radio 3 Listeners Award 2008. *Address:* 704 Belleville Street, Lebanon, IL 62254, USA.

BRICKNER, Szabolcs; Hungarian singer (tenor); b. 6 Dec. 1980, Budapest; m. *Education:* Franz Liszt Acad., Budapest, Hochschule für Musik, Augsburg, private lessons with Nicolai Gedda, Renata Scotto. *Career:* has performed with La Monnaie/De Munt Symphony Orchestra, Orchestra of Opéra Royal de Wallonie, Orchestre Philharmonique du Luxembourg, Nationaal Orkest van België, Nat. Philharmonic Orchestra of Hungary, Budapest Philharmonic Orchestra, Staatsoper München, Oper Frankfurt, Opéra de Rhin, Strasbourg; roles include Tamino in Die Zauberflöte, Nemorino in L'Elisir d'Amore, Lenskij in Eugene Onegin, Romeo in Romeo et Juliette, Orfeo in Orfeo ed Euridice, Jaquino in Fidelio, Alfredo in La Traviata, Belmonte in Die Entführung aus dem Serail. *Honours:* winner, two nat. Hungarian voice competitions, Second Prize, Ferruccio Tagliavini Int. Singing Competition 2004, First Prize, Queen Elisabeth Int. Singing Competition, Belgium 2008. *Current Management:* Alferink Artists Management, Herengracht 340, 1016 Amsterdam, Netherlands. *Telephone:* (20) 6643151. *Fax:* (20) 6752426. *E-mail:* info@alferink.org. *Website:* www.alferink.org.

BRIDEOAKE, Peter, MMus; Australian composer; b. 23 April 1945, Adelaide, SA. *Education:* Adelaide Univ., studied with Richard Meale. *Career:* faculty mem., Elder Conservatory 1975–; commissions from the Australian Chamber Orchestra, Seymour Group and Victoria String Quartet. *Compositions include:* Composition for winds 1971, Music for flute and percussions 1972, Gedatsu for guitar 1972, Chiaroscuro 1978, String Quartet 1980, Interplay for two clarinets and harp 1981, Imagery for string orchestra 1981, Shifting Reflections for chamber ensemble 1982, Canto for Clarinet Alone 1987, A Poet's Lament for soprano and piano 1988. *Honours:* John Bishop Memorial Prize 1976.

BRIDGES, Althea; Australian singer (soprano); b. 11 Jan. 1936, Sydney. *Education:* Sydney Conservatory. *Career:* mem. of Australian Opera Company, 1961–64; sang in Europe from 1964, at first in Austria (Graz); Vienna, Theater an der Wien, in the premiere of Hauer's Die schwarze Spinne, 1966; Stuttgart, 1968, in the premiere of Orff's Prometheus; Landestheater Linz, 1971–83; sang Tosca at Frankfurt and Donna Anna at the Glyndebourne Festival; Bari, Italy, as Ortrud in Lohengrin; other roles include Strauss's Elektra and Marschallin, Marguerite in Faust and Azucena in Il Trovatore; Sang in the premiere of Michael Kohlhaas by Karl Kögler at Linz, 1989; season 2000 at Linz as Baba the Turk in The Rake's Progress and Auntie in Peter Grimes.

BRIGER, Alexander, BMus; Australian/British conductor; *Artistic Director and Chief Conductor, Australian World Orchestra;* b. (Andrew Alexander Briger), 23 April 1969, Sydney, NSW; s. of Andrew Briger and Elizabeth Mackerras; nephew of Sir Charles Mackerras; m. Natascha Eikmeier; three d. *Education:* Sydney Conservatorium, Richard Strauss-Konservatorium, Munich. *Career:* Asst to Sir Charles Mackerras at Edinburgh Festival, including Fidelio and Figaro; has worked closely with Pierre Boulez and Ensemble Contemporain; conducted premieres of works by Arvo Pärt, Mark Anthony Turnage, Simon Holt and Bruno Mantovani; engagements with Royal Opera House, Covent Garden, ENO, Théâtre du Châtelet, Paris, Aix-en-Provence, Royal Swedish Opera, Royal Danish Opera, Komische Oper, Berlin, Canadian Opera Company, Opéra du Rhin, State Opera of South Australia, Philharmonia Orchestra, London Philharmonic, BBC Symphony Orchestra, BBC Scottish Symphony, City of Birmingham Symphony, Royal Liverpool Philharmonic, Bournemouth Symphony Orchestra, RTÉ Nat. Symphony Orchestra, Dublin, Orchestra of the Welsh Nat. Opera, Academy of St Martin in the Fields, Scottish Chamber Orchestra, Northern Sinfonia, Hanover Band, Birmingham Contemporary Music Group, Deutsche Kammerphilharmonie, Konzerthausorchester, Berlin, Frankfurt Radio Symphony Orchestra, Sudwestrundfunk Sinfonieorchester, Stuttgart, Hamburger Symphoniker, Orchestra of the Komische Oper, Berlin, Nordwestdeutscherundfunk Orchester, Orchestra de Paris, Orchestre Philharmonique de Radio France, Orchestre Nat. du Capitole de Toulouse, Strasbourg Philharmonic, Paris Chamber Orchestra, Ensemble Intercontemporain, Monte Carlo Philharmonic, Rotterdam Philharmonic, Gothenburg Symphony, Swedish Radio Symphony, Danish Radio Sinfonietta, Kristiansand Symphony Orchestra, Mozarteum Orchestra, Salzburg, Salzburg Camerata, Belgium Nat. Orchestra, Flemish Radio Symphony, Orquesta Nacional do Porto, Musikkollegium Winterthur, Japanese Virtuoso Symphony Orchestra, Sydney Symphony, Melbourne Symphony, West Australian Symphony, Adelaide Symphony, Queensland Symphony, Tasmanian Symphony, New Zealand Symphony Orchestra; Founder, Artistic Dir and Chief Conductor, Australian World Orchestra 2010–. *Honours:* Winner, Int. Workshop/Competition for Conductors, Czech Repub., Winner, Best Orchestral Concert Australia-wide (Australian World Orchestra) 2011. *Current Management:* c/o Rayfield Allied,

119

Southbank House, Black Prince Road, London, SE1 7SJ, England. *Telephone:* (20) 3176-5500. *Fax:* (700) 602-4143. *E-mail:* info@rayfieldallied.com. *Website:* www.rayfieldallied.com. *Address:* Australian World Orchestra, 770 New South Head Road, Rose Bay, NSW 2029, Australia (office). *Telephone:* (2) 9371-8860 (office). *E-mail:* gthompson@australianworldorchestra.com.au (office); alexbriger@yahoo.com (home). *Website:* www .australianworldorchestra.com.au.

BRIGGS, David, MA, FRCO, ARCM; British organist and composer; *Organist Emeritus, Gloucester Cathedral;* b. 1 Nov. 1962, Bromsgrove; s. of John Rayner Briggs and Jane Angela Briggs; m. Madge Nimocks; three c. *Education:* King's Coll., Cambridge, studied organ with Jean Langlais in Paris. *Career:* Asst Organist, Hereford Cathedral 1984–89; Music Dir Hereford Chamber Choir and String Orchestra 1985–89; Organist and Master of the Choristers, Truro Cathedral 1989–94; Music Dir Gloucester Cathedral 1994–2002, Organist Emer. 2002–; directed Three Choirs Festivals at Gloucester Cathedral, conducting orchestras including the Philharmonia; concert engagements include Nat. Cathedral, Washington, DC, Notre Dame, Paris, Severance Hall, Cleveland, Symphony Hall, Birmingham, UK; has performed improvisation to silent films such as Phantom of the Opera, Nosferatu, King of Kings, Hunchback of Notre Dame, Jeanne d'Arc and Fritz Lang's Metropolis; masterclasses Royal Northern Coll. of Music and Cambridge Univ.; jury chair. Nürnberg 2007. *Commissions include:* Symphony 'Missa pro defunctis', a setting of the Solemn Requiem Mass, Four Concert Etudes, Cello Sonata. *Compositions include:* for choir and orchestra: Creation 2000, Requiem 2003, St John Passion 2005; for choir and organ: Truro Eucharist for SATB and organ 1990, Matin Responsory for SSAATTBB a cappella 1999, The Star-spangled Banner for SATB a cappella 2000, Magnificat and Nunc Dimittis: The Hereford Service for SATB, tenor solo and organ 2000, Messe pour Notre-Dame for SATB and 2 organs 2002, Ave Maria for TTBB and organ 2004, Magnificat and Nunc Dimittis: The Truro Service for SATB and organ 2004, Ave Verum Corpus for SATB and organ 2004, Adam lay y bounden for SATB and organ 2005, I will lift up mine eyes unto the Hills for SATB a cappella 2006, Harvest Anthem for SATB and organ 2006, Ubi Caritas est amor for SSAATTBB a cappella 2006, Jesu, the very thought of thee for SATB and organ 2006; for organ: Marche Episcopale 1999, Variations on 'Laudes Spirituali' 2004, Organ Symphony 'Missa pro defunctis' 2004, Elegy 2004, Fantaisie 2005, Variations on Greensleeves 2005, Four Concert Etudes 2005, Variations on 'Veni Creator' for Organ Duet 2005, Berceuse for Organ 2006; other: Chempinesca for piano duet 2004, Dreamworld, a song cycle for tenor and piano 2005; organ transcriptions. *Honours:* Tournemire Prize, St Albans Int. Organ Improvisation Competition, first prize Int. Improvisation Competition, Paisley, Silver Medal of the Worshipful Co. of Musicians. *Current Management:* Chestnut Music, 36 High Street, Ipswich, MA 01938, USA. *Telephone:* (978) 380-0177 (office). *E-mail:* madge_nimocks@yahoo.com (office). *Address:* 36 High Street, Ipswich, MA 01938, USA (home). *Telephone:* (978) 356-2058 (office). *E-mail:* david@david-briggs.org.uk (office); davidbriggsorganist@gmail.com (office); chestnut_music@yahoo.com (office). *Website:* www.david-briggs.org (home).

BRIGGS, Sarah Beth; British pianist; b. 1972. *Education:* studied with Prof. Denis Matthews in Newcastle, York and Birmingham, Edith Fischer in Lausanne, Switzerland, chamber music with Bruno Giuranna in Blonay, Switzerland. *Career:* professional concert debut aged 12 at Fairfield Hall, Beethoven's 2nd Piano Concerto with New Symphony Orchestra; many recitals and concerto performances throughout England and Scotland, Germany, Switzerland, Austria, France and USA; int. radio and TV broadcasts; Chester Summer Festival 1989, with world premiere of posthumous pieces by Benjamin Britten; London concerto debut at the Barbican 1989, playing Mozart K453; also plays Mozart's 20 other original concertos; further engagements with the Royal Liverpool Philharmonic, Northern Sinfonia, English Chamber Orchestra, Royal Philharmonic, Northern Chamber Orchestra, Ulster Orchestra, Scottish Chamber Orchestra, Manchester Camerata and the London Soloists Chamber Orchestra; US debut 1991, in the San Francisco Stern Grove Festival with the Midsummer Mozart Festival Orchestra, conducted by George Cleve; several further visits to USA for concertos and recitals; QEH debut 1992, performing two Mozart piano concertos with Manchester Camerata; chamber music concerts including series at the Royal Northern Coll. of Music, Manchester; season 1997–98 included debuts with the Hallé and BBC Concert Orchestra; debut Royal Philharmonic Orchestra 2006; formed Trio Melzi with ex-leader and prin. cellist of Manchester Camerata 1999; trio debut at Bridgewater Hall, Manchester 2000; trio featured on BBC Radio 3 and BBC 2; Vienna Chamber Orchestra 2001; mem. Clarion³ensemble with Janet Hilton and Laurence Perkins; mem. Anton Stadler Trio with Janet Hilton and Robin Ireland, Lisney-Briggs Duo with James Lisney; teaches master-classes in UK, Switzerland and USA. *Recordings:* Sarah Beth Briggs plays Haydn, Mozart, Bartók, Brahms, Chopin 2005, Sarah Beth Briggs Plays Beethoven 2013, Appassionata Sonata, Brahms, Handel Variations 2007, Britten and Rawsthorne 2011. *Honours:* First Prize, Surrey Young Pianist of the Year Competition, Third Prize, BBC Young Musician of the Year 1984, First Prize, Yorkshire TV Young Musicians' Awards 1987, Hindemith Scholarship 1987, Jt Winner, Int. Mozart Competition, Salzburg 1988. *Address:* 86 The Green, Acomb, Yorks., YO26 5LS, England (home). *Telephone:* 771749-6506 (mobile). *E-mail:* enquiries@sarahbethbriggs.co.uk. *Website:* www.sarahbethbriggs.co .uk.

BRIGHT, Colin Michael; Australian composer and academic; b. 28 June 1949, Sydney, NSW. *Education:* studied with Mary Egan, Linden Sands, Christopher Nicols and Ton de Leeuw. *Career:* Lecturer for High School Music Teachers from 1987; commissions from Synergy, Seymour Group, Southern Crossings and Sydney Symphony Orchestra. *Compositions include:* Percussion Quartet 1980, Earth Spirit for orchestra 1982, The Dreamtime for baritone and ensemble 1982, Earth, Wind and Fire for saxophone quartet 1982, Long Reef for string quintet and wind quintet 1984, Midnight Tulips song cycle for soprano and large ensemble 1985, The Sinking of the Rainbow Warrior (one-act opera), Tulipstick Talk for percussion 1985, Red Earth for six players 1985, Music for contrabass octet and didjeridoo 1986, Sun is God for string quartet 1989, The Journey (opera) 1991, The Butcher's Apron for four percussion 1991, Young Tree Green: Double Bass Concerto 1993, War and Peace vocal sextet 1994, The Sinking of the Rainbow Warrior (one-act opera) 1994, Oceania orchestral suite 1999, The Wild Boys 1997. *Honours:* Australian Music Centre One-Act Opera Award 1986, Australian Music Centre Award for Best Composition 1997.

BRILOVA, Elena; Russian singer (soprano); b. 9 Feb. 1961, Moscow. *Education:* Moscow Conservatoire. *Career:* sang in concert, 1986–88; Bolshoi Opera Moscow from 1988 as the Queen of Shemakha, Antonida (A Life for the Tsar), Traviata, Rosina and other leading roles; concert appearances as Constanze, Sophie, Oscar, Norina, Lucia, Amina and Leila (Les Pêcheurs de perles); further engagements as the Queen of Night at Cologne and Vienna, Gilda in Oslo and Vienna; Palmide in Il Crociato in Egitto at the 1991 Ludwigsburg Festival; British debut, 1992, as the Queen of Shemakha with the London Symphony Orchestra; Season 1993 as Gilda at the Bergen Festival and in concert performances of Rigoletto at Tel-Aviv, conducted by Zubin Mehta; concert engagements at Brussels and Frankfurt and with such conductors as Bashmet, Simonov, Rostropovich, Rozhdestvensky and Svetlanov; Sang in Berio's Outis at the Théâtre du Châtelet, 1999, and as Rossini's Elvira at Dusseldorf, 2001.

BRÎNDUŞ, Nicolae, MA, PhD; Romanian composer, pianist and musicologist; *Professor, National University of Music, Bucharest;* b. (Nicolae Brânduş), 16 April 1935, Bucharest; s. of Niculae Brânduş and Elena Brânduş; m. 1st Maria Cecylia Ostrowska 1969; m. 2nd Ioana Ieronim 1982; two s. one d. *Education:* Nat. Univ. of Music, Bucharest, Cluj-Napoca Acad. of Music, Ferien Kurse für Neue Musik, Darmstadt, Germany. *Career:* debut: pianist, George Enescu Philharmony of Bucharest 1955, piano soloist 1958–75; concert performances in Romania and abroad; soloist, Ploiesti Philharmonic Orchestra 1959–69; Prof., Nat. Univ. of Music, Bucharest 1969–81, 1992–; Ed. Muzica Review, Bucharest 1981–; compositions printed, recorded, played and broadcast on radio and TV in Bucharest and abroad; mem. Romanian Composers' and Musicologists' Union, Soc. des auteurs, compositeurs et éditeurs de musique, Paris; Pres. Romanian Section, Int. Soc. of Contemporary Music (ISCM) 1992–2002, mem. Exec. Cttee 1991–92, mem. Gen. Assemblies and ISCM World Music Days 1991–2000, Artistic Dir ISCM World Music Days Festival in Romania and Moldova 1999; Visiting Composer and Lecturer in Europe, Asia and USA. *Play:* Bizarmonia instrumental theatre, Bucharest 1988. *Compositions include:* ed and recorded: Pieces for piano 1966, 1984, 7 Psalms 1969, 2006, Mamsell Hus 1977, 2003, Dialo(va)gos, concerto for piano and orchestra 1978, 2003, Rhythmodia 1989, 2010, Ostinato for piano 2003, 2006, Vagues for quintet 2005, 2006, Bowstring for veena solo 2005, 2006; ed: 8 Madrigals for choir a cappella 1968, Sonata for 2 pianos 1978, The Betrothal (opera) 1981, 2008, Languir me fais 1986, Melopedia and Fuga for bassoon 1998. *Recordings include:* Antiphonia for string orchestra 1984, With the Gipsy Girls (opera) 1988, Infrarealism 1998, Second Concerto for piano and orchestra 2002, 2003, Cantus Firmus 2004, Soliloque I & IV 2004, Match II for chamber orchestra 2004, Kitsch-N for clarinet and tapes 2006, Phtora I for orchestra 2010, Tubulatures for orchestra of flutes 2010, SIN-Euphonia II for orchestra and tapes 2010. *Publications include:* Interrelations (musical studies) 1984; contrib. of numerous articles to magazines and journals. *Honours:* Order of Cultural Merit (Bucharest) 1968, Officer 2004; Hon. Mention, Int. Competition Prince Pierre de Monaco 1973, Prize, Romanian Composers and Musicologists Union 1974, 2002, 2005, Georges Enescu Prize, Romanian Acad. 1977, prizes from Romanian radio and TV 1975, 1977. *Current Management:* c/o UCMR, Calea Victoriei 141, 0110071 Bucharest, Romania. *Address:* Street Dr Felix 101, Bl. 19 Sc. A Apartment 42, 011036 Bucharest, Romania. *Telephone:* (21) 3168663. *E-mail:* n.brandus@yahoo .com.

BRINGUIER, Lionel; French conductor and musician (piano, cello); *Chief Conductor and Music Director, Tonhalle Orchestra Zürich;* b. 1986, Nice. *Education:* Conservatoire de Musique, Nice and Conservatoire Nat. Supérieur de Musique, Paris. *Career:* Asst Conductor to John Nelson Ensemble Orchestral de Paris 2005–07; Chef Associé, Orchestre de Bretagne 2006–; Asst Conductor to Esa-Pekka Salonen, Los Angeles Philharmonic 2007–09, Assoc. Conductor 2009–13; Music Dir, Orquesta Sinfónica de Castilla y León 2009–12; Chief Conductor and Music Dir, Tonhalle Orchestra Zürich 2014–; engagements include concerts with Ensemble Modern Acad., Frankfurt, Orchestre Nat. du Capitole de Toulouse, Gurzenich Orchestra, Cologne, WDR Symphony Orchestra, Cologne, Helsinki Philharmonic Orchestra, Staatskapelle Dresden, Leipzig Gewandhaus, Rotterdam Philharmonic Orchestra, Nat. Orchestra of Spain, Madrid. *Honours:* Winner Int. Young Conductors Competition, Besançon 2005. *Current Management:* c/o Mark Newbanks, Fidelio Arts Limited, 103 Whitecross Street, No. 5, London, EC1Y 8JD,

England. *E-mail:* mark@fidelioarts.com. *Website:* www.fidelioarts.com. *Address:* Tonhalle Orchestra Zürich, Gotthardstrasse 5, 8002 Zürich, Germany (office). *Telephone:* (44) 2063440 (office). *Fax:* (44) 2063436 (office). *Website:* www.tonhalle-orchester.ch (office); www.lionelbringuier.com (home).

BRINKMANN, Bodo; German singer (baritone); b. 7 Dec. 1942, Binder, Brunswick. *Education:* Berlin Musikhochschule with Karl-Heinz Lohmann. *Career:* debut at Kaiserslautern 1971; mem., National Theatre Mannheim from 1974; Staatsoper Hamburg in Lohengrin; Munich Staatsoper, notably as Escamillo 1984, and in the 1986 premiere of Reimann's Troades; guest appearances in Berlin, Paris and Strasbourg; Deutsche Oper am Rhein 1987, as Telramund; Munich Olympia Hall 1987, as Prince Igor; Bayreuth Festival 1987–92, Kurwenal, Donner and Gunther; sang Jochanaan in Salome at Barcelona 1989; Cologne Opera 1990, as Wotan in Die Walküre; Düsseldorf 1995–96, as Wolfram and Wotan; season 2000–01 as the Wanderer in Siegfried at Münster and Meinigen. *Recordings include:* The Ring (video, from Bayreuth).

BRIZZI, Aldo; Italian conductor and composer; b. 7 June 1960, Alessandria. *Education:* Bologna Univ. and Milan Conservatorio. *Career:* debut as conductor 1978; Prin. Conductor, Ensemble of Ferienkurse, Darmstadt 1990–94, GMCL, Lisbon 1995–96, Akanthos Ensemble, Italy 1992–99; conducted concerts in Europe, Israel, USA, Central and South America; principal performances with Santa Cecilia Chamber Orchestra of Rome, Philharmonisches Kammermusik Collegium Berlin, Bamberger Symphoniker, Sinfónica Nacional de México, Torino Philharmonic, Lisbon Metropolitan Orchestra, Porto Symphony Orchestra, Caen Orchestra, Menuhin Foundation Orchestra, Bahia Symphony Orchestra, Orchestra Haydn di Bolzano, Israel Chamber Orchestra, Kreisler Strings, London, Ensemble Recherche, Freiburg, Ensemble Itinéraire, Paris; conducted world premieres of Morricone's Viola Concerto, Jesi Festival, numerous works by Scelsi Peixinho, Miroglio and Radulescu; music performed by European Union Youth Orchestra, Bamberger Symphoniker, Baden-Baden Radiosymfonieorkester, Orchestre Philharmonique de Radio France, Arditti String Quartet; wrote Mambo Mistico, Théâtre National de Chaillot, Paris 2005 and Gabriel et Gabriel Théâtre Dunois, Paris 2015. *Compositions include:* The Labyrinth Trial (multimedia concert) 1999, Endless Trails 2002, Mambo Mistico (opera/ musical) (Prix des Souffleurs for Best Theatre Music) 2005, Alter (multimedia opera) 2012. *Recordings include:* The Labyrinth Trial 1998, Brizzi do Brasil 2002, Aço de Açucar 2005, Reis 2008. *Publications include:* Proposte Musicali 1980, La Musica, Le Idee, Le Cose 1981; contrib. to numerous magazines. *Honours:* Venezia Opera Prima 1981, Stipendienpreis, Darmstadt 1984, Young Generation in Europe, Venice, Paris, Cologne 1985, Franco Evangelisti, Rome 1986, Young Composers' Forum, Cologne 1989, Trofeu Caymmi 2003, A. Hepburn Foundation 2004, Beaumarchais, Paris 2013. *Address:* Via Boves 6, Alessandria 15121, Italy. *E-mail:* info@aldobrizzi.net. *Website:* www .aldobrizzi.net.

BRKANOVIC, Zeljko; Croatian composer, conductor and academic; *President, Croatian Composers' Society;* b. 20 Dec. 1937, Zagreb; m. Ivanka Brkanovic 1964; one s. one d. *Education:* Zagreb Music Acad., Skopje Music Acad., Accademia Chigiana Siena, Italy, Hochschule für Musik, Stuttgart, Germany. *Career:* debut with first string quartet in Zagreb 1974; Conductor, Croatian Nat. Theatre Opera, Split and Zagreb 1963–69; Conductor, Nat. Theatre, Split 1964–66; Musical Ed., Croatian Nat. Radio and Television 1969–80; Prof., Music Acad., Zagreb 1966–, Music Acad., Podgorica 1980–; mem. Croatian Composers' Soc., Pres. 2004–. *Compositions:* Nomos, Suite for Strings, Ricercari, Two Symphonies, Concerto for Violin, Concerto for Piano and Orchestra (Josip Slavenski Award 1983), Concerto for Violin, Violoncello and Orchestra, Lyrical Concerto for Piano and Orchestra, Concerto for Percussion and 3 Clarinets (Ministry of Culture Award 1997), Concert Rondo for Piano, Wind and Brass Orchestra; also chamber, piano and organ music. *Recordings:* Tonal Sonata (Porin Award 1999) 1977, Divertimento For Strings 1977, Concerto for Piano and Orchestra 1981, Concerto for Violin 1983, Antependium 1989, Second Symphony 1991, Figures 1995, Song Book 1996; author CDs 1996, 2002. *Publications:* Professor Dr E. Karkoschka, Stuttgart 1991, Bulletin/Croatian Composers' Society 1992; contrib. to Schweinfurtische Nachrichten, Vjesnik Zagreb, Vecernji list Zagreb, Slobodna Dalmacija Split, Piano Journal No. 49 London, op. 46, 1992, Cantus Zagreb 2003, Frankfurter Allgemeine Zeitung 2003. *Honours:* Order of Danica Hrvatska, Croatia 1999; Vladimir Nazor Concert Award 2002. *Address:* 10000 Zagreb, Tomislavov trg 18, Croatia (home). *Telephone:* (1) 4922258 (home). *E-mail:* zeljko.brkanovic@ zg.t-com.hr (home).

BROAD, Daniel; British singer (baritone); b. 1967, England. *Education:* Chetham's School, Manchester, Royal Northern Coll. of Music with Robert Alderson. *Career:* Glyndebourne Chorus from 1996; Keeper of the Madhouse in The Rake's Progress at the Festival 2000; sang Rossini's Figaro at Aix and for Castleward Opera, Yamadori in Butterfly for Clonter Opera, Marcello at Holland Park and Sid in Albert Herring at the Perth Festival; further engagements in Béatrice and Bénédict for European Opera Union and Eugene Onegin in Baden Baden and Paris; other roles include Mozart's Count, Tarquinius in The Rape of Lucretia and Ping in Turandot. *Recordings include:* Anthony in Sweeney Todd (for Opera North). *Honours:* Peter Moores Foundation Scholar.

BROADBENT, Graeme; British singer (bass) and teacher; *Professor of Vocal Studies, Royal College of Music;* b. 18 May 1962, Halifax. *Education:* Royal Coll. of Music with Lyndon Van der Pump; Moscow Conservatoire with Evgeni Nesterenko. *Career:* performed in recital and oratorio throughout the UK and abroad, appearing at all the major London concert halls and at the Proms; repertoire encompasses 115 operatic roles and 52 oratorio and concert works, ranging from Monteverdi's Vespers to Schönberg's Serenade Op 24; debut with Royal Opera, Covent Garden in Salome 1997; 37 roles for the Royal Opera including King Marke in Tristan and Isolde, Nightwatchman in Meistersinger, Timur in Turandot, Colline in La Bohème, Angelotti in Tosca, Leone in Atilla and Capellio in I Capuleti; Glyndebourne Festival debut as Commendatore in 2000, Sarastro for Glyndebourne on Tour and New Zealand Opera; Nilakantha in Lakmé, Gremin in Eugene Onegin and Sulpice in La Fille du Régiment for Holland Park Opera; performed roles including Basilio in The Barber of Seville and the Doctor in Punch and Judy for ENO; world premiere of Jonathan Dove's Pinocchio and Swanhunter for Opera North; performed Powder her Face by Adès in Bremen, the Almeida Festival and Channel 4, Die sieben Todsünden and Mahagonny Songspiel at Théâtre des Champs-Élysées, Falstaff at Festspielhaus Baden-Baden, Pinocchio at Staatsoper Stuttgart, Rossini's Stabat Mater with Royal Liverpool Philharmonic Orchestra, Verdi's Requiem at the Queen Elizabeth Hall, The Dream of Gerontius at the Royal Albert Hall, Beethoven's 9th Symphony at the Barbican; currently Prof. of Vocal Studies, Royal Coll. of Music. *Honours:* Tchaikovsky Conservatoire Postgraduate Diploma.1991. *Address:* Royal College of Music, Prince Consort Road, London, SW7 2BS, England (office). *Telephone:* (20) 7591-4300 (office). *Fax:* (20) 7591-4737 (office). *E-mail:* info@ rcm.ac.uk (office). *Website:* www.rcm.ac.uk (office).

BROADSTOCK, Brenton Thomas, BA, DipMus, MMus, AMusTCL, DMus; Australian composer; b. 12 Dec. 1952, Melbourne, Vic.; m.; three c. *Education:* Monash Univ., Memphis State Univ., USA, Univ. of Sydney, University of Music, Univ. of Melbourne, studied with Peter Sculthorpe. *Career:* Tutor in Music, Faculty of Music, Univ. of Melbourne 1982–84, Sr Tutor in Music 1984–87, Sr Lecturer in Music 1989, then Assoc. Prof.; inaugural composer-in-residence, Melbourne Symphony Orchestra 1988; performances include Melbourne Summer Music Festival 1985, Stroud Festival, England 1985, Adelaide Festival 1986, Spoleto Festival, Melbourne 1986, Nova Festival, Brisbane 1987, Music Today Festival, Tokyo 1988, Int. Soc. for Contemporary Music World Days, Hong Kong 1988, Oslo 1990. *Compositions:* Symphony No. 3, four String Quartets, The Mountain for orchestra, Tuba Concerto, Piano Concerto, Battlements for orchestra, Woodwind Quartet, Aureole 104 for flute and piano, for solo bass clarinet, for oboe and piano, for solo piano, Beast from Air for trombone and percussion, many works for brass band, Symphony No. 1 1988, Symphony No. 2 1989, Bright Tracks for soprano and string trio 1994, Celebration for chamber ensemble 1995, Saxophone Concertino 1995, Dancing on a Volcano for orchestra 1996, Catch the Joy (overture) 1998, I Touched Your Glistening Tears for oboe and piano trio 1998. *Honours:* Paul Lowin Prize 1994. *Address:* 20 Simmons Street, Box Hill North, Vic. 3129, Australia.

BROADWAY, Kenneth; American duo pianist; b. 1950. *Education:* Cleveland Institute of Music with Vronsky and Babin. *Career:* formed piano duo partnership with Ralph Markham and has given many recitals and concerts in North America and Europe; BBC debut recital 1979 and further broadcasts on CBC television, Radio France Musique, the Bavarian Radio and Radio Hilversum in Netherlands; Stravinsky's Three Dances from Petrushka at the Théâtre des Champs Elysées, Paris 1984; season 1987–88 included 40 North American recitals, concert with the Vancouver Symphony and New York debut on WQXR Radio; season 1988–89 included the Concertos for Two Pianos by Mozart and Bruch in Canada and a recital tour of England and Germany; performances of the Bartók Sonata for two pianos and percussion, with Evelyn Glennie and a 1990–91 tour of North America, Europe and the Far East; festival appearances include Newport USA 1988. *Recordings include:* Duos by Anton Rubinstein; Vaughan Williams Concerto for Two Pianos; Bartók Sonata for Two Pianos and Percussion. *Honours:* Musical America Magazine Young Artist of the Year (jtly) 1989.

BROCHELER, John; Dutch singer (baritone); b. 21 Feb. 1945, Vaals, Limburg. *Education:* studied at School of Music, Maastricht under Leo Ketelaars, and in Paris under Pierre Bernac. *Career:* sang at first in concert, notably in Bach Passions, Choral Symphony and Brahms Requiem; Berlin Festival in premieres of Die Erprobung de Petrus Hebraicus by Henri Pousseur 1974 and Mare Nostrum by Kagel 1975; San Diego Opera as Sharpless in Madama Butterfly, Ford in Falstaff and in 1979 premiere of Menotti's La Loca, with Beverly Sills; Netherlands Opera as Germont, Don Giovanni and Marcello, and in Donizetti's Maria Stuarda with Joan Sutherland; Frankfurt Opera 1983, as Amfortas in Parsifal; Glyndebourne 1984, as Mandryka in Arabella; Los Angeles Opera as Nabucco; La Scala Milan 1985, as Jochanaan in Salome and Golaud in Pelléas et Mélisande; Stuttgart 1985, in Henze's König Hirsch; other appearances in Toronto, New York and Paris, Vienna 1988 Goulaud in Pelléas et Mélisande, Bonn 1989; Wolfram, Tannhäuser, Munich 1989; Mathis der Maler, Hindemith; sang Orestes in Elektra at Barcelona 1990; Hindemith's Mathis and Von Einem's Danton at 1990 Munich Festival; sang Barak in Die Frau ohne Schatten for Netherlands Opera 1992; Wozzeck, Stuttgart 1993; Simon Boccanegra, Frankfurt 1993; Wanderer in Siegfried 1994; Dr Schön in Lulu, Salzburger Festspiele 1995 and at Berlin Staatsoper 1997; sang Wanderer at Amsterdam 1998; season 1999–2000 as Dr Schön in Lulu at Salzburg and Amfortas in Munich; Hans Sachs at Covent Garden 2002. *Recordings:* Dichterliebe; Handel's Dettinger Te Deum and Judas Maccabaeus; Kindertotenlieder, Mahler; Des Knaben

Wunderhorn (Mahler); Lucrezia Borgia; Das Paradies und Die Peri. *Address:* Beatrixweg 12, 6285 NC Epen, Netherlands. *Website:* www.johnbrocheler .com.

BROCK, Hannes; German singer (tenor); b. 1 Nov. 1952, Stuttgart. *Education:* studied in Berlin and Wuppertal. *Career:* Berlin Theater des Westens 1978–79; Bach's St Matthew Passion with the Berlin Philharmonic 1981; sang at Opera at Hagen, Essen and Dortmund 1981–95; Eutin Festival 1986 in The Bartered Bride and Zeller's Der Vogelhändler; St Gallen Opera from 1995, with guest appearances at Mannheim, Düsseldorf, Dresden and Hamburg; Dortmund Opera 2001, in Wallenberg by Erkki-Sven Tüür, and as Monostatos; roles have included Mozart's Tamino, Mime in Das Rheingold, Handel's Xerxes, Shuisky in Boris Godunov and Beppe in Pagliacci; modern repertory includes the Captain in Wozzeck, Tom Rakewell, Steva in Jenůfa and Weill's Jim Mahoney.

BRODARD, Michael; Swiss singer (bass-baritone); b. 1 April 1946, Fribourg. *Education:* Fribourg Conservatoire, studied with Vermerk Summa. *Career:* concert singer in France and Switzerland; opera engagements at Geneva, Lausanne, Lucerne, Nancy and Metz; further concerts at Brussels, Marseille, Frankfurt, Barcelona, Lisbon, Buenos Aires, Madrid and Warsaw; repertoire ranges from baroque to modern works; fmr mem. Faculty, Musikhochschule Lucerne. *Recordings include:* L'Enfant et les Sortilèges, Pelléas et Mélisande, Bach's Christmas Oratorio, Haydn's St Theresa Mass, Madrigals and Vespers by Monteverdi, Schubert's E-flat Mass and Vivaldi's Psalm 110; Stravinsky's Renard and Les Noces, Masses by Mozart.

BRODERICK, Kathleen; Canadian singer (soprano); b. 1958, Vancouver. *Education:* studied in Montréal, St Louis and New York. *Career:* sang at Kaiserslautern 1984–88, Saarbrucken 1988–91, Berne 1990 as Dvořák's Rusalka; other roles have included Mozart's Fiordiligi, Pamina, Countess Almaviva; Agathe in Der Freischütz, Violetta, Jenny in Mahagonny; Virginia Opera, Salome, 1993; Minnesota Opera as Turandot, 1994; Hamilton Opera, Canada, as Amelia in Un Ballo in Maschera, 1996; Orlando Opera, USA as Leonora in Il Trovatore, 1997; season 1998 with Turandot for Florida Grand Opera, Turandot and Milada in Dalibor for Scottish Opera and Turandot for Flanders Opera at Antwerp; Long Beach Opera as Judith in Bluebeard's Castle, 1999; Lady Macbeth in the Scottish Opera Macbeth at the Edinburgh Festival, 1999; Turandot, Senta/Flying Dutchman, Elektra/title role at Nationaltheater Mannheim, 2000–03; season 2000–01 as Lady Macbeth in Edinburgh, Bregenz, Vienna and Berlin (Deutsche Oper); Abigaille/Nabucco at Semperoper Dresden, 2001; Brünnhilde in ENO's Ring cycle (Valkyrie/ Siegfried/Twilight of the Gods), 2002–05; frequent concert appearances. *Honours:* Susan Chilcott Award 2005, Maggie Teyte Prize 2006, First Prize Kathleen Ferrier Awards 2007, Guildhall School of Music & Drama's Gold Medal 2007. *Current Management:* Artists Management Zürich, Rütistrasse 52, 8044 Zürich-Gockhausen, Switzerland. *Telephone:* (44) 8218957. *Fax:* (44) 8210127. *E-mail:* schuetz@artistsman.com. *Website:* www.artistsman.com.

BROKAW, James Albert, II, BA, PhD; American musicologist; b. 4 Feb. 1951, Princeton, New Jersey; s. of Richard S. Brokaw and Frances A. Brokaw; m. Mollie Sandock 1984. *Education:* Kenyon Coll., Baldwin Wallace Conservatory, Univ. of Chicago. *Career:* Asst Prof. of Music, Northeastern Illinois Univ. 1989–89; Lecturer in Music, Chicago State Univ. 1986–; Lecturer in Music, Univ. of Chicago Open Programme 1987–; Asst Prof. Music History and Theory, Northeastern Illinois Univ. 1989-1991; Program Annotator, Bowdoin Int. Music Festival 2011; mem. Advisory Bd, Riemenschneider Bach Inst. 1982–86; judge, Mu Phi Epsilon Music History Competition 1988'. *Publications include:* Music of the Baroque 1984, 1987, Programme Notes: The Chicago Symphony Orchestra/Performances for Peace 1984–88, Recent Research on the Genesis and Sources of Bach's Well-Tempered Klavier, II, in Bach: The Quarterly Journal of the Riemenschneider Bach Institute 1985, The Genesis of the Prelude in C Major, in Bach Studies, Cambridge Univ. Press 1989, The Perfectibility of J.S. Bach, or Did Bach Compose the Fugue on a Theme By Legrenzi BWV 574a?, in Bach Perspectives I, University of Nebraska Press 1995, The World of Bach's Mass in B Minor: Genesis, Style, and. Performance, Cresset lxviii, Michaelmas 2004; trans.: Georg von Dadelsen, Friedrich Smend's Edition of the B-Minor Mass by J. S. Bach, Bach: The Quarterly Journal of the Riemenschneider Bach Inst. Vol. XX/2 1989; contributed reviews of scholarly editions of keyboard music of J.S. Bach, C.P.E. Bach and Louis Couperin, in Notes, 1985, 1986, 1989. *Honours:* William H. Scheide Research Grant, American Bach Soc. 2005. *Address:* 222 Pennellville Road, Brunswick 04011, USA (home).

BRONDER, Peter, FRAM, ARAM, LGSM; British singer (tenor); b. 22 Oct. 1953, Herefordshire. *Education:* Royal Acad. of Music with Joy Mammen, Nat. Opera Studio. *Career:* Prin. Tenor with WNO 1986–90; Covent Garden debut as Arturo in Lucia di Lammermoor 1986, also Major Domo in Der Rosenkavalier, Youth in Die Frau ohne Schatten 1992, First Jew in Salome 1995, Kudryash in Katya Kabanova 1989, Andres in Wozzeck 1990, Shepherd in Oedipus Rex 1991, Almaviva 1992–93, Alfred in Die Fledermaus and Italian Tenor in Der Rosenkavalier 1993; further appearances include Netherlands Opera as Ernesto 1989, the Prince in Les Brigands 1992, Glyndebourne Festival 1990, performances for WNO in New York 1989, Milan 1989 and Tokyo 1990; debut at Bavarian State Opera, Munich as Mazal in The Adventures of Mr Brouček, also Narraboth 1994, Pedrillo in Die Entführung at Covent Garden, also Istanbul; sang Pylades in Gluck's Iphigenia auf Tauris, Edinburgh 1996, Alexander in Il Re Pastore for Opera North 1998, Mime for

Longborough Festival 2000, also Loge at Edinburgh and in Dallapicolla's Il Prigioniero for ENO, Bajazet in Tamerlano for Berlin Komische Oper 2001 and Luca in Jenufa 2004, Herod in Salome 2002, Narr in Schatzgraber 2003, Telegrafistu in Voli di Notte 2004, Der Zweng for Oper Frankfurt 2007, Pedrillo in San Francisco 2002, Dr Cains in Falstaff for Metropolitan Opera 2005, Loge in Stuttgart 2005, Herod, Loge for Flanders Opera 2007, Herod in Salome, La Scala 2007; concert appearances in London, Paris, Vienna, Lisbon and for the Australian Broadcasting Company, Perth. *Recordings include:* Mozart Arias with Kiri Te Kanawa, recital recordings of Turco in Italia, Adriana Lecouvreur, Osud, Beethoven 9, La Traviata, Ballo in Maschera, The Rake's Progress, Falstaff, Wozzeck. *Address:* Ivy Cottage, 47 Station Road, Tempsford, nr. Sandy, Beds., SG19 2AU, England.

BRONFMAN, Yefim; Russian pianist; b. 10 April 1958, Tashkent, Uzbekistan. *Education:* Juilliard School of Music, New York, USA, Curtis Inst., Philadelphia, studied with Rudolf Serkin and Arie Vardi. *Career:* debut, Israel Philharmonic with Kostalanetz 1974; soloist with Montreal Symphony Orchestra, Philadelphia, Los Angeles Philharmonic, New York Philharmonic, Minnesota Orchestra, Mostly Mozart Orchestra, English Chamber Orchestra, St Louis Symphony Orchestra, Scottish Chamber Orchestra, Vancouver Symphony Orchestra, Pittsburgh Symphony Orchestra, London Philharmonia, St Paul Chamber Orchestra, Houston Symphony Orchestra, Toronto Symphony Orchestra, Goteborg Symphony Orchestra, Royal Philharmonic, San Francisco Symphony Orchestra, Berlin Philharmonic, Chicago Symphony Orchestra, Baltimore Symphony Orchestra, Rotterdam Philharmonic, Bournemouth Symphony Orchestra, Cleveland Orchestra, Nat. Symphony Orchestra, Rochester Philharmonic, Jerusalem Symphony Orchestra, Winnipeg Symphony Orchestra, Richmond Symphony Orchestra, New Jersey Symphony. *Recordings:* all Fauré; Prokofiev Violin Sonatas with Shlomo Mintz; Musical Heritage, Brahms Sonata in F minor and Scherzo Op 4; Mozart Sonatas for violin and piano with Robert Mann; Prokofiev Piano Sonatas 7 and 8; Mussorgsky, Pictures at an Exhibition, Stravinsky, 3 scenes from Petrushka; Rachmaninov: Piano Concertos 2 and 3, with Esa-Pekka Salonen and Philharmonia Orchestra, 1992; Prokofiev: Piano Concertos 1, 3 and 5, with Zubin Mehta and Israel Philharmonic, 1993. *Honours:* American-Israeli Cultural Foundation Scholarship 1974, Avery Fisher Prize 1991. *Current Management:* Opus 3 Artists, 470 Park Avenue South, 9th Floor North, New York, NY 10016, USA. *Telephone:* (212) 584-7500. *Fax:* (646) 300-8200. *E-mail:* info@opus3artists.com. *Website:* www.opus3artists.com; www .yefimbronfman.com.

BRONK, Stephen; American singer (bass-baritone); b. 1958, Hyannis, Mass. *Education:* Aachen Musikhochschule. *Career:* debut as Justifiar in Kienzl's Evangelimann, Bregenz 1984; appearances in opera at Bremerhaven and Saarbrucken; Bonn Opera from 1993 as Mozart's Osmin, Figaro, Alfonso and Speaker in Die Zauberflöte; Grand Inquisitor in Don Carlos and King in Aida; sang Pizarro in Fidelio at Bonn 1995, and in Janáček's From the House of the Dead at Strasbourg 1996; other roles include Fasolt, Alberich and Hunding in The Ring; concerts include Beethoven's Ninth at Bonn 1994; sang Pizarro in Fidelio and Don Alfonso at Dusseldorf 1999–2000; currently mem. ensemble, Deutsche Oper Berlin. *Address:* Deutsche Oper Berlin, Bismarckstr. 35, 10627 Berlin, Germany. *Website:* www.deutscheoperberlin.de.

BRÖNNIMANN, Baldur; Swiss conductor; *Artistic Director, BIT20 Ensemble. Education:* Basel Music Acad., Royal Northern Coll. of Music. *Career:* has worked closely with composers including Saariaho, Birtwistle, Chin, Adès, with orchestras including Stockholm Philharmonic, Seoul Philharmonic, BBC Symphony and at festivals including Settembre Musicale, Milan, Musica Nova, Helsinki, Ultraschall, Berlin; performs both contemporary and earlier 20th-century repertoire regularly with orchestras including Bergen Philharmonic, Iceland Symphony, Scottish Chamber, Porto Symphony, amongst others; conducted La Fura dels Baus production of Ligeti's Le Grand Macabre at ENO 2009; returned to London's Coliseum to conduct Tom Morris's new production of John Adams's Death of Klinghoffer with ENO 2012; returned to Teatro Colón, Buenos Aires for a double-bill of Schoenberg Erwartung and Szymanowski's rarely heard Hagith 2012; debut at Komische Oper Berlin with Barry Kosky's production of the same work 2013; 2012–13 season highlights included Komische Oper debut, performances of Tan Dun's Marco Polo at Bergen Int. Festival, concerts in Austria and Buenos Aires with Klangforum Wien, a return to the London Sinfonietta, performances of Prokofiev Symphony No. 2 with Malmo Symphony, Nielsen Symphony No. 5 with Bergen Philharmonic, Berlioz Symphonie Fantastique with Iceland Symphony; Music Dir Nat. Symphony Orchestra of Colombia, Bogotá 2009–12, est. an annual symphonic festival and various educational activities;, initiatives included a performance of original version of Falla's El amor brujo with the flamenco singer Carmen Linares, performances with soloists including Valentina Lisitsa, Gabriela Montero, Johannes Moser, Benjamin Schmid, and many Colombian premieres, including Bartók's The Miraculous Mandarin; Artistic Dir BIT20 contemporary music ensemble (Norway) 2011–, season 2012–13 included music by Varese, Zappa, Wallin, amongst others, season 2013–14 programmes included Crumb, Birtwistle, Romitelli, Steen-Andersen; debuts with Oslo Philharmonic, Royal Stockholm Philharmonic, Helsinki Philharmonic, Copenhagen Philharmonic, Orchestre Philharmonique de Strasbourg, Royal Scottish Nat. Orchestra, Philharmonia Orchestra; returns to Teatro Colón for performances of Nono's Promoteo and Lachenmann's Little Match Girl; returns to Klangforum Wien at Theater An Der Wien with Barbara Hannigan and Romitelli's An Index of Metals; participated in Birtwistle's 80th birthday celebrations at the Barbican Centre with Britten Sinfonia; returns to Iceland Symphony, Porto Symphony, London Sinfonietta; conducted Saariaho's L'amour de loin at Norwegian Opera. *Current Management:* c/o Intermusica Artists' Management Ltd, 36 Graham Street, London, N1 8GJ, England. *Telephone:* (20) 7608-9900. *Fax:* (20) 7490-3263. *E-mail:* lgunes@intermusica.co.uk. *Website:* www.intermusica.co.uk. *E-mail:* baldur@baldur.info (home). *Website:* www.baldur.info.

BROOK, Peter Stephen Paul, CH, CBE, MA; British theatre director, film director and writer; b. 21 March 1925, Chiswick, London, England; s. of Simon Brook; m. Natasha Parry 1951; one s. one d. *Education:* Westminster and Gresham's Schools and Magdalen Coll., Oxford. *Career:* joined RSC 1962; Producer, Co-Dir Royal Shakespeare Theatre; f. Centre for Theatre Research, Paris 1970, opened Théâtre des Bouffes du Nord, Paris 1974–2010, Co-Dir with Stéphane Lissner (q.v.) 1998–2005; Dir Int. Centre for Theatre Creations. *Films include:* The Beggar's Opera 1952, Moderato Cantabile 1959, Lord of the Flies 1963, Marat/Sade 1967, Tell Me Lies 1967, King Lear 1969, Meetings With Remarkable Men 1976–77, La Tragédie de Carmen 1983, The Mahabharata 1989 (also producer), The Tragedy of Hamlet 2002. *Productions include:* Dr Faustus 1943, Pygmalion, King John, Lady from the Sea 1945, Romeo and Juliet (at Stratford) 1947, Dir of Productions at Covent Garden Opera 1949–50, Faust (at Metropolitan Opera, New York) 1953, The Dark is Light Enough (London) 1954, House of Flowers (New York) 1954, Cat on a Hot Tin Roof (Paris) 1956, Eugene Onegin (New York) 1958, View from the Bridge (Paris) 1958, The Fighting Cock (New York) 1959, Irma la Douce 1960, King Lear 1963, The Physicists (New York) 1964, The Marat/Sade (New York) 1965, US (London) 1966, Oedipus (Seneca) 1968, A Midsummer Night's Dream 1970, Orghast (Iran) 1971, The Conference of the Birds 1973, Timon of Athens (Paris) 1974, The Ik (Paris) 1975, (London) 1976, (USA) 1976, Ubu (Paris) 1977, Meetings with Remarkable Men (film, also dir screenplay) 1977, Antony and Cleopatra (Stratford and London) 1978, Measure for Measure (Paris) 1978, Conference of the Birds, L'os (Festival Avignon and Paris) 1979, (New York) 1980, The Cherry Orchard (Paris) 1981, (New York) 1988, (Moscow) 1989, La Tragédie de Carmen (opera) (Paris) 1981, (film) 1983, Le Mahabharata (Avignon and Paris) 1985, (world tour) 1988, Woza Albert! (Paris) 1989, La Tempête (Paris) 1990, Impressions de Pelléas (opera) 1992, L'Homme Qui (Paris) 1993, 1997, The Man Who 1994, Oh! Les Beaux Jours (Lausanne) 1995, (Paris) 1996, Don Giovanni (opera) 1998, Je suis un phénomène (Paris) 1998, Le Costume (Paris) 1999, The Tragedy of Hamlet (Paris) 2000, Far Away (Paris) 2002, La Tragédie d'Hamlet (Paris) 2002, La Mort de Krishna (Paris) 2002, Ta Main Dans La Mienne (Paris) 2003, Tierno Bokar (Paris) 2004, Le Grand Inquisiteur (Paris) 2004, Fragments (Paris, London, New York) 2008, Warum Warum 2008, Love Is My Sin (Paris), Eleven and Twelve (London) 2009, Une Flûte Enchantée (opera) (world tour) 2010–11, The Suit (Paris and world tour) 2012. *Publications:* The Empty Space 1968, The Shifting Point: Forty years of theatrical exploration 1946–87, 1987, There Are No Secrets 1993 (appeared in USA as The Open Door: Thoughts on Acting and the Theatre), Threads of Time (autobiog.) 1998, Evoking Shakespeare 1999, The Quality of Mercy: Reflections on Shakespeare 2013. *Honours:* Officier des Arts et des Lettres, Légion d'honneur, Praemium Imperiale; Hon. DLitt (Birmingham), (Strathclyde) 1990; Freiherr von Stein Foundation, Shakespeare Award 1973, Wexner Prize (Ohio State Univ.) 1991, Onassis Int. Award 1993, Times Award 1994, Dan David Prize 2005. *Address:* CIRT, 37 bis boulevard de la Chapelle, 75010 Paris, France (office).

BROPHY, David; Irish conductor; *Principal Conductor, RTÉ Concert Orchestra*; b. Dublin. *Career:* fmr Apprentice Conductor, Nat. Chamber Choir of Ireland; fmr Asst Conductor, RTÉ Nat. Symphony Orchestra of Ireland; Prin. Conductor, RTÉ Concert Orchestra 2007–; has also conducted Vancouver Symphony Orchestra, Nat. Classical Orchestra of Andorra (ONCA), Irish Chamber Orchestra, Ulster Orchestra, Orchestra of the Nat. Concert Hall; has worked with soloists, ensembles and artists including Tasmin Little, Lesley Garrett, Vox21, Crash Ensemble, Paul Brady, Brian Kennedy, The Chieftains, Sharon Shannon; collaborations with opera cos including Co-Opera, Lyric Opera Productions, Opera Theatre Co., Northern Irish Opera; Lecturer, DIT Conservatory of Music and Drama; has given world premieres of works by Irish composers including Frank Corcoran, Raymond Deane, Fergus Johnston, Philip Martin, Ian Wilson. *Address:* c/o Anthony Long, General Manager, RTÉ Performing Groups, Admin Building, RTÉ, Donnybrook, Dublin 4, Ireland (office). *Telephone:* (1) 2082779 (office). *Fax:* (1) 2082511 (office). *E-mail:* anthony.long@rte.ie (office). *Website:* www.rte.ie/orchestras/rteconcertorchestra (office).

BROPHY, Gerard; Australian composer; *Lecturer in Composition, Griffith University*; b. 7 Jan. 1953, Sydney. *Education:* masterclasses with Turibio Santos, NSW State Conservatorium of Music, Accademia Nazionale de Santa Cecilia, Rome, Accademia Chigiana di Siena. *Career:* Composer in Residence, Musica Viva Australia 1983, Australian Chamber Orchestra 1986, Queensland Conservatorium of Music 1987, Pittsburgh New Music Ensemble 1988, Queensland Conservatorium of Music 1989; currently Lecturer in Composition, Grifffith Univ. *Compositions include:* Orchestral Works: Orfeo 1984, Le Reveil de L'Ange 1987, Matho 1987, Forbidden Colours 1988, Les Roses Sanglantes 1990, Lautreamont 1992, Xanthe 1992, Danse de l'extase 2002, Halcyon, ballet in six scenes for orchestra and electronica 2010, The Blue Thread 2010; Ensemble Works: Lace 1985, Mercurio 1985, Spur 1988, Head 1988, Séraphita 1988, Forbidden Colours 1988, Frisson 1989; Vocal Works: Flesh 1987, Shiver 1989; Instrumental Works: Chiarissima 1987, Pink Chair Light Green Violet Violent FLASH 1990, Vorrei Baciarti, for baritone and chamber ensemble 1991, Tweak, for piccolo 1991, Pluck It!, for solo guitar 1992, Twist, for solo clarinet 1993, Tudo Liquido, for wind and percussion 1994, Colour Red... Your Mouth... Heart, for orchestra 1994, Es, for solo flute 1994, Bisoux, for english horn and bass clarinet 1994, Umbigada, Obrigado!, for percussion quartet 1995, Trip, for wind ensemble 1996, Coil 1996, Crimson Songs, for soprano and ensemble 1997, Samba Mauve 1997, Merge–a memoir of the senses for percussion quartet, large orchestra and sound design (commissioned by Melbourne Symphony Orchestra) 1998, Hot Metallic Blues, for electric bass and ensemble 1999, Ru B fogo, for ensemble 1999, Birds of Paradise, for guitar orchestra 1999, Body Map, for ensemble 1999, Yo Yai Pakebi, Man Mai Yapobi, for African percussion and large orchestra 1999, Heavy Metal Boyhood, for ensemble 2000, Pink Edges, for six voices 2000, Abraco, for solo piano 2000, Sheer Nylon Dances, for violin, cello and piano 2001, ...Vision Fugitive, for violin, cello and piano 2001, Danses Veloutées, for solo viola and orchestra 2001, ...Danse de l'Extase, for orchestra 2001, Chorinho Pra Ela, for bass clarinet 2002, Berceuse, for SATB motet 2002, Pas de Deux, for clarinet and cello 2002, Concerto in Blue, for guitar and orchestra 2002, Trance Ripples, for solo marimba 2002, Topolo-NRG, for baritone sax, double bass and piano 2002, mFm, for soprano/baritone sax, bass guitar, marimba and piano 2002, Chi's Cakewalk, for solo bass clarinet 2002, Songo, for percussion quintet 2002, Mantras, for orchestra 2003 Brisbane Drumming, for percussion 2003, Choro Pra Linos, for wind quintet 2003, Phobia, for music theatre performers 2003, Maracatu, for orchestra 2003, Songs of the North, for soprano and ensemble 2004, Cancao, for wind quintet 2004, Frevo, for wind quintet 2004, Wind Around my Heart 2007. *Recordings include:* Hydra, Synergy Percussion; Nadja, Sydney Symphony Orchestra; Shiver, Elision; Head, Het Trio; Nymphe-Echo Morphologique, Laura Chislett; November Snow, Music Box; Forbidden Colours, Queensland Symphony Orchestra; Angelicon, Lisa Moore; Breathless, Laura Chislett; Twist (Philippa Robinson, Floyd Williams, Roslyn Dunlop); Bisous (Barry Davis and Floyd Williams, Philippa Robinson, Roslyn Dunlop, Deborah de Graaff); Pluck It! (Ken Murray, Peter Constant); We Bop (Duo Contemporain, Margery Smith and Daryl Pratt); Charm, Marshall McGuire, Geoffrey Collins and Patricia Pollett; NRG, Henri Bok; Obsidian, Ex Novo Ensemble; Birds of Paradise, Guitarstrophy; Glove, six_new music ensemble; Crimson Songs, Perihelion; Pearl licks, pearl rub, pearl dub, Two Complete Lunatics; the Room of the Saints, Patricia Pollett and Daryl Pratt; Chorinho pra Ela, Henri Bok. *Honours:* numerous grants and fellowships including: Composer Fellowship, Australia Council Music Board, 1982, 1983; Italian Government Scholarship. *Address:* 26 Nott Street, Red Hill, Qld 4059, Australia (home). *Telephone:* (7) 3217-6609 (home). *E-mail:* gerardbrophy@optusnet.com.au (home). *Website:* www.gerardbrophy.com.au (home).

BROS, José; Spanish singer (tenor); b. 1965, Barcelona. *Education:* Barcelona Conservatory. *Career:* debut in Carmina Burana at Palma, 1987; many performances in leading roles at major opera houses, 1992–; Duke of Mantua at Palma and Nadir in Les Pêcheurs de Perles, followed by Percy in Anna Bolena, at Barcelona; leads in La Favorita at Las Palmas, Falstaff and I Capuleti at Lisbon, Lucia di Lammermoor at Zürich, Don Pasquale and Così fan tutte at Bilbao and L'Elisir d'amore (Nemorino, Covent Garden, 1997); further engagements at Hamburg, Vienna, Rome, Naples, Munich, Florence (Edgardo, under Zubin Mehta, at the Maggio Musicale), Bologna and Marseille; Nemorino at Barcelona and Madrid; Edgardo at Barcelona and Donizetti's Roberto Devereux at Hamburg (concert), 2000; recitals and concerts throughout Europe and in London. *Current Management:* Miguel Lerin, La Rambla 54, 2°, 1a, 08002 Barcelona, Spain.

BROSTER, Eileen; British pianist; b. 23 June 1935, London, England; m. R. Chaplin 1972; one s. *Education:* Royal Coll. of Music with Frank Merrick and Cyril Smith. *Career:* debut at Wigmore Hall; performed on BBC radio and television; appeared in all South Bank Halls; toured extensively as soloist in recitals and concerti; performances at Wigmore Hall; mem. Incorporated Soc. of Musicians, EPTA.

BROTT, Boris, OC, FRSA; Canadian conductor; *Music Director, McGill Chamber Orchestra*; b. 14 March 1944, Montréal; m. Ardyth Webster; two s. one d. *Education:* Conservatoire de Musique, Montréal, McGill Univ., Montréal, studied with Pierre Monteux, Igor Markevitch, Leonard Bernstein, Alexander Brott. *Career:* debut as violinist with Montréal Symphony 1949; founder and Conductor, Philharmonic Youth Orchestra, Montréal 1959–61; Asst Conductor, Toronto Symphony Orchestra 1963–65, New York Philharmonic 1968–69; Music Dir, Northern Sinfonia Orchestra, England 1964–69, Royal Ballet, Covent Garden 1966–68, including the Covent Garden premiere of Stravinsky's The Soldier's Tale, Lakehead Univ., Thunder Bay, ON 1967–72, Regina Symphony 1970–73; Conductor and Music Dir, Hamilton Philharmonic Orchestra 1969–90, Ontario Place Pops Orchestra 1983–91; Chief Conductor, BBC Nat. Orchestra of Wales 1972–77, CBC Symphony 1976–83; Pres., Great Music Canada 1977–; Artistic Dir, Stratford Summer Music Festival, ON 1982–84, Brott Music Festivals, Hamilton, ON 1988–95, Nat. Acad. Orchestra 1988–; Conductor, McGill Orchestra, Montréal, QC 1989–; Conductor and Music Dir, Ventura Symphony, Ventura, CA 1990–95; Conductor and Man. Dir, New West Symphony, Los Angeles 1995–; Music Dir, New West Symphony, CA 1996–, McGill Chamber Orchestra 2001–; Prin. Youth and Family Conductor, Nat. Arts Centre Orchestra 2002–; guest conductor at many British orchestras, major Canadian orchestras, and in the USA, Republic of Korea, Japan, Germany, France, Sweden, Israel, Mexico, El

Salvador, Italy, Denmark; Principal Guest Conductor and Music Adviser, Symphony Nova Scotia 1981–; Co-Conductor, McGill Chamber Orchestra 1989; Guest Conductor, Sadler's Wells Opera, Canadian Opera Company, Edmonton Opera; writer, host and conductor of more than 100 television programmes in the UK, USA and Canada; conducted for Pope John Paul II at the Vatican 2000. *Recordings include:* suites from operas by Handel, Dvořák's Serenade op 44, symphonies by Richter, Holzbauer and Cannabich, Sibelius Pelléas, Ravel Le Tombeau de Couperin. *Honours:* Knight of Malta 1990, Order of Ontario 2006; Hon. LLD (McMaster Univ.) 1988; Int. Man of the Year 1992, Nat. Child Day Award (Inst. of Child Health) 2007, City of Hamilton Lifetime Achievement Arts Award 2007. *Telephone:* (905) 525-7664 (office). *Fax:* (905) 526-9934 (office). *E-mail:* boxoffice@brottmusic.com (office). *Website:* www.brottmusic.com (office); www.borisbrott.com.

BROTT, Denis; Canadian cellist; b. 9 Sept. 1950, Québec; s. of Alexander Brott; m. 1976; one s. three d. *Education:* Univ. of Southern California, USA with Gregor Piatigorsky. *Career:* festivals include Marlboro, Aspen, Hampden-Sydney, Orford and Sitka; Artistic Dir, Festival of the Sound, ON 1991; faculty mem., Music Acad. of the West, Santa Barbara 1993–94 summer season, performing chamber music at festivals in Hampden-Sydney, Virginia and Sitka Alaska; jury mem., Evian Int. String Quartet Competition in France 1993, also recitalist, chamber artist and soloist with orchestra; Prof. of Cello and Chamber Music, Conservatoire de Musique de Montréal; established a two-week Festival de Musique de Chambre de Montréal 1995, a celebration of chamber music in the Chateau de Belvedere atop Mont Royal; jury mem., Munich String Quartet Competition 1996; guest lecturer for the Piatigorsky Seminar for Cellists, Univ. of Southern California in Los Angeles 1997. *Recordings include:* 20 chamber music works including the complete string quartets of Beethoven with the Orford String Quartet and Homage to Piatigorsky; works of Alexander Brott, featuring Arabesque for Cello and Orchestra 1993. *Address:* 201 Brock Avenue North, Montréal, QC H4X 2G1, Canada.

BROUGH, Paul; British conductor; *Principal Guest Conductor, BBC Singers*; b. 15 July 1963, London. *Education:* Portsmouth Grammar School, Dulwich Coll., Royal Coll. of Music, St Michael's Coll., Tenbury, Magdalen Coll., Oxford; studied with Colin Metters and George Hurst as RAM Henry Wood Scholar and post-student Fellow; masterclasses with Sir Colin Davis, Ilya Musin and Jeffrey Tate. *Career:* fmr Conductor, Oxford Univ. Chamber Orchestra; Master of the Music, Sheffield Cathedral 1991–94; sang professionally with Schütz Choir, London Voices and BBC Singers; Prin. Conductor, Hanover Band (period orchestra) 2007–10; Prin. Guest Conductor, BBC Singers 2011–; fmr Guest Conductor BBC Philharmonic, BBC Concert Orchestra, Britten Sinfonia, Manchester Camerata, St James's Baroque, Ulster Orchestra; Assoc., Acad. of Music 2007. *Address:* The BBC Singers, Maida Vale Studios, Delaware Road, Maida Vale, London, W9 2LG, England (office). *E-mail:* office@paulbrough.com (office). *Website:* www.paulbrough.co.uk (office).

BROUWER, Leovigildo (Leo); Cuban composer, conductor and classical guitarist; b. 1 March 1939, Havana. *Education:* studied with Isaac Nicola, Peyrellade Conservatoire, Havana, Juilliard School, , USA with Stefan Wolpe and Vincent Persichetti, Hartt Coll. with Isadore Freed. *Career:* debut 1956; Dir Music Dept, Instituto Cubano 1960; teacher, Nat. Conservatory, Havana 1961–67, Dir experimental dept of Cuban film music from 1967; created the Experimentación de Sonidos (with Silvio Rodriguez and Pablo Milanes) 1968; many tours as guitar soloist; guitar competition founded in his honour, Japan 1984; fmr conductor, Orquesta de Cuba; Co-founder, Orchestra de Córdoba, Spain 1992. *Compositions for film:* Historias de la revolución 1960, Papeles son papeles 1966, La Muerte de un burócrata 1966, Hanoi, martes 13 1967, Las Aventuras de Juan Quin Quin 1967, Memorias del subdesarrollo 1968, La Primera carga al machete 1969, La Bataille des dix millions 1971, Un Día de noviembre 1972, Una Pelea cubana contra los demonios 1972, Ustedes tienen la palabra 1973, El Extraño caso de Rachel K 1973, El Hombre de Maisinicú 1973, Rancheador 1975, La Cantata de Chile 1975, El Otro Francisco 1975, La Última cena 1976, Destino manifiesto 1977, Son o no son 1978, El Recurso del método 1978, No hay sábado sin sol 1979, Los Sobrevivientes 1979, La Viuda de Montiel 1979, Una y otra vez 1982, Cecilia 1982, Alsino y el cóndor 1982, Tiempo de amar 1983, Los Refugiados de la cueva del muerto 1983, Amada 1983, La Rosa de los vientos 1983, Hasta cierto punto 1983, La Segunda hora de Esteban Zayas 1984, Jíbaro 1984, Tiempo de morir 1985, Visa USA 1986, Como agua para chocolate 1992, Mátame mucho 1998, Ficción sin ficción 2002, Memorias de Lucía 2003, Lucía y el tiempo 2004, La Persistence de la memoria 2004, Kordavision 2005. *Compositions include:* Homenaje a Manuel de Falla 1958, Sonograms for prepared piano 1963, Balada for flute and orchestra 1963, Tropos for orchestra 1967, Hexahedron for six players 1969, Flute Concerto 1972, Homenaje a Lenin for electronics, five guitar concertos 1972–92, Doble Concierto for violin, guitar and orchestra 1995, Lamento for Rafael Orozco for clarinet and strings 1996, Concierto No.7 La Habana 1998, Concierto No.8 Cantata de Perugia 1999, Viaje a la Semilla 2000, La Danza Imposible for orchestra 2001, Pictures of Another Exhibition 2001, An Idea 2001, Nuevos Estudios Sencillos 2002, Concierto de Benicassim for guitar and orchestra 2002, La Ciudad De Las Columnas 2004, Paisaje Cubano con fiesta 2007, many smaller pieces for guitar. *Honours:* Latin Grammy Award for Best Classical Album (for Integral Cuartetos de Cuerda) 2010. *Current Management:* c/o Chester Music and Novello & Co., 14–15 Berners Street, London, W1T 3LJ, England.

BROWN, Christopher Roland, MA, FRAM; British composer; b. 17 June 1943, Tunbridge Wells, Kent; m. 1st Anne Smillie 1969; one s. one d.; m. 2nd Fiona Caithness 1985; one s. *Education:* Westminster Abbey Choir School, Dean Close School, Cheltenham, King's Coll., Cambridge, Royal Acad. of Music, London, Hochschule für Musik, Berlin, Germany. *Career:* freelance composer 1968–; mem. of faculty, Royal Acad. of Music 1969–; Conductor, Huntingdonshire Philharmonic 1976–91, 1994–95; Composer-in-Residence, Nene Coll., Northampton 1986–88; Conductor, Dorset Bach Cantata Club 1988–; Conductor, New Cambridge Singers 1997–. *Compositions include:* Triptych, The Sun: Rising, Organ Concerto, Festive Prelude, Festival Variations, four operas, two String Quartets, Chamber Music for five instruments, Images, Ruscelli d'oro, La Légende de l'etoile; choral works: David, A Hymn to the Holy Innocents, Three Medieval Lyrics, Magnificat, Chauntecleer, The Vision of Saul, The Snows of Winter, Hodie Salvator Apparuit, Tres Canti Sacri, Landscapes, The Circling Year; numerous songs, carols, church music, Mass for four voices 1991, Christmas Cantata 1992, The Ship of Fools 1992, Star Song I 1994, Summer Winds 1995, Star Song III 1996, Brown the Bear 1997, Star Song IV 1999, Invocation 1999, To the Hills 2000, Dance Variants 2001, Like a Child 2002, Star Song V 2005. *Recordings include:* Laudate Dominum (Dean Close School Choir), Laudate Dominum (Canterbury Cathedral Choir), 'Tis Christmas Time (Huntingdonshire Philharmonic and Canticum), Seascape (British Chamber Choir and Brass Unlimited). *Address:* Halefield Lodge, Oundle Road, Woodnewton, Peterborough, PE8 5EG, England. *Telephone:* (1832) 274226. *E-mail:* cb@cbmusic.freeserve.co.uk.

BROWN, Donna; Canadian/French singer (soprano); b. 15 Feb. 1955, Renfrew, Ont., Canada; d. of Laurence Brown and Florence Yonin; m. James Zaluski. *Education:* studied with Edith Mathis in Salzburg, Noemi Perugia in Paris, Randy Mickelson in Venice, McGill Univ., Montreal, Franz Schubert Institut, Vienna, Austria. *Career:* opera debut in Paris as Michaela in Peter Brook's Tragédie de Carmen; has sung Pamina in Die Zauberflöte, Sophie in Der Rosenkavalier, Almirena in Rinaldo, Gilda in Rigoletto, Nanetta in Falstaff, Rosina in Il barbiere di Siviglia, Servillia in La Clemenza di Tito, Zerlina in Don Giovanni, Morgana in Alcina, Aricie in Hippolyte et Aricie, Scylla in Scylla et Glaucus, Madaleine in Postillon du Longjumeau, and Michaela in Carmen; also appeared as Chimène in world premiere of Debussy's unfinished opera Rodrigue et Chimène; appearances with London Philharmonic, Nat. Arts Centre Orchestra, San Francisco Symphony, Orchestre Nat. de France, Orchestre de Paris, Orquestra Sinfonica Brasileira, Orchestra Santa Cecilia di Roma, and others. *Recordings include:* Rodrigue et Chimène, Brahms' Requiem, Die Schöpfung, Lieder by Fanny Mendelssohn, Debussy Mélodies de Jeunesse, Bachianas Brasileiras. *Current Management:* c/o Opéra et Concerts, 37 rue de la Chaussée d'Antin, 75009 Paris, France. *Telephone:* 1-42-96-18-18. *Fax:* 1-42-96-18-00. *E-mail:* agence@opera-concert.com. *Website:* www.opera-concert.com. *E-mail:* villapamina@magma.ca.

BROWN, Ian; British pianist and conductor; b. 1955, England. *Career:* began as a bassoonist, then became Pianist-in-Residence, Southampton University; concerto soloist with many leading British orchestras including BBC Symphony Orchestra, BBC National Orchestra of Wales, Bournemouth Symphony Orchestra, performing in major European and Scandinavian countries, the Middle East, North and South America, Singapore, Hong Kong and Japan; pianist with Nash Ensemble from 1978, playing in the annual Wigmore series and at all major British festivals; has appeared in duo with Mstislav Rostropovich, Henryk Szeryng, Ruggiero Ricci, Elisabeth Söderström, Felicity Lott, Ralph Kirshbaum, György Pauk, James Galway and others; soloist in Messiaen's Oiseaux Exotiques at the Proms; toured Germany with BBC Philharmonic Orchestra in concerts celebrating Hans Werner Henze's 60th birthday; appearances as conductor with Northern Sinfonia, the City of London Sinfonia, Scottish Chamber Orchestra and Bournemouth Symphony Orchestra and Sinfonietta; London conducting debut at the Barbican (Mahler's Resurrection Symphony with the Salomon Orchestra and London Choral Society). *Recordings:* chamber music from Haydn to the present day, with the Nash Ensemble. *Telephone:* (20) 8459-3589.

BROWN, John, OBE; British violinist; b. 1943, Yorkshire, England. *Education:* Royal Manchester Coll. of Music with Endre Wolf and György Pauk, Salzburg Mozarteum. *Career:* co-Leader, London Symphony Orchestra 1968, Leader 1973; Leader, Orchestra of the Royal Opera House, Covent Garden 1976–96; solo appearances with the BBC Scottish, BBC Symphony and London Symphony Orchestras; plays a Stradivarius violin. *Honours:* prizewinner BBC Violin Competition 1966.

BROWN, Justin; British conductor; *Music Director Laureate, Alabama Symphony Orchestra*; b. 1962, England. *Education:* Trinity Coll., Cambridge, and at Tanglewood with Rozhdestvensky, Ozawa and Bernstein. *Career:* appearances with the London Symphony Orchestra, Royal Philharmonic Orchestra, BBC Symphony, Royal Liverpool Philharmonic, London Symphony, Oslo Philharmonic, Finnish Radio Symphony, Bergen Philharmonic, Lahti Symphony, Dresden Philharmonic, Iceland Symphony, Berlin Symphony, St Petersburg Philharmonic, Swedish Chamber Orchestra, Orchestre National du Capitole de Toulouse, Malaysian Philharmonic, Tokyo Philharmonic, Sydney Symphony, Indianapolis Symphony, Dallas Symphony, ENO, Teatro San Carlo, Lisbon, Staatsoper Stuttgart, Alte Oper Frankfurt, Den Norske Opera; as pianist, chamber music recitals in UK and Scandinavia, concertos (Beethoven, Mozart, Bach) directed from the keyboard; Music Dir Alabama Symphony Orchestra 2006, now Music Director Laureate; Music Dir

Badisches Staatstheater, Karlsruhe 2008–. *Recordings include:* Elgar Cello Concertos with City of Birmingham Symphony Orchestra, Barber Cello Concertos with City of Birmingham Symphony Orchestra, Gershwin's Complete Music for Piano and Orchestra with Dallas Symphony; Bernstein and Candide with Scottish Opera; Tavener's The Protecting Veil with Wallfisch Royal Philharmonic Orchestra, Jesper Koch's Orchestral Works with Odense Symphony Orchestra; works by Elliott Carter, Poul Ruders, Peter Lieberson. *Honours:* winner, London Mozart Players Best Young Conductor 1990. *Current Management:* c/o Patricia Handy, Schmidt Artists International, Inc., 59 East 54th Street, Suite 83, New York, NY 10022, USA. *Telephone:* (212) 421-8500. *Fax:* (212) 421-8583. *E-mail:* mph@schmidtart .com; info@schmidtart.com. *Website:* www.schmidtart.com; www .justinbrownconductor.com.

BROWN, Paul; British stage designer; b. 1960, Vale of Glamorgan, Wales. *Education:* studied with Margaret Harris. *Career:* designs for Monteverdi's Poppea at Bologna, Philidor's Tom Jones and Grétry's Zémire et Azor at Drottningholm; Royal Opera, Covent Garden with Mitridate, The Midsummer Marriage, I Masnadieri and Falstaff 2000; Lulu and Pelléas et Mélisande at Glyndebourne; Parsifal at the Opéra Bastille, Paris; Don Carlos for Opera Australia and Fidelio for ENO; Metropolitan Opera, New York, with Schoenberg's Moses und Aron and Lady Macbeth by Shostakovich; designs for Purcell's King Arthur for the Châtelet, Paris, and Covent Garden 1995; season 2000–01 with Peter Grimes at the Bastille.

BROWN, Rachel; American flautist and recorder player; b. 1962. *Education:* Royal Northern Coll. of Music, England. *Career:* Principal Flautist, King's Consort, the Hanover Band, Acad. of Ancient Music and the Brandenburg Consort; concerto performances on tour in Japan, Europe and America; fmr Prof., RNCM, Manchester, England; teacher, Guildhall School, London and Royal Coll. of Music 2000–; performances with the London Handel Festival 2001. *Recordings include:* Concertos by Vivaldi, Quantz, Handel, Telemann, J.S. and J.C. Bach; Sonatas by Schubert and Boehm; Concertos by Quantz and C.P.E. Bach. *Honours:* winner American Nat. Flute Competition 1984.

BROWNER, Alison, BA; Irish singer (mezzo-soprano); b. 22 Sept. 1958, Dublin; m. Wilhelm Gries, one s. one d. *Education:* Trinity College, Dublin, School of Music, Dublin, studied with Hans Hotter in Munich. *Career:* debut at Ludwigsburger Schloss Festspiele; National Theatre, Mannheim; Appeared at Bayreuth, Stuttgart, Zürich, Brussels, Antwerp, Covent Garden, Wexford Opera Festival, Staatsoper Berlin; Roles include La Cenerentola, Rosina (Barbiere), Cherubino, Hansel, Sesto, Idamante; Season 1995 as Rosina at Santiago and Cherubino at Antwerp; Season 1997–98 appeared at Melbourne and Brisbane Festivals; Extensive tour of Netherlands with St Matthew Passion and Sigiswald Kuijken; Appeared at Madrid Opera, 1999; Engaged to tour in Poland and the Czech Republic with St John Passion also concert performances in Ireland of Messiah and Beethoven's Missa Solemnis, 2000. *Recordings:* Oberto (Verdi) Christmas Oratorio, B Minor Mass, St Matthew Passion (Bach), Hugo Wolf Orchestral Songs with Choir; Lo Speziale (Haydn opera); Mahler 4th Symphony; Konradin Kreutzer 'Faust'. *Current Management:* c/o Neil Dalrymple, Music International, 13 Ardilaun Road, London, N5 2QR, England. *Telephone:* (20) 7359-5183. *Fax:* (20) 7226-9792. *E-mail:* music@musicint.co.uk.

BROWNLEE, Lawrence, Jr, BA, MMus; American singer (tenor); b. 24 Nov. 1972, Youngstown, OH; s. of Larry Brownlee, Sr and Frances Brownlee; m. Kendra Lynn Wilson Brownlee. *Education:* Anderson Univ, Indiana Univ. *Career:* operatic roles include Belfiore/Count Liebenskof in Viaggio a Reims, Almaviva in Il Barbiere di Siviglia, Lindoro in L'Italiana in Algeri, Don Ramiro in La Cenerentola, Argirio in Tancredi, Syme 1984, Arcadio in Florencia en el Amazonas, Giannetto in La Gazza Ladra, Nemorino in L'elisir d'amore, Idreno in Semiramide, Osiride in Mosé in Egitto, Egeo in Medea in Corinto and Narciso in Il Turco in Italia; has appeared at Houston Grand, San Diego, Seattle, Washington Nat. and Metropolitan Operas, with New York and Los Angeles Philharmonic Orchestras, Chicago, Boston, Cincinnati, Cleveland and Detroit Symphonies, at Kennedy Center in several recitals, Teatro alla Scala, Milan, Teatro Comunale di Bologna, Accad. di Santa Cecilia, Théâtre de la Monnaie, Brussels, Teatro Comunale Giuseppe Verdi, Trieste, Teatro Carlo Felice, Genoa, Teatro Real, Madrid, at both the Deutsche Oper and Staatsoper unter den Linden in Berlin, Wiener Staatsoper, Dresden Semperoper, Staatsoper Hamburg, Opernhaus Zürich, Royal Opera House, Covent Garden, London and New Nat. Theatre, Tokyo; concert appearances include Handel's Israel in Egypt (with Cleveland Orchestra), Handel's Messiah (with Baltimore, Houston and Detroit Symphonies), a Martin Luther King Day (with Charlotte Symphony), Bach's Magnificat and Orff's Carmina Burana (with Cincinnati Symphony), Gershwin concerts (with New York Philharmonic and Lorin Maazel), Mozart's Mass in C minor (with American Symphony Orchestra), Carmina Burana (with Berliner Philharmoniker and Sir Simon Rattle, Orchestre Nat. du Capitole de Toulouse, Los Angeles Philharmonic and Boston Symphony), Rossini's Stabat Mater with Orchestre de Chambre de Lausanne; festival appearances have included KlangBogen, Caramoor and Pesaro, amongst others; makes London recital on Rosenblatt Series; future performances include a return to Metropolitan Opera for Barbiere and a role debut, Rinaldo for the Met's first ever production of Rossini's Armida, a return to La Scala, first operatic appearance at Pesaro Festival. *Television:* Live from Lincoln Center, with New York Philharmonic and Lorin Maazel 2002. *Recordings:* Carmina Burana (with Berlin Philharmoniker and Sir Simon Rattle) 2005, Schubert/Verdi/Donizetti/Bellini/

Rossini, Italian Songs 2005, Il Barbiere di Siviglia 2006, Rossini Songs 2008, L'Italiana in Algheri 2009, Rossini's Stabat Mater 2010. *Honours:* Marilyn Horne Foundation Artist 2001, Richard Tucker Career Grant 2003, ARIA Award 2003, Richard Tucker Award 2006, Marian Anderson Award 2006, Opera Co. of Philadelphia's Gisela and Dennis Alter Distinguished Artist Award 2006–07, Seattle Opera Artist of the Year 2008. *Current Management:* c/o Robert Mirshak, Mirshak Artists, 7 West 24th Street, New York, NY 10010, USA. *Telephone:* (917) 282-0687. *Fax:* (718) 784-0143. *E-mail:* robert@mirshakartists.com. *Website:* www.mirshakartists.com. *Current Management:* c/o Federico Tondelli, Prima Fila Artists, Postfach 950145, 81517 Munich, Germany. *Telephone:* (89) 2440-0253; (160) 9504-1215 (mobile). *Fax:* (89) 2440-0253. *E-mail:* info@primafila-artists.com. *Website:* www.primafila-artists.com. *Address:* c/o Karen Krindler Nelson, KKN Enterprises, 277 West End Avenue, Suite 11A, New York, NY 10023, USA (office). *Telephone:* (212) 496-5154 (office). *E-mail:* kknenterp@gmail.com (office). *Website:* www.lawrencebrownlee.com.

BROWNRIDGE, Angela Mary, BMus, LRAM, ARCM; British pianist; b. 24 Oct. 1944, North Humberside, England; d. of Ralph Brownridge and Nelly Brownridge; m. Arthur Johnson 1968; one s. *Education:* Univ. of Edinburgh, studied with Dorothy Hesse, Guido Agosti and Maria Curcio. *Career:* debut, Wigmore Hall, London 1970; appearances in major London concert halls and with major orchestras in UK and abroad; regular broadcaster with BBC Radio 3 and stations world-wide; extensive recital tours in UK, America, Canada, the Far East and Europe; festival appearances at Bath, Edinburgh, Warwick, Grizedale, Newport Rhode Island, Bratislava, Brno, Hong Kong and Maastricht; masterclasses and mem. jury of piano competitions; mem. Incorporated Soc. of Musicians, Musicians' Union, EPTA, Beethoven Piano Soc. of Europe, Liszt Soc.; Founder of the Dean Clough masterclass weekends. *Compositions:* Piano pieces (aged seven). *Recordings include:* complete solo piano music of Barber, Leighton, Gershwin; complete concertos of Saint-Saëns with Hallé Orchestra; 25 CDs. *Honours:* scholarship to Univ. of Edinburgh 1963, Tovey Prize for Performance 1965, Frazer Scholarship 1966, Vaughan Williams Trust Fund 1972, Arts Council Award 1972. *Current Management:* Mary Kaptein, Bouwersdijk 307, 3314 Dordrecht, Netherlands. *Telephone:* (78) 6350-0087. *E-mail:* mckaptein@planet.nl. *Address:* 118 Audley Road, Hendon, London, NW4 3HG, England (home). *Telephone:* (20) 8202-0274. *E-mail:* artangela@btinternet.com.

BROZAK, Daniel; Czech composer, theoretician and violinist; b. 13 April 1947, Písek. *Education:* Prague Conservatory, Royal Conservatory in The Hague, Inst. for Sonology at Utrecht State Univ. *Career:* debut in Prague with own works for solo violin 1973; Leader, Prague Chamber Studio –1969; Musica Intuitiva –1975; theoretical research in the field of 12-tone harmony 1975–84; electronic and computer music 1975–94; mem. IG-Komponisten Salzburg, SEAH Prague, SPNMS, SNH 39815, Artistic Initiative-EKVNM. *Compositions:* Les Voiles 1977, Slunovrat 1978, Equinox 1978, The Seasons 1981, Concerto da Chiesa 1984, Diseased Society 1988, Requiem 1991. *Recordings:* Fresky 1974, Rigorosum 1975, Ave 1978, In Manus Tuas 1987, In A 1988, In the Middle of Nowhere 1988–90, Poetische Stunde 1989, Dopisy Olze 1990, Zbytecná Hudba 1992, Necas Trhovcu 1994, Katolické Radovánky 1996, Privat Sky 1997. *Publications:* Interval Keys 1977, Structural Harmony 1988, Pathology of Music 1991, Zkazena Sul 1997, Liturgie Zbabelych 1998. *Honours:* Wieniawski Composition Competition (Sonata for solo violin, op 52) 1980.

BRUA, Claire; French singer (soprano); b. 1970. *Education:* Nice Conservatoire with Albert Lance, Paris Conservatoire with Rachel Yakar, Gundula Janowitz and William Christie. *Career:* many performances in France and abroad with such conductors of Baroque music as René Jacobs and Jean-Claude Malgoire; appearances with William Christie and Les Arts Florissants include Purcell's Dido, in Paris and Rome; repertory includes Handel, Mozart and Rossini, and recitals of French song; Rinaldo in Jommelli's Armida abandonata at Beaune 1994; Cavalli's Dido at the Paris Opéra Comique 1998; sang Pulcheria in Handel's Riccardo Primo, with Les Talents Lyriques under Christophe Rousset, Fontevraud 1995; Mozart roles, Dorabella in Così fan tutte, Cherubino in Le nozze di Figaro, Zerlina in Don Giovanni, Annio in La Clemenza di Tito, Zweite Dame in Die Zauberflöte. *Recordings include:* Riccardo Primo. *Current Management:* c/o Philippe Kahn-Salmon, Music Talents International, Agence Artistique, Quai de Valmy 59, 75010 Paris, France. *Telephone:* (1) 40-40-94-75. *Fax:* (1) 40-40-94-84. *Website:* pksparis .com.

BRUBAKER, Robert; American singer (tenor); b. 1963. *Career:* sang Henri in Verdi's Vespri Siciliani at Carnegie Hall, New York, 1990; Canadian Opera at Toronto as Cassio in Otello; Season 1993 as Cavaradossi at Seattle and in the title role of Zemlinsky's Der Zwerg at the Spoleto Festival (USA and Italy) and Rome; Sang Pinkerton at Detroit (1994) and Rodolfo at Montreal, 1995; British debut for ENO 1991 as Weill's Jim Mahoney and Don José (returned 1999-2000, as Peter Grimes and as Mao in Nixon in China by John Adams); Washington Opera 1994 in the premiere of Argento's The Dream of Argento; Season 2000-01 as Pierre in War and Peace at the Opéra Bastille and Grimes at Aldeburgh; New York Met as Mephistopheles in Busoni's Faust and Albert Gregor in The Makropoulas Case; Covent Garden debut as Bacchus in Ariadne auf Naxos, 2002; Season 2002–03 in Boris Godunov at the Bastille, Schreker's Der Schatzgräber at Frankfurt and Peter Grimes at Toronto; Siegmund in Madrid, 2003. *Current Management:* IMG Artists, 31–33 rue du Temple, 75004 Paris, France. *Telephone:* 1-44-31-00-10. *Fax:* 1-44-31-44-40.

E-mail: pwiggins@imgartists.com. *Website:* www.imgartists.com; www .robertbrubaker.com.

BRUCE, Margaret, ARCM; Canadian/British concert pianist; b. 28 June 1943, Vancouver, BC, Canada; d. of Mr and Mrs Edward Phillips; m. 1st The Hon. H. L. T. Lumley-Savile 1972 (died 2001); three s. (triplets); m. 2nd Ghislain Pastre 2009. *Education:* Toronto Conservatory of Music, Royal Coll. of Music, London, and in Vienna. *Career:* debut, Wigmore Hall 1968; performances at Wigmore Hall 1968, 1979, Purcell Room 1970, 1975, 1978, 1980, 1983, Barbican, London 1983, 1985, Royal Concert Huddersfield 1982; Italian debut 1983; tours: Czechoslovakia 1968, 1981, Canada 1984, 1987, 1989; originator of new concert series at St John's, Smith Square, London, Canadians and Classics 1986, 1988, 1989, 1990; many other concerts at St John's, including solo and duet; with Royal Philharmonic Orchestra, Barbican 1985; Bulgarian debut 1992; Chomé Piano Trio; many concerts and recordings 1993–; Bruce-Colwell Duo, Edinburgh Festival debut 1994; Bruce/Lyttleton Duo recitals of poetry and piano solos, concerts USA, Canada, Italy, UK 1999; concerts in Bermuda, Italy, Hebden Bridge Arts Festival 2004–07; works have been written for her by Herbert Howells, Lennox Berkeley, Jean Coulthard, Antonin Tucapsky. *Recordings:* CBC Recordings, Canada 1969, 1982, 1984; solo recital, Mozart Concerti K414 and K449, 3 piano concerti written for her, Cello/Piano Duo with Moshe Friedman 2010, Music for piano duet with Peter Gellhorn 2010. *Honours:* Royal Coll. of Music 1962, Sir James Caird Scholarship 1966, Italo-Britanico Soc. Medal. *Current Management:* c/o G. Pastre, Flat 3, 13 Bolton Gardens, London, SW5 0AL, England. *Telephone:* (20) 7373-5068; (790) 003-6035. *Fax:* (20) 7373-5068. *E-mail:* pastre@bluewin .ch. *Address:* 13 Bolton Gardens, London, SW5 0AL, England (home). *Telephone:* (777) 327-8477 (office); (20) 8940-0697 (home). *Fax:* (20) 7373-5068. *E-mail:* margaretbruce333@aol.com. *Website:* www.margaretbruce.com (home).

BRUCE, Neely, DMA; American composer, pianist and conductor; *Professor of Music, Wesleyan University;* b. 21 Jan. 1944, Memphis, TN; m. Phyllis Bruce. *Education:* Univ. of Alabama at Tuscaloosa, with Roy McAllister, Univ. of Illinois with Soulima Stravinsky and Ben Johnston. *Career:* teacher, later Prof. of Music, Wesleyan Univ. 1974–; fmr Visiting Prof. Middlebury Coll., Bucknell Univ., Univ. of Michigan; Conductor, American Music/Theater Group; piano performances of American music, including premieres of works by Cage, Duckworth, Farwell, Brant; New York debut 1968; European debut, Warsaw 1972; directed scenes from American operas at Holland Festival 1982; mem. editorial cttee, New World Records 1974–79; Chair., New England Sacred Harp Singing 1976, 1979, 1982; Sr Research Fellow Inst. for Studies in American Music, Brooklyn Coll. 1980; currently Chorus Dir Connecticut Opera; Co-Dir of Music, South Congregational Church, Middletown. *Compositions include:* Pyramus and Thisbe (chamber opera) 1965, The Trials of Psyche (opera) 1971, Concerto for violin and chamber orchestra 1974, Americana, or A New Tale of the Genii (opera) 1983, The Blades o' Blue Grass Songbook for solo voices and piano 1984–95, Atmo-Rag for chamber orchestra 1987, Santa Ynez Waltz for chamber orchestra 1990, Orion Rising for orchestra 1991, Barnum's Band for large wind ensemble 1992, Tanglewood (oratorio) 1993, Young T.J. 1993, Trio for Bands for three rock bands 1994, Hugomotion (oratorio on texts of Hugo Grotius) 1995, Hansel and Gretel (opera) 1997, Cousins, Brothers and Sisters, Parents (one-act musicals) 1999–2001, Convergence 2000, The Pond 2002, Benedict Arnold: A Brave Revenge 2003, The Bill of Rights 2005, The Portals of St Bartholomew 2008, two one-act operas, five concerti, over 250 solo songs, other orchestral, instrumental, chamber, choral and vocal works. *Recordings:* Eight Ghosts, The Dream of the Other Dreamers, The Plague: A Commentary on the Work of the Fourth Horseman, composed for Electric Phoenix vocal quartet with electronics 1992, Perfumes and Meaning, Illinois Contemporary Chamber Singers with William Brooks 1992, Stanzas for Shep and Nancy, Linda Hirst, mezzo-soprano, composer at piano 1992, For Tom Howell, John Fonville 1992. *Address:* Neely Bruce Music, 440 Chamberlain Road, Middletown, CT 06457, USA (office). *E-mail:* neelybrucemusic@comcast.net (office). *Website:* neelybrucemusic.com.

BRUCE-PAYNE, Sally; British singer (mezzo-soprano); b. 1968, London. *Education:* Royal Coll. of Music, studied with Felicity Palmer. *Career:* concerts include Bach's Choice of Hercules at the Göttingen Festival, the B Minor Mass on tour to Japan and Republic of Korea, English Baroque Soloists; Messiah with the Bach Choir and Bach Cantatas in the USA; season 1998–99 with the St Matthew Passion on tour in Europe, Eryxene in Handel's Poro at Halle and Monteverdi's Ottavia in Japan; European tour of Messiah; Ottone in Handel's Agrippina at St John's Smith Square, Duruflé's Requiem at The Three Choirs Festival and Verdi Requiem with the Philharmonia conducted by David Willcocks; works regularly with major British orchestras, including Royal Liverpool Philharmonic Orchestra, Philharmonia, Bournemouth Symphony Orchestra and Scottish Chamber Orchestra; season 2001–02 included title role in Offenbach's Dick Whittington at the City of London Festival, Elijah with the Philharmonia conducted by Wolfgang Sawallisch, Partenope at the Royal Opera House Linbury Theatre and the Buxton Festival and Messiah at the Lyon Festival. *Recordings:* Schubert's Mass in A flat and Haydn's Theresien and Nelson Masses conducted by John Eliot Gardiner; Vivaldi's operas Ottone in Villa, Tito Manlio and Giustino; Copland's In the Beginning. *Honours:* RCM English Song Prize, Muriel Kistner Prize.

BRÜCK, Markus; German singer (baritone); b. 15 Aug. 1972, Speyer. *Education:* Musikhochschule Mannheim/Heidelberg and Cologne, studied

with Alejandro Ramirez and Kurt Moll. *Career:* joined Theater Hagen 1995; mem. ensemble Opernhaus Kaiserslautern 1997–99, Staatstheater Wiesbaden 1999–2001; mem. Deutsche Oper Berlin 2001–, performing main baritone roles; role debuts in new productions of Parsifal, Peter Grimes and the Love for Three Oranges 2012; US debut as Donner in Das Rheingold and Gunther in Götterdämmmerung at Seattle Opera 2013; soloist in Brahms' Ein Deutsches Requiem with BBC Scottish Symphony Orchestra under Donald Runnicles in Glasgow and Edinburgh, and at Maggio Musicale Fiorentino under Zubin Mehta 2011; other roles include Ottokar in Der Freischutz for Opera Köln 2015, Balstrode in Peter Grimes and Germont in Traviata for Deutsche Oper 2016; has worked with conductors including Marc Albrecht, Vladimir Ashkenazy, Daniel Barenboim, Sylvain Cambreling, Christoph von Dohnányi, Riccardo Muti and Christian Thielemann; numerous recordings. *Honours:* Kammersänger 2011. *Current Management:* Opern-Agentur Kursidem & Tschaidse, Tal 15, 80331 Munich, Germany. *Telephone:* (89) 29161661. *Fax:* (89) 29161667. *E-mail:* tschaidse@opern-agentur.com. *Website:* www .opern-agentur.com; www.markusbruck.com (office).

BRUDERHANS, Zdenek; Czech flautist, university flute professor and writer; b. 29 July 1934, Prague; m. Eva Holubarova 1962; one s. one d. *Education:* Akademicke Gymnasium, Prague, Prague Conservatorium of Music, Prague Acad. of Music. *Career:* debut, Prague 1957; Asst Prin. Flautist, Prague Nat. Theatre 1955–59; Prin. Flautist, Prague Radio Symphony Orchestra 1960–68; represented Czechoslovakia at MIDEM in Cannes, France 1968; Flute Prof., Sweden 1969–73; Lecturer, Adelaide Univ., S Australia, later Sr Lecturer, Reader, Dean of Music 1987–88, 1973–97; flute soloist in 18 European countries, USA, Australia and Asia on radio; recitals, concertos and in festivals. *Recordings include:* 16 recordings including recitals of works by Bach, Mozart, Haydn, Hindemith, Martinů, Messiaen, Berio, Debussy, Varèse, Ravel, Feld and Telemann, Zdenek Bruderhans Almanacs, sonatas by Martinů, Feld, Prokofiev, Flute Anthology. *Radio:* recordings of major flute works for radio in fmr Czechoslovakia, Australia and 16 stations in Europe. *Publications include:* Music, Tectonics and Flute Playing 1997, Fundamentals of Musical Performance, Základy hudebního přednesu; contrib. to Miscellanea Musicologica, The Instrumentalist, Pan and the Flute. *Honours:* Grand Prize, Int. Competition of Wind Instruments, Prague Spring Festival 1959. *Address:* 2 McLaughlan Avenue, Brighton, Vic. 5048, Australia. *Telephone:* (8) 8298-3099. *E-mail:* flute@senet.com.au (home). *Website:* users.senet.com.au/~flute (home).

BRUEGGERGOSMAN, Measha; Canadian singer (soprano); b. 1977, Fredericton, New Brunswick; m. Markus Brueggergosman 1999. *Education:* Univ. of Toronto. *Career:* performances include Beethoven's Symphony No. 9 with National Arts Centre Orchestra and National Symphony Orchestra, Janáček's Glagolitic Mass with London Symphony Orchestra, Berlioz's Les nuits d'été with NDR Hannover Orchestra, Messiaen's Poèmes pour Mi Royal, Concertgebouw Orchestra, Vaughan Williams' A Sea Symphony with Atlanta Symphony, Beethoven's Symphony No. 9 with Cleveland Orchestra, opera arias with Sir Andrew Davis and the New York Philharmonic, Mahler's Des Knaben Wunderhorn and Beethoven's Symphony No. 9 with Toronto Symphony Orchestra, Schönberg's Brettl-Lieder and Mahler's Symphony No. 4 with San Francisco Symphony Orchestra, Gershwin songs with the BBC Scottish Symphony Orchestra, Mahler's Lieder eines fahrenden Gesellen with Israel Philharmonic Orchestra, Strauss' Vier Letzte Lieder with the Gothenburg Symphony Orchestra. *Recordings:* So Much to Tell, Extase, Surprise (Juno Award for Classical Album of the Year: Vocal or Choral Performance) 2008. Beethoven Symphony No. 9. *Honours:* winner, Jeunesses Musicales Int. Competition, Montréal 2002, Wigmore Hall Int. Song Competition, George London Prize, Queen Sonja Int. Music Competition. *Current Management:* IMG Artists, Carnegie Hall Tower, 152 W. 57th Street, 5th Floor, New York, NY 10019, USA. *Telephone:* (212) 994-3500. *Fax:* (212) 994-3550. *E-mail:* bpalant@imgartists.com. *Website:* www.imgartists.com; www .measha.com.

BRUFFY, Charles; American choral conductor; *Artistic Director, Kansas City Chorale and Phoenix Chorale;* b. 1958. *Education:* Missouri Western State Coll., St. Joseph, Mo., Conservatory of Music, Univ. of Missouri Kansas City. *Career:* started career as tenor soloist; performed with Robert Shaw Festival Singers in recordings and concerts in France, and concerts at Carnegie Hall; as conductor, commissioned and premiered works by composers including Jean Belmont, Matthew Harris, Libby Larsen, Zhou Long, Stephen Paulus, Stephen Sametz, Steven Stucky, Eric Whitacre and Chen Yi; conducted Verdi's Requiem at Sydney Opera House, Australia 2009; workshops and clinics across USA; Artistic Dir, Kansas City Chorale 1988–; Artistic Dir, Phoenix Chorale 1999–; Artistic Dir, Kansas City Symphony Chorus 2007–; fmr mem. bd, Chorus America; mem. advisory bd, Atlanta Young Singers of Callanwolde. *Recordings include:* Shakespeare in Song, Eternal Rest, Grechaninov: Passion Week (Grammy Award for Best Engineered Classical Album 2007), Rheinberger: Sacred Choral Works, Spotless Rose: Hymns to the Virgin Mary (Grammy Award for Best Small Ensemble Performance 2008), Life and Breath: Choral Works by René Clausen (Grammy Award for Best Choral Performance 2013). *Honours:* Hon. doctorates (Baker Univ., Missouri Western State Univ.). *Address:* Phoenix Chorale, 100 West Roosevelt Street, Phoenix, AZ 85003, USA (office). *Telephone:* (602) 253-2224 (office). *Fax:* (602) 253-5772 (office). *E-mail:* info@phoenixchorale.org (home). *Website:* phoenixchorale.org (office).

BRUGGER, Janai, MusM; American singer (soprano); b. 1983, Chicago, Ill. *Education:* De Paul Univ. with Elsa Charlston and Univ. of Michigan with Shirley Verrett. *Career:* with Merola Opera Program, San Francisco Opera 2010; Domingo-Thornton Young Artist Program 2011; at LA Opera, sang Barbarina in Le nozze di Figaro under Plácido Domingo, The Page in Rigoletto under James Conlon and other roles 2010–11, also Pamina in Die Zauberflöte 2013; debut at Metropolitan Opera, New York as Liu in Turandot 2011–12, also as Helena in The Enchanted Island 2014; has appeared with Chicago Symphony Orchestra at Ravinia Festival, Palm Beach Opera, Hawaii Opera, Grant Park Music Festival, Chicago, Philadelphia Orchestra, as soloist in Mozart's Requiem at Cincinnati May Festival and High Priestess in Aida under Gustavo Dudamel at Hollywood Bowl. *Honours:* First Prize, Zarzuela Prize and Audience Award, Plácido Domingo Operalia Competition 2012, winner, Metropolitan Opera Nat. Council Auditions 2012. *Current Management:* c/o Deborah M. Sanders, Rayfield Allied, Southbank House, Black Prince Road, London, SE1 7SJ, England. *Telephone:* (20) 3176-5500. *E-mail:* deborah.sanders@rayfieldallied.com. *Website:* www.rayfieldallied.com. *Address:* 1201 Ocean Park Blvd, Suite D, Santa Monica, CA 90405, USA (home). *Telephone:* (773) 401-4887 (home). *E-mail:* jaelysia@gmail.com (home). *Website:* www.janaibrugger.com (office).

BRUHN, Siglind, MA, MM, DrPhil; German pianist and musicologist/music analyst; b. 11 Oct. 1951, Hamburg; m. Gerhold Becker 1985. *Education:* Musikhochschule Hamburg and Stuttgart, Univ. of Munich, master-classes with Wladimir Horbowski, Hans Leygraf, Nikita Magaloff, doctoral studies at Univ. of Vienna. *Career:* debut in 1965; Head of Community Music School, Munich 1978–82; Head, Inst. for Musical Interpretation 1982–87; Dir Pianists Acad., Ansbach 1984–87; Dir of Studies, Univ. of Hong Kong 1987–94; guest Prof., Beijing Central Conservatory of Music 1990, Music Acad. Kraków; Visiting Scholar, Univ. of Michigan 1993–97, Perm. Research Assoc., Inst. for Humanities 1997–; Distinguished Sr Research Fellow, Center for Christianity and the Arts, Univ. of Copenhagen 2002–12; Chercheur invité, Institut d'esthétique des arts contemporains, Univ. of Paris 1 (Sorbonne) 2004–09; performances in most major German cities, Zürich, London, Paris, Lisbon, Venice, Athens, Beirut, Rio de Janeiro, Quito, Johannesburg, Cape Town, Hong Kong, Manila, Beijing, Shanghai, Melbourne, Adelaide, Washington, DC; TV and radio broadcasts worldwide; mem. European Acad. of Arts and Sciences 2001–. *Recordings:* Ravel, Moussorgsky 1984, Dvořák 1986, Hindemith, duo sonatas 1997, Hindemith, piano solo 1997. *Publications include:* Analysis and Interpretation in J. S. Bach's Well-Tempered Klavier 1993, Musikalische Symbolik in Olivier Messiaen's Weihnachtsvignetten 1997, Images and Ideas in Modern French Piano Music 1997, Alban Berg's Music as Encrypted Speech (ed.) 1997, The Temptation of Paul Hindemith: Mathis der Maler as a Spiritual Testimony 1998, Messiaen's Language of Mystical Love (ed.) 1998, Signs in Musical Hermeneutics (ed.) 1998, Frank Martin's Musical Reflections on Death 2011, The Music of Jörg Widmann 2013, Arnold Schoenberg's Journey from Tone Poems to Kaleidoscopic Sound Colors 2015; contrib. to scholarly journals, handbooks and collections in Europe, Asia and USA; also 14 monographs in German. *Honours:* Dr hc (Linnaeus Univ.) 2008. *E-mail:* siglind@umich.edu (home). *Website:* www.personal.umich.edu/~siglind (home).

BRUK, Fridrich, DipMus; Finnish composer; b. 18 Sept. 1937, Kharkov, Ukraine; m. Nadezhda Bruk 1959; one s. *Education:* Kharkov Music Coll. of the Kharkov Conservatory, Conservatory Rimsky-Korsakov, Leningrad. *Career:* debut, The Forty First (opera based on Boris Lavrenev's story) 1961; composer of opera, orchestral works and chamber music, music for theatre and film, popular songs; teaches in various Finnish musical institutes; mem. Soc. of Finnish Composers, Finnish Composers' Copyright Bureau, Guild of Light Music Composers and Authors, Soc. of Russian Composers. *Compositions:* String quartet No. 1 1983; music for children: Spring 1982, Snowdrop 1983, Sleigh Bells 1984, A Glittering Book Mark (fairy-tale musical) 1984, Summer 1985, Golden Autumn 1988, Winter 1988, Sunflecks, suite for orchestra 1987, Five duets for clarinet (B) and violoncello or bassoon 1983, Lyrical images, suite for piano 1985, Variations for piano on the Karelian folk song Strawberry 1985, Concert Variations on An Old Kalevala song, theme for violoncello and piano 1985, The Steppe, suite for woodwind quartet, As Lace Against the Light, 7 songs for 3-voice choir 1986, Sonata for Kantele 1986, String quartet No. 2 1987, Concertino for 2 violins and string orchestra or piano 1987, Sonata for 2 violins 1988, Sonata for violoncello 1989, Sonata for 2 trumpets 1989; music for television films 1988, 1989, Sonata for viola 1990, Sonata for clarinet (B) 1991, Sonata for piano 1994, To the Home Neighbourhood, four songs for mixed choir a cappella 1994, Seven dialogues for oboe and viola 1995, Trio for clarinet (B), viola and violoncello 1996, Symphony No. 1 for orchestra and trombone solo 1998, Symphony No. 2 for orchestra and piano solo 1999, A Wandering Minstrel, oratorio for baritone, soprano, mixed choir and orchestra (poetry by Oiva Paloheimo) 2000, Artist Chagall, Symphony No. 3 for orchestra and tenor 2000, Sounds of Spring, poem for orchestra 2000, Carelia, Symphony No. 4 for soprano, bass, drums, piano, harp and string orchestra (poetry from Kalevala and Eino Leino) 2001, Musik für Quartett 2001, The Hand of God, Christmas oratorio for narrator, soloists, children's choir and instrumental ensemble 2002, Sonata for Piano No. 2 2002, Symphony No. 5 for Orchestra 2002, Birds of Passage, Symphony No. 6 for baritone and orchestra (poetry by Viljo Kajava) 2001–03, The Cat's House (opera for children, libretto by Samuel Marshak) 2003–04, Kalevala, Symphony No. 7 (by artist Axel Gallen-Kallela) 2008, Symphony No. 8 2008, In the Finnish Mode, Symphony No. 9 2008, Poem for Ensemble for ten soloists 2008, Symphony No. 10,

Klezmorim II 2010, Symphony No. 11 The Universe 2011, Symphony No. 12 Turtola's Star 2012, Sonata for Oboe and Xylophone (Marimba) 2013, Sonata for Bassoon and French Horn 2013, Symphony No. 13 Artist Malevich 2014. *Recordings:* Compositions by Fridrich Bruk 1993, Lyrical Images 1994, From Kalevala 1994, The Snowdrop 1996, Dialogues 1996, Artist Chagall, Symphony No. 3 for orchestra and tenor 2002, The Hand of God 2003, The Sunshine 2004, A Wandering Minstrel 2006, Nordic Legends 2008, Christmas Time 2009, In the Finnish Mode 2009, The Search 2010, The Universe 2011, Turtola's Star 2013. *Publication:* One Hundred Friends or A Confession of the Slandered (including CD of Bruk's popular music compositions) (memoir) 2007. *Honours:* Cross of Merit of the Order of the Lion of Finland 1988, Grand Tampere Medal, City of Tampere 2007; various Finnish grants and scholarships. *Address:* Papinkatu 18 A 41, Tampere, 33200 Suomi, Finland. *Telephone:* (3) 2144040. *Fax:* (3) 2144040. *E-mail:* fridrich.bruk@gmail.com.

BRUMBY, Colin James, BMus, DMus; Australian composer, academic and conductor; b. 18 June 1933, Melbourne, Vic. *Education:* Conservatorium of Music, Univ. of Melbourne. *Career:* Lecturer in Music, Kelvin Grove Teachers' Coll. 1960–62; Head of Music Dept, Greenford Grammar School, Middx, UK 1962–64; Lecturer in Music, Univ. of Queensland 1964–65, Sr Lecturer 1966–75, Assoc. Prof. of Music 1976–98; mem. Australian Performing Right Asscn. *Compositions include:* Festival Overture on Australian Themes, Paean, South Bank Overture, Symphony No. 1 (The Sun), The Phoenix and the Turtle, Violin Concerto Nos 1 and 2, Piano Concerto, Charlie Bubble's Book of Hours (cantata), The Vision and the Gap (cantata), Victimae Paschali (cantata), Bassoon Concerto, Bassoon Quintet (Haydn Down Under), Bassoon Sonata, Clarinet Concerto, Clarinet Sonatina, Flute Concerto, Flute Sonatina, Oboe Concertino, Scena for Cor Anglais & String Orchestra, Concerto for Organ & Strings, Piano Quartet, String Quartet, Demotica (three movements for solo piano), Three Italian Songs for high voice and String Quartet, Borromeo Suite for flute and guitar, Gardens of the Villa Taranto for flute & guitar, Cello Concerto, Viola Concerto (Tre aspetti di Roma), Trumpet Concerto, Canti pisani for Medium Voice & Orchestra; operas: Summer Carol, The Heretic. *Publications include:* Missa Canonica 1991, Harlequinade 1987, Of a Rose, a Lovely Rose 1994, Unto us a Baby is Born 2000, In Praise of the Virgin 2000, Priusque gallas cantet 2000, Virgin's Cradle Song 2001, Come, bring a noise 2001, Mater ora filium 2001, Scena for cor anglais and strings 2004, Borromeo Suite 2005. *Honours:* Albert H. Maggs Composition Award 1969, Advance Australia Award (Music) 1981, Don Banks Award 1990. *Address:* 9 Teague Street, Indooroopilly, Qld 4068, Australia (home). *Telephone:* (7) 3378-3761 (office). *E-mail:* cbrumby@bigpond.net.au (office).

BRUMMELSTROETE, Wilke; Dutch singer (mezzo-soprano); b. 1968. *Education:* Royal Acad., The Hague and Britten-Pears School and Mozarteum, Salzburg. *Career:* debut as Purcell's Dido 1991; Netherlands Opera 1992, in Monteverdi's Poppea; Fortuna and Anfinomo in Monteverdi's Ulisse at Brussels, Vienna, Berlin and South Africa; Turno in Bononcini's Il Trionfo di Camilla at Utrecht 1997; Teseo in Handel's Arianna at Göttingen 1999; Juno and Ino in Semele at San Francisco 2000; other roles include Andronico in Handel's Tamerlano, Carmen, and Clothilde in Norma; concerts include Beethoven's Ninth in Lisbon, Mozart's Requiem in Japan and C minor Mass in Florence; Messiah in Vienna, Bach's Magnificat at Barbican and Cantatas at QEH; Elgar's The Kingdom in Buenos Aires, Aldeburgh and Sydney; season 2001–02 with Ruggiero in Alcina at Göttingen, Dido with Irish Chamber Orchestra and concert tour with Israel Camerata. *Current Management:* Ariën Arts & Music Management B.V.B.A, Groot-Brittanniëlaan 27, 9000 Ghent, Belgium. *E-mail:* wilketeb@ision.nl. *Website:* www.wilketebrummelstroete.com.

BRUNNER, Eduard; Swiss clarinettist; b. 14 July 1939, Basle. *Education:* studied in Basle and Paris, France. *Career:* chamber musician in Germany and Switzerland from 1959; soloist with the Bavarian Radio Symphony Orchestra from 1963; collaborations with such musicians as violinist Gidon Kremer (at Lockenhaus), Heinz Holliger (oboe) and Aurèle Nicolet (flute); has premiered works by Jean Francaix, Helmut Lachenmann, Vassily Lobanov and Isang Yun (Concerto 1982, Quintet 1984); Prof. of Clarinet Musikhochschule Saarbrücken 1992–. *Recordings include:* The Art of Playing Clarinet 1995, Stamitz Clarinet Concertos 1998, French Clarinet Concertos 2000, Eduard Brunner 2007, J. X. Lefèvre Clarinet Quartets and Sonatas 2010, Music for Solo Clarinet (ECHO Klassik Award for Instrumentalist of the Year/Clarinet 2012) 2011. *Address:* c/o Christian Obermaier, Bayerischer Rundfunk, Münchner Rundfunkorchester, Rundfunkplatz 1, 80335 Munich, Germany.

BRUNNER, Evelyn; Swiss singer (soprano); b. 17 Dec. 1949, Lausanne. *Education:* Lausanne Conservatory with Paul Sandoz, studied in Milan, and with Herbert Graf in Geneva. *Career:* sang with the Ensemble Vocal de Lausanne under Michael Corboz and with the Orchestre de Chambre de Lausanne under Victor Desrazens; appearances at the Grand Théâtre de Genève as Micaela in Carmen, Marguerite in Faust and Cimarosa's Il Matrimonio Segreto, 1971; sang Mozart's Countess at the Paris Opéra and in Hamburg and Berlin; Opéra du Rhin, Strasbourg, as Elsa in Lohengrin, 1986; engagements at opera houses in Lyon, Toulouse, Avignon and Nantes; other roles include Mozart's Fiordiligi and Donna Anna, Liu in Turandot and Verdi's Elisabeth de Valois and Violetta; many concerts with the Collegium Academicum de Genève. *Recordings:* Rossini's Il Signor Bruschino, conducted by Robert Dunand.

BRUNNER, Heidi; Swiss singer (soprano); b. 1965, Lucerne; m. Bertrand de Billy; one d. *Education:* studied in Lucerne, Zürich and Basle. *Career:* debut as Rossini's Cenerentola; with Vienna Staatsoper 1996–99, with Vienna Volksoper 1996–99; roles include Rosina in Il Barbiere di Siviglia, Idamante in Idomeneo, Zerlina in Don Giovanni, Niklaus in Les Contes d'Hoffman, Sextus in Titus, Aladgisa in Norma, Vitella in La Clemenza di Tito, Marta in Tiefland; season 1998, in Orfeo, Munich Opernfestspiele; in Idomeneo at Wiener OsterKlang 2003; season 2004/05 in Schreker's Irrelohe, Schmidt's Notre Dame, Ursula; season 2005/06 in Schonburg's Erwartung and Wozzeck;season 2006/07 in La Clemenza di Tito, Don Giovanni; season 2007/08 in Tiefland, Dialogues des Carmelites, Parsifal; has performed at Komischen Oper Berlin, Staatsoper Berlin, Bayerische Staatsoper München, the Gran Teatre del Liceu, Barcelona, Nancy, Grand Théatre de Geneve, Wiener Musikverein, Wiener Konzerthaus, Hamburger Staatsoper, in Milan, Paris, Lyon, Zurich, Basel, Lisbon, Helsingborg, Munich, Duisberg; festivals include KlangBogen, Salzburg. *Recordings include:* Cosi fan tutte, Don Giovanni, Le Nozze di Figaro, Tristan und Isolde (excerpts), Heidi Brunner (solo CD) 2004. *Honours:* Migros Study Award. *E-mail:* heidi@heidibrunner .com. *Website:* www.heidibrunner.com.

BRUNNER, Richard; American singer (tenor); b. 1953, Ohio. *Education:* Opera School of Toronto, Academy of Vocal Arts in Pittsburgh. *Career:* sang Ramiro in Cenerentola with Philadelphia Opera (1978), Mime in Das Rheingold (Cincinnati and Dallas, 1981–82), Števa in Jenůfa at the Spoleto Festival, Florestan with Scottish Opera (1991) and roles such as Elemer (Arabella), Narraboth (Salome) and Cassio (Otello) at the Vienna Staatsoper; Denver Opera, 1992, as Walther von Stolzing; other roles include Melot, Sellem (The Rake's Progress) and Eisenstein in Die Fledermaus; Bayreuth Festival 1994–96, as Wagner's Froh; Sang Narraboth in Salome at San Diego, 1998; season 1999–2000 as Strauss's Emperor and Janáček's Albert Gregor at Darmstadt, Sam in Carlisle Floyd's Susannah for Washington Opera. *Current Management:* Pinnacle Arts: Miller Division, 889 Ninth Avenue, Second Floor, New York 10019, USA. *Telephone:* (212) 397-7911. *Fax:* (212) 397-7920. *E-mail:* jmiller@pinnaclearts.com. *Website:* www.pinnaclearts.com.

BRUSA, Elisabetta Olga Laura, DipMus; Italian composer and academic; *Professor of Composition, Milan Conservatoire;* b. 3 April 1954, Milan; d. of Giuseppe Brusa and Joyce Mary Hansford Brusa; m. Gilberto Serembe 1997. *Education:* Conservatorio of Milan with Bruno Bettinelli and Azio Corghi, further studies with Hans Keller in London. *Career:* debut composition performed at Piccola Scala 1982; featured on RAI TV programme on Young Italian Composers 1983; various commissions; worldwide radio and TV broadcasts; performances in Italy, UK, USA, Canada, Australia, Russia, France, Ukraine, Germany, Austria, Switzerland, Korea and Albania, with orchestras such as the BBC Philharmonic, BBC Scottish Symphony Orchestra, CBC Vancouver Orchestra, State Hermitage Orchestra, St Petersburg Symphony Orchestra, Nat. Symphony Orchestra of Ukraine, Philharmonisches Orchestra des Theaters Altenburg-Gera, Aachener Kammerorchester, Virtuosi of Toronto, Boris Brott Festival Orchestra, Radio and TV Symphony Orchestra of Tirana, London Chamber Symphony, New England Philharmonic, Tanglewood Music Center Orchestra, Alea III Ensemble, Contemporary Music Forum of Washington DC, Women's Philharmonic of San Francisco, I Solisti Veneti, Pomeriggi Musicali; *Prof. of Composition,* Conservatorio of Vicenza 1980–82, Conservatorio of Mantova 1982–84, Conservatorio of Brescia 1984–85, Milan Conservatoire 1985–. *Compositions include:* Belsize String Quartet 1981, Fables for chamber orchestra 1983, Marcia Funebre for piano 1984, Suite Grotesque for orchestra 1986, Sonata for piano 1986, Nittemero Symphony for chamber orchestra 1988, Symphony No. 1 for large orchestra 1990, Sonata Rapsodica for violin and piano 1991, La Triade for large orchestra 1992, Firelights for large orchestra 1993, Requiescat for voice and large orchestra 1995, Fanfare for large orchestra 1996, Adagio for string orchestra 1996, Wedding Song for large orchestra 1997, Florestan for large orchestra 1997, Messidor for orchestra 1998, Merlin for large orchestra 2004, Simply Largo for string orchestra 2007, Symphony No. 2 for large orchestra 2000–15. *Recordings:* Orchestral Works Vol. 1, Orchestral Works Vol. 2, Orchestral Works Vol. 3. *Honours:* First Prize, Washington Int. Competition for String Quartet 1982, Fellowship, Tanglewood Music Center 1983, Fulbright Bursary 1983, MacDowell Colony Fellowships 1988, 1989, 1990. *E-mail:* elisabetta.brusa@alice.it (office). *Website:* www.elisabettabrusa.it.

BRUSON, Renato; Italian singer (baritone); b. 13 Jan. 1936, Este. *Education:* studied in Padua. *Career:* debut at Spoleto Festival, 1961; has appeared at all major Italian Opera Houses including La Scala, Milan, Debut 1972; Specialising in Verdi and Donizetti operas in Attila, La Traviata, La Favorita and Lucia di Lammermoor; Other opera houses include Vienna, Hamburg, Berlin, Paris, Brussels etc; Covent Garden debut 1976, as Renato in Un Ballo in Maschera; Appearances in USA include Chicago, New York Metropolitan Opera and San Francisco; Debut as Enrico at the Metropolitan, 1969; Has sung at the Verona Arena 1975–76, 1978–82, 1985; Los Angeles and Covent Garden, 1982, as Falstaff; Also at Parma, 1986; Munich, 1985, as Macbeth; Sang Iago at La Scala, 1987; Don Giovanni at the Deutsche Oper Berlin, 1988; Carnegie Hall, New York, 1990, as Montfort in Les Vêpres Siciliennes; Sang Carlos in Ernani at Parma, 1990, Germont at Turin, Carlos at La Fenice, Venice; Sang Enrico in Lucia di Lammermoor at La Scala, 1992, Germont at the 1992 Macerata Festival and at Covent Garden, 1995; Sang Macbeth at Monte Carlo, 1997; Germont at the 1999 Orange festival; Falstaff at Macerata, 1998; Season 2000–01 at the Vienna Staatsoper as Don Carlo in Ernani, and

Iago. *Recordings:* Luisa Miller; Falstaff; Samson and Delilah etc. Films and television include Don Carlos, La Scala and Luisa Miller, Covent Garden. *Current Management:* Opera Art, Via Isolalta Forette 11, 37068 Vigasio (VR), Italy. *Telephone:* (45) 6649911. *Fax:* (45) 6649912. *E-mail:* info@operaart.it. *Website:* www.operaart.it.

BRUZDOWICZ-TITTEL, Joanna Maria, MA; French/Polish composer, music critic and film producer; b. 17 May 1943, Warsaw, Poland; d. of Konstanty Bruzdowicz and Countess Maria Wilczek; m. Jürgen Tittel; three s. *Education:* Warsaw Conservatory, studied piano with Irena Protasewicz and Wanda Losakiewicz, composition with Kazimierz Sikorski, Nadia Boulanger, Olivier Messiaen, Pierre Schaeffer in Paris. *Career:* Groupe de Recherches Musicales, French Radio and TV, Paris; Groupe Int. de Musique Electroacoustique de Paris; IPEM; electronic studios, Univ. of Ghent, Belgian radio and TV; Founder Jeunesses Musicales, Poland; Founder and Pres. Frédéric Chopin and Karol Szymanowski Soc., Belgium, Int. Music Encounters in Catalonia, Céret, France; Pres., Cat Studios Groupe, Perpignan; Vice-Pres. Int. Fed. of Chopin Socs; advocate of contemporary music; mem. SACD, SACEM (France), Soc. of Authors, ZAiKS, ZKP, Poland; Co-founder and partner Cat.Studios (French film and music production co.). *Honours:* Officer's Cross, Order of Polonia Restituta 2001; Gloria Artis – Golden Medal 2013. *Address:* Mas Terrats, 66400 Taillet, France (home). *Telephone:* (4) 68-87-48-59 (home). *Fax:* (4) 68-87-48-59 (home). *E-mail:* jotibruz@gmail.com. *Website:* www.usc.edu/dept/polish_music/composer/bruzdowicz.html.

BRYAN, John Howard, BA, BPhil, DMus, FHEA; British musician (early instruments) and academic; b. 24 Feb. 1952, Ilford, Essex, England; one s. two d. *Education:* Univ. of York. *Career:* debut 1973; Co-Dir Landini Consort; Dir Rose Consort of Viols; Artistic Adviser, York Early Music Festival; Prof. of Music and Head of Music and Drama, Univ. of Huddersfield 2005–13; has played with I Fagiolini, Consort of Musicke and Musica Antiqua of London; mem. North East Early Music Forum; lecturer, Martin Randall Travel. *Recordings:* with Landini Consort: Nowell, Songs and Dances of Fourteenth Century Italy, The Play of Daniel (also with Pro Cantione Antiqua); with Musica Antiqua of London: A Songbook for Isabella, Music for Henry VIII's Six Wives; with Rose Consort of Viols: Elizabethan Christmas Anthems, Dowland, Lachrimae, Born is the Babe, Ah, Dear Heart, John Jenkins, Consort Music, William Byrd, Consort music, songs and anthems, Orlando Gibbons, Consort music, songs and anthems, John Dowland, Dances and Lute Songs, Purcell, Fantasias and in Nomines, Elizabethan Consort Music, Alfonso Farrebosco I & II Consort Music, John Ward Consort Music, Four Gentlemen of the Chapel Royal, Striggio Mass for 40 Voices, Music from the Dow Partbooks, Mystrelles with Straunge Sunds, Serenissima. *Publications:* contrib. to Music in Education, Compendium of Contemporary Musical Knowledge 1992, Early Music 2008, 2013, Journal of Musicology 2011, Networks of Music and Culture in the Late Sixteenth and Early Seventeenth Centuries 2013. *Address:* 28 Wentworth Road, Scarcroft Hill, York, YO24 1DG, England (home).

BRYARS, Gavin, BA; British composer; b. 16 Jan. 1943, Goole, Yorks., England; s. of Walter Joseph Bryars and Miriam Eleanor Bryars; m. 1st Angela Margaret Bigley 1971 (divorced 1993); two d.; m. 2nd Anna Tchernakova 1999; one s. one step d. *Education:* Goole Grammar School, Univ. of Sheffield, Northern School of Music and pvt composition study with Cyril Ramsey, George Linstead and Benjamin Johnston. *Career:* freelance double bassist 1963–66; Lecturer in Liberal Studies, Northampton Coll. of Tech. 1966–67; freelance composer/performer 1968–70; Lecturer in Music, Portsmouth Polytechnic 1969–70; Sr Lecturer, School of Fine Art, Leicester Polytechnic 1970–78, Sr Lecturer and Head of Music, School of Performing Arts 1978–85; Prof. of Music, De Montfort Univ. 1985–96; Assoc. Research Fellow, Dartington Coll. of Arts 2004–08; collaborations with numerous artists, including Aphex Twin, John Cage, Brian Eno, Tom Waits; mem. Collège de Pataphysique, France 1974–, Regent 2007–, Transcendent Satrap 2015–; Ed. Experimental Music Catalogue 1972–81; British Rep. Int. Soc. for Contemporary Music Festival 1977; Visiting Prof., Univ. of Hertfordshire 1999–2003; Arts Council Comms 1970, 1980, 1982, Bursary 1982; Music Juror, Akademie Schloss Solitude, Stuttgart 1990–92; freelance composer 1994–. *Art exhibitions:* Effervescence, Angers, France 2005, Alvar Aalto Museum, Finland 2006, Underworlds and Overworlds (with Quay Brothers), Leeds 2012. *Compositions include:* The Sinking of the Titanic 1969, Jesus' Blood Never Failed Me Yet 1971, Out of Zaleski's Gazebo 1977, The Vespertine Park 1980, Medea (opera with Robert Wilson) 1982, My First Homage for two pianos 1978, Effarene 1984, String Quartet No. 1 1985, Pico's Flight 1986, By the Vaar for double bass and ensemble 1987, The Invention of Tradition 1988, Glorious Hill 1988, Cadman Requiem 1989, String Quartet No. 2 1990, Four Elements (dance piece) 1990, The Black River for soprano and organ 1991, The White Lodge 1991, The War in Heaven for chorus and orchestra 1993, Epilogue from 'Wonderlawn' for four players 1994, Three Elegies for Nine Clarinets 1994, The North Shore for solo viola and small orchestra 1994, After Handel's Vesper 1995, Cello Concerto 1995, The Adnan Songbook 1996, Doctor Ox's Experiment (opera) 1997, String Quartet No. 3 1998, The Porazzi Fragment for strings 1998, Biped (ballet) 1999, First Book of Madrigals 2000, Violin Concerto 2000, G (opera) 2001, Second Book of Madrigals 2001, Double Bass Concerto 2002, Book of Laude 2003, Writings on Water (ballet) 2003, Third Book of Madrigals 2003, Eight Irish Madrigals 2004, New York (percussion concerto) 2004, From Egil's Saga 2004, Creamer Etudes 2005, New York 2005, Paper Nautilus 2006, The Stones of the Arch 2006, Nothing Like the Sun 2007, Amjad 2007, Nine Irish Madrigals 2007, To Define

Happiness 2007, Sonnets from Scotland 2007–09, Trondúr I Gøtu 2008, Anail Dé 2008–09, St Brendan Arrives at the Happy Land of the Saints 2009, Four Songs from Northern Seas 2009, Four I Tatti Madrigals 2009, At Portage and Main 2009, The First Light (ballet) 2010, The Solway Canal 2010, The Morrison Songbook 2010, Ramble on Cortona 2010, Reverence (ballet) 2011, Dido and Orfeo (after Purcell and Gluck) (ballet) 2011, Lauda 40 and 41 2011, Four Battiferri Madrigals 2011, Children's Songs 2012, The Open Road 2012, Psalm 141 2012, Lauda 42 2012, Three Choral pieces from the Faroe Islands 2012, The Voice of St Columba 2012, After the Underworlds 2012, Through the Halls 2012, The Beckett Songbook 2012–13, Marilyn Forever (opera) 2013, Pneuma (ballet) 2014, The Seasons (ballet) 2014, 11th Floor (ballet) 2014, Peer Gynt (ballet) 2014, The Fifth Century (cantata) 2014, Fifth Book of Madrigals 2009–14, De Profundis Aquarium 2015, Sixth Book of Madrigals 2015–16. *Films:* Sea and Stars (Nat. Film Bd of Canada) 2003, Season of Mists 2008, Our Chekhov 2010, Proezd Serova 2012–13. *Radio:* I Send You This Cadmium Red (BBC Radio 3, with John Berger and John Christie) 2002, Egil's Last Days (BBC Radio 3) 2004, The Pythagorean Comma (BBC Radio 3) 2012. *Television:* Last Summer (CBC TV, Dir Anna Tchernakova) 2000. *Publications:* contribs to Music and Musicians, Studio International, Art and Artists, Contact, The Guardian, Arcana, Modern Painters, Parkett, Open Space (Moscow). *Honours:* Hon. Fellow, Bath Spa Univ. 2008, Birmingham Conservatoire 2015; Dr hc (Plymouth) 2006. *Current Management:* c/o Schott and Co. Ltd, 48 Great Marlborough Street, London, W1F 7BB, England. *Telephone:* (20) 7534-0750. *Fax:* (20) 7534-0759. *E-mail:* sam.rigby@schott-music.com. *Website:* www.schott-music.com. *E-mail:* gbproductions@gavinbryars.com (office). *Website:* www.gavinbryars.com.

BRYN-JULSON, Phyllis, BM, MM; American singer (soprano) and teacher; b. 5 Feb. 1945, Bowdon, ND; m. Donald S. Sutherland; one s. one d. *Education:* Syracuse Univ. *Career:* debut with the Boston Symphony in Berg's Lulu Suite 1966; has given performances of works by George Crumb, David Del Tredici, Lukas Foss, Ligeti, Berg, Webern, Schoenberg (Pierrot Lunaire) and Charles Wuorinen; appearances at the Berlin, Edinburgh, Lucerne and Aldeburgh Festivals; British debut 1975, in Pli selon Pli by Boulez, conducted by the composer; Boulez 60th-birthday celebrations at Baden-Baden 1985; appeared with orchestras, including the New York Philharmonic, the Boston Symphony, Chicago Symphony, Berlin Philharmonic under Abbado; first operatic role as Malinche in Montezuma by Roger Sessions, US premiere, Boston 1976; sang in Stravinsky's Nightingale and Ravel's L'Enfant et les Sortilèges at Covent Garden season 1986–87; tours of Australia, New Zealand, USSR and Japan with Boulez; Ensemble Intercontemporain; tours of the USA with the Los Angeles Philharmonic and of Europe with the BBC Symphony and Berlin Philharmonic; gave masterclasses at the Moscow Conservatoire 1987; took part in the 80th-birthday celebrations for Olivier Messiaen and Elliott Carter 1988; sang in Carter's A Mirror on Which to Dwell, at London's QEH 1991; Schoenberg's Erwartung at the Festival Hall 1991; premiered Marrying the Hangman (one-woman chamber opera) by Ron Caltabiano in New York and San Francisco; staged and televised opera Il Prigioniero by Dallapiccola in Tokyo, with Charles Dutoit conducting; currently Chair. Voice Dept, Peabody Conservatory, Johns Hopkins Univ. *Recordings include:* A Mirror on which to Dwell; Le Visage Nuptial and Le Soleil des Eaux by Boulez, Erato; Il Prigioniero by Dallapiccola, Salonen, Swedish Radio Symphony; Erwartung by Schoenberg, Simon Rattle, City of Birmingham Symphony Orchestra; Schumann's Frauenliebe und Leben, with Leon Fleisher, piano. *Publication:* Inside Pierrot Lunaire (jtly) 2008. *Honours:* Hon. DFA (Concordia Coll., Minn) 1995; Syracuse Univ. Distinguished Alumni Award, Amphion Foundation Award; inducted into Scandinavian/American Hall of Fame 2000. *Current Management:* Howard Stokar Management, 870 West End Avenue, New York, NY 10025-4948, USA. *E-mail:* hstokar@stokar.com. *Website:* www.peabody.jhu.edu/phyllisbrynjulson.

BRYSON, Roger; British singer (bass); b. 1944, London, England. *Education:* Guildhall School, London, London Opera Centre with Walther Gruner and Otakar Kraus. *Career:* Glyndebourne Festival and Touring Opera from 1978 as Neptune in Il Ritorno d'Ulisse, Quince and Bottom in A Midsummer Night's Dream, Osmin in Die Entführung, Rocco in Fidelio and Leporello in Don Giovanni; Kent Opera in Rigoletto, Die Zauberflöte and Don Giovanni; ENO in the British premiere of Ligeti's Le Grand Macabre 1982; Opera North in Die Meistersinger, Werther, La Fanciulla del West and Love of Three Oranges; Scottish Opera as Schigolch in Lulu and Don Alfonso in Così fan tutte; sang at Nancy in the French premiere of Tippett's King Priam and on television in the Midsummer Marriage 1989; as Alvise in La Gioconda for the Chelsea Opera Group, Mephistopheles in Faust for New Sussex Opera 1989, Swallow in Peter Grimes, Don Pasquale for Opera North, Bartered Bride for New Tel-Aviv Opera; sang in concert performances of Ligeti's Le Grand Macabre at the Festival Hall 1989, Don Pasquale for Opera North 1990, premieres of Europeras 3 and 4 by John Cage at the 1990 Almeida Festival, London; sang Quince in A Midsummer Night's Dream, Sadler's Wells, Dikoi in Katya Kabanova for Glyndebourne Touring Opera 1992, Flint in Billy Budd 1992, Claggart in Billy Budd for Opéra de Nancy 1993, Don Basilio in Barber of Seville for Opera Northern Ireland, Calandro in L'Incontro Improvviso by Haydn, for Garsington Festival, and Don Alfonso in Così fan tutte for ENO.

BUCHAN, Cynthia; British singer (mezzo-soprano); b. 1 July 1949, Edinburgh, Scotland. *Education:* Royal Scottish Academy of Music. *Career:* debut in Edinburgh 1968 in Monteverdi's Il Ballo delle Ingrate; has appeared widely in the UK and Europe as Mozart's Cherubino and Dorabella, Massenet's Charlotte, Rossini's Rosina, Verdi's Preziosilla, Tchaikovsky's Olga and as Carmen; in 1987 sang in L'Enfant et les Sortilèges at Glyndebourne, Carmen for Opera North and Mistress Quickly in Peter Stein's production of Falstaff for the Welsh National Opera; guest appearances in Madrid, Munich, Paris as Rosina, Frankfurt as Babette in Henze's English Cat, Adelaide and Hamburg as Miranda in Cavalli's L'Ormindo, and Amsterdam as Varvara in Katya Kabanova; Glyndebourne as Hermia in A Midsummer Night's Dream 1989; sang Despina in Così fan tutte for New Israeli Opera 1994; Maddalena in Rigoletto for WNO 1997; concert appearances in London, Munich, Paris and Lyon; conductors include Gielen, Andrew Davis, Rattle, Ivan Fischer, Knussen, Del Mar, Bernstein and Bertini. *Recordings include:* Bersi in Andrea Chénier (video at Covent Garden) 1985.

BUCHANAN, Alison; British singer (soprano); b. (Alison Harding), 2 Sept. 1969, Bedford. *Education:* Guildhall School of Music and the Curtis Institute, Philadelphia. *Career:* appearances as Clara in Porgy and Bess at the Barbican, in Messiah at Chichester Cathedral, Mozart's Requiem and Bach's Christmas Oratorio at Chelmsford Cathedral and Strauss's Four Last Songs at Curtis Hall; debut with the San Francisco Opera with Western Opera Theatre as Mozart's Countess; season 1995–96 at San Francisco as Mimi, Juliana in Argento's The Aspern Papers, and Micaela; season 1996–97 with Porgy and Bess excerpts in Bruges and Paris and appearances in Elektra, Death in Venice and Rigoletto at San Francisco; other roles include Rosalinde, Mathilde in Guillaume Tell, Helena in A Midsummer Night's Dream and Madame Cortese in Il Viaggio a Reims; sang Giunone in Cesti's Il Pomo d'Oro at Batignano, 1998; title role in Ariadne auf Naxos with Birmingham Opera Co. *Honours:* first place, Maggie Teyte Competition 1991, first prize, Washington Int. Competition 1995, Pavarotti Competition, Philadelphia 1995, Decca Prize, Kathleen Ferrier Competition 1996. *Current Management:* Robert Gilder & Company, c/o Chase Thompson, Pinnacle Arts Management, 889 Ninth Avenue, 2nd Floor, New York, NY 10019, USA. *Telephone:* (212) 397-5299. *Fax:* (212) 397-7920. *E-mail:* cthompson@pinnaclearts.com. *Website:* www.alibuchanan.com.

BUCHANAN, Dorothy Quita; New Zealand composer; b. 28 Sept. 1945, Christchurch. *Education:* Univ. of Canterbury. *Career:* founded music workshops at Christchurch 1973; music educationalist from 1977; composer-in-residence, New Zealand Film Archives, Wellington 1984. *Compositions include:* Five Vignettes of Women for flute and female chorus 1987, other vocal music, Sinfonietta in five Movements 1989, Due Concertante for violin, cello and orchestra 1991, music for stage and screen, The Layers of Time for cello, women's voices and orchestra 1995, chamber music, including Echoes and Reflections for clarinet, guitar, violin and cello 1993.

BUCHANAN, Isobel Wilson; British singer (soprano); b. 15 March 1954, Glasgow, Scotland; d. of Stewart Buchanan and Mary Buchanan; m. Jonathan Stephen Geoffrey King (actor Jonathan Hyde) 1980; two d. *Education:* Cumbernauld Comprehensive High School and Royal Scottish Acad. of Music and Drama. *Career:* professional debut in Sydney, Australia with Richard Bonynge and Joan Sutherland 1976–78; British debut, Glyndebourne 1978; US and German debuts 1979; Vienna Staatsoper debut 1979; ENO debut 1985, Paris Opera debut 1986; now freelance artist working with all major opera cos and orchestras and giving recitals; teaches and regularly gives master-classes and acts as adjudicator in music festivals and competitions. *Recordings:* Beethoven's Ninth Symphony, Werther, Mozart Arias and Duets. *E-mail:* isobel@totalfiasco.co.uk (office).

BUCHBINDER, Rudolf; Austrian pianist; b. 11 Feb. 1946, Leitmeritz. *Education:* studied with Bruno Seidlhofer. *Career:* extensive repertoire of concert pieces, both classical and modern; has performed works rarely played, including The Diabelli Variations, a collection from 50 Austrian composers; has performed a cycle of all 32 Beethoven Sonatas; performances in many major cities in Europe, USA, South America, Australia and Japan; regular guest at major music festivals; has played with all important leading conductors. *Recordings:* over 80 recordings including The Diabelli Variations, Joseph Haydn piano works, Beethoven: The Sonata Legacy (ECHO Klassik Award for Instrumentalist of the Year/Piano 2012) 2011, Beethoven Piano Concertos 1–5 2011. *Honours:* Grand Prix du Disque (for Haydn's piano works).

BUCHLA, Donald Frederick, BA; American composer and electronic instrument designer; b. 17 April 1937, Southgate, CA. *Education:* Univ. of California at Berkeley. *Career:* installed first Buchla synthesizer, San Francisco Tape Music Center, 1966; Founder of Buchla Assocs, Berkeley, 1966; designed and manufactured various electronic instruments; designed electronic music studios including Royal Academy of Music, Stockholm, and IRCAM, Paris; Co-Founder, Electric Weasel Ensemble, 1975; Co-Dir, Artists Research Collective, Berkeley, 1978–. *Compositions include:* Cicada Music for some 2,500 Cicadas, 1963; 5 Video Mirrors for Audience of 1 or More, 1966; Anagnorisis for 1 Performer and 1 Voice, 1970; Harmonic Pendulum for Buchla Series 200 Synthesizer, 1972; Garden for 3 Performers and 1 Dancer, 1975; Keyboard Encounter for 2 Pianos, 1976; Q for 14 Instruments, 1979; Silicon Cello for Amplified Cello, 1979; Consensus Conduction for Buchla Series 300 Synthesizer and Audience, 1981. *Honours:* Guggenheim Fellowship 1978, NEA grant 1981. *Address:* c/o Buchla and Associates, PO Box 10205, Berkeley, CA 94709, USA. *Website:* www.buchla.com.

BUCHNER, Eberhard; German singer (tenor); b. 6 Nov. 1939, Dresden. *Education:* Carl Maria Von Weber-Musikhochschule, Dresden. *Career:* debut at Schwerin 1964 as Tamino; Staatsoper Dresden from 1966, and Staatsoper Berlin from 1968, notably in operas by Strauss, Mozart and Wagner; sang Schubert's Die schöne müllerin in Vienna 1972; appeared at the Vatican 1973 in a concert conducted by Bernstein; sang at Metropolitan Opera 1974, Covent Garden 1975, Hamburg Staatsoper 1983 in a revival of Armadis de Gaule by J.C. Bach, Théâtre de la Monnaie in Brussels, and Salzburg Festival 1985 and 1990 as Flamand in Capriccio; Royal Opera Copenhagen 1986 as Wagner's Lohengrin; sang Adolar in Euryanthe at the Berlin Staatsoper 1986; La Scala Milan 1988 as Erik in Der fliegende Holländer and sang Lohengrin at Lisbon 1990; sang Dionysus in The Bassarids at Hamburg 1994 and as Der Alte in the premiere of Schnittke's Historia von D. Johann Fausten 1995. *Recordings:* Die schweigsame Frau by Strauss; Froh in Das Rheingold; Bach Cantatas; Bach's B minor Mass; Sacred Music by Mozart; Beethoven's 9th Symphony.

BUCHT, Gunnar, PhD; Swedish composer and writer; b. 5 Aug. 1927, Stocksund; m. Bergljot Krohn 1958. *Education:* studied composition with Karl Birger-Blomdahl, Carl Orff, Goffredo Petrassi, Max Deutsch, piano with Yngve Flyckt. *Career:* debut as composer and pianist 1949; Chair. Soc. of Swedish Composers 1963–69; teacher, Stockholm Univ. 1965–69; Vice-Pres. Int. Soc. for Contemporary Music 1969–72; Cultural Attaché, Embassy in Bonn 1970–73; Prof. of Composition, Royal Coll. of Music 1975–85, Dir 1987–93; mem. Royal Acad. of Music. *Compositions include:* 16 symphonies 1952–2012, two cello concertos 1955–90, four string quartets 1951, 1959, 1997, 2011, String Quintet 1950, Sonata for piano and percussion 1955, La fine della diaspora for tenor, chorus and orchestra (Quasimodo) 1957, The Pretenders (opera, after Ibsen) 1966, Symphonie pour la musique libérée for tape 1969, Lutheran Mass 1973, Journées oubliées 1975, Au delà 1977, Violin Concerto 1978, The Big Bang – and After 1979, Georgica 1980, En Clairobscur for chamber orchestra 1981, One Day I Went Out Into The World, novel for orchestra 1983–84, Blad från mitt gulsippeänge for clarinet and piano 1985, Fresques mobiles 1986, Unter Vollem Einsatz for organ and five percussionists 1987, Tönend bewegte Formen for orchestra 1987, Piano Concerto 1994, Coup sur Coup for percussion 1995, Concerto de Marle for viola and orchestra 1996, Movements in Space for orchestra 1996, Panta Rei for soli, chorus and orchestra 1998–99, Alienus' Dream for orchestra 1999, Odysseia (Kazantzakis) half-scenic oratorio for soli, chorus and orchestra, Part One 2000–03, Partita for two violins 2001, Den starkare (Strindberg) monodrama for mezzo-soprano and orchestra 2001, Superstrings for orchestra 2002, The Infinite Melody for orchestra 2004, Notenbüchlein für Duo Gelland for two violins 2008, Wie die Zeit vergeht (Quasi una sinfonia) for orchestra 2009, A la recherche d'une musique inoubliable 2013. *Recordings:* Symphony 7, Violin Concerto, Piano Concerto, Georgica, Cantata, Quatre pièces pour le pianiste, Coup sur Coup, Sections of One Day I Went Out Into the World, Tre per due for two violins. *Publications:* Electronic Music in Sweden 1977, Europe in Music 1996, Född på Krigsstigen (autobiog.) 1997, Rum, rörelse, tid 1999, Pythagoras' String 2005, Rum, Människa, Musik 2009, Quid est tonus 2009, Tankebok: tema musik 2011, Aeolian Harp 2012, Modernism, modernitet, musik 2013, Om det fula i musiken och andra essäer 2013; contrib. to Swedish Journal of Musicology, Nordic Journal of Aesthetics. *Honours:* Royal Medal Litteris et artibus, Royal Acad. of Music Medal for För tonkonstens främjande. *Address:* Rådmansgatan 74, 11360 Stockholm, Sweden. *Telephone:* (8) 736-60-31. *E-mail:* gb.bucht@telia.com. *Website:* www.gunnarbucht.com.

BUCKLEY, Richard Edward, BM, MMus; American conductor; *Principal Conductor, Cleveland Opera*; b. 1 Sept. 1953, New York, NY. *Education:* North Carolina School of the Arts, Winston-Salem, Catholic University of America, Washington, DC, Aspen School of Music, Colorado, Salzburg Mozarteum. *Career:* Asst Conductor and Chorusmaster, Washington Opera Soc. 1973–74; Asst to Music Dir, Seattle Opera 1973–74; Assistant Associate, Resident, and Principal Guest Conductor at Seattle Symphony Orchestra, 1974–85; Music Director, Oakland Symphony Orchestra, California, 1983–86; Guest Conductor, New York Philharmonic Orchestra, Philadelphia Orchestra, Houston Symphony Orchestra, San Antonio Symphony Orchestra, Oregon Symphony Orchestra, Los Angeles Philharmonic Orchestra, Minnesota Orchestra, Indianapolis Symphony Orchestra, BBC Symphony Orchestra, Royal Philharmonic Orchestra, Royal Liverpool Philharmonic Orchestra, Chicago Lyric Opera, Los Angeles Opera, New York City Opera, Houston Grand Opera, Canadian Opera, Netherlands Opera, and Hamburg State Opera, Covent Garden, Paris Opéra Bastille, Berlin Deutsche Oper, Royal Opera, Copenhagen, Teatro Bellini, Teatro San Carlos, Lisbon; Recent operatic premieres include Paulus' The Postman Always Rings Twice with Miami Opera and The Woodlanders at St Louis; US premiere of Sallinen's The King Goes Forth to France, for Sante Fe Opera; Other projects include Les Contes d'Hoffmann with Los Angeles Music Center Opera, Aida at Chicago and Rossini's Il Viaggio a Reims at St Louis; Conducted Il Barbiere di Siviglia for Miami Opera in 1990, and Dvořák's The Devil and Kate at St Louis; Season 1996 with Butterfly at Los Angeles and Aida at Philadelphia; Principal Conductor Opera Cleveland 2006–. *Honours:* prizewinner Besançon Competition 1979, Rupert Foundation Competition 1982. *Address:* c/o Cleveland Opera, 1422 Euclid Avenue, Suite 1052, Cleveland, OH 44115-2063, USA. *E-mail:* mail@clevelandopera.org. *Website:* www.clevelandopera.org.

BUCQUET, Marie-Françoise; French pianist; b. 28 Oct. 1937, Montvilliers; m. Jorge Chaminé. *Education:* Vienna Music Academy, Paris Conservatoire, studied with Wilhelm Kempff, Alfred Brendel and Leon Fleisher. *Career:* debut at Marguerite Long School 1948; attended course by Eduard Steuermann at Salzburg to study music of Schoenberg and followed courses by Pierre Boulez at Basle; Sylvano Bussotti, Betsy Jolas and Iannis Xenakis have written for her; performs works by Bach, Haydn, Stockhausen, Schoenberg and standard repertory music; formed duo with husband, Jorge Chaminé 1979–; Prof. of Accompaniment and Piano Pedagogy, Paris Conservatoire 1986–, Head of Teaching Dept 1991. *Honours:* Edison Award 1976. *Address:* 35 rue Vaneau, 75007 Paris, France (home). *Telephone:* 1-47-05-72-58 (home).

BUCZYNSKI, Walter; Canadian composer and pianist; b. 17 Dec. 1933, Toronto. *Education:* studied with Milhaud, and with Nadia Boulanger at Toronto Conservatory. *Career:* teacher of piano and theory, Royal Conservatory of Toronto 1962; teacher of theory, Univ. of Toronto from 1970. *Compositions include:* Piano Trio 1954, Suite for wind quintet 1955, Divertimento for violin, cello, clarinet and bassoon 1957, Mr Rhinoceros and his Musicians (children's opera) 1957, Do Re Mi (children's opera) 1967, Squares in a Circle for flute, violin, cello and strings 1967, Four Movements for piano and strings 1969, Zeroing In five pieces for various vocal and instrumental groups 1971–72, Three Against Many for flute, clarinet, bassoon and orchestra 1973, Concerto for violin, cello and orchestra 1975, Olympics '75 for brass quintet, From The Buczynski Book of the Dead (chamber opera) 1975, Naked at the Opera 1979, Piano Concerto 1979, Piano Quintet 1984, The August Collection 27 preludes 1987, Litanies for accordion and percussion 1988, songs and piano music.

BUDAI, Livia; Hungarian opera singer (mezzo-soprano); b. 23 June 1950, Esztergom; d. of Ferenc Budai and Martha Budal (née Koszegi); m. Julius Batky. *Education:* Ferenc Liszt Acad. of Music. *Career:* mem. Artistic Staff, Budapest State Opera 1973–75, Gelsenkirchen Music Theatre, Germany 1977–80, Munich State Opera, Germany 1980–83; appearances in Brussels, Royal Opera House, London, Paris, Toronto, Montreal, Metropolitan Opera, New York, San Francisco, Milan, Venice, Florence, Rome, Verona; mem. Bd of Dirs J. B. EM Services Inc., St Laurent, Montreal; numerous recordings and TV appearances. *Television:* FR3: Rusalka, Falstaff, Nabucco; BRT: Tristan and Isolde, Don Carlos, Fl Trubadur. *Honours:* Ravel Prize 1974, Erkel Prize 1976, Kodaly Prize. *Current Management:* c/o Opera Vladarski, Doblingerstr. 57/18, 1190 Vienna, Austria. *Telephone:* (1) 368-69-60. *E-mail:* livbudai@netscape.net. *Website:* www.liviabudai.com.

BUDD, Ruth June; Canadian bassist; b. 20 June 1924, Winnipeg; one s. one d. *Education:* Toronto Conservatory of Music and Univ. of Toronto. *Career:* bassist, Vancouver Jr Symphony, later Vancouver Symphony; bassist, Toronto Symphony Orchestra 1947–52, 1964–89, Vancouver Opera Orchestra 1992–; Founder Toronto Sr Strings 1992–; mandola player, Shevchenko Mandolin Orchestra 1996–; mem. Symphony Six 1952, CBC Symphony; Prin. Bass, Stratford Festival Orchestra, Halifax Symphony Orchestra; Founder and Chair. Org. of Canadian Symphony Musicians; Founding mem. CG Film Soc.; mem. Performing Artists for Nuclear Disarmament. *Honours:* Women of Distinction Award 1984. *Address:* 602 Melita Crescent, Apt 801, Toronto, ON M6G 3Z5, Canada (home). *Telephone:* (416) 536-8506 (home). *Fax:* (416) 536-8518 (home).

BUDIN, Jan; Czech clarinettist; b. 20 May 1950, Prague; m. Vlasta Budínová 1973, one s. one d. *Education:* Acad. of Arts, Prague. *Career:* concert performances in Europe; television performances in the Czech Republic, Poland, Germany, Sweden, Denmark; Ed.-in-Chief, Musical Journal for Blind. *Compositions:* for various chamber ensembles. *Recordings:* František Vincenc Kramár–Quartet B flat major, Op 21, No. 1; Quartet E flat major, Op 21, No. 2; Quintet B flat major, Op 95–Jan Budín with Panocha Quartet; Johannes Brahms–Quintet B minor, Op 115–Jan Budín with Panocha Quartet; František Vincenc Kramar–Symphonia Concertante E flat major, Op 70; Julius Fucik: Chamber music for two clarinets and bassoon; More recordings (especially early Czech music for Czech radio). *Honours:* first prize International Competition of Blind Musicians, Prague 1975.

BUFFLE, Christine; Swiss singer (soprano); b. 1971, Exeter, England. *Education:* Geneva Conservatoire, Guildhall School of Music and Drama, London and Opera Studio, Zürich. *Career:* sang Ninetta in La Finta semplice and Doralice in Scarlatti's Trionfo dell' Onore, Geneva; Musetta, Naiad (Ariadne) Berlin Komische Opera; Coryphée, Gluck's Armide, Versailles; Queen of Night, Scottish Opera; Zürich Opera as Sicle in Cavalli's L'Ormindo, Papagena, High Priestess, Barbarina, Suor Angelica, Echo, Queen of Night and Donna Anna in Gazzaniga's Don Giovanni; season 1999–2000 with Musetta and Naiad for the Komische Oper, Anna in Kurt Weill's Seven Deadly Sins in Geneva; with Landestheater Innsbruck 2003–, roles include Susanna in The Marriage of Figaro 2004, Donna Anna in Don Giovanni 2004, Violetta in La Traviata 2007, Mélisande in Pelléas et Mélisande 2007, Nedda in I Pagliacci 2007, Rose in What Next?, Turin 2008; concerts include Handel's Samson and Haydn's The Seasons; Mozart's C Minor Mass and Requiem; Vivaldi's Gloria; Bach's Magnificat and St John Passion; Honegger's King David, Geneva 2000;, Florent Schmitt's Psaume 47 with BBC Nat. Orchestra of Wales 2006. *Recordings include:* Stravinsky's Les Noces and songs, Massenet's Thaïs 2002, Janacek's Cunning Little Vixen. *Honours:* Eberhardt Waechter Prize 2006. *Current Management:* Intermusica, 16 Duncan Terrace, London N1 8BZ, England. *Telephone:* (20) 7278-5455. *E-mail:* jmaynard@intermusica.co.uk. *Website:* www.christinebuffle.com.

BUFKENS, Roland; Belgian singer (tenor) and academic; b. 26 April 1936, Ronse; m. Simone Deboelpaepe 1961; one d. *Education:* Brussels Conservatoire. *Career:* debut in Germany; German concerts specialising in Bach tradition and also the St John and St Matthew Passions; performances with several German orchestras conducted by Kurt Thomas, Karl Richter, Kurt Redel and Nikolaus Harnoncourt; Berlioz's Romeo and Juliet in a tour of Japan and later in Théâtre des Champs Elysées, Paris, both conducted by Lorin Maazel; other performances include Stravinsky's Mavra in the Concertgebouw of Amsterdam, Martin's Mystère de la Nativité at Madrid Teatro Real (all performances broadcast); Manuel de Falla's Vida Breve conducted by R. F. de Burgos in Palais des Beaux-Arts Bruxelles; participated several times in the Holland Festival, Biennale of Zagreb, Festival of Lourdes, Schwetzinger Festspiele, Festival van Vlaanderen; Prof., Brussels Conservatoire and Lemmens Inst., Leuven. *Recordings include:* works by Schubert, Grétry, Gossec, Lully, Schütz, Bach, Dumont and Carl Orff, compositions by Belgian composers André Laporte and Willem Kersters. *Publications include:* contrib. to Lemmensinstitute Adem, articles for Dutch Singers' Asscn ANZ. *Honours:* Chevalier, Ordre de la Couronne 1978; first prize Brussels Conservatoire 1959, Cecilia Prize for Zemire et Azor, F. M. Grétry, Belgium 1974.

BÜHLER, Urs; Swiss singer (tenor); b. 19 July 1971, Willisau. *Education:* Sweelinck Conservatorium, The Netherlands. *Career:* mem., Il Divo 2003–. *Recordings include:* albums: Il Divo 2004, Ancora 2005, The Christmas Collection 2005, Siempre 2006, The Promise 2008, Wicked Game 2011. *Website:* www.ildivo.com.

BUJARSKI, Zbigniew; Polish composer; b. 21 Aug. 1933, Muszyna. *Education:* Kraków State Coll. of Music with Wiechowicz and Wodiczko. *Compositions include:* Burning Bushes for soprano and chamber ensemble 1958, Triptych for string orchestra and percussion 1959, Synchrony I for soprano and chamber ensemble 1959, II for soprano, chorus and orchestra 1960, Zones for chamber ensemble 1961, Kinoth for orchestra 1963, Chamber Composition for voice and ensemble 1963, Contraria for orchestra 1965, El Hombre for vocal soloists, chorus and orchestra 1969–73, Musica Domestica for 18 strings 1977, Concert for strings 1979, Similis Greco (symphonic cycle) 1979–83, Quartet on the Advent 1984, Quartet for the Resurrection 1990, Pavane for the Distant One for strings 1994, Lumen for orchestra 1997, Five Songs for soprano and strings 1997. *Address:* c/o Society of Authors ZAiKS, 2 Hipoteczna Street, 00 092 Warsaw, Poland (office). *E-mail:* sekretariat@zaiks.org.pl.

BUJEVSKY, Taras; Russian composer; b. 23 June 1957, Kharkiv, Ukraine; m. Jekaterina Tarakanova 1991; one s. one d. *Education:* Moscow State Conservatoire. *Career:* Musical Editor, Russian television, 1993–98; Lecturer, Russian Theatre Academy, 1995–97; music is frequently heard on Russian radio and television, including seven large broadcasts devoted to his life and music 1991–99; mem. Moscow Composers Union, Russian Union of Cinematography. *Compositions:* Symphony, 1989; Repercussions of the Light for string orchestra, 1992; Foreshortenings, chamber symphony for percussion, trumpet, two pianos and mechanical devices, 1993; Post Scriptum for symphony orchestra, 1994; Breathing of Stillness for chamber orchestra, 1995; Eisenstein-Line, Suite for symphony orchestra, 1997; Music for Chamber Ensembles and Solo Instruments includes: Sensus Sonoris for flute and percussion, 1990; Silver Voices for four trumpets, 1991; Pathes of Phonosphere for clarinet; Voice of Loneliness for tenor saxophone, 1993; Mosaics, Suite for grand piano, 1994; Ciao Antonio for flute, oboe, violin, cello, harpsichord and tape; Für Isabella for sextet, 1995; Quartet for oboe, clarinet, bassoon and piano, 1996; Agnus Dei for mixed choir a capella, 1998; Electronic music, music for 30 films and television performances: Participant in international festivals: Moscow Autumn 1990–2003; 5 Capitals, Kiev, 1993; Festival of Contemporary Russian Music in Helsingborg, Sweden, 1994; Festival of Electronic Music, Synthesis-95, Bourges, France;Omen for symphony orchestra, 2000; Aria.ru-monoopera for actress, piano and tape, 2000; Music of Sovok for prepared dustpan and tape, 2000; Largo ricitare for violin and tape, 2001; Dolente cantabile for oboe d'amore, 2002; Das Kolophonium for 12 cellos, 2002; Choirs on poems by K. Vojtyla, 2003; Music for computer's games. *Publications:* Music for S Eisenstein's film The General Line, score for symphony orchestra, 1997; Repercations of the Light, score for string orchestra, 2003; Mosaics, Suite for grand piano, 2004; Collected verses, 2003; Essay About Death but more about Life, 2003. *Honours:* Russian TV TEFI 1999. *Address:* Novoslobodskaja Str 67/69, Apt 113, Moscow 127055, Russia. *E-mail:* buyevsky@mtu-net.ru.

BUKOWSKI, Miroslaw Andrzej, MA; Polish composer and conductor; b. 5 Jan. 1936, Warsaw; m. Hanna Burzynska 1966; one d. *Education:* Acad. of Music, Poznań, Acad. of Music, Gdansk. *Career:* debut at Polish Students Music Festival, Poznań 1957; Asst, Acad. of Music, Poznań 1963–67, Lecturer 1967–80, Asst Prof. 1980–88, Prof. 1988–; Conductor, Wielkopolska Symphony Orchestra 1971–75; Prof., Pedagogical Coll., Zielena Gora, 1984–; mem. Asscn of Polish Composers, Soc. of Authors ZAiKS. *Compositions include:* Requiem for Solo Voices, Mixed Choir and Orchestra, based on Akhmatova's poem; Pastourelle, Interferences for Symphony Orchestra; Concerto for Cello and Orchestra; Ostinato and Mobile for Percussion Ensemble; Swinging Concerto; Symphonic Allegro for Symphony Orchestra; 4 Piano Sonatas; Sonatina for Piano; Expression for Piano; Three Sleepy Poems for Mixed Choir; 2 Cycles of Songs, Znikomosc, Stances.

BULCHEVA, Zlata; Russian singer (mezzo-soprano); b. 1970, St Petersburg. *Education:* St Petersburg Conservatoire. *Career:* appearances with the Kirov Opera from 1996, notably as Olga in Eugene Onegin, Konchakovna (Prince Igor), Carmen, Cherubino, and Erda in Das Rheingold; further engagements

as Ratmir (Ruslan and Lyudmilla), Nezhata (Sadko), Frasya in Prokofiev's Semyon Kotko and Fyodor in Boris Godunov; concerts include Mahler 2nd and 3rd Symphonies; sang with the Kirov Opera at Covent Garden, 2000. *Recordings include:* Boris Godunov. *Honours:* Prizewinner, Young Opera Singer's International Vocal, St Petersburg, 1996, International Rimsky-Korsakov Competition, 1998, and International Tchaikovsky, Moscow, 1999.

BULLOCK, Susan Margaret, CBE, BMus, FRAM; British singer (soprano); b. 9 Dec. 1958, Cheshire, England. *Education:* Royal Holloway Coll., Univ. of London, Royal Acad. of Music and Nat. Opera Studio, London. *Career:* roles with ENO have included Donna Anna, Marguerite in Faust, Alice Ford, Butterfly, Ellen Orford, Princess Natalie in Henze's Prince of Homburg 1996, Desdemona and Isolde; Glyndebourne debut as Jenůfa 1996, followed by Katya Kabanova and Lisa in Queen of Spades; guest appearances with New Israeli Opera and Flanders Opera in Tippett's King Priam; US debut as Butterfly at Portland and title role in British premiere of Die Aegyptische Helena at Garsington 1996; Covent Garden debut as Marie in Wozzeck; other important roles include Wagner's Isolde for Opera North, Oper Frankfurt, Rouen, Düsseldorf and Verona, Brünnhilde in Die Walküre, Siegfried and Götterdämmerung in Tokyo, Brünnhilde in Götterdämmerung at Perth Festival and Lisbon's Teatro São Carlos, Els in Schrecker's Der Schatzgräber, Oper Frankfurt, R. Strauss's Elektra at La Scala, Stuttgart, Frankfurt, Dresden and Rouen, Lady Macbeth in Bloch's Macbeth in Vienna, Magda Sorel in Menotti's The Consul, Spoleto Festival, Italy and Teatro Colon, Buenos Aires, Argentina, Female Chorus in Britten's Lucretia, Munich, Seville, Trittico in Charleston, Ellen Orford in Peter Grimes for ENO and Royal Danish Opera, and Tosca at Royal Albert Hall and debut Wigmore Hall recital; concerts include Berlioz's La Mort de Cléopatre with BBC Philharmonic Orchestra, Schoenberg's Erwartung and Gorecki's Third Symphony with BBC Symphony Orchestra, Mahler's 4th Symphony with Royal Liverpool Philharmonic, Beethoven's Missa Solemnis with Les Arts Florissants, Salome and Elektra with Hong Kong Philharmonic Orchestra, Messiaen's Poèmes pour Mi at the Proms 2004, Prelude and Liebestod from Tristan with Philharmonia, Salome for Opera North; recent appearances as Wagner's Brünnhilde at Wiener Staatsoper, Teatro La Fenice, Teatro Nacional de São Carlos Lisbon, Oper Frankfurt, Opéra de Lyon, New Nat. Theatre, Tokyo and with Canadian Opera Co.; first ever soprano to sing four consecutive cycles of Der Ring des Nibelungen at Royal Opera House, Covent Garden, appearing as Brünnhilde under Sir Antonio Pappano as part of London 2012 Festival; has also performed the role of Isolde in London, Frankfurt, Verona and Rouen; current season highlights include Der Ring des Nibelungen for Opera Australia in Neil Armfield's new production conducted by Pietari Inkinen, performances of Siegfried and Götterdämmerung for Deutsche Oper Berlin under Donald Runnicles, and addition of Owen Wingrave to her repertoire with performances at Aldeburgh Festival; gives recitals with Malcolm Martineau at Melbourne Recital Centre and at Sydney Opera House. *Recordings include:* Hindemith's Sancta Susanna, Menotti's The Consul, Britten's Albert Herring, Chausson's Le Roi Arthus. *Honours:* Hon. Fellow, Royal Holloway Coll. 2004; Royal Philharmonic Soc. Award for Best Singer 2009. *Current Management:* c/o Ian Stones, Harrison Parrott, 5–6 Albion Court, London, W6 0QT, England. *Telephone:* (20) 3725-9104. *Fax:* (20) 7221-5042. *E-mail:* ian.stones@harrisonparrott.co.uk. *Website:* www.harrisonparrott.com.

BULYCHEV-OKSER, Michael, DipMus; Russian pianist and composer; b. 17 Feb. 1981, Moscow. *Education:* Moscow Central Music School for Gifted Children, Moscow State Conservatoire, Juilliard School, USA with Oxana Yablonskaya, New York University with Martin Canin. *Career:* piano and composition debut, Rachmaninov Recital Hall, Moscow Conservatoire 1993; tour, with group of Russian musicians, to Greece, Egypt, Israel and Turkey 1993; moved to USA 1996; performed in numerous different piano recitals; scholarship, Summer Composition Program, La Schola Cantorum, Paris, France 1998; debut on New York radio on Robert Sherman's Young Artists Showcase series Soloist, Manhattan Philharmonic Orchestra 1998; Spring music programme concert, Oyster Bay, Long Island, NY 1999; solo piano recital, Italian Culture Centre of Long Island 1999; Young Musicians' Concert at Weill Recital Hall at Carnegie Hall, New York 1999. *Compositions include:* Sea Landscape, Near Ancient Jerusalem Walls, Kizi: The Dying Sacred Place, Clouds are Over Trinity-St Sergey Monastery, The Areadna's Thread theme and variations, Lullaby for violin and piano, Prelude in C Major for violin and piano, Sonate in D Major for cello and piano, Old Moscow Houses (to words by Marina Zvetaeva). *Recordings include:* Solo Piano Recital 1996, Solo Original Composition Concert 1997, Robert Sherman's Young Artist Showcase performance 1998, Young Musicians' Concert 1999, Michael Bulychev-Okser - Transkriptions of the Past and Future 2012. *Honours:* Richard Kimball Award in Composition 1999, 2000, Carl Owen Award in Piano 1998, First Prize, Young Artists Concerto Competition 1997, First Prize, Piucerda International Piano Competition, Spain 1999, winner, Citta di Gorizia International Piano Competition 2004. *Website:* bulychevokser.com.

BULYCHEVA, Zlata; Russian singer (mezzo-soprano); b. 1970. *Education:* St Petersburg Conservatory. *Career:* appearances with the Kirov Opera from 1996, as Carmen, Olga, Fyodor in Boris Godunov, Cherubino, Konchakovna in Prince Igor and Ratmir in Ruslan and Lyudmilla; Froysa in Prokofiev's Semyon Kotko, Nezhata in Rimsky's Sadko, Polina (The Queen of Spades) and Erda in Das Rheingold; mezzo roles in operas by Verdi, and Maria Bolkonskaya in War and Peace; sang with the Kirov on tour to Covent

Garden, London 2001; concerts include Mahler's 2nd and 3rd Symphonies. *Recordings include:* Boris Godunov. *Honours:* Prizewinner, International Rimsky-Korsakov Vocal competition, St Petersburg, 1993 and International Tchaikovsky, Moscow, 1994.

BUMBRY, Grace; American singer (soprano, mezzo-soprano); b. 4 Jan. 1937, St Louis, Mo.; d. of Benjamin Bumbry and Melzia Bumbry. *Education:* Boston and Northwestern Univs, Music Acad. of the West. *Career:* debut at Paris Opera as Amneris in Aida March 1960; Basel Opera 1960–63; Carmen with Paris Opera and toured Japan; Royal Opera, Brussels; Die Schwarze Venus, Tannhäuser, Bayreuth Festival 1961 and 1962; Vienna State Opera 1963; Covent Garden 1963, 1968, 1969, 1976, 1978, 1988; Salzburg Festival 1964; Metropolitan Opera 1965–85; La Scala 1964–79, Chicago Lyric 1962–78; Porgy and Bess, New York Metropolitan Opera 1985; Hon. Amb., UNESCO. *Honours:* Hon. Citizen of Baltimore, Los Angeles, Philadelphia, St Louis; Commdr des Arts et Lettres 1996, Kammersängerin 2003; Hon. DH (Univ. of St Louis), (Rust Coll.); Hon. DMus (Rockhurst Coll.), (Univ. of Missouri); Richard Wagner Medal 1963, Grammy Award 1979, Royal Opera House Medal 1988, Puccini Award 1990, Kennedy Center Honor 2009. *Current Management:* c/o Jack Mastroianni, IMG Artists, 752 West 57th Street, 5th Floor, New York, NY 70079, USA. *E-mail:* jmastroianni@imgartists.com. *E-mail:* gbumbryoffice@gmail.com. *Website:* gracebumbry.com.

BUNDSCHUH, Dieter; German singer (tenor); b. 10 May 1940, Würzburg. *Education:* Conservatory of Würzburg, also studied with F. Tietjen-Steyer in Wiesbaden. *Career:* chorister, Municipal Theatre of Würzburg 1962–65, soloist 1965–68; soloist, Municipal Theatre of Münster 1968–72, Staatstheater Wiesbaden 1973–82; guest appearances with Cologne Opera House and National Theatre Mannheim; performed at Vienna Staatsoper 1984–87 as Strauss's Matteo and Flamand; Belmonte in Die Entführung and Alfred in Die Fledermaus, Wiesbaden 1981 in premiere of Das Kalte Herz, by Kirchner; guest appearances throughout Germany including Arnold in Guillaume Tell at Mannheim 1987; premiere of Hans Zender's Don Quichotte at Stuttgart 1993; sang Dr Caius in Falstaff at Bonn 1998; other roles include Zemlinsky's Zwerg, Vere in Billy Budd and the Captain in Wozzeck; many concert and broadcast engagements.

BUNDSCHUH, Eva-Maria; German singer (soprano); b. 16 Oct. 1941, Brunswick. *Education:* studied in Chemnitz and Leipzig. *Career:* debut at Bernburg 1967, as Humperdinck's Hansel; sang at Chemnitz 1969–74, Potsdam 1974–77; associated with Staatsoper Berlin from 1976, Komische Oper from 1981; sang first as mezzo, as Dorabella, Carmen and Eboli then soprano repertory from 1978; Olympia and Antonia in Les Contes d'Hoffmann, Wagner's Eva and Freia, Violetta, Musetta and Donna Anna; Berlin Staatsoper roles have included title in premiere of Judith by Siegfried Matthus 1985, Jenůfa 1986, and Isolde 1988; Komische Oper 1987–88, as Donna Anna and Salome; Bayreuth Festival 1988, as Gutrune; further engagements at Amsterdam (Shostakovich's Lady Macbeth 1994), Salzburg, Wiesbaden, Bucharest and Moscow; sang Chrysothemis in new production of Elektra for WNO 1992, Elektra in new production at Netherlands Opera 1996; Gutrune in Götterdämmerung for Netherlands Opera 1998.

BUNGARTEN, Frank; German guitarist; *Professor of Guitar, Hochschule für Musik, Theater und Medien Hannover;* b. 1958, Cologne. *Education:* Acad. of Music, Cologne. *Career:* fmrly taught concert and soloist classes, Musical Coll., Lucerne, Switzerland; played at Berlin Philharmonic, Kunst and Kongresshaus Lucerne, Gasteig Munich, Salzburger Festival, Schwetzinger Musikfestspiele, Schleswig Holstein Festival, MDR Musiksommer, Niedersächsische Musiktage; currently Prof. of Guitar, Univ. of Music, Drama and Media, Hannover; conducts masterclasses world-wide. *Recordings include:* Cancion y Danza (Instrumentalist of the Year (Guitar) Award, ECHO Klassik Awards 2005), Sonatas and Partitas, Fernando Sor Etüden, Sonatas 1923–34, Mario Castelnuovo-Tedesco, Joaquin Rodrigo Guitar Praise – Selected Guitar Works, La Traviata, Serenade to the Dawn, Heitor Villa-Lobos Complete Solo Works, Mauro Giuliani Works for Flute and Guitar, Mauro Giuliani, Works for Flute and Guitar 2011. *Honours:* Int. Guitar Competition, Granada 1981, Audio Reference Prize 1998, Instrumentalist of the Year (Guitar) Award, ECHO Klassik Awards 2011, Preis der Deutschen Schallplattenkritik (German music critic awards). *Address:* Hochschule für Musik, Theater und Medien Hannover, Emmichplatz 1, Room 244, 30175 Hannover, Germany (office). *Telephone:* (511) 3100-1 (office). *Fax:* (511) 3100200 (office). *E-mail:* FrankBungarten@t-online.de (office); post@frankbungarten.de. *Website:* www .hmtm-hannover.de (office); www.frankbungarten.de. *Current Management:* c/o Jörg Schein – Management. *Telephone:* (551) 5317247. *Fax:* 551-5317285. *E-mail:* management@frankbungarten.de.

BUNIATISHVILI, Khatia; Georgian pianist; b. 21 June 1987, Batumi. *Education:* Tbilisi State Conservatoire, Universität für Musik und darstellende Kunst Wien. *Career:* debut as soloist with orchestra aged six; solo recitals and chamber music concerts at halls including London's Wigmore and Festival Halls, Amsterdam's Concertgebouw, Musikverein in Vienna, and Tonhalle Zurich; US concert début at Carnegie Hall (Zankel Hall), performing Chopin's Second Piano Concerto 2008; tours include with Frankfurt Radio Symphony Orchestra under Paavo Järvi, Kremerata Baltica in Japan and Europe, Basel Chamber Orchestra under Krystian Järvi, and US tour including concert series with San Francisco Symphony Orchestra under Vladimir Jurowski; other appearances with Philharmonia under Paavo Järvi, Vienna Symphony Orchestra and Orchestra della Scala, Milan under

Gianandrea Noseda, Orchestre de Paris under Andrey Boreyko; recitals in Singapore, Tokyo and across Europe. *Recordings include:* Liszt (ECHO Klassik Award for Newcomer of the Year/Piano 2012) 2011, Chopin 2012, Motherland 2014. *Honours:* Bronze Medal and Audience Prize, Arthur Rubinstein Piano Master Competition 2008, Borletti-Buitoni Trust Award 2010, Echo Klassic 2012. *Current Management:* c/o Agence Artistique Jacques Thélen, 15 avenue Montaigne, 75008 Paris, France. *Telephone:* 1-56-89-32-00. *E-mail:* jthelen@wanadoo.fr. *Website:* www.jacquesthelen.com.

BUNNING, Christine; British singer (soprano); b. 1960, Luton, England. *Education:* Guildhall School, studied with Irmgard Seefried in Vienna. *Career:* appearances as Verdi's Lady Macbeth, Covent Garden and Edinburgh; Glyndebourne Festival in The Electrification of the Soviet Union (Nigel Osbourne), Katya Kabanova, and Berlioz's Hero for Opera North; Violetta, Mimi, Marenka in The Bartered Bride and Tosca for WNO; Chelsea Opera Group in The Olympians by Bliss, as Chabrier's Gwendoline and as Elena in Mefistofele; other roles include Suor Angelica; Donna Elvira for Opera Factory; Verdi's Abigaille; Medora, Il Corsaro; Amelia, Ballo in Maschera; Rosalinde, Die Fledermaus; ENO as Miss Jessel, Turn of the Screw and in Don Carlos, Street Scene and Trittico; Lady Macbeth for Opera Zuid 1999; Florinda in Schubert's Fierrabras at the Buxton Festival 2000.

BUNTEN, Wolfgang; German singer (tenor); b. 1968, Munich. *Education:* studied in Munich at the Opera Studio in Bavarian State Opera. *Career:* appearances with the Tolzer Knabenchor as a child; sang widely in concerts and oratorios with appearances in France, Spain and Germany; stage debut as Arturo in Lucia di Lammermoor at Munich; Innsbruck, 1992–94 as Fenton in Falstaff, Tom Rakewell, Nemorino and Rodolfo; Mozart's Tamino at Vienna, 1994; Stuttgart, Zürich, 1995 and Brussels, 1996; season 1995–96, as Rodolfo at Basle; in Stravinsky's Rossignol at the Festival Hall, London; Percy in Anna Bolena at Bologna; US debut as Števa in Jenůfa, Cincinnati, 1998; season 1999–2000 at Cologne, as Alfredo, Rinuccio in Gianni Schicchi and Froh in Das Rheingold. *Current Management:* Theateragentur Kühnly, Wörthstrasse 31, 70563 Stuttgart, Germany. *Telephone:* (711) 7802764. *Fax:* (711) 7804403. *E-mail:* Kuehnly@aol.com. *Website:* Agentur-Kuehnly.de.

BURA, Corina, DMusicol; Romanian violinist and academic; *Professor, National University of Music;* b. 15 Feb. 1948, Cluj. *Education:* Lyceum Emil Racovitza, Cluj, Music Lyceum, Cluj, Conservatory of Music, Bucharest. *Career:* debut, soloist with The Philharmonia, Cluj 1967; recitals and concerts with orchestras in Romania; recitals in Germany; TV appearances; radio recordings of Bach, Handel, Telemann, Corelli, Pergolesi, Rameau, Tchaikovsky, Paganini, Szymanowski, Bartók and Romanian music; Prof., Nat. Univ. of Music, Bucharest; mem. Professorial Asscn of the Conservatory of Bucharest, Mihail Yora Foundation, Deutsche Gesellschaft für Musikphysiologie und Musikermedizin. *Recordings:* two albums of Handel music. *Publications:* The 20th Century Violin Concerto 2002; studies about modern music and aesthetics published in the Conservatory's publications; perm. column in Morning Star Literature Review 2001–. *Honours:* Diploma of Chief Promotion, The Music Lyceum 1965, 1966, 1967, Diploma of Chief Promotion, The Conservatory of Bucharest 1972. *Address:* Str. Ecaterina Teodoroiu No. 17, 010971 Bucharest, Romania. *Telephone:* (21) 3108745 (office). *E-mail:* rectorat@unmb.ro (office).

BURCHINAL, Frederick; American singer (baritone); b. 7 Dec. 1948, Wichita, KS. *Education:* Emporia State University, Juilliard School. *Career:* worked with the Metropolitan Opera Studio and made European debut in Floyd's of Mice and Men, at Amsterdam 1976; sang Scrooge in the 1979 premiere of Musgrave's A Christmas Carol, Virginia Opera; New York City Opera, State Theater 1978–88; Metropolitan Opera from 1988 as Macbeth and Rigoletto; other US appearances for the San Francisco Opera, Miami, Houston, New Orleans and San Diego Opera; European appearances for Deutsche Oper am Rhein, Düsseldorf 1988–, also sung in London, Zürich, Berlin and Frankfurt, Cologne; other roles include Rossini's Figaro, Iago, Jack Rance, Tonio, Di Luna, Scarpia, Falstaff, Nick Shadow, Posa in Don Carlos. *Current Management:* Lombardo Associates, 61 West 62nd Street, Suite 6F, New York, NY 10023, USA. *Telephone:* (212) 586-4453. *Fax:* 212) 581-5771. *E-mail:* robert@robertlombardo.com. *Website:* www.rlombardo.com.

BURCHULADZE, Paata; Georgian singer (bass); b. 12 Feb. 1951, Tbilisi. *Education:* Tbilisi Conservatory, La Scala, Italy. *Career:* debut in Tbilisi in 1975 as Mephistopheles in Faust; sang in Russia and Milan; studied further in Italy and began int. career after winning competitions 1981–82; roles include Basilio in Il Barbiere di Siviglia, Leporello, King Rene in Iolantha, Gremin in Eugene Onegin and Boris Godunov; guest appearances at the Bolshoi in Moscow; British debut in Elgar's Dream of Gerontius at the Lichfield Festival 1983; Covent Garden debut as Ramfis in Aida 1984; Salzburg Festival appearances as the Commendatore in Don Giovanni under Karajan; sang Rossini's Basilio at the Metropolitan 1989, and Khan Konchak in Prince Igor at Covent Garden 1990; sang Boris Godunov 1991 and the Inquisitor in Prokofiev's The Fiery Angel 1992; sang King Philip in Don Carlos at Santiago 1994; sang Zaccaria in Nabucco at the Verona Arena and Konchak in Prince Igor at San Francisco 1996; Walter in Luisa Miller for the Royal Opera at Edinburgh 1998; apptd UN Goodwill Amb. 2006, UNICEF Goodwill Amb. 2010; f. Iavnana (charity foundation) 2004. *Recordings include:* Scenes from operas by Mussorgsky and Verdi; Don Giovanni; Fiesco in Simon Boccanegra; Sparafucile in Rigoletto; Ramfis in Aida; Samson et Dalila. *Honours:* awarded title Kammersänger by State Opera of Stuttgart 1998, Honoured Citizen of

Tel-Aviv 2010, Hon. Academician, Georgian Acad. of Science 2015, Hon. Academician, Georgian Business Acad. 2015; Commendatore (Italy) 2010, Austrian Cross of Honour (1st Class) for Science and Art 2014; Dr hc (SDASU) 2014, (Georgian Technical Univ.) 2015; has won several competitions, including Voci Verdiane in Busseto 1981, Gold Medal and First Prize, Tchaikovsky Competition, Moscow 1982, Honoured Artist of Georgia 1983, First Prize, Int. Luciano Pavarotti Competition 1985, First Prize, Maria Callas Competition 1986; numerous awards, including Nat. Artist of Georgia 1985, Zakaria Paliashvili State Award 1991, Shota Rustaveli State Award 1991, Iakob Gogebashvili Award for Charity Activities for Orphans 1991, Vaja-Pshavela Award 1992, M. Tumanishvili Prize 2009, Presidential Order of Excellence of Georgia 2010. *Current Management:* Markus Bendl, Künstleragentur Dr Raab & Dr Böhm GmbH, Plankengasse 7, 1010 Vienna, Austria; Angelo Gabrielli, Prima International Artists Management, Palazzo Zambeccari, Piazza Calderini 2/2, 40124 Bologna, Italy. *Telephone:* (1) 512050110 (Vienna); (5) 1264056 (Bologna). *Fax:* (1) 5127743 (Vienna); (5) 1230766 (Bologna). *E-mail:* bendl@rbartists.at; markusb@cso.at; prima@ primartists.com. *Website:* www.rbartists.at; www.primartists.com; burchuladze.com.

BURDEN, William; American singer (tenor); b. 1965, Florida. *Education:* Indiana Univ. *Career:* appearances with the San Francisco Opera as Belmonte, Count Lerma in Don Carlos and the title role in Bernstein's Candide; European debut as Rodolfo for Opera North (returned as Tamino); further appearances as Rossini's Almaviva with Opera Northern Ireland, Janek in The Makropulos Case at San Francisco, Ali in L'Incontro Improvviso by Haydn at Nice, Ramiro in La Cenerentola in South Africa and Ubalo in Haydn's Armida, at St Louis; season 1995–96 with New York Met debut as Janek, and Tybalt in Roméo et Juliette; Mozart's La Finta Giardiniera for Glimmerglass Opera; season 1997–98 as Tom Rakewell at Genoa, Tamino for Florida Opera, Ali in Bourdeaux and Cimarosa's Il Matrimonio Segreto in Lausanne; sang Tybalt at the Met 1998; concert repertoire from Bach to Bernstein, with Messiah under William Christie. *Current Management:* c/o Opus 3 Artists, 470 Park Avenue South, 9th Floor North, New York, NY 10016, England. *Telephone:* (212) 586-7500. *Fax:* (646) 300-8200. *E-mail:* info@opus3artists.com. *Website:* www.opus3artists.com.

BUREAU, Karen; American singer (soprano); b. 3 Feb. 1951, Glen Ellyn, IL. *Education:* Opera School of the New York Metropolitan Opera. *Career:* debut at New York Met 1982 as Lady in Waiting in Macbeth; sang at Hannover Opera from 1985; as Leonore in Fidelio, Rezia in Oberon; Wagner's Senta, Freia, Elsa and Elisabeth; Leonora in La forza del Destino, Maddalena, Andrea Chenier, and Andromache in Troades by Reimann 1987; Seattle Opera from 1986 as Gutrune and Elisabeth in Tannhäuser; Deutsche Oper Berlin 1991 as Leonore; Brünnhilde in Wagner's Ring at Hannover; Wiesbaden and Flagstaff, Arizona Opera 1996, 1998; other roles include Lady Macbeth, Heidelberg 1995; Aida and the Dyer's Wife in Die Frau ohne Schatten 1997–98, at Kiel Opera; Elettra in Idomeneo; Donna Anna, Weber's Rezia and Euryanthe, Wagner's Eva and Isolde; sang Abigaille in Nabucco at Hannover 1999.

BURGANGER, Judith, MM; American concert pianist and academic; *Professor Emeritus, School of the Arts, Florida Atlantic University;* b. 17 March 1939, Buffalo, NY; d. of Julius Burganger and Berta Burganger (née Kohl); m. 1st; three d.; m. 2nd Leonid Treer 1985. *Education:* Staatliche Hochschule fuer Musik, Stuttgart, Germany, studies with Laura Kelsey, Buffalo NY, Seymour Lipkin, New York City, Rudolf Serkin, Marlboro Music Festival, studies in Germany. *Career:* debut solo recital, Buffalo; orchestral, with Amherst Symphony; early performances 1946–57 as soloist with Buffalo Philharmonic, Toronto Symphony, Nat. Symphony (Washington, DC), Marlboro Festival (Vermont); later performances 1957– as soloist with symphony orchestras throughout USA, Europe and Japan; int. guest performances, solo recitals and collaborations throughout USA, Europe and Canada; performances with Cleveland Orchestra, Chicago Symphony, Bayerischer Rundfunk Sinfonie Orchestra, American Symphony (Carnegie Hall), other major US and Canadian orchestras, most European radio orchestras as a result of winning 1st place in Munich Int. Competition (ARD) 1965, and performances and masterclasses at Beijing and Shanghai music conservatories, People's Repub. of China; created an annual Brahms Festival 1983–2015, performing all chamber music compositions and works for four hands at one piano by Brahms; Founder FAU Chamber Soloists 1984; collaborations with the Cleveland, Emerson, Ridge, Shanghai, Lark, Cavani Alexander, Ciompi and Miami String Quartets; concerts throughout USA, Canada and People's Repub. of China with Leonid Treer: The Art of 4 Hands at One Piano; Artist Teacher, Cleveland Inst. of Music; Assoc. Prof., Artist-in-Residence, Texas Tech. Univ. (Eva Browning Chair); Artist Teacher, Carnegie Mellon Univ.; Assoc. Prof., Florida Atlantic Univ. 1980–83, Prof. 1983–; Dir of Conservatory of Music, Coll. of Liberal Arts, Florida Atlantic Univ. 1993–2003, Prof. and Artist-in-Residence, School of the Arts 2003–13, Prof. Emer. 2013–. *Television:* series of eight short videos of classical four hands at one piano at Flagler Museum, Palm Beach, Fla. *Recording:* Burganger and Leonid Treer, The Art of Four Hands at One Piano 1997. *Honours:* First Prize, Merriweather Post Nat. Competition, Washington, DC 1956, Bronze Medal, Geneva Int. Piano Competition, Switzerland 1958, First Prize, ARD Int. Piano Competition, Munich, Germany 1965, Deutscher Industrie Preis grant 1965. *Address:* Music Department, School of the Arts, Florida Atlantic University,

777 Glades Road, Boca Raton, FL 33481, USA (office). *Telephone:* (561) 297-3329 (office). *E-mail:* burgang@fau.edu (office). *Website:* www.fau.edu (office).

BURGE, John, MMus, DMA, ARCT; Canadian composer; *Professor, School of Music, Queens University;* b. (David Byson), 2 Jan. 1961, Dryden, Ont. *Education:* Royal Conservatory of Music, Toronto, Univ. of Toronto, Univ. of British Columbia. *Career:* Prof. of Composition and Theory, School of Music, Queen's Univ., Kingston, Ont. 1987–, later Assoc. Dir School of Music; mem. Bd of Dirs SOCAN Foundation; Assoc. mem. Canadian Music Centre 1990–; mem. Canadian League of Composers 1993–, Pres. 1998–2006; Fellow, Royal Soc. of Canada 2014. *Compositions include:* Mass for Prisoners of Conscience 1989, Thank You God 1992, Piano Concerto 1993, Divinum Mysterium 1995, Symphony No. 1 1997, Canadian Shield 2000, Trumpet Concerto 2002, Clarinet Concerto 2004, Angels Voices (Asscn of Canadian Choral Conductors' Award for Best New Choral Composition 2006) 2005, Flanders Fields Reflections (Juno Award for Classical Composition of the Year 2009) 2008, Symphony No. 2 2009. *Address:* Queen's University School of Music, Harrison-LeCaine Hall, Room 204, 39 Bader Lane, Kingston, ON K7L 3N6, Canada (office). *Telephone:* (613) 533-2066 (office). *Fax:* (613) 533-6808 (office). *E-mail:* burgej@queensu.ca (office). *Website:* www.queensu.ca/music/people/ biographies/burge (office).

BURGER, Ernst Manfred; German pianist and writer on music; b. 26 March 1937, Munich; m. Dorothea Maillinger 1972; one s. *Education:* Liberal Arts High School, Staatliche Hochschule für Musik, Munich, Künstlerische Staatsprüfung, Pädagogische Staatsprüfung. *Career:* writer on music and researcher on Chopin, Liszt, Schumann and jazz. *Television:* film about Robert Schumann 1999. *Recording:* Swinging Jazz: Playing Erroll Garner. *Publications:* Franz Liszt, A Chronicle of his Life in Pictures and Documents 1986, Frédéric Chopin, A Chronicle of his Life in Pictures and Documents 1990, Carl Tausig 1990, Robert Schumann, A Chronicle of his Life in Pictures and Documents (Deutscher Musikeditions Prize 1999) 1998, Franz Liszt in Contemporary Photography 2003, Erroll Garner: Leben und Kunst eines genialen Pianisten 2006, Franz Liszt: Die Jahre in Rom und Tivoli 2010, Franz Liszt: Leben und Sterben in Bayreuth 2011, Franz Liszt nelle fotografie d'epoca collezione Ernst Burger 2011; contrib. to Die Musik in Geschichte und Gegenwart (MGG) and Süddeutsche Zeitung, music journals, articles about jazz, commentaries for recorded music. *Honours:* Grand Prix de Littérature Musicale 1988, Ordre du Mérite en faveur de la culture polonaise 1991, Robert Schumann Prize, Zwickau 1999, Deutscher Musikeditionspreis 1999, 2011. *Address:* Erhardtstrasse 6, 80469 Munich, Germany (home). *Telephone:* (89) 2016263 (home). *E-mail:* dorotheeburger@gmx.de (home).

BURGESS, Brio, BA; American composer, dramatist, poet and jazz singer; b. 27 April 1943, San Francisco, CA. *Education:* Russell Sage Coll. *Career:* various clerical positions at federal, state, city and county agencies 1972–; performances in Saratoga Springs, NY, San Francisco, San Mateo, CA, Albany, NY, and Troy, NY, of music and words (original works) in various formats; presentation of Street Kids on Radio WRPI, NY and Play with Music, 1992, Radio Free America Broadcast. *Compositions:* Suite for Picasso; Escape, ballet, for Piano, Harp, Feet and Chains; Girl on a Ball, Children's Dance and Toys, piano tunes; Sound Dreams, piano music; Space Visions, including The Painter's Song; Hippy Children's Concentration Camp Blues, for Piano, Harp and Words; Tin Angel Blues, 1990; Purple Hood Suite, 1991–92. *Recordings:* Clear, 1978; Briomindsound, 1979; Ulysses Dog No. 9, 1980; Gathered Hear, 1980; Still, 1981; Ringade, 1982; Grate, 1982; Ether, 1982; Zen Meditations, 1987. *Publications:* poems in Poetalk Publications and BAPC Anthologies, 1989–95; Outlaw Blues, eight song-poems, 1992; Poem in Open Mic: The Albany Anthology, 1994; Street Kids and Other Plays, four opera-musical libretto, 1995, Wail!: An American Journey 2007. *Current Management:* Gail G. Tolley, 5 Cuyler Street, Albany, NY 12202, USA. *E-mail:* streetkids2@aol .com.

BURGESS, Grayston, MA; British conductor and singer (countertenor); b. 7 April 1932, Cheriton, Kent, England; m. Katherine Mary Bryan; three d. *Education:* King's Coll., Cambridge. *Career:* sang with Westminster Abbey Choir 1955–69; sang Oberon in Britten's A Midsummer Night's Dream at Covent Garden; Dowland television programme; performances with Handel Opera Soc. and the Henry Wood Promenade Concerts; numerous radio broadcasts; founder and Dir, Purcell Consort of Voices 1963; debut as conductor at the 1963 Aldeburgh Festival; concerts and recordings with the Purcell Instrumental Ensemble, the Elizabeth Consort of Voices, Musica Reservata, the London Sackbut Ensemble, the Philip Jones Brass Ensemble and the Jaye Consort of Voices. *Recordings include:* Josquin's Deploration sur la Mort de Johannes Ockeghem; Dunstable's Laudi; Ockeghem's Vive le Roy and Ave Maria; Machaut's La Messe de Notre Dame; William Byrd's Church Music; Richard Davy's St Matthew Passion; Music by Schütz, Schein and Scheidt; Doulce Memoire; 16th Century French Chansons; English Madrigals from the Reign of Queen Elizabeth; English Secular Music of the Late Renaissance; The Eton Choir Book; The Triumphs of Oriana; High Renaissance Music in England.

BURGESS, Sally, FRCM; British singer (mezzo-soprano); *Vocal Professor, Royal College of Music;* b. 9 Oct. 1953, Durban, South Africa; d. of Douglas Burgess and Edna Burgess (née Sharman); m. Neal Thornton 1988; one s. *Education:* Royal Coll. of Music, Guildhall School of Music. *Career:* joined ENO 1977–; Glyndebourne debut as Smeraldina in Love for Three Oranges 1983; Covent Garden debut as Siebel in Faust 1983; Metropolitan Opera debut as Carmen 1996; one-woman show, Sally Burgess' Women, Lyric Hammersmith 1997; performances at all major opera houses and festivals; roles include Zerlina in Don Giovanni, the Composer in Ariadne, Carmen, Sextus in Julius Caesar, Orlofsky in Die Fledermaus, Minerva in The Return of Ulysses, Fricka in Die Walküre, Amneris in Aida, Azucena in Trovatore, Eboli in Don Carlos, Judith in Duke Bluebeard's Castle, Dalila, Widow Begbick in Mahagonny, Herodias in Salome, Isabella in The Voyage, Dulcinée in Don Quixote, Ottavia in Poppea, Kabanica in Katya Kabanova, Mère Marie in The Carmelites, Margareta in Genoveva, Baba The Turk in The Rake's Progress, Polinesso in Ariodante, Fortunata in Satyricon, Hanna Glawari in The Merry Widow, Queen Isabella in The Voyage, Mrs Thatcher as Public Opinion in David Pountney's production of Orpheus in the Underworld, Preziosilla in Forza, Tigrana in Edgar, Julie La Verne in Show Boat, and Fricka in Wagner's Ring Cycle, Cavalli's Eritrea, On The Town; concert appearances include Elgar's Dream of Gerontius, Verdi's Requiem, Songs of the Auvergne by Canteloube, premiere of Twice Through the Heart by Mark-Anthony Turnage, premiere of Paul McCartney and Carl Davis' Liverpool Oratorio, Mahler Symphony No. 8, Beethoven Symphony No. 9, Berio's Folk Songs, Monteverdi's Combattimento di Tancredi e Clorinda, Pierrot Lunaire, Walton's Facade, Duke Bluebeard's Castle; numerous jazz performances and recordings; has directed world premieres of Sonya's Story, also Così fan tutte (London, Buxton, Dubrovnik) and Ula; GSMD opera productions include Magic Flute, Poppea, Albert Herring, Marriage of Figaro, Carmelites; Vocal Prof. Royal Coll. of Music; mem. vocal faculties, Guildhall School of Music & Drama; mentor, ROH Jette Parker Young Artist Programme and British Youth Opera; leader, Young Singers Programme, Les Azuriales Opera Festival, Nice and Gnesin Coll. of Music, Moscow; leader, vocal masterclass series for Live Music Now; teaches at Amazwi Omzansi South Aftrica, Durban, also at Univ. of Cape Town; Assoc., Royal Coll. of Music. *Current Management:* c/o Jenny Rose, AOR Management, PMB 221, 6910 Roosevelt Way NE, Seattle, WA 98115, USA. *Telephone:* (206) 729-6160. *Fax:* (206) 985-8499. *E-mail:* aormanagement@gmail.com. *Website:* www.aormanagement.com.

BURIBAYEV, Alan; Kazakhstani conductor; *Chief Conductor, RTE National Symphony Orchestra*; b. 1979. *Education:* Kazakhstan State Conservatory, Hochschule für Musik, Vienna; studied conducting with Uros Lajovic. *Career:* Prin. Conductor, Astana Symphony Orchestra 2003–07; Gen. Musical Dir Meiningen Theatre, Germany 2004–07; Prin. Conductor, Norrköping Symphony Orchestra, Sweden 2007–11; Chief Conductor, Het Brabants Orkest, Netherlands 2008–; Chief Conductor, RTE Nat. Symphony Orchestra 2010–. *Recordings:* albums: Haydn, The Seven Last Words of Our Saviour on the Cross 2006. *Honours:* winner, Lovro von Matacic Conducting Competition 2001, Special Prize, Malko Conducting Competition, Copenhagen 2001, First Prize, Antonio Pedrotti Competition 2001. *Current Management:* c/o Bridget Canniere, IMG Artists, The Light Box, 111 Power Road, London, W4 5PY, England. *Telephone:* (20) 7957-5832. *Fax:* (20) 7957-5801. *E-mail:* bcanniere@imgartists.com. *Website:* www.imgartists.com. *Address:* c/o Helena Plews, Orchestra Manager, RTE National Symphony Orchestra, RTE Performing Groups, Admin Building, RTE, Donnybrook, Dublin 4, Ireland (office). *Telephone:* (1) 2082530 (office). *Fax:* (1) 2082511 (office). *E-mail:* helena.plews@rte.ie (office). *Website:* www.rte.ie/performinggroups (office).

BURMESTER, Pedro; Portuguese pianist; *Artistic and Education Director, Casa da Música, Oporto*; b. 9 Oct. 1963, Oporto. *Education:* Oporto Musical Conservatory, with Helena Sá e Costa, also studied in USA with Sequeria Costa, Leon Fleisher and Dmitri Paperno. *Career:* solo recitalist; debut in 1972; guest soloist with orchestras in Portugal, Spain, Austria, France, Germany, Italy and USA; teacher, Oporto High School of Music; Dir Musical Program for Porto - European Capital of Culture celebrations 2001; Artistic and Educ. Dir, Casa da Música, Oporto 2006–; television appearances in Portugal; various musical festivals in Portugal and Macao; radio broadcasts in Portugal and the USA. *Honours:* 1st Prize, 9th International Vianna da Mota Piano Competition, Lisbon, 1983; Jury Discretionary Award, 8th Van Cliburn International Piano Competition, Fort Worth. *Address:* Casa da Música, Avenida Boavista 604–610, 4149-071 Oporto, Portugal (office). *Telephone:* (22) 0120200 (office). *E-mail:* info@casadamusica.com (office). *Website:* www.casadamusica.com (office).

BURNSIDE, Iain; British pianist and writer; b. 1950, Glasgow, Scotland. *Education:* studied in Oxford, London and Warsaw. *Career:* recital accompanist to Margaret Price, Victoria de Los Angeles, Sarah Walker, Nancy Argenta, Thomas Allen and Stephen Varcoe; Chamber Music performances with Brodsky and Delmé Quartets, Douglas Boyd and Shmuel Ashkenasi; appearances at major British festivals and recitals in Europe, USA, Canada and Japan; devised song series for Schoenberg, The Reluctant Revolutionary concert series on South Bank, London 1988–89; further contributions to French Revolution Festival and Hermann Prey's Schubertiade 1989; Artistic Dir of series of vocal and chamber concerts at St John's Smith Square, London 1989; recitals featuring Karol Szymanowski on South Bank; fmr teacher, Guildhall School of Music and Drama; Int. Visiting Artist, Royal Irish Acad. of Music, Dublin. *Recordings include:* Gurney's Ludlow and Teme with Adrian Thompson and the Delmé Quartet, Remember Your Lovers 2005, On Buying a Horse: The Songs of Judith Weir 2006, Songs of FG Scott: Moonstruck 2007, A Purse of Gold: Irish Songs by Herbert Hughes 2007, Britten Abroad 2008, Beethoven: Lieder und Gesänge 2008, Sonett für Wien: Songs of Erich Korngold 2009, Liszt Abroad 2009. *Website:* www.askonasholt.co.uk/artists/accompanists/iain-burnside.

BURRELL, Diana; British composer; *Artistic Director, Spitalfields Festival*; b. 1948, Norwich. *Education:* Cambridge Univ. *Career:* began career as a teacher, later a freelance viola player; first gained recognition as a composer with Missa Sancte Endeliente for soloists, chorus and orchestra 1980; Artistic Dir Spitalfields Festival, London 2006–; currently Arts and Humanities Research Council Fellow, Royal Acad. of Music. *Compositions:* orchestral: Praeludium 1983, Archangel 1987, Landscape 1988, Landscape with Procession 1988, Scene with Birds 1989, Resurrection 1992, Das Meer so gross und weit ist da wimmelts ohne Zahlgrosse kleine Tiere 1992, Anima 1993, Viola Concerto 1994, Enchaînements 1994, Symphonies of Flocks, Herds and Shoals 1995, Dunkelhvide Månestråler 1996, Clarinet Concerto 1996, Ring 1996, Flute Concerto 1997, The Four Temperaments 2003, Temper 2004; choral: Missa Sancte Endeliente 1980, Come and See the Christ-child 1982, Io Evoe! 1984, Creator of the Stars of Night 1989, Lights and Shadows 1989, You Spotted Snakes 1991, Night Songs 1991, Christo Paremus Cantica 1993, Come Holy Ghost, our Souls Inspire 1993, Benedicam Dominum 1996, Magnificat & Nunc Dimittis 1996, Michael's Mass 1997, Ave Verum Corpus 1998, The St Pancras Evening Canticles 2005, And So the Night Became 2005; for ensemble: Io! 1984, Concertante 1985, Angelus 1986, Untitled Composition 1988, Shadow 1988, Wind Quintet 1990, Barrow 1991, Invocation for Justice 1992, Gulls and Angels 1993, Confession 1996, Gate 1997, Bronze 1998, Earth 1998, Ritual Sentences 1999, Double Image 1999, Athletes 2000, Gold 2001, King Shall Bright Ring Give in Hall 2003, Concerto for Violin with Singer and Three Ensembles 2009; solo and duo: Arched Forms with Bells for organ 1990, Bright Herald of the Morning for clarinet and piano 1992, Tachograph for baritone and piano 1993, Festival for organ 2001, North Star for trumpet and organ 2002, Longtemps ce fut l'eté for soprano and piano 2004, Terce for accordion and piano 2005; opera: The Albatross 1987. *Address:* c/o United Music Publishers Ltd., 33 Lea Road, Waltham Abbey, Essex, EN9 1ES, England (office). *E-mail:* info@ump.co.uk (office). *Website:* www.ump.co.uk (office). *Address:* Spitalfields Festival, 61 Brushfield Street, London, E1 6AA, England (office). *Telephone:* (20) 7377-0287 (office). *Fax:* (20) 7247-0494 (office). *E-mail:* info@spitalfieldsfestival.org.uk (office). *Website:* www.spitalfieldsfestival.org.uk (office).

BURROUGHS, Bruce Douglas, AB, MM; American singer (baritone), educator and writer; b. 12 Nov. 1944, Hagerstown, MD. *Education:* Univ. of California, Los Angeles, New England Conservatory of Music. *Career:* debut as Papageno in Magic Flute, Los Angeles Guild Opera 1965; Metropolitan Opera debut in Einstein on the Beach 1976; more than 40 roles, including title roles of Monteverdi's Orfeo, Mozart's Don Giovanni, Busoni's Arlecchino, Menotti's Bishop of Brindisi; Ed.-in-Chief, The Opera Quarterly; Music Critic, Los Angeles Times; mem. American Guild of Musical Artists. *Publications:* Metropolitan Opera Guide to Opera on Video 1997; contrib. biographical essays to International Dictionary of Opera 1996, contrib. to Collier's Encyclopaedia 1998; articles, features and reviews in Music Journal and Opera News. *Honours:* ASCAP Deems Taylor Award 1991.

BURROWES, Norma Elizabeth, BA, FRAM; British singer (soprano) and academic; b. Bangor, Co. Down, Northern Ireland; d. of Henry Burrowes and Caroline Burrowes; m. 1st Steuart Bedford (q.v.) 1969 (divorced 1980); m. 2nd Emile Belcourt 1987; one s. one d. *Education:* Queen's Univ., Belfast, Royal Acad. of Music. *Career:* début with Glyndebourne Touring Opera singing Zerlina in Don Giovanni 1969, début with Royal Opera House, Fiakermili in Arabella 1976; sings regularly with Glyndebourne Opera, Scottish Opera, Aldeburgh Festival, English Nat. Opera, Welsh Nat. Opera and others; abroad: Salzburg, Paris, Munich, Aix-en-Provence, Avignon, Ottawa, Montreal, New York, Vienna, Chicago, Buenos Aires; has sung with all the prin. London orchestras and on BBC radio and TV; numerous recordings; retd 1982; currently mem. Faculty, Dept of Music, York Univ., Toronto, Canada. *Roles include:* Blöndchen in The Abduction from the Seraglio, Oscar (Ballo in Maschera), Despina (Così Fan Tutte), Woodbird (Siegfried), Sophie (Der Rosenkavalier), Cunning Little Vixen, Manon (Massenet), Titania (Midsummer Night's Dream), Nanetta (Falstaff), Gilda (Rigoletto), Marie (La Fille du régiment), Juliet (Romeo and Juliet), Adina (Elisir d'Amore), Susanna (Nozze di Figaro), Lauretta (Gianni Schicchi). *Honours:* Order of Worshipful Co. of Musicians; Hon. DMus (Queen's Univ., Belfast) 1979. *Address:* Department of Music, York University, Accolade East Building, Suite 371, 4700 Keele Street, Toronto, ON M3J 1P3, Canada (office). *E-mail:* burrowes@yorku.ca (office). *Website:* music.ampd.yorku.ca (office).

BURROWS, Donald (Donwald) James, CertEd, MA, PhD; British academic, writer, conductor, organist and harpsichordist; *Professor Emeritus, Open University*; b. 28 Dec. 1945, London; m. Marilyn Jones 1971; three s. *Education:* Trinity Hall, Cambridge and Open Univ. *Career:* Dir of Music, John Mason School, Abingdon 1970–81; Lecturer in Music, Open Univ. 1982–89, Sr Lecturer in Music 1989–95, Prof. of Music 1995–2015, Head of Music Dept 1991–2002, Prof. Emer. 2015–; Conductor, Abingdon and District Music Soc. 1972–83, Pres. 2012–; Conductor, Oxford Holiday Orchestra 1978–; organist and choirmaster, St Nicholas Church, Abingdon 1972–82; Master of the Music, St Botolph's, Aspley Guise 1985–95; contributor to BBC Radio 3, Radio 4, BBC 2 TV; mem., Editorial Bd, Hallische Händel-Ausgabe 1984–; founder-mem., Handel Inst. 1985–, Chair. of Trustees and Council 1998–; mem. Bd, Georg Friedrich Händel-Gesellschaft 1987–, Vice-Pres. 1999–; mem. Advisory Bd, Maryland Handel Festival, USA 1988–2001; mem.

British Library Advisory Cttee for the Arts, Humanities and Social Sciences 2000–02; mem. Collections Cttee, Gerald Coke Handel Foundation 2007–; mem. Royal Musical Asscn, Royal Coll. of Organists. *Publications:* Handel: 'Messiah' 1991, A Catalogue of Handel's Musical Autographs 1994, Handel 1995 (new edn 2012), The Cambridge Companion to Handel (writer and ed.) 1997, Music and Theatre in Handel's World: The Papers of James Harris 1732–1780 2002, Handel and the English Chapel Royal 2005; as co-author and general ed.: George Frideric Handel: Collected Documents (five vols); as ed.: Handel's Alexander's Feast, The Anthem on the Peace, Foundling Hospital Anthem, Violin Sonatas, Messiah, As Pants the Hart, Songs for Soprano and Continuo, Belshazzar, Imeneo, Samson, Ariodante, Ode for St Cecilia's Day, Te Deum in A major, L'Allegro, il Penseroso ed il Moderato, William Croft Complete Canticles and Anthems with Orchestra, George Frideric Handel: Collected Documents Vols I & 2 (with others) 2014; Elgar pieces for violin and piano; insert notes for recordings, including Handel's Water Music, Anthems, Utrecht Te Deum, Samson, Ode for St Cecilia's Day, Israel in Egypt, Organ Concertos and Messiah; contrib. to The Musical Times, Music and Letters, Early Music, Göttinger Händel-Beiträge, Händel-Jahrbuch. *Honours:* British Acad. research grants 1979, 2004–06, AHRC research grant 2007–10; Vincent H. Duckles Award 1996, Händelpreis der Stadt Halle 2000. *Address:* 126 High Street, Cranfield, Bedford, MK43 0DG (home); Music Department, Faculty of Arts, The Open University, Walton Hall, Milton Keynes, MK7 6AA, England (office). *Telephone:* (1234) 751654 (home); (1908) 653510 (office). *Fax:* (1908) 653750 (office).

BURROWS, (James) Stuart, OBE, DMus; British singer (tenor); b. 7 Feb. 1933, Cilfynydd, Pontypridd, South Wales; s. of Albert Burrows and Gladys Irene Burrows (née Powell); m. Enid Lewis; one s. one d. *Education:* Trinity Coll., Carmarthen. *Career:* stage debut with Welsh Nat. Opera as Ismaele in Nabucco 1963; school teacher until debut at Royal Opera House, Covent Garden 1967; has sung in world's major opera houses, including San Francisco, Vienna, Paris, Buenos Aires (Théâtre Cologne) and Brussels (Théâtre de la Monnaie) as well as Covent Garden and Metropolitan Opera, New York; toured Far East with Royal Opera 1979 and sang with co. at Olympic Festival, Los Angeles 1984; four US tours with Metropolitan Opera; appearances at Aix-en-Provence and Orange Festivals, and at Hamburg, Geneva, Houston (Des Grieux), Santa Fe (Tamino, Alfredo) and Boston; sang Mozart's Titus at Brussels 1982, Covent Garden 1989, Mozart's Basilio at Aix 1991; concert appearances throughout Europe and N America, under Solti, Barenboim, Mehta, Ozawa, Bernstein and Ormandy, including two recitals in Brahmssaal, Vienna; numerous concert appearances in music by Bach and Handel. *Television:* Stuart Burrows Sings (BBC series) 1978–85, BBC TV films of Faust, La Bohème and Rigoletto. *Recordings include:* Die Zauberflöte, Don Giovanni, Die Entführung aus dem Serail, La Clemenza di Tito, La Damnation de Faust, Les Contes d'Hoffmann, Maria Stuarda, Anna Bolena, Eugene Onegin, The Midsummer Marriage, Messiah, Grande Messe des Morts (Berlioz), Les Nuits d'Eté, Das Klagende Lied, Beethoven's 9th (Choral) Symphony and single discs of Mozart arias, Operetta Favourites, German and French songs, popular ballads and Welsh songs, including The Stuart Burrows Edition 2006. *Honours:* Hon. Freedom of the Borough, Rhondda Cynon Taff, South Wales 2008; Hon. DMus (Wales) 1981; Dr hc (Carmarthen) 1989, (Univ. Coll. of Wales, Aberystwyth) 1992; Blue Riband, National Eisteddfod of Wales 1959, Fellowships from Aberystwyth and Cardiff Univs and Trinity Coll., Camarthen, The Stuart Burrows Int. Voice Competition set up in his honour 2006. *Address:* 29 Blackwater Grove, Alderholt, Fordingbridge, SP6 3AD, England (office). *E-mail:* stuartburrows@nicholls.f9.co.uk (office); meryl@nicholls.f9.co.uk (office). *Website:* www.stuartburrows.f9.co.uk (office).

BURT, Robert, AGSM; British singer (tenor) and actor; b. 22 May 1962, England. *Education:* Guildhall School of Music, London. *Career:* has performed with cos including ENO, Opera North, Glyndebourne Festival and Touring Operas, Grange Park Opera, Holland Park Opera, Festival d'Aix-en-Provence, Opera Nat. du Rhin, Deutsche Oper am Rhein, Geneva Opera, Nationale Reisopera, Opera Theatre Co., Chicago Opera Theatre, Teatro Communale di Parma, Teatro Real de Madrid; mem. Nat. Theatre Ensemble 1999–2000, played Father Christmas in The Lion, the Witch and the Wardrobe, and Host of the Garter Inn in Merry Wives the Musical (RSC), Pirelli in Sweeney Todd for Chichester Festival Theatre, transferred to Adelphi Theatre, London 2012; debut at Royal Opera House as the Dancing Master in Manon Lescaut (Puccini) 2014. *Current Management:* c/o Musichall Ltd, Oast House' Crouch's Farm, Hollow Lane, East Hoathly, East Sussex, BN8 6QX, England. *Telephone:* (1825) 840437. *E-mail:* info@musichall.uk .com. *Website:* www.musichall.uk.com.

BURT, Warren Arnold, MA, PhD; American/Australian composer, multimedia artist and writer; *Lecturer in Musicology, Box Hill Institute, Melbourne;* b. 10 Oct. 1949, Baltimore, Md; s. of Raymond Burt and Rose Farkas; m. Catherine Schieve. *Education:* Univ. of California, San Diego, studied with Robert Erickson and Kenneth Gaburo, Univ. of Wollongong, Australia. *Career:* Australian Centre for Arts and Tech. 1994; resident, Mills Coll., Oakland, Calif. 1995, Univ. of Illinois, Urbana-Champaign 2001–02, Univ. of Wollongong 2004–; Australia Council Composer's Fellowship 1998–2000; Lecturer, Illawarra Inst. of Tech. 2006–09; ARC Post Doctoral Research Fellow, Univ. of Wollongong 2007–10; teacher, Bendigo TAFE 2010–13; Lecturer in Musicology, Box Hill Inst., Melbourne 2010–. *Compositions include:* (many with visuals and electronics) Nighthawk 1973–76, Aardvarks

IV 1975, Moods 1978–79, The Wanderer: Pocket Calculator Music II 1983, Woodwind Quintet 1985, Meditations 1986, Voice, Tuning Fork and Accordion 1986, Samples III 1987, String Quartet No. 4 1987, Chaotic Research Music 1990, Some Kind of Seasoning 1990–91, Dense Room 1994, Music for Microtonal Piano Sounds 1992–98, Diversity 1998, Playing in Traffic 2000–01, The Wilson Installations 2002–04, Radio Namings 2005, 17 Pieces for Adelaide 2006, Proliferating Infinities 2006, A Book of Drones 2007, Berries and Gravel 2011, Nightshade Etudes 2012, Moths and Mathematics 2012. *Recordings include:* Aardvarks V 1978, Song Dawn Chords 1981, Four Pieces for Synthesizer 1981, Almond Bread Harmonies II 1985, Chaotic Research Music 1989–90, Three Inverse Genera 1990, Parts of Speech 1992, 39 Dissonant Etudes 1996, Miss Furr and Miss Skeene 1998, Diversity (multimedia theatre) 1998, The Animation of Lists and the Archytan Transpositions 2006, Experience of Marfa: A Book of Drones 2007, Illawarra: The Lake in Winter 2010. *Publications:* Music Talks, 24 pamphlets written or edited for Council of Adult Education, Melbourne 1982–85, Writings from a Scarlet Aardvark – 15 Essays on Music and Art, Critical Vices: The Myths of Post-Modern Theory (with Nicholas Zurbrugg) 1999, Art Performance Media (31 interviews by Nicholas Zurbrugg) 2004, Algorithms, Microtonality, Performance: 11 Musical Compositions 2010. *Honours:* Djerassi Residents' Program 1998, Sounds Australian Award 1998. *Address:* PO Box 1046, Daylesford, Vic. 3460, Australia (office). *Telephone:* (4) 5914-6147 (office). *E-mail:* waburt@melbourne.dialix.com.au (home). *Website:* www.warrennburt .com.

BURTON, Amy; American singer (soprano); b. 14 May 1958. *Career:* Théâtre des Champs Elysées, Paris, as Woglinde and Woodbird in The Ring, 1987, also at Nice; Season 1988 as Adele in Die Fledermaus for Scottish Opera; As Douglas Moore's Baby Doe, for Colorado Opera at Central City; Sang Juliette at Zürich, 1990 and Nannetta in Falstaff at New Orleans; Sophie in Werther at Cincinnati, 1993; Season 1997–98, in Handel's Serse for New York City Opera and Ford's Wife in Falstaff for Glimmerglass Opera; Sang John Musto's Dove Sta Amore with Scottish Chamber Orchestra, 2000; Other roles include Luisa in The Duenna by Prokofiev; Governess in The Turn of the Screw, 2000; La Folie in Rameau's Platée, 2000; Concepcion in L'Heure Espagnole for New York City Opera, 2000; Liù in Turandot for Pittsburgh Opera, 2001. *Recordings include:* Ernst Bacon Songs 2001. *Current Management:* Columbia Artists Management, 1790 Broadway, New York, NY 10019-1412, USA. *Telephone:* (212) 841-9500. *Fax:* (212) 841-9744. *E-mail:* info@cami.com. *Website:* www.cami.com; www.amyburton.com.

BURTON, Humphrey McGuire, CBE, BA, MA; British writer, lecturer and broadcaster; b. 25 March 1931, Trowbridge, Wilts., England; three s. three d. *Education:* Univ. of Cambridge. *Career:* Head of Music and Arts, BBC TV 1965–67, 1975–81; Ed. and Presenter, Aquarius (ITV) 1970–75; presenter of concerts, opera and ballet (BBC) 1975–94; Presenter, Young Musician of the Year 1978–94; Chair. European Broadcasting Union TV Music working party 1976–86; Artistic Dir Barbican Centre 1988–90; Dir Tender is the North, Festival of Scandinavian Arts, Barbican Centre 1992; TV dir 1999–2002, including Flight at Glyndebourne (Channel 4), Falstaff (BBC 2), The Return of Ulysses (Aix/DVD) 2002; broadcaster, Artist in Focus (BBC Radio 3), Walton and Menuhin series (Classic FM), Vincent in Brixton (BBC 4); conducted the Verdi Requiem at Royal Albert Hall 2001; mounted Mozart 2006 and Schubert 2011 festivals at Aldeburgh; lecturer on travel tours and cruise ships 2000–; mem. Royal Philharmonic Soc. *Recordings:* Mozart Harpsichord Duet Sonata K19d (with Erik Smith). *Publications include:* Leonard Bernstein (biog.) 1994, Menuhin (biog.) 2000, Walton –The Romantic Loner: A Centenary Portrait Album (co-author) 2002. *Honours:* Hon. FCSD, Hon. Fellow, Fitzwilliam Coll., Cambridge. *Address:* 13 Linden Road, Aldeburgh, Suffolk, IP15 5JQ, England (home). *Telephone:* (1728) 452548 (home). *E-mail:* humphreyburton@ suffolkonline.net.

BURTON, Stephen; American composer; b. 24 Feb. 1943, Whittier, CA. *Education:* Oberlin Conservatory, Salzburg Mozarteum, Peabody Conservatory, and studied with Hans Werner Henze. *Career:* Dir, Munich Kammerspiel 1963–64; teacher, George Mason Univ., Fairfax, VA 1974–, Heritage Chair in Music (endowed Chair for life) 1996–. *Compositions include:* Concerto da Camera 1963, Ode to a Nightingale for soprano and ensemble 1963, Symphony No. 1 1968, No Trifling with Love (opera) 1970, Stravinskiana for flute and orchestra 1972, Dithyramb 1972, six Hebrew Melodies (after Byron) 1973, String Quartet 1974, Piano Trio 1975, Songs of the Tulpehocken for tenor and orchestra 1976, six Songs for voice and 13 instruments 1977, Ballet Finisterre 1977, The Duchess of Malfi (opera after Webster) 1978, Symphony No. 2 (after Sylvia Plath poems) for mezzo, baritone and orchestra 1979, Variations on a Theme of Mahler for chamber orchestra 1982, Violin Concerto 1983, Aimee (opera) 1983, I Have a Dream cantata for narrator, soprano and orchestra 1987, An American Triptych (three one-act operas after Crane's Maggie, Hawthorne's Dr Heidegger's Experiment and Melville's Benito Cereno) 1989, From Noon to Starry Night for chorus and chamber orchestra 1989, Burning Babe cantata 1999, Brotherhood (music theatre, with Peter Burton) 1992. *Restored film scores:* (with Gillian Anderson) Ben Hur 1997, Passion of St Joan 1998, Ten Commandments 1998, Robin Hood 1999. *Honours:* 30 major commissions and prizes.

BURY, Alison Margaret; British violinist; b. 20 Jan. 1954, Woking, England. *Education:* RCM with Sylvia Rosenberg and Frances Baines, Salzburg with Sándor Végh and Nikolaus Harnoncourt. *Career:* appearances with the Vienna Concentus Musicus, Acad. of Ancient Music 1975–90,

Taverner Players 1976–92, Amsterdam Baroque Orchestra under Ton Koopman 1980–86, the English Baroque Soloists under John Eliot Gardiner (leader from 1983); leader, Orchestra of the Age of Enlightenment 1986–; teacher and Dir, Baroque Orchestra, Royal Coll. of Music, London; chamber recitals with the Chandos Baroque Players 1981–89, L'Ecole d'Orphée 1982–89, Geminiani Trio 1983–90. *Recordings include:* Vivaldi's Four Seasons (with the Acad. of Ancient Music and the Taverner Players), Bach Double Concerto (with Monica Huggett, Elizabeth Wallfisch). *Address:* c/o Royal College of Music, Prince Consort Road, London SW7, England.

BUSCHING, Rainer; German singer (bass); b. 1943, Halle/Saale. *Education:* Felix Mendelssohn Bartholdy Academy of Music, Leipzig. *Career:* guest appearances in Germany then engaged at Landestheater Dessau, 1973–85; Member of the Soloist ensemble at Dresden Staatsoper from 1985 notably as Wagner's Daland, Landgrave and King Henry, Verdi's Zaccaria, Ramphis and Padre Guardiano, Mozart's Sarastro and Commendatore, Weber's Lysiart and Kaspar, Basilio in Il Barbiere di Siviglia, Handel's Giulio Cesare and Gremin in Eugene Onegin; Guest appearances in Italy, Netherlands, Austria, Poland, Brazil and Russia; Sang Sarastro at Lubeck, 1992, at the reopening of the Chemnitz Opera; season 2000 at the Semper Oper Dresden, as Sarastro and the Minister in Fidelio; concert repertory includes St John and Matthew Passions by Bach, Messiah, Die Schöpfung and Jahreszeiten by Haydn, and Schubert's Winterreise. *Current Management:* Agentur Sigrid Rostock, Eugen-Schönhaar-Strasse 1, 10407 Berlin, Germany. *Telephone:* (30) 4257514. *Fax:* (30) 4239136. *E-mail:* sigridrostock@web.de.

BUSSE, Barry; American singer (tenor); b. 18 Aug. 1946, Gloversville, NY. *Education:* Oberlin Coll., Manhattan School of Music. *Career:* has sung as tenor from 1977 in Carlisle Floyd's Of Mice and Men at Houston; created Bothwell in Musgrave's Mary, Queen of Scots for Virginia Opera 1977 and repeated the role at the New York City Opera 1980; sang at Santa Fe 1979 as Alwa in the US premiere of the three-act version of Lulu; European debut 1982 as Don José for Netherlands Opera; further appearances in Toulouse, San Francisco, Santa Fe and Miami; Seattle Opera 1985 as Siegmund in Die Walküre; sang Tichon in Katya Kabanova at Florence 1988 and at Geneva 1989; sang Mephistopheles and Agrippa in Prokofiev's Fiery Angel at the Holland Festival 1990; other roles include Florestan, Cavardossi, Canio, Parsifal at Toulouse 1987, Peter Grimes, Narraboth, Apollo in Daphne, Pollione and Massenet's Des Grieux; created the title role in Nosferatu by Randolph Peters, Toronto 1995; sang Louis Sullivan in Daron Hagen's The Shining Bow, Chicago 1998. *Recordings include:* Mary Queen of Scots.

BUSSI, Francesco, BLit, DipMus; Italian musician and musicologist; b. 14 Sept. 1926, Piacenza; m. Maria Villa 1957; one s. one d. *Career:* Docente di Storia ed Estetica Musicale, Conservatorio di Parma 1955–59; Docente di Storia ed Estetica Musicale, Conservatorio di Piacenza e Bibliotecario 1959–; mem. SIDM, AIBM, AMS, Deputazione di Storia Patria per le Province Parmensi. *Recordings:* Francesco Cavalli: Missa Pro Defunctis (Requiem) a 8 Voci (con il responsorio Libera me, Domine a 5 Voci) 1985, Monumenti Musicali Piacentini e Farnesiani 1987–2004, Gabriele Villani, Toscanelle a 4 voci 1987, Gasparo Villani, Gratiarum Actiones a 20 Voci 1993, La Musica strumentale di Johannes Brahms 1990, Tutti i Lieder di J. Brahms 1999, Giuseppe Allevi detto 'Piacenza', Secondo e Terzo Libro delle Compositioni sacre 2004, La Musica e i musicisti, in Storia di Piacenza 1980–2004, Il Teatro Municipale di Piacenza nei suoi due secoli di storia 1804–2004. *Publications:* Antifonario-Graduale di S Antonino in Piacenza, Umanità e Arte di G. Parabosco, Catalogo dell'Archivio Musicale del Duomo di Piacenza, La Musica Sacra di F. Cavalli in rapporto a Monteverdi, Storia, Tradizione e Arte nel Requiem di Cavalli, L'Opera Veneziana dalla Morte di Monteverdi alla Fine del '600, Tutti i Lieder di Johannes Brahms 1999; contrib. to Jone di Chio, Il Cantore Spagnolo Pedro Valenzuela, Le 'Toscanelle' di Gabriele Villani, La Musica Strumentale di J. Brahms, Tutti i lieder di J. Brahms, Altro Cavalli Sacro Restituito, New Grove Dictionary of Music and Musicians, New Grove Dictionary of Opera, MGG, DEUMM and many others, Moderna Edizione Critica di Pezzi di Girolamo Parabosco, del Requiem di Cavalli, delle Toscanelle e delle Gratiarum Actiones di Villani, delle Composizioni Sacre di G. Allevi detto Piacenza, di Altri Pezzi Sacri e dei 3 Vesperi di Cavalli, Italian edn of vols 2, 4 and 5 of New Oxford History of Music, Storia di Piacenza 1980, 1984, 1997, 1999, 2002, 2003, Francesco Cavalli: tracce della storia della sua fortuna 2003, I Concerti al Teatro Municipale di Piacenza 2004. *Honours:* hon. mem. Rotary Club Piacenza-Farnese 1993; S Antonino d'oro 1990, Premio internazionale L. Illica 1991, Piacentino Benemerito 1998. *Address:* Strada Guastafredda 45, 29100 Piacenza, Italy.

BUSSOTTI, Sylvano; Italian composer, painter, film director and stage designer; b. 1 Oct. 1931, Florence. *Education:* Florence Conservatory with Dallapiccola, Maglioni and Lupi, studied with Deutsch in Paris, Darmstadt courses with Cage, studied in the USA (Rockefeller Foundation grant). *Career:* appearances at music festivals from 1958; co-founder of the exhibition Musica e Segno, seen in Europe and USA 1962; exhibited his own paintings in Italy, USA, Japan, France and Germany; dir and designer of stage works including his own; Prof. of Music Drama, Aquila Acad. of Fine Arts Scuola di Musica di Fiesole 1971–74; Dir, Teatro La Fenice, Venice 1975; Dir, The Puccini Festival, Torre del Lago 1981–85; Bussotti opera-ballet, Scuola Spettacolo 1984–92; designs and production for La Bohème, Turandot, Trittico La Fanciulla del West (Puccini), Aida, Ballo in Maschera, Un giorno di regno, Rigoletto (Verdi), Ulisse (Dallapiccola), Otello, Barbiere (Rossini), Carmen (Bizet), Cavalleria Rusticana (Mascagni), Pagliacci (Leoncavallo) and La Gioconda, Genoa and Florence. *Compositions include:* for stage: Tema-Variazioni, Geographie Francaise 1956, Raramente (mystery play) 1971, Bergkristall (ballet) 1974, Nottetempo (lyric drama) 1976, Le Racine 1980, Fedra (lyric tragedy) 1988, L'Ispirazione 1988, Satiresca 1993, Tieste 1993, Quartettino di Miniature 1996; concert: El Carbonero for five voices 1957, Breve for Ondes Martenot 1958, Sette Fogli 1959, Phrase a Trois for string trio 1960, Torso for solo voices and orchestra 1960–63, Rara for guitar and string trio 1964–67, Julio Organum Julii for speaker and organ 1968, I Semi di Gramsci for string quartet and orchestra 1962–71, Novelletta for piano 1962–73, Opus Cygne for orchestra 1979, Concerto a l'Aquila for piano and nine instruments 1986, Furioso for mezzo and orchestra 1994, Lingue Ignote for voices and chamber orchestra 1994, Madrelingua 1994, Modello for violin and orchestra 1998. *Honours:* Commdr, Ordre des Arts et des Lettres; first prize Italian Section ISCM 1965, 1972, DAAD, Berlin 1972.

BUSTERUD, James; American singer (baritone); b. 1957. *Career:* sang Dandini in La Cenerentola at Philadelphia 1986; season 1987 as Malatesta in Don Pasquale and Mercutio in Roméo et Juliette at Washington; Santa Fe Opera as Sharpless in Butterfly, in Strauss's Friedenstag and Feuersnot; American premiere of Judith Weir's A Night at the Chinese Opera 1989; sang Don Ferdinand in Gerhard's The Duenna, Wexford 1989; in Turandot for Miami Opera; Glimmerglass Opera 1994 as Robert in Tchaikovsky's Iolanta and Portland Opera 1996; as Bassiano in Le Marchand de Venise by Reynaldo Hahn. *Recordings include:* Schaunard in La Bohème.

BUSUIOC, Olga; Moldovan singer (soprano). *Education:* Stefan Neaga Coll. of Music, Chisinau, Acad. of Music, Theatre and Fine Art, Chisinau, Centro Universale del Bel Canto, Modena, Italy with Mirella Freni. *Career:* awarded music scholarship by Irina Bogaciova Foundation, St Petersburg; specializes in Puccini arias; first came to int. prominence after winning second prize and Pepita Embil Domingo Zarzuela Prize at Placido Domingo's Operalia Competition, Moscow 2011. *Address:* c/o Centro Universale del Bel Canto, CUBEC -Musica e Servizio, via Nicolai Ghiaurov 56, 41058 Vignola (MO), Italy. *Telephone:* (059) 7520180. *E-mail:* info@belcanto.it. *Website:* www.belcanto.it/cubec.

BUSWELL, James Oliver, IV, BA; American violinist, conductor and teacher; b. 4 Dec. 1946, Fort Wayne, IN. *Education:* Harvard College, studied with Ivan Galamian at Juilliard School of Music, New York. *Career:* debut as violinist, St Louis 1963; New York recital debut at Philharmonic Hall in 1967; soloist with various orchestras, recitalist and chamber music player; appearances as conductor; Visiting Prof., University of Arizona, Tucson, 1972–73; teacher, Indiana University School of Music, Bloomington, 1974–86, and New England Conservatory of Music, Boston, 1986–; former mem., Buswell Parnas Luvisi Trio; television host for Stations of Bach on PBS Television. *Address:* c/o New England Conservatory of Music, 290 Huntington Avenue, Boston, MA 02115, USA.

BUTLER, Mark; Canadian/British violinist and chamber music coach; b. 5 Feb. 1949. *Education:* Royal Coll. of Music with Leonard Hirsch. *Career:* co-leader, Ulster Orchestra 1970–71; BBC debut in 1971, London debut in 1972; solo recitals in the UK and Canada; Second Violinist of the Chilingirian Quartet 1971–92; resident, Quartet of Liverpool Univ. 1973–76, Sussex Univ. 1978–92, and Royal Coll. of Music 1986–92; Chamber Music Coach, Intercollegiate Awards Scheme, Univ. of Cambridge 2005–; annual series of concerts at the Queen Elizabeth Hall and Wigmore Hall; performances at the Edinburgh, Bath and Aldeburgh Festivals, Munich Herkulessaal, Amsterdam Concertgebouw, Zürich Tonhalle, Vienna Konzerthaus, and Stockholm Konserthuset; New York debut 1976; tours of USA, Canada, Australia, New Zealand, South America and the Far East; represented the UK at the New York Int. Festival Quartet Series; TV and radio appearances throughout Europe on national public radio in USA, and the BBC; mem. Acad. of St Martin-in-the-Fields 1995–. *Recordings include:* The Ten Great Mozart Quartets; Late Schubert Quartets; Debussy and Ravel Quartets; Elgar Quartet and Piano Quintet; Schubert Cello Quintet and Octet; Mozart Clarinet Quintet; Complete Quartets of Bartók and Dvořák; Bartók Piano Quintet. *Address:* c/o Academy of St Martin-in-the-Fields, 8 Baylis Road, London, SE1 7AA, England.

BUTLER, Martin, BMus, PPRNCM, MFA, FRNCM; British composer and academic; b. 1 March 1960, Hampshire. *Education:* Winchester School of Art, Univ. of Manchester, Royal Northern Coll. of Music, Princeton Univ., USA. *Compositions include:* From an Antique Land for ensemble 1982, Concertino for chamber orchestra 1983, Dance Fragments for ensemble 1984, Cavalcade for orchestra 1985, Tin Pan Ballet 1986, arranged as Ballet con Salsa 1987, Bluegrass Variations for violin 1987, Piano Piano for 2 pianos and tape 1988, Graffiti for tape 1989, Jazz Machines for ensemble 1990, O Rio for full orchestra 1990, Chaconne for solo oboe 1991, Down Hollow Winds for wind quintet 1991, Going with the Grain for solo marimba and ensemble 1992, On the Rocks for solo piano 1992, Still Breathing for wind orchestra 1992, Craig's Progress, opera 1994, A Better Place, opera 1999, Suzanne's River Song for violin and piano 1999, Two Rivers for choir and orchestra 2000, Prelude for soprano and trumpet 2001, Siward's River Song for solo cello 2001, Concertino for Piano and Chamber Orchestra 2002, Sequenza Notturna for piano quartet 2003, From the Fairground of Dreams for orchestra 2007, Saxophone Concerto 2009. *Recordings:* Tin Pan Ballet, O Rio. *Publications:* Craig's Progress 1994. *Address:* c/o Repertoire Promotion Department, Oxford University Press, Great Clarendon Street, Oxford, OX2 6DP, England (office). *E-mail:*

repertoire.promotion.uk@oup.com (office). *Website:* www.oup.co.uk/music (office).

BUTT, John, OBE, MA, PhD, FBA, FRCO (CHM), FRSE, ADCM; British musician, musicologist and academic; *Gardiner Professor of Music, University of Glasgow;* b. 17 Nov. 1960, Solihull, England; s. of Wilfrid Butt and Patricia Butt; m. Sally; four s. one d. *Education:* Solihull School, King's Coll., Cambridge (organ scholar). *Career:* Lecturer, Univ. of Aberdeen 1986–87; Research Fellow, Magdalene Coll., Cambridge 1987–89; Prof. of Music and Univ. Organist, Univ. of California, Berkeley, USA 1989–97; Lecturer, Univ. of Cambridge, Fellow, King's Coll. 1997–2001; Gardiner Prof. of Music, Univ. of Glasgow 2001–; Musical Dir Dunedin Consort, Edinburgh 2003–; guest conductor with Philharmonia Baroque Orchestra, Göttingen Handel Festspiele, Berkeley Festival, RSAMD Chamber Orchestra and Chorus, Irish Baroque Orchestra; conducted Bach's Christmas Oratorio with the Orchestra of the Age of Enlightenment 2010; active as a solo organist and harpsichordist; has performed world-wide, including recent trips to Germany, France, Poland, Israel and South Korea; mem. Royal Musical Asscn, Royal Coll. of Organists, American Musicological Soc. *Recordings:* 11 organ, harpsichord and clavichord recordings, Telemann: Fantasies 1999, Bach: Organ Toccatas 2000, Elgar: Organ Works 2002, Handel's Messiah (Gramophone Award for Best Baroque Vocal Recording 2007, Midem Classical Award for Best Baroque Recording 2008) 2006, Bach's St Matthew Passion (ClassicFM Magazine's Recording of the Month) 2008, Handel's Acis and Galatea (Gramophone Editor's Choice and Recording of the Month) 2008, Bach's Mass in B Minor (Gramophone Editor's Choice) 2010. *Publications include:* Bach Interpretation 1990, Bach's Mass in B Minor 1991, Music Education and the Art of Performance in the German Baroque 1994, Playing with History 2002, Cambridge Companion to Bach (ed.), Oxford Companion to Bach (ed.), Cambridge History of Seventeenth Century Music (ed.) 2005, Bach's Dialogue with Modernity, 2010. *Honours:* W. H. Scheide Prize, American Bach Soc. 1991, Dent Medal 2003. *Address:* University of Glasgow, 14 University Gardens, Glasgow, G12 8QQ, Scotland (office). *Telephone:* (141) 330-4571 (office). *Fax:* (141) 330-3518 (office). *E-mail:* john.butt@glasgow.ac.uk (office); j.butt@music.gla.ac.uk (office). *Website:* www.gla.ac.uk/schools/cca/staff/johnbutt (office).

BUTTERFIELD, Adrian, ARCM, MA (Cantab.); British conductor, director, period-instrument violinist and viola d'amore player; *Professor, Royal College of Music;* b. 1965, England; s. of Kenneth Butterfield and Ruth Butterfield; m. Rachel Brown; one d. *Education:* chorister at St Paul's Cathedral, London, St Paul's School, Barnes, Trinity Coll., Cambridge, Royal Coll. of Music. *Career:* numerous appearances as soloist and dir with modern and period-instrument ensembles; Music Dir Tilford Bach Festival; Assoc. Music Dir London Handel Festival; directs London Handel Orchestra, Hanover Band, Theatre of Early Music, Montreal, Southbank Sinfonia across Europe and North America; Leader/Dir London Handel Players and Revolutionary Drawing Room; performances include Beethoven and Mozart concertos with Hanover Band, Mozart Sinfonia Concertante with Stuttgart Baroque Orchestra and London Handel Orchestra, Bach Double Concerto with English Baroque Soloists/John Eliot Gardiner, Vaughan Williams Concerto Accademico; conducted numerous works, including Rameau's Pigmalion, Handel's Alcina, La Resurrezione, Israel in Egypt, Purcell's Fairy Queen, Bach B minor Mass, St John Passion, Magnificat and Cantatas, Cavalieri's Rappresentatione di Anima e di Corpo; Prof., Royal Coll. of Music (RCM), London 2003–; teaches on Aestas Musica Baroque Course in Croatia. *Recordings include:* String Quartets by Boccherini and Donizetti and Mozart Clarinet Quintet, Viennese Quartet Party with Revolutionary Drawing Room, Violin Sonatas by C.P.E. Bach 2003, Bach Oboe and Violin Concerto, Handel Trio Sonatas Op. 5 2005, Handel at Home 2006, Handel Violin Sonatas 2007, Handel Trio Sonatas Op. 2 with London Handel Players, Leclair Op. 1 Sonatas 2009, Geminiani Sonatas Op. 1 2012, Leclair Op. 2 Sonatas 2013. *Current Management:* c/o Jill Davies, Davies Music, 23 Church Street, Tewkesbury, GL20 5PD, England. *Telephone:* (1684) 850112. *E-mail:* daviesmusic@btinternet.com. *Website:* www.adrianbutterfield.com. *Address:* Royal College of Music, Prince Consort Road, London, SW7 2BS, England (office). *Website:* www.rcm.ac.uk (office).

BUTTERLEY, Nigel Henry, AM; Australian composer, pianist and lecturer; b. 13 May 1935, Sydney. *Compositions include:* chamber music: String Quartets No. 1 1965, No. 2 1974, No. 3 1979, No. 4 1995, Trio for Clarinet, Cello and Piano 1979, Forest I, for Viola and Piano 1990, The Wind Stirs Gently, for flute and cello 1992, Forest II, for trumpet and piano 1993, Of Wood, for solo cello 1995, Spindles of the Stars, for flute, clarinet, violin, cello and piano 2005; radiophonic: In the Head the Fire, for choir (Italia Prize 1966), Watershore 1978; piano: Uttering Joyous Leaves 1981, Lawrence Hargrave Flying Alone 1981, Il Gubbo 1987, Two Pianos: Seven Preludes 2011; vocal: The True Samaritan 1958, First Day Covers (with Barry Humphries) 1973, Sometimes with One I Love 1976, The Owl 1983, There Came a Wind like a Bugle, Emily Dickinson 1987, The Woven Light for Soprano and Orchestra, Kathleen Raine 1994, Spring's Ending, Du Fu 1997, Spell of Creation for choir, soloists and orchestra (Lowin Prize 2001) 2000, Paradise Unseen for 6 solo voices 2001, Beni Avshalom 2007, Orphei Mysteria 2008; orchestral: Meditations of Thomas Traherne 1968, Violin Concerto 1970, Fire in the Heavens 1973, Symphony 1980, Goldengrove 1982, In Passing 1982, From Sorrowing Earth 1991, Poverty 1992, Never this Sun, this Watcher 2004; piano: Lawrence Hargrave Flying Alone 1988. *Recordings:* Violin Concerto, Meditations of Thomas Traherne, Goldengrove, From Sorrowing Earth, The Owl,

Laudes, Letter from Hardy's Bay, Uttering Joyous Leaves, String Quartet No. 3, The True Samaritan, There Came a Wind like a Bugle. *Honours:* Hon. DMus (Nat. Coll. of Educ., NSW). *Address:* 57 Temple Street, Stanmore, NSW 2048, Australia (home). *E-mail:* nigelbutterley@bigpond.com (office). *Website:* www.nigelbutterley.info (office).

BUTTERWORTH, (David) Neil, BA, MA; British fmr composer, conductor, writer and broadcaster; b. 4 Sept. 1934, London; m. Anne Mary Barnes 1960; three d. *Education:* Univ. of London, Guildhall School of Music, London, Univ. of Nottingham. *Career:* Lecturer, Kingston Coll. of Tech. 1960–68; Head of Music Dept, Napier Coll., Edinburgh 1968–87; conductor Edinburgh Schools Choir 1968–72, Glasgow Orchestral Soc. 1975–83, 1989–2002, Edinburgh Chamber Orchestra 1983–85; music critic, Times Educational Supplement 1983–97; Winston Churchill Travelling Fellowship 1975; mem. Inc. Soc. of Musicians, Performing Right Soc., Scottish Soc. of Composers. *Compositions include:* two horn concertos, Overture Budapest, A Scott Cantata, Dunblane, In Memory of Auschwitz, Partita, Dances for Dalkeith, Count Dracula (opera), many songs and instrumental works. *Publications:* Haydn 1970, 400 Aural Training Exercises 1970, A Musical Quiz Book 1974, Dvořák 1978, A Dictionary of American Composers 1983, revised edn 2005, Aaron Copland 1984, 20th Century Sight-singing Exercises 1984, Sight-singing Exercises from the Masters 1984, Vaughan Williams 1989, Neglected Music 1991, The American Symphony 1998; contrib. to periodicals, including Classic CD, Classical Music, Musical Opinion, The Scotsman, The Herald, The Sunday Times. *Honours:* Hon. FLCM; Guildhall School of Music and Drama Conducting Prize 1961. *Address:* The Lodge, 42 E High Street, Greenlaw, Berwickshire, TD10 6UF, Scotland (home). *Telephone:* (1361) 810408 (home).

BUWALDA, Sytse; Dutch singer (countertenor); b. 28 Sept. 1965, Zuiderwoude. *Education:* Sweelinck Conservatoire, Amsterdam. *Career:* regular appearances in baroque and classical opera; roles in 20th Century operas; solo ensemble; worked with some of the world's best known conductors and directors; performs theatre shows; performed at festivals throughout Europe and Japan; extensive oratorio and concert repertoire from the Renaissance to the present. *Recordings include:* Sytse Buwalda sings Pergolesi, Vivaldi, Bach, Handel, Bach and Buwalda, Heroic Arias, Airs and Duets, Sacred Arias 2004, About Love 2005, Lust in 4 Gangen 2007; numerous Bach, Handel adn Vivaldi recordings; work with ensembles. *Website:* www.sytsebuwalda.nl.

BYBEE, Luretta; American singer (mezzo-contralto); b. 1965, Midland, Texas. *Career:* Has sung widely in the USA and Europe as Isabella (Cologne and Dublin), Cherubino, Falliero in the US premiere of Rossini's Bianca e Falliero, Meg Page, Farnaces in Mozart's Mitridate at Wexford, Orlofsky, Nicklausse and Maddalena (New Orleans); Season 1993–94 as Dalila with Indianapolis Opera; engagements as Carmen for Dayton Opera (following earlier appearances in Peter Brook's La Tragédie de Carmen), Amneris, Laura (La Gioconda), Venus and Waltraute; Concerts include the Verdi Requiem at Carnegie Hall, Messiah in Texas and the Mozart Requiem at Anchorage, Alaska.

BYCHKOV, Semyon; American conductor; b. 30 Nov. 1952, Leningrad (now St Petersburg), Russia; brother of Yakov Kreizberg; m. Marielle Labèque. *Education:* Leningrad Conservatory (pupil of Musin). *Career:* invited to conduct Leningrad Philharmonic Orchestra; left USSR 1975; debut with Concertgebouw, Amsterdam and Berlin Philharmonic 1984–85; toured Germany with Berlin Philharmonic 1985; Music Dir Grand Rapid Symphony Orchestra 1980, Buffalo Philharmonic Orchestra 1986–87, Orchestre de Paris 1989–98, Semperoper, Dresden 1999–2003; Prin. Guest Conductor Maggio Musicale Fiorentino 1992–96; Chief Conductor WDR Sinfonieorchester Köln 1997–2010; Günter Wand Conducting Chair BBC Symphony Orchestra 2012–; Otto Klemperer Chair of Conducting, RAM, London; guest conductor with New York Philharmonic, Chicago Symphony, Cleveland Orchestra, Philadelphia Orchestra, Los Angeles Philharmonic, Vienna Philharmonic, Royal Concertgebouw Orchestra, Gewandhausorchester Leipzig, Berlin Philharmonic, Munich Philharmonic, London Symphony, Royal Opera House Covent Garden, Teatro Real Madrid, Metropolitan Opera New York, La Scala Milan, Opéra de Paris, Vienna State Opera. *Recordings include:* R. Strauss's Daphne (with Cologne Radio Chorus and Symphony Orchestra) 2005, Elektra (with Chorus and Symphony Orchestra of Westdeutscher Rundfunk, Köln) 2005. *Honours:* Franco Abbiati Prize 1996. *Current Management:* c/o IMG Artists, The Light Box, 111 Power Road, London, W4 5PY, England. *Telephone:* (20) 7957-5800. *Fax:* (20) 7957-5801. *E-mail:* twalton@imgartists .com. *Website:* www.imgartists.com.

BYERS, David, FRSA; British composer and broadcaster; b. 26 Jan. 1947, Belfast, Northern Ireland. *Education:* Queen's Univ., Belfast with Raymond Warren, Royal Acad. of Music with James Iliff, studied with Henri Pousseur in Liège. *Career:* early work as organist and choirmaster, Belmont Presbyterian Church; part-time music teacher, Regent House Grammar School; teacher of organ, theory and aural, City of Belfast School of Music; f. New Belmont Consort 1972; BBC Music Producer 1977–81, Sr Music Producer 1981–97, Chief Producer, Music & Arts 1997–2002 (retd); Northern Ed., Soundpost (then at its successor Music Ireland) 1981–89; Chair. Irish Baroque Orchestra 2012–14; Coulson Gov., Royal Irish Acad. of Music, Dublin 1992–2012; mem. Bd of Dirs National Concert Hall, Dublin 2006–11; mem. Royal Soc. of Musicians of Great Britain 2005. *Compositions include:* Woyzeck (incidental music) 1986, Polyphony for ensemble 1975, Dodecaphony for two organs 1980, At the Still Point of the Turning World for string quartet 1981, Caliban's

Masque for wind band 1982, A Planxty for the Dancer for orchestra 1983, The Wren's Blether for voices and ensemble 1984, The Moon is Our Breathing for narrator and ensemble 1985, Columba and the Crane for tuba and tape 1985, The Deer's Horn for oboe and cello 1988, The Journey of the Magi for string quartet 1990, Out of the Night for orchestra 1991, Medea (incidental music) 1991, Toccata: la morte d'Orfeo for orchestra 1996, Epigrams for piano 1998. *Honours:* several awards at RAM, including Cuthbert Nunn Composition Prize 1971, 1972, Margaret and Sydney Lovett Prize for organ accompaniment 1971, Josiah Parker Composition Prize 1972; Irish Arts Council's Macauley Fellowship in 1972. *Website:* www.byersmusic.com.

BYLES, Edward; British singer (tenor); b. 1935, Ebbw Vale, Wales. *Career:* debut at Glyndebourne 1957, as Brighella in Ariadne auf Naxos; toured with Opera For All and sang with companies, including Royal Opera, and in Europe, Russia, Australia and Ireland; joined ENO 1974, with roles including Monostatos, Mime, Missail in Boris Godunov and Vitek in The Makropulos Case; has sung in Tosca, War and Peace, Madama Butterfly, Orpheus in the Underworld and Pacific Overtures; in 1988 took part in the first British performance of Rimsky-Korsakov's Christmas Eve; season 1992 with ENO as the Broomstick-maker in Königskinder and Trabuco in The Force of Destiny; Spoletta in Tosca for ENO 1994.

BYLSMA, Anner; Dutch cellist and teacher; b. 17 Feb. 1934, The Hague. *Education:* Royal Conservatory of Music, The Hague with Carel Boomkamp. *Career:* principal cellist, Concertgebouw Orchestra, Amsterdam 1962–68; toured throughout the world as soloist with orchestras; recitalist and chamber music player; British debut, Wigmore Hall 1963; many trio appearances with Frans Brueggen and Gustav Leonhardt; teacher, Royal Conservatory of Music, The Hague; Sweelinck Conservatory, Amsterdam; Erasmus Scholar, Harvard Univ. 1982; played Cello Suites by Bach, BBC Lunchtime Concert 1992. *Honours:* winner Pablo Casals Competition, Mexico City 1959, Prix d'excellence, Royal Conservatory of Music 1957.

BYRCHMORE, Ruth, MMus, ARAM; British composer; *Head of Alumni Development, Royal Academy of Music;* b. 1966, Birmingham. *Education:* Royal Acad. of Music. *Career:* Parry Jerusalem Fellow and Composer-in-Residence, Wells Cathedral School 1991; fmrly Head of Open Acad. and Assoc. Head of Composition, Royal Acad. of Music, currently Head of Alumni Devt, also teaches in Academic Studies Dept. *Compositions include:* Marine Night 1990, Baba Yaga (for Kent Opera) 1995, The Fruit of Glory 1996, In Manus Tuas 1996, Manum Suam 1996, Magnificat and Nunc Dimittis 1998, The Glass Piano 1999, A Birthday (St Cecilia's Service, Westminster Abbey) 2004, Ambrose the Green Hippopotamus (for the London Mozart Players), Rock, Seven Little Monsters (for the Wallace Collection), Threads of Gold (trombone concerto), premiered in Birmingham Symphony Hall, Canticles, premiered in St Paul's Cathedral, Quem Pastores, choral (for the Worshipful Company of Musicians) 2006, Adam lay ybounden, choral (for the New Cambridge Singers) 2006. *Honours:* RPS-Radio 3 Award for Education 2004, British Composer Award 2005. *Address:* Alumni Office, Royal Academy of Music, Marylebone Road, London, NW1 5HT, England (office). *Telephone:* (20) 7873-7374 (office). *E-mail:* r.byrchmore@ram.ac.uk (office). *Website:* www.ram .ac.uk (office).

BYRNE, Desmond; Canadian singer (bass-baritone); b. 1965, Montréal. *Education:* McGill University, Montréal. *Career:* season 1989–90 as Leporello at Aldeburgh, under Steuart Bedford, Silvano (Un Ballo in Maschera) at Montréal and Melisso in Alcina at Vancouver; season 1991–92 with Leporello at Seattle, Ravel/Poulenc double bill at the Paris Châtelet, The Dream of Gerontius with the Orchestre National de France, Masetto in Vancouver and Monterone (Rigoletto) at the Opéra Bastille; further engagements in Lucia di Lammermoor at Tours, Massenet's Panurge in St Etienne and Gounod's Romeo in Toulouse 1993–94; sang in Gluck's Armide at Hamburg 1996, as Mozart's Figaro in Dublin and Massenet's Sancho Panza in Nantes 1997; Britten's Bottom in Strasbourg 1998, Créon in Enescu's Oedipe, in Paris and Bucharest, and Thoas in Iphigénie en Tauride at Nantes 1999; season 2000–01 with Rangoni in Boris Godunov, and Balstrode in Peter Grimes at Tours. *Address:* c/o Musicaglotz, 11 rue Le Verrier, 75006 Paris, France. *Telephone:* (1) 42-34-53-40. *Fax:* (1) 40-46-93-77. *E-mail:* general@musicaglotz .com. *Website:* www.musicaglotz.com.

BYRNE, Elizabeth; British singer (soprano); b. 1965, Lancashire, England. *Education:* Royal Northern College of Music and National Opera Studio, London. *Career:* appearances with English National Opera as Oksana in the British premiere of Rimsky's Christmas Eve 1988, Amelia in Un Ballo in Maschera, Madama Butterfly, Tosca, Bianca in Macmillan's Ines de Castro and Brünnhilde in Die Walküre for Scottish Opera 2001; Aida for WNO and Turandot for Mid-Wales Opera; engagements with Lyric Opera Chicago as Tosca, Wagner's Gutrune, and Elena/Margherita in Mefistofele; season 2000–01 as Salome for Glimmerglass Opera, The Duchess of Parma in Busoni's Faust at the Met and Puccini's Minnie for Austin Lyric Opera; sang Brünnhilde in Siegfried for Scottish Opera 2002. *Current Management:* Janice Mayer and Associates, 250 West 57th Street, Suite 2214, New York, NY 10107, USA. *Telephone:* (212) 541-5511. *Fax:* (212) 541-7303. *E-mail:* jmayer@ janicemayer.com. *Website:* www.janicemayer.com.

BYRNE, Nick, MMus; Australian trombonist; b. 1970, Sydney. *Education:* Canberra School of Music, Australian Nat. Univ., De Paul Univ., Chicago with Charles Vernon. *Career:* fmrly solo trombone, Hofer Symphoniker, Germany; joined Sydney Symphony 1996–; has performed with numerous orchestras

including Australian Chamber Orchestra, Australian Opera, Chicago Chamber Orchestra, Civic Orchestra of Chicago, Chicago Symphony; chosen by Sir Georg Solti for his Carnegie Hall Festival Orchestra 1994; performed as chamber musician with Summit Brass, Millar Brass, Chicago Symphony Lower Brass Ensemble, Canberra Trombone Quartet; founding mem. Sydney Symphony Brass Ensemble; co-f. Orchestra Romantique to perform works of the 19th century Romantic masters on period instruments 2009–; Rogen Int. Chair of Trombone, Univ. of NSW 2010–; also performs on and teaches the ophicleide (an early keyed tuba). *Address:* c/o Sydney Symphony Orchestra, PO Box 4972, Sydney, NSW 2001 (office); Orchestra Romantique, PO Box 3088, Redfern, NSW 2016, Australia (office). *Telephone:* (2) 9699-6096 (home); (421) 722883 (mobile) (home). *E-mail:* nick@ophicleide.com (home). *Website:* www.ophicleide.com; www.orchestra-romantique.com.

BYRNE, Peter, ARCM, BMus, MMus; British musicologist, academic and director of music (retd); b. 21 Nov. 1932, Grimsby; m. Anne J. Lavery; one s. two d. *Education:* Nat. Youth Orchestra of GB, Royal Coll. of Music, Goldsmiths Coll., London. *Career:* Dir of Music, Cardinal Wiseman School, Ealing 1959–64, Salvatorian Coll., Harrow 1965–79, Wimbledon Coll., Merton 1979–84; Prin. Lecturer, Goldsmiths Coll., London 1979–87; Academic Prof., Royal Mil. School of Music, London 1986–94; Organist and Choirmaster, Holy Ghost and St Stephen, Shepherds Bush 1960–63, St Benedict's Abbey, Ealing 1963–68; Musical Dir, Cecilians Operatic Soc., Ealing 1969–74; mem. Inst. of Advanced Musical Studies, King's Coll., London 1974–87; mem. Royal Musical Asscn. *Compositions:* Christopher Marlowe (opera) 1972. *Publications:* edn of seven works of Marc-Antoine Charpentier: H394 In Honorem Caeciliae Valeriani et Tiburtii canticum, H397 Caecilia virgo et martyr octo voc[ibus], H413 Caecilia virgo et martyr [I], H415 Caecilia virgo et martyr [II], H415a Prologue de la Ste Caecile après l'ouverture[:] Harmonia coelestis, H240 Motet: O sacrum [convivium] p[ou]r trois religieuses, H491 Dances from Medée [string orchestra]; Les Puys de musique d'Évreux. *Address:* Westgate House, Westgate, Louth, LN11 9YQ, England (home). *Telephone:* (1507) 354388/215 (home).

BYRNES, Garrett, BMus, MMus, DMA; American composer; b. 30 Dec. 1971, Bad Kreuznach, Rheinland-Pfalz, Germany. *Education:* Boston Conservatory, Peabody Conservatory of Music, Indiana Univ., USA. *Compositions include:* orchestral: Concertino for two cellos and string orchestra 1994, Concerto for cello and orchestra 1997, Nordic Realms (Chamber Symphony No. 1) 1998, Episodes for string orchestra 1998, Flames of Imbolc 1999, Dearg Gaelach for orchestra 2000, Nor'easter: Study for orchestra 2001; chamber music: Wraps (music for ballet) for oboe, two clarinets and string quartet 1994, Impressions of the Ocean for flute, violin and piano 1995, Introduction and Scherzo for violin and cello 1997, Three Pieces for flute and guitar 1999, Visions in Twilight for solo harp 2000; vocal music: Sketch of the Peternera song cycle for soprano and guitar (text by Lorca) 1995, Two Poems of Robert Frost for flute, soprano, vibraphone and cello 1998, Twilight Night for treble voice and piano (text by Christina Rossetti) 1999; solo instrumental music: Three Pieces for solo flute 1993, Sonata for solo violoncello 1993, Sonata for violin solo 1994, Nanna's Lament for solo viola 1999; piano music: Fantasy for piano 1994, Piano Sonata 1995, Suite for Piano 1995, Miniature Pictures 1996; has taught composition at Illinois Wesleyan Univ., Indiana Univ.; Asst Prof. of Composition and Theory, Ball State Univ. 2006–07; Owner, Musica Cosmopolita 1999–; Product Development Specialist, Hasbro, Inc. 2013–. *Honours:* awards from American Music Center, Nat. Asscn of Composers, American Art Song Competition, ASCAP, USA Int. Harp Composition Competition, Indiana Univ., California State Univ. at Northridge, Boston Conservatory. *Website:* garrettbyrnes.wordpress.com.

BYRNES-HARRIS, Aleicia; Canadian singer (soprano); b. 1950, Toronto; m. Paul Harris. *Education:* studied in California, at Aspen and San Diego Opera Studio. *Career:* sang in San Diego and Los Angeles as Santuzza, Magda in The Consul and Mme Lidoine in The Carmelites; European engagements from 1981, notably at Oldenburg, Wiesbaden, Nürnberg and Hamburg as Butterfly, Desdemona, Marie in Wozzeck, Irene in Rienzi, Amelia in Ballo in Maschera, Leonore, the Dyer's Wife, Kundry and Isolde; Tosca, Senta, Elektra (Elektra), Ariadne, Rosalinde; appeared at Zürich and Munich National Theatre; title role in Aida by Verdi, Los Angeles Music Center Opera; Die Sängerin in Reigen by Boesmans, Vienna Modern Music Festival; currently teacher, San Francisco Classical Voice; teaches singing, musical and dramatic interpretation at Byrnes-Harris Voice Studio, Karlsruhe, Germany. *E-mail:* Aleiciabyrnes77@gmail.com. *Website:* www.sfcv.org/music-teachers/aleicia -byrnes.

BYRON, Michael, BA; American composer; b. 7 Sept. 1953, Chicago, Ill., USA. *Education:* California Inst. of the Arts with Mario Guarneri, Thomas Stevens and Joe Higgins, York Univ., Canada. *Career:* works in collaboration with the performance art group, Maple Sugar; fmr mem. Faculty, Faculty of Fine Arts at York Univ.; Ed. and Publr Pieces (small press). *Compositions include:* Song of the Lifting up of the Head for piano 1972, Starfields for piano four hands 1974, Morning Glory for percussion 1975, Marimbas 1976, A Living Room at the Bottom of a Lake for orchestra 1977, Music for one piano 1978, Three Mirrors for percussion ensemble 1979, Music of Steady Light, 158 pieces for strings 1979–82, Tidal for ensemble 1981, Double String Quartet 1984. *Honours:* grants from York Univ., Ontario Arts Council, NEA, New York State Council of the Arts.

BYWALEC, Szymon; Polish conductor; b. 1974, Tychy. *Education:* Karol Szymanowski Acad. of Music, Katowice, Music Acad. Kraków, masterclasses with Gianluigi Gelmetti, Lothar Zagrosek, Gabriel Chmura, Kurt Mazur, Zoltán Peskó and Pierre Boulez. *Career:* Perm. Conductor, Orkiestra Musyki Nowej (New Music Orchestra); has performed at festivals of contemporary music including Warsaw Autumn, Musica Polonica Nova, Musica Electronica Nova, Beijing Modern and Velvet Curtain, Lviv; has worked with conductors including Krzysztof Penderecki, Gabriel Chmura, Takuo Yuasa and Paul McCreesh; Guest Conductor, Romanian Nat. Radio Orchestra, Miskolc Symphony Orchestra, Camerata Strumentale Citta de Prato, Orchestra Filharmonica Europea, Ensemble Orchestral Contemporain, Sinfonia Varsovia and Polish Radio Symphony Orchestra; Asst Prof., Karol Szymanowski Acad. of Music, Katowice, Dir Acad. Symphony Orchestra; mem. Repertoire Cttee, Warsaw Autumn Festival 2011–. *Recordings include:* with New Music Orchestra: Ivo Josiporić: Music & Politics, Krzysztof Baculewski: Works for Orchestra 2010, Jakob Kullberg: Momentum (Danish Radio P2 Prize) 2012, Krzysztof Wołek: Elements 2013. *Address:* Orkiestra Musyki Nowej, 41-902 Bytom, ul Jana Matejki 18/2, Poland (office). *Telephone:* (60) 1401224 (office). *Website:* omn.art.pl (office).

C

CABALLÉ, Montserrat; Spanish singer (soprano); b. 12 April 1933, Barcelona; m. Bernabé Marti (tenor) 1964; one s. one d. *Education:* Conservatorio del Liceo. *Career:* studied under Eugenia Kemeny, Conchita Badia and Maestro Annovazi; debut as Mimi (La Bohème), State Opera of Basel; N American début in Manon, Mexico City 1964; US debut in Lucrezia Borgia, Carnegie Hall 1965; appeared at Glyndebourne Festival as the Marschallin in Der Rosenkavalier and as the Countess in The Marriage of Figaro 1965; debut at Metropolitan Opera as Marguerite (Faust) Dec. 1965; frequent appearances at the Metropolitan Opera and numerous other opera houses throughout the USA; has performed in most of the leading opera houses of Europe including Gran Teatro del Liceo, Barcelona, La Scala, Milan, Vienna State Opera, Paris and Rome Operas, Bayerische Staatsoper (Munich), etc. and also at Teatro Colón, Buenos Aires; repertoire of over 40 roles; final performance at the Met in La Bohème 1988; apptd UNESCO Goodwill Amb. 1994. *Recordings include:* Lucrezia Borgia, La Traviata, Salomé, Aida, La Canción Romántica Española (Latin Grammy Award for Best Classical Album) 2007; recorded album Barcelona with Freddie Mercury which went on to be the theme of 1992 Olympic Games. *Honours:* Most Excellent and Illustrious Doña and Cross of Isabella the Catholic 1966, Commdr des Arts et des Lettres 1986; Gold Medal, Gran Teatro del Liceu, Echo Award 2000, Gramophone Lifetime Achievement Award 2007, numerous other awards.

CABELL, Nicole, BM; American singer (soprano); b. 17 Oct. 1977, Panorama City, Calif. *Education:* Eastman School of Music. *Career:* opera highlights: Metropolitan Opera, New York: Pamina (Magic Flute), Adina (Elisir d'Amore), Musetta (La Bohème), Micaela (Carmen); Lyric Opera of Chicago: Musetta, Leila (Pêcheurs de Perles), Micaela, Pamina (Zauberflöte); Royal Opera House, Covent Garden: Eudoxie (La Juive), Musetta, Leila; Deutsche Oper, Berlin: Juliette (Roméo et Juliette), Ilia (Idomeneo), Pamina, Micaela, Donna Elvira (Don Giovanni); orchestra highlights: New York Philharmonic (Opera Arias), Chicago Symphony (A Child of Our Time), Boston Symphony (Beethoven 9th, Porgy and Bess/Clara), Los Angeles Philharmonic (Porgy and Bess/Clara), BBC Symphony (Les Illuminations, A Child of Our Time), BBC Scottish Symphony (Mahler 8th Symphony/Soprano III), Minnesota Orchestra (Gorecki 3rd Symphony), Accad. di Santa Cecilia (Ein Deutsches Requiem, Les Illuminations, Mahler 2nd and 4th Symphonies), Cleveland Orchestra (Ein Deutsches Requiem), Indianapolis Symphony (Mahler 4th Symphony, Les Illuminations, Shéhérazade). *Recordings:* Soprano (solo album), Porgy and Bess (Clara), La Bohème (Musetta), Imelda de' Lambertazzi (Imelda). *Honours:* BBC Cardiff Singer of the World 2005. *Current Management:* c/o Michael Benchetrit, Columbia Artists' Management, 1790 Broadway, New York, NY 10019-1412, USA. *Telephone:* (212) 841-9559 (office). *Fax:* (212) 841-9687 (office). *Website:* www.cami.com (office); www .nicole-cabell.com.

CABEZA, Maia; Canadian musician (violin); b. 1992, Japan. *Education:* Curtis Inst. of Music, Hochschule für Musik Hanns Eisler, Germany, studied with Ulf Wallin; Akad. Berliner Philharmoniker, masterclasses with Ana Chumacenco, Gabor Takacs-Nagy, Christian Tetzlaff and Donald Weilerstein. *Career:* first solo performance with orchestra aged 10; has since performed as soloist in USA with Philadelphia Orchestra, Edmonton Symphony, Reno Philharmonic, Detroit Symphony and Sphinx Chamber Orchestra; as chamber musician, has worked with numerous ensembles and collaborated with musicians including Shmuel Ashkenasi, Carter Brey, Shlomo Mintz, and mems of Cleveland, Guarneri and Orion string quartets; recitals with piano in Canada, USA, Europe, Israel and S America; festival appearances included Music from Angel Fire, Verbier, Schleswig-Holstein, Sarasota Music Festival, Keshet Eilon Mastercourse, Aspen and Marlboro. *Honours:* fellowship from Davidson Inst., First Prize and Mozart Prize, Mozart Int. Violin Competition 2013. *E-mail:* maiacabeza@gmail.com (office). *Website:* www.maiacabeza.com (office).

CABLE, Margaret; British singer (mezzo-soprano); b. 1950, England. *Career:* appearances in Europe, Scandinavia, Israel and the USA; festival engagements at the Bath and Three Choirs Festivals; Promenade concerts in London; performances in Baroque repertoire with ensembles, using original instruments, including Bach's St Matthew Passion under Andrew Parrott and Messiah at the 1985 Lucerne Festival under Christopher Hogwood; broadcasts include Handel's Belshazzar, Tippett's A Child of Our Time, works with orchestra by Arthur Bliss and Robin Holloway; stage roles with Kent Opera included Mrs Grose in The Turn of The Screw, Dorabella, and Marcellina in Le nozze di Figaro, also at the 1986 Vienna International Festival; sang Juno in Handel's Semele at York Early Music Festival 1991; sang in Bach's St John Passion at the Festival Hall, London 1997. *Recordings include:* Haydn Masses with the Academy of Ancient Music; madrigals directed by Peter Pears; works by Mozart and Scarlatti directed by George Guest; Glazunov Songs and Lux Aeterna by William Mathias, with the Bach Choir; Handel's Carmelite Vespers and Messiah with Andrew Parrott and The Taverner Players.

CÁCERES, German; Salvadorean composer and conductor; *Principal Conductor and Music Director, Orquesta Sinfónica de El Salvador*; b. 9 July 1954, San Salvador. *Education:* Juilliard School, New York, Univ. of Cincinnati, USA. *Career:* made debut as oboist-composer at Carnegie Recital Hall, New

York 1978; Conductor, San Salvador Chamber Orchestra 1979–85; Prin. Conductor and Music Dir Orquesta Sinfónica de El Salvador 1985–99, 2002–; taught Music History, Universidad Centroamericana José Simeón Cañas, San Salvador 1993–2002; Dir of Arts and Culture, Univ. of El Salvador 2000–02; Lecturer, at Northridge 2001; Lecturer, Univ. of Southern California 2001; mem. Colegio de Compositores Latinoamericanos de Música de Arte, México, Ateneo de El Salvador, Instituto Bolivariano, Centro Cultural Salvadoreño, Instituto Masferreriano, Fundación Julia Díaz, Instituto Sanmartiniano; Founder and Music Dir El Salvador Contemporary Music Festival. *Compositions:* stage works: Bálsamo (ballet) 1978, El Cristo Negro (three-act opera with libretto by Hugo Lindo) 1998; orchestral: Yulcuicat 1973, Concierto for harp and orchestra 1977, Concierto para Cuerdas for string orchestra 1979, Concierto for piano and orchestra 1981, Sinfonía 1983, Concierto for small orchestra 1988, Diferencias 1988, Concierto for violin and orchestra 1989, Deploración (in memoriam Julián Orbón) 1993, Fanfarria a San Salvador for 12 brass orchestra 1996, Tiento I for small orchestra 1996, Concierto No. 1 for guitar and orchestra 2000, Tiento VII for string orchestra 2000, Concierto No. 2 for guitar and string orchestra 2001, Concierto No. 3 for guitar and orchestra 2001, Doble Concierto for violin, cello and orchestra 2001, Lacónicas II, 2002; chamber music: Cuarteto para cuerdas No. 1 for string quartet 1974, Cuarteto para cuerdas No. 2 for string quartet 1976, Concierto de Cámara No. 1 for flute, oboe, clarinet, French horn, bassoon and piano 1979, Sonata No. 1 for violin and piano 1980, Concierto for viola and ensemble 1980, Sonatina for guitar 1981, Sonata for viola and piano 1982, Sonata for oboe, cello and piano 1983, Tres Piezas for bass clarinet, harp and vibraphone 1987, Cinco Deploraciones for flute 1988, Cuatro Piezas for flute and bassoon 1988, Sonata No. 2 for violin and piano 1988, Concierto de Cámara No. 2 for flute, oboe, clarinet, bassoon, string quartet, double bass and piano 1990, Trío for violin, cello and piano 1991, Partitas for flute, oboe, clarinet, violin, cello and harpsichord 1992, Cuatro Piezas for violin 1993, Concierto de Cámara No. 3 for two violins, cello and harpsichord 1994, Fantasía sobre una Cadencia de Gesualdo for two oboes, two clarinets, two bassoons and two French horns 1994, Cuarteto para cuerdas No. 3 for string quartet 1996, Tiento II for clarinet 1997, Tiento III for cello 1997, Ocho Variaciones sobre un Conjunto de Ocho Notas for guitar 1997, Tiento IV for violin 1999, Tiento V for oboe 2000, Tiento VIII for guitar 2001, Tiento IX for violin, cello and piano 2003, Tiento X for flute and piano 2003; choral works: Tres Cantos for mixed chorus 1981, Cantata for mixed chorus and orchestra 1992, Villancico del Calendario for mixed chorus 1996; vocal works: Tres Canciones for soprano and string quartet 1975, Estáncias for soprano and orchestra 1979, Tres Canciones Epigramáticas for soprano and piano 1979, Cuatro Cantos for soprano and piano 1981, Premisas (cantata) for soprano and string quartet 1982, Cantos de Fácil Palabra for soprano, flute and harpsichord 1985, Tres Canciones for soprano and orchestra 1988, Cantos for soprano and orchestra 1990, Tres Canciones for soprano and piano 1995, El Señor de la Casa del Tiempo for soprano and piano 1996, Lo que dice el Caracol for soprano and orchestra 1997, Siete Canciones for soprano and piano 1999, Cuatro Canciones for soprano and piano 1999, Las Monedas bajo la Lluvia for voice and guitar 1999; piano works: Sonata 1984, Tres Estudios sobre el Silencio 1989, Lacónicas 1993, Tiento VI 2000; other: Tres Piezas 2002. *Honours:* Hon. Pres. Gosau am Dachstein String Festival, Austria 1987, Hon. mem. Research Bd of Advisors, American Biographical Inst. 1999; Ordre des Arts et Lettres 1992, Ordem de Rio Branco, Brazil 1999, Order of Merit, Germany 2008; Guggenheim Foundation Fellowship 1981, Nat. Culture Prize of El Salvador 1982, Int. Gertrud Remdohr Prize, Hamburg, Germany 1986, Fulbright Foundation Fellowship 1987–89, Rockefeller Foundation Fellowship 1991, Distinguished Composer and Conductor Award, Congress of El Salvador. *Address:* Octava Av. Norte No. 228, San Salvador, El Salvador (office). *Telephone:* 2221-2373 (office); 2221-4407 (office). *E-mail:* gcaceres@ cultura.gob.sv (office); gcaceresbuitrago@hotmail.com (home). *Website:* www .germancaceresbuitrago.com.

CACHEMAILLE, Gilles; Swiss singer (bass-baritone); b. 25 Nov. 1951, Orbe. *Education:* Lausanne Conservatoire. *Career:* concert hall appearances 1978–, at the Aix and Salzburg Festivals, at Paris, Lyon, Buenos Aires, Madrid, Strasbourg, Lisbon and Tokyo; repertoire has included the Passions of Bach, L'Enfance du Christ by Berlioz, Franck's Les Béatitudes, Haydn's Schöpfung and Jahreszeiten, works by Monteverdi and songs by Duparc, Poulenc, Schubert and Strauss; debut as mem. of the Lyon Opéra in the stage premiere of Rameau's Les Boréades at Aix, 1982; Lausanne Opéra as Guglielmo, Simone in La Finta Semplice, Mozart's Figaro and Papageno, and Belcore in L'Elisir d'amore, 1988; Mézières in 1988 at Gluck's Orpheus, Leporello at the Hamburg Staatsoper in 1987 and Vienna in 1989; sang in Martinů's Les Trois Souhaits at Lyon, 1990, and Leporello at Houston, 1991; sang Don Giovanni at Glyndebourne, 1994; Merlin in Chausson's Le Roi Arthus, at the Bregenz Festival, 1996; Leporello at Aix-en-Provence, 1998; sang Leporello at Toronto, Figaro (Mozart) at Barcelona and Don Alfonso for Opéra Lyon, 2000–01. *Recordings include:* L'Enfance du Christ; Chausson's Le Roi Arthus; Iphigénie en Aulide; Les Boréades; Gluck's La Rencontre Imprévue; Dominic in Arabella; Golaud in Pelléas et Mélisande; Guglielmo in Così fan tutte under Harnoncourt; Claudio in Béatrice et Bénédict. *Current Management:* Balmer

& Dixon Management AG, Kreuzstrasse 82, 8032 Zürich, Switzerland. *Telephone:* (43) 244-8644. *Fax:* (43) 244-8649. *Website:* www.badix.ch.

CADDY, Ian Graham, LRAM, ARCM, ARAM; British singer (bass-baritone) and stage director; b. 1 March 1947, Southampton, Hants., England; m. Kathryn Dorothy Ash 1979 (divorced 1994); one s. two d.; partner Jacqueline Pischorn 2000–14. *Education:* Royal Acad. of Music, London. *Career:* debut in London 1974; sang with Opera For All, Kent Opera, New Opera Co., Phoenix Opera, Glyndebourne, Scottish Opera, Welsh Nat. Opera, Royal Opera Covent Garden, ENO, Houston Grand Opera, Opéra de Nantes, Opéra d'Angers, Vancouver Opera, Teatro la Fenice; opera, oratorio, festivals and recitals throughout UK and in Austria, Brazil, Canada, at Wexford and Versailles Festivals, in Denmark, Ireland, France, Germany, Hong Kong, Iceland, Netherlands, Spain, USA and Yugoslavia; edited, published, performed and broadcast works by J.S Mayr and Donizetti; staging dir of baroque opera, especially in strict period style; numerous radio and TV broadcasts worldwide; runs own publishing title, Caddy Publishing; Co-founder The Mayr-Donizetti Collaboration 1985–2008. *Recordings include:* L'Amor Coniugale by Mayr, Jigs, Reels and Songs of the Bottle by Holbrooke, Vivaldi's Dixit Dominus, Rameau's Princesse de Navarre and Nais, Schoeck's Notturno, Wallace's Maritana, The Beggar's Opera, Sullivan's The Rose of Persia, Berners' Le Carrosse du Saint-Sacrement, Donizetti's Songs written in the Bass Clef. *Video recordings:* Macbeth, La Fanciulla del West, Intermezzo. *Current Management:* c/o Jill Davies, Davies Music, 23 Church Street, Tewkesbury, GL20 5PD; c/o Music International, 13 Ardilaun Road, London, N5 2QR, England. *E-mail:* jill@daviesmusic.org.uk; music@musicint.co.uk. *E-mail:* info@baroquegestures.com; info@iancaddy.com. *Website:* www .baroquegestures.com; www.caddypublishing.co.uk; www.iancaddy.com.

CADOL, Christine; French singer (mezzo-soprano); b. 1956. *Education:* Paris Conservatoire. *Career:* debut in 1978; appearances as Dalila in Samson et Dalila, Amneris in Aida, Azucena in Le Trouvere, Berta in Il Barbiere di Siviglia, Carmen in Carmen, Charlotte in Werther, Dame Marthe in Faust, Dulcinee in Don Quixote, Enrichetta in I Puritani, Fenena in Nabucco, Giulietta in Les Contes d'Hoffman, Helene in La Belle Helene, Katisha in The Mikado, Maddalena in Rigoletto, Marguerite in La Damnation de Faust, Santuzza in Cavalleria Rusticana, Varvara in Katya Kabanova, Anita in La Navarraise, Suzuki in Madama Butterfly; further guest engagements at Liège, Limoges, Marseilles and Saint-Cere; many concert appearances.

CADUFF, Sylvia; Swiss conductor and academic; b. 7 Jan. 1937, Chur. *Education:* Conservatoire of Lucerne, studied with Karajan at the Berlin Conservatory, and with Kubelik, Matacic and Van Otterloo. *Career:* debut with the Tonhalle Orchestra, Zürich; guest conductor across Europe, USA, Japan, Republic of Korea; appearances with New York Philharmonic, Munich and Berlin Philharmonics, Radio Orchestra Berlin, Royal Philharmonic London; Asst to Bernstein at the New York Philharmonic 1966–67; Music Dir, Solingen 1977–86; taught conducting at the Berne Conservatory 1972–77; Prof. of Conducting and Orchestral Studies; mem. Swiss Musicians' Asscn, Swiss Conductors' Union. *Honours:* second prize Nicolai Malko Competition, Copenhagen 1965, first prize Mitropoulos Competition, New York 1966. *Address:* Belleriverstrasse 29, 6006 Lucerne, Switzerland.

CAETANI, Oleg; Italian conductor; b. 5 Oct. 1956, Lausanne, Switzerland; s. of Igor Markevitch and Topazia Caetani; m. Susanna Stefani Caetani; three d. (two from previous m.). *Education:* studied with Nadia Boulanger, Franco Ferrara in Rome, Kyrill Kondrashin in Moscow and Ilia Mussin in Leningrad. *Career:* Asst to Otmar Suitner, Staatsoper Berlin 1981–84; Deutsche Nat. Theater Weimar 1984–87; Kapellmeister, Städtische Buhnen Frankfurt am Main; Music Dir Wiesbaden 1992–95, leading the Ring, Tristan und Isolde, La Forza del Destino, Otello, Rimsky's Invisible City of Kitezh and Bluebeard's Castle; guest engagements with Semiramide in Vienna, Les Vêpres Siciliennes in Nice, Lucia di Lammermoor and Tosca at Trieste and Verdi's Falstaff at Stuttgart 1996–97; Zurich Opera with Rigoletto, The Nutcracker, La Bohème and Norma; led Tchaikovsky's Maid of Orleans at Strasbourg 1998, Otello and Turandot at La Scala, Don Pasquale in Florence, The Flying Dutchman in Rome etc.; Oslo Opera Madama Butterfly 2012, Lady Macbeth of Mtsensk 2014; with ENO Khovanshchina 2003, Sir John in Love 2006, Madam Butterfly 2012, La Bohème 2013, ROH London Tosca 2014; concert repertoire includes all symphonies by Beethoven, Brahms, Schubert, Schumann, Shostakovich and Tchaikovsky, with soloists such as Martha Argerich, Viktoria Mullova, Shlomo Mintz and the late Sviatoslav Richter; Music Dir, Chemnitz 1996–2001; Chief Conductor Desig., Melbourne Symphony Orchestra 2003–04, Chief Conductor and Artistic Dir 2005–09. *Honours:* winner RAI Competition, Turin 1979, Herbert von Karajan Competition 1982. *E-mail:* caetanioffice@gmail.com. *Website:* www.olegcaetani .com.

CAFORIO, Armando; Italian singer (bass); b. 1956, Civitavecchia. *Education:* studied in Alessandria and the USA. *Career:* debut in Genoa as Count Rodolfo in La Sonnambula 1982; in Florence as Colline in La Bohème 1983, Turin and Martina Franca from 1984; guest appearances 1984–85, in Dublin, Geneva 1987; Torre del Lago and Maggio Musicale Festivals from 1987; Savona 1990, in L'Ebreo by Apollini; Verona 1993, as Rodolfo in Catalani's Loreley; other roles include Rossini's Don Magnifico and Basilio, the Grand Inquisitor, and Loredano in Verdi's Due Foscari; sang Geronte in Manon Lescaut at Catania and Zaccaria in Nabucco at the Verona Arena 2000; sang

Ramphis in Aida at the Teatro dell'Opera, Rome 2005. *Address:* c/o Teatro dell'Opera, Piazza Beniamino Gigli 7, 00184 Rome, Italy.

CAHILL, Teresa Mary, LRAM, AGSM; British singer (soprano); b. 30 July 1944, Maidenhead, Berks.; d. of Henry D. Cahill and Florence Cahill (née Dallimore); m. 1st John Anthony Kiernander 1971 (divorced 1978); m. 2nd Prof. Robert Saxton 2005. *Education:* Notre Dame High School, Southwark, Guildhall School of Music and Drama and London Opera Centre. *Career:* debut at Glyndebourne 1969, Covent Garden 1970, La Scala, Milan 1976, Philadelphia Opera 1981; Prof., Trinity Coll. of Music, London; specialises in works of Mozart, Strauss, Mahler, Elgar and Tippett; has given concerts with all the London orchestras, Boston and Chicago Symphony Orchestras, at Berlin, Vienna and Bath Festivals and throughout Europe, USA and the Far East; Adjudicator, Live Music Now 1988– (Musical Adviser 2000–); Gov. Royal Soc. of Music 2000, Royal Soc. of Musicians of Great Britain 2001–; Prof., Vocal Dept, Trinity Laban Conservatoire of Music and Dance, London; masterclasses, Dartington Festival 1984, 1986, 's-Hertogenbosch 1988, 2000, Univ. of Oxford 1995–96, Peabody Inst. 1999, RAM 2002, Bowdoin Coll. 2004; Patron Opera/UK. *Recordings include:* works by Elgar, Strauss, Mahler, Mozart, Rachmaninov, Saxton and Lutyens. *Publications:* contrib. to 'Divas in their Own Words', compiled by Andrew Palmer; career archive housed in British Library. *Honours:* Worshipful Company of Musicians Silver Medal 1966, John Christie Award 1970. *Address:* 65 Leyland Road, London, SE12 8DW, England (home). *Telephone:* (20) 8852-0847 (home). *E-mail:* tessitura@ btopenworld.com. *Website:* teresacahill.net.

CAHN, Aviel, PhD; Swiss opera administrator; *Artistic Director / Intendant,* Vlaanderen (Flemish Opera); b. 14 June 1974, Zürich. *Education:* Zürich Univ. *Career:* worked for Rudolf Nureyev Foundation; Business and Artistic Dir, Int. Relations, China Nat. Symphony Orchestra, Beijing 2000; Head of Planning and Casting, Nat. Opera of Finland 2001–04; Opera Dir Stadttheater Bern 2004–07; Man. Dir Zürcher Kammerorchester 2007–08; Gen. Man. Vlaamse Opera (Flanders Opera) 2009, currently Artistic Dir/Intendant, Vlaanderen (Flemish Opera); f. Concours Ernst Haefliger (singing competition), Switzerland 2006. *Address:* Vlaanderen, Van Ertbornstraat 8, 2018 Antwerp, Belgium (office). *E-mail:* info@operaballet.be (office). *Website:* operaballet.be/en (office).

CAHOVA, Monika; Czech singer (soprano); b. 20 June 1966, Prague. *Education:* The State Conservatory, Prague. *Career:* debut as Inez in Il Trovatore at the National Theatre, Prague 1988; many appearances at the Opera Theatre Liberec and also sings in the National Theatre of Prague; roles in opera include Marenka in Smetana's The Bartered Bride, Blazenka in The Secret, Vendulka in The Kiss, Titka in Dalibor, Dvořák's Rusalka, Terinka and Julie in Jakobin, Elisabeth de Valois in Don Carlo, Leonora in Il Trovatore, and Amelia in Simon Boccanegra, Mimi in La Bohème, and Tosca, Gioconda in La Gioconda, Marguerite in Faust, Micaela and Carmen in Carmen, Giulietta in Les Contes d'Hoffman and Hélène in La Belle Hélène, Donna Elvira in Don Giovanni and the Countess, Lisa in Tchaikovsky's Queen of Spades, Marica in Kalman's Die Gräfin Maritza, Liza in Das Land des Lächelns and Hana in Die Lustige Witwe; also sang in Britten's War Requiem at the Summer Festival in Olomouc at Zagreb in The Days of Czech Opera, sang Dvořák's Rusalka and Marenka; sang Donna Elvira with the National Theatre of Brno in Italy; also appeared at the Teatro dell'Aquila, Fermo Teatro di Cita, Salerno; Dvořák's Stabat Mater at the Summer Festival in Marianskelazne; sang Mozart's Requiem in Belgium and the Third Lady in Die Zauberflöte in Germany and in Tokyo; regular guest appearances in Germany.

CAINE, Rebecca; Canadian singer (soprano); b. 1962, Toronto. *Education:* Guildhall School of Music, London. *Career:* divides singing between opera and musical theatre; opera debut as Amor in L'Incoronazione di Poppea, Glyndebourne; operatic repertoire includes Pamina, Despina, Susanna, Aminta in Re Pastore, Vixen, Micaela, Musetta, Ophelie, Leila, Marguerite, Violetta, Julietta, Adina, Hanna Glawari in Lehar's Merry Widow, Jezebel, in Playing Away, The Golden Ass, Fotis, Psappha in Mr Emmett Takes a Walk; musical theatre debut as Laurey in Oklahoma, West End, London; performances include Christine in Phantom of the Opera, UK and Canadian tours; created role of Cosette in Les Miserables; vocal tutor, Trinity Coll. of Music. *Recordings include:* Les Miserables, The Phantom of the Opera, Anything Goes, Babes in Toyland, Mr Emmett Takes a Walk; solo: Leading Ladies 2007. *Honours:* Dora Mavor Moore Award 1998. *Current Management:* Cole Kitchenn, 212 Strand, London WC2R 1AP, England. *Telephone:* (20) 7427-5680. *Fax:* (20) 7353-9639. *E-mail:* info@colekitchenn.com. *Website:* www .colekitchenn.com. *E-mail:* rebecca@rebeccacaine.com (office). *Website:* www .rebeccacaine.com.

CAIRE, Patrice; French organist; b. 17 June 1949, Lyon. *Education:* Lyon Conservatory, Conservatoire National Superieur de Musique, Paris, Ecole Normale de Musique, Paris. *Career:* organist, Sainte Croix Church, Lyon 1973–83; organist, St Bonaventure Sanctuary, Lyon 1983–; Keeper, Grandes Orgues de l'Auditorium Maurice Ravel, Lyon 1980–, later Artistic Dir; Commissioner, International Improvisation Competition 1982–83; teacher, Conservatoire National Superieur de Musique, Lyon 1979–; recitals in France, Germany, England, Scotland, Switzerland, Sweden, Spain, Italy, Belgium, USA and Canada; concert performances on radio and television across Europe; with orchestra under S. Baudo, E. Krivine, S. Skrowaczewski, J. Nelson and E. Tchakarov. *Recordings:* two recitals; Ch. M. Widor, Symphony No. 6; A.

Guilmant, Sonata No. 1 REM; six Pieces; Brass; Organ; Percussion; Busser; Litaize; Dupré; Vierne: Gigout, REM; N. J. Lemmens; Fanfare; Priere; Sonatas No. 1, 2, 3, REM; Lemmens, Lefebure Wely, REM; C. Franck et l'orgue du Trocadero, REM; L. Vierne, Finales of six Symphonies; Ch. M. Widor, Symphonies No. 4, 5,; Ch M Widor, Symphonies, No. 1 2; L. Boellmann, Work for Grand Organ; C. Franck, 12 Pieces for Grand Organ; Les Maîtres du Trocadero; Guilmant; Widor; Lemmens; Franck; Dubois; Gigout; Saint-Saëns. *Address:* 73 rue Pierre Corneille, 69006 Lyon, France.

CAIRNS, Christine; British singer (mezzo-soprano); b. 11 Feb. 1959, Ayrshire, Scotland. *Education:* Royal Scottish Acad. of Music and Drama, Glasgow, studied with Neilson Taylor. *Career:* concerts with André Previn and the Los Angeles Philharmonic 1985; Prokofiev's Alexander Nevsky in Los Angeles and with the Cleveland and Philadelphia Orchestras; Royal Philharmonic Orchestra 1988, in Mahler's Kindertotenlieder; tour of the USA with Mahler's 4th Symphony; Festival Hall London 1988, in Schoenberg's Songs Op 22; Promenade concerts London 1989, in Mozart's Coronation Mass, returned 1990; guest appearances throughout the UK and in Athens, Basle, Tokyo, Berlin, San Francisco and Dortmund; touring throughout Spain; guest engagements in Paris, Madrid, Rome, Zürich, Singapore and Rio de Janeiro; staged performances of Monteverdi's Orfeo in Valencia; concerts with Ashkenazy in Berlin and London 1990; Mahler with Simon Rattle and Yuri Temirkanov in Los Angeles 1991; season 1996–97 with Beethoven's Mass in C at the Bath Mozart Festival and Elijah with the Ulster Orchestra. *Recordings:* Mendelssohn's Midsummer Night's Dream, Previn, Vienna Philharmonic; Prokofiev's Alexander Nevsky, Previn, LA Philharmonic; Die Erste Walpurgisnacht, Dohnányi, Cleveland Orchestra. *Current Management:* Carroll Artist Management, 11 Palmerston Place, Edinburgh, EH1L 5AF, Scotland.

CAIRNS, David Adam, CBE, MA, FRSL; British journalist and musicologist; b. 8 June 1926, Loughton, Essex; s. of Sir Hugh William Bell Cairns and Barbara Cairns (née Smith); m. Rosemary Goodwin 1959; three s. *Education:* Dragon School, Winchester Coll., Oxford, Princeton Univ. Graduate Coll., USA. *Career:* Library Clerk, House of Commons 1951–53; critic, Record News 1954–56; mem. editorial staff, Times Educational Supplement 1955–58; music critic, Spectator 1958–63, Evening Standard 1958–63; asst music critic, Financial Times 1963–67; music critic, New Statesman 1967–70; mem. staff, Philips Records, London 1968–70, Classic Programme Co-ordinator 1970–73; asst music critic, Sunday Times 1975–84, music critic 1985–92; Leverhulme Research Fellow 1972–74; Distinguished Visiting Prof., Univ. of California, Davis 1985; Distinguished Visiting Scholar, Getty Center for the History of Art and Humanities 1992; Visiting Resident Fellow, Merton Coll., Oxford 1993; Chair. The Berlioz Soc.; Pres. City Music Soc., Putney Music; Founder-Conductor, Thorington Players (amateur orchestra). *Publications:* The Memoirs of Hector Berlioz (ed. and trans.) 1969 (revised 2002), Responses: Musical Essays and Reviews 1973, The Magic Flute (co-author, ENO Opera Guide) 1980, Falstaff (co-author, ENO Opera Guide) 1982, Berlioz: The Making of an Artist 1803–1832 (ASCAP Deems Taylor Award 2001) 1989, Berlioz: Servitude and Greatness 1832–1869 (Whitbread Biog. of the Year 2000, Samuel Johnson Non-Fiction Prize 2000, Prix de l'Académie Charles Cros 2003) 1999, Mozart and his Operas 2006; contrib. of articles on Beethoven and Berlioz, in Viking Opera Guide 1993. *Honours:* Hon. mem., Royal Acad. of Music; Commdr, Ordre des Arts et des Lettres 2013; Hon. DLitt (Southampton) 2001; British Acad. Derek Allen Memorial Prize 1990, Royal Philharmonic Soc. Award 1990, 1999, Yorkshire Post Prize 1990. *Address:* 49 Amerland Road, London, SW18 1QA, England (office). *Telephone:* (20) 8870-4931 (office). *E-mail:* d03.cairns@btinternet.com (office).

CAIRNS, Janice; British singer (soprano); b. 1955, Ashington, Northumberland. *Education:* Royal Scottish Academy with John Hauxvell, and with Tito Gobbi in Rome. *Career:* debut as Verdi's Desdemona at the Thessaloniki Festival, directed by Gobbi; London debut as Odabella in Attila, for University College Opera; Appearances with Kent Opera as Alice Ford and Donna Anna; Manon Lescaut and Leonora in La Forza del Destino for Chelsea Opera Group; With English National Opera has sung Musetta, Ariadne, Eva, Maria in Mazeppa, Lisa, Maria Boccanegra, Tosca and Amelia; Scottish Opera as Rezia in Oberon, Leonara (Il Trovatore), Aida and Madama Butterfly; For Opera North has sung Aida, Leonore and Helen in the British stage premiere of Verdi's Jerusalem, 1989; Italian debut with Scottish Opera at La Fenice, Venice, as Rezia; Concert engagements include the Verdi Requiem with the London Symphony Orchestra, Odabella at the Concertgebouw, Rachmaninov's The Bells at the Proms and Britten's War Requiem at the Norwich Festival; English National Opera, 1992, as Anna in Street Scene and as Ariadne; Sang Turandot for Welsh National Opera, 1994; Tosca for English National Opera, 1996; Season 1997 with Korngold's Violanta for Opera North and at the London Proms; Foreign Princess in Rusalka for ENO, 1998. *Current Management:* Robert Gilder and Co., 91 Great Russell Street, London WC1B 3PS, England. *Telephone:* (20) 7580-7758. *Fax:* (20) 7580-7739. *E-mail:* rgilder@robert-gilder.com. *Website:* www.robert-gilder.com.

CAIRNS, Tom; British stage director and stage designer; b. 1950, England. *Career:* designed and directed premiere production of Birtwistle's Second Mrs Kong, for Glyndebourne Touring Opera at Glyndebourne, 1994; Other engagements include Tippett's King Priam for Opera North and Flanders Opera, La Bohème at Stuttgart, Don Giovanni for Scottish Opera and Un Ballo in Maschera at Munich; Stage Designs for Mozart's Apollo and Hyacinth at Batignano, Don Giovanni for Opera 80, The Midsummer Marriage, La Finta Giardiniera and Gianni Schicchi for Opera North; The Trojans for Scottish Opera, WNO and Opera North (also seen at Covent Garden): Billy Budd and Beatrice and Benedict for English National Opera; Samson et Dalila at the Bregenz Festival and Benvenuto Cellini by Berlioz for Netherlands Opera, All About My Mother (Old Vic) 2007. *Address:* 505 Bankside Lofts, 65 Hopton Street, London, SE1 9GZ, England.

CALDERÓN, Pedro Ignacio; Argentine conductor; *Music Director, Orquesta Sinfónica Nacional Argentina*; b. 1933, Paraná. *Education:* studied in Buenos Aires, Accademia di Santa Cecilia, Rome, Italy. *Career:* Music Dir, Orquesta de la Universidad Nacional de Tucumán 1958–61; Asst Dir to Leonard Bernstein, New York Philharmonic 1963–64; Music Dir, Orquesta Filarmónica de Buenos Aires 1965–91; f. and Dir, Ensemble Musical de Buenos Aires 1966–; Music Dir, Orquesta Estable del Teatro Colón 1992–93; Music Dir, Orquesta Sinfónica Nacional Argentina 1996–. *Honours:* winner, Dmitris Mitropoulos Int. Competition 1963. *Address:* Orquesta Sinfónica Nacional, Avenida Córdoba 1155, 1055 Buenos Aires, Argentina (office). *Telephone:* (11) 4815-8883 (office).

CALDERON, Rani; Israeli conductor, composer and pianist; *Music Director, Orquesta Filarmónica de Santiago*; b. 1972. *Education:* Rubin Acad. of Music, Jerusalem and Tel-Aviv; studied piano with Prina Salzman, Mendi Rodan, Yitzhak Sadai and Janine Reiss. *Career:* conducted first night of Puccini's Suor Angelica, Teatro Mancinelli 1996; conductor for numerous operas including Don Giovanni in Vienna, Rigoletto and Turandot in Tel-Aviv, Faust in Bilbao, Aida in Avignon and Simon Boccanegra in Strasbourg; Prin. Conductor, Orquesta Filarmonica de Santiago, Chile 2010–; symphonic conductor, Orchestra del Teatro La Fenice, Venice, Orchestre National de Belgique, Brussels, Orchestre National d'Ile de France, Paris, Orchestre National de Montpellier, OSPA, Oviedo, Orchestre Colonne, Paris, I Pomeriggi Musicali, Milan, Sofia Philharmonic, Rishon le-Zion Symphony Orchestra, Ra-anana Symphonette, Ashdod Chamber Orchestra, Israel; numerous piano recitals in Israel and France. *Recordings:* albums: Meyerbeer, Semiramide 2007, Rencontres, Carlo Colombara 2008. *Current Management:* Stage Door s.r.l., Via S. Giorgio 4, 40121 Bologna BO, Italy. *Telephone:* (051) 262126. *Fax:* (051) 271452. *E-mail:* info@stagedoor.it. *Website:* www.stagedoor.it; www.ranicalderon.com.

CALDWELL, John Anthony, BMus, MA, DPhil, FRCO; British lecturer, writer and composer; b. 6 July 1938, Bromborough, England; m. Janet; one s. one d. *Education:* Birkenhead School, Liverpool Matthay School of Music, Univ. of Oxford. *Career:* Asst Lecturer in Music, Bristol Univ. 1963–66; Lecturer in Music, Univ. of Oxford 1966–99, Prof. 1999–2005; Fellow of Jesus Coll., Oxford 1999–2005, Emer. Fellow 2005–; mem. Royal Musical Asscn, Plainsong and Mediaeval Music Soc. (mem. of council). *Compositions:* Paschale mysterium trilogy: Good Friday 1998, The Word 2001, Pascha nostrum 2002; Divertimento for Orchestra 1999, The Story of Orpheus 2004, Mediterranean Creatures 2005, La Corona 2005. *Publications:* English Keyboard Music Before the Nineteenth Century 1973, Medieval Music 1978, Editing Early Music 1985, The Oxford History of English Music (two vols) 1991, 1999; contrib. to Early Music, Music and Letters, The New Grove Dictionary of Music and Musicians 1980, 2002. *Address:* Jesus College, Oxford, OX1 3DW, England (office). *Telephone:* (1865) 310956 (home). *E-mail:* john.caldwell@music.ox.ac.uk (home).

CALLAND, Deborah; British musician (trumpet); *Artistic Director, Hampstead Garden Suburb Chamber Concert Series*. *Education:* Royal Acad. of Music. *Career:* recitals in France, Germany, Denmark, Finland, Iceland, USA, as well as venues throughout the UK; has performed with Singapore Symphony Orchestra, Virtuosi di Kuhmo (Finland), Britten Sinfonia; world premiere performances include Einojuhani Rautavaara's Hymnus 1999, Jonathan Dove's Moonlight Revels 2002, Robin Holloway's Canzona and Toccata 2003, all at the Hampstead and Highgate Festival, London; also Huw Watkins' Three Orations, Cheltenham Festival 2003, Hugh Wood's Cantilena and Fugue, City of London Festival 2004, Sally Beamish's Juno, Chelsea Festival 2005; has also played commissioned pieces by Rhian Samuel, Diana Burrell, Bent Lorentzen, John Hawkins; selected trumpet pieces for syllabus, TCL 2004; Co-Dir Counterpoise Ensemble 2008–; Artistic Dir Hampstead Garden Suburb Chamber Concert Series 2013–. *Publications include:* Top Brass, Onstage Brass, Trumpet All Sorts, Carmen Suite, Fingerprints.

CALLEJA, Joseph; Maltese singer (tenor); b. 22 Jan. 1978. *Career:* studies with Paul Asciak; made professional debut as Macduff in Macbeth, Malta 1997; opera roles include Rodolfo in La Bohème (Toronto, Bregenz Festival, Frankfurt Opera, Dresden Semperoper, Royal Opera House, Covent Garden), The Duke of Mantua in Rigoletto (Royal Opera House debut 2002, Welsh Nat. Opera, Deutsche Oper Berlin, Rotterdam, Zürich Opera, Vienna State Opera, Copenhagen, Metropolitan Opera), Almaviva in Il Barbiere di Siviglia (Washington Opera, Liège), Rinuccio in Gianni Schicchi (Spoleto Festival), Edgardo in Lucia di Lammermoor (Minn. Opera), Leicester in Maria Stuarda (Stockholm, Parma), Alfredo in La Traviata (Opera Nat. du Rhin, Royal Opera House, Vienna Staatsoper), Fenton in Falstaff (Torino), Edoardo di Sanval in Un Giorno di Regno (Bologna), Ernesto in Don Pasquale (Brussels), Don Ottavio in Don Giovanni (Regensburg Festival, Teatre Principal Majorca), Lind in Azio Corghi's Isabella (world premiere, Rossini Opera Festival, Pesaro), Roméo in Roméo et Juliette (Frankfurt), Elvino in La Sonnambula (Vienna State Opera, Zürich Opera), Arturo in I Puritani (Vienna State Opera, Deutsche Oper Berlin), Nemorino in L'Elisir d'Amore (Liceu Barcelona, Vienna Staatsoper), Roberto Devereaux (Vienna Staatsoper),

Nicias in Thaïs (Royal Opera House), Edgardo in Lucia di Lammermoor (Opéra Nat. du Rhin, Strasbourg), Macduff in Macbeth (Royal Opera House), Elvino in La Sonnambula, Arturo in I Puritani, title roles in Tales of Hoffmann and Faust (Metropolitan Opera), Adorno in Simon Boccanegra (Royal Opera House); concert appearances include Hampton Court Festival, Faenol Festival, Sejong Cultural Centre in Seoul, Repub. of Korea, Salzburg Festival, BBC Proms at Royal Albert Hall 2012, Royal Festival Hall, London 2013 and concert tour of leading European halls 2013. *Recordings:* Tenor Arias (Gramophone Magazine Ed.'s Choice) 2004, The Golden Voice 2006, The Maltese Tenor 2011, Be My Love: A Tribute to Mario Lanza 2012. *Honours:* prizewinner Belvedere Hans Gabor competition 1997, winner Caruso Competition, Milan 1998, prizewinner Plácido Domingo's Operalia 1999, Gramophone Award for Artist of the Year 2012. *Current Management:* c/o Judith Neuhoff, Universal Music Classical Management and Productions, Universal Music Group, Bond House, 347–353 Chiswick High Road, London, W4 4HS, England. *Telephone:* (20) 8742-5402. *Fax:* (20) 8742-5445. *Website:* www .josephcalleja.com.

CALLIGARIS, Sergio; Argentine/Italian composer, pianist and academic; b. 1941, Rosario, Argentina. *Education:* Cleveland Inst. of Music, USA. *Career:* concerts in Europe, the Americas, Asia and South Africa 1954–; Chair of Piano, Cleveland Inst. of Music, OH, USA and California State Univ., Los Angeles 1969; teacher at conservatories in Italy from 1974; Arts Dir American Acad. of the Arts in Europe; jury mem. nat. and int. piano competitions in Italy and abroad; musical profile as composer and pianist, Società Aquilana dei Concerti, 40th Anniversary Concert Cycle 1986; works performed on television internationally. *Compositions include:* 24 Studi 1978, 1979, 1980, Il Quaderno Pianistico di Renzo, for piano 1978, Tre Madrigali 1979; published works: Scherzo 1957, Sonata Op. 9, for cello and piano 1978, Passacaglia 1983, Due Danze Concertanti 1986, Suite op. 21 for three pianos 1985, Suite Op. 28 for solo cello 1992, Suite da Requiem Op. 17a, for violin, horn and piano 1983, Scene Coreografiche Op. 30 for 2 pianos (or piano four hands) and string orchestra 1994, Sonata Fantasia Op. 31 for trumpet and piano 1994, and Op. 32 for solo piano 1994, Preludio, Corale e Finale Op. 33 for accordion 1994, Clarinet Quartet No. 1 Op. 34 1995, String Quartet No. 2 Op. 35 1995, Toccata, Adagio and Fugue Op. 36, for string orchestra 1995, Double Concerto Op. 37, for piano, violin and string orchestra 1996, Sonata Op. 38, for clarinet and piano, Sonata Op. 39, for viola and piano, Sonata Op. 40, for violin and piano 1997, Double Concerto Op. 41, for two pianos and orchestra, 2000, Ave Verum Op. 42, for choir and piano, 2000, Ave Verum Op. 42a, for solo piano, 2000, Suite Op. 43, for two pianos and four drums, 2002, Preludio e Toccata Op. 44, for solo piano, 2002, Il Giorno, Suite for youth Op. 45, for chorus, piano, or organ, violin or flute and percussion; recorded works: Ave Maria 1978, Symphonic Dances Op. 26, for large orchestra 1990, Seconda Suite di Danze Sinfoniche Op. 27 for large orchestra 1990, Concerto for piano and orchestra Op. 29 1992, Panis Angelicus Op. 47 for piano, choir and vocal quartet 2005, Sonata Op. 40a for flute and piano 2005, Panis Angelicus Op. 47a for solo piano, Sergio Calligaris 2006, Sonata Fantasia Op. 31a for sax-contralto and piano 2006, Double Concerto Op. 37a for flute, piano and strings orchestra 2006, Double Concerto Op. 37b for cello, piano and strings orchestra 2007, Panis Angelicus Op. 48 for chorus, orchestra and piano, Panis Angelicus, Op. 48a for orchestra and piano, Poema, Op. 49 for voice and piano, Piano Parnassum for piano, Vols 1–6, Sonata, Op. 50 for flute and piano, Sonata, Op. 51 for violin and piano, Concerto Op. 52, for two pianists 2011, Danza Fantastica "Remembrance", Op. 53, for two pianos (or piano four hands) 2011, Imágenes, Op. 54, three movements for string orchestra, Allegro Brutale con Pavana, Op. 55 for piano 4 hands or two pianos, Trio "Meditation", Op. 56 for violin, cello and piano 2015. *Recordings include:* Concerts for Union Européenne Radiodiffusion 1977, 1985, 1987, 1994, 1999, 2001, 2003, 2007, 2008, Sergio Calligaris, recital; album dedicated to him of works by Chopin, Rachmaninov, Vitalini and Calligaris 1993, Piano Concerto Op. 29, Second Suite of Symphonic Dances Op. 27 and Sonata Fantasia for piano Op. 32 1996, Clarinet Quartet No. 1 Op. 34 1999, Double Concerto Op. 37 for violin 1999, Piano and String Orchestra for the Union Européenne Radio Diffusion 1999, Shorts for Spot and Film, contemporary classical music by Sergio Calligaris. *Publications:* contrib. to CD Classica 1995, 1999, Piano Time 1996, 2002, Musica 1996, 2001, Amadeus 1997, Il Giornale della Musica 1997, Suonare News 1999, Geschichte der Klaviermusik 2000, Inarcassa 2003, Terza Pagina 2004, Dizionario di Musica Classica 2005, Suonare News 2009, Il Giornale della Musica 2009, Fanfare 2010, Suonare News 2013, Musica 2013. *Honours:* Giuseppe Verdi Int. Music Prize 2007. *Address:* Via Giovanni Pacini 25, 00198 Rome, Italy (home). *Telephone:* (06) 8547249 (home). *Website:* www .sergiocalligaris.com.

CALM, Birgit; German singer (mezzo-soprano); b. 1959, Lubeck. *Education:* studied in Lubeck and Hamburg. *Career:* sang first at the Kiel Opera, then Osnabruc, 1984–85; appearances at the Bayerische Staatsoper from 1984 include Humperdinck's Hansel, Alkmene in Die Liebe der Danaë and Carlotta in Die schweigsame Frau; guest appearances in concert and opera in Germany and abroad; sang Rossweise and Flosshilde in The Ring at the Salle Pleyel, Paris 1992. *Recordings:* sacred music by Dittersdorf, Third Maid in Elektra (conducted by Sawallisch).

CAMANI, Adrianna; Italian singer (mezzo-soprano); b. 27 March 1936, Padua. *Education:* Padua Conservatory with Sara Sforni Corti. *Career:* debut in Naples 1968, as the Nurse in L'Incoronazione di Poppea; has sung widely in Italy, notably in Genoa, Turin, Trieste, Venice and Naples; sang in the Scala

premiere of Dallapiccola's Ulisse; roles include La Cieca in La Gioconda, Ulrica in Un Ballo in Maschera, Eboli in Don Carlos and parts in Madama Butterfly, Andrea Chénier, Francesca da Rimini and Il Quattro Rusteghi.

CAMBRELING, Sylvain; French conductor; *Principal Conductor, Yomiuri Nippon Symphony Orchestra;* b. 2 July 1948, Amiens. *Career:* conducting debut with Orchestre de Lyon 1975; Prin. Guest Conductor, Ensemble Intercontemporain, Paris 1976; subsequent appearances in Paris with Orchestre de Paris, Nat. Orchestra of France and Ensemble Intercontemporain; has worked regularly at Paris Opéra since conducting Chéreau's production of Les Contes d'Hoffmann; Glyndebourne Opera debut (The Barber of Seville) 1981; Musical Dir Nat. Opera, Théâtre Royal de la Monnaie, Brussels 1981–91; Music Dir Frankfurt Opera 1990s; Chief Conductor SWR Sinfonieorchester Baden-Baden und Freiburg 1999–2012; Prin. Conductor, Yomiuri Nippon Symphony Orchestra 2010–; Gen. Music Dir Staatsoper Stuttgart 2012–; debut at La Scala (Lucio Silla) 1984, Metropolitan Opera, New York (Roméo et Juliette) 1986; has also appeared at Salzburg, Aix-en-Provence and Bregenz festivals; has worked in UK with Hallé and Royal Liverpool Philharmonic orchestras, in Germany with Berlin Philharmonic, Berlin Radio Symphony and other orchestras and in USA. *Honours:* Echo Klassik Conductor of the Year Award 2009, Deutsche Schallplatten Jahrespreise for best orchestral CD (for his recording of Messiaen with the SWR Freiburg and Baden-Baden Symphony Orchestra) 2009, MIDEM Contemporary Music Award (for his recording of Messiaen with the SWR Freiburg and Baden-Baden Symphony Orchestra) 2010. *Current Management:* c/o Peter Railton, Hazard Chase Ltd, 48–49 Russell Square, London, WC1B 4JP, England. *E-mail:* info@hazardchase.co.uk. *Website:* www.sylvaincambreling .com.

CAMERON, Fiona Mary, FRAM; British pianist; b. 4 March 1931, London, England; d. of Douglas Cameron OBE and Lilly Phillips; m. Derek Simpson 1954 (divorced); two s. one d. *Education:* Royal Acad. of Music, London with Harold Craxton, studied in Paris with Yvonne Lefébure. *Career:* debut on piano with Derek Simpson, cello, Recital Room, RFH 1953; broadcasts with Derek Simpson, cello 1955–62, and Carl Pini, violin 1962–64; concerts at music clubs and Wigmore Hall until 1971, including Purcell Room with Diana Cummings, violin 1968; piano teacher, Royal Acad. of Music 1974–86; Royal Ballet School 1963–86; Head of Piano, St Paul's Girls' School, London 1987–92; mem. Incorporated Soc. of Musicians, Royal Soc. of Musicians. *Recordings:* Mendelssohn Sonata in D major for cello and piano (with Derek Simpson), Variations Concertantes; Brahms Sonata in F Major, Sonata in E Minor; Beethoven Sonata in C Major, Sonata in F Major, Sonata in G Minor; Shostakovich Sonata. *Address:* Cremona, 19 Willowhayne Avenue, East Preston, Littlehampton, West Sussex, BN16 1PE, England (home). *Telephone:* (1903) 784629 (home). *Fax:* (1903) 784629 (home). *E-mail:* fionasimpson893@ btinternet.com (home).

CAMILLETTI, Simonetta; Italian classical guitarist; b. 10 Feb. 1962, Civitavecchia, Rome. *Education:* Univ. La Sapienza, Rome, Conservatory A. Casella, L'Aquila, Music Acad., Chigiana, Siena. *Career:* performed for Radiotelevisione Italiana 1987–89, for Swiss TV 1999; Prof. of Guitar, Conservatorio Statale di Musica 2003, Conservatorio F. Torrefranca di Vibo Valentia 2003–07, Conservatorio Statale di Musica S. Cecilia, Rome 2007–. *Compositions include:* songs for voice and guitar: Eagles Fly, This Evening, Beethoven's Street, Look at the Sky, Bagatella, Aria; composed melodies to accompany poems. *Recordings:* Guitar Has a Soul. *Publications include:* Oltre l'Azzurro (fiction), Attimi… (poems); articles in Heitor Villa Lobos and The Guitar; contrib. to biographical dictionary of Italians, including Il Maestro di Chitarra 2012, Guitaromanie (live DVD) 2013. *Honours:* winner, Castel Sant'Angelo's Friends, Rome 1987, Laurea in lettere – Storia della Musica – Diploma Chitarra, Prize, Bereshit Int. 1999. *Address:* Viale Eroi di Rodi 228, 00128 Rome, Italy (home). *Telephone:* 331-4877704 (mobile); (06) 5074425 (office). *E-mail:* simonetta.camilletti@alice.it (office).

CAMM, Rebekah; American singer (soprano). *Education:* Univ. of Michigan, DePaul Univ. *Career:* fmrly with Houston Grand Opera Studio; operatic debut as Micaëla in Carmen with Houston Grand Opera 2005; performed with Cincinnati May Festival, LA Opera, Fort Worth Symphony, San Francisco Opera, Wolf Trap Opera Co. and Nat. Symphony Orchestra; performances include Suor Genovieffa in Suor Angelica and Nella in Gianni Schicchi in her San Francisco Opera debut 2009, Susanna in Le nozze di Figaro for LA Opera, Mozart's Great Mass in C minor and Bach's St Matthew Passion at Cincinnati May Festival, and the title role in Suor Angelica with Lorin Maazel at the Castleton Festival 2010. *Honours:* Judith Raskin Memorial Award 2005, First Prize, Lotte Lenya Competition, Kurt Weill Foundation 2010. *Current Management:* c/o Donna Wolverton, Wolverton Artists Management, 9704 Beach Mill Road, Great Falls, VA 22066, USA. *Telephone:* (703) 757-9477; (703) 477-9477 (mobile). *Fax:* (703) 757-7869. *E-mail:* dwolverton@ wolvertonartists.com. *Website:* www.wolvertonartists.com. *E-mail:* info@ rebekahcamm.com (office). *Website:* www.rebekahcamm.com.

CAMPANELLA, Bruno; Italian conductor; b. 6 Jan. 1943, Bari. *Education:* studied with Piero Bellugi, Hans Swarowsky, Thomas Schippers, Dallapiccola. *Career:* debut at Spoleto Festival, 1967; from 1971, conducted 19th Century Italian opera at La Scala Milan, elsewhere in Italy and in Europe and North America; conducted Rossini's Le Comte Ory at Montréal 1989; Don Pasquale at Covent Garden; Piccinni's La Cecchina at the 1990 Martina Franca Festival; conducted L'Italiana in Algeri at the Teatro Regio Turin,

1992; 1992 at La Scala, Le Comte Ory and Fra Diavolo; Direttore stabile, Teatro Regio, Turin, 1992–; conducted La Fille du Régiment in San Francisco and La Cenerentola in Florence 1993; returned to Covent Garden for Cenerentola in 1994 and Houston in 1995; season 1996–97 at Vienna State Opera with Linda di Chamounix by Donizetti, Don Pasquale and L'Italiana in Algeri; Rota's Italian Straw Hat at La Scala and La Cenerentola, L'Italiana in Algeri and I Capuleti e i Montecchi at the Paris Opéra, 1998; I Capuleti at Covent Garden, 2001. *Recordings:* Il Barbiere di Siviglia; La Fille du Régiment; bel canto arias with Kathleen Battle. *Current Management:* Patricia Greenan and Penelope Marland Associates, 10 Roseneath Road, London, SW11 6AH, England. *Telephone:* (20) 7223-7319. *Fax:* (20) 7771-0675. *E-mail:* penelope@marlandartists.fsnet.co.uk.

CAMPBELL, David, GRSM, ARCM, LRAM; British clarinettist and teacher; b. 15 April 1953, Hemel Hempstead; m. 1981; one s. *Education:* Barton Peveril, Hampshire, Royal College of Music. *Career:* debut at Wigmore Hall, April 1975; solo clarinettist, recitalist and chamber music; has played in 40 countries; concertos with Royal Philharmonic Orchestra, English Chamber Orchestra, City of London Sinfonia, London Mozart Players, BBC Concert and BBC Scottish; BBC National Orchestra of Wales, BBC Philharmonic, Bournemouth Sinfonietta, Quebec Symphony and San Sebastian Symphony; fmr Professor and Head of Woodwind, London College of Music; Head of Woodwind, Westminster School 2002–; Visiting Prof., Canterbury Christ Church Univ. 2006–; Artistic Dir, Musicfest, Aberystwyth; consultant to Buffet-Crampon 2005, Vandoren Reeds 2008; mem. London Metropolitan Orchestra; mem, Incorporated Society of Musicians; Clarinet and Saxophone Society (Chair.). *Recordings:* Mozart Clarinet Concerto with City of London Sinfonia under Hickox, Tributes: Melodies for clarinet and piano, Reflections: Concertos by Finzi, Fitkin and Davis, Brahms and Mozart Quintets, Bliss Quintet, Philip Cannon Quintet, works by Charles Camilleri. *Honours:* Knight of the Order of St John (Malta) 1996; Mozart Memorial Prize 1976, Martin Musical Scholarship 1976. *Address:* 83 Woodwarde Road, Dulwich, London SE22 8UL, England (home). *E-mail:* campbell.music@tiscali .co.uk (home).

CAMPBELL, Ian David, BA; Australian opera director and stage director; b. 21 Dec. 1945, Brisbane, Qld; m. Ann Spira 1985; two s. *Education:* voice studies with Godfrey Stirling, Sydney 1964–72; Univ. of Sydney. *Career:* debut, Australian Opera, Sydney 1967; principal tenor, Australian Opera 1967–74; Sr Music Officer, Australia Council 1974–76; Gen. Man., State Opera of South Australia 1976–82; Asst Artistic Admin., Metropolitan Opera, New York 1982–83; Gen. Dir, San Diego Opera 1983–2014, Artistic Dir 2006–14; Stage Dir, La Bohème 1981, Les Contes d'Hoffmann 1982, State Opera of South Australia; Cavalleria Rusticana/Pagliacci, Santa Barbara Grand Opera 1999; Falstaff 1999, Il Trovatore 2000, Tosca 2002, Katya Kabanova 2004, La Traviata 2004, La Bohème 2005, Don Quichotte 2009 at San Diego Opera; Fellow, Australian Inst. of Management; mem. Kona Kai Club, San Diego, Opera America (bd mem. 1985–93, 1997–2001, Chair. 2001–), San Diego Convention and Visitors Bureau (bd mem. 1997–2001); master-classes, Music Acad. of the West, Santa Barbara 1991–96. *Radio includes:* Producer and Host, At The Opera 1985–97, San Diego Opera Radio Program 1985–97, both on Radio KFSD-FM, San Diego; San Diego Opera radio programme on X-BACH-AM 1997–2001; At the Opera on KPBS-FM 2002–. *Recordings:* War and Peace (television, opening of Sydney Opera House) 1973. *Honours:* Peri Award for services to California opera 1983, San Diego Press Club Headliner of Year 1991, Father of the Year, San Diego 1997, First Place for a Radio Series, Best of Show (Radio) for At the Opera with Ian Campbell 2003, James Wolfensohn Award, Univ. of Sydney 2004.

CAMPBELL, James Kenneth, OC; Canadian clarinettist and academic; *Professor of Music (Clarinet), Jacobs School of Music, Indiana University;* b. 10 Aug. 1949, Leduc, AB. *Education:* Univ. of Toronto, studied with Yona Ettlinger in Paris, Abe Galper, Mitchel Lurie and Daniel Bonade. *Career:* studio performances with Glenn Gould; numerous appearances as concert soloist, including Copland Concerto under the composer 1978–79; engage-ments with Allegri, Amadeus until 1987 and Guarneri quartets, notably in quintets by Mozart and Brahms; quintets written for him by André Prevost and Ezra Laderman; recitals with pianist John York, Univ. of Toronto 1978–87; Artistic Dir Festival of the Sound 1985–; Prof., Indiana Univ. 1988–. *Recordings include:* duos with Glenn Gould and John York. *Honours:* winner, CBC Talent Festival, Jeunesses Musicales, Belgrade 1971, Juno Award (for Stolen Gems), Roy Thomson Hall Award, Canada's Artist of the Year, Queen's Golden Jubilee Medal and Canada's highest honor, the Order of Canada. *Current Management:* GAMI/Simonds, LLC, 42 County Road, Morris, CT 06763, USA. *Address:* Indiana University, Jacobs School of Music, 1201 East Third Street, Bloomington, IN 47405, USA (office). *Telephone:* (812) 855-2618 (office). *E-mail:* campbelj@indiana.edu (office). *Website:* music.indiana.edu (office).

CAMPBELL-WHITE, Martin Andrew, MBE, FRSA; British business execu-tive; *Consultant, Askonas Holt Limited;* b. 11 July 1943, s. of the late John Vernon Campbell-White and Hilda Doris Ash; m. Margaret Mary Miles 1969; three s. *Education:* Dean Close School, Cheltenham, St John's Coll., Oxford, Univ. of Strasbourg, France. *Career:* with Thomas Skinner & Co. Ltd (Publrs) 1964–66, Ibbs & Tillett Ltd (Concert Agents) 1966–72, Dir 1969–72, Harold Holt Ltd (Concert Agents), subsequently Askonas Holt Ltd 1972–, Dir 1973–2014, Deputy Chair. 1989–92, Chief Exec. 1992–98, Jt Chief Exec. 1998–2014, Consultant 2014–; Chair. British Asscn of Concert Agents

1978–81; Council mem. London Sinfonietta 1973–86; Dir Chamber Orchestras of Europe 1983–93; Asst Dir Festival of German Arts 1987; Founding Dir Japan Festival 1991; mem. Bd Première Ensemble 1991–, Riverside Studios 1998–2000; Trustee, Abbado Trust for Young Musicians 1987–2006, Salzburg Festival Trust 1996–2000; Exec. Trustee, Musicians Benevolent Fund 2006–. *Honours:* Hon. mem. Royal Philharmonic Soc. 2014; Sebetia Ter prize for Culture, Naples, Italy 1999. *Address:* Askonas Holt Ltd, Lincoln House, 300 High Holborn, London, WC1V 7JH, England (office). *Telephone:* (20) 7400-1700 (office). *Fax:* (20) 7400-1799 (office). *E-mail:* martin.campbell-white@ askonasholt.co.uk (office). *Website:* www.askonasholt.co.uk (office).

CAMPION, Joanna; British singer (mezzo-soprano); b. 1968, England. *Education:* choral scholar Trinity College, Cambridge, Royal College of Music, Guildhall School, Britten Pears School and the National Opera Studio. *Career:* debut as Ursula in Beatrice et Benedict, for Cambridge Operatic Society; Other roles include title part in Prokofiev's The Duenna, Mrs Page in The Merry Wives of Windsor, Britten's Hermia for Singapore Lyric Opera, and Carmen (British Youth Opera, 1992); Baba the Turk in The Rake's Progress at Glyndebourne, Cenerentola and Hansel for WNO and Rosina for English Touring Opera; sang the Mother in Menotti's Amahl and the Night Visitors at the Spoleto Festival, later released on film directed by Menotti; Season 1998–99, engaged as Feodor in Boris Godunov for Welsh National Opera, Annina in Der Rosenkavalier for Scottish Opera and Sabina in Respighi's La Fiamma at the Wexford Festival; Concerts include Messiah on tour with Les Arts Florissants 1994, Mozart's C minor Mass at St Martin in the Fields, Bach's Passions at St John's Smith Square, Dream of Gerontius, Elijah and the Verdi Requiem at the Royal Albert Hall; Mahler Lieder, Elgar Sea Pictures and the Brahms Alto Rhapsody; Birthday celebrations for Yehudi Menuhin at Buckingham Palace 1996.

CAMPO, Régis; French composer; b. 6 June 1968, Marseille; m. Kanako Abe 1997. *Education:* Aix-en-Provence, Conservatoire de Marseille with Danielle Sainte-Croix, Georges Boeuf, Conservatoire Nat. Supérieur de Paris with Gérard Grisey, studied composition with Edison Denisov. *Career:* works have been commissioned by numerous int. bodies and performed in many festivals or concert seasons world-wide by ensembles including Nieuw Ensemble, Ensemble Intercontemporain, Orchestre Symphonique de Montréal, Orches-tre Nat. d'Île de France, Ensemble Orchestral de Paris, London Sinfonietta, Ensemble Modern, and by performers including Kent Nagano, Felicity Lott, Jay Gottlieb, Jean-Claude Casadesus, Zoltán Kocsis, Laurent Korcia, Quatuor Ysaÿe, Ensemble Chanticleer, Quatuor Parisii, Dominique Visse. *Compos-itions include:* Fabel for piano and ensemble 1994, Commedia for 19 musicians 1995, Anima for 6 musicians 1996, Violin Concerto 1997, Phantasmagoria for orchestra 1997, Les Jeux de Rabelais 1998, Le Livre de Sonates for organ 1997–99, Piano Concerto 1998–99, Nova for 12 voices, choir and large ensemble 1998–99, Livre de fantaisies for cello 1999, Faërie, for orchestra 2000–01, First Book for Piano 2000–02, Lumen for orchestra 2001, Les Heures Maléfiques for string quartet 2005, Lumen II for orchestra 2006–13, String Quartet No. 3 Ombra Felice 2007, Le Bestiaire for soprano and orchestra 2008, Les Quatre Jumelles (opera) 2008, Color! for orchestra 2011, String Quartet No. 5 'Fata Morgana' 2012, Quai Ouest (opera) 2013-2014. *Recordings include:* numerous recordings and monographs. *Honours:* Gaudeamus Prize 1996, First Prize, Special Young Composer Prize and Prix du Public of 3rd Dutilleux Competition 1996, Dugardin Prize, SACEM 1999, Pierre Cardin Prize, Inst. de France 1999, Residency, Villa Medici, Rome 1999–2001, Georges Bizet Prize, Inst. de France 2005, SACEM award 2005, Prix de la fondation Francis et Mica Salabert 2011, Prix de la fondation Simone et Cino del Luca 2014. *Address:* c/o Les éditions Henry Lemoine, 27 boulevard Beaumarchais, 75004 Paris, France (office).

CAMPOS, Anisia; Canadian (b. Brazilian) pianist and educator; b. 1940, Rio de Janeiro; m. Remus Tzincoca. *Education:* Ecole Normale de Musique de Paris, Mozarteum Acad. of Music, Salzburg, Austria, studied with Alfred Cortot, Reine Gianoli and Claudio Arrau. *Career:* recitals in Brazil, Portugal, Romania, France, Germany, England, Canada and Austria; soloist with many orchestras, including Brazilian Symphony Orchestra in Rio de Janeiro, Brazil, Bucharest George Enescu Philharmonic, Radio Television Orchestra in Bucharest, Cluj Philharmonic and Timisoara Philharmonic; gave first performance of Enescu's Sonata No. 1 in numerous cities; collaborated with Remus Tzincoca in discovery and reconstruction of original version, in Romanian language, of Bartók's Cantata Profana 1980s; taught 'École Vincent-d'Indy 1966–71; apptd mem. Faculty, Conservatoire de musique du Québec 1967, apptd Head of Keyboard Dept 1991; taught at Univ. of Ottawa 1972–76, Jeunesses Musicales Canada-Orford Arts Centre 1973–75; Co-founder and Pres. Canadian Enescu Foundation; jury mem. Ecole Normale de Musique de Paris, France. *Publication:* Les Religions sources de l'asservissement des femmes.

CANARINA, John Baptiste, BS, MS; American conductor; b. 19 May 1934, New York. *Education:* Juilliard School, studied with Pierre Monteux, Jean Morel, Arthur Lloyd and Frederick Zimmermann. *Career:* Conductor, 7th US Army Symphony Orchestra 1959–60; Asst Conductor, New York Philhar-monic 1961–62; Music Dir, Jacksonville Symphony Orchestra, FL 1962–69; Dir of Orchestral Activities, Drake Univ. 1973–; Guest Conductor, Royal Philharmonic, Philharmonia Orchestra, Bournemouth Symphony, BBC Nat. Orchestra of Wales and BBC Scottish Symphony, Belgian Radio Orchestra, Slovak Radio Symphony Bratislava. *Publications:* contrib. to Tempo, High Fidelity, Opus and Keynote.

CANAT DE CHIZY, Edith; French composer; b. 26 March 1950, Lyon; d. of Pierre Puvis de Chavannes; m. François Porcile. *Education:* Paris Conservatoire Supérieur de Musique with Maurice Ohana and Ivo Malec. *Career:* Dir, Conservatoires du 15e et 7e arrondissements, Paris 1986–2007, Prof. of Composition, Conservatoire de Région de Paris 2007–; elected mem. Acad. des Beaux-Arts, Paris 2005. *Compositions include:* Yell for orchestra 1985, De noche for orchestra 1991, Hallel for string trio 1991, Siloël for strings 1992, Canciones for 12 solo voices 1992, Tombeau de Gilles de Rais (oratorio) 1993, Exultet (concerto for violin) 1995, Moïra (concerto for cello and orchestra) 1998, Danse de l'Aube 1998, Irisations for solo violin 1999, Vivere 2000, Moving 2001, Quatrains for 12 voices 2004, Dios for choir 2005, Les Rayons du Jour (concerto) 2005, Omen for large orchestra 2006, Pierre d'Eclair 2011, Over the Sea, with electronic disp. 2012, Drift (concerto for clarinet) 2013. *Recordings:* Yell Hallel Canciones de Noche 1994, Tombeau de Gilles de Rais 1995, Exultet Siloël Moïra 1999, Les Rayons du jour 2007, Canciones to Gather Paradise Dios 2008, Livre d'Heures 2008, Times, l'oeuvre pour orchestre 2010. *Honours:* Chevalier des Arts et des Lettres 1994; Officier, Ordre nat. du Mérite 2003; Chevalier, Légion d'honneur 2008; UNESCO Prix de la Tribune Internationale des Compositeurs 1990, SACEM Symphonic Prize 2004. *Current Management:* c/o Editions Henry Lemoine, 27 boulevard Beaumarchais, 75004 Paris, France. *Telephone:* 1-56-68-86-65. *Address:* c/o Académie des Beaux-Arts, Institut de France, 23 Quai Conti, 75270 Paris Cedex 6; 7 place de la Montagne du Goulet, 75015 Paris, France (home). *Telephone:* 1-45-57-50-28 (home). *E-mail:* e.canatdechizy@wanadoo.fr (office). *Website:* www.edithcanatdechizy.com.

CANEV, Borjan; Macedonian conductor; *Principal Conductor, Makedonska Filharmonija*; b. 1973, Skopje. *Education:* Faculty of Music, Skopje, State Acad. of Music, Sofia, Bulgaria, Royal Coll. of Music, London; studied with Fimcho Muratovski, Vasil Kazandijev, Neil Thomson, Sir Simon Rattle, Danielle Gatti and Janos Fürst. *Career:* Assoc. Conductor to Sir Colin Davis; Prin. Conductor, Makedonska Filharmonija (Macedonian Philharmonic Orchestra) 1999–; Asst Prof., Faculty of Music, Skopje 2002–07, Prof. 2007–; Prin. Conductor, Skopje Soloists Chamber Orchestra 2003–06; Prin. Guest Conductor, Sofia Philharmonic Orchestra 2004, 2006–; made debut with Macedonian Nat. Opera 2005. *Honours:* August Mann Prize for Best Young Conductor, Royal Coll. of Music 2001, Composers Asscn of Macedonia Georgi Bozhikov Prize for Best Performance 2010. *Address:* Macedonian Philharmonic Orchestra, Bul. Makedonija b.b., p.f. 507, 1000 Skopje, Macedonia (office). *Telephone:* (2) 311-8450 (office). *Fax:* (2) 316-5753 (office). *E-mail:* makfil@t-home.mk (office); contact@filharmonija.org.mk (office). *Website:* www.filharmonija.org.mk (office).

CANIHAC, Jean-Pierre; French cornet player; b. 16 April 1947, Toulouse; m. Michele Chauzy 1968, one s. one d. *Education:* Conservatoire de Toulouse, Conservatoire de Versailles, Conservatoire National Superieur de Musique, Paris. *Career:* founder, Saqueboutiers de Toulouse; Prof., CNR, Toulouse; Prof., Conservatoire National Superieur de Musique, Lyon; mem. Hesperion XX, La Grande Ecurie et la Chambre du Roi, La Chapelle Royale, Clemencic Consort. *Recordings:* L'Art de Cornet, Schütz, Symphoniae Sacrae, Seven Last Words of Christ, Siècle d'or à Venise, Six Marian Vespers of Monteverdi. *Honours:* first prize Conservatoire de Toulouse 1966, first prize Conservatoire de Versailles 1968, first prize Conservatoire National Superieur, Paris 1970.

CANIN, Stuart V.; American violinist and educator; b. 5 April 1926, New York, NY; m. Virginia Yarkin 1952, two s. *Education:* Juilliard School of Music. *Career:* Fulbright Professor to Freiburg, Germany Staatliche Hochschule für Musik, 1956–57; Prof. of Violin, State University of Iowa, 1953–60, Oberlin Conservatory of Music, 1960–66; Concertmaster, Chamber Symphony of Philadelphia, 1966–68; Concertmaster, San Francisco Symphony, 1970–80; Concertmaster, San Francisco Opera, 1969–72; Artist Faculty, Aspen Colorado Music Festival, 1960–63; Artist Faculty, Music Academy of the West, Santa Barbara, 1983–; Senior Visiting Lecturer, University of California, Santa Barbara, 1983–; Concertmaster, Casals Festival, San Juan, Puerto Rico, 1974–75; Mostly Mozart Festival, New York City, 1980. *Honours:* first prize Paganini International Violin competition, Genoa, 1959.

CANINO, Bruno; Italian pianist and composer; b. 30 Dec. 1935, Naples. *Education:* Milan Conservatory with Calace and Bettinelli. *Career:* piano duo with Antonio Ballista 1953–; career as soloist 1956–, notably in works by Bussotti, Donatoni and Castiglioni; Prof. of Music, Milan Conservatory 1961–85, then in Scuola di Musica di Fiesole, Musikhochschule, Bern, Istituto de Música da Camara, Madrid; played in premieres of Ode by Castiglioni 1966, Tableaux Vivants by Bussotti 1964, Concerto for two pianos and orchestra by Berio 1973; mem., Trio di Milano; accompanist to instrumentalists and singers (Cathy Berberian, Salvatore Accardo, Uto Ughi, Itzhak Perlman, Lynn Harrel, Pierre Amoyal); appearances with András Schiff include Schubert and Janáček Festival, London 1995; juror in int. competitions (Bolzano, Santander, Zürich, Vienna , Moscow, Sendai). *Compositions include:* chamber and instrumental music. *Publications:* Il pianista di musica da camera. *Honours:* Prizes at Piano Competitions of Bolzano and Darmstadt 1956–60. *Current Management:* Via Lodovico Valtorta 1, 20136 Milan; RESIA, via Gioberti 1, 20123 Milan, Italy (office). *Telephone:* (20) 7589-6243 (office). *Fax:* (20) 7581-5269 (office). *E-mail:* info@alliedartists.co.uk (office); resia@resiartists.it (office). *Website:* www.alliedartists.co.uk.

CANN, Antoinette, DipRCM; British pianist; b. 27 Sept. 1963, England; twin sister of Claire Cann; m. Julian Leigh; two d. *Education:* studied piano with Jean Merlow and Robert Pell, duo-piano with Phyllis Sellick at the Royal Coll. of Music, with Anton Kuerti, Jean Paul Sevilla and Gilbert Kalish at the Banff School of Fine Arts, studied arranging with Gerald Gifford. *Career:* duo piano player with twin sister; first major concert aged 13; many appearances in Europe, Canada, USA, New Zealand, Japan and the Middle East; extensive tours of the UK, including concerts at the Royal Festival Hall, Royal Albert Hall, Barbican Hall, Fairfield Halls, London, St David's Hall Cardiff, Glasgow Royal Concert Hall; concertos with the London Philharmonic, Royal Philharmonic, Royal Liverpool Philharmonic, BBC Concert, London Mozart Players, Concert Orchestra of Europa, English Sinfonia, Wren Orchestra, Glasgow Philharmonic; television engagements in the UK, Japan, USA, New Zealand; world premieres of Terry Winter Owens' Homage to Corelli and Pianophoria No. 3; Carey Blyton's Cinque Ports; Michael Elliott's Geminae and Berceuse pour Deux; Timothy Blinko's two-piano concerto with English Sinfonia and Philip Ellis 2003; South Bank premiere of the Max Bruch concerto for two pianos and orchestra, Royal Festival Hall; Chaminade Cycle, Fairfield Halls, London 2007; tour of USA 2009. *Recordings:* albums: Gemini; La Danse; Rhapsody; Reflections; Fantasy; Complete Piano Duet Works of Carey Blyton. *Honours:* Gramophone Critic's Choice, Penguin Rosette Award, Classic FM Critic's Choice, Sound Sense Award, PLG Series, Countess of Munster Trust Awards, RCM President's Rose Bowl. *Current Management:* Appassionata, 5 Engleric, Chrishall, Royston, Herts, SG8 8QZ, England. *Telephone:* (1763) 838367. *E-mail:* gwenhowellmgmt@yahoo.co.uk. *Telephone:* (1763) 261535 (office). *E-mail:* canntwins@btinternet.com (office). *Website:* www.canntwins .com.

CANN, Claire, DipRCM; British pianist; b. 27 Sept. 1963, England; twin sister of Antoinette Cann. *Education:* studied with Jean Merlow, Robert Pell, Phyllis Sellick and Gerald Gifford at the Royal Coll. of Music (RCM), and with Anton Kuerti, Jean Paul Sevilla and Gilbert Kalish at the Banff School of Fine Arts. *Career:* duo piano player with twin sister; first major concert aged 13; many appearances in Europe, Canada, USA, NZ, Japan and Middle East; extensive tours of UK, including concerts at Royal Festival Hall, Royal Albert Hall, Barbican Hall, Fairfield Halls, London, St David's Hall Cardiff, Glasgow Royal Concert Hall; concertos with London Philharmonic, Royal Philharmonic, Royal Liverpool Philharmonic, BBC Concert, London Mozart Players, English Sinfonia, Wren Orchestra, Glasgow Philharmonic; TV engagements in UK, Japan, USA, NZ; world premieres of Terry Winter Owens' Homage to Corelli and Pianophoria No. 3, Carey Blyton's Cinque Ports, Michael Elliott's Geminae and Berceuse pour Deux, Timothy Blinko's two-piano concerto with English Sinfonia and Philip Ellis 2003; South Bank premiere of Max Bruch concerto for two pianos and orchestra, Royal Festival Hall; Chaminade Cycle, Fairfield Halls, London 2007, tour of USA 2009. *Recordings:* albums: Gemini, La Danse, Rhapsody, Reflections, Fantasy, Complete Piano Duet Works of Carey Blyton. *Honours:* Gramophone Critic's Choice, Penguin Rosette Award, Classic FM Critic's Choice, Sound Sense Award, PLG Series, Countess of Munster Trust Awards, Pres.'s Rose Bowl, RCM. *Current Management:* c/o Appassionata, 5 Engleric, Chrishall, Royston, Herts., SG8 8QZ, England. *Telephone:* (1763) 838367. *E-mail:* gwenhowellmgmt@yahoo.co .uk. *Telephone:* (1763) 261535 (office). *E-mail:* canntwins@btinternet.com (home). *Website:* www.canntwins.com.

CANNAN, Phyllis; British singer (soprano); b. 22 Aug. 1947, Paisley, Scotland. *Career:* sang as soprano with most major companies in the UK; soprano repertoire from 1983; first major role in Vivaldi's Griselda, Buxton Festival 1983; sang Gluck's Alceste at the QEH; Kostelnicka in Jenůfa and Katerina in The Greek Passion for WNO; Santuzza, Tosca, Rusalka and Goneril, in the British premiere of Reimann's Lear for ENO; appearances in Der Rosenkavalier and King Priam at Covent Garden; Senta in Der fliegende Holländer at the 1987 Hong Kong Festival; Gerhilde in Die Walküre at the 1989 Promenade concerts; concert engagements include Britten's War Requiem in Belgium; sang the Overseer in Elektra at the First Night of the 1993 London Proms.

CANNE MEIJER, Cora; Dutch singer (mezzo-soprano) and voice teacher; b. 11 Aug. 1929, Amsterdam. *Education:* Amsterdam Conservatory with Jan Keizer and Re Koster, studied with Noémie Perugia in Paris, Alfred Jerger in Vienna. *Career:* debut with Netherlands Opera, Amsterdam 1951; Glyndebourne 1956, as Cherubino and in Die Zauberflöte and Cenerentola; Salzburg 1959, in Haydn's Il Mondo della Luna; Zürich Opera 1960–62; regular appearances at the Holland Festival; has sang at many opera houses, including Vienna, Frankfurt, Brussels, Munich and Hamburg; performed over 65 roles, including Dorabella, Isolier, Rosina, Isabella, Octavian, Marina in Boris Godunov and Carmen; sang in world premiere of Milhaud's La Mère Coupable, Geneva 1966; was also widely in demand as lied, concert and oratorio singer, repertory including works by Stravinsky and Berlioz, Bach's St Matthew Passion, Verdi's Requiem; appeared on television as Carmen and Rosina; for over 20 years has taught at Amsterdam Sweelinck Conservatorium and given masterclasses at home and abroad; produced and directed open-air production of Mozart's Zauberflöte summer 1989; frequent jury mem. for international vocal competitions. *Recordings:* Les Noces by Stravinsky; Der Tag des Gerichts by Telemann; Comte Ory from Glyndebourne; Spanish Folksongs; French and Spanish Songs; Diary of One who Disappeared by Janáček.

CANNON, Philip, FRCM; British composer; b. 21 Dec. 1929, Paris, France; m. 1st Jacqueline Laidlaw (died 1984) 1950; one d.; m. 2nd Baroness Jane Buijs van Schouwenburg 1997. *Education:* Dartington Hall, Devon and Royal Coll. of Music. *Career:* Lecturer in Music, Sydney Univ. 1958–60; Prof. of Composition, Royal Coll. of Music 1960–95; mem. RMA, RPS, ISM, NFMS, PRS, MCPS. *Compositions include:* Te Deum (commissioned by and dedicated to HM The Queen) 1975, three operas, two symphonies, including Son of Man (commissioned by the BBC to mark the UK's entry to the EC), choral works, including Lord of Light (large-scale requiem), chamber music, Piano Quintet 1998, Millennium Symphony 1999. *Publications include:* contrib. of biographical and critical articles to various magazines. *Honours:* Grand Prix, Critics Prize, Paris 1965, Bard of Gorsedd Kernow 1997.

CANONICI, Corrado; Italian double bassist, music agent and producer; *Director, World Concert Artists Ltd*; b. 26 March 1961, Ancona; m. Li Li. *Education:* Rossini Conservatory, Pesaro, double bass masterclasses with Franco Petracchi and Gary Karr, composition masterclasses with Hans Werner Henze and Brian Ferneyhough. *Career:* recitals throughout Europe and USA; chamber music with Ensemble Modern, Music Projects/London, others; radio/TV appearances in Italy, Germany, France, Spain, Romania and USA; master-classes, New York Univ., Harvard Univ., Boston Univ., univs in Los Angeles and Manhattan School of Music, New York, Dartington Int. Summer Music Courses (UK); Performer-in-Residence, New York Univ. 1996; double-bass version of solo work by Karlheinz Stockhausen world premiered in London 4 Oct. 1997; Dir World Concert Artists Ltd, Charlemagne Music Publishing, Festival Asia London 2010–. *Recordings include:* Contrabass, including world premiere recording of Luciano Berio's solo bass piece 1995, Sonage 1997, as a duo with fmr Mingus' trumpeter Jack Walrath 2000, A Roaring Flame (first double bass CD of UK new music) 2004. *Publications:* regular contrib. to The Strad. *Honours:* Freedom of the City of London; Xenakis Award, Paris 1992, Darmstadt Award 1992, Int. New Music Consortium Award 1993, 1997, 1999. *Current Management:* c/o World Concert Artists Ltd, Unit 1, 105 Mayes Road, London, N22 6UP, England. *Telephone:* (20) 3086-9993. *E-mail:* info@worldconcertartists.org. *Website:* www.worldconcertartists.org; www.canonicibass.charlemagnemusicpublishing.com.

CANONICI, Luca; Italian singer (tenor); b. 22 June 1960, Montevarchi, Arezzo, Tuscany. *Education:* studied in Rome with Tito Gobbi and at Pesaro. *Career:* debut at Teatro Sociale Mantua, 1988, as the Duke of Mantua; Sang the Duke in Rome, 1986; Appearances in various Italian theatres, including Bologna and Florence, notably in the Italian premiere of Monteverdi's Ulisse in the version by Henze; Appeared as Rodolfo in the 1987 film version of La Bohème; Other roles include Nemorino and Ernesto, Fernando in Donizetti's Il Furioso all' isola di San Domingo; Frederico in L'Arlesiana; Almaviva and Werther; Bergamo 1990, in Mayr's La rosa bianca a la rosa rossa; Season 1991 as Fenton in Falstaff at Bonn; Pilade in Rossini's Ermione at Rome; Leading role in La Cambiale di Matrimonio at the Pesaro Festival; Sang Max in Leoncavallo's La Reginetta della Rosa, Palermo, 1992; Idreno in Semiramide at Zürich and Tonio in La Fille du Régiment at Rome; season 1996 in the premiere of Berio's Outis at La Scala, as Bellini's Tebaldo at Genoa and Wolf-Ferrari's Filepeto at Parma; sang Mascagni's Fritz at Naples, 1998; season 1999–2000 as Conte Potioski in Donizetti's Gli Esilati di Siberia, at Montpellier, and Nemorino at the Vienna Staatsoper. *Current Management:* Atelier Musicale, Via Caselle 76, San Lazzaro di Savena 40068, Italy. *Telephone:* (51) 19984444. *Fax:* (51) 19984420. *E-mail:* info@ateliermusicale.com. *Website:* www.ateliermusicale.com.

CANTELO, April; British singer (soprano) (retd), singing coach and fmr teacher; b. 2 April 1928, Purbrook, Hampshire; m. Colin Davis 1949 (divorced 1963); one s., one d. *Education:* studied in London with Julian Kimbell, Dartington with Imogen Holst. *Career:* debut as Barbarina in Figaro and Echo in Ariadne auf Naxos with the Glyndebourne Co. at Edinburgh 1950; Glyndebourne Festival 1953, 1963, as Blondchen and Marzelline; English Opera Group 1960–70, notably as Helena in the premiere of A Midsummer Night's Dream and as Emmeline in Purcell's King Arthur; at Sadler's Wells Theatre 1962–66, sang in the premieres of Williamson's Our Man in Havana and The Violins of St Jacques; British premieres of Henze's Boulevard Solitude and Weill's Aufstieg und Fall der Stadt Mahagonny; also created roles in Williamson's The Happy Prince 1965, and Julius Cesar Jones 1966; directed Purcell's The Fairy Queen in New Zealand 1972; made frequent broadcasts and concert appearances; mem. Equity, Inc. Soc. of Musicians, Asscn of Teachers of Singing (AOTOS). *Recordings:* The Indian Queen, Albert Herring and The Little Sweep, Béatrice et Bénédict, 18th-Century Shakespeare Songs, Berlioz' Irelande, Haydn Masses with St John's Coll. Choir, Cambridge, Wagner, Die Feen, Das Liebesverbot, Complete Wagner Operas. *Address:* 1 The Coalyard, All Saints Lane, Sutton Courtenay, Oxon., OX14 4AG, England (home).

CANTINI, Lorenza; Italian director; *Resident Director, Teatro alla Scala*; b. Milan; m. *Education:* Accademia d'Arte Drammatica del Piccolo Teatro, Milan. *Career:* staged Boris Godunov, Florence 1993; Producer, I Due Foscari, Seoul, Leyle und Medjumn, Montepulciano 1993, Orfeo... Cantando Tolse, Favola di Orfeo 1994, L'Elisir d'Amore 1995, Gli Zoccoli in Villa 1996, Passione Secondo Giovanni, Milan 1997, La Forza del Destino, Athens, Il Campanello, Bologna 1998, La Serva Padrona, Florence, La Prova di un Opera Seria, Rome 1999, I Lombardi alla prima Crociata, Cremona 2001, La Serva Padrona, Florence 2001, Bluebeard's Castle 2003, La Fanciulla del West, Baltimore 2004, Perseus and Andromeda 2005 Palermo, Il Piccolo Spazzacamino, La Scala 2013; Resident Dir at La Scala with work in Milan and on tour, including I Capuleti e i Montecchi, Covent Garden 2001, Adriana Lecouvreur, Moscow 2002, Don Giovanni, Moscow 2010, Il Barbiere di Siviglia, La Scala 2010, L'italiana in Algeri, La Scala 2011, Aida, Rigoletto, Falstaff Tokyo 2013, Tosca Astana 2014. *Address:* Teatro La Scala, via Filodrammatici 2, 20121 Milan, Italy (office). *Telephone:* (02) 88792236 (office). *E-mail:* cantini@fondazionelascala.it (office). *Website:* www.lorenzacantini.com.

CANTRELL, Derrick Edward, BMus, MA, FRCO; British cathedral organist; b. 2 June 1926, Sheffield; m. Nancy Georgina Bland; four c. *Education:* Oxford Univ. *Career:* Organist, Manchester Cathedral 1962–77; Lecturer, Royal Northern Coll. of Music. *Recordings:* Manchester Cathedral Organ. *Honours:* Sawyer and Limpus Prizes, Royal Coll. of Organists. *Address:* 36 Parsonage Road, Manchester, M20 4PE, England.

CAPDEPÓN VERDÚ, Paulino, PhD; Spanish musicologist and music educator; *Professor of Musicology and Director of the Aula de Musica, University of Castilla-La Mancha*; b. 6 Oct. 1959, Miranda de Ebro. *Education:* Music Conservatory of Logroño, Univ. of Madrid, Univ. of Hamburg, Germany. *Career:* Assoc. Prof., Univ. of Salamanca 1989–96; Prof. of Musicology and Dir Aula de Música, Univ. of Castilla-La Mancha, Madrid 1996–; Prof., Conservatorio Superior de Música, Madrid 1997–98, Escuela Superior de Canto, Madrid 1998–2005, Univ. of La Rioja 1999–2006; Guest Researcher, European History Inst. and Visiting Prof., Univ. of Mainz, Germany 1998; Dir Aula de Música, Univ. San Pablo-CEU, Madrid 2001–; mem. research group, Historic Music of Castilla-León 1992–; Dir of research groups Historic Music of Valencia 1994–, and Patrimonio Musical de Castilla-La Mancha; mem. Real Academia de la Historia, Real Academia de Doctores, Instituto de Estudios Madrileños, Spanish Soc. of Musicology, Univ. Music Professors Asscn, Int. Musicological Soc., Gesellschaft für Musikforschung (Germany). *Publications include:* Villancicos del padre Antonio Soler (vol. I) 1992, (vol. II) 1992, (vol. III) 1992, (vol. IV) 1992, La música en la Capilla Real de Madrid (Siglo XVIII) 1992, Die Villancicos des Padre Antonio Soler 1994, El Padre Antonio Soler (1729-1783) y el cultivo del villancico en El Escorial 1994, La música en la Catedral de Segorbe (Siglo XVIII) 1996, La música en el monasterio de la Encarnación (Siglo XVIII) 1997, La música en el monasterio de las Descalzas Reales de Madrid (Siglo XVIII) 1999, El padre Antonio Soler (1729-1783): Biografía y obra musical 2000, El compositor castellonense José Pradas y la música de su época 2001, La Música en Irún en el siglo XIX 2012, La música en la Colegiata de Santa María la Mayor de Talavera de la Reina durante el siglo XVIII 2012; contrib. of articles and reviews to nat. (Anuario Musical, Revista de Musicología, Nassarre etc.) and int. journals (Musik und Theorie, Mozart-Jahrbuch, L'orgue etc.) and dictionaries, anthologies and encyclopaedias (Diccionario de la Música española e Iberoamericana 1999, The New Grove Dictionary of Music, Musicians 2001, Lexikon Musik und Gender 2010, Diccionario Biográfico Español 2011, Enciclopedia Auñamendi 2011). *Honours:* numerous awards and fellowships for research including Univ. of Castilla-La Mancha Recognition Award for Research Career 2010. *Address:* Ríos Rosas 32, 6º izq., 28003 Madrid, Spain (home). *Telephone:* (91) 4415795 (home); 6-25852745 (mobile) (home). *E-mail:* paulino.capdepon@uclm.es (office); pcapdepon@telefonica.net (home).

CAPOBIANCO, Tito; Argentine stage director, producer, set and lighting designer and educator; b. 28 Aug. 1931, La Plata; m. Elena Denda; two s. *Career:* Producer and Technical Director, 1964, Producing Director, Technical Director and Set Designer, 1958, Teatro Colón, Buenos Aires; Artistic Director of Santiago Opera Festival; Stage Director of National Ballet of Chile; Professor of Acting and Interpretation at University of Chile, 1956; Stage Director and Lighting Designer of SODRE National Ballet and Opera; Stage Director of SODRE, Montevideo, Uruguay 1957; Artistic Director of Teatro Argentino; Producing Director and Stage Director of National Drama Company of Buenos Aires, 1959; Artistic Director, Cincinnati Opera and Summer Festival; Director of Opera Productions throughout the USA, 1961–65; Producer and Director, International Opera Festival, Mexico City, 1963–65; Founder and General Director of American Opera Centre, Juilliard School of Music, NY 1968–71; Created Opera Department of College of Performing Arts, Philadelphia, 1972; Artistic Director, 1975; General Director 1977; Created Verdi Festival 1978; Young American Conductor's Programme 1980; San Diego Opera; Vice-President and General Director, Pittsburgh Opera, 1983–98; Professor, Opera Department, Yale University 1983; currently Stage Dir, Opera and Ballet Theater, Jacobs School of Music, Indiana Univ. *Compositions:* Libretto of Zapata. *Publications:* The Merry Widow, Franz Lehar, Translation. *Honours:* Cavaliere della Republica, Italy, 1979; Officier dans l'Ordre des Arts et Lettres, France, 1984; Doctor of Music, Duquesne University, 1988; Doctor of Letters, Indiana University of Pennsylvania, 1988; Doctor of Humane Letters, La Roche College, 1989. *Address:* Jacobs School of Music, 1201 East 3rd Street, Merrill Hall 003, Bloomington, IN 47405, USA (office). *Telephone:* (812) 855-9846 (office). *Fax:* (812) 855-9847 (office). *Website:* www.music.indiana.edu/publicity/opera (office).

CAPOLONGO, Paul; French conductor; b. 17 March 1940, Algiers, Algeria. *Education:* Algiers and Paris Conservatories. *Career:* Dir, Quito Symphony 1963–67, Quito Conservatory 1963–66; Asst to Leonard Bernstein at the New York Philharmonic 1967–68; Conductor of Rhine Symphony Orchestra at Mulhouse 1975–85. *Honours:* Mitropoulos Competition winner 1967.

CAPPELLETTI, Andrea; Italian violinist; b. 21 May 1961. *Education:* Naples Conservatory, Liceo Linguistico. *Career:* First Violin, European Community Youth Orchestra 1977; debut in Israel 1984; debut at Royal Festival Hall 1986; Queen Elizabeth Hall 1988; regular appearances with leading orchestras in Italy, France, Germany, Scandinavia; regular appearances in Europe, Australia, USA; Art Dir, United Nations Concerts for the Disabled 1990. *Recordings include:* Koch Int. with 5 Mozart violin concertos, Italian Baroque Concerti, Respighi Concerti and Tartini sonatas for violin solo; for UNICEF Haydn Concerti. *Honours:* Vittorio Veneto 1975, Kiefer Balitzel 1977–78, Fordergemeinschaft 1986.

CAPRIOLI, Alberto; Italian composer, conductor and musicologist; *Professor, Bologna Conservatory of Music*; b. 16 Nov. 1956, Bologna. *Education:* Parma Conservatory with F. Margola, C. Togni, Bologna Conservatory with T. Gotti, Salzburg Mozarteum with B. Schaeffer, Vienna Acad. of Music with O. Suitner, Bologna Univ., studied with E. Raimondi, U. Eco, C. Ginzburg. *Career:* guest conductor with several European orchestras and new music festivals; currently Prof., Bologna Conservatory of Music; fmr mem. Faculty, Centro Interdisciplinare Studi Romantici, Univ. of Bologna; mem. Bd of Dirs Italian Soc. for Comparative Literature; mem. Consiglio Accademico. *Compositions:* Frammenti dal diario for piano 1974, Abendlied for soprano and orchestra 1977, Sonata in memoriam Alban Berg for piano 1982, Sonetti di Shakespeare for child reciter and 10 instruments 1983, Trio for piano, violin and cello 1984, Del celeste confine for string quartet 1985, Serenata per Francesca for six players 1985, A la dolce ombra for piano trio 1985, Dialogue for solo contrabass and two string quartets 1986, Per lo dolce silentio de la notte for piano and computer music tape 1987, Due Notturni d'oblio for 10 players 1988, Symphoniae I, II, III for violin 1988–89, Il vostro pianto aurora o luna for five players 1989, Intermedio I for flute and computer music tape 1989, Vor dem singenden Odem for sextet 1990, Kyrie per Dino Campana for soloists, choir and 29 instruments 1991, John Cage Variations for quintet 1991, A quinze ans for cello 1992, Anges for G-flute, viola and harp, Folâtre (Notturno di rosa) for two guitars 1993, L'ascesa degli angeli ribelli for reciter and 13 players 1994, Dittico baciato for choir and orchestra 1994, Elegia per Carlo Michelstaedter for oboe and 13 instruments 1998, Canto for orchestra and reciter 1998, Era for alto-saxophone and brass quintet 1999, Fiori d'ombra for strings 2001, Verweile... (danza notturna) for reciter and five instruments 2001, Gilles for violin and live electronics 2002, Stelle assenti for chamber orchestra 2004, Senza Tempo for piano 2007, Aria Bizantina for seven players 2007, Due liriche di Sylvia Plath for soprano and piano 2009, Drei Klavierstücke für Boguslaw for piano 2009, Pièce libre pour Gilles Deleuze for viola and quintet 2009, Spazi for viola and live electronics 2010, Fuggente for mezzo-soprano and sextet 2011, Andante adagio for violin 2011, Substanceless blue a Luigi Nono (text by the late Sylvia Plath) 2013, K. Szymanowski's Mythes for violin and orchestra 2014. *Recordings:* nine albums. *Publications include:* Salieri's Falstaff, Shakespeare Yearbook 1994, La musica e le 'favole antiche': la fortuna dell'antichità classica nel Romanticismo musicale 1995, Robert Schumann e l'Italia 1996, L'ultrafilosofia dell'eroe in G. Leopardi e F. Hölderlin 1996, L. Nono's A Carlo Scarpa 1997, John Cage Variations 1997, P. Boulez musicien-écrivain e la letteratura francese del Novecento 1998, The Silent Revolution. La réception de la culture de l'Asie de l'Est 1998, Poésie, musique et critique musicale: Le jeune Schumann 1999, G. Leopardi e la 'nuova musica' 1999, I sogni di Calipso: Musica italiana e romanticismo europeo 2000, Leopardi e Bologna: Nuovi documenti 2001, La profezia del sacro in H Berlioz 2002, Poesia e musica nel giovane Schumann 2001, Il letterato e la musica. Note sull'Italia musicale nell'Europa Romantica 2003, Poesia Romantica in Musica 2005, L'Italia musicale di E. T. A. Hoffmann: mitopolesi e visione 2005, La Fin du Voyage: L'Italia 'refugium spirituale' di F. Liszt 2008, Dalla vetta della Jungfrau all'Italia: Byron interpretato da Schumann 2008, La Morte di Isotta e la gioia ideale: Giosue Carducci 'wagneriano fervente' 2009, Un'inedita fonte italiana di Brahms 2011, La Venezia di Alma Mahler 2011, Il paesaggio romantico musicato e dipinto. Ekphrasis, retorica e straniamento di un modello iconografico 2011, L'oubli de la mémoire. M. Proust et L. Berio 2012, L'anima del Lied 2012, 'La tua morte è una cometa,' Anamnesi dell'Elegia per Carlo Michelstaedter 2014. *Honours:* Premio Leonardo Paterna Baldizzi per la Musica, Accad. Nazionale dei Lincei 2012. *E-mail:* alberto.caprioli@consbo.it (office). *Website:* www.consbo.it (office); www.albertocaprioli.it.

CAPRONI, Bruno; British singer (baritone); b. 1960, Bangor, County Down, Northern Ireland. *Education:* Royal Northern Coll. of Music, National Opera Studio. *Career:* repertoire includes Ezio in Attila, Marcello and Schaunard in La Bohème, Ottokar in Der Freischütz; Renato in Un Ballo in Maschera, roles in Madama Butterfly, Don Carlos, La Forza del Destino, Il Barbiere di Siviglia, Der Freischütz, Otello, Die Meistersinger, Turandot, Rigoletto, Nabucco, Luisa Miller, Cavalleria Rusticana, I Pagliacci, Falstaff, Samson et Dalila; has sung with Opera Northern Ireland, Dublin Grand Opera, Covent Garden, ENO, Welsh National Opera, Vienna Staatsoper, La Scala, Metropolitan Opera, Deutsche Oper Berlin, San Francisco Opera, Houston Grand Opera, Pittsburgh Opera, Dallas Opera, Florida Grand Opera, Cologne Staastoper, Hamburg Staatsoper, Frankfurt Staatsoper, Düsseldorf Staatsoper, Vlaamse Opera, Wexford, Vienna Klangboden and Casals Festivals; sang in Verdi Gala celebrating Luciano Pavarotti's birthday 2002. *Honours:* Vaughan Williams/Frederick Cox Award, Royal Northern Coll. of Music 1987, Ricordi Prize for Opera 1988.

CAPUÇON, Gautier; French cellist; b. 1981, Chambéry; brother of Renaud Capuçon. *Education:* studied with Philippe Muller, Conservatoire National Supérieur de Musique, Paris, with Heinrich Schiff, Univ. of Music and Performing Arts, Vienna, Austria. *Career:* fmr mem., European Community Youth Orchestra under Bernard Haitink, and Gustav Mahler Jugendorchester under Kent Nagano, Daniele Gatti, Pierre Boulez, Seiji Ozawa and Claudio Abbado; has performed as soloist with Philadelphia Orchestra, Orchestre National de France, Houston Symphony, Bayerische Rundfunk Orchestra, Munich Philharmonic, Chamber Orchestra of Europe, Santa Cecilia Orchestra Rome, Orchestre Philharmonique de Monte-Carlo, Orchestre de Paris, Scottish Chamber Orchestra, BBC Nat. Orchestra of Wales, BBC Scottish Symphony Orchestra, working with leading conductors including Christoph Eschenbach, Tugan Sokhiev, Paavo Jarvi, Semyon Bychkov, J. Lopez Cobos, Myung-Whun Chung, Charles Dutoit, Vladimir Fedosseyev; UK debut at Edin. Int. Festival 2004; has performed at Royal Concert Hall (Glasgow), Wigmore Hall, Barbican Hall, QEH (all London); as chamber musician has performed with Martha Argerich, Daniel Barenboim, Yuri Bashmet, Gérard Caussé, Jean-Bernard Pommier, Sarah Chang, Myung Whun Chung, Hélène Grimaud, Stephen Kovacevich, Mikhail Pletnev, Gabriela Montero, Viktoria Mullova, Paul Meyer, Vadim Repin, Pascal Rogé, Jean-Yves Thibaudet, Katia and Marielle Labeque, Maxim Vengerov, Lilya Zilberstein, the Ysaÿe Quartet, and with his brother Renaud; exclusive recording artist with Virgin Classics. *Recordings:* Face à Face: Works for Violin and Cello (with Renaud Capuçon) 2003, Haydn, Cello Concertos 2003, Brahms, Piano Trios (with Renaud Capuçon and Nicholas Angelich) 2004, Schubert, Trout Quintet 2005, Inventions: Works for Violin and Cello (with Renaud Capuçon), Ravel, piano trio, duo violin and cello (with Frank Braley and Renaud Capuçon), Saint-Saens, Carnaval de Animaux, Brahms, double concerto for violin and cello, clarinet quintet (with Renaud Capuçon, Myung-Whun Chung, Gustav Malher Jugend Orchester, Capuçon Quartet, Paul Meyer), Rhapsody: Rachmaninoff cello sonata, Martha Argerich and Friends: Live from the Lugano Festival 2005, 2006, Prokofiev cello sonata (with Gabriela Montero) 2008, Dvořák and Herbert Cello Concertos 2009, Fauré: Complete Chamber Music for Strings and Piano (ECHO Klassik Award for Chamber Music Recording of the Year/Mixed Ensemble – 19th Century 2012) 2011. *Honours:* Victoires de la Musique New Talent of the Year 2001, Borletti-Buitoni Trust award 2004. *Current Management:* c/o Nicholas Curry, Clarion/ Seven Muses, 47 Whitehall Park, London, N19 3TW, England. *Telephone:* (20) 7272-4413 (office). *Fax:* (20) 7281-9687 (office). *E-mail:* nick@c7m.co.uk (office). *Website:* www.c7m.co.uk (office).

CAPUÇON, Renaud; French violinist; b. 1976, Chambéry; brother of Gautier Capuçon. *Education:* Conservatoire National Supérieur de Musique, Paris and studied with Gérard Poulet, Veda Reynolds, Thomas Brandis, Isaac Stern. *Career:* fmr Concertmaster, Gustav Mahler Jugendorchester; has performed with orchestras, including Deutsches Symphonie-Orchester Berlin, Komischer-Oper Berlin, NDR Hamburg Orchester, WDR Köln Orchester, Montréal Symphony, Jerusalem Symphony, Bordeaux, Lille, Lyon, Monte-Carlo, and Toulouse Orchestras, Philharmonique de Radio France, Orchestre National de France, Orchestre de Paris, Ensemble Orchestral de Paris, Copenhagen Royal Orchestra, Swedish Radio Orchestra, Sinfonia Varsovia, Chamber Orchestra of Europe, City of Birmingham Symphony, Mahler Chamber Orchestra, Firenze Maggio Musicale Orchestra, Philharmonic Orchestra of the Scala di Milano, Rome Santa Cecilia Orchestra, Tokyo Philharmonic, NHK Symphony, Lausanne and Zürich Chamber Orchestras; festival appearances include Schubertiade in Schwarzenberg, Ruhr Festival, Spoleto Festival, Lyon, Paris, Naples and Lugano, Montpellier, Geneva, Amsterdam, Antwerpen, Frankfurt, Hamburg, Madrid, Vienna, Innsbruck, Shanghai, Bad Kissingen, Rheingau Musik Festival, Schleswig Holstein Musik Festival; as chamber musician has performed with Martha Argerich, Daniel Barenboim, Elena Bashkirova, Hélène Grimaud, Andre Watts, Yefim Bronfman, Myung-Whun Chung, Stephen Kovacevich, Jean-Yves Thibaudet, Vadim Repin, Katia and Marielle Labèque, Yuri Bashmet, Truls Mork, Paul Meyer, Kremerata Baltica and with his brother, Gautier. *Recordings:* Mendelssohn, Piano Trio No. 1 (with Gautier Capuçon and Martha Argerich), Franck/Rachmaninoff, Violin Sonata in A/Cello Sonata (with Gautier Capuçon, Lilya Zilberstein), Brahms, Violin Sonatas Nos 1, 2 and 3 (with Nicholas Angelich), Brahms, Piano Trios Nos 1, 2 and 3 (with Gautier Capuçon, Nicholas Angelich), Dutilleux, Tout un monde lointain, Face à Face – 20th Century Violin and Cello Duos (with Gautier Capuçon), Le Boeuf sur le toit – French works for violin and orchestra, Mendelssohn/Schumann, Violin Concertos, Ravel, Piano Trio/Violin Sonata (with Gautier Capuçon, Frank Braley), Schubert, Grand Duo (with Jérôme Ducros), Schubert, Trout Quintet, Schumann, Piano Quintet in E-flat Major, Op. 44, Fauré: Complete Chamber Music for Strings and Piano (ECHO Klassik Award for Chamber Music Recording of the Year/Mixed Ensemble – 19th Century 2012) 2011. *Honours:* Berlin Acad. of Arts Prize 1995, Victoires de la Musique New Talent of the Year 2000. *Current Management:* c/o R. Douglas Sheldon, Columbia Artists Management Inc., 1790 Broadway, New York, NY 10019-1412, USA. *Telephone:* (212) 841-9512 (office). *Fax:* (212) 841-9517 (office). *E-mail:* info@cami.com (office). *Website:* www.cami.com (office).

CARBY, Catherine, Adv DipMus, PGDipOpera; Australian singer (mezzo-soprano); *Principal Mezzo-Soprano, Opera Australia*; b. (Catherine Emma Coote), 16 June 1972, Australia; d. of John Walter Coote and Lois Merle Walker; m. Darren Lynch 2006; one d. *Education:* Canberra School of Music, Australian Nat. Univ., Royal Coll. of Music, London. *Career:* currently Prin.

Mezzo-Soprano, Opera Australia; appearances with Victoria State Opera, Opera Queensland, Scottish Opera, English Nat. Opera and Opera Australia; roles include Carmen, Octavian in Der Rosenkavalier, Geschwitz in Lulu, Orlofsky in Die Fledermaus, Baba the Turk in The Rake's Progress, Cornelia in Guilio Cesare, Ruggiero in Alcina, Elvira in Don Giovanni, Romeo in I Capuleti e i Montecchi. *Honours:* winner ABC Young Performer of the Year Awards 1996, STA Australian Nat. Aria Competition, Helpmann Award, Green Room Award, RCM Tait Memorial Trust Scholarships, finalist Kathleen Ferrier and Richard Tauber Awards. *Current Management:* c/o Arts Management, Level 1, 405 Elizabeth Street, Surry Hills, NSW 2010, Australia.

CARD, June; American singer (soprano) and teacher; b. 10 April 1942, Dunkirk, NY; m. Manfred Luetgenhorst. *Education:* Mannes Coll., New York, Univ. of Florida. *Career:* sang on Broadway from 1959, with New York City Opera from 1963; European engagements at Munich; Gartnerplatztheater from 1967; mem., Frankfurt Opera 1969–; appearances in Hamburg, London, Paris, Barcelona, Vienna, Cologne, Met New York, San Carlo (Naples); over 140 roles, including Violetta, Jenůfa, Madama Butterfly, Minnie in La Fanciulla del West and Countess in Die Soldaten by Zimmermann; has sung Janáček's Vixen, Katya and Emilia Marty, Magda in La Rondine, and roles in Schreker's Die Gezeichneten, Henze's Der Junge Lord and Bassarids and The Rake's Progress; Sieglinde and Katerina Izmailova; Frankfurt 1988 in Poulenc's La Voix Humaine; Holland Festival in The Oresteia by Milhaud; produced La Clemenza di Tito at Giessen 1988; Fidelio in France; sang the Mother in Die Wände Adriana Hölsky at Frankfurt 2000; Prof. for Opera and Voice, Univ. of Illinois 1999–; produced Mozart's Figaro and Così fan tutte, Weill's Street Scene, Man of La Mancha, Die Fledermaus. *Recordings include:* Traviata, Gezeichneten. *Honours:* Kammersängerin, Bavarian State Opera and Frankfurt Opera. *Address:* Arabellastrasse 5-1411, 81925 Munich, Germany (home). *E-mail:* cardopera@web.de (home).

CARDEN, Joan Maralyn, AO, OBE; Australian opera singer (soprano); b. 9 Oct. 1937, Richmond, Vic.; d. of the late Frank Carden and of Margaret Carden (née Cooke); m. William Coyne (deceased 2014) 1962 (divorced 1980); two d. *Education:* Trinity Coll. of Music, UK, Stuyvesant Scholar at London Opera Centre, voice studies with Thea Phillips and Henry Portnoj, Melbourne, Vida Harford, London, and David Harper, UK/Australia. *Career:* nat. debut Grisette in Merry Widow with June Bronhill, Melbourne 1960; int. debut, world premiere of Malcolm Williamson's Our Man in Havana, Sadler's Wells 1963; joined Australian Opera (Opera Australia) 1971: Royal Opera, Covent Garden as Gilda in Rigoletto 1974, Glyndebourne as Anna in Don Giovanni 1977, Scottish Opera as Constanze 1977; soloist, Sydney Opera House from opening 1974–2003; US debut at Houston as Amenaide in Tancredi 1977; Metropolitan Opera tour as Anna in Don Giovanni 1978, Kennedy Center 1980, Miami Opera 1981; Singapore Festival 1983; Adelaide Festival 1984; other appearances include Victoria State Opera, Lyric Opera of Queensland, State Opera of South Australia; over 50 major roles including most Mozart heroines, Liu in Turandot, Marguerite in Faust, Gilda in Rigoletto, four heroines in Contes d'Hoffmann, Natasha in War and Peace, Tatyana in Onegin (in English and Russian), Lakmé, Leonora in Forza del Destino/Il Trovatore, Violetta in La Traviata, Alice in Falstaff, Mimi, Musetta in La Bohème, Madama Butterfly, Eva in Die Meistersinger, Feldmarschallin in Der Rosenkavalier, Elisabetta in Maria Stuarda, Médée, Tosca, Public Opinion in Orpheus in the Underworld, Mother Abbess in Sound of Music, Ida Straus in Titanic 2006, Mother Superior in Harp on the Willow 2007; concerts with Australian, Sydney, Melbourne, and Queensland Symphony Orchestras and for Australian Broadcasting Corpn, Sydney Univ. Graduates Choir (sponsors of Joan Carden Award, Sydney Conservatorium 2004–); repertoire includes Mozart Masses, concert arias, choral works, Vier Letzte Lieder (R. Strauss), Britten, works by Australian composers including Peter Sculthorpe, Nigel Butterley, Barry Conyngham, Ross Edwards, Moya Henderson; soloist at numerous state and fed. occasions, including 1988 bicentenary, royal and presidential state visits; est. Joan Carden Award, Sydney Conservatorium of Music 2004. *Recordings include:* Joan Carden Sings Mozart, Great Opera Heroines: Joan Carden, The Australian Opera, Mozart: A Bicentennial Celebration, Stars of The Australian Opera Sing Verdi; Verdi aria in Priscilla, Queen of the Desert, film score. *Honours:* Hon. DUniv (Swinburne Univ. of Tech., Melbourne) 2000, (Australian Catholic Univ., Sydney); Dame Joan Hammond Award for Outstanding Service to Opera in Australia 1987, Australian Govt Creative Fellowship 1993, Australian Govt Fed. Centenary Medal 2001. *Address:* Opera Australia, PO Box 291, Strawberry Hills, NSW 2012, Australia (office). *Telephone:* (2) 9699-1099 (office). *Website:* www.opera -australia.org.au (office).

CARDY, Patrick Robert Thomas, BMus, MMA, DMus; Canadian composer and academic; b. 22 Aug. 1953, Toronto, ON. *Education:* University of Western Ontario, McGill University. *Career:* Professor, School for Studies in Art and Culture, Carleton University, Ottawa, 1977–; performances in Canada, USA and Europe. *Compositions include:* Golden Days, Silver Nights, 1977; Vox Humana, 1977; Jig, 1984; Mirages, 1984; Outremer: The Land Beyond the Sea, 1985; Mimesis, 1987; Qilakitsoq: The Sky Hangs Low, 1988; Tango!, 1989; Tombeau, 1989; The Little Mermaid, 1990; Avalon, 1991; Serenade, 1992; Chaconne, 1992; Autumn, 1992; 'Dulce et decorum est...', 1993; Danses folles et amoureuses, 1993; Et in Arcadia ego, 1994; Fhir a Bhata: The Boatman, 1994; Silver and Shadow, 1994; Te Deum, 1995; Dreams of the Sídhe, 1995; La Folia, 1996; Sans Souci, 1996; Bonavista, 1997; The

Return of the Hero, 1997; '...and in the night the gentle earth is falling into morning...', 1998; Kalenda Maya, 1999; Zodiac Dances, 2000: Trabadores, 2000; Rhythm in Your Rubbish, 2001. *Recordings include:* Virelai; Éclat; Tango!; Tombeau; Dances Folles et Amoureuses; Sans Souci; Liesel, Suse, Ilze and Gerda; Jig; Numerous on major labels. *Address:* 29 Morgan's Grant Way, Kanata, ON K2K 2G2, Canada.

CARELLA, Giuliano; Italian conductor; b. 1956, Milan. *Education:* studied with Franco Ferrara at Siena. *Career:* conductor of opera performances throughout Europe from 1986; engagements at Verona, Munich and Hamburg Staatsoperas, Bologna, Salle Gaveau, Paris, Barcelona and Buenos Aires, L'Italiana in Algeri for the Bayerische Staatsoper, Festival of Martina Franca, with operas by Mercadante, and L'Ultimo Giorno di Pompei, by Pacini 1996, La Morte di Didone at the Rossini Festival Pesaro, and the premiere of Lorenco Ferrero's La Nascite di Orfeo, at the Verona Teatro Filarmonico. *Recordings include:* Les Bijoux (by Sumi Jo) 1999, Caritea regina di Spagna (by Saverio Mercadante) 1999, L'Ultimo Giorno di Pompei (by Giovanni Pacini) 1999, Ave Maria 2000, Ernani (by Guiseppe Verdi) 2001, Elisabetta Regina d'Inghilterra (by Gioachino Rossini) 2002, Le due contesse (by Giovanni Paisiello) 2003, Turandot (by Giacomo Puccini) 2004, Proserpine (by Giovanni Paisiello) 2004, L'esule di Granata (by Jakob Liebmann Meyerbeer) 2005, Bravura Diva (by Jennifer Larmore) 2005, Bel Canto (by Sumi Jo) 2006, Adelaide di Borgogna (by Gioachino Rossini) 2006, Il diluvio universale (by Gaetano Donizetti) 2006, Rossini: Arias (by Jennifer Larmore) 2007, Norma (by Vincenzo Bellini) 2007. *E-mail:* info@giulianocarella.it. *Website:* www.giulianocarella.it.

CAREWE, John Maurice Foxall; British conductor; b. 24 Jan. 1933, Derby, England; two d. *Education:* Guildhall School of Music and Drama, London, Conservatoire National, Paris. *Career:* founded Music Today, New Music Ensemble, 1958; Principal Conductor, BBC National Orchestra of Wales, 1966–71; Musical Director, Principal Conductor, Brighton Philharmonic Society, 1974–87; Principal Conductor, Fires of London, 1980–94; General Music Director of the Opera and the Robert Schumann Philharmonic, Chemnitz, 1993–96. *Recordings:* Stravinsky, Histoire du Soldat; Milhaud, Création du Monde; Bennett, Calendar; Maxwell Davies, Leopardi Fragments; Bedford, Music for Albion Moonlight; Debussy, Ibéria; Falla, Interlude and Dance, La Vida Breve; Bridge, Enter Spring and Oration; Colin Matthews, Landscape and Cello Concerto; Muller-Siemens, Under Neon Light I; Leyendecker, Cello Concerto; Debussy, Pelléas et Mélisande; Dvořák, Symphony No. 8; Brahms, Tragic Overture. *Honours:* Bablock Prize 1960. *E-mail:* service@musicontact.de. *Website:* www.musicontact.de.

CARIAGA, Marvellee; American singer (mezzo-soprano); b. 11 Aug. 1942, California. *Education:* California State Univ. *Career:* sang with San Diego Opera from 1971; Fricka in performances of Der Ring des Nibelungen for Seattle Opera 1975–81; guest appearances at Vancouver 1975–78, San Francisco 1981, and Pittsburgh, Portland and Los Angeles 1987–88; Rio de Janeiro 1979, as Santuzza; Netherlands Opera 1979, 1982; other roles have included Wagner's Venus, Ortrud, Waltraute, Brünnhilde in Siegfried, Isolde and Magdalene; Donna Anna, Amelia in Un Ballo in Maschera, Herodias and Kostelnicka in Jenůfa; Colorado 1986, in the premiere of Pasatieri's The Three Sisters; Los Angeles Music Center Opera 1991, as Mrs Grose in The Turn of the Screw; Mrs Herring at the Dorothy Chandler Pavilion, Los Angeles 1992; currently mem., voice faculty, Bob Cole Conservatory of Music, California State Univ. at Long Beach. *Recordings include:* The Three Sisters. *Address:* Bob Cole Conservatory of Music, California State University, 1260 Bellflower Boulevard, Long Beach, CA 90840-7101, USA (office). *Telephone:* (562) 985-5371 (office). *Website:* www.csulb.edu/~music (office).

CARL, Eugene (Gene) Marion, Jr, BA; American composer and pianist; b. 8 Nov. 1953, Los Angeles, CA. *Education:* Pomona College, Freiburg im Breisgau, Germany, Institute for Sonology, Utrecht State University, Netherlands, Royal Conservatory, The Hague, studied with John Ritter, Geoffrey Madge, Karl Kohn, Konrad Lechner, Jan van Vlymen and Jan Boerman, masterclasses with Padolsky, Voorhies, Kontarsky. *Career:* debut with Beethoven Piano Concerto No. 1, with Sepulveda Orchestra, 1968; composition teaching; (co-)producer for special projects; synthesizer programming and performance De Materie, L. Andriessen and Robert Wilson; Gene Carl band tours, 1995–96, 1996–97, 2000–01; resident at the Djerassi Foundation near San Francisco, 1999. *Compositions include:* Scratch, violin solo, 1985; Gagarin for double orchestra, mixed choir, 2 solo voices, children's choir, synthesizers, tape, 1986–99; Leonardo, Leonardo for violin, electric guitar, tuba, drum kit, synthesizers, tape, voice, 1986; Hommage à Tarkovski for 2 saxophones, violin, synthesizers, percussion, tape, 1987; Claremont Concerto for B-flat clarinet, piano and string quartet, 1987; Roscoe Boulevard for 2 saxophones (doubling bass clarinet and clarinet) and ensemble, 1988; Pink Chinese Restaurants, a cantata for mezzo and 8 instruments, 1990; Laika for solo synthesiser, 1993; Nocturne for tuba, string trio and synthesizer, 1996; Tree of Time for 7 pianos, 1996; Below Paradise for 8 instruments, 1996; Wyoming Elegy, cantata for baritone and 8 instruments (in memoriam Matthew Shepard), 1998–2000. *Recordings:* two albums as member of Hoketus Ensemble; Pianist with 5 UUs; Motor Totemist Guild; Balans, with Hoketus. *Publications:* co-editor or editor: 1976–78, Journal of the Schoenberg Institute; Key Notes, Amsterdam; Cage's Sonatas and Interludes, catalogue, Antiqua Musica, Municiple Museum, The Hague, 1989. *Honours:* Djerassi Resident Artist Program 1999. *Address:* c/o Donemus, Paulus Potterstraat 14, 1071 CZ Amsterdam, The Netherlands.

CARL, Jeffrey, BMus, DipMus; Canadian singer (baritone); b. 1961. *Education:* McGill University, University of Toronto with Louis Quilico, studied in Siena and the Britten-Pears School. *Career:* Nick Shadow in Stravinsky's The Rake's Progress, Vancouver Opera; Ford in Falstaff at the Aldeburgh Festival; Verdi's Germont, di Luna, Macbeth; Puccini's Sharpless, Marcello, Scarpia; Tchaikovsky's Onegin, Mozart's Don Giovanni, Guglielmo; Donizetti's Enrico; Bellini's Riccardo, Gounod's Valentin, Thomas' Hamlet, Bizet's Escamillo as well as Henry VIII (Saint-Saëns), Genoveva (Schumann), Brandenburgers in Bohemia (Smetana) and Gershwin's Blue Monday, Italian debut in 1997; Concerts include: standard repertoire under David Willcocks with the Montreal Symphony, Simon Rattle with the Royal Liverpool Philharmonic and Michael Tippett: Messiah, Carmina Burana, Verdi's Requiem, Beethoven's Ninth, Bach Passions, The Creation, Belshazzar's Feast; Further engagements include: La Gioconda in Toronto, Carmen in Portugal, Child of Our Time in Singapore, Mascagni's Iris in Italy, Ballo in Maschera in Italy, Falstaff (Ford) in London, Mahler Eighth and Scarpia in Verona. *Recordings:* Weill's Firebrand of Florence with Thomas Hampson; La Bohème (Alagna, Ramey, Vaduva, Pappano conducting); The Czarevich with Hadley/Gustafson and Giuditta with Hadley/Riedel conducted by Richard Bonynge; Further recordings include: Caterina Cornaro, Donizetti, with Richard Bonynge. *Address:* Gossage Artists Management, 234 Queen Elizabeth Driveway, Ottawa, Ontario, K1S 3M4, Canada. *Telephone:* (613) 278-2325. *Website:* www.gossageartists.com.

CARLOS, Wendy, AB, MA; American composer, synthesist and recording engineer; b. 14 Nov. 1939, Pawtucket, RI. *Education:* Brown Univ., Columbia Univ. *Career:* worked as a recording engineer, associating with Robert Moog in the development of the Moog Synthesizer 1964; pioneer in utilising the resources of the synthesizer; has delivered papers at New York Univ., Audio Engineering Soc. Digital Audio Conference, Dolby New York City Surround Sound demonstration and panel, and at other music/audio conferences; mem. Audio Engineering Soc., Soc. of Motion Picture and Television Engineers, Nat. Acad. of Recording Arts and Sciences. *Compositions include:* Noah (opera) 1964. *Recordings include:* albums: Switched-on Bach (three Grammy Awards) 1968, The Well-Tempered Synthesizer 1969, Sonic Seasonings 1972, A Clockwork Orange (soundtrack) 1972, Switched-on Bach II 1974, By Request 1975, Switched-on Brandenburgs 1979, The Shining (soundtrack) 1980, Tron (soundtrack) 1982, Digital Moonscapes 1984, Beauty In the Beast 1986, Secrets of Synthesis 1987, Peter and the Wolf (with Al Yankovic) 1988, Switched-On Bach 2000 1992, Tales of Heaven and Hell 1998, Switched-On Boxed Set 1999, Rediscovering Lost Scores 2005. *Website:* www.wendycarlos.com.

CARLSEN, Toril; Norwegian singer (soprano); b. 1954, Oslo. *Education:* studied in Oslo and Budapest, Hungary. *Career:* appearances at the National Theatre, Oslo from 1979, notably as Fiordiligi, Pamina, Adina, Musetta, Micaela and Zdenka; guest at the Berlin Staatsoper from 1989 (Mélisande 1991); many concert appearances. *Recordings include:* Peer Gynt by Grieg.

CARLSON, Claudine; French singer (mezzo-soprano); b. 26 Feb. 1950, Mulhouse. *Education:* studied in California and Manhattan School of Music, New York, with Gertrude Gruenberg, Jennie Tourel and Esther Andreas. *Career:* came to US age 16; professional operatic debut with New York City Opera as Cornelia in Handel's Giulio Cesare 1968; numerous appearances as soloist with orchestras, including Boston Symphony, Detroit Symphony, New York Philharmonic, Minnesota Philharmonic, Los Angeles Philharmonic, St Louis Symphony, National Symphony, London Symphony Orchestra, Orchestre de Paris, Israel Philharmonic; numerous festival appearances; recitalist worldwide. *Honours:* First Prize, Nat. Fed. of Music Clubs Singing Competition, Martha Baird Rockefeller Award.

CARLSON, Lenus Jesse, BA; American singer (baritone) and teacher; b. 11 Feb. 1945, Jamestown, ND; m. Linda Kay Jones 1972. *Education:* Juilliard School with Oren Brown. *Career:* apprentice artist, Central City (Colorado) Opera 1965–66; debut as Demetrius, Midsummer Night's Dream, Minnesota Opera 1968; sang with opera companies in Dallas 1972–73, San Antonio 1973, Boston 1973, Washington, DC 1973, New York (Metropolitan Opera, debut as Berlioz's Aeneas 1973), Amsterdam 1974, and elsewhere; British debut with Scottish Opera, Edinburgh Festival 1975; Covent Garden debut, London, as Valentin 1976; sang at the Deutsche Oper Berlin as Paul in Die tote Stadt by Korngold 1983; Nevers in Les Huguenots 1987, Arcesias in Die toten Augen by d'Albert 1987; premiere of Oedipus by Wolfgang Rihm 1988; sang the Acrobat in Lulu at the Festival Hall, London 1994; Creon in Enescu's Oedipe at the Deutsche Oper 1996 and Klingsor in Parsifal 1998; season 1999–2000 at the Deutsche Oper as the Speaker in Die Zauberflöte, Strauss's Faninal and Kothner in Die Meistersinger; various concert engagements; teacher of voice, Minneapolis 1965–70, New York 1970–.

CARLYLE, Joan Hildred; British singer (soprano) and teacher; b. 6 April 1931, d. of Edgar J. Carlyle and Margaret M. Carlyle; m.; two d. *Education:* Howell's School, Denbigh, N Wales; studied singing with Madame Bertha Nichlass Kempner. *Career:* Prin. Lyric Soprano, Covent Garden 1955–79; has sung at La Scala Milan, Staatsoper Vienna, Munich, Berlin, Teatro Colón Buenos Aires, San Carlo Naples, Monet Monte Carlo, Nico Milan, Cape Town, Brussels, Geneva, Zurich, Amsterdam, Boston, New York; teaches privately and also in London; gives masterclasses, promotes young singers and judges prestigious competitions. *Major roles sung in UK include:* Oscar, Un Ballo in Maschera 1957–58, Sophie, Der Rosenkavalier 1958–59, Nedda, Pagliacci

(Zeffirelli production) 1959, Mimi, La Bohème 1960, Titania, Midsummer Night's Dream, Britten (Gielgud production) 1960, Pamina, Magic Flute 1962, 1966, Countess, Marriage of Figaro 1963, Zdenka, Arabella (Hartman Production) 1964, Suor Angelica 1965, Desdemona, Othello 1965, Arabella 1967, Marschallin, Der Rosenkavalier 1968, Jenifer, Midsummer Marriage 1969, Donna Anna, Don Giovanni 1970, Reiza, Oberon 1970, Adriana Lecouvreur 1970, Rusalka, Elisabetta, Don Carlos 1975. *Major roles sung abroad include:* Oscar, Nedda, Mimi, Pamina, Zdenka, Micaela, Donna Anna, Arabella, Elisabetta and Desdemona. *Recordings include:* Von Karajan's production of Pagliacci as Nedda, Midsummer Marriage as Jenifer, Medea, Pagliacci from Buenos Aires, Mavra, Purcell Anthology, Voice from the Old House (1/11) 2002, (12/29), (30/42) 2003, Complete versions of Otello, Arabella, Suor Angelica, Highlights from La Bohème 2003, complete versions of Arabella and Adriana Lecouvreur, Rusalka, Oberon, complete Ballo 1962, 1971, Benvenuto Cellini 2004, Die Zauberflöte, Samson. *Address:* Laundry Cottage, Hanmer, SY13 3DQ, Clwyd, Wales. *Telephone:* (1948) 830265. *E-mail:* joan@joancarlyle.co.uk (home). *Website:* www.joancarlyle.co.uk (home).

CARMICHAEL, John Russell, MusDip; Australian composer; b. 5 Oct. 1930, Melbourne, Vic. *Education:* Univ. of Melbourne, Paris Conservatoire, studied with Arthur Benjamin, Anthony Milner. *Career:* commission from Friends of the Victorian Opera 1995. *Compositions include:* Concierto Folklorico for piano and strings 1970, Trumpet Concerto 1975, Fantasy Concerto for flute and orchestra 1982, Lyric Concerto for cornet and piano 1982, A Country Flair for clarinet and orchestra 1989, Fêtes Champêtres for clarinet 1989, Monotony for two pianos 1990, When Will the Sun for soprano and piano 1990, Bravura Waltzes for two pianos 1990, Saxophone Concerto 1990, Dark Scenarios for two pianos 1994, From the Dark Side for piano 1995.

CARNEIRO, Joana; Portuguese conductor; *Music Director, Berkeley Symphony Orchestra*; b. Lisbon. *Education:* Academia Nacional Superior de Orquestra, Northwestern Univ., Univ. of Michigan. *Career:* recent debuts with orchestras including Toronto Symphony, Seattle Symphony, São Paulo State Symphony, Ensemble Orchestral de Paris, Saint Paul Chamber Orchestra; past engagements include the Los Angeles Philharmonic, New World Symphony, Grant Park Music Festival, Norrköping Symphony, Prague Philharmonia, Orchestre de Bretagne, Macau Chamber Orchestra, Beijing Orchestra; opened Venice Biennale, Gran Teatro de la Fenice 2009; has worked with Esa-Pekka Salonen, Kurt Masur and Christoph von Dohnányi; fmr Asst Conductor, Los Angeles Chamber Orchestra; Music Dir, Los Angeles Debut Orchestra 2002–05; Principal Guest Conductor, Metropolitan Orchestra of Lisbon 2005–; American Symphony Orchestra League Conducting Fellow, Los Angeles Philharmonic 2005–08; Guest Conductor, Gulbenkian Orchestra 2006–; Music Dir, Berkeley Symphony Orchestra 2009–. *Honours:* Order of the Infante Dom Henrique 2004; Young Musicians Foundation's Nat. Conductor Search 2002. *Current Management:* c/o Bridget Canniere, IMG Artists, The Light Box, 111 Power Road, London, W4 5PY, England. *Telephone:* (20) 7957-5832. *Fax:* (20) 7957-5801. *E-mail:* bcanniere@imgartists.com. *Website:* www.imgartists.com.

CARPENTER, Greg, BMus, MMus; American opera administrator; *General Director, Opera Colorado*. *Education:* Wittenburg Univ., Michigan State Univ., Univ. of Maryland School of Music. *Career:* began career as professional opera singer, performed with Glimmerglass Opera, Central City Opera, Sarasota Opera, Opera Theatre of N Virginia, Cleveland Opera and Lyric Opera Cleveland 1986–88; Artist and Events Services Man., Clarice Smith Performing Arts Center, Univ. of Maryland 1989–2001; Devt Man., Nat. Symphony Orchestra 2001–04; Dir of Devt, Opera Colorado 2004–07, Gen. Dir 2007–. *Address:* Opera Colorado, 695 South Colorado Blvd, Suite 20, Denver, CO 80246, USA (office). *Telephone:* (303) 778-1500 (office). *Fax:* (303) 778-6533 (home). *E-mail:* gcarpenter@operacolorado.org (office). *Website:* www.operacolorado.org (office).

CARR, Colin Michael, ARCM (Hons); British cellist; *Professor of Cello, State University of New York, Stony Brook*; b. 25 Oct. 1957, Liverpool; m. Caroline Carr; three c. *Education:* Yehudi Menuhin School. *Career:* soloist throughout Europe, North America, Australia and Far East with major orchestras, including the Royal Philharmonic Orchestra, Concertgebouw Orchestra, BBC Symphony, Philharmonic, Chicago Symphony, Nat. Symphony Washington, English Chamber Orchestra, Scottish Chamber Orchestra, CBSO, Philadelphia Orchestra, Montréal Symphony; recitals in London, Amsterdam, Paris, New York, Washington, Boston, Los Angeles; TV and radio recordings, throughout Europe and Americas; faculty mem., New England Conservatory, Boston, USA 1983–98; Prof. of Cello, Royal Acad. of Music 1998–, State Univ. of New York, Stony Brook 2002–; also Musician-in-Residence, St John's Coll., Oxford. *Recordings:* Sonatas by Debussy and Franck; Elegie, Romance and Papillon by Fauré; complete Schubert works for Piano Trio; complete Mendelssohn works for Piano Trio; complete Brahms Trios, complete Dvorak Trios with Golub, Kaplan, Carr Trio; Bach Solo Cello Suites; Brahms Sonatas, 20th Century solo cello. *Honours:* Hon. RAM; Winner Young Concert Artists, Piatigorsky Memorial Award, First Prize Naumburg Competition, 2nd Prize Rostropovitch Competition. *Current Management:* c/o Mary Lynn Fixler, Barrett Vantage Management, 505 Eighth Avenue, New York, NY 10018, USA. *Telephone:* (212) 245-3530. *Fax:* (212) 397-5860. *E-mail:* mlfixler@barrettvantage.com. *Website:* www.carolinebairdartists.co.uk. *Address:* Music Department, Stony Brook University, Stony Brook, NY 11794, USA (office). *E-mail:* ccarr@atlas.co.uk (office).

CARR-BOYD, Ann, MA; Australian composer; b. 13 July 1938, Sydney, NSW. *Education:* Univ. of Sydney, studied in London, England with Fricker and Goehr. *Career:* teacher, Univ. of Sydney 1967–73. *Compositions include:* Symphony 1964, two string quartets 1964, 1966, vocal music, including Home Thoughts from Abroad for mezzo and ensemble 1987, instrumental pieces, including Dance Suite for woodwind quintet 1984, Theme and Variations for organ 1989.

CARRERAS, José; Spanish singer (tenor); b. 5 Dec. 1947, Barcelona; s. of José Carreras and Antonia Carreras; m. Ana Elisa Carreras; one s. one d. *Career:* opera debut as Gennaro in Lucrezia Borgia, Liceo Opera House, Barcelona 1970–71 season; appeared in La Bohème, Un Ballo in Maschera and I Lombardi alla Prima Crociata at Teatro Regio, Parma, Italy 1972; US debut as Pinkerton in Madame Butterfly with New York City Opera 1972; debut at Metropolitan Opera as Cavaradossi 1974; debut at La Scala as Riccardo in Un Ballo in Maschera 1975; has appeared at major opera houses and festivals including Teatro Colón, Buenos Aires, Covent Garden, London, Vienna Staatsoper, Easter Festival and Summer Festival, Salzburg, Lyric Opera of Chicago; Pres. José Carreras Int. Leukaemia Foundation 1988–. *Recordings include:* Un Ballo in Maschera, La Battaglia di Legnano, Il Corsaro, Un Giorno di Regno, I Due Foscari, Simone Boccanegra, Macbeth, Don Carlos, Tosca, Thaïs, Aïda, Cavalleria Rusticana, Pagliacci, Lucia di Lammermoor, Turandot, Elisabetta, regina d'Inghilterra, Otello (Rossini). *Films include:* La Bohème, I Lombardi, Andrea Chenier, Turandot, Carmen, Don Carlos, La Forza del Destino, Fedora, Jerusalem, My Life. *Publication:* Singing from the Soul 1991. *Honours:* Hon. Pres. London Arts Orchestra; Hon. mem. RAM 1990, European Soc. for Medicine, Leukaemia Support Group, European Haematology Asscn, German Soc. of Paediatric Oncology and Haematology; Hon. Patron European Soc. for Medical Oncology; Hon. Rector, Hyunghee Hon.; Commdr des Arts et des Lettres, Chevalier, Légion d'honneur, Gran Croce di Cavaliere (Italy), Komandor's Cross of Order of Merit (Poland), Commandeur de la Médaille du Sahametrei (Cambodia), Civil Order Golden Cross of Social Solidarity (Spain), Nat. Order Steaua Romaniei (Romania), Grand Cross, Order of Merit (Germany); Dr hc (Univ. of Barcelona), (Univ. of Loughborough), (Univ. of Sheffield), Univ. Mendeleyev of Moscow), (Univ. of Camerino), (Napier Univ., Edinburgh), (Rutgers Univ.), (Miguel Hernández Univ. of Elche), (Univ. of Coimbra), (National Univ. of Music, Bucharest), Univ. of Marburg), (Univ. of Pécs), (Univ. of Porto); Grammy Award 1991, Sir Lawrence Olivier Award 1993, Gold Medal of City of Barcelona, Albert Schweizer Music Award 1996, ECHO Klassik Lifetime Achievement Award 2008, Classical BRIT Lifetime Achievement Award 2009, Honour Medal of Bavarian Govt, Grand Honour Award of Austrian Republic, Gold Medal of New York Spanish Inst., Hon. Gold Medal of Vienna and Medal of Honour in Gold of the Federal Capital of Vienna, Gold Medal of Fine Arts of Spain, Gold Medal of the Generalitat of Catalunya, Gold Medal of the Gran Teatre del Liceu, Hon. Medal of the City of Leipzig, Prince of Asturias Award 1991, among numerous other awards and prizes. *Address:* c/o José Carreras International Leukaemia Foundation, Muntaner 383, 2nd Floor, 08021 Barcelona, Spain (office). *E-mail:* info@fcarreras.es (office). *Website:* www .fcarreras.org/en (office).

CARRINGTON, Simon Robert, MA; British bass player and and music director; b. 23 Oct. 1942, Salisbury, Wiltshire, England; m. Hilary Stott 1969; one s. one d. *Education:* Christ Church Cathedral Choir School, Oxford, The King's School, Canterbury, King's College, Cambridge, New College, Oxford. *Career:* co-founder and Director of the King's Singers 1968–93, with 3,000 performances world-wide and numerous concerts, radio and television appearances; Freelance Double Bass Player with all major British symphony and chamber orchestras; Since 1994 Professor, Artist in Residence and Director of Choral Activities at the University of Kansas; Monteverdi Vespers, 1994; Britten War Requiem, Tallis 40 part Motet, Tribute to Henry Purcell, 1995; Walton Belshazzar's Feast, Ligeti Lux Aeterna, Josquin Missa Gaudeamus, 1996; Mendelssohn Elijah (staged as an opera), Music from the time of the Mexican Viceroys, Bach Motets, 1997; Director of the Graduate Degree Programs in Choral Directing; Freelance Choral Workshop Director and Choral Competition Judge in the United Kingdom, USA, France, Germany, Netherlands and Hungary; Choral Conductor world-wide including Carnegie Hall performances, 1996 and 1997. *Compositions:* Numerous arrangements for The King's Singers. *Recordings:* Numerous with various labels internationally, 1971–93 including madrigals, motets, folk songs from five centuries. *Publications:* The King's Singers–A Self Portrait, 1981; Video: The Art of The King's Singers. *Address:* Department of Music and Dance, 332 Murphy Hall, University of Kansas, Lawrence, KS 66044, USA.

CARROLI, Silvano; Italian singer (baritone); b. 22 Feb. 1939, Venice. *Education:* Opera School of La Fenice. *Career:* debut in Venice 1964, as Marcello in La Bohème; sang widely in Italy and toured North America with co. of La Scala, 1976; Verona Arena from 1973, in Samson et Dalila, as Ezio in Attila 1985, Renato in Un Ballo in Maschera 1986 and as Amonasro 2000; Washington Opera 1977–78, as Cavaradossi; London, Covent Garden, as Iago and in La Fanciulla del West; Chicago Lyric Opera 1978; Brussels 1980, in revival of Donizetti's Il Duca d'Alba; Barcelona 1983, as Escamillo; Paris Opéra 1984, as Nabucco and in Verdi's Jérusalem; further appearances at Metropolitan Opera and at Deutsche Oper Berlin; Amonasro, Luxor, Egypt, 1987; Iago, Covent Garden, 1990; Scarpia, Arena di Verona; Season 1992, as Gerard in Andrea Chénier at Turin, Scarpia at Covent Garden, Amonasro at

Festival of Caracalla; sang Scarpia at Hanover 1994 and at Verona 1998. *Recordings include:* Video of I Lombardi (Topaz).

CARROLL, Joan; American singer (soprano); b. 27 July 1932, Philadelphia. *Education:* studied in the USA and with Margarethe von Winterfeldt in Berlin. *Career:* debut at New York Opera Company 1957, as Zerbinetta; appearances in North America and in Havana; Santa Fe 1963, as Lulu (US premiere of Berg's opera); European engagements in Belgium, France, Denmark, Switzerland and Netherlands; sang Lulu in Hamburg, Munich and Zürich during the 1960s; mem., Deutsche Oper am Rhein, Düsseldorf, from 1967; sang Mozart's Constanze, Donna Anna and Queen of Night, as well as modern repertory, in Hanover, Berlin, Stuttgart, Cologne and Nuremberg. *Recordings include:* works by Gorecki and Stravinsky.

CARRON, Elizabeth; American singer (soprano); b. 12 Feb. 1933, New York, NY. *Education:* studied in New York. *Career:* debut with New York City Opera 1957, as Madama Butterfly; sang in New York until 1977 and made guest appearances in Cincinnati, Chicago, Pittsburgh, San Francisco and New Orleans; Dallas 1958, as Dirce in Cherubini's Médée; Edinburgh Festival 1984, with the Washington Opera; other roles include Mozart's Constanze, Susanna and Zerlina, Violetta, Micaela, Mimi and Liu, Norina, Strauss's Salome and Daphne, Aïthra in Die Ägyptische Helena and Birdie in Regina by Blitzstein. *Recordings include:* Regina.

CARSEN, Robert; Canadian stage director; b. 23 June 1954, Toronto. *Education:* Upper Canada Coll., York Univ., Toronto, Bristol Old Vic Theatre School. *Career:* Asst Dir, Glyndebourne Festival Opera 1982–85; production of Boito's Mefistofele seen at Geneva 1988 and at San Francisco, Chicago, Houston, Washington and Metropolitan Operas 1989–99; Aix-en-Provence Festival from 1991–96, with A Midsummer Night's Dream, Handel's Orlando, Die Zauberflöte, Semele (French premiere); Salome in Lyon; Bellini's La Straniera for Wexford, A Village Romeo and Juliet for Opera North, Mozart's Finta Semplice and Finta Giardiniera for the Camden Festival, London, and Cendrillon for WNO; Metropolitan Opera debut with Eugene Onegin, European premiere of Blitzstein's Regina for Scottish Opera; Lucia di Lammermoor at Zürich and Munich, Katya Kabanova in Canada and Figaro for Bordeaux, Paris, Israel and Barcelona 1997; seven-part Puccini cycle for the Flemish Opera 1990–96; Otello, Falstaff and Macbeth in Cologne, Die Frau ohne Schatten and Verdi's Jérusalem in Vienna; Alcina, Lohengrin, Nabucco, Capuleti e i Montecchi and Manon Lescaut at the Opéra Bastille, Paris; Carmelites in Amsterdam, Semele at ENO and Antwerp; Tales of Hoffmann for the Paris Opéra, The Ring in Cologne, Jenůfa and Cunning Little Vixen in Antwerp, Dialogues of the Carmelites at La Scala; Capriccio for Paris Opera, Rosenkavalier at Salzburg, La Traviata at Teatro La Fenice, Venice 2004; Elektra for Tokyo Opera Nomuri with Seiji Ozawa, Manon Lescaut at the Vienna Staatsoper, Il Trovatore in Bregenz, Rusalka at Bastille Opera, Le nozze di Figaro in Genova, Jenůfa in Oviedo, Semele in Gent, and Tosca in Hamburg 2005; productions in 2006 include Semele at Vlaamse Opera, Antwerp, Die Walkure at La Fenice, Venice, Orfeo ed Euridice and Iphigenie en Tauride at Chicago Lyric Opera, Kat'a Kabanova at La Scala, Das Rheingold, Die Walkure, Siegfried and Gotterdammerung in Cologne, Salome at Maggio Musicale Fiorentino, Les Dialogues des Carmelites at Teatro Real, Madrid, Il trovatore in Bregenz. *Theatre productions:* The Beautiful Game, Sunset Boulevard. *Honours:* Dr hc (York Univ.) 2005; Carl Ebert Award for directing 1982, French Critics Prize 1992, Grand Prix de la Presse Musicale Internationale 1996; Chevalier, Ordre des Arts et des Lettres 1996. *Address:* Judy Daish Associates Ltd, 2 St Charles Place, London, W10 6EG, England.

CARTER, Barbara; American singer (soprano); b. Columbus, Ohio. *Education:* Capital Univ., Univ. of Toronto, Canada with Louis Quilico, Musical Acad. of the West with Martial Singher. *Career:* sang Violetta and Musetta with Canadian Opera Co. on tour of USA and Canada; European debut with Essen Opera, then appeared as Queen of Night in Die Zauberflöte with Covent Garden Opera on tour to Far East; further appearances in Berlin, Munich, Buenos Aires, Paris, Vienna, Amsterdam, La Scala, Milan, Venice, Barcelona, New York, Ottawa and Bregenz; roles have included Lucia, Gilda, Marie in La Fille du Régiment, Zerbinetta, Sophie, Constanze, Zerlina, Rosina, Elvira in I Puritani, Amenaide in Tancredi, Olympia, Nannetta and Gretel; season 1990–91 as Constanze in Amsterdam and the Italian Singer in Capriccio at Vienna Staatsoper; concert appearances in works by Bach, Mozart, Haydn, Handel, Brahms, Orff, Schubert and Charpentier; Mahler's Symphonies 2, 4 and 8; engagements with Czech Philharmonic, Philharmonia (London) on tour in Japan, Accad. di Santa Cecilia in Rome and Deutsche Oper, Berlin (Fiakermilli in Arabella); recital repertoire includes German lieder and songs in Russian, French, English, Spanish, Italian and Portuguese. *Honours:* Capital Univ. Life Achievement Award, Columbus, Ohio 1996. *Address:* Bruckerstrasse 7, 82284 Grafrath, Germany (home). *Telephone:* (8144) 996565 (office). *Fax:* (8144) 996566 (office). *E-mail:* barbara.carter@soprano.de (home). *Website:* www.soprano.de.

CARTER, Peter John Burnett, ARCM, LRCM, FRSA; South African violinist (retd); b. 30 Jan. 1935, Durban; m. Sally Mackay 1974; one s. one d. *Education:* Royal Coll. of Music, UK, Conservatoire Royale de Musique, Belgium. *Career:* freelanced with Royal Philharmonic and Philharmonia orchestras 1953–56; Founder-mem. and second violin, Dartington String Quartet 1958–68; Dir of Music, Natal Performing Arts Council 1968–69; first violin, Delmé String Quartet, mem. ECO 1969–74; Sr Lecturer, Cape Town 1974–77; Leader and first violin, Allegri String Quartet, Allegri Robles Ensemble 1976–2006, Melos Ensemble 1984; mem. Incorporated Soc. of Musicians. *Recordings include:* Complete Schubert Quartets, 1979–81; Brahms Quartets; Beethoven Quartets and Quintets; Ravel Septet; Stolen Gems, James Campbell, 1986; Leader Bath International Ensemble, 1988; Brahms Clarinet Quintet (James Campbell); Piano Quintet (Rian de Waal), 1992 CALA; Lombardini Sirman 6 Quartets, 1994; Bruch and Brahms 2 Viola Quintets, 1995; Schubert, Newbould, 1996; Haydn Op 33 No. 3, 1996; Ravel, 1996; Haydn, Shostakovich No. 3, 1996; Schubert, Newbould, Stravinsky, Mozart Clarinet quintet, 1997; Beethoven op 131, Britten No. 3, 1998; Romberg and Brandts Buys Quintets (with William Bennett, flute). *Honours:* Hon. DMus (Nottingham) 1994, (Southampton) 1995, (Durham) 2005; Hon. MMus (Hull) 1987. *E-mail:* peter@petercarter.net. *Website:* petercarter.net/biography.

CARTERI, Rosanna; Italian singer (soprano); b. 14 Dec. 1930, Verona. *Education:* studied with Cuisnati and Nino Ederle. *Career:* debut in Rome 1949, as Elsa in Lohengrin; La Scala debut 1951, in La Buona Figliuola by Piccinni; sang in many concerts, notably in Donizetti's Requiem and in the premiere of Pizzetti's Ifigenia (Italian radio 1950); Salzburg Festival 1952, as Desdemona, conducted by Furtwängler; Florence 1953, as Natasha in the premiere of Prokofiev's War and Peace; San Francisco 1954, as Mimi; Chicago Lyric Opera 1955, as Marguerite in Faust; Verona Arena 1958–59; Covent Garden 1960, Mimi; sang in the premiere of Pizzetti's Calzare d'Argento, Milan 1961; premiere, Gilbert Bécaud's Opera d'Aran, Théâtre des Champs-Elysées, Paris 1962. *Recordings include:* La Traviata, Falstaff, Guillaume Tell, Suor Angelica, La Bohème, solo in the Brahms Requiem (conducted by Bruno Walter).

CARVER, Anthony Frederick, BMus, PhD; British university teacher; *Director of Education, School of Music and Sonic Arts, Queen's University, Belfast;* b. 16 Nov. 1947, Brighton; m.; two s. one d. *Education:* Westlain Grammar School, Brighton and Birmingham Univ. *Career:* Lecturer in Music, Queen's Univ., Belfast 1973, Sr Lecturer 1974–, now Dir of Educ., School of Music and Sonic Arts; mem. Royal Musical Asscn, Asscn of Univ. Teachers, Soc. for Musicology in Ireland. *Publications:* Cori Spezzati (two vols) 1988, Irish Church Praise (co-ed.) 1990, contrib. to ACTA Musicologica, Proceedings of the Royal Musical Association, Early Music, Music and Letters. *Address:* School of Music and Sonic Arts, Queen's University, Belfast, BT7 1NN, Northern Ireland (office). *Telephone:* (28) 9097-5208 (office). *Fax:* (28) 9097-5053 (office). *E-mail:* a.carver@qub.ac.uk (office).

CARWOOD, Andrew; British conductor and singer (tenor); *Director of Music, St Paul's Cathedral, London;* b. 30 April 1965. *Education:* St John's Coll., Cambridge. *Career:* fmr lay clerk Christ Church, Oxford and Westminster Cathedral; fmr Dir of Music Brompton Oratory, London; Artistic Dir The Cardinall's Musick 1989–; Dir Edington Music Festival 1992–97, Edington Schola Cantorum 1998–2010; Dir of Music, St Paul's Cathedral, London 2007–; Prin. Guest Conductor BBC Singers 2007–10; has appeared as a singer with numerous ensembles, including The Tallis Scholars, The Orlando Consort, The Parley of Instruments and Pro Cantione Antiqua; solo roles for Sir Roger Norrington, Harry Christophers, Richard Hickox, Paul McCreesh, Phillipe Herreweghe, Robert King and Christopher Hogwood; Assoc., Royal School of Church Music. *Recordings:* 30 recordings with The Cardinall's Musick (including the complete works of Byrd, Fayrfax and Ludford), first recording with St Paul's Cathedral Choir (Mozart) 2010; numerous recordings singing tenor. *Honours:* Hon. Fellow, Royal Acad. of St Cecilia; Preise der Deutsche Schallplatten Kritik 1999, Schallplatten Echo Award 1999, Gramophone Early Music Award 1995, 2006, 2007, 2010, Gramophone Record of the Year 2010. *Current Management:* c/o Rayfield Allied, Southbank House, Black Prince Road, London, SE1 7SJ, England. *Telephone:* (20) 3176-5500. *Fax:* (700) 6024-1439. *E-mail:* info@rayfieldallied .com. *Website:* www.rayfieldallied.com; www.cardinallsmusick.com (office); www.stpaulscathedral.co.uk (office).

CASABLANCAS, Benet, PhD; Spanish composer and musicologist; b. 2 April 1956, Sabadell. *Education:* Vienna Acad. of Music, studied with Friedrich Cerha and Karl Heinz Füssl, Universidad Autónoma de Barcelona, courses with György Ligeti, Elliott Carter, George Benjamin and Magnus Lindberg. *Career:* works performed across Europe and N and S America in halls such as Musikverein, Vienna, Auditorio 400, Madrid, L'Auditori, Barcelona and Miller Theatre, New York, by ensembles including London Sinfonietta, Ensemble Contemporain de Montréal, Arditti Quartet, Ensemble 13 Baden-Baden, Orchestre de Chambre de Lausanne, Leipziger Streichquartett, Ensemble Cantus (Croatia), Orquesta Nacional de España, symphony orchestras of Galicia, Granada, Tenerife, Spanish Radio and Television and Hermitage of St Petersburg, Spanish Nat. Youth Orchestra and BBC Symphony Orchestra; worked with conductors including Lawrence Foster, Vasily Petrenko, Franz-Paul Decker, Timothy Weiss, Ulrich Pöhl, Adrian Leaper, Salvador Mas, Alejandro Posada and Berislav Sipus; fmrly Academic Dir, Catalan Nat. Youth Orchestra (JONC) and Assoc. Prof., Universität Pompeu Fabra de Barcelona and Universidad de Alcalá de Henares; Academic Dir, Conservatori Superior de Música del Liceu, Barcelona 2002–; Composer in Residence, Orquestra Simfònica de Barcelona i Nacional de Catalunya 2013–14, 2014–15. *Compositions include:* Seven Scenes from Hamlet for reciter and chamber orchestra, Epigrams for various formations, Little Night Music and Celebration for chamber ensemble, Haikus for piano solo and small groups, The Dark Backward of Time for orchestra, Alter Klang, impromptu for large orchestra, Darkness visible, Nocturne for orchestra, Sogni ed epifanie

for orchestra. *Recordings:* New Epigrams 1997, Seven Scenes from Hamlet 2008, Piano Music 2010, The Dark Backward of Time 2010, Arditti Quartet String Quartets 2010. *Publications:* El humor en la música 2000; contrib. of articles to The New Grove Dictionary of Music and other publs. *Honours:* numerous awards including prizes from Composers Arena of Amsterdam and Musicians Accord of New York, Nat. Prize Generalitat of Catalonia 2007, Ministry of Culture's Nat. Music Prize 2013. *Address:* Conservatori Superior de Música del Liceu, Calle Nou de la Rambla 88, 08001 Barcelona, Spain (office). *Telephone:* (93) 3271200 (office). *Website:* www.conservatoriliceu.es (office).

CASADESUS, Jean Claude; French conductor; *Director, Lille National Orchestra;* b. (Jean Claude Probst), 7 Dec. 1935, Paris; s. of Lucien Probst and Gisèle Casadesus; two s. one d. *Education:* Paris Nat. Conservatoire and Ecole Normale, Paris. *Career:* solo timpanist, Concert Colonne 1959–68; percussion soloist, Domaine Musical (with Boulez); Conductor, Paris Opéra 1969–71; Co-Dir Orchestre Pays de Loire 1971–76; Founder and Dir Lille Nat. Orchestra 1976–; appears as guest conductor with leading orchestras in UK, USA, France, Germany, Norway, Russia, Czech Repub., int. music festivals etc.; Pres. Musique Nouvelle en Liberté; Musical Dir, Lille Piano Festival. *Recordings include:* works by Dutilleux (1st Symphony), Berlioz, Mahler, Bizet, Stravinsky, Mozart, Beethoven, Ravel, Debussy, Poulenc, Groupe des Six, Prokofiev, Dukas, Massenet, Milhaud, Honneger, Mussorgsky, Franck, Canteloube – Songs of the Auvergne. *Publications include:* Le plus court chemin d'un coeur à un autre 1998, La partition d'une vie 2012. *Honours:* Commdr, Légion d'honneur, Ordre nat. du Mérite, Grand Officier des Arts et des Lettres; Chevalier, Ordre des Palmes académiques; Commdr, Order of Orange Nassau (Netherlands); Officer, Order of Léopold (Belgium); Grand Prix de la SACEM, First Prize in Percussion and Conducting, and several other prizes and awards for recordings. *Address:* Orchestre National de Lille, 30 place Mendès-France, BP 119, 59027 Lille Cedex (office); 2 rue de Steinkerque, 75018 Paris, France (home). *Telephone:* 3-20-12-82-68 (office). *Fax:* 3-20-78-29-10 (office). *E-mail:* rleleu@on-lille.com (home). *Website:* www .onlille.com (home).

CASAPIETRA, Celestina; Italian singer (soprano); b. 23 Aug. 1938, Genoa; m. Herbort Kegel (died 1990). *Education:* Milan Conservatory with Gina Cigna. *Career:* debut at Teatro Nuovo, Milan 1961, in Mese Mariano by Giordano; sang in Genoa, San Remo, Pisa, Venice and Lyon; sang at Staatsoper Berlin from 1985, notably as Elsa, Constanze, Donna Anna, Agathe, Mimi, Micaela, Tatiana in Eugene Onegin and title role in Daphne by Strauss; Salzburg Mozartwochen 1984, as Vitellia in La Clemenza di Tito; Las Palmas 1986, as Elisabeth in Tannhäuser; guest engagements in London, Moscow, Helsinki, Copenhagen, Vienna and Prague; Zemlinsky's Der Kreidekreis, Hamburg 1983, Amsterdam 1989; season 1994 as Tosca at Genoa and Ariadne at Lyon. *Recordings include:* Fiordiligi in Così fan tutte, Mozart's Masses, Orff's Trionfi.

CASCIOLI, Gianluca; Italian pianist, conductor and composer; b. 17 July 1979, Turin. *Education:* Accad. Musicale in Imola, Verdi Conservatory, Turin. *Career:* many recital appearances throughout Italy specializing in classical and contemporary repertory 1994–; engagements with Orchestra della Scala, New York Philharmonic, Boston Symphony, Gustav Mahler Orchestra, Berliner Sinfonie-Orchestre, Orchestra Nazionale della RAI, Orchestra Sinfonica di Santa Cecilia, Camerata Salzburg, Royal Concertgebouw Orchestra Amsterdam, Vienna Philharmonic; has worked with numerous conductors including Claudio Abbado, Peter Rundel, Myung-Whun Chung, Daniele Gatti, Yuri Temirkanov, Riccardo Muti, Daniel Harding, Lorin Maazel, Valery Gergiev, Zubin Metha and Mstislav Rostropovich; concerts in Munich, Vienna, Berlin, Salzburg, Hanover, Frankfurt, Bremen, Hamburg, Paris, London, Barcelona, Lisbon, Athens, Chicago, Tokyo, Beijing. *Compositions include:* Variations for piano 2001, Quintetto per pianoforte e archi 2002, Sonatina per pianoforte 2004, In Memoriam Igor Stravinksy 2007. *Recordings include:* Boulez, Ligeti, Webern and Schoenberg 1996, Bach/Busoni, Beethoven, Debussy, De Falla, Liszt, Prokofiev, Scarlatti 1997, Beethoven variations for solo piano 1999, Schumann Phantasie for piano and orchestra 2002, Chopin 4 Scherzi 2005, Debussy Preludes 2006. *Honours:* First Prize, Umberto Micheli Int. Piano Competition, Milan 1994, named Star of the Year at Munich 1996. *Current Management:* c/o Ibercamera, Gran Via 636 1o 2a, 08007 Barcelona, Spain. *Telephone:* (93) 317-90-50. *E-mail:* ibercamera@ ibercamera.es. *Website:* www.ibercamera.es. *Current Management:* c/o Christoph Boller Artists Management, Magnolienstrasse 3, 8008 Zurich, Switzerland. *Telephone:* (43) 5373913. *Fax:* (44) 4226673. *E-mail:* pierig.escher@ cbamanagement.ch. *Website:* www.cbamanagement.ch. *E-mail:* g.cascioli@tin .it (office). *Website:* www.gianlucacascioli.com.

CASELLA, Elena, DipMus; Italian conductor; b. 28 Jan. 1966, Milan; one d. *Education:* Milano Conservatorio di Musica G. Verdi, masterclasses with Ervin Acél in Italy and Hungary, Julius Kalmar in Vienna, Gustav Kuhn in Italy and Myung-Whun Chung in Italy. *Career:* debut at Sala Verdi, Conservatorio in Milan with Orchestra Pomeriggi Musicali, Milan 1994; teacher of orchestral training, Hungary 1995; Asst to Gustav Kuhn 1994–97; numerous concerts with orchestras, including A. Toscanini (Parma), Pomeriggi Musicali (Milan), Szegend Symphony (Hungary), Novi Musici (Naples), Serenade Ensemble (Trieste); Asst to Ervin Acél in Wiener Musikseminar 1998–. *Compositions:* Eos I and II for solo guitar. *Honours:* Premio Internazionale Sebetia-ter for Music, Naples 1997.

CASHIAN, Philip John, DMus; British composer; b. 17 Jan. 1963, Manchester. *Education:* Univ. of Cardiff, Guildhall School of Music and Drama. *Career:* Northern Arts fellow-in-composition, Univ. of Durham 1993–96; Visiting Lecturer in Composition, Bath Spa Univ. 1997; composer-in-residence, Goldsmiths Coll., London 1999; Lecturer in Composition, Royal Acad. of Music, Royal Holloway; co-founder and Dir, Oxford Festival of Contemporary Music. *Compositions include:* String Quartet 1988, Nightmaze 1991, Dark Inventions 1992, Chamber Concerto 1995, A Sea of Tales 1998, Night Journeys 1998, The Devil's Box 1999, Music for the Night Sky 1999, Tableaux 2003, Caprichos 2003, Spitbite 2004, Three Pieces for chamber orchestra 2004, Piano Concerto 2006. *Recordings:* String Quartet No. 1 (Bingham Quartet, NMC), Music for the Night Sky (Schubert Ensemble, NMC), Dark Inventions (BCMG, Asbury, NMC). *Honours:* Britten Prize 1991. *Address:* Royal Academy of Music, Marylebone Road, London, NW1 5HT, England (office). *Telephone:* (20) 7873-7373 (office). *Website:* www.ram.ac.uk (office).

CASHMORE, John; British singer (baritone); b. 1960, Birmingham, England. *Education:* Birmingham School of Music and the National Opera Studio, London. *Career:* debut singing Guglielmo with Birmingham Music Theatre; opera engagements with English National Opera, Scottish Opera-Go-Round, Wexford Festival, Batignano and the New D'Oyly Carte Opera Company; Guglielmo for Opera Forum in Netherlands, 1991, Figaro in a British tour of Mozart's opera, Marullo in Rigoletto for ENO, 1992, and roles from 1992 at Aachen including Lortzing's Zar and Don Giovanni; Opera galas at the Albert Hall, Festival Hall and in Glasgow; Oratorio engagements include Carmina Burana in Birmingham and Glasgow, Monteverdi Vespers at Coventry Cathedral and Victory's Ultima Rerum in Dublin. *Current Management:* Rudolf W. Vanderhuck, Untere Donnerbergstraße 80, 52222 Stolberg, Germany. *Telephone:* (2402) 863020. *Fax:* (2402) 28136. *E-mail:* vanderhuck@t-online.de. *Website:* www.john-cashmore-entertainment.com.

CASKEL, Christoph; German percussionist; b. 12 Jan. 1932, Greifswald. *Education:* studied in Cologne. *Career:* many performances of modern music at Darmstadt and elsewhere, notably with the brothers Kontarsky in Bartók's Sonata for two pianos and percussion; collaborations with Stockhausen (premiere of Zyklus 1959, and Kontakte), Mauricio Kagel and keyboard player Franz-Peter Goebels; has performed with the Capella Coloniensis and given courses at Darmstadt and Cologne.

CASKEN, John Arthur, BMus, MA, DMus, FRNCM; British composer and academic; *Professor Emeritus of Music, University of Manchester*; b. 15 July 1949, Barnsley, Yorks., England; s. of Arthur Casken and Mary Casken; m. Jeanne Casken. *Education:* Univ. of Birmingham with Peter Dickinson and John Joubert, Warsaw Acad. of Music (Polish govt scholarship) with Andrzej Dobrowolski, consultations with Witold Lutosławski. *Career:* Lecturer, Univ. of Birmingham 1973–79; Research Fellow, Huddersfield Polytechnic 1979–81; Lecturer, Durham Univ. 1981–92; Prof. of Music, Univ. of Manchester 1992–2008, Prof. Emer. 2008–; featured composer, Bath Festival 1980, Musica Nova, Glasgow 1984, Huddersfield Contemporary Music Festival 1986, 1991, Southampton Int. New Music Week 1989, Almeida Festival 1989, 2001, Music Today, Tokyo 1990, St Petersburg 2002, Int. Organ Festival, St Albans 2009; BBC Proms performances 1986, 1989, 1992, 1995, 1998, 2001, 2004, 2009; Composer-in-Asscn with Northern Sinfonia 1990–2000; Artistic Dir Alwinton Church Summer Concerts; Music Dir Coquetdale Chamber Choir. *Compositions include:* orchestral: Tableaux des Trois Ages 1977, Orion Over Farne 1984, Maharal Dreaming 1989, Darting the Skiff for strings 1993, Sortilège 1996, Symphony (Broken Consort) 2004, Restringing for string quartet and orchestra 2005, Concerto for Orchestra 2007; concertos: Masque for oboe 1982, Erin for double bass 1983, Cello Concerto 1991, Violin Concerto 1995, Distant Variations concerto grosso for saxophone quartet and wind orchestra 1997, Après un silence for violin and small orchestra/large ensemble, orchestration of work for violin and piano 1998, That Subtle Knot, double concerto for violin, viola and orchestra 2013; ensemble: Music for the Crabbing Sun for four players 1974, Amarantos for nine players 1978, Firewhirl for soprano and seven players 1980, String Quartet No. 1 1982, Clarion Sea for brass quintet 1985, Vaganza for large ensemble 1985, Piano Quartet 1990, Infanta Marina for cor anglais and six players 1994, Blue Medusa in version for solo bassoon and ensemble 2007, Deadly Pleasures for narrator and ensemble 2009, Winter Reels for sextet 2011; chamber and instrumental: Thymehaze for treble recorder and piano 1976, Salamandra for two pianos 1986, String Quartet No. 2 1994, A Spring Cadenza for solo cello 1994, Après un silence for violin and piano 1998, The Haunting Bough for solo piano 1999, Nearly Distant for saxophone quartet 2000, Piano Trio 2002, Choses en moi for string quartet 2003, Blue Medusa for bassoon and piano 2003, Soul Catcher for marimba and electronic sounds 2004, Shadowed Pieces for violin and piano 2006, Sacrificium for organ 2009, Inevitable Rifts for string quintet 2009, Amethyst Deceiver for solo oboe 2008; vocal and choral: Ia Orana, Gauguin for soprano and piano 1978, To Fields We Do Not Know 1984, Three Choral Pieces 1990–93, Sharp Thorne for four solo male voices 1992, Still Mine for baritone and orchestra (Fondation Prince Pierre de Monaco Composition Prize 1993) 1992, To the lovers' well for four solo male voices 2001, Farness for soprano, solo viola and chamber orchestra 2006, Chansons de Verlaine for soprano and piano 2007, The Dream of the Rood (British Acad. of Composers Award for Best Vocal Composition 2009) 2009, The Knight's Stone for choir and solo flute 2011; opera: Golem (First Britten Award for Composition 1990, Gramophone Award for Best Contemporary Recording 1990) 1986–88, God's Liar (after

Tolstoy) 1995–2000. *Honours:* Hon. DMus (Birmingham) 2011; Hon. DCL (King's Coll., Halifax, NS) 2011; Northern Electric Performing Arts Award 1990, Rockefeller Foundation Award 1992. *Current Management:* c/o Schott Music Publishers, 48 Great Marlborough Street, London, W1F 2BB, England. *Telephone:* (20) 7534-0750. *E-mail:* promotions@schott-music.com. *Website:* www.schott-music.com; www.johncasken.com.

CASOLLA, Giovanna; Italian singer (soprano); b. 1944. *Education:* Conservatorio di San Pietro, Naples. *Career:* debut in Lisbon 1977, as Eboli in Don Carlos; sang at Turin 1978, 1982, Trieste 1979, Buenos Aires 1980, Detroit 1981; San Diego 1982, in the American premiere of Zandonai's Giulietta e Romeo; Metropolitan Opera 1984, as Zandonai's Francesca da Rimini, returned 1986, as Eboli; La Scala Milan 1983 and 1986, as Giorgetta in Il Tabarro; Verona Arena 1986 and 1988, as Maddalena in Andrea Chénier and La Gioconda; Caracalla Festival 1987, 1989, as Tosca; further guest appearances at Vienna and Miami 1988, Deutsche Oper Berlin 1989, Tosca, Stuttgart and Venice Eboli 1991; La Scala and Florence 1991, as Minnie in La Fanciulla del West and Santuzza; Puccini Festival, Torre del Lago 1991, as Giorgetta; other roles include Fedora, Amelia (Ballo in Maschera), Adriana Lecouvreur, Manon Lescaut, Silvana in Respighi's La Fiamma, Bartók's Judith, Maria in Tchaikovsky's Mazeppa and Elena Makropoulos; sang Santuzza at Florence 1996, and Gioconda 1998, Turandot at Barcelona 1999; season 2000 as Tosca at La Scala and Leonora (La Forza del Destino) at the Verona Arena; many concert appearances.

CASONI, Bianca-Maria; Italian singer (mezzo-soprano); b. 1 March 1932, Milan. *Education:* Milan Conservatory with Bruna Jona and Mercedes Llopart. *Career:* debut in Milan 1956, as Mercédès in Carmen; sang widely in Italy after winning La Scala Competition; Salzburg 1960, as Giacinta in La Finta Semplice, 1960; Glyndebourne 1965, as Cherubino; concert performance of Bellini's La Straniera, New York, 1969; appearances at Covent Garden and the Festivals of Aix and Edinburgh; Monte Carlo, Geneva, Barcelona, Philadelphia and the Metropolitan Opera; Turin 1975, in the Italian premiere of Die drei Pintos, Mahler/Weber; Berlin Staatsoper 1981, as Cinderella. *Recordings include:* Mozart's Coronation Mass; La Straniera; Preziosilla in La Forza del Destino.

CASSELLO, Kathleen; American singer (soprano); b. 1958, Wilmington, DE. *Education:* studied with Dan Pressley in Delaware, Wilma Lipp in Salzburg, Sesto Bruscantini in Italy. *Career:* European debut as Queen of Night in Hamburg, 1985; more than 200 Queen of Night performances since in Hamburg, 1986–88, Deutsche Oper and Staatsoper, Berlin, 1986–89, Moscow, 1987, Zürich, Geneva and Salzburg, 1988, Stuttgart, 1990; Staatstheater Karlsruhe Ensemble, 1987–89; Lucia in Karlsruhe, 1989–92, São Paulo, 1989, Marseille, San Sebastian and Zürich, 1990, Malaga, 1992, Treviso, Rome and Palermo, 1993; Traviata in Karlsruhe, 1987–92, Oviedo, 1991, Toulouse, 1992, Festival Orange and Rome, 1993, Tokyo, 1994, and Geneva, 1993; Elvira in Puritani at Marseille, 1991, Malaga, 1993; Gilda in Rigoletto at Marseille, 1992, Mexico City and Nice, 1993, La Scala with Riccardo Muti, 1994; Konstanze in Entführung in St Gallen, 1986–87, Vienna, 1988, Karlsruhe, 1989, Zürich, 1990, Munich National Theater, 1992, Avignon, 1993, Marseille and Hamburg, 1994–; Other roles include: Manon at the Met, 1990; Thaïs at Marseille, 1991; Pamina at Barcelona, 1991; Musetta at the Arena di Verona, 1992; Vitellia in La Clemenza di Tito in Toulouse, 1992, Athens, 1994; Amina in La Sonnambula at Messina, 1993; Elettra in Idomeneo at Venice, 1993; Giulietta in I Capuleti e i Montecchi at Parma, 1994; Amina at Rome, 1996; season 2000 as Constanze and Donna Anna at Dresden, Donizetti's Maria di Rohan at Aachen.

CASSIDY, Paul; British violist; b. 1959, Derry, Northern Ireland. *Education:* Royal Coll. of Music, UK, studied with Brian Hawkins and Orrea Pernel, Univ. of California, Los Angeles, USA, also studied in Detmold, Germany. *Career:* Founder-mem. Brodsky Quartet 1972–; residencies include Univ. of Cambridge four years, Dartington Int. Summer School, Devon; concert engagements include Shostakovich quartets at QEH, London, and performances at Ludwigsburg and Schleswig-Holstein Festivals; New York debut at Metropolitan Museum; further tours of Italy, North America, Australia, Poland, fmr Czechoslovakia and Japan; complete quartets of Schoenberg for BBC 1992; French concerts include visit to Théâtre du Châtelet, Paris. *Recordings include:* Quartets of Elgar and Delius; Schubert A minor and also Schubert D minor and Crumb, Black Angels; Beethoven Op 74; complete quartets of Shostakovich. *E-mail:* brodskyquartet@gmail.com. *Website:* www.brodskyquartet.co.uk.

CASSIS, Alessandro; Italian singer (baritone); b. 1949. *Career:* debut in Florence 1971, in Un Ballo in Maschera; sang in the Maggio Musicale, Florence 1974, La Fanciulla del West; Piccola Scala Milan in La Favola d'Orfeo by Casella; sang Germont at Turin 1977, Amonasro at the Verona Arena 1982; La Scala Milan 1983, as Michele in Il Tabarro, Sharpless in Butterfly 1985; returned to Verona 1986, 1988, as Gérard (Andrea Chénier) and Barnaba (La Gioconda); further appearances at Naples, Genoa, Geneva, Palermo, Trieste and Lisbon; baths of Caracalla, Rome 1991, as Amonasro; other roles include Carlo in La Forza del Destino and Verdi's Luna, Rigoletto and Renato; High Priest in Samson et Dalila; sang Nabucco at Brescia 1994 and Alfonso in La Favorita at Bergamo 1995. *Recordings include:* I Lutuani by Ponchielli, Nerone by Boito.

CASSUTO, Alvaro Leon, MA, PhD; Portuguese conductor and composer; b. 17 Nov. 1938, Oporto. *Education:* Univ. of Lisbon, Vienna Acad. of Music, studied with Arthur Santos, Lopes Graca, courses with Ligeti, Messiaen and Stockhausen in Darmstadt, studied with Karajan, Pedro de Freitas Branco in Lisbon, with Ferrara in Hilversum. *Career:* Asst Conductor, Gulbenkian Orchestra, Lisbon 1965–68, Little Orchestra, New York 1968–70; Perm. Conductor, Nat. Radio Orchestra, Lisbon 1970–75, Music Dir 1975–89; Lecturer, Univ. of California, Irvine 1974–75, Prof. in Music 1975–79; Conductor, Symphony Orchestra; Music Dir, Rhode Island Philharmonic Orchestra, Providence 1979–85, Nat. Orchestra Asscn, New York 1981–87, Nova Filarmonia Portuguesa 1988–93, Orquestra Sinfonica Portuguesa 1993, Israel Raanana Symphony Orchestra 2001–02, Orquestra do Algarve 2002–05, Orquestra Metropolitana de Lisboa 2005. *Compositions:* Sinfonia breve No. 1 1959, No. 2 1960, Variations 1961, Permutations for two orchestras 1962, Concertino for piano and orchestra 1965, Cro(mo-no)fonia for 20 strings 1967, Canticum in Tenebris for soloists, chorus and orchestra 1968, Evocations 1969, In the Name of Peace (opera) 1971, Circle 1971, To Love and Peace (symphonic poem) 1973, Homage to My People suite for band 1977, Return to the Future 1985, The Four Seasons for piano and orchestra 1986; chamber: String Sextet 1962, Song of Loneliness for 12 performers 1972. *Honours:* Koussevitzky Prize, Tanglewood, MA 1969. *Address:* Orquestra Metropolitana de Lisboa, Associação Música-Educação e Cultura, Travessa da Galé 36, 1349-028 Lisbon, Portugal. *Telephone:* (213) 617325. *Website:* www.oml.pt.

CASTELLUCCI, Romeo; Italian stage director and playwright; b. Cesena. *Career:* co-f. avant garde theatre co. Societas Raffaello Sanzio 1981; directed Biennale Teatro, Venice 2005; Assoc. Artistic Dir Festival d'Avignon 2008–; numerous works performed at festivals and theatres in Europe, USA, Australia, Japan including Amleto 1992, Tragedia Endogonidia 2002–04, Inferno/Purgatorio/Paradiso 2008, On the Concept of the Face, Regarding the Son of God (Barbican, London 2009), Persona 2011, The Four Seasons Restaurant 2012, Schwanengesang D744 2013, Natura e origine della mente 2013; operas directed include Parsifal at La Monnaie, Brussels 2011 and Bologna 2014, Orphée et Eurydice at La Monnaie, Brussels and Vienna 2014; other: Le Sacre du printemps: Choreography for 40 Machines to Music by Igor Stravinsky (Ruhrtriennale 2014). *Honours:* Chevalier, Ordre des Arts et des Lettres 2002. *Address:* c/o Societas Raffaello Sanzio, Via Serraglio 2, Cesena, Italy (office). *Website:* www.raffaellosanzio.org.

CASTLE, Joyce, BFA, MM; American singer (mezzo-soprano) and professor of voice; *Professor of Voice, University of Kansas;* b. 17 Jan. 1944, Beaumont, Tex. *Education:* Univ. of Kansas, Eastman School of Music, New York. *Career:* debut in San Francisco as Siebel in Faust 1970; debut, Metropolitan Opera 1985; performances in Die Fledermaus, Eugene Onegin, Puccini, Trittico, Wagner's Ring Cycle, Boris Godunov, Rosenkavalier 14 seasons; debut, New York City Opera 1983, Ballad of Baby Doe, Sweeney Todd, Rake's Progress, Casanova, The Visit of the Old Lady, Candide, etc. 25 seasons; regularly sang with Santa Fe Opera, Seattle Opera, Houston, Dallas, Washington, Montreal; cr. role of Nazimova in Argento's Valentino, Kennedy Center 1994; first performance of Bernstein's Arias and Barcarolles with Bernstein at the Piano; world premiere of Weisgall's Esther, New York 1993; Turin as Madame de la Haltière in Massenet's Cendrillon 1996; season 2000–01 as Orlovsky at Chicago, Herodias (Salomé) in Antwerp and Augusta Tabor in The Ballad of Baby Doe for New York City Opera; Vanessa, Conzertgebouw, Amsterdam; Vanessa, Radio Symphonieorchester, Vienna. *Recordings:* Candide, Old Lady, New York City Opera Recording (Grammy Winner, Sondheim Book of the Month Recording), Vocal Music of Stefan Wolpe, Vocal Music of Joseph Fennimore, Music of Jake Heggie. *Honours:* Distinguished Alumnus, Eastman School of Music, Distinguished Alumnus, Univ. of Kansas Theater. *Current Management:* c/o Janice Mayer, PO Box 515, New York, NY 10577-0515, USA. *E-mail:* jmayer@janicemayer.com. *Website:* www.janicemayer.com. *Address:* School of Music, University of Kansas, Room 420, Lawrence, KS 66045, USA (office). *Telephone:* (785) 864-9741 (office). *E-mail:* jcastle@ku.edu (office). *Website:* www.joycecastle.com.

CASTRO, Carlos José; Costa Rican composer; b. 25 Jan. 1963, San José. *Education:* Castella Conservatory and Univ. of Costa Rica. *Career:* mem., Contemporary Music Centre, San José 1985–; teacher of music, Nat. Univ. School of Dance. *Compositions include:* Gobierno de alcoba (comic opera after play by Samuel Rovinsky), Mambrú se fue a la guerra (after play by Mario Vargas Llosa) 1992, La chunga 1995, Concierto del Sol (Latin Grammy Award for Best Classical Contemporary Composition 2008). *Honours:* Aquileo J. Echevarría Nat. Music Prize. *Address:* c/o Universidad Nacional, Centro de Arte, Segundo Piso, Heredia, Costa Rica (office).

CASTRO-ALBERTY, Margarita; Puerto Rican singer (soprano); b. 18 Oct. 1947, San Sebastian. *Education:* Pablo Casals Conservatory, Accademia di Santa Cecilia, Italy, Juilliard School, USA. *Career:* debut in Santiago 1978, as Amelia in Un Ballo in Maschera; sang at Teatro Colón, Buenos Aires 1979–80; European debut 1980, in La Vida Breve by Falla; Carnegie Hall 1981, as Lucrezia in I Due Foscari; Metropolitan debut 1982, as Amelia; Festival d'Orange 1983, as Aida; guest engagements in Venice, Berlin, Vienna, Nancy, Rome and Toronto; other roles include Donna Anna, Amelia Grimaldi, Nedda, Butterfly, Lucrezia Borgia, Elisabeth de Valois and the Trovatore Leonora; sang at Marseille 1987.

CASTRONOVO, Charles; American singer (tenor); b. Queens, NY; m. Ekaterina Siurina; one s. *Education:* California State Univ., Fullerton. *Career:* resident artist, Los Angeles Opera 1997–99, with debut as First

Priest in Die Zauberflöte 1998, followed by nine other roles, including Baron Rouvel in Fedora, Rodolfo in La Bohème, Remendado in Carmen, Reverend Perris in The Crucible, and Don Basilio in Le nozze di Figaro; European debut in Rossini Stabat Mater, Cologne 1999; sang Tamino in Die Zauberflöte in San Francisco Opera Center's Merola Opera Program; joined Metropolitan Opera Linderman Young Artists Development Program, debut as Beppe in Pagliacci 1999; Don Ottavio in Don Giovanni for Boston Lyric Opera 2000; sang Camille in The Merry Widow for Los Angeles Opera 2001; Ferrando in Così fan tutte at Santa Fe 2003, ROH Covent Garden 2004; sang Germont in La Traviata at ROH, Nadir in The Pearl Fishers for San Francisco Opera 2005; Alfredo in La Traviata San Francisco Opera 2009, Philadelphia Opera 2010, Aix-en-Provence 2011, Staatsoper Vienna 2011–12; Ferrando in Cosi fan tutte, ROH 2010, 2012; other roles include Elvino in La Sonnambula, Ernesto in Don Pasquale, Nemorino in L'Elisir d'Amore, Vincent in Mireille, Mylio in Le Roi d'Ys, Belmonte in Die Entführung aus dem Serail, Tito in La Clemenza di Tito, Rinuccio in Gianni Schicchi, Gonzalve in L'heure espagnole, Pilade in Ermione, Tom Rakewell in The Rake's Progress, Fenton in Falstaff. *Recordings:* Beppe in I Pagliacci 2000, Rossini Stabat Mater (Opus 111) 2001, La Clemenza di Tito 2006. *Current Management:* Zemsky/Green Artists Management, 104 West 73rd Street, Suite 1, New York, NY 10023, USA. *Telephone:* (212) 579-6700. *Fax:* (212) 579-4723. *E-mail:* agreen@zemskygreen.com (office). *Website:* www.zemskygreen.com; www.charlescastronovo.com.

CASULA, Maria; Italian singer (soprano); b. 1939, Cagliari, Sardinia. *Education:* studied in Rome and Venice. *Career:* sang with I Virtuosi di Roma, in concert; Vienna Staasoper 1967, as Vitellia in La Clemenza di Tito; Glyndebourne 1969, Despina; Rome 1978, in the Italian premiere of The Beggar's Opera, arranged by Britten; Cagliari 1987, in Guillaume Tell. *Recordings include:* Il Barbiere di Siviglia, La Clemenza di Tito, Le nozze di Figaro, Leonora by Paer.

CATANI, Cesare; Italian singer (tenor); b. 1970, Ascoli. *Education:* Bergamo Conservatory. *Career:* debut as Kochkarev in The Marriage by Mussorgsky, St Petersburg; appearances in Moise et Pharaon at the Pesaro Rossini Festival, as Edoardo in Verdi's Un Giorno di regno at Parma and as Tebaldo in Bellini's I Capuleti e i Montecchi at Reggio Emilia; Wexford Festival 1997 as Ubaldo in Mercadante's Elena da Feltre; season 1998 as the Doge in Rossini's Otello at Pesaro and as Rodolfo in La Bohème in Tuscany; season 1999 sang Arrigo in Verdi's La battaglia di Legnano at Parma, Piacenza and Modena; Hindemith's Cardillac, as Il cavaliere, in Genoa; Alfredo in La Traviata in Macerata and Gabriele Adorno in Verdi's Simon Boccanegra in Tuscany; debut at La Scala, Milan as Chevalier de la force in Poulenc's Les dialogues des carmelites 2000; Alfredo in La Traviata, Fondazione Toscanini, Moscow 2003, Teatro Bellini, Catania 2003; Ismaele in Verdi's Nabucco, Verona 2005; concerts include Rossini's Petite Messe Solennelle, Salzburg, Rome, Barcelona; Mozart's Requiem, Turin. *Recordings include:* Rossini Petite Messe; Elena da Feltre. *Honours:* winner Angelica Catalani Int. Competition, Senigallia 1995, T. Marchetti Prize for Best Tenor, Busseto 1996. *Current Management:* Lirica International Opera Management, via Albere 19/A, 37138 Verona, Italy. *E-mail:* info@liricainternational.com.

CATHCART, Allen; American singer (tenor) and teacher; b. 2 Aug. 1938, Baltimore, Md. *Education:* Univ. of California, studied with Boris Goldovsky in New York. *Career:* debut at Metropolitan Opera Studio 1961, as Guglielmo in Così fan tutte; European engagements in Brussels, Rome, Zürich, Cologne, Stuttgart and Kiel; WNO in Cardiff; Paris Opéra-Comique, in The Stone Guest by Dargomyzhsky 1985; Paris Opéra as The Drum Major in Wozzeck; other roles include Don José, Florestan, Cavaradossi, the Emperor in Die Frau ohne Schatten, Laca in Jenůfa and parts in operas by Wagner; fmr Prof. of Voice, California State Univ., Sonoma; fmr Artistic Dir and Founder Peninsula Teen Opera; currently Dir South Valley Voice Studio (fmrly Peninsula Voice Studio); has served as judge for numerous vocal competitions, including Metropolitan Opera Nat. Council Auditions. *Recordings include:* Jason in Mayr's Medea in Corinto. *Address:* South Valley Voice Studio, Studio 12 Morgan Hill Downtown Mall, 17470 Monterey Road, Morgan Hill, CA 95037, USA. *E-mail:* southvalleyvoice@gmail.com. *Website:* www.southvalleyvoice.com.

CATLING, Ashley; British singer (tenor); b. 1975, England. *Education:* Guildhall School with William McAlpine, Nat. Opera Studio, London. *Career:* appearances in Friend of the People (premiere) by David Horne for Scottish Opera, Fenton and Ferrando for London Opera Players; Male Chorus in The Rape of Lucretia for The Other Theatre Company, Nemorino, and Steve Reich's video opera Three Tales on European and US tours; concerts include St Matthew Passion at Westminster Cathedral and Carissimi's Jepthé at St John's Smith Square; season 2001–02 as Ferrando and Fenton in Guernsey, and Rossini's Petite Messe; other roles include Sellem in The Rake's Progress and Simon in Birtwistle's The Last Supper. *Address:* 20 Coleshill Drive, Faringdon, Oxon, SN7 7FF, England.

CAUDLE, Mark; British bass violinist, bass violist and cellist; b. 1950, England. *Career:* mem. The Parley of Instruments; Frequent tours in the United Kingdom and abroad, including the British Early Music Network; Performances in Spain, France, Germany, Netherlands, Poland and Czechoslovakia; US debut in New York, 1988; Many concerts with first modern performances of early music in new editions by Peter Holman; Numerous broadcasts on Radio 3 and elsewhere; Repertoire includes Renaissance Violin

Consort Music (Christmas music by Michael Praetorius and Peter Philips, music for Prince Charles I by Orlando Gibbons and Thomas Lupo); Baroque Consort Music by Monteverdi, Matthew Locke (anthems, motets and ceremonial music), Purcell (ayres for theatre), Georg Muffat (Armonico Tributo sonatas, 1682), Heinrich Biber (Sonate tam aris, quam aulis servientes, 1676), Vivaldi (sonatas and concertos for lute and mandolin, concertos for recorders) and J. S. Bach (Hunt cantata No. 208), with Crispian Steele-Perkins, trumpet, and Emma Kirkby, soprano, among others. *Current Management:* The Parley of Instruments, Louise Jameson, 22 Michael Road, London, E11 3DY, England. *Telephone:* (20) 8558-3449. *Fax:* (20) 8926-9188. *E-mail:* louise@earlymusicagency.com. *Website:* www.parley.org.uk.

CAUSSÉ, Gérard; French violist; b. 26 June 1948, Toulouse. *Education:* studied in Toulouse and at the Paris Conservatoire. *Career:* violist, Via Nova Quartet 1989–71, Parrenin Quartet 1972–80; founding mem. and soloist, Ensemble Intercontemporain 1976–; chamber musician from 1982, notably with the Ivaldi Quartet; Artistic Dir, Toulouse Nat. Chamber Orchestra 2002–04, as conductor and soloist; concerto performances with Radio France's Orchestre Nat., Orchestre de la Suisse Romande, Lille Nat. Orchestra (Casadesus), Montpellier Philharmonic (Levi), Malaysia Philharmonic (Baakels), Luxembourg PO (Krivine) and Sao Paulo SO; plays a Gasparo da Salo instrument (1560); Prof., Boulogne Conservatoire 1980, Lyon 1982, Paris 1987–; masterclasses at Mozarteum Salzburg, Queen Sofia Coll., Madrid, Music Acad. of Villecroze and Verbier Festival. *Recordings:* Fauré: Complete Chamber Music for Strings and Piano (ECHO Klassik Award for Chamber Music Recording of the Year/Mixed Ensemble – 19th Century 2012) 2011.

CAUSTON, Richard, BA, MA, ARCM (PG); British composer; b. 12 March 1971, Whitechapel, London, England; m. Jessica Summers 2005; one d. one s. *Education:* Inner London Educ. Authority Centre for Young Musicians, London, Univ. of York, Royal Coll. of Music, London, Civica Scuola di Musica, Milan, Italy. *Career:* music performed by BBC Symphony Orchestra, City of Birmingham Symphony Orchestra, Philharmonia Orchestra, Orchestra of the Age of Enlightenment, Sinfonieorchester Basel, Rundfunk-Sinfonieorchester Saarbrücken, London Sinfonietta, European Union Youth Orchestra, Nash Ensemble, Birmingham Contemporary Music Group and Evelyn Glennie; f. Royal Coll. of Music Gamelan programme; Fellow Commoner in the Creative Arts, Trinity Coll., Cambridge 2003–05; Prof. of Composition, Birmingham Conservatoire 2006–12; Lecturer in Composition, Univ. of Cambridge and Fellow, King's Coll., Cambridge 2012–15, Reader in Composition 2015–; corresp. for Italian Radio (RAI). *Compositions include:* Threnody 1991, Non mi comporto male for piano 1993, The Persistence of Memory for chamber ensemble 1995, Two pieces for clarinet duet 1995, Notturno for chamber ensemble 1998, revised 2001, Millennium Scenes for large orchestra 1998, revised 2001, Concerto for Solo Percussion and Gamelan 2001, Seven States of Rain for violin and piano (British Composer Award for Best Solo/Duo 2004) 2002, Between Two Waves of the Sea for orchestra with sampler 2004, Poems Almost of This World for solo soprano 2005, Jesu, Sweetė Sonė Dear, for unaccompanied choir 2006, Sarabande/The Way the World Ends 2006, Phoenix for quintet (Royal Philharmonic Soc. Award for Chamber-Scale Composition) 2006, Sleep for solo flute 2006, La Terra Impareggiabile song cycle for baritone and piano 2007, As Kingfishers Catch Fire 2007, Chorales for gamelan 2008, Chamber Symphony 2009 (revised 2010), Nocturne for 21 Pianos 2010, Dark Processional 2010, Twenty-Seven Heavens 2012, Out of Your Sleep 2012, Ricercare 2012, De Profundis 2014. *Recordings include:* Two Pieces for two clarinets, Seven States of Rain, Phoenix, Sleep, Cradle Song, English Encouragement of Art, Millennium Scenes, Notturno, The Persistence of Memory, Chamber Symphony, As Kingfishers Catch Fire. *Publications include:* contrib. to Tempo: Berio's Visage and the Theatre of Electroacoustic Music; trans. of Pestalozza's interview with Niccolò Castiglioni; contrib. to The Guardian: Music of the Spheres, article on Concerto for solo percussion and gamelan, The God of Small Things, article on Jeremy Dale Roberts 2004. *Honours:* Fast Forward Composition Prize 1995, First Prize, Third Int. 'Nuove Sincronie' Composition Competition 1996, Mendelssohn Scholarship 1997, SPNM George Butterworth Award 1997, Hon. Mention in Large-Scale Composition category, Royal Philharmonic Soc. Awards 2000, British Composer Award 2004, Winner, Chamber-Scale Composition category, Royal Philharmonic Soc. Awards 2006, International Record Review: Outstanding award 2014. *Address:* c/o Oxford University Press, Repertoire Promotion Department, Great Clarendon Street, Oxford, OX2 6DP, England. *Telephone:* (1865) 355020. *Fax:* (1865) 355060. *E-mail:* repertoire.promotion.uk@oup.com. *Website:* www.global.oup.com.

CAVA, Carlo; Italian singer (bass); b. 16 Aug. 1928, Ascoli Piceno. *Education:* studied in Rome. *Career:* debut at Spoleto 1955, in L'Italiana in Algeri; Netherlands Opera, Amsterdam 1959; Glyndebourne 1961–65, as Seneca in L'Incoronazione di Poppea, as Sarastro, Bartolo in Le nozze di Figaro, Basilio in Il Barbiere di Siviglia and Henry VIII in Anna Bolena; La Scala 1973, as Boris Godunov; appearances in Cairo, Amsterdam, Brussels, Frankfurt, Vienna, Munich, Berlin and Paris. *Recordings include:* Oroveso in Norma, Zaccaria in Nabucco, L'Incoronazione di Poppea, Il Barbiere di Siviglia, Linda di Chamounix.

CAVALLIER, Nicolas; French singer (bass); b. 1964. *Education:* Royal Acad. of Music and Nat. Opera Studio, with Elisabeth Söderström and with Iris dell'Acqua. *Career:* debut, Nancy Opera, 1987, as Cascanda in The Merry Widow; sang Achilles in Giulio Cesare conducted by Trevor Pinnock at RAM; sang Don Fernando (Fidelio) for Glyndebourne Tour 1990, Zuniga for Welsh National Opera and in Alcione by Marais for Les Arts Florissants in Paris; other roles include Don Giovanni, Narbal in Les Troyens, Don Quichotte, Sparafucile and Mozart's Bartolo and Osmin; sang Félix in Donizetti's Les Martyrs at Nancy 1996; sang Lord Sidney in Il Viaggio a Reims at Liège 2000; concert repertoire includes Verdi and Mozart Requiems, A Child of Our Time, Monteverdi Vespers and Die Schöpfung; regular appearances with Seattle Opera. *Honours:* Anne Lloyd Exhibition, Helen Eames Prize, Paton Award, Ricordi Award, RAM . *Current Management:* Agence Artistique Thérèse Cédelle, boulevard Malesherbes 78, 75008 Paris, France. *Telephone:* 1-49-53-00-02. *Fax:* 1-45-63-70-23. *E-mail:* Agence.Cedelle@wanadoo.fr.

CAVE, Penelope, ARAM, GRSM, LRAM, PhD; English harpsichordist, early pianist and musicologist; b. 17 April 1951, Guildford, Surrey; m. Michael Heale 1974; one s. one d. *Education:* Purcell School, Royal Acad. of Music, London, lessons and masterclasses with Kenneth Gilbert, Colin Tilney, Ton Koopman and Gustav Leonhardt, postgraduate studies at Univ. of Southampton. *Career:* debut, Wigmore Hall 1980; solo recitals throughout Europe; live performances for BBC Radio 3, Belgian Radio and Classic FM; regular tutor of harpsichord and chamber music courses, masterclasses and workshops in England and abroad; performing and advisory work with National Trust; presentations, conference papers and articles; mem. Inc. Soc. of Musicians. *Recordings include:* with the Camerata of London, Garth Hewitt and the Feinstein Ensemble, From Lisbon to Madrid (solo CD). *Publications include:* contrib. to Harpsichord Fortepiano magazine, Music Teacher, The Consort, Early Music. *Honours:* Raymond Russell Prize, Winner Nat. Harpsichord Competition, Southport 1970s, Bruges Int. Harpsichord Competition 1983. *Address:* Fridays Hill Cottage, Copyhold Lane, Fernhurst, Haslemere, Surrey, GU27 3DZ, England. *Telephone:* (1483) 652287. *E-mail:* penelope@penelopecave.co.uk. *Website:* www.impulse-music.co.uk/cave.htm.

CAVINA, Claudio; Italian singer (countertenor); *Artistic Director, La Venexiana. Education:* Schola Cantorum Basiliensis with Kurt Widmer, studied with Candace Smith, Cristina Miatello. *Career:* founder La Venexiana vocal ensemble 1995–, serves as Artistic Dir; the ensemble has performed at MusikVerein Golden Hall, Vienna, De Singel, Antwerp, Brugge Festival, Howard Mayer Brown Int. Early Music Series, Chicago, and in Barcelona, Brussels, Utrecht, Strasbourg, Amiens, San Sebastián, Mexico City, Tokyo, New York, Bogotà, San Francisco, Tucson, San Diego, Seattle; solo appearances include La Fenice, Venice, La Scala, Milan, Verona Arena, Concertgebouw, Amsterdam; collaborations with vocal ensembles, including Huelgas Ensemble, La Colombina, Al Ayre Espanol, Clemencic Consort, Elyma Ensemble; gives masterclasses at Belluno Int. Course, Italy, Tsuru Early Music Course, Japan. *Recordings:* Scarlatti, Cantatas and Duets 1994, Marcello, La Stravaganza – Arias & Duets 1999, Aliotti, Il Sansone 2002, De Vitae Fugacitate 2002; with La Venexiana: Sigismondo d'India, Il Terzo Libro de Madrigali 1997, Claudio Monteverdi, Settimo Libro dei Madrigali 1998, Luzzasco Luzzaschi, Quinto Libro de' Madrigali 1999, Luca Marenzio, Il Nono Libro de Madrigali 1999, Sigismondo d'India, Libro Primo de Madrigali 2000, Gesualdo da Venosa, Il Quarto Libro di Madrigali 2001, Marenzio, Il Sesto Libro de Madrigali 2001, Monteverdi, Il Terzo Libro di Madrigali 2001, Giaches de Wert, La Gerusalemme Liberata 2002, Monteverdi, Il Secondo Libro dei Madrigali 2004, Monteverdi Il Sesto Libro dei Madrigali 2005, Monteverdi Ottavo Libro dei Madrigali 2006, Monteverdi L'Orfeo (Gramophone Award for Best Baroque Vocal Recording 2008) 2007, Monteverdi Il Quinto Libro dei Madrigali (Midem Classical Award for Early Music Recording 2009) 2008. *Honours:* with La Venexiana: Premio Cini 1999, Prix Cecilia 1999, Gramophone Award 2000, Cannes Classical Award 2001, Grand Prix du Disque 2004. *Address:* La Venexiana, Viale del Lavoro 56, 47101 Terra del Sole, Italy (office). *Telephone:* (32) 86097309 (office). *Fax:* (32) 86097309 (office). *E-mail:* info@lavenexiana.net (office). *Website:* www.lavenexiana.net (office).

CAZURRA, Anna; Spanish composer and musicologist; b. 1940, Barcelona; m.; one s. one d. *Education:* Barcelona Conservatoire with Josep Soler, Universitat Autonoma de Barcelona. *Career:* Researcher, Universitat Autonoma, Barcelona; Researcher, Centre for 18th-Century Musical Studies, Univ. of Wales, Cardiff; Researcher, Universitat Pompeu Fabra, Barcelona; collaborations with musical asscns and groups. *Compositions:* Poema for brass quintet, Cuatro Evoluciones for piano, Postales de Viaje for piano, string quartets, El Grito for soprano, flute, guitar and cello, Trio for violin, cello and piano, Psalmos for soprano and orchestra. *Publications:* Introducción a la Historia de la Música 1999, Les Obertures de Josep Doran 1995, contrib. articles to New Grove Dictionary, Diccionario de la Música Española, Encyclopedia Catalana de la Música.

CECCARINI, Giancarlo; Italian singer (baritone); b. 19 July 1951, Pisa. *Education:* studied in Pisa and Rome. *Career:* debut at Spoleto 1975, as Belcore in L'Elisir d'amore; appeared widely in Italy as Marcello (La Bohème), Cimarosa's Maestro di Capella and Osmano in L'Ormindo by Cavalli (Venice 1976); performances of Monteverdi's Combattimento at Terni, Bologna, Zürich, Mantua, Cremona and Frankfurt 1980; La Gazetta by Rossini; at Genoa ssng Podestà in Docteur Miracle by Bizet, and Gianni Schicchi; San Remo 1982, as Nabucco; Ping in Turandot at Helsinki 1991. *Recordings include:* I Pazzi per Progresso by Donizetti, Turandot.

CECCATO, Aldo; Italian conductor and music director; b. 18 Feb. 1934, Milan; m. Eliana de Sabata; two s. *Education:* Milan Conservatory, Hochschule für Musik Berlin. *Career:* Musical Dir Detroit Symphony

Orchestra 1973–77, Hamburg Philharmonic 1974–82; Chief Conductor Hannover Radio Orchestra 1985, Bergen Symphony 1985–90, Orquesta Nacional de España 1991–94, Brno Philharmonic Orchestra 1995–2002, now Dir Emer.; Musical Dir I Pomeriggi Musicali orchestra 1999–2004, now Dir Emer. *Honours:* Cavaliere di Gran Croce; Hon. DMus (Eastern Michigan Univ.); Brahms Medal, Senate of Hamburg, Gold Medal, Milan City Council, Mozart Prize, Mozarteum Argentino. *E-mail:* info@aldoceccato.com; maestro.aldo.ceccato@gmail.com. *Website:* www.aldoceccato.it.

CECCHELE, Gianfranco; Italian singer (tenor); b. 25 June 1940, Galliera Veneta. *Education:* studied with Marcello del Monaco in Treviso. *Career:* sang at Catania from 1964; many appearances on the Italian stage; guest appearances in London, Paris, Barcelona, Hamburg, Munich, Nice, Chicago, Philadelphia and Montréal; Carnegie Hall, New York 1968, as Zamoro in a concert performance of Verdi's Alzira; best known in operas by Puccini and Verdi; Verona 1967–84; Rio de Janeiro 1988, as Radames; Mercadante's La Vestale at Split 1987; season 1993–94 as Walter in Catalani's Loreley (Teatro Filarmonico) and Calaf at Viterbo. *Recordings include:* Aroldo by Verdi; Loreley by Catalani; Alzira; Title role in Rienzi by Wagner; Decio in Mercadante's La Vestale, Bongiovanni.

CECCHI, Gabriella; Italian composer; b. 3 Nov. 1944, Ricco del Golfo, La Spezia. *Education:* Lucca Inst., Genoa Conservatory, studied in Siena with Franco Donatoni and in Sargiano-Arezzo with Brian Ferneyhough. *Career:* performances of her music throughout Italy and elsewhere in Europe. *Compositions include:* Kite for chamber orchestra 1981, In proiezione for orchestra 1986, Riverberi for violin and harpsichord 1988, Parvula for ten flutes 1990, Il gallo rosso (small chamber opera) 1992, Doppel atmung for four recorders and percussion 1993, Grig Bian Ner (ballet) for piano, saxophone and percussion 1994, Joueurs for flute, clarinet, violin, cello, saxophone and double bass 1995, ...In un Mare... for soprano, clarinet and piano 1996.

CEELY, Robert Paige, BMus, MA; American composer; b. 17 Jan. 1930, Torrington, Conn.; m. Jonatha Kropp 1962. *Education:* New England Conservatory, Boston, Mills Coll., Calif., Princeton Univ., NJ, studied with Darius Milhaud, Leon Kirchner, Roger Sessions and Milton Babbitt. *Career:* Dir of Electronic Music, Faculty of Composition at New England Conservatory of Music, Boston 1967, now retd. *Compositions:* String Trio 1953, Woodwind Quintet 1954, Composition for 10 instruments 1963, Stratti for magnetic tape 1963, Elegia for magnetic tape 1964, Vonce for magnetic tape 1967, Modules for 7 instruments 1968, Logs for 2 double basses 1968, Hymn for cello and bass 1969, Beyond the Ghost Spectrum (ballet) 1969, Mitsyn for computer-generated tape 1971, Slide Music for 4 trombones 1974, Rituals for 40 flutes 1978, Frames for computer-generated tape 1978, Lullaby for trombone and soprano 1979, Flee, Floret, Florens for 15 solo voices 1979, Piano Piece 1980, Bottom Dogs for 4 double basses 1981, Roundels for large wind ensemble and tape 1981, Piano Variations 1982, Totems for oboe and tape 1982, Dialogue for solo flute 1983, Giostra for oboe and tape 1984, Minute Rag for solo piano 1985, Pitch Dark for jazz ensemble 1985, Synoecy for clarinet and tape 1986, Timeshares for percussion ensemble 1988, Special K Variations for piano 1989, Post hoc, ergo propter hoc for solo bass clarinet 1989, Harlequin for solo double bass and tape 1990, Hypallage for solo trumpet and tape 1990, Asyndeton for piano and tape 1993, Opera from Fernando Arrabal's The Automobile Graveyard 1994, Group Sax for five saxophones 1996, Music for Ten 1996, Enchanted Cycles for computer-generated tape 1996, Auros for five instruments 1997, Wieman's treibt for bass clarinet and tape 1997, Gymel for two oboes 1998, Triple Double for oboe, English horn, bassoon and tape 1998, Mutual Implications for tape 1999, Extensions for solo piano 2000, Five Contemplative Pieces for chorus 2000, Canons for alto flute, clarinet and bassoon 2001, Seven études for piano 2002, Three Satires for orchestra 2002, Carol for mixed chorus and solo trumpet 2003, Three Songs for baritone and piano 2003, Two pieces for string quartet 2004, Whitman (5 songs for soprano and piano) 2005, Metamir for alto flute, bass clarinet, viola and piano 2007, Trio for French horn, flugelhorn and trombone 2008, Negatives for solo piano 2009, Ontology for magnetic tape 2010. *Publications:* A Composer's View of MITSYN 1971, A Composer's Letter to Perspectives of New Music 1972, Electronic Music Resource Book 1979, Compositional Limitation of Current Electronic Music Synthesizers 1980, The Stairs of Sand (fictional autobiog.) 2009. *Honours:* Harvard Univ. Project Zero Lectureship 1971, Northeastern Univ. Artist in Residence 1976; Hobart Coll. Sesquicentennial Award 1972, Cine Golden Eagle Awards for film sound for Incendio and Bleve 1977, Massachusetts Council Grant 1979, Nat. Endowment for the Arts Grant 1986, Brookline Council for the Arts Grant 1986, Margaret Fairbank Jory Grant 1994. *Address:* 33 Elm Street, Brookline, MA, USA (home). *Telephone:* (617) 731-3785 (home). *E-mail:* ceelyinfo@ceelymusic.com (home). *Website:* www.ceelymusic.com (home).

CEGOLEA, Gabriela; Romanian singer (soprano); b. 1950, Northern Moldavia. *Education:* studied in Bucharest, Benedetto Marcello Conservatory, Venice and School of the Royal Opera, Stockholm. *Career:* sang at Taormina Festival; debut in Stockholm 1977, as Tosca; appearances as Tosca at Oslo and as Manon at Venice; La Scala, Milan; further engagements in New York, Berlin, Stuttgart, San Francisco, Naples and Rome; tours of Australia, Brazil and South Korea; Liège 1989, as Maddalena in Andrea Chénier. *Honours:* won several voice competitions including Christine Nilson and Jussi Bjorling Voice Competition, Stockholm and competitions in Lonigo, Peschiera del Garda and Parma, Italy.

CELLI, Joseph, BME, MM; American composer and oboist; b. 19 March 1944, Bridgeport, CT. *Education:* Hartt College of Music, Hartford, CT, Northwestern University, Chicago, Oberlin Conservatory, OH, studied with Ray Still (Chicago Symphony), Albert Goltzer (New York Philharmonic), Wayne Rapier (Boston Symphony Orchestra), John Mack (Cleveland Symphony Orchestra), Fulbright Scholar, Korean Traditional Performing Arts Center, Seoul, Republic of Korea. *Career:* composer, videomaker, performer throughout Europe, Asia, North and South America, 1972–; gave US premieres of Stockhausen's Spiral and Solo for oboe; Exec. Dir, Real Art Ways (contemporary arts center), Hartford, CT 1975–86; CEO/Exec. Dir, New Music America Miami Festival, Florida, 1987–89; Dir of Cultural Programs, Miami-Dade Community College, Miami, FL 1989–90; Dir, OO DISCS Inc. recording company (contemporary American music), 1991–; founder/Dir, Korean Performing Arts Institute, New York/Seoul 1993–; Exec. Dir, founder, Int. Performing Arts; founder, multicultural Black Rock Art Center. *Compositions include:* World Soundprint: Asia for radio (with Jin Hi Kim), 1993; Pink Pelvis: Music for Dance for double reeds, Korean ajeng and Brazilian percussion, 1994; Sunny's piece: Music For Dance with double reeds, Komungo, percussion, 1994; Quintet: for Kayagum, Wx-7 and three kalimba, 1995. *Address:* Black Rock Art Center, 2838 Fairfield Avenue, Bridgeport, CT 06605 (office); 261 Groovers Avenue, Black Rock, CT 06605-3452, USA (home). *Telephone:* (203) 367-7917 (office); (203) 367-9061 (home). *Fax:* (203) 333-0603 (office). *E-mail:* oodiscs@connix.com (office). *Website:* www.internationalperformingarts.com (office).

CEMORE, Alan, BM, MMus; American singer (baritone); b. 1958, Wisconsin; m. Dr Ursula Baumgartner; one s. one d. *Education:* Univ. of Northern Iowa, Indiana Univ., Hochschule für Musik, Frankfurt, Germany, Ogelbay Inst. with Boris Goldovsky, studied voice with Margaret Harshaw and David Smalley. *Career:* leading baritone at the Wiesbaden Opera 1986–88, Basel Opera 1988–90, Graz Opera 1990–97, Bremen Theatre 1998–2002, Schleswig-Holsteinisches Landestheater 2006–11; festivals: Spoleto Festival in Die lustige Witwe 1984, in La Fanciulla del West 1985, Tom in Henze's English Cat at Frankfurt 1986, at Turin and at Edinburgh Festival 1987, as Biagio in Gazzaniga's Don Giovanni and Pantalone in Busoni's Turandot, Wexford Festival 1988, Perth Festival, Australia as Wolfram in Tannhäuser 1999; radio and TV appearances in Europe, Asia and USA; more than 70 leading opera roles in USA and Europe; oratorio soloist in works from Bach to Vaughan Williams; Assoc. Instructor of Voice, Indiana Univ. School of Music 1984–85; mem. Rotary International. *Radio:* ABC, Classic FM Australia, ARD German Radio, Danmarks Radio, DRS Swiss Radio, Hessischer Rundfunk, Nat. Public Radio, USA, N2 Norwegian Radio, ORF Austrian Broadcasting, Radio Bremen, WDR German Radio. *Television:* ARD German TV, CETV Hong Kong, DCTV Washington, Hessischer Rundfunk TV, National Public TV USA, Nat. Video Corpn of Great Britain, NBC Super Channel, ORF Austrian Broadcasting, RAI Italian TV, RTE Irish TV, WDR German TV, WNYC TV 31 New York, WTBS Super Station. *Recordings include:* Die grossmuetige Tomyris by Keiser; Oh wie verfuehrerisch, operatic selections; Happy Birthday George Gershwin!. *Honours:* First Prize, Nat. Asscn of Teachers of Singing Cen. Region Auditions 1977, First Prize, Nat. Fed. of Music Clubs Midwest Dist 1981, Prizewinner, ARD Int. Music Competition, Munich 1984, Rotary International Grad. Fellowship 1981, Cole Porter Memorial Fellowship, Indiana Univ. School of Music 1984, Purple and Old Gold Award for Conspicuous Achievement in Music, Univ. of Northern Iowa. *Current Management:* c/o Music International, 13 Ardilaun Road, Highbury, London, N5 2QR, England. *Telephone:* (20) 7359-5183. *Fax:* (20) 7226-9792. *E-mail:* music@musicint.co.uk. *Website:* www.musicint.co.uk. *E-mail:* alan@cemore.com (home). *Website:* www.cemore.com (home).

CEPICKY, Leos; Czech musician; b. 21 Aug. 1965, Pardubice; m. Katerina Kus 1985, one s. one d. *Education:* Prague Acad. of Arts. *Career:* debut in Prague Spring Quartet Competition 1988; mem., Wihan Quartet, attending music festivals in England, Austria, Germany, France, Italy, Belgium, Spain, Portugal, Singapore, USA, Japan 1985–. *Recordings:* over 25 recordings including Haydn op 64, op 71, Mozart K168, K458, K465, Dvořák Smetana 1, Janáček 1 and 2, Ravel and Britten 2, Beethoven op 59 1, 2, 3, op 14, Dvořák op 51 and op 106, Beethoven: The Late Quartets. *Publications:* contrib. to The Strad. *Honours:* winner, Prague Spring Competition 1988, London Int. String Quartet Competition 1991. *Current Management:* c/o Maureen Phillips, Upbeat Classical Management, PO Box 479, Uxbridge, Middlesex, UB8 2ZH, England. *Telephone:* (1895) 259441. *E-mail:* enquiry@upbeatclassical.co.uk. *Website:* www.upbeatclassical.co.uk. *E-mail:* wihan@wihanquartet.com (office). *Website:* www.wihanquartet.com.

CERAR, Maja, DipMus, MMus, MFA, PhD; Swiss violinist and academic; b. 27 May 1972, Zürich. *Education:* Zürich-Wintertur Conservatory, studied under Aida Stucki-Piraccini, also master-classes with master classes with Zakhar Bron, Franco Gulli, Igor Oistrakh, and Igor Ozim, studied with Dorothy DeLay and Kurt Nikkanen in New York, Columbia Univ., USA. *Career:* debut playing Mozart Violin Concerto K 218 with Symphony Orchestra of Zürich, Zürich Tonhalle 1991; soloist with numerous conductors and orchestras throughout Europe; collaboration with composers such as G. Kurtag and B. Furrer; numerous premieres of contemporary music, USA, Europe; classical recital tours, Europe and USA, including Dame Myra Hess Memorial Concert Series, Chicago; has taught at Rutgers Univ., Fordham Univ.; currently Adjunct Asst Prof., Columbia Univ.; has given violin master-classes and coached chamber music in Skofja Loka, Slovenia; fmr mem. Editorial Bd

Current Musicology journal. *Recordings include:* Recollections, Sonata by U. Krek 1996, Sonatas by Beethoven, Schubert, Brahms, (with pianist Gérard Wyss) 1997, Violin Concerto by Samuel Barber 2000. *Honours:* supported by Swiss Study Foundation for Outstanding University Students 1992, Migros Foundation study grant 1995–97, Fellowship, Columbia Univ. 1999. *Address:* 820 Riverside Drive, #3G, New York, NY 10032, USA. *E-mail:* maja@music .columbia.edu. *Website:* www.majacerar.com.

CERHA, Friedrich, DPhil; Austrian composer; b. 17 Feb. 1926, Vienna. *Education:* Vienna Acad. with Vasa Prihoda and Alfred Uhl, Vienna Univ. *Career:* with Kurt Schwertsik co-founded ensemble, Die Reihe 1958, with performances of contemporary music and works by the Second Viennese School; completion of Act III of Alban Berg's Lulu performed at the Paris Opéra 1979; Opera Baal premiered at the 1981 Salzburg Festival; Der Rattenfänger at Graz 1987; British premiere of Cello Concerto at 1999 Prom concerts, London. *Compositions:* Espressioni fondamentali for orchestra 1957, Relazioni fragili for harpsichord and chamber orchestra 1956–57, Fasce for orchestra 1959, Spiegel I–VII 1960–61, Netzwerk (musical theatre) 1962–80, Exercises for baritone and chamber ensemble 1962–67, Langegger Nachtmusik I and II for orchestra 1969, 1970, III 1991, Double Concerto for violin, cello and orchestra 1975, Baal-Gesänge for baritone and orchestra 1981, Keintate I for voice and 11 instruments 1981–83, II for voice and 11 instruments 1984–85, Requiem für Hollensteiner for baritone, choir and orchestra 1982–83, Eine Art Chansons for voice and three instruments 1985–86, Phantasiestück for cello and orchestra 1989, String-Quartet I 1989, II 1990, III 1992, Impulse for orchestra 1992–93, Concerto for viola and orchestra 1993, Concertino for violin, accordion and ensemble 1994, Requiem for choir and orchestra 1994–2003, Saxophon-Quartett 1995, Acht Sätze nach Hölderlin-Fragmenten für streichsextett 1995, Jahr lang ins Ungewisse hinab für ensemble 1995–96, Concerto for cello and orchestra 1996–97, Lichtenberg-Splitter for baritone and ensemble 1997, Der Riese vom Steinfeld (opera, libretto by Peter Turrini) 1999, Im Namen der Liebe for baritone and orchestra 2000, Hymnus for orchestra 2000–01. *Honours:* Ernst von Siemens Music Foundation Music Prize 2012. *Address:* Kupelwiesergasse 14, 1130 Vienna, Austria.

CERMÁKOVÁ, Vera; Czech composer, pianist and music teacher; b. 17 March 1961, Prague; m. Josef Cermak 1984; one s. *Education:* Prague Conservatoire, studied with Alena Polakova, Oldrich Semerak. *Career:* teaches piano and composition at music school in Kladno; interpretation of piano compositions; performs at festivals of classical and contemporary music; mem. Asscn of Composers, Prague, Atelier 90, Music Studio N. *Compositions include:* Prelude and Rhythmic Fantasia, Piano Solo 1992, Fantasia (piano solo) 1993, Free cycle for 3 String Quartets The Play of Lights 1993, Fragments Nos 1–4 for Symphonic Orchestra 1993, Seven Preludes for Guitar Solo 1994, Ostinato, Melodic No. 2 (piano solo) 1995, Kaleidoskop (piano solo) 1996, Three Bagatelles for Saxophone Quartet 1996, Metamorphosis for Violoncello and Piano 1997, Seclusion of clarinet solo 1997, Reliefs for chamber orchestra 1999, String Quartet No. 4 2000, Genesis for saxophone quartet 2000, Reflections and Meditations for soprano, tenor and chamber orchestra 2001, Solo for soprano saxophone 2002, Solo for alto saxophone 2002, Solo for tenor saxophone 2002, Solo for baritone saxophone 2002, The Spectrum for string orchestra 2004, Sonnets of soprano and piano: A Melancholy Song, These Days 2005, The Year for soprano and flute, Dialogue for soprano and baritone saxophone 2006, Sonnets for soprano and piano: The Song Within, A Winter's Rose 2007, Solo for Hardingfele 2008, Psalms Songs Nos. 1–3 for Hardingfele, Pastorale, The Motion, Lamento, The Unfinished Sound for saxophone quartet, Psalms Nos. 23, 90, 121 for alto and baritone 2009, Psalms Nos. 13, 25, 32, 139 for alto and baritone 2010, Missa No. 1 for solo and choir and organ, Our Father for choir a capella, The Reminiscence for soprano and string quartet 2011. *Honours:* Musica Iuvenis, Prague 1997. *Address:* Karla Tomana 824, 27204 Kladno, Czech Republic (home). *Telephone:* 606-132121 (mobile). *E-mail:* cermakova173@seznam.cz.

CERNY, Florian; German singer (baritone); b. 4 Oct. 1946, Bavaria. *Education:* studied in Australia, Vienna and Munich. *Career:* solo debut with Israel National Opera; Prin. Baritone, Kiel Opera and has sung in Hamburg, Düsseldorf, Hanover and elsewhere in Europe; Geneva Opera as Biterolf in Tannhäuser; with Bayerische Staatsoper, Munich as Bretigny in Manon, Caliph in Der Barbier von Bagdad, Schaunard, and Dominic in Arabella; other roles include Wagner's Dutchman and Kothner, Riccardo (I Puritani), Iago and Don Carlos (La Forza del Destino); sang Wagner's Telramund at Leipzig 1992; sang Wotan in Das Rheingold at Braunschweig 1999.

CERNY, Pavel; Czech organist; b. 9 Oct. 1970, Prague. *Education:* Acad. of Music. *Career:* live television recording 1994; several Czech radio recordings of historic organ; set of historical organ recordings for Dutch radio (KRO) and production; Prague Philharmony (recital 1995); Chartres, Padova, Verona (recitals 1996); Vienna 1994; Salzburg 1994. *Recordings include:* Romantic Organ Repertoire for Four Hands and Four Legs (with Martin Rost) 1997. *Publications:* contrib. to International Organ Dictionary, studies of significant Prague organs 1997. *Honours:* first prize Opava Nat. Competition 1990, first prize Ljublja Competition 1992, first prize Prague Competition 1994.

CERVENA, Sona; Czech singer (mezzo-soprano); b. 9 Sept. 1925, Prague. *Education:* studied with Robert Rosner and Lydia Wegener in Prague. *Career:* joined Janáček Opera Brno 1952–58, Staatsoper Berlin 1958–61, Deutsche Oper Berlin 1962–64, Opera Frankfurt 1964–90; guest appearances in Prague, Vienna, Amsterdam, Brussels, Geneva, London, Milan, Paris, Barcelona, Lisbon, San Francisco, Los Angeles, Chicago; festivals include Bayreuth 1960–66, Salzburg 1961, Glyndebourne 1963–64 as Clairon in Capriccio, Edinburgh 1966–78; season 1987–88 at Frankfurt in Jenůfa and Schreker's Die ferne Klang; numerous roles at Nat. Theatre in Prague. *Publications:* Stýskání zakázáno (autobiography), Můj Václav (My Václav). *Honours:* Hon. mem. State Opera Prague 2010; Freedom of the City of Hradec Králové 2012; Kammersängerin (Berlin and Frankfurt), Thalia Award 2004, Dr František Ulrich Prize 2005, Alfréd Radok Award 2009, Artis Bohemiae Amicis Medal 2011, Gold Medal in the Arts, John F. Kennedy Center, Washington, DC 2013, Medal of the First Degree for Merits in the Arts 2013. *Website:* www.narodni-divadlo.cz.

CERVETTI, Sergio; American/Uruguayan composer and teacher; b. 9 Nov. 1940, Dolores, Uruguay; of Italian and French parentage; partner Kenneth Rinker. *Education:* Peabody Conservatory of Music, USA with E. Krenek and S. Grove. *Career:* Composer-in-Residence, German Artists' Programme, Berlin 1969; mem. Faculty, Tisch School of the Arts, New York Univ. 1970–; numerous commissions; mem. BMI. *Film:* lyrics for 'Fall Of The Rebel Angels' from Natural Born Killers soundtrack (dir Oliver Stone) 1994. *Compositions include:* String Trio 1963, Piano Sonata 1964, Five Sequences for flute, horn, cello, electric guitar, piano, percussion 1966, Orbitas for orchestra 1967, El Carro de Heno 1967, Zinctum 1968, Peripetia 1970, Plexus 1971, Madrigal III 1976, Four Fragments of Isadora 1976, Enclosed Time for electronics 1985, Night Trippers 1986, Inez de Castro (ballet) 1988, Leyenda for soprano and orchestra 1991, four string quartets 1968, 1972, 1990, 1992, Concerto for harpsichord and 11 instruments 1992, The Triumph of Death (song cycle) for piano and soprano, Candombe Alberada and Hard Rock for harpsichord 1993, Candombe II for orchestra 1998, Elegy for a Prince (opera), Yum! (opera), Memoires du Paradis (piano trio), Unbridled for string quartet. *Honours:* grants from Nat. Endowment for the Arts, New York State Council for the Arts, American Music Center, Meet the Composer. *Address:* 212 East Court Street, Doylestown, PA 18901, USA (home). *Telephone:* (215) 489-8716 (office). *E-mail:* kenserg@msn.com (office). *Website:* www.elegyforaprince.com (home); www.sergiocervetti.com.

CHAILLY, Riccardo; Italian conductor; *Principal Conductor, Teatro alla Scala;* b. 20 Feb. 1953, Milan; s. of the late Luciano Chailly and of Anna Marie Motta; m. Gabriella Terragni 1987; two s. *Education:* Giuseppe Verdi and Perugia Conservatories and with Franco Caracciolo and Franco Ferrara. *Career:* Asst to Claudio Abbado, La Scala, Milan 1972–74; debut as Conductor with Chicago Opera 1974; debut, La Scala 1978, Covent Garden (operatic debut) 1979; concert debut with London Symphony Orchestra and Edin. Festival 1979; American concert debut, Los Angeles Philharmonic, CA 1980; Metropolitan Opera debut 1982; Prin. Guest Conductor, London Philharmonic Orchestra 1982–85; Chief Conductor Radio Symphony Orchestra, Berlin 1982–89; Vienna State Opera debut 1983; appearances Salzburg Festival 1984, 1985, 1986; Japan debut with Royal Philharmonic Orchestra 1984; New York Philharmonic Orchestra debut 1984; Music Dir Bologna Orchestra, Teatro Comunale 1986–93; Chief Conductor Royal Concertgebouw Orchestra, Amsterdam 1988–2004, Conductor Emer. 2004–; Prin. Conductor and Music Dir Giuseppe Verdi Symphony Orchestra, Milan 1999–2005, Conductor Laureate 2005–; Chief Conductor Gewandhausorchester Leipzig 2005–15; Music Dir Lucerne Festival Orchestra 2015–; apptd Prin. Conductor La Scala, Milan 2015, Music Dir 2017. *Recordings include:* Beethoven: The Symphonies (ECHO Klassik Award for Conductor of the Year 2012) 2011, Brahms: The Symphonies (Gramophone Award for Recording of the Year) 2014. *Honours:* Hon. mem. RAM; Kt Order of Netherlands Lion 1998, Cavaliere di Gran Croce 1998, Abrogino d'Oro, Comune Milano; Gramophone Award Artist of the Year 1998, Diapason d'Or Artist of the Year 1999; Grand' Ufficiale della Repubblica Italiana. *Address:* Teatro alla Scala, Via Filodrammatici, 2, 20121 Milan, Italy (office). *Telephone:* (02) 88791 (office). *Website:* www.teatroallascala.org/en (office).

CHAITKIN, David, BA, MA; American composer; b. 16 May 1938, New York, NY; m. Carol McCauley 1960; one s. *Education:* Pomona Coll., Univ. of California, Berkeley, studied with Luigi Dallapiccola, Seymour Shifrin, Max Deutsch, Andrew Imbrie and Karl Kohn. *Career:* early experience as a jazz pianist; composed music for film, The Game; comms from Philadelphia Composers' Forum, Sylvan Winds, New Hampshire Music Festival, Da Capo Chamber Players/New York State Council on the Arts, Quintet of the Americas/Chamber Music America, Gordon Gottleib, Pomona Coll. (in honour of its centennial), Anders Paulsson/Gotland (Sweden) Chamber Music Festival, Francesco Trio/Koussevitzky Music Foundation, Stockton (Calif.) Symphony Orchestra, US Marine Band; Prof. of Music, Reed Coll. 1968–69, New York Univ. 1969–76. *Compositions include:* Symphony, Summersong for 23 wind instruments, Etudes for piano, Concerto for flute and strings, Seasons Such as These for mixed chorus a cappella, Serenade for seven players, Scattering Dark and Bright duo for piano and percussion, Quintet for mixed chamber ensemble, Pacific Images for chamber orchestra, Music in Five Parts for septet, Nocturne for woodwind quintet, Impromptu for piano, Poems of Love – Song Cycle for soprano and piano, Three Dances for piano, Rhapsody for cello and piano, Aria for soprano saxophone and strings, Trio for violin, cello and piano, Prelude and Dance for piano solo, Concerto for soprano saxophone and orchestra, Celebration for winds. *Recordings include:* Scattering Dark and Bright, Murray, Stout; Poems of Love, Schadeberg, Fout,

Oldfather, Garrett; Impromptu, Three Dances, Becker; Rhapsody, Chaitkin, Lefebvre; Summersong, Sylvan Winds, Weisbergs. *Publications include:* Celebration, Etudes for piano, Summersong, Impromptu for piano, Nocturne, Quintet, Pacific Images. *Honours:* Nat. Endowment for the Arts grant 1981, Guggenheim Fellowship 1985, American Acad. of Arts and Letters grants 1980, 1994. *Current Management:* Music Publishing Services, 236 West 26th Street, Suite 11–S, New York, NY 10001, USA. *Website:* www.davidchaitkin .com.

CHAKRABARTY, Kaushiki, BA, MA; Indian singer; b. 1980, Kolkata; d. of Pandit Ajoy and Chandna Chakrabarty; m. Partha Desikan. *Education:* Calcutta Univ., Sangeet Research Acad., Shrutinandan School of Music, studied with Gnan Prakash Ghosh and her father. *Career:* performs khayal and thumri forms of Hindustani music; has performed in USA, Canada and Europe; performed QEH, London 2005; contributed to film soundtrack, Deepa Mehta's Water; participated in numerous concerts including Dover Lane Music Conf., ITC Sangeet Sammelans, Spring Festival of Music (Calif.), Parampara Programme (Los Angeles). *Recordings include:* albums: Footsteps 1998, Journey Begins 2002, Pure 2004, The Spiritual Realisation 2005, Kaushiki 2007, Live at Saptak Festival 2008. *Honours:* Jadu Bhatta 1995, Outstanding Young Person 2000, BBC World Music Award for Asia/Pacific 2005. *Address:* Daffodil Greens, Flat # B3A, 17 Chandi Ghosh Road, Tollygunge, Kolkata 700 040, India (office). *Telephone:* (33) 32973311 (home); 9830107 868 (mobile). *E-mail:* contact@kaushiki.net (home); kaushiki.music@gmail.com (home); kaushiki_music@yahoo.com (home). *Website:* www.kaushiki.net.

CHALKER, Margaret, BME, MM; American singer (soprano); b. 1958, Waterloo, NY. *Education:* Baldwin-Wallace Coll., OH and Syracuse Univ. *Career:* Mostly Mozart Festival, New York as Sifare in Mitridate and Giunia in Lucio Silla; Houston Opera as Pamina; Deutsche Oper am Rhein, Düsseldorf from 1985, as Oscar (Ballo in Maschera), Gilda, Celia (Haydn's La Fedelta Premiata) and Lauretta in Gianni Schicchi; Zürich Opera from 1987, as Pamina, Gilda, Jemmy in Guillaume Tell, Sophie (Rosenkavalier) and Janáček's Vixen; other roles include Mozart's Countess and Donna Anna, Micaela, Antonia in Les Contes d'Hoffmann and Helen in Gluck's Paride ed Elena; season 1996 as Puccini's Lauretta at Zürich, Ariadne at Meiningen and the Marschallin in Prague; season 1999 at Zürich as Viclinda in I Lombardi and Freia in Das Rheingold; many concert appearances, notably in works by Bach and composers of the 20th century.

CHALLENGER, Robert; British singer (tenor); b. 1967, South Yorkshire. *Education:* Guildhall School of Music, studied with with Martin Isepp, Suzanne Danco and Hugues Cuenod at Aldeburgh. *Career:* concert appearances as the Evangelist in Bach's Passions, Handel's Messiah and Alexander's Feast; Mozart Requiem and C Minor Mass; Haydn Creation and Mass in Time of War; Britten Rejoice in the Lamb and Cantata Accademica; other concert repertory includes music by Palestrina, Byrd, Cage and Feldman; operatic roles include Beppe in Pagliacci, Brack Weaver in Weill's Down in the Valley and parts in La Jolie Fille de Perth, and Rossini's Il Viaggio a Reims, Covent Garden, 1992. *Honours:* Winner, Young Songmakers' Almanac Competition (recital at St John's Smith Square); Gramophone Prize for recording of Chamber Music, 1992.

CHALMERS, Penelope; British singer (soprano); b. 5 Oct. 1946, Worcester, England. *Education:* Bristol Univ. *Career:* has sung such roles as the Marschallin (Der Rosenkavalier), Leonora (Trovatore), Turandot and Tosca with fringe opera companies; title role in the British premiere of Bruch's Lorelei for University College Opera, Fiordiligi for Pavilion Opera and Rezia in Weber's Oberon at Haddo House, Scotland; London debut at the Prom concerts in Lambert's Rio Grande; appearances as the Dyer's Wife in Die Frau ohne Schatten at Geneva, Helmwige and Ortlinde in Die Walküre at Covent Garden and Emilia Marty in The Makropulos Case at Hagen, Germany; Donna Anna and Lady Billows in Albert Herring for Opera 80, season 1991–92; Judith in Bluebeard's Castle, at ENO 1993; sang title role in Salome with Scottish Opera; national television debut as prima donna in BBC production of Stendhal's Le Rouge et le Noir, 1993.

CHAMAYOU, Bertrand; French pianist; b. 1981, Toulouse. *Education:* studied with Jean-François Heisser, Conservatoire Nat. Supérieur de Musique, Paris, and with Maria Curcio in London. *Career:* has performed in venues including Théâtre des Champs Elysées, New York's Lincoln Center and Mostly Mozart Festival, Herkulessaal, Musikfest Bremen, Wigmore Hall, Lucerne Festival, Rheingau Festival, Rotterdam Gergiev Festival, Klavier-Festival Ruhr, Philharmonie Berlin, with orchestras including Orchestre de Paris, London Philharmonic Orchestra, Rotterdam Philharmonic Orchestra, Deutsche Kammer Philharmonie, Deutsche Radio Philharmonie, Hessischer Rundfunk Sinfonieorchester, WDR Sinfonie Orchester, SWR Sinfonie Orchester, Orchestre Nat. de France, Royal Scottish Nat. Orchestra, Danish Nat. Symphony Orchestra, Orchestre Symphonique de Québec and in 2014 with Deutsches Sinfonie-Orchester, NDR Sinfonie-Orchester Hamburg and Oregon Symphony Orchestra; has worked with conductors such as Pierre Boulez, Leonard Slatkin, Neville Marriner, Semyon Bychkov, Michel Plasson, Louis Langrée, Fabien Gabel, Joshua Weilerstein, Jérémie Rhorer, Stéphane Denève, Ludovic Morlot and Andris Nelson; Artist-in-Residence, Orchestre Nat. de Bordeaux 2013–14; chamber music with artists including Renaud and Gautier Capuçon, Quatuor Ebène, Antoine Tamestit, Baiba Skride, Sol Gabetta and Nicolas Baldeyrou. *Recordings include:* Mendelssohn 2008,

César Franck 2010, Liszt: Années de Pèlerinage (Choc Classica, Diapason d'Or de l'Année, Victoires de la Musique Classique Recording of the Year 2012) 2011, Le Paris des Romantiques 2012. *Honours:* Victoires de la Musique Classique Young Artist of the Year 2006 and Instrumental Soloist of the Year 2011. *Current Management:* Solea Management, 91 rue Lamarck, 75018 Paris, France. *Telephone:* 1-42-36-45-33. *E-mail:* rb@solea-management.com. *Website:* www.solea-management.com.

CHAMPNEY, Wendy; American violist; b. 23 Feb. 1958, USA. *Education:* Indiana Univ., Int. Menuhin Acad., Gstaad, Switzerland. *Career:* Co-founder and violist, Carmina Quartet 1984–; appearances from 1987 in Europe, Israel, USA and Japan; regular concerts at Wigmore Hall from 1987; concerts at South Bank Centre, London, Amsterdam Concertgebouw, Berlin Philharmonie, Berlin, Konzertverein Vienna, and Paris; tours in Australasia, USA, Japan; concerts at Hohenems, Graz, Hong Kong, Montreux, Schleswig-Holstein, Bath, Lucerne and Prague Spring Festivals; collaborations with Dietrich Fischer-Dieskau, Olaf Bär and Mitsuko Uchida; mem. Faculty, Zurich/Winterthur Coll. of Music. *Honours:* jt winner (with Carmina Quartet) Paolo Borciani String Quartet Competition in Reggio Emilia, Italy 1987. *E-mail:* enderle@gmx.ch. *Website:* www.carminaquartet.com.

CHANCE, Michael, CBE; British singer (countertenor); b. 7 March 1955, Penn, Buckinghamshire, England. *Education:* King's Coll., Cambridge. *Career:* appearances with the English Chamber Orchestra, Acad. of Ancient Music, English Concert, Orchestra of St John's, Smith Square, and the Bournemouth Sinfonietta; Handel's Messiah at the Alice Tully and Avery Fisher Halls, New York; concerts with John Eliot Gardiner and the Monteverdi Choir in New York and at the Göttingen and Aix-en-Provence Festivals; operatic roles include Apollo in Cavalli's Jason, Buxton Festival 1983; Andronico in Handel's Tamerlano, Lyon Opéra 1985; Otho in Handel's Agrippina, Bath Festival, Ottone in Monteverdi's L'Incoronazione di Poppea and the Military Governor in the world premiere of Judith Weir's A Night at the Chinese Opera, Kent Opera; Britten's Oberon and Voice of Apollo with Glyndebourne Opera; Paris Opéra debut 1988, as Ptolomeo in Handel's Giulio Cesare; season 1992 as Amphinomous in Monteverdi's Ulisse for ENO, Julius Caesar for Scottish Opera and Britten's Apollo at Glyndebourne; sang in the premiere of Birtwistle's Second Mrs Kong 1994; concerts include Bach cantatas at the Promenade Concerts, London, Messiah at King's Coll., Cambridge, Royal Albert Hall and in Edinburgh; Handel's Theodora at the Paris Opéra 1987; Israel in Egypt in Stuttgart and at La Scala, Milan; Jephtha in London and Göttingen; Bach's St Matthew Passion in Spain and London, B Minor Mass with the Manchester Camerata; world premiere of Bennett's Ophelia 1988; Apollo in Death in Venice with Glyndebourne Touring Opera at Norwich 1989; The Fairy Queen with The Sixteen, Queen Elizabeth Hall 1990; Promenade Concerts, London, Britten's Cantata Misericordium, Mozart's Credo Mass 1991; sang the title role in Gluck's Orpheus for ENO 1997; season 1998 as Monteverdi's Ottone for WNO; season 2000–01 as Gluck's Orpheus at Leipzig and soloist in the St Matthew Passion at La Scala; London Proms Chamber Music 2002. *Recordings:* Bach's St John Passion, Christmas Oratorio and St Matthew Passion, Handel's Messiah, Belshazzar, Oratorium Solomon, Jephtha, Cavalli's Giasone, Bacco and other roles in The Death of Orpheus by Stefano Landi, Handel's Tamerlano, Orfeo settings by Monteverdi and Gluck, Agricola, Buxtehude, Bach Early Cantatas, Vivaldi's Gloria, Klaglied, John Taverner's The Hidden Face. *Current Management:* Ingpen & Williams Ltd, 7 St George's Court, 131 Putney Bridge Road, London, SW15 2PA, England. *Telephone:* (20) 8874-3222. *Fax:* (20) 8877-3113. *E-mail:* info@ingpen.co.uk. *Website:* www.ingpen.co.uk; www.michaelchance.co.uk.

CHANCE, Nancy Laird; American composer; b. 19 March 1931, Cincinnati, OH; m. 1950 (divorced); three s. *Education:* The Foxcroft School, Bryn Mawr Coll., Columbia Univ., studied with William R. Smith, Lilias McKinnon, Otto Luening and Vladimir Ussachevsky. *Career:* performances of her works by Philadelphia Orchestra, St Louis Symphony, The Jupiter Symphony, The American Composers Orchestra, The League ISCM, The Group for Contemporary Music, The New Music Consort, Da Capo Chamber Players, Relache, Continuum, The Goldman Memorial Band and numerous others; world premiere of Planasthai with the Cleveland Chamber Symphony. *Compositions:* Odysseus for solo voice, percussion and orchestra, String Quartet No. 1, Liturgy for orchestra, Elegy for string orchestra, Woodwind Quintet, Domine, Dominus motet for double chorus a capella, Duos III for violin and cello, Exultation and Lament for alto saxophone and timpani, Ritual Sounds for brass quintet and percussion, Daysongs for alto flute and percussion, three Rilke Songs for soprano, flute, English horn and cello, In Paradisum for solo voice, mixed chorus and orchestra, Rhapsodia for marimba quartet, Ceremonial for percussion quartet, Planasthai for chamber orchestra, piano and percussion 1992. *Honours:* ASCAP Rudolph Missim Prize for Orchestral Compositions 1982, 1984, NEA Composer Fellowships 1981, 1983, Sundance Inst. Film Composer Fellow 1988.

CHANG, Han-Na, BA; South Korean cellist and conductor; *Music Director, Qatar Philharmonic Orchestra*; b. Seoul. *Education:* studied privately with Mischa Maisky and Mstislav Rostropovich, Harvard Univ., studied conducting with Lorin Maazel. *Career:* as cellist, has performed in Europe, North America and Asia with orchestras including the Bayerischer Rundfunk Orchestra, Berlin Philharmonic, Dresden Staatskapelle, Cleveland Orchestra, Orchestre de Paris, Orchestre Nat. de France, Israel Philharmonic, London Symphony Orchestra, Maggio Musicale Orchestra, Florence, New York Philharmonic, Boston Symphony, Montreal Symphony, Nat. Symphony

Orchestra, Washington, DC, NHK Symphony, Tokyo, Philadelphia Orchestra, Pittsburgh Symphony, Santa Cecilia Orchestra, Rome, La Scala Orchestra, Milan, San Francisco Symphony, Los Angeles Philharmonic, Sydney Symphony Orchestra, Royal Stockholm Philharmonic Orchestra; has played with Lorin Maazel, Giuseppe Sinopoli, Leonard Slatkin, Charles Dutoit, Antonio Pappano, Herbert Blomstedt, Mariss Jansons, Zubin Mehta, Riccardo Muti, Seiji Ozawa, James Conlon, Mstislav Rostropovich, Myung-Whun Chung and Yuri Temirkanov; currently serves as Goodwill Amb. for Korean Red Cross; founder and Artistic Dir, Absolute Classic Festival, Repub. of Korea 2009–; Music Dir, Qatar Philharmonic Orchestra 2013–. *Recordings include:* Tchaikovsky's Rococo Variations/Saint-Saëns' Cello Concerto No. 1/Fauré's Elégie/Bruch's Kol Nidrei 1995, Haydn Cello Concertos 1998, The Swan 2000, Prokofiev Sinfonia Concertante and Cello Sonata (Gramophone Award for Best Concerto Recording 2003), Shostakovich's Concerto No. 1 and the Cello Sonata 2006, Romance 2007, Vivaldi Cello Concertos 2008. *Honours:* First Prize and Contemporary Music Prize, Rostropovich Int. Cello Competition 1994 (aged 11), ECHO Klassik Prize 1996, 2003, Cannes Classical Award 2003, Gramophone Best Concerto Recording 2003, Caecilia Prize 2003. *Current Management:* c/o Jasper Parrott, Iarlaith Carter, Harrison Parrott, 5–6 Albion Court, London, W6 0QT, England. *Telephone:* (20) 7313-3562. *Fax:* (20) 7221-5042. *E-mail:* iarlaith.carter@harrisonparrott.co.uk. *Website:* www.harrisonparrott.com.

CHANG, Sarah; American violinist; b. 10 Dec. 1980, Philadelphia. *Education:* Juilliard School. *Career:* debut with New York Philharmonic aged eight; debut at Carnegie Hall aged 13; frequent performances with New York Philharmonic, Philadelphia Orchestra, Berlin Philharmonic, Vienna Philharmonic, Los Angeles Philharmonic, London Symphony Orchestra. *Recordings:* albums include: Tchaikovsky Concerto with the London Symphony, Paganini Concerto with the Philadelphia Orchestra, Lalo Symphonie Espagnole with the Royal Concertgebouw Orchestra, Sibelius and Mendelssohn Concertos with the Berlin Philharmonic, Simply Sarah, Lark Ascending with the London Philharmonic, French Sonatas, Fire and Ice with the Berlin Philharmonic, Dvorak Concerto with the London Symphony, Tchaikovsky Souvenir de Florence with the Berlin Philharmonic, Strauss Concerto with the Bayerische Rundfunk, Goldmark concerto with Cologne Gurzenich, Phantasia with Andrew Lloyd Webber, Sweet Sorrow; Shostakovich and Prokofieff Concertos with the Berlin Philharmonic, Vivaldi's Four Seasons with Orpheus, Bruch/Brahms: Violin Concertos. *Honours:* Gramophone Young Artist of the Year 1993, German Echo Schallplattenpreis 1993, International Classical Music Award, Newcomer of the Year 1994, Avery Fisher Prize 1999, Internazionale Accademia Musicale Chigiana Prize 2005, Nan Pa Award. *Current Management:* Opus 3 Artists, 470 Park Avenue South, 9th Floor North, New York, NY 10016, USA. *Telephone:* (212) 584-7500. *Fax:* (646) 300-8200. *E-mail:* info@opus3artists.com. *Website:* www.opus3artists.com. *Current Management:* IMG Artists, The Light Box, 111 Power Road, London, W4 5PY, England. *Telephone:* (20) 7957-5800. *Fax:* (20) 7957-5800. *E-mail:* artistseurope@imgartists.com. *Website:* www.imgartists.com.

CHAPMAN, Janice; Australian singer (soprano) and teacher; b. 10 Jan. 1938, Adelaide. *Education:* Univ. of Adelaide, Royal Coll. of Music, UK, London Opera Centre. *Career:* sang leading roles with Sadler's Wells/ENO, Welsh and Scottish Operas and in numerous European houses; toured Russia with English Opera Group under Benjamin Britten and worked with the composer on roles of Miss Jessel and Mrs Grose in The Turn of the Screw; sang Mrs Julian in stage premiere of Owen Wingrave at Covent Garden 1973; other Britten roles have been Ellen Orford and Lady Billows, and has sung in operas by Mozart, Wagner, Verdi and Puccini; concert engagements with leading orchestras; sang with her trio The Alexandra Ensemble at Women's Music Festival at Beersheba, Israel 1986; appeared as Mrs Grose for New Israel Opera 1990, conducted by Roderick Brydon; Fellow, Guildhall School of Music and Drama 2010, currently mem. Vocal Dept; also Prof. of Voice, London Coll. of Music. *Publication:* Singing and Teaching Singing: A Holistic Approach to Classical Voice 2005. *Honours:* Hon. Pres. Asscn of Teachers of Singing in the UK 2012; winner, Sun Aria Vocal Competition, ABC Concerto and Vocal Competition, Kathleen Ferrier Competition, Medal of the Order of Australia 2004. *Address:* Vocal Department, Guildhall School of Music and Drama, Silk Street, Barbican, London, EC2Y 8DT, England (office). *Website:* www.gsmd.ac.uk/music (office); www.janicechapman.co.uk.

CHAPPLE, Brian, GRSM, ARAM, LRAM; British composer; b. 24 March 1945, London; s. of John and Mildred Chapple; m. Janet Bailey; one step-d. *Education:* Royal Acad. of Music, London. *Career:* commissions and premieres from BBC Proms, London Sinfonietta, London Mozart Players, New London Orchestra, BBC Singers, St Paul's Cathedral, Exeter Cathedral, Dartington Festival, New Music Wells Festival, Highgate Choral Soc., Finchley Children's Music Group and others; Composer in Residence, Exon Singers Festival 2012; mem. Performing Right Soc. *Compositions include:* Scherzos for four pianos 1970, Trees Revisited 1970, Praeludiana 1971, Green and Pleasant 1973, In Ecclesiis 1976, Piano Concerto 1977, Cantica 1978, Venus Fly Trap 1979, Little Symphony 1982, Lamentations of Jeremiah 1984, Piano Sonata 1986, Magnificat 1986, In Memoriam 1989, Berkeley Tribute 1989, Frink Tribute 1990, Requies 1991, Missa Brevis 1991, Three Motets 1992, Songs of Innocence 1993, Ebony and Ivory 1995, The St Paul's Service 1996, A Bit of a Blow 1996, Tribute for Jo Klein 1997, Songs of Experience 1998, Burlesque 2000, Birthday Suite for John 2002, Viola Suite 2004, Tribute for J.M.C. 2004, Bagatelles Diverses 2005, God's Love Come Among Us 2005, Three Sacred Pieces 2006, Three for Two 2007, Swing's the Thing 2007, What Child is This 2009, Missa Brevis Exoniensis 2009, Six Bagatelles 2011, Safe Where I Cannot Lie Yet 2012, Hymn to God the Father 2014, Ecce Lignum Crucis, Passiontide at St Paul's, Burlesque: Piano Duos and Solos; anthems, canticles, children's songs, piano music, instrumental music. *Honours:* BBC Monarchy 1000 Prize 1973, UNESCO Int. Rostrum of Composers 1976. *Current Management:* Music Sales Ltd, 14–15 Berners Street, London, W1T 3LJ, England. *Telephone:* (20) 7612-7400. *Fax:* (20) 7612-7549. *E-mail:* promotion@musicsales.co.uk. *Website:* www.chesternovello.com.

CHAPPUIS, Vincent, MMus; Swiss composer; b. 26 Feb. 1960. *Education:* Inst. of Tech., Zürich. *Career:* numerous int. festivals of contemporary music, mainly in Romania; radio broadcasts with Radio Canada, Radio Belgium, France Musique and Swiss Espace 2; TV with Tele Europe Nova in Romania; Founder-mem. Composers' Asscn Archebole; mem. Swiss Asscn of Musicians. *Compositions include:* Symphonie for big orchestra 1991, Sinfonietta for chamber orchestra 1992, Procession, electro-acoustic piece 1993, Dilemme trio for violin, double bass and piano 1994, Fusions for two pianos and percussion 1995, Quatuor for string quartet 1996, Fusions II for piano and chamber orchestra 1997, Rituels for piano, percussion and clarinet 1998, Symphonie No. 2 for large orchestra and choir 2001, Quatuor No. 2 for string quartet 2002, Nihon trio for piano, flute and percussion 2006, Symphonie No. 3 for choir and orchestra 2010. *Recordings include:* Quatuor, Trio Dilemme, Trio Rituels. *Honours:* Hon. mem. Percussion Ensemble of Cluj, Romania. *Address:* 35 rue Liotard, 1202 Geneva, Switzerland (home). *E-mail:* vincent.chappuis@archebole.com (office). *Website:* www.archebole.com (home).

CHAPUIS, Gérard; French singer (bass); b. 21 Oct. 1931, Lyon. *Education:* Lyon Conservatory. *Career:* sang with the Lyon Opéra 1954–56, Paris Opéra 1956–73; roles include the Minister in Fidelio, Sparafucile, Ramphis, Raimondo in Lucia di Lammermoor, Pistol, Hector in Les Troyens, Sarastro in Die Zauberflöte, Commendatore in Don Giovanni, Osmin in Die Entführung, and in Un Ballo in Maschera and Barbiere di Siviglia; other appearances at the Paris Opéra-Comique; Pres., Des Voix d'Or, Scene Française. *Honours:* Concours de Voix d'Or first prize Caruso 1956.

CHARBONNEAU, Pierre; Canadian singer (bass); b. 14 June 1949, Montréal. *Career:* sang first in Canada, notably at Vancouver from 1974, and then with Canadian Opera at Toronto from 1978; Opéra de Montréal from 1983; guest appearances with Washington Opera 1976, Opéra de Lyon from 1988; sang Jupiter in Orphée aux Enfers at the Paris Opéra 1988, Don Pasquale at Rio de Janeiro 1989; Carnegie Hall 1991, in Boieldieu's La Dame Blanche; other roles include Masetto, Sparafucile, Rocco, Raimondo, Hunding, Arkel, and Timur in Turandot.

CHARD, Geoffrey, AM; Australian singer (baritone); b. 9 Aug. 1930, Sydney; m. Marjorie Margaret Conley 1956 (died 1959). *Education:* New South Wales Conservatory. *Career:* debut in Sydney 1951, in Carmen; moved to England; mem. ENO other appearances with WNO and Glyndebourne and Edinburgh Festivals; Aldeburgh Festival 1967, 1968, in premieres of Berkeley's The Castaway and Birtwistle's Punch and Judy; London Coliseum 1973–83, in British premiere of Penderecki's The Devils of Loudun; Ginastera's Bomarzo and Ligeti's Le Grand Macabre; roles in operas by Gluck, Mozart, Wagner, Britten, Orff, Menotti, Shostakovich, Janáček and contemporary British composers; numerous engagements as concert singer; sang Bartolo in Il Barbiere di Siviglia for Victoria State Opera 1989; Germont in Traviata for Ballarat Opera Festival 1992, Balstrode (Peter Grimes) and Pizarro at Sydney; Tonio in Pagliacci at Sydney 1996.

CHARLTON, David, BA, PhD; British musicologist and academic; *Professor Emeritus, Royal Holloway, University of London*; b. 20 June 1946, London, England; m. Patricia Scholfield. *Education:* Univs of Nottingham and Cambridge. *Career:* Lecturer, Univ. of East Anglia 1970, Reader 1991; Reader, then Prof., Royal Holloway, Univ. of London 1995–2007, later Prof. Emer.; Trustee, The New Berlioz Edition; Trustee, Répertoire Int. de Littérature Musicale (UK); mem. Bd, OPERA edition, Frankfurt. *Radio:* several broadcasts on musical subjects. *Publications include:* Grétry and the Growth of Opéra-Comique 1986, E.T.A. Hoffmann's Musical Writings (collaboration with Martyn Clarke) 1989, Hector Berlioz: Choral Works with Orchestra (ed) 1993, Michel Sedaine 1719–1797: Theatre, Opera, Art (co-ed) 2000, French Opera 1730–1830: Meaning and Media 2000, The Cambridge Companion to Grand Opera (ed) 2003, Théâtre de l'Opéra-Comique, Paris: Répertoire 1762–1972 (collaboration with Nicole Wild) 2005, The Musical Voyager: Berlioz in Europe (co-ed) 2007, Opera in the Age of Rousseau: Music, Confrontation, Realism 2013; contrib. of numerous journal and reference articles on French opera in the New Grove Dictionary of Music and the New Grove Dictionary of Opera; ed Méhul symphonies 1 (A-R Editions), 3, 4, 5 (world premiere editions: Pendragon). *E-mail:* d.charlton@rhul.ac.uk (office).

CHARNOCK, Helen, BA; British singer (soprano) and teacher; b. 1958; m.; two s. one d. *Education:* Univ. of East Anglia, studied at Guildhall School with Laura Sarti. *Career:* Many performances with Opera Factory and London Sinfonietta, including the world premieres of Hell's Angels by Nigel Osborne and Birtwistle's Yan Tan Tethera, 1986; Sang in Weill's Mahagonny Songspiel, Ligeti's Aventures, Nouvelles Aventures and the British premiere of Reimann's Ghost Sonata; Workshops and performances in many venues with the London Sinfonietta's Education Programme, including Holloway Prison and the Huddersfield Contemporary Music Festival; Australian debut in 1986 as Clytemnestra in Iphigénie en Tauride; Sang in the premiere of

Greek by Mark-Anthony Turnage at 1988 Munich Biennale, repeated at Edinburgh Festival in 1988 and ENO 1990; Has sung Britten's Governess and Mrs Coyle at Aldeburgh Festival and has appeared elsewhere as Semele, First Lady, Pamina, Micaela, Butterfly, Titania, Gretel, Adele, Despina and Musetta; TV appearances in works by Birtwistle, Ligeti and Turnage; continues to study singing with Corinne Shirman-Sarti. *Recordings:* Greek by Turnage, 1993. *Honours:* The English Singers and Speakers Prize; two RSA Awards; Inc. Soc. of Musicians Young Artists Award; Ian Fleming Bursary. *Address:* 21 Glengall Road, London SE15 6NJ, England. *Telephone:* (20) 7237-2180 (home). *E-mail:* warrenhelen@hotmail.com.

CHARTERIS, Richard, BA, MA, PhD, FAHA, FRHistS; New Zealand/Australian musicologist, academic, writer and editor; *Professor Emeritus in Historical Musicology, University of Sydney*; b. 24 June 1948, Chatham Islands, New Zealand. *Education:* Victoria Univ., Wellington and Univ. of Canterbury, New Zealand, Univ. of London, UK. *Career:* Research Fellow, Univ. of Sydney, Australia 1976–78, 1981–1990, Sr Research Fellow (Reader) 1991–94, Prof. in Historical Musicology, Music Dept 1995–2008, Prof. Emer. in Historical Musicology 2009–, Dir Centre of Early Venetian Music; Research Fellow, Univ. of Queensland, Australia 1979–80; Australian Acad. of Humanities Travelling Fellow 1979–80; Gov., Dolmetsch Foundation of Great Britain; mem. American Musicological Soc., Australian Acad. of the Humanities, Dolmetsch Foundation of GB, Inst. of Historical Research, London, Int. Musicological Soc., Musicological Soc. of Australia, Nat. Early Music Asscn of GB, Royal Historical Soc., London, Royal Musical Asscn of GB, Viola da Gamba Soc. of America, Viola da Gamba Soc. of GB. *Publications include:* more than 200 books, journal articles and critical and performing edns devoted to the music of Johann Christian Bach, Giovanni Bassano, John Coprario, Giovanni Croce, Alfonso Ferrabosco the Elder, Domenico Maria Ferrabosco, Andrea and Giovanni Gabrieli, Hans Leo Hassler, John Hingeston, Thomas Lupo, Claudio Monteverdi, Daniel Purcell and others, mostly in the series Corpus Mensurabilis Musicae, Musica Britannica, Recent Researches in the Music of the Baroque Era, Fretwork Editions, Baroque and Classical Music Series, Viol Consort Series, Boethius Editions and King's Music Editions; books on composers, music, collectors and early sources in the series Boethius Editions, Thematic Catalogues Series, Annotated Reference Tools in Music, Detroit Studies in Music Bibliography, Musicological Studies and Documents and Altro Polo. *Honours:* Sr Scholar 1970–71, Mary Duncan Scholar 1975, Louise Dyer Award, Royal Musical Asscn 1975, Top Award, Australian Hi Fi FM Classical Music Section 1988, Centenary Medal 2003. *Address:* Arts Music Unit, Seymour Theatre Centre J09, University of Sydney, Sydney, NSW 2006, Australia (office). *Website:* www.richardcharteris.com.

CHASE, Roger, ARCM; British violist; b. 1958, London. *Education:* Royal Coll. of Music with Bernard Shore, studied in Canada with Steven Staryk. *Career:* solo debut with the English Chamber Orchestra 1979; performances internationally from 1976 with such ensembles as the London Sinfonietta, the Esterhazy Baryton Trio and the Nash Ensemble; concerts with the chamber ensemble Hausmusik, featuring works by Mendelssohn, Schubert and Hummel; modern repertoire includes a concerto by Richard Harvey, premiere at the Exeter Festival 1991; toured the USA with Hanover Band 1992, playing Mozart's Sinfonia Concertante; Prof., Guildhall School of Music and Drama; fmr teacher Royal Coll. of Music, Guildhall School, Royal Northern Coll. of Music, Académie Internationale de Music de Chambre, Netherlands, Oberlin Coll., Chicago Coll. of Performing Arts, Roosevelt Univ. *Recordings include:* works by Mendelssohn, Mozart's Concertante and Britten's Lachrymae. *Current Management:* Raymond Weiss Artist Management, 889 9th Avenue, Suite One, New York, NY 10019-1781, USA. *Telephone:* (212) 581-8478. *E-mail:* rwam@rwam.cnc.net. *Website:* www.rogerchase.com (home).

CHASLIN, Frédéric; French conductor, composer and pianist; *Chief Conductor, Santa Fe Opera*; b. 1963, Paris; pnr Nancy Gustafson. *Education:* Paris Conservatoire, Salzburg Mozarteum. *Career:* Asst to Daniel Barenboim at Orchestre de Paris 1987–89, to Pierre Boulez at Ensemble Intercontemporain 1989–91; Music Dir, Rouen Opera and Symphonie 1991–94; guest with the Orchestre National de France 1993, Vienna Symphony Orchestra 1993–95, Orchestre de Paris 1994, Paris Opéra-Comique 1994–95, Paris Opéra Bastille 1997–98, Deutsche Oper Berlin 1997–, Oper Leipzig 2001–02, Metropolitan Opera 2002–, Munich State Opera 2003–, Opera North 2003, Orchestra della Toscana, Florence 2004–, La Scala 2010–, RAI Milan, Scottish Opera, New Israeli Opera, La Fenice, and orchestras of Nice, Marseille, Lyon, Düsseldorf, Stuttgart, Genoa, Parma, Rome, Trieste; Permanent Guest Conductor, Bregenz Festival 1993–, with Nabucco and Fidelio; UK concert debut as guest with Manchester Hallé Orchestra 1996; Chief Conductor, Jerusalem Symphony Orchestra 1999–2002; Chief Conductor, Santa Fe Opera 2010–. *Compositions:* five operas. *Address:* Santa Fe Opera, 17053 US Highway 84/285, Santa Fe, NM 87506, USA (office). *Telephone:* (505) 986-5955 (office). *E-mail:* artsadmin@santafeopera.org (office). *Website:* www.santafeopera.org (office); www.chaslin.com.

CHATEAUNEUF, Paula, BMus; British/American lutenist and early guitar player; b. 1958, USA. *Education:* Univ. of Connecticut, New England Conservatory, with Patrick O'Brien in New York; Fulbright Scholar, Guildhall School of Music, London with Nigel North. *Career:* moved to London in 1982; appearances with many early music ensembles, including the New London Consort, Orchestra of the Age of Enlightenment, English Concert, Sinfonye and the Gabrieli Consort; has worked extensively as soloist and continuo player, particularly in Baroque opera; involved in groups and projects devoted to improvisation and early dance music; tours of Europe, Australia, the Far East and the Americas as soloist and ensemble player, performing at major festivals and recording for radio and TV; lute tutor, Univ. of Birmingham, Arts and Humanities Research Council Fellow in the Creative and Performing Arts, Centre for Early Music Performance and Research 2007–12. *Recordings include:* To the Unknown Goddess: A Portrait of Barbara Strozzi, H. Biber: Rosary Sonatas (with Pavlo Beznosiuk), The Age of Extravagance: Virtuoso Music from Iberia and Italy, J. Blow: Fairest Work of Happy Nature, Monteverdi: Vespro della Beata Vergine (with Gabrieli Consort), Monteverdi: L'Orfeo (with New London Consort),. *Honours:* American Fulbright Scholar to the UK 1982–83, 1983–84. *Address:* 170 Bow Common Lane, London, E3 4HH, England. *E-mail:* paulachateauneuf@gmail.com. *Website:* www.thedivisionlobby.co.uk (home); www.music.bham.ac.uk/cempr (home).

CHAUSSON, Carlos; Spanish singer (bass-baritone); b. 17 March 1950, Zaragoza. *Education:* studied in Madrid and at the Univ. of Michigan. *Career:* debut, San Diego 1977, as Masetto; appearances at Boston, Miami, New York City Opera and Mexico City (as Bartolo in Il Barbiere di Siviglia); sang at Madrid from 1983, Barcelona from 1985; Vienna Staatsoper from 1986, as Paolo in Simon Boccanegra, and Don Alvaro in Il Viaggio a Reims, conducted by Abbado; Vienna Konzerthaus in Les Danaides by Salieri; Parma 1987, as Falstaff, Bologna 1988–89, as Michonnet in Adriana Lecouvreur, Pantaleone in Le Maschere by Mascagni and Sharpless in Butterfly; Barcelona 1989, in the premiere of Cristobal Colón by Baladas, returned 1990 as Paolo; Modena 1990, as Geronte in Manon Lescaut; sang Mozart's Figaro at Madrid, Masetto at the 1990 Vienna Festival; Grand Théâtre de Genève 1991 as Paolo; Madrid 1992 as Bartolo in the new production of Il Barbiere di Siviglia conducted by Alberto Zedda; sang Don Magnifico in Cenerentola at the Palais Garnier, Paris 1996; Giorgio in Paisiello's Nina at Zürich, and John Plake in Wolf-Ferrari's Sly 1998; season 2000–01 as Don Alfonso for Zürich Opera, Fra Melitone (La Forza del Destino) and in La Cenerentola at Madrid; also singing coach, L'Estudi school. *Address:* c/o L'estudi, Calle de la Granja, 08024 Barcelona, Spain (office). *Website:* www.grn.es/estudi (office).

CHEBOTAREVA, Anastasia Savelyevna; Russian violinist; b. 8 Aug. 1972, Odessa, Ukraine; d. of Savely Ignatyevich Chebotarev and Varvara Igorevna Chebotareva. *Education:* Moscow State Conservatory with Irina Bochkova. *Career:* soloist, Moscow State Philharmonic; performed with Russian and European orchestras including Tchaikovsky State Academic Great Symphony under Vladimir Fedoseyev, St Petersburg Philharmonic under Yu Temirkanov, Japan NHK Symphony under Vladimir Ashkenazy, Vienna Chamber Orchestra under Christoph Eberle; performances in leading concert halls include Royal Albert Hall, London, Beethoven Hall, Berlin, Vienna Konzerthaus and Brucknerhaus, Austria Tokyo Metropolitan Art Space Hall, Tokyo Opera City Concert Hall, Suntory Hall, Tokyo, Osaka Symphony Hall, Megaro Hall, Athens, Seoul Art Center Hall, Blackwood Hall, Melbourne, Grand Hall, Giuseppe Verdi Hall, Milan, Moscow Conservatory, St George Hall, Kremlin Palace, Moscow; Asst Prof., Moscow State Conservatory 1999–; Hon. Prof., Kurashiki Sakuyo Univ., Japan 2000–07. *Recordings include:* Carmen–Fantasie 2000, Souvenir de Moscou 2001, Andaluza con Pasion 2002, Arco Tao Iwashiro with Anastasia 2002, Portrait de Fantasie 2003, Tchaikovsky and Mendelssohn Concertos 2003, Tema D'amore Cinema Collection 2004, Valse de Fleur 2005, Zigeunerweisen 2005, Anastasia Violin Best 2007. *Recordings for television include:* Sonagi 2002, Hiiro no Kioku 2003. *Honours:* winner Int. Paganini Competition, Genoa, Italy 1989, Int. Juventus Festival in Europe 1991, First Prize Rodolfo Lipizer Competition, Gorizia, Italy 1992, First Prize Tchaikovsky Competition, Moscow 1994, Merited Artist of Russia 2004. *Address:* Building 27, Gagarinsky Pereulok, Apt 69, Moscow 119034, Russia. *Telephone:* (495) 241-5487. *Fax:* (495) 241-5487. *E-mail:* info@anastasia-chebotareva.com; anastasia-violin@msk.org.ru. *Website:* www.anastasia-chebotareva.com.

CHEDEL, Arlette; Swiss singer (contralto); b. 25 May 1933, Neuchâtel. *Education:* studied in Neuchâtel and at Vienna Musikakademie with Erik Werba. *Career:* concert appearances in works by Schütz, Handel, Bach, Kodály, Frank Martin and Honegger; Radio Lausanne 1974, in premiere of Trois Visions Espagnoles by Gerber; Montreux Festival 1986, in Folie de Tristan by Schibler; guest engagements in Vienna, Prague, Berlin, Rome and Besançon; opera roles included Wagner's Erda, Magdalene and Mary, Mozart's Marcellina, Catherine in Jeanne d'Arc au Bûcher, Nurse in Boris Godunov and Geneviève in Pelléas et Mélisande. *Recordings include:* L'Enfant et les Sortilèges and Les Noces by Stravinsky.

CHEEK, John; American singer (bass-baritone); b. 17 Aug. 1948, Greenville, SC. *Education:* North Carolina School of Arts, Accademia Chigiana in Siena with Gino Bechi. *Career:* sang at the Festivals of Ravinia and Tanglewood and elsewhere in the USA, notably in music by Mozart; Metropolitan Opera debut 1977, as the Doctor in Pelléas et Mélisande: later appeared as Pimen, Ferrando in Il Trovatore, Klingsor, Panthée in Les Troyens, Monterone and Figaro; New York City Opera 1986, as Mephistopheles in Faust; Other roles include Wurm in Luisa Miller; Attila, New York, 1988; Padre Guardiano, Toronto; Metropolitan, La Bohème, 1989; Ramphis in Aida, Cincinnati Opera, 1990; sang Don Pasquale at Cincinnati, 1996; Sang the Berlioz Mephistopheles at Helsinki, 2000; TV appearances and concerts. *Recordings include:* Tosca; Haydn Creation, Stravinsky The Rake's Progress, as Nick Shadow; Messiah; César Franck, Les Béatitudes (Satan), Hänssler. *Honours:* Hon.

DMus 1985; North Carolina Prize 1987. *Current Management:* c/o Wolf Artists International LLC, PO Box 492, Gracie Station, New York, NY 10028, USA. *Telephone:* (212) 319-3614; (646) 744-4581. *Fax:* (646) 863-7149. *E-mail:* Isabel@wolfartists.com; Diane@wolfartists.com. *Website:* www.wolfartists .com.

CHEN, Leland; Taiwanese violinist; b. 8 July 1965. *Career:* made London concerto debut with the London Philharmonia at the Barbican; further concerts with the London Philharmonic Orchestra and London Symphony Orchestra; tour of North America 1985 with the Royal Philharmonic Orchestra; Royal Concert London 1986 playing the Bach Double Concerto with Yehudi Menuhin; tours of Poland and The Netherlands and a 60-city recital tour of the USA; played Vivaldi's Four Seasons at Kennedy Center, Washington, DC, televised by CBS; performances at Gstaad and Schleswig-Holstein festivals; performed throughout Europe with the Netherlands Philharmonic, Polish Chamber Orchestra, Warsaw Sinfonia and Chamber Orchestra of Europe; repertoire includes works by Bartók, Beethoven, Elgar, Mozart, Mendelssohn, Sibelius and Tchaikovsky. *Honours:* Winner Yehudi Menuhin Int. Competition. *Current Management:* c/o Upbeat Classical Management, 170 Thirlmere Gardens, Northwood, HA6 2RU, England. *Telephone:* (1923) 836220. *E-mail:* admin@upbeatclassical.co.uk. *Website:* www.upbeatclassical.co.uk.

CHEN, Mei-Ann, DMusArts; American (b. Taiwanese) conductor; *Music Director, Chicago Sinfonietta;* b. 1973, Taiwan. *Education:* Walnut Hill School, New England Conservatory, Univ. of Michigan with Kenneth Kiesler. *Career:* has lived in USA since 1989; Conductor, Portland Youth Philharmonic 2002–07; Asst Conductor, Baltimore Symphony Orchestra 2009–10, Oregon Symphony, Atlanta Symphony; Music Dir, Memphis Symphony Orchestra 2010–; Music Dir Chicago Sinfonietta 2011–; has worked with numerous orchestras including Chicago Symphony Orchestra, BBC Scottish Symphony, Bournemouth Symphony, Graz Symphony, Norwegian Radio Orchestra, Tampere Philharmonic, Trondheim Symphony, Nat. Symphony of Mexico and Netherlands Philharmonic at Concertgebouw, Amsterdam; has appeared jtly with Marin Alsop and Stefan Sanderling in subscription concerts with Baltimore Symphony, Colorado Symphony and Florida Orchestra. *Honours:* American Soc. of Composers, Authors and Publrs (ASCAP) Award 2004, winner, Malko Int. Conductors Competition 2005, Taki Concordia Fellowship 2007, Sunburst Award 2007, Helen M. Thompson Award, League of American Orchestras 2012. *Current Management:* c/o Patricia A. Winter, Opus 3 Artists, 470 Park Avenue South, 9th Floor North, New York, NY 10016, USA. *Telephone:* (212) 584-7525. *E-mail:* PWinter@opus3artists.com. *Website:* www .opus3artists.com. *Address:* Chicago Sinfonietta, 70 East Lake Street, Suite 226, Chicago, IL 60601, USA (office). *Telephone:* (312) 236-3681 (office). *Fax:* (312) 236-5429 (office). *Website:* www.chicagosinfonietta.org (office); meiannchen.com.

CHEN, Musheng; Chinese composer; b. 25 Jan. 1971, Zhejiang. *Education:* Shanghai Conservatory of Music, Conservatory of Geneva, Switzerland; studied with Chen Mingzhi, Yang Iiqing, Zhao Xiaosheng, Eric Gaudibert, Klaus Huber. *Career:* settled in Europe 2000; Composer in Residence, Cité International des Arts, Paris 2004–05; teacher, Shanghai Conservatory of Music 2006–; commissions from Berliner Philharmoniker, Shanghai Grand Theatre, Emilia Romagna Festival, Italy, Commande d'État, France, Pro-Helvetia, Switzerland. *Compositions include:* Yunnan Capriccio (piano concerto) 2006, A Dream in the Peony Garden for orchestra 2007, Splendid Overture 2008, Les franges du rêve for flute in sol and harp (first prize, ICOMS International Composition Competition, Italy) 2007. *Honours:* First Grand Prize, Concours Dutilleux, France 2004, Young Chinese Composer Award, Amsterdam 2005, Queen Elisabeth Competition Composition Award, Belgium 2006, First Symphony Prize, Ciutat di Tarragona, Spain 2008, winner, Dmitris Mitropoulos Int. Competition 2010. *Address:* Composition Department, Shanghai Conservatory of Music, 20 Fenyang Road, 200031 Shanghai, People's Republic of China (office). *Telephone:* (21) 64312000 (office). *E-mail:* musheng_chen@hotmail.com (home). *Website:* shcmusic.edu .cn (office); www.chenmusheng.com.

CHEN, Pi-hsien, DipMus; Taiwanese pianist; b. 1950. *Education:* studied in Taiwan and at the Cologne Musikhochschule, and with Hans Leygraf, masterclasses with Wilhelm Kempff, Tatiana Nikolayeva and Geza Anda. *Career:* from 1972 performances in London (BBC Proms, South Bank, Barbican), Amsterdam, Zürich, Berlin, Munich, Barcelona and Tokyo; festival appearances at Huddersfield, Lucerne, Schwetzingen, Hong Kong and Osaka; orchestras include London Symphony, BBC Symphony, Royal Concertgebouw, radio orchestras in Austria and Germany, the Züricher Kammerorchester, Tonhalle Orchestra and the Collegium Musicum Zürich; repertory ranges from Scarlatti to Boulez; piano duo performances with Pierre-Laurent Aimard. *Honours:* prizewinner Concours Reine Elisabeth, Belgium 1972, first prize Competition of the Rundfunkanstalten, Munich 1972. *Address:* c/o Naxos, Level 11, Cyberport 1, 100 Cyberport Road, Hong Kong (office).

CHEN, Qigang; French (b. Chinese) composer; b. 1951, Shanghai. *Education:* Cen. Conservatory of Music, Beijing, Univ. of Paris-IV Sorbonne. *Career:* conductor and composer, Zhejiang Symphony Orchestra 1975–78; Asst Prof. of Musical Writing, Cen. Conservatory of Music, Beijing 1983–84; studied with Olivier Messiaen in France 1984–88; training session on composition, Institut de Recherche et Co-ordination Acoustique/Musique (IRCAM), Paris 1987; Artistic Consultant for Festival Présences, Radio France 1996; Music Dir,

Beijing Summer Olympic Games Opening Ceremony 2008. *Compositions include:* Voyage d'un rêve 1987, Yuan 1988, Feu d'ombres 1990, Poème lyrique I 1990, Rêve d'un solitaire 1993, Un instrument de silence 1996, Reflet d'un temps disparu 1998, Poème lyrique II 1998, Wu Xing 1999, Instants d'un opéra de Pékin 2000, Raise the Red Lantern (ballet) 2000, Wu Xing (The Five Elements) 2001, Iris Dévoilée (Iris Unveiled) 2001, Un temps disparu (Reflections of Vanished Time) 2002, Enchantements oubliés 2004, You and Me (duet for male and female voice) (awarded "Five One Programmes" Prize for spiritual and civilization by Publicity Ministry of China) 2008, Er Huang 2009, Theme from Under the Hawthorn Tree (for male voice) 2010, Mother and Childhood (for male voice) 2011. *Recordings:* Iris Dévoilée, Poème lyrique II. *Honours:* first prize, French Ministry of Culture Int. Composition Contest 1986, SACEM (Soc. of Composers and Publishers) Hervé Dugardin Prize 1991, Prize Villa Medicis Hors les Murs 1993, Grand Prize of City of Paris 2000, SACEM Grand Prize for Symphony Music 2005. *Address:* c/o Gérard Billaudot Editeur, 14 rue de l'Echiquier, 75010 Paris, France (office). *Telephone:* 1-47-70-14-46 (office). *Fax:* 1-45-23-22-54 (office). *E-mail:* qigang.chen@wanadoo.fr (home). *Website:* www.chenqigang.com.

CHEN, Ray; Australian violinist; b. 6 March 1989, Taipei, Taiwan. *Education:* Suzuki Music Educ. Queensland, Curtis Inst. of Music, USA. *Career:* moved to Brisbane with family as baby; started playing violin aged four, invited to play solo with Queensland Philharmonic Orchestra aged eight; performed at opening celebration concert, Nagano Winter Olympics, Japan 1998; Russian debut playing Tchaikovsky Violin Concerto with Marinsky (Kirov) Orchestra, St Petersburg 2008. *Honours:* First Prize, Australian Youth Concerto Competition 2002, Australian Music Examinations Bd Sydney May Memorial Scholarship 2003, Australia Nat. Kendall Violin Competition 2005, winner, Sr Div., Menuhin Competition 2008, winner, Queen Elisabeth Competition, Belgium 2009, Young Concert Artists Competition 2009. *Current Management:* c/o Daniel Evans, CAMI Music, LLC, 5 Columbus Circle, 1790 Broadway, 16th Floor, New York, NY 10019-1412, USA. *Telephone:* (212) 841-9500. *Fax:* ((212) 841-9719. *E-mail:* devans@ camimusic.com. *Website:* www.camimusic.com; raychenviolin.com.

CHEN, Shih-hui, DMusA; Taiwanese composer; b. 6 Sept. 1962, Taibei. *Education:* Nat. Acad. of Arts. *Career:* resident in USA 1982–; currently Asst Prof. of Composition and Theory, Shepherd School of Music, Rice Univ. *Compositions include:* String Quartet No. 1 1979, String Quartet No. 2 1987, Water Ink 1988, Mime 1988, 66 Times 1992, Moments 1995, Little Dragonflies 1996, String Quartet No. 3 1998, Fu (Ambush) I 1998, Fu II 1999, 'i' 2001, Jian (Gold) 2002, Twice Removed 2000–02, Shui 2003, Furl 2004, String Quartet No. 4 2004. *Honours:* American Acad. in Rome Prize 1999, Guggenheim Fellowship 2000, Barlow Commission 2001. *Address:* c/o Shepherd School of Music, MS 532, Rice University, PO Box 1892, Houston, TX 77251-1892, USA (office). *Telephone:* (713) 348-3742 (office). *Website:* www.ruf.rice.edu (office).

CHEN, Xieyang; Chinese conductor; *Honorary Music Director, Shanghai Symphony Orchestra;* b. 4 May 1939, Shanghai; s. of Chen Dieyi and Liang Peiqiong; m. Wang Jianying 1973. *Education:* Music High School, Shanghai Conservatory. *Career:* Conductor, Shanghai Ballet 1965–84; studied with Prof. Otto Mueller, Yale Univ., USA 1981–82; Conductor, Aspen Music Festival, Group for Contemporary Music, New York, Brooklyn Philharmonia, Honolulu Symphony, Philippines State Orchestra, Hong Kong Philharmonic, Shanghai Symphony Orchestra, Cen. Philharmonic, Beijing 1981–83, Symphony Orchestra of Vilnius, Kaunas, Novosibirsk, USSR 1985, Tokyo Symphony Orchestra 1986, Orchestre Regional de Cannes 2003; Music Dir and Prin. Conductor Shanghai Symphony Orchestra 1984–2009, Hon. Music Dir 2009–; made recording for Kuklos CBE, France 1983; Dir China Musicians' Asscn; Pres. Shanghai Symphonic Music Lovers' Soc. *Honours:* Excellent Conducting Prize, Shanghai Music Festival 1986. *Address:* Shanghai Symphony Orchestra, 105 Hunan Road, Shanghai 200031, People's Republic of China. *Telephone:* 64335608 (office); 64672915 (home). *Fax:* 64333752 (office). *E-mail:* shso105@sh163.net (office). *Website:* www.sh -symphony.com.

CHEN, Yi, BA, MA, DMA; American (b. Chinese) composer and violinist; *Cravens Millsap Missouri Distinguished Professor in Composition, Kansas City Conservatory of Music and Dance, University of Missouri;* b. 4 April 1953, Guangzhou, China; m. 1983. *Education:* Central Conservatory of Music, Beijing, Columbia Univ., New York. *Career:* Concert Mistress, Beijing Opera Troupe Orchestra, Guangzhou 1970–78; Composer-in-Residence, The Women's Philharmonic, Chanticleer, San Francisco 1993–96; mem. Composition Faculty, Peabody Conservatory, Johns Hopkins Univ. 1996–98; Cravens Millsap Missouri Distinguished Prof. in Composition, Conservatory of Music and Dance, Univ. of Missouri-Kansas City 1998–; works performed and broadcast world-wide 1984–; mem. American Acad. of Arts and Sciences 2005–. *Compositions include:* Duo Ye No. 2 for orchestra, Symphony No. 1, Xian Shi for viola and orchestra, 3 Poems from Sung Dynasty for chorus, Woodwind Quintet, Near Distance sextet for chamber ensemble, As in a Dream for soprano, violin and cello, Overture No. 1 and No. 2 for Chinese orchestra, Piano Concerto, Symphony No. 2, Sparkle for chamber ensemble 1992, Song in Winter (two versions) 1993, Ge Xu (Antiphony) for orchestra 1994, The Linear for orchestra 1994, Shuo for string orchestra 1994, Set of Chinese Folksongs for mixed choir or school choir and strings 1994, Tang Poems Cantata 1995, Chinese Myths Cantata 1996, Golden Flute for flute and orchestra 1997, Spring Dreams for mixed chorus 1997, Fiddle Suite for erhu (Chinese fiddle) and string orchestra or full orchestra, Romance and Dance for string orchestra 1997, Sound of the Five for cello and string quartet, Eleanor's Gift for cello and orchestra 1998, Baban for piano solo, Chinese Poems for girls' chorus, Dunhuang Fantasy for organ and wind ensemble, Spring Festival for children's wind ensemble 1999, Chinese Folk Dance Suite for violin and orchestra 2001, Chinese Mountain Songs for women's choir 2001, Bright Moonlight for soprano and piano 2001, Know You How Many Petals Falling for mixed choir 2001, Ning for violin, cello and pipa 2001, To the New Millennium for mixed choir 2001, as like a raging fire... for chamber ensemble 2002, Burning for string quartet 2002, Singing in the Mountain for piano, Chinese Fables for erhu, pipa, cello, percussion 2002, Ballad, Dance and Fantasy for cello and full orchestra 2003, Caramoor's Summer for chamber orchestra 2003, Landscape for mixed choir 2003, The West Lake for mixed choir 2003, Chinese Ancient Dances for clarinet and piano 2004, Night Thoughts for flute, cello and piano 2004, Happy Rain on a Spring Night for chamber ensemble 2004, Yangko for violin and percussion 2005, Ji-Dong-Nuo for piano 2005, Ancient Dances for pipa and percussion 2005, Si Ji (Four Seasons) for orchestra 2005, Spring in Dresden for violin and orchestra 2005, Looking at the Sea for female choir 2006, The Han Figurines for mixed ensemble 2006, Three Bagatelles from China West for flute and piano or two flutes 2006, The Ancient Beauty for four Chinese instruments and string orchestra 2006, Tunes From My Home for violin, cello and piano 2007, China West Suite for two pianos 2007, The Ancient Chinese Beauty for recorders and string orchestra 2008, From the Path of Beauty for mixed choir and string quartet 2008, Septet for erhu, pipa, percussion and saxophone quartet 2008, Rhyme of Fire 2008, From Old Peking Folklore for violin and piano 2009, Jing Marimba 2009, Dragon Rhyme for symphonic band 2010, Memory for solo violin 2010, Angel Island Passages for children's chorus and string quartet 2010, With Flowers Blooming for women's choir 2010, Spring Rain for mixed choir 2010, Mount a Long Wind for orchestra 2010, Distance Can't Keep Us Two Apart for chorus 2011, Fountains of KC for full orchestra 2011, Jing Diao for orchestra 2011, Early Spring for mixed choir and chamber ensemble 2011, Let's Reach a New Height for mixed choir 2012, Blue, Blue Sky for orchestra 2012, Faith and Perseverance for orchestra 2012, The Soulful and the Perpetual for saxophone and piano 2012, I Hear the Siren's Call for mixed choir 2012. *Honours:* Ives Living Award, American Acad. of Arts and Letters 2001–04. *Current Management:* c/o Theodore Presser Co., 588 North Gulph Road, King of Prussia, PA 19406, USA. *Telephone:* (610) 592-1222. *Fax:* (610) 592-1229. *E-mail:* promotion@presser.com. *Website:* www.presser.com. *Address:* University of Missouri, Kansas City Conservatory, 4949 Cherry, PAC 519A, Kansas City, MO 64110, USA (office). *Telephone:* (816) 235-2911 (office). *Fax:* (816) 235-5265 (office). *E-mail:* cheyi@umkc.edu (office). *Website:* conservatory.umkc.edu/faculty (office); library.newmusicusa.org/ChenYi.

CHEN, Zuohuang, MM, DMA; Chinese/American conductor; *Music Director, China National Centre for the Performing Arts;* b. 2 April 1947, Shanghai, China; s. of Chen Ru Hui and Li He Zhen; m. Zaiyi Wang 1969; one c. *Education:* Cen. Conservatory of Music, Beijing, Univ. of Michigan, USA. *Career:* Musical Dir China Film Philharmonic 1974–76; Assoc. Prof., Univ. of Kansas, USA 1985–87; Prin. Conductor Cen. Philharmonic Orchestra of China 1987–96; Music Dir/Conductor Wichita Symphony Orchestra 1990–2000; Music Dir/Conductor Rhode Island Philharmonic Orchestra 1992–96; Artistic Dir/Conductor China Nat. Symphony Orchestra 1996–2000; Music Dir Orquesta Filarmónica de la UNAM (OFUNAM), Mexico 2002–06, Shanghai Philharmonic Orchestra 2004–08, Incheon Philharmonic Orchestra, South Korea 2006–10, Guiyang Symphony Orchestra 2010–; Artistic Dir China Nat. Centre for the Performing Arts, Beijing 2007–; guest conductor with numerous orchestras including Zurich Tonhalle Orchestra, Vancouver Symphony Orchestra, Budapest Philharmonic Orchestra and State Symphony, Symphony Orchestra of Hungary, Gulbenkian Orchestra, Iceland Symphony Orchestra, Tanglewood Music Festival Orchestra, Colorado Symphony Orchestra, Pacific Symphony Orchestra, Virginia Symphony Orchestra, Alabama Symphony Orchestra, Russian Philharmonic Orchestra, Haifa Symphony Orchestra, Slovak Radio Symphony Orchestra, Hong Kong Philharmonic Orchestra, Singapore Symphony Orchestra, Pusan Philharmonic Orchestra, Mexico Nat. Symphony Orchestra, Mexico City Philharmonic Orchestra, Taipei City Symphony Orchestra, Macao Symphony Orchestra, amongst others.

CHENG, Gloria, DMA; Chinese/American pianist; m. *Education:* Stanford Univ., Univ. of California, Los Angeles, Univ. of Southern California. *Career:* premiered many new compositions, including works composed for her by John Adams, David Raksin, Terry Riley, Esa-Pekka Salonen, Stephen Andrew Taylor, Chinary Ung, John Williams; collaborations with contemporary composers including Thomas Adès, Henry Brant, Earle Brown, Elliott Carter, George Crumb, John Harbison, György Ligeti, Witold Lutosławski, Steve Reich, and Steven Stucky; solo debut with Los Angeles Philharmonic 1998; festivals include Ojai, Tanglewood, Aspen, Bad Gleichenberg, Kuhmo (Finland), Chicago Humanities, Other Minds (San Francisco), and Composer-to-Composer (Telluride) Festivals; solo New York debut recital, Weill Recital Hall 1992; played at Lincoln Center, Radio France, Kennedy Center, Théâtre du Châtelet; collaboration with Calder Quartet; panelist, Minnesota Composers Forum, Coleman Chamber Music Competition, Calif. Arts Council, US Festivals Fund; Bd mem. American Music Center; mem. Music Faculty, UCLA. *Recordings include:* Piano Music of Messiaen, Piano Music of John Adams & Terry Riley, Piano Dance: A 20th-Century Portrait, Piano Music by Salonen, Stucky & Lutosławski (Grammy Award for Best Solo Instrumental Performance 2009) 2008, The Edge of Light: Messiaen/Saariaho 2013.

Honours: winner, League of Composers/ISCM performer competition 1992. *Address:* UCLA Department of Music, 2539 Schoenberg Music Building, Box 951616, Los Angeles, CA 90095-1616, USA (office). *Telephone:* (310) 825-4761 (office). *Website:* www.gloriachengpiano.com.

CHERICI, Paolo; Italian lute teacher; b. 26 March 1952, Naples. *Education:* Milan Conservatoire and Schola Cantorum of Basel. *Career:* concerts of Renaissance and Baroque music as lute soloist and in ensemble in Italy and abroad; appearances on radio and television in Italy and abroad; lute teacher at numerous summer courses; founder of the lute class, Milan Conservatoire. *Recordings:* F. da Milano/P. P. Borrono, Rose e Viole, Benigne de Bacilly, L'art de bien chanter, Vivaldi, Concerti a liuto solo, Monteverdi/Merula etc., Salve, O Regina, Pierre Guédron, Soupirs Meslés d'Amour, J'ay Pris Amours: Chansons au luth du XVIème siècle, Claude le Jeune, Airs et psaumes mesurés à l'Antique, Le intavolature edite da Ottaviana Petrucci. *Publications:* J. S. Bach, Opere per liuto, Opere scelte trascritte per chitarra, Vivaldi, sette concerti trascritti per liuto o chitarra, F. Da Milano, Antologia dalle opere per liuto, Dalza/Spinacino, Antologia delle intavolature di Ottaviano Petrucci, F. Manfredi Concertini per camera, Autori vari, 37 duetti liutistici del Rinascimento inglese, 20 duetti liutistici del Rinascimento italiano. *Honours:* Società Italiana del Liuto. *Address:* Via Ciro Menotti 7, 20129 Milan, Italy (home). *E-mail:* paolo@paolocherici.it (home). *Website:* www .paolocherici.it (home).

CHERNEY, Brian, BMus, MMus, PhD, ARCT; Canadian composer and academic; *Professor, Faculty of Music, McGill University;* b. 4 Sept. 1942, Peterborough, Ont.; s. of Harry Cherney and Sylvia Cherney (née Green); m. Rochelle Terri Soren 1969; one s. one d. *Education:* Univ. of Toronto, studied with Samuel Dolin and John Weinzweig. *Career:* Prof., Faculty of Music, McGill Univ., Montreal 1972–; mem. Canadian League of Composers; Assoc. Composer, Canadian Music Center; Assoc., Royal Conservatory of Toronto. *Compositions:* Chamber Concerto for viola and 10 players 1974, String Trio 1976, Dans le crépuscule du souvenir for piano 1977–80, Adieux for orchestra 1980, In the Stillness Between for wind ensemble 1982, River of Fire for harp and oboe d'amore 1983, In the Stillness of the Seventh Autumn for piano 1983, Into the Distant Stillness for orchestra 1984, String Quartet No. 3 1985, In Stillness Ascending for viola and piano 1986, Illuminations for string orchestra 1987, Shekhinah for solo viola 1988, Oboe Concerto 1989, Transfiguration for orchestra 1990, Et j'entends la nuit qui chante dans les cloches, for piano and orchestra 1990, Apparitions, for cello and 14 musicians 1991, Doppelganger for 2 flutes 1991, In the Stillness of September 1942 for English horn and 9 solo strings 1992, Like Ghosts from an Enchanter Fleeing, for cello and piano 1993, Die klingende Zeit, for flute and chamber ensemble 1993–94, String Quartet No. 4 1994, Et la solitude dérive au fil des fleuves, for orchestra 1995, Tombeau, for piano 1996, Echoes in the Memory for clarinet, cello and piano 1997, Entendre marcher un ange, for flute and percussion 1998, String Quartet No. 5 2000, La princesse lointaine, for harp, English horn and orchestra 2001, Tenebrae, for a cappella choir 2002, Vers minuit, for orchestra 2002, Le miroir des anges, for chamber ensemble and 8 cellos 2003, Die Niemandsrose for a cappella choir 2006, Quelques espaces entre les anges et la terre for wind ensemble 2005, An Unfinished Life (Etty Hillesum) for narrator, voices, choir and instruments 2007, String Quartet No. 6 2008–09, Brahms and the German Spirit for clarinet and cello 2009, Capriccio for solo cello 2010, Twenty-two Arguments for the Suspension of Disbelief for flute, piano and cello 2010. *Recordings include:* Adieux; River of Fire: Into the Distant Stillness; Illuminations. *Publications:* Harry Somers 1975; compositions published by Doberman-Yppan 1970–2004. *Honours:* First Place, String Trio, Int. Rostrum of Composers 1979, Jules Léger Prize for New Chamber Music 1985, Outstanding Teaching Award, McGill Univ. 2005. *Address:* Schulich School of Music, Strathcona Music Building, McGill University, 555 Sherbrooke Street West, Montreal, QC H3A 1E3, Canada (office). *Telephone:* (514) 398-4535 (ext. 00297) (office).

CHERNOMORTSEV, Victor; Russian singer (baritone); b. 1950, Krasnodar. *Education:* Tchaikovsky Conservatoire, Moscow. *Career:* many appearances throughout Russia in opera and concert; Mariinsky Theatre, St Petersburg, from 1994 as Mazeppa, Rigoletto, Prince Igor, Nabucco Tomsky in The Queen of Spades, Amonasro, Count Luna, Scarpia, Alberich in Das Rheingold and Grasnoi in The Tsar's Bride by Rimsky-Korsakov; Tours with the Kirov Opera throughout Europe and to the New York Metropolitan; Other roles include Robert in Iolanta and the Chinese Inspector in Stravinsky's The Nightingale; Sang Matreyev in War and Peace with the Kirov Opera at Covent Garden 2000. *Honours:* Honoured Artist of Russia.

CHERNOUSHENKO, Vladislav; Russian conductor; b. 14 Jan. 1936, Leningrad (now St Petersburg). *Education:* Leningrad State Conservatoire. *Career:* sang with the Boys Choir of Glinka State Capella from 1944; conducted Karelia State Radio Orchestra, then Leningrad Chamber Choir 1962–74; Music Dir Glinka State Capella 1974; directed premiere performance of Rachmaninov's complete Vespers 1974; re-established Symphony Orchestra of Glinka State Capella 1988, and toured in Germany, The Netherlands, Switzerland, Ireland and France, with a repertoire including Haydn, Shostakovich, Brahms, Bruckner, Schnittke and Mozart; Rector, Leningrad-St Petersburg State Conservatoire 1979.

CHERNOV, Alexei; Russian pianist; b. 1982. *Education:* Junior Coll. of Music, Moscow Conservatory (studies with Nina Rogal-Levitskaya and Natali Trull)), Royal Coll. of Music, London (with Vanessa Latarche). *Career:* teaches piano at Cen. Music School, Moscow Conservatory 2006–; currently post-graduate student, Royal Coll. of Music, London; has performed with orchestras led by Mikhail Pletnev, Ravil Martynov, Alexander Sladkovsky, Alexander Anissimov, Vladimir Sirenko, Dmitry Yablonsky, Igor Verbitsky, Enrique Bátiz, amongst others. *Honours:* scholarships from Ministry of Culture and Russian Performing Arts Foundation, Winner, Muse Int. Piano Competition (Greece) 2008, Winner, Morocco Int. Piano Competition, Casablanca 2009, Winner, Int. Piano Competition 'Spanish Composers' 2009, Winner, 13th Jaen Francaix Int. Piano Competition (France) 2010, Winner, 20th AMA Calabria Int. Piano Competition, Valsessia Musica (Italy) 2010, Winner, 4th Campillos Int. Piano Competition (Spain) 2010, Winner, Int. Ettore Pozzoli Piano Competition 2011. *Address:* Royal College of Music, Prince Consort Road, London, SW7 2BS, England. *Telephone:* (20) 7591-4300. *Fax:* (20) 7589-7740. *E-mail:* info@rcm.ac.uk. *Website:* www.rcm.ac.uk.

CHERNOV, Vladimir Kirillovich; Russian singer (baritone) and academic; *Professor of Vocal Studies, University of California, Los Angeles*; b. 1956, Belorechensk; m. Olga Chernova; one s. *Education:* Moscow Conservatory with Georgy Seleznev and Hugo Titz. *Career:* winner of All-Union Glinka Competition, int. competitions: Tchaikovsky (Moscow), Voci Virdiagni (Vercelli), M. Helin (Helsinki); soloist of Kirov (now Mariinsky) Theatre 1990–; debut in USA 1988 (La Bohème, Boston), in UK 1990 (Forza del Destino, Glasgow); perm. soloist of Metropolitan Opera 1990–, Wiener Staatsoper 1991–; guest singer at La Scala, Chicago Lyric Opera, Mariinsky Opera, La Monnaie (Brussels) and other theatres of Europe and USA; leading parts in operas Queen of Spades, Boris Godunov, Barber of Seville, La Traviata, Eugene Onegin, Don Carlos, War and Peace, The Masked Ball, Faust, Rigoletto, Falstaff, Hérodiade (Hérod), La Cenerentola (Dandini), Nabucco (title role); in concerts and recitals performs opera arias, song cycles of Mahler, Tchaikovsky, romances; Regents' Lecturer, Voice and Opera, UCLA 2005, Prof. of Vocal Studies 2007–; Faculty mem. Opera Ischia. *Current Management:* Robert Lombardo and Associates, 61 West 62nd Street, Suite 6f, New York, NY 10023, USA. *Telephone:* (212) 586-4453. *Fax:* (212) 581-5771. *E-mail:* robert@robertlombardo.com. *Website:* www.rlombardo.com. *Address:* UCLA Department of Music, 2539 Schoenberg Music Building, Box 951616, Los Angeles, CA 90095-1616, USA (office). *Telephone:* (310) 794-9501 (office). *Fax:* (310) 206-4738 (office). *E-mail:* musicwebmaster@arts.ucla.edu (office). *Website:* www.music.ucla.edu; www.vchernov.com.

CHERNYKH, Pavel; Russian singer (baritone); b. 1960, Moscow. *Education:* Tchaikovsky Music School, Moscow Conservatoire with Yevgeny Nesterenko. *Career:* stage debut in season 1989–90 as Tchaikovsky's Onegin at the Bolshoi; concerts and recordings with Maly State Symphony, St Petersburg Philharmonic and Moscow Radio Orchestra 1987; further performances as Silvio in Pagliacci, Robert in Tchaikovsky's Iolanta, Yeletsky in The Queen of Spades and Renato (Ballo in Maschera); sang Onegin at Paris Opéra Comique 1987, for Vlaamse Opera in Antwerp 1990; soloist, Bolshoi Theatre 1990–; Stars of Bolshoi Theatre concerts in Germany and Norway 1990; toured with Bolshoi as Onegin in USA 1990 and sang at Wolf Trap Theatre; Edinburgh Festival as Onegin 1991; sang Germont at St Petersburg 1998. *Honours:* second prize, Int. Antonin Dvorak Competition, Czechoslovakia 1987. *Address:* Bolshoi Theatre, Moscow 125009, Theatre Square, 1, Russia. *Website:* www.bolshoi.ru.

CHESWORTH, David Anthony, BA; British composer and sound designer; b. 31 March 1958, Stoke, England. *Education:* La Trobe Univ., Nat. Young Composers' School, Sound Design School. *Career:* freelance composer 1993–; commissions from Paris Autumn Festival 1985, Melbourne Festival 1990–91, Australian Broadcasting Corporation 1993. *Compositions include:* Choral for piano 1982, Stories of Imitation and Corruption for orchestra and tape 1986, Lacuna for chamber opera 1992, Duet I for violin, cello and vibraphones 1993, Exotica Suite for ensemble 1993, The Soft Skin for cello, clarinet and piano 1993, The Two Executioners (chamber opera) 1994, Focal Wall Soundscape 1995, Cosmonart (opera, commissioned by Opera Australia) 1997, Olympic Stadium Sound Environment (commissioned by the Olympic Co-ordination Authority) 1999. *Honours:* Prix Ars Electronica, Austria 1993.

CHEW, Geoffrey Alexander, BA, MusB, PhD; British academic; b. 23 April 1940, South Africa; s. of James Alexander Chew and Florence Hilda Chew; m. Jennifer Comrie 1967; one s. two d. *Education:* Royal Coll. of Music, Caius Coll., Cambridge, Univ. of Manchester. *Career:* Univ. Lecturer, Johannesburg 1968–70, Aberdeen 1970–77, Royal Holloway, Univ. of London 1977–05; mem. Royal Musical Assen, American Musicological Soc., Gesellschaft für Musikforschung, Int. Musicological Soc., Soc. for Music Theory. *Publications:* contrib. to Journal of The American Musicological Society, Music Analysis, Musiktheorie, Cambridge Opera Journal. *Address:* Department of Music, Royal Holloway, University of London, Egham Hill, Egham, Surrey, TW20 0EX (office); The Mount, Malt Hill, Egham, Surrey, TW20 9PB, England (home). *Telephone:* (1784) 443537 (office). *E-mail:* g.chew@rhul.ac.uk.

CHI, Jacob, BA, MM, DMA; Chinese music director, conductor and academic; *Music Director and Conductor, Pueblo Symphony Orchestra*; b. 9 Dec. 1952, Qingdao, Shandong; m. Dr Lin Chang 1987; one s. one d. *Education:* Siena Heights Univ., Univ. of Michigan, Michigan State Univ. with Leon Gregorian, USA. *Career:* Conductor, Qingdao Opera, China 1975–80; Music Dir and Conductor, Pueblo Symphony Orchestra 1991–; Music Dir and Conductor, Miami Univ. Symphony Orchestra 1993–97; Conductor, Colorado Music Festival 1995–; Conductor, Echtenach Int. Music Festival, Luxembourg 1996; Prof., Univ. of Southern Colorado 1991–93, Miami Univ. 1993–97; Prof. of Music, Colorado State Univ.-Pueblo 1997–; Prin. Conductor, Marquette Symphony, Mich.; Artistic and Musical Dir Chihuahua State Philharmonic, Mexico 2005–07; Prin. Guest Conductor and Artistic Adviser, Hua-ou Philharmonic, Qingdao, China; guest conductor with numerous orchestras; mem. Conductors Guild, American Symphony League, Music Teachers Nat. Assen. *Compositions include:* Apricot Field (operetta) 1976. *Honours:* First Prize, Fine Art Composition Contest, Shantung, China 1976. *Address:* Pueblo Symphony Orchestra, 301 North Main, Suite 106, Pueblo, CO 81003, USA (office). *E-mail:* jacob.chi@csupueblo.edu (office). *Website:* www.pueblosymphony.com (office).

CHIARA, Maria; Italian singer (soprano) and actress; b. 24 Nov. 1939, Oderzo; m. Antonio Cassinelli. *Education:* Conservatorio Benedetto Marcello, Austria, with Maria Carbone. *Career:* debut as Desdemona in Otello, Doge's Palace, Venice, 1965, then Rome Opera debut 1965; frequent performances in Italy, including Turandot with Plácido Domingo, Verona 1969; debuts Germany and Austria 1970; début La Scala, Milan as Micaela, Carmen 1972; debut Royal Opera House, Covent Garden, London, Turandot 1973; debut Metropolitan Opera, New York in La Traviata and at Lyric Opera, Chicago in Manon Lescaut 1977; mem. jury, San Marino Int. Voice Competition 2011. *Films include:* Hannah and Her Sisters 1986. *Recordings include:* Aïda, Madame Butterfly, Il Segreto di Susanna and a disc of operatic arias (Decca).

CHICHON, Karel Mark, OBE; Gibraltarian conductor; *Chief Conductor, Deutsche Radio Philharmonie Saarbrücken Kaiserslautern*; b. 1971, London, England; m. Elīna Garanča. *Education:* Royal Acad. of Music, London. *Career:* fmr Asst Conductor to Giuseppe Sinopoli and Valery Gergiev; invited by the Vienna Philharmonic Orchestra to conduct concerts at their Int. Orchestra Inst. in Salzburg 2004, 2005, 2006; regular guest conductor with English Chamber Orchestra 2003–; Chief Conductor Graz Symphony Orchestra 2006–09; Chief Conductor and Artistic Dir Latvian Nat. Symphony Orchestra 2009–12; Chief Conductor Deutsche Radio Philharmonie Saarbrücken Kaiserslautern 2011–; regularly conducts at Wiener Staatsoper, Deutsche Oper Berlin, Bayerisches Staatsoper Munich, Teatro dell'Opera di Roma, Teatro Comunale di Bologna, Teatro Real Madrid, Gran Teatre del Liceu Barcelona and with orchestras including Royal Concertgebouw Orchestra, London Symphony Orchestra, Rundfunk-Sinfonieorchester Berlin, Radio-Symphonieorchester Wien, Wiener Symphoniker, English Chamber Orchestra, Sinfonica Nazionale della RAI, Russian Nat. Orchestra in Vienna, Berlin, Paris, Rome, Turin, Bologna, Munich, Frankfurt, Stuttgart, Madrid and Valencia; debut with Royal Concertgebouw Orchestra, Amsterdam 2010; future debuts include Madama Butterfly at the Metropolitan Opera, New York and La Bohème at Teatro alla Scala, Milan; frequent guest conductor with leading orchestras throughout the world at venues including Berlin Philharmonie, Musikverein Vienna, Konzerthaus Vienna, Concertgebouw Amsterdam, Royal Festival Hall, London, Théâtre des Champs-Élysées, Paris, Munich Philharmonie, Laeiszhalle, Hamburg, Alter Oper, Frankfurt, Great Hall of the Moscow Conservatory, Auditorio Nacional de Musica, Madrid and Seoul Arts Centre, S Korea. *Recordings:* Habanera, Elīna Garanča (with Orchestra Sinfonica Nazionale della RAI) 2010; over the next five years will record complete orchestral works of Dvořák with the Deutsche Radio Philharmonie. *Address:* c/o Liene Lapševska, Gibraltar Philharmonic Society, 72 Prince Edward's Road, PO Box 1479, Gibraltar (office); Deutsche Radio Philharmonie Saarbrücken Kaiserslautern, Funkhaus Halberg, 66100 Saarbrücken, Germany (office). *Telephone:* 56011000 (Gibraltar) (office); (681) 6022210 (Saarbrücken) (office). *Fax:* (681) 602–2243 (Saarbrücken) (office). *E-mail:* tgpsociety@gibtelecom.net (office); info@drp-orchester.de (office). *Website:* www.drp-orchester.de (office); www.philharmonic.gi (office); www.karelmarkchichon.com (home).

CHIHARA, Paul Seiko; American composer; b. 9 July 1938, Seattle, WA. *Education:* Cornell Univ. with Robert Palmer, studied with Nadia Boulanger in Paris, Ernst Pepping in Berlin and with Gunther Schuller at the Berkshire Music Center. *Career:* teacher, Univ. of California, Los Angeles 1966; Assoc. Prof., UCLA until 1974; founder and Dir, Twice Ensemble; Andrew Mellon Prof., California Inst. of Technology 1975; teacher, California Inst. of the Arts 1976; Composer-in-Residence, San Francisco Ballet 1980; commissions from the Boston Symphony Orchestra and the Los Angeles Philharmonic. *Compositions include:* Magnificat for six female voices 1965, Driftwood for string quartet 1967, Branches for two bassoons and percussion 1968, Forest Music for orchestra 1970, Windsong for cello and orchestra 1971, Grass for double bass and orchestra 1972, Ceremony III for flute and orchestra 1973, Shinju (ballet) 1975, Missa Carminum 1975, The Beauty of the Rose is in its Passing for ensemble 1976, String Quartet (Primavera) 1977, two Symphonies 1975, 1980, Misletoe Bride (ballet) 1978, Concerto for string quartet and orchestra 1980, Sinfonia Concertante for nine instruments 1980, The Tempest (ballet) 1980, Saxophone Concerto 1981, Sequoia for string quartet and tape 1984, Shogun the Musical 1990, Forever Escher for saxophone quartet and string quartet 1995, Sonata for viola and piano 1997, Minidoka for chorus, percussion and tape 1998, Concerto for violin, clarinet and orchestra 1999, also film and television scores, arrangements for musicals.

CHILCOTT, Robert (Bob) Lionel; British composer, conductor and fmr singer; *Principal Guest Conductor, BBC Singers*; b. 9 April 1955, Plymouth, Devon, England; m. 1st Polly Ballard 1981; one s. three d.; m. 2nd Kate Ledger 2005; one d. *Education:* Royal Coll. of Music, London. *Career:* mem. Soc. for Promotion of New Music, Royal Soc. of Musicians. *Compositions:* Singing by

Numbers 1995, Fragments From His Dish 1995, City Songs 1996, Organ Dances 1996, Friends 1997, The Elements 1997, Little Jazz Mass, Spells, Jubilate, The Making of the Drum, Canticles of Light, Advent Antiphons, The Modern Man I Sing, Salisbury Vespers 2009, Requiem 2010, Jazz Songs of Innocence 2011, Nidaros Jazz Mass, Angry Planet 2012. *Current Management:* c/o Choral Connections, 14 Stevens Close, Prestwood, Great Missenden, Bucks., HP16 0SQ, England. *Telephone:* (1494) 866389. *E-mail:* val@choralconnections.com. *Website:* www.choralconnections.com. *Address:* c/o Oxford University Press, New Music Promotion, Great Clarendon Street, Oxford, OX2 2DP, England. *E-mail:* bobchilcott@aol.com.

CHILINGIRIAN, Levon, OBE, FRCM, ARCM; British violinist and academic; *Professor, Royal College of Music*; b. 28 May 1948, Nicosia, Cyprus; nephew of Manoug Parikian; m. Susan Paul Pattie 1983; one s. *Education:* Royal Coll. of Music. *Career:* f. Chilingirian String Quartet 1971; has performed in N and S America, Africa, Australasia, Europe and Far East; Prof., Royal Coll. of Music 1980–; Musical Dir Camerata Nordica of Sweden; BBC Beethoven Competition 1969, Munich Duo Competition (with Clifford Benson) 1971. *Recordings include:* 10 Mozart quartets, last three Schubert quartets, Debussy and Ravel quartets, Schubert octet and quintet, six Bartók quartets and piano quintet, late and middle Dvořák quartets, Tippett Triple Concerto; music by Panufnik, Tavener, Pärt, Chausson, Grieg, Vierne, Hahn, Komitas, McEwan, Michael & Lennox Berkeley, Mozart and Eliasson (with Chilingirian Quartet and Camerata Nordica). *Publications:* Edvard Grieg's F Major Quartet 1999. *Honours:* Hon. DMus (Sussex) 1992; Cobbett Medal 1995, Royal Philharmonic Soc. Chamber Music Award 1995. *Current Management:* c/o Ikon Arts Management, Suite 114, Business Design Centre, 52 Upper Street, London, N1 0QH, England. *E-mail:* costa@ikonarts.com. *Address:* 7 Hollingbourne Road, London, SE24 9NB, England. *Telephone:* (20) 7978-9104. *Fax:* (20) 7274-5764. *E-mail:* spplchil@aol.com (home); levon@chilingirianquartet.co.uk. *Website:* www.chilingirianquartet.co.uk.

CHIN, Unsuk; South Korean composer; b. 14 July 1961, Seoul; m. Maris Gothoni; one s. *Education:* Nat. Univ. of Seoul, studied with György Ligeti in Hamburg. *Career:* work features both electronic and acoustic scores; work has been performed worldwide by Ensemble Intercontemporain, Ensemble Modern, Kronos Quartet, London Sinfonietta, Nieuw Ensemble, pianist Rolf Hinds, violinist Viviane Hagner and conductors including Sir Simon Rattle, Gustavo Dudamel, Esa-Pekka Salonen, Kent Nagano, David Robertson, Peter Eötvös and Neeme Järvi; works in electronic studio of the Technische Univ., Berlin 1988–; composer-in-residence, Deutsches Symphonie Orchester, Berlin 2001–02, Seoul Philharmonic 2006–; Artistic Dir, Seoul Philharmonic's Contemporary Music Series and Philharmonia Orchestra's Music of Today. *Compositions include:* Gestalten 1984, Troerrinnen 1986, Gradus ad infinitum 1989, Akrostichon-Wortspiel (Acrostic-Wordplay) for soprano and ensemble 1991–93, Santika Ekatala 1993, Fantaisie mécanique 1994, ParaMetaString 1996, Klavierkonzert 1996–97, Xi for ensemble and electronics (Bourges Electroacoustic Music Prize) 1998, Miroirs des temps 1999, six Piano Etudes 1999–2000, Kalà 2000, Violinkonzert (Grawemeyer Award for Music Composition 2004) 2001, Doppelkonzert 2002, snagS & Snarls 2003–04, Cantatrix Sopranica 2005, Alice in Wonderland (opera) 2007, Rocaná for orchestra 2007, Concerto for Cello and Orchestra (British Composer Award, International category 2010), cosmigimmicks 2012. *Recordings:* Electroacoustic Music 1996, Orchestral Works 2005, Rocaná and Violin Concerto 2009. *Honours:* Schoenberg Prize 2005, Prince Pierre Foundation Music Award 2010, Ho-Am Prize for the Arts 2012. *Address:* c/o Boosey and Hawkes MP Ltd, Aldwych House, 71–91 Aldwych, London, WC2B 4HN, England (office). *Website:* www.boosey.com/chin (office).

CHINGARI, Marco; Italian singer (baritone); b. 1963, Rome. *Career:* sang at Busseto, Italy, 1987–88 in Verdi's Il Corsaro and La Forza del Destino; Appearances at Rome Opera, 1989 in Mascagni's Il Piccolo Marat; Season 1991–92: As Mathieu in Andrea Chénier at Turin and Escamillo in Carmen at Palma; Season 1994–95: As Max in Betly by Donizetti in Bergamo and in Zandonai's Francesca da Rimini at Palermo; Other roles include Michonnet in Adriana Lecouvreur and Verdi's Duke of Mantua; Season 2000 as Tonio in Pagliacci at Bologna and Sharpless in Butterfly at Torre del Lago. *Recordings:* La Fanciulla del West; I Vespri Siciliani. *Honours:* Prizewinner, Voci Verdiane Competition, Busseto. *Current Management:* Agentur Klein, Possartstrasse 8, 81679 Munich, Germany. *Telephone:* (89) 45579931. *Fax:* (89) 45579942. *E-mail:* aklein@agenturklein.de. *Website:* www.agenturklein.de.

CHITTY, Alison Jill, OBE; British stage designer; b. 16 Oct. 1948, d. of Ernest Hedley Chitty and Irene Joan Waldron. *Education:* King Alfred School, London, St Martin's School of Art, Central School of Art and Design, London. *Career:* theatre designer (over 40 productions), Victoria Theatre, Stoke on Trent 1970–79; Co-Dir Motley Theatre Design Course 1992–2000, Dir 2000–; Design Consultant, Rose Theatre, Kingston 2007–08; designs for premiere production of Tippett's New Year, at Houston and Glyndebourne 1989–90, premieres of Birtwistle's Gawain 1991, Goehr's Arianna at Covent Garden, Jenůfa in Dallas, Billy Budd in Geneva, Paris, Los Angeles and London, Giulio Cesare and Der fliegende Holländer in Bordeaux, Khovanshchina for ENO, Turandot in Paris, Otello in Munich, Tristan und Isolde at Chicago and Seattle, Die Meistersinger in Copenhagen, Aida in Geneva, Dialogues des Carmélites for Santa Fe Opera, premiere production of Birtwistle's The Last Supper at Berlin and Glyndebourne 2000–01; Fellow, Birkbeck Coll., London 2011. *Stage:* numerous productions for Royal Nat. Theatre (RNT) including: A Month in the Country, Don Juan, Much Ado About Nothing, The Prince of Homberg, Danton's Death, Major Barbara, Kick for Touch, Tales from Hollywood, Antigone, Martine, Venice Preserv'd, Fool for Love, Neaptide, Antony and Cleopatra, The Tempest, The Winter's Tale, Cymbeline, Cardiff East; productions for RSC including: Tartuffe, Volpone, Breaking the Silence, Romeo and Juliet; other productions including: Old King Cole (Theatre Royal Stratford East), Orpheus Descending (Haymarket), The Rose Tattoo (Playhouse), Ecstasy and Uncle Vanya (Hampstead Theatre), Measure for Measure and Julius Caesar (Riverside Studios), The Way South (Bush Theatre), Carmen Jones and Lennon (Crucible, Sheffield), Remembrance of the Past (RNT) (Olivier Award 2001) 2000, Hamlet (RSC) 2001, Luther (RNT) 2001, Scenes from the Big Picture (RNT) 2003, The Merchant of Venice (Chichester) 2004, The Master and Marguerita (Chichester) 2004, Days of Wine and Roses (Donmar Warehouse) 2005, King Lear (Chichester) 2005, Two Thousand Years (RNT) 2005, The Voysey Inheritance (RNT) (Best Costume Designer, Laurence Olivier Award 2007) 2006, The Vortex (UK tour and Apollo Theatre) 2007–08, Uncle Vanya (Rose Theatre, Kingston, and UK tour) 2008, Ecstasy (Hampstead and West End) 2011, Grief (RNT) 2011, A Provincial Life (NTW) 2012. *Opera:* numerous productions including: The Marriage of Figaro (Opera North), New Year (Houston Grand Opera), Bow Down/Down by the Green Wood Side (South Bank), The Siege of Calais (Wexford), The Vanishing Bridegroom (Saint Louis Opera Theatre), Gawain (Royal Opera House—ROH), Falstaff (Gothenberg Music Theatre), Jenůfa (Dallas Opera) 1994, Billy Budd (Grand Theatre Geneva) 1994, Blond Eckbert (Santa Fé Opera) 1995, Arianna (ROH) 1995, Billy Budd (Bastille Opera Paris) 1996, The Mask of Orpheus (Royal Festival Hall) 1996, Die Meistersinger von Nürnberg (Danish Royal Opera, Copenhagen) 1996, Misper (Glyndebourne) 1997, Turandot (Bastille Opera Paris) 1997, Billy Budd (Dallas Opera and Houston Grand Opera) 1997–98, The Flying Dutchman (Bordeaux Opera) 1998, Tristan and Isolde (Seattle Opera) 1998, The Bartered Bride (ROH at Sadler's Wells) 1998, Julius Caesar (Bordeaux Opera) 1999, Otello (Bavarian Opera Munich) 1999, 2013, Dialogues of the Carmelites (Santa Fé Opera) 1999, Aida (Grand Théâtre, Geneva) 1999, Tristan and Isolde (Lyric Opera Chicago) 2000, The Last Supper (Staatsoper Berlin and Glyndebourne) 2000, Ion (Aldeburgh Festival, Almeida Opera) 2000, Billy Budd (Seattle and Tel Aviv) 2000, Jenůfa (San Francisco) 2000, La Vestale (ENO) 2002, Bacchae (RNT) 2002, Original Sin (Crucible, Sheffield) 2002, Cavalleria Rusticana (Royal Albert Hall) 2002, Pagliacci (Royal Albert Hall) 2002, Khovanshchina (ENO) 2003, L'enfant et les Sortilèges (Maastricht) 2003, Così fan tutte (ENO) 2003, The Flying Dutchman (Vilnius) 2004, The Io Passion (Aldeburgh Festival, Almeida Opera, Bregenz and UK tour) 2004, Billy Budd (Washington) 2004, Jenůfa (Dallas Opera) 2004, Tangier Tattoo (Glyndebourne) 2005, Midsummer Marriage (Chicago Lyric Opera) 2005, Carmen (Greek Nat. Opera) 2007, The Minotaur (ROH) 2008, 2013, The Flying Dutchman (Bergen) 2008, Adrianna's Fall (Cologne) 2008, Hippolyte at Arice (Reis Opera, Netherlands) 2009, Semper Dolors, Semper Dowland/The Corridor (Aldeburgh Festival, Queen Elizabeth Hall, Bregenz) 2009, La Forza del Destino (Holland Park Opera) 2010, Rigoletto (La Fenice Venice, Reggio Emelia) 2010, Betrothal in a Monastery (Toulouse and Paris) 2011, Madame Butterfly (Oslo) 2012, Rigoletto (Venice) 2012, Nabucco (La Scala, Milan, ROH) 2013, Minotaur (ROH) 2013, Parsifal (ROH) 2013, Billy Budd (LA Opera) 2014. *Exhibitions:* Alison Chitty Design Process 1970–2010 Retrospective Exhbn, Nat. Theatre 2010. *Films:* Blue Jean, Aria, Life is Sweet, Black Poppies, Naked, Secrets and Lies (Palme d'Or, Cannes), The Turn of the Screw. *Honours:* Dr hc (Staffordshire) 2005; Mischa Black Award 2007, Young Vic Award 2008, Royal Designer for Industry, RSA 2009. *Current Management:* c/o Allied Artists, Southbank House, Black Prince Road, London, SE1 7SJ, England. *Telephone:* (20) 7589-6243. *Fax:* (20) 7662-1720. *Address:* Watlington House, Stocks Green, Castle Acre, King's Lynn, PE32 2AE, England (home). *E-mail:* ajcoldfield@talktalk.net.

CHIU, Frederic, BS, BMus, MMus; American pianist. *Education:* Indiana Univ., Juilliard School, Ecole Normale de Musique, Paris. *Career:* began career in Paris; has given concerts in Antwerp, Berlin, Brussels, Frankfurt, The Hague, London, Milan, Rome, Warsaw, Africa, Asia, USA; co-f. Consonances Festival, St Nazaire, France. *Recordings include:* 23 recordings including Liszt transcriptions of Schubert's Schwanengesang, Chopin's Etudes and Rondeaux, complete recording of Prokofiev works, Mendelssohn Sonatas, Liszt Symphony No. 5, Liszt Années de pèlerinage, Saint-Saëns Carnival of the Animals. *Honours:* Petscheck Award, American Pianists' Asscn Fellowship and numerous other awards. *Current Management:* c/o Thea Dispeker Inc., 59 East 54th Street, Suite 81, New York, NY 10022, USA. *Telephone:* (212) 421-7676. *Fax:* (212) 935-3279. *E-mail:* galiya@dispeker.com. *Website:* www.dispeker.com. *E-mail:* contact@fredericchiu.com (office). *Website:* www.fredericchiu.com.

CHIUMMO, Umberto; Italian singer (bass-baritone); b. 1970. *Education:* Pescara Conservatoire. *Career:* engagements as Dulcamara at Parma, Enrico in Anna Bolena at Washington and Raimondo in Lucia di Lammermoor for Welsh National and New Israeli Operas; Gounod's Mefistofele at Como, Frère Laurent at the Opéra Comique, Fenicio in Rossini's Ermione at La Monnaie, Brussels, and Alidoro in Houston; Don Giovanni at Sassari, Leporello in Turin and Publio in La Clemenza di Tito for Welsh National Opera; Count in Le nozze di Figaro for Rome Opera, and Bartolo at La Scala, Milan; Ariodate in Xerxes at Monaco and Ircano in Ricciardo e Zoraide at the Rossini Opera Festival, Pesaro; Rossini's Basilio and Mozart's Figaro; Garibaldo in Handel's Rodelinda at the Festival; Raimondo in Toulouse, Leporello in Turin, and Ariodate for the Bayerische Staatsoper, Munich. *Honours:* winner, Concurso

A. Belli. *Current Management:* Stage Door, Via San Giorgio 4, 40121 Bologna, Italy. *Telephone:* (051) 262126. *Fax:* (051) 271452. *E-mail:* info@stagedoor.it. *Website:* www.stagedoor.it.

CHLITSIOS, George, MMus, FLCM; Greek conductor, composer and academic; *Music Director, Tsakalof Symphony Orchestra and Opera;* b. 25 March 1969, Volos, Thessaly. *Education:* Epirotic Conservatory, Ioannina, Rotterdam Conservatorium and Royal (Koninklijk) Conservatorium, The Hague, Netherlands, London Coll. of Music, Thames Valley Univ. and Univ. of Surrey, UK, Aristotle Univ., Thessaloniki. *Career:* debut as Conductor, Tsakalof Youth Symphony Orchestra 1989; Prin. Conductor, Tsakalof Symphony Orchestra 1993–97, Music Dir 1997–; Guest Conductor, LCM Symphony Orchestra 1994, Athens State Orchestra 1997; Prin. Conductor, Epirotiki Opera, Greece 1997–; Guest Conductor, New Sounds Chamber Orchestra 2002, 2006, Plovdiv State Ballet 2002, Tirana Opera Symphony Orchestra 2004, Albanian Radio TV Symphony Orchestra 2005, 2014, 2016, Sofia Philharmonic Orchestra 2006, Cairo Symphony Orchestra 2008, Pazardjik Symphony Orchestra 2009, Thessaloniki Symphony Orchestra 2012; concerts in Greece, Spain, France, UK, Germany, Albania, Bulgaria, Italy, Egypt; conducted world premieres of many symphonic works; appearances on major TV and radio networks in Greece and abroad; Lecturer, North Campus, Yiannena Campus 1994–2001; Lecturer, Central Coll. 2002–10; Prof., Epirotic Conservatory, Ioannina 1996–; Artistic Dir, Municipal Conservatory, Preveza 2003–; Artistic Dir Epirotic Conservatory, Igoumenitsa 2010–14; mem. Inc. Soc. of Musicians, American Symphony Orchestra League, Soc. for Promotion of New Music, American Musicological Soc. *Honours:* Acad. of Athens Scholarship 1993, Rep. Conductor for Greece, VE Day Celebrations, London 1995, Mayor of Ioannina's Medal 1995, Mayor of Kifisia's Medal 1996. *Current Management:* c/o FirstClef, 1022-377 Ridelle Avenue, Toronto, ON M6B 1K2, Canada. *Telephone:* (647) 238-0015. *E-mail:* info@firstclef.com. *Website:* www.firstclef.com. *Address:* Tsakalof Symphony Orchestra, Platia G, Stavrou 5, 454 44 Ioannina, Greece. *E-mail:* gchlitsios@hotmail.com (office). *Website:* www.chlitsios.gr.

CHMURA, Gabriel, DipMus, MA; Polish conductor; *Artistic Director, Poznan Opera;* b. 7 May 1946, Wrocław; m. Mareile Chmura; one s. one d. *Education:* Vienna Acad. of Music, Austria, Ecole Normale de Musique, France, Tel-Aviv Univ. *Career:* grew up in Israel; Asst to Karajan, 1971–73; Generalmusikdirektor, Aachen, 1974–83; Bochum Symphony Orchestra 1983–87; Music Dir-Desig. National Arts Centre Orchestra, Ottawa, Canada, 1986–87, Prin. Conductor and Music Dir 1987–90; Music Dir Polish National Radio Symphony Orchestra, Katowice 2001–12; Artistic Dir Poznan Opera 2012–; Guest Conductor, Berlin Philharmonic Orchestra, Vienna Symphony Orchestra, London Symphony Orchestra, Orchestre Nationale de France, Paris, Tonhalle Orchester, Zürich, North German Radio Symphony Orchestra, Hamburg, Bavarian Radio Symphony Orchestra, Munich, South German Radio Symphony Orchestra, Stuttgart, New York Philharmonic Orchestra, Paris Opéra, Bavarian State Opera, Munich; conducted Werther at Parma, 1990. *Compositions include:* Pièce pour piano, 1968; 3 Songs for soprano and piano; Text James Joyce. *Recordings include:* Mendelssohn Overtures with London Symphony Orchestra; Schubert, Lazarus; Haydn Symphonies 6, 7, 8 with National Arts Centre Orchestra, Canada. *Honours:* Gold Medal, Guido Cantelli Conducting Competition, Milan 1971, 1st Prize, Herbert von Karajan Conducting Competition, Berlin 1971, Prix Mondial du Disque de Montreux 1983. *Address:* Teatr Wielki im. Stanisława Moniuszki, ul. Fredry 9, 61-701 Poznań, Poland. *E-mail:* gabriel@chmura.cc. *Website:* www.opera.poznan.pl; www.chmura.cc.

CHO, Eun-hwa; South Korean composer; b. 1973, Pusan. *Education:* Seoul Nat. Univ., Hochschule für Musik Hanns Eisler, Berlin. *Career:* compositions performed at major music festivals worldwide, including Asian Contemporary Music Festival, Seoul 2002, Ultraschall Festival für neue Musik, Berlin 2003, Acanthesfestival 2003, Int. Ferienkurse für Neue Musik, Darmstadt 2004, Paxos Spring Music Festival, Greece 2006, Music Today 21, Tokyo 2006, by ensembles including Arditti Quartet, Molinari Quartet, Ensemble Modern, Tokyo Sinfonietta, Ensemble TIMF. *Honours:* Hanns Eisler Prize, Berlin 2002, First Prize, Weimarer Frühjahrstage für zeitgenössische Musik 2003, Busoni Composition Prize, Akademie der Künste, Berlin 2008, winner, Queen Elisabeth Competition 2008.

CHODOS, Gabriel, MA; American pianist and teacher; b. 7 Feb. 1939, White Plains, NY. *Education:* Univ. of California, Los Angeles, Akad. für Musik, Vienna, Seoul Nat. Univ., Edward Aldwell Center of the Jerusalem Acad. of Music. *Career:* debut recital at Carnegie Hall, New York 1970; other recitals at Guildhall School of Music and Drama, London, Acad. of Music, Tallinn, Estonia; appearances throughout USA; numerous tours of Europe, Israel and Japan; solo performances with Chicago Symphony Orchestra, Radio Philharmonic Netherlands, Jerusalem Symphony Orchestra and Aspen Chamber Symphony; masterclasses at Aspen Festival, Rutgers Summer Festival, Chautauqua Festival, Hochschule für Musik, Leipzig, Toho Conservatory, Kunitachi Music Univ., Osaka Univ. of Arts and elsewhere throughout Japan, Seoul Nat. Univ., Edward Aldwell Center at Jerusalem Acad. of Music. *Recordings:* Schubert's Sonata in B-flat major and smaller works, Encore Favourites, Bartók's Sonata, Bloch's Visions and Prophecies, Franck's Prélude, Aria et Final, Berlinsky's Sonata for Violin and Piano, Beethoven's Sonata op. 111, Schubert's Moments Musicaux, Schubert's Sonata in G major, Brahms Klavierstücke Op. 76, Beethoven's Sonata, Op. 106, Schumann's Kinderszenen, Schubert's Last Three Sonatas. *Address:* 245 Waban Avenue,

Waban, MA 02468, USA (home). *E-mail:* gabriel.chodos@necmusic.edu (office).

CHOI, Jasmine; South Korean musician (flute); b. Seoul. *Education:* Curtis Inst. of Music, USA, studied with Julius Baker, Juilliard School, with Jeffrey Khaner, and later with Thomas Robertello. *Career:* accepted to study at Curtis Inst. aged 16; aged 22, Assoc. Prin. Flute, Cincinnati Symphony for six years; performed in Rising Stars series, Carnegie Hall's Weill Recital Hall and Philadelphia's Kimmel Center for the Performing Arts; solo recitals at Wigmore Hall, London (debut 2009), Konzerthaus Schubert Saal Vienna, Seoul Arts Center; appeared as soloist in Großer Musikvereinssaal and Konzerthaus Mozart Saal, Vienna, Dvorak and Smetana Halls, Prague, Disney Hall, Los Angeles; featured with Philadelphia Orchestra, Cincinnati Symphony, Buffalo Philharmonic, Juilliard Symphony, Vienna Symphony, St Petersburg Philharmonic, Salzburg Mozarteum, Turku Philharmonic, Riga Sinfonietta, Czech Philharmonic Chamber, Seoul Philharmonic and KBS Symphony, among others; performed at inauguration reception for UN Sec.-Gen. Ban Ki-Moon, New York; soloist with Vienna Symphony for opening concert of Bregenz Festival; featured soloist at Nat. Flute Asscn 40th anniversary concert in Las Vegas, Nev.; engagements for 2015–16 with Berlin Symphony, Baden-Baden Philharmonic, Korean Symphony (New Year's Eve concert in Seoul), George Enescu Philharmonic, Olten Philharmonic; several works composed for her; also writes own arrangements and transcriptions. *Recordings include:* Jasmine Choi Plays Mozart 2006, Fantasy 2011, Claude Bolling Suite for Flute and Jazz Trio 2012, The Telemann Files: 12 Fantasies for Solo Flute 2015; with members of the Vienna Symphony: Mozart: 5 Quartets with Flute. *E-mail:* gisperg@cadenza-concert.at. *E-mail:* jasmine@jasminechoi.com. *Website:* www.jasminechoi.com.

CHOJNACKA, Elisabeth, MA; French harpsichordist; *Professor of Contemporary Harpsichord, Mozarteum Academy of Music;* b. 10 Sept. 1939, Warsaw, Poland; d. of Tadeusz Chojnacki and Edwarda Chojnacka; m. Georges Lesèvre 1966. *Education:* Warsaw Acad. of Music, Ecole Supérieure de Musique and with Aimée van de Wiele, Paris. *Career:* first recital of contemporary harpsichord, L'Arc, Paris 1971; has created new repertoire for solo modern harpsichord, initiated repertoire combining harpsichord with organ, percussion, bandéon, orchestra; soloist with Orchestre de Paris, Cleveland and Minneapolis Orchestras 1974, Suisse Romande Orchestra 1979, Orchestre National de France 1981; Prof. of Contemporary Harpsichord, Mozarteum Acad. of Music, Salzburg 1995–; master-classes; collaborations with choreographer Lucinda Child 1991–; numerous recordings of classical and contemporary music. *Publications:* articles in La Revue Musicale. *Honours:* Chevalier, Légion d'honneur, Officier des Arts et des Lettres, Croix d'Officier, Ordre de Mérite pour la Pologne; First Prize, Int. Harpsichord Competition, Vercelli, Italy 1968, Orphée Prize 1981, 2000, Grand Prix de la SACEM 1983, Polish Union of Composers' Gloria Artis Medal for Culture 2009. *Address:* 17 rue Emile Dubois, 75014 Paris, France (home). *Telephone:* 1-45-89-52-82 (office); 1-45-65-17-20 (home). *Fax:* 1-45-65-31-90 (office). *E-mail:* e.chojnacka@free.fr (office).

CHOO, David Ik-sung, BMus, MMus, DMusA; South Korean conductor; b. 10 Sept. 1962, Seoul. *Education:* California State University, Northridge, University of Southern California, Peabody Conservatory of Music, studied conducting with Frederik Prausnitz, violin with Manuel Compinsky, Miwako Watanabe and Kathleen Lenski, piano with Nobuko Fujimoto. *Career:* debut as Guest Conductor, Aspen Concert Orchestra, 1988; Central Philharmonic Orchestra of China, Beijing, 1991; Conductor: US Chamber (assistant) and Symphony Orchestras (guest); Washington Central Choir and Central Orchestra; Los Angeles Orchestra; The Central Philharmonic Orchestra of China (guest); The Savaria Symphony Orchestra (guest), Hungary, 1992; Ploisti Philharmonic Orchestra (guest), Romania, 1994; St Petersburg Congress Orchestra (Guest), Russia, 1995; Hradec Kralove Philharmonic (guest), Czech Republic, 1995; St Petersburg Hermitage Orchestra (guest), 1997; Seoul Philharmonic Orchestra (guest), 1998; Savannah Symphony Orchestra (guest), 1998; Music Director of Columbia Camerata Musica Chamber Orchestra and Chesapeake Youth Symphony Orchestra; Bavaria Symphony Orchestra. *Publications:* Doctoral Dissertation on Franco Leoni's L'Oracolo: A Study in Orientalism, 1998. *Honours:* Prizewinner, Nicolai Malko Conducting Competition, Copenhagen, 1992. *Address:* 4808 Circling Hunter Dr #203, Columbia, MD 21045, USA.

CHORZEMPA, Daniel Walter, PhD; American/Austrian pianist, organist, harpsichordist, musicologist and composer and conductor; b. 7 Dec. 1944, Minneapolis, Minn., USA; s. of Martin Chorzempa Sr and Henrietta Reiswig. *Education:* Hochschule für Musik, Cologne, Univ. of Minnesota. *Career:* fmr church organist; Organ Instructor, Univ. of Minnesota 1962–65; Fulbright Scholar, Cologne, FRG 1965–66; numerous piano and organ recitals in Germany, Denmark, Italy, Poland, Japan, Mexico, South Africa, Belgium, Holland, Switzerland, Spain, Luxembourg, Greece, USA and UK 1968–; mem. Bd of Dirs, Neue Bach Gesellschaft. *Recordings:* major works of Liszt, J.S. Bach, Mozart, Widor, Vierne, Wagner, Fauré, Saint-Saëns, Haydn, Handel. *Honours:* Hon. mem. Academia Medicea 2004; J.S. Bach Prize, Leipzig 1968, numerous recording awards. *Address:* Via dei Tavolini 7, 50122 Florence, Italy (home). *Fax:* (055) 212334 (home). *E-mail:* daniel@chorzempa.com (home). *Website:* www.chorzempa.com.

CHOU, Wen-Chung; American (b. Chinese) composer and academic; *Director, US-China Arts Exchange, Columbia University;* b. 29 July 1923,

Chefoo (Yentai), China; m. Yi-An; two s. *Education:* New England Conservatory with Slonimsky, Columbia Univ. with Otto Luening, studied with Edgar Varèse, Bohuslav Martinů. *Career:* teacher at several US univs; Prof. of Composition, Columbia Univ., New York 1964–91, Prof. Emer. 1991–, Dir of Center for US-China Arts Exchange 1978–; Dir Fritz Reiner Center for Contemporary Music, School of the Arts 1984–91, Acting Dean, School of Arts 1987, Chair. Music Div. 1969–89; Ed Varèse works, including Amériques 1972, Intégrales 1980, Octandre 1980, Dance for Burgess 1998; ed and completed Varèse works Nocturnal 1972, Tuning Up 1998, Etude pour Espace 2010; mem. Inst. of the American Acad. 1982. *Compositions:* Landscapes for orchestra 1949, All in the Spring Wind for orchestra 1952–53, And The Fallen Petals for orchestra 1956, The Willows are New 1957, Soliloquy of a Bhiksuni for solo trumpet, brass and percussion ensemble 1958, Metaphors for wind orchestra 1961, Cursive for flute and piano 1963, Yü Ko for chamber ensemble 1965, Pien for piano, ten winds and percussion 1969, Yün for winds, two pianos and percussion 1969, Peking in the Mist for 11 players 1986, Echoes from the Gorge for percussion quartet 1989, Windswept Peaks for violin, cello, clarinet and piano 1990, Concerto for violoncello and orchestra 1992, Clouds for string quartet 1997, Streams for string quartet 2003, Twilight Colors for double trio 2007, Eternal Pine for ensemble of traditional Korean instruments 2008, Ode to Eternal Pine 2009, Sizhu Eternal Pine for Chinese instrumental ensemble 2012. *Honours:* Hon. Life mem. Asian Composers' League 1981, Hon. Prof. of Musical Composition, Central Conservatory of Music, Beijing 2004; Officier des Arts et des Lettres 2000; Rockefeller Foundation grant 1954, Guggenheim Fellowships 1955, 1956, Gold Dragon Award for Writers and Artists, Hong Kong 1998. *E-mail:* cwc@spiralismusic.org (office). *Website:* www.chouwenchung.org.

CHOWNING, John MacLeod, BM, DMA; American composer and teacher; *Professor Emeritus, Stanford University*; b. 22 Aug. 1934, Salem, NJ; s. of James Reid Chowning and Louise Chowning (née MacLeod); m. 1st Elisabeth Keller (divorced); one s. one d.; m. 2nd Maureen C. Doody; one s. *Education:* Wittenberg Univ., Springfield, Ohio, studied with Nadia Boulanger in Paris, Stanford Univ. *Career:* teacher, Stanford Univ. 1966–, Dir Computer Music and Acoustics Project 1966–74, inventor of FM sound synthesis 1967, Founding Dir Center for Computer Research in Music and Acoustics 1975, Prof. of Music 1979, Osgood Hooker Professorship in Fine Arts 1992, Hooker Chair School of Humanities and Sciences 1993, currently Prof. Emer.; Fellow, American Acad. of Arts and Sciences 1988. *Compositions:* pieces for computer-generated quadrophonic sound, including Sabelithe 1971, Turenas 1972, Stria 1977, Phone 1981, Voices for Soprano and Electronics 2005 (revised 2011). *Recording:* album: Music with Computers. *Publications:* FM Theory and Applications 1986; contrib. of The Simulation of Moving Sound Sources (to Journal of the Audio Engineering Society) 1972, The Synthesis of Complex Audio Spectra by Means of Frequency Modulation (to Journal of the Audio Engineering Society) 1973. *Honours:* Officier, Ordre des Arts et des Lettres 1995; Hon. DMus (Wittenberg Univ.) 1990; Dr hc (Université de la Méditerranée, Marseille) 2002, (Queen's Univ., Belfast) 2010. *Address:* Center for Computer Research in Music and Acoustics, Music Department, Stanford University, Stanford, CA 94305-8180, USA (office). *E-mail:* jc@ccrma.stanford.edu (office).

CHRÉTIEN, Raphaël; French cellist; b. 17 Feb. 1972, Paris. *Education:* National Superior Conservatory. *Career:* played in Europe at Barbican Hall 1993, Théâtre des Champs Elysées 1994, Basel Symphonic Hall 1995; in the USA at Marlboro Music Festival 1994, 1995; in Japan, touring major halls 1994; appearances with Prague television and radio, Philharmonic Orchestra, Dvořák 1994, Basel Symphony Orchestra, Lalo 1995, Cannes Philharmonic Orchestra, Tchaikovsky 1994; cello teacher, Bordeaux Nat. Conservatory. *Recordings:* Piatti, Caprices for Solo Cello; Brahms Trio Op.114; H. Duparc and G. Ropartz, Sonatas. *Honours:* first prize in cello and chamber music Nat. Superior Conservatory, Paris; Vienna Int. Cello Competition 1993, Prague Int. Cello Competition 1994, Trapani Int. Cello Competition 1995, Belgrade Int. Cello Competition 1995.

CHŘIBKOVÁ, Irena, MgA; Czech organist; *Head Organist and Director of Music, St James' Basilica, Prague*; b. 22 July 1959, Bohumin. *Education:* Kroměří Conservatoire under K. Pokora and at Acad. of Arts in Prague under Prof. M. Šlechta, studied under S. Landale at the Conservatoire Nat. de Rueil-Malmaison, int. organ master classes. *Career:* debut, Prague 1981; solo organ recitals at int. festivals: Olomouc, Paris 1985, Brno, Ljubljana 1987, Paris 1988, Piran, Slovakia 1992, Warsaw, Poland, Auxerre and Bourges, France 1993, Hamburg, Germany 1994, Prague, Czech Repub., Wisla, Warsaw, Frombork, Poland 1995, Sweden (Swedish premiere of Faust, for organ and speaker, by Petr Eben) 1995, Ljubljana (Slovenian premiere of Faust and Four Biblical Dances by Peter Eben) 1995, Berlin, Traunstein, Germany, Monte Carlo, Bourges, Prague, 1996, Berlin, Chartres, France, Serravalle Sesia, Italy, Hannover, Germany 1997; TV broadcasts of concerts in Piran 1992, Warsaw 1995; toured extensively as a concert artist, appearing in many famous European cathedrals and concert halls, as well as in Japan, Russia, Israel and USA; repertoire includes compositions from all music epochs; prefers performing 19th- and 20th-century and contemporary Czech and French organ music; special interest in music of Petr Eben; Czech premiere of The Labyrinth of the World (for organ and speaker) 2004; has led several masterclasses in Slovenia; mem. of juries at several int. organ competitions; concert programmes from the Baroque to contemporary music; discography includes mainly Czech and French organ music; much requested interpreter of contemporary music, especially that of Petr Eben and Jiří Teml; world premiere of Teml's 3rd Organ Concerto with the FOK Orchestra 2012; several recordings for radio and TV; taught at P.J. Vejvanovský Conservatoire 1988–94, Church Conservatoire, Kroměří 1990–94; currently teaches in Prague; mem. jury of several int. organ competitions; f. St James' Int. Organ Festival 1996 and other cycles of sacred organ music. *Recordings include:* Organs and Composing Organists of Prague St James's Basilica 1996, Music of Paris Churches and Cathedrals 2003, Bedřich Antonín Wiedermann (1883–1951) 2005, The Organ of St James's in Prague Live 2008, Petr Eben's The Labyrinth of the World and the Paradise of the Heart 2008, Jiří Teml 2009, St James's Christmas 2010, Sunday at St James' 2013. *Telephone:* 604-208490 (mobile) (office). *E-mail:* info@auditeorganum.cz (office); irena@chribkova.com (home). *Website:* www.auditeorganum.cz (office); www.chribkova.com.

CHRIST, Wolfram; German violist, conductor and teacher; *Professor of Viola, Hochschule für Musik, Freiburg*; b. 17 Oct. 1955, Hachenburg. *Education:* studied at Freiburg. *Career:* numerous solo concertos with conductors such as Abbado, Metha, Karajan, Maazel, Ozawa, Kubelik with Berlin Philharmonic and other orchestras throughout the world; plays regularly at international festivals as soloist and chamber musician; Principal Violist, Berlin Philharmonic Orchestra 1978–99; Artistic Dir and Consultant, Sydney Conservatory of Music 1995–2000; Prof. of Viola, Hochschule für Musik, Freiburg 1999–; Chief Conductor, Kurpfalz Chamber Orchestra, Mannheim 2004–08; Artistic Dir, Accad. Gustav Mahler, Ferrara and Potenza 2005–; Prin. Guest Conductor, Stuttgart Chamber Orchestra 2009–; guest conductor with numerous int. orchestras. *Recordings include:* Bartók's Viola Concerto (with Seiji Ozawa), Berlioz's Harold in Italy, Hindemith's Viola Concerto/Chamber Music No. 5, Hindemith's Concerto for Viola d'Amore/Chamber Music No. 6, Mozart's Sinfonia Concertante, Strauss's Don Quixote, Debussy's Trio for Flute, Viola and Harp (Grand Prix du Disque 1992), Telemann's Concerto for Viola and Strings, Mozart's Divertimento in E Flat Major, Dvořák's String Sextet in A Major. *Honours:* ARD Prize, Munich 1976. *E-mail:* office@musik-und-medien.de. *Address:* Fürstenbergstrasse 5, 79102 Freiburg, Germany (home). *E-mail:* info@wolframchrist.de (home). *Website:* www.wolframchrist.de.

CHRISTENSEN, Dieter, PhD; German ethnomusicologist, anthropologist and academic; *Professor Emeritus, Columbia University, New York*; b. 17 April 1932, Berlin; m. Nerthus Karger (died 2003); one s. one d. *Education:* Berlin State Conservatory, Free Univ., Berlin. *Career:* debut with RIAS Radio, Berlin 1949; taught at Free Univ. of Berlin and Univ. of Hamburg, then at Wesleyan Univ. and CUNY, USA and Universidade Nova, Lisbon, Portugal; Prof. and Dir, Center for Ethnomusicology, Columbia Univ., New York 1971–2006, Prof. Emer. 2006–; Sec.-Gen. UNESCO Int. Council for Traditional Music (ICTM) 1982–2001, Co-Dir UNESCO project The Universe of Music: A History –1993, Gen. Ed. Yearbook for Traditional Music (ICTM/UNESCO) 1982–2001, Ed. UNESCO Collection of Traditional Music 1994–2002. *Recordings:* Lappish folk songs, Kurdish folk music, Yugoslav folk music, Traditional Arts of Oman 1993, A Wedding in Sohar, Oman 1993. *Radio:* numerous features on German radio 1966–70. *Publications include:* Die Musik der Kate und Sialum 1957, Die Musik der Ellice-Inseln (with G. Koch) 1964, Hornbostel Opera Omnia (co-ed.) 1974, Der Ring des Tlalocan 1977, Musical Traditions in Oman 1993, Shauqi's Dictionary of Traditional Music in Oman 1994, Traditional Arts in Southern Arabia (with S. El-Shawan Castelo-Branco) 2009; contrib. to German and international professional journals, book review ed. for Journal of Society for Ethnomusicology. *Address:* Department of Music, Columbia University, New York, NY 10027, USA (office). *E-mail:* dc22@columbia.edu (office). *Website:* www.columbia.edu/~dc22 (office).

CHRISTENSEN, Jesper Boje, DipMus; Danish harpsichordist and musicologist; *Professor, Schola Cantorum, Basel*; b. 3 Dec. 1944, Copenhagen; one s. one d. *Education:* Royal Danish Acad. of Music. *Career:* numerous concerts and masterclasses at most major festivals and centres of early music; Prof., Schola Cantorum, Basel 1988–; Visiting Prof., Conservatoire Supérieur de Musique, Lyon 1989–2000, Centre de Musique Ancienne, Geneva 1989–98, Hochschule für Musik, Würtzburg 1992–95, Dept of Early Music, Kunstuniversität Graz 2004–05, Univ. de Basilicata, Potenza 2005–, Int. Piano Acad., Como 2007–; mem. jury: Festival van Vlaanderen, Int. Harpsichord Competition 1992–2004; Founder and Musical Dir Arcomelo ensemble 1997; Pres. Premio Bonporti, Rovereto 2006–, Early Music Competition, Trossingen 2009–, George Philipp Telemann-Wettbewerb, Magdeburg 2011–. *Recordings:* J. Mattheson: 12 Sonatas for traverso and harpsichord, A. Corelli op. 5 Sonatas for violin and basso continuo, Corelli op. 6 Concerti Grossi, G. Muffat: Armonico Tributo, F. A. Bonporti: Invenzioni op. 10 for violin and basso continuo, F. Geminiani: Six Sonatas for violoncello and basso continuo, Timewave (world music, jazz, flamenco). *Achievements include:* leading authority on basso continuo, also specializing in performance practice, including romantic interpretation as documented on earliest historical recordings. *Publications:* Der Generalbass bei Bach und Händel 1985, Die Grundlagen des Generalbass-Spiels im 18 Jahrhundert 1992, Generalbass (article in new MMG) 1996, Zu einigen Heiligen Kühen des Generalbass-Spiels im 20 Jahrhundert 1995, Francesco Maria Veracini über das Dirigieren 2000. *Honours:* Carl Nielsen Prize, Copenhagen 1971. *Address:* c/o Schola Cantorum, Leonhardstr. 6, Basel 4003, Switzerland.

CHRISTENSEN, Mogens, DipMus, MMus, PhD; Danish composer and academic; b. 7 April 1955, Laesoe; m. Helle Kristensen. *Education:* Royal Acad. of

Music, Århus, Univ. of Århus, Royal Acad. of Music, Copenhagen. *Career:* debut as composer, Denmark 1982; his music has been performed in almost all European countries, in USA and South America; Composer-in-Residence, Copenhagen Philharmonic Orchestra; teacher, Royal Acads of Music at Copenhagen and Århus, Acads of Music in Ålborg and Esbjerg, the Univs of Århus and Ålborg; Asst Prof., Acad. of Music, Esbjerg; mem. Danish Composers' Soc. *Compositions include:* orchestral: Zurvan Akarana 1986, Violin Concerto No. 1: Dreams Within Dreams 1990, Violin Concerto No. 2: Las flores del mar de la muerte 1993, Circulus Stellae 1998, Crystalline Light 1999; chamber works: Orphian Fire Mountains 1988, The Lost Poems of Princess Ateh 1991, The Khazarian Mirrors 1993; vocal works: Hyperions Schicksalslied 1982, Pessimisticum 1993, Systema Naturae (chamber opera) 1998. *Recordings include:* Vocal and Chamber Music Vol. I 1991, vol. II 1993, vol. III 1995, Odriozola and Christensen play Christensen and Odriozola 1995, Music for Solo Instruments Vol. I 1998, Music for Recorder 1999. *Honours:* Artist Prize of the County of Bergen 1991, Artist Scholarship of the Danish State 1993–95, prizewinner UNESCO Composers International Rostrum 1994.

CHRISTESEN, Robert; American singer (baritone); b. 15 Feb. 1943, Washington, DC. *Education:* Manhattan School of Music, Aspen School of Music with Aksel Schiotz and Jennie Tourel. *Career:* debut as Henrik in Maskarade by Nielsen at St Paul, 1972; sang with the Frankfurt and Dortmund Operas (1973–80) and appeared as guest Berlin (Komische Oper), Copenhagen, Budapest, Warsaw, Toulouse, Brno, Prague and in North and South America; Other roles have included Mozart's Count and Don Giovanni, Verdi's Ford, Germont and Luna, Eugene Onegin, Jochanaan, Rossini's Figaro, Kaspar in Der Freischütz and Lescaut in Henze's Boulevard Solitude.

CHRISTIE, Gus (Augustus); British opera administrator; *Executive Chairman, Glyndebourne Productions Limited*; b. 4 Dec. 1963, s. of Sir George Christie and Lady Mary Christie; grandson of John Christie (Founder of Glyndebourne Festival) and Audrey Mildmay; m. 1st Imogen Lycett Green; four s.; m. 2nd Danielle de Niese; one s. *Education:* Eton Coll., King's Coll., London. *Career:* began career working backstage in various theatres, including The Tricycle Co. and Nat. Theatre London; worked with Batignano Opera Festival, Tuscany; with Robert Fox Assocs (film and theatre production co.) 1987–89; Asst Ed. and cameraman, Partridge Films (wildlife film production co.) 1989–91; freelance cameraman from 1991; mem. Bd, Glyndebourne Productions Ltd 1988–, Exec. Chair. 2000–. *Film documentaries include:* A Puffin's Tale 1991, A New Fox in Town 1993, The Lion's Share 1994, Hugo's Diary 1995, Red Monkeys of Zanzibar 1996, The Battle of the Sexes, The Tale of Two Families 1998, Buffalo, The African Boss 1999. *Address:* Glyndebourne Productions Ltd, New Road, Lewes, BN8 5UU, East Sussex, England (office). *Telephone:* (1273) 812321 (office). *E-mail:* info@glyndebourne.com (office). *Website:* www.glyndebourne.com (office).

CHRISTIE, Michael; American conductor; b. 30 June 1974, New York; m. Alexis Christie; one d. *Education:* Oberlin Coll. Conservatory of Music. *Career:* conducting engagements with the Los Angeles and Buffalo Philharmonics, the Lahti Symphony and the Helsinki and Tampere (Finland) Philharmonics, Royal Scottish Nat. Orchestra; UK debut with the City of Birmingham Symphony Orchestra 1996; season 1997–98, Asst to Franz Welser-Möst, Zürich Opera; Apprentice Conductor, Chicago Symphony Orchestra 1995–96; Music Dir, Colorado Music Festival 2000–; Chief Conductor, The Queensland Orchestra 2001–04; Music Dir Phoenix Symphony Orchestra 2005–13, currently Music Dir Laureate; Music Dir Brooklyn Philharmonic Orchestra 2005–10; Music Dir Minnesota Opera 2012–13; engagements with Swedish Radio Symphony, Netherlands Radio Symphony, Royal Liverpool Philharmonic, NDR Hannover, Czech Philharmonic, Orchestre Philharmonique de Luxembourg DSO Berlin, New York Philharmonic, National Symphony, Los Angeles Philharmonic, Dallas Symphony, Atlanta Symphony, Florida Philharmonic. *Honours:* Prize for Outstanding Potential at the First Int. Sibelius Conductors' Competition, Helsinki 1995. *Current Management:* c/o Ron Merlino, MusicVine Management, 2576 Broadway, Suite 239, New York, NY 10025, USA. *Telephone:* (646) 825-9585. *E-mail:* merlino@musicvinearts.com. *Website:* www.musicvinearts.com; www.michaelchristieonline.com.

CHRISTIE, Nan; British singer (soprano); b. 6 March 1948, Irvine, Scotland. *Education:* Royal Scottish Acad. of Music, London Opera Centre. *Career:* repertoire with Scottish Opera includes Britten's Tytania, Rimsky's Queen of Shemakha, The Queen of Night and Zerbinetta in Ariadne auf Naxos; tours to Portugal, Poland, Switzerland and Germany; sang in Mozart's La Finta Giardiniera and the premiere of Oliver's Tom Jones, with English Music Theatre; Tytania with Opera North; Isotta in Die schweigsame Frau and Despina in Così fan tutte, at the Glyndebourne Festival; Zdenka in Arabella, the Queen of Night and Offenbach's Eurydice with ENO; European engagements with Netherlands Opera, Despina; Opéra de Nancy as Pamina; Zürich Opera in the Ponnelle production of Lucio Silla and Frankfurt Opera as Zerbinetta, Marie in Die Soldaten and Susanna; Scottish Opera 1990 as Despina in a new production of Così fan tutte; Birdie Hubbard in the British premiere of Blitzstein's Regina, Glasgow 1991; concerts at the Hong Kong Festival, Hallé Orchestra, BBC Symphony and London Symphony Orchestra, Nash Ensemble and the London Sinfonietta; TV appearances in Mozart's Schauspieldirektor and Ravel's L'Enfant et les Sortilèges; Italian debut in Mitridate by Mozart, La Fenice, Venice, and the Queen of Night in The Magic Flute for ENO 1992; premiere of Jonathan Harvey's Inquest of Love, ENO 1993; sang Third Official in the premiere of The Doctor of Myddfai, by Peter Maxwell Davies, Cardiff 1996. *Recordings:* video: Glyndebourne Festival Così fan tutte, The Gondoliers, The Sorcerer and Princess Ida.

CHRISTIE, Natalie; Australian singer (soprano); b. (Natalie Abrahamson), 17 Jan. 1975, Melbourne. *Education:* Victorian Coll. of the Arts, Guildhall School of Music and Drama, London with Rudolf Piernay. *Career:* appeared in La Bohème, British Youth Opera 1998, Carmen, Clonter Opera 1998, The Carmelites, WNO 1999, Orphee et Eurydice 2000, Der Rosenkavalier 2000, Le Nozze di Figaro 2001, The Magic Flute 2001, Leonore 2001, Adele in Die Fledermaus 2002; St John Passion (soloist), ENO (debut) 2000; Le Nozze di Figaro, Opera Australia 2000; finalist Cardiff Singer of the World 2001; Zerlina in Don Giovanni, Royal Opera House (debut), London 2002; soloist for BBC Nat. Orchestra of Wales, BBC Concert Orchestra, Tasmanian Symphony Orchestra; Roles for WNO 2002–03 Adele in Die Fledermaus, Adina in The Elixir of Love, Zerlina in Don Giovanni and Susanna in Le Nozze di Figaro. *Honours:* Veronica Dunn Singing Competition 20th-Century Aria Prize 1997, Australian Music Foundation Award 1998, WNO Sir John Moores Award 2000.

CHRISTIE, William Lincoln, BA; French/American harpsichordist, conductor and musicologist; *Director, Les Arts Florissants*; b. 19 Dec. 1944, Buffalo, NY; s. of William Christie and Ida Jones. *Education:* Harvard Univ., Yale School of Music, studied harpsichord with Ralph Kirkpatrick, Kenneth Gilbert and David Fuller. *Career:* moved to France 1970; mem. Five Centuries Ensemble 1971–75, René Jacobs' Concerto vocale 1976–80; f. Les Arts Florissants vocal and instrumental ensemble 1979; Prof., Conservatoire Nat. Supérieur de Musique, Paris 1982–95; conducts his own orchestra as well as many leading int. orchestras (Orchestra of the Age of Enlightenment, Glyndebourne 1996, 2005, Berlin Philharmonic, Zurich Opera, Opéra Nat. de Lyon); career highlights include Handel's Theodora, Glyndebourne 1996, Handel's Semele, Aix-en-Provence Festival 1996, Rameau's Hippolyte et Aricie, Paris 1996–97, Lully's Thésée, Barbican, London 1998, Monteverdi's Il ritorno d'Ulisse in patria, Aix-en-Provence 2002, Hercules, Aix-en-Provence 2004, Rameau's Les Paladins, Théâtre du Châtelet 2004, 2006, Brooklyn Acad. of Music 2006, Il Sant'Alessio 2007, The Fairy Queen 2010, Così fan tutte at the Met, etc., Lully's Atys at the Opéra Comique and worldwide tour 2011, La Didone (Théâtre de Caen, Théâtre des Champs Elysées) 2011–12, Charpentier's David et Jonathas (Aix, Edinburgh, Opéra Comique, Théâtre de Caen, Brooklyn Acad. of Music) 2012–13, Rameau's Hippolyte et Aricie, Glyndebourne 2013; Pres. Jury, Concours de Chant Baroque de Chimay, Belgium 2000–; cr. Le Jardin des Voix acad. for young singers in Caen, int. tours 2002, 2005, 2007, 2009, 2011, 2013; Artist-in-Residence (with Les Arts Florissants), Juilliard School, New York 2007–; mem. Royal Acad. of Music, Acad. des Beaux-Arts 2008, Institut de France 2010. *Recordings:* numerous recordings including all works for harpsichord by Rameau, works by Monteverdi, Purcell, Handel, Couperin, Charpentier, Desmarest, Mozart, etc. *Honours:* Commdr, Légion d'honneur 2010; Officier des Arts et des Lettres; Hon. DMus (State Univ. of New York, Buffalo) 1999, (Juilliard School); Prix Edison, Netherlands 1981, Grand prix du disque, Prix mondial de Montreux, Switzerland 1982, Gramophone Record of the Year, UK 1984, 1995, 1997, Deutscher Schallplattenpreis 1987, Grand prix de la Critique (best opera performance) 1987, Prix Opus, USA 1987, Prix int. de musique classique 1992, Prix Grand Siècle Laurent Perrier 1997, Grammy Award for Handel's Acis and Galatea 2000, Grammy and Cannes Classical Awards for Alcina 2001, Harvard Univ. Arts Medal 2002, Royal Philharmonic Award 2003, Liliane Bettencourt Choral Singing Prize, Acad. des Beaux Arts 2004, Prix Georges Pompidou 2005. *Address:* Les Arts Florissants, 46 rue Fortuny, 75017 Paris (office); Secrétariat de William Christie, 11 rue de la Cerisaie, 75004 Paris (office); 32 rue du Bâtiment, Thiré, 85210 Sainte-Hermine, France (home). *Telephone:* 1-43-87-98-88 (Arts Florissants) (office). *Fax:* 1-40-67-17-43 (Secrétariat) (office). *E-mail:* w.christie@orange.fr (home). *Website:* www.arts-florissants.com (office); ww.jardindewilliamchristie.fr.

CHRISTIN, Judith; American singer (mezzo-soprano); b. 15 Feb. 1948, Providence, RI. *Education:* Indiana University. *Career:* sang at first in concert, opera from 1980; Washington Opera from 1981 and at Santa Fe in the US premieres of Weir's A Night at the Chinese Opera, Penderecki's Schwarze Maske and Judith by Matthus; Los Angeles from 1983, San Diego 1984, Philadelphia 1986; New York Metropolitan from 1988, in Eugene Onegin, Faust, Die Zauberflöte, Luisa Miller and Le nozze di Figaro; European career from 1987 (Netherlands Opera); roles have included Despina (Santa Fe 1988–90), the Hostess in Boris Godunov, Suzuki in Butterfly and Carlotta in Die schweigsame Frau; Santa Fe 1996, as Suzuki and Baba the Turk in The Rake's Progress; sang in the premiere of Carlisle Floyd's Cold Sassy Tree, Houston 2000. *Current Management:* Columbia Artists Management, 1790 Broadway, New York, NY 10019-1412, USA. *Telephone:* (212) 841-9500. *Fax:* (212) 841 9744. *E-mail:* info@cami.com. *Website:* www.cami.com.

CHRISTOFF, Dimiter, DrHabil; Bulgarian composer and academic; b. 2 Oct. 1933, Sofia. *Education:* State Music Acad., Sofia with M. Goleminov, study tours in Germany, USA, France, Netherlands. *Career:* teacher, State Music Acad. (now New Bulgarian Univ.) 1960–76, Prof. 1976–; Gen. Sec. Int. Music Council, UNESCO 1975–79; Leader Int. Composers' Workshop (a Bulgarian-Dutch initiative) 1977–2006; Ed.-in-Chief, Scientific Music Magazine, Bulgarian Musicology, Acad. of Sciences 1989–2006; Publr Music, Yesterday, Today 1994; mem. Int. Soc. for Music Educ., Bulgarian Composers' Union (Vice-Pres. 1972–85). *Compositions:* operas: The Game 1978, The Golden Fish Line 1984; orchestral: three piano concertos 1954, 1983, 1994, Sinfonietta for strings

1956, Poem 1957, three symphonies 1958, 1964, 1969, Overture 1961, Symphonic Episodes 1962, three violin concertos 1966, 1996, 1997, Chamber Suite for two piccolos, piano, percussion and strings 1966, Cello Concerto 1969, Concert Miniatures 1970, Overture with Fanfares 1974, Quasi una fantasia-gioco 1981, Game for cellos and orchestra 1983, Perpetui mobili in pianissimi 1987, Groups Troupes 1988, Silent Adagio 1989, Cantilena opra due toni 1990, Merry-go-round of the Suffering 1991, Collapse in the Silence 1992, Crash Down in the Mute 1992, Up High I Look for You 1993, It Streams It Runs Out 1994, I Rise in the Chaos 1995, I Set It Ajar, Peep In 1996, There High it Shines 1997, It Was for Millenniums Predicted 2000, Here is So Silent 2000, Vibrating, Burning 2004, Agitato in Su for piano and orchestra 2005, Toccata Vaganta for piano and orchestra 2007, Triple Concerto for violin, violoncello, piano and orchestra 2008, Shine Through, Rise Slowly Up 2010; chamber: Suite for brass quartet 1953, Two Dances for trumpet and piano 1960, Sonata for solo cello 1965, Concerto for three small drums and five instruments 1967, String Quartet 1970, Quartet for flute, viola, harp and harpsichord 1973, Give Me Solace 1983, piano ensemble music (duo, trio and quartet of piano players), Meditation of a Lonely Violoncello 1991, The Violoncello abandons the Right Hand of the Piano 1992, 32 piano sonatas, 12 piano nocturnes, Blown Away from the Wind for string orchestra 1993, Wait for your Pizzicati for strings 1994, Sad Silk Bows for violin and accompanying viola 1996, Convulsing further for violoncello and harp 2001, Eroica Variations for piano & strings 2002, Cool and Warm for strings 2002, Bow Down for violoncello and strings 2002, 24 etudes for harp 2002–07, Beauty in Two for flute and harp 2006, Sonata for flute and piano 2007, Trio for piano, violin and violoncello 2013, Reminiscences of the Night for violin and piano 2013; choruses and songs. *Publications:* Ideas about Fugue Composition in Well Tempered Klavier by J. S. Bach 1968, Hypothesis about Counterpoint Structure 1970, Theoretical Foundations of the Melodic Structure Vols 1–3 1973, 1982, 1989, Composer & Public Awareness 1975, Introduction in Musicology 1990, Bach's Two-part Inventions: Structure and Process 1995, Analytic and Structural Visualizing Schemes of Canonic Forms: Theory of Polyphonic Composition 1999, Fundamental Preconditions for Composer Imagination: To the Situation at the Beginning of the 21st Century 2004. *Honours:* numerous nat. and int. awards including Int. Acad. for the Arts Award (France) 1999. *Address:* Mavrovets 7, 1415 Sofia-Dragalevtsi, Bulgaria (home). *Telephone:* (2) 967-23-51 (home).

CHRISTOPHERS, Harry, CBE, BA; British conductor; *Conductor, The Sixteen;* b. (Richard Henry Tudor Christophers), 26 Dec. 1953, Goudhurst, Kent; m. Veronica Mary Hayward 1979; two s. two d. *Education:* Canterbury Cathedral Choir School (Head Chorister), King's School Canterbury, Magdalen Coll., Oxford (Academical Clerk). *Career:* f. The Sixteen 1979, The Orchestra of The Sixteen 1986, CORO (own record label) 2001; South Bank debut 1983; Salzburg Festival debut 1989; BBC Proms debut 1990; Lisbon Opera debut 1994; Musikverein, Vienna debut 1998; Concertgebouw, Amsterdam debut 1999; ENO debut 2000; orchestras conducted include BBC Philharmonic, Acad. of St Martin-in-the-Fields, London Symphony Orchestra, Hallé Orchestra, Orchestra of the Age of Enlightenment, Royal Liverpool Philharmonic, English Chamber Orchestra, Northern Sinfonia, City of London Sinfonia, BBC Nat. Orchestra of Wales, Scottish Chamber Orchestra, San Francisco Symphony, St Louis Symphony, Handel and Haydn Soc., Washington Bach Consort, Avanti!, Tapiola Sinfonietta, Lahti Symphony Orchestra, Helsinki Philharmonic, Bergen Philharmonic, Granada Symphony Orchestra, Orquestra Comunidad de Madrid; tours with The Sixteen choir and orchestra throughout Europe, Scandinavia, Israel, Japan, Australia, USA, Brazil; f. The Choral Pilgrimage (musical tour) 2000; apptd Assoc. Artist, Southbank Centre, London 2006; Artistic Dir, Boston Handel and Haydn Soc. 2009–. *Recordings include:* more than 100 recordings, including Taverner's Festal Masses, Vols I–IV 1984–93 and Missa Gloria Tibi Trinitas 1989, Monteverdi's Masses 1987 and Vespers 1988, Handel's Messiah (Grand Prix du Disque) 1989, Chandos Anthems 1990, Alexander's Feast (Deutschen Schallplattenkritik Prize) 1992, Esther 1996, Samson 1997, Italian Cantatas 1998, Byrd's Mass for 5 voices 1989 and Mass for 4 voices 1990, Poulenc's Figure Humaine 1990, Bach's St John Passion 1990, Christmas Oratorio 1993, B Minor Mass 1994, Eton Choir Book Vols I–V 1991–95, Sheppard's Sacred Music Vols I–IV 1990–92, Teixeira's Te Deum (Diapason d'Or 1992) 1991, Britten's Choral Music 1992–93, Stravinsky's Symphony of Psalms (Diapason d'Or) 1995, Messiaen's Cinq rechants 1996, Scarlatti's Stabat Mater 1997, Victoria's Sacred Music Vols I–III 1997–99, Video: Handel's Messiah in Dublin 1992, Tallis: Spem in Alium 2004, Handel Arias: Heroes and Heroines (with Sarah Connolly) 2004, Renaissance (Best Ensemble Album of the Year, Classical BRIT Awards 2005) 2004, Victoria: Requiem 2005, Ikon 2006, A King's Musick 2006, Music for the Sistine Chapel 2007, Brahms: Requiem 2007, A Mother's Love 2007, Treasures of Tudor England 2007, Mozart: Solemn Vespers 2008, Fauré's Requiem 2008, Handel's Messiah (Midem Classical Award 2009) 2008, Handel's Coronation Anthems (Gramophone Award for Best Baroque Vocal Recording) 2009, Bright Orb of Harmony 2009, Guerrero's Missa de la batalla escoutez 2009, Padre Pio's Prayer 2009, Ceremony & Devotion – Music for the Tudors 2010, Monteverdi Selva morale e spirituale 2010, A Traditional Christmas Carol Collection Vol. II 2010, Hail, Mother of the Redeemer 2011, The Victoria Collection 2011, O Guiding Night – The Spanish Mystics 2011, Palestrina Vol. 1 2011, Great British Choral Works 2011, Mozart Requiem 2011, James MacMillan Miserere 2011, Palestrina Vol. 1 (Int. Classical Music Award for Best Early Music Recording 2012) 2011, Palestrina Vol. 2 2012, Monteverdi: Vespers of 1610 2014. *Television:* Sacred Music (multiple series specials, BBC 4), Sacred Music Christmas Special (BBC 4) 2010. *Honours:* Hon. Fellow, Magdalen Coll., Royal Welsh Coll. of Music and Drama; Hon. DMus (Leicester); Gramophone Early Music Award 1992, Classical Brit Award 2005, Gramophone Award for Artist of the Year (with The Sixteen) 2009. *Address:* The Sixteen Ltd, Quadrant House, 10 Fleet Street, London, EC4Y 1AU, England (office). *Telephone:* (20) 7936-3420 (office). *E-mail:* info@thesixteen.com (office). *Website:* www.thesixteen.com (office).

CHRISTOU, Nicolas; Belgian singer (bass-baritone); b. 1943, Alexandria. *Education:* studied in Brussels with Frédéric Anspach. *Career:* made debut at La Monnaie theatre, Brussels 1964–1982; guest appearances throughout Europe, notably at Liège as the Father in Louise, Grandier in The Devils of Loudun and Pizarro in Fidelio 1991–95, also sung in Paris, Madrid, Rome, Parma, Amsterdam, Geneva, Berlin, Copenhagen, Zagreb, Warsaw, Lyon, Nice, Strasbourg; festival engagements at Aix-en-Provence, as the Speaker in Die Zauberflöte and at Wexford; Deutsche Oper am Rhein, Düsseldorf from 1991; other roles have included Mussorgsky's Boris Gudunov, Mozart's Figaro and Leporello, Rossini's Basilio, Wagner's Telramund, Pogner, Amfortas and the Flying Dutchman, Mandryka in Arabella, Ramphis in Aida, Dr Schön in Lulu, Bluebeard in Bluebeard's Castle, Arcangelo Meddaggiero in Genesis, Pizzaro in Fidelio, Escamillo in Carmen, Collatinus in The Rape of Lucretia, Siroco in L'Etoile, Don Candido Gamboa in Cecilia, Golaud in Pelléas et Mélisande, Dulcamara in L'Elisir d'Amore, Raimondo in Lucia di Lammermoor, Agamemnon in Iphigérie en Aulide, Mephisto in Faust, Capulet in Romeo e Julieta, Giulio Cesare, Besenbinder in Handel und Gretel, Tonio in I Pagliacci, Odysseus in Penelope, Alfio in Cavalleria Rusticana, Arthur in Les Trois Souhaits, Père Fotis in La Passion Grecque, Le Roi in Le Cid, Lord Jowler in The Rising of the Moon, Pluto in Orfeo, Don Giovanni, Alfonso in Cosi Fan Tutte, In Conte in Le Nozze di Figaro, Sarastro in Die Zauberflöte, Lindorf in Les Contes d'Hoffman, Marquis de la Force in Dialogues des Carmélites, L'Homme in Les Traveses du Temps, Colline in La Bohème, Scarpia in Tosca, Schicchi in Gianni Schicchi, Michele in Il Tabarco, Le Sultan in Mârouf, Citheron in Platée, Saltan in Tsar Saltan, Basilio in Il Barbiere di Siviglia, Haly in L'Italiana in Algeri, Matt as The Fantasticks, Achilles in Penthesilea, Faninal in Der Rosenkavalier, Mandryka in Arabella, Jochanaan in Salome, Nabucco, Carlo di Vargas in Forza del Destino, Ferrando in Il Trovatore, Filippo II in Don Carlo, Macbeth, Germont in La Traviata, Amonasro in Aida, Iago in Otello, Falstaff, Danton in Dantons Tod, Pogner in Die Meistersinger von Nürenberg, Telramund in Lohengrin, Holländer in Der Fliegende Holländer, Amfortas in Parsifal, Wotan in Rheingold, Wotan in Die Walküre, Gunther in Götterdammerung; concert pieces include Handel's Messiah, The Creation, Bach's Passsions, Frank Martin's Christ of Golgotha, Beethoven's Ninth Symphony, Berlioz's Christ's Childhood, Stravinky's Oedipus Rex, Prokofiev's Ivan the Terrible, Verdi's Requiem; currently Prof., Royal Conservatory, Liège; also solo vocal advisor, Nat. Opera of Estonia, Hélikon Opera, Moscow. *Address:* 40 Chemin de l'Herbe, 1325 Bonlez, Belgium (home). *Telephone:* (10) 68-89-31 (home). *Fax:* (10) 68-89-31. *E-mail:* nicolas@nicolaschristou.com (office). *Website:* www.nicolaschristou.com.

CHU, Wang-Hua, BMus, MMus; Australian composer and pianist; b. 5 Sept. 1941, Jiangsu, China. *Education:* Central Conservatory, Peking, Univ. of Melbourne. *Career:* Piano Dept, Central Conservatory of Music, Beijing 1963–82; freelance composer and pianist in Australia 1982–; mem. Australian Music Centre. *Compositions include:* Seven Piano Preludes, and Three Piano Variations 1961–80, The Yellow River Piano Concerto (co-composer) 1970, The Spring Mirrored the Moon for piano 1972, Sinjiang Capriccio for piano 1977, Piano Sonata No. 1 1981, String Quartet 1983, Ash Wednesday for orchestra 1984, The Borderland Moon for soprano and ensemble 1984, Concerto for Chamber Orchestra 1984, Drinking Alone by Moonlight for soprano and chamber ensemble 1985, The Bamboo for piano and orchestra (Concerto No. 1) 1986, 30 Chinese Folk Songs for piano 1979–86, Barcarolle for piano 1979, Autumn Cry for orchestra 1988, Symphony 1988, Sinfonia for chamber orchestra 1988, The Ancient Battlefield for percussion solo 1989, Piano Concerto No. 2 1989, Fantasia Symphony: The Silk Road 1990, Eva, Beloved Mother, for piano 1993, Air and Variations for choral 1998, A Great River for piano 2001, Fantasia: The Jasmine for piano 2003, Piano Concerto No. 3 2004, The Song of the Island for violin and piano 2004, Piano Sonata No. 2 2006, City Dance for piano four-hand 2007. *Recordings:* The Yellow River Piano Concerto, co-composer, 1970, 1980, 1990; Piano Sonata, 1986; A number of piano works, 1980, 1990. *Honours:* first prize Albert Magg's Composition Competition, Australia 1987. *Address:* 20 Bruce Street, Toorak, Vic 3142, Australia (home). *E-mail:* chu@net2000.com.au (home).

CHUCHROVA, Liubov; Lithuanian singer (soprano); b. 1971, Vilnius. *Education:* studied in Vilnius and Guildhall School, London. *Career:* sang Satirino in La Calisto and Maria in Krenek's Der Diktator at the GSM; Olga in Dargomyzhsky's Rusalka, 1997 Wexford Festival; other roles include Anne Trulove, The Rake's Progress; Tatiana, Marguerite and Mozart's Vitellia, Vilnius Opera; Gorislava in Ruslan and Lyudmilla for Dorset Opera; Spoleto Festival, 1999; War and Peace; Concerts include Vivaldi's Gloria; Bruch's Das Lied von der Glocke; Rossini's Petite Messe at Tel-Aviv; Mozart's Requiem at the Barbican, London. *Honours:* winner GSM Maggie Teyte Competition. *Current Management:* c/o Neil Dalrymple, Music International, 13 Ardilaun Road, London, N5 2QR, England. *Telephone:* (20) 7359-5183. *Fax:* (20) 7226-9792. *E-mail:* music@musicint.co.uk.

CHUDOVA, Tatiana; Russian composer; b. 16 June 1944, Moscow. *Education:* Moscow Central Music School and Conservatory, notably with Khrennikov. *Career:* teacher in Moscow from 1970. *Compositions include:* operas: The Dead Princess and the Seven Heroes, 1967, and To the Village, to Grandfather, 1978; three Suites for orchestra of folk instruments, 1980–82; Symphonic trilogy, 1981–82, and Symphony No. 4, 1988; choral, solo vocal and instrumental music, including two violin sonatas, 1974, 1987. *Address:* c/o RAO, Bolchaia Bronnai 6-1, Moscow 103670, Russia.

CHUNG, David Yu Sum, MPhil, PhD, LRSM, LTCL; Chinese musicologist and academic; *Professor, Hong Kong Baptist University*; b. 10 April 1968, Hong Kong. *Education:* Univ. of Cambridge and Guildhall School of Music and Drama, UK, Chinese Univ. of Hong Kong. *Career:* Asst Prof., then Assoc. Prof. and performance co-ordinator, Hong Kong Baptist Univ. 1998, currently Prof.; harpsichordist and musicologist, with performances in Europe, Asia and USA on a variety of historic and modern keyboard instruments; mem. British Clavichord Soc., Royal Musical Asscn, Southeastern Historical Keyboard Soc., American Musicological Soc. *Publications include:* Jean-Baptiste Lully: 27 Opera Pieces Transcribed for Keyboard in the 17th and 18th Centuries 2004; articles in Early Keyboard Journal 2001, Early Music 2003, Piano Artistry 2003, Journal of Seventeenth-Century Music, Eighteenth-Century Music, Stylus Phantasticus Works for Harpsichord 2003, Music & Letters 2011, Performers' Voice Across Centuries and Cultures 2011, Web Library of Seventeenth-Century Music 2015. *Address:* Department of Music, Hong Kong Baptist University, Kowloon Tong, Hong Kong Special Administrative Region, People's Republic of China (office). *Telephone:* 3411-7871 (office). *Fax:* 3411-7870 (office). *E-mail:* dchung@hkbu.edu.hk (office). *Website:* www.hkbu.edu.hk (office).

CHUNG, Kyung-wha; South Korean violinist; b. 26 March 1948, Seoul; sister of Chung Myung-whun and Chung Myung-wha; m. Geoffrey Leggett 1984; two s. *Education:* Juilliard School, New York with Ivan Galamian. *Career:* started career in USA; European debut 1970; has played with major orchestras, including all London orchestras, Chicago, Boston and Pittsburgh Symphony Orchestra, New York, Cleveland, Philadelphia, Berlin, Israel and Vienna Philharmonics, Orchestre de Paris, Royal Concertegebouw Orchestra, Deutsche Oper, San Francisco Symphony, Orchestre National de Lyon, Pittsburgh Symphony Orchestra, Orchestre Philharmonique de Radio-France, Tonhalle-Orchester Zurich; has toured world; played at Salzburg Festival with London Symphony Orchestra 1973, Vienna Festival 1981, 1984, Edinburgh Festival 1981 and at 80th birthday concert of Sir William Walton March 1982; with Hallé Orchestra, BBC Proms, London 1999; Faculty of Music, Juilliard School, New York 2007–, Pre-College 2008–. *Recordings:* Concertos by Bartók, Beethoven, Bruch, Mendelssohn, Stravinsky, Tchaikovsky, Vieuxtemps, Walton, Vivaldi's The Four Seasons 2001. *Honours:* winner, Leventritt Competition 1968, Medal of Civil Merit (South Korea) 1972, Ho-am Prize 2011. *Current Management:* Opus 3 Artists, 470 Park Avenue South, 9th Floor North, New York, NY 10016, USA. *Telephone:* (212) 584-7500. *Fax:* (646) 300-8200. *E-mail:* info@opus3artists.com. *Website:* www.opus3artists.com. *Address:* The Juilliard School, 60 Lincoln Center Plaza, New York, NY 10023-6588, USA (office). *Telephone:* (212) 799-5000. *Website:* www.juilliard.edu (office).

CHUNG, Mia, BA, MM, DMA; American pianist and academic; *Artist-in-Residence and Professor of Music, Gordon College*; b. 9 Oct. 1964, Madison, WI. *Education:* Harvard Univ., Yale Univ., Juilliard School of Music; studied with Peter Serkin, Boris Berman, Raymond Hanson, Anne Hanson and George Manos. *Career:* debut at Hall of the Americas, OAS Building, Washington, DC 1983; named US Information Agency Amb. 1991; Asst Prof. of Music, Gordon Coll. 1991–2008, Artist-in-Residence 1991–, Prof. of Music 2008–; frequent performer of works by J.S. Bach, Beethoven, Mozart, Felix Mendelssohn and Schumann; appearances with Baltimore Symphony, National Symphony, Alabama Symphony, Corpus Christi Symphony, Billings Symphony, Fort Collins Symphony Orchestra, New Haven Symphony, Harrisburg Symphony, KBS Symphony, Seoul, Seoul Philharmonic; solo recitals and chamber performances at OAS, Alice Tully Hall, National Gallery of Art, the Kennedy Center for Performing Arts, American Acad. of Arts and Sciences, Jordan Hall, Boston, Hoam Art Hall, Seoul, Concertgebouw, Amsterdam, Carnegie Hall, Lincoln Center, and other venues. *Recordings include:* Beethoven Bagatelles, Op 126 and Sonatas No. 16 in G major Op 31, No. 1 and No. 32 in C minor Op 111, Sonata No. 23 in F Minor, Op.57 and No. 30 in E major, Op.109, Schumann's Davidsbundlertanze, Faschingsschwank aus Wien, Novellette, No. 8 in F-Sharp Minor, Bach's Goldberg Variations, Lee Hyla's Riff and Transfiguration. *Honours:* first prize, Johann Sebastian Bach International Competition, New York 1981, first prize, Concert Artist's Guild Competition 1993, US Trust Award 1993, Avery Fisher Career Grant 1997. *Address:* Music Department, Gordon College, Wenham, MA 01984, USA (office). *Telephone:* (978) 867-4864 (office). *Website:* www.miachung.com.

CHUNG, Myung-wha; South Korean cellist; b. 19 March 1944, Seoul; sister of Chung Myung-whun and Chung Kyung-wha. *Education:* Juilliard School with Leonard Rose, Univ. of Southern California masterclass with Gregor Piatigorsky. *Career:* debut with the Seoul Philharmonic before study in New York; has appeared widely in Europe and North America 1971–, notably in England, Italy, Denmark, Germany, Spain, Sweden, Netherlands, Belgium, France, Switzerland, Portugal, Israel and Mexico; festival appearances at Lucerne, Flanders, Spoleto, Palma de Majorca, Birmingham, Evian and Dijon; television programmes in the USA, England, Germany and Switzerland; plays a 1731 Stradivarius cello known as Braga; Goodwill Ambassador for UN Drug Control Programme 1992–; faculty mem., Mannes Coll. of Music, New York and Korean Nat. Inst. of Arts. *Recordings include:* Tchaikovsky Rococo Variations with the Los Angeles Philharmonic under Charles Dutoit, Ten Piano Trio Works with the Chung Trio. *Honours:* First Prize Geneva Int. Music Competition 1971, Nat. Order of Cultural Merit, Republic of Korea 1992. *Address:* 315 West 70th Street, Suite 5G, New York, NY 10023, USA.

CHUNG, Myung-whun; South Korean conductor and pianist; *Music Director, Seoul Philharmonic Orchestra*; b. 22 Jan. 1953, Seoul; brother of Chung Kyung-wha and Chung Myung-wha. *Education:* Mannes Coll. of Music and Juilliard School, New York, USA. *Career:* asst to Carlo Maria Giulini as Assoc. Conductor, Los Angeles Philharmonic 1978–81; moved to Europe 1981, conducting Berlin Philharmonic, Munich Philharmonic, Amsterdam Concertgebouw, Orchestre de Paris, major London orchestras; Music Dir and Prin. Conductor, Radio Orchestra of Saarbrücken 1984–89; in USA has conducted the New York Philharmonic, Nat. Symphony, Washington, DC, Boston Symphony, Cleveland and Chicago Orchestras, Metropolitan Opera, San Francisco Opera 1986–; Guest Conductor, Teatro Comunale, Florence 1987; Musical Dir Opéra de la Bastille, Paris 1989–94; Covent Garden debut, conducting Otello 1997; Music Dir and Prin. Conductor, Orchestra of the Nat. Acad. of Santa Cecilia, Rome 1997–2005; conducted Swedish Radio Symphony Orchestra at London Proms, playing Beethoven's Fourth Piano Concerto and Nielsen's Fifth 1999; Music Dir Asia Philharmonic Orchestra 1997–; Music Dir Radio France Philharmonic Orchestra 2000–; Special Artistic Adviser, Tokyo Philharmonic Orchestra 2001–; Music Dir Seoul Philharmonic Orchestra 2005–; Goodwill Amb. for UNICEF 2008–. *Honours:* Legion d'honneur 1992; Second Prize, Tchaikovsky Competition, Moscow 1974, Abbiati Prize (Italian critics) 1988, Arturo Toscanini Prize 1989, Victoires de la Musique Best Conductor, Best Lyrical Production, Best French Classical Recording 1995, Record Acad. Prize (Japan), Kumkwan (South Korea). *Website:* www.askonasholt.co.uk/artists/conductors/myung-whun-chung. *Address:* c/o Seoul Philharmonic Orchestra, Sejong-ro, Jongno-gu, Seoul 110-821, Korea (office). *Telephone:* (2) 37006300 (office). *Fax:* (2) 37006365 (office). *Website:* www.seoulphil.co.kr/english/main.jsp (office).

CHURCH, Francis; British singer (baritone); b. 1973, Liverpool, England. *Education:* Royal Scottish Acad. with Jeffrey Lawton, National Opera Studio, London, Pears-Britten School with Thomas Allen. *Career:* opera roles include Angelotti in Tosca, Benoit in La Bohème, Britten's Starveling and Sid, Guglielmo, and Sharpless in Madama Butterfly; concerts include Elgar's Coronation Ode, Elijah by Mendelssohn, Messiah, A Child of our Time (Tippett) and Fauré's Requiem. *Honours:* Verdi Prize, National Mozart Competition and John Noble Competition, Scottish Opera.

CHURGIN, Bathia Dina, BA, MA, PhD; American/Israeli musicologist and academic; *Professor Emerita, Bar-Ilan University*; b. 9 Oct. 1928, New York, NY; d. of Prof. Pinkhos Churgin and Rosetta Seligson Churgin. *Education:* Hunter Coll., New York City, Radcliffe Coll., Harvard Univ. *Career:* Instructor to Full Prof., Vassar Coll. 1952–57, 1959–71; Prof. and Founding Head of Dept, Bar-Ilan Univ., Ramat Gan, Israel, 1970–96, Prof. Emer. 1996–; Visiting Prof., Harvard Summer School, Northwestern Univ., Univ. of North Carolina, Chapel Hill, CUNY, Queen's Coll. and Grad. Center, Indiana Univ., Tel-Aviv Univ., The Hebrew Univ., Jerusalem, Rubin Acad. of Music, Jerusalem; Festschrift published in her honour, JM XVIII, 2001; mem. Israel Musicological Soc. (Chair. 1994–95), Int. Musicological Soc.; Corresp. mem. American Musicological Soc. 2007. *Publications:* The Symphonies of G. B. Sammartini, Vol. 1: The Early Symphonies 1968, Thematic Catalogue of the Works of Giovanni Battista Sammartini, Orchestral and Vocal Music (with Newell Jenkins) 1976, Israel Studies in Musicology II (ed.) 1980, G. B. Sammartini, Sonate a tre stromenti, A New Edition with Historical and Analytical Essays 1981, G. B. Sammartini: Ten Symphonies 1984, Israel Studies in Musicology VI (ed.) 1996, Beethoven's Fourth Symphony (ed.) 1998, Beethoven's Third and Fourth Symphonies (ed.), The Symphonic Repertoire Vol. I (co-ed. with Mary Sue Morrow), The Eighteenth-Century Symphony (co-ed. with Mary Sue Morrow); contrib. to professional journals: Francesco Galeazzi's Description (1796) of Sonata Form, JAMS XXI 1968, A New Edition of Beethoven's Fourth Symphony: Israel Studies in Musicology Vol. I 1978, Beethoven and Mozart's Requiem: A New Connection, JM V 1987, Beethoven's Sketches for his String Quintet, Op. 29, LaRue Festschrift 1990, Harmonic and Tonal Instability in the Second Key Area of Classic Sonata Form, Ratner Festschrift 1992, Sammartini and Boccherini: Continuity and Change in the Italian Instrumental Tradition of the Classic Period, Chigiana XLIII 1993, The Andante con moto in Beethoven's String Quartet Op. 130: The Final Version and Changes on the Autograph, JM XVI 1998, Beethoven and the New Development: Theme in Sonata-Form Movements, JM XVI 1998, Exploring the Eroica: Aspects of the New Critical Edition, Tyson Festschrift 1998, Sammartini, Giovanni Battista in New Grove Dictionary of Music 2001, Stormy Interlude: Sammartini's Middle Symphonies and Overtures in Minor in Giovanni Battista Sammartini and his Musical Environment 2004, Recycling Old Ideas in Beethoven's String Quartet Op. 132, Somfai Festschrift 2005, Transcendent Mastery: Studies in the Music of Beethoven 2008. *Honours:* Hon. Lifetime mem. Soc. for Eighteenth Century Music 2009; American Council of Learned Socs Fellowships 1964, 1986, elected to the Hunter Coll. Hall of Fame 1986. *Address:* Department of Music, Bar-Ilan University, Ramat Gan, 52900 (office); Rehov Havazelet 6/3, Kiron 55454, Israel (home). *Telephone:* (3) 531-8405 (office); (3) 534-0205 (home). *Fax:* (3)

738-4104 (office); (3) 534-0205 (home). *E-mail:* churgin@mail.biu.ac.il (home); bathia.churgin@gmail.com (home).

CHYLINSKA, Teresa Wanda, MA; Polish musicologist, music editor and writer on music; b. 20 June 1931, Wojciechowice; m. 1957 (divorced 1960); one s. *Education:* Jagiellonian Univ., Kraków. *Career:* Chief of Dept of Polish Music, Polish Music Publications, Kraków 1954–89; Lecturer, Jagiellonian Univ. and Acad. of Music 1970s; Pres. Karol Szymanowski Music Soc. 1979–80; mem. Scientific Bd Chopin Soc., Warsaw 1982–88. *Radio:* Cykl 22 audycji ożyciu i twórczości Karola Szymanowskiego, styczeń 2002, 2003, 2007. *Publications include:* first critical edn of The Complete Works of Karol Szymanowski (26 vols), complete edn of Szymanowski's correspondence, Vol. 1 1982, Vol. 2 1994, Vol. 3 1997, Vol. 4 2002, Szymanowski's Literary Writings 1989, Szymanowski's Days at Zakopane (fourth edn) 1982, Szymanowski and his Music (popular monograph for young readers, third edn) 1990, Karol Szymanowski, His Life and Works (in English) 1993, K. Szymanowski: Lottery for Husbands 1998, Z kresowych kronik rodzinnych, czyli o Michale von Blumenfeldzie vel Michale Kwiatopolskim 2004, Karol Szymanowski and His Epoch, three vols 2008, Stanisława Szymanowska – Biografia (biog.) 2014; contribs to New Grove Dictionary of Music and Musicians, Encyclopedia Muzyczna PWM, Pipers Enzyklopädie des Musik Theaters, Die Musik in Geschichte und Gegenwart, Polski Słownik Biograficzny. *Honours:* Hon. mem. Polish Composers' Union 2005, Hon. Mayor of Krakow Badge 2006; Gold Cross of Merit 2005, Kt Cross of Polonia Restituta Order 2014; numerous awards including Jurzykowski Foundation Award, New York 1984, Polish Composers' Union Award 1996, Karol Szymanowski Foundation Award 1997, Noweksiazki Award 2002, Gold Medal Gloria Artis for Culture 2006, Medal of the Nat. Museum, Krakow 2007, Polish Cultural Foundation Prize, Krakow 2007, John Dlugosz Award 2009, Golden Muse, Polish Music Asscn Awards 2010, Jagiellonian University Medal 2014. *Address:* ul Boguslawskiego 10.13, 31-038 Kraków, Poland (home). *Telephone:* (12) 422-30-18 (home); 60-4139320 (mobile) (home). *E-mail:* tchylinska@interia.pl.

CICOGNA, Adriana; Italian singer (mezzo-soprano); b. 1955, Este. *Education:* studied in Padua with Gina Cigna. *Career:* engagements from 1983 throughout Italy including Pizzetti's Fedra at Palermo; Donizetti's Sancia di Castiglia at Bergamo and Maddalena in Rigoletto at Florence; La Scala 1987 as Suzuki in Madama Butterfly, also at Torre del Lago 1995; other roles include Fidalma in Il Matrimonio Segreto; Smeton in Anna Bolena and appearances in operas by Monteverdi, Rossini (La Gazzetta) and Mozart; season 1998 at the Teatro Pergolesi, Jesi, as Metalce in a revival of Pergolesi's Il Prigionier superbo. *Recordings include:* Requiem by Pacini.

CIESINSKI, Katherine; American singer (mezzo-soprano); b. 13 Oct. 1950, Newark, DE. *Education:* Curtis Institute, Philadelphia with Margaret Harshaw. *Career:* sang in the US premiere of Berg's three-act Lulu; European debut 1976 at Aix-en-Provence; later sang in Asia, Israel and elsewhere in Europe; In 1988 sang in premiere of Argento's The Aspern Papers at Dallas and La Celestine by Maurice Ohana, Paris; Metropolitan Opera debut 1988, as Nicklausse in Les contes d'Hoffmann, returning as Judith in Duke Bluebeard's Castle by Bartók; Other roles include Waltraute in Götterdämmerung, Strauss's Composer and Octavian, Brangaene in Tristan und Isolde, Britten's Lucretia, Laura in La Gioconda and Barber's Vanessa; Cassandre in Les Troyens for Scottish Opera and at Covent Garden; La Favorite, title role, in revival of original French version, 1991; Santa Fe 1998, as Herodias in Salome. *Recordings:* War and Peace by Prokofiev, Dukas' Ariane et Barbe Bleue; Sapho by Massenet; Pauline in The Queen of Spades. *Current Management:* Columbia Artists Management, 1790 Broadway, New York, NY 10019-1412, USA. *Telephone:* (212) 841-9500. *Fax:* (212) 841 9744. *E-mail:* info@cami.com. *Website:* www.cami.com.

CIESINSKI, Kristine Frances, BA; American singer (soprano); b. 5 July 1952, Wilmington, Del. Delaware; m. Norman Bailey 1985. *Education:* Temple Univ., Univ. of Delaware, Boston Univ. *Career:* New York concert debut as soloist in Handel's Messiah, 1977; European operatic debut as Baroness Freimann in Der Wildschütz at Salzburg Landestheater, 1979, singing there until 1981; Member of Bremen State Opera, 1985–88; guest appearances at Cincinnati Opera, Florentine Opera, Milwaukee in 1983 and 1987, Cleveland Opera, 1985, Scottish Opera, 1985 and 1989, Canadian Opera, 1986, Opera North, Leeds, 1986 and 1988, Augsburg Opera, 1986, Mexico City, 1986, Welsh National Opera, 1987 and 1989, Bregenz Festival, 1987, Zagreb National Opera, 1988, Wexford Festival, 1988, English National Opera, 1989–93, Munich State Opera, 1989, Baltimore Opera, 1989, Winnipeg Opera, 1989 and 1991, Frankfurt State Opera, 1990 and 1993, New Orleans Opera, 1992, Leipzig Opera, 1992, and La Scala Milan in 1992; roles include Medea, La Wally, Eva, Senta, Donna Anna, Tosca, Aida, Ariadne, Salome, Verdi's Lady Macbeth, Shostakovich's Lady Macbeth of Mtsensk, Erwartung, Judith from Bartók's Bluebeard, Berg's Marie, Beethoven's Leonora, Tchaikovsky's Tatiana and Salome, also many concert engagements in a repertory ranging from traditional works to contemporary scores; sang Salome in a new production of Strauss's opera, ENO, 1996 and at Santa Fe, 1998; season 1999–2000 as Wagner's Gutrune in San Francisco and Emilia Marty for Opera Zuid, Netherlands. *Honours:* Gold Medal, Geneva International Competition, 1977; 1st Prize, Salzburg International Competition, 1977. *Current Management:* c/o Artists Management Zurich, Rütistrasse 52, Gockhausen, 8044 Zürich, Switzerland. *Website:* www.artistsman.com.

CIFARIELLO CIARDI, Fabio; Italian composer and academic; *Professor of Composition and Contemporary Music Analysis, Perugia Conservatory;* b. 15 Aug. 1960, Rome; s. of Antonio Cifariello and Marisa Patrizia Giglio; step-s. of Franco Ciardi; m. Antonella Costantino (divorced); two s.; partner Roberta Gottardi. *Education:* Accad. S. Cecilia, Rome, Univ. of Bologna; postgraduate studies with Franco Donatoni at Accad. Nazionale di S. Cecilia, Rome, and Tristan Murail and Philippe Manoury in Paris at IRCAM. *Career:* Composer-in-Residence, EMS, Stockholm 1995; Teacher of Composition and Contemporary Music Analysis, Conservatory of Perugia, now Prof.; mem. Edison Studio (asscn of composers for production of computer music); collaborations with the Research Inst. for Music Theatre, Rome and with RAI-Radio3; comms from Biennale di Venezia, Teatro La Fenice di Venezia, Festival Aperto Reggio Emilia, Ravenna Festival, Fondazione Palazzo Strozzi di Firenze, Festival Transart Bolzano, Società Aquilana dei Concerti B. Barattelli, Agon-Centro Armando Gentilicci, Fondazione S.Cecilia di Portogruaro, Comune di Trento, Orchestra Haydn di Trento e Bolzano, Orchestra Sinfonica di Sanremo, Orchestra MilanoClassica, Orchestra di Roma e del Lazio, Institut für Neue Musik, Freiburg, Singapore Univ., Stockholm Electronic Music Studio, IMEB Bourges; mem. Artistic-Scientific Cttee Federazione Cemat 2002–06, Bd of Analitica Online Journal of Musical Studies. *Compositions include:* Ankaa for clarinet and orchestra, Trame for orchestra, Mirrorshades II for orchestra, S'è desta? for six pianos, Nasdaq Voices (real-time sonification of financial data), Occhi a Maggio (chamber opera), live soundtrack for the silent movies: The Last Days of Pompeii, Das Cabinet des Dr Caligari, Inferno, Blackmail; Coplas for actor, soprano and 4 instruments, Ormond Brasil 10 for actor and piano on a text of F. Dürrenmatt, Tracce I–V for various solo instruments, Finzioni for violin and electronics, Pa(e/s)saggi for viola and electronics, Games for contrabass and electronics, Altri Passaggi for zarb, daf and electronics, Metafore for string quartet, Metri for string quartet, Cara P for voice, 4 intonarumori, radio, chair and electronics, Ab for nine instruments, Ra for eight instruments, Questi Fantasmi for four instruments, Appunti per amanti Simultanei I for trombone, five intonarumori and electronics, Pause for piano, Nasdaq Match 0.1 for flute, clarinet, percussions and sMax (real-time sonification of financial data), Nasdaq Match 0.2 for piano and sMax, Nasdaq Match 0.3 for flute, clarinet, cello, percussion and sMax, Piccoli Studi sul Potere for flute, clarinet, harp, violin, cello and synchronized video (instrumental transcription of Hitler, Emperor Akihito, Bush, Blair and Obama spoken voices), Araba Fenice for flute, clarinet, violin, cello and piano with female voice and chimes. *Television:* Gegenangriff – Wirtschaft im Fadenkreuz der Kunst (Contre-attaque – Quand l'art prend l'économie pour cible) (documentary on his works on real-time sonification of financial data) (Asscn Relative à la Télévision Européenne, ARTE) 2010. *Honours:* Ennio Porrino, Cagliari 1989, L. Russolo, Varese 1992, MusicaNova, Prague 1993, ICMC CD Selection, Tokyo, Japan 1993, Olympia, Athens, Greece 1993, Spectri Sonori 93, Tulane, USA 1993, XXV Concours Int. de Musique Electroacoustique, Bourges, France 1998, Valentino Bucchi, Rome 1999, ICMC Selection, Berlin, Germany 2000, Göteborg, Sweden 2002, Belfast, Northern Ireland 2008, Premio Nuova Musica, 39° Concorso Internazionale di Canto Corale C.A. Seghizzi, Gorizia, Video Evento d'Arte, Turin 2000, ICMC Selection, HK.5 Rimusicazioni Film Festival 2003, Premio Speciale, Associazione Italiana Tecnici del Suono 2011. *E-mail:* info@fabiocifariellociardi.com. *Website:* www .fabiocifariellociardi.com. *Address:* Via Aldo Moro 638, 00067 Morlupo, Rome, Italy (home). *Telephone:* 349-5502571 (mobile). *E-mail:* f.cifariellociardi@ edisonstudio.it (office). *Website:* www.edisonstudio.it (office).

CIOFI, Patrizia; Italian singer (soprano); b. 1967, Casole d'Elsa, Siena. *Education:* Livorno Istituto Musicale, studied in Siena and Fiesole with Carlo Bergonzi, Alberto Zedda and Claudio Desderi. *Career:* debut in Florence 1989, in Gino Negri's Giovanni Sebastiano; appearances throughout Italy as Donna Anna, Gilda, Nannetta in Falstaff, Fulvia in Rossini's La Pietra del Paragone, and Violetta; Martina Franca 1994–96 as Amina in La Sonnambula, Dirce in Cherubini's Médée and Silvia in L'Americano by Niccolo Piccinni; Clorinda in La Cenerentola at Lima and Gilda at Savona and Palermo; other venues include Parma, Trieste and Bologna; Concerts include Mozart's Mass in C minor; Covent Garden debut as Gilda, 2002, also Isabelle in Meyerbeer's Robert le diable 2013. *Honours:* winner Ettore Bastianini Competition, Siena 1991. *Current Management:* Opera Art, Via Isolalta Forette 11, 37068 Vigasio (VR), Italy. *Telephone:* (045) 6649911. *Fax:* (045) 6649912. *E-mail:* info@ operaart.it. *Website:* www.operaart.it.

CIUCIURA, Leoncjusz, BA; Polish composer; b. 22 June 1930, Grodzisk Mazowiecki; m. Sylwia Grelich 1967. *Education:* High School of Music, Warsaw. *Career:* debut concert at High School of Music, Warsaw; Co-founder Polish br. of Jeunesses Musicales movement 1958–62; Founder and Ed. Carmina Academica Musical Publication; Ed. Musical Publication for Contemporary Music 1989; compositions performed world-wide 1964–2011, including Festival ISCM World Music Days, Int. Festival of Music, Warsaw Autumn; numerous int. festivals of contemporary music world-wide; mem. Union of Polish Composers, Soc. of Authors ZAiKS. *Compositions:* Penetrations for orchestral groups, four conductors and composer 1963, Emergenza for choirs and orchestra, three conductors and composer 1963, Spiral Form (in progress); Spirale I per uno 1964–2012, Spirale II per uno e piu 1964–2012, Creatoria I, II 1964–2012, Intarsio I, II 1964–2012, Rencontre I, II 1964–2012, Incidenti I, II 1964–2012, In Infinitum I, II 1964–2012 (all for optional instruments and accompaniment). *Honours:* Ministry of Culture and Art Laureate Prize 1960, Polish Composers Union Competition for Canti al Fresco Prize 1961, Int. Composers Competition (Prague) for Concertino da Camera

Prize 1962, Polish Broadcast and Television Prize for Ornamenti 1963. *Address:* Zwirki and Wigury 5, 05-825 Grodzisk Mazowiecki, Poland (office). *Website:* www.polmic.pt.

CIULEI, Lenuta; Romanian violinist; b. 25 May 1958, Bucharest; m.; two s. *Education:* Bucharest Music Acad., studied in Germany, Belgium and USA, and with Stephan Gheorghiu, André Gertler, Raphael Druian and Ruggiero Ricci. *Career:* debut on Romanian Television broadcast 1967; played concerts with orchestras, recitals as solo violinist and leader of chamber music ensembles in 35 countries throughout Europe, North and South America, Asia; performed at the UN Palais, Geneva, Bartók Memorial House, Budapest, the Great Hall of the Tchaikovsky Conservatory, Moscow, the Lincoln Center's Alice Tully Hall and in Madrid for the Spanish Royal Family; participated in many int. festivals; Assoc. Artistic Dir, Virtuosi de Caracas; gives masterclasses at univs, int. festivals and orchestras in the USA, Venezuela and Europe; violin teacher in Dept of Music, Rowan Univ., USA. *Honours:* first prize in various int. competitions, Pennsylvania Solo Recitalist Award 1994, Order of Brazil for South American Music 1996. *Address:* Department of Music, Rowan University, Wilson Hall, 201 Mullica Hill Road, Glassboro, NJ 08028, USA (office). *E-mail:* atanasiul@rowan.edu.

CLAASSEN, René; Dutch singer (tenor); b. 1937, Helmond. *Education:* Amsterdam Conservatory, The Hague. *Career:* debut at Maastricht 1960; sang at Bremerhaven from 1964, Kassel from 1968 as Wagner's Loge and Mime, Monostatos in Die Zauberflöte, Shuratov in From the House of the Dead, and the Villains in Les Contes d'Hoffmann; appeared in Der Ring des Nibelungen 1989 and sang Aschenbach in Death in Venice; Amsterdam 1986 in Zemlinsky's Der Kreidekreis and as Loge and Mime at Rotterdam 1989; sang Leonard in Nielsen's Maskarade at Kassel 1994; many concert appearances.

CLAMAGIRAND, Fanny; French violinist; b. 12 April 1984, Paris. *Education:* Conservatoire Nat. Supérieur de Musique de Paris with Jean-Jacques Kantorow, Royal Coll. of Music, London with Itzhak Rashkovsky, masterclasses with Ida Haendel, Zakhar Bron, Natalia Gutman, Michèle Auclair, Donald Weilerstein, Shlomo Mintz, Boris Kushnir. *Career:* performed as concert soloist from age nine throughout France and in Europe; also at festivals in France, Germany, Austria, Belarus, Russia, Ukraine, USA, Israel, Switzerland, England and Tunisia; performances at major concert houses including Accademia Santa Cecilia in Rome, Wigmore Hall and Royal Festival Hall in London, Victoria Hall in Geneva, Opera House, Museum of Arts and Blumenthal Center in Tel Aviv, Konzerthaus in Vienna, Opera House in Cairo, Claudion Santoro Opera in Brasilia, Cultural Center in Chicago, Zankel Hall of the Carnegie in New York, Théâtre des Champs Elysées, Paris; appeared as soloist with orchestras including Weimar Symphony Orchestra, Portuguese Radio Symphony Orchestra, Vienna Symphonic Orchestra, Philharmonic Orchestra of Radio France, Symphony Orchestra and Sinfonietta of the London RCM, Philharmonic Orchestra of Monte Carlo, Jerusalem Symphony Orchestra, Teatro La Fenice Orchestra, Chamber Orchestra of Mainz, Royal Chamber Orchestra of Wallonia, Wiener Kammer-Orchester, Israel Chamber Orchestra, Orchestre Nat. du Capitole de Toulouse. *Recordings include:* Ysaye: Sonates pour violon seul, opus 27 2007, Saint-Saëns: Concertos pour violon 2010. *Honours:* First Prize, Louis Spohr Int. Competition 1995, Special Jury Prize, Yehudi Menuhin Int. Competition 2000, Emily Anderson Prize, Royal Philharmonic Soc., London 2004, First Prize, Int. Fritz Kreisler Competition, Vienna 2005, First Prize, Monte Carlo Violin Masters Competition 2007. *Current Management:* c/o Barret Jeremiah, 29 rue Violet, F- 75015 Paris, France. *E-mail:* jeremie .barret@musicaglotz.com. *Website:* www.musicaglotz.com. *E-mail:* info@ clamagirand.com. *Website:* www.fannyclamagirand.com.

CLAMAN, David, BA, MM, MFA, PhD; American composer and academic; b. 1958, Denver, Colo. *Education:* Wesleyan Univ., Conn., Univ. of Colorado, Princeton Univ. *Career:* played electric bass in rock bands in Boston 1980s; fmr Visiting Prof. of Music, Colorado Coll., Colorado Springs; Asst Prof., Coll. of the Holy Cross 2002–04; music has been performed in the USA, Canada, Europe and India; comms from The American Composers Forum (for New York's Cygnus Ensemble), High Altitude Trombone Quartet, New Millennium Ensemble and Princeton Univ.; Fellowship, The American Inst. of Indian Studies 1988–89, residencies at MacDowell Colony 2001 and Rockefeller Foundation's Bellagio Center, Italy 2002. *Compositions:* '70 for computer generated tape 1994, Loose Cannons for three electric guitars 1995, Septet (hip replacement) for trumpets, percussion, electric guitars, bass 1996, Kaavena Kuuvena for South Indian vocal ensemble and soloist 1999, Gone for Foreign for flute, oboe, violin, cello, two guitars 1999, Fifteener for trombone quartet 2000, Unpact for four-hand piano 2003, Loomings for computer generated CD 2003, JGC for flute and piano 2004. *Recording:* Gone for Foreign (with others) 2006. *Honours:* Sr Creative and Performing Arts Fellowship, American Inst. of Indian Studies 1998. *Website:* www.myspace .com/davidclaman.

CLAPTON, Nicholas, MA (Oxon.), MA (London), DLA; British singer (counter-tenor); *Professor of Singing, Royal Academy of Music;* b. 16 Sept. 1955, Worcester, England. *Education:* Magdalen Coll., Oxford and Univ. of London, studied for Doctor of Liberal Arts degree at Liszt Ferenc Music Univ., Budapest, studied singing with David Mason and Diane Forlano. *Career:* debut at Wigmore Hall, London 1984; Aldeburgh Festival 1985; London recital debut Purcell Room 1986; numerous appearances throughout Europe and in

the Far East; operatic roles for ENO, Opera North, Channel 4 TV, Batignano, EBF, ranging from Monteverdi and Handel to world premieres (Barry, Lefanu, Benedict Mason); premieres of concert works by Judith Bingham, Nicola LeFanu, Helen Roe, David Bedford, Simon Holt, Elis Pehkonen, Daryl Runswick, Robin Walker, Jim Aitchison; many recitals (Purcell, Rossini, Romantic song, etc.) with Jennifer Partridge; currently Prof. of Singing, RAM, London; Visiting Prof., Ferenc Liszt Music Univ. (Zeneakadémia), Budapest; mem. Royal Soc. of Musicians of GB, Inc. Soc. of Musicians. *Exhibition:* curator, 'Handel and the Castrati', Handel House Museum, London 2006. *Recordings:* Purcell: Hail, Bright Cecilia, Duruflé: Requiem, Benedetto Marcello: Cantatas, Nicola Porpora: Cantatas, LeFanu: Canción de la Luna, Gerald Barry: operas The Intelligence Park and The Triumph of Beauty and Deceit, two miscellanies of modern English works for countertenor. *Television:* presenter, Castrato (BBC 4). *Publications:* Moreschi: The Last Castrato (biog.) 2004, 2008, Budapest: City of Music 2009; articles for BJECS, Early Music. *Honours:* English Song Award 1987, Winner, Heart of England Int. Competition for Singers 1987, two prizes, Concurso Francisco Viñas, Barcelona 1985. *Address:* Royal Academy of Music, Marylebone Road, London, NW1 5HT, England (office). *E-mail:* bartok@nicholasclapton.com (office); njc@ nicholasclapton.com (office). *Website:* www.nicholasclapton.com.

CLARET, Lluis; Andorran cellist; b. 10 March 1951; m. Anna Mora; one s. *Education:* Liceo Conservatory, Barcelona, Conservatoire European, Paris, Bloomington School of Music, USA, studied with Enric Casals, Radu Aldulescu, Eva Janzer, György Sebok. *Career:* debut with Boccherini Cello Concerto, Barcelona 1968; soloist concerts with National Symphony of Washington and Moscow Philharmonic, Orchestra National de France, English Chamber Orchestra, Czech Philharmonic under Rostropovich, Pierre Boulez, Vaclav Neumman, Witold Lutoslawski; played at closing ceremony of Barcelona '92 Olympic Games; mem. Barcelona Trio. *Recordings:* Bach: Complete Suites for cello solo, 1999; Schubert: Sonata Arpeggione for cello and piano, 1992; Chopin: Sonata for cello and piano; Strauss: Sonata for cello and piano, 1991; Kodály: Sonata for cello, 1990; Schumann: Concerto for cello and orchestra, 1990; Haydn: Concerto No. 1 in C for cello and orchestra; Boccherini: Concerto No. 3 in G minor for cello and orchestra; Dvořák: Trio, Dumky, op. 90, Trio in F minor, 1992; works by Boulez, Mendelssohn and Ravel. *Honours:* first prize Rostropovich Competition 1977, Casals 1978, Bologna Competition 1975. *Address:* c/o Netzel, Pasaie Marimon, 10-4, 08021 Barcelona, Spain.

CLAREY, Cynthia, BMus; American singer (mezzo-soprano); *Professor of Voice, Chicago College of Performing Arts, Roosevelt University;* b. (Viola Cynthia Clarey), 25 April 1949, Smithfield, Va; d. of Waverly Collier and Mildred Cole; m. Jake Gardner 1978 (divorced 2000); one s. *Education:* Howard Univ., Washington, DC and Juilliard School, Postgraduate Diploma. *Career:* sang first with the Tri-Cities Opera Co.; has sung in The Voice of Ariadne by Thea Musgrave with the New York City Opera; Boston Opera Company in the US premiere of Tippett's The Ice Break 1979, and The Makropulos Case 1986; Binghamton, New York 1986, in the premiere of Chinchilla by Myron Fink; British debut at the Glyndebourne Festival 1984, as Monteverdi's Ottavia, followed by Serena in Porgy and Bess 1986; Wexford Festival 1985, 1986 as Polinesso in Ariodante and Thomas's Mignon; has toured with Peter Brook's version of Carmen and appeared in the 1989–90 season in concert versions of Anna Bolena (Concertgebouw, as Jane Seymour), Weill's Lost in the Stars (Almeida Festival, London) and The Ice Break (as Hanna, at the Promenade Concerts, London); has also sung in operas by Cavalli, Mozart, Verdi, Puccini, Menotti and Offenbach; other roles include Monteverdi's Penelope, Cavalli's Diana (La Calisto), Handel's Rinaldo, Zerlina, Isoletta (La Straniera), Preziosilla, Dalila, Butterfly, Nicklausse and Octavian; sang Serena in the Covent Garden premiere of Porgy and Bess 1992, and in Weill/Grosz Concert at the 1993 London Proms; three roles in Berg's Lulu at the Festival Hall, London 1994; sang Gershwin's Bess at Cape Town 1996; sang Kristina in The Makropulos Case at Aix-en-Provence 2000; has sung with major orchestras, including Chicago Symphony, Boston Symphony, Oakland Symphony, New York Philharmonic, BBC Symphony, City of London Sinfonia, Hallé Orchestra and Dallas Symphony; Prof. of Voice, Chicago Coll. of Performing Arts, Roosevelt Univ. 2008–; numerous concert appearances. *Recordings include:* Porgy and Bess, Tippett's The Ice Break, Duffy's A Time for Remembrance, Afrika Songs, Will: Lost in the Stars, Turnage: Somedays, Berg: Lulu. *Current Management:* c/o 132 Leroy Street, Binghamton, NY 13905, USA. *Telephone:* (607) 222-6292 (home). *E-mail:* cyclarey@aol.com. *Website:* www.cynthiaclarey.com.

CLARK, Derek John, Dip MusEd, DipRSAM, BMus; British conductor, coach and accompanist; b. 22 Aug. 1955, Glasgow, Scotland; m. Heather Fryer 1980; one d. *Education:* Dumbarton Acad., Royal Scottish Acad. of Music and Drama, Univ. of Durham, London Opera Centre. *Career:* debut as accompanist, Purcell Room 1976, as conductor with WNO 1982; Staff Conductor, WNO 1976–97; Guest Conductor, Mid-Wales Opera 1989–92; Coach and Conductor, Welsh Coll. of Music and Drama 1992–97; Head of Music, Scottish Opera 1997–; Guest Coach, RSAMD 1998; conducting repertoire includes Tamerlano, Samson, Marriage of Figaro, Così fan tutte, Magic Flute, Die Entführung, La finta giardiniera, Lucia di Lammermoor, Don Pasquale, Count Ory, Beatrice and Benedict, Carmen, La Traviata, Rigoletto, La Bohème, Barber of Seville, Tosca, The Rake's Progress, Noye's Fludde and Maxwell Davies's Cinderella. *Compositions:* three one-act operas for young people: Hardlock House 1988, The Witch of Mawddwy 1993, The Forest Child

1998, songs, choral music and arrangements. *Honours:* Worshipful Company of Musicians Silver Medal 1976.

CLARK, Graham Ronald, MSc, DLC; British singer (tenor); b. 10 Nov. 1941, Littleborough, Lancs., England; s. of Ronald Edward Clark and Annie Clark; m. Joan Barbara Clark 1979; one step-d. *Education:* Loughborough Colls and Univ.; studied singing with Bruce Boyce in London, and in Bologna and Mantua. *Career:* professional debut with Scottish Opera 1975; with ENO 1978–85, subsequent guest appearances (over 200 performances); sang with Royal Opera, Covent Garden, Glyndebourne Festival Opera, Opera North, Welsh Nat. Opera and Northern Ireland Opera 1978–; extensive int. career, appeared at Metropolitan Opera, New York for 15 seasons 1985–2010; Bayreuth Festival 1981–2004 (16 seasons and over 120 performances); numerous appearances in Aix-en-Provence, Amsterdam, Barcelona, Berlin (Deutsche Oper, Deutsche Staatsoper), Bilbao, Biwako, Bonn, Brussels, Catania, Chicago, Dallas, Dublin, Frankfurt, Geneva, Hamamatsu, Hamburg, Los Angeles, Luxembourg, Madrid (Teatro Real, Zarzuela), Matsumoto (Saito Kinen), Milan (La Scala), Munich, Nagoya, Nice, New York (The Met), Paris (Bastille, Champs Élysées, Châtelet, Palais Garnier), Rome, Salzburg, San Francisco, Seville, Stockholm, Tokyo, Toronto, Toulouse, Turin, Vancouver, Vienna (Staatsoper), Yokohama, Zürich 1976–; concerts with many of the world's leading orchestras and at festivals of Amsterdam, Antwerp, Bamberg, Berlin, Brussels, Canaries, Chicago, Cologne, Copenhagen, Edinburgh, London, Lucerne, Milan, Paris, Rome, Tel-Aviv, Washington, DC; has sung over 395 Wagner performances, including over 275 performances of Der Ring des Nibelungen (Loge and Mime); acting debut reciting Plato's Apology, The Trial of Socrates, Luxembourg 2011. *Recordings include:* has recorded with BBC, BMG, Challenge Classics, Chandos, Decca, Deutsche Grammophon, EMI, Erato, Etcetera, EuroArts, Oehms Classics, Opera Rara, Opus Arte, Philips, Profil, Sony, Teldec, The Met New York, United Artists and Warner Classics. *Video recordings include:* Bayreuth performances of Die Meistersinger, Der Fliegende Holländer and 1992 Ring des Nibelungen, the Met's Ghosts of Versailles, Der Ring des Nibelungen from Barcelona and Amsterdam, Wozzeck from Berlin Staatsoper and New York Met, Lady Macbeth of Mtsensk from Barcelona, Khovanshchina from Barcelona, The Makropulos Case from Toronto, The Rake's Progress from Glyndebourne, The Trial of Socrates from the Grand Théâtre, Luxembourg. *Honours:* Hon. DLitt (Loughborough) 1999, Hon. BSc (Loughborough) 2009; Olivier Award (for portrayal of Mephistopheles in Busoni's Doktor Faust, ENO) 1986, Sir Reginald Goodall Prize, London Wagner Soc. 2001, Sherwin Award, Wagner Soc. of Southern California 2009. *Current Management:* c/o Ingpen & Williams, 7 St George's Court, 131 Putney Bridge Road, London, SW15 2PA, England. *Telephone:* (20) 8874-3222. *Fax:* (20) 8877-3113. *E-mail:* info@ingpen.co.uk. *Website:* www.ingpen.co.uk; www.grahamclark.org.

CLARK, Richard J.; American singer (baritone); b. 25 April 1943, Tucson, AZ. *Education:* Academy of Vocal Arts, Philadelphia and Juilliard School, New York. *Career:* debut in San Francisco, as Monterone in Rigoletto; Metropolitan Opera from 1981, as Verdi's Monterone and di Luna, Wagner's Amfortas and Kurwenal, Barnaba in La Gioconda, Michele in Il Tabarro and Gianciotto in Francesca da Rimini by Zandonai.

CLARKE, Adrian; British singer (baritone); b. 1953, Northampton, England. *Education:* Royal College of Music, London and the London Opera Centre. *Career:* appearances with Opera North in Die Fledermaus, The Mikado, Fanciulla del West, The Golden Cockerel, Faust and Carmen (as Escamillo); Don Ferdinand in the British stage premiere of Gerhard's The Duenna, 1994; Rossini's Barber for Scottish Opera and Dublin Grand Opera, Guglielmo and Taddeo in L'Italiana in Algeri for Opera 80; Nick Shadow in The Rake's Progress for New Sussex Opera; Contemporary music includes: Maxwell Davies's Martyrdom of St Magnus for Opera Factory, the premieres of Casken's Golem and Cage's Europera III (London, Berlin and Paris); Gerald Barry's Triumph of Beauty and Deceit for Channel 4 television, the British premiere of Mason's Playing Away (Opera North), Osborne's I am Goya and Rihm's Unsungen (Glasgow and Amsterdam); Season 1995–96 with Rossini's Barber for English Touring Opera, Rigoletto for Mid-Wales Opera and La Bohème for Glyndebourne Touring Opera; Season 2000 as Prince Afron in The Golden Cockerel at Bregenz and the title roles in the premiere of Mr. Emmett Takes a Walk by Peter Maxwell Davies, at Kirkwall. *Current Management:* Musicmakers International Artists Representation, Tailor House, 63–65 High Street, Whitwell, Hertfordshire, SG4 8AH, England. *Telephone:* (1438) 871708. *Fax:* (1438) 871777. *E-mail:* musicmakers@compuserve.com. *Website:* www.operauk.com.

CLARKE, Karin; American singer (soprano); b. 1963, New York. *Education:* Tri-Cities Opera, New York and International Opera Studio, Zürich. *Career:* appearances at the Trier Opera as Giulietta in Hoffmann, Marguerite, Mozart's Countess and Anne Trulove; further engagements at Hagen, Saarbrucken, Munster and Bielefeld notably as Fiordiligi, Saffi (Zigeunerbaron) and Rosalinde in Die Fledermaus; guest at Brussels, Ghent, Liège and Linz, with concert appearances in New York and throughout Germany; other roles include Agathe, Lady (Hindemith's Cardillac), Elvira in Ernani, Marenka in The Bartered Bride and the Marschallin; sang the title role in a revival of Zemlinsky's Sarema, Trier Opera 1996 (first production 20th century). *Recordings include:* Sarema.

CLARKE, Nigel, DMA, ARAM; British composer and musician; b. 1960, Sandwich, Kent. *Education:* RAM, studied with Paul Patterson, Salford Univ.

Career: fmr military bandsman; joined US Embassy exchange programme, with opportunity to experience American musical culture 1997; his work Samurai performed by The President's Own US Marine Band; works played and broadcast world-wide; currently Assoc. Composer, Brass Band Buizingen (Belgium); Composer-in-Residence, Marinierskapel der Koninklijke Marine (Marine Band of Royal Netherlands Navy); Visiting Adjunct Prof., Middle Tennessee State Univ., USA; other positions held have included Tutor in Composition and Contemporary Music, RAM, Head of Composition, London Coll. of Music & Media, Assoc. Composer, Black Dyke Mills Band, Guest Prof., Xinjiang Arts Inst., China, Assoc. Composer, Royal Military School of Music, Kneller Hall, Assoc. Composer, Band of HM Grenadier Guards, Visiting Tutor, Royal Northern Coll. of Music. *Compositions include:* for brass band: When Worlds Collide, Swift Severn's Flood, The Pendle Witches, The City in the Sea, euphonium concerto for brass band, Atlantic Toccata; for concert band: Tilbury Point, Their Finest Hour, Mata Hari, King Solomon's Mines, Heritage Suite, Gagarin, Forgotten Heroes, Fields of Remembrance, Fanfare & Celebrations, Earthrise, Breaking the Century, Battles & Chants, Samurai; other: Winter Music for string orchestra, Spectroscope for solo cello, Solstice for solo piano, Premonitions for solo trumpet, Pernambucco for solo violin, Parnassus for string orchestra, The Miraculous Violin for violin and string orchestra, Loulan for solo violin, The Lindisfarne Stone for violin and piano, Flashpoint for solo viola, Equiano for clarinet quintet, The Devil & the Hemlock Stone for clarinet and electronics, Echo & Narcissus for solo flute, Chinese Puzzles for flute and piano, Work Mysteries of the Horizon, concerto (British Acad. of Songwriters, Composers and Authors Award 2013), two violin concertos (with Peter Sheppard Skaerved); several film scores. *Recordings:* Premonitions 2000, Samurai/Black Fire 2007; works included in collections. *Honours:* Josiah Parker Prize and Queen's Commendation for Excellence (first ever composer), RAM, British Composer Award, wind/brass band categrory 2013. *Address:* c/o Studio Music Company, Cadence House, Eaton Green Road, Luton, LU2 9LD, England (office). *Telephone:* (1582) 432139 (office). *E-mail:* nigel@nigel-clarke.co.uk (office). *Website:* www.nigel-clarke.co.uk (office); www.studio-music.co.uk.

CLARKE, Paul Charles; British singer (tenor); b. 1965, Liverpool. *Education:* Royal College of Music with Neil Mackie. *Career:* many performances throughout the UK, including concerts with Bournemouth Sinfonietta, London Ensemble and Scottish Chamber Orchestra; Duke in Rigoletto, Fenton, the High Priest, Idomeneo and Rodolfo with Welsh National Opera, 1990–93; Paris debut, 1991 as Fenton at Théâtre des Champs Elysées; engagements as Dmitri in Boris Godunov and Rodolfo for Opera North, Alfredo and Nemorino for Scottish Opera, 1993–94; Covent Garden debut, 1994–95; Cassio in Otello; Tybalt in Roméo et Juliette; Alfredo in La Traviata; US debut with Seattle Opera singing the Duke in Rigoletto, 1995; engaged as Faust with Welsh National Opera and Rodolfo at Royal Opera House, Covent Garden, 1996; season 1997–98 as Verdi's Macduff at Monte Carlo, Gabriele Adorno for WNO and the Duke of Mantua for Scottish Opera; Roméo at the Met and Rodolfo at Seattle; sang Alfredo at Cincinnati and Pinkerton for WNO, 1998; season 2000–01 as Verdi's Gabriele Adorno at Wellington, the Duke of Mantua for Santa Fe Opera and Massenet's Des Grieux at Dallas; Don José in Carmen, Copenhagen 2010; Alfred in die Fledermaus, WNO 2011. *Recordings include:* Donizetti, Don Pasquale 1998, Puccini: Madam Butterfly 2001, Donizetti, Lucia di Lammermoor 2002, Mozart, Idomeneo 2002, Smetana, The Bartered Bride 2005. *Honours:* Peter Pears Scholarship and Kathleen Ferrier Memorial Prize. *Address:* c/o Chandos Records Ltd, Chandos House, 1 Commerce Park, Commerce Way, Colchester, Essex CO2 8HX, England (office). *Telephone:* (1206) 225200 (office). *Fax:* (1206) 225201 (office). *E-mail:* enquiries@chandos.net (office). *Website:* www.chandos.net (office).

CLARKE, Stephen David Justin, DipMus, MA, ARCO; British conductor; *Precentor (Director of Music), Radley College;* b. 21 July 1964, Thame, Oxon., England; m. Helen Victoria Morrison; one s. one d. *Education:* New Coll., Oxford, Hertford Coll., Oxford (organ scholarship), Guildhall School of Music and Drama. *Career:* Conductor Oxford Philharmonia 1983–85; Founder St Michael's Sinfonia 1981; Conductor Oxford Univ. Opera Club 1983–85; Conductor Schola Cantorum of Oxford 1985–87; Guest Conductor, Oxford Pro Musica 1985, St Endellion Festival Orchestra 1987; worked with Kent Opera 1988, Geneva Grand Opera 1988, Royal Scottish Acad. of Music and Drama 1988–89; British Youth Opera 1988; Asst Chorus Master, ENO 1990; Head of Music, Scottish Opera 1993; Asst Music Dir New Israeli Opera, Tel-Aviv 1998; performances at Scottish Opera, Opera North 1999–2002; Precentor (Dir of Music), Radley Coll. 2002–; Asst Conductor BBC TV Flashmob Christmas 2003; Head of Music, Garsington Opera 2003. *Honours:* Ricordi Conducting Prize 1985–86. *Address:* 1 Lower Shrubbery, Radley College, Abingdon, Oxon., OX14 2HU, England (home).

CLAXTON, Andrew, MMus, GRSM, ARAM, LRAM, ARCM, PGCE; British composer, instrumentalist (keyboards, low brass), teacher (piano, composition) and piano-broker; *Principal, Oxford School of Music;* b. 22 Jan. 1950, London, England; m.; three s. (one deceased). *Education:* Nat. Youth Orchestra of Great Britain, Royal Acad. of Music, London, Bretton Hall Coll., Univ. of Reading. *Career:* multi-instrumentalist, City of Oxford Orchestra 1974–2000, Dead Can Dance 1987–93, Meltdown 1997–2001; Dir Peacock Press 1985–92; Musical Dir, Gintare 1990–99; apptd Prin., Oxford School of Music 2002; fmr mem. Performing Right Soc., Int. Piano Teachers Group. *Film includes:* Silent Spaces 1998. *Compositions include:* Six 1996, Spires and Spirits 1997, it was…it is…it will be 2001. *Plays:* three professional pantomimes 1980–82, Elements 1988, Fall of The House of Usher 1992. *Television:* Liar 1995, The Big Sleazy 1996, Drug Raped 1998, Silent Spaces 1998, Inside Polygamy 1999, The Forbidden Journey 1999. *Recordings include:* Cobwebs and Cogwheels 2003; collaborations: Dead Can Dance albums: Within The Realm of a Dying Sun 1987, Toward The Within 1994, The Mirror Pool 1995, Dead Can Dance 1981–98 (compilation) 2001. *Publication:* Tuba Technique 1986. *Honours:* winner, Oxford Town Hall Centenary Composers Competition 1997, Finalist, Best Re-Recorded Music Category, British TV Advertising Craft Awards 1998. *Telephone:* (1865) 430409 (office). *E-mail:* principal@oxfordschoolofmusic.org.uk (office). *Website:* www.oxfordschoolofmusic.org.uk (office).

CLAYTON, Beth; American singer (mezzo-soprano); b. 1970, Arkansas. *Education:* Southern Methodist Univ. and Manhattan School of Music, studied with Mignon Dunn. *Career:* sang Don Ramiro in La finta giardiniera at Washington 1996; Cherubino at Caracas, Venezuela; Houston Opera in Roméo et Juliette and Virgil Thomson's Four Saints in Three Acts, also in New York and Edinburgh; season 1998–99 with Cherubino and Nicklausse at Houston, Janáček's Fox at Toronto; Mère Marie in The Carmelites conducted by Seiji Ozawa and Mozart's Sesto in Israel; season 1999–2000 with the premiere of Carlisle Floyd's Cold Sassy Tree at Houston and Carmen for WNO; concerts include Mahler's 8th Symphony with the Montréal Symphony Orchestra 1999–2000; Messiah, Dallas Symphony Orchestra; A Midsummer Night's Dream; sang in British premiere of Saariaho's L'amour de loin, Barbican Hall 2002; as Carmen, Opera Colorado 2005, Santa Fe Opera 2006, New York City Opera 2007. *Current Management:* c/o Matthew A. Horner, IMG Artists, Carnegie Hall Tower, 152 West 57th Street, Fifth Floor, New York, NY 10019, USA. *Telephone:* (212) 994-3500. *Fax:* (212) 994-3550. *E-mail:* mhorner@imgartists.com. *Website:* www.imgartists.com. *E-mail:* beth@bethclayton.info. *Website:* www.bethclayton.info.

CLAYTON, Laura; American composer and pianist; b. 8 Dec. 1943, Lexington, KY. *Education:* Aspen School with Milhaud, New England Conservatory with Wuorinen, Univ. of Michigan. *Compositions include:* Implosure for two dancers, slide and tape 1977, Cree Songs for the Newborn for soprano and chamber orchestra 1987, Panels for chamber ensemble 1983, Sagarama for piano and orchestra 1984, Clara's Sea for women's voices 1988, Terra Lucida for orchestra 1988. *Honours:* NEA awards and Guggenheim Fellowship.

CLEGG, John; British concert pianist; b. 7 Nov. 1928, London. *Education:* Jesus Coll., Cambridge, Royal Coll. of Music, studied piano with Herbert Fryer. *Career:* debut, Wigmore Hall, London 1951; has given recitals, concerts and broadcasts in most countries, with frequent tours of Africa, Middle East and Far East, and concerts in principal European centres; regular performer on BBC radio and television; pianist-in-residence, Lancaster Univ. 1981–93. *Recordings include:* Complete piano music by Alan Rawsthorne 1996, Piano music of Milhaud, Koechlin, Ibert and Schmitt 1998, Music by Chopin-Liszt; Poulenc and Adrian Self 2000, Music by Fauré and Poulenc 2002, Music by Howard Ferguson, William Mathias, Kenneth Leighton 2002. *Honours:* Harriet Cohen Int. Award 1968. *Current Management:* J. Audrey Ellison, International Artists' Management, 135 Stevenage Road, Fulham, London, SW6 6PB, England. *Address:* The Swallow Barn, 3 Lane Foot Farm, Newton, Carnforth, LA6 2PA, England (home). *Telephone:* (1524) 272434 (home). *Fax:* (1524) 272434 (home). *E-mail:* jandjc@hotmail.co.uk (home).

CLEIN, Natalie; British cellist; b. 1977. *Education:* Royal Coll. of Music, Musik Hochschule (Heinrich Schiff), Vienna. *Career:* debut, London Proms Concerts 1997 with Haydn's C major concerto; appearances with Royal Philharmonic, English Chamber, Philharmonia, London Philharmonic and City of Birmingham Orchestras; Elgar Concerto with LPO in Madrid and London; Lutosławski Concerto with Hallé Orchestra; US concerto debut with the California SO, with further engagements at Verbier, Delft and Divonne Festivals, Schwartzenberg Schubertiade, Kronberg, Manchester Cello Festival, Spannungen, Barbican Mostly Mozart; chamber recitals at Wigmore Hall and Cheltenham and Bath Int. Festivals; Schumann Quintet with Martha Argerich; Dvořák Concerto at St Magnus Festival 2001; season 2000–01 with Royal Philharmonic Orchestra, BBC Nat. Orchestra of Wales and tour of UK, including Wigmore Hall recital; New Generation Artists concerts with BBC; recital debuts in Teatro Colón with Buenos Aires Philharmonic 2003, New York Lincoln Centre 2004. *Recordings include:* Taverner (with the English Chamber Orchestra), Dvorat Sextet (with the Nash Ensemble), recital album of Brahms, Schubert (with Charles Owen, piano), Kodály collection 2010. *Honours:* BBC Young Musician of Year 1994, winner Eurovision Competition for Young Musicians, Warsaw 1994, Kronberg Akad. Ingrid zu Solms Cultur Preis 2003, Classical BRIT Award for Young British Classical Performer 2005. . *E-mail:* info@natalieclein.com. *Website:* www.natalieclein.com.

CLEMENCIC, René, PhD; Austrian composer, conductor, recorder player, harpsichordist and clavichord player; *Artistic Director, Clemencic Consort;* b. 27 Feb. 1928, Vienna; m. 1st; one d.; m. 2nd Edda Rischka 1968; one d. *Education:* Univ. of Vienna, studied music with J. Mertin, J. Polnauer, H. U. Staeps, L. Höffer von Winterfeld, W. Nitschke, Eta Harich-Schneider. *Career:* Founder and leader of early music ensemble, Clemencic Consort 1968–, currently Artistic Dir; Ed. Mediaeval Carmina Burana; Baroque opera performances (first modern including: Draghi's L'Eternita Soggetta al Tempo, Peri's Euridice, Leopold I's Il Lutto dell'Universo); TV play; concerts world-wide. *Compositions include:* Maraviglia III and V, Sesostris II and III,

Chronos II, Bicinia Nova, Music for Ariana Mnouchkine's film Molière, Musik zum Urfaust, Tolldrastische Szenen, Stufen, Musik zum Prinzen von Homburg, Missa Mundi, Unus Mundus, Requiem pro Vivis et Mortuis, Musica Hermetica, Drachenkampf, Strukturen, Musica Instrumentalis, Revolution, Opus für Flöte und Streicher 1991, Oratorium Kabbala 1992, Kammeroper Der Berg 1993, Oratorium Apokalypsis 1996, Klaviertrio Jeruschalajim 1997, Emblemata 1998, Reise nach Niniveh 1999, Concerto per Archi 2000, Klavierduo 2000, Stabat Mater 2001, Der Schlüssel zum Paradies 2002, Klaviertrio Das Haus 2004, Lamentations Jeremiae Prophetae 2005, Monduntergang 2006, Kurzoper Nachts unter der steinernen Brücke 2008–09, Operneinakter Harun und Dschafar 2011. *Recordings include:* more than 100 as soloist on recorder and with consort; numerous flute solos; Josquin: Missa Hercules Dux Ferrariae, Musica Sacra; Monteverdi: Missa da Capella, Il Combattimento; Messa a 4 voci; Mediaeval Carmina Burana, Dufay: Missa Ave Regina Coelorum, Missa Sine Nomine, Missa Caput, Missa Ecce Ancilla; Obrecht: Missa Fortuna Desperata; Ockeghem: Requiem; Marcello: Sonate a Flauto; Biber: Fidicinium; Fux: Dafne in Lauro; Carvalho: Testoride; Vivaldi: L'Olimpiade; Pergolesi: Stabat Mater; René Clemencic: Le Combat du Dragon; Kabbala; Apokalypsis; Fux: Requiem; Historic Tablatures: Johannes von Lublin; Dunstable: Sacred Music; Ockeghem: Missa sine Nomine; Biber: Balletti & Sonatas; Fux: Concentus; Dufay: Magnificat; Late Gothic and Renaissance Masterworks (Clavichord): Cabezón, Josquin; Music of the Spanish Renaissance, Tablatures of Amerbach and Waissel. *Publications include:* Alte Musikinstrumente 1968, Carmina Burana 1979, The Clemencic Collection 2003, René Clemencic/Musica Antiqua 2006. *Honours:* Ehrenmedaille in Gold der Bundeshauptstadt Wien 1989, Vienna Music Prize 1997, Anima Mundi Prize Venice Biennale d'Arte Sacra 1997, Zóltán Kodály Prize 2008, Pro Cultura Hungariae Prize 2008. *Address:* Reisnerstrasse 26/7, 1030 Vienna, Austria (home). *Fax:* (1) 712-50-20 (home). *E-mail:* office@clemencic.at (office); clemencic.consort@utanet.at (office). *Website:* www.clemencic.at.

CLEMENTS, Joy; American singer (soprano); b. 1931, Dayton, OH. *Education:* Univ. of Miami, studied in Philadelphia and New York. *Career:* debut at Miami Opera 1956 as Musetta in La Bohème; sang 1959–72 at New York City Opera and in Pittsburgh, Cincinnati, San Diego, Fort Worth, Hawaii; appeared as Mary Warren in premiere of The Crucible by Robert Ward, New York 1961; appearances at Metropolitan from 1963; guest engagements at Tel-Aviv 1963 and Brussels 1975; other roles have included Mozart's Despina, Pamina and Susanna; Verdi's Violetta and Gilda, Gounod's Juliette, Manon, Martha, Gershwin's Bess; many concert appearances.

CLÉMEUR, Marc, MA; Belgian opera company director; *Director General, Opéra National du Rhin;* b. 1952, Antwerp. *Education:* Univ. of Cologne, Germany. *Career:* began career as Asst Producer, Nederlandse Opera, Amsterdam, also worked in Bayreuth and at Deutsche Oper am Rhein, Düsseldorf; worked as classical music radio producer on Flemish Radio and Television VRT 1977; apptd Chief Dramaturge, Opéra des Flandres 1982, Dir Orchestre Philharmonique des Flandres 1984; Dir Gen. Vlaamse Opéra 1989–2008, est. Opéra Studio des Flandres 1998; Dir Gen., Opéra Nat. du Rhin, Strasbourg 2009–. *Publications:* Eine neue Quelle für das Libretto von Verdi 'Don Carlos', Neue Zeitschrift für Musik 1978. *Honours:* Europe Prize 1994, Lieven Gevaert Prize 1997. *Address:* Opéra National du Rhin, 19 place Broglie, PO Box 320, 67008 Strasbourg Cédex, France (office). *Telephone:* (3) 88-75-48-00 (office). *Fax:* (3) 88-24-0-34 (office). *E-mail:* opera@onr.fr (office). *Website:* www.opera-national-du-rhin.com (office).

CLEMMOW, Caroline Anne, ARAM, LRAM, ARCM; British concert pianist, chamber musician, examiner, adjudicator and teacher; b. 10 Feb. 1959, London, England; d. of David Menzies Clemmow and Frances Lilian Clemmow; m. Anthony Goldstone. *Education:* Walthamstow Hall School, Sevenoaks, Royal Acad. of Music. *Career:* leading piano duo with husband, Anthony Goldstone, appearing throughout UK and abroad, including USA; chamber music, including tour of Russia, Ukraine, etc.; collaborations with percussionist Evelyn Glennie; occasional concerto soloist; examiner, Associated Bd; adjudicator and mem. Incorporated Soc. of Musicians. *Recordings include:* approx. 40 piano duo recordings, seven chamber music recordings. *Address:* Walcot Old Hall, Alkborough, North Lincs., DN15 9JT, England (home). *E-mail:* carolineclemmow@aol.com. *Website:* www.divine-art.com/AS/clemmow.htm (office).

CLEOBURY, Nicholas Randall, MA, FRCO; British conductor and academic; *Associate Professor and Head of Opera, Queensland Conservatorium;* b. 23 June 1950, Bromley, Kent; s. of John Frank Cleobury and Brenda Julie Cleobury (née Randall); brother of Stephen Cleobury; m. Heather Kay 1978; one s. one d. *Education:* King's School, Worcester and Worcester Coll., Oxford. *Career:* Asst Organist, Chichester Cathedral 1971–72, Christ Church, Oxford 1972–76; Conductor, Schola Cantorum of Oxford 1973–76; Chorus Master, Glyndebourne Festival Opera 1977–79; Asst Dir, BBC Singers 1977–79; Prin. Opera Conductor, RAM 1980–87; Guest Conductor, Zurich Opera House 1992–; Music Dir, Oxford Bach Choir 1997–2015; Artistic Dir, Aquarius 1983–92, Cambridge Symphony Soloists 1990–92, Britten Sinfonia 1992–2005, Sounds New 1996–2009; Music Dir, Broomhill 1990–94, Artistic Dir, Cambridge Festival 1992, Mozart Ways Canterbury 2003; Artistic Adviser, Berkshire Choral Festival 2007–; Assoc. Dir, Orchestra of the Swan 2004–08; Prin. Conductor, Jam 2007–; Artistic Dir, Mid Wales Opera 2009–; Assoc. Prof. and Head of Opera, Queensland Conservatorium, Griffith Univ., Australia 2015–; Fellow, Christ Church Univ. Coll., Canterbury 2005.

Honours: Hon. RAM 1985. *Current Management:* RayfieldAllied, Southbank House, Black Prince Road, London SE1 7SJ, England. *Address:* Queensland Conservatorium, Griffith University, 140 Grey Street, South Brisbane, Queensland 4101, Australia. *E-mail:* nicholascleobury@btinternet.com (home). *Website:* www.griffith.edu.au/music/queensland-conservatorium (office); www.nicholascleobury.net.

CLEOBURY, Stephen John, CBE, MusB, MA, FRCM, FRCO, FRSCM, FRSA; British conductor and organist; *Fellow, Director of Music and Organist, King's College, Cambridge;* b. 31 Dec. 1948, Bromley, Kent, England; s. of John Frank Cleobury and Brenda Julie Cleobury (née Randall); brother of Nicholas Cleobury; m. 2nd Emma Sian Disley; four d. (two from previous m.). *Education:* King's School, Worcester and St John's Coll., Cambridge. *Career:* Organist, St Matthew's, Northampton 1971–74; sub-organist, Westminster Abbey 1974–78; Master of Music, Westminster Cathedral 1979–82; Dir of Music, King's Coll. Cambridge 1982–, Organist to the Univ. of Cambridge 1991–, also Fellow, King's Coll.; Conductor, Cambridge Univ. Music Soc. 1983–2009, Chorus Dir 2009–; frequent appearances on BBC 2, BBC Radio 3 and Classic FM; freelance conducting and organ playing; mem. Council, Royal School of Church Music 1982–2005; Pres. Inc. Asscn of Organists 1985–87, Cathedral Organists' Asscn 1988–90; mem. Royal Coll. of Organists 1967–2008, Hon. Sec. 1981–90, Pres. 1990–92; Chief Conductor BBC Singers 1995–2007, Conductor Laureate 2007–; Fellow, Royal School of Church Music 2008. *Radio:* A Festival of Nine Lessons and Carols (BBC Radio 3). *Television:* Carols from King's (BBC 2), Easter from King's (BBC 2). *Recordings include:* directing Choir of King's Coll. Cambridge and BBC Singers (Decca, EMI, Priory, King's Coll. Cambridge own label). *Publications:* various musical arrangements and writings. *Honours:* Hon. DMus (Anglia Polytechnic) 2001. *Current Management:* c/o Robin Tyson, Edition Peters Artist Management Ltd, Edition Peters UK, 2–6 Baches Street, London, N1 6DN, England. *E-mail:* robin.tyson@editionpeters.com. *Website:* www.editionpeters.com/london/epamstephencleobury.php. *Address:* King's College, Cambridge, CB2 1ST, England (office). *Telephone:* (1223) 331224 (office). *Fax:* (1223) 331890 (office). *E-mail:* choir@kings.cam.ac.uk (office). *Website:* www.stephencleobury.net.

CLEVENGER, Dale, BFA; American musician (French horn); *Principal Horn, Chicago Symphony Orchestra;* b. 1941; m. Alice Clevenger; two c. *Education:* Carnegie Mellon Univ. *Career:* fmr faculty mem. Northwestern Univ. School of Music; Principal Horn and recording soloist Chicago Symphony Orchestra 1966–; fmr mem. Leopold Stokowski's American Symphony Orchestra and Symphony of the Air directed by Alfred Wallenstein; fmr Principal Horn Kansas City Philharmonic; Music Dir Elmhurst Symphony Orchestra 1992–; currently Prof. of Horn, Roosevelt Univ., Chicago; has appeared as soloist worldwide and at festivals including Santa Fe Chamber Music Festival, Florida Music Festival in Sarasota, Marrowstone Music Festival in Port Townsend, Washington, Affinis Music Festival in Japan, FAME Festival; worked as conductor and teacher with EC Youth Orchestra under Claudio Abbado; masterclasses worldwide. *Recordings:* featured soloist on Martin's Concerto for Seven Winds, Strings, and Percussion, Schumann's Konzertstück for four horns, Britten's Serenade for Tenor, Horn, and Strings, Mozart's Horn Concerto No. 3; played on The Antiphonal Music of Gabrieli (Grammy Award), two Joseph Haydn and Michael Haydn Horn Concertos, Mozart's horn concertos, Mozart and Beethoven Quintets for Piano and Winds (Grammy Award), Brahms's Horn Trio, Tribute to Ellington, Strauss's Horn Concerto No. 1, Op. 11 2000. *Honours:* Hon. DMus (Elmhurst Coll.) 1985. *Address:* The Chicago Symphony Orchestra, Symphony Center, 220 South Michigan Avenue, Chicago, IL 60604, USA (office). *Telephone:* (312) 294-3000 (office). *Fax:* (312) 294-3329 (office). *Website:* www.cso.org (office).

CLINGAN, Judith Ann, AM, BA, DipMusEd; Australian composer, conductor, music educator, music theatre director and artist; *Director, Wayfarers Australia,;* b. 19 Jan. 1945, Sydney; d. of Victor Lawrence William Clingan and Marian Dorothy Clingan (née Tasker); one d. *Education:* Univs of Sydney and New South Wales, Australian Nat. Univ., Canberra School of Music, Kodály Inst. of Music Educ., Hungary. *Career:* composer for Kodály Educ. Inst. 1986; ACT Bicentennial Year 1987, 1988; Creative Arts Fellow, ANU 1989; Composer-in-Residence, Gaudeamus and Young Music Soc. 1990; Australian Council Composer Fellow 1991; Dir of Music, Orana Steiner School Canberra 1991–93, 1997–2000; Founder and Dir Voicebox Youth Opera, South Australia 1994–96, ACT 1997–2002; Dir of Music, Mt Barker Waldorf School, South Australia 1994–96; Dir Imagine Music Theatre 1995–2015, Wayfarers Australia (f. as Waldorf Wayfarers) 1997–, The Variables 1997–2009, Canberra Choral Soc. 2004–05; mem. numerous orgs Founder and Dir Canberra Children's Choir 1967–79, Founder and Dir Young Music Soc. 1969–81; Founder and Dir Gaudeamus 1983–93. *Compositions include:* Songs of Middle Earth 1967–71, 1993, Francis 1986, Nganbra 1988, Terra Beata – Terra Infirma 1989, Kakadu 1990, Seven Deadly Sins 1990, The Birds' Noel 1990, Marco 1991, Songs of Solitude 1991, The Grandfather Clock 1992, The Ring Bearer 1993, Stony Tunes 1994, A Fool Came Riding Along Here 1996, Adam's Rib 1997, The Magician's Nephew 1998, Hobbit Songs 1999, Everyone Sang 2001, Sit, Jessica 2001, Spiritus Sanctus Australia 2002, Esperamus 2002, Seasons of the Soul 2002, The Tree of Life 2003, The Dancing Wombat 2004, Dance on the Wind 2005, Music for The Wind in the Willows 2006, On the Edge of Silence 2007, In This Fateful Hour 2008, Ponder Creation 2009, The Earth Story 2012, Endangered! 2015. *Exhibition:* So Good a Thing, Albert Hall, ACT 2013. *Recordings include:* Choralations 1999, Songs

of the Tree of Life 1999, Short and Sweet 2001, Glimpses 2005, The Floor of Heaven 2007. *Publications include:* The Complete Chorister 1971, So Good a Thing 1981, Music is for Everyone 1984, Songs of the Tree of Life Vol. I 1998, Vol. II 1996, Musicianship Magic 2008. *Honours:* Social Services Award ACT 1980, Canberra Times Artist of the Year 1991, Sounds Australian Award 1991, Art Music Award for Excellence Award by an Individual (ACT) 2014. *Address:* 11 Mirbelia Cres, Rivett, ACT 2611, Australia. *Telephone:* 410-617427 (mobile). *E-mail:* judithclingan@me.com. *Website:* judithclingan.net .au.

CLOSE, Shirley; American singer (mezzo-soprano); b. 1962, Oklahoma. *Education:* University of Southern California. *Career:* sang at the Augusta Opera from 1985; Amneris in Aida for Boston Opera; Mozart's Marcellina at Miami, 1988; Magdalena in Die Meistersinger at Nice, 1986; In Wagner's Ring at Orange, 1988; Cologne Opera, 1989–93 as Wagner's Fricka and Waltraute; Geneviève in Pelléas; Orlofsky in Die Fledermaus and Mary in Der fliegende Holländer; Guest appearances at Munich as Fenena in Nabucco; Bayreuth Festival, Waltraute, 1992 and the Deutsche Oper, Berlin; sang Gluck's Alceste at Strasbourg, 1996. *Recordings:* Elektra, Die Walküre.

CLOZIER, Christian Robert Adrien; French composer and director; b. 25 Aug. 1945, Compiègne; one d. *Education:* National Conservatory of Music, Paris and Practical School for Higher Studies, Paris. *Career:* founder and Dir, IMEB; Dir, Int. Competition of Electro-acoustic Music, Bourges; Hon. Pres., Int. Confederation of Electro-acoustic Music (ICEM); conceptor of electro-acoustic musical instruments. *Compositions include:* La Discordature, A vie (opera), 22 août, Loin la lune, Symphonie pour un enfant seul, A la prochaine, la taupe, Quasars: le chant du monde, Markarian 205, Par Panglos Gymnopède, Le Bonheur: une idée neuve en Europe, Mon nom sous le soleil est France, Le Temps scintille et le songe est savoir, 11 spectacles multimedia, Démotique: de la grève, au loin, Le Clarissophone ont été, Le père, le fils, Pathé Marconi, Lettre à une demoiselle. *Publications:* contrib. to Musique en Jeu No. 8 1970, Faire 2–3 1974, Faire 4–5 1975, Poésie Sonore Internationale. *Address:* Institut International de Musique Electroacoustique, BP 39, Place André Malraux, 18000 Bourges, France. *E-mail:* administration@ime-bourges .org. *Website:* www.imeb.net.

CLURMAN, Judith, BMus, MMus; American conductor; b. 11 March 1953, Brooklyn, NY; m.; one s. *Education:* Oberlin Coll., Juilliard School of Music. *Career:* founder and Dir, New York Concert Singers 1988–; Dir of Choral Activities, The Juilliard School 1989–; Project Youth Chorus 1996–; New York Chamber Symphony Chorus 1996–98; Judith Clurman Choral Workshop 1998–; performed with New York Philharmonic, Boston Symphony, Orchestra of St Luke's, American Composers Orchestra, Mostly Mozart, Classical Band, Lincoln Center's Great Performers series; Musical Dir, 92nd Street Y 'Music of the Jewish Spirit' 1998–2001; Dir of Choral Activities, TodiMusicFest 2001–; conducted numerous premieres, including music by Leonard Bernstein, William Bolcom, John Corigliano, Philip Glass, Aaron Jay Kernis, Libby Larsen, David Diamond, Stephen Paulus, Ned Rorem, Christopher Rouse, Ellen Taaffe Zwilich, Tania Leon, Paul Schoenfield and Robert Beaser; mem. Chorus America, American Choral Directors' Asscn. *Recordings:* Divine Grandeur, The Mask, A Season's Promise. *Honours:* first prize ASCAP, Chorus America Award (with New York Concert Singers) 1992.

CLUTTON, James Charles; British opera and theatre producer; *Director of Opera, Opera Holland Park;* b. 18 Jan. 1966, London, England; s. of Ernest Clutton and Margaret Clutton; m. Angela Edwards. *Career:* Assoc. Producer, Bill Kenwright Ltd 1998–2000; Line Producer, UNICEF The Return Festival, Kosovo 1999; Producer, Opera Holland Park (OHP) 2000–; productions include La forza del destino, L'amico Fritz, Fidelio, Macbeth, Jenůfa, L'amore dei tre Re, Kat'a Kabanova, Roberto Devereux, Fedora, Andrea Chénier, Queen of Spades, Carmen, Don Giovanni, Tosca and approx. 70 others as well producing first OHP production to transfer to another theatre, Tosca to Richmond Theatre 2009; produced, along with Sarah Crabtree, European premiere of Tobias Picker's opera Fantastic Mr Fox 2010, 2011; also worked extensively on OHP's INSPIRE project, taking opera into the community, schools, hosps and Old-Age Pensioner care homes; solo productions include Weill and Brecht's Happy End, Herrmann and Harman's Romance/Romance, Hardy's Far from the Madding Crowd. *Compositions:* Oscar (musical based on life of Oscar Wilde) 1995, Great Things (Thomas Hardy poem set to music) 1997. *Recording:* Oscar 1995. *Address:* Opera Holland Park, Central Library, Phillimore Walk, London, W8 7RX, England (office). *E-mail:* jamesclutton@operahollandpark.com (office). *Website:* www.operahollandpark.com (office).

COAD, Jonathan; British singer (baritone); b. 1958, Crayford, Kent, England. *Education:* Royal Coll. of Music, London. *Career:* many concert appearances, including tours with the Groupe Vocale de France throughout Europe and North America; concert soloist in England and France; sang Pooh-Bah in The Mikado for D'Oyly Carte Opera, and in Bernstein's Candide at the Old Vic 1989; engagements with the Royal Opera, Covent Garden, in Death in Venice, The Fiery Angel, Jenůfa, Tosca, Arabella, and La Bohème; Rigoletto 1997, as Court Usher; sang Cross in Paul Bunyan for the Royal Opera 1997–98. *Recordings include:* albums with Groupe Vocale de France.

COATES, Gloria, BA, BMus, MMus; American composer and actress; b. (Gloria Ann Kannenberg), 10 Oct. 1938, Wausau, Wis.; d. of fmr State Senator Roland Kannenberg and Natalie Zannon; m. Francis Mitchell Coates, Jr 1959–69; one d. *Education:* Columbia Univ., Louisiana State Univ., DePaul Univ., post-graduate composition and musicology with Jack Beeson, Otto Luening and

Alexander Tcherepnin, Mozarteum Summer Acad., Cooper Union Art School, Goodman Theater, Monticello Coll. *Career:* composer of incidental music for Hamlet, Saint Joan, Everyman, Baton Rouge; producer and moderator of TV Programs, WBRZ-TV 1961; music, art and drama critic for State Times of Baton Rouge, La 1962–67; actor, Baton Rouge Little Theater 1961–62; moved to New York City, performed with Schola Cantorum under Hugh Ross and Leonard Bernstein 1966–69; Founder Music Program, Univ. of Wisconsin Int. Programs, Munich-London 1969–99; began experimenting with overtones, glissandi and microtones 1960, developed method of using glissandi and microtones as structural elements in music by 1962; freelance composer, Munich, Germany 1970–; Hon. Organizer-Producer, German-American Contemporary Music Series, Munich and Cologne 1971–84; experimented with vocal multiphonics 1971–74, with demonstration at Int. New Music Summer Acad., Darmstadt 1972; UNESCO World Music Days Prague, Budapest, East Berlin under the American Music Council 1977–83; compositions performed in festivals of new music, including Hanover New Music Festival 1975, Geneva 25th Anniversary Festival 1976, Warsaw Autumn Festival 1978, 1980, Musica Viva, Munich 1980, 1985, 1997, East Berlin Festival 1979, Montepulciano, Dartington, Bonn, Bucharest, New Music America, New York 1989, Passau Festival, March Music–Berlin Festival 2004, New York Microtonal Festival, Other Minds Festival, San Francisco 2012; numerous radio recordings; invited to lecture on her music with concerts, Harvard 1981, Max Mueller Bhavans, Bombay, Calcutta and New Delhi, India 1982, Univ. of Wisconsin-Madison, Brown Univ., Boston Univ., Princeton Univ., Munich Art Acad., New Delhi Conservatory of Music; ensembles include Crash Ensemble Dublin, Talisker Players Toronto, Debussy Trio, Munich Flute Ensemble, Trio con Brio, Berlin Trio, I Solisti Dauni, Italy; conductors include Leif Segerstam, Elgar Howarth, Jerzy Maksymiuk, Dieter Cichewiecz, Michael Finnissey, Kenneth Schermerhorn, Wolf-Dieter Hauschild, Jüergen Wirrmann, Werner Heider, Matthias Kuntzsch, Georg Schmoehe, Jaraslav Opela, Tania Leon, Christoph Poppen, Michael Boder, Olaf Henzold; guest lecturer on Gloria Coates' music with concerts at Harvard, Princeton, Brown, Boston Univs, Univ of the West Indies, Max Mueller Bhavan, New Delhi, Calcutta, Bombay, Univs of Munich and Toruń, Poland. *Solo exhibitions:* Gasteig, Munich, Frauenkirche Museum, Erding, Arabellahaus, Munich, Art and Computer, Goeppingen, Music Conservatory, Erding. *Group exhibitions include:* RAM, London, Stuker Gallery, Zurich; in Munich at: Arabellahaus, Haus der Kunst, America House. *Stage appearances include:* Claire Zachinassian in The Visit (by Durrenmatt), Katherine in The Heiress (by James), Ilona Zsabo in The Play's the Thing (by Molnar), Mary in Journey to Jerusalem (by Maxwell Anderson), Long Winded Lady in Edward Albee's Box and Quotations from Chairman Mao Tse Tung, Miss Holly in Tennessee Williams' Suddenly Last Summer, Medea in Jean Anouilh's Medea, Sidonie in Gigi, and others. *Dance:* Ikarus and Machine Men (Bruno Roveroni), Dreieich-Buchschlag, Germany 1982, Ballet Music for La Voix Humaine (Cocteau), Passau Festival 2010. *Selected compositions include:* 16 symphonies, 10 string quartets; 15 Songs on Poems by Emily Dickinson: (I'm) Nobody 1972, I've Seen a Dying Eye 1972, I Held a Jewel (in my Fingers) 1972, Wild Nights 1972, A Word is Dead 1979, Mine by the Right 1980, Bind Me, I Still Can Sing 1980, If I Can Stop One Heart from Breaking 1980, Now I Lay Thee Down/On the Death of a Child 1980, Will There Really be a Morning? 1984, In Falling Timbers Buried 1984, Vitality, Begun 1993, Bride of the Holy Ghost 1993, After Great Pain 1998; We Have Ears and Hear Not (point counterpoint) 1971, Voices of Women in Wartime for soprano and chamber ensemble 1973, Fragment from Leonardo's Notebooks Anima della Terra for soli chorus and orchestra 1973, Symphony No. 1: 'Music on Open Strings' 1973, 'Planets' for chamber orchestra 1974, May the Morning Star Rise for organ and viola 1974, 'Five Abstractions of the Poems by Emily Dickinson' for woodwind quartet 1975, Fragment from Leonardo's Notebooks 'The Elements' for orchestra and chorus 1975, My Country Tis of Thee for piano four hands 1975, Spring Morning in Grobholz' Garden for flute trio and tape 1982, Auto-Madic Music for cars and motorcycles 1987, Symphony No. 2: Illuminatio in Tenebris 1988, The Force for Peace in War for soprano and chamber ensemble 1988, Fiori and the Princess for alto recorder and tape 1988, for flute and tape 1988, Lichtsplitter for flute, harp, viola and one percussionist 1988, Dramatic Scene (The Swan) for soprano and ensemble 1988, Reaching for the Moon for solo flute 1988, Star Tracks Through Darkness for solo organ 1989, Symphony No. 4 'Chiaroscuro' 1990, Symphony No. 7 1991, Rainbow Across the Night Sky for chorus and chamber ensemble 1991, In the Glacier for 10 flautists and percussion 1991, Wir tönen allein for soprano and chamber ensemble 1991, Royal Anthem (Königshymne) for 10 flautists 1992, Ungeziefer (Insects) for voice and chamber ensemble 1992, Night Music for piano, gongs and saxophone 1993, Castles in the Air for saxophone solo 1993, Time Frozen for chamber orchestra 1994, Blue Monday for percussion and guitar 1994, Sperriges Morgen for soprano and chamber ensemble 1994, The Quinces Quandary: Homage to Van Gogh for orchestra 1994, Symphony No. 9 'The Quinces Quandary' 1994, Lyric Suite for piano, violin and cello 1996, Heinrich von Ofterdingen 'Hommage à Novalis' for chamber ensemble 1996, Fairytale Suite for solo flute 1997, Floating Down the Mississippi for guitar ensemble 1997, Komplementär for voice and piano 1999, Prayers without Words for organ 2002, Mirage for Chamber ensemble and baritone 2003, Entering the Unknown for Multimedia 2004, Abraham Lincoln's Cooper Union Address multimedia 2004, The Books for klavier solo 2004, Along the Yangtze River for flute and piano 2009, Nightscape for double bass and piano 2009, Catch the Wind for soprano and piano 2010, Homeless at the Old Cemetery 2010, trans. of 15 Emily Dickinson Songs into German by Katherina Ponnier premiered 2010, Reaching into

Light for 2 percussionists 2010. *Recordings include:* three albums of 9 String Quartets, Piano Trio and solo violin sonatas, two albums of orchestral music Symphonies No. 1, No. 7 and No. 14, No. 15, Cantata da Requiem, Transitions, Symphony No. 1, No. 2, No. 4, Nr. 7, Homage to Van Gogh, Time Frozen, Leonardo's Anima della Terra: New World Records: Indian Sounds Symphony No. 8, Cette Blanche Agonie, The Force for Peace in War, Wir Toenen Allein, Leonardo's Fonte di Rimini; BIS Records: Reaching for the Moon for solo flute, Cavalli, 15 Emily Dickinson Songs, Wilted Books, and Complementary; Thorofon: Phantom for flute and piano, Lunar Loops for 2 guitars, Pitch CD. *Librettos:* The Portrait, Stolen Identity 2011. *Radio:* numerous programmes on American music in archives of WDR West German Radio Cologne, Open House Sendungen. *Publications:* music: Schott, Moeck, Musik Fabric, Sonoton and self-publication of music compositions; details of works and life in 'Gloria Coates' Komponisten in Bayern, Hans Schneider Verlag Tutzing, Vol. 54 2012; contribs to New Groves, MGG, Bakers etc. and musicological articles in German magazines Die Musik Forschung, Musica, Neue Musikzeitschrift and others. *Honours:* Hon. DMus (Malta) 1988, (Oxford) 1988; Best Actress Theater Award 1960, Best Actress, Flat Rock Playhouse, Best Actress, Baton Rouge Little Theatre 1961, Int. Record Award KIRA (Music on Open Strings) for Symphony No. 1 1986, Medal of Honor, American Biographical Inst. 1987, Louisiana State Univ., Yaddo Colony composition grants, MacDowell Colony Norlin Hewitt Composition Award, Alice Ditson grant, Millay Colony residence, Meet the Composer grants, UNESCO Composition Grant, Columbia Univ., Int. Classical Music Award 2012. *Address:* Tengstr 20, Apt 501, 80798 Munich, Germany (home). *Telephone:* (89) 278-0134 (office). *E-mail:* gloricoates@yahoo.com (office). *Website:* wanadoo.nl/eli.ichie/coates.html.

COATES, Leon; British composer and academic; b. 15 June 1937, Wolverhampton, England; m. 1976. *Education:* St John's Coll., Cambridge. *Career:* various radio broadcasts as pianist, harpsichordist, with Scottish Baroque Ensemble; Conductor, Edinburgh Chamber Orchestra then Edinburgh Symphony Orchestra; organist, Parish Church of St Andrew and St George, Edinburgh 1980-2004; currently Conductor, Edinburgh Studio Orchestra; Lecturer, Univ. of Edinburgh 1965–2002; mem. Scottish Soc. of Composers, Royal Coll. of Organists, Guild of Professional Composers and Songwriters. *Compositions include:* North West Passage (song cycle) 1994, Concerto for viola 1979, Concerto for harpsichord 1984, Music for concert band and choir, Te Deum and Jubilate for choir and organ. *Website:* edinburghstudioorchestra.org.

COATES, Oliver, MPhil; British cellist; b. 19 May 1982, London. *Education:* Royal Acad. of Music, studied cello with Colin Carr, Oxford Univ. *Career:* debut at age 15 playing Haydn's C major Concerto at St John's Smith Square, 1999; recitals and concertos in UK in Aldeburgh, Edinburgh and London, and across Europe and Asia including Japan, Holland, France and Norway: London Soloists' Chamber Orchestra Cello Festival 2002, Paris Chopin Festival, 2003, gala concert, Int. Cello Festival, Manchester 2004, Apeldoorn Chamber Music Festival, The Netherlands, Trasimeno Music Festival Italy, etc; regular performances at major classical music festivals as well as other festivals such as Latitude, Ether and In the Woods; premieres of solo and chamber music by Elena Firsova, Stéphane Altier, Dmitri Smirnov, Graham Williams, Matt Rogers; collaborations with Mira Calix, Ailish Tynan, Julian Bliss, Charles Neidich, Philippe Graffin, Colin Carr, London Mozart Piano Trio; premiere of Nico Muhly's Cello Concerto, Barbican, London 2012; performances with London Sinfonietta and RADIUS (new music ensemble); Artist in Residence, Southbank Centre, London; curator, Southbank Centre Harmonic Series 2011–12; mem. Linden Trio (music group). *Honours:* Dame Ruth Railton Chamber Music Prize at RAM; winner, Douglas Cameron Cello Competition, May Mukle Cello Competition, Montefiore Prize, S&M Eyres Scholarship, Sir John Barbirolli Memorial Prize, Louise Child Prize, Philip and Dorothy Green Award 2006, RPS Young Artists Award 2012. *Address:* Tower Cottage, 1a Parkhill Road, London, NW3 2YJ, England (home). *E-mail:* ollycoates@yahoo.com (home). *Website:* www.olivercoates.com.

COBBE, Hugh Michael Thomas, OBE, MA, FSA; British musicologist and librarian; *Director, Vaughan Williams Charitable Trust;* b. 20 Nov. 1942, Farnham, Surrey; m. Katherine Chichester 1982; two d. *Education:* St Columba's Coll., Dublin and Trinity Coll., Dublin, Ireland, Corpus Christi Coll., Oxford. *Career:* Asst Keeper, Manuscript Dept, British Museum 1967–73 and British Library 1973–78; Head of Publs, British Library 1978–85, Head of Music Collections 1985–2001, Head of British Collections 2001–02; Sr Consultant on Musical Manuscripts, Christie's 2003–08; Deputy Chair. Ralph Vaughan Williams (RVW) Trust 2004–08, Chair. 2008–; mem. Royal Musical Asscn (Pres. 2002–05), Gerald Coke Handel Foundation (Chair. 1996–2013, Trustee 2013–15), The Nat. Folk Music Fund (Chair. 2008–), The Vaughan Williams Charitable Trust (Dir 2008–), The Newbury Spring Festival (Trustee 2014–). *Publications include:* Letters of Ralph Vaughan Williams, 1895–1958 2008; contrib. to Musical Times, Fontes Artis Musicae, New Grove Dictionary of Music and Musicians, Oxford Dictionary of National Biography. *Honours:* G.B. Oldman Prize 2008. *Address:* Fox House, North End, Newbury, Berks., RG20 0AY, England (home). *Telephone:* (1635) 253190 (home). *Fax:* (1635) 253191 (home). *E-mail:* hugh@hughcobbe.com.

COBURN, Pamela; American singer (soprano) and academic; *James B. Stewart Distinguished Visiting Professor of Music, DePauw University;* b. 29 March 1955, Dayton, Ohio. *Education:* De Pauw Univ., Eastman School of Music, American Opera Center of Juilliard School, and studied German Lieder with Elisabeth Schwarzkopf. *Career:* sung at Munich Staatsoper from

1982, Vienna from 1984; Maggio Musicale Florence 1988 as Ellen Orford in Peter Grimes; Los Angeles 1990 as Ilia in Idomeneo; sang Saffi in Der Zigeunerbaron at Zürich and Alice Ford in Falstaff for Miami Opera 1991; Salzburg and Munich Festivals 1991, as Mozart's Countess; sang Ellen Orford in production of Peter Grimes by Tim Albery, Munich 1991; engaged for Giulio Cesare and Das Rheingold at 1997 Munich Festival; other roles include Fiordiligi, Rosalinde in Die Fledermaus and Lauretta in Gianni Schicchi; sang Hanna Glawari at Deutsche Oper Berlin 2000; James B. Stewart Distinguished Visiting Prof. of Music, DePauw Univ. 2005–. *Recordings include:* Honegger's King David; Siebel in Faust, Mozart's L'Oca del Cairo; Marzelline in Fidelio; Zemlinsky's Traumgörge; First Lady in Die Zauberflöte; Flowermaiden in Parsifal conducted by Barenboim. *Honours:* prizewinner, ARD Competition, Munich 1980, Metropolitan Auditions of the Air 1982. *Address:* School of Music, DePauw University, 605 South College Avenue, Greencastle, IN 46135, USA (office). *Website:* www.depauw.edu/music (office).

COBURN, Robert James, BMus, MA, PhD; American composer, performer and educator; *Professor of Composition and Music Theory and Chairman, Department of Music Studies, University of the Pacific*; b. 29 Oct. 1949, Calif.; m. Jeanne Ashby; one s. *Education:* Univ. of Victoria, Canada, Univ. of California, Berkeley, Conservatory of Music, Univ. of the Pacific. *Career:* Prof. of Composition and Music Theory and Chair. Dept of Music Studies, Conservatory of Music, Univ. of the Pacific 1993–, Dir Conservatory Computer Studios for Music Composition; Founding mem. World Forum for Acoustic Ecology; Artistic Dir SoundImageSound Int. Festival of New Music and Visual Image; Fulbright Lecturer, Tokyo Geijutsu Daigaku 2011–12, Fulbright Guest Researcher, Dept of Intermedia Art 2011–12; composition commissions: Sun River Music Festival, San Francisco New Music Ensemble, Oregon Coast Music Festival, Brubeck Festival 2005, 2007; public art commissions: City of Philadelphia Avenue of Arts 1995, Oregon Convention Centre (landscape) 1991. *Art exhibitions:* between... beyond, Reynolds Gallery, Stockton; In the Light of Time Singing, Northwest Artists Workshop; 9 Artists/8 Rooms, Henry Gallery, Seattle. *Compositions include:* The Emptiness Cycle: emptiness [refraction] for computer and video, emptiness [reflection] for alto saxophone, computer and video, In Stillness for violin, computer and video, Fragile Horizon for viola, computer and video, Approaching Twilight for computer, Tranquil Turmoil Dreaming for computer and video, Patterns Luminous for shakuhachi and computer, Traces (Star Map l) for viola and computer sound, Staursahng electroacoustic music and images, Cantos for chamber orchestra, Bell Circles II permanent sound environment (Oregon Convention Center), Luminous Shadows for cello, piano, and percussion 1993, Songs of Solitude for chorus, Shadowbox for clarinet 1994, Ad Vesperum for soprano and 10 instruments. *Sound installations:* between... beyond (site-specific installation for four-channel sound and image boxes), 39 Bells (permanent sound installation, Avenue of the Arts, Philadelphia), Bell Circles II (permanent sound installation, Oregon Convention Center, Portland). *Publications include:* articles in professional journals; contrib. to Portland Review, Prologue; book and CD reviews for Leonardo, Journal of the International Society for the Arts, Sciences and Technology, MIT Press 1993–. *Honours:* Faculty Scholarly and Artistic Research Awards 1996, 1998, 2000, 2004, 2009, 2011, 2014, Eberhardt Teacher/Scholar Award 1999, Dreyfus Undergraduate Research Award 2009, Fulbright Scholars Award for Research/Lecturing in Japan 2011–12. *Telephone:* (209) 946-2186 (office). *Fax:* (209) 946-2770 (office). *E-mail:* rcoburn@pacific.edu (office). *Website:* www1.pacific.edu/~rcoburn (office); fragilehorizon.com.

COCCIANTE, Richard (Riccardo); Italian composer, singer, musician (piano) and arranger; b. Saigon, Viet Nam; m. Catherine Boutet; one s. *Career:* composer, solo artist 1972–; world-wide TV, radio appearances; tour venues include Gran Teatro La Fenice, Venice 1988, Sporting Club, Monaco 1988, 1990, 1995, Teatro dell'opera Caracalla, Rome 1991, Vina del Mar Festival, Chile 1994, Olympia, Paris 1994, 1996, Zenith, Paris 1994, Taj Mahal, Atlantic City 1995, Teatro Sistina, Rome 1988, 1993, 1995, 1997, Théâtre St Denis, Montréal 1994, 1996, Stadsschouwberg, Amsterdam 1995, Vienna Rathaus 1997; collaborated with producers, including Paul Buckmaster, Humberto Gatica, Ennio Morricone, James Newton-Howard, Vangelis; participated in album World War II, interpreting Michelle with London Symphony Orchestra; concert, Christmas In Vienna (with Plácido Domingo, Sarah Brightman and Helmut Lotti) 1997. *Compositions include:* Notre Dame de Paris (musical, Felix Award for Album of the Year, Canada) 1998–99, 2000 (Hymne pour la ville de Lyon) commissioned by Raymonde Barre, Mayor of Lyon, to celebrate the new millennium, Le Petit Prince (musical) 2007. *Recordings include:* albums: (in Italian) Mu 1972, Poesia 1973, Anima 1974, L'alba 1975, Concerto per Margherita 1976, Riccardo Cicciante: A Mano A Mano 1978, ...E Io Canto 1979, Cervo a Primavera 1981, Cocciante (Celeste Nostalgia) 1982, Sincerità 1983, Il Mare dei Papaveri 1985, La Grande Avventura 1987, Se Stiamo Insieme 1991, Eventi e Mutamenti 1993, Un Uomo Felice 1994, Innamorato 1997, Tutti I Miei Sogni 2006, Sulle Labbra E Nel Pensiero 2013; in French: Atlanti 1973, Quand un Amour 1974, Concerto pour Marguerite 1978, Je Chante 1979, Au Clair de tes Silences 1980, Vieille 1982, Sincérité 1983, L'Homme qui vole 1986, Empreinte 1993, L'Instant Présent 1995, La Compilation Italienne 1997, La Compilation Beue 2000; 10 albums in Spanish; three albums in English; film soundtracks: Roma Bene 1971, Tandem 1987, Storia di una capinera 1994, Toy Story 1996, Astérix and Obélix contre César 1999; international hit singles: Bella Senz' Anima (Italy)/ Bella Sin Alma (Spain, Latin America) 1973, Quand un Amour (France, Belgium, Canada) 1974, Margherita (Italy)/Marguerite (France, Belgium, Canada)/Margarita (Spain, Latin America) 1976–78, Coup de Soleil (France, Belgium) 1980, Cervo a Primavera (Italy)/Yo Renascere (Spain, Latin America) 1980, Sincérité (France) / Sincerità (Italy, Holland) / Sinceridad (Spain, Latin America) / Sincerity (USA) 1983, Questione di Feeling (duet with Mina, Italy)/Question de Feeling (duet with Fabienne Thiebeault, France, Belgium, Canada)/Cuestion de Feeling (duet with Melissa, Spain, Latin America) 1985–86, Se Stiamo Insieme (Italy, Belgium, Holland, Brazil) 1991, Pour Elle (France)/Per Lei (Italy, Brazil)/I'd Fly (Italy, France, Belgium, Holland)/Por Ella (Latin America)/Voorbij (Holland) 1993–95, Il ricordo di un istante (Italy, France, Belgium, Canada, Holland), Belle, Le Temps des Cathédrales, Vivre (excerpts from musical Notre Dame de Paris, France, Belgium, Canada) 1998–99, Songs 2005, Tutti i Miei Sogni 2006, Giulietta & Romeo 2007. *Honours:* Grande Ufficiale della Repubblica Italiana (Italy) 1999; Rose d'Or Award (Greece) 1981, Rino Gaetano Award (Italy) 1982, Telegatto (Italy) 1991, Médaille de la Ville de Paris (France) 1998, Victoire de la Musique Award (France) for Song of the Year 1999, for Show of the Year 1999, World Music Award (Monaco) for Best-selling French Artist/Group 1999, Rolf Marbot Award (France) for Song of the Year 1999, Felix Awards (Canada) for Song of the Year 1999, for Show of the Year 1999, for Best-selling Album 1999, for Album of the Year 1999. *E-mail:* riccardo.cocciante@coccianteclub.it (office). *Website:* www.coccianteclub.it.

COCHRAN, William; American singer (tenor); b. 23 June 1943, Columbus, Ohio. *Education:* Curtis Inst. with Martial Singher, studied with Lauritz Melchior and Lotte Lehmann in California. *Career:* sang Wagner roles in San Francisco and Mexico; numerous appearances in Europe from 1967, notably in Hamburg and Frankfurt; roles include Max in Der Freischütz, Jason in Médée, Otello, Herod in Salome and Dmitri in Boris Godunov; concert with New York Philharmonic 1971; Covent Garden debut 1974, as Laca in Jenůfa; San Francisco 1977, as Tichon in Katya Kabanova; appearances in operas by Busoni, Janáček, Zimmermann, Shostakovich and Stravinsky (Tom Rakewell at Frankfurt 1983); sang Bacchus in Ariadne auf Naxos at Metropolitan Opera 1985; Deutsche Oper Berlin 1989 Schreker's Die Gezeichneten; season 1988–89 at Düsseldorf; sang Siegfried in Paris and Brussels 1991; Zimmermann's Die Soldaten at Strasbourg and Tichon (Katya Kabanova), Los Angeles; The Councillor in The Nose by Shostakovich, Frankfurt City Opera; title role in Otello for WNO 1990; season 1992 as Samson at Amsterdam and Schoenberg's Aron (concert performance) at Edinburgh Festival; sang Aegisthus in Elektra at First Night of the 1993 London Proms; Herod in Salome at San Francisco 1997; season 1998 with Aegisthus at Catania and Peter Grimes at Madrid; season 2000–01 as Aegisthus in Elektra at Munich and Shuisky in Boris Godunov at Dusseldorf. *Recordings:* Mathis der Maler and Act I of Die Walküre; Doktor Faust by Busoni; Mahler's 8th Symphony. *Honours:* winner, Lauritz Melchior Heldentenor Foundation Award.

COCKER, Jonathan; British stage director; b. 1963, England. *Education:* Guildhall School of Music and Drama. *Career:* productions of Purcell's Dido and Orfeo et Euridice for Jerusalem Studio Opera; Britten's Turn of the Screw for the Buxton Festival; Carmen and Orfeo for Northern Opera; Martinů's Comedy on the Bridge and Rimsky's Mozart and Salieri at the Ryedale Festival; Nielsen's Maskarade for the Opera North Tour, Purcell's Fairy Queen at festivals of Madrid, Athens and Valencia; also for English Bach Festival at Linbury Theatre, Covent Garden 2001; further engagements with New Israel Opera, Opera North and Opera Studio; musicals and plays in the West End of London and on tours of the UK and Europe.

CODREANU-MIHALCEA, Claudia; Romanian singer (mezzo-soprano); b. 1969. *Career:* many concert and opera engagements in Romania and elsewhere in Europe; repertory includes Mozart's Clemenza di Tito, Rossini's Cenerentola, and songs by Brahms and Mussorgsky; contestant at the Cardiff Singer of the World Competition 1995.

COELHO, Elaine; Brazilian singer (soprano); b. 1950, Rio de Janeiro. *Education:* studied in Rio and Hanover. *Career:* sang at Landestheater Detmold from 1974 as Verdi's Violetta and Nannetta, Mozart's Constanze, Zdenka in Arabella and Liu in Turandot; Stadttheater Bremen from 1976, as Norina in Don Pasquale, Mozart's Susanna, Euridice, Fiorilla in Il Turco in Italia and Lulu; sang at Frankfurt am Main from 1984 and appeared as guest in Turin as Lulu; Further engagements at Aachen, the Vienna Volksoper and the Bregenz Festival, Giulietta in Les Contes d'Hoffmann, 1988; sang Donna Anna in Don Giovanni at the Teatro Municipal, Rio de Janeiro, 1991; Vienna Volksoper 1992, as Abigaille in Nabucco; Season 1995–96 as Salomé in Hérodiade at the Vienna Staatsoper, Donna Elvira and Elettra in Idomeneo at the Munich Staatsoper; season 2000–01 at the Vienna Staatsoper, as Elvira in Ernani and Offenbach's Giulietta.

COELHO DE SOUZA, Rodolfo, MA; Brazilian composer; *Professor of Music Theory and Technology, School of Art and Communication, University of São Paulo*; b. 8 Aug. 1952, São Paulo. *Education:* Univ. of São Paulo, Univ. of Texas, Austin, USA. *Career:* Co-Dir, Santos and São Paulo New Music Festival 1984–96; Dir of Symposium at Winter Festival of Campos do Jordão 1998–93; Chiarosuro premiered by the American Composers Orchestra 1996; Prof. of Composition and Computer Music Technology, Federal Univ. of Paraná 2000–05; Prof. of Music Theory and Technology, Univ. of São Paulo 2005–. *Compositions:* Phantasiestück for string quartet 1982, Carnavalia for orchestra 1983, Rébus for piano 1985, Galáxias for piano and orchestra 1998, Diálogos for marimba and vibraphone 1998, Oblique Rain for ensemble 1992, Luminosidades for orchestra 1993, Fractal Landscapes for ensemble 1993,

Chiaroscuro for piano, tape and two percussionists 1995, Invariants for wind quintet and piano 1995, What Happens Beneath the City While Janis Sleeps (electro-acoustic) 1997, Clariagua for clarinet 1999, Concert for computer and orchestra 2000, Invenções sobre um tema de Gilberto Mendes 2002. *Address:* Universidade de São Paulo, Escola de Comunicações e Artes, Avenida Bandeirantes 3900, Monte Alegre, Riberão Preto, 14040–900 São Paulo, Brazil. *E-mail:* rcoelho@usp.br. *Website:* www.musica.pcarp.usp.br.

COEN, Massimo; Italian violinist and composer; b. 11 March 1933, Rome; m. Mirella Thau; two s. one d. *Education:* Rome Univ., St Cecilia Conservatory, Rome. *Career:* founder of chamber music groups, I Solisti di Roma 1961, Quartetto Nuova Musica 1963, giving concerts and radio performances throughout Europe; tour of USA and Canada as soloist with Cameristica Italiana 1969; founder, Music School, Rome; teacher, Nat. Acad. of Dance; discoverer, editor and performer of numerous ancient Italian musical manuscripts; mem. of professional associations and councils; mem. int. jury, Gaudeamus Foundation Competition, Rotterdam 1976. *Compositions include:* Quartetto II for four temperaments 1987, Divertimento I for flute and strings 1988, Divertimento II: La Marsigliese 1989, Violin Concerto: Saudades de Rio 1991, C'era una Volta 1979, Integrazioni 1980, Dosilado 1983, Nascite 1983, Peav Suite 1983, Didone 1983, La Donna Senz'ombra 1984, Il Rovescio della Medaglia 1984, Sophitour 1985, Introduzione e Valzer in Do 1985, Concerto Grosso for string orchestra 1988, two Divertimenti 1988–89, Fantasia for oboe and string quartet 1993, three Liriche for soprano and violin 1994, Maternidade as Palabras: for soprano and violin (based on poetry by M. L. Verdi) 1994, Crysolith D 12 for violin and accordion 1996, Lolly for string quartet 1996, Le Opere e i Giorni for two violins 1996, L'Anima Negli Occhi for violin and viola 1996, O' Mazzamauriello for violin and cello 1996, Tenores for soprano sax and string quartet 1997, Mneme for soprano, sax soprano and string quartet, Transcriptions of Handel, Haydn, Mozart and Donizetti for voice and string quartet 1998, Accelerazioni, Serpentine e Itaca for string quartet 1999, Mediterraneo for violin, flute, clarinet and saxophone 2000, Nascita di Afrodite for violin, clarinet, alto saxophone and dance 2000, Così fan tutte for violin and actor, Accelerazioni II for violin, percussion and dancers 2001, Lo Sforzo Umano for violin, percussion, actor and dancers 2002, Moby Dick for violin, bass clarinet, percussion and actor 2003, Zampe, Zampette: Ninna Nanna for string quartet and bell 2003, Kleines Quartettsatz for strings 2003. *Recordings:* Baroque and Contemporary Music, Massimo Coen works Edipan Rome, Massimo Coen Live Portrait 2002, Mon Coeur qui Bat 2006. *Publications:* contrib. to Mondo Operaio. *Honours:* Carsulae Award 2002. *Address:* Via Ipponio 8, 00183 Rome, Italy (home). *Telephone:* 67001939 (home).

COERTSE, Mimi; South African singer (soprano); b. 12 June 1932, Durban. *Education:* studied in Johannesburg, and in Vienna, Austria with Josef Witt. *Career:* debut with Vienna Staatsoper in Naples, as Flowermaiden in Parsifal 1955; Basle 1956, as Queen of Night; tour of South Africa; appearances at Salzburg Festival as Constanze in Die Entführung 1956; Glyndebourne Festival 1957, as Zerbinetta; sang at Vienna Staatsoper from 1957; Salzburg 1960, as Queen of Night; Mahler's 8th Symphony; guest appearances in London, Cologne, Brussels, Frankfurt and Munich; sang Mozart's Countess in Pretoria, South Africa 1989. *Recordings include:* Fiakermilli in Arabella.

COGEN, Pierre; French organist, composer and academic; b. 2 Oct. 1931, Paris; m. Michèle Vermesse 1986. *Education:* Cathedral Music School for Children, studied in Paris, with Jean Langlais at Schola Cantorum, CAPES Music Educ. (Secondary), C.A. Professeur d'orgue des conservatoires nationaux. *Career:* Liturgical Organist 1945–94; Director of Boys' Choir 1952–65; concert organist 1959–; Prof. of Organ and Music Educ. 1961–93; Asst to Jean Langlais, Sainte Clotilde and Schola Cantorum 1972–76; Organist, Basilique Sainte Clotilde 1976–94; Pres. Fédération Francophone des Amis de l'Orgue 2003–06. *Compositions include:* Pieces for Organ, published in Das neue Orgelbaum II 1986, Deux Hosannas, Pieces for Organ, in Pedals Only 1988, Psalmodie, Fantaisie sur une Antienne pour orgue à 4 mains 1989, Offrande, 1990, Nocturne 1992, Deux Chorals 1992, Cortège 1996, Introduction, thèmes et variations 2002, Laetare Jerusalem 2004, various unpublished works including L'Epiphanie du Seigneur, L'Exaltation de la Sainte Croix, Lucernaire pour deux orgues, Psaume De profundis pour orgue et cuivres. *Recordings include:* Organ works of Jean Langlais, three recordings; Sept Chorals-Poèmes pour les Sept Paroles du Christ, de Charles Tournemire; Pierre Cogen en concert. *Publications include:* Grand-orgue du Basilique Sainte Clotilde, Les orgues d'Aquitaine, Une Gravure Historique: la Paraphrase-Carillon de Tournemire enregistrée par lui-même en 1931. *Honours:* Chevalier, Ordre des Palmes académiques; numerous prizes for organ and for composition. *Address:* Résidence Lamartine, 23 avenue de Lattre de Tassigny, 33400 Talence, Bordeaux, France (home). *E-mail:* pierre.cogen@wanadoo.fr (office).

COGNET, André; French singer (bass-baritone); b. 1967. *Education:* Marseille Conservatoire, Studio of the Paris Opéra. *Career:* sang Puccini's Schaunard at Toulouse, in Stravinsky's Pulcinella at the Théâtre des Champs Elyseés, Escamillo in Peter Brook's version of Carmen, baritone roles in Les Contes d'Hoffmann and Mozart's Figaro; Wexford Festival appearances as Gaveston in La Dame Blanche and Donizetti's L'Assedio de Calais; Further engagments as Zuniga in Carmen at Munich, Guglielmo at Karlsruhe, Hamlet at Rouen and Zurga for Opera North; Captain in Gulitt's Wozzeck at Rouen, 1997; Season 1997/98 with Les Noces by Stravinsky under Marek Janowski, L'Enfance du Christ by Berlioz in Madrid, and the title role in Paisiello's Il Re Teodoro a Venezia, at the Teatro La Fenice; Verona Arena 1999 as Escamillo in Carmen; Season 2000–2001 as Puccini's Lescaut, with the Israel Philharmonic and Ravel's L'Enfant et les Sortilèges in Berlin; US debut as Gounod's Mephistopheles for Florida Grand Opera, 2002. *Current Management:* Musicaglotz, 11 rue le Verrier, 75006 Paris, France. *Telephone:* (1) 42-34-53-40. *Fax:* (1) 40-46-93-77. *E-mail:* general@musicaglotz.com. *Website:* www.musicaglotz.com.

COGRAM, John; British singer (tenor); b. 1967, Sussex, England. *Education:* Royal College of Music, National Opera Studio and with Janice Chapman, masterclasses with Birgit Nilsson and Luigi Alva. *Career:* Ulm Opera 1994–96, as M. Triquet in Eugene Onegin, Wenzel in The Bartered Bride, Steersman in Fliegende Holländer, Remendado (Carmen) and Bajazet in Handel's Tamerlano; Other roles include Alfredo in La Traviata at Clonter Farm, Pinkerton with English Festival Opera and Rodolfo with English Touring Opera; Oronte in Handel's Alcina in concert performances at Cologne; Basle Opera from 1996, as Pedrillo (Entführung) and Pang in Turandot; Recitals include: Die schöne Müllerin and Dichterliebe. *Honours:* RCM Cuthbert Smith Award.

COHEN, Arnaldo, FRNCM; Brazilian/British/American concert pianist and academic; *Professor of Music (Piano), Jacobs School of Music, Indiana University*; b. 22 April 1948, Rio de Janeiro; s. of Eliazar Cohen and Rachel Cohen; m. Karina Marques; one s. two step-c. *Education:* Engineering Univ. of Rio de Janeiro, School of Music, Federal Univ. of Rio de Janeiro. *Career:* debut at Royal Festival Hall, London 1977; appearances at Royal Albert Hall, Barbican, QEH and Wigmore Hall in London, La Scala Milan, Concertgebouw Amsterdam and Musikverein in Vienna; performed in Amadeus Piano Trio 1988–92; served on juries of Busoni, Liszt and Chopin Competitions; concerts under Menuhin, Tennstedt, Sanderling and Masur; master-classes in Europe, USA and South America; fmr teacher, RAM; currently Prof. of Music (Piano), Jacobs School of Music, Indiana Univ.; apptd to Broadwood Trust Fellowship, Royal Northern Coll. of Music 1992; Artistic Dir, Portland Piano International. *Recordings include:* Liszt Piano Concertos for BIS; Rachmaninov Piano Concertos with Sao Paulo State Symphony; Brasiliana, Three Centuries of Music from Brazil; Liszt recitals including B Minor Sonata, Dante Sonata, Funerailles, Spanish Rhapsody, Vallée D'Obermann, Scherzo and March; Schumann Fantasie Op. 17, Arabesque Op. 18, Brahms Handel Variations; Chopin Scherzo No. 2, Ballade No. 4, Allegro de Concert, Largo and Bolero; recordings for TV and radio, BBC, Dutch, German, Italian, Brazilian and others. *Honours:* First Prize, Beethoven Competition 1970, Busoni Piano Competition, Italy 1972, Royal Northern Coll. of Music Broadwood Fellow in Piano Studies 1991. *Current Management:* c/o Arts Management Group, 130 West 57th Street, Suite 6A, New York, NY 10019, USA. *Telephone:* (212) 337-0838. *E-mail:* bill@artsmg.com. *Website:* www.artsmg.com. *Address:* Merrill Hall, MU220, Jacobs School of Music, 1201 East Third Street, Bloomington, IN 47405, USA (office). *Telephone:* (812) 855-1955 (office). *E-mail:* arncohen@indiana.edu (office); arnaldocohen@gmail.com. *Website:* music.indiana.edu (office); www.arnaldocohen.com.

COHEN, David, BM, MM, PG; Belgian solo cellist, educator, artistic director and chamber musician; *Professor, Conservatoire Royal de Musique de Mons and Trinity Laban, London*; b. Tournai. *Education:* Conservatoire Royal de Bruxelles, Yehudi Menuhin School, Guildhall School of Music and Drama, London with Oleg Kogan, masterclasses with William Pleeth, Melissa Phelps, Lynn Harrell, Daniil Schafran, Natalia Gutman, Gary Hoffman, Bernard Greenhouse, Steven Isserlis, Boris Pergamenschikow, Yehudi Menuhin and Mstislav Rostropovich. *Career:* solo debut with Nat. Orchestra of Belgium aged nine; int. career as a soloist with invitations from St Petersburg Philharmonic Orchestra, BBC Symphony Orchestra, London Soloists Chamber Orchestra, Orchestre Philharmonique de Liège, Orchestre Symphonique de la VRT, Orchestra of the Beethoven Akad., Orchestre Nat. de Lille, Zurich Chamber Orchestra, Orchestre de Chambre de Lausanne, Orchestre Royal de Chambre de Wallonie, Orchestre de la Suisse Romande, Orchestre Symphonique de Grenoble, Polish Philharmonic Orchestra, Sinfonia Varsovia, Philharmonia Orchestra, Seoul Philharmonic, NHK Symphony Orchestra, BBC Concert Orchestra; has performed with leading conductors including Yehudi Menuhin, Mstislav Rostropovich, Walter Weller, Sir Charles Mackerras, Vladimir Ashkenazy, Christophe von Dohnányi, Pedro Halffter and Martin Brabbins, among others; solo debut in Japan with NHK Symphony Orchestra and Vladimir Ashkenazy performing Tchaikovsky Rococo Variations 2007; performed world tour, including at Carnegie Hall, Wigmore Hall, Amsterdam Concertgebouw, Vienna Musikverein, Paris Théâtre des Champs Elysées, Cologne Philharmonie, Palais des Beaux Arts Bruxelles and in Helsinki, Athens and Birmingham; regularly performs chamber music in major festivals; regularly invited to int. chamber music and cello festivals including Kronberg (Germany), Manchester (UK), Cambridge (UK), Beauvais (France), Orpheus Baccheus, Bordeaux (France), Gstaad Festival (Switzerland), West Cork (Ireland), Kuhmo (Finland), Elverum (Norway), Oxford (UK), Sonoro (Romania), amongst others; Artistic Dir Melchior Ensemble, Peterhouse, Cambridge; Founder and Artistic Dir Les Sons Intensifs chamber music festival, Lessines, Belgium; Prin. Cello, Philharmonia Orchestra 2000–08 (youngest ever Prin. Cello in history); Prof., Conservatoire Royal de Musique de Mons and Trinity Laban, London 2000–; plays on the 'Ex-Pergamenschikow cello' (Dominicus Montagnana circa 1735). *Recordings include:* Lalo Cello Concerto, Lutosławski Cello Concerto with the Philharmonia Orchestra, Rococo Variations with NHK Symphony Orchestra and

Vladimir Ashkenazy, Dvořák Cello Concerto with NHK Symphony Orchestra and Vladimir Ashkenazy, Complete Works by Dupuis for Solo Cello and Orchestra (with the Liège Philharmonic), Pieces with Orchestre Royal de Chambre de Wallonie for Forlane, Jeunes solistes francophones (BBC live broadcast), Sophia Gubaidulina Concerto with BBC Symphony Orchestra. *Honours:* Chevalier de la Confrérie des Chevaliers de la Tour 2009; numerous prizes including First Grand Prix, Young Soloist Nat. Competition (Belgium) 1991, First Grand Prix (Sr and Jr divs), Int. Music Competition, Wattrelos (France) 1993, Award, Guilhermina Suggia Gift for Cello (UK) 1996, 1999, First Grand Prix, 11th Int. Cello Competition, Douai (France) 1998, First Grand Prix, Tenuto Nat. Competition (Belgium) 1998, Award, City of Tournai 1999, Award, Fondation S.P.E.S. (Belgium) 1999, Award Winner, KPMG/Martin Musical Scholarship Fund (UK) 2000, 2001, Geneva Int. Cello Competition Special Prize 'Patrick F. Liechti', Fondation SUISA pour la Musique 2000, Award, Belgian Foundation for Young Soloists 2001, Gold Medal, Guildhall School of Music and Drama 2001, ECHO 'Rising Star', Royal Philharmonic Soc. of Belgium and the Concertgebouw 2001, Solti Foundation Award 2002, Octave de la Musique Award for Best Classical Music Album 2002, Borletti Buitoni Fellowship Award 2004, J.S. Bach Int. Competition 2008. *Current Management:* c/o John Owen, Owen/White Management, 22 Brunswick Terrace, Hove, East Sussex, BN3 1HJ, England. *E-mail:* info@owenwhitemanagement.com. *E-mail:* davidcohen007@yahoo.com. *Website:* www.davidcohen.be (home).

COHEN, Joel, MA; American conductor, lutenist, writer and lecturer; *Director, Boston Camerata;* b. 23 May 1942, Providence, RI. *Education:* Brown Univ., Harvard Univ., studied with Nadia Boulanger in Paris. *Career:* Dir Boston Camerata 1968–; guest conductor at various music festivals (Aix-en-Provence, Strasbourg, Tanglewood); Lecturer Early Music Performance at US and European univs and conservatories; specialist in Mediaeval, Renaissance and Baroque music. *Recordings:* with Boston Camerata and Cambridge Consort; Johnny Johnson by Weill, Cantigas de Santa Maria 1999. *Honours:* Grand Prix du Disque 1989. *Current Management:* Aaron Concert Management, 729 Boylston Street, Suite 206, Boston, MA 02116, USA.

COHEN, Robert; British cellist, conductor and teacher; *Professor, Royal Academy of Music;* b. 15 June 1959, London, England; s. of Raymond Cohen and Anthya Rael; m. Rachel Smith 1987; four s. *Education:* Purcell School and Guildhall School of Music (Diploma of Advanced Solo Studies), cello studies with William Pleeth, André Navarra, Jacqueline du Pré and Mstislav Rostropovich. *Career:* started playing cello aged five; Royal Festival Hall debut (Boccherini Concerto) aged 12; London recital debut, Wigmore Hall, aged 17; Tanglewood Festival, USA 1978; recording debut (Elgar concerto) 1979; concerts USA, Europe and Eastern Europe 1979; since 1980, concerts world-wide with major orchestras and with conductors including Muti, Abbado, Dorati, Sinopoli, Otaka, Mazur, Davis, Tilson-Thomas, Marriner and Rattle; Dir Charleston Manor Festival, E Sussex 1989–; regular int. radio broadcasts and numerous int. TV appearances; plays on the 'Ex-Roser' David Tecchler of Rome cello dated 1723; conductor, various chamber orchestras 1990–, symphony orchestras 1997–; Visiting Prof., RAM 1998–, Prof. 2009–; Prof. of Advanced Cello Studies, Conservatorio della Svizzera Italiana di Lugano 2000–12; launched Cello Clinic 2009; cellist, Fine Arts Quartet 2012–; performance/choreographic projects in collaboration with Royal Ballet School 2010–11; Fellow, Purcell School for Young Musicians 1992. *Recordings include:* Elgar Concerto (new Elgar concerto 1993), Dvořák Concerto, Tchaikovsky Rococo Variations, Rodrigo Concierto en modo Galante, Beethoven Triple Concerto, Grieg Sonata, Franck Sonata, Virtuoso Cello Music record, Dvořák Complete Piano trios with Cohen Trio, Schubert String Quintet with Amadeus Quartet, Complete Bach Solo Cello Suites, Howard Blake Diversions, Bliss Concerto 1992, Walton Concerto 1995, Britten Cello Suites 1997, Morton Feldman Concerto 1998, Britten Cello Symphony 1998, Sally Beamish Cello Concerto River 1999, HK Gruber Cello Concerto 2003. *Television includes:* Bach Sarabandes (BBC), Elgar Cello Concerto (BBC), Beamish Cello Concerto (BBC). *Honours:* Hon. RAM 2009; Winner, Suggia Award 1968–72, Winner, Young Concert Artists Int. Competition, New York 1978, English Speaking Union Fellowship 1978, Piatigorsky Prize, Tanglewood Festival 1978, Winner, UNESCO Int. Competition, Czechoslovakia 1981, Robert Helpmann Award (Australia) 2005. *Telephone:* (20) 8444-1065 (office). *E-mail:* office@robertcohen.info (office). *Website:* www.robertcohen.info; www.fineartsquartet.com; www.celloclinic.com.

COHN, James Myron, BS, MS; American composer and musicologist; b. 12 Feb. 1928, Newark, NJ; m. Eileen B. Wions 1979. *Education:* Juilliard School of Music, Hunter Coll., New York, studied with Roy Harris, Wayne Barlow and Bernard Wagenaar. *Career:* musicologist, American Soc. of Composers, Authors and Publishers 1954–84; inventor of various patented control devices for electronic musical instruments; mem. American Federation of Musicians, American Soc. of Composers, Authors and Publishers, Songwriters' Guild of America. *Compositions include:* Symphony No. 1–8, A Song of the Waters (tone poem) for orchestra, The Little Circus, Sonata for flute and piano, Statues in the Park (choral), Concerto da camera, Quintet for winds, Little Overture, Sonatina for clarinet and piano, Serenade for flute, violin and cello, Trio for piano, violin and cello, Mount Gretna Suite for chamber orchestra, Homage (tone poem) for orchestra, Concerto No. 1 for clarinet and strings, Concerto No. 2: Evocations for clarinet and strings, Concerto for piano and orchestra, Concerto for trumpet and strings, Concerto for concertina and strings. *Publications:* contrib. book reviews to Library Journal. *Honours:*

Queen Elisabeth of Belgium Prize (for Symphony No. 2) 1953, AIDEM Prize (for Symphony No. 4).

COHRS, Gunnar, (Benjamin-Gunnar Cohrs), DipMus, DipMusicology, DrPhil; German conductor, music researcher and publicist; *Editor in Chief, Anton Bruckner Urtext Gesamtausgabe Wien;* b. 21 Sept. 1965, Hameln. *Education:* Jugendmusikschule Hameln, Hochschule für Künste Bremen, Univ. of Adelaide, Australia, Univ. of Hamburg, studied conducting with Nicola Samale, Hans-Joachim Kauffmann, musicology with Andrew McCredie. *Career:* Conductor, Jugendstreichorchester Hamelin 1985–90, Bremen String Orchestra 1991–95; several choirs; int. conducting debut with Russian Nat. Orchestra, Moscow 2000; Japanese debut with Royal Flanders Philharmonic, Tokyo 2001; Ed., Bruckner Gesamtausgabe 1995–2010, BGC Manuscript Edn 2010–; Ed. in Chief, Anton Bruckner Urtext Gesamtausgabe Wien 2013–; has appeared with Philharmonia Hungarica, Royal Flanders Orchestra, Sarajevo Symphony Orchestra, Janáček Philharmonic Orchestra, Göttingen Baroque Orchestra, Alsfelder Vokalensemble; mem. Internationale Bruckner Gesellschaft Wien. *Compositions include:* Komm, Herr, segne uns (motet) 1980, Jesu, Deine Passion (organ chorale) 1987, Trois Pastorales for flute and clarinet 1991, Amour Perdu for piano or small orchestra 1993. *Publications include:* Bruckner IX Symphony, Finale (completed performing version) 1983–2012, Frank Martin Sonata da Chiesa (arranged for flute and string orchestra) 1995, Bruckner Studienband zum 2. Satz der IX Sinfonie 1998, Bruckner Two discarded Trios for the Ninth Symphony (completed performing versions) 1998, Bruckner Ninth Symphony (new critical edn and report) 1999, Satie Gymnopedies (arranged for string orchestra), Schubert Unfinished Symphony, Scherzo and Finale 2004, Mozart C-Minor Mass, Completion of Credo and Agnus Dei 2010, Mozart Requiem 2013, Bruckner, VII Symphony (new critical edn) 2015; contrib. to Radio Bremen, Fono Forum, Klassik Heute, BREMER-Die Stadtillustrierte, Weserkurier; programme notes, album booklets, essays, articles, papers at int. confs. *Honours:* Kilenyi Medal, Bruckner Soc. of America 2010. *Address:* Postfach 107507, 28075 Bremen, Germany (office). *E-mail:* info@benjamingunnarcohrs.com. *Website:* benjamingunnarcohrs.com.

COIN, Christophe; French musician (cello, viola da gamba) and conductor; b. 1958, Caen. *Education:* CNSM Paris, Schola Cantorum Basiliensis, studied with André Navarra and Jordi Savall. *Career:* fmr mem. Nikolaus Harnoncourt's Concentus Musicus; Founder-mem. period instrument ensemble Quatuor Mosaïques 1987–; regular performances in halls including Wigmore Hall, London, Wiener Konzerthaus, Concertgebouw Amsterdam, Berlin Philharmonie and Zankel Hall, New York and at festivals such as Edinburgh, Salzburg, Lucerne, Bremen, Bath, Styriarte Graz, Schubertiade Schwarzenberg and Oslo; invited to perform in Spain by King Juan Carlos I using his personal collection of Stradivari instruments 2006; second N America tour 2012; Music Dir Ensemble Baroque de Limoges 1991–2013; guest performances with ensembles including Acad. of Ancient Music, Orchestra of the Age of Enlightenment, le Giardino Armonico and numerous symphony orchestras; has worked as chamber musician with artists including Wieland Kujiken, Jordi Savall, Gustav Leonhardt and Hopkinson Smith; organised int. symposia on period playing techniques and early instrument fabrication, Limoges 1992–; teacher, CNSM Paris and Schola Cantorum Basiliensis 1988–; over 50 recordings. *Recordings include:* with Quatuor Mosaïques: string quartets by Haydn, Beethoven, Boëly, Wölfl, Schubert and Mozart; with Ensemble Baroque de Limoges: Mondonville 1997, Brossard 1997, Bach cantatas for cello piccolo 1994, Telemann 1998. *Honours:* two Gramophone Awards, Diapason d'Or de l'Année. *Current Management:* c/o Rayfield Allied, Southbank House, Black Prince Road, London, SE1 7SJ, England. *Telephone:* (20) 3176-5500. *Fax:* (700) 602-4143. *E-mail:* info@rayfieldallied.com. *Website:* www.rayfieldallied.com.

COKER, Paul; British pianist; b. 1959, London, England. *Education:* Yehudi Menuhin School, studied with Louis Kentner, Tanglewood, USA. *Career:* gave several London recitals, as well as concerts in France, Germany, Belgium, Netherlands, the USA, Canada and India; has played with most leading British orchestras and with the Berlin Philharmonic; The Grieg Concerto with the Belgian National Symphony; many recitals with Yehudi Menuhin in Europe, the USA, Far East and Australia. *Honours:* winner National Federation of Music Societies' Concert Award 1978, Tanglewood Jackson Master Award.

COKU, Alexandru; American singer (soprano); b. 1963. *Education:* Indiana University with Margaret Harshaw. *Career:* has sung in Europe from 1988, notably as Euridice to the Orpheus of Jochen Kowalski at Covent Garden and as Pamina at the rebuilt Frankfurt Opera, 1991; further engagements as Pamina at Vienna, Munich and Düsseldorf; Amsterdam, 1992, as Ismene in Mozart's Mitridate; US appearances as Anne Trulove in The Rake's Progress at Chicago (1990) and Cecilio in Lucio Silla at San Francisco (1991); season 1995–96 as Mozart's Elektra, Offenbach's Antonia and Constanze at Düsseldorf, Romilda in Handel's Xerxes at Cologne, 1998; Giulietta in Les Contes d'Hoffmann; season 2000–01 as Mozart's Countess in Cologne, Ellen Orford at Nancy and Handel's Agrippina for Glimmerglass Opera. *Current Management:* Boris Orlob Management, Jägerstrasse 70, 10117 Berlin, Germany. *Telephone:* (30) 20450839. *Fax:* (30) 20450849. *E-mail:* info@orlob.net. *Website:* www.orlob.net.

COLAIANNI, Domenico, Italian singer (baritone); b. 1964. *Education:* N. Piccinni Conservatory, Bari. *Career:* early appearances as Mengotto in

Piccinni's La Cecchina, Papageno and Schaunard in La Bohème; Enrico in Donizetti's Il Campanello and Slook in Rossini's La Cambiale at Bologna; Cimarosa's Maestro di Capella at Parma, Ping in Turandot at Lecce and Bizet's Don Procopio in Novara; Further engagements in Australia, in Paisiello's Il Barbiere di Siviglia, Rossini's Il Signor Bruschino in Tokyo and Osaka, and Donizetti's Olivio e Pasquale in Germany; Operas by Salieri, Vivaldi and Hasse in Budapest; sang in the first modern performance of I Rantzau, by Mascagni, at Livorno; Festival of Martina Franca in Leo's Amor vuol sofferenza, and as Lisandro in Piccinni's L'Americano, 1996. *Recordings include:* L'Americano (Dynamic). *Current Management:* OPERAdomani, via San Vito 30, 95124 Catania, Italy. *Telephone:* (095) 3521165. *Fax:* (095) 7461401. *E-mail:* info@operadomani.net. *Website:* www.operadomani.net.

COLBERT, Brendan; Australian composer; b. 11 Sept. 1956, Ballarat, Vic. *Education:* Nat. Orchestral Composers School, studied with Brenton Broadstock, Riccardo Formosa. *Compositions include:* Passages for alto saxophone, electric guitar, piano and percussion 1987, Murderers of Calm for ensemble 1987, Agite II for mandolin 1989, Fourplay for viola, cello, clarinet and piano 1991, Agite I for flute 1991, Parallaxis for ensemble 1993, Agite II for piano 1993–95, Mirror, Picture, Echo, Shadow, Dream for cello, flute, percussion and piano 1994, Entfernt for string orchestra 1994, Sphinx for ensemble 1995, Sanctuary for orchestra 1995. *Honours:* Warringah Eisteddfod Young Composers Competiton 1985.

COLDING-JØRGENSEN, Henrik; Danish composer, organist, educator and choral director; *Organist and Choral Director, Hundige-Kildebrønde Parish*; b. 21 March 1944, Riisskov; Christian Colding-Jørgensen and Ruth Colding-Jørgensen (née Lindhard); m. 1st Birgit Nielsen 1966 (divorced); m. 2nd Mette Bramso 1992 (divorced); one d. *Education:* Royal Danish Music Acad. *Career:* organ teacher, teacher of musical theory; producer of radio and TV programmes; Organist and Choral Dir, Kildebrønde, Copenhagen 1975–; Chair. of Bd Holstebro Electronic Music Studio 1977–85; mem. Musical Cttee, Roskilde Co. 1979–87, Cttee of Reps of State Music Council 1981–91, Cttee of Reps of State Art Council 1981–85, Danish Arts Council 1981–84, Bd Danish Composers' Soc. 1981–91, Bd Int. Soc. for Contemporary Music (Denmark) – 1982, Bd Danish Organist and Cantor Soc. 1992–95, Danish Choir Dirs 1996, Swedish Choir Dirs 2003. *Compositions include:* Ave Maria 1974, Balances 1974, To Love Music 1975, Victoria Through the Forest 1975, Boast 1980, Dein Schweigen 1982, Recitativ and Fuga; An Die Nachgeborenen ll 1984, Du Sollst Nicht 1984, Sic Enim 1985, Nuup Kangerlua 1985, Partita, aria e minuetto 1986, Le Alpi Nel Cuore 1988, 2 Songs by Keats 1988, Nunc Est 1989, The Soul and The Butterfly 1990, Babylon 1991, As a Traveller 1992, Krystal, Metamorfose for string quartet 1993, Discourse with Time 1996, Sourires 1997, Four British Songs 1997, Duo Viri in Vestibus Albis 1999, Dolori 2000, Elegie-Wiegenlied 2000, Englens Händ 2001, Primavere 2002, Kyrie Agnus Dei 2002, Osanna! 2003, Angst 2004, Barnet 2004, Screaming Void 2005, Et Recordatus Est 2006, In the Whale 2007, Bach's Christmas 2007, Three Lovesongs 2009–10, Diptychon 2011, Maria am Rosenhag 2012. *Honours:* various bursaries, prizes and comms, Concours Int. de Composition Musicale, Opéra et Ballet, Geneva 1985, European Award for Choral Composers, special mention. *Address:* Gersagerparken 52, 3.mf, 2670 Greve, Denmark (office). *E-mail:* hc-j@hc-j.dk (office). *Website:* www.hc-j.dk.

COLE, Rosamund; British singer (soprano); b. 1968. *Education:* Royal Northern Coll. of Music, Nat. Opera Studio, Cologne Opera Studio, Germany. *Career:* appearances with British Youth Opera 1992, 1993, as Susanna in Le nozze di Figaro and Ninetta in La Gazza Ladra; with Opera North 1996 as Barbarina; at Cologne Opera 1996–98, as Ännchen in Der Freischütz, Priestess in Aida, Johanna in Sondheim's Sweeney Todd, Barbarina, Despina, Zerlina and Gretel in Hänsel und Gretel; Darmstadt Staatstheater 1998–2000, as Serpetta in La Finta Giardiniera, Hannchen in Der Vetter aus Dingsda, Frasquita in Carmen, Valencienne in Die Lustige Witwe and Gretel; concert appearances include Wigmore Hall recital 1994 and Flowermaiden in Parsifal with Cologne Philharmonie with James Conlon. *Honours:* Countess of Munster Award, Sybil Tutton Prize, Wolfson Prize grant.

COLE, Steve; American singer (tenor); b. 1954. *Career:* sang with Washington Opera from 1981, Aix-en-Provence (as Monostatos), 1982, and in Paris, Avignon (Henze's Boulevard Solitude), and Nice; New York Metropolitan debut, 1987, as Brighella in Ariadne auf Naxos; San Francisco Opera from 1990; other modern repertory includes the premieres of Medea by Gavin Bryars (Lyon, 1984) and La Noche Triste by Prodromidès (Nancy, 1989); Other buffo and character roles include Bardolph in Falstaff, Pong in Turandot and Sellem in The Rake's Progress; Sang John Styx in Orphée aux Enfers, Geneva, 1998; Season 1999–2000 as Monostatos in Barcelona and Osmin in Haydn's l'Incontro Improvviso at Eisenstadt. *Current Management:* Columbia Artists Management, 1790 Broadway, New York, NY 10019-1412, USA. *Telephone:* (212) 841-9500. *Fax:* (212) 841 9744. *E-mail:* info@cami.com. *Website:* www.cami.com.

COLE, Tobias, BMus, ARCM; Australian singer (countertenor); b. 1969. *Education:* Univ. of Sydney, Royal Coll. of Music, England. *Career:* appearances included Medoro in Handel's Orlando for West Australian Opera, Eustazio in Rinaldo for Opera Australia and Ulisse in Deidamia for the London Handel Festival; title role in Rinaldo for Abbey Opera; other roles include Farnace in Mitridate and Handel's Julius Caesar; oratorios include St Matthew Passion for City of Bath Bach Choir, Messiah for Queensland and Adelaide Symphonies, Bernstein's Chichester Psalms with the Sydney

Phiharmonia and Handel's Brockes Passion for the London Handel Festival 2000–01; sang in Purcell's Fairy Queen for the English Bach Festival at the Linbury Theatre, Covent Garden 2001. *Current Management:* Arts Management Pty Ltd, Level 1, 405 Elizabeth Street, Surry Hills, NSW 2010, Australia. *Telephone:* (2) 9211 9422. *Fax:* (2) 9211 9466. *E-mail:* enquiries@artsmanagement.com.au. *Website:* www.artsmanagement.com.au.

COLE, Vinson; American singer (tenor); b. 21 Nov. 1950, Kansas City, KS. *Education:* Curtis Institute, Philadelphia. *Career:* debut as Werther in the opera by Massenet while still a student, 1975; sang in the premiere of Jubilee by Ulysses Kay at Jackson, Mississippi, in 1976; European debut, 1976, with Welsh National Opera, as Belmonte in Die Entführung aus dem Serail; Later appearances in Stuttgart, Naples, Salzburg, Paris and Marseilles; St Louis, 1976–80, as Tamino and Rossini's Comte Ory; New York City Opera, 1981, as Fenton in Die lustigen Weiber von Windsor; Other roles include Gennaro in Lucrezia Borgia, Nadir in Les Pêcheurs de Perles, Lenski in Eugene Onegin, Gluck's Orfeo and Gounod's Faust; sang in Mozart's Requiem under Georg Solti at Vienna, 1991; sang Donizetti's Edgardo at Detroit, Ferrando at Seattle, 1992; Nadir in Les Pêcheurs de Perles in Seattle 1994; sang Jason in Cherubini's Medea, Athens 1995; Don Carlo in the French version of Verdi's opera, Brussels, 1996; Renaud in Gluck's Armide, to open the 1996–97 Season at La Scala; Season 1999–2000 as Mozart's Titus at Covent Garden (house debut); season 2000–01 as Gerald in Lakmé at Seattle, the Berlioz Faust at Edinburgh and Cavaradossi in Sydney; Voice Tutor, New England Conservatory of Music; Visiting Artist, Cleveland Inst. of Music 2009–. *Current Management:* Zemsky/Green Artists Management, 730 Fifth Avenue, Suite 1802, New York, NY 10019, USA. *Telephone:* (212) 300-8003. *Fax:* (212) 300-8001. *E-mail:* zgartists@aol.com. *Website:* www.zemskygreen.com.

COLEMAN, Andrea, MMus; American singer (mezzo-soprano). *Education:* Univ. of Kansas, New England Conservatory. *Career:* Young American Artist, Glimmerglass Opera summer 2006, 2007; Resident Artist The Minnesota Opera 2006–, sang Antonia's Mother in The Tales of Hoffmann, Mallika in Lakmé and Marcellina in The Marriage of Figaro. *Honours:* Boston Lyric Opera Stephen Shrestinian Award For Excellence 2006. *Address:* The Minnesota Opera, 620 North First Street, Minneapolis, MN 55401, USA (office). *Telephone:* (612) 333-2700 (office). *Fax:* (612) 333-0869 (office). *E-mail:* mnop@mnopera.org (office). *Website:* www.mnopera.org (office).

COLEMAN, Jeremy (Jaz); New Zealand (b. British) singer, musician (keyboards) and composer; b. 26 Feb. 1960, Cheltenham, Gloucestershire, England. *Career:* Founder-mem. rock band, Killing Joke 1978–; numerous tours worldwide, TV and radio broadcasts; Composer-in-Residence, Auckland Philharmonia Orchestra 1992; arranged Nigel Kennedy's Riders On The Storm, The Doors Concerto 2000; fmr Composer-in-Residence, Prague Symphony Orchestra; Producer, East Meets East 2003; collaboration with Hinewehi Mohu on Oceania 2000; formed record label, Malicious Damage. *Compositions include:* one symphony. *Recordings include:* albums: with Killing Joke: Killing Joke 1980, What's This For? 1981, Revelations 1982, Fire Dances 1983, Night Time 1985, Brighter Than A Thousand Suns 1986, Extremities, Dirt and Various Repressed Emotions 1990, Pandemonium 1994, Democracy 1996, The Unperverted Pantomime 2003, Killing Joke 2003, XYV Gathering: Let Us Prey 2005, Hosannas from the Basements of Hell 2006, Absolute Dissent 2010, MMXII 2012; solo: Outside the Gate (with Anne Dudley) 1988, Songs from the Victorious City 1998. *Current Management:* c/o Christian Bernhardt, The Agency Group Limited, 142 West 57th Street, Sixth Floor, New York, NY 10019, USA. *Telephone:* (212) 581-3100. *Fax:* (212) 581-0015. *E-mail:* ChristianBernhardt@theagencygroup.com. *Website:* www.theagencygroup.com. *Address:* c/o Malicious Damage, 41 Charteris Road, London, NW6 7EY, England. *E-mail:* mail@maliciousdamage.co.uk. *Website:* www.maliciousdamage.biz; www.killingjoke.com.

COLEMAN, Tim; British stage director; b. 30 Oct. 1949, Eastbourne, Sussex, England. *Education:* Univ. of Cambridge and Amsterdam Conservatory. *Career:* wrote incidental music for more than 30 plays; Chief Dramaturg, Netherlands Opera 1986–90; freelance dir 1990–; debut as Dir with Opera Northern Ireland in Die Fledermaus 1990, returned for Le nozze di Figaro 1991 and Rigoletto 1992; US debut with The Beggar's Opera for the Manhattan School of Music; season 1991–92, Tosca for Minnesota Opera and Opera Omaha, Tamerlano for Dublin Opera Theatre, and The Merry Wives of Windsor for the Guildhall School of Music; season 1992–93, L'Italiana in Algeri for Dublin Grand Opera/Opera Ireland, Così fan tutte in Oklahoma City; season 1993–94, Rigoletto in Hong Kong, L'Isola disabitata in New York, Tosca in Indianapolis, Le nozze di Figaro for the Kirov Opera in the Mariinsky Theatre, St Petersburg; festivals of Mikkele, Finland, Schleswig-Holstein, Germany and Beth Shean, Israel; season 1994–95 directed Roméo et Juliette in Shanghai 1995; Chief Dramaturg, Deutsche Oper am Rhein Düsseldorf/Duisburg 1996–99; Artistic Dir Oporto Opera; Swiss debut with production of I Puritani for Ensemble Theater (Biel/Bienne) 2000 and Il Pirata 2002; other recent productions include Stiffelio at Theatre Argentina, La Plata, Madama Butterfly for Opera Holland Park and Cork Opera, La Traviata at Megaron Musiki, Thessaloniki, Die Fledermaus for Opera Cork, Il barbiere di Siviglia for Opera Holland Park, Lucia di Lammermoor for Mississippi Opera, Carousel for Opera Illinois and Kiss Me Kate in Gelsenkirchen.

COLEMAN-WRIGHT, Peter; Australian singer (baritone); b. 1958; m. Cheryl Barker. *Education:* studied in London with Otakar Kraus, Joan

Hammond, Paul Hamburger and Geoffrey Parsons. *Career:* has sung at Glyndebourne as Guglielmo, Demetrius, Dandini, Morales in Carmen and Sid in Albert Herring; ENO as Niels Lyhne in Fennimore and Gerda, Rossini's Barber, Schaunard, Billy Budd and Don Giovanni; Australian Opera as Mozart's Count; Covent Garden, Dandini, then Don Alvaro in Rossini's Il Viaggio a Reims and Papageno; Bordeaux Opera, Guglielmo, Masetto; Victoria State Opera, Wolfram, Papageno, Valentin in Faust; further engagements with Netherlands Opera, La Fenice Venice and the Australian Opera; Grand Théâtre Genève; other roles include Eisenstein and Falke in Die Fledermaus, Masetto, Rossini's Figaro, Wolfram in Tannhäuser, Zurga and the Soldier/Brother in Busoni's Doctor Faust; Lieder recitals at the South Bank, Covent Garden, Théâtre du Châtelet in Paris and the Aix and Spoleto Festivals; Brahms Requiem and Mahler Kindertotenlieder in Austria; concerts in Netherlands, Spain, Germany, Finland, Iceland and for the Australian Broadcasting Commission; premiere of Inquest of Love by Jonathan Harvey, ENO 1993; Wigmore Recital 1993; Bordeaux, Count Almaviva 1993; Australian Opera, Don Giovanni 1993; Staatsoper Munich, Don Giovanni; Marcello, Grand Théâtre de Genève and Covent Garden; Eugene Onegin, ENO and Lyric Opera Queensland; Billy Budd, Covent Garden; Chorèbe in Les Troyens, Australian Opera; sang Escamillo in Carmen at the Opéra Bastille, Paris 1997; sang in premiere production by a British company of Strauss's Die Liebe der Danaë, Garsington 1999; concerts with BBC Symphony including the British premiere of Hindemith's Mörder Hoffnung der Frauen; season 2000–01 with The Prisoner (ENO), Don Giovanni (Vancouver) and Die Liebe der Danaë (New York). *Recordings include:* Oedipus Rex by Stravinsky, Mass of Life, Fennimore and Gerda by Delius, Saint Paul by Mendelssohn, Paul Bunyan, The Pilgrim's Progress. *Honours:* Glyndebourne Touring Prize. *Current Management:* c/o Kathryn Morrison, Kathryn Morrison Management, 1 Mimosa Court, Buxton, Vic. 3711, Australia. *Telephone:* (1) 40987-8016. *E-mail:* kmorrison.work@gmail .com. *Website:* www.kathrynmorrisonmanagement.com. *Address:* 11 Mount Street Walk, Jackson's Landing, Pyrmont, NSW 2009, Australia. *Website:* www.petercolemanwright.com.

COLES, Samuel; British flautist; b. 1964. *Education:* studied with James Galway, at Guildhall School of Music, Paris Conservatoire with Jean-Pierre Rampal. *Career:* solo and chamber music performances in UK and Europe, in Holland with Concertgebouw and The Hague, with Bordeaux Symphony, Monte Carlo Orchestra, London Soloists Chamber Orchestra; Mozart Concerto K313 with Orchestre de Paris at Rampal's Gala Concert, Paris; chamber recitals with mems of European Community Youth Orchestra and duet partnership with harpist Isabelle Courret; concerto engagements with Kenneth Montgomery, Aldo Ceccato and Alain Lombard; as orchestral player has performed under Simon Rattle, Claudio Abbado and Pierre Boulez; has played as guest prin. with London Symphony Orchestra, London Philharmonic Orchestra, Acad. of St Martin in the Fields, BBC Symphony Orchestra, Opera de Paris, Orchestra de Radio France, Bavarian Radio Symphony Orchestra; currently Prin. Flute, Philharmonia Orchestra; teacher, RAM. *Recordings include:* Mozart Concerti with the English Chamber Orchestra under Yehudi Menuhin. *Honours:* Premier Prix, Paris Conservatoire 1987, winner, Scheveningen Int. Flute Competition, Nat. Flute Asscn Young Artists Competition, Second Prize, Jean Pierre Rampal Competition 1987. *Address:* Philharmonia Orchestra, 6th Floor, The Tower Building, 11 York Road, London, SE1 7NX, England. *Website:* www.philharmonia.co.uk.

COLETTI, Paul; American violist, composer and academic; *Professor, Colburn Conservatory, The Colburn School;* b. 21 Dec. 1959, Scotland; s. of Louis Coletti and Guiseppina Coletti; m. Gina Coletti; two d. *Education:* Royal Scottish Acad., Int. Menuhin Acad., Banff Center, Juilliard School, studied with Alberto Lysy, Sándor Végh, Yehudi Menuhin. *Career:* solo concerts at QEH, Geneva, Buenos Aires, Edinburgh, Assisi, Toulon and Harrogate Festivals; recitals at Toronto, Chicago, Cincinnati, Belgrade and Los Angeles; New York debut recital 1983; mem. Menuhin Festival Piano Quartet; chamber performances with Menuhin in Paris, London and Gstaad; mem. Chamber Soc. of Lincoln Center, New York; engagements with Camerata Lysy Ensemble, Los Angeles Philharmonic and playing Bartók's Viola Concerto in Berlin; fmr Prof. of Viola and Chamber Music, Menuhin Acad.; fmr Head of Viola Dept, Peabody Conservatory, Baltimore; fmr Head of Chamber Music, UCLA; fmr Head of String Dept, Univ. of Washington, Seattle; Prof., Colburn Conservatory, The Colburn School, Los Angeles 2003–. *Compositions include:* From My Heart 1994, Viola Tango 1994, Dream Ocean 1995, Circus 1996, Duo for Two Violas 2016. *Address:* Colburn School, 200 South Grand Avenue, Los Angeles, CA 90012, USA (office). *E-mail:* pcoletti@colburnschool.edu (office). *Website:* www.colburnschool.edu (office); www.violacoletti.com (office).

COLGRASS, Michael Charles, BMus; American composer; b. 22 April 1932, Chicago, IL; m. Ulla Damgaard 1966; one s. *Education:* Univ. of Illinois, Berkshire Music Center, Tanglewood with Lukas Foss, studied with Darius Milhaud, Aspen, Colorado Music School, with Wallingford Riegger and Ben Weber. *Career:* freelance solo percussionist with various New York groups 1956–67. *Compositions include:* for stage: Virgil's Dream (music theatre) 1967, Nightingale Inc. (comic opera) 1971, Something's Gonna Happen (children's musical) 1978; orchestral: Auras for harp and orchestra 1973, Concertmasters for three violins and orchestra 1975, Letter from Mozart 1976, Déjà vu for four percussionists and orchestra 1977, Delta for violin, clarinet, percussion and orchestra 1979, Memento for two pianos and orchestra 1982, Demon for amplified piano, percussion, tape, radio and orchestra 1984,

Chaconne for viola and orchestra 1984, The Schubert Birds 1989, Snow Walker for organ and orchestra 1990, Arctic Dreams for symphonic band 1991; chamber: Wolf for cello 1976, Flashback for five brass, Winds of Nagual: A Musical Fable for wind ensemble 1985, Strangers, Variations for clarinet, viola and piano 1986, Folklines for string quartet 1987, piano pieces, The Earth's a Baked Apple for chorus and orchestra 1969, New People for mezzo-soprano, viola and piano 1969, Image of Man for four solo voices, chorus and orchestra 1974, Theatre of the Universe for solo voices, chorus and orchestra 1975, Best Wishes USA for four solo voices, double chorus, two jazz bands, folk instruments and orchestra 1976, Beautiful People for chorus 1976, Mystery Flowers of Spring 1978, Night of the Raccoon 1979. *Publications:* contrib. articles to New York Times. *Honours:* Guggenheim Fellow 1964, 1968, Rockefeller grant 1968, Ford Foundation grant 1972, Pulitzer Prize in Music 1978, Emmy Awards 1982, 1988, Jules Léger Chamber Music Prize.

COLIBAN, Sorin; Romanian singer (bass); b. 1971. *Education:* Bucharest Conservatory. *Career:* debut in Bartók's Bluebeard at Bucharest, 1993; season 1995–96 with Don Giovanni at Athens, Royal Opera debut as Alvaro in a concert performance of Verdi's Alzira, and the Monk in Don Carlos at the London Proms; Season 1996–97 included Colline at Royal Opera House, Covent Garden; In 1997 debut at San Francisco Opera as Mozart's Bartolo; Season 1998–99 Alidoro (La Cenerentola) at Palais Garnier; Capelio in I Capuleti e i Montecchi (Bastille-Paris) and Zuniga at Monte Carlo; 1999–2000 Capulet (Roméo et Juliette) at Covent Garden, Raimondo (Lucia) at San Francisco; Other roles include Procida, Les Vêpres Siciliennes) and Fiesco (Simon Boccanegra). *Honours:* winner of Don Giovanni Competition in Athens and national competitions in Romania. *Current Management:* Theateragentur Erich Seitter, Opernring 8/13, 1010 Vienna, Austria. *Telephone:* (1) 5137592. *Fax:* (1) 5129351. *E-mail:* office@agentur-seitter.at. *Website:* www.agentur -seitter.at.

COLLARD, Jean Philippe; French pianist; b. 27 Jan. 1948, Mareuil-sur-Aÿ (Marne); s. of Michel Collard and Monique Collard (née Philipponnat); m. 2nd Ariane de Brion; three s. (two from previous m.) one d. *Education:* Conservatoire Nat. de Musique de Paris. *Career:* has appeared as soloist with numerous orchestras, including Zürich Tonhalle, Cleveland Orchestra, Philadelphia Orchestra, Minnesota Orchestra, Orchestre de Paris, Orchestre National de Lyon, London Philharmonia Orchestra, Orchestra of St. Luke's, New York Philharmonic Orchestra, BBC Philharmonic Orchestra, Royal Philharmonic Orchestra, Los Angeles Philharmonic Orchestra, Royal Liverpool Philharmonic Orchestra, BBC Scottish Symphony Orchestra, San Francisco Symphony Orchestra, London Symphony Orchestra, Vienna Symphony Orchestra, Pittsburgh Symphony Orchestra, Detroit Symphony Orchestra, Atlanta Symphony Orchestra, Indianapolis Symphony Orchestra, Boston Symphony Orchestra, NHK Symphony Orchestra; has collaborated with numerous conductors, including Semyon Bychkov, Marek Janowski, Eugen Jochum, Seiji Ozawa, André Previn, Simon Rattle, Charles Dutoit. *Recordings include:* music by Bach, Brahms, Debussy, Fauré, Franck, Rachmaninov, Ravel, Saint-Saëns, Schubert, Chopin, Mozart. *Honours:* Chevalier, Ordre des Arts et des Lettres, Chevalier, Ordre nat. du Mérite, Chevalier Légion d'honneur 2003. *Current Management:* Angela Sulivan, Sulivan Sweetland, 1 Hillgate Place, Balham Hill, London, SW12 9ER, England. *Telephone:* (20) 8772-3470. *E-mail:* as@sulivansweetland.co.uk. *E-mail:* pianojpc@aol.com (home). *Website:* www.jeanphilippecollard.com.

COLLI, Federico; Italian pianist; b. 10 Aug. 1988, Brescia. *Education:* Milan Conservatory, at Imola International Piano Acad., at Salzburg Mozarteum, attended master classes with M. Rybicki, E. Virsaladze, J. O'Conor, F. Scala, A. Lonquich and J. Soriano. *Honours:* 1st Prize, Cantù Int. Piano and Orchestra Competition 2008, 1st Prize, Mozart Int. Competition of Salzburg 2011, 1st Prize with Gold Medal, Leeds Int. Piano Competition 2012. *Address:* Via Divisione Acqui 90, 25126 Brescia, Italy (office). *Telephone:* (0347) 6648342 (office). *Fax:* (030) 311079 (office). *E-mail:* colli.operatingoffice@ email.it (office); federicocolli@email.it (home). *Website:* www.federicocolli.org (office).

COLLINS, Finghin, BA, ARCM; Irish pianist; *Artistic Director, New Ross Piano Festival;* b. 31 March 1977, Dublin. *Education:* Royal Irish Acad. of Music, Geneva Conservatoire. *Career:* has performed throughout Europe, the USA and the Far East with orchestras including Chicago Symphony Orchestra, Houston Symphony Orchestra, Seoul Philharmonic Orchestra, London Philharmonic Orchestra, Royal Philharmonic Orchestra, Rotterdam Philharmonic Orchestra, Orchestre de la Suisse Romande, Gulbenkian Orchestra, City of Birmingham Symphony Orchestra; has worked with conductors including Myung-Whun Chung, Christoph Eschenbach, Hans Graf, Emmanuel Krivine, Nicholas McGegan, Gianandrea Noseda, Sakari Oramo, Tadaaki Otaka, Heinrich Schiff, Vassily Sinaisky, Leonard Slatkin; also chamber music; BBC Proms debut, London 2008, second appearance 2010; Artistic Dir, New Ross Piano Festival; Assoc. Artist, RTÉ Nat. Symphony Orchestra of Ireland 2010–; mem. Bd Nat. Concert Hall, Dublin 2001–06, Dublin Int. Piano Competition 2009–. *Recordings:* Mozart's Piano Concerto No. 12, Beethoven's Piano Concerto No. 3 2000, Impromptu 2005, Schumann's Complete Works for Piano, Vol. 1 2006, Vol. 3 2009, Stanford Works for Piano and Orchestra 2010, Mozart Piano Concertos Nos. 13, 18, 20, 22 2013. *Honours:* first prize with distinction, Conservatoire de Genève, Winner, RTÉ Musician of the Future Competition 1994, winner, Classical Category, Nat. Entertainment Awards 1998, first prize, Clara Haskil Int. Piano Competition, Switzerland 1999. *Current Management:* c/o Nicholas

Curry, Clarion Seven Muses, 47 Whitehall Park, London, N19 3TW, England. *Telephone:* (20) 7272-8448. *Fax:* (20) 7281-9687. *E-mail:* nick@c7m.co.uk. *Website:* www.c7m.co.uk. *E-mail:* info@finghincollins.com (office). *Website:* www.finghincollins.com.

COLLINS, Michael Augustus, DipMus; Australian conductor and pianist; b. 16 Oct. 1948, Sydney; m. Lynette Kay Jennings 1971; two s. *Education:* CBHS, St Mary's Cathedral, Sydney, New South Wales State Conservatorium of Music, Hochschule für Musik, Vienna. *Career:* US debut at Carnegie Hall, New York aged 22; Repetiteur and Conductor, Australian Opera 1970–73; Repetiteur, Vienna Staatsoper 1974–77; Repetiteur and Conductor, Württembergische Staatsoper, Stuttgart 1977–79; Musical Dir Stuttgart Ballet 1979–84; Conductor, Bayerische Staatsoper, Munich 1984–90; Kapellmeister, Staatstheater Braunschweig; Guest Conductor, Deutsche Oper, Berlin 1990; Prin. Conductor, City of London Sinfonia 2010–; guest conductor with Philharmonia, Acad. of St Martin in the Fields, London Mozart Players, BBC Scottish Symphony Orchestra, Ulster Orchestra, Kymi Sinfonietta, Auckland Philharmonia, Tasmanian Symphony Orchestra; gave world première of Elena Kats-Chernin's clarinet concerto Ornamental Air with North Carolina Symphony Orchestra 2008; performs with own ensemble London Winds 1988–; performs with musical colleagues such as Belcea and Takács quartets, Martha Argerich, Stephen Hough, Mikhail Pletnev, Lars Vogt, Joshua Bell, Steven Isserlis. *Recordings include:* numerous recordings including Weber Concertos conducted and performed with City of London Sinfonia, British Clarinet Concertos Vol.1, with BBC Symphony Orchestra, British Clarinet Sonatas Vol. 2 recorded with pianist Michael McHale 2013. *Honours:* BBC Young Musician of the Year Competition, Royal Philharmonic Soc. Instrumentalist of the Year Award 2007. *E-mail:* michael@michael -collins.net. *Website:* www.michael-collins.co.uk; www.cityoflondonsinfonia.co .uk.

COLLINS, Michael B., BA, MA, PhD; American academic; b. 26 July 1930, Turlock, CA. *Education:* Stanford Univ. *Career:* faculty mem., Eastman School of Music 1964–68, School of Music at Univ. of North Texas, Denton 1968–2001 (retd); mem. American Musicological Soc. *Publications:* Alessandro Scarlatti's Tigrane (ed.) 1983, Opera and Vivaldi (co-ed.) 1984, Gioachino Rossini's Otello (ed.) 1994; contrib. to Dramatic Theory and the Italian Baroque Libretto, Cadential Structures and Accompanimental Practices in Eighteenth-Century Italian Recitative, Brazio Bracciolo's Orlando furioso: A History and Synopsis of the Libretto, in Opera and Vivaldi; The Performance of Sesquialtera and Hemiolia in the 16th century 1964, The Performance of Triplets in the 17th and 18th Centuries 1966, A Re-examination of Notes inégales 1967, A reconsideration of French Over-dotting, Music and Letters 1969, In Defence of the French Trill 1973, The Literary Background of Bellini's I Capuleti e i Montecchi 1982, in Journal of the American Musicological Society, Bellini and the Pasticcio alla Malibran: A Performance History of I Capuleti e I Montecchi in Note su Note 2002, Mozart's La Clemenza di Tito in the early Ottocento: The Making of a Pasticcio in Mozart-Jahrbuch 2005, Vincenzo Belli's I Capuleti e I Montecchi: Its Debut and Reception in Paris, 1833 in Note su Note 2008. *Honours:* Fulbright-Hays grant for research in Italy 1963–64. *Address:* College of Music, University of North Texas, PO Box 311367, Denton, TX 76203-1367, USA (office). *Telephone:* (940) 565-2791 (office). *Fax:* (940) 565-2002 (office). *E-mail:* mbc0019@unt.edu (office). *Website:* www.music.unt.edu (office).

COLLINS, Michael John, MBE; British clarinettist and conductor; *Principal Conductor, City of London Sinfonia;* b. 27 Jan. 1962, London. *Education:* began clarinet studies aged ten, Royal Coll. of Music, London with David Hamilton, further studies with Thea King. *Career:* Carnegie Hall debut 1984; BBC Promenade Concert debut 1984, with Thea Musgrave's Concerto; 1985 Proms season played the Copland Concerto and was soloist in Bernstein's Prelude, Fugue and Riffs; Prof., Royal Coll. of Music 1985; played the Finzi Concerto with City of London Sinfonia 1987; performances of Weber's 2nd Concerto conducted by Stanislaw Skrowaczewski and Esa-Pekka Salonen; Prin. Clarinet, Philharmonia Orchestra 1988; associated with the Takacs Quartet, The Nash Ensemble and pianists Noriko Ogawa and Kathryn Stott in chamber music; recital partnership with Mikhail Pletnev, piano; played Malcolm Arnold's 2nd Concerto at Last Night of the Proms, London 1993; Stravinsky's Ebony Concerto at South Bank, London 1999; Messiaen's Quartet for the End of Time at BBC Proms 1999; performed premiere of Riffs and Refrains by Mark-Anthony Turnage 2005; Prin. Conductor, City of London Sinfonia 2010–. *Recordings:* Finzi's Concerto, Bernstein's Prelude, Fugue and Riffs and Stravinsky's Ebony Concerto, Quintets by Mozart and Brahms with The Nash Ensemble, Weber Clarinet Concertos and Concertino (play/direct) with the City of London Sinfonia. *Honours:* BBC TV Young Musician of the Year 1978, Frederick Thurston Prize, First Prize, Leeds Nat. Competition, Amcon Award, Concert Artists' Guild of New York 1983, Instrumentalist Award, Royal Philharmonic Soc. 2007. *Current Management:* c/o Peter Railton, Hazard Chase Ltd, 48–49 Russell Square, London, WC1B 4JP, England. *Telephone:* (20) 7636-5440. *Fax:* (20) 7636-5115. *E-mail:* peter .railton@hazardchase.co.uk. *Website:* www.hazardchase.co.uk. *E-mail:* michael@michael-collins.net. *Website:* www.michael-collins.co.uk.

COLLON, Nicholas; British music conductor; *Principal Conductor and Artistic Director, Aurora Orchestra. Career:* Founder and Prin. Conductor Aurora Orchestra; debut at BBC Proms 2010, invited back each successive year with Aurora Orchestra, London Sinfonietta and Birmingham Contemporary Music Group; guest conductor with other ensembles in UK and abroad:

Philhamonia Orchestra, City of Birmingham Symphony Orchestra, London Symphony Orchestra, BBC Philharmonic, Royal Philharmonic Orchestra, Munich Chamber Orchestra, Spanish Nat. Orchestra, Orchestre Nat. d'Île de France, Bournemouth Symphony, BBC Nat. Orchestra of Wales, Northern Sinfonia, Academy of Ancient Music, Auckland Philharmonia and Ensemble Intercontemporain, London Sinfonietta, ENO, Welsh Nat. Opera, Glyndebourne; future debuts with Deutsches Symphonie-Orchester Berlin, Orchestre Nat. du Capitole de Toulouse, Orchestre de Lyon, Royal Liverpool Philharmonic Orchestra, Danish Nat. Chamber Orchestra, Deutsche Radio-Philharmonie, Trondheim Symphony, Ulster Orchestra, Warsaw Philharmonic. *Honours:* Arts Foundation Fellowship 2008, Best Ensemble Award, Royal Philharmonic Soc. Awards 2011, Critics' Circle Award for Exceptional Young Talent 2012. *Current Management:* c/o Janet Marsden, International Classical Artists, The Tower Building, 11 York Road, London, SE1 7NX, England. *Telephone:* (20) 7902-0520. *E-mail:* jmarsden@icartists.co.uk. *Website:* www.icartists.co.uk. *E-mail:* info@auroraorchestra.com (office). *Website:* www.auroraorchestra.com (office); www.nicholascollon.com.

COLOMBARA, Carlo; Italian singer (bass); b. 1964, Bologna. *Career:* debut performances include Silva in Ernani, Teatro dell'Opera, Rome, Seneca in L'Incoronazione di Poppea, Teatro Comunale, Bologna, Creon in Oedipus Rex, Teatro La Fenice, Venice; made debut at La Scala as Procida in I Vespri Siciliani 1989; other roles include Arcibaldo in L'amore dei Tre Re, Zaccaria in Nabucco, Banco in Macbeth, Giorgio in I Puritani, Don Basilio in Il Barbiere di Siviglia, Colline in La Bohème, Raimondo in Lucia di Lammermoor, Alvise Badoero in La Gioconda, Balthazar in La Favorita, Jacopo Fiesco in Simon Boccanegra, Oroveso in Norma, Conte Rodolfo in La Sonnambula, roles in Don Carlo, Aida, La Bohème, Turandot, Verdi roles include Filippo II, Fiesco, Padre Guardiano, Zaccaria, Ramphis, Giovanni da Procida; has performed worldwide for Maggio Musicale Fiorentino, Metropolitan Opera, Chicago Lyric Opera, New National Theatre, Tokyo, New Israeli Opera, Zurich Opernhaus, Bayerische Staatsoper, Arena di Verona, Teatro del Liceu, Barcelona, Deutsche Oper Berlin, Bayerische Staatsoper, Orchestre du Capitole, Toulouse. *Recordings:* solo: Musica Proibita, Opera Arias; operas: La Sonnambula, La Gioconda, Lucia di Lammermoor, Il Trovatore, La Favorite, Handel's Rinaldo, I Masnadieri, La Bohème, Turandot, Stabat Mater, Messa da Requiem, Simon Boccanegra. *Honours:* winner G.B. Viotti International Competition, Vercelli 1986, As.Li.Co. Competition 1987, Premio Lauri Volpi 1994, Premio Orazio Tosi 1995, Premio Cappelli 1999, Premio Matassa d'Oro 2002. *Current Management:* c/o Angelo Gabrielli, Stage Door, Via San Giorgio 4, 40121 Bologna BO, Italy. *Telephone:* (051) 262126. *Fax:* (051) 271452. *E-mail:* info@stagedoor.it. *Website:* www.stagedoor.it; www .carlocolombara.com.

COLOMBET, Pierre; French violinist; b. 1979. *Education:* St-Etienne Conservatory, Boulogne-Billancourt Conservatory, Paris Conservatory with Ysaÿe Quartet, Geneva Conservatory with Gabor Takacs, Hochschule für Musik, Berlin with Eberhardt Feldz. *Career:* mem. Quatuor Ebène (chamber music ensemble) 1999–, joined BBC New Generation Artists Scheme 2006. *Recordings include:* Haydn: Quatuors à Cordes 2006, Bartók: Quatuors 1, 2, 3 2007, Ravel, Debussy and Fauré String Quartets (ECHO Klassik Awards Recording of the Year 2009, Gramophone Awards Recording of the Year and Best Chamber Recording 2009) 2008, Brahms: Piano Quintet No. 1 and String Quartet No. 1 2009, 'Fiction' (Echo Klassik Award) 2010, Mozart: KV 138, KV 421, KV 465 (Echo Klassik Award) 2011, Mozart: Dissonances 2011, Fauré: Quintettes avec Piano, Opp. 89 & 115 2011, Felix & Fanny Mendelssohn (BBC Music Magazine Chamber Award 2014) 2013. *Honours:* First Prize, ARD Int. Competition, Munich 2004, Karl Klinger Foundation Prize, Fondation Groupe Banque Populaire Award, Belmont Prize for Contemporary Music, Fondation Forberg-Schneider 2005, Borletti-Buitoni Trust Award 2007. *Current Management:* c/o Linda Uschinski, Impresariat Simmenauer GmbH, Kurfürstendamm 211, 10719 Berlin, Germany. *Telephone:* (30) 414781717. *Fax:* (30) 414781713. *E-mail:* linda.uschinski@impresariat-simmenauer.de. *Website:* www.impresariat-simmenauer.de (office); www.quatuorebene.com (office).

COLONELLO, Attilio; Italian stage director and stage designer; b. 9 Nov. 1930, Milan. *Education:* studied with Gio Ponti and Ernesto Rogers in Milan. *Career:* designed Traviata for 1956 Florence Festival, Mefistofele at La Scala, 1958; returned to Milan for Don Pasquale, 1965 and 1973, and the premiere of Pizzetti's Clitennestra, 1965; US debut at Dallas, 1962, Otello and L'Incoronazione di Poppea, 1963; Metropolitan Opera, New York, with designs for Lucia di Lammermoor, 1964, Luisa Miller, 1968, and Il Trovatore, 1969; Designs and productions at San Carlo, Naples, 1964–88, for Roberto Devereux, Adriana Lecouvreur, Samson et Dalila, Carmen, La Gioconda and I Puritani; Verona Arena, 1962–84, with Nabucco, Cavalleria Rusticana, La Bohème, Rigoletto, La Forza del Destino, Aida, Un Ballo in Maschera and I Lombardi; Teatro Margherita, Genoa, 1991, Andrea Chénier; Directed the Italian premiere of Rossini's Le Siège de Corinthe at Genoa, 1992, Turandot at 1992 Caracalla Festival.

COLONNA, Monica; Italian singer (soprano); b. 1970, Rome. *Career:* won several int. competitions, including one organized by Opera House, Spoleto, Italy, Int. Zandonai Rovereto and Luciano Pavarotti International; debut 1994; sang in many Italian theatres, including Teatro San Carlo, Naples, Teatro Regio, Turin, Maggio Musicale, Fiorentino, Carlo Felice, Genoa, and abroad in Cologne, Lyon, Brussels, Lausanne, Edinburgh, San Francisco, Minneapolis, Chicago, Detroit, Toronto, Tel-Aviv, Tokyo and Osaka; performed at several int. festivals, including Wexford, Aix-en-Provence and Riva del Garda; has worked with conductors including Abbado, Bonynge, De Bernard, Benini, Rovaris, Lu Ya, Bychkov, Harding, Karabtcheski, Rudner; has worked with directors including Crivelli, Sequi, Gregory, Ronconi, Abbado, Brook, Degli Esposti, Krief, Zaniezcki, Martone, Micheli, Trevisan; has collaborated with artists including Luciano Pavarotti, Andrea Bocelli, Enzo Dara, Carol Vaness, Alfonso Antoniozzi, Carlo Guelfi, Roberto Servile; repertoire includes all the major Mozart roles: Donna Anna and Donna Elvira (Don Giovanni), Fiordiligi (Così fan tutte), The Countess in The Marriage of Figaro and Electra (Idomeneo); also starred as Gilda (Rigoletto by Verdi), Adina (Elisir d'amore by Donizetti), Lei (Notte di un nevrastenico by Nino Rota), Carolina (Matrimonio Segreto by Cimarosa), Lucia (The Rape of Lucretia by Benjamin Britten), Parisina (Parisina by Donizetti), Elena (Elena da Feltre by Mercadante), Agrippina (Agrippina by Handel), Adalgisa (Norma by Bellini), Mimi (La Bohème by Puccini), Violetta (La Traviata by Verdi), Madama Cortese (Viaggio a Reims by Rossini), Elena (Congiurate by Schubert), Nedda (Pagliacci by Leoncavallo), Alice (Falstaff by Verdi); collaboration with dir F. Micheli through the project 'Work Off', which combines opera with pop music, the cinema and theatre since 2009, project staged in several Italian theatres, including Teatro Sociale di Como, Teatro Pavarotti, Modena, Teatro Massimo, Palermo, Sferisterio Festival, Macerata. *Recordings include:* La notte di un nevrastenico 1997, Elena da Feltre 1998, Le congiurate di Schubert 2004. *Honours:* Winner, Modena Competition 1995, Winner, Pavarotti Competition 1995, Winner, Zandonai Competition 1995. *E-mail:* info@monicacolonna.it (office). *Website:* www.monicacolonna.it.

COLPOS, Mariana, BA, DMA; Romanian singer (soprano); b. 1965. *Education:* Bucharest Acad. *Career:* appearances at Bucharest and throughout Europe as Tosca, Aida, Butterfly, Norma, Lucia di Lammermoor and Ariadne auf Naxos; Leonora in Il Trovatore, Marguerite, Donna Elvira, Elisabeth de Valois and Mimi; season 1998 with Norma and Micaela on tour in UK with Moldovan Opera; Atelier Lyrique, Paris as Butterfly; concerts include Mozart, Verdi and Britten's Requiems; Mahler 2nd, 4th and 8th symphonies; Beethoven's 9th; radio and television broadcasts; fmr Artistic Dir Romanian National Opera House; mem. Faculty, Nat. Music Univ. of Bucharest.

COLSON, Andrée; French violinist and conductor; b. 5 Sept. 1924, Paris; d. of Georges Colson and Blanche Colson; m. Charles Meyer 1946; one s. one d. (deceased). *Education:* Conservatoire Nat. Supérieur de Musique, Acad. Chigiana, Italy. *Career:* performed at numerous festivals and concerts world-wide 1955–95; f. chamber orchestra Ensemble Instrumental Andrée Colson 1955, Les Journées Musicales Internationales de Langeais 1975–84, Disques Vernou 1972, also formed recording studio; Pres. Asscn pour la Sauvegarde de la Région de Langeais. *Recordings:* numerous recordings. *Television includes:* numerous programmes recorded for French TV Le Grand Echiquier de Jacques Chancel, Entrée des Artistes de Jacques Martin, Les Grands Maîtres de la Musique. *Honours:* Chevalier, Légion d'honneur 1994, Officier des Arts et des Lettres 1987; Grands Prix du Disque 1972, 1977. *Address:* Vau Godet, 37130 Langeais, France (home). *Telephone:* 2-47-96-80-59 (home). *E-mail:* andree.colson@orange.fr. *Website:* www.vaugodetgitetouraine.fr (home); www.disquesvernou.fr (home); www.orchestre-andreecolson.fr (home).

COMENCINI, Maurizio; Italian singer (tenor); b. 1958. *Education:* Verona Conservatory, La Scala, Milan. *Career:* has sung widely in Italy, notably as Fenton in Falstaff at Parma 1986, in Monteverdi's Ulisse in Florence 1987, and as Belfiore in Mozart's Finta Giardiniera, Alessandria 1991; further engagements at Palermo in Auber's Fra Diavolo, at Genoa 1992 as Neocles in Rossini's Siège de Corinthe and at Lucca as Donizetti's Nemorino; season 1994–95 as Nemorino and Elvino at Genoa, Rossini's Lindoro at Brescia and Almaviva at the Vienna Staatsoper; many radio and other concert engagements. *Honours:* prizewinner Toti del Monte and Maria Callas Competitions. *Current Management:* Living Art Impresariat-Paris, 21 rue Foucher-Lepelletier, 92130 Issy les Moulineaux, France. *Telephone:* (1) 40-93-05-28. *Fax:* (1) 46-38-65-54. *E-mail:* angelika.belamaric@wanadoo.fr.

COMET, Catherine; American conductor; b. Paris, France; m Michael Aiken; one d. *Education:* Conservatoire Nat. Superieur de Musique, France, Juilliard School of Music with Igor Markevitch, Pierre Boulez and Jean Fournet. *Career:* fmr Conductor, Ballet Co. of Theatre Nat. de l'Opera de Paris, Univ. of Wisconsin-Madison Symphony and Chamber Orchestras, St Louis (Mo.) Symphony Orchestra 1981–84; Assoc. Conductor, Baltimore Symphony 1984–86; Music Dir St Louis Youth Orchestra, Grand Rapids (Mich.) Symphony Orchestra 1986–98, American Symphony Orchestra 1989–92; Guest Conductor, San Diego, Boston, Chicago, San Francisco, Toronto, National, Cincinnati, Milwaukee, New Jersey, Indianapolis, Detroit, Seattle and Vancouver Symphony Orchestras, Philadelphia and Minnesota Orchestras, Buffalo and Rochester Philharmonic Orchestras, and St Paul Chamber Orchestra; has appeared in Australia, New Zealand, Singapore, China and Japan, where she conducted Century Orchestra Osaka and Orchestra of the City of Kitakyushu; US Resident Conductor, American/Soviet Youth Orchestra touring fmr Soviet Union, Europe and USA 1990; Guest Conductor with Bochum, Monchengladbach and Hannover Symphony Orchestras, Germany, Bilbao Symphony Orchestra, Spain, and Ensemble Orchestral de Paris, France; has appeared at many summer festivals, including Music Acad. of the West, Santa Barbara, Calif., Peninsula Festival, Wis., Cabrillo Music Festival, Interlochen Arts Festival, Grant Park Music Festival, Chicago, Waterloo Music Festival, New Jersey, Woodstock Mozart Festival, Ill., Peter Britt Festival, Oregon, Minnesota Orchestra's Sommer-

fest, Aspen Music Festival, Colo. *Recordings include:* three discs with Grand Rapids Symphony Orchestra on Koss Classics label. *Honours:* First Prize, Int. Young Conductors' Competition (France) 1966, Award at Dmitri Mitroupolos Int. Contest 1968, Seaver/N.E.A. Conductors' Award.

COMMAND, Michele; French singer (soprano); b. 27 Nov. 1946, Caumont. *Education:* Conservatories of Grenoble and Paris. *Career:* debutin Lyon, 1967, as Musetta in La Bohème; Toulouse 1968, as Fiordiligi; sang in Paris, at the Opéra and the Opéra-Comique, as Mozart's Donna Elvira and Fiordiligi, Gounod's Mireille, Mélisande and Portia in the premiere of Reynaldo Hahn's Le Marchand de Venise; Paris Palais des Sports 1989, as Micaela in Carmen; sang Gounod's Sapho at Saint-Etienne, 1992 (Adriana Lecouvreur and Massenet's Chimène, 1994–95); Compiègne 1996, as Cherubini's Médée. *Recordings:* Pelléas et Mélisande; Ariane et Barbe-Bleue and Fauré's Pénélope; Don Quichotte by Massenet; Orphée aux Enfers by Offenbach, Siebel in Faust; Harawi by Messiaen.

COMPARATO, Marina; Italian singer (mezzo-soprano); b. 1970, Perugia. *Education:* Florence Conservatory. *Career:* appearances as Rossini's Rosina Sesto in La Clemenza di Tito, and Siebel in Faust at Spoleto; Teatro Comunale, Florence, as Isolier in Le Comte Ory, and roles in Elektra, Rimsky's The Tale of Tsar Salten, Orfeo ed Euridice and Les Troyens 2001; Glyndebourne Festival debut 2000, as Cherubino; further engagements as Annio in La Clemenza di Tito at Ferrara, La Cenerentola and Il Viaggio a Reims at Pesaro, Monteverdi's Ulisse in Athens and Boris Godunov at Rome; Flowermaiden in Parsifal at the Opéra Bastille, Paris; concert engagements throughout Europe. *Recordings include:* Vivaldi's Juditha Triumphans (Opus 111).

CONDO, Nucci; Italian singer (mezzo-soprano); b. 15 Jan. 1938, Trieste. *Education:* studied in Rome. *Career:* sang in Vivaldi's Juditha Triumphans at the Queen Elizabeth Hall, London, 1972; New York Kennedy Center, 1972; Glyndebourne Festival, 1972–79, in Le nozze di Figaro, Falstaff, Il Ritorno d'Ulisse and Der Rosenkavalier; Cologne, 1984, as Lucia in La Gazza Ladra; La Scala, 1985, in a revival of Rossi's Orfeo; guest appearances with Netherlands Opera and at the Prague and Dubrovnik Festivals; sang as Ida in Gemma di Vergy at the Teatro Donizetti, Bergamo, 1987; sang Mozart's Marcellina at the Teatro La Fenice, Venice, 1991; concert tours of Yugoslavia, Austria and the USA. *Recordings include:* La Gazza Ladra: Rossini's Otello; Il Ritorno d'Ulisse; Mefistofele by Boito; Video of Le nozze di Figaro, Glyndebourne, 1973.

CONKLIN, John, BA, MFA; American stage designer; *Artistic Adviser, Boston Lyric Opera*; b. 22 June 1937, Hartford, Conn. *Education:* Yale Univ. *Career:* Assoc. Artistic Dir Glimmerglass Opera 1990–2008; currently Artistic Adviser, Boston Lyric Opera; Faculty mem. Tisch School of the Arts, New York Univ.; has designed sets for numerous opera cos including the Metropolitan Opera, San Francisco Opera, Lyric Opera of Chicago, Kennedy Center, Houston Grand Opera, Opera Theatre of St Louis, Seattle Opera, Santa Fe Opera, Dallas Opera, San Diego Opera, Washington Nat. Opera, ENO, London, Royal Opera, Stockholm, Bastille Opera, Paris, De Nederlandse Opera, Amsterdam, Teatro Comunale di Bologna; has designed sets on and off-Broadway as well as for regional theatres including American Repertory Theatre, Goodman Theatre, Long Wharf Theatre, Hartford Stage, Arena Stage, Guthrie Theatre, Center Stage, Baltimore, Actors Theatre of Louisville. *Honours:* Theatre Devt Fund Robert L.B. Tobin Award for Lifetime Achievement in Theatrical Design 2008, Nat. Endowment for the Arts Opera Honors 2011. *Address:* Boston Lyric Opera, 11 Avenue de Lafayette, Boston, MA 02111-1736, USA (office). *Telephone:* (617) 542-4912 (office). *Fax:* (617) 542-4913 (office). *Website:* blo.org (office).

CONLON, James Joseph, BMus; American conductor; *Music Director, Los Angeles Opera*; b. 18 March 1950, New York; s. of Joseph Conlon and Angeline Conlon; m. Jennifer Ringo; two d. *Education:* High School of Music and Art, New York and Juilliard School. *Career:* fmr faculty mem. Juilliard School of Music; since making debut with New York Philharmonic has conducted every major US orchestra and many leading European orchestras; Conductor, New York Philharmonic Orchestra 1974–, Metropolitan Opera, New York 1976–; debut at Metropolitan Opera 1976, Covent Garden 1979, Paris Opera 1982, Lyric Opera of Chicago 1988, La Scala, Milan 1993, Kirov Opera 1994; Music Dir Cincinnati May Festival 1979–, Berlin Philharmonic Orchestra 1979, Rotterdam Philharmonic Orchestra 1983–91, Ravinia Festival 2005–; Musical Advisor to Dir, Paris Opera 1995– (Prin. Conductor 1995–2004); conducted opening of Maggio Musicale, Florence 1985; Gen. Music Dir and Chief Conductor, Cologne Opera 1989–2002; Music Dir Los Angeles Opera 2006– (18); residency at Juilliard School, New York 2007–; has conducted at major int. music festivals and with numerous leading orchestras. *Recordings:* numerous works by Mozart, Liszt, Poulenc etc.; Rise and Fall of the City of Mahagonny (Grammy Awards for Best Classical Album and Best Opera Recording). *Honours:* Commdr, Ordre des Arts et Lettres 1996, Officier, Légion d'honneur 2002; numerous hon. degrees; Premio Galileo Award 2000, Grand Prix du Disque for recording of Poulenc Piano Concertos, Opera News Award 2005, Medal of the American Liszt Soc. 2008, Dushkin Award, Inst. of Chicago 2009, Lifetime Achievement Award, Istituto Italiano di Cultura 2010. *Current Management:* c/o Jonathan Brill, Opus 3 Artists, 470 Park Avenue South, 9th Floor North, New York, NY 10016, USA. *Telephone:* (212) 584-7500. *Fax:* (646) 300-8200. *E-mail:* info@opus3artists.com. *Website:* .opus3artists.com; www.jamesconlon.com.

CONNOLLY, Justin Riveagh; British composer; b. 11 Aug. 1933, London, England. *Education:* Royal Coll. of Music with Peter Racine Fricker and Adrian Boult, studied with Mel Powell. *Career:* teacher, Yale Univ. 1963–66; Prof. of Theory and Composition, Royal Coll. of Music 1966–89; mem. Asscn of Professional Composers; Liveryman Worshipful Co. of Musicians. *Compositions include:* Sonatina in Five Studies for piano, Antiphonies for orchestra, Cinquepaces for brass quintet, Poems of Wallace Stevens I and II for soprano and instruments 1967, 1970, Anima for violin and orchestra 1974, Diaphony for organ and orchestra 1977, Obbligati, Triads and Tesserae (chamber music series) 1966–89, Ceilidh for four violins 1976, Waka for mezzo-soprano and piano 1981, Sestina A and B for ensemble 1978, Verse and Prose for a cappella chorus fourfold from The Garden of Forking Paths for two pianos 1983, Ennead (Night Thoughts) for piano 1983, Spelt from Sibyl's Leaves for six solo voices and ensemble 1989, Nocturnal for flutes with piano, percussion and double bass 1990, Cantata for soprano and piano 1991, Symphony 1991, Sapphic for soprano and seven instruments 1992, Gymel A for flute and clarinet 1993, Gymel B for clarinet and cello 1995, Studies from The Garden of Forking Paths for piano 2000, Piano Trio 2000. *Honours:* Harkness Fellowship 1963–65, The Musicians' Co. Collard Fellowship 1986.

CONNOLLY, Sarah, CBE, FRCM; British singer (mezzo-soprano); b. 1963, Co. Durham, England; m. Carl Talbot 1998; one d. *Education:* Royal Coll. of Music and with David Mason and Gerald Martin Moore. *Career:* concert engagements include Mozart's Requiem under Neville Marriner, Bach's B Minor Mass with Philippe Herreweghe, at Berlin Philharmonia and Honegger's Jeanne d'Arc au Bûcher with the Royal Liverpool Philharmonic, Prom Concerts, London 1997; Wigmore Hall Recital debut with Julius Drake 1998; opera debut as Annina in Der Rosenkavalier for Welsh Nat. Opera 1994; further roles include the Messenger in Orfeo and the Fox in The Cunning Little Vixen (ENO), Charlotte in Massenet's Werther for English Touring Opera and the Musician in Manon Lescaut at the Glyndebourne Festival 1997; season 1997–98 for ENO as Handel's Xerxes, Meg in Verdi's Falstaff; Eduige in Rodelinda for Glyndebourne Touring Opera 1998; world premiere of Rime D'Amore by Matteo D'Amico conducted by Giuseppe Sinopoli in Rome 1998; Ariodante for New York City Opera 1999; Ruggiero in Handel's Alcina, ENO 1999; world premiere of Mark Anthony Turnage's The Silver Tassie, ENO 2000; sang Juno and Ino with San Francisco Opera in Handel's Semele, conducted by Charles Mackerras; role of Nerone in L'Incoronazione di Poppea at Maggio Musicale 2000; further concerts include Bach's St Matthew Passion with the Gabrieli Consort in Spain and with Herreweghe 1998; The Dream of Gerontius in Sydney and Mark Anthony Turnage's Twice Through the Heart, with Markus Stenz in Rome and London; Ravel's L'Heure espagnole at BBC Proms, London 2002; Carnegie Hall debut, Pergolesi Stabat Mater 2003; sang Dido in Dido and Aeneas at BBC Proms 2003, Annio in La Clemenza di Tito at New York Met 2003–04, title role in Giulio Cesare at Glyndebourne Festival 2005, Dido in Purcell's Dido and Aeneas at La Scala, Milan 2006, Octavian in Der Rosenkavalier at Scottish Opera 2006, Handel's Agrippina for ENO 2007; concerts: Mahler's Rückert Lieder with Mark Elder and the Hallé Orchestra, Bridgewater Hall 2006, Mahler's Das Lied von der Erde with Daniel Harding and Concertgebouw Orchestra 2006, Handel's Solomon with Akad. für Alte Musik, Berlin Philharmonie 2006; Octavian in Der Rosenkavalier, ENO 2012 and title role in Medea, ENO 2012; Nerone in L'Incoronazione di Poppea, Festival Enescu, Bucharest 2015; title role in Ariodante, Nat. Opera, Amsterdam 2016. *Recordings include:* Bach Cantatas with Philippe Herreweghe, Les Fêtes d'Hebé by Rameau with Les Arts Florissants and Juditha Triumphans, Vivaldi with the King's Consort, The Exquisite Hour 2006, Sea Pictures: The Music Makers 2006, Mahler Das Knaben Wunderhorn with Dietrich Henschel (Edison Classical Music Award for Best Vocals 2007) 2006, Mozart Mass in C Minor with Paul McCreesh and Gabrieli Consort, Music by John Taverner in film Children of Men 2006, Handel Arias 'Heroes and Heroines' with Harry Christophers and Orchestra of Harmony and Invention, Handel's Solomon with Akad. für Alte Musik, Berlin, Purcell: Dido and Aeneas 2009, Handel: Duets (with Rosemary Joshua) 2010, Britten: A Charm of Lullabies 2011, Elgar The Dream of Gerontius/Sea Pictures (Gramophone Award for Best Choral Recording 2015) 2014. *Honours:* prizewinner, opera section of the 's-Hertogenbosch Competition, Netherlands 1994, Gramophone Award for Baroque Opera 1998. *Address:* c/o Chandos Records Ltd, Chandos House, 1 Commerce Park, Commerce Way, Colchester, Essex, CO2 8HX, England (office). *Telephone:* (1206) 225200 (office). *Fax:* (1206) 225201 (office). *E-mail:* enquiries@chandos.net (office). *Website:* www.chandos.net (office); www.sarah-connolly.com (home).

CONNOLLY, Stephen; British singer (bass); *Head of Vocal Studies, Cheltenham Ladies' College;* b. Yorkshire; two c. *Education:* Guildhall School of Music and Drama. *Career:* mem. The King's Singers 1987–2010, also Co-Dir; has performed at venues including Concertgebouw, Amsterdam, Carnegie Hall, New York, Royal Albert Hall, London, Kennedy Center, Washington, DC, and Suntory Hall, Tokyo; Musical Dir, Int. A Cappella School; Head of Vocal Studies, Cheltenham Ladies' Coll. 2010–. *Recordings:* with The King's Singers: 1605: Treason and Dischord 2005, Sacred Bridges 2005, Six 2005, Thomas Tallis Spem in Alium 2006, Landscape & Time 2006, The Quiet Heart 2007, Live at the Proms 2008, The Golden Age 2008, Simple Gifts (Grammy Award) 2008, Reflections 2008, Romance du Soir 2009, Swimming over London 2010. *Address:* Music Department, Cheltenham Ladies' College, Bayshill Road, Cheltenham, Gloucestershire, GL50 3EP, England (office). *Fax:* (1242) 227882 (office). *Website:* www.cheltladiescollege.org (office).

CONRAD, Barbara; American singer (mezzo-soprano); b. 11 Aug. 1945, Pittsburg, Tex. *Education:* Univ. of Texas. *Career:* operatic debut as Bess in New York City Opera's production of Porgy and Bess 1965; debut at Frankfurt Opera 1978, at Vienna Statsoper 1982 as Azucena in Il Trovatore; with Metropolitan Opera from 1982, as Verdi's Preziosilla and Maddalena, Annina in Der Rosenkavalier and Maria in Porgy and Bess; European engagements at Frankfurt, Vienna, Brussels and Munich; sang at Greater Miami Opera 1989; other roles include Wagner's Fricka and Verdi's Azucena and Eboli; mem. College of Fine Arts Advisory Council, Univ. of Texas 1988–89; Founding Dir American Center For Musical Arts. *Television:* performed as Marian Anderson in Eleanor and Franklin: The White House Years 1976. *Recordings include:* Hamlet (Thomas) and Porgy and Bess. *Honours:* Univ. of Texas Distinguished Alumni Award 1985, Texas Medal of Arts Award for lifetime achievement, Texas Cultural Trust 2011. *E-mail:* JMayer@janicemayer.com. *Website:* www.barbaraconrad.com.

CONSOLI, Marc-Antonio, BMus, MMus, DMA; American/Italian composer, conductor, editor and academic; *Associate Professor of Composition, New York University;* b. 19 May 1941, Italy; partner Jean Feinberg. *Education:* studied with Ernst Krenek, Gunther Schüller, George Crumb. *Career:* commissioned by Fromm and Koussevitsky Foundations, and contemporary music festivals in Royan, France and Steirischer Herbst of Austria; works performed at int. festivals, including Int. Soc. for Contemporary Music in Helsinki 1978, Belgium 1981, New York Philharmonic and Los Angeles Philharmonic; Assoc. Prof. of Composition, New York Univ. 1980–; mem. BMA, American Composers' Alliance. *Compositions include:* Sciuri Novi, Interactions I, II, III, IV, V 1970–71, Isonic 1971, Lux Aeterna 1972, Music for Chambers 1974, Sciuri Novi II 1974, Canti Trinacriani for baritone and chamber orchestra 1976, Memorie Pie 1976, Tre Canzoni 1976, Odefonia 1976, Tre Fiori Musicali 1987, Vuci Siculani 1979, Naked Masks for orchestra 1980, Three Elegies for soprano and orchestra 1981, Orpheus Meditation 1981, The Last Unicorn for orchestra 1981, Afterimages for orchestra 1982, String Quartet 1983, Ancient Greek Lyrics 1985, Musiculi II for female voices and orchestra 1985–86, Reflections 1986, Eyes of the Peacock 1987, Cello Concerto 1988, Greek Lyrics 1988, String Quartet II 1989, Musiculi IV for chorus and orchestra 1990, Musiculi III for orchestra 1992, Games for 2 and 3 1994, Games for 4 1995, Cinque Canti 1995, Varie Azioni 1995, Di-ver-ti-mento 1995, Collected Moments 1996, Sciuri Novi III 1996, Pensieri Sospesi 1997, Rounds and Relays 1997, Varie Azioni II 1998, Varie Azioni III 1999, Passaggi Obbligati (chamber opera) 2000–04, Estratti Obbligati I, II, III 2001, Night Whispers 2002, Varie Azioni IV 2004, Sciuri Novi IV 2004, Collected Moments II 2005, Riti Sicani 2005, Varie Azioni V 2006, U Pupu 'Nnamuratu (ballet) 2007, Musiculi I 2008, El Secreto de Exael 2008, Lunch with Moto (chamber opera) 2009, Two Abstractions 2010, The Divine Crossing (opera in three acts) 2010–11, The Return (opera in four scenes) 2013, The Red Mole (opera in four scenes) 2014. *Honours:* Guggenheim Memorial Fellowships 1971, 1979, Fulbright Scholarship to Poland 1972–74, Nat. Endowment for the Arts grants 1976, 1979, competition prize, Monaco. *Address:* 590 Old Route 82, Craryville, NY 12521, USA (home). *E-mail:* mc29@nyu.edu (office).

CONSTABLE, John Robert, LRAM, FRAM, RAM; British pianist and harpsichordist; b. 5 Oct. 1934, Sunbury-on-Thames, Middx, England; m. Katharine Ingham; two d. *Education:* Royal Acad. of Music, London with Harold Craxton. *Career:* repetiteur, Royal Opera House, Covent Garden, London 1960–72; principal keyboard player, London Sinfonietta since its formation; Prin. Harpsichordist, Acad. of St Martin-in-the-Fields 1984–; Prof., Royal Coll. of Music 1985–; mem. Incorporated Soc. of Music, Musicians' Union. *Recordings:* numerous recordings with London Sinfonietta and Acad. of St Martin-in-the-Fields, playing harpsichord continuo for operas and as accompanist on recital records. *Address:* 13 Denbigh Terrace, London, W11 2QJ, England (home). *Telephone:* (20) 7229-4603 (home). *E-mail:* jkconstable@tiscali.co.uk.

CONSTANTINE, Andrew; British conductor; *Music Director, Reading Symphony Orchestra;* b. 1964, England. *Education:* Accademia Chigiana, Siena, also at Turin Opera and St Petersburg Conservatoire. *Career:* engagements from 1991 with the London Philharmonic in Prokofiev's 5th Symphony, the Hallé and English Chamber Orchestras, the Royal Philharmonic Orchestra and London Mozart Players; Asst Conductor, ENO's Madama Butterfly and Principal Conductor, Sinfonia of Birmingham; further appearances with the St Petersburg and Sofia Philharmonics and the Komische Opera, Berlin; Asst Conductor, Baltimore Symphony Orchestra 2004, Assoc. Conductor 2004–07; Music Dir, Reading Symphony Orchestra, Pennsylvania 2007–. *Honours:* Hon. DMus (Univ. of Leicester); winner Donatella Flick Conducting Competition, London 1991. *Address:* Reading Symphony Orchestra, 147 North 5th Street, Suite 4, Reading, PA 19601-3401, USA (office). *Telephone:* (610) 373-7557 (office). *E-mail:* info@readingsymphony.org (office); constantine2000@comcast.net (office). *Website:* www.readingsymphony.org (office); www.andrewconstantine.com.

CONTE, David, BM, MFA, DMA; American composer and teacher; *Chair and Professor of Composition, San Francisco Conservatory of Music;* b. 20 Dec. 1955, Denver, Colo; s. of Cosmo Conte and Nancy Conte; partner Jacob Lake. *Education:* Bowling Green State Univ., Cornell Univ., studies with Nadia Boulanger in Paris. *Career:* fmr mem. Faculty, Cornell Univ., Colgate Univ., Interlochen Centre for the Arts; Composer-in-Residence, Thick Description theatre co. 1990–; currently Chair and Prof. of Composition, San Francisco Conservatory of Music; Composition faculty, European American Musical

Alliance, Paris; mem. Bd American Composers Forum; mem. The American Soc. of Composers, Authors and Publrs. *Compositions include:* opera: The Dreamers, The Gift of the Magi, Firebird Motel, America Tropical, Famous, Stonewall; musical: The Passion of Rita St James 2003; film scores: Ballets Russes, Orozco: Man of Fire (PBS documentary); instrumental: Sinfonietta for classical orchestra, Of a Summer Evening for guitar duo, Marian Variations for harp, Fantasy for piano, Piano Trio, Cello Sonata, Piano Quintet, Sonatine for piano; organ: Antiphon for organ, two trumpets and two trombones, Christmas Intrada for organ, Meditation on Silent Night for organ, Pastorale and Toccata for organ, Prelude and Fugue for organ, Recollection for organ, Soliloquy for organ; vocal and chorus: Sexton Songs, Three Poems of Christina Rossetti, Everyone Sang (four songs for baritone and piano), Alleluia, Ave Maria, Blessing, Candles in the Wilderness, Cantate Domino, Celia Singing, Charm Me Asleep, The Composer, Elegy for Matthew, An Exhortation, The Great Spirit of Love, The Homecoming, Hosanna, I Love the Lord, In Praise of Music, Invocation and Dance, Irish Blessing, The Nine Muses, Nunc Dimittis, Prayer of St Teresa, O Magnum Mysterium, O Sun, Psalm 121, September Sun, Set Me As a Seal, Silent Night, The Snow Lay on the Ground, A Stable-Lamp is Lighted, Three Sacred Places, Two Hymns in Honor of the Blessed Sacrament, Valediction, The Waking. *Honours:* Fulbright Scholarship 1976, Meet the Composer grant 1983–95, Ralph Vaughan Williams Fellowship, Aspen Music Festival Conducting Fellow, Gerbode Foundation Grant 2004, ACDA Raymond Brock Commission 2007. *Current Management:* c/o ECS Publishing Corporation, 615 Concord Street, Framingham, MA 01702, USA. *Telephone:* (508) 620-7400. *Fax:* (508) 620-7401. *E-mail:* office@ecspub.com. *Website:* ecspublishing.com. *Address:* Department of Composition, San Francisco Conservatory of Music, 50 Oak Street, San Francisco, CA 94102-6011, USA (office). *Telephone:* (415) 863-2070 (office). *E-mail:* davidconte@comcast.net (office). *Website:* www.davidconte.net.

CONTE, Rosario; Italian musician (lute); b. 1966, Taranto. *Education:* N. Piccinni Conservatoire, Bari, Schola Cantorum Basiliensis, Switzerland, studied with Hopkinson Smith. *Career:* mem. period instrument ensembles including Kammerorchester Basel, Accademia Bizantina, Balthasar-Neumann Ensemble, and Freiburger Barockorchester; teacher (lute, theorbo, baroque guitar and basso continuo), N. Piccinni Conservatoire, Bari 2007–. *Recordings:* Une Larme 2010, Piccinini: Works for archlute 2012, L'Univers de Marin Marais 2013, Paganini: La Lanterna Magica 2013. *Address:* Conservatorio di Musica N. Piccinni, Via Cifarelli 26, 70124 Bari, Italy (office). *Website:* nuke.conservatoriopiccinni.it (office).

CONTI, Nicoletta, BMus, MMus; Italian conductor, pianist and academic; *Professor, Bologna Conservatory*; b. 12 July 1957, Bologna. *Education:* Univ. of Bologna, Conservatorio di Musica G.B. Martini, Bologna, Conservatorio Giuseppe Verdi, Milan, Accad. Santa Cecilia, Rome, Tanglewood Music Center, USA. *Career:* debut at Liszt Acad., Budapest 1984; at Aspen Music Festival 1984, Tanglewood Music Center 1985; has made appearances with Orchestra Sinfonica di Bari, Orchestra Regionale Toscana, Orchestra Simphonia Perusina, Orchestra Sinfonica Abrudiese, Orchestra Pro Musica Riminia, Danish Radio Orchestra, Orchestra Arturo Toscanini, Orchestra of the Arena di Verona, the Kyushu Symphony Orchestra, the Hungarian Symphonic Orchestra, Orchestra Sinfonica Città di Ferrara, Orchestra da Camera di Bologna, Orchestra 'I Filarmonici di Bologna', Orchestra Filarmonica di Torino, Orchestra 'I Pomeriggi Musicali di Milano', Stuttgarter Filarmoniker, Tokyo Philharmonic Orchestra, Orchestra Toscanini; Asst Conductor to Antonio Pappano 2000–01, to Georges Prêtre 2002; Prof., Bologna Conservatory; opera masterclasses. *Honours:* Cavaliere della Repubblica Italiana 2006; Concorso da Camera Stresa 1981, Malko Competition for Young Conductors 1986, Minerva Prize for the Arts. *Address:* Via De'Marchi 29, 40123 Bologna, Italy (home). *Telephone:* (051) 334876 (home); 338-9326081 (mobile) (office). *E-mail:* nicolettacnt@gmail.com (home). *Website:* www.nicolettaconti.com.

CONTIGUGLIA, John Joseph, BA, MMus; American pianist; b. 13 April 1937, Auburn, NY; s. of Anthony John Contiguglia and Ida Berrena Contiguglia; twin brother of Richard Contiguglia. *Education:* Yale Univ. and Yale School of Music, studied piano with Dame Myra Hess in London. *Career:* duo recital aged six with brother, Richard; professional debut, Wigmore Hall, London 1962; performed throughout the world as a virtuoso duo; repertoire includes works from the past to contemporary scores, with special emphasis on the piano transcriptions of Liszt; performed with orchestras worldwide, including the Cleveland Orchestra, Pittsburgh Symphony, Atlanta Symphony, National Symphony, Toronto Symphony, Boston Pops Orchestra, Netherlands Chamber Orchestra, Rotterdam Philharmonic and Orquesta Filarmónica de la Ciudad de México; co-founder recording co., Gemini CD Classics LLC. *Recordings include:* Beethoven's 9th Symphony (transcribed for two pianos by Franz Liszt) (Grand Prix Liszt Soc. of Budapest), Schubert Piano Duets: The Final Year, Live from The Holland Liszt Festival: Duos for two pianos and piano four-hands by Franz Liszt, Gershwin. *Honours:* Yale Univ. Charles Seymour Prize. *Address:* 2109 Broadway, Suite 4-43, New York, NY 10023, USA (home). *Telephone:* (212) 874-7227 (home). *Fax:* (212) 874-7227 (home). *E-mail:* Contig@earthlink.net (home). *Website:* www.duopianistscontiguglia.com.

CONTIGUGLIA, Richard, BA, MMus; American pianist; b. 13 April 1937, Auburn, NY; s. of Anthony John Contiguglia and Ida Berrena; twin brother of John Contiguglia. *Education:* Yale Univ., studied with Dame Myra Hess in London. *Career:* duo recital aged six with brother, John; professional debut, Wigmore Hall, London 1962; performed world-wide as a virtuoso duo, including Myra Hess Day, Nat. Gallery, London 2008; appeared in Townsville Chamber Music Festival, Australia 2011; performed in Budapest during Award Presentation Ceremony of Liszt Soc. 2012; repertoire includes works from the past to contemporary scores, with special emphasis on the duos of Bartók, Percy Grainger and two-piano, four-hand piano transcriptions of Liszt, four-hand music of Schubert; performed with orchestras world-wide, including the Cleveland Orchestra, Pittsburgh Symphony, Atlanta Symphony, Nat. Symphony, Seattle Symphony, Toronto Symphony, Boston Pops Orchestra, Netherlands Chamber Orchestra, Rotterdam Philharmonic, Amsterdam Philharmonic and Orquesta Filarmónica de la Ciudad de México; Founder, with brother John, of Adams Foundation Piano Recital Series; Co-founder Gemini CD Classics LLC recording co. *Recordings include:* albums: Beethoven's 9th Symphony, Franz Liszt piano transcription (first-ever recording) (Grand Prix Liszt Soc. of Budapest), Schubert Piano Duets: The Final Year, Live from The Holland Liszt Festival: Duos for two pianos and piano four-hands by Franz Liszt, Gershwin – Grainger, Liszt Operatic Transcriptions and Bartok Suite, Op. 4b (Grand Prix Liszt Soc. of Budapest). *Honours:* Charles Seymour Prize, Yale Univ. *Address:* 2109 Broadway, Suite 6-137, New York, NY 10023, USA. *Telephone:* (212) 724-3972. *E-mail:* rcontiguglia@nyc.rr.com. *Website:* www.duopianistscontiguglia.com.

CONVERY, Robert, BMus, MMus, DMus; American composer; b. 4 Oct. 1954, Wichita, Kan. *Education:* Westminster Choir Coll., Curtis Inst. of Music, Juilliard School; studied with David Diamond, Vincent Persichetti, Ned Rorem and Richard Hundley. *Career:* Resident Composer with Phillips Exeter Acad. 1988, 1991, Dickinson Coll. 1989–90, New York Concert Singers 1991–93; commissions from The Pew Charitable Trusts, Nat. Endowment for the Arts, Opera America, The Rockefeller Foundation, Scandia Symphony, Charleston Symphony, Pro Arte Singers, Musica Sacra, Lesbian and Gay Chorus of Washington, DC, The Bridge Ensemble, Chorale Arts Soc. of Philadelphia, Virginia Chorale, Singing City Choir of Philadelphia, Opera Ebony, O'Neill Theatre Center, Renaissance City Choir, Music Group of Philadelphia; visiting composer appointments at Juilliard School, Columbia Univ., Ithaca Coll., Georgetown Univ., Univ. of Maryland at College Park, Roosevelt Univ., Catholic Univ., Washington and Lee Univ., California State Univ. at Chico, New World School for the Arts, Millersville Univ. *Compositions:* Pyramus and Thisbe, two scenes after Shakespeare (Charles E. Ives Award) 1983, Five Madrigals (Shakespeare) for SATB a cappella 1985, The Blanket, opera in one act 1986, I Have a Dream, cantata for baritone solo, choir, string orchestra 1986, Five carols of the Nativity, cantata for mezzo soprano solo and orchestra 1987, Songs of Children, cantata for choir, strings, piano 1991, The Nativity of Our Lord, cantata for choir, cello and harp 1993, To the One of Fictive Music, cantata for choir, strings, piano 1995, Search, cantata for choir and piano 1998, Clara, opera in five scenes 2004, Not About Cheese, cantata for choir and piano 2004, Glory to the Child, cantata for choir and orchestra 2005, The Owl and the Nightingale, opera in one act 2007, Five Settings of Robert Louis Stevenson, song cycle 2007, Under the Greenwood Tree, cantata for choir and piano 2009, Five Settings of Christina Rossetti, song cycle 2009, As Rivers Seek the Sea, cantata for soprano solo, choir, strings and piano 2010. *Honours:* Charles Miller-Alfredo Casella Award, Samuel Barber Award, Richard Rodgers Fellowship. *Address:* c/o ASCAP, ASCAP Building, 1 Lincoln Plaza, New York, NY 10023, USA (office). *E-mail:* robertconvery@earthlink.net (home).

CONWELL, Julia; American singer (soprano); b. 1954, Philadelphia, Pa; m. Giancarlo del Monaco. *Education:* Curtis Inst. of Music, studied with Margaret Harshaw. *Career:* sang in various US opera houses, notably as Musetta in La Bohème for Michigan Opera; European debut with Munich Staatsoper as Musetta; further appearances as Nedda in Pagliacci, Liu in Turandot, Düsseldorf 1982, and Oscar in Ballo in Maschera, Frankfurt 1984; sang Charpentier's Louise at Nice and Zerlina at Rome 1984; other roles have included Paolina in Poliuto by Donizetti, Rome 1986; Gilda and Salome at Augsburg 1988, and Diana in Iphigénie en Tauride, Deutsche Oper Berlin; mem., Stuttgart Staatsoper from 1985. *Recordings include:* Sandrina in La Finta Giardiniera, Euridice in Orfeo by Gluck, Works by Henze.

CONYNGHAM, Barry Ernest, AM, MA, DMus; Australian composer; b. 27 Aug. 1944, Sydney, NSW. *Education:* Univ. of Sydney, Univ. of California, San Diego, USA and Univ. of Melbourne. *Career:* part-time Lecturer and Tutor, Univ. of New South Wales and Nat. Inst. of Dramatic Art 1968–70; Sr Tutor, Univ. of Western Australia 1971; postdoctoral position, Univ. of California, San Diego 1972–73; Visiting Fellow, Princeton Univ. 1973–74; Composer and researcher-in-residence, Univ. of Aix-Marseille 1974–75; Lecturer, Univ. of Melbourne 1975–79, Sr Lecturer 1979–84, Reader 1984–89; Dean Creative Arts, Univ. of Wollongong 1989–94; Vice-Chancellor, Southern Cross Univ. 1994–; bd mem., Playbox Theatre Co.; Deputy Chair., Opera Australia 1995–. *Compositions:* Crisis: Thoughts in a City 1968, The Little Sheriff 1969, Five Windows 1969, Three 1969, Five 1970, Water... Footsteps... Time 1970, Ice Carving 1970, Edward John Eyre 1971–73, Six 1971, Playback 1972, Without Gesture 1973, From Voss 1973, Snowflake 1973, Ned 1974–77, Mirror Images 1975, Sky 1977, Apology of Bony Anderson 1978, Mirages 1978, Bony Anderson 1978, Concerto for double bass 1979, Basho 1980, Journeys 1980, Viola 1981, Imaginary Letters 1981, Horizons: Concerto for orchestra, Dwellings 1982, Fly 1982–84, Voicings 1983, Cello Concerto 1984, Preview 1984, Antipodes 1984–85, The Oath of Bad Brown Bill 1985, Generations 1985, Recurrences 1986, Vast I: The Sea, II: The Coast, III: The Centre, IV:

The Cities 1987, Glimpses 1987, Bennelong 1988, Matilda 1988, Streams 1988, Monuments: Piano Concerto 1989, Waterways: Viola Concerto 1990, Cloudlines: Harp Concerto 1990, Southern Cross: Concerto for violin and piano 1991, Decades for orchestra 1993, Alterimages for koto and orchestra 1994, Dawning 1996, Nostalgia 1997, Passing 1998, Yearnings 1999, String Quartet 2 1999. *Honours:* Churchill Fellowship 1970, Harkness Fellowship 1972–74, Australia Council Fellowship 1975, Fulbright Sr Fellowship 1982.

COOK, Brian (Robert) Rayner, BA, ARCM (Hons); British singer (baritone); b. 17 May 1945, London; s. of Robert Cook and Gladys Soulby; m. Angela M. Romney 1974; one s. one d. *Education:* Univ. of Bristol, Royal Coll. of Music and privately with Alexander Young (vocal studies) and Helga Mott (repertoire). *Career:* church organist and choirmaster aged 15; major conducting debut (opera) 1966; professional singing debut 1967; has appeared as soloist in oratorio, recitals, music-theatre and opera throughout the UK, Europe, USA, Canada, S America, the Middle East, the Far East and N Africa and has broadcast frequently in UK, Europe and many other countries; has given first performances of various works written for him by distinguished composers; dir singers' workshops, jury mem. int. singing competitions and specialist adjudicator; Visiting Tutor in Vocal Studies and Postgraduate Examiner, Birmingham Conservatoire 1980–99; fmrly Tutor Welsh Coll. of Music and Drama, Cardiff; Specialist Univ. Music Assessor, Higher Educ. Funding Councils of England and of Wales 1994–95; contrib. to RCM Magazine, Music and Musicians. *Recordings include:* opera, oratorio and songs by Schütz, Charpentier, Adam, Fauré, Schumann, Dvořák, Nielsen, Orff, Camilleri, Sullivan, Parry, Elgar, Delius, Butterworth, Vaughan Williams, Holst, Havergal Brian, Coates, Poston, Rubbra, Cruft, Walton, Ferguson and Williamson. *Television:* professional solo debut (BBC) 1970; has since appeared in televised concerts in many European countries in works ranging from Mozart's Requiem to Mahler's 8th Symphony. *Honours:* Kathleen Ferrier Memorial Scholarship 1969 and many other major singing prizes. *Address:* The Quavers, 53 Friars Avenue, Friern Barnet, London, N20 0XG, England. *Telephone:* (20) 8368-3010.

COOK, Deborah; American singer (soprano); b. 6 July 1948, Philadelphia, PA; m. Ronald Marlowe 1985; one s. *Education:* studied with Irene Williams. *Career:* debut, Operatic-Glyndebourne and Covent Garden; Glyndebourne Touring Opera, 1971, as Zerbinetta; 3 years principal soprano in Bremen, 2 years Munich National Theatre; Sang in Sydney, Melbourne, Barcelona, Edinburgh, Geneva, Rome, Paris, Los Angeles, San Francisco, Leipzig, East Berlin; Appeared at Covent Garden Opera House, Hamburg State Opera (from 1981), Deutsche Oper Berlin, Frankfurt Opera, Stuttgart Opera, Deutsche Oper am Rhein; Bonn Opera, 1984–85; Roles include Verdi's Gilda, Strauss's Zerbinetta, Donizetti's Lucia and Mozart's Queen of Night and Constanze; Created role of Rachel in Henze's We Come to the River, Covent Garden, 1976, and Angel of Bright Future in Rochberg's The Confidence Man; Sang Lucia di Lammermoor at the Buxton Festival, 1979. *Recordings:* Dinorah; Ariadne auf Naxos; L'Etoile du Nord.

COOK, Edward; American singer (tenor); b. 30 June 1954, Oxnard, CA. *Education:* New England Conservatory, Boston, studied at Bloomington and with James King. *Career:* sang Gianni Schicchi, Rossini's Figaro and other baritone roles; Froh in Das Rheingold at the Metropolitan; Miami Opera as Siegmund in Die Walküre 1990; further Wagner roles include Parsifal at Wuppertal and Schwerin 1994–95; Siegfried at Essen 1996; Siegmund and Siegfried at Karlsruhe 1994–95; further engagements at Rome and Turin as Gluck's Orestes and Festival Hall, London, as Florestan; other roles include Idomeneo and Strauss's Bacchus.

COOK, Jeff Holland, BM, MA, MM; American music director, conductor and composer; b. 21 Aug. 1940, Chicago, IL; m. Kate Young, 12 May 1974, 1 d. *Education:* Northwestern Univ., Ohio State Univ., New England Conservatory of Music, studied with Pierre Boulez, John Barbirolli, Jean Fournet, Bruno Maderna, Herbert von Karajan, Erich Leinsdorf, Karlheinz Stockhausen, György Ligeti. *Career:* Music Dir and Conductor, Wheeling Symphony Orchestra 1973–85; Music Dir and Conductor, Mansfield Symphony Orchestra, OH 1976–; Assoc. Conductor, Pittsburgh Ballet Theatre 1987–91; Conductor, Louisville Ballet, Kentucky 1990–; guest conductor with Anchorage Symphony, Eastern Music Festival, Rhode Island Philharmonic, North Carolina Symphony, Orquesta Sinfonica Nacional (Santo Domingo), Ballet of Ljubljana (Slovenia), North Bay Music Festival (Ontario). *Compositions include:* Euripides Electra 1972.

COOK, Terry; American singer (bass); b. 9 Feb. 1956, Plainville, TX. *Education:* Texas University. *Career:* sang with the Chicago Lyric Opera from 1980, at Santa Fe (Festival) from 1982, and at the Metropolitan from 1983; Roles have included Dr Grenvil in Traviata, Ferrando, the King in Aida, Oroe in Semiramide and Gershwin's Porgy; Further engagements at Seattle 1985, Théâtre Châtelet, Paris (in Handel's Rinaldo), at the Grand Opéra Paris as Colline in La Bohème and the Opéra-Comique as the Speaker in Die Zauberflöte; Other roles include Achillas in Giulio Cesare, Raimondo in Lucia di Lammermoor and the Minister in Fidelio; sang Oroe in Semiramide at Dallas, 1993; sang Crown in Porgy and Bess at Munich, 2000; many concert appearances. *Current Management:* Thea Dispeker Inc., 59 East 54th Street, Suite 81, New York, NY 10022, USA. *Telephone:* (212) 421-7676. *Fax:* (212) 935-3279. *E-mail:* info@dispeker.com. *Website:* www.dispeker.com.

COOK-MacDONALD, Linda; American singer (soprano); b. 22 Sept. 1947, Twin Falls, Idaho. *Education:* studied in Cincinnati and Mainz. *Career:* debut,

Krefeld, 1971, as Fiordiligi; Sang at such German houses as Krefeld, Wuppertal, Essen and Darmstadt; US appearances at Memphis, Cincinnati, Pittsburgh and Portland; Sang in New York at City Opera; Roles have included Mozart's Constanze, Pamina, Queen of Night and Zerlina, Agathe, Alice Ford, Marguerite, Musetta and Zdenka; Modern repertory has included Thalmar in Leben des Orest by Krenek and Philippe in Penderecki's The Devils of Loudun; many concert appearances.

COOKE, Mervyn John, BA, MPhil, MA, PhD; British composer, musicologist and pianist; *Professor of Music, University of Nottingham*; b. 29 Aug. 1963, Dover, Kent. *Education:* Royal Acad. of Music, London, King's Coll., Cambridge. *Career:* Research Fellow, Fitzwilliam Coll., Cambridge 1987–93; Lecturer in Music, Univ. of Nottingham 1993, Head of Music Dept 1998, Prof. of Music 2000–. *Compositions:* Symphonic Poem Messalina (BBC Concert Orchestra, Radio 3) 1979, Horn Sonata (BBC Radio 3) 1986, incidental scores for Cambridge and Oxford Greek Plays 1983, 1989, 2008, Sixes and Sevens, for soprano saxophone and piano 2013. *Publications include:* Britten and the Gamelan (chapter in Death in Venice, ed by Donald Mitchell) 1987, Britten: Billy Budd 1993, Britten: War Requiem 1996, The Chronicle of Jazz 1997, Britten and the Far East 1998, Jazz 1998, The Cambridge Companion to Benjamin Britten 1999, The Cambridge Companion to Jazz 2002, Letters from a Life: Selected Letters of Benjamin Britten, Vols 3–6 (co-ed) 2004–12, The Cambridge Companion to Twentieth-Century Opera (ed.) 2005, A History of Film Music 2008, The Hollywood Film Music Reader 2010; contrib. to Musical Times, Journal of Musicological Research, Journal of the Royal Musical Association, Music and Letters, Journal of the American Musicological Society, Music Analysis. *Address:* Department of Music, University of Nottingham, Nottingham, NG7 2RD, England (office). *Telephone:* (115) 951-4762 (office). *E-mail:* mervyn.cooke@nottingham.ac.uk (office).

COOKE, Richard; British conductor; b. 1958, England. *Education:* chorister St Paul's Cathedral, King's Coll., Cambridge (choral scholar) with David Willcocks. *Career:* conducted various univ. orchestras; led the chamber ensemble in the War Requiem at the Festival Hall 1984; trained the London Philharmonic Choir in Mahler 8 and for The Kingdom by Elgar; has conducted concerts at the Albert and Festival Halls and throughout South East England; Gothenburg Symphony Orchestra from 1989 in Belshazzar's Feast, the Glagolitic Mass, Dvořák 6 and the Sea Symphony by Vaughan Williams; has also conducted the Brahms Requiem, A Child of Our Time, Monteverdi's Vespers and St Nicolas in Sweden; Verdi Requiem at the Uppsala International Festival 1990, and in Boulogne and Canterbury; Conductor, Chalmers Music Weeks in Sweden; Artistic Dir, St Columb Festival in Cornwall. *Recordings include:* Mahler 8th Symphony and The Kingdom, with the London Philharmonic Choir.

COOKE, Sasha; American singer (mezzo-soprano) and conductor; b. 1982, d. of Brett Cooke and Olga Cooke. *Education:* Rice Univ., Juilliard School. *Career:* completed Young Artist Devt Program, Metropolitan Opera 2009; debuted with many symphony orchestras 2009–10 season including Milwaukee, Hong Kong, Dallas, Colorado, Seattle, Kansas City, San Diego, San Francisco; also appearances with Seattle Opera, Chicago Opera Theatre; concerts as soloist in 2010–11 season include appearances with Deutsches Symphonie-Orchester Berlin, Baltimore Symphony Orchestra, St Paul Chamber Orchestra, Los Angeles Chamber Orchestra, Edmonton Symphony, Houston Symphony, Kansas City Symphony and Seattle Symphony; recitals include appearances at Kennedy Center, Merkin Concert Hall, Univ. of Minnesota, Carnegie Hall, Wigmore Hall, London; operatic appearances include: Doctor Atomic, Falstaff, Giasone, Carmen, Pelléas et Mélisande, Aspern Papers, The Gospel of Mary Magdalene. *Honours:* Rhoda Walker Teagle Debut Prize, Fergus First Prize, Mortimer Levitt Devt Award for Women Artists, Swiss Global Foundation Award, Buffalo Chamber Music Soc. Prize, Embassy Series Prize, Lied Center of Kansas Prize, Orchestra of New England Soloist Prize, Univ. of Georgia Performing Arts Prize, First Prize, Bach Vocal Competition 2005, First Prize, Young Concert Artist Int. 2007, First Prize, Sun Valley Opera Vocal Competition 2007, winner, José Iturbi Int. Music Competition 2010, Marian Anderson Award 2010, Grammy Award for Best Opera Recording (for Doctor Atomic with Alan Gilbert, Meredith Arwady, Richard Paul Fink, Gerald Finley, Thomas Glenn, Eric Owens and Jay David Saks) 2012. *Current Management:* c/o Alec C. Treuhaft, IMG Artists, Carnegie Hall Tower, 152 West 57th Street, 5th Floor, New York, NY 10019, USA. *Telephone:* (212) 994-3500. *Fax:* (212) 994-3550. *E-mail:* atreuhaft@imgartists.com. *Website:* www.imgartists.com. *E-mail:* sashacooke@gmail.com. *Website:* www.sashacooke.com.

COOP, Jane Austin, DipArt, BMus, MM; Canadian pianist; *Professor Emerita, University of British Columbia*; b. 18 April 1950, Saint John, NB; d. of James F. Coop and Ruth A. Coop; m. George Laverock 1984; one d. *Education:* Univ. of Toronto, Peabody Conservatory, Baltimore with Anton Kuerti and Leon Fleisher. *Career:* debuts, St Lawrence Centre, Toronto, Wigmore Hall, London, Carnegie Recital Hall, New York; soloist with all major Canadian orchestras; recitals and concerts in Canada, USA, England, France, Poland, Netherlands, Yugoslavia, Hungary, Czechoslovakia, Russia; major tours of Hong Kong, China, Japan; Faculty Artist: Kneisel Hall Chamber Music Festival, Blue Hill, Me 1996–; Prof. Emer., Univ. of British Columbia 2012–. *Recordings include:* The Romantic Piano, Beethoven Eroica variations and Sonatas Op. 109 and Op. 111, Bach English Suite No. 3 and Partita No. 5, Haydn four Sonatas, Mozart The Piano Quartets, with members of the Orford Quartet, Piano Pieces, Piano Variations (Schumann, Schubert, Brahms),

Chopin Nocturnes and Mazurkas, Chopin The Late Works, Piano Concerti (Bartók, Prokofiev), Piano Concerti (Britten, Ireland, Finzi, Rawsthorne), Chamber Music (Brahms Horn Trio, Jenner Clarinet and Horn Trio), Bax and Bowen Viola Sonatas; Fauré Piano Quartet in C Minor, Brahms Op. 119, Beethoven Op. 7, Chopin Op. 54. *Honours:* Hon. Licentiate, Conservatory Canada; mem. Order of Canada 2012; Distinguished Univ. Scholar 2003; First Prize, CBC Young Performers Competition 1969, Baldwin Prize, Kapell Int. Piano Competition 1975, First Prize, Washington Int. Piano Competition 1975, finalist, Munich Int. Competition 1977, Killam Award for Career Excellence 1989, Queen's Diamond Jubilee Medal 2012. *Current Management:* c/o Andrew Kwan Artists Management, 1315 Lawrence Avenue East, Suite 515, Toronto, ON M3A 3R3, Canada; c/o Lois Scott Management Inc., PO Box 140, Closter, NJ 07624-0140, USA. *Telephone:* (416) 445-4441 (Toronto) (home); (201) 768-6970 (Closter) (home). *Website:* www.janecoop.com.

COOPER, Anna; British singer (mezzo-soprano); b. 1965. *Education:* Royal Acad. of Music, studied at La Fenice, Venice. *Career:* many appearances with leading British opera companies, including Glyndebourne, ENO and English Opera Group; roles have included parts in Albert Herring, Die Walküre, Die Zauberflöte, L'Italiana in Algeri and Dido and Aeneas; appearances with Royal Opera, Covent Garden, as Flora, Lola, the Madrigal Singer (Manon Lescaut), Kate Pinkerton, Grimgerde, Countess Ceprano (Rigoletto) and Annina; Glasa in Katya Kabanova 1997; further engagements in Belgium, Germany, Italy, Greece, Republic of Korea, France, Japan and USA. *Honours:* winner, Kathleen Ferrier Award, scholarship to La Fenice, Venice.

COOPER, Barry Anthony Raymond, MA, DPhil, FRCO; British academic and musicologist; *Professor of Music, University of Manchester*; b. 2 May 1949, Westcliff-on-Sea, Essex; m. Susan Catherine Baynes 1973; four c. *Education:* Univ. Coll., Oxford, studied organ with John Webster, composition with Kenneth Leighton, musicology with John Caldwell, Joseph Kerman. *Career:* Lecturer in Music, St Andrews Univ. 1973–74; Research Officer, Univ. of Aberdeen 1974–78, Lecturer in Music 1978–89, Sr Lecturer in Music 1989–90; Sr Lecturer in Music, Univ. of Manchester 1990–2000, Reader in Music 2000–03, Prof. of Music 2003–; mem. Royal Musical Asscn, Royal Coll. of Organists. *Compositions:* Oratorio, The Ascension; Song-Cycle, The Unasked Question; Wind Band, Mons Graupius; Choral, Organ and Chamber Music. *Publications include:* G. B. Sammartini, Concerto in G 1976, J. C. Schickhardt, Sonata in D 1978, Catalogue of Early Printed Music in Aberdeen Libraries 1978, Englische Musiktheorie im 17 und 18 Jahrhundert (in Geschichte der Musiktheorie, Band 9) 1986, Beethoven's Symphony No. 10, First Movement (Realisation and Completion) 1988, English Solo Keyboard Music of the Middle and Late Baroque 1989, Beethoven and the Creative Process 1990, L. van Beethoven, Three Bagatelles (ed.) 1991, The Beethoven Compendium (ed.) 1991, Beethoven's Folksong Settings 1994, J. Blow, Complete Organ Music (ed.) 1996, D. F. Tovey, A Companion to Beethoven's Pianoforte Sonatas (ed.) 1999, Beethoven (Master Musicians) 2000, Beethoven, The 35 Piano Sonatas (ed.) (Music Industries Asscn Award for Best Classical Publication 2008) 2007, Child Composers and their Works 2009. *Publications:* contrib. to Musical Times, Music and Letters, Music Review, RMA Research Chronicle, Proceedings/Journal of RMA, Recherches sur la Musique Française Classique, Early Music, Acta Musicologica, Beethoven Journal, BBC Music Magazine, Welsh Music History, Irish Musical Studies, Bulletin of the John Rylands University Library of Manchester, New Grove Dictionary of Music and Musicians, Ad Parnassum. *Honours:* Osgood Prize 1972, Halstead Scholarship 1972–74, RSE Research Fellow 1986–87. *Address:* Martin Harris Building (Music), University of Manchester, Coupland Street, Manchester M13 9PL, England (office). *Website:* www.arts.manchester.ac.uk (office).

COOPER, Imogen, CBE; British pianist; b. 28 Aug. 1949, London; d. of the late Martin Du Pré Cooper and of Mary Stewart. *Education:* Paris Conservatoire and in Vienna with Alfred Brendel. *Career:* TV debut at Promenade Concerts, London 1975, has appeared regularly since then; first British pianist and first woman pianist in South Bank Piano series, Queen Elizabeth Hall, London; broadcasts regularly for BBC; performs with New York, Berlin, Vienna and LA Philharmonic orchestras and with Boston, London, Sydney, Melbourne and Concertgebouw Symphony orchestras; gives solo recitals world-wide; performs regularly with Belcea Quartet and cellist Sonia Wieder-Atherton, as Lieder recitalist has had a long collaboration with Wolfgang Holzmair; Humanitas Visiting Prof. in Classical Music and Music Educ., Univ. of Oxford 2012–13. *Recordings include:* Schubert's Schwanengesang, Winterreise, Die Schöne Mullerin and Schumann's Heine Lieder and Kerner Lieder (with Wolfgang Holzmair), Mozart's Concerto for two pianos K.365 (with Alfred Brendel), Schubert four-hand piano music (with Anne Queffélec) 1996, Imogen Cooper and Friends (solo, chamber and lieder) 2004, The Last Six Years of Schubert's piano music 2005, Mozart Concertos (with the Northern Sinfonia) 2006, 2008, 2010, Schubert's Piano Sonata in G Major D. 894 2009. *Honours:* Hon. MusD (Exon) 1999; Paris Conservatoire Premier Prix 1967, Mozart Memorial Prize 1969, Royal Philharmonic Soc. Award for Best Instrumentalist 2008. *Website:* www.imogen-cooper.com.

COOPER, Kenneth, BA, MA, PhD; American harpsichordist, pianist, musicologist, conductor and educator; *Director, Baroque Aria Ensemble, Manhattan School of Music*; b. 31 May 1941, New York, NY; s. of Rudolf Cooper and Florence Cooper; m. Josephine Mongiardo 1969; one s. *Education:* High School of Music and Art, New York, Columbia Univ., Mannes Coll. of Music with Sylvia Marlowe. *Career:* debut at Wigmore Hall 1965, Alice Tully Hall, USA 1973; Academic Instructor, Barnard Coll. 1965–71; Adjunct Asst Prof., Brooklyn Coll. 1971–73; Prof. of Harpsichord, Dir of Collegium, Mannes Coll. 1975–85; Visiting Specialist in Performance Practice, Montclair State Coll. 1977–92; Artist-in-Residence, Columbia Univ. 1983–; graduate seminars in Baroque Performance Practice, Manhattan School of Music 1984–, Dir Baroque Aria Ensemble, Manhattan School of Music 1984–, Chair. Harpsichord Dept 1984–; Grad. Workshops in Performance Practice, Peabody Conservatory of Music 1987–90; grad. workshops at New England Conservatory 2001; many residencies and guest appearances and lectures; performances include premieres of works by Seymour Barab, Noel Lee, Ferruccio Busoni, Paul Ben-Haim, Ernst Krenek, Victoria Bond and others; dozens of modern day revivals; guest appearances and festivals; Harpsichordist and Pianist, Grand Canyon Chamber Music Festival 1985–; Dir Berkshire Bach Ensemble 1991–, Music@Menlo, Chamber Music Northwest, Lincoln Center Chamber Music Soc. *Recordings:* numerous including soundtracks, Van Gogh Revisited, Every Eye Forms Its Own Beauty, Valmont, Louis Cat Orze, Bach: 6 Brandenburg Concerti, Gamba-Harpsichord Sonatas with Yo-Yo Ma, Flute-Fortepiano Sonatas with Susan Rotholz, Silks and Rags, Mother Goose and More, Bach Goldberg Variations, Bach Sonatas for Violin and Fortepiano (with Ani Kavafian), Baroque Fireworks (with Frank Morelli), Should Auld Acquaintance Be Forgot. *Publications include:* Three Centuries of Music in Score, Bach: Two-Part & Three-Part Inventions (Music Publrs Asscn Award) 2004, Beethoven Piano Concerto B flat Cadenza Reconstruction, Schubert Quintet: Adagio and Rondo, Mozart Adagio Quasi Fantasia, Debussy Sonatas Nos 4 and 5; contribs to professional journals. *Honours:* Record of the Year (Cousins) 1977, Paul Revere Awards (Bach Inventions, International Music Co.). *Address:* 425 Riverside Drive, New York, NY 10025, USA.

COOTE, Alice; British singer (mezzo-soprano); b. 10 May 1968, Frodsham, Cheshire. *Education:* Guildhall School of Music and Drama, London, Royal Northern Coll. of Music and Nat. Opera Studio. *Career:* known for performing Strauss, Mahler, Berlioz, Mozart, Händel and Bach with orchestras such as London Symphony Orchestra, Boston Symphony Orchestra, New York Philharmonic, Chicago Symphony Orchestra, OAE, The English Concert, Kammerphilharmonie Bremen, Hallé and Concertgebouw; has collaborated with conductors such as Gergiev, Dohnanyi, Belohavek, Salonen, Elder, Boulez, Jurowski and Järvi; has appeared at opera houses including Opéra de Paris and the Théâtre des Champs-Elysées, in Amsterdam, Geneva, Munich, Frankfurt, and Salzburg in Europe and Chicago Lyric Opera, Seattle, Los Angeles, San Francisco, Toronto and Metropolitan Opera New York in North America; numerous performances with pianist Julius Drake. *Recordings include:* Vaughan Williams' Hugh the Drover 1994, Rossini's Ricciardo e Zoraide 1997, Great Operatic Arias 2002, Verdi's Falstaff 2002, Handel's The Choice of Hercules 2002, Songs 2003, Walton's Gloria, The Choice of Hercules, Orfeo, Elgar's The Dream of Gerontius (Gramophone Award for Best Choral Recording 2009). *Honours:* Brigitte Fassbaender Award for Lieder Interpretation, Decca-Kathleen Ferrier Prize 1992. *Current Management:* c/o Stefania Almansi, IMG Artists, The Light Box, 111 Power Road, London, W4 5PY, England. *Telephone:* (20) 7957-5800. *Fax:* (20) 7957-5801. *E-mail:* salmansi@imgartists.com. *Website:* imgartists.com/artist/alice_coote.

COPE, David Howell; American composer, writer and instrument maker; b. 17 May 1941, San Francisco, CA. *Education:* Arizona State Univ., Univ. of Southern California with Halsey Stevens, Ingolf Dahl and George Perle. *Career:* teacher, Kansas State Coll. 1968–69, California Lutheran Coll., Cleveland Inst., Miami Univ. of Ohio and the Univ. of California, Santa Cruz from 1977; Ed., The Composer 1969–81. *Compositions include:* Tragic Overture 1960, four Piano Sonatas 1960–67, two String Quartets 1961, 1963, Variations for piano and wind 1965, Contrasts for orchestra 1966, Music for brass and strings 1967, Iceberg Meadow for prepared piano 1968, Streams for orchestra 1973, Spirals for tuba and tape 1973, Requiem for Bosque Redondo 1974, Arena for cello and tape 1974, Re-birth for concert band 1975, Rituals for cello 1976, Vectors for four percussion 1976, Tenor Saxophone Concerto 1976, Threshold and Visions for orchestra 1977, Glassworks for two pianos and tape 1979, Piano Concerto 1980, The Way for various instruments 1981, Corridors of Light for various instruments 1983, Afterlife for orchestra 1983.

COPES, Ronald; American violinist; b. Arkansas. *Education:* Oberlin Conservatory, Univ. of Michigan. *Career:* concerto soloist, recitalist and chamber musician; performed at Marlboro, Tanglewood, Bermuda, Cheltenham, Colorado and Olympic Music Festivals; toured with Music From Marlboro ensembles, Los Angeles and Dunsmuir Piano Quartets; mem. (second violinist) Juilliard String Quartet 1997–, concerts throughout Europe, Asia and North America; Prof. of Violin, Univ. of Calif., Santa Barbara 1977–97; mem. faculty, Juilliard School, New York 1997–. *Recordings include:* numerous solo and chamber music works. *Honours:* prizes from Artists' Advisory Council, Merriweather Post, Concours Int. d'Exécution Musicale, Geneva. *Current Management:* c/o Colbert Artists Management, 111 West 57th Street, New York, NY 10019, USA. *Telephone:* (212) 757-0782. *Fax:* (212) 541-5179. *E-mail:* nycolbert@colbertartists.com. *Website:* www.colbertartists.com; www.juilliardstringquartet.org.

COPLEY, John Michael Harold, CBE; British opera director and producer; b. 12 June 1933, Birmingham, West Midlands, England; civil partner John Hugh Chadwyck-Healey 2006. *Education:* Sadler's Wells Ballet School, Central School of Arts and Crafts, London. *Career:* stage man. of opera and ballet cos, Sadler's Wells in Rosebery Avenue 1953–56, musicals, plays, etc.,

London West End; Deputy Stage Man., Covent Garden Opera Co. 1960–63, Asst Resident Producer 1963–65, Assoc. Resident Producer 1966–72, Resident Producer 1972–75, Prin. Resident Producer 1975–88, productions including Suor Angelica 1965, Così fan tutte 1968, 1981, Le nozze di Figaro 1971, Don Giovanni 1973, Faust 1974, Benvenuto Cellini 1976, Ariadne auf Naxos 1976, Maria Stuarda, Royal Silver Jubilee Gala 1977, La Traviata, Lucrezia Borgia 1980, Semele 1982; other productions include numerous operas, London Coliseum, Athens Festival, Netherlands Opera, Belgian Nat. Opera, Wexford Festival, Dallas Civic Opera (US debut 1972, Lucia di Lammermoor), Chicago Lyric Opera, Greek Nat. Opera, Australian Opera, English Opera North, Scottish Opera, English Opera Group, Vancouver Opera, Ottawa Festival, San Francisco Opera, Metropolitan Opera (New York), Santa Fe Opera (La Bohème 1990), Houston Grand Opera, Washington Opera, San Diego Opera, London West End; Dallas production of Hansel and Gretel seen at Los Angeles 1992; directed local premiere of Britten's A Midsummer Night's Dream, Houston 1993; season 1996 with La Rondine at St Louis and Madama Butterfly at Santa Fe; appearances include Apprentice, Britten's Peter Grimes, Covent Garden 1950; soloist, Bach's St John Passion, Bremen, Germany 1965; Co-Dir Fanfare for Europe Gala, Covent Garden 1973. *Address:* 9D Thistle Grove, London, SW10 9RR, England.

CORAL, Giampaolo, DipMus; Italian composer; b. 22 Jan. 1944, Trieste. *Education:* Conservatory of Music B. Marcello, Venice. *Career:* founder and Art Dir, International Contemporary Music Festival, Trieste Prima; Art Dir, International Competition for musical composition, Trieste. *Compositions include:* stage works: Mr Hyde (one-act opera), Schwanengesang (one-act chamber opera), Favola (one-act romantic pantomime); orchestral works: Magnificat for soprano and orchestra, Amras for violin and orchestra, Kubin Zyklus for orchestra, Tout a coup et comme par jeu for flute and orchestra, Requiem for orchestra; chamber music: Osservando Paul Klee for violin, cello and piano, Trakl Lieder for soprano and piano, Second Sonata for piano, Klavieralbum I–III, Raps I–XI for ensemble, Damonen und Nachtgesichte von A. Kubin for ensemble, Modulazioni for piano four hands, Aloe for vocal ensemble and five brass. *Publications:* contrib. to Editio Musica (Budapest), Suvini Zerboni (Milan), Sonzogno (Milan), Curci (Milan), Edipan (Rome), Dictionary: Riemann Musik Lexikon.

CORAZZA, Remy; French singer (tenor); b. 16 April 1933, Revin, Ardennes. *Education:* Toulouse and Paris Conservatories. *Career:* debut at Opéra-Comique, Paris as Beppe in Pagliacci 1959; sang Gonzalve in L'Heure Espagnole at the Paris Opéra 1960; many performances in Paris and elsewhere in France as Pinkerton, Rodolfo, Hoffmann, Nadir and in Mozart roles; Opéra du Rhin, Strasbourg from 1974, Salzburg from 1978, as Monostatos and the Hoffmann buffo roles; Prof., Paris Conservatory 1985; Glyndebourne debut 1987, as Torquemada in L'Heure Espagnole; Nantes Opera 1990 in Le Pré aux clercs by Hérold and Le Roi l'a dit by Delibes.

CORBELLI, Alessandro; Italian singer (baritone); b. 21 Sept. 1952, Turin. *Education:* studied with Giuseppe Valdengo and Claude Thiolas. *Career:* debut in Bergamo, as Marcello in La Bohème 1974; many appearances in the buffo repertory at opera houses in Italy, Vienna, Paris and Germany; Rossini roles include Pacuvio in La Pietra del Paragone (Picco Scala and Edinburgh 1982), Dandini in La Cenerentola (Glyndebourne 1985) and Gaudenzio in Il Signor Bruschino (Paris 1986); Rome Opera 1985–86, as Belcore in L'Elisir d'Amore and Marcello; Covent Garden debut as Taddeo in L'Italiana in Algeri 1988; season 1989–90 in Pergolesi's Lo frate 'nnamorato at La Scala, conducted by Muti, as Don Alfonso at Salzburg Festival and as Germano in La Scala di Seta at Schwetzingen; other roles include Papageno, Ravenna 1986, Guglielmo, Escamillo, Malatesta and the Figaros of Mozart, Rossini and Paisiello; Fabrizio in Crispino e la Comare, Pantaleone in The Love of Three Oranges and Monteverdi's Ottone; season 1992 as Belcore at Parma, Rossini's Martino and Gormano at Cologne, Paris Opéra-Comique and Schwetzingen Festival; sang Leporello at Lausanne 1996 and Alfonso at Covent Garden 1997; Dandini in Cenerentola at Pesaro and Dulcamara at Madrid 1998; season 2000–01 as Rossini's Dandini and Taddeo at New York Met, Leporello at Glyndebourne and Belfiore in Verdi's Un giorno di regno, at Bologna; Dandini at Covent Garden 2003; since 2003 has sung Don Pasquale, Don Magnifico in La Cenerentola, Sulpice in La Fille du Regiment, Don Geronio in Il Turco in Italia and Dr Bartolo in Il Barbiere di Siviglia at Covent Garden; Gianni Schicchi, Dulcamara in L'Elisir d'Amore, Don Magnifico in La Cenerentola at the Met; Don Geronio in Il Turco in Italia in Munich; Dulcamara in L'Elisir d'Amore in Leipzig and Barcelona; Falstaff, Don Magnifico in La Cenerentola at the Champs-Elysées in Paris; Gianni Schicchi and Don Magnifico in La Cenerentola at the Glyndebourne Festival; Dulcamara in L'Elisir d'Amore in Houston and San Francisco. *Recordings include:* eight DVD recordings and numerous opera recordings on CD, including La Cenerentola (conducted by Abbado), L'Italiana in Algeri, Paisiello's Barbiere di Siviglia, La Buona Figliuola by Piccinni. *Current Management:* c/o Patricia Greenan and Penelope Marland Associates, 7 Whitehorse Close, Royal Mile, Edinburgh, EH8 8BU, Scotland. *Telephone:* (131) 557-5872. *Fax:* (131) 556-5825. *E-mail:* patricia@greenanartists.fsnet.co.uk.

CORBETT, Sidney, BA, MM, MMA, DMA; American composer; b. 26 April 1960, Chicago, Ill.; m.; three c. *Education:* Univ. of San Diego, Yale School of Music, Hamburg Acad. of Arts with György Ligeti, studied with Pauline Oliveros, Bernard Rands, Joji Yuasa, Jean-Charles François, Jacob Druckman and Martin Bresnick. *Career:* compositions performed in USA and Europe, including radio broadcasts; composer in Germany 1985–; DAAD Fellow; mem. G. Ligeti Seminar, Hamburg, Germany 1985–87. *Compositions include:* Arien for violin solo 1983, Pastel Nos 1 and 2 for trombone quartet 1984, 1988, Ghost Reveille for orchestra 1984, For Pianos for four pianos 1984, Bass Animation for contrabass with two percussions 1985, Arien IV: Solo Music for guitar 1986, Kandinsky Romance for chamber ensemble 1986, Cactus Flower for solo flute 1988, Pianos' Dream for piano duo 1989, Concerto for trombone and wind orchestra 1989, Lieder aus der Dunkelkammer for soprano, harp and chamber orchestra 1990, Symphony No. 1 Tympan 1991–92, Hamlet Variations (in memoriam John Coltrane) for solo euphonium 1992, Gloucester Epiphonies for chamber ensemble 1993; currently Prof. for Composition, Univ. of Performing Arts, Mannheim. *Current Management:* c/o Stefan Conradi, C. F. Peters Ltd & Co. KG, Stempelfabrik, Hedderichstraße 108-110, 60596 Frankfurt/Main, Germany. *E-mail:* stefan.conradi@editionpeters.com. *Website:* www.sidneycorbett.de.

CORBOZ, Michel; Swiss conductor; b. 14 Feb. 1934, Marsens. *Education:* Ecole Normale in Fribourg. *Career:* Chorus Master, Notre-Dame in Lausanne from 1954, leading such works as the Fauré Requiem; accompanied singers at the organ and worked at various Lausanne churches; founder, Ensemble Vocal et Instrumental de Lausanne 1961, giving notable performances of Monteverdi's Orfeo; conductor of the choirs of the Gulbenkian Foundation in Lisbon from 1969, leading works by Bach, Monteverdi and Vivaldi; conducted Monteverdi's Il Ritorno d'Ulisse at Mézières 1989. *Recordings:* Monteverdi's Orfeo and Vespers, Bach's B minor Mass, Cavalli's Ercole Amante, Charpentier's David et Jonathas, works by Vivaldi and Giovanni Gabrieli.

CORDIER, David John, MA; British singer (countertenor); b. 1 May 1959, Rochester, Kent; m. Ursula Cordier 1990; one s. one d. *Education:* King's College, Cambridge, Royal College of Music, London. *Career:* debut at Wigmore Hall, 1989; Darmstadt (Lear by Reimann), 1990; Handel Opera, Göttingen; Halle and Karlsruhe Festivals; Recital Berlin Philharmonic, 1996; Opera in Amsterdam, Munich, Düsseldorf, Dresden; Innsbruck, Salzburg and Bern; Season 1998 with Ezio at the Halle Handel Festival and Bertarido in Rodelinda for GTO; sang Handel's Radamisto at Halle, 2000; Teacher at Hanns Eisler Hochschule in Berlin (countertenor). *Recordings include:* Bach Matthew Passion, conducted by Gustav Leonhardt; Solo recitals English song. *Current Management:* Robert Gilder and Co., 91 Great Russell Street, London, WC1B 3PS, England. *Telephone:* (20) 7580-7758. *Fax:* (20) 7580-7739. *E-mail:* rgilder@robert-gilder.com. *Website:* www.robertgilder.com.

CORGHI, Azio, DipMus; Italian composer; b. 9 March 1937, Cirie, Turin. *Education:* Turin Conservatory, Milan Conservatory with Bruno Bettinelli. *Career:* freelance composer; teacher of composition, Conservatorio Giuseppe Verdi, Milan, also at Accademia di Santa Cecilia. *Compositions include:* Symbola 1971, Tactus 1974, Actus III (ballet) 1978, Gargantua (two-act opera, after Rabelais, Teatro Regio, Turin) 1984, Mazapegul (ballet) 1986, Blimunda (three-act opera, after Memoriale del Convento by José Saramago, Teatro Lirico, Milan) 1990, Divara (opera, after In nomine Dei by José Saramago, Städtischen Bühnen Münster) 1993, Rinaldo (opera, after Rinaldo by Handel, Catania) 1997, Isabella (opera, after L'italiana in Algeri by Rossini, Pesaro) 1998, Tat'jana (opera, after Tat'jana Repina by Anton Chekhov, Milan) 2000, Dissoluto assoluto (opera) 2005. *Publications:* Critical edns of L'Italiana in Algeri and Tosca. *Address:* c/o Accademia Nazionale di Santa Cecilia, Auditorium Parco della Musica, Largo Luciano Berio 3, 00196 Rome, Italy.

CORIGLIANO, John Paul, BA; American composer and teacher; b. 16 Feb. 1938, New York, NY. *Education:* Columbia Univ., Manhattan School of Music with Otto Luening and Vittorio Giannini, also studied with Paul Creston. *Career:* music programmer, WQXR-FM and WBAI-FM, New York 1959–64; Assoc. Prod., Musical Programmes, CBS-TV 1961–72; Music Dir, Morris Theatre, NJ 1962–64; Teacher of Composition, Coll. of Church Musicians, Washington, DC 1968–71, Manhattan School of Music 1971–78; Teacher of Composition, Lehman Coll., CUNY 1973–, Distinguished Prof. 1986–; composer-in-residence, Chicago Symphony Orchestra 1987–89; Symphony No. 1 premiere, Chicago Symphony, also New York Philharmonic, Boston Symphony, Seattle Symphony; The Ghosts of Versailles premiere, Metropolitan Opera 1991; Symphony No. 2 premiere, Boston Symphony; Symphony No. 3 (Circus Maximus) premiere, Univ. of Texas Wind Ensemble; mem. American Acad. of Arts and Sciences, American Acad. and Inst. of Arts and Letters 1991–. *Compositions:* Kaleidoscope for two pianos 1959, Sonata for violin and piano 1963, Elegy for orchestra 1965, The Cloisters four songs for voice and piano 1965, for voice and orchestra 1976, Christmas at the Cloisters for chorus and organ or piano 1966, Tournaments Overture 1966, Piano Concerto 1968, Poem in October for tenor and eight instruments 1970, for tenor and orchestra 1976, The Naked Carmen for mixed-media opera 1970, Creations (two scenes from Genesis) for narrator and chamber orchestra 1972, Gazebo Dances for band 1973, Aria for oboe and strings 1975, Oboe Concerto 1975, A Dylan Thomas Trilogy for chorus, soloists and orchestra 1960–76, revised 1999, Poem on his Birthday 1976, Etude Fantasy for piano 1976, Voyage for string orchestra 1976, for flute and string orchestra 1983, Clarinet Concerto 1977, Pied Piper Fantasy flute concerto 1981, Three Hallucinations 1981, Promenade Overture 1981, Echoes of Forgotten Rites: Summer Fanfare 1982, Fantasia on an Ostinato for piano 1985, for orchestra 1986, Symphony No. 1 1989–90, The Ghosts of Versailles (opera) 1991, Phantasmagoria (on Themes from The Ghosts of Versailles) for cello and piano 1993, Amen for double a cappella chorus 1994, String Quartet 1996, Chiaroscuro 1997, Fancy on a Bach Air 1997, The Red Violin: Chaconne for violin and orchestra (Acad.

Award 1999) 1998, Troubadours variations for guitar and orchestra 1999, Vocalise 1999, The Mannheim Rocket 2000, Phantasmagoria: Suite from The Ghosts of Versailles for orchestra 2000, Symphony No. 2 (Pulitzer Prize in Music 2001) 2000, Mr Tambourine Man: Seven Poems of Bob Dylan (Grammy Award for Best Classical Contemporary Composition 2009) 2000, incidental music for plays, film scores. *Recordings:* Symphony No. 1, Chicago Symphony/ Barenboim; Pied Piper Fantasy; Fantasia on an Ostinato; Of Rage and Remembrance–Symphony No. 1, 1996; String Quartet, 1996; Video of The Ghosts of Versailles; Phantasmagoria (The Fantasy Album). *Honours:* Dr hc (Manhattan School of Music) 1992, (Ithaca Coll.) 1995, (RCM) 2000, (New England Conservatory) 2001; Guggenheim Fellow 1968–69, NEA grant 1976, American Acad. and Inst. of Arts and Letters Award 1990, L. Grawemeyer Award 1991, Musical American Composer of the Year Winner 1992, Grammy Award for Classical Album of the Year 1996, Grammy Award for Composition of the Year 1996, George Washington Univ. Presidential Medal of Honor 1996, Nat. Arts Club Gold Medal 2002, George Peabody Medal 2004. *Current Management:* The Gorfaine/Schwartz Agency Inc., 4111 W. Alameda Avenue, Suite 509, Burbank, CA 91505, USA. *Telephone:* (818) 260-8500. *Website:* www.gsamusic.com. *Address:* 365 West End Avenue, New York, NY 10024, USA (home).

CORNWELL, Joseph, BA; British singer (tenor); b. 1959. *Education:* York Univ., Guildhall School of Music and Drama. *Career:* sang originally with such early music groups as Consort of Musicke and Taverner Consort; Promenade Concert debut 1982, in Monteverdi's Vespers under Andrew Parrott; tours of The Netherlands and France in Bach Passions; Verdi's Requiem at Albert Hall, conducted by David Willcocks; Bruckner's Te Deum at Festival Hall; appearances at Paris, Bruges, Flanders, Three Choirs and Brighton Festivals; Bach's B minor Mass with London Bach Orchestra at Barbican 1990; opera roles include Fenton in Falstaff, Frederic in Mignon, Jove in The Return of Ulysses (Kent Opera) and parts in Mahagonny and Let's Make an Opera; sang title role in Monteverdi's Orfeo for Oslo Summer Opera, conducted by Andrew Parrott and 1993 for Boston Early Music Festival; also sang Lurcanio in Handel's Ariodante for St Gallen Opera, in Switzerland; Arretro in Peri's Euridice in Rouen 1992–93; sang in King Arthur with The Sixteen, Lisbon 1996; vocal coach, Oundle School 1982–2012. *Recordings include:* St Matthew Passion with Drottningholm Baroque Ensemble, Boyce Peleus & Thetis with Opera Restor'd, Campra Requiem and King Arthur with Le Concert Spirituel, Israel in Babylon with Kantorei Saarlouis, Messiah and Monteverdi Vespers 1610 with Taverner Consort, Acis & Galatea (Gramophone Baroque Vocal CD of 2000), Monteverdi Vespers 1610 and Mozart Mass in C Minor with Les Arts Florissants, Monteverdi Vespers 1610 with Gabrieli Consort, Rossini Petite Messe Solennelle with Jos van Immerseel (BBC Radio 3 Building a Library Choice), Shepherd Oediups Rex with Philharmonia Orchestra, Tamese Arsilda, Regina di Ponto with Modo Antiquo and Fairest Isle with Parley of Instruments.

CORP, Rev. Ronald Geoffrey, OBE, MA, DipTheol; British composer, conductor and ecclesiastic; *Artistic Director, New London Orchestra and New London Children's Choir;* b. 4 Jan. 1951, Wells, Somerset; s. of Geoffrey Charles Corp and Elsie Grace Corp (nee Kinchin); m. J. B. Glass. *Education:* Univs of Oxford and Southampton. *Career:* librarian, producer and presenter, BBC Radio 3 1973–87; Founder and Artistic Dir, New London Orchestra 1988–, New London Children's Choir 1991–; Musical Dir The London Chorus; Conductor, Highgate Choral Soc.; broadcasts for BBC with BBC Singers, BBC Concert Orchestra, Ulster Orchestra, New London Orchestra and New London Children's Choir; BBC Promenade Concerts; Leipzig Philharmonic Orchestra, Royal Scottish Nat. Orchestra, BBC Scottish Symphony Orchestra, Bournemouth Symphony Orchestra, Cape Philharmonic Orchestra; ordained Deacon in the Church of England 1998, ordained Priest 1999; Vice-Pres. Sullivan Soc.; Patron Bracknell Choral Soc., Chantry Dance Co., London Festival of Contemporary Church Music; Pres. Nat. Asscn for Choirs; Deputy Chair. Charity Help Musicians and Chair. Awards Cttee. *Compositions include:* numerous choral, chamber and orchestral works including And All The Trumpets Sounded 1989, Laudamus 1992, Four Elizabethan Lyrics 1994, Cornucopia 1997, Piano Concerto 1997, A New Song 1999, Mary's Song 2001, Adonai Echad 2001, Missa San Marco 2002, Dover Beach 2003, Guernsey Postcards 2004, Forever Child 2004, Christmas Mass 2007, String Quartet No. 1 The Bustard 2007, Quartet No. 2 2009, Symphony 2009, Dhammapada 2010, The Ice Mountain (children's opera) 2010, Quartet No. 3 2011, The Wayfarer 2011, Things I Didn't Say 2011, Songs of the Elder Sisters 2011, The Yellow Wallpaper 2011, Clarinet Quintet 'Crawhall' 2012, Lullaby for a Lost Soul 2012, Sinfonia 4711 2013, Cello Concerto 2013, The Pelican 2014, Fields of the Fallen 2014, An Essex Posy 2015, Dawn on the Somme 2015, Behold, the Sea 2015. *Recordings include:* extensive discography on Hyperion and the Dutton Epoch labels, including Poulenc, Prokofiev, Satie, Milhaud, Virgil Thomson, Boughton, Sullivan, Foulds, Bacewicz and award-winning British, European and American Light Music Series; also numerous recordings of own compositions and orchestral recordings for Stone Records, Naxos Records and Dutton Epoch. *Publication:* The Choral Singer's Companion 1987 (third edn 2006). *Honours:* Hon. DMus (Anglia Ruskin Univ., Univ. of Hull);Freeman of the City of London 2007, Worshipful Co. of Musicians 2007. *Address:* Bulford Mill, Bulford Mill Lane, Cressing, Essex, CM77 8NS, England (home). *E-mail:* info@ronaldcorp.com. *Website:* www.ronaldcorp.com.

CORREAS, Jérôme; French harpsichordist, baroque singer (bass-baritone) and conductor. *Education:* Univ. of Paris (Sorbonne), Conservatoire Nat.

Supérieur de Musique, Paris, studied with Xavier Depraz and William Christie. *Career:* debut at Aix-en-Provence Festival; mem. Les Arts Florissants 1989–93; joined voice school at Opéra de Paris 1991–93; worked in operatic and baroque repertoires on tour and in productions under conductors including Jesus Lopez-Boboz, Sigiswald Kuijken, Christophe Rousset, Jean-Claude Malgoire, Christophe Coin and Marek Janowski; f. baroque vocal and instrumental ensemble Les Paladins 2001; Guest Conductor, Israël Camerata, Musica Petropolitana St Petersburg, Orchestre de l'Opéra de Rouen; teacher, Conservatoire Régional de Toulouse. *Recordings include:* with Les Paladins: Haendel: Cantates & Duos Italiens 2001, Cavalli: L'Ormindo 2007, Le Triomphe de l'Amour 2012, Tenebris/Leçons de ténèbres 2012. *Honours:* Chevalier des Arts et des Lettres 2011;. *Address:* Les Paladins, 46 rue Lacroix, 75017 Paris, France (office). *Telephone:* 1-42-52-75-60 (office). *Fax:* 1-42-52-64-18 (office). *E-mail:* info@lespaladins.com (office). *Website:* www.lespaladins .com (office).

CORSARO, Frank Andrew; American theatre and opera director; b. 22 Dec. 1924, New York; s. of Joseph Corsaro and Marie Corsaro (née Quarino); m. Mary Cross Bonnie Lueders 1971; one s. *Education:* Yale Univ. *Career:* began career as actor 1948, appearing since in productions including Mrs. McThing, Broadway 1951; first film appearance in Rachel 1967; Dir of numerous plays including A Hatful of Rain, Broadway 1955–56, The Night of the Iguana 1961–62, Tremonisha 1975, 1600 Pennsylvania Avenue 1976, Cold Storage, Lyceum 1977–, Whoopee! 1979, Knockout 1979; directed and acted in numerous TV productions; one-man art show 1976; Dir numerous operas with New York City Opera 1958–, Washington Opera Soc. 1970–74, St Paul Opera 1971, Houston Grand Opera 1973–77, Assoc. Artistic Dir 1977–; Artistic Dir The Actors Studio 1977–85; Drama Dir Juilliard Opera Centre 1989, Artistic Dir, Vocal Arts Dept, Juilliard School 1988–2008, Faculty Emer. 2008–. *Theatre productions include:* La Traviata, Madame Butterfly, Faust, Manon Lescaut, A Village Romeo and Juliet, L'Incoronazione di Poppea, The Angel of Fire, Hugh the Drover, Rinaldo, Love for Three Oranges (Glyndebourne 1983), La Fanciulla del West (Deutsches Oper Berlin 1983), Rinaldo (Metropolitan Opera 1983), Fennimore and Gerda (Edinburgh Festival 1983), Where the Wild Things Are, Higglety, Pigglety, Pop! (Glyndebourne 1985), Alcina (Spitalfields 1985), (LA Opera Centre 1986), L'Enfant et les Sortilèges, L'Heure espagnole, Glyndebourne Festival 1987, Hansel and Gretel (Houston, Toronto, Zürich 1997–98), Kuhlhandel (Juilliard 1998). *Publications include:* L'histoire du soldat (adaptation), La Bohème (adaptation), A Piece of Blue Sky (play), Maverick 1978, Libretto: Before Breakfast (music by Thomas Pasatieri), Libretto: Heloise and Abelard (music by Steven Paulus), Kunma (novel). *Honours:* Dr hc (Juilliard School) 2010; Nat. Endowment for the Arts Opera Award 2009. *Address:* c/o Columbia Artists Management Inc., 1790 Broadway, New York, NY 10019-1412 (office); 33 Riverside Drive, New York, NY 10023, USA (home). *Telephone:* (212) 841-9682 (office); (212) 874-1058 (home).

CORTES, Garðar; Icelandic conductor and singer (tenor); b. 1950, Reykjavík. *Education:* Royal Acad. of Music, Trinity Coll. of Music, London. *Career:* has conducted choirs in Iceland and founded the Reykjavík Symphony Orchestra 1985, leading it on a tour of Denmark; with Icelandic Opera has conducted Orpheus in the Underworld, Pagliacci and Die Fledermaus, Noye's Fludde at the Int. Festival in Reykjavík; appearances as singer with Oslo Opera, Royal Swedish Opera, Seattle Opera, Windsor Festival, Opera North and Belfast Festival; Intendant, Gothenburg Opera, Sweden; roles have included Eisenstein, Tamino, Hoffmann, Radames, Cavaradossi, Florestan and Otello.

CORTES, Garðar Thór; Icelandic singer (tenor); b. 2 May 1979, Reykjavík; s. of Garðar Cortes and Krystyna Cortes. *Education:* attended singing school in Reykjavik, Hochschule Vienna, RAM, London, pvt. studies with Andrei Orlowitz in Copenhagen. *Career:* child actor in tv series Nonni and Manni; lived and worked in Denmark for five years; Raoul in Phantom of the Opera, London 1999; has performed roles including José in Carmen Negra, the Italian Tenor in Der Rosenkavalier, Ferrando in Così fan tutte, Rinuccio in Gianni Schicchi, Conte Alberto in L'occasione fa il ladro, Duke of Mantua in Rigoletto; appearances with English Touring Opera, Icelandic Opera, Nordfjord Opera, Norway, Co-Opera Ireland, Nordurop Opera, Rossini Festival, Germany; concert appearances have included Mendelssohn's Elijah, Carnegie Hall, New York, Bach's Mass in B Minor, St Nicolas, Dvořák's Requiem, Verdi's Requiem, Handel's Messiah, Puccini's Missa di Gloria, Rossini's Petite Messe Solennelle and Stabat Mater, Saint-Saëns' Christmas Oratorio and Les Noces; appeared as Passarino in The Phantom of the Opera, Royal Albert Hall, London 2011; appeared as Alfredo in La Traviata, Harpa concert hall, Reykjavik 2014. *Recordings:* albums: Cortes 2007, When You Say You Love Me 2008, Ísland 2011, Rossini: L'occasione fa il ladro 2012. *Play:* L'occasione fa il ladro 2012. *Address:* Believer Music, Bankastraeti 11, Reykjavík 101, Iceland (home). *E-mail:* einar@believer.is (office). *Website:* www.believer.is.

CORTEZ, Luis Jaime; Mexican composer and musicologist; b. 1963, Morelia, Michoacán. *Education:* Univ. of Mexico. *Career:* Dir, Centro Nacional de Investigación, Documentación e Información Musical 1987–1994; Dir, Conservatorio de las Rosas, Morelia 1996–. *Compositions include:* Formas demasiado lejos 1985, Canto por un equinoccio 1989, Lluvias (Symphony No. 1) 1992, En blanco y negro (Symphony No. 2) 1995, Las tentacions de San Antonio (opera) 1996. *Address:* c/o Conservatorio de las Rosas, Santiago Tapia No. 30, Col. Centro, Morelia, CP 58000, Mexico (office).

CORTEZ, Miguel; Mexican singer (tenor); b. 1952. *Education:* studied in Monterrey and New York. *Career:* debut at Metropolitan Opera 1981, as Alfredo; sang with Kentucky Opera as the Duke of Mantua, Rodolfo, Pinkerton, Fenton and Jacquino; European engagements as the Duke at Zürich 1984, Alfredo at Trieste 1985; sang Werther in Mexico City 1985; has also sung in Salzburg (Alfredo 1983), San Francisco (as Pinkerton) and in the Verdi Requiem (at Seattle).

CORTEZ, Viorica; Romanian singer (mezzo-soprano); b. 22 Dec. 1935, Bucium; m. Emmanuel Bondeville 1974 (died 1987). *Education:* Iasi and Bucharest Conservatories. *Career:* debut at Iasi Opera 1960, as Dalila; sang Dalila at Toulouse 1965, Bucharest Opera 1965–70; Covent Garden debut 1968, as Carmen; Italian debut 1969, as Amneris at Naples, La Scala Milan 1970, as Dalila; US debut, Seattle Opera 1971; Metropolitan Opera from 1971, as Carmen, Amneris, Giulietta in Les Contes d'Hoffmann, Adalgisa in Norma and Azucena; Chicago debut 1973, in Maria Stuarda; sang in premiere of Bondeville's Antoine et Cléopatre, Rouen 1974; Paris Opéra 1980, in Bluebeard's Castle, Oedipus Rex and Boris Godunov; sang La Cieca in La Gioconda at the Verona Arena and Barcelona 1988, Gertrude in Hamlet, Turin 1990, and title role in premiere of La Lupa by Marco Tutino at Livorno. *Recordings include:* Carmen, Aida, Il Trovatore, Verdi's Oberto, Donizetti's Requiem, Rigoletto, Video of Rigoletto.

CORTI, Francesco; Italian conductor; b. 17 Oct. 1963, Milan. *Career:* repetiteur Italian theatres; conducting debut (La Traviata) Jesi, Italy 1986; has since performed at opera houses in Italy, France, Spain, Germany, Belgium, Croatia, Switzerland, Korea and Norway including Deutsche Oper, Norwegian Opera, Vienna Volksoper, Gothenburg Opera, Norrköping Opera, Scottish Opera; concerts with orchestras including Rome and Genoa Opera houses, Angelicum, Milan, Hungarian State, Strasbourg Philharmonic, Seville Symphony, Düsseldorf Symphony and Prague Virtuosi; US debut (Il Barbiere di Siviglia) San Francisco Opera 2004; UK debut (Madama Butterfly) Scottish Opera 2007; apptd Kapellmeister Deutsche Oper am Rhein, Düsseldorf 1996; Music Dir Pfalztheater, Kaiserslautern 2000–05; Music Dir Magdeburg Opera, Germany 2006–; Music Dir Scottish Opera 2007–13. *Current Management:* Allied Artists, 42 Montpelier Square, London SW7 1JZ, England. *Telephone:* (20) 7589-6243. *Fax:* (20) 7581-5269. *E-mail:* robert@alliedartists.co.uk. *Website:* www.alliedartists.co.uk. *Address:* c/o Scottish Opera, 39 Elmbank Crescent, Glasgow, G2 4PT, Scotland (office).

CORY, Eleanor; American composer; b. 8 Sept. 1943, Englewood, NJ. *Education:* Columbia Univ., New York with Charles Wuorinen. *Career:* taught at Yale Univ., Manhattan School of Music, Sarah Lawrence Coll. and others. *Compositions include:* Waking for soprano and ensemble 1974, Octagons for ensemble 1976, Tapestry for orchestra 1982, String Quartet 1985, Of Mere Being for chorus and brass quintet 1987, Fantasy for flute, guitar and percussion 1991, Canyons for chamber orchestra 1991.

COSMA, Octavian Lazăr, PhD; Romanian musicologist and academic; *PhD Tutor, National University of Music;* b. 15 Feb. 1933, Treznea, Sălaj; s. of Lazăr Cosma and Aurelia Cosma; m. Elena Cosma 1958 (died 2001); one s. one d. *Education:* N. A. Rimsky-Korsakov Conservatory, St Petersburg, Russia. *Career:* with Muzica journal 1954; Counsellor, Ministry of Culture and Educ. 1959–63; Asst, later Prof., Nat. Univ. of Music, Bucharest 1959–; Ed.-in-Chief Muzica journal 1990–2010; mem. Romanian Acad., Romanian Composers' and Musicologists' Soc. (Sec. 1990, Vice-Pres. 1992, Pres. 2005–10), American Musicological Soc. *Publications include:* Romanian Opera (two vols) 1962, Enescu's Oedipus 1967, The Chronicle of Romanian Music Vols 1–9 1973–91, The Universe of Romanian Music 1995, The Symphonic Concerts of the Romanian Radio Orchestra 1998, The Chronicle of Romanian Opera in Bucharest Vol. 1 2003, The Bucharest Philharmonic in the Light of the Music Review 2005, The National Music University of Bucharest, Vol. 1 2004, Vol. 2 2008, Vol. 3 2010, Romanian Opera in Cluj, Vol. 1 2010, Vol. 2 2011; contribs to various professional journals. *Honours:* Order of Cultural Merit; Dr hc (mult.); Romanian Acad. Ciprian Porumbescu Prize 1962, Romanian Union of Composers Prize 1968, 1975, 1976, 1998, 2003, 2010. *Address:* 5–7 Cotroceni Sos., Bucharest 060111, Romania (office). *Telephone:* (21) 3162864 (home). *E-mail:* olcosma@yahoo.com (office).

COSMA, Viorel; Romanian musicologist and academic; b. 30 March 1923, Timisoara; m. Coralia Cosma. *Education:* Municipal Conservatory, Timisoara and Acad. of Music, Bucharest. *Career:* debut as conductor 1944; musicologist and music critic from 1946; Prof. from 1950. *Publications include:* Bartók 1955, Ion Vidu 1956, Ciprian Porumbescu 1957, Elena Teodorini 1960, Nicolae Filimon 1966, The George Enescu Philharmonic 1968, Romanian Musicians 1970, The Madrigal Choir 1971, Enescu (two vols) 1974, 1981, Enescu Today 1981, Two Millennia of Music 1982, Musicological Exegeses 1984, Musicians of Romania (A–C) 1989, Dinu Lipatti 1991, Romanian Performers 1996. *Honours:* Romanian Composers Prize 1970, 1972, 1978, 1983, 1988, 1991, Acad. of Romania Prize 1971.

COSSA, Dominic, BS, MA, LhD; American singer (baritone) and teacher; b. 13 May 1935, Jessup, PA; m. Janet Edgerton 1957; one s. one d. *Education:* Univ. of Scranton, Univ. of Detroit, Univ. of Scranton, Detroit Inst. of Musical Arts, Philadelphia Acad. of Vocal Arts, studied with Anthony Marlowe, Robert Weede and Armen Boyajian. *Career:* operatic debut as Morales, Carmen, New York City Opera 1961; leading baritone roles, New York City Opera; Metropolitan Opera debut, New York, as Silvio in Pagliacci 1970–76; other Met roles include Masetto, Rossini's Figaro, Marcello and Puccini's Lescaut;

Opéra du Rhin, Strasbourg 1976; sang M. Triquet in Eugene Onegin at Florence 2000; faculty mem., Manhattan School of Music, New York; Chair. of Voice/Opera, Univ. of Maryland, Coll. Park. *Recordings include:* Achilles in Giulio Cesare, conducted by Julius Rudel.

COSSOTI, Max-René; Italian singer (tenor); b. 1950. *Career:* made debut in Rigoletto, Teatro Grande di Brescia; repertoire includes Arlecchino in I Pagliacci, Goro in Madama Butterfly, Gastone in La Traviata, Cajus and Bardolfo in Falstaff, Remendado in Carmen, Edmondo in Manon Lescaut, Arturo in Lucia di Lammermoor, Malatestino in Francesca da Rimini, Pang in Turandot, Abate di Chazeuil in Adriana Lecouvreur, Incredibile in Andrea Chenier, Riccardo in I quatro rusteghi, Blind in Die Fledermaus, Lenski in Eugene Onegin, Maestro di Ballo in Ariadne auf Naxos, Aristeo in Orfeo all'Inferno, Basilio in Le Nozze di Figaro; has also performed in Il Compleanno dell'Infanta, Il Convitato di Pietra, La Vedova Scaltra, Bastiano e Bastiana, La danza delle Llibellule, La Cenerentola, Il Barbiere di Siviglia, Il Turco in Italia, La Rondine, Don Pasquale, L'elisir d'Amore, La Sonnambula, Angéliq, Die lustige Witwe, Les dialogues des Carmélites, Fedora. *Recordings include:* Videos of Ulisse, Falstaff and Il Barbiere di Sivigila from Glyndebourne. *Honours:* winner, XXI As.Li.Co. Competition, XXVI Teatro alla Scala Competition, Voci Verdiane Competition, Premio Abbiati. *Current Management:* Stage Door, Via San Giorgio 4, 40121 Bologna, Italy. *Telephone:* (51) 262126. *Fax:* (51) 271452. *E-mail:* info@stagedoor.it. *Website:* www.stagedoor.it.

COSSOTTO, Fiorenza; Italian singer (mezzo-soprano); b. 22 April 1935, Crescentino; m. Ivo Vinco 1958. *Education:* Turin Conservatory, studied with Ettore Campogalliani. *Career:* debut at La Scala, Milan 1957, in the premiere of Poulenc's Les Dialogues des Carmélites; returned to Milan until 1973, notably as Verdi's Eboli, Amneris and Azucena, and in La Favorite, Les Huguenots, Il Barbiere di Siviglia and Cavalleria Rusticana; sang Jane Seymour in Anna Bolena at Wexford 1958; Covent Garden debut 1959, as Neris in Cherubini's Médée; Chicago Lyric Opera 1964, in La Favorite; Metropolitan Opera debut 1968, as Amneris, returning for Laura in La Gioconda, Adalgisa, Norma, Carmen and Mistress Quickly (Falstaff); sang at Verona Arena 1960–89, notably as Amneris, which she sang at the Metropolitan 1989; sang Dalila at Newark, NJ 1989, the Princess in Adriana Lecouvreur, Rome; sang Santuzza, Piacenza 1990; Ulrica at Lisbon and Amneris at Buenos Aires; sang Ulrica at Genoa 1992. *Recordings:* roles in Andrea Chénier, Norma, Madama Butterfly, La Sonnambula, Macbeth, Don Carlos, Cavalleria Rusticana, Médée and Il Trovatore.

COSTA, Mary; American singer; b. 5 April 1930, Knoxville, Tenn. *Education:* Los Angeles Conservatory of Music. *Career:* debut at Los Angeles Opera 1958, San Francisco Opera 1959, Metropolitan Opera, New York 1964, Bolshoi 1970; performed at opening of J. F. Kennedy Center, Washington DC 1970; appearances at opera houses in UK, Canada, USSR, Portugal; Vice-Pres. Hawaiian Fragrances 1972, California Inst. of the Arts; featured artist at Hollywood Bowl tribute to Walt Disney: 75 Years of Music 2004; apptd by Pres. to Nat. Council on the Arts 2003–06. *Operas include:* La Bohème 1959, Manon 1961, La Traviata 1964, 1970, Candide 1971. *Films include:* Marry Me Again 1953, The Big Caper 1957, Sleeping Beauty (voice of Sleeping Beauty), The Great Waltz 1972; BBC films of La Traviata, Faust, The Merry Widow. *Honours:* Hon. PhD (Hardin-Simmons Univ.) 1973, Hon. DFA (Carson-Newman Coll.) 2007; Los Angeles Woman of Year 1959, DAR Honour Medal 1974, Tennessee Hall of Fame Award 1987, Women of Achievement Award Nat. Women's Bd of Northwood Inst. (Palm Beach, Fla) 1991, Woman of Achievement Award S Birmingham Coll. 1993, Tennessee Achievement Award 1998, Licia Albanese Puccini Foundation Lifetime Achievement Award 1999, Disney Legends Award 1999, TN Woman of Distinction American Lung Asscn 2000, Metropolitan Opera Guild Distinguished Verdi Performance Award 2001. *Telephone:* (415) 362-2787. *E-mail:* don@calartists.com. *Website:* www.calartists.com.

COSTANZO, Anthony Roth, MM; American singer (countertenor) and actor; b. 8 May 1982, Durham, NC. *Education:* Princeton Univ., Manhattan School of Music. *Career:* performed in Amahl and the Night Visitors at Lincoln Center and with Opera Co. of N Carolina aged 12; debut with New Jersey Opera Festival as Miles in Britten's The Turn of the Screw 1994; appeared with Luciano Pavarotti in Philadelphia at Acad. of Music's Opera Extravaganza 1994; debut at Metropolitan Opera in Rodelinda 2009, sang Ferdinand and Prospero in premiere of The Enchanted Island 2012, and Prince Orlofsky in Die Fledermaus 2014; operatic roles with New York City Opera, Glimmerglass Opera, Palm Beach Opera, Boston Lyric Opera, Opera Co. of Philadelphia, Canadian Opera Co., Michigan Opera Theater; debut at Glyndebourne Opera Festival, UK, as Eustazio in Rinaldo 2014; concerts and recitals include Mostly Mozart Festival, Prince Go-Go in Ligeti's Le Grand Macabre with New York Philharmonic, Handel's Messiah with Cleveland Orchestra, Nat. Symphony Orchestra and in Carnegie Hall; featured soloist with orchestras of Indianapolis, Alabama, Detroit, Denver, Seattle and in premiere of John Corigliano's A Dylan Thomas Trilogy with Nat. Symphony Orchestra at Kennedy Center and Carnegie Hall. *Films:* A Soldier's Daughter Never Cries, De particulier à particulier, Lying, Zeferino: The Voice of a Castrato. *Honours:* Lewis Sudler Prize, Hugh Ross Award, Grand Finals winner, Metropolitan Opera Nat. Auditions 2009, George London Award 2010, First Prize, Plácido Domingo Operalia Award 2012. *Current Management:* Opus 3 Artists, 470 Park Avenue South, 9th Floor North, New York, NY 10016, USA. *Telephone:* (212) 584-7500. *E-mail:* info@opus3artists.com. *Website:* www.opus3artists.com; www.anthonyrothcostanzo.com (office).

COSTINESCU, Gheorghe, PhD; Romanian composer, conductor, pianist, musicologist and educator; *Professor Emeritus, Lehman College, City University of New York*; b. 12 Dec. 1934, Bucharest; m. Silvelin von Scanzoni 1971. *Education:* Bucharest Conservatory, Darmstadt and Cologne, Juilliard School, Columbia Univ., studied composition with Mihail Jora in Romania, Luciano Berio in USA, studied with Nadia Boulanger, Karlheinz Stockhausen, Henry Pousseur, Mario Davidovsky and Chou Wen-chung, conducting with Harold Faberman, Maurice Peress and Dennis Russell Davies in USA and with Sergiu Celibidache in Germany. *Career:* debut as composer and pianist, Sonata for violin and piano at Shiraz-Persepolis Festival, Iran 1967; debut as conductor, Washington premiere of Peter Maxwell Davies's Miss Donnithorne's Maggot at the Corcoran art gallery 1979; Prof. Emeritus, Lehmann Coll., CUNY; premieres: Evolving Cycle of Two-Part Modal Inventions for piano, Romanian Broadcast 1964; Past Are The Years for tenor and vocal ensemble with Juilliard Chorus, Lincoln Center, New York 1970; Jubilus for soprano, trumpet and percussive body sounds, commissioned and broadcast by Nat. Public Radio, USA 1981; premiere of stage work: The Musical Seminar at Tanglewood Festival 1982; German premiere at State Opera of Stuttgart 1989; British premiere with Paragon Opera Project at Royal Scottish Acad. of Music, Glasgow 1992; premiere of Pantomime for chamber orchestra at the Romanian Nat. Opera Bucharest 1998; premiere of Paragon 2000 for chamber orchestra, with the Paragon Ensemble of Scotland, Glasgow 2000, full orchestra version with the Concerto Orchestra, Bucharest 2001; first retrospective concert, The Ensemble Sospeso at Miller Theatre, New York 2002. *Recordings:* Composers Recordings Inc, USA; published works: Evolving Cycle for piano 1964, Song of the Rivers vocal symphonic work 1967, Sonata for violin and piano 1968, A Live Retrospective 1952–2002 2007, Gheorghe Costinescu, Music for the Voice; Jubilus & Pantomime (DVD). *Publications:* violin studies and articles on contemporary music, essays on comparative aesthetics. *Honours:* Romanian Acad. George Enescu Prize 1965, Juilliard School Alexandre Gretchaninoff Prize 1970, American Acad. and Inst. of Arts and Letters Music Award 1995, League of Composers/ISCM Competition Music Theater Prize 1986, New York Foundation for the Arts Fellowship Award 1988, NEA Producers and Composers grants 1986, 1989, Fulbright Scholar Award 1997–98. *Address:* 120 Riverside Drive, Apt 6E, New York, NY 10024, USA (home). *Telephone:* (212) 877-3494 (home). *E-mail:* g.s .costinescu@rcn.com (home).

COTRUBAŞ, Ileana; Romanian singer (soprano) (retd); b. 9 June 1939, Galaţi; d. of Vasile Cotrubaş and Maria Cotrubaş; m. Manfred Ramin 1972. *Education:* Scoala Speciala de Musica, Conservatorul Ciprian Porumbescu. *Career:* leading soloist of children's radio chorus 1950; debut as Yniold in Pelléas et Mélisande at Bucharest Opera 1964; Frankfurt Opera 1968–70; Glyndebourne Festival 1968; Salzburg Festival 1969; Staatsoper Vienna 1969; Royal Opera House, Covent Garden 1971; Lyric Opera of Chicago 1973; Paris Opera 1974; La Scala, Milan 1975; Metropolitan Opera, New York 1977; operatic roles include Susanna, Pamina, Norina, Gilda, Violetta, Manon, Antonia, Tatyana, Mimi, Mélisande, Sophie; concerts with all major European orchestras; lieder recitals at Musikverein Vienna, Royal Opera House, Covent Garden, Carnegie Hall, New York, La Scala; retd from public singing 1990; masterclasses worldwide. *Recordings include:* Bach Cantatas, Mozart Masses, Brahms Requiem, Mahler Symphonies 2, 8; complete operas including Le Nozze di Figaro, La finta giardiniera, Così fan tutte, Die Zauberflöte, Hänsel und Gretel, Calisto, Louise, L'Elisir d'amore, Les Pêcheurs de perles, La Traviata, Rigoletto, Alzira, Manon. *Publication:* Opernwahrheiten 1998. *Honours:* Hon. Citizen of Bucharest 1995; Grand Officer, Order of Sant'Iago da Espada (Portugal) 1990; First Prize, Int. Singing Competition,'s-Hertogenbosch, Netherlands 1965, First Prize, Munich Radio Competition 1966; Austrian Kammersängerin 1981.

COTTELI, Honorat; Slovak violinist and composer; b. 4 Jan. 1941, Banska Bystrica; m.; two s. two d. *Education:* Conservatory of Music, Bratislava. *Career:* debut Diploma Concert 1960; Radio Symphony Orchestra, Bratislava 1959; Slovak Philharmonic Orchestra 1960–67; Concertmaster, State Opera Orchestra, Banska Bystrica 1964; Concertmaster, Opera Orchestra, St Gallen, Switzerland 1967–70; Conservatory of Music, Zürich 1976; Opera Orchestra, Zürich 1970; mem. Swiss Musicians Union. *Compositions include:* Music of Stadent 1987, Intrada for strings 1989, Bagatellen for solo instruments and strings 1991, Impressions for strings 1993, Trio burlesco 1994, Preludi for violin and piano 1995, Swing Part for strings 1995, Fantasticherie 1995, Episodi 1996, Orchestino concertino for grand orchestra 1996, Capriccio for violin and piano 1996, Racconti di Faust 1996, five songs for voice 1996–98, Fantasia gioccosa 1997, Partita Slovacca 1997, Brass Quintet 1997, Musica per contrabassi 1997, Favole Slovacche 1998, Suite per tre 1998, Herbstwind 1998, Saloniata 2000, Contrasti 2001, Wasserzauber 2004, Fiori 2005, Tango Breve 2007, Roxy 2007, Frammenti Nuovi 2010, Spievanky 2011. *Honours:* second prize, Composition Competition, Bratislava, Slovakia 1996. *Address:* Cotteli-Musica, Dorfstrasse 71, 8957 Spreitenbach, Switzerland (home). *Website:* www.cotteli-musica.ch.

COULAIS, Bruno; French composer; b. 13 Jan. 1954, Paris. *Compositions for film and TV:* Nuit féline 1978, México mágico 1979, Quidam (TV) 1984, Meurtres pour mémoire (TV) 1985, Bel ragazzo 1986, Lien de parenté 1986, Qui trop embrasse... 1986, La Femme secrète 1986, Les demoiselles de Concarneau (episode in TV series, L'Heure Simenon) 1987, Adieu Christine (TV series) 1989, Juliette en toutes lettres (TV series) 1989, Zanzibar 1989, Le Lien du sang (TV) 1990, La Campagne de Cicéron 1990, Peinture fraîche 1991,

Le Jour des rois 1991, Piège pour femme seule (TV) 1991, Ma soeur, mon amour 1992, Les Équilibristes 1992, Odyssée bidon (TV) 1992, Le Retour de Casanova 1992, Le Petit prince a dit 1992, Vieille canaille 1992, La Place du père (TV) 1992, Siméon 1992, Flight from Justice (TV) 1993, L'Instit (TV series) 1993, Le Juge est une femme (TV series) 1993, Le Fils du requin 1993, L'Ange et le génie - Correspondances Paris-Berlin 1994, Der Grüne Heinrich 1994, Cognacq-Jay (TV) 1994, Mort d'un gardien de la paix (TV) 1994, La Colline aux mille enfants (TV) 1994, Waati 1995, Le Blanc à lunettes (TV) 1995, Un si bel orage (TV) 1995, Des mots qui déchirent (TV) 1995, L'Enfant des rues (TV) 1995, La Rivière Espérance (mini TV series) 1995, Adultère, mode d'emploi 1995, Le Nid tombé de l'oiseau (TV) 1995, Embrasse-moi vite! (TV) 1995, Coeur de cible (TV) 1996, Sixième classique (TV) 1996, Microcosmos: Le peuple de l'herbe 1996, Une fille à papas (TV) 1996, L'Orange de Noël (TV) 1996, J'ai rendez-vous avec vous (TV) 1996, Vice vertu et vice versa (TV) 1996, Victor (TV) 1997, La Mère de nos enfants (TV) 1997, La Belle vie (mini TV series) 1997, Pardaillan (TV) 1997, La Famille Sapajou (TV) 1997, Jeunesse 1997, L'Amour dans le désordre (TV) 1997, Les Héritiers (TV) 1997, Combat de fauves 1997, Flammen im Paradies 1997, Le Dernier été (TV) 1997, Mireille et Vincent (TV) 1997, Deux flics (TV series) 1998, Don Juan 1998, Serial Lover 1998, Déjà mort 1998, Préférence 1998, Le Comte de Monte Cristo (mini TV series) 1998, L'Enfant des terres blondes (TV) 1998, Das Mädchen aus der Fremde 1999, Belle maman 1999, Véga (TV series) 1999, Himalaya - l'enfance d'un chef 1999, Balzac (TV) 1999, Un dérangement considérable 1999, La Débandade 1999, Épouse-moi 2000, Scènes de crimes 2000, Le Libertin 2000, Comme un aimant 2000, Jacqueline dans ma vitrine 2000, Les Fleurs d'Harrison 2000, Les Rivières pourpres 2000, Le Blanc et le rouge (TV) 2000, Zaïde, un petit air de vengeance (TV) 2001, Faut pas rêver (TV series) 2001, Belphégor - Le fantôme du Louvre 2001, De l'amour 2001, Un aller simple 2001, Origine océan - 4 milliards d'années sous les mers 2001, Vidocq 2001, Le Peuple migrateur 2001, Les Ailes de la nature (TV) 2002, Les Tombales 2002, Drengen der ville gøre det umulige 2002, Toute une histoire 2003, Les Parents terribles (TV) 2003, Les Choristes 2004, Agents secrets 2004, Genesis 2004, Milady (TV) 2004, Brice de Nice 2005, Sometimes in April (TV) 2005, Je préfère qu'on reste amis 2005, Les Rois maudits 2005, Gaspard le bandit (TV) 2006, La Planète blanche 2006, L'Affaire Villemin (TV) 2006, Truands 2007, René Bousquet ou Le grand arrangement (TV) 2007, Hellphone 2007, Ulzhan 2007, Max & Co 2007, Le Deuxième souffle 2007, Les Femmes de l'Ombre 2008, MR 73 2008, Villa Amalia 2009, Brendan and the Secret of Kells 2009, Coraline 2009. *Other compositions include:* Mémoires d'un cabotin for nine pianos 1985. *Current Management:* Marsh, Best and Associates, 9150 Wilshire Boulevard, Suite 220, Beverly Hills, CA 90212-3429, USA. *Telephone:* (310) 285-0303. *Fax:* (310) 285-0218. *E-mail:* info@marshbest.com. *Website:* www.sandramarsh.com.

COUROUPOS, Yorgos; Greek composer; b. 1 Jan. 1942, Athens. *Education:* Athens Conservatory, studied with Messiaen in Paris. *Career:* administrative posts at Nat. Lyric Theatre, Athens; Dir, Kalamata Municipal Conservatory from 1985. *Compositions include:* Dieu le Veut 1975, Grisélidis 1977, Pylades (one-act opera, libretto by G. Himonas after Sophocles and Euripides) 1992, Odyssey (ballet) 1995, The Runaways of the Chessboard (opera) 1998.

COUROUX, Marc; Canadian pianist, academic and writer; b. 1970, Montréal. *Education:* McGill Univ. with Louis-Philippe Pelletier. *Career:* repertory includes Night Fantasies by Elliott Carter, Euryali by Iannis Xenakis, 14 Etudes by György Ligeti, other works by Ambrosini, Cage, Donatoni, Lindberg, Messiaen, Nancarrow, Rzewski, Schoenberg, Stockhausen, Szymanowski and Tippett, along with Canadian composers Brégent, Cherney, Gonneville, Tremblay and Vivier; premieres of Envolée by Sean Ferguson and Variations by James Harley 1994; soloist, McGill Symphony Orchestra in the North American premiere of Bengt Hambraeus' Concerto for piano and orchestra 1995; recital of Canadian and Belgian works, ARS Musica Festival Brussels 1995; performed Concerto for piano and orchestra by György Ligeti with CBC Vancouver Orchestra 1996; performed piano solo pieces, Nouvel Ensemble Moderne 1996; artist-in-residence, Banff Centre for the Arts, Princeton and Rutgers Univs, Domaine Forget summer course for new music, St-Irénée, Québec; Lecturer, Univs of New York at Stony Brook, and Buffalo. *Publications:* contrib. several articles in professional journals.

COURTIS, Jean-Philippe; French singer (bass); b. 24 May 1951. *Education:* Paris Conservatoire. *Career:* sang first at the Paris Opéra from 1980, then the Opéra-Comique 1983; appearances at the Aix Festival in Werther, Semiramide, and Ariadne auf Naxos, and guest engagements throughout Europe as Henry VIII in Anna Bolena (Amsterdam, 1989), Don Giovanni (Strasbourg, 1990) and Arkel (Vienna Staatsoper, 1991); sang Méphistophélès in Faust at the Paris Opéra, 1988, and appeared in the 1990 opening of the Opéra Bastille (Les Troyens); Other roles include the Commendatore in Don Giovanni, Don Quichotte, and Frère Bernard in Messiaen's St François d'Assise (premiere, 1983); Season 1994–95 as Falstaff in Le Songe d'une nuite d'été by Thomas, Creon in Cherubini's Médée at Martina Franca and Gounod's Frère Laurent at Houston; Isménor in Rameau's Dardanus at Lyon, 1998; Sang Somarone in Béatrice et Bénédict at Amsterdam, 2001; many concert engagements.

COVELL, Roger David, AM, PhD, FAHA; Australian academic, critic, composer and conductor; *Professor Emeritus, University of New South Wales*; b. 1 Feb. 1931, Sydney, New South Wales; s. of Harold Covell and Margaret Bardsley; m. 1st Sue Catling 1953 (divorced 1964); one s. one d.; m. 2nd Merle Berriman 1965 (divorced 1976); two s.; m. 3rd Patricia Brown 1976. *Education:* Brisbane High School and Univs of Queensland and New South

Wales. *Career:* Chief Music Critic, The Sydney Morning Herald 1960–2001, Sr Music Writer 2002–09; Sr Lecturer and Head Dept of Music, Univ. of New South Wales 1966, Assoc. Prof. 1973, Prof. 1984, Head School of Music and Music Educ. 1993–96, Prof. Emer. 1998–; Artistic Dir Univ. of New South Wales Opera 1968–97; Co-founder Australia Ensemble 1980; mem. Australia Council 1977–83; Pres. Australian Soc. for Music Educ. 1978–81, Musicological Soc. of Australia 1983–84; mem. Council, Australian Acad. of Humanities 1986–88; Fellow, Australian Soc. for Music Educ. 2011. *Music:* Australian Yesterdays (historical musical theatre), Candlepoint and Star (carol cycle). *Publications include:* Australia's Music: Themes of a New Society 1967, Music in Australia: Needs and Prospects 1970, Folk Songs of Australia, Vol. 2 (with J. Meredith and P. Brown) 1987, Edward Geoghegan's The Currency Lass (ed. and arranger); ed. of baroque opera scores. *Honours:* Geraldine Pascall Prize for Music Criticism 1993, Challender Memorial Lecturer 1994, Centenary Medal 2003, APRA-AMC Long-term Advancement of Music Award, Australian Music Centre 2006, Sir Bernard Heinze Memorial Award 2013. *Address:* 9 Kubya Street, Blackheath, NSW 2785, Australia (home). *Telephone:* (2) 4787-6182 (home). *E-mail:* r.covell@unsw.edu.au (office).

COVEY-CRUMP, Rogers, BMus, FRCO, ARCM, LRAM; British singer (tenor); b. 1944, England. *Education:* Royal Coll. of Music, London and Univ. of London. *Career:* concert, broadcasting and commercial recording engagements as a solo artist and as a mem. of the Hilliard Ensemble, Gothic Voices, the Deller and Taverner Consorts and Singcircle (Stockhausen's Stimmung); Promenade Concerts 1984–99, Purcell's Odes, Pärt's Miserere, Bach's St Matthew Passion; premiere of MacMillan's Quickening; performances of Bach, Haydn and Pärt in Finland and Estonia 1985–96, Bach's St John Passion in Vancouver 1997, Bach's Matthew Passion in Stockholm for Swedish radio with Tonu Kaljuste 1997; tours of the UK 1988, 1992, 1998, with Contemporary Music Network in Pärt's Passion, Miserere and Litany; summer schools with the Hilliard Ensemble in UK, Finland, Germany and Austria since 1984; residencies in California and Pennsylvania 1988, 1992; lecturer and writer on aspects of vocal ensemble singing. *Recordings include:* Bach's B Minor Mass and St John Passion, Monteverdi's Vespers and Purcell with Andrew Parrott and the Taverner Players; Bach's St Matthew Passion with Roy Goodman and the choir of King's College, Cambridge; Bach's St Mark Passion with the European Union Baroque Orchestra; Pärt's Passio, Miserere and Litany; Lute Songs, with Paul O'Dette and with Jakob Lindberg; Hilliard Ensemble collaboration with Norwegian saxophonist, Jan Garbarek in the albums Officium and Mnemosyne. *Current Management:* Hazard Chase, 25 City Road, Cambridge, CB1 1DP, England. *Telephone:* (1223) 312400. *Fax:* (1223) 460827. *E-mail:* info@hazardchase.co.uk. *Website:* www.hazardchase.co.uk; www.hilliardensemble.demon.co.uk.

COVIELLO, Roberto; Italian singer (baritone); b. 1958. *Career:* debut in Naples, 1983; sang Guglielmo at Bari, 1984, and Paisiello's Figaro at the 1986 Spoleto Festival; La Scala Milan from 1987, as Don Giovanni and other major baritone roles; Pesaro Festival, 1988–89, in La Scala di Seta and La Gazza Ladra; other roles include Mozart's Figaro, Belcore, Malatesta, Valentin, Mercutio (Roméo et Juliette), Valentin and Ford in Falstaff; season 1990–91 in opera at Bonn, Santiago, Bergamo and Trieste.

COWAN, Sigmund; American singer (baritone); b. 4 March 1948, New York. *Education:* Univ. of Miami, Univ. of Florida, New York Inst. of Finance, Juilliard School, Manhattan School of Music. *Career:* appearances include at New York City Opera, Deutsche Oper am Rhein; Spoleto Festival, Kennedy Center, Miami Opera, Basel, Essen, Wiesbaden, Vienna Festival, Berlin Staatstheater, Brussels, Amsterdam (Opera and Concertgebouw), Carnegie Hall, Mexico City, Dublin, and Calgary and Edmonton (Canada), Rotterdam; sang with Rochester Philharmonic, National Symphony, Baltimore Symphony and at Flagstaff Festival; appeared with National Orchestra, Mexico City, Canadian Opera, L'Opera de Montreal, Baltimore Opera; roles in Nabucco, Rigoletto, Macbeth, Il Trovatore, I Due Foscari, Un Ballo in Maschera, La Forza del Destino, La Traviata. *Recordings include:* Die Gezeichneten with Edo de Waart.

COWIE, Edward, BEd, BMus, DMus, PhD, FRSA; British composer, painter, natural scientist and writer; b. 17 Aug. 1943, Birmingham; m. Heather Jean Johns 1995, two d. (by second marriage). *Education:* Univ. of London, Univ. of Southampton, Univ. of Lancaster. *Career:* Sr Lecturer, Univ. of Lancaster 1973–83; Prof. of Creative Arts, Univ. of Wollongong, NSW, Australia 1983–89; Granada Composer and Conductor, Royal Liverpool Philharmonic Orchestra 1983–86; Prof. of Creative Arts, James Cook Univ., Queensland, Australia 1989–95; Prof. and Dir of Research, Dartington Coll. of Arts, Devon, England 1995–; Artist-in-Residence, Royal Soc. for the Protection of Birds 2002–05; Assoc. Composer, BBC Singers 2002–05; mem. British Ornithologists' Union. *Compositions include:* Commedia (opera) 1979, Concerto for orchestra 1982, five string quartets 1974–95, American Symphony 1983, Choral Symphony 1984, Ancient Voices 1 and 2 1983, 1991, Cello Concerto 1992, Water, Stone, Wood and Breath for chorus and percussion 1996, Between Two Waves for 12 voices 1999, Oboe Concerto 1999, From Moment to Moment for chamber orchestra 2000. *Exhibitions as painter:* 41 exhibitions. *Publication:* Birds Talk 2001. *Honours:* many prizes as composer. *Current Management:* c/o Schott Music, Weihergarten 5, 55116 Mainz, Germany. *Website:* www.edward-cowie.com.

COXON, Richard; British singer (tenor); b. 25 Aug. 1968, Nottingham, England. *Education:* Royal Northern Coll. of Music with John Mitchinson.

Career: debut as Flavio in Norma for Scottish Opera 1993; further roles with Scottish Opera have included Narraboth in Salome, Jacquino, Nemorino, Alfred in Die Fledermaus, Barbarigo in Verdi's Due Foscari, Don Ottavio, Alfredo, and Jiri in The Jacobin by Dvořák; guest appearances for Opera Northern Ireland, Opera Zuid in Maastricht, Glyndebourne Festival Opera, Nationale Reisoper Holland and ENO; concerts include Mendelssohn's St Paul with the Scottish National Orchestra, Messiah with the Bergen Philharmonic Orchestra and engagements with the Hallé Orchestra, BBC Concert Orchestra, BBC Scottish Symphony Orchestra and London Pops Orchestra; Fenton in Falstaff and Young Convict in From the House of the Dead, Painter in Lulu and Nick in The Handmaid's Tale for ENO; Mr By-Ends in Pilgrim's Progress for Royal Opera, in concert; Brighella in Ariadne auf Naxos for Scottish Opera at the Edinburgh Festival and on tour; Edgardo in film version of Lucia di Lammermoor, directed by Don Boyd; Squeak in Billy Budd, Gastone in La Traviata for Royal Opera; Italian Tenor Der Rosenkavalier for Opera North and at the Spolete Festival, Italy; Kudjas in Katya Kabanova for Opera de Montréal, Florida Grand Opera and Scottish Opera. *Honours:* Webster Booth/Esso Award, Clonter Opera Prize, Ricordi Opera Prize.

CRAFTS, Edward James, BMus, MS; American singer (bass-baritone) and opera director; b. 11 Nov. 1946, New York, NY. *Education:* Curtis Inst. of Music, Indiana Univ. and Hochschule für Musik, Hamburg, Germany. *Career:* has sung widely in the USA from 1982, notably at Houston Opera (as Dulcamara), St Louis and the City Opera New York (as Escamillo); Santa Fe 1984; La Scala Milan, 1984, in Bernstein's Trouble in Tahiti; Seattle, 1987, as Iago; New Jersey, 1983; other roles include Falstaff, Scarpia and Mephistopheles; sang Wotan in The Ring for Arizona Opera at Flagstaff, 1996; sang in US premieres of Zemlinsky's Eine Florentinische Tragödie, Wagner's Liebesverbot, Prokofiev's Maddalena and Canadian premieres of Montemezzi's L'Amore doe Tre Re, Hoiby's The Tempest and Weber's Der Freishütz; further appearances at La Scala, Covent Garden, in Vienna, Rome, Monte Carlo, Budapest and Warsaw; previously taught at Univs of Nebraska, Maryland, Peabody Inst., Catholic Univ., Hood Coll., Shenandoah Conservatory; currently Assoc. Prof. of Voice, Univ. of Arkansas at Little Rock; also Dir of Opera Studio, Oblerlin Conservatory. *Recordings include:* Bernstein's A Quiet Place and Trouble in Tahiti, Loeffler's Songs, Verdi's Requiem, Purrfectly Classical. *Telephone:* (646) 591-9721 (mobile) (office). *E-mail:* ejc@edwardcrafts.com (office). *Website:* www.edwardjcrafts.com.

CRAGG, Elizabeth; British singer (soprano); b. 25 Sept. 1976, Birmingham; one c. *Education:* Royal Holloway Coll., London, Royal Coll. of Music with Elisabeth Robson. *Career:* recent operatic roles include Zerbinetta for Garsington Opera, Flowermaiden in Parsifal, Royal Opera, Belinda in Dido and Aeneas, Akademie für Alte Musik Berlin' Clorinda in Il Combattimento di Tancredi e Clorinda, Netherlands Opera and Utrecht, Fauno in Ascanio in Alba, Buxton Festival, Jano in Jenůfa, ENO, Ida in Die Fledermaus, Glyndebourne Festival, The Swan in Jonathan Dove's The Swan on Death's River, Opera North, Ninetta in The Love for Three Oranges, Amsterdam; Salzburg Easter Festival debut under Simon Rattle as First Niece in Peter Grimes; concert performances include engagements with The Acad. of St Martin in the Fields, The Bach Choir, City of London Sinfonia, The English Concert, The Hanover Band, Manchester Camerata, OAE (at BBC Proms) and The Sixteen. *Honours:* RCM Dorothy Silk Prize. *Telephone:* (1825) 840 437. *E-mail:* info@musichall.uk.com. *Website:* www.musichall.uk.com.

CRAIG, Russell; New Zealand stage designer; b. 1948. *Education:* Univ. of Auckland. *Career:* resident designer at New Zealand's Mercury and Downstage theatres; moved to London 1974; designs for Scottish Opera with Savitri, Hedda Gabler, Rossini double bill, Oberon and L'Elisir d'amore 1981–94, WNO with Barber of Seville, Die Entführung, Ariadne and Le Comte Ory 1986–91, and ENO with The Rape of Lucretia and Ariadne auf Naxos 1983; designs for Opera North include Così fan tutte, The Magic Flute, A Village Romeo and Juliet, Acis and Galatea, Showboat, Oberto 1983–94; La Bohème for Glyndebourne Touring Opera 1991; represented Britain at Prague Quadrennial 1983. *Honours:* Queen Elizabeth II Arts Council Award. *E-mail:* russellgcraig@blueyonder.co.uk. *Website:* www.russellcraig.co.uk.

CRANE, Louise; British singer (mezzo-soprano); b. 1965, England. *Education:* Guildhall School of Music, Royal Northern College of Music with Barbara Robotham. *Career:* sang in Opera Factory's Don Giovanni and Dialogues des Carmélites for Opéra de Lyon; further engagements as Third Lady and Mistress Quickly with English Touring Opera, in The Siege of Corinth and The Nightingale for Chelsea Opera Group, Stravinsky's Mother Goose at Aldeburgh and Mozart's Marcellina for European Chamber Opera; English National Opera debut, 1993 in the premiere of Harvey's Inquest of Love; Sang Rita in Zampa for Opera Omnibus, 1996; concert engagements in Rossini's Stabat Mater, Messiah, Beethoven's Ninth and Missa Solemnis, The Dream of Gerontius and Das Lied von der Erde; touring performances of Gilbert and Sullivan. *E-mail:* louisemezzo@aol.com.

CRAWFORD, Bruce, BS; American arts manager and advertising executive; *Non-Executive Chairman, Publicis Omnicom Group;* b. 16 March 1929, West Bridgewater, Mass; m. Christine Crawford 1958. *Education:* Univ. of Pennsylvania. *Career:* entered advertising 1956; CEO BBDO International 1977–, Pres. Batten, Barton, Durstine & Osborn 1978–; joined Bd of Metropolitan Opera 1976, served on Exec. Cttee from 1977, Vice-Pres. 1981, Pres. 1984–85, Gen. Man. 1985–89, now Hon. Dir; Pres. and CEO Omnicom Group 1989–95, Chair. and CEO 1995–97, Chair. 1995–, Chair. Finance Cttee, mem. Exec. Cttee, (merged with Publicis Groupe to form Publicis Omnicom Group 2013), Chair. (non-exec.) 2013–14; Chair. Lincoln Center for the Performing Arts 2002–05, now Chair. Emer.; Dir, Animal Medical Center. *Address:* Publicis Omnicom Group, 437 Madison Avenue, New York, NY 10022, USA (office). *Telephone:* (212) 415-3600 (office). *Fax:* (212) 415-3530 (office). *Website:* www.omnicomgroup.com (office).

CRAWFORD, Timothy Terry; British lutenist, musicologist and academic; *Professorial Research Fellow in Computational Musicology, Goldsmiths College;* b. 11 July 1948, Farnham, Surrey, England; m. Emilia de Grey 1975; two s. one d. *Education:* Univ. of Sussex, Royal Coll. of Music, London. *Career:* Founder-mem. early music ensembles, Ars Nova and Parley of Instruments; frequent appearances with English Baroque Soloists, London Philharmonic Orchestra; Asst Ed., Early Music Magazine 1984–85; Music Co-ordinator, Royal Acad. of Arts; Research Fellow, Dept of Music, King's Coll. London 1989–2002, projects include Electronic Corpus of Lute Music (ECOLM), Online Music Recognition and Searching (OMRAS); researcher, Centre for Computational Creativity, City Univ., London 2002–04; Professorial Research Fellow in Computational Musicology, Dept of Computing, Goldsmiths Coll., London 2004–, projects include MeTAMuSE, Purcell Plus, OMRAS II, Transforming Musicology (AHRC Large Grant 2013–16); mem. Lute Soc. (Cttee mem. 1975–87), Nat. Early Music Asscn (Cttee mem. 1985–86), RMA, Musicians' Union. *Recordings:* Orfeo, Il Ritorno d'Ulisse, Sacred Music of Monteverdi (with Parley of Instruments, Emma Kirkby, Ian Partridge and David Thomas). *Publications:* editor, Lute Society Journal (The Lute) 1979–87, Silvius Leopold Weiss: The Moscow Manuscript 1995, S. L. Weiss: Complete Works, Vols 4–6 (ed.), The Dresden Manuscript (Das Erbe Deutscher Musik) 2002–07, Works from Miscellaneous Manuscripts (Das Erbe Deutscher Musik) Vols 9–10 (co-ed.) 2011–13; contrib. to The Lute, Early Music, Chelys, Journal of the Lute Society of America. *Honours:* Arts Council research grant for continental travel 1976. *Address:* Department of Computing, Goldsmiths College, University of London, London, SE14 6NW, England (office). *E-mail:* t.crawford@gold.ac.uk (office). *Website:* doc.gold.ac.uk/~mas01tc (office).

CREED, Kay, BMus, MPA; American singer, voice teacher and academic; b. 19 Aug. 1940, Oklahoma City; m. Carveth Osterhaus 1975, one d. *Education:* Oklahoma City Univ. and studied in Munich, Germany. *Career:* debut with New York City Opera 1965; created role of Fortuna in Don Rodrigo by Ginastera; Mrs Danton in Danton's Death; opera roles include Carmen, Cenerentola, Dorabella, Hansel, Giulietta, Sextus in Julius Caesar, Ulrica, Urbain (Les Huguenots); solo performances with New York Philharmonic, Chicago Symphony, Philadelphia Orchestra, Carnegie Hall, Les Huguenots; Dallas Symphony; Naumberg Orchestra, Oklahoma City Symphony; mem. Bd of Dirs, Cimarron Circuit Opera 1985; Lecturer in Opera and Voice, Cantor Classes for Catholic Lituigy; founding mem., Oklahoma City Guild of Tulsa Opera; founding mem., Oklahoma Opera and Musical Theater Co.; founding Dir, Edmond Central Historical Opera.

CREED, Marcus; British music conductor; *Artistic Director and Chief Conductor, SWR Vokalensemble Stuttgart;* b. Eastbourne, Sussex. *Education:* King's Coll., Cambridge, Christ Church, Oxford, Guildhall School, London. *Career:* moved to Germany 1976; worked as a coach and chorusmaster at Deutsche Oper Berlin; Artistic Dir RIAS Kammerchor 1987–2001; fmr pianist and conductor, Berlin Scharoun Ensemble; fmr conductor at Berlin Staatskapelle, Symphonie-Orchester Berlin, Akad. für Alte Musik Berlin; Artistic Dir and Chief Conductor, SWR Vokalensemble Stuttgart 2003–; Prof. of Choral Conducting, Hochschule für Musik Köln 1998–; has worked Freiburger Barockorchester and Concerto Köln; gave performances of J.S. Bach's Mass in B minor, Purcell's Dido and Aeneas at Berlin Staatsoper, cycle of George Frideric Handel oratorios (Solomon, Messiah, Jephtha, Israel in Egypt, Alexander's Feast, Theodora, etc.) in Germany; conducted Belshazzar at Göttingen Händel Festival 1996; regularly appears at Berlin Festwochen as well as at festivals including Warsaw Spring, Wien Modern, Salzburg Festspielen, Venice Biennale and at festivals in Montreux, Edinburgh, Lucerne and Innsbruck; in collaboration with Claudio Abbado and Berliner Philharmoniker, conducted Stockhausen's orchestral Gruppen; has worked with other orchestras including Berlin Staatskapelle and Berliner Symphoniker. *Honours:* ECHO Klassik Awards 2011, Edison Award, Diapason d'Or Award, Cannes Classical Award, 20th/21st Century Choral Recording of the Year Award. *Address:* Hochschule für Musik und Tanz Köln, Unter Krahnenbäumen 87, 50668 Cologne, Germany (office). *Telephone:* (221) 9128180 (office). *Fax:* (221) 131204 (office). *E-mail:* MarcusAlan.Creed@hfmt-koeln.de (office). *Website:* www.hfmt-koeln.de (office).

CREFFELD, Rosanna; British singer (mezzo-soprano); b. 1945, England; m. Richard Angas. *Education:* Royal College of Music with Flora Nielsen, studied in Paris with Pierre Bernac, with Vera Rosza in London. *Career:* debut at Glyndebourne 1969, as Second Lady in Die Zauberflöte; Glyndebourne Touring Opera 1969–70, as Dorabella, and as Olga in Eugene Onegin; appearances at Aix-en-Provence, Amsterdam, Strasbourg, Lyon and Bremen; Scottish Opera Glasgow as Dorabella and Cherubino; Monteverdi's Orfeo with the English National Opera; Paris Opéra as Cherubino and as Lucretia in The Rape of Lucretia by Britten; engagements in San Diego 1984, and Pittsburgh 1986; Lausanne 1986, in Honegger's Antigone. *Recordings include:* Matilde in Rossini's Elisabetta Regina d'Inghilterra.

CRESHEVSKY, Noah; American composer; b. 31 Jan. 1945, Rochester, NY. *Education:* Eastman School, Rochester, Juilliard School with Berio, studied with Nadia Boulanger in Paris and with Virgil Thomson. *Career:* teacher, Juilliard and Hunter Coll., New York; Brooklyn Coll. from 1969; Visiting Prof., Princeton Univ. 1987–88 Dir Centre for Computer Music, Brooklyn Coll. 1992–. *Compositions include:* Vier Lieder (stage piece) 1966, Three Pieces in the Shape of a Square for four performers and tape 1967, Monogenesis for voices, chamber orchestra and tape 1968, Variations for four pianists and tape 1969, Mirrors for dancers and tape 1970, Circuit for tape 1971, Broadcast 1973, Chaconne for piano or harp 1974, Guitar 1975, In Other Words: Portrait of John Cage 1976, Great Performances for any two instruments and tape 1977, Great Performances 1978, Portrait of Rudy Perez 1978, Highway 1979, Sonata, Nightscape and Celebration for tape 1980–83, Strategic Defense Initiative 1986, Electric String Quartet 1988, Talea 1991, Private Lives 1993, Coup d'état, Gone Now 1995, Who 1995, Sha 1996, Electric Fanfare 1997, Estancia 1999, Ommagio 2001, I Wonder Who's Kissing Her Now 2003, Brother Tom 2008, La Belle Dame Sans Merci 2009, Götterdämmerung 2009, Happy Ending 2009. *Honours:* NEA grant 1981. *Address:* 301 West 45th Street, Apartment 10L, New York, NY 10036-3831, USA (home). *Telephone:* (212) 247-0265 (home).

CRESSWELL, Lyell Richard, BMus, MMus, PhD; New Zealand composer; b. 13 Oct. 1944, Wellington; m. Catherine Mawson 1972. *Education:* Victoria Univ. of Wellington, Univ. of Toronto, Canada, Univ. of Aberdeen, UK. *Career:* music organiser, Chapter Arts Centre, Cardiff, UK 1978–80; Forman Fellow in Composition, Univ. of Edinburgh 1980–82; Cramb Fellow in Composition, Univ. of Glasgow 1982–85; freelance composer 1985–; Composer-in-Residence, Creative New Zealand/New Zealand School of Music 2006–07; mem. British Acad. of Composers and Songwriters, Composers Asscn of New Zealand. *Compositions include:* Ylur 1990–91, Voices of Ocean Winds, The Pumpkin Massacre, Il Suono di Enormi Distanze, A Modern Ecstasy, Cello Concerto, O!, Salm, Speak for Us, Great Sea, Passacagli, O Let the Fire Burn, Concerto for String Quartet and Orchestra (premiered 1997), Kaea, Trombone Concerto 1997 (premiered 1998), The Voice Inside, concerto for violin and soprano (premiered 2002), Of Smoke and Bickering Flame, concerto for Chamber Orchestra (premiered 2003), Shadows Without Sun (premiered 2003), Ara Kopikopiko (premiered 2005), Canterbury Rhymes (premiered 2006), Alas! How Swift (premiered 2007), The Perfect Woman (premiered 2008), The Money Man (premiered 2010), Piano Concerto (premiered 2011), Triple Concerto (premiered 2012), The Clock Stops (premiered 2014). *Honours:* Hon. DMus (Victoria Univ. of Wellington) 2002; Ian Whyte Award 1978, APRA Silver Scroll 1980, Creative Scotland Award 2001, Inaugural Elgar Bursary 2002, SOUNZ Contemporary Award 2011. *Address:* 4 Leslie Place, Edinburgh, EH4 1NQ, Scotland (home). *Telephone:* (131) 332-9181 (home). *E-mail:* lcress@talktalk.net.

CRIDER, Michèle; American singer (soprano); b. 1963, Illinois. *Education:* Univ. of Iowa, Zürich Opera Studio. *Career:* debut as Leonora in Il Trovatore at Dortmund 1989; US debut in Aida at San Diego Opera 1996; roles include Leonora in Il Trovatore, Leonora in La Forza del Destino, Amelia in Un Ballo in Maschera, Elvira in Ernani, Odabella in Attila, Lucrezia in I due Foscari, Giselda in I Lombardi, Imogene in Il Pirata, Elena and Margherita in Mefistofele, Santuzza in Cavalleria Rusticana and the title roles of Aida, Luisa Miller, Madama Butterfly, Tosca, Norma, La Gioconda; appearances at Teatro alla Scala Milan, Arena di Verona, Florence and Genoa opera houses, Royal Opera House Covent Garden, Deutsche Oper Berlin, the State Operas of Hamburg, Berlin, Vienna, Munich, Stuttgart and Wiesbaden, Bavarian State Opera Munich, Aalto Opera House Essen, Semperoper Dresden, Stadttheater St Gallen and Zürich Opera House, Switzerland, Vienna State Opera, Teatro del Liceu Barcelona, Teatro Real Madrid and Oviedo Opera, Opéra Bastille Paris, New York Metropolitan Opera, San Francisco Opera, Los Angeles Opera, Netherlands Opera, Israeli Opera, Dubai Opera, La Monnaie Brussels, Vlaamse Opera Antwerp; BBC Prom concert with Verdi's Requiem 1997; other concert engagements at Salzburg Festival, Maggio Musicale Fiorentino, Orange, Edinburgh, Macerata and Ravenna Festivals, Royal Albert Hall, Carnegie Hall, Alte Oper Frankfurt, Savonlinna, Salle Pleyel Paris and London Barbican Hall. *Recordings include:* Amelia in Un Ballo in Maschera (under Carlo Rizzi), Elena and Margherita in Mefistofele (under Riccardo Muti), Verdi's Requiem (under Richard Hickox, with London Symphony Orchestra), Gerhilde in Die Walküre (under Christoph von Dohnanyi). *Honours:* winner District Metropolitan Opera Auditions (twice), finalist Luciano Pavarotti Competition 1988, jt first prizewinner Geneva Int. Music Competition 1989, winner Int. Grand Prix 1989, San Francisco Opera Award of Merit 2001, Univ. of Iowa Alumni Asscn Young Alumni Award 2003. *Current Management:* Wolf Piper Artists International, 13 East 69th Street, Suite 3R, New York, NY 10021, USA. *Telephone:* (212) 531-1514. *Fax:* (212) 861-6949. *E-mail:* info@wolfartists.com. *Website:* www.wolfartists.com. *E-mail:* info@michele-crider.com (office). *Website:* www.michele-crider.com.

CRILLY, David Robert, DPhil, MA, LTCL, LLCM; British composer, musician and lecturer; *Head of Creative and Performing Arts, Liverpool Hope University;* b. 3 June 1959, Birkenhead. *Education:* City of Leeds Coll. of Music, Univ. of Southampton, Royal Holloway and Bedford New Coll., Univ. of London, Univ. of Oxford. *Career:* Sr Lecturer in Music and Dir of Research, Anglia Ruskin Univ.; Artistic Dir Cambridge Shakespeare Festival 1988–; Dir Cambridge Acad. of Dramatic Art 2009–. *Compositions:* In that quiet earth, for symphony orchestra, voice and narrator 2000, Leap of faith, for chamber orchestra and voices 2003. *Publications:* Is the application of the principles of semiology to music analysis founded upon a philosophical mistake?, European Journal for Semiotic Studies 2002, Wiggenstein, Music Language – Games, The Open Space issue no. 2, Spring 2002, Elastic form and concrete structure: the analysis of improvised music, in Nikos Mastorakis ed. Mathematics and Computers in Modern Science 2002, Perception of Mathematical Structure and Architectural Design: Form and Forming in Music, in ISAMA 1999 International Society of the Arts, Mathematics and Architecture, The Problem of Form in Analytical Discussions, in Ideas and Production, a journal in the history of ideas Vol. XI. *Address:* 6A Fair Street, Cambridge, CB1 1HA, England (home). *Telephone:* (1223) 321984 (home). *E-mail:* Bartok2571@msn .com (home).

CRIST, Richard LeRoy, BS, MM; American singer (bass) and vocal instructor; *Artist Teacher of Voice and Director of Opera Theater, School of Music, Ohio University*; b. 21 Oct. 1947, Harrisburg, Pa; s. of Robert E. Crist and Mildred C. Crist; m. Yvonne Marie Brennan; two s. one d. *Education:* Messiah Coll., New England Conservatory, Boston, Goldovsky Opera Inst., New York, Special Student – Opera, Curtis Inst., Philadelphia. *Career:* operatic debut with Sarah Caldwell's Opera Co. of Boston, in US stage premier of Berlioz's Les Troyens 1972; gained experience with that co. (appeared in 34 productions 1972–90, 24 for the main co. and ten for the touring co., Opera New England, included two world premieres, five US premieres, five-act version of Don Carlos in French and Shirley Verrett's last performances of Aida), Curtis Inst. of Music and Goldovsky Opera Theater; highlights of nat. and int. performance career include Prin. Artist with Metropolitan Opera, New York City Opera, Santa Fe Opera, San Francisco Opera, San Diego, Opera de Lyon, Bolshoi Opera, Moscow and Wexford and Edinburgh Opera Festivals; numerous PBS 'Great Performances' appearances, including Gian Carlo Menotti's video production with Philadelphia Opera of Tchaikovsky's Queen of Spades; sang at Hamburgische Staatsoper, debut in Rossini's Semiramide with Montserrat Caballé, Marilyn Horne, Samuel Ramey and Francisco Araiza, with conductor Henry Lewis; cr. roles of the Judge in Di Dominica's The Balcony, the King in Lutyen's The Light Princes, Rev. Hooper in The Minister's Black Veil, Haman in Sosin's Esther; also appeared in US premieres of Sessions' Montezuma, Shchedrin's The Dead Souls, Reimann's Melusine, Villa-Lobos' Yerma, Zimmermann's Die Soldaten (also French premiere of this work), Italian and British premieres of Henze's The English Cat; concert appearances with major orchestras, oratorio socs and festivals, including Orchestras of Boston, New York, Philadelphia, Pittsburgh, Cleveland, St Louis, San Francisco, Minnesota, Denver, Washington Chamber Symphony and Kennedy Center Handel Festival, American and Nat. Symphonies; int. appearances include Radio Telefís Éireann Orchestra, London Sinfonia, Nord Deutsche Rundfunk, Sverdlovsk Philharmonic, Yekaterinburg, Russia, Orchestre Nat. de Lyon and Orquesta Sinfónica de Maracaibo; numerous US performances have been broadcast over NPR and PBS; appeared as soloist at Carnegie, Alice Tully and Avery Fisher Halls with orgs including New York Philharmonic, Musica Sacra, Little Orchestra Soc., Opera Orchestra of New York, American Symphony, Clarion Concerts, Voices of Ascension, Mostly Mozart Festival and PBS's Live from Lincoln Center; sang as bass soloist under direction of John Weaver at Madison Avenue Presbyterian Church; also active in Jewish music; London debut at Barbican Centre's 35th Anniversary Rossini Festival in Stabat Mater with Richard Hickox, London Sinfonia and London Symphony Chorus; fmr mem. Voice Faculties of Elizabethtown, Messiah and Smith Colls, Univ. of Arkansas-Fayetteville; fmr Artist-in-Residence/Asst to Sarah Caldwell in the Opera Theater, and at Univ. of Oklahoma-Norman; has taught master-classes at Univ. of Cincinnati Coll. Conservatory of Music, OH, Iona Coll., New York, NY, Kent State Univ., OH, Messiah Coll., Grantham, Pa, State Univ. of NY (SUNY)-Rutgers, New Brunswick, NJ, SUNY-Buffalo, NY, Southern Methodist Univ., Dallas, Tex., Univ. of Arkansas-Fayetteville, Univ. of Missouri Kansas City Conservatory of Music, Mo., Univ. of Missouri-Columbia, Mo., Univ. of Oklahoma-Norman, Univ. of Wisconsin-Madison, Wis., Voice Inst., Sacramento, Calif., Ryder Univ. Westminster Choir Coll., NJ; directed productions of La Bohème, La Traviata, Amahl and the Night Visitors, Hansel and Gretel, A Hand of Bridge, The Turn of the Screw, The Telephone, Comedy on the Bridge, Gianni Schicchi, Die Zauberflöte and Patiencec; currently Artist Teacher of Voice and Dir of Opera Theater, School of Music, Ohio Univ.; mem. American Guild of Musical Artists, Nat. Asscn of Teachers of Singing, Coll. Music Soc., Nat. Music Honor Soc. *Recordings include:* Fiori – Opera-club.net: Pikovaja dama (Queen of Spades) – Tchaikovsky, Opera Company of Philadelphia 1983 (re-released 2009). *Address:* Ohio University School of Music, Room 381, Robert Glidden Hall, Athens, OH 45701, USA (office). *Telephone:* (740) 593-4234 (office). *Fax:* (740) 593-1429 (office). *E-mail:* opera@ohio.edu (office). *Website:* www.finearts.ohio.edu/music (office).

CRNKOVIĆ, Dunja, (Dunja Vejzović); Croatian/German singer (mezzo-soprano); *Professor of Singing, State University of Music and Performing Arts, Stuttgart, Germany*; b. 20 Oct. 1943, Zagreb, Yugoslavia; d. of Jugoslav Crnković and Dragica Crnković-Ocko; m. Christian Romanowski. *Education:* studied in Zagreb, Stuttgart, Weimar and Salzburg. *Career:* sang first at Zagreb, then in Nürnberg, Frankfurt, Basel; debut at Metropolitan Opera as Venus in Tannhäuser 1978; sang at Bayreuth Festival as Kundry in Parsifal 1978–80; other roles include Ortrud in Lohengrin, Hériodade in Hériodade, Senta in Der Fliegende Holländer, Didon in Les Troyens, Venus, Marie in Wozzeck, Florinda in Fierrabras, title roles in Suor Angelica, Salammbo, Medea, Alceste, Hagoromo; has sung in Salzburg, Vienna, Hamburg, Lisbon, Buenos Aires, Bologna, Turin, Tokyo, Houston, Barcelona, Brussels, Paris, Florence; Prof. of Singing, Music Acad. of Zagreb 1998–2000, Hochschule für Musik, Graz 1998–2000, State Univ. of Music and the Performing Arts, Stuttgart, Germany 2000–. *Recordings:* Parsifal (conducted by Karajan), Christus by Liszt, Lohengrin, Der fliegende Holländer, Mort de Cléopatre by Berlioz; Supraphon: Alto by Eschenbach, Rhapsody by Brahms. *Publication:* Dokumenta Dunja Vejzović 2003. *Honours:* Fed. Cross of Merit, Stuttgart 2010; Milka Trnina, Croatia, Prix Fondation Fanny Heldy 1980 1981. *Address:* State University of Music and the Performing Arts, Urban Str. 25, Stuttgart, 70182 (office); Str 43, Heinrich Baumann, Stuttgart, 70190, Germany (home). *Telephone:* (711) 2124620 (office); (711) 9979598 (home). *Fax:* (711) 2845899 (home). *E-mail:* dunja.vejzovica@googlemail.com (home).

CROCKETT, Donald, BM, MM, PhD; American composer, conductor and academic; *Professor of Composition and Chairman, Composition Department, Thornton School of Music, University of Southern California*; b. 18 Feb. 1951, Pasadena, Calif.; m. 1st (divorced); one d.; m. 2nd 1988 (divorced). *Education:* Univ. of Southern California (USC), Univ. of California, Santa Barbara, Thornton School of Music. *Career:* Conductor, USC Thornton Contemporary Music Ensemble; guest conductor with Monday Evening Concerts, Cleveland Chamber Symphony, Pittsburgh New Music Ensemble, Hilliard Ensemble, California EAR Unit; regional and nat. premieres of music by Lutosławski, Davies, Musgrave, Gruber, Ruders, Hartke and others; Composer-in-Residence, Pasadena Chamber Orchestra 1984–87; Prof. of Composition and Chair. Composition Dept, Thornton School of Music, USC; Composer-in-Residence, Los Angeles Chamber Orchestra 1991–97; Sr Composer-in-Residence, Chamber Music Conf. and Composers' Forum of the East 2002–; Conductor, Xtet (Los Angeles-based new music ensemble). *Compositions:* Lyrikos for tenor and orchestra 1979, The Pensive Traveller for high voice and piano 1982, Vox in Rama for double chorus and orchestra 1983, Melting Voices for orchestra 1986, The 10th Muse for soprano and orchestra 1986, Occhi dell'alma mia for high voice and guitar 1977, Array for string quartet 1988, Pilgrimage for piano solo 1988, To Be Sung on the Water for violin and viola 1988, Still Life with Bell for 14 players 1989, Celestial Mechanics for oboe and string quartet 1990, String Quartet No. 2 1993, Roethke Preludes for orchestra 1994, Island for concert band 1998, The Falcon's Eye for solo guitar 2000, The Ceiling of Heaven, commissioned by the Chamber Music Conf. and Composers' Forum of the East 2004, Fanfares and Laments for orchestra, commissioned by the Los Angeles Chamber Orchestra, Winter Variations for solo guitar 2006. *Recordings include:* album: Crockett: Stanford String Quartet 1998. *Publications include:* Still Life With Bell for 14 players, Celestial Mechanics for oboe and string quartet, Roethke Preludes for orchestra, Island for concert band, The Falcon's Eye, The Ceiling of Heaven, To Be Sung on the Water. *Honours:* Kennedy Center Friedheim Award 1991, Goddard Lieberson Fellowship, American Acad. of Arts and Letters 1994, Guggenheim Fellowship 2006, Bogliasco Fellowship 2006. *Address:* Thornton School of Music, University of Southern California, Los Angeles, CA 90089-0851, USA (office). *Telephone:* (213) 740-3126 (office). *Fax:* (213) 740-3217 (office). *E-mail:* dcrocket@usc.edu (office). *Website:* www.donaldcrockett.com.

CROFT, Richard; American singer (tenor); b. 1959, Cooperstown, NY. *Career:* sang Nemorino at Washington and Ramiro in La Cenerentola at St Louis, season 1986–87; European engagements include Mozart's Belfiore, Achille in Gluck's Iphigénie en Aulide and Belmonte at Drottningholm; Strasbourg and Nice, 1990–91, as Don Ottavio and Ferrando; WNO 1989, as Belmonte (repeated at the Metropolitan, 1991); Glyndebourne, 1991, Don Ottavio; Septimus in Handel's Theodora at Glyndebourne, 1996 and Tom Rakewell at Santa Fe; season 1999 with Debussy's Pelléas at Glyndebourne and the London Prom concerts. *Recordings include:* Die Entführung (video). *Current Management:* Columbia Artists Management, 1790 Broadway, New York, NY 10019-1412, USA. *Telephone:* (212) 841-9500. *Fax:* (212) 841-9744. *E-mail:* info@cami.com. *Website:* www.cami.com.

CROLL, Gerhard, PhD; German musicologist; b. 25 May 1927, Düsseldorf. *Education:* University of Gottingen. *Career:* Asst Lecturer, University of Munster, 1958; Chair. of Musicology, Salzburg from 1966; President, International Gluck-Gesellschaft from 1987; mem., Zentralinstitut für Mozart-Forschung. *Publications:* editions of Steffani's Tassilone and Die Entführung aus dem Serail; Gluck's Le Cinesi for the complete edition, 1958, (Editor-in-Chief from 1960) and Alceste 1988; entries on Gluck and Weerbecke in The New Grove Dictionary of Music; articles on Mozart discoveries Larghetto and Allegro in E-flat for two pianos and string quartet arrangement of a Bach fugue, K405; Gluck in Wien (1762), 1997; Rossini in Naples 1998; contributor to the Neue-Mozart-Ausgabe.

CRONIN, Stephen John, PhD; Australian composer; b. 2 Sept. 1960, Brisbane, Qld. *Education:* Univ. of Queensland, studied with Colin Brumby. *Career:* faculty mem., Univ. of Queensland 1984, Queensland Conservatory 1986; commissions from Seymour Group 1993, Synergy 1993, Australian Chamber Orchestra 1995; Vienna Modern Masters Recording Project 1992. *Compositions include:* In Moments Unseen for string quartet 1984, Requiem for chorus, percussion, two pianos and harp 1985, Duo Concertante for clarinet, viola and strings 1986, The Drover's Wife for narrator and orchestra 1987, Piano Concerto 1989, The Snake Pit for ensemble 1990, Eros and Agape for chamber ensemble 1990, House Songs for tenor and ensemble 1991, Eros Reclaimed for ensemble 1992, Carmina Pu for chorus 1992, Cries and Whispers for orchestra 1993, Even Love can Wield a Stealthy Blade for bass clarinet and percussion 1993, Blow for wind octet 1994, Kiss for percussion quartet 1994, Aprilès Nuages for string orchestra 1995.

CROOK, Howard; American singer (tenor); b. 15 June 1947, New Jersey. *Education:* State University, Illinois. *Career:* sang at the Seattle Opera, then appeared as Pelléas and Belmonte at Amsterdam; Paris Opéra-Comique, 1987, as Lully's Atys, Aix-en-Provence, 1987, as Vulcan in Lully's Psyche; Schwetzingen, 1988, in Salieri's Tarare, Versailles, 1988, in Rameau's Pygmalion; Albert Hall, London, 1989, in Daniel Purcell's The Judgement of Paris; Sang in Cesti's Orontea at the 1990 Innsbruck Festival, Rameau's Castor et Pollux at Aix (1991) and Lully's Alceste at the Théâtre des Champs-Elysées, Paris; Sang with Les Musiciens du Louvre in Lully's Acis et Galatée at Beaune, 1996. *Recordings include:* St Matthew Passion and Messiah (DGG); Scylla et Glaucus (Erato); Bach Magnificat and Pygmalion (Harmonia Mundi). *Current Management:* Alferink Artists Management Amsterdam BV, Herengracht 340, 1016 CG Amsterdam, The Netherlands. *Telephone:* (20) 6643151. *Fax:* (20) 6752426. *E-mail:* info@alferink.org. *Website:* www.alferink.org.

CROOK, Paul; British singer (tenor); b. 1943, Blackburn. *Education:* studied in Geneva and London. *Career:* appearances with Geneva Opera and ENO; Royal Opera, Covent Garden from 1975 as Mozart's Monostatos, Mime in Der Ring des Nibelungen and Herod in Salome; other roles in Ariadne auf Naxos, Falstaff, Hoffmann, Die Meistersinger, Tosca, Don Pasquale and Turandot; guest appearances for Deutsche Oper Berlin and San Francisco Opera (as Mime) and in Naples, Warsaw, Paris and Buenos Aires; tours of Japan and South Korea with Royal Opera; sang Pfeifer in English stage premiere of Hindemith's Mathis der Maler, Covent Garden 1995. *Recordings include:* Otello, Werther, La fanciulla del West and Les Contes d'Hoffmann.

CROOM, James; American singer (tenor); b. 1960, North Carolina. *Education:* studied with James Schwabacher. *Career:* appeared for two seasons as apprentice artist with Santa Fe Opera; has sung roles with Scottish Opera, the Glasgow Grand Opera (Calaf 1990), Western Opera Theatre and San Francisco Opera; appearances in Simon Boccanegra, Manon Lescaut, Die Zauberflöte (Monostatos) and Die Meistersinger for Scottish Opera; other roles include Arbace (Idomeneo), Goro (Madama Butterfly) and Mephistopheles in Busoni's Doktor Faust. *Recordings include:* L'Africaine (video from San Francisco Opera). *Honours:* regional finalist Metropolitan Opera Auditions, regional winner Nat. Asscn of Teachers of Singing Competition.

CROSS, Gregory; American singer (tenor); b. 1960. *Career:* European debut as Renaud in Gluck's Armide at Versailles 1992, under Marc Minkowski; further appearances as Rossini's Almaviva for Opéra de Nancy, Ferrando at Strasbourg, Tamino for Greater Miami Opera, Lurcano in Ariodante for Welsh National Opera and in Messiah at San Francisco; sang Iopas in Les Troyens under Colin Davis and Leukippos in Daphne under André Previn, both with London Symphony Orchestra; further concerts include Haydn's Seasons and Mozart's Requiem in Canada, and the Saint Matthew Passion and Mozart's C minor Mass at Kennedy Center, Washington, DC; sang Don Ottavio at Fort Lauderdale, 1997; performed at Baldwin-Wallace Coll. Bach Festival 1995–97; currently mem. ensemble of Metropolitan Opera. *Recordings include:* Les Troyens, under Charles Dutoit. *Website:* www.metopera.org.

CROSSE, Gordon; British composer; b. 1 Dec. 1937, Bury, Lancs., England; s. of Percy Crosse and Marie Crosse. *Education:* Univ. of Oxford with Bernard Rose and Egon Wellesz, Accad. di Santa Cecilia, Rome with Petrassi. *Career:* Tutor in Extra Mural Dept and in Music Dept, Univ. of Birmingham 1964–69; Fellow in Music, Univ. of Essex 1969–74; Fellow, Kings Coll., Cambridge 1974–75; Visiting Prof. of Composition, Univ. of California 1977; freelance composer 1978–, with comms from BBC Symphony Orchestra, Royal Philharmonic Orchestra, London Symphony Orchestra and Festivals of Aldeburgh, Cheltenham and Edinburgh; The Story of Vasco premiered at the London Coliseum. *Compositions:* stage: Purgatory, one-act opera after Yeats 1966, The Grace of Todd (comedy) 1969, Wheel of the World (entertainment on Chaucer's The Canterbury Tales) 1972, The Story of Vasco, opera in three acts 1974, Potter Thompson, one-act music drama 1975; orchestral: Elegy 1959, Concerto da Camera 1962, Symphony No. 1 1964, Ceremony 1966, two Violin Concertos 1962, 1970, Some Marches on a Ground 1970, Ariadne for oboe and ensemble 1972, Symphony No. 2 1975, Epiphany Variations 1976, Wildboy 1977, Thel for ensemble 1978, Symphony for chamber orchestra 1976, Dreamsong, 1979, Cello Concerto 1979, Array for trumpet and orchestra 1986, Quiet, for wind band 1987; vocal: Changes for soprano, baritone, chorus and orchestra 1965, The Covenant of the Rainbow for chorus and organ, For the Unfallen for tenor, horn and strings 1963, Memories of Morning Night for mezzo and orchestra 1971, The New World, poems by Ted Hughes for voice and piano 1978, Dreamcanon I, for chorus, two pianos and percussion 1981, Sea Psalms for chorus, children's voices and orchestra 1990; chamber music: String Quartet 1980, Trio for clarinet, cello and piano 1981, Wave Songs for cello and piano 1983, Piano Trio 1986, Oboe Quintet 1988, Trio for oboe, violin and cello 2009, Viola Concerto 2009, String Quartets 2–4 2010–12, Symphony 3 2011, Symphony 4 2012–13; for children: Meet My Folks 1964, Holly from the Bongs 1974. *Television:* King Lear Incidental Music (Granada TV) with Sir Laurence Olivier 1984. *Address:* Brants Cottage, Blackheath, Wenhaston, Halesworth, Suffolk, IP19 9EX, England. *E-mail:* gordon@crosse.me.uk.

CROSSLEY, Paul Christopher Richard, CBE, MA; British concert pianist and music director; b. 17 May 1944, Dewsbury; s. of the late Frank Crossley and Myra Crossley (née Barrowcliffe). *Education:* Silcoates School, Wakefield, Mansfield Coll., Oxford. *Career:* has performed world-wide as concert pianist; dedicatee and first performer of works by Tippett, Henze, Berio, Takemitsu, Adams, Lindberg, Salonen, Knussen, Benjamin; Artistic Dir London Sinfonietta 1988–94; 15 major films on twentieth-century composers. *Recordings include:* complete piano music of Franck, Fauré, Debussy, Ravel, Poulenc, Janacek, Tippett, Takemitsu; works for piano and orchestra by Franck, Messiaen, Takemitsu, Lutoslawski, Stravinsky, Adams. *Honours:* Hon. Fellow, Mansfield Coll., Oxford 1991. *E-mail:* paul@paulcrossley.org. *Website:* www.paulcrossley.org.

CROSSMAN, (Wallace) Bruce, MMus, MPhil, DCA; New Zealand/Australian composer; *Associate Professor in Music, Western Sydney University*; b. 2 Nov. 1961, Auckland, New Zealand; s. of Wallace Crossman and Rosalie Gillies; m. Colleen Anne Guild 1986; one s. *Education:* Otago Univ., Dunedin, New Zealand, Univ. of York, UK, Univ. of Wollongong, Australia. *Career:* Composer-in-Residence, Nelson School of Music, New Zealand 1987; Fellow in Composition, Pacific Music Festival, Japan 1990; Mozart Fellow, Otago Univ. 1992; Visiting Lecturer in Music, Waikato Univ. 1994; Scholar-in-Residence, David C. Lam Inst. for East-West Studies (LEWI), Hong Kong Baptist Univ. 2010; fmr Sr Lecturer in Composition, Western Sydney Univ., currently Assoc. Prof. in Music; Collaborator, Aichi Univ. of Arts, Japan 2015; mem. Composers Asscn of New Zealand, Australian Music Centre, Australasian Performing Rights Asscn. *Compositions include:* Pezzo Languendo for piano 1984, Expression in Blue for violin and piano 1988, Dual for two violins 1988, Dialogue for Jerusalem for clarinet and piano 1989, Timbres for guitar 1991, Colour Resonances and Dance for orchestra 1996, Rituals for soprano and string quartet 1996, Back to the Centre for piano 1999, Sound Rituals for orchestra 2000, Daragang Magayon Cantata for mezzo-soprano and piano 2001, In Gentleness and Suddenness for shakuhachi 2003, Fierce Tranquility for string trio 2004, Majesty for piano 2005, After Resonance Blues for piano 2005, Double Resonances for piano and percussion 2008, Not Broken Bruised-Reed for violin, percussion and piano 2010, Qi Colour from Hidden Resonances for piano 2010, Gentleness-Suddenness for mezzo-soprano, violin, percussion and piano 2012, Early Spring that No One Sees for viola, percussion and piano 2012, Spirit-Presence for Jiari-shakuhachi and Jinashi-shakuhachi 2012, Resonance of Red for sitar, tabla and harpsichord 2013, Dying of the Light for soprano saxophone 2014, Where are the Sounds of Joy? for trumpet, percussion and piano 2015, Emergence from Darkness for harp 2015, Emergence from Autumn Darkness to Spring for Jiari-shakuhachi and Jinashi-shakuhachi 2015. *Achievements:* compositions selected for: Tunugan/Asian Composers League Festival, Manila, Philippines 1997, Seoul, S Korea, Asian Music Week/Asian Composers League Festival, Yokohama, Japan 2000, Asian Contemporary Music Festival/Asian Composers League 2002, Pacific Rim Music Festival, Santa Cruz, USA 2005, Tongyeong Int. Music Festival, S Korea 2009, Int. Soc. for Contemporary Music World New Music Days, Sydney 2010, Asian Music Festival, Tokyo 2010, Asian Composers League Conf. and Festival, Taiwan 2011, Asian Music Festival, Yokohama and Tokyo 2014. *Recordings include:* Expression in Blue on A Violin and Piano Recital: Mark Menzies and Dan Poynton, The Waiteata Collection of New Zealand Music: Vol. I, Back to the Centre on Hammered: Australian Post-1970 Solo Piano 2000, Double Resonances 2008, Resophonica 2009, Qi Colour from Hidden Resonances on Shadows and Silhouettes 2012, Gentleness-Suddenness DVD Filigree Films 2014. *Publications include:* Personal Creative Process towards a Pacific-European Identity 1999, Intercultural Music: Creation and Interpretation (ed) 2007, Music of the Spirit: Asian-Pacific Musical Identity (ed) 2009. *Honours:* New Zealand Emerging Composers' Award 1984, Corbould Composition Competition Prize 1996, Designated Chief Researcher (DCR), Int. Research Initiatives Scheme — Music of the Spirit Project, UWS 2007–08 with co-researchers Prof. Michael Atherton (UWS) and Prof. Chinary Ung (Univ. of California, San Diego) at Aurora Festival 2008, Highly Commended, Postgraduate Research Training and Supervision, Vice-Chancellor's Excellence Awards, Univ. of Western Sydney 2008, Vice-Chancellor's Professional Devt Scholarship, Univ. of Western Sydney 2009, Presentation and Promotion grant, Australia Council for the Arts 2012, Australia-Japan Foundation Grant 2015. *Address:* Music Area, School of Humanities and Communication Arts, Western Sydney University, Locked Bag 1797, Penrith, NSW 2751, Australia (office). *Telephone:* (2) 4736-0865 (office). *Fax:* (2) 4736-0166 (office). *E-mail:* b.crossman@uws.edu.au (office). *Website:* www.uws.edu.au (office); brucecrossman.wordpress.com.

CROW, Todd, BA, MS; American pianist and academic; *George Sherman Dickinson Professor of Music, Vassar College*; b. 25 July 1945, Santa Barbara, Calif.; m. Linda Goolsby 1967; one s. one d. *Education:* Univ. of California, Juilliard School, Music Acad. of the West. *Career:* debut in London 1975, New York 1981; London orchestral debut, London Philharmonic Orchestra 1986; has given numerous concerts in USA, Europe and South America; Mount Desert Festival of Chamber Music, Maine; Maverick Concerts, Woodstock, New York, Music Mountain, Conn.; radio broadcasts on BBC, Israel Radio, Nat. Public Radio and New York City stations; mem. Faculty, Vassar Coll., Poughkeepsie, NY 1969–, currently George Sherman Dickinson Prof. of Music; New York orchestral debut with American Symphony Orchestra 1992; festivals include Casals Festival, Bard Music Festival, Musica negli Horti (Italy); Music Dir, Mount Desert Festival of Chamber Music, Maine 1996–; performances with St Luke's Chamber Ensemble, Milano Classica, I Solisti Aquilani, Jerusalem Symphony, New York Philharmonic Ensembles, Music of the Spheres, Norfolk and Norwich Chamber Music, Dallas Chamber Music

Series, Brentano String Quartet, Borromeo String Quartet, Shanghai Quartet, Miami String Quartet, Daedalus Quartet, Miró Quartet, Parker Quartet, etc. *Recordings include:* Schubert Piano Sonatas, The Artistry of Todd Crow, Mozart Piano Concerto K467, Liszt E flat Piano Concerto, Berlioz/Liszt Symphonie Fantastique, Ernst Toch Piano Concerto No. 1, complete music for cello and piano by Mendelssohn (with Mark Shuman, cellist), Haydn Piano Sonatas, piano works by Taneyev, Anselm, Josef Hüttenbrenner, Dohnányi, Harold Farberman, BBC recordings of Mendelssohn, Liszt, Schumann and Moscheles, Brahms Piano Concerto No. 2 with American Symphony. *Publications:* Bartók Studies 1976; contrib. to The Compleat Brahms (ed. L. Botstein) 1999, Journal of the American Liszt Society, NOTES, the Journal of the Music Library Association. *Honours:* Univ. of California Distinguished Alumni Award 1986. *Address:* Box 321, Vassar College, Poughkeepsie, NY 12604, USA (office). *E-mail:* tocrow@vassar.edu (office). *Website:* toddcrowpiano.com; www.mtdesertfestival.org.

CROWE, Lucy; British singer (soprano); b. Marchington, Staffs. *Education:* Royal Acad. of Music. *Career:* operatic debut with Scottish Opera as Sophie in Der Rosenkavalier 2006 and with ENO as Poppea in Agrippina 2007; has worked with conductors including Sir John Eliot Gardiner, Lawrence Cummings, Trevor Pinnock, Richard Egarr, Harry Christophers, Richard Hickox, Sakari Oramo, Paul Daniel, Sir Charles Mackerras, Mark Minkowski, Harry Bicket and William Christie; concert engagements include recitals with Scottish Chamber Orchestra, the English Concert, Orchestra of the Age of Enlightenment, The Sixteen, City of London Sinfonia, the King's Consort, City of Birmingham Symphony Orchestra, Monteverdi Choir and Orchestra. *Opera repertoire includes:* Sophie in Der Rosenkavalier, Poppea in Agrippina, Belinda in Dido and Aeneas, Drusilla in L'incoronazione di Poppea, Susanna in Le Nozze di Figaro, title role in The Cunning Little Vixen, Juno in The Fairy Queen. *Recordings:* Memory Takes My Hand 2008, Jacques Offenbach Vert-Vert 2010, Henry Purcell The Fairy Queen (DVD) (BBC Music Magazine Best DVD Award 2011), Handel Il Trionfo del Tempo e del Disinganno 2011, Il caro sassone 2011. *Honours:* Royal Overseas Gold Medal 2002, second prize, Kathleen Ferrier Awards 2005. *Address:* c/o The English Concert, 8 St George's Terrace, London, NW1 8XJ, England.

CROWN, David; British singer (bass-baritone) and conductor; b. 1965. *Education:* Purcell School of Music, King's Coll., Cambridge, master-classes with Graham Johnson and Roger Vignoles, training as baritone with David Pollard. *Career:* early roles (as bass) included Don Giovanni, Leporello, Uberto in La Serva Padrona and Mefistofele; cos included Broomhill Opera, Covent Garden and Batignano festivals, and Pavillion Opera; concerts as baritone include Messiah at Durham Cathedral, Elijah at Truro, Beethoven's Mass in C, Tippett's A Child of our Time and Fauré's Requiem; taught singing at Bristol Univ. and taught singers in Choir of All Saints' Church, Northampton; currently Dir of Chapel Music, Somerville Coll., Oxford; Music Dir Reading Phoenix Choir, The Oxford Singers, The Wychwood Chorale. *Recordings include:* recordings with Choir of Somerville Coll., Oxford, and Reading Phoenix Choir. *Honours:* Wagner Soc. Bayreuth Bursary, Nat. Fed. of Music Socs Award 1997, NFMS/Esso Award, Warwick Artists Young Musicians Trust Competition, Young Songmakers Competition. *Address:* Director of Chapel Music, Somerville College, Woodstock Road, Oxford, OX2 6HD, England. *Website:* www.somervillechoir.com/director-of-music.html; www.david-crown.com.

CROXFORD, Eileen, ARCM, FRCM; British cellist; b. 21 March 1924, Leighton Buzzard, Bucks; m. David Parkhouse (died 1989); two s. *Education:* Royal Coll. of Music, studied with Effie Richardson, Ivor James, Pablo Casals. *Career:* debut in London, Wigmore Hall; BBC Promenade Concerts, Royal Albert Hall; recitalist worldwide with husband, concert pianist David Parkhouse; concertos with leading orchestras; trio with David Parkhouse and Hugh Bean (acclaimed in 1987 as world's longest-standing trio); tours of East and West Europe, North and South America, Far East, Middle East, China and North Africa; Prof. of Cello, Royal Coll. of Music for 40 years; founder mem., Music Group of London; Pres. and founder Shaldon Festival, Devon; Pres. and founder Parkhouse Award (int. chamber music award for piano-based groups, in memory of David Parkhouse); for many years assisted Gerald Moore in his lecture recitals, Am I Too Loud?. *Recordings:* Beethoven: Ghost and Archduke Trios, Irish Songs, Schubert: Trout Quintet, Trios by Bush, Mendelssohn and Ravel, Cello and Piano Sonatas by Dohnányi, Barber, Rachmaninov, Kodály, Debussy, Vaughan Williams: Two Quartets, On Wenlock Edge, Studies on Folk Songs, Warlock: The Curlew, Lennox Berkeley: Sextet, Elgar: String Quartet. *Honours:* Alexander Prize 1945, Queen's Prize 1948, Boise Foundation Award 1949, Cobbett Medal of the Worshipful Co. of Musicians for services to chamber music 1991.

CRUDELI, Marcella; Italian pianist, conservatory director and teacher; b. 16 April 1940, Gondar, Ethiopia; one s. *Education:* Language School, Mozarteum Akademie für Musik, Salzburg, Austria, Hochschule Akademie für Musik, Vienna, Austria, State Conservatory G. Verdi, Milan, Italy. *Career:* debut in Rome 1955; over 2,000 concerts in 85 countries; Dir, State Conservatory 'L. D'Annunzio', Pescara; teacher, Ecole Normale de Musique de Paris 'Alfred Cortot', Academia Pescarese. *Recordings include:* D. Cimarosa, 62 Sonatas; B. Galuppi, 12 Sonatas; R. Schumann, Concerto A Minor, with Symphony Orchestra of Taipei; Glinka, variations on theme of Sonnambula, with Orchestra Rias of Berlin; Beethoven, Sonata Op 81; Mozart, Sonata K576; Schubert, Impromptus Op 90; E. Grieg, Concerto A Minor, with Symphony Orchestra of Taipei. *Publications:* D. Cimarosa: Revision of 62 Sonatas, B. Galuppi: Revision of 12 Sonatas. *Honours:* Cavaliere al Merito della Repubblica Italiana. *Address:* Via Pierfranco Bonetti 90, 00128 Rome, Italy.

CRUM, Alison, BA, LTCL, LRAM, MTC (London); British viol player and academic; *Professor of Viol, Trinity Laban Conservatoire of Music and Dance;* b. 23 Nov. 1949, Derby, England; d. of James Crum and Margaret Crum; m. Roy Marks. *Education:* Shrewsbury High School for Girls, Univ. of Reading, Univ. of London, studied with Wieland Kuijken and Jordi Savall. *Career:* solo viol player, consort player and teacher, with numerous worldwide performances and directing of courses since 1975; Prof. of Viol, Trinity Coll. of Music (now Trinity Laban Conservatoire of Music and Dance) 1987–; Visiting Specialist, West Dean Coll. 1987– and Univ. of Birmingham 1995–; mem. Inc. Soc. of Musicians, Viola da Gamba Soc. of GB (Pres. 1997–). *Recordings include:* more than 100 recordings with many British early music groups, notably with Rose Consort of Viols, Musica Antiqua of London, Consort of Musicke, Dowland Consort; five solo recordings of Bach, Marais, Rogniono, Ortiz. *Publications include:* Play the Viol 1989, seven books of music for viols 1989–, The Viol Rules 2009; contrib. to Chelys, Early Music Today. *Address:* 87 Olive Road, London, NW2 6UR, England (home). *Telephone:* (20) 8452-3254 (home). *E-mail:* alison@alisoncrum.co.uk. *Website:* www.alisoncrum.co.uk.

CRUMB, George, BM, MM, DMA; American composer; b. 24 Oct. 1929, Charleston, W Va; s. of George Henry and Vivian Reed; m. Elizabeth Brown 1949; two s. one d. *Education:* Mason Coll. of Music, Univ. of Illinois, Univ. of Michigan, Hochschule für Musik, Berlin. *Career:* Prof., Univ. of Colorado 1959–63; Creative Assoc., State Univ. of New York at Buffalo 1963–64; Prof. of Composition, Univ. of Pa 1971–83, Annenberg Prof. of the Humanities 1983–97, Emer. 1997–; mem. Nat. Inst. of Arts and Letters 1975–. *Compositions include:* Two Duos for flute and clarinet 1944, Four Songs for voice, clarinet and piano 1945, Sonata for piano 1945, Four Pieces for violin and piano 1945, Poem 1946, Three Early Songs for voice and piano 1947, Gethsemane for orchestra 1947, Alleluja for chorus 1948, Sonata for violin and piano 1949, A Cycle of Greek Lyrics 1950, Prelude and Toccata 1951, Three Pastoral Pieces for oboe and piano 1952, String Trio 1952, Sonata for viola and piano 1953, String Quartet 1954, Sonata for cello 1955, Diptych for orchestra 1955, Variazioni for orchestra 1959, Five Pieces for piano 1962, Night Music I for soprano, piano and two percussionists 1963, Four Nocturnes for violin and piano 1964, Eleven Echoes of Autumn 1966, Madrigals, Books 1–4 1965–69, Songs, Drones and Refrains of Death 1968, Echoes of Time and the River (Pulitzer Prize for Music) 1968, Night of the Four Moons 1969, Ancient Voices of Children 1970, Black Angels for electric string quartet 1970, Vox Balaenae for three masked musicians 1971, Lux Aeterna 1971, Makrokosmos vols I–IV 1972–79, Dream Sequence for violin, cello, piano and percussion 1976, Star-Child for soprano, children's chorus and orchestra (Grammy Award for Best Contemporary Composition 2001) 1977, Apparition 1979, A Little Suite for Christmas 1979, Gnomic Variations for piano 1981, Pastoral Drone for organ 1982, Processional for piano 1983, A Haunted Landscape for orchestra 1984, The Sleeper 1984, An Idyll for the Misbegotten 1986, Federico's Little Songs for Children for soprano, flute and percussion 1986, Zeitgeist for two amplified pianos 1988, Easter Dawning for carillon 1991, Quest for guitar and ensemble 1994, Mundus Canis for guitar and percussion 1998, American Songbooks 2001–04, Unto the Hills 2001, A Journey Beyond Time 2002, Eine Kleine Mitternachtmusik 2002, Otherworldly Resonances 2002, River of Life 2003, Winds of Destiny 2004, Voices from a Forgotten World 2006, Voices from the Morning of the Earth 2007, The Ghosts of Alhambra for baritone, guitar and percussion 2009, Sun and Shadow for soprano, piano 2009, Voices from the Heartland 2010, The Yellow Moon of Andalusi, mezzo-soprano, piano 2013, Yester-Year 2013, Xylophony for Percussion Quintet 2014. *Honours:* Fulbright Scholarship 1955, Rockefeller Grant 1964, Guggenheim Grant 1967, 1973, Koussevitsky Int. Recording Award 1971, UNESCO Int. Rostrum of Composers Award 1971, Fromm Grant 1973, Ford Grant 1976, Prince Pierre de Monaco Prize 1989, Edward MacDowell Colony Medal, Peterborough 1995, Grammy Award (for Star Child) 2000. *Current Management:* c/o Becky Starobin, Bridge Records, Inc., 200 Clinton Avenue, New Rochelle, NY 10801, USA. *Telephone:* (914) 654-9270. *Fax:* (914) 636-1383. *E-mail:* bridgerec@aol.com. *Website:* www.bridgerecords.com. *Telephone:* (610) 565-2438 (home). *Website:* www.georgecrumb.net.

CRUZ, Cláudio; Brazilian conductor and violinist; *Concertmaster and First Violinist, Orquestra Sinfônica do Estado de São Paulo;* b. 16 March 1967, São Paulo; s. of João Cruz; m. *Education:* studied violin with Maria Vishnia, Erich Lehninger, and with Kenneth Goldsmith in USA and conducting with Olivier Toni; masterclasses with Joseph Gingold and Chaim Taub. *Career:* joined Orquestra Sinfônica do Estado de São Paulo (OSESP) 1985, first violinist and concertmaster 1990–, Musical Dir Orquestra Sinfônica Jovem do Estado de São Paulo (youth orchestra) 2012–; Principal Conductor, Orquestra Sinfônica de Campinas 2003–05, Orquestra Sinfônica de Ribeirão Preto 2005–11; Guest Conductor of numerous orchestras including Orquestras Sinfônicas da Bahia, da Curitiba and Brasileira, Orquestra Municipal de São Paulo, YOA Orchestra of the Americas, Orchestre Avignon Provence, Orchestre de Chambre de Toulouse, Metropole Orkest Nederlands, Osaka Chamber Orchestra, Hiroshima Symphony Orchestra, New Japan Philharmonic Orchestra, Northern Sinfonia, Jerusalem Symphony Orchestra; solo violin debut in Europe, with Kammerorchester Berlin 1991; has performed as soloist in France, Italy, Germany, Austria, Hungary, Croatia, Uruguay, Argentina,

Chile, Japan, USA; mem. Quarteto Portinari and Quarteto Amazônia. *Recordings:* several CDs including Adios Nonino (conductor, Latin Grammy Award for Best Classical Album 2002); solo: Dvořák/Bruch, Violin Music in Brazil, Bruch e Tchaikovsky 2010, Flausino Vale e o violino brasileiro (Prêmio Bravo) 2010. *Honours:* Carlos Gomes Prize 2002, 2006. *Address:* c/o Orquestra Sinfônica do Estado de São Paulo, Praça Júlio Prestes 16, CEP 01 218 020, São Paulo, Brazil (office). *Telephone:* (11) 3367-9500 (office). *Website:* www.osesp .art.br; www.claudiocruz.art.br.

CRUZ DE CASTRO, Carlos; Spanish composer, academic and production manager; b. 23 Dec. 1941, Madrid. *Education:* Universidad Central de Madrid, Royal High Conservatory of Music, Madrid, Hochschule Robert Schumann in Düsseldorf, studied with Gerardo Gombau, Francisco Calés, Enrique García Asensio, Milko Kélemen, Gunther Becker and Antonio Janigro. *Career:* participant at the VII Biennial in Paris, representing Spain with his pieces, Mensaje for non-conventional instruments and Pente for wind quintet 1971; co-founder (with Alicia Urreta), Spanish-Mexican Festival of Contemporary Music 1973; took part in Premio Italia representing Spanish National Radio with his work, Mixtitlan 1975 and at the Composers' International Tribune in Paris 1979; with six other composers he established the Spanish Asscn of Symphonic Composers 1976; Prof. of Composition, Counterpoint, Chamber Music, Musical Forms and Aesthetics, Conservatory at Albacete 1983; Production Man., Radio Clásica (Spanish nat. radio); mem. Spanish Asscn of Symphonic Composers. *Compositions include:* Imagenes de infancia for piano, There and Back for guitar, Toccata vieja en tono nuevo, four string quartets 1968, 1975, 1994, 1998, Ida y vuelta, Concierto para guitarra y orquesta de cuerda, Mensaje, Morfologia Sonora No. 1, El Momento de un Instante II (theatrical piece) 1973–74, Concerto for orchestra 1984, Carta a mi hermana Salud (ballet) 1985, Suite No. 1 for guitar 1993, Saxophone Concerto 1997, Canarias Symphony 1998, Barcarola for piano 1999, La Sombra del Inquisitor (opera) 1999. *Honours:* Mexican Union of Theatre and Music Chroniclers Music Prize 1977.

CRUZ-ROMO, Gilda; Mexican singer (soprano); b. 12 Feb. 1940, Guadalajara. *Education:* Mexico City Conservatory with Angel Esquivel. *Career:* debut in Mexico City 1962, in Die Walküre; Metropolitan Opera from 1970 as Madama Butterfly, Puccini's Tosca, Manon and Suor Angelica; Verdi's Leonora (Trovatore and La Forza del Destino), Elisabeth de Valois, Aida, Amelia (Ballo in Maschera) and Violetta; season 1972–73 at Covent Garden and La Scala Milan, as Aida; appearances in Australia, South America and USSR and at Vienna State Opera, Rome Opera, Paris Opéra, New York City Opera and Chicago Lyric Opera; concert appearances in Canada, Mexico, USA, Japan, Israel; Vienna Staatsoper 1979 as Leonora in La Forza del Destino; Ars Musica Chorale and Orchestra, Englewood, NJ, as Santuzza and Matilda in US premiere of Mascagni's Silvana 1988–89. *Recordings include:* Rossini's Stabat Mater, Aida (video at 1976 Orange Festival). *Honours:* Metropolitan Opera Nat. Award 1970.

CSAMPAI, Attila; German musicologist, journalist, author and editor; b. 1949, Budapest, Hungary. *Education:* Ludwig-Maximilians-Universität. *Career:* grew up in Munich; freelance record reviewer for publs such as Hifi-Stereophonie, Neue Musikzeitung, Scala, Amadeo, Musik & Theater, Hifi & Records, Tonart, Musicmanual, Rondo, FonoForum etc 1974–, writer for Stereoplay, Audiophile, Crescendo and HifiStatement.net; Programme Dir Bavarian Radio 1979–83, ed. and presenter on BR-Klassik station 1983–2011; Tech. Dir Toblach Gustav Mahler Music Weeks 1990–; jury chair., Toblach Composition Prize; jury mem., Deutschen Schallplattenkritik Prize (piano category) 2014; fmr Visiting Prof., Mozarteum Salzburg. *Publications include:* as co-ed. and author: Der Konzertführer: Orchestermusik von 1700 bis zur Gegenwart 1987/2005, Der Opernführer 1990/2006, Callas 1993 (15 edns, translated into five languages), Sarastros stille Liebe (essays on opera) 2001. *Address:* c/o Bayerischer Rundfunk, BR-Klassik, Rundfunkplatz 1, 80335 Munich, Germany (office). *E-mail:* info@br-klassik.de.

CSAPO, Gyula, DMus, PhD; Hungarian composer and academic; *Assistant Professor of Composition and Music Theory, University of Saskatchewan;* b. 26 Sept. 1955, Papa; m. Eva Botai 1980, one s. *Education:* Béla Bartók Conservatory, Franz Liszt Acad. of Music, Institut pour la Recherche et Coordination Acoustique/Musique, France, State Univ. of New York, Buffalo, USA, studied with Morton Feldman. *Career:* mem. New Music Studio, Budapest; extensive concert performances, radio recordings and broadcasts with Studio in Budapest, Warsaw, Toruń (Poland), Vienna, Darmstadt, Milan, Rotterdam, London, Frankfurt am Main, Edmonton, Alberta, Canada, Buffalo, New York; associated with Protean Forms Collective, New York; taught at SUNY, Buffalo 1984–86; teacher, Orchestration, Music Theory and Contemporary Music Ensemble, McGill Univ., Montreal 1990–91; Asst Prof. of Composition, Princeton Univ. 1991–94; Asst Prof. of Composition and Music Theory, Univ. of Saskatchewan 1994–; Artistic Co-Dir annual Saskatoon New Music Festival; Fellow, Collegium Budapest Inst. for Advanced Study 1996–97. *Compositions include:* Krapp's Last Tape (after Beckett) 1974–75, Tao Song 1:1/2 1974–77, Fanatritraritrana 1977–81, Handshake After Shot 1977, Hark, Edward... 1979–81, Na'Conxypan 1978–88, Phedre's Hymn to the Sun 1981, Yagul 1987, Infrared Notes No.1 (Prismed Through Darkness) 1986–88, Remnants in White for tape 1989, Choral in Perfect Time for keyboard and bass drum 1993, Phèdre: une tragédie en musique 1996. *Address:* Department of Music, Room 522, Arts Building, University of Saskatchewan, 9 Campus Drive, Saskatoon, SK S7N 5A5, Canada (office).

Telephone: (306) 966-6186 (office). *E-mail:* gyula.csapo@usask.ca (office). *Website:* artsandscience.usask.ca/music (office).

CSAVLEK, Etelka; Hungarian singer and ceramic artist; b. 29 May 1947, Budapest; d. of Andras Csavlek and Etelka Csavlek (née Toth); m. Zoltan Nemeth 1970; two d. *Education:* Budapest Acad. of Arts. *Career:* ceramist 1972–82; opera singer with Hungarian Opera House 1982–; concerts in Italy, Spain, Germany, Switzerland, France and USA; opera repertoire includes Violette in La Traviata, Pamina in Die Zauberflöte, Fiordiligi in Cosi fan Tutte; concert repertoire includes Mozart's Mass in C Minor, Liszt's Mass of Esztergom. *Operas include:* La Traviata, Magic Flute, Così fan Tutte, Fidelio, Tales of Hoffmann. *Recordings include:* works of Wagner, Donizetti, Verdi, Mozart, Beethoven, Offenbach. *Honours:* Ferenc Liszt Prize 1987, Mihály Székely Award 1990, Merited Artist Award 1997. *E-mail:* etelka@csavlek.hu. *Website:* www.csavlek.hu.

CSENGERY, Adrienne; Hungarian singer (soprano); b. 3 Jan. 1946, Bavaria, Germany. *Education:* Bartók Conservatory, Budapest, Franz Liszt Acad. with Eva Kutrucz. *Career:* early engagements at Hungarian State Opera and in Monteverdi's Vespers, conducted by Lovro von Matacic; engagements in Zagreb, Dubrovnik and Palermo; Marzelline in Fidelio at the 1974 Munich Festival; Hungarian State Opera Budapest as Marguerite, Lulu and Anne Trulove; Mozart roles at Munich; Susanna, Pamina, Fiordiligi and Zerlina; appearances at Hamburg, Bayreuth, Cologne, Amsterdam and Bern with Sawallisch, Pritchard, Haitink, Lopez-Cobos, Michael Gielen and Roderick Brydon; Glyndebourne Festival 1976–77 as Susanna and Zerlina, in productions directed by Peter Hall; Wigmore Hall recital 1980, with English Canzonettas by Haydn; performed world premiere of Kurtag's Messages of the Late Miss RV Troussova, with the Ensemble Intercontemporain conducted by Boulez, 1981; later performances of the work in La Rochelle, Milan, Venice, Florence, Budapest, Bath, Edinburgh and London; voice teacher Bartók Int. Seminar and Festival 1995–; mem. Hungarian Music Council (Pres. 1996–2004). *Recordings include:* Wigmore Hall Recital 1980 (Hungaroton); Messages of the late RV Troussova (Erato). *Honours:* winner, Int. Competition, Hertogenbosch, Fauré Competition, Paris, Gramophone Record Prize 1983, Gramophone Contemporary Music Award 1985. *Address:* c/o Bartók International Seminar and Festival, 9700 Szombathely Fő tér 10, Hungary (office).

CUBAYNES, Jean-Jacques; French singer (bass-baritone); b. 14 Feb. 1950, Toulouse. *Education:* Toulouse Conservatory and Paris Opéra studio. *Career:* sang at the Toulouse Opera from 1978, notably as Zuniga, Mephistopheles, Colline and Montrone; Paris Opéra debut 1987, as Publio in La Clemenza di Tito; Opéra Bastille as the Old Hebrew in Samson et Dalila, Samuel in Ballo in Maschera and Zuniga in Carmen, 1991–95; Artistic Director, The Festival Déodat de Severac, Toulouse, France, 1994–; Guest appearances throughout France and in Dublin, Perugia, Liège, Bonn, Karlsruhe, Regensburg and Seville; Other roles have included Don Giovanni in 1988, Lothario in Thomas's Mignon, 1989, Arkel in Pelléas et Mélisande, Gessler in Guillaume Tell, Sparafucile, Daland, and Rodolfo in La Sonnambula; Bregenz Festival 1991, as Zuniga in Carmen; Sang Melcthal in Guillaume Tell at Liège, 1997 and Ramfis in Aida in 1998. *Recordings include:* Gounod's Mireille and Roussel's Padmavati. *Address:* 40 rue Alsace-Lorraine, 31000 Toulouse, France.

CUBERLI, Lella Alice, BMus; American singer (soprano); b. 29 Sept. 1945, Austin, TX; m. Luigi Cuberli 1972. *Education:* Southern Methodist University. *Career:* Debut: European Violetta in La Traviata in Hungary, 1975. Sagra Musicale Umbria in the oratorio La Betulia Liberata by Mozart, 1975; Spoleto Festival concerto da camera with music by Schubert and Beethoven, 1977; Debut at La Scala in Milan in Mozart's Abduction, 1978; Since then regular appearances in operas such as Mozart's Re Pastore, 1979, Handel's Ariodante, 1981 (Opera taken on tour by La Scala to the Edinburgh Festival, 1982), Mozart's Lucio Silla, 1984; Le nozze di Figaro, 1987 and Orfeo by Gluck, 1989; Debut at Festival Woche in Berlin with the Beethoven Missa Solemnis, conductor Herbert von Karajan, 1985, also performed in the Beethoven 9th, 1986, and the Brahms Requiem, 1987, again with Karajan conducting; 1986 debut at Salzburg Festival with Le nozze di Figaro (role of Countess) with James Levine conducting with repeats in 1987 and 1988; 1986 debut at the Mozart Festival in Paris again in Figaro with Daniel Barenboim conducting; 1987, new production of Traviata made especially for her at the Monnaie in Brussels; 1988 debut at Vienna Staatsoper in Viaggio a Reims, Claudio Abbado conducting; 1989 concert at Pesaro Opera, Festival of Beethoven's Schottische Lieder, Pianist Maurizio Pollini; Sang Mozart's Countess at Orchestra Hall, Chicago, 1992; Antonia in Les Contes d'Hoffmann at the Opéra Bastille, the Countess with the Royal Opera in Japan and at Florence, 1992; Sang Donna Anna at the 1996 Salzburg Festival. *Recordings include:* Beethoven, Missa Solemnis, Deutsche Grammophon (Karajan), 1985; Mozart, Da Ponte operas, Erato (Barenboim) Berlin Philharmonic, 1990. *Honours:* Franco Abbiati Italian Critics Award, 1981 and Premio Jovo, 1984; Le Grand Prix du Disque conferred by the Academy of France in Paris and Prix Rossini of Paris and the Maschera d'argento award in Campione d'Italia, 1986; Premio Paisiello in Taranto, Italy, 1987. *Address:* c/o Oldani, Viale Legioni Romane 26, 20147 Milan, Italy.

CUCKSTON, Alan, MusB (Cantab), MA; British harpsichordist, pianist, conductor and lecturer; b. 2 July 1940, Horsforth, Yorks., England; m. Vivien Broadbent 1965; two s. three d. *Education:* Kings Coll., Cambridge. *Career:* debut, Wigmore Hall 1965; BBC recitalist 1964–; solo concerts in Europe,

USA; keyboard accompanist with Acad. of St Martin in the Fields and Pro Cantione Antiqua; Conductor The Alan Cuckston Singers 1961–, City of Bradford Chamber Orchestra, English Northern Philharmonia, New World Ensemble. *Recordings include:* Solo Piano Music of Alan Rawsthorne, William Baines, Eugene Goossens, Edward German, John Field, Sterndale Bennett, Stanford, Corder; Solo Harpsichord Music of Burnett, Kinloch, Farnaby, Tallis, Byrd, Handel, Couperin, Rameau; harpsichord/lute duets and fortepiano/guitar duets with Stuart Willis in recitals and recordings; conductor: English Northern Philharmonia in K. Leighton, M. Hurd, J. Gardner, City of Bradford Orchestra in Rawsthorne, New World Ensemble in Plews and Kimpton. *Publications include:* chapters in William Walton – Music and Literature 1999, Arthur Bliss – Music and Literature 2002, Ronald Stevenson – Music and Literature 2005. *Address:* Turnham Hall, Cliffe, Selby, North Yorks., YO8 6ED, England (home). *Telephone:* (1757) 638238 (office); 7740-516851 (mobile). *E-mail:* alancuckston@email.com (home).

CULLAGH, Majella; Irish singer (soprano); b. 1963, Cork; d. of Tom Cullagh and the late Mrs Cullagh. *Education:* Cork School of Music, Nat. Opera Studio, London. *Career:* appearances with the Royal Danish Opera as Donizetti's Adina, Adèle in Le Comte Ory with the Glyndebourne Tour, Isabella in Wagner's Das Liebesverbot at Wexford and Mozart's First Lady for Opera North; Melissa in Handel's Amadigi at the Covent Garden Festival and New York, and the title role in Medea by Gavin Bryars; concerts include Huit scènes de Faust by Berlioz in Venice, and engagements in the USA; season 2000–01 with Fiordiligi in the Canary Islands, Micaela in Carmen and Countess for Opera North, Donna Anna in Regensburg and Tatiana in Eugene Onegin for Grange Park Opera, Manon for Opera New Zealand, Ninetta in Lagazza Ladra and Arminda in La Finta Giardiniera for Opera North, Violetta in La Traviata and Musetta in La Bohème for Glyndebourne on tour; Nedda in I Pagliacci, Bérénice in L'Occasione Fa Il Ladro and Ghita in Der Zwerg for Opera North. *Recordings include:* Mendelssohn 2nd Symphony, Donizetti's Zoraida di Granata and Rossini's Bianca e Falliero, Don Giovanni, Donizetti's Pia de'Tolomei, Rossini's Elisabetta Regina d'Inghilterra and Mercadante's Zaira, The Thieving Magpie and The Magic Flute. *Telephone:* (7768) 315337 (office). *E-mail:* majellacullagh@yahoo.co.uk (office).

CULLELL MUNIESA, Rosa; Spanish business executive; *Director-General, Gran Teatre del Liceu;* b. 14 March 1958, Barcelona; m.; two c. *Education:* Universidad Autónoma de Barcelona, IESE. *Career:* fmr journalist, working for Mundo Diario, the BBC, TVE-Catalonia and El País; Dir of Communication, La Caixa 1988, later Gen. Man., Exec. Vice-Pres. and Sr Exec. Vice-Pres. –2002, representing La Caixa on the bds of Panrico, Telesp (Telefónica de Sao Paulo) and Port Aventura 2002–; CEO Grup 62 2002–; Dir-Gen., Gran Teatre del Liceu 2005–. *Address:* Gran Teatre del Liceu, La Rambla 51–59, 08002 Barcelona, Spain (office). *Telephone:* (93) 4859900 (office). *Fax:* (93) 4859918 (office). *Website:* www.liceubarcelona.com (office).

CULLEN, Bernadette; Australian singer (mezzo-soprano); b. 1949. *Career:* appearances from 1981 with Australian Opera as Maffio Orsini in Lucrezia Borgia, Nicklausse and Giulietta in Hoffman, Cherubino in Figaro, Angelina in Cenerentola, Ottavia in Poppea, the Secretary in The Consul, Charlotte in Werther and Rosina in Il Barbiere di Siviglia; further performances include Brangaene in a new production of Tristan, Sesto in Clemenza di Tito, Donna Elvira in Don Giovanni, also for Lyric Opera of Queensland; Eboli in Don Carlos and Adalgisa in Norma for Victoria State Opera; Vitellia in concert under Christopher Hogwood, Gala Concert with Joan Sutherland and Richard Bonynge in Perth, Dorabella at Hong Kong and British debut as Isolier in Le Comte Ory for WNO; sang Donna Elvira at the reopening of the Tyl Theatre, Prague, under Charles Mackerras, Leonara in La Favorita for WNO in Cardiff and at Covent Garden, Dido in Dido and Aeneas in Palermo 1994, Cassandre in La Prise de Troie for the Australian Opera, Brangaene in Tristan and Isolde for Scottish Opera; Venus in Tannhäuser at Sydney 1998; concert repertoire includes Mahler's 8th under Charles Dutoit; Rossini Stabat Mater and Petite messe Solennelle, Verdi Requiem in Sydney under Carlo Rizzi and with the Hallé Orchestra, Liverpool Oratorio under Carl Davis, Dream of Gerontius with the Ulster Orchestra and Beethoven's Ninth; season 2000–01 as Eboli at Melbourne and Azucena at Sydney. *Recordings:* Pulcinella with the Australian Chamber Orchestra; The Bohemian Girl, conducted by Richard Bonynge. *Honours:* Vienna State Opera Award, Opera Foundation Australia 1995.

CULLIS, Rita; British singer (soprano); b. 25 Sept. 1952, Ellesmere Port, Cheshire, England. *Education:* Royal Manchester College of Music. *Career:* joined the chorus WNO 1973; Principal, WNO 1976; roles include Leila in The Pearl Fishers, the Countess in Figaro, Titania in A Midsummer Night's Dream, Pamina in The Magic Flute, Ellen in Peter Grimes, Donna Anna in Don Giovanni and Lenio in Martinů's Greek Passion; Buxton Festival 1981, as Elisetta in Cimarosa's Il Matrimonio Segreto; Opera North 1985, as Jenifer in The Midsummer Marriage and as Christine in Strauss's Intermezzo; Season 1986–87 sang the Countess of Tel-Aviv Opera, Ariadne for Opera Northern Ireland and Donna Anna for her debut at the English National Opera, returned for The Fox in Janáček's Cunning Little Vixen; Concert engagements with RAI Milan, Hallé Orchestra, Ulster Radio, Royal Liverpool Philharmonic and the Bournemouth Symphony; Netherlands Opera, Freischütz, 1989–90; Other engagements as the Composer and Fiordiligi, English National Opera, the Fox in The Cunning Little Vixen, Scottish Opera, and the Countess and Donna Anna, debuts with the Canadian Opera Company and San Diego Opera, 1992; Season 1992–93 as the Composer in Ariadne for ENO and Covent Garden debut as Janáček's Fox; Sang Third

Norn in Götterdämmerung at Covent Garden, 1995; Bach's St Matthew Passion at the Festival Hall, 1997; Season 1997–98 with Elisabeth in Tannhäuser for Opera North, Senta for ENO, Ellen Orford and Sieglinde for Royal Opera; Season 1999 as Hecuba in King Priam for ENO, Mozart's Countess at Hamburg and Creusa in the premiere of Param Vir's Ion, at Aldeburgh. *Current Management:* The New Music Partnership Ltd, New Broad Street House, New Broad Street, London, EC2M 1NH, England. *Telephone:* (20) 7840-9592. *E-mail:* lawrence@musicpartnership.co.uk. *Website:* www.musicpartnership.co.uk; www.ritacullis.co.uk.

CULMER-SCHELLBACH, Lona; American singer (soprano); b. 4 Feb. 1954, Miami, FL. *Career:* appeared in the 1986 premiere of Penderecki's Schwarze Maske, at Salzburg; also sang the role of Europa in Die Liebe der Danaë at the Vienna Staatsoper and at Santa Fe, 1988; sang in the premiere of Patmos by Wolfgang von Schweinitz at Munich (1990) and appeared at Kassel from 1989; Lady Macbeth by Shostakovich, 1996; further appearances in Essen, Paris, Berlin and Dresden, as Marie in Wozzeck, Shostakovich's Lady Macbeth, Elsa, Donna Elvira and Ariadne; season 2000–01 as Aida at Heidenheim, Marina in Boris Godunov and Tosca at Kassel, Santuzza for Frankfurt Opera; frequent concert engagements. *Honours:* prizewinner Mozart Competition, Salzburg 1985.

CULVER, (David) Andrew, MM; American composer and performer; b. 30 Aug. 1953, Morristown, NJ. *Education:* composition with Bengt Hambaeus; McGill University. *Career:* founder mem. of SONDE, Canadian music design and performance group; has worked at Yellow Springs Institute for Contemporary Studies, New Music Concerts Toronto, Staten Island Children's Museum 1983 and the Children's Museum of Manhattan 1989–91; collaborations with John Cage 1981–92, including computer assistance with the premiere of Europeras 1 and 2 at the Frankfurt Schauspielhaus 1987; Founder, Anarchic Harmony Foundation 1996–; mem, SOCAN. *Compositions:* Stage works Viti 1981, Music with Tensegrity Sound Source No. 5 1983, Hard Lake Frozen Moon 1989, Quasicrystals, sound sculpture 1989, Ocean 1-95 1994, From Zero (film) 1995, Architonic Space 1996. *E-mail:* AHF@ anarchicharmony.org (office). *Website:* www.anarchicharmony.org (office).

CUMMINGS, Claudia, BA; American singer (soprano); b. 12 Nov. 1941, Santa Barbara, CA; m. 1st H. W. Cummings 1962; m. 2nd Jack Aranson 1973; one d. *Education:* San Francisco Univ. *Career:* debut at San Francisco Opera 1971; San Francisco, New York City, Houston, Seattle, San Diego, Minnesota, Miami, Charlotte Opera Cos; Netherlands Opera; Stuttgart Opera premiere of Satyagraha by Philip Glass 1980; Canadian Opera; sang Countess de la Roche by B. A. Zimmermann 1991 at New York City Opera; other roles have included Violetta, Rosalinda, Lucia di Lammermoor, Lulu, Marguerite, 3 Heroines in the Tales of Hoffmann, Countess in The Marriage of Figaro. *Recordings:* Satyagraha, Philip Glass.

CUMMINGS, Conrad, BA, DMA; American composer, conductor and musician (keyboard); *Member, Composition Faculty, Juilliard School;* b. 10 Feb. 1948, San Francisco, CA. *Education:* Yale Univ., State Univ. of New York, Stony Brook, Columbia Univ., Tanglewood, Computer Music Project, Stanford, IRCAM, Paris. *Career:* teacher Columbia-Princeton Electronic Music Center 1974–76; Electronic Music Co-ordinator, Brooklyn Coll. CUNY 1976–79; Assoc. Prof., Dir Music and Media Program, Oberlin Conservatory 1980–91; Vice-Pres., CFO Hyperspace Cowgirls (children's interactive media co.), New York 1995–2002; mem. composition faculty (evening div.), The Juilliard School 2003–; commissions from the Smithsonian Inst., Oberlin Coll., San Francisco Opera Center, Cleveland Chamber Orchestra, Canadian Brass, Opera Delaware, Brandywine Baroque, Avian Orchestra; panellist, Nat. Endowment for the Arts Opera Music-Theatre Div. 1993, 1994. *Compositions include:* Fragments from 'The Golden Gate' for mezzo soprano, tenor and piano 1985, I Wish They All Could Be... for instrumental octet 1986, Where I Live for soprano, baritone and baroque ensemble 1987, Positions 1956 for amplified voices and instruments 1988, Insertions for amplified voices and instruments 1988, Photo-Op (opera) 1992, Scenes from Tonkin for voices and chamber orchestra 1990, Dénouement for large orchestra 1992, There Is No Hope For Art for soprano, piano and double bass 1992, Tonkin (opera in three acts) 1993, Barnar Venet: Lignes (film score) 1995, 1996, Pierrette Bloch, Boucles (film score) 1997, 1998, Shakespeare in Love for soprano and baritone voices and baroque ensemble 2000, In Memorian Marge Laszlo for chamber ensemble 2004, The Golden Gate (opera) 2008, The Passing Months 2008. *Honours:* MacDowell Colony Fellowships 1981, 1986, Djerassi Foundation Fellowship 1985, grants from the Nat. Endowment for the Arts 1981, 1992, Martha Baird Rockefeller Fund 1980, Opera America 1992, The Rockefeller Foundation 1992. *Address:* 415 W 23rd Street, Apt 11–D, New York, NY 10019, USA (office). *Telephone:* (212) 741-1559 (office). *E-mail:* conrad@conradcummings.com (office). *Website:* www.conradcummings.com.

CUMMINGS, Laurence, MA, ARCM, FRCO; British harpsichordist and conductor; *Music Director, London Handel Festival;* b. 1968, Sutton Coldfield. *Education:* Christ Church Coll., Oxford (organ scholar) and Royal Coll. of Music. *Career:* Head of Historical Performance, Royal Acad. of Music 1996–; Music Dir, London Handel Festival 1999–; Musical Dir, Tilford Bach Soc. 2002–; Artistic Dir, Göttingen Int. Handel Festival 2011–; has performed with the Orchestra of the Age of Enlightenment, The Sixteen, The Gabrieli Consort; regular appearances as conductor including with ENO Semele 2004, Poppea 2007, Messiah 2009, Radamisto 2010; at Glyndebourne Giulio Cesare

2009, Fairy Queen 2009, 2012, Rinaldo 2011; with English Touring Opera Ariodante 2003; at Garsington Opera L'incoronazione di Dario 2008, La Verità in Cimento 2011, L'Olympiade 2012; for the London Handel Festival Atalanta 2008, St Matthew Passion 2009, Jephtha 2009, Rodelinda and Saul 2011; La Spinalba, Casa da Musica, Porto. *Recordings include:* Louis and Francois Couperin keyboard music, Esther 2008. *Honours:* Hon. RAM. *Address:* 81 Chetwynd Road, London NW5 1DA, England. *Website:* www.handel .cswebsites.org.

CUNLIFFE, William (Bill), MMus; American composer, arranger and jazz pianist; b. 26 June 1956, Andover, Mass. *Education:* Duke Univ., Eastman School of Music. *Career:* taught at Central State Univ., Wilberforce; debut with Buddy Rich Big Band; performed with Frank Sinatra, Joe Henderson, Freddie Hubbard, Benny Golson and James Moody; f. own trio, mem. Joe LaBarbera Quintet and duo with flautist Holly Hofmann; also plays with his big band, Latin Band Imaginación, and classical-jazz ensemble Trimotif; composer of big band, chamber, orchestral and choral music; works performed by orchestras including Cincinnati Pops, Illinois Philharmonic, Reading Symphony and Manhattan School of Music; teaches at Vail Jazz Workshop and Skidmore Jazz Inst.; Assoc. Prof. of Music and Distinguished Faculty Mem., Coll. of the Arts, Calif. State Univ., Fullerton; Composer-in-Residence, All Saints Episcopal Church, Pasadena, Calif. *Compositions include:* To Ruth for jazz piano trio and orchestra, Fourth Stream... La Banda, concerto for trumpet and orchestra (premiered at Alice Tully Hall, New York and Verizon Hall, Philadelphia), Overture, Waltz and Rondo for jazz piano, trumpet and chamber orchestra, Symphony #1 Hearts Reaching Upward, tuba and saxophone concertos, Fantasy for jazz piano trio and orchestra, Ballade for trumpet and wind ensemble. *Music for film:* The Northern Kingdom 2009, Split Ends 2009, Janet's Class 2010, On the Shoulders of Giants (documentary about jazz and basketball in 1930s Harlem) 2011. *Recordings include:* A Rare Connection 1994, Satisfaction 1999, Romantic Fantasy 1999, How My Heart Sings 2003, Partners in Crime (with Jim Herschman and Jeff Hamilton) 2005, Imaginación 2005, The Blues and the Abstract Truth, Take 2 2008, Trans-formation 2008, Resonance Big Band Plays Tribute to Oscar Peterson 2009, Nostalgia in Corcovado 2009, Fourth Stream...La Banda 2010, Concerto for Tuba and Orchestra 2011, That Time of Year 2011, Overture, Waltz and Rondo for jazz piano, trumpet and chamber orchestra 2012, Concerto for Tuba and Orchestra 2012, Bill Cunliffe Trio: River Edge, New Jersey 2013; in duo with Holly Hofmann: Just Duet, Vol. 2 2003, Three's Company 2010. *Publications:* Jazz Keyboard Toolbox, Max Blues Keyboard 2004, Jazz Inventions for Keyboard 2005, Uniquely Familiar: Standards for Advanced Solo Piano 2010, Uniquely Christmas 2012. *Honours:* Thelonious Monk Int. Jazz Piano Award 1989, Grammy Award for Best Instrumental Arrangement (for West Side Story Medley), Los Angeles Jazz Soc. Composer/Arranger Award 2010. *Address:* c/o Azica Records, 1645 Eddy Road, Cleveland, OH 44112, USA. *Telephone:* (216) 681-0778. *Fax:* (216) 851-9813. *E-mail:* billcunliffe@me.com (office). *Website:* www.billcunliffe.com (office).

CUNNINGHAM, Thomas (Tom); British composer and conductor; b. 24 March 1946, Edinburgh, Scotland; m. Alison Hannah 1972; two d. *Education:* George Heriot's School, Edinburgh, Univ. of Edinburgh, Morley Coll., London. *Career:* Musical Dir, Brussels Gilbert & Sullivan Soc. 1978–82, Brussels Choral Soc. 1984–2002; composer and Ed. of choral music; mem. Asscn of British Choral Dirs. *Compositions include:* Merry Christmas Jazz, The Saga of the Seven Days, Scotland at Night, Seven Planets and a Cosmic Rock, The Painter's Eye, A Time of Gifts, The Okavango Macbeth (opera), A Tapestry of Many Threads, Fergus of Galloway, Delia (opera). *Recordings include:* Joseph Jongen: Mass Op. 130, Christmas Concert 1988, Festive Joy 2000. *Publications include:* Choral scores of Gustav Mahler: Symphony Nos 2 and 3, Jongen: Mass Op. 130, Deus Abraham, Quid sum Miser, and Three Sacred Songs (ed.). *Address:* 7 Lauder Road, Edinburgh, EH9 2EW, Scotland. *Telephone:* (131) 667-8614. *E-mail:* europa@cflat.co.uk (home). *Website:* www.tomcunningham .org.uk.

CUPER, Philippe; French clarinettist; b. 25 April 1957, Lille. *Education:* Univ. of Paris (Sorbonne), Paris Conservatoire with Guy Deplus, Henri Druart, Guy Dangain, Jacques Lancelot and Gilbert Voisin, Juilliard School, USA with Stanley Drucker. *Career:* fmr Prin. Clarinet, Youth World Orchestra, Lamoureux Orchestra, Paris; Prin. Clarinet, Paris National Opera Orchestra 1984–; has played with Berlin Philharmonic, La Scala de Milano, Bavarian Radio Symphonic, Czech Philharmonic, Moscow Symphonic, Sinfonia Varsovia, Orchestre de Paris, National de France, Ensembles Contemporains, Paris; has played under maestros Sawallisch, Ozawa, Abbado, Maazel, Mehta, Boulez, Prêtre, Dohnanyi, Barenboim, Gergiev, Salonnen, Conlon, Chung, Jordan; Founder Paris Wind Octet; currently Prof., Versailles Nat. Conservatory. *Recordings include:* 40 albums. *Publications:* contrib. to Clarinette magazine, International Clarinet Society magazine, Band Journal (Tokyo), Clarinet and Saxophone Society Magazine (London). *Honours:* prizewinner, Munich International Competition 1982, Geneva 1979, Prague 1986, First Prize Prague 1986, Mravinsky Medal, St Petersburg. *Address:* Conservatoire à rayonnement régional de Versailles, 24 rue de la Chancellerie, 78000 Versailles, France. *Website:* www.operadeparis.fr; www .crr.versaillesgrandparc.fr.

CUPIDO, Alberto; Italian singer (tenor); b. 19 March 1948, Portofino. *Education:* Giuseppe Verdi Conservatory, Milan, Accademia Chigiana, Siena. *Career:* debut in Genoa 1977 as Pinkerton; sang widely in Italy and in Strasbourg, Vienna and Frankfurt; Glyndebourne 1978 as Rodolfo; Munich

Staatsoper 1982 as Faust; US debut San Francisco 1983; Florence 1983 as Rinuccio in Gianni Schicchi; La Scala debut 1984 as Edgardo in Lucia di Lammermoor; returned 1986 as Orontes in I Lombardi; Wiesbaden 1986 in Giulietta e Romeo by Zandonai; further appearances in Cologne, Hamburg, Berlin and Montreal; other roles include Alfredo, Fenton, Duke of Mantua, Fernando in La Favorita and Rodolfo in Luisa Miller; sang Edgardo at Monte Carlo 1987, Faust at Geneva 1988; Teatro Comunale Florence 1989; As Faust in Mefistofele, Rodolfo at Rome, 1990; Gabriele Adorno in a production of Simon Boccanegra at Brussels 1990; debut at Verona Arena as Cavaradossi; Season 1991–92 as Boito's Faust at Lyric Opera Chicago and as Don Carlo at Verona; Enzo in La Gioconda at Berlin 1998. *Honours:* prizewinner, competitions in Parma 1975, Busseto 1976. *Website:* cupido.prosaclick.com.

CURA, José; Argentine/Spanish singer (tenor), conductor, director and stage designer; b. 5 Dec. 1962, Rosario, Santa Fe; m. Silvia Ibarra; two s. one d. *Education:* Rosario Univ., School of Arts, Teatro Colon, Buenos Aires. *Career:* appearances at leading opera houses 1992–; debut at Royal Opera House, Covent Garden in Stiffelio 1995, at Vienna State Opera in Tosca 1996, at La Scala in La Gioconda 1997, at Teatro Colón, Buenos Aires and Metropolitan Opera 1999; Pres. Cuibar Productions; Prof. of Voice, RAM, London 2007–. *Honours:* Hon. Prof., CAECE Univ., Argentina 1999, Hon. Citizen of Rosario, Argentina 1999, of Veszprém, Hungary 2004, Hon. Founding mem. Portuguese Asscn against Leukaemia 2007; Chevalier, Ordre du Cèdre (Lebanon) 2000; Premio Abbiati, Italian Critics' Award, Premio Carrara, Cultura Millenaria 1997, XII Premio Internazionale di Arte e Cultura Cilea 1997, Orphée d'Or, Acad. du Disque Lyrique 1998, ECHO Klassik Award: Singer of the Year, Deutsche Phono-Akad. 1999, Ewa Czeszejko Prize, Sochacka Foundation Award 2002, Giovanni Zanatello Prize for Best Artist of the Year, Arena di Verona 2005, Best Argentinian Opera Singer of the Year, Fundación Teatro Colón 2007, One of the Best 100 Argentinian Artists of the Last 10 Years, Fundación Konex 2009, Österreicher Kammersänger, Austrian Ministry of Culture 2010, Sarmiento Honor, Argentinian Senate. *Address:* José Cura Management, Ronda de la Abubilla 30 bis, 28043 Madrid, Spain (office). *Telephone:* (91) 3000134 (office). *E-mail:* management@josecura.com (office). *Website:* www.josecura.com (office).

CURNYN, Christian; British conductor; *Founder and Music Director, Early Opera Company;* b. 1965, Glasgow. *Education:* York Univ., Guildhall School of Music and Drama, London. *Career:* founder and Music Dir, Early Opera Co. 1994–; productions of Purcell, M. A. Charpentier and Handel, Queen Elizabeth Hall, Wigmore Hall, Buxton, Aldeburgh, Cheltenham, Handel's Saul for Opera North, Handel's Semele and Tamerlano for Scottish Opera, Semele for Budapest Chamber Opera, Orlando and Poppea for Opera Theatre Company, Partenope, Dido and Aeneas and Castor et Pollux for English Nat. Opera, The Beggar's Opera for Royal Opera, Covent Garden, La Calisto for Oper Frankfurt, Partenope and Cosi Fan Tutte for New York City Opera. *Recordings:* Partenope 2005, Semele (Stanley Sadie Handel Prize 2008) 2007. *Current Management:* c/o Ingpen and Williams, 7 St George's Court, 131 Putney Bridge Road, London, SW15 2PA, England. *Telephone:* (20) 8874-3222. *Fax:* (20) 8877-3113. *E-mail:* ds@ingpen.co.uk. *Website:* www.ingpen.co.uk; www.earlyopera.com.

CURPHEY, Margaret; British singer (soprano); b. 27 Feb. 1938, Douglas, Isle of Man. *Education:* studied with John Carol Case in Birmingham, with David Galiver and Joan Cross in London. *Career:* debut at Sadler's Wells Opera 1965, as Micaela in Carmen; sang with Sadler's Wells/ENO in operas by Mozart, Wagner, Verdi and Puccini; sang Eva in new production of The Mastersingers, conducted by Reginald Goodall, Sieglinde in The Valkyrie and Gutrune in The Twilight of the Gods; Camden Theatre 1967, in the British premiere of Mozart's Lucio Silla, guest engagements in Sofia and elsewhere in Europe; sang Brünnhilde at the London Coliseum 1977; Brünnhilde at Santiago and Seattle 1978; season 1981–82 as Rezia in Oberon for Opera North and Jaroslavna in Prince Igor; many appearances as concert singer. *Recordings include:* The Ring of the Nibelung (conducted by Reginald Goodall). *Honours:* prizewinner International Competition, Sofia 1970.

CURRAN, Alvin, BA; American composer; b. 13 Dec. 1938, Providence, RI. *Education:* Brown Univ. with Ron Nelson, Yale Univ. with Elliott Carter. *Career:* co-founder, Musica Elettronica Viva Group, Rome 1966; solo performances in major festivals (new music) 1973–; large-scale environmental works for chorus, orchestra, ship's horns and foghorns 1980–; DAAD Resident Composer in Berlin 1986; Milhaud Prof. of Music Composition, Mills Coll. 1992–. *Compositions:* Songs and Views from the Magnetic Garden, Light Flowers, Dark Flowers, Canti Illuminati, For Cornelius, Maritime Rites 1979–1992 (Music on Water), 1985 A Piece for Peace for three choruses, three speakers, three percussion, cello, violin, saxophone and three accordions 1984, Electric Rags II for saxophone quartet 1989, Notes from Underground/Floor Plan (sound installation) 1991, Animal Behaviour for solo performance live electronics 1992, Schtyx for piano, violin and percussion 1993, Inner Cities 1994, The Twentieth Century 1996, Endangered Species 1996, Caged Notes 1993–96, Erat Verbatim six-part sound work for radio 1989–97, Pittura Fresca Concerto for violin and small ensemble 1997, Rose of Beans for double trio 1998–99, Theme Park x 4 for percussion quartet 1998, Toto Donaueschingen (computer-generated sound installation in large Baroque Park) 1999. *Publications:* Maritime Rites 1984, Maritime Rites: The Lake 1989, Music from the Centre of the Earth 1994. *Honours:* NEA grants 1977, 1983, Prix Italia (for A Piece for Peace) 1985, Ars Acoustica International 1989, Prix Italia (Special Award) 1988, Fromm Foundation award 1998.

CURRAN, Paul; British opera director and fmr ballet dancer; *Artistic Director, Norwegian Opera*; b. 1964, Glasgow. *Education:* Finnish Nat. Opera, Nat. Inst. of Dramatic Art, Sydney, Australia. *Career:* trained as ballet dancer at London Studio Centre and Cen. School of Ballet 1981; fmr Usher ENO; three years as professional dancer with Scottish Ballet; two years as Asst to Baz Luhrmann; debut as ind. freelance opera Dir with The Magic Flute, Bloomsbury Opera 1995; Artistic Consultant, Cen. City Opera, Denver, Colo 2006–08; Artistic Dir Norwegian Opera 2009–. *Opera productions include:* La Cenerentola, A Midsummer Night's Dream 2000, Die Königskinder (Premio Abbiati 2003 for Best Production), Teatro San Carlo, Naples, Ariadne auf Naxos 2002, Daphne 2005, Teatro La Fenice, Venice, Mirandolina, Wexford Festival 2002, La finta Giardiniera, Garsington Opera 2003, Les contes d' Hoffmann, Central City Opera, Denver 2004, Tannhäuser, Teatro alla Scala, Milan 2005, Peter Grimes, Santa Fe Opera 2005, Peter Grimes, Otello, Teatro Giuseppe Verdi, Trieste, Tristan und Isolde for BBC, London, Il Trovatore, Teatro Dell'Opera, Rome, Teatro Comunale, Bologna, A Florentine Tragedy/Miserly Knight, Teatro São Carlos, Lisbon, I Capuleti e I Montecchi, Spoleto Festival, USA, Prince Igor, Kirov Opera, Hamlet with designer Vivienne Westwood for Clerkenwell Music Series, A Midsummer Night's Dream, Pittsburgh Opera and Central City Opera, A Funny Thing Happened on the Way to the Forum, Man of La Mancha (musicals), Covent Garden Festival (also recorded on CD), A Little Night Music, Ohio State Univ. Columbus, Ohio, I Gioielli della Madonna (Wolf-Ferrari) 2000, Univ. Coll. Opera. *Current Management:* c/o Ken Benson, Columbia Artists Management, 1790 Broadway, New York, NY 10019, USA. *Telephone:* (212) 841-9500. *Fax:* (212) 841-9744. *E-mail:* info@cami.com. *Website:* www.cami.com. *Address:* Den Norske Opera & Ballett, Postboks 785, Sentrum, 0106 Oslo, Norway (office). *E-mail:* paulcurr@blueyonder.co.uk (office). *Website:* www.operaen.no (office); www.paulcurran.info.

CURRIE, Colin; British musician (percussion); *Artist-in-Residence, Southbank Centre*; b. 25 Sept. 1976, Edinburgh, Scotland. *Education:* Royal Acad. of Music, London. *Career:* BBC New Generation artist 2003–05; has commissioned 15 percussion concertos; soloist with orchestras including London Philharmonic, Los Angeles Philharmonic, Concertgebouw, Philadelphia and Philharmonia; has performed premieres of works by composers such as Simon Holt, Kurt Schwertsik, Einojuhani Rautavaara, Jennifer Higdon, Alexander Goehr, Elliott Carter, Sally Beamish, Nico Muhly and Kalevi Aho; world premieres with the New York Philharmonic, Swedish and Scottish Chamber Orchestras, Aldeburgh Festival, London Philharmonic and Turku Philharmonic and others; concerto engagements include Gothenburg Symphony, Oslo Philharmonic, Orchestre Nat. du Capitole de Toulouse, Orchestre Symphonique de Montréal, RTVE Symphony Orchestra Madrid, NYYD Festival in Tallinn, Houston Symphony, Utah Symphony with Thierry Fischer, Baltimore Symphony with Marin Alsop for Higdon's Percussion Concerto; chamber performances with percussion ensemble The Colin Currie Group throughout the UK including Southbank Centre London, Sound Festival Aberdeen, Bristol Colston Hall, Birmingham Town Hall and Cheltenham Festival, also performances in Japan and Amsterdam Concertgebouw's Robeco series 2012; duo recital programme with trumpeter Håkan Hardenberger featuring commissions by Lukas Ligeti, Christian Muthspiel and Tobias Brostrom; solo recital programme, Wigmore Hall, London 2014; Artist-in-Residence, Southbank Centre, London 2011–; Visiting Prof., RAM. *Recordings include:* Jennifer Higdon's Percussion Concerto (Grammy Award for Best Contemporary Composition) 2010, Borrowed Time, Rautavaara's Incantations (Gramophone Award for Best Contemporary Recording) 2012, MacMillan's Veni, Veni, Emmanuel 2012. *Honours:* Winner, Percussion Class, BBC Young Musician of the Year 1995, Royal Philharmonic Soc. Young Artist Award for inspirational role in contemporary music-making 2000, Borletti-Buitoni Trust Award 2005, Royal Philharmonic Soc. Instrumentalist of the Year 2014. *Current Management:* c/o Intermusica Artists Management, 36 Graham Street, Crystal Wharf, London, N1 8GJ, England. *Telephone:* (20) 7608-9900. *E-mail:* cgibbs@intermusica.co.uk. *E-mail:* info@colincurrie.com. *Website:* www.colincurrie.com.

CURRIER, Sebastian, DMA; American composer; b. 16 March 1959. *Education:* Juilliard School, Manhattan School of Music. *Career:* wrote Aftersong for violinist Anne Sofie Mutter which she has performed worldwide; also comm. for American Composer Orchestra; works performed in USA and Europe including Carnegie Hall, New York, Symphony Hall, Boston, Barbican Centre, London, Grosses Festspielhaus, Salzburg; currently Asst Prof., Composition Faculty, Dept of Music, Columbia Univ.; residencies at MacDowell and Yaddo colonies. *Compositions include:* Chamber Concerto for violin and string orchestra 1996, Microsymph for orchestra 1997, Night Mass for chorus and orchestra 2003, Nightmaze for chamber ensemble 2005, Remix for mixed chamber ensemble 2005, Crossfade for two harps 2005, Piano Concerto for piano and orchestra 2006, Broken Minutes for harp and string orchestra 2006, Static for chamber ensemble, Aftersong for violin. *Honours:* Berlin Prize, Rome Prize, Guggenheim Fellowship, Nat. Endowment for the Arts Fellowship, Acad. Award, American Acad. of Arts and Letters, Grawemeyer Award for Music Composition 2007. *Address:* Department of Music, Columbia University, 2960 Broadway, MC 1813, New York, NY 10027, USA (office). *Telephone:* (212) 854-3825 (office). *Fax:* (212) 854-8191 (office). *Website:* music.columbia.edu (office); www.sebastiancurrier.com.

CURRY, Diane; American singer (mezzo-soprano); b. 26 Feb. 1942, Clifton Forge, VA. *Career:* sang at the City Opera, New York from 1972, Spoleto Festival from 1975, at Graz 1977; other European engagements at the Deutsche Oper Berlin 1984–88, Hamburg Staatsoper, Köln, Bonn, Brussels, Geneva, Marseille, Nice, Teatro di Bologna and Maggio Musicale di Firenze, Arena di Verona (Amneris); Teatro di Roma; Teatro La Fenice Venice and Théâtre du Châtelet, Paris; returned to the USA at the Metropolitan, New York (Nurse in Die Frau ohne Schatten 1990), San Francisco and Seattle, the Chicago Lyric Opera; other roles include Ulrica, Azucena, Laura and Cieca in La Gioconda, Fricka, Waltraute, Brangaene, Herodias, Clytemnestra, Mère Marie in Dialogues des Carmelites; repertoire includes Erda in Das Rhinegold and Siegfried, the Old Prioress in Dialogues des Carmelites and La Principessa in Suor Angelica; many concert appearances, notably the Mahler Symphonies and the Verdi Requiem. *Honours:* Grammy Award, Gramophone Award 1988.

CURTIN, Phyllis, BA; American singer (soprano); b. (Phyllis Jane Smith), 3 Dec. 1921, Clarksburg, WV; d. of Vernon Smith and Betty Smith; m. Eugene Cook (deceased); one d. *Education:* Wellesley Coll. with Olga Avierino, New England Conservatory and Tanglewood with Boris Goldovsky. *Career:* debut with New England Opera Theater 1946 as Countess in The Marriage of Figaro and Lady Billows in Albert Herring; sang at New York City Opera from 1953, notably in Von Einem's Der Prozess, Salome and in the premieres of Floyd's Susannah and The Passion of Jonathan Wade; also sang Cressida in Walton's Troilus and Cressida, Giannini's The Taming of the Shrew and Poulenc's Les Mamelles de Tirésias; Sante Fe 1958 in premiere of Floyd's Wuthering Heights; Glyndebourne 1959 as Donna Anna; Metropolitan Opera from 1961 as Fiordiligi, Rosalinde, Eva, Mozart's Countess, Violetta and Ellen Orford in Peter Grimes; New York concert performances of Pelléas et Mélisande 1962; guest appearances in Vienna, Buenos Aires, Frankfurt, Milan, Glasgow, Paris and Trieste; other roles include Salome and Alice Ford in Falstaff; sang Rosine in the premiere of Milhaud's La Mère Coupable, Geneva 1966; Ellen Orford at Edinburgh Festival 1968; retired from public singing 1984; teacher, Aspen School of Music and the Berkshire Music Center; artist-in-residence, Tanglewood Music Center 1964–, currently Head of Vocal Studies; Prof. of Music, Yale School of Music 1975–83, Master Branford Coll. 1979–83; also teaches at Boston Univ.; guest teacher, Central Conservatory, Beijing 1987 and Moscow Conservatory 1989; recitalist across USA, Canada, Australia, New Zealand and South America; soloist with major orchestras of USA and other countries; US premieres of Britten's War Requiem with Boston Symphony and Shostakovich's Symphony No. 14 with the Philadelphia Orchestra; Dean Emerita, Coll. of Fine Arts, Boston Univ.; fmrly served on Nat. Council of the Arts. *Honours:* US Govt Ambassador for the Arts; numerous hon. doctorates; Nat. Opera Assn Lifetime Achievement Award, Distinguished Alumnae Award, Wellesley Coll., American Music Center Award for Service to American Music, School of Music Distinguished Faculty Award, Boston Univ. *Address:* 9 Seekonk Road, Great Barrington, MA 01230-1558, USA (home). *E-mail:* curtinphyllis@msn.com (home).

CURTIS, Mark; British singer (tenor); b. 1958, Hertfordshire, England. *Education:* Royal Northern College of Music, National Opera Studio, studied in Italy with Maestro Campogalliani. *Career:* appearances with Glyndebourne Touring Opera in Die Zauberflöte and as Fenton and Jacquino; At Covent Garden in Alceste, Pagliacci (Beppe), Manon Lescaut and Fidelio; Kent Opera as Don Ottavio and Monostatos and in King Priam and Carmen; With Opera North has sung The Steersman, Vasek, Stroh (Intermezzo), Don Basilio (Le nozze di Figaro) and Arv in the British premiere of Nielsen's Maskarade; English National Opera as Amenophis in Mosè, and Don Ottavio, and in the world premiere of Birtwistle's The Mask of Orpheus, 1986; Other roles include Hylas in Les Troyens, the Madwoman in Curlew River and Nadir in Les Pêcheurs de Perles; Sang in the Mozart pasticcio The Jewel Box and King Priam (Hermes) for Opera North, 1991; Has also sung at Bath Abbey and the South Bank Halls and in Dublin, Brussels, Hanover, Berlin, Rome, Palermo, Seville, Hong Kong, Jerusalem, Helsinki and Edinburgh; Many concert appearances with English National Opera, Hilarion in Princess Ida and at Théâtre Royal de la Monnaie, Brussels, Der Soldat in world premiere of Philippe Boesmans, Reigen, 1993; English National Opera in King Priam (Hermes), 1995; Sang Goro in Butterfly for Opera North, 1996; Season 1997–98, sang M. Triquet in Eugene Onegin and Eumeus in The Return of Ulysses for Opera North; Nadir in The Pearl Fishers for English National Opera; Sang with Wiener Symphoniker in Vienna, Hamburg Philharmonic (L'Enfance du Christ), the Bamberg Symphoniker (Beethoven's 9th Symphony) and the Schwetzinger Festival (Beethoven's Missa Solemnis) under Roger Norrington; Sang Don Basilio in Le nozze di Figaro, Garsington Festival Opera, 1999; Goro in Opera Ireland's Madama Butterfly; Rev. Horace Adams in Tours production of Peter Grimes, France; Season 1999–2000 as Hermes in King Priam for ENO, Mozart's Basilio at Garsington and Goro in Butterfly at Dublin. *Recordings include:* Trabuco in La Forza del Destino and Yamadori in Madama Butterfly; Simpleton in Boris Godunov for Opera North conducted by Paul Daniel. *Current Management:* Foxroe Artist Management, 103 Nottingham Road, New Basford, Nottingham, NG7 7AJ, England. *Telephone:* (115) 847-8719. *Fax:* (115) 847-8719. *E-mail:* info@foxroe.com. *Website:* www.foxroe.com.

CURTIS-SMITH, Curtis; American composer and pianist; b. 9 Sept. 1941, Walla Walla, WA. *Education:* Northwest Univ., Tanglewood with Bruno Maderna. *Career:* piano soloist and concerts 1968–; faculty mem., Western Michigan Univ. 1968–. *Compositions:* three string quartets 1964, 1965, 1980, Winter Pieces for chamber orchestra 1974, Belle du Jour for piano and orchestra 1975, Music for handbells 1977, Plays and Rimes for brass quintet 1979, The Great American Symphony for orchestra 1981, Songs and

Cantillations for guitar and orchestra 1984, Float Wild Birds, Sleeping for orchestra 1988, Gold are my Flowers (cantata) 1992, African Laughter for sextet 1994, Violin Concerto 1994. *Honours:* Koussevitsky Prize 1972.

CURZI, Cesare; American singer (tenor); b. 14 Oct. 1926, San Francisco. *Career:* debut at San Francisco 1947 as Pinkerton; sang in San Francisco and elsewhere in North America; moved to Europe 1955 and appeared at opera houses in Kiel, Nuremberg and Frankfurt (Alfredo 1957); Salzburg Festival 1959, in Il Mondo della Luna by Haydn; further engagements in Stuttgart, Hamburg, Berlin and Cologne; Maggio Musicale Florence 1959 and 1973–74; mem., Deutsche Oper am Rhein Düsseldorf from 1965 and sang at Nuremberg until 1986; other roles included Rodolfo, Ferrando in Così fan tutte, Ernesto and the Duke of Mantua. *Recordings:* Rigoletto, Eine Nacht in Venedig, Die Fledermaus.

CVEJIC, Biserka; Croatian singer (mezzo-soprano); b. 5 Nov. 1923, Krilo-Jesenice, Split. *Education:* Belgrade Music Acad. *Career:* debut at Belgrade Opera 1950, as Maddalena in Rigoletto; sang at Belgrade 1954–60, notably as Charlotte in Werther and as Amneris on tour to Vienna 1959; Metropolitan Opera debut 1961, as Amneris; Vienna Staatsoper 1959–79, Zagreb Opera 1975–78; further appearances at Covent Garden, Verona Arena, La Scala and Buenos Aires; sang in Massenet's Marie-Magdalene at Paris, 1977; other roles have included Eboli, Azucena, Carmen and Delilah; retd 1990. *Recordings include:* Eugene Onegin, The Queen of Spades, Prince Igor, Boris Godunov, The Snow Maiden; War and Peace; Zigeunerbaron. *Honours:* Légion d'honneur 2001.

CYNAN JONES, Eldrydd; British singer (soprano); b. 1965, Treorchy, Wales. *Education:* Royal Northern Coll. of Music. *Career:* concerts and recitals throughout Europe, with opera in Wales and England; repertory includes Handel's Giulio Cesare, Turandot and Adriana Lecouvreur; also sings songs by Strauss and Duparc; operatic roles include Madama Butterfly, First Lady in Die Zauberflöte, Sofronie in Gli Equivoci, Berta in Il barbieri di Siviglia, Donna Anna in Don Giovanni, Leonora in Fidelio, Lady Macbeth in Macbeth, Amelia in Un Ballo in Maschera, Musetta in La Bohème; mem. The Opera Stars quartet. *Honours:* winner, Young Welsh Singer Competition 1994. *Current Management:* Chris Davis Management Ltd., Tenbury House, 36 Teme Street, Tenbury Wells, Worcestershire, WR15 8AA, England. *Telephone:* (1584) 819005. *Fax:* (1584) 819076. *E-mail:* info@cdm-ltd.com. *Website:* theoperastars.com (office).

CZAPO, Eva; Hungarian singer (soprano) and teacher; b. Nov. 1944, Budapest. *Education:* Bartók Conservatory, Budapest, studied in Basel and with Elsa Cavelti. *Career:* sang with Trier Opera 1968–69; guest appearances in concert and opera at Basel, Zürich, Lucca 1981, Bologna and Spoleto 1981; appearances at the Salzburg, Lausanne, Lucerne, Lugano, Schwetzingen, Helsinki and Granada festivals; concert repertoire has included Bach's B minor Mass, Beethoven's Ninth, Messiah, Elijah and St Paul by Mendelssohn, Haydn's Schöpfung and Jahreszeiten, Mozart's Requiem and C minor Mass and works by Schoenberg, Nono, Dallapiccola, Stravinsky, Szymanowski, Messiaen and Hindemith; further engagements at Berlin, Hamburg, Munich, Milan, Rome, Turin, Parma and Lisbon; voice teacher at Basel; founder, Divertimento Vocale, Basel 1987. *Recordings:* Bach Cantatas and Cavalieri's Rappresentazione di anima e di corpo; Schoenberg's Moses und Aron, conducted by Gielen; Schubert Masses; Davidde Penitente by Mozart and Carissimi's Dives malus.

D

DA COL, Paolo; Italian singer, organist, choral director, conductor and musicologist. *Career:* fmr mem. Italian vocal groups including Cappella di San Petronio di Bologna and Ensemble Istitutioni Harmoniche; Music Dir, Odhecaton choral ensemble 1998–; leader, Baroque vocal and instrumental ensembles; Co-publisher, L'Organo magazine; music critic and writer; teacher, Conservatorio G. Tartini Trieste. *Recordings include:* with Odhecaton: Heinrich Isaac: Missa La Spagna 2003, Nicolas Gombert: A La Incoronation 2006, O Gente Brunette 2011, Palestrina: Missa Papae Marcelli 2011, Monteverdi: Missa in illo tempore (Diapason d'Or de l'Année, Choc Classica and Grand Prix Int. de l' Acad. du Disque Lyrique) 2012. *Publications:* contrib. of music criticism to magazines including Giornale della Musica, and articles on history of Renaissance and Baroque vocal technique. *Current Management:* c/o Valentina Viola, Studiomusica, via Farini 53, 41121 Modena, Italy. *Telephone:* (59) 245486. *Fax:* (59) 235875. *E-mail:* valentina .viola@studiomusica.net. *Website:* www.studiomusica.net. *E-mail:* info@ odhecaton.it (office).

DA SILVA, Miguel; French violist; b. 1960, Reims. *Education:* Reims Region Conservatoire Nat., Conservatoire Nat. Supérieur de Musique with Serge Collote, studied with Jean-Claude Pennetier and mems of Amadeus and Alban Berg Quartets. *Career:* mem. Ysaÿe String Quartet from 1984; numerous concert performances in France, Europe, America and Far East; festival engagements at Salzburg, Tivoli (Copenhagen), Bergen, Lockenhaus, Barcelona and Stresa; numerous appearances in Italy, notably with Haydn Quartets of Mozart; tours of Japan and USA 1990, 1992; Master-in-Residence, Queen Elisabeth Music Chapel, Belgium; mem. Faculty, Haute École de Musique de Genève 2009–; mem. jury Int. Max Rostal Competition 2015. *Recordings include:* Mozart Quartet K421 and Quintet K516, Ravel, Debussy and Mendelssohn Quartets. *Honours:* Grand Prix Evian Int. String Quartet Competition 1988, special prizes for best performances of a Mozart quartet, Debussy quartet and a contemporary work; 2nd Prize, Portsmouth Int. String Quartet Competition 1988. *Current Management:* Productions Internationale Albert Sarfati, 21, rue Le Peletier, 75009 Paris, France. *E-mail:* contact@migueldasilva.ch. *Website:* www.migueldasilva.ch.

DABH, Halim Abdul Messieh ad-, MM, MFA; American composer and teacher; *Professor Emeritus of African Ethnomusicology, Kent State University;* b. 4 March 1921, Sakakini, Cairo, Egypt. *Education:* Sulcz Conservatory and Univ. of Cairo, Egypt, Berkshire Music Center, Tanglewood with Aaron Copland and Irving Fine, New England Conservatory of Music, Brandeis Univ. *Career:* teacher, Haile Selassie Univ., Addis Ababa 1962–65, Howard Univ. 1966–69; teacher, Kent State Univ. 1969–2012, currently Prof. Emer. of African Ethnomusicology, Co-Dir Center for the Study of World Musics 1979–; cultural and ethnomusicological consultant, Folklife Programs, Smithsonian Inst. 1974–81; composed music for the Sound and Light show performed in several languages at the Sphinx and the Great Pyramids of Giza, Egypt; performed with Ismael (Pops) Mohamed, UNAZI (first African Electronic Music Festival), South Africa 2005. *Compositions include:* The Expression of Zaar 1944, three symphonies 1950–56, String Quartet 1951, Fantasia-Tahmeel for darabukka or timpani and strings 1954, Bacchanalia for orchestra 1958, Clytemnestra 1958, Juxtaposition No. 1 for percussion ensemble 1959, Black Epic (opera-pageant) 1968, Opera Files 1971, Drink of Eternity (opera-pageant) 1981, Concerto for darabukka, clarinet and strings 1981, Tonography III for five winds 1984, Rhapsodia egyptico-brasiliera 1985, Egyptian Calypso, Trinidadian style steel drum ensemble, Symphony for 1000 Drums, also piano pieces and choruses. *Publication:* The Derabucca: Hand Techniques in the Art of Drumming 1965. *Honours:* Dr hc (Kent State Univ.) 2001, (New England Conservatory of Music) 2007; Fulbright Scholarship, two Guggenheim Fellowships. *Address:* c/o Center for the Study of World Musics, Kent University, PO Box 5190, Kent, OH 44242-0001, USA. *E-mail:* info@ halimeldabh.com. *Website:* www.halimeldabh.com.

D'ACCONE, Frank Anthony, BMus, MMus, MA, PhD; American musicologist and academic; *Professor Emeritus of Musicology, UCLA;* b. 13 June 1931, Somerville, MA. *Education:* Boston University, Harvard University; studied with Karl Geiringer, Gardner Read, Nino Pirrotta, A. Tillman Merritt and Walter Piston. *Career:* Assistant, Associate, Professor of Music, State University of New York, Buffalo 1960–68; Visiting Professor, University of California, Los Angeles 1965–66, Professor of Musicology 1968–, now Emer.; Editor, Music of the Florentine Renaissance, Corpus Mensurabilis Musicae series XXXII, 1966–; mem. American Musicological Soc. *Publications:* Alessandro Scarlatti's Gli equivoci nel sembiante: The History of a Baroque Opera, 1985; The Civic Muse: Music and Musicians in Siena during the Middle Ages and the Renaissance, 1997; contrib. articles in many journals and publications including The New Grove Dictionary of Music and Musicians. *Honours:* Guggenheim Fellowship, 1980–81; International Galileo Galilei Prize of the Rotary Club of Italy, 1997. *Address:* Department of Musicology, UCLA, 2443 Schoenberg Music Building, PO Box 951623, Los Angeles, CA 90095-1623, USA (office). *Telephone:* (310) 206-5187 (office). *Fax:* (310) 206-9203 (office). *Website:* www.musicology.ucla.edu (office).

DADÁK, Jaromír; Czech composer and conductor; b. 30 May 1930, Znojmo; m. Ludmila Zapletalová; one s. three d. *Education:* Janáček Acad. of Art, Brno. *Career:* Conductor, Ostrava Radio Orchestra 1960–63, Brno Radio Orchestra 1953–90, Bratislava Radio Orchestra 1982–91; Sec., Czechoslovak Composer Federation 1967–69; Dir, Olomouc State Symphony Orchestra 1969–71; mem. Soc. of Czech Composers (pres. 1993–98), Asscn of Music Artists and Scientists, Soc. for New Music, Přítomnost (founder mem.). *Compositions include:* orchestral: Never More for symphony orchestra 1959, Concerto-Symphony for piano and symphony orchestra 1959, Concertino for dulcimer and orchestra 1965, Concerto for piano four-hands and symphony orchestra 1972, Concerto for alto (viola) and small orchestra 1976, Sonata corta for string orchestra 1977, Concerto for tuba and small orchestra 1982, Four Scanty Honours for bassoon and string orchestra 1991, Ludi for string quartet and symphony orchestra 1991, Benedictum for symphony orchestra 1996; chamber music: Three studies for piano four-hands and percussions 1965, Partita for violin, clarinet and piano 1965, Four Concert Studies for dulcimer 1967, Per aspera ad astra for organ 1971, Four Miniatures for dulcimer 1975, Musica gioccosa for violin, clarinet, violoncello and piano 1980, Sonata for dulcimer 1980, Concerto for alto (with piano) 1983, Sonata for violin and piano 1989, Sonata for violoncello 1992, Transformations for hautboy, clarinet, bassoon and piano 1994, Sonata for piano 1994, Double Sonata for violoncello and piano 1995, Capriccio for piano 1997, Ballad for piano 1998, Small terzet for two for basclarinet and piano with percussions 1998, Exclamatio ad astra for organ 2000. *Publications:* Our Folk Song 1991. *Honours:* Nat. Prize 1960, CMF Prize, Prague 1972, Grand Prix Radio Bratislava 1981. *Address:* Mánesova 13, 120 00 Prague 2, Czech Republic (home). *Telephone:* 737736211 (home). *E-mail:* jdadak@scznam.cz (home).

DAGGETT, Philip; British singer (tenor); b. 1962, Chesterfield, England. *Education:* studied in Chesterfield and at Guildhall School of Music. *Career:* songman at York Minster 1981–85; concert appearances include Bach's Actus Tragicus in Paris and the St John Passion throughout Spain; has sung in Mozart's C Minor Mass and Requiem; Mendelssohn's Lobgesang (Queen Elizabeth Hall debut) and Elijah; Britten's Cantata Misericordium and St Nicolas; operatic roles include Paris in La Belle Hélène, Beppe in Pagliacci, Fernando in Cosi fan Tutte, Count Almaviva in Il Barbiere di Siviglia, Tamino in Die Zauberflöte, Boyar in Boris Godunov, Normanno in Lucia di Lammermoor; sang in premieres of Birtwistle's Gawain at Covent Garden 1991, Maxwell Davies's The Doctor of Myddfai 1996; currently mem. ENO. *Recordings include:* The Fairy Queen with Harry Christophers and The Sixteen; A Festal Mass at the Imperial Court of Vienna and Charpentier's Vespers for the Feast of St Louis with the Yorkshire Baroque Soloists and Peter Seymour. *Address:* English National Opera, London Coliseum, St Martin's Lane, London, WC2N 4ES, England (office). *Telephone:* (20) 7836-0111 (office). *Website:* www.eno.org (office).

DAHL, Tracy; Canadian singer (soprano); b. 1964, Winnipeg, MB. *Education:* Merola Opera Programme. *Career:* sang in the USA from 1986, notably as Offenbach's Eurydice at Houston, Olympia at Chicago (1987), Serpetta in La Finta Giardiniera at St Louis (1988) and Oscar in Ballo in Maschera at San Francisco (1990); also appeared as Oscar at the New York Metropolitan, 1990, returning 1991 in the premiere of The Ghosts of Versailles by Corigliano (repeated, 1995); Toronto Opera, 1992, as Nannetta, Sophie in Werther and Zerbinetta, 1995; season 1999–2000 as Verdi's Oscar and as Lucia di Lammermoor, Servilia in La Clemenza di Tito at New York City Opera. *Current Management:* Thea Dispeker Inc., 59 East 54th Street, Suite 81, New York, NY 10022, USA. *Telephone:* (212) 421-7676. *Fax:* (212) 935-3279. *E-mail:* info@dispeker.com. *Website:* www.dispeker.com.

DAHLBERG, Stefan; Swedish singer (tenor); b. 3 May 1955. *Education:* State Academy of Music, State Coll. of Musical Drama, Stockholm. *Career:* concerts and broadcasts throughout Scandinavia; operatic roles include Rustighello in Lucrezia Borgia by Donizetti, Tamino, Beppe, Count Almaviva, King Charles in The Maid of Orleans by Tchaikovsky and Sextus in Giulio Cesare; Royal Opera Stockholm as Tamino, Sextus, Ferrando and Don Ottavio; Drottningholm 1987, as Titus in La Clemenza di Tito; visited Brighton with the Drottningholm Company, 1987; Season 1988–89 with concert performance of Haydn's Armida in Amsterdam; Grand Théâtre Geneva as Jacquino in Fidelio, conducted by Jeffrey Tate; Gounod's Faust at the Stockholm Opera; Concertgebouw Amsterdam, 1989, as Ubaldo in Rossini's Armida; Drottningholm, 1989, as Tamino; Sang Calaf in Busoni's Turandot at Lyon, 1992; Leading tenor role of Vicente Martin y Soler's Una Cosa Rara; Alfredo in Verdi's La Traviata, Stockholm Royal Opera, 1993; Haydn's Orlando at Drottningholm, 1994; concert repertoire includes Suter's Der Abwesende Gott, Die Schöpfung by Haydn, Le Roi David by Honegger, Messiah, Puccini's Messa di Gloria and works by Thomas Jernefelt and Sven-David Sandström. *Recordings:* Videos of La Clemenza di Tito, Die Zauberflöte and Don Giovanni, from Drottningholm.

DAIKEN, Melanie Ruth; British composer; b. 27 July 1945, London, England. *Education:* Royal Acad., Paris Conservatoire with Loriod and Messiaen. *Career:* Deputy Head of Composition, Royal Acad. from 1986. *Compositions include:* operas: Eusebius 1968, Mayakovsky and the Sun 1971, Viola Sonata 1978, Attica for orchestra 1980, Requiem for piano 1983, Der Gärtner for 13 solo strings and piano 1988, song settings of poems by Lorca, Beckett, Trakl and Baudelaire.

DAÏM, Inès Abdel; Egyptian flautist and orchestra administrator; *Chairman of the National Cultural Centre, Cairo Opera House. Education:* Cairo Conservatoire. *Career:* numerous recitals in France and concerts with Int. UNESCO Orchestra; soloist with Cairo Conservatoire Orchestra, Cairo Symphony Orchestra, Egyptian Chamber Orchestra; has toured Europe, the Middle East, USA, Far East; represented Egypt at int. festivals including Nantes Festival of Arts, France 1995, El Rabat Festival of Arts, Morocco, Salonica Festival of Creative Women, Greece, Mediterranean Orchestra Festival, France; f. class for teaching flute to children, Cairo Opera House 1999; apptd Dir, Cairo Symphony Orchestra 2003; Dean, Cairo Conservatoire 2005–10; Prof., Cairo Acad. of Arts, Vice-Pres. 2010–11; currently first flautist, Cairo Symphony Orchestra; also currently Chair. National Cultural Centre, Cairo Opera House; Artistic Adviser, Al-Nour Wal Amal Orchestra (blind all-women chamber orchestra). *Recordings:* albums: works of Egyptian composer Gamal Abdel-Rahim. *Honours:* Gramophone Certificate of Merit, Kobe Int. Flute Competition, Best Flautist, South Korea Festival of Arts, Creative Prize, Egyptian Ministry of Culture, First Prize, Fédération Nationale des Unions des Conservatoires Municipaux, France 1982, First Prize, Concours générale de musique et d'art dramatique, France 1982, State Prize of Arts, Egypt 2001, Award for Young Artist of the Year 2010. *Address:* Office of the Chairman, National Cultural Centre, Cairo Opera House, El Borg Gezira, Cairo, Egypt (office). *E-mail:* info@cairoopera.org (office). *Website:* www.cairoopera.org (office).

DALAYMAN, Katarina; Swedish singer (soprano); b. 1968. *Education:* Stockholm Royal Coll. of Music. *Career:* debut, Stockholm Royal Opera 1991, as Amelia in Simon Boccanegra; Stuttgart Opera from 1993, as Marie in Wozzeck, Desdemona, Eva in Die Meistersinger and Elisabeth in Tannhäuser 1997; further appearances as Mimi and Marietta in Die tote Stadt at Stockholm, Strauss's Ariadne at the Brussels Opera 1997, Marie at the Maggio Musicale, Florence 1998; season 1998–99 with Parisian debut at the Opéra Nat. as Marie; season 1999–2000 included Ariadne auf Naxos, Tannhäuser and The Queen of Spades in Munich, Dr Faustus at the Met and the Salzburg Festival, Bluebeard's Castle at the Royal Opera House, Covent Garden; concerts include Mahler's 8th Symphony with the London Symphony Orchestra, Sibelius's Kullervo Symphony, under Colin Davis, and Penderecki's Requiem, conducted by the composer; Wagnerian Gala Evening in San Diego and La Damnation de Faust with the Munich Philharmonic and James Levine 1999; appeared with the London Symphony Orchestra and Simon Rattle in concert performances of Ariadne auf Naxos 2000; apptd Hovsångare (singer of the Swedish Court) by His Majesty King of Sweden 2000; season 2001–02 included Wozzeck at the Metropolitan Opera, New York and the Royal Opera House, Covent Garden; Brangäne (Tristan and Isolde) at the Met; Ariadne and Kundry (Parsifal) at the Paris Opéra Bastille; Die Walküre and Lady Macbeth at Covent Garden; Tannhäuser in Brussels; sang title role in Shostakovich's Lady Macbeth of Mtsensk at Covent Garden 2003–04; Pique Dame and Walküre at The Met 2004; Tosca in Stockholm 2004; Tannhauser in Munich 2004; Brünnhilde, Wagner's Ring Cycle, Stockholm 2005–07. *Current Management:* Artistsekretariat Ulf Törnqvist, Sankt Eriksgatan 100, 2 tr, 1133 31 Stockholm, Sweden. *Telephone:* (8) 33-83-23. *Fax:* (8) 33-83-00. *E-mail:* ulf.toernqvist@zeta.telenordia.se.

DALBAVIE, Marc-André; French composer; b. 10 Feb. 1961, Neuilly-sur-Seine. *Education:* Conservatoire national supérieur de musique, Paris. *Career:* researcher, IRCAM 1985–90; worked in Berlin 1992–93, at the Medici Villa, Rome 1995–96; Prof. of Orchestration, Paris Conservatoire 1996–; composer-in-residence, Cleveland Orchestra. *Compositions include:* Les Miroirs transparents for orchestra 1985, Diadèmes for solo viola, electronics and instrumental ensemble 1986, Impressions, mouvements (oratorio) 1989, Logos cycle (including Instances 1991, Seuils 1991), Sextuor 1992–93, In Advance of the Broken Time... 1994, Concertino à une pèce du XVIIème siècle for Baroque orchestra 1994, Offertoire for male choir and orchestra 1995, Concerto pour violon 1995–96, Tactus for orchestra 1996, Non-Lieu for women's choir and instrumental ensemble 1997, Color for orchestra 2001, Palimpseste 2002, Rocks Under the Water 2002, Sinfonietta 2005, Variations orchestrales 2006, La source d'un regard 2007. *Recordings:* Les Paradis mécaniques, Diadèmes and seuils, (Ensemble Intercontemporain, Boulez). *Honours:* Chevalier, Ordre des Arts et des Lettres 2004. *Address:* c/o Gérard Billaudot Editeur, 14 rue de l'Echiquier, 75010 Paris, France (office). *Website:* www.billaudot.com (office).

DALBERG, Evelyn; South African (b. German) singer (mezzo-soprano); b. 23 May 1939, Leipzig. *Education:* Guildhall School of Music with Parry Jones, studied with Annelies Kupper in Munich and with Frederick Dalberg at Cape Town and Mannheim. *Career:* debut in Koblenz 1964, as Venus in Tannhäuser; sang at various provincial German opera houses and in South Africa, notably Cape Town and Johannesburg; other roles have included Verdi's Ulrica, Amneris, Eboli and Mistress Quickly, Nancy in Martha, Giulietta in Les Contes d'Hoffmann, Judith in Bluebeard's Castle, Witch in Hansel and Gretel and Prince Orlofsky in Die Fledermaus.

DALBERTO, Michel; French pianist; b. 2 June 1955, Paris; s. of Jean Dalberto and Paulette Girard-Dalberto. *Education:* Lycée Claude Bernard, Lycée Racine, Conservatoire Nat. Supérieur de Musique, Paris with Vlado Perlemuter and Jean Hubeau. *Career:* started professional career 1975; concerts in major musical centres and at int. festivals including Lucerne, Maggio Musicale Florence, Aix-en-Provence, Vienna, Edinburgh, Schleswig-Holstein, Roque d'Anthéron; has worked with conductors including Leinsdorf,

Sawallisch, Dutoit, Masur, Davis and Dausgaard and with orchestras including Orchestre de Paris, Orchestre Nat. de France, Amsterdam Concertgebouw, Philharmonia, Santa Cecilia in Rome, Oslo Philharmonic, BBC Philharmonic, Orchestras of Beijing, Shanghai and Guangzhou, St Petersburg Philharmonic, Ensemble Orchestral de Paris, Orchestre Philharmonique de Liège; Artistic Dir, Acad.-Festival des Arcs 1991–; as chamber musician, has collaborated with artists including Henryk Szeryng, Lynn Harrell, Renaud and Gautier Capuçon, Dmitri Sitkovetsky, Boris Belkin, Vadim Repin, Yuri Bashmet and Truls Mørk; Pres. Jury, Clara Haskil Competition 1991–. *Recordings include:* albums: Grieg/Strauss 1992, French Melodies (with Barbara Hendricks), Debussy Preludes, Mozart Concerti 2000, Un Piano à l'Opéra (Gramophone Award, Classic FM Award, Diapason d'Or) 2004, Schubert Piano Music (complete recordings) 2006, Brahms Sonatas for cello and piano 2008, Fauré: Complete Chamber Music for Strings and Piano (ECHO Klassik Award for Chamber Music Recording of the Year 2012) 2011. *Honours:* Chevalier, Ordre nat. du Mérite; Clara Haskil Prize 1975; First Prize, Mozart Piano Competition, Salzburg 1975, Leeds Int. Pianoforte Competition 1978; Acad. Charles Cros Award 1980 and Acad. du Disque Français Award 1984 for recordings; Diapason d'Or Award for Best Concerto Recording 1991. *Current Management:* c/o Agence Artistique Jacques Thélen, 15 Avenue Montaigne, 75008 Paris, France. *Telephone:* (1)-56-89-32-00. *Fax:* (1)-56-89-32-01. *E-mail:* thelen@wanadoo.fr (office). *Website:* www .jacquesthelen.com; www.micheldalberto.com.

DALBY, Martin, BMus, ARCM; British composer; b. 25 April 1942, Aberdeen, Scotland. *Education:* Royal Coll. of Music, London with Herbert Howells and Frederick Riddle, studies in Italy. *Career:* BBC Music Producer in London 1965–71; Cramb Research Fellow in Composition, Univ. of Glasgow 1972; Head of Music, BBC Scotland 1972–93; Chair. Composers' Guild of GB 1995–98; mem. Performing Right Soc., PRS for Music, Inc. Soc. of Musicians, British Acad. of Composers and Songwriters; Chair. SW Scotland Centre 2004–10. *Compositions include:* several compositions for cello, piano and string instruments 1965–79; Man Walking octet for wind and strings 1980, Antoinette Alone for mezzo and piano 1980, Chamber Symphony 1982, Nozze di Primavera for orchestra 1984, A Plain Man's Hammer for symphonic wind ensemble 1984, Piano Sonata No. 1 1985, De Patre ex Filio octet for wind and strings 1988, Piano Sonata No. 2 1989, The Mary Bean for orchestra 1991, Path for brass band 1992, Sarabande for St Kevin for organ 1992, Variations for a Fair Maid of Perth for orchestra 1993, Cantata: John Clare's Vision for soprano and strings 1993, The White Maa for orchestra 1994, String Quartet 1995, Piano Sonata No. 3 1998, A Wheen in Doric for symphony orchestra 2000, Three Songs for children and piano 2007. *Publication:* Tender, Troubled Sequences: The Music of Thomas Wilson. *Honours:* Sony Gold Award for Best Classical Music Programme 1993, BASCA Gold Badge Award 1998. *Address:* 23 Muirpark Way, Drymen, Glasgow, G63 0DX, Scotland (home). *Telephone:* (1360) 660427 (home). *Fax:* (1360) 660397 (home). *E-mail:* martindalby@ btinternet.com.

DALE, Clamma, BMus, MS; American singer (soprano); b. 4 July 1948, Chester, PA. *Education:* Juilliard School, New York, Philadelphia Settlement Music School. *Career:* operatic debut as Antonia, Les Contes d'Hoffman, New York City Opera 1975; sang with numerous opera companies; toured as concert singer; roles include Pamina, Countess Almaviva, Nedda, Musetta, Gershwin's Bess at the Theater des Westens, Berlin 1988; Deutsche Oper Berlin 1989, as Liù in Turandot.

DALE, Laurence; British singer (tenor); b. 10 Sept. 1957, Pyecombe, Sussex. *Education:* Guildhall School of Music, Mozarteum, Salzburg. *Career:* debut with ENO as Camille in The Merry Widow, 1981; Covent Garden debut 1982, as Second Noble in Lohengrin; Sang Don José in Peter Brook's La Tragédie de Carmen in Paris, 1981 and on Broadway, 1983; in 1983 sang Gounod's Romeo at Basle and Ramiro at Glyndebourne; Visited Los Angeles with the Royal Opera, 1984, singing Pong in Turandot; English National Opera 1983, as Monteverdi's Orfeo; For Welsh National Opera has sung Mozart's Ottavio and Ferrando and Eisenstein in Die Fledermaus; With Opera North as Mozart's Tamino and Belmonte and Jenik in The Bartered Bride; Further appearances in Lyon, Paris, Hamburg, Amsterdam, Aix, Geneva, Brussels (Tamino and Idomeneo) and Zürich; Other roles include Tchaikovsky's Lensky, Jacquino in Fidelio, Méhul's Joseph and Gonzalve in L'Heure Espagnole; Concert engagements include Mozart's C Minor Mass and Haydn's St Cecilia Mass with the London Philharmonic; Bach's Christmas Oratorio with the Los Angeles Philharmonic; Britten's Spring Symphony at the Festival Hall; The Dream of Gerontius and Liszt's Faust Symphony at the Brighton Festival; Messiah in Vienna, Stravinsky's Pulcinella and Rossini's Stabat Mater; appearances on television in the United Kingdom and Europe; On 27 January 1991 sang Tamino in Die Zauberflöte at the Landestheater Salzburg, to inaugurate the Mozart Bicentenary; Season 1991/92 as Ferrando at Stuttgart and Belfiore in La Finta Giardiniera at the Salzburg Festival; Sang Don Ottavio at Genoa 1993; Pelléas at Brussels, 1996; season 1999 as Chevalier de la Force in Les Dialogues des Carmélites at the London Prom concerts; season 1999–2000 as Monteverdi's Orfeo in Amsterdam and Chicago. *Recordings:* La Tragédie de Carmen; Videos of Princess Ida, Die Zauberflöte from Aix and Cenerentola from Glyndebourne; Mozart's C Minor Mass. *Current Management:* c/o Pelléas Artists, Avenue de la Liberté 36/4, 1081 Brussels, Belgium. *Telephone:* (2) 241-59-88. *Fax:* (2) 241-59-88. *E-mail:* cdrijck@pelleas-artists .com. *Website:* www.pelleas-artists.com.

DALLAPOZZA, Adolf; Austrian singer (tenor); b. 14 April 1940, Bozen. *Education:* studied with Elisabeth Rado in Vienna. *Career:* sang in chorus of Vienna Volksoper while a student; solo debut 1962, as Ernesto in Don Pasquale; sang at Volksoper until 1972, and guested in Munich, Hamburg, Milan, Brussels and Cologne; Bregenz Festival 1972–84; many roles in works by Mozart, Italian Opera and in Operas of Baroque; many appearances in operettas; Wilhelm Meister in Mignon at Vienna Volksoper 1988; season 1990 in Strauss's Intermezzo at Bologna and as Lensky at the Volksoper; sang Dr Caius in Falstaff at the Volksoper 2000. *Recordings include:* Die Fledermaus, Der Vogelhändler; Idomeneo; Intermezzo; Fidelio; Die Meistersinger; Königskinder by Humperdinck. *Honours:* Ehrenzeichen für Verdienste um die Republik Österreich 1998; Kammersänger 1976.

DALLEY, John; American violinist; b. 1 June 1935, Madison, WI. *Education:* Curtis Inst., Philadelphia with Ivan Galamian. *Career:* mem., Oberlin Quartet; fmr teacher at Oberlin Conservatory; performed chamber music with Rudolf Serkin at the Marlboro Festival; prompted by Alexander Schneider to co-found the Guarneri String Quartet 1964–2009; many tours in America and Europe, notably appearances at the Spoleto Festival 1965, to Paris with Arthur Rubinstein and London 1970, in the complete quartets of Beethoven; noted for performances of the Viennese Classics, and works by Walton, Bartók and Stravinsky; season 1987–88 included tour of Japan and concerts at St John's Smith Square and the QEH, London; faculty mem., Curtis Inst., Philadelphia, Univ. of Maryland. *Recordings:* Mozart's Quartets dedicated to Haydn; Complete Quartets of Beethoven; with Arthur Rubinstein, Piano Quintets of Schumann, Dvořák and Brahms; Piano Quartets by Fauré and Brahms. *Honours:* Edison Award (for Beethoven recordings) 1971. *Address:* School of Music, University of Maryland, 2110 Clarice Smith Performing Arts Center, College Park, MD 20742-1620, USA (office). *Telephone:* (301) 405-5549 (office). *Fax:* (301) 314-9504 (office). *E-mail:* jdalley@umd.edu (office). *Website:* www.music.umd.edu/faculty/music_directory/string/john_dalley (office).

DALL'OLIO, Gabriella, DipMus; Italian harpist and academic; b. 7 May 1965, Bologna. *Education:* Conservatories of Bologna and Verona with Anna Loro, Liceo Scientifico, Bologna, master-classes with Pierre Jamet, Jacqueline Borot and Fabrice Pierre in Italy and France, Ecole Normale Supérieure de Paris with Fabrice Pierre and Michael Hentz, Hochschüle für Musik, Würzburg. *Career:* recitals and solo appearances with orchestras and chamber music ensembles throughout Europe and Middle East; live recordings on radio and television in Europe; contemporary music workshops; appearances with several leading chamber ensembles, including Kontraste and Holst Singers; regular appearances as guest prin. harpist with numerous orchestras since 1987, including Chamber Orchestra of Europe, BBC Symphony and Concert Orchestras, Royal Opera House, Bavarian Radio Orchestra, English Chamber Orchestra and numerous regional and festival orchestras; worked under many leading conductors; currently Head of Harp Studies, Trinity Laban Conservatoire of Music and Dance, London; also teaches at Chethams School of Music, Manchester. *Recordings include:* Tema y Variaciones by Joaquin Turina; Two Recitals for Harp with works including Rossini, Handel, Fauré, Bach, Britten, Ginastera, Hindemith, and Roussel; Donatoni; Jean Francaix; Wandering Winds, flute and harp works with Wissam Boustany; Chamber Music Works by Marek; Harp Concerto by Villa-Lobos. *Honours:* Victor Salvi Competition, Italy, Junge Kunstler Prize, Switzerland, prizes in nat. competitions in Alessandria and Latina, Italy. *Address:* Trinity Laban Conservatoire of Music and Dance, Faculty of Music, King Charles Court, Old Royal Naval College, Greenwich, London, SE10 9JF, England (office). *Telephone:* (20) 8305-4444 (office). *E-mail:* g.dall'olio@trinitylaban.ac.uk (office); gabrielladallolio@hotmail.com. *Website:* www.trinitylaban.ac.uk (office).

DALTON, Andrew; Australian singer (countertenor); b. 29 Sept. 1950, Melbourne. *Education:* studied in Brisbane and London, UK. *Career:* debut at Vadstena, Sweden in Provenzale's La Stellidaura vendicata; has sung in Baroque Opera at Venice, Innsbruck, Munich, Berne and Amsterdam; appeared with Scottish Opera in Cavalli's Egisto and at 1987 Buxton Festival as Fernando in Conti's Don Chisciotte in Sierra Morena; season 1988–89 in Jommelli's Fetonte at La Scala, Milan, in Monteverdi's Ulisse with Opera de Lausanne at Mézières, and as Apollo in Death in Venice with Australian Opera at Sydney; engagements in Germany and Switzerland as Britten's Oberon, and has sung in Monteverdi's Orfeo, Handel's Agrippina and Ariodante, and Jommelli's La Schiava Liberata; sang in Purcell's Indian Queen at Barossa Festival, Australia 1995; has appeared with Opera Australia in Death in Venice, L'Incoronazione di Poppea, A Midsummer Night's Dream, Handel's Julius Caesar; has taught at Queensland Conservatorium of Music, Univ. of Queensland; fmr Head of Voice, ANU; currently mem. Faculty, Sydney Conservatorium of Music, Univ. of Sydney. *Honours:* ABC's Instrumental and Vocal Competition. *Address:* Sydney Conservatorium of Music, University of Sydney, Cnr Bridge and Macquarie Street, Sydney, NSW 2000, Australia (office). *E-mail:* andrew.dalton@sydney.edu.au (office). *Website:* music.sydney.edu.au (office).

DAM-JENSEN, Inger; Danish singer (soprano); b. 13 March 1964, Copenhagen; m. Morten Ernst Lassen. *Education:* Royal Danish Acad. of Music, Danish Opera School, studied with Kirsten Buhl Møller. *Career:* roles include Zdenka (Arabella), Ophelia (Hamlet), Norina (Don Pasquale), Sophie (Der Rosenkavalier), Adina (L'elisir d'amore), Susanna (Le Nozze di Figaro), Musetta (La Bohème), Gilda (Rigoletto), Cleopatra (Giulio Cesare), Despina (Così fan Tutte), Lisa (La Sonnambula), Blöndchen (Die Entführung aus dem Serail), Sifare (Mitridate), Pamina (Die Zauberflöte); concert appearances with numerous orchestras, including Danish Radio Symphony, New York Philharmonic, Berlin Philharmonic, Czech Philharmonic, Philharmonia Orchestra, Bastille Orchestra, Sydney Symphony Orchestra, Toronto Symphony Orchestra, Czech Philarmonic Orchestra and Gabrieli Consort; performed closing scene from Strauss' Daphne, London Proms 1999; has performed at Edin. Festival. *Recordings:* Mahler's Fourth Symphony, Grieg's Peer Gynt, Brahms' Ein Deutsches Requiem. *Honours:* winner, Cardiff Int. Singing Competition 1993. *E-mail:* marianne@onstageartists.com. *Website:* onstageartists.com/home.

DAMARATI, Luciano, DipMus; Italian composer, conductor and organist; b. 6 Feb. 1942, Lucca. *Education:* studied with Alessandro Esposito, Fernando Germani, Franco Ferrara, Nino Antonellini, and at Chigiana Acad. of Music, Siena. *Career:* many concerts as organist and orchestral conductor; broadcasts as composer, orchestra conductor and choir conductor on Italian radio and television; mem. Italian Soc. of Musicology. *Compositions:* Impressioni for viola and piano 1968, Fuga for organ 1970, Preludio for organ 1978, Immagini for piano 1980, Contrasti for piano 1980, Preghiera semplice for voice, choir and orchestra 1986, I due fanciulli for voice and piano 1986, Inno di lode a Dio for voice, choir of mixed voices, violin and organ 1988, Le Ciaramelle for voice, violin and piano 1988, La voce for voice, violin and piano 1989, A Silvia for voice and piano 1991, Mottettone for choir of mixed voices, two trumpets, trombone, tam-tam, kettledrums and organ 1995. *Honours:* second prize for composition, Rodolfo del Corona, Leghorn.

DAMIANI, Davide; Italian singer (baritone); b. 1966, Pesaro. *Career:* recital, concert and opera appearances throughout Italy and Europe; contestant at the 1995 Cardiff Singer of the World Competition; repertory includes Le nozze di Figaro and Don Carlo, Lieder by Strauss and Schumann; seasons 1995–99 as house baritone at the Vienna State Opera; WNO 1996, as Don Giovanni; season 2000–01 as Don Giovanni at Toronto and Britten's Tarquinius at Florence. *Current Management:* c/o Musica Management GmbH, Neubauerstrasse 4, 65193 Wiesbaden, Germany. *Telephone:* (611) 2386811. *Fax:* (611) 2386810. *E-mail:* marcus.carl@opernagent.de. *Address:* www.davidedamiani.com.

DAMISCH-KUSTERER, Sieglinde; Dutch singer (soprano); b. 1951, Amsterdam. *Education:* Salzburg Mozarteum, Austria and studied in Vienna with Hilde Konetzni. *Career:* sang at the Vienna Staatsoper from 1979, Salzburg Festival 1981 (Das Buch mit sieben Siegeln by Schmidt); further engagements at Augsburg and elsewhere in Germany as Fiordiligi, Elisabeth de Valois, Tatiana, Jenůfa, Mimi and Pamina; sang Jenůfa at Mönchengladbach 1991; frequent concert appearances.

DAMONTE, Magali; French singer (mezzo-soprano); b. 30 June 1960, Marseille. *Education:* studied in Marseille. *Career:* debut as Zulma in L'Italiana in Algeri at Marseille 1978; many appearances in France with operas by Rossini, Cimarosa and Gounod; Paris Opéra 1980, as Iphise in Rameau's Dardanus; Aix-en-Provence Festival from 1981, as Rosina, Cenerentola and Isaura in Tancredi; at the Opéra de Lyon has sung Aloès in L'Etoile (visit with the company to the Edinburgh Festival 1985); Marseille 1987, as Fidalma in Il Matrimonio Segreto, Théâtre des Champs Elysées, Paris 1989, as Hedwige in Guillaume Tell; other Rossini roles include Isabella, Ragonde (Le Comte Ory) and Marie (Moise); sang Carmen at Covent Garden 1994, and at Vancouver 1996. *Recordings include:* L'Etoile (conducted by John Eliot Gardiner).

DAMRAU, Diana; German singer (soprano); b. 1971, Günzburg an der Donau; m. Nicolas Testé; two s. *Education:* Musikhochschule Würzburg, studied with Carmen Hanganu in Würzburg and Hanna Ludwig in Salzburg. *Career:* began her career with performances in Würzburg, Mannheim and Frankfurt; operatic roles have included Marzelline in Fidelio (Munich) 2002, Small Woman in Cerhas' Der Riese vom Steinfeld (world premiere, Wiener Staatsoper) 2002, Königin der Nacht in Die Zauberflöte (Munich 2003, ROH 2003), Adele in Die Fledermaus (Munich, Dresden) 2003, Sophie in Der Rosenkavalier (Hamburg, Dresden) 2003, Fiakermilli in Arabella (ROH) 2004, title role in L'Europa riconosciuta (Milan) 2004, Zerbinetta in Ariadne auf Naxos (New York Met), Aithra in Die Ägyptische Helena (New York Met), Lorin Maazel's new opera 1984 (world premiere, ROH) 2005, Konstanze in Die Entführung aus dem Serail (Frankfurt, Munich, Vienna) 2006, Zdenka in Arabella (Munich), Gilda in Rigoleto (Opernhaus Zürich 2011, Met Opera 2012), title role in Lucia di Lammermoor, Met tour of Japan 2011, Violetta in La Traviata (ROH 2014, Deutsche Oper 2016), Contessa in Nozze di Figaro (Baden Baden 2015); has performed with leading conductors, including Zubin Mehta, Lorin Maazel, Sir Colin Davis, Christoph von Dohnányi, Adam Fischer, Ivor Bolton, Nikolaus Harnoncourt, Pierre Boulez and Peter Schneider; numerous appearances at Salzburg Festival 2002–, Kissinger Sommer, Munich and Schubertiade Schwarzenberg Festivals; numerous Lied-duo song concerts with Argentinian baritone, Iván Paley. *Recordings include:* Des Knaben Wunderhorn, Schumann's Myrten, Der Riese vom Steinfeld, Mozart's Zaide, Salzburger Liederabend 2005, Schubertiade 2006, Arie di Bravura by Mozart, Salieri and Righini 2007, Mozart's Donna 2008, Liszt Lieder 2011, Forever 2013, Mozart: Die Entführung Aus Dem Serail (with Chamber Orchestra of Europe) 2015. *Honours:* Bayerischer Maximiliansorden für Wissenschaft und Kunst 2010; Bavarian Culture Prize 2006, Bayerische Europa-Medaille 2008, Int. Opera Awards Best Female Singer 2014, Echo Klassik ohne Grenzen Prize 2014. *Current Management:* c/o

Christina Sienel, Hilbert Artists Management, Maximilianstrasse 22, 80539 Munich, Germany. *Telephone:* (89) 29074750. *Fax:* (89) 29074790. *E-mail:* sienel@hilbert.de. *Website:* www.hilbert.de; www.diana-damrau.com.

DANAILOVA, Albena; Bulgarian violinist; *Concertmaster, Vienna Philharmonic*; b. Sofia; d. of Boyan Danailov and Violetta Popova. *Education:* Hochschule für Musik und Theater Rostock. *Career:* with Bayerisches Staatsorchester 2001–03; Concertmaster, London Philharmonic Orchestra 2003–04; First Violin, Vienna Philharmonic Orchestra, now Concertmaster 2010–; as soloist and chamber musician, performed at festivals in Bulgaria, Germany, Israel and USA, with orchestras including Mozart Orchester Hamburg, NDR Sinfonieorchester, Kammerensemle Concertino, Sofia Soloists, Sofia Philharmonics. *Address:* c/o Wiener Philharmoniker, Bösendorferstraße 12, 1010 Wien, Austria (office). *Telephone:* (1) 505-65-25 (office). *Website:* www.wienerphilharmoniker.at (office).

DANBY, Graeme; British singer (bass); b. 1955, Durham, England. *Education:* Royal Academy of Music. *Career:* sang with Scottish Opera until 1995; Appearances with English National Opera in Salome, Boris Godunov, Semele, Rigoletto, Damnation of Faust (Brander), Figaro, Peter Grimes, Poppea and Manon Lescaut; Further engagements with Mid Wales Opera in Aida and Garsington Opera in Le nozze di Figaro; Glyndebourne Tour in Die Entführung and Music Theatre Wales in The Rape of Lucretia and Birtwistle's Punch and Judy; Royal Opera debut 2001, as Marquis d'Obigny in La Traviata; Concerts include Will Todd's oratorio St Cuthbert, at Durham Cathedral, 2001. *Current Management:* Stafford Law, Candleway, Broad Street, Sutton Valence, Kent, ME17 3AT, England. *Website:* www.stafford-law.com.

DANCEANU, Liviu; Romanian composer; *Professor of Composition, University of Music, Bucharest*; b. 19 July 1954; m. Rodica Danceanu 1976. *Education:* Acad. of Music C. Poroumbescu, Bucharest, studied with Stefan Niculescu. *Career:* debut at Acad. of Music C. Porumbescu 1978; concerts in Bucharest and other musical centres, including London, Paris, Rotterdam, Turin, Munich, Warsaw, Prague, Moscow, New York, Salzburg, Vienna, Valencia, Porto, Geneva; broadcasts on nat. and int. radio and television; Leader and Conductor, The Workshop for Contemporary Music ARCHAEUS 1985–; Prof. of Composition, History of Music and Music Aesthetic, Nat. Univ. of Music, Bucharest 1990–; Visiting Lecturer, Acads of Music in Lyon, Munich, Alcoi, Cleveland, Munster, Carbondale, Chisinau, Moscow, Oldenburg, Turin and Dijon. *Compositions:* Les Heros (op 1) 1978, La Rocade de Janus (op 2) 1978, Allegorie (op 3) 1979, Sonate pour Basson (op 4) 1980, In Memoriam Lucian Blaga (op 5) 1981, Angulus Ridet (op 7) 1981, A Cache-Cache (op 8, no. 1) 1982, Steps to Melody (op 8, no. 2) 1982, Ossia (op 9) 1982, To Peace (op 10) 1982, Quasifuga (op 11) 1983, Quasiconcerto (op 12) 1983, Quasisymphonia (Symphony No. 1) (op 13) 1983, Quasiricercare (op 14) 1984, 3 Chansons Infantiles (op 15, no. 1) 1984, 6 Stop-Cadres (op 15, no. 2) 1984, Quasipreludiu (op 16) 1984, Florilège (op 17) 1985, Protocantus (op 18) 1985, Quasipostludiu (Addenda) (op 19) 1985, Glass Music (op 20) 1985, Quasitoccata (op 21) 1985, Rhymes for Archaeus (op 22) 1986, Quasiopera (op 38) 1986, Concerto for bassoon (op 49) 1989, Hexaphonic Melody (op 50, no. 1) 1988, The Great Union (op 50, no. 2) 1988, Trochos (op 51) 1989, L'Effetto Doppler (op 52) 1989, Quasisonata (op 53) 1989, Palimpseste de Couternon (op 54) 1954, Palimpseste 1 & 2 (op 55) 1990, Seven Days (op 56) 1992, Syntiphoniy (op 57) 1991, Concertino Sintoboe (op 58) 1991, Symphony No. 2 (op 59) 1992, Saxas (op 60) 1992, Opus 61 1993, Feast Music (op 62) 1993, Aliquote (op 63) 1994, Andamento (op 64) 1994, Game (op 65) 1994, Climax (op 66) 1995, Chinonic (op 67) 1995, Parallel Musics No. 1 (op 68) 1995, Parallel Musics No. 2 (op 69) 1996, Sega-Nomia (op 70) 1997, History 1 (op 71) 1997, Bas-soon (op 72) 1997, Sifflet en Scène (op 73) 1997, L'Abîme de Pascal (op 74) 1998, History 2 (op 75) 1998, Micro-Pseudo-Requiem (op 76) 1999, Domestic Music (op 77) 1999, History-Rhapsody (op 78) 1999, Opus 79 2000, Opus 80 2000, Tachycardia (op 81) 2000, Panta rei (op 82) 2001, Baclamo (op 83) 2001, Beverdillini (op 84) 2001, Dance by Dance (op 85) 2002, Superbia (op 86) 2002, Lili-Acul (op 87) 2002, One Day of D.G.'s Life (op 88) 2002, Ira (op 89) 2002, Prayer (op 90) 2002, Luxuria (op 91) 2003, Vocabule (op 92) 2003, Tachycardia Again (op 93) 2003, Pietas (op 94) 2003. *Publications:* Implosive Essays I 1998, 'Introduction', in the Epistemology of Music 1999, Implosive Essays II 2001, Book with Instruments 2002, Book with Dances 2002, Seasons of Music – An Elliptic and Didactic History of Music 2003. *Honours:* Romanian Culture Order 2004; Studieen de Toulouse Prize, France 1986, ATM Prize 1987, ACIM Prize 1988, Union of Romanian Composer's Prize 1988, 1990, 1994, 2000, 2003, Romanian Acad. Prize 1989, SOROS Prize 1997. *Address:* Calea Vacaresti No. 276, Bl 63, Apt 49, Sector 4, 040062 Bucharest, Romania (office). *E-mail:* liviud@itcnet.ro (office).

DANCUO-PEHARDA, Mirjana; Croatian singer (soprano); *Singing Teacher, High School of Arts, Oslo*; b. 16 Jan. 1929, Karlovac; m. Zdenko Peharda. *Education:* studied in Zagreb. *Career:* debut with Nat. Opera, Zagreb 1945, as Giannetta in L'Elisir d'amore; sang in Belgrade, Sofia, Brno and elsewhere in Eastern Europe; guest appearances at Teatro Liceo Barcelona, The Vienna Volksoper, Den Norske Opera, Oslo, Stockholm and Gothenburg in Sweden; Herodias in Salome (Strauss); other roles have included Mozart's Countess and Donna Anna, Verdi's Amneris, Amelia in Ballo in Maschera and Trovatore Leonora, La Gioconda, Margherita in Mefistofele, Yaroslavna in Prince Igor, Leonore in Fidelio, Marina in Boris Godunov, Wagner's Sieglinde and Elisabeth, the Marschallin in Der Rosenkavalier, Tosca and Desdemona; Kostelnicka in Jenůfa, Lady Billows in Albert Herring; singing teacher, High School of Arts, Oslo 2001–; mem. Norwegian Opera Singers Assn. *Honours:* Oslo City Culture Prize 1978.

DANEL, Marc; British violinist; b. 1965. *Career:* numerous concerts throughout UK, notably at Aldeburgh Festival, Huddersfield, Andover and Middle Temple; repertoire includes string quartet cycles of Haydn, Beethoven, Schubert, Shostakovich, and Weinberg; Founder-mem. Quatuor Danel 1991, quartet in residence at Univ. of Witten-Herdecke 1996–2006, at CNSM Lyon 2002–04, at Concertgebouw of Bruges 2002–06, Univ. of Manchester 2006–. *Recordings include:* Rosenthal 1995, Gounod to Auvidis 1997, Raskatov 2000, Shostakovich Cycle 2006. *Honours:* prizewinner in competitions at Florence, Evian and London (with Danel Quartet) 1991–94, 1st Grand Prix and prize for best performance of Shostakovich, Shostakovich Competition in St Petersburg 1993. *Current Management:* Ivy Artists, Groot Hertoginnelaan 217, 2517 ES The Hague, The Netherlands. *E-mail:* marc.danel@quatuordanel.eu. *Website:* www.quatuordanel.eu.

DANEMAN, Sophie; British singer (soprano); b. 18 Oct. 1968, d. of Paul Daneman and Meredith Daneman; m. Simon Robson 2001; two s. *Education:* Guildhall School of Music and Drama, studied with Johanna Peters, now studying with Dinah Harris. *Career:* has worked with Christie, Hogwood, Gardiner, Marriner, Prêtre, Biondi, Malgoire, Herreweghe, King, Daniel, Hickox, Fischer, McGegan, Bolton, Hengelbrock, Curnyn, Kraemer and Rattle, amongst others; has sung with RIAS Kammerchor, Philharmonische Staatsorchester Halle, Freibourg Baroque Orchestra, Les Arts Florissants, Scottish Chamber Orchestra, La grande Ecurie, Saint Paul Chamber Orchestra, Berlin Philharmonic, Philharmonia Baroque, Hallé Orchestra, Northern Sinfonia, The Orchestra of the Age of Enlightenment, Gulbenkian Orchestra, Denver Symphony Orchestra, Bournemouth Symphony Orchestra, Apollo's Fire, and others; regular concert appearances, include the South Bank Centre, Wigmore Hall, Maggio Musicale Fiorentino, Concertgebouw, Lufthansa Festival of Baroque Music, Edinburgh, Belfast, Schwarzenberg, Cheltenham, Saintes and Göttingen Festivals; opera title role in Handel's Arianna in Creta and Cleopatra, Göttingen 1999, 2007, Mélisande in Pélleas et Mélisande, Opéra Comique 1999, Euridice and Belinda in Dido and Aeneas, Staatsoper, Munich, Handel's Theodora and Acis and Galatea, Salzburg 2000, Euridice in L'anima del Filosofo, Lausanne 2001, Eileen in Wonderful Town 2004, Susanna in The Marriage of Figaro, Grange Park Opera 2006, Mum in Skellig (Tod Machover), Sage, Gateshead 2008, Phaedra in Hippolyte et Aricie, Reisopera 2009; recitalist at Wigmore Hall, Queen Elizabeth Hall, Carnegie Hall, Concertgebouw, Vienna Concerthaus, Amici della Musica , Schwarzenberg with accompanists including Julius Drake, Eugene Asti, Graham Johnson, Malcolm Martineau, Roger Vignoles and Imogen Cooper; has performed in Schönberg's String Quartet No. 2 with the Tokyo String Quartet. *Films:* Jefferson in Paris, Look at Me. *Recordings include:* Rameau's Castor and Pollux 1993, Rameau's Grand Motets (Gramophone Award) 1994, Purcell's Dido and Aeneas 1995, Charpentier's Médée 1995, Rameau's Les Fêtes d'hébé (Gramophone Award) 1998, Vivaldi's Ottone in Villa 1998, Charpentier: Divertissements, Airs et Concerts 1999, Schumann Lieder 1999, Handel's Acis and Galatea (Gramophone Award) 1999, Mendelssohn songs and duets (three vols) 2000, 2001, Desmaret Grand Motets 2000, Montéclaire's Jephté 2002, Jean-Baptiste Lully's Divertissement de Versailles 2002, Beethoven: Irish and Scottish Songs 2002, Noel Coward duets (with Ian Bostridge) 2002, Handel's Theodora (title role) 2003, Giovanni Pergolesi's Marian Vespers 2003, Charpentier's La Descente D'Orphée 2005, Handel's Rodelinda 2005, Couperin's Lecons de tenebres 2006, Oxford Lieder (live festival recital) 2006, Richard Rodney Bennett: Songs Before Sleep 2010, Blow: Venus and Adonis 2011, Hugo Wolf: the Complete Songs Vol. 1 2011.

DANG, Thai Son, DipMus; Vietnamese/Canadian pianist; b. 2 July 1958, Hanoi; s. of Madame Thai Thi Lien. *Education:* Moscow Tchaikovsky Conservatory, USSR with Vladimir Natanson. *Career:* discovered by Russian pianist Isaac Katz 1974; has performed in more than 40 countries and on concert stages of halls including Lincoln Center, New York, Barbican Centre, London, Salle Pleyel, Paris, Herculessaal, Munich, Musikverein, Vienna, Concertgebouw, Amsterdam, Sydney Opera House and Suntory Hall, Tokyo; appearances at several major festivals, including Berlin, Geneva, Ravinia, Miami, Paris, Brescia, Bergamo, Cannes, Prague Spring, Dubrovnik, Bratislava, Russian Winter, December Nights, Chopin Festival of Nohant, Ruhr Piano Festival; tour of North America 1989; has played with orchestras including Leningrad Philharmonic, Montreal Symphony, BBC Philharmonic, Dresden Philharmonic, Staatskapelle Berlin, Oslo Philharmonic, Warsaw National Philharmonic, Prague Symphony, NHK Symphony, Helsinki Philharmonic, Sydney Symphony, Hungarian Symphony, Moscow Philharmonic; appearances with the Virtuosi of Moscow, the Polish, Moscow and Zürich Chamber Orchestras and with Sinfonia Varsovia; performances with Sir Neville Marriner, Pinchas Zukerman, Mariss Jansons, Ken-Ichiro Kobayashi, Yo-Yo Ma, Seiji Ozawa, Kathleen Battle, Mstislav Rostropovich, Pinchas Zukerman, Murray Perahia, Vladimir Ashkenazy and Isaac Stern; master-classes world-wide; mem. of the jury for piano competitions, including Cleveland, Hamamatsu, Rachmaninoff, Sviatoslav Richter and Arthur Rubenstein competitions; mem. of jury, Chopin Int. Piano Competition 2005, 2010 (performed as a special guest artist for Opening Gala Concert along with Martha Argerich); acclaimed for his interpretations of Chopin; began European tour with several concerts with the Czech Philharmonic Orchestra in Czech Repub. and the 18th Century Orchestra in Poland Feb. 2010, performed at Warsaw Gala Concert 1st March 2010 (Chopin's birthday);

numerous other concerts followed in Russia, Lithuania, Latvia, Macedonia and France; teaches at Univ. of Montreal. *Recordings include:* Dang Thai Son Plays Chopin 1981, Mozart Piano Concertos K.414 & K.467 1984, Concerti for Two Pianos – Mozart and Mendelssohn 1984, Dang Thai Son Plays Chopin Favorites 1986, Chopin Complete Nocturnes 1987, Chopin Preludes, Barcarolle Op. 60 1988, Chopin – 19 Waltzes 1989, Debussy Préludes 1er Livre, Estampes 1990, Chopin Piano Concerto No. 1 & No. 2 1992, Chopin – 4 Ballades, Boléro Op. 19, Tarantelle Op. 43 1993, Chopin – 4 Impromptus, 4 Scherzos 1995, Ravel Pavane pour une infante défunte 1996, Chopin Complete Polonaises 1998, Chopin – The Complete Sonatas 2002, Venetianisches Gondellied – Mendelssohn and Liszt 2002, My Memories – Selections from Chopin, Debussy, Ravel, Mendelssohn and Liszt 2003, Chopin Piano Concertos 1 & 2 2006, Tchaikovsky The Seasons 2007, Complete Mazurkas 2010, Chopin Nocturnes (two versions, one on the 1849 Erard period piano and another one on a Steinway piano) 2010. *Honours:* Hon. Prof., Kunitachi Music Coll., Tokyo; Dr hc (Music Acad., Bydgoczsz, Poland) 2010; First Prize and Gold Medal, Chopin Int. Piano Competition, Warsaw (first Asian) 1980. *E-mail:* danthunga@dangthaison.net (office). *Website:* www.dangthaison.net.

DANGAIN, Guy; French musician (clarinet); b. 12 July 1935, Sains-en-Gohelle. *Education:* Conservatoire National Superieur de Musique, Paris, studied clarinet with Prof. Ulysse Deleclute, chamber music with Prof. Ferrand Oubradous. *Career:* clarinet soloist with National Orchestra of France 1963–93; Prof., Ecole Normale, Paris, Conservatoire National Superieur du Musique, Paris 1975–2000, l'École Normale Int. de Musique, Paris; Dir, Int. Festival, Haut Bugey; Artistic Dir Editions Billaudot; Pres. Artistique, Conseil Nat. Artistique, Confed. Musicale de France; performances with Lorin Maazel, Leonard Bernstein, Neville Marriner, Jean Martinon, Emmanuel Krivine. *Compositions:* over 50 collections of compositions. *Recordings:* Brahms Sonata, Debussy, Rhapsody, Rhapsody with National Orchestra of Martinon, Repertoire from young clarinettist H. Mundi, Creation du Monde, Direction L. Bernstein, Hommage à Louis Cahuzoc, Guisganderie: Hommage à Guisgand, Quinette et Two Songs. *Publications:* Prestige de la clarinette, 1987; A propos de la clarinette, 1991. *Honours:* Officier, Ordre des Arts et des Lettres, Chevalier des Palmes Academiques; Grands Prix du Disque, Académie Charles-Cros. *Address:* 14 Ruelle à Potier, 95590 Nerville la Forêt, France (home). *Fax:* 1-34-69-59-92 (home). *E-mail:* guydangain@aol .com (home).

D'ANGELO, James, BMus, MMus, PhD; American teacher, composer, pianist, organist and workshop leader and writer; *Therapeutic Sound Course Leader, Soundspirit Workshops*; b. 17 March 1939, Paterson, NJ; m. Georgina Joysmith 1970; two d. *Education:* Columbia Univ., New York Univ., Manhattan School of Music, studied with Gunther Schuller, William Russo, John Lewis (MJQ), Jan Gorbaty and Jean Catoire. *Career:* debut, Carnegie Recital Hall, New York 1966; Prof. of Music, CUNY 1970–86; Lecturer, Goldsmiths Coll., London 1987–2003; workshop leader in the Psychology of Musical Performance and Therapeutic Voice Work 1992–, Therapeutic Sound Course Leader, Soundspirit Workshops; mem. Advisory Bd Caduceus Journal 1993–; as composer, works performed at various colls in USA 1968–75, and at various London venues 1985–; song cycle debuted at Carnegie Recital Hall 1971; as pianist, London concerts of own music 1986–; featured composer, Planet Tree Music Festival London 1998, 2000; composer, organ and choral works, Gloucester Cathedral 2009; guest presenter at Findhorn Foundation, Scotland; presenter at Int. Sound Healing Conf., USA 2006, 2008, Yoga Research Soc., USA 2006; guest speaker, Mystics & Scientists Conf., UK 2007. *Compositions include:* Tintinnabulations song cycle for soprano, Toccata for solo percussionist, Songs on poems by e e cummings, The Way of the Spiritual Warrior 1989, The Elements 1990, The Great Happiness 1991, Fool and Angel Entering a City 1993, Fools (three movement suite for flute and percussion) 1997, The Song of Solomon 1998, The Holy City 1998, Tenebrae Factae Sunt 2001, Pater Noster for baritone and string quartet 2003, Songs: The Sacred Clown, Reclamation, Sitting in the Blue Chapel and Elegy 2004–06, Angel Comforting a Fool for oboe/English horn 2005, unaccompanied Missa Brevis 2005, Amen for choir, The Hymn of St Patrick for choir and organ 2007, Ring Out, Wild Bells for choir 2008, Fanfare and Ode to St Kilda for double bass quartet (First Prize in Music Composition, Recital Music Publrs 2010) 2008, Fanfare Fantasia for organ 2009, Introit on Psalm 31 for choir and organ 2009, Tears for soprano, clarinet and piano 2010, Whispers of Heavenly Death & Toward the Unknown Region for soprano and piano 2010, The Holy City for SATB 2010, Magnificat and Nunc Dimittis for SATB and organ 2010, Blow Out Ye Bugles for SATB, trumpet and organ 2011, The Scherzo of Fools for violin 2011, Festival Fanfare for brass, organ and percussion (work commissioned to open the Three Choirs Festival, Gloucester, UK) 2012, The Wounded Angel for five flutes 2013, The Wounded Angel for solo guitar 2013, Angel Comforting a Fool for viola and bassoon 2013, Three Motets on Medieval Lyrics, The Angel of the Flowing Light for orchestra, Three Contemplative songs on Thomas Merton. *Recordings include:* commercial: Fast Cats and Mysterious Cows (including Krishna Portraits) 1999, Virgin Classics: The Holy City, The Sacred Choral Music of James D'Angelo 2014, Gothic Records. *Publications:* Healing with the Voice 2000, The Healing Power of the Human Voice 2005, Essay: A Pathway Towards the One True Religion and Spirituality, in A New Renaissance: Transforming Science, Spirit and Society for Religion and Spirituality 2010, Seed Sounds for Tuning the Chakras: Vowels, Consonants and Syllables for Spiritual Transformation 2012; contrib. to International Dictionary of Opera, Hindemith Jahrbuch, Contemporary Music Review. *Honours:* First Prize in Music Composition, Arklow Music Festival, Ireland 2005. *Address:* 33 Morpeth Street, Gloucester, Glos., G41 4TN, England (home). *Telephone:* (1452) 413220 (office). *E-mail:* jamesdangelomusic@gmail.com (home); info@soundspirit.co.uk (office). *Website:* www.soundspirit.co.uk (office); www.jamesdangelomusic.com (office).

DANIEL, Nicholas, FRAM, FGSM, ARAM; British oboist, conductor and academic; *Professor, Hochschule für Musik, Trossingen*; b. (Jeremy Nicholas Gordon Daniel), 9 Jan. 1962, Liss, Hants., England; s. of the late Jeremy Daniel and Margaret-Louise Daniel; m. 1st Joy Farrall 1986 (divorced 2011); two s.; m. 2nd Piotr Rudkowski 2012. *Education:* Chorister, Salisbury Cathedral School, Purcell School, London, Royal Acad. of Music, London, pvt. studies with Anthony Pay and Hans Keller. *Career:* debut, South Bank 1982; concerto and recital appearances at home and abroad; BBC Proms debut 1990, numerous subsequent appearances; commissioner and first performer of more than 200 new works for oboe; Founder and Dir Haffner Wind Ensemble 1990, Daniel-Drake Duo 1980–; mem. Camerata Pacifica, USA 2007–; regular broadcasts of wide repertoire; tours include USA, Japan, Australia, Scandinavia, Netherlands, Italy, Bulgaria, Spain, France, Switzerland, Germany, S America; performances with Brodsky, Allegri, Brindisi, Vanbrugh, Carducci, Lindsay String Quartets; Prof., Guildhall School of Music and Drama, London 1984–97; Prof. of Oboe, Bloomington, Ind., USA 1997–99; Prince Consort Prof. of Oboe, Royal Coll. of Music, London 1999–2002; Prof., Hochschule für Musik, Trossingen, Germany 2004–; Artistic Dir Osnabruck Kammermusiktage 2001–05; Founder-mem. and Assoc. Artistic Dir Britten Sinfonia 2002–; Artistic Dir Leicester Symphony Orchestra 2001–05, Leicester Int. Music Festival 2004–; Artistic Dir Barbirolli Isle of Wight Int. Oboe Competition 2005; prolific recording artist. *Honours:* Hon. Fellow, RAM, Guildhall School, Purcell School 1988; Queen's Medal for Music 2012; BBC Young Musician of the Year 1980, Gillet Young Artists Prize, Graz 1984, Munich Competition 1986. *Current Management:* c/o Sarah Bruce, Lomonaco Artists, 11 Wotton Court, 6 Jamestown Way, London, E14 2DB, England. *Telephone:* (20) 7538-2203; 7803-923661 (mobile). *Fax:* (20) 7538-2203. *E-mail:* info@lomonaco -artists.com. *Website:* www.lomonaco-artists.com; www.nicholasdaniel.com.

DANIEL, Paul Wilson, CBE; British conductor; *Music Director, Orchestre Nationale Bordeaux Aquitaine*; b. 5 July 1958, Birmingham; m. Joan Rodgers 1988 (divorced); two d. *Education:* choir of Coventry Cathedral, King's Coll., Cambridge, Guildhall School of Music and Drama, London, studied with Franco Ferrara in Italy and with Adrian Boult and Edward Downes. *Career:* mem. music staff, ENO, London 1982–87, Music Dir 1997–2005; Music Dir, Opera Factory 1987–90, Opera North, Leeds 1990–97; Prin. Conductor, English Northern Philharmonia 1990–97; Prin. Conductor and Artistic Adviser, West Australian Symphony Orchestra 2009–13; Prin. Conductor and Artistic Dir, Royal Philharmonic Orchestra of Galicia, Santiago de Compostela 2013–; Music Dir, Orchestre Nat. Bordeaux Aquitaine 2013–; has conducted all the major London orchestras and most of the regional UK orchestras and orchestras in USA, Germany, Netherlands, France and Australia. *Operas conducted include:* (ENO) The Mask of Orpheus, Akhnaten, Tosca, Rigoletto, Carmen, Figaro's Wedding, King Priam, Flying Dutchman, From the House of the Dead, Tales of Hoffmann, Falstaff, Manon, Othello, Boris Godunov, La Traviata, The Carmelites, Nixon in China, The Silver Tassie, War and Peace, Lulu, The Trojans, Twilight of the Gods; (Opera North) Ariane et Barbe-Bleue, Attila, King Priam, Don Giovanni, Der Ferne Klang, Boris Godunov (also at BBC Proms 1992), Rigoletto, Don Carlos, Wozzeck, Gloriana, Baa Baa Black Sheep (world premiere), Playing Away, Il Trovatore, Pelléas et Mélisande, Jenůfa, Luisa Miller; (Royal Opera Covent Garden) Mitridate; has also conducted opera productions in Nancy, Munich, Brussels, Geneva. *Honours:* Olivier Award for Outstanding Achievement in Opera 1997, Gramophone Award for English Music Series 1999. *Current Management:* Ingpen & Williams, 7 St George's Court, 131 Putney Bridge Road, London, SW15 2PA, England. *Address:* Orchestre Nationale Bordeaux Aquitaine, Grand-Théâtre, Place de la Comédie, BP 90095, 33025 Bordeaux Cedex, France (office). *E-mail:* info@onb.fr (office). *Website:* www.onb.fr (office).

DANIELS, Barbara, BA, MA; American singer (soprano); b. 7 May 1946, Granville, OH. *Education:* Ohio State Univ., Univ. of Cincinnati. *Career:* debut in West Palm Beach, FL, as Susanna 1973; sang in Europe from 1974, notably in Innsbruck as Violetta and Cologne as Alice Ford, Rosalinda, Mozart's Countess and Manon Lescaut; appeared in the Michael Hampe productions and films of Agrippina and Il Matrimonio Segreto; Covent Garden from 1978 as Musetta, Donna Elvira, Rosalinde and Alice Ford; Washington, DC 1979, as Donizetti's Norina; San Francisco from 1980, as Zdenka in Arabella and as Violetta, Liu and Micaela; Zürich Opera as the Comtesse, in the Ponnelle production of Le Comte Ory; Metropolitan Opera from 1983, as Musetta, Violetta, Rosalinde, Marguerite and the title role in Les Mamelles de Tirésias; Musetta at Rome 1987; Teatro Regio Turin as Violetta 1988; Rosalinde in Fledermaus at the Metropolitan and Chicago 1990; Jenůfa at Innsbruck 1990; Minnie in La Fanciulla del West at the Metropolitan 1991; sang Senta at Cincinnati 1996; Alice Ford at Baltimore 1997; sang Puccini's Minnie at Nice 2000; concert appearances in Rossini's Mosè at Perugia; Boito's Mefistofele at the Zürich Tonhalle, Schumann's Scenes from Faust with the Berlin Philharmonic and the Missa Solemnis under Giulini at the Maggio Musicale Florence; Prof. of Voice, Salzburg Mozarteum and Innsbruck Conservatory. *Recordings include:* Scenes from Faust, La Bohème (conducted by Bernstein), Mad About Puccini, Fanciulla de West (video), Il Matrimonio

Segreto (video), Agrippina (video). *Honours:* Dr hc (Cincinnati Univ.) 1992. *Current Management:* Opéra et Concert, 1 rue Volney, 75002, Paris, France.

DANIELS, Charles; British singer (tenor); b. 1960, Salisbury. *Education:* King's Coll., Cambridge, Royal Coll. of Music with Edward Brooks. *Career:* numerous appearances in UK, Europe, Canada and USA; Handel's La Resurrezione in Oslo; Saul in Göttingen; Solomon in Halle; L'Allegro at Handel's Church in London; Mendelssohn's Elijah and Puccini's Messa di Gloria under Michel Corboz; Bach St Matthew Passion for De Nederlandse Bach Vereniging; Christmas Oratorio in St Gallen, Lugano, Dublin; regular appearances at BBC Promenade Concerts; Elgar's Dream of Gerontius; Luigi Nono's Canti di Vita e Amore (Edinburgh Festival); Britten's War Requiem (Canterbury Festival); Cavalieri's Anima e Corpo (Schwabische Gmund); Schubert Mass in E Flat with London Phiharmonic Orchestra; Handel's Esther in Hebrew and English in New York; Monteverdi's Orfeo and Purcell's King Arthur in Toronto; premiere of Wojciech Kilar's Missa Pro Pace with Warsaw Philharmonic; mem. of early music vocal ensemble Orlando Consort for 16 years. *Recordings include:* Handel Messiah and Schütz Christmas Story, with Paul MacCreesh; Bach's Easter Oratorio, with Andrew Parrott; Dowland songs, with David Miller; Senfl tenorlied, with Fretwork; Peachum in The Beggar's Opera; The Fairy Queen, under William Christie; many Purcell albums, with the King's Consort; Haydn's St Cecilia Mass; Charpentier Vêpres aux Jésuites, under Michel Corboz. *Honours:* Hubert Parry Prize at GKN English Songs Awards 1986. *Current Management:* Hazard Chase, 25 City Road, Cambridge, CB1 1DP, England. *Telephone:* (1223) 312400. *Fax:* (1223) 460827. *E-mail:* info@hazardchase.co.uk. *Website:* www.hazardchase .co.uk.

DANIELS, Claire; British singer (soprano); b. 1963, England. *Education:* Royal Northern Coll. of Music, studied in Paris with Janine Reiss. *Career:* appearances include Jennie Hildebrand in Street Scene, A Nymph in Rusalka, Niece in Peter Grimes for ENO, Amor in Orfeo ed Euridice for Opera North, Zerlina for Kent Opera; sang in Purcell's King Arthur at the Buxton Festival; Rossini's L'Occasions fa il ladro and L'Italiana in Algeri and Grétry's Le Huron; Vespina, in Haydn's L'Infedeltà Delusa for Garsington Opera; Nannetta, in Falstaff for Opera Zuid in Netherlands; Mozart's Susanna and Servilia and Adina in L'Elisir d'amore for Scottish Opera 1993; The Girl, in Nigel Osborne's Sarajevo, for Opera Factory; Serpetta in La finta giardiniera by Mozart for Klagenfurt Opera in Austria; concert appearances throughout Germany and at Aix-en-Provence, Barcelona and Gothenberg; Mozart's Mass in C Minor with Charles Mackerras; Les Nuits d'Été at Perth Festival; Carmina Burana in Valencia; sang in Peter Grimes with the London Symphony Orchestra under Rostropovich; Mozart's Exsultate Jubilate for concert tour of the UK with the Stuttgart Philharmonic Orchestra.

DANIELS, David; American singer (countertenor); b. 12 March 1966, Spartanburg, SC; m. Scott Walters 2014. *Education:* Univ. of Michigan with George Shirley. *Career:* debut as Nero in L'Incoronazione di Poppea at the Glimmerglass Opera Festival 1994; Handel's Tamerlano at Glimmerglass 1995; followed by Arsamenes in Xerxes with the Boston Lyric Opera season 1995–96, in Israel in Egypt at the Vienna Musikverein, Messiah in Boston and Handel's Saul with the Philharmonia Baroque Orchestra; Salzburg Festival debut as Hamor in Handel's Jephtha 1996; sang Didymus in Theodora at the Glyndebourne Festival 1996; opened 1996–97 season with ENO as Oberon in A Midsummer Night's Dream; London and New York recital debuts at the Wigmore Hall and Lincoln Center 1996; sang in Monteverdi's Ulisse at Los Angeles Opera, as Sesto in Handel's Giulio Cesare for the Royal Opera, London 1997 and Metropolitan Opera, New York 1999; sang Handel's Rinaldo at the London Barbican 2000, at Bavarian State Opera 2001; other roles include Monteverdi's Nero (San Francisco 1998) and Arsace in Handel's Partenope (Glimmerglass 1998); sang Giulio Cesare (Palais Garnier, Paris) 2002, Hercules (Lyric Opera of Chicago) 2011, The Enchanted Island (Metropolitan) 2012, title role in Oscar, Santa Fe Opera 2013, Opera Philadelphia 2015; Prof. of Music in Voice, Univ. of Michigan School of Music, Theatre & Dance 2015–. *Recordings include:* Handel: Operatic Arias 1998, Scarlatti's Cantatas Volume II 1998, Sento Amor 1999, Handel, Rinaldo 2000, Serenade 2000, Handel, L'Allegro, il Pensoroso el il Moderato 2000, Handel, Oratorio Arias 2002, Vivaldi, Stabat Mater 2002, A Quiet Thing 2003, Purcell, Dido and Aeneas 2004, Berlioz, Les Nuits d'Été 2004, Vivaldi, Bazajet 2005, Pergolesi, Stabat Mater 2006, J.S. Bach, Sacred Arias and Cantatas 2008. *Honours:* Opera News Award for invaluable contribution to opera 2012. *Current Management:* c/o Alec Treuhaft, IMG Artists, Carnegie Hall Tower, 152 W. 57th Street, 5th Floor, New York, NY 10019, USA. *Telephone:* (212) 994-3500. *Fax:* (212) 994-3550. *E-mail:* mhorner@imgartists.com. *Website:* www.imgartists.com; www.danielssings.com.

DANILEVSKI, Alexander; Russian composer and lutenist; b. 4 Sept. 1957, St Petersburg; m. Emilia Danilevski 1990, three s. two d. *Education:* Leningrad Conservatoire, Scola Cantorum Basilensis, studied with Galina Ustvolskaya. *Career:* debut with I Sonato for Violin, St Petersburg Philharmonic 1981 and lute recital; solo recitals and concerts throughout Russia; festivals, recitals and concerts in Europe (early music); Founder, Syntagma ensemble of early music; performances of Lauda, Antiphones, Sonata for Cello in Grand Festival des Musiques Slaves, Paris 1996, 1997; numerous concerts of early music given by Syntagma; mem. American Lute Soc. *Compositions include:* Sonatas for violin, violoncello and piano, Missa for choir and orchestra, Seven Words of Christ on the Cross, Strophes enfilees (nai kai), Concerto for organ, harpsichord and piano, Quatuors 1–4 (chamber music),

Lauda for voice and ensemble, Antiphones I for recorder quartet, Antiphones II for string quartet, Revelation for cello 1997, Sonatos 1–3 for piano, Concert and Night Music for two pianos, Seven Words for soprano and ensemble. *Recordings include:* Guillaume Dufay and Music of his time (with Ensemble Pro Anima, St Petersburg), Medieval and Renaissance Music, Johannes Ciaconia and his Time, Solo, Francesco da Milano, Fancies and Ricercars, St Petersburg, Alexandre Danilevski: The Uncertainty Principle 2012. *Publications:* Works for Piano 1997–98, 20 Russian Barocco Songs. *Website:* www .danilevski.info.

DANNA, Mychael; Canadian composer; b. 20 Sept. 1958, Winnipeg, Man. *Education:* Univ. of Toronto. *Career:* has worked with film directors including Atom Egoyan, Catherine Hardwicke, Scott Hicks, Ang Lee, Gillies MacKinnon, James Mangold, Bennett Miller, Mira Nair, Billy Ray, Joel Schumacher, Denzel Washington; fmr Composer-in-Residence, McLaughlin Planetarium, Toronto; Visiting Lecturer, Royal Coll. of Music, London; commissioned by vocal ensemble Chanticleer to write Kyrie for a new mass, And on Earth, Peace, premiered in Temple of Dendur, Metropolitan Museum of Art, Manhattan 2007. *Film scores include:* Family Viewing 1987, Exotica 1994, Lilies 1996, Kama Sutra 1997, The Ice Storm 1997, 8mm 1997, Caribe 1997, Regeneration 1997, The Sweet Hereafter 1997, Girl, Interrupted 1999, Monsoon Wedding 2001, Being Julia 2004, Vanity Fair 2004, Tideland 2005, Capote 2005, Where the Truth Lies 2005, The Nativity Story 2006, Little Miss Sunshine 2006, Surfs Up 2007, Fracture (with Jeff Danna) 2007, Stone of Destiny 2008, Lakeview Terrace 2008, (500) Days of Summer 2009, Chloe 2009, The Whistleblower 2010, Moneyball 2011, Life of Pi (Golden Globe Award for Best Original Score in a Motion Picture 2013, Academy Award for Best Original Score 2013) 2012; TV series: Murder One 1988, Road to Avonlea 1990, Hush Little Baby 1993, Gross Misconduct 1993, Avonlea 1995, At the End of the Day: The Sue Rodriguez Story 1998, The Matthew Shepard Story 2002, Opening Night 2005, New Amsterdam 2008, Dollhouse 2009, Life of Pi 2012. *Honours:* Glenn Gould Composition Scholarship 1985. *Current Management:* c/o First Artists Management, 4764 Park Granada, Suite 210, Calabasas, CA 91302, USA. *E-mail:* admin@mychaeldanna.com. *Website:* www.mychaeldanna.com.

DANTONE, Ottavio; Italian conductor and musician (harpsichord, fortepiano); *Music Director, Accademia Bizantina.* *Education:* Conservatorio Giuseppe Verdi. *Career:* specialist in performance of baroque music; Music Dir Accademia Bizantina, Ravenna 1996–, concerts in Austria, Denmark, France, Germany, Japan, England, Israel, Mexico, Holland, Switzerland, USA, Turkey and Hungary; debut as opera conductor (Giuseppe Sarti's Giulio Sabino at Teatro Alighieri, Ravenna) 1999; La Scala debut (Handel's Rinaldo) 2005, also at Glyndebourne 2011. *Recordings include:* on harpsichord: Scarlatti: Complete Sonatas; as conductor, with Accademia Bizantina: Settecento Veneziano, Sarti: Giulio Sabino, Vivaldi: Tito Manlio, Vivaldi: In Furore/Laudate Pueri/Concerti Sacri 2006. *Honours:* Basso Continuo Prize, Int. Paris Festival 1985, prizewinner, Int. Bruges Festival 1986. *Address:* c/o Laura Crippa, Associazione Accademia Bizantina, Via Fratelli Bedeschi 9, 48012 Bagnacavallo, Italy (office). *E-mail:* lauracrippa@accademiabizantina .it (office). *Website:* www.accademiabizantina.it (office).

DANZ, Ingeborg; German singer (contralto); b. 1961, Witten. *Education:* studied with Heiner Eckels in Detmold. *Career:* has appeared on several opera stages; mainly an oratorio, concert and lieder singer; collaborates closely with Helmuth Rilling and the Internationale Bachakademie Stuttgart and with Collegium Vocale Gent and Philippe Herreweghe; performs repertoire from several musical epochs, especially music by J.S. Bach, also the symphonies of Mahler, Berlioz' Nuits d'été and Schumann's Faust-Szenen, and sacred music by Bruckner and Beethoven; collaborations with conductors including Riccardo Muti, Herbert Blomstedt, Manfred Honeck, Christopher Hogwood, Philippe Herreweghe, Riccardo Chailly, Heinz Holliger, Helmuth Rilling, Ingo Metzmacher and Semyon Bychkov have led her to Teatro alla Scala, Lucerne and Salzburg Festivals and leading orchestras, including Royal Concertgebouw Orchestra Amsterdam, Vienna, Munich and Berlin Philharmonics, Gewandhausorchester Leipzig, Bavarian Radio Symphony Orchestra, Boston Symphony Orchestra, DSO Berlin, NDR Hamburg, Bamberger Symphoniker, SWR Radio Symphony Orchestra Stuttgart, Swedish Radio Symphony Orchestra, NHK Symphony, San Francisco Symphony, Los Angeles Philharmonic, Minnesota Orchestra, Nat. Symphony Orchestra, Washington Symphony and Chicago Symphony orchestras; season 2012–13 at the Lied und Lyrik Festival with Gustav Mahler's Das Lied von der Erde with the Bamberger Symphoniker and a lied matinee for children in Kloster Banz with Michael Gees at the piano; further concerts with Montreal Symphony Orchestra under Kent Nagano, Orchestra Sinfonica Nazionale della RAI under Helmuth Rilling, Concertgebouw Amsterdam with Ivan Fischer, Bruckner Orchestra, Linz and Orchestra Sinfonica do Estado do Brasil under Thomas Dausgaard, amongst others; recent recital tour with Juliane Banse, Christoph Prégardien and Olaf Bär, and later with James Taylor; gave further recital with Olaf Bär at the Rheingau Music Festival; numerous broadcast and TV productions; mem. Bd Neue Bachgesellschaft Leipzig. *Recordings include:* Mozart masses with Nikolaus Harnoncourt, several discs with Philippe Herreweghe, first recital disc with Brahms Lieder, Bach's St Matthew, St John Passion, B Minor Mass and Christmas Oratorio (all with Helmuth Rilling), box set with the complete works of Johannes Brahms, including a recital disc with Ingeborg Danz and the pianist Helmut Deutsch 2008. *Honours:* several prizes and scholarships from Deutscher Musikrat and

Richard Wagner Fed. *Current Management:* c/o Verena Vetter, Kunstler Sekretariat am Gasteig, Rosenheimerstrasse 52, 81669 Munich, Germany. *Telephone:* (89) 44488790. *Fax:* (89) 4489522. *E-mail:* team@ks-gasteig.de. *Website:* www.ks-gasteig.de.

DAOUD, Rageh, BMus; Egyptian composer, musician (piano) and teacher; b. 23 Nov. 1954, Cairo. *Education:* Cairo Conservatoire, Vienna Acad. of Music. *Career:* composer 1978–; teacher and Research Asst, Cairo Conservatoire 1978–81, apptd Assoc. Prof. of Composition 1988, Head, Composition and Conducting Dept 2008–; apptd conductor, Hanager Center Chamber Orchestra, Egyptian Ministry of Culture 1993; Pres. Nat. Cttee, Int. Music Council. *Compositions include:* Egyptian Glimpse for orchestra 1978, Sonata for piano 1978, Lied for soprano and piano 1978, Four Pieces for string orchestra 1981, Fugue for string orchestra 1981, Fantasy for harp, cello and percussion 1982, Four Dances for string quartet 1982, Fantasy for woodwinds and string orchestra 1983, Lied for alto and piano 1984, Takassim for clarinet and orchestra 1984, Quartet for flute, oboe, clarinet and bassoon 1985, Quartet for woodwinds 1985, Der neue Ankommende lied for alto, bass clarinet and vibraphone 1986, Meditation for string orchestra 1986, Portrait No. 1 for string orchestra 1986, Trio for piano, violin and cello 1987, Three Pictures for oboe and piano 1987, Three Children's Pictures for two pianos 1987, Portrait No. 2 for string orchestra 1987, Rhapsody for string orchestra 1988, Nocturne for cello and piano 1989, Nocturne for piano 1989, Requiem for choir and orchestra 1990, Thirty Songs for children and small orchestra 1991, Suite for alto flute solo 1992, Suite for flute and piano 1992, Rhapsody for flute, violin and orchestra 1992, Passacaglia for lute, organ and string orchestra 1993. *Honours:* Ministry of Culture Artistic Creation Prize 1990, Alexandria Film Festival Prize 1991, Film Critics Asscn Prize 1992. *Address:* Committee of Music, Opera and Ballet, Supreme Council of Culture, El Gabalia Street, Opera House, El Gezira, Cairo, Egypt. *Telephone:* (1) 4161141; (2) 5613451. *Fax:* (2) 5877545. *E-mail:* ragehdaoud@hotmail.com; contact@ragehdaoud.com. *Website:* www.ragehdaoud.com.

D'APPARECIDA, Maria; Brazilian singer; b. 17 Jan. 1936, Rio de Janeiro; d. of Sylvio Marques and Dulce Marques (née Adelino). *Education:* Conservatório Brasileiro de Música, Rio de Janeiro, Conservatoire Nat. Supérieur de Musique de Paris, France. *Career:* fmr teacher; radio announcer 1955–58; performed Brazilian songs at Odéon-Théâtre de France 1961; has given recitals and appeared in concerts and at festivals, and has appeared at major opera houses in France. *Recordings include:* Brasileirissimo (Grand Prix Int. de l' Acad. Charles Cros) 1988. *Honours:* Hon. Citizen of Rio de Janeiro 1981, Gold Medal, Soc. d'Encouragement au Progrès, named Gen. Rep. for Brazil 1992; Officier, Ordre des Arts et des Lettres, Chevalier, Légion d'honneur; numerous awards including Médaille d'Argent, Ville de Paris, Orphée d'Or 1969, Grand Prix du Disque Français 1972, Printemps de Suède 1972. *Address:* 19 rue Auguste Vacquerie, 75116 Paris, France (home). *Telephone:* 1-47-20-96-50 (home).

DARA, Enzo; Italian singer (bass); b. 13 Oct. 1938, Mantua. *Education:* studied with Bruno Sutti in Mantua. *Career:* debut at Fano 1960, as Colline in La Bohème; Reggio Emilia 1966, as Dulcamara in L'Elisir d'amore; La Scala Milan debut 1970, as Bartolo in Il Barbiere di Siviglia; sang Bartolo on New York 1982 and Covent Garden 1985 debuts; Pesaro 1984, in revival of Rossini's Il Viaggio in Reims; guest appearances in Naples, Bologna, Moscow, Brussels, Venice, Palermo and Rome; returned to Covent Garden 1987, as Dulcamara; Pesaro Festival 1988, in Il Signor Bruschino; Don Pasquale at Venice 1990; Teatro de la Zarzuela Madrid 1990, in Il Turco in Italia; sang Bartolo at Verona Arena 1996; sang Geronio in Il Turco in Italia and Don Magnifico in Cenerentola at Buenos Aires and Munich 2000. *Recordings include:* Il Barbiere di Siviglia and Il Viaggio a Reims; L'Italiana in Algeri; La Buona Figliuola by Piccinni; Donzetti's L'ajo nell' imbarazzo; Il Turco in Italia.

DARBELLAY, Jean Luc; Swiss composer, conductor and clarinettist; b. 2 July 1946, Berne; m. Elsbeth Darbellay-Fahrer 1971; one s. one d. *Education:* Berne Univ., Berne Conservatory, studied composition with Theo Hirsbrunner, Cristobal Halffter, Dimitri Terzakis, Lucerne Conservatory with Edison Denisov and Klaus Huber, Foundation Ludus Ensemble Berne, studied conducting with Pierre Dervaux and Franco Ferrara. *Career:* concerts throughout Europe as conductor of various orchestras, including Ludus Ensemble, Landesjugendchor Niedersachsen and Quaderni Perugini di Musica Contemporanea, Ensemble Contrechamps, MDR Kammerphilharmonie, John Cage Festival, Perugia. *Compositions include:* Glanum 1981, Amphores 1983, C'est un peu d'eau qui nous separe 1989, Cello Concerto (Radio France recording in Paris with Ensemble Denosjours, dedicated to Siegfried Palm) 1989, Interférences 1991, Before Breakfast (film score) 1991, Pranam III (command of the Quaderni Perugini and Siegfried Palm) 1992, Cantus (command of the Altenburger Orgelkonzerte) 1993, Itinéraires (for St Petersburg Festival) 1994, Elégie 1994, Incanto horn concerto (Plauen) 1995, A la recherche (creation in Moscow), PRANAM IV cello concerto for Siegfried Palm (in Halle), Ein Garten für Orpheus (Bauhaus Dessau) 1996, Écumes for string quartet 1996, Valàre for violin and piano 1997, Lumières 1998, Chant d'adieux 1998, Shadows for percussion ensemble 1999, Gestes-Effleurements for string trio 1999, Messages for piano 2000, Azur 2001, Oyama 2001, A Quattro for four horns and orchestra 2002, Alea concerto for violin 2003, Alani trio for violin, horn and piano 2003, Nocturne 2004, Delphes des trois fois 2004, Postojna 2004, Où irai-je, qui répondra 2004, Espace 2004, Ein Garten für Orpheus 2004, Chant d'adieux 2004, Schwarzwasser 2005, Requiem 2005, Reflets 2005, Par transparence 2005, Hale Bopp 2005, étoile 2005, Concerto Discreto 2005, Al Furioso 2005, 3 Könige 2005, Observatory 2006, Miroirs 2006, Labyrinth 2006, Escales für Horn und Streichchester 2006, Es War Ein Kind, Das Wollte Nie 2006, D'Une Noire Étoile 2006, Alizé 2006. *Recordings:* Leading the Sächsisches Kammerorchester Leipzig: Mozart Divertimento, K251, Violin Concerto, K218, Haydn's Horn Concerto No. 2 and Symphony No. 1, Mozart's Serenade in C minor, K388, Darbellay's Espaces, Sept Poèmes Romands and Wind Octet, Aube Imaginaire with Choeur Novantiqua Sion, Résonances with pieces for violoncello and horn (with Olivier Darbellay) 1997. *Honours:* Chevalier, Ordre des Arts et des Lettres. *Address:* c/o Editors Editions Tre Media, Amalienstrasse 40, 76133 Karlsruhe, Germany (office); Englische Anlagen 6, 3005 Bern, Switzerland (home). *E-mail:* jld@jean-luc-darbellay.ch (home). *Website:* www.jean-luc-darbellay.ch.

D'ARCANGELO, Ildebrando; Italian singer (bass-baritone); b. 1969, Pesaro. *Education:* studied with Maria Vittoria Romano and in Bologna. *Career:* engagements in La Bohème at Chicago, I Capuleti by Bellini at the Berlin Staatsoper, Rossini's Armida and Guillaume Tell at Pesaro and as Mozart's Masetto at the New York Met, Figaro at Salzburg, 1996; Don Giovanni in Bonn and Leporello at the Bayerische Staatsoper; Banquo in Macbeth at Bologna and Colline in La Bohème at Covent Garden 1996; season 1997–98 as Figaro in Rome, Paris and New York, Enrico in Lucia di Lammermoor at the Edinburgh Festival and Leporello in Vienna; Leporello at the Theater an der Wien 1999; sang Rossini's Mosè at Monte Carlo 2000; season 2002–03 in Le nozze di Figaro in Milan, Don Giovanni in Naples. *Recordings include:* Don Giovanni (as Leporello, under John Eliot Gardiner) 1995; Rigoletto 1998 and I Lombardi under James Levine; Otello under Myung Wha Chung; Semiramide; Le nozze di Figaro 2007; Don Carlos; Lucia di Lammermoor (with Mackerras); Don Giovanni (with Abbado); Handel Arie Italiane 2009, Mozart Arias 2011. *Honours:* winner Concorso Internazionale Toti dal Monte, Treviso, Premio della Critica Musicale 'Franco Abbiati' 2003. *Current Management:* Atelier Musicale, via Caselle 76, San Lazzaro di Savena 40068, Italy. *Telephone:* (51) 1998-4444. *Fax:* (51) 1998-4420. *E-mail:* info@ateliermusicale.it. *Website:* www.ateliermusicale.it.

DARLINGTON, Jonathan; British conductor; *Music Director, Vancouver Opera*; b. 1962, England. *Career:* engagements with the Teatro San Carlo, Naples, Hamburg State Opera, Lausanne Opéra and Bordeaux Opera; Principal Guest Conductor, Deutsche Oper am Rhein, Düsseldorf, and concerts with the Orchestra Sinfonia di San Carlo and Swedish Chamber Orchestra; season 2001–02 with the Bochum Symphony, Orchestre Philharmonique de Strasbourg, Orchestre Nat. de L'Ile de France and China Philharmonic Orchestra at the Peking Music Festival; further opera work at the Théâtre des Champs Elysées, Paris, and Vancouver Opera; repertoire includes works by Mozart, Beethoven, Mendelssohn, Schubert and Brahms; choral repertoire includes the Bach Passions and B minor mass, Haydn's Creation, Requiems of Dvoràk and Mozart and the Glagolitic Mass by Janáček; Prin. Conductor, Vancouver Opera –2005, Music Dir 2005–. *Current Management:* c/o IMG Artists, The Light Box, 111 Power Road, London, W4 5PY, England. *Telephone:* (20) 7957-5800. *Fax:* (20) 7957-5801. *E-mail:* aroberts@imgartists.com. *Website:* www.imgartists.com. *Address:* c/o Vancouver Opera, 835 Cambie Street, Vancouver, BC V6B 2P4, Canada. *Website:* www.vancouveropera.ca.

DARLINGTON, Stephen Mark, MA, DMus, FRCO; British organist and academic; *Organist and Tutor in Music, Christ Church, Oxford*; b. 21 Sept. 1952, Lapworth, Warwickshire; m. Moira Ellen Hill 1975; three d. *Education:* Christ Church, Oxford. *Career:* Asst Organist, Canterbury Cathedral 1974–78; Master of the Music, St Alban's Abbey 1978–85; Artistic Dir, Int. Organ Festival, St Albans 1979–85; Organist and Tutor in Music, Christ Church, Oxford 1985–; Choragus, Univ. of Oxford 1998–; Pres., Royal Coll. of Organists 1998–2000. *Recordings include:* Masses by Byrd, Esteves, Lassus, Martin, Palestrina, Poulenc, Taverner, Victoria; Choral works by Haydn, Mathias, Pygott, Tippett, Vaughan Williams, Vivaldi, Walton, Weelkes; Choral Works by Britten, Haydn, Janacek, Goodall; Masses by Aston, Ashwell, Taverner; Music from Eton Choirbook. *Address:* Christ Church, Oxford, OX1 1DP, England (office). *Telephone:* (1865) 276195 (home). *Website:* www.chchchoir.org.

DASCH, Annette; German singer (soprano); b. 1976, Berlin. *Education:* Hochschule für Musik, Munich, Universität für Musik und darstellende Kunst, Graz, masterclasses with Philip Schulze, Wolfram Rieger and Helmut Deutsch. *Career:* debut appearances in Don Giovanni at La Scala, Milan and Il Re Pastore, Salzburg Festival 2006; concert and Lieder recitals include Schubertiade, Schwarzenberg, La Folle Journée de Nantes, performances in Paris, Berlin, Vienna, Monaco, Salzburg, London, Brussels and Naples; has worked with leading conductors including Seiji Ozawa, Daniel Barenboim, Nikolaus Harnoncourt, Sir Simon Rattle, Marek Janowski, René Jacobs, Ivor Bolton, Bertrand de Billy and Fabio Luisi. *Operatic repertoire includes:* Countess in the Marriage of Figaro, Fiordiligi in Cosi fan tutte, Pamina in The Magic Flute, Antonia in Tales of Hoffmann, Freia in Das Rheingold, the Goose Girl in Königskinder, Donna Anna and Donna Elvira in Don Giovanni, Electra in Idomeneo, Rosalinde in Die Fledermaus, Liu in Turandot, Gretel in Hänsel & Gretel, Aminta in Il Re Pastore, Armida. *Recordings:* Armida Arias (Echo Klassik Award for Best Aria Recording 2008) 2007, Mozart Arias 2008. *Honours:* winner Maria Callas Competition, Barcelona 2000, Gold Medal, Robert Schumann Song Contest, Zwickau, Geneva Int. Music Competition 2002. *Current Management:* Italartist Austroconcert Kulturmanagement GmbH, Gluckgasse 1, 1010 Vienna, Austria. *Telephone:* (1) 1-5132657.

E-mail: austroconcert@ia-ac.com. *Website:* www.ia-ac.com; www.annettedasch.de.

D'ASCOLI, Bernard Jacques-Henri Marc; French concert pianist; *Artistic Director, Piano Cantabile;* b. 18 Nov. 1958, Aubagne; one s. *Education:* Marseille Conservatoire. *Career:* became blind 1962; took up music 1970; youngest Baccalauréat matriculate of France 1974; first public appearances on both piano and organ 1974; began int. professional career 1982, following debuts at major London concert halls with Royal Philharmonic Orchestra and first recording; toured Australia with Chamber Orchestra of Europe 1983; debuts: Amsterdam Concertgebouw 1984, Houston Symphony 1985, Musik-verein, Vienna 1986, Tokyo Casals Hall and Bunka Kaikan Hall 1988, Boston Symphony Orchestra 1992, Dresden Philharmonic 1998, Montreal Symphony 1999, English Chamber Orchestra 2004; festival appearances: BBC Proms, Sintra, Besançon, Oviedo, La Roque d'Anthéron, Sydney Olympics cultural festivities; Founder and Artistic Dir Piano Cantabile. *Radio:* numerous BBC Radio broadcasts in recital and as soloist with orchestra. *Television:* South Bank Show, Face the Music. *Recordings include:* Liszt Sonata, Franck Prelude Chorale and Fugue 1982, Schumann and Chopin recordings 1988, 1989, Schumann Quintet with Schidlof Quartet 1999, Chopin Complete Nocturnes, Scherzi and Impromptus 2005, 2006. *Honours:* named best young French talent of the year (Megève) 1976, First Prize, Int. Maria Canals Competition, Barcelona 1979, Prizewinner, Marguerite Long, Paris, Leipzig Bach Competition, Warsaw Chopin Competition 1980, Chopin Prize, Santan-der, Third Prize, Leeds Int. Piano Competition 1981. *Current Management:* c/o Eleanor Harris, Piano Cantabile, 350 Impasse du Baou, 13400 Aubagne, France. *Telephone:* (4) 42-84-02-36. *E-mail:* eleaharr@orange.fr. *Website:* www.bernard-dascoli.com.

DASZAK, John; British opera singer (tenor); b. 24 Feb. 1967, Ashton-under-Lyne, Lancs., England; s. of Bohdan Daszak (Ukrainian) and Ruth Walton (English); m. Jacqueline Miura (soprano); m.; one s. one d. *Education:* Chethams School of Music, Manchester, Guildhall School of Music and Drama, London, Royal Northern Coll. of Music, Manchester, Accad. d'arte lirica, Osimo, Italy, AsLiCo, Milan. *Career:* has sung in many of leading opera houses worldwide, including Royal Opera House, Covent Garden, La Scala, Milan, Staatsoper, Munich, Staatsoper, Berlin, Bastille, Paris, DNO, Amsterdam and Glyndebourne Festival Opera; repertoire ranges from Britten roles of Peter Grimes, Captain Vere and Aschenbach, through Carmen's Don José, Butterfly's Pinkerton, Ballo's Gustavus to major roles in Janáček, Russian repertoire, roles of Alwa, Lulu and Tambourmajor, Wozzeck by Berg and Aron, Moses und Aron by Schönberg; has performed with conductors including Sir Colin Davis, Richard Hickox, Mark Elder, Daniel Harding, Jeffrey Tate, Kent Nagano, Seiji Osawa, Antonio Pappano and Daniel Barenboim; sang role of Loge in Wagner's Rheingold on DVD recording of Ring Cycle from Valencia, Spain with Zubin Mehta; debut at Metropolitan Opera, New York as Captain Vere in Britten's Billy Budd 2010. *Current Management:* c/o Shirley Thomson, Harrison Parrott Ltd, 5-6 Albion Court, Albion Place, London, W6 0QT, England. *E-mail:* shirley.thomson@harrisonparrott.co.uk. *Website:* www.harrisonparrott.com.

DAUCÉ, Sébastien; French conductor, musicologist and musician (organ, harpsichord); *Founder and Artistic Director, Ensemble Correspondances;* b. 4 June 1980. *Education:* CNSM de Lyon, studied harpsichord and basso continuo with Françoise Lengellé and Yves Reschtiener. *Career:* specialist in 17th-century French sacred and secular music; continuo player under Gabriel Garrido (Ensemble Elyma and Académie Baroque d'Ambronay), Raphaël Pichon (Ensemble Pygmalion), Toni Ramon (Maîtrise de Radio France), Françoise Lasserre (Akademia), Geoffroy Jourdain (Les Cris de Paris), Harmut Henschen, Mikko Franck (Orchestre Philarmonique de Radio France); Founder and Artistic Dir Ensemble Correspondances 2008–, per-formances worldwide, at festivals including Ambronay, Pontoise, Sablé, Saintes, Utrecht, tours to Japan and Colombia; researched and co-published (with William Christie) three operas by Marc-Antoine Charpentier; teacher, Pôle Supérieur de Paris 2012–; Assoc. Artist, Fondation Royaumont. *Record-ings include:* with Ensemble Correspondances: O Maria! Psaumes et Motets by Marc-Antoine Charpentier 2011, L'Archange & le Lys, a mass and motets by Antoine Boësset 2012, Meslanges pour la chapelle d'un prince d'Etienne Moulinié (Grand prix int. du disque, Acad. Charles Cros), De Lalande: Leçons de Ténèbres, with Sophie Karthäuser (Diapason d'or 2015), Le Concert Royal de la Nuit (Choc de Classica de l'année) 2015. *Address:* Ensemble Correspondances, 54 rue Taitbout, 75009 Paris, France (office). *E-mail:* sebastien@ensemblecorrespondances.com (office). *Website:* www.ensemblecorrespondances.com (office).

DAUGHERTY, Michael Kevin, BM, MA, DMA; American composer, pianist and teacher; *Professor of Composition, University of Michigan at Ann Arbor;* b. 28 April 1954, Cedar Rapids, Ia; s. of the late Willis Daugherty and Evelyn Daugherty; m. Yopie Prins; one d. *Education:* North Texas State Univ., Manhattan School of Music, Yale Univ. with Jacob Druckman, Roger Reynolds, Bernard Rands and Gil Evans, IRCAM, Paris, studied with Gyorgy Ligeti at Hamburg Musikhochschule. *Career:* Faculty mem. Oberlin Conser-vatory 1986–90; Prof. of Composition, Univ. of Michigan, Ann Arbor 1991–; Composer-in-Residence, Detroit Symphony Orchestra 1999–2003, Louisville Symphony Orchestra 2000, Colorado Symphony Orchestra 2001–02, Cabrillo Festival of Contemporary Music 2001–04, 2006–08, 2011, Westshore Sym-phony Orchestra 2005–06, Eugene Symphony 2006, Henry Mancini Summer Inst. 2006, Music from Angel Fire Chamber Music Festival 2006, Pacific

Symphony 2010–11, New Century Orchestra 2014, Albany Symphony 2015. *Compositions include:* Snap! and Blue Like an Orange 1987 (for 16 players) (Kennedy Center Freidheim Award 1989) 1987, Strut for string orchestra 1989, Firecracker for oboe and six players 1991, Flamingo for chamber orchestra 1991, Desi, Bizarro, and Niagara Falls for symphonic wind band 1991–92, Lex 1991–93, Sing Sing: J. Edgar Hoover for string quartet and tape 1992, Elvis Everywhere for string quartet and tape 1993, Metropolis Symphony 1988–93, Le Tombeau de Liberace for piano and ensemble 1994, Paul Robeson Told Me for string quartet and tape 1994, Motown Metal for brass ensemble and percussion 1994, Lounge Lizards for two pianos and two percussion 1994, Shaken, not Stirred 1995, Timbuktuba 1995, What's That Spell? for two amplified sopranos and 16 players 1995, Jackie's Song for cello 1996, I Loved Lucy 1996, Leap Day 1996, Sinatra Shag 1996, Jackie O (two-act chamber opera) 1997, Route 66 for orchestra 1998, Spaghetti Western for English horn and orchestra 1998, Sunset Strip for chamber orchestra 1999, UFO for percussion solo and orchestra 1999, Hell's Angels for bassoon quartet and orchestra 1999, Route 66 1999, Motor City Triptych 2000, Philadelphia Stories 2001, Pachelbel's Key 2002, Venetian Blinds 2002, Time Machine 2003, Fire and Blood 2003, Once Upon a Castle 2003, Raise the Roof for timpani and symphonic band (Ostwald Award, American Bandmasters Asscn) 2003, Time Machine 2003, Crystal 2004, Tell My Fortune 2004, Brooklyn Bridge 2005, Ghost Ranch 2005, Walk the Walk 2005, Bay of Pigs 2006, Diamond in the Rough 2006, Ladder to the Moon 2006, Regrets Only 2006, Asclepius 2007, March of the Metro 2008, Gee's Bend 2009, Letters from Lincoln 2009, Metropolis Symphony and Deus Ex Machina (Nashville Symphony Orchestra's recording won three Grammy Awards: Best Classical Contemporary Composition, Best Orchestral Performance, Best Engineered Album, Classical 2011) 2009, Trail of Tears for flute and orchestra 2010, Radio City for orchestra 2011, Lost Vegas for symphonic band 2011, The Gospel According to Sister Aimee for organ, brass and percussion 2012, On the Air for symphonic band 2012, American Gothic for orchestra 2012, Fallingwater for violin and strings 2014, Tales of Hemingway for cello and orchestra 2015. *Honours:* Goddard Lieberson Fellowship, American Acad. of Arts and Letters 1991, Nat. Endowment for the Arts Fellowship 1992, Guggenheim Fellowship 1996, Stoeger Prize, Chamber Music Soc. of Lincoln Center 2000, Michigan Gov.'s Award 2004, A.I. duPont Award, Delaware Symphony Orchestra 2007, Outstanding Classical Composer, Detroit Music Awards 2007, 2009, 2010, Grammy Award Best Classical Composition 2011. *Address:* School of Music, Theatre and Dance, University of Michigan, E.V. Moore Building, 1100 Baits Drive, Ann Arbor, MI 48109-2085, USA (office). *Telephone:* (734) 764-5594 (office). *E-mail:* mkd@umich.edu (office). *Website:* www.music.umich.edu (office); www.boosey.com/composer/michael+daugherty; www.michaeldaugherty.net.

DAUSGAARD, Thomas; Danish conductor; b. 1963. *Education:* studied in Scandinavia and London. *Career:* worked with the Oslo, St Petersburg and Royal Philharmonic Orchestras and the Montréal Symphony; Prin. Guest Conductor with Danish Radio Symphony Orchestra 1997– (tour of Germany 2001); conducted Danish Nat. Symphony Orchestra at London Proms 2002; Music Dir, Swedish Chamber Orchestra 1997–; Prin. Guest Conductor, Danish Nat. Symphony Orchestra 2001–04, Chief Conductor 2004–11; guest conductor to the Bayerischer Rundfunk, Dresden Philharmonic, Frankfurt Radio Symphony and Leipzig Gewandhaus Orchestras in Germany and the Orchestre Philharmonique de Radio France in Paris; engagements include conducting the Netherlands Philharmonic Orchestra, the RSB Berlin, the Stockholm and Oslo Philharmonic Orchestras, St Petersburg Philharmonic Orchestra, RAI Turin and La Scala Philharmonic Orchestras. *Recordings include:* Zemlinsky's Seejungfrau and Sinfonietta, complete orchestral works of Beethoven, works of Berwald, Brahms, Grieg, Hamerik, Hartmann, Kunzen, Langgaard, Ligeti, Liszt, Mozart, Nørgård, Riisager, Sibelius, Sinding, Stenhammar, Svendson, Wiren. *Honours:* Music Critics' Circle Prize, Denmark 1993, prizewinner at int. competitions. *Current Management:* IMG Artists, The Light Box, 111 Power Road, , London, W4 5PY, England. *Telephone:* (20) 7957-5800. *Fax:* (20) 7957-5801. *E-mail:* kenticott@imgartists.com (office). *Website:* www.imgartists.com.

DAVENPORT, Glyn, ARCM, LRAM; British singer (bass-baritone); b. 3 May 1948, Halifax, Yorkshire, England; m. Jane Keay 1972; two s. *Education:* Royal Coll. of Music, London, Staatliche Musikhochschule, Hamburg, Germany. *Career:* debut at Wigmore Hall, London, 1973; opera appearances with English Opera Group, English Music Theatre, Scottish Opera, Royal Opera House, Kent Opera, Wexford Festival Opera, Opera Factory, Zürich; recitals for BBC Radio 3, Songmakers' Almanac, British Council in Near and Middle East; oratorio in major London venues and BBC, Switzerland, Germany and Iceland. *Recordings:* The English Cat, Hans Werner Henze. *Honours:* winner, Kathleen Ferrier Memorial Competition, 1972. *Current Management:* Musicmakers International Artists Representation, Tailor House, 63–65 High Street, Whitwell, Hertfordshire SG4 8AH, England. *Telephone:* (1438) 871708. *Fax:* (1438) 871777. *E-mail:* musicmakers@compuserve.com. *Website:* www.operauk.com. *Address:* Wendover, Horsell Rise, Horsell, Woking, Surrey GU21 4BD, England. *E-mail:* glyndavenport@boltblue.com.

DAVERNE, Gary Michiel, ONZM, DipEd, FTCL, LRSM; New Zealand music director, composer, conductor, music producer and fmr schoolteacher; *Music Director Emeritus, Auckland Symphony Orchestra;* b. 26 Jan. 1939, Takapuna, Auckland, North Island; s. of Ron Daverne and Mollie Daverne;

m. Sophia Yang. *Education:* Univ. of Auckland, Auckland Teachers Coll., Trinity Coll. of Music, UK. *Career:* grew up as a rock 'n' roll musician, playing piano and saxophone in New Zealand rock groups; teacher of econs and accountancy 1962–77; began career as a record producer early 1960s, produced more than 40 albums, several hit single records and one platinum and two gold albums; leading musical arranger and dir for Television New Zealand 1970s; now an int. composer and orchestral conductor, having conducted many of the world's major orchestras; Composer in Schools 1978–79; Pres. Composers' Asscn, New Zealand 1979; Founder, Music Dir and Conductor, Auckland Symphony Orchestra 1975–2010, Music Dir Emer. 2010–; Dir of Music, Waitangi Day celebrations 1975; Music Dir Mil. Searchlight Tattoo, New Plymouth 1997; Music Dir/Arranger, Man of Sorrows rock musical 1973; Music Dir for premiere of Jewish oratorio, Hear! O Israel by Cormac O'Duffy, celebrating Israel's 50th nat. birthday. *Compositions include:* recorded more than 100 pop songs, seven children's musicals, operettas, songs for children, three rock operas, concert accordion music, more than 500 TV and radio jingles, film soundtracks; many symphonic works for orchestra (recorded by New Zealand Symphony Orchestra, Moravian Philharmonic), including Rhapsody for Accordion and Orchestra, Gallipoli: Rhapsody for Trumpet and Orchestra. *Recordings include:* ten CDs of original music. *Honours:* Rotary Int. Paul Harris Fellow, Variety Artists Club of New Zealand Scroll of Honour 2000, Confed. Internationale des Accordéonistes Honoured Friend of the Accordion Award 2009, Companion of North Shore City Award 2010, Benny Award, Variety Artist Club of New Zealand 2010. *Address:* 48 Shelly Beach Road, Herne Bay, Auckland 1011, New Zealand (home). *Telephone:* (9) 378-6932 (office). *Fax:* (9) 378-6932 (office). *E-mail:* daverne@ihug.co.nz. *Website:* www.garydaverne.gen.nz.

DAVERSON, Steven, DMus; British composer; b. 11 Jan. 1985, Northampton, Northants., England; s. of Eric John Daverson and Marilyn Joy Daverson (née Gelsthorpe). *Education:* Royal Northern Coll. of Music, studied with David Horne, Royal Coll. of Music, studied with Jonathan Cole and Mark-Anthony Turnage. *Career:* works performed in UK and Europe by groups including Arditti Quartet, Ensemble Recherche, Danel Quartet, BBC Singers, London Philharmonic Orchestra, Ensemble Modern, Klangforum Wien and Moscow Studio for New Music; featured at Aldeburgh Festival 2008, Huddersfield Contemporary Music Festival 2011, Royal Philharmonic Soc.'s Music of Today festival, London 2011; Darmstadt Summer Course for New Music 2012, 2014; Wittener Tage für Neue Kammermusik 2014. *Compositions include:* Kaleidoscopic Negatives for piano and orchestra 2006, Zugunruhe for large ensemble 2008, Tsukimi for Female voice and ensemble 2010, Schattenwanderer for clarinet solo and small ensemble 2011, Clandestine Haze for small ensemble 2011, Escher's Pharmacy for chamber ensemble 2011, Limaçon for solo female voice 2011, Three Rivers from The Navidson Record for string quartet 2012, Giacometti's Razor for solo violin 2014, Filonov's Microscope for ensemble 2014. *Recording:* Shadow Walker 2012. *Honours:* several scholarships, Jurgenson Int. Competition for New Music 2009, Royal Philharmonic Soc. Young Composers Prize 2010, Ernst von Siemens Musikstiftung Komponisten Förderpreis 2011. *Address:* c/o Royal College of Music, Prince Consort Road, London, SW7 2BS, England.

DAVIDOVICH, Bella; American (b. Azerbaijani) pianist; b. 16 July 1928, Baku, Azerbaijan; d. of Mikhail Davidovich and Lucia Ratner; m. Julian Sitkovetsky 1950 (died 1958); one s. *Education:* Moscow Conservatory, USSR. *Career:* studied with Konstantin Igumnov and Jakob Flier; First Prize, Chopin Competition, Warsaw 1949; soloist with Leningrad and Moscow Philharmonics for 28 consecutive seasons; taught piano at Moscow Conservatory 1962–78; toured Europe; went to USA 1978; mem. Faculty, Juilliard School, New York 1983–2003; became US citizen 1984; has performed with world's leading conductors in USA, Russia, Europe and Japan; juror, several int. piano competitions; Prof. Emer., Music Acad. of Baku, Azerbaijan. *Recordings:* numerous recordings on major int. labels. *Honours:* Distinguished Artist of the Russian Soviet Federative Socialist Repub. *Current Management:* c/o KünstlerSekretariat am Gasteig, Elisabeth Ehlers/Lothar Schacke, Rosenheimer Strasse 52, 81669 Munich, Germany. *Telephone:* (89) 4448879-2. *Fax:* (89) 4489522. *E-mail:* verena.vetter@ks-gasteig.de. *Website:* www.ks-gasteig.de.

DAVIDOVICI, Robert, DipMus; Romanian violinist and academic; *Artist-in-Residence and Professor of Violin, Florida International University;* b. 1 Oct. 1946, Sutu-Mare; m. Tamara Golan 1973, two s. two d. *Education:* School of Music No. 1, Bucharest, Conservatorium of Music High School, Australia, Juilliard School, USA. *Career:* debut at Alice Tully Hall, New York, USA 1972; Concertmaster, Fort Worth Symphony Orchestra 1981–91, Vancouver Symphony Orchestra 1991–2002; Artist-in-Residence, North Texas State Univ. 1983–1997; fmr Concertmaster, Grand Teton Music Festival, Chautauqua and Colorado Music Festival Orchestras; Artist-in-Residence and Prof. of Violin, Florida International Univ. 1997–; Guest Prof., Robert Schumann Hochschule, Dusseldorf 1988–, Musashino Academia Musicae, Tokyo 1989–; Founding Artistic Dir Chamber Music Soc. of Fort Worth 1988–; mem. Coll. Music Soc., American String Teachers Asscn, Violin Soc. of America. *Recordings include:* recital with Steven DeGroote of works by Copland, Gunther Schuller, Walter Piston, Hugh Aitken and Paul Schonfield. *Honours:* First Prize, Carnegie Hall Int. American Music Competition 1983, First Prize, Naumberg Competition, New York 1972, Flaggler Award 1973. *Address:* School of Music, Florida International University, Herbert and Nicole Wertheim Performing Arts Center, 10910 SW 17th Street, Miami, FL

33199, USA (office). *E-mail:* rdavidovici@aol.com. *Website:* www.robertdavidovici.com.

DAVIDOVSKY, Mario; American composer and teacher; b. 4 March 1934, Buenos Aires, Argentina; m. Elaine Davidovsky. *Education:* studied with Guillermo Graetzer in Buenos Aires, with Theodore Fuchs, Erwin Leuchter, Ernesto Epstein, and with Aaron Copland and Milton Babbitt at Berkshire Music Center, Tanglewood. *Career:* associated with Columbia-Princeton Electronic Music Center, 1960–; teacher, University of Michigan, 1964; Di Tella Institute, 1969–70; City College of the City University of New York, 1968–80; Columbia University, 1981–; Director, Columbia-Princeton Electronic Music centre, 1981–94; Professor of Music, Harvard University, 1994–; elected mem. Institute of American Academy of Arts and Letters 1982; various commissions. *Compositions include:* Synchronisms No. 1 for flute and electronics, 1963, No. 2 for flute, clarinet, violin, cello and electronics, 1964, No. 3 for cello and electronics, 1965, No. 4 for men's or mixed chorus and electronics, 1967, No. 5 for percussion ensemble and electronics, 1969, No. 6 for piano and electronics, 1970, No. 7 for orchestra and electronics, 1973, No. 8 for woodwind quintet and electronics, 1974; No. 9 for violin and electronics, 1988; No. 10 for guitar and electronics, 1992; Orchestral: Concertino for percussion and strings, 1954; Planos, 1961; Divertimento for cello and orchestra, 1984; Concertante for string quartet and orchestra, 1990; Concertino for violin and chamber orchestra, 1995; Chamber: 4 String Quartets, 1954, 1958, 1976, 1980; Flashbacks for ensemble, 1995; Tape: Electronic Study No. 1, 1961, No. 2, 1962, No. 3, 1965. *Honours:* Guggenheim Fellowships, 1960, 1971; Rockefeller Fellowships, 1963, 1964; American Academy of Arts and Letters Award, 1965; Pulitzer prize in Music, 1971; Naumberg Award, 1972; Guggenheim Award, 1982. *Address:* c/o Music Department, Harvard University, Cambridge, MA, USA (office).

DAVIDSON, Joy; American singer (mezzo-soprano); b. 18 Aug. 1940, Fort Collins, CO. *Education:* studied in Los Angeles, Florida State Univ., and with Daniel Harris. *Career:* debut in Miami 1965 as Rossini's Cenerentola; sang at the opera houses of Dallas, Houston, New Orleans and San Francisco; Santa Fe 1969, in the US premiere of Penderecki's The Devils of Loudun; appearances with the WNO and at Lisbon, Sofia, Vienna, Munich, Milan and Florence; other roles include Carmen, Charlotte in Werther, Dalila, Verdi's Eboli and Preziosilla and Gluck's Orpheus; also heard as concert singer; sang Baba the Turk in The Rake's Progress at the State Theatre, New York 1984.

DAVIDSON, Robert, BMus; Australian composer; b. 17 Dec. 1965, Brisbane, Qld. *Education:* Univ. of Queensland, studied with Terry Riley and LaMonte Young. *Career:* freelance composer; performer in orchestra, including Queensland and Sydney Symphony Orchestras. *Compositions include:* Dodecahedron for string orchestra 1985, Eight for ensemble 1986, Stained Glass for two violins, two cellos, two clarinets and two pianos 1986, Zemar for piano 1987, Sound Panels for flute, string quartet and double bass 1988, Triptych for orchestra 1988, Tapestry for viola, cello, clarinet and piano 1989, Refrains for double bass and piano 1989, Adeney Cycle for violin and viola 1990, Strata for mixed ensemble 1990, Variations and Episodes for piano 1990, Arch for three violins 1992, Conversations for viola, cello and clarinet 1993, Mesh for double bass and piano 1993, Violin Concerto 1994, Three Grounds for ensemble 1994, Chaconne for orchestra 1994, Boombox Pieces for multiple cassette players 1995.

DAVIDSON, Tina, BA; American composer and pianist; b. 30 Dec. 1952, Stockholm, Sweden; m.; one d. *Education:* Bennington Coll., studied with Henry Brant, Vivian Fine, Louis Calabro. *Career:* Assoc. Dir RELACHE ensemble for contemporary music 1978–89; piano instructor, Drexel Univ. 1981–85; residencies at Chamber Music Conference and Composers Forum, Milay Colony for the Arts 1981, Yellow Springs Fellowship of the Arts 1982, Charles Ives Center 1986; Composer-in-Residence, Orchestra Soc. of Philadelphia 1992–94, Opera Delaware Symphony Orchestra, YWCA of Wilmington, Del. 1994–97; Fleisher Art Memorial Composer-in-Residence 1997–99; Founder Philadelphia Chapter of American Composers Forum, Dir 1999–2001; fmr Pres. New Music Alliance. *Compositions include:* Inside and Out for piano and two players 1974, Recollections of Darkness for string trio 1975, Two Beasts from the Forest of Imaginary Beings for narrator and orchestra 1975, Five Songs from The Game of Silence for soprano and viola 1976, Billy and Zelda (music theatre) for eight singers, one actress, string quartet and percussion 1977, Piano Concerto for piano and orchestra 1981, Unicorn/Tapestry for mezzo-soprano, violoncello and tape 1982, Other Echoes for two violins 1982, Wait for the End of Dreaming for two baritone saxophones and double bass 1983–85, Shadow Grief for soprano or alto saxophone 1983, Day of Rage, and I am the Last Witness for piano solo 1984, Blood Memory: A Long Quiet After the Call for cello and orchestra 1985, Bleached Thread Sister Thread 1992, Fire on the Mountain for marimba, vibraphone and piano 1993, They Come Dancing for full orchestra 1994, Cassatt 1994, Over Salt River for soprano 1995, Star Fire for youth orchestra 1996, It is My Heart Singing for string sextet 1996, Of the Running Way for clarinet or alto saxophone and piano 1996, I Hear the Mermaids Singing 1996, Lost Love Songs for solo cello 1997. *Honours:* Pennsylvania Council Fellowship 1983–96, PEN Fellowship 1992–94. *E-mail:* tina@tinadavidson.com. *Website:* www.tinadavidson.com.

DAVIES, Arthur; British singer (tenor); b. 11 April 1941, Wrexham, Wales. *Education:* Royal Northern Coll. of Music, studied under Joseph Ward.

Career: has sung with Welsh National Opera as Nemorino, Albert Herring, Nadir in Les pêcheurs de Perles, Rodolfo, and Don José; Covent Garden debut 1976, in world premiere of We Come to the River by Henze: returned in Lucia di Lammermoor, and as Alfredo, the Italian Tenor in Der Rosenkavalier, Števa in Jenůfa, and Pinkerton; Scottish Opera at Edinburgh Festival as Fox in The Cunning Little Vixen, and David in Die Meistersinger; appearances with ENO as Duke of Mantua, Alfredo, Gounod Faust, and Werther; Opera North as Jenik in The Bartered Bride, Pinkerton, Don José and Nadir; foreign engagements in Chicago, Cincinnati, Connecticut, Ghent, Leipzig, Lisbon, New Orleans, Moscow, Santiago and New York (Metropolitan House with ENO); sang Faust with ENO 1990; Gaston, British stage premiere of Verdi's Jérusalem, Opera North; Cavaradossi and Pinkerton for Scottish Opera; Cincinnati Opera, 1990 as Faust; Edinburgh Festival 1990 as Yannakos in The Greek Passion by Martinů; sang Cavardossi for Opera Pacific at Costa Mesa, 1992; Don José at San Diego and Duke of Mantua for ENO; sang Verdi's Foresto at Buenos Aires 1993; Samson at Metz 1996; concerts include Verdi Requiem at Festival Hall, London, conducted by Giulini. *Recordings include:* Rigoletto, The Dream of Gerontius, with London Symphony Orchestra, Elijah; Rossini's Stabat Mater, The Kingdom of Elgar.

DAVIES, David Somerville; British conductor and artistic director; b. 13 June 1954, Dunfermline, Scotland; m. Virginia Henson 1986. *Education:* Royal Scottish Acad. of Music, Univ. of Edinburgh, Salzburg Mozarteum, Conservatoire National de Marseille. *Career:* Asst Principal Flute, Scottish Nat. Orchestra 1975–80; Principal Flute, Scottish Opera 1980–85; freelance conductor 1985–, working with BBC Scottish Symphony Orchestra, Scottish Chamber Orchestra, Royal Scottish National Orchestra, Royal Liverpool Philharmonic Orchestra in England, Orchestre Philharmonique de Radio France, Opéra de Marseille, Orchestre Philharmonique de Marseille, France, Ensemble Caput, Iceland, and the Stadtorchester Winterthur, Switzerland; Conductor and Artistic Dir, Paragon Ensemble, Scotland, Paragon Opera Projects, Scotland 1985–; Lecturer, Royal Scottish Acad. of Music and Drama 1991–. *Recordings:* two vols of world premiere recordings of Scottish contemporary music 1991, 1993.

DAVIES, Dennis Russell, BMus, MS, DMA; American conductor and pianist; *Chief Conductor and Music Director, Bruckner Orchester Linz;* b. 16 April 1944, Toledo, OH. *Education:* Juilliard School of Music, New York, studied with Berenice B. MacNab, Lonny Epstein, Sascha Gorodnitzki, Jean Morel and Jorge Mester. *Career:* teacher, Juilliard School of Music 1968–71; co-founder (with Luciano Berio) and Conductor, Juilliard Ensemble 1968–74; Music Dir, Norwalk (Conn) Symphony Orchestra 1968–73, St Paul (Minn) Chamber Orchestra 1972–80, Cabrillo (Calif) Music Festival 1974–92, American Composers Orchestra, New York 1977–; Generalmusikdirektor, Wurttemberg State Theatre, Stuttgart 1980–87; Principal Conductor and Dir of Classical Music Programming, Saratoga (NY) Performing Arts Center 1985–88; Generalmusikdirektor, City Theatre and Beethoven Hall Orchestra, Bonn 1987–95; guest conductor with various opera companies and orchestras in North America and Europe; champion of contemporary music; conducted premieres by Luciano Berio, John Cage, Hans Werner Henze, Philip Glass (Akhnaten 1984), Mauricio Kagel, William Bolcom, Joan Tower, Pauline Oliveros, Lou Harrison, Kurt Schwertsik; conducted the premiere of William Bolcom's Songs of Innocence and Experience, Stuttgart 1984; Music Dir, Brooklyn Acad. of Music 1991–93; Principal Conductor, Brooklyn Philharmonic 1991–95; conducted the premiere of Manfred Trojhan's Enrico, Schwetzingen Festival 1991; Chief Conductor, Stuttgart Chamber Orchestra 1995–, Vienna Radio Symphony Orchestra 1996; led Thomson's Four Saints in Three Acts at the 1996 Lincoln Center Festival; season 1998 with Lulu at the Opéra Bastille and Weill's Mahagonny at Salzburg; Chief Conductor, Linz Opera (Landstheater), Austria 2002–; Chief Conductor and Music Dir, Bruckner Orchester Linz 2002–; Music Dir, Sinfonieorchester Basel 2009–; Fellow, American Acad. of Arts and Sciences 2009–. *Recordings include:* Philip Glass: Heroes Symphony 1997. *Honours:* Alice M. Ditson Award for Conductors 1987. *Address:* Bruckner Orchester Linz, Promenade 39, 4010 Linz, Austria (office). *Telephone:* (732) 761-11-95 (office). *E-mail:* office@bruckner-orchester.at (office). *Website:* www.bruckner-orchester.at (office).

DAVIES, Eirian, BA; British singer (soprano); b. 22 May 1954, Llangollen, Wales; one s. *Education:* University College of Wales at Aberystwyth, Royal Academy of Music, London. *Career:* debut as Vivaldi's Griselda, Buxton Festival, and Gounod's La Colombe, 1983; with WNO as Rhinemaiden, in Das Rheingold and Götterdämmerung; Gerhilde, in Die Walküre; Lisa in La Sonnambula; Aenchen in Der Freischütz; with ENO as Pamina in The Magic Flute; Frasquita in Carmen; Orpheus in the Underworld; Opera North Mimi in La Bohème; Christine in Robert Saxton's Caritas (world premiere); at Glyndebourne in world premiere of Nigel Osborne's Electrification of the Soviet Union; Garsington: Rezia in L'Incontro Improvviso, by Haydn; Music Theatre Wales: Dotty in world premiere of Hardy's Flowers; Edinburgh Festival: world premiere of Macmillan's Tourist Variations and Craig Armstrong's Anna; Semur en Auxois Festival; Mozart's Constanze; other performances include Princess Natalie in Der Prinz von Homburg, in Cologne; Gepopo in Le Grand Macabre and Aventures et Nouvelles Aventures, by Ligeti in Zürich; world premiere of Kubo's Rashomon in Graz; Salzburg Festival debut, 1997, in Feldman's Neither, also Wien Moderne Festival in Rihm's Frau Stimme; television and radio broadcasts. *Recordings:* Le Grand Macabre, Caritas by Robert Saxton. *Honours:* Catherine and Lady Grace

James Award; winner, Francisco Vinas International Competition, Barcelona, 1984.

DAVIES, Gareth; British musician (flute); *Principal Flute, London Symphony Orchestra;* b. 1971. *Education:* Guildhall School of Music and Drama. *Career:* apptd Prin. Flute, Bournemouth Symphony Orchestra 1994 aged 23; Prin. Flute, London Symphony Orchestra (LSO) 2000–, also a dir of LSO Woodwind Acad.; teacher and coach of woodwind students at London music colls; master-classes in London, New York, Tokyo and Beijing; performed with students in opening ceremony of 2012 London Olympics; writer, BBC Music Magazine, Classic FM magazine; apptd Prof. of Flute, Royal Coll. of Music, London 2012. *Recordings include:* with Bournemouth Symphony Orchestra: Nielsen Flute Concerto; Karl Jenkins Flute Concerto Quirk (written for him) 2005. *Publications:* The Show Must Go On; also blog. *Address:* London Symphony Orchestra, Barbican Centre, Silk Street, London, EC2Y 8DS, England (office). *Telephone:* (20) 7588-1116 (office). *E-mail:* admin@lso.co.uk (office). *Website:* www.lso.co.uk (office); www.garethdaviesonline.com.

DAVIES, Geraint Talfan, OBE, MA, DL; British opera company director; *Chairman, Welsh National Opera. Education:* Jesus Coll., Oxford. *Career:* Controller BBC Wales 1990–2000, with responsibility for BBC Radio and Chorus of Wales; Chair. Arts Council of Wales 2003–06; Chair. Welsh Nat. Opera 2000–03, 2006–; mem. The Radio Authority 2001–04; fmr mem. Bd Artes Mundi Int. Visual Arts Prize and Wales Millennium Centre Ltd; fmr mem. Bd Sgrin (media devt agency for Wales); fmr Chair. CBAT (arts and regeneration agency); Co-founder and Chair. Inst. of Welsh Affairs 1992–; Chair. Int. Film Festival of Wales 1998–2001; fmr Gov. Welsh Coll. of Music and Drama, fmr mem. Prince of Wales Cttee on the Environment; fmr Trustee UK Cttee European Cultural Foundation; Trustee, Media Standards Trust 2005–. *Publication:* At Arm's Length 2008. *Honours:* Hon. Fellow, Univ. of Wales Inst., Cardiff, Swansea Univ., RIBA; Dr hc (Glamorgan). *Address:* Welsh National Opera, Wales Millennium Centre, Bute Place, Cardiff, CF10 5AL, Wales (office). *Telephone:* (29) 2063-5000 (office); (29) 2062-6571 (home). *E-mail:* geraint.talfan@btopenworld.com (home). *Website:* www.wno.org.uk (office).

DAVIES, Iestyn; British singer (countertenor); b. 16 Sept. 1979, s. of Dr Ioan Charles Glynn Lewis Davies and Diana Wood Davies. *Education:* St John's Coll., Cambridge, Royal Acad. of Music. *Career:* choral scholar at St John's Coll., Cambridge; operatic roles have included Ottone in L'incoronazione di Poppea, Zürich Opera, Glyndebourne Festival Opera, Armindo in Partenope, Voice of Apollo in Death in Venice, English Nat. Opera, Purcell's King Arthur, New York City Opera, English Nat. Opera, Hamor in Jephtha, L'Humana Fragilità and Pisandro in Il ritorno d'Ulisse in Patria, Welsh Nat. Opera, Arsace Partenope, New York City Opera, Oberon in A Midsummer Night's Dream, Houston Grand Opera; debut at Teatro alla Scala, Milan, in concert performance of Bernstein's Chichester Psalms with Orchestra Filarmonica della Scala under Dudamel; has appeared at Wigmore Hall, Barbican, Concertgebouw, Snape Maltings and Théâtre des Champs-Élysées, sung with Orchestra of the Age of Enlightenment, Acad. of Ancient Music, Scottish Chamber Orchestra, London Philharmonic Orchestra, Ensemble Matheus and Bournemouth Symphony Orchestra; debut with New York Met in Handel's Rodelinda 2011, and at Carnegie Hall. *Recordings include:* Handel's Messiah 2006, Vivaldi's Griselda (BBC Music Magazine's Opera Recording of the Year 2007) 2006, Handel's Flavio, Re de'Longobardi 2010, Bach's Easter Oratorio and Ascension Cantata 2010, Porpora: Cantatas 2011, Arias for Guadagni (Gramophone Recital Award 2012). *Honours:* Royal Philharmonic Soc. Award for Best Young Artist 2010. *Website:* www.iestyndavies.com.

DAVIES, Joan; British singer (mezzo-soprano); b. 1940, Swansea, Wales. *Education:* Royal Coll. of Music, London. *Career:* sang with the Glyndebourne Chorus, then with Sadler's Wells until 1969, notably as Offenbach's Hélène and in the premiere of Bennett's A Penny for a Song 1965; debut with WNO as Meg Page in Falstaff; sang Meg Page at Covent Garden and appeared in La Traviata and the premiere of Henze's We Come to the River 1976; other engagements in Munich and Berlin and with Scottish Opera, Opera North, Pheonix Opera, Basilica Opera and Dublin Grand Opera; New Sadler's Wells Opera from 1983 in The Mikado, The Count of Luxembourg, The Merry Widow and works by Gilbert and Sullivan (also in New York); appearances at the Wexford Festival in The Devil and Kate, and Gazzaniga's Don Giovanni 1987; other roles include Mme Popova in Walton's The Bear (Lisbon), Auntie in Peter Grimes at the Royal Opera, Ghent, and Mozart's Marcellina in Bordeaux and Rouen; television appearances as Meg Page, Marcellina and Mary in Der fliegende Holländer; concert engagements with the Royal Liverpool Philharmonic and the Ulster Orchestra.

DAVIES, Menai; British singer (mezzo-soprano); b. 17 Nov. 1939, Wales. *Education:* studied with Gwilyn Gwalchmai Jones and Valetta Jacopi. *Career:* taught music for 14 years; engaged with WNO 1974–86, in repertory from Monteverdi to Britten, to the premiere of Metcalf's The Journey 1981; Mamma Lucia in Cavalleria Rusticana, 1995; Glyndebourne Touring Opera from 1987 (debut in L'Enfant et les Sortilèges) and Festival from 1989, as Grandmother in Jenůfa, Auntie in Peter Grimes and Cleaner in The Makropulos Case 1995; other appearances with Scottish Opera, English National Opera and Opera North's Gloria, H. K. Gruber; Britten's Mrs Herring at Rome and Reggio Emilia, Mrs Grose in Peter Grimes at Cologne, Schwetzingen and Dresden; Théâtre du Châtelet, Paris, in Jenůfa and in premieres of operas by Fenelon and Philippe Manoury; The Makropulos Case at Barcelona and New York;

ideally suited for older roles in modern works. *Current Management:* c/o Harlequin Agency, 203 Fidlas Road, Llanishen, Cardiff, CF14 5NA, Wales. *Telephone:* (29) 2075-0821. *Fax:* (29) 2075-5971. *E-mail:* peter@harlequin -agency.co.uk. *Website:* www.harlequin-agency.co.uk.

DAVIES, Neal; British singer (baritone); b. 1965, Newport, Gwent. *Education:* King's Coll., London, Royal Acad. of Music, Int. Opera Studio, Zürich. *Career:* many roles at the Coburg Opera, Germany, including Papageno in a Brigitte Fassbaender production of Die Zauberflöte; Concerts at the Edinburgh Festival include Prokoviev's Hamlet, Janáček's Sarka, Schubert's Die Freunde von Salamanca, Leonore and Ninth Symphony by Beethoven, and the Scenes from Faust by Schumann, 1992–; Further opera includes Starveling in Midsummer Night's Dream with the London Symphony Orchestra, Handel's Radamisto at Marseilles and Orlando at the City of London Festival, La Bohème with the Oslo Philharmonic Orchestra and Masetto in Don Giovanni for Welsh National Opera; Season 1996–97 as Schaunard for WNO, in Stravinsky's Rossignol under Pierre Boulez for the BBC, Elijah with the Liverpool Philharmonic Orchestra and Messiah with the Gabrieli Consort under Paul McCreesh; Debut with the Royal Opera in Rameau's Platée (also at Edinburgh), 1997; Sang Mozart's Figaro and Handel's Achilla with the Royal Opera, 1998; Season 1999 with Nielsen's Springtime on Funen at the London Prom concerts; Revueltas's la noche de los mayas at the London Proms, 2002; Many recital engagements. *Recordings include:* Britten, A Midsummer Night's Dream 1996; Classics; Elijah; Handel's Messiah 1997; Henri Dutilleux Songs with orchestra; Vivaldi Cantatas with Robert King 1997, Handel's Theodora 2000, Vaughan Williams, The Poisoned Kiss 2003, Barber's Vanessa 2004, Smetana, The Bartered Bride 2005, Janáček: The Makropoulos Case 2007, Handel Saul/Messiah 2008, Handel, Dettingen Te Deum 2008, Handel: Chandos Anthems 2009. *Honours:* winner Lieder Prize at the Cardiff Singer of the World Competition 1991. *Address:* Chandos Records Ltd, Chandos House, 1 Commerce Park, Commerce Way, Colchester, Essex, CO2 8HX, England (office). *Telephone:* (1206) 225200 (office). *Fax:* (1206) 225201 (office). *E-mail:* enquiries@chandos.net (office). *Website:* www.chandos.net (office).

DAVIES, Sir Peter Maxwell, Kt (see MAXWELL DAVIES, Sir Peter)

DAVIES, Ryland; British singer (tenor); b. 9 Feb. 1943, Cwm Ebbw Vale, Monmouthshire (now Gwent); s. of Gethin Davies and Joan Davies; m. 1st Anne Howells 1966 (divorced 1981); m. 2nd Deborah Jane Rees 1983; one d. *Education:* Royal Manchester Coll. of Music. *Career:* voice teacher, Royal Northern Coll. of Music (RNCM) 1987–94, Royal Coll. of Music, London 1999–, also Royal Acad. of Music; Dir Opera Productions RNCM Mananan Festival, Clonter Opera Trust; début as Almaviva in The Barber of Seville, Welsh Nat. Opera 1964; with Glyndebourne Festival Chorus 1964–66; appearances with Scottish Opera, Sadler's Wells Opera, Royal Opera, English Nat. Opera; overseas appearances include Salzburg Festival, Metropolitan Opera, New York, Paris Opera; returned to Covent Garden 1994, 2002, Welsh Nat. Opera 1994, New York Metropolitan Opera 1994, 1995, 2001, Glyndebourne 1997, New Israeli Opera 1997, Chicago Lyric Opera 1998, 2003, Santa Fe Opera 1998, 1999, New Israeli Opera 1998, Netherlands Opera 1998, 1999, 2002, English Nat. Opera 1999, Houston Grand Opera 2002, Japan 2002, Florence 2002, Zauberflote/Monastatos Netherlands 2003, Covent Garden Monostatos 2003, Basilio, Chicago Lyric Opera 2003, Peter Grimes, London Symphony, Barbican and New York, Colin Davis 2004, A Midsummer Night's Dream, La Fenice, Venice 2004, Ein Hurt, La Scala, Milan 2007, 2009; Boise Mendelssohn Foundation Scholarship 1964; Fellow, Welsh Coll. of Music and Drama 1996. *Recordings include:* The Abduction from the Seraglio, L'Amore dei Tre Re (Montemezzi), La Navarraise (Massenet), The Trojans, Saul, Così fan tutte, Thérèse (Massenet), Monteverdi Madrigals, Idomeneo, The Seasons (Haydn), Messiah, L'Oracolo (Leone), Judas Maccabaeus, Pulcinella, Il Matrimonio Segreto, Lucia di Lammamoor, Otello, Mozart's Requiem, C Minor Mass, Credo Mass, Coronation Mass, Messe Solonelle; Oedipus Rex (Shepherd), Il Trovatore (Ruiz), Don Carlo (Conte di Lerma), Le nozze di Figaro (Basilio/ Curzio), Esclarmonde (Massenet). *Video films include:* Don Pasquale, A Midsummer Night's Dream, Die Entführung aus dem Serail, Love of Three Oranges, Trial by Jury, Katya Kabanova. *Television:* Merry Widow, Capriccio (BBC, Glyndebourne), A Goodly Manner for a Song (STV), On Wenlock Edge (BBC Wales), Dido and Aeneas (BBC), Mass in C Minor (BBC Wales). *Achievements include:* played rugby for Wales Schoolboys, two caps 1957–58, Wales Boys Clubs under-18s 1959–60. *Honours:* Hon. Fellow, Royal Manchester Coll. of Music 1971; Ricordi Opera Prize, Royal Manchester Coll. of Music 1963, Imperial League of Opera Prize, Royal Manchester Coll. of Music 1963, First John Christie Award, Glyndebourne 1965. *Current Management:* Hazard Chase Ltd, 25 City Road, Cambridge, CB1 1DP, England. *Address:* Elm Cottage, Loseberry Road, Claygate, Surrey, KT10 9DQ, England (home). *E-mail:* ryland@rylanddavies.info. *Website:* www.rylanddavies.info.

DAVIES, Tansy, PhD; British composer and academic; *Professor of Composition, Royal Academy of Music;* b. 29 May 1973, Bristol. *Education:* Guildhall School of Music and Drama, Royal Holloway Coll. *Career:* commissions include BBC Symphony Orchestra (for Proms 2010), London Sinfonietta, Britten Sinfonia, City of London Sinfonia, Northern Sinfonia, BBC Concert Orchestra, Aldeburgh Festival; works performed internationally by groups including Cantus Ensemble, Grup Instrumental de València, Tiroler Ensemble für Neue Musik, Musiques Nouvelles, Melos Ethos Ensemble, Orchestra of Filharmonia Baltycka, Israel Contemporary Players, Winnipeg Symphony Orchestra,

Orquesta Sinfonica de Chile, Tokyo Symphony Orchestra, Plovdiv Philharmonic; Prof. of Composition, RAM 2012–. *Compositions include:* vocal: This Love, Static, Women in Love, Greenhouses, Destroying Beauty, Christmas Eve, As with Voices and with Tears, requiem for choir, string orchestra and electronics (written to commemorate Remembrance Sunday in Portsmouth Cathedral with London Mozart Players) 2010; chamber: neon, Undertow, Patterning, make black white, Iris saxophone concerto, Falling Angel, Hinterland, Nature; also works for solo, duo, chamber and symphony orchestras. *Recordings include:* Troubairitz 2011, Spine 2012. *Honours:* Dr hc (Colchester Inst.) 2011; BBC Young Composers Award 1996, Paul Hamlyn Award 2009. *Address:* c/o Faber Music, 3 Queen Square, London, WC1N 3AU, England (office). *Telephone:* (20) 7833-7911 (office). *Fax:* (20) 7833-7939 (office). *E-mail:* promotion@fabermusic.com (office). *Website:* www .tansydavies.com (office).

DAVIES, Wyn; British conductor; *Director of Music, NBR New Zealand Opera;* b. 8 May 1952, Gowerton, Wales; m. Jane Baxendale 1975. *Education:* Christ Church, Oxford. *Career:* appearances in concert with BBC Nat. Orchestra of Wales, BBC Scottish Orchestra, Bournemouth Symphony Orchestra, English Chamber Orchestra, Scottish Chamber Orchestra, City of Birmingham Symphony Orchestra, Northern Chamber Orchestra, Orchestra of Opera North, Manchester Camerata, Hallé Northern Sinfonia, Auckland Philharmonia, Belgrade Philharmonic; guest conductor, Opera North, ENO, Scottish Opera, New Sadler's Wells Opera, Welsh Nat. Opera, Opera Australia, Carl Rosa Opera, New Zealand Opera; Asst Conductor, Metropolitan Opera, New York, USA 1985–86; Dir of Music, NBR New Zealand Opera 2005–. *Current Management:* c/o Performing Arts, 6 Windmill Street, London, W1P 1HF, England. *Telephone:* (20) 7255-1362. *Fax:* (20) 7631-4631. *E-mail:* info@performing-arts.co.uk. *Website:* www.performing-arts.co.uk. *Address:* c/o The NBR New Zealand Opera, PO Box 6478, Wellesley Street, Auckland 1141, New Zealand (office); Springmount, Lidgett's Lane, Rainow, Cheshire, SK10 5TG, England. *E-mail:* wyn@polidori.co.uk (office). *Website:* www .nzopera.com (office).

DAVIS, Sir Andrew, Kt, CBE; British conductor; *Musical Director, Lyric Opera of Chicago;* b. 2 Feb. 1944; m. Gianna Rolandi 1989; one s. *Education:* Royal Coll. of Music, King's Coll., Cambridge, studied conducting with Franco Ferrara, Rome. *Career:* continuo player with Acad. of St Martin-in-the-Fields and English Chamber Orchestra; Festival Hall debut conducting BBC Symphony Orchestra 1970; Asst Conductor, Philharmonia Orchestra 1973–77; Prin. Guest Conductor, Royal Liverpool Philharmonic Orchestra 1974–77; Music Dir, Toronto Symphony 1975–88, Conductor Laureate 1988–; Musical Dir, Glyndebourne Festival Opera 1988–2002; Chief Conductor, BBC Symphony Orchestra 1989–2000, Conductor Laureate 2000–, tours with orchestra to Far East 1990, Europe 1992, Japan 1993, 1997, USA 1995, 1998, South America 2001, Far East and Australia 2002; Prin. Guest Conductor, Royal Stockholm Philharmonic 1995–99; Musical Dir, Chicago Lyric Opera 2000–; Chief Conductor and Artistic Dir, Melbourne Symphony Orchestra 2013–; has conducted London Philharmonic, London Symphony, Royal Philharmonic, Boston, Chicago, Cleveland, Los Angeles Philharmonic, New York Philharmonic, Pittsburg Symphony, Orchestre Nat. de France, Frankfurt Radio Orchestra, Royal Concertgebouw Orchestra, Tonhalle Orchestra, Stockholm Philharmonic Orchestra, Israel Philharmonic, Bavarian Radio Symphony and Berlin Philharmonic orchestras, London Sinfonietta, Dallas Symphony and Dresden Staatskapelle orchestras; has conducted at Glyndebourne Festival Opera, Covent Garden Opera, Metropolitan Opera, Washington, DC, Chicago Lyric Opera, Bavarian State Opera, Paris Opéra, La Scala, Milan, Sir Henry Wood Promenade Concerts, maj. British and European music festivals; tours of People's Republic of China 1978, Europe 1983 with Toronto Symphony Orchestra. *Recordings include:* Duruflé's Requiem (Grand Prix du Disque 1978), cycle of Dvořák symphonies, Tippett's The Mask of Time (Gramophone Record of the Year Award 1987, Grand Prix du Disque 1988), Vaughan Williams symphony cycle, Elgar The Dream of Gerontius/Sea Pictures (Gramophone Award for Best Choral Recording 2015) 2014. *Current Management:* Columbia Artist Management Inc., 1790 Broadway, New York, NY 10019-1412, USA. *Telephone:* (212) 841-9500 (office). *Fax:* (212) 841-9744 (office). *E-mail:* cami@cami.com (office). *Website:* www.cami.com (office); www .lyricopera.org; sirandrewdavis.com.

DAVIS, Carl, BA; American composer and conductor; b. 28 Oct. 1936, New York; s. of Isadore Davis and Sara Davis; m. Jean Boht 1971; two d. *Education:* New England Conservatory of Music, Bard Coll. *Career:* Asst Conductor, New York City Opera 1958; Assoc. Conductor London Philharmonic Orchestra 1987–88; Prin. Conductor Bournemouth Pops 1984–87; Prin. Guest Conductor Munich Symphony Orchestra 1990; Artistic Dir and Conductor Royal Liverpool Philharmonic Orchestra, Summer Pops 1993–2000; Guest Conductor Hallé Orchestra, City of Birmingham Symphony Orchestra, Scottish Symphony Orchestra; has created numerous scores for silent films. *Musical theatre:* Diversions (Obie Prize Best Review) 1958, Twists (Arts Theatre London) 1962, The Projector and Cranford (Theatre Royal Stratford East), Pilgrim (Edinburgh Festival), The Wind in the Willows, Peace (Opera North), Alice in Wonderland (Hammersmith) 1987, The Vackees (Haymarket) 1987, The Mermaid. *Incidental music for theatre includes:* Prospect Theatre Co., Nat. Theatre, RSC. *Ballet:* A Simple Man 1987, Lipizzaner 1988, Liaisons Amoureuses (Northern Ballet Theatre) 1988, Madly, Badly, Sadly, Gladly, David and Goliath, Dances of Love and Death (London Contemporary Dance Theatre), The Picture of Dorian Gray (Sadler's Wells Royal Ballet), A

Christmas Carol (Northern Theatre Ballet) 1992, The Savoy Suite (English Nat. Ballet) 1993, Alice in Wonderland (English Nat. Ballet) 1995, Aladdin (Scottish Ballet) 2000, Pride and Prejudice: First Impressions (Central Ballet School Tour) 2002. *Music for TV includes:* The Snow Goose 1971, The World at War (Emmy Award) 1973, The Naked Civil Servant 1975, Our Mutual Friend 1978, Hollywood 1980, Churchill: The Wilderness Years 1981, Silas Marner 1985, Hotel du Lac 1986, The Accountant (BAFTA Award) 1989, The Secret Life of Ian Fleming 1989, Separate but Equal 1991, The Royal Collection 1991, A Year in Provence 1992, Fame in the 20th Century: Clive James 1992, Ghengis Cohn 1993, Thatcher: The Downing Street Years 1993, Pride and Prejudice 1995, Oliver's Travels 1995, Eurocinema: The Other Hollywood 1995, Cold War 1998–99, Goodnight Mr Tom 1998, The Great Gatsby 2000, The Queen's Nose, An Angel for May, Book of Eve 2003, Promoted to Glory 2003. *Operas for TV:* The Arrangement, Who Takes You to The Party?, Orpheus in the Underground, Peace. *Film music:* The Bofors Gun 1969, The French Lieutenant's Woman (BAFTA Award) 1981, Champions 1984, The Girl in a Swing 1988, Rainbow 1988, Scandal 1988, Frankenstein Unbound 1989, The Raft of the Medusa 1991, The Trial 1992, Voyage 1993, Widow's Peak 1994, Topsy Turvy 2000; series of Thames Silents including Napoleon 1980, 2000, The Wind, The Big Parade, Greed, The General, Ben Hur, Intolerance, Safety Last, The Four Horsemen of the Apocalypse 1992, Wings 1993, Waterloo 1995, Phantom of the Opera 1996, 6 Mutuals (Chaplin Shorts) 2004. *Concert works:* Music for the Royal Wedding, Variations on a Bus Route, Overture on Australian Themes, Clarinet Concerto 1984, Lines on London Symphony 1984, Fantasy for Flute and Harpsichord 1985, The Searle Suite for Wind Ensemble, Fanfare for Jerusalem 1987, The Glenlivet Fireworks Music 1988, Norwegian Brass Music 1988, Variations for a Polish Beggar's Theme 1988, The Pigeon's Progress 1988, Jazz Age Fanfare 1989, Everest 1989, Landscapes 1990, The Town Fox (text by Carla Lane) 1990, A Duck's Diary 1990, Paul McCartney's Liverpool Oratorio (with Paul McCartney) 1991. *Recordings include:* Napoleon 1983, Christmas with Kiri (with Kiri Te Kanawa) 1986, Beautiful Dreamer (with Marilyn Horne) 1986, The Silents 1987, Ben Hur 1989, A Simple Man 1989, The Town Fox and Other Musical Tales (text by Carla Lane) 1990, Paul McCartney's Liverpool Oratorio 1991, Leeds Castle Classics, Liverpool Pops at Home 1995. *Publications:* sheet music of television themes. *Honours:* Hon. Fellowship (Liverpool Univ.) 1992; Chevalier, Ordre des Arts et des Lettres 1983, Hon. CBE 2005; Hon. Dr of Arts (Bard, New York) 1994; Hon. DMus (Liverpool) 2002; Special Achievement Award for Music for Television and Film 2003. *E-mail:* admin@threefoldmusic .co.uk (office). *Website:* www.carldaviscollection.com.

DAVISLIM, Steve, BMus; Australian/Irish singer (tenor); b. 1967, Australia. *Education:* studied at the Victorian Coll. for the Arts, Melbourne with Joan Hammond, with John Modenos in Athens, Gösta Windberg in Zürich. *Career:* engaged with the Zürich Opera 1993, as Rossini's Almaviva, the Narrator in The Rape of Lucretia and Ferrando in Così fan tutte, Rossillon in the Merry Widow; further appearances at Hamburg and Berlin as Almaviva, at the Salzburg Festival in concerts, First Prisoner under Solti, as Don Curzio (Figaro) under Harnoncourt and Athens as Don Ottavio 1996, Ludwigsburg Festival as Tamino 1998; Fenton under Abbado in Ferrara, Berlin and Covent Garden under Haitink, Idomeneo at La Scala, Milan 2005; Max in Der Freischütz, Baden Baden, Titus in the Semperoper, Dresden; concerts include Liszt's Faust Symphony, Beethoven's Missa Solemnis (with Roger Norrington, London Prom) and Matthew Passion (Bach), with Riccardo Chailly, appearances at BBC Proms, London with Schumann's Scenes from Goethe's Faust 1999, Mendelssohn's Symphony No. 2 'Lobgesang' 2009, Beethoven's Symphony No. 9 'Choral' 2014; concerts with orchestras such as Chicago Symphony, Tonhalle Orchestra, Zürich, Gewandhaus, Staatskapelle Dresden, Cleveland Symphony, Wiener Philharmoniker, San Francisco BBC Symphony, New York Philharmonic. *Recordings include:* Brahms Rinaldo with Michel Plasson and the Dresden Philharmonie, Bach cantatas and Weber's Oberon with John Eliot Gardiner, Beethoven's Christ on the Mount of Olives and Mozart's Requiem for Opus 111, Rossini's Petite Messe Solennelle and Haydn's Creation (Schöpfung), Holliger's Schneewittchen, Beethoven's Symphony no. 9 with David Zinman, Richard Strauss orchestra songs with Simone Young and the State orchestra of Victoria, Lotario and Rodelinda by Händel with Alan Curtis, also with A.Curtis Grimoaldo in Händel's Rodelina, Mozart Requiem with Christian Thieleman, Lc vin herbé by Frank Martin and several others. *Honours:* Australia Arts Council Grant, Queen Elizabeth II Silver Jubilee Scholarship. *Current Management:* Stefania Almansi, IMG Artists, The Light Box 111 Power Road, London, W45PY, England. *Telephone:* (20) 7957-5800. *E-mail:* salmansi@imgartists.com. *Website:* www .stevedavislim.com.

DAVITASHVILI, Shalva; Georgian composer; b. 1 Jan. 1934, Telavi; m. Nino Zabukidze 1959; one s. one d. *Education:* Tbilisi State Conservatoire. *Career:* debut with The Tiger and the Young Man, symphonic poem, Tbilisi State Conservatoire 1960; Dir music school, Akhalnalexi 1966–68; Georgian television broadcasts 1968–70; teacher music coll. 1970–; Dir, Polioshvili Museum 1992–; mem. Georgian Union of Composers. *Compositions:* two symphonies, three symphonic poems, two ballets, three cantatas, five concertos, two vocal-symphonic cycles, choral works, pieces for piano, pieces for other instruments, incidental music, film scores and songs. *Recordings:* three concertos for clarinet and orchestra, 9th April (symphonic poem), vocal cycles, parts of ballets, Sakartveloze (cantata), songs. *Honours:* Merited Artist of Georgia 1982.

DAWIDOFF, Mikhail; Russian singer (tenor); b. 1960. *Education:* Russian Acad. of the Theatrical Arts, Moscow. *Career:* many appearances with the Bolshoi Opera and elsewhere in Russia; Lucerne Opera as Don José, Pedro in Tiefland and Don Carlos; Radames and Vaudemont in Tchaikovsky's Iolanta at St Gallen; further engagements as Cavaradossi for Palm Beach Opera, Manrico in Il Trovatore at Antwerp and Washington Nat. Opera, Don Carlos in Netherlands and Calaf for Basle Opera; Bolshoi Opera as Alfredo, Lensky, Vladimir in Prince Igor and Verdi's Riccardo, Radames at the Deutsche Opera, Berlin, and Verona; sang Des Grieux in Manon Lescaut at Glyndebourne 1999. *Honours:* prizewinner Tchaikovsky Competition, Moscow 1994.

DAWKINS, Timothy; British singer (baritone); b. 1965, England. *Education:* Royal Coll. of Music. *Career:* appearances with Glyndebourne as Dominik in Arabella and Captain in Eugene Onegin; Leporello at the Batignano Festival, Italy, Mozart's Figaro in the South of France and Switzerland, and the Speaker in Die Zauberflöte on tour to USA; Budd in Albert Herring and Dr Bombasto in Busoni's Arlecchino at Aldeburgh; Colline in La Bohème for European Chamber Opera and roles in Goehr's Arianna; English Bach Festival in Dido and Aeneas, and in The Fairy Queen at the Linbury Theatre, Covent Garden 2001; further engagements with Scottish Opera, Opera North Wexford Festival Opera and Chelsea Opera Group. *Honours:* Erich Vietheer Memorial Award, Glyndebourne.

DAWSON, Anne; British singer (soprano); b. 9 Feb. 1959, Stoke, England. *Education:* Royal Northern Coll. of Music. *Career:* sang Angelica in Handel's Orlando at the Bath Festival 1978, Grenoble Festival 1979; recital tours throughout the UK; with Glyndebourne Touring Opera has sung Eurydice, Susanna and Micaela; WNO as Gilda and Pamina; Marguerite, Gilda and the title role in The Cunning Little Vixen with ENO; Covent Garden debut in Don Carlos 1988; overseas engagements include Gilda in Frankfurt, the Vixen in Vancouver, and appearances with the Netherlands and Lausanne operas; sang Hero in Beatrice and Benedict, London Coliseum 1990; Susanna for WNO; season 1992 as Ninetta in The Thieving Magpie for Opera North, Anne Trulove for Glyndebourne Touring Opera and Chloe in The Queen of Spades at the Festival; Mimi in La Bohème for GTO 1995; Cecilio in Mozart's Lucio Silla for Garsington Opera 1998; sang Polly in The Beggar's Opera at Strasbourg 2000; concert repertoire includes Schubert's Fierrabras, at South Bank conducted by Jeffrey Tate, Carmina Burana, and Mozart's Exsultate Jubilate (Fishguard Festival). *Recordings include:* songs by English composers. *Honours:* John Ireland Festival Centenary Competition and the Gerald Finzi Song Award Competition 1981, Int. 's-Hertogenbosch Singing Competition Soprano Prize 1981, Kathleen Ferrier Memorial Scholarship 1982.

DAWSON, Lynne; British singer (soprano); b. 3 June 1956, York, England. *Education:* Guildhall School of Music, London. *Career:* appearances from 1985 with Trevor Pinnock and the English Concert; John Eliot Gardiner, the Monteverdi Choir and English Baroque Soloists and Christopher Hogwood and the Academy of Ancient Music; Further concerts with Barenboim, Davis, Rattle, Mackerras, Ashkenazy, and Giulini; Tours of Europe and the USA; opera debut as the Countess with Kent Opera, 1986; Monteverdi's Orfeo at Florence, 1988; Festival engagements at Aldeburgh, Edinburgh, Salzburg, Bruges, Aix-en-Provence, Paris, Vienna and Promenade Concerts; Opera career includes Zdenka in Arabella at the Châtelet, Pamina, Berlin Staatsoper; Appearances as Fiordiligi at Naples, Constanze Brussels, Teresa in Benvenuto Cellini for Netherlands Opera, 1991; other roles include, Xiphares in Mitridate (Châtelet, Paris, 1991), Amenaide in Rossini's Tancredi, Berlin Staatsoper, 1994; Shéhérezade at the 1995 London Proms; sang Nitocris in Belshazzar at the 1996 Handel Festival, Göttingen; Opera North 1996 as Gluck's Iphigénie (en Aulide); Sang Libera Me from Verdi's Requiem at the funeral of Diana, Princess of Wales, 1997; sang Dido in Dido and Aeneas at Vlaamse Opera, 1998; engaged for premiere of Elliott Carter's opera What Next?, Berlin, 1999; season 2000 at Lyon and Graz, in Handel's Hercules and Agrippina. *Recordings include:* Bach B Minor Mass, Monteverdi Orfeo, Purcell, Dido and Aeneas; Messiah; Mozart C Minor Mass; Purcell Timon of Athens and Dioclesian, Iphigénie en Aulide; Jephtha; Vespers by Mozart; Mozart's Requiem; Gluck's La Recontre Imprévue; Mozart's Elvira and Constanze, Beethoven 9, Midsummer Night's Dream, Acis and Galatea; Ginevra in Ariadonte; Norina in Don Pasquale; Zaide. *Current Management:* IMG Artists, The Light Box, 111 Power Road, London, W4 5PY, England. *Telephone:* (20) 7957-5800. *Fax:* (20) 7957-5801. *E-mail:* sthomson@imgartists .com. *Website:* www.imgartists.com; www.lynnedawson.com.

DAWSON, Ted, BMus, BEd, MMA, PhD; Canadian composer and educator; *Director, True North Foundation*; b. 28 April 1951, Victoria; s. of William George Dawson and Grace Evelyn Hulett; m. Hemans Yu. *Education:* Victoria School of Music, Univ. of Victoria with Brian Cherney and Rudolf Komorous, McGill Univ. with Bengt Hambraeus and Alcides Lanza, Univ. of Toronto, State Univ. of New York, Buffalo, USA with Charles Wuorinen, Peter Otto, Jan Williams, Jeremy Noble and Martha Hyde. *Career:* Lecturer, Concordia Univ. 1974–78, Vanier Coll., Montreal 1978–80; Asst Prof., Queen's Univ., Kingston, Ont. 1987–88, Brock Univ., St Catherines, Ont. 1988–90; Founder ComPoster Project to promote Canadian music through educ.; Artistic Dir Canadian Music Days Festival of Contemporary Canadian Music, held in Estonia 1993; Organizer The True North Festival, held in Taiwan, 12 concerts of Canadian music and a major contemporary art exhbn 1998; Dir True North Foundation 1998–, The Boreal Orchestra 2006–, Boreal Choir 2009–. *Compositions include:* Pentad for string quartet 1971, Concerto Grosso 1 for tape with/without amplified viola, bassoon, trombone and percussion 1972–74,

Chameleon for amplified flute 1975, The Land of Nurr 1975, The Clouds of Magellan for tape and slides 1976–77, Binaries for four dancers, amplified piano and percussion 1978–80, Joint Actions for solo female dancer and male double bass player 1981, Phantasms for solo piano 1986–87, Portraits in a Landscape for tape 1988, Traces in Glass for orchestra 1986–92, Symphony 1 for orchestra 1992–94, Topographical Sonata for amplified piano and tape 1992–96, Dragon Songs for bass baritone voice and orchestra 1995–98, Piano Concerto Wisteria 2002 (revised 2006), Ice Dreams for wind quintet 2004, Three Estonian Songs on Poems of Andres Ehin for soprano voice and organ 2006 (revised 2011), Dune for brass and percussion ensemble 2009, A Mondrian Triptych for solo piano: I – Chrysanthemums, II – The Winkel Mill in Sunlight, III – The Red Tree 2011–12, Trio for oboe, bassoon and piano 2013–15, Six Preludes for organ 2014, Moon Night Sketches for harpsichord 2015. *Films:* True North Festival in Taiwan 1999, Hidden Identity 2006. *Recordings include:* True North Festival in Taiwan, including Symphony 1 and Dragon Songs performed by the Taipei Symphony Orchestra conducted by Victor Feldbrill. *Publication:* Teacher's Guide to Canadian Music 1991. *Honours:* William St Clair Low Award for Chamber Music Composition 1972, Murray Adaskin Award 1974, Prize for Orchestral Composition at Winnipeg New Music Festival's Canadian Composers Competition, Soc. of Composers, Authors and Music Publrs of Canada (SOCAN) 1995. *Address:* True North Foundation, 516 Eglinton Avenue East, Toronto, ON M4P 1N6 (office); 3420 Bayview Avenue, Toronto, ON M2M 3S3, Canada (home). *Telephone:* (416) 322-5596 (office). *E-mail:* teddawson@gmail.com; teddawson@truenorthfdn .org (office). *Website:* www.truenorthfdn.org (office); www.teddawson .truenorthfdn.org.

DAYMOND, Karl, AGSM; British singer (baritone); *Director, Opera Playhouse*; b. 1965. *Education:* Guildhall School of Music and Drama, Nat. Opera Studio, sponsored by Glyndebourne Festival Opera. *Career:* appeared at Glyndebourne Festival 1992; sang Valentin for Opera Northern Ireland; season 1993 as Schaunard for Welsh Nat. Opera (WNO) and Mountjoy in Gloriana for Opera North; Claudio in Beatrice and Benedict for WNO, Hamlet, Marcello, Papageno, for Opera North; Dandini in Cenerentola at Garsington; Il Trittico and Un Ballo in Maschera for Vlaamse Opera; Anthony in Sweeney Todd for Opera North and Hector in Antheil's Transatlantic for Minnesota Opera; appeared as Purcell's Aeneas for BBC 2 TV 1995; Marcello in La Bohème for Opera North 1996; sang Paride in Cesti's Pomo d'Oro at Batignano 1998; season 1999 in Bernstein's Wonderful Town, at BBC Promenade Concerts, London; sang Kopernikus in premiere of Rêves d'un Marco Polo by Claude Viviers for Netherlands Opera 2000, Wonderful Town with Berlin Philharmonic 2001, Bernstein's Trouble in Tahiti for BBC 2001. *Recordings include:* Méhul's Stratonice with Les Arts Florissants; Wonderful Town; Dido and Aeneas; Weir's A Night at the Chinese Opera 1999, Bernstein's Trouble in Tahiti 2001. *Honours:* British Song Prize 1987, Polonsky Foundation Award 1989. *Address:* c/o Robert Clarke, 1 Worthfarm Cottages, The Street, Worth, Kent, CT14 0DE; 2 The Poplars, Chepstow, Monmouthshire, NP16 7LB, Wales (home). *Telephone:* 7968-950221 (mobile). *E-mail:* karl@ operaplayhouse.com (office). *Website:* www.operaplayhouse.com (office); www .singingclubber.co.uk (office).

DAZELEY, William; British singer (baritone); b. 1966. *Education:* Guildhall School, London. *Career:* season 1990–91 as Onegin with British Youth Opera; season 1991–92 as Schaunard with British Youth Opera and Don Giovanni for Opera North; British premiere of Schreker's Der Ferne Klang, 1992; season 1992–93 with Opera North in Billy Budd and as Mozart's Count and Schaunard, also as Don Giovanni for English Touring Opera; season 1993–94 as Mowgli in world premiere of Michael Berkeley's Baa Baa Black Sheep for Cheltenham Festival, also as Mowgli for Opera North, Harlekin for Broomhill and Papageno for Opera North; season 1994–95 as Rossini's Figaro for Glyndebourne Touring Opera, as Demetrius for Teatro Regio, Turin, and as Pelléas for Opera North; Mozart's Count for GTO at Glyndebourne 1996; Soldier in Busoni's Faust at Salzburg 1999; sang Mercutio in Gounod's Roméo et Juliette at Covent Garden 2000; sang Christ in the premiere of Birtwistle's The Last Supper, Berlin 2000; London Proms 2002. *Recordings include:* Britten, The Rescue of Penelope 1996, Britten, Billy Budd 1998, Leoncavallo, I Pagliacci 1999, Busoni, Doktor Faust 1999, Puccini, La Boheme 1999, Michael Berkeley, Baa Baa Black Sheep 2004, Mozart, Le Nozze di Figaro 2004, Berlioz, L'Enfance du Christ 2007, Leroy Anderson, Suite of Carols 2008, Korngold, Sonnett fur Wien 2009, Verdi, Don Carlos 2009, Billy Budd; Doktor Faust (Erato); La Bohème. *Honours:* Decca-Kathleen Ferrier Prize 1989; Richard Tauber Prize; Winner, Walter Gruner Int. Lieder Competition 1991. *Current Management:* Sue Nicholls, Hazard Chase, 25 City Road, Cambridge, CB1 1DP, England. *Telephone:* (1223) 312400. *Fax:* (1223) 460827. *E-mail:* sue .nicholls@hazardchase.co.uk. *Website:* www.hazardchase.co.uk.

DE BAGHY, Irina; Canadian singer (mezzo-soprano); b. 1981. *Education:* Bishop's Univ., Lennoxville, Schola Cantorum, Paris, France, Sorbonne Paris III, Conservatoire Nat. de Musique de Paris with Peggy Bouveret. *Career:* started singing in musical comedy aged six, moving via jazz to opera; sang Thétis in Andrew MacDonald's Andromache in 2002, Carmen at Poitiers and Châtellerault in 2008, Mozart's Requiem, Haydn's Nelson Mass, Janáček's La petite Renarde rusée in Reims and Liège; recitals in USA, Canada, Germany and France including Amphithéâtre de l'Opéra Bastille, Studio Théâtre de la Comédie Française, Salle Berthier and numerous festivals 2006–. *Honours:* First Prize, Concours Int. de Chant-Piano Nadia et Lili Boulanger 2009.

Address: 15 rue Jacques Louvel Tessier, 75010 Paris, France (home). *Telephone:* 618604568 (mobile) (home).

DE BEENHOUWER, Jozef; Belgian concert pianist; b. 26 March 1948, Brasschaat. *Education:* Univ. of Louvain, Chapelle Musicale Reine Elisabeth Argenteuil, Royal Flemish Conservatory, Antwerp. *Career:* concert pianist with orchestras and solo recitals; chamber music in Vienna (Musikverein, Konzerthaus with Vienna Symphony), Amsterdam (Concertgebouw), Lisbon (Foundation Gulbenkian), London, Berlin (Schauspielhaus), Dresden (Semper-Oper), Rheinisches Musikfest, Flanders Festival, Festival de Paris and in USA; Prof. of Piano, Royal Flemish Conservatory 1983–; Artistic Dir, Brussels Lunchtime Concerts 1990–2015; jury mem. in various int. piano competitions; concerts recorded for radio and TV. *Recordings include:* Schumann's Op 12, Ravel's Gaspard de la Nuit 1982, Peter Benoit's Contes et Ballades and Sonata 1984, Joseph Ryelandt's Piano Works 1986, Clara Schumann's Complete Piano Works 1991, Robert Schumann's Op 16 111 and 133 1994, Robert Schumann's Dichterliebe with Robert Holl 1994, Belgian Piano Music by P Benoit, L Mortelmans, J Jongen, M de Jong and V Legley 1997, Cello Sonatas by A De Boeck and J L Nicodé (with M Van Staalen) 1998, Songs and piano music by Lod Mortelmans 1999, Johannes Brahms, Klavierstücke Op 76 118 and 119 2000, Ludwig Schuncke, Piano Sonata etc. 1986–2000, Hans Pfitzner, Klaviertrios (with Robert Schumann Trio) 2001, Peter Benoit: Liefdedrama – Uit Henriette's Album 2002, Marinus de Jong: Piano Concerto No. 1, piano music 2003, Songs by Wagner, Nystroem and De Boeck (with Nina Stemme) 2004, Robert Schumann: Carnaval, Waldszenen and Kinderszenen 2005, August De Boeck: Piano Concerto, piano music, French Songs 2011. *Honours:* Robert Schumann Prize (Zwickau) 1993. *Address:* Frilinglei 45, 2930 Brasschaat, Belgium (office). *Telephone:* (3) 651-97-72 (home). *E-mail:* jozef .de.beenhouwer@pandora.be.

DE BILLY, Bertrand; French conductor; b. 11 Jan. 1965, Paris. *Career:* Conductor, Orchestre Symphonique des Jeunes, Île de France 1986–91; Prin. Conductor, Anhaltische Theater, Dessau 1993–95, Vienna Volksoper 1996–98; Gen. Music Dir Gran Teatre del Liceu, Barcelona 1999–2004; Chief Conductor and Artistic Dir Vienna Radio Symphony Orchestra 2002–10; has worked with major orchestras and opera houses world-wide, including State Operas of Vienna, Berlin, Hamburg and Munich, Royal Opera House, Covent Garden, La Monnaie, Brussels, Opera Nat. de Paris, Washington, Los Angeles and New York Metropolitan Opera; also collaborated with Musikverein, Vienna, Wiener Konzerthaus, Theater an der Wien. *Recordings include:* Mozart/da Ponte-cycle, d'Albert's Tiefland, excerpts from Wagner's Tristan und Isolde, Ravel and Gershwin piano concertos with Pascal Rogé, Schubert's Symphony in C-Major, Beethoven's Eroica, Puccini's La Bohème with Netrebko and Villazon. *Honours:* Chevalier, Ordre nat. du Mérite, Ordre des Arts et des Lettres, Légion d'honneur; Goldene Ehrenzeichen der Republik Österreich. *Current Management:* c/o Euroartists, Bastiengasse 27, 1183 Vienna, Austria. *Telephone:* (1) 3106096. *Fax:* (1) 3106094. *E-mail:* bueroberlin@opern-agentur.com. *Website:* www.lewin-management.com; www.debilly.com.

DE CALUWE, Peter; Belgian/Flemish opera house director; *Director General/Intendant, Théâtre Royal de la Monnaie/de Munt, Brussels*; b. 26 April 1963, Dendermonde. *Career:* began career at Théâtre Royal de la Monnaie, Brussels; worked with Nederlandse Opera, Amsterdam from 1990, Artistic Dir –2007; Dir Gen./Intendant, Théâtre Royal de la Monnaie/de Munt, Brussels 2007–; Pres. Opera Europe 2011–. *Honours:* Officier, Ordre Léopold II, Order of Merit of the Repub. of Poland, Chevalier des Arts et des Lettres; Master hc (Ecole Supérieure des Arts St Luc, Brussels). *Address:* Théâtre Royal de La Monnaie/de Munt, Rue Léopold/Leopoldstraat 4, Brussels 1000, Belgium (office). *Telephone:* (2) 229-12-02 (office). *Website:* www.lamonnaie.be (office).

DE CANDIA, Roberto; Italian singer (baritone); b. 1968, Molfetta, Bari. *Education:* studied with Sesto Bruscantini. *Career:* debut in Puccini's Messa di Gloria (concert) at the Santa Cecilia, Rome, and in Massenet's Manon at Parma; Engagements as Gianni Schicchi at Turin; Marcello at the Verona Arena, Taddeo (L'Italiana in Algeri) and Masetto in Don Giovanni at the Salzburg Festival; Other roles include: Rossini's Figaro (Paris Opéra-Comique), Parmenione in L'Occasione fa il ladro (Pesaro) and Alcandro in Pacini's Saffo (Wexford Festival); La Scala, Milan, 1996–97, as Ubalde in Gluck's Armide and Poeta (Il Turco in Italia); Glyndebourne Festival 1997, as Lescaut in a new production of Manon Lescaut; Season 1997–98 as Massenet's Lescaut at the Metropolitan, Dandini, and Belcore (L'Elisir d'amore); Season 1998–99 La Bohème; Gala Concert with Luciano Pavarotti at the Metropolitan Opera in New York; Sang in La Forza del Destino and Il Barbiere di Siviglia at La Scala; Season 2000–01 as Rossini's Dandini at Pesaro, Falstaff at Modena and Massenet's Lescaut at the Met. *Recordings:* Saffo; Mascagni's Messa di Gloria; Il turco in Italia with Riccardo Chailly; La Bohème with Riccardo Chailly. *Current Management:* c/o Atelier Musicale, Via Caselle 76, San Lazzaro di Savena 40068, Italy. *Telephone:* (51) 19984444. *Fax:* (51) 19984420. *E-mail:* info@ateliermusicale.com. *Website:* www.ateliermusicale.com.

DE CAROLIS, Natale; Italian singer (bass-baritone); b. 25 July 1957, Anagni. *Education:* Pont Inst. of Vatican State, studied with Renato Guelfi and Maria Vittoria Romano. *Career:* Debut: 1983; La Scala, Milan; Metropolitan Opera, New York; La Fenice, Venice; Maggio Musicale, Florence; Salzburg Festival; La Zarzuela, Madrid; Sydney Opera House; Rossini Opera Festival; Pesaro Teatro Comunale; Bologna Opera; Zürich Opera; Teatro

Massimo, Palermo; Teatro Bellini, Catania; Buenos Aires; Paris; Macerata; S Carlo, Napoli and Bonn; Sang Don Parmenione in a Rossini double bill at Cologne and Schwetzingen, 1992; Count Robinson in Il Matrimonio Segreto at the 1992 Ravenna Festival; Vienna, Musikverein, Staatsoper, Konzerthaus; Frankfurt, Don Giovanni, Figaro, Guglielmo, Belcore; Rome, Teatro Dell"Opera; Hamburg, Berlin, Lausanne, Montpellier, Aix-en-Province, Lisbon, Touloun, Oviedo; Sang Donizetti's Belcore at Covent Garden, 1997; Season 1998 with Guglielmo for the Royal Opera London, and Fernando in Rossini's Gazza Ladra at Venice; Season 2000–01 as Don Giovanni at Glyndebourne and Don Alfonso at Detroit. *Recordings:* Signor Bruschino, Scala di Seta (Rossini); Don Giovanni (Mozart); Rinaldo (Handel); Mozart Recital; L'Occasione fa Il Ladro and L'Inganno Felice (Rossini); Le nozze di Figaro (Mozart); La Ninfa Pazza per Amore (Paisiello); Mozart Recital; Don Giovanni, Così fan tutte, Le nozze di Figaro, Highlights. *Honours:* Spoleto; Baroque Festival Viterbo; Toti Dal Monte (Treviso); Lauri Volpi. *Current Management:* c/o Monaco Music Management, Palais de la Scala, 1263-1Avenue Henry, Dunant, 98000, Monaco. *Website:* www.nataledecarolis.com.

DE CASTRO-ROBINSON, Eve, BMus, MMus, DMus; New Zealand composer and academic; *Senior Lecturer in Composition, University of Auckland*; b. 9 Nov. 1956, London, England. *Education:* Auckland Tech. Inst., Univ. of Auckland. *Career:* Composer-in-Residence with the Auckland Philharmonic, 1991; Sr Lecturer in Composition, Univ. of Auckland; performances of her music with the Karlheinz Company in Auckland and with UNESCO in Paris. *Compositions include:* Fractions 1984, Cross-Hatchings 1985, Desire's Bat 1985, Efflux 1985, Tessellations 1985, Stringencies for 11 solo strings 1986, Spissitudes 1986, Interpolations 1986, Three Emily Dickinson Poems 1986, Peregrinations piano concerto 1987, Undercurrents (Philip Neill Memorial Prize in Music) 1987, Conundrums 1987, Panorama 1987, A Resonance of Emerald 1988, Commemoration for solo cello 1988, Synergy 1988, Countercurrents 1989, Five Responses 1989, Percolations 1990, Aurora 1990, Concerto for 3 clarinets 1991, Noah's Ark 1991, Split the Lark (Philip Neill Memorial Prize in Music 1993) 1991, Instrumental pieces, including Tumbling Strains 1992, Tingling Strings 1993, A Mob of Solid Bliss 1993, Four Marimbulations 1993, Cyprian's Dance 1995, Chaos of Delight I 1995, Chaos of Delight II 1996, A Pink-lit Phase 1997, Chaos of Delight III (Sounz Contemporary Award for Best New Work 2001) 1998, Other Echoes 1998, Kihikihi 1998, Small Blue 1998, Flourish 2001, These Boots (are made for dancing) 2001, Whisper 2001, Len Dances 2002, Ring True 2002, Len Songs 2003, This Liquid Drift of Light 2004, Releasing the Angel 2005, Pearls of the Sea 2005, These Arms to Hold You (Sounz Contemporary Award for Best New Work 2007) 2007. *Recordings include:* A Chaos of Delight 1998, New Zealand Choral Music 1998, Other Echoes 2000. *Address:* School of Music, University of Auckland, Building 250, 6 Symonds Street, Auckland, New Zealand (office). *Telephone:* (9) 3737599 (office). *E-mail:* e.decastro@auckland.ac.nz (office). *Website:* www.creative.auckland.ac.nz/study/programmes/music (office).

DE CLARA, Roberto, BMus; Canadian conductor; *Music Director, Oakville Symphony*; b. Hamilton, ON; m. Anna Colangelo 1983; one s. *Education:* McMaster Univ., Wiener Meisterkurse, Vienna Mozarteum, Salzburg Sommerakademie, Accademia Chigiana, Siena, Aspen Music School, Univ. of Toronto, Royal Conservatory, Toronto. *Career:* debut with Hamilton Philharmonic 1981; Asst Conductor, Opera Hamilton 1979–84, Hamilton Philharmonic 1981–82; Music Dir, Prince George Symphony 1984–87, York Symphony 1990–2003; Israel Vocal Arts, Tel-Aviv 1994–95; Musical Dir, Oakville Symphony 1997–; European Opera debut with Così fan tutte, Nat. Theatre Prague 1998. *Honours:* Heinz Unger Conducting Prize, Toronto 1978, Canada Council Scholarships 1979, 1980, Hans Haring Conducting Prize, Salzburg Mozarteum 1984, Canada-Israel Cultural Foundation grant 1994. *Address:* 129 Sirente Drive, Hamilton, ON L9A 5H5, Canada. *Telephone:* (905) 318-0939. *E-mail:* roberto.declara@sympatico.ca.

DE FUSCO, Laura; Italian concert pianist; b. 1950, Castellammare di Stabia. *Education:* studied at the Conservatorio San Pietro a Maiella, Naples. *Career:* Many concert appearances from 1966, notably in Europe, USA, South America and Japan; Orchestras have included the Detroit Symphony, Philadelphia, Orchestra National de Paris, Budapest Philharmonic, Santa Cecilia Rome, Moscow Symphony, Residentie Den Haag and the Yomiuri Nippon Symphony; Conductors have featured Muti, Mehta, Ceccato, Chailly, Inbal, Maag, De Burgos and Fedoseyev; Marlboro Festival concerts at the invitation of Rudolf Serkin; Debut with the BBC Philharmonic, Feb 1991; piano tutor, Conservatorio San Pietro a Maiella, Naples. *Address:* Conservatorio di Musica San Pietro a Majella, Via San Pietro a Majella, 35, 80138 Naples, Italy (office). *Telephone:* (081) 5644411 (office). *Fax:* (081) 5644415 (office). *E-mail:* conservatorio_di_napoli@sanpietroamajella.it (office). *Website:* www.sanpietroamajella.it (office).

DE GREEVE, Gilbert-Jean; Belgian concert pianist; b. 11 Nov. 1944, St Truiden. *Education:* Studied Piano with Eugene Traey, Royal Conservatory of Antwerp, Belgium, 1958–69; Performing major, with First Prizes in Piano and Chamber Music and a Diplome superieur for Chamber music; Composition major, with First Prizes in Music Theory, Harmony, Analysis, Counterpoint and Fugue; 1970 Peabody Institute of Music, Baltimore, Maryland, USA; Private studies with Rudolph Serkin, Eugene Ormandy and Leonard Pearlmann; 1972, Franz Liszt Academy of Budapest, Hungary. *Career:* Active world-wide as pianist 1970–; Director of the State Music Academy of Antwerp and Professor of the Royal Conservatory of Antwerp, 1970–; Working in a permanent duo with the Belgian soprano Martine De Craene, 1988–,

repertoire of more than 14 hours music from Baroque until today, including 3 books of melodies by Gabriel Fauré; Lieder cycles by composers from Hungary and Canada have been dedicated to and world-created by the Duo. Concerts and Masterclasses in 5 continents; Major foreign tours: Canada, Australia, New Zealand, Africa, Finland, Netherlands, Antilles, Greece. *Compositions:* Chamber Music, a Lieder cycle of 36 Lieder on poems by James Joyce. *Recordings:* Belgian Radio and Television; CBC Canada; Hungarian Radio Budapest. *Address:* Anselmostraat 38, 2018 Antwerpen, Belgium.

DE GROOTE, Philip; South African fmr cellist; b. 25 Dec. 1949, Johannesburg. *Career:* Co-founder and cellist of the Chilingirian Quartet 1971; Resident Quartet of Liverpool Univ. 1973–76, of Sussex Univ. 1978; Resident Quartet of Royal Coll. of Music 1986; performances at Edinburgh, Bath, Aldeburgh Festivals, Munich Herkulessaal, Amsterdam Concertgebouw, Zürich Tonhalle, Vienna Konzerthaus, Stockholm Konserthuset; New York debut 1976; annual coast-to-coast tours of USA and Canada; rep. UK at New York Int. Festival quartet series; New Zealand, South America, the Far East; TV and radio broadcasts throughout Europe, National Public Radio in USA, BBC. *Recordings include:* All Great Mozart Quartets, Late Schubert Quartets, Debussy and Ravel Quartets, Elgar Quartet and Piano Quintet, Schubert Cello Quintet and Octet, Mozart Clarinet Quintet, Complete Quartets of Bartók and Dvořák, Bartók Piano Quintet, Hahn and Vierne Piano Quintets, Grieg Quartets. *Address:* 43 Turney Road, London, SE21 7JA, England (home).

DE JONG, Conrad John, BM, MM; American composer and academic; b. 13 Jan. 1934, Hull, IA. *Education:* North Texas State Univ., Denton, Indiana Univ. School of Music with B. Heiden, studied with T. de Leeuw in Amsterdam. *Career:* Prof. of Music, Univ. of Wisconsin, River Falls 1959–. *Compositions:* Prelude and Fugue for brass trio 1958, three Studies for brass septet 1960, Music for two tubas 1961, Essay for brass quintet 1963, String Trio 1964, Fun and Games for any woodwind, brass or string instrument(s) and piano 1966, Peace on Earth for chorus and organ 1969, Aanraking (Contact) for trombone 1969, Hist Whist for voice, flute, viola and percussion 1969, Grab Bag for tuba ensemble 1970, The Silence of the Sky in My Eyes for 1/2 track stereo tape, musicians, light and optional dance and audience participation 1973, A Prayer for chorus, piano, brass wind chimes and optional audience participation 1975, Ring! My Chimes for chimes, 1/2 track stereo tape and slides 1977, three Short Variation Fanfares for brass quintet 1980, La Dolorosa for English horn 1982.

DE LA GRANGE, Henry-Louis; French writer on music; b. 26 May 1924, Paris; s. of Amaury de la Grange and Emily Sloane. *Education:* studied letters at Aix-en-Provence and the Sorbonne, Paris, Yale Univ. School of Music, studied piano with Yvonne Lefébure and harmony, counterpoint and musical analysis with Nadia Boulanger. *Career:* music critic for French and American publications; guest lecturer at Columbia, Stanford and Indiana Univs 1974–81, Geneva 1982, Leipzig, Juilliard, Univ. of California at Los Angeles 1985, Budapest 1987, Hamburg 1988, Oslo 1993, also Paris Conservatory, Kyoto, Hong Kong, Wellington, Sydney, Canberra, Melbourne, Boulder, San Francisco 1998; taught a DEA Seminar at the Ecole Normale Supérieure, Paris; founded the Bibliothèque Musicale Gustav Mahler, Paris 1986. *Exhibition:* Mahler exhibition, Musée d'Art Moderne, Paris 1985. *Radio:* series of 28 broadcasts on Mahler's biog. *Publications include:* Gustav Mahler: Chronique d'une Vie, 3 vols 1979–84, Vienne, Une Histoire musicale, 2 vols 1990–91, Mahler, Vol. I, England and USA 1973–74, Vols II, III and IV, England and USA 1995–2008. *Honours:* Hon. Pres. Médiathèque Musicale Mahler; Officier, Légion d'honneur 2006, Commandeur, Ordre du Mérite national, Ehrenkreuz für Gesellschaft und Kunst, Austria 2009; Dr hc (Juilliard School) 2010; Deems Taylor Award for Mahler Vol. I 1974, Prize for the Best Book of the Year on Music, Académie Charles Cros 1984, and Syndicat de la Critique musicale et dramatique 1983, Prize of the Royal Philharmonic Soc., London 1996, Charles Flint Kellogg Award in Arts and Letters from Bard Coll., NY 2005, Gold Medal, Vienna Int. Mahler Soc. 2009. *Address:* 8B Chemin du Bochet, 1025 Saint-Sulpice, Switzerland (home); c/o Médiathèque Musicale Mahler, 11 bis, rue de Vézelay, 75008 Paris, France (office). *Telephone:* (21) 691-0295 (home); 1-53-75-16-35 (office). *Fax:* (21) 691-5055 (home); 1-53-75-19-77 (office). *E-mail:* hlg@bluewin.ch. *Website:* www.mediathequemahler.org (office).

DE LA MORA, Fernando; Mexican singer (tenor); b. 1958, Mexico City. *Education:* National Conservatory of Mexico, studying with Leticia Velázquez, Rosa Rimoch and Emilio Perez Casas, also studied in New York, Tel-Aviv and Univ. of North Carolina. *Career:* debut as Borsa in Rigoletto at Mexico City; has appeared widely in Mexico as Pinkerton, Cavaradossi and Alfredo; San Francisco Opera 1988–89, as Gounod's Romeo, and Rodolfo; Alfredo at Vienna Staatsoper and Deutsche Oper Berlin 1989; Faust at Cologne and Verdi Requiem on tour to Moscow with ensemble of La Scala; Milan debut 1990, as Alfredo; Barcelona 1992 as Nemorino; has worked with conductors such as Zubin Mehta, Ricardo Muti, Lorin Maazel, Charles Mackerras, Eduardo Mata, and Richard Bonynge, among others; also performs concerts with mariachi, singing Mexican songs. *Recordings include:* more than 20 recordings including Catan's Rappaccini's Daughter, Lucia di Lammermoor with London Symphony Orchestra, The Artistry of Fernando de la Mora, Love Duets with soprano Youngok Shin. *Website:* tenorfernandodelamora.com.

DE LA PARRA, Alondra, BMus, MA; Mexican conductor; b. 31 Oct. 1980, Mexico City; m. Carlos Zedillo Velasco 2008. *Education:* St Leonards Mayfield School (Royal Acad. of Music), Manhattan School of Music, USA. *Career:* Asst Conductor, St Leonard's Mayfield School Orchestra 1995–96; Founder and Artistic Dir, Philharmonic Orchestra of the Americas 2004–11; Music Dir, Music Festival of the Americas at Stowe 2003–; Prin. Guest Conductor, New Amsterdam Symphony Orchestra 2005–07; Asst Cover Conductor, Manhattan School of Music Symphony 2005–08. *Honours:* Amigos de la Música Music Award 2004, Pablo Casals Award, Manhatthan School of Music 2008, Culture Award 2011, American Business Council 2011, Festspiele Mecklenburg-Vorpommern 2013. *Current Management:* c/o Tanja Dorn, IMG Artists, Theaterstrasse 2 D, 30159 Hanover, Germany. *Telephone:* (511) 20300878. *Fax:* (511) 4378135. *E-mail:* tdorn@imgartists.com; canelaentertainment@gmail.com. *E-mail:* valeria@alondradelaparra.com. *Website:* www.alondradelaparra.com.

DE LA SALLE, Lise; French pianist; b. 8 May 1988, Cherbourg; d. of Anne de la Salle; partner Jean-Philippe Perrot. *Education:* Conservatoire Supérieur de Musique-CNR, Paris, Conservatoire Nat. Supérieur de Musique-CNSM, pvt. lessons with Pascal Nemirovski. *Career:* gave first concert on Radio France aged nine; debut concert appearances in USA, Japan, China, France, Italy, Denmark, Turkey, Portugal and Germany; numerous performances worldwide with major int. orchestras. *Repertoire includes:* Gershwin Concerto in F, Liszt Concerto No. 1, Mozart Concerto No. 9 (Jeunehomme), Mozart Concerto No. 20, Prokofiev Concerto No. 1, Rachmaninov Concerto No. 2, Rachmaninov Rhapsody on a Theme of Paganini, Ravel Sonatine, Ravel Concerto in G Major, Saint Saëns Concerto No. 2, Shostakovitch Concerto No. 1, Haydn Concerto in G Major, Beethoven Concerto No. 2, Beethoven Concerto No. 3, Chopin Concerto No. 2. *Recordings:* Rachmaninov/Ravel 2002, Bach/Liszt 2005, Shostakovitch/Liszt/Prokofiev 2008, Mozart/Prokofiev 2008. *Films:* Lise de la Salle, Majeur!. *Honours:* several awards including First Prize and Bärenreiter Award, Ettlingen Int. Competition, Germany 2000, First Prize, European Young Concert Artists, Paris 2003, Special Prize, Young Concert Artists Int. Auditions, New York 2004. *Current Management:* c/o Dr Hans-Dieter Goehre, Concerto Winderstein München, Postfach 440446, 80753 Munich, Germany. *Telephone:* (89) 38384641. *Fax:* (89) 337938. *E-mail:* goehre@winderstein.de. *Website:* www.winderstein.de; www.lisedelasalle.com (home).

DE LAET, Joris Maurits; Belgian academic; b. 12 July 1947, Antwerp; m. Maria Vervoort 1774, one d. *Education:* Acad. of Antwerp. *Career:* first performances in International Cultural Centre, Antwerp 1974; tape music composition, Parametric; live electronics, video art at festivals in Europe, Canada and Brazil; many radio appearances since 1973; international seminars and lectures; concert organizer of experimental and electronic music and video art; Dir, SEM and Ed. SEM magazine 1975–79; man. sound studio of the Antwerp Music Conservatory and Prof. of Electronic Music Composition; prod. monthly radio programme dedicated to electro-acoustic music 1992–; co-founder and Vice-Pres., BeFEM/FeBeMe, Belgian Federation of Electro-acoustic Music 1994. *Compositions include:* Naderen 1988, Metrokunst 1989, Watertoren-Installatie 1989, Blamis 1990, Transparent Bodies 1991, Penetration 1992, Irreversible, New Environment 1992, Aural Silver 1993, The Shift 1994, Bruit Noir 1995, Soleil Silencieux 1996, Pigeon Piégé 1997, Pièce de Résistance 1998. *Publications:* Documenta Belgicae II (ed. and contrib.) 1985, syllabus on analogue synthesis techniques for Conservatory of Antwerp 1979; contrib. various articles in newspapers and magazines.

DE MAIN, John Lee, BM, MS; American conductor; b. 11 Jan. 1944, Youngstown, OH. *Education:* Juilliard School of Music, New York, studied with Adele Marcus, Jorge Mester. *Career:* Assoc. Conductor, St Paul (Minn) Chamber Orchestra 1972–74; Music Dir, Texas Opera Theater 1974–76; Houston Grand Opera 1979–94, Opera/Omaha 1983–; conducted the local premiere of Britten's A Midsummer Night's Dream, Houston 1993, L'Elisir d'amore at Seattle 1998. *Honours:* Julius Rudel Award 1971, Grammy Award 1977, Grand Prix du Disque 1977.

DE MAISTRE, Xavier; French harpist; b. 1973, Toulon. *Education:* Institut d'études politiques de Paris, LSE, pvt. lessons with Jacqueline Borot and Catherine Michel in Paris. *Career:* solo harpist Bavarian Radio Symphony Orchestra, Munich 1995–98; Prin. Harpist Vienna Philharmonic Orchestra 1998; Prof., Hochschule für Musik, Hamburg 2001–; gives regular masterclasses at Julliard School, New York, Toho Univ., Tokyo, Shanghai Conservatory, Trinity Coll., London; appearances at many festivals including Schleswig-Holstein Festival, Salzburger Festspielen, Rheingau Festival, Wiener Festwochen, Osterklang, Budapest Spring Festival, Schubertiade, Styriarte, Verbier Festival, Würzburg Mozartfest. *Recordings:* Renie Works for Harp 1999, French Concertos for Harp 2002, Concertos for Two Harps and Orchestra 2003, Famous Classics For Harp 2005, Concertos for One and Two Harps 2007, Nuits d'Etoiles 2008. *Honours:* Gold Medal, 4th USA Int. Harp Competition, Bloomington, Ind. 1998. *Current Management:* Baron Artists, Bösendorferstr. 4/12, 1010 Vienna, Austria. *E-mail:* office@baronartists.com. *Website:* www.baronartists.com; www.xavier-demaistre.com.

DE MARCHI, Alessandro; Italian conductor and harpsichordist. *Education:* Accad. di Santa Cecilia, Schola Cantorum Basiliensis, Switzerland. *Career:* fmrly Prof. of Organ and Gregorian Chant, Conservatorio di Musica Cimarosa, pianist with St Louis Big Band, harpsichordist with Italian Baroque Orchestra, Conductor, Chamber Orchestra G. Carissimi; Asst to René Jacobs 1989 (followed by engagements in European theatres, regular guest and harpsichordist at Salzburg Festival) and to Daniel Barenboim at Berlin Staatsoper 1990; has conducted opera productions at Hamburgische Staatsoper (Don Giovanni, Il Barbiere di Siviglia, Giulio Cesare and Keiser's Der Lächerliche Prinz Jodelet), Handel Festspiele Halle (Hercules), Essen (Orlando), Théâtre de la Monnaie, Brussels (Cosí fan Tutte), Opéra de Lyon (Alcine), Nat. Theatre, Prague (La Clemenza di Tito) and Academia Montis Regalis Turin; orchestral conducting has included Munich Chamber Orchestra, Orchestra of Staatsoper Hannover, Orchestre de Chambre de Genève and Orchestra dell' Accad. di Santa Cecilia; regular Guest Conductor, Rossini Festival of Bad Wildbad and Handel Festival Halle; Principal Conductor, Italian baroque orchestra Academia Montis Regalis Turin 1998–; Artistic Dir, Innsbruck Festival of Early Music 2009–. *Recordings include:* as performer: Haendel: Giulio Cesare 1991, Bernardo Pasquini: Virtuoso Music for Two Harpsichords 1992, A Duoi Cembali: Musique allemande pour deux clavecins 1998, Petersen/Kraemer: Speelstukken 1998, Corelli: Concerti Grossi Op. 6 2003; as conductor/leader: Haendel: Cantates Romaines 2000, Rossini: La pietra del paragone 2004, Vivaldi: Orlando finto pazzo 2004, Vivaldi: Operas 2004, Rossini: Torvaldo e Dorliska 2006, Vivaldi: Concerto Rustico 2006, Stradella: San Giovanni Battista 2008, Handel: Il trionfo del Tempo e del Disinganno 2008, Bellini: La Sonnambula 2008, Vivaldi: Motetti 2010, Pergolesi: L'Olimpiade 2011, Handel/Caldara: Carmelite Vespers 1709 2012, Bernardo Pasquini: Caino & Abela 2012, Francesco Provenzale: La Stellidaura vendicante 2013, Rivals: Arias for Farinelli & Co. 2013. *Current Management:* Robert Gilder & Co., 91 Great Russell Street, London, WC1B 3PS, England. *Telephone:* (20) 7580-7758. *Fax:* (20) 7580-7739. *E-mail:* rgilder@robert-gilder.com. *Website:* www.robert-gilder.com.

DE MEY, Guy; Belgian singer (tenor); b. 4 Aug. 1955, Hamme. *Education:* Brussels Conservatory, studied in Amsterdam with Erna Spoorenberg, and with Peter Pears and Eric Tappy. *Career:* has appeared in baroque opera at such centres as Berlin, Hamburg, Strasbourg and Spoleto; Lully's Atys under William Christie in Paris, Florence and New York; Alidoro in Cesti's Orontea at Innsbruck 1986, returning for Aegus in Cavalli's Giasone 1988; Rameau's Hippolyte at Regio Emilia and Eurymachus in Il Ritorno d'Ulisse at Mézières 1989, conducted by Michel Corboz; London 1986 as Monteverdi's Orfeo; Brussels 1988, as the Painter in Lulu; sang Don Polidoro in Mozart's La Finta Semplice at Innsbruck 1991; Lully's Alceste at Opéra Comique, Paris 1992; further engagements at Utrecht Early Music Festival, Zürich, Venice and Bologna; sang in the French version of Don Carlos at Brussels 1996 and Orpheus by Monteverdi for ENO; season 2000–01 as Carrado in A. Scarlatti's Griselda; at Innsbruck, M. Triquet in Eugene Onegin at Brussels and the Schoolmaster in The Cunning Little Vixen, for Netherlands Opera; concert repertoire includes the Evangelist in Bach's Passions. *Recordings:* Le Cinesi by Gluck; A Scarlatti's La Giuditta; Lully's Atys; Der Geduldige Sokrates by Telemann, Monteverdi's Orfeo and Poppea; Cavalli's Xerse and Giasone, Alessandro by Handel, Orontea and Rameau's Platée.

DE MOOR, Chris; Belgian singer (bass); b. 22 June 1946, Antwerp. *Education:* Brussels Conservatory. *Career:* sang throughout Belgium and France, notably as Massenet's Don Quichotte, at Antwerp; Claudius in Hamlet by Thomas and Gounod's Frère Laurent at Antwerp 1996; Zaccaria in Nabucco and Arkel in Pelléas. *Recordings:* Messiah, Mireille by Gounod. *Honours:* Vercelli and Barcelona 1984.

DE NIESE, Danielle; American singer (soprano); b. 1980, Melbourne, Australia; d. of Peter de Niese and Beverley Anderson; m. Gus Christie 2009; one s. *Education:* Colburn School, Los Angeles, Mannes Coll. of Music. *Career:* early career as TV presenter, LA Kids programme; opera debut at age 15 with Los Angeles Opera; joined Lindemann Young Artists Programme, Metropolitan Opera 1998, debut as Barbarina in Le nozze di Figaro; European debut as Cleopatra in Giulio Cesare for Netherlands Opera and Paris Opera 2001; UK debut as Cleopatra, Glyndebourne Festival 2005; Covent Garden debut in Acis and Galatea 2009; Ariel in The Enchanted Island, Metropolitan Opera 2012; Susanna in Marriage of Figaro, Hamburg State Opera 2015; numerous concert recitals including with New York Philharmonic, Cleveland Orchestra, Nat. Symphony, San Francisco Symphony; roles include: Lauretta in Gianni Schicchi, Barbarina and Susanna in Le Nozze di Figaro, Nannetta in Falstaff, Poppea in L'Incoronazione di Poppea, Despina in Cosi fan Tutte, Titania in A Midsummer Night's Dream, Rodelinda, Ginevra in Ariodante; Last Night, BBC Proms, London 2015. *Film:* Hannibal 2001. *Recordings:* Handel Arias (Orphées d'Or Award) 2007, The Mozart Album 2009, Diva 2010, Beauty of the Baroque 2011. *Honours:* Emmy Award for LA Kids TV show. *Current Management:* c/o Alec C. Treuhaft, IMG Artists, Carnegie Hall Tower, 152 West 57th Street, 5th Floor, New York, NY 10019, USA. *Telephone:* (212) 994-3500. *Fax:* (212) 994-3550. *E-mail:* atreuhaft@imgartists.com. *Website:* www.imgartists.com; www.danielledeniese.com.

DE PALMA, Sandro; Italian pianist; b. 14 Feb. 1957, Naples. *Education:* studied with Vincenzo Vitales in Naples. *Career:* debut in Naples; appeared ORF, Vienna 1977, Carnegie Hall, New York 1978; other appearances include Dvořák Hall, Prague, Interforum, Budapest, Gewandhaus, Leipzig, Dresden, Berlin; performances with Italian orchestras, including RAI, Rome, San Carlo, Fenice Venice, Milan; tours of France, Italy, Switzerland, fmr USSR. *Recordings:* Liszt, Muzio Clementi's Gradus ad Parnassum (with Fonit Cetra). *Honours:* first prize Casella Competition, Naples 1976, first prize Bruce Hungerford, New York 1977. *Address:* Via del Colosseo 23, Rome, Italy.

DE PEYER, Gervase Alan, FRCM; British clarinettist and conductor; b. 11 April 1926, London; s. of Esme Everard Vivian de Peyer and Edith Mary Bartlett; m. 1st Sylvia Southcombe 1950 (divorced 1971); one s. two d.; m. 2nd Susan Rosalind Daniel 1971 (divorced 1979); m. 3rd Katia Perret Aubry 1980. *Education:* King Alfred's School, London, Bedales School and Royal Coll. of Music, London. *Career:* served in HM Forces 1945, 1946; studied in Paris 1949; int. soloist 1949–; Founder mem. Melos Ensemble 1950–72; Prin. Clarinet, London Symphony Orchestra 1955–72; Founder and Conductor Melos Sinfonia of Washington 1992; Dir London Symphony Wind Ensemble; fmr Assoc. Conductor Haydn Orchestra of London; solo clarinettist, Chamber Music Soc. of Lincoln Center, NY 1969–89; fmr Resident Conductor Victoria Int. Festival, BC, Canada; Co-founder and Artistic Dir Innisfree Music Festival, Pa, USA; mem. Faculty, Mannes Coll. of Music, NY; also conductor; recording artist with all major companies (most recorded solo clarinettist in the world); gives recitals and master classes throughout the world. *Honours:* Gold Medallist Worshipful Co. of Musicians 1948, Charles Gros Grand Prix du Disque 1961, 1962, Plaque of Honor for Acad. of Arts and Sciences of America for recording of Mozart concerto 1962. *Address:* 42 Tower Bridge Wharf, St Katherine's Way, London, E1W 1UR, England (home). *Telephone:* (20) 7265-1110. *Fax:* (20) 7265-1110. *E-mail:* gdepeyer@aol.com (office). *Website:* www.gervasedepeyer.com (office).

DE PONT DAVIES, Rebecca; British singer (mezzo-soprano); b. 3 July 1962, London. *Education:* Guildhall School of Music and Drama. *Career:* debut, Death in Venice, Glyndebourne Touring Opera, 1989; Gaea in Strauss's Daphne at Garsington Festival, 1995; La Zia Principessa/Zita in Puccini's Il Trittico at Broomhill, 1995; Contemporary works by Judith Weir, Jonathan Dove, Henze, in the United Kingdom and Europe; Concert Appearances at major British venues, Canada and Columbia; 3rd Lady in The Magic Flute, Opera Factory, 1996; Die Muschel in the British premiere of Strauss's Die Agyptische Helena at Garsington, 1997; Moksada in Snatched by the Gods (Param Vir) for Scottish Opera, 1998; Emilia in Verdi's Otello for English National Opera, 1998; Leda in Strauss's Die Liebe der Danaë for Garsington, 1999; Martha/Pantalis in Boito's Mephistopheles, Annina in Der Rosenkavalier and Mrs Sedley in Peter Grimes all for English National Opera, 1999; Geneviève in Pelléas et Mélisande and 3rd Secretary to Chairman Mao in Adams's Nixon in China for English National Opera, 2000; Schwertleite, Die Walküre BBC Proms, 2000; For English National Opera: Flosshilde, Das Rheingold, 2001; Mistress Quickly, Falstaff, 2001; Princess Marya Bolkonskaya, War and Peace, 2001; Ulrica, Un Ballo in Maschera, 2002; Theatre Dresser/School Boy/Groom, Lulu, 2002. *Recordings:* Antigone; Fleurs Jetées; Falstaff, 2001. *Honours:* Many educational prizes including award from Countess of Munster Musical Trust; AGSM; PDVT; Violet Openshaw Memorial Prize for Contraltos; Dorothy Openshaw Prize for Melodie.

DE SARAM, Rohan, ARAM; British cellist; b. 9 March 1939, Sheffield, Yorks., England; s. of Robert de Saram and Miriam Pieris; m.; two c. *Education:* studied in Sri Lanka with Martin Hohermann, in Florence and Siena with Gaspar Cassado, in Puerto Rico with Pablo Casals, further study in London with Sir John Barbirolli. *Career:* gave recitals and concerts in Europe, Asia, Australia, New Zealand, fmr USSR, Canada and USA from age 11; US debut with New York Philharmonic, Carnegie Hall 1960 at the invitation of Dmitri Mitropoulos; as soloist, in addition to standard classical repertoire, has worked personally with, amongst others, Kodály, Walton, Shostakovich, Poulenc; has taught at Trinity Coll. of Music, London, Birmingham Conservatoire, Accad. Chigiana, Siena and Darmstadt Summer School, Germany, Dartington Summer School, as well as masterclasses at numerous other places in Australia, Asia, Europe and America; mem. Arditti Quartet –2005, with repertoire including works by Boulez, Carter, Ferneyhough, Henze, Ligeti and many other contemporary composers; premieres of works by Berio, Bussotti, Cage, Glass, Gubaidulina, Kagel, Lachenmann, Nancarrow, Rihm, Schnittke and many others; as soloist has given British premieres of works such as Bax's Rhapsodic Ballad and Kottos for solo cello by Xenakis; has given world premieres of many works, including Ligeti's Sonata for solo cello, Pousseur's Racine 19 (written for Rohan), Xenakis' Epicycles for cello and ensemble (written for Rohan) and Roscobeck for cello and double bass (written for Rohan and Stefano Scodanibbio), Dillon's Eos for solo cello (written for Rohan), Berio's Sequenza XIV for cello (written for Rohan), and Toshio Hosokawa's 'Chant' for cello and orchestra (written for Rohan), Ton That Tiet's Concerto for cello, percussion and orchestra; Founder, De Saram Clarinet Trio and a duo with his brother Druvi; gives chamber music recitals with a range of artists around the world; interested in music of Sri Lanka and plays Kandyan drum, the rhythms of which Berio uses in Sequenza XIV for solo cello; improvises with a variety of artists. *Publication:* Conversations with Rohan de Saram (with Joachim Steinhauer) 2013. *Honours:* Deshamaniya (nat. honour of Sri Lanka) 2005; Hon. DLitt (Peradeniya Univ., Sri Lanka) 2004; Suggia Award 1957, Ernst von Siemens Prize 1999. *E-mail:* rosiedesaram@hotmail.com. *Website:* www.rohandesaram.co.uk.

DE SIMONE, Bruno; Italian singer (baritone); b. 1957, Naples. *Education:* studied with Sesto Bruscantini. *Career:* made debut as Valentin in Faust and Albert in Werther, Spoleto 1980; made debut at La Scala in Pergolesi's Lo frate 'nnammurato 1990; performances with Teatro di San Carlo, Naples 1991–; repertoire includes Pergolesi's Flaminio, Don Giovanni, Paisiello's L'Idolo cinese, Il Barbiere di Siviglia, Pergolesi's Livietta e Tracollo, Macerata, Haydn's Mondo della Luna, Figaro, Taddeo, Dandini, Magnifico, Rimbaud and Germano, Mozart's Figaro, Alfonso, Guglielmo, Count and Leporello, Donizetti's Dulcamara, Belcore, Sulpice, Geronimo in Il Matrimonio Segreto, Rossini's Bartolo, Cimarosa's Il marito disperatos. *Current Management:* c/o Ariosi Management, Piazzale Gorini, 2, 20133 Milan, Italy. *E-mail:* info@ariosimanagement.com. *Website:* www.ariosimanagement.com; www.brunodesimone.net.

DE SMET, Raoul C., (Simon de Rycke), MPhil; Belgian composer and academic (retd); b. 27 Oct. 1936, Antwerp; m. Marisa Seys 1962; one s. three d. *Education:* Catholic Univ. of Louvain, Univ. of Salamanca, Spain, Music Acad., Deurne, studied composition with A. Verbesselt and Ton de Leeuw, electronic music with L. Goethals, Ipem Gent. *Career:* debut, Darmstadt Ferienkurse Neue Musik; Prof. of Spanish Linguistics and Trans., Kath Vlaamse Hogeschool, Antwerp 1969–97; Founder Orphische Avonden playing concerts of new chamber music 1974–2004; Publr EM-Reeks, new music of Flemish Composers 1981; Founder Orpheus-Prijs Contest for interpretation of new chamber music 1987; mem. Bd of Dirs Unie Belgische Componisten 1995–2012; mem. Soc. d'Auteurs Belge – Belgische Auteurs Maatschappij (SABAM) 1972–, Centre Belge de Documentation Musicale (CeBeDeM), Flemish Composers' Archipel, COMAV, European Composers' Forum; musical corresp., Ambrozijn magazine. *Compositions include:* for chamber opera: Ulrike 1979, 1988, Vincent 1990, Concerto for alto sax, strings, accordion and percussion 1992, Concerto for violin and symphonic orchestra 1993, Three symphonies 1960, 1995, 2010, Three String Quartets, Clarinet and String Quartet, Octopus for eight bass clarinets, Track-Sack-Fantasy for 10 accordions, Logbook 1, cello suite, Gnomons 2 for four trombones and stereotape, Soledad Sonora for alto sax, Concerto for accordion and string orchestra 2000, Ecce Homo, oratorio 2004, Concerto for piano and big band, 15 études de virtuosité for piano 2006–10, Gents Capriccio on Themes of Liszt for piano, organ and strings 2011. *Publications include:* scores published by CeBeDeM (Brussels), Lantro Music, (Grimbergen), Tongermusikverlag (Cologne). *Honours:* Prov. of Antwerp Prize 1985, Fuga Trophy 1995. *Address:* Zilversmidstraat 31 bo 2.2, 2000 Antwerp, Belgium (home). *Telephone:* (32) 32394119 (home). *E-mail:* orpheusprijs@skynet.be.

DE SOUSA DIAS, Antonio, PhD; Portuguese composer, media artist and academic; *Professor, Instituto Superior Autónomo de Estudos Politécnicos*; b. 13 Nov. 1959, Lisbon; s. of António de Macedo and Maria Helena Sousa Dias. *Education:* Lisbon Conservatory with Constança Capdeville, Univ. of Paris VIII with Horacio Vaggione. *Career:* pnr in performance groups, ColecViva, directed by Constança Capdeville 1985–, and Opus Sic; collaboration with Grupo Música Nova, directed by Cândido Lima 1992–, with Les Phonogénistes on Vertiges de l'Espace and Vertiges de l'image project 2009–; Prof. of Composition, Conservatorio de Lisboa 1985–87; Asst Prof. of Composition, Escola Superior de Música, Lisbon 1987–91, Prof. of Composition and Electro-acoustics 1993–2001, Deputy Dir 1995–2001; teacher of electro-acoustic composition, Univ. of Paris 2007–09; seminar tutor, Universidade Católica Portuguesa 2008–; Prof., Instituto Superior Autónomo de Estudos Politécnicos 2009–. *Exhibitions:* Natureza Morta 2010, Tonnetz09B 2011, Vertiges d'image 2011, Monthey04 vrs 2012, A Dama e o Unicornio 2013. *Compositions include:* Estudos para Decoração de Interiores for synthesizers controlled by computer 1987, Para dois pianos No. 1 and 2 1986, 1992, Mise en page for tape 1990, O Jardim das Chuvas de Todo o Sempre for flute, clarinet, guitar, harp, percussion, piano, two violins, viola and cello 1991, Rumbinação, Definitivamente! for two flutes, oboe, two clarinets, soprano, viola, cello and piano 1994, Cinco Circunstancias for clarinet and piano 1995, Komm, tanz mit mir! for five instruments 1997, Gamanço tape 1997, Natureza Morta com Ruídos de Sala, Efeitos Especiais e Claquete for tape 1997, Le blanc souci de notre toile for oboe and cello 1998, . . .uma sombra também for clarinet and electronics 1999, Estranho movimento for tape 2000, Dói-me o luar for flute, clarinet, harp, vibraphone, piano, two violins, viola and cello 2001, Têtrês for tape 2001, Quand trois poules vont au champ for tape 2002, Trois Chansons Inachevées for soprano, tenor sax and tape 2003, Ressonâncias-Memórias for flute, clarinet, vibraphone, piano, violin, viola, cello and tape 2003, Va(lé)riation 1 for two flutes, oboe, two clarinets, bassoon, French horn, trombone and vibraphone 2005, Va(lé)riation 5 for guitar, vibraphone and tape 2005, Va(lé)riation 6: Caravelas for mezzo-soprano and piano 2007, Va(lé)riation 5B for guitar and tape 2009, A Dama e o Unicórno for two speakers and electronics 2009, Vertige de l'espace (with Les Phonogénistes) 2009–, pour un Cadavre Exquis for flute and clarinet in B♭/violin and cello/piano 2010, Keep Smiling for flute, clarinet in B♭/percussion, piano/violin, viola, cello 2012, A Dama e o Unicórnio for voice and electronics 2013, Variação sobre Glosa for flute, clarinet in B♭/violin, cello/piano, electronics 2014. *Music for theatre:* Io Sono Una Bambina o Uno Disegno (with Constança Capdeville) (dance piece) 1988, Estilhaços 1989, Rumor 1996, . . .há dois ou. . . 1998, Ce désert est faux 2012. *Music for film:* Os Abismos da Meia-Noite 1984, Khâlom 1987, Transparências em Prata 1988, Fernando Lanhas, Os Sete Rostos 1988, Transparências em Prata 1988, A Maldição de Marialva 1989, O Altar dos Holocaustos 1992, Chá Forte com Limão 1993, Santo António do Todo o Mundo 1996, Processo Crime 141/53 2000, Natureza Morta – Visages d'une Dictature 2005, 48 2009, Vertiges de l'image (image for) 2011; short films: Detectim 1991, Refléxion faite. . . 2004. *Publications include:* numerous articles in professional journals and conference proceedings. *Honours:* Fernando Lopes Graça Prize 1987, Ministry of Educ. Prize 1990. *Address:* 3 Cité Chaptal, 75009 Paris, France (home). *E-mail:* contact@sousadias.com (office). *Website:* www.sousadias.com.

DE SOUZA, Ralph; British violinist; b. 1959, England. *Career:* Founder mem. and second violinist of the Endellion String Quartet, 1979; numerous concerts in Paris, Amsterdam, Frankfurt, Munich, Salzburg and Rome; appeared at the South Bank Haydn Festival in 1990, the Wigmore Hall Beethoven Series in 1991 and the Quartet Plus Series on South Bank in 1994; Quartet-in-Residence at Cambridge Univ. from 1992; residency at MIT, USA, 1995, 2005, at Royal Northern Coll. of Music, The Venue, Leeds. *Recordings include:* works by Haydn, Bartók, Dvořák, Walton, Smetana, Beethoven, Tchaikovsky, Schubert, Britten, Vaughan Williams, Barber. *E-mail:* James .Brown@hazardchase.co.uk. *Website:* www.hazardchase.co.uk. *E-mail:* info@ endellionquartet.com (office). *Website:* www.endellionquartet.com.

DE VAUGHN, Paulette; American singer (soprano); b. 8 Aug. 1951, California. *Education:* studied with Martial Singher at Santa Barbara, at Juilliard School and in Vienna. *Career:* debut as Elisabeth de Valois at Paris Opéra; appearances at National Theatre Prague from 1980, as Tosca, the Trovatore Leonora, Mimi, Amelia, Ballo in Maschera, Lady Macbeth, Turandot, Violetta and Abigaille; sang Tosca at Stockholm 1988 and in season 1989–90 appeared as Savonlinna, as Tosca at Graz, as Mozart's Electra at Mannheim, Manon Lescaut, Staatsoper Berlin, Elena in I Vespri Siciliani and Komische Oper Berlin, Dresden and Sofia; Saarbrucken as Aida, Salome, Senta, Elsa and Leonore in Fidelio; Sang Aida at Royal Opera Copenhagen, 1991, at the Montpellier Festival 1992 and Alexandria, Egypt, 1995; concerts and lieder recitals in Austria, Germany and Sweden. *Current Management:* c/o Atelier Musicale, Via Caselle 76, San Lazzaro di Savena 40068, Italy. *Telephone:* (051) 19984444. *Fax:* (051) 19984420. *E-mail:* info@ateliermusicale .com. *Website:* www.ateliermusicale.com.

DE VOL, Luana; American singer (soprano); b. 30 Nov. 1942, St Bruno, San Francisco, CA. *Education:* San Diego University, studied with Vera Rozsa in London and with Jess Thomas. *Career:* debut in San Francisco 1983, as Ariadne auf Naxos; European debut Stuttgart 1983, as Leonore in Fidelio; sang the Forza Leonora at Seattle 1983 and appeared at Aachen and Amsterdam; Member of Mannheim Opera from 1986; appearances in Berlin, Staatsoper and Deutsche Oper from 1986 as Euryanthe, Agathe, Rezia in Oberon, Leonore and Senta; Staatsoper, Hamburg 1989, as Irene in Rienzi, Zürich and Vienna 1989 as Ellen Orford in Peter Grimes and Eva in Schreker's Irrelohe; Further engagements in Bologna, Dortmund, Gelsenkirchen and Frankfurt and at Bregenz and Orange Festivals; Sang Amelia in Ballo in Maschera at Stuttgart and Leonore in a concert performances at Festival Hall 1990; Gutrune in Götterdämmerung concert in Rome and Elsa in Lohengrin at Taormina, both conducted by Sinopoli 1991; Sang Marina in Dvořák's Dimitrji at Munich, Leonore at Zürich and Andromache in Reimann's Troades at Frankfurt, 1992; Sang Strauss's Empress at the Paris Châtelet. 1994; Season 1995-96 as Maria in Friedenstag, Amelia (Ballo) and Wagner's Elsa and Isolde at Dresden; Brunswick 1996 and Ghent 1998 as Isolde; Season 2001–02 as the Dyer's Wife in Die Frau ohne Schatten, at Dresden, and Isolde at Antwerp; Other roles include Donna Anna, Isolde, Elisabeth de Valois and Elisabeth in Tannhäuser, Brünnhilde and the Marschallin; Concert reperoire includes the Britten War Requiem and Shostakovich's 14th Symphony. *Recordings include:* Eva in Schreker's Irrelohe. *Current Management:* Hilbert Artists Management, Maximilianstrasse 22, 80539 Munich, Germany. *Telephone:* (89) 2907470. *Fax:* (89) 29074790. *E-mail:* agentur@hilbert.de. *Website:* www.hilbert.de; www .operdiva.com.

DE VRIES, Han Samuel; Dutch oboist; b. 31 Aug. 1941. *Education:* studied in Amsterdam. *Career:* soloist with the Concertgebouw Orchestra and Netherlands Chamber Orchestra; founder mem., Netherlands Wind Ensemble 1960; Danzi Wind Quintet from 1973; concerto soloist and chamber music collaborations throughout Europe, America and the Far East; premiered Bruno Maderna's Third Concerto, and works by Morton Feldman and Louis Andriessen; Lecturer at Amsterdam Conservatory from 1964. *Recordings include:* albums of music by Bach, Mozart and Telemann. *Honours:* Officer Order of Orange Nassau; two Edison Awards for recordings. *Address:* c/o Sweelinck Conservatorium, Van Baerlesstraat 27, 1071 AN Amsterdam (office); Vondelstr. 77, 1054 GL Amsterdam, Netherlands (home). *Telephone:* 206185492 (home). *E-mail:* handevries@hetnet.nl (home). *Website:* www .oboeclassics.com.

DE VRIES, Klaas; Dutch composer; b. 15 July 1944, Terneuzen. *Education:* Rotterdam Conservatory with Otto Ketting, Stuttgart Hochschule für Musik. *Career:* Lecturer at Rotterdam Conservatory, 1979–; Guest Composer at Tanglewood, 1995. *Compositions:* Refrains, for two pianos and orchestra, 1970; Difficulties, for ensemble, 1977; Movements, for 15 instruments, 1979; Areas, for mixed chorus, wind ensemble and orchestra, 1980; Discantus, for orchestra, 1982; Eréndira, opera, 1984; Phrases, for soprano, mixed chorus, wind ensemble and orchestra, 1986; Piano sonata, 1987; Diafonia, la creación for two female voices and ensemble, 1988; Songs and Dances I–IV, for violin and piano, 1989; Eclipse, for ensemble, 1991; De Profundis. for wind orchestra, 1991; String Quartet, 1994; A King, Riding, Scenic oratorio after The Waves by Virginia Woolf, 1996. *Honours:* Mathijs Vermeulen Prize, 1983.

DE WAART, Edo; Dutch conductor; *Music Director, Royal Flemish Philharmonic Orchestra*; b. 1 June 1941, Amsterdam; s. of M. de Waart and J. Rose; one s. one d. *Education:* Amsterdam Music Lyceum with Haakon Stotijn, Hilversum with Franco Ferrara. *Career:* Co-Prin. Oboe, Amsterdam Philharmonic 1961, Concertgebouw Orchestra 1963; Asst Conductor, New York Philharmonic 1965–66, Concertgebouw Orchestra, Amsterdam 1966; Musical Dir Netherlands Wind Ensemble 1966; Conductor Rotterdam Philharmonic 1967, Musical Dir and Prin. Conductor 1973–79; Prin. Guest Conductor San Francisco Symphony Orchestra 1975–77, Music Dir 1977–85; Music Dir Minnesota Orchestra 1986–95; Artistic Dir Nederlandse Omroep Stichting (Dutch radio org.); Chief Conductor Netherlands Radio Philharmonic Orchestra 1989–; Prin. Guest Conductor Santa Fe Opera 1991–92; Artistic Dir and Chief Conductor Sydney Symphony Orchestra 1993–2003; Artistic Dir and Chief Conductor Hong Kong Philharmonic Orchestra 2004–12; Chief Conductor Santa Fe Opera 2007–09; Music Dir Milwaukee Symphony Orchestra 2009–; Artistic Partner, St Paul Chamber Orchestra 2010–; Music Dir Royal Flemish Philharmonic Orchestra 2012–; guest conductor with leading orchestras at venues in USA and Europe and at festivals including Spoleto, Bayreuth and Holland. *Honours:* First Prize, Dimitri Mitropoulos Competition, New York 1964; Hon. AO 2005. *Current Management:* Harrison Parrott, 5–6 Albion Court, London, W6 0QT, England. *Telephone:* (20) 7229-9166. *Fax:* (20) 7221-5042. *E-mail:* info@harrisonparrott.com. *Website:* www .harrisonparrott.com. *Address:* deFilharmonie (Royal Flemish Philharmonic), Filharmonisch Huis, Braziliëstraat 15, 2000 Antwerp, Belgium (office). *Telephone:* 32135420 (office). *Fax:* 32135400 (office). *E-mail:* info@ defilharmonie.be (office). *Website:* www.defilharmonie.be (office).

DEÁK, Csaba; Swedish composer and teacher; b. 16 April 1932, Budapest, Hungary. *Education:* Bela Bartók Conservatory, Budapest, Franz Liszt Acad. of Music, Budapest with Ferenc Farkas, studied with Hilding Rosenberg, Sweden, Ingesund School of Music, Arvika, Stockholm Musikhögskolan. *Career:* teacher, Univ. Coll. of Dance, Stockholm 1969–97, Univ. of Göteborg 1971–74. *Compositions include:* Jubilemus Salvatori chamber cantata 1958, two string quartets 1959, 1967, Duo Suite for flute and clarinet 1960, The Fathers chamber opera 1968, 121 for winds, percussion, double bass 1969, Etude on Spring 1970, Trio for flute, cello, piano 1971, Andante och Rondo for wind quintet 1973, Lucie's Ascent into Heaven astrophonic minimelodrama 1973, Verbunk for brass sextet 1976, Bye-bye, Earth, A Play About Death 1976–77, Hungarian Dances for wind quintet 1977, Octet for wind quintet and string trio 1977, Eden for symphonic band 1978, The Piper's Wedding for wind quintet and symphonic band 1979, Herykon for brass quintet 1981, Vivax for symphony orchestra 1982, Five Short Pieces for symphonic band 1983, Farina Pagus for symphonic band 1984, Massallians for trumpet, trombone, brass ensemble and percussion 1985, Saxophone Quartet 1986, Quintet for alto saxophone and string quartet 1988, Concerto Maeutro for trumpet, euphonium, marimba and symphonic band 1989, Quartet for tubas 1990, Ad Nordiam Hungarica for chamber ensemble 1991, Concerto for clarinet and wind orchestra 1992, Anémones de Felix for symphonic band 1993, Magie Noire for clarinet and string quartet 1993, Novem for saxophone quartet and brass quintet 1994, Memento Mare for mixed choir and wind orchestra 1995, Symphony for wind orchestra 1995, Gloria for mixed choir 1996, Octet for saxophone quartet and string quartet 1998, Mayinka for symphony orchestra 1999, Brassonance for brass band 2000, Symphony No. 2 for wind orchestra 2001, Recollection for wind ensemble 2003, Concerto for flute and string orchestra 2004, Trio Jubilee for flute, clarinet, cello 2006, Divertimento for wind ensemble 2007, Fabula for flute and string quartet 2008, Vindpuszt all'ungherese for saxophone quartet 2008, also piano pieces, pieces for chorus, songs. *Honours:* Atterberg Music Prize 1992, Gustavus Adolphus Fine Art Award 1989. *Address:* Döbelnsgatan 56, 113 52 Stockholm, Sweden (home). *Telephone:* (8) 16-02-17 (home). *Fax:* (8) 16-02-17 (home). *E-mail:* csaba.deak@ comhem.se.

DEAN, Brett; Australian composer and violist; b. 23 Oct. 1961, Brisbane, Qld; m. Heather Betts; two d. *Education:* Queensland Conservatorium of Music, Hochschule der Künste, Berlin. *Career:* debut as violist: Hindemith Concerto with Melbourne Symphony Orchestra (ABC Concerto Competition) 1981; as composer, debut with Ariel's Music with Queensland Symphony Orchestra 1995; as violist, mem. Berlin Philharmonic Orchestra 1985–2000, soloist under Abbado 1995–2000; chamber music at major European festivals including Bath, Aldeburgh and Salzburg; as composer debut with One of a Kind, music for Jiri Kylian Ballet 1998; Artistic Dir, Australian Nat. Acad. of Music 2007–10; Artist-in-Residence, Swedish Chamber Orchestra 2010–11. *Compositions include:* Ariel's Music 1995, Voices of Angels, written for Imogen Cooper 1996, 12 Angry Men, for the 12 cellos of Berlin Philharmonic Orchestra 1996, Intimate Decisions 1996, Carlo, for the Australian Chamber Orchestra 1997, Beggars and Angels, for Melbourne Symphony Orchestra 1999, Pastoral Symphony 2001, Viola Concerto 2004, Wolf Lieder 2007, The Lost Art of Letter Writing (Grawemeyer Award for Music Composition 2009) 2007, Vexations and Devotions 2007, Bliss (opera) 2009, Epitaphs 2010. *Recordings:* Hindemith: Viola d'Amore Concerto, with Frankfurt Radio Symphony Orchestra and Werner Andreas Albert; Frankel: Viola Concerto, with Albert; Brahms and Bruckner: String Quintets, with Brandis Quartet; Dean: Music for 'One of a Kind', with Pieter Wispelwey, cello. *Honours:* first prize ABC Concerto Competition 1981, Queensland Conservatorium Medal for Excellence 1982, selected work at Unesco International Rostrum of Composers, Paris 1999. *Current Management:* Intermusica Artists Management Ltd, 36 Graham Street, Crystal Wharf, London, N1 8GJ, England. *Telephone:* (20) 7608-9900. *Fax:* (20) 7490-3263. *E-mail:* mail@intermusica.co.uk. *Website:* www.intermusica.co.uk.

DEAN, Robert, BMus, ARCM; British conductor, vocal coach and professor of singing; *Professor of Singing, Guildhall School of Music and Drama*; b. 4 Sept.

1954, Surrey, England. *Education:* Durham Univ., Royal Coll. of Music, Royal Northern Coll. of Music, Nat. Opera Studio. *Career:* debut as baritone, as Fiorello in Il Barbiere di Siviglia, Glyndebourne Festival 1979; debut as conductor, Batignano Festival, Leonora 1987; appearances with Covent Garden, ENO, Glyndebourne Festival and Touring, Scottish Opera, Opera North, WNO 1979–87; Scottish Opera 1988; Staff Conductor, Head of Music, Philharmonia Chorus, London 1990–93; Artistic Dir 1988–2007; freelance, with Canadian debut at Edmonton Opera 1993; US debut, Kentucky Opera 1995; Vocal Consultant, Bristol Choral Soc.; currently Prof. of Singing, Guildhall School of Music and Drama. *Recordings:* Coronation Anthems, Rossini Barbiere di Siviglia from Glyndebourne (video), Eustacio Filumena (video). *Current Management:* Musichall Ltd, Oast House, Crouch's Farm, Hollow Lane, East Hoathly, BN8 6QX, England. *E-mail:* info@musichall.uk .com. *Website:* www.musichall.uk.com.

DEAN, Roger Thornton, BA, MA, PhD, DSc; British composer and double bassist; b. 6 Sept. 1948, Manchester, England. *Education:* Univ. of Cambridge, Brunel Univ. *Career:* Prof., Brunel Univ. 1984–88, Univ. of Sydney 1988–. *Compositions include:* Destructures for trumpet and large ensemble 1979, Breaking Worlds for violin, clarinet and double bass 1980, Heteronomy 1–4 for ensemble 1982, BA and BA for brass quintet 1985, Timestrain for clarinet and piano 1989, Reel Choice for ensemble 1989, Time Dance Peace for dancers and eight instruments 1991, It Gets Complicated for speaking pianist 1992, Poet Without Language for voices and electronics 1992, Nuaghic Echoes for voice and electronics 1993, Elektra Pulses for string quartet and tape 1993, Three Bagatelles for piano 1994, Sonopetal for orchestra 1995. *Honours:* Arts Council of Great Britain Development Fellowships.

DEAN, Stafford Roderick; British singer (bass); b. 20 June 1937, Surrey; s. of Eric E. Dean and Vera S. Bathurst; m. 1st Carolyn J. Lambourne 1963; four s.; m. 2nd Anne E. Howells 1981; one s. one d. *Education:* Epsom Coll., Royal Coll. of Music and privately with Howell Glynne and Otakar Kraus. *Career:* Opera for All 1962–64; Glyndebourne Chorus 1963–64, Prin. debut as Lictor in L'Incoronazione di Poppea 1963; under contract to Sadler's Wells Opera/ English Nat. Opera 1964–70; Royal Opera House, Covent Garden 1969–, début as Masetto in Don Giovanni; int. début as Leporello in Don Giovanni, Stuttgart 1971; guest appearances with Metropolitan Opera, New York, Chicago Lyric, San Francisco, Berlin, Munich, Hamburg, Cologne, Frankfurt, Vienna, Paris, Turin operas etc.; specializes in Mozart bass repertoire; bass soloist in world premiere of Penderecki Requiem, Stuttgart 1984; concert appearances in choral works by Beethoven, Shostakovich, Verdi.

DEAN, Timothy; British conductor; b. 1956, England. *Education:* Reading University, Royal College of Music. *Career:* has worked with Opera North, the Buxton Festival Opera and the Royal Opera House, Covent Garden; Kent Opera, 1983–90, conducting Così fan tutte, Agrippina, The Magic Flute, La Traviata, Carmen, Le Comte Ory and Don Giovanni on the company's visit to the Singapore Festival; Conducted Martin's Le Vin Herbé for the London Music Theatre Group and the British premiere of Legrenzi's Guistino for the Chichester Festival; Vivaldi's Juditha Triumphans at the Camden Festival; Acis and Galatea for the English Bach Festival in Italy; Music Director of British Youth Opera, conducting Don Giovanni and The Marriage of Figaro in London and on tour; Music Director of the London Bach Society from 1988, appearing with them at Chichester and City of London festivals and on the South Bank; Season 1990–91, Assistant Music Director of New D'Oyly Carte Opera Company (conducting in the United Kingdom and USA); English National Opera debut, 1991, with Bluebeard's Castle and Oedipus Rex; Scottish Opera debut, 1991, with Barber of Seville; Music Director of The Opera Company, Tunbridge Wells, 1991–94; Also with British Youth Opera, conducting Così fan tutte (1998), Eugene Onegin, La Bohème, Carmen and La Gazza Ladra; In 1994 conducted Kent Opera in The Prodigal Son at major British festivals and for the BBC; Head of Opera at the Royal Scottish Academy of Music and Drama, Glasgow 1994– (L'Assedio di Calais by Donizetti, 1998); conducted British Youth Opera in Albert Herring, 1996; Artistic Dir British Youth Opera 2001–06. *Telephone:* (141) 270-8318. *Fax:* (141) 270-8352. *E-mail:* t.dean@rsamd.co.uk.

DEATHRIDGE, John, MA, DPhil, FRCO; British musicologist; *King Edward Professor of Music, King's College London*; b. 21 Oct. 1944, Birmingham, England; s. of Iris and Leslie Deathridge; m. Victoria Cooper; one d. *Education:* Univ. of Oxford with Egon Wellesz and Frederic Sternfeld. *Career:* conductor, organist and broadcaster in Germany 1970s; Fellow King's Coll., Cambridge 1983–96; Visiting Prof., Princeton Univ., USA 1990–91, Univ. of Chicago 1992; King Edward Prof. of Music, King's Coll. London 1996–; Pres. Royal Musical Assen 2005–; corresponding mem. American Musicological Soc. 2002–. *Publications:* Study of Wagner's Sketches for Rienzi 1977, New Grove Wagner (with Carl Dahlhaus) 1984, Verzeichnis der musikalischen Werke Richard Wagners und ihrer Quellen (with Martin Geck and Egon Voss) 1986, The Wagner Handbook: Essays on Wagner's Life and Work (ed.) 1992, Family Letters of Richard Wagner (ed.) 1991, Critical Edition of Wagner's Lohengrin (three vols) 1996–2000, Documents and Texts of Wagner's Lohengrin 2003, The Invention of German Music c. 1800 2006, Wagner: Beyond Good and Evil 2009; contrib. to Cambridge Opera Journal, New German Critique, TLS; programme notes for Covent Garden, Lohengrin and Der Freischütz 1997–98. *Address:* King's College London, School of Humanities, Department of Music, Strand, London, WC2R 2LS, England (office). *Telephone:* (20) 7848-2793 (office). *Fax:* (20) 7848-2326 (office). *E-mail:* john.deathridge@kcl.ac.uk (office). *Website:* www.kcl.ac.uk (office).

DEBUS, Johannes, BMus; German conductor; *Music Director, Canadian Opera Company*; b. 1974, Speyer. *Education:* Hamburg Conservatory. *Career:* made professional debut conducting Mozart's Die Entführung aus dem Serail, Minden 1996; Répétiteur, Asst Conductor, then Resident Conductor, Frankfurt Opera 1998–2008; Music Dir, Canadian Opera Co. 2009–; Guest Conductor Banff Festival Orchestra 2013; made British debut conducting Philip Glass' Satyagraha, ENO 2007; has also conducted at Bavarian State Opera, Opéra National de Lyon, RSO Stuttgart, Orchestra della RAI Torino, Oper Köln, Bochumer Symphoniker, Staatskapelle Halle, Volksoper, Vienna, Deutsche Oper am Rhein Düsseldorf, Deutsche Oper Berlin, Venice Biennale, Schwetzinger Festspiele, Festival d'Automne Paris, Lincoln Center Festival, Ruhrtriennale, Bergen Festival. *Address:* Canadian Opera Company, 227 Front Street East, Toronto, Ont. M5A 1E8, USA (office). *Telephone:* (416) 363-6671 (office). *Fax:* (416) 363-5584 (office). *E-mail:* info@coc.ca (office). *Website:* www.coc.ca (office).

DECKER, Richard E., BMus, MMus; American singer (tenor); b. 27 April 1958, Montgomery, Pa; s. of Gayle L. Decker and Shirley Wenrick; m. Sabine Lütz; two s. *Education:* Susquehanna Univ., Manhattan School of Music (masterclasses with Judith Raskin, Dan Merriman and Thomas Stewart), Zurich Opera Studio. *Career:* sang with Zurich Opera from 1985; roles include Alwa in Lulu in 14 productions in Europa, USA and S America; has sung Tristan in 92 performances in Frankfurt, Napoli, Rome, Mannheim, Düsseldorf, Tiroler Festspiele, Royal Opera Stockholm, Tokyo, Seoul and Cologne, Parsifal in Venice, Dessau, Naples, Düsseldorf and Enschede; debut as Otello, San Francisco Opera 2002; Samson, Royal Opera, Stockholm; Tannhäuser, Nürnberg State Theater 2009; guest appearances as Ferrando in Così fan tutte in Saarbrucken, the Aix and Macerata Festivals, in Zimmermann's Soldaten at Vienna Staatsoper; has also made frequent concert appearances in Europa and Asia. *Recordings:* Parsifal 2006, Tristan 2008, Götterdämmerung 2010. *Current Management:* c/o Opera-Connection Alste & Mödersheim, Leibnizstrasse 94, 10625 Berlin, Germany. *Telephone:* (30) 31996688. *Fax:* (30) 31809739. *E-mail:* info@opera-connection.com. *Website:* opera-connection.com. *E-mail:* richard@richard-decker.com (office). *Website:* www.richard-decker.com.

DECKERT, Hans Erik, DipMus; Danish cellist and conductor; b. 11 Jan. 1927, Hamburg, Germany. *Education:* Royal Danish Conservatory of Music, Copenhagen, studied with Pablo Casals, Maurice Gendron, Igor Markevitch and Sergiu Celibidache. *Career:* solo cello debut, Royal Conservatory of Music, Copenhagen 1952; cellist, Royal Chapel, Denmark; Docent in Cello, Conducting and Chamber Music, Ingesunds Acad. of Music, Sweden; Docent in Cello and Chamber Music, Esbjerg Acad. of Music, Denmark; Docent in Cello and Conducting, Jutland Acad. of Music, Århus; Founder Cello Acad. (12-part cello ensemble of young European musicians); lectures and gives masterclasses throughout Europe, USA, Japan, S Africa, S America; frequent radio broadcasts as cellist and conductor in Germany and Denmark; mem. ESTA (Danish section) (Founder and Hon. Pres. 1981), Danish Soloists' Union. *Compositions:* Canzona Per Dodici Violoncelli and numerous compositions for choir. *Publication:* Music and Human Beings (articles and essays) 2006. *Address:* Norsmindevej 170, 8340 Malling, Denmark (home). *Telephone:* 86-93-15-85 (home). *E-mail:* hed1155@hotmail.com. *Website:* www.hedmusic.net.

DECOUST, Michel; French composer; b. 19 Nov. 1936, Paris; m. Irene Jarsky 1969, one d. *Education:* Paris Conservatory with Louis Fourestier, Olivier Messiaen, Darius Milhaud, studied with Stockhausen and Pousseur in Cologne, with Boulez in Basle. *Career:* Prof. of Composition, Dartington Coll. summer school, England 1967–69; set up regional French orchestra, Pays de la Loire 1967–70; in charge of musical activities, Maisons de la Culture, Rennes and Nevers 1970–72; founder and Dir, Pantin Conservatory 1972–76; Head Education Dept, IRCAM 1976–79; Chief Inspector for Musical Research, Ministry of Culture and Communications 1979–; music performed at various festivals, Europe, Israel, New York, also broadcast on radio, Italy, Germany, Spain, England, Greece, Switzerland, Poland, USA; Pres., ISCM France. *Compositions:* orchestral, small ensemble, wind band and vocal works, instrumental solos and duos, electro-acoustic music, etc.; Si et Si Seulement for orchestra 1972, L'Application des lectrices aux champs for soprano and orchestra 1977, Eole for flute quartet 1985, Sept chansons erotiques (settings of poems) for soprano and piano 1986, Bleus (text Blaise Cendrars) for soprano and piano 1986, De la gravitation suspendue des memoires for orchestra 1986, Je qui d'autre for three voices and ensemble 1987, Sinfonietta for ten instruments 1983, Sonnet for 15 instruments 1985, One Plus One Equals Four for piano and percussion 1988, Spectre for wind band 1978, Interphone for magnetic tape, Les Galeries de Pierre for alto solo 1984, Le Cygne for flute solo 1982, Lierre for 12 cordes 1986, Cafe-theatre for chant-piano 1985, Violin Concerto 1990, Ligne for clarinet and string quartet 1992, Cent Phrases pour Eventail for six voices and ensemble 1996. *Recordings include:* Releve d'Esquisse, Le Cygne, sinfonietta. *Publication:* Cahiers Perspectives 1987.

DECSENYI, Janos; Hungarian composer; b. 24 March 1927, Budapest. *Education:* studied composition with Rezsö Sugar, Budapest Conservatory, Endre Szervanszky, Budapest Acad. of Music. *Career:* Hungarian Radio, Budapest 1952–92, latterly as Head, Dept of Serious Music and Dir Electronic Music Studio; script ed., Dept of Serious Music 1992–. *Compositions:* stage includes: An Absurd Story (ballet) 1962; orchestral: Divertimento for harpsichord and chamber orchestra 1959, Csontvary Pictures 1967, Melodiae Hominis for chamber orchestra 1969, Thoughts by Day, by Night 1971, Commentaries on Marcus Aurelius for 16 solo strings 1973, Double for chamber orchestra 1974, Variations for piano and orchestra 1976, Concerto Boemo 1976, Concerto Grosso for chamber orchestra 1978, Who Understands the Speech of Crickets?, for chamber orchestra and tape 1983, Cello Concerto 1984, The Third One for 15 solo strings 1985, I Symphony 1986, II Symphony 1993, Keepsake Album, audiovisual oratorio for soprano, bass, chamber choir, chamber ensemble, electronic and projected images 1998, Blind Texts (cantata) 2004, III Symphony 'The Twentythird Letter' for bass solo and mixed choir, to text of 'Book of Jecira' 2006; vocal: Love for soprano and orchestra 1957, Metamorfosi for soprano and piano 1964, Shakespeare Monologues for bass and piano 1968, The Plays of Thought (cantata for soprano and chamber orchestra) 1972, Roads, etudes for soprano and piano 1979, Twelfth Symphony of S.W. for soprano and percussion 1980, 2 Symphonies 1988, 1993, Hyperions Schicksalslied for tenor solo and electronics, to text of poem by F. Hölderlin 2007; chamber: String Trio 1955; Sonatina Pastorale for flute and piano 1962, String Quartet No. 1 1978, String Quartet No. 2 2003, Old Hungarian Texts for soprano, bass and chamber ensemble 1992, Frauengesänge, on German Poems 1998, The Tiger, the Donkey and the Lemmings 1998, Trio divertimento The Three Magi for two clarinets and bassoon 2007; choral music: Incidental music for theatre, films and radio, Electronic: Stones 1987, Prospero's Island 1989, Birds of the Cathedral 1991, Book of Verses, five electro-acoustic sound poems; pedagogical pieces, Farewell to a Far-Away Century (oratorio) 2001, Des Dichters R M Rilke Begegnung mit dem Tod (song cycle) 2001, From the Distance to the Nowadays – cantata to lines from the poems of E. Ady 2003, Four Preludes to Saint-Exupéry, with choir 2003, Homecoming 2005, Concert – from the electro-acoustic cycle 'Narratives' 2006. *Recordings:* several compositions recorded. *Honours:* Merited Artist (Hungary) Bartók-Pásztory Prize 1999. *Address:* Wesselenyi u.65, 1077 Budapest, Hungary (home).

DĚD, Jan; Czech composer; b. 22 June 1936, Plzeň. *Education:* Plzeň Conservatory. *Career:* mem., Music Centre of West Bohemia, Plzeň, Czech Music Society, Prague. *Compositions:* Four songs on the words of folk poetry, chorus, op 1, 1962; Wistful Variations, small ballet for 5 dancers, 5 musicians and reciter, op 38; Short Czech Mass for combined chorus and symphonic orchestra, op 42; Sonatine for Solo Viola, op 43; Great Czech-Latin Mass to Our Lady for combined chorus, soloists, symphonic orchestra and organ, op 44, 1992; Concerto of a serenade in E flat for clarinet in B and piano, op 51, 1996; Christmas Songs for combined chorus and chamber orchestra, op 60, 2002. *Address:* Zelenohorská 2, 32600 Plzeň, Czech Republic. *E-mail:* j.ded@cbox.cz.

DEDEN, Otto; Dutch composer, conductor, organist and choirmaster; b. 19 Nov. 1925, Amsterdam; m. S.A.M. van Dijk, four c. *Education:* studied with Henk Badings. *Career:* appearances in church services on radio and television; choral concerts with various male, female and mixed choirs. *Compositions:* 29 masses, 50 motets, Te Deum, hymns, ballads, oratorios, arrangements of folk songs (commissions), Dirge for soprano with organ 1993, two ballads 1992, Mysteria, Kain, four cantatas for mixed choir and orchestra and solo, Magnificat for mixed choir, organ, flute and alto solo, several cantatas for choir and orchestra preludes and fugues for great organ, Requiem for a Killed Soldier. *Recordings:* Ballade v.d. Bezemsteel (male voices), Maastricht, 1958; Raamconcerto, 1973; Otto Deden Musica Collecta (collection of works). *Honours:* Royal Order of Knighthood of Orange-Nassau 1982, Order of Knighthood of Gregorius Magnus, Vatican, Medal of Honour of the City of Dordrecht, The Netherlands.

DEERING, Richard, GTCL, LRAM, ARCM, PGCA, FTCL; British pianist and adjudicator; b. 15 July 1947, London, England; m. Emma Budgen; four c. *Education:* Trinity Coll. of Music, London. *Career:* debut at Wigmore Hall, London 1973, piano recitals and broadcasts in over 90 countries 1975–; Founder-mem. Piano 40 ensemble (eight hands at two pianos); premieres of several works, with many composers writing and dedicating works to him; examiner worldwide for Trinity Coll., London 1979–; Chair. Croydon Performing Arts Festival 2013–15; piano music reviewer, Music Teacher magazine; mem. Inc. Soc. of Musicians, Adjudicators' Council of British and Int. Fed. of Festivals (Vice-Chair. 2000–02, Fellow 2012). *Recordings include:* Beatles Concerto with Tokyo Symphony Orchestra, English Piano Music, Mediterranean Inspired (Music of Charles Camilleri), Piano 40. *Publications include:* ed. of Music Sales 'Composer' series and 'Century of Piano Music' series; contrib. to Classical Music magazine. *Honours:* Royal Philharmonic Soc. Award for distinguished service to British music 1981, Chair.'s Award for services to Trinity Coll., London 2006. *Address:* 55 Dalmally Road, Croydon, CR0 6LW, England (home). *Telephone:* (20) 8656-6222 (home). *E-mail:* rj .deering@btinternet.com. *Website:* www.impulse-music.co.uk/deering.htm (home).

DEGOUT, Stéphane; French singer (baritone); b. 1975. *Education:* Conservatoire Nat. Supérieur de Musique de Lyon. *Career:* fmr mem. Atelier Lyrique de l'Opéra de Lyon; debut as Papageno at Festival d'Aix en Provence 1999; has appeared at Opéra de Paris (La Bohème, Die Zauberflöte, Ariadne auf Naxos, Iphigénie en Tauride, Nozze di Figaro, Die Tote Stadt), Berlin Staatsoper (Orfeo), Théâtre Royal de la Monnaie (Orfeo, Pelléas et Mélisande, Così fan tutte), Theater an der Wien (Orfeo, Pelléas et Mélisande), Metropolitan Opera, New York (Roméo et Juliette, Die Zauberflöte, Pelléas et Mélisande, Le Comte Ory), Royal Opera House, Covent Garden (debut, La Cenerentola 2007) and Salzburg and Glyndebourne Festivals; concerts and recitals include New York recital debut at Lincoln Center 2004, Théâtre Royal de la Monnaie, Wigmore Hall, London and Concertgebouw Amsterdam. *Recordings include:* Brahms Ein Deutsches Requiem, Fauré Requiem, Werther, Così fan tutte,

Pelléas et Mélisande and La Bohème; solo: Mélodies 2011. *Honours:* Chevalier, Ordre des Arts et des Lettres 2012; 2nd Prize, Plácido Domingo/ Operalia Competition 2002, Prix Gabriel Dussurget, Festival d'Aix en Provence 2007, Prix Victoire for Lyrical Artist of the Year 2012. *Current Management:* c/o Peter Wiggins, IMG Artists, 31–33 rue du Temple, 75004 Paris, France. *Telephone:* 1-44-31-00-10. *E-mail:* pwiggins@imgartists.com. *Website:* www.imgartists.com.

DEKANY, Bela; British violinist; b. 22 April 1928, Budapest, Hungary; m. Dorothy Browning 1961; one s. one d. *Education:* Franz Liszt Acad., Budapest with Prof. Weiner, Acad. of Music, Vienna, Austria with Prof. E. Morawec. *Career:* debut in Budapest 1947; has given recitals and broadcast performances; soloist with orchestras in Hungary, Austria, Switzerland, Australia and the UK; formed Dekany String Quartet, The Netherlands 1960–68; leader, BBC Symphony Orchestra, London 1969–92. *Recordings:* Haydn String Quartets with Dekany String Quartet. *Address:* 68 Woodside Avenue, London, N6 4ST, England (home).

DEKLEVA, Igor, PhD; Slovenian pianist, composer and academic; *Professor of Piano and Piano Duet, Academy of Music, Ljubljana;* b. 30 Dec. 1933, Ljubljana; m. Alenka Dekleva; two s. *Education:* Acad. of Music, Ljubljana, Musical Acad., Munich, studied in Siena, Salzburg. *Career:* concerts, recitals, performances with orchestras in Slovenia and abroad, with repertoire including baroque, romantic and contemporary works; frequent appearances as piano duo with Alenka Dekleva, including first appearance at Opatija Tribune 1967; several concert tours with violinist Michael Grube; directed master-classes in piano in several countries; author, leader and performer, two TV series about piano masterpieces throughout history, and Slovene piano works; Prof. of Piano and Piano Duet, Acad. of Music, Ljubljana 1998–; mem. Asscn of Musical Artists (Vice-Pres.), Kiwanis Int., European Piano Teachers' Asscn of Slovenia (Pres.), Soc. of Composers and Authors. *Compositions include:* many works for piano, chamber orchestra and choirs including Concertino for piano and orchestra 2012. *Recordings include:* some 30 albums. *Publications include:* Slovene National Piano School (eight vols), several piano and piano four-hands compositions, chamber music, orchestral and choral works, Living with Music – A Portrait of Pianist, Pedagogue and Composer Igor Dekleva (auto-biog.) 2006. *Honours:* numerous hon. memberships and fellowships, including Fellowship for Distinguished Service to Music, Madras Philharmonic and Choral Soc. 1984; Dr hc (World Univ. Arizona) 1987; Betetto Prize 1980, Grand Amb. of Int. Achievement 1990, Award of Excellence, Lisbon 2001, Capital City of Ljubljana Award 2004, Lifetime Achievement Award in Education, Govt of Slovenia 2012, Prix Special, Composers Competition, Luxemburg 2013. *Address:* Academy of Music, Stari trg 34, Ljubljana 1000 (office); Hruševo 77, 1356 Dobrova, Slovenia (home). *Telephone:* (1) 3649075 (home). *E-mail:* alenka.dekleva@gmail.com. *Website:* www.drustvo-dss.si; www.sigic.si.

DEL AGUILA, Miguel; Uruguayan/American composer; b. 15 Sept. 1957, Montevideo; s. of Miguel del Aguila and Iris Llordal. *Education:* San Francisco Conservatory of Music, Hochschule für Musik and Vienna Konservatorium, Austria. *Career:* family forced to leave Uruguay 1978; studied in San Francisco then moved to Vienna, Austria; Messages premiered at Musikvereinsaal, Vienna 1983, followed by performances at Konzerthaus and Bösendorfer Hall; piano works performed at New York's Carnegie Recital Hall 1988; works later performed at New York's Lincoln Center, London's Royal Opera House, and in Moscow, Vienna, Zürich, Budapest, Prague, Tokyo, Rome and others; returned to live in Calif. 1992; Conductor, Ojai Camerata 1996–99; Founder-Dir West Coast composer's group Voices; Resident Composer, New York's Chautauqua Inst. Summer Festival 2000–04; Composer-in-Residence, New Mexico Symphony Orchestra 2005–07; works commissioned and regularly performed by more than 100 orchestras and hundreds of chamber ensembles and soloists worldwide. *Compositions include:* chamber music works: Untamed for piano trio, Submerged for harp, flute and violin, Boliviana for guitar and string quartet, Broken Rondo for English horn and piano, Charango Capriccioso for string quartet, piano four-hands, Clarinet Concerto for clarinet and piano, Clocks for piano and string quartet, Conga-Line in Hell for harp, 1 percussion, piano, violin, viola, cello and contrabass, Conga-Line in Hell for flute, clarinet, harp, piano, percussion and 8 cellos, Herbsttag (Autumn Day) for flute, bassoon, harp, Hexen (Witches) for bassoon and piano, Latin Love for wind quintet and piano, Life is a Dream for string quartet, Nostalgica for bassoon and string quartet, Pacific Serenade for clarinet (optional saxophone) and string quartet, Return for violin and piano, Salon Buenos Aires for flute, clarinet, violin, viola, cello and piano, Seduccion for violin and piano, Summer Song for oboe and piano, Sunset Song for bassoon and piano, Tango Trio for violin, cello and piano (optional clarinet, cello and piano), Wind Quintet No. 2 for flute, oboe, clarinet, horn and bassoon, Caribbean Bacchanal for harp, piano and percussion; works for orchestra: Concierto en Tango for cello and orchestra, Chautauquan Summer Overture for orchestra, Clarinet Concerto No. 2 for clarinet and orchestra, Conga for harp and piano, Return to Homeland for violin and orchestra, The Fall of Cuzco for orchestra, The Gian Guitar for orchestra, Time and Again Barelas Overture for orchestra, Time and Again Barelas Choral Suite for choir and orchestra, Time and Again Barelas Suite No. 2 for solo tenor, choir and orchestra, Toccata for large percussion, piano and strings, Violin Concerto for violin and orchestra, Broken Rondo for English horn and orchestra, Caribeña for orchestra for piano-timpani+2 and strings; works for solo piano: Caribbean Bacchanal for 2 pianos/8 hands, Conga-Line in Hell arranged for six pianos,

Four Hand Etude for piano four-hands, Half of Me for piano left hand only, Lieutenant Kije for two pianos four-hands arranged from Prokofiev's Music in a Bottle, Nocturne, Piano Concerto for piano and orchestra, Piano Sonata No. 2, Toccata, Vals Brutal; solo organ/harpsichord works: Bells with a Mission for solo organ, One of You for solo organ, Pictures from America for harpsichord, Toccata for harpsichord; vocal/choral/opera/stage works: Agnus Dei for medium-high voice and piano, Albuquerque for barbershop quartet, Ave Maria for treble chorus and piano (optional harp), Composer Missing (chamber opera for choir, SATB soloists), Cuauhtemoc (full-length opera for soloists, choir and orchestra), Cuauhtemoc Choral Suite for 3 soloists, choir, piano and percussion, Cuauhtemoc Songs for STB soloists and piano, From Darkness to Light for chamber choir, wind quartet, harpsichord, It Is So Cold Tonight for tenor (optional soprano and orchestra), Lacrymosa for medium-high voice and piano, Ophelia in Seville for soprano, tenor, flute, clarinet, trombone, 2 violins, viola and cello, Salva Me for choir a cappella, Time and Again Barelas (opera in two acts for alto, tenor and other soloists, chorus and orchestra), Time and Again Barelas Choral Suite for mixed chorus and orchestra, Time and Again Barelas Choral Suite No. 2 (same plus overture, solo tenor), Troubadours for mixed choir and optional piano. *Recordings:* works on 29 CDs, including 20th Century Dances and Improvisations for Piano 2000, -Line in Hell 2002, Life is a Dream: Music of the Americas 2004, Clocks: Piano Quintets of the Americas 2007, Border Crossings 2008; solo CDs: Music in a Bottle, Summer Song, Salon Buenos Aires. *Honours:* Kennedy Center Friedheim Award 1995, MTC Magnum Opus/Kathryn Gould Award 2008, Peter S. Reed Foundation Award 2008, Lancaster Symphony Composer of the Year Award 2009, awards by The Copland Foundation and Argosy Foundation for Contemporary Music. *Telephone:* (805) 445-9597. *Address:* c/o Peermusic Classical, 250 West 57th Street, Suite 820, New York, NY 10107, USA (office). *Telephone:* (212) 265-3910 (office). *E-mail:* miguel@migueldelaguila.com; m@migueldelaguila.com (office). *Website:* migueldelaguila.com.

DEL BIANCO, Tito (Sergio); Italian singer (dramatic tenor); b. 3 July 1932, Trieste; one s. one d. *Education:* studied with Augusta Rapetti Bassi in Trieste, with Renata Cotogni in Rome. *Career:* debut in New York in Stabat Mater by Rossini, dir Thomas Schippers 1965; in Italy as Otello by Verdi, 8th Festival of Two Worlds, Spoleto 1965; title role of Otello, Teatro Regio Parma 1966–71; Bayerische Staatsoper Munich 1973; May Festival Wiesbaden 1970; Festival Szeged, Hungary 1971; Festival Varna Bulgaria 1972; Maggio Musicale Florence 1980; sang Calaf in Turandot at Naples 1965, Bologna 1969, Parma Regio 1970; Pollione in Norma, Genoa 1967; Faone in Pacini's Saffo, Naples 1967; Radames in Aida at Naples 1968; Ismaele in Nabucco, Trieste 1969; Canio in Pagliacci, Parma Regio 1969; Festival Torre del Lago Puccini 1971; Dir of Studies Centre A. Rapetti Bassi, Trieste; Prof. of Music Acad., Conservatorio in Trieste; Dir, Augusta Rapetti Bassi Studies Centre. *Recordings include:* Rossini's Stabat Mater, Pacini's Saffo, Tito Del Bianco: Opera Arias 2000. *Publications:* A Festival for Giuseppe Verdi in Prima Pagina 1981, La Voce Cantata: Tecnica Vocale ed Espressione dell' Anima 1981, Il Canto e la Psiche 1990, L'Approccio al canto come Terapia 1991, Il Festival Verdiano a Parma 1999, La Forza del Destino e Altre Storie 1999, Verdi e i Segni dei Tempi 2000; contrib. to La Scuola di Canto di Augusta Rapetti Bassi 1988, L'Espressione del Canto Nella Lezione di Reynaldo Hahn 1993, La Parabola di Tristan und Isolde 1993, Misticismo in Musica: Bruckner, Schoenberg e Brahms 1994, Lo Strumento voce: Aspetti, Didattici e docimologici, in Capriccio di Strauss 1996. *Honours:* Commendatore of the Italian Repub. 1998; Gold Medal, Giuseppe Verdi Prize, Parma 1967, Medal, City of Trieste 2003. *Address:* Traude Freudlsperger, Eschenweg 8, Goldensteinau, 5061 Elsbethen, Austria (home).

DEL CARLO, John; American singer (bass-baritone); b. 21 Sept. 1951. *Career:* sang in The Love for Three Oranges at San Diego 1978, and appeared with Western Spring Opera 1980–81; European career from 1980, in Donizetti's Olivo e Pasquale at Barga; member of the Cologne Opera from 1987, and Rossini's Cambiale di Matrimonio at the 1987 Schwetzingen Festival; San Francisco Opera from 1982, as Alidoro in Cenerentola and Wagner's Kothner; sang Donner and Gunther in Ring cycles for Seattle Opera, 1984–92; other roles include the Wanderer in Siegfried (Cologne 1990), Mustafà, Don Alfonso, Dulcamara and Simon Boccanegra; sang Dulcamara at Santiago, 1996; sang Baron di Kelbar in Verdi's Un Giorno di Regno at the Festival Hall, London for the Royal Opera, 1999; sang Rossini's Bartolo at Chicago, 2001. *Recordings include:* La Gioconda, La Cenerentola, La Cambiale di Matrimonio (video). *Current Management:* Opus 3 Artists, 470 Park Avenue South, 9th Floor North, New York, NY 10016, USA. *Telephone:* (212) 584-7500. *Fax:* (646) 300-8200. *E-mail:* info@opus3artists.com. *Website:* www.opus3artists.com.

DEL MAR, Jonathan Rene, MA, ARCM; British conductor and musicologist; b. 7 Jan. 1951, London, England; m. Annabel Teh Gallop 1992; two s. *Education:* Christ Church, Oxford, Royal Coll. of Music, Teatro La Fenice, Venice, Accad. S. Cecilia, Rome. *Career:* debut, London Symphony Orchestra, Barbican 1984; conductor, performed with many British orchestras also throughout Europe; mem Dvořák Soc. *Publications:* Indicatore Anagrafico di Venezia 1996, New Bärenreiter Urtext Edition of Beethoven Symphonies 1–9 1996–2000, Beethoven Cello Sonatas 2004 and Cello Variations 2012, Beethoven String Quartets Op. 18–95 2007–08, Beethoven Violin Concerto 2009 and Violin Romances 2011, Beethoven Triple Concerto 2012, Elgar Cello Concerto 2005, Dvořák Cello Concerto 2011, Dvořák Symphony No. 7 2013,

Beethoven Piano Concertos 1–5 2013–15; contrib. to Tempo, BBC Music Magazine, Beethoven Journal, Das Orchester, Beethoven Forum, Early Music, Nineteenth-Century Music Review, The Strad. *Honours:* Imperial Tobacco Int. Conductors' Award 1978, prize, Nikolai Malko Competition 1980, prize, First Leeds Conductors' Competition 1984. *Address:* Oakwood, Crescent Lane, London, SW4 9QH, England (home). *Telephone:* (20) 7622-2000 (home). *Fax:* (20) 7622-4443 (home).

DEL MONACO, Giancarlo; Italian stage director; b. 27 Dec. 1943, Treviso. *Education:* studied in Lausanne. *Career:* debut in Siracusa 1964, with Samson and Delilah; Asst to Gunther Rennert, Wieland Wagner and Walter Felsenstein at Stuttgart 1965–68; personal asst to the Gen. Dir Vienna Staatsoper 1968–70; Principal Stage Dir, Ulm 1970–73; Intendant at Kassel 1980–82; Dir, Macerata Festival 1986–88; staged Les Huguenots at Montpellier 1990, and at Barcelona, Roberto Devereux, the first of a projected trilogy of Donizetti's Tudor Operas; L'Elisir d'amore at Helsinki 1991, followed by Metropolitan Opera debut with La Fanciulla del West; Intendant and Principal Producer at Bonn 1992–97; further guest engagements at Bayerische Staatsoper, Zürich Opera and Vienna Staatsoper; staged Montemezzi's L'Amore dei tre re at Kassel 1992 and Otello at Reggio Emilia; staged at the Metropolitan Madama Butterfly and Simon Boccanegra 1994–95; La Forza del Destino 1995–96; Verdi's Stiffelio 1997. *Honours:* Bundesverdienstkreuz first class 1987, Cavaliere Ufficiale della Repubblica 1987, Commendatore Dell'Ordine al Merito della Repubblica Italiana 1993, Chevalier, Ordre des Arts et des Lettres, France 1995, Cruzeiro del Sul, Brazil 1995.

DEL POZO, Rodrigo; Chilean singer (tenor); b. 1969. *Education:* studied with Nigel Rogers and David Mason, studied lute with Jakob Lindberg. *Career:* moved to England 1990; sang with most leading groups specializing in Baroque repertoire, including St James' Baroque Players, BBC Proms 1996; Concerto Palatino, Bruges; sang with The King's Consort in Purcell and Blow Anthems and Odes, Bratislava Cantans Festival; Purcell with Tafelmusik, Toronto; sang with Orchestra of the Age of Enlightenment, English Bach Festival Orchestra; Ensemble Baroque de Limoges; performed and recorded Mondonville Motets and Draghi, Mondonville Festival, Versailles; performed Rameau's Anacréon with Les Musiciens du Louvre, Cité de la Musique; sang Monteverdi Madrigals, BBC Proms, Royal Albert Hall, and on tour in USA; performed with Harp Consort, Wigmore Hall; Baroque opera performances have included Oslo Sommeropera and Boston Early Music Festival with Andrew Parrott; Pastore I, in Monteverdi's L'Orfeo, Beaune Festival and Festtage Alter Musik, Stuttgart, with Tragicomedia and Stephen Stubbs; Arcetro, in Peri's Euridice, Drottningholm Theatre and London Lufthansa Baroque Festival with Combattimento; solo roles in Indian Queen with King's Consort, Schwetzinger Festspiele; concerts and recordings across Europe with Gabrieli Consort; The King's Consort, BBC Prom; The Harp Consort, Teatro Lirico; Tragicomedia, Le Parlement de Musique; L'Ensemble Baroque de Limoges, Versailles and on tour in France; performed, Purcell Odes, Les Arts Florissants 1999; tour with King Arthur, Gabrieli Consort and King's Consort; currently Prof., Instituto de Música, Santiago. *Website:* www7.uc.cl/english/prospectus/html/music.html.

DEL PUERTO, David; Spanish composer, musician (guitar) and teacher (composition, analysis); b. 30 April 1964, Madrid; m. Karin Anita Burk 1991; one s. *Education:* studied in Madrid with Alberto Potin (guitar), Jesus Maria Corral (harmony), Francisco Guerrero (composition), Luis de Pablo (composition). *Career:* major works in Almeida Festival, London 1985, Ensemble Intercontemporain Season, Paris 1989, Geneva Summer Festival 1989, Alicante Festival 1991, 1996, Ars Musica Festival, Brussels 1992, 1993, 1996, Gaudeamus Week, Amsterdam 1993, 1996, Takefu Festival, Japan 1993; premiere of Concerto for violin and orchestra in Madison, Wisconsin 1998; Composer-in-Residence, Young Spanish Nat. Orchestra 1999–2000, Strasbourg Festival 1999; premiere of chamber opera Sol de Invierno, Teatro San Joao, Portugal 2002; String Quartet, Liceo de Cámara de Madrid 2002; Symphony No. 1 Boreas, Festival de Canarias 2005 and Prague Festival 2008; Symphony No. 2 Nusantara, Biennale di Venezia 2006; Symphony No. 3, Otoño Musical Soriano 2007, Córdoba 2009; Carmen Replay (ballet), Teatro Real, Madrid 2010, 2011; Céfiro (concerto for guitar and small orchestra) Valencia and New York 2010; Carmen Replay (concert version), Rotterdam 2011, Hamburg 2012; Mistral (double concerto for guitar, accordion and orchestra), ORCAM, Madrid 2012; Simbiosis (educational project for students, ensemble, choir and dancers), Auditorio Nacional Madrid 2012; Symphony No. 4, Mariinsky Theatre, St Petersburg, Russia 2014; Campos de Tauro (concerto for cello and orchestra), Spain 2014; Senda Sur for guitar and orchestra, Spain 2014; Giovanni dei giovani (oratorio), Torino, Italy 2015. *Compositions include:* Corriente Cautiva for orchestra 1991, Concerto for oboe and chamber ensemble (Gaudeamus Prize 1993) 1992, Etude for wind quintet 1993, Vision del Errante for 12 mixed voices 1994, Concerto for marimba and 15 instruments 1996, Intermezzo for string orchestra 1998, Fantasía Primera for orchestra 1998, Mito for 13 instruments 1999, Fantasía Segunda for orchestra 1999, Sol de Invierno, chamber opera for mezzo, baritone and six percussionists (after Ibsen), Alio Modo for piano 2002, Advenit for clarinet, violin, cello and piano 2003, Sobre la noche for soprano and accordion 2003, Symphony No. 1 Boreas (Nat. Music Prize 2005) 2004, Symphony No. 2 Nusantara for piano and orchestra 2005, Carmen Replay, ballet, for soprano, electric guitar and accordion 2009; guitar works: Mirada, 2 Preludes, Winter Suite, Cuaderno de instantes, Páginas de verano, 6 Estudios, Nocturno y toccata, Viento de Primavera, Danza de Otoño, Céfiro for guitar and 14 instruments 2008, 1/6 plugged for electric guitar and 5 instruments 2008, Mistral for guitar accordion and orchestra 2011, A Midsummer Night's Dance for electric guitar, vibraphone, marimba and steel drums 2011, Jardín bajo la luna for violin and guitar 2011, Senda Sur for guitar and orchestra 2014, Guitar Sonatas 1, 2 and 3 2015, Rapsodia for guitar 2015, Melliflui Facti Sunt Caeli for 6-part mixed choir 2011, Symphony No. 4 …donde se baña el viento… 2012, Partita de Santa Marina for organ 2012, Giovanni dei giovani – oratorio for speaker, choir and strings 2014, Cantos de Quirce for mezzo, vocal quartet SATB, oboe, cello and guitar 2015, Costanza for speaker, mezzo and piano 2015. *Recordings:* Concerto for Oboe, by Ernest Rombout, Xenakis Ensemble and Diego Masson (conductor); Invernal and En la luz, by Orquestra del Teatre Lliure, Conductor, J. Pons; Consort, by Quartet de Bec Frullato; Verso III, by José Vicente (percussion); Verso I, Isabelle Duval (flute); Chamber Music, featuring M. Bernat (marimba), E. Rombout (oboe), A. Sukarlan (piano), F. Panisello (conductor); Complete Piano Music/Accordion Solo and Duos featuring A. Sukarlan (piano), C. Gurriarán (soprano), A. L. Castaño (accordion), J. Librado (saxophone), 1st 'Boreas' (1st symphony and orchestral music), featuring Finnish Radio Symphony (S. Oramo), Corporación Radiotelevisión Española (P. Heras), Nusantara and Violin Concerto, featuring A. Sukarlan, M. Guillén, Orquesta y Coro de la Comunidad de Madrid (J. R. Encinar), Mirada, music for solo guitar featuring Eugenio Tobalina. *Honours:* Premio El Ojo Critico (Spanish Nat. Broadcasting) 1993, Gaudeamus Prize (Amsterdam) 1993, Spanish Nat. Music Award 2005. *Address:* Azurita, 9 El Guijo, 28260 Galapagar, Madrid, Spain. *E-mail:* daviddelpuerto_mp@yahoo.es. *Website:* www.daviddelpuerto.com; www .rejoice.es.

DEL TREDICI, David Walter, BA, MFA; American composer and teacher; b. 16 March 1937, Cloverdale, CA. *Education:* Univ. of California at Berkeley, Princeton Univ., studied with Seymour Shifrin, Andrew Imbrie, Arnold Elston, Earl Kim and Roger Sessions. *Career:* debut as piano soloist with the San Francisco Symphony Orchestra aged 16; pianist, Aspen (Colorado) Music Festival 1958, Berkshire Music Center, Tanglewood 1964, 1965; Composer-in-Residence, Marlboro (Vermont) Music Festival 1966, 1967; Teacher, Harvard Univ. 1966–72, State Univ. of New York at Buffalo 1973, Boston Univ. 1973–84, City Coll. and Graduate School of the CUNY 1984–; Composer-in-Residence, New York Philharmonic Orchestra 1988–; Prof., Juilliard School 1993–96; Prof., Yale Univ. 1999. *Compositions:* String Trio 1959, I Hear an Army for soprano and string quartet (after James Joyce) 1963–64, Night Conjure-Verse (after James Joyce) 1965, Syzygy for soprano, horn and chamber ensemble (after James Joyce) 1966, The Last Gospel for soprano, chorus, rock group and orchestra 1967, revised 1984, Pop-Pourri for amplified soprano, mezzo-soprano ad libitum, chorus, rock group and orchestra 1968, revised 1973, An Alice Symphony (after Lewis Carroll) 1969–75, Adventures Underground (after Lewis Carroll) 1971, revised 1977, Vintage Alice: Fantascence on A Mad Tea Party for amplified soprano, folk group and orchestra (after Lewis Carroll) 1972, Final Alice for amplified soprano and orchestra (after Lewis Carroll) 1977–81, March to Tonality for orchestra 1983–85, Haddock's Eyes for soprano and chamber ensemble 1985–86, Ballad in Yellow for piano 1997, Dracula for soprano and ensemble 1998–99, Gay Life for voice and orchestra 2000.

DEL VIVO, Graziano; Italian singer (bass); b. 1 Nov. 1937, Florence. *Education:* Univ. of Florence and Conservatory. *Career:* debut in Spoleto 1961, as Ramphis in Aida; Teatro Regio Parma, as Onofrio in Galuppi's I tre amanti ridicoli 1964, and as Achillas in Handel's Giulio Cesare and Sparafucile in Rigoletto; Florence 1965, in Billy Budd and Katerina Izmailova, returning in Robert le Diable by Meyerbeer 1968, and Spontini's La Vestale, 1970; La Scala Milan as Pluto in Casella's Orfeo; Edinburgh Festival 1969, 1972; sang in The Nose by Shostakovich at Rome and at Genoa and Naples in Verdi Requiem; Pisa 1973, in a centenary concert for Titta Ruffo.

DELACÔTE, Jacques; French conductor; s. of Pierre Delacôte and Renée Wagner Delacôte; m. Maria Lucia Alvares-Machado 1975. *Education:* Music Conservatoire, Acad. of Music, with Prof. Hans Swarowsky, Austria. *Career:* fmrly Asst to Darius Milhaud and Leonard Bernstein; orchestras conducted include Orchestre de Paris, Orchestre Nat. de France, New York Philharmonic, Vienna Philharmonic, Vienna Symphony, Israel Philharmonic, Orchestre Nat. de Belgique, London Symphony, San Francisco, Cleveland, Scottish Chamber, Scottish Nat. Opera, RIAS Berlin, WDR Cologne, SF Stuttgart, SWF Baden-Baden, Bavarian Radio, Munich, English Chamber, BBC, London, London Philharmonic, Royal Philharmonic, London, Japan Philharmonic, Yomiuri Symphony, Dresdner Staatskapelle, Royal Opera House, Covent Garden (including Far East tour, Korea and Japan), English Nat. Opera, Opernhaus Zürich, Teatro Real, Madrid, Teatro Liceo, Barcelona, La Fenice, Venice, Vienna State Opera, Deutsche Oper, Berlin, Pittsburgh Opera, Welsh Nat. Opera, Opéra de Paris, Teatro Colón, Buenos Aires, Canadian Opera Co., Royal State Opera, Copenhagen, State Opera, Hamburg, State Opera, Munich, Chicago Lyric Opera, Semper Oper, Dresden; also recordings with EMI, Philips London and Tring London. *Festivals include:* Flandernfestival, Macerata Festival, Klangbogen Vienna, Dresden Musiktage. *Honours:* First Prize and Gold Medal, Mitropoulos Competition, New York 1971. *Current Management:* Agentur Klein, Hanselmannstr. 11, 80809 Munich, Germany. *E-mail:* aklein@agenturklein.de. *Website:* www.jacques-delacote.com.

DELAIR, Suzy; French actress and singer; b. (Suzanne Pierrette Delaire), 31 Dec. 1917, Paris; d. of Clovis-Mathieu Delaire and Thérèse Delaire (née Nicola. *Plays include:* Deux doux dingues, Adieu Prudence, Croque monsieur, Oscar, Le tube, L'ours, Tricoche et Cacolet, Que les hommes sont bêtes 1968, Nuits de Chine 1971, Le don d'Adèle. *TV appearances:* Hortense Schneider, L'argent par les fenêtres, L'or et la paille, Le manège des amoureux, La mythomane, L'âge vermeil 1984, Traquenard 1987, Les tableaux qui parlent 1988, Ces Chers disparus 1985, La Chance aux Chansons 1988. *Films include:* Le dernier des six 1941, L'assassin habite au 21 1942, Défense d'aimer 1942, La vie de bohème 1942, Copie conforme 1946, Quai des orfèvres 1947, Par la fenêtre 1947, Pattes blanches 1948, Botta e riposta (Je suis de la revue) 1949, Lady Paname 1949, Souvenirs perdus 1950, Atoll K 1951, Le fil à la patte 1954, Gervaise 1955, Le couturier de ces dames 1956, Les régates de San Francisco 1959, Rocco et ses frères 1960, Du mouron pour les petits oiseaux 1962, Les aventures de Rabbi Jacob 1973, Oublie-moi Mandoline 1975. *Operettas:* Ta bouche, Un chien qui rapporte, La chaste Suzanne, Feu d'artifice, Mobylette, La vie parisienne, La Périchole, Boyfriend, Véronique 1980. *Recordings include:* Suzy Delair Chante Offenbach (Grand Prix du Disque 1962), Trois Valses (Prix de l'Acad. Charles Cros). *Honours:* Commdr des Arts et des Lettres, Officier, Ordre nat. du Mérite 1997, Officier, Légion d'honneur 2007. *Address:* 46 rue de Varenne, 75007 Paris, France (home).

DELAMBOYE, Hubert; Dutch singer (tenor); b. 1945, Valkenburg. *Career:* sang in opera at Bielefeld and Wiesbaden 1974–76; Cologne Opera 1979–; in Seattle, Paris and Metropolitan, New York 1986–88, as Mimi in The Ring; Wiesbaden from 1991 in Katya Kabanova and as Wagner's Loge, Siegmund, Siegfried and Tristan; at Salzburg Festival as Mozart's Lucio Silla 1993; in Frankfurt as Cornelius's Nureddin, Loge and Samson 1994; in Brussels as Herod in Salome 1995; other roles include Verdi's Otello; season 1997–98 as Paul in Die Tote Stadt at Wiesbaden, Florestan at the Théâtre des Champs-Elysées, Paris and Tichon in Katya Kabanova at Salzburg; season 2000–01 as Tristan for Reisopera, Netherlands, Lancelot in Le Roi Arthus by Chausson at Edinburgh (concert), in Schoenberg's Die Jakobsleiter at the Vienna Staatsoper and as Tannhäuser at Wiesbaden; season 2004–05 as Filka in From the House of Death, Paris, Madrid, Fidelio, Hamburg, Hauptmann, Barcelona; season 2006–07 in Boulevard Solitude, Barcelona; season 2007–08 as St Francis of Assisi, Amsterdam, London, Paris; concert and broadcast engagements. *Current Management:* Alferink Artists Management Amsterdam BV, Herengracht 340, 1016 CG Amsterdam, The Netherlands. *Telephone:* (20) 6643151. *Fax:* (20) 6752426. *E-mail:* info@alferink.org. *Website:* www .alferink.org.

DELANGE, Claude; French musician (saxophone). *Education:* Conservatoire de Lyon, studied with Serge Bichon, Conservatoire Nat. Supérieur de Musique de Paris, with Daniel Deffayet. *Career:* fmr mem. Quatuor Adolphe Sax, Paris; has worked with composers including Luciano Berio, Pierre Boulez, Toru Takemitsu, Astor Piazzolla and conductors including David Robertson, Peter Eötvös, Kent Nagano, Esa-Pekka Salonen, Myung Whun Chung and George Bernstein; invited saxophonist, Ensemble Intercontemporain 1986–; soloist with numerous orchestras including BBC Symphony, Orchestre Philharmonique de Radio France, Finnish Radio Symphony Orchestra, WDR Sinfonieorchester Köln, Berlin Philharmonic, Kioi Sinfonietta Tokyo; teacher, Conservatoire Nat. Supérieur de Musique, Paris 1988–. *Recordings include:* The Solitary Saxophone 1993, The Japanese Saxophone 1998, A Saxophone for a Lady 1998, A la française 2002, Historic Saxophone 2003, Under the Sign of the Sun 2007, Harmonious Breath 2011, La Création du Monde 2013. *Website:* www.sax-delangle.com (office).

DELFS, Andreas, MMus; German conductor; *Principal Conductor, Honolulu Symphony;* b. 30 Aug. 1959, Flensburg; m. Amy Delfs; four c. *Education:* studied under Aldo Ceccato and Christoph von Dohnanyi at Hamburg Conservatory, Juilliard School of Music. *Career:* began studying piano and music theory aged five; Music Dir, Hamburg Univ. Orchestra 1979; Asst Conductor, Pittsburgh Symphony Orchestra 1984; Chief Conductor, Orchestre Suisse des Jeunes 1984–95; fmr Music Dir, Bern Opera; Gen. Music Dir, City of Hanover 1995–2000; Musical Dir, Milwaukee Symphony Orchestra 1997–2009, Conductor Laureate 2009–; Music Dir, St Paul Chamber Orchestra 2001–04; Prin. Conductor, Honolulu Symphony 2007–; has appeared as guest conductor with many major int. orchestras. *Current Management:* Opus 3 Artists, 470 Park Avenue South, 9th Floor North, New York, NY 10016, USA. *Telephone:* (212) 584-7500. *E-mail:* info@opus3artists.com. *Website:* www.opus3artists.com. *Address:* Honolulu Symphony, 650 Iwilei Rd, Ste 202, Honolulu, HI 96817, USA (office). *Telephone:* (808) 524-0815 (office). *Fax:* (808) 524-1507 (office). *Website:* www.honolulusymphony.com (office).

DELGADO, Alexandre; Portuguese violist and composer; b. 8 June 1965, Lisbon. *Education:* Fundação Musical dos Amigos das Crianças, Lisbon, Conservatório de Música, Lisbon and Nice Conservatoire. *Career:* conductor, Fundação Musical dos Amigos das Crianças string orchestra 1981–86; mem., European Community Youth Orchestra 1988–99; musical asst, Rádio de Portugal 1989–91; mem., Gulbenkian Orchestra 1991–95; hosts weekly television culture programme, A Propósito da Música 1996–; founder mem., Lacerda String Quartet; guest composer, Maastricht Festival 2001; Artistic Dir, Cistermúsica Festival 2006–. *Compositions include:* Prelúdio 1982, Turbilhão 1987, Flute Concerto 1988, Antagonia 1990, String Quartet 1991, Langará 1992, O doido e a morte (chamber opera) 1994, Tresvariacões 1995, Viola Concerto 2000, Little Suite 2001. *Recordings include:* recital with Bruno Belthoise, Arditti String Quartet. *Publications:* Luis de Freitas Branco e o 1°

modernismo português 1990, A Sinfonia em Portugal 2002. *Honours:* Young Musicians Award, Lisbon 1987, João de Freitas Branco Award 1992. *Address:* Av. Luís Bivar 38, 5° esq., 1050-145 Lisbon, Portugal. *Telephone:* (213) 571711. *E-mail:* alexandre.delgado@mail.telepac.pt.

DELLER, Mark Damian, DMus; British singer (countertenor); b. 27 Sept. 1938, St Leonards-on-Sea, Sussex, England; s. of Alfred Deller; m. Sheelagh Elizabeth Benson; three s. *Education:* chorister Canterbury Cathedral, choral scholar St John's Coll., Cambridge. *Career:* Lay Vicar, Salisbury Cathedral 1960–68; founder and Dir, Guildhall Winter Concerts 1962; Artistic Dir, first festival of the arts, Salisbury 1967; Vicar-Choral, St Paul's Cathedral 1969–73; choral conductor; began recording with father Alfred Deller 1962; joined Deller Consort early 1960s; has toured extensively in Europe, USA, Canada and South America, as mem. of Deller Consort and as a solo singer; Dir Deller Consort 1979–; Dir Stour Music 1976–, Canterbury Festival 1988–2003. *Recordings:* mem. Deller Consort, Purcell's The Fairy Queen, King Arthur and The Indian Queen. *Honours:* Hon. DMus (Univ. of Kent) 1995. *Address:* 2 Rural Terrace, Wye, Ashford, Kent, TN25 5AP, England (home). *E-mail:* mark.deller@virgin.net (home).

DELLO JOIO, Justin, BM, MM, DMA; American composer; *Faculty Composer-in-Residence, New York University*; b. 18 Oct. 1960, New York, NY; s. of Norman Dello Joio and Grayce Dello Joio; m. Marianne Bachmann; one d. *Education:* Juilliard School of Music, New York. *Career:* Prof. of Composition, New York Univ., currently Faculty Composer-in-Residence; symphonic, opera, chamber and solo works performed in USA and Europe by orchestras including Detroit Symphony Orchestra, Juilliard Orchestra with Sixten Ehrling, Garrick Ohlsson, Carter Brey, Ani Kavafian, Jeremy Denk, Christopher O'Riley, and by American Brass Quintet, Det Norske Blaseensemble, mems of Mendelssohn String Quartet, and Primavera String Quartet; Piano Sonata premiered at Nat. Gallery of Arts, Washington, DC (also broadcast); collaborated with American novelist, John Gardner, on opera The Holy Sinner. *Compositions include:* String Quartet No. 1, Primavera String Quartet, Sonata for Piano 1986, Musica Humana symphonic poem for orchestra, Two Concert Etudes, Music for Piano Trio, Blue Mountain, one-act opera 2007; works for orchestra, chamber orchestra, string quartet, opera, brass, organ, vocal music and solo piano. *Recordings:* Music of Justin Dello Joio. *Honours:* Charles Ives Scholarship, Nat. Inst. and American Acad. of the Arts, NY State Council on the Arts grant 1983, Nat. Endowment for the Arts grant 1985, New York Foundation for the Arts grant 1986, J. Guggenheim Fellowship 1998, Charles Ives Scholarship 2000, Lakond Award 2000, Acad. Award in Music, American Acad. of Arts and Letters 2004, Composer of the Year, Classical Recording Foundation 2007, Koussevitsky Foundation, Barlow Endowment. *Current Management:* c/o Bridge Records, 200 Clinton Avenue, New Rochelle, NY 10801, USA. *Telephone:* (914) 654-9270. *Fax:* (914) 636-1383. *E-mail:* becky@bridgerecords.com. *Website:* www.bridgerecords.com. *Address:* Department of Music and Performing Arts Professions, 35 West Fourth Street, Suite 777, New York, NY 10012 (office); 400 East 89th Street, New York, NY 10128, USA (home). *Telephone:* (212) 427-8182 (office); (212) 876-9076 (home). *Fax:* (212) 427-8182 (home). *E-mail:* justindellojoio@gmail.com (home). *Website:* justindellojoio.com.

DELOGU, Gaetano; Italian conductor; b. 14 April 1934, Messina. *Education:* Univ. of Catania, studied conducting with Franco Ferrara, Rome and Venice. *Career:* guest conductor, Italian Radio, Rome, Milan, Turin and Naples, London Symphony Orchestra, BBC Orchestra, Royal Opera Covent Garden, Orchestre National de France, Japan Philharmonic, Czech Philharmonic, New York Philharmonic Orchestra and National Symphony Orchestra, Washington, DC, USA 1968–69; conductor, Teatro Massimo, Palermo, Italy 1975–78; Music Dir and Conductor, Denver Symphony, USA 1978–87, Prague Symphony Orchestra 1995–2000, apptd Hon. Dir 2000–. *Recordings include:* Bruckner's Seventh Symphony, Schubert's Great C Major Symphony, Orff's Carmina Burana, Haydn's Symphonies Nos 83 and 101, Mahler's 1st Symphony, Hindemith's Symphonic Metamorphoses and Nobilissima Visione, Smetana's Ma Vlast 2001. *Honours:* first prize Young Conductors' Competition, Florence 1964, Dimitri Mitropoulos Competition, New York 1968.

DELUNSCH, Mireille; French singer (soprano); b. 1962, Mulhouse. *Education:* Strasbourg Conservatoire with Evelyn Brunner. *Career:* sang at Opera du Rhin and in Schoenberg's Moses und Aron, Théâtre du Châtelet, Paris; Pamina at Lyon and Mimi at Bordeaux; Rameau's Hippolyte et Aricie, Palais Garnier; Gluck's Armide, Nice, Amsterdam and Paris; season 1998 with Gluck's Eurydice at Bordeaux and Venus in Rameau's Dardanus at Lyon; season 1999–2000 as La Folie in Rameau's Platée, at Antwerp, and Poppea at Aix and Vienna (Theater an der Wien). *Recordings:* French Cantatas; Lully's Acis et Galatée; Gluck's Armide and Iphigénie en Aulide, under Marc Minkowski.

DEMARINIS, Paul; American composer; b. 8 Oct. 1949, Cleveland, OH. *Education:* Antioch Coll., Ohio and Mills Coll., Oakland with Robert Ashley. *Career:* taught composition and computers at Mills Coll. 1973–78, Wesleyan Univ. 1979–81, San Francisco State Univ. 1987–89; collaborations as a performer with Robert Ashley and David Tudor in New York and Paris and at New Music America Concerts 1980–85; computer audio-graphic systems installed at Museum of Contemporary Art, Chicago and the Wadsworth Atheneum; audio installations at the Exploratorium San Francisco and the Children's Museum, Boston. *Compositions:* computer-processed speech works: Kokole 1985, I Want You 1986; installations: Pygmy Gamelin (Paris, New York and Los Angeles) 1976–80, Music Room, Faultless Jamming (San Francisco and Boston) 1982, Laser Disk (Eindhoven, The Netherlands) 1989.

DEMBSKI, Stephen, BA, MA, MFA, PhD; American composer and academic; *Professor of Composition, University of Wisconsin*; b. 13 Dec. 1949, Boston, Mass. *Education:* Phillips Acad., Clifton Coll., UK, Ecole Normale de Musique, France, Antioch Coll., State Univ. of New York, Stony Brook, Princeton Univ. *Career:* currently Prof. of Composition, School of Music, Univ. of Wisconsin; music presented by UNESCO, Denmark 1978, 5th Int. Festival of Electronic-Acoustic Music, Bourges, France 1976, Int. Soc. for Contemporary Music, Bonn 1976, New York New Music Ensemble, Sequitur, American Composers Orchestra, New York Repertory Orchestra, Silesian Philharmonic, Huddersfield Festival, England, Alan Feinberg, Ursula Oppens, Fred Sherry, Robert Black, Christopher Kendall, Jonathan Faralli, Mauro Castellano, Daniel Druckman, Bert Turetsky, Gregory D'Agostino, Rolf Schulte, William Purves, Gregory Fulkerson, Phyllis Bryn-Julson, Ron Copes, Tony Arnold, Christopher Taylor, Cleveland Contemporary Players, Scott Fields Ensemble, Utah Arts Festival, FLAME Festival, Florence, Italy, Bogliasco Foundation 2013, Ensemble NakedEye. *Compositions include:* recorded: Pterodactyl for piano 1974, Tender Buttons for piano 1977, Trio 1977, Digit for clarinet and computer synthesized tape 1978, Stacked Deck for large chamber ensemble 1979, Alba for chamber ensemble 1980, Spectra for orchestra 1985, Altamira for music box 1994, Of Mere Being for soprano and large orchestra, Sonotropism for saxophone, piano, electric guitar 1996, Being Hearing, Knowing Now for piano 2007, Trio Ju-Ping Song for toy piano 2012; other compositions (selected): Caritas for SATB chorus 1981, Refraction/Refracja for orchestra 1986, So Fine for SATB chorus 1994, Another Day for six percussionists 2001, Only Yesterday for solo percussionist 2001, Pied Beauty for soprano and contrabass 2002, Fool's Paradise: 48 Proverbs of Hell (William Blake) for soprano, violoncello and flute, in virtual reality installation 2004, On Ondine for piano 1991–2000, Three Scenes from Elsaveta (opera) 1992, Memory's Minefield for solo violin 1994, At Baia for soprano and piano, or for soprano, piano, and violin, or for mixed chamber ensemble 1984, Out of my System for solo violin, with clarinet, cello and percussion (bongos, congas and vibraphone) 1995, Brass Attacks for brass quintet 1997, Le Monde Merengue for guitar 1998, Stick for bassoon, and pianist doubling bongo and conga drums 2004, Three Sips of Crow Soup for baritone and piano 2005, Music for Sarod 2006, Raven Songs 2007, Calcium Late, Nate – Marimba 2007, Crow Soup (libretto: Leonora Carrington and Gabriel Weiss-Carrington), Tubular for flute and piano 2009, Transform II for collaborating and improvising bass guitarist 2009, Merengue Manic for piano trio 2009, Aperto Segno (bilingual setting of Guido Cavalcanti's 13th century sonnet 'Tu m'hai…') for two high voices and piano 2009–10, Raven-year for large orchestra 2010, Suite for violoncello solo 1978–2010, Trio (In memoriam Milton Babbitt) for toy piano (and optional clarinet) 2011, Falling for chamber orchestra 2012, In the Fast Lane for two male voices and piano, words of Assotto Saint 2012, Veni Creator Spiritus for handbell choir 2013, NakedEyeCame, for flute (piccolo), Bb clarinet (Eb, Bb bass), pianoforte (toy piano), electric guitar, and contrabass 2014, Gists and Piths for baroque flute and modern flute 2013–14, Moon in the Mirror for mezzo soprano and piano 2015; recorded as conductor: 48 Motives, 96 Gestures, From the Diary of Dog Drexel, all by Scott Fields; published: Sunwood for guitar 1976; arrangements: Prayer – Ernest Bloch's work for cello and piano, arranged for cello choir with solo cello, Ernest Bloch's work for cello and piano. *Publications include:* International Musical Lexicon 1980, Milton Babbitt – Words About Music (with Joseph N. Straus) 1987, Collected Essays of Milton Babbitt (with Peles, Strauss and Mead) 2003, Lexique Musical International (co-author) 1979; numerous articles, including The Context of Composition: The Reception of Robert Morris's Theory of Compositional Design 1989–1990, Misreading Martino 1992, An Idea of Order 2005–06, The Structure of Construction 2008, "…alone. Together." Music Theory by Prof. Tom Moore: Part One 2011, Part Two 2012. *Honours:* American Acad. and Inst. of Arts and Letters Goddard Lieberson Award 1982, Creative Artists Program Service (NYSCA) Fellowship Grant 1983, Chamber Music America commission for 20th Century Consort 1985–86, Howard Foundation Fellowship 1986, Premio Musicale Citta di Trieste, Italy 1990, Pa Council on the Arts commission (Network for New Music) 1995, Romnes Fellowship, Kellet Mid-career Award, Emily Mead Baldwin Award in the Creative Arts, Univ. of Wisconsin-Madison 2012. *Address:* 96 Perry Street, B-22, New York, NY 10014, USA (home). *Telephone:* (608) 263-1900 (office). *E-mail:* sdembski@wisc.edu (office). *Website:* www.stephendembski.com.

DEMETEROVÁ, Gabriela; Czech violinist; b. 17 May 1971, Prague. *Education:* Prague Conservatory, Acad. of Fine Arts, Prague, Royal Acad. of Music, Denmark. *Career:* soloist and Artistic Dir, Czech Philharmonic Collegium ensemble 1995–; has performed with leading Czech orchestras in France, Germany, UK, USA; stringed Autumn Prague 2001, Int. Music Festival Čdeský Krumlov Honour to Baroque 2001; est. Gabriela Demeterová Endowment Fund 2003; f. Collegium of Gabriela Demeterová chamber ensemble 2005. *Recordings include:* selection from Biber's Biblical Sonatas 1996, Italian Baroque, W.A. Mozart – Sonatas for Piano and Violin 2003, Violin Magic, and numerous recordings for Czech Radio. *Honours:* winner Jaroslav Kocián Competition, Yehudi Menuhin Competition 1993. *E-mail:* gabriela@gabrielademeterova.com. *Website:* www.gabrielademeterova.com.

DEMIDENKO, Nikolai; Russian pianist; b. 1 July 1955, Anisimova; m. 1st; one s.; m. 2nd Julya Dougyallo 1994. *Education:* Moscow Conservatoire with Dmitri Bashkirov. *Career:* British debut with Moscow Radio Symphony

Orchestra, 1985; has performed in Russia and abroad in concert and recital from 1976; frequent tours of Japan and concerts with Bolshoi Symphony, Polish Nat. Radio Orchestra, London Philharmonic, BBC Philharmonic and BBC Scottish Symphony, London Proms debut 1992 with Rachmaninov's 4th Concerto; Resident in UK 1990–, teacher at Yehudi Menuhin School; Season, 1992–93 in concerts with the St Petersburg Philharmonic and the Philharmonia Orchestra; recitals in Paris, Milan and the Concertgebouw, Amsterdam; Two-Piano recital with Dmitri Alexeev at Wigmore Hall, March 1993, to mark the 50th Anniversary of Rachmaninov's death; Six Piano Masterworks solo recitals at Wigmore Hall, Jan.–June 1993 recreating concerts given by Alkan and Rubinstein in the 19th Century: The Classicists, The Age of Beethoven, The Early Romantics, The High Romantics, The Baroque Revival and Legacies and Prophecies, Liszt, Berg, Gubaidulina and Messiaen; returned to London for German Romantic concerts 1997. *Recordings:* albums of Bach-Busoni, Chopin and Liszt; Medtner 2nd and 3rd Concertos with BBC Scottish Symphony Orchestra, Medtner and Chopin Concertos with Philharmonia; live recordings at Wigmore Hall Masterworks series, Chopin: 24 Preludes and the Third Piano Sonata (Midem Classical Special Award 2010). *Honours:* medallist Concours Int. de Montréal 1976, Tchaikovsky Int. Competition, Moscow 1978. *Current Management:* c/o Georgina Ivor Associates, 28 Old Devonshire Road, London SW12 9RB, England. *Telephone:* (20) 8673-7179. *E-mail:* info@giamanagement.com. *Website:* www.giamanagement .com.

DEMITZ, Hans-Jürgen; German singer (baritone); b. 1946, Hanover. *Career:* sang in opera throughout North Germany from 1976; Hanover, 1983, as Wagner's Dutchman and Marschner's Hans Heiling; Bayreuth, 1983, as Donner; Season 1985 with the premieres of Boehmer's Dr Faustus in Paris and Sutermeister's Le Roi Berenger in Geneva; Spoleto Festival, 1987, as Amfortas, Cerha's Der Rattenfänger at the Vienna Staatsoper; Other roles include as Wagner's Kurwenal at Trieste and Gunther at Lisbon. *Recordings include:* Zemlinsky's Florentinische Tragödie.

DEMPSEY, Gregory; Australian singer (tenor); b. 20 July 1931, Melbourne. *Education:* studied in Australia with Mavis Kruger and Annie and Heini Portnoj. *Career:* debut at National Opera of Victoria 1954, as Don Ottavio; sang with Sadler's Wells/ENO from 1962, notably as Wagner's Mime and David, Don José, Peter Grimes, Tom Rakewell, and in premiere of Bennett's The Mines of Sulphur 1965; sang in first local productions of Janáček's The Makropulos Case 1966 and The Excursions of Mr Brouček 1979; other roles include Drum Major in Wozzeck, Dionysius in The Bassarids by Henze (British stage premiere), Aeneas in Les Troyens and Shepherd in Szymanowski's King Roger (New Opera Company); US debut, San Francisco 1966, in The Makropulos Case; Aldeburgh Festival 1967, in premiere of Musgrave's The Decision; Covent Garden debut 1972, as Laca in Jenůfa; sang Bob Boles in Peter Grimes, Sydney 1986; Prince Populescu in Countess Maritza at Melbourne 1986. *Recordings include:* Billy Budd, The Ring of the Nibelung (conducted by Reginald Goodall).

DEMPSTER, Stuart Ross, BA, MA; American trombonist, academic and composer; b. 7 July 1936, Berkeley, Calif.; m. Renko Ishida 1964, two s. *Education:* San Francisco State Coll., studied with A.B. Moore, Orlando Giosi and John Klock. *Career:* Prin. Trombonist, Oakland Symphony Orchestra, California 1962–66; mem. performing group Mills Coll. 1963–66; tours as soloist 1962–; teacher, San Francisco Conservatory of Music 1961–66, California State Coll., Hayward 1963–66; Asst Prof., Univ. of Washington, Seattle 1968–78, Assoc. Prof. 1978–85, Prof. 1985–98, Prof. Emer. 1998–; master-classes, International Trombone Workshop 1974–; Instructor, California Inst. of Integral Studies; Founder-mem. Deep Listening Band. *Compositions include:* Sonata for bass trombone and piano 1961, Adagio and Canonic Variations for brass quintet 1962, Chamber Music 13 for voice and trombones 1964, The Road Not Taken for voice, chorus and orchestra 1967, Ten Grand Hosery (mixed media ballet) 1971–72, Pipedream (mixed media piece) 1972, Life Begins at 40 (concert series and musical gallery show) 1976, Standing Waves for trombone 1976, Didjeridervish for didjeridu 1976, Monty for trombone 1979, Fog Calling for trombone and didjeridu 1981, Harmonic Tremors for trombone and tape 1982, Hornfinder for trombone and audience 1982, Roulette for trombone and audience 1983, Aix en Providence for trombones 1983, JDBBBDJ for didjeridu and audience 1983, Don't Worry, It Will Come for garden hoses and audience 1983, Sound Massage Parlor for didjeridu, garden hoses, shell and audience 1986, SWAMI (State of Washington as a Musical Instrument): an Acoustic Guide to the State of Washington for the State's Centennial 1987–89, Milanda Embracing for unspecified mixed ensemble 1993–94, Underground Overlays for conches, chanters and trombone 1994–95, Caprice for Unicycle-Riding Trombonist 1995, Time Piece for solo or mixed ensemble 1998, Alternate Realities for solo flute, various co-compositions with Pauline Oliveros, others in the Deep Listening Band 1988–. *Publications:* The Modern Trombone: A Definition of its Idioms 1979. *Website:* www.deeplistening.org.

DEMUS, Jörg; Austrian concert pianist; b. 2 Dec. 1928, St Pölten, Lower Austria; s. of Dr Otto Demus and Erika Demus (née Budik). *Education:* Vienna State Acad. of Music and studies with various musicians. *Career:* debut at age 14; mem. Gesellschaft der Musikfreunde, Vienna; debuts in London and Switzerland 1950, tour of Latin America 1951, Paris 1953, New York 1955, Japan 1961; has composed music for piano, songs, chamber music, opera; has performed in almost all important musical centres; has made over 450 LP records and CDs. *Publications:* Abenteuer der Interpretation (essays),

co-author of a book on Beethoven's piano sonatas. *Honours:* Dr hc (Amherst Univ.) 1981; Premier Busoni at Int. Piano Competition, Bolzano 1956; Harriet Cohen Bach-Medal 1958; Hon. Prof. of Austria 1977; Beethoven Ring, Vienna Beethoven Soc. 1977; Mozart Medal, Mozartgemeinde, Vienna 1979; several Edison Awards and Grand Prix du Disque; Schumann Award, Zwickau, E Germany, 1986. *Current Management:* Arien-Artists, Groot-Brittanniëlaan 27, 9000 Ghent, Belgium. *Telephone:* (9) 330-39-90. *E-mail:* arien@telenet.be. *Website:* www.arien-artists.com/arien_artists_demus.html.

DENCH, Chris; Australian (b. British) composer; b. 10 June 1953, London, England; m. Diana Palmer; one d. *Career:* became Australian citizen 1992; commissioned by Elision resulting in Driftglass 1990–91, which represented Australia at 1992 International Rostrum of Composers in Paris; commissions from French Ministry of Culture, ABC, BBC, Arditti String Quartet, austraLYSIS, Synergy and others; works performed by Ensemble Accroche Note of Strasbourg, Berlin Radio Symphony Orchestra, Ensemble Exposé, Ensemble Intercontemporain, London Sinfonietta, Music Projects, London, Xenakis Ensemble and such soloists as Andrew Ball, Laura Chislett, James Clapperton, Rolf Hind, Stephanie McCallum; works presented at such events as Brighton Festival, Darmstadt Ferienkurse für Neue Musik, Hong Kong ISCM World Music Days, Insel Musik Berlin, many festivals in France and Italy, Sydney Spring Festival and Venice Biennale. *Compositions include:* four large-scale solo flute works for Laura Chislett, including Sulle Scale della Fenice, Tilt for solo piano, several large ensemble pieces, including Enoncé and Afterimages, quattro frammenti and planetary allegiances, chamber music, atsiluth for heterotic strings, Propriocepts for four voices and orchestra, four Symphonies 1980, 1982, 1987, 1997, Flesh and the Mirror for Elision, Beyond Status Geometry for Synergy 1995, The Heart's Algorithms for piano 1999. *Honours:* Kranichsteiner Musikpreis 1984. *Website:* chrisdench.com.

DENE, Joszef; Hungarian singer (bass); b. 31 March 1938, Budapest. *Education:* studied in Budapest. *Career:* sang at Hungarian State Opera, notably as Alberich in Das Rheingold; many performances at the Zürich Opera, in works by Monteverdi, Berg, Verdi, Janáček and Wagner; Berlin Komische Oper 1975, as Mozart's Figaro; further engagements at La Scala, Bayreuth, San Francisco and Metropolitan (Wagner's Alberich 1981); Paris Opéra 1982, 1985, as Gloucester in Reimann's Lear and as Trithemius in premiere of Boehmer's Docteur Faustus; Opéra du Rhin Strasbourg and Barcelona 1985–96, as Des Grieux in Manon; season 1987 at Graz as Hangman in premiere of Cerha's Rattenfänger and as Taddeo in L'Italiana in Algeri at Schwetzingen Festival; Graz Opera 1988–89, as Alberich in Siegfried and Götterdämmerung; sang Mesner in Tosca at Zürich 2000; other roles include Mozart's Alfonso and Papageno, Don Pasquale, Pizarro, Kurwenal, Klingsor, Leporello and Handel's Claudius (Agrippina). *Recordings include:* Don Giovanni, Boito's Nerone and Juditha Triumphans by Vivaldi; Il Ritorno d'Ulisse, Zürich 1982.

DENES, Istvan; Hungarian conductor and composer; b. 1950, Budapest. *Education:* Franz Liszt Acad., Vienna Musikhochschule (Georg Solti scholarship), Austria. *Career:* joined Hungarian State Opera 1977, now Conductor; Lecturer in Harmony, Franz Liszt Acad. 1980–84; Prin. Conductor, Bremen Opera 1987–95; Gen. Music Dir, Trier Opera, Germany 1995–2008; conducted first production of 20th century of Zemlinsky's first opera, Sarema (Trier Opera 1996); Prin. Guest Conductor, Radio Symphony Orchestra of Budapest. *Compositions include:* Logarithmische Rhythmen for percussion, Trio in Memoriam Bela Bartók for piano, cello and violin, Mohacs 1526: Hommage à Beethoven, Funerailles for orchestra, Fanfár és korál (Fanfare and Coral), Treveris-fantázia (Treveris-fantasy). *Recordings include:* Sarema. *E-mail:* denesistvan@aol.com. *Website:* www.istvandenes.de; www.opera.hu.

DENÈVE, Stéphane; French conductor; *Chief Conductor, Stuttgart Radio Symphony Orchestra* and *Brussels Philharmonic;* b. 24 Nov. 1971, Tourcoing. *Education:* Paris Conservatoire. *Career:* asst to Georg Solti for Bluebeard's Castle with Orchestre de Paris 1995, and Don Giovanni at Paris Opéra 1996; asst to Georges Prêtre with Turandot, Paris Opéra 1997, to Seiji Ozawa with Dialogues des Carmélites, Saito Kinen Festival 1998; has appeared as guest conductor with numerous orchestras, including Orchestre de Paris, Orchestre Nat. de France, Deutsches Symphonie Orchester Berlin, Czech Philharmonic, Hong Kong Philharmonic, Royal Stockholm Philharmonic, Rotterdam Philharmonic, Verdi Orchestra Milan, Cleveland Orchestra, Los Angeles Philharmonic, Boston Symphony, London Symphony Orchestra, NDR Symphony Hamburg and Maggio Musicale Florence; has conducted opera productions at Royal Opera House, Glyndebourne Festival, Opéra Nat. de Paris, Netherlands Opera, La Monnaie, Teatro Comunale Bologna, Cincinnati Opera; Music Dir, Royal Scottish Nat. Orchestra 2005–12; Chief Conductor, Stuttgart Radio Symphony Orchestra 2011–; Prin. Guest Conductor, The Philadelphia Orchestra 2014–; Chief Conductor, Brussels Philharmonic Orchestra 2015–, also Dir Centre for Future Orchestral Repertoire (CffOR) 2015–. *Recordings include:* with Royal Scottish Nat. Orchestra: works of Albert Roussel (Diapason d'Or for Best Orchestral Recording 2007), Stéphane Denève Conducts Debussy (Diapason d'Or for Best Orchestral Recording); with Stuttgart Radio Symphony Orchestra: Poulenc Stabat Mater & Les Biches, Ravel Orchestral Works, Honegger Symphonies Nos 2 & 3. *Honours:* Paris Conservatoire First Prize in Conducting 1995. *Current Management:* c/o Alexander Monsey, IMG Artists, The Light Box, 111 Power Road, London, W4 5PY, England. *Telephone:* (20) 7957-5800. *Fax:* (20) 7957-5801. *E-mail:*

amonsey@imgartists.com. *Website:* www.imgartists.com; www.stephaneneve.com.

DENIZ, Clare Frances, LRAM, MMus, FRSA; British cellist and teacher; b. 7 April 1945, Highgate, London. *Education:* studied briefly with Madeleine Mackenzie, Lilley Phillips, Derek Simpson, Christopher Bunting, Jacqueline du Pré, Antonia Butler, Paul Tortelier, studied at Royal Acad. of Music, Queens Univ., Belfast, London Univ. *Career:* debut at Purcell Room, London 1983; fmr Prin. Cellist with Royal Ballet Orchestra; with Welsh Nat. Opera; sub-prin. cellist with ENO; Prin. solo cellist with Oxford Pro Musica Orchestra 1977–84; played with Northern Sinfonia chamber orchestra; fmr Cellist in Residence, South Hill Park Art Centre; many recitals specializing in British and French music as well as standard repertoire; appeared at Cambridge Festival, Oxford Festival 'Beautiful music in beautiful places', City of London Festival Fringe, Cheltenham Lunchtime Concerts, Fairfield Hall Centenary Concert for Arnold Bax; Concertgebouw Amsterdam debut 1987; recording for BBC Radio Oxford 1987 and recorded a recital of French music 1991; selected to take part in Counterpoint II recital series by Incorporated Soc. of Musicians 1990; three concerts of first performances for the Wessex Composers' Group 1990, organized by Incorporated Soc. of Musicians; children's concerts and workshops; played Haydn's C Major Concerto 1990 and gave a virtuoso recital which included Tschaikowsky Rococo Variations in 1992 for the Jacqueline du Pré Appeal Fund; solo recitals given in Amsterdam 1990, 1992, in Paris 1993; concert given for the EEC Brussels Commission 1994; numerous appearances with London Schubert Players, concerts given with them in Spain Bilbao, Jerez, Cordoba; formed The Belgravia Ensemble of London 2001, performance given at Leominster Festival as string trio; mem. Orama Chamber Ensemble, performances at South Bank London and Alte Oper Frankfurt; recent UK festival appearances include St Albans, Hebden Bridge, St Cuthbert's Festival in Wells, Evesham, Guildford, Du Maurier Festival (now known as Fowey Words and Music Festival), Dawlish, Halifax Festival. *Television:* two BBC television performances 2012, 2013.

DENIZE, Nadine; French singer (mezzo-soprano); b. 6 Nov. 1943, d. of Jean Denize and Christiane Denize; m. Bernard Bovier-Lapierre 1971; one s. *Education:* Conservatoire Nat Supérieur de Musique de Paris. *Career:* singer Opéra and Opéra Comique, Paris 1965–71, Opéra du Rhin, Strasbourg 1974–77, Vienna Opera 1977–79; guest singer Opéra de Paris 1974–89, Opéra Bastille, Paris 1989–93 and major opera houses in Germany, Italy, Portugal, Hungary, Yugoslavia, Netherlands, USA, Argentina, etc.; has performed at the major opera houses and with major orchestras and concert groups in France and worldwide 1974–; appearances at numerous festivals; has performed the works of Wagner, Berlioz, Verdi, Beethoven, Mozart, Schoenberg, Mahler, Mussorgsky, Janacek and Richard Strauss; has recorded works by Wagner, Berlioz, Verdi and Mahler; teacher, Ecole Normale de Musique de Paris Alfred Cortot. *Honours:* Officier, Ordre des Arts et des Lettres, Officier, Ordre Nat. du Mérite. *Current Management:* Robert Gilder & Co., c/o Philippe Grenêche, 44 bis rue de Meaux, 75019 Paris, France. *Telephone:* 1-42-01-84-59. *Fax:* 1-42-01-84-59. *E-mail:* philgren@free.fr. *Address:* 35 rue François Bonvin, 75015 Paris, France (home). *Telephone:* 1-47-34-98-59 (home). *E-mail:* bernard.bovier-lapierre@wanadoo.fr (home).

DENLEY, Catherine, GTCL, FTCL; British singer (mezzo-soprano); b. 1954, Northamptonshire.; m. Miles Golding; three s. *Education:* Trinity Coll. of Music, London. *Career:* sang two years with the BBC Singers; solo performances with major orchestras and conductors throughout Europe and in the USA, Canada, China, Japan and the Ukraine; US appearances at the Tanglewood Festival with the Boston Symphony Orchestra; San Francisco concerts with John Eliot Gardiner; performances of Messiah with the Hallé Orchestra, City of Birmingham Symphony, the English Concert in Belgium and The Sixteen in Finland and Poland; Mozart's Requiem in Salzburg and Innsbruck; Elgar's The Music Makers and the Bliss Pastoral at South Bank; Bach B Minor Mass at Aldeburgh and York; Beethoven's Missa Solemnis at the Windsor Festival; staged performances of L'Incoronazione di Poppea at Spitalfields; operatic roles include Olga in Eugene Onegin at the Aldeburgh Festival, Nutrice in Monteverdi's Poppea, Handel operas Giustino and Radamisto, Mrs Noah in Noye's Fludde; radio and TV recordings in the UK and Europe; TV recordings include appearances in Channel 4 Maestro series and Mahler's 8th Symphony from Dublin; sang Third Lady in Die Zauberflöte 1990; Promenade Concerts; Sisera in Handel's Deborah at the 1993 Proms; Mahler 2 in Kiev and Odessa; Tucapsky Stabat Mater in the Czech Repub.; Haydn Stabat Mater in Madrid and Handel Judas Maccabaeus in Berlin and Halle; Mozart's Requiem and Schumann's Scenes from Faust at the London Prom concerts. *Recordings:* over 50 recordings including Monteverdi's L'Orfeo and L'Incoronazione di Poppea; Handel's Semele, Hercules, Il Duello Amorosa, Ezio, Judas Maccabeus, Alexander Balus, Deborah, Joseph and his Brethren, Ottone and Messiah; Vivaldi's Gloria and Cantatas; Requiem by Bruckner; In the Beginning by Copland; Mozart's Die Zauberflöte. *Current Management:* CDI, Nicholson Proud, Room 31, 23 King Street, Cambridge, CB1 1AH, England. *Website:* www.nicholsonproud.com (office).

DENNER, Bettina; German singer (mezzo-soprano); b. 5 Jan. 1960, Weimar. *Education:* Leipzig Musikhochschule with Hans Christian Polster. *Career:* sang at the Leipzig Opera from 1983, as Zerlina, Carlotta in Die schweigsame Frau, and Nicklause in Les Contes d'Hoffmann; guest at the Berlin Staatsoper from 1987, as Cherubino and on tour to Japan; other roles have included Dorabella, Idamante, Massenet's Charlotte, Hermia in A Midsummer Night's Dream and Orlovsky; sang the Hostess in Boris Godunov at

Leipzig, 1993; many concert engagements, notably at the Leipzig Thomasschule and the Gewandhaus. *Current Management:* c/o Ariën Arts & Music Management, De Boeystraat 6, 2018 Antwerp, Belgium. *Telephone:* (3) 285-96-80. *Fax:* (3) 230-35-23. *E-mail:* arien@pandora.be.

DENNING, Angela; Australian singer (soprano); b. 1952, Sydney, NSW. *Education:* New South Wales Conservatory. *Career:* sang with the State Opera of South Australia from 1976 and with the Australian Opera at Sydney from 1979; English National Opera, 1982–83, Deutsche Oper Berlin, 1984, and the Staatsoper, 1988; sang Clorinda in La Cenerentola at Salzburg, 1988–89, and Dalila in Handel's Samson at the 1988 Göttingen Festival; Other roles included Donna Anna and Meyerbeer's Marguerite de Valois (both in Berlin), Lucia di Lammermoor, Gilda, Nannetta, the Queen of Night and Fiordiligi. *Recordings include:* La Cenerentola (video).

DENNIS, Elwyn, BA; Australian (b. American) composer and sculptor; b. 10 Aug. 1941, Los Angeles, Calif. *Education:* Univ. of California. *Career:* Grad. Asst, Art Dept, Univ. of California 1965; emigrated to Australia 1965; Lecturer, Lecturer, Caulfield Inst. of Technology; Acting Curator, Decorative and Asian Arts, National Gallery of Victoria 1966, Curator of Sculpture and Ethnic Art 1968; Sculptor-in-Residence and Consultant/Lecturer, Dept of Architecture, Univ. of Melbourne 1978; Lecturer, Ballarat Univ. 1990–92; man. of nature conservation area, Clouds; commissions from Asscn of Australia, The Listening Room, ABC-FM. *Compositions include:* Evidence of Origin (performance with sculpture) 1982, Particle Flow 1983, Space of Concern 1983, Clouds Are 1984, Wimmera 1986, A Mother's Day 1987, Time Again 1987, Invention for guitar 1988, Details of a Morning 1988, Dry Country 1992, Waiting Winter Out for tape with harpsichord 1994. *Honours:* Purchase Prize, Mildura Sculpture Triennial 1967, Ampol Special Award for Sculpture 1970, Caulfield Arts Centre Purchase Prize 1979. *Website:* www.elwyndennis.com.

DENNISON, Robert; American pianist; b. 10 June 1960, Philadelphia. *Education:* Philadelphia Music Acad. at Temple Univ., Peabody Conservatory, studied with Claude Frank and Horszowski. *Career:* debut in Philadelphia, with the Shostakovich Second Concerto 1971; concerts and recitals in Washington, Boston, Cleveland, Los Angeles, St Louis and Chicago; Russian tours with concerts in Kiev, St Petersburg, Vilnius, Moscow and Novosibirsk 1991–93; further engagements at Chicago, New Jersey, Colorado, San Francisco, Boston, Essen, Berlin, Hamburg Music Festival, Lucerne Festival and in Hungary, Romania and Czechoslovakia 1992–93; repertoire includes contemporary works by American composers as well as the standard classics.

DENNISTON, Patrick; American singer (tenor); b. 1965, New York. *Education:* Syracuse Univ., Lyric Opera Center, Chicago. *Career:* engagements with the San Francisco Opera, Houston Grand Opera, New York City Opera, Opera Pacific, Kentucky Opera, New Israeli Opera, Bonn Opera and at the Spoleto Festival; further appearances throughout Canada; roles have included Pinkerton, Don Carlos, Don José, Edgardo, Dmitri, Lensky and Alfredo; Glyndebourne Festival 1997, as Des Grieux in a new production of Manon Lescaut; season 1997–98 with Pinkerton and Ismaele in Nabucco at Chicago, Erik in Der fliegende Holländer, and Radames at Houston; Cavaradossi at Madison.

DEPLUS, Guy Gaston Simon; French clarinettist; b. 29 Aug. 1924, Vieux Condé; m. Yvette Vandekerkhove 1946, one s. *Education:* Conservatoire Nat. Supérieur du Musique de Paris. *Career:* Republican Guard Band and Orchestra 1947; concerts Colonne 1950; Domaine Musical, with Pierre Boulez 1953; Ars Nova, with Marius Constant 1963; Paris Octet 1965; Opéra Comique 1968; Opera 1973; Prof. of Chamber Music, Paris Conservatory 1974, of Clarinet 1978; concerts in Berlin, Salzburg, Vienna 1977; adjudicator, int. competitions; Prof., Ecole Normale de Musique de Paris 1991; mem. Int. Clarinet Asscn (French chair.). *Recordings:* Mozart, Concerto, Trio, Quintet; Weber, 1st Clarinet Concerto, Concertino, Grand Duo; Rossini, Introduction, Theme and Variations; Beethoven Septet; Brahms 2 sonatas and trio; Messiaen Quartet. *Publications:* L'Ascèse et la flamme: Guy Deplus Conversations with Bruno Martinez 2013; contrib. to The Clarinet. *Honours:* quoted by Stravinsky in Memories and Commentaries 1959, four Prix de l'Académie du Disque Français, Lifetime Achievement Award, Int. Clarinet Asscn for Outstanding Performance, Teaching, Research and Service to the Clarinet 1999. *Address:* 37 Square Saint Charles, 75012 Paris, France (home).

DĚPOLTOVÁ, Eva; Czech singer (soprano); b. 5 Aug. 1945, Bratislava. *Education:* Univ. of Music Arts, Prague with Zdenka Zika and Elena Obraztsova. *Career:* debut at Prague Nat. Theatre 1974; sang in concert with Czech Philharmonic Orchestra, Vienna Symphony Orchestra and other major orchestras, in Prague, Vienna, Salzburg, Linz, Copenhagen, Vienna, Lyon, Switzerland, Italy, Japan, Germany, Tehran, Istanbul, Taiwan; Dvořák Requiem and Stabat Mater, Janáček Glagolitic Mass, Beethoven, The Ninth Symphony 1976; roles include Lady Macbeth, Marenka, The Bartered Bride, Violetta, La Traviata, Aida, Donna Anna and many others; sang Krasava in Libuše by Smetana at the Nat. Theatre, Prague, 100th anniversary re-opening 1983. *Radio:* Macbeth (Verdi), Il Trovatore (Verdi), Pelléas et Mélisande (Debussy), Mass The Glagolitic Mass (Janáček), Requiem (Verdi). *Television:* Dalibor (Smetana), Libuse (Smetana). *Recordings:* Don Giovanni (Mozart), Dalibor (Smetana), Libuse (Smetana), The Kiss (Smetana), Sarka (Fibich), Eva (Foerster), The Miracles of Our Lady (Martinů), Gilgamesh (Martinů), The Lantern (Novak), The Cunning Peasant (Dvořák), Requiem (Dvořák). Ah, perfido! (Beethoven), The Miracle of Our Lady (Martinu). *Honours:* Union de la Presse Prix Caecilia 1985. *Telephone:* (604) 836271 (office). *E-mail:* eva .depoltova@volny.cz (office). *Website:* depoltova.wz.cz.

DERENZI, Victor; American conductor; *Artistic Director, Sarasota Opera.* *Career:* Artistic Dir and principal conductor, Sarasota Opera 1981–; conductor with Lyric Opera of Chicago, St Louis, Toledo, New Orleans Opera, New York City Opera, and Opéra du Montréal, Un Ballo in Maschera in Canary Islands, and Spoleto Festival; responsible for Sarasota Opera Verdi Cycle, a multi-year project to present all of Verdi's music. *Address:* Sarasota Opera, 61 N. Pineapple Avenue, Sarasota, FL 34236, USA (office). *Telephone:* (941) 366-6645 (office). *Fax:* (941) 955-5571 (office). *E-mail:* info@sarasotaopera.org (office). *Website:* www.sarasotaopera.org (office).

DERNESCH, Helga; Austrian singer (soprano, mezzo-soprano); b. 3 Feb. 1939, Vienna; two c. *Education:* Vienna Conservatory. *Career:* sang numerous operatic roles in Berne 1961–63, Wiesbaden 1963–66, Cologne 1966–69; freelance guest appearances at all major opera houses in Europe 1969–; regular appearances at Bayreuth Festival 1965–69, at Salzburg Easter Festival 1969–73; since 1979 has sung as mezzo-soprano; regular appearances at San Francisco Opera 1982–; debut Metropolitan Opera, New York 1985; has sung in operas and concerts throughout Europe, N and S America, Japan. *Address:* Salztorgasse 8/11, 1013 Vienna, Austria (home).

DEROUBAIX, Jeanne; Belgian singer (mezzo-soprano); b. 16 Feb. 1927, Brussels. *Education:* studied in Brussels. *Career:* sang in ensemble Pro Musica, under direction of Safford Cape 1947–53; toured widely in Europe with repertoire specializing in music of 13th–16th centuries; lieder recitals and programmes of French chansons; often heard in contemporary music; sang in first performances of Stravinsky's Threni, Venice 1958, and A Sermon, a Narrative and a Prayer, Basle 1962; also heard in Schoenberg's Pierrot Lunaire and works by Boulez; Prof., Musikhochschule Detmold from 1957. *Recordings:* Lieder by Brahms; Beethoven's Missa Solemnis; Monteverdi's Orfeo; Le Marteau sans Maître by Boulez.

DESARNAULDS, Edmond Serge, (Serge Arnauld); Swiss composer and writer; b. 16 Nov. 1944, Geneva; s. of Edmond Desarnaulds and Odette Chaïkin; m. 1st Christiane Wirz 1965; two s. one d.; m. 2nd Marie-Odile Dumail 1978; one s. *Education:* studied philosophy with Prof. Vladimir Jankélévitch, Univ. of the Sorbonne, Paris and musical composition with Darius Milhaud, Marcel Landowski, Adrienne Clostre and Louis Saguer. *Career:* radio: Swiss selection for Paul Gilson Prize and Prix Italia with Pugilat 1979, and mini-opera, Masculin-Singulier 1987; films: Jean-Luc Godard's Sauve qui Peut (La Vie) et Passion (participated as actor); musicology: Les Manuscrits de Carpentras, 1979, Scènes de la Vie Judéo-Comtadine, 1980; Founder and Artistic Dir Academies of Rome Int. Music Festival 1984–88; drama consultant, Grand Théâtre de Genève 1989–2001, and for musical Le Petit Prince (music by Richard Cocciante), performed at Casino de Paris 2002; mem. Institut Suisse, Rome 1983. *Compositions include:* Giustiniane (veille-cour-couche-éveil) for mezzo 1983, Le jeu de la Tarasque, ballet-pantomime 1985, L'Esprit de Genève, directed by Jean-Louis Martinoty, to commemorate 450th anniversary of the Reformation in Geneva 1986, Opéra sans le sou: Le double et sa doublure, cabaret songs (with Louis Saguer) 1990, Guillaume Tell, mythe jacobin, to commemorate bicentenary of French Revolution and for 700th anniversary of Swiss Confed. 1991, Trois Lettres, ballet dissocié 1993, Opéra Imaginaire (La Vie à deux) 1999, Le Marchand de sable, monologue (cr. by Michel Kullmann) 2010, Bestiaire cambodgien: Les Pâques khmères, Divinité chtonienne, Enchaînés les uns aux autres, Plat du jour simiesque (cr. by baritone Philippe Huttenlocher and pianist Sylviane Baillif-Beux) 2015; films written: La Chaussure (tant qu'on se croise, on s'aime) 2002, Brothel Eden/need (héraut, comme vous et moi) 2011, Les Cadeaux (L'échappée belle d'Henriette) 2011, Le Chapeau (autobiographie d'un nigaud) 2012, Quatrain du quotidien (les quatre films) 2012, Un Hommage, monologue (cr. by François Rochaix) 2012, Mon intérieur, six récits (cr. by Guy Bovet) 2013, Son extérieur- écart/trace 2014, Duo: l'ours et la course 2015. *Recordings include:* Cantates Ambivalentes, Requiem de Pâques, L'Amour. *Publications include:* La Cotonalité and Le Système Hexacordal 1968–69, Le Chalet dans tous ses états (la construction de l'imaginaire helvétique) 1999–2000, Genève-Oser paraître: Mentalités, goûts et moeurs du regard du théâtre 2004. *Address:* 6 rue de la Mairie, 1207 Geneva, Switzerland (home).

DESCHAMPS, Jérôme; French artistic director, comedian and actor; *Director, Opéra Comique, Paris. Education:* Ecole de la rue Blanche drama school, Conservatoire Supérieur d'Art Dramatique, Paris. *Career:* fmr mem. Comédie Français for three years; writer and dir of numerous stage and TV productions; Co-Dir Compagnie Les Deschiens 1981–; Artistic Dir Théâtre de Nîmes –2006; Dir Opéra Comique, Paris 2007–. *Plays written:* Blanche Alicata 1977, La Famille Deschiens 1978, Les Oubliettes 1978, Les Précieuses ridicules 1997. *Stage productions include:* Baboulifiche et Papavoine 1973, Un peu de musique pour monsieur 1979, La Petite chemise de nuit 1980, Les Précipitations 1980, En avant 1981, Les Blouses 1982, Courts-circuits 1983, La Veillée 1985, C'est dimanche 1985, Les Petits pas 1986, Lapin chasseur 1989, Les Frères Zenitth 1990, Les Brigands 1991, Les Pieds dans l'eau 1992, C'est magnifique 1994, Le Défilé 1995. *Films include:* Tam-Tam (dir) 1985, C'est dimanche (dir) 1987, Lapin chasseur 1989, Les Brigands 1993, C'est magnifique 1993, Les Frères Zenitth 1993, La Séparation 1994, Ligne de vie 1996, Je suis vivante et je vous aime 1998, Les Filles, personne s'en méfie 2003, La Véritable Histoire du chat botté (dir) 2009. *Honours:* Syndicat de la

Critique Prix Révélation Théâtrale 1981, Prix de l' Acad. française pour le Jeune Théâtre 1992, Grand Prix Nat. du Théâtre 1992. *Current Management:* c/o Cinéart, 28 rue de Mogador, 75009 Paris, France. *Telephone:* 1-56-69-33-00. *Fax:* 1-45-61-13-38. *E-mail:* cineart@cineart.fr. *Website:* www.cineart.fr. *Address:* Opéra Comique, 5 rue Favart, 75002 Paris, France (office). *Telephone:* 1-42-44-45-40 (office). *E-mail:* info@opera-comique.com (office). *Website:* www.opera-comique.com (office); www.deschiens-et-compagnie.com.

DESCHÊNES, Bruno, BMus, MMus; Canadian composer, musician and ethnomusicologist; b. 12 Oct. 1955, Cap-Chat, QC; m. Shizuko Toguchi 1981. *Education:* McGill University, Montréal, University of Montréal. *Career:* involved in ethnomusicological studies 1995–, specializing in Japanese traditional music; also performs Japanese music on the shakuhachi (traditional bamboo flute); performing and conducting on radio and concerts 1980–; compositions performed in France, USA, Venezuela, Brazil and Canada 1979–; gives lectures and writes articles on music perception and listening in Canada, USA and Europe; world music reviewer, All-Music Guide (online) 2000–02; journalist, critic and reviewer, specialising in world music, The Scena Musicale (magazine) 2003–. *Compositions:* improvised music: Expansion, Horizon, Pyramide, Chakras; electronic music: Murmures for tape and percussion; for chamber groups: Dimension, Innerance, Prisme, Poèmes Luminescence, Calme en Soi, Double Jeu; for choir: Ondes, Ondes et Particules, Les Vagues for narrator and tape 1994, Le Monde est une bulle d'air for tape 1994; several works for Japanese and Chinese traditional instruments, fusion between Asian and Western instruments. *Publications:* numerous articles on the psychology, sociology and philosophy of music, the history and aesthetic of Japanese traditional music. *Address:* 561 rue Clark, Montréal, QC H2T 2V5, Canada (home). *Telephone:* (514) 277-4665 (home). *E-mail:* bruno@musis.ca (home). *Website:* www.musis.ca.

DESDERI, Claudio; Italian singer (baritone) and conductor; b. 9 April 1943, Alessandria. *Education:* Florence Conservatory. *Career:* sang first in concert; opera debut as Guadenzio in Il Signor Bruschino at the 1969 Edinburgh Festival, with the Maggio Musicale; has sung widely in Italy and in Munich, Salzburg, Paris, Amsterdam, Chicago, Philadelphia and Vienna; best known in opera by Verdi, Berlioz, Monteverdi, Nono, Rossini, Bellini, Mozart, Donizetti and Massenet; regular appearances in the UK from 1981, including Glyndebourne Festival (as Figaro and Alfonso), Promenade and Royal Festival Hall concerts; Covent Garden debut as Mozart's Figaro 1987; Alfonso in Così fan tutte 1989; conducts chamber orchestras in Italy; masterclasses at Musica di Fiesole; conducted Così fan tutte and Le nozze di Figaro at Turin 1989, Piacenza 1990, Royal Coll. of Music, London 1990; sang Don Magnifico in La Cenerentola at Covent Garden 1990; Glyndebourne Festival as Falstaff, Maggio Musicale Florence as Leporello; Met debut 1995, as Rossini's Bartolo; Los Angeles 1995, as Don Pasquale; Sulpice in La Fille du Régiment at Rome 1998. *Recordings include:* Così fan tutte and Le nozze di Figaro (conducted by Haitink). *Current Management:* c/o Atelier Musicale, Via Caselle 76, San Lazzaro di Savena 40068, Italy. *Telephone:* (051) 19984444. *Fax:* (051) 19984420. *E-mail:* info@ateliermusicale.com. *Website:* www.ateliermusicale .com.

DESIMONE, Robert A., BM, MA, DipMus, DMA; American stage director, arts administrator and conductor; b. 1940; m. Angela Carol Bonica 1974, one s. one d. *Education:* Music Academy of the West, University of Southern California, International Opera Centre, Zürich, Switzerland, University of Washington, USA. *Career:* debut as Stage Director, Rome, Italy; Director of Opera, University of Texas, Austin; Director of Opera, College Conservatory of Music, Cincinnati; Assistant Director, School of Music, University of Washington; Executive Director, Visual Arts Center, Anchorage, Alaska; Administrative Co-ordinator, Music Center Opera Association, Los Angeles; Director: City of the Angels Opera, Los Angeles; John F Kennedy Center for the Performing Arts, Washington DC; Lincoln Center for the Performing Arts, New York; Seattle Opera Association, Seattle, Washington; Stage Director: Teatro del' Opera, Rome; Teatro Goldini, Rome; Opernhaus, Zürich, Switzerland; Resident Stage Director, Seattle Opera Association, Seattle, Washington; Guest Director, theatres in Germany, Switzerland, Italy, USA; mem, National Opera Association; Metropolitan Opera Guild; College Music Society; Central Opera Association.

DESJARDINS, Michael Anthony; American pianist; b. 2 Dec. 1959, Boston, Mass. *Education:* National Conservatory of Nice, France, National Superior Conservatory of Paris, Mozarteum, Salzburg, Cleveland Inst. of Music. *Career:* debut piano recital at Princess Grace Theatre, Monte Carlo 1983; performed in major halls and festivals in France, Germany, Italy, Switzerland, Thailand and elsewhere; appearances as soloist with French, Russian and Polish orchestras, such as Philharmonic Orchestras of Nice, Cannes and Czestochowa, Chamber Orchestra of Haute-Normandie, The Moscow Soloists; television appearances include J. Martin's Le Monde est à vous (France 2), A Duault's Portée de Nuit (France 3), on TV 5 Bangkok, and numerous programmes on Télé Monte-Carlo; major radio broadcasts on France Musique, France Inter, Radio Nostalgie, Radio Monte-Carlo; founder and dir of various musical festivals. *Recordings include:* Voyage (musical). *Honours:* Honours Medal, City of Cannes 1971, Grand Prix, City of Nice 1975, Honours Medals, City of St-Jean-Cap-Ferrat 1976, 1999, Lys d'Or Honorary Medal 1996, Honours Medal, J. Rodrigo Anniversary 1999, decorated by Srinakharinwirot Univ., Bangkok 1999.

DESSAY, Natalie; French singer (soprano); b. 19 April 1965, Lyon. *Education:* Bordeaux Conservatoire and Ecole de l'Art Lyrique. *Career:* began career with concert of Mozart arias at La Scala (Milan); has since sung at many leading opera houses in France, Switzerland, Austria, USA and UK. *Operas include:* Don Procopio (Paris Opéra-Comique), Ariadne auf Naxos (Montpellier), Si j'étais Roi (Liège) 1990, Le Roi l'a dit (Nantes) 1990, Schauspieldirektor (Opéra de Lyon) 1991, Die Entführung (Opéra de Lyon), Die Fledermaus (Geneva), Les Contes d'Hoffmann (Opéra Bastille) 1992, (La Scala, Milan) 1994, Ariadne, Der Rosenkavalier (Vienna Staatsoper) 1993, Die Zauberflöte (Aix-en-Provence) 1994, (Opéra de Lyon) 1996, (Salzburg Festival) 1997, Arabella (Metropolitan Opera, New York) 1994, Lakmé (Nimes) 1996, Hamlet (Geneva) 1996, Die Schweigsame Frau (Vienna) 1996, Candide (Glyndebourne Festival) 1997, Alcina (Opera Garnier) 1999, Lulu (Vienna Staatsoper) 2000, Hamlet (Toulouse) 2000, Olympia (Opéra Bastille) 2000, Ophélie (Châtelet) 2000, Queen of Night (Vienna) 2000, Constanze (Geneva Opera) 2000, Aminta (Opéra Bastille) 2000, Hamlet (Royal Opera) 2003, Manon (Geneva) 2003, Roméo et Juliette (Metropolitan Opera) 2005, La Fille du Régiment (Covent Garden) 2006, Lucia di Lammermoor (Metropolitan Opera) 2007, La Sonnambula (Metropolitan Opera) 2009, Giulio Cesar (Opera Garnier, Paris) 2011, La Traviata (Metropolitan Opera) 2012. *Honours:* winner Int. Mozart Competition, Vienna Staatsoper 1990; Premier Prix de Concours Les Voix Nouvelles Competition, Opera News Award 2008. *Current Management:* c/o Agence Artistique Thérèse Cédelle, Boulevard Malesherbes 78, 75008 Paris, France. *Telephone:* 1-49-53-00-02. *Fax:* 1-45-63-70-23. *E-mail:* cedelle@wanadoo.fr. *Website:* www.natalie-dessay.com.

DESSÍ, Daniela; Italian singer (soprano); b. 14 May 1959, Genoa; m. Fabio Armiliato Jacopo. *Education:* Conservatory Arrigo Boito, Parma, Accad. Chigiana di Siena. *Career:* debut with the Comic Opera in La serva padrona by Pergolesi; repertoire of about 60 titles from Monteverdi to Prokofiev, including interpretation of heroines from Mozart and Verdi; considered to be best current interpreter of the 'Verismo' repertoire; Season 1988–89 debut at Teatro Regio di Parma with Don Giovanni, coming back regularly in operas like Falstaff, Don Carlo, Simon Boccanegra, Verdi-Requiem, the concerto Verdi100, Aida and Manon Lescaut; performances in all major opera houses, including Teatro alla Scala of Milan with Riccardo Muti (Don Carlos, Falstaff, Requiem, Così fan tutte and Nozze di Figaro) and in other important productions (Adriana Lecouvreur and Madama Butterfly), Staatsoper of Vienna with Claudio Abbado (Simon Boccanegra and Don Carlos), Metropolitan of New York with James Levine (Pagliacci and Madama Butterfly), Berlin Deutsche Oper and at Dresden with Giuseppe Sinopoli (Aida, Requiem), Bologna with Daniele Gatti (Tosca, Aida, Falstaff and Don Carlos), Bayerische Staatsoper of Munich and in Parma with Zubin Mehta (Falstaff, Requiem, Tosca and Don Giovanni), Philadelphia again with Muti (Pagliacci), Opera of Rome with Gianluigi Gelmetti (Iris, Il Trittico), Festival Rossini of Pesaro again with Gelmetti (Guglielmo Tell), Arena of Verona with Georges Prêtre and Zubin Mehta in Requiem by Verdi and in other productions amongst which are Otello, Aida, Tosca and Madama Butterfly, Zurich with Bruno Bartoletti (La cena delle beffe, Luisa Miller, Pagliacci) and Nicolas Harnoncourt (Aida), Tokyo with James Levine (Pagliacci), Daniele Gatti (Don Carlos) and Gustav Kuhn (La Traviata, La Bohème), again with Bartoletti in Mefistofele at the Comunale in Florence and at the Lyric Opera of Chicago; performed Madama Butterfly in 2001 (first Western performer in Nagasaki, Tokyo and Kobe during the tour organized in cooperation with the Festival Puccini of Torre del Lago); sang Manon Lescaut in Berlin, Tosca and Don Carlo in Vienna 2006; returned to La Scala for performance of Tosca conducted by Lorin Mazel 2006; performed Il Trovatore in a Japan tour with Teatro Comunale di Bologna, Madama Butterfly in Arena di Verona and Tosca in Tokyo, Otzu and Seoul in the 1900 original production by Teatro dell'Opera di Roma. *Recordings include:* Don Carlos (video), Così fan tutte, Adriana Lecouvreur from La Scala, Tosca from Teatro Real Madrid, Aida, Teatro Liceu, Barcellona, Madama Butterfly, Festival Puccini, la Bohème, Don Carlos, Iris, Rigoletto, Pagliacci, Falstaff, Manon Lescaut, Love Duets performed with Fabio Armiliato and Württembergische Philharmonie, conducted by Marco Boemi. *Honours:* First Prize, RAI Int. Competition 1980, Zenatello-Arena di Verona Prize, Giordano Prize, Municipality of Baveno, Puccini Prize, Municipality of Torre del Lago 2000, Cilea Prize, Reggio Calabria, Gigli d'Oro, Municipality of Recanati, Liguria Prize, Municipality of Genoa, E. Mazzoleni Prize, Palermo 2002. *Current Management:* c/o Atelier Musicale, Via Caselle 76, San Lazzaro di Savena 40068, Italy. *Telephone:* (051) 19984444. *Fax:* (051) 19984420. *E-mail:* info@ateliermusicale.com. *Website:* www.ateliermusicale.com. *E-mail:* dessi@danieladessi.com (office). *Website:* www.danieladessi.com.

DESYATNIKOV, Leonid Arkadievich; Russian composer; b. 1955, Kharkov, Ukraine. *Education:* Leningrad State Conservatory, studied with Boris Arapov and Boris Tishchenko. *Career:* Music Dir, Bolshoi Theatre 2009–10; mem. Composers' Union 1979–. *Films:* as composer: Sunset 1990, Lost in Siberia 1991, Capital Punishment 1992, Touch 1992, Moscow Nights 1994, Katia Izmailova 1994, Hammer and Sickle 1994, Giselle's Mania 1995, The Prisoner of the Mountains 1996, The One Who is More Tender 1996, Moscow (Grand Prix, Int. Cinema Music Festival, Golden Ram Prize) 2000, His Wife's Diary 2000, Tycoon: A New Russian 2002, Captive 2008, Target 2011. *Works include:* opera: Poor Lisa, The Children of Rosenthal; ballet: Love Song in Minor, The Children of Rosenthal (special jury prize, Golden Mask National Theatre Prize 2006), Lost Illusions (Golden Mask Prize as Best Composer 2012); tango-operetta: Astor Piazzola's Maria de Buenos Aires; instrumental:

The Right of Winter 1949, Sketches for Sunset 1992, Russian Seasons; vocal: The Gift 1981, Love and Death of a Poet 1989, The Leaden Echo 1990. *Honours:* State Prize of Russia 2003. *Website:* www.leoniddesyatnikov.com (office).

DEUSSEN, Nancy Bloomer, BM; American composer; b. (Nancy Van Norman), 1 Feb. 1931, New York, NY; d. of Horace Van Norman and Julia Van Norman; m. 1st Charles J. Webster 1952; m. 2nd John H. Bloomer 1962; m. 3rd Gary R. Deussen 1982; one s. two d. *Education:* Juilliard School of Music, Manhattan School of Music, Univ. of Southern California School of Music, Univ. of California, Los Angeles, Long Beach State Univ., San Jose State Univ. *Career:* Co-founder and Pres. Emer. Nat. Asscn of Composers, San Francisco Bay Chapter; fmr Assoc. Prof. of Music, Mission Coll., CA; set up Accessibility Music Publishing; comms from Walnut Street Chamber Ensemble, Richard Nunemaker (clarinettist), Angela Koregelos (flautist), Palo Alto Unified School Dist, De Anza Coll. Chorale and Women's Chorus, Mission Chamber Orchestra, Santa Clara Chorale, Choral Project, Mu Phi Epsilon, Soundmoves Chamber Ensemble, Oakland Chamber Orchestra, Semper Virens, US Army TRADOC Band, US Army Band at West Point, Foundation for Universal Sacred Music, Baton Rouge Concert Band, Blackledge Chamber Ensemble, Ron Levy of Palisades Virtuosi, and others; mem. American Music Center, NACUSA, American Composers Forum, BMI, Nat. League of American Pen Women, Fortnightly Music Club. *Compositions:* The Little Hill (ballet music) 1952, Reflections on the Hudson for orchestra 1955, Little Fugue and Harvest Suite for recorders 1956, Missa de Angelis 1957, Suite for clarinet and piano 1959, The Serpent (cantata) 1965, Woodwind Quintet 1983, Three Rustic Sketches for orchestra 1987, Prelude and Cascades for piano 1987, Fanfare and Andante for winds 1988, The Long Voyage for soprano and recorders 1988, Trio for violin, clarinet and piano 1988, San Andreas Suite 1989, Two Pieces for violin and piano 1990, Trio for violin, cello and piano 1993, Peninsula Suite for string orchestra 1994, One of Nature's Majesties 1994, Concerto for clarinet and small orchestra 1995, Musings: Circa 1940 for solo piano 1995, Canticles for brass 1997, Parisian Caper 1997, Ascent to Victory for orchestra 1997, The Pegasus Suite for flute and piano 1998, Tribute to the Ancients for brass quintet 1998, A Silver, Shining Strand suite for orchestra 2001, Celebration Octet 2002, Et in Terra Pax for SATB and piano 2002, Tico for orchestra 2004, The Message for SATB and chamber orchestra 2004, Dawn of Freedom for concert band 2005, American Hymn for orchestra 2005, Solstice Circle for flute, cello and harp 2006, A Field in Pennsylvania for orchestra 2006, A Dream for All People for SATB and piano 2007, Music from the Heartland for flute, violin and cello 2007, Trinity Alps for orchestra 2008, music for Victoria Who? (musical theatre) 2008, Central Coast Concerto for piano and orchestra 2008, Memorabilia for flute, violin and piano 2010, Rondo for Ron for flute, clarinet, piano 2011, Suite for Ingrid for piccolo/ sax quartet 2011, Afternoon in Asbury Park for trumpet/piano 2012. *Honours:* First Prize, Britten-on-the-Bay 1996, Marmor Chamber Music Composition Competition 2002, First Prize, Mu Phi Epsilon Composition Competition 2005, First Prize, Chicago Recorder Soc. Composition Competition 2006, two First Prizes and one Second Prize, Nat. League of American Pen Women Composition Competition 2006. *Address:* 433 Sylvan Avenue #44, Mountain View, CA 94041, USA (home). *Telephone:* (650) 625-8572 (office). *E-mail:* ndeussen@ sbcglobal.net (home); deussen@ix.netcom.com (home). *Website:* www .nancybloomerdeussen.com.

DEUTSCH, Bernd Richard; Austrian composer; b. 15 May 1977, Mödling, Lower Austria. *Education:* Conservatorium Josef Matthias Hauer, Wiener Neustadt, Universität für Musik und darstellende Kunst, Vienna, studied composition with Erich Urbanner and Dieter Kaufmann. *Career:* commissions from ensembles including Die reihe, Reconsil, Klangforum Wien and NÖ Tonkünstlerorchester; worked with ensembles such as Arditti Quartet (premiered Traumspiel and String Quartet No. 2), Ensemble reconsil (premiered the Oboe Concerto) and Tokyo Philharmonic Orchestra (premiered subliminal); works performed at festivals including Wien Modern 2013, which featured five of his works; Composer-in-Residence, Druskininkai Artists Residence, Lithuania 2013. *Compositions include:* Mad Dog for ensemble 2011, Oboe Concerto for oboe and 11 instruments 2011, subliminal for orchestra 2010, Sijo 2012–13, Dr Futurity 2012–13, Konzert for brass trio and orchestra (world premiere, NÖ Tonkünstlerorchester at Vienna Musikverein) 2013–14. *Honours:* Ernst Krenek Prize, City of Vienna 2002, Repub. of Austria Music Prize 2003, Toru Takemitsu Composition Award 2011, Erste Bank Composition Award 2013, Paul Hindemith Prize 2014. *Address:* c/o Antje Müller, Boosey & Hawkes, Lützowufer 26, 10787 Berlin, Germany (home). *Telephone:* (30) 25001323 (office). *Fax:* (30) 25001399 (office). *E-mail:* antje .mueller@boosey.com (office); bernd-richard.deutsch@gmx.net. *Website:* www .boosey.com (office).

DEUTSCH, Helmut; Austrian pianist; b. 24 Dec. 1945, Vienna. *Education:* studied in Vienna. *Career:* chamber musician and accompanist to leading singers; fmr partners include Irmgard Seefried, Rita Streich, Ileana Cotrubas, Grace Bumbry, Barbar Bonney, Hans Hotter, Peter Schreier, Bernd Weikl and Hermann Prey; recital partners include Olaf Bär, Ruth Ziesak, Dietrich Henschel, Juliane Banse, Angelika Kirchschlager, Diana Damrau, Andreas Schmidt, Michael Volle, Jonas Kaufmann, Mauro Peter, Klaus Florian Vogt, Annette Dasch, Camilla Nylund and Bo Skovhus; made his Royal Opera debut 2014; numerous festival appearances; teacher, Vienna Music Acad. 1967–79, Munich Hochschule für Musik 1986–2014; master-classes in Europe and

Japan. *Honours:* Vienna Composition Prize 1967. *E-mail:* hedeutsch@yahoo.com.

DEVIA, Mariella; Italian singer (soprano); b. 1948, Imperia. *Education:* Accademia di Santa Cecilia, Rome. *Career:* debut at Spoleto 1972, as Despina in Così fan tutte; Rome Opera 1973, as Lucia di Lammermoor; guest appearances in Italy and at Munich, Hamburg and Berlin; Has sung Donizetti's Adina in Dallas and Verdi's Oscar in Chicago; Metropolitan Opera from 1979, as Gilda, Constanze in Die Entführung, Nannetta in Falstaff; Concert performance of Lakmé in New York; Sang title role in Donizetti's Elisabetta al Castello di Kenilworth at Bergamo, 1989; Elvira in I Puritani at Rome and Madrid, 1990; Maggio Musicale Florence, 1990 as Donizetti's Parisina; Rossini roles include Adele in Le Comte Ory, Amenaide in Tancredi and Semiramide; Pesaro Festival 1995, Zelmira; Sang Lucia di Lammermoor at Florence, 1996; at Teatro alla Scala: Capuleti e Montecchi, Lodoïska (Cherubini), Lucia di Lammermoor, Die Entführung, La fille du régiment, Turco in Italia 1990–97; Covent Garden: Die Zauberflöte, 1988; Rigoletto, 1990; season 1999–2000 at Covent Garden as Desdemona in Rossini's Otello; season 2000–01 as Donizetti's Adelia at Carnegie Hall, Bellini's Amina and Elvira at Florence, Lucrezia Borgia in Bologna. *Recordings include:* Rossini Adelaide di Borgogna, Donizetti Elisabetta al Castello di Kenilworth, Bellini La Sonnambula and I Puritani (Fonit Cetra); L'Elisir d'amore; Lucia di Lammermoor, with Zubin Mehta. *Current Management:* Atelier Musicale, Via Caselle 76, San Lazzaro di Savena 40068, Italy. *Telephone:* (51) 19984444. *Fax:* (51) 19984420. *E-mail:* info@ateliermusicale.com. *Website:* www.ateliermusicale.com.

DEVICH, Janos; Hungarian cellist and academic; b. 3 April 1938, Szeged; m. Sara Veslelszky 1974; three s. *Education:* Liszt Ferenc Acad. for Music, Budapest. *Career:* concerts regularly across Europe and in the USA, Australia, Japan, People's Republic of China, Republic of Korea; festivals in Besançon, Bath, Estoril, Prague, Warsaw, Babilin, Como, Chamonix, Amiens, Devon; Pres., Magyar Zenemüveszeti Társaság; Vice-Pres., Magyar Muzsikus Forum. *Recordings:* Kodály, Mozart, Dohnányi, Contemporary composers string quartet; String Quartets (Debussy, Ravel, D'Indy); Piano Quintets (Brahms, Schumann, Schubert); Complete Quartets (Schubert, Haydn). *Honours:* Franz Liszt Prize 1970, Merited Artist of Hungary 1990, Bartók-Pasztory Prize 1996.

DEVLIN, Michael Coles, BMus; American singer (bass-baritone); b. 27 Nov. 1942, Chicago, IL. *Education:* Louisiana State Univ., studied with Treigle, Ferro and Malas in New York. *Career:* operatic debut as Spalanzani, Les Contes d'Hoffmann, New Orleans 1963; first appearance with New York City Opera as the Hermit in US premiere of Ginastera's Don Rodrigo 1966; on roster until 1978; British debut as Mozart's Almaviva, Glyndebourne Festival 1974; Royal Opera Covent Garden, London 1975, 1977, 1979; European debut, Holland Festival 1977; Frankfurt Opera and Bavarian State Opera, Munich 1977; Metropolitan Opera debut in New York as Escamillo 1978; San Francisco Opera 1979; Hamburg State Opera and Paris Opéra 1980; Miami Opera and Monte Carlo Opera 1981; Dallas Opera 1983; Chicago Lyric Opera 1984; Los Angeles Opera 1986; other roles have been Don Giovanni, Eugene Onegin, Golaud, Don Alfonso, Ford, Wotan and the villains in Les Contes d' Hoffmann; at Santa Fe has sung Altair in Strauss's Die Aegyptische Helena and the Commandant in Friedenstag; sang Pizarro in Fidelio at Los Angeles 1990; Jochanaan in Salome at Covent Garden 1992; sang Escamillo at Los Angeles 1992 followed by Boris Godunov 1994; Amsterdam 1995, in Schoenberg's Moses und Aron; The Doctor in Wozzeck at the Metropolitan 1997; season 1998 as Dikoy in Katya Kabanova at St Louis; sang in Miss Havisham's Fire by Argento at Saint Louis 2001; numerous appearances as soloist with major orchestras. *Address:* c/o Opera Theatre of Saint Louis, PO Box 191910, 539 Garden Avenue, Saint Louis, MO 63119, USA.

DEVOYON, Pascal; French pianist; b. 6 April 1953, Paris; m. 1992; two s. *Education:* Ecole Normale de Musique Conservatoire de Paris. *Career:* has played with orchestras from 1975, including the Philharmonia, Leningrad Philharmonic, NHK Tokyo; broadcasts over radio and television with Orchestre de la Suisse Romande, Orchestre National d'Espayne, Rotterdam, Stuttgart Philharmonic and RAI of Milan; Debussy Sonatas and Fauré's D Minor Trio for the London Prom concerts at the Victoria and Albert Museum; Prof., Paris Conservatoire 1991, Berlin Hochschule für Musik 1995. *Recordings:* Ravel, Liszt, Tchaikovsky, Bach, Franck, Fauré, Schumann, Grieg, Saint-Saëns. *Honours:* second prize Viotti Competition 1973, Busoni Competition 1974, third prize Leeds Competition 1975, second prize Tchaikovsky Competition 1978. *Address:* 50 Avenue de la Paix, 93270 Sevran, France.

DEW, John; American stage director; *Artistic Director, Darmstadt State Theatre;* b. 1 June 1944, Santiago de Cuba, Cuba. *Education:* studied art history and set design in New York, studied in Germany with Walter Felsenstein and Wieland Wagner. *Career:* grew up in New York; debut in The Rake's Progress at Ulm 1971; directed Mozart and Wagner cycles at Krefeld 1970s; Opera Stage Dir at Bielefeld 1982–95, with Maschinist Hopkins by Brand, Schreker's Irrelohe and Der Singende Teufel, Hindemith's Neues vom Tage, Der Sprung über den Schatten and Zwingburg by Krenek; Bakchantinnen by Wellesz, Fennimore and Gerda, Nixon in China and Boito's Nerone; season 1987–88 at Deutsche Oper, Berlin with Les Huguenots and premiere of Los Alamos by Neikrug; Les Huguenots seen at Covent Garden 1991; other productions include La Juive at Bielefeld and Nuremberg, Clemenza di Tito at Zurich, Death in Venice at Nuremberg 1992, Aida at Hamburg 1993, Puritani,

Vienna 1994, Andrea Chénier, Berlin, Leipzig production of Le nozze di Figaro seen at Israel Festival 1992; Artistic Dir of the Theatres of the City of Dortmund 1995–2001; directed premiere of Schnittke's Historia von D Johann Fausten, Hamburg 1995, Floyd's Susannah at Deutsche Oper, Berlin 1997; season 1998 with Die Königin von Saba at Dortmund and Lehar's Paganini in Vienna; Artistic Dir Darmstadt state theatre 2004–, productions include Oedipus the Tyrant, Antigonae, Apollo et Hyacinthus/The Obligation of the First Commandment, The Wise Woman, Parsifal, La Juive, The Master-singers of Nuremberg, Turandot, Katja Kabanowa, Gisei, the Sacrifice/De temporum fine comoedia, Anatevka, Fidelio, and others. *Address:* Staatstheater Darmstadt, Georg-Büchner-Platz 1, 64283 Darmstadt, Germany (office). *Telephone:* (6151) 2811600 (office). *E-mail:* info@staatstheater-darmstadt.de (office). *Website:* www.staatstheater-darmstadt.de (office).

DEWIS, Michael; British singer (baritone); b. 1970, England. *Education:* Guildhall School and National Opera Studio. *Career:* appearances as Marcello for the Mananan Festival, Escamillo at Dartington and Renato (Un Ballo in Maschera) for Opera Holland Park; Season 1997–98 in Don Carlos and The Golden Cockerel for the Royal Opera; Other roles include Papageno, Jack Rance (La Fanciulla del West) and Don Alfonso; Concerts include Messiah at the Albert Hall, Beethoven's Ninth, Mendelssohn's Elijah, Verdi's Requiem and The Dream of Gerontius. *Honours:* Guildhall Schubert Prize. *Address:* Hinckley, Leics., LE10 0LW, England.

DEXTER-MILLS, Christopher John, BA, MMus, PhD, PGCE; British musicologist, teacher, organist, conductor and composer; *Assistant Director of Music, The Stephen Perse Foundation;* b. 11 Dec. 1956, Boston, Lincs., England; m. Suzanne; one s. *Education:* Dartington Coll. of Arts, Durham Univ. School of Educ., Goldsmiths Coll., London, Univ. of East Anglia. *Career:* asst teacher of music, Ernulf Community School 1980–85; Organist, St Mary's Parish Church, St Neots, Cambs. 1981–83; Head of Music, Soham Village Coll. 1986–94; Conductor Ely Choral Soc. 1992–2000; Dir of Music, The Netherhall School, Cambridge 1995–2011; Asst Dir of Music, The Stephen Perse Foundation 2011–; GCE Examiner, Edexcel Foundation 1996–; mem. Royal Musical Asscn. *Compositions include:* Wind Quintet—Musica Typographia (performed at Cambridge Festival of Ideas) 2013. *Address:* The Stephen Perse Foundation, Union Road, Cambridge, CB2 1HF (office); 123 Nowton Road, Bury St Edmunds, IP33 2NH, England (home). *E-mail:* cdm@stephenperse.com (office); c.dextermills@gmail.com (home).

DEYOUNG, Michelle; American singer (mezzo-soprano); b. 1968, Michigan. *Education:* apprentice with the Santa Fe Opera and the Israel Arts Vocal Inst., Met Young Artist Program. *Career:* concert appearances with orchestras, including New York Philharmonic, Boston Symphony, Chicago Symphony, San Francisco Symphony, LA Philharmonic, Atlanta Symphony, Pittsburgh Symphony, Oregon Symphony, Kansas City Symphony, St Louis Symphony, Vienna Philharmonic, Puerto Rico Symphony, BBC Symphony, Philharmonia, RPO, Orchestre de Paris, Flanders Philharmonic, Bayerische Staatsoper, Chamber Orchestra of Europe; opera engagements have included Venus in Tannhäuser and Dido in Les Troyens (Met Opera), Sieglinde in Die Walküre, Waltraute in Götterdämmerung and Brägane in Tristan und Isolde (Lyric Opera, Chicago), title role in Rape of Lucretia (Glimmerglass), Kundry in Parsifal (Bayreuth Festival), Jocaste in Oedipus Rex and Gertrude in Hamlet (Théâtre du Châtelet), Fricka in Das Rheingold and Die Walküre (Covent Garden, Royal Albert Hall, Birmingham and the Concertgebouw); recitals at the Ravinia Festival, Weill Recital Hall, Alice Tully Hall, SUNY Purchase, Gulbenkian Foundation, Lisbon, Edinburgh Festival, Wigmore Hall, La Monnaie, Brussels. *Recordings include:* Bernstein's Symphony No. 1 with Leonard Slatkin and the BBC SO, Das Klagende Lied with Michael Tilson Thomas and the San Francisco Symphony, Mahler's Symphony No. 3 with Jesus Lopez Cobos and the Cincinnati Symphony, Das Lied von der Erde with the Minnesota Orchestra, Les Troyens with Sir Colin Davis and the LSO (Grammy Awards for Best Classical Album, Best Opera Recording 2001), Mahler's Kindertotenlieder and Symphony No. 3 with Michael Tilson Thomas and the San Francisco Symphony (Grammy Award for Best Classical Album 2004). *Honours:* winner Marilyn Horne Foundation Wings of Song, Marian Anderson Award, Aria Award, Tucker Award, first place Oratorio Competition, winner Met Competition. *Current Management:* c/o Caroline Woodfield, Opus 3 Artists LLC, 470 Park Avenue South, 9th Floor North, New York, NY 10016, USA. *Telephone:* (212) 584-7526. *Fax:* (646) 300-8226. *E-mail:* cwoodfield@opus3artists.com. *Website:* www.opus3artists.com; www.michelledeyoung.com.

DI BELLA, Benito; Italian singer (baritone); b. 1942, Palermo, Sicily. *Education:* Palermo Conservatory, studied in Pesaro. *Career:* sang at Spoleto and elsewhere in Italy before La Scala Milan debut 1971, as Marcello in La Bohème; sang further in Naples, Genoa, Venice and Palermo; Amonasro at 1989 Verona Arena, Jack Rance at the 1985 Macerata festival; further appearances throughout North and South America as Verdi's Luna, Germont, Pietro (Simon Boccanegra) and Rigoletto, Gerard in Andrea Chenier, the Herald in Lohengrin, and Escamillo; Taormina Festival 1990.

DI CESARE, Ezio; Italian singer (tenor); b. 1939, Rome. *Education:* studied in Rome. *Career:* sang with a vocal sextet and made tours of Italy; stage debut 1975, in Bellini's Beatrice di Tenda; many appearances in Italy and elsewhere in Europe as Alfredo, Rodolfo, and Tom Rakewell in The Rake's Progress; La Scala Milan 1980, 1984, in Vivaldi's Tito Manlio and Idomeneo; Arvino, in Verdi's I Lombardi; appearances in The Netherlands and at the Verona Arena;

sang at Rome 1986, in Spontini's Agnese di Hohenstaufen; Teatro Liceo, Barcelona 1987, in the Spanish premiere of Mozart's Lucio Silla; Pesaro Festival 1988, as Iago in Rossini's Otello; sang Carlo in Pergolesi's Lo Frate Innamorato at La Scala 1989; Gabriele Adorno at Cremona; Rome Opera 1990, in Franco Mannino's Il Principe Felice; season 1992 as Iarba in Jommelli's Didone Abbandonata at the Teatro Rossini, Lugo; season 1994 as Ismaele in Nabucco at Verona; La Scala 1995, as Raffaela in Verdi's Stiffelio; Jesi 1998, as Sostrate in Pergolesi's II Prigionero Superbo; sang the High Priest in Idomeneo at Florence 1996; season 2000–01 as Offenbach's Orphée at Turin and the Prince in Lulu at Palermo. *Recordings:* Verdi's Stiffelio, La Finta Giardiniera, Alfano's Cyrano de Bergerac.

DI FRANCO, Loretta; American singer (soprano); b. 28 Oct. 1942, New York, NY. *Education:* studied with Maud Webber and Walter Taussig in New York. *Career:* sang in the chorus of the Metropolitan Opera until 1965; solo appearances in New York in The Queen of Spades, Don Giovanni (Zerlina), Un Ballo in Maschera (Oscar), Gianni Schicchi (Lauretta), Le nozze di Figaro (Marcellina) and Lucia di Lammermoor (title role); Returned to Met 1990, as Marthe in Faust.

DI LOTTI, Silvana; Italian composer; b. 29 Nov. 1942, Aglie Canavese, Turin. *Education:* studied in Turin and Salzburg, in Siena with Berio and Boulez. *Career:* teacher, Turin Conservatory. *Compositions include:* Aragorn for harpsichord and five strings, Contrasti for two clarinets 1981, Capriccio for violin and piano 1981, Duo in Eco for violin and guitar 1982, Conversari for orchestra 1982, Serenata for chamber orchestra 1982, Groups for piano 1983, In Nomine Domini for orchestra 1983, Intonazione for saxophone and piano 1983, Rapsodia for two guitars 1984, Surfaces for organ 1985, Aura for piano 1985, Piano Trio 1986, C'est pour toi seule for mixed choir 1987, Mattutino for harp 1990, A Solo for clarinet and ensemble 1991, Arabesque for cello 1991, E Nessun Tempo a Memoria di Echi Svelati for bass clarinet and harp 1992, Musica per Giocare for piano 1994, Terre Rare for orchestra 1995, Haide for violin, cello and piano, Petite Pièce for string orchestra 2005, Vagheggiar di Eco for soprano, bass, string orchestra and harpsichord (text from 'Sigismondo di Borgogna') 2006. *Address:* c/o Viale Ovidio 5, Gassino, Fr Bardassano, 10090 Turin, Italy. *Telephone:* (011) 9605035. *E-mail:* sildilotti@libero.it (office); maripi@iol.it (office).

DI PIANDUNI, Oslavio; Uruguayan singer (tenor); b. 1939, Montevideo. *Education:* studied in Montevideo. *Career:* appeared at Montevideo 1961–65 as Rinuccio in Gianni Schicchi and Lionel in Martha; Klagenfurt 1968–70 and Alfredo, Riccardo, Hoffmann, Don José, Pinkerton and Calaf at Bielefeld 1970–75; further engagements at Theater am Gärtnerplatz, Munich 1975–76, Vienna Volksoper 1976–78 and Kiel 1979–82; Bremen 1982–84, Zürich 1988 as Edmund in Reimann's Lear; Hanover 1989, as Andrea Chénier; other roles include Luigi in Il Tabarro, Hermann in The Queen of Spades and Otello, Oslo 1999; has also sung in operettas by Lehar, Johann Strauss and Offenbach; numerous concert appearances and lieder recitals.

DI PIETRO, Rocco; American composer; b. 15 Sept. 1949, Buffalo, NY; m. Juli Douglass 1973, one s. *Education:* State Univ. of New York, studied with Hans Hagen, Lukas Foss and Bruno Maderna. *Career:* lecturer on modern music; performances of his compositions have been played in Europe and USA by musicians and ensembles, including Christiane Edinger, Christobal Halffter, Lukas Foss, Bruno Maderna, Bavarian Radio Orchestra, Brooklyn Philharmonic, St Paul Chamber Orchestra. *Compositions:* Overture to Combats for History for percussion orchestra 1980–81, Melodia Arcana for percussion and tarot cards 1980–83, Aria Grande for violin and orchestra 1980, Tratto Bizzaro (opera) 1984, Beauty and the Beast (incidental music for theatre) 1986, Annales after Tasso for madrigal voices and percussion 1987. *Address:* c/o American Percussion Publications, PO Box 436, Lancaster, NY 14086, USA.

DI VIRGILIO, Nicholas; American singer (tenor); b. 1937, New York. *Education:* Eastman School, New York. *Career:* debut as Pinkerton with Chautauqua Opera 1961; sang at Baltimore from 1956, San Francisco 1966–67, Cincinnati, New Orleans 1969–70, San Diego, Pittsburgh and the New York City Opera 1964–71; Metropolitan Opera from 1970, as Pinkerton and as Edgardo in Lucia di Lammermoor; European engagements at Brussels, Amsterdam and Lyon 1968–70; London 1978, in the Verdi Requiem; other roles have included Mozart's Idomeneo, Don Ottavio and Ferrando, Verdi's Alfredo, Fenton and Riccardo, Faust, Rodolfo, Hoffmann, Don José, Laca in Jenůfa and Cavaradossi; voice teacher, Univ. of Illinois.

DIADKOVA, Larissa; Russian singer (mezzo-soprano); b. 1954, Zelenodolsk. *Education:* St Petersburg Conservatory. *Career:* sang with the Kirov Opera, St Petersburg, and elsewhere in Russia as Ratmir in Ruslan and Lyudmila, Konchakovna in Prince Igor, Tchaikovsky's Olga and Pauline and the Duenna in Prokofiev's Betrothal in a Monastery; guest appearances at the Bregenz and Edinburgh Festivals; Florence, 1995 as Verdi's Ulrica, Bolshoi and Metropolitan, 1996 as Marfa in Khovanshchina and Madelon in Andrea Chénier; Lyon and Savonlinna Festival, 1996 as the Countess in The Queen of Spades and Liubov in Mazeppa; Season 1998 as Ulrica at Monte Carlo, in Tchaikovsky's Mazeppa at the New York Met and Marfa with the Kirov Opera at La Scala; Season 2000–01 as Ulrica at the Vienna Staatsoper, Mistress Quickly at Salzburg, Azucena at Verona and Amneris for San Francisco Opera; Jezibaba in Rusalka at Covent Garden (concert) 2003. *Recordings:* Rimsky's Sadko; Mazeppa by Tchaikovsky.

DIANDA, Hilda; Argentine composer; b. 13 April 1925, Cordoba. *Education:* studied with Malipiero and Scherchen, Milan Electronic Music Studios and in Darmstadt. *Career:* teacher at Cordoba until 1971; performances of her music in Europe and North America; educator and lecturer. *Compositions include:* Requiem 1984, Cantico (after St Francis of Assisi) 1985, Trio for clarinet, cello and piano 1985, Encantamientos for tape 1985, Viola Concerto 1988, Paisaje for four percussion 1992, Mitos for percussion and strings 1993, Pitiales for marimba 1994. *Honours:* Cultural Merit Medal, Italy.

DIAZ, Justino; Puerto Rican singer (bass-baritone); b. 29 Jan. 1939, San Juan. *Education:* Univ. of Puerto Rico, New England Conservatory, and studied with Ralph Errolle and Frederick Jagel. *Career:* debut in Puerto Rico 1957, in Menotti's The Telephone; with Metropolitan Opera from 1963, as Monterone and Sparafucile in Rigoletto, Figaro, Rossini's Maometto II and Colline; Festival Casals, Puerto Rico, 1964–65; Spoleto Festival, 1965; Salzburg Festival, 1966, as Escamillo; created Antony in Barber's Antony and Cleopatra, New York Met, 1966; La Scala, Milan, 1969, in Rossini's L'Assedio do Corinto; New York City Opera, 1973, in Ginastera's Beatrix Cenci; Covent Garden, 1976, as Escamillo; guest appearance in Hamburg, Vienna, Mexico City, Chicago and San Francisco; San Francisco and Milan, 1982, as Scarpia and Asdrubalo in La Pietra del Paragone; sang Attila at Cincinnati, 1984, Iago at Covent Garden, 1990; Michele in Il Tabarro at Miami, 1989, Iago and Scarpia at Los Angeles; sang Escamillo at Rio de Janeiro, 1990; debut as Amonasro at Cincinnati, 1990; sang Iago in Zeffirelli's film version of Otello, 1987; Greater Miami Opera, 1992 as Franchetti's Cristoforo Colombo; sang Puccini's Jack Rance at Covent Garden, 1994, Scarpia in 1995 (and for Opera Pacific, 1998); sang Iago for Washington Opera 2000; retd 2003 and now associated with Casals Festival and stages opera. *Recordings include:* Medea and La Wally; Thais by Massenet; L'Assedio di Corinto and Otello; Semele; Videos of Zeffirelli's Otello, and Meyerbeer's L'Africaine, from San Francisco Opera.

DÍAZ, Roberto; Chilean violist and academic administrator; *President and CEO, Curtis Institute of Music. Career:* fmr prin. violist Nat. Symphony under Mstislav Rostropovich; fmr mem. Boston Symphony under Seiji Ozawa, Minnesota Orchestra under Sir Neville Marriner; prin. violist, Philadelphia Orchestra 1996–2006; has performed with orchestras, including Boston Pops, Kansas City Symphony, Curtis Symphony Orchestra, Bavarian Radio Orchestra, Gulbenkian Orchestra, Orquesta Nacional de España, Bilbao Symphony, Netherlands Philharmonic, Russian State Symphony, Saarbrücken Radio Orchestra, Orquesta Simón Bolivar; collaborations with composers, including Edison Denisov, Krzysztof Penderecki, Roberto Sierra; as chamber musician has performed with Emanuel Ax, Yefim Bronfman, Christoph Eschenbach, Yo-Yo Ma, Wolfgang Sawallisch, Isaac Stern, Emerson String Quartet; festival appearances include Kuhmo, Marlboro, Mostly Mozart at Lincoln Center, Spoleto, Verbier; mem., Díaz Trio (with violinist Andrés Cárdenes and cellist Andrés Díaz), touring throughout N and S America and Europe, currently ensemble-in-residence Brevard Music Festival; Pres. and CEO, Curtis Inst. of Music; fmr faculty mem., Peabody Inst., Rice Univ.; mem. American Philosophical Soc. 2013–. *Recordings include:* Druckman, Viola Concerto, Paganini, Music for Strings and Guitar (with Díaz Trio) 1996, Vieuxtemps, Music for Viola and Piano 2004, Díaz Trio Performs Dohnányi, Penderecki, Fine, Beethoven 2005, Primrose, Viola Transcriptions 2006. *Honours:* Hon. mem. Nat. Bd American Viola Soc.; Dr hc (Bowdoin Coll.); prizewinner, Naumburg and Munich Int. Viola Competitions, Philadelphia Orchestra C. Hartman Kuhn Award 2006. *Current Management:* c/o Drew Hemenger, Schmidt Artists International Inc., 59 East 54th Street, Suite 83, New York, NY 10022, USA. *Telephone:* (212) 421-8500 (office). *Fax:* (212) 421-8583 (office). *E-mail:* drew@schmidtart.com (office). *Website:* www .schmidtart.com (office). *Address:* The Curtis Institute of Music, 1726 Locust Street, Philadelphia, PA 19103, USA (office). *Telephone:* (215) 893-5252 (office). *Fax:* (215) 893-9065 (office). *Website:* www.curtis.edu (office); www .robertodiazviola.com.

DIBAK, Igor, Mgr Art, PhD; Slovak composer; *Reader Expert, Academy of Arts, Banská Bystrica;* b. 5 July 1947, Spisska Nova Ves; m. Katarina Ormisova 1970. *Education:* Conservatoire Zilina, Univ. of Arts, Bratislava with Prof. Jan Cikker. *Career:* Ed., Music Dept, Czech TV, Bratislava 1969–79; Ed.-in-Chief, Music Dept, Czech Radio, Bratislava 1979–87, Music Dept, Czech TV 1987–90; Dir, Music School 1990–96; Ed., Music Dept, Slovak TV 1996–98; Reader Expert, Acad. of Arts, Banská Bystrica 1998–; mem. Slovak Music Union, Bratislava, Slovak Protective Union of Authors, Bratislava. *Compositions:* Opera Candlestick, New Year's Eve Party, Ballet Portrait, symphonic works including Accordion Concerto 1996; chamber compositions and compositions for children. *Recordings:* Moments musicaux 1, Fantasy for Viola and Orchestra, Divertimento for Strings, Opera Candlestick, New Year's Eve Party, Ballet Portrait (Czech TV); symphonic and chamber works (Czech Radio Bratislava). *Publications:* Methodics of Piano Improvisation 1981; contrib. to Hudobny zivot (Music Live). *Honours:* Jan Levoslav Bella Award 1979, Union of Slovak Music Composers Award 1987. *Current Management:* c/o Music Fond, Medená 29, 811 02 Bratislava, Slovakia. *Address:* Bajzova 10, 821 08 Bratislava, Slovakia. *Telephone:* (2) 555-72-894 (home). *E-mail:* dibak@ stonline.sk (home).

DIBBLE, Jeremy Colin, BA, PhD, FRSCM, FGCM; British academic; *Professor of Music, Durham University;* b. 17 Sept. 1958, Epping, Essex, England; s. of Colin Dibble and Pamela Miers; m. Alison Jane Manning 1984. *Education:* Trinity Coll., Cambridge, Univ. of Southampton. *Career:* Lecturer in Music,

Univ. Coll., Cork, Ireland 1987–93; Lecturer in Music, Durham Univ. 1993–98, Reader in Music 1998–2003, Prof. of Music 2003–, mem. Soc. of Fellows, Knott/Christopherson Fellowship 2004–; reviewer for the Gramophone; Vice-Pres. Stanford Soc. 2003–; mem. Oxford and Cambridge Club; Fellow, Royal School of Church Music 2011. *Recordings:* consultant, ed. and sleeve-note writer for many recordings of works by Parry, Stanford and others. *Radio:* programmes on Parry and Stanford. *Publications:* C. Hubert H. Parry: His Life and Music 1992, Nineteenth-Century British Music Studies (with Zon) 2002, Charles Villiers Stanford: Man and Musician 2002, Parry Sonatas for Violin and Piano, Musica Britannica Trust, Vol. LXXX 2003, John Stainer: A Life in Music 2007, Michele Esposito 2010, Hamilton Harty: Musical Polymath 2013; contrib. of essays on Vaughan Williams in Perspective, Irish Musical Studies II: Studies in Church Music, King Arthur and Music, Howells Studies, The Ireland Companion (Church Music), Shelley and Music, World Christianity: The Nineteenth Century (Music and the Church), Music and British Culture 1785–1914, Constructions of Nationalism, Nineteenth Century British Music Studies Vols I and II; articles in Journal of the British Institute of Organ Studies, Brio, Journal of the Ralph Vaughan Williams Society, New Grove 2, New Dictionary of National Biography, Thoemmes Dictionary of Nineteenth Century British Philosophers, Musik in Geschichte und Gegenwart, Dictionary of Irish Biography, New Oxford Companion to Music, Grolier's Encyclopaedia of the Victorian Era; reviews in Music and Letters, Notes and Journal of Victorian Studies, Dictionary of Hymnology; Musical Editor, Dictionary of Hymnology. *Address:* Department of Music, Durham University, Palace Green, Durham, DH1 3RL, England (office). *Telephone:* (191) 334-3158 (office). *Fax:* (191) 334-3141 (office). *E-mail:* jeremy.dibble@durham.ac.uk (office). *Website:* www.dur.ac.uk/music (office).

DICHIERA, David, MA, PhD; American arts organization executive; *General Director, Michigan Opera Theater*; b. 8 April 1935, McKeesport, Pa. *Education:* Univ. of California, Los Angeles with Lukas Foss. *Career:* began career as instructor, UCLA; Prof., later Chair. of Music, Oakland Univ., Detroit 1962; cr. Overture to Opera programme of staged opera scenes and one-act operas that he narrated and toured to hundreds of schools and community centers; Founder and Gen. Dir Michigan Opera Theatre 1971–; Founding Dir Music Hall Center for the Performing Arts, Detroit 1973; Artistic Dir Dayton Opera Asscn 1981–93; Founding Gen. Dir Opera Pacific, Orange Co., Calif. 1986–96; est. Detroit Opera House 1996; Chair. of Bd, OPERA America 1979–83. *Honours:* numerous hon. doctorates; Fulbright Scholarship (to Italy), Nat. Endowment for the Arts Opera Honor 2010. *Address:* Michigan Opera Theater, 1526 Broadway, Detroit, MI 48226, USA (office). *Telephone:* (313) 237-3420 (office). *Fax:* (313) 237-3412 (office). *E-mail:* ddd@motopera.org (office). *Website:* www.michiganopera.org (office).

DICHTER, Misha, BS; American concert pianist; b. 27 Sept. 1945, Shanghai, China; s. of Leon Dichter and Lucy Dichter; m. Cipa Dichter 1968; two s. *Education:* Juilliard School under Rosina Lhevinne. *Career:* has performed with leading orchestras and at festivals and given recitals worldwide; also performs with wife as piano duo. *Recordings include:* Beethoven Sonatas, Brahms Variations, music by Gershwin, Liszt, Mussorgsky, Stravinsky, Schumann, Tchaikovsky. *Publications:* articles in New York Times, Ovation and Keyboard magazines. *Honours:* winner, Tchaikovsky Competition 1966, Grand Prix du Disque Liszt 1999. *Current Management:* Shuman Associates, 120 West 58th Street, New York, NY 10019, USA. *E-mail:* shumanpr@shumanassociates.net. *Website:* mishadichter.com.

DICK, James Cordell, BMus; American concert pianist; b. 29 June 1940, Hutchinson, Kansas. *Education:* Univ. of Texas at Austin, Royal Acad. of Music, London; studied with Dalies Frantz, Clifford Curzon. *Career:* debut, Carnegie Hall, New York City, USA; performs professionally throughout the USA and abroad in orchestral, chamber and solo repertoire; performed with conductors Kondrashin, Barbirolli, Ormandy, Maazel, Levine, Comissiona, Lombard, Schwarz, Fleisher, de Priest, Fiedler, Foster, Robert Spano and Christopher Hogwood among others; has performed on radio in England, Germany, France, Netherlands, Switzerland, Mexico and US commissions new music for piano and orchestra; founder and Artistic Dir of Int. Festival-Inst. at Round Top, Texas. *Compositions:* Etudes for piano and orchestra, by Ben Lees, gave world premiere 1975, Shiva's Drum, by Dan Welcher, gave world premiere in 1994, Krishna, from Malcolm Hawkins (England), world premiere in 1996, Rising Light by Chinary Ung. *Recordings:* Beethoven's Concerto No. 4, Tchaikovsky Concerto No. 1, Chopin Concerto No. 1, Prokofiev Concerto No. 3, Saint-Saëns Concerto No. 2, Rachmaninov Rhapsody. *Honours:* Chevalier des Arts et des Lettres 1996; prize-winner, Tchaikovsky Competition, Russia 1965, Leventritt Competition, New York City 1965, Busoni Competition, Italy 1965, Texas State Musician 2003. *Current Management:* c/o Camerata Artists, 4 Margaret Road, Birmingham, B17 0EU, England; Alain Declert & Associates, PO Box 89, Round Top, TX 78954, USA. *Telephone:* (121) 426-6208 (Camerata). *E-mail:* jrhumphreys@yahoo.co.uk. *Address:* Festival Hill, Round Top, TX 78954-0089, USA (office).

DICKERSON, Roger Donald, BA, MM; American composer, musician (piano and double bass) and academic; b. 24 Aug. 1934, New Orleans, LA. *Education:* Dillard Univ., New Orleans, Ind. Univ. at Bloomington, Akademie für Musik und Darstellende Kunst, Vienna, Austria. *Career:* grew up playing jazz and blues in New Orleans; toured with Joe Turner and Guitar Slim 1951–54; mil. service in US Army, based in Ark. and Heidelberg, Germany 1957–59; played double bass with Fort Smith Symphony Orchestra 1957; composer, arranger for US Army in Europe Headquarters Co. Band, Heidelberg 1957–59; performed extensively in French Quarter of New Orleans 1962–; composed for New Orleans Symphony and others 1962–; Program Assoc. and Consultant in Humanities, Inst. for Services to Educ., Washington, DC 1979; private teacher of composition and piano 1962–; Adjunct Prof., Xavier Univ. of La, New Orleans 1979–82; Adjunct Prof., Southern Univ., New Orleans 1979–85; Assoc. Prof. and Co-ordinator of Music, Div. of Fine Arts 1985–; Lecturer in Music, Dillard Univ., New Orleans 1986–; co-f., Creative Arts Alliance of New Orleans (CAANO) 1975; Mayor's Task Force on Arts Policy for the City of New Orleans 1978; Mayor's Advisory Bd Arts and Cultural Affairs for the City of New Orleans 1979; La State Div. of the Arts Grant Cttee 1981; panellist La State Arts Council 1981–, Nat. Endowment for the Arts 1984–; mem. ASCAP. *Compositions include:* Prekussion for percussion 1954, Variations for woodwind trio 1955, Fair Dillard for chorus 1955, Sonatina for piano 1956, Chorale Prelude (Das neugeborne Kindelein) for organ 1956, String Quartet 1956, Music I Heard (vocal) 1956, Music for string trio 1957, Concert Overture for orchestra 1957, Essay for band 1958, Fugue 'n Blues for jazz ensemble 1959, Movement for trumpet and piano 1960, The Negro Speaks of Rivers (vocal) 1961, Quintet for wind instruments 1961, Ten Concert Pieces for beginning string players 1973, A Musical Service for Louis (A Requiem for Louis Armstrong) 1973, Orpheus an' His Slide Trombone for orchestra 1974–75, New Orleans Concerto 1976, Psalm 49 for chorus 1979, African-American Celebration for chorus 1984. *Honours:* Dr hc (Inst. for Minority Nationalities, People's Repub. of China) 1990; Dave Frank Award 1955, American Music Center Award 1972, 1975, New Orleans Bicentennial Comm. Certificate 1977, Citation of Achievement and Key to the City of New Orleans 1977, New Orleans Recreation Dept Louis Armstrong Cultural Devt Fund Memorial Award 1977, Masons Enterprises of New Orleans Outstanding Musicianship Award 1977, City Council of New Orleans Special Commendation 1978, Univ. New Orleans Marcus-Christian Award 1979. *Address:* c/o ASCAP, ASCAP Building, One Lincoln Plaza, New York, NY 10023, USA (office).

DICKIE, Brian James; British opera director (retd) and consultant; *Artistic Adviser, Bertelsmann Stiftung*; b. 23 July 1941, Newark, Notts., England; s. of the late Robert Kelso Dickie and of Harriet Elizabeth Dickie (née Riddell); m. 1st Victoria Teresa Sheldon (née Price) 1968; two s. one d.; m. 2nd Nancy Gustafson 1989; m. 3rd Elinor Rhys Williams 2002; one d. *Education:* Trinity Coll., Dublin. *Career:* Admin. Asst, Glyndebourne Opera 1962–66; Admin. Glyndebourne Touring Opera 1967–81; Opera Man., Glyndebourne Festival Opera 1970–81, Gen. Admin. 1981–89; Artistic Dir Wexford Festival 1967–73; Artistic Adviser, Théâtre Musical de Paris 1981–87, Bertelsmann Stiftung; Gen. Dir Canadian Opera Co. 1989–93; Artistic Counsellor, Opéra de Nice 1994–97; Gen. Dir EU Opera 1997–99, Chicago Opera Theater 1999–2012; Chair. London Choral Soc. 1978–85, Theatres Nat. Cttee Opera Cttee 1976–85; Vice-Chair. Theatres Nat. Cttee 1980–85; Vice-Pres. Theatrical Man. Asscn 1983–85; mem. Bd Opera America 1991–93. *Address:* 4 Bancroft Court, 35 Ackmar Road, London, SW6 4UR, England. *Telephone:* (20) 7736-1031; 7966-467512 (mobile). *E-mail:* briandickie@mac.com. *Website:* www.briandickie.com.

DICKINSON, Meriel, GRSM, ARMCM; British singer (mezzo-soprano); b. 8 April 1940, Lytham St Anne's, Lancs.; m. Robert J.H. Gardner 1991. *Education:* Royal Northern Coll. of Music, Vienna Academy, Austria. *Career:* made professional debut, London 1964; other notable performances included St Matthew Passion at Snape Maltings, Beethoven's Choral Symphony at Vienna Festival; frequent radio broadcasts, two BBC television documentary films; recital programmes with her brother, composer Peter Dickinson throughout Europe; f. Music Deco ensemble 1978; retd from performing 1997; currently private voice tutor and competition judge; mem, Park Lane Group, Incorporated Society of Musicians. *Recordings include:* with Peter Dickinson: An Erik Satie Entertainment, An American Anthology, A Portrait of Lord Berners, Dreamscapes, Rags, Blues and Parodies; solo: Brecht-Weill series with London Sinfonietta. *Honours:* Countess of Munster Musical Trust Scholarship 1964–66.

DICKINSON, Peter, MA, DMus, FRCO, LRAM, ARCM; British composer, writer, pianist and academic; *Professor Emeritus, Keele University and University of London*; b. 15 Nov. 1934, Lytham St Annes, Lancs.; s. of Frank Dickinson and Muriel Dickinson (née Porter); m. Bridget Jane Tomkinson; two s. *Education:* Queens' Coll., Cambridge, Juilliard School of Music, USA. *Career:* various teaching posts in New York, London and Birmingham; First Prof. of Music, Keele Univ. 1974–84, Prof. Emer. 1984–; Prof., Goldsmiths Coll., London 1991–97, Prof. Emer. 1997–; Head of Music, Inst. of US Studies, Univ. of London 1997–2004; performances, broadcasts and recordings as pianist, mostly with sister, mezzo-soprano Meriel Dickinson; Chair. Bernarr Rainbow Trust. *Compositions include:* Satie Transformations for orchestra 1970, Organ Concerto 1971, Piano Concerto 1984, Merseyside Echoes for orchestra 1985, Violin Concerto 1986, chamber music, choral works, songs, keyboard music, church music. *Recordings include:* vocal works to poems of Auden, Dylan Thomas, e. e. cummings, John Heath-Stubbs, Lord Berners, Philip Larkin, Burns, Gregory Corso, Lord Byron, Stevie Smith, Blake, Clare and Hardy; numerous recordings of own music, including as pianist. *Television:* subject of South Bank Show 1987. *Radio:* many BBC Radio 3 recitals talks and documentaries. *Publications include:* 20 British Composers (ed.) 1975, The Complete Songs and The Complete Piano Music of Lord Berners (two vols, ed.) 1982, 2000, Collected Works for Solo Piano of Lennox Berkeley (ed.) 1989, Marigold: The Music of Billy Mayerl 1999, Copland Connotations: Studies and Interviews 2002, The Music of Lennox Berkeley 2003, Cage Talk: Dialogues

With and About John Cage 2006, Lord Berners: Composer, Writer, Painter 2008, Samuel Barber Remembered 2010, Complete Piano Duets of Lord Berners 2010, Lennox Berkeley and His Friends 2012; contrib. to various books, journals and dictionaries. *Honours:* Hon. FTCL; Hon. DMus (Keele Univ.) 1999; Rotary Foundation Fellowship 1958–59. *Address:* c/o Novello and Co., 14–15 Berners Street, London, W1T 3LJ, England. *Website:* www.foxborough.co.uk.

DICKMAN, Stephen Allen, BA, MFA; American composer; b. 2 March 1943, Chicago, IL. *Education:* Bard Coll. with Jacob Druckman, Brandeis Univ. with Arthur Berger and Harold Shapero, Berkshire Music Center, Tanglewood with Ernst Krenek and studied with Golfredo Petrassi in Rome. *Career:* has travelled widely in order to study the music of Asia and the Middle East. *Compositions include:* Musical Journeys, Trees and Other Inclinations for piano 1983, Orchestra by the Sea 1983, The Wheels of Ezekiel for chamber orchestra 1985, Maximus song cycle 1986, Tibetan Dreams (opera, with librettist Gary Glickman) (NEA Artist as Producer of New American Works Award) 1987, Rabbi Nathan's Prayer for soprano and violin 1995, The Violin Maker (musical), King Arthur (theatre) 1996, Cyrano (theatre) 1997, Duets for two singers a capella 1992–98, Four for Tom for piano and baritone 1997, The Music of Eric Zann for baritone solo (on a story by H. P. Lovecraft) 1998, Gilgamesh (chamber opera) 2002, setting of The Yellow Wallpaper by Charlotte Perkins Gillman for soprano, piano and cello 2003. *Recordings:* The Music of Eric Zann; Who Says Works; Four For Tom; Indian Wells; If There Were No Birds and Rabbi Nathan's Prayer, Trees and Other Inclinations and The Wheels of Ezekiel; song cycle for three violins and three sopranos: The Song of the Reed, My Love Makes Me Lonely, Love, the Hierophant. *Honours:* Fulbright Fellowship, Rome 1971–72, CAP Award 1987, 1990, Meet the Composer 1995, SOS grant, East End Arts Council and New York Foundation for the Arts 1995, 1998, 1999, Meet the Composer Fund Award 1990, 1995, 1996, Timeline Suffolk Decentralization grant 1998, American Composers Forum Commission 1998. *Address:* 73 Squaw Road, East Hampton, NY 11937, USA (home). *Website:* sdmusic@optonline.net (office).

DICKSON, Amy; Australian musician (saxophone); b. 1982, Sydney; m. *Education:* Royal Coll. of Music, London, Conservatorium van Amsterdam, studied with Kyle Horch and Arno Bornkamp. *Career:* concerto debut aged 16 in Sydney; moved to London aged 19; performances world-wide in venues including Wigmore Hall and Royal Albert Hall, London, Bridgewater Hall, Manchester, Vienna Konzerthaus and Sydney Opera House; soloist with orchestras including Sydney and Melbourne Symphony Orchestras, Vienna Chamber Orchestra, Philharmonia, London Philharmonic Orchestra and Royal Scottish Nat. Orchestra; performed at Commonwealth Heads of Govt Meetings in Valetta, Malta 2005 and Perth, Australia 2011, and at Scottish Parl., Edinburgh and St James's Palace, London; works written for her by composers including Ross Edwards, Peter Sculthorpe, Graham Fitkin and Huw Watkins; Amb., Australian Children's Music Foundation and The Prince's Trust. *Recordings:* Smile 2008, Glass/Tavener/Nyman 2009, Dusk & Dawn 2013. *Honours:* James Fairfax Australian Young Artist of the Year, Gold Medal, Royal Overseas League Competition, Symphony Australia Young Performer of the Year, Prince's Prize, Classic BRIT Award for Breakthrough Artist of the Year 2013. *Website:* www.amydickson.com.

DICKSON, Grant; New Zealand singer (bass); b. 1940. *Career:* debut at New Zealand Opera 1962, then prin. bass Opera Australia, with appearances as Mozart's Sarastro and Bartolo; Don Basilio, Don Pasquale and Baron Ochs; Rocco, Mephistopheles and Trulove for New Zealand Opera; European engagements from 1991, including Commendatore in Dresden, Pluto in Telemann's Orpheus at Berlin and Boris Godunov for WNO; season 1998–99 with Schigolch in Lulu for De Vlaamse Opera and King Mark in Tristan for WNO; season 1999–2000 in The Greek Passion and La Bohème at Covent Garden; concerts include Verdi Requiem at Albert Hall; returned to New Zealand 2002, now sings with Auckland Choral.

DICTEROW, Glenn; American violinist; *Concertmaster, New York Philharmonic Orchestra;* b. Los Angeles, CA; m. Karen Dreyfus. *Education:* Juilliard School. *Career:* solo debut aged 11 with Los Angeles Philharmonic; Assoc. Concertmaster, then Concertmaster, Los Angeles Philharmonic 1971–79; Concertmaster and solo violin, New York Philharmonic 1980 –; Lecturer, Manhattan School of Music 1982–, Juilliard School 1985–; co-f., Lyric Piano Quartet 1986; guest performances as soloist with symphony orchestras, including Los Angeles, Seattle, San Francisco, Baltimore, Birmingham, Chautauqua, Grant Park, Indianapolis, Kansas City, Mexico City, Miami, Montréal, Omaha, Tampa, Monterey, and with Leipzig Gewandhaus Orchestra, Hong Kong Philharmonic; has played with conductors including Bernstein, Maazel, Kostelanetz, Mehta, Slatkin, Davis, Masur, Gergiev, Sir Colin Davis, Dutoit. *Recordings include:* Copland's Violin Sonata, Largo and Piano Trio, Richard Strauss' Also Sprach Zarathustra, Op. 30/Four Last Songs 1990, Rimsky-Korsakov's Scheherazade 1993, Korngold's Chamber Works 1995, Ives' Chamber Works 1996, Goetz's Chamber Music 1999, New York Legends 1999, Holdridge Conducts Holdridge 2001, Shostakovich's Violin Concerto No. 1, Bernstein's Sonata for Violin and Piano, Serenade, Mozart's Symphonie Concertante. *Honours:* first prize Young Musicians Foundation 1965, first prize Julia Klumke, San Francisco 1966, bronze medal Int. Tchaikovsky Competition 1970. *Address:* New York Philharmonic, Avery Fisher Hall, 10 Lincoln Center Plaza, New York, NY 10023-6990, USA (office). *Website:* www.newyorkphilharmonic.org (office).

DIDONATO, Joyce; American singer (mezzo-soprano); b. 13 Feb. 1969, Kansas; m. Leonardo Vordoni. *Education:* Acad. of Vocal Arts, Phila and Houston Opera Studio. *Career:* continued her postgraduate musical educ. as mem. young artist programmes of San Francisco Opera and Houston Grand Opera, and as a Santa Fe Opera Apprentice (performed Massenet's Cendrillon 2006); repertoire includes operas by Handel, Mozart and Rossini, as well as new works (including world premieres) by Mark Adamo, Todd Machover and Jake Heggie; has sung La Cenerentola in all major opera houses world-wide, also Handel's Dejanjira and Sister Helen Prejean in Jake Heggie's Dead Man Walking, New York City Opera debut 2002; season 2006–07 sang Richard Strauss's Composer in Ariadne auf Naxos, at Teatro Real, Madrid, and Octavian, the Rosenkavalier, at San Francisco Opera; Idamante in new production of Mozart's Idomeneo at Opéra de Paris, Angelina in Rossini's Cenerentola at Houston Grand Opera, Rosina in a new production of Il Barbiere di Siviglia in her second season at Metropolitan Opera, New York; sang Sycorax in The Enchanted Island, Met Opera 2012; has undertaken multi-city recital tours in USA and Europe with regular piano partner Julius Drake; Perspectives Artist, Carnegie Hall 2014/2015 season. *Recordings include:* The Deepest Desire (Bernstein, Copland, Heggie) 2005, Pasión! (with Julius Drake) (Obradors, Granados, Turina, De Falla, Montsalvage) 2006, Furore 2008, Rossini: Colbran, The Muse 2009, Diva Divo (Diapason d'Or 2011, Grammy Award for Best Classical Vocal Solo 2012) 2011, Ercole Sul Termodonte 2011, Drama Queens 2012, Joyce & Tony - Live From Wigmore Hall (with Antonio Pappano) 2015. *Honours:* hon. mem. Royal Academy of Music 2014; Winner, Metropolitan Opera auditions 1996, Richard Tucker Award 2002, Royal Philharmonic Soc. Award for Singer 2006, Second Prize in Placido Domingo's Operalia, prizes from the George London Foundation, the ARIA Awards and the Sullivan Foundation, Metropolitan Opera's Beverly Sills Artist Award 2007, Gramophone Award for Artist of the Year 2010, Echo Klassics Female Singer of the Year 2010. *Current Management:* c/o Simon Goldstone, Intermusica Artists Management Ltd, 36 Graham Street, Crystal Wharf, London, N1 8GJ, England. *Telephone:* (20) 7608-9900. *Fax:* (20) 7490-3263. *E-mail:* sgoldstone@intermusica.co.uk; mail@intermusica.co.uk. *Website:* www.intermusica.co.uk; www.joycedidonato.com.

DIDONE, Rosanna; Italian singer (soprano); b. 13 Feb. 1952, Galliera, Veneta. *Education:* Benedetto Marcello Conservatory, Venice. *Career:* debut in Padua 1978, as Serpina in La Serva Padrona; appearances at Venice in Idomeneo, as Rosette in Manon and Bianca in La Rondine; Clarice in Il Mondo Della Luna at Turin and Frasquita in Carmen at Padau 1982; at Trieste (from 1982) has sung Gnese in Il Campiello, Amor (Orpheus ed Euridice), Barbarina, and Naiad in Ariadne auf Naxos; Rome Opera 1982 and 1988 in Don Carlos and as Mme Silberklang in Der Schauspieldirektor by Mozart; other roles include Musetta, Marie-Louise in Kodály's Háry János, Biancofiore in Francesca da Rimini, Gilda, Susanna, Carolina (Il matrimonio segreto), Norina (Don Pasquale), Oscar, Nannetta, Laura and Despina; guest appearances in The Netherlands and Bulgaria. *Recordings:* Egloge in Mascagni's Nerone, and Francesca da Rimni (Bongiovanni).

DIEMECKE, Enrique Arturo; Mexican conductor, violinist and composer; *Music Director, Orquesta Filarmónica de Buenos Aires.* *Education:* Catholic Univ. of America, Pierre Monteux School for Conductors, USA. *Career:* Music Dir, Opera de Bellas Artes, Mexico 1984–90; Music Dir and Principal Conductor, Flint Symphony Orchestra, Mich. 1990–; Music Dir, Orquesta Sinfónica Nacional de Mexico 1990–2006; Music Dir, Long Beach Symphony Orchestra, Calif. 2001–; Music Dir, Orquesta Filarmónica de Buenos Aires 2005–; guest conductor, BBC Symphony Orchestra, Royal Philharmonic, Columbus Symphony, Los Angeles Philharmonic, Charlotte Symphony, Nat. Symphony Orchestra, USA, Valladolid Symphony, Orchestre de Paris, Orchestre de l'Ile de France, Chautauqua Symphony, Opera Pacific. *Compositions include:* Die-Sir-E 1998, Chacona a Chávez, Guitar Concerto, Camino y Vision 2001. *Honours:* Médaille Orphée d'Or, Acad. du Disque Lyrique, Paris 2000, 2002. *Current Management:* Wolf Artists International, PO Box 492, Gracie Station, New York, NY 10028, USA. *Telephone:* (646) 733-4581. *E-mail:* isabel@wolfartists.com. *Website:* www.wolfartists.com. *Address:* Teatro Colón, Cerrito 618, 1010 Buenos Aires, Argentina (office). *E-mail:* contact@enriquearturodiemecke.com (office). *Website:* www.teatrocolon.org.ar (office); www.enriquearturodiemecke.com.

DIEMER, Emma Lou, BM, MM, PhD; American composer, pianist, organist and academic; *Professor Emerita, University of California, Santa Barbara;* b. 24 Nov. 1927, Kansas City, Mo.; d. of George Willis Diemer and Susie Myrtle Casebolt Diemer. *Education:* Yale School of Music, Eastman School of Music. *Career:* Prof. of Composition, Univ. of California, Santa Barbara 1971–91, now Prof. Emer.; Composer-in-Residence, Santa Barbara Symphony 1990–92; Organist, First Presbyterian Church, Santa Barbara 1984–2000. *Compositions include:* Concerto for marimba 1990, Concerto for piano 1991, Sextet 1992, Four Biblical Settings for organ 1992, Kyrie 1993, Fantasy for piano 1993, Gloria 1996, Psalms for organ and flute, Psalms for organ and trumpet, Psalms for organ and percussion 1998, Mass 2000, Piano Trio 2000, Homage to Tchaikovsky 2001, Songs for the Earth for chorus and orchestra 2005, Homage to Poulenc, Mozart and MacDowell for flute, cello and piano 2005, Poem of Remembrance for clarinet and chamber orchestra 2006, A Requiem for woodwind quintet and string quintet 2006, Suite for violin and piano 2008, Quartet on Themes by Howard Hanson 2010, Piano Trio No. 2 2010. *Recordings include:* Declarations for organ, Toccata and Fugue for organ, Toccata for piano, Summer of 82 for cello and piano, Quartet for piano, violin, viola and cello, Sextet for woodwind quintet and piano, Youth Overture, Encore for piano 1991, Sextet 1993, Concerto in One Movement for piano (Kennedy Center Friedheim Award) 1995, String Quartet No. 1 1995, Santa Barbara Overture 1997, Concerto in One Movement for piano 1998, Fantasy for piano 1998, Suite of Homages, for orchestra 1999, Four Chinese Love Poems 1999, Piano Concerto 2000, Suite of Homages 2001, Santa Barbara Overture 2001, Concerto for Organ 2004, Suite for Violin and Piano (Summer Day) 2008, Quartet for Piano, Flute, Violin, Cello 2010, Piano Trio No. 2 2010, Concerto for Violin 2012. *Publications:* music published since 1957. *Honours:* Hon. DLit (Central Missouri State Univ.) 1999; Fulbright Scholarship 1952–53, American Guild of Organists Composer of the Year 1995. *Address:* 2249 Vista del Campo, Santa Barbara, CA 93101, USA (home). *E-mail:* eldiemer11@gmail.com. *Website:* www.emmaloudiemermusic.com.

DIENER, Melanie; German singer (soprano); b. 1967. *Education:* studied with Sylvia Geszty in Stuttgart, Rudolf Piernay in Mannheim, and at Indiana University. *Career:* concerts include the Brahms Requiem in Paris and Zürich, Mendelssohn's St Paul under Philippe Herreweghe and Mahler's 2nd Symphony at Linz; recitals in Stuttgart and Bonn; Opera debut as Mozart's Ilia at Garsington, England, 1996; season 1996–97 with Elijah at the Berlin Philharmonie, Fiordiligi at Covent Garden and in Paris, First Lady in Die Zauberflöte at the Salzburg Festival; Asberta in Holzbauer's Gunther von Schwarzburg under Ton Koopman at the Amsterdam Concertgebouw; The Strauss Four Last Songs at Turin and the Verdi Requiem at St Gallen; Season 1997–98 with Korngold's Kathrin for the BBC, Agathe in Der Freischütz for the Royal Opera in concert and Donna Elvira at Aix; Elsa in Lohengrin at Bayreuth, 1999; Covent Garden as Donna Elvira, 2002, returned to London 2003, as Elsa. *Honours:* Prizewinner, International Mozart Competition, Salzburg, 1995; Winner, Kirsten Flagstad Prize, Oslo, 1995. *Current Management:* Balmer & Dixon Management AG, Kreuzstrasse 82, 8032 Zürich, Switzerland. *Telephone:* (43) 244-8644. *Fax:* (43) 244-8649. *Website:* www .badix.ch.

DIESSELHORST, Jan; German cellist; b. 1956, Marburg. *Education:* studied in Frankfurt and with Wolfgang Boettcher in Berlin. *Career:* joined the Berlin Philharmonic Orchestra 1979; co-founder, Philharmonic Quartet Berlin, giving concerts throughout Europe, the USA and Japan; British debut 1987, playing Haydn, Szymanowski and Beethoven at Wigmore Hall; Bath Festival 1987, playing Mozart, Schumann and Beethoven (Op. 127); other repertoire includes quartets by Bartók, Mendelssohn, Nicolai, Ravel and Schubert; quintets by Brahms, Weber, Reger and Schumann.

DIETRICH, Karl; German composer and teacher; b. 9 July 1927, Wachstedt/ Eichsfeld; m. Gerda Lins 1952; two d. *Education:* Univ. Jena and High School of Music, Franz Liszt, Weimar. *Career:* Prof. of Composition, High School of Music, Franz Liszt, Weimar; mem. Ordentliches Mitglied Deutscher Komponisten-Interessenverband. *Compositions:* seven Symphonies 1969–92; operas: Die Wette des Serapion 1984, Pervonte 1989; orchestral: three Divertimenti for orchestra 1972–76, Piano Concerto 1964, Concerto for orchestra 1969, Dramatic Scenes for three flutes (one soloist) and large orchestra 1974, Violoncello Concerto 1982, Concertino Giocoso for string orchestra 1962, Konzert-Suite for string orchestra 1967, Memorial for string orchestra (in connection with the choral of J. S. Bach, Vergiá mein Nicht) 1994, Konzertantes Präludium für orchestra 1996; chamber music: Prokofiev-Variationen für Klavier 4-händig 1970, Anregungen für klavier 1974, Etude Capricieuse for cello solo 1993, Ton-triage for flute solo 1986, three Liederzyklen für singstimme und klavier, three Bläserquintette, six Dialoge for two oboes, Divertimento für flöte und streichtrio; organ: Groáe Fantasie für orgel 1981, Vision für flöte und orgel 1984, Rupert-Mayer-Reflexionen für orgel; church music: Psalm 49, Die Vergänglichkeit des Menschen für bariton und orgel 1994, Deutsche Messe für männerchor a cappella 1995, Schöndorfer Messe, lateinischer Text für mittlere singstimme und orgel 1996, Kirchenmusikalische Kompositionen diverser Art für chöre und soli. *Recordings:* Symphony No. 4, contra bellum, SSO Thüringen, Conductor Lothar Seyfarth; Dramatic Szenes, Rundfunk-Sinfonieorchestra Leipzig, Conductor Herbert Kegel; Symphony No. 7, Philharmonie Erfurt, Conductor Wolfgang Rögner. *Honours:* Kunstpreis des FDGB 1971, Kunst Preis der DDR 1975, Kunstpreis der Stadt Weimar 1983.

DIETSCH, James William, BME, MMus; American singer (baritone) and artist manager; b. 21 March 1950, Kansas City, MO; m. Susan Kay Schell 1980; one s. *Education:* Univ. of Missouri, Kansas City, Juilliard School of Music American Opera Center, Vienna Acad. of Music, Austria. *Career:* debut, Fargo-Moorhead Civic Opera 1975; New York Town Hall 1981; Carnegie Hall 1982; leading artist with numerous opera cos and concert appearances in USA and abroad, including San Francisco Opera, New York City Opera, English Opera North, Karlsruhe Badisches Staatstheater, Saarbrucken Saarländiches Staatstheater, Michigan Opera, Milwaukee Opera, Deutsche Oper am Rhein, Minnesota Opera, Hawaii Opera, Staatstheater Essen, Santa Fe Opera, Spoleto Festival USA, New York Philharmonic, Mexico City Philharmonic; founded own artist management co. *Recordings:* Il Corsaro by Verdi, Historical Recording Incorporate, 1981. *Address:* James W. Dietsch International Management, Thierschstrasse 11, 80538 Munich, Germany (office). *Telephone:* (89) 3408-6300 (office). *Fax:* (89) 3408-6310 (office). *E-mail:* jwdietsch@t-online.de (office).

DIJKSTRA, Hebe; Dutch singer (mezzo-soprano); b. 4 Sept. 1941, Tvijzelerheide; m. Jan Alofs. *Education:* Hague Conservatory. *Career:* debut in

Gluck's Orpheus at Enschede 1975; sang Mistress Quickly at Enschede, and appeared in Rimsky's Sadko at Bonn 1976; engaged at Detmold 1976–79, Saarbrucken 1979–80, Freiburg 1981–83; Krefeld 1982–85, Wuppertal 1987–89; Amsterdam 1989, in Der Kreidekreis by Zemlinsky; mem., Staatstheater am Gärtnerplatz, Munich from 1989; sang Rossweise in Die Walküre at Bayreuth 1988–91; Ulrica at Amsterdam 1992; Mary in Der fliegende Holländer at 1992 Bayreuth Festival; other roles include Carmen, Fricka, Waltraute, Nurse in Boris Godunov, and La Comandante in I Cavalieri di Ekebù by Zandonai; sang Margret in Wozzeck at Amsterdam 1994; Witch in premiere of Robert Heppener's Een Ziel van Hout 1998; sang Hecuba in Troades by Reimann at Berlin and Berne 2000.

DIJKSTRA, Peter; Dutch choral conductor; *Artistic Director, Bavarian Radio Choir;* b. 1978. *Education:* Conservatories of The Hague, Köln, Germany and Stockholm, Sweden. *Career:* as boy soprano, solo performances with Netherlands Opera Foundation; as conductor, regular appearances with Netherlands Chamber Choir, BBC Singers, RIAS Chamberchoir Berlin, Collegium Vocale Gent and Danish Radio Choir; Guest Conductor with orchestras including Bavarian Radio Symphony Orchestra, Munich Radio Orchestra, Deutsches Symphonie Orchester Berlin, Sinfonietta Amsterdam, Munich Chamber Orchestra, Arnhem Philharmonic Orchestra, Japan Philharmonic, Akademie für Alte Musik Berlin and Concerto Köln; Artistic Dir, Bavarian Radio Choir, Munich 2005–, collaborating with conductors such as Mariss Jansons, Nikolaus Harnoncourt, Riccardo Muti and Claudio Abbado; Principal Guest Conductor, Swedish Radio Choir 2004–07, Chief Conductor 2007–; Principal Guest Conductor, Netherlands Chamber Choir; Artistic Leader, vocal ensemble MUSA, Utrecht; Artistic Leader/Conductor, vocal ensemble The Gents 1999–2007, First Guest Conductor 2007–; mem. Royal Swedish Acad. of Music 2012–. *Recordings include:* numerous CDs with Swedish Radio Choir, Bavarian Radio Choir, Netherlands Chamber Choir and The Gents. *Honours:* Kersjes-van de Groenekanbeurs for orchestral conducting 2002, First Prize, Eric Ericson Competition (Sweden) 2003, ECHO Klassik Award for Choral Recording of the Year (Fauré Requiem with Bavarian Radio Choir) 2012. *Current Management:* Sorek Artists Management, Burgemeester Patijnlaan 806, 2585 CC The Hague, Netherlands. *Telephone:* (70) 3317902. *E-mail:* info@sorekartists.com. *Website:* www.sorekartists.com; www .peterdijkstra.nl (office).

DILKES, Neville, FRCO, FTCL; British conductor; *Director, L'Ensemble de La Chapelle;* b. 28 Aug. 1930, Derby; m. 1st D. Pamela Walton (died 1979); four d.; m. 2nd Christine M. Allen 1986. *Education:* Birmingham and Peterborough Cathedrals, Birmingham Conservatory, Netherlands Radio Union Int. Conductors' course, studied with Sir Adrian Boult. *Career:* Founder-Conductor, Kettering Symphony Orchestra, Opera Da Camera, English Sinfonia; Assoc. Conductor, Philomusica of London; currently Dir L'Ensemble de La Chapelle; broadcasts on int. radio and TV; mem. Royal Soc. of Musicians of GB. *Recordings:* numerous recordings with special emphasis on British music. *Honours:* Watney-Sargent Award for Conductors 1963. *Address:* La Noue, 85210 La Chapelle-Thémer, France (home). *Telephone:* (2) 51-30-96-34 (home). *Fax:* (2) 51-30-96-34 (home). *E-mail:* ncm-dilkes@wanadoo.fr.

DILLON, James; Scottish composer; b. 29 Oct. 1950, Glasgow. *Education:* Glasgow School of Art, Polytechnic of Central London, Polytechnic of North London. *Career:* works performed and featured at festivals throughout the world, including Antidogma (Turin), Bath, Darmstadt, Gulbenkian (Lisbon), Huddersfield, ISCM (Toronto), La Rochelle, Musica Nel Nostro Tempo (Milan), Music of Eight Decades (London), Paris d'Automne, Warsaw, Zig-Zag (Paris), Châtelet (Paris), Donaueschingen (Germany), Musica Nova (Glasgow), Musica (Strasburg), Ars Musica (Brussels), Ultima (Oslo), Venice Biennale, Sydney Spring, ISCM World Music Days (Toronto, Stockholm, Seoul and Manchester); Guest Lecturer, Univs of Keele, London, New York, Nottingham, Oxford, Central England and Gothenburg; guest composer Darmstadt Ferienkurse 1982, 1984, 1986; jury mem., Gaudeamus Composers' Competition 1985, ISCM Int. 1988 and Besancon Int. Competition 1990. *Compositions:* Spleen 1980, Once Upon a Time 1980, Come Live With Me 1981, Parjanya-Vata 1981, East 11th Street 1982, String Quartet 1983, Sgothan 1984, La Coupure 1986, Helle Nacht 1987, Del Cuarto Elemento 1988, L'Ecran parfum 1988, Shrouded Mirrors 1988, La Femme Invisible 1989, L'Oeuvre au noir 1990, Blitzschlag 1991, String Quartet No. 2 1991, ignis noster 1991–92, Siorram 1992, Vernal Showers 1992, L'Evolution du Vol 1993, Viriditas 1993, Traumwerk Book I 1995, Redemption 1995, Oceanos 1996, Todesengel 1996, The Book of Elements Vol. I 1997, String Quartet No. 3 1998, Hyades 1998, Eos 1998–99, residue… 1999, Vapor 1999, La coupure 2000, Via Sacra 2000, Violin Concerto 2000, Book of Elements Vol. III 2000, La navette 2000–01, Book of Elements Vol. II 2001, Two Studies 2001, Two Studies 2001, Traumwerk Book 2 2001, Traumwerk Book 3 2001–02, Book of Elements Vol. IV 2002, Book of Elements Vol. V 2002, Piano Quintet 2002, New Work 2002–03, The Rape of Philomela 2002–04, The Soadie Waste (British Composer Award for choral work) 2004, String Quartet No. 4 (Royal Philharmonic Soc. Award for Chamber-scale Composition 2006) 2005, Nine Rivers (Royal Philharmonic Soc. Large-scale Composition Award 2011). *Recordings:* helle Nacht; ignis noster; Come Live with me; A Roaring Flame; Sgothan; Ti re-Ti Ke-Dha; Evening Rain; Crossing Over; Spleen; Del Cuarto Elemento; East 11th Street, NY 10003; La femme invisible; Windows and Canopies; Dillug Kefitsah. *Publications:* Problemas Discursivos en La Muska Contemporanea 1989, Speculative Instruments: Timbre, Métaphore pour La Composition 1991. *Honours:* Kranichsteiner Musikpreis (Germany) 1982,

London Times Classical Music Personality of the Year 1989, Royal Philharmonic Soc. Award 1997. *Address:* c/o Peters Edition Ltd, 10–12 Baches Street, London, N1 6DN, England.

DIMITROVA, Anastasia; Bulgarian singer (soprano); b. 16 Nov. 1940, Pernik. *Education:* State Conservatory, Sofia, studied in Zagreb. *Career:* debut in Nabucco at Skopje, 1965; many appearances at opera houses in Bulgaria and Yugoslavia, notably, Belgrade, Sofia, Zagreb and Rijeka; roles have included Verdi's Elisabetta and Leonora (Trovatore), Mimi, Yaroslavna (Prince Igor), Tatiana in Eugene Onegin, Marenka (Bartered Bride), Rusalka, Micaela, Euridice and Marguerite. *Honours:* winner Francisco Vinas Competition, Barcelona 1969, Bussetto Competition.

DINDO, Enrico; Italian cellist; b. 16 March 1965, Turin. *Education:* Conservatorio G. Verdi, Turin and Mozarteum Salzburg with Antonio Sangro. *Career:* debut as First Cellist with La Scala Orchestra 1988; soloist in Beethoven Triple Concerto at La Scala 1996; has played with Orchestre Nationale de France, St Petersburg Philharmonic Orchestra, Orchestra Sinfonica Nazionale RAI, Chicago Symphony and Kirov Chamber Orchestra. *Recordings:* Brahms Cello Sonatas, Haydn Cello Concerti. *Honours:* first prize Rostropovich Cello Competition, Paris 1987. *Current Management:* c/o Luisa Panarello, Resia s.r.l., Via Gioberti 1, 20123 Milan, Italy. *E-mail:* info@enricodindo.com. *Website:* www.enricodindo.com.

DINESCU, Violeta, MA; German (b. Romanian) composer, musician and academic; *Professor of Applied Composition, University of Oldenburg*; b. 13 July 1953, Bucharest; d. of Alfons Dinescu and Elena Dinescu; m. Nicolae Manolache 1993. *Education:* Ciprian Porumbescu Conservatory of Music. *Career:* Instructor of Theory, Piano, Harmony, Counterpoint and Aesthetics, George Enescu Music School 1987–90, Conservatory for Church Music, Heidelberg, Germany 1989–91, Conservatory for Music, Frankfurt, Germany 1989–92, Acad. of Church Music, Bayreuth 1990–94; currently Prof. of Applied Composition, Univ. of Oldenburg, Germany; Special Corresp. Music Section Romania Literară, Muzică 1975–82; European Corresp. Living Music, Calif., USA 1987–; Guest Lecturer at univs in Germany, SA and USA; performances and radio recordings in Romania, Germany, France, UK, USA, Italy, Belgium, Switzerland, Austria, El Salvador, SA, Colombia, Finland, Czech Repub., Sweden, Portugal, Mexico, Luxembourg, Canada etc.; mem. Union of Composers of Romania 1980–, Int. Arbeitskreis Frau und Musik, Germany 1982–, Minnesota Composers' Forum, USA 1984–, Exec. Bd Int. Alliance of Women Composers, USA 1985–, Union of Composers of Germany 1982–; Initiator of Composer Colloquium 1996–, Archive of Music of East Europe 1996, Shifting Times Symposium at Carl von Ossietzky Univ., Oldenburg 2006. *Compositions include:* chamber music: Echoes I, Satya Cicle, Parra Quitarra, Din Cimpoiu, Dies Diem Docet, Scherzo da Fantasia III, Sleep Song, Kata, Ichthys, Figuren III, Stringquartet din Terra Lonhdana, Contraste, Alternances, Festspielfanfare, Fragment V, Letitae, Flutesplay II, In Search of Mozart!, Terra Lonhdana; orchestral music: Transformations, Anna Perenna, Memories, Joc, Fresco, Kybalion; voice and instrumental music: Amont, Quatrain, Psalm 125, Concertino, Fragment I, Euraculos, Arpagic, In my Garden, Spring Song, Latin Sentences, Flower Song, Zori de flori, Bewitch Me into a Silver Bird!, The Play; Pfinstoratorium, Friedensoratorium, Wie Tau auf den Bergen Zions, An den Strömen von Babel; operas: Hunger and Thirst, Der 35 Mai, Eréndira, Schachnovelle, Aus deinem Herzen kannst Du die Liebe nicht ausreissen, Die versunkene Stadt. Eine Geschichte vom Meer; ballet: Der Kreisel, Effi Briest, music for the silent films of Freidrich Wilhelm Murnau: Tabu and Nosferatu, A Symphony of Horror. *Recordings include:* Internationales Festival Heidelberg 1987 1988, Fanny Mendelssohn-Quartet 1988, Internationales Festival Neue Musik 1991; over 50 albums. *Honours:* Composers' Asscn Prize, Romania 1975, 1976, 1980, 1983, First Prize, Int. Eisteddfod Festival, Roodepoort, SA 1991, Gregynog Composers Award, Wales, UK 1993, American-Romanian Acad. of Arts and Sciences Award, Calif., USA 1994, Int. New Music Consortium Award, New York, USA 1996, 1999, Delta Omicron Triennial Composition Competition 1996, Women in Music Award, Ohio, USA 1997, Johann Vaillant Composition Prize, Bergische Biennale für Neue Musik, Remscheid 2010, Johann Wenzel Stamitz Prize, Berlin 2012, and over 70 other awards and prizes. *Address:* University of Oldenburg, Fakultät 3/Musik, 26111 Oldenburg (office); Presuhnstr. 39, 26133 Oldenburg, Germany (home). *Telephone:* (441) 7982027 (office). *Fax:* (441) 7984016 (office); (441) 94904555 (home). *E-mail:* violeta.dinescu@uni-oldenburg.de (office).

DINITZEN, Kim Bak; Danish cellist; b. 24 Oct. 1963, Haderslev; m. Ursula Smith 1993. *Education:* Royal Danish Conservatoire of Music with Erling Blondal Bengtsson, studied in London with Ralph Kirshbaum. *Career:* debut in Copenhagen 1986; Weill Recital Hall at Carnegie Hall, New York 1988; Wigmore Hall, London 1991; soloist with all Danish symphony orchestras; recitals and chamber music concerts throughout Europe; currently prin. cello, Royal Danish Orchestra; mem. Chamber Orchestra of Europe 1990–; teacher, Royal Northern Coll. of Music, UK 1996–; currently teacher, Royal Danish Acad. of Music. *Recordings include:* Benjamin Britten: Complete Works for Cello, G. Fauré: Complete Works for Cello and Piano (with Elisabeth Westenholz, piano), Prokofiev and Schnittke Sonatas (with Paul Coker, piano), Niels W. Gade: String Quintet, Sextet and Octet (with the Johannes Ensemble). *Honours:* Victor Borge Prize, Denmark 1987, first prize for cello Washington Int. Competition 1988, East and West Artists' Prize for New York debut 1988, third prize, Gaspar Cassapo Int. Cello Competition, Florence 1990. *Address:* Chamber Orchestra of Europe, North House, 27 Great Peter Street, London, SW1P 3LN, England. *Website:* www.coeurope.org.

DINNERSTEIN, Simone; American pianist; b. 1972, New York; d. of Simon Dinnerstein and Renée Dinnerstein; m. Jeremy Greensmith; one s. *Education:* Manhattan School of Music, Juilliard School, three years' tuition in London with Maria Curcio. *Career:* New York recital debut, Bach's Goldberg Variations, Carnegie Hall Weill Recital Hall 2005; European recital debut, Berlin Philharmonie 2007; UK debut, Wigmore Hall 2007; has performed as piano soloist at The Kennedy Center for the Performing Arts, Vienna Konzerthaus, Aspen Festival, Ravinia Festival, in Cologne, San Francisco, Paris, London, Copenhagen, Vilnius, Bremen, and at the Stuttgart Bach Festival, with Dresden Philharmonic, Czech Philharmonic, Jerusalem Symphony Orchestra, Stuttgart Radio Symphony Orchestra, New Jersey Symphony Orchestra, New York City's Orchestra of St Luke's, Kristjan Järvi's Absolute Ensemble. *Recordings:* Beethoven: Complete Works for Piano and Cello, Vol. 1 (with Zuill Bailey) 2006 (Classical Recording Foundation Awards 2006, 2007), J. S. Bach: Goldberg Variations (Diapason d'Or) 2007, The Berlin Concert 2008. *Current Management:* c/o Tanja Dorn, IMG Artists, Carnegie Hall Tower, 152 West 57th Street, 5th Floor, New York, NY 10019, USA; IMG Artists, Bandelstrasse 35, 30171 Hannover, Germany. *Telephone:* (212) 994-3540 (USA); (511) 4378134 (Germany). *Fax:* (212) 994-3550 (USA); (511) 4378135 (Germany). *E-mail:* tdorn@imgartists.com. *Website:* www.imgartists.com; www.simonedinnerstein.com.

D'INTINO, Luciana; Italian singer (mezzo-soprano); b. 22 Aug. 1959, San vito al Tagliamento, Pordenone. *Education:* Benedeto Marcello Conservatory, Venice. *Career:* debut singing Azucena in Il Trovatore 1983; appearances as Rossini's Rosina in Marcerata and Naples 1984, 1986; Aida at Cagliari and Trieste; sang Rossini's Ernestina in L'Occasione fa il ladro and Lucia in La Gazza ladra at Rossini Opera Festival of Pesaro 1987, 1989; La Scala Milan from 1987 as Fenena in Nabucco, Guillaume Tell; Jommelli's Fetonte, Princess of Bouillon in Adriana Lecouvreur, Eboli in Don Carlos, Tancredi 1993, Laura Adorno in La Gioconda 1997, Preziosilla in La Forza del Destino 1999, Amneris in Aida 2009, 2011, Santuzza in Mascagni's Cavalleria Rusticana 2011, and as Luggrezia in Pergolesi's Lo Frate 'nnamorato; sang Frederica in Luisa Miller at Rome 1990, Turin as Eboli in Don Carlos and Savona 1991, as Arsace in Rossini's Auerliano in Palmira; sang Preziosilla in Forza del Destino at Naples, Sara in Roberto Devereux at Bologna 1992; Preziosilla at the 1992 Maggio Musicale, Florence; Amneris in Aida at Covent Garden 1994, and at Buenos Aires 1996; sang Eboli at Bologna 1998; season 2000–01 as Rossini's Isabella at Turin and Eboli for Zürich Opera; Verdi Requiem at Florence, Palermo, Rome and Saõ Paulo 2001; at Metropolitan Opera of New York from 2005 as Eboli in Don Carlos, Amneris 2007 and as Azucena in Verdi's Trovatore 2009; season 2005/2006 as La Comandante in Zandonai's I Cavalieri di Ekebù in Catania's Teatro Massimo Bellini and Carmen at Verona Arena; season 2007/2008 as Marina in Boris Godunov at Zürich Opera; sang Azucena at Liceu of Barcelona 2009; Paris Opera from 2010 as Eboli in Don Carlos, Zia Principessa in Puccini's Suor Angelica, Laura in Ponchielli's La Gioconda and Verdi's Amneris. *Recordings include:* Lo Frate 'nnamorato, conducted by Riccardo Muti. *Honours:* winner, Spoleto Singing Competition 1993, Opera Award 2000, 2001. *Current Management:* c/o Stage Door, Via San Giorgio 4, Bologna 40121, Italy. *Telephone:* (051) 262126. *Fax:* (051) 271452. *E-mail:* info@stagedoor.it. *Website:* www.stagedoor.it.

DIVALL, Richard Sydney Benedict, AO, OBE, PhD, FRAS, FRNS; Australian opera conductor, musicologist and academic; *Vice-Chancellor's Professorial Fellow, Monash University*; b. 9 Sept. 1945, Sydney; s. of Frederick Ronald Divall and Dorothy Margaret Johnston. *Education:* Univ. of Melbourne, Conservatorium of Music, Sydney, Univ. of Divinity, Melbourne, King's Coll., UK. *Career:* debut with Handel's Xerxes, Sydney; Producer of Music, ABC 1960–70, guest conductor 1972–; Musical Dir, Queensland Opera 1971–; Music Dir, Victoria State Opera 1972–95, Prin. Conductor 1995–97; Assoc. Prof. of Music, Univ. of Melbourne 1992–; Prin. Resident Conductor, Opera Australia 1997–2002; Vice-Chancellor's Professorial Fellow, Monash Univ. 2011–; Visiting Prof. of Music, King's Coll. London 2014–; ed 18th-century symphonies, 20 vols of early Maltese music, series of 30 vols. of colonial Australian repertoire music and 15 operas; Chair. Marshall-Hall Trust. *Recordings include:* repertoire of more than 150 operas, Early Australian Music. *Publications include:* Music of Carl Linger 1998, Complete Music of Henry Handel Richardson 1999, new edns of three vols of music of Frederick Septimus Kelly, vol. of music of Dom Rosendo Salvado, Alfred Hill, GW Marshall-Hall, Alberto Zelman, Australia's First Piano Music, two Symphonies and two String Quartets of Charles Edward Horsley, one Symphony and String Quartet of Fritz Hart, twenty vols of early Maltese Music, Pergolesi Stabat Mater (Wignacourt MS), Complete Sacred Music of Nicolò Isouard, Complete Works of Michael Christian Festing. *Honours:* KM 1989, Commendatore al Merito 1989, Fra' in the Order of Malta (Cav di Giustizia), Cavaliere Jure Sanguinis, Constantinian Order 2009; Hon. DArtes e Cul (SP) 1987, Hon. DLett (Monash Univ.) 1992, Hon. DUniv (Australian Catholic Univ.); Australian Centenary Medal 2003, Sr Fellowship Inst. for Studies in Australian Music Melbourne Univ., Sr Fellow, State Library of Victoria 2003–04, Sir Bernard Heinze Award 2005. *Address:* 301 Arcadia, 228 The Avenue, Parkville, Vic. 3025, Australia (office). *Telephone:* (3) 9381-0789 (office). *E-mail:* maestro@spin.net.au (office).

DIVES, Tamsin; British singer (mezzo-soprano); b. 1968, England. *Education:* Guildhall School. *Career:* opera appearances with Glyndebourne Festival, ENO, Opera North, Chelsea Opera and Edinburgh and Harrogate Festivals; roles include Fidalma in Il Matrimonio Segreto and Mrs Grose in The Turn of the Screw; concerts with the Hallé Orchestra, Northern Sinfonia and The Nash Ensemble; sang in the British Premiere of Korngold's Die tote Stadt, QEH 1996. *Recordings include:* Davies' The Martyrdom of St Magnus, Macmillan's Visitatio Sepulchri.

DIVOKY, Zdenek; Czech horn player; b. 1954, Brno. *Education:* Janáček Academy in Brno with Frantisek Socl. *Career:* wind section of the State Philharmonic Orchestra Brno; Czech Philharmonic 1979; solo peformer in concert and mem. of such chamber ensembles as the Prague Brass Trio, the Horn Quartet of the Czech Philharmonic, the Collegium Musicum Pragense and the Stamic Quartet; solo engagements in Germany, Australia, England, Spain and Canada; repertoire includes concertos by M. and J. Haydn, Telemann, Mozart, Punto, Rosetti, Schumann, Weber and Strauss; recitalist in Beethoven, Mozart, Reicha, Brahms, Britten, Hindemith and Burghauser; tours with the Czech Philharmonic and with various chamber ensembles to Europe, the USA and Japan. *Honours:* Prizewinner at Prague Spring International Festival and competitions in Munich and Markneukirchen.

DJIOEVA, Irina; Russian singer (soprano); b. 1971, Magadan. *Education:* St Petersburg Conservatoire. *Career:* appearances with the Kirov Opera from 1996, as Verdi's Violetta, Leonora (La Forza del Destino) and Elisabeth de Valois, Glinka's Lyudmilla, and Marfa in Rimsky's The Tsar's Bride; Mozart's Queen of Night, Susanna and Donna Anna, Woglinde in Das Rheingold, Stravinsky's Nightingale and Lucia di Lammermoor; Further roles at the Mariinsky Theatre, St Petersburg, include Amina (La Sonnambula), Volkhova in Rimsky's Sadko, and Mimi; sang in the Verdi season with the Kirov Opera at Covent Garden, 2001; further tours to Italy and the New York Met; Sang Flowermaiden in Parsifal at Salzburg, 1998. *Honours:* Prizewinner, 1995 Mario del Monaco Competition and Rimsky-Korsakov International, 1996.

DJUPSJÖBACKA, Gustav Mikael, DMus; Finnish pianist; *Professor, Sibelius Academy, Helsinki;* b. 21 Dec. 1950, Borgå; m. Lena von Bonsdorff 1977; one s. one d. *Education:* Sibelius Acad., Musical Acad., Prague, Czechoslovakia, Hochschule für Musik, Vienna, Austria. *Career:* debut, Helsinki 1978; keyboard player, Radio Symphony Orchestra of Finland 1977–87; Lecturer in Lied Music, Sibelius Acad. 1987–, Prin. 2004–12, Prof. 2012–; mainly lied recitals in Europe, N and S America with Ritva Auvinen, Monica Groop, Tom Krause, Jorma Hynninen, and others; mem. Yrjö Kilpinen Soc., Madetoja Foundation, Acad. Francis Poulenc, Nordic Music Cttee; Chair, Finland Festivals 2014–, State Music Council 2015–; mem. of jury, Rimski Korsakov Singing Contest, St Petersburg 2002, 2004, Maj Lind Piano Competition 2007; mem. several conservatory evaluation panels. *Recordings:* Winterreise and Sibelius Songs with Tom Krause, Sibelius Songs with Ritva Auvinen, Complete Madetoja Songs with Gabriel Suovanen and Helena Juntunen. *Publications include:* Yrjö Kilpinen's Morgenstern Songs 1992, Aarre Merikanto Songs 2000, Kilpinen Songs 2002, Guide on Finnish Art Songs 2000, Critical Edn of Toïvo Kuula's Songs 2008. *Honours:* Kt Order of the Lion of Finland (Pro Finlandia), Commdr Royal Norwegian Order; Sylvi Kekkonen Scholarship 1975, 1976. *Address:* Sibelius Academy, Töölönkatu 28, 00260 Helsinki (office); Sibelius Academy, PO Box 30, 00097 Art University (office); Töölöntorinkatu 3 A 2, 00260 Helsinki, Finland (home). *E-mail:* gustav.djupsjobacka@uniarts.fi (office).

DJUPSTROM, Michael, BM, MA; American composer and pianist; b. 1980, St Paul, Minn. *Education:* Univ. of Michigan, Curtis Inst. of Music. *Career:* commissions include Philadelphia Orchestra Asscn, Milwaukee Symphony Orchestra, Tanglewood Music Center, Int. Opera Theatre, New York Youth Symphony Chamber Music Program; works performed by ensembles including American Composers Orchestra, Milwaukee Symphony Orchestra, Tokyo Kosei Wind Orchestra, Tanglewood Festival Chorus, Symphony in C, and various new music ensembles including Network for New Music, Brave New Works, Composers, Inc., Sounds New, Aspen Contemporary Ensemble, and New Fromm Players at Tanglewood; Founding mem. Phoenix Trio 2005–08; performs with Philadelphia-based new music ensemble Relâche and as accompanist for Philadelphia Gay Men's Chorus; currently teacher, Curtis Inst. of Music. *Compositions include:* orchestral: Horizon Fragment 2001, Si me tocaras el corazón 2002, Homages for wind ensemble 2002, Prelude to a Forgotten Opera 2006, Gaeng 2006, Puck 2008, Scène et Pas de Deux 2010, Suite from "The Wedding" 2011, The Seahorse and the Crab; solo and chamber music: Remembrances for flute and piano 1998, String Trio 2000, Suite for bassoon and trombone 2001, Incidental music for King Lear 2003, Walimai for alto sax (or viola) and piano (Music Teachers Nat. Asscn/Shepherd Distinguished Composer of the Year 2005, American Viola Soc.'s Gardner Award, inaugural Delius Int. Composition Prize 2012) 2005, Prelude, piano solo 2006; vocal and choral: Berceuse al espejo dormido for SATB chorus a capella 2002, Adam Lay Ybounden for SATB chorus and organ 2007, The Wedding, opera scene for soprano, tenor, baritone, flute, clarinet, violin, violoncello, piano, percussion 2010. *Recording:* Walimai. *Honours:* awards from American Composers Forum, Meet the Composer, ASCAP Foundation, also First Prize and Audience Prize, Great Wall Int. Composition Competition, Chinese Fine Arts Soc. 2006, Charles Ives Fellowship, American Acad. of Arts and Letters 2010. *E-mail:* mdjupstr@yahoo.com (home). *Website:* www.michaeldjupstrom.com (office).

DMITRIEV, Alexander Sergeevich; Russian conductor; *Artistic Director and Chief Conductor, St Petersburg Symphony Orchestra;* b. 19 Jan. 1935,

Leningrad; m.; one s. *Education:* Leningrad Choir School, Leningrad State Conservatory, Vienna Akad. für Musik und darstellende Kunst, Austria. *Career:* Conductor Karelian Radio and TV Symphony Orchestra 1961, Prin. Conductor 1962–71; Prin. Conductor Maly Opera and Ballet Theatre, Leningrad (now St Petersburg) 1971–77, Chief Conductor and Artistic Dir St Petersburg Symphony Orchestra 1977–; Prin. Conductor Stavanger Symphony Orchestra, Norway 1990–98; Prof., Rimsky-Korsakov St Petersburg State Conservatory. *Recordings include:* Handel's Messiah, Haydn's Creation, Schubert's Symphony Nos. 1–9, Tchaikovsky's Symphonies 4, 5, 6, Rachmaninov's Symphony No. 2, Debussy's 3 Nocturnes, Ravel's Valses nobles et sentimentales, Ma Mère l'Oye, Saeverud's Peer Gynt, Symphony dolorosa, Balakirev's Piano Concerto, Medtner's Piano Concerto No. 1, Rachmaninov's Piano Concerto No. 3, Britten's Violin concerto, Sibelius Violin Concerto, Shostakovich and Tchaikovsky Violin Concertos, Shostakovich Symphony No. 7, Scriabin Symphony No. 3. *Honours:* Order of Honour of Cultural and Art Merit; Merited Worker of Arts of Karelian ASSR 1967, People's Artist of USSR 1976, USSR People's Artist, Prize 2nd USSR Competition for Conductors 1966, State Prize of the Russian Fed., Prize of the St Petersburg Govt in Literature, Art and Architecture 2009. *Address:* St Petersburg Symphony Orchestra, St Petersburg 191186, Mikhailovskaya str. 2, Russia (office). *E-mail:* dmitriev@mail.spbnit.ru. *Website:* www.philharmonia.spb.ru (office).

DOANE, Steven, MM; American musician (cello) and academic; *Professor of Violoncello, Eastman School of Music;* b. 1950, New Jersey. *Education:* Oberlin Conservatory, State Univ. of New York at Stony Brook, further studies with Richard Kapuscinski, Bernard Greenhouse, Jane Cowan and Janos Starker. *Career:* apptd Prin. Cellist, Milwaukee Symphony 1976, Rochester Philharmonic 1981; mem. New Arts Trio 1985–86; recitals at festivals and concert series throughout USA and UK; recording series with Eastman pianist Barry Snyder broadcast across N America and by BBC in UK; Carnegie Hall and Kennedy Center debuts (Don Quixote with David Zinman and Rochester Philharmonic) 1983; Tully Hall recital debut 1990; recital appearances at venues including Wigmore Hall, London and Saunders Theater, Boston; mem. Faculty, Eastman School of Music 1981–, Prof. of Violoncello; Assoc. in Cello, Royal Acad. of Music, London 1995–1999, masterclasses and residencies, now Visiting Prof. *Recordings include:* Britten and Frank Bridge: Music for Cello & Piano 1995, Gabriel Fauré: Complete Music for Cello and Piano (Naird Award, Diapason d'Or) 2006, Rachmaninoff Cello Sonata with Barry Snyder 2012. *Honours:* Watson Foundation Grant for overseas study 1975, Naumburg Chamber Music Award (with New Arts Trio) 1980, Piatigorsky Prize in Teaching, New England Conservatory 1986, Eisenhart Award for Excellence in Teaching, Eastman School of Music 1993. *Address:* Eastman School of Music, 26 Gibbs Street, Rochester, NY 14604, USA (office). *Telephone:* (585) 274-1593 (office). *E-mail:* cellodoane@aol.com (office). *Website:* www.esm.rochester.edu/faculty/doane_steven (office).

DOBBER, Andrzej; Polish singer (baritone); b. 26 May 1961, Wiecbok. *Education:* studied in Warsaw and Nuremberg. *Career:* debut as Gremin while a student; sang at Nuremberg Opera 1987–91, debut as Tonio in Pagliacci; Frankfurt Opera from 1991, as Nardo in La finta giardiniera, Luna, the Herald in Lohengrin, Gremin and Marcello; Guest at the Vienna Staatsoper as Escamillo (1992) and frequent concert appearances; Cologne from 1995, as Eugene Onegin and Mozart's Count; Sang Fyodor in The Invisible City of Kitezh at the Komische Oper, Berlin, 1996; Season 2000–01 in Berlin as Danilo in Die Lustige Witwe at the Deutsche Oper, and as Orestes in Elektra at the Komische Oper. *Current Management:* Zemsky Green Artists' Management, 103 West 73rd Street, Suite 1, New York, NY 10023, USA. *Telephone:* (212) 579-6700. *Fax:* (212) 579-4723. *E-mail:* bzemsky@zemskygreen.com. *Website:* www.zemskygreen.com.

DOBSON, John, OBE; British singer (tenor); b. 1930, Derby, England. *Education:* Guildhall School of Music with Norman Walker, studied in Italy with Giovanni Inghilleri. *Career:* debut in Bergamo 1957, as Pinkerton; New Opera Company 1958, in Sir John in Love and A Tale of Two Cities; Glyndebourne Festival 1959, in Der Rosenkavalier; engagements with ENO, WNO and Scottish Opera; Deutsche Oper am Rhein, Düsseldorf, Orange Festival and Maggio Musicale, Florence; Covent Garden 1959–95, in some 100 roles and 2,000 performances: roles included Wagner's David, Mime, Loge and Melot, Beethoven's Jacquino and Mussorgsky's Shuisky; sang Paris in the premiere of Tippett's King Priam, Coventry 1962; sang Luke in the 1977 premiere of Tippett's The Ice Break; with the Royal Opera at La Scala Milan 1976 and the Far East 1979, 1986, 1992; sang Mime in the first Japanese performances of Wagner's Ring with the Deutsche Oper 1987; sang in the British Premiere of Berio's Un Re in Ascolto 1989; Borsa in Rigoletto; Inn Keeper in a new production of The Cunning Little Vixen 1990, the Emperor in Turandot; Dir, Young Singers' Ensemble at Covent Garden; sang Mime in Siegfried 1991, Jakob Glock in a new production of Prokofiev's Fiery Angel 1992; sang Altoun in Turandot at Covent Garden 1994; freelance singer from 1995; Abbate in Andrea Chénier with the Royal Opera at the Festival Hall 1998; retired from singing 1998, after a performance of the Rector (Peter Grimes) with the Royal Opera House at the Savonlinna Festival. *Recordings include:* videos: Peter Grimes, Otello, Samson et Dalila and La Fanciulla del West.

DODD, Geraint; British singer (tenor); b. 1958, Rhosllanerchrugog, Wales. *Education:* Royal Northern College of Music with Joseph Ward. *Career:* appearances with WNO as the Duke of Mantua, Pinkerton and Macduff;

Florestan, Werther and Rodolfo for English Touring Opera; Don José in concert for WNO, 1988, and Radames for Mid Wales Opera; other roles include Pollione in Norma (Neath Opera), Calaf, Cavaradossi in Tosca and Captain Vere in Billy Budd; Concerts include Messiah, the Verdi Requiem and The Dream of Gerontius. *Current Management:* Harlequin Agency Ltd, 203 Fidlas Road, Llanishen, Cardiff, CF14 5NA, Wales. *Telephone:* (29) 2075-0821. *Fax:* (29) 2075-5971. *E-mail:* peter@harlequin-agency.co.uk. *Website:* www.harlequin-agency.co.uk.

DODERER, Gerhard, PhD; German/Portuguese musicologist and organist; *Professor of Musicology, Universidade Nova de Lisboa*; b. 25 March 1944, Kitzingen, Germany; m. C. Rosado Fernandes 1970. *Education:* Univ. of Würzburg, Staatskonservatorium of Würzburg. *Career:* organ recitals since 1970 in Europe and elsewhere; Dir Würzburg Conservatory 1975–80; Prof. of Musicology, Universidade Nova de Lisboa, Portugal 1981–; mem. American, Spanish, Portuguese and German Musicological Socs. *Recordings:* albums of historical Portuguese organs. *Publications:* Portuguese Clavichords of the 18th Century 1971, Organa Hispanica (nine vols) 1971–84, Orgelmusik und Orgelbau in Portugal 1976, Domenico Scarlatti: Libro di Tocate 1991, The Organs at Braga Cathedral 1992, J. de la Té y Sagau: Cantatas Humanas a Solo (1723) 1999, L. Giustini di Pistoia: Sonate de Cimbalo di piano e forte 2002, Portugese String Keyboard Instruments of the 18th Century: Clavichords, Harpsichords, Piano and Spinets (with J. H. van der Meer) 2004. *Address:* Departamento de Ciências Musicais, Universidade Nova de Lisboa, Avenida de Berna, 26 C, Lisbon 1069-061 (office); Rua do Borja 133-B, 3A, Lisbon 1350-046, Portugal (home). *E-mail:* go.doderer@fcsh.unl.pt (office); gdoderer@mail.telepac.pt (home). *Website:* www.fcsh.unl.pt (office).

DODGE, Charles, BA, MA, DMA; American composer; b. 5 June 1942, Ames, IA; m. Katharine Schlefer 1978; one s. one d. *Education:* Univ. of Iowa, Columbia Univ., studied with Richard Hervig, Darius Milhaud, Philip Bezanson, Gunther Schuller, Otto Luening, Godfrey Winheim. *Career:* performances include Tanglewood 1965, 1973, 1986, Warsaw Autumn Festival, Poland 1978, 1985, 1986; New Music, New York Festival 1979; Stockholm Festival of Electronic Music, Sweden 1980, 1982; Venice Biennale, Italy 1981; Calarts Festival 1983; Olympic Arts Festival, Los Angeles 1984; New York Philharmonic 1984; Los Angeles Philharmonic 1984. *Compositions:* Folia, Changes: Earth's Magnetic Field, Speech Songs, Extensions, The Story of Our Lives, In Celebration, Cascando, Any Resemblance is Purely Coincidental, The Waves, The One and the Other for chamber orchestra 1993, That Which I Should Have Done!... for organ and tape 1996, Just Harmonies (for Christian Wolff) 1996. *Recordings include:* Synthetic Speech Music. *Publications:* Computer Music, Synthesis: Composition and Performing (with Thomas A. Jerse) 1985; contrib. 'Musical Fractals' to Byte Magazine 1986.

DOESE, Helena; Swedish singer (soprano); b. 7 Aug. 1946, Göteborg. *Education:* studied in Göteborg, with Luigi Ricci in Rome, with Erik Werba and Gerald Moore in Vienna and with Vera Rozsa in London. *Career:* debut at Göteborg 1971, as Aida; Bern Opera 1972–75, as Jenůfa, Micaela and Donna Anna; Royal Opera Stockholm from 1973 as Liu in Turandot, Mimi, Katya Kabanova and Eva in the Friedrich production of Die Meistersinger; Glyndebourne debut 1974, as Mozart's Countess: Fiordiligi 1975; Covent Garden from 1974 as Mimi, Gutrune in Götterdämmerung, Agathe in Der Freischütz and Amelia in Simon Boccanegra; Tatiana in Eugene Onegin for Scottish Opera; Guest appearances in Marseilles (Elisabeth de Valois), Sydney, (Aida), Paris Opéra, (Fiordiligi), Hamburg, (Agathe), San Francisco, (Countess) and Zürich (Sieglinde); Member of Frankfurt Opera: has sung title roles in Ariadne auf Naxos, Jenůfa and Iphigénie en Tauride, Countess in Capriccio, the Marschallin, and Chrysothemis in Elektra; Deutsche Oper Berlin, 1987, as Agathe followed by the Marschallin at Copenhagen; Sydney, 1988, as Eva in Die Meistersinger; Sang Rosalinde at Oslo, 1988, Tosca 1989; Season 1991/92 as Fidelio at Toronto, Elsa at Frankfurt and Ariadne at Stuttgart; Season 1994–95 sang Chrysothemis at Frankfurt, and Sieglinde; Strauss's Ariadne auf Naxos at the Teatro Colón, Buenos Aires, 1995 and Elisabeth in Tannhäuser by Wagner at Sau Paulo in 1996. *Recordings include:* videos of Glyndebourne Così fan tutte and Covent Garden Bohème.

DOGHAN, Philip, BA; British singer (tenor); *Vocal Coach, Royal College of Music*; b. 1949, London, England. *Education:* Durham Univ. *Career:* sang as a boy in premiere of Tippett's King Priam 1962; has sung roles in Orfeo, Ulysses, Wozzeck, Faust, La Belle Hélène, David Blake's The Plumber's Gift, Busoni's Dr Faustus, Le Duc de Mantoue in Les Brigands, Guillot in Manon, Don Basilio in Le Nozze di Figaro, Mambre in Mosè in Egitto, Aschenbach in Death in Venice, Lohengrin, Guillot de Morfontaine in Manon, Bob Boles in Peter Grimes, Iro in Il Ritorno d'Ulisse; performed in premiere of Adriana Hölszkýs Die Wände at the Oper Frankfurt; has performed at Opera di Roma, La Fenice, the Teatro Massimo di Palermo, Opera du Rhin, Opera de Lausanne, Théâtre du Chatelet, Théâtre des Champs-Elysees, English Nat. Opera, Paris Opera, Covent Garden, Oper Köln, Oper Frankfurt, Opera de Rouen, Theater Lübeck, Los Angeles Opera, Teatro San Carlo di Napoli, New Israeli Opera, Welsh Nat. Opera; festivals include Wexford Int. Festival, Dublin Grand, Aix-en-Provence, Salzburg; currently also Vocal Coach, Royal Coll. of Music. *Honours:* winner Grand Prix, Toulouse 1980.

DOHMEN, Albert; German singer (bass-baritone); b. 1955, Krefeld. *Education:* studied in Cologne and with Gladys Kuchta. *Career:* sang at the Deutsche Oper am Rhein, Düsseldorf 1983–85; Wiesbaden from 1986, Hamburg 1986–87, Vienna Volksoper 1987–90; guest appearances at Stockholm (Assur in Semiramide 1988), Catania (Kaspar in Der Freischütz) and Cairo, in Haydn's La Vera Costanza; sang in the premiere of Bose's Die Leiden des Jungen Werthers at Ludwigsburg 1986 and in the German premiere of La Princesse de Cleve by Jean Francaix; sang Don Giovanni in festivals at Prague and Macerata 1991; returned to Macerata 1992, as Don Parmenione in Rossini's L'Occasione fa il Ladro; other roles include Mozart's Count and Alfonso, Don Magnifico, the Grand Inquisitor and Verdi's Procida and Paolo, Scarpia and Gianni Schicchi, Wagner's King Henry, Biterolf, Wotan, Donner, Gunther and Amfortas; sang Simone in Zemlinsky's Eine Florentinische Tragödie at Florence 1996; season 1998, as Weber's Kaspar at Rome and Jeremiah in Weill's Propheten at the London Proms; season 2000–01 as the Wanderer at Trieste, Wotan in Die Walküre at Geneva, Scarpia for Covent Garden and the Rheingold Wotan at the Vienna Staatsoper, Kothner at Die Meistersinger, Kommandant in Der Friedenstag; concert repertoire includes the Verdi Requiem and Zemlinsky's Sieben Sinfonische Gesänge. *Recordings:* Spirit Messenger in Die Frau ohne Schatten, conducted by Solti. *Current Management:* Opéra et Concert, 37 rue de la Chausée d'Antin, 75009 Paris, France. *Telephone:* 1-42-96-18-18. *Fax:* 1-42-96-18-00. *E-mail:* agence@opera-concert.com. *Website:* www.opera-concert.com. *E-mail:* albertdohmen@aol.com (office).

DOLEŽAL, Karel; Czech violist; *Professor, Prague Conservatory*; b. 16 Jan. 1948, Prague; m. 1974; two s. *Education:* High School of Music, Prague Conservatory with Profs Cerny and Maly. *Career:* f. Doležal String Quartet 1972, viola player 1972–2003; debut in Knights Hall of The Waldstein Palace, Prague 1973; solo performances at Prague Spring Festival 1976, Bratislava Music Festival 1977; music festival performances at Brno, Karlovy Vary, T. Teplice, Poland, GDR, Romania; solo concert, BBC, TV Prague and 12 concerts for Radio Prague; made biographical film with the Doležal String Quartet (Czech Film Corpn), programmes for TV Prague, Radio NY 1981; performances at Wigmore Hall, London, Birmingham, Dublin, Prague Spring Festival, Paris Festival, Bretagne, Tonhalle Zürich, Berlin, Halle; concert tours of Austria, Spain, Scandinavia, Hungary, Tunisia etc.; radio and television programmes for Hamburg, Bremen, Frankfurt, Wiesbaden, Saarbrucken; concert tour of USA 1980; with quartet, concert tours of Japan 1993, Spain 1997, Kangasniemi Festival, Finland 1997; Prof., Prague Conservatory 1993–, Univ. of New York in Prague; concert tour of West Germany 1998–99; masterclasses in Seoul, Daegu, South Korea 2000–07, Dobrichovice String Master Courses 2005–10. *Recordings:* two String Quartets by Dvořák 1983, two String Quartets by Leoš Janáček 1984, five albums of works by Mozart, Dvořák, Janáček, Martinů, Shostakovich, and others; solo: Viola and piano works by: Bloch, Rubinstein, Hindemith, Matousek 1995, Mendelssohn, Reger, Weber 1997; quartet: Quartets by Janáček 1992, two Quartets by Dvořák 1994, Quartets by Smetana, Fibich 1996. *Address:* Za Stodolou 517, 252 31 Všenory-Prague-West, Czech Republic (home). *Telephone:* 257710858 (home); 603821585 (mobile). *E-mail:* violadolezal@seznam.cz (home). *Website:* www.stringmastercourses.net.

DOLLARHIDE, Thomas (Ted), MA, PhD; American composer and musicologist; b. 30 Aug. 1948, Santa Rosa, Calif. *Education:* San Jose State Univ., Univ. of Michigan, studied with Leslie Bassett and William Bolcom, Fulbright Fellowship for study in Paris with composer Eugene Kurtz. *Career:* mem. Faculty, La Trobe Univ. 1981–89; Composer-in-Residence, Santa Rosa Symphony 1980s; fmr Music Dir and Conductor, North Port (Fla) Symphony Orchestra; fmr Coordinator of Music Program, Rogue Community Coll.; fmr Music Dir and Conductor, Southern Oregon Concert Band; mem. Southern Oregon Chapter, Nat. Asscn of Composers. *Compositions include:* Shadows for wind quintet 1973, Theme and Variations for two cellos, flute, clarinet and two speaking voices 1976, Other Dreams, Other Dreamers for orchestra 1976, Shoestrings for flute and clarinet 1977, Pluriels for orchestra 1979, Punk for piano 1980, By Thunder Mill Pond for trombone 1981, Ragings of a One Pot Screamer for piano 1982, A Back Street for violin 1983, Two Pieces for piano 1984, Madness in Paradise for violin, viola, double bass, clarinet, guitar, mandolin and percussion 1986, Aria for cello and piano 1990, The Dark Horse for orchestra 1992. *Honours:* Broadcast Music Award to Young Composers, USA 1975–76.

DOLMETSCH, Jeanne-Marie, LRAM; British recorder player, treble violist and lecturer; b. 15 Aug. 1942, Hindhead, Surrey; d. of Dr Carl Dolmetsch and Mary Douglas Dolmetsch; twin sister of Marguerite Dolmetsch. *Education:* Royal Acad. of Music. *Career:* debut at QEH, London 1973; toured USA, Colombia, Germany, France, Ireland and Sweden with the Dolmetsch Ensemble; recorder soloist and Asst Dir, Haslemere Festival; appearances at Bath Festival, English Bach Festival; Lecturer, Nat. Asscn of Decorative and Fine Arts 1974–; numerous radio broadcasts and television programmes. *Recordings:* collections of early music with the Dolmetsch Ensemble. *Address:* Jesses, Grayswood Road, Haslemere, GU27 2BS, Surrey, England (home).

DOLMETSCH, Marguerite Mabel, LRAM; British recorder player and viola da gamba player; b. 15 Aug. 1942, Hindhead, Surrey; d. of Dr Carl Dolmetsch and Mary Douglas Dolmetsch; twin sister of Jeanne-Marie Dolmetsch; m. Dr Brian E. Blood; two s. one d. *Education:* Royal Naval School, Haslemere, Royal Acad. of Music, London. *Career:* travelled widely with the Dolmetsch Ensemble and Dolmetsch Concertante, touring America, France, Germany, Sweden, South Africa, Colombia; has performed at Three Choirs Festival, Bath Festival and Haslemere Festival; has also appeared at Queen Elizabeth Hall, Purcell Room and Wigmore Hall, London; radio broadcasts and TV programmes in UK, Germany, S Africa and S America. Recitals: various recitals with the Dolmetsch Ensemble; Asst Dir Haslemere Festival; mem. Nat. Fed. of Decorative and Fine Arts Socs. *Recordings:* Choice Consorts for Recorders, A Christmas Tapestry, in Words and Music, A Chest of Viols. *Address:* Jesses, Grayswood Road, Haslemere, Surrey, GU27 2BS, England (home). *Telephone:* (1428) 651473 (home). *E-mail:* marguerite@dolmetsch.com (office). *Website:* www.dolmetsch.com.

DOLTON, Geoffrey; British singer (baritone); b. 30 Dec. 1958, Shrewsbury, England. *Education:* Royal Acad. of Music with Joy Mammen, Nat. Opera Studio, studied in Milan with Peter Moores Foundation. *Career:* debut with Opera North, as Guglielmo in Così fan tutte 1983; further roles with Opera North as Mozart's Count, Lescaut in Massenet's Manon Lescaut and Henrik in the British premiere of Nielsen's Maskarade; with Opera Factory has sung Guglielmo (also televised) and Orestes in Gluck's Iphigenia operas; Manoel Theatre Malta, Figaro in Il Barbiere di Siviglia; season 1992 as Hector in Tippett's King Priam at Antwerp, Monteverdi's Otho for Opera Factory, in Krenek's What Price Confidence? at the Almeida Festival and as Alan in Birtwistle's Yan Tan Tethera; other roles include Papageno for WNO and Opera Northern Ireland; Schaunard in La Bohème for Scottish Opera; Hector in King Priam for Opera North, Malatesta in Don Pasquale for New Israeli Opera and the title role in Grétry's Le Huron at the Buxton Festival 1990; sang Guglielmo in Così fan tutte for ENO 1990; recitals with the pianist Nicholas Bosworth; season 1994, ENO Eisenstein in Die Fledermaus; Opera Northern Ireland, Figaro in the Barber of Seville; Castleward Opera Dandini in La Cenerentola; sang in La Traviata for GTO at Glyndebourne 1996; season 2000, Casey Flood in John Lunn's Zoë for Glyndebourne and Channel 4; First Mate in Billy Budd in Venice; Dr Malatesta in Don Pasquale for Opera Zuid; recent work includes Caius in Merry Wives of Windsor for Buxton Festival and Njegus, The Merry Widow for WNO and BBC 2. *Recordings:* Donizetti's Emilia di Liverpool (with the Philharmonia Orchestra). *Honours:* Peter Pears Prize for Recital Singing at the RAM, Hon. ARAM 1992. *Current Management:* The Music Partnership Ltd, New Broad Street House, New Broad Street, London EC2M 1NH, England. *Telephone:* (20) 7840-9592. *E-mail:* office@musicpartnership.co.uk. *Website:* www.musicpartnership.co.uk.

DOLZHENKO, Irina Igorevna; Russian singer (mezzo-soprano); b. 23 Oct. 1955, Tashkent, Uzbekistan; m.; one d. *Career:* mem. children's troupe, Stanislavsky and Nemirovich-Danchenko Music Theatre, Moscow –1996; soloist, Bolshoi Theare 1996–; sang with Swedish Royal Opera, Deutsche Oper, Berlin, Teatro Colón, Buenos Aires, New Israeli Opera, Tel-Aviv; recitals in Japan, South Korea, USA, Australia, Europe. *Operatic roles include:* Amneris in Aida, Adalgisa in Norma, Amelfa in The Golden Cockerel, Morozova in Oprichnik, Cherubino in Marriage of Figaro, Azucena in Il Trovatore, Ulrica in Un Ballo in Maschera. *Honours:* People's Artist of Russia. *Current Management:* Robert Gilder and Company, 91 Great Russell Street, London, WC1B 3PS, England. *E-mail:* rgilder@robert-gilder.com. *Website:* www.doljenko.ru.

DOMANINSKA, Libuse; Czech singer (soprano); b. 4 July 1924, Brno. *Education:* Prague Conservatory with Hana Pirkova and Bohuslav Sobesky. *Career:* debut in Brno 1946, as Vendulka in The Kiss by Smetana; sang at Brno in operas by Smetana and Janáček (Jenůfa, Katya Kabanova and the Vixen); Prague Nat. Opera 1955–85; visited Edinburgh with the company 1964, as Milada in Dalibor; Komische Oper Brelin 1956, Vienna Staatsoper 1958–68; Holland Festival 1959, as Katya Kababova; roles in Russian operas and in Mozart, Puccini and Verdi; Marenka in The Bartered Bride, Smetana's Libuše, Jenůfa, Aida, Elisabeth de Valois, Euridice and Foerster's Eva; many concert appearances, notably in Janáček's Glagolitic Mass at La Scala; retired 1985. *Recordings:* Glagolitic Mass, The Cunning Little Vixen, The Devil's Wall by Smetana. *Honours:* Artist of Merit 1966, National Artist 1974.

DOMANSKÝ, Hanuš; Slovak composer; b. 1 March 1944, Novy, Hrozenkov. *Education:* Brno Conservatory with Jan Duchan, Bratislava Acad. of Musical Arts with Dezider Kardos, studied with Jaroslav Shanel. *Career:* associated with Czech Radio, Bratislava. *Compositions:* Concerto Piccolo for orchestra 1970, Symphony 1980, Piano Concerto 1984, Music for trumpet, flute and bass clarinet 1966, Musica Giocosa for violin and piano 1971, Dianoia for violin 1976, piano pieces, organ music, About Winter cantata for narrator, children's choir and orchestra 1968, Fiat Lux oratorio for narrator, soprano, chorus and orchestra 1970, Versifying for chorus and percussion 1972, Recruiting Songs for men's chorus 1978, solo songs. *Honours:* Slovak Composer's Award 1983.

DOMARKAS, Juozas; Lithuanian conductor; *Artistic Director and Chief Conductor, Lithuanian National Symphony Orchestra;* b. 28 July 1936, Plunge; m.; two s. *Education:* Klaipeda Simkus Coll. of Music, Lithuanian Acad. of Music, St Petersburg State Conservatory (conducting Symphony Orchestra and Opera, with Prof. Ilja Musin). *Career:* Asst Conductor, Vilnius Band 1957–60; Artistic Dir and Chief Conductor, Lithuanian Nat. Symphony Orchestra 1964–; participated in numerous nat. and int. festivals; teacher, sr teacher, Assoc. Prof., Lithuanian Acad. of Music and Theatre 1968–93, Chair. and Prof. 1993–; mem. of jury for numerous int. competitions for symphony conducting in Russia, Poland and Finland; numerous recordings. *Honours:* Grand Cross, Order of the Lithuanian Grand Duke Gediminas 1998; People's Artist of the USSR 1986, Award of Govt of Lithuania for Merit to Lithuanian Culture 1997, Nat. Prize of Lithuanian Repub. 2000. *Address:* Lietuvos Nacionaline Filharmonija, Ausros Vartu 5, 01129 Vilnius (office); Zydu 4–15, 01131 Vilnius, Lithuania (home). *Telephone:* (5) 266-5210 (office); (5) 262-8461 (home). *Fax:* (5) 266-5266 (office); (5) 262-8461 (home). *E-mail:* info@

filharmonija.lt (office); juozas.domarkas.1@gmail.com (home). *Website:* www.filharmonija.lt (office).

DOMASHENKO, Marina; Russian singer (mezzo-soprano). *Career:* sang Dalila in concert opposite Plácido Domingo and title role in Carmen with San Francisco Opera 2002; debut at Royal Opera House, Covent Garden as Maddalena in Rigoletto 2005; has sung Carmen at Metropolitan Opera, New York, Vienna State Opera, San Francisco Opera, San Diego Opera, Royal Opera House, Covent Garden; repertoire includes Paulina in The Queen of Spades, Olga in Eugene Onegin, Prince Orlofsky in Die Fledermaus, Dorabella in Così fan tutte and Charlotte in Werther; worked with conductors including Sir Colin Davis, Daniel Barenboim, Riccardo Chailly, Fabio Luisi, Myung Whun Chung. *Recordings include:* Marina Domashenko 2001, Tchaikovsky, The Queen of Spades 2002, Prokofiev, Alexander Nevsky 2004, Raffaello 2004, Tchaikovsky Duets: Domashenko and Gutyakova 2006, Verdi, Falstaff (Grammy Award for Best Opera Recording 2006) 2006, Carmen: Duets and Arias 2010. *Honours:* Diva Award of Philadelphia Opera 2002. *Address:* c/o Delos Records, Delos Productions, Inc. PO Box 343, Sonoma, CA 95476, USA (office). *Telephone:* (707) 996-3844 (office). *Fax:* (707) 320-0600 (office). *E-mail:* feedback@delosmusic.com (office). *Website:* www.delosmusic.com (office).

DOMINGO, Plácido, FRCM, FRNCM; Spanish singer (tenor) and conductor; *General Director, Los Angeles Opera;* b. 21 Jan. 1941, Madrid; s. of the late Plácido Domingo and Pepita Domingo (née Embil); m. Marta Ornelas; three s. *Education:* Nat. Conservatory of Music, Mexico City. *Career:* operatic debut at Monterrey, Mexico 1961; with Israel Nat. Opera for over two years; debut at Metropolitan Opera, New York 1968; British debut in Verdi's Requiem at Royal Festival Hall 1969; Covent Garden debut in Tosca 1971, returned to sing in Aïda, Carmen 1973, La Bohème 1974, Un Ballo in Maschera 1975, La Fanciulla del West; has taken leading roles in about 120 operas; with New York City Opera 1965–; Artistic Dir Washington Nat. Opera 1994–2003, Gen. Dir 2003–11; Artistic Dir Los Angeles Opera 2000–03, Gen. Dir 2003–; engagements include Tosca (conducting), Romeo and Juliet at Metropolitan Opera, New York, Aïda, Il Trovatore in Hamburg, Don Carlos in Salzburg, I vespri siciliani and La forza del destino in Paris, Turandot in Barcelona, Otello in Paris, London, Hamburg and Milan, Carmen in Edinburgh, Turandot at the Metropolitan; New York stage debut in My Fair Lady 1988 (213 performances by 2000); Luigi in Il Tabarro at the Met 1989; Otello at Covent Garden 1990, Lohengrin at Vienna Staatsoper, Don José at Rio de Janeiro, Otello at the Met and Barcelona; Don Carlos at Los Angeles, Dick Johnson at Chicago, Riccardo in Un Ballo in Maschera at the 1990 Salzburg Festival; debut as Parsifal at the Met 1991 and 2001, Otello at Covent Garden 1992, Siegmund in Die Walküre at the Vienna Staatsoper 1992; 1997 season included Don José and Siegmund at the Met and Gabriele Adorno in Simon Boccanegra at Covent Garden; 1999 season Herman in the Queen of Spades at the Met, and at Covent Garden 2002; concert performance of Verdi's Battaglia di Legnano with the Royal Opera 2000; Canio in Pagliacci at Covent Garden 2003; Nero in premiere of Monteverdi's Poppea in Los Angeles 2003; Rasputin in premiere of Deborah Drattell's Nicholas and Alexandra, Los Angeles 2003; opened 2002/03 Los Angeles Opera season in Puccini's Fanciulla del West; Maurizio in Adriana Lecouvreur, Metropolitan Opera 2009; sang first baritone title role in Verdi's Simon Boccanegra at Berlin Staatsoper 2009, Covent Garden 2010, the Met 2010; cr. and performed at inaugural Plácido Domingo Festival, Spain 2012; 2015 season included debut in the title role of Verdi's Macbeth, Berlin, Don Carlo in Ernani in New York and title role of Gianni Schicchi in Los Angeles. *Films include:* Madama Butterfly with von Karajan, La Traviata 1982, Carmen 1984, Otello 1986. *Recordings include:* has made well over 100 recordings, including Aïda, Un Ballo in Maschera, Tosca, Tannhäuser 1989, Die Frau ohne Schatten 1993, Gounod's Roméo et Juliette 1996, Merlin by Albeniz 2000, Tristan and Isolde (Critics' Choice Award, Classical Brit Awards 2006), Pasión Española (Latin Grammy Award for Best Classical Album) 2008; has made more than 50 videos. *Publications include:* My First Forty Years (autobiog.) 1983, My Operatic Roles 2000. *Honours:* Commdr, Légion d'honneur, Hon. KBE 2002, Medal of Freedom, Star of the Order of Merit (Hungary) 2005; Dr hc (Royal Coll. of Music) 1982, (Univ. Complutense de Madrid) 1989, Hon. DMus (Univ. of Oxford) 2003, (California State Univ.) 2010, (Harvard) 2013, (Salamanca) 2015; 12 Grammy Awards, European Culture Foundation Culture Prize 2003, Classic FM Gramophone Listeners' Choice Award 2005, Opera News Award 2005, Classic BRIT Award for Lifetime Achievement 2006, Birgit Nilsson Prize 2009, Person of the Year, Latin Recording Acad. 2010, Wolf Foundation Prize in Music (shared with Sir Simon Rattle) 2012, Praemium Imperiale Award, Japan Art Foundation 2013. *Current Management:* c/o Nancy Seltzer and Associates, 6220 Del Valle Drive, Los Angeles, CA 90048, USA. *Telephone:* (323) 938-3562. *E-mail:* nseltzer@nsapr.com. *Website:* www.laopera.org; www.placidodomingo.com.

DOMINGUEZ, Guillermo; Venezuelan singer (tenor); b. 1961, Caracas. *Education:* studied with José Castro in Caracas, then at Rome and Turin. *Career:* debut in Treviso 1984, as Rodolfo; sang Rodolfo at Paris, Amiens and Munich; Zürich Opera as Don Ottavio and Ferrando and in Guillaume Tell; appearances at Monte Carlo as Edgardo in Lucia di Lammermoor and at Innsbruck as Cavaradossi and Duke of Mantua 1988; Nat. Theatre, Mannheim as Alfredo and Puccini's Edgar with Dresden Staatskapelle; engagements in Spain as Duke of Mantua; numerous concert appearances. *Address:* Waldistrasse 22, 8134 Adliswil, Switzerland. *E-mail:* domingueztenor@hotmail.it. *Website:* www.dominguez.ch.

DOMINGUEZ, Ruben; Venezuelan singer (tenor); b. 4 Sept. 1940, Caracas. *Education:* studied in Milan, Italy. *Career:* debut as Cavaradossi, Mexico City 1967; sang throughout USA and in Venezuela as Donizetti's Edgardo, The Duke of Mantua, Alfredo, Riccardo in Un Ballo in Maschera, Rodolfo and Andrea Chénier; Cincinnati 1985–86 as Radames and Manrico; Milwaukee 1988 as Calaf; Opera North 1986 as Ramirez in La Fanciulla del West; Teatro Colón Buenos Aires 1992 as Cavaradossi; other roles include Pollione in Norma, Opéra Nancy.

DONADINI, Giovanna; Italian singer (soprano); b. 1964. *Education:* Accademia di Arte Lirica e Corale di Osimo, also studied with Erika Baechi,. *Career:* debut: Monteverdi's Selve Morale e Spirituale, at La Fenice Venice; Mozart's Countess and Fiordiligi at Treviso, 1990–91; concerts include Pergolesi's Stabat Mater, Bach's Magnificat, Haydn's Stabat Mater, Beethoven's Ninth and Four Last Songs at Treviso and Toulouse. *Honours:* 1994 Concorso Internazionale, Bilbao. *Current Management:* Atelier Musicale, Via Caselle 76, San Lazzaro di Savena 40068, Italy. *Telephone:* (051) 19984444. *Fax:* (051) 19984420. *E-mail:* info@ateliermusicale.com. *Website:* www .ateliermusicale.com.

DONAT, Zdzisława; Polish singer (soprano coloratura); b. 4 July 1939, Poznań. *Education:* studied with Zofia Bregy in Warsaw and Gino Bechi in Siena, Italy. *Career:* debut in Poznań 1964, as Gilda from 1971 in Teatr Wielki, Warsaw; Theater am Gärtnerplatz, Munich, as Queen of Night; Bayerische Staatsoper Munich, Hamburg; Vienna Staatsoper; London Covent Garden; La Scala, Milan; Met-Opera, New York; Teatro Colón Buenos Aires; Deutsche Oper, Berlin; San Francisco Opera; Opera in Moscow, Naples, Zürich, Frankfurt and many others; Festivals in Salzburg, 1979–87; Bregenz, Orange, Munich, Tokyo, Athens, Wroclaw and others; roles include Lucia di Lammermoor, La Sonnambula, Giulia in Capuleti, Norina, Constanze, Blonde, Zerlina, Olympia, Gilda, Violetta, Manon (Massenet), Martha, (Flotow), Queen in Golden Cockerel, La Princesse and Le Feu in L'Enfant et les Sortilèges by Ravel, Hanna (Moniuszko), Marzelline (Beethoven), Adele (Johann Strauss); Warsaw as Giulia in I Capuleti e i Montecchi 1991; television productions, recitals and appearances with symphony orchestras; currently Prof., Frederic Chopin Acad. of Music, Warsaw. *Recordings include:* Die Zauberflöte (conductor J. Levine) (Record of the Year) 1980, Operatic Arias (conductor J. Dobrzanski), Requiem by R. Maciejewski (conductor T. Strugala), Zdzisława Donat (solo album) 1999. *Honours:* Premier Grand Prix, Toulouse; Kammersängerin, Munich 1977. *Address:* Teatr Wielki, Moliere 3, 00-076 Warsaw, Poland.

DONATH, Helen; American singer (soprano); b. 10 July 1940, Corpus Christi, Tex.; d. of Jimmy Erwin and Helen Hamauei; m. Klaus Donath 1965; one s. *Education:* Roy Miller High School, Del Mar Coll., Texas. *Career:* studied with Paola Novikova, later with husband Klaus Donath (by whom all song-recitals are accompanied); début at Cologne Opera House 1962, at Hanover Opera House 1963–68, Bayerische Staatsoper, Munich 1968–72; guest appearances in London (Covent Garden), Vienna, Milan, San Francisco, Lisbon, New York, etc.; has given concerts in all maj. European and American cities. *Major roles include:* Pamina in Die Zauberflöte, Zerlina in Don Giovanni, Eva in Die Meistersinger, Sophie in Der Rosenkavalier, Susanna in Le Nozze di Figaro, Anne Trulove in The Rake's Progress, Ilia in Idomeneo, Micaela in Carmen. *Honours:* Pope Paul Medal, Salzburg 50 Year Anniversary Medal, Bratislava Festival Award, Deutscher Schallplattenpreis and Grosses Lob for her first song recital recording, Lower Saxony Prize for Culture 1990.

DONATI, Walter; German singer (tenor); b. 4 Sept. 1938, Potsdam. *Career:* sang in Italy from 1983, notably at Treviso as Erik in Der fliegende Holländer, at La Scala in Tannhäuser, I Lombardi and Macbeth; Sang Don Carlos at Dublin (1985), Radames at Avignon (1986), and Dick Johnson at Buenos Aires; Further appearances at Venice as Foresto in Attila, at Florence as Dimitri in Boris Godunov, Paris Opéra as Raimbaut in Robert le Diable (1985), returning as Pollione (1988); Manrico at Covent Garden (1990); Baritone from 1995 (Nabucco at Lonigo near Verona); Amonasro at Earl's Court, London, 1998; sang Gleb in Giordano's Siberia at Wexford, 1999, and Nabucco at St Margreth 2000. *Current Management:* c/o Musica Management, Neubauerstrasse 4, 65193 Wiesbaden, Germany. *Telephone:* (611) 2386811. *Fax:* (611) 2386810. *E-mail:* marcus.carl@opernagent.de.

DONCEANU, Felicia; Romanian composer and painter; b. 28 Jan. 1931, Bacau; d. of Alexandru Donceanu and Helena Donceanu. *Education:* Bucharest Conservatory. *Career:* former Ed. of Editura Musicala, Bucharest; mem. Union of Composers and Musicologists of Romania. *Compositions include:* Spinet Sonata 1983, Inscription On A Mast for harp 1989, The Music Lesson (dramatic poem for voice and two pianos) 1992, Moldavian Echoes (suite for chamber orchestra) 2001, Parlando Rubato (concert ballad for harp), Ponti Euxini Clepoydra for oboe, clarinet, soprano, harp and percussion, A Flower's Name (symphonic poem for soprano and orchestra), Blue Hills (trio for clarinet, violin and piano), Singing with Lenachita Vacarescu (cycle of four pieces for soprano, lute, flute, viola da gamba and percussion), Invecatio for soprano, violin, piano and chamber orchestra, The Bells of Fate (cantata for mixed choir and orchestra). *Honours:* ten times winner, Composition Prize, Romanian Composers' Union 1983–2009, George Enescu Prize, Romanian Acad. 1984, winner, Sacred Music Contest, Asscn for Religious Peace 1997. *Address:* 010517 Bucharest, M. Eminescu str. 60, Romania (home); GEMA,

Postfach 301240, 10722 Berlin, Germany (office). *Telephone:* (21) 3194637 (home).

DONNELLY, Malcolm Douglas, AM; Australian teacher (retd) and fmr singer (baritone); b. 8 Feb. 1943, Sydney; m. Dolores Ryles. *Education:* Sydney Conservatory and Opera School, London Opera Centre. *Career:* debut at Australian Opera 1966; Australian Opera, Scottish Opera, ENO, Opera North, Netherlands Opera, Victoria State Opera, State Opera South Australia, Welsh Nat. Opera (WNO), Royal Opera House, Covent Garden, ENO tour, Moscow, Leningrad 1991; Adelaide Festival 1991; appearances at Edinburgh Festival 1975, 1976; Wexford Festival 1977, 1978; Glyndebourne 1979, 1981, 1985; Hong Kong Festival 1987; Brighton Int. Festival 1988; roles include Macbeth, Simon Boccanegra, Rigoletto, Pizarro in Fidelio; sang Kurwenal in Tristan und Isolde for Australian Opera 1990, Macbeth with ENO on tour to Russia, Scarpia with Scottish Opera and Shishkov in From the House of the Dead for WNO 1990; season 1992 in Ovations concert by ENO at the Barbican Hall, Don Carlos in Ernani for WNO and Ford in Falstaff for the ENO; Boccanegra and Iago in Australia; Sharpless, Royal Opera House, Covent Garden; Kurwenal for Australian Opera, Macbeth and Telramund in Lohengrin, ENO 1993; Di Luna in Il Trovatore, Victoria State Opera, Kurwenal in Tristan und Isolde, Scottish Opera; Verdi Requiem, Guildford Cathedral 1994; Scarpia, Lyric Opera of Queensland; Nabucco, Australian Opera; Falstaff, State Opera South Australia 1995; sang Iago at Sydney 1996, Janáček's Forester 1997, Butterfly, Royal Albert Hall, Australian Opera, Alberich in Wagner's Ring Cycle, State Opera of South Australia 1998; currently exam adjudicator and masterclass teacher; Patron Joan Sutherland Soc., Sydney; mem. Music Advisory Bd, Joan Sutherland and Richard Bonynge Opera Foundation; Life mem. Sydney Savage Club. *Recordings include:* videos: Lucia di Lammermoor, Un Ballo in Maschera, Hansel & Gretel (with Australian Opera), Gloriana. *Honours:* Sydney Sun Aria Competition 1969, Australian Opera Auditions Scholarship 1970. *Address:* PO Box 464, Ryde, NSW 2112, Australia (office). *E-mail:* maldel67@tpg.com .au (office).

DONNELLY, Patrick; Australian singer (bass-baritone); b. 15 March 1955, Sydney. *Education:* Conservatorium of Music, Sydney and Guildhall School of Music, UK. *Career:* concert debut at Sydney Opera House in Belshazzar's Feast by Walton; also appeared at Tiresias (Oedipus Rex) and in Monteverdi Vespers; sang with Glyndebourne Chorus on 1983 tour, solo debut as Theseus in A Midsummer Night's Dream 1985; festival and tour appearances in Idomeneo (Neptune), Don Giovanni (Masetto), La Traviata, Le nozze di Figaro (Bartolo) and L'Incoronzione di Poppea; other roles include Mozart's Figaro for Opera 80, First Minister in Cendrillon at Wexford Festival and Bartók's Bluebeard at Barbican; sang Polyphemus in Acis and Galatea on tour in France, Hayden in premiere of 63 Dream Palace by Jurgen Bose in Berlin 1990, and Herald in Lohengrin for Australian Opera 1990; Licone and Caronte in Haydn's Orlando Paladino at Garsington, Oxford; Mozart's Figaro at Grange Park 1998; concerts at numerous London centres, including Stravinsky's Renard at QEH. *Recordings include:* Renard with the Matrix Ensemble, Pergolesi's La Serva Padrona.

DONOHOE, Peter Howard, CBE, BMus, ARCM, FRNCM; British pianist; b. 18 June 1953, Manchester; s. of Harold Donohoe and Marjorie Donohoe (née Travis); m. Elaine Margaret Burns 1980; one d. *Education:* Chetham's School of Music, Royal Manchester Coll. of Music, Univ. of Leeds, studied with Derek Wyndham and Yvonne Loriod, Paris. *Career:* professional solo pianist 1974–; appears several times each season with major symphony orchestras in London and rest of UK and has performed regularly at Promenade Concerts 1979–; performances with LA Philharmonic, Chicago, Boston, Pittsburgh, Cincinnati, Dallas, Detroit and Cleveland orchestras and in Europe with Berlin Philharmonic and Symphony, Leipzig Gewandhaus, Dresden Philharmonic, Vienna Symphony, Czech Philharmonic, Swedish Radio and Radio France Philharmonic orchestras and Maggio Musicale Fiorentino; has also performed at Edin. Festival, Schleswig-Holstein Music Festival, La Roque d'Anthéron, France, and Festival of the Ruhr; Founder and Artistic Dir British Piano Concerto Foundation; Vice-Pres. Birmingham Conservatoire of Music; mem. jury, International Tchaikovsky Competition 2011, 2015. *Recordings include:* Messiaen's Turangalila Symphony 1986, Dominic Muldowney's Piano Concerto 1986, Tchaikovsky's Piano Concerto No. 2 (Gramophone magazine's Concerto of the Year 1988) 1986, Brahms Piano Concerto No. 1, Liszt, Berg and Bartók Sonatas, Beethoven, Diabelli Variations and Sonata Opus 101, Rachmaninov Preludes, Four British Concertos with Northern Sinfonia, Foulds' Dynamic Triptych, pieces by Rawsthorne, Bliss, Darnton, Rowley, Ferguson, Gerhard, Alwyn, Pitfield and Harty. *Honours:* Hon. DMus (Birmingham) 1992, (Univ. of Cen. England), (East Anglia), (Leicester), (Open Univ.); Hon. DLitt (Warwick) 1996; Moscow Int. Tchaikovsky Competition (jt winner,) 1982, Grand Prix Int. du Disque (Liszt), Gramophone Concerto Award (Tchaikovsky). *Current Management:* Ikon Arts Management Ltd, 114 Business Design Centre, 52 Upper Street, London, N1 0QH, England. *Telephone:* (20) 7359-0112. *E-mail:* costa@ikonarts.com. *Website:* www.peter -donohoe.com.

DONOSE, Ruxandra; Romanian singer (mezzo-soprano); b. 2 Sept. 1964, Bucharest. *Education:* Acad. of Music, Ciprian Porumbescu, Bucharest. *Career:* debut in Bellini's Romeo and Varvara in Katya Kabanova at Basle 1991; Rossini's Rosina at Vienna, Hamburg, Toulon and São Paulo; Carmen at Vienna, Leipzig and Prague; Mozart's Cherubino at Dresden, Dorabella in Vienna and Sesto at Covent Garden; Offenbach's Nicklausse and Monteverdi's

Poppea at San Francisco; appearances as Varvara in Vienna, Feodor (Boris Godunov) at Salzburg Festival, Annio in La Clemenza di Tito at Glyndebourne 1998 and Covent Garden 2000; Charlotte in Werther at Covent Garden 2004; soloist at Opera Houses of Constanta, Romania 1989–91, Basel 1991–92, Vienna 1992–98;. *Recordings include:* Das Lied von der Erde and Bach's B minor Mass. *Honours:* Best Young Singer of Romania 1989, ARD Competition, Munich 1990, Marian Anderson Vocal Arts Competition, Special Prize 1991. *Current Management:* c/o Maria Mot, Artist Manager, Vocal and Opera, Intermusica, Crystal Wharf, 36 Graham Street, London, N1 8GJ, England. *Website:* www.ruxandradonose.com.

DOOLEY, Jeffrey Michael, BA; American singer (countertenor) and choral conductor; b. 7 Oct. 1945, Milwaukee, WI. *Education:* Milton Coll., Milton, Wisconsin Conservatory, apprenticeship with Mark Deller, Deller Consort, Canterbury, England. *Career:* debut, Carnegie Hall, 1977; regular appearances in Early Music scene, New York: Basically Bach (Lincoln Center), Clarion Concerts, Amor Artis Ensemble, Waverly Consort, Boston Early Music Festival Orchestra, Milwaukee Symphony Orchestra, Connecticut Symphony; Recital-lecture presentations, The Art of the Counter-Tenor, duo with Richard Kolb, lutenist, founder of The Gotham Consort; Founder, Director, The Stuyvesant Singers, Toronto, Canada; Ongoing appearances with the following Baroque Orchestras: Tafelmusik, Toronto, Ars Musica, Michigan, Levin Baroque Ensemble, Amor Artis Ensemble, Concert Royal, ARTEC Ensemble, New York; European appearances, Madeira Bach Festival, 1981; Stour Music, England, 1985; Amor Artis tour, Switzerland and Italy, 1991; Specialist in the Handel Oratorio, frequently giving masterclasses in interpretation of the arias, and performing; mem, Early Music, America; International Society of Early Music Singers. *Recordings:* Henry Purcell: Airs and Duets, Nonesuch; J. S. Bach: Mass in B Minor, Nonesuch; Johannes Ockeghem: Masses, Nonesuch; G Dufay: Masses, Nonesuch; J. S. Bach: St John Passion, Newport Classic; G F Handel: Acis and Galatea, Newport; H Schütz: St Matthew Passion, Newport. *Publications:* contrib. to The Counter-Tenor Voice Defined, 1977; The Counter-Tenor's Roles in Music, 1982. *Address:* 229 E 11th Street, Apartment 21, New York, NY 10003-7314, USA (home). *Telephone:* (212) 982-7226 (home).

DOOLEY, William; American singer (baritone); b. 9 Sept. 1932, Modesto, Calif. *Education:* Eastman School of Music, studied in Munich with Viktoria Prestel and Hedwig Fichtmuller. *Career:* debut at Heidelberg 1957, as Posa in Don Carlos; sang at Bielefeld 1959–62; mem. Deutsche Oper Berlin from 1962, notably in premieres of Montezuma by Sessions 1964, Gespensersonate by Reimann 1984, Rihm's Oedipus 1987; Salzburg Festival 1964, as Lucio Silla and 1966 in premiere of The Bassarids by Henze; Metropolitan Opera from 1964, as Amonasro, Eugene Onegin, villains in Les Contes d'Hoffmann, Telramund, Orestes (Elektra) and Mandryka; Hamburg Staatsoper 1967, as Iago and 1979 in premiere of Jakob Lenz by Wolfgang Rihm; guest appearances at Royal Opera Stockholm from 1967; other roles include Berg's Wozzeck and Dr Schön, Pizarro, Kothner, Macbeth, Escamillo, Nick Shadow, Captain Mary (Die Soldaten) and Goryanchikov in From the House of the Dead; sang Eagle in premiere of Los Alamos by Marc Neikrug at Berlin 1989; Santa Fe 1991, as Tiresias in Oedipus by Wolfgang Rihm. *Recordings include:* Telramund in Lohengrin, Jakob Lenz.

DOONER, Daniel; Canadian stage director; b. 1960, Ottawa. *Education:* Univs of Toronto and London. *Career:* Assoc. Dir with numerous British opera companies; revivals of Un Ballo in Maschera, Elisir d'Amore, Fidelio, Rigoletto, Simon Boccanegra, Così fan tutte, Don Pasquale and La Traviata for the Royal Opera; Lohengrin for Teatro alla Scala; Owen Wingrave, The Makropoulos Case, Jenůfa, Tristan und Isolde and Katya Kabanova for Glyndebourne Festival, Parsifal for ENO; Così fan Tutte for Canadian Opera Co.; Jenůfa for Israeli Opera; Nikolaus Lehnhoff's Elektra at Salzburg Festival (Co-Dir) 2011; currently Staff Dir Royal Opera House. *Address:* Royal Opera House, Bow Street, Covent Garden, London, WC2E 9DD, England (office). *Website:* www.roh.org.uk/people/daniel-dooner.

DOORNBUSCH, Paul, BMus; Australian composer, sonologist and teacher; *Adjunct Professor, University of Melbourne;* b. 1959, Melbourne. *Education:* Univ. of Melbourne, Royal Conservatory of The Netherlands. *Career:* algorithmic composer of computer and electronic music; staff mem., Royal Conservatory of The Netherlands 1995–99; sound installation Alive, Int. Computer Music Conference 1996; compositional residency for Strepidus Somnus, STEIM, Amsterdam; mem., EU cttee to implement centre for aural art, Macedonia 1998; Sr Sonologist, I-Cubed Virtual Reality Centre, RMIT Univ. 2000; Research Fellow Dept of Computer Science, Univ. of Melbourne 2000, Adjunct Prof.; teacher, New Zealand School of Music 2007–09, Adjunct Prof. 2009–; Pres. Australasian Computer Music Asscn; mem. Int. Computer Music Asscn. *Compositions:* Continuity 1 for electronics, Continuity 2 for recorder, quartet and electronics, Strepidus Somnus for voices and electronics, Oxidization for percussion and electronics, Corrosion for percussion and electronics, Lorenz for piano, ACT 5 for bassoon and percussion, G4 for electronics, MFPG for electronics, Structured Luck for bassoon and electronics, Asfixiation for flute and electronics, On the Fence for medium ensemble and electronics, Iceberg for electronics, Preludes for four voices, M1 and M2 for soloist and electronics, Place Hampi, c1w for ambisonic electronics. *Recording:* Corrosion: The Works of Paul Doornbusch, Thr Frog Peak Collaboration Project. *Publications:* Corrosion, The Frog Peak Collaboration Project 1998, The Music of CSIRAC 2001; contrib. newspaper articles and articles to The Age, Computer Music Journal, Organised Sound, Handbook of

Computer Music. *E-mail:* pauld.doornbusch@gmail.com (office). *Website:* www.doornbusch.net.

DORAN, Seán; Irish/Australian theatre director; b. 1958, Derry, Northern Ireland; m. Ruby Philogene. *Education:* Univ. of East Anglia and Goldsmiths Coll., UK. *Career:* dir of music-theatre co., Bloomsbury, London 1988; Chief Exec. UK Year of Literature and Writing, Wales 1995; Artistic Dir Belfast Festival, NI 1997, 1998; Dir Perth Int. Arts Festival, Australia 2000–2003; Artistic Dir and Chief Exec. ENO, London 2003–05; Founder and Artistic Dir Happy Days, The Enniskillen Int. Beckett Festival 2006–; fmr Founder and Dir Insideworld Imagine Ltd. *Publications include:* Rough Guide to Ireland; music criticism and travel writing for The Times, The Independent, New Statesman. *Honours:* Centenary Medal 2002.

DORDI, Patrizia; Italian singer (soprano); b. 1956. *Education:* Accademia di Santa Cecilia, Rome. *Career:* debut in Rome 1979, in Schumann's Manfred; opera debut in Handel's Ariodante at La Scala 1980; guest at La Fenice, Venice, as Lisa in La Sonnambula and Mathilde in Guillaume Tell; Naples as Elmira in Jommelli's La schiava liberata and at Catania as Amor in Orfeo ed Euridice; other repertory includes Micaela, Sabina in Cimarosa's Gli Orazi ed i Curiazi, Pamina (Ravenna Festival), Mimi and Musetta; Zürich Opera 1992, as Mathilde in Guillaume Tell.

DORFMÜLLER, Joachim, DrPhilHabil; German academic; b. 13 Dec. 1938, Wuppertal; m. Ursula Petschelt 1976; one s. two d. *Education:* Univs of Cologne and Marburg, studied piano and organ with father, Musikhochschule, Cologne. *Career:* teacher of music, mathematics and Latin, Gymnasium 1969–78, Univ. of Duisburg 1978–84, Univ. of Münster 1984–, Music Acad., Cologne 1984–98; founder, Artistic Dir, Wuppertaler Orgeltage 1973–2002; over 2,800 concerts on organ and piano in 21 countries including the USA and Japan; mem. Humboldt-Akademie der Wissenschaften 1990, Norwegian Agder Acad. of Sciences and Letters 2004; Pres., Deutsche Edvard Grieg-Gesellschaft 1993; Research Group of the Norwegian Acad. of Science and Letters 1997. *Recordings include:* Virtuoso organ music of the Romantic period; Famous Organ works by Saint-Saëns; Piano works by Grieg; Meditations: Bach, Bernstein and Messiaen; Bach to Rachmaninov; Bach to Ligeti. *Publications include:* Norweg Klaviermusik 1900–1950, 1968; Zeitgenöss Orgelmusik 1960–84, 1985; 300 Jahre Orgelbau im Wuppertal, 1988; Geschichte des Sinfonieorchesters Wuppertal, 1991; Wuppertaler Musikgeschichte, 1995; Geistl. Musik von Grieg, 2000; Geschichte der Orgelmusik, 2006; contrib. more than 500 articles for Herder-Musiklexikon, Rheinische Musikerbiographien; Musik in Geschichte und Gegenwart; national and international journals. *Honours:* Director of Church Music 1990, Cultural Prize of the Rhineland 1993, Bundesverdienstkreuz 2004. *Address:* Ringelstrasse 22, 42289 Wuppertal, Germany.

DORFMÜLLER, Kurt, DPhil; German musicologist and librarian; b. 28 April 1922, Munich; m. Liselotte Laubmann; two s. *Education:* Univ. of Munich. *Career:* Bavarian State Library 1954–84, including Head of Music Collection 1963, Head of Acquisitions Div. 1969–84, Vice-Dir 1972. *Publications:* Studien zur Lautenmusik in der ersten Hälfte des 16 Jahrhunderts 1967, Beiträge zur Beethoven-Bibliographie 1977, Bestandsaufbau an wissenschaftlichen Bibliotheken 1989, Musik in Bibliotheken 1997, Ludwig van Beethoven Thematisch-bibliographisches Werkverzeichnis (co-author) 2014; contrib. of musicology and library science articles to journals, Festschriften and library exhbn catalogues. *Honours:* Hon. Mem. Int. Asscn of Music Libraries, Int. Inventory of Musical Sources; Verdienstkreuz First Class, Bundesrepublik Deutschland 2003; Ars Jocundissima Festschrift für Kurt Dorfmüller 1984. *Address:* Mälzereiweg 1, 93053 Regensburg, Germany (home). *Telephone:* (941) 6963-3580 (home).

DÖRING, Ute; German singer (mezzo-soprano/lyric-dramatic soprano) and ; b. 4 June 1963, Berlin; m. Wolfgang Florey. *Education:* studied in Berlin with Peter Maus, Peter Iljunas and Dietrich Fischer-Dieskau and in Hannover with Norma Enns. *Career:* sang in opera at Kassel 1990; Ulm 1991–95; roles included Mozart's Cherubino, Idamante and Donna Elvira, Octavian in Der Rosenkavalier, Rossini's Rosina and Angelina; Schubertiade Concerts 1994–97; season 1995 as Flower Maiden in Parsifal at Bayreuth; mem. Cologne Opera 1995–98, guest 1998–2003; roles included Cherubino, Offenbach's Fragoletto in Les Brigands, Niclausse in Les Contes d'Hoffmann, Orlofsky and Gutrune in Götterdämmerung; Wiener Klangbogen: Lieder-Recital and Sycorax in Faust by Spohr 1999; Marie in Wozzeck at Wuppertal 1997, Wiesbaden Maiefstspiele 2003, 2004, 2013, Giessen and Mannheim 2005, Leonore in Fidelio in Osnabrück 2001–02 and Bielefeld 2005, 2nd Dame in Zauberflöte 1998 and Margret in Wozzeck at La Scala, Milan 2002, 2008; US debut with San Francisco Opera as Varvara in Katya Kabanova 2002; mem. Dortmund Opera 2003–04: roles included Octavian and Fenena in Nabucco; mem. Hessisches Staatstheater Wiesbaden 2004–14: roles have included Mozart's Despina, Idamante and Marcellina, Wagner's Sieglinde and Gutrune, Carmen, La Cenerentola, Charlotte in Werther, Orfeo (Gluck), Giulio Cesare, Graefin Geschwitz, Concepción, Meg Page, Giulietta (Les Contes d'Hoffmann), Octavian, Charlotte Haze (R. Shchedrin 'Lolita'), Gertrud (Hansel and Gretel); Hanna Glawari, Preziosilla, Gräfin Karolina von Kirchstetten (Elegie für junge Liebende/Hans-Werner Henze); frequent concert engagements; special engagement for Contemporary Music (in Paris with ensemble intercontemporain 2009); Asian debut as Gräfin Geschwitz in Lulu, Korean Nat. Opera, Seoul 2010; sang Isolde in Tristan und Isolde, Coburg 2013; gives singing lessons at Johannes-Gutenberg Universität/

236

Hochschule für Musik, Mainz 2009–. *Honours:* Bundeswettbewerb Gesang Liedermacher/Chanson/Jazz Förderpreis 1979. *Current Management:* c/o Boris Orlob Management, Jägerstr 70, 10117 Berlin, Germany. *Telephone:* (30) 20450839. *Fax:* (43) 2448649. *E-mail:* natascha@orlob.net. *Website:* www .orlob.net. *Address:* Goebenstrasse 14, 65195 Wiesbaden, Germany (home). *Telephone:* (611) 6901793 (home); 17-76025154 (mobile) (office). *E-mail:* ute -doering@web.de. *Website:* www.ute-doering.de.

DORN, Dieter; German theatre director; b. 31 Oct. 1935, Leipzig. *Education:* Theaterhochschule, Leipzig and Max-Reinhardt-Schule, Berlin. *Career:* actor, producer and dir in Hannover 1958–68; Dir in Essen and Oberhausen 1968–70; Dir at Deutsches Schauspielhaus, Hamburg 1971, Burgtheater, Vienna 1972, 1976, Staatliche Schauspielbühnen, Berlin 1972–75, Salzburg Festival 1974, 1982, 1986; Chief Dir Münchner Kammerspiele (producing works by Lessing, Goethe, Büchner, Shakespeare, etc.) 1976–83, Man. (Intendant) 1983–2001; Man. (Intendant) Bayerisches Staatsschauspiel 2001–11; has also directed opera productions in Vienna, Munich, Kassel, New York and at Salzburg, Bayreuth and Ludwigsburg festivals; mem. Akademie der Künste, Berlin, Bayerische Akademie der Schönen Künste. *Honours:* Grosse Verdienstkreuz mit Stern 2011; Kainz Medal, City of Vienna 1972, German Critics' Prize 1972, Munich Artist of the Year 1976, Cultural Prize of Honour, City of Munich 1993, Bayerische Verfassungsmedaille in Gold 2009.

DORNBUSCH, Hans; Swedish singer (tenor); b. 1946, Gothenburg. *Education:* Stockholm Acad., School of the Royal Opera. *Career:* made debut as Calaf, Stockholm 1969; mem., Royal Swedish Opera, Stockholm 1970–95, notably as Manrico, Otello, Pinkerton, Turiddu, Andres in Wozzeck and the Steuermann in Fliegende Holländer; sang Pope Alexander VII in the premiere of Christina, by Hans Gefors 1986; character roles in Albert Herring and Hansel und Gretel; guest appearances in England and Germany; frequent concert engagements; currently vocal teacher. *Address:* Dreitannenhof 3, 4316 Hellikon, Switzerland (home). *Telephone:* 613210949 (home).

DOROW, Dorothy; British singer (soprano); b. 1930, London, England. *Education:* Trinity Coll., London. *Career:* sang in London from 1958, notably in BBC Invitation Concerts (Webern conducted by John Carewe, and the British premiere of Herzgewächse by Schoenberg 1960); has sung in the premieres of works by Birtwistle, Nono, Maderna, Dallapiccola, Bussotti, Ligeti, Boulez, Goehr and Bennett (The Ledge, Sadler's Wells 1961); sang Hilde Mack in the British premiere of Henze's Elegy for Young Lovers, Glyndebourne 1961; lived in Sweden 1963–77, The Netherlands from 1977; Prof. of Voice, Conservatoire of Amsterdam and The Hague; masterclasses in Europe and Scandinavia; concerts and opera in Italy, at La Scala, Venice, Rome, Florence and Bologna (Le Grand Macabre by Ligeti); repertoire from Monteverdi to the 20th century; Covent Garden debut 1983, as Stravinsky's Nightingale.

DOSS, Mark; American singer (bass); b. 1960, Chicago. *Career:* sang Merlin in Purcell's King Arthur at St Louis 1989; season 1990 as Sarastro at the Glyndebourne Festival and Mozart's Publio at Chicago; New Orleans 1991, as Rossini's Basilio, and Britten's Collatinus at San Diego; season 1992 as Sparafucile in Rigoletto with Canadian Opera, Toronto, and in the premiere of Alice by Anthony Davis, at Philadelphia; Escamillo in Carmen at Brussels; Nourabad in Les Pêcheurs de perles and Water Spirit in Rusalka at San Diego 1993–95; other roles include Hercules in Gluck's Alceste at Chicago; season 1998 as Frère Laurent in Roméo et Juliette at San Diego, Escamillo at San Francisco and High Priest in Samson et Dalila for Cincinnati Opera; sang Escamillo at Chicago and Ravenna, Rossini's Mustafà at Turin 2000. *Honours:* winner George London Competition, Washington 1987.

DOUGLAS, Barry, OBE; Irish pianist and conductor; b. 23 April 1960, Belfast, Northern Ireland; s. of Barry Douglas and Sarah Jane Douglas (née Henry); m. Deirdre O'Hara; two s. one d. *Education:* Royal Coll. of Music, London with John Barstow. *Career:* pvt. study with Maria Curcio; London debut, Wigmore Hall 1981; toured Europe 1986–; regularly performs in USA; other concerts in Japan, USSR, Australia, Iceland, Czechoslovakia; recital debut in Carnegie Hall, New York 1988; Artistic Dir Camerata Ireland; winner of Tchaikovsky Piano Competition, Moscow 1986; tours in USA, S America, Russia, Europe, Australia; has given numerous premieres of contemporary music by Buckley, Wilson, McCabe, Penderecki and O'Leary. *Recordings include:* Tchaikovsky Concertos Nos 1, 2 and 3, Sonata in G, Brahms Concerto No. 1, Piano Quintet in F Minor, Liszt concertos and Sonata in B Minor, Beethoven, Mussorgsky, Prokofiev, Rachmaninov Concerto No. 2, Berg, Reger, Strauss, Debussy, Britten, Corigliano, Penderecki Piano Concerto (with composer conducting), Beethoven Piano Concertos. *Television:* Rhapsody in Belfast (BBC documentary) 1978, After the Gold (ITV) 1987, Playing for Peace (Sky Artsworld) 2001. *Honours:* Hon. FRCM; Hon. DMus (Belfast); Diploma Royal Coll. of Music, Emmy Award for Concerto (Channel 4 TV programme) 1993, Diapason d'Or for Reger/Strauss recording 1998. *Current Management:* c/o IMG Artists, The Light Box, 111 Power Road, London, W4 5PY, England. *Telephone:* (20) 7957-5800. *Fax:* (20) 7957-5801. *E-mail:* lcoles@imgartists.com. *Website:* www.imgartists.com; www.camerata -ireland.com (office); www.barrydouglas.com (home).

DOUGLAS, James, LRAM, ARCM; British composer, organist and accompanist; b. 4 July 1932, Dumbarton, Scotland; s. of James Douglas and Mary Helen Douglas; m. Helen Torrance Fairweather 1968; two s. one d. *Education:* Heriot Watt Coll., Edinburgh, Conservatoire, Paris, Hochschule, Munich, Mozar-

teum, Salzburg. *Career:* debut at Wienersaal, Salzburg 1951; Dir of music: Nicolson Square Church Edinburgh 1953–63, Mayfield Church Edinburgh 1963–69, Reid Meml Church Edinburgh 1969–73; music staff Edinburgh Acad. 1967-79, Dir of Music, Christ Church Edinburgh 1986–91; Founder Dir, Eschenbach Editions, Caritas Records, Caritas Voices and Caritas Ensemble; mem. Performing Right Soc., Mechanical-Copyright Protection Soc., PPL, BPI (British Recorded Music Industry). *Compositions include:* 15 symphonies, 15 string quartets, 20 orchestral works, organ, choral, piano, chamber and instrumental works, including much flute music, 66 works entitled Highlands and Islands Sequence (composed 1968–2006), 75 works entitled The Christ Church Sequence (composed 2001–05). *Recordings include:* A Vision 2000, Cloud of Unknowing 2001, Visions of Glory 2001, Cry of the Deer 2001, 12 albums in the Caritas Live series 2002–11, From the Edge of Mystery 2016. *Honours:* Hon. Prof., Académie des Sciences Universelles, Paris 1992. *E-mail:* eschenbach@caritas-music.co.uk (office). *Website:* www.caritas-music.co.uk/ james_douglas.html (office).

DOUGLAS, Nigel; British singer (tenor), director, writer, broadcaster and academic; b. 9 May 1929, Lenham, Kent; m. Alexandra Roper 1973; one s. two d. *Education:* Magdalen Coll., Oxford and Musikakademie, Vienna, Austria. *Career:* debut as Rodolfo in La Bohème, Vienna Kammeroper 1959; leading roles in opera houses and festivals in Aldeburgh, Antwerp, Barcelona, Basel, Berne, Brussels, Buenos Aires, Catania, Covent Garden, Düsseldorf, Duisburg, Edinburgh, English National Opera, Garsington, Glyndebourne, Hamburg, Lisbon, New York, Paris-Bastille, Sadler's Wells, Scottish Opera, Seoul, , Tokyo, Venice, Vienna Volksoper, Welsh National Opera, Wexford, Zürich and others; repertoire of 80 roles including Peter Grimes, Captain Vere (Billy Budd), Aschenbach (Death in Venice), Eisenstein (Fledermaus), Danilo (Merry Widow), Loge (Rheingold), Herod (Salome), Captain (Wozzeck), Hauk-Sendorf (Makropulos Case); has written and presented over 300 programmes on opera and operetta for BBC Radio 2, 3, 4 and World Service; lectures on various aspects of opera and operetta in London, Edinburgh, Zürich, Vienna, New York, Cleveland, Los Angeles, Sydney, Canberra, Brisbane; regular television appearances in the UK and Europe; directed numerous productions for Sadler's Wells, Australian Opera, Royal Flemish Opera. *Television:* as writer and presenter: Three Legendary Tenors 2003. *Recordings:* Owen Wingrave, Salome, Zigeunerbaron; various recitals. *Publications:* English versions of Die Csardasfürstin (Kalman) 1982, Gräfin Mariza (Kalman) 1983, Merry Widow (Lehar) 1983, Legendary Voices 1992, More Legendary Voices 1994, The Joy of Opera 1997; contrib. of numerous articles to Times Literary Supplement, Opera Magazine, BBC Music Magazine. *Honours:* Worshipful Company of Musicians' Sir Charles Santley Memorial Prize 2003. *Current Management:* c/o Neil Dalrymple, Music International, 13 Ardilaun Road, London, N5 2QR, England. *Telephone:* (20) 7359-5183. *Fax:* (20) 7226-9792. *E-mail:* music@musicint.co.uk. *Address:* Old Church Farmhouse, Barfreston, Kent CT15 7JQ, England (home).

DOUŠA, Eduard, PhD, MGA; Czech composer and teacher; *Vice-Director, Prague Conservatory;* b. 31 Aug. 1951, Prague; m. Eva Benešova 2005; three s. *Education:* gymnasium, Charles Univ., Prague, Acad. of Musical Arts, Prague. *Career:* teacher of theory of music and composition, Charles Univ.; Docent in theory of music (pedagogy), Philosophical Faculty, Prague 1986–, Prague Conservatory 1995–, currently Vice-Dir; Ed. Rytmus music journal 2008–; mem. Soc. of Czech Composers, Collegium (soc. for contemporary music) (chair. 2003–), Pritomnost (soc. for contemporary music). *Compositions include:* Sonata for Organ, Variations on a Baroque Theme for Strings, Miniatures for Piano (for children), Sonatine for clarinet and piano (for children), Rhapsody for Clarinet and Piano, Concertino for trumpet and orchestra, Three short suites for guitar (for children), Concerto for four saxophones and orchestra 1993, Romantic Fantasy for two pianos 1995, Fantasia for trumpet and organ 1995, Uno per quattro per flauto, oboe, chittern ed violoncello 1996, Imaginations for violin and guitar 1997, Motorico for violin solo 1997, Summer Sonatine for soprano saxophone and piano 1999, Sonata drammatica for piano 2001, Sonata brevis accordion 2001, Concerto for violin, accordion, guitar and strings 2000, Concert music for violoncello 2000, Concerto for violin and chamber orchestra 2003, Concert music for violoncello and brass instruments 2003, Quartetto per archi 2005, Sonata: Fantasia for violoncello and piano 2007, Saxonata for saxophone and piano 2009, Little Choirs on the Poetry of Jiří Žáček 2009, PF09 for flute and piano 2009, Sonata for viola solo 2010, Zoo songs for children 2010, Musica Ruvida for violoncello and accordion 2011, Violac concert music for viola and accordion 2012, Sketches for 2 clarinets and bass-clarinet 2012, Mountain Overture for symphony orchestra 2012. *Recordings:* Rhapsody for clarinet and piano 1989, Variations on a Baroque Theme for strings 1988, Miniatures for flute, violin, violoncello and harpsichord 1990, Concerto for four saxophones 1995; many compositions were recorded for Czechoslovak Radio: Concertino for trumpet and orchestra, Sonata for piano, String-quartet, Romantic Phantasy for violin and piano, Rhapsody for clarinet and piano, Dialogue for oboe and piano and many compositions for children, musical fairy tales, songs, choirs; theoretical work on the history of Czech music for children, Czech compositions for children 1945–1995. *Publications:* Czech compositions for children 1945–1995, Short History of Music of the 20th Century (textbook), 200th anniversary of Prague Conservatory (ed.); articles and radio lectures on history of Czech music; dissertation on Charles Univ. *Address:* Pertoldova 3327, Prague 4 (home); Prague Conservatory, Na Rejdišti 1, 110 00 Prague, Czech Republic. *Telephone:* 222326406 (office); 739034313 (office); 777426193 (home). *Fax:* 222326406 (office). *E-mail:* eda.dousa@seznam.cz (home); eduard.dousa@prgcons.cz (office). *Website:* www.prgcons.cz (office).

DOVE, Jonathan; British composer; b. 18 Aug. 1959, London. *Education:* Univ. of Cambridge, studied composition with Robin Holloway. *Career:* began career as rehearsal pianist; spent 10 years with City of Birmingham Touring Opera; fmr Asst Chorus Master, Glyndebourne Festival Opera; Music Adviser, Almeida Theatre 1990–2014; Artistic Dir Spitalfields Festival 2001–06; has written extensively for theatre, TV, community music events; wrote music for opening ceremony of Millennium Dome and fanfare for Millennium Bridge; Assoc., Nat. Theatre. *Compositions include:* L'Augellino Belverde (opera) 1994, Siren Song (opera) 1994, Tobias and the Angel (community opera) 1999, The Palace in the Sky (community opera) 2000, The Passing of the Year (song cycle for double chorus and piano) 2000, When She Died... (Death of a Princess) (TV opera) 2002, His Dark Materials Part I & II (incidental music, Nat. Theatre) 2003, On Spital Fields (community cantata) (British Composer Award) 2005, Flight (Helpmann Award for Best Opera, Adelaide 2006) 2005, The Enchanted Pig (musical theatre) 2006, Man on the Moon (TV opera) (Opera Special Prize, Rose d'Or Festival for TV Programming 2007, Gold Medal, Park City Film Music Festival 2008) 2006, The Adventures of Pinocchio (opera) 2007, Swanhunter 2009, Mansfield Park (opera) 2011. *Honours:* Christopher Whelen Award (jt winner) 1998, Ivor Novello Award for Classical Music 2008. *Current Management:* Peters Edition Limited, Hinrichsen House, 10-12 Baches Street, London, N1 6DN, England. *Telephone:* (20) 7553-4000. *Fax:* (20) 7490-4921. *Website:* www.editionpeters.com.

DOWLING, Richard William, BM, MM, DMA; American concert pianist; b. 6 Sept. 1965, Houston, Tex. *Education:* Univ. of Houston, Yale Univ., Univ. of Texas, Austin with Abbey Simon; additional studies with Jeanne-Marie Darre at Le Conservatoire de Musique, Nice and at Ecole Normale de Musique, Paris, France; Yale Norfolk Summer School and Music Festival, Conn. *Career:* debut with Fort Worth Symphony, Tex. 1981; solo recitals throughout USA; PBS TV solo recital programme debut aired nationally 1986; recital tour, France 1991; concerto appearances with Okla. Symphony, Houston Civic Symphony, Shreveport (La) Symphony, Midland-Odessa (Tex.) Symphony, Brazos Valley (Tex.) Symphony, Yale Trumbull Symphony, Ark. Symphony; concerto appearances with Jupiter Symphony, Tully Hall, Lincoln Center, New York City 1992; first holder of Walles Chair in the Performing Arts, Lamar Univ. 1989–90; Artist Faculty (Piano), The Harid Conservatory of Music, Boca Raton, Fla; recitals: Austria, Australia, SA 1992; second tour of France 1992; Gina Bachaeur Festival, Salt Lake City, Utah 1993; Paris recital debut at Salle Cortot 1994; recitals in Singapore, Kuala Lumpur, Hong Kong 1997, 1998; solo recital, Weill Recital Hall, Carnegie Hall, New York 1998; fifth tour of France, 1998, 6th tour 1999; Season 1998–99 performed all piano solos and works with orchestra by George Gershwin for centennial celebration with West Virginia Symphony; mem. Artist Roster; The Piatigorsky Foundation 1994–. *Recordings:* Richard Dowling Plays Chopin 1997, A Frog He Went A Courting: Pairs of Pieces with cellist Evan Drachman 1999, Sweet and Low-Down, Richard Dowling Plays George Gershwin 2001, Richard Dowling Plays Chopin, Vol. II 2003, World's Greatest Rags 2004, Infinity with cellist Evan Drachman 2005, A Perfect Moment, Silhouettes & Our Song 2006, Romance and Revelation with cellist Evan Drachman 2007, Rhapsody in Ragtime 2007. *Publications:* new critical edn of Maurice Ravel's Trio for Piano, Violin and Cello, 1990; critical edns of complete solo piano works of Ravel, nocturnes of Fauré, and sonatas of Hummel and works of Mendelssohn and Debussy; transcriptions of Gershwin player piano roll performances. *Honours:* Chevalier of the Company of Musketeers of Armagnac, Gascony, France in recognition of dedication to French musical arts 1996; Grand Prix, French Piano Inst. 1993. *Current Management:* c/o Thomas F. Parker, Parker Artists, 382 Central Park West, Suite 9G, New York, NY 10025, USA. *Telephone:* (212) 864-7928. *E-mail:* tom@parkerartists.com. *Website:* www.parkerartists.com. *Address:* 261 West 71st Street, No. 3, New York, NY 10023, USA. *E-mail:* PianistNYC@aol.com (home). *Website:* www.Richard-Dowling.com (home).

DOWNES, Andrew, BA, MA, FRSA, FIBA; British composer; b. 20 Aug. 1950, Handsworth, Birmingham, England; s. of Frank Downes and Iris Downes (née Fennell); m. Cynthia Cooper 1975; two d. *Education:* St John's Coll., Cambridge, Royal Coll. of Music, London, studied singing with Gordon Clinton, composition with Herbert Howells. *Career:* choral scholar, St John's Coll., Cambridge; debut, Wigmore Hall 1969; est. Faculty of Composition, Birmingham Conservatoire 1975, Head of School 1990, Prof., School of Composition and Creative Studies 1992–2005; chaired Symposium on Music Criticism, Indian Music Congress, Univ. of Burdwan 1994; performances of own works include: Berlin Kaiser Willhelm Gedächtniskirche 1980, 2010, Vienna 1983, 1998, 2001, 2002; New York 1993, 1996, 2003, 2009; Calcutta School of Music 1994; Paris 1995, 1996, 1997, 1998, 2001, 2005; Univ. of New Mexico 1995, 1997, 1999; Bombay, Delhi, Calcutta 1996; Chicago 1997; Caracas, Venezuela 1997; Symphony Hall, Birmingham UK 1992, 1997, 2003, 2004, 2005; Rudolphinum, Prague 1998, 2001, 2002, 2005, 2008, 2013; James Madison Univ., Virginia 2000; Phoenix, Ariz. 2001; Genoa 2002; Washington, DC 2002, 2003, 2004; Colo, N Carolina, Mich., Las Vegas, Nev. 2003; N Carolina, Calif., Indiana, Columbia and Nashville, Tenn. 2004; Mexico City 2004; Villa Bertramka, Prague 2005, 2008; Boston, Mass 2000, 2005, 2006, 2007, 2008, 2009; Harvard Univ. 2005, 2006, 2007, 2008, 2009; Tex. 2009; Melbourne, Australia 2009, 2013; Nice, France 2010; W Va 2010; Atlanta, Ga 2010; Norway 2011; New Brunswick, NJ 2011; Beaverton, Ore. 2011; Miami, Fla 2011; Evanson, Ill. 2011; Vancouver, Canada 2011; Czech Repub. 2011; Charlotte, NC 2011; Lviv, Ukraine 2011; Hobart, Tasmania 2011; broadcast on BBC Radio 2, 3 and 4, France Musique, Austrian Radio, Czech Radio, Dutch Radio, Beijing Radio, WHRB Radio, Italian TV; Life Fellow, RSA, Int. Biographical Asscn; Pres. Central Composers' Alliance; Leading Patron, Midland Chamber Players. *Compositions include:* The Marshes of Glynn, for the Royal Opening of the Adrian Boult Hall in Birmingham 1986, Overture for the Three Choirs Festival 1986, Song Cycles for tenor John Mitchinson and for mezzo-soprano Sarah Walker for BBC Radio 3, works for Cantamus Girls' Choir, and for the BBC Radio 4 Daily Service, Centenary Firedances for City of Birmingham's Centenary Festival of Fireworks and Music, Sonata for 8 Horns Opus 54, Univ. of New Mexico comm. 1994, subsequently performed by the Horns of the Czech Philharmonic Orchestra 1998, 2000, 2005, 2008, 2009, Sonata for 8 Flutes, premiered at the USA Nat. Flute Asscn Convention in New York 1996, Songs From Spoon River, performed in New York, at Tanglewood Festival and on Radio 3, Towards A New Age, performed by the Royal Philharmonic Orchestra in Symphony Hall, Birmingham 1997, New Dawn, oratorio based on American Indian texts, performed in Birmingham 2000, and King's Chapel, Cambridge 2001, Sonata for 8 Pianists, Birmingham 2000 and Genoa 2002, Sonata for Horn and Piano and Suite for 6 Horns for the Vienna Horn Soc., 5 Dramatic Pieces for eight Wagner Tubas for the Horns of the Czech Philharmonic Orchestra 2003, Songs of Autumn and Songs of the Skies, commissioned by Symphony Hall, Birmingham, for massed children's choirs 2003, 2004, 2005, Far From the Madding Crowd (opera) for the Thomas Hardy Soc. 2006, Songs of Love (premiered at University Hall, Harvard by Paula Downes and David Trippett) 2006, Forgotten Fields, to commemorate the 80th anniversary of the end of World War I 2007, Sonata for violin, horn and piano for the Brahms Trio, Prague 2008, Concerto for piano and orchestra for Duncan Honeybourne with the Central England Ensemble 2009, Sonata for contrabass flute and piano for Peter Sheridan (premiered in Melbourne, Australia 2010) 2009, Concerto for horn and symphony orchestra for Ondrej Vrabec (Prin. Horn, Czech Philharmonic Orchestra) and Central England Ensemble (premiered in Birmingham Town Hall 2012), Jubilate for 30th anniversary Callington Singers, Cornwall (premiered at Menheniot Parish Church) 2013, Butterfly (commissioned by Cantamus in memory of Pamela Cook , to be premiered in Nottingham) 2014. *Recordings include:* Sonata for 8 Horns by Horns of Czech Philharmonic Orchestra; Concerto for 2 Guitars and Strings, with Simon Dinnigan, Fred T. Baker and Strings from the City of Birmingham Symphony Orchestra; The Marshes of Glynn; Centenary Firedances; Sacred Choral Music, performed by the Chapel Choir of Royal Holloway, Univ. of London; Flute Choir music by USA Flute Choirs; Music for Horns and Piano by the Vienna Horn Soc.; Sonata for Oboe and Piano; Sonata for Violin and Piano; Sacred Mass for Solo Violin; 3 Song Cycles; Piano Music performed by Duncan Honeybourne; Sonata for Violin, Horn and Piano; Music for Horns and Wagner Tubas; O Vos Omnes, motet, Cantamus commission; Sonata for 2 Pianos; Fanfare for a Ceremony; Shepherd's Carol; The Souls of the Righteous, anthem; Sonata for Contrabass Flute and Piano performed Peter Sheridan; DVDs: opera, Far from the Madding Crowd (Thomas Hardy Soc. production), Songs of Love and War (filmed and performed by Paula Downes). *Honours:* Hon. Fellow, Birmingham Conservatoire; Prizewinner, Stroud Int. Composers' Competition 1980, Gold Medal, IMechE 1997. *Current Management:* c/o Lynwood Music, 2 Church Street, Hagley, Stourbridge, West Midlands, DY9 0NA, England. *Telephone:* (1562) 886625. *E-mail:* downlyn@globalnet.co.uk. *Website:* www.lynwoodmusic.co.cc; www.andrewdownes.com.

DOYLE, Grant, BMus, PGDip; British/Australian opera singer (baritone); b. 1971, Adelaide, South Australia. *Education:* Elder Conservatorium, Adelaide, Royal Coll. of Music, London and Vilar Young Artists Programme, Royal Opera House, Covent Garden, UK. *Career:* roles for Royal Opera House include Tarquinius in Rape of Lucretia 2004, Harlequin in Ariadne auf Naxos 2004, Schaunard in La Bohème 2005, Morales in Carmen 2007, Billy in Anna Nicole 2011; other appearances include Schaunard in La Bohème for Glyndebourne on Tour 2004, Demetrius in A Midsummer Night's Dream for Teatro Real, Madrid 2006, Count Almaviva in Le nozze di Figaro 2008, Zurga in Les pêcheurs de perles 2010 and Starbuck in Moby Dick 2011 for State Opera of South Australia, Marcello in La Bohème 2009 and Mr Fox in Fantastic Mr Fox 2010 for Opera Holland Park, London; appears regularly with Opera North, including role of Robin Oakapple in Ruddigore 2011; sang Phillip II in premiere of Isaac Nathan's ballad opera Don John of Austria with Sydney Symphony Orchestra; as concert soloist, performed with Australia Ballet in Australian tour of Carmina Burana/Fauré Requiem; has sung Carmina Burana with the Bach Choir at Royal Festival Hall, Bournemouth Symphony Orchestra, Royal Philharmonic under Daniele Gatti, Ulster Orchestra as well as for Raymond Gubbay at Royal Albert Hall; other performances include Fauré Requiem (Hallé Orchestra, Carl Davis), Judas Maccabeus (King's Lynn Festival), Janáček's Glagolitic Mass (Philharmonia/Brighton Festival), Brahms' Ein Deutsches Requiem with Tasmanian Symphony Orchestra and with the Bach Choir/Philharmonia at Cheltenham Festival and Westminster Cathedral, Britten's War Requiem (Hertfordshire Chorus and Huddersfield Choral Soc.), Tippett's A Child of Our Time (Crouch End Festival Chorus/Barbican), Christus in St John Passion (Irish Chamber Orchestra) and Messiah with the Royal Choral Soc. at the Royal Albert Hall; other roles include the title roles in Britten's Owen Wingrave, Mozart's Don Giovanni and Thomas' Hamlet, Papageno in Die Zauberflöte, Silvio in I Pagliacci, Escamillo in Carmen, Frank/Fritz in Die tote Stadt, Figaro in The

Barber of Seville, Dandini in La Cenerentola, Belcore in L'elisir d'amore, Sid in Albert Herring and Nathan in Nicholas Maw's Sophie's Choice. *Films include:* played lead role in Channel 4/ABC film of The Eternity Man (Rose d'Or Award for Best Performing Arts programme 2009), recorded the Forester for BBC animated film of The Cunning Little Vixen, cr. role of Carlo in Judith Weir's opera Armida for Channel 4 TV. *Honours:* Thomas Elder Overseas Scholarship, Royal Overseas League Trophy, Nat. Mozart Competition for Singers 2000, Madeleine Finden Memorial Trust, Tait Memorial Trust, Arnold Matters Scholarship, Senior Exhibitioner RCM 1999. *Current Management:* c/o Ralph Blackbourn, Rayfield Allied, Southbank House, Black Prince Road, London, SE1 7SJ, England. *Telephone:* (20) 3176-5500. *E-mail:* ralph.blackbourn@rayfieldallied.com; info@rayfieldallied.com. *Website:* www.rayfieldallied.com. *Address:* 140 Earlshall Road, London, SE9 1PN, England (home). *Website:* www.grantdoyle.com.

DOYLE, Niall; Irish opera company executive; *Chief Executive, Opera Ireland;* b. 1960, Co. Waterford. *Education:* Trinity Coll., Dublin. *Career:* played tuba with RTÉ Orchestra, Queensland Symphony Orchestra and Queensland Brass Ensemble, Australia; fmr CEO Music Network; Dir of Music, Exec. Dir Performing Groups Radio Telefís Éireann (RTÉ) 1998–2007; Chief Exec. Opera Ireland 2007–; taught at Dublin Coll. of Music. *Address:* Opera Ireland, West Wing 3, Adelaide Chambers, Peter Street, Dublin 8, Ireland (office). *Telephone:* (1) 4786041 (office). *Website:* www.operaireland.com (office).

DRAGONI, Maria; Italian singer (soprano); b. 1958, Procida, Naples. *Education:* studied in Naples. *Career:* debut as Imogene in Il Pirata at Naples, 1984; appeared in the title role of Pergolesi's Il Flamino at the Teatro San Carlo Naples, 1984; season 1988–89, as Fenena in Nabucco at La Scala, Turandot at Nancy and Ravenna and Aida at Marcerata; Mathilde in Guillaume Tell and Bellini's Norma at the Théâtre des Champs Elysées and Mulhouse, 1989, at Strasbourg 1989; season 1990–91, Semiramide at Strasbourg, as Elisabeth de Valois at Turin and Donna Anna at the Teatro dell Opera at Rome; sang Mimi at Naples and Elisabeth de Valois at the Verona Arena, 1992; other roles include Paolina in Poliuto by Donizetti, Donna Anna, and La Gioconda; sang Aida at Florence, 1996; season 1995–96 as Norma at Zürich and Elvira in Verdi's Ernani at Strasbourg; season 1999–2000 as Elisabeth de Valois in Don Carlos in Metz, at Jesy as Ines de Castro in the opera by Persiani, as Elvira in Ernani at Genoa and as Norma at Savona; Santuzza in Cavalleria at Chieti 2007. *Current Management:* Living Art Impresariat, 21 rue Foucher-Lepelletier, 92130 Issy les Moulineaux, France. *Telephone:* 1-40-93-05-28. *Fax:* 1-46-38-65-54. *E-mail:* angelika.belamaric@wanadoo.fr.

DRAHEIM, Joachim Heinz, PhD; German musicologist, pianist and teacher; *Teacher of Latin and Music, Lessing Gymnasium, Karlsruhe;* b. 26 July 1950, Berlin-Schmargendorf. *Education:* Univ. of Heidelberg, studied piano with Ursula Draheim, violoncello with Annlies Schmidt-de Neveu. *Career:* concerts as solo, chamber music and lieder pianist in Germany, Austria and Switzerland; freelance, many recordings of lieder and piano pieces, Süddeutscher Rundfunk Karlsruhe and Heidelberg, (Südwestrundfunk, Studio Karlsruhe) 1973–; freelance work for several German and foreign music publishers, including Breitkopf and Härtel, Wiesbaden, Schott, Mainz, Ricordi, Berlin, Hofmeister, Leipzig, and Wiener Urtext Edition, and recording companies 1974–; numerous editions, including Brahms und seine Freunde – works for piano, works by Mozart, Haydn, Beethoven, Schubert, Loewe, Fanny Hensel, Liszt, Mendelssohn, Robert and Clara Schumann, Chopin, Carl Reinecke, Woldemar Bargiel, Otto Dessoff, Theodor Kirchner, Brahms, Busoni; first editions: Mendelssohn: Albumblatt in A major, Sonata in D major and Sonata movement in G minor for two pianos; Brahms: Die Müllerin; Schumann: Der Korsar, Piano accompaniment to Bach's Suite in C major for solo cello, Violin setting of Schumann Cello Concerto in A minor op 129, Variations on a nocturne by Chopin for piano, others; teacher of Latin and music, Lessing Gymnasium, Karlsruhe 1978–; works for the Neue Schumann-Gesamtausgabe and the new MGG. *Compositions:* instrumentations and reconstructions of works by Mozart, Schubert, Robert Schumann, Brahms, Puccini, Wilhelm Kienzl, others (Breitkopf and Härtel, Wiesbaden, Ricordi, Berlin). *Publications:* Vertonungen antiker Texte vom Barock bis zur Gegenwart 1981, Karlsruher Musikgeschichte 2004, Eine Musikerfamilie im 19, Jahrhundert 2007; contribs to several encyclopedias and catalogues. *Honours:* Robert Schumann Preis der Stadt Zwickau 2003, Verdienstmedaille der Stadt Baden-Baden 2012. *Address:* Sophienstrasse 165, 76185 Karlsruhe, Germany (home). *Telephone:* (721) 859435 (home). *Fax:* (721) 854507 (home).

DRAHOS, Béla; Hungarian flautist and conductor; b. 1955, Kaposvar. *Education:* Györ Conservatory with Henrik Prohle, Ferenc Liszt Acad., Budapest with Lorant Kovacs, studied with Prof. Carl Osterreicher in Vienna. *Career:* solo flautist with the Budapest Symphony Orchestra from 1976, including many foreign tours; solo flautist with the Hungarian State Orchestra 1990; solo career in Austria, Bulgaria, Belgium, fmr Czechoslovakia, UK, Finland, France, fmr Soviet Union, Switzerland and Germany; concerts with the New Zealand Symphony Orchestra 1988; West Berlin Philharmonie 1989; leader and founder mem., Hungarian Radio Wind Quintet; Music Dir, Kaposvar Symphony Orchestra 1990; Asst Conductor, Hungarian State Symphony Orchestra 1993; guest conductor of leading orchestras in Hungary; conducts operas and concerts in Austria and Germany. *Recordings:* Mozart Concerto K314, Paganini 24 Caprices, Bach 4th Brandenburg Concerto and Concerto for two flutes in F, Vivaldi Concertos, 16 Haydn Symphonies, Beethoven's Symphonies 1–9 and Overtures. *E-mail:* beladrahos@freemail.hu. *Website:* www.beladrahos.com.

DRAKE, George Warren James, PhD; New Zealand academic and musicologist; *Associate Professor of Music, University of Auckland;* b. 4 Aug. 1939, Auckland; m. Carla Maria Driessen, one s. one d. *Education:* Univ. of Auckland, Univ. of Illinois, USA. *Career:* Assoc. Prof. of Music, Univ. of Auckland 1976–, Dean Faculty of Music 1985–88, Head of the School of Music 1988–91; founding Pres., New Zealand Musicological Soc. 1982–85; mem. Musicological Soc. of Australia, Int. Musicological Soc. *Publications:* Liber Amicorum John Steele: A Musicological Tribute (ed.) 1997, Petrucci, Motetti B (Monuments of Renaissance Music XI, Chicago) 2002. *Address:* c/o School of Music, University of Auckland, Auckland, New Zealand (office). *Website:* www.music.auckland.ac.nz (office).

DRAKE, Julius, FRAM; British pianist; *Professor, Kunstuniversität, Graz;* b. 5 April 1959, England; s. of Michael Drake and Jean Drake; m.; two d. *Education:* Purcell School for Young Musicians, Royal Coll. of Music, London. *Career:* specialises in chamber music, working with many leading artists, both in recital and on disc; appears regularly at all major music centres, including Aldeburgh, Edinburgh, Munich, Schubertiade and Salzburg Music Festivals, Carnegie Hall and Lincoln Center, New York, Concertgebouw, Amsterdam, Philarmonie, Berlin, Châtelet and Musée de Louvre, Paris, La Scala, Milan, Liceu, Barcelona, Musikverein and Konzerthaus, Vienna and Wigmore Hall and BBC Proms in London; Dir Perth Int. Chamber Music Festival, Australia 2000–03; Prof., Kunstuniversität, Graz; gives regular masterclasses in Europe and USA. *Radio:* Complete Songs of Fauré (BBC Radio 3). *Television:* Over the Top with Franz (Channel 4), Winterreise (Channel 4). *Recordings include:* Sibelius Songs and Grieg Songs with Katarina Karneus, French Sonatas with Nicholas Daniel, Spanish Song with Joyce Didonato, Mahler Songs and Tchaikovsky Songs with Christianne Stotijn, Schumann Lieder with Alice Coote; live recordings from recitals at Wigmore Hall London for 'Wigmore Live' label have included concerts with Lorraine Hunt Liebersen, Joyce Didonato, Christopher Maltman, Gerald Finley and Matthew Polenzani; recordings with Ian Bostridge, including discs of Schumann, Schubert, Henze, Britten, The English Songbook and La Bonne Chanson; award-winning series of recordings with Gerald Finley: Ives, Barber, Schumann, Ravel and Britten; major project for Hyperion to record the complete songs of Franz Liszt (first three vols with Matthew Polenzani, Angelika Kirchschlager (BBC Music Magazine Award 2012), Schubert's Winterreise (Juno Award for Classical Album of the Year (Soloists with Large Ensemble Accompaniment) 2015) 2014. *Honours:* Gramophone Best Song Disc 1998, (for Barber Songs) 2007, (for Schumann Heine Lieder) 2009, (for Britten Songs) 2011, BBC Best Song Disc 2010, 2012. *Current Management:* c/o Anna Ianni, IMG Artists, The LIght Box, 111 Power Road, London, W4 5PY, England. *Telephone:* (20) 7957-5800. *Fax:* (20) 7957-5801. *E-mail:* a.ianni@imgartists.com. *Website:* www.imgartists.com; juliusdrake.com.

DRAKULICH, Stephen; American singer (tenor); b. 1958, Iowa. *Education:* Boise State Univ., Southern Illinois Univ., apprentice Lyric Opera of Chicago, Northwestern Univ. with Norman Gulbranson. *Career:* sang in The Turn of the Screw, The Rake's Progress and Lucia di Lammermoor at Chicago; Wuppertal Opera as Mozart's Ferrando and Tamino, Rodolfo in Bohème and Britten's Albert Herring, Janáček's Fox, Ramiro (Cenerentola), Lensky, Steuermann in Fliegende Holländer and Jacquino, at Bremen Opera 1982–89; Sergei in Lady Macbeth of Mtensk District, Peter Grimes, Captain Vere (Billy Budd) and Jimmy in Mahagonny, Freiburg Opera 1989–92; guest appearances as Arkenholz in Reimann's Gespenstersonate at Stuttgart and Hamburg; Sergei on tour to Japan with Cologne Opera; Tom Rakewell in Switzerland and Peter Grimes at Glyndebourne Festival 1992; Adam in premiere of Der Garten by Josef Tal 1988; in Lulu, Glyndebourne Festival 1996; currently mem. Faculty, Joop van den Ende Acad., Hamburg, Germany. *Honours:* award winner, Metropolitan Opera Nat. Council auditions.

DRAN, Thierry; French singer (tenor); b. 17 Aug. 1953, Bordeaux. *Education:* Bordeaux Conservatory, studied in Paris with Michel Sénéchal. *Career:* appearances at Paris Opéra-Comique, Berlioz Festival at Lyon (as Benedict), Rouen (Nadir, and in Les Indes Galantes); Marseille (in Capuleti e i Montecchi) and Lyon, as Fenton in Falstaff; Grand Théâtre Geneva, in Offenbach's Les Brigands and Barbe Bleue; sang in Ravel double bill at Glyndebourne 1987–88; Paris Opéra as Don Ottavio and as Mercure in Orphée aux Enfers; guest appearances at Bordeaux, as Jean in Le Jongleur de Notre Dame and Liège (Ernesto, Duke of Mantua and Rossini's Count Almaviva); frequent concert engagements; f. Agence Artistique Thierry Dran. *Recordings include:* Messager's Fortunio and Duc de Mantoue in Les Brigands. *Address:* 298 rue Lecourbe, 75015 Paris, France. *E-mail:* dranthierry@gmail.com. *Website:* thierry.dran.free.fr.

DRASKOVIC, Milimir; Serbian composer, conductor, multimedia artist, producer and publisher; b. 5 June 1952, Sarajevo, Bosnia-Herzegovina; m. Biljana Vasiljevic Draskovic; one s. *Education:* Belgrade Music Acad., studied composition with Vasilije Mokranjac; studied conducting with Borislav Pascan at Belgrade Opera. *Career:* composer of music for numerous ensembles, for film and TV, video, performance installation and for graphics and multimedia packages; performances of work include Gaudeamus, Utrecht 1978; Festival int. des musiques experimentales, Bourges 1982; Radio Biennale, Paris 1982; Esquiss' Art, Almada, Portugal 1982; BITEF, Belgrade 1982; Die Glockenspielen, Essen 1983; New Art in Serbia, Belgrade-Zagreb-

Pristina 1983; video CD, Ljubljana 1983; European Minimal Music Project, Belgrade 1983; Planum '84, Budapest 1984; Different New Music, Belgrade 1984–86; Yugoslav Documentary and Short Film, Belgrade 1986–2000; Festival of Alternative Film, Split 1987; Aut Art Alternativa, Grisignana 1989; Computer Art, Belgrade 1991; Byzanz und Danach, Berlin 1992–95; Eight Weeks, Belgrade 1995; Eine Kleine Geschichtsmusik, Goethe Institut, Belgrade 1996; Oktoih, Belgrade 1997; From the New World, Belgrade 1999; Triosonata, Belgrade 2000; Serbian Music, Kol hamuzika Jerusalim 2001; Draskovic-Oktoih, Outaut, Toronto 2002; Images of Notations, Ljubljana 2003; Open October Salon, Toronto 2003–04; Ars vivendi clavicembalum, Belgrade 2005; Belgrade-Ljubljana express 2005; Days of Serbian Culture in Toronto 2005; Safe & Sound, Belgrade 2006; Lords Day, Toronto 2006; Klavierduo-Abend, Rostock 2007; Ars altera clavicembalum, Belgrade 2007; Homage Nikola Tesla, Toronto 2007; Int. Composers' Review, Belgrade 2008; E-mail Art 2008–09; Minimal Art, Culembourg 2009; Miedzynarodowy Festival, Bialystok 2009, Todaysart, The Hague 2009; Conceptual Belgrade, Toronto 2009; Super Art Market, Berlin 2009, outaut art, Belgrade-Toronto 2010; Retrospective, Belgrade 2011–13; Open October Salon, Toronto 2011, 2012; Ars vivendi clavicembalum, Belgrade 2012–13; The Freedom of Sound, Budapest 2012–13; Retrospective, Toronto 2013; Ginger Ensemble Spring tour 2013; music at numerous film festivals throughout Europe and for radio and TV. *Compositions include:* D'orchestra 1–5, Da camera 1–6, Audiospektar, ADNM 1-5, Musica linea 1–10, HPSCHD 1–9, Eine Kleine Geschichtmusik, Octoechos 1-8, Eight Weeks, From the New World, Opera, Orgelwerke, Sinfonia, Unfinished Symphonies, Chant 1–8, OKTOIH Opus 1-2-3, Octoechos.mus/mid/wav, LP, Music on Long Distance, Triosonata, Duosonata, From the Old World, Surround Music 1–5, Modes 1–8, E-mail Art, WEB Art, NET Art, Surround Art. *Recordings:* Music Program 1979, Opus 4 1981, Ensemble for Different New Music 1981, Film Music 1988, Serbian Music for Harpsichord 1&2 1996, MD: Oktoih-Berlin-Beograd, Vertical Jazz 1997, MD: From the New World 2004, Classic Music 6 2012, Belgrade New Classics 2013. *Publications:* Dirigent 1981, Portrait of a Young Musician 1983, Examples of Ideosemas 1983, Moment 1990, Beorama 1995, Music Minimalism 1998, Triosonata 2000, Opus 4 2001, New Sound 2001, Images of Notation 2003, Impossible Histories: historical avant-gardes 2003, OutAut Gallery 2005, Safe & Sound 2007, The History of Serbian Music 2008, Serbian and Greek Art Music 2009, The History of Serbian Art 2010, Dlanom o stopalo 2010, New Sound 2012, Minimalist and Postminimalist Music 2013. *Address:* Brace Srnic 23, 11050 Belgrade, Serbia. *E-mail:* milimir.draskovic@yahoo.com.

DRATH, Janina (Nina) Irena Drath-Nowicka; Polish pianist; b. 14 Oct. 1954, Katowice; m. Jerzy Bogdan Nowicki 1981; one s. *Education:* Acad. of Music, Warsaw. *Career:* debut with Silesian Philharmonic Orchestra 1968, with WOSPRIT (Great Symphony Orchestra of Radio and Television) 1968; first recital, Katowice 1963; first recital abroad, Ostrava, Czechoslovakia 1965; regular concerts (solo and with orchestra) from age 14; concert tours and performances in Poland, Spain, Italy, Germany, Belgium, France, USA, Mexico, Czechoslovakia; guest artist, Annual Chopin Workshops, Texas A&M Univ., USA 1981–94; Artist-in-Residence, Central State Univ., Okla 1985–87; debut at Carnegie Hall, New York 1998; Founder and Pres. Fryderyk Chopin Soc. of Texas 1990, Int. Chopin Piano Competition, Corpus Christi 1993, Sonata and Sonatina Int. Youth Piano Competition, Corpus Christi 1994; Founder and Artistic Dir Virtuoso Piano Performance Studies; jury mem., Ricardo Vinesz Piano Competition, Lerida, Spain. *Recordings include:* with Vandor Music Group: works of Haydn, Chopin, Petroff and Mozart; three albums of piano music by P. Petroff. *Honours:* prizewinner, Paloma O'Shea Int. Piano Competition, Spain 1976, Int. Piano Competitionin Senigallia, Italy 1979, won Polish piano competition, Slupsk 1979. *Address:* Fryderyk Chopin Society of Texas, 4610 Abner Drive, Corpus Christi, TX 78411, USA. *E-mail:* info@fryderykchopinsocietyoftexas.org. *Website:* www .fryderykchopinsocietyoftexas.org.

DRESHER, Paul Joseph, BA, MA; American composer; b. 8 Jan. 1951, Los Angeles, CA; m. 1986. *Education:* Univ. of California at Berkeley, Univ. of California at San Diego, studied with Nikhil Banerjee, C. K. and Kobla Ladzekpo. *Career:* composer and performer throughout USA, Canada, Europe; commissions from Library of Congress, St Paul Chamber Orchestra, Spoleto Festival, Kronos Quartet, San Francisco Symphony Orchestra, California EAR Unit, Zeitgeist, Walker Arts Center, Meet the Composer, Seattle Chamber Players, Present Music, San Francisco Chamber Orchestra, Chamber Music America, Nat. Flute Asscn, American Music Theater Festival; faculty mem., Cornish Coll. of the Arts, Seattle 1980–83; founder and Artistic Dir, Paul Dresher Ensemble (electro-acoustic chamber ensemble) 1993–; founder, Electro-Acoustic Band chamber group 2004–; has taught at Princeton, Harvard and Stanford univs, Univ. of Wisconsin, Univ. of Iowa, Univ. of California at San Diego, Univ. of California at Riverside, Univ. of California at Berkeley, Columbia Coll. Chicago; mem. BMI, American Music Center, Opera America, Chamber Music America. *Compositions:* This Same Temple 1977, Channels Passing 1981, Night Songs 1981, Liquid and Stellar Music 1981, The Way of How (opera) 1981, Channels Passing for chamber septet 1981, Casa Vecchia for string quartet 1982, Dark Blue Circumstance (electronic) 1982–84, Re:act:ion for orchestra 1984, See Hear (opera) 1984, Other Fire (electronic) 1984, Slow Fire (opera) 1985–88, Water Dreams (electronic) 1986, Power Failure (opera) 1989, Double Ikat for trio 1989, Cornucopia for chamber orchestra 1990, Pioneer (opera) 1991, Opposites Attract 1992, The Gates 1993, Din of Iniquity for six instruments 1994, Stretch for six instruments 1995, Blue Diamonds for solo piano 1995, Cage

Machine and Chorale Times Two concerto for violin 1996, Elapsed Time for violin and piano duo 1998, Sound Stage 2001, Unequal Distemperament 2001–06, Still, Rise, Fall, Again for chamber orchestra 2004–05, The Tyrant (opera) 2004–06, Waterfall 2006, A Slipping Glimpse 2006, To the Lighthouse 2007, Thread (ballet score) 2008. *Honours:* Guggenheim Fellowship 2006. *Address:* 51 Avenida Drive, Berkeley, CA 94708, USA (home).

DREYFUS, George, AM; Australian composer; b. 22 July 1928, Wuppertal, Germany; two s. one d. *Education:* Vienna Acad. of Music, Austria. *Career:* Composer-in-Residence, Tianjin, China 1983, Shanghai 1987, Nanjing 1991. *Compositions include:* Garni Sands, The Gilt-Edged Kid (operas); Symphonies Nos 1, 2 and 3; Symphonie Concertante 1977; Jingles ... & More Jingles; Reflections in a Glasshouse; The Illusionist; The Grand Aurora Australis Now Show; Galgenlieder; Songs Comic & Curious; Music in the Air; From within Looking out; The Seasons; Ned Kelly Ballads; Quintet after the Notebook of J.-G. Noverre; Sextet for Didjeridoo & Wind Instruments; Old Melbourne; several pieces for young people; The Sentimental Bloke (musical) 1985, Lifestyle 1988, Song of Brother Sun 1988 (choral pieces), Rathenau (opera) 1993, Die Marx Sisters (opera) 1994; more than 100 scores for film and TV including The Adventures of Sebastian the Fox 1963, Rush 1974, Great Expectations 1986. *Television includes:* The Gilt-Edged Kid (Australian Broadcasting Corpn/ABC) 1975, Didjeridu in Deutschland (SBS) 1988, Bicycles and Bassoons (SBS) 1989, Life is Too Serious (ABC) 2000. *Publications include:* The Last Frivolous Book (autobiog.) 1984, Being George – And Liking It! 1998, Don't Ever Let Them Get You 2009, Brush Off! 2011; numerous commercial CDs on the Move label. *Honours:* Grosses Bundesverdienstkreuz (Germany); Henry Lawson Award 1972, Prix de Rome 1976, 2004, Mishkenot Sha'ananim, Jerusalem 1980, APRA/AMC Distinguished Services to Australian Music Award 2013. *Address:* 3 Grace Street, Camberwell, Vic. 3124, Australia (home). *Telephone:* (3) 9809-2671 (home). *E-mail:* gdreyfus@bigpond.net.au.

DREYFUS, Huguette Pauline; French harpsichordist and academic; b. 30 Nov. 1928, Mulhouse. *Education:* Ecole Normale de Musique, Conservatoire Nat. Supérieur de Musique, Chigiana Acad., Italy. *Career:* soloist, ORTF and various other radio and TV networks worldwide; harpsichord teacher, Conservatoire Nat. Supérieur de Musique de Lyon, Acad. Musicale de Villecroze, Conservatoire Nat. de Région de Rueil-Malmaison. *Recordings include:* J. S. Bach: Six English Suites, Six French Suites; Rameau: Pièces de Clavecin; Couperin: Pièces de Clavecin; Scarlatti: Chronological Anthology of 70 Sonatas; Seixas: 14 Sonatas; Bartók: Pieces from Mikrokosmos; Chamber music by J.S. Bach, Leclair, Rameau, Haydn, Vivaldi, Corelli, C.P.E. Bach, W.A. Mozart; J.S. Bach: Italian Concerto, Chromatic Fantasy and Fugue, Inventions and Sinfonias, Six Partitas, French Overture, Four Duetti, Praeludium, Fuga and Allegro in E flat major, Goldberg variations; Wilhelm-Friedemann Bach: Nine Fantasien; J.S. Bach Harpsichord Transcriptions of 16 Concerti by various composers; J.S. Bach: The Well-Tempered Clavier, Vol. I; Henri Dutilleux: Les Citations, Diptyque for oboe, harpsichord, double bass, percussion; J.S. Bach: The Well-Tempered Clavier, Vol. II. *Publications include:* Observations sur les termes 'Affectueusement', 'Gracieusement', 'Légèrement', 'Sans Lenteur', 'Tendrement', François Couperin: Nouveaux Regards (ed. Orhan Memed) 1998. *Honours:* Chevalier, Légion d'honneur 1995, Officier 2009, Chevalier, Ordre nat. du Mérite 1973, Officier 1987, Commdr 2004 Chevalier, Ordre des Arts et des Lettres, Officier 1999, Grosse Ehrenzeichen für Verdienste (Austria) 1992; first medal in harpsichord, Int. Competition, Geneva 1958, Prix du Président de la République, Acad. Charles Cros 1985, Médaille de la Ville de Mulhouse 2008, numerous Grand Prix for recordings. *Address:* 91 Quai d'Orsay, 75007 Paris, France (home).

DRISCOLL, F. Paul, BA; American opera director and writer; *Editor-in-Chief, Opera News;* b. 23 Aug. 1954, New York, NY. *Education:* Regis High School, Manhattan, Coll. of the Holy Cross. *Career:* fmr actor, Foothills Theater, Worcester; freelance dir and designer for theatre; worked at departmental store, Lord & Taylor in various roles 1978–85; Product Development Man., Metropolitan Opera Guild retail programme 1985–88; freelance writer and dir 1990–, contributing reviews, stories and essays to publs, including Chamber Music, Musical America, Opera News, Stagebill; Picture Ed., Opera News, Man. Ed. 1998–2000, Exec. Ed. 2000–03, Ed.-in-Chief 2003–; Dir of some 20 musicals and operettas, Coll. Light Opera Co., Falmouth –1998; Artistic Dir, Scarsdale Summer Music Theater; Dir Washington Chamber Symphony, Kennedy Center; Dramatic Dir Blue Hill Troupe 1998–2004. *Television:* host, Opera New York (WNYE) 2002–04. *Publications:* 25 Years at Highfield: A History of the College Light Opera Company 1992, Fantastic Opera (with artist, John Martinez) 1997. *Address:* Opera News, 70 Lincoln Center Plaza, 6th Floor, New York, NY 10023-6593, USA (office). *Telephone:* (212) 769-7080 (office). *Fax:* (212) 769-8500 (office). *E-mail:* info@operanews.com (office). *Website:* www.operanews.com (office).

DRIVALA, Jenny; Greek singer (soprano); b. 4 July 1965, Kálamata. *Education:* Athens and Bremen Conservatories. *Career:* appearances at Vienna Staatsoper, La Scala Milan and in Naples, Rome, Melbourne, Paris Châtelet, Florence and Pretoria; repertoire includes Donizetti's Lucia, Maria Stuarda and Lucrezia Borgia, Violetta, Thais and Mélisande; sang title role in Gluck's Armide for ORF television, Strauss's Daphne and Salome for Greek Radio and Glauce in Médée by Cherubini; season 1994–95 as Massenet's Thais at St Gallen and Glauce in Athens; Strauss concert with Charles Mackerras; sang Anna Bolena at Athens 2000; numerous recordings. *Honours:* First

Prize, V. Bellini Int. Singing Competition. *E-mail:* jenny@drivala.com. *Website:* drivala.com.

DRIVER, Danny, MA (Cantab.), PGDipRCM, ARCM; British pianist and artistic director; b. 1977, London; m. Rebecca Miller; one d. *Education:* Univ. of Cambridge, Royal Coll. of Music, London. *Career:* Hyperion recording artist; recitals across UK, including Wigmore Hall, Bridgewater Hall, Symphony Hall, South Bank Centre, and in USA, Canada, Australia, Hong Kong, Israel and across Europe; teaching includes role in Junior Dept of RAM, London, Asst to Head of Keyboard, Royal Coll. of Music; Artistic Dir Hampstead and Highgate Festival 2009–10. *Recordings:* York Bowen Piano Concertos Nos 3 and 4, York Bowen Piano Sonatas, C.P.E. Bach Keyboard Sonatas, Balakirev Piano Works, Benjamin Dale Piano Sonata, Erik Chisholm Piano Concertos. *Honours:* BBC Radio 2 Young Musician of the Year 2001, Royal Overseas League Coutts Bank Award for Keyboard 2001, Amerada Hess Jr Fellowship, Royal Coll. of Music 2001, Eric Falk Trust Award 2002, First Prize, Robert William and Florence Amy Brant Int. Piano Competition 2004, Soroptimist Prize and Special Prize for Best Performance of the Commissioned Work, Scottish Int. Piano Competition 2004. *Current Management:* c/o Mark Kendall Artists Management, 56 St Anselm's Road, Worthing, West Sussex, BN14 7EN, England. *Telephone:* (1903) 233229. *E-mail:* markkendallartists@mac.com. *Website:* www.markkendallartists.com. *Address:* 146A Audley Road, London, NW4 3EG, England (home). *Telephone:* (20) 8202-9289 (home). *E-mail:* dd@dannydriver.co.uk. *Website:* www.dannydriver.co.uk.

DROBKOVA, Drahomira; Czech singer (mezzo-soprano); b. 28 Feb. 1935, Caslav; d. of Antonin Drobek and Ruzena Benesova; one s. *Education:* Brno Conservatoire, with Prof. Milada Weinbergerova. *Career:* sang with Ostrava Opera 1966–83; roles have included Verdi's Ebol, Amneris and Azucena; Wagner's Ortrud and Adriano; Octavian and Marina, Boris Godunov; Dorabella; with Prague Nat. Theatre, in operas by Puccini, Smetana, Janáček, Strauss, Verdi and Dvořák 1983–; sang Witch in Rusalka, Savonlinna Festival 1991; several concerts in Prague and elsewhere with music by Zelenka, Janáček and Mozart. *Recordings include:* Janáček's Glagolitic Mass; Dvořák's Rusalka; Dvořák's American Flag; Marfa in Dimitrij, Mass D Dur, Spiritual Songs – Ave Maria; B. Martinu, The Prophecy of Isaiah, Hymn to St. James; The Drahomira Drobkova Album. *Honours:* Decoration from Minister of Culture 1986, Thalia 1993. *Address:* Antošovicka 178, Ostrava 2-Koblov 71100, Czech Republic (home). *Telephone:* 77-4046462 (mobile) (office); 77-6239264 (mobile) (office). *E-mail:* robern@quick.cz (office).

DRUCKER, Eugene; American violinist; b. 17 May 1952, Coral Gables, FL. *Career:* founder and co-leader, Emerson String Quartet 1976–; public debut at Alice Tully Hall, New York 1979, playing works by Mozart, Smetana and Bartók; quartet-in-residence, Smithsonian Inst., Washington 1980, and the Hartt School of Music 1981–2002, the Aspen Music Festival 1983, State Univ. of New York at Stony Brook 2002–; faculty mem., SUNY Stony Brook 2002–; European debut at the Spoleto Festival 1981; noted for performances of the quartets of Bartók, including all six works in a single evening; has given the premieres of works by Mario Davidovsky, Gunther Schuller, Richard Wernick, John Harbison, Wolfgang Rihm and Maurice Wright; with Emerson Quartet 100 concerts annually in major musical capitals of Europe, USA and Canada; tours of Japan and Australia; resident quartet, Chamber Music Soc. of Lincoln Center 1982–89. *Recordings include:* with the Emerson Quartet: Bartók complete Quartets, Mozart six Quartets dedicated to Haydn, Schubert Cello Quintet with Rostropovich, Ives and Barber Quartets, Prokofiev Quartets and Sonata for two violins, Complete Beethoven Cycle 1997, Ned Rorem's Quartet No. 4 and Edgar Meyer's Quintet for String Quartet and Double Bass 1998, Mozart and Brahms Clarinet Quintets with David Shifrin 1999, The Complete Shostakovich Quartets 2000, Bach's Art of the Fugue 2003, Haydn's The Last Seven Words of Our Savior on the Cross 2004, Mendelssohn: The Complete String Quartets 2005, Intimate Voices 2006, The Little Match Girl 2006, Brahm's String Quartets 2007, Bach Fugues 2008, Intimate Letters 2009; as soloist: Bach Sonatas and Partitas for violin and complete Duos and Sonatas by Bartók. *Honours:* Naumburg Award for Chamber Music 1978, Gramophone Magazine Award for Best Chamber Music Record and Record of the Year (for Bartók Quartets) 1989, Grammy Award for Best Chamber Music and Classical Record of the Year (for Bartók Quartets) 1990, Grammy Award for Best Chamber Music Album (for Beethoven Quartets) 1998, (for Mendelssohn: The Complete String Quartets) 2005, (for Intimate Voices) 2006, Gramophone Magazine Award for Best Chamber Music Record (for Shostakovich Quartets) 2000, Grammy Awards for Best Chamber Music and Classical Record of the Year (for Shostakovich Quartets) 2001, for Best Chamber Music Performance (for Intimate Letters) 2010. *Current Management:* c/o Matthew Zelle, IMG Artists, 152 W 57th Street, Fifth Floor, New York, NY 10019, USA. *Telephone:* (212) 994-3500. *Fax:* (212) 994-3550. *E-mail:* mzelle@imgartists.com. *Website:* www.imgartists.com; www.emersonquartet.com.

DRUIETT, Michael; British singer (bass); b. 23 Jan. 1967, London. *Education:* European Opera Centre, Belgium, Scuola Superiore, Italy and the National Opera Studio, London. *Career:* appearances with ENO in The Love for Three Oranges, Wozzeck, Gianni Schicchi, Salome, Cunning Little Vixen, Rigoletto, Ariodante, Don Carlos, Masked Ball, Orfeo and Lohengrin; Wozzeck in Paris under Barenboim; Principal Bass with the Royal Opera, Covent Garden 1993–97; season 2000–01 as Donner in Das Rheingold and Ferrando in Il Trovatore for Scottish Opera; further performances Paris Bastille, Toulouse, Bordeaux, Lyon, Dublin, Brussels, Tel-Aviv, WNO; performs regularly with major symphony orchestras. *Recordings:* Floyd's Susannah, with the Opéra de Lyon; Puccini Experience with the Orchestra of the Royal Opera/Downes.

DRUMM, Imelda; Irish singer (mezzo-soprano); b. 1969. *Education:* Dublin City University, Leinster School of Music with Dr Veronica Dunne, National Opera Studio, London. *Career:* roles with Glyndebourne Opera include Cherubino, 1994, Isolier in Le Comte Ory, 1997, Dorabella in Così fan tutte, 1995, Tisbe in La Cenerentola for Opera Ireland and Theodata in Handel's Flavio for OTC Dublin; season 1998 as Cenerentola for English Touring Opera and Abaces in a revival of Artaserses by Terradellas at Barcelona. *Honours:* Richard Lewis/Jean Shanks Award and Esso Touring Award, Glyndebourne Opera.

DU, Ming-xin; Chinese composer and music editor; b. 19 Aug. 1928, Qianjiang Co., Hubei Prov.; m. 1966; one s. one d. *Education:* Yu Cai Music School and Tchaikovsky State Conservatoire, USSR. *Career:* debut solo piano concert, Shanghai 1948; Prof. of Composition, Cen. Conservatory of Music 1978–, also Doctoral Adviser; participated in Asian Composers' Conf. and Music Festival, Hong Kong 1981; travelled to USA for performance of Violin Concerto No. 1, John F. Kennedy Center 1986, and gave lectures in music insts; Exec. Dir Chinese Musicians' Asscn; mem. 11th CPPCC 1997–2002. *Compositions include:* Violin Concerto No. 1, Violin Concerto No. 2, Piano Concerto No. 1, Piano Concerto No. 2, Great Wall Symphony, Luoshen Symphony, Youth Symphony, The South Sea of My Mother Land (symphonic picture), The Goddess of the River Luo (symphonic fantasia), Flapping! the Flags of Army, The Mermaid (ballet suite), The Red Detachment of Women (ballet suite), Wonderful China (film soundtrack) 1982, piano trio, string quartet. *Address:* Central Conservatory of Music, 43 Baojia Street, Beijing 100031, People's Republic of China. *Website:* en.ccom.edu.cn.

DU BOIS, Mark; Canadian singer (tenor); b. 9 Nov. 1953, Toronto. *Education:* studied in Toronto. *Career:* debut with Canadian Opera Company, Toronto; Don Curzio in Le nozze di Figaro 1976; opera roles in Canada and elsewhere have included Tamino, Ramiro in Cenerentola, Fenton, Laerte in Hamlet and Rossini's Almaviva; La Scala, Milan 1982 in Stravinsky's Mavra; Belfast Opera 1983 as Tonio in La Fille du régiment; San Diego Opera from 1987, notably as Ernesto in Don Pasquale; concerts in London and elsewhere. *Address:* 69 Preservation Place, Whitby, ON L1P 1X8, Canada. *E-mail:* markduboistenor@gmail.com. *Website:* www.markdubois-tenor.com.

DU BOIS, Rob; Dutch composer; b. 28 May 1934, Amsterdam. *Education:* studied piano and jurisprudence. *Compositions:* Orchestral: Piano Concerto, 1960, revised, 1968; Cercle for Piano, 9 Winds and Percussion, 1963; Simultaneous, 1965; Breuker Concerto for 2 Clarinets, 4 saxophones and 21 strings, 1968; A Flower Given to My Daughter, 1970; Le Concerto pour Hrisanide for piano and orchestra, 1971; Allegro for strings, 1973; 3 Pezzi, 1973; Suite No. 1, 1973; Violin Concerto, 1975; Skarabee, 1977; Zodiak, 1977; Concerto for 2 violins and orchestra, 1979; Sinfonia da camera for wind orchestra, 1980; Luna, for alto flute and orchestra, 1988; Elegia for oboe d'amore and strings, 1995; Chamber: 7 Pastorales, 1960–64; Trio for flute, oboe and clarinet, 1961; Rondeaux pour deux for piano and percussion, 1962, 2nd series for piano 4-hands and percussion, 1964; Chants et contrepoints, for wind quintet, 1962; Espaces à remplir for 11 musicians, 1963; Oboe Quartet, 1964; String Trio, 1967; Symposium for oboe, violin, viola and cello, 1969; Trio Agitate for horn, trombone and tuba, 1969; Reflexions sur le jour ou Perotin le Grand ressuscitera for wind quintet, 1969; Fusion pour deux for bass clarinet and piano, 1971; Tracery for bass clarinet and 4 percussionists, 1979; Sonata for violin and piano, 1980; Elegia for oboe d'amore, violin, viola and cello, 1980; String Quartet No. 3, 1981; Sonata for Solo Viola, 1981; Ars aequi for 2 double basses and piano, 1984; Autumn Leaves for guitar and harpsichord, 1984; Hyperion for clarinet, horn, viola and piano, 1984; Forever Amber for 2 guitars, 1985; Das Liebesverbot for 4 Wagner tubas; On a Lion's Interlude for alto flute, 1986; Symphorine for flute and string trio, 1987; 4 String Quartets, 1960–90; Gàberbocchus for 4 pianos, 1994; Fleeting for clarinet and ensemble, 1997; Songs for violin, cello and piano, 1998; Die Gretchenfrage for flute and piano, 2004. *Address:* Spruitenbosstraat 21, 2012 LJ Haarlem, Netherlands.

DU PLESSIS, Christian; South African singer (baritone); b. 2 July 1944, Vryheid. *Education:* Potchefstroom and Bloemfontein Univs, studied with Teasdale Griffiths and Esme Webb in South Africa, Otakar Kraus in London. *Career:* debut with PACT Opera in Johannesburg as Yamadori in Madama Butterfly 1967; British debut in Andrea Chénier at Theatre Royal, Drury Lane 1970; Valentin in Faust at Barcelona 1971; Prin. Baritone, ENO 1973–81, notably as Cecil in Maria Stuarda and Verdi's Germont and Posa; USA debut in Les Pêcheurs de Perles, Texas 1984; Covent Garden debut in Rigoletto 1984; recipient, Ernest Oppenheimer Bursary 1968, 1969, 1970; major roles with cos in UK, USA, France, Netherlands, Hong Kong, Ireland; retd 1988.

DUBÉ, Jean; French/Canadian pianist; b. 3 Dec. 1981, Edmonton, Alberta. *Education:* Nat. Conservatory of Nice, National Superior Conservatory of Paris, Royal Irish Conservatory of Music, Dublin; studied under Jacques Rouvier, Jacqueline Robin and John O'Conor. Attended master-classes of L. Naoumov, D. Bashkirov, R. Buchbinder, V. Krainev, O. Yablonskaya, L. Howard, M. Perahia. *Career:* debut at Italian Women's Society Gala, Edmonton, Alberta, Canada aged five; Mozart Concerto No. 5 with Radio France Philharmonic Orchestra, Mozart Bicentenary Gala, Paris aged nine; broadcast on int. radio and television channels, including BBC, France Musiques, NDR, NHK, Fuji, Chicago, Hong Kong; performed in over 34 countries as recitalist, chamber musician and with philharmonic orchestras, including London Philharmonia, Rundfunkorkester, St Petersburg, Györ; performed Int. series, including Lanaudière, Chicago Dame Myra Hess, Olympus, Katia Popova Laureate days, Kiev Musicfest, Bayreuth, Hamilton Great Romantics, Husum, Sion-Valais, Busoni, Rome Pianoforte al Chiaro di Luna, South Africa Pro Musica, Kuhmo, Monterrey Sala Beethoven; currently jury mem. at int. competitions including Città di Pinerolo (Italy), Francis Poulenc, Brive-la-Gaillarde (France). *Radio:* several performances for European, Chinese and Latin-American radio channels: piano recitals as well as Messiaen Turangalila-Symphonie, Ligeti concerto for piano, Mozart concerto n°5, Gershwin "An American in Paris" for piano. *Recordings:* 19 recordings including Liszt, Sibelius, Franck, Cras, Bach, Ciurlionis, Chopin, Rachmaninov, Ravel, Elgar, Brahms, Barber, Messiaen, Komulainen. *Honours:* First Prize, Nat. Conservatory of Nice 1992 (age 10, youngest ever winner), First Prize and Monique de la Bruchollerie Prize, Nat. Superior Conservatory of Paris 1996, First Prize Young Prodigies Mozart in Paris Nat. Competition, First Prize Francis Poulenc Int. Competition, Brive-La-Gaillarde, France 1997, First Prize Jeunesses Musicales Romania, Bucharest 1998, Second Grand Prize, Yvonne Loriod Prize and Editions Durand Prize Messiaen Int. Competition, Paris 2001, Second Prize Takasaki Int. Music Competition, Japan 2000, Bourse Yvonne Lefébure Piano XXème Siècle Orléans Int. Competition 2000, Best Show of the Year (for Turangalila Symphony), Latvia 2001, First Grand Prize and Public Prize, Franz Liszt Piano Competition, Utrecht 2002, Akso Nobel Laureate 2002–03. *Current Management:* Marie Méli, 30 rue du Moulin Joly, 75011 Paris, France. *Telephone:* 1-48-06-99-12 (office). *E-mail:* mariejdmeli@yahoo.fr (office). *E-mail:* jeandube_pn_jc2002@yahoo.fr (office); jeandubepiano@yahoo.fr (office). *Website:* www.jeandube.com (home).

DUBINBAUM, Gail; American singer (mezzo-soprano); b. 15 March, New York, NY; m. John Massaro. *Education:* studied with Herta Glaz and with the Metropolitan Young Artists Program. *Career:* sang at the Metropolitan from 1982, debut in L'Enfant et les Sortilèges; appearances in New York and elsewhere in USA as Rossini's Rosina and Isabella and as Mozart's Dorabella; engagements at Vienna Staatsoper 1986–88; Suzuki in Butterfly for Opera Pacific at Costa Mesa and again at Detroit 1991; sang in the Jeremiah Symphony with Leonard Bernstein conducting Boston Symphony, Los Angeles Philharmonic and Pittsburgh Symphony (40th anniversary of premiere), sang Suzuki and Bach Magnificat with Zubin Mehta and Israel Philharmonic; sang Nefertiti in Akhnaten by Philip Glass at Chicago 2000; sang Nefertiti with Boston Lyric Opera, Suzuki with Phoenix Opera and Maddalena with Montreal Opera; Co-founder (with John Massaro) Phoenix Opera 2006. *Address:* 3120 West Carefree Highway, Suite 1-106, Phoenix, AZ 85086, USA (office). *Telephone:* (623) 363-3327 (office). *E-mail:* gdmaz@cox.net (home). *Website:* www.phoenixopera.org (office).

DUBOSC, Catherine; French singer (soprano); b. 12 March 1959, Lille. *Education:* Strasbourg Conservatory, Ecole Nationale, Paris with Denise Dupleix and Hans Hotter, studied with Eric Tappy at Lyon. *Career:* sang at Lyon Opéra, 1985–87, as Mozart's Despina, Pamina and Susanna, Nannetta, Blanche in Dialogues des Carmélites and Marzelline (Fidelio); sang Gretel at Geneva, 1987 and Isipile in Cavalli's Giasone at Utrecht, 1988, and the Théâtre des Champs Elysées, Paris, 1990; appearances at Montpellier (Pamina, 1991), Avignon, Nancy, Edinburgh and Strasbourg; sang Mélisande at Lausanne, 1992 and at Frankfurt, 1994; sang Blanche in the Danish premiere of Poulenc's Carmelites, Copenhagen, 1997. *Recordings include:* Giasone, The Love for Three Oranges, Campra's Tancrède, Scylla et Glaucus by Leclair and Darande in Gluck's La Rencontre Imprevue.

DUBROVAY, Laszlo; Hungarian composer and teacher; b. 23 March 1943, Budapest. *Education:* Bartók Conservatory, Budapest, Acad. of Music, Budapest, studied with Istvan Szelenyi, Ferenc Szabo, Imre Vincze, Hans-Ulrich Humpert and with Karlheinz Stockhausen in Germany. *Career:* teacher of music Ttheory, Budapest Acad. of Music 1976–; residence in Berlin 1985; Prof. of Theory, Franz Liszt Acad. of Music, Budapest 1998–; mem. Hungarian Arts Acad. *Compositions include:* stage works: The Ransom (one-act opera) 1991, The Sculptor (one-act dance play) 1993, Faust the Damned (dance play) 1998; orchestral: two Concertos for piano 1982, 1998, Concerto for strings 1979, Concerto for flute 1981, Concerto for trumpet 1981, Concerto for violin 1991, Concerto for cimbalom 1994, Triple Concerto for trumpet, trombone and tuba 1989, four suite of Faust the Damned 1989, Hungarian Symphony 1997, Cantata Aquilarum 1999, Timbre Symphony 2000, Concerto for Hungarian folk instruments 2000; symphonic band music: Deserts 1987, March 1990, The Ransom 1992, Buzzing Polka 1993, The Death of Faust 1996, Ballet Suite 1996, Festive Music 2000; chamber music: three string quartets 1970, 1976, 1983, two wind quintets 1968, 1972, three brass quintets 1971, 1980, 1998, Brass Septet 1980, 13 solos for different instruments 1975–2000, Paraphrasis for piano 1999, choruses, tape, live electronic and computer music pieces.

DUDAMEL, Gustavo; Venezuelan conductor, composer and violinist; *Music Director, Orquesta Sinfónica Simón Bolívar; Music Director, Los Angeles Philharmonic Orchestra*; b. 1981, Barquisimento; m. Eloísa Maturén; one s. *Education:* Jacinto Lara Conservatory, Latin American Acad. of Violin. *Career:* began as young violinist with El Sistema music educ. programme, later becoming conductor; Musical Dir Amadeus Chamber Orchestra 1996–99; Musical Dir, Orquesta Sinfónica Simón Bolívar (Simón Bolívar Symphony Orchestra), Venezuela 1999–; currently Music Dir Youth Orchestra of the Andean Countries; attended Int. Conductors' Acad. of the Allianz Cultural Foundation, London 2004–05; Prin. Conductor Gothenburg Symphony Orchestra 2007–11, Hon. Conductor 2013–; Music Dir Los Angeles Philharmonic Orchestra 2009–; has conducted Bamberger Symphoniker, Israel Philharmonic Orchestra, NDR Radio Orchestra Hannover, Royal Stockholm Philharmonic, City of Birmingham Symphony Orchestra, Orchestre Philharmonique de Radio France, Royal Liverpool Philharmonic, Frankfurt Radio Symphony Orchestra, Sächsische Staatskapelle Dresden, Gothenburg Symphony Orchestra at BBC Proms, Los Angeles Philharmonic at Hollywood Bowl (US debut), Philharmonia Orchestra at the Queen Elizabeth Hall 2005–06, Boston Symphony Orchestra, Orchestra del Maggio Musicale Fiorentino, Czech Philharmonic Orchestra, Chicago Symphony Orchestra, Vienna Symphony Orchestra 2006–07, Vienna Philharmonic, New York Philharmonic, Berlin Philharmonic, Berlin Staatskapelle, Leipzig Gewandhaus Orchestra, Orchestre Philharmonique de Radio France, San Francisco Symphony, Philharmonia Orchestra 2007–08. *Recordings include:* Beethoven Symphonies No. 5 and No. 7 2006, Brahm's Symphony No. 4 (Grammy Award for Best Orchestral Performance 2012) 2011, Mahler: Symphony No. 9 2013, Mahler: Symphony No. 7 2014, Wagner (with Orquesta Sinfónica Simón Bolívar) 2015. *Honours:* Winner Bamberger Symphoniker Gustav Mahler Conducting Competition 2004, ECHO Klassik Award for Best New Artist 2007, Premio de la Latinidad, Union Latina 2007, Royal Philharmonic Soc. Award for Best Young Artist 2008, Classical BRIT Award for Male Artist of the Year 2009, Eugene McDermott Award in the Arts, MIT 2010, Gramophone Award for Artist of the Year 2011, Musical America's Musician of the Year 2013. *Current Management:* c/o Mark Newbanks, Fidelio Arts Ltd, 103 Whitecross Street, No. 5, London, EC1Y8JD, England. *E-mail:* mark@fidelioarts.com. *Website:* www.fidelioarts.com; www.gustavodudamel.com.

DUDDELL, Joe, ARAM; British composer; *Professor of Composition, Bath Spa University*; b. 26 July 1972. *Education:* Univ. of Salford, Royal Acad. of Music with Steve Martland. *Career:* comms include London Sinfonietta, BT Scottish Ensemble, ViVA! and BBC, including three works for the BBC Proms, London Symphony Orchestra and Manchester Int. Festival; works performed at Bath, Chester, Huddersfield, Presteigne, Spitalfields, Lichfield, Lucerne and Brisbane Festivals, South Bank and Barbican Centres in London, New York, New Zealand and Moscow, and at tours in Scotland and Taiwan; Reader in Music, Salford Univ. –2012; Prof. of Composition, Bath Spa Univ. 2012–. *Compositions include:* Circle Square (for saxophone quartet) 1997, Dole Stages (for ensemble) 1997, Parallel Lines (for tuned percussion and piano) 1999, The Realside (for soprano, tenor, chorus and optional brass) 1999, Computation (for counter-tenor and ensemble) 1999, Protection (for wind quintet) 1999, The Realside (for solo soprano, solo tenor, SATB chorus and organ or bass) 1999, Alberti Addict (for chamber ensemble) 2000, Intro(m)it (for four trumpets and four trombones) 2000, Shiver and Shake (for trumpet and piano) 2000, Vaporize (for piano 4 hands) 2000, Endgame (for wind quintet) 2001, Fracture (for alto saxophone and piano) 2001, Generation (for harpsichord and strings) 2001, Snowblind (for percussion and strings) 2001, Still Life (for brass quintet) 2001, Two Men Hugging (for soprano saxophone, piano and pre-recorded CD) 2001, Ode to English (for unaccompanied voices) 2002, Ruby (for percussion and orchestra) 2002–03, Scattered black & white (for solo piano) 2002, Shadowplay (for cello and chamber orchestra) 2003, Freaky Dancer (for vibraphone and guitar quartet) 2003), Monotype (for viol consort and lute) 2003), Temporal Keys (for solo organ) 2003, New Dawn Fades (for string orchestra) 2004, Mnemonic (for flute, harp and strings) 2004, Freaky Dancer (for vibraphone and guitar quartet) 2003, Arbor Low (for string quartet) 2004, Hyper-ballad (for double string quartet) 2006, Isolation (for chamber orchestra) 2006, Grace under Pressure (for chamber ensemble) 2007, Four (mere) Bagatelles (for string quartet) 2007, Azalea Fragments (for orchestra) 2007, The Redwood Tree (for symphonic wind band) 2007–08, Cease Sorrows Now (for baritone and piano) 2008, Nightswimming (for piano trio) 2008, Catch (for trumpet and marimba) 2008–09, Elbow Orchestrations (for Elbow, orchestra and children's choir) 2009, Tree Carving (for flute, viola and harp) 2009, All Stars Aligned (for violin and piano) 2010, Magnificat and Nunc Dimittis (for SATB choir and organ) 2011, Ice Interludes (for orchestra and electronics) 2011. *Current Management:* c/o Schott Music Ltd, 48 Great Marlborough Street, London, W1F 7BB, England. *Telephone:* (20) 7534-0750. *Fax:* (20) 7534-0759. *E-mail:* promotions@schott-music.com. *Website:* www.schott-music.com; www.joeduddell.co.uk.

DUDZIAK, Francis; French singer (baritone); b. 1959. *Education:* Paris Conservatoire. *Career:* sang at the Opéra du Rhin, Strasbourg 1982–85; Lyon Opéra 1985–88; guest appearances throughout France in Monteverdi's Orfeo and Ulisse as Mozart's Masetto and Guglielmo, Ramiro in L'Heure Espagnole and in operetta; Saint-Cere Festival 1985 in Dalayrac's L'Amant statue and Maison à vendre; Strasbourg 1991 as Papageno; many concerts in Paris and elsewhere.

DUESING, Dale; American singer (baritone); *Artist-in-Residence in Voice Department, Lawrence University*; b. 26 Sept. 1947, Milwaukee. *Education:* began studies in Milwaukee as a pianist; vocal studies at Lawrence Univ., Wisconsin. *Career:* San Francisco Opera as Britten's Billy Budd and Donizetti's Belcore; Seattle Opera as Wagner's Wolfram and Tchaikovsky's Eugene Onegin; Glyndebourne debut 1976, as Olivier in Capriccio; later sang Guglielmo in Così fan tutte, conducted by Bernard Haitink; Ottone in L'Incoronazione di Poppea, Lysander in A Midsummer Night's Dream, 1989, and Figaro, 1989; Metropolitan Opera debut 1979, as Harlekin in Ariadne auf Naxos; concert engagements with the New York Philharmonic, Berlin

Philharmonic, Boston Symphony, Concertgebouw Orchestra, BBC Symphony and Santa Cecilia of Rome; conductors include Giulini, Levine, Leppard, Ozawa, Sawallisch, Dohnányi and Previn; opera engagements include Ariadne at La Scala, Billy Budd and Peter Grimes at the Metropolitan, Die Meistersinger in Brussels and Così fan tutte at Santa Fe; sang Figaro at Seattle, 1989; Goryanchikov in From the House of the Dead, Brussels 1990; Guglielmo at Barcelona and Olivier, Glyndebourne Festival 1990; solo recitalist in the USA and Europe; world premiere as Wade in Jonathan Wade by Carlisle Floyd, Houston Opera; Così fan tutte at Liceo, Barcelona; Marriage of Figaro, Glyndebourne Opera under Rattle; Metropolitan Opera, New York, Pelléas and Papageno; season 1991/92 as Mozart's Count at Brussels, 'I' in the premiere of Schnittke's Life with an Idiot at Amsterdam and Nardo in La Finta Giardiniera at the Salzburg Festival; Prodocismo in Il Turco in Italia at Théâtre du Champs-Elysées, Paris 1996; Orphée aux Enfers, Brussels 1997; season 1998 as Bill in Mahagonny at Salzburg and Toby Belch in the premiere of Trojahn's Was ihr Wollt at Munich; sang Leontes in the premiere of Wintermärchen by Boesmans, Brussels 1999; Narrator in the premiere of Sophie's Choice at Covent Garden 2002; currently Artist-in-Residence in Voice Dept, Lawrence Univ. *Recordings include:* Don Giovanni and Zemlinsky's Lyric Symphony; Così fan tutte; Arias and Barcaroles, Leonard Bernstein. *Address:* Lawrence University, 711 E Boldt Way, Appleton, WI 54911, USA (office). *Telephone:* (920) 832-7000 (office). *E-mail:* dale.l.duesing@lawrence.edu (office). *Website:* www.lawrence.edu (office).

DUFFIELD, Alan, FTCL, LRAM, ARCM, ABSM; British singer (tenor); b. 1952, Ripon. *Education:* Birmingham School of Music, Nat. Opera Studio, London. *Career:* concerts include Bach's St John Passion and B minor Mass (Lufthansa Festival, London), Handel's Joshua, High Priest in Idomeneo, under Simon Rattle, and Britten's Serenade for tenor, horn and strings (CBSO); Mozart's Requiem and Haydn's Nelson Mass with the London Mozart Players, BBC recital of John Joubert songs; appearances at Glyndebourne in Orfeo (ENO), and as Don Basilio and Don Curzio (Le nozze di Figaro); roles in La Bohème, Madama Butterfly, Der Rosenkavalier, Death in Venice, Samson; Mathis der Maler (Hindemith) for the Royal Opera; chorus mem., Royal Opera, Covent Garden. *Honours:* Dr hc (Birmingham Conservatoire). *Address:* Royal Opera House, Bow Street, Covent Garden, London, WC2E 9DD, England (office). *Telephone:* (20) 7240-1200 (office). *Website:* www.roh.org.uk (office).

DUFOUR, Pierre; Canadian opera company director and producer; *General Director, Opéra de Montréal. Education:* Univ. du Québec, Montréal. *Career:* Production and Tech. Dir Théâtre populaire du Québec 1990–96; took part in several productions at Théâtre de l'Opsis 1993–2002; Production Dir Théâtre du Rideau Vert 1996–98, Théâtre du Nouveau-Monde 1998–2000; Production Dir Opéra de Montréal 2000–, Acting Gen. Dir 2002–03, Gen. Dir 2006–; has overseen production of over 70 theatrical productions, including 30 operas; has taught theatre courses at Theatre Dept Coll. de St-Hyacinthe 1994–, Univ. du Québec 2003. *Address:* Opéra de Montréal, 260 de Maisonneuve Boulevard West, Montréal, PQ H2X 1Y9, Canada (office). *Telephone:* (514) 985-2222 (office). *Fax:* (514) 985-2219 (office). *E-mail:* pdufour@operademontreal.com (office). *Website:* www.operademontreal.com (office).

DUGDALE, Sandra; British singer (soprano); b. 4 Jan. 1946, Pudsey, Yorkshire, England. *Education:* studied in Leeds and at the Guildhall School, London. *Career:* debut with Glyndebourne Touring Opera as Despina in Così fan tutte; has sung with ENO in operas by Mozart, Janáček and Strauss; WNO in The Greek Passion by Martinů; four principal roles with the Handel Opera Soc.; Handel roles with the English Bach Festival; Covent Garden debut 1983 as Fire and The Nightingale in the Ravel/Stravinsky double bill; returned 1985, as Adele in Die Fledermaus; festival appearances include Hong Kong, Camden, Batignano, Wexford and Vienna; frequent broadcasts with the BBC, including the Much Loved Music Show; Lo Speziale by Haydn (for ITV); sang Adele for Opera Northern Ireland at the Grand Opera House, Belfast 1990; Sullivan's Angelina for D'Oyly Carte at Bournemouth 1990; concert engagements with most major British orchestras; regular visits to the USA. *Recordings include:* videos of operettas by Gilbert and Sullivan, 100 Years of Italian Opera (with the Philharmonia Orchestra).

DUIJCK, Johan; Belgian choir conductor, composer and pianist; *Principal Conductor, Gents Madrigaalkoor;* b. 1954. *Career:* Prin. Conductor, Flemish Radio Choir 1997–, Gents Madrigaalkoor, Ghent; Assoc. Conductor, Spanish Radio Television Choir, Madrid 1998–; founder-conductor, European Youth Choir 1994–; Prof., Koninklijk Conservatorium, Ghent, Muziekkapel Koningin Elisabeth, Waterloo; teacher, Dartington Int. Music Schools; directs conducting courses, Euskalerriko Abesbatzen Elkartea, Spain 2000–; Chorus Dir, Acad. of St Martin-in-the-Fields 2002–; pianist, Hans Memling Trio. *Compositions include:* Alma de la música, Cantate Domino canticum novum. *Honours:* Prize of the European Youth Festival, Neerpelt, prizes for vocal composition from East and West Flanders, European Piano Teachers' Asscn composition prize, Haec Olim prize. *Address:* Gents Madrigaalkoor, Albrecht Rodenbachstraat 124, 9040 Sint-Amandsberg (office); Gouden-Boomstraat 51, 8000 Bruges, Belgium (home). *Telephone:* (325) 031-00-28 (home). *E-mail:* secretariaat@gmk.be (office). *Website:* www.gmk.be (office).

DUKES, Philip, FGSM; British violist, conductor and academic; *Professor of Viola, Royal Academy of Music. Education:* Guildhall School of Music, London. *Career:* recital debut 1991; appeared at festivals including Gstaad, Cheltenham, Dartington, Aldeburgh, Colmar, Mecklenburg, Savannah and Schleswig-Holstein; concerto soloist with BBC Philharmonic, London Philharmonic, City of Birmingham Symphony, Royal Philharmonic, Hallé, Philharmonia, Royal Liverpool Philharmonic, Royal Scottish Nat. Orchestra, Bournemouth Symphony, London Mozart Players, Northern Sinfonia, Orchestra of St John's Smith Square, City of London Sinfonia, BBC Scottish Symphony, BBC Nat. Orchestra of Wales, Ulster Orchestra, Warsaw Sinfonia and Swedish Chamber Orchestra; numerous world premieres at BBC Proms, including concerti of Beamish 1995 (Proms debut), Hellawell 1999 and Watkins 2005, and Britten concerto for violin, viola and orchestra at Aldeburgh Festival 1997; soloist in Tippett's Triple Concerto with BBC Symphony Orchestra under Sir Andrew Davies, BBC Proms 2007; recitals across Europe, Canada and USA and at Wigmore Hall and Southbank Centre in London; collaborated as soloist and chamber musician with artists including Daniel Hope, Mischa Maisky, Tasmin Little, Julian Lloyd Webber, Nash Ensemble, The Ruzumovsky Ensemble and mems of Lincoln Centre Chamber Music Soc. of New York; mem. Plane/Dukes/Rahman Trio 1992–; Principal Guest Player, Nash Ensemble 1992–; conducted Southbank Sinfonia, London Mozart Players and City of London Sinfonia 2011; Prof. of Viola, RAM, London; Artistic Dir, Marlborough Coll.; Visiting Prof., McGill Univ., Montreal, Canada. *Recordings include:* solo: Tippett Triple Concerto 2007, Rebecca Clarke Chamber Works 2008; chamber music: string quartets of Beethoven and Brahms, sextets of Brahms and complete viola quintets of Mozart with Nash Ensemble. *Honours:* Hon. ARAM 2007; European Rising Stars Award 1995. *Website:* www.philipdukes.co.uk (office).

DUMAY, Augustin; French violinist; b. 17 Jan. 1949, Paris. *Education:* Paris Conservatoire with Roland Charmy, studied with Arthur Grumiaux. *Career:* debut at Théâtre des Champs Elysées, Paris, 1963; partnerships with Jean-Philippe Collard and Michel Beroff; concert with Karajan and the Berlin Philharmonic 1979 followed by Bartók's 2nd Concerto conducted by Colin Davis; further engagements with L'Orchestre Nat. de France, Suisse Romande Orchestra, London Symphony and English Chamber, and at the Montreux, Bath, Berlin, Lucerne, Monaco, Aix, Leipzig and Montpellier festivals; chamber music collaborations with Maria Joao Pires, Michel Dalberto, Lynn Harrell, Jean-Bernard Pommier, Yo-Yo Ma and Richard Stoltzmann; gave the premiere of Berio's Sequenza 9, for solo violin, and the premieres of the concertos by Marius Constant and Isang Yun; Dir, Nat. Chamber Orchestra of Toulouse 1988–; played a 1721 Stradivarius, formerly belonging to Fritz Kreisler, then a 1744 Guarneri instrument. *Recordings:* Lalo's Symphonie Espagnole, conducted by Michel Plasson, and Chausson's Concerto for piano, violin and string quartet, with Collard and the Muir Quartet; Mozart, Complete Violin Concertos; Tchaikovsky and Mendelsohn, Violin Concertos, London Symphony Orchestra; Mozart, Piano and Violin Sonatas; Brahms, Complete Violin and Piano Sonatas with Maria Joâo Pires. *Current Management:* Kajimoto Concert Management Co. Ltd, Paris Liaison Office, 5 rue Barbette, 75003 Paris, France. *Telephone:* (1) 42-19-92-65. *Fax:* (1) 42-19-92-12. *E-mail:* jerome.delmas@kajimotomusic.com; alison.phillips@kajimotomusic.com. *Website:* www.kajimotomusic.com. *Telephone:* 912502187 (mobile). *E-mail:* augustindumay.contact@gmail.com. *Website:* www.augustindumay.com.

DUMITRESCU, Iancu (Ioan); Romanian composer, music critic, conductor and pianist; b. 15 July 1944, Sibiu; m. 1st Cristina Dumitrescu 1979; m. 2nd Ana-Maria Avram 1988. *Education:* High School of Music, Bucharest, studied with Cici Manta, Alfred Mendelssohn, Stefan Niculescu, Aurel Stroe, and with Sergiu Celibidache in Trier, Germany. *Career:* founder, leader and conductor of chamber music ensemble, Hyperion; pianist specialising in avant garde music; compositions performed on television and radio in Romania, Austria, The Netherlands, France, Italy 1970–; commissions from Radio France, Paris, Commande d'Etat, Minister of Culture, France, Kronos Quartet, San Francisco and G. Enescu Philharmonic Orchestra; world premieres in Amsterdam, Berlin, Bremen, Bucharest, Cluj, Paris (Radio France), London (Royal Festival Hall), Royan, Warsaw, Vienna, Lisbon (Gulbenkian Foundation), Milan (Piccola Scala), Rome, Boston, New York, San Francisco; Head, Radio France, Paris. *Compositions include:* Alternances I and II for string quartet 1968, Multiples for three groups of percussion 1972, Apogeum for orchestra 1973, Reliefs for two orchestras and piano 1975, Orion I and II for three groups of percussion 1978, Perspectives au Movemur for string quartet 1979, Zenith for percussion 1980, Nimbus for three trombones, percussion and tape 1980, Cogito-Trompe L'Oeil for ensemble 1981, Grande Ourse for ensemble 1982, Aulodie Mioritica for double bass and orchestra 1984, Haryphonies (alpha, beta, gamma) for double bass, percussion, harryphono, piano préparé 1985, Holzwege for viola solo 1986, Reliefs for orchestra, Harryphonies (epsilon) for large orchestra 1986, Monades (gamma and epsilon) for six monocords and harryphone 1988, Gnosis for double bass and string ensemble 1988–97, L'Orbite d'Uranus, Astrée Lointaine for bass saxophone and orchestra 1991, L'Empire des Signes 1992, Au de la de Movemur, Clusterum for percussion 1993, Galaxy for three harryphones, three percussions and micro-processor 1993, five Impulsions for large orchestra 1993, A Priori for chamber ensemble 1994, Mythos for chamber ensemble 1994, Kronos/Holzwege for string quartet, Impuls for bass flute and percussion 1994, Mnemosyne for chamber ensemble 1994, Pulsar Perdu (for Kronos Quartet) for string quartet 1995, Fluxus for tapes and large orchestra 1996, Sirius Kronos Quartet for string quartet and tape 1996, Meteorites (electronic music) 1997, Ouranos for distorted spectral sounds, string orchestra and electronic tape 1997, La Chute dans le Temps for six groups of instruments, new distorted spectral sounds and tape 1997, New Meteors, Oiseaux Célestes and Colossus 2000.

DUNCAN, Martin David Anson; British theatre and opera director; b. 12 July 1948, London; s. of Ronald Francis Hamilton Duncan and Margaret Elisabeth Thurlow. *Education:* Durston House, Ealing, Westminster School, London Acad. of Music and Dramatic Art. *Career:* worked as actor 1968–90; Jt Artistic Dir Nottingham Playhouse 1994–99; Jt Artistic Dir Chichester Festival Theatre 2002–06; fmr Dir & Co-writer, National Theatre of Brent; composer of scores for over 50 productions; choreographed several productions for RSC; Bd mem. Mountview Acad. of Theatre Arts 2010–13; Artistic Adviser, London 2012 Festival. *Productions include:* as Dir: The Rocky Horror Show, Munich and Milan 1985; Ariadne auf Naxos, Scottish Opera, Den Norske Opera, Garsington Opera, Edinburgh Int Festival; Die Zauberflöte, Royal Opera House, London; Serse, La Clemenza di Tito, The Rake's Progress and Die Entführung, Bayerische Staatsoper, Munich; L'Heure Espagnole, Gianni Schicchi, The Thieving Magpie, Orpheus in the Underworld, Iolanta, The Nutcracker (with Adventures In Motion Pictures), A Midsummer Night's Dream, Opera North; world premiere production of Birtwistle's The Last Supper, Berlin/Glyndebourne 2000–01; The Comedy of Errors, Gorki Theater, Berlin 2001; world premiere of The Adventures of Pinocchio (Opera North, Oper Chemnitz, Minnesota Opera, Teatr Sats, Moscow, Theater Bonn); The Love for Three Oranges, Cologne, HMS Pinafore, Die Fledermaus, D'Oyly Carte Opera Co., The Gondoliers, ENO, La Traviata, Flanders Opera, Pagliacci/Cavalleria Rusticana for Raymond Gubbay, Royal Albert Hall 2002, Albert Herring for Canadian Opera, Patience, The Yeomen of The Guard, BBC Proms 2009, Artaxerxes, Royal Opera House 2009, Mirandolina, Armida, Il Turco in Italia, Vert Vert, Garsington Opera, La Forza del Destino, Opera Holland Park 2010, Sondheim at 80, BBC Proms 2010; world premiere of Benzin, Oper Chemnitz 2010; Betrothal in a Monastery, Théâtre du Capitole, Toulouse 2011; Dir, world premiere of Moses – The 10 Commandments, Theater St Gallen 2013; world premiere of Alice's Adventures in Wonderland, Holland Park Opera 2013–14; Noye's Fludde, Aldeburgh Education and Aldeburgh Music 2013; Man of La Mancha, Private Lives, Lyceum Theatre Edinburgh 2014. *Current Management:* c/o Tim Menah, Askonas Holt Ltd, Lincoln House, 300 High Holborn, London, WC1V 7JH, England. *Telephone:* (20) 7400-1715. *E-mail:* tim.menah@askonasholt.co.uk. *Website:* www.askonasholt.co.uk; www.martinduncan.com.

DUNDAS-GRANT, Deirdre, FRAM; British fmr bassoon player; b. 28 May 1927, Ewell, Surrey; d. of James H. Dundas-Grant and Katharine Galloway; one d. one s. *Education:* Royal Acad. of Music. *Career:* debut, Bournemouth Municipal Orchestra as Second, then Prin. Bassoon; Prin. Bassoon with BBC Concert Orchestra 1961–69; Prin., London Bach Orchestra, Monteverdi Orchestra, Steinitz Bach Players, Menuhin Festival Orchestra; solo recitals and chamber music with BBC and music clubs; sessions and engagements with all major orchestras; founder mem. Nat. Youth Orchestra and Portia Wind Ensemble; retd from public performing, engaged in examining, adjudication and consultation; mem. British Double Reed Soc. (chair. 1999–2002), Royal Soc. of Music, Court of Assts (retd). *Recordings:* Bach Art of Fugue, Christmas Music from Venice with John Eliot Gardiner, Philip Jones Brass and Ensemble, Bach's B minor Mass with Academy of St Martin-in-the-Fields; many orchestral recordings. *Publications:* arrangements of Bach Trios for Woodwind; Liszt Quintet; contrib. of numerous articles to British Double Reed Notes, Scales and Arpeggios for the Bassoon. *Honours:* Bach, Beethoven Scholarship, Royal Acad. of Music 1947–49. *Address:* 24 Dora Road, London, SW19 7HH, England (office). *Telephone:* (20) 8946-6875 (office).

DUNK, Roderick; British conductor; b. 1959, Birmingham, England. *Education:* Birmingham Conservatory. *Career:* played double bass in the BBC Symphony Orchestra and BBC Concert Orchestra, 1978–90; From 1990 regular guest conductor with the BBC Concert, Royal Philharmonic, London Symphony and Halle Orchestras; Since 1996 conducted London Symphony Orchestra, Royal Philharmonic, Philharmonia, London Philharmonic, Vienna Symphony and Prague Symphony orchestras in several series of Compact Discs; Arranger and Music Director for BBC television, conductor of the London production of Carmen Jones and music director for Travelling Opera; directed numerous performances with London City Ballet and Birmingham Royal Ballet; formed the London Palm Court Orchestra 1986, giving performances of Edwardian and Victorian music. *Current Management:* Manygate Management, Trees, Ockham Road South, East Horsley, Surrey KT24 6QE, England. *Telephone:* (1483) 281300. *Fax:* (1483) 281811. *E-mail:* manygate@easynet.co.uk.

DUNKI, Jean-Jacques; Swiss pianist, composer and writer; *Professor, Musikhochschule Basel*; b. 28 Feb. 1948, Aarau; m. Christine Baader 1994; one d. *Education:* studied in Aarau, Basel, Berlin, Paris, London, Baltimore and New York. *Career:* debut as pianist 1963, as composer 1978; performing in most European countries and USA 1979–, Japan 1993–, Latin America 1997; int. career as fortepianist 1999–; currently Prof., Musikhochschule Basel; Pres. European Piano Teachers Asscn, Switzerland. *Compositions include:* Lutezia 1978, Tú... no tienes imaginación 1979, Prokrustes 1982, Tetrapteron O–IV 1991, Pessoa 1993, Nulla dies 1994, Figures 1997, Kammerstück I–VIII 1985–99, Un Retour de Cythère 2007, Madrigaux (string quartet) 2012. *Recordings include:* Piano Music of Berg, Webern, Schönberg and Zemlinsky; Chamber Music of Grieg, Reger, Schumann; own music, experimental music on the clavichord (also electroacoustic). *Publications include:* Schönberg's Zeichen 2005, Schumann interpretieren 2014; several articles on Schönberg, Schumann, Reger and Webern. *Honours:* First Prize, Arnold Schönberg Piano

Competition 1981. *Address:* Bruderholzallee 12, 4059 Basel, Switzerland (home).

DUNN, Mignon; American singer (mezzo-soprano); b. 17 June 1931, Memphis, TN; m. Kurt Klippstatter 1972. *Education:* Southwestern Univ., Univ. of Lausanne, studied with Karin Branzell and Beverly Johnson in New York. *Career:* operatic debut as Carmen, New Orleans 1955; New York City Opera debut 1956, on roster until 1957, then 1972, 1975; Metropolitan Opera debut, New York as Nurse in Boris Godunov 1958, regular appearances in over 50 major roles, including Ortrud, Mother Marie in Carmélites, Amneris, Azucena, Marina, Fricka, Herodias and Anna in Les Troyens; guest appearances with opera companies in Chicago, San Francisco, Boston, Miami, Berlin, Hamburg, Vienna, Florence and other cities; sang the Kostelnicka in Jenůfa at the 1988 Spoleto Festival; season 1988–89 as the Witch in Rusalka at Philadelphia and Amneris in Chicago; created Madame Irma in the premiere of The Balcony by Di Domenica, Boston 1990; Clytemnestra in Nuria Espert's production of Elektra at Barcelona 1990; Mistress Quickly in Falstaff for New York City Opera 1996; soloist with orchestras in USA and Europe; faculty mem., Univ. of Illinois 1990, Univ. of Texas at Austin, Northwestern Univ., Brooklyn Coll., Manhattan School of Music. *Honours:* Hon. DMus (Southwestern Univ.) 1974. *Telephone:* (212) 749-2802 (office). *E-mail:* mignondunn@aol.com (office).

DUNN, Susan Lorette, BA; Australian singer (soprano) and academic; *Lecturer of Voice, Shepherd School of Music, Rice University*; b. 13 Sept. 1963, Melbourne. *Education:* Hendrix Coll. and Indiana Univ. *Career:* debut as Aida at Peoria (Ill.) Opera Co. 1982; subsequent appearances at La Scala, Milan, Italy, Carnegie Hall, Lyric Opera, Chicago, Vienna Staatsoper, Australian Opera, Washington Opera, San Diego Opera, Teatro Communale Bologna, Metropolitan Opera, New York, Sydney Opera House, Australia; has performed with leading orchestras, including New York Philharmonic, Chicago Symphony, Boston Symphony, Orchestre de Paris, Concertgebouw Orchestra, Netherlands; fmr Lecturer, Queensland Conservatorium of Music, Queensland Univ. of Tech.; currently Lecturer of Voice, Shepherd School of Music, Rice Univ. *Opera roles include:* Aida, Sieglinde in Die Walküre, Elena in I Vespri Siciliani, Elisabeth de Valois in Don Carlo, Leonora in La Forza del Destino, Leonora in Il Trovatore, Amelia in Un Ballo in Maschera, Amelia Boccanegra. *Honours:* Nat. Metropolitan Opera Council Award 1981, Winner Philadelphia Opera Co./Pavarotti Int. Vocal Competition 1981, Winner WGN-III Opera Competition 1983, Dallas Morning News-Dallas Opera G. B. Dealey Prize 1983, Richard Tucker Award 1983. *Address:* 1202 Alice Pratt Brown Hall, Shepherd School of Music, Rice University, 6100 Main Street, Houston, TX 77005-1892 (office); Herbert H. Brelin, Inc., 119 West 57th Street, New York, NY 10019, USA. *Telephone:* (713) 348-4854 (office). *E-mail:* lorette30@hotmail.com. *Website:* music.rice.edu (office).

DÜNNEBACH, Ulrich; German singer (bass-baritone); b. 21 April 1946, Limbach. *Career:* debut at Hagen Opera, 1969; sang in opera at Aachen, 1975–80, Detmold, 1980–85, Nuremberg from 1985; guest appearances at Munich as the Hermit in Der Freischütz, 1995, and at Liège and Rome, 1996, as Rocco in Fidelio; Sang Wagner's Daland at Bologna and Liège, 2000–01; other roles have included Mozart's Figaro, Leporello, Alfonso and Sarastro; Oroveso in Norma, the Doctor in Wozzeck, King Philip in Don Carlos, Banquo and Zaccaria (Nabucco); concerts include Penderecki's Polish Requiem, conducted by the composer. *Current Management:* c/o CANTUS Artists Management, Dorsoduro 121/c, 30123 Venice, Italy. *Telephone:* (41) 5224530. *E-mail:* s.schwarz@tiscali.it.

DUNSBY, Jonathan Mark, ARCM, BA, PhD; British pianist and academic; b. 16 March 1953, Wakefield, Yorkshire, England; m. 1st Anne Davis 1974; one d.; m. 2nd Esther Cavett 1983; one d. *Education:* New Coll., Oxford, Leeds Univ. *Career:* piano debut at Wigmore Hall 1972; regular appearances with violinist, Vanya Milanova; Prof. of Music, Univ. of Reading; Founding Ed., Journal of Music Analysis 1981. *Publications:* Structural Ambiguity in Brahms 1981, Music Analysis in Theory and Practice (with Arnold Whittall) 1987, Schoenberg, Pierrot Lunaire 1992, Performing Music 1995; contrib. to Music and Letters, The Musical Quarterly, Journal of Music Theory, Perspectives of New Music, Journal of the Arnold Schoenberg Institute. *Honours:* bronze medal Geneva Int. Competition 1970, jury prize Munich Int. Competition 1970, winner Commonwealth Competition 1974, Harkness Fellow 1976.

DUPHIL, Monique; French/American pianist; *Professor of Piano, Oberlin Conservatory of Music*; b. 24 April 1936, France; m. Jay Humeston; two d. *Education:* Paris Conservatoire National Supérieur de Musique with Jean Doyen, Rose Lejour, Joseph Calvet and Pierre Pasquier, studied under Marguerite Long. *Career:* debut aged 15 at Paris Théâtre des Champs Elysées with Orchestre des Concerts du Conservatoire (now Orchestre de Paris); solo recitals in over 50 countries; performances with orchestras in Europe, South America, Asia (Taiwan, Hong Kong, Japan, People's Republic of China, Republic of Korea), Australia, New Zealand, USA (Cleveland and Philadelphia Orchestras among many others); has performed with Pierre Fournier, H. Szeryng, R. Ricci, J. P. Rampal, Michel Debost, K. Leister, Oleh Krysa, the St Petersburg and American String Quartet, the Geistag and Mozarteum String Trios; mem., Amici and Villa Lobos Trios; Prof. of Piano, Oberlin Conservatory of Music, Ohio, USA. *Recordings:* J.S. Bach's French Suites, Piano Music by A. Liadov; H. Villa Lobos' Piano Trios Nos 1, 2 and 3 and Piano and Cello Sonata No. 2. *Honours:* Hon. Citizenship, City of Pskov, Russia; Orden Andres Bello

1st Class, Venezuela; Emer. Artist, Ministry of Culture, Brazil. *Address:* c/o Oberlin College, Music Conservatory, Oberlin, OH 44074, USA (office). *Telephone:* (440) 775-8214 (office). *E-mail:* mduphil@oberlin.edu (office). *Website:* www.oberlin.edu/con/faculty/duphil_monique.html (office).

DUPONT, Stephen; American singer (bass); b. 29 July 1958, Houston, TX. *Education:* Memphis State Univ., American Opera Center, New York. *Career:* sang in La Bohème at New York and appeared in operas by Menotti at Spoleto and Palermo 1984; guest appearances at Venice in the Verdi Requiem and Don Carlos, in Paris and San Francisco; Mozart's Commendatore at La Scala 1989, Colline and Ramphis at the Metropolitan 1986–87; sang Gremin at Strasbourg 1990, Sparafucile at Bonn and Banquo for Miami Opera 1992.

DUPRÉ, Heather, LRAM; British pianist; b. 30 March 1949, Channel Islands. *Education:* Royal Acad. of Music. *Career:* debut at Wigmore Hall 1976; solo pianist, recitals in the UK, including several appearances at Edinburgh Festival Fringe, Wigmore Hall and Purcell Room; broadcast on Radio London, 1974; Jr Prof., Royal Academy of Music 1973–76; examiner, Associated Board of Royal Schools of Music 1979–2000; mem., solo performers section, Incorporated Society of Musicians. *Address:* 19c Abercorn Place, St Johns Wood, London NW8 9DX, England (home).

DUPUY, Martine; French singer (mezzo-soprano); b. 10 Dec. 1952, Marseille. *Career:* debut in Aix-en-Province 1975, as Eurydice in Campra's Le Carnaval de Venise; has sung in the coloratura mezzo repertoire in Europe and North and South America; Marseilles Opera 1985, as Bellini's Romeo and as Isabella in L'Italiana in Algeri; Paris Opera 1985, as Neocles in Le Siège de Corinthe; other Rossini roles include Malcolm in La Donna del Lago at Nice 1985 and Bonn 1990, Cenerentola (Lausanne) and Arsace in Semiramide at Valle d'Itria and Nice 1985; Metropolitan Opera debut 1988, as Sextus in Giulio Cesare; sang in the opening concert at the Bastille Opera, Paris 1989; season 1990–91 as Mêre Marie in Les Dialogues des Carmélites for Lyon Opera, Jane Seymour in Anna Bolena at Marseilles and Madrid and Armando in a concert performance of Meyerbeer's Il Crociato in Egitto at Montpellier; other roles include Monteverdi's Nero and Penelope; Mozart's Cecilio in Lucio Silla and Sextus in La Clemenza di Tito; Adalgisa in Norma and Donizetti's Maffeo Orsini in Lucrezia Boria and Ada in Il Diluvio Universale; has also sung in Buenos Aires, Salzburg and Lausanne; Brussels 1996, as Eboli in the French version of Don Carlos; The Prince in Cendrillon at Turin; Cenerentola at Tel-Aviv 1998; sang the Mother in Charpentier's Louise at Toulouse 2000. *Honours:* winner Int. Singing Competition, Peschiera del Garda 1975, Grand Prix Opera International, France 1985.

DÜRMÜLLER, Jörg; Swiss singer (tenor); b. 28 Aug. 1959, Berne. *Education:* studied at Wintherthur Conservatoire, Hochschule für Musik, Hamburg, studied with Christa Ludwig and Hermann Prey. *Career:* first operatic engagements in Bielefeld; fmr permanent mem., Vienna Volksoper; frequent guest appearances with Opera Comique Berlin, in Hamburg, Montpellier, Leipzig, Cologne, Sevilla, Strasbourg, Teatro Real, Madrid, Teatro Regio di Torino; has performed at Royal Albert Hall London (BBC Proms), Auditorio Nacional de España Madrid, Accademia Santa Cecilia Rome, Musikverein Vienna, Théâtre des Champs-Elysées Paris, Théâtre du Châtelet Paris, Philharmony Sao Paulo, Summer Festival Tokyo, Schwetzinger Festspiele, Bach-Fest Leipzig, Epidaurus Festival Athens and the Bachfestival Leipzig; operatic roles include Ferrando in Cosi fan Tutte, Bajazete in Tamerlano, Tamino in the Magic Flute, Don Ottavio in Don Giovanni, Don Ramiro in La Cenerentola, Walther von der Vogelweide in Tannhäuser, Belmonte, Narraboth, Erik in The Flying Dutchman; oratorio repertoire includes works by Bach's St. John Passion, St. Matthew Passion, Handel's Messiah. *Recordings include:* St Matthew Passion, Ernst Krenek's Sardakai (ECHO Klassik Award), Franz von Suppé's Die schöne Galathée. *Current Management:* Alferink Artists Management, Herengracht 340, 1016 CG Amsterdam, The Netherlands. *Telephone:* (20) 6643151. *Fax:* (20) 6752426. *E-mail:* info@alferink.org. *Website:* www.alferink.org.

DÜRR, Karl-Friedrich, PhD; German singer (bass-baritone); b. 1949, Stuttgart. *Education:* studied with Gunther Reich. *Career:* debut as Antonio in Le nozze di Figaro at Ludwigsburg; sang with the Stuttgart Staatsoper from 1980, notably as Rihm's Jakob Lenz, Mozart's Figaro, Leporello, Don Alfonso, Klingsor (Parsifal) and Biterolf (Tannhäuser), Alfio (Cavalleria), Monterone, Zuniga in Carmen, Krishna in Satyagraha by Philip Glass, Faninial (Rosenkavalier); Animal trainer and Athlete in Lulu by Berg; Kothner in Die Meistersinger; appearances at the Ludwisburg and Schwetzingen Festivals and with the ensemble of the Stuttgart Staatsoper on tour to Russia (Zimmermann's Die Soldaten); further engagements as Kaspar in Der Freischütz, Kurwenal, and Wozzeck; concerts in Kassel, Trieste, Berlin and New York 1989; Vienna Festival 1990, as Krenek's Diktator and as the Boxer in Schwergewicht; sang Don Alfonso at Stuttgart 1991; also in Paris, Bastille Opera (Die Soldaten) and Semperoper, Dresden (Leporello) and other German opera houses such as Düsseldorf and Bonn; sang in Debussy's Chute de la Maison Usher at Stuttgart 1996; Sacristan in Tosca and Bartolo in Il Barbiere di Siviglia at Stuttgart 1998; season 2000–01 as Offenbach's Crespel at Stuttgart, and in Donizetti's Le Convenienze and I Pazzi per progetto, Dr Kolenaty in Janáček's Věc Makropulos 2003, Baculus in Lortzing's Der Wildschütz, Bartolo in Mozart's Le Nozze di Figaro, Priestes in Schönberg's Moses und Aron, Humperdinck's Hänsel und Gretel (Father/Peter), Stuttgart 2006, Ruggiero in La Juive, Narbal in Les Troyens, Sprecher in Die Zauberflöte and Lord Davenaut in Marschner's Der Vampir at Opernfestspiele Heidenheim 2006, Faninial in Der Rosenkavalier 2010, Frank in Die Fledermaus at Staufer Festspiele Göppingen and in Stuttgart 2010, Gepetto in Dove's Pinocchio 2010, Lhotsky in Janáček's Osud 2012, Musiklehrer in Ariadne 2013. *Recordings:* Eisenhardt in Die Soldaten, Priester in Schönberg's Moses und Aron; DVD: Philip Glass: Satyagraha (Krishna), directed by D. R. Davis, Stuttgart 1983. *Publications:* Opern nach literarischen Vorlagen: Shakespeares The Merry Wives of Windsor in den Vertonungen von Mosenthal-Nicolai: Die lustigen Weiber von Windsor und G. Verdi: Falstaff 1978. *Honours:* Kammersänger 1998. *Address:* c/o Staatstheater Stuttgart, Oberer Schlossengarten 6, 7000 Stuttgart (office); Paradiesstrasse 27, 70563 Stuttgart, Germany (home). *Telephone:* (711) 7353267 (home).

DÜRR, Walther, PhD; German musicologist and academic; b. 27 April 1932, Berlin; m. Vittoria Bortolotti 1960; two d. *Education:* Tübingen Univ. *Career:* Lecturer, Bologna Univ., Italy, 1957; Asst, Tübingen Univ., Germany, 1962; Gen. Ed., Neue Schubert-Ausgabe, 1965; broadcasts for radio stations Deutsche Welle, Cologne, Südwestfunk, Baden-Baden; collaborator, Internationale Schubert-Gesellschaft, Tübingen; mem. Soc. for Musical Research, Int. Musicological Soc. *Publications:* Rhythmus und Metrum im italienischen Madrigal insbesondere bei Luca Marenzio 1956, Serie IV (Lieder) of Neue Schubert Ausgabe 1966, Franz Schuberts Werke in Abschriften, Liederalben und Sammlungen 1975, Der Kleine Deutsch (with Werner Aderhold and Arnold Feil) 1983, Das Deutsche Sololied im 19 Jahrhundert 1984, Franz Schubert (with Arnold Feil) 1991, Zeichen Setzung Aufsätze zur Musikalischen Poetik 1992, Musik und Sprache 1994, Schubert Handbook (co-ed. with Andreas Krause) 1997, Schubert und das Biedermeier, Festschrift Walther Dürr (co-eds Michael Kube, Werner Aderhold, Walburga Litschaner) 2002, Schubert. Liedlexikon (co-ed. with Michael Kube, Uwe Schweikert, Stefanie Steiner) 2012; contribs to Die Musikforschung, Archiv für Musikwissenchaft, Österreichische Musikzeitschrift; 19th Century Music, MGG, New Grove Dictionary of Music and Musicians; numerous hon. anniversary works and reviews. *Honours:* Hon. Prof., Univ. of Tübingen; Ehrenkreuz 'Litteris et Artibus' der Bundesrepublik Österreich. *Address:* Hausserstrasse 140, 72076 Tübingen, Germany (home). *Telephone:* 707122810 (office); 707163391 (home). *Fax:* 7071687513 (home). *E-mail:* schubert-ausgabe@uni-tuebingen.de (office). *Website:* www.schubert-ausgabe.de (office).

DUSAPIN, Pascal; French composer; b. 29 May 1955, Nancy. *Education:* Université de Paris IV-Sorbonne, attended seminars by Iannis Xenakis. *Career:* works commissioned/performed by La Scala, Milan, Paris Opera, Deutsche Oper Berlin, Berlin Philharmonic, Beethovenfest Bonn, Deutsche Staatsoper (Faustus the Last Night), Ensemble Intercontemporain and Pierre Boulez, Aix en Provence Festival, BBC and Radio France for BBC Proms 2011, Ernst von Siemens Foundation for European Culture Days Festival, Karlsruhe 2012, Arditti Quartet, Ars Musica, Orchestre Philharmonique de Liège and others; works performed across Europe and beyond at venues and festivals including Spoleto, Italy and Lincoln Center, New York; Composer-in-Residence, Orchestre Nat. de Lyon 1993–94; Prof. of Artistic Creation, Collège de France, Paris 2006–07; Corresp. mem., Bayerische Akad. der Schönen Künste, Munich. *Compositions include:* opera: Roméo et Juliette 1984–88, Medeamaterial 1990, To Be Sung 1991–92, Perelà, Uomo di Fumo 2002, Faustus, the Last Night 2006; choral: Niobé 1982, Umbrae Mortis 1997, La Melancholia 1991; orchestral: L'Aven, Go 1992, Seven Solos for Orchestra 1992–2009, Khōra for 60 strings 1993, Extenso 1994, Quad concerto for violin 1996, Celo concerto for cello 1996, Exeo 2003, Reverso 2007, Morning in Long Island concerto 2011; for soloist, duo and small chamber music groups: five string quartets, seven Etudes for piano, Inside for viola 1980, Fist 1982, Hop? 1984, If for clarinet 1984, Item for cello 1985, In and Out for double bass 1989, Trio Rombach 1987. *Recordings include:* Medeamaterial 1998, Extenso/Apex/La Melancholia 1999, Roméo et Juliette 2003, Perelà, Uomo di Fumo 2008, Requiem 2008, 7 Solos for Orchestra 2010, Concertos 2010, 5 String Quartets 2011, Faustus, The Last Night (DVD) (Choc du Monde de la Musique, Victoire de la Musique) 2007. *Honours:* Commdr, Ordre des Arts et des Lettres; Prix Hervé Dujardin, SACEM 1979, Scholarship to Villa Medici, Rome 1981–83, Prix de l' Acad. des Beaux Arts 1993, 2005, Prix Symphonique, SACEM 1994, Grand Prix Nat. de Musique, French Ministry of Culture 1995, Victoire de la Musique for Composer of the Year 2002, Dan David Prize for contrib. to contemporary music 2007. *Address:* c/o Editions Salabert, 4/6 Place de la Bourse, 75002 Paris, France (office). *Website:* www.durand-salabert-eschig.com (office).

DUSSAUT, Thérèse; French pianist; b. 20 Sept. 1939, Versailles; d. of Robert Dussaut and Hélène Covatti; m. Claude Lemaréchal. *Education:* Conservatoire National Supérieur, Paris and Musikhochschule, Stuttgart. *Career:* debut 1951, Salle Gaveau, Paris, with orchestra conducted by Georges Tzipine; regular concert appearances, both solo and orchestral; has undertaken several world tours, including one for the Ravel centenary 1975; Prof., Toulouse Conservatory; mem. juries of int. competitions, including Tchaikovsky (Moscow), Munich, Szymanowski (Poland), Horowitz (Ukraine), Kraïnev (Ukraine); mem. Summer Music Acad., Kiev, Arts-Sciences-Lettres, Paris, Triptyque, Paris. *Compositions:* Rameau Pièces en Concert by Billaudot, Rameau Fêtes d'Hébé by Billaudot. *Recordings:* Rameau complete works, works by Ravel, Tchaikovsky and Shostakovich. *Honours:* first prize Int. Piano Competition, Munich. *Address:* 14 rue Saint Victor, 75005 Paris, France.

DUSSEK, Michael, FRAM; British pianist; b. 1958. *Career:* performed as chamber musician throughout Europe, Japan and Australia, and Canada, notably with such soloists as Cho-Liang Lin, Anne Akiko Meyers, Kurt Nikkanen and Ofra Harnoy; recitals in Amsterdam Concertgebouw, Tokyo, Madrid, Milan and Vienna; engagements throughout UK with cellist Alexander Baillie, oboist Douglas Boyd and violinist Lorraine McAslan; concerto soloist with London Mozart Players at Festival Hall and work for BBC Radio 3 as chamber musician and accompanist; Purcell Room recital 1993 with Markus Stocker, featuring music by Schumann, Brahms, Liszt and Martinů; currently Sr Tutor in Ensemble Piano and Head of Piano Accompaniment, RAM. *Recordings include:* Brahms Piano Trios and Horn Trio with Dussek Trio, contemporary Finnish music with Edymion Ensemble, cello sonatas with Ofra Harnoy and cello sonatas by Reger. *E-mail:* michaeldussek@aol.com. *Website:* www.michaeldussek.co.uk.

DUSSELJEE, Kor-Jan; Dutch singer (tenor); b. 1965. *Education:* Dutch Academy of Arts, masterclasses with Schwarzkopf and Hartmut Holl. *Career:* concerts throughout The Netherlands, from 1988; Besançon and Savonlinna Festivals, Switzerland and Germany; opera engagements in Germany as Wilhelm Meister, Tamino, Don Ottavio, Lancelot in Purcell's King Arthur and Leopold in La Juive; Architect in Reimann's Melusine at Dresden and Munich; season 1998–99 as First Jew in Salome and Francesco in Benvenuto Cellini, both with Rotterdam Philharmonic under Gergiev; further appearances with the Scottish CO, Dresden Staatskapelle and Bamberg Symphony Orchestra. *Current Management:* c/o Dietrich Eberhard Gross Künstleragentur, Eschenweg 19, 61440 Oberursel/Frankfurt, Germany. *Telephone:* (6172) 934144. *Fax:* (6172) 934145. *E-mail:* d.e.gross@grossagentur.de. *Website:* www .grossagentur.de.

DUTOIT, Charles E., OC; Swiss conductor and music director; *Artistic Director and Principal Conductor, Royal Philharmonic Orchestra, London*; b. 7 Oct. 1936, Lausanne; s. of Edmond Dutoit and Berthe Dutoit (née Laederman); one s. one d. *Education:* Conservatoires of Lausanne and Geneva, Accademia Musicale Chigiana, Siena, Italy, Conservatorio Benedetto Marcello, Venice, Italy and Berkshire Music Center, Tanglewood, USA. *Career:* Assoc. Conductor Berne Symphony Orchestra 1964, Prin. and Artistic Dir 1966–78; Assoc. Conductor Tonhalle Orchestra, Zürich 1966; Conductor and Artistic Dir Zürich Radio Orchestra 1964; Artistic Dir Nat. Symphony Orchestra of Mexico and Göteborg Symphony Orchestra 1977–2002; Artistic Dir Montréal Symphony Orchestra 1977–2002; operatic debut Covent Garden (conducting Faust) 1983; Prin. Guest Conductor Minnesota Orchestra 1983–84, 1985–86; Artistic Dir and Prin. Conductor Philadelphia Orchestra summer season, Mann Music Center 1991–2001, Saratoga Springs 1991–2010; Music Dir Orchestre Nat. de France 1990–2001; Prin. Guest Conductor NHK Symphony Orchestra, Tokyo 1996–, Music Dir 1998–2003; Chief Conductor and Artistic Advisor Philadelphia Orchestra 2007–; Artistic Dir and Prin. Conductor Royal Philharmonic Orchestra, London 2009–; guest conductor of major orchestras in USA, Europe, South America, Asia, Australia and Israel. *Recordings include:* over 125 recordings with various orchestras since 1980, winning over 40 int. awards and including Falla's Three Cornered Hat and El amor Brujo, The Planets, Tchaikovsky's 1st Piano Concerto, Saint-Saëns 3rd Symphony, Bizet's L'Arlésienne and Carmen Suites, Gubaidulina Offertorium with Boston Symphony, Symphonies by Honegger, Roussel's Symphonies with French Nat. Orchestra, Saint-Saëns Piano Concertos, Suppé Overtures, Berlioz' Les Troyens. *Honours:* Hon. Citizen of the City of Philadelphia 1991; Commdr, Ordre des Arts et des Lettres 1996, Hon. OC; Dr hc (Montreal) 1984, (Laval) 1985, (McGill); two Grammys, Grand Prix de l'Académie du disque français, High Fidelity Int. Record Critics' Award, Montreux Record Award, Japan Record Acad. Award, Musician of the Year, Canada Music Council 1982, two awards from Canadian Conf. of the Arts, Grand Prix du Président de la République (France), Int. Classical Music Awards Lifetime Achievement Award 2014. *Address:* Royal Philharmonic Orchestra, 16 Clerkenwell Green, London, EC1R 0QT, England (office). *Website:* www.rpo.co.uk (office).

DUTT, Hank, BMus, MMus; American violist; b. (Henry Allan Dutt), 4 Nov. 1952, Muscatine, IA; s. of Frank Dutt and Betty Jane Wienhoff; pnr Greg Dubinsky. *Education:* Indiana Univ. *Career:* joined the Kronos String Quartet 1977–; many performances of contemporary music, including the premieres of works of John Cage (30 pieces for string quartet), Pauline Oliveros (The Wheel of Time) and Terry Riley (G-Song, Sunrise of the Planetary Dream Collector and Cadenzas on the Night Plain); formerly quartet-in-residence at Mills Coll., Oakland; from 1982 resident quartet at Univ. of Southern California; appearances at the Monterey Jazz Festival, Carnegie Recital Hall, San Quentin Prison and London's South Bank; New York debut 1984; noted for 'cross-over' performances of jazz and popular music in arrangement. *Recordings:* over 70 recordings with the Kronos Quartet. *Address:* Kronos Quartet, 1242 Ninth Avenue, San Francisco, CA 94122, USA (office). *Telephone:* (415) 731-3533 (office). *Fax:* (415) 664-7590 (office). *E-mail:* janet@kronosarts.com (office). *Website:* kronosquartet.org (office).

DUTTON, Brenton (Brent) Price, BMus, MMus; Canadian composer, tubist and academic; *Professor of Music, Tuba and Composition, San Diego State University*; b. 20 March 1950, Saskatoon, Sask.; two s. one d. *Education:* Conservatory of Music, Univ. of Regina, Oberlin Conservatory of Music, USA. *Career:* tubist with Cleveland Orchestra 1968–74; L'Orchestra Symphonique de Québec 1971–74, San Diego Symphony 1980; solo recital appearances throughout Canada, USA, Europe; taught tuba, chamber music and composition Laval University 1972–74, Oberlin Conservatory 1974–76, Central Michigan Univ. 1976–81, California Inst. of the Arts 1981–84; Prof. of Music,

Tuba and Composition, San Diego State Univ. 1981–; brass coach for Jeunesses Musicales World Orchestra in Europe, North and South America 1986–92; tubist and Artistic Dir Westwind Brass 1993–. *Compositions include:* Symphony No. 2 1972, Symphony No. 3 1974, Song of the Moon for solo flute, On Looking Back for brass quintet, December Set for woodwind quintet, Dialogues of the Sybarites for three trumpets and organ, Circles song cycle for baritone and chamber ensemble, Chinese Reflections song cycle for baritone and chamber ensemble, A Rolling Silence song cycle for baritone and chamber ensemble, Songs of Love song cycle for baritone and chamber ensemble, Ecq theow Variants for brass quintet, On a Darkling Plain for brass quintet, Song of the Sun for solo viola, Hotel Europejski Suite for violin and piano, Gilgamesh (three-act opera) 1977–78. *Recordings include:* Symphony No. 5 Dark Spirals 1985, Character Dances and Proud Music of the Storm 1986, Carnival of Venice for brass quintet 1983, Olympic Entrance tuba suite 1984, The Siren of Urak for viola and brass quintet 1998, Tuba Concerto I and II 1998, Kraków, Summer for string orchestra, Québec, Spring for string orchestra. *Honours:* Silver Medal for Excellence, Royal Conservatory of Music, Outstanding Prof. of the Year for Music at San Diego State Univ. 1987, 1989, 1993, 2002, elected to Canadian Music Center as Assoc. Composer 1993. *Address:* M236, School of Music and Dance, 5500 Campanile Drive, San Diego, CA 92182-7902, USA (office). *Telephone:* (619) 594-4760 (office). *E-mail:* dutton@mail.sdsu.edu (office). *Website:* music.sdsu.edu (office).

DUTTON, Lawrence; American violist; *Professor of Viola and Chamber Music, State University of New York at Stony Brook, Manhattan School of Music*; b. 9 May 1954, New York; m. Elizabeth Lim-Dutton; three s. *Career:* mem., Emerson String Quartet 1976–; premiere concert at Alice Tully Hall, New York 1977, with works by Mozart, Smetana and Bartók; European debut at Spoleto, Italy 1981; quartet-in-residence Smithsonian Inst., Washington 1980–, at the Hartt School 1981–, and at Spoleto and Aspen Festivals 1981–; first resident quartet at Chamber Music Soc. of Lincoln Center 1982–83; tour of Japan and Australia 1987; many performances of works by Bartók, including all six quartets in a single evening, and contemporary works; premieres include Mario Davidovsky's 4th Quartet and works by Maurice Wright and George Tsontakis; Bartók's 4th quartet and Brahms' C minor, London 2001; currently Prof. of Viola and Chamber Music, State Univ. of New York at Stony Brook, and Manhattan School of Music. *Recordings include:* with the Emerson Quartet: Bartók complete Quartets, Mozart six Quartets dedicated to Haydn, Schubert Cello Quintet with Rostropovich, Ives and Barber Quartets, Prokofiev Quartets and Sonata for two violins, Complete Beethoven Cycle 1997, Ned Rorem's Quartet No. 4 and Edgar Meyer's Quintet for String Quartet and Double Bass 1998, Mozart and Brahms Clarinet Quintets with David Shifrin 1999, The Complete Shostakovich Quartets 2000, Bach's Art of the Fugue 2003, Haydn's The Last Seven Words of Our Savior on the Cross 2004, Mendelssohn: The Complete String Quartets 2005, Intimate Voices 2006, The Little Match Girl 2006, Brahm's String Quartets 2007, Bach Fugues 2008, Intimate Letters 2009. *Honours:* Dr hc (Middlebury Coll., Vermont) 1995; Grammy Awards for Best Chamber Music and Classical Record of the Year (for Shostakovich Quartets) 2001, for Best Chamber Music Performance (for Intimate Letters) 2010. *Current Management:* c/o Matthew Zelle, IMG Artists, 152 W 57th Street, Fifth Floor, New York, NY 10019, USA. *Telephone:* (212) 994-3500. *Fax:* (212) 994-3550. *E-mail:* mzelle@imgartists .com. *Website:* www.imgartists.com; www.emersonquartet.com.

DUVALL, Matthew Lynn; American musician (percussion); b. 5 March 1971, near New Castle, Pa; m.; one s. one d. *Education:* Oberlin Conservatory, Cincinnati Coll.-Conservatory and Northwestern Univ. *Career:* Co-founder and mem. contemporary music ensemble eighth blackbird 1996–; ensemble has commissioned and performed new works by composers such as Steve Reich, Frederic Rzewski, Jennifer Higdon, Stephen Hartke and Steven Mackey, and performed with orchestras including Cleveland Orchestra, Toronto Symphony and Atlanta Symphony; residencies at univs and conservatories worldwide, including Univs of Richmond and Chicago, Oberlin Conservatory, Queensland Conservatorium, Southern Methodist Univ., Colburn School and Curtis Inst. of Music. *Recordings:* thirteen ways 2003, beginnings 2004, fred 2005, strange imaginary animals (Grammy Award for Best Chamber Music Performance 2007) 2006, Paul Moravec: The Time Gallery 2006, Steve Reich: Double Sextet 2010, Jennifer Higdon: On a Wire 2011, Steven Mackey: Lonely Motel: Music from Slide (Grammy Award for Best Small Ensemble Performance) 2011, meanwhile (Grammy Award for Best Chamber Music/Small Ensemble Performance) 2012. *Honours:* winner (with eighth blackbird), Fischoff Chamber Music Competition 1996 and numerous awards including Naumburg Chamber Music Award 2000, ASCAP Award for Adventurous Programming 1998, 2000, American Music Center Trailblazer Award 2007, Meet the Composer Award 2007. *Current Management:* David Lieberman Artists, PO Box 10368, Newport Beach, CA 92658, USA. *Address:* c/o eighth blackbird, 5315 North Clark Street, #104, Chicago, IL 60640-2113, USA (office). *Telephone:* (773) 484-8811 (office). *Fax:* (773) 961-7328 (office). *E-mail:* duvall@eighthblackbird.org (office). *Website:* www .eighthblackbird.org (office).

DUVILLIER-WABLE, Laurent, LLL; French composer; b. 7 Oct. 1947, Nîmes; m. Françoise Gripois 1975; one s. one d. *Education:* studied piano with Suzanne Joly, composition with Michel Puig, René Leibowitz. *Career:* began composing, self-taught 1960; Prof. of Music, Ecole de l'Abbaye au Bois, Paris 1966–68; joined Board, Société des Gens de Lettres 1969, Dir-Gen. 1981–97; Dir-Gen., Société Civile des Auteurs Multimédia 1981–2010; mem. SACEM,

Paris. *Compositions include:* Possibilités I for 2 pianos 1971, Possibilités II for 2 tenor instruments, Possibilités III for violoncello and piano, Possibilités IV, Le chant de l'Unsui, for soprano and piano, 4 hands, Possibilités V, violoncello solo, Possibilités VI for piano, 4 hands (recorded by ORTF, broadcast on France-Culture 1973), Approche I for flute and violin, Approche II for soprano and flute, Variable I for 2 pianos 1973, Variable I, piano solo version 1974, Rite, music for mime and dance 1975, Parcours (film music) 1977, Sonata for flute and percussion 1992, Concertino pour neuf, A mon ami musicien Jean Villatte (commission, recorded by Radio France 1993), Sonata II, De la forêt des stèles 1996, Sonata VI (Harmonologia) 2007, Sonata IV 2010, Preludio for violoncello 2011, 4 Intermezzo and Finale 2014. *Publications:* Sonata II, De la forêt des stèles, Hommage à Edmon Colomer, Sonata VI for piano. *Address:* 150 rue de Tolbiac, 75013 Paris, France (home). *Telephone:* 1-45-81-34-79 (home).

DUYKERS, John; American singer (tenor) and voice coach; *Co-director, First Look Sonoma;* b. 30 Sept. 1944, Butte Montana; s. of Dirk Duykers and Elizabeth Craine Duykers; m. Melissa Weaver; one s. *Education:* Oberlin Conservatory, Univ. of Washington, Merola Opera Program, Santa Fe Apprentice 1965–66, Metropolitan Opera Studio, Centre Lyrique Int., Switzerland. *Career:* Seattle Opera from 1966 (Masetto in Don Giovanni 1968); with Vancouver Opera 1968–, in Edmonton 1969–; sang Mao Tse-tung in premiere productions of Nixon in China by John Adams at Houston, San Francisco, Brooklyn Acad. of Music, Amsterdam, Paris, Frankfurt and Edinburgh 1987–93; Asst Prof., Voice and Opera, Frost School of Music, Univ. of Miami 2007–08; Adjunct Voice Faculty, Cornish Coll. of the Arts (Seattle) 2010–; premieres of Under the Double Moon and Tania, by A Davis, St Louis 1989, Philadelphia 1992; with Chicago Opera, in productions including Tannhauser and Prokofiev's The Gambler 1988–98, with Long Beach Opera 1994–2003; Sellem in The Rake's Progress at the Théâtre du Châtelet, Paris 1996; season 2000–01 in the premiere of In the Penal Colony by Philip Glass, at Seattle, Chicago and New York City, as Strauss's Herod in Philadelphia and Kansas City, and Weill's Fatty at Genoa; other roles include Strauss's Herod and Aegisthus, Britten's Captain Vere in Billy Budd, Philip Glass' Galileo/Galilei, the Captain in Wozzeck with Ensemble Parallelle in San Francisco and more than 100 original productions, including 56 world premieres; currently Co-Dir First Look Sonoma. *Honours:* Garebedian Award, Grammy Award, Emmy Award. *Current Management:* c/o California Artists Management, 564 Market Street, Suite 420, San Francisco, CA 94104-5412, USA. *Telephone:* (415) 362-2787. *Fax:* (415) 362-2838. *E-mail:* don@calartists .com. *Website:* www.calartists.com. *Address:* 1645 Furling Road, Sebastopol, CA 95472, USA (office). *Telephone:* (707) 823-9269 (office); (510) 682-4036. *E-mail:* jduykers@aol.com (office). *Website:* www.firstlooksonoma.com (office); www.johnduykers.com.

DVORSKY, Miroslav; Slovak singer (tenor); b. 16 May 1960, Partizánske, Czechoslovakia (now Slovakia). *Education:* Acad. of Music, Bratislava with Ida Černecká, Teatro alla Scala Milano, Italy with Luciano Silvestri. *Career:* debut in Bratislava, 1983, as Nemorino; sang in 1987 premiere of Cikker's The Insect May and guested at Edinburgh, 1990, as Gounod's Faust; Theater am Gärtnerplatz, Munich, from 1994, notably as Des Grieux in Manon; Rome, 1994, as Prince in Rusalka and Rodolfo in La Bohème; Toronto, 1996, as Duke of Mantua; numerous appearances in operettas by Lehar and Johann Strauss; sang Števa in Jenůfa at Hamburg, 2000, Laca for Washington Opera; Pres. Alzheimer Foundation, Slovakia. *Recordings include:* Das Land des Lächelns; Miroslav Dvorsky–Arias.

DVORSKÝ, Peter; Slovak singer (tenor); *Director, Slovak Institute, Rome;* b. 25 Sept. 1951, Partizánske, Topol'čany Dist; s. of Vendelín Dvorský and Anna Dvorská; m. Marta Varšová 1975; two d. *Education:* State Conservatoire, Bratislava. *Career:* studied with R. Carossi and M. di Luggo, Milan 1975–76; opera soloist, Slovak Nat. Theatre, Bratislava 1972–96, 1999; sang at Metropolitan Opera, New York 1977, Covent Garden, London 1978, Bolshoi Theatre, Moscow 1978, La Scala, Milan 1979; performs regularly at Bratislava, Vienna State Opera, Covent Garden, La Scala, New York Metropolitan Opera, Munich, Berlin, Prague, Geneva, Paris, Buenos Aires, Tokyo and in many other cities throughout the world; numerous radio and TV performances; many recordings; Chair. Council of Slovak Music Union 1991–; Pres. Harmony Foundation 1991–; Dir of Opera, State Theatre, Košice 2006–10; Slovak Nat. Theatre, Bratislava 2010–12; Dir, Slovak Inst., Rome 2013–; performed charity concerts after floods in Czech Repub. 2002; Pres. Dvořak Competition, Karlovy Vary, Czech Repub. *Honours:* awards include Tchaikovsky Competition, Geneva (5th Prize 1974, 1st Prize 1975), Leoš Janáček Memorial Medal 1978, Giuseppe Verdi Medal 1979, Artist of Merit 1981, Nat. Artist 1984, Kammersänger, Vienna 1986, Francisco Cilea Prize 1991, Wilhelm Furtwängler Prize 1992, Association Museum Enrico Caruso Premio Caruso Award, Milan 2013, Citta di Villafranca Giuseppe di Stefano

Award 2013. *Address:* J. Hronca 1A, 841 02 Bratislava, Slovakia. *Fax:* (2) 64287626.

DWORCHAK, Harry; American singer (bass-baritone); b. 1947, Hershey, PA. *Education:* AVA, Philadelphia. *Career:* sang first at the Barcelona Opera (from 1970), then throughout North America, with a 1982 debut at the New York City Opera; Théâtre du Châtelet, Paris, 1982, as Banquo; Welsh National Opera, 1985, as Oroveso; Sang Ferrando in Trovatore at the Metropolitan in 1988, at the Munich Staatsoper, 1992; Der fliegende Holländer, Frankfurt, 1991, Washington, DC, 1995; Scarpia, Covent Garden, 1996; Bayerische Staatsoper, 1997; Sang Jochanaan (Salome), Austin, Texas, 1999; Season 2000–01 engaged as Wotan in Rheingold; Season 2001–02, Metropolitan Opera as Count Waldner in Arabella and Geisterbote in Die Frau ohne Schatten; Der Landgraf in Tannhäuser for Tulsa Opera, 2001; Other roles include the Commendatore, Monteverdi's Seneca, Bellini's Capulet, Mephistopheles (Faust), Don Quichotte, Daland, Wagner's Dutchman, and Dosifey in Khovanshchina; further engagements as Wotan, Rheingold, Augsburg; Wotan, Walküre, Augsburg; Der Wanderer; Pizarro in Fidelio, Buenos Aires, entire Ring Cycle. *Recordings:* Das Schloss, Bayerische Staatsoper, Munich; Don Alfonso in Così fan tutte, European Television Broadcast. *Honours:* Richard Tucker Award 1987, Carnegie Hall Concert 1987. *Current Management:* c/o Pinnacle Arts: Miller Division, 889 Ninth Avenue, Second Floor, New York, NY 10019, USA. *Telephone:* (212) 397-7911. *Fax:* (212) 397-7920. *E-mail:* jmiller@pinnaclearts.com. *Website:* www .pinnaclearts.com; www.harrydworchak.com.

DWORZYŃSKI, Michał; Polish conductor; b. 1979. *Education:* Fryderyk Chopin Music Acad., Hochschule Hanns Eisler, Berlin, Germany. *Career:* Music Dir Bydgoszcz Chamber Orchestra 1995–99; Asst Conductor Nat. Polish Radio Symphony Orchestra, Katowice 2000–; Asst Conductor London Symphony Orchestra 2007–08; has appeared with Warsaw Philharmonic Orchestra, Sinfonia Varsovia, Polish Nat. Radio Orchestras of Katowice and Warsaw, Northern Sinfonia, Berlin Symphony Orchestra, Martinu Philharmonic Zlin, Orchestra Metropolitana, Lisbon, RTE Nat. Orchestra of Ireland, Vienna Chamber Orchestra 2007, London Philharmonic Orchestra 2008, BBC Scottish Symphony 2008. *Honours:* Citizen of Bydgoszcz 1997; Polish Music Critics' Award 1999, Scholarships from Ministry of Culture, Poland 2001, 2003, 2005, winner of conducting competitions in Zagreb 2003 and Suwon 2005, Donatella Flick Conducting Competition 2006. *Current Management:* Intermusica Artists' Management, 16 Duncan Terrace, London, N1 8BZ, England. *Telephone:* (20) 7278-5455. *Fax:* (20) 7278-8434. *E-mail:* mail@ intermusica.co.uk. *Website:* www.intermusica.co.uk.

DYACHKOV, Yegor; Russian cellist; b. 1974, Moscow. *Education:* Moscow Conservatory with Alexander Fedorchenko, studied with Radu Aldulescu in Rome, André Navarra in Vienna, Yuli Turovsky in Montréal, Boris Pergamenschikow in Cologne. *Career:* numerous recitals in the former Soviet Union, Italy, Latin America, Taiwan, USA, Canada; guest soloist with Montréal Symphony Orchestra, Metropolitan Orchestra of Montréal, Orchestre Symphonique de Québec, National Arts Centre Orchestra in Ottawa, I Musici de Montréal; concert performances in Québec, Ontario, New Brunswick; performances at the Lanaudiere Int. Music Festival, Domaine Forget Int. Music Festival, Chamber Music Festival in Ste-Pétronille, Orford Int. Music Festival, Scotia Festival of Music, Mozarteum in Caracas, Vancouver Chamber Music Festival, Evian Festival 1999. *Recordings:* Glazunov's Concerto Ballata, Strauss and Pfitzner Sonatas. *Address:* c/o Latitude 45, Arts Promotion Inc., 109 St Joseph Blvd West, Montréal, QC H2T 2P7, Canada.

DYAKOVSKI, Lubomir; Bulgarian singer (tenor); b. 1 March 1950, Dupnitza; m. Rossitza Ivanova Dyakovska; one s. one d. *Education:* Bulgarian Musical Acad. *Career:* debut as Ernesto in Don Pasquale by Donizetti 1970; permanently engaged in Russe and Pleven; numerous performances throughout Europe; over 40 tenor solo performances in masses, oratorios and requiems, including Lensky in Eugene Onegin, Nadir in the Pearl Fishers by Bizet and Almaviva in Il Barbiere di Siviglia by Rossini; sang with all major symphony orchestras and choruses in Bulgaria; performances with major Bulgarian and European television and radio companies; sang in studio recording of The Suffering of Jesus for Radio Zagreb; participated in opening of Summer Music Festival in Dubrovnik 1991; soloist for Bolshoi Don Kosaken Ensemble, performing throughout Switzerland, Austria and Germany; mem. Rotary Int., Union of Musicians in Bulgaria. *Recordings:* Russian songs and arias; Songs of Petrarca by Liszt, St Matthew Passion, Night of Walpurgis and Bach's Magnificat; The Golden Cockerel, Rimsky-Korsakov; Eugene Onegin; Prince Igor by Borodin; Evangelist in Christmas Oratorio by J. S. Bach; Handel's Messiah. *Honours:* numerous government and state awards.

E

EAGLE, David Malcolm, BMus, MMus, PhD; Canadian composer, flautist and teacher; b. 21 Dec. 1955, Montréal, QC; m. Hope Lee 1980. *Education:* McGill Univ., studied with Cindy Shuter, Bengt Hamnbraeus and Donald Steven, Hochschule für Musik, Freiburg with Klaus Huber and Brian Ferneyhough, Univ. of California at Berkeley. *Career:* works played in Canada, Holland Festival 1985, Germany, Switzerland; broadcasts on CBC Radio Canada, BBC, Hessischer Rundfunk, Swiss Radio, KRO (Netherlands); invited guest composer, Boswil Kunstlerhaus, Switzerland 1985; commissions from Montréal Chamber Orchestra, Array-Music, Toronto Consort, many individuals; Co-ordinator Electro-acoustic Music Studio; Asst Prof. of Composition and Theory, Univ. of Calgary 1990–. *Compositions:* Zhu Fong for string quartet 1978, Strata-Vari for 14 strings 1980, Within for solo cello 1982, Strahlen for organ 1983, Aura for septet 1984, Renew'd at ev'ry glance for variable instruments 1985, Toccare for harpsichord 1986, Luminous Voices for early music ensemble and tape 1987–88, Crossing Currents for orchestra 1991, Hsuan for guzheng and tape 1992, Nohocki for flute and cello 1993, Open This Door for AXIO (midi-controller) 1993, Sounding after Time for violin, cello, piano, computer and synthesizer 1993.

EAGLEN, Jane; British singer (soprano); b. Lincoln, England; d. of Ronald Eaglen and Kathleen Kent. *Education:* Royal Northern Coll. of Music, studied with Joseph Ward. *Career:* debut, ENO in Patience 1984; engagements with ENO as Leonora in Il Trovatore and Elizabeth I in Mary Stuart; Western Australia Opera, Perth, as Tosca; Lyric Opera of Queensland, Brisbane, as Madama Butterfly; Scottish Opera, as Donna Anna; London Promenade Concert debut 1989, as Sieglinde in Act III of Die Walküre; sang Brünnhilde 1991; Tosca for ENO 1990; Donna Anna and Amelia (Ballo), Bologne 1991; sang Mathilde in Guillaume Tell at Covent Garden, Geneva 1992; Scottish Opera as Norma in a new production of Bellini's opera; Tosca, Buenos Aires 1993, then Donna Anna in Don Giovanni, Vienna State Opera, and title role in Norma, Seattle Opera; Brünnhilde in Die Walküre, Opera Pacific, California, and Vienna State Opera 1994; Norma with Riccardo Muti, Ravenna Festival 1994; title role in Ariadne, with ENO 1994; Brünnhilde in Die Walküre, La Scala, Milan 1994, and with Lyric Opera of Chicago 1995; Amelia in Un Ballo in Maschera, Opéra de Paris Bastille 1995; La Gioconda, Chicago, and Tristan and Isolde at Seattle 1998; concert appearances at the Wigmore Hall, Festival Hall and the Barbican Centre; Verdi Requiem and Mahler 8th Symphony; recitals for the Wagner Socs of London, New York and Buenos Aires; sang Isolde and Turandot at the New York Met 2000, 2003, and in Puerto Rico 2004; Turandot at Covent Garden 2001; complete Ring Cycle for Seattle Opera 2001, 2005, Met and Lyric Opera of Chicago 2001–05; London Proms 2002; sang La Vestale for ENO 2003, Ortrud in Lohengrin, and Ariadne, in Seattle 2004, Roselinda in Die Fledermaus, Seattle 2005, Lady Macbeth in Macbeth, Vancouver 2006; Artist in Residence, Univ. of Washington School of Music 2006–07; Prin. Vocal Instructor, Young Artists Program Seattle Opera 2006–. *Recordings:* Die Flammen; Medea in Corinto; Norma, with Muti; Tosca; Turandot; Mozart and Strauss; Bellini and Wagner; Song Cycles by Strauss, Berg and Wagner; Der fliegende Holländer, conducted by Barenboim 2002, Tannhauser (Grammy Award for Best Complete Opera) 2002. *Honours:* Hon. DMus (McGill Univ.), (Bishop Grosseteste Univ. Coll., Lincoln); Peter Moores Foundation Scholarship, Countess of Munster Award, Carl Rosa Trust Award. *E-mail:* management@janeeaglen.com (office). *Website:* www.janeeaglen.com.

EANET, Nick, BM; American violinist; b. Brooklyn. *Education:* Juilliard School. *Career:* invited by Zubin Mehta to appear aged eight as soloist with New York Philharmonic; other solo performances with Minnesota Orchestra with Sir Neville Marriner, New York Youth Symphony, and others; leader and first violinist, Mendelssohn String Quartet 1994–99, performed world-wide in venues such as Carnegie Hall, Avery Fisher Hall, Wigmore Hall, London, Concertgebouw, Amsterdam, Library of Congress; concert master, Metropolitan Opera Orchestra 1999–2009; performed across Europe and Japan; mem. (first violinist), Juilliard String Quartet 2009–11; also performs with Sea Cliff Chamber Players and at Bargemusic; mem. and conductor, Amadeus Virtuosi chamber orchestra; festival appearances include the Mostly Mozart Festival, Sante Fe Chamber Music Festival, Aspen Music Festival, Maui Chamber Music Festival, Steamboat Springs Strings in the Mountains Festival; mem. faculty, Juilliard School 2009–11; also taught at Harvard Univ., Univ. of Delaware, N Carolina School of the Arts. *Current Management:* c/o Colbert Artist Management, 111 West 57th Street, New York, NY 10019, USA. *Telephone:* (212) 757-0782. *Fax:* (212) 541-5179. *E-mail:* nycolbert@colbertartists.com. *Website:* www.colbertartists.com; www.juilliardstringquartet.org.

EARLE, Hobart; American conductor; *Music Director and Principal Conductor, Odesa Philharmonic Orchestra;* b. Caracas, Venezuela. *Education:* Hochschule für Musik, Vienna, Trinity Coll. of Music, London, Princeton Univ.; studied with Ferdinand Leitner, Leonard Bernstein and Seiji Ozawa. *Career:* Founder and Music Dir, American Music Ensemble Vienna and Ensemble for Viennese Music, New York 1987–91, Music Dir and Prin. Conductor, Odesa Philharmonic Orchestra, Ukraine 1991–; guest conductor of numerous orchestras in Europe, North America and Asia. *Recordings:* albums: Music by Theodor Berger and Miguel Del Aguila 1991, Music of Ukraine – Kolessa/Skoryk 1996, Music of Ukraine–Gliere/Stankovych 1997,

American Music Ensemble Vienna 2001, Tchaikovsky Fifth Symphony (JPFolks Music Award for Best Classical Album 2002) 2001. *Honours:* Distinguished Artist of Ukraine, Washington Group Friend of Ukraine Award 1996. *Address:* Odesa Philharmonic Orchestra, 65026 Odesa, vul. I. Bunina 15, Ukraine (office). *Telephone:* (482) 25-01-89 (office). *E-mail:* info@odessaphilharmonic.org (office). *Website:* www.odessaphilharmonic.org (office).

EARLE, Roderick, MA (Hons) (Cantab.); British singer (baritone) and teacher; *Professor of Singing, Royal College of Music;* b. 29 Jan. 1952, Winchester, Hants.; s. of Dennis Earle and Fenella Earle; one s. one d. *Education:* chorister, Winchester Cathedral, St John's Coll., Cambridge, Royal Coll. of Music, London, studied with Otakar Kraus. *Career:* with ENO 1978–80; debut at Royal Opera, Covent Garden as Antonio in Le Nozze di Figaro 1980; joined Royal Opera, sang more than 60 roles, including Schaunard, Abimelech, Orestes, Monterone, the Bonze, Brander, Harasta in Cunning Little Vixen, Kothner, the Philosopher in Cherubin, King Fisher in Midsummer Marriage, Alberich and Siegfried in Götterdämmerung; has appeared with all major British companies, toured to Japan, Repub. of Korea, Greece and Finland with the Royal Opera and appeared in festivals at Edinburgh, Buxton, Israel, Athens, Flanders; has sung Kothner, Rangoni and Abimelech at Teatro Regio, Turin, and Altair in British premiere of Strauss's Die Ägyptische Helena and Ford at Garsington; other appearances include A Midsummer Night's Dream and Turandot (Rome Opera), Der Fliegende Holländer (Opéra de Massy), Amonasro, Alfio and Tonio (Royal Albert Hall), Germont and Scarpia (Holland Park Opera), Ford and the Count in Figaro (New Zealand Opera), Rigoletto (Opera Zuid), Police Inspector in Lady Macbeth of Mtsensk (Royal Opera), Hubbard in Doctor Atomic (ENO), Dancaire in Carmen (Norwegian Opera), Nekrotsar in Le Grand Macabre (Adelaide Festival, Teatro Colón Buenos Aires), Lear in Promised End (English Touring Opera), Monterone (ENO), Klinghoffer (Wuppertal and Oldenburg); sang Melchior in Amahl and the Night Visitors at Sadler's Wells; currently Prof. of Singing, Royal Coll. of Music; Founder and Dir Colchester Chamber Choir 2010. *Films:* appeared in recordings of La Fanciulla del West, Manon Lescaut, Andrea Chénier, Der Rosenkavalier (Solti), Carmen (Mehta), Salome (Downes), Otello and La Traviata (Solti). *Recordings include:* Ferneyhough's Transit; Rossini's Stabat Mater with Richard Hickox; Les Troyens with Sir Colin Davis, soundtrack of film Meeting Venus. *Honours:* Musician of the Year Award, Greater London Arts Assocn, various Grammy Awards. *Address:* 155 Maldon Road, Colchester, Essex, CO3 3BJ, England (home). *E-mail:* roderick.earle1@ntlworld.com (home). *Website:* www.colchesterchamberchoir.org (office).

EAST, Leslie Charles, OBE, BMus, MMus, FGSM; British music publisher, writer, consultant and administrator; *Chairman, Board of Trustees, Association of British Choral Directors;* b. 8 July 1949, Doncaster, South Yorks.; m. Lilija Zobens; two d. *Education:* Kingsbury Co. Grammar School, London, King's Coll., London. *Career:* visiting lecturer and concert organizer, City Univ., London 1973–75; Dir of Music, Guildhall School of Music and Drama, London 1975–87; Publishing Dir, Novello and Co. Ltd 1987–98; Man. Ed., Associated Bd of the Royal Schools of Music (Publishing) Ltd 1998–99, Dir of Publishing 1999–2007, Exec. Dir 2007–13, Chief Exec. 2013–14; Chair. Soc. for the Promotion of New Music 1978–83, New Macnaghten Concerts 1989–99, Early Music Centre and Network 1994–2001, City Music Soc. 1998–; Dir Univ. of York Music Press 2015–; Consultant, Musica Baltica SIA; mem. Arts Council Music Panel 1988–92; mem. Worshipful Co. of Musicians (Master 2007–08), Royal Soc. of Musicians, Royal Philharmonic Soc., Royal Musical Assocn, The Peter Warlock Soc.; Chair. Bd of Trustees, Assocn of British Choral Dirs 2015–; Trustee, London Youth Choir 2015–. *Publications:* Three Betjeman Songs 1984, Songs for Mixed Choir 2009; contrib. of various articles and reviews to The New Grove, The Musical Times, Music and Musicians, Music Teacher. *Honours:* Hon. mem. Royal Coll. of Music; Freeman, City of London 1978, Musicians' Co. 1986; Diploma of World Fed. of Free Latvians 2006.

EASTBURN, Susanna de Martelly, BA, MPhil; British arts executive; *Director of Music Strategy, Arts Council England;* b. 6 Jan. 1969, Truro. *Education:* Penair School, Cornwall, Millfield School, Somerset, King's Coll. Cambridge. *Career:* Int. Promotions Man., Chester Music/Novello & Co. Ltd 1994–2001; Artistic Dir, Huddersfield Contemporary Music Festival 2001–04; Youth Music Fellow, Clore Leadership Programme 2004–05; Exec. Prod., London International Festival of Theatre (LIFT) 2005–08; Dir of Music Strategy, Arts Council England 2008–; non-exec. positions include Yorkshire Regional Arts Council 2002–05; mem. British Arts Festivals Assocns (exec. bd mem.) 2002–04, Réseau Varèse (exec. bd mem.) 2002–04, Soc. for Promotion of New Music (mem. bd, then Chair.) 1998–2007, Int. Soc. for Contemporary Music (chair., British Section) 1999–2002; Gov. Leeds Coll. of Music 2003–05. *Address:* Arts Council England, 14 Great Peter Street, London, SW1P 3NQ, England (office). *Telephone:* (845) 300-6200 (office). *E-mail:* enquiries@artscouncil.org.uk (office). *Website:* www.artscouncil.org.uk (office).

EATHORNE, Wendy, JP, ARAM, LRAM, ARCM; British singer (soprano) and teacher; b. 25 Sept. 1939, Four Lanes, Cornwall, England; one d. *Education:* Royal Acad. of Music. *Career:* West End production, Robert and Elizabeth 1965–67; numerous concert appearances, including Promenade concerts,

London; engagements with the London Bach Choir, London Symphony Orchestra, Hallé Orchestra and other leading British orchestras; repertoire includes works by Handel (Susanna and Belshazzar), Liszt (Missa Solemnis) and Haydn (The Creation); appearances with WNO, ENO and Royal Opera, Covent Garden; Glyndebourne 1969–71, as Sophie in Werther, First Boy in Die Zauberflöte and Atalanta in The Rising of the Moon; Italian debut in Ariadne auf Naxos; repertoire also includes Julia in La Vestale by Spontini and Marguerite in Faust; festival adjudicator; many recitals with the pianist Geoffrey Pratley, programmes include groups of songs by Purcell to modern pieces; Head of Vocal Studies, Opera and Music Theatre, Trinity Coll. of Music 1989–94, Sr Lecturer 1994–. *Recordings:* Masses by Bach; A Village Romeo and Juliet; Monteverdi Madrigals Libro IV; A Scarlatti Clori e Zeffiro and St Cecilia Mass, Schubert Mass in A flat; Vaughan Williams The Pilgrim's Progress and Sir John in Love; Bridge, The Christmas Rose. *Honours:* Hon. FCSM, FTCL, FRSA.

EBBECKE, Michael; German singer (baritone); b. 8 Dec. 1955, Wiesbaden. *Education:* Richard Strauss Conservatory, Munich and Hochshule für Musik Köln with Josef Metternich. *Career:* debut in Stuttgart 1982, as Count in Mozart's Figaro; mem., Staatstheater Karlsruhe 1983–85, Stuttgart Staatsoper 1985–; operatic roles have included Guglielmo, Papageno, Oreste, Don Giovanni, Stolzius, Scerasmin, Ulisse, Falke Heerufer, Wolfram, Germont, Pantalone, Ephraimit/anderer Mann (Moses und Aron), Gorijancikov (Totenhaus), Melisso, Podesta (Gezeichneten), Kotner, Jochanaan, Giuseppe Verdi (Giuseppe e Sylvia); guest appearances at the Berlin Komische Oper (Guglielmo 1984) and Deutsche Oper (Orestes in Iphigénie en Tauride 1988); appearances at Karlsruhe, Paris, Lyon (Wolfram in Tannhäuser) and La Scala Milan (Scherasmin in Oberon 1989); sang Stolzius in Die Soldaten at Stuttgart 1987, Papageno and Escamillo in season 1990–91, Guglielmo 1991–92; season 1995–96 as Pantaleone in The Love for Three Oranges at Stuttgart; Melisso in Handel's Alcina 1998; sang Verdi in the premiere of Adriana Hölszky's Giuseppe Sylvia, Stuttgart 2000; concert engagements include Bach's St John Passion at Amsterdam 1987. *Recording:* Die Soldaten. *Honours:* Kammersänger of Württembergische Staatsoper Stuttgart. *Address:* c/o Stuttgart Staatsoper, Oberer Schlossgarten 6, 70173 Stuttgart, Germany.

EBERLEY, Helen-Kay, MMus; American singer, record company executive and publisher; b. 3 Aug. 1947, Sterling, Ill.; d. of William Elliott Eberley. *Education:* Northwestern Univ. *Career:* debut in Der Rosenkavalier with Lyric Opera, Chicago 1973; has performed jazz with Duke Ellington and Dave Brubeck; numerous solo concerts including Continental Bank Concerts 1981–89; Chair., Pres., Artistic Co-ordinator Eberley-Skowronski Inc., Evanston, Ill. 1973–92; Founder EB-SKO Productions 1976; Exec. Dir and performance consultant E-S Management 1985; Founder HKE Enterprises 1993–; Guest Lecturer at colls and univs, currently Emer.; F. K. Weyerhauser Scholar, Metropolitan Opera 1967; volunteer, Art Inst. of Chicago 1995–. *Operas include:* Così fan Tutte, Le Nozze di Figaro, Dido and Aeneas, Tosca, La Traviata, Don Giovanni, Brigadoon; Producer, Annotator: Gentleman Gypsy 1978; Exec. Producer: Separate But Equal 1976, All Brahms 1977, Opera Lady 1978, Eberley Sings Strauss 1980, Helen-Kay Eberley: American Girl 1983, Helen-Kay Eberley: Opera Lady II 1984, Helen-Kay Eberley: French Lace 1988, Helen-Kay Eberley: Opera Lady III 1989. *Publications:* Angel's Song 1993, The Magdaleva Poems 1994, Chapel Heart 1995, Desert Dancing 1998, Canyon Ridge 2000, River Voice 2002. *Honours:* Milton J. Cross Award, Metropolitan Opera Guild 1968; numerous poetry awards including Best of the Best Award for The Rose Garden, Poets and Patrons, Inc., Chicago, First Prize, Chicagoland Poetry Contest for The Pond. *Address:* HKE Enterprises, 1726 Sherman Ave, Evanston, IL 60201 (office); 2758 Sheridan Road, Evanston, IL 60201, USA (home). *Telephone:* (847) 309-9335 (office).

EBRAHIM, Omar; British singer (baritone); b. 6 Sept. 1956, London, England. *Education:* Guildhall School of Music, London. *Career:* appearances with the Opera Factory in Punch and Judy, The Beggar's Opera, The Knot Garden, and La Calisto; sang in the premieres of Birtwistle's Yan Tan Tethera, South Bank 1986 and Nigel Osborne's The Electrification of the Soviet Union, Glyndebourne 1986; Glyndebourne Touring Opera in Il Barbiere di Siviglia and La Bohème; has sung Hector in King Priam for Kent Opera; with Scottish Opera has appeared in Mahagonny, Die Fledermaus and Iolanthe; Covent Garden 1989, in the British premiere of Un Re in Ascolto by Berio; sang Don Giovanni with Opera Factory at the QEH 1990, Parkhearst in the premiere of Bose's 63: Dream Palace at the 1990 Munich Biennale; The Fool in the premiere of Birtwistle's Gawain, Covent Garden 1991; sang the Voice of Goya in the premiere of Osborne's Terrible Mouth, Almeida Festival 1992; created Vermeer in Birtwistle's The Second Mrs Kong, Glyndebourne 1994; sang Horace Tabor in the British premiere of Moore's The Ballad of Baby Doe, Bloomsbury Theatre 1996; Momo in Cesti's Il Pomo d'Oro at Batignano 1998; television appearances include Yan Tan Tethera, by Birtwistle, The Kiss by Michael Nyman and the title role in a BBC version of Marschner's Vampyr 1992; concert repertoire includes Morton Feldman/Beckett Words and Music, Aventures, Nouvelles Aventures (Ligeti), Enoch Arden (Strauss) and Ode to Napoleon Bonaparte (Schoenberg). *Current Management:* c/o Allied Artists, 42 Montpelier Square, London, SW7 1JZ, England. *Telephone:* (20) 7589-6243. *Fax:* (20) 7581-5269. *E-mail:* info@alliedartists.co.uk. *Website:* www.alliedartists.co.uk.

ECKHARDT, Mária; Hungarian musicologist and choral conductor; *Co-President, Hungarian Liszt Ferenc Society*; b. 26 Sept. 1943, Budapest. *Education:* Liszt Ferenc Acad. of Music, Budapest. *Career:* Librarian and Research Worker, Music Dept, Nat. Széchényi Library, Budapest 1966–73; Research Worker, Inst. of Musicology, Hungarian Acad. of Sciences, Budapest 1973–87; Dir, Liszt Ferenc Memorial Museum and Research Centre at Liszt Acad. of Music, Budapest 1986–2009, Chief Counsellor, Research Dir 2009–13; Co-Pres. Hungarian Liszt Ferenc Soc. 2013–. *Publications:* Franz Liszt und sein Kreis in Briefen und Dokumenten aus den Beständen des Burgenländischen Landesmuseums (with Cornelia Knotik) 1983, Liszt Ferenc Memorial Museum Catalogue 1986, 1996, 2008, Franz Liszt's Estate at the Budapest Academy of Music, I Books 1986, II Music, 1993, Franz Liszt's Music Manuscripts in the National Széchényi Library 1986, Liszt Ferenc válogatott levelei 1824–1861 (selected letters 1824–1861) 1989, Franz Liszt's Weimarer Bibliothek (with Evelyn Liepsch) 1999, Das Album der Prinzessin Marie von Sayn-Wittgenstein 2000, Franz Liszt's Oratorio Christus and the Budapest Academy of Music 2011, Génie oblige! Treasures from the Budapest Liszt Ferenc Memorial Museum (ed.) 2011, Liszt and the Arts, Exhbn Catalogue 2012; contrib. to books on Liszt, Schubert, Chopin, Berlioz and Schumann 1996–2002; Studies on Liszt and 19th-Century Musical Life and Composers, in Studia Musicologica, Magyar Zene, The Hungarian Quarterly, The New Hungarian Quarterly, Journal of The American Liszt Society, The Hungarian View of Liszt, Muzsika and others; exhbn catalogues, forewords to Liszt edns by Henle (Munich), BHKE (Budapest) and Istituto Liszt (Bologna). *Honours:* Award of Excellence, American Liszt Soc. 1985, Erkel Prize 1987, Szabolcsi Prize 2004, MAOE Musical Grand Prize 2004. *Address:* Vörösmarty utca 35, 1064 Budapest, Hungary (office). *Telephone:* (1) 322-9804 (office); (1) 342-1573 (office). *E-mail:* eckhardt.maria@lisztakademia.hu (office). *Website:* www.lisztsociety.hu (office).

ECKHART, Janis Gail, BA; American singer (mezzo-soprano); b. 21 July 1953, CA. *Education:* Univ. of California, Los Angeles and Academia Real de Música, Madrid, Spain. *Career:* debut at New York City Opera 1981; numerous roles at New York City Opera, including Nabucco 1981, Rigoletto 1981, 1984, 1988, 1989, Carmen 1986, 1988; in Rigoletto at Opéra de Monte Carlo 1983, and Aida, Opera Delaware 1984; sang in Il Trovatore 1987, and in Un Ballo in Maschera 1986, both at Nat. Grand Opera; Carmen, Seattle Opera 1982; Samson et Dalila, Nat. Philharmonic of the Philippines 1980; Les Contes D'Hoffmann at the Opera Metropolitana, Caracas 1981; Nabucco, Rigoletto, Teatro de Opera, Puerto Rico 1988; Rigoletto, Opera Carolina 1990; Carmen, Metro Lyric Opera 1992; Carmen, Cairo Opera, Egypt 1992; Mahler's Kindertotenlieder and Songs of a Wayfarer, Nashville Symphony, Verdi's Requiem, New York Chorale Soc. and Plymouth Church of the Pilgrims; concert tour, Instituto Technológico de México 1992; Kismet, Taipei Symphony 1993; Ambassadors of Opera, Far East concert tour 1993; Middle East concert tour 1993; Cavalleria Rusticana, Hong Kong 1994; Carmen, Madrid, Lisbon 1995; Aida, Cairo Opera 1996; Beethoven's 9th Symphony, Avery Fisher Hall 1997; Amneris in Aida, Dicapo Opera Theatre tour 2001; Carmen in Florida 2001, 2003. *Current Management:* c/o J. Dietsch, Pinnacle Arts Management, 889 Ninth Avenue, Second Floor, New York, NY 10019, USA. *Telephone:* (212) 397-7911. *Fax:* (212) 397-7920. *Website:* www.pinnaclearts.com. *Address:* 15 West 72nd Street, New York, NY 10023, USA.

ECONOMOU, Michalis, MusM, MusD; Greek music conductor; *Music Director, Qatar Philharmonic Orchestra*; b. 1973. *Education:* Athens Univ., Nat. Conservatory of Athens, Boston Univ., USA, conducting studies with Jorma Panula and Gianluigi Gelmetti. *Career:* Music Dir Qatar Philharmonic Orchestra 2011–12; has conducted Athens State Orchestra, Kamerata Orchestra of Megaron, Municipal and State Orchestras of Thessaloniki, Nat. Symphony Orchestra of Greek TV, Orchestra of Colours, Contemporary Radio Orchestra of Greece, Qatar Philharmonic Orchestra, Thailand Philharmonic Orchestra, Festival Orchestra di Sofia, ALEA III contemporary ensemble; works have been performed world-wide; commissioned to compose music for Carnegie Hall and Athens Megaron Concert Hall, amongst others; teaches orchestral conducting in Greece; Perm. Conductor, Athens Symphony Orchestra 2000–; Chair. and Artistic Dir, Music Dept, Nat. Tech. Univ. of Athens 2004–. *Honours:* winner of 11 nat. and int. competitions, including ALEA III Int. Composition Competition, Dimitris Mitropoulos Int. Composition Competition. *Address:* Qatar Philharmonic Orchestra, PO Box 5825, Doha, Qatar (office). *E-mail:* info@qatarphilharmonicorchestra.org (office). *Website:* qatarphilharmonicorchestra.org (office).

EDDINS, William; American conductor and pianist; *Music Director, Edmonton Symphony Orchestra*; b. 1964, Buffalo, NY; m.; two s. *Education:* Eastman School of Music with David Effron, Univ. of Southern Calif. with Daniel Lewis. *Career:* fmr Assoc. Conductor Minnesota Orchestra; fmr Asst to Daniel Barenboim at Berlin State Opera; Asst Conductor Chicago Symphony Orchestra 1992, subsequently Assoc. and later the first Resident Conductor of the orchestra; Prin. Guest Conductor RTE Nat. Symphony Orchestra, Ireland 2002–07; Music Dir Edmonton Symphony Orchestra 2005–; founding mem. New World Symphony, Miami; has conducted US symphony orchestras, including San Francisco, Cincinnati, Atlanta, Detroit, Dallas, Los Angeles, Houston, San Antonio, Kansas City, Austin, Hartford, Memphis, Colorado, St Louis, also Los Angeles, Jacksonville and Tulsa Philharmonics; int. appearances as guest conductor of Adelaide SO, Barcelona SO, Bergen Philharmonic, Royal Scottish Nat. Orchestra, RAI Orchestra Sinfonica, Berlin Staatskapelle, Lisbon Metropolitan; regularly conducts from the piano, and has performed as pianist on Chicago Symphony Orchestra's 'Symphony Center Presents' recital series; founder and Artistic Dir Prospect Park Players, Hamline Univ., St

Paul. *Recordings:* piano: Bad Boys Vol. 1 2003. *Honours:* Seaver/NEA Conducting Award 2000. *Address:* Edmonton Symphony Orchestra, 9720-102 Avenue, Edmonton, AB T5J 4B2, Canada (office). *Telephone:* (780) 428-1108 (office). *E-mail:* esofeedback@winspearcentre.com (office). *Website:* www.edmontonsymphony.com (office); www.williameddins.com.

EDDY, Jenifer, OAM; Australian singer (coloratura soprano) and artists' manager; b. 1933, Melbourne, Vic.; m. David Beamish; one s. *Education:* studied in Melbourne with Henri Portnoj and in London with Bertha Nicklauss Kempner and Roy Henderson. *Career:* frequent guest soloist with Australian Broadcasting Corpn in concerts, studio broadcasts and on TV and major choral groups 1953–58; professional stage debut 1954, as Mascha in Chocolate Soldier, Princess Theatre, Melbourne; opera debut 1956, as Nedda in Pagliacci; Elizabethan Opera Co. 1956–57 as Mozart's Susanna, Despina, Papagena and as Polly Peachum, Beggar's Opera; Covent Garden 1959–69, roles including Xenia in Boris Godunov, Amor in Gluck's Orpheus, Fiakermilli in Arabella, Olympia in Tales of Hoffmann, Sophie in Der Rosenkavalier, Tytania in A Midsummer Night's Dream; guest appearances with Sadler's Wells Opera, ENO, Welsh Nat. Opera, Scottish Opera, English Opera Group, Bordeaux Opera, Maggio Musicale, Edinburgh, Leeds, Bath and Schwetzingen Festivals; roles include Despina, Rosina, Norina, Blondchen, Madame Herz in The Impresario, Musetta, Zerbinetta, Adele in Die Fledermaus; appearances for BBC on radio, TV and in concert; Man. Dir Jenifer Eddy Artists' Management, Melbourne 1975–2012; Dir, Lies Askonas Ltd, London 1982–97, consultant, Askonas Holt Ltd 1998–; Assoc., Musical Soc. of Victoria, London Coll. of Music. *Television:* subject of Australian Story (ABC TV) 1999. *Recordings include:* Die Entführung, Gypsy Baron, Hansel and Gretel. *Address:* c/o The Dame Nellie Melba Opera Trust, PO Box 7258, St Kilda Road, Melbourne, Vic. 8004, Australia.

EDDY, Timothy; American violoncellist; b. 1930. *Education:* studied with Bernard Greenhouse. *Career:* mem. Orion String Quartet; fmr mem. Galimir Quartet, New York Philomusica, Bach Aria Group; performed as guest artist with Dallas Symphony, Colorado Symphony, Jacksonville Symphony, North Carolina Symphony, Stamford Symphony Orchestra; has appeared at Mostly Mozart, Ravinia, Aspen, Santa Fe, Marlboro, Lockenhaus, Spoleto and Sarasota festivals; Prof. of Cello, Juilliard School, Mannes Coll. of Music. *Honours:* Gaspar Cassado Int. Violoncello Competition 1975. *Current Management:* Kirshbaum Demler and Associates, 711 West End Avenue, Suite 5KN, New York, NY 10025, USA. *Telephone:* (212) 222-4843. *Fax:* (212) 222-7321. *E-mail:* info@kirshdem.com. *Website:* www.kirshdem.com. *E-mail:* tim@orionquartet.com (office). *Website:* www.orionquartet.com.

EDELMANN, Peter; Austrian singer (baritone); b. 1962, Vienna; s. of Otto Edelmann. *Education:* Vienna Musikhochschule. *Career:* sang Mozart's Figaro on tour in Europe; mem. of Koblenz Opera 1985–, notably in the title role at the premiere of Odysseus by Klaus Arp, 1989; guest appearances in Mannheim, Dortmund, Wuppertal and Krefeld, as Mozart's Don Giovanni and Guglielmo, Marcello, the Forester in Cunning Little Vixen, Rossini's Figaro, Posa and Lord Tristan in Martha; Lieder recitals and concerts in Vienna, Budapest, Salzburg and Wexford; mem. Deutsche Oper Berlin 1990–; sang in the premiere of Desdemona und ihre Schwestern by Siegfried Matthus, Schwetzingen 1991, Theseus in Enescu's Oedipe, Berlin 1996, Albert in Werther, Berlin (concert) 1998, sang Morales in Carmen, Gounod's Valentin and Melot in Tristan at the Deutsche Oper 2000. *Honours:* winner, Belvedere Competition, Vienna 1989. *Current Management:* Bettina Brentano International Management, Avenue Franklin Roosevelt 16, 75008 Paris, France. *Telephone:* 1-42-25-58-34. *Fax:* 1-42-25-64-97. *E-mail:* oia@oia-poilve.com. *Website:* www.oia-poilve.com. *E-mail:* peter@peteredelmann.com. *Website:* www.peteredelmann.com.

EDELMANN, Sergei; Russian pianist; b. 22 July 1960, Lvov. *Education:* Juilliard School, USA with Rudolf Firkusny, Aspen Music School with Claude Frank. *Career:* debut public appearance as soloist, Beethoven Piano Concerto No. 1 with Lvov Philharmonic Orchestra 1970; more than 50 concerts throughout Russia; toured widely in Europe and North America as soloist with leading orchestras and as a recitalist; emigrated to US 1979; Prof. of Piano, New York Univ. 1996–2001; Guest Prof. of Piano, Musashino Music Acad., Tokyo 2002–09; numerous recordings. *Honours:* Hon. Prof., Lvov Music Acad. 2010 Gina Bachauer Memorial Scholarship, Julliard School 1979, winner, Young Concert Artists Int. Auditions, prizewinner, Queen Elizabeth Int. Competition, Belgium, 92nd Street YM-YWHA's Shura Cherkassky Recital Award. *Website:* sergei-edelmann.com.

EDER, Claudia; German singer (mezzo-soprano); b. 7 Feb. 1948, Augsburg. *Education:* studied in Munich and Frankfurt with Marianne Scheck. *Career:* debut in Bielefeld 1973, as Offenbach's Nicklausse; sang at Wiesbaden and Gärtnerplatz Theater, Munich from 1975; Vienna Volksoper from 1982, notably in Christoph Rilke by Matthus; Salzburg Festival 1993, as Octavian, Düsseldorf 1995, as Carmen; other roles include Dorabella, Cenerentola, Meg Page and Hansel; concert engagements throughout Austria and Germany.

EDER, György; Hungarian cellist; b. 2 Feb. 1949, Budapest. *Education:* Franz Liszt Acad., Budapest, Yale Univ., The Banff Centre and Univ. of Wisconsin, USA. *Career:* founder mem., Eder String Quartet 1973–96; mem., Kodály String Quartet 1998–; concert tours worldwide; Principal Cellist, Budapest Symphony Orchestra, later Budapest Festival Orchestra for several years. *Recordings:* over 40 albums. *Honours:* prizewinner Evian Competition 1976, Munich Competition 1977.

EDGAR-WILSON, Richard, MA, ARCM (Hons); British singer (tenor); b. (Richard Wilson), 1963, Ipswich, Suffolk, England; m. Dr Jennifer Barnes. *Education:* Ipswich School, Christ's Coll., Cambridge (choral exhbn), Royal Coll. of Music with Edward Brooks (scholarship). *Career:* opera includes Aschenbach in Death in Venice, Acis, Faust in La Damnation de Faust, Tamino in The Magic Flute, Don Ottavio in Don Giovanni, Orfeo, Madwoman in Curlew River, Quint in Turn of the Screw, Beauty in The Triumph of Beauty and Deceit, Gerald Barry, Channel 4 TV; venues include La Scala Milan, La Monnaie Brussels, Palais Garnier Paris, ENO and Royal Opera House, London; concert repertoire includes Evangelist and arias in Bach Passions, Messiah, War Requiem, Monteverdi Vespers, Mozart's Coronation and C minor Masses and Britten's Serenade; works by Kodály, Stainer, Vaughan Williams, Berio and others; solo appearances all over UK, Europe and N America, Israel, Japan, South Africa, Singapore and NZ; has worked with conductors including Trevor Pinnock, Richard Hickox, Charles Mackerras, Robert King, David Willcocks, Philippe Herreweghe, Jeffrey Tate, Roger Norrington; masterclasses at Dartington Summer School, Britten-Pears School, Univ. of London, USA and Singapore, Wolsey Lecturer, Univ. Campus Suffolk 2015. *Films include:* Suffloesen (Norway), Harry Potter and the Deathly Hallows: Part 1 2010, The Hobbit: An Unexpected Journey 2012, The Hobbit: The Desolation of Smaug 2013, The Croods, 2013; Grand Budapest Hotel 2014, Interstellar 2014; Exodus 2014, Mortdecai 2015. *Radio includes:* numerous broadcasts in UK and abroad. *Television includes:* Triumph of Beauty and Deceit (Channel 4). *Recordings include:* Purcell's Dioclesian, Pinnock; Stradella, San Giovanni Battista, Minkowski (Gramophone Award 1993), Schubert, Die Schöne Müllerin, Coates Orchestral Songs with Sir Thomas Allen, Boyce Odes, Messiah, On Wenlock Edge, two vols of Swiss Romantic Lieder, Sullivan Rose of Persia, Bernard Herrmann Moby Dick, Howard Blake The Passion of Mary, Britten Winter Words. *Publications include:* Ballads and Broadsides: The Poetic and Musical Legacy of the Shannon and the Chesapeake; contrib. to Broke of the Shannon and the War of 1812. *Current Management:* c/o Helen Sykes Artists, 100 Felsham Road, Putney, London, SW15 1DQ, England. *Telephone:* (20) 8780-0060. *E-mail:* helen@helensykesartists.co.uk. *Website:* www.helensykesartists.co.uk. *E-mail:* info@richardedgar-wilson.com. *Website:* www.richardedgar-wilson.com.

EDLUND, Mikael; Swedish composer; b. 19 Jan. 1950, Tranås; two d. *Education:* Univ. of Uppsala, State Coll. of Music, Stockholm with I. Lidholm and A. Mellnäs. *Career:* Producer at Fylkingen, Stockholm 1979; teacher in composition, State Coll. of Music, Gothenburg 1985–87; mem. Soc. of Swedish Composers, Swedish Performing Right Soc., Int. Soc. for Contemporary Music (Swedish Section), Fylkingen (Pres. 1996–98). *Compositions include:* The Lost Jugglery for mezzo-soprano, cello, piano and 2 percussionists 1974–77, Trio Sun for clarinet, bassoon and piano 1980, Leaves for 8 female voices, acoustic piano, electric piano, harp and 7 percussionists 1977–81, Brains and Dancin' for string quartet 1981, Fantasia on a City for piano 1981–86, Jord for 5 percussionists 1982, Små Fötter, a miniature for guitar 1982, Music for double wind quintet 1984, Orchids in the Embers for piano 1984, Ajar for orchestra 1988–91, Blue Garden for piano trio 1992–94, Dissolved Window for 21 strings 1986–96, Fanfara, trumpet solo 1995, Un punto nel cortile for flute 1997, Solo for violin 1998–99, Così ballano i Cinghiali for flute, violin, violoncello and piano 2000, Mannen och flugan for male choir 2002, Accanto for piano and string orchestra 2009. *Recordings:* Brains and Dancin', Trio Sun; Orchids in the Embers, Små Fötter; Leaves, Fantasia on a city, Solo for Violin, Jord; Blue Garden, Music for Double Wind Quintet, The Lost Jugglery, Così ballano i Cinghiali, Fra for jazz ensenble 2002. *Honours:* Christ Johnson 1985. *Address:* Backvägen 2, 19135 Sollentuna, Sweden. *E-mail:* mikedlund@tele2.se.

EDUSEI, Kevin John; German conductor; *Principal Conductor, Theater Augsburg*; b. 1976, Bielefeld. *Education:* Berlin Univ. of the Arts, Royal Conservatory, The Hague, Netherlands. *Career:* Prin. Conductor, Theater Bielefeld 2004–07, Theater Augsburg 2007–; Guest Conductor, Konzerthaus Orchestra Berlin, Beethoven Orchestra, Bonn, The Hague Philharmonic Orchestra, State Orchestra of Hannover and Kassel, Ensemble Modern Frankfurt; festivals include Dresden Festival of Contemporary Music, Musica Viva, Munich, Holland Festival. *Honours:* winner, Dmitris Mitropoulos Int. Conducting Competition 2009. *Address:* c/o Theater Augsburg, Kasernstraße 4–6, 86152 Augsburg, Germany (office). *Telephone:* (821) 324-4933 (office). *Fax:* (821) 324-4521 (office). *E-mail:* theater@augsburg.de (office).

EDWARDS, Joan; British singer (mezzo-soprano); b. 1944, London, England. *Education:* London Opera Centre. *Career:* debut as Schwertleite in Die Walküre at Covent Garden; sang with the English Opera Group in Britain and abroad, often with Benjamin Britten conducting; Opera North from 1978 as Marcellina in Le nozze di Figaro, Third Lady (Magic Flute), Mother in Hansel and Gretel, Juno and Minerva in Orpheus in the Underworld, Berta in Il Barbiere di Siviglia and Mary in The Flying Dutchman; many concert performances; appeared on BBC television in La Traviata.

EDWARDS, Owain Tudor, BMus, MMus, PhD; British musicologist, academic and organist; b. 10 Nov. 1940, Ruabon, Wales; m. Grete Strand 1965; one s. two d. *Education:* Univ. of Wales, Bangor. *Career:* Asst Lecturer, Music Dept, Univ. Coll. of Wales, Aberystwyth 1965, Lecturer 1967; Lecturer in Music, Open Univ. 1970; Lecturer in Music, Univ. of Liverpool 1973; Reader and Head of Music History, Norges Musikkhøgskole, Oslo, Norway 1974, Prof. of Music History 1985–2008; Organist, Kroer Church 1980–2006; mem. Norwegian Acad. of Science and Letters. *Compositions:* Adventsgudstjeneste

1986, 155 orgelsatser til gudstjeneste bruk 1992, Reflective Processional, Triumphant Processional, Festive Recessional, Wedding March: four compositions for organ in 100 Processionals and Recessionals 1995, Commutation, Remembrance, Constancy, Contemplation, four pieces in 100 Communion Interludes 1994, Processional Music for ten-piece brass ensemble or for four trumpets with organ 1995, Woodwind Quintet 2007, Brass Quintet 2012, Four kinds of movement, music for ten-piece brass ensemble 2013. *Publications:* Joseph Parry 1841–1903 1970, Beethoven 1972, People, Instruments and the Continuo 1974, Suite, Sonata and Concerto 1974, Matins, Lauds and Vespers for St David's Day 1990, The Penpont Antiphonal 1997, English Eighteenth-Century Concertos – an Inventory and Thematic Catalogue 2005; contrib. to New Grove Dictionary of Music and Musicians, The Music Review, The Musical Quarterly, Proceedings of the Royal Musical Association, Revue Bénédictine, Cantus Planus, Studia Musicologica Norvegica, Svensk tidskrift för musikforskning, Modern Asian Studies, Flerstemmige Innspill, Nordisk Tidskrift, Edda, Nordic Theatre Studies, Welsh History Review, Oral Tradition, Norges Musikk Historie, Det Norske Videnskaps-Akademi Årbok, Neophilologus, Fund & Forskning, Nasjonalbiblioteks utgivelser.

EDWARDS, Ross, MMus; Australian composer; b. 23 Dec. 1943, Sydney, NSW; m. Helen Hopkins 1974; one s. one d. *Education:* New South Wales State Conservatory of Music, Univ. of Sydney, Univ. of Adelaide. *Career:* International Society of Contemporary Music Festivals, Stockholm, 1966, Basel, 1970; mem., numerous professional organizations. *Compositions:* Sonata for nine instruments, Quem Quaeritis (children's nativity play) 1967, Etude for orchestra 1969, Monos I (cello solo), Monos II (piano solo) 1970, Mountain Village in a Clearing Mist for orchestra, Antifon for voices, brass ensemble, organ and percussion, five Little Piano Pieces, The Tower of Remoteness, Concerto for piano and orchestra, Christina's world (chamber opera), Shadow D-Zone 1977, The Hermit of Green Light 1979, Ab Estasis Foribus 1980, Maninya I 1981, II for string quartet, III 1985, IV 1985–86, V 1986, Kumari (solo piano), Laikan I and II, Ten Little Duets 1982, Marimba Dances 1982, Etymalong 1984, Reflections 1985, Flower Songs 1986, Maninyas for violin and orchestra 1988, Varrageh for solo percussion and orchestra 1989, Aria and Transcendental Dance for horn and string orchestra 1990, Sensing (dance piece) 1993, Guitar Concerto 1994, Veni Creator Spiritus (double string quartet) 1994, Enyato III for orchestra 1995, Binyang for clarinet and percussion 1996. *Publications:* contrib. to Music Now, Australian Contemporary Music Quarterly.

EDWARDS, Sian; British conductor; b. 27 Aug. 1959. *Education:* Royal Northern Coll. of Music, studied with Sir Charles Groves, Norman Del Mar and Neeme Järvi and with Prof. I.A. Musin, Leningrad Conservatoire 1983–85. *Career:* has worked with many leading orchestras in UK including London Philharmonic (LPO), Royal Liverpool Philharmonic, Royal Scottish Orchestra, City of Birmingham Symphony, Hallé, BBC Philharmonic, English Chamber orchestras and London Sinfonietta; also with LA Philharmonic Orchestra, The Cleveland Orchestra, Rotterdam Philharmonic Orchestra and other orchestras; operatic debut, Mahagonny, Scottish Opera 1986; other operatic productions include La Traviata and L'Heure Espagnole (Glyndebourne) 1987–88, Katya Kabanova, New Year (Glyndebourne Touring Opera) 1988–90, The Knot Garden, Rigoletto, Il Trovatore (Royal Opera House, Covent Garden) 1988–91, world premiere Greek (Mark Anthony Turnage), Munich Biennale 1988, Edin. Festival 1988, The Gambler (ENO) 1990, Khovanshchina (ENO) 1994, Mahagonny 1995, La Clemenza di Tito 1998, Eugene Onegin 2000, Peter Grimes (ENO) 2001, Don Giovanni, Danish Royal Opera 2001, The Death of Klinghoffer, La Damnation de Faust, Finnish Nat. Opera 2001; Music Dir ENO 1993–95; frequent collaborations with Ensemble Modern, Germany. *Recordings include:* Tchaikovsky orchestral music (Royal Liverpool Philharmonic Orchestra) and Peter and the Wolf, Young Person's Guide to the Orchestra, Tchaikovsky's Fifth symphony (LPO). *Honours:* won first Leeds Conductors' Competition 1984. *Current Management:* c/o Ingpen & Williams, 7 St George's Court, 131 Putney Bridge Road, London, SW15 2PA, England. *Telephone:* (20) 8874-3222. *Fax:* (20) 8877-3113. *E-mail:* info@ingpen.co.uk.

EDWARDS, Terry; British choral director and conductor; b. 1939, London. *Education:* Trinity Coll. of Music. *Career:* formed and directed such groups as London Sinfonietta Voices, Electric Phoenix and London Voices; concerts and recordings with radio choirs, choral societies and choruses world-wide; Season 1988 with the BBC Singers and Choral Society at the Festival Hall, Bach's B minor Mass at Glasgow; concerts with the London Sinfonietta in the Prom Concerts and festival appearances in Berlin, Geneva and Turin; Chorus Master for Georg Solti in three Verdi concerts in Chicago; directed the chorus at the Michael Vyner Memorial at Covent Garden, 1990; Chorus Dir, Royal Opera, Covent Garden 1992–2004; concerts with the Danish Radio Choir, 1991 and works by Erik Bergmann in Finland; directed Sinfonietta Voices in Stockhausen's Stimmung at the Queen Elizabeth Hall, 1997; concerts in 2004 with Netherlands Radio Choir, NDR Choir, Budapest Radio Choir, Nat. Chamber Choir of Ireland. *Film soundtracks:* Harry Potter, Lord of the Rings, Star Wars. *Recordings include:* Messiaen Cinq Rechants, Rachmaninov and Tchaikovsky Vespers, A Boy was Born by Britten; Verdi Choruses and Otello; La Bohème; Ligeti-A-Capella Music; Holliger; Die Jahreszeiten; Don Carlos; Curlew River, and 200 others.

EDWARDS, Warwick Anthony, BMus, MA, PhD; British academic and instrumentalist (early instruments); b. 22 April 1944, Dewsbury, England; m. Jacqueline Freeman, two d. *Education:* King's Coll., Cambridge. *Career:*

Lecturer, Glasgow Univ. 1971–, Sr Lecturer 1986–; Dir, Scottish Early Music Consort 1976–, Glasgow Int. Early Music Festival 1990–. *Recording as director:* Mary's Music: Songs and Dances from the time of Mary Queen of Scots, Scottish Early Music Consort 1984. *Publications:* Music for Mixed Consort (Musica Britannica 40, ed.) 1977, W. Byrd: Latin Motets (from manuscript scores, ed.) 1984; contrib. to Grove's Dictionary (sixth edn), Music and Letters, Proceedings of the Royal Music Association, Early Music, The Consort, British Book News.

EDWORTHY, Joanne Elizabeth, GMus; British singer (mezzo-soprano), singing teacher and examiner; b. 24 July 1970, Epsom, Surrey, England; m. Robert Allen; one s. one d. *Education:* Royal Northern Coll. of Music (RNCM). *Career:* operatic debut as Hansel, Welsh Nat. Opera (WNO) 1995; Siebel in Faust, WNO; Glyndebourne Co. mem. 1996–2000; opera roles have included Hansel and Meg Page at Queen Elizabeth Hall, Xerxes, Almadigi, Marcellina (Figaro), Ramiro (Finta Giardinera) and Irene (Tamerlano) at New Coll., Oxford and Cherubino (Figaro) at Edinburgh Festival; recitals and oratorio include St Martin in the Fields, St John's, Smith Square, Royal Festival Hall, Sheldonian Theatre, Christchurch Cathedral; TV role of Siebel in Gounod's Faust for WNO; vocal tutor, St Paul's Girls' School, Hammersmith, London and Wycombe Abbey; Int. Examiner for Associated Bd of the Royal Schools of Music. *Honours:* Wingate Foundation Scholarship, Countess of Munster Award, Thurston Memorial Award, RNCM, Oncken Song Prize, RNCM. *Address:* 83 Arundel Road, High Wycombe, Bucks., HP12 4ND, England. *E-mail:* joedworthy@outlook.com.

EENSALU, Marika; Estonian singer (mezzo-soprano); b. 20 Sept. 1947, Tallinn. *Education:* studied in Tallinn and with Irina Arkhipova in Moscow. *Career:* sang at the Estonia Theatre, Tallinn from 1980, as Rosina, Carmen, Dorabella, Bradamante in Alcina, Marfa and Ulrica; Savonlinna Festival 1987, with guest appearances in Moscow and throughout Germany, Denmark and Hungary; concert engagements in works by Estonian composers.

EEROLA, Aulikki; Finnish singer (soprano); b. 1947, Tuusula. *Education:* Sibelius Acad., Helsinki, studied with Hilde Zadek and Erik Werba in Vienna. *Career:* debut in concert in Helsinki 1975; Savonlinna Festival 1977, as Pamina in Die Zauberflöte, and appeared widely in Germany, Austria, England, France and North America as concert soloist.

EFRATY, Anat; Israeli singer (soprano); b. 28 June 1966, Tel-Aviv. *Education:* Rubin Acad., Tel-Aviv, studied with Walter Berry in Vienna. *Career:* debut with Mahler's 2nd Symphony, with the Israel Symphony 1993; New Israeli Opera from 1993, as The Bird in Farber's The Journey to Polyphonia, Britten's Helena, Ninetta in The Love for Three Oranges and other roles; US debut, San Diego 1995, in Vivaldi's Gloria; German debut, Stuttgart 1995, as Flaminia in Haydn's Mondo della luna; Théâtre du Châtelet, Paris 1995, as Tebaldo in Don Carlo; other roles include Frasquita, Sophie in Werther, Nannetta and Despina; season 2000–01 as Lulu and Sophie at the Vienna Staatsoper, Lulu at Palermo. *Current Management:* Guy Barzilay Artists, 6B, 360 W 28th Street, New York, 10001, USA. *Telephone:* (212) 741-6118. *Fax:* (212) 741-2558. *E-mail:* kristin@guybarzilayartists.com. *Website:* www.guybarzilayartists.com.

EFREMOV, Alexander, MMus; Russian pianist; b. 8 July 1962, Tomsk, Siberia. *Education:* Far Eastern Inst. of Arts, Vladivostok, Tchaikovsky Conservatory, studied with Prof. Dimitri Bashkirov. *Career:* debut with Far Eastern Philharmonic, solo concert 1985; Far East television, Russia 1980–85; Radio ORF 1997–; American Broadway music concerts, Tonhalle, Zürich 1993; concert in tribute to Geza Anda, Geza Anda House, Zürich 1993; solo concert at Grossmünster 1993; concert with Bruckner Orchester, Linz 1995; chamber concert at Gasteig, Munich 1996; concert with Yevgeny Nesterenko at Vienna Konzerthaus 1996; concert with Vienna Symphonic Orchestra at Bregenz Festival 1996; concert in Theatre de St Quentin en Yvelines, Paris 1997; Répétiteur and solo pianist, Porgy and Bess with Vienna Symphony Orchestra, Bregenz 1998. *Publication:* Schumann and the Aesthetics of German Romanticism 1990.

EGARR, Richard; British keyboard player and conductor; *Music Director, Academy of Ancient Music. Education:* choirboy York Minster, Chetham's School of Music, Manchester, organ scholar Clare Coll., Cambridge, studied with Gustav Leonhardt. *Career:* has worked with ensembles and orchestras, including Chamber Orchestra of Europe, Dutch Radio Chamber Orchestra, Flemish Radio Symphony Orchestra, Netherlands Wind Ensemble, Orchestra of the 18th Century, Scottish Chamber Orchestra, Tafelmusik Toronto; performances as soloist at major music festivals throughout Europe and Japan; mem. of chamber music duo with violinist, Andrew Manze; Dir Acad. of the Begijnhof, Amsterdam; Assoc. Dir Acad. of Ancient Music 2005–06, Music Dir 2006–. *Recordings include:* works by J.S. Bach, Couperin, Frescobaldi, Gibbons, Purcell, complete keyboard works of Johann Jakob Froberger, Per Cembalo Solo, Bach's Goldberg Variations; with Andrew Manze: violin sonatas by Rebel, Pandolfi (Gramophone Award), Handel, Bach, Corelli (Prix Caecilia), Biber's Rosary Sonatas (Edison Award), Mozart's Auernhammer Sonatas; with the Acad. of Ancient Music: complete Bach harpsichord concertos, Handel's Concerti Grossi Op. 3 (Gramophone Award for Best Baroque Instrumental Recording 2007), Handel Organ Concertos Op. 4 (Midem Classical Award for Concerto Recording 2009) 2008, Purcell's Keyboard Suites and Grounds 2008. *Address:* Academy of Ancient Music, 11b King's Parade, , Cambridge, CB2 1SJ, England (office). *Telephone:* (1223)

301509 (office). *E-mail:* info@aam.co.uk (office). *Website:* www.aam.co.uk (office).

EGERTON, Francis, MBE; British singer (tenor); b. 14 July 1930, Limerick, Republic of Ireland. *Career:* early appearances with Scottish Opera, the Glyndebourne Festival and at Sadler's Wells; Covent Garden from 1972 as Iopas in Les Troyens, Beppe, Flute, the Captain in Wozzeck and roles in Carmen, Les Contes d'Hoffmann and La Fanciulla del West; has sung Mime in Siegfried for Scottish Opera and in San Francisco; other roles include, Pedrillo, Strauss's Scaramuccio at Nice, Italian Tenor at Glasgow and Monsieur Taupe in Capriccio at Glyndebourne, Bardolfo in Falstaff at San Francisco, in concert at Chicago and at Los Angeles, conducted by Giulini; sang Il Conte in Cimarosa's Il Fanatico Burlato at Drottningholm, the Captain in Wozzeck at Edinburgh and Los Angeles; season 1990–91 with Mr Upfold in Albert Herring at San Diego, the four tenor roles in Hoffmann in Paris, Goro in Madama Butterfly and Eumaus in Il Ritorno d'Ulisse in Los Angeles; appearances in Prokofiev's The Fiery Angel at the Proms and Covent Garden 1991–92, as the Doctor; season 1995–96 as M le Comte in La Belle Vivette, after Offenbach, for ENO; M. Taupe in Capriccio at Glyndebourne 1998; Falstaff at the Oper der Stadt in Cologne, Billy Budd at the Bastille, Goro in Los Angeles and Missail for Washington Opera; sang the Emperor in Turandot at Covent Garden 2002.

EGGLESTONE, James; Australian singer (tenor); b. Melbourne. *Education:* Victorian Coll. of the Arts, Melba Conservatorium of Music. *Career:* has performed with Melbourne Opera, Opera Australia, West Australia Opera, Opera Queensland and Victorian Opera; concert appearances with Adelaide Symphony Orchestra, Twilite Orchestra Jakarta, Melbourne Symphony Orchestra, Queensland Orchestra, West Australian Symphony Orchestra, Sydney Philharmonia, Canberra Symphony Orchestra, Auckland Philharmonia; appeared at Belcanto Festival, Netherlands, Puccini Festival of Australia, Castlemaine Festival 2005, Adelaide Festival 2008; roles include Henchman in Batavia, Bird Seller in Der Rosenkavalier, Elvino in La Sonnambula, Don Carissimo in La Dirindina, Tamino in The Magic Flute, Nadir in The Pearl Fishers, Pang in Turandot, Ismaele in Nabucco, Francesco in The Gondoliers, Count Almaviva in The Barber of Seville, Rodolfo in La Bohème. *Honours:* Helpmann Award as Best Male Singer in a Supporting Role (for The Love of the Nightingale) 2007. *Current Management:* Patick Togher Artists' Management, Suite 25, 450 Elizabeth Street, Surry Hills, NSW 2010, Australia. *Telephone:* (2) 9319-6255. *Fax:* (2) 9319-7611. *E-mail:* pjtogher@ozemail.com.au. *Website:* www.patricktogher.com.

EGRI, Monika; Hungarian pianist; b. 17 Oct. 1966, Budapest; m. Attila Pertis 1991. *Education:* Bartók Conservatory, Budapest and Music Acad., Vienna. *Career:* performances at Hungarian Days, London 1989, Musikverein, Vienna 1991, Budapest Spring Festival, Carinthian Summer Festival, Austria; co-f. Egri and Pertis piano duo 1980s. *Recordings include:* Journey Around the World 1995, Liszt: Opera Fantasies and Transcriptions for two pianos 1997–98. *Publications:* contrib. to Die Presse, Kronen Zeitung, Piano Journal. *Honours:* Magistra Artium 1994, Grand Prix Internationale du Disque Liszt 1998, prizewinner at many int. competitions. *Current Management:* Künstlermanagement Till Dönch, Roegergasse 24-26/G2, 1090 Vienna, Austria. *Website:* www.egri-pertis.com.

EHDE, John Martin; Swedish cellist and conductor; b. 25 April 1962, Stockholm. *Education:* Royal Acad. of Music, Århus, Denmark, Hochschule für Musik, Vienna. *Career:* debut recital, Royal Acad., Copenhagen 1987; first appeared on Swedish Radio aged 11; recitals and concertos with orchestras throughout Europe and Canada; radio and television broadcasts in Scandinavia, Iceland, Italy, Viet Nam, Hong Kong, Canada; solo cellist, Helsingborg Symphony Orchestra, Sweden 1989–99; speciality, performing the music of Frederick Delius; Cello Concerto, sonata; Young People's Concerts with most Swedish and Danish symphony orchestras (speaker, cellist, conductor); freelance soloist and chamber musician, with tours in Canada, Hong Kong, Viet Nam, Singapore; conducting appointments with Singapore Symphony, Swedish Chamber Orchestra, Helsingborg Symphony Orchestra, amongst others; currently also teacher of cello, Acad. of Music, Malmö; mem. Leopold Stokowski Soc., London, Frederick Delius Soc., England. *Recordings include:* numerous with The Lin Ensemble and with the pianist Carl-Axel Dominique (Sonatas by Alkan, Debussy and Delius) 1997, Cello Concerto by Olof Lindgren 1997. *Honours:* first prize in many Swedish youth competitions, Malmö Lions Club cultural grant 1974, one-year grant for studies in Vienna, Swedish Inst. for Science and Art 1987, awarded scholarship from Foundation of Swedish Conductor, Sten Frykberg 1990. *Address:* Vestervang 34C, 2500 Valby, Denmark (home). *E-mail:* john@ehde.dk (office). *Website:* www.ehde.dk; www.mixte.dk.

EHNES, James, BMus, DMus; Canadian violinist; b. 1976, Brandon, MB. *Education:* Meadowmount School of Music, The Juilliard School, studied with Francis Chaplin and Sally Thomas, Brandon Univ. *Career:* made his solo orchestral debut with Montréal Symphony Orchestra aged thirteen; has performed with numerous orchestras worldwide, including LSO, Philharmonia, BBC Philharmonic, BBC Symphony, Royal Scottish Nat. Orchestra, Scottish Chamber Orchestra, Deutsche Kammerphilharmonie, DSO Berlin, Gurzenich Orchestra, Orchestre de Lyon, Czech Philharmonic, Budapest Festival Orchestra, Finnish Radio Orchestra, NHK Symphony Orchestra, Malaysian Philharmonic, Sydney Symphony, with almost all North American orchestras including those in New York, Chicago, Cleveland, Boston,

Philadelphia, Los Angeles, San Francisco, Pittsburgh, Cincinnati, St Louis, Detroit, Minnesota, St Paul, Houston, Dallas, Vancouver, Calgary, Toronto and Montréal; Fellow, Royal Soc. of Canada 2007–. *Recordings:* Paganini, 24 Caprices 1995, Prokofiev, The Two Violin Sonatas and Five Melodies 2000, Ravel/Debussy/Saint-Saens (with Wendy Chen) 2000, Bach, The Six Sonatas and Partitas for solo violin (Juno Award 2001, Cannes Classical Award for Young Artist of the Year 2002) 2000, Max Bruch, Violin Concertos Nos 1 and 3 (Juno Award 2002, Canadian Independent Music Award 2002) 2001, French Showpieces 2001, Bruch, Concerto No. 2 and Scottish Fantasy (Juno Award 2003) 2002, Fritz Kreisler 2002, Piano Quintets 2003, Romantic Pieces (works of Janáček, Smetana, Dvořák) 2004, Wieniawski, Sarasate 2004, Dallapiccola 2004, Donhányi 2004, Hummel 2004, John Adams, Road Movies 2005, Dvorak Concertos 2005, Bach Sonatas for Violin and Haprsichord, Vol. 1 2005, Bach Sonatas for Violin and Harpsichord, Vol. 2 2006, Mozart Concertos 2006, Barber, Korngold, Walton: Violin Concertos (Grammy Award for Best Instrumental Soloist Performance 2008, Juno Award for Classical Album of the Year 2008) 2006, Elgar Violin Concerto, with Philharmonia Orchestra (Gramophone Award for Best Concerto Recording 2008) 2007, Schoenfeld 2007, Homage (Juno Award for Classical Album of the Year) 2009, Bartok: Chamber Works for Violin Volume 3 (Juno Award for Classical Album of the Year (Solo or Chamber Ensemble) 2015) 2014. *Honours:* Canadian Music Competition grand prize in strings 1987, first prize in strings 1988, Ivan Galamian Memorial Award, Canada Council for the Arts Virginia Parker Prize 1997, Avery Fisher Career Grant 2005. *Current Management:* Earl G. Blackburn, Opus 3 Artists, 470 Park Avenue South, 9th Floor North, New York, NY 10016, USA. *Telephone:* (212) 584-7514. *E-mail:* EBlackburn@opus3artists.com. *Website:* www.opus3artists.com; www.jamesehnes.com.

EINAUDI, Ludovico; Italian composer and pianist; b. 23 Nov. 1955, Turin; s. of Giulio Einaudi. *Education:* Conservatorio Verdi, Milan, Tanglewood Festival, USA, studied with Luciano Berio. *Career:* took part in Festival of the Desert, Mali 2003. *Film and TV scores include:* Da Qualche Parte in Città 1994, Acquario 1996, Aprile 1998, Treno di Panna 1998, Fuori Dal Mondo 1999, Vita Altrui 2000, Giorni Dispari 2000, Alexandria 2001, Luce Dei Miei Occhi 2001 (Italian Music Award), Le Parole di Mio Padre 2002, Doctor Zhivago (Gold Medal, New York Film Festival) 2002, Sotto Falso Nome (Best Film Score, Avignon Festival) 2004, This Is England 2006, Starfish Tango 2006, I'm Still Here 2010, J. Edgar 2012, The Water Diviner 2014, This is England '90 2015. *Recordings:* Le Onde 1996, Stanze 1997, Eden Roc 1999, I Giorni 2002, Echoes: The Einaudi Collection 2004, La Scala Concert 03.03.03 2004, Una Mattina 2004, Diario Mali 2006, Divenire 2007, Cloud Land 2009, Islands: Essential Einaudi 2011, In a Time Lapse 2013, Elements 2015. *Honours:* Ordine di Merito della Repubblica Italiana. *Website:* www.ludovicoeinaudi.com.

EIRIKSDOTTIR, Karolina, MMus; Icelandic composer; b. 10 Jan. 1951, Reykjavík; m. Thorsteinn Hannesson 1974, one d. *Education:* Reykjavík Coll., Reykjavík Coll. of Music, Univ. of Michigan, USA. *Career:* performances of works across Europe; mem. Soc. of Icelandic Composers. *Compositions include:* Notes for orchestra, Sonans for orchestra, Klifur for orchestra, Five Pieces for chamber orchestra, Rondo and Rhapsody for piano, In Vultu Solis for violin, Trio for violin, cello and piano, Six Poems from the Japanese, Some Days for voice and instruments, Nagon har jag sett (opera), Rhapsody in C, Land Possessed by Poems for baritone and piano, I Have Seen Someone (opera) 1988, Sinfonietta for orchestra 1992, Six Movements for string quartet 1992, Three Paragraphs for orchestra 1993, Concerto for clarinet and orchestra 1994, Living by the Sea (collection of songs) 1997, Man Alive (chamber opera) 1999, also solo pieces for clarinet, harpsichord, cello, violin, guitar, and chamber music.

EISEN, Cliff, BA, MA, PhD; Canadian musicologist and academic; *Professor of Music, King's College London. Education:* Univ. of Toronto, Cornell Univ., USA. *Career:* Assoc. Ed., New Köchel Catalogue; Gen. Ed., Oxford Companion to Mozart; Reader in Historical Musicology, King's Coll., London 1997, now Prof. of Music; served as musicological adviser to Robert Levin, Christopher Hogwood and Acad. of Ancient Music for recordings of the Mozart's piano concertos. *Publications include:* Mozart Studies (ed. and contrib.) 1991, New Mozart Documents 1991, Wolfgang Amadeus Mozart, Symphony K. 425 ('Linz') 1992, Mozarts Streichquintette: Beiträge zum musikalischen Satz, zum Gattungskontext und zu Quellenfragen (co-ed. with W. D. Seiffert, also contrib.) 1994, Orchestral Music in Salzburg, 1750–1780 (co-author) 1994, Mozart Studies 2 (ed. and contrib.) 1997, Four Viennese String Quintets 1998, A Companion to Mozart's Piano Concertos (with Arthur Hutchings) 1998, The New Grove Mozart (with Stanley Sadie) 2000, W. A. Mozart: Piano Concerto in E-flat, KV 271 (with Robert Levin) 2000, Mozart: A Life in Letters (with Stewart Spencer) 2006, The Cambridge Mozart Encyclopedia (with Simon P. Keefe) 2006, Coll' Astuzia, Col Giudizio: Essays in Honor of Neal Zaslaw 2009; contribs to Journal of the Royal Musical Asscn, Early Music, numerous chapters in academic works. *Address:* Department of Music, King's College London, Strand, London, WC2R 2LS, England (office). *Telephone:* (20) 7848-2307 (office). *Fax:* (20) 7848-2326 (office). *E-mail:* cliff.eisen@kcl.ac.uk (office). *Website:* www.kcl.ac.uk/artshums/depts/music/people/acad/eisen/index.aspx (office).

EISMA, Will Leendert; Dutch composer and violinist; b. 13 May 1929, Sungailiat, Indonesia; m. Wilhelmina A. Reeser 1960; one s. one d. *Education:* Conservatory of Rotterdam, Accademia di Santa Cecilia, Rome and Inst. for Sonology, Utrecht. *Career:* violinist, Rotterdam Philharmonic 1953–59,

Società Corelli chamber orchestra 1960–61, Radio Hilversum chamber orchestra 1961–89; mem. electro-instrumental group, ICE; Dir Studio for Electronic Music, Five Roses. *Compositions include:* four Concerti for orchestra (one for two violins and orchestra) 1961, Taurus-A 1963, Volumina for orchestra 1964, Concerti for oboe and horn 1973, chamber and electronic music 1970, Concerto for string trio and orchestra 1974, Concerto for percussion 1979, Concerto for English horn 1981, Concerto for five violas 1982, Du dehors–Du dedans for mezzo-soprano, orchestra and electronics 1983, Silver-Plated Bronze for double bass and orchestra 1986, Te Deum 1988, Passo del Diavolo for orchestra 1988, Mawar jiwa for gamelan 1992, Uguisu for gamelan 1997, String Quartet No. 5 2001, Spijkerboor for winds, guitars and piano 2002, Concerto for violin and orchestra 2006, Lazulite for saxophone quartet 2008, La Salamandre for voice and 16 instruments 2009, String Quartet No. 6 2013. *Address:* Oude Amersfoortsweg 206, 1212 AL, Hilversum, The Netherlands (home).

EJSING, Mette; Danish singer (mezzo-soprano); b. 9 Nov. 1954, Silkeborg. *Education:* studied in Copenhagen with Ulrik Cold and Ingrid Bjoner. *Career:* sang with the Stuttgart Staatsoper 1991–95; St Gallen 1992, as the Countess in The Queen of Spades; Erda in Wagner's Ring at Karlsruhe, Århus, Vienna Staatsoper 1995 and La Scala, Milan 1996; Staatsoper Berlin 1995, in Der Rosenkavalier, Die Zauberflöte and Der fliegende Holländer; Bayreuth Festival in Parsifal and Die Walküre; sang Erda in Siegfried at Helsinki 1998; season 1999–2000 as Erda in Siegfried at Sydney and Trieste, Erda and First Norn at Bayreuth; concerts in San Francisco, Berlin and elsewhere. *Current Management:* c/o Tivoli Artists Management, 3 Vesterbrogade, PO Box 233, 1630 Copenhagen V, Denmark. *Telephone:* 33-75-04-00. *Fax:* 33-75-03-75. *E-mail:* mail@tivoli.dk. *Website:* www.tivoliartists.com.

EK, Harald; Swedish singer (tenor); b. 1936, Jonkoping. *Education:* studied in Gothenburg with G. Kjellertz and R. Jacobson. *Career:* debut in Gothenburg 1966 in Die Lustige Witwe; sang at Drottningholm 1967, as Almaviva in Paisiello's Il Barbiere di Siviglia, Stadtstheater Berne 1969–72, and Bayreuth Festival 1971 in Der fliegende Holländer and Das Rheingold; mem., Staatsoper Hamburg 1972–75, Zürich Opera from 1975; sang Don José at Gothenburg 1988; other roles include Don Ottavio, Tamino, Hoffmann, Comte Ory, Cavaradossi, Tom Rakewell and Alfred in Die Fledermaus. *Recordings include:* Der fliegende Holländer.

EKLÖF, Marianne; Swedish singer (mezzo-soprano); b. 15 March 1956. *Education:* studied in Stockholm, Juilliard School, New York, and in London with Vera Rozsa. *Career:* sang in opera at Malmö from 1985, as Carmen and in the premiere of Werle's Midsummer Night's Dream; Stockholm Folkoperan from 1990, in Samson et Dalila and Les Contes d'Hoffmann; Jutland Opera, Århus 1995, as Waltraute in Götterdämmerung; sang Mme de la Motte in the British premiere of Marie Antoinette by Daniel Börtz, at Brighton; many concert engagements. *Recordings include:* Grieg's Peer Gynt, Sigurd Josalfar. *Current Management:* Ann Braathen Artist Management, Folkskolegatan 5, 11735 Stockholm, Sweden. *Telephone:* (8) 55690850. *Fax:* (8) 55690851. *E-mail:* info@braathenmanagement.com. *Website:* www .braathenmanagement.com.

EKLUND, Anna; Swedish singer (soprano); b. 1964. *Education:* Stockholm Coll. of Music and State Opera School. *Career:* debut at Stockholm Royal Opera as Papagena; sang in staged version of Carmina Burana at Stockholm 1991; roles include Isamene in Haeffner's Elektra at Drottningholm, Novis Elisabeth in Forsell's Riket ar Ditt, the Queen of Night and Serpetta in La Finta Giardiniera; season 1991–92 in the St Matthew Passion under Philippe Herreweghe in Sweden, Barcelona and Madrid, Betty in Salieri's Falstaff at Drottningholm; season 1992–93 as Zémire in Grétry's Zémire et Azor at Drottningholm, and the leading female role in the premiere of Amorina by Lars Runsten at the Royal Opera Stockholm.

ELCHLEPP, Isolde; French singer (mezzo-soprano); b. 1952, Strasbourg. *Education:* Opera School, Bavarian State Opera. *Career:* sang first at Bremen, notably as The Woman in Schoenberg's Erwartung 1985; Wiesbaden from 1986 as Wagner's Venus, Fricka and Waltraute, and Azucena in Il Trovatore; Hanover Opera as Carmen, Ortrud, Santuzza, Octavian, the Composer, Amneris and Kundry; Deutsche Oper Berlin 1990, as Ortrud; guest appearances in Düsseldorf, Mannheim, Brunswick, Karlsruhe, Basle (Herodias in Salome) and Brussels; concert repertory includes Schoenberg's Pierrot Lunaire; guest in Tokyo in Erwartung; also sang Elektra with Oslo Philharmonic; Troades, Frankfurt Opera; Fricka in Das Rheingold and Die Walküre at Hanover 1992 as well as Hostess in premiere of Reimann's Das Schloss, Deutsche Oper Berlin; debut at Bayreuth Festival as Ortrud 1993; sang the Woman in Erwartung for Netherlands Opera; Marie in Wozzeck at Turin 1998; sang Brünnhilde at Hannover 1999, and Elektra at Komische Oper Berlin 2001.

ELDER, Sir Mark Philip, Kt, CBE, BA, MA (Hons); British conductor; *Music Director, Hallé Orchestra;* b. 2 June 1947, Hexham; s. of John Elder and Helen Elder; m. Amanda Jane Stein 1980; one d. *Education:* Bryanston School and Corpus Christi Coll., Cambridge. *Career:* mem. music staff, Wexford Festival 1969–70; Chorus Master and Asst Conductor Glyndebourne 1970–71; mem. music staff, Royal Opera House, Covent Garden 1970–72; Staff Conductor, Australian Opera 1972–74; Staff Conductor, ENO 1974–77, Assoc. Conductor 1977–79, Music Dir 1979–93; Prin. Guest Conductor London Mozart Players 1980–83, BBC Symphony Orchestra 1982–85, City of Birmingham Symphony Orchestra 1992–95; Music Dir Rochester Philharmonic Orchestra, NY

1989–94, Hallé Orchestra, Manchester, UK 2000–; Artistic Dir Opera Rara 2011–; Pres. London Philharmonic Choir 2014–. *Recordings include:* with Hallé Orchestra, Choir and Youth Chorus: Elgar: The Apostles (BBC Music Magazine Choral Award and Recording of the Year 2013, Gramophone Choral Award 2013). *Honours:* Hon. FRNCM; Hon. Fellow, Corpus Christi Coll., Cambridge 2010; Hon. mem. Royal Philharmonic Soc. 2011; Dr hc (Manchester) 2003, (Sheffield) 2006, (Open Univ.) 2009, (RAM) 2012; Olivier Award for Outstanding Contrib. to Opera 1990, Royal Philharmonic Soc. Award for Conductor 2006. *Current Management:* c/o Ingpen & Williams, 7 St George's Court, 131 Putney Bridge Road, London, SW15 2PA, England. *Telephone:* (20) 8874-3222. *E-mail:* info@ingpen.co.uk. *Website:* www.ingpen.co.uk. *Address:* Hallé Concerts Society, The Bridgewater Hall, Manchester, M1 5HA, England (home). *Website:* www.halle.co.uk (office).

ELIAS, Brian David; British composer; b. 30 Aug. 1948, Bombay, India; s. of Albert Elias and Julie Elias. *Education:* Royal Coll. of Music, studied with Elisabeth Lutyens. *Career:* freelance ed., arranger and copyist; clerk and asst statistician 1972–78; full-time composer, with some teaching commitments. *Compositions include:* La Chevelure for soprano and chamber orchestra, Somnia for tenor and orchestra, L'Eylah for orchestra, commissioned by BBC for Promenade Concerts 1984, Tzigane for solo violin, Peroration for solo soprano, Geranos for chamber ensemble, commissioned by The Fires of London 1985, Five songs to Poems by Irina Ratushinskaya for mezzo-soprano and orchestra commissioned by BBC for Winter Season 1989–90, The Judas Tree, ballet score commissioned by The Royal Ballet choreographed by Kenneth MacMillan 1992, Fanfare, Royal Ballet, choreographed by Matthew Hart 1993, Laments for mezzo-soprano, six female voices and orchestra (commissioned by BBC for the Cheltenham Festival 1998), The House That Jack Built for orchestra commissioned by the BBC for Winter Season 2001–02, Three Songs (Christina Rossetti), A Talisman for bass-baritone and chamber orchestra (commissioned by Cheltenham Int. Festival of Music, Doubles for orchestra (British Composer Award, Orchestral category 2010) 2009, Electra Mourns for mezzo soprano, cor anglais & strings (British Composer Award, Vocal Category 2013) 2012. *Recordings:* Peroration, 5 Songs to Poems by Irina Ratushinskaya, The Judas Tree, Laments, Moto Perpetuo, Fantasia, Electra Mourns Proms 2012, Quartet commissioned by Jerusalem String Quartet 2012. *Honours:* Jt Second Prize for Proverbs of Hell, Radcliffe Music Award 1977. *Address:* c/o Chester Music, Music Sales Ltd, 14–15 Berners Street, London, W1T 3LJ, England. *Telephone:* (20) 7612-7400. *E-mail:* promotion@ musicsales.co.uk. *Website:* www.chesternovello.com.

ELIAS, Jorge; Spanish singer (tenor); b. 1973. *Education:* Queen Sofia School of Music, Madrid with Alfredo Kraus. *Career:* appearances throughout Spain from 1995, including Oviedo Opera, Il Barbiere di Siviglia, Bilbao and Madrid; Edgardo in Lucia di Lammermoor at Bergamo 1997; Verdi's I Masnadieri at Piacenza, Don Carlos at Santander Festival; Rodolfo in La Bohème at Lucca; season 1999–2000 with Bruckner's Te Deum at Teatro Comunale in Florence under Zubin Mehta; other concerts include Donizetti's Requiem at Bergamo. *Honours:* Placido Domingo Trophy, first prize Ciudad de Logzaño Opera Contest, second prize, Francisco Slouso Int. Opera Contest. *E-mail:* info@tenorjorgeelias.com. *Website:* www.tenorjorgeelias.com.

ELIAS, Rosalind; American singer and opera director; b. Lowell, MA. *Education:* New England Conservatory, Boston, Accademia di Santa Cecilia, Rome, studied with Daniel Ferro in New York. *Career:* sang with New England Opera 1948–52; Metropolitan Opera from 1954 as Cherubino, Dorabella, Rosina and Hansel, and in the premieres of Barber's Vanessa, and Antony and Cleopatra; Scottish Opera 1970 as Rossini's La Cenerentola; Vienna Staatsoper 1972 as Carmen; Glyndebourne Festival 1975 as Baba the Turk in The Rake's Progress; other appearances in Hamburg, Monte Carlo, Barcelona, Lisbon and Aix-en-Provence; other roles include Verdi's Amneris and Azucena, Massenet's Charlotte and Giulietta in Les Contes d'Hoffmann; sang Herodias in Salome at Houston 1987; produced Carmen at Cincinnati 1988 and Il Barbiere di Siviglia for Opera Pacific, Costa Mesa 1989; sang Mistress Quickly in Falstaff at Boston 1996; Italian debut as Old Lady in Bernstein's Candide, Turin 1997; sang the Baroness in Vanessa at Monte Carlo 2001. *Recordings:* La Gioconda, La Forza del Destino, Il Trovatore, Falstaff, Madama Butterfly, Rigoletto, Der fliegende Holländer.

ELIASSON, Sven Olaf; Swedish singer (tenor); b. 4 April 1933, Boliden. *Education:* Royal Music Acad. *Career:* sang at Oslo from 1961, Stockholm from 1965; guest appearances at Hamburg Staatsoper 1968–74; further engagements at Zürich, Düsseldorf and Frankfurt; Glyndebourne 1967 as Don Ottavio; Drottningholm Opera 1967 as Belmonte in Die Entführung; Zürich Opera 1968 and 1975 as Pfitzner's Palestrina and in premiere of Klebe's Ein Wahrer Held; Stockholm Opera 1970 in premiere of Rosenberg's Hus Med Dubbel Ingang; sang Schoenberg's Aron with Hamburg Staatsoper in Israel 1974; other roles include Don José, Riccardo in Un Ballo in Maschera, Peter Grimes and Tom Rakewell in The Rake's Progress; Dir Oslo Opera from 1983; sang Siegmund at Århus 1987. *Recordings include:* Il Ritorno d'Ulisse in Patria by Monteverdi; Video of Swedish Opera production of Die Meistersinger.

ELLIOTT, Alasdair; British singer (tenor) and teacher; b. 18 July 1954, Hamilton, Scotland. *Education:* Royal Scottish Acad. of Music and Drama, Glasgow, Guildhall School of Music, London with Laura Sarti, Britten Pears School with Peter Pears, Nat. Opera Studio, masterclasses with Graziella Schutti, Elizabeth Schwartzkopf, Hugh Cuenod, Nancy Evans, Thomas Allan and John Copley. *Career:* roles include Mime for Scottish Opera's production of Der Ring; Pong (Turandot) for Teatro Real, Madrid, Royal Opera, Covent Garden and Reisopera, Netherlands; Monostatos (Die Zauberflöte)) for Royal Opera, Covent Garden, ENO, Glyndebourne Touring Opera and in Lisbon; Red Whiskers (Billy Budd) and the Gamekeeper (Rusalka) for Glyndebourne Festival Opera; Bardolpho and Ciaus (Falstaff) for Royal Opera, Scottish Opera, Glyndebourne Festival Opera and with London Symphony Orchestra; First and Fourth Jew (Salome) for Opera Royal de la Monnaie, ENO, Welsh National Opera (WNO) and Netherlands Opera, also recorded for Chandos; other operatic roles include Brighella (Ariadne auf Naxos) for Royal Opera and ENO; Snout (A Midsummer Night's Dream) for Glyndebourne Festival Opera; Goro (Madama Butterfly) for Royal Opera, Opera North and Holland Park Opera; Valzacchi (Der Rosenkavalier) for ENO and Scottish Opera; Guidobald Usodimare (Die Gezeichneten) for Netherlands Opera; David (Die Meistersinger) for Staatstheatre Stuttgart; Vitek (The Makropulos Case) and Shvonder (Dog's Heart) for ENO; Sellem (The Rake's Progress) in Israel and Lille; Andres (Wozzeck) for Royal Opera and Israeli Opera; Red Whiskers (Billy Budd) with London Symphony Orchestra; Nick (Fanciulla del West) for Opera Zuid; Cabaretier (Benvenuto Cellini) with London Symphony Orchestra; Der Bucklige (Die Frau ohne Schatten) with Netherlands Radio Philharmonic; performances of contemporary music, including Festus in world premiere of Legende for Netherlands Opera in the Concertgebouw, Der Kanzler and Der Schreiber in Schreker's Der Schatzgräber for Netherlands Opera; Vova in Schnittke's Life with an Idiot for both ENO and Scottish Opera, and The Servant in world premiere of John Buller's The Bacchae for ENO; has worked with leading conductors including Bernard Haitink, Sir Colin Davis, Sir Charles Mackerras, Valdimir Jurovsky, Sir Richard Armstrong, Sir Andrew Davis, Christian Thielemann, Daniele Gatti and Sir Antonio Pappano; has performed regularly in concert with the London Symphony Orchestra, Monteverdi Choir, English Concert and London Mozart Players; future plans include Bardolpho (Falstaff), Don Curzio (Le Nozze di Figaro) and the Emperor (Turandot) for Royal Opera, Covent Garden; Spoletta (Tosca) for Seattle Opera; (Die Meistersinger von Nürnberg) for Glyndebourne Festival Opera. *Recordings include:* Falstaff (Dr. Ciaus) under Sir Colin Davis (Grammy Award 2005), Rusalka (Gamekeeper), Salome (Fourth Jew), Billy Budd (Red Whiskers) with Daniel Harding and the London Symphony Orchestra, Benvenuto Cellini (Cabaretier) with Sir Colin Davis and the London Symphony Orchestra, Die Meistersinger von Nurenberg for Royal Opera (Heritage Series) with Bernard Haitink. *Current Management:* c/o AOR Management Inc., 6910 Roosevelt Way NE, PMB 221, Seattle, WA 98115, USA. *Telephone:* (206) 729-6160. *Fax:* (206) 985-8499. *E-mail:* aormanagementuk@earthlink.net. *Website:* www.aormanagementuk.com. *E-mail:* alsings@mac.com (office). *Website:* www.alasdairelliott.com.

ELLIOTT, Anthony, BMus; American conductor and cellist; *Professor of Cello, University of Michigan, Ann Arbor;* b. 3 Sept. 1948, Rome, NY; m. Paula Sokol 1975, four d. *Education:* Rome Free Acad., Rome, NY, Indiana Univ. School of Music. *Career:* debut at St Lawrence Centre of Performing Arts, Toronto, ON, Canada; soloist with Detroit Symphony, New York Philharmonic, CBC Toronto Orchestra, Minnesota Orchestra, Vancouver Symphony, Colorado Philharmonic; recitals broadcast on NET, NPR and CBC, including premiere performances of 20th-Century compositions; fmr Musical Dir, Univ. Symphony Orchestra, Western Michigan Univ.; fmr Asst Music Dir, Marrowstone Music Festival; fmr Prof. of Cello, Univ. of Houston; fmr Music Dir, Houston Youth Symphony and Ballet; Visiting Prof., Eastman School of Music, Indiana Univ.; Prof. of Cello, Univ. of Michigan, Ann Arbor; appeared with present and former concertmaster of Berlin Philharmonic, Concertgebouw Orchestra, Philadelphia Orchestra, Chicago Symphony, Minnesota Orchestra, Toronto Symphony, Montréal Symphony, and with mems of Juilliard, Emerson, and Concord String Quartets; also appeared with mems of Chamber Music Soc. of Lincoln Center and with Quarter Canada; conducted: Sphinx Symphony, Sphinx Chamber Orchestra, Scott Joplin Chamber Orchestra, Vancouver Chamber Players, Kent/Blossom Chamber Orchestra, Kitchener-Waterloo Symphony, Prince George's Symphony Orchestra, Plymouth Symphony, All Northwest Orchestra, the All Michigan Honors Orchestra, the Youth Arts Festival Orchestra, the All State Orchestras of Alabama, Alaska, Florida, Maryland, North Carolina, North Dakota, Texas, and Washington. *Recordings:* solo cellist: Ravel's Mother Goose (complete ballet), Ravel's La Valse and Alborada del Gracioso, Rimsky-Korsakov's Russian Easter Overture, Holst's The Planets, Koch International Classics Series (Music by Slav Composers), Lamentations Suite by Coleridge Taylor, Sonata for cello and piano Op No. 3 by Paul Hindemith, Cello music by Rachmaninov 2002, Slavic Music for Cello, French Music for Cello, Music for Cello and Piano by African-American Composers, The Complete Beethoven Sonatas and Variations for Cello and Piano, The Complete Bach Unaccompanied Suites for Cello. *Honours:* gold medal Feuermann Memorial Int. Cello Solo Competition. *Address:* c/o School of Music, University of Michigan, Ann Arbor, MI 48109-2085, USA (office). *E-mail:* aelliot@umich.edu (office). *Website:* www.anthonyelliott.net.

ELLIOTT, Marie; British singer (soprano); b. 1970, Devon, England. *Education:* Guildhall School with Johanna Peters, Royal Acad. of Music, studied with Janet Baker, Sarah Walker and Brigitte Fassbaender. *Career:* solo oratorio appearances in Mozart's Requiem at Gloucester Cathedral; The Apostles by Elgar at Wells, Mendelssohn's Elijah, Pergolesi's Stabat Mater at St Martin-in-the-Fields, and Bach's Christmas Oratorio; opera debut as Teodata in Flavio, for the London Handel Festival 2001; other roles include

Dorabella, Rosina, Britten's Lucretia, and Isolier in Le Comte Ory; solo recital at St James's Piccadilly and Verdi Requiem at Bedford 2001. *Honours:* RAM Lucille Graham Award, RAM Isabel Jay Prize.

ELLIOTT, Paul, BA, MA (Oxon.), CMVT; American/British singer (tenor) and teacher; *Professor Emeritus, Early Music Institute, Jacobs School of Music, Indiana University;* b. (Paul Murray Christopher Elliott), 19 March 1950, Macclesfield, Cheshire, England; s. of William Murray Elliott and Millicent Mason; m. Wendy Gillespie 1982; two s. *Education:* chorister, St Paul's Cathedral, London, The King's School, Canterbury, Magdalen Coll., Oxford, studied with David Johnston and Peter Pears. *Career:* vicar choral, St Paul's Cathedral, London 1972–75; mem. John Alldis Choir 1972–76, Cantores in Ecclesia 1972–76, Schütz Choir of London 1972–78, Monteverdi Choir 1973–78; Founder-mem. Hilliard Ensemble 1974–78, London Early Music Group 1976–79; vocal consort mem. of various consorts; tours of Europe and USA as solo concert artist; operatic engagements include Handel's Acis in St Gallen 1984, Mozart's Belmonte, Indiana Univ. 1988, Mozart's Arbace in Chicago 1988; Artist-in-Residence, Washington Univ., St Louis 1984–85; Visiting Lecturer, Indiana Univ. School of Music, Bloomington 1985–87, Assoc. Prof. of Music 1987–92, apptd Prof. of Music 1992, now Prof. Emer., apptd Dir Early Music Inst., Jacobs School of Music 2009, apptd Chair. 2010; mem. Theatre of Voices 1991–; various workshops and seminars; Pres. McClosky Inst. of Voice, Boston, USA 2003 (Certified McClosky Voice Technician 2000); mem. Nat. Early Music Asscn (UK), Early Music America, Nat. Asscn of Teachers of Singing, American Asscn of Univ. Profs. *Recordings:* as mem. of various vocal ensembles; as soloist with works by Bach, Handel, Purcell. *Honours:* Hon. Fellow, Acad. of St Cecilia (UK) 2007. *E-mail:* elliottp@indiana.edu (office). *Website:* mypage.iu.edu/~elliottp (office).

ELLIS, Brent; American singer (baritone); b. 20 June 1944, Kansas City, MO. *Education:* studied with Daniel Ferro in New York and with Luigi Ricci in Rome. *Career:* debut in Washington, DC 1967 in the premiere of Ginastera's Bomarzo; Santa Fe Opera from 1972 notably as Mozart's Figaro, the 1982 premiere of Rochberg's The Confidence Man and as Kunrad in Strauss's Feuersnot; New York City Opera debut 1974 as Ottone in L'Incoronazione di Poppea; Glyndebourne from 1977 as Ford in Falstaff, Marcello, Don Giovanni and Germont in the Peter Hall production of La Traviata; Metropolitan Opera from 1979 as Silvio in Pagliacci, Rossini's Figaro and Donizetti's Belcore; Opera North, Leeds as Scarpia and Macbeth; WNO as Zurga in Les Pêcheurs de Perles; Cologne Opera from 1984 in La Gazza Ladra, Wozzeck, Rigoletto and Eine Florentinische Tragödie by Zemlinsky; appearances in the premieres of Pasatieri's Washington Square for Michigan Opera and The Seagull for Seattle Opera; sang Germont at Glyndebourne 1987, Santa Fe 1989, also Kunrad in Feuersnot 1988; San Francisco 1989 as Iago, followed by Rigoletto at Covent Garden; season 1992 as Amonasro at Seattle; sang Dandini in Cenerentola at Toronto 1996; sang Macbeth for New Israeli Opera 2000; concert appearances in Mahler's 8th Symphony with the Chicago Symphony and with orchestras in San Francisco, Minnesota, Baltimore, Houston and Denver; Great Woods Festival with Michael Tilson Thomas.

ELLIS, David; British singer (baritone); b. 1970, England. *Education:* Royal Northern College of Music. *Career:* debut as Silvio in Pagliacci with Iceland Opera; Appearances as Don Giovanni with English Touring Opera, and Marcello and Donizetti's Talbot for Scottish Opera; Member of Covent Garden Opera from 1994 in Carmen, Die Meistersinger, Un Ballo in Maschera, Peter Grimes, Fanciulla del West, Salome and Billy Budd; Other roles include Belcore, Guglielmo and Posa in Don Carlos.

ELLIS, David, FRNCM, ARMCM; British composer; b. 10 March 1933, Liverpool, England. *Education:* Royal Manchester Coll. of Music. *Career:* Music Producer, BBC 1964–77, Head of Music 1977–86; Artistic Dir, Northern Chamber Orchestra 1986–94; Assoc. Dir, Orquestra Sinfónica Portuguesa 1994. *Compositions:* Sinfonietta 1953, String Trio 1954, Dewpoint for soprano, clarinet and strings 1955, Piano Sonata, Diversions on a theme of Purcell for strings 1956, Violin Concerto 1958, Piano Concerto 1961, Opera Crito 1963, Magnificat and Nunc Dimittis for choir and organ 1964, Elegy for orchestra 1966, Fanfares and Cadenzas for orchestra 1968, Carols for an Island Christmas 1971, Symphony No. 1 1973, Solus for strings 1973, L for orchestra 1977, Sonata for solo double bass 1977, String Quartet No. 1 1980, Berceuse for clarinet and piano 1981, Aubade for horn and piano 1981, Suite Française for strings 1987, Contraprovisations 1994, Symphony No. 2 1995, String Quartet No. 2 1996, Four Songs 1998, A Little Cantata 1998, Three Note Variables for Piano 1998, Symphony No. 3 1998–99, Shadows in Blue 1999, Epiphany Nocturne 1999, Island Seascape 1999, Old Willows 2000, Attleborough Tuckets 2000, Rondo in Blue Minor for brass band 2001, Contra Partita per Bassi 2001, String Quartet No. 3 2002, Concerto for bassoon and strings 2002, Vetrate di Ricercata for organ 2002. *Recordings:* An Image of Truth 1999, Fast Forward 1999, Old City: New Image 2002. *Honours:* Royal Philharmonic Prize 1956, Royal Coll. of Music Patrons' Award 1956, Theodore Holland Award 1957, Royal Manchester Institution Silver Medal 1957, Ricordi Prize 1957. *E-mail:* delliscomposer@aol.com (office). *Website:* www.davidellis-composer.co.uk.

ELLIS, Gregory Charles, DipRAM, ARAM, MA, FRAM; British violinist; *First Violin and Leader, Vanbrugh String Quartet;* b. 3 Nov. 1960, Preston, Lancs., England; m. Leslie Gail Toney 1985; one s. two d. *Education:* Royal Acad. of Music, London, Northern Illinois Univ., USA with Shmuel Ashkenasi, studied with Carmel Kaine and Frederick Grinke. *Career:* debut in Wigmore Hall,

London; First Violinist and Leader, Vanbrugh String Quartet, resident at Radio Telefis Éireann 1986–; masterclasses in UK, Sweden, Norway, Brazil, China, Singapore, Malaysia, USA; frequent concerto performances on tour in Europe, the Far East, N and S America; broadcasts on radio and TV worldwide; mem. Bd of Dirs West Cork Music 1996–2008; Founder and Dir Vanbrugh Quartet Scholarship Fund. *Radio:* extensive broadcasts on RTÉ (Ireland), BBC, various US and European stations. *Recordings include:* more than 30 CDs on various labels, including complete Beethoven cycle. *Honours:* winner of several prizes, including Royal Soc. of Arts Scholarship, Martin Musical Award, Nat. Entertainment Award (Ireland), London/Portsmouth Int. String Quartet Competition (winner with Vanbrugh String Quartet) 1988. *Address:* Vanbrugh House, Castle Treasure, Douglas, Co. Cork, Ireland (home). *E-mail:* gregoryellis1@me.com (office). *Website:* www.vanbrughquartet.com (office).

ELLIS, James Antony, MA, MMus; British composer and conductor; b. 5 March 1954, Ashton-under-Lyne, England; m. Fiona Anne Johnson 1978, four d. *Education:* King's Coll., Cambridge, King's Coll. London. *Career:* fmr editorial asst, Music Analysis; violinist mem., Royal Philharmonic Orchestra 1977–80, Philharmonia 1980–81; Asst Tutor, King's Coll. London 1982–84; Lecturer in Music, Univ. of Keele 1984–86; composer-in-residence Nat. Centre of Orchestral Studies, Goldsmiths' Coll., London 1986–87; Lecturer in Music, City Univ. 1989–; Conductor, Thames Chamber Players, Oxford Haydn Players; appearances with Nat. Centre of Orchestral Studies, European Community Youth Orchestra, Capricorn. *Compositions include:* chamber: String Quartet No. 1: Summer Song; for piano: Sonata No. 1: Autumn Tale, Serenata, Variations for orchestra 1979, Festive Fanfare, Prelude, Dream Sequence and the Song of the Washerwoman (from the opera, Yerma), The Name of the Rose, Summer Cycle (including Summer Night, Summer's Apotheose), String Quartet No. 2: L'Eveil au Désir, Canti Cantici: Libro 1.

ELLIS, Osian Gwynn, CBE, FRAM; British harpist; b. 8 Feb. 1928, Ffynnongroew, Flintshire, Wales; s. of Rev. T. G. Ellis; m. Rene Ellis Jones 1951; two s. *Education:* Denbigh Grammar School, Royal Acad. of Music. *Career:* Prin. Harpist London Symphony Orchestra 1960–94; mem. Melos Ensemble; Prof. of Harp Royal Acad. of Music 1959–89; recitals and concerts worldwide; radio and TV broadcasts; works written for him include harp concertos by Hoddinott 1957, Mathias 1970, Jersild 1972, Robin Holloway 1985, Rhian Samuel 2000, solos and chamber music by Gian Carlo Menotti 1977, William Schuman 1978 and music by Britten: Suite for Harp 1969, Canticle V 1974, Birthday Hansel 1975, Folk Songs for voice and harp 1976. *Publication:* Story of the Harp in Wales 1991. *Honours:* Hon. DMus (Wales) 1970; Grand Prix du Disque, French Radio Critics' Award and other awards. *Address:* Arfryn, Ala Road, Pwllheli, Gwynedd, LL53 5BN, Wales. *Telephone:* (1758) 612501.

ELMING, Poul; Danish singer (tenor); b. 21 July 1949, Ålborg. *Education:* Conservatories in Ålborg and Århus, and with Paul Lohmann in Wiesbaden. *Career:* debut in recital from 1978; performed baritone roles with Jutland Opera, Århus from 1979; Royal Opera Copenhagen from 1984 in many roles including Mozart's Count, Eugene Onegin, Malatesta and Verdi's Germont and Posa; further private studies at Royal Danish Music Conservatory and the Juilliard, New York; made his tenor debut as Parsifal at the Royal Opera, Copenhagen 1989; has sung Erik in Der fliegende Holländer and Spalanzani in Les Contes d'Hoffmann; Bayreuth Festival, Covent Garden, Deutsche Oper Berlin and the Vienna Staatsoper, Siegmund in Die Walküre and Parsifal in Hannover and Mannheim, Siegmund at Covent Garden, Parsifal at the Bayreuth Festival, Lohengrin in Copenhagen, Siegmund at the Metropolitan Opera, Parsifal at Bayreuth and Covent Garden, Luke in the premiere of The Handmaid's Tale by Poul Ruders, Copenhagen, Loge in Das Rheingold, Copenhagen; many recitals and concerts including appearances with the Danish Radio Symphony Orchestra in Copenhagen; Music Dir, Ålborg Symfoniorkester 2007–10. *Recordings include:* Parsifal (video from the Berlin Staatsoper) 1995. *Current Management:* Ingpen & Williams Ltd, 7 St George's Court, 131 Putney Bridge Road, London, SW15 2PA, England. *Telephone:* (20) 8874-3222. *Fax:* (20) 8877-3113. *E-mail:* jg@ingpen.co.uk. *Website:* www.ingpen.co.uk.

ELMS, Lauris Margaret, OBE, AM; Australian singer (contralto); b. 20 Oct. 1931, Melbourne; d. of Harry Britton and Jean Elms; m. Graeme Ernest de Graaff 1958; one d. *Career:* London debut as Ulrica in Ballo in Maschera, Royal Opera House, Covent Garden 1957; perfomances with Victoria Philharmonic, Sutherland-Williamson Opera Co., Elizabethan Opera Co., Australian Opera Co., Musica Viva, Chamber Music Fed., London Philharmonic, Royal Philharmonic, Israel Philharmonic; retd 1994. *Operas include:* Peter Grimes (also recording), Orfeo, Julius Caesar, Lucretia Borgia, Il Trovatore, Trojans, Bluebeard's Castle, Carmen; numerous recordings for Decca. *Publication:* Singing Elms (autobiog.) 2001. *Honours:* Hon. DMus (Sydney) 1988; Queen's Jubilee Medal 1977.

ELMS, Roderick James Charles, LGSM, ARAM, LRAM, FRCO, FRSA; British pianist, organist, composer and arranger; b. 18 Oct. 1951, Ilford, Essex, England; s. of Jimmy Elms and Hazel Elms; m. Joanna Elms. *Education:* Guildhall School of Music and Royal Acad. of Music, London. *Career:* debut at Wigmore Hall 1975 and Purcell Room 1976; regular soloist on piano and organ; participant in recordings and public concerts given by all major symphony orchestras; many broadcasts on radio and TV; mem. GNAFF Ensemble, which made successful TV debut 1982. *Compositions:* many arrangements and original compositions including Four Season Nocturnes for horn and orchestra 1999, Concertino for Celeste 2001, Cygncopations for cor anglais 2004. *Recordings include:* many solo recordings with London Symphony, London Philharmonic and Royal Philharmonic Orchestras; Organ Music of Percy Whitlock; Christmas Gift, Magnificat, In Dulci Jubilo, Original Music to Love is a Gift (on Just For Today), Frank Martin Ballade for piano and orchestra (with London Philharmonic Orchestra/Bamert) 1995, Nights in the Garden of Spain (with RPO) 2005, Warsaw and Spellbound Concertos; several arrangements and compositions recorded for Dutton-Vocalian under title A Little Fall-ish!; numerous Christmas arrangements and compositions recorded by Naxos under title Festive Frolic. *Publications:* many compositions and arrangements published by Camden Music. *E-mail:* organum.plenum@virgin.net (office). *Website:* www.masterkeyboards.co.uk.

ELOFF, Erica, BMus; South African singer (soprano); b. 1976; m.; two c. *Education:* North-West Univ. at Potchefstroom, Univ. of South Africa (UNISA). *Career:* took masterclasses with Joan Rodgers, Susan Bullock, Catherine Wyn Rogers, Elly Ameling and Helmut Deutsch; numerous concert, opera, oratorio and ensemble performances; since moving to England has sung with British Youth Opera and Garsington Opera; concert performances include recitals at Wigmore Hall, Bearwood Opera; roles include Barbarina in Le nozze di Figaro, Despina, Dorabella and Fiordiligi in Cosi fan Tutte, Adéle in Die Fledermaus, Adina in L'elisir d'amore, Queen of the Night and Fist Lady in the Magic Flute, Frasquita in Carmen, Theodora. *Honours:* winner ATKV Forté (Nat. Classic Music Competition for Young Musicians) 2000, UFAM (Union française des artistes musiciens) Concours Int. de Chant 2003, First UNISA Nat. Singing Competition 2005, special award at Fifth UNISA Int. Singing Competition 2006, Jackdaws Music Educ. Trust Great Elm Vocal Award 2006, winner London Handel Singing Competition 2008. *E-mail:* ericaeloff@hotmail.co.uk (office). *Website:* ericaeloff.com.

ELOY, Jean-Claude; French composer; b. 15 June 1938, Mont Saint Aignan, Seine Maritime; s. of René Eloy and Juliette Eloy (née Lisot). *Education:* Conservatoire Nat. Supérieur de Musique, Paris, studies with Armand Bournonville (Solfège), Lucette Descaves (piano), Pierre Revel (harmony), Noël-Gallon (counterpoint), Jacques Février (chamber music), Maurice Martenot (Ondes Martenot), Darius Milhaud (composition), Music Acad., Basel, master class in composition with Pierre Boulez, followed by courses with Karlheinz Stockhausen, summer courses in Darmstadt with Henri Pousseur, Hermann Scherchen, Karlheinz Stockhausen, Pierre Boulez, Olivier Messiaen. *Career:* concerts and performances at the Domaine Musical, Paris 1962–65; Asst Prof., Music Dept, Univ. of California, Berkeley 1966–68; Cologne Electronic Music Studio with Stockhausen (WDR) 1972–73; producer and collaborator for Radio France 1971–87; Pres. French Section of Int. Soc. for Contemporary Music (ISCM) 1974–75; in charge of music at Festival d'Automne, Paris (in collaboration with ISCM) 1975; Tokyo Electronic Music Studio, NHK 1977–78; Paris, CEMAMu/UPIC (Xenakis) 1979; Utrecht Instituut voor Sonologie 1980; in charge of the CIAMI at Rueil-Malmaison 1981–88; composer at Electronic Music Studio, Sweelinck Conservatory of Music, Amsterdam 1984–86; Cologne Electronic Music Studio, WDR 1990–91; participated at numerous int. music festivals, including Donaueschingen Music Festival 1963, 1964, 1990, Darmstadt Festival 1963, Festival of Royan 1974, Festival d'Automne à Paris 1974, 1979, 1986, 1989, 1992, Festival Musik der Zeit, Cologne, WDR 1975, 1980, 1991, Pan-Music Festival, Tokyo 1976, Festival of La Rochelle 1978, Music Today Festival, Tokyo 1979, Festival Sigma, Bordeaux 1980, 1986, 1996, Holland Festival, Amsterdam 1984, Warsaw Autumn Music Festival 1994, Festival 38e Rugissants, Grenoble 1996, 2001, Présences Festival Radio-France 2000, Musikwissenschaftlisches Institut, Cologne 2001, 2008, 2012, Festival 'Audible', Paris 2012, Festival Présences Electroniques, Paris (GRM) 2013, Festival 'Angelica', Bologna 2013 and many others. *Compositions:* main works: n° 25 – Etude III for orchestra 1962, n° 26 – Equivalences for 18 instrumentalists 1963, n° 30 – Faisceaux-Diffractions for 28 instrumentalists 1970, n° 31 – Kâmakalâ (The Energy Triangle) for three orchestra groups, three choir groups, three conductors 1971, n° 32 – Shânti (Peace) for electronic and concrete sounds (WDR Elektronische Musik Studio, Cologne) 1972–73, n° 33 – Fluctuante-Immuable for large orchestra 1977, n° 34 – Gaku-no-Michi (The Tao of Music, or Ways of Music, a film without images for electronic and concrete sounds, NHK Electronic Music Studio, Tokyo) 1977–78, n° 36 – Etude IV: points-lines-landscapes, electroacoustic, UPIC – computer with graphic interface 1979, n° 37 – Yo-In (Reverberations), sound theatre for an imaginary ritual, with a character-percussionist, electroacoustics, lighting (in four acts), Instituut voor Sonologie, Utrecht) 1980, n° 38 – À l'Approche du Feu Méditant... (Approaching the Meditative Flame...) for 27 instrumentalists from the Gagaku orchestra in Japan, and two Buddhist monk choirs from the Shingon and Tendai sects, with six percussionists 1983, n° 39 – Anâhata (Primordial Vibration) for solo voices of two Buddhist monks, three instrumentalists from the Gagaku orchestra, percussion, electroacoustics, lights 1984–86, n° 41/42 – Butsumyôe and Sappho Hikètis (The Ceremony of Repentance, Sappho Imploring) for two female voices (extended vocal techniques), electroacoustics 1989, n° 43 – Erkos (Song, Praise) for a Satsuma-Biwa soloist and vocalist (using extended Shômyo techniques), with electroacoustics (WDR Elektronic Music Studio, Cologne) 1991, n° 47 – Galaxies for electroacoustics, with vocal solo 1996, integrating the number 48 – ... Kono yo no hoka ... (... This world beyond ...) for solo voice (extended vocal techniques around the Shômyô ones) 1996. *Honours:* Chevalier des Arts et des Lettres 1983; Conservatoire Nat. Supérieur de Musique, Paris: First Prize in Piano 1956, First Prize in

Chamber Music 1958, First Prize in Counterpoint 1959, First Medal in Ondes Martenot 1960, Second Prize in Composition 1961; Prix de la Biennale de Paris 1963, Grand Prix de la musique symphonique de chambre, Soc. des auteurs, compositeurs et éditeurs de musique (SACEM) 1971, Grand Prix Acad. Charles Cros 1974, Grand Prix Nat. de la Musique, Ministère de la Culture 1981, Grand Prix de la musique symphonique, SACEM 1985. *Address:* c/o Studio Eve-Défense, Tour Eve #3011, 1 Place du Sud, 92800 Puteaux, France. *Fax:* 1-47-74-81-90 (office). *E-mail:* levingstone@hors -territoires.com (office); nadia@eloyjeanclaude.com (office). *Website:* www .hors-territoires.com; www.eloyjeanclaude.com.

ELSEN, Gijs; Dutch music executive; *Chief Executive, The English Concert. Education:* St Adelbert Coll., Rijksuniversiteit Groningen. *Career:* worked in artist management in The Netherlands and UK; Gen. Man. The Sixteen 1996–2000; Programmer, Classical Music, The Barbican, London (produced int. classical concert series Mostly Mozart and Great Performers) 2000–11; Chief Exec. The English Concert (baroque orchestra) 2011–. *Address:* The English Concert, 8 St George's Terrace, London, NW1 8XJ, England (office). *Telephone:* (20) 7911-0905 (office). *Fax:* (20) 7911-0904 (office). *E-mail:* gijs@ englishconcert.co.uk (office). *Website:* www.englishconcert.co.uk (office).

ELSNER, Christian; German singer (tenor); b. 1965, Freiburg im Breisgau. *Education:* studied in Frankfurt am Main with Martin Gündler, also studied with Dietrich Fischer-Dieskau. *Career:* performed as Lensky in Eugene Onegin and Macduff in Macbeth at Oper Heidelberg, Tichon in Katya Kabanova, Pedrillo in Entfürung and Idomeneo at Staatstheater Darmstadt, Siegmund in Die Walküre in Weimar, Bari and Semperoper Dresden; concerts include lieder recitals at the Schubertiade Feldkirch, Mozarteum Salzburg and throughout Europe; Mahler's Lied von der Erde in Munich and at the Wiener Festwochen, Bruckner's Te Deum at the Salzburg Festival, Beethoven's Ninth in London and Tokyo, Mendelssohn's Lobgesang, La Scala, Milan, Mozart's Requiem, Carnegie Hall; performed with conductors such as Giulini, Jansons, Harnoncourt, Luisi, Marriner, Norrington, Thielemann and Rattle. *Recordings include:* Schumann's Dichterliebe and Liederkreis op. 39, Mahler's Lieder eines fahrenden Gesellen and Lied von der Erde, Schubert's Winterreise and Schöne Müllerin, Beethoven's Ninth Symphony and Missa Solemnis. *Honours:* winner Int. Walter Gruner Lieder Competition, London 1993, second prize Int. ARD Competition, Munich 1994. *Current Management:* c/o Verena Vetter, Künstler Sekretariat am Gasteig, Rosenheimerstrasse 52, 81669 Munich, Germany. *Telephone:* (89) 44488790. *Fax:* (89) 4489522. *E-mail:* team@ks-gasteig.de. *Website:* www.ks-gasteig.de; www .christian-elsner.de.

ELSTE, (Rudolf Otto) Martin, DPhil; German musicologist, discologist and music critic; *Curator, Staatliches Institut für Musikforschung;* b. 11 Sept. 1952, Bremen. *Education:* Univ. of Cologne, Rheinische Musikschule, Cologne, King's Coll., London, England, Technische Universität, Berlin. *Career:* Curator, Staatliches Institut für Musikforschung Preussischer Kulturbesitz 1982–; Review Ed., IASA Phonographic Bulletin 1982–93; panel mem., German Record Critics Award 1983–, Pres. 2000–08; Chair., IASA Discography Cttee 1992–96; Vice-Pres., IASA 1996–99; consulting musicologist, Bach-Tage Berlin 1986–87; Advisory Bd mem., CIMCIM 1995–2001; Editorial Advisory Bd mem., Music in Performance 1997; Vice-Pres., Verein f. Musik Archiv-Forschung 1998–2001; Consultant Ed., Die Musik in Geschichte und Gegenwart; bd mem. RIdIM Commission Mixte 2004–. *Publications:* Internationale Heinrich Schütz Diskographie 1928–72 1972, Verzeichnis deutschsprachiger Musiksoziologie 1975, Bachs Kunst der Fuge auf Schallplatten 1981, Musikinstrumenten Museum Berlin (contrib.) 1986, Handwerk im Dienste der Musik (contrib.) 1987, 100 Jahre Berliner Musikinstrumenten Museum (contrib.) 1988, Kleines Tonträger-Lexikon 1989, Kielklaviere (contrib.) 1991, Musikalische Interpretation 1992, Modern Harpsichord Music: A Discography 1995, Baines, Lexikon der Musikinstrumente (ed. and trans.) 1996, Bach-Handbuch (contrib.) 1999, Meilensteine der Bach-Interpretation 2000, Ausgezeichnet! (ed.) 2004; contrib. to books and journals, including New Grove, Fono Forum, Fanfare, Die Musikforschung, Basler Jahrbuch für Historische Musikpraxis, Jahrbuch des Staatlichen Instituts für Musikforschung, Jahrbuch Preussischer Kulturbesitz, Klassik heute, Musik in Geschichte und Gegenwart, Frankfurter Allgemeine Zeitung, Die Zeit, Neue Zeitschrift für Musik, Hindemith-Jahrbuch, Beethoven-Lexikon, Mozart-Lexikon. *Honours:* ARSC Award for Excellence in Historical Recorded Sound Research 2001. *Address:* SIMPK, Tiergartenstrasse 1, 10785 Berlin, Germany (office). *Telephone:* (30) 25481132 (office). *Fax:* (30) 25481172 (office). *E-mail:* elste@sim.spk-berlin.de (office). *Website:* www.mim-berlin.de (office); www.martin-elste.de.

ELTS, Olari; Estonian conductor; *Principal Guest Conductor, Scottish Chamber Orchestra and Estonian National Symphony Orchestra;* b. 1971, Tallinn. *Education:* Estonian Music Acad., and privately with Uros Ladjovic in Vienna, Eri Klas in Estonia and Jorma Panula in Finland. *Career:* Founder and Music Dir, NYYD (contemporary music ensemble) 1993–; Prin. Conductor, Latvian Nat. Symphony Orchestra 2001–06; Artistic Adviser, Orchestre de Bretagne 2006–; Prin. Guest Conductor, Scottish Chamber Orchestra 2007–, Estonian Nat. Symphony Orchestra 2007–; has appeared with orchestras including Finnish Radio, Dresden Sinfoniker, SWR Stuttgart, Lucerne Symphony, Orchestre du Capitole de Toulouse, City of Birmingham Symphony, Frankfurt Radio and Cincinnati Symphony, Adelaide Symphony. *Honours:* Winner Jorma Panula Conducting Competition, Finland 1999, Int. Sibelius Conductors' Competition, Helsinki 2000. *Current Management:*

International Classical Artists, The Tower Building, 11 York Road, London, SE1 7NX, England. *Telephone:* (20) 7902-0520. *Fax:* (20) 7902-0530. *E-mail:* info@icartists.co.uk. *Website:* www.icartists.co.uk; www.sco.org.uk; www.erso .ee; www.nyyd.ee.

ELWES, John; British singer (tenor); b. 1946, England. *Education:* Westminster Cathedral with George Malcolm, Royal Coll. of Music. *Career:* chorister at Westminster Cathedral; soloist in Britten's Missa Brevis and Abraham and Isaac; frequent broadcaster for the BBC; repertoire includes baroque, lieder and contemporary music on the concert platform and operas by Gluck, Handel, Mozart and Monteverdi on stage; sang Orfeo in Monteverdi's opera with Phillippe Herreweghe and La Chapelle Royale at the Montpellier opera house and with Flanders Opera, Antwerp 1989–90. *Recordings include:* Orfeo in The Death of Orpheus by Stefano Landi, with Tragicomedia directed by Stephen Stubbs.

EMMERLICH, Gunther; German singer (bass); b. 18 Sept. 1944, Thuringia. *Education:* studied in Weimar and Dresden and with Pavel Lisitsian. *Career:* debut as the Peasant in Die Kluge by Orff at the Dresden Staatsoper 1978; appeared as Kuno in Der Freischütz at the reopening of the Semper Oper, Dresden, and ssng with the Dresden Ensemble at the Vienna Volksoper and in Amsterdam as Don Alfonso 1988; other roles include Osmin in Die Entführung, Geronimo in Matrimonio Segreto, Rocco, Dulcamara and the Hermit in Der Freischütz; many concert appearances. *Recordings:* Der Freischütz, Eugene Onegin.

ENCINAS, Ignacio; Spanish singer (tenor); b. 2 June 1953, Grajal de Campos. *Education:* studied with Enzo Costantini, studied in Madrid, masterclasses with Gianni Poggi and Gino Bechi. *Career:* sang in Trovatore and La Favorita at Santander Festival; Rigoletto at Zarzuela Theatre in Madrid and appeared further in Oviedo, Valladolid and Malaga; at Dijon has sung in Pollione in Norma, Alfredo in Traviata, Rigoletto, and Riccardo in Un Ballo in Maschera; sang in Verdi's Attila at Teatro Romano of Benevento and as Macduff in a concert performance of Macbeth at 1990 Gstaad Festival and at Naples 1998; sang Rodolfo in Luisa Miller for the Royal Opera at Edinburgh 1988. *Honours:* winner of numerous int. competitions.

END, Timothy Francis, BMus (Hons), ARAM; British pianist; b. 22 March 1985, London; s. of Raymond and Vivien End. *Education:* Bancroft's School, Essex (Draper's Music Scholarship), King's Coll., London, Royal Acad. of Music, London with Julius Drake and Patsy Toh. *Career:* wide experience performing chamber music and accompanying singers; specializes in accompanying the brass solo repertoire; appeared on In Tune (BBC Radio 3) accompanying bassoonist Karen Geoghegan performing works by Rossini and Noel Gallon; performed with baritone George Emney at Nat. Opera Studio, Karen Geoghegan at Perth Concert Hall, bass Sir John Tomlinson at Saville Club, Jonathan McGovern at St James's, Piccadilly, recitals in London and Edinburgh with Australian bass-baritone Abraham Singer; debut at Purcell Room for Park Lane Group Artists 2011. *Honours:* DipRAM Award for an outstanding recital 2008, Shinn Fellowship, RAM 2008–09, Parnell Award for an Accompanist, Royal Overseas League Music Competition 2010, Gerald Moore Award for Accompanists 2010, MBF Accompanist Award, Kathleen Ferrier Finals 2011, Jt Winner, Pianist's Prize, Wigmore Hall/Kohn Foundation Int. Song Competition 2011, Jean Meikle Prize for a Duo (with Jonathan McGovern), Accompanists' Prize, Maureen Lehane (fmrly Jackdaws) Vocal Competition Final 2011. *Address:* c/o Breinton, Heath House Road, Woking, GU22 0RD, Surrey, England. *Telephone:* 7742-583927 (mobile); 7789-052028 (Breinton, mobile). *E-mail:* timothyend@gmail.com; soirees@breinton.com. *Website:* www.breinton.com.

ENDERLE, Matthias; Swiss violinist; b. 16 June 1956. *Education:* Winterthur Conservatory, Indiana Univ., USA, Int. Menuhin Acad., Gstaad. *Career:* Co-founder and Leader, Carmina Quartet 1984; appearances from 1987 in Europe, Israel, Japan and USA; regular concerts at Wigmore Hall from 1987; concerts at South Bank Centre, London, Amsterdam Concertgebouw, the Kleine Philharmonie in Berlin, and Konzertverein Vienna; tours of Australasia, USA and Japan; concerts at Hohenems, Graz, Hong Kong, Schleswig-Holstein, Montreux, Bath, Lucerne, and Prague Spring Festivals; collaborations with Dietrich Fischer-Dieskau, Olaf Bär and Mitsuko Uchida. *Honours:* Paolo Borciani String Quartet Competition, Reggio Emilia, Italy (with mems of Carmina Quartet) 1987, Gramophone Prize for Best Chamber Music Recording 1992. *Current Management:* Künstlersekretariat Barbara Golan, Stettbachstrasse 131h, 8051 Zurich, Switzerland. *E-mail:* enderle@ gmx.ch. *Website:* www.carminaquartet.com.

ENDO, Akira, BM, MM; Japanese conductor; b. 16 Nov. 1938, Shido. *Education:* Univ. of Southern California, Los Angeles, USA and studied with Vera Barstow, Eudice Shapiro and Jascha Heifetz. *Career:* Violinist, Trojan String Quartet 1960–62; Second Violinist, Pacific String Quartet 1962–69; Music Dir Long Beach Symphony Orchestra, Calif. 1966–69, West Side Symphony Orchestra, Los Angeles 1968–69; Conductor American Ballet Theatre, New York 1969–79; Resident Conductor Houston Symphony Orchestra 1974–76; Music Dir Austin Symphony Orchestra, Tex. 1975–82, Louisville Orchestra 1980–83; fmr Music Adviser and Prin. Conductor San Antonio Symphony; Music Dir and Prin. Conductor Hamilton Philharmonic in Canada –1997; currently Conductor Colorado Ballet; guest conductor of numerous orchestras, including Dallas Symphony, Detroit Symphony, Houston Symphony, Milwaukee Symphony, Louisiana Philharmonic, Minnesota Orchestra, New York Philharmonic, Philadelphia Orchestra, San

Antonio Symphony, Utah Symphony and orchestras across Europe and S America; Visiting Prof. of Music, Duquesne Univ. School of Music, Pittsburgh, Pa 2000–01; Prof. of Music in charge of orchestral activities and Chair. Dept of Instrumental Performance, Univ. of Miami School of Music for two years; currently Dir of Orchestral Studies, Univ. of Colorado at Boulder; Guest Prof. at insts, including California State Univ. at Long Beach, Rice Univ., Stanford Univ., Univ. of Oklahoma. *Honours:* Third Prize, Dimitri Mitropoulos Int. Competition for Conductors, Carnegie Hall (twice), Award for Adventuresome Programming of Contemporary Music, The American Soc. of Composers, Authors and Publrs (ASCAP) 1982, 1983. *E-mail:* endo@colorado.edu (office).

ENGLICHOVA, Katerina; Czech harpist; b. 13 June 1969, Prague. *Education:* Conservatoire, Prague; Curtis Institute of Music, Philadelphia. *Career:* debut in New York, Weill Recital Hall at Carnegie Hall 1998 Paris 2000; Modern Art Museum, Los Angeles 1996; Paris, France 1994, 1996, 1998, Hong Kong 1998, 2001, Boston 1999, England 1999; The VII World Harp Congress, Prague 1999; festivals include Pacific Music Festival, Japan, Music by the Red Sea, Israel, Tanglewood Music Festival, USA, Rencontres Musicales d'Evian, France, Prague Autumn, Czech Republic; repertoire includes Ravel, Introduction and Allegro, Ginastera Concerto etc.; mem. World Harp Soc. *Recordings:* Britten, Voice and Harp; Hindemith, Sonata; Harmonia Mundi, A. Roussel, with Czech Nonet; Panton, M. Ravel, C. Debussy, Solo and Chamber Recital; Koch, Discover, C. Saint-Saëns, L. Spohr, P. Hindemith, with Josef Suk, Violin; Petr Eben, Music for Harp; Rossetti Sonatas, 2000; Granados-Danzas Espagnolas, Supraphon, 2002. *Honours:* prizewinner E. Herbert Hobin Harp Competition, USA 1993, first prize Concerto Soloists Competition 1994, first prize Pro Musicis Int. Award, New York 1995, European Broadcast Competition 1997, Int. Music Competition, Vienna 1999, Tim Competition, Italy 2002. *Website:* www.englichova.cz.

ENGLISH, Jon Arthur, BM; American composer, trombonist, percussionist and double bass player; b. 22 March 1942, Kankakee, Illinois, USA; m. Candace Natwig. *Education:* University of Illinois with Kenneth Gaburo. *Career:* member of the Harry Partch Ensemble, 1961–62, the Illinois Contemporary Chamber Players, 1963–66 and the Savannah Symphony Orchestra, 1967; Associate Artist of the University of Iowa Center for New Music and New Performing Arts until 1974; has worked from Cologne since 1976; Performances in Europe as soloist, with Candace Natwig, singer, and in new music groups. *Compositions include:* 404 1-2 East Green Street for Tape, 1965; Sequent Cycles for 6 players, 1968;... Whose Circumference Is A Nowhere, 1970; Used Furniture Sale for Tape, 1971; Summerstalks for Performer and Tape, 1973; Shagbolt for Trombone, 1978; Electrotrombonics, 1979; Foursome, 1979; Dog Dreams, 1982; Harmonies For Charlie Mingus, 1983.

ENS, Phillip; Canadian singer (bass); b. 1962. *Career:* debut at Manitoba Opera 1985, as Marchese in La Forza del Destino; numerous appearances throughout Canada as Sarastro, Masetto and Figaro, for Pacific Opera Verdi's Sparafucile and Banquo and Gounod's Frère Laurence; Canadian Opera Company debut 1989 as Don Fernando in Fidelio; US debut 1992 as Sparafucile with Philadelphia Opera; Stuttgart Opera 1993 as Sparafucile, Sarastro, Banquo in Macbeth, Mozart's Commendatore and Pimen in Boris Godunov; Carontes in Monteverdi's Orfeo at Munich and Claggart in WNO's Billy Budd; season 1999–2000 as Padre Guardiano in La Forza del Destino at Deutsche Oper Berlin, Hunding at Metropolitan Opera; Sarastro in Hamburg and Gremin in Eugene Onegin at Brussels; season 2002–03 as Fafner and Hunding in The Ring at Stuttgart; Ramfis in Brussels; Wurm in Metropolitan Opera production of Luisa Miller; Hunding with Lyric Opera of Chicago; concerts include Missa Solemnis in Brussels and Paris, and Mozart Requiem at Salzburg and BBC Proms. *Current Management:* Zemsky/Green Artists Management, 104 West 73rd Street, New York, NY 10023, USA. *Telephone:* (212) 579-6700. *E-mail:* info@zemskygreen.com. *Website:* zemskygreenartists .com/product/phillip-ens.

ENSTRÖM, Rolf; Swedish composer; b. 2 Nov. 1951, Södertälje; m. Karin Enström-Salomonsson 1980; two s. one d. *Education:* Univs of Stockholm and Gothenburg, studied in Örebro. *Career:* debut with multimedia piece, Myr, at the Int. Soc. for Contemporary Music Festival, Athens 1979; as multimedia artist has collaborated with artists in adjacent fields, including photographer Thomas Hellsing; music performed worldwide; Teacher, EMS, Stockholm; summer courses at Nordens Biskops Arnö, near Stockholm; participant in DAAD cultural exchange programme 1991, then Composer-in-Residence, Berlin. *Compositions include:* tape music, music for instruments and electronics and multimedia works, including: Slutförbannelser (text by Elsa Grave) 1981, Fractal (multimedia piece with Thomas Hellsing), Tjidtjag och Tjidtjaggaise (based on Lapp joik) 1987, Skizzen aus Berlin 1991, Asylum (multimedia piece with Thomas Hellsing), Vigil saxophone quartet 1994, In Ice, Mirror 1995, Spin 1995, Charm 1996, Io, intermedia 1996, Open Wide for piano, percussion and tape 1997, Strange 1997, Rama for mixed choir and tape 1998, Kairos 1999, Up 1999, Directions, Final Curses, Dagbrott, Sequence in Blue, Tonal Nagual, Tsentsaks.

ENTREMONT, Philippe; French pianist and conductor; b. 7 June 1934, Reims; s. of Jean Entremont and Renée Entremont (née Monchamps); m. Andrée Ragot 1955; one s. one d. *Education:* Inst. Notre-Dame à Reims, Conservatoire Nat. Supérieur de Musique de Paris. *Career:* has performed with all major orchestras of the world 1953–; Pres. of Acad. Int. de Musique Maurice Ravel, Saint-Jean-de-Luz 1973–80; Musical Dir and Permanent

Conductor, Vienna Chamber Orchestra 1976–; Dir New Orleans Symphony Orchestra 1980–86; Prin. Conductor Denver Symphony Orchestra 1986–88, Paris Orchestre Colonne 1987–90, Netherlands Chamber Orchestra 1993–2002, Israel Chamber Orchestra 1995–; Dir American Conservatory Fontainebleau 1994; f. Santo Domingo Biennial Festival 1997; Prin. Guest Conductor Shanghai Broadcasting Symphony Orchestra 2001–; Prin. Guest Conductor Munich Symphony Orchestra 2005–06, Prin. Conductor 2006; Conductor Super World Orchestra, Tokyo 2006. *Honours:* Officier Ordre nat. du Mérite, Officier, Légion d'honneur, Commdr des Arts et Lettres, Österreichisches Ehrenkreuz für Wissenschaft und Kunst (Arts and Sciences Cross of Honour, Austria); Harriet Cohen Piano Medal 1951, Grand Prix Int. Concours Marguerite Long-Jacques Thibaud 1953, four Grand Prix du Disque Awards, Edison Award 1960, Grammy Award 1972. *Address:* c/o Tim Fox, Columbia Artists Management Inc., 1790 Broadway, New York, NY 10019-1412, USA; c/o Bureau de concerts Dominique Lierner, 17 rue du 4 septembre, 75002 Paris (office); 10 rue de Castiglione, 75001 Paris, France. *Telephone:* 1-42-86-06-08. *Fax:* 1-42-86-86-61 (home).

EŐSZE, László, PhD, CSc; Hungarian pianist, artistic director and musicologist; b. 17 Nov. 1923, Budapest; s. of Rezső Eősze and Janka Kovács; m. 1st 1948; two c.; m. 2nd 1983. *Education:* Ferenc Liszt Acad. of Music, Univ. of Budapest. *Career:* music teacher and pianist; concerts in Hungary and Europe 1946–51; worked as ed. 1952–60; Artistic Dir, EMB music publishing house 1961–87; mem. F. Liszt Soc. (Co-Pres.), Int. Kodály Soc. (Exec. Sec. 1975–95), Hungarian Musicological Soc. 1996–. *Publications include:* Zoltán Kodály élete és munkássága (trans. as Zoltán Kodály, His Life and Work) 1956, Zoltán Kodály élete képekben (trans. as Kodály, His Life in Pictures and Documents) 1957, Az opera utja (History of Opera) 1960, Giuseppe Verdi 1961, Zoltán Kodály 1967, Richard Wagner 1969, Richard Wagner, Eine Chronik seines Lebens und Schaffens 1969, Zoltán Kodály, életének krónikája 1977, 119 római Liszt dokumentum 1980, Selected Studies on Zoltán Kodály 2000, The Family of Zoltán Kodály 2007, Kodály, the Conductor 2012, Verdi és Wagner világa (The World of Verdi and Wagner) 2012, Intermezzo (memoirs) 2015, Tristan and Aida (selected essays) 2015; contribs to essays and articles in various languages to numerous professional publications; contribs to The New Grove Dictionary of Music and Musicians, Brockhaus Riemann Musiklexikon. *Honours:* Erkel Prize 1977, Gramma Award 1978, Medium Cross of the Order of the Hungarian Republic 1998, Medal for Merit of the Pres. of the Repub. 2003, Grand Prize of the Nat. Soc. of Creative Artists 2003, Széchemyi Award 2013. *Address:* 1012 Budapest, Attila ut 133, Hungary. *Telephone:* (1) 212-2526. *E-mail:* eosze.laszlo@chello.hu.

EÖTVÖS, Peter; German (b. Hungarian) composer, conductor and academic; b. 2 Jan. 1944, Székelyudvarhely, Hungary; s. of László Eötvös and Ilona Szücs; m. 1st Piroska Molnár 1968; one s.; m. 2nd Pi-Hsien Chen 1976; one d.; m. 3rd Maria Mezei 1995. *Education:* Budapest Music Acad., Musikhochschule, Cologne. *Career:* played in Stockhausen's Ensemble, Cologne 1968–76; composer and producer at WDR Electronic Music Studio, Cologne 1971–79; Conductor and Musical Dir Ensemble Intercontemporain, Paris 1979–91; Prin. Guest Conductor BBC Symphony Orchestra, London 1985–88, Gothenburg Symphony Orchestra 2003–07; First Guest Conductor, Budapest Festival Orchestra 1992–95, ORF Radio Symphony Orchestra, Vienna 2009–12; Chief Conductor Netherlands Radio Chamber Orchestra 1994–2005; Prof., Musikhochschule Karlsruhe, Germany 1992–98, 2002–08, Cologne 1998–2001; f. Peter Eötvös Contemporary Music Foundation 1991; mem. Akad. der Künste, Berlin, Szechenyi Acad. of Art, Budapest, Sächsische Akad. der Künste, Dresden, Royal Swedish Acad. of Music, Stockholm. *Compositions include:* for orchestra: Chinese Opera, Psychokosmos 1993, Atlantis, Ima, Jet Stream, CAP-KO, Zeropoints, Two Monologues, Replica, Konzert für zwei Klaviere, Levitation; for ensemble: Intervalles-Intérieurs, Windsequenzen, Steine, Triangel 1993, Shadows 1996, Octet, Sonata per sei; for string quartet: Korrespondenz, Encore, Da Capo 2014; for vocal ensemble: Three comedy madrigals, Schiller: energische Schönheit; for percussion: Psalm 151, Speaking Drums; for violin: Seven (Prix de Composition Musicale, Fondation Prince Pierre de Monaco 2008), Doremi; for violoncello: Cello Concerto Grosso; for musical theatre/opera: Radames, Harakiri, Three Sisters, As I Crossed a Bridge of Dreams 1998–99, Le Balcon 2001–02, Angels in America 2002–04, Lady Sarashina 2008, Love and Other Demons 2008, Die Tragödie des Teufels 2010, Paradise Reloaded, Der goldene Drache 2013–14. *Honours:* Commdr, Ordre des Arts et des Lettres 2003; Bartók Award, Budapest 1997, Stephan Kaske Prize, Munich 2000, Kossuth Prize, Hungary 2002, Royal Philharmonic Soc. Music Award 2002, Midem Classical Award 'Living Composer', Cannes 2004, European Composing Prize 2004, Frankfurt Music Prize 2007, Prince Pierre of Monaco Prize in Musical Composition 2008, Golden Lion Award for Lifetime Achievement 2011, Echo Klassik Award for Choral Recording of the Year – 20th/21st Century (for Ligeti Requiem) 2012, Gramophone Recording of the Year 2013, Echo Klassik Prize 2013. *Current Management:* c/o Harrison Parrott, 5–6 Albion Court, Albion Place, London, W6 0QT, England. *Telephone:* (20) 7229-9166. *Fax:* (20) 7221-5042. *E-mail:* info@harrisonparrott.co.uk. *Website:* www.harrisonparrott.com. *E-mail:* eotvos@eotvospeter.com (home). *Website:* www.eotvospeter.com (home).

EPSTEIN, Matthew A., BA; American opera administrator and academic; b. 23 Dec. 1947, New York, NY. *Education:* Univ. of Pennsylvania. *Career:* Vice-Pres. Columbia Artists Man. 1973–99, now Dir Columbia Artists Vocal; Artistic Dir Brooklyn Acad. of Music 1987–90; consultant, Santa Fe Opera 1980–; Artistic Dir Welsh Nat. Opera 1991–94; mem. Faculty, Voice and Vocal

Piano, Music Acad. of the West, Santa Barbara, Calif. 1997–2009, 2011, 2012, then Auditions and Career Guidance; Artistic Dir Lyric Opera of Chicago 1999–2005; Vice-Pres., Dir of Vocal Divisions, Columbia Artists Management Inc. 2005–10; Artistic Dir Kennedy Center Gala honouring George London 1981; Dir Rossini 200th Birthday Celebration Gala, Lincoln Center 1990; Artistic Consultant, Celebration of the American Musical, Lincoln Center 1997. *Address:* Music Academy of the West, 1070 Fairway Road, Santa Barbara, CA 93108-2899, USA (office). *E-mail:* info@musicacademy.org (office). *Website:* www.musicacademy.org (office).

EPSTEIN, Selma; American pianist and musicologist; b. 14 Aug. 1927, Brooklyn, NY; d. of the late Samuel Schechtman and Tillie Schechtman (née Schneider); m. Joseph Epstein 1950; two s. two d. *Education:* Juilliard School and privately. *Career:* debut as concert pianist, Carnegie Hall, New York 1942; many concert tours in USA and worldwide, including People's Repub. of China 1992–93; many concert tours with US Information Agency in Europe, the Far East and Australasia promoting music by 20th century, black and women composers 1964–; teacher, Newcastle Conservatory of Music, NSW, Australia 1972–75; Dir of Publications Chromattica USA 1981–; art exhbns in USA and Canada 1991–92. *Recordings include:* Selma Epstein plays Percy Grainger 1981. *Publications:* eight group piano-teaching books 1975–, guide to researching music by women 1991, ed. two historical anthologies of duets 1992. *Address:* Chez Quatre Minous, 2443 Pickwick Road, Dickeyville, MD 21207, USA. *Telephone:* (410) 448-3334. *Fax:* (410) 448-1433.

EPSTEIN, Steve, BSc; American record producer and record company executive. *Education:* Hofstra Univ. *Career:* fmrly worked as music ed. with CBS Masterworks; Sr Exec. Producer, Sony Classical 1973–2005; produced over 100 albums and worked with leading artists, including Isaac Stern, Yo-Yo Ma, Wynton Marsalis (both classical and jazz), Midori, Lorin Maazel, Claudio Abbado, Itzhak Perlman, Murray Perahia, Emanuel Ax, Placido Domingo, Andre Previn, Bobby McFerrin, Vienna, Berlin and New York Philharmonic Orchestras, Chicago, Cleveland, London, Conzertgebouw, Philadelphia, Pittsburgh and Los Angeles Symphony Orchestras; Owner, Steven Epstein Productions, Inc.; Adjunct Prof., Dept of Music Research, Schulich School of Music, McGill Univ. *Honours:* Grammy Award for Classical Producer of the Year 1985, 1996, 1998, 1999, 2001, 2004, 2010. *Current Management:* McKenna Group Productions, PO Box 88, Pomona, NY 10970, USA. *Address:* Steven Epstein Productions, Inc., 489 Shelley Hill Road, Stanfordville, NY 12581, USA.

EQUILUZ, Kurt; Austrian singer (tenor); b. 13 June 1929, Vienna. *Education:* studied in Vienna with Adolf Vogel. *Career:* sang as chorister in Vienna from 1945; solo career at the Vienna Staatsoper from 1957, notably as Mozart's Pedrillo, Beethoven's Jacquino and in operas by Strauss; sang at the Salzburg Festival in the premieres of Liebermann's Penelope 1954, Martin's Le Mystère de la Nativité 1960 and Wagner-Régeny's Das Bergwerk zu Falun 1961; performed the Narrator in Schnittke's Historia von D. Johann Fausten, Vienna 2001; many concert appearances as lieder singer and in religious music; Prof., Graz Musikhochschule 1971–; Prof. of Lieder and Oratorio, Acad. for Music in Vienna 1982–. *Recordings:* Monteverdi's Orfeo and Il Ritorno d'Ulisse, Cantatas by Bach and the St John and St Matthew Passions, Cavalieri's La Rappresentazione di Anima e di Corpo.

ERBE, Teresa; German singer (soprano); b. 1958, Oberschesien. *Education:* studied in Katowice. *Career:* sang at Gdansk from 1981; Bremerhaven Opera 1986–87, and Bremen 1987–92, as Salome, Arabella and Elisabeth de Valois; Essen from 1992, as Bartók's Judith, the Marschallin and Giulietta in Les contes d'Hoffmann 1996; season 1999–2000 as Salome at Freiburg, and Natasha in Three Sisters by Peter Eötvös; further appearances in Rusalka, and operetta; guest engagements in Prague, Stockholm, Copenhagen and St Petersburg.

ERBEN, Valentin; Austrian cellist; b. 14 March 1945, Pernitz. *Education:* Munich Acad. of Music with Walter Reichardt, also studied with Tobias Kühne in Vienna and André Navarra at Conservatoire in Paris, studied chamber music with Jean Hubeau and Joseph Calvet. *Career:* Co-founder and cellist, Alban Berg Quartet 1971–2008; numerous concert engagements worldwide, including complete cycles of Beethoven Quartets in 15 European cities 1987–88, 1988–89 seasons; Bartók/Mozart cycle in London, Vienna, Paris, Frankfurt, Munich, Geneva and Turin 1990–91; annual concert series at Vienna Konzerthaus and festival engagements worldwide; Assoc. Artist, South Bank Centre, London; US appearances in Washington, DC, San Francisco and Carnegie Hall, New York; cellist, Lucern Festival Orchestra 2004–07; Prof., Musikhochschule, Vienna –2013 (retd). *Recordings include:* Complete Quartets of Beethoven, Brahms, Berg, Webern and Bartók; Late Quartets of Mozart, Schubert, Haydn and Dvořák; Quartets by Ravel, Debussy and Schumann; Live recordings from Carnegie Hall playing Mozart and Schumann, Konzerthaus in Vienna, and Opéra-Comique in Paris, playing Brahms. *Honours:* winner, nternational cello competition ARD, Munich 1968, Grand Prix du Disque, Deutsche Schallplatenpreis, Edison Prize, Japan Grand Prix, Gramophone Award. *Address:* Argentinierstraße 42/38, 1040 Vienna, Austria. *Website:* www.valentin-erben.at.

ERDÉLYI, Csaba, DipMus; Hungarian violist and conductor; b. 15 May 1946, Budapest; m. Ju-Ping Chi 1989, three s. *Education:* Franz Liszt Acad. of Music, studied with Pál Lukács, Yehudi Menuhin, Bruno Giuranna. *Career:* Franz Liszt Chamber Orchestra 1968–72; Eszterházy Baryton Trio 1973–78; Principal Viola, Philharmonia Orchestra, London 1974–78; Prof. of Viola,

Guildhall School of Music, London 1980–87; Chilingirian String Quartet 1981–87; Prof. of Viola, Indiana Univ., Bloomington 1987–91, Rice Univ., Houston, TX 1991–95; soloist in RFH, Promenade Concerts; frequent pnr with Yehudi Menuhin; masterclasses worldwide, including RAM London, Aldeburgh, Alaska, Beijing, Mexico, Budapest, USA; annual summer classes in Gubbio Festival, Italy; jury mem., BBC Young Musician of the Year and Lionel Tertis Viola Competition, Isle of Man; first US performance of Brahms/Berio Sonata for viola and orchestra; opening recital at Int. World Viola Congress in Redlands, CA 1989, and Vienna 1992; mem. Inst. for the Development of Intercultural Relations through the Arts, Geneva. *Recordings:* Hoddinott Viola Concerto, Strauss Songs with Jessye Norman. *Honours:* first prize Carl Flesch Competition 1972.

ERDING-SWIRIDOFF, Susanne; German composer; b. 16 Nov. 1955, Schwabisch Hall; m. Paul Swiridoff 1988. *Education:* Stuttgart Univ., Yale Univ., USA, Université de Montréal, Canada, Stuttgart Acad. of Music with Milko Kelemen, Int. Summer School of Music with Peter Maxwell Davies, Dartington, England, summer courses at Univs of Oxford and Cambridge, England, studied with Dieter Acker in Munich, Agosto Benjamin Rattenbach in Buenos Aires. *Career:* many television appearances 1983–88. *Compositions include:* orchestra: Yellan 1981, Event 1985, Il Visconte Dimezzato 1994; concertos: Konzert 1983, Tierra Querida 1986; operas: Joy (chamber opera) 1983, Die Wundersame Geschichte des Peter Schlemihl (marionette opera) 1991; ballet: Yellan 1981; piano: Klaviersuite 1982, Maske und Kristall IV 1992; chamber music: Grotesques Arabesques 1980, Rotor 1982, Homage to the City of Dresden 1985, Variations Serieuses, Fayence 1986, Labirinto del Sole 1987, Gioielli Rubati 1987, Blumen und Blut 1988, Zeitstimmen 1993; vocal: Okteondo 1979, Initialen 1986, Maske und Kristall X 1993, XII 1994.

ERICSON, Barbro; Swedish singer (mezzo-soprano); b. 2 April 1930, Halmstad. *Education:* studied in Stockholm with Arne Sunnegard. *Career:* debut in Stockholm 1956, as Eboli in Don Carlos; guest appearances in London, Berlin, Hamburg, Edinburgh, Helsinki, France, The Netherlands and Italy; sang at Paris Opéra 1964 as Venus in Tannhäuser, Bayreuth Festival from 1964 as Kundry and Venus, and Salzburg Easter Festival 1967 in Die Walküre under Karajan; Metropolitan Opera debut 1968 as Fricka, returning to New York 1976 as Herodias in Salome; sang in premiere of Ligeti's Le Grande Macabre 1978. *Recordings include:* Die Walküre, Requiem and other works by Ligeti.

ERKOREKA, Gabriel, Dip RAM, MMus, ARAM; Spanish composer and artistic director; *Composition Teacher, Musikene-Basque Country Superior Conservatoire;* b. 27 Feb. 1969, Bilbao. *Education:* Conservatorio Superior de Música, Bilbao, Royal Acad. of Music, UK. *Career:* performances include Venice Biennale 2004, Musikverein in Vienna, ISCM World Music Days Manchester 1998, Hong Kong 2007, Wigmore Hall, ICA and South Bank Centre, London, Festival Internacional de Alicante, Auditorio Nacional de Música, Chicago, New York, Amsterdam, Paris, Rome, Sydney, Tokyo; Composition Teacher, Musikene-Basque Country Superior Conservatoire; Artistic Dir Ciclo de Conciertos de Música Contemporánea Fundación BBVA, Bilbao. *Compositions:* more than 65 pieces, including Krater for chamber ensemble, Kantak for piccolo and chamber ensemble, Bizitiza for mezzo soprano and ensemble, Izaro for piano quintet, Duduk I for solo soprano saxophone, Afrika for solo marimba and orchestra, Océano for orchestra, Veni Creator for choir, organ and percussion, Fuegos for Orchestra, Hamar for the 10th anniversary of the Guggenheim Museum, Bilbao, Tres Sonetos de Michelangelo for countertenor and orchestra, Ekaitza, concerto for cello and orchestra. *Recordings include:* Kantak, Krater, Nubes, Cuatro Diferencias for accordion, Fuegos, Ekaitza. *Honours:* SGAE Prize 1996, Basque Govt Prize 1999, INAEM Prize 2001, Spanish Acad. Rome Prize 2001, Premio Reina Sofia 2007. *Address:* c/o Music Department (repertoire promotion), Oxford University Press, Great Clarendon Street, Oxford, OX2 6DP, England. *Telephone:* (1865) 355021. *Fax:* (1865) 355060. *E-mail:* repertoire.promotion@oup.com. *Website:* www .erkoreka.com.

EROD, Ivan; Hungarian composer, academic and pianist; b. 2 Jan. 1936, Budapest; m. Marie-Luce Guy 1969; three s. two d. *Education:* Acad. of Music, Budapest, Acad. of Music, Vienna. *Career:* debut in Budapest; coach for Vienna State Opera 1962–64; concert pianist, with performances worldwide; appearances include Salzburg Festival, Vienna Philharmonic with Karl Bohm; Prof. of Composition and Music Theory, Hochschule für Musik und Darstellende Kunst, Graz 1971–89, Hochschule für Musik, Vienna 1989–2004; Guest Prof., Liszt Ferenc Acad. of Music, Budapest 2004–05; mem. Széchenyi Irodalmi it Müvészeti Akadémia 2009–. *Compositions include:* two operas, orchestral works, concertos, chamber music, cantatas, lieder, chorus works. *Recordings include:* as pianist, 10 albums with Rudolf Schock, tenor, Pierrot Lunaire (Die Reihe, Vienna) recordings in 10 countries; as composer, numerous radio recordings for BBC. *Publications:* contrib. articles to Osterreichische Musikzeitschrift. *Honours:* Hon. mem. Österreichischer Komponistenbund 2006; Ehrenzeichen für Verdienste um die Republik Österreich 2001; several Austrian state prizes, Bartók Pasztory Prize 1993. *Website:* www.ivan-eroed.at.

ESCAICH, Thierry; French composer and organist; b. 8 May 1965, Nogent-sur-Marne. *Education:* Conservatoire Nat. Supérieur de Musique, Paris. *Career:* compositions performed by Orchestre Nat. de Lille, Orchestre de Bretagne, Orchestra Nat. de Lyon, Philadelphia Orchestra, Chicago Symphony Orchestra, Berlin Konzerthaus Orchestra, Orchestre Philharmonique de Radio France, Mariinsky Theater Orchestra and Orchestre de Paris, and by Christoph Eschenbach, Lothar Zagrosek, Claire-Marie Le Guay, Paul Meyer, Iveta Apkalna, John Mark Ainsley, Trio Dali and Quatuor Voce, BBC Choir and Radio France Choir; numerous int. tours as concert organist, combining classic repertoire with own compositions and improvisations; Prof. of Composition and Improvisation, Paris Conservatoire 1992–; Organist, Église St-Étienne-du-Mont, Paris 1997–; Composer-in-Residence, Orchestra Nat. de Lyon 2007–11; fmr Composer-in-Residence, Orchestre Nat. de Lille and Orchestre de Bretagne; Associated Composer, Ensemble Orchestral de Paris 2011–. *Compositions include:* over 100 works, including La Barque Solaire (The Sun Boat) for organ and orchestra, Le Chant des ténèbres (The Song of Darkness), saxophone concerto, Le Dernier Évangile (The Last Gospel), oratorio for double choir, organ and orchestra 1999, Chaconne for orchestra 2000, Ad ultimas laudes for mixed choir, Choral's Dream for piano and organ 2003, Scènes de bal for string quartet, Vertiges de la croix (Awe and Wonder at the Cross) for orchestra 2004, Les Nuits hallucinées for mezzo-soprano and orchestra 2008, Violin Concerto, The Lost Dancer ballet for orchestra 2010, Études-Chorals for organ 2010, Questions de Vie for mixed voices and accordion 2011, Ground IV for four clarinets 2011. *Recordings include:* as organist: Le Chant des Ténèbres 1996, Escaich Joue Escaich 2001, Chorus 2003, Organ Spectacular 2008, Tanz-Fantasie, organ and trumpet (with Éric Aubier) 2009, Live Improvisations 2010; as composer: Le Dernier Évangile 2002, Organ Concerto No. 1 (Diapason d'Or de l'année) 2002, Exultet 2006, Miroir d'ombres (Monde de la Musique magazine Choc de l'année award) 2007, Lettres mêlées 2009, Les Nuits hallucinées (Classica magazine Choc award) 2011. *Honours:* Blumenthal Prize, Fondation franco-américaine Florence Blumenthal 1989, Prix des Lycéens 2002, Composer of the Year, Victoires de la Musique Classique 2003, 2006, 2011, Grand Prix de la Musique symphonique, SACEM 2004. *Current Management:* Karen McFarlane Artists, 33563 Seneca Drive, Cleveland, OH 44139, USA. *Website:* www.concertorganists.com; www.escaich.org.

ESCHENBACH, Christoph; German conductor and concert pianist; b. 20 Feb. 1940, Breslau (now Wrocław, Poland). *Education:* Musikhochschulen, Köln and Hamburg. *Career:* Musical Dir of Philharmonic Orchestra, Ludwigshafen 1979–83; Chief Conductor Tonhalle Orchestra, Zürich 1982–86; Co-Artistic Dir Pacific Music Festival 1992–98; Artistic Dir Schleswig-Holstein Music Festival 1999–2002; Musical Dir Houston Symphony Orchestra 1988–99 (Conductor Laureate 1999–), Ravinia Festival 1994–2003; Prin. Conductor NDR Symphony Orchestra 1998–2004; Musical Dir Orchestre de Paris 2000–10, Philadelphia Orchestra 2003–08; Music Dir, Nat. Symphony Orchestra, includes role as Music Dir, Kennedy Center 2010–17; has appeared as conductor Boston Symphony, Chicago Symphony, Houston Symphony, LA Philharmonic, New York Philharmonic, Philadelphia Orchestra, San Francisco Symphony (US conducting debut 1975), Berlin Philharmonic, Danish Nat. Radio Orchestra, Hamburg NDR Symphony Orchestra, Kirov Orchestra, all five London orchestras, Orchestre de Paris, Vienna Philharmonic; as pianist with Atlanta Symphony, Radio Orchestras of Munich and Stuttgart, Israel Philharmonic and Israel Chamber Orchestras, NHK Orchestra Tokyo; operatic engagements include Bayreuth, Houston Grand Opera, NY Metropolitan Opera, Hessian State Theatre, Darmstadt (operatic conducting debut 1978); festivals include Bayreuth, Ravinia and Schleswig-Holstein. *Recordings include:* Mozart: The Piano Sonatas 1967, Schubert: Music for Piano Duet II 1997, Rachmaninov: Piano Concertos Nos. 1-4 2007, Tchaikovsky: Symphony No. 6, 'Pathétique' 2008, Hindemith: Violinkonzert; Symphonic Metamorphosis; Konzertmusik (Grammy Award for Best Classical Compendium 2014) 2013. *Honours:* Officer's Cross with Ribbon, German Order of Merit 1990, Commdr's Cross 1993, Officer's Cross with Star of the German Order of Merit 2002, Chevalier de la Légion d'honneur 2002; 1st Prize, Steinway Piano Competition 1952, Munich Int. Competition 1962, Clara Haskil Competition 1965, Leonard Bernstein Award, Pacific Music Festival 1993. *Current Management:* Opus 3 Artists, 470 Park Avenue South, 9th Floor North, New York, NY 10016, USA. *E-mail:* info@opus3artists.com. *Website:* www.opus3artists.com; www.christoph-eschenbach.com.

ESCHKENAZY, Vesko, BMus, MMus; Bulgarian violinist; *Concertmaster,* ; b. 3 March 1970, Sofia. *Education:* L. Pipkov Nat. Music School, Sofia, P. Vladiguerov State Music Acad., studied violin with Angelina Atanassova and Prof. Petar Hristoskov, Guildhall School of Music, London with Prof. Ifra Neaman. *Career:* appeared as an orchestra leader as a child; Concertmaster, Youth Philharmonic Orchestra of Prof. Vladi Simeonov aged 11; Concertmaster, Koninklijk Concertgebouworkest 2000–; performs extensively in Europe, USA, South America, India, China and in festivals of Midem in Cannes, Montpellier and Atlantic (France), Music Festivals in Nantes and Rheims, New Year Music Festival in Sofia and Varna Summer and Apolonia Festival; soloist with the Royal Concertgebouw Orchestra, London Philharmonic Orchestra, English Chamber Orchestra, Monte Carlo Philharmonic, Sofia Philharmonic Orchestra, Mexico City Symphony, Netherlands Philharmonic Orchestra, Prague Symphony Orchestra, Nat. Symphony Orchestra of Ireland, Bach Chamber Orchestra, Berlin, etc.; has performed alongside Montserrat Caballé, Plácido Domingo, Alexis Weissenberg, Yuri Bashmet and Mstislav Rostropovich; has played under the direction of Mariss Jansons, Bernard Haitink, Riccardo Chailly, Kurt Masur, Sir Colin Davis, Carlo-Maria Giulini, Seiji Ozawa and Emil Tchakarov; concert performances include Violin Concerto in A major by Mozart under Mariss Jansons, Dvorak Violin Concerto under Sir Colin Davis, Barber Violin Concerto under Jaap van Zweden, Bruch

Violin Concerto in G minor under Ankush Kumar Bahl 2012, all with Royal Concertgebouw Orchestra; performed extensively with his brother, conductor Martin Panteleev, with whom he performed the Dvorak Violin Concerto with Orkest van het Oosten, Mozart's A major Concerto with Concertgebouw Chamber Orchestra and many other works 2009, also toured to Sofia and Istanbul with Concertgebouw Chamber Orchestra; season 2010–11: open air performance in centre of Sofia with Sofia Philharmonic Orchestra; Artist-in-Residence, Bulgaria Hall, Sofia with four recitals and a performance of the Bruch Violin Concerto in G minor with Sofia Philharmonic 2009; as a chamber musician, joined pianist Ludmil Angelov to perform sonata duos 1995, numerous concerts in Europe, performed complete Mozart sonatas for violin and piano, recital in Bulgaria Hall broadcast live by Bulgarian TV 2007; season 2012–13: formed a duo with pianist Marietta Petkova; has played a Guarneri del Gesu violin from 1738 since 2000. *Recordings include:* with Concertgebouw Chamber Orchestra: Concertos by Mozart, Mendelssohn and Schubert (Rondo), Bach Violin Concertos No. 1 & 2; Concerto for 2 Violins 2012; chamber music: joint Russian Music album with Ludmil Angelov, second album, The Fascinating George Gershwin 2013. *Honours:* Laureate, Int. Violin Competition 'Wieniawski' (Poland), China Int. Violin Competition, Beijing, Carl Flesch Competition, London, Musician of the Year, Bulgarian Nat. Radio 2010. *E-mail:* info@hbartistmanagement.com. *Website:* hbartistmanagement.com/?page_id=117. *Address:* Stichting Koninklijk Concertgebouworkest, Jacob Obrechtstraat 51, 1071 KJ Amsterdam, Netherlands (office).

ESCHRIG, Ralph; German singer (tenor); b. 2 April 1959, Dresden. *Education:* Musikhochschule Dresden. *Career:* sang at the Dresden Staatsoper 1984–87, notably in the local premiere of The Nose by Shostakovich; lyric tenor at the Berlin Staatsoper from 1987, notably as Mozart's Ottavio, Belmonte, Tamino and Ferrando, Fenton by Nicolai and in the Singspiels Erwin und Elmire by Reichardt and Zar und Zimmerman by Lortzing; concert appearances as the Evangelist in Bach's Passions, Lieder by Schubert and Schumann and The Diary of One who Disappeared by Janáček; engagements with the Dresden Kreuz Choir and Chorus of St Thomas's Leipzig and broadcasting stations in Germany and Finland. *Recordings include:* Mendelssohn Motets and Bastien und Bastienne by Mozart. *Honours:* prizewinner Int. Bach Competition 1984, Mozart Competition at Salzburg 1987.

ESCOT, Pozzi, BS, MS; American composer, teacher, writer on music and editor; *Professor of Graduate Theoretical Studies and Composition, New England Conservatory;* b. 1 Oct. 1933, New York, NY. *Education:* Juilliard School of Music, New York, Hamburg Hochschule für Musik, Germany with Philipp Jarnach. *Career:* teacher, New England Conservatory of Music, Boston 1964–67, Prof. of Grad. Theoretical Studies and Composition 1980–; Ed. Sonus Journal 1980, now Ed.-in-Chief; Visiting Lecturer, Harvard Univ., Princeton Univ., Univ. of Chicago, Columbia Univ., Stanford Univ., Univ. of California, Berkeley, Univ. of Illinois, Northwestern Univ., also Univ. of London, Univ. of Edinburgh, Univ. of Nice, Catholic Univ. of Eichstätt-Ingolstadt, Univ. of Augsburg, Univ. of Helsinki, Univ. of Hamburg, Univ. of Leuven, Sorbonne, Dublin Inst. of Tech., Univ. of Darmstadt, Univ. of Milan, Univ. of Paris, Beijing Univ., Shanghai Univ., Hanyang Univ., Yonsie Univ., Kunitachi Univ., Hiroshima Univ.; Pres. Int. Soc. of Hildegard von Bingen Studies 1993–; Woodrow Wilson Visiting Fellow 1999–; exhibited math. models at Univ. of Ancona, Nat. Museum of Fine Arts, Hungary, Harvard Univ., Univ. of Edinburgh, State Univ. of New York, Southwestern Coll., New England Conservatory. *Compositions:* six Symphonies 1952–2009, five string quartets, A Trilogy for chamber ensembles, concertos for piano, violin, saxophone, clarinet, diverse chamber and solo works, Three Poems of Rilke for narrator and string quartet, 1959, Three Movements for violin and piano 1959–60, Lamentus, Trilogy No. 1 for soprano and 8 players 1962, Visione, Trilogy No. 3 for soprano, speaker and 5 players 1964, Sands… for orchestra 1965, Neyrac Lux for two guitars and electric guitar 1978, Eure Pax for violin 1980, Concerto for piano and chamber orchestra 1982, Trio In Memoriam Solrac for violin, cello and piano 1984, Jubilation for string quartet 1991, Mirabilis III for low voice, three flutes and three violins 1995, Visione 97 for chorus 1997, Piano pieces and pieces for instrument and tape, Fifth Symphony 2000, Sixth Symphony 2001. *Publications:* Sonic Design: The Nature of Sound and Music (with Robert Cogan) 1976, Sonic Design: Practice and Problems (with Robert Cogan) 1981, The Poetic Simple Mathematics in Music 1999, Oh How Wondrous: Hildegard von Bingen Ten Essays; contrib. to Mystics Quarterly, Interface, New York Theory Society Music and Practice, Edinburgh University Musical Praxis, Perspectives of New Music, Stanford University Humanities Review, University of Leuven, Belgium. *Honours:* Radcliffe Inst., Rockefeller, Bellagio, Ford, Marshall Plan, Metropolitan Wash. Bd of Trade Certification of Award 1965, New York Acad. of Sciences Recognition 1986, Int. Cultural Diploma of Honor 1997, City of Cambridge/ Council Resolution Honor 2003, Int. Musician of the Year, Cambridge, UK 2004, Mass House of Reps Tribute for Lifetime Musical Achievement 2006, Outstanding Educator of America, Woman of the Year 2008, Certificate of AAAS 2013. *Address:* 24 Avon Hill, Cambridge, MA 02140, USA (home). *Telephone:* (617) 585-1374 (office); (617) 868-0215 (home). *Fax:* (617) 868-0215 (home). *E-mail:* pozzi.escot@necmusic.edu (office). *Website:* www.newenglandconservatory.edu (office); www.sonicdesign.org (office).

ESCRIBANO, María; Spanish composer and pianist; b. 24 Jan. 1954, Madrid. *Education:* Real Conservatorio Superior de Música de Madrid with Cristobal Halffter, Tomas Marco and Carmelo A. Bernaola, Curso Internacional de Música Manuel de Falla de Granada with Rodolfo Halffter, Darmstadt Int. Courses. *Career:* premiere of first work for instrumental ensemble 1975; resided in France as mem., Roy Hart Theatre, as composer, actress and pianist 1978–80; toured France, Belgium and Spain 1980; co-founder of theatrical group, Agada 1983; composition and music teaching 1989–; mem. Society of Authors. *Compositions include:* Muñecas de mimbre 1974, Sin Seso 1978, Concierto para Imma 1976, L'histoire d'un s. 1978, Cuentos y canciones de la media lunita 1987, Madrid de noche 1992, El sonido viajero 1992, Memoria del viento 1992, Desde la otra orilla 1993, Sortilegio 1993, Solar 1994. *Publications:* contrib. to Dictionary of Iberoamerican Music. *Honours:* several scholarships.

ESFAHANI, Mahan; Iranian/American musician (harpsichord); b. 1984, Tehran. *Education:* studied musicology (with George Houle) and history as a President's Scholar at Stanford Univ., also in Boston with Peter Watchorn, in Milan with Lorenzo Ghielmi, and in Prague with Zuzana Růžičková. *Career:* BBC New Generation Artist (first harpsichordist) 2008–10; Wigmore Hall solo debut in 2009; recitalist and concerto soloist at major European halls and with such orchestras as Acad. of Ancient Music, Orchestra of the Age of Enlightenment, The English Concert, Hamburg Symphony, Hanover Band, Arion Baroque Orchestra, BBC Symphony, BBC Nat. Orchestra of Wales, BBC Scottish Symphony, and B'Rock under conductors including Thierry Fischer, Martyn Brabbins and Jiří Bělohlávek; first ever solo harpsichord recital at BBC Proms 2011; invited to direct his own orchestration of J.S. Bach's Art of Fugue for Acad. of Ancient Music 2012; solo tour of Japan and appearances at Vienna Konzerthaus, Cologne Philharmonie, Cardiff's Hoddinott Hall, Prague Symphony Chamber Concerts, Musica Antiqua Festival of Bruges, Frick Collection, Leeds International Concert Season, Istanbul Bach Days, Maastricht Musica Sacra Festival, Copenhagen's Garnisonskirken, Vancouver Early Music, and others; collaborates regularly with recorder player Michala Petri; Fellow, New Coll., Oxford 2008. *Recordings include:* Byrd/Bach/Ligeti 2013, Rameau complete solo harpsichord works (2 CDs) 2013, C. P. E. Bach Württemberg Sonatas (Gramophone Award for Best Baroque Instrumental Recording) 2014, Corelli La Follia (with Michala Petri) 2014. *Honours:* Hon. Mem. Keble Coll., Oxford 2010; Borletti-Buitoni Trust Fellowship 2009–11. *Current Management:* c/o Rayfield Allied, Southbank House, Black Prince Road, London, SE1 7SJ, England. *Telephone:* (20) 3176-5500. *Fax:* (700) 602-4143. *E-mail:* ben.rayfield@rayfieldallied.com. *Website:* www.rayfieldallied.com; www.mahanesfahani.com.

ESHAM, Faith; American singer (soprano); b. 6 Aug. 1948, Vanceburg, Kentucky, USA. *Education:* Studied at Juilliard School with Jennie Tourel and Beverly Johnson. *Career:* Debut: New York City Opera in 1977 as Cherubino; European debut as Nedda in Nancy; Sang Cherubino at Glyndebourne in 1981 and at La Scala in 1982; Vienna Staatsoper in 1984 as Micaela in Carmen; Geneva Opera in 1984 as Mélisande; New York City Opera as Pamina in Die Zauberflöte, Leila in Les Pêcheurs de Perles, Marguerite in Faust and Massenet's Cendrillon; Washington DC as Zerlina in Don Giovanni; Pittsburgh Opera as Gilda; Las Palmas as Antonia in Les Contes d'Hoffmann; Metropolitan Opera debut in 1986 as Marzelline in Fidelio; Season 1990–91 as Musetta at Cologne, Pamina for Washington Opera and Susanna at Fort Lauderdale; Micaela for Cincinnati Opera, Butterfly at St Louis and Cherubino at the Dallas Opera, 1992; Sang Butterfly for Welsh National Opera, 1995; Concert appearances at the Mostly Mozart Festival, New York, Requiem and Schubert's A flat Mass, and Fauré's Requiem with the Pittsburgh Symphony under Charles Dutoit. *Recordings include:* La nozze di Figaro conducted by Haitink; Video of Carmen, with Domingo. *Honours:* Young Artists Award from the National Opera Institute, 1978–79; Concours International de Chant de Paris Prize, 1981.

ESPERIAN, Kallen; American singer (soprano); b. 8 June 1961, Waukegan, IL. *Education:* Univ. of Illinois. *Career:* sang in various opera houses and concert halls in the USA; toured with Pavarotti to China, singing Mimi in La Bohème; further appearances as Mimi at the Berlin and Vienna Staatsopers 1986, the Lyric Opera of Chicago and the Metropolitan, New York 1989; returned to the Metropolitan as Elena in I Vespri Siciliani; has sung Verdi's Luisa Miller in Vienna 1986, Verona and Geneva 1993; sang Desdemona at the Opéra Bastille in Paris and Reggio Emilia 1992, Mozart's Countess at St Louis, the Trovatore Leonora at Chicago and Nedda for Connecticut Grand Opera; San Francisco 1991 as Donna Elvira in Don Giovanni; sang Desdemona at Covent Garden 1997, and Amelia in the original version of Simon Boccanegra; season 1999–2000 as Alice Ford in Falstaff at Chicago and Elisabeth de Valois at Munich. *Honours:* winner Pavarotti Competition 1985. *E-mail:* ghproductions@comcast.net (office). *Website:* www.kallenesperian.com.

ESPERT ROMERO, Nuria; Spanish actress and director; b. 11 June 1935, Hospitalet (Barcelona); m. Armando Moreno 1955; two d. *Career:* professional actress since 1947; first maj. success in Medée aged 19; created her own co. 1959; has appeared in works by Calderón, Shakespeare, O'Neill, Lope De Vega, Genet, Lorca, Espriu, Valle Inclán, Sartre etc.; Dir The House of Bernarda Alba (Lorca) with Glenda Jackson and Joan Plowright, London 1986 (Evening Standard Drama Award); has also directed operas Madame Butterfly, Elektra, Rigoletto, La Traviata and Carmen at Covent Garden and in Scotland, Brussels, Israel and Japan; Artistic Dir Turandot, Liceo Theater, Barcelona 1999. *Theatre includes:* The Seagull 1997, Master Class 1998, Who's Afraid of Virginia Woolf 1999, 2000, Medée 2002. *Publications:* numerous int. theatre publications. *Honours:* more than 100 Spanish honours

and awards; 17 int. awards. *Address:* Pavia 2, 28013 Madrid, Spain. *Fax:* (91) 3511177 (office); (91) 5474501 (home). *E-mail:* interludio@portalatino.net (home).

ESPOSITO, Valeria; Italian singer (soprano); b. 10 April 1961, Naples. *Education:* Salerno Conservatoire. *Career:* debut at Teatro del Giglio in Lucca as Zerlina in Don Giovanni 1986; appeared in concert productions at La Scala of Riccardo III by Flavio Testi and Berg's Lulu; Amsterdam 1987 as Nausicca in Ulisse by Dallapiccola; Lucca 1987 in Domenico Puccini's Il Ciarlatano; Teatro Lirico Milan as Sophie in Werther; US debut at Houston 1988 in Werther; Teatro San Carlo Naples 1988 as Amor in Orfeo e Euridice; La Scala 1989 in Pergolesi's Lo Frate Innamorato; Radio France 1989 in the title role of Linda di Chamounix by Donizetti; WNO 1989 as Amina in La Sonnambula; sang Ippodamia in Paer's Achille at Lugo di Romagna 1988; sang Amina at the 1992 Macerata Festival and at Rome 1996; season 1995–96 as Adina at Rome, Rossini's Fiorilla at Catania and Constanze at the Vienna Staatsoper; Offenbach's Olympia at Catania 1998; Lucia di Lammermoor at Toulouse 1998; sang Gilda at St Gallen and the Queen of Night at Barcelona 2000. *Honours:* Winner Aslico Competition, Milan 1987, Winner Cardiff Singer of the World Competition 1987. *Current Management:* c/o Lirica International via Croce Bianca 31, 37139 Verona, Italy. *Telephone:* (045) 8104688. *Fax:* (045) 810-0353. *E-mail:* info@liricainternational.com. *Website:* www .liricainternational.com; www.valeriaesposito.com.

ESSWOOD, Paul Lawrence Vincent, ARCM; British singer (countertenor) and conductor; b. 6 June 1942, Nottingham; s. of Alfred W. Esswood and Freda Garatt; m. 1st Mary L. Cantrill 1966 (divorced 1990); two s.; m. 2nd Aimée Désirée Blattmann 1990; one s. one d. *Education:* West Bridgford Grammar School and Royal Coll. of Music. *Career:* Lay Vicar, Westminster Abbey 1964–71; Prof., Royal Coll. of Music 1973–85, Royal Acad. of Music 1985–; Co-founder Pro Cantione Antiqua – A Cappella 1967; opera debut in L'Erismena, Univ. of Calif., Berkeley 1968; debut at La Scala, Milan with Zürich Opera in L'Incoronazione di Poppea and Il Ritorno d'Ulisse 1978; Scottish opera debut in Dido and Aeneas 1978; world premiere in Penderecki's Paradise Lost, Chicago Lyric Opera 1979, Philip Glass's Akhnaton, Stuttgart 1984, Herbert Will's Schlafes Bruder, with Zurich Opera 1996; world première in Schnittke's Faust Cantata, Vienna, 1986; Handel's Riccardo Primo, Covent Garden, 1991; specialist in performing baroque music and has made many recordings of works by Bach, Handel, Purcell, Monteverdi, Cavalli, Britten (Abraham and Isaac), folksongs, others; Prof. at 'Maîtrise de Notre Dame', Paris, conducting debut at Chichester Festival with Purcell's The Fairy Queen 2000, Kraków, Poland 2001. *Honours:* Hon. RAM 1990; Handel Prize (Germany) 1992. *Address:* Jasmine Cottage, 42 Ferring Lane, Ferring, West Sussex, BN12 6QT, England (home). *Telephone:* (1903) 504480 (home). *Fax:* (1903) 504480 (home). *Website:* www.esswood.co.uk.

ESTEP, Craig; American singer (tenor); b. 1962. *Career:* sang Rinuccio in Gianni Schicchi at Charlotte Opera 1987; San Francisco Opera as Ferrando in Così fan tutte, Alfredo, Nemorino, and Noburo in the 1991 US premiere of Henze's Das verratene Meer; Washington Opera 1992–95, as Nemorino, and Tonio in La fille du Régiment; Calgary Opera 1994, as Edgardo; Cologne 1995, as Anfinomo in Monteverdi's Ulisse; other roles include Pong in Turandot, Cassio in Otello and Ernesto in Don Pasquale.

ESTES, Simon; American singer (bass-baritone); b. 2 March 1938, Centerville, Ia. *Education:* Univ. of Iowa with Charles Kellis, Juilliard School, New York. *Career:* sang at various German opera houses from 1965 with debut at Deutsche Oper Berlin as Ramfis in Aida; mem. Zürich Opera 1976; Metropolitan Opera from 1976 in roles including Oroveso in Norma, La Scala 1977 as Arkel in Pelléas et Mélisande, Hamburg Staatsoper 1978 as King Philip in Don Carlos, Bayreuth Festival from 1978 as the Dutchman and Amfortas, Geneva Opera 1984 as Jochanaan in Salome, and Covent Garden debut 1986 as Wagner's Dutchman; sang Wotan in new productions of Der Ring des Nibelungen at Berlin 1984–85 and the Metropolitan 1986–88; appearances at San Francisco, Glyndebourne Festival, Paris Opéra, Munich and Vienna; other roles include the Villains in Les Contes d'Hoffmann, Escamillo, King Mark, Mephistopheles, the Pharoah in Rossini's Moses and Boris Godunov; concert engagements include US premiere of 14th Symphony by Shostakovich with Philadelphia Orchestra; other concerts with New York Philharmonic, Chicago Symphony, Boston Symphony and Berlin Philharmonic; BBC Promenade Concerts debut, London 1989 in Act III, Die Walküre; sang title role in the musical King, London 1990; season 1992 included Macbeth for Greater Miami Opera and Wotan at Bonn; sang Zaccaria in Nabucco at Orange Festival 1994, Porgy at Cape Town 1996; debut at The Washington Opera 1998 as Simon Boccanegra and at Los Angeles Opera 2000 as Amonasro; numerous recitals in Austria, France, Germany, Japan, Spain, Switzerland and USA. *Recordings include:* Simon Boccanegra, Oberto by Verdi, Mahler's 8th Symphony, Fauré's Requiem, Flying Dutchman, Parsifal, Carmen, Messiah, Beethoven's 9th, Mozart's Requiem, Verdi's Requiem, Oedipus Rex, Broadway's Greatest Hits, Spirituals. *Current Management:* c/o Personal Artists Management, Gudrun Rohrbach Sierichstrasse 99, 22299 Hamburg, Germany. *Telephone:* (40) 488147. *Fax:* (40) 4801247. *E-mail:* grohrbach@arcor.de.

ETTINGER, Daniel; Israeli conductor, singer (baritone) and pianist; *Music Director and Principal Conductor, Nationaltheater Mannheim*; b. 1971. *Education:* Tel-Aviv Univ., Rubin Acad. of Music, Jerusalem. *Career:* debut as opera singer in recital with Israel Philharmonic Orchestra 1993, went on to perform numerous opera roles including Papageno in The Magic Flute, Figaro in Il Barbiere di Seviglia, Don Giovanni and Masetto in Don Giovanni, Lescaut in Manon, Albert in Werther, Ottone in L'incoronazione di Poppea, Marullo in Rigoletto, Silvano in Un Ballo in Maschera, Hermann and Schlemil in The Tales of Hoffmann, Demetrius and Starveling in A Midsummer Night's Dream, Farfarello in The Love for Three Oranges, Dancairo in Carmen, Marquese D'Obigny in La Traviata; conducting debut with Jerusalem Symphony Orchestra 1999, Chief Guest Conductor 2002–03; Conductor-in-Residence, Israeli Opera 1999–2003; Kapellmeister, Staatsoper Unter den Linden, Berlin 2003–; Music Dir and Prin. Conductor, Israel Symphony Orchestra 2005–; appearances as guest conductor with Staatsoper Berlin 2003–04, 2005–07, Tokyo New Nat. Theater 2004–05, 2006–07, Los Angeles Opera 2005, Tokyo Philharmonic Orchestra 2006, Wiener Staatsoper 2007–08, Washington Nat. Opera 2008–09; Music Dir and Prin. Conductor, Nationaltheater Mannheim 2009–; Chief Conductor, Tokyo Philharmonic Orchestra 2010–. *Honours:* Israel Cultural Excellence Foundation Award 2003. *Current Management:* ArtPro, POB 22044, Tel Aviv 61220, Israel. *Telephone:* 9-9505816. *Fax:* 9-9505817. *E-mail:* urizur@artpro.co.il. *Website:* www.artpro.co.il.

EUBA, Akin, PhD; Nigerian composer, musician (piano) and lecturer; *Andrew W. Mellon Professor of Music, University of Pittsburgh*; b. 28 April 1935, Lagos; one s. one d. *Education:* CMS Grammar School, Lagos, Trinity Coll. of Music, London, England, Univ. of Calif., Los Angeles, and Univ. of Ghana, Legon. *Career:* Sr Programme Asst, Nigerian Broadcasting Corpn 1957–60, Head of Music and Music Research 1960–65; performer, numerous recitals in Europe, USA, Africa; organizer, numerous concerts of African music at home and abroad; lecturer in Africa and abroad 1966–; teacher, Univ. of Lagos 1966–68, Univ. of Ife 1968–77; Dir Center for Cultural Studies, Univ. of Lagos 1978–81; Dir Elekoto Music Centre, Lagos 1981–86; Research Scholar, Univ. of Bayreuth, Germany 1986–91; Dir Centre for Intercultural Music Arts, London 1988–; Hon. Visiting Prof., Dept of Music, City Univ., London 1993–96; Andrew W. Mellon Prof., Univ. of Pittsburgh, PA, USA 1997–; Overseas Fellow, Churchill Coll., Cambridge 2000–01; composer-in-residence, Ensemble Noir, Toronto, Canada 2003; World Music Scholar-in-Residence, Azusa Pacific Univ. 2004; Dir, Centre for Intercultural Musicology, Churchill Coll., Cambridge 2006–. *Compositions include:* Introduction and allegro 1956, String Quartet 1957, Two Yoruba Folk Songs 1959, The Wanderer for cello 1960, Igi nla so 1963, Five Pieces for English Horn and Piano 1963, Dance to the Rising Sun for chamber orchestra 1963, Three Songs for voice, piano and Iyalu drum 1963, Four Pieces 1964, Four Pictures from Oyo Calabashes for piano 1964, Impressions from an Akwete Cloth for piano 1964, Saturday Night at the Caban Bamboo for piano 1964, Tortoise and the Speaking Cloth (dramatic music) 1964, Abiku I (incidental music, for Iya–Abiku) 1965, Four Pieces for African Orchestra 1966, Legend 1966, Olurounbi: A Symphonic Study on a Yoruba Legend 1967, Wind Quartet 1967, Abiku II 1968, The Fall of the Scales 1970, Dirges 1970, Chaka (opera) 1970, The Laughing Tree 1970, Scenes from Traditional Life for piano 1970, Music for violin, horn, piano and percussion 1970, Ice Cubes for string orchestra 1970, Six Yoruba Folk Songs 1975, Two Tortoise Folk Tales in Yoruba 1975, FESTAC 77 1977, Black Bethlehem (opera) 1979, West African Universities Games Anthem 1981, Two Songs for orchestra with chorus 1983, Bethlehem (opera) 1984, Time Passes By 1985, Seven Modern African Poems 1987, Two Modern African Poems 1987, Wakar Duru: Studies in African Pianism Nos 1–3 1987, Themes from Chaka No. 1 1996, Orunmila's Voices 2002, Study in African Jazz No. 3 2002, Themes from Chaka 2 2003, Below Rusumo Falls 2003. *Honours:* first prize in piano performance Nigerian Festival of the Arts 1950–52, Fed. Govt of Nigeria Scholarship 1952–57, Rockefeller Foundation fellowship for study at Univ. of Calif., Los Angeles 1962–64. *Address:* Room 204, Music Building, Department of Music, University of Pittsburgh, Pittsburgh, PA 15260, USA (office). *E-mail:* aeuba@pitt.edu (office). *Website:* www.pitt.edu/~musicdpt (office).

EULER, Christian, BMus, MMus; German violist; b. 12 May 1956, Kassel; m.; one s. *Education:* Juilliard School of Music, USA. *Career:* Philadelphia Orchestra, under Riccardo Muti 1984–91; mem., Philadelphia Chamber Ensemble; Prof. of Viola and Chamber Music, Universität für Musik und darstellende Kunst, Graz, Austria 1991–; solo and chamber music appearances in Europe.

EVAN, Allan; American singer (baritone); b. 1941, Macon, GA. *Education:* Juilliard, New York and studied in Munich, Salzburg and Vienna. *Career:* sang at Trier and elsewhere in Germany from 1968, as Crown in Porgy and Bess; Bremen Opera 1973–76, Zürich 1976–79, Basle 1977–87, Mannheim from 1987; other roles have included Escamillo and Pizarro (at Graz), Don Giovanni, Amonasro (Wiesbaden 1996), Wotan, Amfortas and Scarpia in Tosca (Mannheim 1994); Strauss's Barak and D. Schnyder's The Tempest, Berne 1996; sang Dr Schön in Lulu at Mannheim 1998.

EVANGELATOS, Daphne; Greek singer (mezzo-soprano); b. 1952, Athens. *Education:* studied in Athens, Munich and Vienna. *Career:* sang first at the Bayerische Staatsoper, Munich then in Vienna, Cologne, Frankfurt, Hamburg and Vienna; Théâtre de la Monnaie Brussels 1982 in La Clemenza di Tito; Hamburg Staatsoper 1984 in Cavall's L'Ormindo; Salzburg Festival 1985 in Henze's version of Monteverdi's Il Ritorno d'Ulisse, as Melanto; Cologne 1986 as the Prince in Massenet's Cendrillon; other roles include Octavian in Der Rosenkavalier, Mozart's Cherubino, Sextus and Annius, Preziosilla in La Forza del Destino, the Composer in Ariadne auf Naxos and Wagner's Waltraute; sang Tisbe in La Cenerentola at the 1988 Salzburg Festival; Wolf-Ferrari's Le Donne Curiose at the 1990 Munich Festival; has also appeared in Campra's Tancrède, at Aix, Ramiro in La Finta Giardiniera, Orpheus, Mozart's Annius and Sextus, Fricka, Waltraute, and Varvara in Katya Kabanova.

EVANGELIDES, Petros; Cypriot singer (tenor); b. 1949, Limasol. *Education:* studied in Athens and Vienna. *Career:* sang at Klagenfurt 1973–74 and as Ernesto on tour in Switzerland, Germany and The Netherlands 1974; Stadttheater Berne 1976–82, Nat. Theatre Mannheim 1982–84, Glyndebourne Festival 1983 as Pedrillo in Die Entführung, Deutsche Oper Berlin as Monostatos and Pedrillo; further appearances in Stuttgart, Amsterdam and Berlin, returned to Glyndebourne 1984–91, in L'Incoronazione di Poppea, Falstaff, Die Entführung and Carmen; Vienna Staatsoper from 1984, notably in 1986 tour to Japan in Manon Lescaut and Tristan und Isolde; La Scala debut in 1986 as Monostatos; sang Johannes in the premiere of Der Rattenfänger by Friedrich Cerha, Graz 1987; guest engagements at Hamburg as Brighella in Ariadne, Bonn, Zürich as Singer in Rosenkavalier, Strasbourg and Vichy. *Recordings include:* L'Incoronazione di Poppea (film).

EVANS, Dame Anne, DBE; British singer (soprano); b. 20 Aug. 1941, London, England. *Education:* Royal Coll. of Music, London and Conservatoire de Musique, Geneva. *Career:* Prin. Soprano, ENO 1968–78; debut as Mimi in La Bohème, then Mozart's Fiordiligi, Verdi's Violetta, Strauss's Marschallin, Wagner's Elsa and Sieglinde and Smetana's Mlada; with Welsh Nat. Opera sang Strauss's Chrysothemis, Empress and Dyer's Wife, Beethoven's Leonore, Mozart's Donna Anna; has sung extensively in Germany, Italy, France and America, including Brünnhilde in Berlin, Nice, Paris, Turin, Zürich, Vienna, Buenos Aires and at the 1989–92 Bayreuth Festivals; Isolde in Brussels 1994, Berlin 1996, Dresden 1997 and Paris 1998; Sieglinde in San Francisco; Elsa in Buenos Aires; Leonore in Stuttgart; made Metropolitan debut with Elisabeth in Tannhäuser 1992 and returned for Leonore in Fidelio 1993; recitals at Edinburgh Festival 1993 and Wigmore Hall 1995; sang Brünnhilde in Siegfried 1995, and Götterdämmerung 1996 at Covent Garden; Ariadne in Ariadne auf Naxos (original version), Edinburgh Festival 1997; Madame Lidoine in Les dialogues des Carmélites, Glimmerglass Opera Festival 2002; now teaching, coaching and adjudicating; trustee, Countess of Munster musical scholarships 2009–. *Recordings:* Helmwige and Third Norn in ENO Ring under Goodall, Brünnhilde's Immolation scene, Brünnhilde in Der Ring des Nibelungen from Bayreuth, Mrs Grose in The Turn of the Screw, Chrysothemis in Elektra, Brünnhilde in Die Walküre, Siegfried and Götterdämmerung, Bayreuth (DVD). *Honours:* Hon. DMus (Kent) 2005. *Current Management:* c/o Ingpen & Williams, 7 St George's Court, 131 Putney Bridge Road, London, SW15 2PA, England. *Telephone:* (20) 8874-3222. *Fax:* (20) 8877-3113. *E-mail:* info@ingpen.co.uk. *Website:* www.ingpen.co.uk.

EVANS, Damon; American singer (tenor); b. 1960, Baltimore, MD. *Education:* Interlochen Arts Acad. *Career:* sang Amon in Akhnaten by Philip Glass at the New York City Opera 1985; Virginia Opera Association 1985 as Benji in the premiere of Musgrave's Harriet: The Woman Called Moses; Glyndebourne Festival 1986 as Sportin' Life in Porgy and Bess; has also sung Sportin' Life at Charleston, Boston, London with Philharmonic Orchestra and Moscow with the Finnish Nat. Opera 1988; concert engagements include Beethoven's Ninth and Pulcinella, conducted by Simon Rattle; Bernstein's West Side Story at the Usher Hall in Edinburgh and a Bernstein Celebration at Alice Tully Hall in New York; sang in the British premiere of Blitzstein's Airborne Symphony with the London Symphony, A Child of Our Time at the City of London Festival and Weill's three Concert Suites at the Almeida Festival; Carnegie Hall debut 1989 in the premiere of a suite from Weill's Lost in the Stars; has also sung Janáček's Diary of One Who Disappeared with Matrix at the QEH; sang Don José in Carmen Jones in London 1991; sang in Porgy and Bess at Covent Garden 1992 and in the Weill/Grosz concert at the 1993 London Proms; sang Sporting Life at Costa Mesa, CA 1996.

EVANS, (D.) John O., BMus, MA, PhD; British broadcaster and musicologist; *President and Executive Director, Oregon Bach Festival*; b. 17 Nov. 1953, Morriston, Wales. *Education:* Univ. Coll., Cardiff, Univ. of Wales. *Career:* First Research Scholar, Britten-Pears Library and Archive, Red House, Aldeburgh 1980–85; Music Producer, BBC Radio 3 1985–89, Chief Producer (series) 1992–93, Head of Music Dept 1993–97, Head of Classical Music 1997–2000, Head of Music Programming 2000–07; Postgraduate Music Tutor, Univ. Coll., Cardiff 1986–87; Artistic Dir, Volte Face Opera Project 1986–89; Exec. Trustee, Peter Pears Award 1989–92; Artistic Dir, Covent Garden Chamber Orchestra 1990–93; Pres. and Exec. Dir Oregon Bach Festival 2007–; guest lecturer, Nat. Film Theatre, ENO, Fairfield Halls, Croydon, Britten-Pears School, Aldeburgh Festival, Royal Coll. of Music, Goldsmiths' Coll. London, Hull Univ., Camden Festival, Bath Festival, Int. Brown Symposium on Benjamin Britten at Southwestern Univ., Georgetown, TX, USA; Chair., Royal Philharmonic Soc. Awards Opera Jury; juror Int. Conductors' Competition, Lisbon 1995, Kondrashin Conducting Competition 1998, BBC Singer of the World Competition, Cardiff 2003–, Tosti Int. Singing Competition; Dir, Britten Estate; Trustee, Britten Pears Foundation; Chair., Concentric Circles Theatre Bd. *Publications:* Benjamin Britten: Pictures from a Life 1943–1976 (with Donald Mitchell) 1978, Benjamin Britten: his Life and Operas (ed.) 1982; contrib. to A Britten Companion 1984, A Britten Source Book 1987, ENO, Royal Opera and Cambridge Opera Guides on Britten's Peter Grimes, Gloriana, The Turn of the Screw, Death in Venice; articles in magazines, including Opera Quarterly. *Honours:* Prix Italia 1989, Charles Heidsieck Award 1989, Royal Philharmonic Soc. Award 1994, Sony Radio

Award 1997, Vienna TV Award 2004. *Address:* c/o Oregon Bach Festival, University of Oregon, Eugene, OR 97403, USA (office). *Telephone:* (541) 346-1000 (office). *E-mail:* bachfest@uoregon.edu (office). *Website:* www.oregonbachfestival.com (office); www.uoregon.edu (office).

EVANS, Joseph; American singer (tenor) and academic; *Coordinator, Voice Studies Area and Professor of Music, Moores School of Music, University of Houston;* b. 13 Aug. 1945, Brookhaven, Miss. *Education:* North Texas State Univ. *Career:* sang with the New York City Opera in Les Pêcheurs de Perles, Maria Stuarda, Don Giovanni, The Love for Three Oranges, Attila and La Traviata; appearances with the Opera Company of Boston in Don Pasquale, Rigoletto, Benvenuto Cellini, War and Peace, I Capuleti e i Montecchi, Ruslan and Lyudmilla, Die Soldaten by Zimmermann, Montezuma by Sessions and Orphée aux Enfers; has also sung with Houston Grand Opera and with opera companies in San Diego, Palm Beach, Cincinnati, Cleveland, Hawaii, Fort Worth and Colorado; sang in The Love for Three Oranges in Geneva, The Prodigal Son in Venice, Persephone by Stravinsky at Nancy, and Guidon in Rimsky's Tsar Saltan at La Scala; season 1988–89 with The Devil and Kate and Marschner's Der Templer und die Jüdin at Wexford; sang Alwa in Lulu for Opéra de Nantes, and Max in Der Freischütz for WNO; concert engagements with Bernstein and the New York Philharmonic, Lukas Foss and the Brooklyn Philharmonic and with Julius Rudel and Michael Tilson Thomas; has also sung with the Pittsburgh, Atlanta and Indianapolis Symphony Orchestras and appeared in concerts with the Orchestre de l'Ile de France; sang Lucas Wardlaw in Floyd's Passion of Jonathan Wade, Santa Fe 1996; sang Captain Vere in Billy Budd at Seattle 2001; Teacher, Voice and Choral Studies, The Hockaday School, Dallas 1971–74; Guest Instructor, Univ. of Texas, March-May 1992, Visiting Lecturer 1992–93; Assoc. Prof., Univ. of Miami 1994–98; Prof. of Music, Moores School of Music, Univ. of Houston 1998–, also Coordinator, Voice Studies Area; Dir Brevard Music Center High School Voice Program 2014. *Current Management:* John Gingrich Management, Inc., PO Box 1515, New York, NY 10023, USA. *Address:* Moores School of Music, University of Houston, 3333 Cullen Blvd, Room 120, Houston, TX 77204-4201, USA (office). *Telephone:* (713) 743-3149 (office). *E-mail:* jsevans@uh.edu (office). *Website:* www.uh.edu/class/music (office).

EVANS, Peter; British singer (tenor); b. 1962, England. *Education:* Royal Northern Coll. of Music, Royal Scottish Acad. *Career:* South Bank debut as Purcell's Aeneas with the English Chamber Orchestra 1988; further concerts with the Bournemouth Sinfonietta, London Bach Orchestra and Royal Liverpool Philharmonic; repertory has included Elijah, Messiah (at Gdańsk, Poland), Mozart's Requiem (Aix Festival), Purcell's King Arthur with the English Concert and Hindemith's Das Nusch-Nuschi with the BBC Symphony Orchestra 1995; sang Monteverdi's Orfeo at the Aldeburgh Festival 1993; First Shepherd with ENO 1996; Covent Garden Festival as Mozart's Schauspieldirektor and Lurcanio in Handel's Ariodante 1996–97; concert venues include the QEH, St John's Smith Square and the Wigmore Hall. *Honours:* NFMS Concert Artists Award 1987.

EVANS, Peter Angus, BA, BMus, MA, DMus, FRCO; British fmr musicologist; b. 7 Nov. 1929, West Hartlepool; s. of Rev. James Mackie Evans and Elizabeth Mary Fraser; m. June Margaret Vickery 1953 (died 2011). *Education:* Durham Univ. with Arthur Hutchings and A. E. F. Dickinson. *Career:* Music Master, Bishop Wordsworth's School, Salisbury 1951–52; Lecturer, Durham Univ. 1953–61; Prof. of Music, Southampton Univ. 1961–90; Conductor, Southampton Philharmonic Soc. 1965–90. *Compositions:* Sonata for oboe and piano 1953, Three Preludes for organ 1955, Concerto for clarinet and string orchestra 1957, Stabat Mater for chorus and orchestra 1958. *Publications include:* The Vocal Works in Michael Tippett: A Symposium (chapter) 1965, Music of the European Mainstream 1940–60 (chapter in New Oxford History of Music, Vol. X: The Modern Age) 1974, The Music of Benjamin Britten 1979 (expanded edns 1989, 1996), Instrumental Music (chapter in Blackwell History of Music in Britain, 20th-century vol.) 1995; contrib. of articles on Britten and Jonathan Harvey in Tempo and The Musical Times, articles on Britten and Rawsthorne in The New Grove Dictionary of Music and Musicians 1980. *Honours:* Hon. mem. Guildhall School of Music 1998; Limpus Prize, Reid Prize. *Address:* Pye's Nest Cottage, Parkway, Ledbury, Herefordshire, HR8 2JD, England (home). *Telephone:* (1531) 633256 (home).

EVANS, Peter Geoffrey, BMus, ARCM; British pianist, teacher and conductor; b. 13 Jan. 1950, Redhill, Surrey, England; m. Ulrike Fenner. *Education:* Univ. of Edinburgh, Hochschule für Musik, Vienna, Austria. *Career:* performances as solo pianist and in various duos and ensembles throughout UK, including Aldeburgh and Edinburgh Festivals, London's South Bank and Wigmore Halls, St John's Smith Square, also in Austria, Denmark, Germany, France, Netherlands, Poland, Ireland, USA, fmr USSR, Japan, Kenya 1974–; appearances on Scottish, Tyne-Tees and BBC TV, including BBC 2 Beethoven cello/piano sonata series; recordings for French and Swedish Radio and BBC Radio 3; soloist with all major orchestras in Scotland; Prin. Conductor, Edinburgh's Meadows Chamber Orchestra 1972–; conducting debut in Spain at Festival of Torroella de Montgri, Catalonia 1986; close association with Int. Musicians Seminar, Cornwall 1982–93; master classes, Oberlin Coll., Ohio, USA 1980, Deal Summer Music Festival 1985–88; mem. London-based Premiere Ensemble 1990–; Artistic Co-Dir of Hebrides Ensemble 1991–2003; workshops and concerts in Kenya, including conducting Nairobi Orchestra 2005, 2007, 2010; teacher of piano and jazz, Aberdeen City Music School 2009–. *Recordings:* Brahms and Martinů sonatas for cello and piano, with Steven Isserlis, cello; Cello and piano recital, with Alexander Baillie, cello, 1988; Solo piano in Britten's Young Apollo, with Scottish Chamber Orchestra, Serebrier, 1990; Recital of French music for cello and piano; Works by Webern, Lutosławski and Rachmaninov for cello and piano, with William Conway; more than 80 recordings for BBC, including a large number for Radio 3. *Address:* 49/6 Spottiswoode Road, Edinburgh, EH9 1DA, Scotland. *Telephone:* (131) 447-6414. *Fax:* (131) 447-6414. *E-mail:* peterevans49@hotmail.com.

EVANS, Rebecca Ann; British singer (soprano); b. 19 Aug. 1963, Neath, Wales. *Education:* Guildhall School of Music and Drama, London. *Career:* debut as Gretel in Hansel and Gretel, WNO 1990; has appeared in television series, Encore and Rebecca Evans; roles include Ilia in Idomeneo, Oscar in Un Ballo in Maschera, Inez in La Favorita, the title role in Massenet's Cendrillon, and the Countess in Rossini's Count Ory; season 1994 as Strauss's Sophie and Berlioz's Hero for WNO, Marzelline in Leonore at the Edinburgh Festival; Janáček's Vixen with Scottish Opera, 1997; season 1998 as Susanna for the Royal Opera, Massenet's Cendrillon at Ghent and Nannetta at the London Proms; season 2000–01 as Anne Trulove at San Francisco and Sophie at Munich (also Susanna, and Zdenka in Arabella); sang Zerlina at Covent Garden, 2002, Nannetta in 2003. *Recordings:* Mabel in The Pirates of Penzance; Belinda in Dido and Aeneas; Barbarina in Le nozze di Figaro; Nannetta in Falstaff conducted by John Eliot Gardiner; Italian Song Recital; Delius, Requiem; Finzi, Dies Natalis, Humperdinck's Hansel and Gretel (Grammy Award for Best Opera Recording 2008) 2008. *Honours:* Hon DMus (Glamorgan) 1997, (Wales) 2009; Prizewinner, BP Peter Pears 1990, Young Welsh Singer of the Year 1991, Théâtre du Châtelet Paris Prix Hélène Rochas 2001, Sir Geraint Evans Music Prize 2009. *Address:* 203 Fidlas Road, Llanishen, Cardiff CF14 5NA, Wales.

EVANS, Tecwyn; New Zealand chorus master, conductor and composer; b. 1971, Auckland. *Education:* University of Otago, University of Kansas with Brian Priestman. *Career:* debut, Dunedin Sinfonia, 1997; led Die Fledermaus for Kansas University Opera; Chorus Master at Glyndebourne Festival, from 1999–2002; engagements with Netherlands Radio Choir, and choral workshops in New Zealand, USA and England; Assistant Conductor at Glyndebourne 2001 for Otello (Festival) and Le nozze di Figaro (Tour); Fidelio at the Paris Châtelet, 2000. *Compositions include:* Waikareiti 1990, Where is my Green Pasture? 1990, My Father Today 1991, Gerauschvoll 1994, Heedless Conclusions 1994, Point of Farewell 1994, Quartet No. 1 1994, Set me as a Seal upon thine Heart 1994, The Graduate Fanfare 1994, Onward 1995, Akaroa 1995, Fires of Light 1996, Three Miniatures and a Cadenza 1996, God Be in My Head 1997, Every Other Day in Sunshine 1998, I Will Betroth Thee 1998, Psalm 100 1998, To See the World 1998, Cat on the Mat 2000, The Lamb 2002, Hymn to the Virgin 2004, Dedica. *Honours:* Fulbright Fellowship.

EVANS, Wynne, BMus, AGSM; British singer (tenor); b. 1972, Carmarthen, Wales; s. of David Evans and Elizabeth Evans MBE; m. Tanwen 1999; one s. one d. *Education:* Guildhall School, Nat. Opera Studio, London. *Career:* performances as a principal tenor with Welsh Nat. Opera include Duke in Rigoletto, Cassio in Otello, Naraboth in Salome, Rodolfo in La Bohème, Tamino in Die Zauberflöte, Alfredo in La Traviata, Jaquino in Leonore, Schoolmaster in Cunning Little Vixen, Chevalier in Les Dialogues de Carmelites, Italian Tenor in Rosenkavalier, First Jew in Salome, Liberto in L'Incoronazione di Poppea, Brighella in Ariadne auf Naxos and Alfred in Die Fledermaus; other roles include Alfredo La Traviata, Spoletta in Tosca, Second Jew in Salome for ENO, Fenton in Falstaff , Prunier in La Rondine, Paulino in The Secret Marriage for Opera North, Tamino in Die Zauberflöte and Italian Tenor in Der Rosenkavalier for Scottish Opera, Fracasso in La Finta Semplice for the Classical Opera Company, Orpheus in Orpheus in the Underworld for Opera Holland Park, Peacock in Param Vir's Broken Strings for the Almeida Festival (recorded for BBC), Vasek in The Bartered Bride for Neath Opera, Rodolfo for Castleward Opera, Arvino il Lombardi and Foresto Attila for the Chelsea Opera Group, Don Ottavio, Don Giovanni and the title role in Robinson Crusoe for British Youth Opera; concert performances include Vaughan William's Serenade to Music at the televised opening night of the 2001 BBC Proms, Elgar's The Dream of Gerontius at the Welsh Proms in St David's Hall, Tippett's A Child of our Time in France, La mort d'Orfée with the Hanover Band, Third Jew Salome with the Bournemouth Symphony Orchestra conducted by Andrew Litton, soloist in a special televised performance of Karl Jenkins' Mass for Peace: The Armed Man, conducted by the composer in celebration of his 60th birthday, Verdi's Requiem at Royal Albert Hall, London, Handel's Messiah at St David's Hall, Cardiff and a recital at the Wigmore Hall, London; tour of Sweden with the pianist Robert Wells 2004; currently Prof., Royal Welsh Coll. of Music and Drama. *Honours:* Commdr, order of St John. *Current Management:* Christopher Broom, Athole Still International, Forresters Hall, 25-27 Westow Hill, London, SE19 3RY, England. *Telephone:* (20) 8771-5271 (office). *Fax:* (20) 8771-8172 (office). *E-mail:* chris@atholestill.co.uk (office). *Website:* www.atholestill.com (office). *E-mail:* wynne@wynneevans.co.uk. *Website:* www.wynneevans.co.uk.

EVERETT, Paul Joseph, BMus, PhD; British academic; b. 6 May 1955, London; m. Margaret Mary Bernadette McLoughlin 1979, one s. *Education:* Univ. of Sheffield, Univ. of Liverpool. *Career:* Lecturer in Music, Univ. of Liverpool 1980–81; Lecturer in Music, Univ. Coll., Cork 1981–; mem. RMA. *Publications:* editor of various modern editions of music by D. Purcell, J. C. Schickhardt, J. B. Loeillet and several works by Vivaldi for the Istituto Italiano Antonio Vivaldi; scholarly articles on Italian sources, especially those of Vivaldi's music; The Manchester Concerto Partbooks (two vols) 1989; contrib. to Music and Letters, Musical Times.

EVERSON, Terry, MM; American musician (trumpet), composer, conductor and academic; *Associate Professor of Music, College of Fine Arts, Boston University. Education:* Ohio State Univ., studied with Richard Burkart; also lessons with Frank Kaderabek. *Career:* fmr mem. Faculty, Asbury Coll., Univ. of Kentucky, Philadelphia Biblical Univ. (now Cairn Univ.), Las Vegas Music Festival and Lutheran Music Program; currently Prin. Trumpet, Boston Modern Orchestra Project and Peninsula Music Festival, Door County, Wis., and Soprano Cornettist Brass Band of Battle Creek; Assoc. Prof. of Music, Coll. of Fine Arts , Boston Univ. and Tanglewood Inst. 1999–; premiered major works by composers Richard Cornell, John Davison, Stanley Friedman, Jan Krzywicki, Elena Roussanova-Lucas and Gary Ziek; appears frequently as recitalist and at workshops, and as soloist with orchestras, wind ensembles and brass bands; has appeared in concert with Boston Symphony and Pops, Philadelphia Orchestra, Boston Ballet, Boston Modern Orchestra Project, Chestnut Brass Company, Philadelphia Natural Trumpet Ensemble, Lexington Philharmonic, Lexington Brass Band, Kentuckiana Brass and Percussion Ensemble, Ray Charles, Manhattan Transfer, Kentucky Jazz Repertory Orchestra, and as conductor of Costa Rica Nat. Symphony Brass and Percussion and the Boston Univ. and Univ. of Kentucky Trumpet Ensembles in various venues, including three int. brass conferences; three recordings of notable modern works with pianist Susan Nowicki; recorded as soloist with New England Brass Band, Lexington Brass Band and Eastern Wind Symphony; as composer, commissions from Wizards! double reed ensemble, Texas Tech Trombone Choir, Lutheran Music Program brass quintet, and Messiah Coll. and Philadelphia Biblical Univ. trumpet ensembles; mem. Exec. Cttee Nat. Trumpet Competition; Life mem. Int. Trumpet Guild. *Honours:* Hon. mem. New England Brass Band; winner, Baroque/Classical and 20th Century categories of inaugural Ellsworth Smith Int. Trumpet Competition 1988, First Prize, Louise D. McMahon Int. Music Competition 1990, Metcalf Award for Excellence in Teaching, Boston Univ. 2014. *Address:* Boston University College of Fine Arts, Room 420A, 855 Commonwealth Avenue, Boston, MA 02215 (office); 7 Angela Road, Framingham, MA 01701, USA (home). *Telephone:* (617) 353-3376 (office); (508) 788-7344 (home). *E-mail:* teverson@bu.edu (office); treverson@treversonmusic.com (home). *Website:* www.bu.edu/cfa/music/faculty/everson (office).

EVROVA, Ekaterina (Katia), DipMus; French/Bulgarian pianist; *Titular Professor of Piano and Chamber Music, School of Music, Pays de Langres, France;* b. 5 Oct. 1947, Sofia. *Education:* Bulgarian Superior Conservatoire of Music, Sofia, Debussy Conservatoire, Paris. *Career:* first appearance with Yova Kallova, teacher of piano, Sofia 1952; fmr Dramaturg, Sofia Weeks of Music, Bulgarian Int. Festival; concerts as mem. of violin and piano duo and trio with piano 1976–81; concerts as violin and piano duo with Vladimir Lazov 1983–89, performances include cycle of Schubert sonatas 1987, cycle of 19 sonatas for piano and violin by Mozart 1989; concert tours, Europe and Asia; piano teacher, Chaumont, France 1989; f. Mezzo-Forte Ensemble (piano, flute, classical guitar) with Franck Douvin and Gérard Montaudoin 1989; piano and chamber music teacher, School of Music, Pays de Langres 1991–; concerts with the Mezzo-Forte Ensemble at Chaumont and European Congress of Jewish Studies, Troyes 1990; debut, cycle of Mozart works for piano and violin as duo with Svetoslav Marinov 1990; tours of Brazil and Mexico 1991, France 1992, 1993, Brazil 1993; concerts in France in duo with Svetoslav Marinov 1994, 1995; concerts 1996, and all of Beethoven's sonatas for piano and violin, duo with S. Marinov 1997; concert tour as soloist with Orchestral Ensemble of the Sofia Philharmonia 1998 at Sofia; concert tours in France as Duo Amadeus 91 (with S. Marinov) at Arc-en-Barrois 1999, 2002, Chaumont and Joinville 2000; concert tour with Vocalys Ensemble in Rossini's Petite messe solennelle, France 2003, with Duo Amadeus 2004, with Vocalys 2005, 2006, in Langres 2005–08; concerts in chamber groups in France 2008–12. *Address:* 28 rue du Château Paillot, 52000 Chaumont, France. *Telephone:* (3) 25-03-54-24. *E-mail:* evrova.ekaterina@free.fr.

EVSTATIEVA, Stefka; Bulgarian singer (soprano); b. 7 May 1947, Rousse. *Education:* Sofia Conservatoire with Elena Kiselova. *Career:* mem. Rousse Opera 1971–79; roles have included Verdi's Amelia, Elisabeth de Valois, Aida and Desdemona, Margarita in Mefistofele, Yaroslavna in Prince Igor, Puccini's Mimi and Suor Angelica; mem. Bulgarian Nat. Opera in Sofia from 1978; guest appearances in Vienna, Frankfurt, Munich, Hamburg, New York, Berlin, Milan, Verona, Madrid and Paris; roles include, Leonora in Il Trovatore, Elvira in Ernani, Madeleine de Coigny in Andrea Chénier, Donna Elvira in Don Giovanni and Lisa in Queen of Spades; Royal Opera debut in Manchester as Desdemona in Otello; London 1983 as Elisabeth de Valois; Metropolitan debut 1983 as Elisabeth de Valois; San Francisco 1984, 1986 as Aida; Toronto 1989–90 as Tosca, Mimi, Leonora in La Forzo del Destino and Desdemona; appeared at Nimes 1986 as Medora in French premiere of Verdi's Il Corsaro; sang at Savonlinna Festival 1990 as Aida; season 1991–92 as Amelia in Ballo in Maschera at Antwerp, Tosca at Buenos Aires and Forza Leonora at Florence; sang Giordano's Maddalena at Buenos Aires 1996; Elisabeth de Valois at Trieste 1997. *Recordings include:* Rimsky-Korsakov's Boyartinya Vera Sheloga and The Maid of Pskov; two recitals of Italian arias.

EWENS, Craig Russell Rupert, AGSM, FGMS; British piano teacher and pianist; b. 26 March 1966, Wokingham, Berks., England. *Education:* Royal Coll. of Music Jr Dept, Guildhall School of Music and Drama. *Career:* debut at St John's Smith Square, London 1988; many recitals for nat. music socs and in London; solo recitals at St John's Smith Square, Barbican Centre, St Martin-in-the-Fields, St James's Piccadilly, St Bride's Fleet Street, Purcell Room; currently pvt. piano teacher, Craig Ewens Piano Tuition Ltd; mem. Inc. Soc. of Musicians, European Piano Teachers' Asscn; Fellow, Guild of Musicians and Singers. *Recordings:* Prokofiev 2nd Piano Concerto, Rachmaninov 2nd and 3rd Piano Concertos, Chopin E Minor Concerto, Liszt A Major Concerto, Beethoven Sonatas Op. 57, 81a, 109, 110, Mozart Sonata K457, Chopin Ballades, Schubert Wanderer Fantasy, Schumann Fantasy Op. 17, Prokofiev Sonatas Nos 2, 3 and 6, Berg Sonata Op. 1, Liszt Variations on Weinen, Klagen, Sorgen, Zagen, Ravel's Gaspard de la Nuit. *Honours:* Concert Recital Diploma (Premier Prix), GSMD 1990, Teresa Carreño Memorial Piano Prize 1984. *Address:* Flat 16, Howitt Close, London, NW3 4LX, England. *Telephone:* (20) 7483-4405 (home). *E-mail:* ewenscraig@gmail.com.

EWING, Alan; British singer (bass); b. 1959, Northern Ireland. *Education:* Univ. of East Anglia, choral scholar Norwich Cathedral Choir, Guildhall School of Music with Rudolf Piernay. *Career:* roles at the Guildhall School of Music, London include Sarastro, Colline, Bottom, Collatinus in The Rape of Lucretia, and Falstaff in The Merry Wives of Windsor; has sung widely with renaissance and baroque groups, notably with the Consort of Musicke at major festivals in USA, Australia, Japan, Israel and Europe; has sung in oratorios throughout Europe and with 1989 Young Songmakers' Almanac Concert; appearances in The Rape of Lucretia at Aldeburgh Festival and as the Voice of Neptune in Idomeneo with Rattle at Queen Elizabeth Hall, London; sang Trulove in The Rake's Progress conducted by John Lubbock and in Kopernicus by Claude Vivier in a Pierre Audi production at Almeida Festival; sang Osmin in Die Entführung at 1991 Buxton Festival; sang Rocco in Fidelio for Opera Northern Ireland 1996; season 1998 as the Priest in The Cunning Little Vixen at Spoleto and Vengeance in Rameau's Zoroastre on tour with Les Arts Florissants; season 2000–01 in premiere of Rêves d'un Marco Polo at Amsterdam, as Handel's Polyphemus at Salzburg Easter Festival and as Britten's Collatinus at Florence. *Current Management:* c/o Katrin Sillem Konzertagentur, Agricolastrasse 19, 80687 Munich, Germany. *Telephone:* (89) 51513932. *Fax:* (89) 58958865. *E-mail:* ks@sillem-konzertagentur.de. *Website:* www.sillem-konzertagentur.de.

EWING, Maria Louise; American singer (soprano); b. 27 March 1950, Detroit, Mich.; d. of Norman I. Ewing and Hermina M. Veraar; m. Sir Peter Hall 1982 (divorced 1989); one d. *Education:* Cleveland Inst. of Music. *Career:* debut at Metropolitan Opera, New York singing Cherubino in The Marriage of Figaro 1976, closely followed by debuts with major US orchestras, including New York Philharmonic and at La Scala Milan; regular performances at Glyndebourne including the Barber of Seville, L'Incoronazione di Poppea and Carmen; repertoire also includes Pelléas et Mélisande, The Dialogues of the Carmelites, Così fan Tutte, La Perichole, La Cenerentola, The Marriage of Figaro (Susanna); performed Salome at Covent Garden 1988, 1992, Carmen at Earl's Court, London 1989, Tosca in Los Angeles 1989, Salome in Washington 1990, Madame Butterfly in Los Angeles, Tosca in Seville, Tosca in Los Angeles and Chicago, Salome in San Francisco, Madame Butterfly and Tosca in Vienna, The Trojans at the Metropolitan, New York 1993–94; also appears as concert and recital singer; debut Promenade Concerts, London 1987, Lady Macbeth of Mtsensk with Metropolitan Opera 1994. *Current Management:* c/o David Godfrey, Mitchell-Godfrey Management, 48 Gray's Inn Road, London, WC1X 8LT, England; c/o Herbert Breslin, 119 West 57th Street, Room 1505, New York, NY 10019, USA (office).

EYSER, Eberhard; Swedish composer and violist; b. 1 Aug. 1932, Marienwerder, Prussia, Germany (now Kwidzyn, Poland). *Education:* Akad. für Musik und Theater, Hannover, Mozarteum Salzburg, Accad. Chigiana, Siena, Italy. *Career:* violist, Royal Swedish Opera Orchestra. *Compositions:* about 400 works, including chamber and orchestral music, vocal and electronic music, computer music; operas and chamber operas include Molonn 1970, The Death of a Bird 1971, A Man's Dream 1972, Last Voyage 1973, King of Hearts 1973, Abu Said 1976, Summer's Day 1979, The Deep Water 1980, Bermuda Triangle 1981, The Ravens 1982, The Unaccomplished Flyswat 1982, The Red Book Mystery 1984, Twilight in Granada 1984, It Was Raining Yesterday 1985, The Picture of Dorian Gray 1986, The Aspern Papers 1989, Charley McDeath 1992; orchestral works: Metastrophy, Persistence Pays Overture, Macbeth Overture, Itabol, Anacrón, 3 Symphoniettas 1976, 1979 and Hidden Nightingale 2010; chamber music: The Nightingale Was Singing All Night Long (quintet, London Schubert Players Competition) 2008, seven saxophone quartets. *Television:* Charly McDeath (chamber opera). *Recordings:* King of Hearts, Last Voyage, The Deep Water, Persistence Pays Overture, Circus Overture, Anacrón, Duo 3 C, The Bard, Correlazioni, Flux. *Honours:* 50th Anniversary Competition Award, Prague Broadcast Orchestra 1965, Light Music Award, Stockholm 1976, First Prize, Carl-Maria-von-Weber Award, Dresden 1978, 1986, First Prize, Florilège Vocal Awards, Tours 1990, Balearic Music Foundation Award, Palma de Mallorca 1990, Gregynog Award (Wales) 1994, Oare String Orchestra Award, Kent 1995, Stockholm Culture Capital of Europe Award 1998. *Address:* Karlbergsvag 71B, 11335 Stockholm, Sweden (home). *Telephone:* (8) 308425 (home). *E-mail:* eyser.eb@ swipnet.se (home). *Website:* www.stim.se; www.mic.se.

EZZAT, Mohammed Amin; Iraqi conductor and composer; *Conductor, Baghdad Symphony Orchestra. Compositions include:* Three Fragments, Back to Reality. *Address:* Iraqi National Symphony Orchestra, Baghdad Convention Center, Green Zone, Baghdad, Iraq.

F

FABBRI, Franca; Italian singer (soprano); b. 28 May 1935, Milan. *Education:* studied in Milan with Adelina Fiori, Adelaide Saraceni and Giuseppe Pais. *Career:* debut in Spoleto 1963 as Violetta; has sung widely in Italy and in Berlin, Hamburg, Cologne, Budapest, Warsaw, San Francisco and Aix-en-Provence; sang in the premieres of L'Idiota and Riva delle Sirti by Chailly, Orfeo Vedovo by Savino and Al Gran Sole Carico d'Amore by Nono 1975; repertoire included Lucia di Lammermoor, Musetta, Nedda, Fiordiligi, Gilda, Marguerite de Valois in Les Huguenots, the Queen of Night and Pamira in L'Assedio di Corinto by Rossini; roles in operas by Britten, Shostakovich, Maderna and Malipiero.

FABBRICINI, Tiziana; Italian singer (soprano); b. 1961, Asti, Piemonte. *Education:* studied in Milan and other centres in Italy. *Career:* made debut as Violetta in La Traviaita under Riccardo Muti, La Scala 1990; has sung the role of Violetta around the world in New York, Vienna, Berlin, Paris, Hamburg, Tel Aviv and Tokyo; other roles include Fiorilla in Il Turco in Italia, in Il Viaggio, Ivanhoe, Don Giovanni, La Muette de Portici, Lucia di Lammermoor, Ariadne in Naxos, La Serva Padrona, Anna Bolena, Maria Stuarda, Adriana Lecouvreur, Macbeth, Attila, Tosca, Manon Lescaut, Cavalleria Rusticana, Messa in Requiem. *E-mail:* postmaster@tizianafabbricini.com (office). *Website:* www.tizianafabbricini.com.

FABER, Lothar; German oboist; b. 7 Feb. 1922, Cologne. *Education:* Cologne Musikhochschule, Paris Conservatoire, France. *Career:* played with the WDR Orchestra, Cologne from 1946; has made many appearances at festivals throughout Europe: Berlin, Venice, Warsaw, The Netherlands and Darmstadt; has premiered works by Maderna, K. Mayer, Baird, Fortner, Schuller and Zimmermann; gave summer courses at Darmstadt and Siena 1972–77.

FABIAN, Marta; Hungarian dulcimer player; b. 1946, Budapest. *Education:* Béla Bartók Conservatory, Ferenc Liszt Academy of Music, Budapest. *Career:* soloist with Budapest Chamber Ensemble; has made numerous guest performances in Austria, Belgium, Bulgaria, Czechoslovakia, Finland, France, Germany, the UK, the Netherlands, Italy, Latin America, Mexico, Poland, Russia, Spain, Sweden, Switzerland, Turkey, USA and Yugoslavia and appeared at the Bratislava, Darmstadt, Netherlands, Lucerne, IGNM (SIMC) of Athens and Graz Festivals, Warsaw Autumn Festival of Modern Music, the Witten Festival and the Zagreb Biennial Festival of Modern Music. *Recordings include:* Cimbalom recital. *Honours:* Grand Prize, French National Record Academy, 1977; Liszt Prize.

FAERBER, Jorg; German conductor and composer; b. 18 June 1929, Stuttgart. *Education:* Hochschule für Musik, Stuttgart. *Career:* theatre conductor and composer in Stuttgart and Heilbronn 1952–60; founder, Württemberg Chamber Orchestra 1960; tours to Austria, the UK, France, Italy, USA and South Africa; many performances in the Baroque repertory; appearances with the European Community Chamber Orchestra, various BBC Orchestras, the Bournemouth Sinfonietta, the Thames Chamber Orchestra and the Northern Sinfonia; festival engagements at Swansea and with the English Bach Festival. *Recordings:* Bach Brandenburg Concertos; Boyce Symphonies; Vivaldi Four Seasons and other concertos; Bassoon Concertos by Weber, Graun, J. C. Bach, K. Stamitz, Boismortier and Mozart; Concertos for cello, clarinet, viola and flute by Stamitz; Trumpet concertos by Torelli, Albinoni, Biber, Stölzel and Manfredini; Mozart piano concertos K413 and K450, violin concertos K218 and K219, flute concertos, Sinfonia Concertante K297b and overtures.

FAGEN, Arthur; American conductor; *Music Director, The Atlanta Opera;* b. New York. *Education:* Wesleyan Univ., Curtis Inst. with Max Rudolf, Hans Swarowsky and Laszlo Halasz. *Career:* fmrly Prin. Conductor in Kassel and Brunswick, Chief Conductor, Flanders Opera of Antwerp and Ghent, Music Dir Queens Symphony Orchestra, mem. conducting staff, Lyric Opera of Chicago and Metropolitan Opera; Music Dir Dortmund Philharmonic Orchestra and Dortmund Opera 2002–07; Music Dir The Atlanta Opera 2010–; conducts opera and symphony repertoire of over 75 operas; has performed with Munich State Opera, Semper Opera Dresden, Hamburg State Opera, Deutsche Oper Berlin, Staatsoper Berlin, Teatro Regio Torino, Opera Capitole de Toulouse, New York City Opera, Metropolitan Opera; regular guest conductor, Vienna State Opera 1998–2002; has conducted Tokyo Philharmonic, Orchestre de la Suisse Romande, Schleswig-Holstein Festival, Deutsche Kammerphilharmonie, Bamberg Symphony, RAI Orchestras of Italy, Jerusalem Symphony Orchestra and Baltimore Symphony Orchestra; conducted Dortmund Philharmonic at Concertgebouw in Amsterdam, Palais de Beaux Arts in Brussels, and in Salzburg, Beijing and Shanghai; Prof. of Orchestral Conducting, Indiana Univ. *Recordings include:* six symphonies of Bohuslav Martin, Martinů Piano Concerti (Gramophone Magazine Editor's Choice March 2010). *Honours:* winner, Baltimore Symphony Orchestra Int. Conducting Competition. *Address:* The Atlanta Opera Center, 1575 Northside Drive, NW Building 300, Suite 350, Atlanta, GA 30318, USA (office). *Telephone:* (404) 881-8801 (office). *Fax:* (404) 881-1711 (office). *E-mail:* info@atlantaopera.org (office). *Website:* www.atlantaopera.org (office).

FAGÉUS, Kjell; Swedish clarinettist; b. 25 July 1949, Lönneberga; m. Lena Fagéus 1993, two s. *Education:* Royal Music Acad., Stockholm, Juilliard School of Music, New York with Stanley Drucker. *Career:* debut at Waldemars

udde, Stockholm 1974; Principal Clarinet, Royal Opera, Stockholm 1976–90; chamber music and solo performances throughout the world; coach in mental training, Royal Acad., Stockholm, and for professional musicians at SAMI; mem. SYMF, SAMI Sweden. *Recordings include:* three albums with Stockholm Wind Quintet, Mozart Clarinet Concerto and Swedish Concertos with Royal Opera Orchestra, Mozart and Brahms Clarinet Quintets. *Publications:* Lek på fullt allvar 1998; contrib. Visions of Excellence (to Int. Soc. for Mental Training and Excellence). *Honours:* ten-year Swedish Govt scholarship.

FAGGIONI, Piero; Italian opera producer; b. 12 Aug. 1936, Carrara. *Career:* worked under Jean Vilar and Luchino Visconti in Italy; debut producing La Bohème at Venice 1964; produced Alceste at La Scala 1972, La Fanciulla del West in Turin 1974 and at Covent Garden, Norma at Vienna 1977, Carmen at Edinburgh 1977, Macbeth at Salzburg 1984, Francesca da Rimini at Metropolitan Opera, New York 1984, Boris Godunov at Barcelona; staging of Massenet's Don Quichotte seen at Paris Opéra 1986, Florence and Monte Carlo 1992; produced Il Trovatore at Covent Garden 1989; Principal Guest Producer at Covent Garden until 1990; Don Quichotte at the Rome Opera 1997.

FAHBERG, Antonia; Austrian singer (soprano); b. 19 May 1928, Vienna. *Education:* Vienna Music Acad. *Career:* sang at Innsbruck from 1950, and Munich from 1952; opera engagements in Hamburg, Vienna, Brussels and Amsterdam; radio and television broadcasts; interpreter of works by Rossini (Stabat Mater), Beethoven (Christ at the Mount of Olives), Bruckner (Te Deum) and Bach. *Recordings include:* St Matthew Passion and Cantatas by Bach, Alexander Balus by Handel, Il Ritorno d'Ulisse and L'Incoronazione di Poppea, Diana in Gluck's Iphigénie en Tauride.

FÄHNDRICH, Walter; Swiss violist and composer; *Professor of Improvisation, Musikhochschule, Basel;* b. 1 April 1944, Menzingen; one d. *Education:* studied in Lucerne. *Career:* int. activities as viola player, composer and improviser; solo concerts; music installations: Music for Spaces, Improvisation; Prof. of Improvisation, Musikhochschule, Basel 1985–; Organizer Int. Congresses for Improvisation, Lucerne 1990–2005; mem. Schweizerischer Tonkünstler-Verein. *Compositions:* works for viola solo, Music for Spaces, musical landscape projects, chamber music, electro-acoustic music, music for radio plays, theatre, ballet. *Recordings:* Viola, Spaces, Music for Spaces, various radio and TV recordings. *Publications:* Musik für Räume 1986, 1995, Musik und Raum 1989, 2000, Klang Bewegung Raum 1990, Improvisation 1992, Improvisation II 1994, Improvisation III 1998, Zur geschichte und gegenwart der Elektronischen Musik 1999, Improvisation IV 2001, Ein paar lockere, nichtsdestotrotz grundsätzliche Gedanken zur (musikalischen) Improvisation 2003, Improvisation V 2003, Improvisation VI 2007, various publications on music and space. *Address:* Piodina 20, 6614 Brissago, Switzerland (office). *Website:* www.musicforspaces.ch.

FAIRBAIRN, Clive Stuart; British conductor; b. 21 April 1946, London, England; m. Nicola Swann 1979, one d. *Education:* Royal Acad. of Music, London. *Career:* debut at St Johns, Smith Square, London 1977; Principal Conductor, New Mozart Orchestra 1977–, Lindstrom Philharmonic Orchestra 1984–; guest appearances include London Symphony Orchestra, London Philharmonic, Philharmonia and Wren Orchestra; has broadcast with New Mozart Orchestra, London Symphony Orchestra, and Wren Orchestra; conducted in Germany, Switzerland, Turkey and Portugal; mem. Incorporated Soc. of Musicians.

FAJTOVÁ, Marie; Czech singer (soprano). *Education:* Prague Conservatory, studied piano with Jan Novotný and opera singing with Jiří Kotouč. *Career:* with Musica Bohemica ensemble 1998–2003; mem. J. K. Tyl Theatre, Pilsen 2005–06; soloist, Prague State Opera 2006–07; concert recitals in many countries including Spain, Poland, Germany, The Netherlands, Japan; roles include: Angelica in Orlando Furioso, Norina in Don Pasquale, Donna Elvira in Don Giovanni, Esmeralda in The Bartered Bride, Despinio in The Greek Passion, Violetta in La Traviata, Susanna in Le nozze di Figaro, Pamina in Die Zauberflöte, Frasquita in Carmen. *Honours:* first prize, B. Smetana Int. Piano Competition 1994, Grand Prize for Female Vocalist, Barbara Hendricks Int. Vocal Competition, Strasbourg 2008. *Current Management:* arte management s.r.o, Slezská 130, 130 00 Prague 3, Czech Republic. *Telephone:* 608333603. *E-mail:* ytannenberger@artemanagement.com. *Website:* www.artemanagement.com. *E-mail:* info@mariefajtova.com (office). *Website:* www.mariefajtova.com.

FALCON, Ruth, BMus, MFA; American singer (soprano); b. 2 Nov. 1946, Residence, LA; m. Douglas W. Meyer. *Education:* Loyola Univ., Tulane Univ., studies in Italy with Tito Gobbi and Luigi Ricci. *Career:* debut, New York City Opera in 1974 as Micaela in Carmen; Title role in Mayr's Medea in Corinto, Bern, 1975; Bayerische Staatsoper Munich, 1976–80 as Leonora in Trovatore and La Forza del Destino, and Mozart's Countess and Elettra; Guest artist in New York, Canada, Germany and France as Puccini's Manon Lescaut and Weber's Agathe; Paris Opéra debut in 1981 as Mozart's Donna Anna; Covent Garden and Vienna Staatsoper in 1983 as the Trovatore Leonora; Sang Anna Bolena at Nice in 1985; Nancy Opéra in 1986 as Norma; Aix-en-Provence Festival as Ariadne; Covent Garden in 1987 and Metropolitan in 1989 as the Empress in Die Frau ohne Schatten; Buenos Aires 1993 as Turandot; Sang the

Trovatore Leonora at New Orleans, 1997; concert repertory includes Mahler's 8th Symphony, Beethoven's Missa Solemnis, Verdi's Requiem and works by Handel, Mozart, Brahms, Dvořák and Strauss; mem. Voice Faculty, Mannes Coll. The New School of Music 1991–. *Recordings include:* Die Walküre; Götterdämmerung. *Address:* Mannes College The New School of Music, 150 West 85th Street, New York, NY 10024, USA (office). *Telephone:* (212) 580-0210 (office). *Fax:* (212) 580-1738 (office). *Website:* www.newschool.edu/mannes (office).

FALEWICZ, Magdalena; Polish singer (soprano); b. 11 Feb. 1946, Lublin. *Education:* Warsaw Conservatory with Olga Olgina and Maria Kuninska-Opacka. *Career:* mem. Warsaw Chamber Opera 1971–72; solo debut as Oscar in Un Ballo in Maschera at Komische Oper Berlin 1973; sang Madama Butterfly with WNO 1978 and for ENO at London Coliseum 1986; mem. Staatsoper Berlin from 1984, with guest appearances in Frankfurt, Leipzig and USA, Bulgaria, Finland and The Netherlands; Dresden Staatsoper 1985 as Countess in premiere of Siegfried Matthus' Weise von Liebe und Tod des Comten Christoph Rilke; Mozart's Countess at Dresden 1988. *Recordings include:* Schubert's Alfonso und Estrella, Amor in Gluck's Orfeo ed Euridice, Die Kluge by Orff.

FALK, Elizabeth Moxley; American opera and theatre producer; b. 21 Sept. 1942, Memphis, Tenn.; d. of the late Warren Luke Moxley and of Elizabeth Moxley (née Beshears); m. 1st Lee Harrison Falk 1977 (died 1999); m. 2nd Martin Piecuch 2001. *Education:* Blytheville High School. *Career:* actress and singer 1961; Marketing Exec. BBDO Advertising 1970–86; Producer, New York Town Hall; Stage Man., later Producer New York Vineyard Opera and Co. Man. New Artists' Coalition 1986–88; Founder, Producer and Artistic Dir Pala Opera Asscn 1989–; Fellow, Accad. Rossiniana, Pesaro. *Achievements include:* created concept of putting Hamlet on trial with real judges and lawyers, witnesses and the defendant can only respond with lines from the play. *Productions include:* The Tempest, The Soldier's Tale, Il Viaggio a Reims, La Gazza Ladra 1990, The Quicksilver Celebration 1991, Othello Meets Otello 1991, La Donna del Lago 1992, Hail Macbeth! 1992, Rigoletto, The Fool 1992, Waking in New York 2002; int. directorial debuts include those with The International Hamlet Festival of Seoul: Hamlet, opera by Amboise Thomas with Seoul Nat. Symphony Orchestra 2005, Hamlet On Trial, Sedong Center for the Performing Arts, Seoul 2005. *Publications include:* White Tie and Veils, Goldsmith's Last Rites. *Address:* 7 West 81st Street, Suite 12C, New York, NY 10024, USA. *Telephone:* (212) 269-8760. *Fax:* (212) 769-8760. *E-mail:* elizabethfalk@usa.net. *Website:* www.elizabethfalk.com.

FALKMAN, Carl Johan; Swedish singer (baritone); b. 24 July 1947, Stockholm. *Education:* studied in Stockholm and with Gino Bechi in Florence. *Career:* debut in Stockholm 1973, in the premiere of Werle's Tintomara; Drottningholm Festival from 1973, as Guglielmo, Pacuvio in Kraus's Proserpina; Guest engagements in Scandinavia and elsewhere as Dandini in La Cenerentola, Mozart's Figaro and Masetto, Eugene Onegin and Marcello; Don Giovanni at the Prague bicentenary performances, Prague, 1987; Grétry's Zémire et Azor at Drottningholm, 1993; Sang Wozzeck and Papageno at the Royal Opera Stockholm, 2000. *Current Management:* c/o Ann Braathen Artist Management AB, Folkskolegatan 5, 11735 Stockholm, Sweden. *Telephone:* (8) 556-908-50. *Fax:* (8) 556-908-51. *E-mail:* info@braathenmanagement.com. *Website:* www.braathenmanagement.com.

FALLETTA, JoAnn; American conductor; *Music Director, Buffalo Philharmonic Orchestra*; b. 27 Feb. 1954, New York, NY. *Education:* Juilliard, Queens Coll. and Mannes Coll. *Career:* soloist with orchestras on classical guitar, lute, mandolin; has conducted leading orchestras at Denver, Indianapolis, Phoenix, St Paul, Richmond, Toledo, Tucson and Columbus; European engagements in Italy, France, Switzerland and Denmark; Music Dir, Long Beach Symphony Orchestra 1989, Virginia Symphony Orchestra 1991–, with guest appearances with the Symphony Orchestras of San Francisco, Savannah, Delaware, Hamilton and Antwerp; German debut with the Mannheim Nat. Theatre Orchestra, in works by Barber, Gershwin and Brahms; Music Dir, Buffalo Philharmonic Orchestra 1998–; Principal Conductor, Ulster Orchestra 2011–. *Honours:* Stokowski Award 1985, Toscanini Award 1985, Bruno Walter Award 1982–87. *Current Management:* c/o Ron Merlino, Columbia Artists Management Inc., 1790 Broadway, New York, NY 10019-1412, USA. *Telephone:* (212) 841-9560. *Fax:* (212) 841-9552. *E-mail:* rmerlino@cami.com. *Website:* www.cami.com; www.bpo.org; www.joannfalletta.com.

FALLOWS, David Nicholas, BA, MMus, PhD, FBA; British musicologist and academic; b. 20 Dec. 1945, Buxton, Derbyshire; m. 1st Paulène Oliver 1976 (divorced); one s. one d.; m. 2nd Dagmar Hoffmann-Axthelm 2013. *Education:* Jesus Coll., Cambridge, King's Coll., London, Univ. of California, Berkeley, USA. *Career:* Asst, Studio der Frühen Musik, Munich 1967–70; Lecturer in Music, Univ. of Wisconsin, Madison, USA 1973–74; Lecturer in Music, Univ. of Manchester 1976–82, Sr Lecturer 1982–92, Reader in Music 1992–97, Prof. of Musicology 1997–2010; Reviews Ed., Early Music 1976–95, 1999–2000; Visiting Assoc. Prof., Univ. of North Carolina, Chapel Hill, USA 1982–83; Founder and Gen. Ed. Royal Musical Asscn Monographs 1982–98; Visiting Prof. of Musicology, École Normale Supérieure, Paris, France 1993; Corresp. mem. American Musicological Soc. 1999–; mem. Int. Musicological Soc. (Vice-Pres. 1997–2002, Pres. 2002–07), Royal Musical Asscn (Vice-Pres. 2000–08). *Publications include:* Dufay 1982, Chansonnier de Jean de Montchenu (co-author) 1991, Companion to Medieval and Renaissance Music (co-ed.) 1992, The Songs of Guillaume Dufay 1995, Oxford Bodleian Library MS Canon

Misc. 213: Late Medieval and Early Renaissance Music in Facsimile (Vol. 1) (ed.) 1995, Songs and Musicians in the Fifteenth Century 1996, The Songbook of Fridolin Sicher 1996, A Catalogue of Polyphonic Songs 1415–1480 1999, Josquin 2009, Composers and their Songs, 1400–1521 (Variorum Collected Studies Series) 2010, The Henry VIII Book 2014, Secular Polyphony 1380–1480 (Musica Britannica vol. 97) 2014; contrib. to reference works, scholarly books and professional journals, including Gramophone, The Guardian, Early Music, New Grove Dictionary of Music and Musicians 1980, 2001. *Honours:* Chevalier, Ordre des Arts et des Lettres 1994; Dr hc (Univ. of Tours) 2010; Ingolf Dahl Prize in Musicology 1971, Dent Medal 1982. *Address:* Martin Harris Centre for Music and Drama, University of Manchester, Manchester, M13 9PL, England. *Telephone:* 7714-184655 (mobile). *E-mail:* david.fallows@manchester.ac.uk.

FALVAY, Attila; Hungarian violinist; b. 7 Sept. 1958, Budapest; s. Károly Falvay and Molnár Zsóka Falvayné; m. Maria Farnadi 1983, two d. *Education:* Liszt Ferenc Acad. of Music, Budapest with Prof. Semyon Snitkowsky, Vienna Music Acad. with Prof. Josef Sivo. *Career:* First Violinist, Kodály Quartet 1980–; Leader, Budapest Symphony Orchestra 1989–2005; Concertmaster, Hungarian Nat. Philharmonic Orchestra 2005–. *Recordings include:* Complete Haydn Quartets, Complete Beethoven Quartets, Complete Schubert Quartets, Ravel, Debussy, d'Indy Quartets 1 and 2, Schumann, Brahms Piano Quintet, Schubert Forellen Quintet, Hofstetter Quartets 1–6, Brahms, Weber Clarinet Quintets, Kodály Quartets 1 and 2, Mendelssohn, Bruch Octets, Mozart Horn Quintet, Oboe Quartet, Musical Joke, Bartók Piano Quintet, Dubrovay Violin Concerto, Spohr Potpourri, op. 22. *Honours:* second prize Szigeti Competition, Budapest 1978, Hubay Prize 1980, Merited Artist of Hungary 1990, Bartók-Pásztory Prize 1996. *Address:* 1121 Budapest, Kázmér utca 40, Hungary (home). *E-mail:* falvay@kodalyquartet.com (office). *Website:* www.kodalyquartet.com (office).

FALVO, Robert, BM, MM, DMA; American percussionist; b. 27 Aug. 1963, New York, NY. *Education:* State Univ. of New York, Fredonia, Manhattan School of Music, studied with Fred Hinger, Christopher Lamb, James Presiss, Claire Heldrich, Lynn Harbold and Theodore Frazeur. *Career:* performances with the New Music Consort, New York 1987–, NOA, Carnegie Hall, New York 1988–, English Chamber Orchestra with US tour 1988, Pierre Boulez and the Scotia Festival Orchestra, Nova Scotia, Canada 1991, Frick Hawkins Dance Co. Orchestra with tour to Tokyo, Shanghai, Hong Kong and throughout USA from 1991, and Tokyo Symphony with world tour 1991; has also appeared with Erie Chamber Orchestra, Hudson Valley Symphony Orchestra and New Music Orchestral Project; xylophone soloist with Fredonia Symphony Orchestra; many contemporary music recitals in New York area, including Carnegie Hall, Merkin Hall, Miller Hall, Hubbard Hall and Town Hall; has conducted the Manhattan School of Music Contemporary and Percussion Ensembles; frequent lectures on contemporary composition techniques for percussion instruments; Asst Prof. of Music in the School of Music, Appalachian State Univ., NC.

FANDREY, Birgit; German singer (soprano); b. 1963, Vorpommern. *Education:* Carl Maria von Weber Musikhochschule, Dresden. *Career:* associated with the Opera Studio of the Dresden Staatsoper, then appeared with the main company from 1987 notably as Mozart's Susanna, Papagena, Pamina and Zerlina, Euridice, Mimi, Gretel, Sophie Scholl in Udo Zimmermann's Die Weisse Rose and in parts in operas by Siegfried Matthus; Sang Handel's Galatea at the Halle Festival in 1987, Amor in Orfeo ed Euridice at the Leipzig Gewandhaus, Mozart's Constanze at Amsterdam and Pamina at St Gallen; Constanze at Munich, 1993; lieder recitals in works by Schubert, Schumann, Brahms and Strauss; concert repertoire includes Beethoven's Mass in C at Amsterdam Concertgebouw, Bach's St John Passion, Messiah and Mozart's Exsultate Jubilate. *Current Management:* Agentur Sigrid Rostock, Eugen-Schönhaar-Strasse 1, 10407 Berlin, Germany. *Telephone:* (30) 4257514. *Fax:* (30) 4239136. *E-mail:* sigridrostock@web.de.

FANNING, David John, BMus, PhD, GNCM, FRNCM; British academic and pianist; *Professor of Music, Manchester University*; b. 5 March 1955, Reading, Berkshire, England; m. 1st 1975 (divorced 1994); one s.; m. 2nd 1994 (divorced 2004). *Education:* Manchester Univ., Royal Northern Coll. of Music. *Career:* fmr Reader, Manchester Univ., Prof. of Music 2004–; mem. Royal Musical Asscn. *Publications:* The Breath of the Symphonist: Shostakovich's Tenth 1988, Carl Nielsen Symphony No. 5 1997, Shostakovich: String Quartet No. 8 2004; contrib. to Gramophone, Music and Letters, The Daily Telegraph. *Address:* Martin Harris Centre for Music and Drama, University of Manchester, Coupland Street, Manchester, M13 9PL, England (office). *Telephone:* (161) 275-4989 (office). *Fax:* (161) 275-4994 (office). *E-mail:* david.fanning@manchester.ac.uk (home). *Website:* www.arts.manchester.ac.uk.

FARBACH, Kent, BMus, MMus; Australian composer; b. 2 Aug. 1961, Southport, Qld. *Education:* Queensland Conservatory. *Career:* Sr Teacher, Forte Music School, Queensland Conservatory 1992–. *Compositions include:* Mini Overture with Fanfares for brass septet and organ 1989, Beneath the Forest Canopy for ensemble 1989, Life Stratum for orchestra 1990, Tears for string orchestra 1991, 1845: An Irish Elegy for orchestra 1992, From Quiet Places for violin, cello, flute, clarinet, wind chimes, percussion and piano 1993, Into the Landscape for orchestra 1994; commissions from the Melbourne and Sydney Symphony Orchestras 1992, Queensland Symphony Orchestra 1994, Sydney Philharmonia Choir 1995. *Honours:* Adelaide Chamber Orchestra Prize 1992.

FARBERMAN, Harold, BS, MS; American conductor and composer; b. 2 Nov. 1929, New York, NY; m. Corinne Curry 1958; one s. one d. *Education:* Juilliard School of Music, New England Conservatory of Music, Boston. *Career:* percussionist, Boston Symphony Orchestra 1951–63; Conductor, New Arts Orchestra, Boston 1955–63, Colorado Springs Philharmonic Orchestra 1967–68, Oakland Symphony Orchestra, CA 1971–79; Principal Guest Conductor, Bournemouth Sinfonietta 1986–; founder and first Pres., Conductors' Guild 1975; founder, Conductors' Inst., Univ. of West Virginia 1980 (relocated to Univ. of South Carolina 1987). *Compositions include:* opera: Medea 1960–61; for mixed media: If Music Be 1965; ballets, film scores; orchestral: Concerto for bassoon and strings 1956, Timpani Concerto 1958, Concerto for alto saxophone and strings 1965, Violin Concerto 1976, War Cry on a Prayer Feather 1976, Shapings for English horn, strings and percussion 1984, Concerto for cello and orchestra 1998–99; chamber: Variations for percussion and piano 1954, Music Inn Suite for six percussion 1958, Quintessence for woodwind quintet 1962, Images for five brass 1964, Alea for six percussion 1976, Concerto for flute and chamber orchestra 1996, Little Boy and the Tree Branch 1998; vocal works. *Recordings include:* Symphonies by Mozart, Schumann and Beethoven; Bartók's Divertimento and Sonata for two pianos and percussion; Schoenberg/Handel Concerto; Bassoon Concertos by Weber and Hummel; Mahler, 1, 2, 4, 5, 6, 10; 22 Michael Haydn Symphonies; Glière No. 3, Bournemouth Symphonietta. *Publication:* The Art of Conducting Technique: A New Perspective 1997. *Honours:* winner Belgium St Helena Award for best recording of the year.

FARINA, Franco; American singer (tenor); b. 1957, Connecticut. *Career:* sang widely in opera in USA from 1986; Tamino at Cincinnati, Pinkerton at Pittsburgh (1989); Houston, Chicago and New Orleans; European engagements at the Paris Opéra (Pollione in Norma at the Bastille, 1996), Glyndebourne (Stravinsky's Tom Rakewell, 1989) and Frankfurt (Duke of Mantua, 1990); Metropolitan Opera from 1990 as Rodolfo, Alfredo and Pinkerton (1995); Toulouse, 1993, as Lensky in Eugene Onegin, Deutsche Oper Berlin, 1995, as Riccardo; Season 1998 as Manrico at Geneva, Cavaradossi in Cincinnati and Carlo in Verdi's Masnadieri for the Royal Opera at Baden-Baden, Edinburgh and Savonlinna; Cavaradossi at the New York Met, 2002; season 2002–03 as Carlo in I Masnadieri at Covent Garden, Manrico at the Met, Radames at Barcelona and Gabriele Adorno for the Vienna Staatsoper; concerts include the Verdi Requiem and Beethoven's Missa Solemnis. *Current Management:* Zemsky/Green Artists Management, 730 Fifth Avenue, Suite 1802, New York, NY 10019, USA. *Telephone:* (212) 300-8003. *Fax:* (212) 300-8001. *E-mail:* zgartists@aol.com. *Website:* www .zemskygreen.com.

FARKAS, Andras; Hungarian conductor; b. 14 April 1945, Budapest; m. Françoise Viquerat 1973; one s. one d. *Education:* Béla Bartók Acad., Budapest, Franz Liszt Acad., Budapest, Akademie für Musik und Darstellende Kunst, Vienna with Hans Swarowsky. *Career:* debut in Budapest 1973; settled in Switzerland 1974 and performed in concerts throughout Europe; guest conductor, Orchestra of Hungarian Radio, Budapest Philharmonic, Orchestre de la Suisse Romande, Orchestre de Chamber de Lausanne, Orchestra of Slovakian Radio, Bratislava, Orchestra of Pilzn Radio, Orchestre de Seville; Dir Choeur J.S. Bach 1979–; Artistic Dir and founder, Nouvel Orchestre de Montreux 1987; mem. Swiss Musicians' Asscn, Centre Europeen de la Culture, Geneva; founder Acad. Int. de Choeurs d'Eté 2004. *Honours:* Vermeil Medal des Arts, Sciences et Lettres, Paris 1990. *Address:* Choeur J.S. Bach, Chemin des Bouvreuils 12, 1009 Pully, Switzerland (office). *Telephone:* 17284727 (office). *E-mail:* info@choeurbach.ch (office). *Website:* www .choeurbach.ch (office).

FARKAS, Andrew, BA, MLS; American librarian, educator and author; *Library Director Emeritus, University of North Florida;* b. 7 April 1936, Budapest, Hungary; s. of Miklós Farkas and Renée Schwartz; m. (divorced). *Education:* Eötvös Lóránd Univ. of Law, Hungary, Occidental Coll., Univ. of California, Berkeley. *Career:* Gift and Exchange Librarian, Chief Bibliographer and Asst Head, Acquisitions Dept, Univ. of California, Davis 1962–67; Music Ed. Daily Democrat, Woodland, Calif. 1965–67; Asst Man. Walter J. Johnson Inc., New York 1967–70; Dir of Libraries and Prof. of Library Science, Univ. of North Florida, Jacksonville 1970–2003, Distinguished Prof. 1991, Library Dir Emer. 2003–; Advisory Ed. of 42-vol. series Opera Biographies 1977, Series Ed. 1989–2003; Contributing Ed., The Opera Quarterly 1993–2005; life mem. American Library Asscn. *Publications:* Titta Ruffo – An Anthology 1984, Opera and Concert Singers – An Annotated International Bibliography 1985, Lawrence Tibbett, Singing Actor (ed.) 1989, Enrico Caruso – My Father and My Family (co-author with Enrico Caruso Jr) 1990, Jussi (co-author with Anna-Lisa Björling) 1996, Librarians' Calendar and Pocket Reference (annual) 1984–2005; adviser and contrib. to International Dictionary of Opera 1993; book chapters and bibliographies. *Honours:* Outstanding Faculty Scholarship Award 2000. *Address:* Office of the Library Director Emeritus, University of North Florida, Thomas G. Carpenter Library, 1 UNF Drive, Jacksonville, FL 32224-7699, USA (office). *E-mail:* afarkas@unf.edu (office).

FARKAS, Katalin; Hungarian singer (soprano); b. 5 Jan. 1954, Budapest. *Education:* studied in Budapest. *Career:* singer at the Hungarian State Opera from 1982 as Rosina, Sophie (Werther), Sophie (Der Rosenkavalier), Mozart's Blondchen, Belinda, Nannetta (Falstaff), Oscar, Norina and Flotow's Martha; Glyndebourne Festival debut 1985 as Zdenka in Arabella; season 1986–87 in Liszt's Don Sanche at Naples and Amaryllis in Il Pastor Fido at the Göttingen Festival; other roles include Beethoven's Marzelline, Donizetti's Gianetta (L'Elisir d'amore) and Serafina (Il Campanello), Zerbinetta; Göttingen 1990 in Handel's Floridante. *Recordings include:* world premiere recordings with Hungaroton, Handel: Terpsicore-Erato (conductor Nicholas McGegan, with Derek Lee Ragin), Handel: Atalanta (title role, conductor Nicholas McGegan), Telemann: Der geduldige Socrates-Erato (conductor Nicholas McGegan, with Paul Esswood, Guy de Mey), Don Sanche (Liszt, under Tamás Pál), recorded as Serpina (Pergolesi: La serva padrona), Amarilli (Handel: Il pastor fido, also with Esswood and McGegan).

FARLEY, Carole, MusB; American singer (soprano); b. 29 Nov. 1946, Le Mars, Ia; d. of Melvin Farley and Irene Farley (née Reid); m. José Serebrier 1969; one d. *Education:* Indiana Univ. and Hochschule für Musik, Munich (Fulbright Scholar). *Career:* operatic debut in USA in title role of La Belle Hélène, New York City Opera 1969; debut at Metropolitan Opera as Lulu 1977; now appears regularly in leading opera houses world—wide and in concert performances with major orchestras in USA and Europe; Metropolitan Opera premiere of Shostakovich's Lady Macbeth of Mtsensk (Katerina Ismailova); Wozzeck (Marie), Toulouse Opera, Teatro Colón; mem. American Guild of Musical Artists. *Recordings include:* Le Pré aux Clercs, Behold the Sun, French songs by Chausson, Duparc, Satie and Fauré, Prokofiev songs, Poulenc's La Voix Humaine, Menotti's The Telephone, Britten's Les Illuminations, Prokofiev's The Ugly Duckling, Kurt Weill songs, Milhaud songs (with John Constable), Strauss Songs and the Four Last Songs, Strauss Final Scenes from Daphne and Capriccio, Tchaikovsky opera arias, Delius songs with orchestra, Les Soldats Morts 1995 (Grand Prix du Disque), Grieg songs with orchestra, Serebrier Symphony No. 3, Ned Rorem Songs with Ned Rorem, Piano, Der Wampyr by Marschner, Songs of William Bolcom, Classic American Love Songs. *Roles include:* Monteverdi's Poppea, Massenet's Manon, Mozart's Idomeneo, Don Giovanni, Entführung, Die Zauberflöte, Verdi's La Traviata, Puccini's La Bohème, Tosca, Lehar's The Merry Widow, Strauss' Zigeunerbaron, Berg's Lulu, Wozzeck, Weill's Mahagonny, Offenbach's Tales of Hoffmann, La Belle Hélène, Strauss's Salome, Capriccio, Die Frau ohne Schatten, Elektra, Shostakovich's Lady Macbeth of Mtsensk, Wagner's Parsifal, Die Walküre, Schönberg's Erwartung, Janáček's Macropoulos Case, Jenůfa, Katya Kabanova. *Honours:* numerous awards and prizes including Grand Prix du Disque for Les Soldats Morts (by A. Lemeland) 1995 and Diapason d'Or (France) 1997, Abbiati Prize for Best Production of an Opera in Italy (for Berg's Lulu, Turin). *Current Management:* c/o Robert Lombardo Associates, Suite 6F, 61 West 62nd Street, New York, NY 10023, USA. *Telephone:* (212) 586-4453. *Fax:* (212) 581-5771. *Website:* www .lombardoassociates.org. *E-mail:* carole@carolefarley.com (home). *Website:* www.carolefarley.com.

FARMAN, Raphaëlle; French singer (soprano); b. 1965. *Education:* Paris Conservatoire, Opera School of the Opéra Bastille. *Career:* debut in Mozart's Susanna 1989; Gilda in Rigoletto and Bellini's Elvira for Radio France; appearances in The Queen of Spades and Carmen (as Frasquita) at the Opéra Bastille; Arminta in La Finta Giardiniera at Nantes, Gluck's Euridice at Lille, Mozart's Countess in Rennes, Poulenc's Blanche in St Etienne, and Micaela for Opera La Havana, Cuba 2001; British debut as Massenet's Esclarmonde, for Chelsea Opera Group, London; engagements as Offenbach's Antonia, and the Countess, at Tours, Anna in La Dame Blanche, Poulenc's Thérèse and Donna Anna for the Opéra Comique, Paris; season 2001–02 as Venus in Cherubini's Anacreon in Venice, Donna Anna at Toulon, and Mozart's Sandrina at the Opéra Comique; concerts with Armin Jordan, Charles Dutoit, Michel Plasson and Myung Whun Chung. *E-mail:* raphaelle-farman@easynet .fr. *Website:* www.raphaelle-farman.com.

FARNES, Richard; British conductor; *Music Director, Opera North;* b. 1964, England. *Education:* King's Coll., Cambridge, Nat. Opera Studio, Royal Acad. of Music, Guildhall School of Music and Drama. *Career:* music staff, Glyndebourne and with Scottish Opera and Opera Factory; English Touring Opera with Falstaff, La Bohème and The Barber of Seville; Gloriana, Figaro, Giovanna D'Arco, La Traviata, The Nightingale's to Blame (Simon Holt) and The Secret Marriage for Opera North; Bastien und Bastienne and La Serva Padrona for European Chamber Opera; Macbeth for City of Birmingham Touring Opera; season 1997–98 with The Makropulos Case at Glyndebourne, Die Entführung, Figaro and La Bohème for Glyndebourne Touring Opera; The Magic Flute, Param Vir double bill and world premiere of David Horne's Friend of the People for Scottish Opera 1999; also Nabucco for New Israeli Opera, Tel-Aviv, Albert Herring at Guildhall School 1998 and The Rake's Progress in Dublin 1999; founded Equinox 1992, for the performance of modern chamber ensemble pieces; Music Dir, Opera North 2004–. *Honours:* RAM Henry Wood and Philharmonia Chorus conducting scholarships. *Current Management:* c/o Ingpen & Williams, 7 St George's Court, 131 Putney Bridge Road, London, SW15 2PA, England. *Telephone:* (20) 8874-3222 (office). *Fax:* (20) 8877-3113. *E-mail:* info@ingpen.co.uk (office). *Address:* Opera North, Grand Theatre, 46 New Briggate, Leeds, LS1 6NU, England (office). *Website:* www.operanorth.co.uk (office).

FARNON, David Graham, MA, LRAM, ARCM, LMusTCL; British composer, conductor and producer; b. 12 Oct. 1956, London, England; m. Susie Best 1989; two s. *Education:* Univ. of Cambridge, Royal Acad. of Music, Royal Coll. of Music, Trinity Coll. of Music, London. *Career:* performances at The Barbican, Royal Festival Hall, London Palladium, the QEH with orchestras, including London Symphony Orchestra and London Philharmonic Orchestra; numerous television and radio appearances. *Compositions include:* two Pieces for orchestra 1980, Overture: London By Day 1981, Songs for Loving Swingers (musical) 1991, Beyond the Furthest Star (for the Royal Choral Soc.) 1993, Pastourelle for violin and orchestra 1993, ten Pieces for wind band 1989–94, 30 Pieces for woodwind ensemble 1988–94, various shows, television and radio commissions. *Recordings:* Conducting with the Royal Philharmonic Orchestra, including Holst, Elgar, Strauss, Albinoni and various operatic arias; first performance of Robert Farnon's Piano Concerto, Cascades to the Sea, with the Bratislava Radio Symphony Orchestra. *Address:* Les Villets Farm, Les Villets, Forest, Guernsey GY8 0HP, UK. *Telephone:* (1481) 265712. *E-mail:* david@farnon.co.uk.

FARNSWORTH, Marcus, MusB (Hons), MA, Dip RAM, ARAM; British singer (baritone); b. 19 Oct. 1983, Nottingham; s. of Barry Farnsworth and the late Alison Willett. *Education:* The Minster School, Southwell, Chetham's School of Music (studied trumpet and jazz piano, vocal training with Martin Bussey), Manchester, Univ. of Manchester, Royal Acad. of Music (studied with Glenville Hargreaves and Audrey Hyland), previous teachers include David Lowe, currently studies with Gary Coward in London. *Career:* began his musical training as a chorister at Southwell Minster, Notts.; in charge of Manchester Univ. Chamber Choir 'Ad Solem' for two years, Conductor Manchester Univ. Chorus 2005–09; began freelancing in oratorio, opera and recital work; was also a lay clerk at Manchester Cathedral and mem. BBC Daily Service Singers; operatic roles include The Novice's Friend/Billy Budd (ENO), Eddy/Turnage's Greek (Music Theatre Wales), Owen/Owen Wingrave (Nuremberg Int. Chamber Music Festival), Sid/Albert Herring (RAO), Oreste/Cavalli's Giasone (Royal Acad. Opera–RAO), Dandini/La Cenerentola (Clonter Opera), Guglielmo/Così fan tutte (RAO), Meredith/Maxwell Davies' Kommilitonen! (RAO, world premiere), and in concert Killian/Der Freischütz for the London Symphony Orchestra with Sir Colin Davis, and Aeneas/Dido and Aeneas for the Early Opera Company with Christian Curnyn at Wigmore Hall; recital, Lammermuir Festival and BBC Radio 3 with Joseph Middleton, Wigmore Hall recital with James Baillieu and further recitals with Simon Lepper, Iain Burnside, Elizabeth Burgess and Graham Johnson; further recitals include Britten War Requiem with the Adelaide Symphony Orchestra; Dvořák Te Deum with the Royal Liverpool Philharmonic Orchestra; Monteverdi Vespers, on tour, including Lille and Essen with Emmanuelle Haïm; Haydn Paukenmesse with BBC Scottish Symphony Orchestra and Bernard Labardie, and Peter Maxwell Davies Eight Songs for a Mad King on a UK tour with the Hebrides Ensemble; sings Son in a new work by David Sawer, Flesh and Blood with the BBC Symphony Orchestra and Ilan Volkov; European tour and recording of Thomas Larcher's Die Nacht der Verlorenen for baritone and ensemble 2013; sang Nielsen Symphony No. 3 with the London Symphony Orchestra and Sir Colin Davis; Bach Ich habe Genug with Acad. of Ancient Music throughout UK and on tour to France, also sang Bach St John Passion (arias) in London and Cambridge; other concert appearances have included Eight Songs for a Mad King with the Wermlands Opera Orchestra, Karlstad, Sweden and Bach St John and St Matthew Passions (Christus and bass arias) with the Gabrieli Consort and Paul McCreesh; season 2012–13 included English Clerk/Death in Venice (ENO) and a revival of Eddy/Greek (MTW); further recitals include debuts at the Concertgebouw, Amsterdam and La Monnaie, Brussels with Mark Padmore and Julius Drake and Tit for Tat at Wigmore Hall with Malcolm Martineau and Canticles with Julius Drake as part of 2012 Britten Festival; recital of Hugo Wolf for the Oxford Lieder Festival 2013; concerts with the Carducci Quartet, including Finzi By Footpath and Stile and Barber Dover Beach; sang with Myrthen Ensemble at the Wigmore Hall 2013; Royal Opera House debut as Eddy (Greek) for Music Theatre Wales 2013; Brahms Requiem Aldeburgh Voices, Snape Maltings 2014; Così fan tutte, ENO 2014; Solaris, Dai Fujikura, Opéra de Lille 2015; Górecki - Symphony no. 2 'Copernican', Barbican Hall 2015; Così fan tutte, The Ministry of Operatic Affairs, Antwerp 2016; Bach - St Matthew Passion, London Oratory School 2016. *Honours:* Winner, Wigmore Hall/Kohn Foundation Int. Song Competition 2009, Song Prize, Kathleen Ferrier Awards 2011. *Current Management:* c/o Maxine Robertson Management Ltd, 14 Forge Drive, Claygate, Surrey, KT10 0HR, England. *Telephone:* (20) 7993-2917. *E-mail:* mr@maxinerobertson.com. *Website:* www.maxinerobertson.com; www.marcusfarnsworth.com.

FARR, Gareth, BMus; New Zealand composer and percussionist; b. 29 Feb. 1968, Wellington. *Education:* Victoria Univ., Wellington, Auckland Univ., Eastman School of Music. *Career:* Composer-in-Residence, Chamber Music New Zealand 1993–; also performs as Lilith Lacroix in Drumdrag shows. *Compositions include:* Pembukaan 1990, works for Javanese gamelan, including Kebyar moncar and Reongan, Lilith's Dream of Ecstasy 1995, From the Depths Sound the Great Sea Gongs 1996, Hikoi 1998, Te Papa 1998, Concerto for four percussionists 2005. *Recordings include:* album: Ruaumoko, Beowulf, Orakau, Rangitoto and Te Papa played by New Zealand Symphony Orchestra. *E-mail:* gareth@drumdrag.com (office). *Website:* www.garethfarr.com.

FARRALL, Joy; British clarinettist; *Professor of Clarinet, Guildhall School of Music and Drama. Education:* GSMD, studied in Melbourne, Australia with Isobel Carter, with Nigel Keates, Yona Ettlinger and Antony Pay in England. *Career:* fmr mem., Nat. Youth Orchestra; founder mem., Haffner Wind Ensemble; has performed as a soloist with orchestras, including the Philharmonia, English Chamber Orchestra, City of London Sinfonia, London Mozart Players, Ulster Sinfonia, Britten Sinfonia; appearances as guest soloist with string quartets including Vanbrugh, Kreutzer, Medea, Brindisi,

New Leipzig, Schidloff, Pellegrini; numerous recitals with pianists Julius Drake and Graham Johnson at Wigmore Hall, Purcell Rooms and in Spain, Australia, Finland and Norway; festival appearances include Leicester, Cambridge, Aldeburgh, Cheltenham, Stockholm, Kuhmo, Finland; tour of Norway with Alpaca Trio 2006; works written for her include Simon Bainbridge's Double concerto and Clarinet Quintet, Edward Cowie's Elysium, works by Oliver Knussen and John McCabe; currently Prof. of Clarinet, GSMD. *Recordings:* Mercadante, Clarinet Concerto in B Flat, Mozart, Clarinet Concerto, The Daniel Trio, Rossini, Woolrich, Mozart, Divertimenti for Three Bassett Horns, Britten, The Prince of the Pagodas 1990, Mozart, Clarinet Masterworks 1993, Mozart, Clarinet Quartets 1993, Robert Simpson, String Quartets and two Clarinet Quintets 1993, Alwyn, Chamber Works 1994, Francaix, String Trio/Wind Quintet No. 1 1995, Beethoven, Trio for Clarinet, Cello and Piano (with The Ambache Chamber Ensemble) 1997, Mozart, Wind Concertos 2001, Richard Strauss, Horn Concertos 2002. *E-mail:* joy@engage.plus.com (office). *Website:* www.joyfarrall.co.uk (office).

FARRELL, Eibhlis; Irish composer; b. 27 July 1953, Rostrevor, Co. Down. *Education:* Queen's Univ., Belfast and Bristol Univ. *Career:* Deputy Principal, Coll. of Music, Dublin Inst. of Technology 1983. *Compositions include:* Concerto Grosso 1988, Sinfon for orchestra 1990, Exultet oratorio 1991, Exaudi Voces and a Garland for the President for solo voices and chorus 1991, Soundshock for concert band 1993; solo vocal music: The Silken Bed for mezzo, violin, cello and harpsichord 1993, Caritas Abundar for two sopranos and chorus 1995, Island of Women for orchestra 1996; chamber and instrumental pieces: Earthshine for harp 1992.

FARREN-PRICE, Ronald William, DipMus; Australian pianist and academic; b. 2 July 1930, Brisbane; m. Margaret Lillian Cameron 1982, three s. two d. *Education:* Univ. of Melbourne, studied with Claudio Arrau in London and New York. *Career:* debut with Melbourne Symphony Orchestra, Concerto 1947; Wigmore Hall, London 1955; has played in over 50 countries, including 12 concert tours of the former USSR and many performances at London's Wigmore Hall, QEH, Purcell Room and St John's Smith Square; performances at Carnegie Recital Hall, New York, Nat. Gallery, Washington, and Tchaikovsky Hall, Moscow; Reader in Music, Univ. of Melbourne 1975, Dean of Faculty of Music 1986–90, Head of Keyboards 1991–97, Assoc. Prof. 1989–, Sr Assoc. of the Faculty 1998–, Fellow of Queen's Coll. 1991–, Council Mem. of Queen's Coll. 1986–, Music Patron Trinity Coll. Music Foundation; Patron St Paul's Cathedral Old Christians Ascn; Dir, Australian Nat. Acad. of Music 1999; Federal Examiner for the Australian Music Examinations Bd 1984–85, 1994–97; has performed concertos with many leading conductors; has broadcast recitals in many countries and also appeared in television recitals; mem. Melbourne Club, Univ. House, Univ. of Melbourne. *Address:* c/o Faculty of Music, University of Melbourne, Parkville, Victoria 3052, Australia.

FARRER, John; American conductor; b. 1950. *Career:* numerous performances with leading orchestras in USA, notably San Francisco Symphony Orchestra; Music Dir Roswell Symphony Orchestra, New Mexico; mem. Faculty, conducting workshops, American Symphony Orchestra League; London debut in 1986 with London Philharmonic; Sr Guest Conductor, English Sinfonia, and concerts with Royal Philharmonic Orchestra and Bournemouth Symphony Orchestra. *Recordings include:* Tchaikovsky album with the London Philharmonic, Dvořák with the RPO and Copland and Gershwin with the Bournemouth Symphony Orchestra. *Current Management:* John Gingrich Management, PO Box 1515, New York, NY 10023, USA. *E-mail:* johnfarrerconductor@gmail.com. *Website:* johnfarrerconductor.com.

FASHAE, Alycia; British singer (soprano); b. 1970. *Education:* Royal Northern Coll. of Music with Ryland Davies and Honor Shepherd, L'Opéra National de Paris. *Career:* appearances in Paris as Mozart's Servilia, Pamina and Fiordiligi; Adina in L'Elisir d'Amore, Lucia di Lammermoor, Gounod's Juliette, Micaela, Bizet's Leila, Massenet's Sophie and Cendrillon, Violetta, Gilda and Nannetta; engagements on tour of Britain as Violetta, with European Chamber Opera and Pamina with Diva Opera; Leila in The Pearl Fishers for ENO; season 2001–2002 as Donna Anna and Offenbach's Antonia with Diva Opera, Frasquita in Carmen for ENO and Gilda for European Chamber Opera; tour of USA as Hanna Glawari in Merry Widow.

FASOLIS, Diego; Swiss organist and conductor; *Principal Conductor, Choir of Radiotelevisione Svizzera*; b. 1958. *Education:* Musikhochschule Zürich, masterclasses with Gaston Litaize and Michael Radulescu. *Career:* mem. Radiotelevisione Svizzera Italiana 1986–, Conductor 1993–, Music Dir, Choir of Radiotelevisione Svizzera 1993–; Founder and Principal Conductor, period instrument orchestras Ensemble Vanitas 1995– and I Barrochisti 1998–; Guest Conductor, several Swiss orchestras, RIAS Kammerchor Berlin, Sonatori della Gioiosa Marca, Concerto Palatino, Real Orquesta Sinfónica de Sevilla, Orchestra and Chorus of La Scala, Milan, Rome Opera, Orchestra dell'Arena di Verona and Teatro Comunale di Bologna; as organist, has performed the complete works of Bach, Buxtehude, Mozart, Mendelssohn, Franck and Liszt. *Recordings include:* with Concerto Köln: Vinci: Artaserse (ECHO Klassik Award for Opera Recording of the Year 2013); with I Barrochisti: Mission (ECHO Klassik Award for World Premiere Recording of the Year 2013), St. Petersburg (with Cecilia Bartoli) 2014. *Address:* c/o Coro della Radiotelevisione Svizzera, Via Canevascini, 6903 Lugano, Italy (office). *Telephone:* (91) 8039576 (office). *E-mail:* coro@rsi.ch (office); barocchisti@gmail.com (office). *Website:* www.retedue.rsi.ch (office).

FASSBAENDER, Brigitte, FRNCM; German singer (mezzo-soprano) and artistic director; b. 3 July 1939, Berlin; d. of the late Willi Domgraf-Fassbaender and Sabine Peters. *Education:* Nuremberg Conservatoire and studied with father. *Career:* debut at Bavarian State Opera, Munich 1961; has appeared at La Scala Milan, Vienna State Opera, Covent Garden London, Metropolitan Opera, New York, San Francisco and Salzburg; Teacher of Solo Vocal Music Musikhochschule, Munich; soloist, Dir of Opera, Brunswick 1995–97; Intendantin (Artistic Dir), Tiroler Landestheater, Innsbruck 1999–2012. *Recordings:* over 100 recordings since 1964. *Honours:* Bundesverdienstkreuz am Bande, Bayerischer Verdienstorden. *Address:* c/o Tiroler Landestheater und Orchester GmbH, Rennweg 2, 6020 Innsbruck, Austria.

FAST, George Allen, BMusA; Canadian singer (countertenor), academic and writer on music; b. 27 March 1954, Leamington, ON. *Education:* Univ. of Western Ontario. *Career:* debut with Waverly Consort, Kennedy Center, Washington DC, USA 1979; soloist with Tafelmusik Baroque Orchestra, The Bach Ensemble, Nat. Arts Centre Orchestra (Ottawa), CBC Vancouver Orchestra, Smithsonian Chamber Players, New York Oratorio Soc., Oregon Symphony, Opera Atelier (Toronto), Casals Festival, Madeira Bach Festival, Wratislavia Cantans, Pacific Opera Victoria, Les Violons du Roy, Studio de Musique Ancienne de Montréal, L'Orchestre de la Nouvelle France, Edmonton Symphony, Louisville Bach Soc. and others; Asst Prof. of Early Music Voice, Dir of Cappella Antica, McGill Univ.. *Recordings include:* The Christmas Story (with The Waverly Consort) 1983, Renaissance Favorites (with The Waverly Consort) 1985, Bach Cantatas 8, 78 and 99 (with Bach Ensemble, Joshua Rifkin) 1989, Complete Alto Cantatas of Buxtehude 1989.

FATH, Karl; German singer (bass); b. 1941. *Career:* Sang at Giessen, 1963–67, Koblenz, 1968–72, Brunswick, 1972–74 and Saarbrucken, 1974–77; Engaged at Gelsenkirchen from 1977 and has made guest appearances at Stuttgart, Karlsruhe, Frankfurt, 1984–86 and Cologne, 1987–88; Tour of Brazil in 1982 singing in Jakob Lenz by Wolfgang Rihm; Appeared as Don Magnifico in La Cenerentola at Bielefeld, 1989, Lunardo in I Quattro Rusteghi by Wolf-Ferrari at Hannover in 1991; Sang Truffaldino in Ariadne auf Naxos at Hannover, 2000; Many lieder recitals and concert appearances. *Recordings:* Petite Messe Solennelle by Rossini. *Address:* c/o Niedersachsiche Staatstheater, Opernplatz 1, 3000 Hannover, Germany.

FAULKNER, Julia; American singer (soprano); b. 1962, St Louis, Mo. *Education:* studied with Margaret Harshaw at Bloomington. *Career:* sang Arminda in Mozart's Finta Giardiniera at Lyon, returning for Alice Ford in Falstaff; Mozart and Strauss roles at Munich Staatsoper (Marschallin 1995); Vienna 1993–95, as Arabella and Countess in Capriccio; Miami Opera 1991, as Fiordiligi; sang Marianne in Der Rosenkavalier at Met 2000; other roles include Ariadne and Wagner's Gutrune (Vienna Staatsoper); further engagements at Hamburg, Amsterdam, Geneva and Stockholm; Prof. of Voice, Univ. of Wisconsin for 10 years; currently voice instructor, Patrick G. and Shirley W. Ryan Opera Center, Lyric Opera of Chicago; Founder Julia Faulkner Voice Studio. *Recordings include:* Die Zauberflöte and Pergolesi's Stabat Mater. *E-mail:* juliafaulkner1@me.com. *Website:* juliafaulkner.net.

FAUST, Isabelle; German violinist. *Education:* Colls of Music in Saarbrücken, Detmold and Berlin, studied with Christoph Poppen. *Career:* played with major orchestras, including Hamburg Philharmonic (conducted by Yehudi Menuhin), Berlin Philharmonic, Munich Philharmonic, Orchestre de Paris, Boston Symphony Orchestra, BBC Orchestras and Mahler Chamber Orchestra; performances under conductors including Claudio Abbado, Charles Dutoit, Daniel Harding, Heinz Holliger, Mariss Janson, among others. *Recordings:* Bartók's Solo Sonata for Violin, Mozart's Violin Concerto in A Major, Prokofiev's Concerto No. 1, Dvořák's Violin Concerto in A Minor 2003, Mendelssohn's Violin Concerto in E Minor, Bruch's Violin Concerto in G Minor, Beethoven Violin Concerto 2007, Beethoven Sonatas for Piano and Violin (with Alexander Melnikov) (Gramophone Award for Best Chamber Music Recording 2010) 2009, Bach Partitas and Sonatas 2010, Beethoven/Berg Violin Concertos (Gramophone Award for Best Concerto Recording, ECHO Klassik Award for Instrumentalist of the Year/Violin) 2012). *Honours:* First Prize, Int. Leopold Mozart Competition for Violinists, Augsburg 1987, Premio Quadrivio for Outstanding Musical Achievement, Rovigo, Italy 1990, First Prize, Paganini Competition, Genoa, Italy 1993, Prize for Highly Talented Young Artists in Nordrhein-Westfalen 1994. *Current Management:* c/o Impresariat Simmenauer, Schlueterstrasse 36, 10629 Berlin, Germany. *Telephone:* (30) 414781720. *E-mail:* juliette.dufau@impresariat-simmenauer.de. *Website:* www.impresariat-simmenauer.de.

FAUST, Michael; German flautist; *Professor of Flute, Robert-Schumann-Hochschule, Düsseldorf*; b. 16 Jan. 1959, Cologne; one s. one d. *Education:* Hochschule für Musik, Hamburg. *Career:* Prin. Flautist with the Santa Cecilia Orchestra in Rome, Hamburg Philharmonic (conductor C. von Dohnányi), Stuttgart Opera (conductor D. R. Davis), Munich Philharmonic (conductor S. Celibidache), Cologne Radio Symphonie (conductors Gary Bertini, Hans Vonk and Semyon Bychkov); major solo concerts in New York, St Louis, Boston, Tokyo, Moscow and Paris; Ibert Concerto with the Moscow Symphony, conductor V. Fedosseyew 1985; Gunther Schuller's Flute Concerto with the St Louis Symphony Orchestra 1998; premiere of Mauricio Kagel's Flute Concerto, Das Konzert 2003; Founding mem. Ensemble Contrasts Köln and Zephyr Bläserquintett; Prof. for Flute, Robert-Schumann-Hochschule, Düsseldorf. *Recordings:* H. W. Henze El Cimarron, J. S. Bach to Mozart, 20th Century Flute Concertos, Ibert, Bernstein, Nielsen, Elliott Carter, French

Flute Music. *Honours:* prizes and awards at competitions in Bonn, Rome, Prague, Pro Musicis Award, New York. *Current Management:* Rolf Sudbrack, Hamburg. *E-mail:* rolf-sudbrack@t-online.de. *Address:* Hittorfstrasse 2, 50735 Köln, Germany. *E-mail:* mfaust@post.com. *Website:* www.mfaust.de.

FEATHERSTONE, Gary Maxwell; Australian composer and pianist; b. 2 Sept. 1949, Sydney. *Education:* Sydney Conservatorium. *Career:* debut, Radio 2CH, Sydney, aged 15; performances in England, France, Poland, Germany and Australia; recordings for ABC Radio and 2MBS, FM Radio, Sydney. *Compositions:* Piano Pieces for Children 1989, Idyll, for flute and piano 1990, Prelude in E Flat major, for piano 1990, Improvisation, for piano 1993, Pieces for Musical Children 1993, I Need Love, for voice and piano 1995, Four Nocturnes 1995, The Waltzes, for piano 1995, Barcarolle, for piano 1995, Berceuse, for piano 1996, Scherzo, for piano 1996, Two Dance Songs, piano 1997, 24 Preludes, piano 1999, Piano Concerto No. 1, Piano Concerto No. 2, Rhapsody on Original Theme for Piano and Orchestra, Serenade for Strings 1999, Symphonic Fantasia – Peter Ibbetson (full orchestra) 2000, Romance for Violin and Piano 2001, Dance in the Moonlight, for oboe and piano 2002. *Recordings:* Serenade for Strings (Nevsky Quartet, St Petersburg, Russia), Symphonic Fantasia (Peter Ibbetson, Slovak Radio Orchestra), Australian Piano Music (three compositions), Barcarolle (for ABC-FM, Australian Composers Concert) 1995. *Address:* 29 Balmain Road, McGraths Hill, NSW 2756, Australia (home).

FEDDERLY, Greg; American singer (tenor); *Principal Artist, Los Angeles Opera*; b. 1961, California. *Education:* Univ. of Southern California. *Career:* appearances with Los Angeles Opera have included Britten's Albert Herring, Mozart's Monostatos, Pinkerton, Hylas in Les Troyens and Arturo in Lucia di Lammermoor 1988–, currently Prin. Artist; European debut as Tom Rakewell, Aldeburgh Festival 1992; engagements at the Théâtre du Châtelet, Paris, in Die Frau ohne Schatten and Moses und Aron; Philidor's Tom Jones at the Drottningholm Festival 1995; Gluck's Orpheus 1996; further roles include Mozart's Ferrando, Alfredo in La Traviata, Washington 1996, Rossini's Almaviva, Seattle 1997 and David in Die Meistersinger at Los Angeles, season 1997–98; sang in the premiere of Florencia of the Amazons, Houston Opera 1996; Tamino at Los Angeles 1998; saeason 1999–2000 included Telemaco in Ulisse at Glimmerglass; concerts of The Creation, Barcelona; Alfredo in La Traviata at Los Angeles Opera and Pinkerton in Madama Butterfly in Santa Barbara; San Francisco Opera debut 2002 as Brighella in Ariadne aux Naxos; Metropolitan Opera debut 2003 as Basilio in Marriage of Figaro and has subsequently appeared at the Met as Goro in Madama Butterfly; 2009–10 season engagements included Monostatos in Die Zauberflöte and Don Basilio in Le nozze di Figaro at the Metropolitan Opera, Brighella in Ariadne auf Naxos for Washington Nat. Opera, cameo appearance in The Play of Daniel for LA Opera; 2010–11 engagements included Borsa in Rigoletto and Noble in Lohengrin with LA Opera. *Recordings include:* The Rake's Progress, for Swedish Television. *Honours:* first recipient of the Marilyn Horne Scholarship at UCLA. *Address:* c/o LA Opera, Dorothy Chandler Pavilion, 135 North Grand Avenue, Los Angeles, CA 90012, USA (office). *Telephone:* (213) 972-7219 (office). *Fax:* (213) 687-3490 (office). *E-mail:* wehelpyou@laopera.com (office). *Website:* www.laopera.com (office).

FEDER, Donn-Alexandre, BS, MS, DMA; American pianist and teacher; b. 23 June 1935, Philadelphia, PA; m. Janet Landis 1960, one d. *Education:* Juilliard School of Music, studied with Rosina Lhevinne, Kabos and Gorodnitzki, Eastman School of Music with Jorge Bolet. *Career:* debut at New York Town Hall 1963; extensive concert tours throughout Europe, Mexico, Canada and USA, and for NBC and ABC television and BBC, England; appearances with major European and American orchestras; faculty mem., Philadelphia College of Performing Arts, 1971–81; Piano Faculty, Manhattan School of Music, 1978–; mem., two-piano team, Feder and Gilgore; co-director of Musicisti Americani Festival and Institute, Rome and Sulmona, Italy; Artist-Teacher, Taiwan International Festival, China, 1988 and 1989. *Recordings:* with the Netherlands Radio Philharmonic under Allers and Van Otterloo. *Recordings include:* Szymanowski Piano Music, Excursions for Two Pianos, Music of Barber, Copland and Gershwin (with Elisha Gilgore), Bartók Sonata for 2 Pianos and Percussion, Stravinsky's Concerto for 2 Solo Pianos, with Elisha Gilgore. *Address:* c/o Manhattan School of Music, Piano Faculty, 120 Claremont Avenue, New York, NY 10027, USA.

FEDIN, Alexander; Russian singer (tenor); b. 11 Sept. 1954. *Career:* sang at first in concert, then appeared at the Bolshoi, Moscow, from 1986, notably as Werther, Rossini's Almaviva and the Holy Fool in Boris Godunov; Guested with the Bolshoi at Glasgow, 1990, as the King in Tchaikovsky's Maid of Orleans, and at Rome, 1989, in a concert performance of Rachmaninov's Aleko; Berlin Staatsoper, 1991, as the Duke of Mantua; Further appearances at the Vienna Staatsoper, in Dortmund and at the Teatre Liceu, Barcelona; Cologne Opera 1995–96 as Tamino, Steuermann and Cassio; Season 2000–01 as Faust at Essen, Wagner's Erik at Freiburg and the Prince in The Love for Three Oranges at Cologne.

FEDOSEYEV, Vladimir Ivanovich; Russian conductor; *Principal Conductor and Artistic Director, Tchaikovsky Academy Symphony Orchestra*; b. 5 Aug. 1932, Leningrad; s. of Ivan Fedoseyev and Elena Fedoseyeva; m. Olga Dobrokhotova; two c. *Education:* Gnesins Musical Academy, Tchaikovsky Conservatory with Leo Ginzburg. *Career:* mem. CPSU 1963–91; Artistic Dir and Chief Conductor Moscow Radio Symphony Orchestra of USSR Radio Network (now Tchaikovsky Acad. Symphony Orchestra) 1974–; Music Dir

Vienna Symphony Orchestra 1997–2005; apptd Perm. Guest Conductor Tokyo Philharmonic Orchestra 1996, Zürich Opera 1997, Radio France Orchestra 2001; Prin. Conductor Orchestra Sinfonica di Milano Giuseppe Verdi 2009–; works with Bolshoi and Mariinsky Theatres, opera productions and concerts abroad, including Italy, France, Austria, Germany, Japan, Switzerland, Spain, UK, USA. *Recordings include:* Symphonies by Beethoven, Mahler, Shostakovich, Mussorgsky, Sviridov, Russian operas. *Honours:* People's Artist of USSR 1980, RSFSR State Prize 1989, Crystal Award of Asahi Broadcasting Corpn, Osaka 1989, Golden Orpheus, for recording of opera May Night, Gold Medal, Int. Gustav Mahler Soc. 2007, among others. *Address:* 121069 Moscow, Malaya Nikitskaya 24, Russia (home). *Telephone:* (495) 229-57-68 (Moscow) (home); (1) 503-84-77 (Vienna) (home). *Website:* www.fedoseyev.com (office); www.bso.ru (office).

FEENEY, Angela; British singer (soprano); b. 19 Oct. 1954, Belfast, Northern Ireland. *Education:* studied at Belfast, Dublin and Munich. *Career:* debut with Irish Nat. Opera 1977, as Cherubino; ENO from 1978, as Micaela, Marenka in The Bartered Bride, Nedda, and Donna Elvira 1986; Munich Staatsoper 1983–86, as Papageno, Gretel, and Ingrid in Egk's Peer Gynt; Deutsche Oper Berlin 1985, as Butterfly; Dublin Grand Opera 1986, as Gluck's Euridice; Wexford Festival 1986, as Giulietta in Verdi's Un giorno di Regno; other roles include Mimi and Leonore in Il Trovatore; Tutor of Singing, Queen's Univ. Belfast 2003–, est. Belfast Classical Music Bursaries. *Honours:* Dr hc (Queen's Univ. Belfast) 2006.

FEGRAN, Espen; Norwegian singer (baritone); b. 1960, Oslo. *Education:* Oslo Acad. with Nicolai Gedda. *Career:* sang at Norwegian Nat. Opera in Oslo as Papageno 1987, Marcello, Guglielmo, Mozart's Count and similar repertory; moved to Hessian State Theatre, Wiesbaden 1988, performed as Eugene Onegin, Belcore, Beckmesser, and in Henze's Verratene Meer; Bonn 1992, in Jakob Lenz by Rihm; Leipzig 1996, in Greek by Turnage; with Staatstheater Kassel 2009–. *Current Management:* c/o Thomas Weiler, Weiler Artists Management Berlin, Kaiserin-Augusta-Allee 47, 10589 Berlin, Germany. *E-mail:* weiler@weiler-artists.de. *Website:* www.staatstheater-kassel.de/espen-fegran,p11058.html.

FEIGIN, Joel, BA, MM, DMA; American composer; *Professor of Composition, University of California, Santa Barbara;* b. 23 May 1951, New York, NY; s. of Dr Irwin Feigin and Mollie Kanowitz Feigin; m. Severine Neff 1986. *Education:* Columbia Univ., studied with Charles Wuorinen, Harvey Sollberger and Patricia Carpenter, Juilliard School, studied with Roger Sessions and Renee Longy, Fontainebleau Conservatoire Americaine, studied with Nadia Boulanger, Mellon Fellowship to Cornell Univ., Aaron Copland-American Soc. of Composers, Authors and Publrs Fellowship to Tanglewood Music Center. *Career:* Prof. of Music, Univ. of California, Santa Barbara 1997–; Sr Fulbright Scholar, Moscow Conservatory, Russia 1998–99; comms from Fromm Music Foundation, Santa Barbara Youth Symphony, Long Leaf Opera Co., Theatre Cornell, Voices of Change, Golden Fleece Ltd, Zen Mountain Monastery, Leonard Stein, Margaret Mills. *Compositions:* Mysteries of Eleusis (opera), Twelfth Night (opera), Festive Overture for orchestra, Elegy in Memoriam Otto Luening for orchestra, Janfare for small orchestra, Aviv: Concerto for piano and chamber orchestra, Concerto Grosso: Catastrophe, Lamentation and Prayer for string orchestra, Mosaic in Two Panels for string orchestra, Dirge for brass ensemble, The Lament Cycle: Lament with Ghosts for solo viola and a consort of six violas, Lament for solo viola, Ghosts for six violas, Shifting Spirits for violin and cello, Mel's Song for two recorders, Echoes of the Holocaust for chamber ensemble, Transience for oboe and percussion, Nexus for flute and piano, Four Poems of Linda Pastan for soprano and ensemble, Five Ecstatic Poems of Kabir for soprano and ensemble, Veränderungen for violin and piano, gently flowing for violin and piano, Variations on a Theme by Arnold Schoenberg for piano, Festive Overture for orchestra, Music for Mountains and Rivers Trio for piano, violin and cello, Tapestry for French horn, violin and piano, Meditations from Dogen for piano, An Empty Boat Floating Adrift, Five Poems of Tu FU for contralto, piano and percussion, Lament for solo viola, Ghosts for six violas, Lament with Ghosts for solo viola and six voices, Variations on Empty Space for piano, Lament for solo cello, Montecito Variation for solo violin, music for 'Mountains and Rivers' video by John Daido Loori Roshi, music for 'Old Plum Mountain: The Berkeley Zen Center: Life Inside the Gate' a video by Ed Herzog. *Recordings:* Transience (includes 10 chamber and vocal works). *Publications:* Transience for oboe and percussion 1997; contrib. to Stil oder Gedanke? Die Schoenberg-Nachfolge in Europa und Amerika, Roger Sessions Newsletter Vol. I, Perspectives of New Music Vol. 12. *Honours:* Mellon Foundation Fellowship 1983–85, Sr Fulbright Fellowship, Moscow Conservatory, Fromm Comm. 2007, prizes from Speculum Musicae, Auros Group for New Music, Quinto Maganini Competition, Int. Chamber Music Competition, New York City Opera Showcase. *Current Management:* c/o Jeffrey James Arts Consulting, 45 Grant Avenue, Farmingdale, NY 11735, USA. *Telephone:* (516) 586-3433. *E-mail:* jamesarts@att.net. *Website:* www.jamesarts.com. *Address:* 2673 Moreton Bay, Lane #5, Goleta, CA 93117 (office); 173 Wintersage, Pittsboro, NC 27323, USA (office). *Telephone:* (805) 681-9705 (office); (919) 542-6219 (office). *E-mail:* feigin@music.ucsb.edu (office). *Website:* www.joelfeigin.com.

FEJER, András; Hungarian cellist; b. 1950; m.; three c. *Education:* Franz Liszt Acad. with András Mihaly, studied with Amadeus Quartet and Zoltán Szekeley. *Career:* Founder-mem. Takacs Quartet 1975; numerous concert appearances in all major European centres and USA; tours include New Zealand, Japan, England, Sweden, Belgium and Ireland; Bartók Cycle for

festival at South Bank, London 1990, Théâtre des Champs-Elysées, Paris 1991; Great Performers series at Lincoln Center and Mostly Mozart Festival at Alice Tully Hall, New York; visits to Japan 1989, 1992; Mozart Festivals at South Bank, Wigmore Hall and Barbican Centre, London 1991; Beethoven cycles at Zürich Tonhalle, Dublin, at Wigmore Hall and in Paris 1991–92. *Recordings include:* Schumann Quartets, Opus 41, Mozart String Quintets with Denes Koromzay, 6 Bartók Quartets, Schubert's Trout Quintet with Zoltán Kocsis, Haydn, Opus 76, Brahms, Opus 51, Nos 1 and 2, Chausson Concerto with Joshua Bell and Jean-Yves Thibaudet; Works by Schubert, Mozart, Dvořák and Bartók. *Honours:* winner, Int. Quartet Competition, Evian 1977, Portsmouth Int. Quartet Competition 1979. *Current Management:* Christa Phelps Artist Management, 7 Merchant House, 184-186 Sutherland Avenue, Little Venice, London, W9 1HR, England. *E-mail:* info@takacsquartet.com. *Website:* www.takacsquartet.com.

FELCIANO, Richard James, DipMus, MA, PhD; American composer and teacher; *Professor Emeritus, University of California at Berkeley;* b. 7 Dec. 1930, Santa Rosa, CA. *Education:* Mills Coll., Oakland, CA with Milhaud, Paris Conservatory with Milhaud and Ple-Caussade, studied with Dallapiccola in Florence, Univ. of Iowa with Bezanson. *Career:* Composer-in-Residence, Nat. Center for Experiments in Television, San Francisco 1967–71, City of Boston 1971–73; Chair of Music Dept, Lone Mountain Coll., San Francisco 1959–67; Prof., Univ. of California, Berkeley 1967–2004, Prof. Emer. 2004–; founder Center for New Music and Audio Technologies, Univ. of California, Berkeley 1987. *Compositions include:* chamber opera: Sir Gawain and the Green Knight 1964; orchestral: Mutations 1966, Galactic Rounds 1972, Orchestra 1980, Concerto for organ and orchestra 1986, Symphony for strings 1993, Overture Concertante for clarinet and orchestra 1995; chamber: Evolutions for clarinet and piano 1962, Glossolalia for baritone, organ, percussion and tape 1967, Chod for violin, cello, double bass, piano, percussion and live electronics 1972, In Celebration of Golden Rain for Indonesian gamelan and organ 1977, Alleluia to the Heart of Stone for reverberated recorder 1984, Shadows for flute, clarinet, violin, cello, piano and percussion 1987, Palladio for violin, piano and percussion 1989, Responsory for solo male voice and live electronics 1991, Camp Songs for chamber orchestra of 15 instruments 1992, Cante Jondo for bassoon, clarinet and piano 1993, String Quartet 1995, An American Decameron (song cycle on texts from interviews of Stubs Terkel) 2001; piano pieces and various choral works. *Publications:* analysis and commentary on sketches for Edgard Varèse's Poème électronique in Space Calculated in Seconds (Treib) 1997. *Honours:* Fulbright Fellowship 1958, Guggenheim Fellowship 1969, American Acad. of Arts and Letters Award 1974, various grants and commissions, Library of Congress Koussevitzky Commission 1999. *Address:* c/o Music Department, University of California, Berkeley, CA 94720 (office); 1326 Masonic Avenue, San Francisco, CA 94117, USA (home). *E-mail:* felciano@cnmat.berkeley.edu (office).

FELDHOF, Gerd; German singer (baritone); b. 29 Oct. 1931, Radvormwald, Cologne. *Education:* studied in Detmold. *Career:* debut at Essen 1959 as Mozart's Figaro; guest engagements at Buenos Aires 1960; sang at Städtische Oper Berlin and Frankfurt Opera from 1961 and Metropolitan Opera from 1961, with debut as Kaspar in Der Freischütz; further appearances in Helsinki, Hamburg, Copenhagen, Amsterdam, Montreal, Mexico City, Japan and Korea; Bayreuth Festival 1968–78, notably as Amfortas; also sings Barak in Die Frau ohne Schatten (Karlsruhe 1992); Deutsche Oper Berlin 1996, as Wagner's Kurwenal. *Recordings include:* Lulu; Kothner in Die Meistersinger; Beethoven's 9th Symphony; Jonny Spielt Auf by Krenek; Hindemith's Mathis der Maler.

FELDMAN, Jill; American/French singer (soprano) and teacher; *Professor in Baroque Singing, Zürcher Hochschule der Künste and Royal Conservatory, The Hague;* b. 21 April 1952, Los Angeles, Calif.; m. Kees Boeke; one d. *Education:* studied in San Francisco, Basel and Paris, Univ. of California, Santa Barbara. *Career:* has sung in Europe and the USA in many performances of early music; US opera debut as Music in Monteverdi's Orfeo 1979; European opera debut as Clerio in Cavalli's Erismena at Spoleto 1980; mem. William Christie's ensemble, Les Arts Florissants 1981–, concerts include Charpentier's Médée at Salle Pleyel, Paris 1984, Bach Magnificat at Palais Garnier, Paris Opera, Edinburgh Festival and Opéra de Versailles in Charpentier's Actéon and Rameau's Anacréon 1985; premiere of Hildegard Von Bingen's Ordo Virtutum with Ensemble Sequentia for West Deutsche Rundfunk in Cologne; sang Belinda at Opéra du Rhin, Strasbourg; tours in USA with Nicolas Megegan and Philharmonia Baroque Orchestra; London BBC Handel Carmelite Vespers with Andrew Parrot; solo recitals in Wigmore Hall, London and Cité de la Musique, Paris; sang Minerva in Monteverdi's Ritorno d'Ulissi in Patria, Concertgebouw, Amsterdam; sang Vita in first modern revival of Marco Marazzolli's La Vita Humana, at the Tramway, Glasgow, with Scottish Early Music Consort 1990; sang The Aunt in Mariken in der Tuin der Lusten, Opera2Day 2015; Co-founder (with her husband), Olive Music (music co.) 2003–; vocal teacher, Academia de Música Antiga de Lisboa, Portugal, Amici della musica di Firenze, Italy; Prof. in Baroque Singing, Royal Conservatory, The Hague, Zürcher Hochschule der Künste. *Recordings include:* more than 50 recordings, including four solo recitals, Udite amanti by Monteverdi, D'India, Rossi, Strozzi, Carissimi, Henry Purcell: Ayres from Orpheus Britannicus with lutenist Nigel North, and Henry Purcell: Harmonia Sacra with organist Davitt Moroney, Pianger di dolcezza: Italian poetry set to music by Giulio Caccini and Sigismondo D'India

(Stradivarius); Olive Music: Trecento (Machaut, Jacopo da Bologna, Matteo da Perugia, Ciconia), Ténèbres (Charpentier, DeLalande, Couperin), William Byrd and his Contemporaries, Dufay Chansons, Squarcialupi codex, Chantilly codex (Ensemble Tetraktys), and with pianist Jeannette Koekkoek, Songs of Charles Ives; Charpentier's Médée (Gramophone Award 1985, Grand Prix Charles Cros, Grand Prix du Disque de Montreux) 1984, 1999, Schutz's Il primo libro de madrigali 1992, Charpentier's Les Arts Florissants 1992, Campra's Cantatas Françaises 1992, Purcell's Dido and Aeneas 1992, Rameau's Anacréon 1992, Handel's Susanna 1992, Mozart's Ascanio in Alba 1995, Monteverdi's Il Ballo delle Ingrate 1996, Handel's Carmelite Vespers 1999, Handel's Clori, Tirsi e Fileno 2003, Charpentier's Actéon, Cesti's Orontea, Cavalli's Xerse, incidental music for Molière's Le Malade Imaginaire, Ensemble Mala Punica, Van Eyck: French and English Lute Songs. *Honours:* Gramophone Award 1984. *Address:* Località Campodalti, 52020 Pergine Valdarno, Italy (home). *Telephone:* (057) 5897010 (home). *Fax:* (057) 5897180 (home). *E-mail:* jill.feldman40@gmail.com (home); jillann52@me.com (office). *Website:* www.o-livemusic.com (home).

FELENCHAK, Vladimir; Russian singer (tenor); b. 1972, Yalta. *Education:* Glinka Academic Choir School, St Petersburg Conservatoire. *Career:* Young Singers' Academy at the Mariinsky Theatre, St Petersburg, from 1998; appearances with the Kirov Opera as Mozart's Basilio, the Duke of Mantua, Alfredo, the Indian Merchant in Sadko and Rimsky-Korsakov's Kaschchei and Berendai (The Snow Maiden); sang Tamino and Monostatos in Die Zauberflöte in Midia, Lithuania, 1998; Other roles include the Simpleton in Boris; sang with the Kirov Opera in summer season at Covent Garden, 2000.

FÉLIX, Loïc; French (b. French Guiana) singer (tenor). *Education:* Conservatoire Nat. Supérieur de Musique, Paris, masterclasses with Michel Sénéchal, Régine Crespin and Renata Scotto. *Career:* fmr mem. Petits Chanteurs à la Croix de Bois, Paris (boys' choir); mil. service with Choeur de l'Armée Française (French army choir, part of Garde républicaine); has sung with opera cos in Vienne, Aix en Provence, Monte Carlo, Luxembourg, Rennes, Théâtre du Châtelet, Paris, Opéra de Montpellier, Opéra Nat. du Rhin, Opéra de Marseille, Glyndebourne Festival. *Opera repertoire includes:* Monostatos in Die Zauberflöte, title role in Albert Herring, Don Basilio in Le Nozze di Figaro, Alfred in Die Fledermaus, Albazar in Il Turco in Italia, Pluto in Orpheus in the Underworld, Remendado in Carmen, Pedrillo in Die Entführung aus dem Serail. *Recordings include:* Mozart's Die Entführung aus dem Serail (DVD) 2007, Offenbach Opera Extracts 2007, Rossini's Ermione (Gramophone Award for Best Opera Disc 2011) 2010, Offenbach Vert-Vert 2010. *Current Management:* Le bureau François Rousseau, 20 rue milton, 75009 Paris, France. *Telephone:* 1-45-26-79-36 (office). *E-mail:* mmassonnat@fr-lebureau.com (office). *Website:* www.fr-lebureau.com (office).

FELLER, Carlos; Argentine singer (bass); b. 30 July 1922, Buenos Aires. *Education:* Teatro Colón Opera Studio. *Career:* debut singing the Doctor in Pelléas et Mélisande, Buenos Aires 1946; sang widely in South America and toured Europe with Argentine Chamber Orchestra 1958; resident in Germany from 1958, notably at Cologne Opera where he has sung Don Pasquale, Dulcamara, Dr Bartolo, Leporello and Don Alfonso; Glyndebourne Festival 1959–60, as Don Alfonso, Figaro, the Speaker in Die Zauberflöte and Dr Bombasto in British premiere of Busoni's Arlecchino; appearances at Salzburg, Edinburgh and Holland Festivals and in major opera houses in Europe and Americas; Metropolitan Opera debut 1988, as Don Alfonso, followed by Dr Bartolo 1990; Buenos Aires and Santiago 1990–91; other roles in Il Matrimonio Segreto, Venice and Washington; Wozzeck at Seattle; Zar und Zimmermann, Der Rosenkavalier, La Cambiale di Matrimonio and Il Signor Bruschino at Cologne; sang Schigolch in Lulu, Opéra Bastille 1998; season 2000–01 included La Nozze di Figaro at the Brussels Opera, Merry Widow at Teatro Colón Buenos Aires and La Bohème in Florence; season 2001–02 sang in Tales of Hoffmann in Geneva. *Recordings include:* Don Alfonso and Mozart's Bartolo with the Drottningholm Ensemble, conducted by Arnold Oestmann; Videos of Il Barbiere di Siviglia, Il Matrimonio Segreto, La Gazza Ladra and Agrippina.

FELLNER, Till; Austrian pianist; *Professor, Zürcher Hochschule der Künste*; b. 9 March 1972, Vienna. *Education:* Vienna Conservatory with Helene Sedo-Stadler, studied with Alfred Brendel and Oleg Maisenberg. *Career:* performances with numerous orchestras, including Acad. of St Martin-in-the-Fields, Boston Symphony Orchestra, Camerata Salzburg, Chicago Symphony Orchestra, Israel Philharmonic Orchestra, London Philharmonia, Los Angeles Philharmonic, Munich Philharmonic, Orchestre de Paris, Orchestre Nat. de France, Pittsburgh Symphony, Royal Concertgebouw Orchestra, San Francisco Symphony, Vienna Philharmonic, Vienna Symphony; has worked under numerous conductors, including Claudio Abbado, Vladimir Ashkenazy, Herbert Blomstedt, Semyon Bychkov, Christoph von Dohnányi, Bernard Haitink, Nikolaus Harnoncourt, Heinz Holliger, Sir Charles Mackerras, Sir Neville Marriner, Kurt Masur, Kent Nagano, Jonathan Nott, Franz Welser-Möst and Hans Zender; chamber work with Alban Berg Quartet, Belcea Quartet, Lisa Batiashvili, Adrian Brendel, Mark Padmore, Heinrich Schiff; appearances at BBC Proms, Schubertiade Schwarzenberg, Wiener Festwochen, Mostly Mozart in New York, Tanglewood Music Festival, Edinburgh Festival, Festival de La Roque d'Anthéron, Festival Montreux-Vevey, Klavier-Festival Ruhr, Salzburg Festival and others; one-year sabbatical 2012; began teaching at Hochschule der Künste, Zürich, Switzerland 2013; debut with Berlin Philharmonic 2015. *Film:* Pianomania 2009. *Recordings include:* Schubert: Four Impromptus for Piano, Schoenberg: Suite für Klavier Op.

25, Beethoven: Piano Sonata in F minor, Op. 57, Mozart: Piano Concerto K482, Rondo in A minor, K511, Beethoven: Piano Sonata in C minor Op. 10/1, Schumann: Kreisleriana Op. 16, Reubke: Sonata in B minor, Schubert: Sonata in A minor D784, Moments musicaux D780, Grazer Walzer D924, Mozart: Piano Concertos No. 25, K503 and No. 19, K459, Beethoven: The Complete Works for Cello and Piano (with Heinrich Schiff), J. S. Bach: The Well-Tempered Clavier Book 1, Inventions and Sinfonias, French Suite No. 5, Beethoven: Piano Concertos Nos 4 and 5, Thomas Larcher: 'Böse Zellen', H. Birtwistle: Chamber Music. *Publication:* Alfred Brendel als Lehrer 2008, About Alfred Brendel 2010, Subversion und Stille – Zur Musik in den Filmen von Luis Bunuel 2013. *Honours:* First Prize, Clara Haskil Int. Competition 1993, Mozartinterpretationspreis, Mozartgemeinde Wien 1998. *Current Management:* c/o Künstlermanagement Till Dönch, Rögergasse 24–26/G2, 1090 Vienna, Austria; c/o Ingpen & Williams, 7 St George's Court, 131 Putney Bridge Road, London, SW15 2PA, England. *Telephone:* (20) 8874-3222 (London). *Fax:* (20) 8877-3113 (London). *E-mail:* management@doench.at; info@ingpen.co.uk. *Website:* www.doench.at; www.ingpen.co.uk; www.tillfellner.com.

FELTSMAN, Vladimir; Russian/American pianist and teacher; b. 8 Jan. 1952, Moscow. *Education:* Central Music School, Moscow, studied with Yakov Flier at Moscow Conservatory, St Petersburg Conservatory. *Career:* debut as soloist with Moscow Philharmonic 1963; toured Russia and Eastern Europe from 1971; played in Japan in 1977 and France in 1978; moved to USA 1987; New York recital debut at Carnegie Hall 1987; Prof., SUNY, New Paltz 1987–, currently Distinguished Chair of Piano; founder and Artistic Dir, Int. Festival-Inst. Piano Summer at New Paltz. *Honours:* first prize Prague Concertino Competition 1967, jt first prize Marguérite Long-Jacques Thibaud Competition, Paris 1971. *Current Management:* Arts Management Group, 37 West 26th Street, Suite 403, New York, NY 10010-1006, USA. *Telephone:* (212) 337-0838. *Fax:* (212) 924-0382. *E-mail:* info@artsmg.com. *Website:* www.artsmg.com; www.feltsman.com.

FENNELLY, Brian Leo, BMechEng, BA, MMus, PhD; Irish-American composer, theorist, pianist and academic; *Professor Emeritus, School of Arts and Science, New York University*; b. 14 Aug. 1937, Kingston, NY; s. of Leo Paul Fennelly and Florence Agnes Fennelly; m. 1st; one s.; m. 2nd Jacqueline Burhans Baczynsky. *Education:* Union Coll., Yale School of Music, Yale Univ. Grad. School. *Career:* USAF 1958–61; teacher, Union Coll. and Yale Univ. Faculty 1962–68; Prof., School of Arts and Science, New York Univ. 1968–97, Prof. Emer. 1997–; Co-Dir Washington Square Contemporary Music Soc. 1976–; Ed. Contemporary Music Newsletter 1969–77, Composers' Forum 1968; performances in USA, Europe, Canada, Japan, Korea, S America and Int. Soc. for Contemporary Music Int. Festival 1973, 1980, 1981, 1984, 2011, Warsaw Autumn Festival1980, 1984; comms from Koussevitsky Foundation 1983, 1999, Hudson Valley Philharmonic 1984, Meet the Composer 1992, Fromm Music Foundation 1999; Rockefeller Foundation Bellagio Center residency 1999; Camargo Foundation residency 2002; Copland House residency 2004. *Compositions include:* SUNYATA 1970, String Quartet in 2 Movements 1971–74, Tesserae I–IX 1971–80, In Wildness is the Preservation of the World 1976, Sonata Seria 1976, Quintuplo 1977–78, Tropes and Echoes 1981, Canzona and Dance 1982–83, Thoreau Fantasy No. 2 1985, Corollaries I–IV 1986–2002, Brass Quintet No. 1 1987, Keats on Love 1988–89, Lunar Halos 1990, A Sprig of Andromeda 1991–92, On Civil Disobedience 1993, Locking Horns (Brass Quintet No. 2) 1993–94, Skyscapes I–IV 1996–2006, Chrysalis 1997, Sonata Serena 1997–98, Velvet and Spice (Brass Quintet No. 3) 1999–2000, Three's Company 2000, Arias and Interludes (String Quartet No. 2) 2001, Quincunx 2003, Sasquatch 2003–04, String Quartet No. 3 (Sigol: Thirty Flowers) 2005, 'Sigol' for Strings 2007, Sigol for Two 2008, Sinfonia Concertante 2009, The Other Side of Time 2009, Sacred Songs 2010–11, Kythera Variations 2012, Tableaux 2013–14. *Recordings:* Wind Quintet, Evanescences, String Quartet in 2 movements, In Wildness Is The Preservation Of The World, Sonata Seria, Scintilla Prisca, Prelude and Elegy, Empirical Rag, Tesserae VII, For Solo Flute, Concerto for saxophone and string orchestra, Tesserae VIII, Tesserae II, Fantasy Variations, Two Poems of Shelley, On Civil Disobedience, A Sprig of Andromeda, Paraphrasis, Chrysalis, Thoreau Fantasy No. 2, Concert Piece for Trumpet and Orchestra, 'Reflections/Metamorphoses', Lunar Halos, 'Sigol' for Strings, Fantasia Concertante, Tropes and Echoes, Corollary III, The Other Side of Time. *Publications:* contrib. to Dictionary of Contemporary Music 1974, New Grove Dictionary of Music and Musicians, Perspectives of New Music, Journal of Music Theory, Notes. *Honours:* Nat. Endowment for the Arts Composer Fellowships 1977, 1979, 1985, Guggenheim Foundation Fellowship 1980, first prizes Shreveport Symphony Competition 1981, Louisville Orchestra Competition 1986, Int. Trumpet Guild 1990, New Ariel Competition 1995, American Acad. of Arts and Letters Lifetime Achievement Award 1997, Bogliasco Foundation Fellowship 2002, New York Composers' Circle Competition 2008, Fauxharmonic Orchestra Competition 2009, Outstanding Eng Alumnus Award (for career in music), Union Coll. 2013. *Address:* 2 Schryver Court, Kingston, NY 12401, USA (home). *Telephone:* (845) 331-3228 (office). *E-mail:* FennellyBL@aol.com (home); Brian.Fennelly.MUS.65@aya.yale.edu (office). *Website:* library.newmusicusa.org/brianfennelly; composers.com/brian-fennelly; www.washingtonsquaremusic.org.

FENOUILLAT, Christian; French set designer; b. 1940, Grenoble. *Career:* stage designs include Fidelio and Gluck's Orpheus for WNO; Bellini's I Capuleti at Lisbon, Gluck's Armide and Mozart's Clemenza di Tito at the

Théâtre des Champs Elysées and Jenůfa at Spoleto; Wozzeck, Hamlet by Thomas, Der Rosenkavalier and Wagner's Ring, for Geneva Opera; Pelléas et Mélisande at Brussels and Ariane et Barbe-Bleue by Dukas for Opéra de Lyon; designs for La Cenerentola at Covent Garden, Hamlet at Barcelona and Lucia di Lammermoor for Chicago Lyric Opera 2001–02 season.

FERGUS-THOMPSON, Gordon, FRCM; British pianist and academic; *Professor of Piano, Royal College of Music*; b. 9 March 1952, Leeds, Yorks., England; s. of the late George Thompson and Constance Webb. *Education:* Temple Moor Grammar School, Leeds and Royal Northern Coll. of Music. *Career:* debut at Wigmore Hall 1976; has appeared as soloist with orchestras including Orchestra of the Hague, Gothenburg Symphony Orchestra, Royal Liverpool Philharmonic, The Philharmonia, City of Birmingham Symphony, Hallé, BBC Symphony; extensive tours in Europe, N America, Australia, Far East and S Africa; Prof. of Piano, Royal Coll. of Music 1996–; Gulbenkian Foundation Fellowship 1978. *Recordings include:* The Rachmaninov Sonatas 1987, Balakirev and Scriabin Sonatas 1987, Complete Works of Debussy (five vols), Complete Works of Scriabin (five vols) 1990–2001, Rachmaninov's Etudes-Tableaux 1990, Bach Transcriptions 1990, Complete Works of Ravel (two vols) 1992, Headington: Piano Concerto 1997. *Honours:* MRA Prize for Best Instrumental Recording of the Year 1991, 1992. *Address:* 44 Courtfield Rise, West Wickham, BR4 9BH, Kent, England (home). *Telephone:* (7590) 515-645 (office). *E-mail:* gfergusthompson@rcm.ac.uk (office). *Website:* www.gordonfergusthompson.com.

FERMANI, Simone; Italian conductor, composer and academic; *Full Professor of Conducting and Score Reading, Conservatory of Music G. Verdi, Milan*; b. (Simone Francesco Maria Ferdinando Fermani), 3 Dec. 1954, Appignano (Macerata); great-great-grandson of Giuseppe Verdi and Giuseppina Strepponi; m. Alberta Girardi; one d. *Education:* Conservatory Francesco Morlacchi, Perugia, Conservatory of Music Santa Cecilia, Rome, advanced conducting studies with Franco Ferrara in Rome, Leonard Bernstein in Vienna and Rome, Peter Maag in Bologna, Padua, Venice and Bern, Catholic Univ. of Milan, Liceo Giacomo Leopardi, Macerata. *Career:* began playing and studying piano aged six; professional conductor since 1989; debut in opera conducting Rossini's The Barber of Seville at Opera Marseille; has conducted at Teatro Massimo, Palermo, Teatro Regio, Parma, 49th Int. Summer Festival of Liubljana, Belgrade Nat. Opera, Santa Fe, Argentina; has also conducted Puccini's Suor Angelica, Pergolesi's La serva padrona and Menotti's The Telephone; invited by Youth Orchestra of Nat. Acad. Santa Cecilia, Rome, Haydn Orchestra of Bolzano, Orchestra of Lyric Theatre, Cagliari, Orchestra Capella Cracoviensis, Kraków, Orquesta Sinfonica de Santa Fe, Argentina, Symphony New Brunswick, Canada, Symphony Orchestra of the Nat. Opera Theatre of Maribor, Slovenia, Symphony Orchestra Gioachino Rossini of Pesaro, Milan, Rome Theatre of Terme di Caracalla, Florence, Montreal, Ottawa, Bangkok, Würzburg, Strasbourg, Belfort (France), Neuchâtel, Murcia, Cartagena, Santander Palacio de Festivales (Spain), Belgrade; Founder Orchestra Filarmonica Marchigiana, Ancona, Artistic and Musical Dir 1978–80; Founder Symphony Orchestra of Catholic Univ. of Milan, Artistic and Musical Dir 1991–2001, designed, managed and conducted nine symphonic seasons of 55 concerts (with Susanna Mildonian, Maxence Larrieu, Rocco Filippini, Francesco Manara, Vincenzo Balzani and others), 20 Italian tours, eight European tours in France, Germany, Switzerland, Spain and Slovenia and tours in Thailand and Canada; conducted premiere of Abendlied, composed by Niccolò Castiglioni 1995; opened the Verdi & Wagner Festival at Helikon Opera, Moscow conducting Un ballo in maschera by Verdi 2013; taught score reading at Conservatories of Cagliari 1999–2000, Alessandria 2000–06, score reading and orchestral conducting at Conservatory of Music G. Cantelli, Novara 2006–07; Prof. of Score Reading, Conservatory of Music Giuseppe Verdi, Milan 2007–; Prof. of Conducting and Score Reading, Conservatory of Music G. Verdi, Milan 2009–; master class for opera and symphonic conductors at Scuola Musicale di Milano 2010–; master class for opera conductors and singers at Latvian Acad. of Music Jazep Vitols, Riga 2011, 2012, Lithuanian Acad. of Music, Vilnius 2011, Conservatorio Superior de Musica of La Coruña, Spain 2011, Conservatorio Superior de Musica of Vigo, Spain 2012; Academic mem. Accad. Georgica 2013. *Achievement:* rediscovered, from the original score, and rebuilt the sistrum, an instrument that Rossini designed and indicated for his opera The Barber of Seville; instrument used for the first time following its rediscovery in performances at Opéra Marseille 1998–. *Recordings include:* Rossini's The Barber of Seville at Opéra Marseille (DVD) 1998, Luigi Cherubini's Requiem in C Minor for Choir and Orchestra with the Symphony Orchestra of Università Cattolica and Choir of the Municipality of Milano 1999, Giuseppe Verdi's Requiem with Orquesta Sinfonica e Coro Provincial de Santa Fe, Argentina (DVD), 2005, Rossini: Overtures from Famous Operas with Symphony Orchestra G. Rossini (DVD) 2010. *Honours:* Hon. mem. Annuario Musicale Italiano, CIDIM-Roma (sections: Conductors and Artistic Direction) 1991, Artistic Council of Int. Cultural Centre (YUBIN), Belgrade 2003; J.F. Perrenoud Prize for Conducting, Fifth Vienna Int. Music Competition, Vienna 1995, winner of three competitions held by Italian Ministry of Educ. for Full Profs in Italian Conservatories of Music 1999. *Current Management:* c/o Massimilano Becco, Athole Still Opera, 25-27 Westow Street, London, SE19 3RY, England. *Telephone:* (20) 87686617; 607-848426 (mobile). *E-mail:* max@atholestill.co.uk. *Website:* www.atholestill.com. *Address:* Via Nicola Romeo 5, 20142 Milan, Italy (home). *Telephone:* (02) 89300074; 349-8342776 (mobile). *Fax:* (02) 89300074. *E-mail:* simone@simonefermani.it. *Website:* www.simonefermani.it.

FERNÁNDEZ, Nohema, DipMus, BMus, MMus, DMA; Cuban pianist; b. 23 May 1944, Havana; one d. *Education:* Conservatorio Internacional, Havana, DePaul, Northwestern and Stanford Univs, USA, studied with Jorge Bolet, Adolph Baller and duo-pianists Vronsky and Babin. *Career:* debut in Havana 1960; New York debut at Carnegie Recital Hall 1983; appearances at Festival de Música Latino-Americana, Mexico City, Cabrillo Festival, and Sunriver Festival and recitals in Glasgow, Edinburgh, Vienna, Amsterdam, New York, Miami and San Francisco; radio broadcasts in Mexico City, New York and San Francisco and television appearances in Chicago and San Jose; soloist with orchestras in USA, Republic of Korea; recitals in Cuba, USA, Canada, Europe, South America; mem., Jaffe-Fernández Duo (cello and piano); radio broadcasts in Mexico, USA, Republic of Korea; Dean of the Claire Trevor School of the Arts and Prof. of Music, and Claire Trevor Dean's Endowed Chair, Univ. of California at Irvine 2003–. *Recordings include:* Latin-American music for the Saarländisches Rundfunk. *Publications:* contrib. articles to Piano Quarterly and Latin American Music Review. *Honours:* NEA Solo Recitalist Award 1990–91, La Rosa Blanca Distinction of Honour, Los Angeles 1996. *Address:* 200 Mesa Arts Building, Department of Music, University of California, Irvine, CA 92697-2775, USA (office). *Website:* www.nohemafernandez.com.

FERNANDEZ, Wilhelmenia; American singer (soprano); b. 5 Jan. 1949, Philadelphia, PA. *Education:* studied in Philadelphia and at the Juilliard School. *Career:* debut with Houston Opera, 1977, as Gershwin's Bess; sang in Porgy and Bess on tour in the USA and Europe; Paris Opéra, 1979, as Musetta in La Bohème; appearances at the New York City Opera, in Boston and Michigan, and at Toulouse as Aida; Opéra du Rhin, Strasbourg, and Liège, 1987–88, as Marguerite; Theater des Westens, Berlin, 1988, as Bess; Bonn Opera, 1989, as Aida; sang the title role in Carmen Jones, London, 1991; National Indoor Arena, Birmingham, 1992; 1994–96, Aida at Deutsche Oper Berlin; other roles include Mozart's Countess and Donna Anna, Purcell's Dido and the title role in Luisa Miller; concert engagements include Beethoven's Ninth; recital at Kensington Palace in the presence of HRH Princess of Wales; regular recitalist throughout Europe and USA. *Film appearance:* Diva. *Honours:* Evening Standard Award for Best Actress in a Musical. *Current Management:* Bureau de Concerts de Valmalète, 7 rue Hoche, 92300 Levallois Perret, France. *Telephone:* 1-47-59-87-59. *Fax:* 1-47-59-87-50. *Website:* www.valmalete.com.

FERNANDEZ-GUERRA, Jorge; Spanish composer; b. 17 July 1952, Madrid. *Education:* Madrid Conservatory. *Career:* from 1970 worked as musician, composer and actor in the independent theatre movement; opera 'Sin demonio no hay fortuna', based on the Faust legend and performed at Madrid's Sala Olimpia 1987. *Compositions include:* Sin demonio no hay fortuna (opera), incidental music to plays by Aeschylus, Wilde, Beckett, Brecht and others, chamber and orchestral music.

FERNEYHOUGH, Brian John Peter, DMus, ABSM, ARAM, FRAM, FBC; British composer and academic; *William H. Bonsall Professor in Music, Stanford University*; b. 16 Jan. 1943, Coventry, West Midlands, England; s. of Frederick George Ferneyhough and Emily May Ferneyhough (née Hopwood); m. 4th Stephanie Hurtik 1990. *Education:* Birmingham School of Music, Royal Acad. of Music, Sweelinck Conservatory, Amsterdam, Music Acad., Basle. *Career:* composition teacher, Musikhochschule, Freiburg, Germany 1973–78, Prof. of Composition 1978–86; Prin. Composition Teacher, Royal Conservatory of The Hague 1986; Prof. of Music, Univ. of California, San Diego 1987–99; Leader of Master Class in Composition, Civica Scuola di Musica, Milan 1982–86, Fondation Royaumont, France 1990–; Visiting Artist, DAAD, Berlin 1976–77; Guest Prof., Musikhögskolan, Stockholm 1980, 1981, 1982, 1985; Visiting Prof., Univ. of Chicago 1986; Lecturer in Composition, Darmstadt Int. Courses 1976–96, 2008–; Guest Prof. of Poetics, Mozarteum, Salzburg, Austria 1995; William H. Bonsall Prof. in Music, Stanford Univ. 2000–; Visiting Prof., Harvard Univ. 2007–08, S.L. Lee Visiting Professorial Fellow, Univ. of London 2012; Corresp. Mem. Bayrische Akademie der Schönen Künste 2005–; mem. Akademie der Künste, Berlin 1996–; mem. Bd Perspectives of New Music 1995–; Jury mem. Kranichsteiner Preis Jury, Darmstadt 1978–96. *Compositions include:* Sonatas for String Quartet 1967, Firecycle Beta 1969–71, Transit 1972–74, Time and Motion Study III 1974, La Terre Est Un Homme 1976–79, Second String Quartet 1979–80, Lemma-Icon-Epigram 1981, Carceri d'Invenzione 1981–86, 3rd String Quartet 1987, Kurze Schatten II 1988, La Chute d'Icare 1988, Fourth String Quartet 1989–90, Allgebrah 1991, Bone Alphabet 1991, Terrain 1992, On Stellar Magnitudes 1994, String Trio 1995, Incipits 1995–96, Flurries 1997, Unsichtbare Farben 1999, Doctrine of Similarity 2000, Opus Contra Naturam 2000, Stele for Failed Time 2001, Shadowtime (opera) 2004, Plötzlichkeit 2005, Fifth String Quartet 2006, Dum transisset I–IV 2007, Exordium 2008, Chronos-Aion 2008, Renvois/Shards 2008, Sisyphus Redux 2008, Sixth String Quartet (Royal Philharmonic Soc. Chamber-scale Composition Prize 2011) 2009, Liber Scintillarum 2012, Finis Terrae 2012, Quirl 2013, Schatten aus Wasser und Stein 2013, Silentium 2013, Contraccolpi 2015. *Publications include:* Complete Writings on Music 1994, Collected Writings 1996; various articles published separately. *Honours:* Hon. DMus (Goldsmiths Coll.) 2011; Chevalier des Arts et des Lettres 1984; Koussevitsky Prize 1979, Grand Prix du Disque 1978, 1984, Ernst von Siemens Prize for Lifetime Achievement 2007, and other awards and prizes. *Address:* Office 231A, Department of Music, Braun Music Center, Stanford University, 541 Lasuen Mall, Stanford, CA 94305-3076, USA (office). *Telephone:* (650) 725-3102 (office). *Fax:* (650) 725-

2686 (office). *E-mail:* brian.ferneyhough@stanford.edu (office). *Website:* music.stanford.edu (office).

FERRAND, Emma, ARAM, FRNCM; British cellist; *Senior Lecturer, Royal Northern College of Music*; b. 1 Oct. 1948, London, England; m. Richard Deakin 1969; three c. *Education:* Int. Cello Centre, London, Royal Acad. of Music, London and studied with Pierre Fournier in Geneva. *Career:* debut at Wigmore Hall 1974; solo concerts; BBC recordings; BBC television with Elgar Concerto 1975; chamber music concerts; mem., Deakin Piano Trio and Deakin Chamber Players; Sr Lecturer, Royal Northern Coll. of Music, Manchester 1983–; Artist-in-Residence, Stowe Summer School and Lake District Summer Music 1999–; Visiting Prof., Eastman School of Music, New York, USA 1994; appearances on BBC 2, Radio 3; tour and masterclasses in USA 2001; concerts throughout Canada and UK 2003; currently Visiting Prof., Univs of Georgia and Oslo; masterclasses Banff Centre 2003–05; works commissioned for her: Suite for solo cello by Hywel Davies 2005 and Recit & Aria for Violin & Cello by John Manduell 2010; jury mem., South Africa Int. String Competition, Antonio Janigro Int. Cello Competition 2008, Beethoven Hradec Int. Cello Competition 2010. *Recordings:* C. Hubert Parry's complete piano trios, piano quartet; Parry's Chamber Works with Piano; Bach Suites for Solo Cello Vols I and II 2005, Northern Lights: English Cello Sonatas 1920–1950 2009. *Current Management:* c/o J Audrey Ellison International Artists' Management, 135 Stevenage Road, Fulham, London SW6 6PB, England. *Telephone:* (20) 7381-9751. *Fax:* (20) 7381-2406. *E-mail:* audrey@ellison-intl.freeserve.co.uk. *Website:* www.ellison-intl.freeserve.co.uk. *Address:* Ings Cottage, Berrier, Nr Penrith, Cumbria CA11 0XD, England. *E-mail:* deakinmusic@aol.com (home). *Website:* www.emmaferrand.co.uk.

FERRANDIS, Bruno, MA, Post-Grad. Dip; French conductor; b. 1960, Algiers. *Education:* Guildhall School, London and Juilliard School, New York, studied with Leonard Bernstein and Franco Ferrara. *Career:* Assoc. Conductor, Juilliard Opera Center –1993; Resident Conductor, Canadian Opera Co., Toronto 1993–; Music Dir, Santa Rosa Symphony Orchestra, USA 2006–07; repertoire includes Lulu, Pelléas, Jenůfa, Katya Kabanova, Erwartung, Fidelio, and works by Verdi, Puccini and Strauss; Dir of New York ensemble, Music Mobile –1996, Contemporary Opera Training in Banff –2001; symphonic repertoire with BBC Northern, Polish Radio, Monte Carlo and Jerusalem Symphony, Hong Kong and Seoul Philharmonics, Madrid RTVE, French orchestras particularly Radio France Philharmonique; specialist in Gurlitt's Wozzeck and Die Soldaten. *Recordings:* albums: Yves Prin: Dioscures 2001, MFA Collection: Claude Ballif/Ahmed Essyad. *Honours:* Grand Prix de la Critique 1997. *Address:* c/o Musicaglotz, 11 rue le Verrier, 75006 Paris, France. *Telephone:* 1-42-34-53-46 (office). *E-mail:* music@glotz.com (office).

FERRARI, Elena; British singer (soprano); b. 1970, England. *Education:* Nat. Opera Studio, London. *Career:* appearances with Opera North as Musetta (1996) and Bice in Korngold's Violanta (also at the 1997 London Proms); Mozart's Countess for English Touring Opera 1997 and Fiordiligi for Opera North 1997–98; other roles include Adina (L'Elisir d'amore), Violetta, Donna Elvira, Marguerite, Mélisande, Cherubini's Medea and Polly Peachum in The Threepenny Opera; Jenny in Weill's Mahagonny Songspiel at the London Proms 1997; season 1998, as Cinna in Mozart's Lucio Silla for Garsington Opera; other concerts include the Verdi Requiem, Elijah, Italian Songs and French Melodies. *Honours:* Nat. Opera Studio Gerald McDonald Award.

FERRÉ, Susan Ingrid, BA, BM, MM, DMA; American organist, harpsichordist and conductor; *Director, Music in the Great North Woods*; b. 5 Sept. 1945, Boston, Mass; d. of Gustave A. Ferré and Dorothy Fredericks Ferré; m. Kenneth Charles Lang 1980; one s. *Education:* Texas Christian Univ., Diplôme d'Orgue et Improvisation, Schola Cantorum, Paris, France, Eastman School of Music, North Texas State Univ., studied with Jean Langlais, Marcel Dupré, Maurice Duruflé in France and Emmet Smith, David Craighead and Don Willing in USA. *Career:* fmr mem. Adjunct Faculty, North Texas State Univ., Southern Methodist Univ.; Dir Texas Baroque Ensemble 1980–2005; Dir of Early Music at Round Top Festival 1986–2000; organ and harpsichord performances in N and S America, Europe and Scandinavia; Featured Artist, Lahti Organ Festival, Finland and at WCC, Switzerland; recitals at Cathedral of Notre-Dame, Paris; Past Dean, Dallas Chapter, American Guild of Organists 1991–93; Visiting Asst Prof. of Music and Univ. Organist, Pacific Lutheran Univ. 2001–02; Bd Pres. Westfield Center for Keyboard Studies 1999–2004; currently Dir Music in the Great North Woods, Gorham, NH; mem. Bd Jehan Alain Soc. 2002–04. *Compositions:* numerous compositions published and recorded by Avant Quart Company, France. *Recordings include:* Works of Langlais on the Cavaillé organ at Ste Clotilde, Paris; Messe Solennelle by Louis Vierne; Preludes & Postludes for the year beginning 9-11-2001; Stories From the Human Village: War and Peace (ninetydays.com); recordings for nat. radio and TV in France, Hungary, Sweden, Finland, USA; works by Karg-Elert, Langlais, Alain, Duruflé, Fanny Mendelssohn, Liszt, Ethel Smyth, Tournemire, Messiaen and Bolcom, organ recitals. *Publications:* numerous articles in The American Organist, The Diapason, Westfield Center Journal, The Tracker, Old West Society Journal. *Honours:* Hon. Alumna, Perkins School of Theology, Southern Methodist Univ.; Fulbright Scholar 1968–69; Distinguished Alumna Award, Univ. of N Texas School of Music 2001. *Telephone:* (580) 624-0160. *Website:* www.iconcertartists.com. *Address:* 290 Gorham Hill Road, Gorham, NH 03581, USA (home). *Telephone:* (603) 466-2865 (office). *E-mail:* susanferre@earthlink.net. *Website:* www.susanferre.com; www.musicgnw.org (home).

FERRERO, Lorenzo; Italian composer; b. 17 Nov. 1951, Turin. *Education:* studied with Massimo Bruni and Enore Zaffiri and at Univ. of Turin. *Career:* collaboration with Musik Dia Licht Galerie, Munich from 1974, producing multimedia works; Artistic Consultant, Puccini Festival, Torre del Lago 1980–84; Artistic Dir Arena di Verona 1991–94, Festa della Musica, Milan 1999–2003, Ravello Festival 2004–06; Vice-Pres. Società Italiana degli Autori ed Editori 2007–11; Pres. Int. Council of Music Authors (Cisac) 2011–. *Compositions include:* Piano Concerto 1991, Tempi di quartetto 1996–98, Three Baroque Buildings, concertino for trumpet, bassoon and strings 1997, Second Piano Concerto 2009; theatre pieces: Rimbaud, Avignon 1978, Marilyn, Rome 1980, La Figlia del Mago, Montepulciano 1981, Charlotte Corday, Rome 1989, Le Bleu-blanc-rouge Et Le Noir, Paris, Centre Georges Pompidou 1989, Nascita di Orfeo, Verona Filharmonico 1996, La Conquista, Prague National Opera, Le Piccole Storie, Modena 2007, Franca Florio, Teatro Massimo, Palermo 2007, Risorgimento! Modena and Bologna 2011. *Address:* Via Lanfranchi 17, 10131 Turin, Italy (home). *E-mail:* lor.ferrero@gmail.com (office); annamaria.macchi@umusic.com (office). *Website:* www.freebase.com/view/en/lorenzo_ferrero.

FERREYRA, Beatriz Mercedes; Argentine composer; b. 21 June 1937, Córdoba; d. of Jorge Enrique Ferreyra and Maria Angelica Fanny LLambi Campbell. *Education:* studied with C. Bronstein in Buenos Aires, with Nadia Boulanger, Edgardo Canton, with György Ligeti and Earle Brown in Darmstadt, Groupe de Recherches Musicales (GRM), Paris and Radiotelevisione Italiana (RAI) with Pierre Schaeffer. *Career:* debut with GRM, Paris 1964; Asst Prof. 1965–70, Groupe de Musique Expérimentale de Bourges (GMEB) 1973; B. Baschet Musical Instrument Devt 1971; Music Therapy 1973–76, 1989; Dartmouth Coll. Computer System 1975; jury mem., fourth Int. Music Competition, GMEB 1976, second Int. Radiophonic Competition Phonurgia Nova, Arles 1987, Royal Conservatory of Music, Mons, 'Metamorphoses' 2000–01, 2003; numerous musical confs, courses, records, musical comms since 2003. *Compositions:* Demeures Aquatiques 1967, Médisances (Diplôme du meilleur disque pour 'Loisir des Jeunes', Paris 1971) 1968, L'Orvietan 1970, Etude aux sons flegmatiques 1971, Le Récit 1971, Antartide (film score) (Prix du Centre Nat. du Cinéma Français 1972) 1971, Siesta Blanca (Third Prize, Electronic Music Competition, Fylkingen 1975) 1972, Mutations (film score) 1972, A la lueur de la lampe (ballet) 1973, Canto del Loco 1974, Homo Sapiens (for television) (Prix Rissolli della Prima Opera, Italy 1978) 1974, Tierra Quebrada 1976, Echoes 1978, La Baie St James (for TV) 1980, Jeux des Rondes 1980–84, Musiques en Feu (for TV) 1981, Cercles des Rondes 1982, La Calesita 1982, Boucles, rosettes et serpentines 1982, Bruissements 1983, Arabesque autour d'une corde raide 1984, Passacaille débôitée pour un lutin 1984, Petit Poucet Magazine (Concours Int. de Création Radiophonique Phenourgia Nova Prix France Culture de l'Innovation, Arles 1986) 1985, The UFO Forest (hon. mention, Concours Int. du GMEB, Bourges 1987) 1986, L'Autre... ou le chant des marécages 1987, Souffle d'un petit Dieu distrait (Lauréat du concours UPIC dans le cadre des Journées d'Informatique Musicale, Paris 1999) 1988, 1997, Brise sur une fourmillère 1988, Tata, tocame la toccata 1990, Remolinos 1990, Mirage Contemplatif? 1991, Ríos de Sueño: No. 1 Río de los pájaros (Concours int. de musique et d'art sonore electroacoustique Prix Magisterium, Bourges 2000) 1998, No. 2 Río de los pájaros escondidos 1999–2000, No. 3 Río de los pájaros azules 1993, 1998, Jazz't for Miles 2001, La Ba-balle du chien-chien à la mé-mère 2001, Cantos de antes (Radio Bulgarie second prize 2004) 2002, Les Chemins du vent des glaces 2002, Murmureln 2003, Le Solfegiste solfegé 2003, Dans un Point Infini 2006, Sourires d'Automne 2006, L'Autre Rive 2007, Deux Dents Dehors 2007, Un fil invisible 2009, Pas de 3... et plus 2009, Flotando 2010, Vuelo de signos y remolinos 2010, Les rétrouvailles 2010, Les larmes de l'inconnu 2011, Improvisations with Christine Groult: Duo 2013 and Nahash 2014–15. *Exhibition:* Grand Marché d'Art Contemporain, Paris 2015. *Publications:* Le solfège sonore de Pierre Schaeffer et la composition musicale (article in LYRE magazine, Dec. 1999), Le 'groupe solfège' du G.R.M. et le Traité des Objets Musicaux (article in Du sonore au musical of Sylvie Dallet and Anne Veitl) 2001, Musikhören: Theorie und Praxis Elektroakustischer Musik, and Klänge und Klangstrukturen – Finden, Erfinden, Verarbeiten (two chapters in Welt Musik) 2004, Clio, Histoire, Femmes et Sociétés 2007, Portraits polychromes Pierre Schaeffer (article) 2008, Revue Maldoror (article) 2009, L'Espace du son III (article) 2010, Cahiers d'Histoire de la Radiodiffusion (article) 2011, Herencia de Pierre Schaeffer (article) 2011, Filigrane (article) 2012, Memoire de Mondes (article) 2014, Fragments d'un enseignement ... (article, INA-GRM) 2014; contrib. to articles, reports and album notes. *Honours:* Hon. mem. Int. Confed. of Electroacoustic Music 2014. *Address:* 600 Chemin des Logis, Hameau de Hodeng, 76270 Nesle Hodeng, France. *Telephone:* (2) 32-97-10-16. *E-mail:* beatriz.ferreyra@neuf.fr. *Website:* www.beatrizferreyra.odavia.com.

FIALA, George (Joseph), DMus; Canadian composer, pianist and conductor; b. 31 March 1922, Kiev, Ukrainian SSR, USSR. *Education:* Tchaikovsky State Conservatory, Akademische Hochschule für Musik, Berlin with Hansmaria Dombrowski and Wilhelm Furtwängler, Conservatoire Royal de Musique with Leon Jongen. *Career:* began studying piano aged seven; took piano lessons from K. Mikhailoff 1934; active mem. Séminaire des Arts Brussels; participated in many musical events as composer, pianist and conductor; settled in Montreal, Canada 1949, where active as composer, pianist, organist and teacher, naturalised Canadian citizen 1955; producer for Radio Canada International; more than 200 compositions. *Compositions include:* soloist with orchestra: Capriccio 1962, Divertimento Concertante 1965, Musique Concertante 1968, Sinfonietta Concertata 1971; voices with orchestra: Canadian

Credo 1966; orchestral: Autumn Music 1949, Symphony in E Minor 1950, Shadows of Our Forgotten Ancestors 1962, Eulogy 'In Memory of President J.F. Kennedy' 1965 (revised 1985), Montreal 1967, Ouverture burlesque 1972, Symphony No. 4 'Ukrainian' 1973, Ukrainian Triptych 1971, Overtura buffa 1981, Symphonie No. 5 'Sinfonia breve' 1981, The Kurelek Suite 1982, Festive Overture 1983, Music for Strings No. 1 and 2 1985, 1989, OVERture AND OUT 1989, Flute Concerto 1991, Sinfonico II 1992; chamber music: Cantilena and Rondo 1963, Duo Sonata for violin and harp 1971, Concertino Canadese 1972, Partita Concertata 1982, Quintet 1982, Musique à sept 1992; voice: Four Russian Poems 1968, My Journey 1982, Requiem 1995; piano solos and duos.

FIALKOWSKA, Janina, OC; Canadian pianist; b. 7 May 1951, Montreal, Quebec; m. Harry Oesterle. *Education:* Univ. of Montreal, studied in Paris with Yvonne Lefébure, Juilliard School with Sasha Gorodnitzki, and with Arthur Rubinstein. *Career:* has performed with all major N American orchestras and many major European and Asian orchestras; recitals worldwide; premiered Liszt's Concerto No. 3 Opus posthumus with Chicago Symphony 1990; premiered Andrzej Panufnik Concerto in N America; premiered piano concertos by Libby Larsen, Marian Mozetich and John Burge; renowned for Chopin, Mozart and Liszt interpretations and promotes 20th century Polish and Canadian music; Founder of Piano Six, a group of internationally renowned Canadian pianists committed to a programme that brings affordable important recitals to areas throughout Canada where classical music performances are a rarity, Founder of Piano Plus (successor to Piano Six), now also including singers and other instrumentalists. *Films:* The World of Janina Fialkowska (CBC) 1992, An Evening with Janina Fialkowska (CBC) 2013. *Recordings:* Chopin's Piano Concertos (chamber version and with orchestra), Etudes Nos 10 and 25, Sonatas Nos 2 and 3, Impromptus, Polonaises, Mazurkas, Waltzes, Nocturnes, Preludes, Barcarolle, 1st Scherzo, 3rd Ballade; Liszt's Piano Concertos, 12 Transcendental Etudes; works by Szymanowski, Moszkowski's La Jongleuse, Mozart's Piano Concertos, Paderewski's Piano Concerto, Moszkowski's Piano Concerto, Koprowski's Piano Concerto, Chopin: Polonaise in E flat, Preludes, Mazurkas etc (BBC Music Magazine Instrumental Award 2013). *Honours:* Dr hc (Acadia Univ.) 2006, (Queen's Univ.) 2011, (Wilfrid Laurier Univ.) 2013; top prizewinner A. Rubinstein Piano Competition 1974, Opus Award 1998, Paul de Hueck and Norman Walford Career Achievement for Keyboard Artistry 2007, Gov.-Gen.'s Performing Arts Awards for Lifetime Artistic Achievement 2012. *Current Management:* c/o PRO by Harry Oesterle, 86356 Neusaess, Germany. *E-mail:* info@fialkowska.com. *Website:* www.fialkowska.com.

FIDDES, Ross Ashley, AMusA, DipLaw; Australian composer and conductor; b. 20 Nov. 1944, Newcastle, NSW. *Career:* solicitor 1968–; Founder and Musical Dir Novocastrian Arts Orchestra 1991–95; Principal Conductor and Artistic Dir Opera Hunter 1992–95; Conductor, Artistic and Musical Dir The Sound Construction Company 1988–. *Compositions include:* Four Ceremonies for piano 1982, Kids Bits piano solos for children 1982, The Proposal (one-act chamber opera after Chekov) 1985, Suite for brass quintet 1985, Sonata for trumpet and piano 1985, Ceremony for symphonic wind band 1987, Image and Refraction for clarinet, bassoon, horn and string quintet 1987, Bird Song (song cycle) for soprano and clarinet 1991, Abelard and Heloise (musical drama in two acts) (City of Newcastle Drama Award (CONDA) for outstanding achievement in Newcastle Theatre 1997, CONDA for Excellence in Professional Achievement 2002) 1997–2002, Playing Post Office (chamber opera), The Man In The Other Room (song cycle) premiered 2015, These Men (song cycle), premiered 2015. *Honours:* Festival of Emerging Composers, USA 1995. *E-mail:* ross@rossfiddesmusic.com. *Website:* www.rossfiddesmusic.com.

FIELD, Helen; British singer (soprano); b. 14 May 1951, Wrexham, Clwyd, Wales. *Education:* Royal Northern Coll. of Music, Royal Coll. of Music, also studied in FRG. *Career:* roles with Welsh Nat. Opera include Musetta, Poppea, Kristina, Gilda, Marzelline, Mimi, Tatyana, Jenůfa, the Vixen, Marenka and Desdemona; has also appeared with Opera North and Scottish Opera; debut at Royal Opera House, Covent Garden as Emma in Khovanschina 1982; debut with ENO, as Gilda 1982, at Metropolitan Opera, New York, also as Gilda; has also appeared with Netherlands, Cologne and Brussels opera cos; concert performances with several leading orchestras and regular radio and TV appearances. *Recordings include:* Rigoletto, A Village, Romeo and Juliet, Osud, Greek Passion, Rossini Stabat Mater, Hiawatha. *Honours:* won triennial Young Welsh Singers' Competition 1976. *Current Management:* c/o Robert Gilder and Co., N102, Westminster Business Square, 1-45 Durham Street, London, SE11 5JH, England. *Telephone:* (20) 7580-7758. *Fax:* (20) 7580-7739. *E-mail:* rgilder@robert-gilder.com. *Website:* www.robert-gilder.com. *E-mail:* info@helenfield.co.uk. *Website:* www.helenfield.co.uk.

FIELDSEND, David; British singer (tenor); b. 1947, Yorkshire, England. *Education:* Guildhall School of Music and Drama. *Career:* debut as Vanja in Katya Kabanova at the 1972 Wexford Festival; appearances with Scottish Opera as Jacquino in Fidelio, Arturo in Lucia di Lammermoor and Rossini's Almaviva; further engagements with the D'Oyly Carte Opera, Opera North, Travelling Opera, Chelsea Opera Group and Dorset Opera; Covent Garden debut 1983, in Der Rosenkavalier, Bardolph in Falstaff, Paris and Borsa in Rigoletto, Jerusalem; concerts and oratorios with orchestras and choral societies throughout the United Kingdom and Europe. *Recordings include:* five operetta albums with the D'Oyly Carte Opera. *Honours:* GSMD Gold Medal, London.

FIERENS, Guillermo; Argentine classical guitarist; b. 1940, Argentina. *Education:* studied with Andrés Segovia. *Career:* debut in Spain 1963; US debut in 1965 with concert tour of Mexico in 1967; Regular engagements in the United Kingdom with the London Symphony Orchestra, Hallé Orchestra, English Chamber, Royal and London Philharmonics, Philharmonia and Orchestra of the Welsh National Opera; Played at Queen's Hall in Edinburgh in 1983 and festival appearances at Norwich, St Andrews, Harrogate, Lichfield, Newbury and Belfast; Further concerts in Netherlands, Switzerland, Spain, Hong Kong, Czechoslovakia, USA, Italy and Canada. *Recordings:* Music by Castelnuovo-Tedesco, Albeniz, Turina, Sor and Villa-Lobos. *Honours:* Caracas International Guitar Competition 1967; Citta d'Alessandria Competition in Italy; Gold Medal, Villa-Lobos Competition, Rio de Janeiro, 1971.

FIFIELD, Christopher George, MusB, GRSM, ARCO, ARMCM; British conductor, music historian, lecturer and broadcaster; *Music Director, Lambeth Orchestra*; b. 4 Sept. 1945, Croydon, Surrey; s. of Frederick William Fifield and Ursula Paschen; m. 1st Judith Weyman 1972 (divorced); two c.; m. 2nd Anna Milton 2007; two c. *Education:* Univ. of Manchester, Royal Manchester Coll. of Music, Guildhall School, Cologne Musikhochschule, Germany, Univ. of Bristol. *Career:* fmr Deputy Dir of Music, Capetown Opera; mem. music staff, Glyndebourne for 12 years; fmr Music Dir London Contemporary Dance Theatre; fmr Dir Northampton Symphony Orchestra, Central Festival Opera, Reigate and Redhill Choral Soc. and Jubilate Choir; fmr Conductor, Guildhall School of Music, Trinity Coll. of Music; Dir of Music, Univ. Coll. London 1980–90; fmr Chorus Master, Chelsea Opera Group; currently Music Dir and Conductor, Lambeth Orchestra; conducted British opera premieres of Verdi's Oberto 1982, Chabrier's Gwendoline 1983, Bruch's Die Loreley 1986, Smetana's The Devil's Wall 1987, world premiere of Diana Burrell's The Albatross, Spitalfields Festival, London 1997. *Recordings include:* Frederic Cliffe: Symphony No. 1, Xaver Scharwenka: Symphony in C minor, Andreas Hallén: Gustaf Wasas Saga, Philipp Scharwenka: Three Works for Orchestra, Schnyder von Wartensee, Franz Xaver: Symphony No. 3, 'Militärsinfonie' and Overture in C minor, Richard Franck: Orchestral Works, Robert Hermann: Symphonies 1 & 2. *Publications include:* Max Bruch: his Life and Works 1988, 2005, Wagner in Performance 1992, True Artist and True Friend: A Biography of Hans Richter 1993, 2016, Letters and Diaries of Kathleen Ferrier 2003, 2012, Ibbs and Tillett: The Rise and Fall of a Musical Empire 2005, The German Symphony between Beethoven and Brahms: The Fall and Rise of a Genre 2015; contrib. to reference books and journals, including Viking Opera Guide, International Opera Guide, New Grove Dictionary of Opera 1992, Grove 7, Dictionary of National Biography, Oxford Companion to Music. *Address:* 80 Wolfington Road, London, SE27 0RQ, England (home). *Telephone:* (20) 8761-3600 (home); 7752-273558 (mobile). *E-mail:* cgfifield@btinternet.com. *Website:* www.lambeth-orchestra .org.uk (office).

FIGUEROA, Rafael, BM; American cellist; b. 27 March 1961, San Juan, PR; m. Irma I. Justicia 1987. *Education:* Indiana Univ. School of Music, studied with Janos Starker and Gary Hoffman. *Career:* recital debut at Terrace Theater, Kennedy Center for The Arts, Washington, DC; recitals in major concert halls including Library of Congress, Kennedy Center, National Gallery of Art, Jordan Hall, Shriver Hall, Merkin Hall, Caslas Hall in Tokyo, Carnegie Recital Hall; numerous radio broadcasts on national public radio. *Recordings:* F. Mendelssohn's Concerto for Violin and Piano with Orpheus Chamber Orchestra, 1989; Schoenberg's Verklärte Nacht, 1990; Strauss's Le Bourgeois Gentilhomme and Divertimento Op 86, 1992; Weber's Clarinet Concertos and Rossini's Variations, 1992. *Publications:* contrib. to The Strad Magazine, Strings Magazine.

FILATOVA, Ludmila Pavlovna; Russian singer (mezzo-soprano); b. 6 Oct. 1935, Orenburg; d. of Pavel Filatov and Valentina Semoylova; m. Rudakov Igor 1971. *Education:* Faculty of Mathematics, Leningrad Univ. *Career:* mem. CPSU 1969–91; began singing in choir; mem. Kirov Opera choir 1958–60; soloist with Kirov (now Mariinsky) Opera 1962–; teacher of singing, Leningrad Conservatoire 1973–; gives chamber concerts: Shostakovich, Tchaikovsky, Rachmaninov, Glinka etc. *Major roles include:* Lyubasha in A Bride for the Tsar, Marfa in Khovanshchina, Carmen, Marta-Ekaterina in Petrov's Peter I, Countess in The Queen of Spades. *Honours:* Glinka Prize 1960, People's Artist of USSR 1983. *Address:* Mariinsky Theatre, Teatralnaya pl. 1, St Petersburg, Russia.

FILIANOTI, Giuseppe; Italian singer (tenor); b. 11 Jan. 1974, Reggio Calabria. *Education:* Acad. La Scala, Milan with Alfredo Kraus, Conservatorio Francesco Cilea, Reggio Calabria with Anna Gaggiotti. *Career:* debut in Donizetti's Dom Sébastien at Bologna 1998; appearances at La Scala in Gluck's Armide and Paisiello's Nina and as Donizetti's Edgardo at Turin; Alfredo at Florence, Tokyo and Covent Garden 2001; engagements in Rossini's Le Siège de Corinthe and Tancredi at Pesaro, Un giorno di regno by Verdi at Bologna and La Favorita at Las Palmas 2001; season 2001–02 as Tamino and Rinuccio in Gianni Schicchi at Rome, and Fenton in Falstaff at Bologna; as Edgardo in Lucia di Lammermoor at Metropolitan Opera 2005; as Nemorino at Los Angeles Opera 2009, Lyric Opera of Chicago 2010; US recital debut on Harriman Jewell Series 2012; as La clemenza di Tito at Metropolitan Opera 2012. *Honours:* winner Francisco Viñas and Plácido Domingo Operalia Competitions, Franco Abbiati Italian Critics' Prize 2004. *Current Management:* c/o Neil Funkhouser, 105 Arden Street, #5G, New York, NY 10040-1119, USA. *Telephone:* (212) 304-3796. *Fax:* (212) 304-4507. *E-mail:* neil@

funkhouserartists.com. *Website:* www.funkhouserartists.com; giuseppefilianoti.com.

FILIP, Ana Felicia; Romanian singer; b. 1959. *Education:* Bucharest Acad. *Career:* debut as Antonia in Les Contes d'Hoffmann, with Romanian Opera; sang at first at Brasov, then at Nat. Opera in Bucharest, debut as Antonia in Les Contes d'Hoffmann 1986; guest appearances in Basle (as Violetta 1991), Frankfurt and elsewhere, including Covent Garden 1994; at Nancy as Violetta 1998; season 2000–01 as the Trovatore Leonora at Dortmund and Contessa de Folleville in Il Viaggio a Reims, at Liège and Bologna; numerous concert engagements.

FILIPOVA, Elena; Bulgarian singer (soprano); b. 2 Dec. 1957, Pasardjk. *Education:* Sofia Music High School, Sofia Music Conservatory. *Career:* debut as Marenka in Bartered Bride, Bad Staatstheater Karlsruhe 1981; Badisches Staatstheater 1981–86; sang at Salzburg Festival 1983; guest performances at Hamburg, Frankfurt, Barcelona, Luxemburg, Hannover as Violetta 1988, Bern, Vienna and Nuremberg; has also sung Donna Anna, Amelia Boccanegra and Tatiana, and sang Aida at Hanover 1990; concerts in Germany, Austria, France, Italy, and Switzerland; television appearances on ORF Salzburg Festival 1983, ZDF, Berlin 1983, SWF, Baden Baden 1985, with Mozart and Handel arias; sang Manon Lescaut at Sydney 1998; sang Puccini's Minnie at Toronto 2001. *Honours:* first prize Karajan Foundation, Salzburg Festival 1982.

FILIPOVIC, Igor; Slovenian singer (tenor); b. 18 April 1951, Ljubljana. *Education:* studied in Ljubljana and in Italy. *Career:* debut as Ernesto in Don Pasquale 1976; mem. Vienna Kammeroper 1976–77, Lucerne Opera 1977–78; guest appearances in Europe, USA and Canada as Rossini's Amenofi in Mosè in Egitto and Arnoldo in William Tell, Arturo in I Puritani, Edgardo in Lucia di Lammermoor, Enrico in Maria di Rudenz, Tonio in La Fille du Régiment, the Duke of Mantua in Rigoletto, Alfredo in La Traviata, Riccardo in Un Ballo in Maschera, Rodolfo in Luisa Miller, Cavaradossi in Tosca, and Don José in Bregenz Festival 1992; also sang at Prague, Venice, Milan, Rome, Turin, Palermo, Vienna Staatsoper and Volksoper, Stuttgart, Mannheim, Frankfurt, Brussels, Chicago and New York at the City Opera; Verdi's Riccardo at Ljubljana 1998; broadcasting engagements throughout Europe.

FILJAK, Martina; Croatian pianist; b. 1979, Zagreb. *Education:* Music Acad. of Zagreb, Vienna Conservatory, Hochschule für Musik und Theater, Hannover, Como Piano Acad., Italy. *Career:* made professional debut aged 12, with Zagreb Soloists; solo engagements at Concertgebouw, Amsterdam, Hotel de Ville, Brussels, Philharmonic Hall, Ljubljana, Salle Cortot, Paris, Palais des Congrès, Strasbourg, Nat. Palace of Culture, Sofia, Boesendorfer Saal, Vienna, Steinway Hall, New York; has appeared with orchestras including Strasbourg Philharmonic, Croatian Symphony Orchestra, Morocco Philharmonic, Belgrade Philharmonic, Streicherakademie Bozen, Turin Philharmonic Orchestra, Chamber Orchestra of S Africa, Orquestra Simfónica del Vallés, Moscow State Symphony Orchestra, Barcelona Symphony Orchestra, Bilbao Symphony Orchestra, Orchestra Sinfonica di Savona, Zagreb Philharmonic Orchestra and Croatian Chamber Orchestra; recital performances in France, Germany, Italy, Greece and Japan and tours of Spain, Argentina and China. *Honours:* winner, Boesendorfer Prize, Vienna; Special Prize, Okiden Competition; first prize, Johannes Brahms Competition; winner, M. Masin Competition; winner, Int. Keyboard Inst. Competition, New York; first prize, Int. Viotti Piano Competition 2007; first prize and Gold Medal, Maria Canals Int. Piano Competition, Barcelona; winner, Cleveland Int. Piano Competition 2009. *Current Management:* Konzertdirektion Lee, Potsdamer Platz 11, 10785 Berlin, Germany. *Telephone:* (30) 25894074. *Fax:* (30) 25894100. *E-mail:* mail@konzertdirektion-lee.de. *Website:* www.konzertdirektion-lee.de; www .martinafiljak.com.

FINCH, Catrin; British harpist and composer; b. 1980, Llanon, Ceredigion, Wales; m. Hywel Wigley 2003. *Education:* Purcell School, Royal Acad. of Music. *Career:* performed at BBC proms aged 11, while mem. of Nat. Youth Orchestra; Royal Harpist to HRH, the Prince of Wales 2000–04; has performed in concerts with Bryn Terfel and Sinfonia Cymru in Dublin and Birmingham, English Chamber Orchestra, London Acad. Symphony Orchestra, RPO, Acad. of St Martin-in-the-Fields, London Mozart Players, Nat. Polish Radio Symphony Orchestra, BBC Nat. Orchestra of Wales, Manchester Camerata Orchestra, European Union Chamber Orchestra, Peoria Symphony, Canton Symphony, Cedar Rapids Symphony Orchestra, North Carolina Symphony Orchestra, Yakima Symphony Orchestra, Boston Pops, Charlotte Symphony; has given recitals at Wigmore Hall, Carnegie Hall, Young Concert Artists Series, New York and Boston; formed the Catrin Finch Band 2005–, debut performance Koh Samui Festival, Thailand 2005. *Recordings include:* Little Angels, Harp Recital 2000, Carnaval de Venise 2001, From Coast to Coast 2002, Crossing the Stone 2003, The Harpist 2004, Unexpected Songs 2006, String Theory 2008, Bach: Goldberg Variations 2009, Drift Away 2010, Clychau Dibon (with Seckou Keita) 2013, Lullabies 2013, Tides 2015. *Honours:* Hon. Fellowship, Royal Welsh Coll. of Music and Drama 2005, Univ. of Wales 2006; Royal Overseas League Music Competition Marisa Robles Harp Prize, London 1999, first prize Lily Laskine Int. Harp Competition, France 1999, winner Young Concert Artists Int. Auditions 2000, Princeton Univ. Concerts Prize 2000, Echo Klassik Award for Best Crossover Artist in Germany 2004. *Current Management:* c/o Hazard Chase Limited, 25 City Road, Cambridge, CB1 1DP, England. *Telephone:* (1223) 312400. *Fax:*

(1223) 460827. *E-mail:* info@hazardchase.co.uk. *Website:* www.hazardchase .co.uk; www.catrinfinch.com.

FINCKEL, David; American cellist; b. 6 Dec. 1951, Kutztown, PA. *Career:* mem. Emerson String Quartet 1977–(2013); premiere concert at Alice Tully Hall in New York 1977, with works by Mozart, Smetana and Bartók; European debut at Spoleto, Italy 1981; quartet-in-residence, Smithsonian Inst., WA 1980, at the Hartt School 1981, and the Spoleto and Aspen Festivals 1981; first resident quartet, Chamber Music Soc. of Lincoln Center 1982–83, co-Artistic Dir; many performances of works by Bartók, including all six quartets in a single evening, and contemporary works; premieres include Mario Davidovsky's 4th Quartet and works by Maurice Wright and George Tsontakis, Beethoven series at South Bank, London 1996; Haydn, Beethoven, Razumovsky Quartets 2001; co-founder and Artistic Dir, Music@Menlo (chamber music festival) 2003–; f. own label, ArtistLed. *Recordings include:* with the Emerson Quartet: Bartók complete Quartets, Mozart six Quartets dedicated to Haydn, Schubert Cello Quintet with Rostropovich, Ives and Barber Quartets, Prokofiev Quartets and Sonata for two violins, Complete Beethoven Cycle 1997, Ned Rorem's Quartet No. 4 and Edgar Meyer's Quintet for String Quartet and Double Bass 1998, Mozart and Brahms Clarinet Quintets with David Shifrin 1999, the complete Shostakovich Quartets 2000, Bach's Art of the Fugue 2003, Haydn's The Last Seven Words of Our Savior on the Cross 2004, Mendelssohn: The Complete String Quartets 2005, Intimate Voices 2006, The Little Match Girl 2006, Brahm's String Quartets 2007, Bach Fugues 2008, Intimate Letters 2009. *Honours:* Grammy Awards for Best Chamber Music and Classical Record of the Year (for Shostakovich Quartets) 2001, for Best Chamber Music Performance (for Intimate Letters) 2010. *Current Management:* c/o Matthew Zelle, IMG Artists, 152 W 57th Street, Fifth Floor, New York, NY 10019, USA. *Telephone:* (212) 994-3500. *Fax:* (212) 994-3550. *E-mail:* mzelle@imgartists.com. *Website:* www.imgartists.com; www.emersonquartet.com.

FINDLAY, Jane; British singer (mezzo-soprano); b. 1960, England. *Education:* Royal Northern Coll. of Music, studied with Peter Harrison and Paul Hamburger. *Career:* sang with the Glyndebourne Festival Chorus, then as Hermia and Dorabella with the Touring Opera, and Third Boy in Die Zauberflöte at the Festival; sang Dorabella with the Northern Ireland Opera Trust in Belfast and with Opera 80 in tour; appearances at the Wexford Festival and with Opéra Nancy; sang in Margot-la-Rouge at the Camden Festival in 1984 and in Monteverdi's L'Orfeo at Florence under Roger Norrington; tour of Germany with the Monteverdi Choir in 1985, including Irene in Handel's Tamerlano at the Göttingen Festival and concert performances in Cologne; Season 1987–88 in Opera 80's Cenerentola and appearances in The Gondoliers and La Belle Hélène for New Sadler's Wells Opera; WNO debut in 1989 in La Traviata and Covent Garden debut in 1990 as Magdalena in Die Meistersinger; concert repertoire includes The Dream of Gerontius, Shéhérazade by Ravel, Bach's Christmas Oratorio and Messiah. *Honours:* South East Arts Award; Miriam Licette Award 1985.

FINDLAY, Paul Hudson Douglas, BA; British opera director; b. 26 Sept. 1943, New Zealand; s. of the late John Niemeyer Findlay and Aileen May Findlay (née Davidson); m. Françoise Christiane 1966; one s. one d. *Education:* Univ. Coll. School, London, Balliol Coll., Oxford, London Opera Centre. *Career:* Production and Technical Man. New Opera Co. 1967; Dir London Sinfonietta 1967–; Stage Man. Glyndebourne Touring Opera and English Opera Group 1968; Asst Press Officer, Royal Opera House, Covent Garden 1968–72, Personal Asst to Gen. Dir 1972–76, Asst Dir 1976–87, Opera Dir 1987–93; Man. Dir Royal Philharmonic Orchestra 1993–95; Planning Dir European Opera Centre 1997; Arts Man. Kirov Ballet; Chair. Opera 80 1987; fmr Gen. Man. Mariinsky Theater, St Petersburg, Russia; Co-founder and Vice-Pres. Performing and Visual Arts, Global Music Network –2002, Vice-Pres. GMN Europe 1998–2001; mem. Bd of Dirs Nat. Youth Music Theatre, English Touring Opera, Arts Educational Trust, Arts Education London, Welsh National Opera. *Honours:* Cavaliere Ufficiale del Ordine al Merito della Repubblica Italiana; Chevalier des Arts et des Lettres 1991.

FINE, Wendy; South African singer (soprano); b. 19 Dec. 1943, Durban. *Education:* studied with John van Zyl in Durban, with Christian Mueller, Erik Werba and Maria Hittorf at Vienna Music Acad. *Career:* debut at Stadttheater Berne as Madama Butterfly; appearances at opera houses in London, Hamburg, Munich, Stuttgart, Berlin, Lisbon, Vienna and Geneva; sang at Bayreuth Festival 1971; roles include Nedda, Micaela, Marguerite, Mimi, Sophie in Der Rosenkavalier, Desdemona, Fiordiligi, Donna Elvira, Pamina, Luise in Der Junge Lord (British premiere 1965), Ophelia in Szokolay's Hamlet, and Maria in The Miracles of Our Lady by Martinů; sang at Covent Garden 1971–77 as Musetta, Gutrune, Donna Elvira, Fiordiligi and Jenůfa, and at La Scala Milan 1977 as Berg's Marie.

FINGERHUT, Margaret; British pianist; b. 30 March 1955, London, England. *Education:* Royal College of Music, London and Peabody Conservatory, Baltimore. *Career:* performed in the UK, America, Europe, Scandinavia, Africa, India, Turkey and Israel; played with London Symphony, Royal Philharmonic, London Philharmonic and Philharmonia Orchestras; broadcasts for BBC radio and WFMT, Chicago; appeared on film and television; Prof. of Piano, Royal Northern College of Music, 1998–. *Recordings:* several with the London Philharmonic and London Symphony Orchestras, including world premiere recording of Arnold Bax's Winter Legends; music by Grieg, Dukas, Falla, Howells, Suk, Stanford and Moeran; collections of Russian and

French composers. *Honours:* Hopkinson Gold Medal, 1977; Boise Foundation Scholarship, 1977; Greater London Arts Association, Young Musician of the Year, 1981. *Telephone:* (117) 973-2038. *E-mail:* jillwhitemusic@aol.com. *Website:* www.margaretefingerhut.co.uk.

FINK, Bernarda; Slovenian singer (mezzo-soprano); b. 29 Aug. 1955, Buenos Aires, Argentina; m.; two c. *Education:* Instituto Superior de Arte del Teatro Colón, Argentina, and studied with Michel Corboz in Europe. *Career:* sang Rossini's Cenerentola at Buenos Aires 1986; concerts of Baroque music with Michel Corboz as conductor in Paris, Geneva, Berlin, Lisbon and Tokyo; sang Penelope in Monteverdi's Ulisse at Innsbruck 1993, Montpellier and Barcelona (also the Messenger in Orfeo); Amsterdam as Proserpina in Orfeo 1995; Cenerentola at the Berlin Staatsoper 1994; season 2000 as Dorabella at Aix-en-Provence and European tour as Gluck's Orpheus, with René Jacobs; recitals at Carnegie and Wigmore Halls, Paris, Vienna and Sydney Opera Houses; sang Cecilio in Lucio Silla at Theater an der Wien 2005–06, Sesto in a concert version of La Clemenza di Tito 2005; has worked with leading conductors including Blomstedt, Bychkov, Gardiner, Gergiev, Harnoncourt, Herreweghe, Jansons, Marriner, Minkowski, Muti, Norrington, Welser-Möst; festival appearances include Salzburg Festival and Mozartwochen, Wiener Festwochen, Schubertiade Schwarzenberg, Prague Spring Festival, Tokyo Summer Festival and Montreux Festival; regularly holds masterclasses at Wiener Meisterkurse, Young Singers Project, Salzburg, Acad. of the Festival in Aix-en-Provence, Schubert-Institut, Baden; mem. jury, International Song Competition, Wigmore Hall, London, Bach Wettbewerb Leipzig; expert, BBC Cardiff Singers of the World. *Recordings include:* Caldara's Maddalena ai Piedi di Cristo (Gramophone Award), Dvořák songs (solo recital) (Diapason d'Or), Rossini's Zelmira and Handel's Amadigi, Handel's Giulio Cesare and Flavio, Monteverdi's Orfeo and Ulisse, Messiah. *Honours:* Austrian Hon. Medal for Art and Science 2006, Prešeren-foundation Award (with her brother Marcos Fink) for their recording Slovenija! and related concerts 2013. *Current Management:* c/o Helga Machreich-Unterzaucher, Machreich Artists Management GmbH, Beatrixgasse 26/5/42, 1030 Vienna, Austria. *E-mail:* machreich@machreich-artists.com (office). *Website:* www.machreich-artists .com (office).

FINK, Manfred; German singer (tenor); b. 15 April 1954, Frankfurt am Main. *Education:* studied in Frankfurt. *Career:* chorus of the Cologne Opera, 1979–81 then soloist with the Mainz Opera from 1981 with debut as Tamino; Deutsche Oper am Rhein, Düsseldorf, from 1982 as Mozart's Ferrando, Belmonte and Don Ottavio; Guest appearances from 1984 at Buenos Aires, Venice, Rome, Nice, Florence as David in Die Meistersinger in 1985, Frankfurt and Vienna; Other roles have included Edgardo in Lucia di Lammermoor, Des Grieux in Manon Lescaut, Rinuccio and Nemorino; Sang the Steuermann in Der fliegende Holländer for Cologne Opera in 1991, and Pedrillo in Die Entführung at the Schwetzingen Festival in 1991; Sang Verdi's Macduff at the Komische Oper, Berlin, 1997. *Recordings include:* Handel Dettingen Te Deum. *Current Management:* c/o Künstleragentur Tobias Kade, Ammonstraße 72, 01067 Dresden, Germany. *Telephone:* (351) 4906794. *Fax:* (351) 4906793. *E-mail:* tobias-kade@gmx.de. *Website:* www.kuenstleragentur -kade.de.

FINK, Marcos; Slovenian singer (bass-baritone); b. 29 Nov. 1950, Buenos Aires, Argentina; m. Cristina Vovk; one d. *Education:* studied with Ivan Ivanov and Victor Srugo. *Career:* began career as Lecturer in Agrarian Zoology, Univ. of Buenos Aires; early musical experience with several vocal ensembles including Argentine Nat. Polyphonic Choir, Karantania (Slovene vocal group), Musicamara, Camerata Monteverdi, Camerata Vocal, Carlos Vilo Group, Bach Acad. of Buenos Aires; invited by Salzburger Landestheater to appear in Europe 1990, opera debut in Othello, Grosses Festspielhaus Salzburg 1990; regularly participates in performance and recording of oratorios with Slovenian Philharmony, Slovenian RTV Symphonic Orchestra, Slovenian Chamber Choir; numerous solo performances in concert halls worldwide including Buenos Aires, Paris, Vienna, Madrid, Barcelona, Geneva, Prague, Bratislava, Ljubljana, Strasbourg, Lisbon, Milan, Zagreb and Tokyo. *Opera repertoire includes:* Figaro in Le nozze di Figaro, Leporello in Don Giovanni, Don Alfonso in Cosi fan tutte, Orator in Die Zauberflöte, Colas in Bastien and Bastienne. *Recordings include:* Leopold I: Sacred Works 1998, Canciones Argentinas 2006, Rossini: Petite Messe Solennelle 2008, Mozart Requiem, Schubert Die schöne Müllerin, Die Winterreise and Schwanengesang, Die Zauberflöte (BBC Music Magazine Award, Opera Category 2011) 2010. *Address:* c/o Harmonia Mundi, Mas de Vert, BP 20150, 13631 Arles, France (office).

FINK, Myron S.; American composer; b. 19 April 1932, Chicago. *Education:* Juilliard School with Bernard Wagenaar and Castelnuovo-Tedesco, Burrill Phillips at the University of Illinois, Cornell University with Robert Palmer and in Vienna. *Career:* former teacher at Alma College, the Curtis Institute; faculty mem. Hunter College, CUNY 1966–91. *Compositions:* Chamber Music: Twelve Etudes for Piano 1962, Triptych 1964, Sinfonia 1965, Sonata 1974, Canto 1974, String Quartet No. 1 1975, Trio 1975, Piano Quartet No. 1 1976, Brass Quartet 1977, Sextet 1977, String Quartet No. 2 1978, Sonata 1983, Twelve Expressions 1985, Brass Quintet 1986, String Quartet No. 3 1987, Divertimento 1987, Suite 1988, Sinfonietta 1989, Sonata No. 1 1990, Elegy 1990, Rhapsody 1991, Variations 1992, Sonata for Flute and Piano 1992, Divertimento for Brass Trio 1993, Sextet 1995, Sonata No. 2 1995, Six Miniatures 1998, Stiring Quartet No. 4 1999; for Orchestra: Piano Concerto No. 1 1972, Scherzo 1979, Violin Concerto 1986, Symphony No. 1 1987,

Symphony No. 2 1989, Piano Concerto No. 2 1991, Symphony No. 3 1996, Symphony No. 4, A Bintel Lieder 1999; Operas: The Boor, after Chekhov 1955, Susanna And The Elders 1955, Jeremiah 1962, Judith And Holofernes 1978, Chinchilla 1986, The Island Of Tomorrow 1986, The Conquistadors 1997, Edith Wharton: A Self Portrait 2003; Vocals: Incidental Music 1955, Fifteen Songs 1961, Christmas Anthem 1963, Anne Rutledge 1975,Five Songs 1981, Two Epitaphs 1982, Four Psalms 1983, Psalm 23 1988, Psalm 46 1989, Prayer of St. Francs 1995, Spoon River Portraits 1998. *Honours:* Woodrow Wilson Memorial Fellowship 1954. *E-mail:* myron@myronfink.com (home). *Website:* www.myronfink.com (home).

FINK, Richard-Paul; American singer (dramatic baritone) and conductor; b. 23 March 1955. *Education:* Kent State Univ., Oberlin Coll. *Career:* worked and performed with the Houston Symphony, Pops, Houston Ballet; other productions include Falstaff, Boris Godunov, Eugene Onegin at Houston Opera, Scarpia at Bremer Stadt Theater in Germany 1988, Jokanaan in Salome, Enrico in Lucia di Lammermoor and Tchelio in The Love for Three Oranges at Bremen Opera 1988–89, Kaspar in Der Freischütz 1988–89, Escamillo in Carmen and as Rigoletto for Welsh National Opera 1990–91, the Water Gnome in Rusalka and Klingsor in Parsifal at Houston Grand Opera 1991–92; 1992–93 season opened as Sid in Albert Herring with the Atlanta Opera, Kurwenal in Tristan, Count di Luna in Il Trovatore, Pizarro in Fidelio and Sebastiano at the Washington Opera Kennedy Center's staging of D'Albert's Tiefland; sang Wagner's Dutchman at Sydney 1996; The Forester in The Cunning Little Vixen at Toronto 1998; Alberich in Wagner's Ring Cycle (Met, Dallas, Seattle) 1999, 2000, 2001; title role in Flying Dutchman in Sydney, Toronto and Mexico City; leading roles with Metropolitan Opera, New York, Opéra Bastille, Paris, Seattle, Dallas, Los Angeles and others; engaged for Rigoletto for Opéra du Montréal 2003. *Honours:* Grammy Award for Best Opera Recording (for Doctor Atomic with Alan Gilbert, Meredith Arwady, Sasha Cooke, Gerald Finley, Thomas Glenn, Eric Owens and Jay David Saks) 2012. *Current Management:* Zemsky/Green Artists Management, 730 Fifth Avenue, Suite 1802, New York, NY 10019, USA. *Telephone:* (212) 300-8003. *Fax:* (212) 300-8001. *E-mail:* zgartists@aol.com. *Website:* www.zemskygreen .com; www.richardpaulfink.com (home).

FINK, Walter; Austrian singer (bass); b. 1949, Vienna. *Education:* Vienna Conservatory. *Career:* mem. Vienna Staatsoper 1977–; regular performer at Bregenz Festival 1989–95, repertoire includes Baron Ochs in Der Rosenkavalier, Daland in The Flying Dutchman, Rocco in Fidelio, in Rossini's La Donna del Lago, Osmin and Pogner in Die Meistersinger, Kaspar in Der Freischütz, Wagner's Landgrave and Hunding, Sarastro, Ramphis in Aida, Orestes and La Roche in Capriccio, the Father in Il Figliol Prodigo, Colonna in Rienzi, General Polkan in The Golden Cockerel, Sarastro in Die Zauberflöte. *Recordings include:* Fafner in Das Rheingold. *Current Management:* Opéra et Concert, 37 rue de la Chaussée d'Antin, 75009 Paris, France. *Telephone:* 1-42-96-18-18. *Fax:* 1-42-96-18-00. *E-mail:* agence@opera-concert.com. *Website:* www.opera-concert.com.

FINKE, Martin; German singer (tenor); b. 1948, Rhede bei Bocholt. *Education:* Folkwang Hochschule Essen with Hilde Wesselman. *Career:* sang first at opera houses in Augsburg, Cologne Stuttgart, at Bayreuth Festival 1975; sang at Barcelona 1983 as Jacquino in Fidelio and Bregenz Festival 1984; sang David in Die Meistersinger at the Théâtre de la Monnaie, Brussels 1985, at Salzburg Festival 1986 in the premiere of Penderecki's Die Schwarze Maske; other roles include Mozart's Pedrillo and Monostatos and Mime in Der Ring des Nibelungen, Nice Opéra 1988; Cologne Opera 2000, as Hauk in The Makropulos Case and Mime in Das Rheingold; concert singer in the Passions of Bach, Messiah and the Missa Solemnis. *Recordings:* Pagliacci, Intermezzo and Ariadne auf Naxos; Die Verschworenen by Schubert; Operettas by Lehar.

FINKO, David; Russian/American composer and conductor; b. 15 May 1936, Leningrad (now St Petersburg). *Education:* Rimsky-Korsakov School of Performing Arts, Leningrad Conservatory. *Career:* early training as engineer; moved to USA 1979; Visiting Lecturer, Univ. of Pennsylvania 1979–81; Lecturer and Composer-in-Residence, Univ. of Texas, El Paso 1981; also taught at Yale Univ. *Compositions include:* Polinka (after Chekhov) 1965, In a Torture Chamber of the Gestapo 1970, The Enchanted Tailor 1983; orchestral: six Tone Poems 1965–78, Symphony No. 1 1969, Piano Concerto 1971, Viola Concerto 1971, Symphony No. 2 1972, Double Concerto for violin, viola and orchestra 1973, Double Concerto for viola, double bass and orchestra 1975, Harp Concerto 1976, Concerto for three violins and orchestra 1981, Pilgrimage to Jerusalem 1983; Hear, O Israel for soloists, chorus and orchestra 1987; Violin Concerto 1988; chamber: Piano Sonata 1964, Mass Without Words for violin and organ 1968, Lamentations of Jeremiah for violin 1969, Fromm Septet 1983. *Honours:* ASCAP grants and fellowships, Fromm Foundation and Memorial Foundation of Jewish Culture. *E-mail:* david@davidfinko.org. *Website:* www.davidfinko.org.

FINLEY, Gerald Hunter, OC, MA (Cantab.), ARCM, FRCM; Canadian singer (baritone) and conductor; b. 1960, Montreal; s. of Eric Gault Finley and Catherine Finley; m. 1st Louise Winter 1990 (divorced 2009); two s.; m. 2nd Heulwen Keyte 2010. *Education:* Glebe Collegiate Inst., Univ. of Ottawa, Royal Coll. of Music, UK, Nat. Opera Studio, London, King's Coll., Cambridge. *Career:* chorister, St Matthew's Church, Ottawa 1969–78; mem. Ottawa Choral Soc., Cantata Singers, Ont. Youth Choir 1977–78; Glyndebourne Festival Chorus, UK 1986–89; professional debut as opera soloist, Antonio (Le nozze di Figaro), Ottawa 1987 and Papageno (Die Zauberflöte), London 1989; debut at Glyndebourne with Glyndebourne Touring Opera as Kuligin (Katya Kabanova) 1988, Sid (Albert Herring) 1989, English Clerk (Death in Venice) 1989, Fiorello, Figaro (Il barbiere di Siviglia) 1989, Papageno 1990, with Glyndebourne Festival Opera as the Count Dominik (Arabella) 1989, Guglielmo 1990, 1992, Figaro at opening of new Glyndebourne opera house 1994, Owen Wingrave 1997, Olivier (Capriccio) 1998, Nick Shadow (The Rake's Progress) 2000, Agamemnon (Iphigénie en Aulide) 2002, Don Giovanni 2010, Hans Sachs (Meistersinger) 2011; debut at Canadian Opera Co. as Sid 1991, Figaro 1993; debut at Amsterdam as Demetrius (A Midsummer Night's Dream) 1993, Count 2001; debut at Covent Garden as Figaro 1995, Achilla (Giulio Cesare) 1997, Pilgrim (Pilgrim's Progress) 1997, Creonte (L'anima del filosofo) 2001, Forester (Cunning Little Vixen) 2003, Don Giovanni 2005, 2012, Count (Le nozze di Figaro) 2006, Yeletsky (Pique Dame) 2006, Golaud (Pélléas et Mélisande) 2008, Onegin (Eugene Onegin) 2008, Frank/Fritz (Die tote Stadt) 2009, Zurga (Les pêcheurs de perles) 2010, Howard K. Stern (Anna Nicole) 2011; debut at Opéra de Paris Valentin (Faust) 1997, Sharpless (Madama Butterfly) 1998, Papageno 2001, Figaro 2003, Don Giovanni 2003, Count Almaviva 2003; debut at Metropolitan Opera, New York as Papageno 1998; Papageno 2000, Marcello 2001, 2010, Don Giovanni 2005, Golaud 2010; Don Giovanni at Tel-Aviv 2000, Vienna 2006, Prague 2006, Budapest 2006, Rome 2006; debut at Los Angeles Opera as Figaro 1995, Belcore (L'elisir d'amore) 1996, Mr Fox (Fantastic Mr Fox) 1998; debut at ENO as Harry Heegan (The Silver Tassie) 2000, Onegin 2005, Balstrode (Peter Grimes) 2009; debut at San Francisco Opera as J. Robert Oppenheimer (Dr Atomic) 2005, Amsterdam 2007, Chicago 2008, Metropolitan Opera 2008, Atlanta 2008, ENO 2009; debut at Salzburg Festival as Conte (Nozze di Figaro) 2007, 2009, Don Giovanni 2011, Don Alfonso 2013; debut at Bayerische Staatsoper as Don Giovanni 2010, Escamillo (Carmen) 2011; Iago (Otello), London Symphony Orchestra, London 2009; Guillaume Tell, Accad. di Santa Cecilia 2010; title role in Falstaff, Canadian Opera Co. 2014; performed world premiere of True Fire by Kaija Saariaho 2015; concert soloist and lieder singer; Visiting Prof., Royal Coll. of Music 2000–. *Films include:* Owen Wingrave 2001, L'amour de loin 2006, Doctor Atomic 2008. *Recordings:* albums include: Papageno, Guglielmo, Sid, Masetto, Haydn's Creation, Brahms' Requiem, Handel Messiah, Bach Weihnachtsoratorium, Silver Tassie, Pilgrim's Progress, Dido and Aeneas, Songs of Travel 1998, Schubert Complete Songs 1817–1821, Complete Songs of Henri Duparc 2002, Songs of Charles Ives 2005, 2008, Stanford – Orchestral Songs (Editor's Choice Award, Gramophone Awards) 2006, Barber – Songs (Gramophone Award for Best Solo Vocal 2008), Schumann – Dichterliebe, etc. (Gramophone Award for Best Solo Vocal Performance 2009), Ravel – Songs 2009, Opera Arias in English (Juno Award 2011) 2010, Otello 2010, Britten Songs & Proverbs of William Blake (Gramophone Award for Best Solo Vocal Recording) 2011, The Ballad Singer 2011, Schubert's Winterreise (with Julius Drake) (Juno Award for Classical Album of the Year (Soloists with Large Ensemble Accompaniment) 2015) 2014. *Radio:* numerous recordings with BBC, CBC, ORF and BR. *Achievements include:* climbed Mount Kilimanjaro in 2014 to raise funds for UK-based Musicians' Charity. *Honours:* John Christie Award, Glyndebourne 1989, Juno Award for Best Vocal Performance (Canada) 1998, 2011, Singer Award, Royal Philharmonic Soc. 2001, Opera News Award 2009, Grammy Award for Best Opera Recording (for Doctor Atomic with Alan Gilbert, Meredith Arwady, Richard Paul Fink, Sasha Cooke, Thomas Glenn, Eric Owens and Jay David Saks) 2012. *Current Management:* c/o IMG Artists, The Light Box, 111 Power Road, London, W4 5PY, England; Alison Pybus, 10395 Wetherburn Rd., Ellicott City, MD 21163, USA. *Telephone:* (20) 7957-5800 (London); (410) 480-2095 (home). *Fax:* (20) 7957-5801 (London); (212) 994-3550 (New York). *E-mail:* salmansi@imgartists.com; alisonpybus73@gmail.com. *Website:* www.imgartists.com; www.geraldfinley.com; www.geraldfinley.info.

FINNIE, Linda Agnes; British singer (mezzo-soprano); b. 9 May 1952, Paisley; d. of William Finnie and Agnes Finnie. *Education:* John Neilson Inst., Paisley, Carrick Acad., Maybole, Royal Scottish Acad. of Music and Drama. *Career:* concert performances in many European countries, Australasia, the Far East and USA and regular radio broadcasts; has sung with all the maj. British orchestras and with Chicago, Boston, Pittsburgh and San Francisco Symphony orchestras, Hong Kong Philharmonic, Orchestre de Paris, Orchestre Philharmonique de Radio France, RAI Orchestra (Turin) and Danish Radio Orchestra, under many leading conductors, including Claudio Abbado, Lorin Maazel, Daniel Barenboim, André Previn, Michael Tilson-Thomas, Jeffrey Tate, Sir John Pritchard, Sir Colin Davis, Simon Rattle, Andrew Davis, Esa Pekka Salonen, Neemi Jarvi and Richard Hickox; opera roles with ENO include Amneris, Eboli, Brangäne and Ulrica, with Royal Opera House, Waltraute, Mme. Larina, Second Norn; has also sung at Geneva, Nice, Bayreuth and Frankfurt; Hertogenbosch Concours, John Noble Bursary, Countess of Munster Scholarship. *Recordings include:* Alexander Nevsky, Elijah, Beethoven's 9th Symphony, Songs of the British Isles, Armide, La Rondine and l'Enfant et les Sortilèges. *Honours:* Kathleen Ferrier Memorial Award, Kathleen Ferrier Prize. *Address:* 16 Golf Course, Girvan, Ayrshire, KA26 9HW, Scotland.

FINNILA, Birgit; Swedish singer (contralto); b. 20 Jan. 1931, Falkenberg; m. Allan Finnila, two s. three d. *Education:* studied in Goteborg with Ingalli Linden, Royal Acad. of Music, UK with Roy Henderson. *Career:* concerts in Sweden from 1963; London debut 1966, followed by concerts in Berlin, Hamburg, Hanover, Stuttgart and Düsseldorf; tours of USA, Australia, Russia

and Israel from 1968; opera debut at Goteborg 1967 as Gluck's Orpheus; guest appearances at La Scala Milan and Munich Staatsoper; Salzburg Easter Festival 1973–74 as Erda in The Ring, under Karajan; sang Brangaene in Tristan und Isolde at Paris Opéra 1976. *Recordings include:* Cimarosa's Requiem; Mozart's Betulia Liberata; Bach's Magnificat; Bruckner's Te Deum; Dvořák's Requiem; Strauss's Aegyptische Helena; Bach's B minor Mass; Vivaldi's Tito Manlio. *Honours:* Grand Prix du Disque for Juditha Triumphans by Vivaldi.

FINNIS, Edmund, DMus; British composer; b. 1984. *Education:* King's Coll., London, Guildhall School of Music and Drama; studied with Julian Anderson, Paul Newland and Rozalie Hirs. *Career:* commissions include London Symphony Orchestra, London Sinfonietta, Carnegie Hall Weill Music Inst., Mercury Quartet, Aldeburgh Festival, Spitalfields Music Festival, British Film Inst.; works performed worldwide by ensembles including Chicago Symphony Orchestra, Sibelius Acad. Symphony Orchestra, Helsinki, Isafold Chamber Orchestra, Reykjavik, Fromm Players, Tanglewood, clarinettist Mark Simpson and viol-player Liam Byrne. *Compositions include:* Flicker for full orchestra 2008, Speak, Memory for six cellos 2009, Music for Two Pianos 2009, Echolalia for chamber ensemble 2010, Focus/Pull for chamber ensemble 2011, Veneer for solo viola with live electronics 2011, Frame/Refrain for chamber ensemble 2011, rev. 2012, Unfolds for chamber ensemble 2011, rev. 2012, Sister for string duo 2012, Brother for string duo 2012, Quartet in Three Parts for chamber ensemble 2012, Relative Colour for string septet 2012, Four Duets for clarinet and piano 2012, Variation on a theme by Andrzej Panufnik 2012. *Honours:* First Prize, Int. Composer Pyramid 2011, Paul Hamlyn Award 2012. *E-mail:* erfinnis@hotmail.com (office). *Website:* www.edmundfinnis.com (office).

FINNISSY, Michael Peter, FRCM; British composer; *Chair in Composition, University of Southampton;* b. 17 March 1946, London, England. *Education:* Royal Coll. of Music, London. *Career:* Dir of Music, London School of Contemporary Dance 1969–74; Lecturer, Chelsea Coll., Chelsea School of Art, Dartington Summer School; guest artist, The Victorian Coll. of The Arts, Melbourne 1982–83; composition teacher, Winchester Coll. 1987–, Sussex Univ. 1989–2000; Chair in Composition, Univ. of Southampton 1999–; Sr Fellow, KBC-Chair. in New Music, Catholic Univ. of Leuven 2000–02; Royal Acad. of Music 1991–2001; Chair., British Section ISCM 1989–90; Pres., ISCM 1991–96, Exec. Councillor 1990–96; Pres. Steyning Music Soc. 2013; Pres. Norfolk Composers' Group 2014–; hon. mem., Int. Soc. for Contemporary Music. *Compositions include:* World 1968–74, Folk-Song Set 1969–70, Tsuru Kame 1971–73, Mysteries 1972–79, Cipriano 1974, seven piano concertos 1975–81, Offshore 1975–76, Mr Punch 1976–77, English Country Tunes 1977, Alongside 1979, Sea and Sky 1979–80, Kelir 1981, Dilok 1982, Whitman 1981–2005, Vaudeville 1983, Ngano 1983–84, String Quartet 1984, Cabaret Vert 1985, The Undivine Comedy, stage work 1988, Red Earth 1987–88, Gershwin Arrangements and More Gershwin 1975–90, Obrecht Motetten 1988–, Unknown Ground 1989–90, Thérèse Raquin, stage work 1992–93, Folklore 1993–95, Shameful Vice, stage work 1994, Liturgy of Saint Paul 1995, The History of Photography in Sound 1995–2001, Onbevooroordeeld Leven 2000–01, four organ symphonies 2002–, Verdi Transcriptions (for Book 4, British Composer Award, Instrumental category, British Acad. of Composers and Songwriters 2005) 1972–2005, Molly-House (Making Music Award, British Composer Awards 2005), Koralforspill 2011–12, Gesualdo Sesto Libro 2012–13, Remembrance Day 2013–14. *Current Management:* c/o Music Department, Oxford University Press, Great Clarendon Street, Oxford, OX2 6DP, England. *Website:* www.michaelfinnissy.info.

FINSCHER, Ludwig, PhD; German musicologist, lexicographer and academic (retd); b. 14 March 1930, Kassel. *Education:* Univ. of Göttingen. *Career:* Asst Lecturer, Univ. of Kiel 1960–65, Univ. of Saarbrücken 1965–68; Ed. Die Musikforschung 1961–68, Co-Ed. 1968–74; Prof. of Musicology, Univ. of Frankfurt am Main 1968–81, Univ. of Heidelberg 1981–95; mem. Akad. der Wissenschaften, Heidelberg, Akad. der Wissenschaften und der Literatur, Mainz, Academia Europaea; Corresp. mem. American Musicological Soc. *Publications:* Collected Works of Gaffurius (ed., two vols) 1955, 1960, Collected Works of Compère (ed., five vols) 1958–72, Loyset Compère (c. 1450–1518): Life and Works 1964, Geschichte der Evangelischen Kirchenmusik (co-ed., second edn) 1965, Studien zur Geschichte des Streichquartetts: I, Die Entstehung des klassischen Streichquartetts: Von den Vorformen zur Grundlegung durch Joseph Haydn 1974, Collected Works of Hindemith (co-ed. with K. von Fischer) 1976–, Renaissance-Studien: Helmuth Osthoff zum 80. Geburtstag (ed.) 1979, Quellenstudien zu Musik der Renaissance (ed., two vols) 1981, 1983, Ludwig van Beethoven (ed.) 1983, Claudio Monteverdi: Festschrift Reinhold Hammerstein zum 70. Geburtstag (ed.) 1986, Die Musik des 15. und 16. Jahrhunderts: Neues Handbuch der Musikwissenschaft (ed., Vol. 3/1–2) 1989–90, Die Mannheimer Hofkapelle im Zeitalter Carl Theodors (ed.) 1992, Die Musik in Geschichte und Gegenwart (ed., second edn, 26 vols) 1994–2007, Joseph Haydn 2000, Geschichte und Geschichten: Ausgewählte Aufsätze zur Musikhistorie 2003; contrib. editorially to the complete works of Mozart and Gluck, contrib. to scholarly books and journals. *Honours:* Hon. mem. Int. Musicological Soc., Gesellschaft für Musikforschung; Hon. Foreign mem. Royal Musical Asscn, London 1978; Ordre pour le Mérite 1994, Grand Order of Merit (Germany) 1997; Dr hc (Athens) 2002, (Zürich) 2003, (Saarbrücken) 2009; Akad. der Wissenschaften Prize, Göttingen 1968, Balzan Prize 2006. *Address:* Am Walde 1, 38302 Wolfenbüttel, Germany (home). *Telephone:* (5331) 32713 (home). *Fax:* (5331) 33276 (home).

FINSTERER, Mary, BMus, MMus, PhD; Australian composer; b. 25 Aug. 1962, Canberra. *Education:* studied with Brenton Broadstock and Riccardo Formosa in Melbourne, Louis Andriessen in Amsterdam, Univ. of Melbourne. *Career:* lecturer at various univs, including Montréal, Dusquene in Pittsburgh, Wollongong, Melbourne and Victorian Coll. of Arts, Australia; work has been performed at major festivals and concerts throughout the world, including New York, Paris, Amsterdam, Pittsburgh, Los Angeles, Montréal, Zürich, Essen, Berlin, Frankfurt, Manchester, London, Sydney and Melbourne; numerous commissions and performances from leading ensembles in Australia, Europe, Canada and the USA, including Queensland, Melbourne and Sydney Symphony Orchestras, Australian Chamber Orchestra, Le Nouvel Ensemble Modern, Ensemble Modern, Arditti String Quartet and Ensemble Intercontemporain; numerous film scores; Composer–in–Residence, Campbelltown Performing Arts Centre 2009; Vice-Chancellor's Professorial Fellow, Monash Univ. *Film music includes:* Fish Kiss, Tatlin, Matchbox, Die Hard 4, South Solitary. *Compositions include:* Scat for chromatic harmonica and orchestra 1992, Catch for soprano saxophone, bass clarinet and piano 1992, Omaggio alla Pieta for six voices, double bass (optional) and percussion 1993, Tract for solo cello 1993, Constans violin concerto 1995, Nyx concerto grosso 1996, Magnet for solo tuba and tape 1997, Ether for solo flute 1998, The Door in the Wall for solo piano with multimedia 1999, Pascal's Sphere for chamber orchestra and multimedia 1999. *Honours:* Le Nem Forum 1991, Paris Rostrum 1992, represented Australia in four ISCM World Music Day Festivals in Switzerland 1991, Germany 1995, England 1997 and Romania 1998. *Current Management:* Australian Music Centre, PO Box N690, Grosvenor Place, Sydney, NSW 1220, Australia. *E-mail:* info@australianmusiccentre.com.au. *Website:* www.australianmusiccentre.com.au/artist/finsterer-mary; maryfinsterer.com.

FIORILLO, Elisabetta; Italian singer (mezzo-soprano); b. 1960, Naples. *Career:* appeared as Ulrica at Naples, Musetta in Leoncavallo's Bohème at Venice and Azucena at Zürich, Macerata, Turin, Verona, and Parma, 1984–; guest appearances in Berlin, Hamburg, Verona and Philadelphia as Amneris in Aida, 1993–96; Preziosilla in La Forza del Destino at Barcelona, Azucena at Munich, Eboli in Turin and Fenena in Nabucco at Naples; sang Eboli at Trieste, 1997; concert repertory includes the Verdi Requiem and song recitals; further engagements at the Vienna Staatsoper and the Caracalla Festival, Rome. *Honours:* winner Mattia Battistini Competition, 1983; Prizewinner, Voci Verdiane Competition Busseto and the Vincenzo Bellini Competition, 1984. *Current Management:* Hilbert Artists Management, Maximilianstrasse 22, 80539 Munich, Germany. *Telephone:* (89) 2907470. *Fax:* (89) 29074790. *E-mail:* agentur@hilbert.de. *Website:* www.hilbert.de.

FIRSOVA, Elena Olegovna; Russian composer; b. 21 March 1950, Leningrad (now St Petersburg); d. of Oleg Borisovich Firsov and Victoria Evgenievna Firsova; m. Dmitri Smirnov 1972; one s. one d. *Education:* Moscow Conservatory with Alexander Pirumov and Yury Kholopov, also studied with Edison Denisov. *Career:* mem. Composers' Union, Russia 1976–; British debut with Petrarch's Sonnets 1980; moved to UK 1991; freelance composer 1991–; Prof. and Composer-in-Residence, Keele Univ. 1993–; Tutor in Composition, Royal Northern Coll. of Music, Manchester 1999–2001; featured composer, Park Lane Group 2004. *Compositions include:* String Quartet No. 1 1972, String Quartet No. 2 1974, Violin Concerto No. 1 1976, Chamber Concerto for flute and strings 1978, String Quartet No. 3 Misterioso 1980, Chamber Concerto for cello and orchestra 1982, Violin Concerto No. 2 1983, Earthly Life cantata for soprano and ensemble 1984, Fantasie for violin solo 1985, Chamber Concerto for piano and orchestra 1985, Music for 12 1986, Piano Sonata 1986, Forest Walks for soprano and ensemble 1987, Chamber Concerto for horn and ensemble 1987, Augury for orchestra and chorus 1988, Autumn Music 1988, Monologue for bassoon 1989, Nostalgia for orchestra 1989, String Quartet No. 4 Amoroso 1989, Stygian Song for soprano and ensemble 1989, Odyssey for seven performers 1990, Verdehr-Terzett for violin, clarinet and piano 1990, The Nightingale and the Rose (chamber opera after Wilde) 1991, Seven Haiku for voice and lyre 1991, Far Away, for saxophone quartet, Sea Shell for voice and ensemble 1991, Whirlpool for voice, flute and percussion 1991, Silentium for voice and string quartet 1991, String Quartet No. 5 Lagrimoso 1992, Secret Way for orchestra and voice 1992, Distance for voice and ensemble 1992, Meditation in the Japanese Garden for flute, viola and piano 1992, You and I for cello and piano 1992, Starry Flute 1992, Vigilia for violin and piano 1992, Otzvuki for flute and guitar 1992, Cassandra for orchestra 1992, Phantom for four viols 1993, The Night Demons for cello and piano 1993, Crucifixion for cello and bayan 1993, Hymn to Spring for piano 1993, Monologue for solo saxophone 1993, The Enchanted Island 1993, Album Leaf for cello and piano 1993, Piano Trio No. 2 Mad Vision 1993, Insomnia for four singers 1993, Before the Thunderstorm for soprano and ensemble 1994, String Quartet No. 6 1994, String Quartet No. 7 Compassione 1995, String Quartet No. 8 The Stone Guest 1995, String Quartet No. 9 The Door is Closed 1996, Chamber Concerto for cello and orchestra 1996, Temple of Mnemosyne chamber concerto for piano and orchestra 1996, The River of Time for mixed chorus and chamber orchestra 1997, The Secrets of Wisdom for soprano, flute, recorder and percussion 1997, The Sound of Time Passing for orchestra 1997, The Captivity for wind orchestra, Leaving for strings, Equinox for choir, The Scent of Absence for bass, harp and flute 1998, String Quartet No. 10 La Malinconia 1998, Frozen Time for piano quartet, Winter Elegy for counter-tenor and string trio, The Singing Forest for four recorders and strings, Das Erste ist vergangen for soprano, bass, mixed choir and chamber orchestra, Vernal Equinox for violin and piano 1999, Perpetual Return for ensemble 2001, The Rest is Silence for cello (from poem by Mandelstam), Epitaph for string trio, Romantische Fragmente for ensemble, Prrok (Prophet) for baritone, chorus and accordion, Euphonisms for euphonium and piano 2003, Requiem on Anna Akhmatova Poem 2003. *Current Management:* Boosey & Hawkes PLC, First Floor, Aldwych House, 71–91 Aldwych, London, WC2B 4HN, England. *Telephone:* (20) 7299-1919. *Fax:* (20) 7299-1991. *E-mail:* moboosey@music-exchange.co.uk. *Website:* www.boosey.com/firsova.

FIRTH, Tazeena Mary; British stage designer and costume designer; b. 1 Nov. 1935, Southampton; d. of Denis Gordon Firth and Irene Firth (née Morris). *Education:* St Mary's School, Wantage and Châtelard School, Switzerland. *Career:* Stage Design with Timothy O'Brien 1961–80; ind. stage designer 1980–; has designed for numerous plays and operas in Europe, USA, Australia, etc. for cos including RSC, Nat. Theatre, Royal Opera House, Covent Garden and ENO. *Stage designs include:* The Bartered Bride 1962, The Girl of the Golden West 1962, Tango 1966, All's Well that Ends Well 1967, The Merry Wives of Windsor 1968, The Latent Heterosexual 1968, Women Beware Women 1969, As You Like It 1973, Next of Kin 1975, The Marrying of Ann Leete 1976, The Force of Habit 1977, Evita 1979, Bedroom Farce 1979, The Rape of Lucretia 1982, A Doll's Life 1982, Turandot 1983, La Traviata 1986, Rigoletto 1987, Romeo and Juliet 1988, Dido and Aeneas 1989, 1995, From the House of the Dead 1990, Macbeth 1990, La Bohème 1991, Don Giovanni 1991, Rigoletto 1992, Carmen 1993, Magic Flute 1993, Peter Grimes 1993, Don Giovanni 1995, Oh Come ye Sons of Art, Bluebeards Castle, Jenůfa, Copenhagen 1995, Peter Grimes, Göteborg and Finnish Nat. Opera, and Jenůfa, Copenhagen 1998. *Honours:* Gold Medal for Set Design, Prague Quadriennale 1975. *Address:* Faraway, Keyhaven Marshes, Lymington, SO41 0TR, England. *Telephone:* (1590) 643265.

FIRTICH, Georgy Ivanovich; Russian composer; b. 20 Oct. 1938; m. (divorced); two s. one d. *Education:* Leningrad Music Coll., Leningrad Conservatoire. *Career:* debut in Leningrad 1953, as composer and musician; composer of symphonies, film scores, and music for radio and theatre; Chair., St Petersburg Asscn of Modern Music; Prof. of Music, St Petersburg State Pedagogical Univ.; mem. Composers' Union of St Petersburg, Asscn of Modern Music, St Petersburg. *Compositions include:* seven Sonatas for piano and for viola and piano 1960–90, Bug (ballet) 1961, Return (ballet) 1964, About Motherland (symphony) 1963, Baths (opera) 1971, Concerto-Symphony 1986, Vocal Cycle for baritone 1988, Vocal Cycle for soprano and piano 1990; choral works: Leningrad cantata in six movements for soprano, baritone, chorus and symphony orchestra 1976, ten Sonatas for piano and for flute and piano 1996–99, Concerto Fantasia for two pianos 1997, Quintet-fantasia Music Therapy 1999, Young Ignoramus (musical play) 1999, The Reminiscences of Mikhailovskoye (symphonic poem) 1999. *Films:* as composer: Delovye lyudi 1962, Mimo okon idut poezda 1963, Deti Don-Kikhota 1965, Papa, slozhi! 1966, If I Had a Million Rubles 1968, Gold 1969, Samye krassyvye korably 1973, Vozle etikh okon 1973, Utrenniy obkhod 1974, Nebo so mnoi 1974, Yesli khochesh byt schastlivym 1974, Priklyucheniya kapitana Vrungelya 1976, Armed and Dangerous: Time and Heroes of Bret Harte 1977, Versiya polkovnika Zorina 1978, Priyezzhaya 1978, Story of an Unknown Man 1980, Smert na vzlyote 1982, Zaryazhennye smertyu 1991. *Recordings include:* Adventures of Captain Vrungel 1986; Edwards; Sonata No. 4 for piano 1985; Concerto-symphony for piano and symphony orchestra 1986; Doctor Aibolit 1999. *Honours:* laureate of Leningrad Competitions, Honoured Worker of Arts, Russia 1993. *Address:* 193012 St Petersburg, Novoalexandrovskaya Street 11-29, Russia (home).

FISCH, Asher; Israeli conductor; *Principal Guest Conductor, Seattle Opera*; b. 1965, Jerusalem. *Career:* engagements with Don Giovanni at Munich, Tristan and La Forza del Destino at Copenhagen and Katya Kabanova at Houston; British and US debuts 1995–1996, with Der fliegende Holländer at Los Angeles and Gala with the Royal Opera; Music Dir, Vienna Volksoper – 2000, with Die Meistersinger and Zemlinsky's Der König Kandaules; Vienna Staatsoper performances include Parsifal, Tosca, and Eugene Onegin; Metropolitan Opera debut 2000, with The Merry Widow; season 2001–02 with Parsifal for Seattle Opera, Les Contes d'Hoffmann in Berlin and The Ring in Adelaide (Helpmann Award for Best Musical Dir 2005) 2004–05; Music Dir, New Israeli Opera, Tel-Aviv 2001–08, with Otello, Aida and Norma; concerts with the Munich, Israel and Radio France Philharmonics, Detroit Symphony, Philharmonica Hungarica and NHK SO, Japan; Principal Guest Conductor, Seattle Opera 2007–; Principal Conductor designate, West Australian Symphony Orchestra (2014–). *Current Management:* Opus 3 Artists, 470 Park Avenue South, 9th Floor North, New York, NY 10016, USA. *Telephone:* (212) 584-7500. *Fax:* (646) 300-8200. *E-mail:* info@opus3artists.com. *Website:* www.opus3artists.com.

FISCHER, Adam; Hungarian conductor; *Music Director, Austro-Hungarian Haydn Orchestra*; b. 9 Sept. 1949, Budapest, Hungary; m. Doris Fischer 1979; one s. one d. *Education:* Budapest School of Music. *Career:* conducting and composition studies in Budapest and Vienna with Swarowsky; held posts at Graz Opera, Karlsruhe; Gen. Music Dir Freiburg; work with Bavarian State Opera; regular conductor with Vienna State Opera 1973–, and with Zurich Opera; major debuts Paris Opera 1984, La Scala 1986, Royal Opera House 1989, ENO 1991, San Francisco Opera 1991, Chicago Lyric Opera 1991, Metropolitan Opera, New York 1994; has conducted many world-class orchestras, particularly Helsinki Philharmonic, Boston and Chicago Symphonies and LA Philharmonic and Vienna Chamber Orchestra; concert tours to Japan and USA; Music Dir Kassel Opera 1987–92, founder and Artistic Dir, first Gustav Mahler Festival, Kassel 1989; f. Austro-Hungarian Haydn Orchestra (AHHO) and Festival, Eisenstadt, Austria 1987, later Music Dir AHHO; Chief Conductor, Danish Nat. Chamber Orchestra 1999–; Conductor, Bayreuth Festival (Ring Cycle) 2001; Music Dir, Orchestra of the Hungarian Radio 2004–; f. Wagner Days festival 2006; Music Dir, Hungarian State Opera 2007–10, Prin. Guest Conductor 2010–. *Film:* BBC TV film of Bartók's Bluebird's Castle with London Philharmonic Orchestra (Italia Prize 1989 and Charles Heidsieck Prize). *Recordings include:* complete Haydn symphonies, Lucio Silla and Des Knaben Wunderhorn with Danish Radio Sinfonietta. *Honours:* first prize (jtly) Milan Cantelli Competition 1973. *Current Management:* c/o Angelika Csillag, Raab und Böhm Agentur, Plankengasse 7, 1010 Vienna, Austria. *Telephone:* (1) 5120501. *Fax:* (1) 5127743. *E-mail:* csillag@rbartists.at. *Website:* www.rbartists.at.

FISCHER, György; Hungarian conductor, pianist and harpsichordist; b. 12 Aug. 1935, Budapest. *Education:* Franz Liszt Academy, Budapest and Salzburg Mozarteum. *Career:* Asst to Karajan at the Vienna State Opera where he conducted Die Zauberflöte and Die Entführung; Principal Conductor at the Cologne Opera, notably in a Mozart cycle produced by Jean Pierre Ponnelle; Bavarian State Opera with Don Giovanni, Idomeneo and Die Zauberflöte in South America, and Cimarosa's Le Astuzie Femminili at Wexford; British debut with the WNO 1973 returning for Così fan tutte and Le nozze di Figaro; London debut in 1979 with the British premiere of Mozart's Mitridate at the Camden Festival; English Chamber Orchestra from 1980; Debut with Australian Opera, 1987–88, conducting Così fan tutte in 1990; Don Giovanni for Vancouver Opera in 1988; Season 1992 with Le nozze di Figaro at Sydney; Accompanist to leading singers including his former wife, Lucia Popp. *Recordings include:* Mozart Arias for soprano voice with Kiri Te Kanawa, Teresa Berganza and Cecilia Bartoli.

FISCHER, Hanne; Danish singer (mezzo-soprano); b. 1968. *Education:* Royal Danish Acad. of Music, Copenhagen, studied with Ingrid Bjoner and Vagn Thordal. *Career:* debut, Royal Opera, Copenhagen 1993, as Cherubino in Le Nozze di Figaro; engaged as mem. of the ensemble at the Opera in Kiel, Germany 1993–97, where she sang Siebel in Faust, Second Lady in The Magic Flute, Dorabella in Così fan tutte, Cherubino in Le Nozze di Figaro, Hänsel in Hänsel and Gretel, Angelina in La Cenerentola and Idamante in Idomeneo; guested at the Royal Opera, Copenhagen, singing Rosina (The Barber of Seville) 1993, 1994, Dorabella in Così fan tutte 1995, and Zerlina in Andreas Homoki's staging of Don Giovanni 1996; debut at the Glyndebourne Festival as Annio in Nicholas Hytner's staging of La Clemenza di Tito 1995, reinvited to sing Isolier in Le Comte Ory 1997, 1998; further engagements at the Flemish Opera, Antwerp, as Annio 1997, Idamante in Idomeneo 1998; mem. of the ensemble at the Royal Opera, Copenhagen 1997–, where she has sung Suzuki in Madama Butterfly, Idamante in Idomeneo, Der Komponist in Ariadne auf Naxos, Dorabella in Così fan tutte, Cherubino in Le Nozze di Figaro, Offred's Double in The Handmaid's Tale, Pauline in Queen of Spades, Amando in Le Grand Macabre and Marchesa Melibea in Il Viaggio a Reims; numerous concerts all over Europe, several of which broadcast on radio and TV, including the title role in Offenbach's Perichole and the final gala concert at Euromusicale, Munich; soloist in the first performance of Vølvens Spaadom by Andy Pape, with Copenhagen Philharmonic Orchestra 2000; soloist in the Philharmonie Berlin with the RSO Berlin in the performance of Franz Léhar's opera Tatjana 2001; season 2000–01 at the Flemish Opera, Antwerp and Gent, singing The Fox in Robert Carsen's staging of The Cunning Little Vixen by Janáček, also guested at the Staatsoper Hamburg and the Opera in Bonn; season 2002–03, debut at the Théâtre des Champs-Elysées, Paris as The Fox in The Cunning Little Vixen, at the Flemish Opera singing Dorabella in Guy Joosten's staging of Così fan tutte, with both the Copenhagen Philharmonic and the Danish National Radio Symphony Orchestra as soloist in Mahler's Rückert-Lieder, and with the Royal Opera, Copenhagen singing Waltraute in Kasper Holten's new production of Die Walküre; season 2003–04 debut as Sextus in David McVikar's La Clemenza di Tito, and performances in Il Viaggio a Reims, Das Rheingold, and The Handmaid's Tale at the Royal Opera, Copenhagen. *Recordings:* Tatjana (with the RSO, Berlin) 2001, The Handmaid's Tale 2000, Archipel des solitudes (with the Danish National Radio Symphony Orchestra and Leif Segerstam) 2000, Des Sänger's Fluch (with the Danish National Radio Symphony Orchestra and Michael Schönwandt) 1999, Vom Pagen und der Königstochter (with the Danish National Radio Symphony Orchestra and Michael Schönwandt) 2000. *Honours:* Noilly Prat Music Prize. *E-mail:* mail@hannefischer.com (office). *Website:* www.hannefischer.com.

FISCHER, Iván; Hungarian/Dutch conductor; *Music Director, Budapest Festival Orchestra;* b. 20 Jan. 1951, Budapest; s. of Sándor Fischer and Evelin Boschán; two s. two d. *Education:* B. Bartók Music Conservatory, Budapest and Wiener Hochschule für Musik under Hans Swarowsky, Mozarteum, Salzburg under Nikolaus Harnoncourt. *Career:* Jt Music Dir Northern Sinfonia of England, Newcastle 1979–82; Music Dir and Artistic Dir, Kent Opera 1982–2000; Prin. Guest Conductor Cincinnati Symphony Orchestra 1989–96; Music Dir Lyon Opera House 2000–03; Prin. Conductor Nat. Symphony Orchestra, Washington, DC 2008–10; Co-founder and Music Dir Budapest Festival Orchestra 1983–; also Music Dir Konzerthaus and Konzerthausorchester, Berlin; concerts with London Symphony Orchestra, Berlin Philharmonic Orchestra, Concertgebouw Orchestra etc.; main performances in USA: Los Angeles Philharmonic, Cleveland, Philadelphia, San Francisco Symphony and Chicago Symphony Orchestras; operas: Idomeneo,

Don Giovanni, Julius Caesar, La Bohème, La Clemenza di Tito, Marriage of Figaro, Magic Flute in London, Paris, Vienna; Founder Hungarian Mahler Soc.; Patron British Kodály Acad. *Compositions include:* The Red Heifer 2014. *Honours:* Hon. Citizen of Budapest, Hon. Mem. Royal Acad. of Music, UK 2013; Chevalier des Arts et des Lettres; Premio Firenze 1974, Rupert Foundation Award, BBC, London 1976, Gramophone Award for Best Orchestral Recording of the Year (for The Miraculous Mandarin) 1998, Golden Medal, Republic of Hungary 1998, Crystal Award, World Econ. Forum 1998, Kossuth Prize 2006, Gramophone Editor's Choice Award (for Mahler's Second Symphony) 2007, Royal Philharmonic Soc.'s Conductor Award 2011, Dutch Ovatie Prize 2011. *Address:* Budapest Festival Orchestra, Alkotás utca 39/c., 1123 Budapest, Hungary (office). *Telephone:* (1) 489-4330 (office). *Fax:* (1) 355-4049 (office). *E-mail:* bfofound@mail.datanet.hu (office). *Website:* www.bfz.hu (office).

FISCHER, Julia; German violinist; b. 1983, Munich. *Education:* Leopold Mozart Conservatory, Augsburg with Lydia Dubrowskaya, Munich Acad. of Music with Ana Chumachenco. *Career:* has performed with orchestras in USA, Japan, Brazil and throughout Europe, including New York Philharmonic, Boston Symphony Orchestra, Acad. of St Martin-in-the-Fields, RPO, Berlin Radio Symphony Orchestra, Bavarian Radio Symphony Orchestra, Gewandhaus Orchestra, Dresden Philharmonic, Real Orquesta Sinfónica de Sevilla; chamber music pnrs include Christoph Eschenbach, Jean-Yves Thibaudet, Daniel Müller-Schott, Tabea Zimmermann, Gustav Rivinius, Lars Vogt, Oliver Schnyder, Milana Chernyavska. *Recordings:* Brahms, Piano Quartets 2003, Russian Violin Concertos (Gramophone magazine Editor's Choice 2005) 2004, Bach, Sonatas and Partitas for Solo Violin 2005, Mendelssohn's Piano Trios (with Daniel Müller-Schott and Jonathan Gilad) 2006, Tchaikovsky Violin Concerto 2007, Bach Concertos 2009, Paganini 24 Caprices 2010. *Honours:* first prize and special prize Int. Yehudi Menuhin Competition 1995, Eurovision Competition for Young Instrumentalists 1996, Foundation of European Industry Prix d'Espoir 1997, Gramophone Award for Artist of the Year 2007, Midem Classical Award for Instrumental Artist of the Year 2009. *Current Management:* Mastroianni Associates Inc., 161 West 61st Street, Suite 17E, New York, NY 10023, USA. *Telephone:* (212) 586-6210 (office). *Fax:* (212) 586-5963 (office). *E-mail:* info@jfmartists.com (office). *Website:* www.jfmartistsonline.com (office). *E-mail:* julia@juliafischer.com. *Website:* www.juliafischer.com.

FISCHER, Klaus Peter, DipMus, PhD; German musicologist; b. 16 Jan. 1937, Breslau, Silesia. *Education:* Franz-Liszt Hochschule, Weimar, Cologne Univ. *Career:* German Historical Inst., Rome, Italy 1970–72; German Research Asscn 1972–76; scientific collaborator, Inst. for Hymnological and Ethnological Studies, Cologne-Maria Laach, Germany 1977–78; Lecturer, Univ. of Pavia, Italy 1982–87, Assoc. Prof. 1988–; mem. Gesellschaft für Musikforschung, Int. Musicological Soc., Società Italiana di Musicologia, Associazione fra Docenti Universitari Italiani di Musica. *Publications:* Die Psalmkompositionen in Rom um 1600 (ca 1570–1630) 1979; contrib. to Analecta Musicologica, Archiv für Musikwissenschaft, Studi Musicali, Die Musikforschung, New Grove Dictionary of Music and Musicians (various edns), Kirchenmusikalisches Jahrbuch, Die Musik in Geschichte und Gegenwart (MGG, second edn), Congress Reports.

FISCHER, Miroslav; Slovak stage director and opera regisseur; b. 6 Dec. 1932; m. 1st Olga Hanakova 1977; m. 2nd Jitka Saparova 1977; one s. one d. *Education:* School of Musical Arts, Bratislava. *Career:* debut with La Traviata, at Slovak National Theatre, Bratislava, 1955; more than 130 operas and operettas performed in Bratislava, Banska, Bystrica, Kosice, Brno, Plzeň, Ankara, Bilbao, Brussels, most notably: The Consul, 1956; Fliegende Holländer, 1957; Pelléas et Mélisande, 1958, Fidelio, 1960; Midsummer Night's Dream, 1963; La Forza del Destino, 1964; The Greek Passion, 1969; Salome, 1976; Lohengrin, 1976; Falstaff, 1978, Elektra, 1980; Don Carlos, 1981; Katarina Izmailova, 1984; Un Ballo in Maschera, 1985; Wozzeck, 1985; Donizetti's Caterina Cornaro at Bratislava, 1997.

FISCHER, Norman; American cellist; b. 25 May 1949, Plymouth, MI. *Education:* Interlochen Arts Acad., Oberlin Coll. Conservatory with Richard Kapuscinski. *Career:* mem., Concord String Quartet from 1971; nationwide performances in a wide repertory, including many works by American composers; George Rochberg has written his Piano Quintet, String Quintet and String Quartets Nos 3–7 for the ensemble; other composers premiered include Lukas Foss (Third Quartet), Ben Johnston (Crossing) and Jacob Druckman (Third Quartet); Quartet-in-Residence, Dartmouth Coll., New Hampshire from 1974. *Recordings include:* Fourth, Fifth and Sixth Quartets by George Rochberg. *Honours:* Naumburg Award 1971.

FISCHER, Thierry; Swiss conductor; *Principal Conductor, BBC National Orchestra of Wales;* b. 1957, Livingstone. *Education:* studied with Aurèle Nicolet. *Career:* fmr flautist with Zürich Opera; fmr Prin. Flute, Chamber Orchestra of Europe, where he also began conducting; devoted career solely to conducting from 1994; fmr Prin. Conductor Netherlands Ballet Orchestra 1997–2001; Prin. Conductor, Ulster Orchestra 2001–06; Prin. Conductor, BBC Nat. Orchestra of Wales 2006–; Chief Conductor, Nagoya Philharmonic Orchestra, Japan 2008–11; Music Dir, Utah Symphony Orchestra 2009–; has appeared as guest conductor with orchestras including the Philharmonia, CBSO, Halle, BBC Symphony, Bournemouth Symphony, Scottish Chamber, Northern Sinfonia, Philharmonique de Radio France, WDR Köln, SWR Freiburg/Baden-Baden, Hanover Radio, Düsseldorf Symphoniker, Berlin

Symphony, Sinfonica di Milano, Stavenger Symphony, Copenhagen Philharmonic, Monte-Carlo, RSI Lugano Chamber, Zürich Chamber, Australian Chamber; made N American debut with Nat. Arts Centre Orchestra, Ottawa and Colorado Symphony 2003–04; tours with Ulster Orchestra include Prague and New York, also BBC Proms 2005; tours with BBC Wales to USA, Prague, Spain, Italy, China. *Recordings:* Frank Martin, Polyptyque 1992, Mozart, Serenades 1997, Netherlands Wind Ensemble plays Janáček 1999, Stravinsky, Mavra and Chamber Works 1999, Prokofiev, Violin Concerto No. 2 2003, Jean Françaix, Symphony in G Major, Françaix, Orchestral Works 2004, Françaix, Le Roi Nu and Les Demoiselles de la Nuit 2005, Stravinsky, The Firebird 2010, Stravinsky, Petrushka; Liadov, Kikimora 2010, Stravinsky Rite of Spring 2011, Martin Der Sturm (Int. Classical Music Award for Best Opera Recording 2012) 2011. *Current Management:* c/o Intermusica Artists Management Ltd, 36 Graham Street, Crystal Wharf, London, N1 8GJ, England. *Telephone:* (20) 7608-9900. *Fax:* (20) 7490-3263. *E-mail:* mail@intermusica.co.uk. *Website:* www.intermusica.co.uk.

FISCHER-DIESKAU, Julia, (Julia Varady); German/Romanian singer (soprano); *Professor, Hochschule für Musik Hanns Eisler, Berlin;* b. (Julia Töszer), 1 Sept. 1941, Oradea, Romania; m. Dietrich Fischer-Dieskau 1977 (died 2012). *Education:* studied in Cluj with Emilia Popp and in Bucharest with Arta Florescu. *Career:* debut, Cluj as Fiordiligi 1962; guest appearances at the Budapest and Bucharest Operas; moved to Frankfurt 1971; in Munich from 1973, as Vitellia in La Clemenza di Tito, Il Trovatore, Otello, Butterfly, Giorgetta in Il Tabarro, Elektra in Idomeneo, Santuzza, Liu, Leonora in La Forza del Destino, Elisabeth de Valois and Cordelia in the premiere of Lear by Reimann 1978; Scottish Opera 1974, as Gluck's Alceste; Metropolitan Opera 1978, Donna Elvira; tours of Japan, Israel and the USA; appearances at the Berlin, Edinburgh, Munich and Salzburg Festivals and at the Promenade Concerts London; La Scala Milan 1984, in Idomeneo; other roles include Countess Almaviva, Judith (Bluebeard's Castle), Tatiana, Desdemona and Rosalinde; sang Wagner's Senta at Munich 1990, Covent Garden 1992; Vitellia in La Clemenza di Tito at the Queen Elizabeth Hall 1990; appeared as Abigaille in Nabucco at the 1990 Munich Festival; season 1992–93 as the Trovatore Leonora at Munich and Elisabeth de Valois at the Deutsche Oper Berlin; returned to Berlin 1997, as Senta; Aida at the 1997 Munich Festival; concert repertoire includes arias by Mozart and Beethoven, Vier Letzte Lieder by Strauss, Britten's War Requiem, the Verdi Requiem, the Faust oratorios of Schumann and Berlioz; Requiem by Reimann (premiere 1982); soloist in the Verdi Requiem at Berlin 2000; recital in Madrid 2003; Prof., Hochschule für Musik Hanns Eisler, Berlin 1999–; Visiting Prof., Opernstudio der Staatsoper Unter den Linden, Berlin, Hochschule für Musik, Karlsruhe. *Recordings include:* Lucio Silla by Mozart, Die Fledermaus, Il Matrimonio Segreto, Lear, Idomeneo, La Clemenza di Tito, Duke Bluebeard's Castle, Gli Amori di Teolinda by Meyerbeer, Cavalleria Rusticana, Les Contes d'Hoffmann, Arabella, Don Giovanni, Handel's Saul, Mozart's Le Nozze di Figaro, works by Verdi and Richard Strauss, Wagner's Wesendonk Lieder. *Honours:* first winner of the Music Prize of the Kulturstiftung, Dortmund. *Address:* Lindenallee 22, 14050 Berlin, Germany.

FISCHER-MÜNSTER, Gerhard; German composer, conductor, soloist (piano, clarinet) and academic; *Lecturer, Peter Cornelius Konservatorium, Mainz;* b. 17 Nov. 1952, Münster-Sarmsheim; s. of Theo Fischer and Vera Fischer; m. Bettina Fischer-Münster 1979; one s. one d. *Education:* Peter Cornelius Konservatorium, Mainz, Staatliche Musikhochschule und Johannes Gutenberg Universität, Mainz, seminar for conducting, Bingen; Staatsexamen (Musikdozent, Dirigent, Solist). *Career:* first compositions in 1965; concerts as soloist (piano, clarinet); concerts as conductor of various orchestras and ensembles; radio and TV performances and recordings in Germany, Italy, Austria, Switzerland, France, Belgium, Colombia, USA and Japan; Guest Conductor with European Symphony Orchestra, Luxembourg 1993; Guest Lecturer, Universität Mainz and various insts; f. wind chamber ensemble 1981; Founder, Symphonic Wind Orchestra of Mainz Conservatory 1991; Lecturer, Peter Cornelius Konservatorium, Mainz (clarinet, piano improvisation, composition, symphonic wind orchestra, wind chamber ensemble) 1975–; Ed. Komponisten-Atelier, Loosmann Verlag 2011, 2013, 2016. *Compositions include:* symphonies: Psychodrom, Im Anfang war das Wort, Symphony 5 'Connections', Daliphonie, Haiku-Lieder, Psalm 99, Schizophonie; Geldschein-Sonate, Piano Concertino, Symphonic Pictures; sonatas, lieder and orchestral works. *Recordings include:* Haiku-Lieder, Philosophie eines Filous, Musique de table, Süd-Freak-Idyll, Schizophonie, Adoration, chamber music and more. *Radio:* in Germany, Switzerland, Austria, France, Italy and elsewhere, several stations in USA. *Television:* appearances on ZDF, SWR, TV Turkey. *Publications include:* Harmonie aus dem Einklang, Lehrplan Klarinette, Kreativ Üben. *Honours:* numerous prizes in Germany, Switzerland, France, UK, USA . *Address:* Auf den Zeilen 11, 55424 Münster-Sarmsheim, Germany (home). *Telephone:* (6721) 46727 (home). *E-mail:* fischer-muenster@gmx.de. *Website:* www.pckmainz.de (office); www.fischer-muenster.de; www.fischer-münster.de.

FISET, Marianne; Canadian singer (soprano); b. 1979, Québec. *Career:* debut with Opéra de Montréal as Adza in L'Étoile 2005; mem. Atelier Lyrique, Opéra de Montréal seasons 2005–06, 2006–07; Artist-in-Residence, Radio Canada 2008; European recital debut, St John's Smith Square, London and Salons de Boffrand, Palais du Luxembourg, Paris 2007; performed at Cleveland Art Song Festival 2006, Toronto Luminato Festival 2007; took part in opening ceremony, Québec 400th anniversary celebrations 2008; roles

include: Adza in L'Étoile, Miss Jessel in The Turn of the Screw, Dolcina in Suor Angelica, Amante in Il tabarro, Annina in La Traviata, Clarice in Il Mondo della Luna. *Recordings:* Ravel: Shéhérazade, Debussy: Proses Lyriques 2008. *Honours:* numerous prizes including Bourse d'Excellence de la Ville de Québec 2004, first prize and Radio Canada Prix Étoile Galaxie, Trois-Rivières Symphony Orchestra Competition 2004, Prix Opus de la Découverte 2006–07, first prize, Montréal Int. Music Competition 2007, Prix Jean A. Chalmers for Best Canadian Artist, Prix Joseph Rouleau for Best Québec Artist, Prix Poulenc and Public Prize 2007. *Current Management:* Philippe Cuisinier, Aria Management, 75 rue de Lourmel, 75015 Paris, France. *Telephone:* 1-46-05-46-57. *Fax:* 1-46-05-46-91. *E-mail:* ariamngt@aol.com. *Website:* www.ariamanagement.com. *E-mail:* info@mariannefiset.com (office). *Website:* www.mariannefiset.com.

FISHER, Gillian; British singer (soprano); b. 1955, England; m. Brian Kay. *Education:* Royal Coll. of Music with John Carol Case, studied with Jessica Cash. *Career:* appearances in the world's leading concert halls, including Royal Albert, Festival and Barbican Halls, London, Amsterdam Concertgebouw, Lincoln Center, New York and Suntory Hall, Tokyo, Handel Festivals in London and in Maryland, USA; frequent broadcasts with repertoire ranging from Baroque music to the vocal symphonies of Milhaud; featured in television series Man and his Music; sang in Theodora and other works by Handel for tercentenary year 1985; sang in Messiah with Ton Koopman and the Amsterdam Baroque Orchestra, Japan 1987; appearances in Italy, Japan and Australia with vocal group The Sixteen; Gluck's Euridice at Covent Garden 1989. *Recordings include:* Purcell's King Arthur and Dioclesian with John Eliot Gardiner and the Monteverdi Choir; The Triumph of Time and Truth by Handel with Denys Darlow and the London Handel Orchestra; Great Baroque Arias and Pergolesi's Stabat Mater with the King's Consort and Michael Chance; Purcell's Fairy Queen and Bach cantatas with The Sixteen and Harry Christophers and Handel duets with the King's Consort and James Bowman. *Address:* Bell Cottage, Church Lane, Fulbrook, Burford, OX18 4BA, England. *Telephone:* (1993) 823193. *E-mail:* gillykay.kay@btinternet.com.

FISHER, John; British artistic director; b. Scotland. *Career:* Music Dir, Welsh Nat. Opera 'Music For All' project 1972; subsequently worked at Théâtre de la Monnaie, Brussels and Netherlands Opera; fmr Head of Music and Artistic Admin., La Scala, Milan; Artistic Dir, Teatro alla Fenice, Venice 1989–94; Dir of Opera and Vocal Productions and Exec. Producer, Deutsche Grammophon 1994–97; Dir of Music Admin, Metropolitan Opera, New York 1997–2006; Gen. Dir, Welsh Nat. Opera 2006–11.

FISHER, Jonathan; British singer (baritone); b. 1963, England. *Education:* Guildhall School, London with Bernard Dickerson, Cologne Musikhochschule. *Career:* appearances for the Royal Opera, Covent Garden, in The Pilgrim's Progress and La Battaglia di Legnano (concert), Chérubin by Massenet, Der Rosenkavalier, Simon Boccanegra and The Midsummer Marriage; Henry Higgins in My Fair Lady for the Covent Garden Festival; Associated with Royal Opera House education projects. *Recordings:* The Pilgrim's Progress, Peter Grimes, Christmas from Covent Garden. *Publications:* By George, musical about the Gershwins. *Honours:* Painter prize, Guildhall School.

FISHER, Norma Ella, FRNCM; British pianist and academic; *Professor of Piano, Royal College of Music, London;* b. 11 May 1940, London, England; d. of Julius Fisher and Anne Hertz; m. Barrington Saipe 1967; two s. *Education:* Guildhall School of Music with Sidney Harrison, pvt. studies with Ilona Kabos in London and Jacques Février in Paris, protegée of Gina Bachauer. *Career:* debut at Wigmore Hall 1956, Proms, Royal Albert Hall 1963; performances worldwide in recitals, concertos and chamber music; regular performer for BBC; represented UK twice at Int. Jeunesses Musicales Congress; jury mem. of numerous int. piano competitions; invited to give masterclasses world-wide; f. London Master Classes 1988; Prof. of Piano, Royal Northern Coll. of Music, Manchester, Royal Coll. of Music, London. *Honours:* Second Prize, Busoni Int. Piano Competition, Italy 1961, Piano Prize (jt holder with Vladimir Ashkenazy), Harriet Cohen Int. Awards 1963. *Address:* 5 Lyndhurst Gardens, Finchley, London, N3 1TA, England (home). *Telephone:* (20) 8346-7088 (office). *Fax:* (20) 8343-3669 (office). *E-mail:* ns@londonmasterclasses.com (office). *Website:* www.londonmasterclasses.com (office).

FISHER, Stephen Carey, BA, PhD; American musicologist; b. 18 May 1948, Norfolk, VA. *Education:* Univ. of Virginia, Univ. of Pennsylvania. *Career:* Asst Prof., Widener Univ. 1985–87; Lecturer, Univ. of Pennsylvania 1989–; mem. American Musicological Soc., Int. Musicological Soc., Music Library Asscn. *Publications:* The Symphony 1720–1840, series B, vol. IX 1983, Joseph Haydn Werke series 1, vols 9, Sinfonien um 1777–79 2002; contrib. to Haydn-Studien, Mitteilungen der Internationalen Stiftung Mozarteum, Current Musicology, Haydn Studies 1975, The Haydn Yearbook, The Eighteenth Century: A Current Bibliography, Eighteenth-Century Studies, Journal of Musicology, New Grove Dictionary of Opera, Notes, Journal of the American Musicological Society, New Grove Dictionary of Music. *Honours:* Fulbright-Hays grant 1976–77. *Address:* c/o Department of Music, University of Pennsylvania, 201 South 34th Street, Philadelphia, PA 19104-6313, USA. *E-mail:* docsfisher@aol.com (home); fisher@pobox.upenn.edu (office).

FISICHELLA, Salvatore; Italian singer (tenor); b. 15 May 1943, Catania, Sicily; m. Fiorella Botta; one s. one d. *Education:* studied in Catania and Rome. *Career:* debut at Spoleto Festival, as Werther; sang in Rigoletto and I Puritani at the Rome Opera and appeared widely in Europe and America as Arturo, Arnoldo in Guillaume Tell and Gualtiero in Il Pirata; New York Met debut as Arturo, opposite Joan Sutherland; engagements at Zürich Opera under Nello Santi in I Puritani, Il Pirata and Guillaume Tell; further leading roles in La Traviata, Butterfly, La Favorita, Roberto Devereux, Faust, Mefistofele and Attila; season 1996–97 as the Duke of Mantua at Zürich, Pinkerton and Alfredo at Palermo, Edgardo in Lucia di Lammermoor at La Scala and Fernando in La Favorita at Catania; further roles in Rossini's Mosè in Egitto and Otello, I Capuleti e i Montecchi, and The Two Widows; season 2000–01 as the Duke of Mantua at St Gallen and Gualtiero in Bellini's Pirata at Catania. *Honours:* Cavaliere della Repubblica Italiana, Cavaliere di Malta OSI; Premio Bellini d'Oro in Catania, Premio Internazionale Giacomo Lauri Volpi, Rome, Premio Francesco Tamagno 2013. *Address:* via Quasimodo 19-Sant'Agata li battiati, Catania, Sicily, Italy (office). *Telephone:* (039) 095212866 (office). *E-mail:* opera@salvatorefisichella.it (office). *Website:* www.salvatorefisichella.it.

FISK, Eliot Hamilton, MA; American classical guitarist and academic; *Professor, Salzburg Mozarteum*; b. 10 Aug. 1954, Philadelphia, PA. *Education:* Yale Univ., Aspen Music School with Oscar Ghiglia, studied with Andres Segovia, Ralph Kirkpatrick, Albert Fuller. *Career:* solo recital debut, Alice Tully Hall, New York 1976; toured throughout the world as soloist with orchestras, as recitalist and chamber music performer; teacher, Aspen Music School 1973–82, Yale Univ. 1977–82, Mannes Coll. of Music 1978–82; Prof., Cologne Hochschule für Musik 1982–89, Mozarteum, Salzburg 1989–, New England Conservatory, Boston 1996–; prepared transcriptions of works by J. S. Bach, Scarlatti, Mozart, Paganini, Mendelssohn, E. Halffter, I. Albeniz, E. Granados, for guitar; new works for guitar composed for him by Robert Beaser, Luciano Berio, Cristóbal Halffter, Nicholas Maw, Xavier Montsalvatge, George Rochberg, Kurt Schwertsik, Leonardo Balada, Daniel Bernard Romaine. *Recordings:* first recordings of Paganini Caprices Op. 1, Rochberg: Caprice Variations, Balada: Concierto Magico, Segovia: Canciones Populares, Berio: Sequenza XI, Beaser: Mountain Songs, Rochberg: Muse of Fire, Castelnuovo-Tedesco: Suite Op. 133, J. S. Bach BWV 1001–1006, BWV 525–529, BWV 1014–1019, Mozart K. 439. *Publications:* transcriptions of Bach, Mozart, Frescobaldi, Scarlatti, Paganini; edns of Beaser, Berio, Rochberg, Halffter, Montsalvatge, Maw and others. *Honours:* winner Int. Classical Guitar Competition, Gargnano, Italy 1980. *Current Management:* c/o Vantage Artists, 131 Varick Street, Suite 937, New York, NY 10013, USA. *E-mail:* probles@vantageartists.com. *Website:* www.vantageartists.com; www.eliotfisk.com.

FISSORE, Enrico; Italian singer (bass); b. 23 Jan. 1939, Piemonte. *Education:* Milan and Turin Conservatories. *Career:* debut, Teatro Nuovo Milan 1964, as Don Giovanni; Many appearances in Europe and North America in Italian operas of the 17th and 18th centuries; Glyndebourne debut 1967, as Schaunard in La Bohème; USA debut at San Francisco, as Rossini's Bartolo; La Scala Milan 1979, in Vivaldi's Tito Manlio; Further engagements as Verdi's Melitone and Dulcamara in L'Elisir d'amore at the Metropolitan, Don Magnifico in La Cenerentola with Florida Opera and Leporello at Portland 1997–98; other appearances at the Chicago Lyric Opera, Vienna Staatsoper, Opéra Bastille, Salzburg Festival and Munich; Glyndebourne 1997, as Bartolo in Le nozze di Figaro, followed by Puccini's Trittico in Brussels. *Current Management:* Robert Gilder & Co., 91 Great Russell Street, London, WC1B 3PS, England. *Telephone:* (20) 7580-7758. *Fax:* (20) 7580-7739. *E-mail:* rgilder@robert-gilder.com. *Website:* www.robertgilder.com.

FITKIN, Graham, BA, MA; British composer; b. 19 April 1963, Crows-an-Wra, Cornwall. *Education:* Univ. of Nottingham, Koninglijk Conservatorium, The Hague with Louis Andriessen. *Career:* Co-founder piano ensemble The Nanquidno Group 1985; Programme Dir, Soc. for the Promotion of New Music 1993; PRS Composer in Education 1995, 1996, 1998; Composer-in-Residence, Royal Liverpool Philharmonic Orchestra 1994–96; Founder sextet Graham Fitkin Group 1996; Composer-in-Residence, The Harbourside Centre, Bristol 1997–98, The Lemon Tree, Aberdeen 2000, 2001, London Chamber Orchestra 2008–09; featured composer for Park Lane Group and at Presteigne Festival 1999, at Mixing Music Festival 2000, at Int. Guitar Festival 2001; various collaborative projects with different orgs, including The Geography Project, Scotland 1999–, Tokyo Symphony Orchestra, Hallé Orchestra, BBC Philharmonic, dance cos including New York City Ballet, Royal Ballet, Wayne McGregor's Random Dance, Shobana Jeyasingh, San Francisco Ballet, artists including Kathryn Stott, Yo-Yo Ma, John Patitucci, Noriko Ogawa; commissioned to write a piece of music for the 2012 Cultural Olympiad; composed Birch for European City of Culture Umea with Fitkin Group 2014, toured Disco (composition) 2015–16. *Compositions include:* Drum (music theatre) 1989, Loud 1989, Log 1990, Line 1991, Nasar 1992, Ghosts (opera) 1993, Huoah 1994, Length 1994, Metal 1995, Henry 1995, Granite 1995, Bebeto 1995, North 1998, Bob 1998, Timber 2000, Ending 2000, Ascendant 2001, Circuit concerto for two pianos 2002, Circuit 2003, Kaplan 2004, Still Warm 2006, Passing 2006, Piano Solos 2007, Circuit 2007, Glass 2007, Subterfuge 2007, Reel (British Composer Award for Best Stage Work 2009) 2008, Chain of Command 2008, Ruse 2009, Sinew 2009, PK (British Composer Awards for Outreach 2011), Track to Track 2012, Helical Strake (for pianist Kathryn Stott and trumpeter Tine Thing Helseth) 2012, Birch 1871 (for orchestra) 2014, Lost 2014, Disco 2015. *Honours:* Hon. Fellow, Falmouth Univ.; Int. Grand Prix Music for Dance Video Award 1994, British Composer Award 2010, 2011, Hon. Music Award, Univ. of Nottingham 2013. *Telephone:* (151) 513-2716. *E-mail:* jane@wardmusic.co.uk. *E-mail:* info@fitkin.com. *Website:* www.fitkin.com.

FITZGERALD, Daire; Irish cellist; b. 1966, Dublin. *Education:* studied with Rostropovich, Menuhin School with William Pleeth, Menuhin Academy with Radu Aldulescu. *Career:* concerts throughout Western Europe, China, India, Israel and Czechoslovakia, while a student at the Society of Lincoln Center, New York, and concerts with such orchestras as the Royal Philharmonic, Warsaw Sinfonia, Central Philharmonic of Peking, Hallé and Berlin Radio Symphony; soloist with the Camerata Lysy Gstaad on tour to Japan and Canada; Berlin debut with the Saint-Saëns A minor concerto; New Year's Concert for Finnish television, tour of USA playing chamber music with Menuhin and participation on Julian Lloyd Webber's Cellothon at South Bank, London; currently mem., St Luke's Chamber Ensemble. *Address:* St Luke's Administrative Offices, 330 West 42nd Street, Ninth Floor, New York, NY 10036, USA (office). *Website:* www.oslmusic.org.

FITZPATRICK, Martin; British musician, conductor and music administrator; *Head of Music, English National Opera*; b. 10 July 1967, London, England; m. Emer McGilloway 2001; one s. one d. *Education:* Balliol Coll., Oxford, Guildhall School of Music, London, Nat. Opera Studio. *Career:* Head of Music, Royal Danish Opera 1998–2001; Chorus Master, Opera North 2001–05; Head of Music, ENO 2003–, conducting at ENO includes The Magic Flute, Falstaff, La Bohème, Turn of the Screw, Don Giovanni, Carmen, La Traviata. *Address:* English National Opera, London Coliseum, St Martin's Lane, London, WC2N 4ES, England (office). *Telephone:* (20) 7845-9412 (office). *Fax:* (20) 7845-9296 (office). *Website:* www.eno.org (office).

FLANAGAN, Leslie John; Australian singer (baritone); b. 1969, Rockhampton. *Education:* studied in Australia and at Scottish Acad. of Music. *Career:* appearances at Mananan Festival as Schaunard in La Bohème and as Malatesta in Don Pasquale for Clonter Opera; Junior Principal with ENO 1999–2000 season; other roles include Papageno, Demetrius (A Midsummer Night's Dream), Don Giovanni and Escamillo; concerts include Fauré and Brahms Requiems, Mendelssohn's St Paul, Elgar's Apostles and Puccini's Messa di Gloria. *Honours:* Marianne Mathy Award 1996.

FLECK, William; American singer (bass); b. 28 Aug. 1937, Tyrone, Pa. *Education:* Eastman School and at the Manhattan School of Music. *Career:* sang widely in USA, first as guest in Boston, Minneapolis and Hawaii; Metropolitan Opera from 1980, in Die Zauberflöte, Tannhäuser, Traviata, Bohème and Tosca; sang Rocco at Mexico City 1983; sang in US premiere of Ruslan and Lyudmilla, Boston and elsewhere as Leporello, Alfonso, Don Magnifico, and Morosus in Die schweigsame Frau; Baron Ochs in Der Rosenkavalier, directed by Jonathan Miller, New York City Opera debut 1996. *Current Management:* c/o Sardos Artists Management, 180 West End Avenue, Suite 22B, New York, NY 10023, USA. *Telephone:* (212) 874-2559. *Fax:* (212) 721-7815. *E-mail:* info@ritasardos.com. *Website:* www.ritasardos.com. *E-mail:* ellsler13@sbcglobal.net (office).

FLEET, Marlene Rose, LRAM, ARCM; British pianist; b. 13 Feb. 1942, Grimsby, South Humberside, England; m. Harry Terence Harvey Taylor 1972. *Education:* Grimsby Technical Coll., Royal Acad. of Music. *Career:* debut at Wigmore Hall 1964; numerous concerts in the UK, Europe and America; appearances at Wigmore Hall, Purcell Room, QEH, Royal Festival Hall, London; plays regularly for BBC and has performed on BBC television; played with most of the leading British orchestras and with many distinguished conductors. *Honours:* winner many solo pianist prizes Royal Acad. of Music 1960–65, Countess of Munster Scholarship, Martin Musical Scholarships.

FLEISCHER, Tsippi, PhD; Israeli composer; b. 20 May 1946, Haifa; one s. *Education:* Tel-Aviv and New York Univs, Rubin Acad. of Music, Bar Ilan Univ., Ramat Gan, Israel. *Career:* lecturer, Tel-Aviv and Bar-Ilan Univs; Prof. in Music Dept, Levinsky Inst., Tel-Aviv; mem., Levinsky Inst. Pedagogical Cttee. *Compositions include:* A Girl Named Limonad (music theatre) 1977, Girl-Butterfly-Girl song cycle for soprano and ensemble 1977, Lamentation for soprano, women's chorus, two harps and percussion 1985, In the Mountains of Armenia for children's chorus 1988, Ethnic Silhouettes 1988–98, Cantata, Like Two Branches 1989, Oratorio 1492–1992 1992, Four Old Winds (four multimedias in ancient Semitic language) 1993–96, Medea (chamber opera) 1995, Salt Crystals (first symphony) 1995, The Train Symphony (second symphony) 1998, Regarding Beauty (third symphony) 1998, A Moving Shadow (fourth symphony, incl. folk wind and percussion) 2000, Cain and Abel (opera) 2001, Lead Life song cycle 2001, An Israeli-Jewish Collage (fifth symphony) 2002–03, Victoria (opera) 2003–04, Ancient Love for boys choir and lute 2006, Oasis (children's opera) 2010. *Recordings include:* Tsippi Fleischer Vocal Music 1992, Tsippi Fleischer Art Music Settings of Arab Poetry 1993, Around the World with Tsippi Fleischer 1997, Israel at 50: A Celebration of the Music of Tsippi Fleischer 1999, Symphonies I–V 2004, Girl-Butterfly-Girl 2005, Lieder (double album) 2009. *Publications:* Harmonization of Songs (two vols) 2005, Matti Caspi 2012. *Honours:* ACUM Prize for Music 1994, Prime Minister's Award for Composers (50th Anniversary of the State of Israel) 1998, ACUM Prize for lifetime achievement in composition for the concert hall 2002. *Address:* PO Box 8094, Haifa 31080, Israel (home). *E-mail:* info@tsippi-fleischer.com. *Website:* www.tsippi-fleischer.com.

FLEISHER, Leon; American pianist and conductor; *Andrew W. Mellon Chair in Piano, Peabody Institute, Johns Hopkins University*; b. 23 July 1928, San Francisco, CA. *Education:* studied with Artur Schnabel, Pierre Monteux. *Career:* debut public recital 1934; played Liszt's A Major Concerto with the San Francisco Symphony 1942; Brahms D Minor Concerto in San Francisco and New York 1943, 1944; international career from 1952; gave concerts with

George Szell and the Cleveland Orchestra; faculty mem., Peabody Inst. of Music, Johns Hopkins Univ. 1959–, currently Andrew W. Mellon Chair. in Piano; premiered Leon Kirchner's Concerto, Seattle 1963; lost use of right hand 1965, and later played Piano Left Hand repertoire; Co-Director of the Kennedy Center Theater Chamber Players, Washington, DC 1968; Assoc. Conductor, Baltimore Symphony Orchestra 1973–78; guest engagements as conductor with leading orchestras in the USA; resumed bimanual solo pianist career 1982; Music Dir Annapolis Symphony Orchestra, Tanglewood Music Center 1986–97. *Publication:* My Nine Lives: A Memoir of Many Careers at the Keyboard (with Anne Midgette) 2010. *Honours:* Dr hc (San Francisco Conservatory of Music), (Boston Conservatory), (Cleveland Inst. of Music); winner, Queen Elisabeth Piano Competition, Belgium 1952, President's Medal, Johns Hopkins Univ., Kennedy Center Honor 2007, Royal Philharmonic Soc. Instrumentalist Award 2011. *Address:* Peabody Institute, Johns Hopkins University, 1 East Mount Vernon Place, Baltimore, MD 21202, USA (office). *Telephone:* (410) 659-8100 (office). *Website:* www.peabody.jhu.edu/405 (office).

FLEMING, Renée, MMus; American singer (soprano); b. 14 Feb. 1959, Indiana, Pa; d. of Edwin Davis Fleming and Patricia (Seymour) Alexander; m. Richard Lee Ross 1989 (divorced 2000); two d. *Education:* Potsdam State Univ., Eastman School of Music of Univ. of Rochester, Juilliard School American Opera Center. *Career:* debuts Houston Grand Opera in Marriage of Figaro 1988, Spoleto Festival, Charleston and Italy 1987–90, New York City Opera in La Bohème 1989, San Francisco Opera, Metropolitan Opera, Paris Opera at Bastille, Teatro Colón, Buenos Aires all in Marriage of Figaro 1991, Glyndebourne in Così fan tutte 1992, La Scala Milan in Don Giovanni 1993, Vienna State Opera in Marriage of Figaro 1993, Lyric Opera of Chicago in Susannah 1993, San Diego Opera in Eugene Onegin 1994, Paris Opera 1996, Massenet's Thaïs at Nice and Gounod's Marguerite at the Met 1997, Floyd's Susannah at the Met 1999, Louise at Barbican Hall, London and the Marschallin at Covent Garden 2000; premiered Previn's A Streetcar Named Desire 1998; recital tour with Jean-Yves Thibaudet 2001–02; London Proms 2002, Dvořák's Rusalka in concert at Covent Garden 2003, Bellini's Il Pirata at the Met 2003; Fulbright Scholar to Germany 1984–85; sang The Star-Spangled Banner (first opera singer), Super Bowl opening ceremony 2014. *Plays:* Living on Love (Williamstown Theatre Festival 2014, Broadway debut in Longacre Theatre 2015). *Recordings include:* Sacred Songs 2005, R. Strauss's Daphne (with Cologne Radio Chorus and Symphony Orchestra) 2005, Love Sublime (with Brad Mehldau) 2006, Homage: The Age of the Diva 2006, Four Last Songs 2008, Verismo Arias (Grammy Award for Best Classical Vocal Performance) 2009, Dark Hope 2010, Ravel/Messiaen, Dutilleux: Poèmes (ECHO Klassik Award for Female Singer of the Year) (Grammy Award for Best Classical Vocal Solo 2013) 2012, Christmas in New York 2014. *Publication:* The Inner Voice: The Making of a Singer (autobiog.) 2005. *Honours:* Hon. mem. RAM 2003; Chevalier, Légion d'honneur 2005; Dr hc Juilliard School, New York 2003, Hon. DMus (Harvard) 2015; Fulbright Scholar 1984–85, George London Prize 1988, Richard Tucker Award 1990, Solti Prize, Acad. du Disque Lyrique 1996, Prix Maria Callas Acad. du Disque Lyrique 1997, 2004, Musical America Vocalist of the Year 1997, Prize Acad. du Disque Lyrique 1998, Grammy Awards 1999, 2002, 2010, creation of the dessert 'La Diva Renée' by Master Chef Daniel Boulud 1999, Classical BRIT Awards for Top-selling Female Artist 2003, for Outstanding Contribution to Music 2004, LOTOS Medal of Merit 2005, Polar Music Prize 2008, Opera News Award 2008, Nat. Medal of Arts 2012. *Current Management:* c/o Alec C. Treuhaft, IMG Artists, Carnegie Hall Tower, 152 West 57th Street, 5th Floor, New York, NY 10019, USA. *Telephone:* (212) 994-3500. *Fax:* (212) 994-3550. *E-mail:* atreuhaft@imgartists.com. *Website:* www.imgartists.com; www.renee-fleming.com.

FLETZBERGER, Matthias; Austrian pianist; b. 24 Aug. 1965, Vienna. *Education:* Hochschule für Musik, Vienna. *Career:* Musikverein Wien; Mozarteum Salzburg Festival; festivals in Puerto Rico, Lockenhaus, Athens, Naples; soloist, Israel Philharmonic, Orchestre de Bordeaux, R. Schumann Philharmonie, Hochschulorchester Vienna, Orquesta Sinfonica de Chile; recitals in Europe, America, Australia; Musical Asst to Elisabeth Schwarzkopf and Renata Tebaldi; Musical Dir and Principal Conductor, Superstiltheater, Vienna. *Television:* The Magic Flute at the Vienna Festival (conductor) 1991.

FLIMM, Jürgen; German theatre director; *Director, Staatsoper im Schiller Theater*; b. 17 July 1941, Giessen; s. of Werner Flimm and Ellen Flimm; m. Susanne Ottersbach 1990. *Career:* early work at the Munich Kammerspiele; Dir Nationaltheater, Mannheim 1972–73; Prin. Dir Thalia Theater, Hamburg 1973–74, 1985–2000; Dir Cologne Theatre 1979–85; Acting Dir Salzburg Festspiele 2001–06, Artistic Dir 2006–10; Artistic Dir Festival Ruhrtriennale 2005–08; Dir Staatsoper im Schiller Theater, Berlin 2010–; Pres. German Bühnenverein 1999–2003; mem. Acad. of Arts in Hamburg, Munich, Berlin, Frankfurt. *Films:* Wer zu spät kommt – die letzten Tage des Politbüros 1990, Käthchens Traum 2004. *Publications:* Theatergänger 2004. *Honours:* Bundesverdienstkreuz 1992; Dr hc (Hildesheim) 2002; Konrad-Wolf-Preis 1995, Grimme Prize, Medal for the Arts and Sciences of Free Hanseatic City of Hamburg, Max-Brauer-Prize, Alfred Toepfer Foundation F.V.S. *Address:* Staatsoper im Schiller Theater, Bismarckstrasse 110, 10625 Berlin, Germany (office). *Website:* staatsoper-berlin.de (office).

FLITER, Ingrid; Argentine pianist; b. 1973, Buenos Aires; m. Anton Dressler 2014. *Education:* Hochschule für Musik, Freiburg, and with Carlo Bruno in Rome, Acad. Incontri col Maestro, Imola. *Career:* debut Teatro Colon, Buenos Aires at age 16; has performed with orchestra and in recital at major halls including Concertgebouw, Amsterdam, Suntory Hall, Tokyo, Liszt Conservatory Hall, Budapest, Philharmonia, San Petersburg, Teatro Colón, Buenos Aires, Alte Oper, Frankfurt, Conservatorio Giuseppe Verdi, Milan, Grosses Festspiele-Haus, Salzburg, Cologne Philharmonic with orchestras including the Berlin Symphony, Netherlands Philharmonic, Hungarian Nat. Philharmonic, St Petersburg Symphony Orchestra, Giuseppe Verdi Orchestra, Milan, Nat. Symphonic and Nat. Philharmonic Orchestras of Buenos Aires; US orchestra debut with Atlanta Symphony under Donald Runnicles 2006. *Honours:* first prize Cantu Int. Competiton, Ferruccio Busoni Competiton, Italy, Silver Medal Frédéric Chopin Competition, Warsaw 2000, Gilmore Artist Award 2006. *Current Management:* Harrison Parrott, 5–6 Albion Court, London, W6 0QT, England. *Telephone:* (20) 7229-9166. *Fax:* (20) 7221-5042. *E-mail:* jennifer.spencer@harrisonparrott.co.uk. *Website:* www.harrisonparrott.com. *E-mail:* info@ingridfliter.com (office). *Website:* www.ingridfliter.com.

FLOR, Claus Peter; German conductor; b. 16 March 1953, Leipzig; adopted s. of Richard Flor and Sigrid Langer. *Education:* Music School, Weimar and High School of Music, Weimar/Leipzig, studied under Rolf Reuter, Rafael Kubelik and Kurt Sanderling. *Career:* studied violin and clarinet before commencing conducting studies; Chief Conductor, Music Dir Berliner Sinfonie Orchester (now Konzerthausorchester Berlin) 1984–92; Artistic Adviser, Zürich Tonhalle Orchestra 1991–96; Prin. Guest Conductor, Philharmonia Orchestra, London 1991–94, Dallas Symphony Orchestra 1999–2008, Orchestra Sinfonica di Milano Giuseppe Verdi 2003–08; Music Dir, Malaysian Philharmonic Orchestra 2008–14; regular appearances with Vienna Symphony, Orchestre de Paris, Royal Concertgebouw, Rotterdam Philharmonic and major German orchestras; frequent guest engagements with leading orchestras in UK, USA, Canada etc.; conductor of opera at many German opera houses including Berlin Staatsoper and Deutsche Oper, Berlin. *Recordings include:* Mendelssohn, Cherubini, Dvořák, Mozart, Shostakovich. *Current Management:* c/o IMG Artists, The Light Box, 111 Power Road, London, W4 5PY, England. *Telephone:* (20) 7957-5800. *Fax:* (20) 7957-5801. *E-mail:* pmartin@imgartists.com. *Website:* www.imgartists.com.

FLÓREZ, Juan Diego; Peruvian singer (tenor); b. 13 Jan. 1973, Lima; m. Julia Trappe. *Education:* studied in Lima and at Curtis Inst., Philadelphia, USA. *Career:* debut in Matilde di Shabram at Rossini Opera Festival, Pesaro 1996; signed exclusive contract with Decca Music Group 2001; appearances include La Scala, Milan (in Armide, Falstaff, Cappello di Paglia di Firenze, Barbiere di Siviglia, Nina Pazza per Amore, La Sonnambula, Fille du Régiment), Comunale, Firenze (in Le Comte Ory, Falstaff), Covent Garden, London (in Elisabetta by Donizetti, Otello by Rossini, La Cenerentola, Don Pasquale, Fille du Régiment, Matilde di Shabran, Barbiere di Siviglia), Metropolitan Opera, New York (Barbiere di Siviglia, Don Pasquale, Cenerentola, Italiana in Algeri, Fille du Regiment, Sonnambula), Salzburg Festival (Donna del lago, Recital), Konzerthaus, Vienna (in La Semiramide), Carlo Felice, Washington Nat. Opera (in Italiana in Algheri), Genoa (in La Cenerentola, Le Comte Ory, Donna del lago), Regio, Turin (in La Sonnambula, Maria Stuarda, L'Elisir d'Amore), La Maestranza, Seville (in Donizetti's Alahor in Granata), Filarmonico, Verona (in Italiana in Algeri), Vienna Staatsoper (in Barbiere di Siviglia, Italiana in Algeri, Gianni Schicchi, La Sonnambula, I Puritani, Fille du Régiment), Opera di Roma (in Barbiere di Siviglia, Italiana in Algheri), Bologna (Comte Ory, Puritani), Las Palmas (in Italiana in Algeri, Fille du regiment, L'Elisir d'Amore, I Puritani), Vienna Musikverein (in Stabat Mater), Bayerische Staatsoper (in Italiana in Algeri), Gran Teatro del Liceo, Barcelona (in Stabat Mater, Maria Stuarda, Semiramide, La Cenerentola), Opera Nat., Paris (in Italiana in Algeri, Donna del lago), Bilbao (in Barbiere di Siviglia, Sonnambula, Fille du regiment), Rossini Opera Festival (Matilde di Shabran, Donna del lago, Barbiere di Siviglia, Cenerentola, Viaggio a Reims, Comte Ory, Otello, Zelmira), Edgardo in Lucia di Lammermoor (Liceo, Barcelona 2015); f. Sinfonía por el Perú. *Recordings include:* more than 20 recordings of operas including Il barbiere di Siviglia 1997, La Cenerentola 2000, Le Comte Ory 2003, La Fille du régiment 2007, Orphée et Eurydice 2010, La sonnambula 2010; recital recordings include Great Tenor Arias 2004, Arias for Rubini 2007, Bel Canto Spectacular 2009, Santo 2010. *Honours:* Gran Cruz, Orden del Sol (Peru) 2007; Abbiati Prize 2000, Rossini d'Oro (Pesaro) 2000, Opera Actual magazine Award for Best Tenor 2005, Plácido Domingo Prize, World Econ. Forum Crystal Award 20i4. *Current Management:* c/o Ernesto Palacio, Via Donizetti 11, Lurano, Italy. *Telephone:* (035) 800645. *Fax:* (035) 4877767. *E-mail:* ernestopalacio@ernestopalacio.com. *Website:* www.ernestopalacio.com; www.juandiegoflorez.com.

FLOROS, Constantin, DrPhil; German musicologist and academic; *Professor Emeritus, University of Hamburg*; b. 4 Jan. 1930, Salonika, Greece. *Education:* Vienna Music Acad., Vienna Univ., Austria. *Career:* Prof. of Musicology, Univ. of Hamburg 1972–95, Prof. Emer. 1995–; Pres. Gustav Mahler Vereinigung, Hamburg 1988; mem. European Acad. of Sciences and Arts 2002. *Compositions:* works for chamber music, choir, organ. *Publications include:* György Ligeti 1996, Anton Bruckner 2004, Neue Ohren für neue Musik 2006, Peter Tchaikovsky 2006; other books include three vols on medieval notations, three-vol. treatise on Gustav Mahler, two vols on Johannes Brahms, two vols on Alban Berg, Der Mensch die Liebe und die Musik 2000, Hören und verstehen/Die Sprache der Musik und ihre Deutung 2008; eight books have been translated into English. *Honours:* Dr hc (Athens)

1999, (Salonika) 2004, Golden Dr Diploma (Vienna) 2005; Gustav Mahler Medal 2010. *Address:* Mac Lean, Loehrsweg 1, 20249 Hamburg, Germany (office). *Telephone:* (40) 4605108 (office). *Fax:* (40) 4605108 (office). *E-mail:* music-contact@floros.de (office); macleanofcoll@web.de (office). *Website:* www.floros.de (office).

FLOWERS, Kate; British singer (soprano); b. 1950, Cheshire, England. *Education:* Northern School of Music, Royal Northern College of Music, studied in Paris. *Career:* Glyndebourne Festival from 1976, as Despina, Isotta in Die schweigsame Frau, Norina in La Fedeltà Premiata and the title role in The Cunning Little Vixen; Appearances with Opera North as Gretel, Despina, Susanna, Zerlina, Aennchen in Der Freischütz and Thérèse in Les mamelles de Tirésias; Polly Peachum in The Beggar's Opera for Scottish Opera; Micaela, Marenka and Jenůfa for the Welsh National Opera; Concert engagements in Europe, and on London's South Bank with the Philharmonia, the English Chamber Orchestra, Royal Philharmonic, Hallé Orchestra, London Philharmonic and the Academy of St Martin in the Fields; Sang Jenny in The Threepenny Opera for Opera North, 1990; Sang Mrs Ford in Falstaff with City of Birmingham Touring Opera, 1995; Sang Marianne in Der Rosenkavalier at Covent Garden, 2000. *Honours:* John Christie Award, Royal Soc. of Arts Scholarship 1977. *Current Management:* Musicmakers International Artists Representation, Tailor House, 63–65 High Street, Whitwell, Hertfordshire SG4 8AH, England. *Telephone:* (1438) 871708. *Fax:* (1438) 871777. *E-mail:* musicmakers@compuserve.com. *Website:* www.operauk.com.

FLOYD, Carlisle, BA, MA; American composer; b. 11 June 1926, Latta, SC. *Education:* Converse Coll., Spartenberg, Syracuse Univ. with Ernest Bacon, studied piano with Rudolf Firkusny and Sidney Foster. *Career:* teacher, Florida State Univ. 1947–76; M. D. Anderson Prof. of Music, Univ. of Houston 1976–. *Compositions:* operas: Slow Dusk 1949, Susannah 1951, Wuthering Heights 1958, The Passion of Jonathan Wade 1962, The Sojourner and Mollie Sinclair 1963, Markheim 1966, Of Mice and Men 1969, Bilby's Doll 1976, Willie Stark 1981, Cold Sassy Tree 2000; other: Pilgrimage (song cycle) 1956, Piano Sonata 1957, The Mystery (song cycle) 1960, Flower and Hawk monodrama for soprano and orchestra 1972, Citizen of Paradise (song cycle) 1983, A Time to Dance for baritone, chorus and orchestra 1994, Cold Sassy Tree (musical play) 2000. *Honours:* Nat. Medal of Honour 2005, Nat. Endowment for the Arts Opera Award 2008. *Current Management:* Boosey & Hawkes, Aldwych House, 71–91 Aldwych, London, WC2B 4HN, England. *E-mail:* composers.uk@boosey.com. *Website:* www.boosey.com/floyd.

FLURY, Urs Joseph; Swiss composer, violinist and conductor; b. 25 Aug. 1941, Bern; s. of Richard Flury and Rita Gosteli. *Education:* Univ. of Bern, Univ. of Basel, Conservatoires of Biel and Basel. *Career:* stage appearances, TV and radio broadcasts in Switzerland and other European countries. *Compositions include:* chamber music: Variations on a Christmas Carol, Fantasia and Sonata for violin solo, Two Suites for violin and piano, Variations and Duo for violin and viola, String Trio, Wind Quintet, Quartet for oboe, violin, viola and cello, Lieder; orchestral works: Vineta (Symphonic Poem), Three Suites, The Little Mermaid, Concerto di carnevale for rag band and orchestra, Three Fantasies on Carols for organ and strings; instrumental concertos: Concertino Veneziano for violin and strings, Concerto for violin in D, Romance for violin and orchestra, Cello Concerto; piano concerto; vocal music: Christmas Cantata, Christmas Oratorio, Passion, three masses, salve regina. *Recordings include:* as violinist and conductor: Cello Concerto, Concertino Veneziano, Concerto for violin in D, Sonata for Violin Solo, Suite Nostalgique, Christmas Oratorio, The Little Mermaid, Vineta, Lieder, Quartet for oboe, violin, viola and cello, Duo for violin and viola. *Publications include:* Pahlen Kurt: Oratorien der Welt 1985, Pahlen Kurt, Neue Musikgeschichte der Welt 1990, Hartnack Joachim: Grosse Geiger unserer Zeit 1983, Schweizer Chorkomponisten 1999, Musik in Geschichte und Gegenwart 2002; contrib. to several professional journals and magazines. *Honours:* Music Prize, Canton Solothurn 1993. *Address:* Zelglistrasse 5, 4562 Biberist, Switzerland (office). *Telephone:* (32) 6723288 (office). *E-mail:* urs.joseph.flury@bluewin.ch. *Website:* www.ujflury.ch; www.richardflury.ch.

FOCCROULLE, Bernard; Belgian organist, composer and theatre director; *Director, Aix-en-Provence Festival*; b. 1953, Liège. *Education:* Conservatoire de Liège, studied organ under Hubert Schoonbroodt, Xavier Darasse, Bernard Lagacé, Gustav Leonhardt. *Career:* fmr teacher of musical analysis; has toured worldwide as a soloist; mem. Ricercar Consort early music ensemble from 1982; Dir-Gen. Théâtre Royal de la Monnaie, Brussels 1992–2007; Dir Aix-en-Provence Festival 2007–; f. Culture and Democracy arts org. 1993; Pres. Opera Europa 2006–; Prof., Brussels Conservatory. *Recordings:* J. S. Bach's complete works for organ, Mozart, Keyboard Works 1992, Bruhns/Reinken, Sämtliche Orgelwerke 2002, Organ Recital at Grenzing Organ Brussels Cathedral 2003, Tunder, Organ Works 2004, Dietrich Buxtehude complete works for organ 2007. *Publications:* Entre Passion et Résistance 2005, La naissance de l'individu dans l'art 2005. *Honours:* Fondation Alfred Töpfer Prix Montaigne 2001, Grand Prix, Académie Charles Gros 2007. *Address:* Festival Aix-en-Provence, 11 rue Gaston de Saporta, 13100 Aix-en-Provence, France (office). *Telephone:* 4-42-17-34-34 (office). *Fax:* 4-42-63-13-74 (office). *E-mail:* bernard.foccroulle@festival-aix.com (office). *Website:* www.festival-aix.com (office).

FOCILE, Nuccia; Italian singer (soprano); b. 25 Nov. 1961, Militello, Sicily. *Education:* Turin Conservatory. *Career:* season 1986–87, as Oscar in Ballo in Maschera at Turin and Philadelphia, Thalia in Rameau's Platée at Spoleto, Elvira (L'Italiana in Algeri) at Schwetzingen and Mistress Ford in Salieri's Falstaff at Peralade; further engagements at Buenos Aires as Musetta, Valencienne in The Merry Widow at Venice and Nannetta at Covent Garden, 1988; Rio de Janeiro in 1989 as Rossini's Rosina, and Oscar at Naples, and Ascanio in Pergolesi's Lo frate 'nnamorato at La Scala; returned to Milan in 1990 as Servilia in La Clemenza di Tito and appeared at Bergamo as Eleanora in Donizetti's L'Assedio di Calais; Pesaro Festival, 1990, as Giulia in La Scala di Seta, Teatro Valle Rome as Countess in Paisiello's Don Chisciotte; returned to Philadelphia 1991, as Norina, sang Mozart's Susanna at Houston and appeared at the Opéra Bastille, Paris, as Ilia in Idomeneo; Barcelona and Dallas, 1992, as Adina in L'Elisir d'amore, Oscar at the Opéra Bastille, Paris, Tatiana at the Théâtre du Châtelet and Carolina (Matrimonio Segreto) at the 1992 Ravenna Festival; sang Gounod's Juliette at the Paris Opéra-Comique, 1994; La Traviata for WNO 1995; season 1996–97 with Mozart's Ilia at Florence, Liù and Susanna for the Royal Opera, Mimi in Paris and Tel-Aviv, and Amelia Boccanegra for WNO; season 2000–01 as Amelia Grimaldi at Wellington, Susanna for WNO and Mimi at the Met; season 2009–10 as Mimi in La Bohème for Deutsche Oper Berlin, Despina in Cosi fan tutte for Dallas Opera, Violetta in La Traviata at Seattle Opera, the Countess in Le nozze di Figaro at the New Zealand Opera Auckland, concerts of Rachmaninoff's The Bells with San Francisco Symphony conducted by Semyon Bychkov; season 2010–11 as Rosalinde in Die Fledermaus for WNO and La Voix Humaine at Covent Garden; season 2011–12 as Donna Elvira in Don Giovanni for WNO and Musetta in La Bohème at Covent Garden. *Recordings include:* Lo frate 'nnamorato (Pergolesi) and L'Assedio di Calais (Donizetti); Le nozze di Figaro, Così fan tutte and Don Giovanni with Charles Mackerras. *Honours:* Turin International Competition, 1983; Pavarotti Competition, Philadelphia, 1986. *Current Management:* Askonas Holt Ltd, Lincoln House, 300 High Holborn, London, WC1V 7JH, England. *Telephone:* (20) 7400-1700. *Fax:* (20) 7400-1799. *E-mail:* info@askonasholt.co.uk. *Website:* www.askonasholt.co.uk.

FOLAND, Nicolle, BMus, MMus; American singer (soprano); b. 1968, Des Moines. *Education:* University of Northern Iowa. *Career:* appearances with San Francisco Opera 1995–, as Clorinda in La Cenerentola, Gerhilde, Musetta, multiple roles in the premiere of Harvey Milk; Micaela with Cincinnati Opera, Musetta with Los Angeles Music Center Opera and Seattle Opera 1996–97; Micaela, San Francisco Opera 1998; Countess at Boston Lyric Opera and Opera Company of Philadelphia, Desdemona at Minnesota Opera, Violetta at Houston Grand Opera 1999; Donna Anna and Kitty Hart in Dead Man Walking at San Francisco Opera 2000, Violetta at Michigan Opera Theater, Sifare in Mitridate at Santa Fe Opera 2001, Mimi at Minnesota Opera and Boston Lyric Opera, Countess at New York City Opera 2002, Micaela at New York City Opera and Donna Anna at Thessaloniki 2003, Mimi at Arizona Opera 2004, Alceste at Opera Boston, Micaela at Arizona Opera 2005, Drusilla in Poppea at Central City Opera, Violetta at Utah Opera 2006; concerts include Plácido Domingo special, San Francisco. *Current Management:* Guy Barzilay Artists, 360 West 28th Street #6B, New York, NY 10001, USA. *Telephone:* (212) 741-6118. *Fax:* (212) 741-2558. *E-mail:* guybar@aol.com. *Website:* guybarzilayartists.com; nicollefoland.com.

FÖLDES, Imre; Hungarian musicologist and academic; *Professor of Music History and Theory, Ferenc Liszt University of Music*; b. 8 March 1934, Budapest; grandson of writer and dramatist Imre Földes; m. Dr Zsuzsa Vadász; one d. *Education:* Ferenc Liszt Univ. of Music, Budapest. *Career:* musicologist and Prof. of Music History and Theory, Ferenc Liszt Univ. of Music, Dept of Teacher Training; lecturer on music for general public and radio; mem. Hungarian Musicians' Asscn, Soc. for Propagating Sciences and Arts, Hungarian Ferenc Liszt Soc., Hungarian Kodály Soc., Lajos Bárdos Soc., Magyar Újságírók Szövetsége. *Publications:* Harmincasok, Beszélgetések magyar zeneszerzökkel (Generation of the Thirties: Conversations with Hungarian Composers) 1969, Life and Works of J. S. Bach 1976, The Melody Dies Irae 1977; contrib. to Az ének-zene tanítása, Muzsika, Parlando. *Honours:* Kt's Cross, Order of Merit of Hungary 2004; Art Prize for Socialist Culture 1974, Art Prize, Nat. Council of Trade Unions 1975, Szabolcsi Prize 1977, Ferenc Erkel Prize 1986, Moholy-Nagy Prize 2010, Artisjus Prize 2011. *Address:* 1132 Budapest, Kresz Géza utca 26, Hungary. *Telephone:* (1) 349-8332; 30-581-1794 (mobile). *E-mail:* foldesimre2@gmail.com.

FOLWELL, Nicholas David, ARAM; British singer (baritone); b. 11 July 1953, s. of Alfred Thomas Folwell and Irmgard Gertrude Folwell; m. Susanna Folwell; one s. *Education:* studied with Raimund Herncx; Royal Acad. of Music and London Opera Centre. *Career:* sang with Welsh Nat. Opera (WNO) from 1978 as Mozart's Figaro and Leporello, Pizarro, Melitone, Escamillo, The Poacher in The Cunning Little Vixen, Alberich in The Ring of the Nibelung (also at Covent Garden with WNO 1986) and Wagner's Melot and Klingsor; other roles include Villains in The Tales of Hoffmann, Tonio, Beckmesser, Schaunard, Creon and The Messenger in Oedipus Rex, Alberich, Papageno, in Weill's Seven Deadly Sins with the London Sinfonietta 1988, Alberich in Rheingold, Figaro, Cecil in Maria Stuarda, Alberich in Siegfried, Sancho Panza in Don Quixote, Paulus, the Bosun in Billy Budd, the Host of the Garter in Sir John in Love, Antonio in The Marriage of Figaro, Mr Kallenbach in Satyagraha, Don Alfonso in Così fan tutte, Bartolo in Il Barbiere di Siviglia, The Doctor in Punch and Judy, The Commissar of Police in Der Rosenkavalier, Mumlal in The Two Widows; sang Dreieinigkeits Moses in Aufstieg und Fall der Stadt Mahagonny for Opera Angers/Nantes in France; Alberich in Das Rheingold for Nationale Reisopera in Enschede, The Netherlands; concerts in France, Italy, Austria and Germany 1987–90; cr. roles of Koroviev in York Höller's Master and Margarita in Paris 1989, Ekbert in Blonde Ekbert 1994, Mutius in Timon of Athens 1991, Van Tricasse in Dr Ox's Experiment 1998, Idraote in Armida 2005, The Beggar and Bishop Foliot in Stephen Barlow's King 2006, Pope Clement VI in Light Passing 2006, Charles Frieth in For You 2009, Alberich in Das Rheingold in the Netherlands 2010; recital tour with Lesley Garrett 2010; sang Brander in The Damnation of Faust for ENO 2011, Alberich in Siegfried in the Netherlands 2011, Longborough Festival Opera and in Bergen, Norway with Kent Nagano, Alberich in Das Rheingold for Opera North 2011, Nachtigal in Die Meistersinger von Nürnberg for Royal Opera House, Covent Garden 2011, Antonio in Le Nozze di Figaro for Glyndebourne Festival Opera and Alberich in Götterdämmerung in the Netherlands 2012, Der Theatre Direktor and Bankier in Lulu for WNO 2013, Tiger Brown in Dreigroschenoper with London Philharmonic Orchestra and Vladimir Jurowsky 2013, more performances as Antonio for Glyndebourne Festival Opera 2013 and Alberich and Gunther in Der Ring der Nibelungen for Opera de Dijon 2013, Mr Kallenbach in Satyagraha for ENO 2013, Filip in The Jakobin for the Buxton Festival 2014, various roles in the World Premier of The Trial by Pillip Glass for Music Theatre Wales 2014. *Recordings:* solo: A Dream of Paradise; also appears in recordings of Tristan and Isolde and Parsifal, conducted by Reginald Goodall, The Cunning Little Vixen, The Mikado. *Current Management:* c/o Helen Sykes Artists' Management, 100 Felsham Road, London, SW15 1DQ, England. *Telephone:* (20) 8780-0060. *Fax:* (20) 8780-8772. *E-mail:* info@helensykesartists.co.uk. *Website:* www.helensykesartists.co.uk.

FONDRAY, Alain; French singer (baritone); b. 1932, Bangolet. *Education:* studied in Paris. *Career:* debut as Tonio in Pagliacci, Cherbourg 1968; sang in many provincial French opera houses 1970s; appearances at the Paris Opéra 1985, 1991, in Jerusalem by Verdi and as the High Priest in Samson et Delila; Royal Opera House, Covent Garden, in La Fanciulla del West, La Scala Milan as Amonasro, Metropolitan Opera in Cavalleria Rusticana; sang Scarpia at San Francisco, returning 1990 as Renato in Un Ballo in Maschera; Vienna Staatsoper and Barcelona 1991, as the High Priest and Scarpia; festival engagements include Orange 1992, as Count Luna, and Bregenz 1993, as Nabucco; sang Massenet's Sancho Panza at Toulouse 1992, and Count Luna at Orange; La Scala 1993, as Scarpia; sang in Massenet's Thais at Nice 1997; season 2000–01 as Iago at Brussels, Comte de Toulouse in Verdi's Jérusalem at Genoa, and in the premiere of Cecilia by Charles Chayne at Monte Carlo; Amonasro at Maastricht and Massenet's Hérode at St Etienne. *Recordings include:* Sancho Panza in Don Quichotte, conducted by Michel Plasson.

FONTANA, Carlo; Italian opera house director, journalist and arts executive; *Executive Director, Teatro Regio di Parma*; b. 15 March 1947, Milan; s. of Ciro Fontana; m. Roberta Cavallini. *Education:* Univ. Statale di Milano. *Career:* journalist 1968–77; responsible for youth activities, Piccolo Teatro di Milano 1968–71; Asst to Gen. Man. Teatro all Scala, Milan 1977–79, mem. Admin. Council 1980–84; Deputy Admin. Fonit Cetra 1979–84; Pres. Associazione Lirica Concertistica Italiana 1980–83; Dir Music Section, Venice Biennale 1983–86; Dir Ente Autonomo Teatro Comunale di Bologna 1984–90; Sovrintendente, Teatro alla Scala, Milan 1990–2005; Senator (cultural) 2006–08; Exec. Dir Teatro Regio di Parma 2012–; Pres. AGIS (Associazione Generale Italiana dello Spettacolo) 2013–; Prof., Univ. of Pavia in 1990s; Adjunct Prof., Univ. of Milan 2005–07; Pres. Associazione Nazionale Enti Lirici e Sinfonici 1986; mem. Commissione Centrale Musica, Consiglio Nazionale dello Spettacolo. *Publication:* A scena aperta 2007. *Honours:* Grande Ufficiale della Repubblica Italiana, Ambrogino d'Oro, Milan 1999. *Address:* Teatro Regio di Parma, strada Garibaldi, 16/a, 43121 Parma, Italy (office). *Website:* teatroregioparma.it (office).

FONTANA, Gabriele, MA; Austrian singer (soprano); *Professor of Lied and Oratorio, University of Music and Performing Arts, Vienna*; b. (Gabriele Pietschnigg-Fontana), 11 Feb. 1960, Innsbruck; d. of Wilhelm Pietschnigg and Maria Fontana; m. Peter Weber. *Education:* Gymnasium Sillgasse Innsbruck, Hochschule für Musik und Darstellende Kunst Wien with Ilse Rapf and Dr Erik Werba, master classes with Elisabeth Schwarzkopf and Peter Pears. *Career:* mem. Opera Studio, Vienna State Opera; debut as Pamina at Frankfurt Opera House aged 21; mem. Hamburg State Opera, sang roles including Pamina, Konstanze, Sophie (Rosenkavalier), cr. role of Sophie Scholl in Zimmermann's Weisse Rose; subsequently invited to Bavarian State Opera (Contessa, Rosalinde), Vienna State Opera (Pamina, Sophie, Zdenka, Rosalinde), Glyndebourne Festival (Contessa, Fiordiligi), BBC Proms (Contessa), Bregenz Festival (Pamina), Salzburg Festival and Mozartwoche, Festwochen Vienna, and to opera houses in Berlin, Dresden, Amsterdam, Prague, Israel, USA and Japan; has worked regularly with conductors including Boulez, Barenboim, Sir Colin Davis, von Dohnányi, Haitink, Leinsdorf, Masur, Mehta, Sawallisch, Tate, Welser-Möst; has appeared in recitals and concerts in New York, Washington, DC and Philadelphia (Sawallisch), Manchester, Prague and Tel-Aviv (Four Last Songs), Vienna Musikverein, Accad. di Santa Cecilia, Rome with Mahler 8 (Chung) and Das Paradies und die Peri (Sawallisch), and was invited to Macerata Festival with Maria Stuart Recital; since 2003, major debuts with Euryanthe in Amsterdam, Edinburgh, Dresden, Cologne and Brussels, Senta in Marseille, Elsa, Sieglinde in Marseille and Lyon, Arabella in Graz, Marschallin at Staatsoper Berlin, Leipzig, Dresden, Taipei and Marseille, Kaiserin in Frankfurt and Amsterdam, Chrysothemis in Amsterdam and Dresden, Capriccio in Amsterdam, Dresden and Edinburgh Festival, Maria Stuarda/Maria in Geneva and Baltimore, and Fidelio in Lyon, Leipzig, Tokyo, Moscow, St Petersburg, Baden-Baden, Barcelona and Frankfurt; debut as Gutrune (Götterdämmerung) in new Ring production at Bayreuth with Thielemann 2006; debut with Ellen Orford in Geneva 2009 and Dresden 2010; Prof. of Lied and Oratorio, Univ. of Music and Performing Arts, Vienna 2007–; mainly concerts and recitals world-wide since 2009 and master-classes and opera workshops in Stift Altenburg, Jerusalem, Savonlinna, Amsterdam, Minneapolis, New York, Izmir, Cairo, Taiwan and Tokyo. *Recordings include:* Schubert Lieder and Bach Cantatas (Münchinger), Idomeneo, Arabella/Zdenka (with Kiri Te Kanawa and Geoffrey Tate), Rheintochter in Das Rheingold with Christoph von Dohnányi and Cleveland Symphony Orchestra, Gluck's Paride ed Elena, Die Weisse Rose by U. Zimmermann, Die grossmütige Tomyris by Reinhard Keiser, complete Fledermaus (Rosalinde) by Johann Strauss, Complete Songs by Clara Schumann, Last Songs by Strauss and Hugo Wolf, Das Buch mit 7 Siegeln by Franz Schmidt with Horst Stein, Von deutscher Seele by Hans Pfitzner, 2nd Symphonie by Gustav Mahler, 'Wer einsam ist, der hat es gut' by Alfred Uhl, Operettas by Lehar, Strauss and Kalman, Beethoven 9th Symphony with Kristjan Järvi, 'Prinzessin Traurigkeit oder das Känguruh im Schnee' by G.von Einem. *Radio:* all over in Europe, USA and Japan. *Television:* shows with Anneliese Rothenberger on ZDF, ORF, RAI and in France. *Honours:* Kammersängerin; Mozart Interpretationspreis (Austria), Richard Tauber Memorial Prize, Bach Preisträgerin, Int. Bach Competition, Leipzig 1980. *Current Management:* c/o Haydn Rawstron Ltd, First Floor, 29A High Street, West Wickham, Kent, BR4 0LP, England. *Telephone:* (20) 8777-6070. *Fax:* (20) 8777-4073. *E-mail:* enquiries@haydn-rawstron.com. *Website:* www.haydnrawstron.com. *Address:* Universität für Musik und Darstellende Kunst Wien, Institut 9, Penzingerstrasse 7, 1140 Vienna, Austria (office). *Website:* www.gabriele-fontana.com.

FONTYN, Jacqueline; Belgian composer; b. 27 Dec. 1930, Antwerp; m. Camille Schmit (deceased); two c. *Education:* studied piano with Ignace Bolotine, theory and composition with Marcel Quinet; studied in Paris with Max Deutsch and conducting in Vienna with Hans Swarowski. *Career:* Prof. of Music Theory, then Prof. of Composition, Koninklijk Conservatorium and Conservatoire Royal de Bruxelles 1963–90; has given lectures and seminars around the world; commissions from the Serge Koussevitzky Music Foundation, Library of Congress, Washington DC; mem. Royal Acad. of Belgium. *Compositions include:* symphony orchestra: Danceries 1956, Six Ebauches 1964, Evoluon 1972, Frises II 1976, Quatre Sites 1977, Créneaux 1982, Arachné 1983, In the Green Shade 1988, On a Landscape by Turner 1992, L'Anneau de Jade 1996, Goeie Hoop 1998, Au Fil des Siecles 2000, Ein (Kleiner) Winternachstraum 2002; chamber or string orchestra: Digressions 1964, Galaxie 1965, Colloques 1970, Per Archi for string orchestra 1973; solo and orchestra: Mouvements Concertants for two pianos and strings 1957, Violin Concerto 1974, Halo for harp and 16 instruments 1978, Colinda for cello and orchestra 1991, Vent d'Est for classical accordion and strings, Es ist ein Ozean concerto for flute, harpsichord and string orchestra 1999; symphonic band: Frises 1975, Créneaux 1983, Aratoro 1992, Blake's Mirror 1993; vocal music: Psalmus Tertius for baritone, choir and orchestra, Ephémères for mezzo-soprano and orchestra 1979, Alba for soprano, clarinet, cello, harp or percussion and piano 1981, Pro and Antiverb(e)s for soprano and cello 1984, Cheminement for soprano and and eight players 1986, Rosa, Rosae for soprano, contralto, clarinet, violin, harp and piano 1986, Rose des Sables for mezzo-soprano, speaker, female choir and orchestra 1990, Sieben Galgenlieder for soprano or mezzo-soprano, oboe or clarinet, cello and piano 1994, Ich Kannte Meine Seele Nicht for six mixed voices or six female voices 1997, Naïra for mezzo and piano 2000; solos and duos: Capriccio 1954, Ballade 1963, Le Gong 1980, Aura 1982, Spirales for two pianos 1971, Six Climats for cello and piano 1972, Controverse for bass clarinet and percussion 1983, La Devinière for violin and piano 1987–88, Polissonnerie for percussion and piano 1991, La Quinta Stagione for violin solo 1991, Analecta for two violins 1981; instrumental and chamber music: Piano Trio 1957, Horizons for string quartet 1977, Zones for flute, clarinet, cello, percussion and piano 1979, Meglio Tardi for flute, bass clarinet and piano 1994, La Fenêtre Ouverte for traverso, gamba and harpsichord 1996, Aube for flutes, guitar and piano 1998, En luminures for organ 2000, Koba for violin and piano 2000, Ein (Kleiner) Winternachtstraum 2002, Battements d'ailes 2001, Rivages Solitaires 1989, Virus Alert (opera) 2002, Eole 2005, L'Etanée 2006, Lieber Joseph 2007. *Recordings:* Spirales, Ballade, AUa, Capriccio, Le Gong, Mosaici, Bulles, Robert Groslot and Daniel Blumenthal; Ephémères, Per Archi, Halo, Psalmus Tertius, Aulos; Créneaux, Blake's Mirror, Aratoro, Frises, Grand Orchestre d'Harmonie 'Musique Royale des Guides', Norbert Nozy, WWM; Alba, Intermezzo, Mime 5, Fougères, Filigrane sul Cuor Della Terra, Compagnon de la Nuit, Ottavo Records; Pro and Antverb(e)s, Sieben Galgenlieder, Le Gong, Six Climats, Mosaïques, Musica a Quattro, Mime 2, Cyprès. *Honours:* Oscar Espla Prize, Fondation de France Prix Arthur Honegger 1988; awarded title of Baroness by the King of Belgium in recognition of her artistic merits. *Address:* POM, Rue Léon Dekaise 6, 1342 Ottignies, Belgium (office). *Telephone:* (10) 414695 (office). *Fax:* (10) 414695 (office). *E-mail:* performourmusic@yahoo.fr (office). *Website:* www.jacquelinefontyn.be.

FOO, Mei Yi; Malaysian pianist; b. 1980. *Education:* Royal Coll. of Music, Royal Acad. of Music, studied with Yonty Solomon, Christopher Elton and Alexander Satz. *Career:* has played at Royal Festival Hall and Wigmore Hall, London, Finlandia Hall, Helsinki, Salle Gaveau, Paris, Hong Kong City Hall, Verona Filarmonica, Megaron Athens and Zürich Kammerorchester Haus and with orchestras including BBC Concert Orchestra, Forth Worth Symphony, Helsinki Philharmonic, Hong Kong Sinfonietta and London Chamber

Orchestra; appearances at festivals worldwide including Lorin Maazel's Castletown Festival, Mänttä Festival Finland, Pharos Arts Foundation in Cyprus, Britten-Pears in Aldeburgh with Mitsuko Uchida, Lucerne, Huddersfield and Poznań Spring; has performed at Vienna's Schoenberg Centre, Park Lane Group at Southbank, Ultraschall Festival, Berlin and Pinakothek der Moderne in Munich; chamber music with musicians including Dimitri Ashkenazy, Shlomy Dobrinsky, Patricia Kopatchinskaya and Ashley Wass; keyboard teacher, Royal Welsh Coll. of Music 2013–. *Recordings:* Recital, Musical Toys 2013. *Honours:* Setiawan Tuanku Muhriz medal 2011; Maria Callas Grand Prix 2008, Newcomer of the Year, BBC Music Awards 2013. *Current Management:* c/o Elise Maingot, Athole Still Ltd, Foresters Hall, 25–27 Westow Street, London, SE19 3RY, England. *Telephone:* (20) 8768-6603. *Fax:* (20) 8771-8172. *E-mail:* elise@atholestill.co.uk. *Website:* www .atholestill.com. *E-mail:* info@meiyifoo.com (office). *Website:* www.meiyifoo .com (office).

FORBES, Rupert Oliver; British singer (tenor), conductor and stage director; b. 27 Jan. 1944, London, England; m. Elisabeth Burnett 1976, two s. *Education:* St John's Coll., Cambridge, Opera Studio, Zürich, studied with Pierre Bernac in Paris, Luigi Ricci in Rome, Arturo Merlini in Milan. *Career:* sang at the Zürich Opera 1970–75; engaged at the Stadttheater Basel from 1975, singing Mozart's Monostatos and Pedrillo, Jacquino in Fidelio, Tybalt in Roméo et Juliette, Lindoro, (Haydn's La Fedeltà Premiata), the comic roles in Les contes d'Hoffmann, Wagner's Steuermann, Hauptmann in Wozzeck (Berg) and Lord Barrat in Der Junge Lord; guest appearances in Mannheim, Wiesbaden, Kassel, Bremen and Freiburg; since 1990, freelance singer with Covent Garden, Scottish Opera, Glyndebourne, Rome, Wexford; stage director, Of Mice and Men (Carlisle Floyd) Opéra de Nantes; many engagements in concert and oratorio, notably in works by Bach. *Recordings:* as tenor: Visitatio Sepulchri by James MacMillan, Salome by Strauss; as conductor: Fauré Requiem, Opera Choruses, My Fair Lady, Fiddler on the Roof, Oliver, Carmen.

FORBES, Sebastian, BMus, MA, MusD, ARAM, LRAM, ARCO, ARCM; British composer, conductor and academic; *Emeritus Professor of Music, University of Surrey;* b. 22 May 1941, Amersham, Bucks; s. of Watson Forbes; m. 1st Hilary Spaight Taylor; two d.; m. 2nd Tessa Brady 1983; one s. one d. *Education:* Royal Acad. of Music, Kings Coll., Cambridge. *Career:* treble soloist 1953–56; BBC Producer 1964–67; organist, Trinity Coll., Cambridge 1968, East and West Clandon 2006–; Lecturer, Bangor Univ. 1968–72; Conductor, Aeolian Singers 1965–69, Seiriol Singers 1969–72, Horniman Singers 1981–90, Univ. of Surrey orchestras and choirs 1972–2006, Surrey Cantata 2008–, Vox Chamber Choir 2010–; Lecturer, Univ. of Surrey 1972–81, Prof. of Music 1981–06, Prof. Emer. 2006–; mem. PRS. *Compositions:* Essay for clarinet and orchestra (for Proms) 1970, Symphony (for Edinburgh Festival) 1972, Sinfonia I–III 1979, 1989, 1990, eight ensemble sonatas 1976–2001, organ and piano music, including Sonata-Rondo for piano 1996, chamber music, including five string quartets 1969, 1979, 1982, 1996, 2000, numerous works of church music. *Recordings:* String Quartet No. 1 1971, Capriccio for organ 1980, Bristol Mass 1992, Hymn to St Etheldreda 1996. *Honours:* McEwen Memorial Prize 1962, Clements Memorial Prize 1963, Radcliffe Music Award 1969, SPNM Carl Flesch Prize 1980. *Address:* Octave House, Boughton Hall Avenue, Send, Woking, Surrey, GU23 7DF, England (home). *Telephone:* (1483) 211785 (home). *E-mail:* s.forbes@surrey.ac.uk. *Website:* www .sebastianforbes.com; www.surreycantata.com.

FORBES-LANE, Andrew; British singer (tenor); b. 1960, Walton-on-Thames. *Education:* Manchester University, Royal Northern College of Music with Nicholas Powell. *Career:* appearances with Opera North, City of Birmingham Touring Opera, and Crystal Clear Opera; English National Opera 1993, in the premiere of Jonathan Harvey's Inquest of Love; Roles have included Don José, Alfredo, Tamino, Pinkerton, Lensky, Jenik in The Bartered Bride, Ferrando, Rodolfo, and Tichon in Katya Kabanova; Glyndebourne Festival and Tour debut 1999, as Ringmaster in The Bartered Bride; Don Curzio in Le nozze di Figaro, 2000; concerts with the RTE, Dublin, Hanover Band, London Proms, Salisbury Festival and in Antwerp. *Current Management:* c/o Neil Dalrymple, Music International, 13 Ardilaun Road, London, N5 2QR, England. *Telephone:* (20) 7359-5183. *Fax:* (20) 7226-9792. *E-mail:* music@musicint.co.uk.

FORD, Andrew, DCA; British/Australian composer, conductor, writer and broadcaster; b. 18 March 1957, Liverpool, England; s. of Alexander Douglas Ford and Marjorie Evans; m. 1st Margaret Morgan 1984; m. 2nd Anni Heino 2000; one d. *Education:* Univ. of Lancaster, UK, studied composition with Edward Cowie and John Buller, Univ. of Wollongong, NSW, Australia. *Career:* Fellow in Music, Univ. of Bradford 1978–82; Founder, Music Dir and performer, Big Bird Music Theatre 1982; Lecturer, Faculty of Creative Arts, Univ. of Wollongong 1983–95; presenter, The Music Show (ABC Nat. Radio) 1995–; many world and Australian premieres with the faculty's contemporary music ensemble, SCAW 1984–90, including Stockhausen's Stimmung 1986; Conductor, Australia Ensemble, Seymour Group, Magpie Musicians, Australian Chamber Orchestra; Composer-in-Residence, Bennelong Programme, Sydney Opera House 1985; own works played in Australia, Europe, South Africa, America, SE Asia; commissions; writer and broadcaster on music; featured composer at many festivals, including Aspekte, Salzburg 1984, Ferrara 1985, Istanbul, Buffalo, Up-Beat to The Tate, Liverpool, Aspen 1988, Adelaide 2000, 2004, Melbourne 2001, 2003, 2004, Australian Festival of Chamber Music 2009; Composer-in-Residence and Conductor, Australian

Chamber Orchestra 1993–94; Composer-in-Residence, Australian Nat. Acad. of Music 2009. *Compositions include:* music theatre: From Hand to Mouth 1984–85, Poe (opera) 1981–83, Whispers 1990, Casanova Confined 1995, Night and Dreams: The Death of Sigmund Freud 1999, Rembrandt's Wife (opera) 2007–09; children's opera: The Piper's Promise 1986–87, The World Knot 1987–88; orchestral: Concerto for orchestra 1980, Prologue, Chorale and Melodrama 1981, Epilogue to an Opera 1982, The Big Parade 1985–86, Imaginings for piano and orchestra 1991, The Widening Gyre for chamber orchestra 1993, The Great Memory for cello and orchestra 1994, The Unquiet Grave for viola and chamber orchestra 1998, The Furry Dance 1999, Sad Jigs for string orchestra 2005, Scenes from Bruegel for chamber orchestra and pre-recorded sound 2006, Headlong 2006; chamber ensemble: Chamber Concerto No. 1 1979, No. 2: Cries in Summer 1983, No. 3: In Constant Flight 1988, No. 4: 2003, Boatsong 1982, Four Winds for saxophone quartet 1984, Foolish Fires 1985, String Quartet No. 1 1985, No. 2: A Reel, a Fling and a Ghostly Galliard 2006, Ringing the Changes 1990, Pastoral 1991, Dance Maze for large ensemble 1996, Tattoo for 12 timpani and four pianos 1998, Icarus drowning for seven instruments; solo instruments: Like Icarus ascending for violin 1984, A Kumquat for John Keats for piano 1987, Swansong for viola 1987, ... les débris d'un rêve for piccolo and reverb 1992, The Waltz Book for piano (Jean Bogan Memorial Prize 2003) 2002, Thin Air for piano 2007; vocal: The Laughter of Mermaids for vocal ensemble, Insomnia for chorus and ensemble, Harbour for tenor and strings 1992, Dancing with Smoke for high voice and harp 1995, The Past for counter-tenor, flute and strings 1997, Learning to Howl for soprano and ensemble (Australian Music Centre Award for Best Composition, Paul Lowin Song Cycle Prize 2004) 2001, Tales of the Supernatural for folk singer and string quartet (APRA Award 2005) 2002, An Die Musik for chamber choir 2005, Elegy in a Country Graveyard for choir, brass band and backing track 2007, Domestic Advice for soprano and piano 2007, Symphony 2008, A Singing Quilt for choir, percussion and pre-recorded interviews 2008, Rembrandt's Wife (opera) 2009, Bright Shiners for solo violin and string orchestra 2009, Willow Songs for soprano, mezzo-soprano and ensemble 2009, The Musical Child for actor, piano duet and strings 2009, A Dream of Drowning for baritone and orchestra 2009, Rauha for large ensemble 2009, The Rising for brass band 2010, The Scattering of Light for violin, viola, cello and piano 2010, You Must Sleep, But I Must Dance for viola and percussion 2010, Waiting for the Barbarians for choir 2011, Blitz for orchestra, pre-recorded voices and optional chorus 2011, String Quartet No. 3 2012, String Quartet No. 4 2012, On Reflection for two pianos 2013, String Quartet No. 5 2013, Last Words for soprano and piano trio 2013, Uproar for 11 trombones and four bass drums 2013, Untuning the Sky radiophonic 2013, Common Ground for two string quartets 2014, The Drowners for baritone and orchestra 2015, Missa brevis for choir and organ 2015, Contradance for 11 instruments, Raga for electric guitar and orchestra 2016. *Radio includes:* Illegal Harmonies 1997, Dots on the Landscape 2001, Music and Fashion 2005, The Sound of Pictures 2006–09, Earth Dances 2015. *Publications include:* Composer to Composer 1993, Illegal Harmonies 1997, Undue Noise 2002, Speaking in Tongues: the Music of Van Morrison (with Martin Buzacott) 2005, In Defence of Classical Music 2005, The Sound of Pictures 2010, Try Whistling This 2012, Earth Dances 2015. *Honours:* Peggy Glanville-Hicks Composer Fellowship 1998–2000, Ian Potter Commission 2001, Australia Council Music Bd Fellowship 2005–06. *Address:* c/o The Music Show, ABC Radio National, GPO Box 9994, Sydney, NSW 2001, Australia. *Website:* www .andrewford.net.au.

FORD, Anthony Dudley, BMus; British musician; b. 19 Sept. 1935, Birmingham; m. Diane Clare Anwyl; one s. one d. *Education:* Birmingham Univ. *Career:* Sr Lecturer in Music, Univ. of Hull 1964–99; conductor, Hull Bach Choir 1969–; freelance harpsichordist and pianist; mem. Royal Musical Assocn. *Compositions:* various songs and choral pieces. *Publications:* editions: Giovanni Bononcini: When Saul was King, Aeterna Fac, Arias from the Vienna Operas; Purcell: Fantazias and In Nomines; contrib. to The Musical Times, Proceedings of the Royal Musical Association, Current Musicology, Die Musik in Geschichte und Gegenwart, Dictionary of National Biography. *Honours:* Barber Post-graduate Scholarship in Music 1957.

FORD, Bruce; American singer (tenor); b. Lubbock, Tex.; m. H. Ypma 1982; one s. *Education:* West Texas State Univ., Texas Tech. Univ., Houston Opera Studio. *Career:* sings in major opera houses in N America and Europe, specializing in Mozart and bel canto composers; Rossini's Otello (Covent Garden), Ermione (Glyndebourne), Zelmira, Ricciardo e Zoraide (Pesaro) revived for him; concert appearances include La Scala, Edinburgh Festival, Covent Garden, San Francisco Opera, Düsseldorf Symphonic, Chicago Lyric Opera and Amsterdam Concertgebouw; extensive recording career including many rare 19th century operas. *Honours:* Seal of Texas Tech. Univ. 1997. *Current Management:* c/o Athole Still Opera Ltd, 25–27 Westow Street, London, SE19 3RY, England. *Website:* www.atholestill.co.uk. *E-mail:* tenorbruceford@gmail.com; hetty.ford@gmail.com. *Website:* tenorbruceford .com.

FORD, Trevor, ARAM, FRSCM, FRSA, FISM, Dip RAM; British music administrator, writer, lecturer, flautist and choral director; b. 28 Nov. 1951, London; m. Marianne Barton 1979; two s. *Education:* Royal Acad. of Music. *Career:* orchestral flautist 1976–2006; Personnel Man., English Sinfonia 1979–2003; Orchestral Man., Philomusica of London 1981–2002, Midland Philharmonic 1982–96, Ambache Chamber Orchestra 1984–89; Gen. Man., English Festival Orchestra 1984–; Finance Admin., Concerts from Scratch 2002–12; Dir

Gander Music Ltd 2002–12; Prof., Guildhall School of Music and Drama 1996–, Birmingham Conservatoire 1999–2004; mem. Bd of Dirs Asscn of British Orchestras 1985–88, mem. Council 2004–06; Dir of Music, St John's Church, Palmers Green 1992–2008; Chair. Organists' Working Party 1993–95; mem. Council and Exec. and Treas. Royal Coll. of Organists (RCO) 1995–2004; mem. Council and Vice-Chair. Royal School of Church Music (RSCM), London 2001–08, Chair. RSCM London Area 2012–; Chair. London Youth Choir 2012–; Dir Scratch Concerts Ltd 2012–; mem. Council, Inc. Soc. of Musicians (Treas. 1996–2003, 2009–15), Musicians' Union, Asscn of British Choral Dirs, Church Music Soc.; Trustee, Newham Music Trust 2009–. *Publications:* The Musician's Handbook (ed.) 1986, 1991, 1996, The Art of Auditioning 1988, Church Music Quarterly 1989–2000. *Honours:* Hon. mem. Royal Coll. of Music; Hon. RCO. *Address:* 151 Mount View Road, London, N4 4JT, England (home). *Telephone:* (20) 8341-7809 (office). *Fax:* (20) 8340-0021 (office). *E-mail:* tfordandco@aol.com (office).

FORSBERG, Bengt; Swedish pianist; b. 1952, Edsleskog. *Education:* Gothenburg Music Acad., studied in London with Peter Feuchtwanger, in Copenhagen with Herman D. Koppel. *Career:* chamber musician and accompanist to leading soloists; Chamber Music Soc. of Lincoln Center, New York concerts 1999–2000 with Anne Sofie von Otter, featuring music by Korngold; further engagements at Wigmore Hall, London, Lisbon, Paris Châtelet, Graz and Gothenburg; other repertoire includes Mozart and Martinů Concertos, Bach's Well-Tempered Klavier, and works by Grieg, Sibelius, Fauré and Franck; numerous collaborations with Anne Sofie von Otter. *Recordings include:* Songs by Stenhammar and Sibelius, with Anne Sofie von Otter; Schumann's Frauenliebe und Leben, Lieder by Berg, Korngold, Strauss and Schubert; Songs by Grieg and Weill; Albums with Mats Lidström, cello. *Current Management:* Helena Friberg Artists Management, Nibblevägen 25, 2 tr, 177 36 Järfälla, Sweden. *Website:* www.hfam.se/Artister/BFs.html.

FORSBERG, Roland, DipMus; Swedish music director and organist; b. 18 Sept. 1939, Stockholm; m. 1st Margaretha Widlund 1967; m. 2nd Lisbeth Carlborg 1992; two s. one d. *Career:* Prof. of Music, Royal Acad. of Music, Stockholm 1961; Dir of Music, Norrmalm Church, Stockholm 1964–89; organist, Immanuel Church, Stockholm 1989–; musical expert, Swedish State Psalm Cttee 1976–86; mem. Kammarmusikföreningen Samtida Musik, Föreningen Svenska Tonsättare, Stockholm. *Compositions include:* Liten Svit for organ 1959, Passacaglia for organ 1960, Verbum Christi for voice 1963, 12 Sacred Songs 1964, Musica Solenne for organ 1965, Orgeljojk for two organs 1975, Sicut Cervus Organ Symphony 1977, Sonata Lapponica for violin and piano 1980, Sonatina da cappella for violin and organ 1983, three piano sonatas, concertos for flute and oboe, Sacred Concertos for solo voices and organ, songs, hymns, motets, cantatas, oratorios, masses and other choral works, eight organ suites, Psalm Sonata for mixed chorus (English words) 1984, Credo Triptych for organ 1988, Memoria for violin and piano or organ 1988, Symphonic Pictures for Archipelago for organ and brass orchestra 1995, Missa in Millennium Immanuel 1998–99. *Recordings:* Kärlekens musik, Tre orglar i Västervik, En gång blir allting stilla, Sjögrens Legender, Autography: Swedish Composers Play Their Own Works, Orgelmusik i Sjövik, Skärgårdsorgel, Archipelago the Mid-Eighteenth Century Organ of Utö. *Honours:* STIM Composers' Scholarships, Stockholm 1974, 1981, 1985, Föreningen Svenska Tonsättare 1996.

FORST, Judith Doris, OC, BMus; Canadian singer (mezzo-soprano); b. 7 Nov. 1943, New Westminster, BC; d. of Gordon Stanley and Euna Jessie Lumb; m. Graham N. Forst 1964; one s. one d. *Education:* Univ. of British Columbia. *Career:* has appeared in USA with New York Metropolitan Opera, New York City Opera, Seattle Opera, San Francisco Opera, New Orleans Opera, Fort Worth Opera, Santa Fe Opera, Washington, DC Opera, Miami Opera, Baltimore Opera and San Diego Opera Soc., in Canada with Canadian Opera Co. (Toronto), Vancouver Opera, Calgary Opera, Montréal Symphony Orchestra, Vancouver Symphony Orchestra and Hamilton Symphony Orchestra, and in Europe with Munich State Opera (Germany), Symphony Orchestra of Barcelona (Spain) and Orchestre de Radio France (Paris); Guest Lecturer, Univ. of British Columbia, Univ. of Montréal; mem. Asscn of Canadian TV and Radio, American Guild of Musical Artists. *Honours:* Hon. LLD (Univ. of British Columbia) 1992; Hon. DMus (Univ. of Victoria) 1995; Order of BC 2001; won Metropolitan Opera auditions 1968, CBC Cross-Canada Talent Contest 1968, Canadian Woman of the Year 1978, Greater Miami Opera Asscn Performer of the Year 1980, Univ. of British Columbia Distinguished Alumnus of the Year 1986, Freeman City of Port Moody 1992. *Address:* 428 Princeton Ave, Port Moody, BC V3H 3L3, Canada (home). *Telephone:* (604) 939-8323 (home).

FORSTER, Andreas; German singer (baritone); b. 17 Sept. 1949, Naumberg. *Education:* studied in Berlin and in Essen with Gladys Kuchta. *Career:* debut in Detmold 1974, as Schaunard in La Bohème; sang at Kaiserslautern 1975–76, Saarbrucken 1976–78, Nuremberg 1978–88; Staatstheater Hanover from 1988; guest appearances at the Staatsoper Berlin, Düsseldorf, Cologne, Dortmund, Stuttgart, Munich, Wiesbaden and Orlando, Florida, USA; roles have included Verdi's Nabucco, Rigoletto, Macbeth and Simon Boccanegra, Germont, Renato, Iago and Amonasro, Rodrigo, Luna, Donizetti's Enrico, Belcore and Dulcamara, Gerard, Escamillo, Eugene Onegin, Wolfram, Amfortas, Marcello, Olivier in Capriccio and Mozart's Don Giovanni and Count; concert engagements in works by Bach, Handel, Beethoven, Brahms, Mahler and Penderecki; lieder recitals and broadcast concerts in Germany,

France and Italy; sang Grigoris in The Greek Passion and Telramund in Lohengrin at Hannover 2000.

FORSYTH, Malcolm Denis, OC, BMus, MMus, DMus; Canadian composer, conductor and trombonist; b. 8 Dec. 1936, Pietermaritzburg, South Africa; s. of Claude McLean Forsyth and Doris Bertha Relph; m. Lesley Eales 1965 (divorced 1984); one d. *Education:* Univ. of Cape Town, Canford Summer School of Music. *Career:* Conductor, Chamber Choir and Orchestra, Univ. of Cape Town 1962–64, St Cecilia Orchestra 1977–86, Edmonton Wind Sinfonia 1978–79, West Wind Chamber Ensemble 1980–83, Chamber Choir, Univ. of Witwatersrand 1983, Mill Creek Colliery Band 2002–10; guest conductor, Cape Town, CAPAB and Edmonton Symphony Orchestras, Alberta Ballet Orchestra, National Orchestra, SABC, Johannesburg; Asst Principal Trombonist, Cape Town Symphony Orchestra 1961–67; co-Principal Trombonist, CAPAB Symphony Orchestra 1971–72; Principal Trombonist, Edmonton Symphony Orchestra 1973–80; Jr Lecturer, Coll. of Music, Univ. of Cape Town 1967; Asst Prof., Univ. of Alberta, Edmonton, Canada 1968–71, Assoc. Prof. 1971–77, Prof. of Music 1977–, Dir, Concert Activity 1984–86, Artistic Dir Music Dept 1987–89; McCalla Prof. 1990–91; Visiting Prof., Cape Town and Witwatersrand Univs, Univ. of Saskatchewan 2009–10; Composer-in-Residence, Banff Centre 1975–78, Festival of the Sound 1991, Univ. of Alberta 1996–2002, Saskatchewan New Music Festival 1997; commissions include Canada Council, CBC and Univ. of Cape Town; Fellow Camargo Foundation, Cassis, France 1993. *Compositions:* 150 works for orchestra, band, ensembles, piano, vocal solos and choir, including three symphonies, Atayoskewin, Suite for Orchestra 1984, Trumpet Concerto 1987, Valley of a Thousand Hills for orchestra 1989, These Cloud Capp'd Towers for trombone and orchestra 1990, Evangeline for soprano, trumpet and chamber orchestra 1994, Electra Rising for cello and chamber orchestra 1995, Accordion Concerto 1998, Double Concerto for viola, cello and orchestra 2004. *Honours:* Composer of the Year, Canada 1989, JUNO Award for Best Classical Composition 1987, 1995, 1998, Queen's Jubilee Medal 2003. *Address:* 9259 Strathearn Drive, Edmonton, AB T6C 4E1, Canada (home). *Telephone:* (780) 469-4992 (home). *Fax:* (780) 468-1935 (office). *E-mail:* composer@shaw.ca (office). *Website:* members.shaw.ca/composer (office).

FORTE, Cinzia; Italian singer (soprano); b. 1968. *Career:* appearances at La Scala Milan as Lisette in La Sonnambula, as Pamina at La Coruña, Gilda in Rigoletto in Venice and Lucia di Lammermoor; Teti in Rossini's Le nozze di Teti e di Peleo at Pesaro, La Traviata in Modena, Lisette in Puccini's La Rondine at Covent Garden, Corina in Rossini's Il viaggio a Reims in Oviedo, Lucia in Tokyo and Adina in L'elisir d'amore at Venice; other roles include Susanna and Musetta; Baroque repertory includes Vivaldi's Farnace, Messiah, Te Deum by Charpentier and Pergolesi's Stabat Mater. *Current Management:* c/o Angelo Gabrielli, Stage Door, Via San Giorgio 4, 40121 Bologna, Italy. *Telephone:* (051) 262126. *Fax:* (051) 271452. *E-mail:* info@stagedoor.it. *Website:* www.stagedoor.it. *E-mail:* info@cinziaforte.it (office). *Website:* www.cinziaforte.it.

FORTIN, Lyne; Canadian singer (soprano); b. 28 April 1962, Québec. *Education:* studied in Québec and with Marlena Malas. *Career:* sang with Canada Piccola Opera 1985–; frequent concert appearances; Voice Teacher, Montréal Opera Apprentice Programme. *Opera appearances include:* Susanna in Marriage of Figaro and Gilda in Rigoletto at Québec Opera 1987, 1989, Montréal Opera 1990–, including Olympia in Les Contes d'Hoffman, Gounod's Juliette and Leila in The Pearl Fishers 1996, Norina in Don Pasquale at Philadelphia 1991, Micaela in Carmen at Portland Opera 1994, Adina in Elisir d'Amore at Seattle and Countess in Marriage of Figaro at Montréal 1988, Donna Anna in Don Giovanni with Scottish Opera 2001, Countess in Marriage of Figaro and Electra in Idomeneo at Vlaamse Opera, Antwerp. *Recordings include:* Les Grands Duos d'Amour de l'Opéra Française (with Richard Margison) 1987, Noel 1993, Lyne Fortin Live 1995, Mozart 1999. *Honours:* special prize CBC Nat. Competition for Young Performers 1986, winner Pavarotti Int. Vocal Competition 1988, first prize and grand prize CIBC Nat. Competition Festival of Music, Concourse de musique de Québec, Medal of 125th Anniversary of Canada for contribution to community 1992. *Current Management:* Pinnacle Arts Management, 889 Ninth Avenue, 2nd Floor, New York, NY 10019, USA. *Telephone:* (212) 397-7915. *Fax:* (212) 397-7920. *Website:* www.pinnaclearts.com. *E-mail:* kaskou@sprint.ca (office).

FORTIN, Viktor, Mag. Dr; Austrian composer and academic; *Professor Emeritus, Kunst Universität, Graz;* b. 14 May 1936, Fohnsdorf, Styria; s. of Viktor Fortin and Maria Fortin; m.; one s. *Education:* Steiermärkisches Landes Konservatorium, Univ. of Vienna, Akad. für Musik und Kunst, Graz, Karl Franzens Univ., Graz. *Career:* Prof. Emer., Kunst Univ., Graz 2004–; mem. Osterreichischer Komponistenbund, Steirischer Tonkünstlerbund. *Compositions include:* Appalachian sonata for flute and piano 1970, Happy Suite for strings, piano and percussion 1978, Maja's Orchestra for strings and piano, five Love Songs with texts from Erich Fried, Marginals to the Spring 1986, Ohhh Pinocchio! (Opera House, Graz 1994–95, Tartu, Estonia 1999, Kraków, Poland 2005), Concerto for speaker and orchestra, with texts from Mozart letter (Graz 1994, Lublin 1997, Quito, Ecuador 1998), Archibald's Adventures for two speakers and orchestra 1997, 1998 (Cairo and Graz 1999), Der Kleine Klabautermann, Blacksmith Variations, Concerto for soprano recorder and strings, Hafer Quartet, Konzert für Alphorn und Blasorchester 2005, Borderline Sonata for trombone and piano 2005, Opera Franz Jaegerstaetter 2006, Tausendblütennarr 2013, Cantata Jeder Ton ist wie eine Stern 2007, Psalm 104 2007, Hengsberger Sinfonie 2008, Abenteuer

Ohrwurm for clarinet, choir, speaker and piano 2009, Sparkling Duet for violin and piano, Pinocchio, the flute-player for orchestra and solo recorder 2010, Alice in Wonderland for orchestra, solo violin and speaker 2011, Kinder Quartett for violin, viola and cello, Klavier, Sinfonietta for strings, Grosse Verneigung vor Felix for viola, clarinet and piano 2012, Musica liquida for recorder quintet 2012, Philharmonisches aus Salvador al Bahia de Todos os Santos for two violins, Desioso sogno per la melodia for string quartet, Vier-Flöten-Trio for recorders (soprano, alto, tenor, bass – one player), violin and piano, Remember Holidays for soprano recorder, treble recorder and guitar, Sestetto nel blu for two violins, two violas and two cellos, Scherzo Bambini for violin, viola and violoncello, Sechs Kinderlieder for children's choir, Vier blecherne Bagatellen for trumpet, trombone and piano 2013, Concerto for Steirische Harmonika and orchestra 2013, Concerto for recorder and wind orchestra 2013, Blasorchester 2013, Romanze für Violoncello und Klavier 2014, Elf Würfe für junge Streicher 2014, Pinocchio-Blues 2014, Liebeserklärungen an die Blockflöte 2015. *Plays include:* Ohhh Pinocchio! 1994, Viktor Fortin and Friends 1996, Franz Jägerstätter, Oper in 10 Bildern und einem Vorspiel, Tausendblütennarr (children's opera) 2013. *Recordings include:* Ohhh Pinocchio! 1994, Viktor Fortin and Friends 1996, Archibald's Adventure 2000, Missa duri montis 2003, Concertino for bassoon and strings 2004, Concert amusant (flute and strings) 2004, Sinfonietta for strings 2008. *Publications include:* Doblinger, Vienna, Concert for soprano recorder and string orchestra 1992, Brass Light, Not Easy, Moeck Germany, Lambsborner Nuesse for recorder-orchestra 1997, Mitteilungen des Steirischen Tonkünstlerbundes 2004; contrib. to Musik aus Österreich 1998. *Honours:* Hon. Pres. Steirischer Tonkunstlerbund; Goldenes Ehrenzeichen des Landes Steiermark 1995. *Address:* Halmweg 13, 8054 Graz, Austria (home). *Telephone:* 650-6898587 (mobile) (home). *Fax:* (316) 296207 (office). *E-mail:* fortin@aon.at. *Website:* www.fortin.at.

FORTUNATO, D'Anna, BMus, MM; American singer (mezzo-soprano); *Professor of Voice, New England Conservatory;* b. 21 Feb. 1945, Pittsburgh, PA. *Education:* New England Conservatory with Frederick Jagel and Gladys Miller, Berkshire Music Center with Phyllis Curtin. *Career:* concert appearances in Pittsburgh, Detroit, Louisville, Atlanta and Minnesota; recitals with the Chamber Music Soc. of Lincoln Center and with the Boston Musica Viva ensemble; taught at Longy School of Music, Cambridge 1974–; mem., Liederkreis Ensemble; European debut, Paris 1980, as Purcell's Dido with the Boston Camerata; sang in the premiere of John Harbison's opera Full Moon in March, New York 1979; New York recital debut 1981; New York City Opera debut 1983, as Ruggiero in Handel's Alcina; has sung as soloist with many leading US orchestras, including Ravel's L'Enfant et les Sortilèges and Verdi's Falstaff with Seiji Ozawa and the Boston Symphony Orchestra, Handel's Messiah with the Nat. Symphony, Mozart's Requiem with Nat. Arts Center Orchestra, Ottawa, Gluck's Orfeo with the Philadelphia Orchestra, Berlioz's Roméo et Juliette with Minnesota Orchestra and the San Francisco Symphony, Ah, Perfido! with the Pittsburgh Symphony, Honegger's Jeanne d'Arc au Bucher with New York Philharmonic and Kurt Masur, Berio's Folksongs with New Jersey Symphony and Omaha Symphony; has sung in world premieres of works by John Harbison, Stephen Jaffee, Stephen Albert, John Heiss; Prof. of Voice, New England Conservatory. *Recordings include:* Handel's Deidamia (role of Achille), Honegger's Jeanne d'Arc au Bucher (Heavenly Voice, with New York Philharmonic), Victorian Baseball: Hurrah for our National Game, Amy: Beach Songs (New York Magazine, Boston Globe, New York Post CD of the Year), Dido and Aeneas (with the Boston Camerata), David Schiff's Gimple the Fool, Marilyn Ziffrin's Songs & Arias. *Honours:* Distinguished Alumni Award New England Conservatory, Bucknell Univ., co-winner Naumburg Chamber Music Prize 1980, Jacobo Peri Award, New England Opera Club 2000. *Address:* 33 Sycamore Street, Boston, MA 02131 (home); Thea Dispeker Inc., 59 East 54th Street, Suite 81, New York, NY 10022, USA (office). *Telephone:* (617) 469-4880 (home); (212) 421-7676 (office). *E-mail:* dannateach@aol.com (home); info@dispeker.com (office). *Website:* www.dispeker.com (office).

FORTUNE, George; American singer (baritone) and voice teacher; b. 13 Dec. 1931, Boston, Mass. *Education:* Brown Univ., Providence, Boston Univ., studied with Todd Duncan, Georgetown Univ., Musikakademie Vienna. *Career:* debut at Ulm 1960, as Fluth in Die Lustigen Weiber von Windsor; guest appearances in Bordeaux, Brussels, Strasbourg, Hamburg and Munich; Glyndebourne 1964, as the Count in Le nozze di Figaro; Santa Fe 1967, in the US premiere of Henze's Boulevard Solitude; mem. Deutsche Oper Berlin 1965–; roles include Mozart's Figaro and Guglielmo, Rigoletto, Giulio Cesare, Iago, Amonasro, Posa, Scarpia, Gerard and Wolfram; further appearances in Düsseldorf, Frankfurt, Milan and Zürich; debut at the Metropolitan Opera New York in 1985 with Tonio, further parts include Jack Rance and Alfio; sang Scarpia at the Teatro San Carlos, Lisbon 1988, the High Priest in Samson et Dalila at the Deutsche Oper Berlin 1989; Barnaba in La Gioconda 1998; season 2000–01 as Scarpia at the Prague State Opera, Gounod's Capulet at Strasbourg, Count Luna for the Deutsche Oper; numerous concert engagements. *Recordings include:* Thérèse by Massenet, Olympie by Spontini, Christus by Liszt, Armida by Dvořák, La Vita Nuova by Wolf Ferrari. *Honours:* Kammersänger of Berlin 1990; Howard Foundation Grant, Grad. School of Brown Univ., First Prize, Int. Competition of Radio Stations of Germany, Munich 1961. *Address:* Keithstrasse 12, 12307 Berlin, Germany (home). *E-mail:* fortune.berlin@gmail.com (home).

FOSTER, Catherine; British singer (soprano); b. 1975, Nottingham, England. *Education:* Royal Northern College of Music, National Opera Studio. *Career:* appearances as Britten's Governess in Nottingham, Donna Anna at Dartington and Musetta for the Mananan Festival; WNO and ENO with the Queen of Night; concerts include Mozart's Requiem and C Minor Mass, Schubert's Mass in G, Elijah, the Brahms Requiem and Haydn's Theresienmesse, 1999–2000 season. *Honours:* Dame Eva Turner Award, 1997; Mario Lanza Opera Prize. *Current Management:* Dietrich Eberhard Gross Künstleragentur, Eschenweg 19, 61440 Oberursel/Frankfurt, Germany. *Telephone:* (61) 72934144. *Fax:* (61) 72934145. *E-mail:* d.e.gross@grossagentur.de. *Website:* www.grossagentur.de.

FOSTER, Donald H., BS, MusM, PhD; American academic; *Professor Emeritus, Univ. of Cincinnati;* b. 30 April 1934, Detroit, Mich. *Education:* Wayne State Univ., Univ. of Michigan. *Career:* mem. of music faculty, Olivet Coll., Mich. 1960–67; Prof. of Musicology, Coll.-Conservatory of Music, Univ. of Cincinnati, Ohio 1967–99, Prof. Emer. 1999–; mem. American Musicological Soc., American Asscn of Univ. Profs. *Publications include:* L'histoire de la femme adultère by Louis-Nicolas Clérambault 1974, Louis-Nicolas Clérambault 1676–1749: Two Cantatas for Soprano and Chamber Ensemble 1979, Symphonies concertantes of Jean-Baptiste Davaux, Overtures of Franz Beck, Jean-Philippe Rameau: A Guide to Research 1989, Sourcebook for Research in Music (co-author) 1993; contrib. to Symphony Orchestras of the USA: Selected Profiles 1986, Opera Quarterly, Recherches sur la musique française classique, The Diapason, Acta Musicologica, Current Musicology, L'orgue–cahiers et mémoires. *Honours:* Fulbright Grant 1962. *Address:* 393 Amazon Avenue, Cincinnati, OH 45220, USA (home).

FOSTER, Jillian; British singer (soprano); b. 1970, England. *Education:* Royal Acad. of Music. *Career:* has sung with Kent Opera, Wexford Festival, Dublin Grand Opera and the Richard Strauss Soc.; roles have included Tosca, Mimi, Donna Elvira, Violetta, Agathe and Arabella; sang Garsenda in Francesca da Rimini with the Chelsea Opera Group and Messiah and Beethoven's Ninth with the Tokyo Philharmonic. *Honours:* winners' concert at the Pavarotti Competition 1992.

FOSTER, Lawrence Thomas; American conductor; b. 23 Oct. 1941, Los Angeles, Calif.; m. Angela Foster 1972; one d. *Education:* studied with Fritz Zweig and Karl Böhm and at Bayreuth Festival and Tanglewood Master Classes. *Career:* Music Dir, Young Musicians Foundation, Los Angeles 1960–64; Conductor, San Francisco Ballet 1960–64; Asst Conductor, LA Philharmonic Orchestra 1965–68; Chief Guest Conductor, Royal Philharmonic Orchestra, London 1969–74; Music Dir, Houston Symphony Orchestra 1971–78; Music Dir, Orchestre Philharmonique, Monte Carlo 1978–96; Music Dir, Duisburg Orchestra, FRG 1982–86; Music Dir, Chamber Orchestra of Lausanne 1985; conductor, Jerusalem Symphony Orchestra 1990; Music Dir, Aspen Music Festival and School 1990–96; Music Dir, Orquestra Ciutat de Barcelona 1995–2002, Prin. Guest Conductor 2002–; Artistic Dir, Georg Enescu Festival 1998–2001; Music Dir, Gulbenkian Orchestra, Lisbon 2002–13, Orchestre et Opéra Nat. de Montpellier 2009–12, Opéra de Marseille and Orchestre Philharmonique de Marseille 2013–. *Film appearance:* Belle toujours 2006. *Honours:* Pres.'s decoration for services to Romanian music 2003; Koussevitsky Memorial Conducting Prize, Tanglewood 1966, Orfée d'Or, Académie National du Disque Lyrique (for his recording of Vincent D'Indy's L'Etranger with Opera et Orchestre National de Montpellier Languedoc Roussillon) 2013. *Current Management:* c/o Opus 3 Artists, Pariser Straße 62, 10719 Berlin, Germany. *Telephone:* (30) 88910150. *Fax:* (30) 88910152. *E-mail:* info.berlin@opus3artists.com. *Website:* www.opus3artists.com/artists/lawrence-foster.

FOU, Ts'ong; British (b. Chinese) pianist; b. 10 March 1934, s. of the late Fu Lei; m. 1st Zamira Menuhin 1960 (divorced 1970); one s.; m. 2nd Hijong Hyun 1973 (divorced 1978); m. 3rd Patsy Toh 1987; one s. *Education:* studied in China with Mario Paci, Warsaw Conservatory with Zbigniew Drzewiecki. *Career:* debut with Shanghai Municipal Orchestra, playing Beethoven's Emperor Concerto 1951; gave 500 concerts in E. Europe while studying in Poland 1953–58; moved to UK 1958, London debut 1959; solo appearances in Europe, Scandinavia, the Far East, Australia and New Zealand, North and South America; currently Visiting Prof., Int. Foundation for Pianists, Como, Italy and Shanghai Conservatory, China. *Solo piano CDs:* Bach, Chopin, Debussy, Handel, Mozart, Scarlatti, Schubert and Schumann. *Piano concerto CDs:* Chopin and Mozart. *Honours:* Dr hc (Hong Kong Univ.); Third Prize, Bucharest Piano Competition 1953, Int. Chopin Competition, Warsaw 1955. *Address:* 62 Aberdeen Park, London, N5 2BL, England (home). *Telephone:* (20) 7226-9589 (home). *Fax:* (20) 7704-8896 (home). *E-mail:* foutoh@yahoo.co.uk (home).

FOUCHECOURT, Jean-Paul; French singer (tenor); b. 10 Aug. 1958, Blanzy. *Education:* trained as conductor and saxophone player; vocal studies under the influence of Cathy Berberian. *Career:* many appearances with such early music groups as Les Arts Florissants, and Les Musiciens du Louvre; Rameau's Les Indes Galantes, Les Fêtes d'Hébé and Zoroastre, Lully's Atys and Charpentiers's David et Jonatas under the direction of William Christie, concerts in France and on tour throughout Europe, America and Japan; Rameau's Hippolyte et Aricie and Lully's Phaëton under Marc Minkowski; further engagements in Purcell's Fairy Queen at the Aix Festival, Monteverdi's Orfeo under René Jacobs at Salzburg, L'Incoronazione di Poppea with Christophe Rousset for Netherlands Opera and Monteverdi's Ulisse with

Michel Corboz at Geneva; other repertory includes the Berlioz Roméo et Juliette (with John Eliot Gardiner), Offenbach's Orphée aux Enfers, Mozart's Nozze di Figaro and Poulenc's Les Mamelles de Tiresias with Seiji Ozawa (on tour to Japan 1996); season 1997–98 in the title role of Rameau's Platée with the Royal Opera and at Edinburgh; L'Enfant et les Sortilèges at Florence 1998; Debut at the Met in New York with Tales of Hoffmann; season 1999–2000 included Golden Cockerel at Covent Garden, Madama Butterfly with Boston Symphony Orchestra, Poppea at Aix en Provence Festival and Platée at the Bastille; Arnalta in Poppea for Netherlands Opera 2001; Ravel's L'Heure Espagnole, London Proms 2002, Rameua's Platée, Santa Fe Opera 2007. *Recordings include:* Lully's Atys and Phaëton; Mondonville's Titon et L'Aurore and Les Fêtes de Paphos; Rameau's Les Indes Galantes, Pygmalion and Hippolyte et Aricie; Socrate by Satie; Les Mamelles de Tiresias, Orphée et Euridice 2005. *E-mail:* pleintelev@aol.com. *Website:* www.fouchecourt.com.

FOUNTAIN, Ian; British pianist and professor of piano; *Professor of Piano, Royal Academy of Music*; b. 15 Oct. 1969, Welwyn Garden City, Herts., England. *Education:* chorister at New Coll., Oxford, Winchester Coll., Royal Northern Coll. of Music, Manchester with Sulamita Aronovsky. *Career:* has performed widely in UK, in major London recital halls and in Europe and USA from 1986, with recitals at festivals including Sintra, Stresa, Montpellier, Davos, Kuhmo, Berlin, Schleswig-Holstein, Prague Spring and Ravello; worked with leading orchestras, including London Symphony Orchestra, Czech Philharmonic, Israel Philharmonic, City of Birmingham Symphony Orchestra, Philharmonic Orchestra, Bournemouth Symphony Orchestra, English Chamber Orchestra, Royal Liverpool Philharmonic Orchestra, Britten Sinfonia, Deutches Symphonie-Orchester, Singapore Symphony Orchestra, Polish Nat. Radio Symphony, Slovak Philharmonic and Jerusalem Symphony; Prof. of Piano, RAM, London 2001–. *Recordings include:* 20th Century Works for Piano, Beethoven Diabelli Variations, 'Non-Beethoven' Diabelli Variations. *Honours:* Hon. ARAM 2005, Hon. RAM 2014; winner, Viotti-Valsesia Int. Piano Competition (Italy) 1986, jt winner, Arthur Rubinstein Int. Piano Competition 1989. *Current Management:* c/o Connaught Artists Management Ltd, Penhurst House, 352–356 Battersea Park Road, London, SW11 3BY, England. *Telephone:* (20) 7978-0144. *Fax:* (20) 7978-0134. *E-mail:* patrick@connaughtartists.com. *Website:* www.connaughtartists.com. *Address:* Royal Academy of Music, Marylebone Road, London, NW1 5HT, England (office). *Telephone:* (20) 7873-7373 (office). *Fax:* (20) 7873-7374 (office). *Website:* www.ram.ac.uk (office).

FOUNTAIN, Primous, III; American composer; b. 1 Aug. 1949, St Petersburg, FL. *Education:* DePaul University, Chicago. *Career:* freelance composer from 1968, including association with the Arthur Mitchell Dance Theatre of Harlem. *Compositions include:* Manifestations for orchestra, 1969; Grudges for orchestra, 1972; Ritual Dance of the Amaks for orchestra, 1973; Duet for flute and bassoon, 1974; Cello Concerto, 1976; Ricia for violin, cello and piano, 1980; Harp Concerto, 1981; Symphony No. 1, Epitome of the Oppressed, 1984. *Honours:* BMI Composition Award, 1968; Guggenheim Fellowships, 1974, 1977; Award, American Academy and Institute of Arts and Letters.

FOURNIER, Brigitte; Swiss singer (soprano); b. 14 June 1961, Nendaz. *Education:* studied in Berne, Essen and Lausanne. *Career:* sang in concert in works by Bach, Handel, Mozart, Schubert, Rameau and Honegger; concert and lieder venues at the Aix and Montpellier Festivals, and throughout Switzerland; sang Musetta in La Bohème at Biel/Solothurn, Naiad in Ariadne auf Naxos at Lausanne and Zerbinetta at Klagenfurt (1991), Toulouse 1995, as Constance in Dialogues des Carmélites, Geneva 1996, as Mozart's Blondchen; season 2000–01 as Lucia in The Rape of Lucretia at Lausanne and the Woodbird in Siegfried at Geneva. *Recordings include:* Zelenka Requiem. *Current Management:* c/o Caecilia Lyric Department, Rennweg 15, 8001 Zürich, Switzerland. *Telephone:* 2213388. *Fax:* 2117182. *E-mail:* caecilia@caecilia-lyric.ch. *Website:* www.caecilia.ch.

FOURNILLIER, Patrick; French conductor; b. 26 Dec. 1954, Neuilly-sur-Seine. *Education:* studied with Louis Fourestier and Pierre Dervaux in Paris, Strasbourg Conservatoire with Jean-Sebastian Bereau, Salzburg Mozarteum with Leopold Hager, studied with Franco Ferrara at the Accademiana Chigiana, Siena. *Career:* Asst Conductor to Jean Claude Casadesus, Orchestre National de Lille 1983–85, Artistic Dir –1986; Music Dir, Nouvel Orchestre de St Etienne 1988–; Dir, Sinfonietta d'Amiens 1989–92; Music Dir, Massenet Festival, St Etienne 1988–; important revivals of such neglected Massenet operas as Amadis, Thérèse, Cléopâtre, Esclarmonde and Grisélidis; Le Roi de Lahore by Massenet 1997; premieres have included Quatre-Vingt-Treize by Antoine Duhamel 1989. *Honours:* Hans Haring Prize, Salzburg, 1982; Second Prize, Besancon Int. Conductors Competition, 1984; Prizewinner, Vaclav Talich Competition Prague, 1985; Second Prize, Grzerorz Fitelberg Competition at Katowice, 1987. *Current Management:* The Music Partnership, New Broad Street House, New Broad Street, London, EC2M 1NH, England.

FOWKE, Philip Francis, FRAM; British concert pianist; b. 28 June 1950, Gerrards Cross, Bucks.; s. of Francis H.V. Fowke and Florence L. (née Clutton) Fowke. *Education:* Downside Abbey School. *Career:* began piano studies with Marjorie Withers 1957; awarded RAM Scholarship to study with Gordon Green 1967; Wigmore Hall debut 1974; UK concerto debut with Royal Liverpool Philharmonic 1975; Royal Festival Hall debut 1977; BBC Promenade Concert debut 1979; US debut 1982; debuts in Denmark, Bulgaria, France, Switzerland, Hong Kong, Belgium and Italy 1983; Austrian debut at Salzburg Mozart week 1984; German debut 1985; New Zealand debut 1994; now appears regularly with all the leading orchestras in UK and gives regular recitals and concerto performances for BBC Radio; Prof., RAM 1984–91, Welsh Coll. of Music and Drama 1994; Head of Keyboard Dept, Trinity Coll. of Music, London 1995–98, Sr Fellow 1998; recordings of Bliss, Chopin, Delius, Finzi, Rachmaninoff and Tchaikovsky piano concertos; Recitalist and Piano Tutor, Dartington Int. Summer School 1996, 1997, 2000; concerto appearances with the Hallé Orchestra and in USA 1997; 50th Birthday Recital, Wigmore Hall, London 2000; soloist, BBC Proms 2001; mem. London Piano Quartet; Vice-Chair. European Piano Teachers' Asscn (UK) presenter and contrib. to music programmes on BBC Radio and to nat. press. *Recordings include:* Hoddinott Piano Concerto, CD album of film scores 1998. *Publications:* reviews and obituaries in nat. press. *Honours:* Countess of Munster Musical Trust Award 1972, Nat. Fed. of Music Socs. Award 1973, BBC Piano Competition 1974, Winston Churchill Fellowship 1976 and numerous other awards and prizes. *Current Management:* Patrick Garvey Management, 40 North Parade, York YO30 7AB, England. *Telephone:* (1904) 621222. *Fax:* (1723) 330050. *E-mail:* patrick@patrickgarvey.com. *Website:* www.philipfowke.co.uk.

FOWLER, Bruce; American singer (tenor); b. 1965, West-Monroe, LA. *Career:* Chicago Opera from 1990, notably as Nemorino in L'Elisir d'amore; Lindoro in Il Turco in Italia at Cleveland and Tonio in La Fille du régiment at Toronto (1994); Pesaro Festival, 1993, as Carlo in Rossini's Armida, and as Ferrando in Così fan tutte at Catania; Bonn Opera, 1995–96, in La Rondine and as Rossini's Almaviva; Sang Ferrando for Palm Beach Opera, 1998; Season 2000–01 as Rossini's Lindoro at the Deutsche Oper Berlin, Idreno in Semiramide at St Paul and Ramiro in Cenerentola at Cincinnati; Alfredo for Finnish National Opera. *Recordings include:* Armida. *Current Management:* c/o Atelier Musicale, Via Caselle 76, San Lazzaro di Savena 40068, Italy. *Telephone:* (51) 19984444. *Fax:* (51) 19984420. *E-mail:* info@ateliermusicale.com. *Website:* www.ateliermusicale.com.

FOWLER, Jennifer, BA, DipEd, BMus; Australian/British composer; b. 14 April 1939, Bunbury, Western Australia; m. Bruce Patterson; two s. *Education:* Univ. of Western Australia, Studio for Electronic Music, Utrecht, Netherlands. *Career:* resident in London 1969–; music teacher in schools 1962–72; freelance composer; mem. Women in Music, Int. Alliance for Women in Music, British Acad. of Composers, Songwriters and Authors. *Compositions include:* Hours of the Day for four mezzos, two oboes and two clarinets (Berlin Acad. of the Arts Prize 1970) 1968, Chimes, Fractured for ensemble 1971, Veni Sancte Spiritus for chamber choir 1971, Chant with Garlands for orchestra 1974, Voice of the Shades for soprano and ensemble 1977, Piece for EL for solo piano 1981, Line Spun with Stars for piano trio 1983 (revised 2006), When David Heard… for choir and piano 1983 (revised 2007), Blow Flute for solo flute 1983, Letter from Haworth for mezzo, clarinet, cello and piano 1984 (revised 2005), Answer Echoes for four flutes 1986, Lament for baroque oboe and bass viol 1987, Restless Dust for cello and piano 1988, And Ever Shall Be for mezzo and ensemble 1989, Reeds, Reflections… for oboe and string trio 1990, Plainsong for Strings for string orchestra 1992 (revised 2000), Lament for Mr Henry Purcell for ensemble 1995, Singing the Lost Places for soprano and orchestra 1996, Lament for Dunblane for chamber choir 1996, Eat and Be Eaten for six singers and harp 2000, Freewheeling for solo harp 2001, Echoes… for flute, cello, violin and piano 2001, Magnificat & Nunc Dimittis 2002, Hymn for St Brigid for SATB 2002, Apsaras Flying for three recorders, cello and harpsichord 2003, Towards Release for violin and marimba 2003, Echoes from an Antique Land for four woodwind and four tuned percussion 2004, Streaming Up for flute, oboe, clarinet, cello and piano (also for four bassoons and piano) 2004, Bone Dance for four trombones 2006, Threaded Stars 2 for harp 2006, An Apple Taken for chamber choir and brass quintet 2006, Lament for three viols 2007, Concerto for alto saxophone and orchestra 2010, Uncoiling for oboe and piano 2011, Three Cellos for 3 cellos 2012, Magnificat 3 for soprano, flute, cello and piano 2013. *Recordings include:* Chimes Fractured on Australian Festival of Music Vol. 10, Blow Flute on the Flute Ascendant, Threaded Stars on Awakening, Echoes from an Antique Land on Mizu to Kori, Veni Sancte Spiritus on Sydney Dreaming. *Publications include:* contrib. to New Music Articles Vol. 4 1985, Contemporary Music Review Vol. II 1995, Journal of International Alliance for Women in Music, Vol. 12, Nos 1 & 2 2006. *Honours:* Radcliffe Award 1971, First Prize in Chamber Music, Int. Contest for Women Composers, Mannheim 1974, Miriam Gideon Prize 2003, Christopher Bodman Memorial Composition Award 2006, Sylvia Glickman Memorial Prize 2009, Marin Goleminov Composition Contest 2008. *Address:* 21 Deodar Road, London, SW15 2NP, England. *E-mail:* 100611.2060@compuserve.com. *Website:* www.impulse-music.co.uk/fowler.htm.

FOWLER, John; American singer (tenor); b. 1956. *Career:* sang in the USA as Edgardo in Lucia di Lammermoor, and in Norma; European engagements from 1983, including Rodolfo at Cologne and Hoffmann at Liège, 1985; Vienna Staatsoper, 1984–85, as Des Grieux, Leicester in Maria Stuarda and Arturo in I Puritani; Hamburg Staatsoper, 1984–85, in Rosenkavalier, Traviata and La Bohème; Welsh National Opera, 1986–87, as Edgardo and as Tonio in La Fille du Régiment; Further appearances in New Orleans, Houston (as Faust), Miami (Hoffmann, 1989), with Edmonton Opera (Duke of Mantua) and Liège (Gounod's Romeo, 1988); Concert showings in works by Respighi, Verdi (Requiem) and Mendelssohn (Elijah); Sang Percy in Anna Bolena at Barcelona and Donizetti's Edgardo at Dublin, 1991; Sang Hoffmann at Cincinnati, 1992; Gounod's Faust at Saint Louis, 1998. *Honours:* winner Metropolitan Opera

Auditions 1981. *Current Management:* c/o Pinnacle Arts: Miller Division, 889 Ninth Avenue, Second Floor, New York, NY 10019, USA. *Telephone:* (212) 397-7911. *Fax:* (212) 397-7920. *E-mail:* jmiller@pinnaclearts.com. *Website:* www.pinnaclearts.com.

FOWLES, Glenys; Australian singer (soprano); b. 4 Nov. 1946, Perth, WA. *Education:* studied with Margarita Mayer in Sydney, Kurt Adler in New York and Jani Strasser in London. *Career:* debut as Oscar (Ballo in Maschera), Australian Opera in Sydney 1969; sang in the USA 1974–81, notably at the New York City Opera as Poppea, Susanna, Mélisande 1976, Mimi and Micaela; European engagements have included Ilia in Idomeneo at Glyndebourne 1974, Sophie and Titania for Scottish Opera (A Midsummer Night's Dream); other roles include Gounod's Juliette, Mozart's Zerlina and Pamina, Marzelline, Marguerite (Faust), Nannetta, Anne Trulove, Mimi and Lauretta; sang Liu in Turandot for Australian Opera 1991; Marschallin 1992.

FOX, Christopher, DPhil; British composer; *Research Professor in Music, Brunel University;* b. 10 March 1955, York. *Education:* Univs of Liverpool, Southampton and York, studied composition with Hugh Wood, Jonathan Harvey and Richard Orton. *Career:* staff mem. Darmstadt New Music Summer School 1984–94; guest on DAAD Berlin Artists Programme 1987; joined Music Dept, Univ. of Huddersfield 1994, fmr Prof. of Composition; Research Prof. in Music, Brunel Univ. 2006–; compositions have included concert works, multimedia installations and experimental music; frequent collaborations with The Ives Ensemble, Apartment House, EXAUDI, The Clerks; British Chair. Int. Soc. for Contemporary Music; fmr Ed. Contact magazine. *Compositions include:* Second Eight for solo piano 1978–80/1982, Magnification for female voice and tape 1978–80, American Choruses for voices and electric organs 1979–81, L for four male voices 1980, Alleluia for five male voices 1981, 1997, Bewegung for three bamboo pipes 1981, Recirculation for bass trombone and tape 1981–82, Contraflow for amplified bass flute 1983, Etwas Lebhaft for ensemble 1983, Threnos for amplified male voice 1983, Winds of Heaven for amplified tenor recorder and 12-second delay 1984, Broadway Boogie for three cors anglais or cor anglais and tape 1984, ...or just after for solo harp 1984, The Missouri Harmony for organ 1985, Dead Fingers Talk for solo percussion 1985, A Kind of Prayer for two pianos 1986, Heliotropes – a cycle of six works 1985–90, More Light for solo piano 1987–88, A-N-N-A Blossom-time for voice and piano 1987–88, stone.wind.rain.sun for saxophone quartet 1989, Leap Like the Heart for percussion and ensemble 1989, The Science of Freedom for baroque flute, baroque violin, percussion, harpsichord and viola da gamba 1990, Straight Lines in Broken Times for organ 1991, Louisiana for voice and piano 1991, Sing for the Muses and Myself for piano and voice 1991, A Glimpse of Sion's Glory for chorus 1992, You, Us, Me (Habañera) for solo piano 1992, Striking Out for solo viola 1993, Trummermusik for mezzo soprano and hurdy-gurdy 1993, MERZ-sonata for tape 1993, 1998, More Things in the Air than are Visible for piano and tape 1993–94, 27 Fanfares (new heaven, new earth) for organ 1994, Paired Off for solo piano 1995, Complementary Forms for solo piano 1996, Alarmed and Dangerous (four works which may also be performed separately) 1996, Prime Site for solo piano 1997, How Time Passes for solo baroque violin 1997–98, The Art of Concealment for four percussionists 1997–98, Liquid Architecture (24 autonomous sound-producing devices) 1998, Vanished Days for voice and piano 1995–98, Notes from a Cold Front for voice, recorder, lute and dulcimer 1996–98, Skin for violin, viola and cello 1998–99, The Grain of Abstraction for electric guitar and tape 1997–99, My First Century for ensemble 1997–99, Everything You Need to Know installation for ensemble and voice (a series of component works which may also be performed separately) 1999–2001, Strangers in Our Midst for tenor saxophone, euphonium, accordion, banjo, cello and video cameras 1999–2001, Shadow Cast for string ensemble 2001, An der Schattengrenze for ensemble 2001–02, BLANK for three or more sustaining instruments 2002, Phonogrammatische Inventionen for solo percussionist 2002, Canonic Breaks for six percussionists 2002–03, ZONE (Zeit-Ort-Name) for ensemble, electric guitar and electronic drones 2002–04, Republican Bagatelles for solo piano 2000–03, Seven Serious Pieces for flute, violin, accordion and piano 2000–05, Open the Gate for choir 2004, She's Texting. He's Dancing for three melody instruments, voice (optional), keyboard and wood-block 2004, Terra Incognita 2005, De Grote Muziek for ensemble 2004–05, Iridescence for solo violin 2005, Susan's Purple for solo cello 2005, 1-2-3 for string quartet 2005–06, Schwebende Zeit for clarinet, electric guitar, viola and cello 2005–06, hearing not thinking for four instruments 2007, Extended Play for chamber orchestra 2009, drift drag for chamber orchestra 2010, L'ascenseur for piano 2012, Widerstehen for singer, actress and ensemble 2012. *Publications:* Von Kranichstein zur Gegenwart (co-ed.), Uncommon Ground (co-ed.) 1998; contrib. to Contact, Contemporary Music Review, Musical Times, Tempo, The Guardian. *Honours:* Composition Prize, Performing Right Soc. of GB 1981. *Address:* School of Arts, Brunel University, Uxbridge, Middx, UB8 3PH, England (office). *E-mail:* christopher .fox@brunel.ac.uk (office). *Website:* www.foxedition.co.uk (home).

FOX, Donal Leonellis; American composer and jazz and classical musician (piano); b. 17 July 1952, Boston, Mass; m. Dr Karen L. Mapp. *Education:* New England Conservatory of Music, Berklee Coll. of Music, Berkshire Music Center, Tanglewood; piano with Jeanette Giguere and Margaret Chaloff, theory and counterpoint with Avram David, composition and harmony with T. J. Anderson, composition and orchestration with Gunther Schuller. *Career:* debut, premiere of Refutation and Hypothesis II for chamber orchestra, Festival of Contemporary Music at Tanglewood 1983; piano and improviser,

world premiere of Oliver Lake's Movements Turns and Switches for violin and piano, Library of Congress, Washington, DC 1993; piano and improviser, world premiere, The Demon, Int. Ottawa Jazz Festival, Nat. Gallery of Canada 1995; piano and improviser, world premiere of Anthony Kelley's Africamerica for piano and orchestra 1999; piano and improviser, world premiere of T.J. Anderson's Fragments 2006; Composer-in-Residence, St Louis Symphony Orchestra 1991–92; publisher and writer, BMI 1993–; Pres., Leonellis Music 1994–, Harry Fox Agency Inc. 1996–; Artist-in-Residence, Tyrone Guthrie Centre, Northern Ireland 2003, Oberfäzer Künstlerhaus, Schwandorf, Germany 2004; Visiting Artist, Fusion Arts Exchange, US State Dept 2007; mem. Massachusetts Cultural Council (educational collaborative) 1984–. *Television includes:* Donal Fox and David Murray in Session 1993, The Fox/Troupe Project (PBS) 1993, Say Brother (WGBH) 1993, Donal Fox Plays T.J. Anderson Concerto (PBS) 2006. *Compositions include:* Refutation and Hypothesis I: a Treatise for piano solo 1981, Dialectics for two grand pianos 1988, Variants on a Theme by Monk for alto saxophone and piano 1990, Jazz Sets and Tone Rows for alto saxophone and piano 1990, Vamping with T. T. for bass clarinet and piano 1993, T-Cell Countdown for voice, piano and double bass 1993, River Town Packin House Blues, The Old People Speak of Death, Following the North Star Boogaloo for piano and poet 1993, Gone City: Ballet in Three Movements for clarinet, piano and double bass 1994, The Scream 1996, Toccata on Bach 2001, Hear de Lambs A-Cryin for baritone and orchestra 2005, Peace Out, My Brother for voice and piano 2006, Duetto II for clarinet and piano 2008, Star-Spangled Banner Fractured 2008. *Recordings include:* Boston Duets 1992, Videmus 1992, Ugly Beauty 1995, Donal Fox: Mellow Mood 1996, Donal Fox: Gone City 1997, Donal Fox Quartet: Scarlatti Jazz Suite Project 2008. *Honours:* American Acad. of Arts and Letters Award in Music 2008. *Address:* Leonellis Music, 14 Highland Park Avenue, Boston, MA 02119, USA (office). *Telephone:* (617) 821-0145 (office). *Fax:* (617) 427-6539 (office). *E-mail:* dfoxmu@aol.com. *Website:* www.leonellismusic.com (office).

FOX, Erika, ARCM; British composer; b. (Erika Roth), 3 Oct. 1936, Vienna, Austria; d. of Ezekiel Kanner and Dina Roth-Hager; m. Manfred Fox 1961 (died 2006); one s. one d. *Education:* scholarship to Royal Coll. of Music, London, studied piano with Angus Morrison, composition with Bernard Stevens, private study with Jeremy Dale Roberts and Harrison Birtwistle. *Career:* numerous commissions from leading contemporary music groups; works performed at London's South Bank, Canada, Greece, Turkey, fmr Czechoslovakia, festivals and broadcasts; worked with Menuhin School; teaching includes Centre for Young Musicians, Pimlico; Jr Dept, Guildhall School of Music and Drama; composition workshops in various schools and privately; sometime ballet pianist for Arts Educational Schools; lectures in New Zealand and Sydney; Visiting Composer-in-Residence, Univ. of Auckland; performance in Trieste, Italy 2015. *Compositions include:* Lamentations for Four 1973, The Slaughterer (chamber opera) 1975, Paths Where the Mourners Tread 1980, Litany for strings 1981, Movement for string sextet 1982, Shir 1983, Kaleidoscope 1983, Quasi una Cadenza 1983, Nick's Lament 1984, Osen Shomaat 1985, Silver Homage 1986, Rivka's Fiddle 1986, On Visiting Stravinsky's Grave at San Michele 1988, Hungarian Rhapsody 1989, The Bet (puppet music drama) 1990, The Dancer Hotoke (chamber opera, Garden Venture commission) 1992, The Moon of Moses 1992, Singender Steige 1994, Tuned Spheres 1995, Davidsbündler Lieder for flute and piano 1999, Remembering the Tango 1999, Sonnet 2000, Malinconia Militare 2003, Café Warsaw 1944 2005. *Honours:* Finzi Award 1983. *Address:* 394 Goldhawk Road, London, W6 0SB, England (home). *Telephone:* (20) 8748-5152 (office); 7967-628559 (mobile) (home). *E-mail:* erika3fox@gmail.com (office).

FOX, Frederick (Fred) Alfred, BMus; American composer; b. 17 Jan. 1931, Detroit, MI. *Education:* Wayne State Univ., Univ. of Michigan, Indiana Univ., Bloomington with Bernhard Heiden. *Career:* teacher, Franklin Coll., Indiana and Sam Houston State Univ., Huntsville, TX; worked in Minneapolis as composer-in-residence, Asst, Contemporary Music Project, Washington, DC; teacher, California State Univ., Hayward 1964–74, Indiana Univ. 1974–1997, Chair of Composition Dept 1980–1997; mem. ASCAP, American Music Center, Composers' Forum. *Compositions include:* A Stone, A Leaf, an Unfound Door for soprano and ensemble 1966, BEC for chamber ensemble 1968, The Descent for chorus and percussion 1969, Violin Concerto 1971, Matrix for cello, strings and percussion 1972, Ternion for oboe and orchestra 1973, Variables No. 5 for orchestra 1974, Variables Nos 1–4 and 6 for instruments 1976, Time Excursions for soprano, speaker and instruments 1976, Beyond Winterlock for orchestra 1977, Ambient Shadows for eight instruments 1978, Night Ceremonies for orchestra 1979, Sonaspheres Nos 1–5 for chamber ensemble 1980–83, Nilrem's Odyssey for baritone, speaker and chorus 1980, Tracings for orchestra 1981, Bren for 13 brass 1982, Januaries for orchestra 1984, Shaking the Pumpkin for saxophone, piano and percussion 1988, Auras for chamber ensemble 1989, Nightscenes for strings and percussion 1989, Devil's Tramping Ground for chamber ensemble 1991, Echo Blues for orchestra 1992, Dreamcatcher for 13 players 1994, Impressions for orchestra 1995, When the Thunder Speaks for saxophone and piano 1998. *Recordings:* Music of Frederick Fox Vol. I, Vol. II, Shaking the Pumpkin. *Address:* 711 South Clifton Street, Bloomington, IN 47401, USA (home). *Telephone:* (812) 334-1645.

FOX, Sarah; British singer (soprano); b. 1973, Giggleswick, Yorkshire. *Education:* Univ. of London with Margaret H. Clark, Royal Coll. of Music with Margaret Kingsley. *Career:* debut at Wigmore Hall recital with Roger

Vignoles, 1998; St John's Smith Square recital debut with Malcolm Martineau, March 1999; recitals for BBC Radio 3; concerts and festival engagements throughout the UK and abroad including BBC Proms, Edinburgh Festival, San Francisco Symphony Orchestra, Berlin Philharmonic and tours of Israel and Japan. *Recordings include:* Boccherini's Stabat Mater with the King's Consort, Vivaldi Sacred Music with King's Coll., Cambridge, Mozart's The Magic Flute with LSO/Mackerras, Vaughan Williams' Christmas Music with CLS/Hickox. *Operatic appearances include:* Woglinde in Wagner's Ring Cycle, Covent Garden, Salzburg; Susanna in Le Nozze de Figaro, Glyndebourne; Zerlina in Don Giovanni, Glyndebourne, Cincinnati Opera and Covent Garden, Asteria in Tamerlano, Munich. *Honours:* numerous prizes including Thomas Allen Opera Scholarship 1997, Royal Coll. of Music Queen Elizabeth Rose Bowl 1998, Kathleen Ferrier Award 1997, John Christie Award, Glyndebourne 2000. *Current Management:* Stafford Law, Candleway, Broad Street, Sutton Valence, Kent, NE17 3AT, England. *Telephone:* (1622) 840038. *E-mail:* staffordlaw@btinternet.com. *Website:* www.stafford-law.com.

FOX, Tom; American singer (baritone); b. 1950, USA. *Education:* College Conservatory of Music in Cincinnati Opera Company. *Career:* appeared with Texas Opera Theater 1974, then with Houston Grand Opera; resident mem., Cincinnati Opera 1976–80; Frankfurt Opera 1981–82; repertoire includes Amonasro in Aida, Escamillo in Carmen, Don Pizarro in Fidelio, Scarpia in Tosca, Iago in Otello, Thoas in Iphigénie en Tauride, Ford in Falstaff, Nick Shadow in The Rake's Progress, Jochanaan in Salome, the Four Villains in Les Contes d'Hoffmann, Gérard in Andrea Chénier, Barnaba in La Gioconda, the Music Master in Ariadne auf Naxos, Bluebeard in Bartok's Bluebeard's Castle, Prus in The Makropoulos Case, and Dr. Schoen in Lulu, Golaud in Pelléas et Mélisande, Boris in Lady Macbeth of Mzentsk, Wotan in Das Rheingold, Die Walküre, and Siegfried, The Dutchman in Der fliegende Holländer, Alberich in Der Ring des Nibelungen, Kurwenal in Tristan und Isolde, Telramund in Lohengrin, Klingsor in Parsifal, Biterolf in Tannhäuser, Hans Sachs in Die Meistersinger, Lescaut in Boulevard Solitude, Biteroff in Tannhäuser; has performed with Metropolitan Opera, San Francisco Opera, Lyric Opera of Chicago, Washington Opera, Los Angeles Opera, Houston Grand Opera, San Diego Opera, Pittsburgh Opera, Cincinnati Opera, Minnesota Opera, Austin Lyric Opera, Vancouver Opera, and Canadian Opera Company, Teatro alla Scala, Milan, Bayerische Staatsoper, Munich, Deutsche Oper, Berlin, Wiener Staatsoper, Vienna, Oper Frankfurt, L'Opera de Paris, Teatro dell'Opera, Rome, Opera de Nice, Opera de Montpellier, Opéra National du Rhin, Strasbourg, Festspielhaus und Festspiel Baden-Baden, Teatro Comunale di Bologna, Teatro Reggio di Torino, Opéra National de la Monnaie, Brussels, Teatro Colón, Buenos Aires, Teatro Municipal, Santiago, at he Salzburg Festival and Savonlinna Festival. *Current Management:* Columbia Artists Management, 1790 Broadway, New York, NY 10019-1412, USA. *Telephone:* (212) 841-9500. *Fax:* (212) 841 9744. *E-mail:* info@cami.com. *Website:* www.cami.com.

FRACCARO, Walter; Italian singer (tenor); b. 1968. *Career:* numerous appearances at leading opera houses from 1993; season 1994–95 as Ismaele in Nabucco at Barcelona, Cavaradossi at Valencia and Lisbon, and Raffaele in Stiffelio at Madrid; further engagements as Alfredo at Lisbon, Radames at Pittsburgh, Riccardo in Ballo in Maschera at Tenerife and Marseilles; Alfredo and the Verdi Requiem at Int. Festival of Peralada in Spain; season 1996–97 as Faust in Mefistofele at Pittsburgh, Radames at San Francisco, Pinkerton at the Metropolitan Opera and Verdi's Macduff in Hamburg; Don José at San Francisco 1998; performed Turandot at Met in New York and in Seoul, Madama Butterfly in Nice and Athens, Aida in San Diego, Otello in Como, Il trovatore in Belem (Brazil) and Mexico City 2013. *Honours:* winner, Concorso di Vorallo Valesia (Jury Prize from Carlo Bergonzi) 1993, Placido Domingo Prize Concorso Internazionale di Canto Francisco Vinas, Barcelona 1993. *Current Management:* Atelier Musicale, Via Caselle, 76, 40068, San Lazzaro di Savena, Bologna, Italy.

FRACKENPOHL, Arthur Roland, BA, MA, DMus; American composer and academic; b. 23 April 1924, Irvington, NJ. *Education:* Eastman School of Music with Bernard Rogers, Berkshire Music Center, Tanglewood with Darius Milhaud, McGill Univ., Montréal, studied with Nadia Boulanger at Fontainebleau. *Career:* teacher, Crane School of Music, State Univ. of New York at Potsdam 1949–61, Prof. 1961–85; mem. ASCAP. *Compositions:* chamber opera: Domestic Relations (To Beat or Not to Beat) 1964; orchestral: A Jubilant Overture 1957, Largo and Allegro for Horn and Strings 1962, Short Overture 1965, Concertino for Tuba and Strings 1967, Suite for Trumpet and Strings 1970, Concerto for Brass Quintet and Strings 1986; band music: Brass Quartet 1950, 5 Brass Quintets 1963, 1972, 1986, 1994, 1997, Trombone Quartet 1967, Brass Trio 1967, String Quartet 1971, Breviates for Brass Ensemble 1973, Suite for Brass Trio and Percussion 1973, Trio for Oboe, Horn and Bassoon 1982, Tuba Sonata 1983; Concerto for bassoon and band 1998; choral works: Te Deum 1962, Gloria 1968, Mass 1990; piano pieces; song cycles; solo songs. *Publication:* Harmonization at the Piano 1962. *Address:* c/o 13 Hillcrest Drive, Potsdam, NY 13676, USA (home).

FRANCES-HOAD, Cheryl, MA, MPhil, PhD; British composer; b. 1980, Essex, England. *Education:* Yehudi Menuhin School, Gonville and Caius Coll., Cambridge with Robin Holloway, King's Coll., London with George Benjamin. *Career:* Leverhulme Trust Artists in Residence Fellowship, Univ. of Cambridge 2008; apptd first DARE Cultural Fellow in Opera Related Arts, Univ. of Leeds 2010; Music Fellow, Rambert Dance 2012–13. *Compositions include:* for orchestra: Rhapsody on a Theme by Ralph Vaughan Williams 2000, Many Moons 2007; for soloist and orchestra: Concertino 1996, A Refusal to Mourn 2000, The Dreams That Fly From Me 2003, Piano Concerto 2009; small ensemble works: Three Fragments 2000, Melancholia 2002, My Fleeting Angel for piano trio (Robert Helps Prize 2006) 2005, My Day in Hell 2008, Stapleton Castle 2010, The Madness Industry for brass quintet 2012; solo and duo works: The Prophecy 1998, In Glass Houses 2002, Excelsus 2002, The Snow Woman 2007, Stolen Rhythm (BASCA British Composer Award 2010) 2009; other: Psalm No.1 for SATB chorus and organ (BASCA British Composer Award 2010) 2009, Love Bytes (short opera) 2011, Beowulf song cycle for mezzo soprano and piano 2012, Amy's Last Dive (opera) 2012. *Recording:* The Glory Tree 2011. *Honours:* winner, BBC Young Composer Competition 1996; numerous other awards including Cambridge Composer's Competition 2001, Bliss Prize 2002, Int. String Orchestra Competition (Malta) 2006, Royal Philharmonic Soc. Composition Prize 2007, Sun River Composition Prize (China) 2007, Wicklow Co. Council Per Cent for Arts Comm. (Ireland) 2008. *Address:* c/o Cadenza Music, 48 Ridgeway Avenue, Newport, NP20 5AH, Wales. *Website:* www.cherylfrancoshoad.co.uk.

FRANCESCH, Homero; Swiss-Uruguayan concert pianist; *Professor*, *Zürcher Hochschule der Künste*; b. 6 Dec. 1947, Montevideo, Uruguay. *Education:* studied in S America and with Hugo Steurer and Ludwig Hoffmann at the Munich Acad., Germany. *Career:* numerous appearances as concert soloist throughout Europe, notably with the Ravel concertos and in premiere of Henze's Tristan, London 1974; has played with the major orchestras and conductors world-wide; frequent radio and TV appearances; Prof., Zürcher Hochschule der Künste, Switzerland. *Honours:* Prix Italia 1973, Deutscher Schallplatten Preis 1978, Goldene Note, Zürich 2008. *Current Management:* c/o Arteclass GmbH, Konzertbüro, Grabenstrasse 3, 8200 Schaffhausen, Switzerland. *Telephone:* (52) 6400985. *E-mail:* info@arteclass.ch. *Website:* www.homerofrancesch.com.

FRANCESCHETTO, Romano; Italian singer (bass-baritone); b. 26 May 1957. *Education:* Conservatorio di Parma. *Career:* has sung widely in Italy 1981–, notably at La Scala, Milan, Rome, Parma, Verona, Venice, Turin, Palermo, Bologna, Trieste and Catania; further engagements in Hamburg, London, Dresden, St Petersburg, Bordeaux, Tel-Aviv, Rio de Janeiro, Seoul, Brooklyn Acad. of Music and elsewhere; has performed all the major buffo roles such as Don Bartolo, Dulcamara, Don Magnifico; Leporello; Geronimo; Don Pasquale; Gianni Schicchi; also leading roles in many baroque and classical operas; currently voice tutor, Conservatorio di Parma. *Recordings include:* Morlacchi's Barbiere di Siviglia (Bongiovanni), Paisiello's Don Chisciotte, Rossini's Adina, Salieri's Falstaff. *Address:* Via Cavour Camillo Benso Conte 110, 43036 Fidenza, Italy. *Telephone:* (0524) 527662.

FRANCH-BALLESTER, José; Spanish clarinettist; b. 1960, Moncofa, Valencia. *Education:* Conservatorio Superior de Música Joaquín Rodrigo, Valencia, Curtis Inst. of Music, Philadelphia, USA, studied with Donald Montanaro. *Career:* has played with various artists including Charles Wadsworth, Arnold Steinhardt, Warren Jones, Ida Kavafian, Frederica von Stade and David Shifrin, the Saint Lawrence and Jupiter String Quartets, also as soloist with Orquesta de la Radiotelevisión Española, I Musici of Montréal, Orchestra of Saint Luke's, New York, City of London Sinfonia; festivals include Int. Music Festival of Cartagena de Indias, Colombia, Chamber Music Northwest, Skaneateles Festival, Bridgehampton Chamber Music Festival, Music from Angel Fire, Usedomer Musikfestival, Verbier Festival; commissioned and worked with contemporary composers such as Kenji Bunch, Paul Schonfield, Edgar Meyer, William Bolcom, George Tsontakis, John B. Hedges, David Schiff, Jake Heggie and Kevin Puts; mem. Chamber Music Soc. Two, Lincoln Center, New York; Founding mem. Nuevo Tango Zinger Septet (Valencia), performing and recording music of Latin America throughout Spain. *Honours:* First Prize, Young Concert Artists Int. Auditions, New York 2004, Avery Fisher Career Grant 2008, Midem Classical Award for Outstanding Young Artist 2010. *Address:* c/o Young Concert Artists, Inc., 250 West 57 Street, Suite 1222, New York, NY 10107, USA (office). *E-mail:* jose@josefranchballester.com (home). *Website:* www.josefranchballester.com.

FRANCI, Carlo; Italian composer and conductor; b. 18 July 1927, Buenos Aires, Argentina. *Education:* Rome Conservatory, Academy of St Cecilia with Fernando Previtali. *Career:* conducted symphonic music at first, then Hänsel und Gretel at Spoleto 1959; appearances at many opera houses in Italy and abroad, including the Vienna Staatsoper; led the Company of Rome Opera in Rossini's Otello at the New York Metropolitan 1968, returning as guest 1969–72; other repertoire includes Spontini's Fernand Cortez and Verdi's Nabucco, Berne 1990; conducted the Seven Stars concert at the Baths of Caracalla 1991; Verdi's I Masnadieri at Piacenza 1998. *Compositions include:* L'Imperatore (opera, produced at Bergamo) 1958.

FRANCI, Francesca; Italian singer (mezzo-soprano); b. 1962, Rome. *Education:* studied with Rodolfo Celletti and Tito Gobbi. *Career:* debut singing Mahler's Lieder eines fahrenden Gesellen at Verona, 1984; appeared as Maddalena in Rigoletto at Genoa and Naples, Rosina at Bari and Suzuki in Bologna, 1988; Festival della Valle d'Itria 1988 in Donizetti's Maria di Rohan, as Armando; Edvige in Guillaume Tell at La Scala, Milan, returning as Fatima in Oberon; sang Ernestina in Rossini's L'Occasione fa il Ladro at Pesaro; further engagements at Rome and Naples (from 1987), Florence, Monteverdi's Otho, 1992, Paris and Wiesbaden; France 1992 as Stephano in

Gounod's Roméo et Juliette; sang Verdi's Preziosilla at Verona Arena and Adalgisa in Norma at Catania, 2000. *Recordings include:* Maria di Rohan.

FRANCIS, Alun; British conductor; b. 1943, Kidderminster, England. *Education:* Royal Manchester Coll. of Music. *Career:* played the horn in Hallé and Bournemouth Symphony Orchestras; from 1966 conducted more than 60 orchestras in over 20 countries; guest conductor at the Vienna Festival, Hong Kong Arts Festival with the BBC Scottish Symphony, Århus Festival in Denmark with the Philharmonia Hungarica, Promenade Concerts, London, with the Royal Philharmonic, and Festival Hall 1983, in Henryk Szeryng Golden Jubilee concert; Chief Conductor and Artistic Dir, Ulster Orchestra 1966–67, Northern Ireland Opera Trust 1974–84; Dir, Northwest Chamber Orchestra, Seattle 1980–85; Dir and Artistic Adviser, Overijssells Philharmonic, The Netherlands 1985–87; Chief Conductor, Nordwest Deutsche Philharmonie; Principal Conductor, Berlin Symphony from 1989; repertoire includes Bel Canto opera (1978 revival of Donizetti Gabriella di Vergy, premiere of revised version at Belfast), 20th-century music ranging from Berio to Stockhausen; has composed music for the concert hall, films and theatre. *Recordings:* Donizetti's Ugo, Conte di Parigi, with the Philharmonia Orchestra; Offenbach's Christopher Columbus, with the London Mozart Players (Opera Rara); albums with the London Symphony, Royal Philharmonic, English Chamber and Northwest Chamber Orchestras.

FRANCIS, Jeffrey; American singer (tenor); b. 1958, Poplar Bluff, MO. *Education:* studied in Seattle. *Career:* sang at the Berlin Staatsoper from 1990, as Lentolo in Graun's Cleopatra e Cesare, Tamino, Paolino in Il Matrimonio Segreto, Jupiter in Semele 1996, and in Gassmann's L'Opera Seria; Rossini Festival at Pesaro 1993–95, as Gernando in Armida and Rodolphe in Guillaume Tell; season 1993–94 as Evander in Alceste at Vienna, Argirio in Rossini's Tancredi in Berlin and Rossini's Almaviva at Santa Fe; season 1998 with Rossini's Ramiro in Tel-Aviv and Chapelou in Le Postillon de Lonjumeau at the Berlin Staatsoper; season 2000 in Roméo et Juliette by Berlioz at Salzburg and as Almaviva at the Vienna Staatsoper. *Recordings include:* Armida.

FRANCIS, Sarah Janet, ARCM, FRCM; British oboist, academic and tutor; b. 11 Jan. 1939, London; d. of John and Millicent Francis; m. Michael D. C. Johnson; two d. *Education:* Royal Coll. of Music (RCM), London; studied with Pierre Pierlot, Paris. *Career:* debut, BBC 1959; Prin. Oboe, BBC Nat. Orchestra of Wales; BBC recitalist; soloist, chamber music and orchestral player; Prof. of Oboe, RCM, London 1974–2015; Dir London Harpsichord Ensemble; dedicatee of many concert and chamber music works; solo recordings on Heritage, Hyperion, Chandos and Naxos; master classes in Amsterdam, Cologne, Geneva, Moscow, Copenhagen and Stockholm Conservatoires; Juror, Prague Spring Competition, Fernand Gillet Competition; mem. British Music Soc., Royal Soc. of Musicians; fmr Chair. British Double Reed Soc. *Compositions:* Seven Dedications: Gordon Jacob, Seven Bagatelles 1971, Gordon Crosse, Ariadne for solo oboe and 12 players 1972, Phyllis Tate, The Rainbow and the Cuckoo for oboe quartet 1975, Crosse, Little Epiphany Variations for oboe and cello 1977, Anthony Payne, Concerto 1980, William Mathias, Oboe Concerto 1989, Stephen Dodgson, Oboe Quartet 1994. *Recordings include:* numerous solo recordings of 18th-century music and British 20th-century music, including Britten Metamorphoses; Gordon Crosse Concerto Ariadne; Boccherini Quintets; Crusell, Reicha Quintets; Howells, Rubbra Sonatas; Rutland Boughton Oboe Concerto, RPO; Mozart and Krommer Concertos, LMP; Britten complete oboe music; Bax, Holst Quintets; Moeran, Jacob Quartets; Complete Albinoni, Handel and Telemann Concertos LHE; Vanhal Quartets; Telemann Complete Oboe Sonatas; Krommer Quintets & Quartets; Jacob Trio, Sonata & Quartet; Alwyn Sonata; Lennox Berkeley: Chamber Works for Wind Strings and Piano 2011, Epiphany variations with Rohan de Saram, Dodgson Oboe Quartet with Tagore Trio Howells Sonata with Peter Dickinson Jacob Bagatelles 2014, English Music for Oboe 2014. *Publications:* Going Solo 1995, Oboe Music to Enjoy 1996, Unbeaten Tracks; contrib. to Joy Boughton: A Portrait, Double Reed News. *Honours:* RCM Somerville Prize for Wind Instruments 1959, Boise Foundation Scholarship, French Govt scholarship. *Address:* 10 Avenue Road, London, N6 5DW, England (home). *Telephone:* (20) 8340-5461 (home). *Fax:* (20) 8347-5907 (home). *Website:* www.sarahfrancisoboe.co.uk.

FRANCK, Michel; French concert promoter; *General Director, Théâtre des Champs-Elysées;* b. 6 March 1957. *Career:* began career in family fashion business Franck et Fils; Co-Dir Jeanine Roze Production 1987–95, responsible for running Sunday morning classical concerts, Assoc. Dir 1995–2008; Gen. Dir Théâtre des Champs-Élysées 2008–. *Honours:* Chevalier des Arts et des Lettres 2006. *Address:* Théâtre des Champs-Élysées, 15 avenue Montaigne, 75008 Paris, France (office). *Telephone:* 1-49-52-50-00 (office); 1-49-52-50-11 (office). *Fax:* 1-49-52-07-41 (office). *E-mail:* rp@theatrechampselysees.fr (office). *Website:* www.theatrechampselysees.fr (office).

FRANCK, Mikko; Finnish conductor; *Music Director, Orchestre National de Belgique;* b. 1979, Helsinki. *Education:* Sibelius Acad. and studied in New York, Israel and Sweden. *Career:* children's chorus mem., Finnish Nat. Opera; appeared as the young Sibelius at the Helsinki Swedish Theatre 1992; conductor with several Finnish orchestras, including the Vaasa, Lappeenranta, Pori and the Chamber Orchestra of the Sibelius Acad., Helsinki; season 1997–98 with the Turku Philharmonic, Tapiola Sinfonietta, Tampere Philharmonic and Netherlands Radio Philharmonic; Japanese tour with the Sibelius Acad. Symphony Orchestra; conductor, The Magic Flute at the

Finnish Nat. Opera; US debut at the Aspen Festival; season 1999–2000 included return visits to the Stockholm Philharmonic, Finnish Radio Symphony, Swedish Radio Symphony, Bergen Philharmonic and a tour of Japan with the Bamberg Symphony in 2000; Music Dir and Chief Conductor of the Orchestre Nat. de Belgique 2002–; season 2002–03 debuts with Chicago, San Francisco Symphony and Berlin Philharmonic orchestras and tour of Japan with the Orchestre Nat. de Belgique; concerts with the Scottish Chamber, BBC Nat. Orchestra of Wales, Hessischer Rundfunk, Stuttgart Opera and Tokyo Symphony Orchestras; premiere of Rautavaara's Rasputin, Helsinki 2003; 2003–04 season included concerts with Hamburg Staatsoper Orchestra, La Scala Orchestra, Milan, Staatsoper Berlin, Munich Philharmonic, Israel Philharmonic; Gen. Music Dir, Finnish Nat. Opera 2006–07. *Recordings:* Sibelius En Saga and Lemminkainen Legends (with the Swedish Radio Symphony), Tchaikovsky's Sixth Symphony. *Current Management:* Harrison Parrott, 5–6 Albion Court, London, W6 0QT, England. *Telephone:* (20) 7229-9166. *Fax:* (20) 7221-5042. *E-mail:* info@harrisonparrott.co.uk. *Website:* www.harrisonparrott.com.

FRANDSEN, John, MMus; Danish composer and organist; b. 13 March 1956, Aalborg; m. Kirsten Grove 1985, one d. *Education:* Aalborghus Statsgymnasium, Århus Univ., Royal Acad. of Music, Århus. *Career:* Teacher, Århus Univ. 1979–83, Royal Acad. of Music, Århus 1980–; organist, Ellevang Church 1982–84, Holy Ghost Church, Århus 1984–; Conductor, Cantilena Choir 1983–; mem. Young Nordic Music (Danish Section, chair. 1983–87), Århus Unge Tonekunstnere (chair. 1983–), Danish Composers' Soc. *Compositions:* String Song for string quartet 1980, Wo Immer Wir Soielen for mixed choir 1982, Songs of Innocence for soprano and guitar 1984, Amalie Lever (opera) 1984, Avers/Revers for wind quintet 1985, Deux Poèmes sur le temps for mixed choir 1985, Amalie Suite for chamber orchestra 1985, Stabat Mater for tenor and organ 1986, Petite Suite for guitar 1986, De/Cadences for wind quintet 1987.

FRANG, Vilde; Norwegian violinist; b. 1986. *Education:* Barratt Due Music Inst., Oslo, Musikhochschule Hamburg (Germany) with Kolja Blacher, Kronberg Acad. (Germany) with Ana Chumachenco. *Career:* has performed with Mahler Chamber Orchestra, Kremerata Baltica, Acad. of St Martin in the Fields, BBC Symphony, Symphonieorchester des Bayerischen Rundfunks, Konzerthausorchester Berlin, HR-Sinfonieorchester Frankfurt, Tonhalle Orchester Zürich, Russian Nat. Orchestra, Rotterdam Philharmonic, NHK Symphony, Tokyo, Orchestre Philharmonique de Monte Carlo; debut with London Philharmonic Orchestra 2007; has worked with conductors including Ivan Fischer, Paavo Järvi, Vladimir Ashkenazy, Mariss Jansons, David Zinman, Vassily Sinaisky, Esa-Pekka Salonen, Gianandrea Noseda, Jukka-Pekka Saraste; performed at festivals in Schleswig-Holstein, Mecklenburg-Vorpommern, Rheingau, Lockenhaus, Gstaad, Verbier, Lucerne; collaborations with musicians including Gidon Kremer, Yuri Bashmet, Martha Argerich, Julian Rachlin, Leif Ove Andsnes, Maxim Vengerov, Anne-Sophie Mutter, Michail Lifits. *Recordings:* Prokofiev & Sibelius: Violin Concertos 2010, Bartók/Grieg/Strauss Violin Sonatas 2011, Nielsen/Tchaikovsky Violin Concertos 2012. *Honours:* EMI Classics Young Artist of the Year 2010, Best Newcomer, Edison Klassiek Award 2010, 2012, Classic BRIT Award for Best Newcomer 2010. *Current Management:* c/o Askonas Holt, Lincoln House, 300 High Holborn, London, WC1V 7JH, England; Opus 3 Artists, 470 Park Avenue South, 9th Floor North, New York, NY 10016, USA. *Telephone:* (20) 7400-1740 (Askonas Holt); (212) 584-7518 (Opus 3). *E-mail:* jilly.clarke@askonasholt.co .uk; jbrill@opus3artists.com. *Website:* www.askonasholt.com; www .opus3artists.com; www.vildefrang.com (office).

FRANK, Gabriela Lena, BA, MA, DMA; American composer; b. 1972, Berkeley, Calif. *Education:* Rice Univ., Univ. of Michigan. *Career:* music inspired by Bela Bartók and Alberto Ginastera; work has been commissioned and performed by artists including Sharon Isbin, Silk Road Ensemble, Chiara Quartet, San Francisco Chamber Orchestra, the King's Singers. *Compositions:* Manhattan Serenades 1995, Las Sombras de los Apus 1998, Ríos Profundos 1999, Cuatro Canciones Andinas 1999, Elegia Andina for orchestra 2000, Sonata Andina 2000, Leyendas: An Andean Walkabout for string orchestra 2001, Sueños de Chambi 2002, Hombre Errante for chorus 2002, Three Latin American Dances for orchestra 2003, Havana Jila for violin and orchestra 2003, Khazn's Recitative for violin 2003, Illapa: Tone Poem for Flute and Orchestra 2004, Ccollanan Maria for chorus 2004, Inkarri 2005, Manchay Tiempo for orchestra 2005, Why Am I So Brown? for children's chorus 2005, Ritmos Anchinos 2006, Cinco Danzas de Chambi 2006, Canto de Harawi 2005, Ghosts in the Dream Machine for piano quintet 2005, Jalapeño Blues 2006, Requiem for a Magical America: El Día de los Muertos for ensemble 2006, Cuatro Bosquejos Pre-Incaicos 2006, Danza de los Saqsampillos 2006, Pollerita Roja for chorus 2006, Compadrazgo for piano, cello and orchestra 2007, La Llorona: Tone Poem for viola and orchestra 2007, Dos Canciones de Cifar for baritone and piano 2007, Quijotadas 2007, Adagio para Amantani for cello and piano 2007, Soliloquio Serrano for pipa 2007, New Andean Songs 2007, Inca Dances (Latin Grammy Award for Best Classical Contemporary Composition 2009) 2008, Two American Portraits for orchestra 2008, Hypnagogia 2008, Two Mountain Songs for chorus 2008, Peregrinos for orchestra 2009, Canto y Danza 2009. *Honours:* Raymond and Beverly Sacker Composition Prize 2002, Brillante Prize, Hispanic Scholarship Foundation 2008, Guggenheim Fellowship 2009. *Address:* c/o G. Schirmer Inc., 257 Park Avenue South, 20th Floor, New York, NY 10010, USA (office). *Telephone:* (212)

254-2100 (office). *Fax:* (212) 254-2013 (office). *E-mail:* katy.tucker@schirmer.com (office). *Website:* www.schirmer.com (office).

FRANK, Pamela; American violinist; *Professor of Violin, Curtis Institute of Music;* b. 20 June 1967, New York; d. of Claude Frank and Lilian Kallir. *Education:* Curtis Institute, Philadelphia and studied with Szymon Goldberg and Jaime Laredo. *Career:* debut at Carnegie Hall, New York, with the New York String Orchestra, conducted by Alexander Schneider 1985; many appearances with leading orchestras worldwide, including Boston Symphony, Cleveland Orchestra, Tonhalle Orchestra (Zürich) and Orchestre de Paris; soloist with the Acad. of St Martin-in-the-Fields, London, and leader of Acad. Chamber Ensemble; engagements with chamber musicians, including Peter Serkin and Yo-Yo Ma, and frequent recital tours with her father; contemporary repertoire includes music by Takemitsu, Ellen Taafe Zwilich and Aaron Jay; Prof. of Violin Curtis Inst. of Music 1999–, Peabody Conservatory 2002–, SUNY Stony Brook 2002–. *Recordings include:* albums with the Academy of St Martin-in-the-Fields, Czech Philharmonic, Zürich Tonhalle Orchestra, Claude Franck, Yo-Yo Ma, Emmanuel Ax, Peter Serkin. *Honours:* Avery Fisher career grant 1988, Avery Fisher Prize 1999. *Current Management:* Opus 3 Artists, 470 Park Avenue South, 9th Floor North, New York, NY 10016, USA. *Telephone:* (212) 584-7500. *Fax:* (646) 300-8200. *E-mail:* info@opus3artists.comnk. *Website:* www.opus3artists.com. *Current Management:* IMG Artists, The Light Box, 111 Power Road, London, W4 5PY, England. *Telephone:* (20) 7957-5800. *Fax:* (20) 7957-5801. *Website:* www.imgartists.com.

FRANK, Susanne; Swiss violinist; b. 2 Nov. 1962. *Education:* Winterthur Conservatory, Paris and Int. Menuhin Acad. *Career:* second violin, Carmina Quartet from 1987; appearances from 1987 in Europe, Israel, Japan and the USA; regular concerts at Wigmore Hall from 1987; concerts at South Bank Centre, London, Amsterdam Concertgebouw, the Kleine Philharmonie in Berlin, Konzertverein Vienna; four engagements in Paris 1990–91, seven in London; tours to Australasia, USA, Japan, and concerts at the Hohenems, Graz, Hong Kong, Montreux, Schleswig-Holstein, Bath, Lucerne and Prague Spring Festivals; collaborations with Dietrich Fischer-Dieskau, Olaf Bär and Mitsuko Uchida. *Honours:* winner (with Carmina Quartet) Paolo Borciani String Quartet Competition in Reggio Emilia, Italy 1987, Gramophone Prize for best recording of chamber music 1992. *Address:* Vogelsangstrasse 9, 8006 Zurich, Switzerland. *E-mail:* susanne.frank@carminaquartet.com. *Website:* www.carminaquartet.com.

FRANKE-BLOM, Lars-Åke (Harry); Swedish composer; b. 4 April 1941, Norrköping, Sweden; m. Gunilla Marie-Louise Dalin 1965; one s. two d. *Education:* Univ. of Uppsala, Logopede, Karolinska Inst., Stockholm, studied composition with Nils Eriksson and Daniel Börtz. *Career:* debut with orchestral work Motions 1975; active in Norrköping, collaborating with the local symphony orchestra on several occasions; mem. Asscn of Swedish Composers 1978. *Compositions:* Motions for orchestra 1973, Music for Mobile for orchestra 1975–77, Concertos for violoncello 1977, viola 1980, contrabasso 1983, The Troll Battle (opera for children, commissioned and performed by Folkopera, Stockholm 1979) 1979, The Well of the Virgins (ballet, commissioned by Swedish TV) 1982, four symphonies 1982, 1993, 1994, 2009, The Web of Yearning (symphonic poem, commissioned by Norrköping Symphony Orchestra 1984, presented on Swedish TV 1988) 1984, Impossible Reality, chamber music 1986, HP (opera in two acts, commissioned by the Royal Theatre, Stockholm in 1990, first performance 2001) 1990–95, Music for Art, chamber music 1991, Symphony No. 3: Fire on Earth (commissioned and performed by the Swedish Radio Symphony Orchestra) 1998, music for the film Bathers (presented on Swedish TV) 1999, A Mansion Tale (opera, commissioned and performed by Värmlandsoperan, Karlstad) 2004, Piano Concerto No. 1 2005–07, Symphony No. 4: The Pope 2009, Luceafarul (symphonic poem), first performance Pitesti Philarmonic Orchestra, Romania 2012, The Career of Florenzo Waldweibel-Hostellii, Chamber Opera, first performance Gothenburg Music High School 2014. *Recordings include:* Endymion, Music for Mobile, The Web of Yearning, music and TV film, Music for Art, several radio recordings. *Honours:* Prizewinner, Int. New Music Composers' Competition 1989–90. *Address:* Björkbacken 7, 605 80 Svärtinge, Sweden (home). *Telephone:* (1) 131-98-46 (home). *Fax:* (1) 131-98-46 (home). *E-mail:* lasse@frankeblom.nu. *Website:* www.frankeblom.nu.

FRANKL, Peter; British pianist and academic; *Professor of Piano, School of Music, Yale University;* b. 2 Oct. 1935, Budapest, Hungary; s. of Tibor Frankl and Laura Frankl; m. Annie Feiner 1958; one s. one d. *Education:* Franz Liszt Acad. of Music, Budapest with Profs Hernadi, Kodály and Weiner. *Career:* began career on int. circuit 1960s, London debut 1962, New York debut with Cleveland Orchestra 1967; has performed with numerous orchestras in USA (Chicago, Philadelphia, Boston, Washington, Los Angeles, San Francisco, Pittsburgh etc.), Berlin Philharmonic, Leipzig Gewandhaus, Amsterdam Concertgebouw, Orchestre de Paris, Israel Philharmonic, all London orchestras and many others in Europe and all parts of the world; has appeared with conductors including Abbado, Ashkenazy, Barbirolli, Blomstedt, Boulez, Chailly, Davis, Dorati, Fischer, Haitink, Kempe, Kertesz, Leinsdorf, Maazel, Masur, Muti, Sanderling, Solti, Szell, among others; numerous tours to Japan, Australia, NZ and South Africa, playing with orchestras, in recitals and in chamber music concerts; more than 20 appearances at BBC Promenade Concerts, London; regular participant at Edinburgh, Cheltenham, Aldeburgh, Verbier, Kuhmo, Naantali and Casals Festivals; highlights at Edinburgh Festival include Britten Concerto under baton of the composer and opening televised concert with the Philharmonia Orchestra under Riccardo Muti;

soloist at Enescu Festival, Bucharest with Budapest Festival Orchestra at one of the last concerts Yehudi Menuhin ever conducted; regular guest artist at summer festivals in Aspen, Chautauqua, Hollywood Bowl, Marlboro, Norfolk, Ravinia, Santa Fe and Yellow Barn, USA; toured with Frankl-Pauk-Kirshbaum Trio world-wide; frequent performances with string quartets including Amadeus, Bartók, Borodin, Fine Arts, Guarneri, Lindsay, Panocha, Takacs, Tokyo and Vermeer; master-classes world-wide, including RAM and Royal Coll. of Music, London, Liszt Acad., Budapest, Van Cliburn Inst., Texas, in Berlin, Madrid, Beijing, Hong Kong and Seoul; mem. numerous jury panels at int. piano competitions, including Van Cliburn, Rubinstein, Leeds, Santander, Hilton Head, William Kappell, Hong Kong, Clara Haskil, Paderewski, Marguerite Long, Cleveland, Shanghai, Manchester and Brussels (Queen Elisabeth); mem. Faculty, Yale Univ. School of Music 1987–, now Prof. of Piano. *Recordings include:* complete Schumann and Debussy piano works (with Andras Schiff, the Schumann two-piano and four-hand repertoire); both Brahms Concerti and the Violin Sonatas (with Kyung Wha Chung) and Piano Trios; Piano Concerti, Violin Sonatas and four-hand works by Mozart; Bartók solo and violin pieces; Piano Quintets by Brahms, Schumann, Dvořák, Martinů and Dohnányi. *Honours:* Hon. Prof., Franz Liszt Acad. of Music; Officer's Cross and Middle Cross (Hungary) 1972; won first prize in several int. competitions. *Address:* 5 Gresham Gardens, London, NW11 8NX, England (home). *Telephone:* (20) 8455-5228 (home). *Fax:* (20) 8455-2176 (home). *E-mail:* info@peterfrankl.co.uk. *Website:* www.peterfrankl.co.uk; music.yale.edu/faculty/frankl-peter.

FRANKLIN, James (Jim), PhD; Australian lecturer in music technology, composer and musician (shakuhachi performer); b. 14 Feb. 1959, Sydney, NSW. *Education:* Univ. of Sydney; Shihan (master performer), Int. Shakuhachi Research Centre, Japan, 1996; studies with Peter Sculthorpe 1978–81, Milko Kelemen 1982–85, Ton de Leeuw 1985–86, Riley Lee 1988–98, Katsuya Yokoyama 1996. *Career:* Univ. of Sydney 1987–93; Lecturer in Music Tech., Univ. of Western Sydney 1994–2003; Founder-mem. OHM, electronic music group; freelance composer, shakuhachi performer and music educator 2003–. *Compositions include:* Corno Inglese for choir 1979, Talisman for piano 1980, Three Glimpses of Aquilon for piano 1980, Across the Swan's Riding for piano and orchestra 1981, The Unliving Seed (chamber opera) 1983, Boundaries for the Child of Flame for string quartet 1984, Fragments of a Broken Land for orchestra 1984, Triptych for 8 voices and ensemble 1984, Dream Within a Dream for tape 1988, Raising Dust for synthesizer 1988, The Hours of the Sea-Bird for voices, keyboard, synthesizer, sampler and sequencer 1988, Fountain of Light for Shakuhachi and electronics (with Riley Lee) 1991, Middle Dance for voices and ensemble 1992, Naratic Visions (dance theatre) 1993, Heart for shakuhachi, voice and live electronics 1994, Three Treasures: Columns and Webs for koto quartet, percussion, shakuhachi and electronics 1996, Peace Bell for 3 shakuhachi and collaged pre-recorded bells 1996, Songs for the Not-Born #1 for shakuhachi and live electronics 1996, Water Spirits for koto, shakuhachi and electronics (with Satsuki Odamura) 1994–96, Thoughts of Distant Clouds for koto and shakuhachi 1998, Butsuga for shakuhachi 1999, Moon Road to Dawn (with Antony Wheeler) 1999, Abundance (with Michael Atherton) 2001, Flötenspiel for shakuhachi 2002, Songs for the Not-Born #2 for shakuhachi, theremin and live electronics 2002, #3 2003, A Lattice of Winds for shakuhachi and koto 2003, Aurora for shakuhachi, koto, ruined piano, guitars, marimba and double bass (with Michael Atherton) 2003, Zen-Geschicthen for shakuhachi and narrator 2004. *Publications:* The Ongaku Masters – An Anthology of Japanese Classical Music (ed. five CDs and booklets) 2004. *Honours:* Best Original Soundtrack, Munich Int. Multi-Media Festival 1990. *Address:* 2 Garden Square, Faulconbridge, NSW 2776, Australia (home); Ottensooser Weg 1, 91207 Lauf, Germany (home). *E-mail:* dr_jim_franklin@hotmail.com.

FRANKLIN, Peter Robert, BA, DPhil; British academic; b. 19 Dec. 1947, London, England. *Education:* Univ. of York. *Career:* Teacher of Music and German, Harlaxton Coll., Lincolnshire 1974–79, William Jewell Coll., Liberty, MO, USA 1979; Lecturer Dept of Music, Univ. of Leeds 1980–95. *Publications:* Natalie Bauer-Lechner: Recollections of Gustav Mahler (ed., annotator) 1980, The Idea of Music, Schoenberg and Others 1985; contrib. on Mahler and Schreker to many journals, including The Music Review, Music and Letters, Opera 1992, The Musical Quarterly, The Musical Times; programme notes (e.g. Pfitzner's Palestrina at Covent Garden 1997), article on Mahler in New Grove Dictionary 2001.

FRANOVA, Tatiana; Slovak pianist; b. 3 Aug. 1945; m. Eduard Ihring 1966, one d. *Education:* Bratislava Conservatoire, Acad. of Music and Dramatic Arts, Bratislava, Music Acad., Vienna, Austria. *Career:* concert tours in Austria, Brazil, Cuba, Egypt, France, Germany, Hungary, India, Italy, Luxembourg, Poland, Romania, Spain, Gran Canaria, Switzerland, Sweden, USSR; Prof., Acad. of Arts, Cairo, Egypt 1983–87; Prof. of Piano, Acad. of Music Arts, Bratislava 1987–; mem. Slovak Music Union. *Recordings:* Brahms: Sonata in F sharp minor Op 2, 1975; Rachmaninov: Sonata in B minor Op 36, 1975; Etudes–Chopin, Liszt, Scriabin, Rachmaninov, 1978; Rachmaninov: Concerto No. 1 in F sharp minor, 1982; De Falla: Nights in the Gardens of Spain, 1982; Complete works of Glazunov, 1991. *Honours:* first prize Radio Competition, Young People's Studio 1964, silver medal Int. Festival, Bordeaux 1974, F. Kafenda Prize 1980.

FRANTZ, Justus; German pianist and conductor; b. 18 May 1944, Hohensalza. *Education:* under Prof. Eliza Hansen in Hamburg, Wilhelm Kempf in Positano and Wilhelm Brückner-Rüggeberg in Hamburg. *Career:*

since 1969 has appeared at all major European concert venues and toured USA, Far East and Japan; US debut with Leonard Bernstein and the New York Philharmonic Orchestra 1975; has made many tours and recordings in piano duo with Christoph Eschenbach and received Edison Int. Award for their recording of Schubert marches 1983; Prof. Hamburg Musikhochschule 1985–; Co-founder Schleswig-Holstein Music Festival 1986, Dir 1986–94; Founder and Chief Conductor Philharmonia of the Nations 1995–; Musical Dir Israel Sinfonietta Beer-Sheva 2013–; performed complete cycle of Mozart concertos in several European cities 1987–88; Special Amb. for UNHCR 1989. *Recordings include:* works by Scarlatti, Beethoven, Mozart and concertos for two, three and four pianos by J. S. Bach. *Honours:* Grosse Bundesverdienstkreuz 1989; prizewinner, Int. Music Competition, Munich 1967. *Address:* K. u. J. Managementgesellschaft für Konzertveranstaltungen, Mittelweg 20, 20148 Hamburg, Germany (office). *Telephone:* (40) 41622-387 (office). *E-mail:* info@justusfrantz.net (office). *Website:* www.justus-frantz.de (office); english.isb7.co.il (office).

FRANZÉN, Olov Alfred; Swedish composer, cellist and recitalist; b. 22 Jan. 1946, Umeå; m. Ingeborg Axner 1977. *Education:* Stockholm Music Acad., studied cello with Gunnar Norrby, composition with Ingvar Lidholm. *Career:* debut as composer, A Wind Quintet in Lund 1963, as cellist, Nyström 1971; cellist in Norrköping Symphony Orchestra 1971–72; Harpans Kraft, Stockholm 1971–77; Swedish TV film, Sundcreme with Harpans Kraft 1976; freelance in Härnösand and Founder, HND Ensemble 1977–92; cellist, Sundsvall Chamber Orchestra 1983–90; teacher of composition, Kapellsberg Music School, Härnösand 1983–92; started Faimo Edition for publishing music scores and recordings 1986; freelance in Skokloster 1992–; hundreds of solo recitals throughout Sweden 1993–; has played with Harpans Kraft and HND in Sweden, Finland, Austria on radio; compositions played in all Nordic countries and abroad; cellist, Duo Franzén 1978–, Skokloster Chamber Soloists 1994–97, Trio Concordia 1999–. *Compositions include:* Cytoplasma for song and piano 1968, Fiesta for percussion ensemble 1982, Har for soprano and harp 1983, The Vacuum State for symphony orchestra 1983, From The Junction Point for bassoon and live electronics 1985, Suite for three flutes 1986, Agnim for symphony orchestra 1987, It's Getting Sunny for brass band 1988, Gaps for violin and piano 1990, Apmel for flute, clarinet, percussion, piano and string quartet 1992, The Unseen Present for cello and reciter 1993, Opus NN for mezzo soprano, guitar and cello 1994, Clouds on Blue Sky for symphony orchestra 1995, Organic music No. 2 for cello solo 1995, String Quartet 1996, Lamentode for soprano, bass clarinet and piano 1997, Autumn Duo for two violins 1997, Four Realities for reciter and symphony orchestra 1998, La terza via for cello solo 2000, In Fondo for mezzo-soprano, flute and cello 2001, Organic Music No. 4 for string sextet 2002, Strigi Aluconi Gratias for saxophone quartet 2003, Suite Grande for cello solo 2004, Incanto for organ 2005, Concert Overture No. 2 for symphony orchestra 2006, Lamento di Terra for symphony orchestra 2007, Il Dimenticato for bassoon 2007, Organic Music No. 5 for two violins and orchestra 2009, Vintergata for reciter, flute, guitar and cello 2010, Sei Miniature for flute and cello 2011, Lingue d'Ottoni for brass quintet 2011, Chamber Duo for trombone and percussion 2012, Monolit for piano 2012, Quiete inquieta for string quintet 2013, Organic Music No 6 for clarinet and bassoon 2014, Sjung min flöjt (Sing my flute) for reciter and flute 2015. *Recordings include:* Beyond (with six pieces for winds and piano) 1991, Gaps 1997, Four Realities 2000, La Terza Via (four pieces for solo cello) 2002, Piece for Guitar 2013. *Address:* Abbotvägen 18, 74695 Skokloster, Sweden (home). *Telephone:* (18) 386268 (office). *E-mail:* olov.franzen@telia.com (office). *Website:* www.olovfranzen.se.

FRANZETTI, Carlos; American composer and conductor; b. 1948, Buenos Aires, Argentina. *Education:* Conservatório Nacional de Buenos Aires, Juilliard School, New York. *Career:* jazz and classical composer; compositions performed at Teatro Colón, with Orquesta de la Plata, Boston Pops Orchestra, Nat. Symphony Orchestra, Washington, DC, St Louis Symphony, Brooklyn Philharmonic, Buffalo Philharmonic, Nat. Symphony of Mexico, Nat. Symphony of Argentina, Orquesta Filarmónica de Buenos Aires, Czech Nat. Symphony, City of Prague Philharmonic, Modus Chamber Orchestra, Janáček Philharmonic, Bratislava Radio Orchestra, orchestras in Mexico, Venezuela, Spain, Sweden, Norway and France. *Compositions include:* Gauchito and the Pony (children's opera), Concierto del Plata for guitar and chamber ensemble, Millennium Concerto for flute and orchestra, Piano Concerto No. 2, Sinfonia No. 1. *Recordings include:* Tropic of Capricorn 1993, Portraits of Cuba with Paquito d'Rivera (Latin Grammy Award for Best Latin Jazz Album) 1997, Remembrances 1999, Obsesión 1999, Tango Fatal (Latin Grammy Award for Best Tango Album) 2001, Tango Bar 2002, Poeta de Arrabal 2003, You Make Believe in Spring 2004, Reflexiones 2004, Promises Kept 2004, Corpus Evita: An Opera in Two Acts 2005, Carlos Franzetti and the Jazz Kamerata 2005, Songs for Lovers 2006, Graffiti 2007, Duets with Eddie Gomez (Latin Grammy Award for Best Instrumental Album) 2009, Mambo Tango 2009, Galaxy Dust, Alborada, Pierrot et Colombine. *Publication:* The Cuchifrito Circuit and Other Stories 2009. *Honours:* Yamaha Composers Award, Trofeu Laus, Spain, Clio Award, Pensario Award, Premio Konex, Argentina. *Address:* 14 Dartmouth Road, Cranford, NJ 07016, USA (office). *Telephone:* (908) 709-0937 (office). *Fax:* (908) 709-0938 (office). *E-mail:* yumba@aol.com (office). *Website:* www.carlosfranzetti.com.

FRASER, Malcolm Henry; British opera director; b. 1 Aug. 1939, Kingston-upon-Thames; m. 1964; four s. *Career:* Assoc. Dir, Lincoln Repertory 1966–68; Resident Dir, WNO 1968–76; Sr Lecturer, Royal Northern Coll. of Music

1976–87; founder and Artistic Dir, Buxton Int. Festival 1979–87, Assoc. Artistic Dir 1988–91; J. Ralph Corbett Distinguished Prof. of Opera, Univ. of Cincinnati 1986–2003, Prof. Emer. 2003–; Guest Dir, London Opera Centre, New Sadler's Wells Opera, Portland Opera, Seattle Opera, Calgary Opera, Edmonton Opera, Virginia Opera, Arkansas Opera –1990; Permanent Guest Dir, Arkansas Opera 1988–91; Florentine Opera of Milwaukee; Artistic Dir, Opera Theatre of Lucca 1996–2003; directed world premiere of Hermann's Wuthering Heights for Portland Opera, and Falstaff with Sir Geraint Evans and Don Giovanni with James Morris for the same co. *Honours:* Churchill Fellow 1969, Prague Int. Television Festival Prize for Mise-en-Scène 1975, Hungarian Government Kodály Medal 1982, 14 times winner Nat. Opera Asscn Prize for best college production in USA, Manchester Evening News Award and Sunday Times (London), Post-Corbett Award, Award for Excellence, Univ. of Cincinnati. *Address:* 3 The Cottages, King Sterndale, Buxton, Derbyshire SK17 9SF, England (home). *Telephone:* (1298) 214383 (home). *E-mail:* m.hf@btopenworld.com (home).

FREDERIKSEN, Joel David, MMus; American singer (bass) and musician (lute); *Musical Director, Ensemble Phoenix Munich;* b. 17 April 1959, Minnesota; m. Carolina Mora Cordero; two c. *Education:* Oakland Univ., master-classes with Helena Lazarska at Salzburg Mozarteum, ind. studies at New York Univ. and pvt. studies with William Schumann and Myron McPherson. *Career:* career includes appearances in opera, oratorio and in concert on stages world-wide; solo appearances at operatic festivals including Salzburg Summer Festival (under Dennis Russell Davies in Kurt Weill's Aufstieg und Fall der Stadt Mahagonny), Vancouver Summer Festival (role of Plutone in Monteverdi's Orfeo under Paul O'Dette and Stephen Stubbs), Hong Kong Arts Festival (performed in Monteverdi's L'incoronazione di Poppea and Orfeo with Ensemble for Early Music, New York); performed in staged medieval music dramas Lazarus as well as Daniel and the Lions at Australia's Brisbane Arts Festival and in New York and Washington, DC; appeared at Passau Music Festival with Orpheus Choir of Munich singing Giacomo Carissimi's Jephthe and as narrator/bass soloist in premiere of Be Still, composed by Lawrence Traiger on theme of 'September 11'; as oratorio soloist, sang Bach's B-minor Mass with Jordi Savall and La Capella Reial de Catalunya in Spain; has closely cooperated with orchestras including New York's Fairfield Orchestra and Atlanta Baroque Orchestra, with which he appeared as Jesus in Bach's St John Passion and Polyphemus in Georg Friedrich Handel's Acis and Galatea; performed Monteverdi's Marienvespers and Biber's Requiem with the Freiburger Baroque Orchestra and Orlando di Lasso Ensemble; bass singer with numerous ensembles, including Huelgas Ensemble, Ensemble Gilles Binchois and Musica fiata; mem. Waverly Consort, Boston Camerata, toured extensively with both and recorded more than a dozen CDs during 1990s; has made a speciality of the self-accompanied lute song; regular guest around Europe with programmes of English, French and Italian music for bass voice and Renaissance lute and archlute; Musical Dir Ensemble Phoenix, Munich. *Recordings include:* Orpheus, I Am 2004, The Elfin Knight 2007, O felice morire (German Critics' Prize) 2008, Rose of Sharon 2011, Requiem for a Pink Moon – An Elizabethan Tribute to Nick Drake 2012; contribs to albums by Ensemble Unicorn, Musica Fiata, Josquin Capella, Huelgas Ensemble, Orpheus Choir Munich, Vox Resonat, Boston Camerata, Ensemble for Early Music, Waverly Consort. *Honours:* Distinguished Musicianship Award, Oakland Univ. 1990, 2012, Alumnus of the Year in Music, Oakland Univ. 2003, Classical Musician of the Year, Munich Evening News 2008, Orphée d'Or, Acad. du Disque Lyrique, Opéra Bastille, Paris for his basso profondo singing with Dame Emma Kirkby 2011. *Current Management:* c/o Magda Wallner, Dvořák Artists International, Kalouskova 13, 683 01 Rousinov, Czech Republic. *Fax:* (517) 371573. *E-mail:* magdalena.dvorakova@dvorakartists.com. *Website:* www.dvorakartists.com. *Address:* Hohenzollernstrasse 21, 80801 Munich, Germany (office). *Telephone:* (160) 7249633 (office). *E-mail:* info@joelfrederiksen.com (office). *Website:* www.ensemble-phoenix.com (office); www.joelfrederiksen.com.

FREDMAN, Myer, LRAM; British conductor and author; b. 29 Jan. 1932, Plymouth, Devon, England; m. Jeanne Winfield 1954; two s. *Education:* Dartington Hall and The Opera School, London. *Career:* debut in Cork; Glyndebourne Festival with operas by Mozart, Verdi, Maw and Von Einem; Glyndebourne Touring Opera 1968–74; State Opera of South Australia; Seymour Group; guest conductor throughout Europe, America and Australia; BBC television; Wexford, Perth and Adelaide Festivals also at Hong Kong Fest; conductor in Poland, Belgium, Romania and Germany; conducted Cavalli's L'Ormindo at Brussels 1972, Bizet's Carmen in Hamburg 1973 and Il Barbiere di Siviglia in Sydney 1974; season 1992 with La Bohème for the Canadian Opera Company, Toronto and Le nozze di Figaro in Sydney; Head of Opera at the New South Wales Conservatorium 1981–92, including the premiere of Lawrence Hargrave by Nigel Butterfly in 1988; Assoc. Artist, The Australian Opera 1991–99; concert debut South America 1992 at Montevideo and Buenos Aires; conducted Australian premieres of Midsummer Marriage, Death in Venice and One Man Show; Dialogues des Carmélites 1997. *Recordings:* Bax Symphonies 1 and 2, London Philharmonic Orchestra, No. 3 with Sydney Symphony; H. Brian Symphonies 16 and 22 with London Philharmonic Orchestra; Delius Paradise Garden with London Philharmonic Orchestra; Benjamin Overture to an Italian Comedy; Respighi Sinfonia Drammatica, Piano Concerto with Sydney Symphony; Puccini Le Villi with Adelaide Symphony; Britten and Delius recordings. *Publications:* The Conductor's Domain 1999, From Idomeneo to Die Zauberflöte 2002, The Drama of Opera 2003, Maestro, Conductor or Metro-Gnome 2005. *Honours:*

bronze medal Italian Government 1965. *Current Management:* c/o Grant Rogers Musical Artists' Management, 8 Wren Crescent, Bushey Heath, Hertfordshire WD23 1AN, England. *Telephone:* (20) 8950-2220. *Fax:* (20) 8950-3570. *E-mail:* info@ngrartists.com. *Website:* www.ngrartists.com. *Address:* 18A Nietta Road, Lindisfarne 7015, Tasmania (home). *Telephone:* (3) 6243-1368. *E-mail:* mfredman@netspace.net.au. *Website:* www.netspace .net.au/~mfredman.

FREDRIKSSON, Karl-Magnus; Swedish singer (baritone); b. 6 Feb. 1968, Stockholm. *Education:* Music High School, Opera High School, studied with D Fischer-Diskau. *Career:* debut at Stockholm Royal Opera, 1996; recital at Wigmore Hall, 1994, 1995; Recitals at Helsinki Opera Stage, 1996; and in Stockholm Opera Stage, 1997; Die Lustige Weiber von Windsor, Stockholm Opera, 1997; Radio Opera in Swedish Radio, 1997; Several tours with Eric Ericson in Europe; Figaro in Il Barbiere di Siviglia, Royal Opera Stockholm, 1998; mem. The Swedish Theatre Order. *Recordings include:* Kullervo (Sibelius) with Colin Davis; Die Lustige Witwe (Lehar) with John Eliot Gardiner; Nordic Romances (solo recording); Summer Night, 1999. *Honours:* major soloist prize from the Swedish Royal Music Acad., 1993; Miriam Helin Competition in Helsinki. *Address:* c/o Göran Eliasson, Eliasson Artists, Skeppargatan 86, 114 59 Stockholm, Sweden. *Telephone:* (8) 667-24-03. *E-mail:* goran@eliassonartists.com. *Website:* www.eliassonartists.com; www .fredrikssonthesinger.com.

FREEDMAN, Gertrud; German singer (soprano); b. 1933. *Education:* Augsburg Conservatory. *Career:* sang at Passau and Mainz 1957–60, Munich Staatsoper 1960–80; guest appearances at Lisbon and Barcelona as Sophie and Blondchen, Komische Oper Berlin as Rosina in Paisiello's Barbiere di Siviglia; other roles include Mozart's Papagena and Despina, Anna in Intermezzo, Zdenka, Oscar, Musetta, and Adele in Die Fledermaus.

FREEDMAN-MILLER, Amelia, CBE, FRAM; British music administrator; *Founder and Artistic Director, Nash Ensemble;* b. 21 Nov. 1940, d. of Henry Freedman and Miriam Freedman (née Claret); m. Michael Miller 1970; two s. one d. *Education:* St George's School, Harpenden, Henrietta Barnet School, London. *Career:* music teacher, King's School, Cambridge, Perse School for Girls, Cambridge, Chorleywood Coll. for the Blind, Sir Philip Magnus School, London 1961–72; founder and Artistic Dir Nash Ensemble 1964–; Artistic Dir Bath Int. Festival 1986–93, Bath Mozartfest 1995–; Musical Adviser Israel Festival 1989–; Programme Advisor Philharmonia Orchestra 1992–95; Head of Classical Music, South Bank Centre 1995–; chamber music consultant for numerous projects at the Barbican and South Bank Centre, London. *Honours:* Hon. DMus (Bath Univ.) 1993; Chevalier, Ordre des Arts et des Lettres, Chevalier, Ordre Nat. du Mérite 1996; Worshipful Company of Musicians Cobbett Gold Medal 1996, Royal Philharmonic Soc./Performing Right Soc. Leslie Boosey Award 2000. *Current Management:* c/o Matthew Brailsford, 14 Cedars Close, Hendon, London, NW4 1TR, England. *E-mail:* nash_ensemble@ lineone.net (office). *Website:* website.lineone.net/~nash_ensemble; www .southbankcentre.org.uk (office).

FREEMAN, David; Australian stage director; b. 1 May 1952, Sydney; m. Marie Angel. *Career:* f. Opera Factory, Sydney 1973, in Zürich 1976, with 20 Swiss productions; productions for Opera Factory, London 1981–98 included The Knot Garden, Punch and Judy, The Beggar's Opera, Cavalli's La Calisto, Birtwistle's Yan Tan Tethera (world premiere 1986); Eight Songs for a Mad King by Peter Maxwell Davies, Ligeti's Adventures/Nouvelles Aventures and Reimann's The Ghost Sonata; Mozart's three Da Ponte operas presented at QEH as part of bicentenary celebrations; has also produced Osborne's Hells Angels; f. Opera Factory Films 1991; directed Prokofiev's The Fiery Angel for Marinsky Theatre, St Petersburg, Covent Garden and Metropolitan, New York; operas by Birtwistle, Maxwell Davies, Ligeti and Mozart have been shown on BBC and Channel 4 television, UK; for ENO has produced Orfeo, Akhnaten by Glass (British premiere), The Mask of Orpheus (world premiere) and The Return of Ulysses; productions elsewhere have included La Bohème for Opera North, Manon Lescaut at the Opéra-Comique, Paris, and work in Germany, Houston and New York; The Magic Flute, for Opera Factory 1996; Butterfly and Tosca, Raymond Gubbay 1998–2001; Nabucco for Opera Australia 2005. *Honours:* Chevalier, Ordre des Arts et des Lettres 1985. *Current Management:* Athole Still Ltd, Foresters Hall, 25-27 Westow Street, London, SE19 3RY, England.

FREEMAN-ATTWOOD, Jonathan, BMus, MPhil, FKC, FRNCM; British educator, musician (trumpet), producer and writer; *Principal, Royal Academy of Music;* b. 4 Nov. 1961, Woking, England; m. Henrietta Parham; one s. one d. *Education:* Univ. of Toronto, Christ Church, Oxford. *Career:* Dean of Undergraduate Studies, RAM 1991–95, Vice-Prin. and Dir of Studies 1995–2008, Prin. 2008–; Prof., Univ. of London 2001–; Fellow, King's Coll., London; mem. Bd, Garsington Opera 2012–, Chair. Artistic Cttee; Trustee, Associated Bd of the Royal Schools of Music, Young Classical Artist Trust, SAGA Trust British Library and Countess of Munster Trust. *Recordings:* numerous recordings as producer for ind. labels (ASV, BIS, Sony, Harmonia Mundi, Channel Classics, Naxos, Avie, Simax, Hyperion, Chandos); recordings as trumpet soloist: Albinoni Sonatas and Concertos with Ian Simcock, Bach Connections with Colm Carey, Rheinberger and Elgar with John Wallace and Colm Carey, La Trompette Retrouvée and Trumpet Masque, Romantic Trumpet Sonatas, A Bach Notebook for Trumpet, The Neoclassical Trumpet with Daniel-Ben Pienaar. *Radio:* broadcaster and reviewer for BBC Radio 3. *Publications:* contrib. to New Grove (second edn), Music and Letters,

Musical Times, Early Music, Gramophone. *Honours:* Diapason d'Or and Gramophone Awards as producer 1995–2015. *Address:* Royal Academy of Music, Marylebone Road, London, NW1 5HT, England (office). *Telephone:* (20) 7873-7377 (office). *Fax:* (20) 7873-7314 (office). *E-mail:* k.mckiernan@ram.ac .uk (office).

FREIBERG, Christine; British singer (soprano); b. 1966, England; m.; two c. *Education:* Royal College of Music with Marion Studholme, studied in Paris with Bruce Brewer. *Career:* Clori in Cavalli's L'Egisto for St James's Opera; First Niece in Peter Grimes in Nantes and Cologne; Cherubino for Reisopera in The Netherlands; appearances with Opéra de Nantes in Ariadne auf Naxos; Kullervo by Sallinen; Götterdämmerung and Parsifal; season 1998–99: Flower Maiden in Parsifal for Reiseopera, Netherlands; Italian Singer in Capriccio for Opera Nantes; Nele in Till Eulenspiegel for Nantes, 1999; Fyodor in Boris Godunov for Opera Ireland, 1999; Il re pastore: Aminta, for Musiek theater, Transparant, Belgium, 2002 and 2003 tour; many concert appearances. *Current Management:* Music International, 13 Ardilaun Road, London, N5 2QR, England. *Telephone:* (1727) 766432. *E-mail:* pc.raymond@virgin.net.

FREIER, Jurgen; German singer (baritone); b. 3 Feb. 1943, Danzig. *Career:* debut at Dresden Staatsoper 1973, as Silvio in Pagliacci; Dresden until 1980, as Papageno, Rossini's Figaro and Belcore; guest appearances throughout Eastern Europe; Berlin Staatsoper from 1980, notably as Lysiart in Weber's Euryanthe, in the title role of Graf Mirabeau by Matthus (premiere 1989) and Eugene Onegin; Düsseldorf 1991, in Schreker's Die Gezeichneten; Hamburg 1995, in the premiere of Schnittke's Historia von Dr Johann Fausten, Munich 1996, in the premiere of Bose's Schlachthof 5; Komische Oper Berlin as Pizarro and Cologne Opera as Kurwenal 1998; season 1999–2000 as Wagner's Donner and Gunther at Hamburg, Kurwenal for Cologne Opera, and Alberich at Chemnitz.

FREIRE, Nelson; Brazilian pianist; b. 18 Oct. 1944, Boa Esperança. *Education:* studied with Nise Obino and Lúcia Branco in Brazil, with Bruno Seidlhofer in Vienna. *Career:* debut at Vienna Acad. of Music, performing Brahms' Sonata in F sharp minor 1959; duo partner Martha Argerich; has appeared with orchestras, including the Berlin Philharmonic, Munich Philharmonic, Bayerische Rundfunk, Concertgebouw Orchestra of Amsterdam, Rotterdam Philharmonic, Tonhalle Orchestra of Zurich, Vienna Symphony, Royal Philharmonic, London Symphony, London Philharmonic, Israel Philharmonic, Mariinsky, St Petersburg Philharmonic, Czech Philharmonic, Orchestre National de France, Orchestre de Paris, Radio France Philharmonic, Monte Carlo Orchestra, Orchestre de la Suisse Romande, Leipzig Gewandhaus Orchestra, New York Philharmonic, Cleveland Orchestra, Boston Symphony, Chicago Symphony, Los Angeles Symphony, San Francisco Symphony, Montreal Symphony; signed exclusive recording contract with Decca 2001; Chair. jury, Marguerite Long Competition 2001. *Recordings include:* Chopin 24 Préludes (Edison Prize 1972, Diapason d'Or, Grand Prix de l'Académie Charles Cros, Choc du Monde de la Musique) Villa-Lobos/ Tchaikovsky Concerto, Grieg Concerto, Schumann Concerto, Liszt Totentanz, Brahms Piano Concertos (Gramophone Award for Best Recording 2007), Piano duos with Martha Argerich/Chopin's The Nocturnes 2010, Chopin Études Op.10 and Op.25, Debussy Préludes/Schumann Selected Works, Beethoven 4 Sonatas, Liszt Selected Works, Nelson Freire Brasileiro, Chopin Sonatas. *Honours:* Dr hc (Universidade Federal do Rio de Janeiro); Légion d'Honneur 2011, Commdr, Ordre des Arts et des Letters 2007, Ordem do Rio Branco; prize winner, Int. Piano Competition of Rio de Janeiro 1957, Dinu Lipatti Medal, London 1964, First Prize Vianna da Motta Competition, Lisbon 1964, Diapason d'Or, Grand Prix de l'Académie Charles Cros. *Current Management:* Agence Artistique Jacques Thelen, 15 avenue Montaigne, 75008 Paris, France. *Telephone:* (1) 56-89-32-00. *Fax:* (1) 56-89-32-01. *E-mail:* jthelen@wanadoo.fr. *Website:* www.jacquesthelen.com. *Address:* c/o Decca Music Group, 8 St James's Square, London, W14 8NS, England. *E-mail:* nelsonfreirepiano@gmail.com. *Website:* www.nelsonfreire.com.

FREITAG, Erik; Austrian composer and violinist; b. 1 Feb. 1940, Vienna. *Education:* Vienna Hochschule für Musik, studied with Karl-Birger Blomdahl in Stockholm. *Career:* violinist, Swedish Radio 1964–66, Philharmonic Orchestra, Stockholm 1967–1970; section leader, Conservatory of Vienna; Composer-in-Residence, Northwestern Michigan Coll., USA (in asscn with Int. Festival Earth/Arts Traverse City, Mich.) 1996; has performed with Chamber Orchestra of Belarus, Berliner Symphoniker (Frühbeck de Burgos), Orquesta Sinfonica de Madrid (López Cobos), Orchestra Novaya Russia, Tchaikovsky Orchestra Moscow (Eugeny Bushkov); Composer-in-Residence, Moulin d'Andé, France 1997; mem. Austrian Soc. of Composers, Int. Soc. for Contemporary Music (Austrian Section), Ensemble Wiener Coll. (Admin.). *Compositions:* Quintet for clarinet, horn, violin, cello and piano, Circuits Magiques for string quartet, Limericks: five songs for medium voice and six instruments, Immagini for violin solo, flute, oboe, violin, viola, cello, double bass and piano, Yoziguanatzí for orchestra, five Triaphonies for various instruments, Concerto for marimba and string orchestra, Quintet for flute and string quartet, Marsyas and Apollo for flute and guitar, García Lorca Canciones Españoles Antiguas for orchestra, Guridi (six Spanish songs) for orchestra, En svensk jullegend for celesta, harp and string quartet, Icnocuicatl (five Indian songs) for chamber orchestra, Strindberg-ljus och skugga for chamber ensemble. *Recordings:* Helle Nacht for strings 1990, Sonata for cello and piano 1990, Triaphonie I for horn, violin and piano 1995, Soul-Sky for violin solo 1995, El retablo de la catedral de Tarragona for chamber ensemble 1992, Yoziguanatzí for orchestra 1994, 2009, Triaphonie II for saxophone, violin and piano, Passages in the Wind: Poems by John Gracen Brown for baritone and seven instruments, Reflections in Air for string trio, three pieces for string quartet, Strindberg-ljus och skugga for chamber orchestra, Idun for violin and piano, Sonata Nachtstücke for violin and viola, Canciones Españolas Antiguas by García Lorca, Novelette (Fantasie on two Belarusian themes) for strings 2010, Björnlunda-serenad for flute and two guitars 2011, Zwei Nachtstücke for orchestra 2014, Mussorgsky/Freitag Orchestration of Sunless 2015. *Radio:* Austrian Radio, Radio Sweden, Radio Berlin, Radio Clásica de España. *Television:* TV2 (France). *Honours:* Hon. mem. Samtida Musik, Stockholm 2005; Competition Prize, Nordelbische Tage, Hamburg 1975, Austrian Ministry of Educ. Prize 1975, City of Vienna Prize 1979, Theodor Körner Prize 1981. *Address:* Schippergasse 20, 1210 Vienna, Austria (home). *Telephone:* 650-406-3409 (mobile) (office). *Fax:* (1) 294-5108 (office). *E-mail:* erik.freitag@aon.at (home).

FRÉMAUX, Louis Joseph Félix; French orchestral conductor; b. 13 Aug. 1921, Aire-sur-la-Lys; m. 1st Nicole Petitbon 11948; four s. one d.; 2nd Cecily Hake 1999. *Education:* Conservatoire Nat. Supérieur de Musique, Paris. *Career:* Musical Dir and Perm. Conductor of Orchestre Nat. de l'Opéra de Monte-Carlo, Monaco 1955–66; Prin. Conductor, Rhône-Alpes Philharmonic Orchestra, Lyon 1968–71; Prin. Conductor and Musical Dir, City of Birmingham Symphony Orchestra 1969–78; Chief Conductor, Sydney Symphony Orchestra 1979–81, Prin. Guest Conductor 1982–85; guest appearances in Austria, Belgium, Holland, France, Italy, New Zealand, Norway, Switzerland, South America and Germany. *Honours:* Hon. mem. RAM 1978; Chevalier, Légion d'honneur; Croix de Guerre (twice); Hon. DMus (Univ. of Birmingham) 1978; 8 Grand Prix du Disque Awards; Koussevitsky Award. *Address:* 21 rue de la Place, 41500 Avaray, France. *Telephone:* (2) 54-81-73-42.

FRENI, Mirella; Italian singer; b. (Mirella Fregni), 27 Feb. 1935, Modena; d. of Ennio Fregni and Gianna Fregni (née Arcelli); m. 1st Leone Magiera 1955; one d.; m. 2nd Nicolai Ghiaurov (died 2004). *Career:* debut 1955 as Micaëla in Carmen, debut at Glyndebourne Festival 1961, Royal Opera House, Covent Garden 1961, La Scala, Milan 1962, Metropolitan Opera, NY 1965; has sung at Vienna State Opera, Rome Opera, Barcelona Gran Teatro del Liceo, Boston Opera, La Scala and at Salzburg Festival and leading opera houses throughout the world; retd from the stage 2005; frequent master-classes, including extended classes in voice at Acad. of Vocal Studies, Vignola, Italy. *Recordings include:* Carmen, Falstaff, La Bohème, Madame Butterfly, Tosca, Verdi Requiem, Aïda, Don Giovanni. *Major roles include:* Nanetta in Falstaff, Mimi in La Bohème, Zerlina in Don Giovanni, Susanna, Adina in L'Elisir d'amore, Violetta in La Traviata, Desdemona in Otello. *Honours:* Midem Classical Award for Lifetime Achievement 2010, Opera News Award for invaluable contribution to opera 2012. *Current Management:* c/o Jack Mastroianni, IMG Artists, Carnegie Hall Tower, 152 West 57th Street, 5th Floor, New York, NY 10019, USA. *Telephone:* (212) 994-3525. *E-mail:* jmastroianni@imgartists.com. *Website:* imgartists.com/artist/mirella_freni.

FREUD, Anthony Peter, OBE, LLB; British/American opera administrator and barrister; *General Director, Lyric Opera of Chicago;* b. 30 Oct. 1957, London, England; s. of the late Joseph Freud and Katalin Freud (née Löwi); partner Colin Ure. *Education:* King's Coll. School, Wimbledon, King's Coll., London. *Career:* trained as barrister before becoming theatre man. at Sadler's Wells Theatre Co. 1980–84; Co. Sec., Welsh Nat. Opera 1984, Head of Planning 1989–92, Gen. Dir 1994–2005; Chair. Opera Europe 2001–05; Gen. Dir and CEO Houston Grand Opera, Tex., USA 2006–11; Gen. Dir Lyric Opera of Chicago 2011–; Exec. Producer, Opera, Philips Classics 1992–94; Chair. OPERA America 2008–12; Jury Chair., BBC Cardiff Singer of the World Competition 1995–2005; Trustee, Nat. Endowment for Science, Tech. and the Arts 2004–05. *Honours:* Hon. Fellow, Univ. of Cardiff 2002, Royal Welsh Coll. of Music and Drama 2005. *Address:* Lyric Opera of Chicago, 20 North Wacker Drive, Chicago, IL 60606, USA (office). *Telephone:* (312) 827-3550 (office). *Fax:* (312) 332-0503 (office). *E-mail:* afreud@lyricopera.org (office). *Website:* www.lyricopera.org (office).

FREUDENTHAL, Otto; Swedish composer and pianist; b. 29 July 1934, Gothenburg; s. of Heinz Freudenthal and Elsbet Freudenthal; one s. *Education:* Trinity Coll., London, UK, studied piano with Ilona Kabos. *Career:* debut as pianist, Wigmore Hall, London; recitals and concerts in UK, Germany, Switzerland, The Netherlands, Scandinavia, Japan, China, USA; broadcasts; teacher, Royal Northern Coll. of Music, Manchester; asst to Otto Klemperer –1973; mem. Swedish Soc. of Composers, Svenska Tonsättares Internationella Musikbyrå. *Compositions:* chamber music, viola concerto, concert piece for trombone and orchestra, In Highgate Cemetery for strings, chamber opera, A BankoMat cantata, The Song about Our Town, a cantata to Linköping's 700 year jubilee, string quartet 1991, Saxophone Quartet 1992, Adagio for strings 2012. *Recordings include:* Wir Wandelten (with Cheryl Jonsson, soprano), Sudden Fire, Music for Viola. *Publications:* Music and Equity (essay, with Irene Lotz), Chamber Music, Plucked String Music (49th edn). *Honours:* Harriet Cohen Memorial Medal for interpretation of Beethoven, Swedish State Cultural Stipend 1977, 1987. *Address:* 6 Hillsborough, Corris Uchaf, Powys, SY20 9RG, Wales. *Telephone:* (1654) 761405. *E-mail:* mail@ottofreudenthal.co.uk. *Website:* www.ottofreudenthal.co.uk.

FREY, Alexander James, BMus, MMus; American organist, pianist, music director and conductor; b. 5 Oct. 1961, Chicago, IL. *Education:* Univ. of Michigan, Ann Arbor, studied with Gavin Williamson, Robert Glasgow, Gustav Meier, Dietrich Fischer-Dieskau in Berlin. *Career:* appeared as pianist and organist with Berlin Philharmonic Orchestra, Hollywood Bowl Orchestra, Deutsches Sinfonie Orchester, Rundfunk-Sinfonie Orchester Berlin, Brandenburg Chamber Orchestra (also Guest Conductor 1993–94), Ars Longa Chamber Orchestra of Germany (also Principal Guest Conductor 1991–94), Ensemble Europa (also Conductor 1995), mems of Chicago Symphony Orchestra (under Mauceri, Abbado and others); annual worldwide recital tours; Music Dir, Hamburg Kammerspiele Theater 1992–93, Berliner Ensemble 1992–95, collaborating with Peter Zadek; Music Dir, Antony and Cleopatra at Edinburgh Festival, Vienna Festwochen, Holland Festival, Berlin 1994, Das Wunder von Mailand, Venice Festival, Fifth European Festival, Berlin 1995, Ich bin das Volk, Heidelberg Festival, Berlin 1995; conducted Ensemble Europa, Israel, Berlin to commemorate end of World War II 1995; chamber music with Ruggiero Ricci, Vermeer Quartet and Donald McInnes; various film and television appearances, radio broadcasts; Principal Conductor, Philharmonia Orchestra of Berlin 1995–; Principal Conductor, Artist-in-Residence and Artistic Adviser, Festival Ruidoso 1995–. *Current Management:* Artist Recitals, 3427 Fernwood Avenue, Los Angeles, CA 90030, USA.

FREY, Hans-Joachim; German theatre director; *General Director, Theater Bremen;* b. 10 June 1965, Gehrden, Hannover; s. of Dietrich Frey and Christa Frey; m. Kirsten Blanck; one d. *Career:* Artistic Dir Theater Eisenach 1993–95, Bremer Theater 1995–97; Opera Dir Sächsischen Staatsoper Dresden 1997–2007; Gen. Dir Theater Bremen 2007–; Chair. Int. Forum for Business and Culture; teaches at Hochschule für Musik Franz Liszt, Weimar. *Address:* Theater Bremen, Goetheplatz 1-3, 28010 Bremen, Germany (office). *Telephone:* (42) 136530333 (office). *Fax:* (42) 13653332 (office). *E-mail:* info@theaterbremen.de (office). *Website:* www.theater-bremen.de (office).

FREYER, Achim; German stage director and theatre designer; b. 30 March 1934, Berlin. *Education:* Akademie der Kunste, Berlin. *Career:* designed sets and costumes for the Ruth Berghaus production of Il Barbiere di Siviglia at the Berlin Staatsoper 1967; created designs for Cardillac and Pelléas et Mélisande at the Cologne Opera 1973–75; directed and designed Iphigénie en Tauride at the Munich Staatsoper 1979 (seen at Amsterdam and Basle 1990); Philip Glass's Satyagraha and the premiere of Akhnaten at the Stuttgart Staatsoper 1981, 1984; Orfeo ed Euridice at the Deutsche Oper Berlin 1982, Die Zauberflöte at Hamburg (seen at the Vienna Festival 1991); Iphigénie en Tauride at the Deutsche Staatsoper 1994; Die Zauberflöte at Salzburg 1997; Don Giovanni at Schwetzingen 1998; Genoveva for Opera Leipzig 2000, L'anima del filosofo for Schwetzinger Festspiele 2001, Mesaa da Requiem for Deutsche Oper Berlin 2001, Bach's H-moll Messe 2002, Wagner's Ring cycle, Los Angeles Opera 2009. *Current Management:* c/o Julia Lukjanova, Balmer and Dixon Berlin, Laubacherstrasse 11, 14197 Berlin, Germany. *Telephone:* (30) 20658470. *Fax:* (30) 206584719. *E-mail:* lukjanova@badix-berlin.de. *Website:* www.badix.ch; www.freyer-ensemble.de.

FRIED, Anneliese; German singer (mezzo-soprano); b. 1962. *Education:* studied in Karlsruhe. *Career:* sang at Aachen Opera 1985–91, Munster 1991–93, Cologne from 1993; guest appearances at Düsseldorf (Mistress Quickly in Falstaff 1995), Dresden (Fidalma in Il Matrimonio Segreto 1996), Paris, Zürich and Geneva; other roles have included Mary in Der fliegende Holländer, Ericlea in Monteverdi's Ulisse, Mrs Sedley in Peter Grimes, and Orlofsky in Die Fledermaus; Prof., Cologne Musikhochschule from 1995.

FRIED, Joel Ethan, BMus, MMus, DMA; American conductor; b. 22 April 1954, California; m. Mary Anne Massad 1990; one step-d. *Education:* Univ. of Southern California. *Career:* debut at Hidden Valley Opera 1978; European debut, Heidelberg Castle Festival 1981; Asst Conductor, New York City Opera 1980–82; resident Conductor, Heidelberg Castle Festival 1981–; Studienleiter, Saarland State Theatre 1983–86; Chorusmaster, Cleveland Opera 1990–92; Chorusmaster and Music Administrator, Pittsburgh Opera 1992–; conducting appearances with Zürich Opera, Fort Worth Opera and Cleveland Opera. *Honours:* second prize American Conductors' Competition 1978, Hans Swarowsky Int. Conducting Competition Special Prize for Contemporary Music, Vienna 1984.

FRIED, Miriam; Israeli (b. Romanian) violinist; b. 9 Sept. 1946, Satu-Mare. *Education:* Rubin Acad. Acad. of Music, Israel, Juilliard School, USA with Ivan Galamian. *Career:* debut at Carnegie Hall, New York 1969; Royal Festival Hall, England; appearances with orchestras worldwide, including Los Angeles Philharmonic, Philadelphia, Cleveland, Chicago, Boston Symphonies, New York Philharmonic, Berlin and Munich Philharmonics, Vienna Symphony, Zürich Tonhalle, Orchestre Nationale de France; appearances include Stuttgart Radio Orchestra (conducted Neville Marriner), Danish Radio (Kurt Sanderling), Jerusalem Symphony at Berlin Festival, Orchestre Nationale, Belgium, Philharmonic Orchestras, Monte Carlo, Stuttgart, Nuremburg, Nouvel Orchestre Philharmonique, Paris; opened Helsinki Festival (with Helsinki Philharmonic conducted by Gennadi Rozhdestvensky) 1988; Hollywood Bowl (Yuri Temirkanov) 1988; Cleveland Orchestra (Mariss Jansons) 1989; Santa Cecilia (Temirkanov) 1989; Orchestre de Paris (Kurt Sanderling) 1989; frequent engagements with Royal Philharmonic Orchestra and frequent solo concerto appearances with Chicago Symphony Orchestra; BBC television and Promenade concerts; Edinburgh Festival; Scottish Nat. Orchestra; Bournemouth Symphony; numerous recitals; fmr first violinist, Mendelssohn String Quartet; Artistic Dir Steans Music Inst., Ravinia Inst. 1993–. *Recordings include:* album of recital, solo violin works, Bach, Sibelius Violin Concerto, Helsinki Philharmonic (Okko Kamu) 1988. *Honours:* First Prize, Paganini Int. Competition, Genoa, Italy 1968, First Prize, Queen

Elisabeth of Belgium Int. Competition 1971. *Current Management:* Opus 3 Artists, 470 Park Avenue South, 9th Floor North, New York, NY 10016, USA. *Telephone:* (212) 584-7500. *Fax:* (646) 300-8200. *E-mail:* info@opus3artists .com. *Website:* www.opus3artists.com/artists/miriam-fried.

FRIEDE, Stephanie; American singer (soprano); b. 1959, New York. *Education:* Juilliard School, Oberlin Conservatory. *Career:* debut at Houston Opera 1985, as Siebel in Faust; sang further at Houston as Zerlina, Micaela and Manon; European debut at Stuttgart 1987, as Adina; Amsterdam 1987, as Massenet's Cendrillon; engagements at Buxton Festival as Eleanore d'Este in Torquato Tasso by Donizetti, at Cologne as Violetta and elsewhere in Europe as Gounod's Juliette, Anne Trulove, and Mimi. *Current Management:* c/o Konstantin Unger, Balmer & Dixon Management AG, Kreuzstrasse 82, 8032 Zurich, Switzerland. *E-mail:* unger@badix.ch. *Website:* www.stephaniefriede .com.

FRIEDEL, Martin Kurt, BSc, PhD; German composer; b. 3 Aug. 1945, Warwateil. *Education:* Univ. of Melbourne. *Career:* fellowships and residences in Australia and Germany 1976–95; commissions from theatres in Australia and from Adelaide Festival of the Arts 1992. *Compositions include:* Sin (seven-act opera for four voices and orchestra) 1978, Two Songs for soprano and ensemble 1982, South of North (one-act chamber opera) 1985, Conversations Before the Silence (cantata) 1989, Foxy (one-act chamber opera) 1991, The Heaven Machine and Seduction of a General (one-act operas for soprano and electronics) 1991, Four Choral Fragments for Walter Benjamin 1992, Songs from the Astronauts for soprano, baritone and ensemble 1994, The Third Planet (oratorio) 1995, Three Night Pieces from string quartet 1995. *Honours:* Chicago International Film Festival Award for Best Score 1994. *Current Management:* Australian Music Centre, PO Box N690, Grosvenor Place, Sydney, NSW 1220, Australia. *E-mail:* info@australianmusiccentre.com.au. *Website:* www.australianmusiccentre.com.au/artist/friedel-martin.

FRIEDERICH, (Albert) Matthias; German oboist, recorder player and composer; b. 16 June 1954, Heidelberg; m. Margaret Joy Stone 1980; one s. *Education:* Cologne Music College with G. Hoeller, H. Hucke and A. Meidhof. *Career:* debut, recorder soloist, Vivaldi's Sopranini Recorder Concerto in C major, Heidelberg, 1966; Concerts with George Malcolm, Amadeus Quartet, Mozarteum Quartet, Munich String Trio, and Sinfonia Varsovia, Poland; Since 1988, member of Pifferari di Santo Spirito Trio, Heidelberg (with Margaret Friederich and Peter Schumann); Concerts, Berlin, Paris, Dallas and Tokyo; mem, International Double Reed Society. *Compositions:* Happy Birthday Variations, 1989; Highstreet Dixie, 1990; Enigma Blues for FGB, 1991; Jubilee Stomp, 1992; Amusement, 1994. *Recordings:* Music for Fun, 1991; Pifferari Safari, 1993. *Publication:* contrib. article, Jazz on the oboe and the cor anglais, to Rohrblatt. *Address:* Floringasse 2, 69117 Heidelberg, Germany.

FRIEDLI, Irene; Swiss singer (mezzo-soprano); b. 1965, Rauchlisberg. *Education:* Basle Music Acad. with Kurt Widmer, masterclasses with Dietrich Fischer-Dieskau and Brigitte Fassbaender. *Career:* Shepherd and Hope in Monteverdi's Orfeo and Dryad in Ariadne auf Naxos, Lucerne Opera 1993–94; Zürich Opera as Gertrude in Roméo et Juliette, Suzuki, Third Lady in Die Zauberflöte, Mercédès (Carmen) and the title role in L'Enfant et les Sortilèges 1994; opera and concert engagements with such conductors as Helmuth Rilling, Horst Stein, Michel Corboz and Neeme Järvi; has appeared widely as guest in Switzerland and abroad, notably in contemporary concert music. *Honours:* prizewinner Hugo Wolf (Stuttgart), Schubert (Graz) and Othmar Schoeck (Lucerne) Competitions.

FRIEDMAN, Jefferson, MM; American composer and musician; b. 1974, Swampscott, Mass. *Education:* Columbia Univ., Juilliard School with John Corigliano; also studied with George Tsontakis and Christopher Rouse. *Career:* works performed throughout USA and abroad including at Kennedy Center for the Performing Arts, Lincoln Center's Alice Tully Hall and Avery Fisher Hall, Carnegie Hall, Hollywood Bowl, Bowery Ballroom and (Le) Poisson Rouge; repeat commissions from Leonard Slatkin and Nat. Symphony Orchestra (NSO); performances by NSO, Chicago Symphony, Chiara Quartet, Corigliano Quartet, American Contemporary Music Ensemble; performed with rock bands including Shudder To Think; collaborated with electronic music duo Matmos. *Compositions include:* orchestral: Elusion for flute, French horn, bassoon, piano 1994, Spindle for oboe, violin, viola, cello 1995, The Gift of the Tongue, chamber opera 1996, Pull for violin, percussion, 6 dancers 2000, Sacred Heart: Explosion for orchestra 2000/07, March for orchestra 2001, Paper Song/Epithalamion for soprano and string trio 2002, The Throne of the Third Heaven of the Nations' Millennium General Assembly 2004, 3 string quartets, 78 for flute, clarinet, piano, violin, cello 2006, On In Love for rock vocalist, amplified and processed flute, clarinet, string quartet, piano, percussion 2009–11. *Recordings include:* Corigliano/ Friedman: String Quartets 2009, Jefferson Friedman: Quartets 2011. *Honours:* Rome Prize in Musical Composition 2004, ASCAP Leo Kaplan Award, BMI Student Composer Award, ASCAP Morton Gould Young Composer Award, Palmer-Dixon Prize. *Current Management:* c/o Christina Jensen PR, 394 Broadway, 5th Floor, New York, NY 10013, USA. *E-mail:* christina@ christinajensenpr.com. *E-mail:* jeffeff@jeffersonfriedman.com (office). *Website:* jeffersonfriedman.com (office).

FRIEDRICH, Reinhold; German musician (trumpet); b. 14 July 1958, Weingarten, Baden; m. Annette Friedrich; two s. *Education:* studied with Edward Tarr, Pierre Thibaud in Paris. *Career:* debut with Berlin Philhar-

mony; numerous television and live performances, including the EBU Opening Concerto with B. A. Zimmermann's Nobody Knows De Trouble I See, Biennale Berlin 1997; Trumpet Concerto by Benedict Mason; Hummel's First Recordings of the Concerto in E Major with the Historical Keyed Trumpet 1996; Prof., Hochschule fur Musik, Karlsruhe; Docent, Hochschule Musik und Theater Zürich; mem. Int. Trumpet Guild. *Recordings:* B. A. Zimmermann's Nobody Knows De Trouble I See, Hummel and Puccini Recordings with the Historical Keyed Trumpet, Sequenza X by Berio, Gubaidulina's Trio. *Honours:* first prize German Music Competition 1981, winner ARD Competition, Munich 1986. *Address:* Künstlersekretariat Astrid Schoerke, Grazer Strasse 30, 30519 Hannover, Germany (office).

FRIEND, Caroline; British singer (soprano); b. 1950, England. *Career:* concert appearances in the UK, Switzerland, Belgium, France, Germany and The Netherlands; repertoire includes Handel's Oratorios, Bach's Oratorios and Cantatas, Schubert's A flat Mass, Britten's War Requiem under Stephen Cleobury in King's Coll., Vaughan Williams' Sea Symphony, Howells' Hymnus Paradisi, Rossini's Stabat Mater, Dvořák's Stabat Mater; Mahler's 4th Symphony and Les Nuits d'Eté with the Netherlands Philharmonic under Franz-Paul Decker; appearances with the Songmakers' Almanac in England and Ireland, performing Robin Holloway's Women in War; sang Diane in Rameau's Hippolyte et Aricie for the English Bach Festival under Jean-Claude Malgoire in Athens and Versailles and at Covent Garden; other roles include Mozart's Donna Anna, Susanna, Pamina, Countess and Fiordiligi (Pavilion Opera), Rosalinde (Die Fledermaus), Norina (Don Pasquale), Hannah in The Merry Widow, Tosca and Mimi, (Puccini), Berta in The Barber of Seville and performances of Balfe's The Siege of Rochelle; engagements in all the major London concert halls and with many choral societies.

FRIEND, Lionel; British conductor; b. 13 March 1945, London; s. of Norman A. C. Friend and Moya L. Dicks; m. Jane Hyland 1969; one s. two d. *Education:* Royal Grammar School, High Wycombe, Royal Coll. of Music, London, London Opera Centre. *Career:* with Welsh Nat. Opera 1969–72, Glyndebourne Festival/Touring Opera 1969–72; Second Kapellmeister, Staatstheater Kassel, West Germany 1972–75; Conductor ENO 1976–89; Musical Dir New Sussex Opera 1989–96; Conductor-in-Residence, Birmingham Conservatoire 2003–10; Guest Conductor BBC Symphony, Philharmonia, Royal Philharmonic, Nash Ensemble, Scottish Chamber, Royal Ballet etc. and in Australia, Belgium, Brazil, Denmark, France, Germany, Hungary, the Netherlands, NZ, Norway, Spain, Sweden, USA. *Honours:* Hon. Fellow, Birmingham Conservatoire. *Current Management:* c/o Robert Gilder & Co., N102 Westminster Business Square, 1-45 Durham Street, London, SE11 5JH, England. *Telephone:* (20) 7580-7758. *Fax:* (20) 7580-7739. *E-mail:* rgilder@robert-gilder .com. *Website:* www.robert-gilder.com. *Address:* 136 Rosendale Road, London, SE21 8LG, England (home). *Telephone:* (20) 8761-7845 (home). *E-mail:* lionelfriend@hotmail.com. *Website:* lionelfriend.com.

FRIGERIO, Ezio; Italian stage designer; b. 16 July 1930, Como. *Education:* Milan Polytechnic. *Career:* costume designer, Giorgio Strehler's Piccolo Teatro d'Arte from 1955; collaborations with Strehler, Eduardo de Filippo and other directors in Italy and elsewhere; designed Don Pasquale at the Edinburgh Festival 1962, Tosca at Cologne 1976, Carmen at Hamburg 1988; collaborations with Nuria Espert for Madama Butterfly and Traviata at Scottish Opera 1987, 1989, Rigoletto at Covent Garden 1988, Elektra at Barcelona 1990; La Scala Milan 1990, with Fidelio and The Queen of Spades; designs for Il Turco in Italia and Anna Bolena at Madrid season 1990–91; Andrea Chénier for Buenos Aires 1996; Aida at Palermo 1998; frequent associations with costume designer, Franca Squarciapino.

FRIMMER, Monika; German singer (soprano); b. 1955, Marburg. *Education:* studied in Hanover. *Career:* Staatstheater, Hanover 1981–93, notably in operas by Mozart and the Baroque repertory; Herrenhausen Festival 1981, as Morgana in Handel's Alcina; Hanover 1989, as Matilde in a revival of Steffani's Enrico Leone; Deutsche Oper Berlin 1991–92; sang in Handel's Radamisto at Göttingen 1993; concert engagements throughout Europe, and in the USA and Israel. *Recordings include:* Messiah, Mozart Masses and Pergolesi Stabat Mater; Radamisto.

FRISCH, Walter M., BA, MA, PhD; American academic; b. 26 Feb. 1951, New York, NY; m. Anne-Marie Bouché 1981, two s. *Education:* Yale Univ., Univ. of California, Berkeley. *Career:* Asst Prof. of Music, Columbia Univ. 1982–88, Assoc. Prof. 1988–94, Prof. 1994–; Co-Ed., 19th Century Music 1984–92; research in music of 19th and 20th centuries, especially the Austrian tradition (Schubert, Brahms, Schoenberg); mem. American Musicological Soc., American Brahms Soc. *Publications:* Brahms' Alto Rhapsody (ed. facsimile edn) 1983, Brahms and the Principle of Developing Variation 1984, Schubert: Critical and Analytical Studies (ed.) 1986, The Early Works of Arnold Schoenberg 1993. *Honours:* ASCAP Deems Taylor Award for outstanding books on music 1985, 1995.

FRISELL, Sonja; British stage director; b. 5 Aug. 1937, Richmond, Surrey. *Education:* Guildhall School. *Career:* associated with Carl Ebert at Städtische Oper Berlin and at Glyndebourne; staff producer, La Scala, solo producer in North and South America and Europe; directed La Favorite at 1977 Bregenz Festival, Vivaldi's Tito Manlio at La Scala 1979, and Handel's Agrippina at Venice 1985; Marriage of Figaro, San Francisco 1982; directed Carmen at Buenos Aires 1985, Aida at Metropolitan 1988; Lyric Opera of Chicago 1989–90; Don Carlos, Khovanshchina at San Francisco 1990; Don Giovanni,

Capetown 1991; directed Die Zauberflöte for Washington Opera at Kennedy Center 1991 (revived 1998), Forza del Destino at San Francisco 1992, Otello at Washington, DC 1992, Ballo at Chicago 1992, Rigoletto at Gothenburg 1993, Trovatore at Chicago 1993, Lucia at Calgary 1994, Eugene Onegin, Calgary 1996, La Gioconda, La Scala 1997, Elena da Feltre, by Mercadante, Wexford 1997, Turandot at Seville 1998, and at Trieste, Cagliari, Santander and Cordoba 1999, Eugene Onegin, Phoenix 2000, Otello, Washington 2000, Eugene Onegin with Arizona Opera 2000, La Traviata in Rio de Janeiro 2001, Don Carlos, Washington, DC 2001, Carmen, Iceland 2001, Otello, Tokyo 2002, Salome with Arizona Opera 2003, Turnadot in Helsinki 2004; mem. AGMA. *Current Management:* Columbia Artists Management Inc., 1790 Broadway, New York, NY 10019-1412, USA. *Telephone:* (212) 841-9500. *Fax:* (212) 841-9744. *E-mail:* info@cami.com. *Website:* www.cami.com.

FRITH, Benjamin, BA; British pianist; b. 11 Oct. 1957, Sheffield, England; m. Donna Sansom 1989, three d. *Education:* studied with Fanny Waterman, Univ. of Leeds. *Career:* official London debut in recital at Wigmore Hall 1981, sponsored by Countess of Munster Trust; performing career of recitals, concertos and participation in chamber music ensembles in London and the provinces including South Bank, Wigmore Hall, Usher Hall Edinburgh, Aldeburgh, Harrogate and many major festivals; television and radio appearances; concerts in Italy, Spain, Germany, Poland, Israel and America; mem. Incorporated Soc. of Musicians. *Recordings:* Diabelli and 32 variations by Beethoven; chamber music; Schumann piano music, Davidsbündlertänze (opus 6), Fantasiestücke (opus 12); Martin Ellerby, piano and chamber works, and Collage, French and English, clarinet and piano music with Linda Merrick; Mendelssohn, complete solo piano works and complete works for piano and orchestra; Messiaen, Visions de l'Amen, with Peter Hill, Malcolm Arnold, complete piano works. *Honours:* jt first prize Busoni Int. Pianoforte Competition 1986–, gold medal and jt first prize Arthur Rubinstein Int. Piano Masters Competition 1989. *Current Management:* Michael Brewer Artists Management, 2 Beech Avenue North, Worcester, WR3 8PX, England. *Telephone:* (1905) 454361. *E-mail:* michaelbrewer@mbam.co.uk. *Website:* www.mbam.co.uk.

FRITTOLI, Barbara; Italian singer (soprano); b. 1967, Milan. *Education:* Giuseppe Verdi Conservatory, Milan. *Career:* sang first at the Teatro Comunale, Florence, and has appeared as Mozart's Countess under Abbado, Fiordiligi in Vienna and Ravenna 1996; Donna Elvira at Naples; Desdemona with Antonio Pappano at Brussels and with Abbado at the Salzburg Easter Festival 1996; New York Met and Covent Garden debuts as Mimi and Micaela; Medora in Verdi's Il Corsaro, Turin 1996; concerts include Strauss's Vier Letzte Lieder in Milan, Rome and London, Rossini's Stabat Mater, Ein Deutsches Requiem and the Verdi Requiem; sang Fiordiligi in Così fan tutte at Covent Garden and Glyndebourne 1998; season 1999–2000 in new production of Falstaff at Covent Garden; season 2002–03 as Donizetti's Maria Stuarda at Edinburgh (concert) and Vitellia in La Clemenza di Tito at Covent Garden, returning for Luisa Miller; toured Japan with Metropolitan Opera in La Bohème 2011. *Recordings include:* Il Trittico, with Mirella Freni; Il Barbiere di Siviglia; Pergolesi's Stabat Mater, with Riccardo Muti. *Honours:* Winner of several international competitions. *Current Management:* DM Artist Management, Via Al Fiume 16/A, 6963 Pregassona, Switzerland; Monaco Music Management, Palais de la Scala, 1 Avenue Henry Dunant, Monte-Carlo, 98000, Monaco. *Telephone:* (91) 9401185 (Monaco); 607936063 (Switzerland). *Fax:* (91) 9402367 (Monaco). *E-mail:* office@dmartist.com; info@3m.mc; monacomusicmanagement@gmail.com. *Website:* www.dmartist.com; www.3mcmusic.com; www.frittolibarbara.com (home).

FRITZSCH, Johannes; German conductor; *Chief Conductor, The Queensland Orchestra*; b. 1960, Meissen. *Education:* studied with his father and Carl Maria von Weber Music Acad., Dresden. *Career:* second Kapellmeister, Rostock Opera 1982–87; conducted Il Barbiere di Siviglia and Il Matrimonio Segreto at the Semper Opera Dresden 1987; Kapellmeister, Staatsoper Dresden 1987–, with more than 350 opera and ballet performances; guest conductor, Royal Swedish Opera, Stockholm; regular orchestra concerts in fmr E Germany; West German debut 1990 with Beethoven's Fifth Piano Concerto and the New World Symphony with the Nat. Theatre Orchestra, Mannheim; Danish debut with the Orchestra of Danish Radio at Copenhagen 1991; also Don Giovanni, Royal Opera, Stockholm 1991; Rialto Theatre, Copenhagen 1991; Entführung, Nozze di Figaro and Don Giovanni, Royal Opera, Stockholm 1991; La Traviata, Hanover 1991; Hansel and Gretel at Sydney, with Australian Opera 1992; Kapellmeister, Staatsoper Hannover 1992–93; Die Bassariden at Freiburg 1993; Der Freischütz at Cologne 1997; Music Dir and Chief Conductor, Städtische Bühnen and the Philharmonische Orchester, Freiburg 1992–99; guest appearances with orchestras, including Berliner Sinfonie Orchester, Copenhagen Radio Orchestra, Düsseldorfer Sinfoniker, Hamburger Sinfoniker, Nationaltheater-Orchester Mannheim, Norddeutsche Philharmonie Rostock, Orchestre Philharmonique Montpellier, Orchestre Philharmonique Strasbourg, Orchestre Philharmonique Toulouse, Oslo Radio Orchestra, Philharmonie Essen, Staatskapelle Dresden, Staatskapelle Schwerin, Staatsorchester Halle, State Orchestra of Victoria, Stockholm Radio Orchestra, Sydney Symphony Orchestra, Tasmanian Symphony Orchestra, West Australian Symphony Orchestra; and with opera cos, including Bastille Opera Paris, Deutsche Oper Berlin, Komische Oper Berlin, Opera Australia, Opera Cologne, Opera Malmö, Royal Opera Stockholm; Conductor of Der Rosenkavalier, Barber of Seville for Opera Australia in Sydney, La Bohème for Royal Opera Stockholm and The Rake's Progress and Entführung for Staatsoper Dresden 2004; Conductor of Don Giovanni in Sydney, Falstaff in Dresden and Der Rosenkavalier in Graz 2005; Chief Conductor, Philharmonisches Orchester Graz and Grazer Oper 2006–; Chief Conductor, The Queensland Orchestra 2008–. *Current Management:* c/o Haydn Rawstron Ltd, 29a High Street, First Floor, West Wickham, Kent BR4 0LP, England. *Telephone:* (20) 8777-6070. *Fax:* (20) 8777-4073. *E-mail:* enquiries@haydn-rawstron.com. *Website:* www.haydnrawstron.com. *Address:* c/o Oper Graz, Theater Graz, Kaiser Josef Platz 10, 8010 Graz, Austria (office). *Telephone:* (316) 8008 (office). *Website:* www.theater-graz.com/opernhaus (office).

FRONTALI, Roberto; Italian singer (baritone); b. 1963. *Career:* sang at Rome Opera from 1986, in Spontini's Agnese di Hohenstaufen, Valentin in Faust and Massenet's Albert; season 1992–93 as Belcore at Dallas and Ford in Falstaff at La Scala; sang Rossini's Figaro at Florence and Naples 1993; San Francisco 1993, as Riccardo in I Puritani; season 1995–96 with Marcello in La Bohème at Metropolitan; Florence 1996, as Enrico in Lucia di Lammermoor; other roles include Nottingham in Roberto Devereux by Donizetti, Verdi's Miller and Puccini's Sharpless; season 1998 with Alphonse in La Favorite at Rome and Rossini's Figaro at Genoa and for Royal Opera, London; season 2000–01 as Count Luna at the New York Met, Eugene Onegin at Florence, Germont for the Opéra Bastille, Falstaff at Frankfurt and Ernesto in Il Pirata by Bellini at Catania. *Recordings include:* Falstaff, L'Elisir d'amore. *Current Management:* Zemsky/Green Artists Managment, 104 West 73rd Street, New York, NY 10023, USA. *Website:* www.robertofrontali.it.

FRÖST, Martin; Swedish clarinettist. *Education:* studied with Hans Deinzer in Hannover and Sölve Kingstedt in Stockholm. *Career:* has appeared as soloist with orchestras, including BBC Symphony, Chamber Orchestra of Europe, Rotterdam Philharmonic, BBC Philharmonic, Acad. of St Martin-in-the-Fields, City of Birmingham Symphony, Czech Philharmonic, Stuttgart Radio Orchestra, NHK Symphony, Gothenburg Symphony, Swedish Radio Symphony; has performed at Concertgebouw, Amsterdam, Konzerthaus and Musikverein, Vienna, Louvre, Paris, Palais des Beaux Arts, Brussels, Carnegie Hall and Lincoln Center, New York and at festivals, including Schubertiade, Feldkirch, Vancouver, Mondsee, Trondheim 2005, Bremen Festival 2006, Baltic Sea Festival 2006, Verbier Festival 2006, Kamermuziek Festival, Trondheim 2005, Bremen 2006, Baltic Sea Festival 2006, Kamermuziek Festival, Utrecht 2006; has collaborated with musicians, including Mitsuko Uchida, Leif-Ove Andsnes, Roland Pöntinen, Heinrich Schiff, Christian Tetzlaff, Tabea Zimmermann, Janine Jansen, the Jerusalem Quartet; BBC New Generation Artist 2003–05; Dortmund Konzerthaus Junge Wilde (group of young artists) 2006–09; Artistic Dir Musik i Dalarna's Vinterfest 2007; has created music programmes, including No Strings Attached, Dance to Black Pipe, Beyond All Clarinet History, Voices and Wings, which combine choreography, theatre and music; performed world premieres of Krzysztof Penderecki's Concerto for Three Clarinets 2004, Anders Hillborg's Peacock Tales, Aho's Clarinet Concerto 2006, Sandström's Clarinet Concerto 'Marche funebre – Be Still My Child'; future debuts include orchestras in Oslo, Los Angeles, Seoul and return visits to the BBC Symphony, Residentie, Gothenburg (both in Sweden and on tour) and Rotterdam. *Recordings include:* French Beauties and Swedish Beasts 1994, Krysztof Penderecki Chamber Works for strings and clarinet (with The Tale Quartet) 1994, Close Ups (with Niklas Brommare) 1996, Concertos dedicated to Benny Goodman 1998, The Pied Piper of the Opera 2000, Schumann 2002, Mozart, Clarinet Concerto and Quintet 2003, Brahms, Clarinet Sonatas and Trios 2005, Weber Clarinet Concertos 2006, Aho and Nielsen Clarinet Concertos 2007, Works by Bernhard Henrik Crusell 2008, Fröst & Friends 2010, Dances to a Black Pipe (Int. Classical Music Award for Best Concerto 2013) 2011. *Honours:* Winner, Borletti-Buitoni Trust 2003, Nippon Music Award, Akzo Nobel Music Award, Léonie Sonning Music Prize 2014. *Current Management:* c/o Jennifer Spencer, Harrison/Parrott Ltd, 12 Penzance Place, London, W11 4PA, England. *Telephone:* (20) 7313-3531. *Fax:* (20) 7221-5042. *E-mail:* jennifer.spencer@harrisonparrott.co.uk. *Website:* www.harrisonparrott.com; www.martinfrost.se.

FROUNBERG, Ivar, MA, DipComp; Danish composer and academic; *Professor Emeritus, Norwegian Academy of Music*; b. 12 April 1950, Copenhagen; m. 1st Inge Sínderskov Madsen (divorced 2005); one s.; m. 2nd Ann Holstvoll 2008. *Education:* State Univ. of NY, USA, Royal Danish Acad. of Music. *Career:* Lecturer, Electro-acoustic Music 1986–90, Asst Prof., Musical Composition 1991–99, Royal Danish Acad. of Music; mem. Bd Danish Composers' Soc. 1982–94, KODA 1988–94; Music Co-ordinator ICMC 1994; Chair. Int. Soc. for Contemporary Music Festival 1996, DIEM 1998–2000; Councillor, Danish Arts Council 1999–2001; Sr Prof., Norwegian Acad. of Music, Oslo 2000–12, Prof. Emer. 2012–. *Compositions:* Drei-Klang 1982, Henri Michaux preludes 1985, Embryo 1985, Multiple Forms 1986, A Dirge: Other echoes inhabit the Garden 1988, What Did the Sirens Sing as Ulysses Sailed By? 1989, A Pattern of Timeless Motion 1989, Time and the Bell 1990, SHâTaLè 1991, World Apart 1992–94, . . . to arrive where we started 1993, Hydra 1996, Droemmespor 1997, The Anatomy of a Point 1990–95/97, Hoodoos 1997, Quasi una sonata 1998, Cancion, no cantado 1998, Voyelles 1999, SAXO 2000, Prélude-Voyage-Jotunheim 2002, Logogriphes 2003, . . .and sank in tumult into a lifeless ocean 2005, Grenzland 2006, Waves and Velocities 2007, Friction and Transformation 2009, The Quantum Mechanics of My Life 2010, Three Cognitive Objects and Improvisations 2011. *Recordings:* A Pattern of Timeless Motion, What did the Sirens Sing as Ulysses sailed by?, A Dirge: Other Echoes Inhabit the

Garden, Worlds Apart, ... to arrive where we started. *Publications:* Theory and Praxis in the compositional methods of Iannis Xenakis–an exemplification; Komponisten Pierre Boulez, 1985; Ein Schwebender Stein... Positionen 37; contrib. to Dansk Musiktidskrift, Nutida Musik. *Honours:* Ancker Grant 1994, three-year grant, Danish State Arts Council 1994–96, Prize in Honour of Carl Nielsen 1995, Poul Schierbeck Prize of Honour 1998. *Address:* PO Box 5190, Gydasvei 6, Majorstua 0302 (office); Betzy Kjelsbergsvei 14C, 0486 Oslo, Norway (home). *Telephone:* 90-94-67-19 (home). *E-mail:* ivar@frounberg.dk (home). *Website:* www.frounberg.dk/ivar.

FU, Haijing; Chinese singer (baritone) and academic; b. 1960. *Education:* studied in London and New York. *Career:* concert engagements include Mozart's Requiem with Montreal Symphony Orchestra, Zemlinsky's Lyric Symphony, Beethoven's Ninth, Carmina Burana with Pacific Symphony and Cleveland Orchestra, Verdi's Requiem in Geneva; Mendelssohn's Erste Walpurgisnacht with Boston Symphony and Mozart's C minor Mass with Cincinnati Orchestra; Metropolitan Opera debut 1990, as Germont, followed by Sir Richard Forth in I Puritani; Renato with Atlanta Opera, Enrico and Verdi's Miller at Philadelphia and Filippo in Bellini's Bianca e Fernando at Catania, Italy, 1992; appearances as Rigoletto with San Diego and Edmonton Opera companies; other roles include Marcello in La Bohème, and Posa in Don Carlos; sang Germont at Philadelphia, 1992; currently Prof. and Vice-Pres. Peking Univ. Acad. of Opera. *Honours:* Second Prize, Benson and Hedges Gold Award Int. Competition, London 1987, winner, Metropolitan Opera Nat. Council Competition 1988. *E-mail:* hsifh@pku.edu.cn. *Website:* opera.pku.edu .cn.

FUCHS, Barbara; Swiss singer (soprano); b. 1959, Zürich. *Education:* studied in Frankfurt and Zürich, masterclasses with Erik Werba, Sena Jurinac and Elisabeth Schwarzkopf. *Career:* sang at the Ulm Opera, 1983–85, as Blondchen, Adele, Olympia, Rosina and Susanna; Gelsenkirchen, 1985–87, as Sophie, the Queen of Night and Annina in Eine Nacht in Venedig; Frankfurt from 1990, as Zerbinetta, Helena in Reimann's Troades and other coloratura roles; guest appearances throughout Germany and frequent concert engagements.

FUCHS, Olivia, BA (Hons); British opera director; b. 15 Aug. 1963, London, England; m. Nigel Robson; one s. one d. *Education:* Westfield Coll., London and Drama Studio, London. *Career:* debut with Johnny Johnson by Kurt Weill for Opera Factory, Zurich 1992; Britten's Turn of the Screw, for Bath Theatre Royal 1993; Handel's Arminio for London Handel Soc. 1996; Mozart's Marriage of Figaro at Queen Elizabeth Hall 1996; La Bohème 1997 and Il Trovatore 1998, both for Opera South, Ireland; Mozart's Apollo and Hyacinth for the Classical Opera Co. 1998; premiere of John Lunn's The Maids for ENO/Lyric Theatre, Hammersmith 1998; Britten's The Turn of the Screw for the Brighton Festival 2000; Verdi's La Traviata for English Touring Opera 2001–02; Janáček's Osud and Sarka for Garsington Opera 2002; Beethoven's Fidelio for Opera Holland Park 2003; Wolf's Italian Songbook for Royal Opera House 2003; Dvořák's Rusalka for Opera North 2003; Tchaikovsky's Cherevichki for Garsington Opera 2004; Verdi's Luisa Miller for Opera Holland Park 2004; Peter Sellar's Theodora for Opera du Rhin 2004; Don Giovanni for Opera North 2005; Macbeth for Opera Holland Park 2005; Roméo et Juliette for British Youth Opera 2005; Pied Piper for Opera North 2005; Midsummer Night's Dream for Royal Opera House 2005, 2008; Marriage of Figaro for ENO 2006; Maynight for Garsington Opera 2006; Rigoletto for Danish Nat. Opera 2007; Rusalka for Opera Australia 2007; Jenůfa for Opera Holland Park 2007; The Rake's Progress for Garsington Opera 2008; Katya Kabanova for Opera Holland Park 2009; La Traviata for Danish Nat. Opera 2009; Rusalka for Opera North 2010; Pelleas and Melisande for Opera Holland Park 2010; Fidelio for Opera Holland Park 2010; Magic Flute for Garsington and Oviedo 2011; Saul for Buxton Festival 2011; Pelléas et Mélisande for Teatro Colón, Buenos Aires 2011; Il Trovatore for Danish Nat. Opera 2011; fmr Assoc. Dir, Glyndebourne and Opera Factory; mem. Directors' Guild of GB. *Honours:* Helpmann Award for Best Opera 2007, Green Room Awards for Best Opera and Best Direction 2007. *Current Management:* c/o Musichall Ltd, Oast House' Crouch's Farm, Hollow Lane, East Hoathly, East Sussex, BN8 6QX, England. *Telephone:* (1825) 810437. *E-mail:* info@musichall.uk.com. *Website:* www.musichall.uk.com.

FUGE, Katharine; British singer (soprano); b. 1968, Jersey. *Education:* City Univ., London. *Career:* engagements with English Bach Soloists, notably on Bach Cantata Pilgrimage tour 2000, throughout Europe and in New York; St Matthew Passion with De Nederlande Bachvereniging 2001; Handel and Zelenka with Collegium Vocal Gent, Handel's Athalia with Frieder Bernius in Göttingen, Acis and Galatea in Denmark; repertory includes Poulenc's Gloria, Stabat Mater by Stanford and Pergolesi, and Messiah; sang First Mermaid in Weber's Oberon at the Barbican Hall, London 2002. *Recordings include:* albums: Bach Cantata Pilgrimage, Vivaldi Gloria and Handel Dixit Dominus, Dvořák Mass in D. *Website:* www.katharinefuge.com.

FUGELLE, Jacquelyn; British singer (soprano); b. 1949, London, England; m. George Johnston 1975; one d. *Education:* Guildhall School of Music, Vienna Academy, studied in Rome. *Career:* debut at Wigmore Hall, London, 1975; extensive repertoire in oratorio, recital and opera; appearances in England, Canada and Europe; Television and radio appearances in the Netherlands, Sweden and for the BBC; Debut at Royal Opera House, Covent Garden, 1991 as Arbate in Mozart's Mitridate; other roles at Royal Opera House include Falcon, in Die Frau ohne Schatten; Debut with Scottish Opera, 1993; major

oratorio performances include Elijah with London Philharmonic Orchestra, conducted by Kurt Masur; broadcasts include Messiah in Norway, Mendelssohn's 2nd Symphony in Paris and B Minor Mass in Iceland; mem. ISM, Equity. *Recordings:* Operatic Favourites with Joan Sutherland, Luciano Pavarotti; Music by Bottesini with Tomas Martin on double bass and Anthony Halstead on piano. *Honours:* Silver Medal, Worshipful Company of Musicians; Countess of Munster; Royal Society of Arts Scholarships; 2nd Prize, Kathleen Ferrier Competition. *E-mail:* jacquelyn@fugelle.fsworld.co.uk. *Website:* jacquelynfugelle.com.

FUJIKAWA, Mayumi; Japanese violinist; b. 27 July 1946, Asahigawa City. *Education:* Toho Conservatoire, Tokyo, Antwerp Conservatory, Belgium, and studied with Leonid Kogan in Nice. *Career:* concerts with leading orchestras in South America, Australia, Israel, Asia, Japan and Europe; American orchestras in Philadelphia, Boston, Chicago, Pittsburgh and Cleveland; festival engagements at Aldeburgh with Previn, Edinburgh with the Concertgebouw Orchestra and Kondrashin; other conductors include Barenboim, Dutoit, Foster, Haitink, Levine, Ormandy, Sanderling and Rattle; TV appearances playing the Mozart Concertos with Scottish Chamber Orchestra; BBC Promenade Concerts, London in Mozart's Sinfonia Concertante 1991. *Recordings:* Mozart Concertos with the Royal Philharmonic conducted by Walter Weller, Beethoven's Kreutzer and Franck's Sonata with Michael Roll, Tchaikovsky and Bruch Concertos with the Rotterdam Philharmonic, Sonatas by Prokofiev and Fauré. *Honours:* Second Prize, Tchaikovsky Int. Competition, Moscow 1970, First Prize, Henri Vieuxtemps Competition, Verviers, Belgium 1970. *Current Management:* c/o Harrison Turner Artists Management, 53 Ticknell Piece Road, Charlbury, Oxon., OX7 3TN, England. *Telephone:* (1608) 810330. *Fax:* (1608) 811331. *E-mail:* artists@harrisonturner.co.uk. *Website:* www.harrisonturner.co.uk.

FUJIOKA, Sachio; Japanese conductor; *Principal Conductor, Kansai Philharmonic Orchestra*; b. 1962, Tokyo. *Education:* studied in Japan with Kenichiro Kobayashi and Akeo Watanabe, Royal Northern Coll. of Music, UK. *Career:* Asst Conductor, BBC Philharmonic 1994; Conductor, Japan Philharmonic and Prin. Conductor, Manchester Camerata 1995–2000; Prin. Conductor, Kansai Philharmonic Orchestra 2001–; guest conductor, Royal Philharmonic, Hallé Orchestra, Bournemouth Symphony, Royal Liverpool Philharmonic, Swedish Chamber Orchestra, Norrköping Symphony, Gavle Symphony, Orchestre Nat. du Capitole de Toulouse, Moscow Radio Symphony, New Zealand Symphony, Melbourne Symphony, West Australian Symphony, Tasmanian Symphony, Queensland Orchestra, Stavanger Symphony, Singapore Symphony, Opera de Oviedo. *Recordings include:* several recordings of works by Takashi Yoshimatsu with BBC Philharmonic. *Honours:* Charles Grove Conducting Fellowship 1993. *Current Management:* c/o IMG Artists, The Light Box, 111 Power Road, London, W4 5PY, England. *Telephone:* (20) 7957-5800. *Fax:* (20) 7957-5801. *E-mail:* nmathias@imgartists .com. *Website:* www.imgartists.com.

FUKAI, Hirofumi; Japanese violist; b. 10 Feb. 1942, Saitama. *Education:* Juilliard School, USA with Ivan Galamian, Toho School, Tokyo, Basle Conservatory, Switzerland. *Career:* soloist with the Berne Symphony and the Hamburg Philharmonic 1970–87; NDR Symphony from 1988; concert performances throughout Europe, notably in the premieres of works by Zimmermann, Rihm and Henze (Compases para preguntas ensimismadas); Prof., Hamburg Musikhochschule from 1974. *Current Management:* Svensk Konsertdirektion AB, Danska vägen 25B, 41274 Göteborg, Sweden.

FUKASAWA, Ryoko; Japanese pianist; b. 22 June 1938, Togane City, Chiba Prefecture; m. Tomoyuki Fukasawa 1967 (deceased). *Education:* Hochschule für Musik und darstellende Kunst, Vienna, Austria. *Career:* debut recital in Tokyo with Tokyo Symphonia Orchestra 1953; recital in Vienna 1959; regular concerts with Tonkünstler Orchester conducted by E. Merzendorfer, Musikverein 1960; NHK Symphony Orchestra conducted by S. Ozawa in Tokyo 1963; Wiener Kammerorchester conducted by A. Quadri 1965; NHK Symphony Orchestra conducted by L. von Matacic 1966; concert tours of Switzerland, Hungary and Japan 1965–68, of Europe, South America and Asia; television and radio appearances in Japan and Europe; numerous premieres of contemporary music in Japan and Europe. *Recordings:* albums: Encore 1988, Piano Recital 1989, Beethoven Violin Sonata 1991, Schubert and Beethoven 1992, Trout Quintet (with Wiener Kammer Ensemble) 1992, Moments Musicaux 1997, Mozart Recital 1999. *Publications:* Diary for the Piano 1955, Diary from Vienna 1957, Schubert and Vienna (pocketbook on music) 1980, The Piano and Me 1991. *Honours:* first prize Student Music Competition, Japan 1950, first prize Japan Music Competition (organised by NHK and Mainich newspaper) 1953, first prize Geneva Int. Music Competition 1961.

FUKUHARA, Kan; Japanese flautist; b. Nagoya. *Education:* Tokyo Fine Arts Univ., studied with Sanzaemon Takara. *Career:* specializes in traditional Japanese music, often playing the nokan, a double-barrelled flute. *Recording:* Splendour of the Shamisen 1999. *Address:* c/o Playasound Records, Sunset France Productions, 96 rue du Château, Boulogne 92100, France (office).

FULGONI, Sarah; British singer (mezzo-soprano); b. 1970, London, England. *Education:* Royal Northern Coll. of Music. *Career:* has sung with the WNO from 1994 as Prince Charming in Cendrillon and Beatrice in Beatrice and Benedict; season 1995 as Dorabella with ENO, Strauss's Composer at Broomhill Opera, Celia in Haydn's Fedeltà Premiata at Garsington and Hyppolita in A Midsummer Night's Dream at the Ravenna

Festival; further engagements at the Harrogate and Schleswig-Holstein Festivals, at La Scala in Elektra and in Berlin in Mahler's Third Symphony; sang Carmen with WNO 1997 and Ino in Semele for Flanders Opera 1998; engaged in Carmen at Santa Fe; other roles include Charlotte in Werther (at Tel-Aviv), Monteverdi's Penelope (Geneva) and Leonora in La Favorita (Nice); sang Berlioz's Béatrice for WNO and Netherlands Opera 2001; Covent Garden debut as Federica in Luisa Miller 2003. *Honours:* Frederic Cox Award, Curtis Gold Medal, runner-up in Kathleen Ferrier Awards 1993.

FULKERSON, James Orville, MM; American composer and trombonist; b. 2 July 1945, Manville, Illinois. *Education:* Illinois Wesleyan University, University of Illinois. *Career:* fellow, Center for Creative Performing Arts, State University of New York at Buffalo 1969–72; residencies at the Deutscher Akademischer Austauschdienst in Berlin 1973, the Victorian College of the Arts, Melbourne 1977–79; resident at Dartington College, South Devon 1981–. *Compositions include:* Guitar Concerto 1972, To See a Thing Clearly for orchestra 1972, Co-ordinative systems Nos 1–10 1972–76, Orchestral Piece 1974, Music for Brass Instruments Nos 1–6 1975–78, Raucasity and the Cisco Kid or, I Skate in the Sun, theatre piece 1978, Concerto for amplified cello and chamber orchestra 1978, Vicarious Thrills for amplified trombone and pornographic film 1979, Symphony 1980, Force Fields and Spaces for trombone, tape and dancers 1981, Cheap Imitations IV for soloist, tape and films 1982, Put Your Foot Down Charlie for three dancers, speaker and ensemble 1982, Rats Tale for six dancers, trombone and ensemble 1983, Faust for tape 1992, Antigone, tape 1993, Eden, electronics 1992, Wood-Stone-Desert for trumpet, live electronics and tape 1996, Mixed-media works, television and film music; various instrumental pieces under the titles Space Music, Patterns, Metamorphosis and Chamber Musics. *Current Management:* c/o Sylvia Junge Management, 7 Elton Close, Kingston-upon-Thames, Surrey KT1 4EE, England. *Telephone:* (20) 8977-9613. *E-mail:* sylviajunge@hotmail.com.

FULLER, David Randall, AB cum laude, AM, PhD; American musicologist, organist and harpsichordist; b. 1 May 1927, Newton, Mass; s. of Joseph Cheever Fuller and Ruth Brodhead Fuller. *Education:* Harvard Univ., private organ study with E. Power Biggs, William Self and André Marchal, harpsichord with Albert Fuller. *Career:* served in USN 1945–46; Instructor, Robert Coll., Istanbul 1950–53; Asst Prof., Dartmouth Coll. 1954–57; Prof. of Music, State Univ. of New York, Buffalo 1963–98; mem. American Musicological Soc., American Guild of Organists, Soc. for Seventeenth-Century Music, American Bach Soc., Organ Historical Soc., Westfield Center for Early Keyboard Studies, Asscn Aristide Cavaillé-Coll. *Recordings include:* music by Armand-Louis Couperin (with William Christie), organ music of Widor, Reubke, Liszt, Stehle, Wagner and Fährmann. *Publications include:* A Catalogue of French Harpsichord Music 1699–1780 (with Bruce Gustafson) 1990, edns of keyboard works by Armand-Louis Couperin and Handel; contrib. of over 150 articles and chapters on French baroque music and historical performance to The New Grove Dictionary of Music and Musicians 1980, 2001, The New Harvard Dictionary of Music 1986, musicological journals and books. *Honours:* Hon. mem. Société Philharmonique d'Istanbul; John Knowles Paine Travelling Fellowship, Harvard 1960–61, Nat. Endowment for the Humanities Sr Fellowship 1976–77, CIES-Fulbright Research Award (Western European Regional Research Programme) 1985, Westrup Prize of the Music and Letters Trust 1997, Festschrift: The Worlds of Harpsichord and Organ, Liber Amicorum David Fuller 2014. *Address:* 54 Norwood Avenue, Buffalo, NY 14222, USA (home). *E-mail:* drfuller@buffalo.edu.

FULLER, Louisa; British violinist; b. 1964, England. *Education:* Royal Acad. of Music with Emanuel Hurwitz, studied with David Takeno. *Career:* extensive tours of Europe as principal second violin of the Kreisler String Orchestra, winner in 1984 of Jeunesses Musicales Competition in Belgrade; co-founder and Leader, Duke String Quartet 1985–, performing throughout the UK, with tours of Germany, Italy, Austria and Baltic states, and South Bank series 1991 with Mozart's early quartets; recorded soundtrack for Ingmar Bergman documentary, The Magic Lantern (Channel 4 television) 1988; BBC debut feature, features for French television 1990–91, playing Mozart, Mendelssohn, Britten and Tippett works, Brahms Clarinet Quintet for Dutch radio with Janet Hilton; Live Music Now series with concerts for disadvantaged people, The Duke Quartet invites... at the Derngate Northampton 1991 with Duncan Prescott and Rohan O'Hora; Resident Quartet of the Rydale Festival 1991; Residency at Trinity Coll., Oxford, with tours to Scotland and Northern Ireland and a concert at QEH 1991; extensive work with choreographers, Bunty Mathias, Union Dance and Rosas 1994–95. *Recordings include:* with Duke Quartet: Quartets by Tippett, Shostakovich and Britten, Dvořák (American) Barber Quartet and Kevin Volans Works 1995. *Honours:* RAM Poulet Award.

FULLJAMES, John; British opera director; *Associate Director of Opera, Royal Opera House. Education:* Christ's Coll. *Career:* fmr Asst, Glyndebourne, Royal Opera House and Grand Theatre de Genève; Co-founder and Artistic Dir The Opera Group 1997–2011, Adviser 2011–; Assoc. Dir Opera, Royal Opera House 2011–. *Productions include:* The Bear 1997, Triptych 1997, Die Feuersbrunst 1998, The Martyrdom of Saint Magnus 1999, Boys and Girls Come Out to Play 1999, The Nose 2000, Parthenogenesis 2000, The Threepenny Opera 2001, The Bluebird's Castle 2001, The Young Man with the Carnation 2002, Die Walküre 2002, Candide 2003, Girl of Sand 2003, Tobias and the Angel 2004, Bake for One Hour 2004, Hansel and Gretel 2005, The Birds 2005, Gentle Giant 2006, The Enchanted Pig 2006, Mavra & Gianni

Schicci 2007, Nabucco 2007, The Shops 2007, Varjak Paw 2008, Romeo et Juliette 2008, Into the Little Hill 2009, Das Portrait 2010, The Lion's Face 2010, The Adventures of Mr Broucek 2010, The Knight's Crew 2010, Street Scene 2011, From the House of the Dead 2011, Seven Angels 2011, Von Heute auf Morgen (Schoenberg) 2012, Sancta Susanna (Hindemith) 2012, La Clemenza di Tito 2013. *Address:* Royal Opera House, Covent Garden, London, WC2E 9DD (office); The Opera Group, Room 23SWB, King's College London, The Strand, London, WC2R 2LS, England. *Telephone:* (20) 7240-1200 (office); (20) 7848-7314. *Fax:* (20) 7848-2326. *E-mail:* info@roh.org.uk (office); enquiries@theoperagroup.co.uk. *Website:* www.roh.org.uk (office); www.theoperagroup.co.uk.

FURIC LEIBOVICI, Stéphane, DipMus; French composer and musician (double bass); b. (Stéphane Furic), 15 July 1965, Paris; s. of Simon Salomon Leibovici and Zelia Leibovici; partner, Corinne Pautard; two s. from previous relationship. *Education:* Berklee Coll. of Music, USA, double bass studies with William H. Curtis, improvisation studies with John LaPorta. *Career:* concerts include int. jazz festivals, tours, radio and TV shows, recordings for series of albums releases (Europe, N America, Asia), as leader of ensemble including Chris Cheek, Patrick Goraguer, Lee Konitz, Chris Speed, Jim Black; mem. SACEM, BMI (as composer and publr); written pieces for Dag Gabrielsen, Robert Schumann, Lee Konitz. *Major compositions include:* Kishinev (suite for quartet) 1990, Dances (suite for septet) 1994, Penelope: her hands 2002, Les Nuits de la Chapoulie-Nocturnal 2004, Clair-Obscurs I–V 2004, Le Feuillage des Gestes 2004, Phongsaly 2004, Quatre Intermezzi 2004, Siddartha (A Music of Tranquillity) 2005, (...les Astres sont anciens mais la nuit est nouvelle...) 2005, Vier Orchesterstücke 2005, Concertino for Piano 2005, Fragmente 2006, Erste Sinfonie 2007. *Recordings include:* Kishinev 1991, The Twitter-Machine 1993, Crossing Brooklyn Ferry 1995, Music for 3, vol. 1 2003, Phongsaly 2005, Starry Nights 2005. *Publication:* Downshifting—Capturing Music Performance. *Address:* Château de Fressanges, 87260 Vicqsur-Breuilh, France (home). *Telephone:* 6-33-97-27-22 (home). *E-mail:* stephane.furic@gmail.com. *Website:* www.stephanefuric.com.

FURLANETTO, Ferruccio; Italian singer (bass); b. 16 May 1949, Pordenone, Sicily. *Education:* studied with Campogaliani and Casagrande. *Career:* sang at Vicenza 1974 as Sparafucile in Rigoletto; Trieste 1974, as Colline in La Bohème, with José Carreras and Katia Ricciarelli; appearances at La Scala, Banquo, Turin, Leporello, and San Francisco as Alvise in La Gioconda; Metropolitan Opera 1980; Salzburg Festival from 1986, as Philip II and Leporello 1990, conducted by Riccardo Muti; San Diego and Covent Garden, 1988, as Mephistopheles and Leporello; sang Mozart's Figaro at Geneva and Fernando in La Gazza Ladra at the Pesaro Festival 1989; season 1991–92 included Le nozze di Figaro in Paris, London, Salzburg and New York; sang in Semiramide and Don Giovanni at the Metropolitan; concert performances of Mozart's Da Ponte operas with Chicago Symphony; other roles include Philippe II, Don Giovanni, Leporello with Karajan, Figaro (Salzburg), Figaro, Bastille, Procida in Vespri Siciliani, Scala; festival appearances 1996 at Salzburg (Don Giovanni) and Florence (Orestes); Philip II in Don Carlos for Royal Opera at Edinburgh 1998; season 2000–01 as Don Giovanni at Salzburg, Gremin in Eugene Onegin at Florence, Leporello for New York Met and Attila at Trieste; season 2014–15 as Philipp II in Don Carlo. *Recordings include:* Don Alfonso in Così fan tutte, conducted by James Levine; roles in Mozart's Da Ponte operas, conducted by Daniel Barenboim; videos of Don Carlos, Metropolitan and Salzburg, Rigoletto, Metropolitan, Vespri Siciliani at La Scala, and Don Giovanni at the Metropolitan and Salzburg; also many films. *Honours:* UN Hon. Amb. of Honour. *E-mail:* Daniel.Lombard@musicaglotz.com. *Website:* www.ferrucciofurlanetto.com.

FURLANETTO, Giovanni; Italian singer (bass-baritone); b. 1958. *Career:* sang in Italian opera houses from 1982; Trieste, 1989, in Donizetti's Linda di Chamounix, Florence, 1989, as Mozart's Figaro; Philadelphia Opera as Wurm in Luisa Miller; Season 1990 as Leporello at Trieste and Ircano in Rossini's Ricciardo e Zoraide at Pesaro; Salzburg Festival, 1995, as Masetto; Season 1995–96 as Escamillo at Nice and Wurm in Santiago; Mozart's Figaro at San Francisco, 1997; Season 1998 as Nonancourt in Rota's Italian Straw Hat, at La Scala; Sang Mozart's Figaro at Hamburg and Leporello in Baltimore, 2000. *Current Management:* Atelier Musicale S.r.l., Via Caselle 76, 40068 San Lazzaro di Savena (Bo), Italy. *Telephone:* (051) 199844 44. *Fax:* (051) 199844 20. *E-mail:* info@ateliermusicale.it. *Website:* www.ateliermusicale.it. *E-mail:* giovannifurlanetto@giovannifurlanetto.com. *Website:* www.giovannifurlanetto.com.

FURMANSKY, Abbie; American singer (soprano); b. 1969; m. Daniel Sutton; one s. *Education:* Juilliard School, New York and Santa Fe Opera School. *Career:* New York City Opera from 1993, as Micaela, Musetta, Janáček's Fox, and Lisette in La Rondine; engagements with Canadian Opera, and at Frankfurt, Washington (Esmerelda in The Bartered Bride) and New Jersey; Deutsche Oper Berlin from 1995, as Pamina, Zerlina, Sophie in Werther, Gretel, and Junge Mädchen in Schoenberg's Moses and Aron (season 1999–2000); concerts include Elijah, Haydn's Lord Nelson Mass, Mahler's 4th Symphony, Beethoven's Missa Solemnis and Mozart's Requiem and Vespers; Schoenberg's 2nd Quartet and Rossini's Petite Messe; Carnegie Hall debut, Oct. 2012; teacher of vocal technique, Berlin Staatsoper Opera Studio 2010–. *Recordings:* Ines in La Favorite by Donizetti. *Honours:* prizewinner Francesco Vinas Competition, Barcelona 1999. *Current Management:* c/o Robert Gilder and Co., N102, Westminster Business Square, 1-45 Durham Street, London, SE11 5JH, England. *Telephone:* (20) 7580-7758. *Fax:* (20)

7580-7739. *Website:* www.robert-gilder.com. *E-mail:* info@abbiefurmansky .net (office). *Website:* www.abbiefurmansky.net.

FURRER, Beat; Austrian (b. Swiss) composer, conductor and academic; *Conductor, Klangforum Wien;* b. 6 Dec. 1954, Schaffhausen, Switzerland. *Education:* Hoschschule für Musik und Darstellende Kunst, studied with Roman Haubenstock-Ramati (composition) and Otmar Suitner (conducting). *Career:* moved to Vienna in 1975 to study; co-f. Klangforum Wien ensemble, Music Dir 1985–1992, now Conductor; Prof. of Composition, Univ. of Music and Dramatic Arts, Graz 1991–; Guest Prof. in Composition, Hochschule für Musik und Darstellende Kunst, Frankfurt 2006–09; co-f. impuls, ensemble and composers' acad. for contemporary music; works include solo and ensemble music, orchestral and choral works and opera. *Compositions include:* String Quartet No. 1 1984, Poemas for mezzo-soprano, guitar, piano and marimba 1984, Retour an Dich for violin, cello and piano 1986, Voicelessness—The Snow Has No Voice for piano 1986, Aer for piano, clarinet and cello 1991, Nuun for 2 pianos and ensemble 1996, a due for viola and piano 1997, Risonanze for orchestra in 3 groups, Schleedoyer for string quartet, Spur for piano and string quartet 1998, Begehren Musiktheater 2003, Chiaroscuro für R.H.R., for orchestra, Ensemble for 4 clarinets, 2 piano, vibraphone and marimbaphone, Face de la chaleur for flute, clarinet, piano and orchestra in 4 groups, Phasma for solo piano 2002, Fama, opera in 8 Scenes (Golden Lion, Venice Biennale 2006) 2004–05, String Quartet No. 2, String Quartet No. 3 2004, Für Alfred Schlee for string quartet, Gaspra for ensemble, Illuminations for soprano and chamber ensemble, Madrigal for orchestra, Narcissus-Fragment for 2 narrators and 26 players, Piano Concerto 2007, Studie 2—à un moment de terre perdue for ensemble, Studie— Übermalung for large orchestra, Tiro mis tristes redes for orchestra, Trio for flute, oboe or saxophone and clarinet, Ultimi cori for mixed chorus and 3 percussionists, Wie diese Stimmen for 2 cellos, opera: Die Blinden (Wiener Staatsoper commission) 1989, Narcissus 1994, Begehren (music theatre) 2003, Invocation 2003, Wüstenbuch 2010, La Bianca Notte 2015. *Honours:* mem. Akad. der Künste, Berlin 2005; City of Vienna Music Prize 2003, Grosser Österreichischer Staatspreis 2014. *Address:* c/o Andreas Karl, Reinprechts- dorferstrasse 54/14, 1050 Vienna, Austria (office). *E-mail:* office@beatfurrer .com. *Website:* www.beatfurrer.com.

FUSSELL, Charles Clement, BM, MM; American composer, conductor and teacher; b. 14 Feb. 1938, Winston-Salem, NC. *Education:* studied with Clemens Sandresky in Winston-Salem, with Thomas Canning, Wayne Barlow, Bernard Rogers, José Echaniz, Eastman School of Music, Rochester, NY with Herman Genhart, Berlin Hochschule für Musik with Boris Blacher. *Career:* teacher of theory and composition, Univ. of Massachusetts 1966, founder and Dir of its group for new music 1974, later renamed Pro Musica Moderna; teacher of composition, North Carolina School of the Arts, Winston- Salem 1976–77; Boston Univ. 1981; Conductor, Longy School Chamber Orchestra, Cambridge, MA 1981–82; Artistic Dir, New Music Harvet/Boston (city-wide contemporary music festival) 1989. *Compositions:* orchestral: Symphony No. 1 1963, No. 2 1964–67, No. 3: Landscapes 1978–81, three Processionals 1972–73, Northern Lights for chamber orchestra 1977–79, four Fairy Tales 1980–81, Dance Suite for five players 1963, Ballades for cello and piano 1968, revised 1976, Greenwood Sketches for string quartet 1976, Free- fall for seven players 1988, Julian (drama) 1969–71, Voyages for soprano, tenor, women's chorus, piano, winds and recorded speaker 1970, Eurydice for soprano and chamber ensemble 1973–75, Resume (song cycle) for soprano and three instruments 1975–76, Cymbeline (drama) for soprano, tenor, narrator and chamber ensemble 1984, The Gift for soprano and chorus 1986, five Goethe Lieder for soprano or tenor and piano 1987, for soprano or tenor and orchestra 1991, A Song of Return for chorus and orchestra 1989, Wilde Symphony No. 4 for baritone and orchestra, Last Trombones for five percussionists, two pianos and six trombones 1990, Symphony No. 5 for large orchestra 1994–95, Night Song for piano solo 1995, Specimen Days (cantata) for baritone solo, chorus and orchestra 1993–94, Being Music (Whitman) for baritone solo and string quartet 1993, Venture (four songs) for baritone and piano 2001, Right River for cello solo and string orchestra 2001, Infinite Fraternity for baritone solo, chorus, flute and viola 2002, High Bridge choral symphony 2003–04. *Honours:* Ford, Fulbright, Copland grants and commis- sions.

FUTRAL, Elizabeth; American singer (soprano); b. 1968, Louisville, Ky. *Education:* Opera Center of Chicago Opera. *Career:* debut at New York City Opera 1992, as Gilda; sang Bella in The Midsummer Marriage, and Lakmé at City Opera; season 1995–96 as Gounod's Juliette at Miami, Valencienne in The Merry Widow at the City Opera and Lucia di Lammermoor at Florence; Rossini's Matilde di Shabran at Pesaro, Musetta at Covent Garden and Catherine in Meyerbeer's Etoile du Nord, at Wexford 1996; other roles include Tytania in A Midsummer Night's Dream; season 1999 with Gounod's Juliette at Chicago, Gilda at Pittsburgh and Brussels, Susanna at Munich and Strauss's Zerbinetta at Santa Fe; season 2000–01 as Donizetti's Adina for Chicago Opera, Gilda at Santa Fe, Nannetta in Munich and Baby Doe in the Opera by Douglas Moore for New York City Opera; Lucia di Lammermoor at New Orleans; season 2013–14 as Vera Donovan in Picker's Dolores Claiborne for San Francisco Opera, Alice B. Toklas in Ricky Ian Gordon's 27 for Opera Theatre St. Louis, role debut as Zdenka in Arabella for Minnesota Opera. *Honours:* New York City Opera Award for Artistic Excellence 2007. *Current Management:* c/o Lee Prinz, Colbert Artists, 307 7th Avenue, #2006, New York, NY 10001, USA. *Website:* www.elizabethfutral.com.

G

GABARASHVILI, Tamar; Georgian cellist and music teacher; b. 22 July 1937, Tbilisi; d. of Boris Gabarashvili and Buda Gabarashvili; m. Irakli Khomeriki 1980. *Education:* Tbilisi Cen. Musical School and Moscow Tchaikovsky Conservatoire. *Career:* soloist with Mosconcert 1966–90, then with Tbilisi Symphonic Orchestra; teacher, Chair. in Tbilisi Conservatoire. *Film:* Pastorali (cellist) 1975. *Recordings:* numerous recordings of solo concerts 1962–. *Honours:* Gold Medal, Int. Cello Competition, Helsinki 1962, Third Prize, Int. Pablo Casals Competition, Budapest 1963, Laureate, Third Int. Tchaikovsky Competition, Moscow 1966. *Address:* Griboedor str. 8, 0108 Tbilisi (office); Larsi Str. 2–6, 380079 Tbilisi, Georgia (home). *Telephone:* (32) 987186 (office); (32) 226420 (home). *Fax:* (32) 221103 (office); (32) 987187. *E-mail:* interrelation@conservatoire.ge (office); hydro_tgu@yahoo.com (home).

GABBITAS, Christopher Alan, BA (Hons), MA, PGDL; British singer (baritone); *Member, The King's Singers;* b. 15 May 1979, Cornwall, England; s. of Brian Gabbitas and Evelyn Gabbitas; m. Stephanie Seales 2006; one d. *Education:* Uppingham School, St John's Coll., Cambridge, Postgraduate Diploma in Law. *Career:* practised as a solicitor 2001–03; has sung since the age of eight in various choirs including Rochester Cathedral, St John's Coll., Cambridge and Christ Church Cathedral, Oxford; performed with groups including Polyphony, The English Concert, The King's Consort, and in the inaugural concert of European Voices; joined The King's Singers as second baritone 2003–; has performed at venues including Concertgebouw, Amsterdam, Carnegie Hall, New York, Royal Albert Hall, London, Kennedy Center, Washington, DC and Suntory Hall, Tokyo. *Recordings:* with The King's Singers: 1605: Treason and Dischord 2005, Sacred Bridges 2005, Six 2005, Thomas Tallis Spem in Alium 2006, Landscape & Time 2006, The Quiet Heart 2007, Live at the Proms (MIDEM Award 2009) 2008, The Golden Age 2008, Simple Gifts (Grammy Award) 2008, Reflections 2008, Romance du Soir 2009, Swimming over London 2010; with Eric Whitacre, the Eric Whitacre Singers, Christopher Glynn, Laudibus and the Pavão Quartet: Light and Gold (Grammy Award for Best Choral Performance 2012) 2010. *Honours:* CARA Award 2009. *Current Management:* c/o Alec C. Treuhaft, IMG Artists, Carnegie Hall Tower, 152 West 57th Street, 5th Floor, New York, NY 10019, USA. *Telephone:* (212) 994-3500. *Fax:* (212) 994-3550. *E-mail:* atreuhaft@imgartists.com. *Website:* www.imgartists.com. *Address:* c/o Claire Long, The King's Singers, Music Productions Ltd, Unit 14, 21 Wadsworth Road, Perivale, Middx, UB6 7JD, England (office). *Telephone:* (1753) 646100 (office). *E-mail:* christopher@kingssingers.com (office). *Website:* www .kingssingers.com (office).

GABETTA, Sol; Argentine cellist; b. 1981, Córdoba. *Education:* Escuela Superior de Musica Reina Sofia, Madrid, Musik Akademie, Basel, Switzerland, Hanns Eisler Musikhochschule, Berlin. *Career:* won first competition in Argentina; studied with Ivan Monighetti and David Geringhas; made debut with Vienna Philharmonic Orchestra under Valery Gergiev, Lucerne Festival 2004; teacher, Musik Akademie, Basel 2005–; guest appearances with numerous orchestras including Munich Philharmonic, Vienna Symphony Orchestra, SWR Stuttgart, Nat. Symphony Orchestra of Washington, Calgary Philharmonic Orchestra, Seoul Philharmonic, City of Birmingham Symphony Orchestra, Philadelphia Orchestra, Detroit Symphony Orchestra, Royal Philharmonic Orchestra, Het Residentie Orkest, Trondheim Soloists, orchestras of Euskadi, Tenerife and Seville; regularly performs with Basel Symphony Orchestra; Founder and performer, Solsberg chamber music festival, Switzerland; recordings with Münchner Rundfunkorchester, Sonatori de la Gioiosa Marca, Münchner Philharmoniker, Prague Philharmonic Orchestra. *Recordings:* albums: Sol Gabetta: Tchaikovsky, Saint-Saëns, Ginastera (Echo Klassik Award for Instrumentalist of the Year 2007) 2006, Il Progetto Vivaldi 2007, Shostakovich (Echo Klassik Award for Concerto Recording of the Year 2009) 2008, Cantabile 2008, Hofmann, Haydn, Mozart 2009, Elgar Cello Concerto 2010, Duo (with Hélène Grimaud) (Diapason d'Or for Best Chamber Music Recording) 2012. *Honours:* Gramophone Award for Young Artist of the Year 2010. *Current Management:* c/o Sabine Frank, Harrison/Parrott GmbH, Johannisplatz 3a, 81667 Munich, Germany. *Telephone:* (89) 45726154. *Fax:* (89) 45726150. *E-mail:* info@harrisonparrott.de. *Website:* www.harrisonparrott.de. *Address:* c/o Sony Music Entertainment, Schlegelstraße 26b, 10115 Berlin, Germany (office). *Telephone:* (30) 138887364 (office). *Fax:* (30) 138887389 (office). *E-mail:* presse_classical@ sonymusic.com (office). *Website:* www.sonymusic.com (office); www.solgabetta .com.

GADD, Stephen; British singer (baritone); b. 18 Sept. 1964, Berkshire, England. *Education:* St John's College, Cambridge and Royal Northern College of Music. *Career:* Ping in Turandot at Covent Garden; Yeletsky in Queen of Spades for Scottish Opera; Count in Marriage of Figaro for Scottish Opera; Marcello (La Bohème), Peking Festival; Escamillo (Carmen) for BBC; Other appearances at Geneva Opera, Châtelet (Paris), Opéra Comique (Paris), New Israeli Opera and Opéra du Rhin; Concert repertoire includes: Britten, War Requiem; Walton, Belshazzar's Feast; Mendelssohn, Elijah. *Recordings include:* Mozart's Coronation Mass; Purcell's Dioclesian for DGG with Trevor Pinnock and the English Concert; La Bohème and Madama Butterfly (excerpts) with RPO; Hamish Maccun Works. *Honours:* Kathleen Ferrier Memorial Scholarship. *Telephone:* (23) 8045-4570. *E-mail:* manager@ ruttergadd.co.uk. *Website:* www.ruttergadd.co.uk.

GADDES, Richard, ; British opera administrator and director; b. 23 May 1942, Wallsend, England. *Education:* Trinity Coll. of Music, London. *Career:* co-founder, Wigmore Hall lunchtime concerts 1965; emigrated to USA 1969; Artistic Administrator, Santa Fe Opera 1969–76, Gen. Dir 2000–08; founder, Opera Theater of St Louis 1976, Gen. Dir 1976–85; production of Britten's Albert Herring for WNET and BBC television 1978; visited Edinburgh with the St Louis Co. 1983, with Fennimore and Gerda by Delius and The Postman Always Rings Twice by Stephen Paulus (the first American opera to be performed at the Edinburgh Int. Festival); American premiere of Saariaho's L'Amour de loin 2002; world premiere of Sheng's Madame Mao 2003; mem. Bd of Dirs Pulitzer Foundation for the Arts, Vilcek Foundation, George London Foundation. *Honours:* Hon. DMusA (St Louis Conservatory) 1983, Hon. DFA (Univ. of Missouri, St Louis) 1984, Hon. DA (Webster Univ.) 1986; Nat. Endowment for the Arts Opera Award 2008. *Address:* 480 Park Avenue, New York, NY 10022, USA (home).

GADENSTÄTTER, Clemens; Austrian composer, conductor and teacher; *Professor of Music Theory, Analyses and Composition, University of Music and Performing Arts, Graz;* b. 26 July 1966, Zell am See. *Education:* Universität für Musik und darstellende Kunst, Vienna, composition with Erich Urbanner, flute with Wolfgang Schulz, Musikhochschule, Stuttgart, composition with Helmut Lachenmann. *Career:* Founder (with Florian Müller), Ensemble Neue Musik, Vienna 1990; Lecturer, Darmstadt Ferienkurse für Neue Musik 1994; teacher, Universität für Musik und darstellende Kunst, Vienna 1995–; Prof. of Music Theory, Analyses and Composition, Univ. of Music and Performing Arts, Graz 1998–; teaches composition at International Summercourses for New Music Darmstadt 2014, Impuls Acad. 2013, 2015, Kiev Courses for contemporary music 2015; Co-Ed. bi-annual journal Ton 1995–2000; concerts and premieres include Donaueschingen Music Days 2001, 2005, 2012, Berliner Festival, Salzburg Festival 1999, 2005, Vienna Modern 2001, 2007, 2012, 2014, Summer 07 – Festival for New Music/Stuttgart, Int. Courses for Contemporary Music, Darmstadt 1996, 2006, 2007, Festival Ultraschall, Berlin 2007, 2012, 2014, Musikbiennale, Salzburg, Arcana Festival, RAI-Nuova Musica, Turin, Festival 'rainy days', Luxembourg Philharmonie, Musikprotokoll-Graz, Festival Styrian Autumn 1999, 2011, etc; commissions from Salzburg Festival 1999, 2005, Musikprotokoll, Graz 1999, 2011, Donaueschingen Music Days 2001, 2005, 2012 (SWR Baden Baden), Berlin Festival, Konzerthaus, Berlin 2002, 2007, Wien Modern 2002, 2007, 2011, 2013, Salzburg Biennale 2011, Festival for Contemporary Chamber Music, Witten 2015, Musik der Jahrhunderte, Stuttgart, Vienna Konzerthaus, ORF/ RSO-Wien, Ensemble Modern, Frankfurt, Ensemble Conterchamps – Genève, Klangforum Wien, Ensemble Nikel, JACK Quartett, Ensemble Recherche, Trio Accanto, L'Instant Donné, Paris, Ensemble asamisimasa, Oslo, Ensemble Ascolta, Stuttgart, Neue Vocalsolisten, Stuttgart, Gewandhaus Leipzig, Mendelssohn Kammerorchester, Leipzig, Int. Soc. for Contemporary Music; collaborations with orchestras and ensembles including Radio Symphony Orchestra, Vienna, Radio Symphony Orchestra, Berlin, Orchestra Sinfonica Nazionale della RAI, Torino, Klangforum Vienna, Arditti Quartet, Ensemble Ascolta, Stuttgart, Ensemble asamisimasa, Oslo, Ensemble Nickel, Amsterdam/Tel-Aviv, Ensemble Talea, New York, Ensemble Mosaik, Berlin, Trio Accanto, Stuttgart, Basel, Freiburg im Breisgau, SWR Vokalensemble, Stuttgart, Neue Vocalsolisten, Stuttgart, etc; collaborations with conductors including Peter Eötvös, Hans Zender, Peter Rundel, Sian Edwards, Pascal Rophé, Johannes Kalitzke, Marc Foster, Dennis Russell-Davies, Dominique My, Jonathan Stockhammer, Luca Pfaff, Ernst Kovacic, Jürg Henneberger, Arturo Tamayo, Beat Furrer and others; collaborations with soloists including Salome Kammer, Yukiko Sugawara, Teodoro Anzellotti, Markus Weiss, Ernst Kovacic, Jürgen Ruck, David Moss, Eva Furrer, Anette Bik, Andreas Lindenbaum, Krassimir Sterev, Sarah Sun, Andreas Fischer, Frank Wörner, Yaron Deutsch, Florian Müller, Anna Maria Pammer, Duo Pascal Meyer, Xenia Pestova, Theo Nabicht and others. *Compositions include:* Trio 1990, Musik für Orchesterensembles 1990–94, Versprachlichung: dreaming of a land an arm's length away – die arie des vogelnestaushebers (with film installation by Joseph Santarromana) 1992–94 (version without film entitled Versprachlichung) variationen und alte themen 1996, Ballade L 1997, Polyskopie 2000–01, Wir müssen einzelne irgendwann bitten, alle jetzt aufzupassen (electroacoustic) 2001, Comic sense 2002–03, powered by emphasis 1–3 (orchestra, choir, soloists, electronic), Songbook No. 1–11, Semantical Investigations 1, 2 (ensemble), Iconosonics 1–3 (various chamber groups), Fluchten/Agorasonie 1 (orchestra soloists), häuten – Paramyth 1, schlitzen – Paramyth 2 (string quartet). *Recordings include:* Polyskopie, Streichtrio II, Variationen und alte themen, Comic sense, Versprachlichung, schniTt, Musik für Orchesterensembles, ES for ensemble, voice-over and film 2011, Sad Songs for four instruments 2012. *Publications include:* tag day. ein schreibspiel (with Lisa Spalt) 2000; contrib. to Stellwerk I 2002; co-ed. book series Musik. Theorien der Gegenwart 2007–; numerous essays. *Honours:* winner, Forum junge Komponisten competition, WDR 1992, Publicity Prize, SKE-Fond 1997, Vienna Förderungspreis 1997, First Prize 2003, Erste Bank Composition Prize 2003, DAAD scholarship (Berlin Artists Programme) 2006. *E-mail:* mailport@inode.at. *Address:* Universität für Musik und Darstellende

Kunst Graz, Leonhardstrasse 15, PO Box 208, Palais Meran, 8010, Austria (office). *Telephone:* (316) 389-0 (office). *Fax:* (316) 389-1101 (office). *E-mail:* clemens.gadenstaetter@kug.ac.at (office). *Website:* www.kug.ac.at (office); www.gadenstaetter.info.

GAEDE, Daniel; German violinist; b. 25 April 1966, Hamburg; m. Xuesu Liu 1992. *Education:* Studienstiftung des Deutschen Volkes and Abbado European Musicians Trust, studied with Thomas Brandis in Berlin, Max Rostal in Switzerland, Josef Gingold in USA. *Career:* regular performances as soloist and chamber musician in Europe, Asia, N and S America; soloist with Philharmonia Orchestra, London, City of London Sinfonia, Vienna Philharmonic Orchestra; taught at University of the Arts, Berlin 1991–94; leader, Vienna Philharmonic Orchestra 1994–2000; Prof. Hochschule für Musik Nürnberg-Augsburg 2000–. *Honours:* winner, German National Competition, Jugend musiziert 1983, Prizewinner, Carl Flesch Competition, London and Artist International Competition, New York, Eduard Söring Prize 1987, Joseph Joachim Prize 1989. *Address:* Hochschule für Musik Nürnberg-Augsburg, Veilhofstrasse 34, 90489 Nürnberg, Austria (office). *Telephone:* (911) 2318443 (office). *Fax:* (911) 2317697 (office). *E-mail:* hfm-rektorat@stadt .nuernberg.de (office). *Website:* www.hfm-n-a.de (office).

GAETA, Luis; Argentine singer (baritone); b. 1953, Buenos Aires. *Education:* studied in Buenos Aires and with Tito Gobbi. *Career:* many appearances at the Teatro Colón, Buenos Aires, notably as Verdi's Rigoletto, Posa (1996) and Germont, Marcello, Jack Rance (La Fanciulla del West), Valentin and Rossini's Figaro; Prus in The Makropulos Case, Mozart's Count and the Villains in Les Contes d'Hoffmann; Premieres of works by local composers and guest appearances throughout South America; Season 1998 as Malatesta in Don Pasquale; Many concert engagements; Season 2000 as Puccini's Sharpless at Buenos Aires and Donizetti's Enrico at Córdoba. *Website:* www .geocities.com/luisgaetabaritono.

GAFFIGAN, James, MMus; American conductor; b. 1979, New York City; m. Lee Taylor Gaffigan. *Education:* LaGuardia High School of Music and Art, Juilliard School Prep. Div., New England Conservatory of Music, Shepherd School of Music at Rice Univ., Houston with Larry Rachleff. *Career:* Asst Conductor, Cleveland Orchestra, working under Franz Welser-Moest 2003–06; Assoc. Conductor, San Francisco Symphony, where he assisted Michael Tilson Thomas, led subscription concerts and was Artistic Dir of orchestra's Summer in the City Festival 2007–10; Chief Conductor, Lucerne Symphony Orchestra 2011–; Prin. Guest Conductor, Netherlands Radio Philharmonic Orchestra 2011–; has conducted major orchestras throughout USA, also City of Birmingham Symphony Orchestra, Orchestra of the Age of Enlightenment, Gürzenich Orchestra Cologne, Tonhalle Orchestra and the Camerata Salzburg, Munich and Rotterdam Philharmonics, Deutsches Symphony Orchestra Berlin, Bournemouth Symphony, Leipzig and Stuttgart Radio Orchestras, Dresden Staatskappelle, Sydney Symphony and the Tokyo Metropolitan Symphony Orchestra; professional opera debut (La Bohème) at Zürich Opera 2005; festival performances of Don Giovanni at Aspen Music Festival, and Falstaff for Glyndebourne on Tour 2009; Marriage of Figaro at the Houston Grand Opera and debut at Vienna State Opera (La Bohème) 2011. *Honours:* First Prize, Sir Georg Solti Int. Conducting Competition, Frankfurt, Germany 2004; Robert Harth Conducting Award, American Acad. of Conducting, Aspen 2006; conducting fellowship to study at the Tanglewood Music Center. *Current Management:* c/o Nicholas Mathias, IMG Artists, The Light Box, 111 Power Road, London, W4 5PY, England. *Telephone:* (20) 7957-5800. *Fax:* (20) 7957-5801. *E-mail:* nmathias@imgartists.com. *Website:* www .imgartists.com. *Address:* Lucerne Symphony Orchestra, Pilatusstrasse 18, 6003 Luzern, Switzerland (office). *Telephone:* (41) 2260510 (office). *Fax:* (41) 2260520 (office). *E-mail:* info@sinfonieorchester.ch (office). *Website:* www .jamesgaffigan.com.

GAGE, Irwin; American pianist; b. 4 Sept. 1939, Cleveland, Ohio. *Education:* Univ. of Michigan with Eugene Bossart, Yale Univ. with Ward Davenny, Vienna Akademie with Erik Werba, Klaus Vokurka and Hilde Langer-Rühl. *Career:* accompanist to numerous singers, including Hermann Prey, Dietrich Fischer-Dieskau, Christa Ludwig, Gundula Janowitz, Jessye Norman, Elly Ameling, Lucia Popp, Brigitte Fassbaender, Tom Krause, Arleen Auger, Anna Reynolds, René Kollo, Peter Schreier and Edita Gruberova, and younger singers François Le Roux, Cheryl Studer, Thomas Hampson, Siegfried Lorenz and Francisco Araiza; festival appearances at major festivals worldwide; Prof., Zürich Conservatory 1979–2005; master-classes worldwide; anniversary concerts of Brahms, Ravel, Schubert and Mendelssohn 1997. *Recordings:* over 50 recordings. *Honours:* Gramophone Award (three times), Grand Prix du Disque, Deutsche Schallplatten Preis (five times), Edison Prize, recording prizes from Spain, Belgium, Finland and Japan, Ovation-MUMM Award (USA).

GAGNÉ, Marc, DLit; Canadian academic and composer; b. 16 Dec. 1939, Saint Joseph de Beauce, QC; m. Monique Poulin 1969, one s. two d. *Education:* Univ. Laval, QC and School of Music of Univ. Laval with Jacques Hétu, José Evangélista and Roger Matton. *Career:* Symphonie de chants paysans created at Moncton Choralies Internationals 1979; Symphonie-itineraire was principal work by Québec Symphony Orchestra at Festival marking 375th anniversary of the discovery of Canada; L'opéra Menaud was given on television in the form of a scenic Cantata 1992. *Compositions:* Les Chansons de la tourelle (in the folklore mode) 1975, Jeu a deux faces Piano Sonata No. 1, Ceremonial d'orgue pour la fête du Tres Saint-Sacrement 1976, Deux chorals

pour la temps de la Passion for organ 1976, Les Jeunes Filles a marier suite for a capella choir on folklore themes 1977, Short Mass, du Peuple de Dieu 1981, Messe, des enfants de Dieu 1993, Sonate du roi Renaud for alto saxophone and piano 1983, Vari-anes et moulin-ations for solo marimba 1983, Symphonie-itineraire 1983–84, Menaud (opera in three acts and a prologue) 1984–86, Évangéline et Gabriel (two-act opera) 1987–90, Le Père Noël la sorcière et l'enfant (conte de Noël) for chamber orchestra, choir and soloists 1993, Les Verdi (three-act opera) 1999, Trio with piano No. 1: Le Rossignol y chante 1999, Trio with piano No. 2: Au bois du rossignolet 1999, Horn Sonata The Winter 1999.

GAGNON, Alain; Canadian composer; b. 1938, Trois-Pistoles, Quebec. *Education:* Ecole de Musique, Laval Univ., studied with Jeanne Landry, Jocelyne Binet, Roger Matton, Ecole Normale de Musique, Paris with Henri Dutilleux, Ecole César-Franck, Paris with Olivier Alain, Geneva Conservatory with André-François Maresconi, Univ. of Utrecht. *Career:* works performed in France, Switzerland, Germany, Latin America and Canada and several have been recorded or published; sat on several juries, including Competition for Young Composers 1980; Teacher of Techniques of Composition, Ecole de Musique, Laval Univ. 1967, Dir of Composition Programme 1977–. *Compositions include:* works for orchestra, chamber music, string quartets and piano; Trio pour flûte, violon et violoncello, Septuor, Les oies sauvages, Prélude pour orchestra 1969, ballet score 1983. *Honours:* Prix d'Europe 1961.

GAHL, Dankwart Arnold, DipMus; German cellist and academic; b. 18 Dec. 1939, Korbach; m. Irmgard Schuster 1964 (died 1996); one s. one d. *Education:* Akademie für Musik und darstellende Kunst, Vienna, studied with Johannes Koch/Kassell, Wilfried Boettcher, Erwin Ratz. *Career:* founder mem., Vienna Soloists 1959, touring worldwide, participating in many festivals, including Prades Festival; originating from this same ensemble is the Alban Berg Quartet and the Austrian String Quartet, of which mem. since 1972; quartet-in-residence, Mozarteum, Salzburg 1972–, holder of the cello class 1972–; founder mem. piano trio, Trio Amade, Salzburg 1979; Ordinary Prof., Hochschule 1984–; concerts in the USA and several tours to the Far East; guest classes in Republic of Korea on many occasions; has given classes with the quartet at Salzburg Summer Acad., Mozarteum for many years; invited jurist of int. chamber music competitions on many occasions; mem., Vienna Symphony Orchestra. *Honours:* Studienstiftung des Deutschen Volkes scholarship.

GÄHMLICH, Wilfried; German singer (tenor); b. 14 July 1939, Halle. *Education:* Musikhochschule Freiburg, studied with Alfred Pfeifle in Stuttgart. *Career:* debut in Giessen 1968, as Pedrillo in Die Entführung; sang at Wuppertal 1973, in premiere of Blacher's Yvonne, Prinzessen von Burgund; appearances in Düsseldorf, Zürich, Vienna, Stuttgart, Wiesbaden and London; Salzburg 1983, in Dantons Tod by Von Einem; other roles include Florestan, Drum Major in Wozzeck, Tamino, Andrea Chénier, Don José and Max in Der Freischütz; Bregenz Festival 1987–88, in Les Contes d'Hoffmann; sang Pedrillo in Die Entführung at the Theater an der Wien, Vienna 1989; The Sailor in Krenek's Orpheus und Eurydike for Austrian Radio; Salzburg Festival 1992, as The Hunchback in Die Frau ohne Schatten; Valzacchi in Der Rosenkavalier at the Opéra Bastille; sang in premiere of K… by Philippe Manouri at Opéra Bastille 2001. *Recordings include:* Dantons Tod; Die Entführung; Video of Elektra conducted by Abbado (as the Young Servant).

GAIDA, Natalia V.; Belarusian singer; b. 1 May 1939, Sverdlovsk; m. Youri Bastrikov 1965; one d. *Education:* Law Inst., Sverdlovsk and Conservatoire, Sverdlovsk. *Career:* debut, Sverdlovsk Opera 1965; singer, Belarus Musical Comedy 1970; Prof., Minsk Acad. of Arts 1994–; mem. Cen. Cttee Cultural Workers' Union 1978–82, Presidium Union of Theatrical Players 1982–. *Operas and shows include:* La Bohème, Don Juan, Fille de Neige, Silver, Maretza and the Princess of the Circus, My Fair Lady, Hello Dolly; over 60 operettas and 15 operas. *Film:* La soirée de gala avec les italiens 1970. *Honours:* Order of the Insignia of Honour 1986; People's Artist of the Repub. of Belarus 1980, Kryštalnaja Paŭlinka Prize 1995. *Address:* vul Ramanaŭskaya Slabada 9-76, 220004 Minsk, Belarus. *Telephone:* (172) 202153.

GAILIS, Viesturs; Latvian conductor; *Music Director, New Chamber Orchestra of Rīga;* b. 20 March 1955, Rīga. *Education:* Latvian Acad. of Music, St Petersburg Conservatory, Vienna Conservatory. *Career:* Conductor, Orchestra of the Latvian Nat. Opera 1984–91, Artistic Dir and Prin. Conductor 1991–94; Prof. of Music and Head, Opera Dept, Latvian Acad. of Music 1994–; Conductor, Latvian Nat. Symphony Orchestra 1998–2001; Music Dir New Chamber Orchestra of Rīga 2001–; guest conductor with Tampere Philharmonic Orchestra, Vienna Pro Arte Orchestra, North Hungary Philharmonic Orchestra, Liepaja Philharmonic. *Honours:* winner, Young Conductors Competition, Latvia, Int. Conducting Competition S. Wagner Stipendiumstiftung, Germany, Int. Conducting Competition of Music of 20th Century, Austria. *Telephone:* 7211-297 (office). *Fax:* 7281-737 (office). *E-mail:* viesturs.gailis@apollo.lv (office); chamberorchestra@music.lv (office). *Website:* www.music.lv/chamberorchestra.

GAJEWSKI, Jaromir Zbigniew, MA; Polish conductor, musician and composer; b. 2 April 1961, Pryzyce. *Education:* Acad. of Music, Poznań. *Career:* debut in Poznań 1986; Teacher of Conducting, Composition and Harmony, 1988–; Founder of Academy Orchestra, 1991–; mem. Polish Composers' Soc., Polish Soc. for Contemporary Music. *Compositions include:* Altana–Songs for voice and piano, 1986; 2 String Quartets, 1986, 1988;

Penetration for symphony orchestra, 1989; From Dawn to Dusk for orchestra, 1989; In Cage, opera, 1990; Overture, 1993; 3rd string quartet, 1995; Requiem Symphony, 1997; Fantasy, 1998; Why Has Thou Forsaken Me?, 1999. *Recordings include:* Altana–Songs; 2 String Quartets.

GAL, Zahava; Israeli singer (mezzo-soprano); b. 29 Aug. 1948, Haifa. *Education:* Rubin Acad., Jerusalem, Juilliard School with Jennie Tourel and Daniel Fero. *Career:* Feodor in Boris Godunov, La Scala, 1979; Salzburg Easter Festival production of Parsifal, 1980; Angelina in La Cenerentola, Netherlands Opera, Amsterdam, 1980; Feodor in Boris Godunov, Carmen, Paris Opéra, 1981; Sang Carmen in Peter Brook's Carmen, Hamburg, Zürich; Rosina in Barber of Seville, Washington DC (2 seasons), Glyndebourne Festival Opera, at Santiago de Chile, Scottish Opera in Lyon, Avignon, Nantes, Dario Fo's Amsterdam production, Frankfurt Opera (2 seasons); Isolier in Le Comte Ory, Pesaro, Italy; Cherubino in Marriage of Figaro at Monte Carlo, Vienna Staatsoper and Santa Fe Festival; Ariodante in Nancy, Paris, Lausanne, Dejanira in Hercules, title role in Teseo, Covent Garden, Siena, Athens Summer Festival, Handel Year, 1985; Nicklausse, Rosina, Carmen with New Israeli Opera, 1988–89; Rinaldo, Paris; Elmira in Floridante with Tafel Baroque Orchestra in Toronto, San Francisco; Zerlina in Don Giovanni, Nancy; Concert repertoire includes Schéhérazade, L'Enfant et les Sortilèges (Ravel), Songs of a Wayfarer, 3rd and 4th Symphonies (Mahler), Romeo and Juliet (Berlioz), Requiem, C-minor Mass (Mozart), Bruckner's Te Deum, Beethoven's 9th, Pergolesi's Stabat Mater; Has sung with Mehta and Israel Philharmonic, Barenboim and New York Philharmonic, Abbado with La Scala Orchestra and Chicago Symphony, Armin Jordan and Orchestre de la Suisse Romande, Mata with Pittsburgh and Dallas Symphonies; Television appearances in Switzerland, Italy, France, Israel. *Recordings include:* Mussorgsky's choral works with Abbado; Amaltea in Moses in Egypt; L'Incoronazione di Poppea; Duet selection; Donizetti cantata. *Honours:* Grand Prix, 1st Prize, Mélodie Française Concours International de Chant, Paris; Top Prize, Lieder, Munich International Competition; 1st Place, Kathleen Ferrier Young Artists Award.

GAL, Zoltan; Hungarian violist; b. 1960. *Education:* Franz Liszt Acad., Budapest, studied with Sandor Devich, György Kurtág and András Mihaly. *Career:* mem., Keller String Quartet from 1986, debut concert at Budapest 1987; played Beethoven's Grosse Fuge and Schubert's Death and the Maiden Quartet at Interforum 87; series of concerts in Budapest with Zoltán Kocsis and Deszo Ranki (piano) and Kalman Berkes (clarinet); further appearances in Nuremberg, at the Chamber Music Festival La Baule and tours of Bulgaria, Austria, Switzerland, Italy (Ateforum 88, Ferrara), Belgium and Ireland; concerts for Hungarian radio and television. *Honours:* second prize Evian Int. String Quartet Competition 1988.

GALANTE, Inessa; Latvian singer (soprano); b. 1959, Riga. *Education:* Riga Conservatory. *Career:* sang at the Riga National Opera, 1982–91, notably as Gilda, Adina, L'Esilir d'Amore, Rosina, Micaela, Rimsky's Snow Maiden, Marguerite, Lucia di Lammermoor and Olympia in Les Contes d'Hoffmann; guest appearances at St Petersburg as Lucia and Marguerite; Mannheim Opera from 1991 as Pamina, Nedda, Freia in Das Rheingold, Mimi, and Gluck's Euridice; Sang Micaela at Frankfurt, 1993 and Donna Elvira at Düsseldorf, 1996; Violetta at Nancy, 1998; sang Mimi for Miami Opera, 1999; concert repertory in Russia, Germany and North America includes requiems by Brahms, Faure, Verdi and Mozart; Beethoven Ninth. *Current Management:* Guy Barzilay Artists, 360 West 28th Street #6B, New York, NY 10001, USA. *Telephone:* (212) 741-6118. *Fax:* (212) 741-2558. *E-mail:* guybar@aol.com. *Website:* guybarzilayartists.com.

GALÁS, Diamanda; American singer and poet; b. San Diego, Calif. *Education:* Univ. of California. *Career:* played in her father's band at mil. bases and bars from age 13; first live performance, Festival d'Avignon, France 1979; performed lead in opera Un Jour Comme un Autre, Avignon 1980; performed at Théâtre Gerard Philippe Saint-Denis; solo tour at European festivals including Donaueschingen, Inventionen, Biennale de Paris, Musica Oggi, Festivale de la Voce; performed at Int. AIDS Conf., San Francisco 1990, Olympic Festival, Barcelona, Spain 1990, Helsinki Festival, Festival delle Colline, Italy, Serious Fun Festival, Lincoln Center, USA 1993, Royal Festival Hall (RFH), London, UK 1996, Defixiones, London 1999, La Serpenta Canta, RFH, London 2001. *Recordings include:* The Litanies of Satan 1982, Panoptikon, The Masque of the Red Death (triptych) 1989, Plague Mass (trilogy), Wild Women with Steak Knives, Tragouthia apo to Aima Exon Fonos (Song from the Blood of those Murdered), Vena Cava 1992, The Divine Punishment, Saint of the Pit, There are No More Tickets to the Funeral, The Singer, Insekta 1993, The Sporting Life 1994, Schrei X Live/Schrei 27 1996, Malediction & Prayer 1998, La Serpenta Canta 2003, Defixiones, Will and Testament 2003, Guilty Guilty Guilty 2008, The Cleopatra Set 2009. *Publications include:* The Shit of God 1996. *Address:* c/o Asphodel Records, 763 Brennan Street, San Francisco, CA 94103, USA (office). *E-mail:* garth@diamandagalas.com (office). *Website:* www.diamandagalas.com (office).

GALE, Elizabeth; British singer (soprano); b. 8 Nov. 1948, Sheffield, Yorks. *Education:* Guildhall School of Music, London with Winifred Radford. *Career:* debut with the English Opera Group, in Purcell's King Arthur; appeared in The Turn of the Screw with the EOG; Scottish Opera (Glasgow) as the Queen of Shemakha in The Golden Cockerel and Despina and Tytania; WNO (Cardiff) as Blondchen in Die Entführung; Glyndebourne 1973–86, as Barbarina, Papagena, Susanna, Nannetta, Zerlina, Marzelline in Fidelio,

Drusilla in L'Incoronazione di Poppea, Titania in A Midsummer Night's Dream and Miss Wordsworth in Albert Herring; also Amor in Orfeo; Marzelline at the Paris Opéra and the Vienna Staatsoper; Covent Garden as Zerlina and as Adele in Die Fledermaus, also as Woodbird in Siegfried and Xenia in Boris Godunov; Zürich Opera as Susanna, Ilia in Idomeneo, Ismene in Mitridate, Nannetta, Drusilla and Marzelline; Frankfurt 1980, in Castor et Pollux by Rameau also as Aennchen in Freischütz and Marzelline; guest appearances in Amsterdam, Geneva and Cologne; sang at San Diego, in La Voix Humaine by Poulenc 1986, US debut; appeared with Chelsea Opera Group at the QEH 1989, as Massenet's Thais; Glyndebourne Festival 1990, as Miss Wordsworth, repeated at Los Angeles 1992; sang in Owen Wingrave at Glyndebourne 1997; season 1998 as Alice Ford at Garsington and Despina for Glyndebourne Touring Opera; sang Susanna, Tytania and Oscar in Ballo at Hong Kong Festival; Despina in Los Angeles and Donna Elvira in Belfast; sang Despina at Glyndebourne 2000; many concert engagements, in particular in works by Handel; guest at opera houses in Vienna and Paris. *Recordings include:* Le nozze di Figaro and Don Giovanni; Amor in Orfeo ed Euridice; Israel in Egypt; Handel's Messiah, Saul, and Jephtha conducted by Harnoncourt; Dido and Aeneas; Semele in Die Liebe der Danaë, in a BBC recording of Strauss's opera; recital of Bliss Songs with Nash Ensemble. *Honours:* John Christie Award, Glyndebourne 1973. *Address:* c/o Musichall Ltd, Oast House, Crouch's Farm, Hollow Lane, East Hoathly, BN8 6QX, England.

GALL, Jeffrey Charles, BA, MPhil; American singer (countertenor); *Professor of Music, Montclair State University*; b. 19 Sept. 1950, Cleveland, OH; m. Karen Rosenberg 1978. *Education:* Princeton University, Yale University with Blake Stern, Arthur Burrows. *Career:* member, Waverly Consort, 1974–78; Debuts: Brooklyn Academy of Music in Cavalli's Erismena, Spoleto Festival, Italy, 1980, La Scala, 1981, Edinburgh Festival, 1982, San Francisco Opera, 1982, La Fenice, 1984, Teatro di San Carlo Naples, 1984, Canadian Opera, 1984, Handel Festival at Carnegie Hall, 1984, Chicago Lyric Opera, 1986, Sante Fe Opera, 1986, and Metropolitan Opera, 1988; Has sung in operas by Jommelli, Lully, Pergolesi, Cesti, Purcell, Scarlatti and Mozart; Television appearances include the title role in Handel's Giulio Cesare; Season 1992 included Britten's Oberon at Los Angeles and in Conti's Don Chisciotte at the Innsbruck Festival of Early Music; Performed Oberon in Britten's Midsummer Night's Dream with the Frankfurt Opera, Ottone in Monteverdi's Poppea for the Cologne Opera, David in Handel's Saul with the Boston Caecelia Society, 1993; Returned to Metropolitan Opera in Britten's Death in Venice in 1994; Sang Medieval Carmina Burana for Clemencic Consort, Oberon in for the New Israeli Opera and Ottone for the Dallas Opera, repeated at Amsterdam, 1996; currently Prof. of Music and Voice Program Co-ordinator, Montclair State Univ.; founding mem. Il Terzo Suono vocal ensemble. *Recordings include:* Flavio conducted by René Jacobs. *Honours:* First Prize, Bodky Award for Performance of Early Music, 1977. *Address:* School of Music, Montclair State University, Montclair, NJ 07043, USA (office). *Telephone:* (973) 655-7213 (office). *E-mail:* gallj@mail.montclair.edu (office). *Website:* www.montclair.edu/Music (office).

GALLA, Jan; Slovak singer (bass); b. 21 Dec. 1955, Nova Zahky, Czechoslovakia. *Education:* Bratislava Conservatory. *Career:* mem. Nat. Theatre Bratislava, in Italian and Slavonic opera repertory; guest appearances in Rio de Janeiro (as Ramphis in Aida 1986), Paris Opéra and Opéra-Comique, and Opera North, Leeds; sang Verdi's Attila with Bratislava co. at Edinburgh 1990; season 1992–93 as Donizetti's Raimondo in Dublin and Commandant in From the House of the Dead at Barbican Hall; Bratislava 1995, as Massenet's Don Quichotte.

GALLARDO-DOMÂS, Cristina, MMus; Chilean/Spanish singer (lyric soprano); b. 20 Aug. 1967, Santiago, Chile; m. Justo Garzón Ortega; one s. one d. *Education:* Escuela Moderna de Musica, Santiago (Intérprete Superior en Canto), Juilliard School, New York. *Career:* debut at Santiago Opera as Madama Butterfly, Municipal Theatre, Santiago 1990; European debut at Spoleto Festival as Suor Angelica 1993, repeated role in Willy Decker production, Cologne; La Rondine, La Scala 1993; debuts at main European houses: La Scala (Contes d'Hoffmann, Faust, Manon, Turandot, Traviata and La Bohème); Met (Traviata, Bohème, Turandot); Vienna (Pagliacci, Turandot, Traviata, Contes d'Hoffman, Bohème, Simon Boccanegra); Paris (Traviata, Boheme, Contes d'Hoffmann, Capuletti e I Montechi, Faust, Otello); Covent Garden (Turandot, Bohème, Madama Butterfly); Zurich (Bohème, Manon Lescaut); Munich (Traviata, Bohème, Simon Boccanegra, Otello); Berlin (Traviata, Otello, Suor Angelica, Madama Butterfly); Concertgebow, Amsterdam (Pagliacci, Suor Angelica, Le Villi); Teatro Colon (Suor Angelica, Mefistofele); Salzburg Festival (Turandot); Maggio Musicale Fiorentino (Turandot); Tokyo (Traviata); Zurich (Bohème); Ravinia Festival (Otello) has performed with leading conductors, including Chailly, Muti, Mehta, Conlon, Pappano, Harnoncourt, Thielemann, Levine, Prêtre, Gergiev, Luisi, Maazel; has worked with stage directors including Zeffirelli, Poutney, Kupfer, Stein, Decker, Flimm, Carsen, Leiser-Caurier, Wagner, Asagaroff, among others; sang Madame Butterfly in new production at Covent Garden 2003, 2005; protagonist of New York Met's Opening Night with new production of Madame Butterfly under Anthony Minghella 2006. *Recordings:* Aria recital 'Bel Sogno' (Teldec), Aida, conducted by Harnoncourt (Teldec), Suor Angelica conducted by Pappano (EMI), Verdi Sacred Pieces, conducted by Chailly, La Bohème, conducted by Bartoletti (TDK), Simon Boccanegra, conducted by Gatti (TDK), Verdi's Requiem conducted by Domingo (Glor). *Honours:* Dr hc

(Universidad Andres Bello, Santiago); Gran Cruz Lazo de Dama Gabriela Mistral 2001, Medalla Apostol Santiago 2003, Laurence Olivier Award for Outstanding Achievement in Opera 2004, Opera Actual magazine Premio de la Mejor Soprano 2005, Merito a la Trayectoria Musical, Instituto Cultural de Providencia (Chile) 2007, Medalla de Oro del Instituto Cultural de Providencia, Puccini Int. Award 2008; Hija Adoptiva Municipalidad de Providencia (Chile), Placido Domingo Award 2007, Puccini Int. Award 2008, Luigi Illica Int. Award 2009, Premio Internacional Luigi Illica, among others. *E-mail:* gallardodomas@live.com (office). *Current Management:* c/o DM Artist Management, Mario Dradi, Alte Landstraße 40, 8702 Zollikon, Switzerland; c/o José Velasco Management, S.L. c/Gran Via 62, 7° 28013 Madrid, Spain. *Telephone:* 434994363 (Zollikon); (91) 5593327 (Madrid). *Fax:* 434994364 (Zollikon); (91) 5480280 (Madrid). *E-mail:* alessandro.ariosi@dmartist.com; jvelasco@velascointernational.com. *Website:* www.dmartist.com; www.velascointernational.com. *Address:* Canarias Lyric S.L., c/ Secretario Artiles nº 36, Derecha 2°, 35007 Las Palmas de Gran Canaria, Spain (office). *Telephone:* (928) 22-41-13 (office). *Fax:* (928) 22-55-68 (office). *E-mail:* garzon_gallardodomas@yahoo.es (office). *Website:* www.gallardo-domas.com.

GALLEGO, Maria; Spanish singer (soprano); b. 1962, San Fernando. *Education:* Conservatorio Superior Manuel de Falla, Conservatorio del Liceo with Jaime Francisco Puig. *Career:* debut in Barcelona 1985 as Sidonie in Gluck's Armide; appearances at Barcelona as Celia in Mozart's Lucio Silla, Monica in Respighi's La Fiamma and in Strauss's Capriccio; Telemaco by Gluck 1987; guest appearances in Bologna and Ravenna as Rosaura in Le Maschere by Mascagni 1988; Pisa and Madrid; Bonn Opera 1991–92; other roles include Betty in Salieri's Falstaff. *E-mail:* manager@mariagallego.com. *Website:* www.mariagallego.com.

GALLI, Dorothea; Swiss singer (soprano); b. 11 Nov. 1951, Zürich; m. Rudolf Bamert. *Education:* studied with Elsa Cavelli and Elisabeth Schwarzkopf and at the Salzburg Mozarteum. *Career:* sang at the Zürich Opera 1976–78, Kaiserlautern 1978–79, Gelsenkirchen 1979–82; guest appearances at the Deutsche Oper am Rhein Düsseldorf, Karlsruhe, Mannheim, Dortmund, Heidelberg and Amsterdam; roles have included Mozart's Donna Elvira, Fiordiligi and Ramiro in La Finta Giardiniera, Leonore, Marguerite, Mimi, Tatiana, the Marschallin, Arabella, Emilia Marty and Giorgietta in Gianni Schicchi; many Lieder recitals and performances of oratorio. *Address:* Friedheimstrasse 54, 8057 Zürich, Switzerland (office). *Telephone:* 443127039 (office). *E-mail:* dorogalli@gmx.ch (office). *Website:* www.dorotheagalli.ch.

GALLIANO, Richard; French accordionist, composer and arranger; b. 12 Dec. 1950, Le Cannet, Côte d'Azur; s. of Lucien Galliano (Italian-born accordion teacher). *Education:* studied with Claude Noel, studied harmony, counterpoint and trombone at Nice Conservatoire. *Career:* renowned for creating a fusion of jazz, classical and traditional styles of accordion music; began playing the accordion aged four; was introduced to jazz through discovery of music of Clifford Brown aged 14; became interested in Brazilian accordionists including Sivuca and Dominguinhos; discovered American jazz specialists (Tommy Gumina, Ernie Felice and Art Van Damme), and leading Italian players, Felice Fugazza, Volpi and Fancelli; moved away completely on traditional style of playing that dominated in France; moved to Paris 1973; composer, arranger and conductor with Claude Nougaro Orchestra 1973–76; played on numerous recordings by popular French artists, including Barbara, Serge Reggiani, Charles Aznavour and Juliette Gréco, and on film scores; played with, and improvised alongside, jazz musicians from all backgrounds, including Chet Baker (in Brazilian repertoire), Steve Potts, Jimmy Gourley, Toots Thielemanns, cellist Jean-Charles Capon (with whom he cut his first disc) and Ron Carter, with whom he paired up to make an album in 1990; returned to his roots, on advice of Astor Piazzolla, and traditional repertoire of Valses-Musette, Javas, Complaintes and Tangos 1991; travelled to USA to record New York Tango with George Mraz, Al Foster and Biréli Lagrène 1996; other collaborations have included Enrico Rava, Charlie Haden and Michel Portal, accordionist Antonello Salis, Italy, and organist Eddy Louiss 2001; played in trio with Daniel Humair and Jean-François Jenny-Clarke 1993–98, returned to this format with a 'New York' rhythm, made up of Clarence Penn and Larry Grenadier 2004; one-off collaborations with Jan Garbarek, Martial Solal, Hermeto Pascoal and Anouar Brahem, Paolo Fresu and Jan Lundgren and Gary Burton, among others; presented own compositions, with chamber orchestra accompaniment, together with pieces by Astor Piazzolla 1999; played with Brussels Jazz Orchestra 2008; solo appearances at Paris Concert from the Châtelet 2009. *Recordings:* New Musette (with Aldo Romano, Pierre Michelot and Philip Catherine for Label bleu) (Django Reinhardt Prize for French Musician of the Year, Acad. du Jazz 1993) 1992, Spleen 1993, Viaggio 1993, Panamanhattan, Live, with Ron Carter (Classical and Jazz Award for Best Jazz Album 1996) 1994, Laurita 1995, New York Tango (with George Mraz, Al Foster and Biréli Lagrène) (Victoire de la Musique 1996) 1996, Blow Up (Victoire de la Musique 1997, Classical and Jazz Award for Best Jazz Album 1997) 1997, French Touch (with Wynton Marsalis) (Musica Jazz Award for Best Int. Jazz Album) 1998, Passatori 1999, Concerts Inédits 2000, Blues Sur Seine (with Jean-Charles Capon) 2001, Gallianissimo 2001, Face to Face (with Eddy Louiss) 2001, Piazolla Forever 2003, Concerts (with Michel Portal) 2004, Blue Hat (with Josephine Cronholm) 2005, Ruby My Dear 2005, Solo 2006, Luz Negra 2007, Mare Nostrum (with Paolo Fresu and Jan Lundgren) 2008, Love Day (with Gonzalo Rubalcaba, Charlie Haden and Mino Cinelu) 2009, Ten Years Ago (with Brussels Jazz Orchestra) 2008, Tribute to Billie Holliday and Edith Piaff with the Wynton Marsalis Quintet 2010, The JS Bach Project 2010, Tribute to Nino Rota 2011, Southern Exposure with Christian Howes 2012, Vivaldi Four Seasons 2013, Sentimentale 2014. *Publication:* co-author (with father Lucien) of accordion method (SACEM Prize for Best Pedagogical Work) 2009. *Honours:* Officier des Arts et des Lettres, Légion d'honneur. *Current Management:* c/o Jean Michel de Bie, Ginga Productions, Chaiseray, 72310 Vancé, France. *Telephone:* (2) 43-35-92-52. *Fax:* (2) 43-35-92-53. *E-mail:* ginga@wanadoo.fr; gingaproductions@yahoo.fr. *Website:* www.richardgalliano.com.

GALLO, F. Alberto, LLD, PhD; Italian academic; b. 17 Oct. 1932, Verona. *Publications include:* Antonii Romani Opera 1965, Mensurabilis Musicae Tractatuli 1966, Il Codice Musicale 2216 della Biblioteca Universitaria di Bologna 1968–70, Franchini Gafurii Extractus Parvus Musicae 1969, Petrus Picardus Ars Motettorium Compilata Breviter 1971, Johannes Boen Ars Musicae 1972, La Prima Rappresentazione al Teatro Olimpico 1973, Italian Sacred Music 1976, Storia della Musica: Il Medioevo 1977, Il Codice Musicale Panciatichi 26 della Biblioteca Nazionale di Firenze 1981, Geschichte der Musiktheorie 1984, Music of the Middle Ages 1985, Musica e Storia tra Medio Evo e Età Moderna 1986, Italian Sacred and Ceremonial Music 1987, Musica nel Castello Bologna 1992, Il Codice Squarcialupi 1992.

GALLO, Lucio; Italian singer (baritone); b. 9 July 1959, Taranto; m. Claudia Benvenuti; two d. *Education:* Conservatorio G. Verdi, Turin. *Career:* sang Marcello to Pavarotti's Rodolfo in Peking, People's Republic of China; Escamillo in Turin and Leporello at the Vienna Staatsoper 1989; returned to Vienna as Valentin in Faust, Marcello, and Paolo in Simon Boccanegra; further appearances at the Hamburg Staatsoper as Mozart's Count (also at Covent Garden), Dandini in Cenerentola at Bologna and Don Alvaro in Il Viaggio a Reims at Pesaro; Metropolitan Opera New York debut 1991, as Guglielmo; Mozart's Figaro 1992, with the Covent Garden co. on tour to Japan; sang Dallapiccola's Prigioniero at Florence 1996; Puccini's Lescaut at La Scala 1998; season 2000–01 at the Deutsche Oper Berlin as Eugene Onegin and Macbeth at the Staatsoper; Amonasro at Macerata, Rigoletto and Wozzeck in Palermo, Mozart's Count at Munich and Ford in Falstaff for the Salzburg Easter Festival; Covent Garden 2001, 2003, 2005, Dandini and Sharpless; 2006 Scarpia at La Scala and at the Vienna Staatsoper; Golaud and Telramund in Bologna; Posa and Simone in Florence; Macbeth in Dresda; Hollaender in Frankfurt and Hamburg; concert repertory includes Les Béatitudes by Franck, Winterreise, and Lieder by Wolf. *Recordings include:* Bartolo in Il Barbiere di Siviglia, Figaro and Count in La Nozze di Figaro, Don Alvaro in Viaggio a Reims, Lescaut in Manon, Paolo in Simone Boccanegra, Lieder of Shsumann, Respighi, Wolf-Ferrari and Tosti. *Current Management:* c/o Atelier Musicale, Via Caselle 76, San Lazzaro di Savena 40068, Italy. *Telephone:* (51) 19984444. *Fax:* (51) 19984420. *E-mail:* info@ateliermusicale.com. *Website:* www.ateliermusicale.com. *E-mail:* luciogallo@hotmail.it.

GALOUZINE, Vladimir; Belgian/Russian singer (tenor); b. 1957, Novosibirsk, Siberia. *Education:* Novosibirsk Conservatoire. *Career:* sang at the Novosibirsk Opera 1988–90, Kirov Theatre St Petersburg 1990–; tours with the Kirov to Spain, Italy, France and the Edinburgh Festival; appearances as Otello in St Petersburg and as Guest in Stuttgart, Dresden, Amsterdam, Brussels and Japan; Grishko in the Kupfer production of Rimsky's Invisible City of Kitezh (Bregenz 1995), and Sergei in the Graham Vick production of Lady Macbeth of the Mtsensk District, at the Metropolitan 1996; season 1996–97 as Pinkerton at Cologne and Alexei in The Gambler by Prokofiev at La Scala; many engagements at the Vienna Staatsoper (debut as Hermann in The Queen of Spades); season 1997–98 with Otello at Brussels and for the New Israeli Opera, Lensky in Eugene Onegin at Buenos Aires; other roles include Radames, Don Carlos, Calaf, Cavaradossi, Chevalier des Grieux, Andrei in Tchaikovsky's Mazeppa and Vladimir in Prince Igor; season 1998 as Khovansky in Khovanshchina at La Scala and Calaf at Madrid; returned to Madrid 2000, for Alvaro in La Forza del Destino; season 2000–01 as Pinkerton, Shostakovich's Sergei and Alexei in The Gambler by Prokofiev at the New York Met; Cavaradossi at Orange, Radames at the Verona Arena and Hermann in The Queen of Spades at Covent Garden. *Recordings include:* Boris Godunov, The Gambler (title role), Rimsky's Sadko (title role, video). *Address:* c/o IMG Artists Paris – Vocal Division, 44 rue Blanche, 75009 Paris, France (office). *Telephone:* 1-44-31-00-10 (office). *Fax:* 1-44-31-44-01 (office). *E-mail:* galouzine@skynet.be (home); artistsparis@imgartists.com (office). *Website:* www.galouzine.com (home).

GALSTIAN, Juliette; Armenian singer (mezzo soprano); b. (Julietta Galstyan), 21 Dec. 1971, Yerevan; m. G. A. Everts. *Education:* Yerevan Conservatoire (class of her grandmother, Marianna Harutiunian), State Conservatoire Diploma (piano and voice, both with honours). *Career:* appearances in Armenia as piano recitalist and concert soloist; from season 1996 engagements at leading opera houses, including Mimi in the centenary production of La Bohème at Turin, Zerlina in Don Giovanni at La Fenice, Susanna in Le nozze di Figaro and Xenia in Boris Godunov at Turin, Flowermaiden in Parsifal at the Opéra Bastille, Paris, Valencienne in The Merry Widow at Royal Opera, Covent Garden, London, Xerxes, Cornelia in Giulio Cesare, Minerva in Il Ritorno d'Ulysse, Rinaldo, Mélisande etc.; repertoire includes Carmen, Charlotte in Werther, Marina in Boris Gudunov, Orphée in Orphée et Eurydice, Rinaldo, Ariodante, Ottavia in L'Incoronazione di Poppea, Meg Page in Falstaff Suzuki in Madama Butterfly; large repertoire of German, Russian etc. lieder. *Recordings include:* Iphigénie en Tauride (DVD), Theodora (CD). *Honours:* First Prize, Viotti Int. Competition, Italy, prizewinner, Maria Callas Grand Prix, Athens, prizewinner José Carreras Competition, Pamplona. *E-mail:* juliette@juliettegalstian.com. *Website:* www.juliettegalstian.com.

GALVANY, Marisa; American singer (soprano); b. 19 June 1936, Paterson, NJ. *Education:* studied with Armen Boyajian. *Career:* debut at Seattle Opera 1968, as Tosca; New York City Opera from 1972, as Elizabeth I in Maria Stuarda, Anna Bolena, Médée, Santuzza and Violetta; Mexico City and San Francisco 1972–73, Aida; New Orleans 1974, as Rachel in La Juive; guest appearances in Philadelphia, Warsaw, Prague, Belgrade and Rouen; Metropolitan Opera from 1979, as Norma, Ortrud, and the Kostelnicka in Jenůfa; other roles include Verdi's Hélène, Abigaille and Elvira, Turandot, Mozart's Countess, Massenet's Salomé and Tchaikovsky's Iolanta; sang Verdi's Ulrica in New York Central Park 2000. *Recordings include:* title role in Medea in Corinto by Giovanni Simone Mayr.

GALVEZ-VALLEJO, Daniel; Spanish singer (tenor); b. 1967. *Education:* studied in Spain and Italy. *Career:* many appearances in Italy as Alfredo and Rodolfo in La Bohème; Montpellier Festival, 1991–95, as Igor in Bizet's Ivan IV, and in Sacchini's Oedipe a Colone; Riccardo in Verdi's Oberto; sang in Les Brigands by Offenbach at the Paris Opéra, Bastille, 1994; Season 1995 as Hoffmann at Lyon and Don José at Lille; other roles include Pollione in Norma and Wagner's Steersman. *Recordings include:* Samson et Dalila. *Current Management:* c/o Agence Artistique Thérèse Cédelle, Boulevard Malesherbes 78, 75008 Paris, France. *Telephone:* 1-49-53-00-02. *Fax:* 1-45-63-70-23. *E-mail:* Agence.Cedelle@wanadoo.fr.

GALWAY, Sir James, Kt, KBE, FRCM, FRCO, FGSM; British flautist and conductor; b. 8 Dec. 1939, Belfast; s. of James Galway and Ethel Stewart Galway (née Clarke); m. 1st 1965; one s.; m. 2nd 1972; one s. two d. (twins); m. 3rd Jeanne Cinnante 1984. *Education:* Mountcollyer Secondary School, Royal Coll. of Music, Guildhall School of Music, Conservatoire National Supérieur de Musique, France. *Career:* first post in Wind Band of Royal Shakespeare Theatre, Stratford-on-Avon; later worked with Sadler's Wells Orchestra, Royal Opera House Orchestra, BBC Symphony Orchestra; Prin. Flute, London Symphony Orchestra and Royal Philharmonic Orchestra; Prin. Solo Flute, Berlin Philharmonic Orchestra 1969–75; int. soloist 1975–; soloist/conductor 1984–; Prin. Guest Conductor, London Mozart Players 1997–; performances worldwide include appearances in The Wall, Berlin, and at Nobel Peace Prize Ceremony, 1998; as conductor, toured Germany with Wurttembergisches Kammerorchester and Asia with Polish Chamber Orchestra, 2000–01; has premiered many contemporary flute works commissioned by and for him; f. First Flute online educational network 2013; Amb. to European Brain Council; James Galway Rose named after him by David Austin. *Recordings include:* Vivaldi The Four Seasons, Sometimes When We Touch, Mozart Concerto No. 1, Andante and Concerto for Flute and Harp, Song Of The Seashore 1979, Annie's Song 1981, Man With The Golden Flute 1982, The Wayward Wind 1982, Nocturne 1983, James Galway Plays Mozart 1984, In The Pink 1984, In Ireland 1986, Christmas Carol 1986, J.S. Bach Suite No. 2 Concerto - Trio Sonatas 1987, Mercadante Concertos 1987, James Galway Plays Beethoven 1988, The Enchanted Forest 1988, James Galway Plays Giuliani 1988, Quantz 4 Concertos 1989, C.P.E. Bach 3 Concertos 1989, The Concerto Collection 1990, Over The Sea To Skye 1990, J.S. Bach Suite No. 2 Concerto for Flute, Violin and Harpsichord 1991, Italian Flute Concertos 1991, In Dulci Jubilo 1991, The Wind Beneath My Wings 1991, Mozart Flute Quartets 1991, Mozart Concerto for Flute and Harp and Sonatas for Flute and Piano 1992, At The Movies 1992, The Magic Flute 1992, Danzi 1993, Dances For Flute 1993, Seasons 1993, The Classical James Galway 1993, Bach Sonatas 1993, Pachelbel Canon 1994, Wind Of Change 1994, The Lark In The Clear Air 1994, The French Recital 1994, Mozart Concerto for Flute and Harp, Concerto No. 1 and Concerto No. 2 1995, Bach Vol. 2 Trio Sonatas 1995, The Celtic Minstrel 1996, James Galway plays the music of Sir Malcolm Arnold 1996, Music for my Friends 1997, James Galway plays Lowell Liebermann 1997, Legends 1997, Flute Sonatas 1997, Meditations 1998, Serenade 1998, Tango del Fuego 1998, Winter's Crossing 1998, Unbreak My Heart 1999, Sixty Years-Sixty Flute Masterpieces Collection 1999, Love Song 2001, Hommage à Rampal 2001, A Song of Home: An American Musical Journey 2002, The Very Best of James Galway 2002, Music for my Little Friends 2002, Wings of Song 2004, My Magic Flute 2006, Ich war ein Berliner 2006, The Essential James Galway 2006, Celebrating 70: A Collection of Personal Favourites 2009, James Galway Plays Flute Concertos (12-cd set) 2011. *Film music:* flute soloist, soundtrack of Lord of the Rings – Return of the King. *Publications:* James Galway: An Autobiography 1978, Flute (Menuhin Music Guide) 1982, James Galway's Music in Time 1983, Flute Studies – Boehm 12 Grand Studies 2003. *Honours:* Hon. MA (Open Univ.) 1979, Hon. DMus (Queen's Univ., Belfast) 1979, (New England Conservatory of Music) 1980, (St Andrew's Univ.); Officier, Ordre des Arts et des Lettres 1987; Grand Prix du Disque 1976, 1989, Nat. Acad. Recording, Arts & Sciences Pres. Merit Award 2004, Classical BRIT Award for Outstanding Contribution to Music 2005, Artist Laureate, Ulster Orchestra 2009, Gramophone Award for Lifetime Achievement 2014. *Current Management:* c/o Elizabeth Sobol Gomez, IMG Artists, Carnegie Hall Tower, 152 West 57th Street, 5th Floor, New York, NY 10019, USA. *Telephone:* (212) 994-3541. *Fax:* (212) 994-3550. *E-mail:* esobol-gomez@imgartists.com. *Website:* www.imgartists.com; jamesgalway.com.

GAMBA, Piero; Italian conductor; b. 16 Sept. 1936, Rome. *Education:* studied piano and score reading with his father. *Career:* conducted Beethoven's 1st Symphony at Rome Opera House aged 8; tours of Europe and North and South America as a child; British debut 1948, conducting Beethoven and Dvořák in London; moved to Madrid 1952; guest engagements in London 1959–63, often with London Symphony Orchestra; Musical Dir Winnipeg Symphony Orchestra, Canada 1970–81, also Music Dir Australian Broadcasting Corporation and National Symphony Orchestra of Uruguay; Prin. Conductor, Adelaide Symphony Orchestra 1982–88. *Recordings include:* Rossini's Overtures with the London Symphony Orchestra, Beethoven's Piano Concertos with Julius Katchen as soloist. *Honours:* Arnold Bar Memorial Medal. *Website:* www.pierogamba.com.

GAMBA, Rumon; British conductor; *Chief Conductor and Music Director, NorrlandsOperan Symphony Orchestra*; b. 24 Nov. 1972, England. *Education:* Royal Acad. of Music, with Colin Metters. *Career:* Assoc. Conductor, BBC Philharmonic Orchestra 1998–2002; Chief Conductor and Music Dir, Iceland Symphony Orchestra 2002–11; Chief Conductor and Music Dir, NorrlandsOperan Symphony Orchestra 2009–; appearances with all the BBC Orchestras, City of Birmingham Symphony Orchestra, Britten Sinfonia, Bournemouth Symphony Orchestra and Royal Scottish Nat. Orchestra; season 2001–02 with Munich Philharmonic Orchestra, Toronto Symphony Orchestra, Bergen Philharmonic Orchestra, London Philharmonic, Melbourne and Dusseldorf Symphonies and NDR Hannover; season 2002–03 with US debut (Florida Philharmonic), New York Philharmonic youth series concerts and 2003 Sydney Festival (most leading Australian orchestras); further engagements with Barcelona and Basle Symphonies, Orquesta de Valencia and Singapore SO; Blue Peter concerts with the BBC Philharmonic Orchestra at the London Proms 2002. *Recordings include:* Malcolm Arnold Symphonies; ballet and film music by Vaughan Williams, Auric, Bliss, Alwyn, Spoliansky, Bernard Herrmann and Richard Rodney Bennett; orchestral works by d'Indy, Matthews, Rozsa. *Current Management:* Harrison/Parrott Ltd, 5–6 Albion Court, London, W6 0QT, England. *Telephone:* (20) 7229-9166. *Fax:* (20) 7221-5042. *E-mail:* info@harrisonparrott.com. *Website:* www.harrisonparrott.com.

GAMBERONI, Kathryn; American singer (soprano); b. 11 June 1955, Pennsylvania. *Education:* Curtis Inst. *Career:* debut in St Louis 1981 as Gerda in the US premiere of Fennimore and Gerda by Delius; sang with the St Louis Company at the Edinburgh Festival 1983 as Margot la Rouge by Delius; Seattle Opera from 1985 as Adina, Despina, Adele, Juliette, Zerbinetta and Marzelline 1991; Santa Fe 1985 in the US premiere of The English Cat by Henze, returning 1989 in Judith Weir's A Night at the Chinese Opera and as Satirino in La Calisto; guest appearances in Paris, Dallas, Cologne, Chicago and Melbourne; other roles include Mozart's Blondchen, Susanna and Papagena, and Fanny in Rossini's La Cambiale di Matrimonio; sang Rosina in Paisiello's Il Barbiere di Siviglia for Long Beach Opera 1989 and the title role in The Cunning Little Vixen at the New York City Opera 1991.

GAMBILL, Robert; American singer (tenor); b. 11 March 1955, Indianapolis, IN. *Education:* Hamburg Musikhochschule with Hans Kagel. *Career:* debut in Milan 1981 as Michael in the premiere of Stockhausen's Donnerstag aus Licht; sang at Frankfurt from 1981 notably in Die Gezeichneten by Schreker; sang at Wiesbaden as Ernesto, Tamino, Don Ottavio and Nicolai's Fenton; Glyndebourne 1982–85 as Almaviva in Il Barbiere di Siviglia and Don Ramiro in La Cenerentola, La Scala Milan 1982, Teatro La Fenice, Venice as Ferrando in Così fan tutte 1983; sang David in Die Meistersinger at the renovated Zürich Opera 1984; Geneva and Aix-en-Provence 1984 as Rossini's Lindoro and Almaviva; season 1987–88 as Belmonte at Buenos Aires and the Steersman in Fliegende Holländer at La Scala, also at the Metropolitan 1989; Schwetzingen Festival 1987 as Rossini's Almaviva, Theater an der Wien, Vienna 1988 in Schubert's Fierrabras, sang Almaviva at Munich 1990 and Wagner's David at Covent Garden; other roles include Mozart's Ferrando, Renaud in Armide, Verdi's Fenton and Iopas in Les Troyens; sang in Rossini double bill at Cologne and Schwetzingen 1992; sang Offenbach's Barbe-bleue at Stuttgart 1996; season 1997–98 with Max at Frankfurt and Florestan at Stuttgart; sang Tannhäuser at Dresden 2001; London Proms 2002; engaged as Tristan at Glyndebourne 2003. *Recordings include:* Rossini's Stabat Mater; Evander in Gluck's Alceste ed Euridice; Tenor Solo in Messiah.

GAMMON, Philip Greenway, ARCM, ARAM, FRAM; British pianist and conductor; *Guest Pianist, The Royal Ballet*; b. 17 May 1940, Chippenham, Wilts., England; s. of S.A.J. Gammon and P.J. Gammon; m. Floretta Volovini 1963; two s. *Education:* Royal Acad. of Music, pupil of Harold Craxton, Badische Musikhochschule, pupil of Yvonne Loriod. *Career:* joined Royal Ballet, Covent Garden 1964; apptd Deputy teacher, Royal Scottish Acad. of Music, Glasgow, Royal Acad., London 1964; Prin. Pianist, Ballet for All 1968–71; teaching appointments at Watford School of Music and Trinity Coll.; returned to Royal Ballet 1972; solo pianist for many ballets including Elite Syncopations, A Month in the Country and Return to the Strange Land; conducting debut with Ballet for All at Richmond Theatre 1970; at Covent Garden 1978, Sleeping Beauty; BBC Radio 3 broadcasts in recitals as soloist and accompanist; debut at Royal Festival Hall and Barbican Hall in 1984 as piano soloist; solo pianist for Rhapsody, Mr Worldly Wise, Ballet Imperial, Concerto, La Fin du Jour, Winter Dreams; The Concert, Marguerite and Armand; guest conducting with English Nat. Ballet, Hong Kong Ballet 1996 and Nat. Ballet of Portugal 1997 and 1998; Prin. Pianist and Conductor Royal Ballet 1999–2005, Guest Pianist 2005–; presents a lecture-recital, Music and Reminiscence, A Pianist's Life with the Royal Ballet; recent performances include Dances of a Gathering 2008, Bach's Goldberg Variations, Royal Opera House 2009; solo pianist at Entente Cordiale Gala, Palais Garnier, Paris 2004, Gala des Etoiles, La Scala, Milan 2004, Winter Dreams Tour, Japan 2006.

Recordings: Elite Syncopations, with musicians from the Covent Garden Orchestra, A Month in the Country, Chopin/Lanchbery, Winter Dreams, DVD of Marguerite and Armand (Liszt Sonata) 2004. *Publications:* first orchestral arrangement of La Chatte Metamorphosée en femme, premiered in 1985 at Royal Opera House. *Honours:* Recital Diploma 1960, MacFarren Gold Medal 1961, Karlsruhe Culture Prize 1962, Badische Musikhochschule Diplom 1963, Royal Ballet Gold Medal 2011. *Address:* 19 Downs Avenue, Pinner, Middx, HA5 5AQ, England (home). *Telephone:* (20) 8866-3260 (home). *E-mail:* pggammon@hotmail.com.

GANASSI, Sonia; Italian singer (mezzo-soprano); b. 1967, Reggio Emilia. *Career:* debut, Spoletto 1991 as Rossini's Cenerentola; Rome Opera from 1992, as Rossini's Isabella and Rosina; season 1995 as Rosina at Venice, Adalgisa in Norma at Bologna, Carmen at Monte Carlo and Emma in Zelmira at Pesaro; US debut Washington 1993 as Cenerentola; season 1996 as Isabella at Genoa; Giovanna in Anna Bolena at Bologna and as Mascagni's Zanetta at Florence; season 1997–98 as Rosina for the Royal Opera in London; Bellini's Romeo at Reggio Emilia and Maffeo Orsini in Lucrezia Borgia at La Scala; other roles include Elisabetta in Maria Stuarda, Dorabella, Nicklausse in Les Contes d'Hoffmann and Massenet's Charlotte; season 2001–02 as Cenerentola, and Romeo in I Capuleti e i Montecchi at Covent Garden; Adalgisa at Turin, Donizetti's Leonora at Bologna, Cenerentola in Madrid, Milan and San Francisco, Elisabetta in Barcelona; London Proms 2002. *Recordings:* Il Barbiere di Siviglia, Rossini's Sigismondo. *Current Management:* All'Opera Artists Management, Viale Giuseppe Mazzini 41, 00195 Rome, Italy. *Telephone:* (06) 3215772. *Fax:* (06) 3215252. *E-mail:* info@allopera.net. *Website:* www.allopera.net.

GANATRA, Simin, BMus; American violinist; b. Los Angeles. *Education:* Oberlin Conservatory of Music; studied with Idell Low, Robert Lipsett, Roland Vamos, Almita Vamos. *Career:* Founder mem. Pacifica Quartet 1994–, Faculty Quartet-in-Residence, Univ. of Illinois, Champagn/Urbana 2003–, Quartet-in-Residence, Metropolitan Museum of Art 2009–; Faculty mem., Univ. of Illinois, Champagn/Urbana 2003–, Univ. of Chicago. *Recordings:* with The Pacifica Quartet: String Quartets by Easley Blackwood 1999, Dvořák: String Quartet No. 13 in G Major and String Quintet in E-flat Major 2001, Mendelssohn: The Complete String Quartets 2005, Declarations: Music Between the Wars 2006, Elliott Carter: String Quartets Nos 1 and 5 (Grammy Award for Best Chamber Music Performance 2009) 2008. *Honours:* Louis Kaufman Prize for Outstanding Performance in Chamber Music, Oberlin Conservatory, first prize, Union League of Chicago Competition, Pasadena Instrumental Competition, Minnesota Sinfonia Competition, Schubert Club Competition, Grand Prize, Coleman Chamber Music Competition 1996, Walter F. Naumburg Chamber Music Award 1998, Chamber Music America's Cleveland Quartet Award 2002, Avery Fisher Career Grant 2006, Musical America Award for Ensemble of the Year 2009. *Current Management:* Melvin Kaplan Inc., 115 College Street, Burlington, VT 05401, USA. *Telephone:* (802) 658-2592. *Fax:* (802) 658-6089. *E-mail:* music@melkap.com. *Website:* www .melkap.com. *E-mail:* pacificaquartet@yahoo.com (office); sganatra@ ameritech.net (home). *Website:* www.pacificaquartet.com.

GANTER, Martin; German singer (baritone); b. 15 May 1965, Freiburg. *Education:* Staatliche Hochschule für Musik, Karlsruhe with Prof. Kern. *Career:* debut in Mozart's Count at Coblenz 1989; sang in premiere of Henze's Das verratene Meer, Berlin 1990; mem. ensemble of Bavarian State Opera 1993–2007; appearances at Bavarian State Opera, Munich from 1991, as Ned Keene in Peter Grimes, Schaunard (La Bohème), Papageno, Silvio and Malatesta; Guglielmo (Così fan tutte) in Basle, Barcelona and Dresden 1997; Don Giovanni at Hof and Rossini's Figaro at Baden-Baden 1985, Dandini in La Cenerentola at Dresden Staatsoper 1996; toured Italy with Zubin Mehta 2002; sand Kurwenal in Tristan und Isolde in Zurich 2008; sang Hoopoe in The Birds with Los Angeles Opera 2009; sang Beckmesser in Die Meistersinger von Nürnberg with Zurich Opera 2012, 2013; debut at Metropolitan Opera as Kothner 2014. *Honours:* winner, VDMK Competition, Berlin 1988, named Kammersänger by Bavarian State Opera 2005. *Current Management:* Hilbert Artists Management, Maximilianstrasse 22, 80539 Munich, Germany. *E-mail:* agentur@hilbert.de. *Website:* www.hilbert.de.

GARANČA, Elīna; Latvian singer (mezzo-soprano); b. 16 Sept. 1976, Riga; m. Karel Mark Chichon; two d. *Education:* studied with her mother at Latvian Acad. of Music, also with Irina Gavrilovici in Vienna and Virginia Zeani in USA. *Career:* began as Resident Artist, Südthüringischer Staatstheater, Meiningen, and later Frankfurt Opera; originally specialised in Mozart roles, now equally noted for bel canto and Romantic repertoire; has appeared at major opera houses and concert halls and with symphony orchestras world-wide including Deutsche Oper Berlin, La Scala, Wiener Staatsoper (over 140 performances of 18 roles since her 2003 debut there, notably in the roles of Carmen, Sesto, Giovanna Seymour, Charlotte and Oktavian), Opéra de Paris, Royal Opera House Covent Garden (debut 2007), Metropolitan Opera (debut as Rosina 2008, her Carmen was broadcast in over 1,000 cinemas world-wide in 2009 and reprised in 2015), Bayerische Staatsoper Munich, Concertgebouw Amsterdam, Vienna Musikverein, Vienna Philharmonic, Theater an der Wien, Théâtre des Champs-Elysées, Festspielhaus Baden-Baden; festivals, gala concerts and recitals in Europe and USA, including Verdi Requiem at Salzburg Festival; past concert appearances have included Berg's Seven frühe Lieder with Vienna Philharmonic, Dvořák's Requiem with Bayerische Rundfunk, Beethoven's Missa Solemnis with Orchestre Nat. de France, Rossini's Stabat Mater with Helsinki Philharmonic, Mozart's Requiem at

Staatsoper Vienna. *Recordings include:* solo: Aria Cantilena (Echo Klassik Award for Singer of the Year) 2007, Bel Canto (Echo Klassik Award for Singer of the Year) 2009, Habanera (Orchestra Sinfonica Nazionale della RAI/Karel Mark Chichon) 2010, Romantique (Echo Klassik Award Solo Recording of the Year 2013) 2012, Meditation 2014; other: I Capuleti e i Montecchi 2009, Carmen 2012, La Cenerentola 2013. *Publications:* Wirklich wichtig sind die Schuhe (The Shoes Are Really Important) (memoir) 2014. *Honours:* Three Star Order, Latvia 2007; prizewinner, Mirjam Helin Singing Competition, Finland 1999, Great Music Award, Latvia 2000, 2010, European Culture Prize 2006, Musical America Award for Vocalist of the Year 2010, Midem Classical Award for Singer of the Year 2010, Kammersängerin, Wiener Staatsoper 2013. *Current Management:* Ernesto Palacio, InArt Artists Management, Via San Gregorio 53, 20124 Milano, Italy. *Telephone:* (2) 97374166. *Fax:* (2) 97374233. *E-mail:* ernestopalacio@tiscali.it. *Website:* www.askonasholt.co.uk/ artists/singers/mezzo-soprano/elna-garana; www.inartmanagement.com; elinagaranca.com.

GARAZZI, Peyo; French singer (tenor); b. 31 March 1937, St Jean Pied de Port, Basses Pyrénées. *Education:* studied in Bordeaux and Paris. *Career:* sang first at Théâtre de la Monnaie in Brussels; sang at Royal Opera Ghent 1962 as Nadir in Les Pêcheurs de Perles, Paris 1977 in Gwendoline by Chabrier and guest appearances in Bordeaux, Munich and Berlin; Covent Garden Opera 1983 as Don Carlos in French-language revival of Verdi's opera; other roles include Florestan, Aron in Moses und Aron by Schoenberg and parts in operas by Delibes, Donizetti, Offenbach and Puccini. *Recordings include:* Don Quichotte by Massenet.

GARBER, J. Ryan, BMus, MMus, DMus; American composer; *Associate Professor of Music, Carson-Newman College;* b. 1973, Harrisonburg, Va. *Education:* James Madison Univ., Florida State Univ., studied composition with John S. Hilliard, Ladislav Kubik. *Career:* began studying piano aged four; Assoc. Prof., Carson-Newman Coll. 2001–; performs in Garber-Scruggs Duo; plays bassoon with Knoxville Wind Symphony; Organist and Adult Choir Dir, All Saints Church, Morristown 2008–. *Compositions include:* for orchestra: Out of the Silent Planet 2003, Magnificat 2004, Concerto for Piano and Orchestra 2005, Concertino 2005; for choir: Peace on Earth 2001, Te Deum 2002, Tu Es Christus 2003, Magnificat 2004; instrumental: Sonata for Cello and Piano 1995, Trio for Oboe, Clarinet, and Bassoon 1997, Piano Quintet 2000, Resonances 2003, Valley Breezes 2003, Parabolisms 2005, Light Shines in the Darkness 2005, Fantasie auf Ein Feste Burg 2006, Concurrently Colliding Sonorities 2006, Another Twist 2006, Quadrasonare 2007; vocal: Songs for My God 2001, The Lord's Prayer 2004, A Carol 2004, An American Song Cycle 2007. *Recordings:* A Mighty Fortress 2004, Resonances 2007, Kettle Music 2007, Another Twist, Concertino. *Honours:* Tennessee Composer of the Year 2002, Carson-Newman Creativity Award 2003, Excellence in Teaching and Leadership Award 2003. *Address:* Music Faculty, Carson-Newman College, 1646 Russell Avenue, Jefferson City, TN 37760, USA (office). *Telephone:* (865) 471-3410 (office). *E-mail:* rgarber@cn.edu (office); info@ryangarber.com (office). *Website:* cnweb.cn.edu/music/rgarber.html (office); www.ryangarber.com.

GARCIA, Jose; American singer (bass); b. 1959. *Career:* season 1987 as Sarastro for Pennysylvania Opera and Commendatore in Peter Sellars production of Don Giovanni; season 1988–89 as Grand Inquisitor in Don Carlos at Bologna; Polidoro in Rossini's Zelmira at Venice; Gounod's Frère Laurent at Seattle; season 1990 as Roger in British premiere of Verdi's Jérusalem for Opera North; Sarastro for Glyndebourne Touring Opera. *Recordings include:* Zelmira.

GARCIA, Navarro Luis; Spanish conductor; b. 30 April 1941, Chiva, Valencia. *Education:* Valencia and Madrid Conservatories, studied in Italy with Franco Ferrara, Vienna Acad. with Hans Swarowsky. *Career:* founded the Spanish Univ. Orchestra 1963; Permanent Conductor, Valencia Symphony 1970–74; Musical Dir, San Carlos Theatre at Lisbon 1980–82; Principal Guest Conductor, Radio Symphony Orchestra, Stuttgart 1984–87; Vienna State Opera 1987–91, Tokyo Philharmonic Orchestra 1992–; Generalmusik-direktor, Stuttgart State Opera 1987–91; Musical and Artistic Conductor, Barcelona Symphony Orchestra 1991–93; Permanent Guest Conductor, Deutsche Oper Berlin 1992–; appearances in most major int. opera theatres, including Covent Garden La Bohème 1979 and Tosca 1983, La Scala Milan, Madama Butterfly in 1987, Vienna State Opera, Falstaff, La Bohème, Tosca, La Forza del Destino and Andrea Chénier; has conducted leading orchestras, including the Vienna Philharmonic, London Symphony and Philharmonia, Leningrad Philharmonic, Chicago Symphony, Pittsburgh Symphony, Los Angeles Philharmonic; mem. Royal Acad. of San Carlos, Spain. *Honours:* first prize Madrid Conservatory 1963, prizewinner Int. Competition Besançon 1967, Gold Medal, Paris 1983.

GARCÍA, Orlando Jacinto, DMA; American (b. Cuban) composer; *Professor of Music and Director, School of Music, Florida International University;* b. 1954, Havana, Cuba. *Education:* Univ. of Miami. *Career:* migrated to USA in 1961; over 140 compositions of new music commissioned and/or performed by soloists, ensembles and orchestras worldwide; Founder and Dir of int. festivals including New Music Miami Festival and Music of the Americas Festival; Founder and Artistic Dir NODUS Ensemble and Florida Int. Univ. (FIU) New Music Ensemble; Prof. of Music and Dir School of Music, FIU. *Compositions include:* fragmentos del pasado 2001, imagenes sonidos congelados for violin and electronics 2001, Auschwitz (nunca se olvidaran) for orchestra and choir 2003, resonancia for solo piano 2003, vientos fragmentados for bass clarinet and trombone 2005, Music for Italy for piccolo doubling bass flute and piano 2006, Otro mundo sonoro for wind ensemble 2006, Islas for flute ensemble, solo flute, electronics 2007, Transcending Time for chamber ensemble, mezzo soprano soloist, 4 singers, cajas sonoras for guitar ensemble, video, electronics 2009, Dreaming Amazonia for electronics 2009. *Recordings include:* solo albums: La Belleza del Silencio, Celestial Voices, Sombras iluminadas, Fragmentos del Pasado, Temporal 2008. *Honours:* Rockefeller residencies, Fulbright fellowships, Cintas Foundation and State of Florida Council for the Arts fellowships, First Prize, Nuevas Resonancias Composition Competition, Mexico, First Prize, Joyce Dutka Arts Foundation Composition Competition 2001. *Address:* Florida International University School of Music, University Park, Miami, FL 33199, USA (office). *E-mail:* orlando@orlandojacintogarcia.com (home). *Website:* www .orlandojacintogarcia.com.

GARCÍA ALARCÓN, Leonardo; Argentinian conductor, musicologist and musician (harpsichord, organ); b. 1976, La Plata. *Education:* La Plata Nat. Univ., Conservatoire and Centre for Ancient Music, Switzerland. *Career:* mem. Elyma ensemble and asst to Gabriel Garrido; Founder and Dir, La Cappella Mediterranea 1999–; organist, Chapelles d'Anières-Vésenaz, Geneva 2000–; Artistic Dir, La Nouvelle Ménestrandie ensemble 2005–; Artistic Dir, Choeur de Chambre de Namur 2010–, Co-Dir, harpsichordist and organist, Ensemble Clematis; has performed with his groups at festivals including Chaise-Dieu, Teatro Massimo in Palermo, Beaune and Ambronay, and as chamber musician with Christophe Coin, Maurice Bourgue, Sergio Azzolini, Manfredo Kraemer and Andrea De Carlo; has conducted works including Rameau's Les Fêtes de Ramire, Scarlatti's La Dirindina, Offertorio by Giovanni de Giorgis and Monteverdi's La Selva Morale, Giuseppe Zamponi's opera Ulisse nell'Isola di Circe; has also appeared as soloist; musicologist specialising in voice; teacher, Haute Ecole de Musique, Geneva and at Festival d'Ambronay. *Recordings include:* with La Cappella Mediterranea: Andalusian Music in Mexico in the 17th Century 2003; with Ensemble Clematis: Nicolaus à Kempis: Symphoniae, Carolus Hacquart: Cantiones & Sonate, Carlo Farina: Capriccio stravagante, Frescobaldi: Il Regno d'Amore, Matheo Romero: Romerico Florido, Giovanni Giorgi: Ave Maria, Bach–Böhm, Vitali Ciaconna, Carmina Latina. *Address:* c/o Choeur de Chambre de Namur, Avenue Jean 1er, 2, 5000 Namur, Belgium (office). *Telephone:* 81711500 (office). *E-mail:* secretariat@cavema.be (office). *Website:* choeur-chambre -namur.be (office).

GARCÍA ASENSIO, Enrique; Spanish conductor and academic; b. 22 Aug. 1937, Valencia; m. Maria Isabel del Castillo Mendía; three d. *Education:* Royal Conservatory of Music, Madrid, Munich Higher School of Music with Profs Lessing, Eichhorn and Mennerich, Accad. Chigiana, Siena, Italy with Sergiu Celibidache. *Career:* has conducted all leading Spanish orchestras; Music Dir and Conductor, Las Palmas Philharmonic, Canary Islands 1962–64, Valencia Municipal Orchestra 1964–65, Spanish Radio and Television Orchestra, Madrid 1966–84; Asst Conductor, Nat. Symphony Orchestra, Washington, DC 1967–68; Prin. Guest Conductor, Valencia Orchestra; Conductor and Music Dir Madrid Municipal Symphonic Band 1994–98, 2001–12; Music Dir and Conductor, Radio Television Symphony Orchestra 1998–2001; asst to Celibidache at master-classes, Bologna, Munich; master-classes at Festival Celibidache 100, Bucharest 2012; Prof. of Conducting, Royal Conservatory of Music, Madrid 1970–85, also at Musikene (Higher School of Music of the Basque Country); int. master-classes, the Netherlands and Dominican Repub.; presenter, El Mundo de la Música (educational TV programme) 1976–80; mem. Valencia Cultural Council 1986–. *Recordings include:* more than 60 recordings, including: Zarzuela, Teresa Berganza and English Chamber Orchestra 1976, Ernesto Halffter, English Chamber Orchestra 1991, Banda Sinfónica Municipal de Madrid, Orquesta Sinfónica RTVE. *Honours:* granted title of Predilect Son of the City, Municipality of Valencia 2012; RAI Conducting Prize 1962, Gold Medal, Royal Conservatory of Music, Madrid, Gold Medal, Dimitri Mitropoulos Int. Competition, New York 1967. *Current Management:* c/o Edificio Foro de Somosaguas, planta 1, oficina 26 Urbanización Pinar de Somosaguas nº 89 bis Pozuelo de Alarcón, 28223 Madrid, Spain. *Telephone:* (91) 5913290; 609-242404 (mobile). *Fax:* (91) 5913291. *E-mail:* musiespana@musiespana.com. *Website:* www.musiespana .com. *Telephone:* (91) 6302572 (home). *Fax:* (91) 6303810 (home). *E-mail:* maestro@garciaasensio.com (office); gasensio@hotmail.com. *Website:* www .garciaasensio.com.

GARCISANZ, Isabel; Spanish singer (soprano); b. 29 June 1934, Madrid. *Education:* studied with Angeles Ottein in Spain, with Erik Werba in Vienna. *Career:* debut at Vienna Volksoper 1964 as Adèle in Le Comte Ory; sang in Paris at the Opéra and the Opéra-Comique; guest appearances in Bordeaux, Marseille, Nancy, Nice, Cologne, Barcelona and Miami; Glyndebourne 1966–68, 1970 as Concepcion in L'Heure Espagnole, Nerillo in L'Ormindo and Zaida in Il Turco in Italia; Toulouse 1972–73 in the premieres of operas by Casanova and Nikiprowetsky; Strasbourg 1974 in the premiere of Delereue's Medis et Alissio; engagements with French Radio, Paris, in the first performances of works by Mihalovici; was the first singer of Hahn's Sybille; sang in the premiere of Le Château des Carpathes, by Philippe Hersant, Montpellier 1993; mem. Acanthes, Union des Femmes Artists Musiciennes. *Recordings:* L'Ormindo; Le Maître de Chapelle by Paer; Le Roi Malgré Lui by Chabrier; Cantigas; Sybille; Mass by Ohana; Three Centuries of Spanish Melodies; Spanish Songs by Rodrigo, Falla, and Garcia. *Address:* c/o Opéra du Rhin, 19 Place Broglie, 67008 Strasbourg Cédex, France.

GARD, Robert, OBE; British singer (tenor); b. 7 March 1927, Cornwall, England. *Education:* Guildhall School of Music with Dino Borgoli and Walter Hyde, studied with Kaiser Breme in Bayreuth. *Career:* debut with English Opera Group in Lennox Berkeley's Ruth 1957; sang for Welsh Opera, then at Aldeburgh and in Australia as Britten's Peter Quint in the Turn of The Screw, Albert Herring, Male Chorus and Aschenbach; sang Anatol in War and Peace at the opening of the Sydney Opera House 1973, appearing on television in this production, and Charpentier's Louise and Manon; sang Aschenbach in a film version of Britten's Death in Venice 1981, commissioned by the Britten Foundation; other roles included Aegisthus, Herod, Loge, Siegmund, Tamino, Števa in Jenůfa, Peter Grimes, Tom Rakewell, and Le Mesurier in the premiere of Meale's Voss 1986; sang Mr Upfold in Albert Herring at Sydney 1996.

GARDELLA, Federico; Italian composer; b. 1979, Milan. *Education:* Milan Conservatoire, Universität der Künste, Berlin, Accad. Nazionale di Santa Cecilia, Rome, Accad. Chigiana, Siena. *Career:* commissions from Divertimento Ensemble, Fondazione Spinola Banna per l'Arte, Orchestra I Pomeriggi Musicali, Résonance Contemporaine, Takefu Int. Music Festival and Trieste Prima; works performed at major festivals and concert houses in Europe and Japan by ensembles including Latvian Nat. Symphony Orchestra, Łódź Philharmonic Orchestra, Neue Vocalsolisten Stuttgart, Divertimento Ensemble, Ensemble Algoritmo, Freon Ensemble, Talea Ensemble and Trio di Parma; Composer-in-Residence, Fondazione Spinola Banna per l'Arte 2010, Compagnie Nationale de Théâtre Lyrique et Musical ARCAL, Paris. *Honours:* Takefu Int. Composition Award 2009, Toru Takemitsu Award for Composition 2012. *Address:* via Organdino 6, 20146 Milan, Italy (home). *E-mail:* federico .gardella@libero.it (home). *Website:* www.federicogardella.it (office).

GARDINER, Ian, MA; British composer, arranger and academic. *Education:* Royal Holloway Coll., London and Univ. of Keele. *Career:* Lecturer, Royal Holloway Coll., London 1987–90, Salford Univ. 1992–96, Liverpool Inst. for the Performing Arts 1996–2002, Univ. of Liverpool 2002–; specializes in composition and analysis of music for film and television; Researcher, Goldsmiths Coll., London, British Film Inst.; commissions from Endymion Ensemble, Ensemble 10:10, Harmonie Band, Trio Phoenix; fmr Dir, George W. Welch Ensemble; as arranger and orchestrator, has worked with Elmer Bernstein, John Harle, Willard W. White, Evelyn Glennie, Will Gregory from Goldfrapp, Royal Shakespeare Co. *Compositions:* Lift Music, Bold St, The Desert Island Variations, Monument (Prix Italia Special Prize for Music Programmes 1994, Sony Radio Award 1994), Annabelle Dancing 1995. *Compositions for television:* The Media Show theme (Channel Four), The History of Britain (BBC), The Ship (BBC). *Compositions for film:* scores for silent films: Fétiche, The Cabinet of Dr Caligari. *Address:* School of Music, University of Liverpool, 80 Bedford Street South, Liverpool, L69 7WW, England (office). *Telephone:* (151) 794-3096 (office). *Fax:* (151) 794-3141 (office). *E-mail:* music@liv.ac.uk (office). *Website:* www.liv.ac.uk (office).

GARDINER, Sir John Eliot, Kt, CBE, MA, FRSA; British conductor and music director; *President, Bach-Archiv Foundation;* b. 20 April 1943, Fontmell Magna, Dorset; s. of the late Rolf Gardiner and of Marabel Gardiner (née Hodgkin); m. 1st Cherryl Anne ffoulkes 1971 (divorced 1981); m. 2nd Elizabeth Suzanne Wilcock 1981 (divorced 1997); three d.; m. 3rd Isabella de Sabata 2001. *Education:* Bryanston School, King's Coll., Cambridge, King's Coll., London, and in Paris and Fontainebleau with Nadia Boulanger. *Career:* Founder and Artistic Dir Monteverdi Choir 1964, Monteverdi Orchestra 1968, the English Baroque Soloists 1978, Orchestre Révolutionnaire et Romantique 1990; concert debut Wigmore Hall, London 1966; youngest conductor at Henry Wood Promenade Concerts, Royal Albert Hall 1968; operatic debut Sadler's Wells Opera, London Coliseum 1969; Prin. Conductor CBC Vancouver Orchestra 1980–83; Musical Dir Lyon Opera 1982–88, Chef fondateur 1988–; Artistic Dir Göttingen Handel Festival 1981–90, Veneto Music Festival 1986; Prin. Conductor, NDR Symphony Orchestra, Hamburg 1991–94; residency at Théâtre du Châtelet, Paris 1999–2003; Bach Cantata Pilgrimage, with performances throughout Europe 2000; Guest Conductor, Royal Opera House, Covent Garden, La Scala, Milan; regular guest conductor with London Symphony Orchestra, and other major orchestras in Amsterdam, Paris, Dresden, Leipzig, Prague, Vienna, Berlin, Chicago, Cleveland, Pittsburgh; Domaine privé, Cité de la musique, Paris 2007; appearances at European music festivals, including Aix-en-Provence, Aldeburgh, Bath, Berlin, Edinburgh, Flanders, Netherlands, London, Salzburg, BBC Proms; Pres., Bach-Archiv Foundation, Leipzig 2014–; Visiting Fellow, Peterhouse Coll., Cambridge 2007–08; Christoph Wolff Distinguished Visiting Scholar, Harvard Univ. 2015. *Recordings include:* over 250 albums including Bach Cantatas (Gramophone Award for Specialist Achievement 2011, J. C. Bach: Welt, gute Nacht (ECHO Klassik Award for Choral Recording of the Year – 16th/17th Century 2012) 2011, Bach Motets (Gramophone Award for Baroque Vocal 2013). *Publications:* Music in the Castle of Heaven: A Portrait of Johann Sebastian Bach 2013. *Honours:* Hon. Fellow, King's Coll., London 1992, Royal Acad. of Music 1992, King's Coll., Cambridge 2015; Commdr, Ordre des Arts et des Lettres 1997, Officer's Cross of the Order of Merit (Germany) 2005, Chevalier, Légion d'honneur 2011; Dr hc (Univ. Lumière de Lyon) 1987, (Complutense Univ. of Madrid) 2001, (New England Conservatoire) 2005, (Pavia) 2006; Hon. DMus (St Andrews) 2014, (Cambridge) 2015; 17 Gramophone awards, including Record of the Year 1991, 2005, Artist of the Year

1994, eight Edison Awards, four Grands Prix du Disque, three Prix Caecilia, two Arturo Toscanini Music Critics' awards, two Grammy Awards, three Deutscher Schallplattenpreis, Buxtehude Prize Lübeck 1994, Robert Schumann Preis Zwickau 2001, Halle Handel Prize 2001, La Medalia Internacional Complutense Univ. of Madrid 2001, Classic FM Gramophone Award 2005, Léonie Sonning Music Prize 2005, City of Leipzig and Bach Archiv Bach Medal for lifetime achievement in the performance of music by J. S. Bach 2005, Royal Acad. of Music/Kohn Foundation Bach Prize 2008, Diapason d'Or de l'année 2011, Harvard Glee Club Medal 2015. *Current Management:* Intermusica Artists' Management Ltd, 36 Graham Street, Crystal Wharf, London, N1 8GJ, England. *Website:* www.intermusica.co.uk/gardiner.

GARDNER, Edward, OBE; British conductor; *Music Director, English National Opera;* b. 22 Nov. 1974, Gloucester. *Education:* King's Coll., Cambridge and Royal Acad. of Music. *Career:* fmr Asst Conductor Hallé Orchestra; Music Dir Glyndebourne Touring Opera 2004–06, with productions including La Bohème 2004, La Cenerentola 2005, The Turn of the Screw 2006, Fidelio 2006; has conducted Camerata Salzburg, London Philharmonic, Melbourne Symphony, Belgrade Philharmonic, Royal Scottish Nat. Orchestra, BBC Symphony Orchestra, Philharmonia, Alabama Symphony, Orchestre de Bretagne; season 2005–06 appearances included BBC Scottish Symphony Orchestra, BBC Nat. Orchestra of Wales, Vancouver Symphony, Orquestra Nacional do Porto, MDR Leipzig, Orchestre Philharmonique de Liège; opera highlights include Tchaikovsky's Eugene Onegin with Glyndebourne Touring Opera 2002, Meyerbeer's L'Africaine with Strasbourg Opera 2004, Mozart's Così fan tutte with ENO 2005, Adams' The Death of Klinghoffer with Scottish Opera 2005, Weill's Seven Deadly Sins with Paris Opéra 2005, Royal Opera debut Il re pastore 2006, Donizetti's L'Elisir d'amore, Paris Opéra 2006, Stravinsky's The Rake's Progress, Paris 2007–08; Music Dir, ENO 2006–; Prin. Guest Conductor, City of Birmingham Symphony Orchestra 2011–; Guest Conductor, Bergen Philharmonic Orchestra, Chief Conductor 2015–; co-f. (with tenor Toby Spence) song recital series Wardsbrook Concerts 2013. *Honours:* Royal Philharmonic Soc. Award for Best Young Artist 2005, for Best Conductor 2008, Olivier Award for Outstanding Achievement in Opera 2009. *Website:* www.askonasholt.co.uk. *Address:* English National Opera, London Coliseum, St Martin's Lane, London, WC2N 4ES, England (office). *Website:* www.eno.org (office).

GARDNER, Jake; American singer (bass-baritone); b. 14 Nov. 1947, Oneonta, NY; m. Jill Gardner. *Education:* State Univ. of New York, Potsdam, Syracuse Univ. *Career:* spent first ten years of career studying and performing with Tri-Cities Opera, Binghamton, New York; sang Valentin in Faust at Houston 1975; Carnegie Hall 1976, in concert performance of Le Cid by Massenet; sang James Stewart in premiere of Thea Musgrave's Mary, Queen of Scots 1977 Edinburgh Festival, and repeated role at Norfolk, Va 1978 and elsewhere; appeared with Boston Opera 1979 US premiere of Tippett's The Ice Break and has sung at opera houses in Washington, Detroit, San Diego, San Francisco, New Orleans and St Louis; has sung Mozart's Guglielmo and Figaro with Netherlands Opera, Escamillo in Peter Brook's version of Carmen throughout Europe and at Lincoln Center; Wexford Festival debut 1987 as Valdeburgo in La Straniera; has also sung title role of Il Ritorno d'Ulisse conducted by Nicholas McGegan for Long Beach Opera and in premiere of Musgrave's Incident at Owl Creek Bridge, for BBC Radio 3; prin. baritone at Cologne Opera from 1989, as Valentin, Nardo in La Finta Giardiniera, Mozart's Count, Puccini's Lescaut and Marcello, Belcore in L'Elisir d'amore; concert performances of Figaro and the Glagolitic Mass, conducted by Simon Rattle; Glyndebourne Festival debut 1991, as Guglielmo; other roles in Shostakovich The Nose for Cologne Opera and title role in Don Giovanni for Dresden Opera 1994; Ned Keene in Peter Grimes, Châtelet 1995; Schwetzingen Festival 1995, in Salieri's Falstaff; sang Kolenaty in The Makropulos Case at Aix 2000; season 2013–14 included debut with North Carolina Opera as Don Alfonso in Mozart's Così fan tutte and with Eugene Opera as Giorgio Germont in Verdi's La Traviata, role debut in title role of Wagner's Der Fliegende Holländer with Piedmont Opera. *Recordings include:* El Cid, Mary, Queen of Scots, An Occurrence at Owl Creek Bridge. *Current Management:* Uzan International Artists, 250 West 57th Street, Suite 1932, New York, NY 10107, USA. *Website:* bassbaritonejakegardner.com.

GARDOW, Helrun; German singer (mezzo-soprano); b. 8 Jan. 1944, Eisenach. *Education:* studied in Berlin and Milan and with Josef Metternich in Cologne. *Career:* sang at Bonn Opera 1969–76, Zürich Opera 1976–87, in various roles, including Orpheus and Dorabella; appeared in premieres of Kelterborn's Ein Engel Kommt nach Babyon 1977 and Der Kirschgarten 1984; guest appearances at Copenhagen, Düsseldorf, Edinburgh, Berlin, Dresden, Munich, Milan and Vienna; concert engagements at Frankfurt, Madrid, Amsterdam, Cologne and Naples; active in Seoul, South Korea from 1987, as singer and dir of Art-Com, in computer visual art and music, returned to Europe 1990s. *Recordings include:* Minerva in Il Ritorno d'Ulisse; L'Incoronazione di Poppea; Dido and Aeneas; Bach Cantatas and Magnificat; Haydn's Theresa Mass; Mozart's Missa Brevis in D.

GARETTI, Helene; French singer (soprano); b. 13 March 1939, Roanne, Loire. *Education:* Paris Conservatoire, studied with Régine Crespin. *Career:* sang first at Nice then Paris Opéra from 1968 as Marguerite, Iphigénie en Tauride, Médée, Chrysothemis 1987 and Desdemona 1988; sang Massenet's Grisélidis at Strasbourg 1986; appearances at the Paris Opéra-Comique as Mimi, Butterfly, Katya Kabanova and Donna Elvira 1988; sang Sieglinde at

Rouen and elsewhere in France; other roles have included Leonore, Ariadne and Marguerite in Damnation de Faust.

GARIBOVA, Karine; Russian violinist; b. 1965, Moscow. *Education:* Central Music School, Moscow. *Career:* co-founder, Quartet Veronique 1989; many concerts in the former USSR and Russia, notably in the Russian Chamber Music Series and the 150th birthday celebrations for Tchaikovsky 1990; masterclasses at the Aldeburgh Festival 1991; concert tour of the UK 1992–93; repertoire includes works by Beethoven, Brahms, Tchaikovsky, Bartók, Shostakovich and Schnittke. *Recordings include:* Schnittke's 3rd Quartet. *Honours:* winner All-Union String Quartet Competition, St Petersburg 1990–91, third place Int. Shostakovich Competition, St Petersburg 1991 (both with Quartet Veronique).

GARIFULLINA, Aida; Russian singer (soprano); b. 30 Sept. 1987, Kazan, Tartarstan. *Education:* Musikhochschule Nürnberg, Germany with Siegfried Jerusalem, Universität für Musik und darstellende Kunst, Austria with Claudia Visca. *Career:* debut, Mariinsky Theatre at invitation of Valery Gergiev, as Susanna in Le nozze di Figaro and Adina in L'elisir d'amore 2013; signed with Decca Records, London. *Honours:* First Prize, Plácido Domingo Operalia Competition 2013. *E-mail:* avtoledi-40@mail.ru (office). *Website:* www.askonasholt.co.uk.

GARILLI, Fabrizio, DipMus; Italian pianist and composer; b. 29 July 1941, Monticelli d'Ongina, Placenza; m. Anna Paola Rossi 1968, one s. *Career:* debut as piano soloist with orchestra, Beethoven's 3rd Concerto, Teatro Municipale, Piacenza; concerts as solo pianist with orchestra and chamber music; Conservatory Dir. *Compositions:* Fantasie for piano, Cantico delle Creature for soloists, choir and organ, Contrappunti Su Temi Gregoriani for organ and orchestra, Metamorfosi for two pianos and percussion, Laude for female choir, narrator and orchestra. *Recordings:* albums: Music of 17th-Century Italians, Ciampi, Galuppi and Scarlatti, and J.S. Bach Well-Tempered Klavier. *Honours:* first prize FM Neapolitano Composition Competition, Naples, second prize Pedrollo, Milan, Assisi Prize.

GARINO, Gérard; French singer (tenor); b. 1 June 1949, Lançon, Provence. *Education:* Bordeaux Conservatoire and studied in Italy. *Career:* debut in Bordeaux, 1977 as Rossini's Almaviva; appearances at Bordeaux as Gerald in Lakmé and in La Dame Blanche and Gounod's Mireille; further engagements as Mozart's Ferrando at Toulouse and Nadir in Les Pêcheurs de Perles at Aix; Paris Opéra and Liège 1981, in Il Matrimonio Segreto and Don Pasquale in Ernesto; returned to Liège 1982 and 1987, as Idomeneo and in Grétry's Zemire; Portrait de Manon, Monte Carlo 1989; season 1991, as Nadir at the Opéra-Comique, Paris, Pylades in Iphigénie en Tauride by Piccinni at Rome and Masaniello in La Muette de Portici at Marseille; Other roles include Tonio in La Fille du Régiment, Macduff, Ismaele in Nabucco and Nicias in Thais; Traviata and Romeo and Juliette at Liège, Bohème at Toulouse, Thérèse in Massenet at Monte Carlo, 1989; Manon in Massenet at Bordeaux, Anna Bolena at Marseille, 1990; Werther at Festival Massenet and Festival de La Coruna, Spain, 1993; St Gallen 1994, as Nicias in Thais by Massenet. *Recordings:* L'Abandon d'Arianne by Milhaud; Don Sanche by Liszt; Messiaen's St François d'Assise; Il Pitor Parigino by Cimarosa; Video of Carmen (as Remendado); La Mort d'Orphée, Berlioz. *Honours:* Winner, 1973 Enrico Caruso Competition. *Current Management:* c/o Musicaglotz, 11 rue le Verrier, 75006 Paris, France. *Telephone:* 1-42-34-53-40. *Fax:* 1-40-46-93-77. *E-mail:* general@musicaglotz.com. *Website:* www.musicaglotz.com.

GARNER, Françoise; French singer (soprano); b. 17 Oct. 1933, Nérac, Lot-et-Garonne. *Education:* Paris Conservatoire, Accademia di Santa Cecilia, Rome and in Vienna. *Career:* debut, Paris Opéra-Comique in 1963 in premiere of Menotti's Le Dernier Sauvage; sang in Paris as Rosina, Leila, Lakmé and Olympia; Paris Opéra as Gilda and Lucia di Lammermoor, and Aix-en-Provence Festival in 1971 as Queen of Night in Die Zauberflöte; sang Marguerite in Faust at La Scala Milan in 1977, and at Verona Arena as Butterfly and Gounod's Juliette, 1977–79; numerous performances in France and Italy in operas by Bellini; Metropolitan Opera 1986 as Elvira in I Puritani.

GARO, Edouard; Swiss chorus master, composer and academic; b. (Edouard Roland), 6 July 1935, Nyon; m. Verena Rellstab 1963; one s. one d. *Education:* Univ. of Lausanne, Acad. of Music Lausanne, studied singing with Pierre Mollet in Geneva and Sylvia Gähwiller in Zurich. *Career:* Founder and Conductor, Ensemble Choral de la Côte; Music Master, Gymnase Cantonal de Nyon; Prof., Séminaire Pédagogique de l'enseignement secondaire, Lausanne; mem. ASM, SUISA, SSA. *Compositions include:* Prospectum for piano and tape 1971, Les Sept contre Thèbes for eight female voices and percussion 1978, Incantation à trois for clarinet solo and tape 1980, Agamemnon (opera) 1982, Le Masque blanc sur fond rouge (opera-ballet) 1984, Un Instant seul 1989, Petra cantat 1994, Joutes 1996, La Grande Eclipse 1996, String Quartet No. 1 1993–97, No. 2 1995–97, No. 3 1998, Violin Concerto 1999, Joutes rhapsodiques for cello, clarinet and piano 2001, Requiem for STB solo, mixed and boys' choir and instrumental ensemble 2001. *Publication:* Invention for Music Teaching: SOLMIPLOT. *Honours:* Grand Prix UFAM with Medal, Ville de Paris 1972, Silver Medal, Int. Exhbn of Inventions and New Techniques, Geneva 1974. *Address:* 16 rue de la Porcelaine, 1260 Nyon, Switzerland (home). *Telephone:* (22) 3614945 (home). *Fax:* (22) 3614945 (office). *E-mail:* garo.ed@gmail.com. *Website:* www.garo-ed.ch. *Current Management:* c/o Centre de documentation et de recherche Niedermeyer, BP 1117, 1260 Nyon 1, Switzerland. *E-mail:* niedcov@gmail.com. *Website:* www.niedermeyer-nyon .ch.

GARRETT, David; American/German violinist; b. 4 Sept. 1980, Aachen, Germany. *Education:* studied with Itzhak Perlman at Juilliard School, New York. *Career:* first violin lessons aged four; first public concert with Hamburger Philharmoniker under Gerd Albrecht aged 10; began working with Polish violinist Ida Haendel 1992; has played in all major cities in Europe, USA and Japan with leading orchestras and conductors, including London Philharmonic Orchestra, Los Angeles Philharmonic Orchestra, Israel Philharmonic Orchestra, Russian Nat. Orchestra, Orchestre Nat. de Paris, Mozarteum Orchester, Chamber Orchestra of Europe, Staatskapelle Dresden and numerous others; has performed with Claudio Abbado, Zubin Mehta, Giuseppe Sinopoli, Herbert Blomstedt, Charles Dutoit, Eliahu Inbal und Mikhail Pletnev, amongst others; performed Elgar Violin Concerto with Royal Philharmonic Orchestra under Sir Yehudi Menuhin in Wiener Musikverein 1996; moved to New York 1998; repertoire includes Bach and Mozart, violin concerts of Beethoven, Brahms, Sibelius and Tchaikovsky and rarely played violin concerts by Conus, Schumann and Dvořák, and virtuoso pieces by Waxman, Ravel and Saint-Saëns; invited to various concerts world-wide, including in Israel with Israel Philharmonic Orchestra under George Pehlivenian (11 concerts, Mozart's G Major Conzert, Vivaldi's Four Seasons and Paganini's Concerto No. 2 La Campanella) 2007; played La Campanella under George Pehlivenian in Ljubljana and Villach 2008; further engagements with orchestras including Orchestre Nat. de Lyon under Jun Märkl and Orchestre Philharmonique du Luxembourg under Sir Neville Marriner and performances in Portugal, Spain, Italy, France, Luxemburg, Croatia, Israel, USA, Brazil and Japan; toured USA with Israel Chamber Orchestra 2008; performed Elgar Violin Concerto with Dmitrij Kitajenko 2008; duo recital at Festival 2008; guest performances at Brabants Orkest (Brahms Violin Concerto), Bergen Philharmonic Orchestra (Bruch Violin Concerto), Deutsche Staatsphilharmonie Rheinland-Pfalz (Beethoven Violin Concerto), Philharmonisches Orchester Kiel (Bartók Violin Concerto No. 1), Moscow State Symphony Orchestra (Beethoven Violin Concerto) and at Hong Kong Sinfonietta, as well as with Zurich and Prague Chamber Orchestras; plays chamber music with pianists Julien Quentin, Itamar Golan, Daniel Gortler and Milana Chernyavska, guest performances at BBC Proms, Bemus Festival, Belgrade, Verbier Festival; trio concerts with Jean-Yves Thibaudet and Gautier Capuçon at Schleswig-Holstein Music Festival and Ludwigsburger Schlossfestspiele 2009; Artistic Consultant, Saar Music Festival 2009; signed exclusive contract with Deutsche Grammophon aged 13 (youngest artist) 1994; exclusive artist of Decca 2007–; Beethoven Violin Concerto with Royal Philharmonic Orchestra and Ion Marin; invited by Russian Nat. Philharmonic Orchestra and Vladimir Spivakov, Vienna Symphony Orchestra and Andrey Boreyko 2011; played at Enescu Festival, Bucharest, Verbier Festival and several crossover shows together with his band and orchestra; season 2012 included crossover shows, recitals with Julien Quentin and invitations from orchestras including Basle Symphony Orchestra conducted by Dennis Russell Davies and Orchestra Sinfonica di Milano Giuseppe Verdi conducted by John Axelrod. *Film:* David Garrett Live – In Concert & In Private 2009. *Recordings include:* Mozart Violin Concerts with Claudio Abbado 1995, 24 Paganini Caprices 1997, Violin Concertos by Tchaikovsky and Conus with Russian Nat. Orchestra under Mikhail Pletnev 2001, Pure Classics (compilation of his first recordings) 2002, Virtuoso (ECHO Klassik Award in category 'Classical Music Without Borders', Germany 2008) 2007, Encore 2008, Classic Romance (including Mendelssohn Violin Concerto and works arranged by himself) 2009, Rock Symphony 2010, Legacy (including Beethoven Violin Concerto and works by Fritz Kreisler) 2011, Timeless (with Israel Philharmonic and Zubin Mehta) 2014. *Current Management:* c/o Weigold & Boehm International Artists & Tours GmbH, Thünefeldstrasse 5, 82299 Türkenfeld, Germany. *Telephone:* (8193) 2361200. *Fax:* (8193) 2361209. *E-mail:* agentur@weigold-boehm.de. *Website:* www.weigold-boehm.de; www.david-garrett.com.

GARRETT, Lesley, CBE, FRAM; British singer (soprano); b. 10 April 1955, d. of Derek Arthur Garrett and Margaret Wall; m. 1991; one s. one d. *Education:* Thorne Grammar School, Royal Acad. of Music, Nat. Opera Studio. *Career:* performed with Welsh Nat. Opera, Opera North, at Wexford and Buxton Festivals and at Glyndebourne; joined ENO (Prin. Soprano) 1984; Gov. RAM. *Television:* appeared in BBC TV series Lesley Garrett... Tonight, The Lesley Garrett Show. *Major roles include:* Susanna in The Marriage of Figaro, Despina in Così Fan Tutte, Musetta in La Bohème, Jenny in The Rise and Fall of The City of Mahagonny, Atalanta in Xerxes, Zerlinda in Don Giovanni, Yum-Yum in The Mikado, Adèle in Die Fledermaus, Oscar in A Masked Ball, Dalinda in Ariodante, Rose in Street Scene, Bella in A Midsummer Marriage, Eurydice in Orpheus and Eurydice and title roles in The Cunning Little Vixen and La Belle Vivette; numerous concert hall performances in UK and abroad (including Last Night of the Proms). *Recordings include:* albums: Diva! A Soprano at the Movies 1991, Prima Donna 1992, Simple Gifts 1994, Soprano in Red 1995, Soprano in Hollywood 1996, A Soprano Inspired 1997, Lesley Garrett 1998, I Will Wait for You 2000, Travelling Light 2001, The Singer 2002, So Deep is the Night 2003, When I Fall in Love 2007, Amazing Grace 2008, You'll Never Walk Alone: The Collection 2010, A North Country Lass 2012, Centre Stage: The Musicals Album 2015. *Publication:* Notes From a Small Soprano (autobiog.) 2001. *Honours:* Hon. DArts (Plymouth) 1995; winner Kathleen Ferrier Memorial Competition 1979, Gramophone Award for Best Selling Classical Artist 1996. *Current Management:* The Music Partnership Ltd, Eaton House, 126A Chester Road, Helsby, Cheshire, WA6 0QS, England. *Telephone:* (20) 7840-9590. *E-mail:* office@musicpartnership.co.uk. *Website:* www.musicpartnership.co.uk; www.lesleygarrett.co.uk.

GARRISON, Jon; American singer (tenor); b. 11 Dec. 1944, Higginsville, MO. *Career:* has sung widely in North America notably at opera houses in Houston, Montréal, Santa Fe and San Diego; Metropolitan Opera from 1974 in Death in Venice, Manon Lescaut, Così fan tutte as Ferrando and Die Zauberflöte as Tamino; New York City Opera from 1982 as Adméte in Alceste, Don Ottavio, Rodolfo, Nadir, the Duke of Mantua, Tom Rakewell, Tamino and Nicholas in the premiere of Reise's Rasputin 1988; sang Prince Edmund in the premiere of Stewart Copeland's Holy Blood and Crescent Moon at Cleveland 1989, and sang Shuratov in the US stage premiere of From the House of the Dead, in New York 1990; sang the title role in Oedipus Rex at the Festival Hall, London 1997; Idomeneo at the 1996 Garsington Festival.

GARRISON, Kenneth; American singer (tenor); b. 6 Dec. 1948, West Monroe, La. *Education:* Salzburg Mozarteum, studied with Hans Hopf in Munich. *Career:* spent 13 years as clarinetist then studied singing; debut in Regensburg 1977, as Mozart's Basilio; sang at Regensburg 1977–80, Oldenburg 1980–82, Karlsruhe 1982–84 (Wagner's Mime and Steersman); Munich Staatsoper from 1984, as Luzio in Wagner's Das Liebesverbot, Dvořák's Dimitri, the Prince in Love for Three Oranges, Max and Narraboth; guest engagements as Strauss's Emperor at Karlsruhe, Radames at Saarbrucken and Parsifal at Brunswick and Essen; Mainz 1990, as Otello; season 1993 at Brunswick as Strauss's Emperor, Strasbourg 1996 in From the House of Death; numerous concert appearances, notably in Beethoven's Ninth and Rossini's Stabat Mater; season 2000–01 as Mime in Siegfried at Mannheim and Tannhäuser at Cape Town. *E-mail:* info@kenneth-garrison.com. *Website:* kenneth-garrison.com.

GASDIA, Cecilia; Italian singer (soprano); b. 14 Aug. 1960, Verona. *Education:* studied in Verona. *Career:* debut in Florence 1982 as Giulietta in I Capuleti e i Montecchi by Bellini; La Scala 1982 as Anna Bolena in the opera by Donizetti; Perugia and Naples 1982 in Demophoon by Cherubini and as Amina in La Sonnambula; Paris Opéra debut 1983 as Anais in Moise by Rossini; Pesaro 1984 in a revival of Il Viaggio a Reims by Rossini; US debut in Philadelphia 1985 as Gilda in a concert performance of Rigoletto; Chicago Lyric Opera and Metropolitan Opera 1986 as Giulietta and as Gounod's Juliette; other roles include Violetta, Liu in Turandot, Hélène in Verdi's Jérusalem and Mrs Ford in Salieri's Falstaff; sang Rosa in Fioravanti's Le Cantatrici Villane, Naples 1990; season 1991–92 as Adina at Chicago, Mimi at Bonn, Nedda at Rome, Elena in La Donna del Lago at La Scala and Rosina at the Festival of Caracalla; Pesaro Festival 1994, as Semiramide; Zürich 1997, as Gounod's Marguerite; season 1998 as Euridice at Florence, Giulietta in Un Giorno di Regno at Parma, Handel's Cleopatra at Glimmerglass, New York, and Suzel in L'Amico Fritz at Naples; season 2000–01 as Jean in Le Jongleur de Notre Dame by Massenet in Rome, Elcia in Rossini's Mosè in Egitto at Verona and as Suzel in Mascagni's L'Amico Fritz. *Recordings include:* Catone in Utica; Motets by Vivaldi; Il Viaggio a Reims; Video of Turandot; Rossini's Armida and Ermione.

GASSIEV, Nikolai Tengizovich; Russian singer (tenor); b. 2 Feb. 1952, Tskhinvali, Georgia. *Education:* Leningrad State Conservatory. *Career:* soloist, Mariinsky Opera and Ballet Theatre 1990–; debut in Metropolitan Opera as Yurodivy (Boris Godunov) and Agrippina (Fairy Angel) 1992, Dresdner Staatsoper 1993, Brooklyn School of Music 1995, Edinburgh Festival 1995, Albert Hall 1995, La Scala 1996. *Honours:* Prize of Union of Theatre Workers Best Actor of the Year 1994. *Address:* Mariinsky Theatre, Teatralnaya pl. 1, St Petersburg, Russia. *Telephone:* (812) 315-57-24. *Website:* www.mariinsky.ru.

GASTEEN, Lisa, AO; Australian singer (soprano); b. 1957, Queensland. *Education:* Queensland Conservatorium with Margaret Nickson, studied in San Francisco, London Opera Studio. *Career:* debut, Lyric Opera of Queensland as the High Priestess in Aida and Diana in Orpheus in The Underworld 1985; appearances with Australian Opera as Miss Jessel in The Turn of the Screw, Frasquita, Madame Lidoine in Carmelites, both Leonoras, Elsa, Donna Elvira and Leonore in Fidelio; Victorian State Opera as Elisabeth in Tannhäuser, Elisabeth de Valois and Desdemona, Leonora Trovatore 1993; season 1991–92 as the Trovatore and Forza Leonoras for Scottish Opera, Amelia in Un Ballo in Maschera for WNO and Washington Opera, Donna Anna in Prague and Fidelio Leonore in Stuttgart; concert repertoire includes Rossini's Stabat Mater and Elijah for the Sydney Philharmonia, Beethoven's Ninth in Sydney, Melbourne and Tasmania, Tokyo Philharmonic; sang Verdi's Requiem for Hungarian radio 1993, Maddelena in Andrea Chénier for Deutsche Oper Berlin 1994, Aida for Australian Opera 1995; sang the Trovatore Leonora at Sydney 1996; sang the Empress in Die Frau Ohne Schatten for Melbourne Festival 1996; season 1999–2000 as Brünnhilde in Siegfried at Stuttgart, Verdi's Elisabeth de Valois and Strauss's Chrysothemis at Sydney; season 2001–2002 all three Brünnhilde at Meiningen and Isolde for Opera Australia in Melbourne; sang Brünnhilde at Covent Garden 2005. *Honours:* Covent Garden Scholarship 1984, Metropolitan Opera Educational Fund grant winner Australian Regional Finals Metropolitan Opera, NY Competition 1982, Advance Australia Award 1991, winner Cardiff Singer of the World Competition 1991, Helpmann Award (for role of Isolde with Opera Australia) 2002. *Current Management:* Jenifer Eddy Artists' Management, Suite 11, The Clivedon, 596 St Kilda Road, Melbourne 3004, Vic., Australia.

GASTINEL, Anne; French cellist; b. 14 Oct. 1971, Lyon. *Education:* Conservatoire de Musique, Lyon, Conservatoire Nat. Supérieur de Musique, Paris. *Career:* TV debut as concert soloist aged ten; toured as solo performer in major concert halls of Europe, Africa, Asia and America 1990–; has performed with Kurt Sanderling, Emmanuel Krivine, Louis Langrée, Semyon Bychkov, Vladimir Spivakov, Pinchas Steinberg, Yuri Bashmet, Max Rabinovitsj, Yehudi Menuhin; Patron, Festival des Rencontres de Musique de Chambre de Lyon 2000–. *Recordings include:* Beethoven: Cello & Piano Sonatas 2, 4, & 5 (with François-Frédéric Guy) 2003, Cello Concertos 2004, Elgar and Barber Cello Concertos 2004, Schubert: Arpeggione 2005. *Honours:* First Prize, Int. Competition of Scheveningen 1989, Victoire de la Musique Award for Young Talent 1994, Victoire de la Musique Award for Best Recording of the Year 1995, Prix FNAC 1995, 2000, 2003, Prix de l' Acad. du disque et Classique d'or RTL 1996, 1998, Choc du Monde de la Musique/Télérama Award 1998, 2000, 2001, 2002, Femme en Or 2002, Victoire de la Musique Award for Soloist of the Year 2006. *Current Management:* TransArt, 7 rue Hoche, 92300 Levallois Perret, France. *Telephone:* 1-47-59-87-09. *Fax:* 1-47-59-87-00. *E-mail:* transartuk@transartuk.com. *Website:* www.transartuk.com.

GASZTOWT-ADAMS, Helen Catriona; Australian singer (soprano); b. 29 Sept. 1956, Geelong, Vic. *Education:* Victorian Coll. of the Arts, Melbourne, Nat. Opera Studio, UK, studied with Audrey Langford and Janice Chapman. *Career:* debut as Pamina in Die Zauberflöte, State Opera of South Australia 1983; sang in Don Giovanni, Manon, Countess Maritza, and Figaro for State Opera of South Australia 1985–86; debut with Australian Opera as Nanetta 1986, then in Suor Angelica, Il Tabarro, Médée, Poppea and Carmen; London debut in Anna Bolena at Nat. Opera Studio Showcase, QEH 1989; BBC Cardiff Singer of the World finals 1989; European concert debut, Grusse aus Wien, Robert Stolz Club, recorded for Belgian radio and television 1990; sang Gilda in Rigoletto, Australian Opera 1990; ENO debut as Donna Elvira 1991; other appearances include Rossini's Petite Messe Solennelle, Netherlands and Belgian tour, Strauss's Vier Letzte Lieder, Koninklijk Ballet van Vlaanderen, Antwerp, Belgium, Mozart's Requiem, English String Orchestra, Bath Mozart Festival, and as Pamina in Die Zauberflöte, Victoria State Opera, Melbourne; extensive radio and television recital and concert work, including Handel's Messiah, Mendelssohn's Elijah, A Midsummer Night's Dream, Orff's Carmina Burana, and Vier Letzte Leider; performed with Melbourne and Sydney Symphony Orchestras, Australian Chamber Orchestra and opera and concert performances in UK, Barbados, Australia, France and Spain.

GATES, Crawford, BA, MA, PhD; American conductor and composer; b. 29 Dec. 1921, San Francisco, CA; m. Georgia Lauper 1952; two s. two d. *Education:* San Jose State Coll., Brigham Young Univ., Eastman School of Music, Univ. of Rochester, and studied conducting with Eleazar de Carvalho and Hans Swarowsky. *Career:* debut at Stanford Univ. as composer 1938; Utah Symphony as conductor; Chair Music Dept and Conductor, Symphony Orchestra and Opera, Brigham Young Univ. 1960–66; artist-in-residence, Prof. and Chair of Music Dept, Beloit Coll., Beloit, Wisconsin 1966–89; Music Dir, Beloit Janesville Symphony 1966–1999, Quincy Symphony 1969–70, Rockford Symphony Orchestra 1970–86. *Compositions include:* six stage works, seven symphonies, Tone Poems, Suites, Concertos, numerous choral arrangements, four major choral works, trumpet concertino and horn sonata, Pentameron for piano and orchestra (commissioned by Grant Johannesen). *Recordings:* Symphony No. 2, Orchestral Setting of Beloved Mormon Hymns, included on Philadelphia Orchestra Album, The Lord's Prayer and A Jubilant Song, Music to the New Hill Cumorah Pageant 1988, Promised Valley. *Address:* 2108 Scenic Drive, Salt Lake City, UT 84109, USA (home). *Telephone:* (801) 486-3976 (home). *E-mail:* gatescr@aol.com (home).

GATI, Istvan; Hungarian singer (tenor); b. 29 Nov. 1948, Budapest. *Education:* Franz Liszt Acad., Budapest. *Career:* mem., Hungarian State Opera from 1972, notably in the premieres of Csongor and Tunde by Attila Bozay 1985 and Ecce Homo by Sandor Szokolay 1987; appearances at the Vienna Staatsoper from 1986; sang Don Giovanni at Liège 1988, Nick Shadow at the Deutsche Oper Berlin 1989 and Antonio in Le nozze di Figaro at the 1991 Vienna Festival; season 1999–2000 as Ruggiero in Halévy's La Juive and Marco in Gianni Schicchi; guest appearances in Italy, France, Poland, Spain, The Netherlands and Austria and concert engagements in works by Bach, Handel, Mozart, Beethoven and Liszt. *Recordings include:* Cantatas by Bach, Don Sanche and The Legend of St Elisabeth by Liszt; Salieri's Falstaff; Paisiello's Barbiere di Siviglia; Don Pasquale; Simon Boccanegra; Telemann's Der Geduldige Sokrates; Balthazar and Jonas by Carissimi; Ein Deutsches Requiem; Mahler's Lieder eines Fahrenden Gesellen; Oronte in Handel's Floridante. *Honours:* competition winner at Salzburg, Vienna, Trevisto and Moscow at Tchaikovsky Int. 1974.

GATTI, Daniele; Italian conductor; *Music Director, Orchestre Nationale de France*; b. 6 Nov. 1961, Milan. *Education:* Giuseppe Verdi Conservatory. *Career:* debut at La Scala, Milan with Rossini's L'occasione fa il Ladro 1987–88 season; US debut with American Symphony Orchestra, Carnegie Hall, New York 1990; Covent Garden debut with I Puritani 1992; Music Dir Accad. di Santa Cecilia, Rome 1992–97; Prin. Guest Conductor, Royal Opera House, Covent Garden 1994–97; debut at Metropolitan Opera, New York with Madama Butterfly 1994–95 season; debut with Royal Philharmonic Orchestra 1994, Music Dir 1995–2009, Conductor Laureate 2009–; debut with New York Philharmonic 1995; Music Dir Teatro Communale, Bologna 1997–2007; Music Dir, Orchestre Nat. de France 2008–; Music Dir, Opernhaus Zürich 2009–12; apptd Chief Conductor Royal Concertgebouw Orchestra 2014; has led many orchestras in Europe and USA, including Vienna Philharmonic, Concertgebouw Amsterdam, Staatskapelle Dresden, Bavarian Radio Symphony, Munich Philharmonic, London Philharmonic, New York Philharmonic, Boston and Chicago Symphonies, Filarmonica della Scala, Milan and Accademia Santa Cecilia, Rome. *Recordings include:* Tchaikovsky's Fourth and Fifth Symphonies, Pathétique Symphony No. 6 2005. *Address:* Orchestre Nationale de France, c/o Radio France, 116 avenue du Président Kennedy, 75220 Paris, France (office). *Telephone:* 1-56-40-29-07 (office). *Fax:* 1-56-40-43-33 (office). *E-mail:* info@danielegatti.eu. *Website:* maisondelaradio.fr (office); danielegatti.eu.

GATTI, Giorgio; Italian singer (bass-baritone); b. 1 April 1948, Poggio a Caino; m. Maria Teresa Conti. *Education:* studied in Florence and Rome. *Career:* opera engagements throughout Italy 1994–; in La Bohème; opera and concert appearances across Italy, in France, Germany, Switzerland, Japan and North America; mem. Recitar Cantando group 1980–90; repertoire includes Count Ceprano in Rigoletto, Sagrestano in Tosca, Marquis d'Obigny in La Traviata. *Recordings include:* Anfossi's Il Barone di Rocca antica, Fioravanti's La Servascaltra. *Honours:* winner, Concorso A. Belli 1971.

GAUCI, Miriam; Maltese singer (soprano); b. 3 April 1957, Vittoriosa; d. of Carmel Cutajar and Rosette Tabone; m. Michael Laus 1987; one d. *Education:* Conservatorio G. Verdi and Centro di Perfezionamento Artisti Lirici, Milan, Italy. *Career:* debut at La Scala, Milan in La Sonnambula, L'Orfeo, Die Frau ohne Schatten; debut in USA in Madame Butterfly at Santa Fe 1987; appeared in La Bohème with Plácido Domingo in Los Angeles, USA and Hamburg, Germany; in La Traviata in Geneva, Switzerland and Dresden, Germany; also sang in Madrid, Lisbon and Berlin, Manon at Vienna Staatsoper 1996 and in Boito's Mefistofele with Riccardo Muti; in Falstaff at the Hamburg Staatsoper 1997, Mimi at the New York Met 2001; Contessa in Le Nozze di Figaro at La Scala, Milan 2006; Stage Dir, Rigoletto, Die Zauberflöte, Malta. *Video:* Carmen 1989. *Recordings include:* Madame Butterfly 1992, Manon Lescaut, Pagliacci, La Bohème, Deutsche Requiem, Verdi's Requiem, Egmont, Operatic Arias. *Honours:* Nat. Order of Merit (Malta) 1993, Cavaliere della Repubblica (Italy) 2010; first prize in various int. competitions, including Treviso, Bologna, Milan, Italy 1979. *Address:* 360 Salini Street, Marsascala, Malta (home). *E-mail:* michael.laus@maltaorchestra.com (office).

GAVANELLI, Paolo; Italian singer (baritone); b. 1959, Monselice, near Padua. *Career:* debut as Leporello at the Teatro Donizetti, Bergamo in 1985; season 1988–89 as Mephistopheles at Barcelona and Marcello in La Bohème in Madrid; Further engagements as Marcello at Venice, Bologna and the State Operas of Munich and Vienna in 1991; Sang Luna in Trovatore at the Metropolitan in 1990 returning in Puritani and as Germont in 1992; Sang Gerard in Andrea Chénier at San Francisco and Stuttgart, Renato in Un Ballo in Maschera at Chicago and Verdi's Falstaff at the Rome Opera; Festival appearances at Pesaro as Germano in La Scala di Seta, 1990 and the Arena Verona; Has also appeared at La Scala from 1991 and Genoa as Renato; Other roles include Rossini's Figaro and Verdi's Iago, Rigoletto and Amonasro; Festival appearances 1996 at Ravenna (as Alfio) and Rome (Gerard); Renato (Ballo in Maschera) at Verona, 1998; Season 2000–01 at the Munich State Opera as Riccardo in I Puritani, Germont, and Posa; Nabucco at Verona, Falstaff at Covent Garden and Simon Boccanegra for San Francisco Opera; Germont for the Royal Opera, 2002. *Recordings:* Marcello in La Bohème. *Current Management:* c/o Hilbert Artists Management, Maximilianstrasse 22, 80539 Munich, Germany. *Telephone:* (89) 2907470. *Fax:* (89) 29074790. *E-mail:* agentur@hilbert.de. *Website:* www.hilbert.de.

GAVIN, Julian, BMus; Australian singer (tenor); b. 1965, Melbourne, Vic. *Education:* Univ. of Melbourne, National Opera Studio, London. *Career:* has appeared widely in the United Kingdom and Ireland as Alfredo, Des Grieux, Nemorino, Rodolfo, Tamino, Don José and the Duke of Mantua; Further appearances in Franck's Hulda, Alvaro in La Forza del Destino, Ismaele in Nabucco, Arrigo in Verdi's Battaglia di Legnano, Pinkerton, and Laca in Jenůfa (Opera North, 1995); Pollione in Norma at Lucerne, 1996; Steersman in The Flying Dutchman, Alfredo in La Traviata for Australian Opera, 1996, 1997; Concert repertoire includes Messiah, Rossini's Stabat Mater, The Dream of Gerontius, the Verdi Requiem with David Willcocks, Mahler's 8th Symphony at the Festival Hall; Tippet, A Child of Our Time, Ulster Orchestra; Sang Beaumont in Maw's The Rising of the Moon for the BBC; Season 1996–97 as the Duke of Mantua, Alfredo and Pinkerton for ENO; Sang Hoffmann, 1998; Carlo VII in Verdi's Giovanna d'Arco for Opera North, Don Carlos in Leeds, at the Edinburgh Festival and for the Royal Opera, 1998 with Haitink, and for Opera Australia, 1999; Season 1999–2000, Roméo in Gounod's Roméo et Juliette and Don José in Carmen, Puccini's Des Grieux at Genoa, with the ENO Rodolfo in La Bohème and the title role in Ernani; Pinkerton for Opera North; Concert performances of Kodàly's Psalmus Hungaricus with the BBC Symphony Orchestra and Berlioz Roméo et Juliette with the Sydney Symphony Orchestra; Manrico for ENO 2001; mem, International Society of Musicians. *Recordings:* Godvino in Verdi's Aroldo; Don José in Carmen; Roméo et Juliette; Les Contes d'Hoffmann. *Honours:* University of Melbourne Lady Turner Prize 1978, Hon. LMusA 1985.

GAVRILOV, Andrei Vladimirovich; Russian pianist and conductor; b. 21 Sept. 1955, Moscow. *Education:* Moscow Conservatory, studied with Lev Naumov. *Career:* int. debut at Salzburg Festival 1974; London debut with Paavo Berglund and Bournemouth Symphony Orchestra, Royal Festival Hall 1976; Carnegie Hall debut 1985; has performed with orchestras in New York, Los Angeles, Detroit, Cleveland, Chicago, Philadelphia, Montreal, Toronto, London, Vienna, Paris, Berlin, Munich, Amsterdam, Tokyo, Moscow, St Petersburg and many others; has performed in UK with Philharmonia,

London Philharmonic, Royal Philharmonic, BBC Symphony and London Symphony Orchestras; has performed with numerous conductors including Abbado, Haitink, Muti, Ozawa, Svetlanov, Tennstedt, Rattle, Neville Marriner; recorded with Sviatoslav Teofilovich Richter. *Publication:* Tchainik, Fira and Andrey (autobiog.) 2011. *Honours:* winner, Tchaikovsky Competition in Moscow 1974; Gramophone Award 1979, Deutschen Schallplattenpreis 1981, Grand Prix Int. du Disque de l'Academie Charles Cros 1985, 1986, Int. Record Critics Award 1985, Premio Internazionale Accademia Musicale Chigiana 1989. *E-mail:* contact@andreigavrilov.ch. *Website:* www.andreigavrilov.com.

GAWRILOFF, Saschko; German violinist; b. 20 Oct. 1929, Leipzig. *Education:* Leipzig Conservatory with Gustav Havemann, studied with Martin Kovacz in Berlin. *Career:* Leader, Dresden Philharmonic 1947–48, Berlin Philharmonic 1948–49, Berlin Radio Symphony 1949–53, Museum Orchestra of Frankfurt am Main 1953–57, Hamburg Radio Symphony 1961–66; teacher, Nuremberg Conservatory 1957–61; Prof., North-West German Music Acad. 1966–69, Folkwang-Hochschule Essen 1969, fmr Prof. Hochschule Detmold, also conducted master-classes at Cologne Musikhochschule –1996, now Emer.; appearances include concerts in Vienna, Milan, Madrid, Rome, Paris, India and Japan; has given premieres of works by Maderna, Dieter Kaufmann and Schnittke; formed trio with Alfons Kontarsky and Klaus Storck 1971; mem. Robert Schumann Trio (with Johannes Goritzki and David Levine); contemporary music with Siegfried Palm and Bruno Canino; currently teacher, Hanns Eisler School of Music, Berlin. *Honours:* winner, Int. Competitions at Berlin and Munich 1953, Genoa Paganini Competition and City of Nuremberg Prize 1959, Grammy Award for best chamber music interpretation with György Ligeti's horn trio 1997. *Address:* Hochschule für Musik Hanns Eisler Berlin, Charlottenstr. 55, 10117 Berlin, Germany. *Website:* www.hfm-berlin.de/en/school/people/sachko-gawriloff/details.

GAYER, Catherine; American singer (soprano); b. 11 Feb. 1937, Los Angeles, Calif. *Education:* studied in Los Angeles before moving to Berlin for further study. *Career:* sang in premiere of Nono's Intolleranza 1960, at Venice 1961, Covent Garden 1962 as Queen of Night; Deutsche Oper Berlin from 1963, notably as Hilde Mack in Henze's Elegie für Junge Liebende, Berg's Lulu and Marie in Zimmermann's Die Soldaten and Nausicca in 1968 premiere of Dallapiccola's Ulisse, and Scottish Opera from 1968 as Susanna, Hilde Mack, Queen of Shemakha in The Golden Cockerel and in 1975 premiere of Orr's Hermiston; sang at Schwetzingen Festival 1971 in premiere of Reimann's Melusine, at Edinburgh Festival 1972 with Deutsche Oper Berlin in Die Soldaten; sang leading role in premiere of Joseph Tal's Der Versuchung at Munich 1976; other roles include Ulisse at La Scala, Zerbinetta, Gilda and Mélisande, sang Woman in Schoenberg's Erwartung at Komische Oper Berlin 1988, songs by Reimann and Szymanowski at 1990 Aldeburgh Festival, Berlin Kammeroper 1991 with Berio's Sequenza III, Tal's Die Hand, The Medium by Maxwell Davies and Weisgall's The Stronger; sang at Stuttgart 1992 as Grand-Mother in Dinescu's Eréndira and in Rag Time, an arrangement of Joplin's Treemonisha at 1992 Schwetzingen Festival and in two productions of Schoenberg's Pierrot Lunaire; sang in Manon at Deutsche Oper 1998; taught singing at Folkwang Hochschule Essen. *Recordings include:* Woodbird in Siegfried; Elegie für Junge Liebende; Die Israeliten in Der Wüste by CPE Bach; Il Giardino d'Amore by Scarlatti. *Honours:* winner, San Francisco Opera auditions 1960, Berlin Kammersängerin 1970.

GAYFORD, Christopher; British conductor; b. 1963, Wilmslow, Cheshire, England. *Education:* Royal Coll. of Music, London with Christopher Adey, John Forster and Norman del Mar, Royal Northern Coll. of Music (RNCM), Manchester with Timothy Reynish. *Career:* Repetiteur, Graz Opera 1987; Jr Fellow in Conducting, RNCM 1988; conducted Don Carlos and A Midsummer Night's Dream at RNCM 1990; debut with London Mozart Players at Barbican Hall 1990; L'Elisir d'amore for RNCM, Don Giovanni for Opera North, Aida for Scottish Opera; Asst Conductor to Royal Liverpool Philharmonic Orchestra 1990–91; conducted Così fan tutte for British Youth Opera at Sadler's Wells 1992; engagements and tours with Scottish Chamber Orchestra, BBC Scottish Symphony Orchestra, Ulster Orchestra, BBC Philharmonic, Manchester Camerata, BBC Concert Orchestra, Britten Sinfonia, City of Sheffield Youth Orchestra, Royal Philharmonic Orchestra and Orchestra of the Royal Opera House, Covent Garden; research in music psychology 1996–; Research Fellow Trinity Coll. of Music 2001–03; Hon. Research Fellow, Keele Univ. 2004–06; Visiting Researcher, RNCM 2006–07. *Honours:* First Prize, Besançon Int. Competition for Young Conductors 1989. *Website:* www.feelingsound.net.

GEBHARDT, Horst; German singer (tenor); b. 17 June 1940, Silberhausen. *Education:* studied in Weimar and Berlin. *Career:* debut at Schwerin 1972 as Chateauneuf in Lortzing's Zar und Zimmermann; Sang at Leipzig, the Staatsoper Dresden and Berlin; Member of the Leipzig Opera from 1985 including role as Erik in Fliegende Holländer in 1989, and has made guest appearances in France, Italy, Spain, England, Yugoslavia, Russia, Poland, Japan and Cuba; Other roles have included Max, Mozart's Belmonte, Ottavio, Titus, Tamino and Ferrando, Lensky, Fenton, Strauss's Narraboth and Flamand, Jacquino in Fidelio, David in Die Meistersinger, Alfredo and Sextus in Giulio Cesare; Kiel Opera 1991, in Vincent by Rautavaara. *Recordings:* Idomeneo; Parsifal; Palestrina; Alfonso und Estrella. *Honours:* Prizewinner, International Bach Competition, Leipzig and National Opera Competition, Germany, 1972.

GEDDA, Nicolai; Swedish singer (tenor); b. 11 July 1925, Stockholm; s. of Michael Ustinov and Olga Ustinov (née Gedda); m. Anastasia Caraviotis 1965; one s. one d. *Education:* Musical Acad., Stockholm. *Career:* debut, Stockholm 1952; concert appearances Rome 1952, Paris 1953, 1955, Vienna 1955, Aix-en-Provence 1954, 1955; first operatic performances in Munich, Lucerne, Milan and Rome 1953, Paris, London and Vienna 1954; Salzburg Festival 1957–59, Edin. Festival 1958–59; with Metropolitan Opera, NY 1957–2001, Tokyo Opera 1975–2003; worldwide appearances in opera, concerts and recitals; numerous recordings. *Address:* Valhallavagen 110, 114 41 Stockholm, Sweden.

GEDGE, Nicholas Paul Johnson, MA; British singer (bass-baritone); b. 12 March 1968, Brecon, Wales; m. Kate Robinson 1995, one d. *Education:* St John's Coll., Cambridge, Royal Acad. of Music. *Career:* debut as Theseus in Midsummer Night's Dream, Covent Garden Festival 1994; sang Leporello at Royal Acad. of Music, Charon at Batignano, Dr Bartolo and Don Magnifico with English Touring Opera; concerts with London Philharmonic Orchestra, Ulster Orchestra, CLS; recitals at Buxton Festival and Wigmore Hall. *Honours:* Royal Acad. of Music Queen's Commendation for Excellence.

GEDIZLIOĞLU, Zeynep; Turkish composer; b. 1977, Izmir. *Education:* State Conservatory of Mimar Sinan Univ., studied composition with Theo Brandmüller at Hochshule für Musik Saar, Germany, and with Wolfgang Rihm in Karlsruhe, Ivan Fedele in Strasbourg, and Daniel Teruggi and François Donata at Groupe de Recherches Musicales, Paris. *Career:* music performed throughout Turkey and Europe by ensembles including Ensemble Recherche, Arditti Quartet, Navarra Symphony Orchestra, and Ensemble Accroche Note; festivals include Musica Strasbourg, Mediterranean Contemporary Music Festival and ISCM World Music Days. *Compositions include:* Dengesiz Denklemler (Unequal Equations) for clarinet and cello 2006, Akdenizli (The Mediterranean) for violin, viola and piano 2007, Susma (Do Not Be Silent) string quartet 2007, Kesik (Cut) for 12 instruments 2010, Yol (The Path) for ensemble, Along the Wall, Mut for four cellos. *Recordings include:* Kesik (with Ensemble Modern and Arditti Quartet) 2012. *Honours:* several scholarships, prizes and residencies including IRCAM Paris, Ernst von Siemens Foundation Composers Prize 2012. *Address:* c/o Col Legno, Schottengasse 4/V/32, Vienna 1010, Austria. *Website:* www.col-legno.com.

GEERTENS, Gerda; Dutch composer; b. 11 Aug. 1955, Wildervank. *Education:* studied with Klaas de Vries. *Career:* performances of works at the Concertgebouw in Amsterdam, in Darmstadt, Israel, Ireland and the USA. *Compositions include:* Mexitli for mixed choir and ensemble 1982, Trope for cello 1987, As En Seringen for ensemble with percussion 1988, String Trio 1990, Contrast for saxophone quartet 1990, Heartland for symphony orchestra 1994, Transitions for flute trio 1998, New Era (electronic music) 2001. *E-mail:* geertens@ggvision.com. *Website:* www.gegee.nl.

GEFORS, Hans, DipMus, Litteris et Artibus, PhD; Swedish composer and professor in composition; b. 8 Dec. 1952, Stockholm. *Education:* studied with Per-Gunnar Alldahl, Maurice Karkoff, Stockholm Acad. of Music with Ingvar Lidholm, Jutland Conservatory of Music with Per Norgård. *Career:* Prof. of Composition, Malmö Coll. of Music 1988; mem. STIM, Royal Acad. of Music, FST (Soc. of Swedish Composers). *Compositions:* operas: The Poet and the Glazier 1979, Christina (premiere at Royal Opera, Stockholm) 1986, Der Park (premiere at Wiesbaden Festival 1992) 1991, Vargen Kommer (Cry Wolf, premiere at Malmö Opera) 1997, Clara (premiere at 100th anniversary of the Opéra Comique, Paris) 1998, Skuggspel 2005, Cleansing of the Soul through Fun and Games 2010; music theatre: Me Morire en Paris 1979, The Creation No. 2 1988; orchestral: Slits 1981, Christina Scenes 1987, Twine 1988, Die Erscheinung im Park 1990, Lydias Sånger for mezzo and orchestra 1996, Njutningen for soprano, baritone, choir and orchestra 2002, The Knight of the Boy's Gaze 2003, Sweet Sounds for soprano and orchestra 2009; chamber: Aprahishtita 1970–71, La Boîte Chinoise 1976, L'Invitation au Voyage for voice, guitar and violin 1981, Krigets Eko for percussionist 1982, Tjurens Död 1982, Flickan och den Gamle 1983, Galjonsfiguren 1983, One Two 1983, A Hunting for the Wind for organ 1994; vocal: Sånger om Förtröstan for voice and guitar 1970, Whales Weep Not! for 16-part choir 1987, En Obol (sonnets) for voice, clarinet, cornet, cello and piano 1989, Total Okay 1992. *Publication:* The Twofold Rhythm of Duration in Opera – The Musical Dramaturgy of the Car Radio Opera 'Cleansing of the Soul through Fun and Games' (doctoral dissertation) 2011. *Honours:* Christ Johnson Fund Prize 1994, 2002, Prix Italia 2011. *Address:* Svensk Musik Swedmic AB, Box 17092, 104 62 Stockholm, Sweden (office). *Telephone:* (8) 783-88-00 (office). *E-mail:* info@svenskmusik.org (office). *Website:* www.mic.stim.se (office).

GEIGER, Ruth; American pianist and teacher; b. 30 Jan. 1923, Vienna, Austria. *Education:* studied in Vienna with Hans Gal and Julius Isserlis, Juilliard School, New York with Josef Lhevinne. *Career:* debut at the Town Hall, New York 1944; recitals and appearances with orchestras in USA; radio and television broadcasts in New York; annual concert tours of Europe from 1957; performances with orchestras including Suisse Romande, New Philharmonia, English Chamber Orchestra; BBC Series, My Favourite Concertos; appearances on BBC solo recital series at St John's Smith Square, London; numerous live broadcasts include concerto broadcasts with Glasgow BBC Orchestra; complete Schubert Sonatas for Basel Radio; toured Sweden, Netherlands, Belgium, Switzerland, Austria, England; masterclasses at Univ. of Sussex 1971; chamber music with the Allegri Quartet; concert and teaching one-week residency at Yale Univ., USA; appearances on Live BBC Concert series; lunchtime recital at St David's Hall, Cardiff 1992; live broadcast of lunchtime recital at St John's Smith Square, London 1992; 1995 included recital on Sunday Morning Coffee Concerts, Wigmore Hall, London; masterclass and recital, Newton Park Coll., Bath; solo recitals in Tours, France 1995, 1997, also collaboration in Tours with French mezzo-soprano Agnès Lécossois in Lieder by Schubert and Brahms. *Recordings include:* Schubert Sonatas, works by Haydn, Beethoven and Schumann. *Honours:* Naumburg Award, New York 1943, finalist Leventritt Competition 1944 and Rachmaninov Competition 1948. *Address:* 160 W 73 Street, New York, NY 10023, USA (home).

GELB, Peter; American business executive, film and television producer and arts administrator; *General Manager, Metropolitan Opera*; b. 1953, s. of Arthur Gelb and Barbara Gelb; m. Keri-Lynn Wilson; two s. (from a previous m.). *Career:* fmr Man., Vladimir Horowitz; Pres. Sony Classical USA 1993–95, Pres. Sony Classical Int. Operations 1995–2005; Gen. Man. Metropolitan Opera, New York 2006–. *Honours:* Officier, Ordre des Arts et des Lettres 2010, Chevalier, Légion d'honneur 2013; Dr hc (Macaulay Honors Coll., CUNY) 2008; Emmy Award for Outstanding Classical Program in the Performing Arts 1987, 1990, 1991, Emmy Award for Outstanding Individual Achievement in Int. Programming 1991, Int. Documentary Asscn Award 1991, Grammy Award 2002, Diplomacy Award, Foreign Policy Asscn 2012, Sanford Prize, Yale School of Music 2013. *Address:* The Metropolitan Opera, Lincoln Center, New York, NY 10023, USA (office). *Telephone:* (212) 799-3100 (office). *Website:* www.metoperafamily.org (office).

GELLMAN, Steven D.; Canadian composer, pianist and academic; b. 16 Sept. 1947, Toronto; m. Cheryl Gellman 1970, one s. one d. *Education:* Juilliard School of Music, New York, USA and Conservatoire de Paris, France. *Career:* soloist with CBC Symphony Orchestra in own Concerto for piano and orchestra aged 16; compositions performed in USA, Canada, France, Europe, South America and Japan; European tour with Toronto Symphony 1983; Gellman's Awakening performed throughout Europe; Universe Symphony, inaugurated the International Year of Canadian Music 1986; Prof. of Composition and Theory, Faculty of Music, Univ. of Ottawa 1994–; Assoc. of Canadian Music Centre; mem. Canadian League of Composers. *Compositions include:* orchestral: Odyssey 1971, Symphony No. 2 1972, Chori 1976, Deux Tapisseries 1980, Awakening 1982, The Bride's Reception 1983, Universe Symphony for large orchestra and synthesizers 1984–85, Love's Garden for soprano and orchestra 1987, Piano Concerto 1988–89, Canticles of St Francis for choir and orchestra 1989, Jaya Overture 1995, Fanfare for the New Millennium 1999; chamber music: Mythos II for flute and string quartet 1968, Wind Music for brass quintet 1978, Dialogue for solo horn 1978, Transformation 1980, Chiaroscuro 1988, Concertino for guitar and string quartet 1988, Red Shoes 1990, Musica Eterna, for string quartet 1991, Child-Play, for chamber orchestra 1992, Sonata for cello and piano 1995, Viola Concerto 2004; piano: Melodic Suite 1972, Poeme 1976, Waves and Ripples 1979, Keyboard Triptych for piano-synthesizer 1986, Piano Quartet 2003; opera: Gianni 1996–99. *Honours:* Composer of the Year 1987. *Telephone:* (613) 562-5800 (office). *E-mail:* sgellman@uottawa.ca (office); s.gellman@sympatico.ca (home).

GELMETTI, Gianluigi; Italian conductor and composer; b. 11 Sept. 1945, Rome. *Education:* Accademia di Santa Cecilia, Rome with Franco Ferrera, studied with Sergiu Celibidache and in Vienna with Hans Swarowsky. *Career:* Musical Director, Pomeriggi Musicali, Milan, and teacher at the Conservatory –1980; Artistic Director, RAI Symphony Orchestra, Rome 1980–84; Musical Director, Rome Opera 1984–85; Chief Conductor, Stuttgart Radio Symphony Orchestra 1989–98; Musical Director, Orchestre Philharmonique of Monte Carlo 1990–92; has conducted the first performances of Castiglioni's Sacro Concerto 1982, Donatoni's In Cauda 1983 and Henze's 7th Symphony 1984; Royal Opera premiere of Rossini's Otello, Covent Garden 2000, returned to Covent Garden for La Rondine and Turandot 2002; teacher and Head of Orchestra, Accademia Chigiana, Siena 1997–; Chief Conductor, Teatro dell'Opera, Rome 2000–08; Chief Conductor and Artistic Director, Sydney Symphony Orchestra 2004–08, Guest Conductor 2008–. *Compositions include:* In Paradisum Deducant Te Angeli, Algos, Prasanta Atma, Cantata della Vita. *Recordings include:* operas by Rossini, Puccini and Mozart, orchestral work by Ravel, Mozart, Stravinsky, Berg, Webern, Varèse, Rota, Bruckner. *Honours:* Chevalier, Ordre des Arts et des Lettres, Cavaliere, Gran Croce della Repubblica Italiana; Premio Rossini d'Oro 1999. *Current Management:* c/o Patrizia Garrasi, Resia Artists, Via Gioberti 1, 20123 Milan, Italy. *Telephone:* (02) 654161. *Fax:* (02) 6597851. *E-mail:* resia@resiartists.it. *Website:* www.resiartists.it.

GELT, Andrew Lloyd, BM, MM, MPD, DMA, PhD; American composer, conductor and musician (woodwinds); b. 2 Feb. 1951, Albuquerque, NM; s. of Philip Alfred Gelt and Martha Ann Ambrose. *Education:* Univ. of New Mexico, Univ. of Southern California (USC), Univ. of Miami, Univ. of Denver, Princeton Univ., student of Mitchell Lurie, Stanley Drucker, Frederick Fennell, Kurt Frederick (Mozarteum) Hans Beer, Daniel Lewis (USC). *Career:* Prof. at several colls and univs, including Univ. of Miami, Univ. of North Carolina, Richmond Tech. Coll., Temple Univ., Princeton Univ.; specialized in analysis of microprocessor devices as applied to music; main expertise in theory and composition of music in eclectic vein; mem. The College Music Soc., Soc. of Composers, Inc., Int. Clarinet Soc., Int. Alban Berg Soc., Nat. Asscn of Jazz Educators, Nat. Asscn of Composers, Phi Mu Alpha Sinfonia (Hon. Eta Beta), American Soc. of Univ. Composers, American Music Center (Composer mem.), American Fed. of Musicians, AFL-CIO; Fellow, Univ. of Miami Dean's Appointment, Temple Univ.; currently working in psychoacoustics developing neurological diagnostic methodology utilizing physiological responses to musical just intervals. *Compositions include:* Symphony No. 1 (Op. 34) The Art of Eclecticism (premiered by Frederick Fennell), Lamento for strings (Op. 22), Homage to Gesualdo (Op. 33), Suite Eclectique (Op. 35), Concerto-Quintet for Five Clarinets Assorted (Op. 19), Sonatina Veehemente (Op. 26) 'Armageddon'. *Honours:* Univ. of New Mexico 1969–73: Woodward Academic Scholarship, Mu Phi Epsilon Scholarship, Music Activity Award, Music Dept Academic Scholarship; John Philip Sousa Award for Band 1969, Nat. Fed. of Music Clubs SW Dist Winner (Clarinet) 1970, 1971, 1972, Pennsylvania Composers Project Performance Grant 1981, Winner, Int. Music Prize, Nat. Acad. of Music 2011, Diploma of Excellence in Music Composition 2011. *Address:* 3700 NW 7th Court, Delray Beach, FL 33445-1902, USA (home). *Telephone:* (561) 396-3766 (office); (954) 415-4358 (office). *E-mail:* andrew@gelt.net (office). *Website:* gelt.net.

GEMROT, Jiri; Czech composer; b. 15 April 1957, Prague; m. 1982; one s. two d. *Education:* Prague Conservatorium, Acad. of Musical Arts, Prague, Accad. Chigiana, Siena, Italy. *Career:* Producer, Radio Prague 1982–86, Chief Producer 1990–; Ed., Panton Publishing House 1986–90; teacher of Composition, Prague Conservatory 2001–. *Compositions include:* Sonata for piano No. 1 1981, Tributes for orchestra 1983, Five Lyrical Songs to Poems by Ingeborg Bachmann for soprano and piano 1984, Inventions for violin and viola 1984, Sonata for piano No. 2 1985, Maxims for 15 strings 1986, Rhapsody for bassoon and piano 1986, Preludium and Toccata for harpsichord 1988, Rhapsody for oboe and piano 1988, Sonatina for violin and piano 1990, Inventions for cello and double bass 1991, Concerto for flute and orchestra 1992, Psalmus 146 for mixed chorus and orchestra 1992, Lauda, Sion for baritone and wind orchestra 1994, Schalmeiane for six oboes 1996, IV Sonata for piano 1996, The American Overture 1996, Concertino for orchestra 1997, Bachman lieder for soprano and orchestra 1998, Concertino for harp and orchestra 1998, V Sonata for piano 1999, Quintet for piano and strings 2001, Sonata for cello and piano 2001, Trio for violin, cello and piano 2001, Concertino for flute, timpani, bagpipes and orchestra 2002, Double-Concerto for cello, piano and orchestra 2002, Lullaby for mezzo-soprano, cello and piano 2002, Sapporiana for flute and guitar 2003, Piano Concerto 2003, Plays for harpsichord 2003, Concertino for cello, piano and orchestra 2004, Romance for violin and piano 2004, String Quartet 2005, Sonata for violin and piano 2005, Quintet for clarinet and strings 2005, Small Suite for piano 2006, Sonatina for flute and harpsichord 2007, Symphony for small orchestra 2007, Concerto for cello and chamber orchestra 2009, String Quartet No. 2 2010, Trio for oboe, harp and piano 2010, Variations on Dvořák's Theme for cello and piano 2011, Capriccio for cello and piano 2011, Mourning Music for violin and string orchestra 2012, Lamento for cello and stings 2012, Second Symphony 2013. *Recordings include:* Tributes; Dances and Reflections; Cello Concerto; Sonata for harp; Bucolic for string quartet; Meditation for viola and organ; Invocation for Violin and Organ; Sonatina for flute and piano; Maxims for 15 strings; Piano Sonatas. *Address:* Kostelni 6, 170 00 Prague 7, Czech Republic (home). *Telephone:* (603) 820306 (office). *E-mail:* jiri.gemrot@seznam.cz (home).

GENAUX, Vivica A., BA; American singer (mezzo-soprano); b. 10 July 1969, Fairbanks, Alaska; d. of Charles Genaux and Hanna Genaux; m. Massimo Patella 2003. *Education:* Indiana Univ. *Career:* noted for her singing of Baroque and bel canto operas; numerous worldwide performances of Rosina in Il Barbiere di Siviglia, Angelina in La Cenerentola and Isabella in L'Italiana in Algeri (all Rossini); other appearances include Hasse's Marc Antonio e Cleopatra in Brussels and Paris, Scarlatti's oratorio La Santissima Trinità in Paris, Palermo and Lyon, Gluck's Orfeo ed Euridice at Los Angeles Opera, Mendelssohn's A Midsummer Night's Dream with the Orchestre Nat. de France in Paris and Hong Kong, Hassem in Donizetti's Alahor in Granata, in Seville, Selimo in Hasse's Solimano for the Deutsche Staatsoper, Berlin, Penelope in Monteverdi's Il ritorno d'Ulisse at the Bayerische Staatsoper; performances have included Vivaldi's Bajazet with Europa Galante in many European cities, both on stage and in concert, tour of S America with Concerto Köln, the Caramoor Festival for Semiramide, BBC Proms debut 2009, Tancredi and Il mondo della Luna in Vienna 2009, Cenerentola at Théâtre des Champs Elysées (TCE), Paris 2010, concert tour in France and Italy with Fabio Biondi and Europa Galante featuring Vivaldi Arias; Salzburg Whitsun Festival debut in Hasse's Piramo e Tisbe 2010, repeated in Montpellier, also Juno/Ino in Semele at the TCE and Barbican, London 2010, Isabella in L'Italiana in Algeri at Opera Nat. de Paris, Edemondo in Meyerbeer's Emma di Resburgo at Wiener Konzerthaus; concerts in Berne, Paris, Versailles, Brussels, Lucerne, Wiesbaden and Copenhagen, Il Piacere in Handel's Il trionfo del Tempo e del Disinganno and a concert Tribute to Faustina Bordoni, both in Vienna, Galatea in Handel's Acis, Galatea e Polifemo in Berlin and Salzburg, San Macario in Leonardo Leo's Sant' Elena al Calvario in Kraków, Isabella in L'italiana in Algeri in Vienna and a tour in France and Germany with Concerto Köln; season 2011–12: two US concert tours, one in San Francisco area with Philharmonia Baroque and the other a six-city tour with frequent performance and recording colleagues, Fabio Biondi and Europa Galante; stage debut at Opéra du Rhin, Strasbourg; concerts at Concertgebouw, Amsterdam, Hindsgavl, Denmark and Gluck Festival, Nuremburg, Germany; Dido in Dido and Aeneas, Versailles 2014; title role in Cenerentola, Musikfest Bremen 2015. *Film:* Fracture (vocal segment). *Recordings:* Donizetti's Alahor in Granata/Almaviva 1999, Michael Ellison's Before All Beginning/MMC 1998, Handel's Arminio/Virgin 2001, Rinaldo/Harmonia

Mundi 2003, Rossini's An Evening of Arias & Songs/EPCASO 1999, Rossiniana/Agora 1998, Scarlatti's La Santissima Trinità/Virgin 2004, Vivaldi's Bajazet/Virgin 2005, L'Atenaide/Naïve 2007; Arias for Farinelli – Baroque Arias 2002, Bel Canto Arias – Donizetti & Rossini 2003, Handel & Hasse: Opera Arias & Cantatas 2006, Pyrotechnics (all Vivaldi Arias) 2009, Hasse's Sanctus Petrus and Sancta Maria Magdalena, Haydn's Il mondo della luna, Vivaldi's L'oracolo in Messenia, Patrick Cassidy's Mass, Hasse's Marc'Antonio e Cleopatra, Hasse/Handel recording with Andres Gabetta. *Honours:* ARIA Award 1997, Dresden Music Festival, Artist of the Year 1999, Florentine Opera-Marie Z. Uihlein Artist Fund 2004, New York City Opera Christopher Keene Award for Artistic Excellence 2007, Pittsburgh Opera Maecenas Award 2008. *Current Management:* c/o Dominique Riber, Opéra et Concert, 37 rue de la Chaussée d'Antin, 75009 Paris, France. *Telephone:* 1-42-96-18-18. *Fax:* 1-42-96-18-00. *E-mail:* d.riber@opera-concert.com. *Website:* www.opera-concert.com. *E-mail:* contact@vivicagenaux.com (office). *Website:* vivicagenaux.com.

GENIUŠAS, Lukas; Russian pianist; b. 1 July 1990, Moscow; s. of Petras Geniušas and Xennia Knorre. *Education:* F. Chopin Music Coll., Moscow State Conservatory. *Career:* has appeared with numerous orchestras including Hamburg and Duisburg Symphony Orchestras, BBC Scottish Symphony, Kremerata Baltica, Lithuanian State Orchestra, Warsaw Philharmonic; collaborations with conductors including Andrey Boreyko, Saulius Sondeckis, Antoni Wit, Roman Kofman, Dmitry Liss, Jonathan Darlington and others; concert tours to France, Italy, Spain, Poland, Lithuania, Japan, South Korea, USA, Germany and other countries; extensive repertoire ranging from Baroque to works by modern composers; chamber music performer in duets, trios and quintets; regular participant in The New Names Foundation Concerts. *Recordings include:* Sergej Rachmaninov, Frederic Chopin (1810–1849). *Honours:* grants from Vladimir Spivakov Foundation and Mstislav Rostropovich Foundation, Fed. grants from Russian Fed. 'Young Talents' 2005, The Gifted Youth of XXI Century 2007; Winner, Int. Piano Competition, St Petersburg 2002, Winner, First Open Competition of Cen. Music School, Moscow 2003, Second Prize, Moscow Int. Chopin Youth Piano Competition 2004, Second Prize, Gina Bachauer Youth Piano Competition, Salt Lake City 2005, Second Prize, Scottish Int. Piano Competition 2007, Gold Medal, 7th Youth Delphic Games Russia 2008, Second Prize, 'Musica Viva' III Piano Competition, San Marino 2008, Winner, Int. Piano Competition 'Musica della Val Tidone', Pianello (Italy) 2009, Winner, Gina Bachauer Int. Artists Competition, Salt Lake City 2010, Second Prize, 16th Chopin Int. Piano Competition, Warsaw 2010. *Current Management:* c/o Artists Management Co., Piazza R. Simoni 1, 37122 Verona, Italy. *Telephone:* (045) 8014041. *Fax:* (045) 8014980. *E-mail:* panozzo@amcmusic.com. *Website:* www.amcmusic.com. *E-mail:* lukasgeniusas@gmail.com. *Website:* www.geniusas.com.

GENS, Véronique; French singer (soprano); b. 19 April 1966, Orléans. *Education:* Paris Conservatoire. *Career:* has sung with Les Arts Florissants from 1986; solo engagements include Mozart's Cherubino and Vitellia, under Jean-Claude Malgoire, the Countess with Opéra de Lyon 1994, and Donna Elvira at Tourcoing; sang Venus in King Arthur with Les Arts Florissants in Paris and at Covent Garden 1995; Mozart's Idamante in Lisbon 1995; has also worked with such conductors as William Christie, Marc Minkowski and René Jacobs; season 1996 with Les Talens Lyriques at the Versailles Baroque Days as Venus in Les Fêtes de Paphos by Mondonville, Beaune Festival with Les Musiciens du Louvre as Lully's Galatée; solo engagements include Fiordiligi with Vlaamse Opera, Belgium 1997 and Donna Elvira at Aix-en-Provence, Milan, La Monnaie and Tokyo with Claudio Abbado and Peter Brook 1998–99; as Vitellia (Clemenza di Tito) in Madrid 1999 and Fiordiligi there 2002; Wigmore Hall, London recital 2000, 2006, 2008; Alcina in Hamburg 2002; Donna Elvira in Don Giovanni, Glyndebourne 2002 and Liceu Barcelona 2003, Fiordiligi in Tokyo 2005, Vitellia (Clemenza) in Dresden 2005, La Finta Giardiniera in Salzburg 2006, Alice in Falstaff in Baden-Baden 2007, La Calisto in Munich and London 2008, Die Meistersinger in Barcelona 2009, Don Giovanni in Vienna 2009, Iphigénie en Tauride, Vienna 2010. *Recordings:* Dido and Aeneas; Les Arts Florissants, William Christie; Hippolyte et Aricie by Rameau; Les Musiciens du Louvre, Marc Minkowski; Campra Motets, Requiem and Te Deum; Charpentier David et Jonathas, Miserere and Missa Assumpta Est; Jommelli Armida Abbandonata and Lamentations; Lully Acis et Galatée, Alceste, Armide, Atys, Phaeton; Marais, Alcyone; Mondonville Les Fêtes de Paphos; Mozart's Così fan tutte and Don Giovanni; Purcell King Arthur and Fairy Queen; Rameau Castor et Pollux, Dardanus and Platée; Mozart Arias; Handel's Cantatas; Cosí fan Tutte with Jacobs; French Songs with Roger Vignoles; Berlioz: Les Nuits d'Eté, Les chants d'Auvergne under J. C. Casadesus, Orchestre de Lille 2004, Tragédiennes (Gramophone Award for Best Recital Recording) 2006, Canteloupe with Orchestre de Lille 2007, Lamenti 2008, Tragédiennes 2 2009, Tragédiennes 3 (Int. Classical Music Award for Best Vocal Recital Recording 2012) 2011. *Honours:* Chevalier des Arts et des Lettres 2007; Révélation Musicale de l'année 1995, Artiste Lyrique of the Year 1999. *Current Management:* Hilbert Artists Management, Maximilianstrasse 22, 80539 Munich, Germany. *Telephone:* (89) 290747-0. *Fax:* (89) 290747-30. *E-mail:* agentur@hilbert.de. *Website:* www.hilbert.de.

GENTILE, Ada, DipMus; Italian composer; b. 26 July 1947, Avezzano; m. Franco Mastroviti 1972. *Education:* S. Cecilia Conservatoire, Rome, Accademia di Santa Cecilia with Goffredo Petrassi. *Career:* works performed throughout Europe, Canada, USA, China, Japan and Australia; invited to festivals of contemporary music, including Huddersfield, Århus, Zagreb, Warsaw, Alicante, Bacau and Kassel; commissions from RAI, French Ministry of Culture, opera theatre in Rome and Accademia di Santa Cecilia; Artistic Dir, G. Petrassi Chamber Orchestra 1986–88, Nuovi Spazi Musicali Festival, Rome; teacher, S. Cecilia Conservatoire; presenter of contemporary music festivals for RAI-Radiotre. *Compositions:* some 60 published works and several recorded works. *E-mail:* ada.gentile@tin.it. *Website:* www.adagentile.it.

GENTILE, Louis; American singer (tenor); b. 2 Sept. 1957, Connecticut. *Education:* studied in New York. *Career:* guest appearances in opera and broadcasting houses in Europe and the USA; sang at Darmstadt, 1983–86; Krefeld, 1986–88 as Alfredo, among other roles; Netherlands Opera at Amsterdam, 1988, in Fidelio, Berlin Staatsoper, 1986, in Judith by Siegfried Matthus; Appeared at the Deutsche Oper Berlin 1990, as Schwalb in Mathis der Maler; Pedro in Tiefland at the Theater am Gärtnerplatz, Munich, 1991; Sang Don José at Oslo, 1991; Other roles include Tamino, Rossini's Almaviva, Boris in Katya Kabanova, Cavalli's Ormindo, Rodolfo, and Erik in Der fliegende Holländer; Sang Bibalo's Macbeth for Norwegian Opera at Oslo, 1992; Season 1995 at Bielefeld in the premiere of Der Sturz des Antichrist by Ullmann and at Leipzig as Boris in Katya Kabanova; Wagner's Tristan at Ghent, 1998; sang Max at Bonn and Tristan in Antwerp, 2001. *Honours:* winner Young Talent Presents, Competition 1981. *Current Management:* Matthias Vogt Artists Management, 211 Gough Street #115, San Francisco, CA 94102, USA. *Telephone:* (415) 788-8073. *Fax:* (415) 276-1780. *E-mail:* matthias.vogt@usa.net. *Website:* www.matthiasvogt.com; www.louisgentile.com.

GEORG, Mechthild; German singer (mezzo-soprano); b. 1956. *Education:* Robert-Schumann-Hochschule, Düsseldorf with Ingeborg Reichelt and at Cologne Opera Studio. *Career:* sang at first in concert, then at Essen Opera from 1989; guest engagements throughout Germany as Monteverdi's Octavia and Penelope, Cherubino, the Composer in Ariadne auf Naxos, Flosshilde (Hamburg 1992) and Henrietta in Graf Mirabeau by Matthus; concerts in Belgium, Austria and Switzerland; sang Atalanta in Handel's Serse at Copenhagen 1996; Magdeburg Telemann Festival 1996, in Der Neumodische Liebhaber Damon. *Recordings include:* Suor Angelica and Gianni Schicchi; Messiah and Schumann Requiem; Udolin in Schubert's Die Verschworenen. *E-mail:* mail@mechthild-georg.de. *Website:* www.mechthild-georg.de.

GEORGE, Alan Norman, MA; British violist, teacher, writer and lecturer; *Violist/Manager, Fitzwilliam String Quartet*; b. 23 Dec. 1949, Newquay, Cornwall; s. of Norman George and Joyce George; m. Lesley Schatzberger 1976; one s. two d. *Education:* King's Coll., Cambridge. *Career:* debut as mem. of Fitzwilliam Quartet, Sheffield Festival 1972; mem. Fitzwilliam Quartet 1968– (also Man.), Quartet in Residence, Univ. of York 1971–74, 1977–86, Univ. of Warwick 1974–77, Fitzwilliam Coll., Cambridge 1998–, Univ. of Wales, Bangor 1999–2005; Affiliate Artist, Bucknell Univ., USA 1978–86, 1998–; Lecturer, Univ. of York, 1986–88; tutor in viola/chamber music, Royal Northern Coll. of Music, Manchester 1998–2003; participant, first performance of quartets by Sebastian Forbes (No. 2), Edward Cowie (No. 1), Colin Matthews (No. 1), David Matthews (No. 3), David Blake (Nos 2 and 5), Bernard Rands, John Paynter, Michael Blake (No. 1), Rachel Stott, Matthew King (Nos 1 and 2), Liz Johnson (Nos 1, 3, 4 and Tide Purl), Jeremy Thurlow (No. 1 and Fantasia), Peter Dyson, Steve Crowther, Duncan Bruce (No. 4 and Palimpsest), John Ramsay (No. 4), John Gibson (No. 1), David Power, Simon Morecroft, Alex West; Long Hidden, Ghosts, Threnody by Jackson Hill, More Fools Than Wise by Jonathan Rathbone, Susato Dances, The Dance Master by Marcus Heathcock, The Mystic Ring, Fantasy in G by Carolyn Sparey, Clarinet Quintet by David Blake, Nun Danket Alle Gott by Jacques Cohen, A Distant Kiss by Peter McCarthy, Clarinet Quintet, Piano Quintet by Michael Blake, Journey to the East, Genesis, Absolutely, Epiphany Fantasia by Uwe Steinmetz, Clarinet Trio by William Sweeney; first British and US performances, Shostakovich Quartets 13, 14, 15, Alfred Schnittke Canon in Memory of I. F. Stravinsky; Prin. Viola, English Baroque Soloists/Orchestre Révolutionnaire et Romantique 1988–99, Classical Opera Co. 2002–07, Southern Sinfonia 2008–11; mem. Finchcocks Quartet 1992–96, Yorkshire Baroque Soloists, New London Consort, King's Consort, Lumina contemporary music group; concerts and recordings, London Classical Players, Orchestra of the Age of Enlightenment, Acad. of Ancient Music, Hanover Band. *Recordings:* Shostakovich Quartets Nos 1–15, Franck Quartet in D, Borodin Quartets Nos 1 and 2, Delius Quartet, Sibelius Voces Intimae, Brahms Clarinet Quintet with A. Hacker, Wolf Italian Serenade, Schubert String Quintet with C. van Kampen, Beethoven Quartets Op. 127, 130, 132, 133, 135, Shostakovich Piano Quintet with V. Ashkenazy, Mozart Clarinet Trio with A. Hacker and K. Evans, Schumann Piano Quintet and Piano Quartet with R. Burnett, Mozart Clarinet Quintet with L. Schatzberger, chamber version of Beethoven's Piano Concerto No. 4, with R. Levin, Purcell Anthems with New College Choir/E. Higginbottom, Haydn Seven Last Words from the Cross, chamber versions of Mozart Piano Concertos K413, K415 and Piano Quartet K452a, with Richard Burnett, Haydn Quartets Op. 1/6, 71/2, 77/2, Brahms Clarinet Quintet/Mozart/Glazunov/Sweeney with L. Schatzberger, Vaughan Williams' On Wenlock Edge, Gurney Ludlow & Teme, Bliss Elegaic Sonnet, Warlock the Curlew with J. Gilchrist and A. Tilbrook, John Ramsay Quartets Nos 1–4, Uwe Steinmetz Absolutely & Epiphany Fantasia, Bruckner Quartet & Quintet with J. Boyd, Liz Johnson Quartets Nos 1–4 (with L. Lixenberg) & Tide Purl, Purcell and Humfrey Anthems with St Salvator's Chapel Choir/T. Wilkinson. *Publications include:* Shostakovich Chamber Music, Performing

Haydn's Quartets 2001, Russian and Soviet Quartets in the 20th Century 2001. *Honours:* Hon. DMus (Bucknell, USA) 1981; Hon. DUniv (York) 2006. *Address:* 10 Bootham Terrace, York, YO30 7DH, England (home). *Telephone:* 7878-672190 (mobile) (office). *Fax:* (20) 8521-7657 (office). *E-mail:* fitzwilliam .quartet@ntlworld.com (office). *Website:* www.fitzwilliamquartet.org (office).

GEORGE, Donald; American singer (tenor); b. 13 Sept. 1955, San Francisco, Calif. *Education:* Louisiana State Univ., studied in Berlin and with Josef Metternich in Munich. *Career:* sang lyric tenor roles at Theater am Gärtnerplatz, Munich, Brussels and the Vienna Staatsoper, 1986, in premiere of Das Schloss by André Laporte and as Belmonte; Deutsche Oper Berlin, 1988–89, as Bernstein's Candide and as Fenton in Die Lustigen Weiber von Windsor; guest appearances at Madrid in local premiere of Lulu, Würzburg (as Belmonte), Komische Oper Berlin (Tamino); Leopold in La Juive (Bielefeld 1989); Giessen (Mozart's Titus) and Bregenz (Steuermann in Der fliegende Holländer); other roles include Faust, Ferrando, Leukippos (Daphne), Jason in Médée and Jenik in The Bartered Bride; sang Antonio in Prokofiev's The Duenna at 1989 Wexford Festival; title role in Rossini's Aureliano in Palmira at Bad Wildbad, 1996; The Prince in The Love for Three Oranges, Komische Oper Berlin, 1998; season 1999–2000 as Mozart's Ferrando at Naples and Bob Boles in Peter Grimes at La Scala; concerts at Barbican Hall, London; other repertoire includes works by Bach, Handel, Orff and Vaughan Williams; currently Prof. of Voice, Crane School of Music, SUNY Potsdam; fmr Guest Artist, West Virginia Univ. *Recordings include:* Alzira by Verdi. *Honours:* Honored Prof., Shenyang Conservatory, China. *Address:* Bishop Hall C321, Crane School of Music, SUNY at Potsdam, 44 Pierrepont Avenue, Potsdam, NY 13676, USA. *E-mail:* georged@potsdam.edu; donald-george@donald -george.com. *Website:* www.potsdam.edu/academics/Crane/MusicBusiness/ index.cfm; www.donaldgeorge.de.

GEORGE, Michael; British singer (baritone); b. 10 Aug. 1950, Thetford. *Education:* chorister King's Coll., Cambridge, Royal Coll. of Music, London. *Career:* debut in The Maltings, Snape, in Handel's Saul 1972; solo engagements and as mem. of leading early music ensembles in the UK and across Europe; sang in Handel's L'Allegro at the 1988 Promenade Concerts, Brahms Requiem with the London Symphony Orchestra and Kurt Sanderling, Haydn's Creation in Madrid, Beethoven's Missa Solemnis and Choral Symphony with the Hanover Band, Purcell's Dioclesian with John Eliot Gardiner, and performances of Messiah with The Sixteen in London, Italy, Spain, Poland and France; engagements at the Three Choirs Festival, Royal Festival Hall, Oslo, Brussels and tour of Austria, Germany and Yugoslavia with the Orchestra of St John's; 20th-century repertoire includes Threni by Stravinsky for the BBC, A Child of Our Time with the Bournemouth Symphony Orchestra, the premiere of John Metcalf's The Boundaries of Time for the BBC at the Swansea Festival and Christus in the St John Passion by Arvo Pärt during a tour of the UK with the Contemporary Music Network; sang in three Promenade Concerts 1990, and in Bach's Cantata Herz und Mund und Tat und Leben, Bonfire of the Vanities and Janáček's Glagolitic Mass; sang Abinoam in Handel's Deborah at the 1993 Proms; Grimbald in Purcell's King Arthur at Rome 1996; sang in Oswald von Wolkenstein concert at the Purcell Room, London 1997; sang in staged version of Bach's St John Passion for ENO 2000; Handel's Samson at the London Proms 2002. *Recordings include:* Medieval Carmina Burana; Monteverdi's Vespers of 1610 and Orfeo; At The Boar's Head by Holst; Purcell's St Cecilia Ode; Handel's Ottone; Complete Purcell Odes with the King's Consort. *Current Management:* Hazard Chase, 25 City Road, Cambridge, CB1 1DP, England. *Telephone:* (1223) 312400. *Fax:* (1223) 460827. *E-mail:* sue.nicholls@ hazardchase.co.uk. *Website:* www.hazardchase.co.uk.

GEORGIADIS, John, FRAM, FGSM; British conductor and fmr violinist; b. 17 July 1939, Rochford, Essex, England; s. of Alexander Georgiadis and Nancy Ethel Warren; m. Monica Georgiadis; two s. one d. *Education:* Royal Liberty, Romford, Essex, Royal Acad. of Music, London. *Career:* Concertmaster (Leader), City of Birmingham Symphony Orchestra 1962–65, London Symphony Orchestra 1965–79, Oxford Philomusica 1999–2007; Music Dir and Prin. Conductor, London Virtuosi 1972–, Bristol Sinfonia 1982–84, Bangkok Symphony Orchestra 1994–96; First Violin, Gabrieli Quartet 1987–90; numerous guest conductor appearances world-wide; numerous compositions, arrangements and orchestrations. *Film:* Quartet (played part of Bill) 2012. *Recordings:* with London Symphony Orchestra, Gabrieli Quartet and London Virtuosi Chamber Orchestra. *Honours:* Dr hc (Essex) 1990; Dove Prize 1960, Gulbenkian Award 1960, Queen's Prize 1960. *E-mail:* john.georgiadis@ hotmail.com. *Website:* www.musiciansgallery.com; www.tuesdaytour.org.uk; www.cavalrybarracks.org.uk; www.johngeorgiadis.com.

GEORGIAN, Karine; Russian cellist; b. 5 Jan. 1944, Moscow; m. Anthony Philips 1990, one s. *Education:* Gnessin School, Moscow Conservatory with Mstislav Rostropovich, studied with Armen Georgian. *Career:* regular appearances with leading Soviet, European and American orchestras and festivals; debut tour 1969 at Carnegie Hall with Chicago Symphony, returning 1970 in performance of Khatchaturian Cello Rhapsody; recital at Prague 1970; played with Berlin Philharmonic Orchestra 1970, Leningrad Philharmonic Orchestra 1973, and Royal Philharmonic Orchestra 1982; played at BBC Proms, Henry Wood Promenade Concerts 1985, 1990, and with Philadelphia Orchestra 1990; Prof. of Cello, Musikhochschulen Detmold, Germany 1982–2002; currently teaches at Royal Northern Coll. of Music, Manchester, UK. *Recordings include:* Brahms Trio in B with Dmitri Alexeyev and Liane Isakadze; Denisov Concerto in C with Moscow Philharmonic and Dmitri

Kitayenko; Khatchaturian Cello Rhapsody with Bolshoi Radio Symphony and Aram Khatchaturian; Sonatas by Shostakovich and Locatelli, Aza Amintayeva; Couperin Music for two cellos with Natalia Gutman; Brahms Trio in A minor with Thea King and Clifford Benson. *Honours:* First Prize, All Union Music Competition 1966, First Prize and Gold Medal, Tchaikovsky Int. Competition, Moscow 1966. *Address:* Shona Galletly Public Relations, 3 Salisbury Place, Calverley, Leeds, LS28 5PX, England. *E-mail:* cellogold@ karinegeorgian.com. *Website:* www.karinegeorgian.com.

GERBER, Steven Roy, BA, MFA; American composer and pianist; b. 28 Sept. 1948, Washington, DC. *Education:* Haverford Coll., Princeton Univ., studied composition with Robert Parris, Milton Babbitt, J. K. Randall, Earl Kim, piano with Robert Parris, Agi Jambor, Irwin Gelber. *Career:* world premiere of his compositions Symphony No. 1 and Serenade for string orchestra during tour of Russia 1990, returning 1991 to perform several more concerts of orchestral and chamber works, including a concert at Tchaikovsky Hall, Moscow; since then has returned numerous times; commissions include Piano Trio for Kindler Foundation, Spirituals for Concertante Chamber Players, Five Canonic Duos for The Lark Ascending; mem. several professional orgs. *Compositions include:* Duo in Three Movements for violin and piano (American Composers' Alliance 50th Anniversary recording award), Dirge and Awakening for orchestra (premiered by the Russian Nat. Orchestra under Mikhail Pletnev), Violin Concerto (written for the American violinist Kurt Nikkanen who premiered it in Moscow and Novosibirsk 1994 and Kennedy Center, Washington with Nat. Chamber Orchestra 1995), Spirituals for clarinet and string quartet 2001, Symphony No. 1 (premiered by the Louisville Orchestra and Robert Franz) 2002, Fanfare for the Voice of A-M-E-R-I-C-A 2003, Triple Overture (premiered by the Long Island Philharmonic) 2003–04, String Quartet No. 5 (premiered by the Amernet String Quartet) 2003–04, Symphony No. 2 (premiered by the Skokie Valley Symphony) 2006, Music in Dark Times (premiered by San Francisco Symphony) 2009. *Recordings include:* Une Saison en Enfer; CDs on Chandos, Koch Int., Arabesque, Naxos. *Honours:* Princeton Univ. Fellowship, winner of competitions held by The New Music Consort with String Quartet No. 2 and Musicians' Accord with Concertino, Aaron Copland Fund recording grant. *Address:* 639 West End Avenue 10D, New York, NY 10025, USA (home). *Website:* www.stevengerber .com.

GERELLO, Vassily; Ukrainian singer (baritone); *Principal Artist, Mariinsky Theatre*; b. 1950, Chernivtsi. *Education:* St Petersburg Conservatory. *Career:* sang as professional while a student, and with Kirov Opera as Verdi's Germont and Posa, Valentin (Faust), Napoleon in War and Peace, Balearalz in Mussorgsky's Salammbô and the Venetian Guest in Rimsky's Sadko; on tour to Edinburgh Festival 1991; season 1993–94 as Papageno and Mozart's Figaro in St Petersburg, Rossini's Figaro with Netherlands Opera; season 1994–95 as Paolo in Simon Boccanegra at Bastille Opéra and Covent Garden; Eugene Onegin for Toronto Opera and the Vienna Staatsoper 1998; Yeletsky in The Queen of Spades at Buenos Aires and Posa at the São Paulo Opera; season 1995–96 with Bohème, Giulio Cesare and Boccanegra at the Bastille Opéra; New York Met debut as Alfio in Cavalleria Rusticana 1997; Rachmaninov's Aleko at London Proms 1999; currently Prin. Artist, Mariinsky Theatre. *Recordings include:* Dr Pustrpalk in Salatán by Pavel Haas; Tchaikovsky's Moscow Cantata. *Current Management:* c/o State Academic Mariinsky Theatre, 1 Theatre Square, 190000 St. Petersburg, Russia. *Telephone:* (812) 326-41-41. *Website:* www.mariinsky.ru/en.

GERGALOV, Alexander; Russian singer (baritone); b. 1960. *Career:* performances at the Kirov Opera, St Petersburg from 1990 including Eugene Onegin; Robert in Tchaikovsky's Iolanta; Yeletsky in The Queen of Spades; Andrei in War and Peace; Germont; Yeletsky at Lyon Opéra, 1996; Other roles include: Figaro in Il Barbiere di Siviglia; Don Carlo in La Forza del Destino; Renato in Un Ballo in Maschera; Papageno; Rodrigo in Don Carlos; Many guest engagements in Europe with the Kirov Company; Numerous concert appearances. *Recordings:* The Queen of Spades; Rimsky's Sadko; War and Peace (Bolkonsky); Betrothal in the Monastery (Ferdinand); Kashchey the Immortal (Ivan Korolevich).

GERGIEV, Valery Abesalovich; Russian conductor; *General Director and Artistic Director, Mariinsky Theatre*; b. 2 May 1953, Moscow; m. Natalia Gergieva; two s. one d. *Education:* Leningrad Conservatory. *Career:* Chief Conductor Armenian State Orchestra 1981–84; Asst Conductor (to Yuriy Temirkanov) Kirov Opera, Leningrad; Music Dir Kirov (now Mariinsky) Opera Theatre Orchestra 1988–, also Artistic and Gen. Dir 1996–; Prin. Guest Conductor Rotterdam Philharmonic 1989–92, Prin. Conductor 1992–2008, Music Dir 1995–2008; Prin. Guest Conductor New York Metropolitan Opera 1998–2008; Prin. Conductor London Symphony Orchestra 2007–15; Chief Conductor, Munich Philharmonic 2015–; Artistic Dir St Petersburg Stars of the White Nights Festival, Moscow Easter Festival, Gergiev Festival Rotterdam, Mikkeli Int. Festival, Finland; tours extensively in Europe and the USA; has guest-conducted Berlin Philharmonic, Dresden Philharmonic, Bayerischer Rundfunk, Royal Concertgebouw, London Philharmonic, City of Birmingham Symphony, Royal Philharmonic, London Symphony, Orchestra of Santa Cecilia, Japan Philharmonic, orchestras of Boston, Chicago, Cleveland, New York, San Francisco and Toronto, operas at Covent Garden, Metropolitan and San Francisco; Dean of the Faculty of Arts, St Petersburg State Univ. 2010–. *Recordings:* numerous recordings of operas and ballets including Shostakovich War Symphonies (No 4-9) 2005, Prokofiev Complete Symphonies (Gramophone Award for Best Orchestral Recording 2007) 2006,

Tchaikovsky Swan Lake 2007, Shostakovich The Nose 2009, Wagner Parsifal 2010. *Honours:* Hon. Pres. Edinburgh International Festival 2011; Dr hc (Moscow State Univ.) 2012; prize winner at All-Union Conductors' Competition, Moscow (while still a student) and at Karajan Competition, Berlin, State Prize of Russia 1994, 1999, Musical Life Magazine Musician of the Year 1992, 1993, Classical Music Award 1994, Musical America Yearbook Conductor of the Year 1996, People's Artist of Russia 1996, Triumph Prize 1999, Order of Friendship, Russia 2000, Order of St Mesrop Mashtots, Armenia 2000, Russian Presidential Prize 2002, UNESCO Artist of the World 2003, Nat. Pride of Russia Award 2003, For Work and the Fatherland Award 2003, World Econ. Forum Crystal Prize 2004, People's Artist of Ukraine 2004, Royal Swedish Acad. of Music Polar Music Prize 2005, Royal Philharmonic Soc. Award for Best Conductor 2009, Hero of Labour of the Russian Federation 2013. *Current Management:* Columbia Artists Management, 1790 Broadway, New York, NY 10019-1412, USA. *Telephone:* (212) 841-9500. *Fax:* (212) 841-9744. *E-mail:* info@cami.com. *Website:* www.cami.com. *Address:* Mariinsky Theatre, Teatralnaya pl. 1, St Petersburg, 190000, Russia. *Telephone:* (812) 326-41-41. *Fax:* (812) 314-17-44. *E-mail:* post@mariinsky.ru. *Website:* lso.co .uk; mariinsky.us/valery-gergiev.

GERGIEVA, Larissa; Moldovan pianist; b. 1959, Beltsy. *Education:* Vladikavkas with Zarama Lolaeva. *Career:* repetiteur at the Vladikavkas Opera, then at the Tchaikovsky Opera House Perm, 1987–; Russian recitals at Moscow and St Petersburg and partnerships with leading singers in Italy, Germany, USA and UK (Edinburgh, Wigmore Hall and Queen Elizabeth Hall); season 1994–95 included recitals at the Edinburgh Festival with Olga Borodina and Galina Gorchakova, and at the Wigmore Hall in the Wigmore/ Kirov series; coaching engagements have included The Fiery Angel and Ruslan and Ludmila with the San Francisco Opera 1994–95; accompanied Kirov artists in Shostakovich Songs for the BBC 1995; masterclasses for singers at Perm, and Gen. Dir of Rimsky-Korsakov Competition for singers at St Petersburg; currently Artistic Dir Mariinsky Acad. of Young Singers. *Recordings include:* Tchaikovsky Songs, and the Mighty Handful, with Olga Borodina. *Honours:* First prize at the Kazan and Tallinn National Competitions. *Current Management:* James Fox Artist Management, LLC, One Riverplace Drive, Suite 420, La Crosse, WI 54601, USA. *Telephone:* (310) 531-0213. *E-mail:* peter@jfartists.com. *Website:* www.jfartists.com.

GERHAHER, Christian; German singer (baritone); b. 1969, Straubing. *Education:* received a medical degree; Munich Music Acad., masterclasses with Dietrich Fischer-Dieskau and Elisabeth Schwarzkopf. *Career:* began career at Municipal Theatre Würzburg 1998–2000; operas include The Magic Flute at Strasbourg Opera, Ruhr Triennale, Gärtnerplatztheater Munich, Salzburg Festival, Così fan tutte at Baden-Baden Festival, Freischütz with Capella Coloniensis, Orfeo and Tannhäuser at Opera Frankfurt, Marriage of Figaro in Munich 2010; concert appearances with the Berlin Philharmonic singing various Schubert cycles, Britten's War Requiem; debut with Royal Concertgebouw Orkest, Amsterdam, singing Dvorak's Biblical Songs 2004; regular performances at Wigmore Hall, London, including Schubert recital; other concert performances with Gewandhausorchester, Leipzig, Vienna Philharmonic, Bayerische Rundfunk, Philharmonie Cologne, Boston Symphony Orchestra, and numerous nat. and int. festivals. *Recordings include:* Abert, Ekkehard 2000, Weber, Der Freischütz 2002, Schubert, Winterreise 2002, Mahler, Kindertotenlieder 2002, Schubert, Die Schöne Müllerin 2003, Schubert, Schwanengesang 2003, Haydn, The Creation 2004, Schubert, Song Cycles 2004, Schumann, Lieder 2004, Orff, Carmina Burana 2005, Abendbilder – Schubert Lieder (Winner Gramophone Awards Solo Vocal Category 2006) 2005, Melancholie Songs of Robert Schumann (with Gerold Huber) (BBC Music Magazine Award for Best Vocal Recording 2009) 2008, Othmar Schoeck, Notturno 2009, Mahler, Lieder 2010, Romantic Arias (Int. Opera Awards Best Operatic Recital CD Award 2013), Schubert Nachtviolen Lieder (Gramophone Award for Best Solo Recording 2015) 2014. *Honours:* Prix Int. Pro Musicis, Paris/New York 1998, Midem Classical Award for Singer of the Year 2010. *Current Management:* c/o Verena Vetter, KünstlerSekretariat am Gasteig, Rosenheimer Str. 52, Munich 81669, Germany. *Telephone:* (89) 444-8879-2 (office). *Fax:* (89) 448-9522 (office). *E-mail:* team@ks-gasteig.de (office). *Website:* www.gasteig.de (office).

GERHARDT, Alban, MMus; German cellist; b. 25 May 1969, Berlin; s. of Axel Gerhardt and Johanna Gerhardt; m. Gergana Gergova Gerhardt; two s. *Education:* Cincinnati Conservatory, Musikhochschule Köln. *Career:* debut with Berlin Philharmonic under Semyon Bychkov aged 21; has worked with 160 orchestras worldwide, under conductors such as Kurt Masur, Christoph von Dohnányi, Christoph Eschenbach, Sir Neville Marriner, Marek Janowski, Sir Colin Davis, Leonard Slatkin, Fabio Luisi, Sakari Oramo, Paavo and Neeme Järvi; recent debuts include Boston Symphony, Nat. Symphony and NDR Hamburg (all under C.von Dohnányi), Philadelphia Orchestra, San Francisco Symphony, Los Angeles Philharmonic at Hollywood Bowl and Disney Hall, Cleveland Orchestra; has collaborated with composers including Unsuk Chin and Matthias Pintscher; also recitals and chamber music at numerous festivals worldwide including Edinburgh, Aldeburgh, Cheltenham, Schleswig-Holstein, Schubertiade, Bad Kissingen, Prague Autumn, Weimar, Colmar, Kuhmo, Spoleto (USA) and Newport. *Recordings include:* Kodàly, Debussy, de Falla, Kreisler, Paganini 1992, Wandering Soul 1992, Brahms, Franck 1992, Schubert, Schumann 1993, Bach, Brahms Schubert 1997, Brahms Sonatas (Echo Klassik Prize 1998) 1998, Spanish Encores 1999, Anton Rubinstein (Echo Klassik Prize 2003) 2003, Berkeley Lennox and Michael 2003, Frank Bridge, Orchestral Works, Vol. 4 2004, Bach, Britten, Kodály 2004, The Romantic Cello Concerto Vol. I: Dohnányi, Enesco & d'Albert (Midem Classic Award 2006, Best Orchestra Recording BBC Music Magazine) 2005, Shostakovich & Schnittke: Cello Sonatas 2006, The Romantic Cello Concerto Vol. 2, Schumann, Volkmann, Gernsheim & Dietrich 2007. *Honours:* Winner Univ. of Maryland Int. Leonard Rose Cello Competition 1993. *E-mail:* Grace.Ko@harrisonparrott.co.uk. *Website:* www.albangerhardt .com.

GERINGAS, David; Russian cellist and conductor; b. 29 July 1946, Vilna; m. Tatiana Schatz. *Education:* Moscow Conservatoire with Rostropovich. *Career:* concert tours of Germany 1970 and Hungary 1973; many recitals with pianist, Tatiana Schatz; played in the orchestra of the North German Radio and has given solo performances of works by Honegger, Milhaud, Hindemith and Kabalevsky; premiered the Sonata for Solo Cello by Gottfried von Einem in 1987; piano trio performances with Gerhard Oppitz and Dmitri Sitkovetsky; Also plays the baryton and has formed the Trio Geringas with the violinist, Vladimir Mendelssohn and the cellist, Emil Klein; Concerts with the Berlin PO, Vienna SO, Montreal SO, Philadelphia Orchestra, Chicago Symphony, NHK SO (Tokyo), London PO, Philharmonia and Israel PO, with conductors such as Ashkenazy, Gerd Albrecht, Eschenbach, Kondrashin, Leitner, Rattle, Rostropovich, Sawallisch and Tilson Thomas; as conducor performances include with North German Radio Symphony, Orchestra da Camera di Padova and the Forum Philharmonic in Netherlands; currently guest conductor of the South-West German CO in Pforzheim and the Lithuanian CO; Active career in chamber music working with his wife pianist Tatjana Geringas and British pianist Ian Fountain; Commissioned works from composers including Sofia Gubaidulina, Peteris Vasks, Erkki Sven Tüür, and was a pioneer in introducing the music of many Russian avant-garde composers to the west, including Gubaidulina, Denisov and Schnittke; Prof. of Cello, Musikhochschule in Lübeck 1980–2000, Hochschule für Musik 'Hanns Eisler' 2000–. *Recordings include:* Gubaidulina Offertorium with the Boston Symphony under Dutoit; Concertos by Boccherini and Pfitzner. *Honours:* winner Tchaikovsky International Competition 1970, Preis der Deutschen Schallplattenkritik 1994. *Current Management:* c/o Grant Rogers Musical Artists' Management, 8 Wren Crescent, Bushey Heath, Hertfordshire, WD23 1AN, England. *Telephone:* (20) 8950-2220. *Fax:* (20) 8950-3570. *E-mail:* info@ ngrartists.com. *Website:* www.ngrartists.com.

GERMAIN, Alan; French stage director, choreographer, author and set and wardrobe designer; b. 1948. *Education:* studied in Paris. *Career:* f. dance and theatre company 1972, for historically authentic performances throughout France; Productions include Mozart's Requiem at the Opéra Comique 1995; Opéra Côté Costume at the Palais Garnier 1995; Le Triomphe de la Vertu at the Musée National du Moyen Age 1999; Cesti's Il Tito at the Opéra du Rhin, Strasbourg, with Les Arts Florissants; Lehar's The Merry Widow at the Opéra de Saint-Etienne, Opéra de Vichy 1999/2003, Opéra de Massy 2003; Productions for the English Bach Festival include Gluck's Iphigénie en Tauride at the Royal Opera and for Athens Festival; Rossini's Le Siège de Corinthe in Madrid and Oresteia by Xenakis at the Linbury Studio Theatre, Covent Garden 2000; Lully/Molière Bourgeois Gentilhomme at the Château de Chambord 1995, and at the Linbury 2001, Château de Blois and Grand Théâtre de Reims 2002; Gluck's Telemaco at the Covent Garden and the Athens Festival 2003, Charpentier/Molière Le Malade imaginaire, Château de Blois and Grand Théâtre de Reims; Gounod/Molière Le Médicin malgré lui, Opéra de Tours, Massy, Vichy, Tourcoing, Limoges. *Exhibitions:* Costumes de scène en liberté, Grand Théâtre de Reims 2001, Memoires de scène, Bibliotheque de l'Opéra de Paris 2003, Fantômes d'opéra, Reims 2004. *Publications include:* Le Tour du Monde en 80 Langues 1995, Les Origines de l'Homme 1997, La Ville Invisible 1999, Les Grenouilles de Saint-Pierre 2001 L'Affaire Callas 2002, Meurtre à la Française 2004, Fantômes d'opéra 2004. *Honours:* Fondation de la Vocation Prize 1978. *Address:* 29 rue de Paradis, 75010 Paris, France (home). *Telephone:* 1-42-46-37-83 (home). *Fax:* 1-42-46-67-85 (home). *E-mail:* compagnie@alaingermain.com (office). *Website:* www.alaingermain.com.

GERSHON, Grant; American choral director and singer (tenor); b. Alhambra, Calif.; m. Elissa Johnston; one s. one d. *Education:* Thornton School of Music, Univ. of Southern California. *Career:* Asst Conductor, Los Angeles Philharmonic 1994–97; Music Dir, Los Angeles Master Chorale 2001–; over 100 performances at Walt Disney Concert Hall; world premieres of major works by composers such as John Adams, Louis Andriessen, Christopher Rouse, Steve Reich and Chinary Ung; fmr Asst Conductor/ Principal Pianist, Los Angeles Opera, currently Resident Conductor; operas included La Traviata (debut) 2009, Daniel Catán's Il Postino 2010, Handel's L'Allegro, il Penseroso ed il Moderato 2011, Puccini's Madame Butterfly 2012, Carmen 2013; toured with Los Angeles Chorale and Los Angeles Opera 2013, to London, Lucerne, Paris and New York (Adams' The Gospel According to the Other Mary); conducting appearances at festivals including Berkshire Choral, Ravinia (also sang David Lang's The Little Match Girl in quartet), Aspen, Edinburgh, Helsinki and Vienna, and in Great Performers series at Lincoln Center and Making Music series at Zankel Hall, New York; Guest Conductor, Minnesota Opera 2007, Santa Fe Opera 2010; hon. bd mem. Los Angeles Children's Chorus 2005; mem. bd of advisors, Thornton School of Music, Univ. of Southern California 2006–. *Films:* Lady in the Water 2006, Charlie Wilson's War 2007, I Am Legend 2007. *Recordings include:* with Los Angeles Master Chorale: Lauridsen: Lux Aeterna 1998, Argento-Duruflé 2001, Glass-Salonen 2002, Steve Reich: You Are 2005, Steve Reich: Daniel Variations 2008, Glass:

Itaipú 2010, A Good Understanding 2010, Górecki: Miserere 2012. *Address:* Los Angeles Master Chorale, 135 North Grand Avenue, Los Angeles, CA 90012, USA (office). *Telephone:* (213) 972-3110 (office). *Fax:* (213) 972-3136 (office). *E-mail:* lamc@lamc.org (office). *Website:* www.lamc.org (office).

GERSTEIN, Kirill, MMus; American (b. Russian) pianist; b. 1979, Voronezh. *Education:* Berklee Coll. of Music, Boston, Manhattan School of Music with Solomon Mikowsky, also with Dmitri Bashkirov in Madrid and Ferenc Rados in Budapest. *Career:* moved to USA aged 14 to study music; has performed with Chicago Symphony Orchestra under Charles Dutoit, Atlanta Symphony, Saint Paul Chamber Orchestra, Rochester Philharmonic, Los Angeles Philharmonic, Nat. Arts Centre Orchestra, Ottawa, Detroit, Houston, Oregon, San Francisco, Baltimore, Dallas, Indianapolis, Vancouver, Oregon and Utah Symphonies, Philadelphia Orchestra at Mann Music Center, Cleveland Orchestra at Blossom Music Festival and Chicago's Grant Park Festival; recitals in Boston, New York, Cincinnati, Detroit, Vancouver, Kansas City, Portland, and Washington's Kennedy Center; has appeared with NHK Symphony Orchestra and Dutoit in Tokyo, Hanover's NDR Orchestra in Austria and Italy, in Caracas with Gustavo Dudamel and the Simon Bolívar Youth Orchestra, Munich, Rotterdam and Royal Philharmonics, City of Birmingham Symphony Orchestra, Staatskapelle Dresden, Zurich's Tonhalle, Finnish and Swedish Radio Symphony Orchestras, WDR Symphony Orchestra Cologne, and Deutsches Symphonie-Orchester Berlin; also recitals in Paris, Prague, Hamburg, London's Wigmore and Queen Elizabeth Halls, Liszt Acad. in Budapest, Salzburg Festival (debut) playing solo and two-piano works with András Schiff 2008; collaborates in chamber groups with artists including cellists Steven Isserlis and Clemens Hagen, violinist Joshua Bell, flutist Emmanuel Pahud and clarinettist Martin Frost; teaches at Musikhochschule Stuttgart 2006–. *Honours:* First Prize, Arthur Rubinstein Piano Competition, Tel-Aviv 2001, Gilmore Young Artist Award 2002, 2010. *Current Management:* c/o David Sigall, Ingpen & Williams, 7 St George's Court, 131 Putney Bridge Road, London, SW15 2PA, England. *Telephone:* (20) 8874-3222. *Fax:* (20) 8877-3113. *E-mail:* ds@ingpen.co.uk. *Website:* www.ingpen.co.uk; www.kirillgerstein.com.

GESSENDORF, Mechthild; German singer (soprano); m. Ernö Weil. *Career:* performances with Bayerische Staatsoper (Munich), Hamburgische Staatsoper, Deutsche Oper (Berlin), Wiener Staatsoper (Vienna), Royal Opera House (Covent Garden, London), Grand Opéra (Paris), La Scala (Milan), Metropolitan Opera (New York), Monte Carlo Opera etc.; numerous appearances at int. festivals including Salzburg (Austria), Aix-en-Provence (France) and Edinburgh (UK). *Operas include:* Der Rosenkavalier, Ariadne auf Naxos, Lohengrin, Die Walküre, Der fliegende Holländer, Jenufa, Die Frau ohne Schatten, Tannhäuser. *Address:* Nibelungen Str. 23, 75179 Pforzheim, Germany.

GESSI, Romolo; Italian conductor; b. 25 March 1960, Trieste; m. Alessandra Carani 1995, one d. *Education:* State Conservatoire, St Petersburg with Kukuskin, Wiener Meisterkurse, Vienna with Kalmar, Accademia Musicale, Pescara with Renzetti. *Career:* debut at Teatro Rossetti, Trieste (symphonic) 1991, Teatro Lirico di Spoleto with Puccini's La Bohème (operatic) 1995; Music Dir, Chamber Orchestra of Friuli Venezia-Giulia 1991–, Serenade Ensemble 1994–2000; Prof. of Conducting, State Conservatoire, Milan 1995; Prof. of Chamber Music, State Conservatoire, Trieste 1997–; Prof., European Masterclass in Spoleto; Conductor, Orchestra del Teatro Lirico di Spoleto; guest conductor with Milano Classica, Filarmonia Veneta; numerous concerts in Italy, Austria, Spain, Hungary, Russia, Sweden, Switzerland, Slovenia and Croatia. *Recordings:* Rimsky-Korsakov, Dvořák, Strauss and Music in the 20th Century, with Serenade Ensemble. *Honours:* second prize Gusella Conducting Competition, Pescara 1993, first prize Austrian-Hungarian Int. Conducting Competition, Vienna and Pécs 1994.

GESTER, Martin; French conductor, musician (organ, harpsichord, piano) and musicologist. *Education:* Conservatoire de Strasbourg, Université de Strasbourg. *Career:* f. Le Parlement de Musique vocal and instrumental ensemble 1990–; has conducted performances on four continents and at venues including Théâtre des Champs Elysées and festivals of Ambronay, Lourdes, Halle and Zamora (Spain); collaborated and toured with Polish Baroque orchestra Arte dei Suonatori and with vocal ensembles Les Pages et les Chantres de la Chapelle Royale de Versailles and Maîtrise de Bretagne; has performed as soloist and as guest conductor with ensembles including New York Collegium, Nederlandse Bach Vereniging, Collegium Vocale Gent, La Chapelle Royale de Paris, Musica Aeterna Bratislava, Sächsisches Sinfonieorchester Chemnitz, Camerata Antiqua de Curitiba and Orchestre du Pays de Savoie; over 40 recordings as soloist or with Le Parlement de Musique; teacher, Acad. Supérieure de Musique and Conservatoire de Strasbourg; master-classes (Studio Baroque de Versailles, Jeunes Voix du Rhin, Stanford Univ., USA and Academia Mexicana de Música Antigua). *Recordings include:* with Le Parlement de Musique: Nicolaus Bruhns: Organ Works and Cantatas 1999, Scarlatti: La Giuditta 2006, Monteclair/Clérambault: Le Retour de la Paix 2011, Nicola Porpora: Vespro per la Festività dell'Assunta 2012; with Arte dei Suonatori: Handel: Twelve Grand Concertos op. 6 2007, Telemann: Ouvertures pittoresques 2013; with Aline Zylberajch: Caprices 2012, Mozart: Grandes Sonates à 4 mains 2014; other: Bach Partitas 2014. *Honours:* Chevalier, Ordre des Arts et des Lettres 2001, Polish Order of Merit. *Address:* c/o Le Parlement de Musique, 17 Grand rue, 67000 Strasbourg, France (office). *Telephone:* 3-88-31-47-75 (office). *E-mail:* info@

martingester.com (office). *Website:* www.martingester.com (office); www.leparlementdemusique.com (office).

GESZTY, Sylvia; Hungarian singer (soprano); b. 28 Feb. 1934, Budapest. *Education:* Budapest Conservatory, Budapest Music Acad. with Erszébet Hoor-Tempis. *Career:* sang at Berlin Staatsoper from 1961 with debut as Amor in Orfeo ed Euridice, Komische Oper Berlin 1963–70, and Hamburg Staatsoper 1966–72; Covent Garden and Salzburg Festival debuts 1966, 1967 as Queen of Night; sang at Stuttgart Opera from 1971, Glyndebourne Festival 1971–72 as Zerbinetta and Constanze, Luzern Festival in Paisiello's Barbier, Los Angeles 1973 with co. of New York City Opera as Sophie in Der Rosenkavalier and Schwetzingen Festival 1976 as Gismonda in Cimarosa's Il Marito Desperato; sang Rosina in Haydn's La Vera Costanza at Vienna 1984; guest appearances in Buenos Aires, Vienna, Paris, Amsterdam, Moscow, Cairo, Helsinki, Stockholm, Lisbon, Venice and Rome; numerous concert appearances. *Recordings include:* Ariadne auf Naxos; Die Israeliten in der Wüste by C.P.E. Bach; Cantatas by J.S. Bach; La Rappresentazione di Anima e di Corpo by Cavalieri; Die Zauberflöte; Così fan tutte; Barbier von Bagdad by Cornelius; Mozart's Die Schuldigkeit des Ersten Gebotes; Handel's Imeneo; Mozart's Kolatur-Konzertarien; Songs by Debussy, Ravel, Kodály, Bartók; Dessau Lieder; Beethoven's Christus am Ölberg; Television productions: Hoffmann's Erzählunen; Barbier von Bagdad; Eine Nacht in Venedig. *E-mail:* Contact@SylviaGeszty.com. *Website:* www.sylviageszty.de.

GEYER, Gwynne; American singer (soprano); b. 1965. *Career:* season 1991 as Tatiana in Eugene Onegin at St Louis; Rosalinde in Die Fledermaus at Toronto and Nedda at the New York City Opera; season 1993–94 as Rusalka at the Metropolitan Opera; Smetana's Marenka at Toronto and Mimi in Geneva; sang in Kalman's Gräfin Mariza at Santa Fe, 1995; Musetta at the Opéra Bastille, Paris and the title role in Landowski's Galina at Lyon; sang Jenůfa at Cincinnati, 1998; many concert appearances. *Current Management:* Wolf Piper Artists International, 13 East 69th Street, Suite 3R, New York, NY 10021, USA. *Telephone:* (212) 531-1514. *Fax:* (212) 861-6949. *E-mail:* info@wolfartists.com. *Website:* www.wolfartists.com.

GEYER, Roland; Austrian opera house director; *Intendant, Theater an der Wien;* b. Vienna. *Career:* fmr Musikintendant in Vienna; co-founder and Intendant, OsterKlang and KlangBogen Festivals, Vienna 1997–2005; Intendant, Theater an der Wien 2006–. *Address:* Theater an der Wien, Linke Wienzeile 6, Vienna 1060, Austria (office). *Telephone:* (1) 5883-0660 (office). *Fax:* (1) 5883-0650 (office). *E-mail:* oper@theater-wien.at (office). *Website:* www.theater-wien.at (office).

GHAZARIAN, Sona; Austrian singer (soprano); b. 2 Sept. 1945, Beirut, Lebanon. *Education:* Armenian Coll., Beirut, American Univ., Beirut, masterclasses Accademia Chigiana, Siena and Accademia Santa Cecilia, Rome. *Career:* mem., Vienna Staatsoper 1972–, notably as Oscar in Un Ballo in Maschera and Violetta in La Traviata, during the same period appeared in the title role in Lucia di Lammermoor at the Grand Théâtre of Geneva; guest appearances in Hamburg, Paris, Brussels, Verona, Barcelona, Geneva, Salzburg and New York; sang in J.C. Bach's Adriano in Siria for Austrian Radio, conducted by Charles Mackerras; operatic roles include Aennchen in Der Freischütz, Musetta in La Bohème, Susanna in Nina, Barbarina in Le Nozze di Figaro, Marzelline in Fidelio. *Recordings:* Il Re Pastore by Mozart, Marzelline in Fidelio, Un Ballo in Maschera, Mozart Gala in Tokyo, Beethoven's Missa Solemnis–Live Concert at the Vatican. *Honours:* many int. prizes. *Address:* Köstlerg 5, 1060 Vienna, Austria (home). *Telephone:* 1-587-81-35 (home). *Website:* www.sonaghazarian.com.

GHEORGHIU, Angela; Romanian singer (soprano); b. 7 Sept. 1965, Adjud; m. 1st Andrei Gheorghiu 1988; m. 2nd Roberto Alagna (q.v.) 1996. *Education:* Bucharest Acad., studied with Mia Barbu. *Career:* debut at Bucharest as Solveig in Grieg's Peer Gynt 1983; appearances at Covent Garden from 1992, Met debut 1993, and in Washington, Vienna, Monte Carlo, Berlin, Nat. Opera Cluj; repertoire includes Zerlina, Mimi, Nina (all in Cherubin), Suzel (L'Amico Fritz), Juliette (Roméo et Juliette), Magda (La Rondine), Nedda (Pagliacci), Tosca, Manon, and roles in Don Giovanni, La Bohème (Mimi), Turandot, Carmen, La Traviata (Violetta), L'Elisir d'Amore, Falstaff. *Recordings include:* La Traviata (as Violetta) 1994, Casta Diva 2001, Tosca (solo) 2001, Diva 2004, Manon 2007, Live From La Scala 2007, My Puccini 2008, Madama Butterfly 2009, Puccini Opera Arias 2010, Fedora 2011, Homage to Maria Callas 2011, Solti: The Legacy 1937–97 2012, Tosca (Puccini) (BBC Music Magazine DVD Performance Award 2014) 2012, O, ce veste minunata! Colinde romanesti 2013. *Honours:* Officier, Ordre des Arts et Lettres, Chevalier, Ordre des Arts et Lettres, Nihil Sine Deo 2012; Dr hc (Univ. of Arts, Iasi); Belvedere Prize, Vienna, Schatzgraber-Preis, Hamburg State Opera, Gulbenkian Prize, La Medaille Vermeille de la Ville de Paris, Star of Romania 2010, European Culture Award 2015. *Current Management:* c/o IMG Artists, Carnegie Hall Tower, 152 West 57th Floor, 5th Floor, New York, NY 10019, USA. *Telephone:* (212) 994-3500. *Fax:* (212) 994-3550. *Website:* www.imgartists.com. *E-mail:* agerdanovits@gmx.net. *Website:* www.angelagheorghiu.com.

GHEORGHIU, Stefan; Romanian violist; b. 13 Aug. 1951, Constanta; m. Cornelia Gheorghiu 1975; two s. *Education:* Music High School, Bucharest, Music Academy, Bucharest. *Career:* debut recital, 1973; first concert as soloist (Arad) 1975; soloist with George Enescu, Philharmonic Orchestra, 1976; mem. of George Enescu Philharmonic Orchestra 1974–, First Viola 1985–; solo career in Romania and Italy; founder member of Romantica String Trio;

Professor at Darmstadt Summer Courses for Contemporary Music 1986–; Professor at the Music Academy, teaching viola 1993–; President, Romanian Federation on the Musicians Union; President, Union of Interpretative Creation of Romanian Musicians. *Recordings:* 1975–95 recordings as Soloist and Chamber Music at Romanian Radio and Television Broadcasting System; 1984, Mozart-Sinfonia Concertante for violin and viola. *Honours:* Medal, Markneukirchen (DDR), 1977; Special Prize for Interpretation of a French Piece, Evian, France, 1979; Prize, Darmstadt, Germany, 1984. *Address:* Str Frumoasa 52, et 4, ap 18, 78116 Bucharest, Romania.

GHEZZO, Dinu, DipEd, DipComposition, PhD; American/Romanian composer and conductor; *Professor Emeritus of Composition, New York University;* b. 2 July 1941, Tuzla, Romania; m. Marta Ghezzo 1961; one d. *Education:* Romanian Conservatory, Univ. of California at Los Angeles. *Career:* Program Dir, Composition Dir, Prof. of Composition, now Emer., New York Univ.; Dir, George Enescu Int. Composition Competition; co-Dir, New Repertory Ensemble of New York; Pres. Int. New Music Consortium, Int. Composers and Interactive Artists. *Compositions include:* Music for Flutes and Tape 1972, Kanones 1973, Aphorisms 1979, Structures 1980, Sketches, Breezes of Yesteryear, Sound Shapes I and II, From Here to There, Two Prayers for soprano and tape, A Book of Songs, Ostrom, Doina, Five Village Scenes for chamber ensemble 1995, Checkmate for John Cage for ensemble and dancers 1995, Wind Rituals 1995, In Search of Euridice for saxophone, piano and tape 1995, Five Corrado Songs for bass and tape 1996, Three Italian Love Songs 1997, Sound and Etchings for clarinet 1997, Imaginary Voyages for clarinet, cello and percussion 1997, Eyes of Cassandra 1997, In Search of Euridice 1999, Contraste 2001, Alba 2002, Eastern Rituals 2003, Samson Agonistes 2003, Colinde 2005, Shadow Dances 2007, Citicabs. *Publications:* contrib. to Tomis, Living Musician. *Honours:* Commdr, for Faithful Service, Romania; Dr hc (Ovidius Univ., Romania); ASCAP Awards, CAPS Awards, UCLA Chancellor's Fellow, Gus Kahn Award. *Address:* 87–27 Santiago Street, Holliswood, NY 11423, USA (home). *E-mail:* ghezzomusic@gmail.com (home); dinu.ghezzo@nyu.edu (office). *Website:* www.ghezzomusic.com.

GHIELMI, Vittorio; Italian musician (viola da gamba); b. 1968, Milan. *Education:* studied with Roberto Gini at Accademia Internazionale della Musica Milan, Wieland Kuijken at Conservatoire Royale Brussels and Christophe Coin in Paris. *Career:* specialist researcher into old musical traditions; one of few gamba players regularly invited to play as solo performer with orchestras; has appeared as soloist or conductor with numerous orchestras including Los Angeles Philharmonic, London Philharmonia, Vienna Philharmonic, Il Giardino Armonico, Freiburg Baroque Orchestra; has performed in duo with his brother, Lorenzo Ghielmi and with Luca Pianca; soloist in world premieres of many new compositions including Kevin Volans; Uri Caine's Concerto for viola da gamba and orchestra was composed for him (first performed at Amsterdam Concertgebouw); f. early music ensemble Il Suonar Parlante; has performed with jazz players such as Kenny Wheeler, Uri Caine, Jim Black, Don Byron, Markus Stockhausen and Nguyn Le; has collaborated with traditional Asian musicians such as Afghan virtuosi of Ensemble Kaboul (Khaled Arman); teaches at Conservatorio Luca Marenzio, Brescia and has given master-classes in numerous acads and univs. *Recordings include:* Bagpipes from Hell 2009, Barbarian Beauty 2011, The Passion of Musick (Echo Klassik Award for Best Chamber Music Recording 2015) 2014. *Honours:* winner, Concorso Internazionale Romano Romanini per strumenti ad arco, Brescia 1995, Erwin Bodky Award 1997. *Current Management:* Maria Goded Music Management, Calle Codolosa 8, 28200 San Lorenzo de El Escorial, Madrid, Spain. *Telephone:* (918) 969035. *Website:* mariagoded.com. *E-mail:* vghielmi@gmail.com.

GHIGLIA, Oscar; Italian classical guitarist; b. 13 Aug. 1938, Livorno; m. Anne-Marie d'Hauteserre 1966; one d. *Education:* Santa Cecilia Conservatory, Rome. *Career:* concert tours in N America 1965–; performed with Juilliard, Tokyo, and Emerson String Quartets, Julius Baker, Victoria de los Angeles, and Jean Pierre Rampal; performances worldwide include Turkey, Israel, Japan, Australia and New Zealand; artist-in-residence, Hartt School of Music, Univ. of Hartford, USA, and Musik Akademie de Stadt, Basel 1983–2004; summer instructor at Aspen, Colorado Music Festival 1969, Academia Musicale Chigiano, Siena, Italy 1976, and Banff Centre for the Arts, Canada 1978–. *Recordings include:* Paganini Sonata, The Guitar in Spain, The Spanish Guitar of Oscar Ghiglia. *Address:* Helfenberg Strasse 14, Basel 4059, Switzerland. *Address:* 197 South Quaker Lane, West Hartford, CT 06119, USA (office); Helfenberg Strasse 14, Basel 4059, Switzerland.

GHINDIN, Alexander; Russian pianist; b. 1977, Moscow. *Education:* Tchaikovsky State Conservatory, Moscow. *Career:* concert and recital engagements in Russia, USA and Europe from 1994; festival appearances in Stockholm, Luxembourg, Moscow and Brussels; soloist with the Moscow State Philharmonic 1999–, the London Philharmonic Orchestra under Ashkenazy, Philharmonic de Liège, St Petersburg Camerata and Philharmonia, London; has performed with London Philharmonic Orchestra, Munich Philharmonic Orchestra, Berlin Symphony Orchestra, Orchester der Stadt Freiburg, New Japan Philharmonic, Philharmonie de Liège, Flemish Radio Orchestra, the Swedish Royal Festival Orchestra, Orchestre National de Belgique, Rotterdam Symphony Orchestra, Philharmonique de Monte-Carlo, Orchestre National de Montpellier, Philharmonie de Luxembourg, Israel Chamber Orchestra, the Moscow Virtuosi, the St Petersburg Camerata; recitals under the auspices of UNESCO, for the Pope and British royalty.

Recordings: over 15 albums. *Honours:* winner, Moscow Young Pianists' Competition 1991, Tchaikovsky Int. Competition 1994, second prize, Queen Elisabeth Competition 1999, winner, Cleveland Int. Piano Competition 2007.

GHONEIM, Mauna, BMus; Egyptian composer, musician (piano) and academic; *Associate Professor of Composition, Cairo Conservatoire;* b. 21 Aug. 1955, Cairo. *Education:* Cairo Conservatoire, Hochschule für Musik und darstellende Kunst Vienna, Austria. *Career:* composer from 1977; teacher and Research Asst Cairo Conservatoire 1978–81, Assoc. Prof. of Composition 1988–. *Compositions include:* Sonata for piano 1977, Aria for voice and piano 1977, Fantasy for piano and strings 1978, Sahara Safari 1978, Hadith El Hajar (Talking Stones) 1979, Hadith El Karya (The Village) 1979, El Adkar El Dameya (Blood Density) 1980, Small Pieces for percussion instruments 1984, Concerto for piano and orchestra 1984, Two Pieces for woodwinds and string orchestra 1984, String Quartet 1985, String Trio 1985, Lied for soprano and piano 1985, Suite for flute, oboe and string orchestra 1986, Piano Pieces for two voices 1986, Quartet for woodwinds 1986, Tanz für klavier and zwei schlagzeuger (Dance for piano and two percussionists) 1988, El Mashrabia for string orchestra 1988, Two Portraits for string orchestra 1988, Die Däume der Nacht for voice with instrumental ensemble 1988, Elegy for orchestra 1990, Sunlight Fishing 1990, Little Songs for Children 1991, Nacht Bäume Suite for flute solo 1991, Three Pieces for two pianos 1993, Suite for flute and harp 1993. *Honours:* winner Syndicate of the Arts Prize 1991, Acad. of Arts Award 1991, Ismaelia Festival Prize for Film Music 1990. *Address:* Cairo Conservatoire, Avenue of the Pyramids, Giza, Egypt (office).

GIACOLONE, Nicolo Alessandro, (Daniel Knight), BFA; British/Canadian singer (bass, bass-baritone, baritone, counter tenor), voice teacher, artistic director and conductor; b. 28 Nov. 1956, Montreal, Quebec; s. of Antonino Giacalone and Emmy Hummel; adopted father Karl Steiner; m. Janaina de Souza Fernandes; two s. *Education:* Marianopolis Coll., McGill Univ., Conservatoire de Musique, Québec, Concordia Univ.; studied singing with Benjamin Luxon, Vera Rozsa, James Bowman, Rita Streich, Max van Egmond, Daniel Ferro and Emma Kirkby, postgraduate studies in 17th- and 18th-century music and Baroque vocal performance practice. *Career:* Dir Dido and Aeneas, Waltham Abbey 1995; singing, St John's Smith Square, London 1997; BBC radio debut, Glenn Gould, Bach; modern world premiere singing title role of full staged complete performance of Purcell's Dioclesian, Dartington and Croatia 1995, 19th- and 20th-century Austrian Lieder to mark Austria's Thousand Years 1996; Artistic Dir and Founding mem. Handel Opera Co. Ltd, London 1995–, Musical Dir, Artistic Dir and Chair.; f. Belleville Bach Choir and Believable Baroque Ensemble in Canada; recital and voice masterclass, Houston, Tex., USA 1999; private singing teacher, masterclasses in Canada, USA, Ireland, UK 1974–; Adjunct Voice Teacher, Queens Univ., Kingston, Ont.; Head of Voice and Music, Birmingham School of Speech and Drama, UK; Voice Teacher, Univ. of Essex, UK; Visiting Voice Teacher, Univ. of Cambridge, UK; Replacement Voice Instructor, Cardiff Univ., UK. *Film:* Loose Cannon/Lewis Cannon, music by Steiner. *Radio:* took part in CBC Nat. Audition Series for Best Canadian Singer and Musician 1985, Between the Ears (BBC Radio 3). *Television:* Pushy Parents (produced by Monkey Kingdom for Channel 5, UK and Sky Television Worldwide). *Recordings:* Music of the Second Generation 1995, Dioclesian by H. Purcell 1995, Baroque Opera Arias for Bass 1997. *Publications:* A. Scarlatti Cantatas and Serenatas 1997, articles on singing in NODA London News. *Honours:* Strand Scholarship, King's Coll. London, Pauline Donald Memorial Scholarship, Concord Univ., Montreal, Dean's commendation for saving the life of female student at McGill Univ. *Address:* Suite 122, 203 Abbot Street, Gastown, Vancouver, BC V6B 2K7, Canada (home). *Telephone:* (604) 353-0000 (home). *E-mail:* daniel.knightrider@gmail.com (office).

GIACOMINI, Giuseppe; Italian singer (tenor); b. 7 Sept. 1940, Veggiano, Padua. *Education:* studied with Elena Fava Ceriati in Padua, Marcello del Monaco in Treviso and Vladimiro Badiali in Milan. *Career:* debut in 1966 as Pinkerton in Madama Butterfly; sang in Berlin and Vienna from 1972, Hamburg from 1973, La Scala debut 1974, Paris Opéra debut 1975, and US debut at Cincinnati Opera from 1976 as Alvaro in La Forza del Destino, Verdi's Macduff, Don Carlos and Manrico, Puccini's Cavaradossi and Canio in Pagliacci; further appearances in Barcelona, Boston, Budapest, London, Munich and Tokyo; sang Verdi's Otello at San Diego 1986; season 1992 as Alvaro at Naples, Canio at Rome and Radames at festival of Caracalla; other roles include Puccini's Calaf, Luigi, Rodolfo and Des Grieux, Pollione in Norma, Turiddu in Cavalleria Rusticana, Giordano's Andrea Chénier, Verdi's Radames in Aida, and Ernani; sang Radames at Verona Arena, Manrico at Vienna Staatsoper and Calaf at Covent Garden 1996; season 2000–01 as Canio in Pagliacci at the Vienna Staatsoper and Cavaradossi at Covent Garden; toured China 2010. *Recordings include:* Norma; Fausta by Donizetti; Manon Lescaut; Cavalleria Rusticana; Il Tabarro and Tosca, recorded in Philadelphia under Riccardo Mutio. *Honours:* prizewinner, competitions in Naples, Vercelli and Milan.

GIAIOTTO, Bonaldo; Italian singer (bass); b. 25 Dec. 1932, Ziracco, Udine. *Education:* studied in Udine and with Alfredo Starno in Milan. *Career:* debut at Teatro Nuovo Milan 1957; sang widely in Italy, then appeared as Rossini's Bartolo at Cincinnati 1959; Metropolitan Opera debut 1960 as Zaccaria in Nabucco and sang in New York for 25 years in 300 performances, notably as Ramphis, Raimondo and Timur; further engagements in Paris, London, Bordeaux, Rome, Geneva, Vienna, Hamburg and Madrid; concert tour of

South America 1970; season 1985 as Banquo in Zürich, Attila at the Verona Arena and in revival of Donizetti's Il Diluvio Universale at Geneva, as Noah; La Scala Milan debut 1986 as Rodolfo in La Sonnambula; season 1988–89 as Ramphis in Aida at Chicago, Fiesco in Simon Boccanegra at Piacenza and Padre Guardiano in Miami and Verona; sang Timur in Turandot at Turin 1990; season 1992 as Alvise in La Gioconda at Rome and Philip II and Ramphis at Verona Arena; sang in French version of Don Carlos at Brussels 1996. *Recordings including:* Ferrando in Il Trovatore; Brogni in La Juive; Luisa Miller; Aida; La Traviata; Turandot; La Cieco in Massenet's Iris conducted by Patanè. *Website:* www.bonaldogiaiotti.it.

GIANNATTASIO, Carmen; Italian singer (soprano); b. 24 April 1975, Avellino, Campania. *Education:* Univ. of Salerno, Conservatoire Domenico Cimarosa, Avellino under vocal teachers Cecilia Valdenassi, Barbara Lazotti and Marilena Laurenza, Accad. di Perfezionamento per Cantati Lirici del Teatro alla Scala, Milan; masterclasses with Leyla Gencer. *Career:* operatic debut at Teatro Fraschini di Pavia in La Cecchina ossia a bona figliola; int. debut with Los Angeles Opera as Desdemona in Otello conducted by Plácido Domingo 2003; has performed at leading int. opera houses including Teatro alla Scala, Milan (Carmen, Un Giorno di Regno, Ugo Conte di Parigi), La Fenice, Venice (Maometto II), Teatro Comunale Bologna (Il Trovatore, Simon Boccanegra), Teatro Regio, Turin (Turandot, Edgar), Opernhaus Zürich (Il Trovatore, Il Corsaro), Staatsoper Berlin (La Traviata, L'Incoronazione di Poppea), Deutsche Oper, Berlin (La Traviata), Staatsoper Munich (La Bohème), Théâtre de la Monnaie, Brussels (L'Incoronazione di Poppea), Aix en Provence Festival (La Clemenza di Tito), Metropolitan Opera (Il Trovatore), Royal Opera House, Stockholm (La Traviata), Royal Opera House, Covent Garden (La Bohème); concert performances of Verdi's Requiem at Théâtre de la Wallonie, St Petersburg Philharmonie, Tchaikovsky Hall, Moscow, Monte Carlo. *Recordings include:* Rossini's La donna del lago 2007, Donizetti's Parisina 2009, Rossini's Ermione (Gramophone Award for Best Opera Recording 2011) 2010, Bellini's Il Pirata 2012. *Honours:* First Prize and Audience Award, Plácido Domingo's Operalia Competition, Paris 2002. *Current Management:* Opera Art, Via Isolalta-Forette 11, 37068 Vigasio (VR), Italy. *Telephone:* (45) 6649911. *E-mail:* info@operaart.it. *Website:* www .carmengiannattasio.com (office).

GIBAULT, Claire; French conductor; b. 31 Oct. 1945, Le Mans; d. of Louis and Suzanne Gibault. *Education:* Conservatoire du Mans and Conservatoire Nat. Supérieur de Paris. *Career:* at Opéra de Lyon 1971–74, Conductor 1990–; fmr Dir Office de Radiodiffusion-Télévision Française (ORTF) Orchestra, Orchestre du Conservatoire de Paris, and Toulouse, Angers, Nantes and Mulhouse orchestras; Dir Opéra de Chambéry; conductor at concerts in France and abroad, and with orchestras including Orchestre de la Suisse Romande, Monte-Carlo, Nice-Provence-Côte-d'Azur, Turin, Rome, Lausanne, Brussels, Québec and San Francisco orchestras, at Royal Opera House, Covent Garden, London, Berlin Philharmonic Orchestra (first woman conductor) etc. *Works conducted include:* The Magic Flute 1974, 1994, L'enlèvement au sérail 1987, Pelléas et Mélisande 1993, La station thermale (world première) 1995; numerous contemporary works. *Recordings:* Les mariés de la Tour Eiffel 1990, Les Brigands d'Offenbach (laser video). *Honours:* Chevalier de l'Ordre Nat. du Mérite; Prix de la Fondation de la Vocation 1969 and numerous prizes from Conservatoire du Mans and Conservatoire Nat. Supérieur de Paris. *Current Management:* c/o Owen/ White Management, Flat 6, 22 Brunswick Terrace, Hove, East Sussex BN3 1HJ, England. *Telephone:* (1273) 727127. *Fax:* (1273) 527038. *E-mail:* info@ owenwhitemanagement.com. *Website:* www.owenwhitemanagement.com.

GIBBONS, Jack; British pianist; b. 2 March 1962. *Career:* London solo debut 1979; numerous solo and concert appearances from the age of 10; annual solo concert at QEH, London since 1990; performances at Barbican, London, Symphony Hall, Birmingham, New York and Washington, DC debuts 1994; debut, Lincoln Center, New York 1997; numerous appearances on BBC radio, television and Classic FM radio, and with various orchestras. *Compositions include:* solo piano arrangements of Gershwin's concert works and overtures, and transcriptions of Gershwin's original piano improvisations from recordings and piano-rolls. *Recordings include:* The Authentic George Gershwin vols 1, 2, 3 and 4, Alkan's Complete Opus 39 Etudes vols 1 and 2, Lambert's Rio Grande with English Northern Philharmonia Orchestra, Opera North, conductor David Lloyd-Jones. *Honours:* First Prize, Newport Int. Pianoforte Competition 1982, MRA Award for best solo instrumental recording (for The Authentic George Gershwin) 1993. *E-mail:* management@jackgibbons.com. *Website:* www.jackgibbons.com.

GIBSON, Jon Charles; American flautist, saxophonist and composer; b. 11 March 1940, Los Angeles, CA. *Education:* Sacramento and San Francisco State Univs. *Career:* co-founder, New Music Ensemble 1961; associated with minimalist group of composers, including participation in the premiere of Terry Riley's In C 1964; mem., Philip Glass Ensemble 1968; visual arts involved in compositions, some of which written for dancers; solo appearances as instrumentalist in the USA and Europe. *Compositions include:* opera: Voyage of the Beagle 1985, Who Are You for vocal and tape delay, Visitations: An Environment Soundscape and Radioland for tape 1966–72, Instrumental: Multiples 1972, Song I–IV 1972–79, Melody I–IV 1973–75, Cycles for organ 1973, Recycle I and II 1977, Call 1978, Return and Variations both for small ensemble 1979–80, Extensions (dance score) 1980, Relative Calm (dance score) for small ensemble and tape 1981, Interval for video tape 1985, Southern Climes for ensemble 1993, Chorales from Relative Calm for

ensemble 1993, Chrome 1995, Lines for ensemble 1996, Unfinished Business I for small ensemble 1997, A Rose It Isn't for solo instrument 1997. *Recordings include:* Einstein On The Beach (with the Philip Glass Ensemble). *Honours:* Creative Artist Public Service Program grant 1974, 1981, Rockefeller Foundation grant 1982.

GIEBEL, Agnes; German singer (soprano); b. 10 Aug. 1921, Heerlen, Netherlands; m. Herbert Kanders; one s. two d. *Education:* Folkwang-Schule Essen with Hilde Wesselmann. *Career:* gave first public concert 1933 with Lieder by Strauss and Reger; career from 1947 giving numerous concerts and recitals in Europe and North America; Bach Cantatas series with Karl Ristenpart for Berlin Radio 1950–51; church concerts in Cologne until 1982, duet concert there 1989; repertoire included 20th-century works, Mozart arias and baroque music. *Recordings include:* Bach's Christmas Oratorio; St Matthew Passion; St John Passion; Beethoven's Missa Solemnis; Die Schöpfung; Bach Cantatas; Ein Deutsches Requiem; Song recitals, and album with Hermann Prey and Celibidache.

GIELEN, Michael Andreas; Austrian fmr conductor and composer; b. 20 July 1927, Dresden, Germany; s. of Josef Gielen; m. Helga Augsten 1957; one s. one d. *Education:* Univ. of Buenos Aires, studied composition under E. Leuchter and J. Polnauer. *Career:* early career as pianist in Buenos Aires; on music staff, Teatro Colón 1947–50; with Vienna State Opera 1951–60, Perm. Conductor 1954–60; First Conductor, Royal Swedish Opera, Stockholm 1960–65; conductor and composer in Cologne 1965–69; Musical Dir Nat. Orchestra of Belgium 1969–73; Chief Conductor, Netherlands Opera 1973–75; Music Dir and Gen. Man. Frankfurt Opera House 1977–87; Music Dir Cincinnati Symphony 1980–86; Prin. Conductor, SWF Radio Orchestra, Baden-Baden 1986–99, Hon. Conductor 2002–; Prof. of Conducting, Mozarteum, Salzburg 1987–95, Prof. Emer. 1995–; Chief Guest Conductor, BBC Symphony Orchestra 1979–82; Perm. Guest Conductor, Berlin State Opera and Berlin Symphony Orchestra 1998. *Compositions include:* Au vieux souvenirs (string quartet) 1983. *Recordings:* as conductor: Schöenberg, Moses und Aron, Gurre-Lieder, complete Beethoven symphonies, complete Mahler symphonies. *Publications:* Mahler im Gesprach 2002, Unbedingt Musik (autobiog.) 2005. *Honours:* Dr hc (Berlin Hochschule der Künste) 2000; State Prize, Hessen 1985, Adorno Prize, Frankfurt 1986, Vienna Music Prize 1997, Frankfurt Music Prize 1999, MIDEM Prize for Lifetime Achievement 2002, Der Faust Prize for Lifetime Achievement 2007, ECHO Klassik Prize 2008, Ernst von Siemens Music Foundation Music Award 2010. *Address:* Niedersee 49, 5311, Innerschwand am Mondsee, Austria (home). *Telephone:* (6232) 2082 (home).

GIERHARDT, Heike; German singer (soprano); b. 8 Aug. 1964, Frankfurt. *Education:* Frankfurt Musikhochschule. *Career:* sang at the Mannheim Opera 1987–92; Essen from 1992; roles have included Nicolai's Frau Fluth, Mozart's Constanze, Donna Anna, Pamina and Fiordiligi; Marenka in The Bartered Bride, Freia in Das Rheingold and Saffi in Der Zigeunerbaron; guest engagements at Dresden, Frankfurt, Dortmund and Weimar; season 1998 as Mme Lidoine in Les Dialogues des Carmélites at Essen; season 1999 as the Empress in Die Frau ohne Schatten at Essen and Barcelona; numerous concert appearances.

GIERLACH, Robert; Polish singer (bass-baritone); b. 1965. *Education:* Chopin Conservatoire, Warsaw. *Career:* appearances in title role of Szymanowski's King Roger at Carnegie and Festival Halls and at Salzburg Festival; Rossini's Basilio and Alidoro for Rome Opera; Mozart's Count in Venice and Trieste, Faraone in Rossini's Mosè in Egitto at Verona, Don Giovanni at Amsterdam and Don Profondo in Il Viaggio a Reims at Bologna; Stravinsky's Oedipus Rex (as Creon) in Paris, and Pulcinella; Mozart's Figaro at Glyndebourne (debut, 2001), Florida, Geneva and Detroit. *Honours:* Winner, Viotti Contest at Vercelli and Alfredo Kraus Competition, Las Palmas. *Current Management:* Pinnacle Arts Management, Uzan Division, 889 Ninth Avenue, 2nd Floor, New York, NY 10019, USA. *Telephone:* (212) 397-7926. *Fax:* (212) 397-7920. *E-mail:* yuzan@pinnaclearts.com. *Website:* www .pinnaclearts.com.

GIERZOD, Kazimierz; Polish pianist; *Professor, The Fryderyk Chopin University of Music;* b. 6 Aug. 1936, Warsaw; m. Jolanta Zegadlo 1974. *Education:* The Fryderyk Chopin Univ. of Music, Warsaw, with Prof. Margerita Trombini-Kazuro, Accad. Chigiana, Siena, Italy with Prof. Guido Agosti. *Career:* regular recitals and concerts in Europe, Canada, China, Cyprus, Japan, USA, S America, Australia and Kuwait from 1964; tutor, The Fryderyk Chopin Univ. of Music, Warsaw 1969–73, Asst Prof 1973–86, Prof. 1986–, Dean of Piano Dept 1975–87, elected Rector of Acad. 1987, 1990–93; lectures on musical interpretation, masterclasses in Poland, Japan, South Korea, USA, Venezuela, Cyprus, China, Germany, Taiwan and Lithuania; radio and TV commentator during Int. Frederic Chopin Piano Competition, Warsaw 1985, 1990; radio and TV interviews and interviews for local and foreign press; Visiting Prof., Soai Univ., Osaka, Japan 1988–; Chief of Piano Chair 1999–2006; mem. Jury of Piano Competition, Europe, Japan and Venezuela; Pres. Frederic Chopin Int. Foundation, Warsaw, Poland 1992–98; Vice-Pres. Frederic Chopin Soc., Warsaw 1997, Pres. 2002–. *Recordings:* archival recordings for Polish radio of Polish music, recordings for American, Cypriot, Polish and Japanese radio and television, album released in Poland and Germany. *Publications:* numerous articles in music journals, including Ruch Muzyczny. *Honours:* Officer's Cross, Order of Polonia Restituta 2002; First Prize, Gdansk Piano Competition 1964, Ministry of Culture Medals for

Artistic and Pedagogic Achievements. *Address:* The Fryderyk Chopin University of Music, 2 Okolnik str., 00-368 Warsaw (office); ul Sygietynskiego 36, 05-805 Otrebusy, Poland (home). *Fax:* (22) 8278308 (office); (22) 7585562 (home). www.chopin.edu.pl (office).

GIETZ, Gordon; Canadian singer (tenor); b. 1968. *Education:* studied in Calgary, Toronto and New York. *Career:* Artist-in-Residence with Opéra de Montréal; sang Don Ottavio in Don Giovanni, Opéra National de Paris; Števa in Jenůfa, Grand Théâtre de Genève; Tamino in Die Zauberflöte, De Nederlandse Opera; Idamante in Idomeneo, Chevalier in Dialgoues des Carmélites and Benedict in Beatrice and Benedict, all with Santa Fe Opera; Sam Polk in Susannah, Grand Théâtre de Genève; Tom Rakewell in The Rake's Progress, Edmonton Opera, Duke in Rigoletto, Hennessy Opera, Beijing and Hanoi; Fenton in Falstaff, New York City Opera; Alfredo in La Traviata, Opera Company of Philadelphia; Hoffmann in Les Contes d'Hoffmann and Tamino in Die Zauberflöte, l'Opéra de Montréal; Roméo in Roméo et Juliette, Western Australia Opera; Danceny in Dangerous Liaisons, Washington Opera; Recent concert engagements: Sang Števa in Jenůfa, Philadelphia Orchestra, Carnegie Hall; Das Lied von der Erde, Mainly Mozart Festival; Klaus-Narr, Gurre lieder, Ravinia Festival; Beethoven's Ninth Symphony, Houston Symphony and at BBC Proms, Royal Albert Hall; Jacquino in Fidelio, New York Philharmonic; Schubert's Mass in E Flat, Philadelphia Orchestra; Mahler's Eighth Symphony, Winnipeg Symphony; Frère Massée in Saint François d'Assise, VARA Radio Orchestra, Concertgebouw; season 2000–01 as Lysander in Britten's A Midsummer Night's Dream, Glyndebourne Festival Opera; Carmina Burana, Tanglewood Festival; engaged to sing Jack in The Midsummer Marriage, Royal Opera House, Covent Garden; Valinace in Arshak II, San Francisco Opera; Števa in Jenůfa, Théâtre du Châtelet; Camille in Thérèse Raquin, Dallas Opera; Rinuccio in Gianni Schicchi, De Vlaamse Opera; Duke in Rigoletto, Edmonton Opera; Covent Garden debut as Stingo in the premiere of Sophie's Choice, 2002. *Recordings include:* L'Enfance du Christ and Berlioz's Lelio; Les Mamelles de Tirésias. *Current Management:* IMG Artists, Carnegie Hall Tower, 152 West 57th Street, 5th Floor, New York, NY 10019, USA. *Telephone:* (410) 480-2095. *Fax:* (410) 994-3550. *E-mail:* apybus@imgartists.com. *Website:* www.imgartists.com; www.gordongietz.com.

GIFFORD, Anthea; British classical guitarist; b. 17 Feb. 1949, Bristol, England; m. John Trusler 1970; one s. one d. *Education:* Accademia Musicale Chigiana, Siena, Italy, Royal College of Music, London. *Career:* debut, Purcell Room, London; Many solo recitals and over 30 programmes on BBC Radio 3 with violinist, Jean-Jacques Kantorow; Recitals at the Purcell Room, Wigmore Hall, Fairfield Hall, Barbican Centre, Queen Elizabeth and Festival Halls; Television appearances on Channel 4, BBC 2, and TSW among others, frequent chamber music recitals with Delmé String Quartet and adjudicator for Overseas League; Performances in Italy, France, Spain and Germany; Director of Droffig Recordings; mem, Incorporated Society of Musicians; Overseas League. *Recordings:* Paganini and his Contemporaries by Kantorow-Gifford Duo, 1991; Solo Recital, 1991; Paganini Ensemble, 1991; Kantorow-Gifford Violin and Guitar Duos, 1993; Dodgson Duo Concerto with Northern Sinfonia, 1994. *Publications:* contrib. to Guitar International. *Honours:* Young Musician of the Year, Greater London Arts Association Award.

GIFFORD, Helen, BMus; Australian composer; b. 5 Sept. 1935, Melbourne. *Education:* Melbourne Univ. Conservatorium of Music. *Career:* Composer-in-Residence, Melbourne Theatre Co. 1970–; commissions from Melbourne Chorale, Astra Chamber Music Soc., Australian Broadcasting Comm., Australian Percussion Ensemble. *Compositions include:* chamber music: Fantasy for flute and piano 1958, Skiagram for flute, viola and vibraphone 1963, String Quartet 1965, Canzone for chamber orchestra 1968, Sonnet for flute, guitar and harpsichord 1969, Overture for chamber orchestra 1970, Images for Christmas for speaker, electric guitar, small organ with percussion, celesta and effects for five players 1973, Point of Ignition for mezzo and orchestra 1997, The Western Front, World War I for choir and ensemble 1999; piano: Piano Sonata 1960, Waltz 1966, Cantillation 1966; orchestral: Phantasma for string orchestra 1963, Imperium 1969; vocal/choral: As Dew in Aprille, Christmas carol for boy or female soprano, piano or harp or guitar 1955, Vigil a cappella 1966, Bird Calls from an Old Land for five soprano soloists and a cappella female choir 1971; brass: Company of Brass for ensemble 1972; theatre: incidental music and songs, Jo Being (one-act opera) 1974, music for the Adonia theatre 1992. *Current Management:* Australian Music Centre, PO Box N690, Grosvenor Place, Sydney, NSW 1220, Australia. *E-mail:* info@australianmusiccentre.com.au. *Website:* www.australianmusiccentre.com.au/artist/gifford-helen.

GILAD, Jonathan; French pianist; b. 1981, Marseille. *Education:* Marseille Conservatory, studied with Dimitri Bashkirov in Colmar and Madrid. *Career:* concerts with the Israel Philharmonic under Zubin Mehta, Monte Carlo Philharmonic Orchestra, The Ulster Orchestra and Lausanne Chamber Orchestra; US debut, 1996 with the Chicago Symphony Orchestra, returned 1997 with the Chopin E minor Concerto; Berlin recital debut, 1988; season 1998–99 included USA tour with the St Petersburg Philharmonic Orchestra; Boston Symphony Orchestra concerts, appearances with the Israel Philharmonic Orchestra and at the Maggio Musicale, Florence; Schumann Concerto with the Chicago Symphony Orchestra in Berlin under Daniel Barenboim; Wigmore Hall debut 2000. *Recordings include:* numerous including Mendelssohn's Piano Trios (with Julia Fischer and Daniel Müller-Schott) 2006.

Honours: Prizes at Paris Mozart Competition 1991, Salzburg Mozarteum Competition 1992. *Address:* Münchner Konzertdirektion Hörtnagel Berlin GmbH, PO Box 860520, 81632 Berlin, Germany.

GILBERT, Alan; American conductor; *Music Director, New York Philharmonic;* b. 23 Feb. 1967, New York; s. of Michael Gilbert and Yoko Takebe; m. Kajsa William-Olsson; two c. *Education:* Fieldston School, Harvard Univ., Curtis Inst. of Music, Juilliard School. *Career:* Chief Conductor and Artistic Adviser, Royal Stockholm Philharmonic Orchestra 1999–2008; Music Dir, Santa Fe Opera 2003–07; Principal Guest Conductor, NDR Hamburg Symphony Orchestra 2003–; Music Dir New York Philharmonic 2009–; guest conducting engagements include performances with the Bayerischer Rundfunk, Orchestre de Paris, Tonhalle, New York Philharmonic, Los Angeles Philharmonic, NHK Symphony, Royal Concertgebouw Orchestra debut 2003, BBC Proms debut with the Mahler Chamber Orchestra 2003, debut with Zurich Opera 2003, with Deutsches Symphonie-Orchester 2006, with Vienna State Opera 2007. *Honours:* First Prize in the Int. Competition for Musical Performance, Geneva 1994, Seaver/Nat. Endowment for the Arts Conductors Award 1997. *Current Management:* c/o Alec C. Treuhaft, IMG Artists, Carnegie Hall Tower, 152 West 57th Street, 5th Floor, New York, NY 10019, USA. *Telephone:* (212) 994-3500. *Fax:* (212) 994-3550. *E-mail:* atreuhaft@imgartists.com. *Website:* www.imgartists.com; nyphil.org.

GILBERT, Anthony, MA, DMus; British composer; b. 26 July 1934, London, England; s. of Joseph William John Gilbert and Doreen Vera Gilbert; two s. one d. *Education:* Morley Coll., London, studied composition with Anthony Milner, Mátyás Seiber, Alexander Goehr, conducting with Lawrence Leonard; additional studies with Gunther Schuller, Tanglewood; Univ. of Leeds. *Career:* House Ed., Contemporary Music, Schott & Co. Ltd 1965–70; Lecturer in Composition, Goldsmiths' Coll., London 1968–73; Composer-in-Residence, Lancaster Univ. 1970–71; Lecturer in Composition, Morley Coll. 1972–75; Sr Lecturer in Composition, Sydney Conservatorium, Australia 1978–79; Composer-in-Residence, City of Bendigo, Vic. 1981; Head of School of Composition and Contemporary Music, Royal Northern Coll. of Music, Manchester –1999; mem. Performing Right Soc., Mechanical Copyright Protection Soc., Inc. Soc. of Musicians. *Compositions include:* operas: The Scene-Machine 1971, The Chakravaka-Bird 1977; orchestral: Symphony, Sinfonia, Ghost and Dream Dancing, Crow Cry, Towards Asavari, On Beholding a Rainbow violin concerto 1997, Another Dream Carousel, Sheer, Palace of the Winds, Groove, Perchants 2007, Triptych 2014; for wind orchestra: Dream Carousels; chamber: five string quartets, String Trio 2008, Haven of Mysteries for string quintet 2014, Saxophone Quartet, Quartet of Beasts, Nine or Ten Osannas, Vasanta with Dancing; instrumental: Ziggurat, Reflexions, Rose Nord, Moonfaring, Dawnfaring, three piano sonatas, Spell Respell, The Incredible Flute Music, Treatment of Silence, Osanna for Lady O, Rapprochement; vocal: Certain Lights Reflecting, Love Poems, Inscapes, Long White Moonlight, Beastly Jingles, Ondine, Vers de Lune 1999, Encantos, En Bateau d'après Watteau, Those Fenny Bells; music theatre: Upstream River Rewa 1991; choir: Handles to the Invisible for chorus 1995. *Recordings include:* Beastly Jingles, Towards Asavari, Igorochki, Quartet of Beasts, Six of the Bestiary, Farings. *Honours:* Hon. FRNCM 1981. *E-mail:* gilbertcomp@btinternet.com. *Website:* www.anthonygilbert.net (home).

GILBERT, Kenneth Albert, OC, DMus, FRCM, FRSC; Canadian/Austrian harpsichordist, organist and academic; *Adjunct Professor of Harpsichord and Organ, Faculty of Music, McGill University;* b. 16 Dec. 1931, Montreal; s. of Albert George Gilbert and Reta Mabel (née Welch). *Education:* Conservatoire de Musique, Montréal and Conservatoire Nat. Supérieur de Musique, France. *Career:* Prof., Conservatoire de Musique, Montreal 1965–72; Assoc. Prof., Laval Univ., Québec 1970–76; Guest Prof., Royal Antwerp Conservatory, Belgium 1971–73; Dir Early Music Dept Conservatoire de Strasbourg, France 1981–85; Prof., Staatliche Hochschule für Musik, Stuttgart, Germany 1981–89, Paris Conservatoire 1988–96; Prof., Hochschule Mozarteum, Salzburg, Austria 1984–2000, Prof. Emer. 2000–; Adjunct Prof. of Harpsichord and Organ, McGill Univ., Montreal 1998–; Visiting Prof., RAM and Royal Coll. of Music, London; instructor at other music acads, summer schools etc.; Pres. Editions de l'Oiseau-Lyre, Monaco 2001–12. *Recordings include:* complete harpsichord works of F. Couperin, Scarlatti and Rameau, Suites and Partitas of J.S. Bach, Well-Tempered Clavier and Concertos for 2, 3 and 4 Harpsichords by Bach. *Publications:* editions of complete harpsichord works of Couperin, Scarlatti and Rameau, Bach's Goldberg Variations, Frescobaldi Toccatas, Kapsberger's lute works transcribed for harpsichord. *Honours:* Hon. RAM; Hon. FRCO; Officier des Arts et des Lettres, Cross of Honour 1st Class (Austria); Hon. DMus (McGill), (Melbourne), (Laval); Fellowships from Canada Council 1968, 1974, and Calouste Gulbenkian Foundation 1971, Prix Opus Québec 2006. *Address:* Strathcona Music Building, 555 West Sherbrooke Street, Montreal, PQ H3A 1E3, Canada (office). *E-mail:* kenneth.gilbert@mcgill.ca (office). *Website:* www.mcgill.ca/music (office).

GILCHRIST, Diana; Canadian singer (soprano); b. 1970, Edmonton, Alberta; m. Shelley Katz. *Education:* Carleton Univ., Banff School of Fine Arts, private vocal studies in Los Angeles with Seth Riggs and then in New York with Robert Leonard. *Career:* sang at Koblenz Opera from 1989, notably as Susanna, Janáček's Vixen and Gilda; sang Mozart's Blondchen with Mainz Opera, followed by Zerbinetta; Bielefeld 1991 as Grétry's Zemire, Vienna Volksoper 1992 as the Queen of Night, returning as Offenbach's Olympia; concerts in Canada and Germany include Orff's Carmina Burana; Founder, Opera Lyra, Ottawa, served four years as Artistic Dir; Musicians-in-Residence (with husband), Bader International Study Centre, Queen's Univ. 1997–. *E-mail:* s.katz@mac.com. *Website:* dianagilchrist.com.

GILCHRIST, James; British singer (tenor); b. 1970. *Education:* chorister New Coll., Oxford, choral scholar King's Coll., Cambridge. *Career:* began career in medicine; full-time singer 1996–; concerts include Haydn's Creation at the QEH, London, Elijah at St David's Cathedral, Solomon in Buxton and Mozart's Requiem at the Barbican with the English Chamber Orchestra; engagements with the King's Concert in Purcell Odes at the Wigmore Hall, and Bach's B minor Mass at the QEH 2000; Messiah in Oslo, Bach's Magnificat with The Sixteen in Spain and the Christmas Oratorio in Italy; opera includes Mozart's Ferrando and Strauss's Scaramuccio, under Richard Hickox, and Gomatz in Mozart's Zaide in Istanbul; season 2000–01 with the Britten War Requiem in King's Coll. Chapel, Monteverdi Vespers and Messiah with The Sixteen, Bach Passions with the Australian Chamber Orchestra and various Bach touring projects, notably with the Monteverdi Choir and Orchestra. *Current Management:* c/o Sue Nicholls, Hazard Chase, 25 City Road, Cambridge, CB1 1DP, England. *Telephone:* (1223) 312400. *Fax:* (1223) 460827. *E-mail:* sue.nicholls@hazardchase.co.uk. *Website:* www.hazardchase .co.uk; www.jamesgilchrist.co.uk.

GILES, Alice; Australian concert harpist; b. 9 May 1961, Adelaide. *Education:* studied with June Loney and Alice Chalifoux. *Career:* extensive concert performances in Australia, the USA, Israel and Germany; festival engagements at Schleswig-Holstein, Bayreuth (International Youth Festival) and Düsseldorf New Music Festivals, Adelaide (Britten's Canticles with Barry Tuckwell and Gerald English), Sydney, Marlboro Music Festival (USA), and Bath Mozartfest; New York Merkin Hall debut, 1983, 92nd Street 'Y' Concert, 1988; Wigmore Hall debut, June 1989, and tour with Luciano Berio; Featured Soloist at festivals including Salzedo Centennial, Austin, Texas, World Harp Congress, Copenhagen, and World Harp Festival, Cardiff, Wales; Frankfurt Hochschule, 1990–98; School of Music at Canberra, Australia, 1999–; Concertos with Collegium Musicum Zürich, Badische Staatskapelle Karlsruhe, English Symphony Orchestra, all major symphony orchestras in Australia and tour of North and South America with Australian Youth Orchestra; Chamber concerts with violinist Thomas Zehetmair and pianist Arnan Wiesel; mem, Co-Founder, Director, EOLUS–International Salzedo Society. *Recordings include:* Recital, Fauré's Impromptu in D flat major, 2 Preludes of Debussy, Tournier's 2nd Sonatine, 5 Preludes of Salzedo; Recital of works for solo harp by Carlos Salzedo; Chamber music for flute and harp with Geoffrey Collins, flute. *Honours:* Churchill International Fellowship, 1980; Winner, International Harp Competition, Israel, 1982. *Current Management:* Arts Management Pty Ltd., Level 1, 405 Elizabeth Street, Surry Hills, Sydney, NSW 2010, Australia. *Telephone:* (2) 9211-9422. *Fax:* (2) 9211-9466. *E-mail:* enquiries@artsmanagement.com.au. *Website:* www .artsmanagement.com.au; www.ganyarharps.com.au.

GILFRY, Rodney; American singer (baritone); b. 11 March 1959, California. *Career:* sang in opera at Los Angeles as Guglielmo, Mozart's Figaro, the Villains in Contes d'Hoffmann and Ford in Falstaff, 1990; European engagements as Figaro at Hamburg, Tel-Aviv and Zürich; Frankfurt Opera from 1989, as Gounod's Mercutio, Ernesto (Il Pirata) and Massenet's Herod; Lescaut in Manon Geneva 1988; US premiere of Oedipus by Rihm, Santa Fe 1991; concert engagements include Bach's B minor Mass in Paris and at La Scala, Milan; season 1992 as Guglielmo in Barcelona and at the Holland Festival, Don Giovanni at the Opéra de Lyon; sang Sharpless in Butterfly at Los Angeles 1996; Guglielmo at Covent Garden 1997; Met debut as Demetrius in A Midsummer Nights Dream 1997; season 1998 as the Count in Capriccio at Glyndebourne and Stanley in the premiere of Previn's A Streetcar Named Desire at San Francisco; season 2000–01 as Billy Budd and Dandini at Los Angeles, Valentin in Faust at Munich and Guglielmo for the New York Met; Nathan in the premiere of Sophie's Choice, Covent Garden 2002, Edward Gaines in Margaret Garner, Opera Co. of Philadelphia, Cincinnati Opera and Michigan Opera Theatre 2005–06, Prospero in The Tempest, Santa Fe Opera 2006, Falke in Japanese tour of Die Fledermaus 2008, as Lancelot in Camelot 2009, as Emile de Becque in South Pacific 2009. *Recordings:* Ein Deutsches Requiem; Così fan tutte. *Current Management:* Robert Lombardo and Associates, 61 West 62nd Street, Suite 6F, New York, NY 10023, USA. *Telephone:* (212) 586-4453. *Fax:* (212) 581-5771. *E-mail:* Robert@ RobertLombardo.com. *Website:* www.rlombardo.com. *E-mail:* rod@rodgilfry .com (home). *Website:* www.rodgilfry.com (home).

GILHOOLY, John, OBE, BA; Irish music administrator; *Director, Wigmore Hall;* b. 15 Aug. 1973, Castleconnell, Co. Limerick; s. of Owen Gilhooly and Helen Conway. *Education:* Univ. Coll. Dublin, Dublin City Coll. of Music and Leinster School of Music and Drama. *Career:* fmr history teacher, Univ. Coll. Dublin; man. positions include with Harrogate Int. Centre, ExCel in Docklands, London, Univ. Coll. Dublin Admin and Services Dept; Exec. Dir Wigmore Hall, London 2000–05, acting Artistic Dir 2005, now has overall title of Dir 2005–; Chair. Royal Philharmonic Soc. 2010–; has appeared as a tenor soloist on TV and radio in Ireland; fmrly presented radio programmes for Lyric FM, Ireland. *Publications:* A History of Castleconnell 1988, A History of Woodland House 1990. *Address:* Wigmore Hall, 36 Wigmore Street, London, W1U 2BP, England (office). *Telephone:* (20) 7258-8200 (office). *Fax:* (20) 7258-8201 (office). *E-mail:* info@wigmore-hall.org.uk (office). *Website:* www .wigmore-hall.org.uk (office).

GILL, Timothy; British cellist; b. 1960, England. *Career:* co-founder, Chagall Piano Trio at the Banff Centre for the Arts in Canada, resident artist; debut concert at the Blackheath Concert Halls in London 1991; further appearances at the Barbican's Prokofiev Centenary Festival, the Warwick Festival and the South Place Sunday Concerts at the Conway Hall in London; Purcell Room London recitals 1993 with the London premiere of piano trios by Tristan Keuris, Nicholas Maw and Ethel Smyth (composed 1880); premiere of Piano Trio No. 2 by David Matthews at the Norfolk and Norwich Festival 1993; Malvern Festival 1994.

GILLES, Marie-Louise; German singer (mezzo-soprano); b. 1937, Duren. *Education:* Folkwang-Hochschule Essen with Hilde Wesselmann. *Career:* Wiesbaden Opera from 1962 as Octavian, Dorabella and the Composer in Ariadne auf Naxos; Staatsoper Munich, 1964–66, Bremen, 1966–68 and from 1968 at Hannover notably as Azucena, Brangaene, Eboli, Waltraute, Fricka, Ortrud, Berg's Marie and Countess Geschwitz, and Santuzza; Bayreuth Festival, 1968–69, appearances at the Dubrovnik and Salzburg Easter festivals and concert engagements in Washington, New York, Vienna, Paris and Lisbon; Prof., Hannover Musikhochschule from 1982. *Recordings:* Petite Messe Solennelle by Rossini; Bach Cantatas; Hans Heiling by Marschner. *Address:* Hochschule für Musik und Theater, Emmichplatz 1, 3 Hannover, Germany.

GILLESPIE, Neil; British singer (tenor); b. 1968, Glasgow, Scotland. *Education:* Royal Scottish Acad. with Duncan Robertson, Britten-Pears School and European Centre for Opera and Vocal Studies, Belgium, studied with Nicolai Gedda. *Career:* appearances with Opéra de Lyon, New Israeli Opera and ENO; Royal Opera, Covent Garden in Mathis der Maler by Hindemith, Verdi's Il Corsaro, Luisa Miller, Paul Bunyan and The Pilgrim's Progress; Giuseppe in La Traviata 2001; other roles include Bacchus in The Olympians by Bliss, Rossini's Almaviva, Tamino, and Sailor in Dido and Aeneas.

GILLESPIE, Rhondda Marie, BMus; British concert pianist; b. 3 Aug. 1941, Sydney, Australia; d. of David Gillespie and Marie Gillespie; m. Denby Richards 1972. *Education:* NSW Conservatorium with Alexander Sverjensky and in London with Louis Kentner and Denis Matthews. *Career:* debut on Australian radio aged eight 1949; first public recital 1953; winner NSW Concerto Competition, Sydney 1959; European debut in London with Tchaikovsky Piano Concerto No. 2 1960; since then has played with major orchestras throughout UK, Netherlands, Germany, Scandinavia, Far East and USA and made many festival appearances. *Address:* 50 Collinswood Drive, St Leonards-on-Sea, East Sussex, TN38 0NX, England (home). *Telephone:* (1424) 715167 (home). *Fax:* (1424) 712214 (office). *E-mail:* rhonmus@aol.com (home).

GILLESPIE, Wendy, BA; American viola player and academic; b. 1950, New York. *Education:* Wellesley Coll. *Career:* mem. Fretwork with first London concert at Wigmore Hall 1986; appearances in Renaissance and Baroque repertoire across Europe; tour of Russia 1989 and Japan 1991; festival engagements in UK; repertory includes In Nomines and Fantasias by Tallis, Parsons and Byrd, dance music by Holborne and Dowland, including Lachrimae, six-part consorts by Gibbons and William Lawes, songs and instrumental works by Purcell; collaborations with vocal group, Red Byrd in verse anthems by Byrd and Tomkins, London Cries by Gibbons and Dering, Resurrection Story and Seven Last Words by Schütz; gave George Benjamin's Upon Silence at QEH 1990; Wigmore Hall concerts 1990–91, with music by Lawes, Purcell, Locke, Dowland and Byrd; currently Prof. of Music (Viola da gamba) and Chair, Early Music Dept, Jacobs School of Music, Indiana Univ.; fmr Pres. Viola da Gamba Soc. of America; mem. Higher Educ. Cttee, Early Music America. *Recordings include:* Heart's Ease, late Tudor and early Stuart; Armada, courts of Philip II and Elizabeth II; Night's Black Bird by Dowland and Byrd; Cries And Fancies (fantasias, In Nomines and The Cries Of London by Gibbons); Go Nightly Cares, consort songs, dances and In Nomines. *Honours:* Early Music America's Thomas Binkley Award 2011, Alumnae Achievement Award, Wellesley Coll. 2012. *Address:* Merrill Hall, MU210, 1201 East Third Street, Bloomington, IN 47405, USA. *Telephone:* (812) 855-7594. *E-mail:* wendygil@indiana.edu. *Website:* music.indiana.edu/ departments/academic/early-music.

GILLETT, Christopher, MA; British singer (tenor), writer and director; b. 16 May 1958, London, England; s. of Sir Robin Gillett, Bt and Lady Elizabeth Gillett (née Findlay); m. 1st Julia Holmes 1984 (divorced 1996); one s. one d.; m. 2nd Lucy Schaufer 1996. *Education:* studied at King's Coll., Cambridge, Royal Coll. of Music with Robert Tear and Edgar Evans, Nat. Opera Studio, London. *Career:* debut at Sadler's Wells as Edwin in The Gypsy Princess 1981; sang with New Sadler's Wells Opera in Gilbert and Sullivan; has appeared with Glyndebourne Touring Opera as Ferrando and Albert Herring; Hermes in King Priam for Kent Opera; Royal Opera House Covent Garden from 1984 as Flute in A Midsummer Night's Dream, Roderigo in Otello, Dov in Knot Garden, Pang and Hermes and in Parsifal, Un Re in Ascolto and Idomeneo; Nooni in The Making of the Representative for Planet 8 by Glass at London Coliseum, Amsterdam; season 1990–91 with Martyrdom of St Magnus by Maxwell Davies, London, Glasgow; Mozart's Ferrando at Garsington Manor and Arbace with English Bach Festival at Covent Garden, Vichy Festival, France; Pysander in Netherlands Opera Ulysses; sang Musil in premiere of Broken Strings by Param Vir, Amsterdam 1992; Tichon in Katya Kabanova for Glyndebourne Touring Opera and Britten's Flute at the 1992 Aix-en-

Provence Festival; concert engagements include Tippett's Mask of Time with Hallé; Bach's St John Passion in Hong Kong, King's Coll., Cambridge, Greenwich, and Elijah with Bach Choir 1995, world premiere of A King Riding at La Monnaie Brussels 1996, ENO, Netherlands Opera; season 1997 with Britten's Flute and Pirzel in Die Soldaten for ENO and M Triquet for Netherlands Opera; season 1999 as Britten's Flute, Rome Opera and in premiere of Rêves d'un Marco Polo by Claude Vivier at Amsterdam; Oliver Knussen's Where the Wild Things Are and Higglety, Pigglety, Pop! at BBC Proms, London 2002; since 2002: Netherlands Opera (200 performances), ENO (The Trojans, Sir John in Love, Figaro, Poppea, Madam Butterfly, Dr Atomic), Teatre Liceu, Barcelona, Teatro Real, Madrid, Los Angeles Opera, Montpellier Opera, Suntory Tokyo (world premiere Tan Dun's TEA), Brooklyn Acad. of Music, La Scala, Milan, Covent Garden, Teatro Petruzzelli, Bari, Teatro Reggio Emilia, Theater An Der Wien; concerts with London Symphony Orchestra, Bach Choir (Evangelist, St Matthew Passion 2000–07), London Sinfonietta (Henze's Voices at 2006 Proms), Philharmonia, Royal Philharmonic Orchestra, London Philharmonic Orchestra, English Chamber Orchestra, Royal Scottish Nat. Orchestra, BBC Symphony Orchestra, Cleveland Orchestra, Berlin Philharmonic, Michael Nyman Band, Schoenberg Ensemble, Philadelphia Orchestra, CBSO, Berlin Radio Orchestra, Les Journées Ravel, Kymi Sinfonietta; War Requiem sung in Stuttgart, Rotterdam, Amsterdam, Buenos Aires, Taipei, Aachen, Nijmegen, Bratislava, Berlin. *Exhibition:* photo collage in Bradford on Avon and for Manchester Food and Drink Festival 2005. *Radio:* numerous broadcasts for the BBC. *Television:* many broadcasts in Europe. *Recordings include:* CDs: Albert Herring, Billy Budd, Peter Grimes, Elegy For Young Lovers, Beggar's Opera, Martyrdom of St Magnus, Rosa, a Horse Drama, HMS Pinafore, The Kingdom, Where the Wild Things Are, Higglety Pigglety Pop!, Elegy for Young Lovers; DVDs: TEA, A Midsummer Night's Dream, Il Ritorno d'Ulisse, King Priam, Peter Grimes. *Publications include:* Who's My Bottom? 2011, Scraping the Bottom 2013, Lexibography 2014; contrib. to Private Eye, The Observer; contribs as Columnist: Sinfinimusic.com, Opernwelt, BBC Music Magazine. *Honours:* winner, Grimsby Singing Competition 1980, Countess of Munster Award 1981. *Current Management:* c/o Musichall Ltd, Oast House, Crouch's Farm, Hollow Lane, East Hoathly, East Sussex, BN8 6QX, England. *Telephone:* (1825) 840437. *E-mail:* peter@musichall.uk.com. *Website:* www.musichall.uk .com; www.christophergillett.co.uk.

GILLIES, Malcolm George William, BA, DipEd, MA, MMus, PhD, DMus; Australian academic and university administrator; *Vice-President (Development), Australian National University*; b. 23 Dec. 1954, Brisbane; s. of Frank Douglas Gillies and Beatrice Mary Belle Gillies (née Copeman). *Education:* Australian Nat. Univ., Univ. of Queensland, Royal Coll. of Music, London, Univs of Cambridge and London, UK, Univ of Melbourne. *Career:* Tutor in Music, Univ. of Melbourne 1981–83; Lecturer in Music, Victorian Coll. of Arts 1983–86; Lecturer in Music 1986–90, Sr Lecturer, Univ. of Melbourne 1991–92; Prof. of Music, Univ. of Queensland 1992–99; Exec. Dean, Humanities and Social Sciences and Pro-Vice-Chancellor, Univ. of Adelaide 1999–2001; Deputy Vice-Chancellor (Educ.) ANU 2002–; Fellow, Australian Acad. of the Humanities 1992, Pres. 1998–2001; Pres. Nat. Acads Forum, Australia 1998–2002, Australian Council for Humanities, Arts and Social Sciences 2004–. *Publications include:* Bartók in Britain 1989, Notation and Tonal Structure in Bartók's Later Works 1989, Bartók Remembered 1990, Bartók im Spiegel Seiner Zeit 1991, The Bartók Companion (ed.) 1993, Halsey Stevens's The Life and Music of Béla Bartók (3rd edn) 1993, The All-Round Man: Selected Letters of Percy Grainger (co-ed.) 1994, Northern Exposures 1997, Grainger on Music (co-ed.) 1999, Gen. Ed. (series) Oxford Studies in Musical Genesis, Structure and Interpretation, Portrait of Percy Grainger (co-author) 2002, El Mundo de Bartók 2004, Self-Portrait of Percy Grainger (co-ed.) 2006. *Honours:* Centenary Medal (Australia) 2003. *Address:* Chancelry, Australian National University, ACT 0200 (office); 1501 Capital Tower, 2 Marcus Clarke Street, Canberra City, ACT 2601, Australia (home). *Telephone:* (2) 6125-9403 (office); (2) 6262-5498 (home). *Fax:* (2) 6125-9614 (office). *E-mail:* malcolm.gillies@anu.edu.au (office). *Website:* www.anu.edu.au (office).

GILLINSON, Sir Clive Daniel, Kt, CBE, ARAM, FRAM, FRNCM; British cellist and arts administrator; *Executive and Artistic Director, Carnegie Hall*; b. 7 March 1946, Bangalore, India; m. Penny Gillinson; one s. two d. *Education:* Frensham Heights School, Queen Mary Coll., Univ. of London, Royal Acad. of Music, London. *Career:* played in Nat. Youth Orchestra of GB 1963–65, Philharmonia Orchestra –1970, London Symphony Orchestra 1970–84; elected to Bd of Dirs London Symphony Orchestra 1976–79, 1983–, Finance Dir 1979, Man. Dir 1984–2005; Exec. and Artistic Dir Carnegie Hall, New York 2005–; owned an antique shop, Hampstead, London 1978–86; Chair. Asscn of British Orchestras 1992–95; Gov. and mem. of Exec. Cttee Nat. Youth Orchestra 1995–2004; Founding Partner, Masterprize 1997–; Founding Trustee, Nat. Endowment for Science, Tech. and the Arts 1998–2004; mem. Int. Music Council of the Children's Hearing Inst., New York 1998–, Brubeck Inst. Hon. Bd 2007–, Curtis Inst. Bd of Overseers 2007–08. *Honours:* Hon. GSMD 1992, Freeman of the City of London 1993; Dr hc (City Univ.) 1995, (Curtis Inst.) 2007; Hon. DHumLitt (Skidmore Coll.) 2010; RAM May Mukle Cello Prize, ABSA Garrett Award 1992, Luminary Award, Eastman School of Music 2010, Int. Citation of Merit, Int. Soc. for the Performing Arts 2012. *Address:* Carnegie Hall, 881 Seventh Avenue, New York, NY 10019-3210, USA (office). *Telephone:* (212) 903-9820 (office). *Fax:* (212) 903-0820 (office). *E-mail:* cgillinson@carnegiehall.org (office). *Website:* www.carnegiehall.org (office).

GILMORE, Gail Varina, MMus; American singer (mezzo-soprano); b. 21 Sept. 1951, Washington, DC. *Education:* Xavier Univ., New Orleans and Univ. of Indiana at Bloomington. *Career:* appearances at Oper am Rhein (Düsseldorf, Germany), Teatro la Fenice (Venice, Italy), Arena di Verona (Italy), Opernhaus Frankfurt (Germany), Houston Opera (TX), Metropolitan Opera (New York), Bolshoi Theatre (Moscow); performances with José Carreras; Teacher, S.M.U. Gesangs Schule, Munich. *Operas include:* Les Troyens, Carmen, Orfeo ed Euridice, Cavalleria Rusticana, Ariadne auf Naxos, Der Rosenkavalier, Aida, Macbeth, Il Trovatore, Don Carlos, Tannhäuser, Parsifal, Lohengrin. *Address:* Gilmore Music Productions, Apollolaan 123, 1077 AP Amsterdam, Netherlands. *Telephone:* (20) 6626691. *Fax:* (20) 4710577. *E-mail:* info@gilmore.nl. *Website:* www.gilmore.nl.

GILMOUR, Russell Scott, BA; Australian composer; b. 21 May 1956, Penrith, NSW. *Education:* Univ. of New England, Australian Chamber Orchestra Composer Workshop. *Career:* faculty mem., All Saints Coll., Bathurst 1987–90, Canterbury Coll., Qld 1990–; commissions from Bathurst City and chamber orchestras 1987, 1989. *Compositions include:* A Peaceable Kingdom for chamber orchestra 1987, Mud for tuba 1989, Songlines for orchestra 1989, Edge for flute 1990, Wood Dance for marimba 1991, Point II for recorder 1991, Blowpipes for flute quartet 1993, Cantate Domino for choir 1993, String Quartet: The Art of Reckoning 1993, A Way Along for choir and marimba 1994.

GILTBERG, Boris; Israeli (b. Russian) pianist; b. 1984, Moscow, Russia. *Education:* studied with Arie Vardi. *Career:* moved to Tel-Aviv in early childhood; several tours of S America 2002–; debut with Israel Philharmonic 2005, regular appearances with major orchestras and recital series in Israel; debut, Philharmonia 2007; regular performer at Royal Festival Hall, London; BBC Proms debut with BBC Scottish Symphony 2010; first concerto appearance at Concertgebouw Amsterdam with Netherlands Philharmonic Orchestra 2012; debut, London Philharmonic 2012; guest performances with several UK orchestras and appearances with DSO Berlin, Frankfurt Radio Symphony, Orchestre Nat. du Capitole de Toulouse, Royal Flemish Philharmonic, Swedish and Danish Radio Symphonies, Prague Symphony, St Petersburg Philharmonic; Tokyo debut 2005, first China tour 2007; N American orchestra debut with Indianapolis Symphony 2007; has collaborated with conductors including Marin Alsop, Martyn Brabbins, Christoph von Dohnányi, Neeme Järvi, Nicola Luisotti, Vasily Petrenko; recitals in halls including Amsterdam Concertgebouw, Vienna Konzerthaus, Munich Herkulessaal, Paris Louvre, Zürich Tonhalle, Wigmore Hall, London, Teatro San Carlo Naples, Leipzig Gewandhaus, Palais des Beaux Arts, Brussels, Southbank Centre, London; festivals include Klavierfest am Ruhr, Schwetzingen, Lucerne, Piano aux Jacobins and Cheltenham. *Recordings include:* solo: Prokofiev War Sonatas, Romantic Sonatas (Rachmaninov, Liszt, Grieg). *Honours:* First Prize and Audience Prize, Santander Awards 2002, First Prize, Queen Elisabeth Competition, Brussels 2013. *Current Management:* c/o Intermusica, 36 Graham Street, Crystal Wharf, London, N1 8GJ, England. *Telephone:* (20) 7608-9900. *Fax:* (20) 7490-3263. *E-mail:* mail@intermusica.co.uk. *Website:* www.intermusica.co.uk.

GILVAN, Raimund; British singer (tenor); b. 1938, Manchester, England. *Education:* Cologne Musikhochschule. *Career:* sang at the Mainz Opera from 1961, Mannheim 1963–74; roles include Capito in Mathis der Maler, Lensky, Henze's Junge Lord, Adrasto in Traetta's Antigone, David in Die Meistersinger and Pfitzner's Palestrina; many concert appearances. *Recordings:* Beethoven Missa solemnis, Bach B minor Mass, Lieder by Wolf.

GIMÉNEZ, Eduardo; Spanish singer (tenor); b. 2 June 1940, Mataro, Barcelona. *Education:* studied with Carmen Bracons de Clomer and Juan Sabater in Barcelona, Vladimiro Badiali in Rome. *Career:* debut at Reggio Emilia 1967 as Nemorino in L'Elisir d'amore; has sung widely in Italy and at the Teatro Liceo, Barcelona; Holland Festival in 1970 in La Fedeltà Premiata by Haydn; Guest appearances in Brussels, Nice, Monte Carlo, Venice, Budapest, Bordeaux, Tel-Aviv, Seattle and Washington; Sang at Pesaro and La Scala Milan, 1984–85 in a revival of Rossini's Il Viaggio a Reims; Well known in operas by Cimarosa, Bellini, Paisiello, Galuppi, Mozart, Verdi and Puccini; Has sung in Paisiello's Il Barbiere di Siviglia at Leningrad, and at Barcelona in 1988 in the premiere of Libre Vermell by Xavier Benguere, returning as Ferrando in Così fan tutte in 1990; Covent Garden debut 1990, as Ernesto; season 1992 as Rossini's Don Ramiro at the Semper Oper Dresden and in Barcelona. *Recordings include:* Elvino in La Sonnambula; Don Pasquale; L'Atlantida by Falla; Rossini's Armida.

GIMÉNEZ, Raul; Argentine singer (tenor); b. 14 Sept. 1950. *Education:* studied in Buenos Aires. *Career:* debut at Teatro Colón, Buenos Aires 1980, as Ernesto in Don Pasquale; sang in concert and opera throughout South America before his European debut as Filandro in Cimarosa's Le Astuzie Femminili at the 1984 Wexford Festival; sang in Paris and Venice as Roderigo in Rossini's Otello and appeared as Elvino in La Sonnambula 1989 at the Théâtre des Champs-Elysées; season 1987 sang at the Pesaro Festival in Rossini's L'Occasione fa Il Ladro, at Amsterdam as Ernesto and as Alessandro in Il Re Pastore at Rome; Aix-en-Provence 1988 as Gernando and Carlo in Rossini's Armida; Toronto and Zürich 1989 as Almaviva; US debut at Dallas as Ernesto, Lisbon 1989 as Tonio in La Fille du Régiment and Covent Garden 1990–93 as Almaviva, Ernesto and Ramiro; season 1990 with appearances as Argirio in Tancredi at Geneva, Così fan tutte at Buenos Aires and Salieri's Les Danaides at the Ravenna Festival as Lyncée; debuts at Vienna State Opera

1990 as Almaviva, La Scala 1993 as Argirio in Tancredi, and at Florence 1993 in La Cenerentola; further guest appearances in Munich, Rome Geneva, Naples, Bologna, Verona, Turin, Frankfurt, Toulouse, Monte Carlo, Lausanne, Schwetzingen Festival and Brussels; season 1996 sang Appio in Pacini's L'Ultimo giorno di Pompei, Martina Franca; Lindoro in L'Italiana in Algeri at the Vienna State Opera 1996; season 1998 debut at Paris Opéra Bastille as Tebaldo in Capuleti ed i Montecchi and Edgardo in Lucia di Lammermoor, as Il Turco in Italia at Monte Carlo and Almaviva at Geneva; season 2000 as Don Ottavio at La Coruña and as Ramiro in La Cenerentola at the Met and in Madrid. *Recordings include:* Arias by Mozart, Rossini, Bellini and Donizetti; Les Danaides; L'Occasione fa il Ladro conducted by Michelangelo Veltri; Il Turco in Italia; Rossini's Messa di Gloria, 1992; Il Barbiere di Siviglia; Viaggio a Reims; La Cenerentola; L'italiana in Algeri; L' Inganno Felice; Rossini's Stabat Mater; La Sonnambula.

GIMSE, Havard; Norwegian pianist; b. 15 Sept. 1966, Kongsvinger. *Education:* Norway State Acad. of Music, Bergen Music Conservatory, Mozarteum, Salzburg and Musikhochschule, Berlin. *Career:* debut with Trondheim Symphony Orchestra 1981; soloist with Scandinavian orchestras, including Oslo Philharmonic, Bergen Philharmonic, Helsinki Radio from 1981; concerts in Europe, North and South America; several chamber music appearances; Oslo Philharmonic tour of the UK 1995–96; Schleswig-Holstein Festival 1997; Valdemossa Chopin Festival 1997, Baltimore Symphony Orchestra, City of Birmingham Symphony Orchestra, Royal Philharmonic Orchestra. *Recordings:* Liszt: Piano Sonata, Chopin: Piano Music, Grieg: Piano and chamber music, Tveitt: Piano Music, Sibelius: Piano Music. *Honours:* Princess Astrid Music Prize 1985, Robert Levin Festival Prize 1986, Jugend Musiziert Frankfurt 1987, Steinway Prize, Berlin 1995, Grieg Prize, Norway 1996. *Current Management:* Pro Arte A/S, John Lunds Pl. 1, 5007 Bergen, Norway. *Telephone:* 55-31-94-35. *E-mail:* kjell@proarte.no. *Website:* www.proarte.no. *Address:* Mikael Hertzbergs Vei 2b, 0495 Oslo, Norway (home).

GINTY, Eugene, BA; British singer (tenor); b. 10 Dec. 1965, London, England. *Education:* Durham University, studied with Ian Barr. *Career:* debut in Japan and France 1994; Don Jose 1997; Cavaradossi, for Midwales Opera 1997; Don Ramiro for English Touring Opera 1997; Sandy, The Lighthouse 1998; Tonio, La Fille du Régiment for English Touring Opera 1998; numerous broadcasts on BBC Radio 2, Radio 3, Radio 4; concert repertoire includes Evangelist (St John), Sheffield Cathedral (St Matthew), Durham Cathedral and St Anne's, Belfast; Britten's Abraham and Isaac, Eton College, 1994; Bach Cantata 191 at Queen Elizabeth Hall, 1995; Schubert's Mondschein at Wigmore Hall under Stephen Cleobury; Britten's Serenade for Tenor, Horn, and Strings, Cleveland Chamber Orchestra, 1996; Elgar's Dream of Gerontius, Guildford Civic Hall, 1998; mem. Equity, Pamra. *Recordings:* Psalms and Part Songs, BBC Singers/Jane Glover; Pärt and Tormis, BBC Singers/Bo Holton; Richard Strauss, BBC Singers/Stephen Cleobury. *Current Management:* c/o Judith Newton, Opera and Concert Artists, 75 Aberdare Gardens, London, NW6 3AN, England. *Telephone:* (20) 7328-3097. *Fax:* (20) 7372-3537. *E-mail:* enquiries@opera-and-concert-artists .co.uk.

GINZER, Frances; Canadian singer (soprano); b. 19 Sept. 1955, Calgary. *Education:* Calgary, North Texas State and Toronto Univs. *Career:* debut with Canadian Opera, Toronto, as Clothilde in Norma; Sang Antonia in Les Contes d'Hoffmann at Toronto, followed by the Verdi Requiem, Messiah, Beethoven's Ninth and Die Schöpfung; European opera debut Karlsruhe, 1983 as Antonia; Engaged at Düsseldorf from 1987 and has made guest appearances at Hamburg, Stuttgart, Cologne, Bonn, London (English National Opera), Munich State Opera, Frankfurt, Zürich, Warsaw, Maastricht, Vancouver, Calgary, Edmonton, Winnipeg and US debut in Dallas, Tex.; WNO 1991, as Violetta; Duisburg 1991, as Frau Fluth in Die Lustige Weiber von Windsor; Washington Opera 1995, as Senta; Brünnhilde in Siegfried at Düsseldorf, 1996; Elsa in Lohengrin at Tokyo, 1997; Early roles included Micaela, Constanze, Donna Anna and Mozart Countess; Lucia, Cleopatra, Sophie in Der Rosenkavalier, Aminta (Die schweigsame Frau), Jenůfa, Leila (Les Pêcheurs des perles) and Mimi; Present Repertoire includes Turandot, Ariadne, Senta and Tosca; Sang Brünnhilde for San Francisco and Dallas Opera, 1999–2000; Turandot at Covent Garden, 2002; mem. Advisory Cttee Music Performance Program, Mount Royal Univ., Calgary. *Recordings include:* Handel's Rodrigo; Adriana Lecouvreur. *Address:* c/o Mount Royal University, Music Performance Program, 4825 Mount Royal Gate SW, Calgary, AB T3E 6K6, Canada.

GIORDANI, Marcello; Italian singer (tenor); b. 1963, Catania, Sicily. *Career:* debut at Spoleto Festival 1986, as Duke of Mantua; La Scala debut 1988, as Rodolfo, and US debut at Portland, as Nadir; season 1991 in Live from Lincoln Center (New York) concert and debut at the Verona Arena, as the Duke; engagements as Nemorino, Rodolfo and Alfredo at the Metropolitan (season 1996–97), Pinkerton, Edgardo and Gounod's Roméo at Houston, Alfredo at Covent Garden under Georg Solti, Tonio (La Fille du Régiment) and Hoffmann at Portland and Faust at the Opéra Bastille, Paris; engagements at San Francisco Seattle, Chicago, Vienna (in Rosenkavalier and I Puritani), Hamburg, Munich and Berlin; season 1997–98 as Werther at the Metropolitan, in Lucrezia Borgia at La Scala, L'Elisir d'amore in Dallas and as Pinkerton at San Francisco; season 2000–01 as Faust at Los Angeles, Gabriele Adorno for San Francisco Opera, Rodolfo at the Met, Cavaradossi for Chicago Opera and Raoul in Les Huguenots at Carnegie Hall. *Current Management:*

Opera Art, via Isolalta Forette 11, 37068 Vigasio (VR), Italy. *Telephone:* (045) 6649911. *Fax:* (045) 6649912. *E-mail:* info@operaart.it. *Website:* www .operaart.it; www.marcellogiordani.com.

GIOVANINETTI, Christoph; French violinist; b. 1960. *Education:* Paris Conservatoire with Jean-Claude Pennetier, studied with the Amadeus and Alban Berg Quartets. *Career:* mem., Ysaÿe String Quartet from 1984; many concert performances in France, Europe, America and the Far East; festival engagements at Salzburg, Tivoli in Copenhagen, Bergen, Lockenhaus, Barcelona and Stresa; many appearances in Italy, notably with the Haydn Quartets of Mozart; tours of Japan and the USA 1990, 1992. *Recordings:* Mozart Quartet K421 and Quintet K516; Ravel, Debussy and Mendelssohn Quartets. *Honours:* Grand Prix Evian Int. String Quartet Competition 1988, special prizes for best performances of a Mozart quartet, the Debussy quartet and a contemporary work, second prize Portsmouth Int. String Quartet Competition 1988.

GIRAUD, Suzanne; French composer; b. 31 July 1958, Metz. *Education:* Strasbourg and Paris Conservatoires, studied with Claude Ballif, Tristan Murail, Hugues Dufourt, Marius Constant, Accademia Chigiana, Siena with Franco Donatoni, Internazionales Musikinstitut, Darmstadt with Brian Ferneyhough, in Rome with Giacinto Scelsi. *Career:* Prof. of Piano, Conservatoire Nat. de Région de Strasbourg 1976–81; Prof. of Composition, Ecole Municipale de Musique de Conflans-Ste-Honorine 1981–88, Ecole Nat. de Musique de Fresnes 1982–84; Prof. of Harmony and Counterpoint, Conservatoire Nat. Supérieur de Musique de Paris 1988–93; Lecturer in Composition, Internationales Musikinstitut Darmstadt 1994–98; masterclasses at Conservatoire de Genève 2005; Dir Conservatoire Municipal du 20è arr. Paris 1993–. *Compositions include:* Tentative-Univers for percussion 1983, String Quartet 1983, Terre Essor for orchestra 1984, Ergo Sum for 15 instruments 1985, L'Offrande à Venus for eight instruments 1985, Le Rouge des Profondeurs for six instruments 1990, L'Oeil et le Jour for percussion 1990, String Trio 1991, Envoûtements I for violin 1996, Petraca for six voices 1996, Envoûtements IV for string quartet 1997, Ton Coeur sur la Pente du Ciel for orchestra 1998, To One in Paradise for mezzo-soprano and orchestra 1999, Zéphyr for piano 1999, Au Commencement était le Verbe for 16 voices and six percussionists 2002, Le Bel été for baritone and piano 2002, Envoûtements V for guitar and string quartet 2001, Duos pour Prades for clarinet and cello 2002, Envoûtements VI for six percussionists 2003, Le Vase de Parfums (opera) 2004, Concerto for cello and orchestra 2004, Envoûtements VII for soprano and six instruments 2005, Envoûtements VIII for eight cellos (cello octet) 2005, Pianoconcerto Stereo Space 2006, Clarinet concerto 4 Fluides 2007, Orchestral work Echo-Réplique 2008, Psalm CXXXVII for mixed choir 2008, 926,5 opera miniscule for four singers and piano 2010. *Publication:* La musique nous vient d'ailleurs, book of interviews. *Honours:* first prizes Paris Conservatory, Diploma from the Accademia Chigiana in Siena for Composition, Villa Medici residency, Rome, SACEM George Enesco Prize 1987, Acad. des Beaux-Arts Georges Bizet Prize 1987, UNESCO Prix de la Tribune Internationale 1988. *Current Management:* c/o Yutha Tep, Agence des Concerts Parisiens, 23 rue Bergère, 75009 Paris, France. *Telephone:* 6-61-88-64-78. *E-mail:* ytep@concertsparisiens.fr. *E-mail:* suzanne.giraud@free.fr (office). *Website:* www.suzannegiraud.com.

GIRAULT, Benoît; French conductor; *Artistic Director and Chief Conductor, Orchestre Philharmonique du Maroc;* b. 1961, Paris. *Education:* Conservatoire National Supérieur de Musique, Paris, studied with Robert Delacroix and Franco Ferrara. *Career:* began career as Music Dir Choeurs et Orchestres des Grandes Ecoles; Music Dir Musique de la Police Nationale 1992–2006; Music Dir Ensemble Prisme 2001; Music Dir Orchestra National d'Harmonie des Jeunes 2004–05; currently Artistic Dir and Chief Conductor, Orchestre Philharmonique du Maroc; regular guest conductor, Orchestre Pasdeloup; mem. jury, Concours International de Piano du Maroc. *Address:* Orchestre Philharmonique du Maroc, Théâtre Guéliz, 40000 Marrakesh, Morocco (office). *Website:* www.opm.ma (office).

GIROLAMI, Renato; Italian singer (baritone); b. 1959, Amelia, Torino. *Education:* studied in Germany with Ernst Haefliger and Dietrich Fischer-Dieskau, in Italy with Sesto Bruscantini. *Career:* sang Mozart's Figaro and Leporello at Passau, Germany, St Gallen, Switzerland and at Salzburg Landestheater 1987–89; from 1989 with ensemble at Vienna Volksoper singing Figaro, Leporello and Guglielmo in Così fan tutte; mem., Vienna Staatsoper from 1991, where he added Bartolo in Barber of Seville; also in Stuttgart 1992–94, Belcore in L'Elisir d'amore, Sharpless in Madama Butterfly and Taddeo in L'Italiana in Algeri; other roles include Somarone in Béatrice et Bénédict with Neville Marriner in London 1990, Papageno at Barcelona 1991, the Count in Le nozze di Figaro at Bari 1991, Schaunard in La Bohème at Naples 1992, and at Tokyo 1993, and Enrico in Lucia di Lammermoor at Marseille 1994; sang at Essen 1999–2000 as Don Alfonso and Don Pasquale.

GISCA, Nicolae, DMus; Romanian conductor and academic; *Professor of Conducting and Orchestration, George Enescu University of Arts;* b. 30 Sept. 1942, Tibirica; m. Elena Gisca 1965; one d. *Education:* Music Conservatory George Enescu, Iasi, Romania Univ. of Music. *Career:* conducting debut with Conservatory Choir 1962; conductor of over 1,000 choral, chamber and symphony concerts with Conservatory Symphony and Chamber Orchestras, Conservatory Choir and Chamber Choir, Bacau and Botosani Philharmonic Orchestras; performances and tours of concerts in Romania, Austria, Belgium,

Finland, France, Germany, Italy, Luxembourg, Mexico, Spain, Switzerland, USA, Wales, with Chamber Choir, Cantores Amicitae; TV and radio appearances; Prof. of Conducting and Orchestration, George Enescu Univ. of Arts 1965–, Rector 1990–2000. *Compositions include:* arrangements and choral processing of Romanian, European, American, African and Asian folksongs for choir; 145 musical pieces. *Recordings include:* The Tour of The World in 16 Melodies 1981, Winter Songs From Everywhere 1982, Romanian Christmas Carols 1992, Romanian Choral Music 1993, Cantores Amicitiae Sing to the World 1994, Christmas Carols from Romania and From the World 1995, Krieppenspiel 1996, Romanian Choral Music 1 1997, Die Schönsten Weihnachtslieder 1997, P. Constantinescu: The Byzantine Oratorio for Christmas 1999, Negro Spirituals 2003, The Liturgies of the World 2004, Romanian Choral Music 2 2008, Orthodox Music 2008, Noel/Weihnachten/ Christmas 2009, Musik aus aller Welt/La musique du monde/The World Music 2012. *Publications include:* The Conductor's Art 1982, The Treaty of Instruments Theory Vol. I 1987, Vol. II 1998, The Conductor of the Choir 1992, The Interpretation of Choral Music 2004, Unity and Variety in Christian Spirituality Reflected in Choral Liturgical Music 2004, George Enescu Conservatoire of Music, Iasi 1960–70 2010, Dew Eternity (in collaboration with Gregory Vieru, Stephen Andronic) 2010. *Honours:* six first prizes at Nat. Festival of Singing, Romania 1979, 1981, 1983, 1985, 1987, 1989, First Prize, Youth and Music Int. Competition, Vienna 1980, Third Prize, Int. Music Eisteddfod, Llangollen, Wales 1991, Second Prize 1995, Excellent Mention, Int. Competition, Montreux 1995, Special Prize, Int. Music Festival, Cantonigros, Spain 1995, two First Prizes, World Music Int. Music Festival, Fivizzano, Italy 2002, Third Prize, Int. Choirs Competition, Spittal an der Drau, Austria 2005, Second Prize Folklore Music, Third Prize Mixed Choirs, Int. Choir Competition, Germany 2006, Golden Stamp (First Prize), Tampere Vocal Music Festival, Finland 2007, George Enescu Univ. of Arts Prize 2008, Golden Diplom (First Prize), Anton Bruckner Int. Choir Competition , Linz, Austria 2013, Grand Prix, Int. May Choir Competition, Bulgaria 2014, First prize and Grand Prix at the Int. Choirs Competition, Romania 2014. *Fax:* (232) 212551 (office). *E-mail:* ngisca@arteiasi.ro (office). *Website:* www .cantoresamicitiae.ro.

GITECK, Janice; American composer and pianist; b. 27 June 1946, New York. *Education:* Mills Coll. with Darius Milhaud and Morton Subotnick, Paris Conservatoire with Olivier Messiaen, Aspen School with Milhaud and Charles Jones. *Career:* teacher, Hayward State Univ., Univ. of California at Berkeley 1974–76, Cornish Inst., Seattle from 1979; co-Dir, Port Costa Players 1972–79; commissions from soloists and ensembles. *Compositions include:* Piano Quintet 1965, two String Quartets, How to Invoke a Garden cantata 1968, Traffic Acts for four-track tape 1969, Sun of the Center cantata 1970, Magic Words 1973, Messalina 1973, Helixes for ensemble 1974, A'gita (opera) 1976, Sandbars on the Takano River 1976, Thunder Like a White Bear Dancing 1977, Callin' Home Coyote (burlesque) 1978, Far North Beast Ghosts the Clearing 1978, Peter and the Wolves for trombone with actor and tape 1978, Breathing Songs from a Turning Sky 1980, When the Crones Stop Counting for 60 flutes 1980, Tree (chamber symphony) 1981, Hopi: Songs of the Fourth World 1983, Loo-Wit for viola and orchestra 1983. *Honours:* California Arts Council grant 1978, NEA grants 1979, 1983.

GITLIS, Ivry; Israeli violinist; b. 22 Aug. 1922, Haifa; m. Paule Deglon. *Education:* Ecole Normale de Musique, Paris, studied with Flesch, Enescu and Thibaud. *Career:* first played in public aged eight in Israel; worked in British Troop entertainment during the War; debuts with the London Philharmonic, BBC Symphony and other British orchestras during the 1940s; Paris debut in 1951, Israel debut in 1952 and US debut in 1955; many recitals and concert appearances with leading orchestras; often heard in works by 20th-century composers. *Recordings include:* concertos by Berg, Stravinsky, Bartók and Tchaikovsky. *Honours:* Thibaud Prize 1951. *Current Management:* c/o Transart UK, Cedar House, 10 Rutland Street, Filey, N Yorks., YO14 9JB, England. *Telephone:* (1723) 515819. *E-mail:* transartuk@transartuk.com.

GIURANNA, Bruno; Italian violist and conductor; *Viola Professor, Fondazione Stauffer, Cremona;* b. 6 April 1933, Milan. *Education:* Coll. S. Giuseppe and Conservatorio di Musica Santa Cecilia, Rome and Conservatorio di Musica S. Pietro a Maiella, Naples. *Career:* Founder-mem. I Musici 1951–61; Prof., Conservatorio G. Verdi, Milan 1961–65, Conservatorio S. Cecilia, Rome 1965–78, Accad. Chigiana, Siena 1966–83, 2004–, Nordwest-deutsche Musikakademie, Detmold, Germany 1969–83, Hochschule der Künste, Berlin 1981–98, Fondazione Stauffer, Cremona 1985–, RAM, London 1994–96, Accad. S. Cecilia, Rome 1995–97; mem. Int. Music Competition jury, Munich 1961–62, 1967, 1969, Geneva 1968, Budapest 1975; soloist at concerts in festivals including Edinburgh and Holland Festivals, and with orchestras including Berlin Philharmonic, Amsterdam Concertgebouw and Teatro alla Scala, Milan; Artistic Dir Orchestra da Camera di Padova 1983–92; Academician of Santa Cecilia 1974; Pres. European String Teachers Asscn 2011. *Honours:* Cavaliere, Gran Croce della Repubblica Italiana 1987; Hon. DLit (Univ. of Limerick) 2003. *Address:* Via Bembo 96, 31011 Asolo, Treviso, Italy. *Telephone:* (0423) 55734. *Fax:* (0423) 529913. *E-mail:* brgiuranna@gmail.com. *Website:* www.giuranna.com.

GIVONY, Ronen, MLitt; American concert promoter; *Founder and Artistic Director, Wordless Music;* b. 1979. *Education:* Yale Univ. *Career:* Grants Manager, New World Symphony 2002–03; Grant Writer, Chamber Music Soc., Lincoln Center 2005–07; Founder and Artistic Dir, Wordless Music (series of concerts presenting different genres of music on the same bill) 2006–;

Editorial Co-ordinator, Nonesuch Records 2007–; Music Dir, Le Poisson Rouge 2008–. *Address:* 188 Sackett Street, Brooklyn, New York, NY 11231, USA (office). *E-mail:* illtemperedclavier@gmail.com (office). *Website:* www .ronengivony.com; wordlessmusic.org.

GIZBERT STUDNICKA, Bogumila, DipMus, MMus; Polish harpsichordist; b. 16 March 1949, Kraków; one s. *Education:* Acad. of Music, Kraków, Conservatoire Royal, Antwerp, Belgium with Jos Van Immersel, masterclasses with Zuzana Ruzickova, Kenneth Gilbert and Ton Koopman. *Career:* numerous concert appearances, including with Polish Orchestra of Wojciech Rajski, Poland and other European countries; active participant in many chamber music ensembles; Asst Prof. Depts of Harpsichord and Early Instruments, and of Chamber Music, Acad. of Music, Kraków; mem. Polish Soc. of Musicians. *Recordings:* Concertos of Antonio Vivaldi, J.S. Bach's transcriptions, Polskie Nagrania Musa, recordings for Polish and Belgian radio and television and Dutch radio. *Honours:* prize Polish Piano Festival, Slupsk 1974, prize with distinction Int. Harpsichord Competition, Bruges, Belgium 1977.

GJEVANG, Anne; Norwegian singer (contralto) and arts administrator; *Casting Director and Deputy Director of Opera, Norwegian Opera;* b. 24 Oct. 1948, Oslo. *Education:* Conservatorio Santa Cecilia (Rome) and Hochschule für Musik und Darstellende Kunst (Vienna). *Career:* operatic debuts in Austria and Germany, Bayreuth Festival 1983, Metropolitan Opera, New York 1987, Victoria Music Festival, London 1991; mem. Zurich Opera House 1983–88; guest performer Berlin and London Philharmonics, Chicago Symphony Orchestra, USA, Orchestre de Paris; also performed at Covent Garden, London, La Scala, Milan; performed with famous conductors including Solti, Barenboim, von Karajan, Giulini, Abbado, Chailly, Albrecht, Perick, Haitink and Pappano; renowned for appearances as Erda in Wagner's Ring des Nibelungen; Casting Dir and Deputy Dir of Opera, Norwegian Opera, Oslo 2009–. *Recordings include:* Anne Gjevang in Recital, Mahler's 3rd Symphony, Schumann's Das Paradies und die Peri, Handel: Messiah 1985, (Arias and Choruses) 1990, (Highlights) 1998; DVDs: Der Ring der Nibelungen. *Films:* Mitridate, rè di Ponto 1986. *Honours:* Norsk Kritikerpris 1986. *Address:* Den Norske Opera and Ballett, Kirsten Flagstads plass 1, 0150 Oslo, Norway. *Website:* www.operaen.no.

GLANERT, Detlev; German composer; b. 6 Sept. 1960, Hamburg; s. of Heinz Paul Glanert and Brigitte Glanert. *Education:* studied with Diether de la Motte, Günther Friedrichs, with Hans Werner Henze in Cologne, with Oliver Knussen, Tanglewood Music Festival. *Career:* co-organizer, Cantiere Internazionale d'Arte, Montepulciano 1989–93, Artistic Dir 2009–11; taught composition workshops, Genoa 1996, Aspen 1997, Montepulciano 1999, Melbourne 2000, Jakarta 2000; Villa Aurora Fellowship, Los Angeles 1999; mem. Freie Akad. der Künste, Hamburg 2002; Composer-in-Residence, Mannheim 2003, Sapporo 2005, WDR in Cologne 2008–09, Amsterdam Concertgebouw Orchestra 2011–. *Compositions include:* Symphonie 1 1984, Mahler/Skizze for ensemble 1989, Der Spiegel des großen Kaisers (opera) (Rolf Liebermann Opera Prize 1993) 1989–93, Klavierkonzert 1 1994, Symphonie 3 1996, Katafalk for orchestra 1997, Joseph Süß (opera) 1997–99, Scherz, Satire, Ironie und tiefere Bedeutung (opera) (Bavarian Theatre Prize 2001) 1999–2000, Burleske for orchestra 2000, Chamber Sonata No. 3 Geheimer Raum 2002, Die drei Rätsel (opera) 2002–03, Argentum et Aurum 2004, Theatrum Bestiarum for orchestra 2004–05, Vier Präludien und Ernste Gesänge for baritone and orchestra 2004–05, Caligula (opera) 2004–06, Doppelkonzert for two pianos and orchestra 2007, Nijinsky's Tagebuch (opera) 2007–08, Fluss ohne Ufer for orchestra 2008–09, Drei Gesänge ohne Worte for orchestra 2008–09, Das Holzschiff (opera) 2009–10, Insomnium for orchestra 2010, Solaris (opera) 2011–12. *Recording:* Portrait. *Honours:* Bach Prize Fellowship, Hamburg 1987, Berlin Senate Fellowship for Istanbul 1988, Rolf Liebermann Opera Prize Fellowship 1989, 1993, Berlin Senate composition grant 1990. *Address:* c/o Boosey and Hawkes, Komponisten Abt., Lützowufer 26, 10787 Berlin, Germany (office). *E-mail:* composers.germany@boosey.com (office). *Website:* www.boosey.com/glanert (office).

GLANVILLE, Mark; British singer (bass); b. 24 May 1959, London, England. *Education:* Univ. of Oxford and Royal Northern Coll. of Music. *Career:* debut singing the 2nd Soldier in Les Troyens and the Doctor in Macbeth for Opera North 1987; has sung Nourabad (Les Pêcheurs de Perles), the King (Aida), the King of Clubs in The Love for Three Oranges, Hobson in Peter Grimes and Betto di Signa in Gianni Schicchi for Opera North; Scottish Opera debut 1988, as the Commendatore in Don Giovanni; Radio Vara, Amsterdam, as Lord Rochefort in Anna Bolena; Omaha Opera as Ferrando in Il Trovatore; sang Iago at Haddo House 1996; concert engagements include Bruckner's Te Deum for the Hallé Orchestra and Messiah with the Royal Liverpool Philharmonic; opera includes King (Oranges) in Lisbon 1991, Father (Jewel Box) for Opera North 1991, New Israeli Opera 1992; concerts of Beethoven 9 (Ulster Orchestra conducted by Tortelier and Netherlands Philharmonic, conducted by Menuhin); Mozart Requiem, Bournemouth Sinfonietta conducted by Menuhin, City of London Orchestra conducted by Judd, Stravinsky's Oedipus (RAI Milano conducted by Gatti). *Recordings include:* Donizetti's L'Assedio di Calais, Schubert's Mass in G. *Honours:* Scholarships from the Peter Moores Foundation and the Countess of Munster and Ian Fleming Trusts; Ricordi Opera Prize and Elsie Sykes Fellowship, Royal Northern College of Music.

GLANVILLE, Susannah; British singer (soprano); b. 1964. *Education:* studied with Margaret Field at the Birmingham Conservatoire and with

Margaret Kingsley at the Royal College of Music; further study at the National Opera Studio. *Career:* season 1994–95 with Glyndebourne Touring Opera singing Musetta in La Bohème; Mimi for English Touring Opera; Luisa Miller at Opera North; European debut in Nice as Mozart's Countess; season 1996–97 Fiordiligi in Così fan tutte for Opera North and Mozart's Pamina for ENO; season 1998–99 sang Verdi's Giovanna D'Arco for Opera North; American debut as Blanche Dubois in André Previn's Streetcar Named Desire with San Francisco Opera; title role in Strauss's Arabella for Opera North and Vitellia in Mozart's La Clemenza di Tito for Glyndebourne Touring Opera; concert appearances include Britten's War Requiem with the Bournemouth Symphony Orchestra, Hindemith's Das Nusch-Nuschi and Mörder, Hoffnung der Frauen with the BBC Symphony Orchestra and Andrew Davies; Verdi's Requiem with the English Northern Philharmonia and Paul Daniel and Blanche Dubois in Streetcar Named Desire Suite with André Previn at the Tanglewood Festival; sang Schumann's Genoveva for Garsington Opera 2000: First Lady in Die Zauberflöte at Covent Garden 2003, Metropolitan Opera 2006, title role in Tosca for Scottish Opera 2012. *Current Management:* Robert Clarke, Hazard Chase, 25 City Road, Cambridge, CB1 1DP, England. *Telephone:* (1223) 312400. *Fax:* (1223) 460827. *E-mail:* robert.clarke@ hazardchase.co.uk. *Website:* www.hazardchase.co.uk.

GLASS, Paul Eugène, BMus; American composer; b. 19 Nov. 1934, Los Angeles, CA; m. Penelope Margaret Mackworth-Praed 1977. *Education:* Univ. of Southern California, studied with Boris Blacher, Ingolf Dahl, Hugo Friedhofer, Goffredo Petrassi at Accademia di Santa Cecilia, with Roger Sessions at Princeton Univ., with Witold Lutoslawski in Warsaw. *Career:* first public performance of compositions 1956; composer of concert music, film and television music; Prof., Conservatorio di Musica della Svizzera Italiana and Franklin Coll., Switzerland. *Compositions:* (all works published) orchestral works include: Sinfonia No. 3 1986, No. 4 1992, Lamento dell'acqua 1990, Quan Shi-qu 1994, Corale per Margaret 1995, Omaggio for piano 1995, How to Begin, for orchestra 1995, Sinfonia No. 5 ad modum missae 1999; chamber works include: Quartet for flute, clarinet, viola, violoncello 1966, Wie ein Naturlaut for 10 instruments 1977, Saxophone Quartet 1980, String Quartet No. 1 1988; vocal works include: 3 Songs for baritone and piano 1954, 5 chansons pour une Princesse errante for baritone and piano 1968, baritone and orchestra 1992, Sahassavagga, for children's chorus (text from the Dhammapada) 1976, Un sogno, for children's chorus (text Alberto Nessi) 1981, Deh, spiriti miei, quando mi vedete for chorus (text Guido Cavalcanti) 1987, Pianto de la Madonna for soprano, baritone, chorus, orchestra (text Jacopone da Todi) 1988; film scores include: The Abductors 1957, Lady in a Cage 1962, Bunny Lake is Missing 1965, Catch My Soul 1972, Overlord 1974, The Late Nancy Irving 1983, Die Abzocker 2000, Kakapo, ballet pour enfants 2001, Soggetti migranti for three percussionists and orchestra 2002, Prisma for solo dancer and jazz ensemble 2002, Sinfonia No. 6: quinto giorno 2003. *Recordings:* Portrait Paul Glass; Sinfonia No. 3, Quartetto I, 5 pezzi per pianoforte, Lamento dell'acqua; Jan Fryderyk, 2 concerts, Cologne; Concerto per pianoforte estemporaneo e orchestra; I Cantori della Turrita, Guilys; Sahassavagga; many for Swiss radio. *Address:* Presso Conservatorio della Svizzera Italiana, via Soldino 9, 6900 Lugano-Besso, Switzerland.

GLASS, Philip; American composer; b. 31 Jan. 1937, Baltimore, Md; s. of Benjamin Glass and Ida Glass (née Gouline); m. 1st JoAnne Akalaitis (divorced); m. 2nd Luba Burtyk (divorced); one s. one d.; m. 3rd Candy Jernigan (died 1991); m. 4th Holly Critchlow 2001; two s. one d. *Education:* Peabody Conservatory, Univ. of Chicago and Juilliard School of Music. *Career:* Composer-in-Residence, Pittsburgh Public Schools 1962–64; studied with Nadia Boulanger, Paris 1964–66; f. Philip Glass Ensemble 1968; f. record co. Chatham Square Productions, New York 1972, Dunvagen Music Publishers, Orange Mountain Music record co. 2002; mem. ASCAP. *Film scores include:* North Star 1977, Koyaanisqatsi 1983, Mishima 1985, Powaqqatsi 1987, The Thin Blue Line 1988, Hamburger Hill 1989, Mindwalk 1990, A Brief History of Time 1991, Anima Mundi 1991, Candyman 1992, The Voyage 1992, Orphée 1993, Candyman II: Farewell to the Flesh 1994, Monsters of Grace 1998, Bent 1998, Kundun 1998, The Hours (BAFTA Anthony Asquith Award 2003, Classical BRIT Award for Contemporary Music 2004) 2002, Cassandra's Dream 2007, Mr Nice 2010, They Were There 2011, Fantastic Four 2015. *Compositions include:* String Quartets (1–4), Violin Concerto, Low Symphony, The Palace of the Arabian Nights, Einstein on the Beach 1976, Madrigal Opera: The Panther 1980, Satyagraha 1980, The Photographer 1982, The Civil Wars: A Tree Is Best Measured When It Is Down 1983, Akhnaten 1983, The Juniper Tree 1985, A Descent Into The Maelstrom 1986, In The Upper Room 1986, Violin Concerto 1987, The Light for Orchestra 1987, The Making of the Representative for Planet 8 1988, The Fall of The House Of Usher 1988, 1,000 Airplanes on the Roof (with David Henry Hwang) 1988, Mattogrosso 1989, Hydrogen Jukebox (with Allen Ginsberg) 1989, The White Raven 1991, Orphée, chamber opera after Cocteau 1993, La belle et la bête, after Cocteau 1994, Witches of Venice (ballet) 1995, Les enfants terrible (dance opera) 1996, The Marriages Between Zones Three, Four and Five 1997, Symphony No. 5 1999, Symphony No. 6 (Plutonian Ode) 2000, In the Penal Colony (theatre) 2000, Tirol Concerto, piano and orchestra 2000, Concerto Fantasy for two timpanists and orchestra 2000, Voices for Organ, Didgeridoo and Narrator 2001, Concerto for Cello and Orchestra 2001, Danassimo 2001, The Man in the Bath 2001, Passage 2001, Diaspora 2001, Notes 2001, Galileo Galilei (opera) 2002, Waiting for the Barbarians (opera) 2005, Appomattox (opera) 2007, The American Four Seasons 2010, The Perfect American 2013. *Publications:* Music by Philip Glass 1987, Opera on the Beach 1988, Words Without Music:

A Memoir 2015. *Honours:* BMI Award 1960, Lado Prize 1961, Benjamin Award 1961, 1962, Ford Foundation Young Composer's Award 1964–66, Fulbright Award 1966–67, Musical America Magazine Musician of the Year 1985, New York Dance and Performance Award 1995, Nat. Endowment for the Arts Opera Honor 2010, Glenn Gould Prize 2015. *Current Management:* Dunvagen Music Publishers, 40 Exchange Place, Suite 1906, New York, NY 10005, USA. *Telephone:* (212) 979-2080 (office). *Fax:* (212) 473-2842 (office). *E-mail:* info@dunvagen.com (office). *Website:* www.philipglass.com.

GLASSMAN, Allan; American singer (tenor, baritone); b. 1950, Brooklyn, NY. *Education:* Hartt College of Music and Juilliard School. *Career:* sang as a baritone at Michigan Opera from 1975, then at Philadelphia, Washington and the City Opera, New York; Roles have included Dandini in La Cenerentola, Rossini's Figaro, Belcore, Enrico in Lucia di Lammermoor, Ford and Schaunard; Studied further in New York and sang tenor roles at the Metropolitan from 1985 with debut as Edmondo in Manon Lescaut; Further appearances in USA and at Frankfurt as Tybalt in Roméo et Juliette, Cassio, Bacchus, Alfredo, Hoffman, Faust and Eisenstein; Sang Tichon in Katya Kabanova at the Metropolitan in 1991, Marcello in Leoncavallo's La Bohème at St Louis, Dimitri in Boris Godunov at Pittsburgh in 1991, and Arrigo in I Vespri Sicilani at Nice in 1997; Season 1995–96 as Kardinal Albrecht in Mathis der Maler, and Cavaradossi at the New York City Opera, Bacchus in Ariadne auf Naxos for Miami Opera; Tichon at Dallas, 1998; Sang Boris in Katya Kabanova at Montreal, 2000. *Address:* 1704 Garnet Lane #3002, Fort Worth, TX 76112, USA.

GLAUSER, Elisabeth; Swiss singer (mezzo-soprano); b. 1 June 1943, Interlaken; d. of Eva Zurbrügg (violinist). *Education:* studied in Berne, Stockholm and Italy. *Career:* sang in Pforzheim 1971–73, Freiburg 1973–75, Dortmund 1975–82, Staatsoper Stuttgart 1982–88; sang Rossweise at Bayreuth Festival 1976–81, Adelaide in Arabella at Glyndebourne Festival 1985, 1989; guest appearances at Rome Opera as Herodias in Salome 1988, and Komische Oper Berlin in Düsseldorf, Zurich, Bologna, Venice, Cologne, Lisbon, Hanover, Schwetzingen Festival and Lucerne Festival; other roles include Marcellina, Maddalena, Santuzza, Kundry, Fricka, Waltraute, Octavian, Clytemnestra and the Countess Geschwitz in Lulu; concert soloist in classical and contemporary repertory; recordings for RIAS Berlin, WDR Cologne, RAI Roma; Prof., Hochschule der Künste, Berne 1988–2010; Pres. Jury, KHS/ASM Competition; mem. Bd, Kiefer-Hablitzel-Stiftung 1999–2011. *Website:* www.elisabethglauser.com.

GLAZER, Gilda, BA, MA; American pianist; b. 1949, New York, NY; m. Robert Glazer. *Education:* Queens Coll., CUNY, Columbia Univ., studied with Nadia Reisenberg. *Career:* debut at Kaufman Concert Hall, New York; resident keyboardist, Chicago Symphony, St Louis Symphony; guest soloist, Chicago, St Louis, North Carolina Symphonies; resident soloist, New York String Symphony; pianist, Glazer Duo 1970–; pianist, New York Piano Quartet; guest pianist with Mendelssohn Quartet; world premieres of works by Leo Ornstein, David Ott; mem. piano faculty, Hartt Coll. of Music, Chicago Musical Coll.; extensive solo tours; appearances in Lincoln Center, Carnegie Hall and Ravinia Festival; pianist, New Friends of Chamber Music, New York; judge Heida Hermanns Int. Competition. *Recordings:* piano solos and chamber music of Leo Ornstein, Joaquin Turina, Easley Blackwood and David Amram. *Address:* Prestige Concerts International, 14 Summit, Englewood, NJ 07632, USA.

GLAZER, Robert, BMus, MMus; American violist and conductor; b. 1945, Anderson, IN; m. Gilda Glazer. *Education:* Chicago Musical Coll., studied with William Primrose, Franco Ferrara. *Career:* mem. string faculty, Columbia Univ.; mem., Chicago Symphony; co-Principal Viola, St Louis Symphony; violist, Hartt String Quartet; Music Dir, New York String Symphony; violist of Glazer Duo 1970–; guest soloist, St Louis Symphony, Louisville Orchestra, Hartford Symphony; guest violist, Lenox Quartet, Manhattan and Mendelssohn Quartets; extensive solo tours; world premieres of works by David Epstein and Leo Ornstein; Conductor, American Chamber Orchestra, Brevard Music Festival; judge, Washington Int. Competition, Primrose Memorial Competition. *Recordings:* Soloist, Morton Gould Viola Concerto with Louisville Orchestra; Violist, Lyric by George Walker; works by Joaquin Turina and Easley Blackwood. *Honours:* Tanglewood Award. *Address:* Prestige Concerts International, 14 Summit, Englewood, NJ 07632, USA.

GLENN, Bonita; American singer (soprano); b. 1960, Washington. *Education:* Philadelphia Academy of Music. *Career:* sang with the Philadelphia Orchestra under Eugene Ormandy, the Oakland Symphony, Toronto Symphony and Rochester Orchestra; recitals at Carnegie Hall, Avery Fisher Hall, Tully Hall, and Kennedy Hall and in Canada and Costa Rica; sang in La Bohème with Philadelphia Grand Opera and in Turandot at the Salzburg Landestheater under Leopold Hager; sang Manon in Houston and Pamina with Santa Fe Opera; appeared as Musetta, Suppé's Galatea, and Corilla in Viva La Mamma at Berne and St Gallen in Switzerland; concert engagements in Europe, Canada and the USA, in Germany with the Nuremberg Symphony Orchestra, the Stuttgart Symphony in Four Last Songs under Neville Marriner, and the Bavarian Radio Symphony Orchestra; sang Clara in Porgy and Bess with the Royal Liverpool Philharmonic conducted by Libor Pešek and with the Scottish Chamber Orchestra under Carl Davis, 1989–90. *Honours:* winner Philadelphia Orchestra Vocal Competition.

GLENNIE, Dame Evelyn Elizabeth Ann, DBE, GRSM, FRAM, FRCM, FRNCM; British percussionist, composer, consultant and motivational speaker; b. 19 July 1965, Aberdeen, Scotland; d. of Isobel Glennie and Herbert Arthur Glennie. *Education:* Ellon Acad., Aberdeenshire, Royal Acad. of Music, London. *Career:* solo debut at Wigmore Hall, London, 1986; concerto, chamber and solo percussion performances worldwide; gave Promenade concerts' first-ever percussion recital 1989; numerous TV appearances, three documentaries on her life including Touch the Sound 2004 (BAFTA Award); composer of music for TV and radio; many works written for her by composers, including Bennett, Rouse, Heath, Macmillan, McLeod, Muldowney, Daugherty, Turnage and Musgrave; Munster Trust Scholarship 1986. *Films:* wrote and played music for The Trench, Touch the Sound (Critics' Prize, Locarno Int. Film Festival), Golf in the Kingdom. *Play:* Playing from the Heart. *Recordings include:* Rhythm Song, Dancin', Light in Darkness, Rebounds, Veni Veni Emmanuel, Wind in the Bamboo Grove, Drumming, Her Greatest Hits, The Music of Joseph Schwantner, Sonata for Two Pianos and Percussion (Bartók), Last Night of the Proms – 100th Season, Street Songs, Reflected in Brass, Shadow Behind the Iron Sun, African Sunrise, Manhattan Rave, UFO: The Music of Michael Daugherty, Bela Fleck-Perpetual Motion, Oriental Landscapes, Fractured Lines, Michael Daugherty: Philadelphia Stories/UFO, Philip Glass: The Concerto Project 2004, Christopher Rouse 2004, Touch the Sound soundtrack 2004, Margaret Brouwer: Aurolucent Circles 2006. *Television includes:* music for Trial and Retribution 1–5 (Yorkshire TV), music for Mazda commercial Blind Ambition, Survival Special (Anglia) and others. *Publications:* Good Vibrations (autobiography) 1990, Great Journeys of the World, Beat It!, African Dances, Marimba Encores, 3 Chorales for Marimba. *Honours:* Hon. DMus (Aberdeen) 1991, (Bristol, Portsmouth) 1995, (Leicester, Surrey) 1997, (Queen's, Belfast) 1998, (Southampton) 2000, (Williams Coll., USA) 2005, (Binghampton) 2007, (Edinburgh Napier Univ.) 2009, (Cambridge) 2010, Hon. DLitt (Warwick) 1993, (Loughborough) 1995, (Salford) 1999, Hon. LLD (Dundee) 1996, Hon. DUniv (Essex, Durham) 1998, (Open) 2007, (Queen Margaret, Edinburgh) 2008; many int. prizes and awards, including Shell/LSO Music Gold Medal 1984, Queen's Commendation Prize at RAM 1985, Grammy Award 1988, Scotswoman of the Decade 1990, Charles Heidsieck Soloist of the Year, Royal Philharmonic Soc. 1991, Personality of the Year, Int. Classical Music Awards 1993, Young Deaf Achievers Special Award 1993, Best Studio Percussionist, Rhythm Magazine 1998, 2000, 2002, 2003, 2004, Best Live Percussionist, Rhythm Magazine 2000, Classic FM Outstanding Contribution to Classical Music 2002, Walpole Medal of Excellence 2002, Musical America 2003, Tartan Clef Award 2005, Scotland with Style Classical Award 2005, Best Orchestral Percussionist, Drummies Readers' Poll Awards 2005, 2009, Incorporated Soc. of Musicians Distinguished Musician Award 2006, Sabian Lifetime Achievement Award 2006, inducted into PASIC Hall of Fame 2008, Percuaction Lifetime Achievement Award 2014, Grammy Award 2014, Polar Music Prize 2015. *Address:* Evelyn Glennie Office, Unit 6, Ramsay Court, Hinchingbrooke Business Park, Huntingdon, Cambs., PE29 6FY, England (office). *Telephone:* (1480) 459279 (office). *Fax:* (1480) 451610 (office). *E-mail:* admin@evelyn.co.uk (office); brenda@evelyn.co.uk (office). *Website:* www.evelyn.co.uk (office).

GLENNON, Jean; American singer (soprano); b. 1960. *Career:* professional career from 1983; many appearances with opera companies in Miami, Virginia and New York; season 1993 gave British concert debut with the Academy of St Martin in the Fields and further concerts at Düsseldorf, Brescia and Montreux; season 1994 with Musetta at Antwerp, Aida at Würzburg, and Mimi in Dortmund; concerts of the Verdi Requiem at Bordeaux and Beethoven's Ninth in Strasbourg; season 1995–96 as Tosca at St Gallen, Butterfly at Malmö and Donna Anna for New Zealand Opera. *Recordings include:* Floyd's Susannah, with Opéra de Lyon; sang Turandot at Auckland 1997. *Honours:* winner Metropolitan Opera Auditions 1983.

GLOBOKAR, Vinko; French composer and trombonist; b. 7 July 1934, Anderny, Meurthe et Moselle; m. Tatjana Kristan 1963, two s. *Education:* Ljubljana Conservatory, Conservatoire National de Musique, Paris, studied with René Leibowitz, Luciano Berio. *Career:* trombone soloist; conductor; played with group for new music, Buffalo University, 1966; teacher of trombone, Staatliche Hochschule für Musik, Cologne, 1968–76, and composition, New Music Courses, Cologne; founder, New Phonic Art Quartet, 1969; Director of Department for Instrumental and Vocal Research, IRCAM, Paris, 1973–79; Professor, Scuola di Musica, Fiesole-Florenna, 1983–; solo performer of works written for him by Stockhausen, Berio, Kagel and others; British premiere with Heinz Holliger of Gemeaux by Toru Takemitsu, Edinburgh, 1989; played his Kolo at Dartington Summer School, 1992. *Compositions include:* Accord for soprano and ensemble 1966, Concerto Grosso for five instruments, chorus and orchestra 1970, Laboratorium for ensemble 1973, Les Emigrés 1982–86, Labour 1992, Blinde Zeit for ensemble 1993, Dialog Über Feuer 1994, Dialog Über Erde 1994, Dialog Über Wasser 1994, Dialog Über Luft 1994, Masse, Macht und Individuum 1995. *Publications:* Vzdih-Izdih, Einatmen-Ausatmen Komposition und Improvisation by Vinko Globokar; contrib. some 30 articles to musical magazines. *Honours:* first prize for trombone, Paris 1959, Gaudeamus for Composition 1968, Radio Yugoslavia 1973.

GLOVER, Jane Alison, CBE, MA, DPhil, FRCM; British conductor; *Director of Opera, Royal Academy of Music;* b. 13 May 1949, d. of the late Robert Finlay Glover and Jean Muir. *Education:* Monmouth School for Girls and St Hugh's Coll., Oxford. *Career:* Jr Research Fellow, St Hugh's Coll. 1973–75, Lecturer in

Music 1976–84, Sr Research Fellow 1982–84; Lecturer, St Anne's Coll., Oxford 1976–80, Pembroke Coll. 1979–84; mem. Univ. of Oxford Faculty of Music 1979–; professional conducting debut at Wexford Festival 1975; operas and concerts for BBC, Glyndebourne 1982–, Royal Opera House 1988–, Covent Garden, ENO 1989–, London Symphony Orchestra, London Philharmonic Orchestra, Royal Philharmonic Orchestra, Philharmonia, Royal Scottish Orchestra, English Chamber Orchestra, Royal Danish Opera, Glimmerglass Opera, New York 1994–, Australian Opera 1996– and many orchestras in Europe and USA; Prin. Conductor London Choral Soc. 1983–2000; Artistic Dir London Mozart Players 1984–91; Prin. Conductor Huddersfield Choral Soc. 1989–96; Music Dir Music of the Baroque, Chicago, USA 2002–; Dir of Opera, RAM 2009–; mem. BBC Cen. Music Advisory Cttee 1981–85, Music Advisory Cttee, Arts Council 1986–88; Gov. RAM 1985–90, BBC 1990–95. *Television:* documentaries and series and presentation, especially Orchestra 1983, Mozart 1985. *Radio:* talks and series including Opera House 1995, Musical Dynasties 2000. *Publications:* Cavalli 1978, Mozart's Women: His Family, His Friends, His Music 2005; contribs to The New Monteverdi Companion 1986, Monteverdi 'Orfeo' Handbook 1986; articles in numerous journals. *Honours:* Hon. DMus (Exeter) 1986, (CNAA) 1991, (London) 1992, (City Univ.) 1995, (Glasgow) 1996; Hon. DLitt (Loughborough) 1988, (Bradford) 1992; Dr hc (Open Univ.) 1988, (Brunel) 1997. *Current Management:* Music International, 13 Ardilaun Road, Highbury, London, N5 2QR, England. *E-mail:* neil@musicint.co.uk. *Address:* Royal Academy of Music, Marylebone Road, London, NW1 5HT, England (office). *Telephone:* (20) 7873-7373 (office). *E-mail:* j.glover@ram.ac.uk (office). *Website:* www.ram.ac.uk (office); www.janeglover.co.uk; www.baroque.org.

GLUBOKY, Pyotr; Russian singer (bass); b. 1947, Gordiyenki, near Volgograd. *Education:* Moscow Conservatoire and the Bolshoi Theatre. *Career:* appearances at the Moscow Bolshoi from 1975, as Rossini's Bartolo and Basilio, Leporello and Alfonso, Pimen, King Philip, Mendoza in Prokofiev's Betrothal in a Monastery and parts in his War and Peace; Guested with the Bolshoi at the 1991 Edinburgh Festival as Panas in Rimsky-Korsakov's Christmas Eve; Concert appearances in Greece, England, Canada, USA, Australia, France, Italy and Japan.

GLUSHCHENKO, Fedor Ivanovich; Russian conductor; *Principal Guest Conductor, National Symphony Orchestra of Ukraine;* b. 29 March 1944, Rostov Region; m. 1st; one s. one d.; m. 2nd Galina Baryshnikova; one d. *Education:* Moscow and Leningrad State Conservatories, Vienna Acad. of Music; studied under Herbert von Karajan. *Career:* Chief Conductor, Karelian Radio and TV Symphony Orchestra, Petrozavodsk 1971–73; Chief Conductor and Artistic Dir, Ukrainian State Symphony Orchestra, Kiev 1973–87; British debut in 1989 with BBC Scottish Symphony, also appeared with Royal Liverpool Philharmonic and Scottish Chamber Orchestra; Conductor, Istanbul State Opera 1990–91; Prin. Guest Conductor, Nat. Symphony Orchestra of Ukraine 2010–; fmr Chief Conductor and Artistic Dir J.S. Bach Chamber Orchestra, Yekaterinburg; Guest Conductor, Moscow Philharmonic Orchestra, Russian State Symphony Orchestra, Moscow Symphony, Ministry of Culture Orchestra and orchestras in Riga, Vilnius, Leningrad (now St Petersburg), Sverdlovsky, Tbilisi and Tashkent; tours in UK, Sweden, Italy, Denmark, China, Germany, France, Spain, Netherlands, Greece, Turkey, Portugal, Slovenia, Ireland, Poland. *Honours:* Artist of Ukraine 1979, People's Artist of Ukraine 1982. *Address:* 105037 Moscow, 1st Pryadilnaya str. 11, Apartment 5, Russia. *Telephone:* (499) 165-49-46; 903-1142086 (mobile). *E-mail:* f.glushchenko@mail.ru.

GLUZMAN, Vadim; Israeli (b. Ukrainian) violinist; b. 1973; m. Angela Yoffe. *Education:* Juilliard School with the late Dorothy DeLay and Masao Kawasaki, also studied with Roman Šne in Latvia, Zakhar Bron in Russia, Yair Kless in Israel and Arkady Fomin in USA. *Career:* grew up in Riga, Latvia; moved to Israel 1990; appearances worldwide with orchestras including Chicago Symphony, London Philharmonic, Israel Philharmonic, London Symphony, Leipzig Gewandhaus, Munich Philharmonic, San Francisco Symphony, Minnesota Orchestra, St Louis Symphony and NHK Symphony under conductors including Neeme Järvi, Michael Tilson Thomas, Andrew Litton, Marek Janowski, Itzhak Perlman, Tugan Sokhiev, Paavo Järvi, Rafael Frühbeck de Burgos, Hannu Lintu and Peter Oundjian; festival appearances at Verbier, Ravinia, Lockenhaus, Pablo Casals, Colmar, Jerusalem and North Shore Chamber Music Festival, Northbrook, Ill. (co-founder with wife); live and recorded premieres of contemporary music by composers including Giya Kancheli, Peteris Vasks, Lera Auerbach, Sofia Gubaidulina, Michael Daugherty and Balys Dvarionas; Creative Partner and Principal Guest Artist, ProMusica Chamber Orchestra, Columbus 2013–. *Recordings include:* Richard Rodney Bennett, Hindemith/Beethoven/Brahms, Auerbach, time... and again, Pärt – Spiegel im Spiegel, Ballet for a Lonely Violinist, Glazunov/Tchaikovsky Violin Concertos 2008, Fireworks, Remembrance, Barber/Bernstein/Bloch, Korngold – Dvarionas Violin Concertos, Bruch Concerto pour violon no.1 (Diapason d'Or de l'année 2011), Gubaidulina In Tempus Praesens/Glorious Percussion, Bach/Auerbach/Ysaÿe Partitas 2011, Prokofiev Violin Sonatas Number 1&2 2013. *Honours:* Choc de Classica. *Current Management:* c/o Sonia Simmenauer, Impresariat Simmenauer, Kurfürstendamm 211, 10719 Berlin, Germany. *Telephone:* (30) 414781718. *Fax:* (30) 414781713. *E-mail:* sonia.simmenauer@impresariat-simmenauer.de. *Website:* www.impresariat-simmenauer.de. *E-mail:* vadim@vadimgluzman.com (office). *Website:* www.vadimgluzman.com (office).

GLYNN, Gerald, BA, MA; Australian composer; b. 3 Sept. 1943, Brisbane. *Education:* University of Queensland, University of Sydney, electronic studios of French Radio, studied with Peter Maxwell Davies, Olivier Messiaen, Larry Sitsky, composition seminars with Iannis Xenakis and Henri Pousseur. *Career:* NSW Conservatory, 1981; Commissions from Seymour Group (1982) and Symeron (1992). *Compositions include:* Masses, for organ, 1972; Chanson de Ronsard, for soprano, countertenor and percussion, 1974; Changes, for cello, 1975; Syntheses, for string quartet, 1977; Interplay for cello and piano, 1980; William Blake Triptych for chorus, 1981; Chamber Concerto, 1982; Love's Coming, song cycle for medium voice and piano, 1986; Toccata-Sonata, for piano, 1989; Filigrees 1, 2 and 3, for piano, 1981–91; The Rose of Amherst, song cycle for medium voice and piano, 1991; Strata for violin and piano, 1994; Filigrees 4 for piano, 1997.

GNAM, Adrian, BMus, BS, MMus, DMus; American conductor, music director, oboist and academic; b. 4 Sept. 1940, New York; m. Catharine Dee Morningstar 1983; one s. one d. *Education:* Coll. Conservatory of Music, Cincinnati, Univ. of Cincinnati. *Career:* debut at Carnegie Recital Hall and Town Hall, New York 1962; Principal Oboe, American Symphony Orchestra (under Stokowski), Cleveland Orchestra (under Szell), Heritage Chamber Quartet, Carnegie Wind Quintet, Chamber Arts Ensemble; mem. Faculty, Univ. of Cincinnati Coll. Conservatory of Music 1967–76, Ohio Univ. 1969–76, currently mem. Faculty, Georgia Southern Univ.; Distinguished Artist-in-Residence, Mercer Univ. 2001; guest conductor throughout the USA and for orchestras in Romania, Yugoslavia, Venezuela, Mexico, Japan, Italy, Brazil and Spain; Congress of Strings, Temple and Georgetown Univs, Peabody Conservatory, Univs of Michigan, Georgia and Houston, Colorado Philharmonic; Asst Music Dir, Nat. Endowment for the Arts 1976–82, Music Dir 1982–84; Principal Guest Conductor, Philadelphia Concerto Soloists Chamber Orchestra 1977–88; Music Dir, Midland Symphony, Mich. 1982–86, Macon Symphony, Ga 1983–, Eugene Symphony, Ore. 1985–89, Tuscaloosa Symphony, Ala 1993–96; Music Dir, Macao Sinfonia 2000; Pres. Conductors' Guild; mem. AFM, American Symphony Orchestra League. *Address:* Department of Music, Georgia Southern University, PO Box 8052, Statesboro, GA 30460, USA (office). *Telephone:* (912) 478-5396 (office). *Fax:* (912) 478-1295 (office). *E-mail:* agnam@georgiasouthern.edu (office). *Website:* class.georgiasouthern .edu (office).

GOBLE, Theresa; British singer (mezzo-soprano); b. 1970, England. *Education:* Guildhall School, Nat. Opera Studio, Britten-Pears School and European Opera Centre with Vera Rozsa and Nicolai Gedda. *Career:* concert repertoire includes the Verdi Requiem, Rossini Stabat Mater and Petite Messe, Messiah, Dvořák Stabat Mater and Tippett's Child of Our Time; created the Aunt in Param Vir's Snatched by the Gods, for ENO Contemporary Opera Studio; sang Flosshilde in Das Rheingold for Scottish Opera, and appeared as Baba the Turk in The Rake's Progress at the QEH 1997; Ulrica in Un Ballo in Maschera for Opera Holland Park; other roles include Dorabella, Verdi's Amneris, Eboli and Mistress Quickly, Charlotte in Werther, Carmen, Adalgisa, Leonora in La Favorita and Laura in La Gioconda.

GOCKLEY, (Richard) David, BA, MBA; American opera director; *General Director, San Francisco Opera;* b. 13 July 1943, Philadelphia, Pa; s. of Warren Gockley and Elizabeth Gockley; m. Adair Lewis; one s. two d. *Education:* Brown Univ., Columbia Univ., New England Conservatory. *Career:* Dir of Music, Newark Acad. 1965–67; Dir of Drama, Buckley School, New York 1967–69; Box Office Man., Santa Fe Opera 1969–70; Asst Man. Dir Lincoln Center, New York 1970; Business Man., Houston Grand Opera 1970–71, Assoc. Dir 1971–72, Gen. Dir 1972–2006; Co-founder Houston Opera Studio 1977; Gen. Dir San Francisco Opera 2006–; mem. Bd of Dirs Texas Inst. of Arts in Educ.; mem. Opera America (Pres. 1985–); fmr Chair. Houston Theater Dist. *Operas produced include:* Pasatieri's The Seagull 1974, Porgy and Bess (Grammy Award 1977) 1976, Floyd's Bilby's Doll 1976, Willie Stark 1981, Harvey Milk (by Stewart Wallace and Michael Korie), Philip Glass's Akhnaten 1984, John Adams' Nixon in China (Emmy Award 1988) 1987, Tippett's New Year 1989, The Passion of Jonathan Wade 1991, Meredith Monk's Atlas 1991, Robert Moran's Desert of Roses 1992, Florencia en el Amazonas, Treemonisha, A Quiet Place, Resurrection, Carmen. *Honours:* Hon. DHL (Univ. of Houston) 1992, Hon. DFA (Brown Univ.) 1993; League of New York Theaters and Producers Tony Award 1977, Columbia Business School Dean's Award 1982, Nat. Inst. of Music Theater Award 1985, Brown Univ. William Rogers Award 1995. *Address:* San Francisco Opera, 301 Van Ness Avenue, San Francisco, CA 94102-4509, USA (office). *Telephone:* (415) 861-4008 (office). *Website:* www.sfopera.com (office).

GODAR, Vladimir; Slovak composer; b. 16 March 1956, Bratislava. *Education:* Bratislava Conservatory, Acad. of Music and Drama. *Career:* Ed., OPUS Publishing House. *Compositions include:* Trio for oboe, violin and piano 1973, Fugue for string orchestra 1975, Three Songs 1977, Overture for symphony orchestra 1978, Symphony 1980, Wind Quintet 1980, Trio for violin, clarinet and piano 1980, Ricercar 1980, Melodarium (20 dances) 1980, Melodarium (72 duets) 1981, Lyrical Cantata 1981, Partita 1983, Talisman 1983, Grave Passacaglia for piano 1983, Four Serious Songs 1984, Orbis Sensualium Pictus (oratorio) 1984, Concerto Grosso per archi e cembalo 1985, Sonata in Memoriam Viktor Shklovski 1985, Symphony No. 2 1992, Via Lucis for orchestra 1994, Déploration sur la mort de Witold Lutoslawski (piano quintet) 1994, Tombeau de Bartók for orchestra 1995. *Honours:* Slovak Music Fund Jan Levoslav Bella Prize.

GODFREY, Daniel Strong, BA, PhD; American composer and academic; b. 20 Nov. 1949, Bryn Mawr, PA; m. Diana Carol Bottum 1976; one s. *Education:* Yale Univ., Yale School of Music, Univ. of Iowa. *Career:* Dir, Yale Russian Chorus, including tours of USA and USSR 1969–72; Visiting Asst Prof. of Music Composition and Theory, Univ. of Pittsburgh, PA 1981–93, Asst Prof. 1983–88, Assoc. Prof. 1988–93, Prof. 1993–, Dir 1997–99; Composer-in-Residence, Syracuse Univ. School of Music, Syracuse, NY 2002–. *Compositions:* String Quartet 1974, Progression 1975, Trio 1976, Five Character Pieces for viola and piano 1976, Celebration for solo piano 1977, Music for marimba and vibraphone 1981, Scrimshaw for flute and violin 1985, Concentus for small orchestra 1985, Intermedio for string quartet 1985, Dickinson Triptych for soprano and piano 1986, Three Marian Eulogies for high voice, viola and piano 1987, Mestengo for orchestra 1988, Numina for six instruments 1991, Clarion Sky for orchestra 1992, String Quartet No. 2 1993, Two Scenes in Chiaroscuro for ten performers 1994, Serenata Ariosa for clarinet, viola and piano 1995, Festoons for piano solo, From a Dream of Russia for clarinet, violin and piano 1996, Jig for wind ensemble/concert band 1996, Sinfonietta for string orchestra 1996, Lightscape for orchestra 1997, Symphony in Minor 1999, String Quartet No. 3 2000, revised 2001, Shindig for solo horn and wind ensemble 2000, revised 2001, Breath and Shadow for bassoon and string quintet 2001, Romanza for string quartet 2001, Concerto for piano and chamber winds 2003, Pomp and Revelry for wind quintet 2004. *Publications:* Music Since (with Elliott Schwartz) 1945; contrib. to Elliott Carter's String Quartet No.3: A Unique Vision of Musical Time (in Sonus, Vol. 8, No. 1). *Honours:* New York Foundation for the Arts Award 1991, winner Spirit of Today West Competition 1991, Indiana State Univ. Festival Award 1992, American Acad. of Arts and Letters 1998, Barlow Endowment for Music Composition 1999, Big Ten Band Directors' Asscn 1999, Koussevitzky Music Foundation Award 2000, J. S. Guggenheim Foundation Award 2001–02. *E-mail:* cynthia@artists.com. *Address:* 222 Kensington Place, Syracuse, NY 13210, USA. *E-mail:* dsgodfre@syr.edu.

GODSON, Daphne, LRAM, ARAM; British violinist; b. 16 March 1932, Edinburgh, Scotland. *Education:* Royal Acad. of Music, London and Brussels Conservatoire. *Career:* principal soloist, Scottish Baroque Ensemble 1969–87; principal, Scottish Chamber Orchestra 1974–76; mem., Bernicia Ensemble, Scottish Early Music Consort; Leader, Edinburgh Bach Players; soloist, BBC Scottish, Scottish Nat. Orchestra and the Bournemouth Symphony Orchestra; teacher, RSAMD, City of Edinburgh Music School; mem. Incorporated Soc. of Musicians, Soroptimist Int. *Honours:* premiere prize Brussels Conservatoire 1956.

GODZISZEWSKI, Jerzy, MA; Polish pianist; b. 24 April 1935, Wilno. *Education:* Superior Music School, Warsaw; summer masterclasses in piano with Benedetti Michelangeli, Arezzo, Italy. *Career:* regular appearances as soloist and with orchestras in Poland and abroad; performed complete piano works of Maurice Ravel 1975, of Karol Szymanowski 1982; chamber music appearances; teacher of piano, Superior Music School, Wroclaw 1967–77; teacher of piano 1978–, Prof. 1988–, Acad. of Music, Bydgoszcz; appearances in int. music festivals, including Warsaw Autumn, Chopin festivals; mem. Polish Artists' and Musicians' Asscn. *Recordings:* piano works of Chopin, Szymanowski, Debussy, Ravel, Prokofiev and others for Polish radio and television, and for Muza and Wifon record companies; Complete Piano Works of K. Szymanowski. *Honours:* Distinction, Sixth Chopin Int. Piano Competition, Warsaw 1960, Szymanowski Memorial Foundation Award 1998, Fryderyk Prize for Best Solo Record for Complete Piano Works of K. Szymanowski 1998. *Current Management:* Maria Blaszczak Artists' Management, ul. Ogrody 13/246, 85-870 Bydgoszcz, Poland. *Telephone:* (52) 3713211. *Fax:* (52) 3713211. *E-mail:* iamb@bzi.pl. *Website:* www.iamb.bzi.pl. *Address:* ul. W. Lokietka 54, 85-200 Bydgoszcz, Poland. *E-mail:* iamb@lazi.pl.

GOEBBELS, Heiner; German composer and director; *Professor, Institute for Applied Theatre Studies, Justus Liebig University;* b. 17 Aug. 1952, Neustadt an der Weinstraße, Rhineland-Palatinate. *Education:* studied sociology and music in Frankfurt. *Career:* co-founded Duo Heiner Goebbels Alfred Harth 1976–88; Music Dir, Frankfurt Schauspiel 1978–88; founded performance group, Cassiber 1982; Prof., Inst. for Applied Theatre Studies, Justus Liebig Univ., Giessen 2006–, Man. Dir 2003–11; Pres. Theatre Acad. of Hesse; Artistic Dir Ruhrtriennale –Int. Festival of the Arts 2012–14; Fellow, Inst. for Advanced Studies, Berlin 2007; Artist in Residence, Cornell Univ., USA 2010; mem. of several acads of arts, including Berlin, Frankfurt, Düsseldorf, Mainz, Munich. *Exhibitions include:* documenta 8, 1987, documenta X 1997, Centre Pompidou, Paris 2000, Museum Mathildenhöhe, Darmstadt 2012, Musée d'Art Contemporain, Lyon 2014, Artangel, London 2008, 2012, Albertinum, Dresden 2016. *Compositions include:* Red Run 1988–91, Befreiung for narrator and ensemble 198, Surrogate Cities for orchestra, eight movements 1994, Industry and Idleness, for chamber orchestra 1996, Nichts Weiter, for orchestra 1996, Walden 1998, From a Diary 2002, Songs of Wars I Have Seen 2007, etc. *Music theatre includes:* Ou bien le débarquement désastreux 1993, Repetition 1995, Black on White 1996, Nichts Weiter, for orchestra 1996, Eislermaterial 1998, Max Black 1998, Hashirigaki 2000, Landscape with Distant Relatives 2002, eraritjaritjaka 2004, Stifters Dinge 2007, I Went to the House but Did Not Enter 2008, When the Mountain Changed its Clothing 2012. *Radio includes:* Verkommenes Ufer 1984, Die Befreiung des Prometheus 1986, Wolokolamsker Chausee 1989, Schliemanns Radio 1990, Shadow-Landscape with Argonauts 1991, Roman Dogs 1996. *Publications:* Komposition als Inszenierung 2002, Aesthetics of Absence: Texts on Theatre

2015. *Honours:* Hon. Fellow, Dartington Coll. of Arts, Central School of Speech and Drama, London; Dr hc (Birmingham); Prix Italia 1986, 1992, 1996, Karl Szcuka Award 1984, 1990, 1992, European Theatre Award 2001, Ibsen Award (Norway) 2012, Excellence in Teaching Award 2012, Premio Franco Quadri Milano 2015. *E-mail:* mail.hg@gmail.com. *Website:* www.heinergoebbels.com.

GOEBEL, Reinhard; German violinist; b. 31 July 1952, Siegen, Westphalia. *Education:* studied in Cologne and Amsterdam with Maier, Gawriloff and Leonhardt. *Career:* founder of Musica Antiqua Köln 1973, for the performance of early music, touring in Europe, North and South America, the Far East and Australia; London debut at the QEH 1978; played in a concert at the 1989 York Festival in England with music by Legrenzi, Schmelzer and Biber; season 1996 with Gluck's Orphée et Eurydice at Drottningholm and Handel's Serse at Copenhagen; tour of N and S America for 30th anniversary of ensemble 2003. *Recordings include:* Bach's Art of Fugue and Musical Offering; Biber's Mensa Sonora and Solo Violin Sonata in A; Orchestral Suites by Telemann (ECHO Award for Sinfonia Spituosa 2002); soundtrack of Gérard Corbiau's film, Le Roi danse, with music by Lully (ECHO Award 2001); Bachiana (music by the Bach family); Charpentier's Musique Sacrée, Biber's Harmonia Artificiosa. *Publications:* Johann David Heinichen: Sacred Vocal Music 2003, Johann David Heinichen: Lamentations Jeremiae. *Address:* Brüsseler Str. 94, 50672 Köln, Germany (office). *Telephone:* (221) 9232030 (office). *Fax:* (221) 9232031 (office). *E-mail:* management@musica-antiqua-koeln.de (office). *Website:* www.musica-antiqua-koeln.de (office).

GOEHR, Alexander, MA; British composer and academic; *Professor Emeritus of Music, University of Cambridge*; b. 10 Aug. 1932, Berlin, Germany; s. of Walter Goehr and Laelia Goehr; m. 1st Audrey Baker 1954; m. 2nd Anthea Felicity Staunton 1972; m. 3rd Amira Katz; one s. three d. *Education:* Berkhamsted School, Royal Manchester Coll. of Music, Paris Conservatoire (with Olivier Messiaen) and privately with Yvonne Loriod. *Career:* composer, teacher, conductor 1956–; held classes at Morley Coll., London; part-time post with BBC, responsible for production of orchestral concerts 1960–; works performed and broadcast world-wide; awarded Churchill Fellowship 1968; Composer-in-Residence, New England Conservatory, Boston, Mass. 1968–69; Assoc. Prof. of Music, Yale Univ. 1969–70; Prof., West Riding Chair of Music, Univ. of Leeds 1971–76; Prof. of Music, Univ. of Cambridge 1976–99, Prof. Emer. 1999–, Fellow of Trinity Hall, Cambridge 1976–; Reith Lecturer 1987. *Compositions include:* Songs of Babel 1951, Sonata 1952, Fantasias 1954, Capriccio 1957, The Deluge 1957–58, La belle dame sans merci 1958, Four Songs from the Japanese 1959, Sutter's Gold 1959–60, Suite 1961, Hecuba's Lament 1959–61, A Little Cantata of Proverbs 1962, Two Choruses 1962, Virtutes 1963, Little Symphony 1963, Little Music for Strings 1963, Five Poems and an Epigram of William Blake 1964, Pastorals 1965, Piano Trio 1966, Arden muss sterben (Arden Must Die, opera) 1966, Warngedichte 1967, Romanza 1968, Naboth's Vineyard 1968, Nonomiya 1969, Paraphrase 1969, Symphony in One Movement 1970, Shadowplay 1970, Sonata about Jerusalem 1970, Concerto for Eleven Instruments 1970, Chaconne for Wind 1974, Lyric Pieces 1974, Metamorphosis/Dance 1974, Fugue on the Notes of the Fourth Psalm 1976, Romanza on the Notes of the Fourth Psalm 1977, Prelude and Fugue for three clarinets 1978, Chaconne for organ 1979, Das Gesetz der Quadrille 1979, Babylon the Great is Fallen 1979, Behold the Sun 1984, Two Imitations of Baudelaire 1985, Symphony with Chaconne 1986, Eve Dreams in Paradise 1987, Carol for St Steven 1989, ...in real time 1989, Sing, Ariel 1989, Still Lands 1990, Bach Variations 1990, The Death of Moses 1991, The Mouse Metamorphosed into a Maid 1991, Colossus or Panic 1992, I Said, I Will Take Heed 1993, Cambridge Hocket 1993, Arianna (opera) 1995, Schlussgesang 1997, Kantan (opera) 2000, Piano Quintet 2001, Second Musical Offering (GFH) 2002, Marching to Carcassonne 2003, Adagio (Autoporträt) 2003, Dark Days 2004, Fantasie 2005, Broken Lute 2006, Since Brass, Nor Stone (British Composer Award for Best Chamber Music Composition 2009) 2008, manere2008, Broken Psalm 2009, TurmMusik/Tower Music 2009–10, from Shadow of Night 2009–10, Hymn to Night 2010, When Adam Fell 2010–11, Cities and Thrones and Powers 2011, Pomfret. The Dungeon of the Castle 2012, Largo Siciliano 2012, To These Dark Steps/The Fathers Are Watching 2012, ...between the Lines/...zwischen den Zeilen 2013, Seven Impromptus 2014, Vanishing Word 2014–15. *Honours:* Hon. Prof., Beijing Univ. 2001; Hon. mem. American Acad. and Inst. of Arts and Letters; Hon. ARCM 1976; Hon. FRNCM 1980; Hon. FRCM 1981; Hon. DMus (Southampton) 1973, (Manchester), (Nottingham) 1994, (Siena) 1999; Dr hc (Cambridge) 2000. *Address:* c/o Schott Music, 48 Great Marlborough Street, London, W1F 7BB, England. *E-mail:* promotions@schott-music.com. *Website:* www.schott-music.com.

GOERGEN, Viviane, BMus; Luxembourg/Swiss pianist; b. 17 June 1948, Paris, France. *Education:* Conservatoire de la Ville de Luxembourg, Conservatory of Nancy, France, Paris Conservatory and Ecole Nationale de Musique, Paris. *Career:* debut in Luxembourg; first appeared, Paris, 1971; London, 1973; Zürich, 1974; Bonn, 1975; Brussels, 1976; Prague, 1978; Vienna, 1979; Frankfurt, 1982; Madrid, 1983; Berlin, 1991; since 1978 has taken part in regular foreign tours; numerous radio appearances; first performances of works, partly especially composed for her; devotes attention to the music of Claude Debussy and to reviving pianoworks of forgotten composers; lectured in Berlin, Frankfurt, Cythira and Madeira 2000–05; founder mem. Center for the Mental Training of Musical Performers, 1994. *Recordings:* Schumann: Davidsbündlertänze, Drei Romanzen op 28; Johannes Brahms: Sonata op 5 and Sonata op 38; César Franck: Sonata in A Major; Ludwig van Beethoven: Sonatas op 5; Dimitri Shostakovich: Sonata op 40.; Lyonel Feiniger, The Piano Works, 1994; Kurt Dietmar Richter, Feiniger Impulse, 1994; Claude Debussy, Images, 1997; Erwin Schulhoff, 3rd Sonata for piano, 1997; Ernst Toch, 10 recital and 10 concert studies (op 56 and 55), Burlesques (op 31), 1999. *Film:* film of the Center for the Mental Training of Musical Performers (RTL) 2002. *Honours:* Order of Merit for artistic achievements, Luxembourg 1993. *Address:* Nelkenstr. 1, 63322 Rödermark, Germany. *E-mail:* viviane.goergen@gmx.net (office).

GOERNER, Stephan; Swiss cellist; b. 23 Oct. 1957. *Education:* Winterthur Conservatory, Juilliard School, USA and International Menuhin Acad., Gstaad. *Career:* co-founder and cellist, Carmina Quartet 1984, with appearances from 1987 in Europe, Israel, Japan and USA; regular concerts at the Wigmore Hall from 1987 and at the South Bank Centre in London, Amsterdam Concertgebouw, the Kleine Philharmonie in Berlin, and Konzertverein Wien in Vienna; four engagements in Paris 1990–91, seven in London and tours to Australasia, USA, and Japan with concerts at the Hohenems, Graz, Hong Kong, Montreux, Schleswig-Holstein, Bath, Lucerne, and Prague Spring Festivals; collaborations with Dietrich Fischer-Dieskau, Olaf Bär and Mitsuko Uchida. *Honours:* winner Paolo Borciani String Quartet Competition, Reggio Emilia, Italy (with Carmina Quartet) 1987.

GOERTZ, Harald, OBE, DrPhil; Austrian conductor, musicologist, pianist, manager and academic; *Vice-President, Österreichische Gesellschaft für Musik*; b. 31 Oct. 1924, Vienna; m. Carola Renner; one s. one d. *Education:* Univ. of Vienna, advanced piano studies with Wührer and conducting studies with Reichwein, Krips and Swarowsky, Acad. of Music, Vienna. *Career:* asst to Herbert von Karajan, Scala di Milano, Lucerne and others; Music Dir opera and concerts, Ulm, Germany 1955–63; Guest Conductor, Stuttgart, Vienna, Berlin and elsewhere; teacher, Acad. of Music, Stuttgart and Salzburg Mozarteum; Prof. and Leader of Conductor's Class, Opera Section, Hochschule für Musik, Vienna and seminars for interpretation; Chorus Dir Vienna Opera –1991; Pres. Austrian Soc. of Music 1963–97; writer and commentator, Austrian TV and Salzburger Festspiele; organizer, British Music Week, Vienna 1969. *Publications:* Österreichisches Musikhandbuch (ed.), Dictionary of Contemporary Austrian Composers (ed.) 1989, Mozart's Dichter Lorenzo da Ponte 1988, Gerhard Wimberger (monograph) 1990, Österreichische Komponisten der Gegenwart (ed.) 1994, Hanns Eisler Symposion (ed.) 2000, Verdi für Opernfreunde 2001, Musikhandbuch für Österreich 2003, Anthology: 17 studies 2010; contribs to Grove Dictionary of Music and Musicians. *Honours:* Bundesverdienst-Kreuz, Germany. *Address:* Österreichische Gesellschaft für Musik, Hanuschgasse 3, 1010 Vienna (office); Wiedner Hauptstrasse 40, 1040 Vienna, Austria (home). *Telephone:* (1) 5123143 (office); (1) 5876406 (home); (676) 6052706 (Mobile) (home). *Fax:* (1) 5123143 (office). *E-mail:* office@oegm.org (office). *Website:* www.oegm.org (office).

GOLAN, Itamar; Israeli pianist; b. 1970, Vilnius, Lithuania. *Education:* studied in Israel with Lara Vodovoz and Emmanuel Krasovsky, and in Boston, USA. *Career:* recitals and chamber music performances in Israel and the USA 1977–; collaborations with Mischa Maisky, Ivry Gitlis and the Aurora Piano Quartet; appearances at the Ravinia, Edinburgh, Besançon, Ludwigsburg and Wyoming Festivals; concert partners have included Maxim Vengerov, Shlomo Mintz and Tabea Zimmerman; trio formation with Mintz and Mat Haimovitz (violin and cello); solo engagements with the Israel Philharmonic under Zubin Mehta and the Jerusalem Symphony Orchestra with David Shallon; faculty mem., Manhattan School of Music 1991–; Prof. of Chamber Music, Paris Conservatoire 1994–. *Address:* c/o Conservatoire National Supérieur de Musique et de Danse, 209 ave Jean Jaurès, 75019 Paris, France (office).

GOLANI, Rivka; Canadian/Israeli violist and painter; b. 22 March 1946, Israel; d. of Jacob Gulnik and Lisa Gulnik; m. Jeremy Fox 1993; one s. *Education:* Univ. of Tel-Aviv, Rubin Music Acad., studied with Oedon Partos. *Career:* concerts as soloist world-wide; has inspired many new works including viola concerti by Holloway, Hummel, Fontajn, Colgrass, Holmboe, Yuasa and Turner, solo works by Holliger, Holmboe and others; has collaborated with composers as a visual artist in presenting multimedia performances; art exhbns in Israel, UK, Germany and N America; Artistic Director of the Fort Macleod International Chamber Music Festival; currently mem. Faculty, Strings Dept, Trinity Laban Conservatoire of Music and Dance, London; named Amb. of Canadian Music by Canadian Music Centre. *Recordings include:* three-album set of solo works by J. S. Bach. *Publication:* Birds of Another Feather (book of drawings). *Honours:* Grand Prix du Disque 1985, Medal Pro Artibus, Artijus Foundation. *Current Management:* Marilyn Gilbert Artists Management, 705 King Street West, Suite 1713, Toronto, ON M5V 2W8, Canada. *Address:* Trinity Laban Conservatoire of Music and Dance, Faculty of Music, King Charles Court, Old Royal Naval College, Greenwich, London, SE10 9JF, England (office). *E-mail:* r.golani@trinitylaban.ac.uk (office). *Website:* www.trinitylaban.ac.uk (office).

GOLDBERG, Reiner; German singer (tenor); b. 17 Oct. 1939, Crostau. *Education:* Carl Maria von Weber Hochschule für Musik, Dresden with Arno Schellenberg. *Career:* debut as Luigi in Il Tabarro at Dresden 1966; Dresden State Opera 1973–77 and Deutsche Staatsoper East Berlin from 1977; roles include Florestan, Turiddu, Cavaradossi, Hermann in The Queen of Spades, Aron in Schoenberg's Moses und Aron, and Sergei in Katerina Izmailova; guest appearances in Leipzig, Leningrad, Vienna, Prague and Italy; toured Japan with Dresden Company 1980; Covent Garden debut 1982 as Walther in

Die Meistersinger; Paris 1982 in a concert performance of Strauss's Die Liebe der Danaë; Bayreuth Festival 1988 in a new production of The Ring produced by Harry Kupfer; New York debut 1983 in a concert performance of Strauss's Guntram; La Scala Milan 1984 as Tannhäuser; Teatro Liceo, Barcelona 1985 as Siegfried; sang Walther at Covent Garden 1990, Erik in Der fliegende Holländer at Bayreuth 1990 and Bayreuth Festival 1992, Florestan and Tannhäuser at the Metropolitan 1992; Aegisthus in Elektra at Florence 1996; Tannhäuser at the Berlin Staatsoper 1999; season 2000–01 as Max in Der Freischütz at the Berlin Staatsoper and Walther von Stolzing in Madrid. *Recordings:* Drum Major in Wozzeck; Parsifal in the film version of Wagner's opera by Syberberg, with role mimed by a woman; Max in Der Freischütz; Guntram; Siegmund in Haitink's recording of Die Walküre.

GOLDENTHAL, Elliot; American composer; b. 2 May 1954, New York. *Education:* Manhattan School of Music with John Corigliano. *Career:* freelance composer of theatre, film and choral music; collaborations with Yo-Yo Ma, Julie Taymor and Neil Jordan; mem. American Soc. of Composers, Authors and Publishers. *Compositions include:* Brass Quartet 1983, The Transposed Heads (musical after Thomas Mann) 1987, Pastime Variations for chamber orchestra 1988, Shadow lay Scherzo for orchestra 1988, Juan Darien, A Carnival Mass 1988, Fire Water Paper: A Vietnam Oratorio 1995, Concerto for trumpet and piano 1996, Othello (for San Francisco Ballet) 2003, , incidental music for A Midsummer Night's Dream, The Taming of the Shrew, The Tempest, Titus Andronicus. *Film scores:* Cocaine Cowboys 1979, Blank Generation 1980, Drugstore Cowboy 1989, Pet Cemetery 1989, Grand Isle 1991, Alien 3 1992, Demolition Man 1993, Interview with the Vampire 1994, Golden Gate 1994, Cobb 1994, Voices 1995, Batman Forever 1995, Heat 1995, Michael Collins 1996, A Time to Kill 1996, Batman & Robin 1997, The Butcher Boy (Los Angeles Film Critics Asscn Award for Best Original Score) 1998, Sphere 1998, In Dreams 1998, Titus 1999, Final Fantasy: The Spirits Within 2001, Frida (Golden Globe for Best Score 2003, Acad. Award for Best Original Score) 2002, The Good Thief 2002, S.W.A.T. 2003, Across the Universe 2007, Public Enemies 2009, The Tempest 2009. *Television music:* Criminal Justice 1990, Fool's Fire 1992, Behind the Scenes (series) 1992, Roswell 1994. *Honours:* Stephen Sondheim Award in Music Theater, Arturo Toscanini Award. *Current Management:* Gorfaine/Schwartz Agency Inc., 4111 West Alameda Avenue, Suite 509, Burbank, CA 91505, USA. *Telephone:* (818) 260-8500. *Website:* www.gsamusic.com.

GOLDSMITH, Barry, BM, MM, DMA; American pianist; b. 4 June 1959, New York. *Education:* Peabody Conservatory of Music, Johns Hopkins University, Indiana University School of Music, Manhattan School of Music. *Career:* debut at Carnegie Recital Hall, New York City, 1982; solo recitals in USA, Canada and Europe, including New York, Philadelphia, Washington, DC, Baltimore, San Francisco, Vancouver, London, Oslo, The Hague, Brussels, Milan; performed in major concert halls, including Carnegie Recital Hall, New York; Wigmore Hall, London; Diligentia Hall, The Hague; University Hall, Oslo; solo recitals at Interlochen Arts Academy; guest appearances at univs on the east coast and midwest USA; soloist with Peabody Symphony, The Queensborough Symphony and Orchestras in New York; live performances on WNYC FM Radio in New York; taped performances on Nat. Public Radio, USA; solo recitals in Edinburgh (Scotland) and with orchestras in New York's Town Hall (USA); Prof. of Piano, Queensborough Community College, New York. *Compositions:* works for piano, voice or violin and piano, The Heritage, Suites for violin and piano. *Address:* 75-07 171 Street, Flushing, NY 11366, USA.

GOLDSMITH, Harvey, CBE; British music promoter; b. 4 March 1946, London; s. of Sydney Goldsmith and Minnie Goldsmith; m. Diana Goldsmith 1971; one s. *Education:* Christ's Coll. and Brighton Coll. of Tech. *Career:* joined Big O Posters, Kensington Market 1966; organized open-air free concerts, Parliament Hill Fields 1968; in partnership with Michael Alfandary opened Round House, London 1968; organized 13 Garden Party concerts at Crystal Palace, London 1969; merged with John Smith Entertainment 1970–75; formed Harvey Goldsmith Entertainment promoting rock tours by Elton John, Rolling Stones etc.; in partnership with Ed Simons, rescued Hotel Television Network 1983; formed Allied Entertainment Group as public co. 1984–86; returned to pvt. ownership 1986; subsidiary Harvey Goldsmith Entertainment promotes some 250 concerts per year; formed Classical Productions with Mark McCormack, promoting shows at Earls Court including Pavarotti concert and productions of Aida 1988, Carmen 1989, Tosca 1991; produced Bob Dylan Celebration, New York 1992, Mastercard Masters of Music (Hyde Park), The Eagles (Wembley), Three Tenors (Wembley), Lord of the Dance (world tour) 1996, Music for Montserrat (Royal Albert Hall), Boyzone (tour), Paul Weller (tour), Pavarotti (Manchester), Cirque du Soleil (Royal Albert Hall) 1997, Alegria (Royal Albert Hall), The Bee Gees (Wembley), Ozzfest (Milton Keynes Bowl), Paul Weller (Victoria Park) 1998; Chair. Nat. Music Day; Vice-Chair. Prince's Trust Bd; Vice-Pres. React 1989–; Trustee, Gret, Band Aid 1985–, Live Aid Foundation 1985–; Dir Pres.'s Club, London First, London Tourist Bd; Amb. for London Judges Award 1997; Chair. Ignition International 2006–; mem. Advisory Group Red Cross. *Honours:* Music Industry Trust Award 2006, Queen's Diamond Jubilee Award 2012. *Address:* Harvey Goldsmith Entertainments Ltd , 3rd Floor, 113 Great Portland Street, London, W1W 6QQ, England (office). *Telephone:* (20) 7224-1992 (office). *Fax:* (20) 7580-1853 (office). *Website:* www.harveygoldsmith.com.

GOLDSTEIN, Malcolm, MA; American/Canadian composer and violinist; b. 27 March 1936, Brooklyn, NY; two s. *Education:* Columbia Coll., Columbia Univ. with Otto Luening. *Career:* worked at Columbia-Princeton Electronic Music Center 1959–60, Columbia Univ. 1961–65, New England Conservatory 1965–67, Goddard Coll., Vermont 1972–74, and Bowden Coll., Brunswick, Maine 1978–82; with Judson Dance Theater 1960s; Co-Dir of the concert series, Tone Roads, 1963–69, giving performances of works by Ives, Varese and Cage; Dir of the New Music Ensemble and Collegium at Dartmouth Coll. 1975–78; Dir, Ensemble for New Music, Hessen Radio 1990s; has toured Europe and North America as composer and violinist. *Compositions include:* Emanations for violin and cello 1962, Ludlow Blues for winds and tape 1963, Illuminations from Fantastic Gardens for vocal ensemble 1964, Sirens for Edgard Varese 1965, Death: act or fact of dying for vocal ensemble 1967, Frog Pond at Dusk 1972, Upon the String, within the bow....breathing for string ensemble 1972, Yosha's Morning Song Extended 1974, Hues of the Golden Ascending for flute ensemble 1979, Marin's Song, Illuminated 1979/82, On the First Day of Spring There Were 40 Pianos 1981, A Breaking of Vessels, Becoming Song (flute concerto) 1981, The Seasons, Vermont 1980–82, Of Sky Bright Mushrooms Bursting in My Head for ensemble 1984, Cascades of the Brook (Bachwasserfall) violin concerto 1984, That hung like fire on heaven for chamber ensemble 1985, Soweto Stomp for ensemble 1985, qernerâq: our breath as bones for voice and instrumental ensemble 1986, Through Deserts of Time for string quartet 1990, Gentle Rain Preceding Mushrooms for violin and voice 1992, An enactment of absence for violin and piano 1995, Configurations in Darkness for instrumental ensemble 1995, As it were for violin, contrabass and percussion 1996, Regarding the Tower of Babel for ensemble 1997, Hardscrabble songs for violin and voice 2000, A New Song of many faces for In These Times for string quartet 2002, What can be said of our differences? 2005; radio/acoustic art works, including Ishi/timechangingspaces 1988, between (two) spaces 1993, As it Were, Another 1998, Fragments of the Wall (music theatre) 2007, The Sky has Many Stories to Tell 2010. *Publications include:* From Wheelock Mountain, scores and writings 1977, Edition of the String Quartet No. 2 by Ives; book: Sounding the Full Circle: concerning music improvisation and other related matters 1988. *Honours:* Artists Foundation Fellowship in Music Composition, Boston 1984, Prix Acustica Int., West German Radio, Cologne 1994; numerous commissions and grants from Mass Council on the Arts, Canada Council for the Arts. *Address:* PO Box 134, Sheffield, VT 05866, USA (home).

GOLDSTONE, Anthony Keith, GRSM, ARMCM; British pianist; b. 25 July 1944, Liverpool, England; s. of Myer Charles Maurice Goldstone and Rose Goldstone; m. Caroline Clemmow 1989. *Education:* Royal Manchester Coll. of Music. *Career:* debut at Wigmore Hall, London 1969; appearances throughout England with all major symphony orchestras and in recital; many festivals; several BBC Promenade Concerts in London including the Last Night in 1976; very frequent broadcaster; tours to N and S America, Africa, Asia, Europe, Australasia; regular piano duo with wife, Caroline Clemmow, and numerous chamber activities, including founding Musicians of the Royal Exchange 1978; Fellow, Royal Manchester Coll. of Music; mem. Inc. Soc. of Musicians. *Recordings include:* solo piano: Mozart, Beethoven, Schubert, Lyapunov, Arensky, Glière, Rebikov, Parry, Elgar, Holst, Lambert, Mussorgsky, Schumann, Britten, Kodály, Enescu, Bridge, A. Moyzes, operatic and ballet transcriptions and others; chamber: Beethoven, Sibelius, Mendelssohn, Holst and others; piano duo: two-piano works by Chopin, Holst (Planets), Brahms (Sonata), Gershwin, Ravel, Gál, Britten, George Lloyd, Mozart, Grieg, Soler, Leighton, A. Moyzes, B. Chapple and others; piano duets by Schubert (complete), Alkan (complete), Dvořák, Mendelssohn, Herzogenberg, Rimsky-Korsakov, Tchaikovsky, Stravinsky, Elgar; virtuoso variations, romantic sonatas, others; concertos: Beethoven (from BBC Promenade Concerts), Alkan, Saint-Saëns, Pitfield. *Honours:* prizes, Int. Piano Competitions, Munich, Vienna 1967, BBC Piano Competition 1968, Gulbenkian Fellowship 1968–71. *Address:* Walcot Old Hall, Alkborough, North Lincs., DN15 9JT, England. *E-mail:* AKGoldstone@aol.com. *Website:* www.divine-art.com/AS/goldstone.htm.

GOLDTHORPE, (John) Michael, MA, PGCE; British singer (tenor), lecturer, teacher and conductor; *Musical Director, Lymington Choral Society*; b. 7 Feb. 1942, York, North Yorks., England; two s. two d. *Education:* Trinity Coll., Cambridge, King's Coll., London, Guildhall School of Music and Drama, London. *Career:* debut at Purcell Room, London 1970; Paris debut 1972; Opera Royal, Versailles 1977; Royal Opera, Covent Garden and BBC TV 1980; regular broadcaster, BBC Radio; US debut, Miami Festival 1986; appearances in Singapore, Iceland and most countries in Western Europe; Concertgebouw, Amsterdam 1986; directed Medieval Concert in Rome 1987; noted Bach Evangelist and exponent of French Baroque; Lucerne Festival's performance of Frank Martin's Golgotha 1990; series of concerts for the Sorbonne, Paris 1992; Examiner, Trinity Coll. of Music and Royal Coll. of Music, London; fmr Lecturer and Teacher, Univ. of Roehampton, London; Founder and Artistic Dir specialist Victorian music group and charity The Bold Balladiers 1995; Musical Dir, Lymington Choral Soc. 2006–; mem. Royal Soc. of Musicians of GB 1999–. *Recordings include:* Rameau: Hippolyte et Aricie, La Princesse de Navarre and Pygmalion, Charpentier: Missa Assumpta est Maria, Mondonville Motets, Cavalli: Ercole Amante, Delius: Irmelin, Monteverdi: L'Incoronazione di Poppea, Madrigali, Blanchard: Cantatas, Stuart Ward: St Cuthbert of Lindisfarne and Other Songs. *Honours:* Hon. Fellow, Cambridge Soc. of Musicians 1993; Choral Exhbn, Cambridge 1961, Lieder Prize, Guildhall School of Music 1967, Young Musicians Award, Greater London Arts Asscn, Young Musicians Award, Inc. Soc. of Musicians, Young Musicians Award, Park Lane Group early 1970s, Wingate Scholarship 1994, SEDA accreditation as Teacher in Higher Educ. 2000. *Address:* 77 Southampton Road, Lymington, Hants., SO41 9GH, England (home). *Telephone:* (1590) 677258 (home); (7761) 247617 (home). *E-mail:* info@michaelgoldthorpe.com (office). *Website:* www.michaelgoldthorpe.com.

GOLESORKHI, Anooshah; American singer (baritone); b. 1962, Tehran, Iran. *Education:* studied in California, USA. *Career:* debut at Opera Pacific Costa Mesa 1988 as Amonasro in Aida; sang Escamillo at Bergen Opera, Norway; Iago on tour with the Company in Israel 1993; Connecticut Opera 1991 as Garriso in Massenet's Navarriase; San Jose Opera as Rossini's Figaro and Marcello in La Bohème; St Gallen 1993 as Barnaba in La Gioconda and Canterbury Opera, New Zealand as Scarpia; other roles include Verdi's Nabucco, Renato, Luna and Macbeth and Gerard in Andrea Chénier. *Current Management:* c/o Organisation Internationale Artistique, 16 Avenue Franklin D. Roosevelt, 75008 Paris, France; c/o Pinnacle Arts: Miller Division, 889 Ninth Avenue, Second Floor, New York, NY 10019, USA. *Telephone:* 1-42-25-58-34 (OIA); (212) 397-7911 (Pinnacle). *Fax:* 1-42-25-64-97 (OIA); (212) 397-7920 (Pinnacle). *E-mail:* oia@oia-poilve.com; jmiller@pinnaclearts.com. *Website:* www.oia-poilve.com; www.pinnaclearts.com.

GOLIGHTLY, David Frederick, BA, AMusM, PGAS, PGCE; British composer; *Director, Modrana Music Publishers;* b. 17 Nov. 1948, Co. Durham, England; s. of Joyce Bewley. *Education:* Univ. of Huddersfield, Guildhall School of Music and Drama, London, Univs of Leeds and Nottingham. *Career:* Dir, Modrana Music Publrs 1980–; Chair. North-West Composers Asscn 1994–2000; mem. Bd of Dirs British Acad. 1999–2001, The Composers' Guild of GB 1998; mem. Advisory Group, Performing Right Soc. 1998. *Compositions include:* The Eye, a Chamber Opera premiered 1992, Symphony No. 1, Rites of Passage and The St Petersburg Mass premiered 1994 in the State Capella Hall, St Petersburg, Russia, Frontiers (five arrangements of American folk songs for male voice choir), Songs of the Cliff Top for baritone and piano, Star Flight, Northumbrian Fantasy, Crimond arrangement, and A Weardale Portrait for brass band, Septet for brass, Little Suite for brass quintet, Three Pieces for trombone quartet (Vols 1 and 2), Concert Fanfare for brass and percussion, Four Preludes for flute and guitar, Three Shadow Portraits for piano, Piano Sonata No. 1, Flute concerto, Trumpet concerto, Concerto for strings, Three Pan Love Songs for solo flute, Piano Trio Letters of Regret, Dances for Showgirls for piano trio, Prelulada Contrapontala for string orchestra, Piano Trio Immemorial, Symphony No. 2, premiered St Petersburg 2006, Bassoon Concerto, Three Impressionist Impressions for oboe and piano, Three Preludes and Fugues, Into My Heart song cycle, Three Houseman settings, Seven Preludes and Fugues on the DFG Codes, Songs of Time and Place, Songs of an Evening Sea, Variations on Psalm 33 for organ and SATB, Cornish Fishermen for TTBB and piano, The Christmas Rose for SATB, The Rose for TTBB and piano, Cello Sonata, Violin Sonata, Three Dance Episodes for viola and piano, Tuba Sonata, Fantasy on a Theme of Thomas Morley for piano, Three Tuba Jollies, Three Folk Song Settings for mezzo soprano and string trio; music for the theatre and film. *Publication:* two-vol. Compositional Tutorial (includes 205 original music examples). *Honours:* Second Prize (for Symphony No. 1 recording), 'Just Plain Folks' Best Classical Album 2006. *Address:* Modrana Music Promotions Ltd, Mill Isle House, 4 The Batts, Frosterley, Wear Valley, Bishop Auckland, Co. Durham, DL13 2SB, England (office). *Telephone:* (1388) 527068 (office). *Fax:* (1388) 527068 (office). *E-mail:* info@modranamusicpromotions.com (office). *Website:* www .modranamusicpromotions.com (office).

GOLIJOV, Osvaldo, PhD; Argentine composer; *Composer-in-Residence, Chicago Symphony Orchestra;* b. 5 Dec. 1960, La Plata. *Education:* Jerusalem Rubin Acad., Univ. of Pennsylvania, Tanglewood Inst., studied with Gerardo Gandini in La Plata, Mark Kopytman in Jerusalem, George Crumb in Pennsylvania, Oliver Knussen at Tanglewood. *Career:* moved to USA 1986; numerous collaborations with the Kronos Quartet, including a series of arrangements of music from all over the world; collaborations with artists including Taraf de Haïdouks, Mexican rock band Café Tacvba, Klezmer master David Krakauer, tabla virtuoso Zakir Hussain, Argentine musician and prod. Gustavo Santaolalla, Mexican film dir Alejandro González Iñarritu; composer-in-residence posts include Merkin Hall, New York, Spoleto Festival, Los Angeles Philharmonic Music Alive series, Marlboro Music Festival, Ravinia Festival; teacher Coll. of the Holy Cross, Worcester, MA 1991–, currently Assoc. Prof.; Visiting Lecturer Boston Conservatory, Tanglewood Music Center; composer-in-residence Chicago Symphony Orchestra 2006–(08). *Compositions include:* Yiddishbbuk for string quartet 1992, The Dreams and Prayers of Isaac the Blind for klezmer clarinet and string quartet 1994, K'vakarat for clarinet and string quartet 1994, Last Round for string orchestra 1996, Oceana (choral work) 1996, Din for bells and ensemble 1998, Doina for string quartet 1999, Mariel for cello and marimba 1999, St Mark Passion for soloists, chorus, percussion and orchestra 2000, Tenebrae for soprano, clarinet and string quartet 2002, Three Songs for soprano and orchestra 2002, Ainadamar (one-act opera) (Grammy Award for Best Classical Contemporary Composition 2007) 2003, Ayre for soprano and ensemble 2004, Tekyah for klezmer ensemble 2004. *Film soundtracks:* The Man Who Cried 2000, Darkness 2002. *Current Management:* c/o Jonathan Brill, ICM Artists, 40 W 57th Street, New York, NY 10019, USA. *Telephone:* (212) 556-5620 (office). *Fax:* (212) 556-5677 (office). *E-mail:* jbrill@icmtalent.com (office). *Website:* www.icmtalent.com (office). *E-mail:* nfo@osvaldogolijov.com. *Website:* www.osvaldogolijov.com.

GÖLLNER, Theodor, PhD, DrPhil, Habil.; German musicologist; *Professor Emeritus and Director, Commission of Music History, Bavarian Academy of Sciences;* b. 25 Nov. 1929, Bielefeld; s. of Friedrich Göllner and Paula Brinkmann; m. Marie Louise Martinez 1959; one s. one d. *Education:* Univs of Heidelberg and Munich. *Career:* Lecturer, Univ. of Munich 1958–62, Asst Prof. 1962–67, Assoc. Prof. 1967; Prof., Univ. of Calif., Santa Barbara 1967–73; Prof. and Chair. Inst. of Musicology, Univ. of Munich 1973–97; Prof. Emer. and Dir Comm. of Music History, Bavarian Acad. of Sciences 1982–; mem. European Acad. of Sciences and Arts 1991–. *Publications:* Formen früher Mehrstimmigkeit 1961, Die mehrstimmigen liturgischen Lesungen 1969, Die Sieben Worte am Kreuz 1986, Et incarnatus est in Bachs h-moll-Messe und Beethovens Missa solemnis 1996, Die Tactuslehre in den deutschen Orgelquellen des 15. Jahrhunderts 2003, Münchner Veröffentlichungen zur Musikgeschichte (ed.) 1977–2006, Münchner Editionen zur Musikgeschichte 1979–97, Die psalmodische Tradition bei Monteverdi und Schütz 2006. *Address:* Institute of Musicology, University of Munich, Geschwister-Scholl-Platz 1, 80539 Munich (office); Bahnweg 9, 82229 Seefeld, Germany (home). *Telephone:* (1089) 21802364 (office). *E-mail:* TheodorGoellner@aol.com (home).

GOLOVIN, Andrei; Russian composer and conductor; b. 11 Aug. 1950, Moscow. *Education:* Moscow Conservatoire. *Career:* teacher of composition, Gnesins' State Musical College 1975–, Gnesins' Russian Academy of Music 1989–; mem. Russian Composers' Union. *Compositions:* Cadence and Ostinato for five timpani, bells, tam-tam and piano, 1979, Concerto Symphony for viola, cello and symphony orchestra, 1980, Sonata for oboe and cembalo, 1980, Sonata for piano, 1981, Duet for violin and piano, 1981, Duet for viola and cello, 1981, Sonata Breve for viola and piano, 1982, Japanese edition, 1992, 2 Pieces for piano, 1982, Sonata for cello solo, 1983, 2 Pieces for flute and piano: Portrait, and, Landscape, 1983, Prelude for vibraphone, 1984, Legend for piano, 1984, 3 Easy Pieces for piano, 1985, 1st Quartet for 2 violins, viola and cello, 1986, Music for string quartet, 1986, Sonatina for piano, 1986, Japanese edition, 1991, Fairy-Tale for horn and piano, 1987, Concert Symphony for viola, piano and orchestra, 1988, Symphony for full symphony orchestra, 1990, Elegy for cello solo, 1990, Poeme Nocturne for viola and piano, 1991, Plain Songs: Canata to Verses by N Rubtsov for mezzo-soprano, bass, piano and chamber orchestra, 1991, Remote Past for piano, 1991; Symphony No. 4, for cello and orchestra, 1992; On the Hills of Georgia, chorus, 1992; Spring Song for trombone and piano, 1993; First Love, opera after Turgenev, 1996. *Recordings:* Simple Songs: Cantata, Elegy for cello solo; Sonata Breve for viola and piano; Elegy for cello solo; Concert Symphony for viola, piano and orchestra; Quartet for 2 violins, viola and cello; 2 Pieces for flute and piano; Music for strings. *Address:* Shumkin Street 3, k2, Ap 45, Moscow 107113, Russia.

GOLUB, David; American pianist and conductor; b. 22 March 1950, Chicago. *Education:* studied with Alexander Uninsky in Dallas, with Beveridge Webster at the Juilliard School, New York. *Career:* debut with Dallas Symphony Orchestra 1964; appeared with orchestras in Philadelphia, Cleveland, Dallas, St Louis, Pittsburgh, Cincinnati, Chicago, Minnesota, Washington and Atlanta; solo appearances also with orchestras of Toronto, Ottawa, Edmonton, Montréal, Calgary and Vancouver; has performed at all major North American music festivals; European engagements with orchestras in London, Rome, Paris, Milan, Geneva, Florence, Rotterdam, Amsterdam and Prague; appeared in film From Mao to Mozart, which documented tour to China 1979 with Isaac Stern; formed a piano trio with Colin Carr and Mark Kaplan. *Recordings:* Gershwin and Rachmaninov with London Symphony Orchestra and complete piano trios of Schubert, Mendelssohn and Brahms; Haydn's L'Isola Disabitata, as conductor; The Complete Trios of Dvořák, Rachmaninov with Golub-Kaplan-Carr Trio.

GOMBRICH, Carl; British singer (bass); b. 1975, England. *Education:* Guildhall School of Music and Drama, Nat. Opera Studio, London with Neil Howlett, King's Coll. London. *Career:* with Morley Opera sang Tom in Un Ballo in Maschera, Mephistopheles in Faust, Sparafucile (Rigoletto) and Guglielmo (Così fan tutte); joined Pavilion Opera 1998, singing Dr Bartolo in Le nozze di Figaro, Un Fraate and Il Grande Inquisitore in Don Carlo, Commendatore in Don Giovanni , the title role in Don Pasquale, and Oroveso in Norma; Blansac in La Scala di Seta at the Wexford Festival 1999; Mozart's Osmin in The Escape from the Seraglio, for British Youth Opera (Linbury Studio Theatre, Covent Garden) 2000; Zaretsky in Eugene Onegin with Grange Park Opera 2000; Raimondo in Lucia di Lammermoor for Millennium Opera 2000; Il Bonze in Madama Butterfly and the Sergeant of Police in The Pirates of Penzance for Open Air Music Theatre Co. 2000; mem., European Opera Centre, with roles including Collatinus in The Rape of Lucretia; sang Der Kammersanger in Intermezzo, returning in 2002 to sing Masetto in Don Giovanni, for Garsington Opera.

GOMEZ, Jill, FRAM; British singer (soprano); b. 21 Sept. 1942, New Amsterdam, British Guiana. *Education:* St Joseph's Convent, Trinidad, St Maur's Convent, Surrey, Royal Acad. of Music, Guildhall School of Music, studied with Luigi Ricci in Rome. *Career:* operatic debut as Adina in L'Elisir d'Amore with Glyndebourne Touring Opera 1968 and has since sung leading roles with Glyndebourne Festival Opera including Mélisande, Calisto and Ann Truelove in The Rake's Progress; has appeared with The Royal Opera, ENO, English Opera Group, and Scottish Opera in roles including Pamina, Ilia, Fiordiligi, the Countess in Figaro, Elizabeth in Elegy for Young Lovers, Ann Trulove, Tytania, Lauretta in Gianni Schicchi and the Governess in The

Turn of the Screw; cr. the role of Flora in Tippett's The Knot Garden, at Covent Garden 1970 and of the Countess in Thea Musgrave's Voice of Ariadne, Aldeburgh 1974; sang title role in Massenet's Thaïs, Wexford 1974 and Jenifer in The Midsummer Marriage with Welsh Nat. Opera 1976; cr. title role in William Alwyn's Miss Julie for radio 1977; performed Tatiana in Eugene Onegin with Kent Opera 1977; Donna Elvira in Don Giovanni, Ludwigsburg Festival 1978; cr. title role in BBC world premiere of Prokofiev's Maddalena 1979; Fiordiligi in Così fan tutte, Bordeaux 1979; sang in première of the Eighth Book of Madrigals in Zürich Monteverdi Festival 1979; Violetta in Kent Opera's production of La Traviata, Edin. Festival 1979; Cinna in Lucio Silla, Zurich 1981; The Governess in The Turn of the Screw, Geneva 1981; Cleopatra in Giulio Cesare, Frankfurt 1981; Teresa in Benvenuto Cellini, Berlioz Festival, Lyon 1982; Leila in Les Pêcheurs de Perles, Scottish Opera 1982–83; Governess in The Turn of the Screw, ENO 1984; Helena in Glyndebourne's production of Britten's A Midsummer Night's Dream; Donna Anna in Don Giovanni, Frankfurt Opera 1985 and with Kent Opera 1988; Rosario in Goyescas by Granados 1988, Helena in Midsummer Night's Dream, London Opera 1990; cr. role of Duchess of Argyll in Thomas Adès's Powder Her Face, Cheltenham Int. Music Festival and London 1995; regular engagements including recitals in France, Austria, Belgium, Netherlands, Germany, Scandinavia, Switzerland, Italy, Spain, USA; festival appearances include Aix-en-Provence, Spoleto, Bergen, Versailles, Flanders, Netherlands, Prague, Edin. and BBC Promenade concerts; master-classes at Pears-Britten School, Aldeburgh, Trinity Coll. of Music, London, Dartington Summer Festival, Meridian TV. *Recordings include:* Vespro della Beata Vergine 1610 (Monteverdi), Ode for St, Cecilia's Day (Handel), Acis and Galatea (Handel), Admeto (Handel), A Child of Our Time (Tippett), three recital discs of French, Spanish and Mozart songs with John Constable, Quatre Chansons Françaises (Britten), Trois Poèmes de Mallarmé (Ravel), Chants d'Auvergne (Canteloube), Les Illuminations (Britten), Bachianas Brasileiras No. 5 (Villa Lobos), Cabaret Classics with John Constable, Knoxville-Summer of 1915 (Barber), South of the Border (Down Mexico Way...) arranged by Christopher Palmer for Jill Gomez, Britten's Blues (songs by Britten and Cole Porter); premiere recordings of Quatre Chansons Françaises (Britten), Cantiga – The Song of Inês de Castro commissioned by her from David Matthews, Seven Early Songs (Mahler), A Spanish Songbook (with John Constable), The Knot Garden (Tippett), Miss Julie (William Alwyn), Powder Her Face (Thomas Adès).

GOMEZ-MARTINEZ, Miguel-Angel; Spanish conductor and composer; b. 17 Sept. 1949, Granada. *Education:* Granada and Madrid Conservatories, studied in the USA and in Vienna, Austria with Hans Swarowsky. *Career:* conducted opera in Lucerne, Berlin, Frankfurt, Munich and Hamburg, at Covent Garden in London, Paris, Geneva, Berne, Houston, Chicago, Florence, Rome, Venice and Palermo; Resident Conductor Berlin Deutsche Oper 1973–77, Vienna Staatsoper 1977–82; festivals in Berlin, Vienna, Munich, Macerata in Italy, Granada, Santander, San Sebastián, Savonlinna in Finland and Helsinki; repertoire of over 50 operas including works by Mozart, Puccini, Rossini, Verdi and Wagner; Conductor Radiotelevision Española Orchestra 1984–87; Artistic Dir and Chief Conductor, Teatro Lirico Nacional Madrid 1985–91; Gen. Music Dir, Nationaltheater Mannheim and Chief Conductor of the Nationaltheater Orchestra 1990–93; Chief Conductor, Hamburg Symphony 1992–; Gen. Music Dir, Finnish National Opera, Helsinki 1993–96; Chief Conductor, Orchestra of Valencia –2004; Music Dir, Opera Bern 2000–04; concerts with most major orchestras in Europe, Far East and America. *Compositions include:* Sinfonia del Descubrimiento, first performed in 1992, at Mozart Saal, Rosengarten, Mannheim, Five Canciones sobre poemas de Alonso Gamo, for soprano and orchestra, first performed Grosse Musikhalle, Hamburg, 1996, Suite Burlesca, first performed Palau de la Música, Valencia 1999, Sinfonia del Agua 2007. *Honours:* Orden del Mérito Civil 1996; Gold Medal, City of Grenada1984, Citizen of the Century, City of Grenada 2000, numerous others. *Current Management:* Balmer & Dixon Management AG, Kreuzstrasse 82, 8032 Zürich, Switzerland. *Telephone:* (43) 244-8644. *Fax:* (43) 244-8649. *Website:* www.badix.ch.

GONDEK, Juliana, MM; American singer (soprano/mezzo-soprano) and academic; *Professor of Voice and Opera, The Herb Alpert School of Music, University of California, Los Angeles;* b. Pasadena, Calif.; one d. *Education:* studied piano and violin, Univ. of Southern California School of Music, Britten-Pears School of Advanced Musical Studies, Aldeburgh, UK, San Diego Opera Center Young Artist Program. *Career:* debut with San Diego Opera as Doralice in Il Trionfo dell'Onore 1979; sang Contessa in Le nozze di Figaro with Netherlands Opera 1986, Heroines in The Tales of Hoffmann 1986, Alcina at Opera Theatre of St Louis 1987, Fiordiligi in Così fan tutte at Hawaii Opera 1989; debut with Metropolitan Opera as Marianne in Der Rosenkavalier 1991, 1992, 1993; First Lady in Die Zauberflöte with Metropolitan Opera 1991, 1992, 1993; Vitelia in La Clemenza di Tito for Scottish Opera in 1991; title role in Beatrice di Tenda 1991; Elvira in Don Giovanni at Seattle Opera 1991; Gismonda in Handel's Ottone, Göttingen Handelfestspiel and Halle Handelfestspiel 1992; Zenobia in Handel's Radamisto, Göttingen Handelfestspiel and Halle Handelfestspiel 1993; title role in Handel's Esther, Göttingen Handelfestspiel 1994; Ginevra in Handel's Ariodante, Handelfestspiel and Halle Handelfestspiel 1995; Aspasia in Mozart's Mitridate, Mostly Mozart Festival, New York 1993; Leyla in Bright Sheng's The Song of Majnun with San Francisco Symphony 1992; Paquette in Bernstein's Candide with San Francisco Symphony 1992; triple role of Diane Feinstein/Harvey's Mama/The Hooker in world premiere of Harvey Milk with Houston Grand Opera, New York City Opera and San Francisco Opera 1994–96; title role in the world

premiere of Hopper's Wife by Stewart Wallace and Michael Korie, Long Beach Opera 1997, Ginevra in Handel's Ariodante with Dallas Opera 1998; Gertrude Stein in Blood on the Dining Room Floor by Jonathan Sheffer 1999; Autonoe in The Bassarids, Amsterdam Concertgebouw 2002, La Madre (Blood Wedding) in Lorca, Child of the Moon by Ian Krouse, Los Angeles 2005; title role in Purcell's The Fairy Queen, Astoria Music Festival 2009; appeared in concerts in Canada, USA, China, Japan and in Europe; appeared as soloist at Edinburgh, Caramoor, Marlboro, Mostly Mozart, Newport, Lincoln Center, Bard, Bowdoin, Hawaii, Göttingen, Avignon and Winter Park Bach Festivals and as recitalist throughout USA, Japan, China and Europe; has performed with over 150 orchestras and opera companies worldwide; Prof. of Voice and Opera, The Herb Alpert School of Music, UCLA 1997–, Chair. Div. of Voice Studies 2002–08, Chair. Div. of Music Performance 2007–10; Head of Voice Faculty Hawaii Performing Arts Festival 2006–; Founder and Artistic Dir Baroque Opera Boot Camp, Accad. Europea di Firenze, Florence, Italy 2011–; Artist in Residence, Hong Kong Acad. for Performing Arts; Nat. Peer Reviewer in Music, Fulbright Foundation, US State Dept; master classes; judge in numerous int. and US opera and singing competitions. *Recordings include:* Yoav Chamber Ensemble (Yehudi Menuhin Foundation Prize) Orion 1979, Bernstein's West Side Story conducted by Leonard Bernstein 1984, Handel's Ottone (Gismonda) 1992, Live From The Met (video), Die Zauberflöte (1st Lady) with Metropolitan Opera 1992, Handel's Radamisto (Zenobia) 1993, Handel's Giustino (Fortuna) 1994, Handel's Ariodante (Ginevra) (Gramophone magazine Record of the Year) 1995, Mozart concert arias, Harvey Milk with San Francisco Symphony Orchestra and Chorus under Donald Runnicles (premiere) 1997, Bright Sheng's Songs from the Sung Dynasty with Hong Kong Philharmonic under Samuel Wong (premiere) 2003, Complete Songs of Karol Szymanowski (premiere) (Polish Recording Industry Record of the Year 2005, Polish Nat. Gramophonic Soc. 'Fryderyk' Award for Best Recording of Polish Music 2005) 2004, Weisgall's Esther (title role) with Seattle Symphony under Gerard Schwarz (premiere) 2006, Paul Chihara's Magnificat 2007, Roger Bourland 18 Songs 2013, This is What I Know 2015. *Honours:* Hon. Lifetime mem. Pasadena Fine Arts Club; Grad. Teaching Fellowship in Music Theory, Univ. of Southern California School of Music 1975–77, Unanimous Gold Medal, Geneva Int. Singing Competition 1983, Prix Patek Philippe 1983, Gold Medal, Barcelona 'Viñas' Int. Singing Competition 1984, Nat. Endowment for the Arts Solo Recitalists Award; prizes in Montreal Int., Metropolitan Opera, San Francisco Opera, Baltimore and New York Oratorio Soc. Competitions. *Current Management:* c/o California Artists Management, 564 Market Street, Suite 420, San Francisco, CA 94104-5412, USA. *Telephone:* (415) 362-2787. *Fax:* (415) 362-2838. *E-mail:* don@calartists.com. *Website:* calartists.mymcn.org. *Address:* Herb Alpert School of Music, Schoenberg Hall, University of California, Los Angeles, CA 90095-1616, USA (office). *Telephone:* (310) 794-9269 (office). *E-mail:* jgondek@ucla.edu. *Website:* www .julianagondek.com; www.napamusic.org.

GONG, Dong-Jian; Chinese singer (bass); b. 1 Dec. 1957, Nanchang. *Education:* Shanghai Conservatory of Music, Indiana University, USA, Opera Music Theatre International, USA. *Career:* debut as Colline in La Bohème, Vienna Staatsoper, 1991; Colline, Opera de Nice, France, Sparafucile in Rigoletto, Bilbao, Spain, Ramfis in Aida with Palm Beach Opera, Giorgio in I Puritani with Opera Malaga, Spain and as Timur with the Teatro Municipal in Santiago, 1992–93; Asdrubila, an opera premiered at 1993 Barcelona Summer Festival; Zaccaria in Nabucco with the Opera de Bellas Artes in Mexico City, Ferrando in Il Trovatore with Minnesota Opera, Raimondo in Lucia di Lammermoor with the New Jersey State Opera, Il Frate in Don Carlos in Bilbao, 1993–94; Sparafucile in Rigoletto, Timur in Turandot and Colline in a new production of La Bohème, he also appeared with the Virginia Opera as Basilio in Il Barbiere di Siviglia, performed the Boatsman in Bruch's Odysseus with the American Symphony Orchestra at Avery Fisher Hall, soloist in the Verdi Requiem with the Kennedy Opera, 1995–96; Returned to Vancouver Opera as Zaccaria in Nabucco, concert appearances included a performance of Beethoven's Missa Solemnis with the Richmond Symphony, 1994–95; Performances of Philip II in Don Carlos with the Kentucky Opera, the Grand Inquisitor in Don Carlos with Opéra de Lyon and Opéra de Nice, Ramfis with Oper der Stadt Köln and performances in Munich, Amsterdam and Hong Kong in the role of Kublai Khan in Marco Polo, 1996–97; Oper der Stadt Köln for performances of Ramfis in Aida, 1997–98; Ramfis at the Deutsche Oper Berlin, performances of Beethoven's Symphony No. 9 with the Columbus Symphony Orchestra, Biterolf in Tannhäuser in Seville, Oroveso in Norma with Opera Memphis, soloist in the Verdi Requiem with the Nashville Symphony, 1998–99. *Recordings:* Marco Polo by Tan Dun as Kublai Khan. *Current Management:* Pieter G. Alferink Artists Management Amsterdam BV, Apollolaan 181, 1077 AT Amsterdam, Netherlands.

GONLEY, Stephanie, FGSM; British violinist; *Leader, English Chamber Orchestra;* b. 1966. *Education:* Chetham School of Music, Guildhall School of Music, with Dorothy DeLay at Juilliard School and in Berlin. *Career:* Mozart Concertos with Manchester Camerata, Mendelssohn, Walton, Brahms and Bruch with Royal Philharmonic, Walton with the London Philharmonic Orchestra and Beethoven in the Netherlands with Adrian Leaper; Further engagements with English Chamber Orchestra (ECO) in 1990, Philharmonia and Halle, at Montpellier Festival and in Hong Kong, Belgium and Canada, played Vivaldi's Four Seasons with English Chamber Orchestra at Festival Hall in 1993; Prom Debut in 1995 with BBC Scottish Symphony Orchestra; Leader, English Chamber Orchestra 1991–; (Masterclasses at Banff, Canada, Aspen, USA and Prussia Cove, Cornwall, England); Co-Founded the Vellinger

String Quartet in 1990; (Particpated in master classes with the Borodin Quartet, Pears-Britten School in 1991); Concerts at Ferrara Musica Festival in Italy and debut on South Bank with the London premiere of Roberts Simpson's 13th Quartet; BBC Radio 3 debut in 1991; Season 1994–95 with concerts in London, Germany, Austria at Sweden, Paris, at Davos Festival, Switzerland; Played at Wigmore Hall several times (with Haydn Op 54 No. 2, Gubaidulina and Beethoven Op 59 No. 2), and at the Purcell Room with Haydn's Seven Last Words. *Recordings include:* Elgar's Quartet and Quintet with Piers Lane, Dvorak Romance with ECO and Charles Mackerass, Sibelius Concerto with Adrian Leaper and Orchestra of Gran Canaria, Schubert Quintet with Bernard Greenhouse. *Honours:* Winner of London International String Quartet Competition 1994. *Current Management:* c/o Robert Gilder & Company, 91 Great Russell Street, London, WC1B 3PS, England. *Telephone:* (20) 7580-7758. *Fax:* (20) 7580-7739. *E-mail:* rgilder@ robert-gilder.com. *Website:* www.robert-gilder.com.

GONNEVILLE, Michel, BMus, DMus; Canadian academic and composer; b. 1950, Montréal. *Education:* Ecole de Musique Vincent-d'Indy, Univ. of Montréal, Conservatoire de Musique de Montréal with Giles Tremblay; studied with Stockhausen, Frederic Rzewski and Joh Fritsch. *Career:* worked in the Electronic Studio at Cologne Musikhochschule; student and personal asst to Henri Pousseur at Liège; returned to Canada 1978; lectured on analysis and composition at Montréal and Rimouski Conservatories and at the Univs of Montréal and Ottawa; Prof. of Composition and Analysis, Conservatoire de Musique de Montréal; composed works for Louis-Philippe Pelletier, Michael Laucke, Robert Leroux, Gropus 7, L'Ensemble d'Ondes de Montréal, the SMCQ and a recent work premiered by the Orchestre des Jeunes du Québec; his works have been performed in Montréal, Québec, Toronto, Metz, Cologne, Bonn, Liège and Paris and several have been recorded, including Adonwe and broadcast by CBC and WDR in Cologne. *Compositions include:* Chute/Parachute for piano and band 1989, Adonwe for piano and orchestra 1994, Attiré vers le haut par le menu for alto solo 1995, Le Cheminement de la baleine 1998.

GONZAGA, Otoniel; singer (tenor); b. 1944, The Philippines. *Career:* appeared at opera houses in Europe and North America 1967–; engaged at Trier 1973–77, Frankfurt am Main 1977–88; mem., Cologne Opera 1988–; guest engagements at Stuttgart, Munich (Theater am Gärtnerplatz), Vienna (Volksoper), Barcelona, Berne and Genoa; sang Otello at Aachen, Edgardo in Lucia di Lammermoor at Cincinnati 1990; other roles have included Ferrando, Faust, Almaviva and Luigi in Il Tabarro; season 1993–94 as Calaf at Bergen and Manrico at Cincinnati; many concert appearances.

GONZALES, Dalmacio; Spanish singer (tenor); b. 12 May 1945, Olot. *Education:* studied in Barcelona and at the Salzburg Mozarteum with Arleen Auger and Paul Schilharsky; Further study with Anton Dermota in Vienna. *Career:* debut at the Teatro Liceo Barcelona in 1978 as Ugo in Parisina by Donizetti; New York City Opera and San Francisco in 1979 as Alfredo and in Rossini's Semiramide and Tancredi; Metropolitan Opera from 1980 as Ernesto in Don Pasquale and later as Almaviva, Fenton and Nemorino; Sang at La Scala Milan and Aix-en-Provence in 1981 in Ariodante and Tancredi, at Pesaro and La Scala, 1984–85 in a revival of Rossini's Il Viaggio a Reims and further appearances in Rome, Los Angeles, Chicago, Berlin, Zürich, Trieste and London; Sang Ford in Salieri's Falstaff at Parma in 1987 and at Munich Festival in 1990 as Catullus in Catulli Carmina by Orff; Sang Ugo at the 1990 Maggio Musicale, Florence; Other roles include Rossini's Argiro in Tancredi, Idreno in Semiramide, Lindoro, James V in La Donna del Iago and Rinaldo in Armida; Season 1992 as Nemorino at Barcelona and Demetrio in Rossini's Demetrio e Polibio at Martina Franca; Madrid 1995, as Stravinsky's Oedipus; Sang Calaf in Turandot at the reopening of the Teatre Liceo, Barcelona, 1999. *Recordings:* Verdi's Requiem, Falstaff and Il Viaggio a Reims; La Donna del Lago by Rossini.

GONZALEZ, Carmen; Spanish singer (mezzo-soprano); b. 16 April 1939, Valladolid. *Career:* Madrid Conservatory, studied with Magda Piccarolo and Rodolfo Celetti in Milan. *Recordings:* Orlando Furioso by Vivaldi, Anacreon by Cherubini.

GONZALEZ, Manuel; Spanish singer (baritone); b. 30 April 1944, Madrid. *Education:* Madrid Conservatoire. *Career:* debut at the Théâtre de la Monnaie, Brussels in the lyric baritone repertoire at opera houses in Brussels, Antwerp, Ghent and Liège; guest engagements in Dortmund, Essen, Frankfurt, Hamburg, Stuttgart and Mannheim, Barcelona, Lisbon, Paris, Nice, Marseilles and Geneva, and at the Vienna Volksoper; sang roles in operas by Donizetti, Bizet, Mozart, Puccini, Rossini, Massenet and Verdi; Wagner's Wolfram von Eschenbach and Tarquinius in Britten's The Rape of Lucretia; Wexford Festival 1973, in Donizetti's L'Ajo nell'imbarazzo (The Tutor in a Fix); many concert appearances.

GONZÁLEZ, Pablo; Spanish conductor; *Music Director, Orquestra Simfònica de Barcelona i Nacional de Catalunya*; b. (Pablo González Bernardo), 1975, Oviedo. *Education:* Guildhall School of Music and Drama, UK. *Career:* fmrly Asst Conductor, London Symphony Orchestra (collaborated with Sir Colin Davis on the recording of Berlioz's The Trojans), Bournemouth Symphony Orchestra and Bournemouth Sinfonietta 1998–2000 and Nat. Youth Orchestra of Spain; Prin. Guest Conductor, City of Granada Orchestra 2008–; Music Dir Orquestra Simfònica de Barcelona i Nacional de Catalunya 2010–; has worked with soloists including Maxim Vengerov, Truls Mørk, Rudolf Buchbinder, Renaud Capuçon, Viviane Hagner, Eldar Nebolsin, Alban

Gerhardt, Ainhoa Arteta, Jacques Zoon, Asier Polo, Florian Uhlig; has conducted Orchestre de Chambre de Lausanne, Deutsche Radio Philharmonie, Danish Radio Sinfonietta, City of London Sinfonia, Sinfonieorchester Basel, Orchestre Nat. de Belgique, Wiener Kammerorchester, Orchestre Philharmonique de Strasbourg, Royal Flemish Philharmonic, Hamburger Symphoniker, Orchestre Philharmonique de Liège, Winterthur Musikkolegium, Radio Svizzera Italiana de Lugano, Orquesta Sinfónica Nacional de Colombia, Orquestra Sinfónica del Estado de São Paulo and most of the orchestras in Spain. *Recordings include:* Robert Schumann: Complete Works for Violin and Orchestra. *Honours:* Jt Winner, Donatella Flick Conducting Competition 2000, First Prize, 8th Int. Cadaqués Orchestra Conducting Competition 2006. *Current Management:* c/o Liz Sam, International Classical Artists, The Tower Building, 11 York Road, London, SE1 7NX, England. *Telephone:* (20) 7539-2640. *Fax:* (20) 7902-0530. *E-mail:* lsam@icartists.co.uk. *Website:* www.icartists.co.uk. *Address:* Entitat Autónoma Orquestra Simfònica de Barcelona i Nacional de Catalunya, Lepant 150, 08013 Barcelona, Spain (office). *Telephone:* (93) 2479300 (office). *Fax:* (93) 2479301 (office). *E-mail:* informacio.obc@auditori.cat (office).

GOODALL, Howard Lindsay, CBE, MA, ARCO, FRSA; British composer and broadcaster; b. 26 May 1958, London; s. of Geoffrey Goodall and Marion Goodall; m. Val Fancourt. *Education:* chorister, New Coll., Oxford, Lord Williams' School, Thame; music scholar, Christ Church Coll., Oxford. *Career:* Nat. Amb. for Singing, England 2007–11; presenter and Composer-in-Residence, Classic FM 2008–; mem. British Acad. of Songwriters, Composers and Authors. *Compositions for theatre:* Wayne Sleep's Dash 1985–89, The Hired Man (with Melvyn Bragg) (Ivor Novello Award for Best Musical 1985, John Kraaijkamp Musical Award, Netherlands 2001, seven Waterford Int. Musical Festival awards, TMA Award for Best Musical 2004) 1984, Girlfriends 1986, As You Like It (score) 1989, King Lear (score) 1989, Days of Hope 1990, Measure for Measure (score) 1990, The Tempest (score) 1991, Silas Marner 1993, Catwalk 1994, The Kissing-Dance 1999, The Dreaming 2001, A Winter's Tale 2005, Two Cities 2006, Requiem (ballet), Rambert Dance Company 2008, Love Story (Duchess Theatre, West End) 2010, Bend it Like Beckham – The Musical 2015. *Compositions for film:* Bernard and the Genie 1991, Mr Bean 1997, Blackadder Back and Forth 2000, The Gathering Storm 2002, Johnny English 2003, Mr Bean's Holiday 2007, Into the Storm 2009. *Compositions include:* choral works: Psalm 23, Missa Aedis Christi 1993, We Are the Burning Fire 1997, Love Divine 2000, Remember Bethlehem and other carols 2000, In Memoriam Anne Frank 2001, O Lord God of Time and Eternity 2003, We Are God's Labourers 2003, To See Another Sun 2003, Jason and the Argonauts for organ, narrator, tenor and percussion 2004, Saved (based on Wendy Cope's poem) 2005, Of the Dark Past 2005, Ecce Mater Tua 2005, Winter Lullabies 2007, Requiem 2008, Eternal Light: A Requiem by the Rambert Dance Company (choral-orchestral ballet and concert work commissioned by London Musici) 2008, Enchanted Voices (setting of the Beatitudes) (No. 1 on Specialist Classical CD chart for six months) 2009, A Song of Hope, for the Nat. Holocaust Memorial Event in London's Guildhall 2010, More Tomorrows 2013, Steadfast 2014. *Radio:* presenter, Young Chorister of the Year (BBC Radio 2), Howard Goodall's Classical Connections (BBC Radio 2), Howard Goodall Saturday Show (Classic FM) 2008–. *Television:* presenter: Choir of the Year competition (BBC) 1990–2002, Young Musician of the Year (BBC); writer and presenter: Howard Goodall's Organ Works (Channel 4) (Royal TV Soc. Award for Best Music 1997) 1996, Howard Goodall's Choir Works (Channel 4) 1998, Howard Goodall's Big Bangs (Channel 4) (BAFTA Huw Weldon Award 2001, Peabody Award for Journalism & Mass Communication, USA 2001, IMZ Vienna TV Award for Best Documentary 2001) 2000, Howard Goodall's Great Dates (Channel 4) 2002, Howard Goodall's 20th-Century Greats (Channel 4) (Royal TV Soc. Award for Educ. 2005) 2004, South Bank Show: Musical Nation (BBC) 2004, How Music Works (Channel 4) 2006, The Truth About Christmas Carols (BBC 2) 2008, Hallelujah! The Story of Handel's Messiah 2009, Music Room (Sky Arts) 2010, The Story of Music (BBC 2) 2013. *Television themes include:* Mr Bean, Blackadder, The Vicar of Dibley, Red Dwarf, QI, The Catherine Tate Show, Island Parish, Seaside Parish, Country House, 2.4 Children, The Thin Blue Line, The Borrowers, Chalk, A Time to Dance, The Adventure of English, The Land of the Lakes. *Recordings:* numerous, including The Seasons, with the Tippett Quartet 2010, Pelican in the Wilderness: Songs from the Psalms 2010, Enchanted Voices 2010. *Publication:* Big Bangs: Five Discoveries that Changed Musical History 2000. *Honours:* Hon. DMus (Bishop Grosseteste Univ. Coll., Lincoln) 2006; Hon. Dr Arts (Bolton) 2011; Ivor Novello Award for Best Musical 1984, British Television Advertising Craft Award for Best Original Music (for Timebank/ BBC Turned Tables advertisement) 2001, TMA Award for Best Musical 2004, British Acad. of Composers and Songwriters Gold Badge Award 2006, Naomi Sargant Memorial Voice of the Viewer Listener Award for Outstanding Contrib. to Educ. in Broadcasting 2006, Royal Television Soc. Judges' Award for Outstanding Contrib. to Educational TV 2007, Making Music/Sir Charles Grove Prize for Outstanding Contrib. to British Music 2007, Classical BRIT Award for Composer of the Year 2009, Karl Haas Prize for Music Educ. 2009, MIA/Classic FM Award for Outstanding Contrib. to Music Educ. 2009, Primetime Emmy® Award (Creative Arts) for Outstanding Music Composition for a Miniseries, Movie or a Special (Original Dramatic Score), Classical Brits Award Composer of the Year 2009. *Current Management:* c/o PBJ Management, 22 Rathbone Street, London, W1T 1LA, England. *Telephone:* (20) 7287-1112. *Fax:* (20) 7287-1191. *E-mail:* general@pbjmgt.co.uk. *Website:*

www.pbjmgt.co.uk. *Telephone:* (20) 7376-3342 (office). *E-mail:* prubouverie@btinternet.com (office). *Website:* www.howardgoodall.co.uk.

GOODALL, Valorie, BM, MM; American singer (soprano), voice teacher and opera director; b. 23 Sept. 1936, Waco, TX; m. William P. Mooney 1962; two s. *Education:* Baylor Univ., Univ. of Colorado. *Career:* debut at Graz Opera House, Austria; leading lyric soprano, roles of Mimi, Micaela, Mélisande, Zdenka, Composer, Fiordiligi, Cherubino, Graz Opera; performances at opera houses of Graz, Geneva, Bern, Theater an der Wien in Vienna, Prague; singer and producer, State Museum tour of Venus and Adonis with early instruments, New Jersey 1981; founder and Dir, Opera at Rutgers; performer in oratorio, song recital and musical theatre; resident Stage Dir, New England Lyric Operetta, Stamford, CT. *Recordings include:* Land des Lächelns by Lehar.

GOODE, David, MPhil; British musician (organ, keyboard); *Organist and Head of Keyboard, Eton College;* b. 1971. *Education:* Eton Coll., King's Coll., Cambridge. *Career:* Sub-Organist Christ Church Coll., Oxford 1996–2001, 2004–; freelance performer 2001–03; Organist-in-Residence, First Congregational Church, Los Angeles 2003–06; has appeared as soloist at many leading UK venues including BBC Proms at the Royal Albert Hall, Royal Festival Hall, Symphony Hal), across Europe and in Canada, USA, S Africa, S Korea, Australia and Singapore; Visiting Prof., William Jewell Coll. 2002; Organist and Head of Keyboard, Eton Coll. 2005–. *Recordings include:* French Showpieces from King's, The Great Organs of First Church, Vol. 2 2004, Organ Works of Max Reger Vol. 1 2004, A Bach Christmas 2005. *Honours:* First Prize St Albans Interpretation Competition 1997, Recital Gold Medal and Encore Prize Calgary Int. Organ Competition 1998. *E-mail:* info@valfancourt.com. *Website:* www.valfancourt.com. *Address:* Eton College, Windsor, SL4 6DW, England (office). *E-mail:* message@goodeorganist.co.uk (office). *Website:* www.goodeorganist.co.uk.

GOODE, Richard Stephen, DipMus, BSc; American pianist; *Co-Artistic Director, Marlboro Music;* b. 1 June 1943, New York City; m. Marcia Weinfeld 1987. *Education:* Mannes Coll. of Music, Curtis Inst., studied with Nadia Reisenberg and Rudolf Serkin. *Career:* debut, New York Young Concert Artists 1962; Carnegie Hall recital début 1990; mem. Boston Symphony Chamber Players 1967–69; Founding mem. Chamber Music Soc. of the Lincoln Center 1969–79, 1983–89; mem. Piano Faculty, Mannes Coll. of Music 1969–; concerts and recitals in USA, Europe, Japan, South America, Australia, Far East; has played with Baltimore, Boston, Chicago, Cleveland, New York, Philadelphia, Berlin Radio, Finnish Radio and Bamberg Symphony Orchestras, New York, Los Angeles, Baltimore, Orpheus, Philadelphia, ECO and Royal Philharmonic Orchestras; currently co-Artistic Dir with Mitsuko Uchida, Marlboro Music (series of chamber music festivals). *Honours:* Young Concert Artists Award, First Prize Clara Haskil Competition 1973, Avery Fischer Prize 1980, Grammy Award (with clarinettist Richard Stoltzman), Jean Gimbel Lane Prize Northwestern Univ. School of Music 2006. *Address:* Marlboro Music, Box K, Marlboro, VT 05344 (office); Marlboro Music, 121 West 27th Street, Suite 703, New York, NY 10001 (office); 12 East 87th Street, Apt 5A, New York, NY 10128, USA (office). *Telephone:* (212) 581-5197 (NY) (office). *Fax:* (212) 581-4029 (NY) (office). *Website:* www.marlboromusic.org (office).

GOODING, Julia; British singer (soprano); b. 1965, England. *Education:* Guildhall School. *Career:* opera appearances at the Innsbruck Festival and the Opéra-Comique, Paris; Dido and Aeneas in Mexico; concerts with such conductors as Malgoire, Minkowski, Leonhardt, Bruggen and Mackerras in Europe, North America and the Far East. *Recordings include:* King Arthur, Handel's Belshazzar, Handel's Teseo, Purcell Odes, Monteverdi's Orfeo, Blow Venus and Adonis.

GOODLOE, Robert; American singer (baritone); b. 5 Oct. 1936, St Petersburg, FL. *Education:* Simpson Coll. Indianola, IA, studied with Harvey Brown and Armen Boyajian. *Career:* debut in Des Moines, Iowa 1963, as Mozart's Figaro; has sung principally at the Metropolitan Opera, also in Hartford, Baltimore, Philadelphia and San Francisco; roles include Puccini's Scarpia, Michele and Marcello; Enrico (Lucia di Lammermoor); Mercutio in Roméo et Juliette; Germont in La Traviata and Paolo in Simon Boccanegra.

GOODMAN, Craig Stephen, BA, MM; American flautist, conductor and educator; b. 6 July 1957, Pittsburgh, PA. *Education:* Yale Univ., Yale School of Music, studied with Marcel Moyse and Narcis Bonet. *Career:* debut at Konzerthus, Vienna, Austria 1975; solo flutist, Opera Company, Philadelphia 1978–79; freelance, American Symphony, New York City Ballet, St Luke's Chamber Orchestra, Musica Aeterna 1979–86; solo engagements in Australia, Europe, USA; Musical Dir, The Players of the New World, New York; chamber music performances with L'Ensemble, New York, Bach Aria Group, New York, and Ensemble i, Vienna, Austria. *Recordings:* Bach Aria Group, Bach Brandenburg Concerto No. 4 with James Buswell, Samuel Baron and Festival Strings, Ensemble I recording, Bach Trio Sonata in G for two flutes and continuo; Musical Heritage Society recording, Morton Gould's Concerto for wind quartet, piano and violin.

GOODMAN, Erica; Canadian harpist; *Solo Harp, Hamilton Philharmonic Orchestra* and *Esprit Orchestra;* b. 19 Jan. 1948, Toronto, Ont.; d. of Hyman Goodman; one s. *Education:* Royal Conservatory of Music, Canada, Nat. Music Camp, Interlochen, Mich., USA, Univ. of Southern California, Curtis Inst. of Music. *Career:* debut at Alice Tully Hall-Lincoln Center, New York 1972; child prodigy, accompanied opera singer Teresa Stratas on nat. TV aged 13 1961; played for Pres. Kennedy at White House 1962; youngest musician ever to join Toronto Musicians' Asscn 1962; mem. Toronto and CBC Symphony Orchestras 1962–66; conducted by Igor Stravinsky 1964; soloist, Philadelphia Orchestra 1968; toured Japan with flautist Robert Aitken at invitation of Toru Takemitsu to perform his work 1995; performed at Royal Palace in Stockholm with horn player Sören Hermansson 1996; active studio harpist and played on numerous scores of films, TV and radio productions; plays with contemporary ensembles Esprit Orchestra, New Music Concerts, Soundsteams, Trio Désirée (soprano, cello and harp), also with Hamilton Philharmonic; gives master-classes and adjudicates at Glenn Gould School, Toronto; performs regularly at Festival of the Sound and Shaw Festival in Canada. *Recordings include:* Erica Goodman In Concert, Erica Goodman And Friends, The Virtuoso Harp, Flute and Harp, Erica Goodman Plays Canadian Harp Music, Horn And Harp Odyssey, Trio Lyra; CDs feature the music of Berio, Takemitsu, Crumb and Elliott Carter. *Honours:* Grand Prix du Disque, Gramophone Editor's Choice Award, Juno Award. *E-mail:* erigo78@hotmail.com; ericagoodman.tripod.com.

GOODMAN, Roy, ARCO, FRCO, ARCM, FRCM; British conductor, director and violinist; *Principal Guest Conductor, English Chamber Orchestra;* b. 26 Jan. 1951, Guildford, Surrey; s. of Peter Goodman and Mary Sheena Goodman; m. 1st Gillian Dey 1970 (divorced 1992); two s. one d.; m. 2nd Sally Jackson 1992 (divorced 1999). *Education:* chorister, King's Coll., Cambridge, Royal Coll. of Music, London, Berkshire Coll. of Educ. *Career:* Head of Music, Alfred Sutton Boys' School, Reading, Berks. 1971–74, Bulmershe Comprehensive School, Reading 1974–76; Founder and Dir Brandenburg Consort 1975–2001; Sr String Tutor for Berks. 1976–78; Co-founder and Co-Dir The Parley of Instruments 1978–86; Co-founder London Handel Orchestra 1981; Dir of Music, Univ. of Kent, Canterbury 1986–87; Prin. Conductor The Hanover Band 1986–94; Dir of Early Music, RAM, London 1987–89; Musical Dir European Union Baroque Orchestra 1989–2004; Prin. Conductor Händel Festspiele at Badisches Staatstheater, Karlsruhe 1990–98, Umeå Symphony Orchestra and Swedish Northern Opera 1995–2001, Holland Symfonia and Dutch Nat. Ballet 2003–06; Music Dir Manitoba Chamber Orchestra, Winnipeg 1999–2005; Prin. Guest Conductor Västerås Sinfonietta 1995–2011, English Chamber Orchestra 2004–, Auckland Philharmonia Orchestra 2007–11; Artistic Leader and Conductor Bachkoor Holland with Royal Concertgebouw Kamerorkest 2006–10; seven tours of USA, including Lincoln Center and Carnegie Hall 1988–94; Guest Conductor with Finnish, Norwegian and Swedish Radio, NDR Hannover, WDR Cologne, SWR Stuttgart, MDR Leipzig, Royal Concertgebouw, Lahti, Tampere, Ulster, Norrköping, Reykjavík and Stavanger Symphony Orchestras, Royal Liverpool, BBC, Hallé, Royal Scottish Nat. and Rotterdam Philharmonic Orchestras, English Northern Philharmonia, Orchestre de Bretagne, New Queen's Hall Orchestra, Scottish, English, Swedish, Netherlands Radio, Netherlands, Geneva, Lausanne and Manitoba Chamber Orchestras, City of London Sinfonia, Västerås Sinfonietta, German Handel Soloists, Orchestra of the Age of Enlightenment, Freiburg Baroque Orchestra, Netherlands Wind Ensemble and the Amsterdam Bach Soloists; conducted complete Beethoven Symphonies in Hanover, Handel's Tamerlano in Paris and Aldeburgh and with Opera North in Leeds, Scipione, Tamerlano, Ezio and Amadigi in Karlsruhe, Mozart's Bastien and Bastienne in Portugal, Don Giovanni in Belfast, La Clemenza di Tito for Flanders Opera, Gluck's Orfeo for ENO at the London Coliseum and Trädgården by Jonas Forssell at the Drottningholm Court Theatre, Sweden, Handel's Rodelinda, Mozart's Figaro in Stuttgart and San Francisco; revival of Arne's Artaxerxes, London 1995; conducted New Queen's Hall Orchestra at Barbican Hall, London 1997, La Clemenza di Tito at Antwerp 1997; debut at Sydney Opera House 2010. *Recordings include:* as conductor, violinist and keyboard player, has directed some 120 recordings of repertoire ranging from Monteverdi to Holst, including major orchestral works by Purcell, Corelli, Bach and Handel, and the symphonies of Haydn, Beethoven, Schubert, Weber, Berwald and Schumann. *Honours:* Hon. DMus (Hull) 2002. *Address:* 38 Blackbrook Road, Newark, Notts., NG24 2ST, England (home). *Telephone:* (1636) 703064. *E-mail:* roy@roygoodman.com. *Website:* www.roygoodman.com.

GOODWIN, Paul; British conductor; *Music Director and Conductor, Carmel Bach Festival;* b. 2 Sept. 1956, England. *Education:* City of London School, Temple Church Choir, Nottingham Univ., Guildhall School of Music, Vienna Hochschule für Musik. *Career:* Assoc. Dir, Acad. of Ancient Music; Dir, Dartington Festival Baroque Orchestra and the Royal Coll. of Music Baroque Orchestra; Prin. Guest Conductor, English Chamber Orchestra 1998–2003; Prin. Guest Conductor, Kammerorchester Basel; Music Dir and Conductor, Carmel Bach Festival 2011–; guest engagements with Ulster Orchestra, Hallé, BBC Symphony Orchestra, Scottish Chamber Orchestra, RTE Dublin, CBSO, English Chamber Orchestra, Swedish Chamber Orchestra, Komische Oper Berlin, Lyon Opera Orchestra, Nurenburg Philharmonic, SWR Rundfunk Orchester, Hessiche Rundfunk Orchester, Orchestra Nat. de Lille, European Baroque Orchestra, and in the USA with the Portland Baroque Orchestra and St Pauls Chamber Orchestra; conducted staged production of the Bach St Matthew Passion in collaboration with Jonathan Miller; opera productions include Karlsruhe Opera, Opernhaus Halle and Opera North and at the Megaron, Athens; conducted Handel's Poro at Halle and Il Re Pastore at Leeds 1998; London Proms 1999 with Haydn's 64th Symphony and excerpts from Handel's Triumph of Time and Truth; featured at the London Proms 1999, 2002 and 2004 with the Acad. of Ancient Music. *Recordings:* solo oboe:

Bach, Telemann, Albinoni, Vivaldi, Haydn, Mozart; as conductor with the Acad. of Ancient Music: Mozart, Handel, Schütz and Tavener, Elgar's Nurdery Suite, Ikon of Gros (Taverner), Lotorio (Handel), album of Christmas Music (with SWR Kaiserslautern Orchestra). *Honours:* Handel Prize, City of Halle 2007. *Address:* Carmel Bach Festival, PO Box 575, Carmel, 93921, USA (office). *Telephone:* (831) 624-1521 (office). *Fax:* (831) 624-2788 (office). *E-mail:* info@bachfestival.org (office). *Website:* www.bachfestival.org (office); www .paulgoodwinconductor.com (home).

GORBENKO, Pavel; Russian violinist; b. 1956, Moscow. *Education:* Gnessin Music Inst. with Dr Kiselyev. *Career:* co-founder, Amistad Quartet 1973, later Tchaikovsky Quartet; many concerts in Russia with repertoire including works by Haydn, Mozart, Beethoven, Schubert, Brahms, Tchaikovsky, Borodin, Prokofiev, Shostakovich, Bartók, Barber, Bucci, Golovin and Tikhomirov; concert tours to Mexico, Italy, Germany. *Honours:* winner Bela Bartók Festival (with Amistad Quartet) 1976, Bucchi Competition, Rome (with Amistad Quartet) 1990.

GORCHAKOVA, Galina Vladimirovna; Russian singer (soprano); *Artistic Director, Mariinsky Academy of Young Singers;* b. 1962, Beltsy, Moldova; m. Nikolai Petrovich Mikhalsky (divorced); one s. *Education:* Novosibirsk State Conservatory. *Career:* soloist, Sverdlovsk (now Yekaterinburg) Theatre of Opera and Ballet 1987–91, Kirov (now Mariinsky) Theatre 1990–96; Gen. Dir Rimski-Korsakov competition 1992; leading roles in opera productions Madam Butterfly, Prince Igor, The Invisible City of Kitezh, Queen of Spades, Aida, Don Carlos, Tosca, Cavalleria Rusticana; regularly performs in European and American opera theatre including Covent Garden (debut Renata, The Fiery Angel by Prokofiev 1991), Royal Opera House, La Scala, Metropolitan Opera, Opera Bastille, San Francisco Opera, also in Tokyo; Artistic Dir Mariinsky Acad. of Young Singers 1998–, Summer Acad. at Mikkeli Int. Music Festival; gives masterclasses in Europe, USA, Canada and Japan. *Honours:* Merited Artist of Russia, prizes in more than 30 nat. and int. competitions. *Current Management:* c/o Robert Gilder and Co., 91 Great Russell Street, London, WC1B 3PS, England. *Website:* www.galinagorchakova.com.

GORDEI, Irina; Russian singer (soprano); b. 1968. *Education:* Belarus State Academy. *Career:* Ekaterinburg Opera and Ballet Theatre from 1993, as Tosca, Aida, Amelia (Un ballo in Maschera), Lisa (The Queen of Spades) and Verdi's Elisabeth and Lady Macbeth; Teatro Comunale, Floreance, 1994 as Amelia (repeated at Vienna Staatsoper 1995); appearances with Kirov Opera, St Petersburg, from 1999, including Verdi season at Covent Garden, 2001; concert repertoire includes Verdi Requiem and works by Shostakovich (Festival Medal, 1997). *Honours:* Prizewinner, International F. Vignas Competition, Barcelona, 1993.

GORDIEJUK, Marian Stanislaw Wlodzimierz; Polish composer, academic, music journalist and musicologist; b. 9 Feb. 1954, Bydgoszcz; m. 1977; one s. two d. *Education:* State Coll. of Music, Łódź, studied with Antoni Kedra, Prof. Franciszek Wesolowski, Prof. Zygmunt Gzella, Prof. Jerzy Bauer. *Compositions include:* Suite, Birds for two transverse flutes 1976, Games for flute and harp 1987, Children's Quart Miniature for oboe or flute and piano 1987, String Quartet with amplifier 1991.

GORDON, Alexandra; New Zealand singer (soprano); b. 1945, Dannevirke. *Education:* London Opera Centre (Friends of Covent Garden scholarship), studied with Walter Midgley. *Career:* debut as First Boy in Die Zauberflöte and Despina in Così fan tutte for New Zealand Opera aged 19; sang with Opera for All at Glyndebourne and with Scottish Opera, notably as the Queen of Night and Flotow's Martha, and in The Nightingale by Stravinsky; many concert appearances and radio broadcasts; sang Delia in new production of Rossini's Il Viaggio a Reims, Covent Garden 1992.

GORDON, David Jamieson; American singer (tenor); b. 7 Dec. 1947, Philadelphia; m. Barbara Bixby 1969. *Education:* Coll. of Wooster, McGill Univ., Conservatoire de Québec, Canada. *Career:* made debut in Der Rosenkavalier with Lyric Opera of Chicago 1973; opera repertoire includes 59 roles; frequent appearances with North American and European orchestras and opera companies, including Metropolitan Opera, Lyric Opera of Chicago, San Francisco Opera, Hamburg Staatsoper, Boston Symphony, Philadelphia Orchestra, Cleveland Orchestra, Los Angeles Philharmonic; specialist in music by J. S. Bach; also appears regularly as master class teacher and lecturer; has performed at Bach Festivals of Bethlehem, Carmel, Oregon and Winter Park, Stuttgart, Tokyo; currently Educ. Dir, Carmel Bach Festival; also runs own vocal studio. *Recordings:* Bach Magnificat–R Shaw/Atlantic Symphony; Acis and Galatea, Seattle Symphony; Pulcinella, St Paul Chamber Orchestra; other recordings on Telarc, London Decca, Delos, RCA Red Seal and Nonesuch/Electra. *Address:* David Gordon Voice Studio, PO Box 4832, Carmel, CA 93921-4843, USA (office). *Telephone:* (831) 238-4843 (office). *E-mail:* website11@spiritsound.com (office). *Website:* www.spiritsound.com.

GORDON, Michael Zev; British composer and academic; *Professor of Composition, Music Department, University of Birmingham;* b. 1963, London. *Education:* studied with Robin Holloway, Oliver Knussen and John Woolrich. *Career:* works performed/commissioned by artists including Britten Sinfonia, London Sinfonietta, BBC Scottish Symphony Orchestra, Birmingham Contemporary Music Group, EXAUDI, Composers' Ensemble, Orkest de Volharding, Endymion, Carducci Quartet, New Music Players, Concordia, Cheltenham Music Festival, Choir of King's Coll., Cambridge and Sarah Leonard, Huw Watkins and cellist Anton Lukoszevieze; works performed at

Aldeburgh, Lichfield, Brighton, Huddersfield and Spitalfields Music Festivals; featured composer, Park Lane Group series, Southbank Centre, London and CoMA summer school; taught at Univ. of Southampton and Royal Coll. of Music; Prof. of Composition, Music Dept, Univ. of Birmingham 2012–. *Compositions include:* Plain Hunting 2000, A Pebble in the Pond, large-scale radiophonic work on the subject of memory (Prix Italia 2004) 2003, Fragments of a Diary 2005, The Fabric of Dreams, oboe concerto 2006, This Night for choir (British Composer Award 2008) 2007, Allele for 40 voices (British Composer Award 2011) 2010, Bohortha 2012, Glass Mountain (commissioned for CHROMA's 15th birthday celebrations at King's Place) 2012. *Recordings include:* On Memory (Andrew Zolinsky, piano) (The Times top 10 contemporary albums 2010) 2009. *Honours:* PRS Award 1995, Gemini Fellowship 1996. *Address:* Arts Building, University of Birmingham, Edgbaston, Birmingham, B15 2TT, England (office). *E-mail:* m.z.gordon.1@bham.ac.uk (office). *Website:* www.birmingham.ac.uk/music (office).

GORITZKI, Ingo; German oboist and academic; *Professor of Oboe, Staatliche Musikhochschule, Stuttgart;* b. Berlin. *Education:* Detmold Music Acad., studied flute with Gustav Schech, piano with E. Picht-Axenfeld, oboe with Helmut Winschermann. *Career:* fmr prin. oboist, Basel Symphony Orchestra, Frankfurt Radio Symphony Orchestra; apptd Prof., Staatliche Hochschule für Musik und Theater, Hannover 1976; currently Prof., Staatliche Musikhochschule, Stuttgart; co-founder, Musikalische Akademie Stuttgart; Artistic Dir Sommersprossen Festival, Rottweil; has appeared at numerous int. festivals, including Oregon Bach Festival, USA, Kasarsu Festival, Japan, Isang Yun Festival, Korea, Crusell Festival, Finland; gives masterclasses at Int. Bach Acad., Stuttgart and worldwide. *Recordings include:* Bach, Orchestral Suites Nos 1–3 1990, Hindemith, Sonatas, Vol. 5 1996, Oboe Concertos from Bohemia 1999, Mozart, Oboe Concertos 1999, R. Strauss, Wind Concertos 1999, Bach, Restored Oboe Concerti 2000, Bach, Oboe Works 2000, Bach, Sonatas, The Art of Fugue 2002. *Address:* Staatliche Musikhochschule, Raum 6.26, Landhausstr. 20, Stuttgart 70190, Germany (office). *Telephone:* (711) 523763 (office). *Fax:* (711) 524010 (office). *E-mail:* ingogoritzki@netscape.net (office). *Website:* www.mh-stuttgart.de/studium/ fachgruppen/vita/goritzki (office).

GORMLEY, Clare; Australian singer (soprano); b. 1969. *Career:* frequent concert and recital appearances throughout Australia and in Europe; repertory includes Lieder by Mozart and Schumann, Bach's St Matthew Passion and Goyescas by Granados; contestant at the 1995 Cardiff Singer of the World Competition; season 1995–96 as Alexandra in the premiere of The Eighth Wonder, at Sydney and Gretel at Brisbane (also at the Met); debut with Royal Opera, London as Despina 1998, also at the New York Met. *Honours:* winner Metropolitan Opera Auditions.

GÖRNE, Matthias; German singer (baritone); b. 1967, Weimar. *Education:* Leipzig Univ. of Music and Theatre 'Felix Mendelssohn Bartholdy' with Prof. Hans-Joachim Beyer, then with Dietrich Fischer-Dieskau and Elisabeth Schwarzkopf. *Career:* performed with the children's choir at Chemnitz Opera; sang in Bach's St Matthew Passion under Kurt Masur, Leipzig 1990; appearances with NDR Symphony Orchestra Hamburg; further engagements under Horst Stein, with Bamberg Symphony Orchestra and in Hindemith's Requiem under Wolfgang Sawallisch; concerts at Leipzig Gewandhaus under Helmuth Rilling and in Amsterdam and Paris; Lieder recitals and records with pianists Eric Schneider, Vladimir Ashkenazy, Alfred Brendel, Christoph Eschenbach and Leif Ove Andsnes at Wigmore Hall, London, Carnegie Hall, New York, festivals in Edinburgh, Lucerne, and Salzburg; sang title role in Henze's Prinz von Homburg, Cologne 1992, Marcello in La Bohème at Komische Oper, Berlin 1993, Wolfram in Tannhäuser, Cologne 1996, Die Schöne Müllerin, Bath 1997; Papageno in Die Zauberflöte, Salzburg Festival 1997; Wozzeck at The Royal Opera House, Covent Garden 2002; role of Kasim in Henze's L'Upupa 2003, Salzburg Festival 2003, repeated in Teatro Real, Madrid 2004; Wozzeck at Saito Kinen Festival with Ozawa in 2004; Papageno at Metropolitan Opera 2005; debut at Vienna State Opera as Wolfram 2010; Bluebeard in Bartók's Duke Bluebeard's Castle at Saito Kinen Festival 2011 and Maggio Musicale in Florence 2012; debut as Kurwenal at Bavarian State Opera, Munich 2012; roles of Kurwenal, Amfortas, and Wozzeck at Vienna State Opera, 2013–14; "Wozzeck", Metropolitan Opera New York 2014; debut as Wotan in Wagner's Rheingold in Hong Kong; concert performances with all major orchestras in Europe and US including Amsterdam Concertgebouworkester, Berliner Philharmoniker, Boston Symphony, Chicago Symphony, London Symphony, London Philharmonic, Los Angeles Philharmonic, New York Philharmonic, Orchestre de Paris; tour with Wiener Philharmoniker 2011; Prof. of Lieder Interpretation, Schumann Hochschule, Dusseldorf 2001–05. *Recordings include:* Matthäuspassion 1994, Winterreise 1997, Entarte Musik, Arias, J.S. Bach Cantatas, Eisler's Deutsche Sinfonie, The Hollywood Songbook, Mahler's Des Knaben Wunderhorn, Mendelssohn's Paulus Oratorio op. 36, Schubert's Schwanengesang, Die Schöne Müllerin, Winterreise, Goethe-Lieder, Messe D950, Liederkreis, Schumann's Dichterliebe; Performances and recordings: of Bartók's Bluebeard and Britten's War Requiem, first performances of works by Hans Werner Henze L'upupa, Thomas Larcher Böhmen liegt am Meer, and Marc-André Dalbavie; championing 20th century composers Karl Amadeus Hartmann (Gesangsszene) and Bernd Alois Zimmermann (Ekklesiastische Aktion). *Current Management:* Michael Kocyan Artists Management, Alt-Moabit 104A, 10559 Berlin, Germany. *Telephone:* (30) 31004940. *Fax:* (30) 31004984. *E-mail:* artists@ kocyan.de. *Website:* www.kocyan.de; www.matthiasgoerne.de.

GOROKHOVSKAYA, Yevgena; Russian singer (mezzo-soprano); b. 1944, Baku. *Education:* Leningrad Conservatory. *Career:* debut at Maly Theatre, Leningrad, as Lehl in The Snow Maiden by Rimsky-Korsakov, 1969; mem., Maryinsky Opera Leningrad (later St Petersburg), 1976–; roles have included Lubasha in The Tsar's Bride by Rimsky, Eboli (Don Carlos) and Azucena; Guest appearances, Germany, Romania, Spain, France, Greece, USA, Switzerland, Czechoslovakia; on tour to the UK 1991, sang Mme Larina in Eugene Onegin at Birmingham and Marfa in Khovanshchina at Edinburgh Festival; Salzburg Easter Festival 1994 as the Nurse in Boris Godunov.

GORRARA, Riccardo (Richard), DipMus; French classical guitarist, lutenist and conductor; b. 29 May 1964, Metz. *Education:* studied in Italy and England, Guildhall School of Music, Royal Academy of Music, Paris Music College. *Career:* debut in Genoa Cathedral, Italy; appeared in most European halls and festivals, Milan, Rome, Turin, London, Paris, Madrid; Paris Festival, Edinburgh Festival; mem, Royal Philharmonic Society; National Early Music Association; Lute Society; Dutch Lute Society; Brussels Philharmonique Society. *Compositions:* Varied; Music for guitar and lute from 15th Century to present, including Dowland, Frescobaldi, Ferrabosco, Couperin, Weiss, Bach, Sor, etc. *Recordings:* Various major recordings for guitar and lute, particularly works from 15th Century to 20th Century rarely played; 7 Gramophone recordings, also for radio broadcasting; Various national radio stations in Italy, Denmark, Switzerland. *Publications:* contrib. various reviews of Guitar and lute method, technique, interpretation for Italian guitar and music magazines.

GORTON, Susan; British singer (mezzo-soprano); b. 1946, Cheshire, England. *Education:* Royal Manchester College of Music. *Career:* debut as Feklusha in Katya Kabanova for the Glyndebourne Tour, 1992; further appearances with GTO, as Filippyevna in Eugene Onegin and Marcellina in Le nozze di Figaro; Glyndebourne Festival 1995–97, as the Chambermaid in The Makropulos Case; Further engagements as Mistress Quickly and Mrs Sedley in Peter Grimes, for English National Opera; Florence Pike in Albert Herring for English Touring Opera, Martha in Faust and Mamma Lucia in Cavalleria Rusticana for Welsh National Opera; Premieres include Julian Grant's A Family Affair for the Almeida Festival and The House of Crossed Desires by John Woolrich for Music Theatre Wales, 1996; Season 1997–98 as the Hostess in Boris Godunov and Grandmother in Jenůfa for WNO, and Mrs Sedley for the Lyric Opera, Chicago. Season 1998–99 Mrs Sedley in Peter Grimes and Mamma Lucia in Cavalleria Rusticana for Welsh National Opera and Chambermaid in The Makropulos Case for Gran Teatre del Liceu; Grandmother Burja in Jenůfa and Auntie in Peter Grimes for Glyndebourne Festival Opera, 2000; Countess in The Queen of Spades, Welsh National Opera, 2000; Mary in Der fliegende Holländer, Lyric Opera of Chicago, 2001; Mrs Herring, Glyndebourne Festival Opera, and Florence Pike, GTO, in Albert Herring, 2002. *Current Management:* c/o Harlequin Agency Ltd, 203 Fidlas Road, Llanishen, Cardiff, CF14 5NA, Wales. *Telephone:* (29) 2075-0821. *Fax:* (29) 2075-5971. *E-mail:* peter@harlequin-agency.co.uk. *Website:* www.harlequin-agency.co.uk.

GORTSEVSKAYA, Maria; Russian singer (mezzo-soprano); b. 1965. *Career:* many appearances in solo recitals in France, Belgium, Germany and Spain; Mariinsky Theatre, St Petersburg, from 1990, as Siebel in Faust, Fyodor in Boris Godunov, Rossini's Rosina, Bizet's Mercédès and roles in The Fiery Angel and War and Peace; sang Adjutant to Marshal Murat in War and Peace with the Kirov Opera at Covent Garden, 2000; appearances as guest with the Kirov in Japan and the USA (Metropolitan Opera).

GORZYNSKA, Barbara, MA; Polish violinist; b. 4 Dec. 1953, Cmielow; d. of Zygmunt Gorzynski and Janina Gorzynski (née Nowak); m. Ryszard Rasinski 1982; one s. *Education:* Acad. of Music, Łódź. *Career:* debut with Great Symphony Orchestra of Polish Radio 1969; performances as soloist with London Philharmonic Orchestra, Royal Philharmonic Orchestra (UK), Staatskapelle Dresden (Germany), Warsaw Philharmonic Orchestra, English Chamber Orchestra, Halle Orchestra (Germany) 1981–; London debut Royal Festival Hall 1981; Prof. of Violin Acad. of Music, Łódź; Visiting Prof., Hochschule für Musik und Darstellende Kunst, Graz, Austria; currently also teacher of Music Performance, Inst. for Int. Educ. of Students. *Recordings include:* Chopin's Trio in G Minor 1986, Wieniawski's Pieces for Violin and Piano 1988, Mozart's Violin Concerto in D 1991. *Honours:* First Prize and Henryk Szeryng Special Prize Zagreb Int. Violin Competition 1977, First Prize Carl Flesch Int. Violin Competition 1980. *Address:* The Institute for the International Education of Students, Johannesgasse 7, 1010 Vienna, Austria (office). *Telephone:* (1) 226-0127 (office). *Fax:* (1) 22601 (office). *E-mail:* ies@ies.ac.at (office). *Website:* www.ies.ac.at (office).

GOSMAN, Lazar, DipMus; violinist and conductor; b. 27 May 1926, Kiev, USSR; m. Eugenia Gosman 1950, one s. *Education:* Central Music School, Moscow, Tchaikovsky Conservatory of Music, Moscow. *Career:* violinist, Leningrad Philharmonic Orchestra; Music Dir, Leningrad Chamber Orchestra 1962–77; Assoc. Concertmaster, St Louis Symphony, USA 1977–82; Music Dir, Tchaikovsky Chamber Orchestra, formerly Soviet Emigré Orchestra; Prof. of Violin, State Univ. of New York, Stonybrook. *Recordings:* over 40 with Leningrad Chamber Orchestra, two albums with Tchaikovsky Chamber Orchestra. *Address:* 3 East Gate Street, Setauket, NY 11733, USA.

GOSSETT, Philip, BA, MFA, PhD; American musicologist, academic and writer; *Robert W. Reneker Distinguished Service Professor Emeritus, University of Chicago*; b. 27 Sept. 1941, New York; s. of Harold Gossett and Pearl Gossett (née Lenkowsky); m. Suzanne S. Gossett 1963; two s. *Education:* Amherst Coll., Columbia Univ., Princeton Univ. *Career:* Asst Prof., Univ. of Chicago 1968–73, Assoc. Prof. 1973–77, Prof. 1977–84, Chair Dept of Music 1978–84, 1989, Robert W. Reneker Distinguished Service Prof. 1984–2010, Prof. Emer. 2010–, Dean Division of Humanities 1989–99; Visiting Assoc. Prof., Columbia Univ. 1975; Direttore dell'edizione, Edizione critica delle Opere di Gioachino Rossini 1978–2005; Meadows Visiting Prof., Southern Methodist Univ. 1980; Assoc. Prof., Universitá degli Studi, Parma 1983; Visiting Prof., Univ. of Paris 1988; Five-Coll. Visiting Prof. 1989; Gauss Seminars, Princeton Univ. 1991; Prof. di chiara fama, Univ. Roma, La Sapienza 2004–11; 'Consulenza musicologica', Verdi Festival, Parma 2000–01; Hambro Visiting Prof. of Opera Studies, Univ. of Oxford 2001; Visiting Scholar, Phi Beta Kappa 2002–03; mem. Bd of Dirs American Inst. of Verdi Studies, American Musicological Soc. (Pres. 1994–96), Int. Musicological Soc. (Directorium 2006–), Società Italiana di Musicologia, Soc. for Textual Scholarship (Pres. 1993–95); Corresp. Fellow, British Acad. 2008–; Foreign mem. Ateneo Veneto 2001; Fellow, American Acad. of Arts and Sciences 1989, American Philosphical Soc. 2008–. *Publications include:* The Operas of Rossini: Problems of Textual Criticism in Nineteenth-Century Opera (two vols) 1970, Treatise on Harmony, by Jean-Philippe Rameau (trans. and ed.) 1971, The Tragic Finale of Tancredi 1977, Early Romantic Opera (ed. with Charles Rosen) 1978–83, Le Sinfonie di Rossini 1981, Rossini Tancredi (critical edn) 1983, Italian Opera 1810–1840 (ed., 25 vols) 1984–92, 'Anna Bolena' and the Maturity of Gaetano Donizetti 1985, Il barbiere di Siviglia 1992, Rossini Ermione (with P. Brauner) 1995, Don Pasquale 1999, Semiramide (with A. Zedda) 2001, Divas and Scholars: Performing Italian Opera 2006, Petite messe solennelle (with P. Brauner) 2009, Dive e maestri 2009; Gen. Ed. The Works of Giuseppe Verdi 1981–2014; Gen. Ed. Works of Gioachino Rossini (Bärenreiter-Verlag) 2006–; Sr Ed. The Works of Giuseppe Verdi 2014–; contribs to reference works, scholarly books and professional journals. *Honours:* Hon. mem. Accad. Filarmonica di Bologna 1992, Accademico Onorario, Accad. di Santa Cecilia Rome 2003, Foreign mem. Royal Soc. of Music in Sweden 2008; Grand Ufficiale dell'Ordine al Merito 1997, Cavaliere di Gran Croce 1998, Order of Rio Branca, Brazil 1998; Hon. DHL (Amherst Coll.) 1993, (New England Conservatory) 2013; Woodrow Wilson Fellowship 1963–64, Fulbright Scholar, Paris 1965–66, Martha Baird Rockefeller Fellowship 1967–68, Alfred Einstein Award, American Musicological Soc. 1969, Guggenheim Fellowship 1971–72, Nat. Endowment for the Humanities Sr Fellowship 1982–83, Medaglia d'Oro prima classe (Italy) 1985, Deems Taylor Award, American Acad. of Composers, Authors and Publrs 1986, 2007, Mellon Distinguished Achievement Award 2004, Serena Prize, British Acad. 2008, Kinkeldey Award, American Musicological Soc. 2008, Palisca Award, American Musicological Soc. 2009, Cavaliere di Verdi, Club del 27, Parma 2013, Award from the Packard Inst. for the Humanities 2014–19. *Address:* Department of Music, University of Chicago, 1010 East 59th Street, Chicago, IL 60637 (office); 5810 S Harper Avenue, Chicago, IL 60637, USA (home). *Telephone:* (773) 834-4181 (office); (773) 955-3738 (home); (773) 710-7074 (mobile) (home). *Fax:* (773) 955-0247 (home). *E-mail:* phgs@uchicago.edu (office).

GOTHÓNI, Ralf; Finnish pianist, conductor, composer and academic; *Professor, Musikhochschule Karlsruhe*; b. 2 May 1946, Rauma; m. 4th Suzan Saber; two s. from previous m. *Education:* Sibelius Acad., Folkwang-Hochschule, Germany, with Ervin Laszlo in Switzerland and Max Martin Stein in Düsseldorf. *Career:* soloist with leading orchestras, recitals and chamber music concerts world-wide; guest at major festivals; debut at Jyvaskyla Festival; Artistic Dir Savonlinna Opera Festival 1984–87; Prin. Guest Conductor, Turku Philharmonic 1994–2000; Artistic Dir Forbidden City Music Festival, Beijing 1996–98; Artistic Dir Musical Bridge Egypt-Finland in Cairo 2004–; Prin. Conductor, English Chamber Orchestra 2000–09; Music Dir Northwest Chamber Orchestra, Seattle, Wash., USA 2001–06; Guest Conductor, Deutsche Kammerakademie 2004–; Artistic Dir Musical Bridge Azerbaijan–Finland, Baku 2011–; Prof. of Chamber Music, Musikhochschule Hamburg, Germany 1986–96, Sibelius-Acad., Helsinki 1992–2007, Hanns Eisler Hochschule, Berlin, Germany 1996–2000, Instituto de Musica de Camara, Reina Sofia, Madrid, Spain 2006–13, Musikhochschule Karlsruhe 2012–. *Compositions:* three chamber operas, chamber music and songs. *Recordings include:* more than 100 recordings, including music by Britten: Piano Concerto, Rautavaara: two piano concertos, Villa Lobos: Chorus XI, Schubert: Chamber music and piano sonatas, Brahms: Piano quartets; music by Sallinen and Schnittke, etc. *Publications include:* The Moment of Creativity 1997, Does the Moon Rotate 2001, With the Grand Piano 2003, The Spider 2014. *Honours:* Order Pro Finlandia 1992; Schubert Medal (Austria) 1977, Hon. Prize, Finnish Cultural Foundation 1984, Gilmore Artist Award (USA) 1994, Hon. Prize, Queen Sofia of Spain 2012. *E-mail:* gothoniweb@mac.com. *Website:* www.gothoni.com.

GOTO, Masataka; Japanese pianist. *Education:* Showa Grad. School of Music with Fumiko Eguchi, Piano Art Acad. *Career:* recital at RAM, London 2003; concert tour of Europe and USA 2005; has appeared with orchestras including Japan Philharmonic Orchestra, Kraków State Philharmonic Orchestra, Philharmonic Orchestra of Silesia; debut at Concertgebouw, Amsterdam with Netherlands Radio Philharmonic Orchestra under Jaap van Zweden 2011; concert appearances in Russia with State Hermitage Orchestra, in Poland at Duszniki Festival and in Latvia with Latvian Nat. Symphony Orchestra 2011; concert tours in USA, Indonesia, Europe, Japan and China 2011. *Honours:* Winner, 28th Competition of the Japanese Piano

Teachers' Nat. Asscn Grand Prix 2004, Winner, Ennio Porrino Int. Piano Competition (Italy) 2005, Winner, 9th Int. Franz Liszt Piano Competition 2011, Van Lanschot Bankiers Audience Award 2011. *Address:* c/o Liszt Competition Foundation, PO Box 550, 3500 AN Utrecht, Netherlands. *Telephone:* (30) 286-2258. *Fax:* (30) 231-6522. *E-mail:* info@liszt.nl. *Website:* www.masatakagoto.com.

GOTSINDER, Mikhail; Russian violinist; b. 1950, Moscow. *Education:* Moscow Conservatoire with David Oistrakh. *Career:* co-founder, Amistad Quartet 1973, later Tchaikovsky Quartet; many concerts in Russia with repertoire, including works by Haydn, Mozart, Beethoven, Schubert, Brahms, Tchaikovsky, Borodin, Prokofiev, Shostakovich, Bartók, Barber, Bucci, Golovin and Tikhomirov; concert tours to Mexico, Italy, Germany. *Recordings include:* all Tchaikovsky's quartet works. *Honours:* winner Bela Bartók Festival (with Amistad Quartet) 1976, Bucchi Competition, Rome (with Amistad Quartet) 1990.

GOTTLIEB, Gordon, BMus, MMus; American percussionist, conductor and composer; b. 23 Oct. 1948, Brooklyn, NY. *Education:* High School of Performing Arts, Juilliard School of Music, studied with James Wimer, Saul Goodman. *Career:* extensive performing with New York Philharmonic, including solo appearances 1974 and 1986; commissioning and performing new works for piano and percussion with brother Jay, active in contemporary music and has played with Contemporary Chamber Ensemble, Speculum Musicae, the Juilliard Ensemble, the Group for Contemporary Music and others; as conductor performed the New York premiere of Vesalii Icones by Peter Maxwell Davies and made his Carnegie Hall debut conducting William Walton's Facade with Anna Russell narrating 1981; conducted Histoire du Soldât of Stravinsky with L'Ensemble and Shaker Loops of John Adams at the Santa Fe Chamber Musical Festival 1986; performed with Stevie Wonder, Ray Charles, Patti LaBelle, Tony Bennett, Paula Abdul, Michael Bolton, Bette Midler, Sarah Vaughan, Quincy Jones, Al Jarreau, Paul Winter; mem. Percussive Arts Soc., NARAS, Recording Musicians' Asscn. *Compositions:* Graines gemellaires (improvisation 1), Traversées (improvisation 2) Saudades do Brasil, The River Speaker, Improvisations with Jay Gottlieb, Ritual Dancer, Fanfare (with Paul Winter), various jingles. *Recordings:* History, Michael Jackson; Kingdom of the Sun, film with Sting; Bulletproof Heart, with Grace Jones; A Secret Life, with Marianne Faithfull; Romulus Hunt, My Romance, with Carly Simon; Sostice Live!, Prayer for the Wild Things, with Paul Winter; Pete, Pete Seeger; many films and jingles; Bartók, Sonata for 2 Pianos; Histoire du Soldât, I Stravinsky; Two Against Nature, Steely Dan (four Grammy awards, including Album of the Year 2001); Everything Must Go, Steely Dan, 2003, Something to Be, Rob Thomas 2005, Morph the Cat, Donald Fagen 2006, Circus Money, Walter Becker 2008, Duets II, Tony Bennett 2011. *Publications:* The Percussion of Carnival, for Modern Percussionist magazine 1984, World Influences: Africa and South India 1985, contrib. three articles on studio playing 1985. *Honours:* Martha Baird Rockefeller grant 1980, four Grammy Awards (including for Paul Winters, Prayer for the Wild Things 1994, Pete Seeger, Pete), NARAS Most Valuable Player Award, New York Studios 1989, Meet the Composer grant 1989. *E-mail:* gorgot@earthlink.net.

GOTTLIEB, Jay Mitchell, BA, MA; American pianist and composer; b. 23 Oct. 1954, New York. *Education:* Hunter Coll., Harvard Univ., Chatham Square Music School, Juilliard School, Conservatoire Americain de Fontainebleau, France with Nadia Boulanger, festivals of Tanglewood and Darmstadt with Messiaen, Loriod, Ligeti, Kontarsky. *Career:* recitals in New York: Alice Tully Hall, Merkin Hall, Carnegie Recital Hall, Third Street Settlement, Cooper Union, New School, Mannes Coll., Radios WQXR, WNYC, New York Univ., Théâtre des Champs-Elysées, Centre Pompidou, Paris, Alte Oper, Frankfurt; soloist with Boston Symphony, Orchestra della Radiotelevisione in Italy, Nouvel Orchestre Philharmonique, Paris, Orchestre Philharmonique d'Europe, Paris, Ensemble Orchestral de Paris, Percussions de Strasbourg, Orchestre du Rhin, Geneva and radio and television in New York, Boston, Washington, Paris, Switzerland, Frankfurt, Cologne, Rome; festivals of Berlin, Rome, Milan, Venice, Paris, Almeida, Aldeburgh, Autumn in Warsaw, Moscow Forum, Musica in Strasbourg, Avignon, Toulouse, Frankfurt, Amsterdam; Int. Piano Festival of La Roque d'Anthéron, France, Int. Keyboard Inst. and Festival, New York; Guest Prof., Paris Conservatory, France, American Conservatory of Fontainebleau, Ecole Normale, Paris, Music School of Indiana Univ., Bloomington; mem. jury for int. piano competitions; mem. Advisory Bd, Swiss Global Artistic Foundation, Washington Int. Piano Arts Council, Jury of Hamamatsu Int. Piano Competition. *Compositions include:* Synchronisms for two percussionists and tape, Sonata for violin and piano, Improvisations for piano and percussion, Essay for orchestra, La Discrète (film soundtrack). *Recordings include:* Trois Contes de L'Honorable Fleur/Maurice Ohana, Lys de Madrigaux, Piano and Percussion (with Gordon Gottlieb), Appello/Barbara Kolb; Harawi/Messiaen, Figure/Michèle Reverdy, La Discrète soundtrack, Arcane/Allain Gaussin, Concord Sonata and short works for piano/Ives, Piano Works/John Adams, Piano Sonata/Solbiati, Piano Works of John Cage, Piano Works of Philip Glass, Recital for Signature series Radio-France, Jazz Connotation/Bruno Mantovani, Piano Music of Nicolas Obouhov, Piano Concerto/Regis Campo, Piano Concerto/Dmitri Yanov-Yanovsky/Piano works of George Gershwin. *Publication:* Dix ans avec le piano du XXe siècle 1998. *Honours:* C.D. Jackson Prize, Berkshire Music Center, Tanglewood 1975, First Prize, Int. Improvisation Competition, Lyon, France 1976, Martha Baird Rockefeller Foundation grant

1980, NEA grant 1980, Laureate Yehudi Menuhin Foundation 1982, Grand Prix du Disque 1995, 2002, 2004, Le Monde de la Musique Recording of the Month 1998, 1999, 2000, Diapason d'Or 2001, Steinway Artist. *Address:* 29–31 rue des Boulets, 75011 Paris, France. *Telephone:* 1-43-48-59-71. *Fax:* 1-43-48-58-30. *E-mail:* jaygottlieb35@gmail.com. *Website:* jaygottliebpiano.com.

GOTTLIEB, Peter; French singer (baritone); b. 18 Sept. 1930, Brno, Czechoslovakia. *Education:* studied in Rio de Janeiro and in Florence with Raoul Frazzi. *Career:* sang at first in Brazil, Italy, Belgium and North America; Paris Opéra, premiere of L'Opéra d'Aran by Becaud 1962, and as Don Giovanni, Figaro, Papageno, Scarpia and Wozzeck 1985; Glyndebourne Festival 1966–79 as Albert in Werther, Barber in Die schweigsame Frau, Mercurio in the first modern performance of Cavalli's Calisto 1970 and Zastrow in premiere of The Rising of the Moon by Nicholas Maw; Théâtre de la Monnaie Brussels 1983, in premiere of La Passion de Gilles by Boesmans; Opéra du Rhin, Strasbourg in premiere of H.H. Ulysses by Jean Prodromidès 1984; other roles include Iago, Don Carlos in La Forza del Destino and the Count in Capriccio; sang 120 roles, most performed part Escamillo in Carmen; Prof., Paris Conservatoire 1982–95. *Recordings include:* La Calisto, Opéra D'Aran, La Passion de Gilles, H.H. Ulysses, La Cocarde de Mimi Pinson, La Traviata, Roméo et Juliette. *Address:* 361 rue Lecourbe, 75015 Paris, France (home).

GÖTZ, Cornelia; German singer (soprano); b. 2 March 1965, Waiblingen. *Education:* Coll. of Music, Karlsruhe, studied with Ruthilde Boesch and at Max Reinhard Seminar, Vienna, with Astrid Varnay at opera sudio of Bavarian State Opera of Munich, and with Martino Stamos Vogiatsis in Nürnberg. *Career:* first major role as Mozart's Zaide, at Munich Staatsoper; appearances as the Queen of Night in Die Zauberflöte throughout Germany and at Wiener Festwochen; Nuremberg Opera 1992–94, as Mozart's Serpetta and Zerlina, Suppe's Galathée, and Rosina; further roles include Mozart's Papagena, Blondchen and Constanze; Adele in Die Fledermaus and Olympia, First Flower Maiden in Parsifal at Covent Garden; sang in Zimmermann's Die Weisse Rose at Vienna Odeon 1998; concerts include Bach Passions, Handel's Messiah, Haydn Creation and Seasons, Mozart's C Minor Mass and Carl Orff's Carmina Burana; Schoenberg's Herzgewäcsche and Second String Quartet with Bavarian Radio; Season 1999–2000 as Constanze at Kassel and Frasquita in Carmen for Deutsche Oper Berlin; Season 2000–01 as Zerbinetta in Tokyo under Sinopoli with Vienna State Opera 2000, Queen of the Night in Leipzig, Antwerp and Munich, and as Cunigonde (Candide of Loriot) in Munich; Season 2003–04, Queen of the Night in The Magic Flute at Glyndebourne Festival; US debut as the Queen of the Night for Lyric Opera of Chicago 2005. *Recording:* Bach's St Matthew Passion with Rolf Schweizer. *Address:* c/o Lyric Opera of Chicago, North Wacker Drive, #860, Chicago, IL 60606, USA. *Telephone:* (312) 332-2244.

GÖTZ, Werner; German singer (tenor); b. 7 Dec. 1934, Berlin. *Education:* studied with Friedrich Wilcke and W. Kelch in Berlin. *Career:* debut at Oldenburg 1967, as Alvaro in La Forza del Destino; sang in Düsseldorf, Karlsruhe, Munich, Stuttgart and Hamburg; roles included Wagner's Erik, Lohengrin and Parsifal, Mozart's Tamino, Lionel in Martha by Flotow and parts in operas by Puccini, Janáček and Verdi; further engagements in London, Zürich, Łódź, Barcelona, Amsterdam and Frankfurt; Munich Opera 1978, in the premiere of Lear by Reimann; Karlsruhe Opera until 1984. *Recordings include:* Lear (Deutsche Grammophon); Melot in Tristan und Isolde; Eine Florentinische Tragödie by Zemlinsky (Fonit-Cetra).

GÖTZEN, Guido; German singer (bass); b. 1959, Düsseldorf. *Education:* studied in Cologne with Joseph Metternich. *Career:* sang first at the Cologne Opera Studio and at Berne, as Angelotti in Tosca, the Major Domo in Capriccio, Hobson in Peter Grimes, and Sarastro 1988–89; Bayerische Staatsoper Munich, as the King in Aida, Colline, Masetto and roles in Palestrina, Meistersinger, Mathis der Maler, Parsifal, Orff's Trionfi, Dvořák's Dimitri and The Love for Three Oranges 1989–94; Zürich Opera as Sparafucile in Rigoletto (under Nello Santi), Mozart's Commendatore and Sarastro, and the Bonze in Madama Butterfly from 1994; Zürich Opera 2000 as Lamoral in Arabella and Schigolch in Lulu. *Recordings include:* Die Meistersinger (conducted by Sawallisch). *Honours:* prizewinner Belvedere Competition 1987.

GOULD, Clio; British violinist; *Leader, Royal Philharmonic Orchestra*; b. 1968, England. *Education:* studied with Emanuel Hurwitz, Pauline Scott and Igor Ozim. *Career:* concerto debut at Royal Festival Hall, aged 17; recitalist and soloist at Bath, Cheltenham, Harrogate, Spitalfields (London) and Huddersfield festivals; Artistic Dir of the BT Scottish Ensemble 1993–2005; Leader, Royal Philharmonic Orchestra 2002–; currently principal violinist of the London Sinfonietta; concerto soloist with the Ulster Orchestra; Nat. Symphony Orchestra of Ireland and Royal Philharmonic (Barbican Hall, London); Proms debut 1999, with Inside Story by Piers Hellawell; Festival d'Automne, Paris, and chamber recitals in Japan; season 2000–01 with European tour of the Weill Concerto (London Sinfonietta) and concertos with the London Philharmonic Orchestra, Ulster Orchestra and Royal Scottish Nat. Orchestra; teaches violin masterclasses, Royal Acad. of Music. *Recordings include:* Tears of the Angels, by John Tavener. *Honours:* Hon. RAM 1999. *Address:* Royal Philharmonic Orchestra, 16 Clerkenwell Green, London, EC1R 0QT, England (office). *Telephone:* (20) 7608-8800 (office). *Fax:* (20) 7608-8801 (office). *E-mail:* info@rpo.co.uk (office). *Website:* www.rpo.co.uk (office).

GOULD, Stephen; American singer (heldentenor); b. Virginia. *Education:* New England Conservatory of Music, Lyric Opera of Chicago Center for American Artists. *Career:* sang for eight years in musical theatre; sang Tannhäuser under Franz Welser-Möst, both Siegfrieds in the Ring cycle under Christian Thielemann and Bacchus in Ariadne auf Naxos at Vienna State Opera, both Siegfrieds and Eric in Der fliegende Holländer at Metropolitan Opera, New York, and Der Kaiser in Die Frau ohne Schatten at Salzburg Summer Festival; other appearances include Tristan in Tristan and Isolde in Tokyo and Dresden, Lohengrin in Hamburg and Trieste, Parsifal in Vienna, Otello and Fidelio in Tokyo, Tannhäuser in Paris, Las Palmas and Geneva, Peter Grimes in Dresden and Geneva, Les Troyens, Fidelio and Otello in Florence and Tannhäuser, Siegfried and Götterdämmerung at Bayreuth Festival (debut 2004); performed under conductors including Daniel Barenboim, Pierre Boulez, Riccardo Chailly, Myung-Whun Chung, Daniele Gatti, Valery Gergiev, Zubin Mehta, Seiji Ozawa, Donald Runnicles and Esa-Pekka Salonen; concerts included Tannhäuser at Opera Nomori Spring Festival in Tokyo, Das Lied von der Erde in Prague, Beethoven's 9th Symphony with Atlantic Symphony Orchestra in Berlin and Munich, Beethoven's Missa Solemnis with Chicago Symphony, Schönberg's Gurrelieder in Montreal, Berlin, Brussels, Amsterdam, Helsinki and Lucerne Festival, Mahler's Eighth Symphony at Bergen Festival, Carnegie Hall and in Leipzig, Paris, Vienna and Budapest, and Stravinsky's Oedipus Rex in London. *Current Management:* c/o Caecilia Lyric Department, Rennweg 15, 8001 Zürich, Switzerland. *E-mail:* caecilia@caecilia-lyric.ch. *Website:* www.stephengould.org.

GOURLAY, Andrew; British conductor; b. Jamaica. *Education:* Univ. of Manchester, Royal Northern Coll. of Music, Royal Coll. of Music. *Career:* grew up in Jamaica, the Bahamas, Philippines, Japan and UK; as professional trombonist until his twenties, played with the Philharmonia, London Sinfonietta, Hallé Orchestra, BBC Philharmonic, BBC Nat. Orchestra of Wales, Opera North; toured S America and Europe as mem. Gustav Mahler Jugendorchester under Claudio Abbado; Asst Conductor to Sir Mark Elder, Hallé Orchestra 2010–12; Prin. Guest Conductor, Symphony Orchestra of Castile and León (Orquesta Sinfónica de Castilla y León) 2014–15, Music Dir 2016–; has conducted BBC Symphony, BBC Philharmonic, London Symphony, London Philharmonic, London Sinfonietta, Philharmonia, Hallé, BBC Scottish Symphony, BBC Nat. Orchestra of Wales, Royal Flemish Philharmonic, Royal Liverpool Philharmonic Orchestra, Melbourne Symphony, Irish Chamber, numerous orchestras throughout Spain; opera engagements include UK premiere of Luca Francesconi's Quartett, Royal Opera House and new production by Graham Vick of Tippett's The Ice Break with CBSO. *Honours:* winner, Cadaques Int. Conducting Competition 2010, Gramophone magazine 'One to Watch' 2010, BBC Music Magazine 'Rising Star: Great Artists of Tomorrow' 2011. *Current Management:* c/o Jonathan Groves, Ingpen & Williams, 7 St George's Court, 131 Putney Bridge Road, London, SW15 2PA, England. *Telephone:* (20) 8874-3222. *Fax:* (20) 8877-3113. *E-mail:* jg@ingpen.co.uk. *Website:* www.ingpen.co.uk; andrewgourlay.com.

GOWLAND, David; British music coach; *Artistic Director, Jette Parker Young Artists Programme, Royal Opera House;* b. 1963. *Education:* Royal Coll. of Music and Nat. Opera Studio, London. *Career:* mem., Glyndebourne music staff 1987, as pianist, repetiteur and asst conductor in a wide repertory; Paris Opéra with La Clemenza di Tito and La Bohème, pianist in Porgy and Bess; Head of Music Staff at the Geneva Opera 1989–96, and appointments with Royal Danish Opera, Netherlands Opera, Covent Garden and Dublin Grand Opera; Festivals of Aix, Orange and Wexford; Weill's Threepenny Opera at RADA, London; concerts include Edinburgh and Aldeburgh Festivals, London Proms and with BBC orchestras; The Ring in Australia 1998; Lucia di Lammermoor and Turandot at Orange; La Traviata for the Opéra Bastille, Paris; Artistic Dir of the Jette Parker Young Artists Programme, Royal Opera House; visiting tutor, Nat. Opera Studio. *Honours:* Jani Strassi Award, Glyndebourne 1988. *Address:* Jette Parker Young Artists Programme, Royal Opera House, Covent Garden, London, WC2E 9DD, England (office). *Telephone:* (20) 7212-9192 (office). *Fax:* (20) 7212-9497 (office). *E-mail:* youngartistsprogramme@roh.org.uk (office). *Website:* www.roh.org.uk (office).

GRAEBNER, Eric (Ric) Hans, MA, PhD, ARCO; British composer, pianist, lecturer and conductor; *Director, Resurge Studio;* b. 8 Jan. 1943, Shrewsbury, Shropshire, England; one s. *Education:* Univs of Cambridge and York. *Career:* Lecturer in Music, Univ. of Southampton 1968–98; Visiting Fellow, Princeton Univ., USA 1973, 1981–82, 1983; Asst Prof., William Paterson Coll., New Jersey 1981–82; Dir Resurge Studio 1998–; mem. EMAS (Sonic Arts Network), Performing Right Soc., NMB (New Music Brighton); Fellow, Salzburg Seminar of American Studies 1976. *Compositions include:* Aspects of Three Tetrachords 1973, Thalia 1975, Between Words 1976, String Quartet No. 1 1979, Four Songs and an Aria 1980, Quintet 1981, String Quartet No. 2 1984, La mer retrouvée 1985–86, 3rd String Quartet 1985, Dollbreaker 1987, Trapeze Act 1988, Berenice 1990–91, Introduction and Passacaglia 1993, Venus in Landscape 1995, Resurge 1997, Conversation with Clarinet 1999, Morphologies 2001, Wind Quintet 2002, Naughty Plautus 2002, Nothing but Bonfires 2004, The Reckless Sleeper 2006, 4th String Quartet 2009, Sinfonietta Concertante 2010, Piano Trio 2 2012. *Recordings include:* Divertimento of the Statues 1993, Resurge 1997, Venus in Landscape 1998, Fulminar 1998. *Publications:* New Berlioz Edition 1971–72; contrib. to Soundings, Perspectives of New Music, In Theory Only, Music Analysis. *Honours:* Fulbright-Hayes Fellowship 1973, Dio Award 1977. *Address:*

Resurge Studio, 30 Dyke Road Drive, Brighton, East Sussex, BN1 6AJ, England (office). *Website:* www.ricgraebner.co.uk (office).

GRAF, Hans; Austrian conductor and music director; b. 15 Feb. 1949, Linz; m. Margarita Graf; one d. *Education:* Bruckner Conservatory, Linz, Acad. of Music, Graz, studied in Italy with Franco Ferrara and Sergui Celibadache and in Russia with Arvid Jansons. *Career:* Music Dir Iraqi Nat. Symphony Orchestra 1975–76, Mozarteum Orchestra, Salzburg 1984–94, Calgary Philharmonic Orchestra 1995–2003 (Music Dir Laureate 2003–), Orchestre Nat. de Bordeaux-Aquitaine 1998–2004, Opéra de Bordeaux 1998–2004, Houston Symphony 2001–13 (Conductor Laureate 2013–); guest conductor with several orchestras including Vienna Symphony, Vienna Philharmonic, Orchestre Nat. de France, Leningrad Philharmonic, Pittsburgh Symphony, Boston Symphony, Royal Concertgebouw Orchestra, Deutsches Symphony Orchestra, Bavarian Radio Orchestra; currently Prof. of Orchestral Conducting, Univ. Mozarteum Salzburg. *Honours:* Chevalier, Légion d'Honneur 2002, Grand Honour in Gold (Austria); First Prize, Karl Böhm Conductors Competition, Salzburg 1979. *Current Management:* CM Artists, 127 West 96th Street, 13B, New York, NY 10025, USA. *Telephone:* (212) 864-1005. *Website:* www.cmartists.com/artists/hans-graf.htm.

GRAF, Judith; Swiss singer (soprano); b. 1967. *Education:* studied in Zürich, at Juilliard, New York and in London. *Career:* sang at Biel Opera from 1989 in Gianni Schicchi and as Donna Elvira, Monteverdi's Poppea, Anne Trulove, Pamina, Fiordiligi, Mozart's Vitellia, the Composer in Ariadne and Tchaikovsky's Tatiana; Pforzheim 1991 as Marguerite in Faust; Landstheater Slazburg 1993 in the premiere of Glaube, Liebe, Hoffnung by G. Schedle; Biel 1995 as Sonja in Der Zarewitsch; concert appearances throughout Switzerland.

GRAF, Maria; German singer (mezzo-soprano); b. 1929. *Education:* Vienna Acad. with Anny Konetzni. *Career:* sang in the chorus of the Vienna Staatsoper 1950–55, solo debut at Innsbruck 1955; sang at Munster and Frankfurt, then Karlsruhe Opera 1969–69; guested at Bayreuth 1955 (as Flosshilde and Rossweise) and Italy in operas by Wagner (Die Walküre at La Scala 1963); sang Helen in the German premiere of Tippett's King Priam 1963; other roles included Mozart's Marcellina, Herodias in Salome, Marie (Wozzeck) and Mistress Quickly (Falstaff); Teatro La Fenice, Venice 1968, in the Ring.

GRAF, Peter-Lukas; Swiss flautist and conductor; b. 5 Jan. 1929, Zürich. *Education:* Paris Conservatoire with Marcel Moyse and Eugene Bigot. *Career:* first flautist with the Winterthur Orchestra, 1951–57; Conductor at the Lucerne State Theatre 1961–66; played in the Lucerne Festival Orchestra 1957–, and toured as soloist with the Edwin Fischer and Gunther Ramin; Performances with the English Chamber Orchestra, the Academy of St Martin in the Fields and the Lucerne Festival Strings; as soloist and conductor, tours of Europe, South America, Australia, Japan and Israel; teacher, Basle Conservatory 1973–. *Recordings include:* Spohr Concertante for violin, harp and orchestra; Bach A minor Triple Concerto and Saint-Saëns A minor Concerto (English Chamber Orchestra); Mozart Flute Concertos and Concerto K299 (Lausanne Chamber Orchestra); Swiss music with Orchestra della Radio Svizzera, and the Zürich Tonhalle. *Honours:* first prizes in flute and conducting, Paris Conservatory, 1950, 1951; Winner, International ARD Competition, 1953; Bablock Prize, Harriet Cohen International Music Award, London, 1958.

GRAFFMAN, Gary; American pianist; b. 14 Oct. 1928, s. of Vladimir and Nadia (Margdin) Graffman; m. Naomi Helfman 1952. *Education:* Curtis Inst. of Music, Philadelphia under Mme. Isabelle Vengerova. *Career:* professional début with Philadelphia Orchestra 1947; concert tours all over the world; appears annually in America with major orchestras; Dir Curtis Inst. 1986–, Pres. 1995–2006; year offstage to correct finger injury 1980–81; gramophone recordings for Columbia Masterworks and RCA Victor including concertos of Tchaikovsky, Rachmaninoff, Brahms, Beethoven, Chopin and Prokofiev. *Publication:* I Really Should be Practising (autobiog.) 1981. *Honours:* several hon. degrees; Leventritt Award 1949. *Current Management:* Opus 3 Artists, 470 Park Avenue South, 9th Floor North, New York, NY 10016, USA. *Telephone:* (212) 584-7500. *Fax:* (646) 300-8200. *E-mail:* info@opus3artists.com. *Website:* www.opus3artists.com.

GRAHAM, Alasdair; BMus; British pianist and academic; b. 19 April 1934, Glasgow, Scotland. *Education:* Edinburgh Univ., Vienna Hochschule für Musik, Royal Acad. of Music with Peter Katin. *Career:* debut at Bishopsgate Hall 1958; soloist with Scottish Nat. Orchestra, London Philharmonic Orchestra, BBC Symphony Orchestra (Proms 1963), Royal Liverpool Philharmonic, Hallé Orchestra, Sydney Symphony Orchestra, Melbourne Symphony Orchestra (Australian tour) 1967; recitals for BBC TV (UK), and in Turkey, India; as accompanist with Elisabeth Söderström, Josef Suk, John Shirley-Quirk; Prof., Royal Coll. of Music, London; mem. Royal Soc. of Musicians of Great Britain. *Recordings:* Schubert: Sonata in B flat, 8 Ecossaises. *Honours:* Harriet Cohen Commonwealth Medal 1963, Hon. RCM 1973.

GRAHAM, Peter John, MMus, PGCE, PhD; British composer, arranger and academic; *Chair of Composition, University of Salford;* b. 5 Dec. 1958, Bellshill, Scotland; m. Janey Buchan; one s. one d. *Education:* Univ. of Edinburgh, Moray House Coll., Goldsmiths Coll., Univ. Salford. *Career:* arranger, composer, New York 1983–86, London 1986–91; Lecturer, Univ. of

Salford 1991–97, Sr Lecturer 1997–2001, Reader in Composition 2001–04, Chair. of Composition 2004–. *Compositions:* numerous publs for brass and, wind including Dimensions 1983, Montage 1994, Harrison's Dream 2000, Journey to the Centre of the Earth 2005; arrangements for BBC Radio and TV, commercial TV. *Recordings:* various recordings, including Reflected in Brass, Evelyn Glennie meets the Black Dyke Band. *Honours:* American Bandmasters Asscn/Ostwald Composition Prize 2002, Iles Medal 2009. *Address:* c/o Gramercy Music, PO Box 41, Cheadle Hulme, Cheshire, SK8 5HF, England.

GRAHAM, Susan; American singer (mezzo-soprano); b. 23 July 1960, Roswell, NM. *Education:* Manhattan School of Music, Texas Technical Univ. *Career:* sang Massenet's Chérubin while a student; engagements with St Louis Opera as Erika in Vanessa, Charlotte and at Seattle as Stephano in Roméo et Juliette; season 1989–90 included Chicago Lyric Opera debut as Annius in La Clemenza di Tito, Sonia in Argento's Aspern Papers at Washington, Dorabella and the Composer at Santa Fe; Carnegie Hall debut in Des Knaben Wunderhorn and Bernstein concert in New York; created Sister Helen Prejean in Jack Heggie's Dead Man Walking, San Francisco 2000; season 2001 as Mignon at Toulouse and Dorabella at the New York Met. *Recordings include:* Falstaff conducted by Solti, La Damnation de Faust conducted by Kent Nagano, Béatrice et Bénédict conducted by John Nelson, Stravinsky's Pulcinella, Charles Ives Songs (Grammy Award for Best Classical Vocal Performance 2005) 2004, Poèmes de l'amour 2005, Mozart – La Clemenza di Tito, Massenet: Werther 2006, Un Frisson Francais 2008, Virgins Vixens & Viragos 2012. *Honours:* Opera News Award 2005. *Current Management:* Glenn Petry, 21C Media Group, 162 West 56th Street, Suite 506, New York, NY 10019; IMG Artists, Carnegie Hall Tower, 153 West 57th Street, 5th Floor, New York, NY 10019, USA. *E-mail:* gpetry@21cmediagroup.com. *Website:* www.susangraham.com.

GRAHAM-HALL, John, MA (Cantab.); British singer (tenor); b. (John Hall), 23 Nov. 1963, Middx; s. of the late Leonard Graham Hall and Betty Hall (née Minns); m. Helen Williams; two d. *Education:* King's Coll., Cambridge, Royal Coll. of Music. *Career:* debut with Opera North, as Ferrando in Così fan tutte 1983; has sung Albert Herring at Covent Garden and Glyndebourne, Pedrillo for Kent Opera, Cassio for Welsh Nat. Opera and Don Ottavio for Opera Northern Ireland; Glyndebourne Touring Opera as Britten's Aschenbach, Lysander, Basilio and Ferrando; ENO debut as Basilio 1991, returning as Cyril in Princess Ida, Tanzmeister in Ariadne and Schoolmaster in Cunning Little Vixen; engagements at Lyon as Lensky and Frère Massée in Messiaen's St François d'Assise, Vancouver as Ferrando, Brussels and Lisbon as Cassio and Antwerp as Achilles in King Priam; Glyndebourne Festival as Kudrjas in Katya Kabanova and Flute in Midsummer Night's Dream; Scottish Opera as Eisenstein, and Schoolmaster in Cunning Little Vixen; Aix-en-Provence as Lysander and Bordeaux as Tanzmeister in Ariadne; Amsterdam as Basilio and Curzio; concert career with major British orchestras, including Pulcinella with BBC Symphony 1993; further appearances include Moses and Aron in Amsterdam, La Belle Hélène with ENO, and Shapkin in House of the Dead in Nice; season 1996 with Narciso in Il Turco in Italia at Garsington and in Moses and Aron at Salzburg; Basilio in Figaro for the Royal Opera, London; season 2000–01 in the premiere of The Silver Tassie by Turnage, for ENO, and as Monostatos and Mime; Britten's Bob Boles at Amsterdam; Alwa and Herod for ENO 2002, Dancing Master in Ariadne at Covent Garden 2002; Perelà at Paris Bastille 2003, Man and Boy: Dada at Almeida 2004, Podestà in La Finta giardiniera, Salzburg 2006, Michel in Julietta for Paris Opera 2006; Aschenbach in Death in Venice 2009, Brussels 2009, La Scala, Milan 2011, ENO and Netherlands Opera 2013; Adventures of Mr Broucek, Opera North 2009 and Scottish Opera 2010, Zivny in Janáček's Osud, Stuttgart 2012–13; Peter Grimes at La Scala 2012, Nice 2015; Basilio at Aix-en-Provence and Met, New York 2012; Kaufmann in Jakob Lenz Stuttgart 2014; Shuisky in Boris Godunov, Toulouse 2014. *Recordings include:* Albert Herring, Katya Kabanova, La Finta Giardiniera, Carmina Burana, L'Incoronazione di Poppea, A Midsummer Night's Dream, as Bob Boles in Peter Grimes, songs of Lloyd-Webber; for Chandos Opera in English: Herod (Salome), Monostatos (Magic Flute), Alwa (Lulu), Basilio (Figaro), Peter Grimes La Scala 2012, Aschenbach Death in Venice (ENO) 2013. *Publication:* My Wife the Diva (debut novel) 2013. *Honours:* Franco Abbiati Prize for Best Male Singer in Italy for Death in Venice at La Scala 2011. *Current Management:* c/o Musichall Ltd, Oast House, Crouch's Farm, Hollow Lane, East Hoathly, East Sussex, BN8 6QX, England. *Telephone:* (1273) 840437. *E-mail:* info@musichall.uk.com. *Website:* www.musichall.uk.com.

GRAHN, Ulf Ake Wilhelm, BMus, MM; Swedish composer; b. 17 Jan. 1942, Solna; m. Barbro Dahlman 1969, one s. *Education:* SMI, Stockholm, Catholic Univ., Washington, DC, Uppsala Univ., Sweden. *Career:* music instructor, Stockholm and Lidingo Schools 1964–72; teaching asst, instructor, Catholic Univ., Washington 1972–76; founder and Music Dir, Contemporary Music Forum 1973–85; Lecturer, Northern Virginia Community Coll. 1975–79; Lecturer, then Assoc. Prof., George Washington Univ. 1983–87; founder and Artistic Dir, The Aurora Players 1983–; Artistic and Man. Dir, Lake Siljan Festival Sweden 1988–90; composer-in-residence, Charles Ives Center, USA 1988; publisher and owner, Edition NGLANI 1985–; mem. STIM Sweden, Soc. of Swedish Composers. *Compositions include:* Symphonies Nos 1 and 2, concertos for piano, guitar and double bass, chamber and choral music, solo works for guitar, piano, violin, Cinq Preludes, Snapshots, Sonata for piano with flute and percussion, In the Shade, Caprice, Sonata for piano, Three Dances with Interludes 1990, Blå Dunster (instrumental opera) 1990, As Time Passes By for orchestra 1993, Aron's Interlude for six instruments 1994, Summer '61 for ensemble 1995, Morning Rush for orchestra 1995, Cikadas for four instruments 1996. *Publications:* contrib. articles and reviews to publications in Europe, and to Tonfallet, Musik Revy, Ord och Ton. *Honours:* Stockholm Int. Organ Days 1973, League Int. Soc. for Contemporary Music Piano Competition 1976, first prize in music Dalarna Composition Contest (for Toccata for carillon) 1990.

GRANDISON, Mark, BMus, MMus; Australian composer; b. 9 Dec. 1965, Adelaide, SA. *Education:* Univ. of Adelaide, studied with Richard Meale. *Career:* teacher and co-ordinator, Marryatville Special Interest Music Centre, Adelaide 1992–93; Kambala School, Sydney 1994–; commissions from the Adelaide Chamber Orchestra, Vrizen and Australian Broadcasting Asscn. *Compositions include:* Four Poems of Wilfrid Owen for contralto and ensemble 1985, Contrasts for orchestra 1987, Night Interiors for orchestra 1988, Los Caprichos for chamber orchestra 1989, Five Blake Songs for soprano and piano 1990, Toccata for chamber ensemble 1992, Three Dances for string orchestra 1993, Surface Tension for string quartet 1996, Kinetica for youth orchestra 1997, Tarantella for orchestra 1998. *Honours:* South Australia Young Composer's Award 1993.

GRANGE, Philip Roy, BA, PhD; British composer and academic; *Professor of Composition, University of Manchester*; b. 17 Nov. 1956, London; m. Elizabeth Caroline Hemming 1986; two c. *Education:* Univ. of York, Dartington Summer School of Music. *Career:* BBC Promenade Concert debut 1983; Fellow in the Creative Arts, Trinity Coll., Cambridge 1985–87; Northern Arts Fellow in Composition, Univ. of Durham 1988–89; Lecturer in Composition, Univ. of Exeter 1989–95, Reader in Composition, 1995–99, Prof. of Composition 1999–2000; Prof. of Composition, Univ. of Manchester 2001–, Head of Music Dept 2008–11; MacDowell Fellow 1996; Bogliasco Fellow 2015; performances of music at most major festivals in UK and in Europe, USA and Far East; British Council sponsored tour of Taiwan as both composer and lecturer 1997, 2000; featured composer, TWCAT Conf., Taiwan 2003, Music Factory Festival, Bergen, Norway 2003, Durham Music Festival 2003, Gemini Music Festival, London 2007, Monterrey, Mexico 2013, 2014, 2015, Pan Music Festival, Seoul, South Korea 2014; performed at WASBE confs in Ireland 2007, Taiwan 2011. *Compositions include:* Cimmerian Nocturne 1979, Sextet 1980, The Kingdom of Bones 1983, La Ville Entière 1984, Variations 1986, Out in the Dark 1986, In Memorian HK 1986, The Dark Labyrinth 1987, Concerto for orchestra, Labyrinthine Images 1988, In a Dark Time 1989, Changing Landscapes 1990, Focus and Fade 1992, Lowry Dreamscape 1992, Piano Polyptich 1993, Bacchus Bagatelles 1993, Des fins sont des commencements 1994, Piano Trio: Homage to Chagall 1995, A Puzzle of Shadows for soprano, violin and piano 1997, Sky-Maze with Song Shards 1999, Lament of the Bow 2000, Clarinet concerto 2000, Daedalus's Lament 2001, String Quartet 2003, Duet Movement 2003, Eclipsing 2004, A Spectre Scene 2004, Prelude in Memoriam Karrlin Field 2005, The Sleep of Reason Brings Forth Monsters 2006, Carillon Ritual 2007, Tiers of Time 2007, Time Softly Treads 2008, First Known When Lost 2008, Cloud Atlas (Symphonic Wind Band) (BASCA Award in wind band/brass band category 2010) 2009, Elegy 2009, Adopted Path 2010, To the Borders of Sleep 2011, Ghosts of Great Violence 2012–13, Prelude and Nocturne 2013, In Midnight Sleep 2014, Sick Moon 2014. *Recordings include:* La Ville Entière for clarinet and piano, Dark Labyrinths (recording of six pieces) (Classic Album of the Week in Music Week and Critic's Choice, Gramophone 2000), Horizons (recordings of Diptych and The Knell of Parting Day), Darkness Visible (recording of three pieces) (Critic's Choice, Gramophone 2006), Zeitgeist (recording of four pieces), Borderlands (recording of Piano Trio), Piano Polyptych (recording of eponymous piece), Cloud Atlas (recording of symphonic wind band music and wind quintet), New Sounds from Manchester (recording of Ghosts of Great Violence). *Current Management:* c/o Peters Edition Ltd, Hinrichsen House, 2–6 Baches Street, London, N1 6DN, England. *Website:* www.edition-peters.com. *Address:* Martin Harris Centre for Music and Drama, University of Manchester, Coupland Street, Manchester, M13 9PL, England (office). *Telephone:* (161) 275-4990 (office). *E-mail:* philip.grange@manchester.ac.uk (office).

GRANT, Allison Jean, BMus; Canadian actress, singer, director and choreographer; b. 23 Nov. 1958, Vancouver, BC; d. of Ian Van Felson and Antoinette Suzanne Grant. *Education:* Banff School of Fine Arts, Alberta, Univ. of Western Ontario, Morley Coll. and The Dance Centre, UK. *Career:* mem. Stratford Festival Acting Co. seven years; co-writer musical featuring Gilbert and Sullivan compositions; Resident Dir Showboat Festival five years; teacher, dir and choreographer, Opera Division, Univ. of Toronto; currently Artistic Dir Theatre Athena, Waterloo, Ont. *Stage appearances include:* Private Lives, Double Double, Sylvia, Much Ado About Nothing, Cats, The Drunkard, Desert Song, The Magic Flute, Heat, Brigadoon, Not Available in the Stores (premiere), Guys and Dolls, They're Playing Our Song, The Secret Garden (world premiere) (Dora Mavor Moore Award for best actress in a musical) 1986, Carousel (as Julie Jordan) 1991, The House of Martin Guerre (world premiere) 1993. *Television includes:* Iolanthe 1984, The Pirates of Penzance 1985. *Productions as Director:* A Meeting of Minds at Canstage, All Grown Up, Carmen (Opera Ontario), Cinderella (Canadian Opera Co.), Così fan tutte (Vancouver Opera), Die Zauberflöte, Double Double, Figaro, Figaro, Figaro (Vancouver Opera), L'Italiana in Algeri (L'Opéra de Montréal), Smokey Joe's Cafe (Stagewest Calgary), The Boyfriend (University of Toronto Opera School), The Long Weekend (Showboat Festival Theatre), The Pirates of Penzance (Canadian Children's Opera Chorus), This is a Changing World –

A Noel Coward Revue, When the Reaper Calls, Don Giovanni, The Brothers Grimm, Private Lives, Bach at Leipzig. *Choreography:* Eugene Onegin, Queen of Spades, Dido and Aeneas (Canadian Opera Co.), Die Fledermaus (Vancouver Opera, Kentucky Opera, Opera Hamilton), Die Lustige Witwe (Hawaii Opera Theatre, Opera Hamilton, Edmonton Opera), La Fille du Régiment, Carmen (Opera Ontario), Le Nozze di Figaro (Opera Saskatchewan), Lullaby of Broadway, Pretty Woman, Roll Over Beethoven (Showboat Festival Theatre). *Honours:* Tyrone Guthrie Awards, Stratford, Ont. 1982, 1983, 1985. *Current Management:* Dean Artists Management, 204 St George Street, Toronto, Ont. M5R 2N5, Canada. *Telephone:* (416) 969-7300. *Fax:* (416) 969-7969. *E-mail:* deanarts@interlog.com. *Website:* www.deanartists.com.

GRANT, Clifford Scantlebury; Australian singer (bass); b. 11 Sept. 1930, Randwick, North South Wales; m. 1st Jeanette Earle; one s. two d.; m. 2nd Ruth Anders 1992. *Education:* Sydney Conservatorium with Isolde Hill, Melbourne with Annie Portnoj, studied in London with Otakar Kraus. *Career:* debut with New South Wales Opera Co., as Raimondo in Lucia di Lammermoor 1952; sang with Sadler's Wells/ENO from 1966, debut as Silva in Ernani; leading roles in Oedipus Rex, The Mastersingers, Peter Grimes, The Magic Flute, Madama Butterfly, The Barber of Seville, The Ring of the Nibelung, Don Giovanni, The Coronation of Poppea, Don Carlos; sang in San Francisco 1966–78; Glyndebourne Festival as Nettuno in Il Ritorno d'Ulisse 1972; further engagements with Covent Garden Opera, Welsh Nat. Opera and in Europe; sang in Sydney from 1976, as Nilakantha (Lakmé) 1986; season 1990 as Marcel in Les Huguenots with Australian Opera; returned to UK 1992 and sang Alvise in new production of La Gioconda, Opera North 1993; numerous concert appearances. *Recordings:* Don Giovanni, Rigoletto, Esclarmonde, L'Oracolo, Fafner in The Rhinegold and Hunding in The Valkryie, conducted by Reginald Goodall, Bartolo in Le nozze di Figaro, Il Corsaro, The Apostles by Elgar, Tosca, Les Huguenots. *Honours:* Medal of the Order of Australia. *Address:* c/o Opera Australia, Sydney Opera House, Bennelong Point, Sydney, NSW 2000, Australia (office). *E-mail:* ruthanders51@gmail.com (office).

GRANT MURPHY, Heidi; American singer (soprano); b. 1962. *Education:* studied in New York. *Career:* mem. Met Opera's Young Artist Devt Program 1988; Met debut in Die Frau ohne Schatten (1989) followed by Xenia (Boris Godunov), Papagena, Oscar, Nannetta, Sophie in Der Rosenkavalier, Soeur Constance (Carmélites), Ilia; Servilia (La Clemenza di Tito), Pamina and Susanna in season 1997–98; Santa Fe debut 1991, as Susanna; European debut at Brussels 1991, in La Favorita, followed by Monteverdi's Drusilla with Netherlands Opera, Mozart's Celia (Lucio Silla) and Ismene (Mitridate) at Salzburg, Servilia at the Paris Opéra and Ilia at Frankfurt; concerts include Mozart's C Minor Mass (Houston Symphony), Mahler's Eighth Symphony (Atlanta Symphony and Vienna Philharmonic); New York Philharmonic debut 1996, in Honegger's Jeanne d'Arc au Bûcher; Semire in Les Boréades by Rameau, London Prom concerts 1999; sang Strauss's Sophie at the New York Met, 2000; conductors have included Levine, Ozawa, Robert Shaw, Masur, Michael Tilson Thomas and Charles Dutoit. *Recordings include:* Idomeneo, from the Met (DGG); Haydn's Die Schöpfung (Teldec), Lullabies and Nightsongs 2009. *Honours:* winner Metropolitan Nat. Council auditions 1988, Distinguished Alumni Award from West Washington Univ. 2005. *Current Management:* Kirshbaum Demler & Associates, Inc., 711 West End Avenue, Suite 5KN, New York, NY 10025, USA. *Telephone:* (212) 222-4843. *Fax:* (212) 222-7321. *E-mail:* info@kirshdem.com. *Website:* www.kirshdem.com.

GRÄSBECK, Manfred, MMus; Finnish violinist; b. 16 July 1955, Åbo; m. Maija Lehtonen 1989; one s. one d. *Education:* Åbo Konservatorium, Acad. Internationale de Musique with Maurice Ravel Acad. Internationale d'été, Nice, France, Tjajkovskij-konservatoriet, Kiev, Ukraine, Sibelius Academy, postgraduate studies, Sibelius-Akademin, Helsingfors. *Career:* debut, Ludwig van Beethoven sonatas Nos 5, 7 and 9, Salle Gaveau, Paris, 1978; as soloist with orchestras: Århus 1972, Copenhagen 1972, Bordeaux 1972, Toulouse 1973, 1974, Västerås 1977, Stockholm 1983, Hamburger Symphoniker 1983 Reykjavík 1986 Volgograd 1990; Beethoven Violin Concerto (with cadenzas by M. Gräsbeck), Vilnius and Kaunas 1992; mem. Liszt Gesellschaft Ky, Helsinki; attended Prof. Jorma Panula Conducting Competition, Vaasa, Finland 2003. *Compositions:* seven symphonies, six violin concertos, HRF Op. 23 and Integrity Op. 34, film music and others. *Recordings:* Ellis B Kohs: Conductor, Passacaglia K 11 for organ and strings, Piano and organ, Kreisler with Love, Vols 1 and 2, with Maija Lehtonen, Paganini Caprices Op. 1, K. Aho Violin Concerto, L. Bashmakov Violin Concerto No. 2, Manfred Gräsbeck Plays Sibelius 2005. *Current Management:* J. Audrey Ellison International Artists' Management, 135 Stevenage Road, Fulham, London, SW6 6PB, England. *Telephone:* (20) 7381-9751. *Fax:* (20) 7381-2406. *E-mail:* audrey@ellison-intl.freeserve.co.uk. *Website:* www.ellison-intl.freeserve.co.uk. *Address:* Nallebackavägen 1B, 00700 Helsinki, Finland.

GRAUBART, Michael, BSc; British composer, conductor, writer and academic; *Tutor, Morley College, London;* b. 26 Nov. 1930, Vienna, Austria; s. of Siegfried Graubart and Oda Graubart; m. 1st Ellen Barbour Clark 1962; one s. two d.; m. 2nd Valerie Coumont 1996. *Education:* Univ. of Manchester, England, studied with Matyas Seiber, Geoffrey Gilbert and Lawrence Leonard. *Career:* Conductor, Ars Nova Chamber Orchestra 1960, Hampstead Chamber Orchestra 1962–66; Music Dir, Focus Opera Group 1967–71; Dir of Music, Morley Coll., London 1969–91, currently Tutor (part-time); Adjunct Prof. of Music, Syracuse Univ. London Centre 1989–91; Sr Lecturer, School of Academic Studies, Royal Northern Coll. of Music, Manchester 1991–96; performances of compositions in UK, USA, Canada, Austria and Italy; broadcasts in UK and Canada. *Compositions include:* Sinfonia à 10 for 10 winds, Quintet for flute, clarinet, viola, cello and vibraphone, Canzonetta for triple chamber orchestra, Declensions for 10 instruments, To a Dead Lover for soprano and seven instruments, Untergang for baritone, chorus and 11 instruments, Quasi una Sonata for piano, Three Bagatelles for cello and piano, Sure I am only of Uncertain Things for a cappella chorus, Two Songs for mezzo-soprano and piano, Concertino da Camera for viola and four woodwinds, Diptych (The Seed and the Harvest, Broken Mirror) for four winds, Scena and Capriccio for piano, Variants and Cadenzas for orchestra, Nightfall for chorus and piano, Elegy for orchestra, Speculum Nocturnum for nine winds, cello and bass, Scena II and Finale for euphonium, two flutes, viola and cello 1992, 1995, Ricordanze for recorders and piano 1994, 1996, String Quartet 2000, Sonata for cello and piano, The Meridian Angel for countertenor, two tenors and baritone, Scena III for solo cello, Prelude, Duets and Arias for solo flute 2004–07, Aria II for violin, cello and four trombones 2006, Multum in Parvo for string quartet 2006, Interval Music for violin and piano 2012; edns of music by Pergolesi, Dufay and Josquin. *Publications include:* four articles on Leopold Spinner, including one for the revision of New Grove Dictionary of Music; numerous other articles and reviews on Bach, Beethoven, Schubert, Mendelssohn, Schoenberg, Berg, Webern and Ullmann for Tempo and Musical Times. *Address:* 18 Laitwood Road, Balham, London, SW12 9QL, England. *E-mail:* michael.graubart@btinternet.com. *Website:* www.michaelgraubart2010.musicaneo.com; www.basca.org.uk/directory/355.

GRAVES, Denyce; American singer (mezzo-soprano); b. 7 March 1964, Washington, DC. *Education:* Oberlin Coll. Conservatory and New England Conservatory. *Career:* early roles included Maddalena at Wash. and Giuletta in Les Contes d'Hoffmann at the Spoleto Festival; further engagements as Dalila in Philadelphia and Montréal, Honegger's Antigone, the High Priestess in La Vestale at La Scala, Adalgisa in Zürich and Donizetti's Leonora (La Favorita) at Catania; appearances as Carmen at San Francisco, Vienna, the Bergen Festival, Covent Garden, Berlin, Zürich, Houston, Los Angeles, Buenos Aires and Munich; season 1995–96 as Carmen in Zürich and at the Met, Dalila in Wash., Carmen at San Francisco 1998; season 2000 as Carmen at Chicago, Amneris in Cincinnati, Dalila at the Met and Dulcinée in Don Quichotte for Wash. Opera; The Nation's Favourite Prom at the London Proms 2002; created title role in Richard Danielpour's Margaret Garner 2005; concert repertory includes Messiah, the Verdi Requiem, Rossini's Stabat Mater, Ravel's Shéhérazade and Mahler's Kindertotenlieder; currently Faculty, Peabody Conservatory, John Hopkins Univ. *Recordings include:* Gertrude in Hamlet by Ambroise Thomas, Emilia in Otello, Angels Watching over Me, Héroïnes de l'Opéra Romantique Français, Voce di Donna 1999, The Lost Days 2003, Church 2003, Kaleidoscope 2004, French Opera Arias 2005. *Honours:* Grand Prix du Concours Int. du Chant de Paris, Marian Anderson Award. *Address:* Peabody Institute of The Johns Hopkins University, 1 East Mount Vernon Place, Baltimore, MD 21202, USA (office). *Telephone:* (41) 0234-4500 (office). *E-mail:* m.bell@jhu.edu (office). *Website:* www.peabody.jhu.edu (office); www.denycegraves.com.

GRAVS, Leonard; Dutch singer (bass-baritone); b. 28 Jan. 1944, Maastricht. *Career:* debut as Sparafucile in Rigoletto at Maastricht 1966; sang with Netherlands Opera, Opéra de Wallonie at Liège 1973–82, Hannover Opera 1982–86, Saarbrucken 1986–88, Geneva 1988–94; guest appearances at Marseille, Cologne (Pallante in Agrippina) 1985, Montréal; roles include Puccini's Colline and Angelotti, Nourabad in Les Pêcheurs de perles and the Minister in Fidelio, at Liège 1996; Zuniga in Carmen, Verdi's Zaccaria, Grand Inquisitor and Ramphis; Escamillo and Kaspar; season 1997–98 as Gessler in Guillaume Tell at Liège.

GRAY, George; American singer (tenor); b. 26 May 1947. *Career:* sang Cavaradossi at Colorado Springs 1984, Cairo and Radames with North Carolina Opera 1986, 1988; New Jersey Festival 1987, as Bacchus, Seattle 1987, as Otello; Tristan at Columbus, Ohio; season 1988 in Schoenberg's Gurrelieder at Frankfurt, and Pollione in Norma; Tristan at Nancy 1990, with Aeneas at the opening of the Bastille Opéra, Paris; sang Parsifal at Chicago 1990, Siegfried at Zürich 1988; further appearances as Bacchus at Kassel, in Schreker's Schatzgräber at the Holland Festival and Meyerbeer's Vasco da Gama at the Berlin Staatsoper 1992; Lohengrin at Leipzig; season 1999–2000 at the San Francisco and Dallas Operas as Siegfried.

GRAY, James, BA, MA, LRAM, LTCL; British singer (counter-tenor), keyboard player and conductor; *Director of Music, Santa Felicita, Florence;* b. 1 Jan. 1956, London, England; m. Junko Ishikawa. *Education:* Royal Acad. of Music, London, studied with Maria Curcio in London and Clive Britton in Florence, Acad. of Fine Arts, Prague, Centro Studio Musicali Rinascimento, Florence, Open Univ., Laulukoulu, Finland. *Career:* debut at Czech Philharmonic Soc., Prague 1976; Guest Dir Prague Madrigalists 1980–81 (Berlin TV debut 1981); repétiteur, Nationaltheater, Mannheim 1981–82; La Chaise-Dieu Festival 1984 (French TV); Domenico Scarlatti Tercentenary Celebrations 1985 (Radio Madrid, Spanish TV); Dir Horti Annalenae (Baroque) 1989–, Mayfair Quartet/Quintet (Ragtime) 2004–; Piccadilly Piano Quintet; Organist at Basilica di Santo Spirito, Florence 2008–13; Artistic Dir of Organa sonent!, Palazzo Pitti, Florence 2008–; Dir of Music, The Global Theatre Project 2010–; Dir of Music, Santa Felicita, Florence 2013–. *Recordings include:* Domenico Scarlatti 5 Cantate inedite 1985, Monteverdi: Lamento d'Arianna 1985, O Primavera 2002, Guillaume de Machaut: La Messa de Nostre Dame 1989, Benedetto

Marcello, Cantate a 1, 2, 3 voci 1990. *Honours:* Grand Prix 'Discobole pour l'Europe' 1985, Grand Prix d'Honneur (chamber music), 85ème Concours Int. de Musique Léopold Bellan. *Address:* Via Romana 34, 50125 Florence, Italy (home). *E-mail:* horti.annalenae@gmail.com (office).

GRAY, Linda Esther; British singer (soprano); b. 29 May 1948, d. of James Gray and Esther Gray; m. Peter McCrorie 1971; one d. *Education:* Greenock Acad. and Royal Scottish Acad. of Music and Drama. *Career:* with London Opera Centre 1969–71, Glyndebourne Festival Opera 1972–75, Scottish Opera 1974–79, ENO 1979, Welsh Opera 1980; debut American performance in 1981; appeared Royal Opera House, London 1982, 1983. *Operas include:* Tristan und Isolde, die Walküre, Tosca, Parsifal, Fidelio. *Recordings:* Tristan und Isolde 1981, Die Feen 1983. *Publication:* A Life Behind Curtains: A Singer's Silent Sounds (autobiog.) 2007. *Honours:* Cinzano Scholarship 1969, Goldsmith Scholarship 1970, James Caird Scholarship 1971, Christie Award 1972, Kathleen Ferrier Award 1972. *Address:* 35 Green Lane, New Malden, Surrey, KT3 5BX, England.

GREAGER, Richard; New Zealand singer (tenor); b. 5 Nov. 1946, Christchurch; m. Rosemary Greager Andrew Greager; one s. one d. *Education:* Melbourne Univ. Conservatorium of Music. *Career:* Jr Prin., Covent Garden – 1975; lyric tenor, Scottish Opera 1975, then sang widely in Germany, notably at Hanover, Dortmund, Wiesbaden, Cologne, Karlsruhe and Bonn; roles include Don Ottavio, Ferrando, Tamino, Rodolfo, the Duke of Mantua, Fenton and Ernesto; Australian Opera from 1980, as The Painter in Lulu, Edgardo (opposite Sutherland's Lucia), Peter Grimes, Lensky, Don José and Peter Quint (The Turn of the Screw); guest appearances at the Grand Théâtre Geneva as Peter Quint, the Painter and the Negro in Lulu (Jeffrey Tate conducting) and Edgardo; Opéra de Lyon as Huon in Oberon; season 1988–89 as Rodolfo at Melbourne and Covent Garden; Eisenstein in Die Fledermaus for Scottish Opera; Peter Quint in Schwetzingen and Cologne; Covent Garden 1991 as Arthur in the world premiere of Gawain by Harrison Birtwistle; other roles include Tonio (La Fille du Régiment) and Werther; season 1991–92 as Arbace in Idomeneo at Helsinki, Herod in Salome at Wellington and Mozart's Basilio with the Royal Opera in Japan; sang Don José and Don Ottavio for Wellington City Opera 1997; Torquemada in L'Heure Espagnole at Auckland 1998; Captain in Wozzeck (Barrie Kosky's production), Sydney; Dr Caius in Falstaff for NBR New Zealand Opera, Roger in Love in the Age of Therapy for OzOpera, Melbourne and Sydney Festivals 2001; Prince Shuisky in Boris Godunov for NBR New Zealand Opera; Herod in Salome for Opera Australia 2003; Mime in Der Ring des Nibelungen, South Australian Opera 2004; Herodes in Salome, Brisbane 2006; Candide, Perth Festival 2006; Herodes in Salome Auckland 2008. *Recordings:* DVD: Gawain, Lucia di Lammermoor, La Traviata, Un Ballo in Maschera, Turn of the Screw, Dialogue of the Carmelites; also recorded Berlioz's Requiem and Schubert's Six Masses. *Honours:* winner Sun Aria Competition, Sydney and Melbourne, Australia, Winner Best Supporting Singer Aust. Green Room Awards for Wozzeck 2003. *Current Management:* Arts Management Pty Ltd, Level 1, 405 Elizabeth Street, Surry Hills, NSW 2010, Australia. *Telephone:* (2) 9211 9422. *Fax:* (2) 9211 9466. *E-mail:* enquiries@artsmanagement.com.au. *Website:* www .artsmanagement.com.au.

GREEN, Anna, ARCM; British singer; b. 27 Jan. 1933, Southampton, England; m. Howard Vanderburg 1965. *Education:* Royal Coll. of Music. *Career:* debut as Amelia in Verdi's Un Ballo in Maschera, Deutsche Oper am Rhein, Düsseldorf 1961; sang Aida, Tosca and Abigaille; later sang German roles, including Fidelio, Marschallin, Isolde, Brünnhilde and Elektra; appeared as Hecuba in King Priam at Royal Opera House, Covent Garden, London, Brünnhilde for ENO and WNO, Elektra for Vienna State Opera and in Karslruhe and Mannheim, Brünnhilde in Barcelona, Florence, Naples, Nice, Warsaw, Lisbon, Hamburg, Stuttgart and Cologne, Isolde in Berlin, Mannheim, Karlsruhe and Wiesbaden, Kostelnicka in Jenůfa in Stuttgart; also sang in Canada and USA, as Brünnhilde at founding of Pacific Northwest Wagner Festival and in subsequent four seasons; concert appearances include Stravinsky's Les Noces at Albert Hall, London, under Pierre Boulez, Schoenberg's Erwartung in Scotland, under Gari Bertini, Altenberg Lieder for RAI, Rome, Wagner concert with Los Angeles Philharmonic conducted by Zubin Mehta; mem. Genossenschaft Deutscher Bühnen. *Recordings:* Aus dem Essener Musikleben; Betulia Liberata KV 118 Mozart.

GREEN, Barry, BMus, MMus; American bassist, academic and writer; *Professor of Bass, University of California, Santa Cruz;* b. 10 April 1945, Newark, NJ; m. Mary Tarbell Green 1984; two s. one step-s. *Education:* Indiana Univ. School of Music, Univ. of Cincinnati, Performers Certificate. *Career:* Prin. Bassist, Nashville Symphony 1965–66, Cincinnati Symphony 1967–95; Faculty, Univ. of Cincinnati 1967–95; Prof. of Bass, Univ. of California, Santa Cruz 1996–; Dir Young Bassist Program, San Francisco Symphony Educ. Dept 1995–2011; Casals Festival Orchestra 1979–87; int. workshops 1982–86; Founder-Dir and Life mem. American String Teachers Asscn; Founder-Exec. Dir Int. Soc. of Bassists. *Recordings:* solos: Baroque Bass, Romantic Music for Double Bass, New Music for Double Bass, Bass Evolution, Sound of Bass, Vol. 1 (Chamber Music Recordings) Heritage Chamber Quartet, Music Now, What of My Music Opus One, Ole-Cool, Live from St Croix, Seat of the Pants. *Publications:* Fundamentals of Double Bass Playing; Advanced Techniques of Double Bass Playing 1976, Inner Game of Music 1986, The Mastery of Music, Ten Pathways to True Artistry (also DVD) 2003, Bringing Music to Life 2008 (also DVD 2010); contrib. to Suzuki Journal, American Music Teacher, Instrumentalist, Bass World. *Honours:* Recognition

Award (Young Bassist Amb.), Int. Soc. of Bassists 2007. *Current Management:* c/o Price Rubin & Partners, 520 Geary Street, Suite 605, San Francisco, CA 94102, USA. *Website:* www.pricerubin.com. *Address:* 2654 San Marcos Avenue, San Diego, CA 92104, USA (home). *Telephone:* (619) 795-7565 (home). *Fax:* (619) 795-6980 (home). *E-mail:* barry@innergameofmusic.com (home). *Website:* www.innergameofmusic.com; www.greenartsnetwork.com.

GREEN, Barton; American singer (tenor); b. 1967, New Orleans. *Education:* Washington and Yale Univs. *Career:* sang Tamino at Tacoma Opera 1986; Pinkerton for Sarasota Opera 1994; season 1995 with Alfredo for Pittsburgh Opera; Faust at Conneticut; Rossini's Almaviva for Da Capo Opera and Tonio in La Fille du régiment for Augusta Opera; Eugene Opera, 1996 as Rodolfo, and Gennaro in Lucrezia Borgia at Manhattan Opera; Giessen Opera, 1996 as Edgardo in Lucia di Lammermoor; Alfred in Die Fledermaus for Florida Grand Opera, 1998. *Honours:* Richard Tucker Award 1994.

GREEN, Paul Jay, BA, MS, JD, LLM; American clarinettist; b. 19 Dec. 1948, New York; m. Lisa Dolinger Green 1993. *Education:* Yale College, Juilliard School of Music, Brooklyn Law School, New York University, studied with Leon Russianoff, Keith Wilson, Joseph Allard. *Career:* debut with Young Concert Artists, Carnegie Recital Hall 1966; soloist: New York Philharmonic; Hartford Symphony Orchestra; New Haven Symphony Orchestra; Colorado Music Festival; Festival of Two Worlds in Spoleto, Italy; International Festival of Contemporary Music, Kraków, Poland; The Days of New Music Festival in Chisinau, Moldova; chamber music performances with: Jacqueline Du Pré; Richard Goode; The Lark Quartet; The Borromeo Quartet; The Ying Quartet; The Alexander Quartet; The St Lawrence Quartet; The Miami String Quartet; The Eroica Trio; founder and Artistic Dir, Gold Coast Chamber Music Festival; principal clarinettist, New Haven Symphony Orchestra 1989–90; Colorado Music Festival Orchestra; Symphony of the Americas; American Sinfonietta; Atlantic Classical Orchestra; Assoc. Prof. of Music, Clarinet and Chamber Music, Conservatory of Music, Lynn Univ., Boca Roton, FL 1992–; Instructor of Music, Clarinet and Chamber Music, School of Music, Florida Int. Univ., Miami, FL 1996–. *Recordings:* Carnival of the Animals with Leonard Bernstein and the New York Philharmonic; Return to the Concert Stage, 1990; Quintet for Clarinet and Strings with the Miami String Quartet, 2001. *Address:* 717 Heron Drive, Delray Beach, FL 33444, USA.

GREENAN, Andrew, MA; British singer (bass-baritone); b. 5 Feb. 1960, Birmingham; m. Susannah Davies 1989; two s. one d. *Education:* St Marys Coll., Liverpool, St Johns Coll., Cambridge, Royal Northern Coll. of Music with John Cameron. *Career:* debut at La Scala, Milan 1983; Bayreuther Festspielchor 1985–87; British Opera debut, Mozart's Bartolo Opera 80 1989; Principal Bass, ENO 1992–97; roles include King Henry, Sarastro, Rocco, Commendatore, Timur, Sparafucile, Swallow; other engagements include Bottom in Midsummer Night's Dream at Teatro Regio, Turin 1995; Landgraf in Tannhäuser at QEH; For Royal Opera Covent Garden: Swallow with Mackerras, Ataliba in Alzira with Elder, 1st Nazarene in Salome with Dohnányi, Pietro in Simon Boccanegra with Solti, Rocco for WNO, Abimélech in Samson et Dalila for New Israeli Opera 1998, Swallow for Hamburg State Opera and WNO; concert work includes Verdi Requiem with Belgian National Orchestra and appearances with the English Chamber and BBC Symphony Orchestras. *Recordings:* The Nightingale by Stravinsky, with the Philharmonia and Robert Craft; video recordings of Peter Grimes with ENO and Salome with the Royal Opera; appeared as Raymond/Larimondo in the film Lucia based on Donizetti's opera. *Current Management:* Hazard Chase, 25 City Road, Cambridge CB1 1DP, England. *Telephone:* (1223) 312400. *Fax:* (1223) 460827. *E-mail:* info@hazardchase.co.uk. *Website:* www.hazardchase.co.uk. *Address:* 3 Wheatsheaf Gardens, Lewes, East Sussex BN7 2UQ, England (home).

GREENAWALD, Sheri Kay; American singer (soprano); b. 12 Nov. 1947, Iowa City, IA. *Education:* Univ. of Northern Iowa with Charles Matheson, studied with Hans Heinz, Daniel Ferro and Maria DeVarady in New York, with Audrey Langford in London. *Career:* debut at Manhattan Theater Club 1974, in Les Mamelles de Tirésias by Poulenc; sang in the premieres of Bilby's Doll by Carlisle Floyd and Washington Square by Thomas Pastieri (Houston and Detroit 1976); European debut with Netherlands Opera as Susanna in Le nozze di Figaro 1980; regular concert appearances with the St Louis and San Francisco Symphony Orchestras and the Rotterdam Philharmonic; sang in the premiere of Bernstein's A Quiet Place, Houston 1983; other roles include Violetta, Ellen Orford (Peter Grimes), Mozart's Despina and Zerlina, Sophie in Werther and Norina in Don Pasquale; season 1991–92 at Chicago as Pauline in the US stage premiere of Prokofiev's The Gambler and Mozart's Donna Anna, Fiordiligi at Seattle; sang the Marschallin with WNO 1994; Susa's Transformations at St Louis 1997; Los Angeles Opera debut 1998 as Catán's Florencia.

GREENBAUM, Stuart Geoffrey Andrew, BMus, MMus, PhD; Australian composer; b. 25 Dec. 1966, Melbourne. *Education:* Univ. of Melbourne, studied with Brenton Broadstock and Barry Conyngham. *Career:* debut with Upon the Dark Water (text by Ross Baglin), premiered at Sydney Opera House 1990, by the Song Company; works performed by groups, including The Modern Wind Quintet, I Cantori di New York, The Song Company, Melbourne Symphony, The Oxford University Philharmonia, The Arcadian Singers, Ormond Coll. Choir, The Pacific Ocean Symphony Orchestra; mem. AMC, FAC, CPCF. *Compositions:* Ice Man for solo piano 1993, The Killing Floors for orchestra 1995, Four Minutes in a Nuclear Bunker for orchestra 1995, Nelson for soprano, baritone and string quartet 1997, The Foundling for choir, string quartet and vibraphone 1997. *Recordings:* albums: Upon the Dark Water, Greenbaum, Hindson, Peterson anthology, Music for Theatre, Portrait and Blues Hymn, Polar Wandering, Fairfield Days. *Honours:* ANA Composition Award 1991, Dorian Le Galliene Composition Award 1993.

GREENBERG, Sylvia; Israeli singer (soprano); *Professor of Voice Studies, Hochschule für Musik und Theater München; Konservatorium Wien Privatuniversität;* b. 1952, Romania. *Education:* Tel-Aviv Acad. of Music, Int. Opera Studio, Zurich. *Career:* debut in a Tel-Aviv concert, conducted by Zubin Mehta; stage debut as Queen of Night, Zurich 1977; later sang Zerbinetta, Olympia in Les Contes d'Hoffmann, and in operas by Monteverdi; guest appearances in Hamburg, Berlin, Vienna, Munich and Cologne; Glyndebourne Festival 1978, Die Zauberflöte; US debut in Die Schöpfung, Chicago, conducted by Solti 1981; Bayreuth Festival as Waldvogel in Siegfried 1983; Salzburg Festival in premiere of Un Re in Ascolto by Berio 1984; at La Scala sang Queen of Night 1985; Aix-en-Provence as Ilia in Idomeneo 1986; sang in Doktor Faustus by Giacomo Manzoni at La Scala 1989; Olga in Fedora at Bologna 1996; sang Donna Elvira for New Israeli Opera 2000; currently Prof. of Voice Studies, Hochschule für Musik und Theater, Munich and Konservatorium Wien Privatuniversität. *Recordings include:* Die Schöpfung, Te Deum by Bizet, Poulenc's Gloria, Carmina Burana, Haydn: L'anima dell filosofo, Mozart: Die Entführung aus dem Serail, Hausmusik (songs by Korngold, Bruno Walter, Zemlinsky, Mahler). *Current Management:* c/o Franz Hainzl Artists' Management, Postfach 17, 1043 Vienna, Austria. *Telephone:* (1) 586-4536. *Fax:* (1) 585-5551. *E-mail:* office@hainzl.net. *Website:* www.sylviagreenberg.com.

GREENLAW, Kevin; American singer (baritone); b. 1965. *Education:* Interlocken Arts Academy; Eastman School of Music; Opera School of the Royal Scottish Academy. *Career:* Early appearances as Mozart's Guglielmo and Nardo, Schaunard in La Bohème, Britten's Tarquinius, and Papageno (at Aldeburgh); Concerts include Carmina Burana, Des Knaben Wunderhorn by Mahler, Messiah and the Fauré Requiem; Paris Opéra Bastille in Manon, Parsifal, Don Carlos and War and Peace; Ned Keene in Peter Grimes at Montpellier 2001; Elsewhere in France as Belcore, Ramiro in L'Heure Espangole and Odoardo in Handel's Ariodante at the Paris Palais Garnier, 2001; Juan in Massenet's Don Quichotte and Morales in Carmen at the Bastille; Has sung at Dortmund Opera as Don Giovanni and Marcello; Festival engagements at Edinburgh (Fringe), Isle of Mann, Aldeburgh and Orange. *Current Management:* Musicaglotz, 11 rue le Verrier, 75006 Paris, France. *Telephone:* (1) 42-34-53-40. *Fax:* (1) 40-46-93-77. *E-mail:* general@musicaglotz.com. *Website:* www.musicaglotz.com.

GREENWOOD, Andrew; British conductor; b. 1954, Todmorden, Yorks., England. *Education:* Clare Coll., Cambridge and London Opera Centre. *Career:* Opera for All 1976; mem. music staff, Covent Garden 1977–84, studying with Edward Downes and conducting the Dutch Radio and Television Orchestra; Prin. Guest Chorus Master, Philharmonia Chorus 1981–91; concerts with Previn, Davis, Giulini, Sinopoli and Solti; conducted Rossini's Petite Messe Solennelle at Istanbul Festival 1985; Chorus Master, Welsh Nat. Opera 1984–90, and has conducted performances of operas by Mozart, Bizet, Puccini, Verdi, Berlioz (The Trojans), Beethoven, Strauss and Smetana; numerous concerts on BBC Radio 2 and Radio 3, notably with BBC Nat. Orchestra of Wales; debut with Rotterdam Philharmonic 1990, Cologne Opera 1990, The Bartered Bride and Die Fledermaus; ENO 1990–92, The Magic Flute and Madama Butterfly; conducted Manon Lescaut for Chelsea Opera Group 1992, Don Giovanni for ENO; Royal Danish Opera, Così, Barbiere, Turandot, Entfuhrung, Don Giovanni; Music Dir English Touring Opera 1996–2002, Figaro, Fidelio, Manon, Macbeth, Fille du Régiment, Rake's Progress; Artistic Dir Buxton Festival 2006–11, (for Buxton) Roberto Devereux, Lucrezia Borgia, Mignon, Luisa Miller, Maria di Rohan; Aïda, Royal Albert Hall 2012; Wexford Festival, Foroni Cristina Regina di Svezia 2013. *Current Management:* c/o Athole Still International Ltd, Foresters Hall, 25–27 Westow Street, London, SE19 3RY, England. *Telephone:* (20) 8771-5271. *Fax:* (20) 8771-8172. *E-mail:* enquiries@atholestill.co.uk. *Website:* www.atholestill.com; www.andrewgreenwood.org.uk.

GREEP, Francis, MusM, DMus; Australian conductor and pianist; *Head of Music Staff and Music Director, Houston Grand Opera Studio. Education:* Univ. of Cincinnati Coll.-Conservatory of Music, Univ. of Western Australia. *Career:* perm. mem. of music staff, serving as rehearsal coach, Asst Conductor, Chorus Master and Children's Chorus Master, Opera Australia 1995–2005; Head of Music and Asst Conductor, West Australian Opera 2006–10, Artistic Dir Young Artist Program 2006–; Head of Music Staff and Music Dir, Houston Grand Opera Studio 2010–; teaching and coaching credits include Sydney Conservatorium, Univ. of Western Australia and Western Australian Acad. of Performing Arts, Opera Festival of Lucca, Houston Grand Opera; Chorus Master for Australian premiere of John Adam's A Flowering Tree 2007. *Operas include:* La Sonnambula (Bellini), Peter Grimes (Britten), The Girl of the Golden West (Puccini), Tristan und Isolde (Wagner), Tales of Hoffman (Offenbach), Pelléas et Mélisande (Debussy), Wozzeck (Berg), Dead Man Walking (Jake Heggie), The Love of the Nightingale (Richard Mills). *Address:* Houston Grand Opera, 510 Preston Street, Houston, TX 77002, USA (office). *Telephone:* (713) 546-0200 (office). *Website:* www.houstongrandopera.org (office).

GREER, David Clive, BA, MA, MusD, FRSA; British professor of music; *Professor Emeritus of Music, Durham University;* b. 8 May 1937, London, England; s. of William MacKay Greer and Barbara Avery; m. 1st Patricia Regan 1961 (died 1999); two s. one d.; m. 2nd Harriet Marling 2002. *Education:* Dulwich Coll., Univ. of Oxford, Univ. of Dublin. *Career:* Lecturer in Music, Univ. of Birmingham 1963–72; Hamilton Harty Prof. of Music, Queen's Univ., Belfast 1972–84; Prof. of Music, Univ. of Newcastle 1984–86; Prof. of Music, Durham Univ. 1986–2001, Prof. Emer. 2001–; Coll. Tutor, Univ. Coll., Durham 2008–; Mellon Visiting Fellow, Huntington Library, Calif. 1989, Mayers Visiting Fellow 1991, 2007; Folger Visiting Fellow, Folger Shakespeare Library, Washington DC 1994, 1998, 2008, 2014; Chair. Accreditation Panel, Hong Kong Baptist Univ. 1994; Ed. Journal (fmrly Proceedings) of the Royal Musical Asscn, Vols 103–115. *Publications:* English Madrigal Verse (co-ed. with F. W. Sternfeld, third edn) 1967, English Lute Songs (facsimile series) 1967–71, Hamilton Harty, his Life and Music 1979, Songs from Manuscript Sources 1979, Collected English Lutenist Partsongs (Musica Britannica, Vols 53–54) 1987–89, A Numerous and Fashionable Audience: The Story of Elsie Swinton 1997, John Dowland: Ayres for Four Voices (Musica Britannica, Vol. 6) 2000, Musicology and Sister Disciplines 2000, Musica Transalpina (The English Madrigalists, Vol. 42) 2011, Manuscript Inscriptions in Early English Printed Music 2015; contrib. to Music and Letters, Proceedings of the Royal Musical Asscn, Lute Soc. Journal, Musical Times, Shakespeare Quarterly, English Studies, Notes and Queries, Early Music, Music Review. *Address:* 20 Haldane Terrace, Jesmond, Newcastle upon Tyne, NE2 3AN, England (home). *Telephone:* (191) 334-3140 (office); (191) 281-6766 (home). *Fax:* (191) 334-3141 (office). *E-mail:* d.c.greer@durham .ac.uk (office). *Website:* www.dur.ac.uk/music/staff (office).

GREGSON, Edward, BMus, FDCA, FRAM, FRNCM, FRCM, GRSM, LRAM; British composer; *Professor Emeritus, Royal Northern College of Music;* b. 23 July 1945, Sunderland; s. of Edward Gregson and Elizabeth May Eaves; m. Susan Carole Smith 1967; two s. *Education:* Royal Acad. of Music, London, Goldsmiths Coll., Univ. of London. *Career:* Lecturer, Rachel McMillan Coll. 1970–76, Goldsmiths Coll. 1976, Reader in Music 1989, Prof. of Music 1994; Prin. Royal Northern Coll. of Music 1996–2008, Prof. Emer. 2008–, Fellow 1999, Companion 2008; Chair. Conservatoires UK 2004–08; Dir Associated Bd of the Royal Schools of Music 1996–2008, Performing Right Soc. for Music 1995–; Gov. Chetham's School of Music, Manchester 1996–, Hallé Orchestra 1998–2004; Fellow, Dartington Coll. of Arts 1997, RAM 1999, Royal Coll. of Music 2000, Leeds Coll. of Music 2008; Trustee, Nat. Foundation for Youth Music 1999–2003, PRS for Music Foundation 2009–; as composer, commissioned by numerous orchestras, orgs and ensembles, in UK and abroad 1970–, including English Chamber Orchestra 1968, York Festival 1976, RSC 1988, 1990, Bournemouth Festival 1991, Royal Liverpool Philharmonic 1991, BBC Radio 3 (for BBC Philharmonic) 1994, Hallé Orchestra 1999, Mahler in Manchester festival (for BBC Philharmonic) 2010, Nat. Centre for Orchestral Studies, Wren Orchestra of London; extensive judging panel work, including BBC Young Musician of the Year and Royal Philharmonic Soc., Stresa Festival, amongst others. *Plays:* The Plantagenets Trilogy (RSC) 1988, Henry IV parts 1&2 (RSC) 1990. *Compositions include:* orchestral: Music for chamber orchestra 1968, Horn Concerto 1971, Tuba Concerto 1976, Trombone Concerto 1979, Metamorphoses 1979, Concerto for orchestra 1983, revised 2001, Trumpet Concerto 1983, Celebration 1991, Blazon 1992, Clarinet Concerto 1994, Concerto for piano and wind 1995–97, And the Seven Trumpets 1998, Violin Concerto 2000, Saxophone Concerto 2006, A Song for Chris, concerto for cello and chamber orchestra 2007, Goddess for string orchestra 2009, Dream Song 2010, Aztec Dances – concerto for flute and ensemble 2013; choral and vocal: In the Beginning 1966, Five Songs of Innocence and Experience 1980, Missa Brevis Pacem 1988, Make a Joyful Noise (anthem) 1988, A Welcome Ode 1997, The Dance, Forever the Dance 1999, Three John Donne Settings 2013; instrumental and chamber: Divertimento for trombone and piano 1967, Brass Quintet 1967, Six Little Piano Pieces 1982, Equale Dances for brass quintet 1983, Piano Sonata in one movement 1986, Alarum for solo tuba 1993, Three Matisse Impressions for recorder and piano or string orchestra, harp and percussion 1993, Serenata Notturna for violin and piano 1999, Serenata Notturna for cello and piano 2004, Shadow of Paradise for oboe and percussion 2005, Tributes for clarinet and piano 2010, Aztec Dances for recorder or flute and piano 2010, An Album for my Friends (piano) 2012; brass band: Essay 1971, Variations on Laudate Dominum 1976 (revised 2008), Connotations 1977, Dances and Arias 1984, Of Men and Mountains 1990, The Trumpets of the Angels 2000, 2016, An Age of Kings 2004, Rococo Variations 2008, Symphony in two movements 2012, Of Distant Memories (Music in an Olden Style) 2013, Cornet Concerto 2015; symphonic wind band: Festivo 1985, The Sword and the Crown 1991, The Kings Go Forth 1997; also educational music, TV and theatre music. *Publications include:* The Contemporary Repertoire of Brass Bands in the 20th Century 1979, Composers on composing for bands, My New Music - Dream Song for Orchestra 2010, Arnold the Symphonist 2011. *Honours:* Hon. DMus (Sunderland) 1996, (Lancaster) 2006, (Manchester) 2008, (Chester) 2009, Dr hc (Manchester Metropolitan) 2003, Hon. DUniv (Central England) 2007; BUMA Int. Brass Award 2013. *Current Management:* c/o Novello and Co. Music Publishers, 14–15 Berners Street, London, W1T 3LJ, England. *Telephone:* (20) 7612-7400. *Fax:* (20) 7612-7545. *E-mail:* music@musicsales.co .uk. *Website:* www.musicsales.co.uk; www.edwardgregson.com.

GREILSAMMER, David; Israeli pianist and conductor; *Music Director, L'Orchestre de Chambre de Genève;* b. 1977, Jerusalem. *Education:* Rubin

Conservatory, Juilliard School, New York. *Career:* New York debut, Lincoln Center under James Conlon 2004; London debut, Wigmore Hall 2007; regularly invited to perform in major int. concert halls under leading conductors; performed complete Mozart piano sonatas, Verbier Festival, France 2008; recitals in Beijing, Bologna, Hong Kong, Lisbon, London, Madrid, Mexico City, Montpellier, Paris, Saitama, Shanghai, Tel-Aviv, Toulouse, Venice and Yokohama 2008; has performed with many leading orchestras including Orquestra Metropolitana, Portugal, Orchestre du Capitole de Toulouse, France, Kanagawa Philharmonic, Japan (pianist and conductor), Orchestre Nat. d'Ile de France, Jerusalem Symphony, Israel Chamber Orchestra, Haifa Symphony, Princeton Symphony, Minsk Symphony, Nordwestdeutsche Philharmonie, Cuba Nat. Symphony, Taipei Philharmonic; Music Dir L'Orchestre de Chambre de Genève, Suedama Ensemble. *Recordings:* Mozart Early Concertos 2006, fantaisie_fantasme 2007, Mozart Piano Concertos Nos 22 & 24, Tansman/Boulanger/Gershwin 2010. *Honours:* First Prize, Juilliard Concerto Competition 2004, Young Musician of the Year, French Music Awards 2008. *Current Management:* c/o IMG Artists, The Light Box, 111 Power Road, London W4 5PY, England. *Telephone:* (20) 7957-5800. *Fax:* (20) 7957-5801. *E-mail:* arance@imgartists.com. *Website:* www.imgartists.com. *E-mail:* contact@davidgreilsammer.com (office). *Website:* www.davidgreilsammer.com.

GRELA-MOZEJKO, Piotr, MA, MMus; Polish composer and music critic; b. 15 March 1961, Bytom; m. Kasia Zoledziowski 1990. *Education:* Univ. of Silesia, Katowice, studied composition with Dr Edward Boguslawski in Katowice, Dr Boguslaw Schaeffer in Kraków, Dr Alfred Fisher at Univ. of Alberta, Edmonton. *Career:* debut in The Silesian Tribune of Composers, 1982; first performance of work, 1977; works performed at major festivals such as Warsaw Autumn Festival, Poznań Music Spring Festival, Gdansk Meetings of Young Composers; founder, Fascinating Music Festival, Katowice, 1983–86; co-founder, J. S. Bach Festival, Kraków-Katowice, 1985; took part in many exhibitions of musical scores, Institut Polonais, Paris, RAM, London, Warsaw, Salzburg, Katowice; numerous interviews, Polish tv and radio, also CBC; Polish tv documentary on activities and the Fascinating Music Festival, 1992. *Compositions include:* Archival radio recordings, Poland, Canada, USA: Ravenna, harpsichord; minimum-optimum-maximum, chamber ensemble; en attendant Bergson, string quartet; The Dreams of Odysseus, tape (performed in Warsaw, Poland, as part of the first exhibition of Polish artists in exile, Jestesmy); Epitaph for Jerzy, for tape included in A BEAMS Compilation; Xylotet Concerto, saxophone, orchestra; Horror Vacui, strings; Ordines, saxophone, organ, cello; Melodramas I–VI, solo instruments; Festivals: Canada, Pacific Market, Fringe, The Edmonton Music Festival, Warsaw.

GRIBENSKI, Jean; French musicologist; *Professor, Poitiers University*; b. 5 Aug. 1944, Castelmoron-sur-Lot, Lot-et-Garonne; m. Isabelle Serrand 1980, one s. three d. *Education:* Sorbonne, Univ. of Paris. *Career:* teacher of history of music, Sorbonne, Université de Paris IV 1970–2003, Université de Poitiers 2003–; Editor-in-Chief, Revue de Musicologie 1974–86; mem. Société française de musicologie (bd of dirs 1974–, pres. 1995–2001). *Publications:* thèses de doctorat en langue française relative à la musique/French language dissertations in music 1979, D'un opéra l'autre 1996, Catalogue des éditions françaises de Mozart (1764–1825) 2006. *Address:* 41 rue Boulard, 75014 Paris, France (home). *E-mail:* jean.gribenski@wanadoo.fr (home).

GRICE, Garry Bruce, BA; American singer (tenor); b. 25 Jan. 1942, Dayton, OH; m. Patricia A. Michael 1983, one s. two d. *Education:* University of Dayton, studied with Hubert Kockritz in Cincinnati and Adelaide Saraceni in Milan. *Career:* debut at National Opera, USA, 1970–71; eight seasons in German and Swiss opera houses, including at Stadttheater, St Gallen, Switzerland, 1974, Bavarian State Opera, 1974; as Don José in Carmen, Florentine Opera, Milwaukee, 1980; Bacchus in Ariadne auf Naxos, Des Moines Metro Opera, 1980; at New York City Opera, 1981; Bermuda Festival, 1981; in Chicago as Don José in Carmen, 1983; with Calgary Opera Association, 1985; in Cairo, 1990; has sung with conductors Kleiber, Prêtre, Guadagno, Keene and Rescigno; appeared in over 50 roles including Otello, Florestan, Bacchus, Canio, Max and Radames; sang throughout USA, also Canada, Bermuda and Europe mainly Germany, Austria, Switzerland; faculty of voice and opera, University of Notre Dame, 1991; Artistic Dir, Indian Opera North from 1990; New Orleans debut, Verdi Requiem, 1992. *Recordings:* title role in Otello, 1984; Turiddu in Cavalleria Rusticana, 1985. *Publications:* translations into English of Otello, II Trovatore and Tales of Hoffmann. *Current Management:* Warden Associated Inc., 127 W 72nd Street, Suite 2-R, New York, NY 10023, USA. *Website:* www.garrygrice.ipfox.com.

GRIER, Francis, FRCO; British organist, pianist and composer; b. 1955, England. *Education:* chorister at St George's Chapel, Windsor Castle, Eton Coll., organ scholar at King's Coll., Cambridge, studied with Joseph Cooper, Fanny Waterman, Bernard Roberts, Gillian Weir, studied in India. *Career:* Asst Organist to Simon Preston, at Christ Church Cathedral, Oxford, organist and Dir of Music 1981; organ recitals throughout the UK; first organ recital at the BBC Promenade Concerts 1985; worked with mentally handicapped in London and Bangalore, India; works as psychodynamic counsellor. *Compositions:* Advent Responsories (for King's Coll. Chapel) 1990, Mass with Motets (for Westminster Abbey), Sequences of Readings and Music for Ascension (for the 550th anniversary of Eton Coll.) 1990, The Cry of Mary (for BBC2) 1992, St Francis (opera, for Eton Coll. and Nat. Youth Music Theatre) 1993, Mass in Time of Persecution for soloists, chorus and orchestra (including poems of Ratushinskaya) 1994, My Heart Dances (settings of Tagore) for soloists, chorus and orchestra (commissioned by 3 Choirs Festival) 1995, Missa Brevis (British Composer Award for Liturgical Music 2012). *Recordings:* Bach, Mendelssohn, Couperin, Franck, Messiaen: Messe de la Pentecôte and L'Ascension (all on the Rieger organ at Christ Church Cathedral).

GRIEVES-SMITH, Jonathan Mark, BA; British conductor and artistic director; *Artistic Director and Principal Conductor, Melbourne Chorale*; b. 14 Dec. 1962, Kendal, England; m. Sally; two s. one d. *Education:* Kingswood School, Bath and Univ. of Sussex. *Career:* Artistic Dir and Prin. Conductor, Melbourne Chorale 1998–2003, 2004–; Artistic Admin., The Queensland Orchestra 2003; fmr Music Dir, Brighton Festival Chorus; Chorus Master, Huddersfield Choral Soc., Halle Choir, Reading Festival Chorus; guest conductor, Royal Philharmonic Orchestra, Royal Liverpool Philharmonic, London Mozart Players, Bournemouth Symphony Orchestra, New Zealand Symphony Orchestra, Melbourne Symphony Orchestra, Orchestre Nat. de Lille, Bochum Symphoniker, Europa Cantat in Denmark and Austria, Dartington Int. Summer School; Conductor Emer., Melbourne Chorale. *Recordings:* as chorus master for Bax/Handley, Beethoven/Menuhin, Walton/Previn, Tippett/Previn, Martin/Bamert, Lloyd/Lloyd, Patterson/Simon. *Address:* Melbourne Chorale, Horti Hall, 31 Victoria Street, Melbourne, Vic. 3000 (office); 14 Lambert Road, Toorak, Vic. 3142, Australia (home). *Telephone:* (3) 9639-8810 (office). *E-mail:* jgs@melbournechorale.com.au (office). *Website:* www.melbournechorale.com.au (office).

GRIFFEL, Kay; American singer (soprano); b. 26 Dec. 1940, Eldora, IA; m. Eckhard Sellheim. *Education:* Northwestern Univ., IL, studied in Berlin and at Santa Barbara with Lotte Lehmann. *Career:* debut, Chicago 1960, as Mercédès in Carmen; sang at the Deutsche Oper Berlin and in Bremen, Mainz, Karlsruhe, Hamburg and Düsseldorf; Salzburg 1973 in the premiere of De Temporum fine Comoedia by Orff; Glyndebourne Festival 1976–77, as Alice Ford in Falstaff; tour of Japan with the Staatsoper Berlin 1977, as the Marschallin, Donna Elvira and Mozart's Countess; Lisbon 1978, Eva in Die Meistersinger; Metropolitan Opera from 1982, as Electra in Idomeneo, Rosalinde, Arabella, Tatiana and the Countess; further appearances in Brussels, Moscow, Cologne and at the Orange Festival; sang Eva in Die Meistersinger at Wellington, New Zealand 1990. *Recordings:* Janáček Diary of One who Disappeared, De Temporum fine Comoedia, Italian Arias. *Honours:* Hon. DFA (Simpson Coll., Indianola, IA) 1982.

GRIFFEY, Anthony Dean, BMus, MMus; American singer (tenor); b. 1968, High Point, North Carolina; s. of Raymond Griffey and Joyce Wishon Griffey. *Education:* Metropolitan Young Artist Development Program, Juilliard School, Eastman School of Music, Wingate Univ. *Career:* debut, New York Met 1995, as First Knight in Parsifal; appearances at the Met in Manon, Don Carlos, Aida, Billy Budd, Salome, Boris Godunov and The Queen of Spades; further engagements as Peter Grimes and Sam Polk in Floyd's Susannah at the Met, Mitch in Previn's A Streetcar named Desire at San Francisco, and Mozart's Idomeneo for the Mainly Mozart Festival, New York; season 2000–01 with Peter Grimes at Glyndebourne, Ferrando in Così fan tutte and Laca in Jenůfa at the Saito Kinen Festival, Japan, and The Dream of Gerontius with the New York Philharmonic; other concerts include Britten's War Requiem, at Tanglewood. *Recordings include:* Amy Beach, Cabildo 1995, Verdi, I Lombardi 1997, A Streetcar Named Desire 1998, Poulenc, Les Mamelles de Tirésias 1999, Britten, War Requiem 2006. *Current Management:* c/o Elizabeth Sobol-Gomez, IMG Artists, Carnegie Hall Tower, 152 West 57th Street, 5th Floor, New York, NY 10019, USA. *Telephone:* (212) 994-3550. *Fax:* (212) 994-3550. *Website:* www.imgartists.com; www.anthonydeangriffey.com.

GRIFFIN, Judson, DMA, BM, MM; American violist and violinist; b. 7 Sept. 1951, Lewes, DE; m. Mara Paske 1988. *Education:* Juilliard School of Music, Eastman School of Music. *Career:* debut at Carnegie Recital Hall, New York 1981; violist, Rochester Philharmonic Orchestra 1970–73; freelance violist, New York 1973–77; Asst Prof., Univ. of North Carolina at Greensboro 1977–79; principal viola, Aspen Chamber Symphony 1977–80; freelance violinist and violist, New York 1979–; violist, Smithson String Quartet and Smithsonian Chamber Players (Smithsonian Institution, Washington, DC); Atlantis Ensemble (Europe); violinist of Four Nations and Sonata a Quattro (New York); regular appearances with many period-instrument organizations in USA. *Recordings:* chamber music, many radio recordings.

GRIFFITH, Lisa; American singer (soprano); b. 1959. *Education:* Indiana Univ. and the Cincinnati Conservatory. *Career:* debut at Seattle Opera 1984; sang at Wiesbaden Opera 1984–89, Hanover 1989–91, notably as Zerbinetta; Deutsche Oper am Rhein, Düsseldorf from 1991, as Susanna in The Marriage of Figaro and Sophie in Rosenkavalier 1993; other roles include Gilda and Pamina; guest at the Munich Staatsoper, the Komische Oper Berlin and Staatsoper Stuttgart; frequent concert appearances; sang in premiere production of Beuys by Franz Hummel, Vienna, Berlin and Düsseldorf 1998; sang Irina in Three Sisters by Peter Eötvös at Dusseldorf 1999, and Gounod's Juliette at Lubeck 2000.

GRIFFITH-SMITH, Bella; American singer and conductor; b. 1920. *Education:* studied with Howard Thain, Franco Iglesias, Dr Paul Csonka. *Career:* debut at the Civic Opera of the Palm Beaches; appeared with Louis Quilico, Metropolitan artist, Robert Merrill, Giuseppe Campora; television: Concert Version-Spanish Translation, Channel 2, Miami; Madama Butterfly; radio: La Traviata; leading roles in Madama Butterfly; La Bohème, Tosca, Cavalleria Rusticana, Pagliacci, Suor Angelica, Il Tabarro, Faust, Carmen (Micaela), Così fan tutte (Fiordiligi), Tales of Hoffmann (Antonia), Don Pasquale-Norina,

L'Oca del Cairo (Celidora), La Traviata, Oratorio-Elijah, L'Enfant Prodigue, Messiah, Vivaldi's Gloria, Stabat Mater, Rossini; concerts: Salome, Otello, Turandot, with Alain Lombard/Greater Miami Philharmonic; guest soloist; Pres., Coral Gables Civic Opera and Orchestra, Inc. *Address:* Coral Gables Opera, 700 Santander Avenue, Coral Gables, FL 33134, USA (office). *Telephone:* (305) 443-7370 (office). *Website:* www.coralgablesopera.com (office).

GRIFFITHS, Graham Charles Thomas, BMus, PGCE; British conductor, pianist and lecturer; b. 13 May 1954, Tiverton, England; m. Miriam Regina Zillo 1985, two s. *Education:* Bryanston School, Univ. of Edinburgh, Univ. of Cambridge. *Career:* Founder-mem., Edinburgh Experimental Arts Soc. 1972–76, Grand Toxic Opera Co., Edinburgh 1974–76; mem., Cambridge Contemporary Music Ensemble 1976–78; Marketing/Education Officer, Scottish Nat. Orchestra 1978–81; co-administrator, Int. Musica Nova Festival, Glasgow 1978–81; arts journalist, Scottish Television 1981–86; Principal Conductor, Glasgow Chamber Orchestra 1985–86; Lecturer in 20th-Century Music, São Paulo State Univ., Brazil 1987–89; founder-Dir, Jardim Musical Arts Centre 1987–; founder-Conductor, Ensemble Grupo Novo Horizonte 1988–; Dir of Education, Mozarteum Brasileiro 1987–; Conductor, Choir of Cultura Inglesa, São Paulo 1988–90; Choral Dir, Nat. Festival of Brazilian Colonial Music (Juiz de Fora) 1990; Guest Conductor, Campos do Jordao Festival 1990, Orquestra Sinfonica e Madrigal da Universidade Federal da Bahia, Salvador 1990–; Dir of Conducting Course, Festival Seminarios Internacionais Salvador 1991; lecture and recital piano tours include Bridges Across Time (Brazil, Denmark, UK) 1990, New World Experience (Brazil, Denmark) 1991; co-founder and Dir, Mostra de Musica Contemporanea, Ouro Preto 1991; regular broadcasts on Radio e Televisao Cultura, São Paulo 1988–; Visiting Lecturer, Federal Univs of Rio de Janeiro 1990, Bahia 1990–91, Uberlandia 1992; Guest Conductor, Camerata Antigua de Curitiba 1993. *Compositions:* sacred choral works include: Anglican Hymn Collection 1988–, The Lord's Prayer 1990, Ta Voix 1991, Cançao de Quatá for trombone quartet 1993. *Address:* Rua Angatuba 97, Pacaembu, 01247-000 São Paulo, SP, Brazil.

GRIFFITHS, Hilary; British conductor; b. 18 March 1949, Leamington Spa, Warwicks.; s. of Rev. Leonard Griffiths and Eileen Griffiths; m. Andrea Andonian 1978, two s. *Education:* King's Coll. Choir School, Cambridge, Uppingham School, Trinity Coll., Oxford, Univ., Royal Acad. of Music, London Opera Centre, Conservatorio G. Verdi, Milan, Accad. Chigiana, Siena. *Career:* fmr Prin. Staff Conductor, Cologne Opera, with appearances also in Dresden, Düsseldorf, Nuremberg and Basle; fmr Music Dir, Oberhausen Opera, with further engagements in Oslo, Antwerp, Leeds (Opera North), Reykjavik, Bogotá, Barcelona, Eindhoven and at Edinburgh, Prague and Schwetzingen Festivals; Conductor, State Opera Prague 1992– (13 productions by Zemlinsky, Strauss, Leoncavallo, d'Albert, Schoenberg, Verdi, Mozart, Britten, Mascagni, Wagner); Music Dir, Regensburg 1993–97, Eutin Opera Festival 1991–2006; festival appearances include five productions for Tenerife Opera Festival, six productions for Nat. Opera of Colombia, Don Giovanni at the Perth Festival, Australia, Un Ballo in Maschera at Hong Kong Int. Arts Festival, Der Prinz von Homburg at Wiesbaden May Festival; concerts with Deutsche Oper, Rotterdam Philharmonic, BBC Nat. Orchestra of Wales, West German Radio Orchestra, Virtuosi di Praga, Czech Nat. Symphony Orchestra, Colombia Nat. Symphony; Prof., Mannheim Univ. for Music and Fine Arts 2004–07; Guest Conductor, Nationaltheater Mannheim 2006–07; Chief Conductor and Music Dir, Wuppertal Opera 2009–12; US debut with La porta della legge (Sciarrino), Lincoln Center Festival, New York 2010; new production of Tannhäuser, State Opera, Prague 2014. *Television:* Il matrimonio segreto (Cimarosa) from the Schwetzingen Festival 1986, Der Freischütz (Weber) from the Eutin Festival 2005. *Recordings include:* albums: Jommelli, Mass in D and Te Deum, Leoncavallo, La Bohème, Tiefland, I vespri siciliani, Complete Piano Duets by Weber, Bluthochzeit (Fortner) (DVD) 2013. *Current Management:* c/o Neil Dalrymple, Music International, 13 Ardilaun Road, London, N5 2QR, England. *Telephone:* (20) 7359-5183. *Fax:* (20) 7226-9792. *E-mail:* music@musicint.co.uk. *Website:* www.musicint.co.uk. *Address:* Graf-Adolf-Str. 28, 51065 Cologne, Germany (home). *E-mail:* griffiths@hilarygriffiths.com (office). *Website:* www.hilarygriffiths.com.

GRIFFITHS, Howard Laurence, MBE, ARCM; British conductor; b. 24 Feb. 1950, Hastings, England; m. Semra Griffiths 1971; one s. one d. *Education:* Royal Coll. of Music, London with Cecil Aronowitz, studied conducting with Leon Barzin, Paris, Erich Schmid, Zürich. *Career:* debut at QEH, English Chamber Orchestra 1989; Royal Festival Hall, Royal Philharmonic Orchestra 1991; Principal Viola, Ankara State Opera until 1979; mem., Lucerne String Quartet; Principal Guest Conductor, Oxford Orchestra da Camera 1994; Dir and Principal Conductor, Zürich Chamber Orchestra 1996–; has conducted many prominent orchestras, including Royal Philharmonic Orchestra, English Chamber Orchestra, Warsaw Philharmonic Orchestra, Basel Radio Symphony Orchestra, Istanbul State Symphony Orchestra, Northern Sinfonia of England, Stadtorchester Winterthur, Polish Chamber Orchestra, Tonhalle Orchestra Zürich, Nat. Orchestra of Spain, London Mozart Players, Slovak Radio-Symphony Orchestra, Tchaikovsky SO of the Moscow Radio, Orchestre Nationale de Paris, Orchestre Philharmonique de Montpellier, Tapiola Sinfonietta; repertory includes music by Henze (Requiem), Crumb, Kagel and Pärt; Artistic Dir, Allensbach Chamber Music Festival, Germany 1992–98; Artistic Director, Orpheum Foundation for the Promotion of Young Soloists 2000–. *Recordings include:* 18th Century Swiss Composers Stalder and Reindl, English Chamber Orchestra; Instrumental Works of Othmar

Schoeck, English Chamber Orchestra; Mozart Horn Concertos, Kalinski and Polish Chamber Orchestra; works of Max Bruch, Royal Philharmonic Orchestra; three albums of music by Turkish composers Saygun, Erkin, Rey, with Northern Sinfonia of England; Baroque Oboe Concertos and Mozart Sinfonia Concertante; Caspar Fritz Violin Concerto, English Chamber Orchestra; Ferdinand Ries Complete Symphonies 1–8 with Zürich Chamber Orchestra. *Current Management:* Konzertgesellschaft, Hochstrasse 51, Postfach, 4002 Basel, Switzerland.

GRIFFITHS, Paul Anthony, OBE, BA, MSc; British music critic and writer; b. 24 Nov. 1947, Bridgend, Glam., Wales; s. of Fred and Jeanne Griffiths; m. Anne West Griffiths; two s. *Education:* Lincoln Coll., Oxford. *Career:* music critic for various journals 1971–; Area Ed. 20th Century Music, New Grove Dictionary of Music and Musicians 1973–76; music critic, The Times 1982–92, New Yorker 1992–96, New York Times 1997–; compiled Mozart pasticcio The Jewel Box for Opera North 1991, Purcell pasticcio Aeneas in Hell 1995; guest lecturer City Univ. of New York Graduate Center 2013. *Publications:* A Concise History of Modern Music 1978, Boulez 1978, A Guide to Electronic Music 1979, Cage 1981, Peter Maxwell Davies 1982, The String Quartet 1983, György Ligeti 1983, Bartók 1984, Olivier Messiaen 1985, New Sounds, New Personalities: British Composers of the 1980s 1985, An Encyclopedia of 20th Century Music 1986, Myself and Marco Polo 1987, The Life of Sir Tristram (novel) 1991, The Jewel Box (opera libretto) 1991, Stravinsky 1992, Modern Music and After 1995, opera libretti for Tan Dun's Marco Polo 1996 and Elliott Carter's What Next? 1999, Leda 2000, A Concise History of Western Music 2006, Horizons Touched: The Music of ECM (Ed., with Steve Lake) 2007, Let Me Tell You 2008, La musica del novecento, Einaudi, 2014, Gulliver (libretto) 2014. *E-mail:* paul@disgwylfa.com. *Website:* www.disgwylfa.com.

GRIFFITHS, Paul Wayne; British conductor; b. 1958, England. *Education:* Royal Northern College of Music and London Opera Centre. *Career:* conducted The Judgement of Paris by John Woolrich in Royal Opera House Garden Venture Series, Orchestra of Royal Opera at Windsor Festival and Symphony Hall, Birmingham; Paris debut at Théâtre du Champs Elysées, with Orchestre du Conservatoire National; further concerts with Royal Philharmonic, English Chamber Orchestra and Tokyo Philharmonic; season 1992–93 with Il Trovatore for Scottish Opera, L'Elisir d'amore at Gothenburg, concert in Athens with Grace Bumbry and London with Josephine Bartsow and Montserrat Caballé; Covent Garden debut with Rigoletto 1994, returning for La Bohème and Turandot; Artistic Dir and Accompanist of Luciano Pavarotti masterclass; recital accompanist with Geraint Evans, José Carreras, Katia Ricciarelli, James King, Thomas Allen and Yevgeny Nesterenko; staff conductor, Royal Opera House, Covent Garden.

GRIGOREV, Alexei; Russian singer (tenor); b. 1968. *Education:* Sweelinck Conservatory, Netherlands Int. Opera Studio. *Career:* appearances throughout Europe in Billy Budd, Antwerp, The Nose, Leipzig, Mozart's Mitridate at Lyon, Meistersinger, Parsifal and Figaro, Netherlands; Season 1998–99 in Moses und Aron, Die Zauberflote and La finta giardiniera, Darmstadt, Marzio, Mozart's Mitridate, Lyon 1998; Season 1999–2000 at Châtelet, Paris, Amsterdam and Antwerp; sang Innkeeper, Benvenuto Cellini, Festival Hall Concert 1999; Season 2000–01: Le grand macabre, Antwerp, Boris Godounov, Capriccio, DNO, Amsterdam, Don Pasquale, Luxembourg, Three Sisters by Eötvös, Bastien und Bastienne, Concertgebouw, Amsterdam; Season 2001–02: Le Coq d'or in Nantes, Three Sisters by Eötvös in Brussels, Lyon and Vienna, Pulcinella in Brussels and Amsterdam, Lucia di Lammermoor in Basel, Dido and Aeneas, Netherlands, Lustigen Weiber; concert repertory includes Bach's St John and St Matthew Passions, Berlioz Messe solennelle and Mahler's Klagende Lied; Season 2001–02: Orff's Carmina Burana, Rossini's Stabat Mater, Debussy's L'invocation, Shostakovich's From Jewish Folk Poetry; Season 2005–06: Puccini's La Rondine, Musiekcentrum Vredenburg, Utrecht 2005. *Address:* Sleewijkstraat 78, 1107 TW Amsterdam, Netherlands (home). *E-mail:* a.grigorev@freeler.nl (home).

GRIGORIAN, Gegam; Armenian singer (tenor); b. 29 Jan. 1951, Yerevan. *Education:* Opera School of La Scala, Milan. *Career:* debut at Lvóv Opera, 1989, as Cavaradossi; Kirov Opera, St Petersburg, from 1990, notably as Vladimir in Prince Igor and Dimitri in Boris Godunov; Amsterdam from 1991, as Gennaro in Lucrezia Borgia, Andrea Chénier and Cilea's Maurizio; Pierre in War and Peace at the Opéra Bastille, Paris; Covent Garden debut, 1993, as Lensky; Season 1994–95, as Radames at Rome, Pollione in Norma at Genoa and Rimsky's Sadko in Paris; Sang Verdi's Riccardo at Santiago, Cavaradossi at Wiesbaden and Turiddu at Florence; Metropolitan Opera debut as Hermann in The Queen of Spades, 1995; Season 1998 as Riccardo at Monte Carlo, Vasily Golitsin in Khovanshchina at La Scala (Kirov Opera) and Alvaro in La Forza del Destino at St Petersburg (also televised); Sang Canio at Buenos Aires, 2000, Golitsin on tour with the Kirov to Covent Garden, and Pierre in War and Peace at La Scala.

GRIGSBY, Beverly; American composer; b. 11 Jan. 1928, Chicago, IL. *Education:* studied in California with Ernst Krenek and Ingolf Dahl, Stanford Univ., Royal Coll. of Music, London. *Career:* teacher, California State Univ., Northridge 1963–92. *Compositions include:* stage works: Augustine the Saint 1975, Moses 1978, The Vision of St Joan 1987; other: Trio for violin, clarinet and piano 1984, Wind Quintet 1990, Keyboard Concerto 1993, Concerto for orchestra 1994; also computer music. *E-mail:* beverly.grigsby@csun.edu. *Website:* www.beverlygrigsby.org.

GRIMAUD, Hélène; American (b. French) pianist; b. Aix-en-Provence, France. *Education:* studied in Marseille with Pierre Barbizet, Conservatoire Nat. Supérieur de Musique, Paris, studied with Jacques Rouvier, Gyorgy Sandor and Leon Fleischer. *Career:* Paris debut recital 1987; performances at MIDEM, Cannes, and at La Roque d'Anthéron Piano Festival 1987; has performed with orchestras worldwide, including Boston Symphony, Cleveland Orchestra, Los Angeles Philharmonic, New York Philharmonic, Philadelphia Orchestra, Montréal Symphony, London Symphony Orchestra, City of Birmingham Symphony Orchestra, London Philharmonic Orchestra, English Chamber Orchestra, Berlin Philharmonic, Bavarian Radio Symphony, Deutsches Symphonie-Orchester, Gewandhausorchester Leipzig, Tonhalle Zurich, Göteborg Symphony, Oslo Philharmonic, Tokyo NHK Symphony, St Petersburg Philharmonic, Concertgebouw Orchestra, Rotterdam Philharmonic, Orchestre Philharmonique de Radio France, Orchestre de Paris; performances include the première of a work for piano and orchestra by Arvo Pärt at the Tate Modern gallery, London, concerts in Amsterdam, London, Paris and Japan with the Czech Philharmonic and Ashkenazy, performances with the Philharmonia Orchestra under Christoph von Dohnányi, the Danish National Radio Symphony under Thomas Dausgaard, Detroit Symphony under Neeme Järvi and Netherlands Radio Philharmonic under Peter Eötvös; season 2003–04 appearances included performances with Orchester der Bayerische Staatsoper, San Francisco Symphony, Deutsches Symphonie Orchester Berlin, Tokyo Philharmonic, and tours with the Australian Youth Orchestra, the Chamber Orchestra of Europe and the Philharmonia Orchestra. *Recordings include:* Rachmaninoff's Sonata No. 2 (Grand Prix du Disque 1986) 1985, Ravel Concerto in G and Rachmaninov Concerto No.2 with the Royal Philharmonic and Jesus Lopez-Cobos, Schumann Concerto and Strauss Burleske with David Zinman and the Deutsches Symphonie-Orchester Berlin, Brahms opus 116–119 1996, Gershwin Concerto in F and the Ravel Concerto in G with David Zinman and the Baltimore Symphony, Brahms Piano Concerto No.1 with Berlin Staatskapelle Orchester and Kurt Sanderling (Cannes Classical Recording of the Year 1999) 1997, Beethoven sonatas opus 109/110 and concerto No.4 with the New York Philharmonic under Kurt Masur 1999, Rachmaninov Etudes-Tableaux and concerto No.2 with the Philharmonia Orchestra and Vladimir Ashkenazy 2001, Credo 2002, Bartók Piano Concertos (with Zimerman and Andsnes) (Midem Classical Music Award for Concertos 2006), Bach 2009, Duo (with Sol Gabetta) (Diapason d'Or for Best Chamber Music Recording) 2012. *Honours:* Officier, Ordre des Arts et des Lettres 2002. *Current Management:* c/o Kathryn Enticott, IMG Artists, The Light Box, 111 Power Road, London, W4 5PY, England. *Telephone:* (20) 7957-5800. *Fax:* (20) 7957-5801. *E-mail:* kenticott@imgartists.com. *Website:* www.imgartists.com; www.helenegrimaud.com.

GRIME, Helen, BMus (Hons), MMus; British composer; *Associate Composer, The Hallé*; b. 1981. *Education:* studied oboe with John Anderson and composition with Julian Anderson and Edwin Roxburgh at Royal Coll. of Music, London, Tanglewood Music Center, USA (studies with John Harbison, Michael Gandolfi, Shulamit Ran and Augusta Read Thomas). *Career:* wrote short opera Doorstepping Susanna for ENO Studio and Tête à Tête Opera; Oboe Concerto premiered by Meadows Chamber Orchestra, conducted by Peter Evans, with composer as soloist 2003; has worked with orchestras including London Symphony Orchestra, Philharmonia, BBC Symphony Orchestra, BBC Scottish Symphony Orchestra, Britten Sinfonia, Birmingham Contemporary Music Group, Composers' Ensemble, Hebrides Ensemble, Kungsbacka Trio; Chasing Butterflies for 100 violas commissioned by BBC Radio 3 2003; attended Britten-Pears Contemporary Performance and Composition course 2005, 2006, Aldeburgh Opera Writing workshops; Legal & General Jr Fellow, Royal Coll. of Music 2005–07; Assoc. Composer, Hallé 2011–; a work for solo clarinet and ensemble performed at Festival of Contemporary Music 2009. *Compositions include:* Virga (orchestral piece) commissioned by LSO in partnership with UBS 2007, Into the Faded Air (for the Britten Sinfonia) 2008, A Cold Spring for Ten Instruments (commissioned by Aldeburgh Festival for the BCMG under Oliver Knussen) 2009, Seven Pierrot Miniatures (commissioned by the Hebrides Ensemble) 2009, Clarinet Concerto 2010, To See the Summer Sky for violin and viola 2010. *Recordings include:* Romance, for violin and piano, performed by Alexandra Wood and Huw Watkins, Nobody Comes, for voice and piano, performed by Jean Rigby and Huw Watkins. *Honours:* British Composer Awards (Making Music category with Oboe Concerto) 2003, Intercollegiate Theodore Holland Composition Prize as well as all major composition prizes at Royal Coll. of Music 2003, Leonard Bernstein Fellowship to study at Tanglewood Music Center 2008, Lili Boulanger Memorial Fund 2010. *Address:* Hallé Concerts Society, The Bridgewater Hall, Manchester, M1 5HA, England (office). *Telephone:* (16) 1907-9000 (office). *E-mail:* info@halle.co.uk (office). *Website:* www.halle.co.uk (office).

GRIMM, Hans-Gunther; German singer (baritone) and academic; b. 1925. *Education:* studied in East Berlin. *Career:* sang at Berlin Staatsoper 1950–52, Bremen 1952–54, Mannheim 1954–60, Cologne 1960–64, Theater am Gartnerplatz, Munich 1964–66, Dortmund 1966–70; sang in Cologne 1961, in German premiere of Nono's Intolleranza 60; guest appearances as concert and opera singer in Japan, N America, France and Spain; roles included Mozart's Count, Don Giovanni, Guglielmo and Papageno, Malatesta, Marcello, Wolfram, Escamillo, Don Fernando in Fidelio and Carlos in Forza del Destino; Prof., Maastrich Conservatory, The Netherlands 1973–82. *Recordings include:* Undine by Lortzing; Eine Nacht in Venedig; Rossini's Petite Messe solennelle; Beethoven's Ninth.

GRIMSLEY, Greer; American singer (bass-baritone); b. 1962, New Orleans, LA; m. Luretta Bybee; one d. *Education:* Loyola Univ. and The Juilliard School. *Career:* sang Jochanaan in Salome with Scottish Opera 1988; Saratoga Opera 1988, as Alfonso in Così fan tutte and Wexford Festival in Der Templer und die Jüdin by Marschner; tour of Australia, Canada and Europe in Peter Brook's La Tragédie de Carmen; Bregenz Festival 1991, as Escamillo; Santa Fe in US premiere of Henze's English Cat and appearances with Lake George Festival as Pizarro and Don Giovanni; Italian debut, Bologna as Escamillo 1995; Metropolitan Opera as Balstrode (Peter Grimes) and Jochanaan 1995–96; Escamillo at Vancouver 1996; engaged as Donner and Gunther in The Ring, Seattle 2001; Seasons 2003–04 and 2004–05: Metropolitan Opera as Kurwenal in Tristan und Isolde, Jack Rance in La Fanciulla del West and Telramund in Lohengrin with Seattle Opera, title role in Der Fliegende Holländer with Pittsburgh Opera, title role in Duke Bluebeard's Castle with Montreal Opera, Scarpia in Tosca with Austin Lyric Opera and Michigan Opera Theatre, Jokaanan in Salome with Orlando Opera, Amphortas in Parsifal in Barcelona, and debut as Wotan in Stephen Wadsworth's Ring Cycle with Seattle Opera 2005; Season 2005–06: Metropolitan Opera as Scarpia in Tosca, Telramund in Lohengrin and Amfortas in Parsifal, Wotan in Die Walkure in Venice, Jokanaan in Salome with Michigan Opera Theater and Santa Fe Opera, as well as Scarpia in Tosca with Portland Opera and Pittsburgh Opera; Verdi's Requiem with Atlanta Symphony at Carnegie Hall and Scarpia in Tosca with Deborah Voight and Minnesota Orchestra; Gala Concert, New Orleans Opera 2006. *Honours:* Artist of the Year Seattle Opera 2006. *Current Management:* c/o Pinnacle Arts Management, 889 Ninth Avenue, 2nd Floor, New York, NY 10019, USA. *Telephone:* (212) 397-7915. *Fax:* (212) 397-7920. *Website:* www.pinnaclearts.com.

GRIN, Leonid; American (b. Ukrainian) conductor; *Artistic Director and Chief Conductor, Orquesta Sinfónica de Chile*; b. Ukraine; two c. *Education:* Dnipropetrovsk Coll. of Music, Moscow Conservatory, Russia, studied composition and conducting under Leo Ginsburg and Kiril Kondrashin. *Career:* gave his first piano recital aged seven; Assoc. Conductor, Moscow Philharmonic 1977, led concerts throughout fmr Soviet Union and on tours of Spain, Mexico and Canada; guest conductor with Soviet ensembles, including Leningrad (now St Petersburg) Philharmonic, Moscow State Radio Orchestra, Estonian State Symphony, Georgian State Symphony, Moscow Chamber Orchestra; immigrated to USA 1981; chosen by Leonard Bernstein for first Los Angeles Philharmonic Inst.; fmrly Gen. Music Dir Saarlandisches Staatstheater, Saarbrucken, Germany; Music Dir San Jose Symphony 1992–2001; Prin. Guest Conductor, Tampere Philharmonic Orchestra, Finland 1988–90, Music Dir 1990–94; Prin. Guest Conductor, City of Dortmund Opera and Orchestra 1999–2000; has conducted numerous orchestras, including Göteborg Symphony, Berlin Radio Orchestra, Frankfurt Radio Orchestra, Helsinki Philharmonic, Kuoppio Symphony, Belgrade Philharmonic, Nürnberg Philharmonic, Tenerife Symphony Orchestra, Kiel Philharmonic, Gran Canaria Philharmonic, Gulbenkian Orchestra in Lisbon; also concerts with Orquesta Philharmonica de Buenos Aires at Teatro Colon, Philharmonia Hungarica, Hong Kong Philharmonic, Nat. Symphony of China; debut with Los Angeles Philharmonic 1999; other US engagements have included with Nat. Symphony, Houston, San Diego, Cincinnati Symphony and Vancouver Symphonies; gives master-classes at Neeme Järvi Summer Acad. 2009–; Chief Conductor, Orquesta Sinfónica de Chile 2013–, Artistic Dir 2014–. *Recordings:* recordings with Berlin Radio Orchestra and Tampere Philharmonic Orchestra include music of Prokofiev, Tchaikovsky, Shostakovich and Mellartin; recordings of complete symphonies of Finnish composer Erkki Mellartin with Tampere Philharmonic Orchestra. *Honours:* Exxon Endowment Conductors Fellowship, ASCAP Award for commitment to contemporary American music 1999. *Current Management:* Mark Stephan Buhl Artists Management, Geylinggasse 1, 1130 Vienna, Austria. *E-mail:* mark@msbuhl .com. *Address:* Orquesta Sinfónica de Chile, Centro de Extensión Artística y Cultural de la Universidad de Chile, Av. Providencia 043, Providencia, Chile (office). *Website:* leonidgrin.com.

GRINDENKO, Tatyana Tikhonovna; Russian violinist; *Artistic Director, OPUS-POST Ensemble*; b. 29 March 1946, Kharkov, Ukraine; m. 1st Gidon Kremer; m. 2nd Vladimir Martynov. *Education:* Moscow State Conservatory. *Career:* repertoire includes baroque, avant-garde, jazz, rock, experimental music; Co-founder (with A. Lyubimov) and Artistic Dir Moscow Acad. of Ancient Music; est. OPUS-POST Ensemble 1999, now Artistic Dir. *Honours:* First Prize and Golden Medal at World Int. Youth Competition in Bulgaria 1968, Winner at IV Int. Tchaikovsky Competition 1970, winner Wieniawski Competition in Poland 1972, People's Artist of Russia 2002, State Prize of the Russian Fed. 2003. *Address:* Mariinsky Theatre, St Petersburg, 190000, Theatre Square, 1, Russia (office). *Website:* www.mariinsky.ru (office).

GRINGOLTS, Ilya; Russian violinist; b. 2 July 1982, St Petersburg; m. Anahit Kurtikyan; one d. *Education:* St Petersburg Special Music School with Tatiana Liberova and Jeanna Metallidi, Juilliard School, New York with Itzhak Perlman and Dorothy Delay. *Career:* appearances with St Petersburg Philharmonic Orchestra, Moscow Symphony and BBC Scottish Symphony Orchestras; further engagements 1999–2000 with Nat. Symphony Orchestra, Wash., Melbourne Symphony Orchestra, Minnesota Orchestra, Royal Liverpool Philharmonic Orchestra and Tapiola Sinfonietta, Finland; recitals for the BBC's Verbier Festival, The Louvre, Palais des Beaux Arts and Oleg Kagan Festival; concerto tour of Italy with Moscow Soloists and Yuri Bashmet 2000; Shostakovich's Concerto No. 1 at BBC Proms, London 2002; engagements include performances with Chicago Symphony Orchestra under Daniel Barenboim, UBS Verbier Orchestra/Kurt Masur and Mstislav Rostropovich, Israel Philharmonic with Zubin Mehta, St Petersburg Philharmonic Orchestra and Yuri Temirkanov, Deutsche Symphonie Orchester Berlin, at the Proms with BBC Philharmonic and Vassily Sinaisky, Rotterdam Philharmonic with Vladimir Jorowski, London Philharmonic, Atlanta Symphony, City of Birmingham Symphony, BBC Symphony, Warsaw Philharmonic, Swedish Chamber Orchestra, Minnesota Orchestra and New Zealand Symphony Orchestra; currently Int. Violin Fellow, Royal Scottish Acad. of Music and Drama. *Recordings include:* Paganini Concerto No. 1, works by Ysaÿe, Ernst and Schnittke, Tchaikovsky and Shostakovich No. 1 Concertos and Solo Bach, Ernst Solo Works, Tanyev and Arensy Violin Concertos, Schumann: Violin Sonatas 1-3, Schumann: Piano Trios Nos. 1-3, Schumann: Chamber Works, Paganini: 24 Caprices for Solo Violin, Op. 1. *Honours:* winner International Violin Competition 1998, Premio Paganini. *Current Management:* c/o Xenia Groh-Hu, Karsten Witt Musikmanagement, Leuschnerdamm 13, 10999 Berlin, Germany. *Telephone:* (30) 214594227. *Fax:* (30) 214594101. *E-mail:* xh@karstenwitt.com. *Website:* de.karstenwitt.com; www.ilyagringolts .com.

GRIST, Reri, BA (Music); American singer (coloratura soprano) and professor of voice; b. 29 Feb. 1932, New York, NY; d. of Arthur Grist and Ena Grist; m. Dr Ulf Thomson 1966; one d. *Education:* High School of Music and Art, Queens Coll., New York, pvt. voice teacher Claire Gelda. *Career:* early childhood roles included musicals on Broadway, Cindy Lou in Oscar Hammerstein II's Carmen, Consuelo in original cast of West Side Story 1957, introduced the song Somewhere; soloist in Mahler's Fourth Symphony with Leonard Bernstein and New York Philharmonic 1959; opera debut as Blondchen in Mozart's Die Entführung aus dem Serail and as Adele in Die Fledermaus, Santa Fe Opera 1959; appeared as Cindy Lou (Micaela) in adaptation of Carmen at New York City Opera 1959, Metropolitan Opera, New York 1966–77, Vienna State Opera, Austria 1963–88, Munich State Opera, Germany 1965–83, San Francisco Opera Asscn 1963–76, 1983, 1990, Royal Opera House, Covent Garden, London 1962–1974, La Scala, Milan 1963, 1977–78, Opernhaus Zürich, Switzerland 1960–66, Netherlands Opera, Amsterdam 1990–91, Chicago Lyric Opera 1964, Teatro Colón, Buenos Aires 1970, Deutsche Oper, Berlin, Washington Opera Soc.; European debut as Queen of the Night in Mozart's Die Zauberflöte in Cologne, Germany 1960; festival appearances include debut as Zerbinetta in Ariadne auf Naxos by Richard Strauss, Salzburg Festival, Austria 1964–77, Munich Festival 1967–83, Vienna Festival 1963–80, Holland Festival 1963, Glyndebourne Festival 1962, Spoleto Festival, Italy 1961; repertoire includes Mozart: Susanna, Queen of Night, Despina, Zerlina, Blondchen, Papagena, Madame Herz; R. Strauss: Zerbinetta, Sophie, Aminta, Italian Singer; Verdi: Gilda, Oscar, Nannetta; Donizetti: Adina, Norina, Marie; Rossini: Rosina, Fanny, Elvira; J. Strauss: Adele; Offenbach: Olympia; Delibes: Lakmé; Poulenc: Constance; D. Moore: Baby Doe; Britten: Titania; Morton Feldman: The Woman (Neither); Stravinsky: Le Rossignol; Massenet: Manon; Orff: Carmina Burana; concert appearances with Leonard Bernstein, Pierre Boulez, Michael Gielen, Leopold Stokowski, Igor Strawinsky, Wolfgang Sawallisch, Friedrich Cerha, New York Philharmonic, Wiener Philharmoniker, Boston Symphony, Munich Philharmonic, NDR Sinfonieorchestrer Hamburg, Die Reihe and others; concert repertoire includes Nono's Canti di Vita ed Amore, Webern Op. 13, 15, 16, Schoenberg's Herzgewächse, Mozart's Mass in C Minor, Requiem, Bach's Cantatas, Fauré's Requiem; song recitals in Austria, France, Germany and USA; Prof. of Voice, Indiana Univ., Bloomington 1981–83, Hochschule für Musik, Munich, Germany 1984–95, master classes at Int. Opernstudio Zurich Opera 2007, Metropolitan Opera Lindemann Young Artist Devt Program 2008, Escuela Superior de Música della Reina Sofia, Madrid 2008–10, Opernstudio Staatsoper Hamburg 2008, 2013, Steans Inst., Ravinia, Ill., Santa Fe Opera 2011, 2012, Hochschule für Musik und Theater, Hamburg 2012, among others; pvt. voice teacher and vocal coach; master classes in opera, oratorio and song repertoire. *Films:* DVDs: Salzburger Festspiele: Ariadne Auf Naxos, Le Nozze di Figaro, Die Entführung aus dem Serail, Così fan tutte; Covent Garden: Un Ballo in Maschera; Bayerische Staatsoper: Die Schweigsame Frau; Bayerische Rundfunk: Reri Grist – Singer/Director Axel Corti, The Pleasure Gardens/Dir Peter Windgassen, Don Pasquale; NET: Le Rossignol; Bayerische Rundfunk: Da Capo/August Everding; Pars Nova/ Marieke Schroeder: Oper ist Theater/Opera is Theatre, Aida's Brothers and Sisters. *Television:* Tatort 'Aïda' (Bayerische Rundfunk). *Recordings:* Marriage of Figaro, Don Giovanni, Die Entführung, Così fan tutte, The Impresario, Il re pastore, Ariadne auf Naxos, Ballo in maschera, Rigoletto, Scarlatti's Endimione e Cintia, Le Rossignol, West Side Story, Mahler's Fourth Symphony, Fauré Requiem. *Honours:* Bayerische Kammersängerin 1976; Queens Coll. Alumni Award 1970, American Opera Asscn Legacy Award 2001, Lifetime Achievement Award, Licia Albanese Foundation 2003. *Website:* www .rerigrist.com.

GRITTON, Peter William, MA, LRAM; British composer, arranger, accompanist, singer and teacher; *Director of Music, James Allen's Girls' School, London;* b. 7 Dec. 1963, Redhill, Surrey, England; m.; one s. one d. *Education:* chorister at Salisbury Cathedral, Reigate Grammar School, Clare Coll., Cambridge. *Career:* Prin. Horn, Nat. Youth Orchestra; countertenor lay clerk, Christ Church Cathedral, Oxford 1985–87; has sung with The Sixteen, Hanover Band, I Fagiolini, Gabrieli Consort, The Light Blues, Tenebrae, Flash Harry, Cambridge Singers; accompanist to Ian Partridge, Henry Herford, Nicholas Clapton, Christopher Purves; Dir of Music, St Paul's

Boys' School, London; Dir of Music, James Allen's Girls' School, London 2012–. *Compositions:* Run with Torches, Away in a Manger, Stille Nacht: Portraits of Peace, Love Songs, Mary Seacole, Jones: The Musical, Pitch Perfect, The GREAT BIG Little Symphony. *Publications:* Follow that Star (Christmas Songs), With a little help from my friends (Beatles), Encores for Choirs (two vols), G & S for Choirs, Folksongs from around the world (India, Far East, Caribbean and Australia and the South Pacific), Simply Classics (three vols); contrib. to The Faber Carol Book, Jazz Piano Time, Spooky Piano Time, Fingerprints, Here's a Howdy-do. *Address:* 70 Hydethorpe Road, Balham, London, SW12 0JB, England. *E-mail:* petergritton@gmail.com.

GRITTON, Susan; British singer (soprano); b. 31 Aug. 1965, Reigate. *Education:* Univs of London and Oxford. *Career:* debut in Mozart Requiem, Wigmore Hall 1994; many engagements in such repertory as Mozart's C Minor Mass, Brahms Requiem, Handel's Theodora and Schubert's Der Hirt auf dem Felsen, with orchestras including the London Symphony Orchestra under Colin Davis, London Philharmonic Orchestra under Haitink, Hallé under Nagano, City of London Sinfonia under Hickox, Gothenburg Symphony under Järvi and the Orchestra of the Age of Enlightenment under Steuart Bedford; opera roles include Mozart's Susanna and Zerlina at Glyndebourne, Marzelline for Rome Opera; Fulvia in Handel's Ezio at Théâtre des Champs-Elysées; Tiny in Britten's Paul Bunyan for ROH, Atalanta in Xerxes and Xenia in Boris Godonov at English Nat. Opera; Sister Constance in The Carmelites 1999; other ENO roles include Caroline in The Fairy Queen, Pamina, Monteverdi's Drusilla, Nannetta and Janáček's Vixen; season 2001–02 with Euridice and Marenka for the Royal Opera, Handel's Cleopatra and Romilda (Xerxes) at Munich; Bach's St Matthew Passion at the London Proms 2002. *Recordings include:* Messiah and Solomon, Haydn's Nelson's Mass, Miss Wordsworth in Albert Herring; Holst Songs, Handel, Vivaldi, Purcell, Handel's Theodora, Vivaldi's Ottone in Villa 1998, Weckmann: Sacred Concerti and Harpsichord Music 1999, Verdi, Falstaff 2002, Verdi, Aida 2002, Howells: Choral Works 2006, Mendelssohn: Paulus 2009, Sings Britten/Finzi/Delius 2010, Britten: War Requiem (BBC Music Magazine Choral Award 2014). *Honours:* winner, Kathleen Ferrier Memorial Prize 1994, Arts Foundation Fellowship 1994. *Website:* www.askonasholt.co.uk.

GRIVNOV, Vsevolod; Russian singer (tenor); b. 1968. *Education:* Russian Chorus Acad., Russian Music Acad. *Career:* soloist with the New Opera company of the Moscow Municipal Theatre 1990–; roles have included Bayan in Ruslan and Lyudmilla, Lensky (Eugene Onegin) and Leicester in Maria Stuarda; concerts with the Toscanini Orchestra, Italy, under Rudolf Barshai, with Beethoven's Missa solemnis and Bach's B minor Mass, 1991–92, Ghent 1992, as Don José in Peter Brook's Tragédie de Carmen; Fenton in Falstaff at Copenhagen 1997; engaged in Rachmaninov's Aleko at the 1999 London Proms. *Recordings include:* filmed version of Eugene Onegin 1993, Verdi Arias 2002, Tchaikovsky's Opricnik 2003, Raffaello 2004, Tchaikovsky Duets 2006. *Address:* c/o Delos Productions, Inc., PO Box 343, Sonoma, CA 95476, USA (office). *Telephone:* (707) 996-3844 (office). *Fax:* (707) 320-0600 (office). *E-mail:* feedback@delosmusic.com. *Website:* www.delosmusic.com.

GROBEN, Françoise; Luxembourg cellist; b. 4 Dec. 1965. *Education:* Köln Musikhochschule with Boris Perganenshikov, Amadeus (also William Pleeth, Daniel Shafran). *Career:* debut, Musikverein, Vienna, Festspielhaus, Salzburg; Major concert halls in Europe, Russia, Japan and Israel including Suntory Hall, Tokyo, St Petersburg Philharmonic Hall, Hamburg Musikhalle, Brussels Palais des Beaux Arts, Berlin Philharmonie; Soloist of St Petersburg Philharmonic Orchestra, Moscow Radio-TV Orchestra, Russian State Orchestra, NHK Orchestra, Tokyo; Jerusalem Philharmonic Orchestra, Conductor, Svetlanov, Kitajenko, Rostropovich; Bavarian Radio Sinfonia; Festivals: Berliner Festwochen, Schleswig-Holstein Festival, Radio France Montpellier, Kuhmo, St Petersburg Spring, Wallonie, MDR, Bratislava; mem. Zehetmair String Quartet 1998–, the Alloys Ensemble. *Recordings:* many radio and television recordings, Busoni and Poulenc cello music; Zemlinsky Chamber Music. *Honours:* 2nd Prize (Silver Medal) International Tchaikovsky Competition, Moscow, 1990; Several special prizes. *Current Management:* Konzertdirektion Andrea Hampl, Karl-Schrader-Str.6, 10781 Berlin, Germany. *Telephone:* (30) 4782699. *Fax:* (30) 4783792. *E-mail:* hampl@ konzertdirektion.de. *Website:* www.konzertdirektion.de.

GROOP, Monica, BA, MA; Finnish singer (mezzo-soprano); b. 4 April 1958, Helsinki. *Education:* Conservatory and Sibelius Acad., Helsinki, Helsinki Univ., masterclasses with Kim Borg, Hartmut Holl, Mitsuko Shirai and Erik Werba. *Career:* appeared with the Savonlinna Opera Festival from 1986 and Finnish Nat. Opera in Helsinki from 1987; sang Dorabella in a production of Così fan tutte conducted by Salvatore Accardo at Naples 1989; concert performance of Così fan tutte in Rome 1991; concert engagements with leading Finnish and other Scandinavian orchestras under Erich Bergel, Jukka-Pekka Saraste, Leif Segerstam and Walter Weller; tour of West Germany 1989 with the Drottningholm Baroque Orchestra in Bach's St John Passion (Bachwoche Ansbach Festival); season 1989–90 with the Bach B minor Mass and St John Passion in Stockholm, Berlin and Edmonton, Canada; Mozart's Betulia Liberata with the Bachakademie in Stuttgart under Helmuth Rilling 1991; Mahler/Schoenberg project with Philippe Herreweghe and the Ensemble Musique Oblique; season 1991/92 with Cherubino at Aix-en-Provence, Wellgunde and the Walküre Waltraute at Covent Garden (debut), the Missa Solemnis at Aix 1992; tour of Così fan tutte with Sigiswald Kuijken to Spain, France and Portugal and appearances with the Drottningholm Theatre at the Barbican; season 1993 with Cherubino at Toulouse, the

Composer at the Paris Opéra Comique and Bach's St John Passion in Spain, Lucerne and Stockholm; sang Mélisande for Netherlands Opera 1996, Cherubino for the Royal Opera 1998, Sesto in La Clemenza di Tito at Glyndebourne Festival 1999; sang in the premieres of works by Olli Kortekangas and Kalevi Aho at Savonlinna 2000; Dorabella at Tokyo 2001; Wigmore Hall recital 2002; Prof. and Chair. Vocal Dept, Sibelius Acad. 2009–13; mem. Royal Swedish Music Acad. 2001. *Honours:* Culture Prize in Music, Gloria Magazine 1995, Culture Prize, Foundation for Finnish Culture 1995, Sibelius Home Town Medal (with Sir Colin Davis) 1998, Culture Prize, Foundation for Culture in Sweden and Finland 1999, Cultural Prize, Foundation for Swedish Culture 2001, Pro Finlandia Medal 2006. *Current Management:* c/o Opéra et Concert, 37, rue de la Chaussée d'Antin, 75009 Paris, France. *Telephone:* 1-42-96-18-18. *Fax:* 1-42-96-18-00. *E-mail:* agence@opera-concert.com. *Website:* www.opera-concert.com; www.monicagroop.com.

GROSCHEL, Werner; German singer (bass); b. 18 Sept. 1940, Nuremberg. *Education:* Richard Strauss Conservatory, Munich with Marcel Cordes and Josef Metternich. *Career:* debut in Flensburg 1967, as Fiesco in Simon Boccanegra; mem., Zürich Opera from 1972, as Rocco, Mephistopheles, Falstaff (Nicolai) and Dikoy in Katya Kabanova; Mozart's Osmin, Don Giovanni and Sarastro; Verdi's King Philip, Silva (Ernani) and Zaccaria (Nabucco); Wagner's Daland, Landgrave, King Henry and Pogner; sang in the 1975 premiere of Klebe's Ein Wahrer Held and the premiere of Kelterborn's Ein Engel kommt nach Babylon 1977; guest appearances elsewhere in Switzerland and in Germany; sang Don Inigo in Ravel's L'Heure Espagnole at the Zürich Opera 1996; sang the Theatre Director in Lulu at Zürich 2000; many concert engagements, notably in music by Bach and Monteverdi. *Recordings include:* Plutone in Monteverdi's Orfeo, L'Incoronazione di Poppea and Il Ritorno d'Ulisse.

GROSGURIN, Daniel, MMus; Swiss concert cellist and professor of cello; *Professor of Cello, Schola Cantorum de Paris;* b. 13 July 1949, Geneva; s. of Dr Jean Grosgurin and Madeleine Grosgurin; m. Ferhan Güraydin 1990. *Education:* Collège Calvin and Conservatoire de Musique, Geneva, Indiana Univ. School of Music, Bloomington, Ind., USA. *Career:* debut at Wigmore Hall, London 1976; Lucerne Festival 1975; Festival Strings, Lucerne 1975–78; appearances with orchestras such as Orchestre de la Suisse Romande, Orchestre du Capitole, Stuttgart Philharmonic 1978–; chamber music with several well-known artists; Salzburg Festival 1990; London Festival Hall with LSCO 1991; Tibor Varga Festival 1991; Eastern Music Festival, USA 1992–98; Founder and Artistic Dir Les Solistes de Genève 1995–2005; Prof. of Cello, Musikhochschule, Heidelberg-Mannheim, Germany 1978–90; Prof. of Cello, Geneva Conservatory of Music (Haute Ecole de Musique de Genève) 1990–2014; Guest Prof., Menuhin, Acad., Vevey 2008–10, State Music Univ., Freiburg, Germany 2011–13; Prof. of Cello, Schola Cantorum de Paris 2014–; master classes in Europe, Asia and the Americas. *Recordings:* works by G. Cassadó: Pièces favorites (Dante), Violoncelle et Opéra (Gallo), Bach Beethoven and Krenek with Beethoven String Quartet (Dabringhaus & Grimm), Schubert fragments (Naxos). *Publications:* Cello: A User's Guide (internet publ.) 2013; transcriptions and cadenzas. *Honours:* Hon. Prof., Ministry of Culture, Baden-Württemberg 1980; laureate of int. competitions in Geneva 1975, Florence ('Cassadó') 1977. *Address:* 15 route de Florissant, 1206 Geneva, Switzerland (office). *Telephone:* (79) 4370930 (office). *E-mail:* danielgrosgurin@netcourrier.com (home).

GROSS, Ruth; German singer (soprano); b. 1959, Kleve. *Education:* studied in Essen and with Edda Moser in Cologne. *Career:* debut at Regensburg, as Leonore in Fidelio 1987; sang at Ulm 1988–89, notably in Golem by d'Albert and in operetta; Bayreuth Festival 1989–90, as Ortlinde in Die Walküre; sang Leonore at Basle 1989; has appeared at Staatsoper Stuttgart 1989–, as Iphigénie (in Aulide), Arabella and Elsa in production of Lohengrin conducted by Silvio Varviso; season 1995–96 at Kaiserslantern as Wagner's Elisabeth and in the premiere of Gesualdo by Franz Hummel.

GROSSNER, Sonja Elizabeth, MA, PhD; British violinist and composer; b. 14 Dec. 1942, Maidenhead; one d. *Education:* Berkshire Junior Music School, Reading, Carl Maria von Weber Hochschule für Musik, Dresden, Germany, DeMontford Univ., Leicester, Birmingham Conservatoire. *Career:* violinist, State Theatre Orchestra, Freiberg Sachsen 1968–73; music teacher and violinist, Dresden 1974–84; teaching appointments, Leicestershire 1985–87; self-employed music teacher, Loughborough 1986–88; peripatetic violin and viola teacher, Derbyshire LEA 1988–91; instrumental teacher, Bedfordshire LEA 1991–92; violin and viola teacher, Nottingham LEA 1992–95; Northamptonshire Music Service 1996–97; private music teacher; mem. Incorporated Soc. of Musicians, British Acad. of Composers and Songwriters, Central Composers' Alliance. *Compositions include:* Sad Prelude and Carefree, for orchestra 1992, Summer Suite, for string orchestra 1993, Musical Moments, for five clarinets, Fantasy Fragments, for trumpet solo and electroacoustics 1996, Parody, for two pianos and percussion 1996, To each other strangers, for woodwind quintet, Elegy 2, for full orchestra, Dark Adagio, String Quartet No. 3 1999, Appassionato, for cello and piano, Destiny, for full orchestra. *Publications include:* Sonata for viola and piano in one movement 1996, Four Kinds, for four clarinets 1997, I Am Nobody, four songs of poems by Emily Dickinson 1998. *Honours:* Birmingham Chamber Music Prize 1999, Almira String Quartet Prize 2002. . *Website:* www.duba3generations.webs.com.

GROSVENOR, Benjamin, BMus; British pianist; b. 8 July 1992, Essex. *Education:* Royal Acad. of Music, also studied with Christopher Elton, Leif Ove Andsnes and Stephen Hough. *Career:* mem. BBC New Generation Artists Scheme 2010–12; has performed worldwide with orchestras including London Philharmonic, RAI Torino, New York Philharmonic, Philharmonia, Tokyo Symphony in venues such as Royal Festival Hall, Barbican Centre, Singapore's Victoria Hall, The Frick Collection and Carnegie Hall; has worked with conductors including Vladimir Ashkenazy, Jiří Bělohlávek, Semyon Bychkov and Vladimir Jurowski; BBC Proms with BBC Symphony Orchestra (youngest ever First Night soloist) 2011, with Royal Philharmonic Orchestra and Charles Dutoit 2012; recital appearances at Sydney Opera House, Concertgebouw, Berlin Konzerthaus, Festival de la Roque d'Anthéron, Salle Gaveau, Piano aux Jacobins, Nat. Concert Hall Dublin, Southbank Centre, London and tour of USA; also chamber music collaborations with Elias String Quartet, Escher String Quartet and Endellion String Quartet. *Recordings include:* This & That 2009, Chopin, Liszt & Ravel (Gramophone Award for Best Instrumental Recording 2012, Diapason d'Or Award for Most Talented Young Artist 2012, Classic Brits Critics Choice Award 2012) 2011, Rhapsody in Blue 2012. *Honours:* Winner, Keyboard Class, BBC Young Musician of the Year 2004, Gramophone Young Artist of the Year Award 2012, UK Critics Circle Award for Exceptional Young Talent 2012. *Current Management:* Hazard Chase Ltd, 25 City Road, Cambridge, CB1 1DP, England. *Telephone:* (1223) 312400. *Fax:* (1223) 460827. *E-mail:* james .brown@hazardchase.co.uk. *Website:* www.hazardchase.co.uk; www .benjamingrosvenor.co.uk.

GROT, Alexandra; Russian flautist; b. 31 Aug. 1981, Moscow. *Education:* Gnessin Music School, Moscow, Conservatoire Nat. Supérieur de Musique, Paris, Musikhochschule Munich. *Career:* tours in Eastern Europe and France; recitals in Auditorium du Louvre, Musée d'Orsay and Théâtre de la Ville de Paris; festivals include Colmar, Sion, Juventus, Grenoble, Sorø and Copenhagen; chamber music partners include Marie-Pierre Langlamet, Alexandre Tharaud, Alexei Ogrintchouk, Quatuor Parisii; played as soloist with Cappella Symphony Orchestra in St Petersburg, Nat. Philharmonic Orchestra of Ukraine in Kiev, Bad Reichenhaller Philharmonic Orchestra and Georgische Kammerorchester in Germany, and Odense Symfoniorkester in Denmark. *Recordings:* 20th century Russian music for flute and piano 2006, Théâtre pour deux: Music by Hao-Fu Zhang (with others) 2009. *Honours:* First Prize, Int. Competition Jeunesses Musicales, Bucharest 1997, Juventus Prize 2004, First Prize and three Special Prizes, Carl Nielsen Int. Competition 2006, Konzertverein Ingolstadt Prize 2008, Special Prize, Int. Kobe Competition 2009. *Address:* Blücherstrasse 11A, 41564 Kaarst, Germany. *E-mail:* grotsasha@freenet.de. *Website:* www.alexandragrot.com.

GROTH, Konradin; German musician (trumpet) and academic; *Professor of Trumpet, Hochschule der Künste, Berlin. Career:* joined the Berlin Philharmonic Orchestra 1968, prin. trumpet 1974–98 (performed world premiere of Siegfried Matthaus' Concerto for trumpet 1984), trumpet teacher Orchestra Akademie 1974–; prin. trumpet German Opera 1971–74; Prof. of Trumpet, Hochschule der Künste, Berlin 1998–; lectures and masterclasses worldwide, including 6th Hamamatsu Int. Wind Instrument Acad. and Festival, Japan 2000, Int. Trumpet Guild Conf., New York 2000; has recorded with ensembles, including German Brass, Berlin Philharmonic Brass Ensemble, Berlin Philharmonic Brass Quintet. *Recordings:* Brass in Berlin 1990, Christmas Adagio 1996, Das Deutsche Blechbläserquintett 2004. *Publication:* Etudes on New Tonguing and Breathing Techniques 1990. *Address:* Hochschule der Künste, Universität der Künste, Ansprechpartner/-in, Postfach 12 05 44, Berlin 10595, Germany (office).

GROVES, Glenys; British singer; b. 28 July 1949, Hillingdon, Middlesex. *Education:* studied with Mavis Bennett and Eduardo Asquez. *Career:* debut with D'Oyly Carte Opera Co. 1968; Royal Opera House, Covent Garden 1988; regular work with Ambrosian Singers 1967–; West End shows include The Great Waltz (Drury Lane) 1970, The Card, Tom Brown's School Days, Chichester Festival 1983, Justinus 1984, The Lily Maid, Wexford Festival 1984, 1985, 1987; Royal Opera, Covent Garden, as Chief Hen, Cunning Little Vixen, Lady in Waiting, Les Huguenots; solo voice, Prince Igor; Newspaper Seller, Death in Venice; Modestina, Il Viaggio a Reims; Milliner, Der Rosenkavalier; Page, Lohengrin; Olga, Merry Widow; Ida, Die Fledermaus; BBC radio, roles in Gilbert and Sullivan operettas; Songs from the Shows, Friday Night is Music Night; regular guest soloist with Black Dyke Band; extensive concert and oratorio repertoire; performances throughout the UK and Europe with The Garden Party; mem. The Friends of Robert Stolz. *Recordings:* with Royal Opera: Cunning Little Vixen, Prince Igor; Vox Ottone, Trumpet and Soprano in Duet. *Address:* Marlings, 42 Southdean Close, Middleton on Sea, West Sussex, PO22 7TH, England (home).

GROVES, Paul; American singer (tenor); b. 24 Nov. 1964, Los Angeles; m. Charlotte Hellekant. *Education:* Louisiana State Univ., Juilliard Opera Center. *Career:* debut as Steuermann in Der fliegende Holländer, Metropolitan Opera, 1992; Appearances in New York as Mozart's Ferrando and Verdi's Fenton, and roles in Ariadne, Death in Venice, Les Troyens, Parsifal, Die Zauberflöte and The Ghosts of Versailles; European debut as Belfiore in La Finta Giardiniera, for Welsh National Opera; Mozart's Don Ottavio at Salzburg, Idamante at Geneva and Tamino at Munich; Season 1995–96 with Tamino at La Scala, Tom Rakewell for WNO and New York recital debut at Alice Tully Hall; Season 1996–97 with Tom Rakewell at the Paris Châtelet, Nemorino, Flamand in Capriccio and Rossini's Almaviva at the Vienna

Staatsoper; Recitals throughout the USA; further roles include Nadir for Vancouver Opera, Lensky at St Louis and Arturo in I Puritani for Boston Lyric Opera; sang Des Grieux in Manon at Berlin, 1998; Berlioz Faust at Salzburg, 1999; season 2000–01 as Bellini's Arturo at Munich, Gluck's Pylades at Salzburg and Ferrando at the Met; Haydn's the Creation at the London Proms, 2002; engaged as Tamino at Covent Garden, 2003. *Recordings include:* Rigoletto, Alceste, Parsifal and Idomeneo, Der fliegende Holländer, Manon Lescaut, Elgar's The Dream of Gerontius (Gramophone Award for Best Choral Recording 2009). *Current Management:* c/o Opus Artists, 470 Park Avenue South, 9th Floor North, New York, NY 10016, USA. *Telephone:* (212) 584-7500. *E-mail:* info@opus3artists.com. *Website:* www.opus3artists.com.

GRUBE, Michael; German violinist and violin teacher; b. 12 May 1954, Überlingen; s. of Max-Ludwig Grube. *Education:* studied with his father and with Henryk Szeryng, Ivan Galamin and Gunther Becker. *Career:* debut in Berlin 1964; concert soloist in countries worldwide, performances before HM King Tupou IV of Tonga; concerts and festival performances in Vienna, Copenhagen, Prague, Warsaw, Leningrad, Moscow, New York, Washington, DC, Jerusalem, Caracas, Buenos Aires, Canberra, Singapore, Osaka, Bangkok, Bogota, São Paulo, Delhi, Panama City, Madrid, Istanbul; mem. Pro Musica International USA. *Compositions:* Souvenir de Senegal for solo violin, Hommage a Colville Young an Olanchito 1986–87. *Recordings:* Violin Concertos by Bruch, Mendelssohn, Mozart, Violin Music by Dvořák, Smetana, Suk, Handel, Paganini, Reger, Haas, collaborations with Max Ludwig Grube (violin) and Helen Grube (piano).

GRUBER, Andrea; American singer (soprano); b. 1965, New York, NY. *Career:* debut with Scottish Opera 1990, as Leonore in Forza; sang Third Norn in Götterdämmerung at the Metropolitan 1990, followed by Elisabeth de Valois and Aida at the Met; Amelia (Ballo), Amelia (Simon Boccanegra); opera debut as Leonora in Forza with Scottish Opera; professional debut as soprano soloist in Verdi's Requiem with James Levine, Chicago Symphony, Ravinna Festival 1989; Seattle Opera 1992, as Aida, Cologne 1993, as Amelia (Ballo in maschera); further guest appearances in Toronto, at the Vienna Staatsoper and in Italy; Covent Garden debut 1996, Arabella; sang Chrysothemis in Elektra at Seattle 1996; season 1998 as Amelia (Ballo in Maschera) at Monte Carlo; Elvira (Ernani) at Marseilles 1999; sang Odabella in Attila at Chicago 2001. *Recordings include:* Götterdämmerung.

GRUBER, Heinz Karl; Austrian composer; b. 3 Jan. 1943, Vienna. *Education:* Vienna Hochschule für Musik and with Gottfried von Einem. *Career:* sang in Vienna Boys' Choir 1953–57; double bass player in ensemble Die Reihe from 1961; Prin. Double Bass, Tonkünstler Orchestra 1963–69; Co-Founder, MOB Art and Tone ART ensemble 1968–71; has worked with Austrian Radio, Vienna 1969–; conducted premiere of his opera Gomorra at Vienna Volksoper 1993; Trumpet Concerto premiered at BBC Proms, London 1999; Der Herr Nordwind (opera) premiered in Zurich 2004; composer and Conductor, BBC Philharmonic Orchestra 2009–. *Compositions:* 4 pieces for solo violin 1963, Manhattan Broadcasts 1962–64, 5 Kinderlieder for female voices 1965, revised 1980, The Expulsion from Paradise for speakers and 6 solo instruments 1966, revised 1979, 3 MOB Pieces for 7 instruments and percussion 1968, revised 1977, 6 Episodes from a Discontinued Chronicle for piano 1967, Frankenstein !! for baritone, chansonnier and orchestra 1976–77, ensemble version, 1979, Phantom-Bilder for small orchestra 1977, Violin Concerto 1977–78, Demilitarized Zones for brass band 1979, Charivari for orchestra 1981, Castles in the Air for piano 1981, Rough Music, concerto for percussion and orchestra 1982, Anagram for 6 cellos 1987, Nebelsteinmusik (2nd Violin Concerto) 1988, Cello Concerto 1989, Gomorra (opera), 1992, Gloria von Jaxtberg, music theatre, 1992–94, Trumpet Concerto, 1998; TV appearances include Nekrophilius the Pawnbroker in Bring Me the Head of Amadeus (for the Mozart Bicentenary, 1991), Dancing in the Dark for orchestra 2002, Der Herr Nordwind (opera) 2004, Zeitfluren for ensemble 2004. *Current Management:* c/o Boosey & Hawkes Ltd, First Floor, Aldwych House, 71–91 Aldwych, London, WC2B 4HN, England. *Telephone:* (20) 7054-7200. *Fax:* (20) 7054-7293. *E-mail:* composers.uk@boosey.com. *Website:* www.boosey.com/gruber.

GRUBEROVA, Edita; Slovak singer (soprano); b. 23 Dec. 1946, Bratislava. *Education:* studied with Maria Medveckà in Prague and with Ruthilde Boesch in Vienna. *Career:* debut in Bratislava 1968, as Rosina; Sang at the Vienna Staatsoper 1970, as the Queen of Night; sang Zerbinetta in Vienna 1976; Glyndebourne Festival 1973; Salzburg Festival from 1974, as the Queen of Night, conducted by Herbert von Karajan; Metropolitan Opera debut 1977, as the Queen of Night; Covent Garden 1984, as Giulietta in a new production of I Capuleti e i Montecchi by Bellini; Guest appearances at the Bregenz Festival and at La Scala, the Munich Staatsoper (Massenet's Manon) and the Hamburg Staatsoper; Other roles include Gilda, Lucia, Constanze and Violetta; Sang Lucia at La Scala, 1984, Chicago 1986 and Barcelona 1987; La Scala 1987, Donna Anna, Zürich Opera 1988, as Marie in La Fille du Régiment; Metropolitan Opera 1989, as Violetta; Sang Rossini's Rosina and Semiramide (concert) at Munich 1990; Barcelona 1990, as Ariadne; Vienna Staatsoper Oct 1990, as Elizabeth I in Donizetti's Roberto Devereux, season 1992 as Lucia at Munich and Semiramide at Zürich; Linda di Chamounix, 1995; Anna Bolena at the 1997 Munich Festival; season 1997–98 as Linda di Chamounix at Vienna and La Scala, Milan; season 2000–01 as Anna Bolena at Zürich, Elvira in Puritani at the Vienna Staatsoper and Elizabeth I in Roberto Devereux in Hamburg (concert). *Recordings:* Video of Rigoletto, with Luciano Pavarotti; Lucia di Lammermoor; La Traviata; I Puritani; Roberto Devereux; Linda di Chamounix; La Fille du Régiment; Don Giovanni; Die Zauberflöte.

GRUBERT, Naum; Russian pianist; b. 1951, Riga, Latvia. *Education:* Riga Conservatory, studied with Prof. Gutman in Moscow. *Career:* performed first in Russia, Eastern Europe, Italy and Finland; emigrated from USSR 1983; has performed with the London Symphony, the Hague Philharmonic, Netherlands Philharmonic Orchestre de la Suisse Romande, Helsinki Philharmonic and orchestras in Germany and Spain; further engagements with the Rotterdam Philharmonic, the Tonkunstler Orchestra Vienna and the Scottish Nat. Orchestra. *Honours:* second prize Int. Piano Competition, Montréal 1977, prizewinner Tchaikovsky Competition, Moscow 1978.

GRUDZEIŃ, Jacek; Polish composer; b. 7 Feb. 1961, Warsaw. *Education:* Akademii Muzycznej, Warsaw with Włodzimierz Kotoński (composition) and Szabolsca Esztényi (piano improvisation), studied composition at Darmstadt, Patras, Kazimierz and Dartington, studied in London with Paul Paterson and Giles Swayn, electronic studio work with Barry Anderson. *Compositions include:* Tristaniana 1984, Turdus musicus 1984, Movement I 1984, Muzyka z okna 1985, Mechaniczny ogród 1985, Dla Elizy czyli Straszny sen pewnego pianisty (For Elise, or The Terrible Dream of a Certain Pianist) 1985, Sonosfera 1985, Androvanda, gui 1986, Interludium 1986, Koncert skrzypcowy 1986, Dźwięki nocy (Night Sounds) 1987, Lumen, chorus 1987, Hologram II 1988, Somnus 1988, Drzewa (Trees) 1992, Missa brevis 1992, Movement II 1992, Tritonos 1993, Wiatr od morza (Wind from the Sea) 1993, Pavana 1994, Hyacinth Girl 1995, One Jubilee Rag 1995, Gagliarda 1996, Nonstrom 1996, Saxophone Concerto 1996, Światła Pochylenie 1997, Postludium 1998, Studium przedmiotu 1999, Oktet 2000, Ad Naan 2002, Leanyka 2003, Piosenka 2005. *Recordings include:* Vivienne Spiteri, Wiatr od morza. *Honours:* Konkursu Młodych Kompozytorów Polskich 1988, Ogólnopolskiego Konkursu Kompozytorskiego 1995. *E-mail:* Jacek.Grudzien@ddg.art.pl (office). *Website:* all.art.pl/all.art.pl/on-line/Grudzien/Jacek.html.

GRUENBERG, Erich, OBE, FRCM, FGSM; British violinist and music teacher; b. 12 Oct. 1924, Vienna, Austria; s. of Herman Gruenberg and Kathrine Gruenberg; m. Korshed Madan 1956; two d. *Education:* in Vienna, Jerusalem and London. *Career:* Leader, Philomusica of London 1954–56, Stockholm Philharmonic Orchestra 1956–58, London Symphony Orchestra 1962–65, Royal Philharmonic Orchestra 1972–76; Leader, London String Quartet and mem. Rubbra-Gruenberg-Pleeth Piano Trio in 1950s; now appears as soloist with leading orchestras in UK and abroad; taught at Royal Coll. of Music 1960–65, Guildhall School of Music and Drama; Prof., RAM 1988–; int. masterclasses; Chair. of Jury, Fritz Kreisler Int. Violin Competition, Vienna 2005, Yehudi Menuhin Int. Violin Competition; Chair. Bd of Trustees, Mattori Foundation. *Honours:* Hon. RAM, Hon. Pres. Stamford Int. Music Festival 2007; Winner, Carl Flesch Int. Violin Competition. *Address:* 22 Spencer Drive, Hampstead Garden Suburb, London, N2 0QX, England (home). *Telephone:* (20) 8455-4360 (home). *Fax:* (20) 8455-6234 (home).

GRUENBERG, Joanna; Swedish pianist; b. 1957, Stockholm. *Education:* studied with Fanny Waterman, Louis Kentner and Peter Frankl, Guildhall School of Music with James Gibb. *Career:* appearances at the Aldeburgh and Harrogate Festivals, at the Fairfields Hall, Croydon and for the City Music Society, London; Festival Hall debut 1978, with the Royal Philharmonic Orchestra; recital tours with her father, Erich Gruenberg; concerts with the GLC series at Ranger House and visits to Ireland and Spain; played with the Bournemouth Symphony and Sinfonietta 1983–85; Barbican Centre with Tchaikovsky's 1st Concerto and the Grieg Concerto with the Royal Liverpool Philharmonic, 1984–85; further engagements with the Hallé Orchestra (Mendelssohn's 1st Concerto, 1988) and the Philharmonia at the Barbican. *Honours:* RAOS Silver Medal 1980.

GRUESSER, Eva; German violinist; b. 1965, Black Forest. *Education:* Freiburg Hochschule, Rubin Acad., Jerusalem and Juilliard School, USA. *Career:* Leader, Lark Quartet, USA; concert tours to Australia, Taiwan, Hong Kong, People's Republic of China, Germany, The Netherlands; US appearances at Lincoln Center (New York), Kennedy Center (Washington, DC), Boston, Los Angeles, Philadelphia, St Louis, San Francisco; repertoire includes quartets by Haydn, Mozart, Beethoven, Schubert, Dvořák, Brahms, Borodin, Bartók, Debussy and Shostakovich. *Honours:* with Lark Quartet: Gold Medals at 1990 Naumberg and 1991 Shostakovich Competitions, prizewinner Premio Paulio Borciani, Reggio Emilia 1990, Karl Klinger Competition, Munich 1990, London Int. String Quartet Competition 1991, Melbourne Chamber Music Competition 1991.

GRUFFYDD JONES, Angharad; British singer (soprano); b. 1973, Wales. *Education:* Univ. of Cambridge, Royal College of Music with Margaret Kingsley. *Career:* concert engagements with conductors Ivor Bolton, Richard Hickox, Roy Goodman and Roger Norrington; Mozart Exsultate Jubilate at Greenwich and York Minster, Messiah in Spain with Harry Christophers and the Monteverdi Vespers at Washington, DC; song recitals in London (Purcell Room) and elsewhere; opera appearances in Orlando by Handel for the Cambridge Handel Opera Group, and Fidalma in Muzio Scevola for the London Handel Festival, 2001; sings with chamber choirs The King's Consort, The Sixteen and the Monteverdi Choir; soloist in John Eliot Gardiner's Bach Cantata Pilgrimage, 2000. *Honours:* prizewinner Young Welsh Singer of the Year Competition 2000.

GRUNDHEBER, Franz; German singer (baritone); b. 27 Sept. 1937, Trier. *Education:* studied in Trier and Hamburg, Indiana Univ., USA, Music Acad. of the West, Santa Barbara. *Career:* singer, Hamburg Staatsoper 1966–; frequent guest performances with Bavarian State Opera, Munich, Semperoper, Dresden and Deutsche Oper, Berlin; has appeared in many European opera houses including Paris, Barcelona, Madrid, Oviedo, Athens, Rome, Milan, Verona, Florence, Turin, Copenhagen, Helsinki, Moscow, Brussels, Amsterdam; guest appearances at Metropolitan Opera, New York 1999, 2001, 2004; several tours of Japan; has sung with many conductors including Herbert von Karajan, Kurt Masur, Seiji Ozawa, Colin Davis, Giuseppe Sinopoli, Claudio Abbado and Semyon Bychkov. *Performances include:* Vienna Staatsoper 1983, as Mandryka in Strauss's Arabella; Salzburg Festival 1985, as Olivier in Strauss's Capriccio; Mozart's Masetto in Don Giovanni and Guglielmo in Puccini's Le Villi, Faninal in Strauss's Der Rosenkavalier, and Escamillo in Bizet's Carmen; Salzburg and Savonnlina Festivals 1989, as Orestes in Strauss's Elektra, and Amonasro in Verdi's Aida; Barak in Strauss's Die Frau ohne Schatten at the Holland Festival 1990; Germont in Verdi's La Traviata, Barcelona 1992; Berg's Wozzeck at the Châtelet, Paris, and Verdi's Macbeth at Cologne; Wozzeck at Chicago 1994; Verdi's Rigoletto at Covent Garden 1997; Wozzeck at the Vienna Staatsoper 2000–01, Verdi's Simon Boccanegra in Munich 2000–01, Amfortas in Wagner's Parsifal for the San Francisco Opera 2000–01, Scarpia in Puccini's Tosca, Hamburg 2000–01; Simon Boccanegra, Santiago de Chile 2001 (Chilean Critics' Award for Int. Opera); Dr Schön in Berg's Lulu at Vienna, 2002; Rigoletto and Wozzeck at Metropolitan Opera, NY 1999, 2001 and 2004; Wagner's Flying Dutchman, Rome Opera 2004; Scarpia, Santiago de Chile 2004; Orestes, Tokyo Opera Nomori 2005, Gurrelieder, Saito Kinen Festival, Japan 2005; Rigoletto, Hamburg 2005, Scarpia, Hamburg 2005, Flying Dutchman, Hamburg 2005, Macbeth, Dresden 2005, Jago in Verdi's Otello, Dresden 2005, Orestes, Munich 2005, Simon Boccanegra, Hamburg 2006, Moses in Schönberg's Moses und Aron, Vienna 2006, Munich 2007, Amonasro, Dresden 2009, Cardillac, Paris 2008, Barak in Die Frau ohne Schatten, Hamburg 2008, Schigolch in Lulu, Madrid, Barcelona, Salzburg, Paris 2009/2010/2011, Gerard in Andrea Chénier, Hamburg 2010, Simon Boccanegra, Frankfurt 2011. *Recordings include:* video of Elektra (role of Orestes) conducted by Abbado; Alban Berg's Wozzeck, conducted by Abbado (Prix Georges Till) 1997; several works by Strauss including roles of Olivier, Faninial, Mandryka, Jupiter, Barak and Orest. *Honours:* Kammersänger and Hon. mem. Hamburg State Opera, Vienna State Opera. *Current Management:* c/o Artists Management Zürich, Rütistrasse 52, 8044 Zürich, Switzerland. *Telephone:* 821-89-57.

GRUNEWALD, Eugenie; American singer (mezzo-soprano); b. 1962. *Career:* appearances as Amneris in Aida at Michigan, Orlando, Austin, Miami and for the San Francisco Opera 1997; European debut as Giovanna Seymour in Anna Bolena at Barcelona; Dido in Les Troyens at Toulouse and Athens, Tchaikovsky's Joan of Arc and Lyubov (Mazeppa) with the Opera Orchestra of New York; Azucena and Wagner's Venus with Austin Lyric Opera, the mezzo roles in Puccini's Trittico with the Chicago Lyric Opera and Santuzza with Tulsa Opera; Fenena in Nabucco with Connecticut Opera, Preziosilla at Barcelona and the Nurse in Dukas' Ariane et Barbe-bleue at Hamburg (1997); Concerts with the New World Symphony under Michael Tilson Thomas, the Boston Philharmonic, Little Orchestra Society and the Pacific Symphony at the Aspen Festival. *Current Management:* c/o John Miller, Pinnacle Arts Management, 889 Ninth Avenue, Suite 1, New York, NY 10019, USA. *Telephone:* (212) 397-7911. *Fax:* (212) 397-7920. *E-mail:* jmiller@pinnaclearts.com. *Website:* www.eugeniegrunewald.com.

GRUSKIN, Shelley; American flautist and recorder player; b. 20 July 1936, New York. *Education:* Eastman School, Rochester. *Career:* mem., New York Pro Musica 1961–74, playing recorder and other early wind instruments; associated with such singers as Charles Bressler, Bethany Beardslee, Jan De Gaetani, Russel Oberlin; premiere of liturgical drama, The Play of Herod at the Cloisters, New York 1963; tour of Europe 1963, USSR 1964; final performances with group in Marco da Gagliano's La Dafne 1974; formed Philidor Trio 1965, with soprano Elizabeth Humes and harpsichordist Edward Smith; performances with group until 1980; teacher of music history and early music performance practice at various institutions; artist-in-residence, Coll. of St Scholastica, Duluth, MN 1978–1998, faculty emerita 1998–; Pres., American Recorder Soc. 1980–88. *Recordings include:* albums with New York Pro Musica and Philidor Trio.

GRUZIN, Boris; Russian conductor; b. 1940, Tashkent. *Education:* Moscow Conservatoire. *Career:* Principal Conductor of the Novosibirsk and Odessa Opera and Ballet Theatres; Mariinsky Theatre, St Petersburg, from 1993; Professor at the St Petersburg Conservatoire 1986–; Repertoire includes Tchaikovsky's Mazeppa, Eugene Onegin, Swan Lake and Sleeping Beauty, Prince Igor, The Maid of Pskov by Rimsky-Korsakov and Giselle; season 1999–2000 with War and Peace at St Petersburg and the Kirov Ballet at Covent Garden; other ballet repertoire includes Romeo and Juliet and Le Corsaire; symphonic concerts in Moscow, Odessa, Kiev, Tomsk and abroad. *Honours:* Honoured Artist of the Russian Federation 1992.

GUACCERO, Giovanni, BA; Italian composer; b. 25 Sept. 1966, Rome. *Education:* Conservatory of Santa Cecilia, La Sapienza Univ., Rome. *Career:* debut in Rome, Folkstudio 1991; mem. Nuova Consonanza; Lecturer, Conservatorio F. Cilea, Reggio Calabria, Scuola Populare di Musica di Testaccio; has collaborated with artists including Giovanna Marini, Ennio Morricone, Enzo Siciliano, Rosalia de Souza. *Compositions include:* Filottete (stage music) 1991, Salmo Metropolitano for chorus and orchestra 1995, Trane's Way 1996, Infedelis Peregrinatio 1996, Flute Dance 1997, Per Versi Diversi 1997, Il Canto dei Popoli 1998, Alquimia (for radio) 1998, Ascoltate e capire la luna 1999, Dal Centro del Corpo 1999, Danza No. 2 1999, Pincelada 1999, Uno dei Tanti Epiloghi for orchestra 2000, Musica per le Montagne 2002, Se Essere Uomo for orchestra 2007, Le Isole Felici (stage play with music) 2008. *Recordings:* Salmo Metropolitano 1998, Musica per le Montagne 2004. *Honours:* Nuove Generazioni project of Nuova Consonanza 1997. *Address:* Via Segesta 1, 00179 Rome, Italy (home). *Website:* www.giovanniguaccero.com.

GUARNERA, Piero; Italian singer (baritone); b. 1962, Rome. *Education:* studied with Maria Carbone and Maria Vittoria Romano. *Career:* debut: Spoleto 1984, as Belcore in L'elisir d'amore; appeared at Teatro dell'Opera in Rome as Masetto in Don Giovanni under Peter Maag 1984; appeared as Guglielmo in Così fan tutte; appearances at Teatro dell'Opera di Roma (Ifigenia in Tauride, Malatesta in Don Pasquale, Ford in Falstaff, Miserere di Bartolucci for opening of concert season 1996), Teatro di San Carlo in Naples (Il barbiere di Siviglia under the baton of Bartoletti, The Rape of Lucretia, staged by Corbelli), Teatro alla Scala (Idomeneo, conducted by Muti, Arabella under Sawallish), Teatro Regio di Torino (Enrico in Il campanello, conducted by Carminati, Il barbiere di Siviglia, under Corrado Rovaris), Teatro Massimo di Palermo (Marcello in La Bohème, under Renzetti), Teatro La Fenice di Venezia (title role of Falstaff under Kabaratchevsky), Teatro Carlo Felice di Genova (cover of Raimondi in role of Sir John Falstaff), Opernhaus in Zurich (Marcello in La Bohème), Opéra de Montecarlo (Falstaff), as well as in Spoleto (Enrico in Lucia di Lammermoor, Don Pasquale), Pisa (Le nozze di Figaro, Don Pasquale under Benini), Jesi (Adriana Lecouvreur), Malaga (La Cenerentola), Bordeaux and Maastricht (La Bohème), Santiago de Compostela (La scala di seta), and in Tokyo, Como, Salerno, Sanremo, Tours; participated in several festivals, singing Re Teodoro a Venezia by Paisiello conducted by Mega at Festival di Montepulciano, world première of Amor vuol dire sofferenza by Leo, Il barbiere di Siviglia (Figaro) staged by Daniele Abbado at Arena Festival in Avenches and at Opera Festival in Bellinzona, Così fan tutte (Guglielmo) at Las Palmas Festival, role of Lui in Le parole al buio by Furlani conducted by Enrique Mazzola in Spoleto and more recently L'armida immaginaria and Proserpine at Festival della Valle d'Itria in Martina Franca; has recently performed in L'elisir d'amore at Opernhaus in Graz, and La traviata at Teatro Manoel in Malta; debuts in Adina ovvero il Califfo di Bagdad at Teatro Sao Carlos in Lisbon, Orleanskaya Deva at Teatro Regio di Torino and at Teatro Massimo di Palermo, under Stefano Ranzani; tour to Pisa, Prato and Siena in title role in The Marriage of Figaro at Teatro Lirico di Cagliari in Capriccio under Rafael Frübeck de Burgos; debut in Il turco in Italia at Teatro Marruccino di Chieti, and sang in role of Figaro in Il barbiere di Siviglia at Teatro La Fenice di Venezial has recently returned to Cagliari for Turandot and Hans Heiling by Marschner, L'elisir d'amore in Lisbon and Covenienze e inconvenienze teatrali at the Teatro Massimo in Palermo; sang in I Cavalieri di Ekebù at Teatro Bellini in Catania 2006. *Recordings include:* Rossini: The Turk in Italy, Donizetti: Il Campanello, Salieri: La Locandiera 1993, Cimarosa: Armida Immaginaria 1996. *Honours:* Winner, Spoleto International Competition 1984, Treviso Toti dal Monte Competition 1995. *Current Management:* Atelier Musicale, Via Caselle 76, San Lazzaro di Savena 40068, Italy. *Telephone:* (051) 1998-4444. *Fax:* (051) 1998-4420. *E-mail:* info@ateliermusicale.com. *Website:* www.ateliermusicale.com.

GUBAIDULINA, Sofia Asgatovna; Russian (b. Tatar) composer; b. 24 Oct. 1931, Chistopol; d. of Asgat Gubaidulin and Fedossia Gubaidulina; m. Peter Meshchaninov; one d. *Education:* Kazan and Moscow Conservatories, pvt. studies with Nikolai Peiko, Vissarion Shebalin and Grigori Kogan. *Career:* first noticed abroad, Paris 1979; UK debut (Symphony in 12 Movements) 1987; freelance composer in Moscow 1963–91, in Germany 1991–. *Compositions include:* instrumental: Piano quintet 1957, Allegro rustico for flute and piano 1963, Five Etudes for harp, double bass and percussion 1965, Vivente non vivente for synthesizer 1970, Concordanza for chamber ensemble 1971, String Quartet No. 1 1971, Fairytale Poem 1971, Stufen (The Steps) 1971, Detto II for cello and ensemble 1972, Rumore e Silenzio for percussion and harpsichord 1974, Quattro for 2 trumpets and 2 trombones 1974, Concerto for bassoon and low strings 1975, Sonata for double bass and piano 1975, Light and Darkness for solo organ 1976, Dots, Lines and Zigzag for bass clarinet and piano 1976, Revue for orchestra and jazz band 1976, Duo-Sonata for 2 bassoons 1977, Quartet for 4 flutes 1977, Misterioso for 7 percussionists 1977, Te Salutant capriccio for large light orchestra 1978, Introitus concerto for piano and chamber orchestra 1978, Detto I sonata for organ and percussion 1978, De profundis for solo bayan 1978, Sounds of the Forest for flute and piano 1978, In Croce for cello and organ 1979, Jubilatio for 4 percussionists 1979, Offertorium concerto for violin and orchestra 1980, Garten von Freuden und Traurigkeiten for flute, harp and viola (speaker ad lib) 1980, Rejoice sonata for violin and cello 1981, Descensio for ensemble 1981, Seven Words for cello, bayan and strings 1982, In the Beginning there was Rhythm for 7 percussionists 1984, Et exspecto sonata for solo bayan 1985, Quasi Hoquetus for viola, bassoon, cello and piano 1985, Stimmen… vetummen…, symphony in 12 movements 1986, Answer without Question collage for 3 orchestras 1988, Pro et Contra for large orchestra 1989, Silenzio 5 pieces for bayan, violin and cello 1991, Even and Uneven for 7 percussionists 1991, Tatar dance for 2 double basses and bayan 1992, Dancer on a Tightrope for violin and piano

1993, Meditation on the Bach-Choral Vor deinen Thron tret ich hiermit for harpsichord, 2 violins, viola, cello and double bass 1993, Early in the Morning, Right Before Waking for 7 kotos 1993, The Festivities at Their Height for cello and orchestra 1993, Now Always Snow for chamber ensemble and chamber choir on poems of Gennady Aigi 1993, 2nd cello concerto 1994, In anticipation... for saxophone quartet and 6 percussion 1994, Zeitge-stalten symphony in 4 movements 1994, Quaternion for 4 cellos 1996, Galgenlieder à 3 15 pieces for mezzo, double bass and percussion 1996, Galgenlieder à 5 1996, Ritorno perpetuo for harpsichord 1997, Canticle of the Sun for cello, chamber chorus and 2 percussionists 1997, Im Schatten des Baumes for koto, bass-koto, cheng and orchestra 1998; vocal: Phacelia vocal cycle for soprano and orchestra 1956, Night in Memphis cantata for mezzo-soprano, male chorus and chamber orchestra 1968, Rubaiyat 1969, Roses 5 romances for soprano and piano 1972, Counting Rhymes 5 children's songs 1973, Hour of the Soul for mezzo-soprano and large orchestra 1976, Perception for soprano, baritone and 7 string instruments 1981, Hommage à Marina Tsvetava, suite in 5 movements for chorus a cappella 1984, Hommage à T. S. Eliot for soprano and octet 1987, Witty Waltzing in the style of Johann Strauss for soprano and octet 1987, Two Songs on German Folk Poetry for soprano, flute, harpsichord and cello 1988, for piano and string quartet 1989, Jauchzt vor Gott for chorus and organ 1989, Aus dem Stundenbuch for cello, orchestra, male chorus and female speaker 1991, Johannes Passion 2000, Johannes Ostern 2001, Risonanza for chamber ensemble 2001, Reflections on the theme B-A-C-H 2002, Mirage: the Dancing Sun for eight violoncelli 2002, On the Edge of the Abyss for seven violoncelli and two waterphones 2002, The Rider on the White Horse for large orchestra and organ 2002, The Light of the END for large orchestra 2003, Under the Sign of Scorpio for bayan and large orchestra 2003, Verwandlung for trombone, saxophone quartet, cello, contra basso and tam-tam 2004, The Deceitful Face of Hope and Despair for flute and large orchestra 2005, Feast during a Plague for large orchestra 2006, Die Leier des Orpheus for violin, string orchestra and percussion 2006, Ravvedimento for cello and guitar quartet 2007, In Tempus Praesens for violin and orchestra 2007, Glorious Percussion concerto for percussion and orchestra 2008, Fachwerk concerto for bayan, percussion and strings 2009, Sotto voce for viola, double bass and two guitars 2010. *Honours:* Hon. DHumLitt (Univ. of Chicago) 2011; Great Distinguished Service Cross of the Order of Merit (FRG) 2002; numerous awards including Prix de Monaco 1987, Koussevitzky Int. Record Award 1989 and 1994, Premio Franco Abbiati 1991, Heidelberg Artists Prize 1991, Russian State Prize 1992, Premium Imperiale 1998, Léonie Sonning Music Prize 1999, Goethe Medal, City of Weimar 2001, Royal Swedish Acad. of Music Polar Prize 2002, Living Composer Prize, Cannes Classical Awards 2003, European Culture Prize 2005, Bach Prize, Hamburg 2007. *Address:* Ziegeleiweg 12, 25482 Appen, Germany (home). *Telephone:* (41) 2281875 (home).

GUBBAY, Raymond, CBE, FRSA; British music promoter; *Chairman, Raymond Gubbay Ltd;* b. 2 April 1946, London, England; s. of the late David Gubbay and Ida Gubbay; m. Johanna Quirke 1972 (divorced 1988); two d. *Education:* Univ. Coll. School, Hampstead. *Career:* concert promoter 1966–; Founder, Man. Dir and Chair. Raymond Gubbay Ltd 1966–; presents regular series of concerts at major London and regional concert halls including Royal Albert Hall, Royal Festival Hall, Barbican Centre, Symphony Hall Birmingham, Bridgewater Hall Manchester, Royal Concert Hall Glasgow and in Ireland, Belgium, Germany, Austria, Switzerland, Netherlands and Scandinavia; has presented productions of: (operas and operettas) The Ratepayer's Iolanthe 1984, Turandot 1991–92, La Bohème (centenary production) 1996, 2004, 2006, Carmen 1997, 2002, 2005, 2009, 2010, 2013, Madam Butterfly 1998, 2000, 2003, 2011, The Pirates of Penzance 1998–99, 2000, Tosca 1999, Aïda 2001, Cavalleria Rusticana and Pagliacci 2002; (ballets) Swan Lake 1997, 1999, 2002, 2004, 2007, 2010, 2013, Romeo and Juliet 1998, The Sleeping Beauty 2000; D'Oyly Carte Opera Co. seasons 2000–03, Follies 2003, On Your Toes 2004, Savoy Opera 2004, Showboat 2006, Carmen Jones 2007, Strictly Gershwin 2008, 2011, The King and I 2009, Aïda (new production) 2012; mem. Bd Royal Philharmonic Orchestra, Bd Govs Cen. School of Ballet. *Honours:* Hon. FRAM 1988, Hon. FTCL 2000, Gold Badge Award, British Acad. of Songwriters, Composers and Authors 2009. *Address:* Dickens House, 15 Tooks Court, London, EC4A 1QH, England (office). *Telephone:* (20) 7025-3750 (office). *E-mail:* info@raymondgubbay.co.uk (office). *Website:* www .raymondgubbay.co.uk (office).

GUBRUD, Irene Ann; American singer (soprano); b. 4 Jan. 1947, Canby, MN. *Education:* St Olaf Coll., Northfield, MN and Juilliard School, New York. *Career:* concert engagements with leading US orchestras; tour of Germany with the Baltimore Symphony; premiere of Star-Child by George Crumb with the New York Philharmonic conducted by Pierre Boulez 1977; European engagements with the Stuttgart and Bavarian Radio Orchestras; opera debut 1981, as Mimi with the Minnesota Opera, St Paul; recitals at Lincoln and Kennedy Centers 1981; appearances at the Aspen, Blossom and Meadowbrook Festivals; teacher, Washington Univ., St Louis 1976–81. *Honours:* first prize Concert Artists' Guild competition 1970, Ford Foundation performance competition 1971, Rockefeller and Minna Kaufmann Ruud competitions 1972, winner Naumburg Int. Voice Competition 1980.

GUDBJORNSSON, Gunnar; Icelandic singer (tenor); b. 1965, Reykjavík. *Education:* New Music School, Reykjavík, studied with Hannelore Kuhse in Berlin, with Nicolai Gedda in London. *Career:* debut at Icelandic Opera as Don Ottavio 1988; sang Clotarco in Haydn's Armida at Buxton Festival 1988; appearances with Opera North and WNO; opera galas at St David's Hall,

Cardiff, and with Royal Philharmonic; sang the Lawyer in Punch and Judy at Aldeburgh Festival and engaged with Wiesbaden Opera as Almaviva, Ottavio and Tamino; concert repertoire includes St Matthew Passion (Queen's Hall, Edinburgh), Britten's Serenade, Die schöne Müllerin; recitals at Covent Garden and Wigmore Hall 1993; further appearances at the BBC Proms (Les Noces 1996), the Opéra Bastille, Bregenz Festival, Aix-en-Provence, Geneva and Lisbon; Wagner's Steersman at Lille 1998; season 2000–01 as Don Ottavio at the Deutsche Oper Berlin, Belmonte, and Fenton in Falstaff at the Berlin Staatsoper; radio recordings for BBC, Radio France and Hessische with broadcasts in most of Europe. *Recordings include:* Die schöne Müllerin; albums in Mozart complete edition. *Honours:* Gunnar Thoroddson Scholarship 1987, Léonie Sonning Prize 1988.

GUDMUNDSEN-HOLMGREEN, Pelle; Danish composer; b. 21 Nov. 1932, Copenhagen; m. 1st Gunvor Kaarsberg 1959; one s. one d.; m. 2nd Karin B. Lund 1997. *Education:* studied Theory and History of Music at Royal Danish Conservatory of Music. *Career:* teacher, Royal Danish Acad. of Music, Århus 1967–73; compositions performed world-wide. *Compositions include:* Frère Jacques for orchestra 1964, Recapitulations for small ensemble 1965, Je ne me tairai Jamais, for voices and instruments 1966, Piece by Piece for chamber orchestra 1968, Tricolore IV for orchestra 1969, Terrace in 5 Stages for woodwind quintet 1970, Plateaux pour Deux for cello and percussion 1970, Mirror II for orchestra 1973, Songs Without for mezzo soprano and piano 1976, Symphony, Antiphony 1977, Prelude to Your Silence, octet 1978, Your Silence, septet and soprano 1978, Mirror Pieces for clarinet trio 1980, String Quartet V Step by Step 1982, VI Parting 1983, VII Parted 1984, Triptycon, concerto for percussion 1985, String Quartet VIII Ground 1986, Concord, Sinfonietta 1987, Octopus for organ and two players 1989, Trois Poèmes de Samuel Beckett for vocal group 1989, Concerto Grosso for string quartet and symphonic ensemble 1990, The Creation, the 6th day, for double choir and violin solo 1991, For Piano 1992, Turn for guitar, bass flute, harp and soprano 1993, Traffic, Sinfonietta 1994, Double for violin and piano 1994, Album for saxophone quartet 1994, For Cello and orchestra 1996, Blow on Odysseus for vocal soloists, choir, trombones and percussion 1998, Stepping Still for string sextet 1999, Still, Leben for organ 2000, Countermove I–III for organ 2000, In Triplum for organ 2000, Sound/Sight for choir 2001, Two/Four Madrigals for vocal ensemble 2001, For Violin and Orchestra 2002, Three Stages for vocal ensemble 2003, Moving, Still. Hans Christian Andersen 200 for baritone and string quartet 2004, Portrait for saxophone quartet and bass drum 2004, Plateaux pour piano et orchestre 2005, Last Ground for string quartet and ocean 2006, Moments musicaux for violin, cello and piano 2006, Again for vocal ensemble 2006, Convex-Concave-Concord (sextet) 2008, Play (sinfonietta) 2010, Song for vocal quartet 2010, Company for vocal quartet and sinfonietta 2010, Incontri for orchestra 2010, Near Still Distant Still for violin, horn and piano 2010, Sounds I and Sounds II for vocal quartet 2011, New Ground for string quartet 2011, Green for vocal quartet 2011, New Ground Green for string quartet and vocal quartet 2011, No Ground for string quartet 2011, No Ground Green for string quartet and vocal quartet 2011, Run for ten musicians 2012, Og for sinfonietta 2012, Chacun son son for recorder and orchestra, the sun goes up the sun goes down (opera) 2013, Music for 13 strings 2014, String Quartets 12+13+14 = All in one 2014, On one note for vocal quartet 2015, Ad Cor for choir and chamber orchestra 2015. *Recordings including:* Symphony-Antiphony for Cello and Orchestra, Frère Jacques, Concerto Grosso for string quartet and orchestra, Triptycon for percussion and orchestra, Plateaux pour piano et orchestre, Music for voices and instruments, chamber music, music for solo instruments, organ music and music for choir; Music is a Monster (DVD). *Publications include:* contrib. to Dansk Musiktidsskrift. *Address:* Bartholinsgade 7 st.tv., 1356 Hellerup, Denmark (home). *Telephone:* 51-93-63-93 (mobile) (home); 86-59-68-48 (home). *E-mail:* pelle.gh@gmail.com.

GUÉRINEL, Lucien; French composer; b. 16 Aug. 1930, Grasse; m. Marie-Claire 1958; one s. *Education:* studied with Yvonne Studer and Marcel Prévot in Marseille, with André Jouve and Louis Saguer in Paris. *Career:* mem. Sciences, Letters and Arts Acad. of Marseille. *Compositions:* Sept Fragments d'Archiloque for 12 voices, Quatre poèmes de E. Montale for 12 voices, Quatre chants pour un visage for 12 voices and four instruments, Canti Corali Ungaretti for choir and orchestra, Les Sept Portes for choir, 16 strings and two percussionists, Prendre corps for string quartet with soprano and mezzo-soprano, Séquence for reeds trio. *Recordings:* String Quartet No. 2: Strophe 21, Ce chant de brume for cello, Sept Fragments d'Archiloque, Quatre poèmes de E. Montale, Quatre chants pour un visage, Chants-Espaces for two pianos, Huit préludes for piano, Appels for vibraphone, Cadence for harpsichord, Six Bagatelles for wind quintet, Soleil ployé for violin. *Publications:* poetry: La Parole échouée 1969, La Sentence nue 1973, Acte de présence 1997; contrib. music criticism to La Provence. *Honours:* second prize Philip Morris Competition for String Quartets, Paris 1983, finalist Int. Piano en Creuse Competition 1990, 1994.

GUERRERO, Giancarlo; Costa Rican conductor; *Music Director, Nashville Symphony Orchestra;* b. 14 March 1969, Managua, Nicaragua. *Education:* Baylor Univ., Tex., Northwestern Univ., Ill. *Career:* early musical training as mem. Costa Rica Youth Symphony Orchestra; fmr Music Dir Tachira Symphony, San Cristobal, Venezuela; Assoc. Conductor, Minnesota Orchestra 1999–2004; Music Dir Eugene Symphony, Ore. 2001–08; Music Dir Nashville Symphony Orchestra 2009–; Prin. Guest Conductor, Cleveland Orchestra's Miami Residency 2011–; regular appearances with Orquesta Sinfónica Simón

Bolívar, Venezuela; has also worked with several American orchestras including the Philadelphia Orchestra, Boston Symphony, Baltimore Symphony, Seattle Symphony, Los Angeles Philharmonic, Dallas Symphony Orchestra; fmr Guest Conductor with Gulbenkian Orchestra, Polish Nat. Radio Symphony Orchestra, Royal Scottish Nat. Orchestra, Brussels Philharmonic, BBC Scottish Symphony Orchestra, BBC Nat. Orchestra of Wales, Strasbourg Philharmonic, Monte Carlo Philharmonic. *Recordings include:* Daugherty: Metropolis Symphony: Deus Ex Machina (Grammy Awards for Best Orchestral Performance and Best Classical Contemporary Composition 2011) 2009, Piazzolla: Sinfonia Buenos Aires 2010, Schwantner: Percussion Concerto-Morning's Embrace-Chasing Light? (Grammy Award for Best Classical Instrumental Solo 2012) 2011. *Honours:* Helen M. Thompson Award, American Symphony Orchestra League 2004. *Current Management:* Intermusica Artists Management Ltd, 36 Graham Street, Crystal Wharf, London, N1 8GJ, England. *Telephone:* (20) 7608-9900. *Fax:* (20) 7490-3263. *E-mail:* mail@intermusica.co.uk. *Website:* www.intermusica.co.uk.

GUERRIER, David; French trumpeter; *Principal Horn, Orchestre National de France*; b. 2 Dec. 1984, Pierrelatte, Drôme. *Education:* studied with Pierre Dutot and Jean-François Madeuf at Conservatoire Nat. Supérieur de Musique, Lyon. *Career:* began to learn trumpet aged seven; mem. Mediterranean Youth Orchestra 1998; took part in the summer tour, EU Youth Orchestra 1999, 2000; US debut at Kennedy Center, Washington DC 2004; concerto appearances with Camerata de Coahuila, Mexico, Basel Symphony Orchestra and Geneva Chamber Orchestra, Switzerland, Vogtland Philharmonic, Germany, Chamber Orchestra of Venice, Italy, Ensemble Musica Viva, Portugal, Košice Festival Orchestra, Slovakia; has also appeared as soloist with several French orchestras including Colonne Orchestra, Paris, Lyon Chamber Orchestra, Lorraine Philharmonic, Nat. Orchestras of Bordeaux and Toulouse; Prin. Horn, Orchestre Nat. de France 2005–; mem. Turbulences (brass quintet). *Honours:* numerous prizes, including First Prize, Maurice André Int. Trumpet Competition, Paris 2000, First Prize, Int. Trumpet Guild Competition, New York 2002, St Vincent Coll. Concert Series Prize 2003, John and Esther Browning Memorial Prize 2003, First Prize Munich Int. Music Competition of the ARD 2003. *Current Management:* Young Concert Artists Inc., 250 West 57th Street, Suite 1222, New York, NY 10107, USA. *Telephone:* (212) 307-6655. *Fax:* (212) 581-8894. *E-mail:* yca@yca.org. *Website:* www.yca .org.

GUHL, Helmut; German singer (baritone); b. 1945, Hamburg. *Education:* studied in Hamburg. *Career:* debut at Eutin Festival 1973, as the Count in Lortzing's Wildschütz; sang with Oldenburg Opera 1974–78, notably as Sharpless, Papageno, Germont and Wolfram; Eutin Festival as Guglielmo, Rossini's Figaro and Belcore; Hanover Opera from 1978, as Don Giovanni, Orpheus, Rossini's Mosè 1991, and Beckmesser; guest appearances at the Deutsche Oper am Rhein, Düsseldorf, and in Hamburg, Mannheim and Stuttgart.

GUIDARINI, Marco; Italian conductor; b. 1952, Genoa. *Education:* studied with Franco Ferrara and at the Acad. of Pescara. *Career:* led regional orchestras in Italy, then assisted John Eliot Gardiner at the Lyon Opéra, making debut 1986 with Falstaff; Wexford Festival and London 1988–89, with the local premieres of Mercadante's Elisa e Claudio and Mozart's Mitridate; season 1990–91 with Tosca at ENO, Figaro for WNO, La Bohème for Scottish Opera and Manon Lescaut in Dublin; Vancouver and Sydney debuts with Don Pasquale and Tosca; season 1993–94 with La Traviata at Stockholm, I Lombardi at Bologna and Il Barbiere di Siviglia at the Berlin Staatsoper; season 1997 with Don Giovanni at Copenhagen, Rigoletto in Geneva, Barbiere at Los Angeles (US debut) and Don Carlos in Marseilles; other repertory includes Così fan tutte (Australian Opera), Die Zauberflöte, Un Ballo in Maschera and Nabucco (Nice Opéra); Bellini's Capuleti at Reggio Emilia, 1998. *Address:* Via Maragliano 3, Apartment 15, Genoa, 16121, Italy. *Website:* www.marco-guidarini.com.

GUILLOU, Jean; French organist, composer and pianist; *Organist, Eglise Saint Eustache, Paris*; b. 18 April 1930, Angers. *Education:* Paris Conservatoire with Dupré, Duruflé and Messiaen. *Career:* Prof., Instituto de Alta Cultura, Lisbon 1953–57; recitalist in residence in Berlin 1958–62; organist, St Eustache, Paris 1963; Prof. with int. masterclass in Zürich 1970–2005. *Compositions include:* Toccata for organ (op 9) 1962, Sagas for organ (op 20) 1968, Symphonie Initiatique for organ 1969, La Chapelle des Abimes for organ 1970, Scènes d'Enfants for organ (op 28), Judith-Symphonie for mezzo and orchestra, Concerto Grosso (op 32), Andromeda for soprano and organ (op 39), Peace for eight voices and organ (op 43), Hyperion for organ (op 45), Aube for 12 voices and organ (op 46), Concerto No. 5 King Arthur, Missa Interrupa (op 51), Eloge for organ (op 52), Alice au Pays de l'orgue for organ 1995, Fête for clarinet and organ (op 55), Instants for organ (op 57), Colloque No. 2 for piano and organ, Colloque No. 4 for piano and organ, Colloque No. 5 for piano and organ, Concerto for cello and organ, Concerto for violin and organ, Concerto Héroïque, Concerto 2000 (op 62), Concerto for trumpet and organ (op 64), Epitases for two pianos (op 65), Colloque No. 7 for piano and organ (op 66), Colloque No. 8 for marimba and organ (op 67), Concerto No. 6 for organ and orchestra (op 68), Concerto No. 7 for organ and orchestra (op 70), La Révolte des Orgues for organs and percussion. *Recordings:* J. S. Bach, Complete Organ Works, Goldberg Variations, Musical Offering; Vivaldi, Five Concertos; C. Franck, Complete Organ works; Mussorgsky, Pictures at an Exhibition; Stravinsky, Petrushka; Julius Reubke, piano and organ sonatas; Guillou Plays Guillou (seven vols), Guillou plays Mozart. *Publication:* L'orgue,

souvenir et avenir, Die Orgel: Erinnerung und Zukunft 2005. *Honours:* Gramophone Critics Prize 1980, Int. Performer of the Year, USA 1980, Liszt Acad. Prize, Budapest 1982, Diapason d'Or, Le Monde Prix Choc 1991. *Address:* 179 rue Saint-Jacques, Paris 75005, France (home). *Telephone:* 1-43-25-78-36 (home). *Fax:* 1-40-46-00-67 (home). *E-mail:* suzanne.varga@orange .fr (home). *Website:* www.jeanguillou.org.

GULEGHINA, Maria; Belarusian/Armenian/Ukrainian singer (soprano); b. (Maria Meytargian), 9 Aug. 1959, Odessa, Ukraine; two c. *Education:* Odessa Conservatory (studied with Yevgeni Ivanov). *Career:* professional debut at Minsk Opera Theatre 1986; has performed more than 160 times at Metropolitan Opera, New York, performing title roles in Aida, Tosca, Norma, Adriana Lecouvreur, also roles in Macbeth, Nabucco, Andrea Chenier, Pique Dame, etc. 1991–; frequently performs in all major opera houses world-wide, including Vienna State Opera, Covent Garden, Opera Bastille, Bavarian State Opera, Deutsche Opera Berlin, Mariinsky Theatre, Teatro Liceu, Teatro Colon, etc.; opera roles include title roles in Tosca, Aïda, Manon Lescaut, Norma, Fedora, Adriana Lecouvreur, Turandot, as well as Lady Macbeth in Macbeth, Abigaille in Nabucco, Leonora in Il Trovatore, Oberto in La Forza del Destino, Elvira in Ernani, Elisabetta in Don Carlo, Amelia in Simon Boccanegra, Un Ballo in Maschera, Lucrezia in I due Foscari, Desdemona in Otello, Santuzza in Cavalleria Rusticana, Maddalena in Andrea Chénier, Lisa in Pique Dame, Odabella in Attila, others; UNICEF Int. Goodwill Amb.; sang at Winter Paralympics opening ceremony, Sochi 2014. *Television:* Nabucco (Vienna Met), Andrea Chenier, Tosca, Manon Lescaut, Macbeth (all at La Scala), Verdi Arias, Italian Arias (both for NHK), Macbeth and Il Trittico (the Met), Nabucco (Arena di Verona). *Recordings include:* albums include: Tabarro, Oberto, Francesca di Rimini, Pique Dame, Passion of Verismo (live concert recording), Passion of Rachmaninov; video-audio includes: Tosca, Manon Lescaut, Macbeth (all at La Scala, Milan), Andrea Chenier, Nabucco (both at Metropolitan Opera, New York), Andrea Chenier (DVD, Teatro Communale di Bologna), Macbeth (DVD, Liceu in Barcelona), Nabucco with James Levine (DVD, Metropolitan Opera). *Honours:* Hon. Bd mem. Int. Paralympic Cttee; Order of Holy Olga, from Patriarch Alexis of Russia; numerous prizes and awards, including First Prize All-Union Glinka Competition 1984, Giovanni Zanatello Prize for her debut at Arena di Verona 1997, Maria Zamboni Gold Medal, Gold Medal, Osaka Festival 1999, Bellini Prize 2001, Arte e Operosita nel Mondo Prize, Milan. *Current Management:* c/o Impresario e.K., Herzog-Welf-Str. 94, 85604 Zorneding, Germany. *Telephone:* (8106) 248808. *Fax:* (8106) 375960. *E-mail:* impresarioek@gmail.com. *Website:* www.impresario-art.com. *E-mail:* info@mariaguleghina.com. *Website:* www .mariaguleghina.com.

GULKE, Peter, PhD; German conductor; b. 29 April 1934, Weimar. *Education:* Franz Liszt Hochschule, Weimar, Friedrich Schiller Univ., Jena and Karl Marx Univ., Leipzig. *Career:* Repetiteur, Rudolstadt Theatre 1959; Music Dir, Stendal 1964 and Potsdam 1966; Stralsund 1972–76; Kapellmeister, Dresden Opera 1976; Musical Dir, Weimar 1981; Musicologist, Technical Univ., Berlin 1984; Musical Dir, Wuppertal Opera 1986–96; work as musicologist includes edition of Symphonic Fragments by Schubert, from sketches, broadcast at the Schubert Congress in Detroit 1978; Lecturer, Hochschule für Musik in Dresden; conducted Poulenc's Dialogues des Carmélites at Wuppertal 1989, to commemorate the bicentenary of the French Revolution, and numerous other operas including the Ring at Wuppertal, Graz, Kassel; Prof., Staatliche Hochschule für Musik, Freiburg 1996–2000. *Recordings include:* Beethoven Piano Concerto of 1784 and Udo Zimmermann's Der Schuhu und der fliegende Prinzessin, works by Schreker, Ravel, Schoenberg, Berg, Webern, Baird; Symphonic Fragments by Schubert, Schumann. *Publications:* Bruckner, Brahms, Zwei Studien, 1989; Schubert und seine Zeit, 1991; Fluchtpunkt Musik, 1994; Triumph der neuen Tonkunst. Mozarts späte Sinfonien und ihr Umfeld, 1998. *Address:* Zum Rebberg 10, 79112 Freiburg, Germany.

GULLBERG JENSEN, Eivind; Norwegian conductor; *Chief Conductor, NDR Radiophilharmonie*; b. 1972. *Education:* studied in Trondheim, Stockholm and Vienna with Jorma Panula and Leopold Hager, masterclasses with Kurt Masur. *Career:* has conducted orchestras including Oslo Philharmonic, Wiener Symphoniker, Rotterdam Philharmonic, Gothenberg Symphony, Bamberger Symphoniker, Orchestre Philharmonique du Luxembourg, Orchestre Nat. de Belgique, Konzerthausorchester Berlin, Münchner and Berliner Philharmonikers, WDR Sinfonieorchester, Deutsches Symphonie-Orchester Berlin, London Philharmonic Orchestra, Orchestre Nat. de France, Danish Nat. Symphony Orchestra, Bergen Philharmonic (world premiere of Bent Sørensen's Sounds Like You), with musicians including Truls Mørk, Tabea Zimmermann, Martin Fröst, Julia Fischer and Vadim Repin; debut in Japan at Pacific Music Festival, Sapporo 2012; as opera conductor, productions included Jenůfa at ENO, Rusalka, Eugene Onegin and La Bohème at Den Norske Opera, Rusalka at Opernhaus Zürich and Fidelio at Bayerische Staatsoper; Chief Conductor, NDR Radiophilharmonie 2009–. *Recordings include:* Nielsen/Tchaikovsky: Violin Concertos (Preis der Deutschen Schallplattenkritik) 2012, Wolfgang Rihm: Über die Linie II 2012, Grieg: Piano Concerto/Norwegian Dances/Lyric Suite 2012. *Current Management:* Harrison Parrott Ltd, 5–6 Albion Court, Albion Place, London, W6 0QT, England. *Address:* NDR Radiophilharmonie, Rudolf-von-Bennigsen Ufer 22, 30169 Hannover, Germany (office). *E-mail:* eivind@eivindgullbergjensen.com; radiophilharmonie@ndr.de (office). *Website:* www.ndr.de/orchester_chor/ radiophilharmonie (office); www.eivindgullbergjensen.com.

GULYAK, Sofya; Russian pianist; b. 1979, Kazan. *Education:* Kazan State Conservatory, École Normale de Musique, Paris, Incontri col Maestri Piano Acad., Imola, Italy. *Career:* concerts in Russia, Poland, France, Morocco, Norway, Italy and Portugal. *Recording:* La Primavera. *Honours:* winner, William Kapell Int. Piano Competition 2007, winner, Schumann Int. Piano Competition, Pistoia 2008, first prize and Audience Favourite Award, Tivoli Int. Piano Competition, Copenhagen 2008, winner, Leeds Int. Piano Competition 2009.

GULYÁS, Dénes; Hungarian singer (tenor) and politician; b. 31 March 1954, s. of Dénes Gulyás and Mária Szitár; m. Judit Szekeres; two s. one d. *Education:* Liszt Ferenc Acad. of Music. *Career:* joined State Opera, Budapest 1978; debut as Rinuccio in Gianni Schicchi; debut in USA, Carnegie Hall and Avery Fisher Hall, New York; numerous tours in the USA; teacher, Liszt Ferenc Music Conservatory; mem. Országgyülés (Parl.) (Fidesz) for Pest Co. 10th dist 2006–. *Repertoire includes:* Faust, des Grieux (Manon), Werther, Hoffman, Titus (La Clemenza di Tito), Percy (Anne Boleyn), Ernesto (Don Pasquale), Duke of Mantua (Rigoletto), Fenton (Falstaff), Ferrando (Così fan tutte), Don Ottavio, Tamino, Alfredo (La Traviata), Edgardo (Lucia di Lammermoor), Nemorino, Rodolfo (La Bohème), Tom Rakewell (The Rake's Progress). *Recordings include:* Caldara, Albinoni, Sammartini, Vivaldi: Magnificat, Erkel: Hunyadi László 1994. *Honours:* 1st Prize, Parma 1979, won Luciano Pavarotti singing competition, Philadelphia 1981, Franz Liszt Prize 1982, Artist of Merit 1985, Kiváló művész 2000, Hungarian Heritage Award 2014. *Address:* Országgyülés (National Assembly), 1055 Budapest, Kossuth Lajos tér 1–32 (office); 2094 Budapest, Nagykovácsi Pf. 93, Hungary. *Telephone:* (1) 441-4000 (office); (1) 131-2550 (office). *Fax:* (1) 441-5000 (office). *E-mail:* denes.gulyas@parlament.hu (office). *Website:* www.parlament.hu (office).

GUNDE, Peter; Hungarian conductor; b. 1942, Budapest. *Education:* Budapest Conservatory, Franz Liszt Acad., Budapest, took seminars in Weimar and Petersburg with Arvid Jansons. *Career:* oboist, Nat. Orchestra, Budapest 1961–63; Kapellmeister in Miskolc, Hungary 1972–73; Opera Kapellmeister, Hungarian State Opera 1973–75; founder and Dir, Corelli Chamber Orchestra, Budapest 1975–77; Conductor and Artistic Dir of Chorus and Orchestra, Kapisztran and Palestrina Choir, Budapest 1973–77; Dir of the Chamber Orchestra and Lecturer, Int. Youth Festival, Bayreuth 1975–77; Asst to Peter Maag, Christoph von Dohnànyi, Herbert von Karajan, Salzburg Festival 1977–78; Lecturer, Univ. of Bielefeld and Univ. of Osnabrück; guest conductor in Stavanger, Oslo and Hungary 1981–83, and in Tokyo and Israel; concerts with the Sudwesteutschen Kammerorchester in Pforzheim and Reutlingen, Philharmonie Südwestfalen; concerts in Hungary and the USA 1984; broadcasts with the Westdeutschen Rundfunk Cologne 1985–89; concert tour with the Hungarian Virtuosi Orchestra 1990–93. *Address:* Kastanienweg 2, 32139 Spenge, Germany (home).

GUNN, Jacqueline; British stage designer; b. 1959, Scotland. *Career:* opera designs have included The Rake's Progress for Opera Integra, La Voix Humaine at the Bloomsbury Festival, La Pietra del Paragone at Wuppertal, Tannhäuser for New Sussex Opera, Henze's Labirinto at the Munich Biennale, Otello, L'Elisir d'amore and Trovatore for Lucerne Opera and Così fan tutte for ENO 1994.

GUNN, Nathan; American singer (baritone); b. 1970. *Education:* Univ. of Illinois. *Career:* debut, New York Met 1995, as Morales in Carmen; appearances at the Metropolitan include Guglielmo, Paris in Roméo et Juliette, Strauss's Harlequin and Schaunard in La Bohème; European debut as Prince Andrei in Prokofiev's War and Peace at the Opéra Bastille, Paris; season 2000–01 as Guglielmo at Glyndebourne, Mozart's Count in Brussels and Harlequin for the Royal Opera, Covent Garden; concerts with the Chicago Symphony and Cleveland Orchestras and recitals at the Wigmore Hall. *Recordings include:* American Anthems 2009, Just Before Sunrise 2010. *Honours:* Metropolitan Opera Beverly Sills Artist Award 2006. *Current Management:* c/o Opus 3 Artists, 470 Park Avenue South, 9th Floor North, New York, NY 10016, USA. *Telephone:* (212) 584-7500. *Fax:* (646) 300-8200. *E-mail:* info@opus3artists.com. *Website:* www.opus3artists.com; www .nathangunn.com.

GUNS, Jan; Belgian bass clarinettist and basset hornist; *Professor of Bass Clarinet, Royal Flemish Conservatorium, Antwerp* and *Lemmensinstituut, Leuven*; b. 22 Nov. 1951, Antwerp; one s. two d. *Education:* Royal Flemish Conservatorium, Antwerp, summer courses in Nice, France. *Career:* debut with Royal Flemish Opera, Antwerp 1971; Asst Prof. of Clarinet, Royal Conservatorium, Gent 1979; bass clarinet, Opera of Flanders 1980; solo bass clarinet, BRT Philharmonic Orchestra 1983–2010; Assoc. Prof., Royal Flemish Conservatorium, Antwerp 1984, Prof. of Bass Clarinet 1991–; bass clarinet, Gemini Ensemble 1990–; Prof. of Bass Clarinet/Basset Horn, Flanders Centre, Osaka, Japan 1995–; teacher, Int. Music Course, Vitoria-GasteIz, Spain 2006–, Metropolis Music Summer Course, Bornem, Belgium; Prof. of Bass Clarinet, Lemmensinstituut, Leuven 2010–; Conductor, Cor de Clarinets de Valencia 2011–. *Recordings:* Introduction and Concertante for Bass Clarinet and Clarinet Choir, opus 58 (Norman Heim), with Walter Boeykens Clarinet Choir 1986, Harry's Wonderland for Bass Clarinet and two tapes (André Laporte) 1987, Mladi sextet (Leoš Janáček), with Walter Boeykens Ensemble 1992, Spotlights on the Bass Clarinet, Concerto for Bass Clarinet and Concert Band (Jan Hadermann), with Concert Band of the Belgian Guides, conducted by N. Nozy 1993; with Gemini Ensemble: Sonata (Frits Celis) 1993, Van

Heinde en Verre (Wilfried Westerlinck) 1993, Due Concertante (Ivana Loudova) 1993, Giuco per Due (Dietrich Erdmann) 1993, Exercises (Jean Segers) 1993, Tango (Frédéric Devreese) 1993; with Moscow Chamber Soloists: Trio Classicum and Gemini Ensemble 2000, Elegie (Dirk Brossé), Zebus (Johan Favoreel), Divertimento (Alain Craens), Pierrot (Wilfried Westerlinck), Fantasy Quintet (York Bowen), Divertimento (Akira Yuyama), Duo-Sonata (Charles Camilleri), Experience (Alain Craens); with Hans Ryckelynck: Lied for bass clarinet and piano (Francois Rasse) 2005, Sonatine for bass clarinet and piano (Bohuslav Martinu) 2005, Sonate for bass clarinet and piano (Paul Hindemith) 2005, Cyclus for bass clarinet and piano (August Verbesselt) 2005, Sonate for bass clarinet and piano (Othmar Schoeck) 2005; Klage for bass clarinet solo (Terry Winter Owens) 2005, Da uno a cinque for bass clarinet and string quartet (Frits Celts) 2005, Look, a bass clarinet in my garden! for bass clarinet solo (Wilfried Westerlinck) 2005, Tre Sentimenti, Three Moods for Bass Clarinet and Symphonic Band (Jan Van der Roost) with Tokyo Kosei Wind Orchestra conducted by Douglas Bostock 2005, Suite for bass clarinet and piano (Dirk Brossé) with Anastasia Kozhushko 2010, Suite for bass clarinet and symphonic band (Dirk Brossé), Spotlights on the Bass Clarinet, Concerto for bass clarinet and concert band (Jan Hadermann) with La Armónica (Buñol, Valencia) conducted by Frank De Vuyst 2013. *Honours:* Fugue Trophy, Union of Belgian Composers 2010. *Address:* Hagelandstraat 48, 2660 Hoboken (Antwerp), Belgium. *Telephone:* (3) 288-9184. *E-mail:* guns .jan@telenet.be. *Website:* www.janguns.be.

GUNSON, Ameral Blanche Tregurtha, AGSM; British singer (mezzo-soprano) and voice teacher; *Professor of Vocal Studies, Guildhall School of Music and Drama*; b. 25 Oct. 1948, London; d. of Charles Cumbria and Auriol Cornwall; m. 1st Maurice Powell 1969 (divorced 1974); m. 2nd Philip Kay 1979; two s. *Education:* Convent of Jesus and Mary, London and Guildhall School of Music and Drama. *Career:* freelance singing career 1972–74, with BBC Singers 1976–80; solo singing career in Britain and abroad, Proms Seasons 1979, 1985, 1988, 1989, 1990; Prof. of Vocal Studies, Guildhall School of Music and Drama 2004–09; Prof. of Vocal Studios, Trinity Laban 2007–12; runs "Singing and Imagination" courses, Jackdaws Trust; teacher, AIMS Int. Courses. *Recordings:* Britten's Peter Grimes (Gramophone Award 1997), The Rape of Lucretia, Verdi's Requiem, Copland's In the Beginning; numerous BBC recordings. *Honours:* Lubslith Asscn Award for vocal teaching (Finland) 1997. *Address:* 40 Brooklands Way, Redhill, Surrey, RH1 2BW, England. *Telephone:* (1737) 762726.

GUNSON, Emily Jill, BMus, PhD, LMusA, LRAM, LGSM, ARCM; Australian flautist and musicologist; b. 28 Jan. 1956, Melbourne, Vic. *Education:* Univ. of Western Australia, studied with William Bennett. *Career:* concerto debut 1973; Prin. Flute, West Australian Arts Orchestra 1982–83; performances with West Australian and Sydney Symphony Orchestras; Artistic Dir, Leader, Australian chamber ensembles, W.A. Mozarteum, Wendling Quartet, Cambini Quintet, Emanuel Ensemble, Music'Autentica, performing on both modern and historical flutes; Dir Avon Valley Spring Chamber Music Festival 2004–; guest artist, Mozart Gesellschaft Kurpfalz; Dir Mozart 250th Anniversary Concert Series, Perth 2006; musicological research in field of 18th century flute history, performance and repertoire; int. authority on flautist and composer Johann Baptist Wendling and Wendling family of musicians and singers in 18th century Mannheim and Munich. *Publications include:* Johann Baptist Wendling (1723–1797): Life, Works, Artistry and Influence, Including a Thematic Catalogue of all his Compositions 1999; contrib. to The Court of Carl Theodor: A Paradise for Flautists, in Quellen und Studien zur Geschichte der Mannheimer Hofkapelle, Vol. 8 2002; seven articles in New Grove Dictionary (second edn); RISM errata; 18th and 19th Century Flute Music (ed.). *Honours:* Médaille d'honneur de la Ville de Ribeauvillé (France) 2000. *Current Management:* c/o Flutissimo, PO, Clackline, WA 6564, Australia. *Telephone:* 417-984887 (mobile). *Website:* www.flutissimo.com.au. *Telephone:* (8) 9574-1591 (home). *E-mail:* emily@emilygunson.com. *Website:* www.emilygunson.com.

GUNTER, John Forsyth, DipAD; British fmr stage designer and costume designer; b. 31 Oct. 1938, England; s. of Herbert Gunter and Charlotte Gunter; m.; two d. *Education:* Cen. School of Art and Design (now Central St Martin's School of Art), London. *Career:* Head of Theatre Dept, Cen. School of Art and Design; Head of Design, Nat. Theatre, London; opera designs for the Glyndebourne Festival include Albert Herring, Simon Boccanegra, Porgy and Bess (British Co. premiere 1986), La Traviata and Falstaff; Le nozze di Figaro 1994, revived 1997, Peter Grimes and Otello (also for Chicago Lyric Opera); further engagements with ENO, WNO, Scottish Opera, Opera North and the Salzburg Festival; La Scala, Milan and opera houses at Munich, Cologne, Hamburg, Buenos Aires, Sydney and Los Angeles; original 1857 version of Simon Boccanegra for Covent Garden 1997; season 1996–97 with Samson et Dalila for Queensland Opera; also Ernani for Nat. Reise Opera, The Netherlands, and Der fliegende Holländer for Covent Garden; revival of Albert Herring at Glyndebourne Festival and tour with GTO 2002 (from 1985 production at Glyndebourne); musicals, Guys and Dolls and Anything Goes at Royal Nat. Theatre 2002, revived for the West End; Roméo et Juliette, for Los Angeles Opera, revived for Lyric Opera, Chicago; revival of Otello for Glyndebourne Festival 2005; Peter Grimes, for Salzburg (sets and costumes) 2006; Don Carlo for Los Angeles Opera; Sir John in Love at ENO; Porgy and Bess The Musical, Savoy Theatre 2006, DOUBT for Tricycle Theatre 2007, Der Fliegende Holländer for Mariinksy Theatre, St Petersburg 2008, Simon Boccanegra for Covent Garden and Albert Herring for Glyndebourne 2008;

numerous designs for theatre productions worldwide and several designs for dance and ballet. *Honours:* SWET Award for Best Designer (for Guys and Dolls, Nat. Theatre) 1982, Olivier Award for Best Designer (for Wild Honey, Royal Nat. Theatre) 1984, Primetime Emmy Award for Best Design (for Porgy and Bess) 1994, Best Set Designer, Theatregoers' Choice (for Anything Goes and Love's Labour's Lost, Royal Nat. Theatre) 2004.

GUO, Lanying; Chinese singer; b. 31 Dec. 1930, Ping Tao Co., Shanxi Prov.; d. of Guo Yingjie and Liu Furong; m. Wan Mingyuan 1962; one s. two d. *Education:* People's Univ., Beijing. *Career:* mem. Chinese Opera 1946–49, Leading Actress 1949–78; Pres. Chinese Art Cttee and mem. Council of China and Foreign Countries' Friendship Asscn 1949–78; Deputy 1st to 6th NPC; mem. Cttee Chinese Literature and Art Asscn 1955–88; Prof. China's Music Coll. 1980–82; mem. Council Chinese Music Asscn, Drama Asscn 1980–82; f. Guo Lanying Art School, Guangdong 1986; Dir China's Nat. Opera; Pres. Chinese Nat. Folk Art Coll. of Guangzhou 1986. *Films include:* Xiao Erhei's Marriage 1952, The East is Red 1964, Embroidering Silk Banner With Words of Gold 1965. *Recordings include:* The White-haired Girl, The Unjust Verdict of Widow Du E, The Best of Guo Lanying 1990. *Publication:* Selected Songs of Guo Lanying 1980. *Honours:* Stalin Prize 1954. *Address:* Chinese National Folk Art College of Guangzhou, Fei E Ling, Shatou, Panyu Co., 511490 Guangzhou, Guangdong, People's Republic of China. *Telephone:* (20) 4870408 (office); (20) 4878200 (home).

GUO, Wenjing; Chinese composer; b. 1 Feb. 1956, Chongqing; one d. *Education:* Central Conservatory of Music, Beijing. *Career:* violinist, Dance and Choral Ensemble of Chongqing 1970–77; Dean and Prof., Composition Dept, Central Conservatory of Music, Beijing 1983–; works performed at major festivals in Europe and by orchestras world-wide, including BBC Scottish Symphony Orchestra, China National Symphony Orchestra, Cincinnati Percussion Group, Göteborg Symphony Orchestra, Hong Kong Chinese Orchestra, Hong Kong Philharmonic Orchestra, HuaXia Chinese Ensemble, Lincoln Center Chamber Music Soc., London Sinfonietta, New York Music Consort, Nieuw Ensemble, Taiwan Symphony Orchestra; Visiting Scholar, Asian Cultural Council, USA; guest lecturer, Swedish Royal Inst. of Music, Univ. of Cincinnati, Manhattan School of Music; mem. Asscn of Chinese Musicians. *Film appearance:* Broken Silence. *Composition for film and television includes:* Hong fen 1994, Yangguang Canlan de Rizi 1994, Riding Alone for Thousands of Miles 2005. *Compositions include:* Ba 1982, The River of Sichuan 1981, Concerto 1986, Shu Dao Nan 1987, Shou Kong Shan 1991, Yun Nan 1993, The Wolfcub's Village (opera) 1993 (orchestral suite) 1994, Drama op. 23 1995, Inscriptions on Bone op. 24 1996, Concertino pour violoncelle et ensemble op. 26 1997, Echoes of Heaven and Earth op. 31 1998, The Night Banquet (opera) 1998, Journeys 2004. *Address:* c/o Central Conservatory of Music, 43 Baojia Street, Xicheng District, Beijing 100031, People's Republic of China. *Telephone:* (10) 6641 2585. *Fax:* (10) 6641 3138. *E-mail:* imecwy@public.bta.net.cn. *Website:* www.ccom.edu.cn.

GUO, Yue; Chinese flautist and composer; b. 1958, Beijing; m. Clare Farrow. *Education:* Guildhall School of Music, UK. *Career:* plays traditional Chinese bamboo flute and silver flute; left China 1982; soloist 1990–; also performs with brother Guo Yi as Guo Brothers at int. festivals including WOMAD; performed bamboo flute concerto with BBC Concert Orchestra, WOMAD 1999; played on soundtrack of several films including The Killing Fields 1984, The Last Emperor 1987; has worked with numerous musicians including Peter Gabriel and the Chieftains. *Recordings include:* Yuan (with Guo Yi and Guo Xan) 1990, Trisan (with Joji Hirota and Pol Brennan) 1992, Red Ribbon (with Joji Hirota) 1995, Music, Food and Love 2007. *Publications include:* Music, Food and Love (with Clare Farrow) 2006, Little Leap Forward 2008. *Address:* 76A Mount Ararat Road, Richmond, Surrey, TW10 6PN, England (office). *E-mail:* guoyue@mac.com (office).

GUPTA, Rolf; Norwegian conductor and composer; b. 14 Jan. 1967, Uppsala, Sweden. *Education:* Sweelinck Conservatorium Amsterdam, Sibelius Acad., studied composition with Per Nørgård. *Career:* Chief Conductor, Norwegian Radio Orchestra 2003–05, Norwegian Baroque Orchestra 2004–06; Chief Conductor, Kristiansand Symphony Orchestra 2006–13, Artistic Dir 2006–; worked with orchestras and ensembles including RSO Frankfurt, BBC Symphony Orchestra, Konzerthausorchester Berlin, Stuttgart Radio Symphony, Gothenburg Symphony, Orchestra della Toscana, MDR Symphony Orchestra Leipzig, Finnish Radio Symphony, Sydney Symphony, Klangforum Wien and Ensemble Intercontemporain; worked closely with composers including Berio, Lindberg, Grisey, Nørgård, Wallin, Benjamin and especially Henze, whose works he conducted with Scharoun Ensemble of Berlin Philharmonic, Oslo Philharmonic, Russian Nat. Orchestra, WDR Symphony Orchestra and Radio Symphony Orchestra Berlin; conducted world premieres of operas including Gerhard Lang's Der Alte vom Berge at Schwetzingen Festival and Theater Basel; opera productions include Finnish Nat. Opera and Norwegian Opera, La Traviata for Nationaltheater Mannheim, Henze's Der Prinz von Homburg for Nationale ReisOpera, Grieg's Peer Gynt with Swedish Radio Symphony, Norwegian Opera and the Mariinsky Choir at the White Nights Festival, La Traviata and Die Zauberflöte for Frankfurt Opera and Jonathan Miller production of Don Giovanni; festival appearances include Radio France Présences, Moscow Easter, Ultima and Savonlinna Opera Festival; fmrly Artistic Dir, MAGMA2002 Berlin. *Compositions include:* Chiaroscuro. *Recordings include:* Tango Ballet, Thommessen's BullsEye, Francesconi's Cobalt Scarlet: Two Colours of Dawn, Chiaroscuro, Arne Nordheim Epitaffio 2011. *Current Management:* c/o Konzertdirektion Martin

Müller, Uhrs Knäppken 8, 59320 Ennigerloh-Ostenfelde, Germany. *Telephone:* (2524) 263480. *Fax:* (2524) 263481. *Website:* www.kdmueller.eu. *E-mail:* rolfgupta@gmail.com.

GÜRA, Werner; German singer (tenor); b. 1964, Munich. *Education:* Salzburg Mozarteum, studied in Basel with Kurt Widmer and in Amsterdam with Margreet Honig. *Career:* mem. Semperoper, Dresden 1994–99; Guest Artist, Staatsoper Berlin 1998–; well-known for Lieder interpretations, performing recitals at Wigmore Hall, London, Amsterdam Concertgebouw, Lincoln Center, New York, Schubertiade, Schwarzenberg; concert performances include Salzburg Festival, Rheingau Musik Festival 2004, 2009, 2011, Innsbruck Festival, Lucerne Festival 2011; teaches voice and chamber music, Zürcher Hochschule der Künste. *Recordings include:* Bach's Christmas Oratorio 1997, St Matthew Passion 1998, Bach's cantata Wir danken dir, Gott, wir danken dir 2007, Schubert's Die Winterreise (BBC Music Magazine Award, Vocal Category 2011) 2010, Schubert: Willkommen und Abschied (ECHO Klassik Award for Song Recording of the Year) 2012. *Address:* Zürcher Hochschule der Künste, Florhofgasse 6, 8001 Zürich, Switzerland (office). *Telephone:* 434465140 (office). *Website:* www.zhdk.ch (office).

GURIAKOVA, Olga; Russian singer (soprano); b. 1971, Novokuznetsk. *Education:* Moscow Conservatoire. *Career:* appearances at the Stanislavsky Musical Theatre, Moscow, from 1994; Kirov Opera, St Petersburg, from 1996, as Mimi, Natasha in War and Peace, Tatiana, Maria in Tchaikovsky's Mazeppa, Donna Anna, Desdemona and Elvira in Ernani; Further engagements as Gorislava in Ruslan and Lyudmilla and Militrissa in Rimsky-Korsakov's Tsar Saltan; Tours of Europe, Israel and the Far East with the Kirov; Tchaikovsky's Maria at the New York Met and Iolanta at Carnegie Hall, 1998; Season 1999–2000 with Maria and Donna Anna in St Petersburg and Natasha at the Opéra Bastille, Paris; sang with the Kirov at Covent Garden, 2000. *Honours:* winner Rimsky-Korsakov International Competition, Russian Golden Mask and Casta Diva Competition 1996.

GUSCHLBAUER, Theodor; Austrian conductor; b. 14 April 1939, Vienna. *Education:* Vienna Acad. of Music. *Career:* conducted the Vienna Baroque Ensemble 1961–69; Asst at the Vienna Volksoper 1964–66; Conductor of the Salzburg Landestheater 1966–68, Lyon Opéra 1969–75; General Musik-Direktor, Linz-Bruckner Symphony Orchestra and the Landestheater Linz 1975–83; Chief Conductor, Strasbourg Philharmonic 1983–97, Rhineland-Palatinate Philharmonic 1997–2001; guest appearances at many festivals, including those at Salzburg, Aix-en-Provence, Prague, Bregenz, Flanders, Oxford, Lucerne, Montreux, Ascona, Maggio Musicale Fiorentino; regular guest conductor with the Vienna and Hamburg Operas, Geneva, Paris (Bastille), Munich, Cologne, Lisbon and Zürich. *Recordings:* Symphonies by Mozart, Haydn, Schubert and Beethoven; Concertos by Strauss, Mozart, Haydn, Mendelssohn and Weber; Mozart's Divertimento K287, Cassation K99, Masses K194 and K220, Vesperae Solennes, Sinfonia Concertante K297b, Bassoon Concerto, Flute Concertos (Rampal), and Piano Concertos K271, K453 and K467 (Maria Joao Pires); K415; K488; Strauss Burleske, Horn Concerto No. 2 and Oboe Concerto; Beethoven's 6th Symphony and Schubert's Ninth, with the New Philharmonia; Bruckner 7, D'Indy, Hindemith, Grieg, Rachmaninov, Waldteufel, Dvořák, Scriabin, Vieuxtemps. *Honours:* Chevalier, Légion d'honneur 1997; seven Grand Prix du Disque; Mozart Prize, Goethe Foundation, Basel 1988.

GUSSMANN, Wolfgang; German stage designer and costume designer; b. 9 Aug. 1952, Oldenburg. *Career:* freelance stage and costume designer 1979–; has worked almost exclusively with stage directors Willy Decker and Andreas Homoki, principally in the opera houses of Vienna, Munich, Paris, Amsterdam, Brussels, Zürich, Dresden, Berlin, Hamburg, Leipzig and Cologne; in collaboration with Willy Decker, has designed new productions of Capriccio at Maggio musicale Fiorentino, Billy Budd and Lulu in Vienna, Eugene Onegin, Der fliegende Holländer and Lulu in Paris, Wozzeck, Elektra, Katja Kabanowa, Boris Godunov in Amsterdam, Der Freischutz, Don Giovanni, Die Soldaten, Lear and Der Ring des Niebelungen in Dresden, Riemann's Das Schloss at Deutsche Oper Berlin and in Munich, Pelléas et Mélisande, Katja Kabanowa and Salome in Hamburg, Tristan und Isolde and Dr Faustus in Leipzig, Tosca in Stuttgart, La Bohème, Le finta giardiniera, Der fliegende Hollander, Billy Budd, Eugene Onegin, Il Trittico in Cologne and La Traviata at the Salzburg Festival; productions with Willy Decker include Pique Dame in Hamburg, Der Rosenkavalier and Don Carlos in Amsterdam, Die tote Stadt at the Salzburg Festival, Vienna, Amsterdam and Barcelona, Albert Herring at Komische Oper and Dresden, Moses und Aron in Vienna and Roméo et Juliette in Salzburg; in collaboration with Andreas Homoki, has designed new productions of Die Frau ohne Schatten and Orphée in Geneva, Idomeneo, Arabella and Manon Lescaut in Munich, Carmen, Lulu and Capriccio in Amsterdam, Hansel and Gretel in Frankfurt and in Berlin for Deutsche Oper, Die Frau ohne Schatten in Paris, Rigoletto in Hamburg, Macbeth in Leipzig, Tannhäuser in Paris and Die lustige Witwe and Der Zwerg/Eine florentinische Tragödie at Komische Oper Berlin; productions with Andreas Homoki include Der Zwerg/Eine florentinische Tragödie in Brussels, Turandot in Dresden, Roméo et Juliette and Königskinder in Munich and Eine florentinische Tragödie in Milan. *Honours:* Chevalier des Arts et des Lettres 2002. *Address:* Ziegelhofstrasse 40, 26121 Oldenburg, Germany (home).

GUSTAFSON, Nancy; American singer (soprano); b. 27 June 1956, Evanston, IL; m. Brian Dickie. *Education:* studied in San Francisco (Adler Fellowship Programme). *Career:* San Francisco Opera debut as Freia in Das

Rheingold: returned as Musetta in La Bohème and Antonia in Les Contes d'Hoffmann and Elettra in Idomeneo; Opera Colorado as Donna Elvira; Minnesota Opera as Leila in Les Pêcheurs de Perles; Canadian debut as Violetta for Edmonton Opera; Festival performances as Rosalinda in Sante Fe and Britten's Helena for Chataugua Opera; European debut as Rosalinde in Paris, season 1984–85; Glyndebourne debut as Donna Elvira, while tour to Hong Kong: Festival appearances as Katya Kabanova, in a new production of Janáček's opera, 1988, returned 1990; Chicago Lyric Opera debut as Marguerite in Faust; Covent Garden debut 1988, as Freia; Scottish Opera 1989, as Violetta; Metropolitan Opera debut 1989, as Musetta; sang Freia in Rheingold at Munich, 1990; Seattle Opera 1989, as Elettra in Idomeneo, Antonia in Les Contes d'Hoffmann 1990; sang Eva at La Scala and Amelia in a new production of Simon Boccanegra at Brussels 1990; Sang Lisa in The Queen of Spades at Glyndebourne 1992; Season 1991–92 as Violetta and Alice Ford at Toronto; Sang the Letter Scene from Eugene Onegin at the 1993 London Proms; Eva in a new production of Die Meistersinger at Covent Garden, 1993; Concert engagements in Mahler's 8th Symphony, with the San Francisco Symphony, and at the Carmel Bach Festival, California; Engaged as Floyd's Susannah, Houston, 1996; Returned to Covent Garden as Eva, 1997; Season 2000–01 as Laurie Moss in Copland's The Tender Land, at the Barbican, Ellen Orford in Los Angeles, and Mathilde in Guillaume Tell for the Vienna Staatsoper. *Current Management:* Zemsky/Green Artists Management, 730 Fifth Avenue, Suite 1802, New York, NY 10019, USA. *Telephone:* (212) 300-8003. *Fax:* (212) 300-8001. *E-mail:* zgartists@aol.com. *Website:* www .zemskygreen.com.

GUSTAVSSON, Jan; Swedish musician (trumpet); b. 8 Dec. 1959, Vadstena; m. Jessica Gustavsson 1996, one s. *Education:* Gothenburg Music Conservatory. *Career:* debut in Lisbon, Portugal 1989; principal trumpet, Norrköping 1982–92, Royal Stockholm Philharmonic Orchestra 1992–; trumpet soloist appearances in Sweden, Portugal, Austria and Switzerland. *Recording:* Leopold Mozart, Giuseppe Tartini trumpet concertos (as soloist with Winterthur Stadtorchester) 1989. *Honours:* second prize Budapest Int. Trumpet Solo Competition 1984.

GUTH, Martha Angeline, BMus, MMus; Canadian singer (soprano); b. Lancaster, UK; d. of DeLloyd Guth and Katherine Guth; m. Ricardo Lugo. *Education:* Oberlin Conservatory of Music, Cincinnati Coll. Conservatory of Music. *Career:* began career with the Canadian Opera Company; Young Artist, Santa Fe Opera 2006–07; performances include Cornelia in Giulio Cesae in Egitto with the Canadian Opera Company, the first lady in The Magic Flute with the Grazer Oper in Graz, Austria, the Countess in Marriage of Figaro in Mallorca, Spain, Pamina in The Magic Flute, Konstanze in The Abduction in Augsburg, Germany, Alcina in Handel's Alcina in Lucca, Italy, Micaela in Bizet's Carmen, Poulenc's La Voix Humaine; faculty mem., Vancouver Int. Song Inst. *Honours:* winner, Jeunesses Musicals Int. Competition, Montréal 2001, Wigmore Hall/Kohn Foundation Int. Song Competition 2007, Cincinnati Coll. Conservatory of Music Fellowship, Canada Council for the Arts Grant. *Current Management:* c/o John Miller, Pinnacle Arts Management, 889 Ninth Avenue, 2nd Floor, New York, NY 10019, USA. *Telephone:* (212) 397-7915. *Fax:* (212) 397-7920. *E-mail:* jmiller@pinnaclearts .com. *Website:* www.pinnaclearts.com. *E-mail:* marthaguth@hotmail.com (office).

GUTIERREZ, Horacio; Cuban pianist; b. 28 Aug. 1948, Havana; m. Patricia Asher. *Education:* Juilliard School of Music, USA. *Career:* debut aged 11 with Havana Symphony Orchestra; performed most major symphony orchestras as soloist in recitals throughout the world; appearances on BBC television and also in France and USA; tours in USA, Canada, Europe, South America, Israel, USSR, Japan. *Recordings include:* Rachmaninov Piano Concertos No. 2 and 3 with Lorin Maazel and Pittsburgh Symphony, Brahms Nos 1 and 2, Tchaikovsky No. 1. *Honours:* second prize Tchaikovsky Competition 1970, Avery Fisher Prize 1982. *Address:* 3426 Springhill Road, Latayette, CA 94549, USA.

GUTMAN, Natalia Grigorievna; Russian/German cellist; b. 14 Nov. 1942; m. Oleg Kagan (deceased); three c. *Education:* Gnessin Music School, Moscow under R. Shaposhnikov, Moscow Conservatory under Prof. Kozolupova and postgraduate studies in Leningrad under Mstislav Rostropovich. *Career:* tours include visits to Europe, USA and Japan, appearing with the Berlin Philharmonic Orchestra, Vienna Philharmonic Orchestra, London Symphony Orchestra, Orchestre Nat. de France and Orchestre de Paris; played chamber music in USSR and Europe with Eliso Virsaladze and Oleg Kagan; played sonatas, trios and quartets with Sviatoslav Richter; plays sonata and concerto written for her by Alfred Schnittke; solo tours include USA with USSR State Symphony Orchestra and Yevgeny Svetlanov, Italy with BBC Symphony and Yuri Temirkanov, USSR with Sir John Pritchard; performed with Royal Philharmonic Orchestra under Yuri Temirkanov, Royal Festival Hall, London, Concertgebouw, London Philharmonic, Munich Philharmonic, Berlin Philharmonic, Orchestre Nat. de France, Los Angeles Philharmonic under André Previn, Chicago Symphony under Claudio Abbado 1988–89; fmr teacher at Moscow Conservatory; Prof., Stuttgart Conservatory 1997–2004; f. Oleg Kagan Music Festival, Kreuth and Moscow. *Honours:* Winner, Vienna Student Festival Competition, Dvořák Competition, Prague, ARD Competition, Munich. *Address:* Natalia Gutman's Office, c/o Tallafocs els Ferros 7, 46012 Valencia, Spain. *Telephone:* 6-9380483 (mobile). *E-mail:* cellogutman@ gmail.com.

GUTTLER, Ludwig; German musician (trumpet), conductor and academic; b. 13 June 1943, Sosa. *Education:* Leipzig Hochschule für Musik with Armin Mennel. *Career:* debut as soloist with orchestra 1958; solo trumpeter, Handel Festival Orchestra, Halle 1965–, and Dresden Philharmonic 1969–81; founder and Dir, Leipziger Bach-Collegium 1976–, Blechbläserensemble Ludwig Guttler 1978–; Virtuosi Saxoniae 1985–; solo tours worldwide; Lecturer, Dresden Hochschule für Musik 1972–80, Prof. 1980–, Head of masterclasses in wind instruments 1982–; guest teacher at Weimar Int. Music Seminar 1977–, also in Austria, Japan and the USA. *Recordings:* more than 21 albums. *Honours:* GDR Nat. Prize 1978, German Phonoakademie Recording Prize 1983, Music Prize, City of Frankfurt 1989.

GUTTMAN, Albert; Romanian pianist; b. 12 Oct. 1937, Galati. *Education:* Conservatoire of Music, Bucharest, Florica Musicescu, studied with Dagobert Buchholz, Santa Cecilia Conservatoire, Rome with Guido Agosti. *Career:* Prof. of Piano, Chamber Music and Piano Accompaniment, Bucharest Conservatoire of Music 1960–76; Official Asst for Chamber Music, Santa Cecilia Nat. Acad., Rome 1972; invited by Yehudi Menuhin to teach chamber music at Int. Menuhin Acad. of Music, Gstaad, Switzerland 1982–84; taught summer courses in Italy and Switzerland 1969–83; Prof. of Piano, Musikschule Saanenland, Gstaad and Prof. of Piano Accompaniment, including permanent masterclass for graduate pianists specializing in piano accompaniment, Musik Akademie der Stadt Basel 1983–; worldwide tours and participant in numerous festivals; radio and TV recordings worldwide; recitals with Radu Aldulescu and Silvia Marcovici, and frequent performances with Yehudi Menuhin, Pierre Fournier, Ruggiero Ricci, Enrico Mainardi, Jean Pierre Rampal, Christian Ferras, Lola Bobesco, Pina Carmirelli, Ivry Gitlis, Raphael Sommer. *Recordings include:* Beethoven, Complete Edition Five Sonatas for Piano and Cello, Radu Aldulescu on cello; Schumann, Frauen Liebe und Leben; De Falla, Siete Canciones Populares Españolas, Elena Cernei, mezzo; Shostakovich Sonata Op 40 for Cello and Piano; Hindemith Sonata Op 11 No. 3 for Cello and Piano, Radu Aldulescu on Cello; Bach Sonata No. 4 for Violin and Piano BWV 1017; Beethoven Sonata Op 30 No. 3 for Piano and Violin, Lola Bobesco on Violin; Brahms Sonata No. 2 Op 100 in A major and No. 3 Op 108 in D minor for Piano and Violin, Angela Gavrila Dieterle on Violin; Beethoven Seven Variations in E flat WoO46 for Piano and Cello, Mirel Iancovici on Cello. *Honours:* Hephzibah Menuhin Int. Prize for Pianists 1981. *Address:* Chalet Bel Air, Appartement 216, 3780 Gstaad, Switzerland.

GUY, Barry John, AGSM; British musician (double bass, baroque bass) and composer; b. 22 April 1947, Lewisham, London; m. Maya Homburger. *Education:* Guildhall School of Music and Drama. *Career:* freelance bassist; Prin., City of London Sinfonia, Academy of Ancient Music, London Classical Players –1995; solo recitalist; Artistic Dir London Jazz Composers Orchestra, Barry Guy New Orchestra; plays with improvisation focused groups Parker/ Guy/Lytton, Guy/Gustafsson/Strid/Marilyn Crispell/Guy/Lytton, Cecil Taylor, Bill Dixon Quartet, Marilyn Crispell, Homburger-Guy Duo, Demierre/Guy/ Niggli, Vandermark/Guy/Sanders, Fernandez/Guy/Lopez, Turkmani/Guy Duo; mem. Musicians Union, PRS, MCPS, BACS. *Compositions include:* Statements ll 1972, String Quartet III 1973, Anna 1974, Play 1976, EOS for double bass and orchestra 1977, Details 1978, Hold Hands and Sing 1978, Waiata 1980, Pfiff 1981, Flagwalk 1974, Voyages of the Moon 1983, RondOH! 1985, Circular for solo oboe 1985, The Road to Ruin 1986, Harmos 1987, The Eye of Silence 1988, UM 1788 1989, Look Up! 1990, Theoria 1991, After the Rain 1992, Bird Gong Game 1992, Mobile Herbarium 1992, Portraits 1993, Witch Gong Game 1993, Witch Gong Game ll 1994, Un Coup Dés 1994, Buzz 1994, Celebration 1995, Ceremony 1995, Three Pieces for orchestra 1995, Concerto for orchestra, Fallingwater 1996, Double Trouble Two 1996, Holyrood 1998, Redshift 1998, Bubblets 1998, Remembered Earth 1998, Octavia 1999, Dakryon 1999, Inscape (Tableaux) 2000, Nasca Lines 2001, Switch 2001, Inachis 2002, Aglais 2002, Anaklasis 2002, Folio 2002, Oort-Entropy 2004, Lysandra 2004, Only Today 2006, Convergence 2006, Magical Mobiles and a Meditation 2006, Aglais Ex 2007, Radio Rondo, ihi, Horizontal Blue, Phases of the Night, Hommage à Max Bill, Schweben -ay, but can ye? Four Edo Songs, 2008, Marsyas 2009, fff (Fixed, Fragmented, Fluid) 2010, Amphi 2010, Tales of Enchantment 2010, Nig(ra) Z(s)um 2011, Time Passing... 2012–13. *Recordings include:* Ode 1972, Endgame 1979, Incision 1981, Tracks 1983, Zürich Concerts 1988, Double Trouble 1990, Elsie jo Live 1992, Theoria 1992, After the Rain 1993, Fizzles 1993, Portraits 1994, Vade Mecum 1994, Imaginary Values 1994, Witch Gong Game ll 1994, Cascades 1995, Obliquities 1995, Iskra 1903 1995, Three Pieces for orchestra 1997, Sensology 1997, Frogging 1997, Natives and Aliens 1997, Bingo 1998, Double Trouble Two 1998, At the Vortex 1998, Ceremony 1999, In Darkness Let Me Dwell 2000, Melancholy 2000, Nailed 2000, Dividuality 2001, Inscape – Tableaux 2001, Odyssey 2002, Symmetries 2002, Celebration 2002, Inachis 2003, Ithaca 2004, Gubbröra 2004, Brainforest 2004, Dakryon 2005, Folio 2005, Stringer 2005, Zafiro 2005, Aurora 2006, Stringer 2006, Falkirk 2006, Topos 2007, Portrait 2007, Tarfala 2008, Aglais 2008, Phases of the Night 2008, Fox Fire 2009, The Moment's Energy 2009, Crossing Borders 2009, Sinners Rather Than Saints 2009, Radio Rondo 2009, Set 2009, Flashback 2009, Multitude 2010, Prayer for Peace 2010, Nightwork 2010, Valencia 2010, Scenes in the House of Music 2010, Morning Glory 2010, Attikos 2010, Polisation 2010, Harmos (DVD) 2011, Syzygy 2011, Goldsmiths 2011, Lysandra 2011, Spiegel 2011, Games and Improvisations 2012, METAL! 2012, Hexentrio 2012, Hasselt 2012, Tales of Enchantment 2012, Schwaben - Ay, But Can Ye? 2012, Lava 2012, Buxton Orr 2012, Brigantin 2012, One Four and Two Twos 2012, Mad Dogs 2013, Live at Maya Recordings Festival –

Parker/Guy/Lytton 2013, The Dowland Project – Night Sessions 2013, Iskra 1903, South on the Northern 2013, A Moment's Liberty 2013, Barry Guy New Orchestra: Amphi/Radio Rondo 2014, Slip, Slide and Collide 2014. *Honours:* Radcliffe Award 1st Prize 1973, Royal Philharmonic Prize for Chamber Scale Composition 1991, Jt Prizewinner, Hilliard Composition Prize 1994, Abendzeitung (Munich) Sterne des Jahres 1999, Choc de l'année 2001, 2005. *Address:* POB 52, 8477 Oberstammheim, Switzerland (home). *Telephone:* (52) 7402971 (home). *Fax:* (52) 7402972 (home). *E-mail:* barry@aglais.ch (home). *Website:* www.maya-recordings.com (home).

GUYER, Joyce; American singer (soprano); b. 1961. *Career:* sang Mozart's Constanze at Washington 1987; Chicago Opera 1988, as Gluck's Euridice; Buxton Festival 1989, as Livia in Cimarosa's L'Italiana in Londra; Metropolitan Opera, New York from 1993, in Jenůfa, Ariadne auf Naxos, Parsifal and Idomeneo; season 1991 at Montpellier and Nice, as Constanze and Donna Anna; Bayreuth Festival 1995–96, in The Ring and Parsifal. *Recordings include:* videos of Parsifal and Idomeneo.

GUZMAN, Hector, BM, MM; American (b. Mexican) conductor and organist; *Music Director, Plano Symphony Orchestra*; b. 27 Sept. 1956, Zacatecas, Mexico; s. of Efren Guzmán and Ofelia Mejía; m. Daisy Piantini; one s. one d. *Education:* Conservatory of Music in Mexico City, Univ. of North Texas, Southern Methodist Univ. in Dallas, Accademia Musicale Chigiana, Siena, Italy. *Career:* studied organ with Alfred Mouledous and Robert Anderson; studied conducting with Anshel Brusilow, Helmuth Rilling, Carlo Maria Giulini, Eduardo Mata; as a soloist, performed in many venues including Meyerson Symphony Hall, Dallas, Morelia Cathedral, Guadalajara Cathedral, Chartres Cathedral; Music Dir, Plano Symphony Orchestra, Tex. 1982–; Music Dir Irving Symphony Orchestra, Tex. 1991–; Dir San Angelo Symphony Orchestra, Tex. 2002–; Music Dir Jalisco Philharmonic Orchestra, Mexico 2004–; guest conductor with numerous orchestras, including Monterrey Symphony, Xalapa Symphony, State of Mexico Symphony, UNAM Philharmonic, Philharmonic Soc. Orchestra, Bellas Artes Chamber Orchestra, San Antonio and Dallas Symphonies, Wheeling Symphony, Nat. Symphony of the Dominican Republic, Mexico City Philharmonic, Nat. Symphony of Mexico, Vivaldi Orchestra of Mexico City, Collegium Orchestra of Prague, Czech Republic, Japan Philharmonic, Amadeus Orchestra, Ruffano, Pomeriggi Musicale, Bari Symphony, Milano Classica Orchestra, Italy, orchestras in Spain, Poland, South Korea. *Honours:* Mozart Medal, Embassy of Austria in Mexico City 2008; Winner, solo competitions at Southern Methodist Univ. and Univ. of North Texas, Chamber Soloists Competition First Prize, Manuel Ponce Nat. Organ Competition First Prize, Outstanding Nat. Young Artist Award, Govt of Mexico, Mexican Union of Musicians Golden Lyre Award, Southern Methodist Univ. Meadows Award, Dir par Excellence Award, DeVry Inst., Seven Conductors-One Baton Int. Conducting Competition Winner 2004, Artistic Merit Gold Medal, Govt of Mexico 2005, Artistic Silver Medal, Govt of Zacatecas 2006, "For the Love of Art" Lifetime Achievement Award 2012. *Current Management:* c/o Alexander Djinov, Virtuoso Artists Management, PO Box 250664, Plano, TX 75025-0664, USA. *Telephone:* (469) 682-1842. *Fax:* (972) 208-1880. *E-mail:* djinov@gmail.com. *Website:* virtuosoartistsmanagement.com. *Address:* Plano Symphony Orchestra, 5236 Tennyson Parkway, Building 4, Suite 200, Plano, TX 75024, USA (office). *Telephone:* (972) 473-7262 (office). *Fax:* (972) 473-4639 (office). *E-mail:* info@planosymphony.org (office). *Website:* www.planosymphony.org (office); www.irvingsymphony.com (office).

GWYNNE, David; British singer (bass); b. 1945, Pontnewydd, Cwmbran, Wales. *Education:* Guildhall School, London. *Career:* appearances with Welsh National Opera as Verdi's Zaccaria, and Grand Inquisitor, Wagner's Daland, Pimen in Boris Godunov, Mozart's Basileo and Rocco in Fidelio; Scottish Opera in The Trojans, Peter Grimes, Schnittke's Life with an Idiot, Katya Kabanova, Aida, Oedius Rex and Don Giovanni, as the Commendatore; Engagements with English National Opera in Henze's The Prince of Homburg and Gianni Schicchi; Opera North in Katya Kabanova, Attila, The Love for Three Oranges, Fidelio (Fernando) and Gloriana; Arkel in Pelléas et Mélisande, Ferrando in Il Trovatore and Hermit in Der Freischütz are other roles: Glyndebourne Festival 2000, as Antonio in Le nozze di Figaro.

GYSELYNCK, Jean-Baptiste; Belgian academic; b. 22 March 1946, Ghent; m. Bruyneel Arlette 1946, one s. one d. *Education:* Royal Atheneum of Ghent, Royal Music Conservatory of Ghent and Conservatory of Brussels. *Career:* teacher of counterpoint, Royal Flemish Music Conservatory of Antwerp 1970; Prof. of Harmony, Counterpoint and Composition, Lemmens Inst. of Louvain 1970–79; Prof. of Written Harmony, Royal Music Conservatory of Brussels 1970–, Prof. of Harmony 1974–75. *Compositions include:* Simfonia da Camera 1975, Intermezzi for wood instruments 1977, Trio for strings 1979, Adagio en Allegro for alto saxophone 1979, Diptyque for violin and piano 1980, Illuminatio, Music (for six poems written by Johan Daisne). *Honours:* International Music Competition Queen Elisabeth Laureat of Composition 1980, silver prize of HM Queen Fabiola Composition Competition Sabam 1980.

H

HAAN, Richard; Slovak singer (baritone); b. 1959, Kosice. *Career:* sang at Usti nad Labem and Olomouc, Slovak Nat. Opera at Bratislava 1990–93, Janáček Opera at Brno and Nat. Theatre, Prague, as guest (Verdi's Amonasro and Renato 1994–96); Edinburgh Festival 1990, as Valentin in Faust, Salzburg 1992, in Janáček's From the House of the Dead; US debut 1996, at Virginia Opera, Norfolk, as Wagner's Dutchman; sang Mathis in The Polish Jew by Karel Weis at the Prague State Opera 2001; other roles include Don Giovanni and Gershwin's Porgy; numerous concert appearances.

HAAS, Kenneth, BA; American orchestra executive; b. 8 July 1943, Washington, DC; m. 1st Barbara Dooneief 1964 (divorced 1990); two d.; m. 2nd Signe Johnson 1990; one s. *Education:* Columbia Coll. *Career:* Asst to Managing Dir, New York Philharmonic 1966–70; Asst Gen. Man., Cleveland Orchestra 1970–75, Gen. Man. 1976–87; Gen. Man., Cincinnati Symphony Orchestra 1975–76; Managing Dir, Boston Symphony Orchestra 1987–; Chair. Orchestra Panel, NEA 1982–85, Co-Chair. of Music Overview Panel, NEA 1983–85; Chair. of Challenge Grant Panel, Ohio Arts Council 1985–86; mem. American Symphony Orchestra League (exec. cttee 1980–82, bd of dirs 1993–94), Managers of Major Orchestras, USA (chair. 1980–82).

HAAS, (Benjamin) Michael; British classical producer; *CEO, Coralfox Ltd;* b. 23 Oct. 1954, Charlotte, NC, USA; s. of Douglas Taylor Haas; partner Kevin Bell. *Education:* Vienna Conservatory, Vienna Music Acad. *Career:* fmr Recording Producer and Exec., Decca/London record co., many productions for Sir Georg Solti; fmr Recording Producer and Exec., Sony Classical, later Vice-Pres. A&R, New York, worked with Claudio Abbado and Berlin Philharmonic; worked with many leading classical artists, including Christoph von Dohnanyi, Bernard Haitink, Zubin Mehta, Riccardo Chailly, Mstislav Rostropovich, Hans Werner Henze, Valery Gergiev, Sir Simon Rattle, Radu Lupu, Vladimir Ashkenazy, Alicia de Larrocha, Andras Schiff, Lynn Harrell, Pinchas Zukerman, Maxim Vengerov, Alfred Brendel, Luciano Pavarotti, Plácido Domingo, Kiri Te Kanawa, Cecilia Bartoli, Joan Sutherland, Renée Fleming, Anna Tomowa-Sintow, Hildegard Behrens, Monserat Caballé, Mirella Freni, Christa Ludwig, Lucia Popp, Jessye Norman, Matthias Goerne, Sumi Jo, Bryn Terfel, Ian Bostridge, Barbara Bonney, Samuel Ramey, Angela Gheorghiu, Roberto Alagna; independent prod. 2000–, projects include Entartete Musik series (recordings of works banned in Nazi Germany), series of 19th-century Spanish Grand Opera; has worked with Forum for Suppressed Music, Jewish Music Inst.; fmr Dir Musica Prohibita Festival of Entartete Musik, Barcelona; fmr consultant to Dutch broadcaster, VARA on series of matinee concerts in Concertgebouw, Amsterdam; Music Curator, Jewish Museum of Vienna; CEO Coralfox Ltd (classical music production co.); lectures and seminars at institutions, including Jewish Theological Inst., Columbia Univ., Musik Hochschule, Hamburg Univ., Univ. of Virginia, Lincoln Centre Festival, SOAS, London; mem. Faculty, The Banff Centre, Canada. *Achievement:* initiated first retrospective by a major label of works banned by the Third Reich, the recording series 'Entartete Musik' won wide int. recognition over its ten year run and some 30 individual recordings. *Publication:* Cambridge Book on Conducting – The Conductor in the Studio. *Honours:* Jewish Music Inst. David Uri Fellowship 2002, four Grammy Awards, including first two Grammy Latinos ever awarded; all other major recording awards. *Address:* Coralfox Ltd, 65 Riverside Court, 20 Nine Elms Lane, London, SW8 5BY, England (office). *Telephone:* 7768-465923 (mobile) (office). *Fax:* (20) 7720-3732 (office). *E-mail:* michaelhaas@coralfox.com (office). *Website:* www.coralfox.com (office).

HABBESTAD, Kjell Helge; Norwegian teacher and composer; *Professor in Theory, Norwegian Academy of Music;* b. 13 April 1955, Bomlo, Hordaland; m. Inger Elisabeth Brammer 1976, one s. two d. *Education:* Norwegian Acad. of Music. *Career:* Organist, Snaroya Church, Baerum 1977–81, Langhus Church, Ski 1986–87; teacher of harmony, counterpoint and composition, Bergen Conservatory of Music 1981–86, Ostlandets Conservatory of Music, Oslo 1986–96; Prof. in Theory, Norwegian Acad. of Music 1996–; festival composer, Festival of Northern Norway 1995; mem. Norwegian Soc. of Composers (bd mem. 1987–96, vice-chair. 1990–96, chair. advisory bd 1996–); chair. of bd Composers' Remuneration Fund 2002–05; Chair. TONO (Norwegian Performing Rights Soc.) Evaluation Cttee 2005–. *Compositions:* three Cantica (Magnificat, Nunc Dimittis, Benedictus Dominus) for choir and soloists 1978–83, Lament for soprano and orchestra 1981, Mostraspelet for baritone solo, choir, orchestra and mediaeval instruments 1983, Ave Maria Concerto for organ and string orchestra 1984, Something New – Below Ground Concerto for tuba and brass band 1985, Mostrasuite for baritone solo, unison choir and orchestra 1986, Introduction and Passacaglia (over a theme by Fartein Valen) for organ solo 1987, Hammerklavier for piano solo 1989, Orpheus for flute, piano and ballet dancer 1993, One Night on Earth (oratorio) 1993, Hans Egedes Natt (opera) 1995, Ibsen Songs for singer and piano 1996, Ego Clamavi for choir and solo soprano 1998, The Maid of Norway (opera) 2000, Havet (The Ocean) for choir 2000, Den fagraste rosa (The Fairest Rose) for choir and soloists 2000, Etwas Neues unter der Sonnen! for symphonic band and Hardanger fiddle 2000, Mysteriet (The Mystery), The Passion according to Arnold Eidslott for vocal quartet SSAA and instruments 2001, Angeli – XVIII imagines angelorum Antiqui et Novi Testamenti (IDACD 3) 2001, Un rêve Norvégien Concerto for saxophone and symphonic band 2002,

Voluspå for choir 2003, Psalmi for choir 2003, Das Lied von der Glocke for choir TTBB/SATB, soprano and baritone soloists, percussion, strings and organ (texts Friedrich Schiller Psalms 31 and 13) 2004, Terje Vigen a melodrama for flute, violin, cello, piano and recitation (text Henrik Ibsen, trans. William H. Halverson) 2005, Exaudi for viola and organ 2005, A solis ortus cardine for organ 2006; also liturgic dramas/church plays, choral works, chamber music, cantatas, organ chorals, motets. *Publications:* Cantate – Handbook of Norwegian Sacred Choral Works 1989, Themes, Trends and Talents, 25 Years of Contemporary Norwegian Music (co-ed.) 1992, Arrangements, Arenas and Actors in Contemporary Norwegian Music 1992, Yearbook of Contemporary Norwegian Music 1996–97. *Honours:* first prize TONO Competition for Choral Worlks 1978, first prize Jubal in competition for a new organ, Borgund Church 1981, Oslo City Cultural Stipendium 1994. *Address:* Wesselsvei 5, 1412 Sofiemyr, Norway (home). *Telephone:* 66805459 (home). *Fax:* 66805445 (home). *E-mail:* kjell@habbestad.no (home). *Website:* www.notam02.no/~khabbest/.

HABEREDER, Agnes; Swiss/German singer (soprano); *Leader of Singing Department, Leopold-Mozart-Zentrum, Augsburg University;* b. 1957, Kelheim, Germany. *Education:* studied in Munich and Florence. *Career:* sang at Augsburg Mozart Festival, 1979 as Mozart's Donna Anna; guest appearances at Florence and Paris as Wagner's Gutrune, 1981; Semperoper Dresden Musikfestspiele 1984–89, Marie in Berg's Wozzeck; Zürich Opera from 1984 as Strauss's Empress, Wagner's Senta, and Ursula in Hindemith's Mathis der Maler; Bayreuth Festival 1983–86, in The Ring; Salzburg Festival 1986, as Leonore in Fidelio; other roles include Salome, Korngold's Marietta and Cassandre in Les Troyens (Zürich, 1990); other guest appearances at Vienna, Munich, Mannheim, RAI Turin; concert performances all over the world; teacher at Augsburg Music High School 1993–, Munich Music High school 1993–; currently Leader of Singing Dept, Leopold-Mozart-Zentrum, Augsburg Univ.; mem. Bund Deutsche Gesangspädagogen, Muenchner Tonkuenstler EV; owner Gestnet Kirchberg, working with UNICEF. *Film:* played Cassandre in Hector Berlioz by Tony Palmer. *Recordings:* Kantate, Von deutscher Seele, by Hans Pfitzner, Düsseldorfer Symphoniker, conductor Heinrich Hollreiser. *Honours:* winner of Mozart Competition in Würzburg, Deutscher Musikrat Competition, Berlin. *Address:* Leopold-Mozart-Zentrum, University of Augsburg, Maximiliaustr. 59, 86150 Augsburg (office); Stillnau 52, 86657 Bissingen, Germany (home). *Telephone:* (1702) 061054 (home); (821) 45041617 (office). *E-mail:* labelagemusic@hotmail.com (office). *Website:* www.gestuet.kirchberg.de (office); www.agnes-habereder.de.

HABERMANN, Michael Robert, AAS, BA, MA, DMA; American pianist, piano instructor and composer; b. 23 Feb. 1950, Paris, France. *Education:* Nassau Community College, Garden City, NY, Long Island Univ., Greenvale, NY, Peabody Conservatory, Baltimore, MD. *Career:* debut, Carnegie Recital Hall 1977; appearances at American Liszt Festival 1978, 1982, 1993, Int. Piano Festival, Univ. of Maryland 1979, Grand Piano Programme, Nat. Public Radio recital 1981, McMaster Univ., Hamilton, Ont., Canada 1983, Rocky River Chamber Music Soc., Ohio 1984–2001; Lecturer, Elder Hostel Program, Peabody Conservatory, Baltimore 1990–; Int. Concert Series, Hempstead, New York 1999; Performing Arts Center, Purchase, New York 2000. *Recordings:* Sorabji: A Legend in His Own Time, Sorabji: Le Jardin Parfumé, Sorabji: Piano Music, Vol. 3, Sorabji: The Legendary Works, Sorabji: Transcriptions and other works, Piano Music of Alexandre Rey Colaço Educo. *Publications:* Kaikhosru Shapurji Sorabji in The Piano Quarterly 1983; The Exotic Piano Masterpieces of Sorabji in Soundpage and Score, Keyboard Magazine 1986; A Style Analysis of The Nocturnes for Solo Piano by Kaikhosru Shapurji Sorabji, with special emphasis on Le Jardin Parfumé, University Microfilms International; Sorabji's Piano Music, in Sorabji: A Critical Celebration 1993; Essay for Remembering Horowitz: 125 Pianists recall a legend 1993. *Address:* 4208 Harford Terrace, Baltimore, MD 21214, USA (home). *E-mail:* mrh@charm.net (office).

HADARI, Omri, FGSM; Israeli conductor; b. 10 Sept. 1941; m. Osnat Hadari 1965; one s. one d. *Education:* Tel-Aviv Music Coll., Guildhall School of Music and Drama, London. *Career:* debut, London 1974; conductor, London Lyric Orchestra; Principal Guest Conductor, Adelaide Symphony Orchestra; conducted Shostakovich's New Babylon in London 1982, New York and Helsinki and at the Flanders Festival; debut with Australian Opera 1988 in La Bohème; Music Dir and Principal Conductor, Cape Town Symphony Orchestra, S Africa 1989–; Guest Conductor for Royal Philharmonic Orchestra, London Symphony Orchestra, City of Birmingham Symphony Orchestra, Australian Opera, Sydney Symphony Orchestra, Melbourne Symphony Orchestra, South Australia Symphony Orchestra, Queensland Symphony Orchestra, Israel Chamber Orchestra, Jerusalem Symphony Orchestra, Beer-Sheva Sinfonietta, Het Brabant Symphony Orchestra, Dutch Nat. Ballet, Victorian State Opera, Ulster Orchestra, Nat. Symphony Orchestra of S Africa, Natal Philharmonic, Columbus Symphony Orchestra, Ohio, San Francisco Chamber Orchestra, Orchestra of Radio City New York, Lahti Symphony Orchestra, Avanti Orchestra, Tasmania Symphony Orchestra; mem. Incorporated Soc. of Musicians. *Honours:* Dr Leo Kestenberg Prize, Israel 1969, Guildhall School of Music Conducting Prize 1974, Capsalic Cup for Conducting 1974. *Current Management:* c/o J. Audrey Ellison International Artists' Management, 135 Stevenage Road, Fulham, London SW6 6PB, England. *Telephone:* (20) 7381-9751. *Fax:* (20) 7381-2406. *E-mail:* Audrey@ellison-intl.freeserve.co.uk. *Website:* www.ellison-intl.freeserve.co .uk. *Address:* PO Box 128, Shdeima 76855, Israel. *Telephone:* (8) 869 3041. *E-mail:* hadario@013.net. *Website:* www.hadarimaestro.com.

HADDOCK, Marcus Jerome; American singer (tenor); *Instructor in Applied Voice, Hobart William Smith Colleges;* b. 19 June 1957, Fort Worth, Tex. *Education:* Baylor Univ., Waco, Tex. with Carol Blaickner-Mayo, Texas Tech. Univ. with John Gillas, Boston Univ. with Phyllis Curtin. *Career:* roles include Count Almaviva in Il Barbiere di Siviglia, Ramiro in La Cenerentola, Lindoro in L'Italiana in Algeri, Tonio in La Fille du Régiment by Donizetti; International debut in Bordeaux as Ford in Salieri's Falstaff; Nemorino in L'Elisir d'amore; Festival appearances in Aachen, Karlsruhe and Bonn in La Bohème and Lucia di Lammermoor, La Traviata, Madama Butterfly, Werther and Les Contes d'Hoffmann; Debut with Opéra Paris de Bastille as Arbace in Idomeneo; 1992 debut with Teatro alla Scala as Matteo in Arabella; 1994–95 season as Lenski in Eugene Onegin for Lausanne Opera, then Rodolfo in La Bohème in Geneva, Pinkerton in Madama Butterfly in Los Angeles and Don Carlo in Antwerp; Season 1995–96 included Ruggero in La Rondine, Roméo in Roméo et Juliette in Geneva and appearance in Gran Teatro la Fenice to sing Don Carlo in Warsaw; Season 1996–97 included appearance with Deutsche Oper Berlin as Faust, Tebaldo in I Capuleti e i Montecchi at Opera de Bastille and Lenski in debut with Nederlandse Opera in Amsterdam; Verdi Requiem with Orchestre de Paris; Season 2000–01 as Puccini's Ruggiero in Los Angeles, Julien in Louise at Toulouse, Pinkerton at the Teatro Colón, Buenos Aires, and the Duke of Mantua for Dallas Opera; in 2002 sang Don José at Glyndebourne, Hoffmann with Los Angeles Opera and Paris Opera de Bastille, Don Carlo in Cologne 2002; in 2003 sang Faust with Chicago Lyric Opera, Pinkerton at Royal Opera House, London, Alfredo and Faust at Metropolitan Opera, New York, Tosca and Romeo in Munich, Hoffmann in Paris, Adorno in Simon Boccanegra in Santa Fé, Hoffmann at La Scala, Milan, Don Carlo in Florence; in 2005 sang Carmen in Rome, Tosca in Florence, Hoffmann in Orange and Dallas, Ballo in Maschera in Philadelphia; concert repertoire includes Missa Solemnis, Verdi Requiem, Dream of Gerontius and Beethoven's 9th, Aenaeus in Les Troyens, Boston Symphony, James Levine, Tanglewood. *Recordings:* Orazi e Curiazi with London Philharmonic Orchestra, Il Guarany, with Oper der Stadt Bonn, Werther with Orchestre de Lille, La Bohème, with Atlanta Symphony Orchestra, Carmen with Glyndebourne Opera (DVD). *Honours:* Winner, Metropolitan Opera Nat. Council Auditions. *Current Management:* c/o CAMI, 1790 Broadway, New York, NY 10019, USA. *Telephone:* (212) 841-9680. *E-mail:* marjehad@verizon.net (home). *Website:* www.marcushaddock.com.

HADELICH, Augustin; German violinist; b. 4 April 1984, Cecina, Italy. *Education:* Istituto Mascagni, Livorno, Italy, Juilliard School, New York, USA. *Career:* studied with Joel Smirnoff; performed as a soloist with Alban Gerhardt and Fort Worth Symphony Orchestra, New York String Orchestra, Cleveland Orchestra, New York Philharmonic Orchestra, Los Angeles Philharmonic Orchestra, Atlanta Symphony Orchestra, Baltimore Symphony Orchestra, Cincinnati Symphony Orchestra, Phoenix Symphony Orchestra, Seattle Symphony Orchestra, Utah Symphony Orchestra, Vancouver Symphony Orchestra. *Recordings:* albums: Haydn, Violin Concertos 2008, Telemann, Twelve Fantasies for Solo Violin 2009, Flying Solo 2009, Dutilleux: Violin Concerto, L'Arbre des Songes 2015. *Honours:* Gold Medal, Int. Violin Competition of Indianapolis 2006, Avery Fisher Grant Winner 2009. *Current Management:* Schmidt Artists International Inc., 59 East 54th Street, Suite 83, New York, NY 10022, USA. *Telephone:* (212) 421-8500. *Fax:* (212) 421-8583. *E-mail:* info@schmidtart.com. *Website:* www.schmidtart.com. *E-mail:* augustin@augustin-hadelich.de. *Website:* www.augustin-hadelich.de.

HADJINEOPHYTOU, George Constantinou; British composer and musician (mandolin); b. 28 Oct. 1965, London; m. Eleni Hadjineophytou 1994. *Education:* Trinity Coll. of Music, London. *Career:* performances and compositions for BBC TV and radio, City of London Sinfonia, Royal Shakespeare Co., Shakespeare's Globe, Nat. Theatre. *Recordings include:* Psyche and Eros (animation), Channel 4; Grandmother's Hands (short film for TV), Under the Stars (film soundtrack). *Honours:* Isabelle Bond Gold Medal.

HAEBLER, Ingrid; Austrian pianist; b. 20 June 1929, Vienna. *Education:* Vienna Acad., Salzburg Mozarteum and Geneva Conservatory. *Career:* specializes in Haydn, Mozart, Schubert and Schumann; mem. Faculty, Salzburg Mozarteum 1969–; concerts with Concertgebouw Orchestra, London Symphony, Royal Philharmonic, Vienna and Berlin Philharmonics, Boston Symphony, Lamoureux Orchestra, Stockholm and Warsaw Philharmonics, London Mozart Players; has appeared in festivals worldwide. *Honours:* won 1st Prize, Int. Competition Munich 1954; Mozart Medal, Vienna 1971, Mozart Medal, Salzburg 1979, Gold Medal of Honour, Vienna 1986, Gold Medal 'Viotti d'oro', Vercelli, Italy 2000.

HAEFLIGER, Andreas; Swiss pianist; b. Berlin, Germany; m. Marina Piccinini. *Education:* Juilliard School, USA, studied with Herbert Stessin. *Career:* has appeared with numerous orchestras in N America, Europe and Japan; numerous recital appearances including Great Performers Series, Lincoln Center, New York, Wigmore Hall, London and in Germany, Austria, France and Italy; has performed regularly at BBC Proms, London; performs in USA with Takacs String Quartet; performs frequently with baritone Matthias Goerner. *Recordings include:* Mozart Piano Sonatas, Schumann's Davidsbün-

dlertanze and Fantasiestücke, Schubert's Impromptus, music by Sofia Gubaidulina, Schubert's Goethe Lieder (with Matthias Goerne), Perspectives I–IV (including works by Schubert, Adès, Mozart and Beethoven). *Honours:* twice won Gina Bachauer Memorial Scholarship, Preis der Deutschen Schallplattenkritik (for recording of Schubert's Goethe Lieder). *Current Management:* c/o Susie McLeod, Intermusica Artists Management Ltd, Crystal Wharf, 36 Graham Street, London, N1 8GJ, England. *Telephone:* (20) 7608-9920. *Fax:* (20) 7490-3263. *E-mail:* mail@intermusica.co.uk. *Website:* www.andreashaefliger.com.

HAEFLIGER, Michael, BMus, MBA; German musician; *Artistic and Executive Director, Lucerne Festival;* b. 2 May 1961, Berlin. *Education:* Juilliard School of Music, St Gallen Univ., Harvard Business School. *Career:* Artistic and Exec. Dir Davos Music Festival 1986–98, Lucerne Festival 1999–; mem. Int. Soc. of Performing Arts, Lions Club. *Honours:* World Econ. Forum Global Leader for Tomorrow 2000, European Cultural Initiative Award 2003. *Address:* c/o Lucerne Festival, Hirschmattstr 13, 6002 Lucerne (office); Spissenstr 2, 6047 Kastanienbaum, Lucerne, Switzerland (home). *Telephone:* 412264400 (office). *Fax:* 412264460 (office). *E-mail:* m.haefliger@ lucernefestival.ch (office). *Website:* www.lucernefestival.ch (office).

HAEGGANDER, Mari Anne; Swedish singer (soprano); b. 23 Oct. 1951, Troekoerna. *Education:* Opera School, Gothenburg. *Career:* debut as Micaela in Carmen, Ponelle production, Royal Opera, Stockholm; has sung Cherubino, Elisabetta in Don Carlo at Savonlinna in Finland, Pamina and the Countess in Figaro at Bonn and Buxton Festival, Eva in Meistersinger at Bayreuth 1981, Mimi at Stockholm and Hamburg, Eva at the Metropolitan 1985, and Elsa in Lohengrin at San Francisco; guest appearances include Berlin, Munich, Paris, Brussels, Vienna, New York, Seattle and Toronto; other roles include Butterfly, Amelia in Un Ballo in Maschera and Simon Boccanegra, Marschallin, Tatiana in Eugene Onegin, Lisa in The Queen of Spades, Sieglinde, Arabella, and Donna Anna; Prof. of Singing, Opera Coll., Stockholm. *Recordings:* Das Rheingold with Levine; Peer Gynt with Blomstedt; Several lieder and sacred music recordings. *Honours:* Royal Court Singer to HM the King of Sweden 1991. *Current Management:* c/o Artistsekretariat Ulf Tornqvist, Sankt Eriksgatan 100 2 tr, 113 31 Stockholm, Sweden.

HAENCHEN, Hartmut; German conductor; *Artistic Director, Dresden Music Festival;* b. 21 March 1943, Dresden. *Education:* Dresden Hochschule für Musik. *Career:* fmr mem., Dresden Kreuzchor under Rudolf Mauersberger; directed the Robert-Franz-Singakademie and the Hallé Symphony 1966–72; Music Dir, Zwickau Opera 1972–73; Guest Conductor, Deutsche Staatsoper Berlin 1972–86; Permanent Conductor, Dresden Philharmonic 1973–76, Philharmonic Chorus of Dresden 1974–76, 1985–1987; Musical Dir, Schwerin Staatstheater and conductor of the Mecklenburg Staatskapelle 1976–79; Permanent Guest Conductor, Berlin Komische Oper 1980–96; Prof. of Conducting, Dresden Musikhochschule 1980–86; guest appearances in Europe, USA, Canada, Japan and China, at leading opera houses in Europe, New York, and at Kirishima Festival, Japan; Artistic Dir, C.P.E. Bach Chamber Orchestra, Berlin 1980–, Prof. 1985–; Musical Dir, Netherlands Opera, Amsterdam 1986–99, First Guest Conductor 1999–2006; Chief Conductor, Netherlands Philharmonic Orchestra and the Netherlands Chamber Orchestra 1986–2002; Artistic Dir, Dresden Music Festival 2002–. *Recordings include:* Gluck's Orfeo ed Euridice (Preis der Deutschen Schallplatten). *Publications:* Doubt as Weapon 1996, Von der Unvereinbarkeit von Macht und Liebe 2004, Mahler's Fictitious Letters (in 14 vols) 1999. *Honours:* mem. Akademie der Künste, Saxony; Hon. Conductor, Staatskapelle, Hallé 2005; Knight in the Order of the Netherlands Lion, Cross of Merit (Germany) 2008; first prize Carl Maria von Weber Conducting Competition, Dresden 1971, Netherlands Artist of the Year 2000, Lawrence Olivier Award 1990, 1992. *Current Management:* International Classical Artists, The Tower Building, 11 York Road, London SE1 7NX, England. *Telephone:* (20) 7902-0520. *Fax:* (20) 7902-0530. *E-mail:* info@icartists.com. *Website:* www.icartists.com. *Address:* Dresden Music Festival, An der Dreikönigskirche 1, PO Box 10 04 53, 01097 Dresden, Germany (office). *Fax:* (351) 47856-23 (office). *E-mail:* hartm@ haenchen.net (office). *Website:* www.musikfestspiele.com; www.haenchen .net.

HAENDEL, Ida, CBE; British (b. Polish) violinist; b. 15 Dec. 1928, Chelm, Poland. *Education:* Warsaw Conservatoire, pvt. tuition in Paris and London. *Career:* studied with Carl Flesch and Georges Enescu; London debut at Queen's Hall with Sir Henry Wood, Queen's Hall 1937; USA debut 1946; moved to Montréal, Canada 1952, Miami, Fla, USA 1979; performances throughout world with many noted conductors including tour with London Philharmonic Orchestra to first Hong Kong Festival of Arts and China and three tours of USSR; participated in centenary anniversary Festival of Bronislav Huberman, Tel-Aviv 1982; celebrated 50th anniversary of debut at Promenade Concerts, London 1987; numerous recordings of works by all the major composers. *Publication:* Woman with Violin (autobiog.) 1970. *Honours:* Hon. mem. RAM 1982–; Dr hc (Royal Coll. of Music) 2000; Sibelius Medal (Finland) 1982. *Address:* c/o Ernest Gilbert Associates, 109 Wheeler Avenue, Pleasantville, NY 10570, USA. *Telephone:* (914) 769-3691. *Fax:* (914) 769-5407. *E-mail:* ejgilbert@msn.com (office).

HAENEN, Tom; Dutch singer (bass); b. 1959, Amsterdam. *Education:* Amsterdam Conservatoire. *Career:* debut as Don Alfonso in Così fan tutte for Netherlands Opera; appearances in the Netherlands and elsewhere as the General in Prokofiev's The Gambler, Arkel in Pelléas et Mélisande and

Ferrando in Il Trovatore, Osmin in Die Entführung for Opera North and Leporello and Geronte in Manon Lescaut in Dublin; further engagements as Sparafucile in Rigoletto at Barcelona, Don Cassandro in La Finta Semplice and Tom in Un Ballo in Maschera for Flanders Opera in 1992; guest appearances at Spoleto, Israel and Las Palmas Festivals. *Honours:* Prizewinner at the International 's-Hertogenbosch and Rio de Janeiro Competitions.

HAFIDH, Munther Jamil; Iraqi musician (viola, cello); m. *Career:* founding mem. and viola player, Baghdad Symphony Orchestra 1959–. *Address:* Iraqi National Symphony Orchestra, Baghdad Convention Center, Green Zone, Baghdad, Iraq.

HAGEGÅRD, Erland; Swedish singer (baritone); b. 27 Feb. 1944, Brunskog; m. Anne Terelius. *Education:* studied in Sweden with Arne Sunnegaard, with Erik Werba and Gerald Moore in Vienna. *Career:* debut at Vienna Volksoper 1968, in Trois Opéras Minutes by Milhaud; sang with Frankfurt Opera 1971–74; mem., Hamburg Staatsoper from 1974; guest with the Vienna Staatsoper from 1976; appearances at the Drottningholm Court Opera in Sweden; Danish television in Xerxes by Handel; roles include Escamillo, Valentin, Don Giovanni, Eugene Onegin, Albert in Werther and Germont in La Traviata; lieder singer in works by Schubert; television appearances include Suppé's Boccaccio.

HAGEGÅRD, Håkan; Swedish singer (baritone); b. 25 Nov. 1945, Karlstad; m. Barbara Bonney (divorced); two c. *Education:* Music Acad. of Stockholm, studied with Tito Gobbi in Rome, Gerald Moore in London and Erik Werba in Vienna. *Career:* debut as Papageno in The Magic Flute, Royal Opera, Sweden 1968; Metropolitan Opera debut 1978 as Donizetti's Malatesta; mem., Royal Opera Stockholm; appeared with major opera companies throughout Europe, in film of The Magic Flute 1975 and at Glyndebourne from 1973 as the Count in Figaro and Capriccio and as Mozart's Guglielmo; created role of Crispin in Tintomara, Royal Opera Stockholm 1973; Covent Garden debut 1987 as Wolfram in Tannhäuser, also at Chicago 1988; Metropolitan Opera 1988 as Guglielmo; sang Eisenstein in Die Fledermaus at Chicago 1989; created Beaumarchais in The Ghosts of Versailles by Corigliano at the Metropolitan 1991; Deutsche Oper Berlin 1992 as Wolfram; season 1996 at the Met as Prus in The Makropulos Case and in April Gala; The Officer in the US premiere of Lindberg's A Dream Play, Santa Fe 1998; sang Scarpia at Sydney 2000; recitalist. *Recordings include:* Die Zauberflöte, Don Giovanni (title role, from Drottningholm).

HAGEN, Christina, DipMus; German singer (mezzo-soprano); b. 1956, Hamburg. *Education:* Hochschule für Musik und Darstellende Kunst, Hamburg, studied with Naan Pold, Hilde Nadolowitsch, masterclasses with Sena Jurinac, International Studio for Singing, Herbert von Karajan Stiftung with Christa Ludwig. *Career:* engaged at Staatstheater Oldenburg 1983–84, then Deutsche Oper am Rhein, Düsseldorf-Duisburg 1984–; guest appearances in Germany at Berlin, Hamburg and Cologne, at Bolshoi Theatre in Moscow, Antwerp, Amsterdam and Staatsoper Berlin, National Theater Munich; participant at Bayreuth Festival 1989, 1990, 1991; has sung Rosina in Barber of Seville, Micha in Samson by Handel, Judith in Bluebeard's Castle by Bartók and Jocasta in Oedipus Rex at Oldenburg, Olga in Eugene Onegin and Second Woman in Die Zauberflöte at Oldenburg and Düsseldorf, the Composer in Ariadne auf Naxos, Dorabella in Così fan tutte, Nicklausse in Tales of Hoffmann, Orlowsky in Die Fledermaus, Maddalena in Rigoletto, Fatima in Weber's Oberon, Sextus in Julius Caesar by Handel, Flosshilde, Erda and Fricka in Rheingold and in Walküre, Second Norn and Waltraute, Fenena in Nabucco, Britten's Lucretia, Olga in Das Schloss, Ottavia in Monteverdi's L'Incoronazione di Poppea, Eboli at Düsseldorf, Clytemnestra (Gluck) at Düsseldorf and Berlin, Fricka in Walküre at Munich, Santuzza in Cavalleria Rusticana at Eutiner Festival; season 1995–96 at Düsseldorf as Wagner's Venus and Fricka; many lieder recitals and concert appearances.

HAGEN, Daron Aric, MMus; American composer, pianist, conductor and stage director; b. 4 Nov. 1961, Milwaukee, Wis.; s. of Earl Hagen and Gwen Johnson; partner Gilda Lyons. *Education:* Univ. of Wisconsin, Curtis Inst., Juilliard School. *Career:* comms from New York Philharmonic, Philadelphia Orchestra, Nat. Symphony, Seattle Opera; Milwaukee, Buffalo, New Mexico, Denver and Albany Symphony Orchestras; composition teacher, Bard Coll. 1986–98, Curtis Inst. 1996; Pres. Lotte Lehmann Foundation, New York 2004–07; Composer-in-Residence, Princeton Univ. Atelier 1997, 2005; Lifetime mem. Corpn of Yaddo; Trustee, Douglas Moore Fund for American Opera. *Plays:* Shining Brow, Bandanna, Vera of Las Vegas, Amelia, New York Stories, the Antient Concert. *Compositions include:* 30 orchestral works including four symphonies, seven concertii, massive works for chorus and orchestra, seven operas, 15 song cycles, 45 chamber works. *Honours:* Kennedy Center Friedheim Prize, the Bearns, Barlow and ASCAP-Nissim Prizes, two Rockefeller Bellagio Residencies, the Camargo Residency, multiple residencies at VCCA and MacDowell, scholarships and devt grants from American Acad. of Arts and Letters, Nat. Endowment for the Arts, Meet the Composer, Opera America. *E-mail:* daron@daronhagen.com (home). *Current Management:* c/o Burning Sled Music, 3505 Broadway, Suite 52, New York, NY 10031, USA. *Telephone:* (347) 684-1640. *E-mail:* info@burningsled.org. *Website:* www.burningsled.org. *E-mail:* daron@daronhagen.com (home). *Website:* www.daronhagen.com.

HAGEN, Reinhard; German singer (bass); b. 1966, Bremen. *Education:* studied in Karlsruhe. *Career:* sang at Kassel Opera, 1989–90, Dortmund,

1991–94, Deutsche Oper Berlin from 1993; Season 1991 as Sarastro at the Landestheater Salzburg and at Brussels; Salzburg Festival, 1993, as Plutone in Monteverdi's Orfeo; German premiere of Casken's The Golem, 1993; Season 1996 as Cadmus in Semele at Aix-en-Provence, Gounod's Frère Laurent at Geneva and Ferrando in Il Trovatore at Berlin; Sang Titurel in Parsifal at the Deutsche Oper, 1998; Season 2000–01 as Verdi's Banquo and Count Walter at the Deutsche Oper, King Henry in Lohengrin at San Diego, Sarastro in Barcelona, Rocco at Glyndebourne and bass solos in the St Matthew Passion for La Scala, Milan. *Recordings include:* Les Béatitudes, by Franck. *Current Management:* Organisation Internationale Artistique, 16 Avenue Franklin D. Roosevelt, 75008 Paris, France; c/o Musiespaña, Calle José Maranón 10, 28010 Madrid, Spain. *Telephone:* 1-42-25-58-34 (France); (91) 5913290 (Spain). *Fax:* 1-42-25-64-97 (France); (91) 5913291 (Spain). *E-mail:* oia@oia-poilve.com; horan@musiespana.com. *Website:* www.oia-poilve.com.

HAGEN-GROLL, Walter; German choral conductor; b. 15 April 1927, Chemnitz. *Education:* Stuttgart Musikhochschule. *Career:* Asst Conductor, Stuttgart Opera 1952; Chorus Master, Heidelberg Opera 1957; Deutsche Oper Berlin 1961; directed the chorus of the Berlin Philharmonic from 1961; assisted Wilhelm Pitz at Bayreuth 1960–62; Chorus Master, Salzburg Festival from 1965, Philharmonia Chorus, London 1971–74, Vienna Staatsoper 1984, Vienna Singakademie 1987; Choral Dir, Salzburg Mozarteum from 1986.

HÄGER, Claus; German singer (baritone); b. 1963, Wuppertal. *Education:* studied in Cologne and Freiburg, masterclasses with Dietrich Fischer-Dieskau. *Career:* Hamburg Staatsoper 1991–92; sang Papageno at the Berlin Staatsoper 1994; Schwetzingen Festival 1995; other roles have included Mozart's Guglielmo, Silvio in Pagliacci, Puccini's Schaunard and Falke in La Bohème; broadcast and concert engagements; season 1998 as Marquis de Corcy in Le Postillon de Lonjumeau at the Berlin Staatsoper. *Honours:* prizewinner Oberdörfer Competition, Hamburg 1992.

HAGER, Leopold; Austrian conductor; b. 6 Oct. 1935, Salzburg; m. Gertrude Entleitner 1960, one d. *Education:* High School for Music (Mozarteum), Salzburg. *Career:* Asst Conductor, Staedtische Buhnen, Mainz, Germany 1957–62; Principal Conductor, Landestheater, Linz 1962–64, Opernhaus, Cologne, Germany 1964–65; Gen. Music Dir, Staedtische Buhnen, Freiburg, Germany 1965–69; Principal Conductor, Mozarteum Orchestra, Salzburg 1969–81; has conducted many performances of early operas by Mozart; led the first modern performance of Mitridate, Salzburg 1971; Symphony Orchestra, Radio Luxembourg 1981–96; guest conductor, Vienna Opera, Munich Opera, Metropolitan Opera, Royal Opera Covent Garden, Teatro Colón Buenos Aires, Berlin and Vienna Philharmonics; conducted Così fan tutte at the Metropolitan, New York 1991, Figaro 1997. *Recordings:* Mozart Piano Concertos (with Karl Engel), Bastien and Bastienne, Lucio Silla, Il re Pastore, Ascanio in Alba, Mitridate Re di Ponto, La Finta Semplice 1990. *Honours:* Ehrenkreuz 1 klasse für Kunst und Wissenschaft, Austria.

HAGLEY, Alison; British singer (soprano); b. 9 May 1961, London, England. *Education:* Guildhall School of Music, National Opera Studio. *Career:* sang in Handel's Rodelinda at the Aldeburgh Festival and Handel's Flavio with Musica nel Chiostro at the 1985 Batignano Festival in Italy; Camden Festival 1986 in La Finta Giardiniera by Mozart; sang Clorinda in Opera 80s 1987 production of La Cenerentola; Glyndebourne debut 1988 as the Little Owl in L'Enfant et Les Sortilèges, returning in Jenůfa and as Susanna, Nannetta, Papagena and Zerlina; Glyndebourne Tour as Varvara in Katya Kabanova, Despina and Papagena; Covent Garden as a Flowermaiden in Parsifal and in Peter Grimes; ENO 1991 as Lauretta in a new production of Gianni Schicchi and Gretel in Hansel and Gretel; Scottish Opera appearances as Musetta in La Bohème and Adele in Die Fledermaus; sang Mélisande 1992 with Boulez and Peter Stein, WNO; sang Nannetta for ENO 1992; Glyndebourne 1994, as Susanna; Covent Garden 1997, in Massenet's Chérubin; Bella in The Midsummer Marriage at Munich 1998; Munich Opera Festival 2000. *Honours:* National Opera Studio FPC Opera Singer of the Year.

HAHM, Shinik; Korean/American conductor; *Chief Conductor, KBS Symphony Orchestra.* *Education:* Rice Univ., Eastman School of Music, Rochester, NY. *Career:* Music Dir Abilene Philharmonic Orchestra 1993–2003; Music Dir Yale Symphony Orchestra 1995–2004; Music Dir Tuscaloosa Symphony Orchestra 2000–10; Artistic Dir and Prin. Conductor Daejeon Philharmonic Orchestra, Korea 2004–06; Music Dir Philharmonia Orchestra of Yale 2004–; Prof. of Conducting, Yale Univ. 2004–; debuted with Petersburg Symphony Orchestra, Russia 2005; debuted in Geneva, Switzerland and Besançon, France 2006–07; many collaborations with Mexican orchestras 2006–, including Mexico Nat. Symphony and Xalapa Symphony Orchestra; conducted European tour of Nordwestdeutsche Philharmonie Orchestra 2009. *Recordings:* albums: with Polish Nat. Radio Symphony Orchestra: Shostakovich, Symphony No. 5, Brahms, Symphony No. 4, Prokofiev, Piano Concerto No. 3; with Yale Symphony Orchestra: Orff, Carmina Burana 1998. *Honours:* Hon. Prof., Hwa Gong Univ., China; Winner, Fourth Gregor Fitelberg Int. Competition for Conductors 1991, Eastman School of Music Walter Hagen Conducting Prize, Rice Univ. Shepherd Soc. Award, Arts and Culture Medal from Korean Govt 1995. *Address:* KBS Symphony Orchestra, KBS Hall, 18 Yeouido-dong, Yeongdeungpo-gu, Seoul, 150-790, South Korea (office); Yale University, PO Box 201945, New Haven, CT 06520-1945, USA (office). *Telephone:* (2) 781-2240 (office); (2) 781-2246 (office); (2) 781-2251 (office); (2) 781-2255 (office). *Fax:* (2) 781-2249 (office). *E-mail:* webmaster@kbs.co.kr (office); ShinikHahm@yahoo.com (office). *Website:* kbsso.kbs.co.kr/eng/main .php (office); www.yale.edu (office); www.shinikhahm.com.

HAHN, Barbara; German singer (mezzo-soprano); b. 1965, Stuttgart. *Education:* studied in Stuttgart and at Salzburg Mozarteum. *Career:* sang at Bielefeld from 1987 as Dorabella, Cherubino and Orlofsky; Nicklausse in Les contes d'Hoffmann at Bregenz Festival, 1987; Appeared as Dorabella and Nicklausse at Hanover, 1988; Sang Grimgerde in Die Walküre at Bologna; Angelina, in La Cenerentola at Passau; Freiburg Opera, 1989–91, as Octavian, Idamantes, Hansel and Sonja in Der Zarewitsch; Concert performance of Schreker's Der ferne Klang in Berlin, 1990; Frankfurt Opera, 1992–, debut as Dorabella. *Recordings:* Der ferne Klang, conducted by Gerd Albrecht. *Address:* Steinachstr. 2, 97082 Würzburg, Germany. *E-mail:* pphahnpp@gmx .de. *Website:* barbarahahn.de.

HAHN, Hilary, BMus; American violinist; b. 27 Nov. 1979, Lexington, Va; m.; one d. *Education:* Curtis Inst. of Music, Philadelphia. *Career:* debut aged six, Baltimore 1986; first full recital, aged 10 1990; major orchestra debut with Baltimore Symphony Orchestra 1991; Utah and Florida Symphonies 1992; Philadelphia Orchestra 1993; New York Philharmonic Orchestra and Cleveland Orchestra 1994; European concerto debut in Budapest, with Budapest Festival Orchestra, and European recital debut at Festival de Sully et d'Orleans, France 1994; German debut at 15 playing Beethoven Violin Concerto with Bavarian Radio Symphony Orchestra and Lorin Maazel, Munich 1995; Carnegie Hall debut at 16 with Philadelphia Orchestra and Christoph Eschenbach 1996; concerto debuts in Berlin, Frankfurt, Hannover and Rotterdam 1996; recital debuts in Kennedy Center (DC), Alice Tully Hall, New York, Munich, Rotterdam and Paris 1997; concerto debuts in London, Glasgow, Birmingham, Zürich and Vienna with Bavarian Radio Symphony, and in Paris with French Radio Symphony Orchestra 1998; as chamber musician appears regularly at Marlboro Music Festival, Skaneateles Festival and with the Chamber Music Society of Lincoln Center, New York. *Recordings include:* Hilary Hahn plays Bach 1997, Beethoven Violin Concertos/Bernstein Serenade 1999, Barber and Meyer Violin Concertos 2000, Brahms and Stravinsky Violin Concertos (Grammy Award for Best Instrumental Soloist Performance with Orchestra) 2001, Mendelssohn and Shostakovich Concertos 2002, Bach Concertos 2003, Elgar Violin Concerto and Vaughan Williams The Lark Ascending 2004, Mozart Violin Sonatas 2005, Paganini and Spohr Concertos 2006, Birthday Concert for Pope Benedict XVI 2007, Schoenberg and Sibelius Concertos (Grammy Award for Best Instrumental Soloist Performance 2009) 2008, Bach: Violin and Voice 2010, Higdon & Tchaikovsky: Violin Concertos 2010, Charles Ives Four Sonatas (ECHO Klassik Award for Chamber Music Recording of the Year/Strings – 20th/21st Century) 2012, Silfra (with Hauschka) 2012. *Honours:* Avery Fisher career grant 1995, Grammy Award 2001, Gramophone Award for Artist of the Year 2008. *Current Management:* IMG Artists, Carnegie Hall Tower, 152 West 57th Street, 5th Floor, New York, NY 10019, USA. *Telephone:* (212) 994-3500. *Fax:* (212) 994-3550. *E-mail:* ksymon@imgartists.com. *Website:* www.imgartists .com; www.hilaryhahn.com.

HAIDER, Friedrich; Austrian pianist and conductor; *Chief Conductor, Oviedo Filarmonia;* b. 1961. *Education:* Acad. of Music, Vienna and Mozarteum, Salzburg. *Career:* theatrical debut in Klagenfurt, with Johann Strauss's Wiener Blut 1984; Chief Conductor of the Opéra du Rhin, Strasbourg 1991–95, with Il Trovatore, Rigoletto, La Traviata and Madama Butterfly; debut in Vienna Staatsoper in Die Fledermaus 2003–04; Chief Conductor, Oviedo Filarmonia, Spain 2004–; guest appearances at Nice, with Faust and Tristan und Isolde, Barcelona with Lohengrin, Beatrice di Tenda, Lisbon with Norma, I Puritani, Hamburg with Don Giovanni, Cologne with I Capuleti e I Montecchi, Venice with Freischütz, Tokyo with Salome, Copenhagen with Otello, Verona with Macbeth, New York with Rigoletto; concerts in Tokyo, Amsterdam, London, Dresden, Munich, Milan and Budapest; recital accompanist to Renata Scotto, Charlotte Margiono, Vesselina Kasarova and Rainer Trost. *Recordings include:* Il segreto di Susanna, Brahms Serenade op.11, Donizetti/Roberto Devereux, Schubert/ Die schöne Müllerin with Rainer Trost, Strauss/ Die Fledermaus, Richard Strauss: Eine Alpensinfonie, Ein Heldenleben, Till Eulenspiegel. *Honours:* Preis der Deutschen Schallplattenkritik 1998. *Current Management:* Theateragentur Dr G. Hilbert, Maximilianstrasse 22, 80539 Munich, Germany. *Telephone:* (49) 892907470. *Fax:* (49) 8929074790. *E-mail:* agentur@hilbert .de. *Website:* www.hilbert.de.

HAIGH, Andrew Wilfred, LRAM, ARCM; British pianist and teacher; *Head of Piano, Kent Music Academy;* b. 26 April 1954, Lagos, Nigeria. *Education:* Royal Coll. of Music, London, Royal Acad. of Music, studied with Cyril Smith, Phyllis Sellick, Albert Ferber. *Career:* debut with London Philharmonic Orchestra, Royal Festival Hall 1965; Wigmore Hall 1971; soloist with all major British orchestras, including London Symphony, London Philharmonic, Philharmonia, Royal Philharmonic, BBC Philharmonic Orchestra; soloist, Herbert von Karajan Festival, Berlin 1970; recitals in Europe; Head of Piano, Kent Music Acad. (fmrly Kent Centre for Young Instrumentalists); Examiner, Trinity Coll. of Music, and Adjudicator. *Honours:* Gold Medallist 1969, winner BBC Mozart Competition 1969, winner Royal Overseas Competition, Nat. Piano Competition, Hopkinson Silver Medal 1973, RCM Dannreuther Concerto Prize. *Address:* 15 Dornden Drive, Langton Green, Tunbridge Wells, Kent TN3 0AA, England (home). *Telephone:* (1892) 862187 (home).

HAILSTORK, Adolphus Cunningham, MMus, PhD; American composer; b. 17 April 1941, Rochester, NY. *Education:* Howard Univ., Washington DC, Manhattan School, Michigan State Univ., with Nadia Boulanger in France. *Career:* teacher, Michigan State Univ. 1969–91, Youngstown State Univ. 1971–76, Norfolk Virginia State Coll. 1977–. *Compositions include:* The Race For Space, theatre piece 1963, Phaedra, tone poem 1966, Horn Sonata 1966, Statement, Variation And Fugue for Orchestra 1966, Sextet for Strings 1971, Violin Sonata 1972, Bagatelles for Brass Quintet 1973, Pulse for Percussion Ensemble 1974, Bellevue and Celebration, both for Orchestra 1974, Concerto for Violin, Horn and Orchestra 1975, Spiritual for Brass Octet 1975, American Landscape, Nos 1, 3 and 4 for Orchestra 1977–84, Five Friends 1977, Out of the Depths 1977, American Landscape for Violin and Cello 1978, The Cloths of Heaven 1979, Piano Sonata 1981, Eight Variations on Shalom Haverim 1981, Sport of Strings 1981, Variations for Trumpet 1981, American Guernica 1983, Arise my Beloved 1983, An American Fanfare 1985, Essay for strings 1986, Three Smiles for Tracy 1989, I Will Life up Mine Eyes 1989, Shout for Joy 1990, Break Forth 1990, Four Spirituals 1991, Intrada 1991, Piano Concerto 1992, Consort Piece 1993, Lachrymosa 1995, Sanctum 1995, Symphony No. 2 1996, Bassoon Set 1996, Trumpet Sonata 1996, Let the Heavens be Glad, for chorus 1996, Flute Set 1996, Two Romances 1997, Go Down, Moses 1998, Second Symphony 1999, Joshua's Boots 1999, Baroque Suite 1999, Two Romances 1999, Motherless Child 2000, Songs of Innocence 2000, Falling Leaves 2002, Little Diversions for Lord Byron's Court 2002, Little David Play on yo' Harp 2003, Missa Brevis 2003, Wade in de Wadduh 2003, Ride on King Jesus 2003, Earthrise 2006, Three Studies on Chant Melodies 2006, Whitman's Journey 2006, Rise for Freedom 2007, Serenade 2008, Set Me on a Rock 2008. *Honours:* Dr hc (Coll. of William and Mary) 2001; Ernest Bloch Award 1971, Virginia Cultural Laureate Award 1992, first place, Univ. of Delaware Festival of New Music 1995, Governor's Award for the Arts, Virginia 2000. *Address:* 521 Berrypick Lane, Virginia Beach, VA 23462-1927, USA (home). *Telephone:* (757) 499-6709 (home).

HAÏM, Emmanuelle; French conductor, harpsichordist and pianist; *Artistic Director, Le Concert d'Astrée;* b. 1967, Paris. *Education:* studied with Kenneth Gilbert and Christophe Rousset. *Career:* coach and assistant to William Christie, Simon Rattle (Les Boréades by Rameau, Salzburg, 1999), Mark Minkowski and Christophe Rousset; founded Paris-based early music group, Le Concert d Astrée, 2000, now Artistic Dir; conducted Rodelinda for the Glyndebourne Tour, 2001; season 2002–03 with Handel's Agrippina in Chicago and Poro at the Edinburgh Festival; guest conductor with Les Muses Galantes and the Orchestra of the Age of Enlightenment; appearances at the Beaune and Poitiers Festivals, recitals with Natalie Dessay, Sandrine Piau and Patricia Petibon; engaged for Theodora with GTO for 2003, and Rodelinda at the 2004 Festival; conducted Monteverdi's Orfeo at the London Barbican, 2003 and engaged for European and US tours 2004–05; Handel's Tamerlano for Opéra Lille 2004–05; Giulio Cesare for Lyric Opera of Chicago 2007; Rameau's Hippolyte at Aricie for Opéra de Paris 2010; Giulio Cesare for Opéra Garnier 2011. *Recordings include:* Handel Arcadian Duets and Cantata Aci Galatea e Polifemo; Purcell's Dido and Aeneas, with Ian Bostridge and Susan Graham. *Honours:* Hon. mem. RAM, London; Chevalier, Légion d'Honneur 2009, Chevalier des Arts et des Lettres. *Address:* Le Concert d'Astrée, 28 rue des Jardins, 59000 Lille, France. *Telephone:* 3-20-74-28-78. *Fax:* 3-20-74-28-73. *E-mail:* management@leconcertdastree.fr. *Website:* www.leconcertdastree .fr.

HAIMOVITZ, Matt; Israeli cellist; b. 3 Dec. 1970, Tel-Aviv; m. Luna Pearl Woolf; one d. *Education:* Juilliard School, New York, Collegiate School, New York, Princeton Univ. and Harvard Univ., studied with Gabor Rejto, Leonard Rose, Carl Schahter. *Career:* appeared with Israel Philharmonic Orchestra under Zubin Mehta at Mann Auditorium, Tel-Aviv, broadcast on Israel nat. TV 1984; London debut with English Chamber Orchestra under Barenboim at the Barbican 1985; appearances with many conductors and orchestras and regular recitals throughout USA and Europe since 1985; debut with Philharmonia Orchestra and Giuseppe Sinopoli at Royal Festival Hall in London 1987; debut with Chicago Symphony Orchestra under James Levine at Ravinia Festival 1988; first tour to Japan 1988, to Europe 1989, and to Australia with Sydney and Melbourne Symphony Orchestras 1991; live concert appearance, The Performing Arts Pay Tribute to Public Television (PBS) 1988; first American recital tour 1990; debut with Berlin Philharmonic under James Levine in Berlin 1990; Lucerne Festival debut with solo recital programme 1990; recital debuts with solo cello repertoire at Montreux Festival, Washington, DC, New York and Paris 1991; debut with Dallas Symphony 1992; Prof. of Cello, Schulich School of Music, McGill Univ. *Recordings include:* Lalo and Saint-Saëns Concerti with Chicago Symphony under Levine 1988, Haydn, C.P.E. Bach, Boccherini: Cello Concertos 1990, Suites and Sonatas for Solo Cello 1991, Solo Cello in works by Reger, Britten, Crumb and Ligeti 1991, Trios with Rob Wasserman 1993, The 20th Century Cello, Vol. I 1995, Vol. II 1997, Portes Ouvertures 1999, Under Tree 1999, J.S. Bach: Six Suites for Cello Solo 2000, Lemons Descending 2001, The Rose Album 2002, Hadyn Mozart 2003, Hyperstring Trilogy 2003, Anthem 2003, Goulash! 2005, Epilogue 2006, Aprés Moi, le Déluge 2006, Mozart the Mason 2006, VinylCello 2007, Odd Couple 2008, Bach's Goldberg Variations 2008, Figment 2009. *Honours:* Avery Fisher Career Grant Award 1986, Grand Prix du Disque 1991, Premio Intenazionale Accademia Musicale Chigiana 1999. *Address:* Department of Performance, Schulich School of Music, McGill University, Strathcona Music Building, 555 Sherbrooke Street West,

Montréal, Québec, H3A 1E3, Canada (office). *Telephone:* (514) 398-4535 (office). *Fax:* (514) 398-8061 (office). *Website:* www.mcgill.ca/music (office).

HAITINK, Bernard John Herman, KBE; Dutch conductor; *Conductor Emeritus, Boston Symphony Orchestra*; b. 4 March 1929, Amsterdam. *Career:* Conductor Netherlands Radio Philharmonic Orchestra 1955–61; appeared regularly as Guest Conductor for Concertgebouw Orchestra, Amsterdam 1956–61, Jt Conductor 1961–64, Chief Conductor and Musical Dir 1964–88, Hon. Conductor 1999–; Prin. Conductor London Philharmonic Orchestra 1967–79, Artistic Dir 1970–78, Pres. 1990–; Musical Dir Glyndebourne Festival Opera 1978–88, Royal Opera House, Covent Garden 1987–2002, European Union Youth Orchestra 1994; Prin. Guest Conductor Boston Symphony Orchestra 1995–2004, Conductor Emeritus 2004–; Chief Conductor and Music Dir, Sächsische Staatskapelle, Dresden 2002–04; Prin. Conductor Chicago Symphony Orchestra 2006–10; Conductor Laureate, European Union Youth Orchestra 2015–; tours with Concertgebouw in Europe, N and S America, Japan, with London Philharmonic in Europe, Japan, USA; Guest Conductor Los Angeles Philharmonic, Boston Symphony, Cleveland, Chicago Symphony, New York Philharmonic, Berlin Philharmonic, Vienna Philharmonic, Dresden Staatskapelle, Concertgebouw and other orchestras; Conductor Laureate, Concertgebouw 1999; Hon. mem. RAM, London 1973, Int. Gustav Mahler Soc.; records for Philips, Decca and EMI. *Honours:* Royal Order of Orange-Nassau, Chevalier des Arts et des Lettres, Officer, Order of the Crown (Belgium), CH Concertgebouw 2002–; Hon. DMus (Oxford) 1988, (Leeds) 1988; Medal of Honour, Bruckner Soc. of America 1970, Gold Medal of Int. Gustav Mahler Soc. 1971, Erasmus Prize 1991, Gramophone Award for Lifetime Achievement 2015. *Address:* c/o Boston Symphony Orchestra, Symphony Hall, 301 Massachusetts Avenue, Boston, MA 02115, USA (office). *Telephone:* (617) 266-1492 (office). *Website:* www.bso.org (office).

HAJDU, Andre; Israeli composer and academic; b. 5 March 1932, Budapest. *Education:* studied with Kodály, Kosa, Szabo and Szervanszky in Budapest and with Milhaud and Messiaen in Paris. *Career:* teacher, Tel-Aviv Acad. of Music 1967–92, School for Excellency, Jerusalem 1992–2005; Prof., Bar Ilan Univ. 1970–2000. *Compositions:* Plasmas 1957 for piano, Petit enfer for orchestra 1959, Journey Around My Piano 1963, 2 piano concertos 1968, 1990, Ludus Paschalis for soloists, chorus and 9 instruments 1970, Mishnayoth for voice, choir, orchestra and piano 1972–73 Terouath Melech for clarinet and strings 1974, The Unbearable Intensity of Youth for orchestra 1976, Bashful Serenades, clarinet and orchestra 1978, Instants suspendus, preludes for solo violin or viola or cello 1978, On Light and Depth for chamber orchestra 1983, The Story of Jonas, opera for children 1985–86, Sonatina for flute and clarinet 1990, Book of Challenges (three vols) 1991–99, Dreams of Spain, cantata for orchestra and choir, Symphonie concertante for 6 soloists and strings 1994, Ecclesiaste for narrator, solo cello and cello ensemble 1994, Continuum, for piano and 15 instruments 1995, Merry Feet, nursery songs 1998, Birth of a Niggum for flute, clarintet and piano 1999, B.A.C.H. D.I.E.S. for 17 instruments, A late sonata, for piano 2005. *Publications:* Milky Way (four vols piano pedagogic) 1975, The Art of Piano Playing, piano pedagogic 1987, Book of Challenges (three vols) 1991–99, Die Dritte Hand 2001, 'Where Swim the Salmons?' (autobiog. with Mira Zakai). *Honours:* Dr hc (Hebrew Univ., Jerusalem) 2005; Israel Prize for Composition 1997. *Address:* c/o ACUM Ltd, PO Box 14220, Acum House, Rothschild Blvd 118, Tel-Aviv 61140; 14 Rechov Aviad, Jerusalem 93703, Israel (home). *Telephone:* (2) 6787769 (home). *Fax:* (2) 6783513 (home). *E-mail:* hajdu@013.net.il (home).

HAJOSSYOVA, Magdalena; Czech singer (soprano); b. 25 July 1946, Bratislava. *Education:* Bratislava Music Acad. *Career:* debut at Slovak National Theatre, Bratislava 1971, as Marenka in The Bartered Bride; sang at the National Theatre Prague and elsewhere in the former Czechoslovakia; Berlin Staatsoper from 1975, as Mozart's Pamina, Fiordilgi, Contessa, Donna Anna, Handel's Alcina, Wagner's Eva, Elsa, Strauss's Arabella, Marschallin, Capriccio, Dvořák's Rusalka; has also sung in the operas of Jan Cikker; guest appearances as opera and concert singer in England, Belgium, Spain, The Netherlands, Greece, Italy, France, USA, Japan, Russia, Austria, Iran and Germany. *Recordings include:* The Cunning Little Vixen, Don Giovanni and Mahler's 4th Symphony; Erindo by Sigismund Kusser; Beethoven's 9th Symphony; Mozart's Requiem; Dvořák's Requiem, Stabat Mater; Britten: Illuminations; Janáček: Missa Glagolitica; Dvořák: Dimitri; Mahler's 2nd Symphony; Schumann: Paradies und der Peri; Gounod: Margarethe in Faust; Wagner: Wesendonk-Lieder; Strauss: Brentano-Lieder, 4 Letzte Lieder; Bruckner: Te Deum, and F minor Mass; Schubert: G major Mass and Stabat Mater; H Wolf, Italienisches Liederbuch; Mahler G and Alma: Lieder; Brahms, Lieder. *Address:* Kopenicker Str 104, Berlin 19179, Germany.

HAKALA, Tommi; Finnish singer (baritone); b. 9 Aug. 1970, Riihimäki. *Education:* Sibelius Acad. and Staatliche Hochschule für Musik, Karlsruhe. *Career:* early engagements included several opera houses in Germany and Finland and a guest contract with Finnish Nat. Opera; held positions with Nuremberg Opera 1998–2001, 2001–04; now freelance artist; repertoire includes such roles as Marcello, Papageno, Guglielmo, Graf/der Wildschütz, Dandini, the Count and Figaro in Le nozze di Figaro, Besenbinder/Hänsel und Gretel, Wolfram/Tannhäuser, Schaunard/La Bohème and Silvio/Pagliacci; has given concerts in Finland, Belgium, Estonia, Germany, Italy and the USA; recent guest engagements have included Finnish Nat. Opera, Helsinki, Savonlinna Opera Festival, Bayerische Staatsoper, Aalto Theater, Essen, Semperoper, Dresden, among others; future projects include concerts in Madrid, Barcelona, Aalborg as well as the recording of a Sallinnen Opera with the Helsinki Philharmonic Orchestra. *Recording:* Great Baritone Arias 2005. *Honours:* Matti Salminen Grant, scholarship from the Richard Wagner Foundation, First Prize, Merikanto Singing Competition 2001, Winner, BBC Cardiff Singer of the World Int. Singing Competition 2003. *Current Management:* c/o Pekka K. Pohjola, Allegro Artist Management, Kimmeltie 3, 02110 Espoo, Finland. *Telephone:* (9) 4123012. *E-mail:* allegro@allegroartist.com. *Website:* www.allegroartist.com.

HAKHNAZARYAN, Narek; Armenian cellist; b. 1988, Yerevan. *Education:* Sayat-Nova School of Music, Yerevan with Zareh Sarkisyan, Moscow Conservatory, Russia with Alexey Seleznyov, New England Conservatory of Music, USA with Laurence Lesser. *Career:* concerts in Russia, Europe, UK, Greece, Turkey and Canada; New York debut in Young Concert Artists Series at Carnegie's Zankel Hall and in Washington, DC at Kennedy Center; has performed with int. orchestras including the Verdi Orchestra, Milan, Jerusalem Symphony, Tokyo Symphony at Suntory Hall; recitals throughout USA and with US orchestras including the Boston 'Pops', Pasadena Symphony and Naples Philharmonic under Jorge Mester; invited to perform in Europe at Verbier Festival, Switzerland, Beethoven Festival, Warsaw, Tivoli Festival, Denmark; chamber music performances with Boston Chamber Music Soc. and at Ravinia's Steans Inst., Caramoor Festival's 'Rising Stars' series; 2011–12 season included first concerto appearance at Lincoln Center's Alice Tully Hall with Orchestra of St Luke's under Ryan McAdams on the Young Concert Artists Gala, performances with London Symphony Orchestra and Mariinsky Orchestra under Valery Gergiev, a five-concert European tour with Moscow Philharmonic. *Honours:* scholarships from Rostropovich Russian Performing Arts Fund, Winner, Aram Khachaturian Int. Competition 2006, Winner, Johansen Int. Competition for Young String Players 2006, Winner, Young Concert Artists Int. Auditions 2008, First Prize and Gold Medal, XIV Int. Tchaikovsky Competition, Moscow also Prize for Best Performance of Chamber Concerto and Audience Prize 2011, Artist Diploma, New England Conservatory of Music 2011. *Current Management:* c/o Opus 3 Artists, 470 Park Avenue South, 9th Floor North, New York, NY 10016, USA. *Telephone:* (212) 584-7500. *E-mail:* info@opus3artists.com. *Website:* www.opus3artists.com.

HAKIM, Naji Subhy Paul Irénée; Lebanese/French organist, composer and academic; *Professor of Music Analysis, Conservatoire à Rayonnement Régional de Boulogne-Billancourt*; b. 31 Oct. 1955, Beirut, Lebanon; s. of Subhy Hakim and Katy Nammour; m. Prof. Dr Marie-Bernadette Dufourcet; one s. one d. *Education:* Conservatoire Nat. Supérieur de Musique, Paris, École Nationale Supérieure des Télécommunications, studied with Jean Langlais, Roger Boutry, Jean-Claude Henry, Marcel Bitsch, Rolande Falcinelli, Jacques Castérède and Serge Nigg. *Career:* Organist, Basilique du Sacré-Coeur, Paris 1985–93, Église de la Trinité 1993–2008; Prof. of Musical Analysis, Conservatoire à Rayonnement Régional de Boulogne-Billancourt 1988–; Visiting Prof., RAM; Composer-in-Residence, Trinity Coll. of Music, London, UK 2004–; French mem. Consociatio Internationalis Musicae Sacrae, Vatican City 2000–; mem. Comm. Consultative des orgues de la Ville de Paris 1983–90; Vice-Patron Acad. of St Cecilia, London 2003–. *Compositions:* orchestral: Fantaisie Celtique 1985, Concerto No. 1 for organ and strings 1988, Les Noces de l'Agneau 1996, Hymne de l'universe 1997, Seattle Concerto 1999, Concerto pour violon et orchestre à cordes 2002, Concerto No. 3 for organ and string orchestra 2003, Ouverture Libanaise 2004, Phèdre 2004; vocal: Saul de Tarse for choir 1991, Missa Resurrectionis 1994, Missa Redemptionis 1995, Phèdre 1997, Messe Solennelle 1999, Children 1999, Magnificat 1999, Trois Noëls 2001, Gloria 2002, Ave Maris Stella 2003; chamber: Prélude et Fugue for bassoon quartet 1983, Divertimento for guitar quartet 1987, Sextuor for piano and string quintet 1988; solo organ: Symphonie en trois mouvements (Prix Amis de l'Orgue) 1984, Hommage à Igor Stravinski 1986, Fantaisie sur Adeste Fideles 1986, The Embrace of Fire (first prize Int. Organ Competition Anton Heiller, Southern Missionary Coll., Collegedale, USA) 1986, Memor 1989, Rubaiyat 1990, Variations on Two Themes 1991, Le Tombeau d'Olivier Messiaen 1993, Mariales 1993, Vexilla Regis Prodeunt 1994, Canticum 1995, Pange Lingua 1996, Sinfonia in Honore Sancti Ioannis Baptistæ 1996, Chant de Joie 1997, Bagatelle 1997, Te Deum 1997, The Last Judgement 1999, Quatre Etudes 2000, Ouverture Libanaise 2001, Le Bien-aimé 2001, In Organo Chordis et Choro 2001, Agapê 2001, Gregoriana 2003, Bach'orama 2003, Gregoriana 2003, Salve Regina 2004, Sakskobing Praeludier 2005, Mit seinem Geist und Gaben 2006, Esquisses grégoriennes 2006, Glenalmond Suite 2007, All my Founts Shall be With You 2007, Ich liebe die farbenreiche Welt 2008, Arabesques 2009, Fanfare for Nottingham 2010; solo instrument: Jeu for harp 1987, Sonata for violin 1994; duo: Rondo for Christmas for trumpet and organ 1988, Duo Concertant for organ and piano 1988, Rhapsody for organ duet 1992, Sonata for trumpet and organ 1994, Caprice en Rondeau for flute and piano 1998, Sonate for violin and piano 2000, Suite Rhapsodique for trumpet and organ 2002; ensemble: Old Hundredth for organ and brass 1987, Hymne au Sacré-Coeur for seven trumpets and organ 1993. *Honours:* Augustae Crucis Insigne pro Ecclesia et Pontifice from Pope Benedict XVI 2007; Dr hc (Pontifical Univ. Saint-Esprit of Kaslik, Lebanon) 2002; Prizewinner, Int. Organ Competitions at Haarlem, Beauvais, Lyon, Nuremberg, St Albans, Strasbourg and Rennes, Académie des Beaux-Arts Prix de Composition Musicale André Caplet 1991. *Address:* Conservatoire National de Région de Boulogne-Billancourt, 22 rue de la Belle-Feuille, Boulogne-Billancourt 92100, France (office). *E-mail:* mail@najihakim.com (office). *Website:* www.najihakim.com.

HÄKKINEN, Aapo; Finnish harpsichordist, music director and conductor; *Artistic Director, Helsinki Baroque Orchestra. Education:* Sibelius Acad., studied with Bob van Asperen at Amsterdam Sweelinck Conservatoire, and with Pierre Hantäi in Paris. *Career:* chorister, Helsinki Cathedral; has appeared as soloist world-wide, in halls and at festivals including La Roque d'Anthéron, Konzerthaus Berlin, Brühler Schlosskonzerte, Dresdner Musikfestspiele, Wartburgkonzerte Eisenach, Göttinger Handel-Festspiele, Kölner Philharmonie, Rheingau, Flanders, Bachfest der Neuen Bachgesellschaft, Musica Bayreuth, Washington Library of Congress, Copenhagen Tivoli, St Petersburg Early Music Festival, Semana Santa Madrid, Semana de Música Antigua de Estella, Bolzano Festival, Zagreb Baroque Festival, Helsinki and Turku Festivals, Lahti Organ Festival; chamber music concerts in Europe with numerous ensembles and artists; conducted Handel's Acis and Galatea and Haydn's L'isola disabitata for Finnish Chamber Opera, Carissimi's Jephte for Kokkola Opera and Pergolesi's La serva padrona for Croatian Nat. Theatre; Artistic Dir, Helsinki Baroque Orchestra; writer and broadcaster on early music; ed. of series of 17th century Florentine keyboard music for Ut Orpheus Edizioni; teacher, Sibelius Acad. and master-classes. *Recordings include:* numerous recordings including Couperin: Suites 2013; with Helsinki Baroque Orchestra: Monteverdi 2005, Franz Xaver Richter: Grandes Symphonies 1–6 2007, 7–12 2009, Agrell Orchestral Works 2010, Dussek: Four Symphonies 2012, Bach Harpsichord Concertos Vol. 1 2012, Vol. 2 2013. *Honours:* Special Prize, Norddeutscher Rundfunk 1997, VRT Prize, Bruges Int. Harpsichord Competition 1998. *Address:* Helsinki Baroque Orchestra, Box 34, 00131 Helsinki, Finland (office). *Telephone:* (50) 4924339 (office). *E-mail:* aapo.hakkinen@hebo.fi. *Website:* www.aapohakkinen.com.

HAKOLA, Riikka; Finnish singer (soprano); b. 1962. *Education:* Sibelius Acad., Helsinki, studied in Italy and in Berlin, New York and London. *Career:* sang in the 1989 premiere of The Knife by Paavo Heininen, at the Savonlinna Festival; National Opera, Helsinki 1990, as Lucia di Lammermoor; guest artist in London in Haydn's opera Orfeo; sang Marzelline in Fidelio at Savonlinna 1992; other roles have included Rosina, Gilda, Susanna, the Queen of Night and Violetta; debut at the Bolshoi in Moscow 1995; frequent concert engagements in Finland and abroad; Turku 1996, as Zetulbe in Crusell's The Little Slave Girl; has sung in several world premieres by Finnish contemporary composers at Savonlinna Opera Festivals, including the title role in Frieda by Tikka and Hilda in Alexis Kivi by Rautavaara; sang Jenny in Weill's Mahagonny and First Nymph in Linkola's Angelika in recordings for Finnish television.

HALA, Tomás; Czech conductor and composer; b. 6 Sept. 1963, Prague. *Education:* Prague Conservatory, Prague Acad. of Music. *Career:* Conductor, Opera House Ceskè Budejovice 1990–91; Conductor, Prague Nat. Theatre Opera from 1991, including Mozart's Don Giovanni (Asst to Charles Mackerras), Die Zauberflöte, Le nozze di Figaro, Verdi's La Forza del Destino; mem. Czech Musical Fund. *Compositions:* Vejstupny Syn (chamber opera), Rough Sea for baritone solo, Variations for cello, Piano Concerto.

HALBREICH, Harry Leopold; musicologist; b. 9 Feb. 1931, Berlin, Germany; m. Helène Chait 1961, one s. two d. *Education:* Geneva Conservatory, Ecole Normale de Musique, Paris with Arthur Honegger, Paris Conservatoire. *Career:* teacher of musical analysis, Royal Conservatory, Mons, Belgium 1970–; Gen. Musical Adviser to the Brussels Philharmonic Soc., with some 180 concerts annually; numerous lectures and seminars in Italy, including Turin, Cagliari and Venice, in Spain at Madrid and Granada, in Japan at the Akiyoshidai Festival of Contemporary Music, and elswhere; Artistic Bd mem. (programme adviser), Venice Biennale for Contemporary Music; int. jury mem., International Record Critics' Award, High Fidelity, New York, Academie Charles-Cros, Paris, Prix Cecilia, Brussels, and for several composition competitions at Parma, Turin and Cagliari; regular producer of radio programmes for RTB, Brussels and RSR, Geneva; co-founder and co-Ed. of music magazine, Crescendo, Brussels. *Publications include:* Edgard Varèse 1970, Olivier Messiaen 1980, Claude Debussy 1980, Arthur Honegger: un musicien dans la cité des hommes 1992, L'Oeuvre d'Arthur Honegger 1993, Arthur Honegger 1995; contrib. to Fayard Music Guides: Piano Music 1987, Chamber Music 1989, Choral Music 1993, contrib. to several titles in the L'Avant-Scène Opéra series, including Moses und Aron; contrib. to Harmonie 1965–84, Le Monde de la Musique 1982–89, Encyclopaedia Universalis.

HALE, Robert; American singer (bass-baritone); b. 22 Aug. 1943, Kerrville, TX; m. Inga Nielsen. *Education:* New England Conservatory of Music with Gladys Miller, Boston Univ. with Ludwig Bergman, Oklahoma Univ., studied with Boris Goldovsky in New York. *Career:* debut with New York City Opera 1967; Metropolitan debut in the title role in Der Fliegende Holländer 1990, returning there as Wotan in Die Walküre 1993, 1996, Pizzaro in Fidelio 1993, Orest in Elektra 1994; performances as Wotan in Richard Wagner's Der Ring des Nibelungen include Vienna, La Scala, Paris, Berlin, Munich, Hamburg, Cologne, Tokyo, Sydney, San Francisco, Washington, DC and New York; other roles include Pizzaro in Fidelio, Salzburg Festival 1990, Barak in Die Frau ohne Schatten at the Easter and Summer Festival (televised) 1992, the title role in Béla Bartók's Bluebeard's Castle at the Summer Festival 1995, Handel's Saul at the Ludwigsburg Festival 2000–01; sings regularly with Vienna State Opera, Royal Opera Covent Garden, La Scala Milan, Paris, Munich State Opera, Deutsche Oper Berlin, Hamburg State Opera; guest appearances include performances with the orchestras of Boston, Philadelphia, Cleveland, Chicago, San Francisco, New York, Houston, Dallas, Los Angeles, Washington, DC, Toronto and Montréal, the Berliner Philharmonie, Musikverein Vienna, the Royal Albert Hall and the Barbican Centre in London, Concertgebouw Amsterdam; festival engagements include Ravinia, Tanglewood, Cincinnati and Wolftrap in the USA, and Salzburg, Munich, Bregenz, Bergen, Lausanne, Orange, Bordeaux, Ravenna and Athens in Europe. *Recordings include:* Der Fliegende Holländer, Das Rheingold, Die Walküre, The Messiah, Siegfried, Verdi Requiem, Das Paradies und die Peri, Song of Love (with Inga Nielsen) 1997, Salome 1999. *Video recordings include:* Die Frau ohne Schatten, Der Fliegende Holländer, Der Ring des Nibelungen. *Honours:* Singer of the Year, Nat. Asscn of Teachers of Singing. *Current Management:* Dr Germinal Hilbert Theateragentur, Maximillianstrasse 22, 80539 Munich, Germany.

HALEVI, Hadar; Israeli singer (mezzo-soprano); b. 1966. *Career:* appearances in Israel and throughout Europe in concerts and opera; repertory includes Carmen, Bizet, Werther, Massenet, Il Barbiere, Rossini, Mozart operas, Ravel; contestant at the 1995 Cardiff Singer of the World Competition. *Current Management:* Zemsky/Green Artists Management, 730 Fifth Avenue, Suite 1802, New York, NY 10019, USA. *Telephone:* (212) 300-8003. *Fax:* (212) 300-8001. *E-mail:* zgartists@aol.com. *Website:* www.zemskygreen.com.

HALFFTER, Cristobal; Spanish composer and conductor; b. 24 March 1930, Madrid; m. Maria Manuela Caro; two s. one d. *Education:* Real Conservatorio de Música, Madrid with Del Campo, studied with Alexander Tansman, Conrado del Campo. *Career:* teacher of composition and musical forms, Real Conservatorio de Música, Madrid 1961–66, Dir 1964–66; Lecturer, Univ. of Navarra 1970–78, Internationale Ferienkurse für Neue Musik at Darmstadt 1976–78; Pres., Spanish section of the ISCM 1979; Artistic Dir Studio for Electronic Music, Heinrich Strobel-Stiftung in Freiburg 1980; Principal Guest Conductor, Nat. Orchestra, Madrid from 1989; conductor of the chief orchestras in Europe and America from 1970; mem. Real Academia de Bellas Artes, Akademie der Künste, Berlin, Kungl Musikaliska Akademien, Stockholm, Sweden, Royal Acad. of the Fine Arts San Fernando, Madrid, European Acad. of Science, Arts and Humanities, Paris. *Compositions:* stage: Ballet Saeta 1955; orchestral: Piano Concerto 1955, 5 Microformas 1960, Rhapsodia española de Albeniz for piano and orchestra 1960, Sinfonia for three instrumental groups 1963, Secuencias 1964, Lineas y Puntos for 20 winds and tape 1967, Anillos 1968, Fibonaciana for flute and strings 1970, Plaint for the Victims of Violence 1971, Requiem por la libertad imaginada 1971, Pinturas negras 1972, Processional 1974, Tiempo para espacios for harpsichord and strings 1974, Cello Concerto 1975, Elegias a la muerte de tres poetas españoles 1975, Officium defunctorum 1979, Violin Concerto, Tiento 1980, Handel Fantasia 1981, Sinfonia Ricercata 1982, Versus 1983, Parafrasis 1984, Cello Concerto No. 2 1985, Double Concerto for violin, viola and orchestra 1984, Tiento del Primer tono y Batalla Imperial 1986, Concerto for cello and orchestra No. 2 1986, Dortmund Variations 1987, Piano Concerto 1988, Preludio and Nemesis 1989, Concerto for saxophone quartet and orchestra 1989, Violin Concerto No. 2 1991, Daliniana for chamber orchestra 1994, Odradek, Homage à F. Kafka for orchestra 1996; vocal: Regina Coeli 1951, Misa Ducal 1956, In exspectatione resurrectionis Domini 1962, Brecht-Lieder 1967, Symposium 1968, Yes Speak Out 1968, Noche pasiva del sentido 1971, Gaudium et Spes for 32 voices and tapes 1972, Oracion a Platero 1975, Officium Defunctorum 1978, Noche Pasiva del Sentido 1979, Leyendo a Jorge Guillen 1982, Dona Nobis Pacem 1984, Tres Poemas de la Lirica Española 1984–86, Dos Motetes para caro a cappella 1988, Muerte, Mudanza y Locura for tape and voices (text by Cervantes) 1989, La del alba seria (after Cervantes) for solo voices, chorus and orchestra 1997; opera, Don Quijote (premiered at Madrid, Teatro Real) 2000; chamber: two String Quartets 1955, 1970, Solo Violin Sonata 1959, Codex for guitar 1963, Antiphonismoi for seven players 1967, Noche activa del espiritu 1973, Mizar for two flutes and electronic ensemble 1980, String Sextet 1994; piano music. *Honours:* Ford Foundation and Berlin (DAAD) scholarships, King Juan Carlos of Spain Gold Medal for Fine Arts 1983. *Address:* Bola 2, Madrid 28013, Spain (office). *Telephone:* 987540296 (office). *Fax:* 987542648 (office).

HALFVARSON, Eric, MMus; American singer (bass), conductor and teacher; b. 1953, Aurora, Illinois; s. of Sten Halfvarson and Lucille Halfvarson; two d. *Education:* Houston Opera Studio, Univ. of Illinois. *Career:* made debut as Basilio in Il Barbier di Siviglia, Lake George Opera Festival 1973; sang at Houston from 1977, notably as Sarastro 1980; Carnegie Hall, New York, in Hamlet by Ambroise Thomas 1981; San Francisco 1982–, notably as Hagen in The Ring 1990; sang Spoleto in European premiere of Barber's Antony and Cleopatra 1983; further appearances at Chicago, Toronto, Miami, St Louis (US premiere of Il Viaggio as Reims, 1986) and Dallas (premiere of The Aspern Papers by Dominick Argento, 1988); sang Raimondo in Lucia di Lammermoor at Washington 1989, Wagner's King Henry at Dallas and the Landgrave in Tannhäuser at Montpellier 1991; engagements at Santa Fe as Baron Ochs 1989, 1992, and Morosus in Die schweigsame Frau 1991; other roles include Ramphis in Dallas 1991, Banquo, Rocco, Sparafucile at New York Met, 1995, the Commendatore in Don Giovanni, Puccini's Colline, Alvise in La Gioconda, Gremin in Eugene Onegin, the King in Schreker's Der Schatzgräber at Holland Festival 1992, Fafner and Hagen in The Ring Cycle, Bayreuth Festival 1994, Pogner in Die Meistersinger, Bayreuth Festival 1996, Hagen, Buenos Aires 1998; sung as Fafner and Hunding at the Met, Sarastro and the Grand Inquisitor at the Vienna Staatsoper, Claggart at Covent Garden and King Henry in Lohengrin at Bayreuth, Sparafucile in Rigoletto at Covent Garden, Doctor in Wozzeck, Grand Inquisitor in Don Carlos and Dalland in

Der Fliegender Hollaender, Barcelona, Rocco in Fidelio at Covent Garden, Sarastro in Die Zauberfloette, Hyogo, Japan, Landgraf in Tannhaeuser with San Francisco Opera, Banco in Macbeth with Dallas Opera, Grande Inquisitor in Don Carlos in Valencia, K. Marke in Tristan und Isolde, Lodovico in Otello with Los Angeles Opera, Hagen in Götterdaemmerung, Vienna State Opera 2009, Budapest Opera. *Recordings include:* Antony and Cleopatra, Royok, Don Carlos, Billy Budd, Gotterdammerung, The Flying Dutchman, Boris Godunov, Die Walküre, Siegfried, Rigoletto, Tristan und Isolde. *Current Management:* c/o Jack Mastroianni, IMG Artists, Carnegie Hall Tower, 152 West 57th Street, 5th Floor, New York, NY 10019, USA. *Telephone:* (212) 994-3550. *Fax:* (212) 994-3500. *E-mail:* jmastroianni@imgartists.com. *Website:* www.imgartists.com. *Address:* 1264 Harwood Road, Suite 100, Bedford, TX 76021, USA (office). *Telephone:* (646) 431-1823 (office). *E-mail:* halfvarson@aol.com (office). *Website:* www.erichalfvarson.com.

HALGRIMSON, Amanda; American singer (soprano); b. 28 Nov. 1956, Fargo, ND. *Education:* Northern Illinois Univ. *Career:* appearances at opera houses across the USA, notably as Fiordiligi, Norina, Clarice in Il Mondo della Luna and Rosalinde; sang with Texas Opera on tour 1987–88, as Lucia di Lammermoor; European debut 1988, as the Queen of Night with Netherlands Opera; further engagements in Vienna (Volksoper and Staatsoper), St Gallen and Düsseldorf; concert performances include Mozart's Schauspieldirektor and Salieri's Prima la musica, poi le parole with Houston Symphony; sang the Queen of Night in a new production of Die Zauberflöte at the Deutsche Oper Berlin 1991; mem. ensemble of the Deutsche Oper Berlin 1992–93; sang Beethoven's Missa Solemnis with the Boston Symphony Orchestra under Roger Norrington 1993; sang Beethoven's 9th Symphony at the reopening of the Liederhalle in Stuttgart under G. Gelmetti 1993; Schumann's Faust/Gretchen with the Minnesota Orchestra, as well as Beethoven's Missa Solemnis with the Boston Symphony Orchestra at the Tanglewood Festival; sang Donna Anna with the Birmingham Symphony Orchestra under Simon Rattle 1993; concerts of Mozart's Requiem in London, Berlin and Paris with the Chamber Orchestra of Europe 1993; Queen of Night at the Grand Théâtre de Genève 1994; sang the Trovatore Leonora and Donna Anna at the Deutsche Oper Berlin 1996; other roles include Strauss's Empress (Berlin 1998) and Aithra in Die Aegyptische Helena; season 2000 as Trovatore Leonora at Bonn and the Empress in Die Frau ohne Schatten at Essen; mem. Deutsche Oper, Berlin 1992–2001. *Honours:* prizewinner Voci Verdiana (Bussetto) Competition 1985, Metropolitan Auditions 1987.

HALIM, Mohammed; Indonesian composer; b. 1963, Bukittinggi, Sumatra. *Education:* Acad. for Indonesian Performing Arts, Padangpanjang, and in Surakarta. *Career:* collaboration with dance ensemble, Gumarang Sakti 1990–; concert tours to Europe, America and Asia 1994; teacher of composition, Acad. for Indonesian Performing Arts (Sekolah Tinggi Seni Indonesia), Padangpanjang. *Compositions include:* Amai-Amai 1992, Awuak Tongtong 1993. *Address:* Sekolah Tinggi Seni Indonesia, Padangpanjang, West Sumatra, Indonesia (office). *E-mail:* mitramus@indo.net.id (office).

HALL, Aled; British singer (tenor); b. 1970, Pencader, Wales. *Education:* studied in Aberystwyth and London, National Opera Studio. *Career:* sang as boy soprano then at Wexford Festival, 1995–96 in Pacini's Saffo and Meyerbeer's L'Etoile du Nord; Appearances in Falstaff and Le Pescatrici for Garsington Opera; Carmen and Poppea for Welsh National Opera and as Monostatos for Scottish Opera; Butterfly and Tosca for Raymond Gubay productions; Concerts include Janáček's Diary at Wexford; Messiah at the Festival Hall and Mozart's Requiem. *Honours:* Royal Academy Joseph Maas Prize. *Current Management:* c/o Harlequin Agency Ltd, 203 Fidlas Road, Llanishen, Cardiff, CF14 5NA, Wales. *Telephone:* (29) 2075-0821. *Fax:* (29) 2075-5971. *E-mail:* peter@harlequin-agency.co.uk. *Website:* www.harlequin-agency.co.uk.

HALL, Janice; American opera singer (soprano) and actor; b. 28 Sept. 1953, San Francisco, Calif. *Education:* Boston Conservatory. *Career:* performed with New York City Opera (Dido and Aeneas, Falstaff, Le Nozze di Figaro, La Traviata, La Bohème), Houston Grand Opera (La Perichole), Chicago Lyric Opera (Le Nozze di Figaro), Santa Fe Opera Festival (The Barber of Seville, Don Pasquale, La Traviata, Ariodante, The Beggar's Opera), Washington Nat. Opera (La Bohème, La Sonnambula), Opera Pacific (The Pearl Fishers), Fort Worth Opera (Angels in America, Turn of the Screw, Dialogues of the Carmelites); European debut with Hamburg Opera (Il Barbiere di Siviglia) 1982; also performed with Cologne Opera (Lucia di Lammermoor, La Traviata, Gianni Schicchi, La Finta Giardiniera, Turandot), Komische Oper Berlin (La Bohème, Madama Butterfly), Zurich (Carmen), Vienna (Il Barbiere), Venice (Il Matrimonio Segreto) and Drottningholm (Agrippina); performed at Salzburg Festival as Fortuna in premiere of Henze's version of Il Ritorno d'Ulisse 1985, Schwetzingen Festspiele (Agrippina, La Cambiale di Matrimonio), Kurt Weill Fest, Dessau (Street Scene) and Micaela at Eutin Festival 1995; world premiere performances and recording of opera, Before Night Falls 2010; also performing as actor and cabaret artist in New York 2010–. *Honours:* Emmy Award, Best Cultural Program (for La Traviata, Live from Lincoln Center) 1995. *Current Management:* c/o Nick Netos, Alpha Artists Management LLC, 889 Ninth Avenue, New York, NY 10019-1781, USA. *Telephone:* (212) 397-7921 (ext. 13); (646) 479-5263 (mobile). *Fax:* (212) 397-7920. *E-mail:* alphaartists@pinnaclearts.com. *Website:* www.alpha-artists.com; www.janice-hall.com.

HALL, John; British singer (bass); b. 1956, Brecon, Wales; m. Julie Crocker; one s. two d. *Education:* Birmingham School of Music, Royal College of Music with Frederick Sharp. *Career:* sang Rossini's Basilio and Mozart's Bartolo for Opera 80; appearances with the English Bach Festival at Covent Garden and the Athens Festival; Glyndebourne Festival from 1981; Glyndebourne Touring Opera as Masetto in Don Giovanni (Hong Kong 1986), Mozart's Figaro and Quince in A Midsummer Night's Dream; Théâtre du Châtelet, Paris, 1985, in The Golden Cockerel; Opera North, 1986, in The Trojans and Madama Butterfly, and returned in Carmen, Tosca, Nielsen's Maskarade and Don Giovanni (as Leporello); Kent Opera, 1989, in The Return of Ulysses; Almeida Festival, 1989, in the premiere of Golem by John Casken; Glyndebourne Touring Opera, 1989–90, as Basilio and Rocco in Fidelio; Covent Garden, 1991, in Boris Godunov, as Mitiukha; English National Opera, 1992, in Return of Ulysses, as Time, Antinous; throughout France in Midsummer Night's Dream, 1993–94; premiere of Gruber's Gloria at Huddersfield Contemporary Music Festival, 1994; Midsummer Night's Dream at Torino and Ravenna, 1995; sang Mozart's Antonio for GTO at Glyndebourne, 1996; concert repertory includes Vaughan Williams's Serenade to Music (Last Night of the Proms, 1987), Messiah and Elijah. *Recordings:* title role in Casken's Golem. *Address:* Ivydene, Vicarage Way, Ringmer, East Sussex BN8 5LA, England.

HALL, Peter John, BA, MA; British singer (tenor); b. 7 April 1940, Surbiton, England. *Education:* King's College, Cambridge (choral scholarship), studied with Arthur Reckless, John Carol Case. *Career:* lay Vicar, Chichester Cathedral, 1965–66; Vicar-Choral, St Paul's Cathedral, London, 1972–2001; mem. of various professional choral groups, including John Alldis Choir, Schütz Choir of London, London Sinfonietta Voices; sang Ugo and Il Prete in La Vera Storia (Berio), Florence 1986, un Prete and Reduce in Outis (Berio) at La Scala, Milan, 1996 and Dr Chebutykhin in Three Sisters (Eötvös) in Lyon, 1998 at the composers' personal request; mem. Incorporated Society of Musicians. *Recordings:* Carmina Burana (Orff), with Hallé Orchestra; Transit (Ferneyhough), with London Sinfonietta; At the Boar's Head (Holst), with Royal Liverpool Philharmonic Orchestra; Christmas Vespers (Monteverdi) with Denis Stevens; Prometeo (Nono) with the Ensemble Modern, Frankfurt and The Flood (Stravinsky) with the London Sinfonietta. *Current Management:* c/o Rachel Nicholson, Concert Directory International, POB 53911, London, SW15 2UX, England. *Telephone:* (870) 742-4011. *Fax:* (870) 742-4012. *E-mail:* rachel@nicholsonproud.com. *Website:* www.nicholsonproud.com.

HALL, Sir Peter Reginald Frederick, Kt, CBE, MA; British theatre director and film director; b. 22 Nov. 1930, Bury St Edmunds, Suffolk; s. of late Reginald Hall and Grace Hall; m. 1st Leslie Caron 1956 (divorced 1965); one s. one d.; m. 2nd Jacqueline Taylor 1965 (divorced 1981); one s. one d.; m. 3rd Maria Ewing 1982 (divorced 1989); one d.; m. 4th Nicola Frei 1990; one d. *Education:* Perse School and St Catharine's Coll., Cambridge. *Career:* produced and acted in over 20 plays at Cambridge; first professional production The Letter, Windsor 1953; produced in repertory at Windsor, Worthing and Oxford Playhouse; two Shakespearean productions for Arts Council; Artistic Dir Elizabethan Theatre Co. 1953; Asst Dir London Arts Theatre 1954, Dir 1955–57; formed own producing co., Int. Playwright's Theatre 1957; Man. Dir Royal Shakespeare Co., Stratford-upon-Avon and Aldwych Theatre, London 1960–68 (resgnd), Assoc. Dir –1973; mem. Arts Council 1969–73; Co-Dir, Nat. Theatre (now Royal Nat. Theatre) with Lord Olivier April-Nov. 1973, Dir 1973–88; f. Peter Hall Co. 1988; Artistic Dir Glyndebourne 1984–90; Artistic Dir The Old Vic 1997; Wortham Chair in Performing Arts, Houston Univ., Tex. 1999; Chancellor, Kingston Univ. 2000–; fmr Dir Kingston Theatre, now Dir Emer.; Assoc. Prof. of Drama, Warwick Univ. 1964–67; Patron, Canon's Mouth; mem. Bd Playhouse Theatre 1990–91; acted in The Pedestrian (film) 1973. *Productions include:* Blood Wedding, The Immoralist, The Lesson, South, Mourning Becomes Electra, Waiting for Godot, Waltz of the Toreadors, Camino Real, Gigi, Love's Labours Lost, Cymbeline, Twelfth Night, A Midsummer Night's Dream, Coriolanus, Two Gentlemen of Verona, Troilus and Cressida, Ondine, Romeo and Juliet, The Wars of the Roses (London Theatre Critics' Award for Best Dir 1963), Becket, Cat on a Hot Tin Roof, The Rope Dancers (on Broadway), The Moon and Sixpence (opera, Sadler's Wells), Henry VI (parts 1, 2 and 3), Richard III, Richard II, Henry IV (parts 1 and 2), Henry V, Eh?, The Homecoming (London Theatre Critics' Award for Best Dir 1965, Antoinette Perry Award for Best Dir 1966), Moses and Aaron (opera, Covent Garden), Hamlet (London Theatre Critics' Award for Best Dir 1965), The Government Inspector, The Magic Flute (opera), Work is a Four Letter Word (film) 1968, Macbeth, Midsummer Night's Dream (film) 1969, Three into Two Won't Go (film) 1969, A Delicate Balance, Perfect Friday (film) 1971, La Calisto (opera, Glyndebourne Festival) 1970, The Knot Garden (opera, Covent Garden) 1970, Eugene Onegin (opera, Covent Garden) 1971, Old Times 1971, Tristan and Isolde (opera, Covent Garden) 1971, All Over 1972, Il Ritorno d'Ulisse (opera, Glyndebourne Festival) 1972, Alte Zeiten (Burgtheater, Vienna) 1972, Via Galactica (musical, Broadway) 1972, The Homecoming (film) 1973, Marriage of Figaro (opera, Glyndebourne) 1973, The Tempest 1973, Landscape (film) 1974, Akenfield (film) 1974, Happy Days 1974, No Man's Land 1975, Judgement 1975, Hamlet 1975, Tamburlaine the Great 1976, Don Giovanni (opera, Glyndebourne Festival) 1977, Volpone (Nat. Theatre) 1977, Bedroom Farce (Nat. Theatre) 1977, The Country Wife (Nat. Theatre) 1977, The Cherry Orchard (Nat. Theatre) 1978, Macbeth (Nat. Theatre) 1978, Betrayal (Nat. Theatre) 1978, Così Fan Tutte (opera, Glyndebourne) 1978, Fidelio (opera, Glyndebourne) 1979, Amadeus (Nat. Theatre) 1979, Betrayal (New York)

1980, Othello (Nat. Theatre) 1980, Amadeus (New York) (Tony Award for Best Dir 1981) 1980, Family Voices (Nat. Theatre) 1981, The Oresteia (Nat. Theatre) 1981, A Midsummer Night's Dream (opera, Glyndebourne) 1981, The Importance of Being Earnest (Nat. Theatre) 1982, Other Places (Nat. Theatre) 1982, The Ring (operas, Bayreuth Festival) 1983, Jean Seberg (musical, Nat. Theatre) 1983, L'Incoronazione di Poppea (opera, Glyndebourne) 1984, Animal Farm (Nat. Theatre) 1984, Coriolanus (Nat. Theatre) 1984, Yonadab (Nat. Theatre) 1985, Carmen (opera, Glyndebourne) 1985, (Metropolitan Opera) 1986, Albert Herring (opera, Glyndebourne) 1985, The Petition (New York and Nat. Theatre) 1986, Simon Boccanegra (opera, Glyndebourne) 1986, Salome (opera, Los Angeles) 1986, Coming in to Land (Nat. Theatre) 1986, Antony and Cleopatra (Nat. Theatre) 1987, Entertaining Strangers (Nat. Theatre) 1987, La Traviata (Glyndebourne) 1987, Falstaff (Glyndebourne) 1988, Salome (Covent Garden) 1988, Cymbeline (Nat. Theatre) 1988, The Winter's Tale (Nat. Theatre) 1988, The Tempest 1988, Orpheus Descending 1988, Salome (opera, Chicago) 1988, Albert Herring 1989, Merchant of Venice 1989, She's Been Away (TV) 1989, New Year (opera, Houston and Glyndebourne) 1989, Born Again (musical) 1990, The Homecoming 1990, Orpheus Descending (film) 1990, Twelfth Night 1991, The Rose Tattoo 1991, Tartuffe 1991, The Camomile Lawn (TV) 1991, Four Baboons Adoring the Sun (New York) 1992, All's Well That Ends Well (RSC) 1992, The Gift of the Gorgon (RSC) 1992, The Magic Flute (LA) 1993, Separate Tables 1993, Lysistrata 1993, She Stoops to Conquer 1993, Piaf (musical) 1993, An Absolute Turkey (Le Dindon) 1994, On Approval 1994, Hamlet 1994, Jacob (TV) 1994, Never Talk to Strangers (film) 1995, Julius Caesar (RSC) 1995, The Master Builder 1995, The Final Passage (TV) 1996, The Oedipus Plays (Nat. Theatre at Epidaurus and Nat. Theatre) 1996, A School for Wives 1995, A Streetcar Named Desire 1997, The Seagull 1997, Waiting for Godot 1997, 1998, King Lear 1997, The Misanthrope 1998, Major Barbara 1998, Simon Boccanegra (Glyndebourne) 1998, Amadeus 1998, Kafka's Dick 1998, Measure for Measure (Los Angeles) 1999, A Midsummer Night's Dream (Los Angeles) 1999, Lenny (Queens Theatre) 1999, Amadeus (Los Angeles, New York) 1999, Tantalus (Denver, Colo) 2000, Japes 2000, Romeo and Juliet (Los Angeles) 2001, Japes 2001, Troilus and Cressida (New York) 2001, A Midsummer Night's Dream (Glyndebourne) 2001, Otello (Glyndebourne) 2001, Japes (Theatre Royal) 2001, The Royal Family (Theatre Royal) 2001, Lady Windermere's Fan (Theatre Royal) 2002, The Bacchai (Olivier Theatre) 2002, Design for Living (Theatre Royal, Bath) 2003, Betrayal (Theatre Royal, Bath) 2003, The Fight for Barbara (Theatre Royal, Bath) 2003, As You Like It (Theatre Royal, Bath) 2003, Cuckoos (Theatre Royal, Bath) 2003, The Marriage of Figaro (Lyric Opera of Chicago) 2003, Happy Days (Arts Theatre, London) 2003, Man and Superman (Theatre Royal, Bath) 2004, Galileo's Daughter (Theatre Royal, Bath) 2004, The Vortex 2007, An Ideal Husband 2008, Pygmalion 2009. *Publications:* The Wars of the Roses 1970, Shakespeare's three Henry VI plays and Richard III (adapted with John Barton), John Gabriel Borkman (English version with Inga-Stina Ewbank) 1975, Peter Hall's Diaries: The Story of a Dramatic Battle 1983, Animal Farm: a stage adaptation 1986, The Wild Duck 1990, Making an Exhibition of Myself (autobiog.) 1993, An Absolute Turkey (new trans. of Feydeau's Le Dindon, with Nicki Frei) 1994, The Master Builder (with Inga-Stina Ewbank) 1995, Mind Millie for Me (new trans. of Feydeau's Occupe-toi d'Amélie, with Nicki Frei), The Necessary Theatre 1999, Exposed by the Mask 2000, Shakespeare's Advice to the Players 2003. *Honours:* Hon. Fellow, St Catharine's Coll., Cambridge 1964; Chevalier, Ordre des Arts et des Lettres 1965; Dr hc (York) 1966, (Reading) 1973, (Liverpool) 1974, (Leicester) 1977, (Essex) 1993, (Cambridge) 2003, (Bath) 2006; Hon. DSocSc (Birmingham) 1989; Hamburg Univ. Shakespeare Prize 1967, Evening Standard Special Award 1979, Evening Standard Award for Outstanding Achievement in Opera 1981, Evening Standard Best Dir Award for The Oresteia 1981, Evening Standard Best Dir Award for Antony and Cleopatra 1987, South Bank Show Lifetime Achievement Award 1998, Olivier Special Award for Lifetime Achievement 1999, New York Shakespeare Soc. Medal 2003, Lifetime Achievement Award, Theater Hall of Fame 2006.

HALL, Vicki; American singer (soprano); b. 13 Nov. 1943, Jefferson, TX. *Education:* studied in New York and with Josef Metternich in Cologne. *Career:* sang at New York City Opera 1970–; made guest appearances in Vienna (Volksoper), Munich (Theater am Gärtnerplatz), Cologne, Wuppertal and Bregenz; roles have included Mozart's Susanna and Blondchen, Carolina in Matrimonio Segreto, Frau Fluth in Die Lustige Weiber von Windsor, Olympia, Strauss's Sophie, Adele in Fledermaus, Gretel, and Janáček's Vixen; many concert appearances.

HALLGRÍMSSON, Haflidi; Icelandic composer and cellist; b. 18 Sept. 1941, Akureyri; m. 1975; three s. *Education:* The Music School, Reykjavík, Accad. Santa Cecilia, Rome, Italy, Royal Acad. of Music, London, UK; pvt. studies in composition with Alan Bush and Peter Maxwell Davies. *Career:* mem. Haydn String Trio 1967–70, English Chamber Orchestra 1971–76; Prin. Cellist, Scottish Chamber Orchestra 1977–83, Mondrian Trio 1984–88; numerous recitals; appeared as soloist with numerous symphony orchestras and performed on BBC Radio 3; teacher, St Mary's Music School, Edinburgh, UK 2000–; mem. Soc. of Promotion for New Music, Soc. of Scottish Composers, Performing Right Soc. *Compositions include:* Poemi, Verse I, Five Pieces for Piano, Seven Folksongs from Iceland, Fimma, Scenes from Poland, Your Image, Words in Winter, Níunda Stund Offerto, Ríma, Herma, Still-Life, Hljómsveitarmyndir, Bagatelles, Fley, Ombra, Myrtuskógur, Symphony No. 1, Mini-Stories, Ombra, Notes from a Diary, Botticelli Fragments for viola and

cello, Too Loud a Solitude. *Recordings include:* Strond, Poemi, Vers I, Daydreams in Numbers, Tristia, Jacob's Ladder, String Quartet No. 1, String Quartet No. 2, solitaire, Offerto, Seven Epigrams, Intarsia, The World of Incidences (D. Kharms), Cello Concerto No. 2, Passia (choral work), Homage to Mondrian (piano solo), La Serenissima, Narratives from the Deep North, Sonnambulo, Noðurdjúp, Svíta, Hymnos. *Honours:* Order of the Falcon (Iceland); Suggia Prize for Cello playing 1967, Viotti Prize, Italy 1975, Nordic Council Prize 1986. *Address:* 5 Merchiston Bank Gardens, Edinburgh, EH10 5EB, Scotland. *Telephone:* (131) 447-5752 (home). *E-mail:* haflidi@hallgrimsson.org.uk.

HALLIN, Margareta; Swedish singer (soprano), composer and academic; b. 20 Feb. 1931, Karlskoga. *Education:* Royal Stockholm Conservatory with Ragnar Hulten. *Career:* sang at the Royal Opera, Stockholm 1954–84, in the premieres of Blomdahl's Aniara 1959 and Drommen om Therese 1964 and Tintomora 1973, by Werle; also as Constanze, Blondchen, Lucia di Lammermoor, Gilda and Leonora in Il Trovatore; sang Anne Trulove in the Swedish premiere of The Rake's Progress 1961; Glyndebourne Festival 1957, 1960, as the Queen of Night; Covent Garden 1960, with the Stockholm Co. in Alcina by Handel; Drottningholm Court Opera from 1962, notably in the Abbé Vogler's Gustaf Adolf och Ebba Brahe 1973; appearances in Florence, Edinburgh, Hamburg, Zürich, Rome and Munich; later in career sang Elsa, Elisabeth de Valois, Mathilde in Guillaume Tell, the heroines in Les Contes d'Hoffmann, Violetta, Donna Anna, Senta, Butterfly and the Marschallin; sang Cherubini's Médée 1984; Drottningholm 1991, as Clytemnestra in Electra by Haeffner; Prof. of Singing, Kungliga Musikaliska Akademien, Stockholm 2001–. *Compositions include:* Miss Julie, The Stronger (operas after Strindberg), Elektra (opera after Sophocles), The Pig-farmer (opera after H. C. Andersen), Julkantat 2008. *Honours:* Swedish Court Singer 1966; Order Litteris et artibus 1976. *Address:* Kungliga Musikaliska Akademien, Blasieholmstorg 8, 111 48 Stockholm, Sweden (office). *Telephone:* (8) 407-18-02 (office). *Fax:* (8) 611-87-18 (office). *E-mail:* adm@musakad.se (office).

HALLSTEIN, Ingeborg; German singer (coloratura soprano); b. 23 May 1939, Munich; one d. *Education:* studied with her mother, Elisabeth Hallstein. *Career:* Mem. Bayerische Staatsoper 1961–73; numerous guest appearances in Germany and abroad, including Teatro Colón (Buenos Aires), Wiener Staatsoper (Vienna), Royal Opera House (Covent Garden, London), Royal Opera House (Stockholm), Deutsche Oper (Berlin), Staatsoper (Hamburg and Stuttgart), Concertgebouw (Amsterdam), Teatro La Fenice (Venice); has performed at many festivals in Austria (Salzburg), Germany, the Netherlands and Ireland; has performed operas, operettas and oratorios for radio and TV broadcasts; Prof. Hochschule für Musik, Würzburg 1979–2006; title Bayerische Kammersängerin conferred. *Operas include:* Die Schweigsame Frau, Die Zauberflöte, Le Nozze di Figaro, Der Rosenkavalier, Ariadne auf Naxos, Idomeneo, La Traviata, Rigoletto, Les Contes d'Hoffmann, Fidelio, Così fan tutte, L'Italiana in Algieri, Die Liebe zu den drei Orangen, Die Bassariden, Entführung, Le Boheme, Oberon, Capriccio, In seinem Garten liebt Don Perlimplin Belisa, Carmina Burana, La Finta Giardiniera, Il Re Cervo, Die Schweigsame Frau, Frau Ohne Schatten, Zaide, Der Türke in Italien, Aucassin und Nicolette, Fledermaus, Il Re Teodoro, I Commedianti, La Cenerentola. *Film:* Wälsungenblut. *Honours:* Bundesverdienstkreuz 1976, 1996, Bayerischer Verdienstorden 1999. *Address:* Tengstrasse 35, 80796 Munich, Germany (home). *Telephone:* (89) 2718338 (home). *Fax:* (89) 2722846 (home).

HALMEN, Petre; Romanian stage designer, costume designer and stage director; b. 14 Nov. 1943, Talmaciu. *Education:* studied in Berlin. *Career:* worked at Kiel and Düsseldorf, then collaborated with director Jean-Pierre Ponnelle at Zürich from 1975 in cycles of operas by Monteverdi and Mozart; Munich 1978–, with premieres of Reimann's Lear and Troades, 1986, Das Liebesverbot by Wagner and Berg's Lulu, 1985; Designs for Aida at Berlin; Chicago and Covent Garden 1982–84; Parsifal at San Francisco 1988 and 2 Ring Cycles; Designed and Directed Lohengrin at Düsseldorf 1987, Paer's Achille at Bologna 1988, La Straniera at Spoleto Festival, Charleston, 1989, and Nabucco for Munich Festival, 1990; Designs for Parsifal seen at Mainz 1991, Mozart's Lucio Silla at Vienna Staatsoper; Directed The Golden Cockerel at Duisburg, 1991, La Clemenza di Tito at Toulouse, 1992; Directed and designed Turandot at Deutsche Oper am Rhein, Düsseldorf, 1993; Directed and designed: Aida at Staatsoper Berlin, 1995, Turandot at Opéra de Nice, France, 1995, Don Giovanni at Staatsoper Hamburg, 1996, Rosenkavalier at Staatstheater Darmstadt, 1997, Orfeo by Gluck at Opernhaus Halle, 1997, Ariadne auf Naxos at Toulouse, France, 1988, Idomeneo at Salzburg Festspielhaus, 1998 and Ezio by Handel at Festspiele Halle, 1998, La Clemenza di Tito, Madrid, Oedipus Rex, Trier, Ariadne auf Naxos, Naples, The Tales of Hoffmann and Turandot, Lulu, Toulouse. *Address:* Tengstrasse 26, 80798 Munich, Germany.

HALMRAST, Tor, BMus, MSc; Norwegian composer and academic; *Associate Professor, Department of Musicology, University of Oslo;* b. 26 April 1951, Sarpsborg. *Education:* Univ. of Trondheim, Oslo Conservatory, Sweelinck Conservatory, Amsterdam, The Netherlands. *Career:* Composer-in-Residence, Music Conservatory, Tromsø 1988–90; Festival Composer, Northern Norwegian Festival 1990; in charge of acoustic design of several buildings for music, concerts and theatres, and studios; Head of Acoustics, Statsbygg; currently Assoc. Prof., Univ. of Oslo; mem. Bd Norwegian Network for Tech., Acoustics and Music (NoTAM); mem. Soc. of Norwegian Composers (Vice-Chair.). *Compositions:* works for symphony orchestra, chamber works, solo works, music for television, films and records and sound installation, including the music for the Norwegian Pavillion at the World Fair, Expo92, for ice/music sculpture for the Winter Olympics, Lillehammer 1994, Alfa and Romeo (radio opera for Norwegian Radio) (Prix Italia/European Broadcasting Union Prize) 1997. *Recordings:* Hemera 2901, Music for Expo92 and other electro-acoustic works: Aquaduct, Icille, Oppbrudd, Varang, Motgift. *Publications:* several papers on room acoustics in Journal of Sound and Vibration, Journal of the Acoustical Society of America. *Honours:* AM Prize for Best Sound Installation/Composition, World Fair, Expo92, Seville, Spain 1992. *Address:* University of Oslo, Department of Musicology, PO Box 1017, Blindern, 0315 Oslo (office); Spaangberg v 28A, 0853 Oslo, Norway (home). *Telephone:* 95-19-16-75 (office). *E-mail:* torhalm@online.no. *Website:* www.tor.halmrast.no.

HALSEY, Simon Patrick, CBE, MA; British conductor; *Chorus Director, London Symphony Orchestra and Chorus*; b. 8 March 1958, Kingston, Surrey; m. Lucy Lunt 1986. *Education:* King's Coll., Cambridge, Royal Coll. of Music. *Career:* Conductor, Scottish Opera-Go-Round 1980, 1981; Dir of Music, Univ. of Warwick 1980–88; Chorus Dir, City of Birmingham Symphony Orchestra 1982–; Assoc. Dir, Philharmonia Chorus 1986–97; Music Dir, Birmingham Opera Co. 1987–2000; Wagner's Ring 1990–91; Britten's Church Parables in London and elsewhere 1997; Dir, Acad. of Ancient Music Chorus 1988–92; Dir, Salisbury Festival 1989–93; Chorus Dir, Flanders Opera, Antwerp 1991–95; Artistic Dir, BBC Nat. Chorus of Wales 1995–2000; Consultant Ed., Faber Music Ltd 1996–; Int. Chair of Choral Conducting, Royal Welsh Coll. of Music and Drama 2008–14; Artistic Dir, Berlin Philharmonic Youth Choral Programme 2012–; Dir, BBC Proms Youth Choir 2012–; Chorus Dir, London Symphony Orchestra and Chorus 2012–; Prof. and Dir of Choral Activities, Univ. of Birmingham 2012–; Artistic Advisor, Schleswig-Holstein Musik Festival Choir Acad. 2014–; Guest Conductor, Chicago Symphony Chorus 1993–94; Prin. Guest Conductor, Netherlands Radio Choir 1995–2002, Chief Conductor 2002–08; Prin. Guest Conductor, Sydney Philharmonic Choirs 1997–2001; Prin. Conductor, Berlin Radio Choir 2001–; performed at BBC Proms, leading choirs in Michael Tippett's A Child of Our Time 2012, Ralph Vaughan-Williams' A Sea Symphony 2013, Benjamin Britten's War Requiem 2014. *Publication:* Vom Konzept zum Konzert 2011. *Honours:* Bundesverdienstkreuz 2010; Dr hc (Central England) 2000, (Birmingham) 2009, (Warwick); Diapason d'Or (France), BBC Music Magazine award, several German Echo Klassik Awards, Gramophone Record of the Year 1989, Deutsche Schallplatten Prize 1993, Grammy Awards 2008, 2009, 2011, Queen's Medal for Music 2015. *Current Management:* c/o Intermusica Artists Management Ltd, 16 Duncan Terrace, London, N1 8BZ, England. *Telephone:* (20) 7608-9900. *Fax:* (20) 7490-3263. *E-mail:* mail@intermusica.co.uk. *Website:* www.intermusica.co.uk.

HALSTEAD, Anthony George, FRNCM, FGSM; British conductor, horn player, keyboard player, composer and inventor; *Director, Halstead Music*; b. 18 June 1945, Manchester, England; m. 1st Lucy Mabey 1969; two s.; m. 2nd Ellen O'Dell 1985; one d. *Education:* Chetham's School, Royal Manchester Coll. of Music, studied with Sydney Coulston, Dr Horace Fitzpatrick, Myron Bloom, George Malcolm, Sir Charles Mackerras and Michael Rose. *Career:* mem. Bournemouth Symphony Orchestra 1966, BBC Scottish Symphony Orchestra 1966–70, London Symphony Orchestra 1970–73, English Chamber Orchestra 1972–86; Prof., Guildhall School of Music 1971–99; mem. Musicians' Union, Royal Soc. of Musicians, Inc. Soc. of Musicians. *Compositions:* Divertimento Serioso 1973, Prologue and Passus 1976, Serenade for oboe and strings 1977/1978, Concertino Elegiaco 1983, Suite for solo horn or trumpet 1978, Shakespeare Songs for Soprano, Recorder and Piano 2005. *Recordings:* Weber Horn Concertino 1986, Mozart Horn Concertos 1987, 1993, Haydn Horn Concertos 1989, Britten Serenade 1989, 12 harpsichord and 15 fortepiano concertos by J. C. Bach, 22 albums of J. C. Bach's complete orchestral works. *Honours:* Hon. mem. British Horn Soc., Int. Horn Soc. *Address:* 6 The Orchids, Etchinghill, Folkestone, Kent, CT18 8AR, England (office). *Fax:* (871) 989-5641 (office). *E-mail:* tony@halsteadmusic.co.uk (office). *Website:* www.halsteadmusic.co.uk (office).

HALTON, Richard; British singer (baritone); b. 1963, Devon, England; m. Julie Gossage. *Education:* Univ. of Kent at Canterbury, Guildhall School of Music, London with Johanna Peters, studied with Renato Cappecchi in USA. *Career:* has performed with all major British opera cos and on London West End stage; roles in London include Ravenal (Showboat) at London Palladium in RSC/Opera North production (Olivier Award), Harry Easter (Street Scene, also for BBC TV), Novice's Friend and understudy of Billy Budd (Billy Budd) for ENO, Diener (Capriccio), Paris (Romeo et Juliette) (also on video), understudy of The Traveller (Death in Venice) and Agravain (Gawain) all for Royal Opera, title role and Monsieur André in The Phantom of the Opera at Her Majesty's Theatre 1997–2003, Count Danilo (The Merry Widow) for English Touring Opera at New Sadler's Wells and on tour, Macheath (The Beggar's Opera) in The Great Hall, Lincoln's Inn, Mercury/Littore in David Alden's award-winning production of Poppea for Welsh Nat. Opera at The Shaftesbury Theatre (as seen on BBC 2), title role (The Emperor of Atlantis) at the Queen Elizabeth Hall, Max (Betly), Figaro (Il Barbiere di Siviglia), Silvio (Pagliacci) and Silvano (Ballo in Maschera) all at Holland Park Open Air Theatre, Jean (Miss Julie) and Barabashkin in Shostakovich's Cheryomushki at The Lyric, Hammersmith, The Shrink (Terminatrix) for Royal Nat. Theatre, Vox (Bad Times) and Marcello (Exposition of a Picture) at The Young Vic and Holofernes in world premiere of Ian McQueen's Line of Terror at the Almeida Festival; outside London, has sung Danny in Girl Crazy, Papageno (Magic Flute), Ned Keene (Peter Grimes), Counsel (Trial by Jury) and title role in Eugene Onegin, all for Scottish Opera, Jason in Gavin Bryar's Medea with BBC Scottish Symphony Orchestra at The Tramway, Marcello (La Bohème) and Mercury (Poppea) for Welsh Nat. Opera, Schaunard (La Bohème) and Welko (Arabella) for Glyndebourne, title role in Don Giovanni at Aldeburgh, Harlequin (Ariadne auf Naxos), Sid (Albert Herring), Perrucchetto (La Fedelta Premiata) and Guglielmo (Così fan tutte), all for Garsington Festival Opera, Tony in West Side Story at Derngate Theatre, Northampton, Fritz (plus six other characters) in Stephen Oliver's A Man of Feeling (also co-directed) and The White Voice in Akin Euba's Chaka both for City of Birmingham Touring Opera; has performed numerous concerts and oratorios, both at home and abroad, notably in Spain, Portugal, Italy, Belgium and Ireland; formed Bux Vox Singing Studio with his wife 2004, runs singing courses and Summer School for young people; mem. Faculty, Guildford School of Acting; pvt. teaching practice. *Television:* The Mill on the Floss (BBC TV), The Phantom of the Opera for Warner Bros/Really Useful Films/Sony. *Recordings include:* soundtrack for Fakers, a film by Richard Janes, music by Kevin Sargent; Inspector Morse; Collections of Broadway songs and Gilbert & Sullivan arias and duets for Pickwick; Chaka; The Brothers Grimm, a film by Terry Gilliam and most recently 'Writing on Water' a new collaboration by composer David Lang and film dir Peter Greenaway with the London Sinfonietta at the Queen Elizabeth Hall and Concertegebouw, Bruges (also on DVD); music theatre: Man of La Mancha; I Love You, You're Perfect, Now Change; The Wild Party; Parade. *Honours:* Walter Hyde Memorial Prize, Schubert Prize, Lawrence Classical Singing Bursary. *E-mail:* thelamphouse@onetel.com (office). *Website:* www.richardhalton.co.uk.

HALTON, Rosalind, BA, DPhil; New Zealand harpsichordist and musicologist; *Associate Professor, University of Newcastle*; b. 4 Oct. 1951, Dunedin; m. David Halton 1979. *Education:* Otago Univ., St Hilda's Coll., Oxford, UK, studied harpsichord with David Ledbetter and Colin Tilney. *Career:* research and editing Cantatas and Serenatas of Alessandro Scarlatti (2 A-R edns); concerts of 17th and 18th century chamber music using period instruments; solo performances on harpsichord and pianos of 18th and early 19th centuries; Lecturer in Performance, Univ. of New England, Armidale, NSW, Australia 1986–90, Sr Lecturer 1990–99; Sr Lecturer in Performance and Musicology, Univ. of Newcastle, NSW 1999–2010, Assoc. Prof. 2010–; mem. Musicology Soc. of Australia. *Recordings:* The French Harpsichord: Music by F. and L. Couperin 1996, Venere, Adone et Amore, Serenatas and Cantatas by Alessandro Scarlatti 2007 (three-CD set). *Publications:* edns of music by Alessandro Scarlatti, including Venere, Adone et Amore 2009, Solo Serenatas by A. Scarlatti (co-ed. with Marie-Louise Catsalis) 2011; online edns for the Web Library for 17th-century Music (WLSCM); 4 Sonatas a Quattro; contrib. of reviews to Music and Letters, Musicology Australia; papers on Alessandro Scarlatti, including articles in Eighteenth-Century Music (with Michael Talbot) 2015, Studi Musicali 2015. *Honours:* Hon. FAHA; Soundscapes Award 1997. *Address:* The Conservatorium, University of Newcastle, Auckland Street, Newcastle, NSW 2300 (office); 26 Rhondda Road, Teralba, NSW 2284, Australia (home). *E-mail:* r.halton@newcastle.edu.au (office).

HÄMÄLÄINEN, Jari; Finnish conductor, opera company director and pianist; *Artistic Director, Savonlinna Opera Festival*; b. 1963. *Education:* Sibelius Acad. *Career:* Asst to Gen. Music Dir Finnish Nat. Opera, Helsinki 1985–90, coach and conductor Savonlinna Festival 1985–90; worked at various German opera houses including Braunschweig State Opera, as pianist, chorus master and conductor 1990–97; Gen. Music Dir Pforzheim Opera 1997–, Gen. Dir 2003–; Artistic Dir Savonlinna Opera Festival 2008–; has conducted over 45 operas; Guest Conductor at Finnish Nat. Opera 2002, 2004, Frankfurt Opera; has conducted Munich Philharmonic, Frankfurter Museumsorchester, Stuttgart Philharmonic, Württemberg Philharmonie Reutlingen, Südwestdeutsche Philharmonie Konstanz and Philharmonic Orchestra Regensburg; engagements have included Sibelius Anniversary Concert with Mexico City Philharmonic 2007 and Rigoletto in Macau, China 2007. *Current Management:* c/o Brian Jauhiainen, Bel Canto Global Arts, 89 Scribner Avenue, Staten Island, NY 10301, USA. *Telephone:* (917) 734-6849. *Fax:* (718) 273-5918. *E-mail:* brian@belcantoglobal.com. *Website:* www.belcantoglobalarts.com. *Address:* Savonlinna Opera Festival, Olavinkatu 27, 57130 Savonlinna, Finland (office). *Telephone:* (15) 476750 (office). *Fax:* (15) 4767540 (office). *E-mail:* info@operafestival.fi (office). *Website:* www.operafestival.fi (office).

HAMARI, Julia; Hungarian/German singer (mezzo-soprano); b. 21 Nov. 1942, Budapest; d. of Sándor Hamari and Erzsébet Dokupil. *Education:* Franz Liszt Music Acad. of Budapest, Hochschule für Musik, Stuttgart, Germany. *Career:* debut as soloist, Bach's St Matthew Passion in Vienna under Karl Richter 1966; specializes in Rossini, Mozart, Bellini; lieder recitalist and oratorio performer; has appeared world-wide with conductors including Herbert von Karajan, Sergiu Celibidache, Rafael Kubelik, Georg Solti, Karl Böhm, Pierre Boulez, Carlo M. Giulini, Nikolaus Harnoncourt, Claudio Abbado, Riccardo Muti and Mariss Jansons; debut in USA as soloist with Chicago Symphony Orchestra 1967; opera debut at Salzburg Festival as Mercedes in Bizet's Carmen 1967 and as Carmen in Stuttgart 1968; has appeared with Deutsche Oper am Rhein in various baroque and classical operas; has appeared at major opera houses including La Scala, Covent Garden, Vienna State Opera, Metropolitan Opera; opera roles include Celia in La fedeltia premiata (J. Haydn), Orpheus (Gluck), Dorabella and Despina (Così fan tutte), Angelina in La Cenerentola (Rossini), Rosina in Il Barbiere di

Siviglia (Rossini), Sesto in La clemenza di Tito (Mozart), Cherubino in Le Nozze di Figaro (Mozart), Sinaide in Mosé in Egitto (Rossini), Romeo in I Capuleti ed I Montecchi (Bellini), Farnace in Mitridate (Mozart); Prof., Staatliche Hochschule für Musik, Stuttgart 1989–2009; performed in festivals of Edinburgh, Glyndebourne, Florence (Maggio Musicale), Netherlands (Schleswig-Holstein Musik, Schwetzingen). *Recordings include:* Bach's St John and St Matthew Passion 2006, Bach's Mass in B Minor, Oratorios, Cantatas, Oberon by Weber, Il matrimonio segreto by Cimarosa, Giulio Cesare by Handel, Roméo et Juliette by Berlioz, Mozart's Requiem, Mass in C major by Beethoven, Ernani by Verdi, Tito Manlio, Cavalleria rusticana, Juditha Triumphans by Vivaldi, I Puritani by Bellini, Beethoven's 9th Symphony, Mahler's Second and Eighth Symphonies, Orpheus by Gluck, Stabat Mater by Haydn and Pergolesi, Don Sanche by F. Liszt, Mosé in Egitto by Rossini, Prima la musica by A. Salieri, Eugen Onegin (also video), Meistersinger, Zigeunerlieder 1967, Lieder 1969, Bartók Songs 1973, Nausikaa Lieder Recital 1982, Lieder der Romantik 1982–94, Handel German Arias 1990, Julia Hamari Operatic Recital 1983–2000. *Honours:* Offizierskreuz (Hungary) 2002; prizewinner, Erkel Int. Singing Competition, Budapest 1964, Kodály Prize 1987. *Address:* Max Brod-Weg 14, 70437 Stuttgart, Germany (office). *Fax:* (711) 8403625 (home). *E-mail:* julia.hamari@live.de (home).

HAMBLETON, Tristan, BA (Hons), MA (Hons), Adv. Dip.; British singer (bass/baritone); b. 4 Dec. 1988, London, England; s. of Hale Hambleton and Diana Mitchell. *Education:* St Paul's Cathedral School, London, The King's School, Canterbury, St John's Coll., Cambridge, Univ. of Heidelberg, Germany, Royal Acad. of Music Opera School, London. *Career:* as a treble soloist performed with Accademia Nazionale di Santa Cecilia in Rome, Les Arts Florissant in France and at BBC Proms, Royal Opera House, Covent Garden; roles include Achilla in Giulio Cesare, Guglielmo & Don Alfonso in Così fan tutte, Masetto & Leporello in Don Giovanni, Publio in La clemenza di Tito, Don Magnifico in Cenerentola, Nick Shadow in The Rake's Progress and Superintendent Budd in Albert Herring; invited by Sir Mark Elder to sing role of Hermann Ortel in the Halle's concert performance of Die Meistersinger Act III at the Bridgewater Hall for Wagner bicentenary 2013; has since been invited back to sing the Bass solos in Mozart Requiem at Bridgewater Hall with the orchestra; has appeared as Re di Scozia in Handel's Ariodante for RAO directed by Paul Curran and conducted by Jane Glover, Figaro in Le Nozze di Figaro for Hampstead Garden Opera directed by Bruno Ravella, Somnus in Semele for Jackdaw's and Bottom in Britten's Midsummer Night's Dream at Edinburgh Fringe for Shadwell Opera; has appeared with orchestras including Orchestra of the Age of Enlightenment, Hallé, London Mozart Players at venues including Sheldonian Theatre, Wigmore Hall, Cadogan Hall, Bridgewater Hall, Birmingham Symphony Hall and Concertgebouw, Amsterdam; Glyndebourne debut creating role of Karl in David Bruce's opera Nothing as part of a Glyndebourne/ROH joint commission 2016; also sang the role of Balthazar in Donizetti's La favourite for UCO at London's Theatre Royal, Stratford 2016; Josephine Baker Trust Artist, Jackdaws Young Artist, Samling Artist. *Recordings:* as treble soloist: Karl Jenkins' The Armed Man, A Mass for Peace 2001, Boys Air Choir – Boys Gregorian; as bass-baritone: The Crypt Choir, Canterbury – In Quires and Places 2007, The Gentlemen of St John's – A Gentle Christmas 2009, St John's College Choir – Hear My Words 2010, Laudent Deum 2011. *Honours:* Associated Bd of the Royal Schools of Music UK Postgraduate Scholarship to study at RAM, London 2011–13, D'Oyly Carte Memorial Trust Scholarship 2013–15, Countess of Munster Trust 2014. *E-mail:* tristanhambleton@googlemail.com (office).

HAMEENNIEMI, Eero Olavi, DipMus; Finnish composer; b. 29 April 1951, Valkeakoski; m. Leena Peltola 1977 (divorced 1989), one d. *Education:* Sibelius Acad., State Higher School of Music, Kraków, Eastman School of Music, Rochester, NY. *Career:* commissions for the Finnish Radio Symphony Orchestra, Swedish RSO, Helsinki Festival, Finnish National Ballet; works also performed by Scottish National Orchestra, Malmö Symphony Orchestra, Gothenburg Symphony Orchestra; Sr Lecturer, Sibelius Acad. 1982–. *Compositions:* Symphony 1982–83, 1984, Dialogue for piano and orchestra 1987, Sonata for clarinet and piano, Loviisa (two-act ballet) 1987, Second Symphony 1988, two String Quartets 1989, 1994, Leonardo (two-act ballet), The Bird and the Wind for strings, soprano and two Indian classical dancers (choreography by Shobana Jeyasingh) 1994, The Dances of the Wind for strings 1994, Nattuvanar for male voice choir (UNESCO Rostrum of Composers Award) 1994, Valkalam for two viols and harpsichord 1996, Chamber Concerto 1997. *Recordings:* Duo l, for flute and cello; Pianosonata, 1979; Sonata for clarinet and piano, 1987. *Publications:* ABO – johdatus uuden musiikin teoriaan (an introduction to the theory of contemporary music) 1982, Tekopalmun alla (under an artificial palm tree, essays).

HAMELIN, Marc-André, OC; Canadian concert pianist and composer; b. 1961, Verdun; m. 1st Judy Karin Applebaum; m. 2nd Cathy Fuller. *Education:* Vincent d'Indy School of Music and Temple Univ., Philadelphia. *Career:* recitals in Montréal, Toronto, New York and Philadelphia; concerto appearances in Toronto, Québec, Ottawa, Albany, Detroit, Indianapolis, Minneapolis, New York (Manhattan Philharmonic and Riverside Symphony) and Philadelphia; toured with the Montreal Symphony to Spain, Portugal and Germany 1987; duo partnership with cellist, Sophie Rolland from 1988; Beethoven cycles in New York, Washington, Montréal and London (Wigmore Hall 1991); soloist, Turangalîla Symphony with the Philadelphia Orchestra and Andrew Davis 1996–97; played with the Tokyo Philharmonic, conducted by Okko Kamu; gave a recital in Seoul 2004; Hong Kong Arts Festival debut, with the Hong Kong Philharmonic 2004. *Compositions include:* 12 Études in all of the minor keys (for piano), Con Intimissimo Sentimento (7 pieces for piano), Tico-Tico No Fubá, Fanfares For Three Trumpets. *Recordings include:* Works by Leopold Godowsky, William Bolcom Twelve New Etudes, Stefan Wolpe Battle Piece and Ives Concord Sonata, Sorabji Sonata No. 1, Rzewski The People Will Never Be Defeated, Albéniz's Iberia 2005, Alkan Concerto for Solo Piano (Juno Award for Classical Album of the Year: Solo or Chamber Ensemble 2008) 2006, Marc-André Hamelin in a State of Jazz 2008, Haydn's Piano Sonatas 2009, F. Busoni: Die späten Klavierwerke (Echo Klassik Award for Best Pianist of the Year 2014) 2013. *Honours:* first prize Carnegie Hall Int. American Music Competition 1985, Virginia P. Moore Prize, Canada 1989. *Current Management:* Colbert Artists Management, 111 West 57th Street, New York, NY 10019, USA. *Telephone:* (212) 757-0782. *Fax:* (212) 541-5179. *E-mail:* nycolbert@colberartists.com. *Website:* www.colbertartists.com.

HAMILTON, David; American singer (tenor); b. 1960. *Career:* appearances with opera companies at Philadelphia, San Diego, Tulsa, Sarasota, Hawaii, New York (City Opera), Milwaukee and St Louis; Metropolitan Opera debut, season 1986–87; season 1991–92, as Tamino for Opéra de Nice, Lensky with Manitoba Opera, and Pinkerton with Chattanooga Opera; season 1992–93, as Tamino with Vancouver Opera, Peter Quint in Turn of the Screw for Edmonton Opera and Lensky with Scottish Opera; concert repertoire includes Messiah, Rinaldo by Brahms, Mozart's Requiem, Dvořák's Stabat Mater, the Berlioz Roméo et Juliette and Schumann's Scenes from Faust; Soloist with Israel Philharmonic, Baltimore Symphony, Mostly Mozart Festival Orchestra and Indianapolis Symphony under Raymond Leppard; as recitalist gave premiere of Hugo Weisgall's cycle Lyric Interval; sang Belmonte in Die Entführung with the Metropolitan Opera. *Honours:* winner Paris International Voice Competition 1984. *Current Management:* Dorothy Cone Artists Representatives, 150 West 55th Street, New York, NY 10019, USA. *Telephone:* (212) 765-7412. *Fax:* (212) 765-7443. *E-mail:* dcone@ix.netcom.com. *Website:* www.dorothyconeartistrep.com.

HAMILTON, Ronald; American singer (tenor); b. 1947, Hamilton, Ohio. *Career:* sang in opera at Ulm 1975–77, Düsseldorf 1977–85; guest appearances throughout Germany and in Stockholm, Geneva and Paris; Metropolitan Opera 1988, as Alwa in Lulu, and Salzburg Festival 1990, as Krenek's Orpheus; Paris Opéra Bastille 1992, in Messiaen's St François d'Assise; Brussels 1993, in From the House of the Dead, and the premiere of Reigen by Boesmans; Trieste and Montpellier 1996, as Tristan; other roles include Florestan, Wagner's Lohengrin and Walther, Strauss's Emperor and Bacchus, and Enée in Les Troyens; sang Tannhäuser at Palermo 1998; season 2000–01 as Tristan at Hamburg and Wagner's Erik in Trieste.

HAMMES, Lieselotte; German singer (soprano) and academic; b. 1932, Siegburg. *Education:* studied in Cologne. *Career:* debut in Cologne, as Amor in Orfeo ed Euridice 1957; guest appearances at Stuttgart, Hamburg, Berlin (Deutsche Oper), Naples, Rome, Lisbon and Paris 1971; Glyndebourne Festival 1965, as Sophie in Der Rosenkavalier; sang at Cologne until 1975 as Mozart's Pamina, Susanna and Papagena, Marzelline, Mimi, Manon Lescaut, Nedda, Marenka in The Bartered Bride and Anne Trulove in The Rake's Progress; teacher at Bonn then Siegburg from 1973; Prof., Cologne Musikhochschule 1985–.

HAMON, Deryck; British singer (bass); b. 24 Sept. 1946, Guernsey. *Education:* Royal Northern Coll. of Music, Rose Bruford Coll. of Speech and Drama. *Career:* concert performances throughout the UK of Messiah, Elijah, Samson, Haydn's Nelson Mass, Five Elizabethan Songs by Vaughan Williams and the Mozart and Fauré Requiems; mem., D'Oyly Carte Opera, notably as The Mikado; Rossini's Basilio and Escamillo for Travelling Opera, Dikoy in Katya Kabanova at the Opera Theatre, Dublin, and Banquo in Macbeth for City of Birmingham Touring Opera; other roles include Mozart's Sarastro, Commendatore and Alfonso, Rossini's Bartolo, Puccini's Angelotti (Tosca) and Colline (La Bohème). *Current Management:* James Black Management, The Old Grammar School, High Street, Rye, East Sussex TN31 7JF, England. *Telephone:* (1797) 224668; (7810) 436773 (mobile). *Fax:* (1797) 224668. *E-mail:* james@jamesblackmanagement.com. *Website:* www.jamesblackmanagement.com.

HAMPE, Christiane; German singer (soprano); b. 1948, Heidelberg. *Education:* studied in Heidelberg and in Munich with Annelies Kupper. *Career:* sang at the Hagen Opera 1971–73, Basle 1974–76, Wuppertal 1976–78, and Karlsruhe 1979–80; Bregenz Festival 1974, as Clarice in Haydn's Il mondo della luna, Vienna Staatsoper as Susanna and further guest appearances in Hamburg, throughout Europe and in the USA; Prof., Karlsruhe Musikhochschule from 1988. *Recordings include:* Lortzing's Undine (Capriccio).

HAMPE, Michael, DPhil; German stage and television director, actor and academic; *Professor, Hochschule für Musik und Tanz, Cologne*; b. 3 June 1935, Heidelberg; s. of Hermann Hampe and Annemarie Hampe; m. Sibylle Hauck 1971; one d. *Education:* Falckenberg Schule, Munich, Univs of Vienna and Munich, Syracuse Univ., USA. *Career:* Deputy Dir Schauspielhaus, Zürich 1965–70; Dir Nat. Theatre, Mannheim 1972–75, Cologne Opera 1975–95, Salzburg Festival 1984–90, Dresden Music Festival 1992–2000; has directed opera at La Scala, Milan, Covent Garden, London, Paris Opera, Salzburg and Edin. Festivals, Munich, Stockholm, Cologne, Geneva, San Francisco, Sydney, Los Angeles, Buenos Aires, Tokyo; has directed drama at Bavarian State Theatre, Munich Schauspielhaus, Zürich, etc; dir and actor in film and TV; Prof., State Music Acad., Cologne and Cologne Univ.; mem. Bd European

Acad. of Music, Vienna; theatre-bldg consultant; Prof., Hochschule für Musik und Tanz, Cologne; teaches at Vienna Univ., UCLA, Univ. of Southern California and Yale Univ., USA, Kunitachi Coll. of Music and Studio, New Nat. Theatre, Tokyo, Universität der Künste, Berlin. *Productions include:* Don Giovanni, Così fan tutte, le Nozze di Figaro, Il Ritorno d'Ulisse in Patria, La Cenerentola for Salzburg Festival, Andrea Chénier for Royal Opera House, Covent Garden 1984, Il Barbiere di Siviglia for Royal Opera House, Covent Garden 1985, La Gazza Ladra for Cologne Opera 1987, L'Italiana in Algeri 1987, Die Meistersinger von Nürnberg 1988, Il Barbiere di Siviglia 1988, Così fan tutte 1989, La Cenerentola for Royal Opera House, Covent Garden 1990, Don Giovanni 1991, Falstaff at Schwetzingen Festival 1996, world première of Farinelli, oder die Macht des Gesangs at Karlsruhe 1998, Così fan tutte in Santiago and in Genoa, Fidelio for San Francisco Opera 2005, Die Zauberflöte at Megaron, Athens, Die Frau ohne Schatten for Helsinki Opera, Die Zauberflöte at New Nat. Theatre, Toyko, Dallas and San Diego, La clemenza di Tito for Washington Opera 2006, Così fan tutte at Teatro Colón, Buenos Aires 2006, Maometto II at Pesaro 2008, Trovatore at Semperoper, Dresden, Elektra, Aïda, Teatro Municipal, Santiago, etc. *Publications include:* 20 Jahre Kölner Oper 1995, Alles Theater, Reden und Aufsätze 2000; articles in newspapers and periodicals. *Honours:* Bundesverdienstkreuz, Commendatore Ordine al Merito (Italy), Goldenes Ehrenzeichen des Landes Salzburg; Olivier West End Award 1983. *Address:* Carl Spitieler Strasse 105, 8053 Zürich, Switzerland.

HAMPSON, (Walter) Thomas, BA; American singer (baritone); b. 28 June 1955, Elkhart, Ind.; s. of Walter Hampson and Ruthye Hampson; one d. *Education:* Eastern Washington Univ., Fort Wright Coll., Music Acad. of West. *Career:* with Düsseldorf Ensemble 1981–84; title role in Der Prinz von Homburg, Darmstadt 1982; debut in Cologne, Munich, Santa Fé 1982–84, Metropolitan Opera, New York, Vienna Staatsoper, Covent Garden 1986, La Scala, Milan, Deutsche Oper, Berlin 1989, Carnegie Hall, San Francisco Opera 1990; Artist-in-Residence, New York Philharmonic; has performed with Vienna Philharmonic, New York Philharmonic, London Philharmonic and Chicago Symphony orchestras; Special Advisor to the Study and Performance of Music in America, US Library of Congress; f. The Hampsong Foundation 2003; mem. American Acad. of Arts and Sciences 2010–. *Recordings include:* Schubert's Winterreise 1997, Das Lied von der Erde 1997, Belshazzar's Feast 1998, Operetta Album with London Philharmonic 1999, No Tenors Allowed: Opera Duets (with Samuel Ramey) 1999, Verdi Arias with Orchestra of the Age of Enlightenment 2001, Wagner's Tannhäuser 2002, Cole Porter's Kiss Me Kate 2002, Forbidden and Banished 2006, I Hear America Singing 2006, Simon Boccanegra 2006, Don Giovanni 2006, Doktor Faust 2007, Athanaël 2008, Mozart Gala From Salzburg 2008, Wondrous Free—Song of America II 2009, Mahler: Des Knaben Wunderhorn 2011, Brahms: Ein Deutsches Requiem 2011, Schubert: Winterreise 2011, Puccini: Tosca 2011, Verdi: La Traviata 2011. *Honours:* Hon. mem. RAM 1996, Freunde der Wiener Staatsoper 2004, Wiener Konzerthausgesellschaft 2005, Hon. Prof., Univ. of Heidelberg; Chevalier des Arts et des Lettres, Officer of the Order Pro Merito Melitensi (Malta) 2006; Dr hc (Whitworth Coll., Washington, San Francisco Conservatory, Manhattan School of Music); Edison Prize, Netherlands 1990, 1992, Grand Prix du Disque 1990, 1996, Cannes Classical Award 1994, Echo Klassik 1995, EMI Artist of the Year 1997, Deutsche Schallplattenkritik Award 1999, Cecilia Award 2000, Diapason d'Or Award 2000; Citation of Merit, Vienna Kammersänger 1999, Edison Award for Life Achievement 2005, Grammy Award for Best Opera Recording 2006, Deutsche Schallplatten Prize 2008, Distinguished Artistic Leadership Award, Atlantic Council 2009, Award for Distinguished Achievement in the Arts, Third Street Music School Settlement 2009, Living Legend Award, Library of Congress 2010, Concertgebouw Prize 2011, Venetian Heritage Award 2013, inducted to Hall of Fame by Gramophone 2013. *Current Management:* c/o Centre Stage Artist Management, Stralauer Allee 1, Raum 1.11, 10245 Berlin, Germany. *Telephone:* (30) 520071762. *Fax:* (20) 87425682. *E-mail:* jonathan.letts@umusic.com; judith.neuhoff@umusic.com. *Address:* 1841 Broadway, Suite 1204, New York, NY 10023, USA (office). *Telephone:* (212) 767-0074 (office). *E-mail:* office@thomashampson.com (office). *Website:* www.thomashampson.com (office); www.hampsong.com.

HAMVASI, Sylvia; singer (soprano); b. 1972, Budapest, Hungary. *Education:* Franz Liszt Acad. and Leo Weiner Conservatory, Budapest. *Career:* roles with Budapest Youth Opera have included Mozart's Blonde and Mme Herz, Serpina in La Serva Padrona and Olympia; concert tour with the Youth Opera Studio to Kuwait; repertoire includes Bach's St John Passion, Christmas Oratorio and Masses, Mozart, Liszt and Kodály Masses, Carmina Burana and Handel's Messiah, Dixit Dominus and Solomon. *Recordings include:* album with the Hungarian Radio Youth Orchestra (conducted by Tamas Vasary). *Honours:* Hommage á Lucia Popp Competition European Mozart Foundation Award, Bratislava 1996.

HAN, Derek; American pianist; b. 1951. *Education:* Juilliard School, New York. *Career:* many appearances in USA, Europe and the Far East from 1976 notably with Moscow Philharmonic, Berlin Symphony, Sinfonia Varsovia (conducted by Yehudi Menuhin), Frankfurt State Orchestra, Moscow State Symphony Orchestra and London Philharmonic; also with Warsaw Philharmonic, Budapest Symphony, Bolshoi Symphony, Residentie Orchestra, the Hague, St Louis Symphony, Giuseppe Verdi Orchestra of Milan, Royal Philharmonic Orchestra, Philharmonia der Nationen and Camerata Salzburg; further concerts with Philharmonie der Nationen. *Recordings include:*

Complete Concertos of Haydn, Mozart, Beethoven, Mendlessohn and Chopin; Tchaikovsky, Shostakovich and Rachmaninov Concertos; Complete Mozart Violin and Piano sonatas, with Joseph Silverstein. *Honours:* winner Athens Int. Piano Competition 1977. *Current Management:* c/o Arts Management Group, 37 West 26th Street Suite 403, New York, NY 10010-1006, USA. *Telephone:* (212) 337-0838. *Fax:* (212) 924-0382. *E-mail:* info@artsmg.com. *Website:* www.artsmg.com.

HANANI, Yehuda; cellist; b. 19 Dec. 1943, Jerusalem, Israel; m. Hannah Glatstein 1971; one s. *Education:* Rubin Acad. of Music, Juilliard School, USA. *Career:* guest performer with Chicago Symphony, Philadelphia Orchestra, Baltimore Symphony, St Paul Chamber Orchestra, Berlin Radio Symphony, Israel Philharmonic, BBC National Orchestra of Wales and others; Aspen Music Festival; Chautauqua; Marlboro; Artistic Dir Chamber Music Series, Miami Center for the Fine Arts; mem. cello faculty, The Peabody Conservatory and Cincinnati Coll.-Conservatory. *Recordings:* Miaskovsky Cello Sonatas; Alkan Cello Sonata; Vivaldi Cello Sonatas; Aleksander Obradovic Cello Concerto; Leo Ornstein Sonata; Samuel Barber Sonata; Lukas Foss Capriccio. *Honours:* three Martha Baird Rockefeller grants for music, America Israel Cultural Foundation Award.

HANCOCK, Gareth, ARAM; British pianist and conductor; b. 1960, England. *Education:* Clare Coll., Cambridge, Royal Acad., London. *Career:* engagements as repetiteur at English National Opera, playing harpsichord in The Barber of Seville; conducted Rigoletto for English Touring Opera 1996, and Misper for Glyndebourne Education 1997; repetiteur and assistant at Glyndebourne from 1995, including Chief Coach for Jonathan Dove's Flight 1999; teacher at the Royal Academy; Lieder recital accompanist in Britain, France, Germany and USA. *Recordings include:* The Barber of Seville, ENO. *Address:* Royal Academy of Music, Marylebone Road, London, NW1 5HT, England (office). *Telephone:* (20) 7873-7383 (office). *E-mail:* voice@ram.ac.uk (office). *Website:* www.ram.ac.uk (office).

HANCOCK, John; American singer (baritone); b. 1968, New York, NY; m. Jane Gilbert. *Education:* Juilliard Opera Center, New York. *Career:* sang Oreste in Iphigénie en Tauride at Strasbourg, 1993, Rossini's Dandini in Kansas City and Raimbaud for the Spoleto Festival, USA; La Haine in Lully's Armide in Paris and Antwerp, Marcello in La Bohème at Glyndebourne and with the Canadian Opera Company, 1995, Rossini's Barber for the New Israeli Opera and Valentin in Philadelphia; Other roles include Silvio in Pagliacci, Malatesta and Tarquinius; Sang Lord Henry Wootton in the premiere of Lowell Liebermann's The Picture of Dorian Gray, Monaco, 1996; Belcore for Florida Grand Opera, 1998; Concert repertoire includes Mahler's Kindertotenlieder at Alice Tully Hall and Des Knaben Wunderhorn. *Current Management:* Columbia Artists Management LLC, 1790 Broadway, New York, NY 10019-1412, USA. *Telephone:* (212) 841-9500. *Fax:* (212) 841-9744. *E-mail:* info@cami.com. *Website:* www.cami.com.

HANCOCK, Paul, BMus, MA; British composer; b. 6 May 1952, Plymouth, Devon, England; m. Joan Baigent 1986; three step-s. one step-d. *Education:* Trinity Hall, Cambridge. *Career:* composer and private music teacher in Plymouth 1976–79, York 1979–83, Oxford 1983–85, Cambridge 1985–87; first London recital at BMIC 1986; mem. Composers' Guild of Great Britain. *Compositions include:* 24 Preludes for piano solo 1979–81, String Quartet 1982, Who? Songs for children 1981, With the Mermaids for wind quartet 1983, The Gift of a Lamb (children's opera) 1985, Maen Tans-Boskednan for piano solo 1984, Silent Love (song cycle) 1985, Zennor for clarinet and viola 1986, Little Gidding Variations for orchestra 1985–86, Viola Concerto 1986, The Mermaid of Zennor (opera) 1986–88, ...O Very Most the Hidden Love... (song cycle) 1986, The Voice of the Hidden Waterfall for ensemble 1987, Nocturne for Ragnhild for soprano and piano duet 1988, Dancing on a Point of Light for ensemble 1988, Round 12 O'Clock Rock for baritone and piano, Sea Change for percussion ensemble 1989, Vespers of St Mary Magdalene for soprano and organ 1990, Piano Sonata No. 1, No. 2 and No. 3 1990–91, Ogo Pour for percussion solo 1991, Matrice for piano duet 1991, The Ring of Fire for piano solo 1992, Journey Out of Essex for baritone and ensemble 1993. *Recordings:* two albums of piano music.

HANCORN, John; British singer (baritone); b. 1954, Inverness, Scotland. *Education:* Trinity Coll. of Music, National Opera Studio; further studies with Hans Hotter in Munich and London. *Career:* debut, Edinburgh 1981, as Masetto in Don Giovanni; Aldeburgh from 1981 in Albert Herring, The Rape of Lucretia and Eugene Onegin; Glyndebourne Touring Opera from 1983 in The Love of Three Oranges, Kent Opera as Masetto in Don Giovanni and Fidelio; Debut at Covent Garden as Hermann in Les Contes d'Hoffmann; Tour of Italy 1986 with Monteverdi's L'Orfeo conducted by Roger Norrington; Concert performance of Charpentier's Médée with the Orchestra of the Age of Enlightenment 1987; Season 1989–90 with Welsh National Opera as Kilian in Der Freischütz, Hector in King Priam with Musica nel Chiostro in Batignano, Italy, Handel's Israel in Egypt with the Royal Choral Society, 1990; Concert repertory also includes the Brahms Requiem; Appearances with the Royal Philharmonic Orchestra, Scottish Chamber Orchestra, Bournemouth Sinfonietta and at the festivals of Camden, Greenwich, Brighton, Aldeburgh, Flanders and Frankfurt; Sang in Weber's Oberon at the Edinburgh and Tanglewood Festivals and at the Alte Oper, Frankfurt, conducted by Ozawa; Season 1992–94 worked with Welsh National Opera and English National Opera in many major roles; Sang Jove in Semele by John Eccles, for Mayfield Chamber Opera, 1996; The Devil in Ordo Virtutum by

Hildegard of Bingen for Vox Animae at the 1996 York Early Music Festival; currently Choral Conductor, East Sussex Acad. of Music, Musical Dir East Sussex Bach Choir. *Recordings:* with Consort of Musicke and Anthony Rooley, 1994. *E-mail:* vswinslade@ukonline.co.uk (office). *Website:* www.bachchoir.org.uk (office).

HAND, Richard, ARAM; British musician (guitar); b. 27 Nov. 1960, Marsden, Yorks., England. *Education:* Royal Acad. of Music, London. *Career:* mem. English Guitar Quartet (tour of Israel), flute and guitar duo, The Light-fingered Gentry (tours of Germany, Holland, Egypt, Dubai, Brunei, Malaysia), guitar duo, Hand/Dupré (tours of Norway, Poland, India, Bangladesh, Sri Lanka, Philippines, Malaysia, Indonesia, Singapore, Hong Kong, USA, Turkey, Azerbaijan), Pro Arte Trio (tour of Sweden), Tetra Guitar Quartet (tour of Saudi Arabia, India); concerts in Wigmore Hall, St John's Smith Square, Purcell Room, Barbican and BBC Proms at Royal Albert Hall; numerous TV and radio broadcasts world-wide; has performed premieres of new works by Peter Dickinson, Tim Souster, Jonathon Lloyd, David Bedford, Roger Steptoe, Michael Ball, Brian May, Judith Bingham, Wilfred Josephs; mem. Inc. Soc. of Musicians. *Recordings:* Carey Blyton: Complete Guitar Music, Lyric Pieces (Hand-Dupré Duo), Scenes from Childhood (with Pro Arte Guitar Trio), Summer Waves (with English Guitar Quartet), Carmen (with Tetra Quartet); world premieres of works by Edward Cowie, Malcolm Williamson, Peter Dickinson, David Bedford, Tim Souster. *Honours:* RAM Open Scholarship 1979, RAM Julian Bream Prize 1981, RAM String Players' Prize 1981, RAM John Munday Prize 1981. *Address:* 61 Balcombe Street, Marylebone, London, NW1 6HD, England. *E-mail:* info@richardhand.net. *Website:* www.richardhand.net.

HANDEL, David, BMus, MMus; American conductor; *Principal Guest Conductor, Moscow City Symphony. Education:* Univ. of Michigan at Ann Arbor. *Career:* Asst Conductor, Leipzig Gewandhaus Orchestra 1988–90; Rehearsal Conductor, Civic Orchestra of Chicago 1991; Prin. Guest Conductor, Chicago Youth Symphony Orchestra 1991–93; Music Dir, Orquesta Sinfónica Nacional de Bolivia 1997–; Artistic Advisor, Orquesta Sinfónica Nacional de Guatemala 2000–01; Music Dir, UNCuyo Symphony Orchestra 2005–; Founder, Artistic and Gen. Dir, Guadalquivir Festival 2006–; Prin. Guest Conductor, Moscow City Symphony 2011–; int. concert engagements: Atlantic Classical Orchestra, Cayuga Chamber Orchestra, Lafayette Symphony Orchestra, Amherst Symphony Orchestra, Owensboro Symphony Orchestra, El Paso Symphony Orchestra, Riverside Symphonia, La Jolla Symphony Orchestra, Acadiana Symphony Orchestra, Waukesha Symphony Orchestra, Buffalo Philharmonic Orchestra, New York Philharmonic, Chicago Youth Symphony Orchestra, Nat. Opera Asscn and De Paul Univ. Symphony, Civic Orchestra of Chicago, Bucharest Symphony Orchestra, Russian Philharmonic, La Serena Symphony Orchestra (Chile), San Juan Symphony Orchestra (Argentina), Milan Academic Symphony Orchestra (Italy), Espiritu Santo Symphony Orchestra (Brazil), Nat. Symphony Orchestra of Bolivia, Koszalin State Philharmonic (Poland), Nat. Symphony Orchestra of Malta, Nat. Symphony Orchestra of Ecuador, Sergipe Symphony Orchestra (Brazil), IPN Symphony Orchestra (Mexico), Mendoza UNCuyo Symphony Orchestra (Argentina), Nat. Symphony Orchestra of Argentina, Guadalquivir Festival Orchestra (Bolivia), Nat. Symphony Orchestra of Colombia, Nat. Symphony Orchestra of Brazil UFF, Amazon Philharmonic (Brazil), Nat. Symphony Orchestra of Iraq, Venezuela Symphony Orchestra, Oaxaca Symphony Orchestra (Mexico), Nat. Symphony Orchestra of Peru, Nat. Symphony Orchestra of El Salvador, Baku Opera Radio and Television Symphony Orchestra (Azerbaijan), Nat. Symphony Orchestra of Guatemala, Coyoacan Symphony Orchestra (Mexico), Matanzas Symphony Orchestra (Cuba), Michoacan Symphony Orchestra (Mexico), Jalisco (Guadalajara) Philharmonic (Mexico), Xalapa Symphony Orchestra (Mexico). *Honours:* Decoration of Illimani (Bolivia) 1998, Municipal Medal of Honour 'Pedro Domingo Murillo' (Bolivia) 2004, Coat of Arms of the City of La Paz 2008, 'Nilo Soruco Arancibia' Nat. Medal of Honour 2012; Marguerite Lapp Memorial Scholarship 1982, Chicago Artists Int. Award 1995, 1997, Fulbright Fellowship 1998, 1999, UNESCO Pro-Santa Cruz Culture Prize 2001. *Current Management:* c/o Jeffrey James Arts Consulting, 45 Grant Avenue, Farmingdale, NY 11735, USA. *Telephone:* (516) 586-3433. *Fax:* (516) 586-3433. *E-mail:* jamesarts@worldnet.att.net. *Website:* www.jamesarts.com.

HANDT, Herbert; singer (tenor), conductor and musicologist; b. 26 May 1926, Philadelphia, PA, USA. *Education:* Juilliard School, New York and Vienna Acad. *Career:* debut at Vienna Staatsoper 1949; sang in the premieres of Venere Prigioniera by Malipiero (Florence 1957) and Maria Golovin by Menotti (Brussels 1958); appeared in the Italian and French premieres of works by Henze, Berg, Busoni and Britten; debut as conductor, Rome 1960; founded own opera group and gave revivals of works by Boccherini, Rossini and Geminiani; also heard in Haydn's Orfeo ed Euridice (L'Anima del Filosofo); settled in Lucca, Italy and founded the Associazione Musicale Lucchese and the Lucca Chamber Orchestra. *Recordings:* Maria Golovin, Don Giovanni, Haydn's Orfeo, Idomeneo, Giuseppe, Figlio di Giacobbe by Luigi Rossi, Rossini's Otello, Temistocle by J.C. Bach, Sesto in Giulio Cesare by Handel. *Publications include:* performing editions of early Italian vocal music.

HANKEY, Tom; British violinist; b. 1975, England. *Education:* Royal Coll. of Music, London. *Career:* co-founder, Tavec String Quartet at RCM 1999; coached by Simon Rowland-Jones and the Chillingirian Quartet; performances at St Martin-in-the-Fields, Serpentine Gallery (BBC Proms) and National Gallery, London; music society concerts throughout Britain; festival

engagements at Lower Wye Valley Chamber Music Festival 2000–01; workshops and concerts in educational establishments; concert at the National Gallery, London 2001, with Octet by Schubert and Strauss's Till Eulenspiegel; mem. and leader, Piros Ensemble 2000–. *Honours:* winner Helen Just String Quartet Prize, Rio Tinto Ensemble Prize, NET4 Music Prize.

HANLEY, Regina; singer (soprano); b. 1970, Dublin, Ireland. *Education:* Dublin Coll. of Music, Royal Northern Coll. of Music, England. *Career:* appearances with Glyndebourne Festival Opera as Micaela, Jenůfa, Katya Kabanova, Nedda and Tatiana; season 1998–99, as Janáček's Emilia Marty for Scottish Opera, Go Round and Donna Anna for the Perth Festival; concerts include Beethoven's Mass in C, Messiah, Verdi Requiem, Vivaldi's Gloria, Mozart Mass in C Minor, Strauss's Four Last Songs and Rossini's Stabat Mater.

HANLON, Kevin Francis, DMA; American composer; b. 1 Jan. 1953, South Bend, IN. *Education:* Indiana Univ., Eastman School of Music, Univ. of Texas, studied with Mario Davidovsky at the Berkshire Music Center. *Career:* teacher, Univ. of Kentucky 1982–83; mem. composition and electronic music faculty, Univ. of Arizona, Tucson; Dir of the Arizona Contemporary Music Ensemble; appearances as singer and conductor. *Compositions include:* Through to the End of the Tunnel for low voice and tape delay 1976, revised 1980, Second Childhood for soprano and ensemble 1976, Cumulus numbus for orchestra 1977, Variations for alto saxophone and tape delay 1977, Toccata for piano 1980, String Trio 1981, An die ferne Geliebte for low voice and piano 1980, Lullaby for my Sorrows for chamber orchestra 1982, Ostinato Suite for harpsichord 1982, Centered for chamber ensemble and tape 1983, A. E. Housman Song Cycle for low voice and chamber ensemble 1982, Choral Introits for chorus and ensemble 1982, Trumpet Sonata 1983, Sratae for orchestra 1983, Relentless Time for small orchestra 1984, Kaleidoscopic Image for orchestra 1986, On an Expanding Universe 1986, Chronological Variations for strings 1987, The Lark of Avignon for wind ensemble and piano 1993, Clarion for orchestra 1997. *Honours:* Joseph H. Bearns Prize 1978, Koussevitzky Prize 1981.

HANLY, Brian Vaughan, DipMus; violinist and academic; b. 3 Sept. 1940, Perth, Australia; m. Jeri Ryan Hanly 1968; two s. *Career:* violinist in Arts Trio, in residence at Univ. of Wyoming and Univ. of Houston, TX, USA; numerous tours with Western Arts Trio, to Europe, USA, Mexico, also concerts throughout South America and Australia; soloist with orchestras throughout Australia, Mexico, USA, with particular success with Beethoven and Prokofiev Concertos. *Recordings:* Claude Debussy's piano trio, seven albums with Western Arts Trio. *Honours:* winner Australian Broadcasting Commission Concerto Competition.

HANNAH, Ron, BSc, BMus, MMus, EdDip; Canadian composer and teacher; b. 14 Dec. 1945, Moose Jaw, Saskatchewan. *Education:* Univ. of Alberta, Edmonton, studied with Violet Archer, Manus Sasonkin, Malcolm Forsyth. *Career:* mem., Da Camera Singers 1973–; Instructor Dept of Extension, Univ. of Alberta 1975–76; Instructor in Harmony and Ear Training, Red Deer Coll. 1977–78; Music Instructor, Edmonton public schools 1980–; founder and owner, Composer Publications, Edmonton 1989; commissions from Edmonton Symphony Orchestra and Canadian Broadcasting Corporation; founding Ed., The Alberta New Music Review (magazine of Edmonton Composers' Concert Soc.); co-founder and co-ordinator, Edmonton New Music Festival. *Compositions include:* From Song of Solomon for SATB and piano 1972, An Immorality for SATB and piano 1972, The Dinner Party song cycle for soprano, clarinet and piano 1973, String Quartet No. 1 1973, Sonata for violoncello and piano 1973, Three African Songs for tenor and piano 1974, The Shrine of Kotje for chorus and orchestra 1975, Variations on a Theme of Violet Archer for piano 1975, Concert Piece for flute and piano 1975, Visions of Nothingness for piano sonata in two movements 1975, Sonata for French horn and piano 1976, Prelude and Meditation on Coventry Cathedral for trumpet and organ 1978, Five Preludes for organ 1978, Songs of Myself for song cycle, soprano, violin, piano and French horn 1979, The Lonely Princess for flute and guitar 1981, Suite for Elan for piano 1982, Piano Trio No. 1 1982, Four Canons for Three Voices for mixed chorus and piano 1983, Mademoiselle Fifi (chamber opera) 1983, Three Songs on Poems of Robert Graves for voice and electronic tape 1984, Fantasia on Ein Feste Burg for organ 1984, Hypatia (a play with songs) 1984, Three Romantic Madrigals 1985, Concerto for piano and tape 1986, Morning's Minion (four songs after G. M. Hopkins) for soprano and piano 1987, Alleluia for SATB 1989, Credo for mezzo-soprano, viola and piano 1990, Divertimento for strings 1991, Pastoral Suite for solo guitar 1992–93, Suite of Orchestral Dances 1992, Toccatissimo! for two pianos and two percussionists 1993–94.

HANNAN, Michael Francis, BA, PhD; Australian composer, writer, educator and keyboard player; b. 19 Nov. 1949, Newcastle, NSW. *Education:* Univ. of Sydney. *Career:* teacher, Univ. of New South Wales 1975–76, Univ. of Sydney 1977–83; Lecturer in Composition, Queensland Conservatorium of Music 1985–86; Head of Music, Northern Rivers Coll. of Advanced Education 1986–; research as post-doctoral scholar, Univ. of California, Los Angeles 1983–84; research affiliate, Univ. of Sydney 1985–. *Compositions:* Voices in the Sky for piano 1980, Rajas for solo cello 1982, Zen Variations for piano 1982, Island Song for recorders, percussion and organ 1983, In the Utter Darkness for solo flute 1983, Callisto for piano 1986. *Recording:* The Piano Music of Peter

Sculthorpe 1982. *Publications:* Peter Sculthorpe: his Music and Ideas 1929–79 1982; contrib. to various publications.

HANNIGAN, Barbara, MusM; Canadian singer (soprano) and conductor; b. 1971. *Education:* studied with Mary Morrison at Univ. of Toronto, vocal studies with Meinard Kraak at Royal Conservatory of The Hague and privately with Neil Semer, conducting studies with Jorma Panula. *Career:* has given numerous world premieres of contemporary music, including new works written especially for her and orchestra by composers such as Gerald Barry, Peter Eötvös, Magnus Lindberg, Unsuk Chin and Salvatore Sciarrino; worked with composers including Ligeti, Dutilleux, Benjamin, Dusapin, Abrahamsen, Andriessen, Barry, Hosokowa, Luca Francesconi, Stockhausen, Eötvös and Oliver Knussen; frequent guest of Berlin Philharmonic, and has performed with numerous leading orchestras and ensembles, with conductors including Andris Nelsons, Pierre Boulez, Kent Nagano, Yannick Nézet-Séguin, Sir Simon Rattle, Reinbert de Leeuw, Esa-Pekka Salonen, Lorin Maazel, Kurt Masur, Alan Gilbert, Jonathan Nott, Susanna Mälkki, Jukka Pekka Saraste, Ingo Metzmacher, Pablo Heras-Casado, Thomas Adès, Peter Oundjian, Oliver Knussen, John Storgårds, Michael Gielen and Peter Eötvös; conducting debut (Stravinsky's Renard), Théâtre du Châtelet, Paris 2010; has since conducted Gothenburg Symphony, WDR Symphony Orchestra, Prague Philharmonic, London Sinfonietta, Accad. Naz. di Santa Cecilia and Gulbenkian Orchestra, Lisbon and Britten Sinfonia; has sung Ligeti's Mysteries of the Macabre at Lincoln Center, Berlin Philharmonie, Châtelet Paris, Salzburg, Disney Hall, Amsterdam Concertgebouw, Vienna Konzerthaus; also appeared at La Monnaie in Brussels, Barcelona's Liceu, BBC Proms; sang Agnes for the world premiere of George Benjamin's Written on Skin at the Aix-en-Provence Festival; other operatic world premieres include Pascal Dusapin's Passion (Lei) at Aix-en-Provence Festival, title role in Hosokawa's Matsukaze at La Monnaie, Louis Andriessen's Writing to Vermeer (Saskia) for Netherlands Opera and Barry's The Bitter Tears of Petra von Kant (Gabrielle) for English National Opera; sang Berg's Lulu in La Monnaie's new production, directed by Warlikowski. *Recordings include:* Andriessen: Writing to Vermeer 2006, Kris Defoort: The House of the Sleeping Beauties 2009, Ligeti: Requiem and Apparitions 2013, Britten 2013, Dutilleux: Correspondances (Victoires de la Musique Classique award 2014, Gramophone Award for Best Contemporary Recording) 2013, George Benjamin: Written on Skin (Agnès) (Gramophone Award for Best Contemporary Recording 2014) 2013. *Honours:* Musical Personality of the Year, Syndicat de la Presse Française 2012, Opernwelt Singer of the Year 2013, 2012. *Current Management:* c/o Jasper Parrott, Harrison Parrott Ltd, 5-6 Albion Court, Albion Place, London, W6 0QT, England. *Telephone:* (20) 7229-9166. *Fax:* (20) 7221-5042. *E-mail:* info@harrisonparrott.co.uk. *Website:* www.harrisonparrott.co.uk; www.barbarahannigan.com.

HANNIKAINEN, Ann-Elise; Finnish composer and pianist; b. 14 Jan. 1946, Hangö; d. of Heikki Hannikainen and Marianne Vennström; pnr Ernesto Halffter 1974–89. *Education:* Academia Moderna de Música, Peru, Sibelius Acad., Finland, studied with Ernesto Halffter in Spain. *Career:* debut as composer, orchestral piece, Anerfálicas, Valencia, Spain 1973; tournée as pianist, Andalucia 1975; performance, world premiere, Piano Concerto, Helsinki 1976; Anerfálicas, Teatro Real, Madrid, Spain 1977; Finnish and Spanish radio broadcasts; piano recitals; Festival Kuhmoinen, Andalucia, Madrid and others; mem. Société des Auteurs, Compositeurs et Editeurs de Musique (SACEM), Paris, Soc. of Finnish Composers. *Compositions include:* Anerfálicas for orchestra 1973, Pensamientos for piano 1974, Toccata Fantasia for piano 1975, Concerto for piano and orchestra (in memoriam Manuel de Falla's 100th anniversary) 1976, Cosmos for orchestra 1977, Trio Sextetto 1979, Chachara for flute and piano 1980, Solemne for solo piano 1982, Zafra for violin and piano 1986. *Honours:* first prize Contest for Young Composers, JJMM Barcelona 1980. *Address:* Kyläkirkontie 6–10B, 00370 Helsinki 37, Finland (home). *Telephone:* (9) 3405016 (home); 408363877 (mobile).

HANNULA, Kaisa; Finnish singer (soprano); b. 1959. *Education:* Sibelius Acad., Helsinki, studied in London and Vienna. *Career:* sang at first in concert and appeared at the 1989 Savonlinna Festival, in the premiere of The Knife by Paavo Heininen; Savonlinna 1991, as Marenka in The Bartered Bride and Helsinki 1992, in Pohjalaisia by Madetoja; other roles include Marguerite and Violetta; sang Schoenberg's Erwartung at Savonlinna 1995; Princess in the premiere of Erik Bergman's The Singing Tree, Helsinki 1995; season 2000–01 as Papageno at Savonlinna and Wagner's Gunther in Bonn.

HANNULA, Tenno; singer (baritone); b. 1950, Vehmaa, Finland. *Education:* studied in Finland with P. Salomaa, in Rome with Luigi Ricci and at the Musikhochschule Vienna. *Career:* sang Escamillo and Posa in Don Carlos at Kaiserslautern 1976; Nationaltheater Mannheim from 1977, as Wolfram, Enrico, Counts Luna and Almaviva, Eugene Onegin, Marcello, Rossini's Figaro and Lortzing's Tsar; sang Almaviva at Ludwigsburg 1980–81, Savonlinna Festival 1981–89, as Papageno and in the 1984 premiere of Sallinen's The King Goes Forth to France; Stuttgart Staatsoper 1982–, notably in the 1984 premiere of Akhnaten by Philip Glass; guest appearances at Hamburg, Hanover, Karlsruhe, Aachen, Vienna, Moscow, Leningrad and Munich; Finnish National Opera, Helsinki, as Rigoletto, Deutsche Oper Berlin as Thoas in Iphigénie en Aulide; sang Blancsac in La Scala di Seta at Stuttgart Staatsoper 1991; Forester in The Cunning Little Vixen at Karlsruhe 1996, and Dunois in The Maid of Orleans 1998. *Recordings include:* Akhnaten.

HANSELL, Kathleen Amy Kuzmick, BA, MMus, PhD; American musicologist and music editor; *Music Editor, University of Chicago Press*; b. (Kathleen Amy Kuzmick), 21 Sept. 1941, Bridgeport, Conn.; one s. one d. *Education:* Wellesley Coll., Mass, Univ. of Illinois, Urbana, Univ. of California, Berkeley, studied piano, organ and harpsichord privately. *Career:* Instructor in Music History, by correspondence, Univ. of Illinois 1967–68; Organist, Lutheran Church of the Good Shepherd, Sacramento, Calif. 1969–71, Gloria Dei Lutheran Church, Iowa City 1973–74; Instructor in Musicology, Harpsichord and Organ, Grinnell Coll., Ia 1975–76; Instructor in Music History, Cornell Coll., Mt Vernon, Ia 1979; Archivist, Swedish Music History Archive, Stockholm, Sweden 1982–88; Co-ordinator, RISM libretto cataloguing project, Stockholm 1985–88; Chair. Editorial Bd Monumenta Musicae Svecicae 1986–88; Docent in Musicology, Uppsala Univ., Sweden 1987–88; In-house Ed. for critical edns, G. Ricordi and Co., Milan, Italy 1988–92; Music Ed., Univ. of Chicago Press, Chicago, Ill. 1992–; Man. Ed., The Works of Giuseppe Verdi 1992–; mem. American and Italian Musicology Socs, American Inst. for Verdi Studies. *Publications:* as editor: Mozart: Lucio Silla for Neue Mozart Ausgabe 1986 (critical commentary 2009), Franz Berwald Complete Works, Vol. 14, Duos 1987, Verdi: Stiffelio for The Works of Giuseppe Verdi 2003, Rossini: Zelmira, for Tutte le opere di Gioachino Rossini (with Helen Greenwald) 2005; as author: 'Ballet in Stockholm during the Later 18th Century and Its Relationship to Contemporary Trends on the Continent' in Svensk Tidskrift för Musikforskning 1984, 'Il balletto e l'opera italiana', in Storia dell'opera italiana 1988, 'Gluck's Orpheus och Euridice in Stockholm: Performance practices on the way from Orpheo to Orphée', in Gustavian Opera: An Interdisciplinary Reader in Swedish Opera Dance and Theatre, 1771–1809 1991, En uti Harmonie öfvad på Clav-Cymbal: A Critical Edition of Johan Helmich Roman's Swedish Translation (1753) of Francesco Gasparini's 'L'Armonico pratico al cimbalo' (1708) (with Eva Nordenfelt 1993, 'Gaetano Gioia, il ballo teatrale e l'opera del primo Ottocento', in Creature di Prometeo: Il ballo teatrale dal divertimento al dramma 1996, 'Compositional Techniques in Stiffelio: Reading the Autograph sources', in Verdi's Middle Period: Source Studies, Analysis and Performance Practice 1997, 'Mozart's Milanese Theatrical Works', in Music in the Theater, Church, and Villa: Essays in Honor of Robert Lamar Weaver and Norma Wright Weaver, 2000, 'Ballet in Italy: The Background to Verdi' in Verdi in Performance (co-ed. Alison Latham and Roger Parker) 2001, 'Theatrical Ballet and Italian Opera', in The History of Italian Opera 2002, 'Eighteenth-Century Italian Theatrical Ballet: The Triumph of the Grotteschi', in The Grotesque Danser on the Eighteenth-century Stage: Gennaro Magri and his World 2005; contrib. to numerous professional magazines and publs, including Grove's Dictionary (sixth edn), The New Grove Dictionary of Opera, The International Encyclopedia of Dance, The Cambridge Verdi Encyclopedia. *Honours:* Willliam Billings Prize in Music, Wellesley Coll. (for performance as organist) 1963, Alfred Hertz Memorial Fellowship in Music, Univ. of California, Berkeley (dissertation research grant) 1971–72, Anne Louise Barrett Fellowship in Music, Wellesley Coll. (dissertation research grant) 1971–72, Internationale Stiftung Mozarteum, Salzburg (travel grant to Kraków to study Mozart autograph scores) 1980, Stina & Erik Lundberg Stiftelse, Stockholm (research grant) 1984–85, Lorenzo Gori-Mazzoleni Memorial Fund for Musicological Studies Abroad, Stockholm (research and travel grant) 1987, Univ. of Louisville, Ky (travel grant for conf.) 1989, Internationale Stiftung Mozarteum, Salzburg (travel grant for conf.) 1991. *Address:* Editorial Department, The University of Chicago Press, 1427 East 60th Street, Chicago, IL 60637, USA (office). *Telephone:* (773) 702-0427 (office). *Fax:* (773) 702-2705 (office). *E-mail:* khansell@press.uchicago.edu (office). *Website:* www.press.uchicago.edu (office).

HANSFORD, Andrew, BA, BMus, MA, ARCM, ARCO, LRSM, LGSM, LTCL, FLCM, FRSA; British pianist, organist and harpsichordist; b. 25 May 1973, Taplow, Berks., England. *Education:* Univ. of Surrey, Guildford, Univ. of Bristol, Open Univ., Univ. of Cardiff. *Career:* principally a piano accompanist, also accomplished solo pianist, organist and harpsichordist; performance work as a professional keyboard accompanist, choral accompanist, continuo player, chamber/orchestral pianist and piano duet player; has performed with numerous groups including Bath Philharmonia, Cleeve Chorale, Bridgwater Choral Society, Charlton Kings Choral Society, Cheltenham Choral Society, Cirencester Choral Society and Jubilate Chamber Choir in Bath, Cheltenham, Cirencester and Edinburgh; UK/int. examiner, Associated Bd of the Royal Schools of Music; mem. Oxford and Cambridge CT ABRSM Mentor Panel; UK/int. adjudicator mem., British and Int. Fed. of Festivals for Music, Dance and Speech; previous positions include pianist, Royal Ballet School, tutor/piano accompanist, Morley Coll., London, visiting piano/jazz piano tutor, Cheltenham Coll., part-time Lecturer in Music, Univ. of Bath in Swindon, examiner for the Oxford and Cambridge Board; currently tutor/piano accompanist, Cirencester Coll.; also resident organist, local Gloucestershire church; mem. Royal Coll. of Organists, RSA. *Address:* Flywheel House, The Estate Yard, Westonbirt, nr Tetbury, Glos. GL8 8QH, England (home). *Telephone:* (1666) 880099 (home). *E-mail:* andhmusic@yahoo.co.uk (home).

HANSLIP, Chloë; British concert violinist; b. 1987, Guildford; d. of Martin and Averil Hanslip. *Education:* studied with Natasha Boyarskaya, 1991–; masterclasses in Vienna with Zakhar Bron, 1993– and Gerhard Schulz 2004–; further studies in Cologne and Madrid. *Career:* played child violinist in 1996 film, Onegin (Devil's Trill Sonata); recitals in Europe, Scandinavia and the USA; TV appearances at Europe, Russia and Israel; Bruch First Concerto at the Barbican, London, 2002; Sarasate's Carmen Fantasy at the 2002 London

Proms; Wigmore Hall concert and concertos with the London Mozart Players; European premiere of Sir John Taverner's Ikon of Eros, Chichester 2005; opened season with Bayrische Rundfunk and Mariss Janson with Sibelius, Gasteig, Munich 2005; Prussia Cove Tour 2006; Chamber Music Festival at Blonay, Switzerland with Seiji Ogawa 2006; Kuhmo Chamber Music Festival, Finland 2006. *Recordings include:* Paganini and Bloch (with John Williams) 2002, Bruch I and III (with LSO), 2003, American Works (with Leonard Slatkin) 2006, Juno Hubay Violin Concertos 2009. *Honours:* First Prize, Junior Int. Competition; Novosibirsk, 1997; Scholarship with Sibelius Foundation, 2001. *Current Management:* Agence Artistique Ludmila Lincy, 35 Avenue des Champs Elysées, 75008 Paris, France. *Website:* www.chloehanslip.com.

HANSMANN, Christine; singer (mezzo-soprano); b. 1964, Thuringia, Germany. *Education:* studied in Leipzig. *Career:* sang at Weimar Opera from 1989; guest appearances at Leipzig, Kassel and elsewhere in Germany, as Mozart's Dorabella and Cherubino, Fricka, Ottavia in Poppea, the Composer in Ariadne auf Naxos and Hansel; Leipzig Opera from 1993 in Le Grand Macabre by Ligeti, Satyricon by Maderna and Schoenberg's Moses und Aron; other roles include Wagner's Kundry and Brangaene; concerts with the Leipzig Gewandhaus Orchestra, including US debut at New York in the Wesendonck Lieder.

HANSON, George; American conductor and pianist; *Music Director, Tucson Symphony Orchestra*; m. Petra Boehm; three s. *Education:* Vienna Acad. of Music, Curtis Inst., Indiana Univ., Concordia Coll. *Career:* served as an asst to Leonard Bernstein; Resident Conductor, Atlanta Symphony Orchestra 1988–93; assisted Kurt Masur at New York Philharmonic Orchestra 1993–2000; Music Dir Tucson Symphony Orchestra 1996–; fmr Gen. Music Dir Wuppertal Symphony Orchestra and Opera, Germany; performed with Lang Lang, Yo-Yo Ma, Joshua Bell, Peter Serkin, Alicia de Larrocha, André Watts, Emmanuel Ax, Tony Bennett, Dizzy Gillespie, Roberta Flack; has led nearly 100 symphony orchestras and opera companies, including New York Philharmonic, Phoenix Orchestra, Indianapolis Orchestra, Charlotte Symphony Orchestra, radio orchestras of Berlin and Hamburg, Berlin's Komische Opera, Vienna's Kammeroper, Warsaw Philharmonic, Mexico's Nat. Symphony, orchestras of Osaka and Seoul, Anchorage Symphony. *Honours:* Winner, Budapest Int. Conducting Competition, Winner, Stokowski Competition, New York, Echo Klassik Award 2003. *Address:* Tucson Symphony Center, 2175 North Sixth Avenue, Tucson, AZ 85705-5606, USA (office). *Telephone:* (520) 792-9155 (office). *Website:* tucsonsymphony.org (office).

HANSON, Robert Frederic, BA, PhD, ARCO, FRSA; British composer, conductor, lecturer and teacher; b. 24 Oct. 1948, Birmingham; m. Judith Hanson; two s. one d. *Education:* Univ. of Southampton. *Career:* revived and conducted Univ. of Southampton Chamber Orchestra 1970–72; analytical research into music of Webern 1970–73; Lecturer in Music, Dartington Coll. of Arts 1974–91; degree course leader 1983–91, then Acting Head of Music, Dir of Music, Morley Coll. 1991–2007; Conductor, Morley Chamber Choir 1991–2009, Hythe Singers 2008–15, Borough Chamber Choir 2009–; now freelance conductor, composer, lecturer and teacher; mem. Sound and Music, Performing Right Soc.; Trustee, Matyas Seiber Trust. *Compositions include:* Metaphysical Verses for soprano and orchestra 1980, Changes for string orchestra 1982, Piano Trio 1984, Chamber Concerto 1986, Violin Sonata 1987, Song Cycles: Auguries of Innocence 1988, Clarinet Concerto 1991, Thanksgiving Music 1994, String Quartet 1997, Exequiae Musiciae 1999, Motet in 40 Parts: And There Shall Be No Night There 2002, Surrexit Dominus 2006, Beyond that Dim Horizon 2008, Reconnection for jazz quartet 2008, Ave Maria, Four British Folksongs 2009, Magnificat & Nunc Dimittis 2013, Te Deum 2015. *Recording:* Thanksgiving 2013. *Publications:* contrib. to Tempo, Lutoslawski's Mi-Parti, Music Analysis, Webern's Chromatic Organisation. *Address:* 12 Nutfield Road, Mersham, Surrey, RH1 3EW, England (home). *Telephone:* (1737) 646124 (home). *E-mail:* rfhanson@btinternet.com.

HAO, Jiang Tian; American (b. Chinese) singer (bass); b. 1954, Beijing. *Education:* Central Conservatory of Music, Beijing, Univ. of Denver. *Career:* began career at Cen. Philharmonic Soc. of China; moved to USA to study; debut at Metropolitan Opera 1991 season, has since appeared in 26 operas at the Metropolitan in every subsequent season; has sung over 1,300 performances of 40 operatic roles worldwide; int. appearances include Berlin State Opera, Teatro Comunale, Florence, Teatro Carlo Felice, Genoa, Arena di Verona, Teatro Colon, Buenos Aires, Chicago Lyric Opera, Canadian Opera Co., Washington Nat. Opera, and other opera houses in France, Spain, Netherlands, Portugal, Chile, Japan and China; concert appearances with Philadelphia Orchestra, Cleveland Orchestra, Colorado Symphony, Orchestra of St Martin-in-the-Fields, Orchestra of Radio Vara, China Philharmonic, Shanghai Symphony Orchestra, Hong Kong Philharmonic; roles include: General Wang in the First Emperor, Chang the Coffin Maker in The Bonesetter's Daughter, Philip II and Grand Inquisitore in Don Carlos, Procida in I Vespri Siciliani, Mephistopheles in Faust, Le Comte in Manon, Raimondo in Lucia di Lammermoor, Ramfis and King in Aida, Oroveso in Norma, Colline in La Boheme, Sparafucile in Rigoletto, Don Basilio in Il Barbiere di Siviglia, Oroveso in Norma, Count Walther in Luisa Miller, Silva in Ernani. *Recordings:* Operatic Arias 2006, Across the Ocean. *Publications:* Along the Roaring River: My Wild Ride from Mao to the Met (auto-biog.) 2008. *Honours:* winner of numerous int. singing competitions, including Rosa Ponselle Foundation, Bel Canto Voice Competition, Sullivan Foundation Voice Competition of New York, San Francisco Opera Competition; Denver Univ. Alumni Professional Achievement Award 2008. *Current Management:* Zemsky/Green Artists Management, 104 West 73rd Street, Suite 1, New York, NY 10023, USA. *Telephone:* (212) 579-6700. *Fax:* (212) 579-4723. *E-mail:* bzemsky@zemskygreen.com. *Website:* www.zemskygreen.com. *E-mail:* marthaliao@gmail.com (office). *Website:* www.tianhaojiang.com.

HARA, Kazuko; Japanese composer; b. 10 Feb. 1935, Tokyo. *Education:* studied in Japan, with Dutilleux in Paris and with Tcherepinn, Venice Conservatory, studied Gregorian Chant in Tokyo. *Career:* operas have been successfully performed in Tokyo. *Compositions include:* operas: The Casebook of Sherlock Holmes: The Confession 1981, On the Merry Night 1984, A Selection for Chieko 1985, Sute-Hime: The Woman Who Bit off a Man's Tongue 1986, A Love Suicide at Sonezaki 1987, Beyond Brain Death 1988, Yosakoi-bushi: Junshin and Omma 1990, Princess Iwanaga 1990, Pedtro Kibe: recanted not 1992, Nasuno-Yoichi 1992, Tonnerre's Miraculous Tree 1993, The Life of the Virgin Mary (oratorio) 1993, Lord Sansho 1995, Princess Nukata 1996, Crime and Punishment (after Dostoyevsky) 1998.

HARADA, Sadao; Japanese cellist; b. 4 Jan. 1944, Tokyo. *Education:* Juilliard School. *Career:* cellist of the Tokyo Quartet 1969–99; regular concerts in the USA and abroad; first cycle of the complete quartets of Beethoven at the Yale at Norfolk Chamber Music Festival, 1986; repeated cycles at the 92nd Street Y (NY), Ravinia and Israel Festivals and Yale and Princeton Universities; season 1990–91 at Alice Tully Hall, the Metropolitan Museum of Art, New York and in Boston, Washington DC, Los Angeles, Cleveland, Detroit, Chicago, Miami, Seattle, San Francisco, Toronto; tour of South America, two tours of Europe including Paris, Amsterdam, Bonn, Milan, Munich, Dublin, London, Berlin; Quartet-in-Residence at Yale University, the University of Cincinnati College-Conservatory of Music. *Recordings:* Schubert's Major Quartets; Mozart Flute Quartets with James Galway and Clarinet Quintet with Richard Stoltzman; Quartets by Bartók, Brahms, Debussy, Haydn, Mozart and Ravel; Beethoven Middle Period Quartets (RCA). *Honours:* Grand Prix du Disque du Montreux; Best Chamber Music Recording of the Year from Stereo Review and the Gramophone; Four Grammy Nominations. *Current Management:* Kajimoto Concert Management, 8-6-25 Ginza, Chuo-ku, Tokyo, 104-0061, Japan.

HARBISON, John Harris, BA, MFA; American composer and conductor; *Institute Professor, Massachusetts Institute of Technology*; b. 20 Dec. 1938, Orange, NJ. *Education:* Harvard Coll. with Walter Piston, Berlin Hochschule für Musik with Boris Blacher, Princeton Univ. with Roger Sessions and Earl Kim, Berkshire Music Center, Tanglewood, MA with Eleazer de Carvalho, studied in Salzburg with Dean Dixon. *Career:* teacher, MIT 1969–82, currently Inst. Prof.; Conductor, Cantata Singers and Ensemble 1969–73, 1980–82; composer-in-residence, Reed Coll. 1968–69, Pittsburgh Symphony Orchestra 1982–84, Berkshire Music Center 1984; New Music Adviser, Los Angeles Philharmonic Orchestra 1985–86, Composer-in-Residence 1986–88; Co-Artistic Dir, Token Creek Chamber Music Festival 1989–; Pres. Aaron Copland Fund for Music 1997–2010; commissions include the opera The Great Gatsby, performed at the Metropolitan 2000. *Compositions include:* operas: The Winter's Tale 1974, Full Moon in March 1977, The Great Gatsby 1999; ballet: Ulysses 1984; instrumental and orchestral: Sinfonia for violin and double orchestra 1963, Confinement for chamber ensemble 1965, Elegiac Songs for mezzo-soprano and chamber orchestra 1973, Descant-Nocturne 1976, Diotima 1976, Piano Concerto 1978, Snow Country for oboe and strings 1979, Violin Concerto 1980, Symphony No. 1 1981, Deep Potomac Bells for 250 tubas 1983, Remembering Gatsby 1985, Viola Concerto 1989, Symphony No. 2 1987, Oboe Concerto 1991, David's Fascinating Rhythm Method 1991, Symphony No. 3 1991, 14 Fabled Folksongs for violin and marimba 1992, Suite for cello 1993, Flute Concerto 1993, Cello Concerto 1993, The Most Often Used Chords for orchestra 1993, Emerson for double chorus 1995, Four Psalms for vocal soloists, chorus and orchestra 1999, Partita 2001, Darkbloom 2004, Canonical American Songbook 2005, The Great Gatsby Suite 2007, Mary Lou 2008; chamber: Serenade for six instruments 1968, Piano Trio 1969, Bermuda Triangle for amplified cello, tenor saxophone and electric organ 1970, Die Kurze for five instruments 1970, Woodwind Quintet 1979, Organum for Paul Fromm for chamber group 1981, Piano Quintet 1981, Exequien for Carlo Simmons for seven instruments 1982, Overture, Michael Kohlhass for brass ensemble 1982, Variations for clarinet, violin and piano 1982, String Quartet No. 1 1985, No. 2 1987, No. 3 1993, Fanfare for a Free Man 1997, Six American Painters 2000, Chaconne 2001, Cucaraccia and Fugue 2003, French Horn Suite 2006, Deep Dances 2006, Abu Ghraib 2006, Cortège 2008; also choral pieces and songs. *Honours:* Guggenheim Fellowship 1978, Pulitzer Prize in Music 1986. *Address:* Department of Music and Theater Arts, Massachusetts Institute of Technology, 4-246, 77 Massachusetts Avenue, Cambridge, MA 02139-4307 (office); Token Creek Chamber Music Festival, PO Box 55142, Madison, WI 53705-8942, USA (office). *E-mail:* harbison@mit.edu (office); info@tokencreekfestival.org (office). *Website:* web.mit.edu/music/facstaff/harbison.html (office); www.tokencreekfestival.org (office).

HARBOTTLE, Guy; British singer (baritone); b. 1960, England. *Education:* Royal Coll. of Music, London. *Career:* appearances with Kent Opera, Wexford Festival, European Chamber Orchestra and Travelling Opera as Bizet's Escamillo and Zurga, Germont, Amonasro, Gianni Schicchi, Marcello and Belcore; further engagements with British Youth Opera, Pavilion Opera, at Gothenburg and the Edinburgh Festival; sang Fritz in the British premiere of Korngold's Die tote Stadt (concert) at the QEH 1996; Orestes in the British premiere of Oresteia by Xenakis for the English Bach Festival, Linbury

Studio, Covent Garden 2000; Britten roles include Balstrode, Sid (Albert Herring) and Tarquinius in The Rape of Lucretia.

HARDENBERGER, Håkan; Swedish musician (trumpet); *Professor, Malmö Conservatoire;* b. 27 Oct. 1961, Malmö. *Education:* studied with Bo Nilsson in Malmö, Royal Coll. of Music, Malmö, Paris Conservatoire with Pierre Thibaud, studied in Los Angeles with Thomas Stevens. *Career:* regular performances with leading int. orchestras including Chicago Symphony, Wiener Philharmoniker, Orchestra Nat. de France, London Symphony, The Philharmonia, Symphonieorchester des Bayerische Rundfunks, NHK Symphony Orchestra; regular collaborations with conductors including Pierre Boulez, Daniel Harding, Neeme Järvi, Andris Nelsons, Antonio Pappano, Esa-Pekka Salonen, John Storgårds and David Zinman; has performed numerous world premieres including Hard Pace by Luca Francesconi with Accademia Nazionale di Santa Cecilia, Rome 2008; repertory includes works by Sir Harrison Birtwistle, Hans Werner Henze, Rolf Martinsson, Olga Neuwirth, Arvo Pärt, Mark Anthony Turnage, HK Gruber; as recitalist collaborates with pianists Aleksandar Madar and Roland Pöntinen, Swedish poet Jacques Werup, actress Pernilla August, jazz pianist Jan Lundgren, percussionist Colin Currie; currently Prof, Malmö Conservatoire; 2009 season includes include performances with SWR Radio orchestra, Cologne and Paris, Bamberger Symphoniker, Danish Nat. Symphony, Munich and Royal Stockholm Philharmonics, Gustav Mahler Youth Orchestra, Berliner Philharmonie, Wiener Musikverein, Royal Scottish Nat. Orchestra. *Repertoire includes:* pioneer of new trumpet works as well as classical repertoire. *Recordings include:* Concertos by Haydn, Hummel, Hertel, Stamitz and Telemann, Birtwistle Endless Parade Concertos by Davies and Watkins, Mysteries of the Macabre, Baroque Trumpet Recital, At the Beach, Turnage, Gruber, Neuwirth, Martinsson Francesconi, and Eotvös trumpet concertos. *Honours:* RPO Charles Heidseele Music Award for best instrumentalist 1988, 1989. *Current Management:* Konzertdirektion Schmid UK Ltd, 40 St Martin's Lane, London, WC2N 4ER, England. *Telephone:* (20) 7395-0910. *Fax:* (20) 7395-0911. *E-mail:* pia.sikorski@kdschmid.co.uk. *Website:* www.kdschmid.de; www.hakanhardenberger.com.

HARDING, Daniel; British conductor; *Music Director, Mahler Chamber Orchestra;* b. 31 Aug. 1975, Oxford; m. Beatrice Muthelet (separated); two c. *Education:* Univ. of Cambridge. *Career:* season 1993–94 conducted The Miraculous Mandarin Suite with the City of Birmingham Symphony, followed by Schnittke's Viola Concerto with Yuri Bashmet; other CBSO repertory includes Das Lied von der Erde, The Rite of Spring and Stockhausen's Gruppen; season 1994–95 with the Rotterdam Philharmonic, London Symphony, Scottish Chamber Orchestra and BBC Philharmonic Orchestra; tour of the UK 1995 with the Birmingham Contemporary Music Group in The Soldier's Tale; further engagements with the Netherlands Wind Ensemble and the Jeunesse Musicales World Orchestra; London Proms debut 1996 (as youngest ever conductor), Prin. Conductor, Trondheim Symphony Orchestra 1997, Prin. Guest, Norköpping Symphony Orchestra; conducted Don Giovanni at Aix and Jenüfa for WNO 1998; guest conductor, Santa Cecilia Orchestra of Rome, Royal Stockholm Philharmonic, Frankfurt Radio Symphony Orchestra and the Residentie Orchestra of the Hague 1997–98; season 1998–99 conducted the London Philharmonic and Leipzig Gewandhaus Orchestras; Music Dir Deutsche Kammerphilharmonie, Bremen 2000–03; further engagements include returns to the City of Birmingham and London Symphony Orchestras, Berlin Philharmonic and the Frankfurt and Swedish Radio Orchestras; debut at the Royal Opera House with Turn of the Screw 2001; season 2001–02 with San Francisco Symphony Orchestra, Philadelphia Orchestra, Los Angeles Philharmonic Orchestra, London Symphony Orchestra, Gewandhaus Orchestra, Dresden Staatskapelle and Concertgebouw Orchestra; Wozzeck at Aix 2003; co-f. and Music Dir, Mahler Chamber Orchestra 2003–; prin. guest conductor LSO 2004, 2006–07; opened 2005–06 season with Mozart's Idomeneo at La Scala, Milan; season 2007–08 included engagements with Vienna Philharmonic, Amsterdam Concertgebouw, New Japan Philharmonic, Deutsches Symphonie-Orchester Berlin, Tokyo Philharmonic, La Scala, Staatskapelle Dresden, Bayerischer Rundfunk Munich orchestras; Music Dir Swedish Radio Symphony Orchestra 2007–12. *Recordings:* works by Lutoslawski with soprano Solveig Kringelborn and the Norwegian Chamber Orchestra, works by Britten with Ian Bostridge and the Britten Sinfonia 1998, The Turn of the Screw (Gramophone Opera Award 2003) 2002, Britten: Billy Budd (Grammy Award for Opera 2010) 2008, Orff: Carmina Burana 2010, Beethoven Piano Concertos Nos 3 & 4 (Gramophone Award for Best Concerto Recording 2015) 2014. *Honours:* Royal Philharmonic Soc. Best Debut award 1994, Choc de L'Année 1998, Le Monde de la Musique 1998; Chevalier, Ordre des Arts et des Lettres 2002. *Current Management:* c/o CAMI Music LLC, 1790 Broadway, 16th Floor, New York, 10019, USA. *Telephone:* (212) 841-9500. *Fax:* (212) 841-9744. *E-mail:* info@cami.com. *Website:* www.cami.com. *Address:* Mahler Chamber Orchestra e. V. Hasenheide 54, 10967 Berlin, Germany (office). *Telephone:* (30) 41-71-79-0 (office). *Fax:* (30) 41-71-79-29 (office). *E-mail:* mco@mahler-chamber.de (office). *Website:* www.mahler-chamber.de (office); www.danielharding.com (home).

HARDY, Janet, BM; singer (soprano); b. 1940, Atlanta, GA, USA. *Education:* Mississippi Southern and Louisiana Colls, Louisiana Coll. and studied with Dorothy Hulse, Dominique Modesti, Gladys Kuchta and Hilde Zadek. *Career:* has sung in Gelsenkirchen, Kassel and Augsburg as Elektra, Ortrud, Leonore in Fidelio, the Kostelnicka in Jenüfa, Kundry, Isolde, Senta and Turandot; guest appearances in Frankfurt, Salzburg, Copenhagen, the Berlin Staatso-

per, Trieste, Leipzig, Berne, Mannheim, Toulon and Düsseldorf; season 1988–89 with the title role in new productions of Mona Lisa by Schillings in Augsburg and Elektra in Innsbruck; sang Elektra at the Vienna Staatsoper 1991; Brünnhilde in Die Walküre at Liège, the Dyer's Wife in Die Frau ohne Schatten at Augsburg 1991; sang Elektra with WNO 1992; sang with the Augsburg Opera until end of season 2000–01.

HARDY, Rosemary; British singer (soprano); b. 1949, England. *Education:* Royal Coll. of Music, Franz Liszt Acad., Budapest. *Career:* performances with Roger Norrington, Michel Corboz and John Eliot Gardiner in The Baroque repertoire; solo cantatas with the Drottningholm Baroque Ensemble, Sweden, at the Berlin Staatsoper and the Wigmore Hall; sang in Jonathan Miller's production of Orfeo by Monteverdi; modern repertoire includes Webern's music for voice at the Venice Biennale 1983 and the Cheltenham Festival; Webern recital at the Vienna Konzerthaus 1983; Schoenberg's 2nd Quartet (Arditti) for the Maggio Musicale, in Geneva and in London (BBC); premieres of Jonathan Harvey's Passion and Resurrection and Song Offerings; tours of France with Ensemble Intercontemporain, performing Boulez, Ravel, Varèse and Kurtag (Scenes from a Novel); has also given Kurtag's Sayings of R. V. Troussova; appearances at the Glyndebourne Festival in Knussen's Where the Wild Things Are and Higgelty Piggelty Pop; concert showings with the Hallé, City of Birmingham, San Diego, Danish Radio, BBC Symphony and London Symphony Orchestras; has sung in Henze's The English Cat for the BBC, and in Frankfurt and Italy; concert with the Schoenberg Ensemble and the Nieuw Ensemble at the Holland Festival; Pierrot Lunaire in Milan 1991; tour with Capricorn on the Contemporary Music Network; has also sung in Schubert Masses with the London Philharmonic, Mozart and Handel concert for the Cambridge Festival and concerts at the Aldeburgh Festival; Knussen's Where the Wild Things Are and Higglety Pigglety Pop at the London Proms 2002. *Recordings:* Cavalli's Ercole Amante, Monteverdi's Combattimento, Il Ballo delle Ingrate and Scherzi Musicale. *Honours:* Artijus Prize, Hungary 1983.

HARE, Ian Christopher, MA, MusB, FRCO, ADCM, ARCM; musician and organist; *Director of Music, Crosthwaite Church, Keswick and Organist and Honorary Fellow, Lancaster University;* b. 26 Dec. 1949, Kingston upon Hull, England; m. (divorced 2002); two d. *Education:* Hymers Coll., Hull, King's Coll., Cambridge, Royal Coll. of Music. *Career:* Lecturer in Music, subsequently Organist, Lancaster Univ.; Organist and Master of Choristers Cartmel Priory 1981–89; sub-organist Carlisle Cathedral 1989–95; founder and Musical Dir Lancaster Singers 1975–89; currently Dir of Music Crosthwaite Church; directs the Keswick Choral Soc.; Chorus Master Cumbria Rural Singers; Associated Bd examiner; adjudicator for organ competitions; performed in Britain and abroad, including France, Germany, USA as organ recitalist and accompanist; played at many of the major London venues, including the Proms at Royal Albert Hall; mem. Incorporated Soc. of Musicians, Royal Coll. of Organists, Incorporated Asscn of Organists. *Compositions:* Thou, O God Art Praised in Sion, anthem 1973, Beethoven's Hymn to Joy, organ arrangement 1974, A Child is Born, anthem 1987, Three Dances for Organ, Except the Lord build the house, anthem for SATB and organ, many others for choir and organ. *Recordings:* Handel's Messiah, Bach Cantata 147 and motets, Britten's Missa Brevis, St Nicholas, Once in Royal David's City, Hymns for all Seasons, King's Coll. Choir Cambridge 1968–72; In Pastures Green (The Organ of Crosthwaite Church, Keswick). *Honours:* Hon. Fellow, Lancaster Univ. 2006. *Current Management:* J. Audrey Ellison, International Artists' Management, 135 Stevenage Road, Fulham, London, SW6 6PB, England. *Telephone:* (20) 7381-9751 (office). *Fax:* (20) 7381-2406 (office). *E-mail:* Audrey-Ellison@Intel.freeserve.co.uk (office). *Address:* The Porch, Skiddaw Lodge, Crosthwaite Road, Keswick, Cumbria, CA12 5QA, England (home). *Telephone:* (1768) 773342. *Fax:* (1768) 773342. *E-mail:* ian.c.hare@gmail.com. *Website:* www.ianhare.org.uk.

HARGAN, Alison; British singer (soprano); b. 1943, Yorkshire, England. *Education:* Royal Northern Coll. of Music. *Career:* debut with WNO, as Pamina in Die Zauberflöte; concert performances of music by Strauss and Mahler, Four Last Songs and Resurrection Symphony, and Verdi (Requiem); appearances include Tippett's A Child of our Time with Neville Marriner, the Fauré Requiem with the Royal Philharmonic Orchestra and Bach's B Minor Mass in Lisbon; Britten's War Requiem with the Boston Symphony Orchestra and Mahler's 8th Symphony at La Fenice, Venice, conducted by Eliahu Inbal; worked with orchestras, including the Vienna Philharmonic, Munich Philharmonic and Los Angeles Philharmonic, as well as leading orchestras in the UK.

HARGITAI, Géza; Hungarian violinist; b. 1940. *Education:* Franz Liszt Acad., Budapest. *Career:* second violinist, Bartók Quartet 1985–; performances in nearly every European country and tours of Australia, Canada, Japan, New Zealand and the USA; festival appearances at Adelaide, Ascona, Aix, Venice, Dubrovnik, Edinburgh, Helsinki, Lucerne, Menton, Prague, Vienna, Spoleto and Schwetzingen; tours of the UK, including concerts at Cheltenham, Dartington, Philharmonic Hall Liverpool, RNCM Manchester, the Wigmore Hall, Sheldonian Theatre, Oxford, Harewood House and Birmingham; repertoire includes standard classics and Hungarian works by Bartók, Durko, Bozay, Kadosa, Soproni, Farkas, Szabo and Lang. *Recordings include:* complete quartets of Mozart, Beethoven and Brahms, major works of Haydn and Schubert, Complete quartets of Bartók. *Address:* Nippon Artists Management Inc., 5-4-10-3F Koishikawa Bunkyo, Tokyo 112-0002, Japan.

HARGREAVES, Glenville, BMus, GRSM, ARMCM, FRSA, FHEA; British singer (baritone); *Senior Professor of Singing and LRAM Tutor, Royal Academy of Music*; b. 26 July 1947, Bradford, Yorks. *Education:* York St John's Univ., York, Royal Northern Coll. of Music, Manchester, London Opera Centre, Univ. of Liverpool. *Career:* debut in title role, Il Barbiere di Siviglia 1981; Covent Garden debut in Les Contes d'Hoffmann 1982; with ENO 1982–, notably in Magic Flute, War and Peace, Salome; modern repertory includes The Old Man, in Purgatory by Gordon Crosse; Walworth in Wat Tyler by Alan Bush; Ullmann's Emperor of Atlantis; Mittenhofer in Henze's Elegy for Young Lovers (QEH, London and Opéra de Lausanne); Sir Charles Keighley in John Metcalf's Tornrak (creation 1990); appeared with Opera North as The Dark Fiddler in A Village Romeo and Juliet, Kothner in Meistersinger and roles in Tosca, The Bartered Bride and La Traviata (Germont) 2004; WNO debut as Marcello in La Bohème, also the Guardian in Elektra, Don Pasquale 1992 and Ankarstroem 1993; debut as Falstaff with City of Birmingham Touring Opera; Don Alfonso and Musicmaster in Ariadne 2003 for English Touring Opera; other roles include Nick Shadow, Sharpless (Cork Opera and Paris), Tonio, Scarpia and Michele (Holland Park); concert repertory includes Elijah, Judas Maccabaeus, The Kingdom, Messiah, Sea Drift by Delius, Gerontius, Lieder eines fahrenden Gesellen by Mahler, Bach Passions, Carmina Burana; has sung with Hallé Orchestra, Nat. Orchestra of Spain, Royal Philharmonic Orchestra, Royal Liverpool Philharmonic Orchestra, Nat. Orchestra of Argentina, BBC Philharmonic, Bournemouth Symphony Orchestra; frequent broadcasts; appearances at Garsington Opera: Musiklehrer in Ariadne 1993, Count Capriccio 1994, Schumann's Genoveva 2000; Rigoletto for Pimlico Opera, English Touring Opera 1996, Roubaix 1997, Belfast 2004; for Grange Park Opera: André in Messager's Fortunio 2001, Mountararat in Iolanthe 2003; Opera Holland Park seasons: Michele in Il Tabarro 1997, Baldassare in L'Arlesiana 1998, Don Alfonso 2000, Tonio in I Pagliacci 2003; The Rake's Progress for Opéra de Lausanne and Opéra de Bordeaux 2003; for the Netherlands: Kolenaty in Macropulos Case 2001, all seven Traveller roles in Death in Venice 2002; Sr Tutor in Vocal Studies, Royal Northern Coll. of Music 1986–99; Sr Prof. of Singing, RAM, London 1997–, Head of Opera Studies, Postgraduate Opera Course 2008–11, LRAM Tutor 2011–, mem. Academic Bd and Governing Body; Fellow, Higher Educ. Acad. 2011. *Recordings include:* Old Man, in Purgatory, Andrea, in Catarina Cornaro (Donizetti). *Honours:* Hon. ARAM . *Current Management:* c/o Musichall Ltd, Oast House, Crouch's Farm' Hollow Lane, East Hoathly, East Sussex, BN8 6QX, England. *Telephone:* (1825) 840437. *E-mail:* info@musichall.uk.com. *Website:* www .musichall.uk.com.

HARJANNE, Jouko; Finnish musician (trumpet); *Artistic Director, Lieksa Brass Week*; b. 21 June 1962, Rauma. *Education:* Tampere Conservatory with Raimo Sarmas, studied with Henri Adelbrecht and Timofey Dokshitser. *Career:* concerto debut with Finnish Radio Symphony Orchestra 1978; co-prin. trumpeter, Tampere Philhamonic Orchestra 1978–84; prin. trumpet, Finnish Radio Symphony Orchestra 1984–; chamber musician with many ensembles, including Finnish Brass Ensemble, Brasstime Quartet and Protoventus Ensemble; Prof., Sibelius Acad., Helsinki 1989–; Artistic Dir, Lieksa Brass Week 1996–; has given first performances of concertos by Segerstam 1984, Gruner 1987, 1992, Linkola 1988, 1993, Wessman 1991, Bashmakov 1992, European premiere of Schedrin's Concerto 1995. *Recordings include:* Angel Music, Velvet Trumpet, Slavonic Fantasy, Finnish Trumpet Concertos 1989, Total Trumpet 1990, Trumpet Concertos with RSO 1994, Trumpet Experience 1994, Virtuoso Trumpet 1994, Trumpet Adagio 1995, American Trumpet Sonatas 1997, Proclamation 1998, Trumpet Aria 2000, Festive Trumpet 2005, Symbiosis 2006, Concert Pieces 2006, Dramatic Legend 2007, Elegy 2007, Narva 2007, Romantic Trumpet 2007, What a Wonderful Christmas 2008, Trumpet Rhapsody 2009, Great Trumpet Sonatas 2009, The Russian Trumpet 2009. *Honours:* second prize Prague Spring Int. Competition 1987, Lieksa Brass Week Brass Player of the Year Award 1989, first place Int. Trumpet Guild Ellsworth Smith Trumpet Competition 1990. *Current Management:* Alarik Repo Management, Hermistostigen 15, 21660 Nagu, Finland. *Telephone:* (7) 73106. *E-mail:* alarik@plyms.fi. *Website:* www.joukoharjanne.com.

HARLE, John Crofton, ARCM, FGSM; British saxophonist, composer, arranger, producer and academic; *Professor of Saxophone, Guildhall School of Music and Drama*; b. 20 Sept. 1956; m. 1st Julia Jane Eisner 1985 (divorced 2003); m. 2nd Riccarda Anne Kane 2010; two s. *Education:* Royal Coll. of Music Foundation School, studied in Paris. *Career:* Leader, Myrha Saxophone Quartet 1977–82; formed duo with pianist John Lenehan 1979; saxophone soloist 1980–, with major int. orchestras, including London Symphony Orchestra, English Chamber Orchestra, Basel Chamber Orchestra, San Diego Symphony Orchestra; Prin. Saxophone, London Sinfonietta 1987–; Prof. of Saxophone, GSMD 1988–; formed Berliner Band 1983, John Harle Band 1988; premiered Birtwistle's Panic at Last Night of the London Proms 1995; Opera Angel Magick premiered at BBC Proms 1998; world premiere of The Little Death Machine at BBC Proms 2002; mem. of several ensembles 1983–, including London Brass and London Symphony Orchestra; frequent composer and soloist on TV and feature films; regular broadcaster on BBC Radio; featured in One Man and his Sax (BBC 2) 1988; works written for him by Dominic Muldowney, Ned Rorem, Richard Rodney Bennett, Luciano Berio, Michael Nyman, Gavin Bryars, Mike Westbrook and Stanley Myers; tour with Marc Almond (The Tyburn Tree) 2014; duo with pianist Steve Lodder 2016. *Publication:* John Harle's Saxophone Album 1986. *Honours:* RCM Dannreuther Concerto Prize 1980, GLAA Young Musician 1979, 1980. *Website:* www.johnharle.com.

HARMS, Kirsten; German opera company director; *Artistic Director, Deutsche Oper Berlin*; b. 25 June 1956, Hamburg. *Education:* Univ. of Hamburg. *Career:* co-founder Mimesis drama co.; Asst Producer, Städtische Bühnen Dortmund 1985–88; worked as freelance producer in Bremen, Hannover, Kiel, Saabrücken, Darmstadt, Innsbruck and Mainz; Assoc. Lecturer for Music Production, Coll. of Music and the Arts, Hamburg 1992–; Artistic Dir, Theater Kiel 1995–2003; Artistic Dir, Deutsche Oper Berlin 2004–(12). *Productions include:* Madame Butterfly 1990, Lohengrin 1992, L'elisir d'Amore 1993, Mignon 1993, La Sonnambula 1994, Turandot 1995, Die Frau ohne Schatten 1996, Das Rheingold 1997, The Magic Flute 1997, Die Walküre 1998, Der Schimmelreiter 1998, Siegfried 1999, Götterdämmerung 2000, Die Liebe der Danae 2001, Die Schweigsame Frau 2001, Christophorus oder 2002, Das Spielwerk und die Prinzessin 2003, Semiramide 2003, Anatevka 2003, Romeo and Juliet 2004. *Address:* Deutsche Oper Berlin, Richard Wagner Strasse 10, 10585 Berlin, Germany (office). *Telephone:* (30) 34384901 (office). *Website:* www.deutscheoperberlin.de (office).

HARNONCOURT, Nikolaus; Austrian cellist and conductor; b. 6 Dec. 1929, Berlin, Germany; s. of Eberhard Harnoncourt and Ladislaja Harnoncourt (née Meran); m. Alice Hoffelner 1953; three s. one d. *Education:* Matura Gymnasium, Graz, Acad. of Music, Vienna. *Career:* cellist with Vienna Symphony Orchestra 1952–69; solo concerts on viola da gamba; int. debuts 1966; Prof., Mozarteum and Inst. of Musicology, Univ. of Salzburg 1972–93; Founder-mem. Concentus Musicus, Ensemble for Ancient Music 1953; as conductor has performed in leading concert halls worldwide, including in Amsterdam, Berlin, Vienna, Zürich, London, New York, Tokyo, Salzburg Festival and Styriarte Festival, Graz. *Recordings include:* more than 450 recordings with period instruments and music from 1200–1950; many works with Concentus Musicus, notably Handel's Messiah, Mozart's early symphonies, Bach's Brandenburg Concertos and Cantatas, Beethoven symphonies with Chamber Orchestra of Europe, Mozart and Schubert symphonies with Concertgebouw Orchestra Amsterdam, recordings with Berlin and Vienna Philharmonic Orchestras, Arnold Schoenberg Choir. *Publications include:* Musik als Klangrede, Wege zu einem neuen Musikverständnis 1982, Der musikalische Dialog 1983, Was ist Wahrheit 1995, Mozart-Dialoge 2005, Töne sind höhere Worte 2007. *Honours:* Officier de la Légion d'honneur 2012; several hon. doctorates including Hon. DMus (Edin.) 1987; Erasmus Prize (jtly) 1980, H. G. Nägeli Medal, Zürich 1983, Polar Prize, Stockholm 1994, Ernst von Siemens Music Prize 2002, Grammy Award (for recording of Bach's St Matthew Passion) 2002, Kyoto Prize (arts and philosophy category, for life's work) 2005, Gramophone Lifetime Achievement Award 2009, RPS Gold Medal 2012, Echo Klassik Lifetime Achievement Award 2014. *Address:* 38 Piaristengasse, 1080 Vienna, Austria (home). *Website:* www.harnoncourt.info. *Current Management:* c/o Styriarte, Steirische Kulturveranstaltungen GmbH, Sackstraße 17, 8010 Graz, Austria. *E-mail:* presse@styriarte.com.

HARNOY, Ofra, CM; Israeli/Canadian cellist; b. 31 Jan. 1965, Hadera, Israel; d. of Jacob Harnoy and Carmela Harnoy; m. Robert S. Cash. *Education:* studied with her father in Israel, William Pleeth in London, Vladimir Orloff in Toronto and in master-classes with Mstislav Rostropovich, Pierre Fournier and Jacqueline du Pré. *Career:* immigrated to Canada at age six; professional debut with Boyd Neel Orchestra, Toronto aged 10; solo appearances with many major orchestras in USA, Canada, Japan, Europe, Israel and Venezuela; TV appearances in Canada, UK and other European countries, Japan and Australia; played world premiere performance Offenbach cello concerto, N American premiere Bliss cello concerto, world premiere recording of several Vivaldi cello concertos; many solo recordings. *Honours:* prizes and awards include JUNO Award for Instrumental Artist of the Year (Canada) 1987/88, 1988/89, 1991, 1992, 1993, First Prize, Montreal Symphony Competition 1978, Canadian Music Competition 1979, Concert Artists Guild, New York 1982, Young Musician of the Year, Musical America magazine, USA 1983, Grand Prix du Disque, Critics' Choice, Best Records of the Year, The Gramophone, UK 1986, 1988, 1990. *Address:* c/o Robert S. Cash, Suite 1000, 121 Richmond Street West, Toronto, ON M5H 2K1, Canada (office). *E-mail:* management@ofraharnoy.com (office). *Website:* www.ofraharnoy.com (office).

HARPER, Heather, CBE, FRCM; British singer (soprano); b. 8 May 1930, Belfast; d. of Hugh Harper and Mary Eliza Harper; m. 2nd Eduardo J. Benarroch 1973. *Education:* Trinity Coll. of Music, London. *Career:* cr. soprano role in Britten's War Requiem, Coventry Cathedral 1962; toured USA with BBC Symphony Orchestra 1965, USSR 1967, soloist opening concerts at the Maltings, Snape 1967, Queen Elizabeth Hall 1967; annual concert and opera tours USA 1967–91 (retd); prin. soloist BBC Symphony Orchestra on 1982 tour of Hong Kong and Australia; prin. soloist Royal Opera House USA visit 1984; also concerts in Asia, Middle East, Australia, European Music Festivals, S. America; prin. roles at Covent Garden, Bayreuth Festival, La Scala (Milan), Teatro Colón (Buenos Aires), Edinburgh Festival, Glyndebourne, Sadler's Wells, Metropolitan Opera House (New York), San Francisco, Frankfurt, Deutsche Oper (Berlin), Japan (with Royal Opera House Covent Garden Co.), Netherlands Opera House, New York City Opera; renowned performances of Arabella, Ariadne, Chrysothemis, Kaiserin, Marschallin (Richard Strauss); TV roles include Ellen Orford (Peter Grimes), Mrs. Coyle (Owen Wingrave), Ilia (Idomeneo), Donna Elvira (Don Giovanni), La Traviata, La Bohème; 25 consecutive years as prin. soloist at the Promenade concerts; Dir Singing Studies at the Britten-Pears School for Advanced Musical Studies, Aldeburgh, Suffolk 1986–; Prof. of Singing and Consultant Royal Coll. of Music, London 1985–93; First Visiting Lecturer in Residence, Royal

Scottish Acad. of Music 1987–; retd from operatic stage 1986 (operatic farewell, Teatro Colón, Buenos Aires 1986), from concert stage 1991; mem. BBC Music Panel 1989, Royal Soc. of Arts 1989–. *Recordings include:* Les Illuminations (Britten), Symphony No. 8 (Mahler), Don Giovanni (Mozart), Requiem (Verdi) and Missa Solemnis (Beethoven), Seven Early Songs (Berg), Marriage of Figaro, Peter Grimes, Four Last Songs (Strauss), 14 Songs with Orchestra. *Honours:* Hon. Fellow, Trinity Coll. of Music; Hon. mem. RAM; Hon. DMus (Queen's Univ.); Edison Award 1971, Grammy Award 1979, 1984, 1991.

HARPER, John Martin, MA, PhD; British academic; *RSCM Research Professor of Music and Liturgy and Director, International Centre for Sacred Music Studies, University of Wales;* b. 11 July 1947, Staffordshire; m. Sally Harper. *Education:* King's Coll. School, Cambridge, Clifton Coll., Selwyn Coll., Cambridge, Univ. of Birmingham. *Career:* music tutor, West Bromwich Arts Centre 1970–71; Dir Edington Festival 1971–78; Dir of Music, St Chad's Cathedral, Birmingham 1972–78; Lecturer in Music, Univ. of Birmingham 1974–75, 1976–81; Asst Dir of Music, King Edward's School, Birmingham 1975–76; Fellow, organist, Informator Choristarum and tutor in music, Magdalen Coll., Oxford, Lecturer, Univ. of Oxford 1981–90; Lecturer, Univ. Coll. of North Wales, Univ. of Wales, Bangor, Prof. of Music 1991–98; Resident Prof. in Christian Music and Liturgy and Dir Gen., Royal School of Music 1998–2007; RSCM Research Prof. of Music and Liturgy and Dir, Int. Centre for Sacred Music Studies, Univ. of Wales, Bangor 2007–; Leverhulme Fellow 1997–98; Dir, Centre for Advanced Welsh Music Studies 1994–; Ed. Welsh Music History 1996–; mem. Plainsong and Medieval Music Soc. (chair. 1998–), Guild of Church Musicians, Cathedral Organists Asscn (sec. 1998–), Cathedral Music Working Party, Early English Organ Project (trustee 1999–), Panel of Monastic Musicians (adviser 1976–), General Synod Liturgical Commission (consultant mem. 2001–07). *Compositions include:* Choral Compositions 1974–. *Recordings include:* The English Anthem 1993–98. *Publications include:* as (Ed): Orlando Gibbons Consort Music 82, The Forms and Orders of Western Liturgy 1991, Hymns for Prayer and Praise 1996, 2011–12, RSCM Music for Common Worship Series 2000–07, Sarum Customary Online 2012–, Experience of Worship in late medieval Cathedral and Parish Church 2012–. *Honours:* Hon. Fellow Guild of Church Musicians 1996; Hon. DMus 2010. *Address:* School of Music, Univ. of Wales, College Road, Bangor, Gwynedd LL57 2DG, Wales (office). *Telephone:* (1248) 490176 (office). *E-mail:* jharper@icsmus.org (office). *Website:* www.bangor.ac.uk/music/staff/harper (office).

HARPER, Thomas; American singer (tenor); b. 1950, Oklahoma. *Education:* studied in Los Angeles, Kansas City, Paris and Italy. *Career:* sang in opera at Coburg, 1982–85, Kaiserslautern, 1985–87, in buffo and character roles; Stadttheater Hagen, 1987–, as the Duke of Mantua, Radames, Almaviva, Don Ottavio, Alwa in Lulu and Daniel in Belshazar by David Kirchner; sang Fritz in Der Ferne Klang by Schreker, 1989; Seattle Opera, 1991 and 1995, as Mime in Der Ring des Nibelungen; Dortmund Opera, 1991–92, as Mime and in premiere of Sekunden und Jahre des Caspar Hauser, by Reinhard Febel; sang Mime in Siegfried at Turin, 1998; season 2000–01 as Mime for Dallas and Geneva Operas. *Recordings include:* Der Ferne Klang (Marco Polo).

HARRELL, Lynn; American cellist and academic; b. 30 Jan. 1944, New York; s. of Mack Harrell and Marjorie Fulton; m. 1st Linda Blandford-Kate; one s. one d.; m. 2nd Helen Nightengale; one s. one d. *Education:* Juilliard School of Music, Curtis Inst. of Music. *Career:* principal cellist, Cleveland Orchestra (under George Szell) 1963–71; now appears as soloist with various orchestras; Piatigorsky Prof. of Cello, Univ. of Southern California 1987–93; Prof. of Int. Cello Studies, RAM, London 1988–93, 1993–95; Artistic Dir LA Philharmonic Inst. 1988–92; Music Advisor, San Diego Symphony Orchestra 1988–89; soloist, Memorial Concert for Holocaust Victims, Vatican 1994; Prof. of Cello, Shepherd School of Music, Rice Univ. 2002–09; collaborations with Anne-Sophie Mutter, André Previn; f. HEARTbeats Foundation (charity) 2010. *Recordings include:* works by J.S. Bach, Beethoven, Bloch, Boccherini, Brahms, Bruch, Debussy, Dutilleux, Dvořák, Elgar, Fauré, Haydn, Herbert, Hindemith, Lalo, Mendelssohn, Prokofiev, Rachmaninov, Rosza, Saint-Saëns, Schoenberg, Schubert, Schumann, Shostakovich, Strauss, Tchaikovsky, Villa-Lobos, Vivaldi, Walton. *Honours:* two Grammy Awards, Avery Fisher Award 1975, Piatigorsky Award, Ford Foundation Concert Artists' Award, others. *Current Management:* R. Douglas Sheldon, Columbia Artists Management, 1790 Broadway at 5 Columbus Circle, New York, NY 10019, USA. *E-mail:* rdsheldon@cami.com. *Website:* www.lynnharrell.com; www .heartbeatsforchildren.org.

HARRHY, Eiddwen; singer (soprano); b. 14 April 1949, Trowbridge, Wiltshire, England; m. Gregory Strange 1988; one d. *Education:* Royal Manchester Coll. of Music, studied in London and Paris. *Career:* debut at the Royal Opera House, Ring Cycle 1974; ENO 1975, Marriage of Figaro, Magic Flute, Carmen, Le Comte Ory; appeared with all the major British orchestras and opera companies; sang in Europe (Paris, Amsterdam, Berlin, Barcelona and many other venues), USA, Hong Kong, Sydney and Wellington; vocal tutor, Welsh Coll. of Music and Drama 1996–2001; Prof., Royal Coll. of Music, London 2001–; mem. Musicians' Benevolent Fund. *Recordings:* Handel's Alcina and Amadigi, Beethoven's 9th Symphony, Fairy Queen. *Honours:* Miriam Licette 1972, RMCM Imperial League of Opera 1972.

HARRIES, Kathryn, ARAM, GRSM, BMus, FRAM; British singer (soprano); *Director, National Opera Studio;* b. 15 Feb. 1951, Hampton Court, Middx,

England; d. of Stanley Harries and Gwynneth Harries. *Education:* Royal Acad. of Music with Constance Shacklock, Univ. of London. *Career:* presented BBC TV series Music Time; Festival Hall, London debut 1977; concert repertoire ranges from Monteverdi to the 20th century; operatic debut with Welsh Nat. Opera 1983, as Leonore; returned as Sieglinde and Gutrune (also at Covent Garden 1986), Adalgisa, and the Composer in Ariadne auf Naxos; ENO as Eva, Female Chorus in The Rape of Lucretia, Irene (Rienzi) and Donna Anna in The Stone Guest by Dargomyzhsky; appearances with Scottish Opera as Leonore, the title role in the premiere of Hedda Gabler by Edward Harper, and Senta; Metropolitan Opera 1986, as Kundry in Parsifal; returned 1989, as Gutrune in a new production of Götterdämmerung; sang Dido in the first complete performance of Les Troyens in France, Lyon 1987, Senta for Paris Opéra, Sieglinde in Nice and Paris and Leonore in Buenos Aires; Covent Garden debut 1989, in the British premiere of Un Re in Ascolto by Berio; returned 1991 as Gutrune in a new production of Götterdämmerung; Dido in Les Troyens for Scottish Opera 1990, also at Covent Garden; season 1990–91 with Katya Kabanova at ENO, Bartók's Judith for Scottish Opera, Dukas' Ariane, Netherlands Opera, Massenet's Cléopâtre in St Etienne and Giulietta in Les Contes d'Hoffmann at the Châtelet in Paris; season 1992 with the Berlioz Dido in Brussels and Carmen at Orange; sang Brangaene for Scottish Opera 1994, 1998; Kundry in Parsifal at the Opéra Bastille, Paris 1997; Kostelnička in Jenůfa at Chicago 2000; season 2000–01 in the premieres of Rêves d'un Marco Polo by Claude Vivier, at Amsterdam, and David Sawyer's From Morning to Midnight, for ENO; Kostelnička at San Francisco 2001, Genoa 2003, Glyndebourne 2004, Lyon 2005, Nantes 2007; Mme Croissy in Dialogues des Carmelites, Hamburg 2002, Bilbao 2007; Kabanicha in Kát'a Kabanová, Antwerp 2004; A Wedding by William Bolcom (world premiere), Chicago Lyric 2005; Die Soldaten, Ruhr Triennale Festival 2006, The Heron in Stephen McNeff's Tarka The Otter, the Two Moors Festival, 2006; cr. Coverwood Concerts at Coverwood Lakes, Surrey 1991; Dir, Nat. Opera Studio 2009–; Admin., Carlisle Summer Festival of Classical Music 2009–; Prof. of Singing, Guildhall School of Music and Drama 2009–. *Honours:* Hon. DMus (Kingston). *Address:* Ingpen & Williams Ltd, 7 St George's Court, 131 Putney Bridge Road, London, SW15 2PA, England (office). *Telephone:* (20) 8874-3222 (office). *Website:* www.ingpen.co.uk. *E-mail:* kathrynharries@gmail.com (home). *Website:* www.kathrynharries.co.uk.

HARRINGTON, David; American violinist; b. 9 Sept. 1949, Portland, Ore. *Education:* Univ. of Washington. *Career:* Founder mem. and Artistic Dir Kronos Quartet 1973–; Quartet-in-residence, State Univ. of New York, Geneseo 1975–77, Mills Coll., Oakland 1977–, Univ. of Southern Calif. 1982–. *Recordings:* albums with Kronos Quartet: In Formation 1982, Monk Suite: Kronos Quartet Plays Music of Thelonious Monk (with Ron Carter) 1985, Terry Riley: Cadenza on the Night Plain 1985, Music of Bill Evans 1986, Kronos Quartet 1986, White Man Sleeps 1987, Winter Was Hard 1988, Steve Reich: Different Trains/Electric Counterpoint (as contributors) 1989, Kronos Quartet Plays Terry Riley: Salome Dances for Peace 1989, Black Angels (Australian Broadcasting Company Classic FM Best International Recording of the Year 1991) 1990, Five Tango Sensations 1991, Górecki: Already It is Dusk 1991, Pieces of Africa (Edison Award in Popular Music, Netherlands) 1992, Short Stories 1993, Górecki, String Quartets Nos. 1 and 2 1993, At the Grave of Richard Wagner 1993, Morton Feldman, Piano and String Quartet (with Aki Takahashi) 1993, Night Prayers 1994, Kronos Quartet Performs Philip Glass 1995, Howl, USA 1996, Osvaldo Golijov: The Dreams and Prayers of Isaac the Blind 1997, Tan Dun: Ghost Opera 1997, Early Music (Lachrymæ Antiquæ) 1997, Kronos Quartet Performs Alfred Schnittke: The Complete String Quartets 1998, John Adams, John's Book of Alleged Dances 1998, Caravan (Edison Award for Chamber Music 2001) 2000, Terry Riley: Requiem for Adam 2001, Steve Reich, Triple Quartet 2001, Nuevo 2002, Alban Berg, Lyric Suite (Grammy Award for Best Chamber Music Performance 2004) 2003, Musical America (Musicians of the Year 2003, Grammy Award for Best Chamber Music Performance 2004) 2003, Harry Partch, Mugam Sayagi: Music of Franghiz Ali-Zadeh 2005, You've Stolen My Heart: Songs from R.D. Burman's Bollywood (with Asha Bhosle) 2005, Górecki, String Quartet No. 3 2007, Kronos Quartet Plays Sigur Rós 2007, Terry Riley, The Cusp of Magic 2008, Floodplain 2009. *Honours:* San Francisco Focus Award for Best Contemporary Music 1984, Western Alliance of Arts Administrators Distinguished Service Award 1989, Kenwood Classical Music Award for Chamber Group of the Year 1994, Nat. Public Radio New Horizon Award for Significant contrib. to Classical Music in America 1996, 1998, Nat. Asscn of Recording Arts and Sciences, San Francisco Chapter, Gov.'s Award for Lifetime Achievement 2002. *Address:* Kronos Quartet, PO Box 225340, San Francisco, CA 94122-5340; c/o Nonesuch Records, 1290 Avenue of the Americas, 23rd Floor, New York, NY 10104, USA (office). *E-mail:* info@nonesuch.com (office); nonesuch.uk@warnermusic.com (office); talk@kronosquartet.org. *Website:* www.nonesuch.com (office); kronosquartet.org.

HARRIS, Donald, BMus, MMus; American composer and musicologist; b. 7 April 1931, St Paul, MN; m. Marilyn Hackett 1983; two s. (from previous m.). *Education:* Univ. of Michigan, studied with Paul Wilkinson at St Paul, Minnesota, with Ross Lee Finney at Univ. of Michigan, with Nadia Boulanger, Max Deutsch and André Jolivet in Paris, France. *Career:* administrator, New England Conservatory 1968–77; Dean, Hartt School of Music, Univ. of Hartford 1980–88; Dean, College of Fine Arts, Ohio State Univ. 1988–97; Prof. of Composition and Theory School of Music 1997–. *Compositions include:* Piano Sonata, Violin Fantasy, Symphony in Two Movements, On Variations, For the Night to Wear, Balladen, Little Mermaid (opera), Two String

Quartets, Ludus I, Ludus II, Of Hartford in a Purple Light, Les Mains (Marguerite Yourcenar), Second String Quartet, Lyric Fanfare for Orchestra, Five Tempi (Ludus III). *Publications:* Correspondence Between Alban Berg and Arnold Schoenberg (co-ed.); contrib. to Journal of the Arnold Schoenberg Institute, Perspective of New Music, newsletter, International Alban Berg Society, Music Journal, Alban Berg Studien, Universal Edition. *Address:* c/o School of Music, Ohio State University, 110 Weigel Hall, 1856 College Road, Columbus, OH 43210, USA (office). *Telephone:* (614) 688-4728 (office). *E-mail:* harris.27@osu.edu (office).

HARRIS, Ellen T., BA, MA, PhD; American musicologist and academic; *Class of 1949 Professor Emeritus of Music, Massachusetts Institute of Technology*; b. (Ellen Turner), 4 Dec. 1945, Paterson, NJ. *Education:* Brown Univ. with Ivan Waldbauer, Univ. of Chicago with Robert Marshall, Edward Lowinsky and Howard M. Brown. *Career:* at Columbia Univ., New York 1977–80; joined Faculty at Univ. of Chicago 1980, Prof. 1988; Prof., MIT 1989–2011, Class of 1949 Prof. of Music 1996–2011, Prof. Emer. 2011–; Visiting Prof., Julliard School 2016; consultant, Santa Fe Opera 2001, Renée Fleming 2003, La Risonanza 2005–10; mem. Inst. for Advanced Study 2004; Fellow, American Acad. of Arts and Sciences 1998, Phi Beta Kappa Visiting Lecturer 2013-14; Pres. American Musicological Soc. 2014–16. *Publications include:* Handel and the Pastoral Tradition 1980, Henry Purcell's Dido and Aeneas 1987, Handel as Orpheus: Voice and Desire in the Chamber Cantatas 2001, George Frideric Handel: A Life with Friends 2014; editions: Purcell, Dido and Aeneas (ed.) 1987, The Librettos of Handel's Operas (ed.) 1989, G. F. Handel, Alto Cantatas (ed.) 2001; articles: The Italian in Handel 1980, Handel's London Cantatas 1984, Shakespeare in Music 1985, Integrity and Improvisation in the Music of Handel 1990, Handel's Ghost: The Composer's Posthumous Reputation in the Eighteenth Century 1992, Why Study the Arts – Along with Science and Math 1992, Harmonic Patterns in Handel's Operas 1994, King Arthur's Journey into the Eighteenth Century 1995, Twentieth Century Farinelli 1997, Metastasio and Sonata Form 1999, James Hunter, Handel's Friend 2000, Mozart's Mitridate: Going Beyond the Text 2004, Handel the Investor 2004, With Eyes on the East and Ears in the West: Handel's Orientalist Operas 2005, Silence as Sound: Handel's Sublime Pauses 2005, Butler's Narcissus: 'A Tame Oratorio' 2007, Cantate, que me veux-tu? or: Do Handel's Cantatas Matter? 2007, Handel is Fired 2008, Joseph Goupy and George Frideric Handel: From Professional Triumphs to Personal Estrangement 2008, Handel and his Will 2009, Viardot Sings Handel (with thanks to George Sand, Chopin, Meyerbeer, Gounod and Julius Rietz) 2010, Sacred and Profane Love: Handel and the Roman Cardinals 2010, Courting Gentility: Handel at the Bank of England 2010, Pamphilj as Phoenix: Themes of Resurrection in Handel's Italian Works 2011, The Cantata as Narrative: Serials, Colloquies and Commemoratives 2013, Music Distribution in London during Handel's Lifetime: Manuscript Copies vs. Prints 2013, , Taking the Oaths: The Directors of the Royal Academy of Music Swear Allegiance to King and Country 2015. *Honours:* Hon. mem. American Musicological Soc. 2011; American Council of Learned Socs Fellowship 1980–81, Nat. Endowment for the Humanities Fellowship 1988–89, 2006–07, Bunting Inst. Fellowship 1995–96, Otto Kinkeldey Award, American Musicological Soc. 2002, Louis Gottschalk Prize, American Soc. for Eighteenth Century Studies 2003, Westrup Prize 2004, Gyorgy Kepes Prize, MIT 2005, ASCAP-Deems Taylor Award 2015. *Address:* Music and Arts Theater Section, 4-246, 77 Massachusetts Avenue, Cambridge, MA 02139, USA (office). *Telephone:* (617) 253-5882 (office). *E-mail:* eharris@mit.edu (office). *Website:* web.mit.edu/music/facstaff/harrise.html (office).

HARRIS, Hilda; American singer (mezzo-soprano); b. 1930, Warrenton, NC. *Education:* North Carolina State Univ., studied in New York. *Career:* sang in musicals on Broadway; opera debut at St Gallen, Switzerland 1971, as Carmen; returned to New York 1973, as Nicklausse in Les Contes d'Hoffmann at City Opera and in Virgil Thomson's Four Saints in Three Acts (as St Theresa) at the Metropolitan; further roles at the Met have included the Child in L'Enfant et les Sortilèges, Cherubino, Hansel, Stephano in Roméo et Juliette and parts in Lulu; sang Nicklausse at Seattle 1990, Cherubino at the 1990 Spoleto Festival; frequent concert appearances.

HARRIS, Matthew, BM, MM, DMA; American composer; b. 18 Feb. 1956, North Tarrytown, NY; m. 1988. *Education:* New England Conservatory with Donald Martino, Fontainbleau School, France with Nadia Boulanger, Juilliard School of Music and Harvard Graduate School. *Career:* performances include New York New Music Ensemble 1983, Houston Symphony 1986, Minnesota Orchestra 1987, League/ISCM, New York 1987, Florida Symphony Orchestra 1988, Alea III, Boston 1988; Asst Prof., Fordham Univ. 1982–84; Instructor, Kingsborough Coll., CUNY 1985; Music Ed., Carl Fischer Inc. 1987–; mem. BMI, Composers' Forum, American Music Center; bd mem., League-International Soc. for Contemporary Music. *Compositions:* Music After Rimbaud, Songs of the Night for soprano and orchestra, Ancient Greek Melodies for orchestra, As You Choose (monodrama), Starry Night for piano trio, Invitation of the Waltz for string quartet, String Quartet No. 7. *Recordings:* Music After Rimbaud, Opus One Commissions: Casa Verde Trio, 1984; Haydn-Mozart Orchestra, 1985; Scott Stevens: Leigh Howard Stevens, marimbist, 1986; Minnesota Composers Forum: Omega String Quartet, 1988; The Schubert Club; Anthony Ross, cellist, 1988.

HARRIS, Paul, GRSM, LRAM, ARAM, FRAM ARCM, MTC (Lond), FRSA; British composer, teacher, performer and writer; *Lecturer, Royal Academy of Music*; b. London, England. *Education:* Haberdashers' Aske's School, Royal Acad. of Music, Univ. of London. *Career:* Head of Wind and Brass, Stowe School; examiner, Associated Bd of the Royal Schools of Music (ABRSM); adjudicator, BBC Young Musicians; Conductor, Charwell Youth Sinfonia; Dir Malcolm Arnold Festival; Lecturer, RAM and Acad. of Music and Dramatic Arts, Denmark. *Compositions include:* five Buckingham Concertos, Trombone Concerto, Clarinet Concerto 2008, Arrows of Desire (ballet), The Meal (children's opera); series: Improve Your Sight Reading, Improve Your Scales, Improve Your Practice, Improve Your Aural, Improve Your Theory; numerous shorter educational works, Music Through Time series, Chocolate Box (flute and piano), Adagio for clarinet and piano, Swiftly for clarinet and piano, Visions for clarinet and piano, The Unhappy Aardvark (Wind Quintet), Clarinet Quintet, Sonatinas for clarinet, piano, cor anglais, numerous other chamber and educational works. *Recording:* Paul Harris: A Musical Celebration 2012. *Publications:* The Music Teachers' Companion 2001, Clarinet Basics 2002, Malcolm Arnold – Rogue Genius (co-author) 2004, Improve your teaching 2006, Malcolm Williamson: Mischievous Music (co-author) 2007, Teaching Beginners 2008, The Virtuoso Teacher 2012, The Practice Process 2014, Simultaneous Learning: The Definitive Guide 2014, You Can Read Music 2014; contrib. to Libretto (ABRSM), ICA Magazine, The Strad, BBC Music Magazine, ISM Journal, Clarinet and Saxophone Soc. Magazine, Beckus (Malcolm Arnold Soc.). *Honours:* Hon. TCL; MIA Winner, Music Teacher's Companion 2001. *Address:* 15 Mallard Drive, Buckingham, Bucks., MK18 1GJ, England (home). *Telephone:* (1280) 813144 (home). *E-mail:* pauldavidharris@icloud.com. *Website:* www.paulharristeaching.co.uk.

HARRIS, Ross; New Zealand composer; b. 1 Aug. 1945, Amberley. *Education:* Univ. of Canterbury, studied with Douglas Lilburn at Victoria Univ., Wellington. *Career:* Assoc. Prof., Victoria Univ. from 1989; freelance composer, notably with electronic resources. *Compositions include:* Trio for flute, viola and harp 1973, To a Child for tape 1973, Shadow Music 1977, Skymning 1978, Echo 1979, The Hills of Time for orchestra 1980, Incantation for soprano and tape 1981, Life in Peace for choir and synthesizer 1983, Waituki (opera) 1984, Evocation for flute, cello and synthesizer 1985, Flüchtig for flute and tape 1986, Kaiku 1987, Dreams, Yellow Lions for baritone and chamber ensemble 1987, Mosaic (Water) 1990, Tanz der Schwäne (chamber opera) 1989, Wind Quintet 1989, Harmonicity 1991, Horn Call on Makara Cliff for horn and tape 1991, two string quartets 1991, 1998, two chamber concertos 1994, 1996, Piano Trio 1995, Sinfonietta for strings 1996, Inharmonicity for piano and tape 1998.

HARRISON, Jonty, DPhil; British composer and academic; *Professor of Composition and Electroacoustic Music, University of Birmingham*; b. 27 April 1952, Scunthorpe, Lincs., England; m. Alison Warne 1985; two d. *Education:* Univ. of York, British Youth Symphony Orchestra, Nat. Youth Orchestra of GB; studied composition with Bernard Rands, Elisabeth Lutyens, David Blake. *Career:* Nat. Theatre, London; Visiting Composer, Univ. of East Anglia Recording and Electronic Music Studio 1978; Visiting Lecturer, City Univ., London 1978–80; Lecturer, later Sr Lecturer in Music, Univ. of Birmingham 1980–, Reader in, later Prof. of Composition and Electroacoustic Music; Dir Electroacoustic Music Studio and BEAST (Birmingham ElectroAcoustic Sound Theatre); Visiting Composer at Hungarian Radio 1982, IRCAM 1985, Groupe de Recherches Musicales, Paris 1986, 1993, Groupe de Musique Expérimentale de Bourges 1987, 1995, Musik-Akad. Basel 2006, Studio Metamorphoses d'Orphee, Musiques et Recherches, Ohain, Belgium 2006; mem. Music Sub-panel Research Assessment Exercise 2008. *Compositions:* Q 1976, Lunga 1977, Pair/Impair 1978, SQ 1979, Rosaces 3 1980, EQ 1980, Monodies 1981, Rosaces 4 1982, Klang 1982, Sons transmutants/sans transmutant 1983, Hammer and Tongs 1984, Paroles hérétiques 1986, Tremulous Couplings 1986, Farben 1987, Aria 1988, Concerto Caldo 1991, . . .et ainsi de suite. . . 1992, Ottone 1992, Hot Air 1995, Unsound Objects 1995, Sorties 1995, Hot Air 1996, Surface Tension 1996, Splintering 1997, Abstracts 1998, Streams 1999, Ellipsis 2000, Rock 'n' Roll 2004, Force Fields 2004–06, Internal Combustion 2005–06, Free Fall 2006, Undertow 2006, Afterthoughts 2007, Phantom Power 2007–08, BEASTtory 2010. *Recordings:* Klang 1984, Sons transmutants/sans transmutant (Fine Arts Brass Ensemble) 1985, EQ (Daniel Kientzy) 1986, Klang, EQ (Stephen Cottrell) 1996, Pair/Impair, . . .et ainsi de suite. . ., Unsound Objects, Aria, Hot Air 1996, Sorties 1997, Unsound Objects 1997, EQ (Stephen Cottrell) 2000, Klang, Sorties, Surface Tension, Splintering, Streams 2000, Abstracts 2001, . . .et ainsi de suite. . . 2004; solo CDs: Articles indéfinis, Evidence matérielle; solo DVD: Environs. *Publications:* Articles indéfinis (Pair/Impair, Aria, Unsound Objects, ...et ainsi de suite..., Hot Air) 1996, Évidence matérielle (Klang, Sorties, Surface Tension, Splintering, Streams) 2000, Environs (Undertow, ReCycle, Rock'n'Roll, Internal Combustion, Free Fall, Streams, Afterthoughts) 2007, Q, Sons transmutants/sans transmutant, Hammer and Tongs, Concerto Caldo, Rosaces 4, Paroles hérétiques, Paroles plus hérétiques, Tremulous Couplings, EQ, Ottone 1996; contribs to Electro-Acoustic Music, Music and Letters, The Musical Times, Lien (Musiques et Recherches, Belgium), Upbeat to the Tate 88, Liverpool (programme book), The Journal of Electro-acoustic Music, Organised Sound. *Honours:* Arts Council of GB Composition Bursary 1978, Bourges Int. Electroacoustic Music Awards, France: Euphonie d'or 1992, Prizes 1981, 1983, 1996, 2001, 2008, Prix Ars Electronica, Linz, Austria 1993, 1997, Musica Nova Prize, Prague 1994, Performing Right Soc. Prize for Electroacoustic Composition 1979, Lloyds Bank Nat. Composers' Award 1985, Leverhulme Research Grant 1990–91, Arts and Humanities Research Bd Small Research Grants 1999, 2002. *Address:* Music Department, College of Arts and Law, University of

Birmingham, Edgbaston, Birmingham, B15 2TT, England (office). *Telephone:* (121) 414-5787 (office); (121) 449-2461 (home). *Fax:* (121) 414-5668 (office). *E-mail:* d.j.t.harrison@bham.ac.uk (office); jonty.harrison@blueyonder.co.uk (home). *Website:* artsweb.bham.ac.uk/harrison (office); www.beast.bham.ac .uk (office); www.electrocd.com/bio.e/harrison_jo.html (home).

HARRISON, Sally, GRNCM, PPRNCM; British singer (soprano); b. 6 April 1968, d. of Barbara Harrison; m. Stuart Hickmott; one s. *Education:* Royal Northern Coll. of Music and Nat. Opera Studio. *Career:* sang Morgana in Alcina, Manon and Gilda in Rigoletto with Royal Northern Coll. of Music 1987–88; engagements with ENO: Giannetta in The Elixir of Love, Romilda in Xerxes, Despina in Così fan tutte, Pamina in The Magic Flute, Yum-Yum in The Mikado, Chloe in The Queen of Spades, Flowermaiden in Parsifal and Micaela in Carmen 2005; other operatic engagements have included Lucia in Lucia di Lammermoor for Stowe Opera, Poppea in Agrippina at the Buxton Festival, Galatea in Acis and Galatea for the English Bach Festival, Despina in Così fan tutte and Polly Peachum in The Threepenny Opera for Scottish Opera and Musetta in La Bohème for the Opera Society of Hong Kong; concert engagements have included St John Passion at Birmingham Symphony Hall, Esther at the Greenwich Festival, Messiah with the Bournemouth Sinfonietta, Mozart Mass in C Minor at the Harrogate Festival and Carmina Burana at the Hallé Proms; contemporary work has included Boulez's Improvisations sur Mallarmé with the Bavarian Radio Symphony Orchestra and Maggie/Edith in Deidre Gribbbins' Hey! Persephone for Almeida Opera; specialist in the music of Henze, has sung Minette in The English Cat in Benin, Gütersloh, London and at the Montepulciano Festival, Being Beauteous with the ECO, Cantata della fiaba estrema with the Scharoun Ensemble of Berlin, Novae de infinite laudes with the London Sinfonietta and Whispers of Heavenly Death with the Ensemble Modern of Frankfurt; starred as Carlotta in The Phantom of the Opera at Her Majesty's Theatre, London 2004–05; other roles include Countess Almaviva in Le nozze di Figaro for OTC, Dublin and Yum-Yum in The Mikado at La Fenice, Venice, Fiordiligi in Così fan tutte and Musetta in La Bohème for Cork Opera, Ireland, Brahms Requiem for Tonbridge Philharmonic Soc., Dvořák Te Deum for Brighton Orpheus Choir, The Kingdom for Folkestone Choral Soc., Messiah for Aberdeen Choral Soc., Saul for Imperial Coll. Choir, Elijah for Ashtead Choral Soc. and Billingshurst Choral Soc., Mozart Mass in C Minor in Beverley Minster and for the Athenaeum Singers, Rossini Stabat Mater for Billingshurst Choral Soc., Four Last Songs with the Sussex Symphony Orchestra and Watford Philharmonic Soc., Verdi Requiem in Rochester Cathedral and A Sea Symphony in Sheffield Cathedral, A Sea Symphony, Tokyo Symphony Orchestra, Missa Solemnis, Durham Cathedral. *Recordings include:* Mercedes in Carmen, Sultana Rose-in-Bloom in The Rose of Persia. *Honours:* Peter Moores Foundation Scholarship. *Address:* 52 Aynsley Gardens, Church Langley, Harlow, CM17 9PD, England (home).

HART-DAVIS, Michael; British singer (tenor); b. 1968, Worcester, England. *Career:* Glyndebourne Festival from 1995, as Atallo in Rossini's Ermione, Messenger in Theodora, Lamplighter in Manon Lescaut, and Thomas in The Last Supper by Birtwistle, 2001; Glyndebourne Tour as Mozart's Don Curzio, Janek in The Makropulos Case and Rossini's Comte Ory; Further appearances as Don Curzio for Netherlands Opera, Agenor in Il Re Pastore for Opera North and Rossini's Almaviva for English National Opera and Mid-Wales Opera; Chelsea Opera Group as Innkeeper in Benvenuto Cellini and Pallas in Cherevichki by Tchaikovsky; Concerts include Messiah at the Albert Hall under David Willcocks, and engagements at Verbier, Geneva, Lyon and Annecy; Season 2001–2002 as Ramiro in La Cenerentola for Opera Zürich. *Current Management:* Musicmakers International Artists Representation, Tailor House, 63–65 High Street, Whitwell, Hertfordshire SG4 8AH, England. *Telephone:* (1438) 871708. *Fax:* (1438) 871777. *E-mail:* musicmakers@ compuserve.com. *Website:* www.operauk.com.

HARTELIUS, Malin; Swedish singer (soprano); b. 1966, Malmö; one s. one d. *Education:* Vienna Conservatory with Margarethe Bence. *Career:* with Vienna State Opera 1989–91, with Zurich Opera 1991–; made debuts at Ludwigsburger Festspiele 1990, Schwetzinger Festspiele 1991, Salzburg Festival 1992; recital debut, Théâtre du Châtelet, Paris 1993; roles include Adina in Liebestrank at Opera Frankfurt, Najade in Ariadne auf Naxos, Sophie in Der Rosenkavalier, Adele in Die Fledermaus, Pamina in Die Zauberflöte, Marzellina in idelio, Konstanze, Donna Elvira, Contessa in Le Nozze di Figaro, Gretchen in Szenen aus Goethes Faust, Christine in Intermezzo, La Princesse Eudoxie in La Juive, Armida in Rinaldo; has sung with Opera Frankfurt, State Opera Unter den Linden, Berlin, Opéra National de Paris, Munich State Opera, Vienna Philharmonic Orchestra, Bayerische Staatsoper München, Hamburgische Staatsoper, Concertgebouw Amsterdam, Accademia Santa Cecilia, Cleveland Orchestra, Gewandhaus Orchestra, London Symphony Orchestra, Orchester des Bayerischen Rundfunks, Orchestra Giuseppe Verdi, Philharmonia Orchestra, Rundfunk-Sinfonie-Orchester Berlin, Tonhalle Orchestra, Orchestre Philharmonique de Monte-Carlo, Dresdner Philharmonic, Combattimento Consort; sang in John Eliot Gardiner's Bach Cantata Pilgrimage 2000. *Recordings:* Bach's Alle Mit Gott, Cantatas Vol. 21, Cantatas Vol. 7, Cantatas Vol.8, Haydn's Die Schöpfung, Handel's Messiah, Mozart's Die Entführung aus dem Serail, Il Sogno de Scipione. *Current Management:* General Manager, Boris Orlob Management, Jägerstrasse 70, 10117 Berlin, Germany. *Telephone:* (30) 20450839. *Fax:* (30) 20450849. *E-mail:* info@orlob.net. *Website:* www.orlob.net.

HARTEROS, Anja; German singer (soprano); b. 1972. *Education:* studied in Cologne. *Career:* professional debut at Gelsenkirchen 1996; debut at Wiener Staatsoper and Nationaltheater München 1999; debut at Opéra Nat. de Paris 2002; debut at Salzburger Festspiele 2000; debut at Metropolitan Opera New York 2003; debut at La Scala di Milano 2006; debut at Royal Opera House, London 2008; roles include Mozart: Contessa, Elettra, Donna Anna, Fiordiligi; Wagner: Eva, Elsa, Elisabeth; Strauss: Arabella, Marschallin, Ariadne; Verdi: Aida, Desdemona, Amelia Grimaldi, Leonora in Trovatore and Forza del destino, Alice Ford, Traviata, Elisabetta; Puccini: Mimi, Tosca. *Honours:* Winner Cardiff Singer of the World Competition 1999, Cologne Opera Prize 2010. *Current Management:* c/o Künstleragentur Seifert, Postfach 38 02 57, 14112 Berlin, Germany.

HARTKE, Stephen Paul, BA, MA, PhD; American composer; b. 6 July 1952, Orange, New Jersey; m. Lisa Stidham 1981; one s. *Education:* Yale Univ., Univ. of Pennsylvania, Univ. of California, Santa Barbara, studied composition with James Drew, George Rochberg and Edward Applebaum. *Career:* Fulbright Prof. of Composition, Univ. of São Paulo, Brazil 1984–85; Prof. of Composition, Univ. of Southern California 1987–; composer-in-residence, Los Angeles Chamber Orchestra 1988–92; mem. American Music Center, American Acad. of Arts and Letters 2009–. *Compositions include:* Symphony No. 1 1976, Four Madrigals on Old Portuguese Texts 1976–81, Caoine 1980, Two Shetland Bridal Tunes 1981, Songs for an Uncertain Age 1981, Canções Modernistas 1982, Iglesia Abandonada 1982, Alvorada 1983, Sonata Variations 1984, Oh Them Rats is Mean in My Kitchen 1985, Maltese Cat Blues 1986, Precession 1987, Post-Modern Homages 1987–92, The King of the Sun 1988, Pacific Rim 1988, Night Rubrics 1990, Symphony No. 2 1990, Wir Küssen Ihnen Tausendmal die Hände 1991, Un Tout Petit Trompe-L'Oreille 1992, Auld Swaara (concerto for violin and orchestra) 1992, The Piano Dreams of Empire 1994, Wulfstan at the Millennium 1995, The Ascent of the Equestrian in a Balloon 1995, Sons of Noah 1996, The Horse with the Lavender Eye 1997, Sonata 1998, The Rose of the Winds 1998, Gradus 1999, Tituli 1999, Cathedral in the Thrashing Rain 2000, Beyond Words 2001, Landscape with Blues (concerto for clarinet and orchestra) 2001, Prelude to a Shadow Play 2003, Symphony No. 3 2003, The Greater Good 2003–06, Suite for Summer 2004, Percolative Processes 2005, Three Soliloquies from the Greater Good 2006, Boule de Suif 2006, Meanwhile (Grammy Award for Best Contemporary Classical Composition 2013) 2007, A Brandenburg Autumn 2007, Precepts 2007. *Publications:* contrib. to Caderno de Musica 1985, Minnesota Composers Forum Newsletter 1988. *Honours:* Rome Prize 1992, American Acad. of Arts and Letters Award 1993, Chamber Music Soc. of Lincoln Center Stoeger Award 1997, Guggenheim Fellowship 1997–98, Charles Ives Living Award, American Acad. of Arts and Letters 2004, 2008. *Current Management:* 21C Media Group, 162 West 56th Street, Suite 506, New York, NY 10019, USA. *Telephone:* (212) 245-2110. *Fax:* (212) 245-1965. *E-mail:* info@21cmediagroup.com. *Website:* 21cmediagroup.com. *E-mail:* stephenhartke@earthlink.net (office). *Website:* www.stephenhartke.com.

HARTLIEP, Nikki; singer (soprano); b. 22 Sept. 1955, Naha, Okinawa, Japan. *Education:* San Francisco Conservatory. *Career:* debut with Western Opera, San Francisco 1982; appearances at Chicago Opera 1987–88, as Ellen Orford in Peter Grimes (Tatiana in Eugene Onegin 1990); Madama Butterfly at San Francisco Opera and elsewhere from 1989 (Dublin 1990); other roles include Micaela, Antonia in Les contes d'Hoffmann, Alice Ford (Long Beach Opera 1994) and Mimi; numerous concert engagements.

HARTMAN, Vernon, DipA; American singer (baritone) and opera producer; *President, Impresario Productions LLC;* b. 12 July 1952, Dallas, TX. *Education:* Southwest Texas State Univ., North Texas State Univ., Acad. of Vocal Arts, Philadelphia. *Career:* debut as Rigoletto, Shreveport 1975; sang with New York City Opera from 1977 and made guest appearances at Cincinnati, San Antonio and Seattle; Spoleto Festival 1977–78, as Guglielmo; Cincinnati 1990, as Enrico in Lucia di Lammermoor; Metropolitan Opera from 1983, as Rossini's Figaro, Count Almaviva, Eisenstein and Ping; other roles have included Scarpia, Malatesta, Silvio, Marcello, Frank in Die Tote Stadt and Falke in Fledermaus; sang Almaviva and Marcello at Milwaukee 1991; created title role in Boston Lyric Opera's Elmer Gantry; sang the role of Fred Moore in the world premiere of Anton Coppola's epic Sacco and Vanzetti for Opera Tampa; frmly Gen./Artistic Dir, Opera Birmingham, Artistic Adviser, Boheme Opera, NJ; guest dir for numerous companies and organizations throughout the USA; currently Prod. of Opera for Opera Tampa, Evansville Philharmonic Orchestra, Indiana, and Bardavon 1869 Opera House, Poughkeepsie; founder and Pres., Impresario Productions LLC, opera, musical theatre and concert production co. *Address:* Impresario Productions LLC, 2582 Church Lane, Kintnersville, PA 18930, USA (office). *Telephone:* (267) 980-3961 (office). *Fax:* (610) 847-7014 (office). *E-mail:* vernon@ impresarioproductions.com (office). *Website:* www.impresarioproductions.com (office).

HARTMANN, Will; German singer (tenor); b. 1968, Siegen. *Education:* Musikhochschule, Cologne. *Career:* Opera Studio, Cologne 1991–93; roles at Cologne Opera 1993–96, including Papageno, Guglielmo, Schaunard, Morales (Carmen) and Harlequin in Ariadne auf Naxos; Hannover State Opera from 1996 as Dandini in Cenerentola, Monteverdi's Orfeo, Marcello and Rossini's Figaro; further appearances at Munich, Bonn, Leipzig, Rome and Orange; Royal Opera debut 1998 as Da-ud in Die Aegyptische Helena (concert); title role in Birtwistle's Gawain 2000; concerts with Sinopoli, Janowski and Christian Thielemann; season 2002 engaged as Stewa in Jenůfa and Tom

Rakewell in The Rake's Progress in Hannover, Macduff in Macbeth at Covent Garden; season 2003 engaged as Tamino in Die Zauberflöte at Covent Garden and Pelléas in Pelléas et Mélisande in Hannover. *Honours:* winner Alexander Girandi Competition, Coburg, Int. Wagner Singing Competition, Strasbourg. *Current Management:* c/o Haydn Rawstron, 29a High Street, First Floor, West Wickham, Kent BR4 0LP, England. *Telephone:* (20) 8777-6070. *Fax:* (20) 8777-4073. *E-mail:* enquiries@haydn-rawstron.com. *Website:* www.haydnrawstron.com.

HARVEY, Keith; British cellist; b. 1950, England. *Education:* Royal Academy of Music with Douglas Cameron, studied with Gregor Piatigorsky in Los Angeles. *Career:* formerly youngest ever principal cellist of London Philharmonic Orchestra, then principal of English Chamber Orchestra; plays cello by Montagnana of 1733, formerly belonging to Bernard Romberg; founder mem., Gabrieli Ensemble, with chamber music performances in the UK and abroad; co-founder, Gabrieli Quartet 1967, and toured with them to Europe, North America, Far East and Australia; festival engagements in the UK, including Aldeburgh, City of London and Cheltenham; concerts every season in London, participation in Barbican Centre Mostly Mozart Festival; Resident Artist at University of Essex, 1971–; has co-premiered by William Alwyn, Britten, Alan Bush, Daniel Jones and Gordon Crosse, 2nd Quartets of Nicholas Maw and Panufnik (1983, 1980) and 3rd Quartet of John McCabe (1979); British premiere of the Piano Quintet by Sibelius, 1990. *Recordings include:* early pieces by Britten, Dohnányi's Piano Quintet with Wolfgang Manz, Walton's Quartets and the Sibelius Quartet and Quintet, with Anthony Goldstone. *Honours:* Emmy Award for solo playing in films.

HARVEY, Peter; British singer (baritone); b. 1958, England. *Education:* Choral Scholar at Magdalen College Oxford, Guildhall School of Music. *Career:* concert appearances with the St James Baroque Players in Telemann's St Matthew Passion at Aldeburgh and London; Visit to Lisbon with The Sixteen; Concerts of Monteverdi and Purcell in Poland and the Flanders Festival with London Baroque; Sang with Joshua Rifkin and the Bach Ensemble at St James Piccadilly, 1990; Engagements with La Chapelle Royale and Collegium Vocale in Belgium, France and Spain; Bach Cantatas for French television and tour of Messiah with Le Concert Spirituel; Other repertoire includes the War Requiem, Elijah and the Five Mystical Songs of Vaughan Williams; St John in The Cry of the Ikon by John Tavener (also televised); Bach's St John Passion (Westminster Abbey) and Christmas Oratorio; Schubert's E flat Mass; Visited Brazil 1989 with The Sixteen for Messiah; Belgium 1991 in Teixeira's Te Deum, conducted by Harry Christophers; Sang with Les Talens Lyriques at Versailles Baroque Days in Mondonville's Les Fêtes de Paphos, 1996. *Recordings:* Dido and Aeneas; Sacred music by CPE Bach with La Chapelle Royale (Virgin Classics); Gilles Requiem with Le Concert Spirituel. *Honours:* Walther Gruner International Lieder Competition, 2nd Prizewinner; Nonie Morton Award (leading to Wigmore Hall debut). *Current Management:* c/o Tivoli Artists Management, 3 Vesterbrogade, PO Box 233, 1630 Copenhagen, Denmark. *Telephone:* 33-75-04-00. *Fax:* 33-75-03-75. *E-mail:* artistsmanagement@tivoli.dk. *Website:* www.tam.dk. *E-mail:* enquire@peterharvey.info. *Website:* www.peterharvey.com.

HARVEY, Richard Allen, ARCM; British composer, conductor and recorder player; b. 25 Sept. 1953, London, England. *Education:* Royal Coll. of Music. *Career:* debut as Conductor, London Symphony Orchestra, Barbican Centre 1985; founder, London Vivaldi Orchestra; guest conductor, Royal Philharmonic and London Symphony Orchestras; toured with guitarist, John Williams 1984–; conductor and instrumentalist with English Chamber Orchestra, Barbican Centre, London 1987. *Compositions:* Concerto Antico for guitar and orchestra, Reflections on a Changing Landscape (viola concerto), Plague and the Moonflower (eco-oratorio), A Time of Miracles (children's opera), compositions for films and television include Game, Set and Match, G.B.H, Jake's Progress, Defence of the Realm. *Recordings:* Italian Recorder Concertos; The Genteel Companion; Brass at La Sauve-Majeure; Four Concertos for Violins and Recorder; G.B.H. (soundtrack); Jake's Progress (soundtrack).

HARWOOD, Richard; British cellist; b. 8 Aug. 1979, Portsmouth. *Education:* Royal Northern Coll. of Music, Manchester with Prof. Ralph Kirshbaum; cello with Joan Dickson, Steven Doane, David Waterman, Heinrich Schiff; piano with Diana Bell and Joyce Rathbone. *Career:* debut, Kabalevsky op49 in G minor at Adrian Boult Hall, Birmingham 1990; Purcell Room debut with Julius Drake 1999; performed concerti in Royal Albert Hall, Queen Elizabeth Hall, St John's Smith Square and St George's Brandon Hill; collaborated with conductors, including David Parry, En Shao, and Yehudi Menuhin; soloist with numerous orchestras, including Bournemouth Symphony Orchestra and Philharmonia; toured New Zealand with Elgar Concerto 1993; recital performances include Schoenbrunn Palace Theatre, Vienna 1997, Wigmore Hall Recital debut 1998, Purcell Room debut 1999. *Recordings:* Elgar Concerto (BBC Radio 3) 1993, Tchaikovsky's Variations on a Rococo Theme (BBC Radio 3). *Honours:* Audi Junior Musician (youngest ever winner) 1992, Pierre Fournier Award for cellists 2004, numerous scholarships winner Pierre Fournier Award 2004, Bachpreisträger XIV Internationaler Johann-Sebastian-Bach-Wettbewerb, Leipzig 2004. *E-mail:* office@richardharwood.com (office). *Website:* www.richardharwood.com.

HASELBÖCK, Martin; Austrian organist and conductor; b. 23 Nov. 1954, Vienna. *Education:* Musikhochschule, Vienna, studied with Jean Langlais and Daniel Roth in Paris. *Career:* debut at Konzerthaus, Vienna, 1973; Organist at Augustinekurche, Vienna, 1976; Vienna Hofkapelle, 1977; solo appearances with leading orchestras in Berlin, Vienna and elsewhere in Europe; premieres of organ concertos by Ernst Krenek Cristobàl Halffter and William Albright; Prof. of Organ, Lubeck Musikhochschule, 1986–2003; Vienna Music Univ., 2003–; founded the Wiener Akademie 1985, giving many performances of baroque and early classical music; guest conductor with the Vienna Symphony, Philadelphia, Los Angeles, Pittsburgh Orchestra and many other orchestras; opera engagements in Prague (Mozart Festival) and Zürich. *Recordings include:* works by Haydn, Mozart, Bach, Biber and Telemann, with the Wiener Akademie; complete organ works of Bach, Schoenberg and Liszt. *Honours:* winner Vienna-Melk International Organ Competition 1992, Deutscher Schallplattenpreis, Ehrenkreuz für Wissenschaft und Kunst, Vienna 1997; Dr hc (Luther Coll., Iowa, USA) 2003. *Address:* c/o Universität für Musik, 1030 Vienna, Germany. *E-mail:* haselboeck@chello.at.

HASHIMOTO, Eiji, BM, MA, MM; American (b. Japanese) harpsichordist and academic; *Professor Emeritus of Harpsichord, College-Conservatory of Music, University of Cincinnati;* b. 7 Aug. 1931, Tokyo, Japan; m. Ruth Anne Laves 1963; one s. two d. *Education:* Tokyo Univ. of Fine Arts and Music, Univ. of Chicago, Yale Univ. School of Music. *Career:* Instructor in Harpsichord, Toho Gakuen School of Music, Tokyo 1966; Asst Prof. of Harpsichord and Artist-in-Residence, Coll.-Conservatory of Music, Univ. of Cincinnati 1968–72, Assoc. Prof. of Harpsichord and Artist-in-Residence 1972–77, Prof. of Harpsichord and Artist-in-Residence 1977–2001, Prof. Emer. of Harpsichord 2001–; recitals and solo appearances in Australia, Austria, Belgium, Brazil, Canada, Chile, China, Finland, France, Germany, Iran, Italy, Japan, Luxembourg, Mexico, Netherlands, New Zealand, Philippines, Spain, Switzerland, UK, USA and Venezuela. *Recordings include:* 18 recordings (including eight CDs) of solo, solo with orchestra, conducting and ensemble performances. *Publications include:* D. Scarlatti, 100 Sonatas in three vols 1975 and 1988, C.P.E. Bach, Sonatas in three vols 1984, 1988, J.B. Loeillet, Pièces pour Clavecin 1985, D. Scarlatti, 90 Sonatas in three vols 1999–2002 (new version 2012), A Performer's Guide to Baroque and Post-Baroque Music 2005, Practical and Logical Use of Baroque Keyboard Fingering 2011. *Honours:* Prize of Excellence, Japanese Ministry of Cultural Affairs 1978, 1982, Rockefeller Foundation Bellagio Residency Grant 1998, 2009, Distinguished Research Professorship, Univ. of Cincinnati 1998. *Address:* 4579 English Creek Drive, Cincinnati, OH 45245, USA (home). *E-mail:* eiji.hashimoto@uc.edu (office). *Website:* www.eijihashimoto.com.

HASKIN, Howard; American singer (heldentenor) and voice teacher; b. 19 Jan. 1953, Kansas City; s. of Howard D. Haskin Sr and Olene M. Brown Singleton; pnr Joshua L. Sigal. *Education:* studied at Bloomington, Illinois and Zürich, Wichita State Univ., Indiana Univ. Bloomington, lessons with Arthur Newman, Margaret Harshaw, Marie-Henriette Dejean. *Career:* has sung some 50 roles including Don José, Peter Grimes, Otello (Verdi), Bacchus (Ariadne auf Naxos), Vova (Life with an Idiot), Samson, Oedipus, Parsifal, Siegmund, Jason (Cherubini's Médée), Orphée (Gluck's Orphée et Euridice); numerous concerts works including Das Lied von der Erde, Beethoven IX, Verdi Requiem, Mozart Requiem; since European debut at Opernhaus Zürich has sung with many leading int. opera companies; several recitals at Wigmore Hall, London. *Current Management:* c/o Alexandra Mercer, APA Artists' Management, Studio 1, 79 Bedford Gardens, London, W8 7EG, England. *Telephone:* (20) 7794-7633. *Fax:* (20) 7431-4344. *E-mail:* alexandra@mercer.uk.com. *Website:* www.apaartistsmanagement.com; www.howardhaskin.com (home).

HASSON, Maurice; French/Venezuelan violinist; b. 6 July 1934, Berck-Plage, Pas de Calais; m. Jane Hoogesteijn 1969; one s. three d. *Education:* Conservatoire Nat. Supérieur de Musique, Paris, further studies with Henryk Szeryng. *Career:* concert artist in major concert halls worldwide, also in TV and radio performances; Prof. of Violin, RAM, London 1986–2015. *Recordings include:* Concerto No. 1 (Paganini), Concerto No. 2 (Prokofiev), Debussy Sonatas, Fauré Sonatas, Concerto No. 1, Scottish Fantasy (Bruch), Concerto for 2 and 4 violins (Vivaldi), Double Concerto (Bach), Concerto (Brahms), Brilliant Showpieces for the Violin, Tzigane (Ravel), Rondo Capriccioso (Saint Saëns), Poème (Chausson), Gypsy Airs (Sarasate), Violin Concerto (Castellanos-Yumar), Sonata (Franck), virtuoso pieces. *Honours:* Hon. mem. RAM, Orden Andrés Bello, First Class, Orden Tulio Febres Cordero, First Class (Venezuela), refused Orden Francisco de Miranda, First Class as a political statement against Pres. Hugo Chavez of Venezuela, Médaille de Vermeil de la Ville de Paris; First Prize Violin, Prix d'Honneur and First Prize Chamber Music, Conservatoire Nat. Supérieur de Musique, Paris 1950, Int. Prize Long Thibaut 1951, Int. Prize, Youth Festival, Warsaw 1955, Grand Prix Musique de Chambre 1957. *Address:* 18 West Heath Court, North End Road, London, NW11 7RE, England (home). *Telephone:* (20) 8458-3647 (home). *E-mail:* jdehasson@btinternet.com.

HATRÍK, Juraj; Slovak composer and professor of music; *Professor of Composition and Music Theory, Academy of Music and Dramatic Arts, Bratislava;* b. 1 May 1941, Orkucany, Presov; m. 1965; two s. *Education:* Acad. of Music and Dramatic Arts, Bratislava. *Career:* debut, Sinfonietta 1963; Lecturer in Musical Educ., Aesthetics and Psychology of Music, Acad. of Music and Dramatic Arts, Bratislava, Prof. of Composition and Music Theory 1997–; mem. Slovak Roma Club. *Compositions include:* Double Portrait for Orchestra 1971, Da Capo al Fine for Orchestra 1976, Diary of Tanja Savitchova for brass quintet and soprano 1976, television version 1983, Happy Prince, opera after

Oscar Wilde 1978, Sans Souci, 1st symphony 1979, Vox Memoriae, cycle for 4 instruments 1983, Canzona for organ, alto and viola, (after John Roberts), after R. Tagore 1984, Submerged Music for soprano and strings 1985, Moment Music avec J. S. Bach for soprano and chamber group 1985, Victor, 2nd symphony 1988, compositions for children, choirs and 4 monologues for accordion, Adam's Children, chamber opera after Slovak national proverbs and bywords 1991, Diptych for violin, cello and piano 1989, The Lost Children for string quartet with basso solo after Gregory Orr 1993, The Brave Tin Soldier, musical by Hans Andersen 1994, An die Musik, sonata-dépêche for Schubert for clarinet, violin, cello and piano 1995–96, Requiem for Iris, for actress and chamber ensemble 1998, Skatingring 1951, 1998, Liebe, Sinn und Not, sonata for contrabasso and piano (in memoriam R. M. Rilke) 1999, Litany of While (after Arthur Lundkvist, symphonic poem for large orchestra) 2001, Ecce quod Natura…, concerto for piano and orchestra 2002, Dolcissima mia vita…, poem for string quartet 2004, Vision, for accordion, violoncello and guitar 2005, Two Ballads after F. Villom, for mixed choir 2005. *Recordings include:* Piano Music for Children 2004. *Publications include:* Jewel of Music: Pedagogical texts about music 1997, Voice of Memory: Dialogues and Other Texts about Music and Life 2003; contrib. to Slovak Music, Musical Life. *Honours:* Premio di città Castelfidardo (Composition for Accordion Solo) 1993. *Address:* Academy of Music and Dramatic Arts, Ventúrska 3, 81301 Bratislava (office); Dubnická 2, 85102 Bratislava, Slovakia (home). *Telephone:* (2) 59383546 (office); (2) 63838733 (home). *E-mail:* hatrik@vsmu.sk (office).

HATTORI, Joji; Japanese conductor and violinist; *Associate Guest Conductor, Vienna Chamber Orchestra*; b. 1969. *Education:* studied violin with Rainer Küchl, Yehudi Menuhin, Vladimir Spivakov, Herman Krebbers and Michel Schwalbé, studied conducting with Lorin Maazel, studied sociology at St Antony's Coll., Oxford. *Career:* performances as concert violinist with major orchestras throughout Europe and Japan 1989–2002; Assoc. Guest Conductor Vienna Chamber Orchestra 2004–; Prin. Resident Conductor, Opera House, Erfurt, Germany 2007–08; Music Dir Tokyo Ensemble 2001–; Dir open-air Summer Festival, Schloss Kittsee, Austria 2009–11; Guest Conductor with Philharmonia Orchestra, London, Vienna Symphony Orchestra, Slovakian Philharmonic, Düsseldorfer Symphoniker, Yomiuri Symphony Orchestra, Japan, etc.; collaboration with soloists including Maria João Pires and Piotr Anderszewski; debut as opera conductor at Tokyo New Nat. Theatre 2005, Vienna State Opera with three performances of The Magic Flute 2009; mem. Jury and Pres. Int. Yehudi Menuhin Violin Competition; Assoc. Guest Conductor, Vienna Chamber Orchestra. *Recordings:* Bach Violin Concertos with the Scottish Chamber Orchestra 1997, Kreisler Pieces with Joseph Seiger 1998, Mozart Violin Concertos with London Mozart Players 2001. *Honours:* Hon. RAM; First Prize, Menuhin Int. Violin Competition, UK 1989, Young Musician of the Year (Japan) 1992, Prizewinner, Maazel-Vilar Conducting Competition, New York 2002. *Current Management:* Künstersekretariat Bachmann, Schachnerstrasse 27, 1220 Vienna, Austria. *E-mail:* rudolf@bachmann.at. *Address:* Girardigasse 2/51, 1060 Vienna, Austria (home). *E-mail:* office.at@jojihattori.com (office). *Website:* www.jojihattori.com.

HATZIANO, Markella; Greek singer (mezzo-soprano); b. 1960, Athens. *Education:* Athens National Conservatory with Gogo Georgilopoulu, studied with Tito Gobbi in Rome. *Career:* sang Eboli in Don Carlos with the National Opera of Greece and made her US debut, as Azucena at Boston, in 1987; Returned to Boston as Suzuki, Amneris, Neris in Cherubini's Médée and in Verdi's Requiem; French repertory includes Carmen (Mexico 1992, under Enrique Batiz), Massenet's Charlotte (Malaga, 1993) and Marguerite in La Damnation de Faust (Trieste, 1993); sang Dido in Les Troyens with the London Symphony Orchestra at the Barbican Hall, under Colin Davis, 1993; further appearances as Judith in Bluebeard's Castle at the Salzburg Festival, Dido at La Scala, 1996, Amneris at Florence, under Zubin Mehta; sang Dalila and Amneris at Covent Garden, 1996; concert repertory includes Mahler's Das Lied von der Erde, Kindertotenlieder and 2nd and 3rd Symphonies; season 1996–97 concerts with the New York Philharmonic, Chicago Symphony Orchestra, Los Angeles Philharmonic and the Orchestre de la Suise Romande; debut with the London Symphony in Schoenberg's Erwartung, 1997; season 2000–01 with Giovanna Seymour in Anna Bolena at Athens and the Verdi Requiem for the Granada Festival. *Recordings include:* Verdi Requiem, with the London Symphony Orchestra under Richard Hickox. *Honours:* winner Tito Gobbi International Competition, 1983; American-Israel Competition, 1987. *Current Management:* Organisation Internationale Artistique, 16 Avenue Franklin D. Roosevelt, 75008 Paris, France. *Telephone:* 1-42-25-58-34. *Fax:* 1-42-25-64-97. *E-mail:* oia@oia-poilve.com. *Website:* www.oia-poilve.com; www.markella.com.

HATZIS, Christos, PhD; Canadian composer and academic; *Professor of Composition, University of Toronto*; b. 21 March 1953, Volos, Greece; s. of Panagiotis Hatzis and Maria Hatzis; m. 1st Rania Hatzis 1984; one d.; m. 2nd Beverley Johnston. *Education:* Hellenic Conservatory, Greece, Eastman School of Music, State Univ. of New York at Buffalo. *Career:* emigrated to Canada in 1982; currently Prof. of Composition, Faculty of Music, Univ. of Toronto; Composer-in-Residence, Winnipeg New Music Festival, Scotia Festival of Music, Festival of the Sound 2007, Toronto Summer Music Festival 2009, Scotia Bank Northern Lights Festival 2012; has composed major works for all media; best-known work Constantinople opened Int. Festival of Arts and Ideas, New Haven, Conn. 2005, followed by several int. performances including at Royal Opera House, Covent Garden, London 2007; recent comms from Hilary Hahn, Royal Winnipeg Ballet, Orchestre symphonique de Montréal, Dame Evelyn Glennie, Afiara String Quartet, Pacifica Quartet, CityMusic Cleveland, Suzie Leblanc, TorQ, Winnipeg Symphony Orchestra, Thunder Bay Symphony Orchestra. *Compositions include:* String Quartet No. 1 (Juno Award for Classical Composition of the Year 2006), Constantinople (multimedia music theatre piece) (Juno Award for Classical Composition of the Year 2008) 2004, The Troparion of Kassiani, Old Photographs, Dance of the Dictators, From the Book of Job 2006, Wormwood (cantata) 2006, Mystical Visitations for vocalist 2006, Sepulcher of Life for soloists, choir and orchestra, Concerto for Piano and Orchestra in the Spirit of W. A. Mozart 2007, Tongues of Fire for percussion and orchestra 2007, Rebirth for viola and orchestra 2008, From the Song of Songs for vocalists, baroque orchestra and choir 2008, Psalm 91 for choir 2008, Water (Irish folk instruments and multiple children's choirs) 2008, In the Fire of Conflict for cello, percussion and dance 2008, Pauline (chamber opera) (with Margaret Atwood) 2009, Arabesque for violin, piano and string orchestra 2009, Mirage for vibraphone, cloud gongs and string orchestra 2009, Redemption: Book 1 for string quartet and orchestra 2009, Coming To for violin and piano and Dystopia for solo violin (commissioned by Hilary Hahn) (Grammy Award 2015) 2009, Credo for rebetiko baritone and orchestra (commissioned for George Dalaras) 2010, Extreme Unction for bass clarinet and string orchestra 2010, Four Songs on Poems by Elizabeth Bishop (commissioned by Suzie LeBlanc) 2011, Okiatsâsiujut for women's choir and Inuit throat singers (commissioned by Lady Cove) 2011, Mysterion Xenon for youth choir (commissioned by Nat. Youth Choir of Canada) 2011, Departures: Concerto for Flute and String Orchestra 2011 (premiered by Susan Hoeppner and Kyoto Symphony, and Patrick Gallois and Thessaloniki State Symphony Orchestra 2011), Lamento for pop singer and symphony orchestra (commissioned by CBC for Sarah Slean and Symphony Nova Scotia, and released as CBC video) 2012, Redemption: Book 3 for full orchestra (commissioned by the Winnipeg Symphony Orchestra) 2012, Atonement for cello and piano (commissioned by the Women's Musical Club of Toronto for Yegor Dyachkov and Jean Saulnier) 2012, The Isle is Full of Noises (commissioned by Orchestre symphonique de Montréal) 2013, String Quartet No. 3 (The Questioning) (commissioned by the Afiara String Quartet) 2013, Going Home Star – Truth and Reconciliation (ballet, based on the subject of the Indian Residential Schools commissioned by Royal Winnipeg Ballet under the auspices of the Truth and Reconciliation Commission of Canada 2015, touring Canada 2016. *Publications:* several essays about music. *Honours:* Jules Léger Prize for chamber music 1996, Prix Italia Premio Speciale 1996, Jean A. Chalmers Nat. Music Award 1998, Prix Bohemia Radio 1998, New Pioneer Award 2002, Juno Award for Classical Composition of the Year 2006, 2008, Jan V. Matejeck Concert Music Award (Soc. of Composers, Authors and Music Publrs of Canada) 2008, Hellenic Heritage Foundation Life Achievement Award 2014. *Current Management:* c/o Promethean Editions Ltd, PO Box 10143, Wellington, New Zealand. *Telephone:* (4) 473-5033. *Fax:* (4) 473-5066. *E-mail:* info@promethean-editions.com. *Website:* www.promethean-editions.com. *Address:* Faculty of Music, University of Toronto, Edward Johnson Building, 80 Queen's Park, Toronto, ON M5S 2C5, Canada (office). *Telephone:* (416) 978-5774 (office). *E-mail:* christos@hatzis.com (office). *Website:* www.reverbnation.com/christoshatzis (office); www.hatzis.com.

HAUBOLD, Ingrid; German singer (soprano); b. 1943, Berlin; m. Heikki Toivannen. *Education:* studied in Detmold, Munich Musikhochschule with Annelies Kupper. *Career:* sang at the Munich Theater am Gärtnerplatz 1965–66, Detmold Landestheater 1970–72, Bielefeld 1972, Lubeck from 1979; guest engagements at Hanover from 1981, Karlsruhe 1981–84; sang Isolde at Madrid 1986, Turin and Berlin 1988, Lucerne Festival 1989, Kassel 1992; has also appeared at the Teatro Massimo Palermo, Teatro Comunale Bologna, the Vienna Staatsoper, Schwetzingen Festival (Ariadne 1989) and the Metropolitan Opera 1990–91; other roles include Senta (Savonlinna Festival 1990), Pamina, Wagner's Elsa, Elisabeth, Brünnhilde (Wiesbaden 1996), Gutrune, Eva, Freia, Sieglinde, Irene (Rienzi) and Ada (Die Feen); Leonore, Strauss's Chrysothemis and Marschallin, Janáček's Jenůfa and Katya Kabanova; many concert appearances.

HAUDEBOURG, Brigitte; French harpsichordist, pianofortist and teacher; b. 5 Dec. 1942, Paris; m. Paul Cousseran; one s. one d. *Education:* studied piano with Marguérite Long and Jean Doyen, masterclass with R. Veyron-Lacroix. *Career:* debut in Paris; numerous radio and TV and appearances in France, USA, Canada, Europe, Russia, Tunisia, Hong Kong, Bangkok, Tahiti; Artistic Dir French baroque festival in Tarentaise. *Recordings:* 70 albums and CDs, including, Daquin, Dandrieu, two albums of suites; Devienne, for flute and harpsichord, Chevalier de St Georges, for violin and harpsichord, Jean Pierre Baur, for harp and harpsichord, W. F. Bach, two albums, Nos 1, 3, 4, 5; CDs include Louis Couperin for harpsichord, Josse Boutmy for harpsichord, world premiere, Padre Antonio Soler, J. Schobert for pianoforte, J. A. Benda for pianoforte, E. N. Mehul for pianoforte, J. G. Eckardt for pianoforte, L. Kozeluh for pianoforte. *Publications include:* 2nd book of Josse Boutmy (harpsichord). *Address:* 10 Avenue F. Roosevelt, 92150 Suresnes, France.

HAUG, Halvor; Norwegian composer; b. 20 Feb. 1952, Trondheim. *Education:* Conservatory of Music, Veitvet, Oslo, Sibelius Acad., Helsinki, studied with Kolbjörn Ofstad in Oslo, and in London. *Career:* performances in Norway and abroad with major musicians and orchestras; numerous radio and television performances in Norway and overseas; mem. Soc. of Norwegian Composers. *Compositions include:* orchestra: three Symphonies 1982, 1984,

1991–93, Symphonisk Bilde 1976, Stillhet for strykere 1977, Poema Patetica 1980, Poema Sonora 1980, Cordiale 1982, Menneskeverd og fred 1985, Exit 1985, Insignia 1994, Glem aldri henne (song cycle) for mezzo-soprano and orchestra 1997, Il Preludio dell'Ignoto 2000; chamber: Brass Quintet 1981, Essay 1986, two String Quartets 1985, 1996, Piano Trio 1995. *Address:* Røsslyngen 30, 2743 Harestua (home); Warner Chappell Music Norway, PO Box 576, Sentrum, 0105 Oslo, Norway (office).

HAUGSAND, Ketil; Norwegian musician (harpsichord), conductor and academic; *Associate Professor, Royal Danish Academy of Music. Education:* Oslo Music Acad. (now Norwegian Acad. of Music), Amsterdam Conservatory, studied with Gustav Leonhardt. *Career:* debut Oslo 1969; has appeared at numerous festivals and concert series in Europe, USA and Israel, as soloist with orchestra, recitalist and chamber musician; Artistic Dir and Conductor, Norwegian Baroque Orchestra, Arte Real Ensemble, Stavanger Symphony Orchestra, Oslo Radio Orchestra; mem. jury, int. harpsichord competitions at Leipzig, Warsaw and Prague; festivals include Utrecht Festival voor Oude Muziek, Paris Festival Estival, Bergen Festival, Stavanger Int. Chamber Music Festival, Stavanger Symphony Orchestra, Berlin Komische Oper, Tage Alte Musik Berlin, Regensburg Tage Alte Musik, St Paul Schubert Club, Minneapolis Lyra Concert Baroque Orchestra, Berkeley Early Music Festival, Jerusalem Festival, Lisboa Expo '98, Açores Festival; Asst Prof., Norwegian State Acad. of Music, Oslo 1974–94; apptd Prof. of Harpsichord, Hochschule für Musik, Köln 1994, now Prof. Emer.; Assoc. Prof., Royal Danish Acad. of Music 2013–. *Recordings include:* Bach: Goldberg Variations and works by Rameau, Marchand, Seixas, Sousa Carvalho. *Honours:* prizewinner, int. harpsichord competitions in Paris 1979 and Bruges 1980. *Address:* Royal Danish Academy of Music, Rosenoerns Allé 22, 1970 Frederiksberg C, Denmark (office). *E-mail:* ketil@haugsand.com.

HAUNSTEIN, Rolf; singer (baritone); b. 18 Jan. 1943, Dresden, Germany. *Education:* studied with Johannes Kemter in Dresden and Kurt Rehm in Berlin. *Career:* sang in Bautzen, Freiberg and Cottbus, before engagement at the Dresden Staatsoper 1971; roles include Germont, Posa, Ford, Scarpia, Beckmesser, Rigoletto, Pizarro, Klingsor, Telramund, Onegin and Wagner's Dutchman; guest engagements at Leipzig, the Komische Oper Berlin, Kiel, Wiesbaden and Strasbourg; mem., Zürich Opera from 1991; season 1996–97, Telramund, the Minister in Fidelio and Dikoj in Katya Kabanova; sang Kdenatý in The Makropulos Case, Toulouse 1998; sang the Animal Trainer and Athlete in Lulu at Zürich 2000.

HAUPTMANN, Cornelius; German singer (bass); b. 1951, Stuttgart. *Education:* Stuttgart Musikhochschule, Berne Conservatoire with Jakob Stämpfli, studied with Dietrich Fischer-Dieskau in Berlin and masterclasses in Salzburg with Eric Tappy and Elisabeth Schwarzkopf. *Career:* sang at Stuttgart from 1981, notably as Masetto; Heidelberg Opera 1985–87, as King Philip in Don Carlos and Osmin; Stadttheater Karlsruhe from 1987, as Sparafucile (Rigoletto), Plutone (Orfeo), Sarastro and Mozart's Figaro; Festival appearances at Lucerne, Salzburg, Singapore, Sapporo, Schwetzingen (1983 premiere of Henze's The English Cat) and Ludwigsburg (recital 1991); Further engagements in Munich, Paris, Berlin, Leipzig, Orleans, London, Lyon and Amsterdam (Publio and Sarastro in concert performances of La Clemenza di Tito and Die Zauberflöte, 1990); Sang Sarastro at Ludwigsburg, 1992; Conductors include John Eliot Gardiner, Hogwood, Janowski, Tilson Thomas, Masur, Barenboim, Maazel, Lothar Zagrosek, Roger Norrington, Neville Marriner, Pierre Boulez, Philippe Herreweghe; Concert performances include the St Matthew Passion (Gardiner) and Mozart's Requiem (Bernstein) in 1988; Frequent Lieder recitals, and other concerts under Nikolaus Harnoncourt, Trevor Pinnock, Helmut Rilling and Gary Bertini; Sang Rocco in a concert performance of Fidelio at Lyon, 1996; Gave masterclasses in Wales, Japan and England (Britten-Pears School of Advanced Music Studies, Aldeburgh). *Recordings:* Bach St John and St Matthew Passion, Mozart C minor Mass, Idomeneo, La Clemenza di Tito, and Die Entführung, with Gardiner and Mozart Requiem and C minor Mass (Bernstein) for Deutsche Grammophon; Beethoven: Missa Solemnis (Herreweghe); Schoenberg's Jakobsleiter (Inbal); Haydn Stabat Mater, with Pinnock (DG) and Die Zauberflöte with Norrington; Enescu Oedipe with Foster (EMI); Akhnaten by Philip Glass (CBS); Lieder by Loewe, Mozart, Schubert, Mendelssohn, Monteverdi; Schütz with Frieder Bernius. *Current Management:* c/o Ariën Arts & Music Management, De Boeystraat 6, 2018 Antwerp, Belgium. *Telephone:* (3) 285-96-80. *Fax:* (3) 230-35-23. *E-mail:* arien@pandora.be.

HAUSCHILD, Wolf-Dieter; German conductor; b. 6 Sept. 1937, Greiz. *Education:* Franz Liszt Musikhochschule, Weimar with Ottmar Gerster and Hermann Abendroth, studied with Hermann Scherchen and Sergiu Celibidache. *Career:* Conductor, Deutsche National Theater Weiners and from 1963 Chief Conductor of the Kleist Theatre at Frankfurt Oder (also of Frankfurt Philharmonic); Chorus Master for RDA Radio 1971–74, joint conductor of Berlin Radio Symphony Orchestra 1974–78; Chief Conductor, Symphony Orchestra of Radio Leipzig 1978–85; Prof. of Conducting, Musikhochschule of Berlin and Leipzig from 1981; guest conductor of Berlin Symphony Orchestra; Chief Conductor, Stuttgart Philharmonic Orchestra 1985–91; Prof. of Conducting, Karlsruhe Musikhochschule 1988; Artistic Dir and Chief Conductor, Essen Opera 1991–98 (1806 Version of Fidelio 1998); guest appearances at Berlin Staatsoper and Komische Opera and the Semper-Oper Dresden; conducted a new production of Tristan und Isolde at Essen 1992.

HAUSER, Alexis; Austrian music director; *Artistic Director, Orchestre Symphonique McGill de Montréal;* b. 1947, Vienna. *Education:* Conservatory and the Acad. of Music and Performing Arts, Vienna, masterclass with Prof. Hans Swarowsky, studied with Franco Ferrara in Italy and Herbert von Karajan at Salzburg Mozarteum. *Career:* conducting debut with the NTO Tonkünstler Orchester 1970; debut with Vienna Symphony 1973, several subsequent concerts and broadcasts with Vienna Symphony; invitations to conduct many other European orchestras, including the Berlin RIAS Symphony, Belgrade Philharmonic and the Vienna Chamber Orchestra; invited by Seiji Ozawa to spend summer of 1974 in Tanglewood, USA; US debut with the Atlanta Symphony 1975, later appearing with New York City Opera; Canadian debut with Orchestre Symphonique de Montréal 1976; Music Dir, Orchestra London Canada 1981–88, including European tour to the Festival Internationale dell Aquila in Italy; Principal Conductor, Int. Mozart Festival, Cluj, Romania 1992–98; Artistic Adviser to the Niederösterreich International contemporary music festival, Austria 1994–96; Artistic Dir, Orchestre Symphonique McGill de Montréal 2001–; guest engagements with orchestras across Europe and America, including as Principal Guest Conductor Budapest Philharmonic 1991–95, Ensemble Wiener Collage 1999–. *Honours:* winner Int. Hans Swarowsky Conducting Competition, Vienna, Koussevitzky Conducting Prize at Tanglewood 1974, Canadian Performing Right Organization Award of Merit (with Orchestra London Canada) 1984. *Current Management:* c/o Dr Josef Tichy, Kuenstleragentur Dr Raab & Dr Boehm, Plankengasse 7, 1010 Vienna, Austria. *Telephone:* (1) 512 05 01 12. *Fax:* (1) 512 77 43. *E-mail:* tichy@rbartists.at. *Website:* www.rbartists.at; www.alexishauser.com.

HÄUSERMANN, Ruedi; Swiss composer; b. 1948, Lenzburg; m.; two c. *Education:* studied econs and classical flute. *Career:* advocate of free improvisation style of performance; founding mem. Immervollesäle trio; began Der Schritt ins Jenseits solo project 1993–; works performed at Luxemburg-Platz, Berlin, Neumarkt theater and Schauspielhaus, Zürich, Theater Basel, Staatstheater Hannover, Steierisches Fall, Graz, Schauspielhaus and Burgtheater, Vienna, Munich Opera Festival; currently teaches at Universität der Künste, Berlin. *Film-score:* Leo Sonnyboy 1990. *Honours:* Bavarian Theatre Prize 2000. *Address:* Universität der Künste Berlin, KlangKunstBühne, Postfach 12 05 44, 10595 Berlin, Germany (office). *Telephone:* (30) 31852701 (office). *Fax:* (30) 31852710 (office). *E-mail:* klangkunstbuehne@udk-berlin.de (office). *Website:* www.udk-berlin.de (office).

HAUTA-AHO, Teppo; Finnish composer and musician (bass); b. 27 May 1941. *Education:* Sibelius Acad., studied with Prof. Frantisek Posta. *Career:* bassist Helsinki Philharmonic 1965–72, Finnish Nat. Opera 1975–2000; played with numerous artists including Seppo Paakkunainen in early 1960s, Juhani Vilkki, Kaj Backlund Big Band, Pekka Pöyry Quartet, Tuohi Quartet; leader own group, Kalmisto-Klang; mem. Quintet Moderne 1980s–; also classical and chamber musician; performed at annual festivals in Kuhmo; now concentrating on composing; duos with singer/pianist Carita Holmström, pianist/composer Eero Ojanen, violinist/composer Phil Wachsmann; mem. Cecil Taylor European Quintet. *Compositions include:* Fantasy for trumpet and orchestra, Kadenza for contrabass (used as set piece in int. bass competitions) 1990–99. *Honours:* Royal Acad. Composer's Prize, Stockholm, winner EBU competition for jazz groups, Montreux (with Tuohi Quartet) 1971, first prize Reine Marie José competition, Geneva 1986, Int. Soc. of Bassists Recognition Award for composition 2003, British and Int. Bass Forum Award for Lifetime Achievement 2004. *Address:* Mechelininkatu 27 B, 00100 Helsinki, Finland.

HAUTZIG, Walter; Austrian pianist; b. 28 Sept. 1921, Vienna; m. Esther Rudomin 1950, one s. one d. *Education:* State Acad. of Vienna, Jerusalem Conservatory, Curtis Inst., Philadelphia, studied with Mieczyslaw Munz, Artur Schnabel. *Career:* debut at Town Hall, New York 1943; recitals and orchestral appearances worldwide; soloist with Berlin Philharmonic, Orchestra National Belgique, Oslo, Stockholm, Copenhagen, Helsinki, Zürich, New York, Baltimore, St Louis, Buffalo, Vancouver, Honolulu, Tokyo, Sydney, Melbourne, Auckland, Wellington, Mexico, Bogotá, Jerusalem and Tel-Aviv; played for BBC, Australian, New Zealand, Japanese, USA and Canadian Radio; Prof. of Piano, Peabody Conservatory of Johns Hopkins Univ., Baltimore, USA 1960–87. *Publications:* Playing Around: A Pianist Remembers 1996; contrib. to Musical America, American Record Guide.

HAVERINEN, Margareta; Finnish singer (soprano); b. 1951. *Education:* studied with Pierre Bernac in Paris, Anita Välkki in Helsinki, Gladys Kuchta in Düsseldorf and Vera Rozsa in London. *Career:* after winning the 1978 Geneva International Competition sang in opera at Helsinki and Oslo as Gilda, Violetta, Tosca and Donna Anna; Welsh National Opera, 1988, and Dublin, 1992, as Tosca; London, 1992, in the British premiere of Sibelius's opera The Maiden in the Tower; Savonlinna Festival, 1994, as Judith in Bluebeard's Castle; Many concerts and Lieder recitals in Europe and the USA (Carnegie Hall, New York, and the Westminster Artsong Festival in Princeton).

HAVLAK, Lubomir, MgA; Czech violinist; *Leader, Martinů Quartet and Chamber Orchestra of National Theatre, Prague;* b. 27 Feb. 1958, Prague; m. Jarmila Havlakova 1983; one s. one d. *Education:* Conservatoire in Prague, Acad. of Music in Prague, master-classes with Nathan Milstein in Zürich and with leading ensembles, including Amadeus, Alban Berg, Guarneri, Juilliard and Tel-Aviv Quartets. *Career:* debut at Prague Spring Festival 1980; mem. Martinů Quartet, leader, Havlak and Martinů Quartet; performances at Prague Spring Festival, UNESCO Hall in Paris, Kuhmo Festival (Finland), Wigmore Hall, London, Bath Festival, Brighton Festival; festivals in Dartington, Evian (France), Arjeplog (Sweden), Bratislava (Slovakia), Orlando Festival (Netherlands), Frankfurter Sonoptikum; concerts in Europe, USA and Japan; Leader, Talich Chamber Orchestra 2008–09, Chamber Orchestra of Nat. Theatre, Prague 2010–; numerous performances on radio and TV; lecturer, Charles Univ., Prague 2014–. *Film:* Meeting with Segerstam. *Recordings include:* Martinů Quartets Vols 1, 2 (MIDEM Award, France 2004) and 3, Debussy, Martinů, Early Czech Composers – Krommer, Richter; Dvořák, Smetana-String Quartets, Antonin Wranitsky – Concertante Quartets, Janáček String Quartets, Honegger, Bodorová/Stevenson 2003, Dvořák String Quartets 2012, Škroup String Quartets 2012, Taneyev Complete Quintets 2015. *Honours:* with Havlak Quartet: Second Prize, Prague Spring Competition 1979, First Prize, Contemporary Music, Evian 1978, Second Prize, Portsmouth 1982, Second Prize, Munich 1982, Second Prize, Florence 1984. *Address:* Pod Vlastnim Krovem 27, 182 00 Prague 8, Czech Republic (home). *Telephone:* (2) 42485154 (home); 606-888373 (mobile). *E-mail:* lubomir.havlak@volny.cz. *Website:* www.martinuquartet.eu.

HAVLIK, Jiri; Czech horn player; b. 20 July 1956, Tabor; m. Helena Havlikova 1978, two d. *Education:* Prague Conservatoire, Acad. of the Musical Arts. *Career:* mem., Czech Philharmonic 1979–, Horn Trio Prague 1985–; chamber and solo performances in Czech Republic, Switzerland, The Netherlands, Japan, Canada; founder, Horn Music Agency, Prague 1991. *Compositions:* Concerto for horn and orchestra 1976, The Cycle of the Piano Compositions 1978, Three Fugues for three horns and piano 1997. *Recordings:* Czech Philharmonic Horn Section 1989, Old Czech Concertos for two and three horns 1992. *Honours:* second prize Concertino Prague Int. Competition 1970, Czech Ministry of Culture Special Prize 1978, third prize Prague Spring Int. Competition 1978. *Address:* Na Spravedlnosti 1152, 27101 Nove Straseci, Czech Republic.

HAWES, Patrick, MA, FRCO; British composer; b. 1958, Lincs., England; civil partner Andy Berry. *Education:* Durham Univ. *Career:* fmr conductor, Durham Univ. Chamber Choir and Symphony Orchestra; fmr music and English teacher, Pangbourne Coll.; fmr Composer-in-Residence Charterhouse, Classic FM 2006–07; own choir, Conventus. *Compositions include:* A King's Ransom (children's opera, with Andrew Hawes), The Land (folk song-based choral work, with Andrew Hawes), The Wedding at Cana, The Far Seeing Land, The Call (song cycle), Quanta Qualia, Song of Songs, Lazarus Requiem, Highgrove Suite (for HRH The Prince of Wales), Te Deum, Three Welsh Songs (for Elin Manahan Thomas), Eventide (In Memoriam Edith Cavell), I Hear the Music (based on the Wilfred Owen poem), Angel. *Film scores:* The Incredible Mrs Ritchie 2002, Prima Primavera. *Recordings:* albums: Blue in Blue 2002, Towards the Light 2006, Song of Songs 2009, Fair Albion 2009, Highgrove Suite 2010, Lazarus Requiem 2012, Angel 2014. *Publications:* The Wedding at Cana 1989, The Call 1997, Quanta Qualia 2004, Reflexionem, Tres Amores 2005, When Israel Was a Child 2005, O Lord Our Governor 2005, Violin Lullaby 2005, Lazarus Requiem 2005, Cantate Domino 2006, Highgrove Suite 2008, Song of Songs 2009, Te Deum 2011. *Current Management:* c/o Andy Berry at Hawes Music Ltd. *E-mail:* andyberry@ hawesmusic.com. *E-mail:* patrick.hawes@googlemail.com. *Website:* www .patrickhawes.com.

HAWKES, Tom, RAM DipEd, LRAM, ARAM, GSMD; British stage director; b. 21 June 1938, England. *Education:* Royal Acad. of Music. *Career:* resident staff producer, Sadler's Wells 1965–69; Artistic Dir Northampton Festival Opera until 2004, directed 22 productions; Dir of Productions Handel Opera Soc.; Artistic Dir Phoenix Opera; Dir Morley Opera; Dir of Productions Lyric Theatre Singapore; Dir of Productions Castleward Opera; has directed over 280 new and different productions of 157 operas as well as plays, pantomimes and jazz evenings; opera productions worldwide in countries including Austria, Belgium, Canada, Ireland, Malaysia, New Zealand, Trinidad, USA and Yugoslavia. *Opera productions include:* for Castleward Opera: L'Etoile, Martha, Lucia di Lammermoor, La Rondine, Rigoletto, La Bohème, Così fan tutte, Die Fledermaus; for Handel Opera Soc.: new productions of Esther, Ezio, Hercules, Partenope, Radamisto, Rodrigo, Xerxes and premiere of Alan Bush's Wat Tyler (all at Sadler's Wells Theatre); for ENO: five productions including Un Ballo in Maschera, La Gazza Ladra and La Vie Parisienne; for The English Bach Festival: Castor et Pollux, Platée, Alceste, Oreste, Riccardo Primo, Teseo, Orphée, Mitridate, Idomeneo and Dido & Aeneas at venues including Royal Opera House, Covent Garden, in Paris, Monte Carlo and Versailles and at festivals in Athens, Madrid, Granada, Peralada, Bologna, Siena, Viterbo, Vichy and Dijon; for Opera Holland Park: 12 productions including Iris, L'Arlesiana, Adriana Lecouvreur, Werther, Eugene Onegin, The Merry Widow, Lakmé, Orpheus in the Underworld and La Rondine. *Honours:* Hon. MA (Nene Univ., Northampton) 1998; Ivan Lukačić Prize (for Cavalli's Pompeo Magno, Varazdin Baroque Festival) 2002. *Address:* Norfolk House, 113 Knatchbull Road, London, SE5 9QY, England (home). *Telephone:* (20) 7274-9639 (home). *E-mail:* thomhawkes@aol.com.

HAWKINS, Brian, FRCM; British violist and fmr teacher; b. 13 Oct. 1936, York, Yorks., England; m. Mavis Spreadborough 1960; one s. one d. *Education:* St Peter's School, York, Nat. Youth Orchestra, Royal Coll. of Music. *Career:* chamber music, Edinburgh Quartet, Martin Quartet, Vesuvius Ensemble, Nash Ensemble, London Oboe Quartet, Gagliano String Trio; mem. English Chamber Orchestra, Acad. of St Martin-in-the-Fields, London Sinfonietta, London Virtuosi; apptd Prof. of Viola and Chamber Music, Royal Coll. of Music 1967, String Faculty Adviser 1989, Head of String Faculty 1992–2000; Cttee mem. European String Teachers' Asscn; Jury Chair., Lionel Tertis Int. Viola Competition; examiner and adjudicator; mem. Royal Soc. of Musicians, Inc. Soc. of Musicians. *Recordings include:* with Nash Ensemble, London Virtuosi, London Oboe Quartet and Gagliano Trio, London Sinfonietta, English Chamber Orchestra, Acad. of St Martin-in-the-Fields, Nat. Philharmonic Orchestra. *Honours:* Silver Medal, Worshipful Co. of Musicians 1960. *Address:* The Old Vicarage, 129 Arthur Road, London, SW19 7DR, England. *Telephone:* (20) 8946-4511. *E-mail:* violahawk@waitrose.com.

HAWKINS, John, MMus; Canadian composer and pianist; b. 26 July 1944, Montréal, Canada. *Education:* McGill Univ. and studied with Istvan Anhalt. *Career:* teacher of theory and composition in faculty of music, Univ. of Toronto 1970–; active as pianist and performs frequently in the concerts of Societe de Musique Contemporaine du Québec, as well as Toronto's New Music Concerts; Conductor, Pierre Boulez conducting seminar, Switzerland 1969; mem. of bd of dirs New Music Concerts. *Compositions include:* pieces for harpsichord and organ, Music for an Imaginary Musical for chamber ensemble 1994, Night Song for baritone, marimba and string quartet 1995, If There are Any Heavens for soprano and chamber ensemble 1996. *Honours:* John Adaskin Memorial Fund Award 1968, BMI Student Composers' Award 1969.

HAWKSLEY, Deborah, GRNCM; British singer (mezzo-soprano); b. Singapore. *Education:* Royal Northern Coll. of Music, Manchester, Guildhall School of Music and Drama, London. *Career:* roles include Third Lady (The Magic Flute), Prince Orlofsky (Die Fledermaus), The Composer (Ariadne on Naxos), Marfa in Mussorgsky's Khovanchina, Annina in Der Rosenkavalier, Serena Joy in The Handmaid's Tale and Katisha in Jonathan Miller's Mikado (ENO), Katisha (Mikado) at Savoy Theatre, London, title role in La Belle Hélène for Castleward Opera, Dinah in Bernstein's Trouble in Tahiti for Opéra Décentralisé, Geneva, The Strolling Player (Death in Venice) for Glyndebourne Touring Opera, Cherubino (Marriage of Figaro) and title role in Cenerentola for European Chamber Opera, Mrs Peachum in The Beggar's Opera (Britten realisation) and Florence Pyke (Albert Herring) for the Opera Project, Annina (La Traviata) and Third Lady (Die Zauberflöte) for Diva Opera, Prince Orlofsky and Flora (La Traviata) at Holland Park Opera, The Duchess of Plazatoro (The Gondoliers) for Buxton G&S Festival, Baba The Turk (The Rake's Progress) at Aldeburgh Festival and for Opera East, The Forrester's Wife and The Owl in The Cunning Little Vixen at Longborough Opera Festival, Mistress Quickly in Verdi's Falstaff for the Opera Project, Madam Larina (Onegin) for Iford Opera and Prince Orlofsky for Castleward Opera at Wexford Opera House, Ireland; performed and recorded Prince Orlofsky for D'Oyly Carte Opera; regular Promenade soloist with City of London Sinfonia, appearing with them in Promenade Concerts in Berlin, Düsseldorf and Hamburg; also performed Promenade concerts with Sudwestfalen Orchester in Cologne and at Neuen Palais in Sanssouci Park, Potsdam. *Current Management:* c/o Music International, 13 Ardilaun Road, Highbury, London, N5 2QR, England. *Telephone:* (20) 7359-5183. *Fax:* (20) 7226-9792. *E-mail:* Dan@musicint.co.uk. *Website:* www.musicint.co.uk.

HAWLATA, Franz; German singer (bass-baritone); b. 26 Dec. 1963, Eichstatt. *Education:* Munich Musikhochschule with Ernst Haefliger, Hans Hotter and Erik Werba. *Career:* debut at Gärtnerplatztheater, Munich, 1986; engagements at the Komische Oper Berlin and in Munich, with guest appearances as Altoum in Busoni's Turandot in Dortmund; Baron Ochs in Der Rosenkavalier at Würzburg, for Welsh National Opera, New York Metropolitan 1995 and the Paris Opéra Bastille 1998; Peneios in Strauss's Daphne at Hamburg, Wozzeck at Bad Urach, Rocco in Beethoven's Leonore, on tour with John Eliot Gardiner, Leporello at Covent Garden and Osmin in Die Entführung at Salzburg (1996); Vienna State Opera 1994–95 as Nicolai's Falstaff, Kaspar, Don Pasquale, Sarastro and Baron Ochs; The Monk in Don Carlos at the Opéra Bastille, 1998, and Kecal in The Bartered Bride for the Royal Opera; Ochs at Covent Garden, 2000; season 2001 as the Dutchman in Chicago and Wotan in Meiningen. *Recordings include:* Mephisto in Spohr's Faust, from the Bad Urach Festival. *Honours:* Prizewinner, 1987 Belvedere International Singing Competition, Vienna. *Current Management:* c/o William G. Guerri, Columbia Artists Management Inc., 1790 Broadway, New York, NY 10019-1412, USA. *Telephone:* (212) 841-9680. *Fax:* (212) 841-9516. *E-mail:* info@cami.com. *Website:* www.cami.com. *Current Management:* Aria's di Novella Partacini & Alexandra Plaickner, Rappresentanza Artisti, Via Josef Weingartner 4, 39022 Lagundo, Italy. *Telephone:* (0473) 200200. *Fax:* (0473) 222424. *E-mail:* info@arias.it. *Website:* www.arias.it.

HAYASHI, Yasuko; singer (soprano); b. 19 July 1948, Kanagawa, Japan; m. Giannicola Piglucci. *Education:* studied in Tokyo with Shibata and Rucci, with Lia Gurani and Campogalliani in Milan. *Career:* debut at La Scala 1972, as Madama Butterfly; appearances in Florence, Rome, London, Venice, Turin, Barcelona, Chicago and Aix-en-Provence; other roles include Donna Anna, Fiordiligi, Carolina in Il Matrimonio Segreto, Luisa Miller, Anne Trulove and Liu, in Turandot; Turin 1976, in Bianca e Fernando by Bellini; sang Donna Anna at reopening of Stuttgart Staatsoper 1984; Genoa 1985, in a revival of Il Diluvio Universale by Donizetti; season 1987–88 as Butterfly at Verona and Leonora in La Forza del Destino in Tokyo; appearances on television and in concert. *Recordings:* I Lituani by Ponchielli; Rachel in La Juive; Requiem by Bottesini, Fonit-Cetra; video of Madama Butterfly from La Scala.

HAYASHI, Yusuke; Japanese violinist; b. 5 Sept. 1984. *Education:* Vienna Univ. of Music and Performing Arts with Dora Schwarzberg. *Career:* began studying violin aged four and won several music competitions in Japan shortly thereafter; youngest laureate of the 69th Japan Violin Competition 2000. *Honours:* Winner, Int. String Competition of Upbeat, Hvar (Croatia) 2003, Winner, Yehudi Menuhin Int. Competition for Young Violinists 2004, Winner, Romano Romanini Int. Competition, Brescia (Italy) 2004, Winner, Dr Luis Sigall Int. Competition (Chile) 2005, Stefanie-Hohl Violin Competition, Vienna 2005, Winner, Int. Violin Competition 'Citta di Brescia' 2010. *Address:* Vienna University of Music and Performing Arts, Anton-von-Webern-Platz 1, 1030 Vienna, Austria. *Telephone:* (1) 711-55. *Fax:* (1) 711-55-19-9. *Website:* www.mdw.ac.at.

HAYES, Jamie; stage director; b. 1959, England. *Career:* productions of The Gondoliers, The Magic Flute and Midsummer Night's Dream at Freemason's Hall; Aida, Opera Northern Ireland; Il Barbiere di Siviglia and La Cenerentola for Garsington Opera, Thieving Magpie, Figaro, Così fan tutte and Albert Herring for British Youth Opera at Sadler's Wells and Edinburgh; fmr Dir of Productions, Clonter Opera For All, with La Traviata, La Bohème and Carmen; Buxton Festival with L'Italiana in Algeri, Le Huron and L'Italiana in Londra; Wexford Festival with Zaza and Le Rencontre Imprévue; other productions include Alcina for Royal Northern Coll. of Music and The Pearl Fishers for Victorian State Theatre, Robinson Crusoe, British Youth Opera, The Bear, RSAMD; Dir of Productions, British Youth Opera 1996; La Bohème, for BYO 1998.

HAYES, Malcolm Lionel Fitzroy, BMus; British music journalist, writer and composer; b. 22 Aug. 1951, Overton, Marlborough, Wiltshire. *Education:* St Andrews Univ., Univ. of Edinburgh. *Career:* music critic, The Times 1985–86, The Sunday Telegraph 1986–89, The Daily Telegraph 1989–95; regular freelance writer The Sunday Telegraph 1989–, BBC Music magazine 1997–, Classic FM magazine 1995–2013; frequent broadcasts (talks) for BBC Radio 3 1985–, and Radio 4 1986–; music performed at Bath Festival 1985, ICA, London 1985, BBC, London 1986, 2006, 2007, 2012, 2013, Viitasaari Festival, Finland 1987; Edinburgh Contemporary Arts Trust 2002, New Coll., Oxford 2007. *Compositions:* Into the Night for unaccompanied chorus 1984, Stabat Mater for soloists and orchestra 2001, Odysseus Remembers for soloists and orchestra 2004, Alleluia Nativitas for unaccompanied chorus 2005, From the Paradiso of Dante for solo piano 2006, The Wild Swans of Coole for unaccompanied chorus 2010, May Magnificat for unaccompanied chorus 2010, Byzantium for orchestra 2012, Violin Concerto 2014. *Publications:* New Music 88 (co-ed.) 1988, Anton von Webern 1995, 20th-Century Music (6 vols) 2001, Selected Letters of William Walton 2002, Liszt 2011; contributed numerous articles to Tempo 1982–92, The Listener 1985–89, Musical Times 1985–86, International Opera Guide 1987, New Music 87 1987, Opera Now 1991–1996, Classic FM Magazine 1995–2013, BBC Music Magazine 2002–, BBC Proms Guide 1999–, BBC Proms and orchestras programme notes 1992–. *Honours:* Edinburgh Univ. Tovey Prize for Composition 1974. *E-mail:* malcolmhayes@btinternet.com (office). *Website:* www.malcolmhayes.co.uk.

HAYES, Quentin; British singer (baritone); b. 27 Nov. 1958, Southend, Essex. *Education:* studied at Dartington Coll., Guildhall School with Arthur Reckless and Rudolph Pernay, and at Nat. Opera Studio. *Career:* cr. Eddy in Mark-Anthony Turnage's Greek, Munich 1988, repeated it at Edinburgh and London Coliseum; Rossini's Figaro with Glyndebourne Touring Opera, Verdi's Ford for CBTO, Morales in Carmen for Welsh Nat. Opera, and Angelotti for Scottish Opera; Ford, Papageno and Marcel Proust in Schnittke's Life with an Idiot for ENO 1995; concerts include Britten's War Requiem at Amsterdam Concertgebouw, Elijah in Wells Cathedral, L'Enfance du Christ in Spain and music by Purcell with Collegium Vocale; Season 1997 with The Dream of Gerontius at Bath, Handel's Semele at Berlin Staatsoper, Britten's Church Parables for CBTO and Henze's Elegy for Young Lovers with London Sinfonietta; Frère Léon in Messiaen's St François d'Assise for Concertgebouw, Amsterdam; Season 2003 at Covent Garden as Yamadori in Butterfly and the Herald in Lohengrin, Where teh Wild Things Are with Berlin Philharmonic; Season 2004: Ned Keene in Peter Grimes and Ping in Turandot, Royal Opera House, Covent Garden; Season 2005: Zuniga in Carmen with City of Birmingham Symphony Orchestra, Ping in Turandot, Second Apprentice in Wozzeck, Royal Opera House, Vaughn Williams' Sea Symphony in Exeter Cathedral and at Snape Maltings, Aldeburgh. *Recordings include:* Pepusch Death of Dido for BBC; Greek; Britten, Rejoice in the Lamb; Where the Wild Things Are, Knussen; Donald in Billy Budd with Hickox and the London Symphony Orchestra, King in Wallace's Maritana with Radio Telefís Eireann Concert Orchestra. *Honours:* Winner, Vara Dutch Radio Prize, Belvedere Singing Competition, Vienna 1992, 1993. *Address:* c/o Royal Opera House (contracts), Bow Street, Covent Garden, London, WC2E 9DD, England. *Telephone:* (20) 7240-1200 (office).

HAYMON, Cynthia; American singer (soprano); b. 6 Sept. 1958, Jacksonville, Fla; m. Barrington Coleman. *Education:* Northwestern Univ. *Career:* debut at Santa Fe Opera, as Diana in Orpheus in the Underworld, 1985; Sang Xanthe in US premiere of Die Liebe der Danaë, Santa Fe, 1985; has sung Micaela for Seattle Opera and Liu in Boston; Created Harriet, A Woman Called Moses, Virginia, 1985; European debut, 1986, as Gershwin's Bess at Glyndebourne; With Covent Garden has sung Liu on tour to Far East and Mimi in London; State Operas, Hamburg, Munich, as Liu, Theatre de la Monnaie, Brussels, as Gluck's Amor; Israel Philharmonic as Micaela, conducted by Zubin Mehta; season 1988–89 with Eurydice at Glyndebourne, Mimi for Baltimore Opera, Marguerite with Opera Grand Rapids; Season 1989–90 included Susanna for Seattle Opera, Canadian Opera debut as Micaela; Coretta King opposite Simon Estes, West End; 1990–91 highlights: Lauretta in Gianni Schicchi at Seattle, Liu in Miami, and Mozart's Pamina at Bastille Opéra, Paris; 1991–92 highlights: San Francisco Opera debut as Micaela in Carmen, premiere of Rorem's Swords and Plowshares with Boston Symphony, Pamina at Opéra Bastille, Liu at Royal Opera House, Covent Garden, Gershwin in concert at Teatro La Fenice, Venice, recital at Northwestern Univ., Carmina Burana with Detroit Symphony Orchestra, Mendelssohn's Symphony No. 2 for RAI, Rome, Gershwin and Tippett concert with London Symphony Orchestra, Gala concert, Glyndebourne Festival, 1992–93 highlights: Bess in Porgy and Bess, Royal Opera House, Pamina at Opéra Bastille, Micaela in Birmingham and Dortmund, Marguerite at Deutsche Oper Berlin, Mimi at Santa Fe Opera; sang Musetta at Amsterdam, 1996; Liu in Turandot at Dallas, 1997; Sang Gluck's Euridice at Leipzig, 2000; concert engagements in Brahms Requiem conducted by Kurt Masur, Rossini's Stabat Mater (London debut) with London Symphony Orchestra conducted by Michael Tilson Thomas. *Recordings include:* Tippett's A Child of Our Time, London Symphony Orchestra, Richard Hickox, conductor; Bess in Porgy and Bess, Glyndebourne Festival Opera, Simon Rattle, conductor. *Honours:* Grammy Award 1990. *Address:* 3302 Lake Shore Drive, Champaign, IL 61821, USA (office). *E-mail:* haymonco@illinois.edu (office).

HAYRABEDIAN, Roland; French conductor; *Founder and Conductor, Ensemble Musicatreize*; b. 19 May 1953. *Career:* f. Choeur Contemporain d'Aix-en-Provence 1978; Founder and Conductor, Ensemble Musicatreize 1987–; fmr guest conductor, orchestra of Spoleto Festival, St Petersburg Philharmonic, Chorus of Radio France, Orchestre Philharmonique des Pays de Loire, Orchestre Philharmonique de Lorraine, Orchestre d'Avignon; Music Dir, Orchestre des Jeunes et de la Méditerranée 2002–05; lecturer, Conservatoire Nat. de la Région Marseilles; has also performed with Les Percussions de Strasbourg, Musique Vivante, Musique Oblique, 2e2m, tm+ and many foreign ensembles; teaches choral and instrumental conducting at CNR, Marseille. *Concert series include:* Musiques en 13 2000, Les Tentations 2003–05, Les sept contes de Musicatreize, Trois cantates policières. *Recordings include:* (as conductor): Liszt: Via Crucis 1970, Ohana—Llanto por Ignacio Sanchez Mejias 1992, French Choral Music Vol. 3 2007, Cantigas, Avoaha, Messe, Sundown Dances, Ohana—Trois contes de l'honorable Fleur, Mantovani—L'enterrement de Mozart, Strasnoy—Un retour. *Honours:* Victoire de la musique "Meilleur ensemble" 2007. *Address:* Ensemble Musicatreize, 53 rue Grignan, 13006 Marseille, France (office). *Telephone:* 4-91-00-91-31 (office). *Fax:* 4-91-55-03-93 (office). *E-mail:* r.hayrabedian@musicatreize.org (office). *Website:* www.musicatreize.org (office).

HAYS, Sorrel Doris; American composer, pianist and multimedia artist; b. 6 Aug. 1941, Memphis, Tenn.; d. of Walter Ernest Hays and Christina Doris Fair. *Education:* Hochschule für Musik, Munich, Germany, Univ. of Wisconsin, Cadek Conservatory, studied with Hilda Somer, Paul Badura-Skoda, Harold Cadek, Hedwig Bilgram, Friedrich Wuhrer, Arthur Plettner. *Career:* in 1980s added film and video to media art; comms from West German Broadcasting, Cologne; film, music video production shown at Museum of Modern Art, New York and Stedelijk Museum, Amsterdam; premiered Henry Cowell's Concerto for Piano and Orchestra 1978; comms from Westdeutscher Rundfunk, Cologne 1988; Echo, Whatchasay Wie Bitte 1989; The Hub, Megopolis Atlanta and Sound Shadows, commissioned as opening work for Whitney Museum Acoustica Festival 1990; Bits, NY City premiere 1993, Merkin Hall; performances of Opera, The Glass Woman, NYC, Encompass Theater and Interart Theater 1993; premiere, The Clearing Way, Chattanooga Symphony 1992; comm./premiere A Birthday Book for baritone, oboe, tuba, Cowell Centennial Festival, Merkin Hall 1997; Queen Bee-ing, The Bee Opera, comic opera 1997 commissioned by Cary Trust, premiered by Medicine Show Theater, New York City 2003; opera Our Giraffe featured in New York City Opera VOX Festival 2008; comic cantatera TOOWHOPERA commissioned by Georgia Music Teachers' Asscn; 1970s music featuring southern roots: Southern Voices for Soprano and Orchestra commissioned by Chattanooga Symphony, Tunings for string quartet, first concert of women's music at Library of Congress, Sunday Nights for piano; mem. American Soc. of Composers, Authors and Publishers. *Films:* Flowing Quilt, C.D., The Ritual of Civil Disobedience, M.O.M. 'n P.O.P., Touch of Touch. *Compositions:* Southern Voices for Orchestra and Soprano 1982, Celebration of No, tape, Soprano, Violin, Piano, Cello 1983, Sunday Nights for piano 1979, HUSH for soprano and two percussion 1986, The Clearing Way for orchestra, contralto, SATB chorus, The Glass Woman, opera (Opera America Award) 1993, Sound Shadows for oboe, didjeridu, dancer, video, synth, Whitney Museum 1990, Mapping Venus, opera 1998, The Bee Opera (Cary Trust Grant, Arts Int. Award 2005) 2003, Our Giraffe, opera in three acts (American Music Center Composer Award) 2008, Rocker Parts for two pianos, TOOWHOPERA, a cantatera for eight voices and orchestra 2009, Wednesday Nights (piano, clarinet and trombone) 2010, Houston Light Guard March (for brass band) 2011. *Recordings:* Dreaming the World, Voicings (Smithsonian Folkways), Sorrel Hays Plays Henry Cowell (Townhall), Past Present, pno (Opus One), MOM 'N POP 3 pnos,Bits, MIDIklavier (Opus One). *Plays:* Disarming the World, WNYC (radio play). *Radio:* Etwas Tun, Traum in ihrem Kopf, Westdeutscher Rundfunk, Köln, Liebe im All, WDR Köln. *Publications:* Tunings for string quartet, Southern Voices for Soprano and Orchestra, Blues Fragments for Soprano and piano, TOOWHOPERA. *Honours:* Nat. Endowment for the Arts Fellowship 1981, 1987, 1992, New York Foundation on the

Arts Fellowships 1985, 1998, Carey Grant 2003, American Music Center 2008, Composer Grant 2008. *Address:* 266 Carnes Road, Buchanan, GA 30113, USA (home). *Telephone:* (770) 646-5442 (office); (212) 663-6164 (office). *E-mail:* hays2ries@mindspring.com (office). *Website:* www.sorrelhays.com.

HAYWARD, Robert; British singer (bass-baritone); b. Nov. 1956, Surrey, England. *Education:* Guildhall School of Music and the National Opera Studio. *Career:* sang Falstaff and Mozart's Figaro while at college; Glyndebourne Touring Opera, 1986, as Don Giovanni; Has sung Figaro, Don Giovanni, Marcello, Count and Sharpless for WNO; Theseus and Haushofmeister (Capriccio) for Glyndebourne Festival; English National Opera appearances as Tomsky in The Queen of Spades, Escamillo 1995, and Jochanaan 1996; US debut as Figaro for Houston Grand Opera, 1988; German debut, 1990, as Don Giovanni for the Bayerische Staatsoper on tour to Teatro Liceo Barcelona; For Opera North Guglielmo, Figaro, Count, Escamillo, Don Giovanni, Malatesta, Marcello, Robert in Iolanta, Debussy's Golaud; For Royal Opera House, Spirit Messenger (Frau); For Glyndebourne Tour Count and Onegin; Sang Germont for GTO at Glyndebourne, 1996; Sang Iago in Otello for ENO, 1998; Concert engagements include Messiah with the Royal Liverpool Philharmonic, Hallé and London Philharmonic Orchestras; The Mask of Time, Elijah, Beethoven's Ninth and the Brahms Requiem with the Hallé; Das klagende Lied and Gurrelieder with the English Northern Philharmonia; The Dream of Gerontius with the Scottish National Orchestra; Haydn's Creation with the Bournemouth Sinfonietta and the Philharmonia conducted by Claus Peter Flor; Mozart Requiem with Georg Solti; New Israeli Opera as: Malastesta, Guglielmo, season 2000–01 as Escamillo for WNO, Golo in Pelléas for ENO and Jochanaan in Salome at Glasgow. *Recordings:* Beethoven's 9th Symphony; Das klagende Lied.

HAYWOOD, Lorna; British singer (soprano); b. 29 Jan. 1939, Birmingham, England; m. Paul Crook. *Education:* Royal Coll. of Music with Mary Parsons and Gordon Cinton, Juilliard School with Sergius Kagen and Beverly Johnson. *Career:* debut at Juilliard 1964, as Katya Kabanova; Covent Garden debut 1966, in Die Zauberflöte: sang Jenůfa 1972; ENO from 1970, notably Janáček's The Makropulos Case and Katya Kabanova; appearances with WNO and at the Glyndebourne Festival; guest engagements in Prague, Brussels, New York, Chicago, Dallas, Washington and Seattle; roles include Marenka in The Bartered Bride, Mimi, Micaela in Carmen, Sieglinde, Elizabeth Zimmer in Elegy for Young Lovers, Mozart's Countess, Madama Butterfly, Ariadne, the Marschallin and Lady Billows in Albert Herring (Los Angeles 1992); masterclass for Ohio Light Opera 1996.

HAZELL, Andrea; British singer (mezzo-soprano); b. 1965, Southampton, England. *Education:* Royal Acad. of Music. *Career:* many appearances throughout the UK in oratorio; sang Second Witch in Dido and Aeneas for Amersham Festival, Offenbach's Perichole in Reading and Dorabella at the 1990 Cheltenham Festival; sang in Carmen at Earl's Court 1989, and on tour to Japan; mem., Royal Opera Chorus, Covent Garden 1990–, in Les Huguenots and Die Frau ohne Schatten and as Tefka in Jenůfa 1993; other roles include Marcellina in Le nozze di Figaro. *Address:* c/o Royal Opera Chorus, Royal Opera House, Bow Street, Covent Garden, London, WC2E 9DD, England.

HAZELL, Richard; British singer and actor; b. (Charles Richard Hazell), 5 Aug. 1939, Staffs., England; s. of Raymond Hazell and Eileen Hazell. *Education:* Royal Coll. of Music, London. *Career:* debut in film Phantom of the Opera 1961; theatre and TV work –1973; appearances with Royal Opera, Covent Garden, in Manon, Carmen, The Merry Widow, Andrea Chénier, La Rondine, Der Rosenkavalier, La Bohème, La Traviata and Paul Bunyan; Orge in British premiere of Henze's Policino; int. tours with National Reisopera, Netherlands 2001–02, D'Oyly Carte Opera Co. 2002–05; M. Firmin in Phantom of the Opera, London; regular mem. Ambrosian singers; fmr Chair. Amici di Verdi and Founding mem. Royal Opera House Educ. Advisory Council 1961–97. *Television:* Monty Python's Flying Circus, The Two Ronnies, The Goodies, Broaden Your Mind, Milligan in Spring, Blue Peter, Katherine Mansfield, La Vida Breve, Otello, Peter Grimes, The Flying Dutchman, The Tales of Hoffmann, numerous direct relays from the Royal Opera House, Covent Garden. *Current Management:* c/o Jaffrey Management Ltd, 74 Western Road, Romford, Essex, RM1 3LP, England. *Telephone:* (1708) 732350. *E-mail:* castings@jaffreyactors.co.uk. *Website:* www.jaffreyactors.co.uk.

HAZLEWOOD, Charles; British conductor and music director; m.; three c. *Education:* Christ's Hospital, Univ. of Oxford. *Career:* Music Dir Broomhill Opera 1993–96; jt Artistic Dir Wilton's Music Hall, London 1999–2003; co-founder and jt Artistic Dir Dimpho Di Kopane Opera Co., Cape Town, South Africa 2000–06, conducting Carmen and West Side Story, conceived music for Yiimimngaoliso (The Mysteries), Ibali Loo Tsotsi (The Beggar's Opera), The Snow Queen; collaborations with Steve Reich, Peter Maxwell Davies, Badly Drawn Boy and Goldfrapp; Music Dir and Conductor, Excellent Device and Harmonieband chamber orchestras; Carnegie Hall debut 2003; Prin. Guest Conductor, BBC Concert Orchestra 2005–; BBC Proms debut, London 2006; launched own music festival Orchestra in a Field, Somerset 2009; conducts own period instrument orchestra Army of Generals. *Films:* Music Dir on U-Carmen e-Khayelitsha (Golden Bear for Best Film, Berlin Film Festival 2005), The Son of Man. *Television:* Presenter, Author and Conductor, Vivaldi Unmasked, The Genius of Mozart, The Genius of Beethoven, the Genius of Tchaikovsky (all BBC). *Radio:* Presenter, Charles Hazlewood Discovering Music (BBC Radio 3), The Charles Hazlewood Show (BBC Radio 2). *Honours:*

Winner, European Broadcasting Union conducting competition 1995, Sony Award 2005, 2006. *Current Management:* c/o Theia Nankivell, KBJ Management, 7 Soho Street, London, W1D 3DQ, England. *Telephone:* (20) 7434-6837. *Fax:* (20) 7287-1191. *E-mail:* Sadie@kbjmanagement.co.uk; Charlie@kbjmanagement.co.uk. *Website:* www.kbjmgt.co.uk; www.charleshazlewood.com.

HAZUCHOVA, Nina; Slovak singer (mezzo-soprano); b. 24 May 1926. *Education:* Conservatory, Bratislava. *Career:* appeared with Slovak National Theatre; roles included: Carmen, Amneris in Aida; Azucena in ll Trovatore; Eboli in Don Carlos; Maddalena in Rigoletto; Suzuki in Madama Butterfly; Rosina, in The Barber of Seville; Marina in Boris Godunov; Cherubino in The Marriage of Figaro; Nancy in Martha; Isabella in The Italian Girl in Algiers; Catherine in The Taming of the Shrew; appeared as a Concert Singer performing with the best Czech orchestras; Has toured many countries including USSR, Germany, Austria, Belgium, Italy, Yugoslavia, Arabia, China, Mongolia; Vocal-Teacher, Academy of Music Arts (Vysoka skola muzickych umeni) Bratislava; mem. Slovak Music Foundation, Bratislava. *Honours:* Meritorious Artist 1968.

HEADLEY, Erin; American lirone player and viola da gamba player; b. 1948, Texas. *Career:* mem., Tragicomedia, three musicians performing in the Renaissance and Baroque repertory; concerts in the UK and at leading European early music festivals; gave Stefano Landi's La Morte d'Orfeo at the 1987 Flanders Festival; Francesca Caccini's La liberazione di Ruggiero dall'isola d'Alcina at the 1989 Swedish Baroque Festival, Malmö. *Recordings include:* Proensa (troubadour songs), My Mind to me a Kingdom is (Elizabethan ballads, with David Cordier); A Musicall Dreame (duets from Robert Jones's 1609 collection); Biber's Mystery Sonatas; Concert programmes include The Lyre of Timotheus (incidental music by Handel, Bach, Vivaldi and Abel); Orpheus I Am (music based on the Orpheus myth by Landi, Monteverdi, Lawes and Johnson); Il Basso Virtuoso (songs by Landi, Monteverdi, Strozzi, Huygens and Purcell, with Harry van der Kamp); Three Singing Ladies of Rome; Monteverdi Madrigals from Book VIII and L'Orfeo; Early Opera: Peri's Euridice, Landi's La Morte d'Orfeo and Rossi's Orfeo.

HEALEY, Derek; composer; b. 2 May 1936, England. *Education:* Univ. of Durham with Harol Darke and Herbert Howells, Royal Coll. of Music, studied with Petrassi and Celibidache in Italy. *Career:* tutor, Univ. of Victoria, BC, Australia 1969–71, Coll. of Arts, Univ. of Guelph 1972–78; Prof. of Composition and Theory, Univ. of Oregon 1979; returned to the UK 1988. *Compositions include:* Seabird Island (opera) 1977, Mr Punch (children's opera) 1969; ballets: Il Carcerato 1965, The Three Thieves 1967; orchestral: The Willow Pattern Plate 1957, Concerto for organ, strings and timpani 1960, Butterflies for mezzo and chamber orchestra 1970, Arctic Images 1971, Tribulation 1977, Music for a Small Planet 1984, Mountain Music 1985, Gabriola (A West Coast Canadian Set) 1988, Salal (An Idyll) 1990, Triptych 1996; chamber: String Quartet 1961, Cello Sonata 1961, Mobile for flute and ensemble 1963, Laudes for flute and ensemble 1966, Maschere for violin and piano 1967, Wood II for soprano and string quartet 1982, English Dances for percussion sextet 1987; piano music: Lieber Robert 1974; three organ sonatas 1961, 1992, 1996.

HEARTZ, Daniel Leonard, AB, MA, PhD; American educator; b. 5 Oct. 1928, Exeter, NH. *Education:* Univ. of New Hampshire, Harvard Univ. *Career:* Asst Prof. of Music, Univ. of Chicago 1957–60; Asst Prof. of Music, Univ. of California at Berkeley 1960–64, Assoc. Prof. 1964–66, Prof. 1966–, Chair of Music Dept 1968–72; Fellow American Acad. of Arts and Sciences 1988; mem. American Musicological Soc. (vice-pres. 1974–76), IMS, RMA, Société Française de Musicologie, Gesellschaft für Musikforschung. *Publications:* Pierre Attaingnant, Royal Printer of Music 1969, Edition of Mozart's Idomeneo, Neue Mozart Ausgabe 1972, Mozart's Operas 1990, Haydn, Mozart and the Viennese School 1740–1780 1995, Music in European Capitals: The Galant Style 1720–1780 2003, From Garrick to Gluck: Essays on Opera in the Age of Enlightenment 2004, Mozart, Haydn and Early Beethoven 1781–1802 2009; contrib. to professional journals, including The Beggar's Opera and opéra-comique en vaudevilles 1999. *Honours:* RMA Dent Medal 1970, American Musicological Soc. Kinkeldey Prize 1970, 2004, Guggenheim Fellowship 1967–68, 1978–79. *Address:* 1098 Keith Avenue, Berkeley, CA 94708, USA (home).

HEASTON, Nicole; American singer (soprano); b. 1965, Ohio. *Education:* University of Akron, Ohio and Cincinnati Conservatory. *Career:* debut at Houston Grand Opera as Gounod's Juliette; as Pamina, Washington Opera; Anne Trulove, The Rake's Progress, European debut at Montpellier, 1997; concerts with Marc Minkowski at Halle, Brussels and Barcelona, 1995; created Jacqueline Onassis in Michael Dougherty's Jackie O at Houston; concert repertory includes works by Handel and Bach. *Recordings include:* Une Bergère in Gluck's Armide. *Honours:* William Matheus Sullivan Foundation Award 1998. *Current Management:* Zemsky/Green Artists Management, 730 Fifth Avenue, Suite 1802, New York, NY 10019, USA. *Telephone:* (212) 300-8003. *Fax:* (212) 300-8001. *E-mail:* zgartists@aol.com. *Website:* www.zemskygreen.com.

HEATER, Claude; singer (tenor); b. 1930, Oakland, CA, USA. *Education:* studied in Los Angeles, and in Europe with Mario del Monaco and Max Lorenz. *Career:* sang at first as baritone, on radio and TV and in Broadway musicals; Bayerische Staatsoper 1964, in König Hirsch by Henze; sang Wagner roles in Amsterdam, Brussels, Hamburg, Berlin and Milan; Bayreuth Festival 1966, as Siegmund and Melot; other roles included Turiddu, Otello,

Florestan and Samson; guest appearances in South America; sang Tristan at Spoleto 1968 and appeared at Dresden 1968, Barcelona, Bordeaux and Geneva 1968–69; Budapest and Venice 1970. *Recording:* Melot in Tristan und Isolde (conducted by Karl Böhm).

HEBERT, Bliss; American stage director; b. 30 Nov. 1930, Faust, NY. *Education:* Syracuse Univ. with Robert Goldsand, Simone Barrere, Lelia Gousseau. *Career:* debut as Stage Dir, Santa Fe 1957; Gen. Man., Washington Opera Soc. 1960–63; Stage Dir, New York City Opera 1963–75, Metropolitan Opera, New York 1973–75 (debut with Les Contest d'Hoffmann); guest Dir, Juilliard School 1975–76; Dir of opera cos of San Francisco 1963, Washington 1959, Houston 1964, Fort Worth 1966, Caramoor Festival, Katonah, NY 1966, Seattle Opera 1967, Cincinnati 1968, La Gune Festival 1968–, Portland, Oregon 1969, Vancouver 1969, San Diego 1970, New Orleans 1970, Toronto 1972, Baltimore 1972, Tulsa 1975, Miami, FL 1975, Charlotte, NC 1975, Dallas 1977, Shreveport, Los Angeles 1977, Chicago 1983, Montréal 1984, Boston 1984, Cleveland 1988, Opera Northern Ireland 1988, Virginia Opera 1991, Opera Mexico City 1993, Austin Opera 1993, Florentine Opera, Milwaukee 1994; Don Giovanni 1996; Roméo et Juliette at San Diego 1998. *Address:* Pinnacle Arts Management Ltd, 889 Ninth Avenue, Second Floor, New York, NY 10019, USA. *Telephone:* (212) 397-7915. *Fax:* (212) 397-7920.

HEBERT, Pamela; American singer (soprano); b. 31 Aug. 1946, Los Angeles, CA. *Education:* Juilliard School with Maria Callas, Tito Capobianco, Margaret Hoswell and Boris Goldovsky. *Career:* debut in New York City Opera 1972, as Donna Anna; appearances in New York as Mimi, title role in L'Incoronazione di Poppea, Vespina in Haydn's L'Infedeltà delusa and the Composer in Ariadne auf Naxos; frequent concert engagements.

HECHT, Joshua; singer (baritone); b. 1928, New York, NY, USA. *Education:* studied with Lili Wexberg and Eva Hecht in New York and with Walter Tassoni in Rome. *Career:* debut in Baltimore 1953, as Des Grieux in Manon; sang in Boston, Chicago, Miami, Pittsburgh, San Francisco, Seattle and New Orleans; Metropolitan Opera from 1964; further appearances at the New York City Opera and in Graz, Johannesburg, Barcelona, Bucharest, Dublin and Vancouver; roles include the Wanderer in Siegfried, Amfortas, Rigoletto, Iago, Scarpia and the title role in Einstein by Dessau (Gelsenkirchen 1980); sang Prospero in Martin's Der Sturm (The Tempest), Bremen 1992; Australian Opera at Sydney 1994, as Schigolch in Lulu.

HECKMANN, Harald, DPhil; German musicologist; b. 6 Dec. 1924, Dortmund; s. of Dr W. Gg. Heckmann and Marie Heckmann (née Schulte); m. Elisabeth Dohrn 1953; one s. *Education:* Gymnasium, Dortmund and Univ. of Freiburg/Breisgau. *Career:* teacher of church music history, Coll. of Music, Freiburg/Breisgau 1950–54, Asst to Wilibald Gurlitt 1952–54; Dir German History of Music Archives, Kassel 1954–71; Dir German Broadcasting Archives, Frankfurt am Main 1971–91; mem. and Hon. Pres. Int. Asscn of Music Libraries, Int. Inventory of Musical Sources; Bd mem. Robert-Schumann Soc.; Co-Pres. Int. Repertoire of Music Iconography; mem. History of Music Comm., Germany. *Publications include:* Deutsches Musikgeschichtliches Archiv, Katalog der Filmsammlung 1955–72, W. A. Mozart, Thamos, Koenig in Aegypten, Choere und Zwischenaktmusiken 1956, W. A. Mozart, Musik zu Pantomimen und Balletten 1963, Ch. W. Gluck, La Rencontre imprévue (ed. and critic) 1964, Elektronische Datenverarbeitung in der Musikwissenschaft 1967, Das Tenorlied (three vols, co-ed.) 1979–86, Musikalische Ikonographie (co-ed.) 1994; various essays on musicology, including La Sventurata musica 1996, Nachschlagewerke zur Musik 1998; articles about music iconography, music documentation etc. *Honours:* Hon. mem. Int. Schubert Soc., Rotary; Stadtmedaille der Stadt Kassel 1979, Goldene Mozart Medaille der Int. Stiftung Mozarteum, Salzburg 1993, Bundesverdienstkreuz (First Class) 2000. *Address:* Im Vogelshaag 3, 65779 Ruppertshain /Ts, Germany (home).

HEDGES, Anthony John, BMus, MA (Oxon.), LRAM; British composer and academic (retd); b. 5 March 1931, Bicester, Oxon., England; m. Delia Joy Marsden 1957; two s. two d. *Education:* Keble Coll., Oxford. *Career:* teacher, Lecturer, Royal Scottish Acad. of Music 1957–63; Lecturer in Music, Univ. of Hull 1963, Sr Lecturer 1968, Reader in Composition 1978–95; Founder-Conductor The Humberside Sinfonia 1978–81; Chair. Composers' Guild of GB 1972, Jt Chair. 1973, Exec. Cttee mem. 1969–73, 1977–81, 1982–87, Council mem.; mem. Westminster Cen. Music Library. *Compositions include:* orchestral: Comedy Overture 1962, Sinfonia Semplice 1963, Expressions 1964, Concertante Music 1965, Variations on a theme of Rameau 1969, An Ayrshire Serenade 1969, Festival Dances 1976, Symphony No. 1 1972–73, Sinfonia Concertante 1980, Scenes from the Humber 1981, Showpiece 1985, Symphony No. 2 1997, Divertimento for String Orchestra 1997; choral: Gloria, unaccompanied 1965, Epithalamium for chorus and orchestra, to text by Spenser 1969, Bridge for the Living, for chorus and orchestra, to text by Philip Larkin 1976, The Temple of Solomon for chorus and orchestra 1979, I Sing The Birth, for chorus and chamber orchestra 1985, I'll Make Me a World, chorus and orchestra 1990, The Lamp of Liberty, chorus and orchestra 2006; chamber: Five preludes for piano 1959, Ten Bagatelles for piano 2005, Sonatinas for flute, viola, bassoon, trumpet and trombone 1982, Flute Trios 1985, 1989, Piano Quartet 1992; many other chamber works, anthems, partsongs, albums of music for children; music for TV, film and stage. *Recordings include:* Scenes from the Humber, Kingston Sketches, Bridge for the Living, Four Breton Sketches, Four Miniature Dances, Overture: Heigham Sound, Cantilena, Divertimento for string orchestra, An Ayrshire Serenade, Fiddlers Green, A

Cleveland Overture, Festival Dances, Saturday Market Overture, Showpiece, Variations on a Theme of Rameau, Piano Sonata; various solo and chamber works. *Publications include:* Basic Tonal Harmony 1987, Comprehensive Archive in Hull Central Music Library; regular contrib. to The Guardian, The Scotsman, The Glasgow Herald, The Musical Times 1957–63, The Yorkshire Post 1963–73. *Honours:* Hon. DMus (Hull) 1997. *Address:* Malt Shovel Cottage, 76 Old Walkergate, Beverly, East Yorks., HU17 9ER, England (home). *Telephone:* (1482) 860580. *E-mail:* ahedges@westfieldmusic.karoo.co.uk. *Website:* www.westfieldmusic-anthonyhedges.co.uk.

HEDWALL, Lennart, PhD; Swedish composer, conductor and musicologist; b. 16 Sept. 1932, Gothenburg; m. Ingegerd Henrietta Bergman 1957; four s. *Education:* Royal Coll. of Music, Stockholm; studied composition and conducting in Darmstadt, Vienna, Hilversum and Paris. *Career:* debuts, as composer 1950, as professional conductor, Messiah 1954; Conductor, Riksteatern 1958–60, Great Theatre Gothenburg 1962–65, Drottningholmteatern 1966–70, Royal Theatre 1967–68, Örebro Orchestra Soc. 1968–74; teacher, Dramatic School in Gothenburg 1963–67, State Opera School 1968–70, 1974–80, 1985–97; Dir Swedish Nat. Music Museum 1981–83; Dean, Stockholm Univ. 1997; mem. Royal Swedish Acad. of Music, Accad. Filarmonica of Bologna. *Compositions include:* operas: Herr Sleeman Kommer and America, America, The Dress of Birgitta (church opera), Symphony 1 (retrospettiva), 2 (elegiaca), 3 (semplice), 4 (seria), Sagan (symphonic phantasy), Legend, Pezzo pastorale and Intrada for orchestra, Jul igen, a Christmas Rhapsody; several works for string orchestra; concertos for flute, oboe, clarinet, bassoon, violoncello; chamber music: three string quartets and two string trios, and others; organ and piano works; several song cycles; choral pieces and cantatas; stage and TV works; numerous edns of old Swedish music. *Recordings include:* as conductor with Orebro Chamber Orchestra, Värmland Sinfonietta, Musica Vitae and Östersunds Serenade Ensemble; as accompanist, several song recitals; also others as organist and pianist. *Publications include:* Hugo Alfvén (monograph) 1973, Operettas and Musicals 1976, The Swedish Symphony 1983, Wilhelm Peterson-Berger, a biography in pictures 1983, The Concert Life in Åbo 1872–76 1989, Hugo Alfvén, a biography in pictures 1990, The Musical Life in the Manors of Vermland 1770–1830 1992, Form Structures in Roman's Sinfonias 1995, A Survey of The Music in Vermland 1995, Swedish Music History 1996, The Composer Erik Gustav Geijer 2001, Oscar Byström, a biography 2003, Streaks of Light: a Geijer Anthology 2006, Pathos and Tradition (biog. of conductor Tor Mann) 2011, The Tone Poet Carl Jonas Love Almqvist 2014. *Publications:* contrib. to Dagen Nyheter 1957–78, Musikrevy and others. *Honours:* numerous awards including Hon. medal, Royal Swedish Acad. of Music. *Address:* Mårdvägen 37, 16756 Bromma, Sweden (home). *Telephone:* 8269450 (home). *E-mail:* lhedwall@msn.com.

HEELEY, Desmond; stage designer; b. 1 June 1931, West Bromwich, England. *Education:* studied at Shakespeare Memorial Theatre, Stratford. *Career:* debut in La Traviata for Sadler's Wells 1960; productions for Glyndebourne (I Puritani 1960) and ENO (Maria Stuarda 1973); work for the Metropolitan Opera includes Norma 1970, Pelléas et Mélisande 1972, Don Pasquale 1978 and Manon Lescaut 1980; Chicago designs for La Traviata seen at Detroit and Seattle 1996.

HEFTI, David Philip; Swiss composer and conductor; b. 1975, St Gallen. *Education:* Conservatoires of Zürich and Karlsruhe, studied composition, conducting, clarinet and chamber music with Wolfgang Rihm, Cristóbal Halffter, Wolfgang Meyer, Rudolf Kelterborn and Elmar Schmid. *Career:* has appeared at festivals including Ultraschall, Berlin, Wien Modern, Steirischer Herbst, Graz, Menuhin Festival, Gstaad, EuroArt, Prague, Musica de Hoy, Madrid, Beijing Modern, Suntory Festival, Tokyo; Composer-in-Residence, Moritzburg Festival and with Heidelberg Philharmonic; worked with soloists including Fabio Di Càsola, Thomas Grossenbacher, Viviane Hagner, Wolfgang Meyer, Christian Poltéra, Hartmut Rohde, Baiba Skride, Jan Vogler, Antje Weithaas, with conductors including Peter Eötvös, Howard Griffiths, Kent Nagano, Jonathan Nott, Michael Sanderling, Jac van Steen, Mario Venzago and David Zinman, and with Bavarian Radio Symphony Orchestra, German Symphony Orchestra Berlin, Bamberg Symphony Orchestra, German Radio Philharmonic Orchestra, Zurich Tonhalle Orchestra, Vienna Radio Symphony Orchestra, Montreal Symphony Orchestra, Tokyo Sinfonietta, Leipzig String Quartet, Neue Vocalsolisten Stuttgart, Ensemble Modern Frankfurt and Collegium Novum, Zurich; taught at Musikhochschule, Zurich. *Compositions:* compositions for large orchestra, chamber orchestra, string orchestra, chamber music, solo pieces, vocal music, opera. *Honours:* winner of numerous composition competitions including Gustav Mahler in Vienna, Pablo Casals in Prades and George Enescu in Bucharest, Siemens Foundation Composers Prize 2013, Hindemith Prize 2015. *Current Management:* c/o Gabriele Schiller, PR2 Classic, Kreuznacher Strasse 63, 50968 Cologne, Germany. *Telephone:* (221) 381063. *Fax:* (221) 383955. *E-mail:* office@pr2classic.de. *Website:* www.pr2classic.de. *E-mail:* info@hefti.net (office). *Website:* www.hefti.net (office).

HEGAARD, Lars, DipMus, BA; Danish composer; b. 13 March 1950, Svendborg; m. Susanne Taub 1984; four s. *Career:* has played at major festivals in Denmark and Scandinavia, often recorded for radio; has several comms through Danish Arts Foundation. *Compositions include:* orchestra: Symphony No. 1, Symphony No. 2, Space Even More than Time, Letter To My Son, Symphony No. 3, To Populate a Plain, Symphony No. 4, Beings of Light and Darkness; chamber orchestra: Decet, Intersections, The Rolling Force Cello Concerto, The Seasons According to I Ching, Triptych with Objects,

Twine for nine instruments; chamber works: Five Fragments for string quartet, The Four Winds for clarinet, cello and piano, Music for Chameleons for wind quintet, Configurations for alto flute and guitar, Six Studies for two guitars, Song-lines for guitar trio, 13 short pieces for flute, viola and harp, Dreamtracks for flute, clarinet, horn, percussion, guitar and cello, Four Square Dances for saxophone quartet, Partials' Play for flute, guitar and cello, Inside for bass clarinet, percussion and electronics, Beings for flute, clarinet, vibraphone, piano, guitar, violin and cello, Rituals for solo guitar, flute, clarinet, percussion, piano, violin and cello, Four Visions for string quartet, Invocations for organ and two saxophones, Short Cuts for oboe, clarinet, saxophone and bassoon, Singing Sculpture for recorder, violin, cello and guitar, Ambient Voices for violin, clarinet, cello and piano, Octagonal Room for guitar and string quartet; solo works: Variations for guitar, The Conditions of a Solitary Bird for guitar, Canto for cello, The Great Beam... for piano, Worldes Bliss for organ, Labyrinthus for electric guitar, Chains for organ; vocal: Hymns for baritone and sinfonietta, Haiku for soprano, violin and piano, Far Calls, Coming Far for mezzo-soprano, electric guitar and percussion (text by James Joyce), The Dimension of Stillness for soprano, flute, guitar and cello (text by Ezra Pound), Night Flower, Four Poems by Sylvia Plath for mezzo-soprano, percussion, piano, viola and double bass, Nogle Lykkelige Sekunder: Four Poems by Poul Borum for organ and bass, Rituals for guitar and ensemble, Emanations Four Movements for cello and piano 2009, Close Encounters for viola and piano 2009, Four Ways of Looking at One Thing – Four Pieces for violin and piano 2009–10, Like a Cube of Silence – Five Movements for piano trio 2010. *Honours:* Danish Arts Foundation three-year stipendium 1983, Carl and Anne Marie Carl-Nielsen grant 2007. *Address:* Danish Composers' Society, Lautrupsgade 9. 5., 2100 Copenhagen Ø (office); Edition-s, Worsaaesvej 19, 5., 1972 Frederiksberg C, Denmark. *Telephone:* 33-13-54-45 (office). *Fax:* 33-93-30-44 (office). *E-mail:* sales@edition-s.dk (office). *Website:* www.edition-s.dk (office).

HEGARTY, Mary; Irish singer (soprano); b. 1960, Cork. *Education:* Cork School of Music, Aldeburgh and the National Opera Studio in London, studied with Josephine Veasey. *Career:* has sung for Radio Telefis Eireann in Britten's Quatres chansons Françaises and the Brahms Requiem; Bach's Christmas Oratorio with Harry Christophers; Recitals in Ireland, the USA and at the Aix-en-Provence Festival (Une Heure avec Mary Hegarty); Covent Garden debut as a Flowermaiden in Parsifal, followed by Pousette in Manon; English National Opera as Nannetta and Naiad (Ariadne); Appearances with Opera Factory in La Calisto; With Opera North as Leonora in the British premiere of Nielsen's Maskarade (1989) in Ariane et Barbe-Bleue, the Mozart pasticcio The Jewel Box (1991) and as Frasquita; Buxton Festival 1991, in Mozart's Il Sogno di Scipione; Requiem for RTE; Princess Laula in Chabrier's Etoile, (Opera North); Papagena in Magic Flute (ENO); Eurydice in Orpheus in The Underworld, (D'Oyly Carte); Adele in Die Fledermaus, (Dublin Grand Opera Society); Eurydice in Orpheus In the Underworld; Cherubino in The Marriage of Figaro, Elisa in Mozart's Il Re Pastore, The Italian Soprano in Strauss's Capriccio and Gloria in world premiere of Gloria-A Pigtale, Nerina in La Fedeltà Premiata, Tanterabogus in The Fairy Queen; 1996–97 with the English National Opera included Norina in Don Pasquale, Blonde in Die Entführung aus dem Serail and Elvira in L'Italiana in Algeri; Fiorilla in Il Turco In Italia for Garsington in 1996; Susanna in The Marriage of Figaro at Grange Park, 1998; Season 2000 as Jessie in the premiere of Turnage's The Silver Tassie, for ENO, Puccini's Lisette and Donizetti's Adina for Opera North. *Recordings:* solo album: A Voice is Calling; title role in Gilbert and Sullivan's Patience; Eurydice in Offenbach's Orpheus in the Underworld; Mendelssohn Lobgesang. *Honours:* Winner, Golden Voice of Ireland, 1984; Bursary for study at Aldeburgh; Irish Life, Sunday Independent Classical Music Award, 1988; Allied Irish Bank, RTE National Entertainments Award for Classical Section, 1987.

HEGEDUS, Olga; British fmr cellist; b. 18 Oct. 1920, London, England. *Education:* London Violoncello School, studied privately with Pierre Fournier. *Career:* debut recital at Wigmore Hall, London; solo recitals; many television appearances with trios, chamber ensembles and others; mem. Incorporated Soc. of Musicians, Musicians' Union. *Recordings:* Art of Fugue, Bach, and Musical Offering, with Tilford Festival Ensemble; The Curlew, Warlock, with Haffner Ensemble; Vivaldi Motets with Teresa Berganza and English Chamber Orchestra; Dvořák Serenade, with English Chamber Orchestra Ensemble; Schubert Quintet in C, with Gabrieli Quartet. *Publications:* contrib. to A Pictorial Review, English Chamber Orchestra 1983. *Address:* 8 Kensington Place, London, W8 7PT, England (office). *Telephone:* (20) 7727-4463 (home).

HEICHELE, Hildegard; German singer (soprano); b. Sept. 1947, Obernburg am Main; m. Ulrich Schwalb. *Education:* Munich Musichochschule. *Career:* debut at Klagenfurt, as Jennie in Aufstieg und fall der Stadt Mahagonny; Munich Staatsoper from 1971, notably as Mozart's Zerlina, Despina, Susanna and Ilia; Appearances in Vienna, Cologne (as Gretel), Karlsruhe (as Adina), Berlin, Zürich and Barcelona; Covent Garden 1977, 1983, as Adele in Die Fledermaus; Frankfurt 1981, in the Symphony of a Thousand, by Mahler; Monte Carlo 1982, Brussels 1984, as Susanna; Bayreuth Festival 1984, as the Woodbird in Siegfried; Sang at Kassel and Hanover 1988, as Elsa and Elisabeth; Concert engagements in Vienna, Graz and Venice (1985). *Recordings include:* Mahler's 8th Symphony; Egisto by Cavalli; Bach Magnificat, Handel Dettinger Te Deum; Video of Die Fledermaus (Covent Garden 1983).

HEIDEMANN, Stefan; German singer (baritone); b. 1961. *Education:* studied in Hanover and with Joseph Greindl. *Career:* sang at Nuremberg Opera, 1988–91, Düsseldorf from 1991; Komische Oper Berlin, 1993, as Guglielmo, Ford in Falstaff, 1996; Season 1995–96 at Düsseldorf as Wagner's Wolfram, Falke in Die Fledermaus, and in the premiere of Gervaise Macquart by Klebe; Other roles include Lortzing's Tsar Peter, Mozart's Count, Nicolai's Herr Fluth, and Marcello in La Bohème; Guest engagements in concert and opera throughout Germany; Sang in the premiere production of Beuys by Franz Hummel, Düsseldorf and Vienna, 1998. *Current Management:* c/o Opernagentur Inge Tennigkeit, Kempener Strasse 4, 40474 Düsseldorf, Germany. *Telephone:* (211) 5160060. *Fax:* (211) 51600616. *E-mail:* opera@tennigkeit-ag.de. *Website:* www.tennigkeit-ag.de.

HEIDSIECK, Eric; French pianist; b. 21 Aug. 1936, Reims. *Education:* Ecole Normale de Musique, Paris, Paris Conservatoire with Marcel Ciampi, studied with Alfred Cortot and Wilhelm Kempff. *Career:* many appearances in London, France and elsewhere from 1955; Mozart's last 12 concertos in Paris, 1964, and the Beethoven Sonatas (1969, 1979); frequent chamber music engagements, notably with Paul Tortelier; repertory also includes the Suites of Handel; Prof., Lyon Conservatoire 1980–98. *Recordings include:* Le Tombeau de Couperin, by Ravel; concertos by Mozart and Beethoven's Sonatas. *Publications include:* Cadenzas to Mozart's Piano Concertos. *Honours:* Paris Conservatoire Premier Prix 1954.

HEIFETZ, Daniel Alan; American violinist and teacher; b. 20 Nov. 1948, Kansas City, MO. *Education:* studied with Theodore Norman, Los Angeles Conservatory with Sascha Jacobson, Israel Baker and Heimann Weinstine, Curtis Inst. of Music, Philadelphia with Efrem Zimbalist, Ivan Galamian and Jascha Brodsky. *Career:* debut as soloist in the Tchaikovsky Violin Concerto with the National Symphony Orchestra of Washington, DC, on tour in New York; thereafter regular tours of North America and the world; faculty mem., Peabody Conservatory of Music, Baltimore 1980. *Honours:* first prize Merriweather-Post Competition, Washington, DC 1969, fourth prize Tchaikovsky Competition, Moscow 1978.

HEIFETZ, Robin Julian, DMA; American composer; b. 1 Aug. 1951, Los Angeles, CA. *Education:* UCLA with Paul Chihara and Roy Travis, Univ. of Illinois with Salvatore Martirano and Ben Johnston. *Career:* Composer-in-Residence, Shiftelsen Electronic Studio, Stockholm 1978–79; worked at various music depts in Canada and the USA; Dir of the Centre for Experimental Music, Hebrew Univ. of Jerusalem 1980. *Compositions include:* two Pieces for piano 1972, Leviathan for piano 1975, Chirp for euphonium and piano 1976, Susurrus for computer and tape 1978, Child of the Water for piano 1978, For Anders Lundberg Mardrom 29 30 10 for tape 1979, A Clear and Present Danger for tape 1980, Spectre for tape 1980, Wanderer for synthesizer 1980, The Unforgiving Minute for nine instruments 1981, In the Last, Frightened Moment for tape 1980, The Vengeance for synthesizer 1980, The Arc of Crisis for tape 1982, A Bird in Hand is Safer than one Overheard for two or more performers 1983, At Daggers Drawn for tape 1983. *Honours:* awards at the Concours International de Musique Electro-Acoustique, Bourges, France 1979, 1981, International Computer Music Competition, Boston 1983.

HEILGENDORFF, Simone, Mag. Art, MA, DrPhil; German violist and musicologist; *Reader and Researcher, University of Salzburg;* b. 4 April 1961, Opladen. *Education:* Staatliche Hochschule für Musik im Rheinland, Cologne, Albert-Ludwigs-Univ., Freiburg, Univ. of Michigan, USA, Humboldt Universität zu Berlin. *Career:* fmr mem. symphonic orchestras Junge Deutsche Philharmonie, Serenata Basel (chamber orchestra), Work in Progress; performances of contemporary music with Ensemble Modern (ISCM-Ens), Aventure Freiburg, Contemporary Ensemble (Aspen Music Festival 1991); Founder-mem. Kairos Quartet, specializing in contemporary music, Berlin 1996; performances of early music with Ensemble für Alte Musik, Dresden and Concerto Köln; Visiting Prof. of Musicology, Univ. of Potsdam 2004–06; Full Prof. of Applied Musicology, Univ. of Klagenfurt, Austria 2007–13; Visiting Prof. of Musicology, Hochschule für Musik, Detmold April–Sept. 2013; mem. Scholarly-Artistic Bd, John Cage Organ Foundation, Halberstadt 2006–, Advisory Bd, Österreichische Musikzeitschrift 2011–; Reader and Researcher, int. research project, New Music Festivals as Agorai – Their Formation and Impact of Warsaw Autumn, Festival d'Automne in Paris and Wien Modern Since 1980, Univ. of Salzburg, Austria 2013–. *Recordings:* numerous CD productions, including Georg Friedrich Haas String Quartets Nos 1 and 2 (German Critics' Award 2005) 2004. *Publications:* various musicological publs; Experimentelle Inszenierung von Sprache und Musik, Vergleichende Analysen zu Dieter Schnebel und John Cage 2002. *Address:* Ringstrasse 41/42, 12205 Berlin, Germany (home). *E-mail:* simoneheilgendorff@gmx.net (office). *Website:* www.uni-salzburg.at/newmusic (office); www.kairosquartett.de (office).

HEILMANN, Uwe; singer (tenor); b. 7 Sept. 1960, Darmstadt, German; m. Tomoko Nakamura. *Education:* studied in Detmold with Helmut Kretschmar. *Career:* sang at Detmold from 1981 as Tamino, Don Ottavio and the Italian Singer in Rosenkavalier; Stuttgart Staatsoper from 1985, notably as Tamino, Belmonte, Don Ottavio, Cassio in Otello and Max in Der Freischütz; Munich Staatsoper as Don Ottavio, Vienna as Tamino; sang Pylades in Iphigénie en Tauride at the Deutsche Oper Berlin; appearances at the Salzburg and Ludwigsburg Festivals 1988–89, including Max; concert engagements and lieder recitals, notably in works by Schubert and Wolf; sang Cassio in Metropolitan Opera Gala 1991; season 1993–94 as Belmonte at La Scala and

Steuermann at the Met. *Recordings include:* Tamino in Die Zauberflöte, conducted by Solti; Belmonte in Die Entführung conducted by Hogwood; Die schöne Mullerin, with James Levine; Haydn's Orfeo ed Euridice, with Cecilia Bartoli (L'Oiseau Lyre 1997).

HEIMANN, Robert; singer (baritone); b. 1958, Boston, USA. *Education:* Stanford Univ., studied in New York. *Career:* sang in musicals on Broadway from 1981; concert appearances at Carnegie Hall, including Linda di Chamounix 1993; European debut, Belfast Opera 1991, as Mozart's Figaro; Leipzig Opera from 1991, as Rossini's Figaro, Guglielmo, Papageno, Count Luna in Il Trovatore, and Leporello; guest engagements in Brussels 1992, Israel and Brunswick (as Silvio in Pagliacci).

HEININEN, Paavo; Finnish composer; b. 18 Jan. 1938, Järvenpää. *Education:* Sibelius Acad., Helsinki, Coll. of Music, Cologne, Germany and Juilliard School of Music, New York, USA. *Career:* teacher of theory and composition, Turku Inst. of Music, Turku, Sibelius Acad., Helsinki 1966–. *Compositions include:* orchestral works: Symphony No. 1 1958, revised 1960, Piano Sonata, Symphony No. 3 1969, revised 1977, Dia 1979; works for solo instrument: Gymel for bassoon and tape 1978, Concerto for piano and orchestra No. 3 1981, Cello Concerto 1985, Violin Concerto 1993, Lightings 1998, Muraski in Casa Ando 1998, What an Evening, What a Lightning for ensemble 1999, Bluekeys for piano 1999; chamber music: Jeu I and II 1980; vocal and choral works: The Silken Drum (opera) 1980–83, Floral View with Maidens Singing (folk melody) 1980–83, Dicta (computer music) 1980–83, Another Heaven, Blooming Earth for male chorus 1999. *Recordings include:* Adagio with Royal Philharmonic Orchestra under Walter Süsskind; Da Camera Magna; Sonatine, 1957; Sonatina Della Primavera; The Autumns, Finnish Radio Chamber Choir under Harald Andersén; Maiandros, tape composition; Discantus I; Touching; Concerto III with Paavo Heininen on Piano, the Sibelius Symphony Orchestra under Ulf Söderblom.

HEINIÖ, Mikko, PhD; Finnish composer, musicologist and academic; b. 18 May 1948, Tampere; s. of Seppo Heiniö and Marja Heiniö; m. Riitta Pylvänäinen 1977; one s. one d. *Education:* Univ. of Helsinki, Hochschüle der Künste, West Berlin, Sibelius Acad. *Career:* composer 1972–; teacher, Univ. of Helsinki 1977–85; Prof. of Musicology, Univ. of Turku 1985–2005; Pres. Finnish Composers' Soc. 1992–2010; mem. Bd, Teosto (Finnish Copyright Soc.) 1984–2014, Vice-Pres. 1999–2014. *Compositions include:* orchestral: nine piano concertos, Concerto for French horn and orchestra 1978, Concerto for Orchestra 1982, Possible Worlds (Symphony No. 1) 1987, Dall'ombra all'ombra 1992, Trias 1995, Symphony No. 2 (Songs of Night and Love) 1997, On the Rocks for orchestra 1998, Minne for string orchestra 1996, Envelope for Haydn's Trumpet Concerto 2002, Sonata da chiesa for brass and percussion 2005, Alla madre, violin concerto 2007, Maestoso 2008, Event Horizon for wind orchestra 2012, Concerto for organ and orchestra 2012–13; chamber music: Duo for Violin and Piano 1979, Brass Mass 1979, Piano Trio 1988, In G for violoncello and piano 1988, Wintertime for harp and marimba/ vibraphone 1990, Piano Quintet 1993, Relay for cello and violin 1998, Treno della notte for clarinet, violin, cello and piano 2000, Sextet for baritone, flute, clarinet, violin, cello and piano 2000, Café au lait for flute, clarinet, violin, cello and piano 2006, Canzona for string trio 2006, Piano Quartet (The Voice of the Tree) 2006; vocal: Landet som icke är for children's choir and piano 1980, The Shadow of the Future for soprano and brass instruments 1980, Vuelo de alambre for soprano and orchestra 1983, La for piano and four voices 1985, Genom kvällen for piano, mixed choir and string orchestra (Piano Concerto No. 4) 1987, Wind Pictures for choir and orchestra 1991, Three Morning Songs for baritone and piano 2003, Moon Concerto for mezzo soprano, piano and orchestra (Piano Concerto No. 8) 2007–08, Song of Late Summer for baritone and orchestra 2010, Maria Suite for mixed choir 2011, Concerto for organ and orchestra 2013, Five Preludes for guitar 2013, Evening for mixed choir, clarinet and cello 2014, Through Green Glass for guitar 2014, April Evenings for Black Twins (sonata for two pianos) 2015; works for the stage: Hermes for piano, soprano, string orchestra and dance theatre 1994 (Piano Concerto No. 6) 1994, The Knight and the Dragon, church opera 2000, Khora for piano, five percussionists and dance theatre (Piano Concerto No. 7) 2001, The Hour of the Snake, opera in two acts 2003–05, Eric XIV, opera in three acts 2008–10. *Recordings include:* Notturno di fiordo for flute and harp, Genom kvällen, Vuelo de alambre, Possible Worlds, Wind Pictures, Duo for Violin and Piano, Piano Quintet, Hermes, Piano Trio, In G, Wintertime, The Knight and the Dragon, Sextet, Symphony No. 2, Alla Madre, Café au Lait, Deductions, Ritornelli, Three Folk Songs, Luceat, Framtidens skugga, Landet som icke är, Pikavuaro Turkku, Eric XIV, Lindgreniana, Festive March for Quiet Men, Mind of Dust, Minimba 1, Maria Suite, Evening, Five Preludes for guitar, Through Green Glass. *Publications:* Contemporary Finnish Composers and their background 1981, Contemporary Finnish Music 1982, The Idea of Innovation and Tradition 1984, The Reception of New Classicism in Finnish Music 1985, The Twelve Tone Age in Finnish Music 1986, Postmodern Features in New Finnish Music 1988, Contextualisation in the research of art music 1992, Finnish Composers (co-author) 1994, Finnish Music History 4: Music of Our Time 1995, From Tones to Words 1997, The Reception of New Finnish Operas 1975–1985 1999. *Honours:* mem. Royal Swedish Acad. of Music 2004; Finlandia Prize for non-fiction 1997, Suomi Prize 2007. *Address:* Mustainveljestenkuja 2A, 20700 Turku, Finland. *E-mail:* mikko.heinio@ composers.fi. *Website:* www.fimic.fi/fimic/heinio+mikko.

HEINRICH, Siegfried; German conductor and director; b. 10 Jan. 1935, Dresden. *Education:* studied in Dresden and Frankfurt am Main. *Career:* debut as Sänger im Dresdner Kreuzchor 1948; Conductor Frankfurt Chamber Orchestra 1957; Artistic Dir Hersfeld Festival operas and concerts from 1961; Lecturer, Music Acad. of Kassel; Künstlerischer Leiter des J.S. Bach-Institutes und Bachchores Frankfurt (M) 2000; Conductor Radio Symphony Orchestras of Prague, Frankfurt am Main, Hanover, Luxemburg, ORTF, France, Budapest, Warsaw, Katowice, Kraków, Venice, Stuttgart; concert tours throughout Europe; new interpretations of Bach's The Art of the Fugue, Beethoven's opera Fidelio with parts of Leonore I, Handel's Messiah, Monteverdi's Marian Vespers, Orfeo, Poppea, Il ritorno d'Ulisse; Künstlerischer Direktor für Oper und Festspielkonzerte, Bad Hersfeld. *Recordings:* Bach, Beethoven, Bizet, Brahms, Britten, Bruckner, Carissimi, Dvořák, Honegger, Liszt, Mahler, Mozart, Monteverdi, Ockeghem, Spohr, Telemann, Weber. *Publications:* prospectuses and press reviews from Jubilate Schallplatten, Bärenreiter. *Honours:* Hon. Prof.; Bundesverdienstmedaille 1976, Goethe-Medaille 1983, Bundesverdienstkreuz 1988. *Address:* Arbeitkreis für Musik e V, Nachtigallenstr 7, 36251 Bad Hersfeld, Germany.

HEINRICH, Susanne; German viola da gamba player. *Education:* Meistersinger Conservatory, Nuremberg, Frankfurt State Acad. of Music, study with Wieland Kuijken at Royal Conservatory of The Hague. *Career:* founder mem., Charivari Agréable 1993; mem. baroque ensemble The Palladians 1994–; Chief Ed. Charivari Agréable Publications; fmr Prof. for Viols and Violone, Guildhall School of Music and Drama, London; has performed and recorded with leading period-instrument ensembles of Europe, including the English Concert, Taverner Consort, King's Consort, Parley of Instruments, Orchestra of the Age of Enlightenment. *Recordings:* over 15 recordings with Charivari Agréable, including Modus Phantasticus: Viol Music from 18th Century Germany 2003; Palladians: The Devil's Trill, Bach, Brandenburg Concertos, La Guitarra Espanola 2007, Mr Abel's Fine Airs: Music for Solo Viola da Gamba (Gramophone Editor's Choice Award) 2008. *Publications:* contribs to various journals including The Consort, Chelys. *Telephone:* (1865) 744128 (office). *E-mail:* enquiriesSH@susanneheinrich.co.uk (office). *Website:* www .susanneheinrich.co.uk.

HEINSEN, Geerd, PhD; German journalist; b. 29 Jan. 1945, s. of Hans Adolf Heinsen. *Education:* studies in Berlin, Freiburg, Harvard Univ. and UCLA, USA, Berlin Free Univ. *Career:* Ed. Orpheus Oper International magazine. *Address:* Orpheus, Charlottenstrasse 53, 14059 Berlin, Germany (office). *E-mail:* heinsenorpheus@t-online.de (home); info@orpheusoper.de (office). *Website:* www.orpheusoper.de (office).

HEISSER, Jean-François; French pianist, conductor and artistic director; *Artistic Director, Orchestre Poitou Charentes*; b. 7 Dec. 1950, St Etienne. *Education:* Paris Conservatoire with Vlado Perlemuter. *Career:* many appearances in Europe and North America 1975–; recital engagements with violinist Regis Pasquier 1976–; soloist with the Nouvel Orchestre Philharmonique de Radio-France 1976–85; Prof. Paris Conservatoire 1991–; Pres. Maurice Ravel Acad., Saint-Jean-de-Luz 1993–; repertory includes Beethoven, Schubert, Dukas, Berio and Schoenberg; Artistic Dir, Orchestre Poitou Charentes 2001–; also Artistic Dir Soirées Musicales d'Arles. *Recordings include:* Albeniz Iberia, Beethoven Sonatas, Bagatelles and Diabelli Variations, Paul Dukas Piano Works, Granados, Turina, Falla, and Martinů Double Concerto. *Honours:* six Premier Prix, Paris Conservatoire 1973, winner, International Competition at Jaén, Spain 1974. *Current Management:* Caroline Martin Musique, 126 rue Vieille du Temple, 75003 Paris, France. *Telephone:* 1-42-74-49-01. *Fax:* 1-42-74-49-17. *E-mail:* caroline.martin .musique@orange.fr. *Website:* www.caroline-martin-musique.com; www .jeanfrancoisheisser.com.

HÉJA, Domonkos; Hungarian conductor and percussionist; *Music Director, Danubia Youth Symphony Orchestra*; b. 20 Dec. 1974, Budapest. *Education:* Bartók Conservatory, Ferenc Liszt Acad. of Music. *Career:* debut in Budapest 1993; founder and Music Dir, Danubia Youth Symphony Orchestra 1993–; Asst Conductor, Budapest Festival Orchestra 1995–96; Principal Conductor, Robert Schumann Philharmonie Chemnitz 2005–; regularly conducts Budapest Philharmonic Orchestra, Budapest Symphony Orchestra, Matáv Symphony Orchestra, Budapest Opera; has also conducted Slovak Philharmonic, Kosice State Symphony, Macedonian Philharmonic, Deutsche Symphonie Orchester Berlin, Tokyo City Philharmonic, Orchestra di Lazio Roma, Orchestra of Antwerp Conservatory. *Recording:* M. Haydn St Theresienmesse. *Honours:* first prize National Percussion Competition 1990, first prize Int. Conductors Competition, Budapest 1998, Caripodis Prize, Mitropoulos Competition, Athens 1998, Ferenc Liszt Prize 2003, Artisjus Prize 2005, László Lajtha Prize 2006. *Current Management:* c/o Monika Ott, Berliner Konzertagentur, Dramburgerstrasse 46, 12683 Berlin, Germany. *Telephone:* (30) 5144858. *Fax:* (30) 5142659. *E-mail:* berlinkonzert.ott@t-online.de. *Website:* www.berlinkonzert-ott.de.

HELD, Alan; American singer (bass-baritone); b. Washburn, Ill. *Education:* Millikin Univ., Wichita State Univ. *Career:* appearances with nearly every major opera house in the world since his professional debut in 1986; has appeared nearly 200 times at Metropolitan Opera, New York in numerous roles, including title role in Wozzeck 2005, 2011; noted specialist in Wagner and Strauss, has appeared at Royal Opera House, Covent Garden, Paris Opera, Vienna Opera, Bavarian State Opera, Lyric Opera of Chicago, San Francisco Opera, Teatro Liceu, La Monnaie, Teatro Real, Hamburg State Opera, Frankfurt Opera, Teatro alla Scala and Washington Nat. Opera (more than 20 roles); has appeared with leading orchestras, including Vienna

Philharmonic, Berlin Philharmonic, Chicago Symphony, Los Angeles Philharmonic, Cleveland Orchestra, Nat. Symphony Orchestra, Pittsburgh Symphony Orchestra; vocal teacher and clinician, regularly gives public masterclasses at Yale Univ. *Recordings include:* Hänsel und Gretel, Cardillac, Rusalka, Das Rheingold, Fidelio. *Honours:* Hon. DHumLitt (Millikin Univ.); numerous awards, winner of several vocal competitions, including the Birgit Nilsson Prize 1991. *Current Management:* c/o Caroline Woodfield, Opus 3 Artists, 470 Park Avenue South, New York, 10016, USA. *E-mail:* cwoodfield@opus3artists.com. *Website:* www.opus3artists.com; www.alanheld.com.

HELESFAI, Andrea; Hungarian/Swiss violinist; b. 18 Nov. 1948, Budapest, Hungary. *Education:* Béla Bartók Conservatoire, Franz Liszt Univ. of Music; studied with Vilmos Tátrai, András Mihály, Johanna Martzy and Henryk Szeryng. *Career:* debut in Budapest aged 11; mem. Hungarian Nat. Philharmonie, Hungarian Chamber Orchestra, Budapest Chamber Ensemble (often as soloist), Zürich Chamber Orchestra 1973–75; First Violinist, Tonhalle Orchestra, Zurich 1975–2013; frequent int. concert tours with the Tonhalle Orchestra; second concert master in Camerata Zurich, Barock Strings; numerous appearances as soloist in Germany, Switzerland, UK and Brazil; frequent appearances on radio and TV; Founder Trio Turicum, chamber music with piano with Werner Bärtschi, Zsuzsanna Sirokay, Walter Prossnitz, Patrizio Mazzola (Duo Bern-Budapest); tutor of violin at Music Acad. of Basel 1991–94, of violin and chamber music at Hochschule Hottingen/Zurich 1998–2013; numerous CD, radio and TV recordings; mem. various professional ensembles, extemporized music and albums of own compositions. *Recordings:* Béla Bartók: 44 Duos for 2 Violins (with Christopher Whiting and E. von Dohnányi), Serenade Op. 10 (with Trio Turicum), M. J. Rumi: Where Everything is Musik (Reshad Feild recites Poems of Rumi with music extemporized and composed by Andrea Helesfai), Inspiration music for violin (extemporized, composed and played by Andrea Helesfai), For My Friends (works by Frank Martin, Heinz Marti and Charles Ives). *Honours:* Award Winner, Int. Mozart Violin Competition, Salzburg. *Current Management:* c/o Roland Meier, Kultur Erleben. *Telephone:* (44) 2520012. *E-mail:* kultur-erleben@bluewin.ch. *Website:* www.kultur-erleben.ch. *Address:* Lerchenhalde 20, 8703 Erlenbach, Switzerland. *Telephone:* (44) 361-7939. *E-mail:* ah@andreahelesfai.ch; andrea@helesfai.ch. *Website:* www.andreahelesfai.ch.

HELEY, John; British cellist; b. 1948, London, England. *Education:* Guildhall School of Music with William Pleeth. *Career:* sub-Prin. Cellist, Royal Philharmonic Orchestra 1970–80; Prin. Cello, Orchestra of St John's, Smith Square 1977–; freelance career from 1981, with chamber recitals with London Sinfonietta and other ensembles; Assoc. Prin. Cellist, Academy of St Martin-in-the-Fields from 1986, including solo appearances, Second Cello, Academy of St Martin-in-the-Fields Chamber Ensemble 1997–. *Address:* c/o Academy of St Martin in the Fields, 8 Baltic Street East, London, EC1Y 0UP, England (office). *Telephone:* (1353) 615665 (home). *E-mail:* johnheley@ntlworld.com (home).

HELFRICH, Paul M., BMus, MMus, DMA; American composer; b. 5 May 1955, Philadelphia. *Education:* Pennsylvania State University, Temple University, studied with Clifford Taylor and Maurice Wright. *Career:* owner, Nu Trax Recording Studio, Upper Darby, PA, 1981–; Sr Project Manager, 1987–91, Asst Dir, Exhibit Development, 1991–, Franklin Institute Science Museum, PA. *Compositions include:* Sine Nomine for brass chorale, 1974; Metamorphosis 1 for string orchestra, 1976; Theme and Five Variations for string orchestra and percussion, 1977; Five Short pieces for piano, 1977; Sonata Allegro in G for symphonic wind ensemble, 1978; Winds from a longer Distance, for tape and seven dancers, 1989; Song for healing, tape and solo dancer, 1990; The Robot Game Show, for tape, 1990; Movie soundtracks: Spirits in the Valley II, 1991, The Alchemist's Cookbook, 1991. *Address:* 130 Cunningham Avenue, Upper Darby, PA 19082, USA.

HELIN, Jacquelyn, BM, MA, DMA; pianist; b. 24 Sept. 1951, Chicago, IL, USA. *Education:* Univ. of Oregon 1973, Yale Univ. School of Music, Stanford Univ., Univ. of Texas. *Career:* performances at Wigmore Hall, London, The Chagall Museum, Nice, American Embassy, Paris, Merkin Hall and Town Hall, New York, Dumbarton, Oaks, The Corcoran Gallery, Hirshhorn Museum, Washington, DC and The Brooklyn Coll. Conservatory of Music; the Dame Myra Hess Series; the Beethoven Discovery Series, the Aspen Music Festival; featured artist, PBS television programme honouring Virgil Thomson's 90th birthday; premiered Joan Tower's Piano Concerto with Hudson Valley Philharmonic 1986; numerous radio broadcasts. *Recordings:* For Musical Heritage, Virgil Thomson Ballet and Film Scores for Piano.

HELLAWELL, Piers, BA, MA; British composer and academic; b. 14 July 1956, Chinley, Derbyshire, England. *Education:* New Coll., Oxford. *Career:* composer-in-residence, Queen's Univ. Belfast 1981–85, Lecturer in Music 1986–; Northern Ireland Co-ordinator, European Music Year 1985; regular broadcasts on BBC Radio 3. *Compositions:* Xenophon 1985, How Should I Your True Love Know 1986, Sound Carvings from Rano Raraku 1988, Das Leonora Notenbuch 1989, The Erratic Aviator's Dance 1989, Memorial Cairns 1992, River and Shadow 1993, Victory Boogie-Woogie 1993, High Citadels 1994, Truth or Consequences 1994, Camera Obscura 1994, Sound Carvings from the Ice Wall 1995, Takla Makan 1995, Do Not Disturb for youth chorus 1996, Let's Dance for percussion 1996, Sound Carvings from the Water's Edge for 11 strings 1996, The Building of Goves for piano quartet 1998. *Address:* c/o Department of Music, Queen's University Belfast, Belfast, BT7 1NN, Northern Ireland.

HELLEKANT, Charlotte; Swedish singer (mezzo-soprano); b. 15 Jan. 1962, Hogalid. *Education:* Eastman School of Music with Jean DeGaetani, Curtis Inst. *Career:* opera engagements include Cherubino for Portland and Washington Operas, Dorabella for the Canadian Opera Company, Charlotte and the Composer in Ariadne for Glimmerglass Opera and Musetta in Leoncavallo's Bohème at St Louis; season 1995–96 as Bartók's Judith with the Orchestre de Paris, Charlotte at Washington, the Page in Salome for the Metropolitan Opera (debut role) and Ino in Semele at Aix-en-Provence; Contemporary roles include Lotte in Bose's Werther at Santa Fe, Erika in Barber's Vanessa, Cherubino in Corigliano's Ghosts of Versailles at Chicago, the leading role in Bergman's The Singing Tree, for Finnish National Opera and Nastassja in Krasa's Verlobung in Traum; Concerts include Marguerite in La Damnation de Faust (Stockholm Philharmonic Orchestra), Mahler's 2nd Symphony (San Francisco Symphony Orchestra), Les Nuits d'Eté (Cleveland) Mahler's Rückert Lieder and Das Lied von der Erde (Netherlands Radio Philharmonic Orchestra); Berlioz L'Enfance du Christ with John Nelson and Mozart's Requiem under Neeme Järvi; Berio's Epiphanies with the composer conducting, Des Knaben Wunderhorn with the Swedish Radio Symphony Orchestra and Le Martyre de Saint Sebastien; Season 1997 as Cherubino at the Opéra Bastille, Salzburg debut as Amando in Ligeti's Le Grand Macabre, and Charlotte for New Israeli Opera; season 1999–2000 as the Berlioz Marguerite at Salzburg, Nicklausse in Hoffmann at Antwerp and Varvara in Katya Kabanova at Amsterdam. *Recordings include:* Krasa's Verlobung in Traum; Mahler's 2nd Symphony; Ligeti's Le Grand Macabre. *Current Management:* c/o Shirley Thomson, Harrison Parrott Ltd, 5-6 Albion Court, Albion Place, London, W6 0QT, England. *E-mail:* shirley.thomson@harrisonparrott.co.uk. *Website:* www.harrisonparrott.com.

HELLELAND, Arild; singer (tenor); b. 29 Nov. 1949, Norway. *Education:* studied in Oslo, Bergen and Gothenburg. *Career:* concert appearances throughout Scandinavia; Norwegian State Opera at Oslo from 1989, as Janek in The Makropulos Case, Eisenstein in Die Fledermaus, and Mime in Wagner's Ring (also at Helsinki 1996); Deutsche Oper Berlin 1994–95, as Shuisky in Boris Godunov, Monostatos in Die Zauberflöte; Royal Opera, Stockholm in A Dreamplay by Lidholm; Sellem in The Rake's Progress on Swedish television; Edinburgh and other festival engagements; sang Mime in Siegfried at Helsinki 1998.

HELLER, Richard Rainer, DipMus; composer; b. 19 April 1954, Vienna, Austria; m. Shihomi Inoue 1980. *Education:* Hochschule für Musik und Darstellende Kunst, Vienna. *Career:* numerous performances of own works in Argentina, Austria, Belgium, Bulgaria, Czechoslovakia, Denmark, Egypt, France, Germany, Greece, Hungary, Italy, Japan, Kazakhstan, The Netherlands, Romania, Russia, Switzerland, Spain, Saudi Arabia, South Africa, Turkey, Uruguay, Yugoslavia; teacher of composition and music theory, Music Acad., Augsburg, Germany 1979–. *Compositions include:* Concerto for violin, Concerto for two pianos and orchestra, Sinfonietta for wind orchestra, Concerto for bass clarinet, Concerto for marimba, Concertino for orchestra, Concerto per fiati, Toccata for wind orchestra, Novelette for piano trio, Trois Moments musicaux for guitar quartet, String Quartet, Cellophonie for eight violoncellos, Statement for string trio, Elegy on texts out of Duineser Elegien by R. M. Rilke, Ballade for piano four hands, various pieces for chamber ensembles, songs, solo pieces for piano, organ, bass clarinet. *Recordings:* Augsburger Gitarrenquartett; Organ-piano; numerous music recordings.

HELLERMANN, William, MA, DMA; American composer; b. 15 July 1939, Wisconsin; m. 1985; one s. one d. *Education:* Columbia Univ. School of Arts, private study with Stefan Wolpe. *Career:* Composer in Residence, Center for Culture and Performing Arts, State Univ. of New York at Buffalo 1977; mem. BMI, ACA. *Compositions include:* Time and Again, for orchestra 1967, Anyway..., for orchestra 1976, But the Moon..., for guitar and orchestra 1975, Tremble, for solo guitar, Squeek for desk chair 1978, Post/Pone for guitar and 5 instruments 1990, Hoist by Your Own Ritard 1993. *Recordings include:* Ariel, for electronic tape 1967, At Sea, Ek-Stasis I, Passages 13–The Fire. *Publications include:* Beyond Categories, 1981; Experimental Music, 1985; Scores: Row Music, Tip of the Iceberg, Time and Again for symphony orchestra; Long Island Sound; Distances/Embraces; Circle Music 2 and 3; Passages 13–The Fire; To the Last Drop; Ek-Stasis I; numerous articles published. *Honours:* Prix de Rome, American Academy 1972, Nat. Endowment for the Arts Fellowship 1976–79.

HELLMANN, Claudia; German singer (mezzo-soprano); b. 1931, Berlin. *Education:* studied in Berlin. *Career:* debut at Oper Munster 1958–60; Stuttgart Staatsoper 1960–66, Nuremberg 1966–75; appearances at Bayreuth Festival 1958–61, as Wellgunde and a Flower Maiden; La Scala Milan 1963, as Flosshilde; sang in concert at the Salzburg Festival 1961–85; Hamburg Staatsoper from 1960, Théâtre de la Monnaie Brussels 1963–67; other roles have included Marcellina, Magdalena in Die Meistersinger, Mistress Quickly, Fidalma in Matrimonio Segreto and Frau von Hufnagel in Henze's Der Junge Lord; many concert and oratorio appearances. *Recordings:* Ismene in Orff's Antigonae, Bruckner's F minor Mass; Die Walküre; Bach's Easter Oratorio; Bach Church Cantatas.

HELLWIG, Klaus; German pianist and educator; b. 3 Aug. 1941, Essen; m. Mi-Joo Lee. *Education:* Folkwang Hochschule Essen with Detlek Kraus, in Paris with Pierre Sancan; summer courses with Guido Agosti and Wilhelm Kempff. *Career:* concerts throughout Europe, USA, Canada, Asutralia, Brazil, Far and Middle East, all German radio stations, BBC London, NHK Tokyo;

Prof., Univ. of the Arts, Berlin. *Recordings:* FX Mozart Concerti in C and E Flat, Cologne Radio Orchestra, conductor Roland Bader (Schwann); Haydn Concerto in D, Mozart Concerto KV 537; Bach Inventions; recordings of 20 other works; Carl Reinecke: The Four Piano Concerti. *Honours:* Prize at the Concours Internationale M. Long–J. Thibaud, Paris 1965, First Prize, Concorso Internazionale G. B. Viotti, Vercelli, Italy 1966. *Address:* Mommsenstrasse 58, 10629 Berlin, Germany (home). *E-mail:* hellwig.lee@t-online.de (home); hellwig.lee@gmx.de (home).

HELM, E(rnest) Eugene, BME, MME, PhD; American musicologist and academic; b. 23 Jan. 1928, New Orleans, LA. *Education:* Southeastern Louisiana Coll., Louisiana State Univ., North Texas State Univ. *Career:* faculty mem., Louisiana Coll. 1953–55, Wayne (Neb) State Coll. 1958–59, Univ. of Iowa 1960–68; Assoc. Prof. of Music, Univ. of Maryland 1968–69, Prof. of Music 1969–, Chair Musicology Division 1971–87; Co-ordinating Ed., Carl Philipp Emanuel Bach Edition 1982–89. *Publications:* Music at the Court of Frederick the Great 1960, Words and Music (with A. Luper) 1971, A Thematic Catalogue of the Works of Carl Philipp Emanuel Bach 1987, The Cannon and the Curricula 1994; contrib. articles to numerous periodicals and other publications. *Address:* c/o University of Maryland School of Music, 2110 Clarice Smith Performing Arts Center, College Park, MD 20742-1620, USA.

HELM, Hans; singer (baritone); b. 12 April 1934, Passau, Germany. *Education:* studied with Else Zeidler and Franz Reuter-Wolf in Munich, Emmi Muller in Krefeld. *Career:* debut at Graz 1957, in Boris Godunov; sang in Vienna, Cologne, Frankfurt, Munich, Düsseldorf and Hanover; Salzburg Festival 1973, in the premiere of De Temporum fine Comoedia by Orff; Glyndebourne Festival 1976, as the Count in Le nozze di Figaro (also at Covent Garden 1976, 1991); Vienna Staatsoper 1987, 1990, as Agamemnon in Iphigénie en Aulide, and in Die Soldaten; Munich 1989, as Faninal in Der Rosenkavalier; sang The Forester in The Cunning Little Vixen at the Vienna Volksoper 1992; season 1995–96 as Donner in Das Rheingold at Vienna and Strauss's Faninal in Munich; many concert appearances. *Recordings:* Otello, De Temporum fine Comoedia, Die Frau ohne Schatten.

HELMS, Dietrich, MA, DrPhil, Habil., Priv. Doz.; German musicologist; *Professor of Music History, University of Osnabrück;* b. 23 July 1963, Westfalen. *Education:* Westfälische Wilhelms Universität Münster, St Peter's Coll., Oxford, UK. *Career:* editorial work for the Hallesche Händel-Ausgabe 1996–97; Lecturer, Institut für Musik und Musikwissenschaft, Dortmund Univ. 1997–2006; Prof. of Music History, Univ. of Osnabrück 2006–, Head of Music Dept 2008–12, Dean of Dept of Educational and Cultural Sciences 2012–14; lectureships at Univs of Münster, Hamburg and Bremen; mem. Gesellschaft für Musikforschung, Royal Musical Asscn, Arbeitskreis Studium Populäre Musik, Arbeitskreis musikpädagogische Forschung. *Publications:* Heinrich VIII und die Musik: Überlieferung, musikalische Bildung des Adels und Kompositionstechniken eines Königs 1998, Beiträge zur Popularmusikforschung (ed.), Samples: Notizen, Projekte und Kurzbeiträge zur Popularmusikforschung (ed.); contrib. to Die Musikforschung, Beiträge zur Popularmusikforschung, Hamburger Jahrbuch für Musikwissenschaft, Musical Quarterly. *Address:* Institut für Musikwissenschaft und Musikpädagogik, Fachbereich 03, Universität Osnabrück, Schloss/Neuer Graben 29, 49069 Osnabrück, Germany (office). *Telephone:* (541) 969-4510 (office). *Fax:* (231) 969-4775 (office). *E-mail:* dietrich.helms@uni-osnabrueck.de (office). *Website:* www.musik.uni-osnabrueck.de (office).

HELMS, Joachim; singer (tenor); b. 24 June 1943, Rostock, Germany. *Education:* Franz Liszt Musikhochschule Weimar and in Dresden. *Career:* debut in Erfurt 1974, as Ernesto in Don Pasquale; sang at Erfurt 1974–83, as Mozart's Ferrando and Tamino, the Duke of Mantua, Nemorino, Don Carlos, Max in Der Freischütz and Sergei in Katerina Izmailova; Dresden Staatsoper from 1984, as Rodolfo, Alfredo and Don Ottavio; guest appearances in the former Soviet Union, Poland, Bulgaria, Austria and Switzerland; sang Ernesto at Leipzig 1989; many concert appearances and broadcasting engagements.

HELSETH, Tine Thing; Norwegian trumpeter; b. 1987, Oslo. *Career:* has performed with orchestras including Zurich Chamber, Dresden Philharmonic, Royal Philharmonic, Royal Liverpool Philharmonic, Ulster Orchestra, Munich Symphony, Prague Radio Symphony, Sioux City, Oslo and Copenhagen Philharmonics, Stavanger Symphony and Kristiansand Symphony; BBC Proms concerto debut, Royal Albert Hall (London premiere of Matthias Pintscher's Chute d'Étoiles with BBC Scottish Symphony Orchestra) 2013; has premiered works of contemporary composers including Bent Sørensen and Britta Byström; as recitalist, tours of UK, Norway, France and Finland with Kathryn Stott, appearing at Wigmore Hall, among others; f. brass ensemble tenThing 2007, performances included festivals in Germany, UK, Italy and China and concerts in Switzerland, Austria, and at Int. House of Music, Moscow 2014; f. jazz/tango fusion ensemble Tine Thing Helseth Quintet (TTHQ) 2010. *Recordings:* solo: Classical Trumpet Concertos (Aftenposten Classical Recording of the Year) 2007, My Heart is Ever Present 2009, Storyteller 2012, Tine 2013; with tenThing: 10 2012. *Honours:* Borletti-Buitoni Trust Fellowship, Norwegian Grammy Awards Newcomer of the Year 2007, ECHO Klassik Awards Newcomer of the Year 2013. *Current Management:* c/o Kathryn Enticott, IMG Artists, The Light Box, 111 Power Road, London, W4 5PY, England. *Telephone:* (20) 7957-5834. *E-mail:* kenticott@imgartists.com. *Website:* www.imgartists.com. *E-mail:* post@tenthing.no (office). *Website:* www.tinethinghelseth.com (office); www.tenthing.no (office).

HELTAY, Laszlo Istvan, BLitt, MA; British (b. Hungarian) conductor; b. 5 Jan. 1930, Budapest, Hungary. *Education:* Franz Liszt Acad. of Music, Budapest with Kodály and Bardos, Merton Coll., Oxford, England. *Career:* Dir of Music, Merton Coll., Oxford 1960–64; founded the Kodaly Choir, and Schola Cantorum of Oxford (subsequently Collegium Musicum Oxoniense) 1960 and gave premiere of Kodaly's The Music Makers 1964; Assoc. Conductor, New Zealand Broadcasting Corporation Symphony Orchestra 1964–65; Musical Dir, New Zealand Opera Co. 1964–66; Conductor, Phoenix Opera Co., London 1967–69, 1973; Conductor, Collegium Musicum of London 1970–89; Dir of Music, Gardner Centre, Sussex Univ. 1968–78; founder and Music Dir, Brighton Festival Chorus 1967–94, Conductor Emeritus 1994–; Music Dir, Chorus of the Acad. of St Martin-in-the-Fields 1975–99; Dir, Royal Choral Soc. 1985–94; Dir, Coro de RadioTelevision Española, Madrid 1997–2000; concerts with Norddeutscher Rundfunk Chor, the Philharmonia, the Royal Philharmonic, London Philharmonic and Dallas Symphony Orchestras; masterclasses for young choral conductors in Europe and USA; Chorus Dir for film, 'Amadeus'. *Recordings:* choral works of Kodály, Respighi, Rossini and Haydn (Stabat Mater and Salve Regina), Paco Peña: Misa Flamenca. *Honours:* Hon. DMus (Univ. of Sussex) 1995, Hon. Fellow Merton Coll., Oxford 1997; International Kodály Medal 1982.

HEMM, Manfred; Austrian singer (baritone); b. 1961, Mödling; m. Amanda Roocroft 1995. *Education:* Vienna Conservatory with Waldemar Kmentt. *Career:* debut at Klagenfurt 1984, as Mozart's Figaro; sang at Augsburg 1984–86, Graz 1986–88, notably as Papageno, Leporello and Polyphemus in Acis and Galatea; Vienna Staatsoper from 1988 (title role in the premiere of Von Einem's Tuliphant 1990); guest appearances as Bayreuth, Basel, Berne, Zürich, Salzburg (Figaro 1989–91) and Orange; sang Figaro at the Deutsche Oper Berlin 1990, Aix-en-Provence Festival 1991; Metropolitan Opera debut 1991, as Papageno; Salzburg Festival 1992, as the One Eyed Brother in Die Frau ohne Schatten; Philadelphia 1995, as Giorgio in I Puritani; Sang Kuno in Der Freischütz in concert with the Royal Opera 1998; sang Amfortas for Scottish Opera and Mozart's Figaro in Munich 2000; frequent Lieder recitals and concert appearances. *Current Management:* c/o Boris Orlob Management, Jägerstrasse 70, 10117 Berlin, Germany. *Telephone:* (30) 20450839. *Fax:* (30) 20450849. *E-mail:* info@orlob.net. *Website:* www.orlob.net.

HENCK, Herbert; German pianist and writer on music; b. 28 July 1948, Treysa, Hesse. *Education:* studied in Mannheim and Stuttgart, Hochschule für Musik, Cologne with Aloys Kontarsky. *Career:* many appearances in Germany and elsewhere in 20th-century repertoire, notably with music by Cage, Stockhausen, Boulez and Schoenberg; leader of courses at Darmstadt, Cologne and other avant-garde centres. *Recordings include:* Boulez Sonatas; Music of Changes, Cheap Imitation and Music for Piano, 1–84, by John Cage; Stockhausen's Klavierstücke I–IX; Les Heures persanes, by Koechlin; Music by Schoenberg and Charles Ives. *Publications include:* Neuland, Ansätze zur Musik der Gegenwart 1980–85, Experimentelle Pianistik 1994.

HENDERSON, Gavin Douglas, CBE, BFA, MA, DipAD; British arts administrator and college principal; *Principal, Royal Central School of Speech & Drama, University of London;* b. 3 Feb. 1948, Brighton; m. 1st Jane Williams 1973 (divorced 1977); m. 2nd Carole Becker 1983 (divorced 1992); m. 3rd Mary Jane Walsh 1992; two s. *Education:* Brighton Coll. of Art, Kingston Art Coll., Slade School of Fine Art, Univ. Coll. London. *Career:* debut as soloist, Wigmore Hall 1972; performer, BBC radio and television, festivals including City of London, Brighton; Artistic Dir, Brighton, York, Portsmouth, Crawley, Bracknell (jazz, folk and early music), Bournemouth festivals; Chief Exec., the New Philharmonia and Philharmonia Orchestra 1975–79; Chair., Music Panel, Arts Council of England; Vice-Pres., British Arts Festivals Asscn; Vice-Pres., European Festivals Asscn, Pres. 2004–06; Prin. and Chief Exec., Trinity Coll. of Music and Trinity Laban, London 1994–2006; Prin., Royal Central School of Speech & Drama, Univ. of London 2007–; Artistic Dir, Dartington Int. Summer School 1985–2010; Chair., Nat. Foundation for Youth Music 1998–2007; mem. RSA, ISM, Musicians' Union, Worshipful Co. of Musicians, RSM. *Art Exhibitions:* Picasso and the Theatre 1982, Curtain Up – The New Europe 1990, Court in the Act, Royal Acad. of Art 1993. *Television:* A View Of... (BBC series). *Publications:* Picasso and the Theatre 1982, Festivals UK Arts Council 1986, National Arts and Media Strategy (Festivals Section) 1991; contrib. to Musical Times, Classical Music, Tempo, The Listener, The Stage, Resurgence, Music Journal (ISM), Piers. *Honours:* Hon. FRCM, Hon. FRNCM, Hon. CTL, Hon. FBCM, CCIM, Hon. Fellow, Sussex Univ. and Univ. of Brighton; Hon. MA (Sussex); East Sussex County Council Europe Award 1992, Sir Charles Groves Award (for Making Music 2005), BACS Gold Award 2007. *Address:* Royal Central School of Speech & Drama, Eton Avenue, London, NW3 3HY, England (office). *Telephone:* (20) 7559-3903 (office). *E-mail:* gavin.henderson@cssd.ac.uk (office). *Website:* www.cssd.ac.uk.

HENDERSON, Katherine; singer (mezzo-soprano); b. 1970, Cape Town, South Africa. *Education:* Univ. of Cape Town, National Opera Studio. *Career:* debut with Beethoven's Choral Fantasia, Cape Town Symphony Orchestra 1994; sang title role in Peter Brook's La Tragédie de Carmen, Cape Town; concert for Nelson Mandela 1996; appearances at Cape Town as Lola in Cavalleria Rusticana and as Maddalena in Rigoletto; Carmen for Castleward Opera, Belfast; Bess in Porgy and Bess Suite, Peterborough; Mercédès in Carmen for Opera North and Mozart's Requiem at Basingstoke; season 1999 at Mercedes, at Leeds; The Kingdom by Elgar, Isle of Wight; further concerts. *Honours:* winner Wendy Fine Opera Prize Competition 1994.

HENDERSON, Moya; Australian composer; b. 2 Aug. 1941, Quirindi, NSW. *Education:* Univ. of Queensland, studied with Maurice Kagel in Cologne. *Compositions include:* Sacred Site for organ and tape 1983, The Dreaming for strings 1985, Celebration 40,000 (piano concerto) 1987, Currawong: A Symphony of Bird Sounds 1988, Waking Up the Flies for piano trio 1990, Wild Card for soprano, cello and piano 1991, Anzac Fanfare for soprano and orchestra 1995, Lindy (opera) 1997, In Paradisum for chorus 1997, I Walked into my Mother (music drama for radio) 1998, also music theatre pieces, chamber and vocal music.

HENDRICKS, Barbara Ann, BSc, BMus; Swedish (b. American) singer (soprano); b. 20 Nov. 1948, Stephens, Ark., USA; d. of M. L. Hendricks and Della Hendricks; m. Ulf Englund 1978; one s. one d. *Education:* Univ. of Nebraska-Lincoln and Juilliard School of Music, studying with Jennie Tourel. *Career:* operatic debut, San Francisco Opera (L'Incoronazione di Poppea) 1976; has appeared with opera companies of Boston, Santa Fe, Glyndebourne, Hamburg, La Scala (Milan), Berlin, Paris, Los Angeles, Florence and Royal Opera, Covent Garden (London), Vienna; recitals in most major centres in Europe and America; toured extensively in USSR and Japan; concert performances with all leading European and US orchestras; has appeared at many major music festivals including Edinburgh, Osaka, Montreux, Salzburg, Dresden, Prague, Aix-en-Provence, Orange and Vienna; nominated Goodwill Amb. for Refugees at UNHCR 1987; Founder Barbara Hendricks Foundation for Peace and Reconciliation 1998; f. record label Arte Verum 2006; Artist-in-Residence, Pitea, Sweden 2008. *Film appearances:* La Bohème 1988, The Rake's Progress 1994. *Recordings:* nearly 90 recordings. *Honours:* Hon. mem. Inst. of Humanitarian Law, San Remo, Italy 1990; Commdr des Arts et des Lettres 1986, Chevalier, Légion d'honneur 1993; Hon. DMus (Nebraska Wesleyan Univ.) 1988; Dr hc (Univ. of Louvain, Belgium) 1990, 1993, (Dundee) 1992, (Univ. of Paris VIII) 1999, (Juilliard School) 2000, (Liege) 2004; Laurent Perrier Champagne Award for Service to the Community and to French Culture 1988, Prince of Asturias Foundation Award 2000, Lions Club International Award for the Defense of Human Rights 2001, Premio Internacional Xifra Heras, Univ. of Gerona, Spain 2004, La Medaille D'Or de la ville de Paris 2004, Creu de Sant Jordi, Catalunya, Spain 2006, Medal of the City of Sarajevo 2007, Prize Save the Children, Spain 2009. *Address:* B H Office, Fondberg Produktion, Dalagatan 48, 11324, Stockholm, Sweden (office). *E-mail:* bh.office@bluewin.ch (office). *Website:* www.barbarahendricks.com (office).

HENDRICKS, Marijke; singer (mezzo-soprano); b. 18 April 1956, Schinveld, The Netherlands. *Education:* studied in Maastricht and Cologne. *Career:* sang at Cologne Opera 1981–85, notably as Nancy in Martha, Cherubino, Hansel, Meg Page and Olga in Eugene Onegin; sang the Marchesa in Musgrave's The Voice of Ariadne at the 1982 Edinburgh Festival; guest appearances at Geneva 1985, as Cherubino, Salzburg 1986 as Second Lady in Die Zauberflöte and Innsbruck 1986 in the title role of Cesti's Orontea; Bordeaux and Lyon 1987, as Ramiro in La Finta Giardiniera; Amsterdam 1987, in a concert performance of Tancredi, as Isaura; visits to the Orange Festival and to Israel with the company of Cologne Opera 1984; Antwerp 1988, as Dulcinée in Massenet's Don Quichotte; Maastricht 1989 in La Belle Hélène; television appearances in Austria and Switzerland.

HENDRICKS, Scott; American singer (baritone); b. 1968, San Antonio, Texas. *Education:* Univ. of Arkansas. *Career:* performs both bel canto as well as contemporary repertoire; notable interpreter of Verdi operas; held position with Houston Grand Opera Studio; joined Oper der Stadt Köln, Germany where he spent three years on a Fest contract building his repertoire, performed Rodrigo, Marquis di Posa in new production of Don Carlo; engagements have incuded Enrico/Lucia di Lammermoor and Germont/La Traviata at Opera Colorado, Marcello/La Bohème at San Francisco Opera and San Diego Opera, appearances in three consecutive summer seasons at Santa Fe Opera as Eugene Onegin, Ford/Falstaff and Robert/Intermezzo, and debut at Klangbogen Festspiel in Vienna as King Vladislav in Dalibor; other engagements have included title role in Richard III, Giorgio Battistelli's world premiere opera for De Vlaamse Opera, The Captain in The Death of Klinghoffer with Rotterdam Philharmonic, and as Chucho in Salsipuedes with Houston Grand Opera; role of Il Conte di Luna in new production of Il Trovatore for Bregenzer Festspiele 2005, 2006; sang role of Posa in new production of Don Carlos with WNO 2006; future engagements include debuts at Netherlands Opera, the Liceu in Barcelona, Washington Opera and Opera Nat. de Lille. *Current Management:* c/o Simon Goldstone, Intermusica Artists Management Ltd, 36 Graham Street, Crystal Wharf, London, N1 8GJ, England. *E-mail:* sgoldstone@intermusica.co.uk. *Website:* www.intermusica.co.uk.

HENKEL, Kathy, BA, BM, MA; American composer, writer and lecturer; b. 20 Nov. 1942, Los Angeles, CA; d. of Norman Nicholas Henkel and Lila Rhea Lee; m. Michael E. Manes (divorced). *Education:* Univ. of California at Los Angeles; California State Univ. at Northridge. *Career:* music reviewer, Los Angeles Times 1979; scriptwriter and producer for radio station, KUSC-FM 1984–89; programme annotator, education co-ordinator, Chamber Music/LA Festival 1987–95; programme annotator, Los Angeles Chamber Orchestra 1988–98; liner notes writer, Pro Piano Records 1993–2003; owner, Sign of the Silver Birch Music 2003–; Principal Guest Composer, 28th Annual New Music Festival, Dana School of Music, Youngstown State Univ., Ohio 2012; works premiered and performed at Gubbio Music Festival, Italy, Montevarchi Festival, Italy, Alaska Women Festival, Fairbanks, Dana Festival, Ohio,

Toronto Guitar Soc., live broadcasts on KFAC, Los Angeles, in London, England, Greenwich Village, New York; commission from State of Alaska 1993; mem. Phi Beta Kappa, Nat. Acad. of Recording Arts and Sciences. *Compositions:* Pioneer Song Cycle 1968, Trumpet Sonata 1979, Lost Calendar Pages 1984, Moorland Sketches 1985, Piano Sonata 1986, Bass Clarinet Sonata 1987, River Sky for solo guitar 1988, Book of Hours for solo harp 1990, Sonata for flute and piano 1992, Sea Songs 1997, Suite Spice for clarinet, bassoon and piano 2001, Gotta Minute Suite 2003, Tango for bassoon and piano 2005, Elements for solo oboe 2006, Christmas Ave for harp and soprano 2006, Summer's Echo for English horn and piano 2009, Ritual for clarinet and bassoon 2010, Salve Regina for soprano and harp 2010, Remembrance of Miracles for Flute 2012, Tintagel Dreams for Bass Clarinet 2013, Passing Doble for String Ensemble 2014, Samantha's Song for solo trombone 2014. *Publications:* contrib. to Performing Arts Magazine. *Address:* 2367 Creston Drive, Los Angeles, CA 90068-2201, USA (office).

HENKEL, Susanna Yoko; German/Japanese violinist and academic; *Professor of Violin, Cologne University of Music;* b. 1975, Freiburg im Breisgau. *Education:* Acad. of Music, Freiburg with Rainer Kussmaul, Munich Acad. with Ana Chumachenco. *Career:* began playing the violin aged two; chamber music partners include Pavel Gililov, Lauma Skride, Itamar Golan, Milana Chernyavska, Jing Zhao, Maxim Rysanov; has worked with Berlin Radio Broadcasting Orchestra, Radio Symphony Orchestras of SWR and MDR Leipzig, Symphony Orchestras of Aachen and Duisburg, Orchestra of the Beethovenhalle Bonn, Stuttgart Chamber Orchestra, Symphony Orchestra of the Mozarteum Salzburg, KBS Symphony Orchestra, Seoul; has performed at Ansbacher Bachwoche, Ludwigsburger Schlossfestspiele, Rheingau-Musik-Festival, concerts in the Théâtre du Châtelet, Paris; f. Zagreb Int. Chamber Music Festival 2006; Artist-in-Residence, Duisburg Philharmonic 2009–10; Prof. of Violin, Cologne Univ. of Music 2010–. *Recordings include:* complete recordings of Johann Sebastian Bach's Sonatas and Partitas for solo violin, chamber music works of Maurice Ravel, Sergei Prokofiev and Richard Strauss, solo works of Ysaÿe, Bartók and Isang Yun, duo works for violin and violoncello by Handel/Halvorsen, Eisler, Schulhogg and Kodály, Tchaikovsky Violin Concerto with Duisburg Philharmonic Orchestra 2010, Mozart Violin Concertos 2011. *Honours:* Winner, Queen Elisabeth Competition, Brussels 1997, German Music Competition, Berlin 1998, Mozart Competition, Salzburg 1999, Int. Violin Competition, Markneukirchen 1999, 19th Century Recording of the Year (Violin), ECHO Klassik Awards 2011. *Address:* The Spot Music, Torstrasse 41, 10119 Berlin (office); Hochschule für Musik und Tanz Köln, Standort Aachen, An den Frauenbrüdern 1, 52064 Aachen, Germany (office). *Telephone:* (30) 28873818 (Spot); (241) 4757120 (HFMTK) (office). *Fax:* (30) 28873819 (Spot); (241) 4757129 (HFMTK) (office). *E-mail:* susanna@susanna-yoko-henkel.com (office). *Website:* www.hfmt-koeln.de (office); www.susanna-yoko-henkel.com (office).

HENN, Brigitte; singer (soprano); b. 21 Oct. 1939, Freudenthal, Czechoslovakia; m. Raymond Henn. *Education:* studied in Frankfurt, in Wiesbaden with Helena Braun, and in Basle. *Career:* sang at the Basle Opera 1968–75, Deutsche Oper Berlin 1976–80; guest appearances at Basle from 1982, and in Düsseldorf, Frankfurt, Zürich and Hanover; roles have included Mozart's Countess, Donna Anna and Fiordiligi, Agathe, Euridice, Marenka in The Bartered Bride, Wagner's Senta, Elsa and Sieglinde, Elisabeth de Valois, Alice Ford and Amelia in Un Ballo in Maschera; operetta engagements in works by Lehar and Zeller; many concert appearances.

HENRY, Antoni Garfield; British singer (tenor); b. 1970, England. *Education:* studied with Ludmilla Andrew and Nicholas Powell. *Career:* debut as Luigi in Il Tabarro for Broomhill Opera; appearances as Don José for Opera North 1999; Rodolfo for European Chamber Opera and at Holland Park 1998–99; The Duke of Mantua for English Touring Opera; Canio in Pagliacci for Central Festival Opera; Alfred in Die Fledermaus and Pinkerton for European Chamber Opera; Carmen Jones, Old Vic and West Side Story for Pimlico Opera.

HENRY, Claire; British singer (mezzo-soprano); b. 1970, England. *Education:* Trinity Coll., London, studied with Ryland Davies. *Career:* appearances as Mozart's Sesto, Bloomsbury Theatre; Cherubino for Clonter Opera; Périchole for Dorset Opera; Kate Pinkerton, ENO; in Die Meistersinger, Covent Garden; concerts include Elgar's The Kingdom; Messiah and works by Haydn, Mendelssohn, Bach, Mozart and Vivaldi; season 1999 with Herr Mozart and Doctor Strauss for the Covent Garden Festival. *Honours:* first prize English Song Competition, TCM.

HENRY, Didier; French singer (baritone); b. 24 May 1953, Paris. *Education:* Paris Conservatoire and the studio of the Grand Opéra. *Career:* sang at St Etienne 1988, in a revival of Massenet's Amadis; Aix-en-Provence 1989, in The Love for Three Oranges and in Belfast as Valentin the same year; season 1990 as Marc-Antoine in Massenet's Cléopâtre at St Etienne, followed by Blondel in Grétry's Richard Coeur de Lion; has sung in Moscow in Pelléas et Mélisande, in Marseille as Pietro in La Muette de Portici by Auber and at the Paris Théâtre du Châtelet in L'Enfant et les Sortilèges; other roles include Gluck's Orestes (La Scala 1991), Puccini's Lescaut, Pelléas and Hamlet; Marquis de la Force in Poulenc's Carmelites at the 1999 London Proms; sang Gluck's Oreste at Marseille 2000; teacher of vocal interpretation, l'Académie Musicale Internationale de Bayonne 1985–97, Hochschule für Musick, Karlsruhe 2006–. *Recordings include:* Debussy's Pelléas et Mélisande (Grammy Award 1991), Ravel's L'Enfant et les Sortilèges, Chabrier's Gwendoline, Prokofiev's

The Love for Three Oranges, Massenet's Amadis, Cléopâtre, Griséldis, Mascagni's: Il Piccolo Marat, Komives' Le muet au couvent, Gounod's Romeo et Juliette, Duruflé's Requiem, Ropartz's Le martyr de Saint Nicolas, Saint-Saëns' La Lyre et la Harpe, Mélodies de Ravel, Massenet, Poulenc, Leguerney, Max d'Ollone, Hahn, Berliioz and Saint-Saëns. *Current Management:* c/o Philippe Cuisinier, Aria Management. *Telephone:* 1-46-05-46-57. *E-mail:* ariamngt@aol.com. *Telephone:* 6-7-87-30-39 (office). *E-mail:* didier.henry@ free.fr (office). *Website:* didier.henry.free.fr.

HENRYSON, Svante; Swedish musician (cello, double bass, bass guitar) and composer; b. 22 Oct. 1963, Stockholm. *Education:* Ingesund Coll. of Music, Acad. of Performing Arts, Prague. *Career:* played double bass in Oslo Philharmonic Orchestra, becoming Asst Prin. Double Bassist 1983–86; Prin. Bassist, Norwegian Chamber Orchestra 1987–89; moved to US and played bass in Yngwie Malmsteen's rock band 1989–92; performer on jazz and classical scenes in numerous collaborations; has worked with musicians such as Martin Fröst, Anne Sofie von Otter, Elvis Costello, Roland Pöntinen; Landsdelsmusikernes Artist-in-Residence 2010–12; currently Artistic Dir Umeå Chamber Music Festival. *Recordings include:* Enkidu 1999, Night Song 2011, High, Low or In Between 2016. *Compositions include:* works range from an oratorio, Vidderna inom mig (Wide Open Spaces Within Me), set to lyrics by Nils-Aslak Valkepää, a Sámi poet from the North of Norway, to solo violin sonatas. *Honours:* Jazz Musician of the Year, Swedish Radio in 2014, Nordic Council Music Prize 2015. *Address:* c/o ECM Records, Postfach 600 331, 81203 Munich, Germany (office). *E-mail:* ecmrecords@ecmrecords.com (office). *Website:* www.henryson.net.

HENSCHEL, Dietrich; German singer (baritone); b. 1967, Berlin. *Education:* studied with Hanno Blanschke in Munich and with Dietrich Fischer-Dieskau in Berlin. *Career:* debut at the Munich Biennale in Michèle Reverdy's Le Précepteur 1990; concert appearances in festivals at Stuttgart, Urach and Feldkirch (Schubertiade); Kiel Opera 1993–96, as Mozart's Papageno and Count, Rossini's Figaro, Valentin in Faust, Pelléas, Henze's Prince of Homburg, and Monteverdi's Orfeo; engagements with leading orchestras in Germany, Netherlands and Austria; numerous guest appearances at opera houses from 1996, including in Bonn, Stuttgart, Lyon, Staatsoper Komische Oper and Deutsche Oper Berlin (debut in title role of Hans Werner Henze's Der Prinz von Homburg 1997), Amsterdam, Brussels, Madrid, Vienna, Zurich, Geneva, Florence, Milan, Théâtre du Châtelet and Opéra, Paris; other opera roles include the title role of Œdipe, Don Giovanni, Wozzek, Beckmesser in Die Meistersinger von Nürnberg, Tuzenbach in premiere of Trois Soeurs by Peter Eötvös, Olivier and Count in Capriccio, the Barber in Die schweigsame Frau, Monteverdi's Ulisse and Faust in Busoni's Doktor Faust; concert repertory includes Messiah, Carmina Burana, all Bach's oratorios, War Requiem, Brahms Requiem, Wunderhorn Lieder, Das Lied von der Erde and various Lied recitals. *Recordings include:* Carmina Burana, Handel's Messiah, Humperdinck's Königskinder, Brahms's German Requiem, Haydn's Four Seasons, Mahler orchestral songs (with Kent Nagano and the Hallé Orchestra), Bach's St Matthew Passion (with Nikolaus Harnoncourt and Concentus Musicus Wien), Korngold Lieder (with Helmut Deutsch), Schubert's Die Winterreise (with Irwin Gage) 2000, Mahler's Des Knaben Wunderhorn (with Sarah Connolly, Philippe Herreweghe and the Orchestre des Champs-Elysées) (Edison Classical Music Award for Best Vocals 2007) 2006, Wolf Mörike-Lieder, Schubert's Schwanengesang (with Fritz Schwinghammer), Beethoven Lieder (with Michael Schäfer), Wagner's Meistersinger (Beckmesser). *Honours:* Grammy Music Award. *Current Management:* c/o Christian Lange, Langemusic, Ludwig-Behr-Str. 7, 82327 Tutzing, Germany. *Telephone:* (81) 581832. *Fax:* (81) 58852. *E-mail:* chrlange@langemusic.eu. *Website:* www.langemusic.eu; www.dietrichhenschel.de.

HENSCHEL, Jane Elizabeth, BA; American singer (mezzo-soprano); b. 2 March 1952, Appleton, Wis.; d. of Lester Haentzschel and Betty Haentzschel (née Lau). *Education:* Univ. of Southern California. *Career:* debut with Netherlands Opera as the Nurse in Die Frau ohne Schatten 1992; ensemble mem. Aachen Oper 1977–80; joined Wuppertal Opera, Germany 1980, later with Dortmund and Düsseldorf Operas; appearances at Glyndebourne, Salzburg and Saito Kinen Festivals and at La Scala, Milan, Deutsche Oper, Berlin, Amsterdam Opera, Paris Opera, Bayerische Staatsoper, Munich, Staatsoper, Berlin, Royal Opera House, Covent Garden, London and San Francisco Opera; has performed with numerous conductors, including Seiji Ozawa, Sir Colin Davis, Daniel Barenboim, Bernard Haitink, Riccardo Muti, Christian Thielemann, Sir Andrew Davis, Lorin Maazel; Baroque repertoire includes Vivaldi's oratorio Juditha Triumphans (Radio France). *Operatic roles include:* Die Amme (the nurse) in Die Frau ohne Schatten (Netherlands Opera, Royal Opera House, London 1992, Los Angeles, Bavarian State Opera, Munich, Vienna, Paris, Deutsche Oper Berlin, Metropolitan Opera), Fricka in Das Rheingold and Die Walküre (Royal Opera House, London 1996), Ulrica in Un Ballo in Maschera (Royal Opera House, London), Klytemnestra in Elektra (Bavarian State Opera, Munich, Royal Opera House, London), Herodias in Salome (Bavarian State Opera, Munich, La Scala, Milan, San Francisco Opera), Brangäne in Tristan und Isolde (Orange Festival, Los Angeles Music Center Opera, Paris Opera), Queen of Sheba in Königin von Saba (Concertgebouw, Amsterdam), Genevieve in Pelléas et Mélisande (Japan), Cassandre in Les Troyens (La Scala, Milan), Waltraute in Götterdämmerung (Royal Opera House, London), Mrs Grose in The Turn of the Screw (Royal Opera House, London), Judy in Birtwistle's Punch and Judy (Netherlands Opera 1993), Kostelnicka in Jenufa (Japan), Mistress Quickly in Falstaff

(Vienna, Munich, with the London Symphony Orchestra), The Witch in Rusalka, Ottavia in L'Incoronazione di Poppea (Aachen Oper), Erda in Ring (Royal Opera House, London) 2004, Auntie in Peter Grimes (Salzburg) 2004, Mistress Quickly (Los Angeles Opera) 2004; Amneris, Eboli, Ortrud, Carmen, Azucena, Venus. *Recordings include:* Mahler's 8th Symphony with CBSO and Simon Rattle, The Rake's Progress with Ozawa 1997, Krasa's Die Verlobung im Traum with Daniel Harding 2002, Humperdinck's Hansel und Gretel 2006, Janácek's Katya Kabanova 2007. *Honours:* Grammy Award 2001, Gramophone Award 2003.

HEPPNER, Thomas Bernard (Ben), CC, DMus; Canadian singer (tenor); b. 14 Jan. 1956, Murrayville, BC. *Education:* Univ. of British Columbia. *Career:* many oratorio and concert performances in Canada; Opera Bacchus in Ariadne auf Naxos; Canadian Opera Co. as Zinovy in Lady Macbeth of Mtsensk; American debut in Tannhäuser at the Chicago Lyric Opera 1988; has sung the Prince in Rusalka with the Philadelphia Opera Co., Seattle Opera 1990, and at the Vienna State Opera 1991; European debut as Lohengrin at the Royal Opera Stockholm 1989; sang Walther von Stolzing on his La Scala and Covent Garden debuts 1990, and in Seattle; San Francisco Opera debut as Lohengrin 1989; season 1991–92 with Janáček's Laca at Brussels, the Emperor in Die Frau ohne Schatten at Amsterdam and the premiere of William Bolcom's McTeague in Chicago; season 1992 with Dvořák's Dimitrij at Munich, Mozart's Titus at Salzburg; sang Lohengrin at Seattle 1994, Walther at the Met, New York 1995, Peter Grimes at Royal Opera, Covent Garden 1995; debut as Tristan at Seattle 1998 and under Abbado at Salzburg 1999; sang Aeneas in Les Troyens with the London Symphony Orchestra at the Barbican Hall 2000, Otello at Lyric Opera, Chicago 2001, Schoenberg's Gurrelieder at the BBC Proms, London 2002. *Recordings:* Fidelio (conducted by Colin Davis) 1996, two of Die Meistersinger (conducted by Wolfgang Sawallisch and by Solti) 1997, Rusalka (conducted by Charles Mackerras) 1998, Les Troyens (conducted by Sir Colin Davis) 2001, Fidelio (DVD) (conducted by James Levine in 2000) 2003, Tristan and Isolde (DVD) (conducted by James Levine in 1999) 2004, Die Meistersinger von Nurnberg (DVD) (conducted by James Levine in 2001) 2004. *Honours:* Hon. LLD; Hon. LittD; Birgit Nilsson Prize 1988, ECHO Deutscher Schallplatten-preis for Singer of the Year 1993, Juno Awards for Best Classical Album, Vocal or Choral Performance 1996, 2000, Seattle Opera Artist of the Year 1996, Grammy Awards for Best Opera Recording 1998, Best Opera Recording and Best Classical Album 2002, Royal Philharmonic Soc. Award for Best Singer 2005, Metropolitan Opera Guild Opera News Award 2006. *Address:* Ben Heppner Administrative Office, 35 Kearney Drive, Toronto, ON M9W 5J5, Canada (office). *Telephone:* (416) 743-2761 (office). *E-mail:* eldonmcbride@ sympatico.ca (office). *Website:* www.benheppner.com. *Current Management:* Columbia Artists Management, 165 W 57th Street, New York, NY 10019, USA.

HERAS-CASADO, Pablo; Spanish conductor; *Principal Conductor, Orchestra of St Luke's;* b. 21 Nov. 1977, Granada. *Education:* Univ. de Granada; studied conducting at Univ. de Alcalá de Henares, and with Harry Christophers, Sylvain Cambreling, Peter Eötvös and Pierre Boulez. *Career:* Founding Dir Capella Exaudi vocal-instrumental early music ensemble 1995–2007; f. Sonóora ensemble at Granada Conservatoire to explore and perform Webern and Varèse, experiments with new music 1999–2001; Asst Conductor Nat. Youth Orchestra of Spain 2000–01, Opéra de Paris 2006–07; Deutsche Oper Berlin 2006; f. Orquesta Barroca de Granada 2002; Founder and Artistic Dir Int. Choral Conducting Masterclass, Valle de Ricote (Murcia), teaching alongside Harry Christophers 2004–06; f. Compañía Teatro del Principe, period instruments orchestra devoted to neglected theatrical repertoire of the Spanish Court in the XVIII century 2007; Prin. Conductor Orquesta de Girona 2005–08; Prin. Conductor Orchestra of St Luke's, New York 2012–, Carnegie Hall debut 2013; Prin. Guest Conductor Teatro Real Madrid 2014–; as guest conductor with numerous orchestras including Berliner Philharmoniker, Gewandhausorchester Leipzig, Royal Concertgebouw, Rotterdam Philharmonic, Tonhalle-Orchester Zürich, New York Philharmonic, Los Angeles Philharmonic, Boston Symphony and Cleveland orchestras; regular collaborations with Ensemble Intercontemporain and Freiburger Barockorchester; Guest Conductor, Opéra Nat. de Bordeaux (Offenbach's La Périchole), ENO (L'elisir d'amore), Canadian Opera Co. (John Adams' Nixon in China, Gluck's Iphigénie en Tauride), Mariinsky Theatre, St Petersburg (Carmen), Festspielhaus Baden-Baden (L'elisir d'amore, La traviata), Frankfurt Opera (Verdi's Les vêpres siciliennes), Los Angeles Philharmonic (Eötvös's Angels in America), Metropolitan Opera (Rigoletto, Carmen), Teatro Real Madrid (Catán's Il Postino, world premiere of Mauricio Sotelo's El Publico), Deutsche Oper Berlin (Rigoletto) and Dutch Nat. Opera with Sasha Waltz & Guests (Orfeo); appearances at Salzburger Festspiele and Festival d'Aix-en-Provence; invited annually for Dialogue Festival and Mozartwoche at Mozarteum Salzburg; conducted annual televised Advent Concert of Staatskapelle Dresden. *Recordings include:* Giuseppe Bonno: L'isola disabitata (with Compañía Teatro del Príncipe) 2009, Weill: Rise and Fall of the City of Mahagonny (DVD) (Diapason d'Or) 2011, Plácido Domingo: Verdi 2013, Schubert: Symphony No. 3 and No. 4 (with Freiburger Barockorchester) (Echo Klassik Award 2014) 2013, Mendelssohn: Symphony No. 2 (with Symphonieorchester des Bayerischen Rundfunks) 2014, El Maestro Farinelli 2014. *Honours:* Richard Wagner Soc. Fellowship, winner, Lucerne Festival Conductors Competition 2007, Rodriguez Acosta Foundation Medal of Honour 2012, Golden Medal of Merit, Council of Granada 2012,

Musical America Conductor of the Year 2014. *Current Management:* c/o Lydia Connolly, Harrison Parrott Ltd, 5–6 Albion Court, London, W6 0QT, England. *Telephone:* (20) 7229-9166. *Fax:* (20) 7221-5042. *E-mail:* lydia.connolly@harrisonparrott.co.uk. *Website:* www.harrisonparrott.com. *E-mail:* fernando@pabloherascasado.com.

HERBERT, Trevor, BA, DLitt, PhD, ARCM; British musician (trombone), musicologist and academic; *Professor of Music, The Open University*; b. 18 Oct. 1945, Cwmparc, Wales; s. of Trevor Herbert and Megan Herbert; m. Helen Grace Barlow. *Education:* Tonypandy Grammar School, St Luke's Coll., Exeter, Royal Coll. of Music, Open Univ. *Career:* trombone player (modern and period instruments), BBC Symphony Orchestra, Royal Philharmonic Orchestra, Nat. Orchestra of Wales, Musica Reservata, Taverner Players, Wallace Collection 1969–76; Music Dept, Open Univ. 1976–, Prof. of Music 1998–; freelance performer, writer, composer and broadcaster; mem. Royal Musical Asscn, American Musicological Soc., Historic Brass Soc., Galpin Soc. *Compositions include:* several TV scores, including Wales! Wales? (BBC 1993) and Under Milk Wood (Syriol/BBC 1992). *Recordings include:* with major orchestras, Taverner Players, Musica Reservata. *Publications include:* Cambridge Companion to Brass Instruments (co-ed with J. Wallace) 1997, The British Brass Band: A Musical and Social History 2000, Music in Words: A Guide to Researching and Writing About Music 2001, The Cultural Study of Music: A Critical Introduction (co-ed with M. Clayton and R. Middleton) 2003, The Trombone 2006; contrib. to The New Grove Dictionary of Music and Musicians 2000, Continuum Encyclopedia of Popular Music of the World 2003–, The Oxford Dictionary of National Biography 2004–, The Trombone 2006, Music and the British Military (with Helen Barlow). *Honours:* Hon. FRCM 2007; Hon. Fellow, Leeds Coll. of Music 2007; Foundation scholar, Royal Coll. of Music 1967, Martin Scholarship 1968, Christopher Monk Award, Historic Brass Soc. 2002. *Address:* Faculty of Arts, The Open University, Milton Keynes, MK6 7AA, England (office). *Telephone:* (1908) 655798 (office). *E-mail:* trevor.herbert@open.ac.uk (office). *Website:* www.open.ac.uk/Arts/music/therbert.shtml (office).

HERBIG, Gunther; German conductor; b. 30 Nov. 1931, Aussig, Czechoslovakia; s. of Emil Herbig and Gisela Herbig (née Hieke); m. Jutta Czapski 1958; one s. one d. *Education:* Franz Liszt Conservatory for Music, Weimar. *Career:* conductor, Nat. Theatre, Weimar 1957–62; Music Dir Hans Otto Theatre, Potsdam 1962–66; Conductor Berlin Symphony Orchestra, Berlin, GDR 1966–72, Gen. Music Dir 1977–83; Gen. Music Dir Dresden Philharmonic, Dresden, GDR 1972–77; Music Dir Detroit Symphony Orchestra, Detroit, Mich, USA 1984–90, Toronto Symphony Orchestra 1988–94, Toronto, Ont., Canada 1990–91; Prin. Guest Conductor Dallas Symphony Orchestra, Dallas Tex. 1979–81, BBC Philharmonic Orchestra, Manchester, UK 1981–84; Chief Conductor Saarbrucken Radio Symphony Orchestra 2001–06; Music Advisor and Prin. Guest Conductor Nat. Philharmonic Orchestra of Taiwan 2008–10, now Conductor Laureate; Prin. Guest Conductor Orquesta Filarmonica de Gran Canaria. *Honours:* Theodor Fontane Prize 1964, Cultural Award (GDR) 1970. *Current Management:* c/o Harrison Turner Artists Management, 53 Ticknell Piece Road, Charlbury, Oxon., OX7 3TN, England. *Telephone:* (1608) 810330. *Fax:* (1608) 811331. *E-mail:* artists@harrisonturner.co.uk. *Website:* www.harrisonturner.co.uk.

HERCHERT, Jörg; German composer; b. 20 Sept. 1943, Dresden. *Education:* Dresden and East Berlin Conservatories, Berlin Acad. with Paul Dessau. *Career:* freelance composer from 1975; Prof. of Composition, Dresden Conservatory 1992–. *Compositions:* Ode an eine Nachigall for soprano and oboe 1972, Komposition for soprano, baritone and 12 instruments 1975, Seligpreisungen I–VIII for organ 1974–85, Flute Concerto 1976, Sextet 1978, Das Geistliche Jahr cantata cycle (nine works for soloists, chorus and ensemble with percussion) 1978–96, Horn Concerto 1980, Octet 1984, two String Quartets 1981, 1986, Nonet 1990, Nachtwache (opera) 1993, Abraum (opera) 1997, Namen Gottes I–XXI for organ 1990–97.

HERFORD, (Richard) Henry, MA; British singer (baritone) and voice teacher; *Vocal Tutor, Royal Northern College of Music*; b. 24 Feb. 1947, Edinburgh, Scotland; s. of P. H. Herford and E. J. Herford (née Hawkins); m. Lindsay John 1982; two s. one d. *Education:* Trinity Coll., Glenalmond, King's Coll., Cambridge, Univ. of York, Royal Northern Coll. of Music, Manchester. *Career:* Glyndebourne Chorus 1977–78; Glyndebourne Touring Opera: Forester in Janáček's Cunning Little Vixen; roles with Royal Opera House, Covent Garden, Scottish Opera, Handel Opera, Chelsea Opera Group, Batignano, Nancy, English Bach Festival; frequent concerts with leading orchestras in the UK, Europe and N and S America; appearances with many ensembles and on radio and TV (Maxwell Davies, The Lighthouse, BBC 2); numerous recitals and oratorios on BBC Radio 3; concerts and operas on BBC and ITV; Prof., Royal Coll. of Music, London; Vocal Tutor, Royal Northern Coll. of Music, Birmingham Conservatoire. *Recordings:* Recital of American Songs; High Priest in Rameau's Castor and Pollux; Handel, Messiah, excerpts with Scottish Chamber Orchestra and George Malcolm; Peter Dickinson, A Dylan Thomas Song Cycle (with Robin Bowman); Handel, Dixit Dominus and Israel in Egypt with King's Coll. Cambridge Choir; John Joubert, The Instant Moment with English String Orchestra; Vaughan Williams, Five Tudor Portraits, Five Mystical Songs; Britten, A Midsummer Night's Dream; Charles Ives, Songs, two vols (with Robin Bowman); Songs with Instruments, with Ensemble Modern; Maxwell Davies, Resurrection; Bridge, The Christmas Rose; Michael Berkeley, Père du doux repos; George Lloyd, Iernin; Stravinsky, Pulcinella; Edward Gregson, Missa Brevis Pacem; Bliss, Com-

plete Songs; John Manduell, Songs of the Renaissance, Peter Dickinson, Larkin's Jazz. *Honours:* Curtis Gold Medal, Royal Northern Coll. of Music, First Prize, Benson & Hedges Gold Award (Snape), First Prize, Int. American Music Competition, New York, British Retailers Record of the Year. *Address:* Pencots, Northmoor, Oxford, OX29 5AX, England (home). *Telephone:* (1865) 300884 (home). *E-mail:* the.herfords@btinternet.com.

HERINCX, Raimund (Raymond Frederick); British singer (bass-baritone) and voice teacher and therapist; b. 23 Aug. 1927, London; s. of Florent Herincx and Marie Cheal; m. Margaret J. Waugh (known as Astra Blair) 1954; one s. two d. *Education:* Thames Valley Grammar School and Univ. of London; studied singing in Antwerp, Brussels, Barcelona and London with Giovanni Valli, Samuel Worthington and Harold Williams 1949–53. *Career:* Educ. Officer, Household Cavalry 1946–48; mem. Royal Opera House chorus; joined Welsh Nat. Opera 1956; Prin. Baritone, Sadler's Wells Opera 1957–67; debut Royal Opera House, Covent Garden 1968; joined Metropolitan Opera House, New York 1976, subsequently appeared in most major US opera houses mainly in works of Wagner and Richard Strauss; opera and concert appearances in South America 1976–81; numerous operatic performances in Europe in Wagner's Ring Cycle and other heldenbaritone roles; frequent European appearances 1974–87 in concert performances of British composers Elgar, Britten, Tippett, Walton and Vaughan-Williams; last professional performances: opera: Dalua in Rutland Boughton's The Immortal Hour, Glastonbury Festival 1998; concert: Verdi's Requiem, Wells Cathedral 2001; Prof. of Voice RAM 1970–77; Sr Visiting Prof. and Voice Teacher, North East of Scotland Music School 1979–; voice therapist 1979–; voice teacher, Trinity Coll. of Music, London 1993–95; Lecturer, Univ. Coll., Cardiff 1984–87; music critic, Music and Musicians. *Honours:* Hon. RAM 1971; Hon. DMus (Aberdeen) 1991; Opera Medal, Int. Music Awards 1968. *Address:* North East of Scotland Music School, Dorothy Hately Music Centre, 21 Huntly Street, Aberdeen, AB10 1TJ, Scotland (office). *Telephone:* (1224) 649685 (office). *Fax:* (1224) 649685 (office). *E-mail:* nesms@dsl.pipex.com. *Website:* www.nesms.org.uk.

HERLITZIUS, Evelyn; German singer (soprano); b. 27 April 1963, Osnabrück. *Education:* Musikhochschule Hamburg, studied with Hans Kagel and Eckart Lindemann. *Career:* debut as Elisabeth in Wagner's Tannhäuser, Landestheater Flensburg; mem. Hamburgische Staatsoper, Semperoper Dresden 1997–2000 where she performed Janáček's Jenůfa, Elisabeth and Venus in Tannhäuser, Sieglinde and Brünnhilde in Wagner's Der Ring des Nibelungen, Kundry in Parsifal, Dyer's Wife in Die Frau ohne Schatten by Richard Strauss, Salome and Puccini's Turandot, regular returns since including as Elektra (Faust Award) 2013 and Leonore in Fidelio 2014/15; has performed regularly at Bayreuth Festival since her debut there as Brunnhilde in Wagner's Ring 2002, also with Wiener Staatsoper, Deutsche Oper Berlin, Opernhaus Zurich, Teatro alla Scala Milan, and at European opera houses such as Badisches Staatstheater Karlsruhe, Saarländisches Staatstheater Saarbrücken, Bregenzer Festspiele, Bayerische Staatsoper, Accademia di Santa Cecilia in Rome and Aalto Theatre in Essen, Théâtre de la Monnaie Brussels and at Aix-en-Provence. *Recordings include* Elektra (Gramophone Award for Best Opera Recording 2015). *Honours:* Christel-Goltz-Prize 1999, Kammersangerin 2002, Deutsche Theaterpreis Faust 2006. *Current Management:* Bühnen- und Konzertagentur Marianne Böttger, Wittelsbacherstr. 21, 10707 Berlin, Germany. *E-mail:* agency@boettger-berlin.de. *Website:* www.boettger-berlin.de.

HERMAN, Silvia; singer (soprano); b. 1954, Vienna, Austria. *Education:* studied in Vienna with Anton Dermota. *Career:* worked at the Opera Studio of the Vienna Staatsoper 1976–79; appearances in Vienna 1979–82, Hamburg 1983–85; guest engagements in Stuttgart, Geneva, Barcelona, Madrid and Cologne 1989–90; Salzburg Festival 1978–81; Bayreuth Festival 1978 as a Flowermaiden 1985–88, as Wellgunde and Waltraute in Die Walküre; Bruckner Festival in Linz 1982–88, and elsewhere, in lieder recitals and concert showings. *Recordings:* Das Rheingold and Die Walküre (conducted by Haitink), Schumann's Das Paradies und der Peri.

HERMAN, Witold Walenty, MA, DPhilMus; Polish cellist; *Professor, State Academy of Music, Kraków*; b. 14 Feb. 1932, Toruń; s. of Alojzy and Marguerite Grosser; m. Catherine Bromboszcz 1970; one s. one d. *Education:* Szymanowski Conservatory, Toruń, Acad. of Music, Kraków, Ecole Normale de Musique, Paris, France, World Univ., Tucson, AZ, USA. *Career:* debut with State Philharmonie, Kraków, May 1954; cello concerts with orchestras, cello recitals, masterclasses in Poland and other European countries; Prof., Music Acad., Kraków, Dir of Cello and Double Bass Dept; Visiting Prof., Franz Liszt Musik Akademie in Weimar 1972; mem. of jury Int. Pablo Casals Cello Competition, Budapest 1968, Int. Cello Competition Markneukirchen, Germany. *Recordings:* for radio and television in Poland and the rest of Europe including Radio Luxembourg; as a solo cellist with major symphony orchestras. *Publication:* Notes for Cello, edited in Poland, Polish Music Edition. *Honours:* Chevalier Cross of the Order of Polonia Restituta; Special Prizes of the Polish Minister of Culture, Golden Cross of Merit, Poland, Excellence in Teaching Award Palm Beach Univ., Florida (USA) 2001, Honoured Guest Tchaikovsky Competition, Moscow (Russia), J. S. Bach Competition, Leipzig (Germany), Ray Robinson Excellence in Teaching Award. *Address:* ul Friedleina 49 m 5, 30-009 Kraków (home); Academy of Music, ul sw. Tomasza 43, 31027 Kraków, Poland (office). *Telephone:* (12) 634-53-73 (home); (12) 422-32-50 (office). *Fax:* (12) 422-66-94 (office).

HERMANN, Roland; singer (baritone); b. 17 Sept. 1936, Bochum, Germany. *Education:* studied with Paul Lohmann, Margarethe von Winterfeldt and Falmino Contini. *Career:* debut in Trier 1967 as Count Almaviva; mem., Zürich Opera from 1968; guest appearances in Munich, Paris, Berlin and Cologne; Buenos Aires 1974, as Jochanaan in Salome and Wolfram in Tannhäuser; US debut 1983, with the New York Philharmonic; La Scala Milan debut 1986, with Claudio Abbado; roles include Don Giovanni, Amfortas, Germont, Gunther in Götterdämmerung and the title roles in Karl V by Krenek and Doktor Faust by Busoni; Apollo (L'Orfeo), Cinna (Lucio Silla), Morald (Die Feen), Forester (The Cunning Little Vixen); Mauregato (Alfonso und Estrella); Beckmesser, Achille (Penthesilea); Vendramin (Massimila Doni), Orff's Prometheus; took part in the European stage premiere of Die Jakobsleiter by Schoenberg (Hamburg 1983) and the world premiere of Kelterborn's Der Kirschgarten (Zürich 1984); sang in the premiere of Krenek's Oratorio Symeon der Stylites at the 1988 Salzburg Festival, conducted by Lothar Zagrosek; BBC London 1989, in the title role of Der Prinz von Homburg by Henze; sang the Forester in The Cunning Little Vixen at Zürich 1989, The Master in the premiere of York Höller's Der Meister und Margarita (Paris 1989) and Gunther at a concert performance of Götterdämmerung at the Holland Festival; sang Busoni's Doktor Faust at Leipzig 1991; season 1992 as Nekrotzar in Le Grand Macabre at Zürich, followed by the Count in Capriccio; sang Paolo in Simon Boccanegra at Zürich 1996; Gurlitt's Wozzeck at Florence 1998; many lieder recitals and concert appearances. *Recordings include:* Penthesilea by Schoeck, Prometheus and Trionfi by Orff, Die Meistersinger, C.P.E. Bach's Magnificat, Moses und Aron by Schoenberg, Zemlinsky's Der Kreidekreis, Mathis der Maler by Hindemith, Peer Gynt by Werner Egk, Der Vampyr by Marschner, Schumann's Genoveva.

HERMANOVA, Vera, MMus, PhD; Czech organist; b. 9 Sept. 1951, Brno; m. Zdenek Spatka 1977. *Education:* Brno Conservatoire, Janáček Acad. of Performing Arts, Brno, Conservatoire National de Saint-Maur, Paris with Prof. Gaston Litaize, Masaryk Univ., Brno. *Career:* special attention to French and Czech organ music of all periods; masterclass with prominent European organists (Gaston Litaize, Piet Kee, Lionel Rogg); radio and television recordings in Czech Republic, Denmark, Germany, Austria, Slovenia; organ recitals in a number of European culture centres, including Prague, Paris, Vienna, Linz, Berlin, Munich, Hamburg, Dresden, Copenhagen, Oslo, Ljubljana, Haarlem, Utrecht, and in festivals at home and abroad (the UK, Germany, Denmark, The Netherlands, Austria); mem. Asscn Jehan Alain, Romainmôtier, Switzerland. *Recordings:* French Organ Works (Messiaen, Dupré, Alain); Les Grandes Orgues de Notre Dame de Chartres (French Organ Music); Musica Nova Bohemica (Eben, Kohoutek); Musik der Gegenwart (Bodorová); Czech Organ Music of the 18th Century; Czech Organ Music of the 20th Century; F. X. Brixi (1732–1771) Organ Concertos (with authentic period instruments), 1999. *Honours:* finalist Int. Organ Competition, Bologna 1975, Premier Prix à l'Unanamité, Saint-Maur 1981, Czech Music Fund Prize, Prague 1992.

HERNANDEZ, Cesar; American singer (tenor); b. 13 Oct. 1960, Puerto Rico. *Career:* debut in New Jersey 1989, as Rodolfo in La Bohème; Spoleto Festival 1991, in Menotti's Goya; appearances in opera houses at Trieste, Catania and Genoa; season 1995 as Pinkerton at Hamburg, Alfredo at Vienna and Cavaradossi at Helsinki; further engagements as the Duke of Mantua at Tel-Aviv and for Miami Opera, Edgardo in Lucia di Lammermoor and San Diego as Cavaradossi 1996; sang Paco in La Vida Breve at Brussels 1998; season 2000 as Pinkerton at the Deutsche Oper Berlin, Cavaradossi in Brussels, Faust at the Salzburg Landestheater and Falla's Paco at Venice; concerts include the Verdi Requiem.

HERNANDEZ-IZNAGA, Jorge; Cuban violist; b. 1950, Havana; m. Lozano Carola 1972; one s. one d. *Education:* National School of Art, Havana, Conservatory Tchaikovsky, Moscow. *Career:* debut at Havana 1972; Prof. of Viola, Conservatory Roldan, Havana 1972–76, Superior Inst. of Arts, Havana 1983–92; Principal Viola, National Symphonic Orchestra of Cuba; founder, The Havana String Quartet; television and radio broadcasts in Cuba 1972–92, Russia 1977, 1979, Hungary 1979, Argentina 1987, 1988, Uruguay 1988, Republic of Korea 1988, Bulgaria 1990, Mexico 1990, Spain 1992–97; co-principal, Orchestra of Cordova, Spain; mem. Writers' and Artists' Union of Cuba, Chamber Music of America. *Recordings:* Havana String Quartet, L. Brouwer's Quartets and M. Ravel-H. Villa Lobos No. 1. *Honours:* Chamber Music Festival of Havana Interpretive Mastery Prize 1987. *Address:* Basilica No. 18, Madrid 28020, Spain.

HERNANDEZ-LARGUIA, Cristian; Argentine choir conductor; b. 6 Oct. 1921, Buenos Aires; m. Eugenia Barbarich 1953. *Education:* studied with T. Fuchs, E. Leuchter, R. Shaw, N. Greenberg and G. Graetzer. *Career:* debut with Madrigal Group, Asoc Ros de Cultura Inglesa 1941; Conductor, Coro Estable de Rosario, since 1946; founder and Conductor, Pro Musica de Rosario, 1962; appearances in concert tours to North, Central and South America and Europe, 1967–92, Hunter College, NY, Coolidge Auditorium, Washington DC and St Martin in the Fields, London; Prof. of Choir Conducting, Musical Morphology and Acoustics, University of Litoral, University Rosario; performances include Mass in B Minor, Bach's first version with Argentine cast, 1985; St John Passion, Bach, 1977; First Argentine performance of complete and original version Messiah, 1973, Brocke's Passion, 1980, Handel. *Recordings:* 35 albums. *Honours:* awards with Pro Musica and CER, as well as National Culture Glory 1984, illustrious citizen

1985, Concorso Internazionale Guido d'Arezzo, Italy 1967–81. *Address:* San Luis 860, 4J, 2000 Rosario, Argentina.

HERNON, Paul; British theatre director and designer; b. 1947, Northumberland, England. *Career:* co-founder, London Music Theatre Group 1982, and directed the British stage premieres of Martin's Le Vin Herbé and Vivaldi's Juditha Triumphans at the Camden Festival, London; British premieres of Salieri's Prima la Musica and Ward's The Crucible; directed a tercentenary production of Handel's Acis and Galatea for the English Bach Festival in Reggio Emilia, Seville and Madrid; in Northern Ireland has directed Don Giovanni, Così fan tutte, Le nozze di Figaro, Die Zauberflöte and Der Schauspieldirektor and works by Haydn, Donizetti, Puccini and Purcell; has designed productions of Hansel and Gretel at Sadler's Wells, La Favorita in Dublin, Offenbach operas in Belfast and Crispino e la Comare at the Camden Festival; designed the Yuri Lyubomov productions of Jenůfa (first in Zürich 1986) and Das Rheingold at Covent Garden 1986, 1988; Eugene Onegin for Bonn 1987, and Tannhäuser for Stuttgart 1988.

HERR, Karlheinz; German singer (bass); b. 27 Dec. 1933, Zellhausen. *Education:* studied with Paul Lohmann in Frankfurt. *Career:* sang first in opera at Mainz 1959, then appeared at Darmstadt 1960–63, Mannheim 1963–88; among best roles have been Klingsor, Osmin, Mozart's Bartolo, Leporello, Rocco, Daland, and Varlaam in Boris Godunov; guest appearances at the Paris Opéra 1974, Bayreuth Festival 1974, and in The Ring at Warsaw 1988–90; concert engagements in Haydn's Seasons and Creation, Messiah, Rossini's Stabat Mater and the Verdi and Fauré Requiems.

HERREWEGHE, Philippe; Belgian conductor and choral director; b. 2 May 1947, Ghent. *Education:* Ghent Conservatory. *Career:* founder, Collegium Vocale of Ghent 1975, La Chapelle Royale 1977, Orchestre des Champs Elysées 1991, Ensemble Vocal Européen; performances include St Matthew's Passion, Bach, with La Chapelle Royale; C Minor Mass and Requiem, Mozart; Elias, Paulus, A Midsummer Night's Dream, Mendelssohn; Missa Solemnis, Beethoven; German Requiem, Brahms; Les Nuits d'Eté, L'Enfance du Christ, Berlioz; guest conductor with many orchestras, including Concertgebouw Orchestra, Rotterdam Philharmonic Berlin Philharmonic, Leipzig and Vienna Philharmonic; Artistic Dir, Saintes Festival 1982–; Cultural Ambassador for Flanders 1993–; Musical Dir, Royal Flanders Philharmonic Orchestra 1998. *Recordings include:* music by Rameau, Lalande and Lully, Mahler's Des Knaben Wunderhorn (with Orchestre des Champs-Elysées) 2005, Schütz's Opus ultimum (Schwanengesang) 2007. *Honours:* Officier, Ordre des Arts et des Lettres; Dr hc (Leuven Univ.) 1997. *Address:* c/o Stephane Maciejewski, 10 rue Coquillère, 75001 Paris, France.

HERRICK, Christopher; British organist. *Career:* fmr organist Westminster Abbey, London; freelance concert organist 1984–; numerous int. performances, including complete organ works of J. S. Bach at Lincoln Center Festival, USA 1998, BBC Proms, London, St Olav's Festival, Norway, Stockholm Int. Festival, Sweden, Eskilstuna Kloster, Sweden, Toledo Int. Organ Festival, Spain, concerts and tours in New Zealand, Australia, Canada, Denmark, Switzerland. *Recordings:* Organ Fireworks Vols 1–10 1984–2004, Bach, The Six Trio Sonatas 1990, Bach, The Orgelbüchlein 1994, Daquin, Douze Noëls 1995, Bach, The Italian Connection 1995, Bach, Organ Miniatures 1997, Organ Dreams I 1998, Bach, Organ Cornucopia 1999, Bach, The Clavierübung Chorales 1999, Organ Dreams II 2000, Bach, Attributions 2000, Organ Dreams III 2002, Bach's Complete Organ Works (16 CDs) 2002, Sweelinck, Keyboard Music 2003, Organ Dreams IV 2005. *E-mail:* enquiries@herrick.musician.org.uk (office). *Website:* www.herrick.musician.org.uk.

HERRMANN, Anita; singer (mezzo-soprano); b. 1947, Karlsruhe, Germany. *Education:* studied in Strasbourg and with Joseph Metternich in Cologne. *Career:* sang with the Bonn Opera 1971–79, Karlsruhe 1980–86, with further engagements at the Staatsoper Stuttgart, the Berlin Deutsche Oper and the Vienna Volksoper; Bregenz Festival 1987–90, in Contes d'Hoffmann and Fliegender Holländer; roles have included Mozart's Marcellina, Ino in Semele, Mistress Quickly in Falstaff, Lubasha in Sadko, Carolina in Elegy for Young Lovers and Mirza in Judith by Matthus (Berne 1992); sang Strauss's Annina at Deutsche Oper, Berlin 1993.

HERRMANN, Arnulf; German composer; b. 12 Dec. 1968, Heidelberg. *Education:* Dresden Univ. of Music, Paris Consevatoire with Gérard Grisey and Emanuel Nunes, IRCAM. *Career:* worked closely with contemporary music ensembles including Ensemble Intercontemporain, Klangforum Wien and Ensemble Modern; festivals include Donaueschinger Musiktagen, Wittener Tage für neue Kammermusik, Wien Modern, Ultraschall Berlin, Eclat Festival Stuttgart and Musica Strasbourg; Lecturer in Composition, Hochschule für Musik Hanns Eisler, Berlin. *Compositions include:* for orchestra: Herzbergwerk 2009, durchbrochene Arbeit 2012; for ensemble: direkt entrückt 2003, Fictive Tänze Vols 1 & 2, for wind ensemble 2008, 2009; for solo instrument with ensemble: Anklang 2004, Monströses Lied 2007; also chamber music and works for solo instruments. *Recordings include:* Wasser (with Ensemble Modern). *Honours:* grants and fellowships include Villa Massimo, Rome, Hanns Eisler Composition Prize 2001, Stuttgart Composition Prize 2003, Förderpreis Musik 2008, Ernst von Siemens Music Foundation Composers Award 2010. *Current Management:* c/o Edition Peters, 2–6 Baches Street, London, N1 6DN, England. *Telephone:* (20) 7553-4000. *Fax:* (20) 7490-4921. *Website:* www.editionpeters.com. *E-mail:* info@arnulfhermann.com (office).

HERRMANN, Karl Ernst; German stage director and stage designer; b. 1936, Neukirch, Upper Lusatia; m. Ursula Herrmann. *Education:* Hochschule für Bildende Kunst, Berlin. *Career:* designed for theatre at Ulm from 1961 and associated with Peter Stein at Bremen and Berlin 1969–78; worked with Claus Peymann at the Württembergisches Staatsschauspiel 1974–80, with Bochumer Ensemble 1980–85 and at the Vienna Burhtheater 1986–2000; teacher of stage design, Akademie der Bildenden Künste München 1994–2000; designed Das Rheingold and Die Walküre at the Paris Opéra 1976; Théâtre de la Monnaie, Brussels, from 1978, with a cycle of seven operas by Mozart, La Traviata and Orfeo ed Euridice; Eugene Onegin at Hamburg 1979; Die Zauberflöte at the Salzburg Landestheater, to inaugurate the Mozart Bicentenary 1991; Die Entführung at the Vienna Staatsoper 1991; Brussels productions of La Clemenza di Tito and La finta Giardiniera seen at Salzburg Festival 1992; designed sets for the Peter Stein production of Pelléas et Mélisande at Welsh National Opera 1992. *Address:* Grollmannstrasse 58, 10623 Berlin, Germany (home).

HERSANT, Philippe; Italian composer; b. 21 June 1948, Rome. *Education:* Paris Conservatoire, studied with André Jolivet in Madrid, Villa Médici, Rome. *Career:* Producer, Radio France, 1973–; Composer-in-Residence with the Orchestre National de Lyon, 1998–2000. *Compositions include:* Les Visites Espacées, chamber opera, 1982; Stances, for orchestra, 1992; Aztlan, for orchestra, 1983; String Quartet no. 1, 1985; Missa Brevis, 1986; Nachtgesang, for clarinet, violin, cello and piano, 1988; String Quartet No.2, 1988; 2 Cello Concertos, 1989, 1997; Sextet, 1994; Le Chateau des Carpathes, opera, 1991; Landschaft mit Afgonauten, cantata, 1994; L'Infinito, for 12 voices, 1994; 5 Pièces, for orchestra, 1997; Piano Trio, 1998; Paysage avec ruines, for mezzo and orchestra, 1999. *Honours:* Prix Arthur Honegger, 1994; Prix Maurice Ravel, 1995; Grand Prix de la Musique Symphonique, 1998.

HERZOG, Mathieu; French violist. *Education:* Boulogne-Billancourt Conservatory, Paris Conservatory with Ysaÿe Quartet, Geneva Conservatory with Gabor Takacs, Hochschule für Musik, Berlin with Eberhardt Feldz. *Career:* mem. Quatuor Ebène (chamber music ensemble) 1999–2014, joined BBC New Generation Artists Scheme 2006. *Recordings include:* Haydn: Quatuors à Cordes 2006, Bartók: Quatuors 1, 2, 3 2007, Ravel, Debussy and Fauré String Quartets (Echo Klassik Award for Recording of the Year 2009, Gramophone Award for Record of the Year 2009) 2008, Brahms: Piano Quintet No. 1 and String Quartet No. 1 2009, 'Fiction' (Echo Klassik Award 2011) 2010, Mozart: KV 138, KV 421, KV 465 (Echo Klassik Award 2012) 2011, Fauré: Quintettes avec Piano, Opp. 89 & 115 2011, Felix & Fanny Mendelssohn (BBC Music Magazine Chamber Award 2014) 2013. *Honours:* first prize, ARD Int. Competition, Munich 2004, Karl Klinger Foundation Prize, Fondation Groupe Banque Populaire Award, Belmont Prize for Contemporary Music, Fondation Forberg-Schneider 2005, Borletti-Buitoni Trust Award 2007. *Current Management:* c/o Linda Uschinski, Impresariat Simmenauer GmbH, Kurfürstendamm 211, 10719 Berlin, Germany. *Telephone:* (30) 414781717. *Fax:* (30) 414781713. *E-mail:* linda.uschinski@impresariat-simmenauer.de. *Website:* www.impresariat-simmenauer.de.

HESS, Andrea, Dip. RAM, ARAM; British cellist; b. 7 May 1954, London, England; m. John Leonard 1985. *Education:* Royal Acad. of Music, London, Nordwestdeutschemusikakademie, Detmold, Germany. *Career:* debut at Wigmore Hall, London 1979; numerous performances as a soloist throughout UK, Europe, Canada and Far East; performed as mem. of several chamber ensembles, notably the Kreisler Trio of Germany and Raphael Ensemble; appeared on stage as solo cellist in Nat. Theatre production of The Elephant Man 1980–81; solo cellist for RSC 1982–87; Artistic Dir Glenilla Arts Foundation 1986–2008; appearances in drama productions for BBC and major ind. TV cos; several broadcasts for BBC Radio 3; composer and on-stage solo cellist, Nat. Theatre and West End for Arthur Miller's Broken Glass 1994–95, at Nat. Theatre for The Enchantment 2007. *Recordings:* Volker David Kirchner Trio, Wergo; Chopin cello works and Chamber Music with the Kreisler Trio, Pantheon; Hyperion recordings of both Brahms sextets, Dvořák Quintet and Sextet, Korngold Sextet and Schoenberg's Verklärte Nacht, Martinů and Schulhoff Sextets, Arensky Quartet, and Tchaikovsky's Souvenir de Florence Sextet, Strauss Sextet from Capriccio, Bruckner Quintet, Schubert String Trio and Double Cello Quintet and both Brahms Quintets and the Mendelssohn Quintets; Frank Bridge Quintet and Sextet with the Raphael Ensemble. *Address:* 10 Belsize Park, London, NW3 4ES, England.

HESSE, Ruth; German singer (mezzo-soprano); b. 18 Sept. 1936, Wuppertal. *Education:* studied with Peter Offermans in Wuppertal and with Hildegard Scharf in Hamburg. *Career:* sang in Lubeck from 1958; Hamburg Staatsoper from 1960; operas by Wagner, Verdi and Strauss at the Deutsche Oper Berlin from 1962; Bayreuth Festival as Mary, Magdalene and Ortrud; Berlin 1965, in the premiere of Der junge Lord by Henze; Vienna Staatsoper 1966, Ortrud, Brangaene and Eboli; Paris Opéra 1966, 1972, as Kundry and as The Nurse in Die Frau ohne Schatten; Salzburg Festival 1974–75, as The Nurse; sang Clytemnestra in Elektra at the Deutsche Oper Berlin 1988; concert and oratorio appearances. *Recordings:* Die Meistersinger, Die Frau ohne Schatten, Der junge Lord, Fricka in Der Ring des Nibelungen, Violanta by Korngold.

HESSE, Ursula; German singer (mezzo-soprano); b. 1970, Cologne. *Education:* Berlin Musikhochschule with Ingrid Figur and Gundula Hintz-Lukas, masterclasses with Hilde Rössl-Majdan and Brigitte Fassbaender, studied with Aribert Reimann. *Career:* Komische Oper Berlin, in the song cycle Love, Life and Death by Siegfried Matthus, 1995; toured Brussels, London, Dresden

and Copenhagen in Mozart concert arias for the ballet Un Moto di Gioa, 1995; concerts at the Berlin Festival with the Berlin Singakademie and with the New Bach Collegium in Brussels and Amsterdam; season 1996–97 as Carmen at Lubeck and in Die Zauberflöte at Brussels; Alcina, Handel, Amsterdam. *Recordings include:* Webern Lieder, with Aribert Reimann. *Honours:* Prizewinner, Paula-Saloman-Lindberg Lieder Competition, 1993; Deutscher Musikweitbewer, 1995. *Current Management:* c/o Stafford Law, Candleway, Broad Street, Sutton Valence, Kent ME17 3AT, England. *Telephone:* (1622) 840038. *Fax:* (1622) 840039. *E-mail:* staffordlaw@btinternet.com. *Website:* www.stafford-law.com.

HETHERINGTON, Hugh; British singer (tenor); b. 1958. *Education:* Guildhall School of Music, St John's Coll., Cambridge, studied with Frederick Cox in Manchester and with Audrey Langford. *Career:* with Glyndebourne Festival and touring companies has sung Dr Caius (Falstaff), Truffaldino (Love of Three Oranges), Where the Wild Things Are and Idomeneo; appearances with Scottish Opera as Dema in Cavalli's L'Egisto, Pang in Turandot, The Devil in The Soldier's Tale, Basilio in Le nozze di Figaro and roles in Iolanthe, Lulu, La Vie Parisienne and Eugene Onegin; with ENO as Piet in Ligeti's Le Grand Macabre and in The Return of Ulysses and L'Orfeo 1992; Covent Garden from 1985 in King Priam and Samson et Dalila; further engagements with University Opera, New Sussex Opera, Opera Factory, Zürich and London Sinfoniettas, the Singers' Company, Channel 4 television and the Endymion Ensemble double bill of Monteverdi and Michael Nyman 1987; New York debut 1989, in HMS Pinafore with New Sadler's Wells Opera at the City Center Theater; concerts with the City of Birmingham Symphony and the Matrix Ensemble.

HETHERWICK, Gilbert; American label manager; b. Shreveport, La. *Education:* Louisiana State Univ. *Career:* played guitar in New Orleans clubs; fmr regional sales man., PolyGram Classics; fmr Gen. Man. Angel Records/EMI Classics USA; fmr man. at Sony Classical and Telarc Records; Vice-Pres. and Gen. Man. BMG Classics 2003–05; Pres. Sony BMG Masterworks Classical Division 2005–06, responsible for labels, including RCA Red Seal, Sony Classical, Odyssey, Deutsche Harmonia Mundi, Arte Nova. *Telephone:* (845) 246-1852 (office). *E-mail:* hetherwick@mac.com (office). *Website:* www.gilberthetherwick.com.

HEUCKE, Stefan; German composer; b. 24 May 1959, Gaildorf. *Education:* studied with Prof. Renate Werner in Stuttgart, with Prof. A. von Arnim, Prof. G. Schafer at Musikhochschule Dortmund. *Career:* debut in the premiere of Vier Orchesterstücke, op 5, performed by Saarland State Orchestra, Saarbrucken 1985; Dozent (Univ. Lecturer) in Theory of Music, Musikhochschule Dortmund 1989–; production and editing live for WDR, SDR and Saarlandischer Rundfunk broadcasting stations; numerous performances in Germany, Russia, The Netherlands, France and Chile; mem. GEMA, Interessenverband Deutscher Komponisten. *Compositions include:* Vier Orchesterstücke (op 5) 1983, Variations on a theme of Webern for orchestra (op 10) 1988, Piano trio (op 11) 1989, Symphony No. 1 (op 12) 1990, Abendgebete (op 14), Symphony No. 2 (op 19) 1993, The Selfish Giant for narrator and orchestra (op 20) 1994, Sonata for bass clarinet and piano (op 23) 1995, Quintet for violin, viola, violoncello, double bass and piano (op 25) 1995, The Happy Prince: 21 Easy Piano Pieces (op 28). *Honours:* Forum of Young German Composers Competition Prize 1985, City of Dortmund grant 1990.

HEWITT, Angela, CC, OBE, ARCT, BMus, FRSC; Canadian pianist; b. 26 July 1958, Ottawa, Ont.; d. of the late Godfrey Hewitt and Marion Hogg. *Education:* Royal Conservatory of Music, Toronto, Univ. of Ottawa. *Career:* first recital aged nine; US debut, Kennedy Center, Washington, DC 1976; Wigmore Hall debut 1985; BBC Proms debut, London 1990; recitals and concerto appearances throughout N America, Europe, the Far East, Australia, New Zealand, Mexico, etc; numerous radio and TV broadcasts in UK and overseas; performed J. S. Bach's The Well-Tempered Clavier in 26 countries 2007–08; Artistic Dir Trasimeno Music Festival, Umbria, Italy 2004–. *Recordings include:* all the major keyboard works of J.S. Bach 1994–2005; twice recorded Bach's complete Well-Tempered Clavier; Bach Performance on the Piano (DVD), The Art of Fugue 2014; also recorded solo works of Couperin, Rameau, Scarlatti, Beethoven, Schumann, Chabrier, Fauré, Debussy, Messiaen, Ravel; Mozart Concerto cycle begun in 2011; works for piano and orchestra by Robert Schumann with DSO Berlin, conductor Hannu Lintu 2012. *Publications include:* Angela Hewitt's Bach Book 2010. *Honours:* Hon. DMus (Ottawa) 1995; Hon. LLD (Queen's, Kingston) 2002, (Toronto) 2009; Hon. DUniv (Open) 2006; First Prize, Toronto Int. Bach Piano Competition 1985, Juno Award for Best Instrumental Recording of the Year (Canada) 1999, 2001, 2004, Gov. Gen.'s Award for Performing Arts 2002, Listeners' Award, BBC Radio 3 2003, Artist of the Year, Gramophone Awards 2006, Instrumentalist of the Year, MIDEM, Cannes 2010, Gramophone Hall of Fame 2015. *Current Management:* c/o Harrison Parrott, 5–6 Albion Court, Albion Place, London, W6 0QT, England. *Telephone:* (20) 7313-3502. *Fax:* (20) 7221-5042. *E-mail:* info@harrisonparrott.co.uk. *Website:* www.harrisonparrott.com; www .angelahewitt.com; www.trasimenomusicfestival.com.

HEYDE, Neil, MMus, PhD, LMusA; British musician (cello) and academic; *Professor, Royal Academy of Music. Career:* cellist, Kreutzer Quartet; Prof., Univ. of London at RAM 2013–, Head of Postgraduate Programmes; as soloist and chamber musician, has appeared throughout Europe and broadcast on BBC, WDR, ORF, Radio France, Netherlands Radio. *Film:* Electric Chair Music (documentary). *Recordings include:* Ferneyhough: Time and Motion

Study II for solo cello and electronics 1973–76; with Kreutzer Quartet: Michael Finnissy: Second and Third String Quartets 2012, Quartet Choreography – String Quartets by Stravinsky, Lutosławski, Ligeti and Finnissy 2012, Grieg Piano Quintet and Finnissy Grieg-Quintettsatz (with Roderick Chadwick, piano) 2013, Anton Reicha – Complete String Quartets, Vol. Two, op. 48 no. 3 and op. 49 no. 1 2014, Unfold, Australian String Quartets of the 1960s and '70s 2014. *Publications include:* critical editions for Faber Music; articles in journals. *Honours:* Hon. RAM. *Address:* Royal Academy of Music, Marylebone Road, London, NW1 5HT, England (office). *Telephone:* (20) 7873-7395 (office). *Website:* www.ram.ac.uk (office).

HEYER, John Hajdu, BMus, MA, PhD; American musicologist and conductor; b. (John H. Hajdu), 4 Jan. 1945, Altoona, PA; m. Sandra Lee Heyer 1973; two s. *Education:* DePauw Univ., Univ. of Colorado, studied with Nadia Boulanger. *Career:* teacher, Univ. of Colorado 1971–73; teacher, 1973–87, Chair., Music Department, 1980, Univ. of California, Santa Cruz; Lecturer, Programme Annotator, Carmel Bach Festival, 1979–; Dean, Coll. of Fine Arts, Indiana Univ. of Pennsylvania, Indiana, PA, 1987–; mem. of International Committee preparing the New Collected Works of Jean-Baptiste Lully for publication; Pres., Rocky Ridge Music Center Foundation, 1989–; Dean, Coll. of Arts and Communication, Univ. of Wisconsin, Whitewater, 1997–. *Recordings:* Conducted J. Gilles, Messe des Morts, Musical Heritage Society, 1981. *Publications:* Critical Edition: Jean Gilles, Messe des Morts, 1983; Lully and the Music of the French Baroque, 1989; Critical edition: J.-B. Lully, Notus in Judaea, 1996; Lully Studies, 2000; contrib. to Notes; The New Grove. *Address:* College of Arts and Communication, University of Wisconsin Whitewater, Whitewater, WI 53190, USA.

HICKEY, Angela; British singer (mezzo-soprano); b. 1949. *Education:* Guildhall School of Music. *Career:* appearances with Royal Opera House, English National Opera, Scottish Opera, Opera North, Glyndebourne, City of Birmingham Touring Opera, Opera Northern Ireland, Monte Carlo Opera, Teatro Carlo Felice, Genoa; Roles include: Verdi's Preziosilla, Mistress Quickly and Azucena; Kabanicha in Katya Kabanova; Jocasta in Oedipus Rex; Carmen; Hélène in War and Peace with ENO; Annina in Der Rosenkavalier with Monte Carlo Opera; Mrs Sedley in Peter Grimes; Madame Larina in Eugene Onegin; Marcellina in Figaro with Opera Northern Ireland, 1991, Glyndebourne, 1992, Opera North, 1996; Mother Goose at Glyndebourne, 1994; Sang Mrs Sedley at Genoa, 1998; Mrs Trapes in Beggar's Opera in Caen and Rouen, 1999; Concerts include: Stabat Mater, Rossini; Requiem, Verdi; The Dream of Gerontius and Sea Pictures, Elgar; Ninth Symphony and Missa Solemnis, Beethoven; 2nd Symphony, Mahler; Nuits d'Eté; Appearances throughout Spain, France, Germany, Italy, Brazil, Czech Republic and Denmark. *Recordings include:* Hippolyte et Aricie, Rameau; Street Scene, Weill; Arianna, Alexander Goehr; Sea Pictures, Elgar.

HICKS, Sarah, BA; American conductor; *Principal Conductor of Pops and Presentations, Minnesota Orchestra;* b. Tokyo, Japan; m. Paul LaFollette. *Education:* Harvard Univ., Curtis Inst. of Music, studied with Otto Werner-Müller. *Career:* founder and Music Dir, Hawaii Symphony Orchestra 1991–96; faculty mem., Curtis Inst. of Music 2000–05; Staff Conductor 2005–; Asst Conductor, Minnesota Orchestra 2006–09; Principal Conductor of Pops and Presentations 2009–; Assoc. Conductor, North Carolina Symphony Orchestra 2009–; guest conductor with Los Angeles Philharmonic, San Francisco Symphony Orchestra, Detroit Symphony Orchestra, Milwaukee Symphony Orchestra, Prime Philharmonic of Korea, Delaware Symphony Orchestra, Chamber Orchestra of Philadelphia, South Carolina Philharmonic, East Slovak State Opera. *Honours:* Thomas Hoopes Prize, Doris Cohen Levy Prize, Harvard Univ. *Address:* Minnesota Orchestra, Orchestra Hall, 1111 Nicollet Mall, Minneapolis, MN 55403, USA (office). *Telephone:* (612) 371-5600 (office). *E-mail:* shhicks@hotmail.com (office); info@mnorch.org (office). *Website:* www .minnesotaorchestra.org (office); www.sarahhicksconductor.com.

HIDALGO, Manuel; Spanish composer; b. 4 Feb. 1956, Antequera, Andalusia. *Education:* Zürich Conservatory with Hans Ulrich Lehmann, studied in Hannover and Stuttgart with Helmut Lachenmann. *Career:* freelance composer 1982–, with performances at Donaueschingen, Stuttgart, Saarbrücken and elsewhere. *Compositions include:* Hacia for string quartet 1980, Harto for orchestra 1982, Al componer for viola, cello, double bass and orchestra 1986, Alegrias (piano concerto) 1987, Gloria for six voices and orchestra 1989, Trio esperando 1989, Física for orchestra 1991, Vomitorio (stage piece) 1991, Desastres de la guerra (after Goya) for narrator and 19 instruments 1996, Des Kaisers neues Kleid (after Andersen) 1996, String Quartet No. 2 1996, Musik nach Gedichten for soprano, alto and orchestra 1996, Dalí (opera) 1999.

HIDJOV, Plamen; singer (bass); b. 20 March 1953, Sofia, Bulgaria. *Education:* studied in Sofia, and in Rome with Boris Christoff. *Career:* National Opera, Sofia 1981–88, Kaiserslautern from 1994; Prokofiev's Napoleon in War and Peace, Theatre Champs-Elysées, Paris, Teatro Massimo, Palermo 1986; Wexford Festival and QEH, London 1988, in Mercadante's Elisa e Claudio; Scottish Opera 1989 and Madrid 1991, as Leporello; other roles include Rossini's Bartolo, Basilio, Don Magnifico, Donizetti's Dulcamara, Don Pasquale, Raimondo, Verdi's Philip II, Procida, Attila and Mussorgsky's Boris Godunov, Pimen, Dosifey and Varlaam; Wagner's Daland, King Marke and Wotan, Baron Kelbar in Verdi's Un Giorno di Regno, Kaiserslautern 1996; Glinka's Ivan Susanin at Kaiserslautern 1997; concerts include Bach's B minor Mass, Messiah, and Mozart's Coronation Mass; Beethoven's 9th

Symphony at Paris and Medellin, Colombia 1987; Liszt Festival Tour, Oratorio Christus 1990; Verdi's Requiem in Granada 1993.

HIELSCHER, Ulrich; German singer (bass); b. 29 April 1943, Schwarzengrund. *Education:* studied in Düsseldorf and with Paul Lohmann in Wiesbaden. *Career:* sang at Essen from 1967, mem., Cologne Opera from 1974; guest appearances at Hamburg, Hanover, Wuppertal, Frankfurt, Düsseldorf, Stuttgart and the Vienna Staatsoper, Ghent Opera 1984–85, and further appearances as concert singer in The Netherlands, Belgium, France, Switzerland and Colombia; further guest appearances, Stadtstheater Schwerin, Staatsoper Berlin, Staatsoper Dresden, Theatre in Kiel and Freiburg; opera roles have included Mozart's Osmin, Figaro, Leporello, Alfonso, Sarastro and Speaker, Verdi's Falstaff and Padre Guardiano, Kecal in The Bartered Bride, Mephistopheles in Faust, Plunket in Martha; Wagner's Daland, Hagen and Gurnemanz, Baron Ochs, the Doktor in Wozzeck, Don Pasquale, Rodrigo in Lulu, Rocco in Fidelio, Pogner in Die Meistersinger and Massenet's Don Quichotte; season 1994–95 at Schwerin as Don Quichotte and Pogner; season 2000–01 at Cologne in Werther, Billy Budd, Falstaff, Carmen and The Love for Three Orange; concerts of works by Bach, Handel, Haydn, Mozart, Beethoven and Bruckner; lied repertoire includes Schubert, Schumann, Beethoven, Richard Strauss, Wolf, Brahms, P. Cornelius, Dvořák, F. Martin, C. Loewe, Paul Gräner, Hans Pfitzner, Moussorgsky, Mendelssohn and Robert Franz. *Recordings include:* Messa di Gloria by Puccini.

HIERHOLZER, Babette, DipMus; German pianist; b. 27 March 1957, Freiburg im Breisgau; m. D. Michael Simpler 1990. *Education:* studied with Elisabeth Dounias-Sindermann in Berlin, with Herbert Stessin at Juilliard School of Music, New York, with Lili Kraus at Texas Christian Univ., Fort Worth, with Wolfgang Saschowa in Berlin, with Maria Tipo in Florence, Italy, with Paul Badura-Skoda at Folkwang-Hochschule Essen and in Vienna, with Bruno Leonardo Gelber in Buenos Aires, Argentina. *Career:* debut with orchestra at Philharmonic Hall, Berlin aged 11; regular appearances with orchestra and solo recitals in Berlin, Hamburg, Bonn, Frankfurt, Munich, Salzburg, Lausanne, Torino, Bordeaux, Caracas, Santiago, New York, Chicago, St Louis, Pittsburgh, Washington, DC; numerous engagements with the Berlin Philharmonic Orchestra; USA debut with Pittsburgh Symphony Orchestra 1984; recital debut at Carnegie Hall, New York 1991; Canadian debut with Saskatoon Symphony Orchestra 1994; several performances of the Clara Schumann Piano Concerto (on the occasion of the 100th anniversary of Clara Schumann's death) in Berlin, Winnipeg, Ottawa, festivals at Merida and Maracaibo, Venezuela; solo recitals with an original recital programme of Clara Schumann at Schumann Houses at Bonn and Zwickau; co-f., with pianist Jürgen Appell, Duo Lontano 2004; Artistic Advisor, German Forum; invited to play Mozart's Concerto for two pianos in Venezuela under conductor Gustavo Dudamel and the Orquesta Nacional Sinfónica de la Juventud Venezolana Simón Bolivar 2010. *Film:* played on soundtrack and double for Clara Wieck (played by Natassja Kinski) in the Schumann movie, Spring Symphony (by Peter Schamoni). *Recordings:* albums of music by Couperin, Debussy, Schumann, Mozart, Schubert, Scarlatti Piano Sonatas Vols. 1, 2 and 3, Kinderszenen 1999, Ferdinand Ries Music for Cello and Piano, Vol. 1, J.S. Bach Concerto Transcriptions and a live recording of Mozart Concerto No. 23 in A Major KV 488 with the Berlin Philharmonic Orchestra under Klaus Tennstedt. *Address:* 46 Aspinwall Road, Red Hook, NY 12571, USA. *Website:* www.babettehierholzer.com; www.duolontano.com; www.germanforum.org.

HIESTERMANN, Horst; German singer (tenor); b. 14 Aug. 1934, Ballenstadt, Harz. *Career:* Stadttheater Brandenburg from 1957, debut as Pedrillo in Die Entführung; sang in Leipzig, Weimar, Berlin and Dresden; Deutsche Oper am Rhein Dusseldorf 1976–84; Salzburg Festival from 1978 as Monostatos, as the Dancing Master in Ariadne auf Naxos, and as Robespierre in Dantons Tod 1983; Dallas Opera 1982, as Loge in Das Rheingold; Tokyo 1983, as Mime in Siegfried; other appearances in Geneva, Rouen, Amsterdam, Houston and New York (Metropolitan Opera); Barcelona 1984, as Aegisthus in Elektra; mem., Zürich Opera from 1984; Deutsche Oper Berlin 1984, in the premiere of Reimann's Gespenstersonate; Vienna Staatsoper 1987, as Herod in Salome; sang Mime in a new production of The Ring at the Metropolitan 1988–90; Shuisky in Boris Godunov at Barcelona 1990; Herod in Berlin; sang Aegisthus at Athens 1992; other roles include the Captain in Wozzeck (Catania 1998) and David in Die Meistersinger. *Recordings:* Wozzeck, The Duenna by Prokofiev, Puntila by Dessau, Carmina Burana, Trionfi by Orff, Die Zauberflöte, Karl V by Krenek, Die Meistersinger conducted by Karajan. *Publication:* E: Mime bist du so witzig? 2000.

HIETIKKO, Jaakko; Finnish singer (bass); b. 16 May 1950, Kurikka. *Education:* Helsinki Sibelius Acad. *Career:* sang in the chorus of the Finnish Nat. Opera from 1975 and apptd as a soloist 1980; has appeared in most of the classical bass roles; has specialised in such modern repertory as The Red Line by Sallinen (premiere 1978), Vincent by Rautavaara (premiere 1990); sang in the premiere of The Book of Jonah by Olli Kortekanges, Helsinki 1995 and The Last Temptations by Kokkonen; many appearances at the Savonlinna Festival and as a concert singer.

HIGDON, Jennifer, BM, MA, PhD; American composer; b. 31 Dec. 1962, Brooklyn, NY. *Education:* Bowling Green State Univ., Univ. of Pennsylvania. *Career:* composer-in-residence, American Composers' Forum Continental Harmony Project 2000, Nat. Youth Orchestra Festival 2002, Bravo! Vail Valley Music Festival 2002, 2003, Tanglewood Festival of Contemporary

Music 2002, Bard Conductor's Inst. 2003, Cabrillo Festival of Contemporary Music 2004, Composers' Conference at Bennington Coll. 2004, The Philadelphia Singers 2004–05, Pittsburgh Symphony Orchestra 2005–06, Green Bay Symphony Orchestra 2006–07; featured composer, Tanglewood Festival of Contemporary Music 2003, Midwest Int. Band and Orchestra Clinic 2006; Visiting Composer, Univ. of Texas at Austin 2006; Karel Husa Visiting Prof., Ithaca Coll. 2006–07; mem. composition faculty, Curtis Inst. of Music, currently Milton L. Rock Chair in Composition Studies. *Compositions include:* Autumn's Cricket 1987, Autumn Reflection 1994, Shine 1995, Autumn Music 1995, Blue Cathedral 1999, Wind Shear 2000, Celestial Hymns 2000, Ceremonies 2001, Dark Wood 2001, DASH 2001, City Scape 2002, Amazing Grace 2002, Concerto for Orchestra 2002, Machine 2002, Bentley Roses 2002, Piano Trio (Ithaca Coll. Heckscher Prize) 2003, Impressions 2003, Dooryard Bloom 2004, Logo 2004, Bop 2004, An Exaltation of Larks 2005, Percussion Concerto (Grammy Award for Best Classical Contemporary Composition 2010) 2008, Violin Concerto (Pulitzer Prize for Music 2010) 2009. *Recordings include:* Blue Cathedral (with Atlanta Symphony Orchestra) 2003, City Scape and Concerto for Orchestra (with Atlanta Symphony Orchestra) 2004, Percussion Concerto 2005, Splendid Wood 2006, String Poetic 2006, Piano Trio, Voices and Impressions (with Cypress String Quartet) 2006, Strange Imaginary Animals (with Eighth Blackbird) 2006, International Connections (with Verdehr Trio) 2006. *Honours:* winner ASCAP Foundation Commission Project 1995, Pennsylvania Council on the Arts Fellowship 1996, 2000, American Acad. of Arts and Letters Charles Ives Fellowship 1997, Guggenheim Fellowship 1997, Musical Fund Soc. Grant 1998, Meet the Composer Grant 1998, Pew Fellowship 1999, Pennsylvania Council on the Arts Artist's Fellowship 2000, Bowling Green State Univ. Distinguished Alumni Award 2001. *Address:* c/o Cheryl Lawson (Artist Representative), Lawdon Press, 1008 Spruce Street, Suite 3F, Philadelphia, PA 19107, USA (office). *Telephone:* (215) 592-1847 (office). *Fax:* (215) 592-1095 (office). *E-mail:* lawdonpress@aol.com (office). *Website:* jenniferhigdon.com.

HIGGINBOTTOM, Edward, BMus, MA, DPhil, FRCO; British university lecturer; *Director of Music, New College, Oxford*; b. 16 Nov. 1946, Kendal, Cumbria; m. Caroline M.F. Barrowcliff 1971; three s. four d. *Education:* Corpus Christi Coll., Cambridge. *Career:* worked in Paris 1970–72; Research Fellow, Corpus Christi Coll., Cambridge 1973–76; Dir of Music and Fellow, New Coll., Oxford 1976–. *Recordings:* more than 80 recordings ranging over Renaissance and Baroque music, plus a significant contrib. to 20th century repertory. *Publications:* various edns of 17th and 18th cenutry music, contribs to Grove 6 and 7, Musical Times, Organists Review, Music and Letters. *Honours:* Hon. Fellowships, Royal School of Church Music 2002, Guild of Church Musicians 2003; Commdr, Ordre des Arts et Lettres; Royal Coll. of Organists Harding and Read Prizes, John Stewart of Rannoch Univ. Prize in Sacred Music. *Address:* New College, Holywell Street, Oxford, OX1 3BN, England (office). *E-mail:* edward.higginbottom@new.ox.ac.uk (office). *Website:* www.newcollegechoir.com (office).

HILEY, David, BA, PhD; British academic; b. 5 Sept. 1947, Littleborough, Lancs.; m. Ann Fahrni 1975; two d. *Education:* Univs of Oxford and London. *Career:* Asst Music Master, Eton Coll. 1968–73; Lecturer, Royal Holloway Coll., London 1976–86; Prof., Regensburg Univ., Germany 1986–; mem. Plainsong and Mediaeval Music Soc., Gesellschaft für Musikforschung, American Musicological Soc., Academia Europaea. *Publications:* New Oxford History of Music II (co-ed.) 1990; Western Plainchant: A Handbook 1993; Die Offizien des Mittelalters (co-ed.) 1999; Das Repertoire der normanno-sizilischen Tropare I: Die Sequenzen 2001. *Address:* Sonnenstrasse 10, 93152 Nittendorf, Germany (home). *E-mail:* david.hiley@psk.uni-regensburg.de (office).

HILL, David Neil, MA, FRAM, FRCO, FRSCM; British organist, conductor and academic; *Principal Conductor, Schola Cantorum and Professor of Choral Conducting, Yale University*; b. 13 May 1957, Carlisle, Cumbria, England; s. of Brian Hill and Jean Hill; m. 1st Hilary Llystn Jones 1979; one s. one d.; m. 2nd Alice Mary Wills 1994; one d. one s. *Education:* Chetham's School of Music, Manchester, St John's Coll., Cambridge. *Career:* Conductor, Alexandra Choir, London 1979–80, Musical Dir 1980–87; Sub-Organist, Durham Cathedral 1980–82; Organist and Master of Music, Westminster Cathedral 1982–88; Organist and Dir of Music, Winchester Cathedral 1988–2002; Artistic Dir, Philharmonia Chorus 1990–98; Musical Dir, Waynflete Singers 1988–2002; Musical Dir, The Bach Choir 1998–; Dir of Music, St John's Coll., Cambridge 2003–07; frequently directs choral workshops and summer schools in UK, USA and Australia; Chief Conductor Southern Sinfonia; Chief Conductor BBC Singers 2007–; Musical Dir Leeds Philharmonic Soc. 2006–; Prin. Conductor Schola Cantorum and Prof. of Choral Conducting, Yale Univ.; Fellow, Royal School of Church Music. *Recordings:* numerous albums with Westminster and Winchester Cathedral Choirs, St John's College Choir, Cambridge, Bournemouth Symphony Orchestra/Waynflete Singers, Bournemouth Symphony Orchestra/Bach Choir and other groups. *Publications:* Giving Voice (co-author) 1995; regular contrib. of articles on choir training in Choir and Organ. *Honours:* Hon. DMus (Southampton); Gramophone Award 1985, Grammy Award 1997. *Current Management:* c/o Rayfield Allied, Southbank House, Black Prince Road, London, SE1 7SJ, England. *Telephone:* (20) 3176-5500. *E-mail:* catherine.strange@rayfieldallied.com.

HILL, George R., AB, AM, PhD; American musicologist and music bibliographer; *Associate Professor of Music, Baruch College, City University of New York*; b. 12 July 1943, Denver, Colo. *Education:* Stanford Univ., Univ. of Chicago, New York Univ. *Career:* Librarian, Music Div., New York Public Library 1966–70; Asst Music Librarian, New York Univ. 1971–72; Fine Arts Librarian, Univ. of California, Irvine 1972–73; Assoc. Prof. of Music, Baruch Coll., CUNY 1973–. *Publications:* A Thematic Locator for Mozart's Works as Listed in Kochel's Chronologisch-Thematisches Verzeichnis, 6th Edition (principal author) 1970, A Preliminary Checklist of Research on the Classic Symphony and Concerto to the Time of Beethoven (excluding Haydn and Mozart) 1970, A Thematic Catalogue of the Instrumental Music of Florian Leopold Gassmann 1976, Florian Leopold Gassmann, Seven Symphonies 1981, Joseph Haydn Werke, Floetenuhrstuecke 1984, A Handbook of Basic Tonal Practice 1985, Index to Printed Music: Collections and Series (database ed.-in-chief) 2004–; contrib. of articles and reviews to various professional journals, including The New Grove Dictionary of Music and Musicians. *Address:* 84 Highgate Terrace, Bergenfield, NJ 07621-3922, USA (home). *Telephone:* (201) 387-1258 (home). *E-mail:* george.r.hill@att.net (home).

HILL, Jackson, AB, MA, PhD; American composer and academic; *Professor Emeritus of Music, Bucknell University*; b. 23 May 1941, Birmingham, Ala; m. Martha Gibbs 1966; one s. *Education:* Univ. of North Carolina, studied with Iain Hamilton, Roger Hannay. *Career:* Asst Prof., then Assoc. Prof. of Music, Bucknell Univ., Lewisburg, Pa 1968–80, Head of Dept of Music 1980–90, Assoc. Dean of Faculty 1990–95, Presidential Prof. 1996–2000, Prof. Emer. of Music 2008–; Conductor, Bucknell Symphony Orchestra 1969–79; mem. Research Unit, Manchester Coll. Oxford, UK 1975; Visiting Scholar and Choral Asst, Exeter Coll. Oxford 1974–75; Hays/Fulbright Fellow, Japan 1977; Visiting Fellow, Clare Hall Cambridge, UK 1982–83. *Compositions include:* Serenade 1970, Three Mysteries 1973, Paganini Set 1973, Missa Brevis 1974, English Mass 1975, By the Waters of Babylon (sonata) 1976, Whispers of the Dead 1976, Streams of Love 1979, Enigma Elegy 1987, Symphony No. 1 1990, Symphony No. 2 1993, Symphony No. 3 1997, Long Hidden Deep 2001, Philomel 2002, In Winter's Keeping 2002, Remembered Love 2004, When Spring is Born 2004, Sky of Birds 2005, Summer Dreams 2006, A Haunted Melancholy 2008, Bucknell Fantasy 2008, Klavierstuck 2009. *Recordings:* Sonata: By the Waters of Babylon, Ecce vidimus eum, Rhapsody 1995, Tholos 1998, Tango 1998, Tango II 2002, Voices of Autumn 2003, Ma fin est mon commencement 2009, El Duelo (The Mourning) 2010, The Silent Ground 2010, Still, In Remembrance 2011, No Traveler More Blest 2012. *Publications:* The Music of Kees van Baaren 1970, The Harold E. Cook Collection of Musical Instruments; contrib. of numerous articles on music and mysticism, Japanese music and Buddhist liturgical music; contribs to Ethnomusicology, Studia Mystica, Notes. *Honours:* Harriman Award 2004, grants, Exxon Foundation, Fulbright, Nat. Endowment for the Humanities. *Address:* Department of Music, Bucknell University, Lewisburg, PA 17837, USA (office). *Telephone:* (570) 577-1239 (office). *Fax:* (570) 577-1215 (office). *E-mail:* jhill@bucknell.edu (office). *Website:* www.jacksonhillmusic.com (office).

HILL, Jenny; British singer (soprano); b. 20 June 1939, London; m. (divorced); two d. *Education:* Nat. School of Opera, London Opera Centre. *Career:* debut, Sandman, Hansel and Gretel, Sadler's Wells Opera Company (now known as ENO); English Opera Group with Benjamin Britten performing in London, Russia and Canada; created role of Pretty Polly in Punch and Judy premiere, Aldeburgh and Edinburgh Festivals 1968, and Mrs Green in Birtwistle's Down by the Greenwood Side, premiere at the London and Brighton Festivals 1969; repertory operas performed include Traviata, Lucia, La Sonnambula, Rigoletto, Marriage of Figaro, Magic Flute; other appearances include: The Rape of Lucretia (Lucia), A Midsummer Night's Dream (Titania), The Makropoulos Case (Kristina), Hansel and Gretel; concert appearances include A Mother Goose Primer, with the Pierrot Players, and Petrassi's Magnificat, with Giulini, both British premieres at the Royal Festival Hall 1972; City of London Festival Opening Concert, Bach's B minor Mass with Giulini at St Paul's Cathedral; opening concert, English Bach Festival, Blenheim Palace; performances on radio and television as well as numerous song recitals of classical and avant-garde music; fmr Prof. of Singing, Skalkottas Conservatory, Athens, Greece; now teaching singing from home as well as performing; mem., Equity, Incorporated Society of Musicians, Asscn of Singing Teachers. *Recordings include:* The Rape of Lucretia, as Lucia; Schumann's Faust; Bach's St John Passion, Bach's B Minor Mass(Giulini); other recordings now available in Italy of concerts and performances with Giulini (EMI) and Britten (Universal). *Honours:* Leverhulme Scholarship 1960–63, Gulbenkian Fellowship for Most Outstanding Young Performer 1969–72. *Address:* 155 Boston Manor Road, Brentford, Middlesex, TW8 9LE, England (home). *Telephone:* (20) 8560-4758 (home). *E-mail:* jennyhillsinging@googlemail.com (home).

HILL, Martyn, ARCM; British singer (tenor); b. 14 Sept. 1944, Rochester, Kent, England; m. Julie Ann Moffat. *Education:* Royal College of Music, studied with Gerald English, Audrey Langford. *Career:* known worldwide as an opera singer, concert and oratorio soloist and recitalist; repertoire includes Elgar's Dream of Gerontius, Berlioz's Damnation of Faust, Brucker's Te Deum, Verdi's Requiem and Mahler's Das Lied von der Erde; Performs regularly the works of Benjamin Britten; Glyndebourne 1985 and 1988, as Idomeneo and Belmonte; sang War Requiem with the Sydney Symphony and Edo de Waart, Spring Symphony with the Hallé Orchestra and Kent Nagano, and Serenade with the Czech Philharmonic and Christopher Seaman; Evangelist in Bach's St John Passion; Prometeo with Berlin Philharmonic; sang Eumete in Monteverdi's Ulisse at Florence 1999, in Turandot, Die

Meistersinger, Madama Butterfly, Salome at Covent Garden; premiere of Haas' Melancholia, Paris 2008; Tosca and Un Ballo in Maschera, Covent Garden, world premiere of Kagel's Der Matrazengruft, Munich 2009. *Recordings include:* over 200 classical recordings. *Honours:* Hon. DMus (Leicester) 2009. *Current Management:* c/o Owen/White Management, Flat 6, 22 Brunswick Terrace, Hove, East Sussex, BN3 1HJ, England. *Telephone:* (1273) 727127. *Fax:* (1273) 527038. *E-mail:* info@owenwhitemanagement .com. *Website:* www.owenwhitemanagement.com.

HILL, Peter, MA; British pianist and academic; b. 14 June 1948, Lyndhurst, England; m. Charlotte Huggins 1981, two d. *Education:* Univ. of Oxford and Royal College of Music. *Career:* debut at Wigmore Hall, London, 1974; regular broadcasts, BBC; international festival appearances include: Harrogate, Bath, English Bach, Dublin, Stuttgart; Founder Member, Ensemble Dreamtiger; Prof., University of Sheffield. *Recordings:* Complete Piano Music of Havergal Brian; Dreamtiger; East-West Encounters; Nigel Osborne: Remembering Esenin; Piano Works by Nigel Osborne, Douglas Young, Howard Skempton; Messiaen: The Complete Piano Music; Beethoven: Diabelli Variations; The Complete Piano Works of Schoenberg, Berg and Webern; Stravinsky: Music for Four Hands; Stravinsky: Solo Piano Music. *Publications:* The Messiaen Companion (editor); Stravinsky: The Rite of Spring; contrib. to Tempo. *Honours:* Chappell Gold Medal, Royal College of Music, 1971; 1st Prize, Darmstadt Ferienkurs, 1974. *Telephone:* (114) 230-2309. *Fax:* (114) 263-0231. *E-mail:* p.hill@shef.ac.uk.

HILL, Robert Stephen, DipMus, LTCM, MA, PhD; harpsichordist, fortepianist and musicologist; b. 6 Nov. 1953, The Philippines. *Education:* Amsterdam Conservatory, Trinity Coll. of Music, London, Harvard Univ. *Career:* tours with Musica Antiqua Köln; radio and television broadcasts for German, British, Dutch, Belgian and French networks, and National Public Radio and CBC, USA. *Recordings:* J. S. Bach. Sonatas for violin and harpsichord with Reinhard Goebel, J. S. Bach, Art of Fugue, early version; Solo Harpsichord. *Publications:* contrib. to Early Music, Bach Jahrbuch. *Honours:* Erwin Bodky Award 1982, NEA Solo Recitalist Award 1983, American Musicological Soc. Noah Greenberg Award 1988.

HILL SMITH, Marilyn, AGSM; British singer (soprano); b. 9 Feb. 1952, Carshalton, Surrey; d. of George Smith and Irene Smith. *Education:* Nonsuch High School, Ewell and Guildhall School of Music and Drama. *Career:* cabaret, pantomime, concerts 1971–74; toured Australia and NZ with Gilbert & Sullivan for All 1974, USA and Canada 1976; Prin. Soprano, ENO Opera 1978–84; Covent Garden début in Peter Grimes 1981; has appeared at several major European music festivals including Versailles, Granada, Aldeburgh, London Promenade Concerts etc., also with New Sadler's Wells Opera, Canadian Opera Co., Welsh Nat. Opera, Scottish Nat. Opera, New D'Oyly Carte Opera, Lyric Opera of Singapore, etc. and on television and radio and has made several recordings particularly of operetta; Patron Cen. Festival Opera, Epsom Light Opera, Ivor Novello Appreciation Bureau; singing teacher and adjudicator for music festivals. *Plays:* The Sound of Music (as Mother Abbess), UK tour 2010–. *Honours:* Hon. Life mem. Johann Strauss Soc. of GB; Young Musician of the Year 1975 and other prizes.

HILLEBRAND, Nikolaus; singer (bass); b. 1948, Oberschlesien, Germany. *Education:* studied with Rolf Dieter Knoll in Cologne and Hanno Blaschke in Munich. *Career:* debut with Lubeck 1972; Israel 1972, as Mosè in the opera by Rossini; Salzburg Easter Festival 1974, in Die Meistersinger; Vienna Staatsoper 1974; Bayreuth Festival 1974–75, in Parsifal and Die Meistersinger; further engagements in Munich (Lohengrin), Karlsruhe, London, Paris, Rome and Brussels; Taormina Festival 1991, as Telramund; many concert appearances, notably in music by Bach. *Recordings include:* Stefano Colonna in Rienzi; St John Passion by Bach; Egisto by Cavalli; Romeo und Julia by Sutermeister; Reger's Requiem.

HILLEBRANDT, Oskar; German singer (baritone); b. 15 March 1943, Schopfheim, Baden. *Education:* Cologne Musikhochschule with Josef Metternich. *Career:* sang at the Stuttgart Staatsoper from 1969; appearances at Saarbrucken, Kiel and Brunswick from 1971; mem., Dortmund Opera from 1985; guest appearances at Hamburg, Munich, Düsseldorf, Mannheim and Zürich; La Scala Milan as Telramund and the Teatro Zarzuela Madrid as Achillas in Giulio Cesare by Handel; Seattle Opera as Alberich in the Ring; further engagements in Antwerp, Copenhagen and at the Santander Festival, Marseilles and Turin 1986, as Kaspar and Donner; British debut 1989, as Mandryka at the Glyndebourne Festival; other roles include Pizarro, Scarpia, Count Luna, Amonasro, Simon Boccanegra and Jochanaan in Salome; Wagner's Dutchman, Amfortas and Klingsor; sang Alberich at Santiago 1996; season 1995–96 as Wotan at Dortmund, Pizarro at Rome and Alberich in Oslo; sang Alberich and Gunther in Götterdämmerung at Buenos Aires 1998; sang Alberich in Siegfried, and Falstaff at the Komische Oper Berlin 2000; concert showings in Paris, London, New York, Barcelona and Rome.

HILLEBRECHT, Hildegard; singer (soprano); b. 26 Nov. 1927, Hannover, Germany. *Education:* studied with Margarethe von Winterfeld, Franziska Martianssen Lohmann and Paul Lohmann. *Career:* debut in Freiburg 1951, as Leonora in Il Trovatore; sang at Zürich 1952–54, notably in the premiere of the revised version of Hindemith's Cardillac 1952; Düsseldorf 1954–59, Cologne 1956–61; sang Maria in Strauss's Friedenstag at Munich 1961; many appearances at the State Operas of Vienna, Hamburg and Munich; Salzburg Festival 1946, 1964, as Ilia, Chrysothemis and Ariadne; Deutsche Oper Berlin 1968, in the premiere of Ulisse by Dallapiccola; Covent Garden 1967, as the

Empress in Die Frau ohne Schatten; Metropolitan Opera 1968–69; sang with the Zürich Opera from 1972; appearances in Rio de Janeiro, Paris, Rome, San Francisco, Edinburgh, Copenhagen, Barcelona, Dresden, Brussels and Prague; repertoire includes works by Wagner, Puccini (Tosca), Verdi and Strauss, Elena in I Vespri Siciliani, Elisabeth de Valois, Desdemona, Sieglinde, Jenůfa and Ursula in Mathis der Maler. *Recordings:* excerpts from Don Giovanni and Tannhäuser; Cavalleria Rusticana; Der Rosenkavalier; Ariadne auf Naxos; Don Giovanni; Duchess of Parma in Doktor Faust by Busoni; Die Zauberflöte.

HILLER, Wilfried; German composer; b. 15 March 1941, Weissenhorn, Swabia. *Education:* Munich Musikhochschule with Günther Bialas, studied with Boulez and Stockhausen at Darmstadt, and with Carl Orff. *Career:* founded concert series Musik Unserer Zeit, 1968; Ed., Bavarian Radio from 1971; Composition Department of the Richard Strauss Conservatory, Munich, from 1993. *Compositions include:* Katalog I–V for percussion 1967–74, An diesem heutigen Tage, theatre 1973, Schumamit, from the Song of Songs, for soloists, choruses and orchestra 1977–93, Niobe, theatre 1977, Der Josa mit der Zauberfiedel, for speaker, violin and chamber orchestra 1985, reconstruction of Karl Amadeue Hartmann's Chaplin-Ford-Trott (from Waxworks), opera 1930/87, Das Traumfresserchen, singspiel 1990, Chagall-Zyklug, for clarinet and chamber orchestra 1993, Der Rattenfänger, opera 1993, Peter Pan, theatre 1997, Der Schimmelreiter, stage 1997, Der Geigenseppel, melodrama for marionettes 1999, Eduard auf dem Seil, opera 1999, Aias, after Sophocles and Ovid, for mezzo, baritone, speaker and orchestra 2000, Pinnochio, opera 2001, Wolkenstein, opera 2003, Augustinus, oratorio for 2 sopranos, boy soprano, 6 male voices, choir and ensemble 2004. *Honours:* Richard Strauss Prize, Munich, 1968; Schwabinger Arts Prize, 1978. *Current Management:* Schott & Co Ltd, 48 Great Marlborough Street, London, W1F 7BB, England.

HILLIER, Paul Douglas, OBE, AGSM; British singer, conductor and writer; *Director, Theatre of Voices;* b. 9 Feb. 1949, Dorchester, Dorset, England; m. 2nd Else Torp; two d. from previous m. *Education:* Guildhall School of Music, London. *Career:* debut at the Purcell Room, London 1974; Vicar-Choral, St Paul's Cathedral, London 1973–74; Dir Hilliard Ensemble 1973–90; Early Music masterclasses, York, London, Vancouver, Canada; Visiting Lecturer, Univ. of California, Santa Cruz, USA 1980–81; TV debut, Music in Time 1983; Copland Fellow, Amherst Coll., Mass, USA 1984; Founder and Dir Theatre of Voices 1989–; Prof. of Music, Univ. of California, Davis 1990–96; Dir Early Music Inst., Indiana Univ. School of Music 1996–2003; Prin. Conductor, Estonian Philharmonic Chamber Choir 2001–07; Artistic Dir and Chief Conductor, Ars Nova Copenhagen 2003–, Nat. Chamber Choir of Ireland 2008–, Coro Casa da Musica, Porto 2009–. *Recordings:* more than 100 solo and ensemble CDs. *Publications:* 300 Years of English Partsongs 1983, Romantic English Partsongs 1986, The Catch Book 1987, Arvo Pärt 1997, Steve Reich: Writings On Music (ed.) 2002, On Pärt 2005, John Cage and the Music of Always 2007. *Honours:* Order of the White Star (Estonia) 2007; Edison Klassik 1986, Grammy Award 2008, 2010. *Current Management:* c/o Theatre of Voices Management, Livjaergergade 40, 2100 Copenhagen Ø, Denmark. *Telephone:* 28-14-14-85. *E-mail:* contact@paulhillier.net (office). *Website:* www.paulhillier .net.

HILTON, Janet, ARNCM, FRCM; British clarinettist and academic; *Professor of Clarinet, Royal College of Music;* b. 1 Jan. 1945, Liverpool; d. of H. Hilton and E. Hilton; m. David Richardson 1968; two s. (one deceased) one d. *Education:* Belvedere School, Liverpool, Royal Northern Coll. of Music, Vienna Konservatorium. *Career:* BBC concerto debut 1963; appearances as clarinet soloist with major British orchestras including Royal Liverpool Philharmonic, Scottish Nat., Scottish Chamber, City of Birmingham Symphony Orchestra (CBSO), Bournemouth Symphony, Bournemouth Sinfonietta, City of London Sinfonia, BBC Scottish and Welsh Symphony, BBC Philharmonic; guest at Edinburgh, Aldeburgh, Bath, Cheltenham, City of London Festivals, BBC Henry Wood Promenade concerts; appearances throughout Europe and N America; Prin. Clarinet Scottish Chamber Orchestra 1974–80, Kent Opera 1984–88; teacher Royal Scottish Acad. of Music and Drama 1974–80, Royal Northern Coll. of Music 1983–87; Head of Woodwind, Birmingham Conservatoire 1992–; Prof. of Clarinet, Royal Coll. of Music, London 1998–, Head of Woodwind 1998–2010; Prof., Univ. of Central England 1993; Dir Camerata Wind Soloists; works composed for her by Iain Hamilton, John McCabe, Edward Harper, Elizabeth Maconchy, Alun Hoddinott, Malcolm Arnold; Reger Clarinet Sonatas with Jakob Fichert, piano 2009; int. master classes in Paris, Vienna, Wrocław, Singapore, Hong Kong, USA (Chicago, Indiana and Michigan), Australia (Sydney and Melbourne); Pres. Clarinet and Saxophone Soc. of GB. *Recordings include:* several recordings for Chandos, including all of Weber's music for clarinet with the CBSO, Lindsay Quartet and Keith Swallow, the Nielsen and Copland Concertos with the Scottish Nat. Orchestra, Stanford Clarinet Concerto with Ulster Orchestra, Mozart Clarinet Quintet with the Lindsay Quartet 1998; Dedications— concertos by McCabe, Harper, Maconchy and Hoddinott with BBC Scottish Symphony Orchestra, Reger Clarinet Sonatas with Jakob Fichert, piano. *Honours:* Hon. Fellow, Birmingham Conservatoire 2009. *Address:* Royal College of Music, Prince Consort Road, London, SW7 2BS (office); Holte End, Whitehall Lane, Checkendon, Oxon., RG8 0TN, England (home). *Telephone:* (1491) 682853 (home). *E-mail:* jhilton@rcm.ac.uk (office). *Website:* www .impulse-music.co.uk/hilton.htm.

HIMMELBEBER, Liat; singer (mezzo-soprano); b. 27 April 1956, Stuttgart, Germany. *Education:* studied in Berlin, in Hamburg with Judith Beckmann, masterclasses with Aribert Reimann and Dietrich Fischer-Dieskau. *Career:* sang at the Eutin Festival 1982–83, Oldenburg 1984–85, and from 1985 as mem. Theater am Gärtnerplatz, Munich; roles include Rosina, Mozart's Dorabella and Cherubino, and Hansel; guest with the Hamburg Staatsoper and appearances with the Augsburg Opera from 1992; concerts include premieres of works by Reimann, Von Bose and Manfred Trojahn; sang also in the Munich 1987 premiere of Miss Julie by A. Bibalo.

HIND, Rolf, BMus; British pianist and composer; b. 1964, England. *Education:* Royal College of Music with John Constable and Kendall Taylor, studied Los Angeles with Johanna Harris-Heggie. *Career:* has premiered works by Ligeti, Kurtag, Berio, Ruders, McMillan, Holt, Unsuk Chin and many others; played in festivals and major venues throughout Europe and Australasia under conductors including Sir Simon Rattle, Oliver Knussen, Vladimir Ashkenazy and Franz Welser-Most. *Compositions:* composed works for piano and for ensemble, BBC Radio and WDR; chamber collaborations with cellist Frances-Marie Uitti and David Alberman. *Recordings include:* solo works by Messiaen, John Adams, Poul Ruders, Per Norgard, Robert HP Platz, Ligeti, Carter. *Current Management:* c/o Clarion/Seven Muses, 47 Whitehall Park, London, N19 3TW, England. *Telephone:* (20) 7272-4413. *Fax:* (20) 7281-9687. *E-mail:* admin@c7m.co.uk. *Website:* www.rolfhind.com.

HINDS, Esther; singer (soprano); b. 3 Jan. 1943, Barbados, West Indies. *Education:* studied with Clyde Burrows in New York and at Hartt Coll., Hartford with Helen Hubbard. *Career:* debut at New York City Opera 1970, as First Lady in Die Zauberflöte; has sung in New York as Donna Elvira, Madama Butterfly and Gershwin's Bess (on Broadway); engagements at opera houses in Houston, Cincinnati and San Diego; other roles include Liu (Turandot) and Micaela; Spoleto Festival 1983, as Cleopatra in Antony and Cleopatra by Samuel Barber; many concert performances.

HINDS, Geoffrey William John, BA, BDiv, MPhil (Mus), LRSM; New Zealand composer and piano teacher; b. 2 April 1950, Auckland. *Education:* studied in Auckland, Melbourne Coll. of Divinity. *Compositions include:* Sonata for viola and pianoforte 1975, Suite for string quintet 1975, String Quartet 1976, Wellington Motet for the Lord has Purposed 1980–81, Overture into a Broad Place 1981, String Quartet 1981, And His Name Shall Be Called 1981, Cantata Upon This Rock 1982, Symphonic Moments of our Time 1982, Through the Grapevine 1982, Water Water Everywhere (song cycle) 1985, Pieces of Peace (song cycle) 1986, Colyton Overture 1986–87, String Quartet 1983–84, Innocence and Experience (song cycle) 1987, Blowing in the Wind for wind quintet 1987, Nine Mystical Songs (song cycle) 1988–89, Godzone Re-evaluated for youth orchestra 1989, Great Outdoors Suite for piano 1989, String Quartet 1989, St Barnabas Ballads Symphony for tenor and piano, Creation Cantata, The Good Life (musical) 1990, Piano Sonata, Two-Edged Sword (song cycle) for soprano and piano, Sonata for trombone and organ 1991, Flights of Fancy for clarinet and string quartet, Gardens for SATB, Suite for viola, Our Good Keen Men (song cycle) for tenor and piano 1992, A Tree for All Seasons for soprano, cello and piano, City of... (song cycle) for tenor and piano 1993, String Quartet No. 2 1995, The Mind canticle for soprano and piano 1995, Reflections 1995, From the Rising of the Sun 1996, Solitude: A Pilgrim's Progress, Creation in Reverse 1997, Spiritual Suite for guitar 1997, From Dawn to Dusk for wind quintet 1997, Piano Suite 1997, At Akito for SATB, three trombones and timpani 1997, Tension for alto, tenor and pianoforte 1997, The Cave for SATB 1998, Rhapsody in White for clarinet, trombone and pianoforte 1998, On Watching the Sailboats for tenor and pianoforte (words by J. G. Brown) 1998, String Quartet No. 6: ...of Ages 1998, Bully Boys for tenor solo, men's chorus, three trombones and percussion 1999.

HINTERHÄUSER, Markus; Austrian conductor; *Artistic Director, Wiener Festwochen and Salzburg Festival;* b. 30 March 1958, La Spezia, Italy. *Education:* Vienna Conservatory with Elisabeth Leonskaja, Mozarteum Univ. of Salzburg with Oleg Maisenberg. *Career:* has performed as pianist in orchestral concerts, as recitalist and also in chamber concerts in major concert halls including Carnegie Hall, New York, the Muiskverein and Konzerthaus, Vienna, La Scala, Milan; festival appearances including Salzburg Festival, Schubertiade in Hohenems, Lucerne Festival, Wien Modern, Festival d'Automne, Holland Festival, Berlin Festival; performed with Arditti Quartet; worked with Brigitte Fassbaender as lied accompanist; known for interpretation of Second Viennese School and 20th century works, especially works by Luigi Nono, Karlheinz Stockhausen, Morton Feldman, John Cage, Galina Ustwolskaja and György Ligeti; worked with Christoph Marthaler, Johan Simons and Klaus Michael Grüber on music theatre productions; Co-founder (with Tomas Zierhofer-Kin) Zeitfluss series as part of Salzburg Festival 1993–2001; fmr Artistic Dir Zeit-Zone Project, Vienna Festival; Concert Dir Salzburg Festival 2006–11, Interim Artistic Dir 2011, Artistic Dir 2016–; apptd Dir Wiener Festwochen (Vienna Festival). *Recordings include:* several radio and TV recordings and CDs of entire piano works of Schoenberg, Berg and Webern as well as compositions by Feldman, Nono, Scelsi, Ustwolskaya and Cage. *Address:* Wiener Festwochen, Lehárgasse 11/1/6, 1060 Vienna, Austria. *Telephone:* (1) 589-22-0. *E-mail:* festwochen@festwochen.at. *Website:* www.festwochen.at/en.

HINTERMEIER, Margareta; Austrian singer (mezzo-soprano); b. 11 April 1954, St Polten; one s. *Education:* studied in Vienna with Hilde Konetzi. *Career:* Peter Musikus at Theater an der Wien 1972; engaged at Wiener

Staatsoper from 1976; debut as Hirte in Tosca 1976; roles include the Composer in Ariadne auf Naxos, Clairon in Capriccio, Lola, Annio, Dorabella, Orlofsky, Federica in Luisa Miller, Wagner's Magdalena, Cherubino, Silla, Lucrezia Borgia, Fricka in Das Rheingold and Die Walküre, Octavian, Jocaste, Emilia, Herodias, Venus in Tannhäuser, Adriano in Rienzi; guest appearances include the opening of Dresden Opera, Salzburg Festival, Schubert Festival Hohenems, Carinthia Summer, Istanbul Festival, Altafulla (Barcelona, Spain), Flanders Festivals. *Recordings include:* Maidservant in video of Elektra, conducted by Abbado; Die Walküre; Beethoven's Ninth. *Honours:* Preis der Freunde der Wiener Staatsoper, Kammersängerin 1991. *Address:* c/o Staatsoper, Opernring 2, 1010 Vienna, Austria (office).

HIRAI, Motoki, BPhil, MA; Japanese pianist and composer; b. Tokyo; s. of Takeichiro Hirai. *Education:* Keio Univ., Tokyo, Royal Acad. of Music, City Univ. and Guildhall School of Music and Drama, London. *Career:* numerous concert appearances in Japan; UK concert appearances include St George's, Bristol, Duke's Hall, St James's, Piccadilly, St John's, Smith Square, St Martin-in-the-Fields, Wigmore Hall, South Bank Centre; concert appearances in USA, Austria, France, Italy, Spain; performed a programme of own works, Nagano Piano Convention, Japan 1994; has performed with Kalman Berkes, Michael Cox, Barry Craft, Takeichiro Hirai, John Pearce; apptd artistic emissary by Japanese govt, overseas visits in this capacity include Sri Lanka 1994, Portugal 1996, Malaysia 1998; concert tour of Europe and Japan 2005. *Compositions include:* Valse Pathétique 1993, Hommage à Chopin 1999, Scenes from a Native Land. *Recordings include:* Piano Compositions: Canto Amoroso 2007. *Honours:* Sir Jack and Lady Lyons Performance Award. *E-mail:* info@motokihirai.com (office). *Website:* www.motokihirai.com (office).

HIROKAMI, Jun'ichi; Japanese conductor; *Chief Conductor, Kyoto Symphony Orchestra;* b. 5 May 1958, Tokyo. *Education:* Tokyo Music University. *Career:* debut with Israel Philharmonic Orchestra 1988, London debut, London Symphony Orchestra 1989; Assistant Conductor, Nagoya Philharmonic Orchestra 1983; international career from 1984; conducted the NHK Symphony Orchestra 1985, Orchestre National de France 1986; Royal Philharmonic Orchestra 1990; further engagements with Stockholm Philharmonic, Norrkoeping Symphony Orchestra, Principal Conductor 1991–95; Malmö and Gothenburg Symphony Orchestras and radio orchestras in Netherlands and Italy; operatic debut 1989, Un Ballo in Maschera followed by Rigoletto and La Forza del Destino, all with Australian Opera; international concert activities spread to other countries: Spanish National Orchestra, Berlin Radio Symphony, Royal Concertgebouw Amsterdam, Montréal Symphony and with many European orchestras; Principal Guest Conductor, Japanese Philharmonic Orchestra 1991; Principal Guest Conductor, Royal Liverpool Philharmonic Orchestra 1997–2000; Music Dir, Columbus Symphony Orchestra 2006–08; Chief Conductor, Kyoto Symphony Orchestra 2008–. *Recordings:* debut with the London Symphony Orchestra, subsequent recordings with his own Norrkoping Symphony Orchestra. *Honours:* winner International Kondrashin Conducting Competition, Amsterdam 1984. *Address:* Kyoto Symphony Orchestra, 1–26 Shimogamo Hangi-cho, Sakyo-ku, Kyoto, 606-0823, Japan (office). *Telephone:* (75) 711-3110. *Website:* www.kyoto-symphony.jp.

HIRSCH, Michael; German musician and composer; b. 1958, Munich. *Career:* composer 1976–; mem. several groups for contemporary music; collaborations with Dieter Schnebel, Josef Anton Reidl, Helmut Lachenmann; performances and broadcasts for European radio and television; actor, stage director at several European theatres and festivals; translates works from music to speech, theatre to music; work performed at several international festivals, including Donaueschingen Festival, Klangaktionen, Musica Viva, in Munich; Witten Festival for new chamber music, Grenzenlos; Berlin in Moscow 1996; XIII Cigle de música del segle XX, Barcelona; Dresden Festival for Contemporary Music; Music Biennale, Berlin. *Compositions include:* Il Viaggio (music theatre) 1982–83, Memoiren 1 Buch for string quartet 1983–85, Memoiren 3 Buch concerto for six instruments 1986–91, Beschreibung eines Kampfes (music theatre) 1986–92, Hirngespinste nocturnal scene for two players and accordion 1996, Odradek (novel for chamber ensemble) 1994–97, Passagen/Szenen for flute, clarinet, piano and string trio 1997, Le Carnet d'esquisse for chamber ensemble 1997–98, Das stille Zimmer (opera) 1998–99.

HIRSCH, Peter; German conductor; b. 1956, Cologne. *Education:* Hochschule, Cologne. *Career:* Asst to Michael Gielen at the Frankfurt Opera 1979; First Conductor, Frankfurt Opera 1983–87; debut at La Scala with Prometeo by Luigi Nono; world premiere of Stephen Climax by Hans Zender 1986; guest conductor at many German theatres as well as WNO, ENO, Netherlands Opera; Chief Conductor, Jeune Philharmonie de Belgique 1993–95; regular guest amongst others at Staatsoper unter den Linden, Berlin, Deutsches Symphonie-Orchester Berlin, Berliner Sinfonie-Orchester, Residentie Orkest Den Haag, Orchestre National de Belgique, Bournemouth Symphony, Radio Orchestras of WDR Cologne and MDR Leipzig, ensemble recherche, at Bologna Festival, Berliner Festwochen and Munich Biennale; many world premieres of works by Nono, Lachenmann, Zender, Knaifel and others. *Recordings include:* Mahler 5th Symphony, Nono, Brahms, Schoenberg.

HIRSCH, Rebecca; British violinist. *Education:* Royal Coll. of Music, London with Jaroslav Vanecek. *Career:* debut with the London Sinfonietta at the Barbican, playing Strauss' Bougeois Gentilhomme; has appeared as soloist with numerous orchestras in the UK and elsewhere in Europe, including Ålborg Symphony Orchestra, Bournemouth Symphony Orchestra, BBC Concert Orchestra, BBC Philharmonic, BBC Scottish Orchestras, Danish National Radio Symphony Orchestra, London Sinfonietta, Philharmonia, Ulster Orchestra. *Honours:* English Speaking Union scholarship 1984.

HIRST, Grayson; singer (tenor); b. 27 Dec. 1939, Ojai, CA, USA. *Education:* Music Acad. of the West with Martial Singher, Juilliard School with Jennie Tourel. *Career:* debut as Cavalli's Ormindo with the Opera Soc. of Washington 1969; sang Tonio in La fille du régiment at Carnegie Hall 1970; New York City Opera debut 1970, in Britten's The Turn of the Screw; Kennedy Center, Washington, in the premiere of Ginastera's Beatrix Cenci; other premieres include works by Robert Aitken, Ned Rorem, Robert Starer, Virgil Thomson (Lord Byron) and Jack Beeson; sang Tonio in Pagliacci at Carnegie Hall, New York 1990; further appearances in France, Brazil, England and Switzerland; other roles include Don José, Pelléas, Faust and Mozart's Tamino, Ferrando and Belmonte. *Recordings include:* Schubert's Die schöne Müllerin.

HIRST, Linda Margaret, AGSM, AGSM (flute), FDCA, FRSA; British singer (mezzo-soprano) and academic; *Head of Vocal Studies, Trinity Laban Conservatoire of Music and Dance;* b. 19 Nov. 1947, Yorks., England; d. of Harold Bruce Hirst and Margaret Hirst (née Binns); m. 1st Terry Edwards; one s. one d.; m. 2nd Gillean Weston Craig. *Education:* Greenhead High School, Huddersfield, Guildhall School of Music, London. *Career:* joined Swingle Singers and often appeared with Cathy Berberian; concerts with the London Sinfonietta with Berio, Ligeti and Henze conducting their works; premiere performances of Muldowney's Duration of Exile, Osborne's Alba, Simon Holt's Canciones and Judith Weir's The Consolations of Scholarship; performances of Schoenberg's Pierrot Lunaire in Paris and Florence and for Channel 4 TV; Glyndebourne Festival debut in Knussen's Where the Wild Things Are 1985; world premiere of Osborne's The Electrification of the Soviet Union 1986; appearances at Bath and Almeida Festivals; Frankfurt Opera, Henze's Elegy for Young Lovers; Arts Council Network tour with the London Sinfonietta; also performs earlier music such as Incoronazione di Poppea in Spitalfields for Opera London; sang in premiere of Vic Hoyland's La Madre (written for her), London 1990; numerous premieres, comms, recordings, broadcasts on radio and TV; masterclasses and education workshops worldwide; worked with visual artist Terry Smith in Venice Biennale 2007, 2009; Head of Vocal Studies, Trinity Laban Conservatoire of Music and Dance, London. *Recordings:* Songs Cathy Sang; Ottavia in L'Incoronazione di Poppea; recordings with Pink Floyd, Ivor Cutler, Non-Classical improvisation night with Mercury Quartet. *Honours:* Hon. DLitt. *Telephone:* (20) 7937-9490. *Fax:* (20) 8305-4476. *E-mail:* lhirst@tcm.ac.uk (office).

HIRSTI, Marianne; singer (soprano); b. 1958, Oslo, Norway. *Education:* studied in Oslo and Lubeck. *Career:* sang at Kiel 1980–81; Staatsoper Hamburg 1981–85; Cologne 1985–87; Staatsoper Stuttgart from 1987; San Meroe in Reinhard Keiser's Die grossmütige Tomyris at Ludwigshafen, followed by Constanza in Bononcini's Griselda and Blondchen in Die Entführung; Cologne Opera as Maire in Zar und Zimmermann; Ludwigsburg Festival as Susanna in Le nozze di Figaro; Théâtre de la Monnaie, Brussels, as Berta in Il Barbiere di Siviglia 1992; other roles have included Despina, Marzelline, Gretel, Sophie in Werther and Tytania in A Midsummer Night's Dream; many lieder recitals and concert appearances, including Wigmore Hall, London 1988. *Recordings include:* Beethoven Missa Solemnis; Die Grossmütige Tomyris; Der Zwerg by Zemlinsky; Blondchen in Die Entführung, conducted by Hogwood.

HIRVONEN, Anssi, DipMus; Finnish singer (tenor); b. 1948. *Education:* Sibelius Acad., Helsinki, Conservatoire of Tampere, Helsinki, studied with Jolanda di Maria Petris and in Berlin and Vienna. *Career:* appearances as oratorio and concert soloist in Finland, Sweden, Germany, Hungary, USA, Estonia, Russia, Latvia and the Faroe Islands; opera debut at Tampere Opera 1975; solo engagements at the Heidelberg Opera 1979–80, the Savonlinna Opera Festival 1978–, the Finnish Nat. Opera 1980–, and provincial operas in Finland; sang in the world premieres of Ilkka Kuusisto's The War of the Light 1982, Rautavaara's Thomas 1986 and his Vincent 1990, Atso Almila's 30 Silver Coins 1988; guest soloist at the operas of Stockholm and Tallinn; numerous television and radio appearances and recordings; Prof. and Lecturer of Singing, Sibelius Acad.; guest soloist, Finnish Nat. Opera; sang Don Ottavio in Don Giovanni for St Michael Opera 1999. *Recordings include:* Contemporary Finnish Choir Music; Sacred Songs of C. Franck, T. Kuusisto, Y. Karanko, E. Linnala, A. Maasalo and L. Madetoja; Christmas Songs of O. Kotilainen, A. Maasalo, S. Palmgren and S. Ranta; Musica Humana, Sacred Songs of P. Kostiainen and J. Sibelius; Rautavaara's Vincent, 1986 and Thomas, 1990; Jean Sibelius: The Tempest op 19, 1992. *Honours:* Director Musices 1998.

HIRZEL, Franziska; Swiss singer (soprano); b. 28 Nov. 1952, Zürich. *Education:* studied in Basel, Fribourg, Frankfurt am Main and Zürich. *Career:* sang at Darmstadt Opera from 1980, notably in the 1983 premiere of Klebe's Die Fastnachtsbeichte and as Mozart's Blondchen, Donna Elvira, Fiordiligi and Pamina, Micaela, Martha, Euridice, Gilda, Musetta and Gretel; concert repertoire has included sacred works by Bach, Beethoven, Mozart, Haydn and Schoenberg; many Lieder recitals and broadcasting engagements; guest appearances at concert halls and opera houses throughout Germany; sang Marie in Gurlitt's Wozzeck at Turin 2000.

HJORTSO, Merete; Danish singer (soprano); b. 1944. *Education:* studied in Copenhagen and Vienna. *Career:* debut at Royal Opera Copenhagen 1971 in Kagel's Halleluja; sang frequently with the Jutland Opera at Århus, notably in the 1983 premiere of Det guddommelige Tivoli by Norgaard; major roles have included Marguerite in Faust, Susanna and Cherubino in Le nozze di Figaro, Zdenka, Micaela, Massenet's Thaïs and Leonora in Nielsen's Maskarade; guest engagements in Strasbourg, Brussels and elsewhere; frequent concert appearances. *Recordings include:* Nielsen's Maskarade.

HO, Allan Benedict, BA, MA, PhD; American musicologist; b. 30 March 1955, Honolulu, HI. *Education:* Univ. of Hawaii, Univ. of Kentucky. *Career:* discovered a copy of the lost full score of Wilhelm Stenhammar's First Piano Concerto (manuscript of which believed destroyed during WWII); mem. American Musicological Soc. *Publications:* A Biographical Dictionary of Russian/Soviet Composers 1989, Music for Piano and Orchestra: The Recorded Repertory, critical edns of the two-piano score and full score of Wilhelm Stenhammar's First Piano Concerto, Shostakovich Reconsidered 1998; contrib. to Journal of the American Liszt Society, Notes, The New Grove Dictionary of American Music, New Grove Dictionary of Opera, New Grove Dictionary of Women Composers, New Grove Dictionary. *Address:* Box 1771, Music Department, Southern Illinois University, Edwardsville, IL 62026, USA.

HOARE, Peter; British singer (tenor); b. 1965, Bradford, England. *Education:* Huddersfield School of Music. *Career:* appearances with Welsh National Opera from 1992, as Jacquino, Mozart's Tito, Arbace and Basilio, and the Shepherd in Tristan und Isolde; Nemorino for Mid Wales Opera and Sellem in The Rake's Progress at Lausanne; Bardolfo in Falstaff at Covent Garden, 1999; concerts include the Mozart and Berlioz Requiems, Messiah with George Malcolm, Bach's Christmas Oratorio, Britten's Serenade and the Verdi Requiem; Season 1999 with Vitek in The Makropulos Case at Aix-en-Provence. *Current Management:* Harlequin Agency Ltd, 203 Fidlas Road, Llanishen, Cardiff, CF14 5NA, Wales. *Telephone:* (29) 2075-0821. *Fax:* (29) 2075-5971. *E-mail:* peter@harlequin-agency.co.uk. *Website:* www.harlequin -agency.co.uk.

HOBKIRK, Christopher; British singer (tenor); b. 1965, Henley-on-Thames, England. *Education:* Royal Scottish Academy, Royal College of Music with Neil Mackie. *Career:* concert engagements in Finland and Norway with Britten's St Nicolas and Bach's St John Passion; Bach's Magnificat with the Las Palmas Philharmonic, the B minor Mass at Edinburgh and Telemann's Luke Passion at St John's Smith Square; created Eochd in Edward McGuire's opera The Loving of Etain, 1990, at Glasgow; season 1991 with Britten's Serenade at Palma, Bach's St Matthew Passion at Darmstadt and Bergen, Mozart's Requiem with the Manchester Camerata and the B minor Mass conducted by William Boughton; sang Misael in The Burning Fiery Furnace for St James's Opera, 1991.

HOBSON, Ian, BA, MA, DMus; pianist and conductor; b. 1953, Wolverhampton, England; m.; four s. one d. *Education:* Magdalene College, Cambridge, Yale University. *Career:* Finalist in 1978 Baltimore Symphony Conducting Competition; Silver Medals at Artur Rubinstein and Vienna-Beethoven Competitions; 1st Prize, Leeds International Piano Competition, 1981; Soloist with Royal Philharmonic Orchestra, Philharmonia and Scottish National Orchestra; USA with Orchestras of Chicago, Philadelphia, Pittsburgh, St Louis, Baltimore, Indianapolis and Houston; Complete cycles of Beethoven's Sonatas; Founded Sinfonia da Camera, 1984; The Age of Anxiety for Bernstein's 70th birthday, 1988; As conductor led Mozart's Concertos from the keyboard with English National Orchestra on its Far Eastern tour; Illinois Opera Theatre in Così fan tutte and Die Fledermaus; 1988–89 season engagements with San Diego Chamber Orchestra and in Israel; Professor, University of Illinois, 1983–. *Recordings:* Chopin/Godowsky Etudes and the complete piano sonatas of Hummel; Strauss's Burleske and the Paregon on the Symphonia Domestica, with the Philharmonia; Concertos by Français, Saint-Saëns and Milhaud, with the Sinfonia da Camera; 24 Chopin Etudes, Rachmaninov Transcriptions and Mozart's Concertos Nos 23 and 24. *Telephone:* (20) 8894-0391. *Fax:* (20) 8287-9428. *E-mail:* howard@howardgreenwood.freeserve.co .uk.

HOCH, Beverly; American singer (soprano); b. 1956, Kansas City, Kansas; m. Mike Steinel. *Education:* Friends Univ., Wichita, Oklahoma State Univ., Wichita State Univ., later studied in New York. *Career:* concert performances from 1980, notably at Carnegie Hall, New York, and the Kennedy Center, Washington; European concerts in Madrid, Gothenburg and Brussels; opera appearances at Spoleto, the Wexford Festival (Philine in Mignon), and Santa Fe; best known role is Mozart's Queen of Night, which she sang at the 1991 Glyndebourne Festival; Adjunct Asst Prof. of Voice, Texas Woman's Univ. 1999–. *Recordings include:* Carmina Burana, The Art of the Coloratura, Handel's Imeneo, Mozart's Die Zauberflöte. *Address:* Department of Music, Texas Woman's University, PO Box 425768, Denton, TX 76204-5768, USA (office). *Telephone:* (940) 898-2499 (office). *Fax:* (940) 898-2494 (office). *E-mail:* beverlyhoch@hotmail.com (office). *Website:* www.twu.edu/soa/music/faculty/ hoch (office).

HOCH, Francesco; Swiss composer and academic (retd); b. 14 Feb. 1943, Lugano; m. 1971; two s. *Education:* Giuseppe Verdi Conservatory, Milan and studied in Padua, Darmstadt. *Career:* Prof. of Music, Lugano; Asst to Composition Course, Chigiana Acad., Siena, Italy 1974; invited to Int. Lab., Venice Biennale 1975; Founder Oggimusica Asscn of Contemporary Music

1977; regular radio broadcasts of compositions in Europe, Israel, Canada, USA, Australia, Japan, Russia, Latin America, and TV recordings. *Compositions include:* Dune for three instruments, two percussion and two voices 1972, L'Oggetto Disincantato for 13 instruments 1974, Trittico for clarinet and viola, Leonardo e/und Gantenbein (opera-ballet) 1980–82, Ostinato Variabile I for bass clarinet 1981, II for bass clarinet and piano, III for two guitars, IV for piano and violin 1982, Sans for oboe and orchestra 1985, Un Mattino for two flutes 1986, Der Tod ohne des Mädchen for string quartet 1990, Memorie da Requiem for choir and orchestra 1989–91, Postludio degli Spettatori for choir 1991, Péché d'outre-tombe for clarinet and string quartet 1993, La Passerelle des Fous (opera) for three sopranos, five actors and eight instruments 1994–95, Canti e danze dai nuovi gironi for 13 instruments 1995, Der hoffnungsvolle Jean und der Moloch for narrator and chorus 1995, Suite Palomar for five instruments 1995–97, L'Isola dell'amore for three voices and mandolin orchestra 1997–98, The Magic Ring (opera) for six voices, three electronic guitars, three percussions, electronic tape and video scenes 1995–2000, Su Gentile Invito for violin and cello 2000, Es ist Zeit for flute 2000, Doppio Concerto for cello, piano and orchestra 2001–02, Duo dal doppio for cello and piano 2002, Ave lucanum for choir 2003, Percorso novecento for three voices, three actors and four instruments 2003–04, Josef K – Il processo continua (opera) 2005–07, Trio Ischia for violin, cello, piano 2007–08, Poema Orchestrale for six percussion ensembles 2008, Imago for women's choir and string quartet 2009, Flashback for piano 2010, Ex Antiquo for two pan flutes and string orchestra 2010–11, Consumo di Donna for soprano and 13 instruments 2013, Piume di Senso for flauto dolce, ArCADiA 15 for orchestra 2015. *Recordings include:* Chamber and orchestral works 1997, Il Mattino Dopo 2000, Memorie da Requiem 2002, Fantasia da L'isola dell'amore 2003, The Magic Ring 2004, Duetti 2005, Flashback 2014; video recordings: Trasparenza per nuovi elementi 1977, Leonardo e/und Gantenbein 1985, F. Hoch: Ritratto and Suite Palomar 2001. *Honours:* First Prize, Angelicum Int. Orchestral Composition Competition Milan 1975, Jubileo UBS Prize for his complete works 1991, Kammersprechchor Zürich Prize 1995, EPTA-ESTA Prize 1996, Concerti monografici per il 70esimo compleanno, Geneva, Lugano, Bellinzona, Savosa 2013. *Address:* Campo dei Fiori 9, 6942 Savosa, Switzerland (home). *Telephone:* (91) 9660220 (home). *Fax:* (91) 9660220 (home). *E-mail:* hoch.francesco@sunrise.ch (home).

HOCKNEY, David, OM, CH, RA; British artist, stage designer and photographer; b. 9 July 1937, Bradford, Yorks.; s. of the late Kenneth Hockney and Laura Hockney. *Education:* Bradford Grammar School, Bradford Coll. of Art, Royal Coll. of Art, London. *Career:* taught at Maidstone Coll. of Art 1962, Univ. of Iowa 1964, Univ. of Colorado 1965, UCLA 1966 (Hon. Chair. of Drawing 1980), Univ. of California, Berkeley 1967; has travelled extensively in Europe and USA; many works now housed in Salts Mill, Saltaire, nr Bradford; mem. Advisory Bd Standpoint (political magazine) 2008–; Assoc. mem. Royal Acad. 1985. *Film:* A Bigger Splash (autobiographical documentary) 1974. *Solo exhibitions include:* first solo exhbn, Kasmin Gallery, London 1963; subsequent exhbns at Museum of Modern Art, New York 1964, 1968, Laundau-Alan Gallery, New York 1964, 1967, Kasmin Gallery 1965, 1966, 1968, 1969, 1970, 1972, Stedeljik Museum, Amsterdam 1966, Palais des Beaux-Arts, Brussels 1966, Studio Marconi and Galleria dell'Ariete, Milan 1966, Galerie Mikro, Berlin 1968, Whitworth Art Gallery, Manchester 1969, André Emmerich Gallery, New York 1972–96, Gallery Springer, Berlin 1970, Kestner-Gesellschaft, Hanover 1970, Whitechapel Gallery (retrospective exhbn), London 1970, Kunsthalle, Bielefeld 1971, Musée des Arts Décoratifs, Louvre, Paris 1974, Galerie Claude Bernard, Paris 1975, Nicholas Wilder, Los Angeles 1976, Galerie Neundorf, Hamburg 1977, Warehouse Gallery 1979, Knoedler Gallery 1979, 1981, 1982, 1983, 1984, 1986, Tate Gallery (retrospective exhbn) 1980, 1986, 1988, 1992, Hayward Gallery (photographs) 1983, 1985, Museo Tamayo, Mexico City 1984, LA County Museum of Art (retrospective) 1988, 1996, Metropolitan Museum of Art (retrospective), New York 1988, Knoedler Gallery, London 1988, LA Louver Gallery, Calif. 1986, 1989–95, 1998, 2005, 2007, 2009, Venice 1982, 1983, 1985, 1986, 1988, Nishimura Gallery, Tokyo, Japan 1986, 1989, 1990, 1994, Royal Acad. of Arts, London 1995, Hamburger Kunsthalle 1995, Manchester City Art Galleries (retrospective exhbn) 1996, Nat. Museum of American Art, Washington, DC 1997, 1998, Museum Ludwig, Cologne 1997, Museum of Fine Arts, Boston 1998, Centre Georges Pompidou, Paris 1999, Musée Picasso, Paris 1999, Annely Juda Fine Art 2003, 2006, 2009, Nat. Portrait Gallery 2003; touring show of prints and drawings Munich, Madrid, Lisbon, Tehran 1977, Saltaire, Yorks., New York, LA 1994, Royal Acad. (drawings), Royal Acad. of Arts 1995–96, 1999, 2002, 2004, 2005, 2007, Kunsthalle Würth, Schwäblisch Hall 2009, A Bigger Picture (Royal Acad. of Arts) 2012; has painted hundreds of portraits, still lifes and landscapes using the Brushes iPhone and iPad application since 2009, Fleurs fraîches (Fresh Flowers), La Fondation Pierre Bergé, Paris 2011, Fresh-Flowers, Royal Ontario Museum, Toronto 2011, 25 Trees and Other Pictures Salts Mill, Saltaire, West Yorkshire, UK 2014. *Group exhibitions include:* ICA, Second and Third Paris Biennales of Young Artists, Musée d'Art Moderne 1961, 1963, Third Inst. Biennale of Prints, Nat. Museum of Art, Tokyo 1962, London Group Jubilee Exhbn 1914–1964, Tate Gallery 1964, Painting and Sculpture of a Decade, Gulbenkian Foundation, Op and Pop, Stockholm and London 1965, Fifth Int. Exhbn of Graphic Art, Ljubljana 1965, First Int. Print Biennale, Kraków 1966, São Paulo Biennale 1967, Venice Biennale 1968, Pop Art Redefined, Hayward Gallery, London 1969, 150 Years of Photography, Nat. Gallery, Washington, DC 1989–90. *Stage design:* set: Ubu Roi, Royal Court Theatre, London 1966, Rake's Progress, Glyndebourne 1975, Die Zauberflöte, Glyndebourne 1978, La Scala 1979, Nightingale, Covent Garden 1983, Varii Capricci, Metropolitan Opera House, New York 1983, Tristan and Isolde, LA Music Centre Opera, LA 1987, Turandot, Lyric Opera 1992–, San Francisco 1993, Die Frau Ohne Schatten, Covent Garden, London 1992, LA Music Centre Opera 1993, The Performing Arts Museum, Melbourne (Green Room Award for Stage Design in Opera 1997) 1997; costume and set: Les Mamelles de Teresias, Metropolitan Opera House, New York 1980, L'Enfant et les sortilèges, Metropolitan Opera House, New York 1980, Parade, Metropolitan Opera House, New York 1980, Oedipus Rex, Metropolitan Opera House, New York 1981, Le Sacre du Printemps, Metropolitan Opera House, New York 1981, Le Rossignol, Metropolitan Opera House, New York 1981. *Radio:* guest ed., Today programme (BBC Radio 4) to air his views as a pro-tobacco campaigner Dec. 2009. *Publications include:* Hockney by Hockney 1976, David Hockney, Travel with Pen, Pencil and Ink (autobiog.) 1978, Paper Pools 1980, Photographs 1982, China Diary (with Stephen Spender), 1982, Hockney Paints the Stage 1983, David Hockney: Cameraworks 1984, Hockney on Photography: Conversations with Paul Joyce 1988, David Hockney: A Retrospective 1988, Hockney's Alphabet (ed. by Stephen Spender) 1991, That's the Way I See It (autobiog.) 1993, Off the Wall: Hockney Posters 1994, David Hockney's Dog Days 1998, Hockney on Art: Photography, Painting and Perspective 1999, Hockney on 'Art': Conversation with Paul Joyce 2000, Secret Knowledge: Rediscovering the Lost Techniques of the Old Masters (British Book Design and Production Award 2002) 2001, Hockney's Pictures 2004; illustrated Six Fairy Tales of the Brothers Grimm 1969, The Blue Guitar 1977, Hockney's Alphabet 1991; contributed original sketches to launch edn of Standpoint magazine June 2008. *Honours:* Foreign Hon. mem. American Acad. of Arts and Sciences 1997; Freedom of the City of Bradford 2000; Hon. PhD (Aberdeen) 1988, (Royal Coll. of Art) 1992; Hon. DLitt (Oxford) 1995, (Leeds) 2000, (Cambridge) 2007; hon. degree from Acad. of Fine Arts, Florence 2003; Guinness Award 1961, Graphic Prize, Paris Biennale 1963, First Prize 8th Int. Exhbn of Drawings and Engravings, Lugano 1964, prize at 6th Int. Exhbn of Graphic Art, Ljubljana 1965, Cracow 1st Int. Print Biennale 1966, First Prize, 6th John Moores Exhbn 1967, Hamburg Foundation Shakespeare Prize 1983, Progress Medal, Royal Photographic Soc. 1988, Praemium Imperiale, Japan Art Asscn 1989, Fifth Annual Gov.'s Award for Visual Arts in Calif. 1994, Kulturpreis, Deutsche Gesellschaft für Photographie E.V. 1997, Mario Tamayo Award for Outstanding Dedication in the Visual Arts, Los Angeles Contemporary Exhbns 1998, Charles Wollaston Award, Royal Acad. of Arts, Summer Exhbn, London 1999, Commendation by the Gov. of Calif., Gray Davis, for Efforts on Behalf of People Living with HIV/AIDS 1999, Centenary Medal, Royal Photographic Soc. 2003, Lorenzo De' Medici Lifetime Career Award, Florence Biennale 2003, Orthopaedic Ward at The Yorkshire Clinic, W Yorks. named 'The Hockney Ward' 2003, La Rosa D'Oro Award, Palermo, Italy 2004, Bannister Fletcher Award 2004. *Website:* www.hockneypictures.com.

HODGES, Nicolas; British composer and pianist; b. 4 June 1970, London, England. *Education:* Univ. of Cambridge, studied at Dartington and Winchester with Morto Feldman and Michael Finnissy, and with Robert Bottone and Susan Bradshaw. *Career:* as pianist, premieres including music by Finnissy, Weir, Skempton, Toovey, Powell, Holloway, Bill Hopkins, some as part of the Bach project, broadcast on Radio 3. *Compositions include:* Piano Studies for solo piano 1988–92, Small Shadows 1990, Twothreefourfive for violin and piano 1991–92, Do I detect a silver thread between you and this young lady for solo viola 1993, Concertino 1993, Scripture for soprano, oboe d'amore and two percussion 1994. *Recordings include:* over 20 recordings, including Bach Project. *Publications:* contrib. various articles and reviews to Tempo, Musical Times, including The Music of Bill Hopkins 1993, The Music of Luigi Nono 1950–58 - Analytical investigations. *Current Management:* c/o Earl Blackburn, Opus 3 Artists, 470 Park Avenue South, 9th Floor North, New York, NY 10016, USA. *Telephone:* (212) 584-7514. *Fax:* (646) 300-8214. *E-mail:* eblackburn@opus3artists.com. *Website:* www.opus3artists.com; www.nicolashodges.com.

HODGSON, Julia; violist; b. 1960, England. *Career:* mem., Fretwork, first London concert at the Wigmore Hall, London 1986; appearances in the Renaissance and Baroque repertoire in Sweden, France, Belgium, The Netherlands, Germany, Austria, Switzerland and Italy; radio broadcasts in Sweden, The Netherlands, Germany and Austria; televised concert on ZDF, Mainz; tour of Soviet Union 1989, and Japan 1991; festival engagements in the UK; repertory includes In Nomines and Fantasias by Tallis, Parsons and Byrd; dance music by Holborne and Dowland (including Lachrimae); six-part consorts by Gibbons and William Lawes; songs and instrumental works by Purcell; collaborations with vocal group Red Byrd in verse anthems by Byrd and Tomkins, London Cries by Gibbons and Dering, Resurrection Story and Seven Last Words by Schütz; gave George Benjamin's Upon Silence at the QEH 1990; Wigmore Hall concerts 1990–91, with music by Lawes, Purcell, Locke, Dowland and Byrd. *Recordings:* Heart's Ease (late Tudor and early Stuart); Armada (Courts of Philip II and Elizabeth I); Night's Black Bird (Dowland and Byrd); Cries and Fancies (Fantasias, In Nomines and The Cries of London by Gibbons); Go Nightly Care (consort songs, dances and In Nomines by Byrd and Dowland).

HODKINSON, Juliana, MA; composer; b. 17 March 1971, Exeter, England. *Education:* King's Coll., Cambridge, Sheffield Univ., studied with Hans Abrahamsen and Per Norgård. *Career:* debut professional performance of composition Recalling Voices of the Child, Capricorn ensemble, ICA, London

1994; works performed at ICA, London, Den Anden Opera, Copenhagen, Nordic Music Days 1998, Stockholm, Musikhalle, Hamburg, Paul Gerhardt Kirche and Neuköllner Saalbaum, Berlin, Tokyo Univ. of Fine Arts, La Machine à Eau, Mons, Belgium; works performed by Capricorn (London), Athelas Sinfonietta (Copenhagen), Sonanza (Stockholm), Orchestre Royal de Chambre de Mons (Belgium), Contemporary Alpha (Tokyo), Matthias Arter (Zürich), Prisma (Berlin), Ensemble 2000 (Denmark), Danish Radio Concert Orchestra; mem. Dansk Komponist Forening, Koda-NCB, Denmark. *Compositions:* In Slow Movement 1994, Water Like a Stone 1996, Machine à Eau 1998, Music for Gilles Requiem 1999. *Publications:* contrib. to Dansk Musik Tidsskrift 1994, 1997, Japanese Society Proceedings 1996. *Honours:* Danish Arts Council grants 1994, 1998, 1999, Daiwa Foundation scholarship 1995–97, Pépinières Européens Jeunes Artistes residency 1997–98, Kongegaarden Centre for Music and Visual Arts residency 1999.

HOEL, Lena; Swedish singer (soprano); b. 1957. *Education:* Stockholm Music High School. *Career:* sang at the Stockholm Royal Opera from 1984 as Gilda, Sophi in Der Rosenkavalier and in the premieres of Backanterna by Daniel Börtz 1991; Festival of Drottningholm from 1989; in Soliman II by J.M. Kraus and Isme in Elektra by J.C. Haeffner; Mozart: Pamina/Magic Flute, Fiordiligi/ Così fan tutte; Puccini: Mimi/La Bohème; Bizet: Carmen; Janáček: The Cunning Little Vixen; Lidholm: A Dreamplay/Indra's Daughter; Sandström: Staden/Cecilia; other roles in Aniara by Blomdahl; sang Dorinda in Handel's Orlando at Stockholm 2000; recitals and chamber music as well as oratorios. *Recordings:* Sandström/The High Mass, Blomdahl/Aniara, Börtz/The Bac- chantes. *Honours:* Jenny Lind Scholarship until 1983. *Address:* c/o Kungliga Operan, PO Box 16094, 10322 Stockholm, Sweden.

HOELLE, Matthias; German singer (bass); b. 8 July 1951, Rottweil am Neckar. *Education:* studied in Stuttgart with Georg Jelden and in Cologne with Josef Metternich. *Career:* sang first in concerts and oratorios; sang in opera at Cologne from 1976; at Ludwigsburg Festival as the Commendatore in Don Giovanni 1978; has appeared at the Bayreuth Festival as the Night- watchman, Titurel, Fasolt and Hunding (1988 in Der Ring des Nibelungen, conducted by Daniel Barenboim) 1981–, as King Marke 1993–, as Pogner 1998–, as Gurnemanz 2000–; King Marke in Tristan und Isolde at Bologna 1983, Florence 1989 and Cologne 1990; sang in premiere of Stockhausen's Donnerstag 1981, cr. Lucifer in Stockhausen's Samstag aus Licht at Palazzo dello Sport, La Scala, Milan 1984; guest appearances in Hannover, Geneva, Tel-Aviv and New York (Fidelio at the Metropolitan 1986), as Don Fernando in Fidelio at Brussels, Daland in Stuttgart and the Commendatore at Parma, Hunding at Bonn and Bayreuth Festival, Fafner in The Ring, Covent Garden, Hermit in Der Freischütz, Rome, Marke in Tristan and Isolde, Munich, Seneca in L'Incoronazione di Poppea, Athens Concert Hall, Sarastro in Die Zauberflöte, Barcelona, Fasolt, Toulouse, Penderecki's Credo and Seven Gates of Jerusalem in Madrid and Valencia, Fidelio and Missa Solemnis, Granada Festival, Hunding, Deutsche Oper Berlin and Liceu, Barcelona, Don Quichotte, Cologne Opera, Fidelio, Genova, Parsifal, Venice, Seven Gates of Jerusalem in Paris and Caracas; Romeo et Juliette, São Paulo, Parsifal, Deutsche Oper am Rhein, Düsseldorf, world premiere of Nunes' opera Das Märchen, Lisbon 2008; further guest appearances include at Deutsche Oper and Komische Oper in Berlin, Düsseldorf, Naples, Genova, Venice, Barcelona, Sevilla, Tokyo (with Salzburg Easter Festival); concerts in Philadelphia, New York, Caracas, São Paulo, Moscow, St Petersburg and Paris as well at the festivals in Ludwigsburg, Warsaw, Granada and Gran Canaria. *Recordings include:* Mozart's Requiem, Haydn's Seven Last Words on the Cross, Handel's Saul, Bruckner's Mass No. 3 in F-minor, Mendelssohn's Walpurgisnacht, Lieder by Schumann, Stockhausen's Samstag- und Donnerstag aus Licht, Seneca in L'Incoronazione di Poppea, Commendatore in Don Giovanni, Gurnemanz in Parsifal, Nachtwächter and Pogner in Die Meistersinger, Marke in Tristan, Fasolt in Das Rheingold, Hunding in Die Walküre, Eremit in Der Freischütz, Rocco in Fidelio. *Honours:* Kammersänger of the Stuttgart State Opera; Felix Mendelssohn-Bartholdy Prize, Stiftung Preußischer Kulturbesitz. *Current Management:* c/o Lore-M. Schulz International Artists Management, Zittelstrasse 8, 80796 Munich, Germany. *Telephone:* (89) 3087092. *Fax:* (89) 3087093. *E-mail:* artists@lore-m-schulz.com. *Website:* www.lore-m-schulz.com.

HOELSCHER, Ulf; German violinist; b. 17 Jan. 1942, Kitzingen. *Education:* studied with Bruno Masurat, Max Rostal in Cologne, in USA with Josef Gingold at Indiana Univ. and with Ivan Galamian at Curtis Inst., Philadelphia. *Career:* mem., International Geiger Elite; Violin Concertos of Kirchner with Berlin Philharmonic, 1984; Franz Hummel's Violin Concerto, Baden-Baden, 1987; performed Double Concerto by Aribert Reimann, with Wolfgang Reimann, Hannover, 1989; performances and recordings from a wide repertoire featuring Frankel, Tchaikovsky, Schumann, Mendelssohn, Richard Strauss, Brahms and Beethoven, and the chamber music of Bartók, César Franck, and Szymanowski. *Recordings:* Hummel's Violin Concerto, with USSR State Symphony Orchestra. *Current Management:* Connaught Artists Management Limited, Artiller House, 35 Artillery Lane, London, E1 7LP, England. *Telephone:* (20) 7426-5503. *Fax:* (20) 7247-0440. *E-mail:* patrick@connaughtartists.com. *Website:* www.connaughtartists.com; www .ulfhoelscher.de.

HOENE, Barbara; singer (soprano); b. 4 Feb. 1944, Cottbus, Germany. *Education:* Leipzig Musikhochschule, studied with Johannes Kempter. *Career:* debut in Dessau 1966 as Laura in Der Bettelstudent; sang at Halle/ Saale 1968–73; with the Dresden Opera roles have included Mozart's

Fiordiligi and Pamina, Sophie in Der Rosenkavalier, Carolina in Il Matrimonio segreto, Orff's Die Kluge and Verdi's Nannetta; many further roles in operas by Handel; guest appearances in Berlin, St Petersburg, Italy, France and Japan; season 1994–95 as Marcellina in Le nozze di Figaro; sang in the premiere of Reimann's Melusine; sang in the premiere of Celan by Peter Ruzicka at Dresden 2001; lieder recitals and oratorios by Bach and Handel.

HOEPRICH, Thomas Eric, AB, DipMus; clarinettist; b. 5 Sept. 1955, Baltimore, MD, USA. *Education:* Harvard Univ., Royal Conservatory of Music, The Netherlands. *Career:* Principal Clarinet, Orchestra of the 18th Century 1983–; founder mem., Amadeus Winds, Stadler Trio (basset horns), Nachtmusik and Trio d'Amsterdam; regular appearances with London Classical Players, Tafelmusik and the Orchestra of the Handel and Haydn Soc.; Prof., Royal Conservatory of Music, The Netherlands. *Recordings:* Mozart Clarinet Concerto and Quintet with Orchestra of the 18th Century, soloist recordings with Taverner Players, Musica Antiqua Cologne. *Publica- tions:* contrib. to Early Music, Tibia, Galpin Society Journal, NOTES.

HOFFMAN, Gary; Canadian cellist; b. 1956, Vancouver. *Education:* Indiana University School of Music. *Career:* faculty mem., Bloomington, Indiana 1980s; soloist with major orchestras in Chicago, London, San Francisco, Montréal, Cleveland, Philadelphia; English Moscow and Los Angeles Cham- ber Orchestras, Orchestre National de France, Suisse Romande and Rotterdam Philharmonic; festival engagements at Ravinia, Aspen, Marlboro, Bath, Helsinki, New York (Mostly Mozart) and Verbier; chamber music as guest with the Emerson, Tokyo, Brentano and Ysaye String Quartets; artist mem., Lincoln Center Chamber Music Society, New York. *Honours:* winner Rostropovich International Competition, Paris 1986.

HOFFMAN, Irwin; conductor and violinist; b. 26 Nov. 1924, New York, NY, USA; m. Esther Glazer Hoffman; three s. one d. *Education:* Juilliard School of Music. *Career:* Conductor, Vancouver Symphony, BC, Canada 1952–64; Assoc. Conductor and Acting Music Dir, Chicago Symphony, IL 1964–70; Music Dir, The Florida Orchestra 1968–87; Chief Permanent Conductor, Belgian Radio and Television Symphony 1972, 1976; guest conductor for various leading orchestras in Europe, North America, Israel and South America.

HOFFMAN, Joel Harvey, BM, MM, DMA; composer, pianist and teacher; b. 27 Sept. 1953, Vancouver, BC, Canada; m. 1988. *Education:* Univ. of Wales, Cardiff, Juilliard School, New York, USA. *Career:* graduate teaching asst, Juilliard School, New York 1976–78; Prof. of Composition, Coll.-Conservatory of Music, Univ. of Cincinnati, OH 1978–; commissions from NEA, Cincinnati Symphony Orchestra 1993, Shanghai String Quartet 1993, National Chamber Orchestra 1993, Golub-Kaplan-Carr Trio 1991; Artistic Dir, Music Ninety- eight, Music Ninety-nine and Music 2000 Festivals. *Compositions:* Variations for violin, cello and harp 1975, Music from Chartres for ten brass instruments 1978, September Music for double bass and harp 1980, Chamber Symphony 1980, Sonata for harp 1982, five Pieces for two pianos 1983, Double Concerto 1984, Violin Concerto 1986, Fantasia Fiorentina for violin and piano 1988, Hands Down for piano 1986, Crossing Points for string orchestra 1990, Partenze for solo violin 1990, Each for Himself for piano solo 1991, Cubist Blues for violin, cello and piano 1991, Music in Blue and Green for orchestra 1992, Metasmo for percussion trio 1992, Self-Portrait with Mozart for violin, piano and orchestra 1994, Music for chamber orchestra 1994, ChiaSsO for orchestra 1995, L'Immensitá dell'Attimo (song cycle) for mezzo and piano 1995, The Music Within the Words 1996, Portogruaro Sextet 1996, Millen- nium Dances for orchestra 1997, Self-Portrait with Gebirtig for cello and orchestra 1998, Kraków Variations for viola solo 1999, Reyzele: A Portrait for chamber ensemble 1999. *Recordings:* Duo for viola and piano 1991, Partenze 1992, Music for two oboes 1995, Tum-Balalayke 1996, Fantasy Pieces 1999. *Honours:* BMI Award 1972, Columbia Univ. Bearns Prize 1978, American Acad. Inst. of Arts and Letters 1987.

HOFFMAN, Stanley, BSc; violinist and violist; b. 8 Dec. 1929, Baltimore, MD, USA. *Education:* studied with Arthur Grumiaux in Belgium, Juilliard School of Music, studied with Mischa Mischakoff, Raphael Bronstein and Oscar Shumsky. *Career:* debut at Carnegie Recital Hall, New York; regular mem., New York Philharmonic Orchestra under Leonard Bernstein 1961–64, Jerusalem Radio Symphony Orchestra, Israel 1981–83; Bohemians, New York; Local 802 Asscn Federation of Musicians. *Recordings:* Vocal Chamber Music, Vol. I with Susan Reid-Parsons as soprano, 1971, Vol. II with Elinor Amlen and Rose Macdonald, sopranos, 1973; Taping session for Radio Kol Israel, 1984, 1986; Solo violin sonatas, Béla Bartók, Honegger, Hindemith, Ralph Shapey, Paul Ben-Haim, Bach C Major, Roger Sessions.

HOFFMANN, Anke; German singer (soprano); b. 19 Sept. 1969, Siegen. *Education:* Musikhochschule Cologne. *Career:* Deutsche Oper am Rhein, Düsseldorf from 1990 as Gounod's Juliette, Papagena in Die Zauberflöte, Nicolai's Anne, Frasquita in Carmen and Olympia in Les contes d'Hoffmann; Wiesbaden 1992, in the premiere of Der Park by Hans Gefors; further guest engagements in Mainz, as Zerbinetta and in Henze's Der junge Lord at Saarbrucken, as Zerlina, and at Bremerhaven, as Gilda; other roles include Mozart's Blondchen and Queen of Night, Nannetta, Adele, and Philene in Mignon; Bonn Opera from 1993; sang Aennchen in Der Freischütz at Eutin 2000; concerts include Bach's Passions, Handel's Messiah and Joshua, Mozart's Requiem and Mendelssohn's Elijah. *Honours:* medal winner Com- petitions at Berlin and Salzburg 1990, 1993.

HOFFMANN, Horst; singer (tenor); b. 13 June 1935, Oppeln, Germany. *Education:* studied with Thilde Amelung in Hildesheim and Otto Kohler in Hanover. *Career:* debut at Hanover 1961, in Zar und Zimmermann; has sung at the Stuttgart and Munich State Operas and the Deutsche Oper am Rhein, Düsseldorf; Komische Oper Berlin and the Opéra du Rhin, Strasbourg; Bayreuth Festival 1967–68; further appearances in Cologne, Lisbon, Zürich, Vienna (Volksoper) and Sydney 1984 (Lohengrin and Siegmund 1987, 1989); Teatro Regio, Turin 1987, as Don Ottavio; Otello, Sydney and Melbourne 1988, and in Sydney 1992; From the House of the Dead, Cologne, Germany 1992; sang Florestan at Sydney 1992; Tristan and Isolde, Sydney and Melbourne 1993, and Essen, Germany 1993; Die Meistersinger, Sydney 1993; roles include Tamino, Belmonte, Nemorino, Edgardo, Pinkerton, Alfredo in La Traviata and Alfred in Die Fledermaus; sang Otello at Sydney, Lohengrin at Dresden, Walküre at Düsseldorf and Tristan at Trieste 1996; season 1997–98 Tannhäuser at Sydney and Melbourne, Bacchus in Ariadne and Samson at Sydney, and Erik in The Flying Dutchman in Melbourne; season 1999–2000 Florestan in Fidelio in Capetown, Andres in Wozzeck and Aegisthus in Elektra in Sydney and Tristan in Sydney and Melbourne; season 2003: Gurrelieder in Perth; Messiah in Tampa 2004. *Recordings include:* Bruckner Te Deum, Great Opera Heroes 1996. *Address:* 2504 Gulf Blvd #506, Indian Rocks Beach, FL 33785, USA.

HOFFMANN, Martin; German arts organization executive, television producer and lawyer; *Director, Berlin Philharmonic Orchestra*; b. 1959, Nussloch. *Education:* Univs of Saarbrücken, Lausanne and Hamburg. *Career:* faculty mem., Max Planck Inst. for Int. Civil Law, and practising lawyer in Hamburg –1993; head of office management, private television channel Sat.1, later head of Business Affairs (programming) 1994–97, Man. Dir, Sat.1 Boulevard TV GmbH and Sat.1 SatellitenFernsehen 1997–2003; CEO, MME Moviement AG (television production co.) 2004–; Dir, Berlin Philharmonic 2010–. *Address:* MME Moviement AG, Gotzkowskystr. 20–21, 10555 Berlin, Germany (office). *Telephone:* (30) 5200760 (office). *Fax:* (30) 520076500 (office). *E-mail:* mhoffmann@mmemoviement.de (office). *Website:* www .mmemoviement.de (office).

HOFFMANN, Richard; American/Austrian composer, musicologist and educator; *Professor Emeritus, Oberlin College*; b. 20 April 1925, Vienna, Austria. *Education:* Univ. of New Zealand, Univ. of California at Los Angeles, studied with Arnold Schoenberg. *Career:* Sec. and Asst to Schoenberg 1947–51; teacher, Univ. of California at Los Angeles 1951–52, Oberlin Coll. 1954–2005; Visiting Prof., Univ. of California at Berkeley 1965–66, Harvard Univ. 1970, Univ. of Iowa 1976, Columbia Univ. summer programme, Paris 1977, Vienna Univ. 1985; co-editor complete works of Schoenberg 1961, edited score of Von Heute auf Morgen. *Compositions include:* Prelude and Double Fugue for strings 1944, Piano Sonata 1946, Violin Concerto 1948, six String Quartets 1947, 1950, 1974, 1977 (with computer-generated tape) 1995, 1998, 3 Songs 1948, Duo for violin and cello 1949, 3 Songs 1950, Piano Quartet 1950, Fantasy and Fugue for organ 1951, Piano Sonatina 1952, Piano Concerto 1954, Cello Concerto 1956–59, Orchestra Piece 1961, String Trio 1963, Memento Mori for male voices and orchestra 1966–69, Music for strings 1971, Decadanse for 10 players 1972, Changes for 2 chimes, 4 performers 1974, Souffleur for orchestra 1976, In memoriam patris for computer-generated tape 1976, Les Adieux for chorus (SATB) and orchestra 1980–83, two poems from Albert Giraud's Pierrot lunaire for Pierrot Ensemble 1986, two songs (text Rückert and Heine) for soprano and chamber orchestra 1991, Lacrymosa 91 for chorus and orchestra 1991, Mono/Poly for piano 1994, Notturno for double string quartet 1995, Die Heimkehr (texts Georg Trakl) for baritone, orchestra and double chorus 1997, String Quartet #6 1998. *Honours:* Nat. Inst. of Arts and Letters Award 1966, DAAD Fellowship, Berlin 1968, Guggenheim Fellowships 1970, 1977, NEA Grants (MIT, Cambridge) 1976, 1978, 1979, Sr Fulbright Grant 1984, Ehrenzeichen für Kunst und Kultur 1991. *Current Management:* BMI, 40 West 57th Street, New York, NY 10019, USA.

HOFFMANN-ERBRECHT, Lothar, DrHabil; German academic; b. 2 March 1925, Strehlen Schlesien; m. Margarete Fischer; two d. *Education:* Acad. of Music, Weimar, Univs of Jena and Frankfurt. *Career:* Prof. of Musicology, Univ. and Acad. of Music of Frankfurt am Main, Tech. Univ. Darmstadt; mem. Soc. for Music Research, Int. Musicological Soc. *Publications include:* Deutsche und italienische Klaviermusik zur Bachzeit 1954, Thomas Stoltzer, Leben und Schaffen 1964, Thomas Stoltzer, Ausgewaehlte Werke II–III, Heinrich Finck, Ausgewaehlte Werke, I–II, Beethoven Klaviersonaten (with Claudio Arrau), Henricus Finck-musicus excellentissimus, 1445–1527 1982, Musikgeschichte Schlesiens 1986, Jüdische Musiker aus Breslau 1996, Schlesisches Musiklexikon 2001; contribs to various professional journals. *Honours:* Bundesverdienstkreuz 1997. *Address:* 9 Amselweg, 63225 Langen, Germany (home).

HOFMAN, Srdjan; Serbian composer; b. 4 Oct. 1944, Glina, Yugoslavia. *Education:* Belgrade Acad. *Career:* Asst Prof., Belgrade Acad. of Music 1974, Prof. 1986–; electronic music festivals at Bourges and Helsinki; further performances at ISCM festivals in Essen and Stockholm. *Compositions include:* Symphony in Two Movements 1969, Concerto Dinamico 1971, Konzertanntne epizode for violin and orchestra 1972, The Legal Code of Succession for clarinet and two string sextets 1974, Cantus de Morte for speaker, mezzo and orchestra 1978, Who Am I? fairy tale for actors, mezzo, female chorus ensemble and tape 1986, Rebus I and II for electronics 1988–89, Replika for violin and piano 1990, Koncertatna muzika for piano, 13 strings

and electronics 1993, Duel for piano and live electronics 1996. *Honours:* first prize Belgrade Int. Composers' Forum 1994, 1995.

HOFMANN, Manfred; singer (bass); b. 10 Oct. 1940, Kahl am Main, Germany. *Education:* Frankfurt Musikhochschule. *Career:* sang at Saarbrucken 1970–71, Lucerne 1972–74, Mainz Opera 1974–77, St Gallen 1977–80, and Berne 1980–84; mem., Graz Opera from 1985, notably in the 1987 premiere of Der Rattenfänger by Friedrich Cerha; major roles have included Mozart's Bartolo, Alfonso and Sarastro, Rocco in Fidelio, Donizetti's Raimondo and Dulcamara, Rossini's Bartolo, Alidoro in La Cenerentola and Geronimo in Il Turco in Italia; Waldner in Arabella, the Grand Inquisitor in Don Carlo and Wagner's Landgrave; many buffo and character roles.

HOFMANN, Rosmarie; singer (soprano); b. 1 July 1937, Lucerne, Switzerland. *Career:* concerts throughout Europe, overseas; appeared at many regular int. festivals; many world premieres, including works composed for her; extensive repertoire. *Recordings include:* Phyllis und Thirsis, C. P. E. Bach; Canzonette amorose, Rossi; Stabat Mater, Dvořák; Sacred music, J. and M. Haydn; Bach cantatas; Mozart motets, Scholar Cantorum Basiliensis Orchestra, conductor Peter Sigrist; Quiteria (main role), Die Hochzeit des Camacho, 1993.

HOFMEYR, Hendrik Pienaar, DMus; South African composer and academic; *Associate Professor, University of Cape Town*; b. 20 Nov. 1957, Cape Town; s. of Arend Hermanus Hofmeyr and Estelle Christine Pienaar. *Education:* Univ. of Cape Town, Conservatoires of Florence and Bologna, Italy. *Career:* freelance composer in SA and elsewhere 1986–; Lecturer, Univ. of Stellenbosch 1992–; Sr Lecturer, Univ. of Cape Town 1998–2000, Assoc. Prof. 2001–. *Compositions include:* The Fall of the House of Usher (opera) 1987, Vala (ballet, after William Blake) 1998, Missa Sancti Ignatii de Loyola. for soprano, chorus and orchestra 1989, The Land of Heart's Desire (opera, after W. B. Yeats) 1990, Alice (ballet) 1991, Lumukanda (opera) 1995, Raptus for violin and orchestra 1996, Alleenstryd for medium voice and piano 1997, String Quartet 1998, Flute Concerto 1999, Piano Concerto 1999, Of Darkness and the Heart for soprano and orchestra 2000, Concerto for Violin and Flute 2001, Die Laaste Aand (opera) 2002, Sinfonia africana 2003, Die Stil Avontuur for soprano and piano 2003, Vier gebede by jaargetye in die Boland for voice and piano 2004, Concerto for two pianos 2005, Concerto for cello 2006, String Quartet II 2006, Partita africana for piano 2006, Flute Sonata 2006, Alto Saxophone Concerto 2007, Violin Sonata 2008, Trio 2008, Saartjie (opera) 2009, Baritone Saxophone Concerto 2009, Ek maak 'n hek oop in my hart for voice and piano 2010, Trio for flute, clarinet and piano 2010, Piano Sonata 2011, Kasi – An Introduction to the Orchestra 2011. *Honours:* Winner, Queen of Belgium Composition Competition 1997, Winner, Dimitri Mitropoulos Competition (Greece) 1997, Kanna Award (SA) 2008. *Address:* SA College of Music, UCT Private Bag, Rondebosch 7701, South Africa (office). *Telephone:* (21) 650-2651 (office); (21) 492-3202 (home). *Fax:* (21) 650-2627 (home). *E-mail:* hendrik.hofmeyr@uct.ac.za (office).

HÖFS, Matthias; German musician (trumpet) and academic; *Professor, Hochschule für Musik und Theater Hamburg*; b. 1965, Lübeck. *Education:* Hochschule für Musik und Theater Hamburg, studied with Peter Kallensee, Karajan Acad. of the Berlin Philharmoniker with Konradin Groth. *Career:* solo trumpeter, Philharmoniker Hamburg 1984–2000; mem. German Brass Ensemble 1985–; concert performances as soloist and chamber musician; Prof., Hochschule für Musik und Theater Hamburg 2000–; Guest Prof., Tchaikovsky Moscow State Conservatory, Acad. of Schleswig-Holstein Musik Festival, Royal Danish Music Acad. Copenhagen, Conservatoire Nat. Supérieur de Musique et Danse Paris, Guildhall School of Music and Drama London; workshops in Mexico, Spain and Japan. *Recordings include:* solo albums: Un concerto italiano 1995, Trumpet Acrobatics 2007, The Trumpet Shall Sound 2009, Solo de Concours 2010, Adventures of a Trumpet 2011, Hommage! C. P. E. Bach 2014; other: An English Concert (with Matthias Janz) 2002, Bassoon Concertos (20th century) 2005, Gansch Meets Höfs (with Hans Gansch) 2006, over 20 recordings with German Brass. *Honours:* Eduard-Söhring-Prize 1988, German Music Council/Mozartgesellschaft scholarship 1989, First Prize, Int. Music Competition Markneukirchen 1990. *E-mail:* office@musik-und-medien.de. *Address:* Hochschule für Musik und Theater Hamburg, Harvestehuder Weg 12, 20148 Hamburg, Germany (office). *E-mail:* info@matthiashoefs.de. *Website:* www.matthiashoefs.de.

HÖGMAN, Christina; Swedish singer (soprano); b. 18 Feb. 1956, Danderyd; d. of Claes Högman and Anna-Brita Högman; m. Nils-Erik Sparf 1991; two s. *Education:* Univ. of Uppsala, Royal Music Acad., Stockholm, State Opera School, Stockholm, master classes with Elisabeth Schwarzkopf, Nicolai Gedda, Geoffrey Parsons, Vera Rozsa. *Career:* debut at Drottningholm Court Theatre 1985; sang with Hamburg State Opera, Germany 1986–88; guest contracts 1988–97, at Basel Opera, Innsbruck Opera, Opéra du Rhin, Strasbourg, Monte Carlo Opera, Montpellier Opera, Royal Opera in Stockholm; major roles include Donna Elvira in Don Giovanni, Contessa and Cherubino in Le Nozze di Figaro, Despina in Così fan tutte, Annio in La Clemenza di Tito, Vitige in Flavio, Angelica in Orlando, Elisabetta in Don Carlos; sang title role in premiere of Marie Antoinette by Daniel Börtz, Stockholm 1998, Sivan in premiere of Jeppe by Sven David Sandström, Stockholm 2001, Dodi in premiere of Zarah by Anders Nilsson, Stockholm 2007. *Recordings:* Donna Elvira in Don Giovanni, Vitige in Flavio (Handel), Telemacho in Il Ritorno d'Ulisse in Patria and Valetto in L'Incoronazione di Poppea (Monteverdi), English Lute Songs with Jakob Lindberg, Lieder by

Clara Schumann, Les Illuminations by Britten, Second String Quartet by Schoenberg, Matthew Passion and John Passion (Bach), Neun Deutsche Arien (Handel). *Publication:* Marie och Musiken 2002. *Current Management:* Good Company AB, Upplandsgatan 62, 113 28 Stockholm, Sweden. *Telephone:* (8) 545-805-54. *Fax:* (8) 34-43-54. *E-mail:* maria@goodcompany.se. *Website:* www .goodcompany.se.

HÖH, Volker; German guitarist and guitar teacher; *Guitar Teacher, Landesmusikgymnasium Rheinland-Pfalz, Montabaur;* b. 24 April 1959, Altenkirchen, Pfalz; m. Jutta Maria Höh 1980; two d. *Education:* Univ. Rheinland-Pfalz, Koblenz, Staatliche Hochschule für Musik, Westfalen-Lippe, Münster. *Career:* recitalist and soloist with orchestras; radio and TV engagements; performed in most major cities and festivals; guitar teacher, Landesmusikgymnasium Rheinland-Pfalz, Montabaur 1994–, Univ. of Rheinland-Pfalz, Koblenz 1998–2011; master-classes and workshops; jury -mem. at int. competitions and festivals; ed. of pedagogic and chamber music guitar literature; mem. EGTA, BDZ. *Recordings include:* solo: Cantos de Cuba, Danzas Fantásticas, Triops-Botschaft, Matthias Drude: Kammermusik, Zypern-Variationen, Gala d'Opera (Mozart, Rossini, Verdi on historic instruments), Dreams of Love (Romantic love songs), J. S. Bach: Ich ruf zu dir Herr Jesu Christ, Cenas Brasileiras: Villa-Lobos and Savio; duets: Calliope-Calls (with Christina Ascher), Annette Schlünz: Kammermusik, 7. und 8. Dresdner Tage der zeitgenössischen Musik; played on The Straits of Magellan (Turfan Ensemble), Fünf Stücke op. 10 (RSO Frankfurt), Zwei Suiten für Jazzorchester (RSO Frankfurt), Von Heute Auf Morgen (RSO Frankfurt), Die Jakobsleiter (RSO Frankfurt), Cristoforo Colombo (RSO Frankfurt), German composers for 1, 2, 3 and 4 guitars, Ein Tango für Gardel, Tango with music and text, with Raphaela Crossey. *Publications include:* contrib. of articles on guitar to music periodicals. *Honours:* stipends and scholarships from Kultusministerium Rheinland-Pfalz, Darmstädter Ferienkurse, Richard Wagner Verband, Deutscher Musikrat, Deutscher Orchesterwettbewerb (with guitar ensemble cantomano) 2000, 2004, 2008, 2012, 2016, Glücksspirale Prize 2013. *Address:* Taunusstrasse 14, 56410 Montabaur, Germany (office). *Telephone:* (2620) 9506667 (office). *E-mail:* volker.hoeh@t-online.de. *Website:* www.volker-hoeh.de.

HOHEISEL, Tobias; German stage designer; b. 1956, Frankfurt. *Education:* Hochschule der Künste, Berlin. *Career:* collaborations with dir Nikolaus Lehnoff include Janáček Trilogy (Katya, Jenůfa and Makropulos Case) at Glyndebourne and Pfitzner's Palestrina at Covent Garden (season 1996–97, also seen at the Metropolitan, New York); debut as set and costume designer with Salome at Rio de Janeiro; Britten's Death in Venice for the Glyndebourne Tour, La Bohème, and the Tales of Hoffmann for ENO 1997–98; further engagements at Berlin (Deutsche Oper and Deutsche Staatsoper), Vienna, La Scala Milan, San Francisco, Chicago, Amsterdam, Antwerp, Zürich and Cologne; Lohengrin at Théâtre de la Monnaie Brussels, for Anja Silja's debut as producer; season 1997 with Der Freischütz in Berlin, Ariadne at Brussels; Macbeth in Hamburg and Don Carlos at the Opéra Bastille, Paris; designs for Henze's Boulevard Solitude at Covent Garden 2001; has also worked with New York City Opera, Santa Fe Opera, Glimmerglass Festival, Hamburg Staatsoper, Bayerische Staatsoper Munich, Deutsche Oper am Rhein Düsseldorf, Drottningholm Festival, Bregenz Festival, Wiener Festwochen, Maggio Musicale, Festival für alte Musik Innsbruck, Styriate Graz, Opera North, Scottish Opera, WNO; co-directed and designed Ariodante 2002, Madama Butterfly 2004, Die Entführung aus dem Serail 2007 for Nationale Reisopera, The Netherlands, Two Widows for Edinburgh Int. Festival 2008, Die Meistersinger for Oper Köln, Serse at Theater an der Wien 2011, Arabella for Santa Fe Opera 2012, Don Carlo Bolshoi Theatre, Moscow 2013. *Address:* 124 Leighton Road, London, NW5 2RG, England. *Website:* tobiashoheisel.co .uk.

HÖHN, Carola; singer (soprano); b. 3 March 1961, Erfurt, Germany. *Education:* Franz Liszt Musikhochschule, Weimar. *Career:* sang at Eisenach 1984–87, Altenburg 1987–88; Berlin Staatsoper from 1988, notably as Marie Antionette in the 1989 premiere of Graf Mirabeau by Siegfried Matthus; other roles have included Antonia, Mozart's Fiordiligi and Pamina, Gretel, Marie in Zar and Zimmermann and Sophie in Der Rosenkavalier; Agathe, Eva, the Countess in Capriccio and Albertine in Die Brautwahl by Busoni; concert repertoire includes Carmina Burana by Orff; guest engagements elsewhere in Germany and broadcasting commitments; Pamina in Die Zauberflöte at Bordeaux 1992; season 2000–01 in Berlin as Eva and Donna Elvira.

HOJSGAARD, Erik; Danish composer; b. 3 Oct. 1954, Århus. *Education:* Royal Acad. of Music, Århus with Per Norgård, Royal Acad. of Music, Copenhagen. *Career:* music copyist 1977–82; Asst Prof. (Ear Training), Royal Acad. of Music, Copenhagen 1982–88, Assoc. Prof. 1988–2002, Prof. 2002–; works performed at various music festivals in the Nordic countries, also at Int. Soc. for Contemporary Music festivals 1980, 1983. *Compositions:* orchestral: Untitled symphony 1974, Cello Concerto 1975, Refleksion 1977, Scherzo e notturno 1982, Piano Concerto 1984–85, Four Sketches 1990, Nocturne 1994, Fragment 1995, Symphony No. 1 2000, Symphony No. 2 2003; chamber music: Dialogues 1972, Solprismer 1978, The Sunflower 1978, Intrada 1981, Fantasy Pieces 1982–84, Watercolours 1983, Intermezzi 1983, Carillon 1986, Two Mobiles 1990, Paysage blême 1991, Paysage triste 1994, Equali 1996, Four Small Pieces 1996, Paysage 1997, Images oubliées I–III 2004, Picture at an Exhibition 2008; solo instruments: Cendrée 1976, Sonata in C major 1980, C'est la mer mêlée au soleil 1981, Corellage 1992, Epreuve 1993, Violin Sonata 1997, Etude 1999, Three small pieces 2000; solo voice with instruments:

Landet som icke är 1974, Tuan's Songs 1976, Variations: 6 Songs of Autumn 1976, Vise, ballad 1977, Täglich kommt die gelbe Sonne 1977, Joyous 1979, Fragments 1979, The Lost Forest 1980, Summer Songs 1981, The Rose 1981, Two Songs 1985, Two songs for mixed choir 1985–86, Don Juan kommt aus dem Krieg, opera 1989–92, rev. 2005–07, Songs on poems by Ole Sarvig 2007. *Honours:* Carl Nielsen Prize 1993. *Address:* Rued Langgaards Vej 25, 2300 Copenhagen S, Denmark (home). *E-mail:* erikhojsgaard@gmail.com (home). *Website:* www.hojs.dk.

HOLDEN, Amanda Juliet, MA (Oxon.), LRAM, ARCM, LGSM; British musician, translator, writer and librettist; b. 1948, London; d. of Sir Brian Warren and Dame Josephine Barnes; m. (divorced); three s. *Education:* Univ. of Oxford, Guildhall School, American University, Washington, DC. *Career:* freelance accompanist and Teacher at Guildhall School, 1973–86; freelance translator and writer; piano tuner for Nigel Osborne 2005. *Publications:* opera translations include: Haydn's Armida, Handel's Ariodante and Alcina, Rameau's Les Boréades; Verdi's Rigoletto, Un Ballo in Maschera, Aida and Falstaff; Wagner's Lohengrin, Mozart's La finta giardiniera, Il re pastore, Idomeneo, Die Entführung, Le nozze di Figaro, Don Giovanni and La clemenza di Tito, Rossini's La Cenerentola, The Barber of Seville, Puccini's La Bohème, Tosca, Madama Butterfly and Il Trittico, Donizetti's L'Elisir d'amore and Mary Stuart, Gounod's Faust, Bizet's The Pearl Fishers and Carmen, Massenet's Werther, Rachmaninov's Francesca da Rimini; Gen. Ed. The Viking Opera Guide 1993, The Penguin Opera Guide 1995, The New Penguin Opera Guide 2001, The Penguin Concise Guide to Opera 2005, librettos for The Silver Tassie by Mark Anthony Turnage, English National Opera 2000, Family Matters, Tête-à-Tête 2005; contrib. to The Mozart Compendium 1990. *Honours:* Olivier Award for Outstanding Achievement in Opera 2001.

HOLDORF, Udo; German singer (tenor); b. 10 July 1946, Bonn. *Education:* studied in Cologne with Josef Metternich, and in Düsseldorf. *Career:* debut at Würzburg 1971, as Otello; Deutsche Oper am Rhein, Düsseldorf, from 1973 as Edgardo in Lucia di Lammermoor, Puccini's Calaf and Luigi (Il Tabarro), Strauss's Herod and Matteo, the Captain in Wozzeck and Janáček's Boris, Albert Gregor and Mr Brouček; Guest appearances in Frankfurt, Stockholm, Paris and Lisbon; sang in the 1985 Duisburg premiere of Goehr's Behold the Sun and at Bayreuth, 1981–88, in Die Meistersinger; US engagements in New York, Atlanta and Los Angeles; season 1995–96 in Athens as Berg's Captain and at Amsterdam in The Nose by Shostakovich; Sang Jack in Weill's Mahagonny at Salzburg, 1998; season 2000–01 as Vitek in The Makropulos Case at Dusseldorf and Aegithus in Elektra at Essen; many concert engagements. *Recordings include:* Der Silbersee by Weill.

HOLECEK, Sebastian; Austrian singer (baritone); b. 1965, Vienna. *Education:* studied in Vienna. *Career:* Vienna Volksoper, 1987–90, notably in Die Weise von Liebe und Tod by Matthus; Theater am Gärtnerplatz, Munich, 1990–92; Monte Carlo, 1991, as Papageno; The Speaker in Die Zauberflöte at Ludwigsburg, 1993; Further appearances in Paris, Santiago and Turin; Vienna Volks and Staatsoper, from 1992; Other roles include Mozart's Masetto and Figaro; Schaunard in La Bohème; Sang Papageno at St Margareth, 1999. *Recordings:* Irrelohe by Schreker. *Current Management:* c/o Opera Vladarski Döblinger, Hauptstraße 57/18, 1190 Vienna, Austria. *Telephone:* (1) 368-6960/6961. *Fax:* (1) 368-6962. *E-mail:* opera.vladarski@ utanet.at.

HOLEK, Vlastimil; Czech violinist; b. 1950. *Education:* Prague Conservatory. *Career:* founder mem., Prazak String Quartet 1972–; tour of Finland 1973, followed by appearances at competitions in Prague and Evian; concerts in Salzburg, Munich, Paris, Rome, Berlin, Cologne and Amsterdam; tour of the UK 1985, including Wigmore Hall debut; tours of Japan, the USA, Australia and New Zealand; tour of the UK 1988, and concert at the Huddersfield Contemporary Music Festival 1989; recitals for the BBC, Radio France, Dutch Radio, the WDR in Cologne and Radio Prague; appearances with the Smetana and LaSalle Quartets in Mendelssohn's Octet. *Honours:* winner, Chamber Music Competition of the Prague Conservatory 1974, Grand Prix, International String Quartet Competition, Evian Music Festival 1978, National Competition of String Quartets in Czechoslovakia 1978, Best String Quartet of the Prague Spring Festival 1978. *Current Management:* c/o Světlana Jahodová, Jahoda Artists Management. *Telephone:* 603293985. *E-mail:* info@jahoda-arts.cz. *Website:* www.jahoda-arts.cz; www .prazakquartet.com.

HOLENDER, Ioan; Romanian opera house director; b. 18 July 1935, Timisoara; m.; two s. one d. *Education:* Timisoara Polytechnic Inst., Vienna Conservatory, Austria. *Career:* expelled from Romanian higher educ. system on political grounds 1956; worked as tennis trainer and stage dir's asst 1956–59; moved to Vienna and began singing studies 1960; opera singer, Vienna and Klagenfurt 1962–66; joined Starka Theater Agency 1966, later took control of agency and renamed it Holender Opera Agency; Gen. Sec. Vienna Staatsoper and Vienna Volksoper 1988–92, Dir Vienna Volksoper 1992–96, Gen. Dir Vienna Staatsoper 1992–2010; Guest Lecturer, Univ. of Vienna, Donau-Universität Krems 2008–; Artistic Adviser, Teatro Massimo Bellini, Catania 2008–; Artistic Consultant, Metropolitan Opera 2010–, Spring Festival Tokyo; Artistic Dir and Pres. Enescu Music Festival; Host, kulTOUR with Holender (ServusTV). *Publications:* Ioan Holender: Der Lebensweg des Wiener Staatsoperndirektors (autobiog.) 2004, Ioan Holender: Ich bin noch nicht fertig 2010. *Honours:* Hon. mem. Romanian Acad., Hon. Citizen of Timisoara; Vienna Municipality Golden Medal of Merit, Golden

Medal for Services to Vienna Community, Grand Golden Hon. Medal of Austrian Repub., Austrian Hon. Cross for Science and Art, First Class, Officier, Ordre des Artes et des Lettres; Dr hc (Gheorge Dima Music Acad.); Vienna Philharmonic Franz Schalk Gold Medal. *Website:* www.holender.at.

HOLICKOVA, Elena; Slovak singer (soprano); b. 1950. *Education:* Conservatory of Music, Bratislava and Acad. of Music and Drama, Bratislava. *Career:* Slovak Nat. Theatre; Musetta in La Bohème, Lisa in The Queen of Spades, Rusalka in Rusalka, Jenůfa, Julietta, Adriana in Adriana Lecouvreur, Marina in Dimitriy; Verdi's Gilda; Feodor in Mussorgsky's Boris Godunov; Small Shepherd in Suchon's The Whirlpool; Nuri in The Lowlands; Queen in Dance over the Crying; Swallow in The Happy Prince; A Servant in Elektra; Marenka in The Bartered Bride; Orphan in The Siege of Bystrica; Amelia Grimaldi in Simon Boccanegra 1984–85. *Recordings:* Songs by Mikulus Schneider-Trnavsky; Cycles by Alexander Moyzes; Glimpse into the Unknown; Mutations by Ilja Zeljenka, 1980; Ode to Joy, 1983. *Honours:* Slovak Music Fund Prize 1984.

HÖLL, Hartmut; German pianist; *Dean, Hochschule für Musik, Karlsruhe*; b. 24 Nov. 1952, Heilbronn. *Education:* studied in Stuttgart, Milan and Munich. *Career:* many lieder recitals since 1972 worldwide with Mitsuko Shirai and other leading singers; accompanist for Dietrich Fischer-Dieskau 1982–92; chamber music engagements with violist Tabea Zimmermann 1985–; toured with Renée Fleming in Europe, Asia, USA 2001–; worked with Thomas Hampson, Jochen Kowalski, Christoph Prégardien, Hermann Prey, David Wilson Johnson, Urszula Kryger, Jadwiga Rappé, Peter Schreier, Roman Trekel; fmr Prof. Frankfurt, Cologne; Prof. Karlsruhe; masterclasses in Finland, Weimar Int. Music Seminar, Schleswig-Holstein Festival, Salzburg Mozarteum, in Jerusalem and USA; Visiting Prof. Helsinki 1998–99, Salzburg Mozarteum 1994–2003, Zurich 2004–; Dean, Hochschule für Musik, Karlsruhe 2007–; Dir Int. Hugo Wolf Acad. for Chant, Poetry and Lieder Art, Stuttgart; mem. jury Robert Schumann Contest, Zwickau, Naumburg Competition, New York and Int. ARD Music Contest, Munich. *Recordings include:* over 70 recordings including lieder albums with Mitsuko Shirai and Dietrich Fischer-Dieskau; Sonatas and others by Brahms and Shostakovich with Tabea Zimmermann and Sabine Meyer. *Honours:* Hon. mem. Robert Schumann Soc., St Petersburg Philharmonia Soc.; jt winner Hugo Wolf Competition, Vienna, Robert Schumann Competition, Zwickau 1974, 1990, prizes at Athens and 's-Hertogenbosch, Netherlands 1976, Louvre Carte Blanche, Paris (with Mitsuko Shirai) 1993, ABC Int. Music Award (with Mitsuko Shirai) 1997. *Address:* Hochschule fur Musik Karlsruhe, Postfach 6040, 76040 Karlsruhe, Germany (office). *Telephone:* (721) 7202029 (office). *E-mail:* kivisaari@aol.com (office).

HOLL, Robert; singer (bass-baritone); b. 10 March 1947, Rotterdam, The Netherlands. *Education:* studied with Jan Veth and David Hollestelle. *Career:* sang with the Bayerische Staatsoper Munich from 1973; concentrated on concert career from 1975; appearances at the Vienna, Holland and Salzburg Festivals, the Schubertiade at Hohenems; Salzburg Mozartwochen 1981–83 as the Priest in Thamos, König in Ägypten, as the Voice of Neptune in Idomeneo and Cassandro in La Finta Giardiniera; many engagements as a singer of lieder, in music by Schubert, Brahms and Wolf; concert appearances with Bernstein, Giulini, Harnoncourt, Jochum, Karajan, Sawallisch, Stein and De Waart; Promenade Concerts, London 1987, in the Choral Symphony; judge, Walter Gruener Int. Lieder Competition, London 1989; sang in Schubert's Fierrabras at the Theater an der Wien, Vienna 1988; season 1992 at Zürich, as Assur in Semiramide and La Roche in Capriccio; sang Hans Sachs at the Bayreuth Festival 1996–2002; Vienna Festival 1997, Schubert's Des Teufels Lustschloss; season 2000–01 as Hans Sachs at Bayreuth, Mozart's Commendatore and Wagner's Daland at the Berlin Staatsoper; future engagements include the part of Gurnemanz (Parsifal) at the Weiner Staatsoper and Bayreuth Festival 2004. *Recordings include:* Mozart's Requiem, Mozart and Salieri by Rimsky-Korsakov, Lieder by Pfitzner, Requiems by Bellini and Donizetti, Mozart's Zaide and La Finta Semplice, St Matthew Passion by Bach, Die Schöpfung, Utrecht Te Deum by Handel, Mozart's Mass in C Minor, Bach Mass in B Minor, Wagner's Die Meistersinger von Nuremberg (Sachs), Wagner's Der Fliegende Holländer (Daland). *Honours:* winner Munich Int. Competition 1972.

HOLLAND, Ashley; British singer (baritone); b. 1969, England. *Career:* many concert and opera engagements throughout the UK; opera repertory includes Handel's Giulio Cesare and Walton's The Bear; also sings Mahler's Rückert Lieder; Contestant at the 1995 Cardiff Singer of the World Competition; season 1998 in Mozart's Grabmusik for the Classical Opera Company and Cecil in Mary Stuart for ENO; has appeared with BBC Proms, BBC Scottish Symphony Orchestra, SWF Sinfonie Orchester, BBC Philharmonic, Orchestra National de Lille, London Symphony Orchestra, Hallé Orchestra, Orchestra of the Age of Enlightenment, Concertgebouw; has worked with many conductors and Dirs, including Mark Elder, Sir Andrew Davis, Johannes Erath, Christopher Alden, Sebastian Weigle, Kent Nagano, David Parry and Paul Daniel. *Recordings:* UIN-SCI L'Oracolo, Caligula (title), Belcore in L'Elisir d'Amore and Ford in Falstaff. *Current Management:* c/o Chris Broom, Athole Still Limited, Foresters Hall 25-27 Westow Street , London, SE19 3RY, England. *Telephone:* (20) 8771-5271. *Fax:* (20) 8771-8172. *E-mail:* Christoper@atholestill.co.uk. *Website:* www.atholestill.com. *Telephone:* (20) 8768-6604. *E-mail:* mail@ashleyholland.com. *Website:* www .ashleyholland.com.

HOLLAND, Mark; British singer (baritone); b. 19 Sept. 1960, Salford. *Education:* Royal Northern Coll. of Music with John Cameron, and with Roberto Benaglio in Italy. *Career:* joined Welsh Nat. Opera in 1984 and has appeared as Rossini's Figaro, Mozart's Count, Eugene Onegin, Schaunard in La Bohème, Don Carlo in Ernani and Enrico in Lucia di Lammermoor; Sonora in La Fanciulla del West 1991; festival engagements include Piccinni's La Buona Figliola at Buxton; season 1989–90 as Falke in Fledermaus for Opera Northern Ireland and Masetto for Dublin Grand Opera; season 1990–91 as Ford in Falstaff at the Théâtre des Champs-Elysées, tour to Japan with La Bohème and Carmina Burana with the Royal Philharmonic; sang Puccini's Marcello and Mozart's Allazim (Zaide) with the City of Birmingham Touring Opera 1991–92; Bregenz Festival 1992, as Morales in Carmen; Minister in Fidelio at Bregenz 1995; sang Andrei in Three Sisters by Peter Eötvös at Hamburg 2000. *Current Management:* c/o Robert Gilder & Co., N102, Westminster Business Square, 1–45 Durham Street, London, SE11 5JH, England. *Telephone:* (20) 7580-7758. *Fax:* (20) 7580-7739. *E-mail:* rgilder@ robert-gilder.com. *Website:* www.robert-gilder.com.

HOLLANDER, Julia; stage director; b. 1965, Bristol, England. *Education:* St Catherine's Coll., Cambridge, studied in Paris. *Career:* opera productions have included Orfeo ed Euridice for the Cambridge Arts Theatre, Les Mamelles de Tiresias at the Edinburgh Festival, Giovanna d'Arco at the Bloomsbury Theatre, London, Samson and Delilah for Northern Opera in Newcastle, The Rake's Progress for Aldeburgh, Acis and Galatea for Gregynog and Manchester Festivals, Turn of the Screw at the Britten Theatre, London, La Bohème for Mid-Wales Opera, La Wally at the Bloomsbury Theatre and Love of Three Oranges in London; Staff Producer, ENO 1988–91, working on numerous productions and reviving Xerxes, Lear and Macbeth in London and abroad; solo production debut for ENO with Fennimore and Gerda 1990, returning for the premiere of John Buller's Bakxai 1992 and Eugene Onegin 1994; directed Margareta Hallin's Miss Julie for Operate at Hammersmith 1996.

HOLLANDER, Lorin D.; American pianist; b. 19 July 1944, New York, NY. *Education:* studied with Eduard Steuermann at the Juilliard School, and with Leon Fleisher and Max Rudolf. *Career:* debut at Carnegie Hall, 1955; has performed with leading orchestras in the USA including the New York Philharmonic, Philadelphia Orchestra, Washington National and Chicago Symphony Orchestra; European engagements with the Warsaw Philharmonic, Orchestre de la Suisse Romande, London Philharmonic and Concertgebouw; has performed in prisons, hospitals and other institutions; series of programmes on television; adviser to the Office of the Gifted and Talented for the US Government; lecturer on psychological aspects of musical performance. *Current Management:* Thomas F. Parker, Parker Artists Managers & Consultants, 382 Central Park West, #9G, New York, NY 10025, USA. *E-mail:* tom@parkerartists.com. *Website:* www.lorinhollander .com.

HÖLLER, York; German composer; *Professor of Composition, Cologne Musikhochschule*; b. 11 Jan. 1944, Leverkusen. *Education:* studied at Cologne Musikhochschule with B.A. Zimmermann and Herbert Eimert and at Ferienkurse Darmstadt with Boulez. *Career:* worked at the Electronic Music Studios, Cologne with Stockhausen; freelance composer 1965–; first orchestral work, Topic, performed at Darmstadt 1970; invited by Boulez to work at the studios of IRCAM 1978; piano concerto given French premiere by Daniel Barenboim, Paris 1988; Der Meister und Margarita last new production at the Paris Opera, Salle Garnier, before the opening of the Opéra de la Bastille; Prof. of Analysis and Music Theory, Cologne Musikhochschule 1975–89; Dir Electronic Studio at WDR Cologne 1990–2000; Prof. of Composition, Cologne Musikhochschule 1995–; mem. Berlin Acad. of the Arts, Free Acad. of the Arts, Hamburg. *Compositions include:* Five Pieces for piano 1964, Diaphonie for two pianos 1965, Topic for orchestra 1967, Sonate informelle 1968, Cello Sonata 1969, Epitaph for violin, piano 1969, Chroma for orchestra 1972–74, Horizont for electronics 1972, Tangens for ensemble 1973, Klanggitter for ensemble 1976, Antiphon for string quartet 1977, Arcus for orchestra 1978, Moments Musicaux for flute, piano 1979, Umbra for orchestra 1979–80, Mythos for orchestra 1979–80, Résonance for orchestra, tape 1981–82, Schwarze Halbinseln for orchestra, tape 1982, Traumspiel for soprano, orchestra, tape 1983, Piano Concerto No. 1 1983–84, Magische Klanggestalt for orchestra 1984, Improvisation sur le nom de Pierre Boulez 1985, Der Meister und Margarita, opera 1985–89, Piano Sonata No. 2, Hommage à Franz Liszt 1986, Fanal for trumpet, orchestra 1989, Pensées for piano, orchestra, electronics 1991, Aura for large orchestra 1992, Monogramme 1995–2003, String Quartet No. 2 1997, Zwiegestalt for string quartet and piano 1997–98, Aufbruch for orchestra 1999, Der Ewige Tag for chorus, orchestra and electronics 2001, Ex Tempore for 9 players 2001, Trias for saxophone, percussion and piano 2001, Klangzeichen for piano and wind quartet 2003, Scan for solo flute 2004, Feuerwerk 2004, Fluchtpunkte 2006, Sphären for orchestra (Grawemeyer Award for Music Composition 2010) 2001–06, Movements for cello and piano 2009, Doppelspiel for piano four hands 2010–11, Crossing for ensemble and live electronics 2012, Cello Concerto 2012. *Recordings:* Schwarze Halbinseln, Résonance, Arcus, Mythos, Traumspiel, Fanal, Pensées, Der Meister und Margarita, Aufbruch, Der ewige Tag, Sphären. *Publications:* Composition of the Gestalt or the making of an organism 1984, B.A. Zimmermann: Moine et Dionysios 1985, Auf der Suche nach dem Klang von Morgen 1990. *Honours:* Chevalier des Arts et des Lettres; Bernd Alois Zimmermann Prize, City of Cologne, Promotion Prize, State of

North Rhine-Westphalia, Prize of Int. Composers' Forum of UNESCO, Rolf Liebermann Prize for Opera Composition, Special Prize, Asscn of French Theatre and Music Critics. *Address:* c/o Boosey & Hawkes Bote & Bock, Lützowufer 26, 10787 Berlin, Germany. *E-mail:* hoeller.york@netcologne.de (office); composers.germany@boosey.com. *Website:* www.boosey.com/holler; www.yorkhoeller.de.

HOLLEY, William; American singer (tenor); b. 4 Dec. 1930, Bristol, FL. *Education:* studied in Florida. *Career:* debut as Gounod's Faust, Salzburg Landestheater, 1961; sang as Gelsenkirchen Opera, 1962–65; Deutsche Oper Berlin, 1971–79; Bavarian State Opera, 1971–76; Stuttgart, 1973–82; Deutsche Oper am Rhein, Düsseldorf, 1966–84; guest appearances in San Francisco, Don Ottavio, 1968; Vienna, Copenhagen, Barcelona and Houston; Salzburg Festival, 1969–71 in Cavalieri's La Rappresentazione di Anima e di Corpo; other roles have included Mozart's Tamino, Ferrando and Belmonte, Verdi's Duke of Mantua and Alfredo, Hoffman, Froh in Das Rheingold, Puccini's Cavaradossi and Calaf, Andrea Chénier, Don José, Lensky and Laca in Jenůfa; Des Grieux in Manon Lescaut, Don Carlos and Verdi's Riccardo.

HOLLIDAY, Melanie; singer (soprano); b. 12 Aug. 1951, Houston, TX, USA. *Education:* Indiana Univ., Graz Acad. of Music. *Career:* sang at Hamburg and Klagenfurt from 1973; Basle Opera as Zerbinetta in Ariadne auf Naxos; Vienna Volksoper from 1976, as Olympia in Les Contes d'Hoffmann, Frau Fluth, Constanze, Philine in Mignon, Adele (Die Fledermaus), Valencienne (Die Lustige Witwe) and in Die Schöne Galatea by Suppé; tours of Japan with the Volksoper 1979, 1982, 1985; guest appearances in Germany, Italy, The Netherlands, Spain and Switzerland; Vienna Staatsoper; Houston Opera 1983; operetta tour of Germany with René Kollo 1984; Theater am Gärtnerplatz, Munich 1986, as Musetta in La Bohème; Turin and Berlin 1994, 1996, Adele and Valencienne. *Recordings include:* Die Fledermaus, L'Elisir d'amore (film).

HOLLIER, Donald Russell, DMus; Australian composer and conductor; b. 7 May 1934, Sydney. *Education:* NSW State Conservatorium, RAM, London, Univ. of London. *Career:* Head of Academic Studies, Canberra School of Music 1967–84; Musical Dir Canberra Choral Soc. and Canberra Opera; Australian premieres of works by Vaughan Williams, Walton, Britten and Poulenc. *Compositions include:* nine Concertos 1966–89, The Revelation of St John the Divine (oratorio) 1974, The Heiress (opera) 1975, seven Psalms and Lamentations of David 1979, seven New Psalms 1986, The Beggar's Bloody Opera 1991, All Between the Earth and Sphere for orchestra 1991, For the Term of his Natural Life 1993, Myra Breckinridge, Variations on a theme of Debussy for trumpet and piano 1998, three Symphonies 1999, 2002, 2004, many songs and piano pieces. *Honours:* Churchill Fellowship 1973. *Address:* c/o Australian Music Centre Ltd, First Floor, Argyle Stores, 18 Argyle Street, The Rocks, Sydney, NSW 2000, Australia.

HOLLIGER, Heinz; Swiss oboist, composer and conductor; b. 21 May 1939, Langenthal; m. Ursula Holliger. *Education:* in Berne, Paris and Basel under Emile Cassagnaud (oboe) and Pierre Boulez (composition). *Career:* Prof. of Oboe, Freiberg Music Acad. 1965–; has appeared at major European music festivals and in Japan, USA, Australia, Israel, etc.; conducted Chamber Orchestra of Europe, London 1992, London Sinfonietta 1997; Composer-in-Residence, Lucerne Festival 1998; recorded over 80 works, mainly for Philips and Deutsche Grammophon. *Compositions include:* Der magische Tänzer, Trio, Siebengesang, Wind Quintet, Dona nobis pacem, Pneuma, Psalm, Cardiophonie, Kreis, String Quartet, Atembogen, Die Jahreszeiten, Come and Go, Not I. *Recordings include:* Koechlin's Vocal works with orchestra (Midem Classical Award for Vocal Recitals 2006). *Honours:* Frankfurt Music Award 1988, Ernst von Siemens Music Award 1991, Prix de Composition Musicale de la Fondation Prince Pierre de Monaco 1994, Zurich Festival Award 2007, Rheingau Musikpreis 2008, among others. *Address:* c/o Colbert Artists Management, 307 Seventh Avenue, Suite 2006, New York, NY 10001, USA; Konzertgesellschaft, Hochstrasse 51/Postfach, 4002 Basel, Switzerland. *Website:* www.heinzholliger.com.

HOLLINGWORTH, Robert Matthew; British conductor; *Music Director, I Fagiolini.* *Education:* New Coll., Oxford. *Career:* chorister, Hereford Cathedral; Founder and Music Dir, vocal ensemble I Fagiolini 1986–; debut at BBC Proms 2013, projects with I Fagiolini included Simunye, The Full Monteverdi, Tallis in Wonderland, How Like an Angel (with Australian contemporary circus group Circa) 2012–13; Guest Conductor, BBC Singers, English Concert, Nederlands Kamerkoor, NDR Chor, Academy of Ancient Music, St James Baroque, BBC Concert Orchestra, Dartington Summer School; Artistic Adviser, York Early Music Festival 2006–10, Trigonale Festival, Austria 2009; directed period instrument ensembles Florilegium and The Bach Players; writer/presenter for BBC radio (Record Review, Music Restored, Discovering Music and The Early Music Show). *Films include:* Quills. *Recordings include:* with I Fagiolini: Insalata 1998, Tomkins: Music Divine 2002, Monteverdi: Flaming Heart 2006, Gabrieli: The Madrigal in Venice 2006, The Triumphs of Oriana 2006, Monteverdi: Fire & Ashes 2008, Monteverdi: Sweet Torment 2009, Striggio: Mass in 40 Parts (Gramophone Award for Best Early Music Recording, Diapason d'Or de l'Année) 2011, 1612 Italian Vespers 2012. *Honours:* Royal Philharmonic Soc.'s Ensemble Award (with I Fagiolini) 2005. *Current Management:* Percius, Advice Hub, 66 Devonshire Road, Cambridge, CB1 2BL, England. *E-mail:* info@percius.co.uk. *Website:* www.percius.co.uk; www.ifagiolini.com (office).

HOLLOP, Markus; German singer (bass); b. 1968, Berlin. *Education:* Munich Musikhochschule. *Career:* major roles with the opera studio of the Bayerische Staatsoper, from 1991; Sarastro in Die Zauberflöte and Rossini's Basilio in Gorlitz; Ulm Opera as the King in The Love for Three Oranges, Offenbach's Crespel at Wiesbaden and engagements with the Bayerische Staatsoper, from 1993; Further appearances in Schumann's Genoveva (Zürich), Hamlet and Wozzeck (Geneva) and Salome (Paris Châtelet, under Semyon Bychkov, 1997); Concerts include Weill's Ozeanflug in Munich and Solo Voice in Schoenberg's Moses und Aron with the Philharmonia Orchestra under Christoph von Dohnányi at the Festival Hall, London, 1996. *Honours:* winner Carl Maria von Weber Competition, Munich, 1993. *Current Management:* c/o Opera Vladarski Döblinger, Hauptstraße 57/18, 1190 Vienna, Austria. *Telephone:* (1) 368-6960/6961 (Austria). *Fax:* (1) 368-6962 (Austria). *E-mail:* opera.vladarski@utanet.at.

HOLLOWAY, David, BA, MA; singer (baritone) and teacher; b. 12 Nov. 1942, Grandview, MO, USA; m. Deborah Seabury 1975, four s. one d. *Education:* Univ. of Kansas, studied with Luigi Ricci in Rome, Richard Torigi in New York, with Janine Reiss, Jacqueline Richard and Frank Eggermann. *Career:* debut with Kansas City Lyric Opera 1968; sang with Deutsche Oper am Rhein 1981–91, Metropolitan Opera 1974–87, New York City Opera 1972–80, Glyndebourne Opera Festival 1985, 1987, Chicago Lyric Opera, Dallas Opera, Houston Opera, National Opera Center, Ottawa, Canada, Santa Fe Opera, Central City Opera Festival, San Francisco, Cincinnati Opera; mem. of voice/opera faculty, North Park Univ. and Music Inst. of Chicago. *Recordings:* Escamillo in Carmen with Glyndebourne Festival Opera; The Face on the Barroom Floor by Mollicone; Songs by Frederick Rzewski; Songs by Karl and Vally Weigl. *Honours:* winner San Francisco Opera audition 1968, Martha Baird Rockefeller Docent 1970, Tanglewood Festival HiFidelity/Musical America Award 1971, National Opera Institute grant 1973–74.

HOLLOWAY, John; British violinist and academic; *Professor, Guildhall School of Music, London*; b. 19 July 1948, Neath, Wales. *Education:* Guildhall School, London with Yfrah Neaman, studied with William Pleeth, Sándor Végh and Sigiswald Kuijken. *Career:* Leader of Kent Opera Orchestra 1972–79, Taverner Players 1977–91, London Classical Players 1978–92; f. L'Ecole d'Orphée 1975, with numerous performances of Baroque music in London and elsewhere; Prof., Guildhall School of Music, London and Guest Prof., Schola Cantorum, Basel and Indiana Univ., USA; Prof., Musikhochschule, Dresden, Germany 1999–2014. *Recordings include:* Chamber Music by Handel, with L'Ecole d'Orphée; Biber's Mystery Sonatas; Buxtehude Chamber Music, with Jaap ter Linden and Lars Ulrik Mortensen; for ECM sonatas by Schmelzer, Biber, Leclair, Veracini, Bach (solo sonatas and partitas), Castello and Fontana, Dowland 'Lachrimae Pavans', Purcell Fantazias; also Corelli Sonatas, Telemann 'Paris Quartets'. *Honours:* Gramophone Award 1991, Danish Grammy Award 1995, 1998, ICMA 2014. *Telephone:* 702173579 (mobile, Czech Repub.). *E-mail:* jholloway@gmx.de. *Website:* www.johnholloway.org.

HOLLOWAY, Robin Greville, PhD, DMus; British composer, writer and fmr academic; b. 19 Oct. 1943, Leamington Spa; s. of Robert Charles Holloway and Pamela Mary Holloway (née Jacob). *Education:* St Paul's Cathedral Choir School, King's Coll. School, Wimbledon, King's Coll., Cambridge, New Coll., Oxford. *Career:* Lecturer in Music, Univ. of Cambridge 1975, Reader in Musical Composition 1999, Prof. of Musical Composition 2001–11; Fellow, Gonville and Caius Coll., Cambridge 1969. *Compositions include:* Garden Music (Opus 1) 1962, First Concerto for Orchestra 1969, Scenes from Schumann (Opus 13) 1970, Evening with Angels (Opus 17) 1972, Domination of Black (Opus 23) 1973, Clarissa (opera) (Opus 30) 1976, Second Concerto for Orchestra (Opus 40) 1979, Brand (dramatic ballad) (Opus 48) 1981, Women in War (Opus 51) 1982, Seascape and Harvest (Opus 55) 1983, Viola Concerto (Opus 56) 1984, Peer Gynt 1985, Hymn to the Senses for chorus 1990, Serenade for strings 1990, Double Concerto (Opus 68), The Spacious Firmament for chorus and orchestra (Opus 69), Violin Concerto Opus 70 1990, Boys and Girls Come Out To Play (opera) 1991, Winter Music for sextet 1993, Frost at Midnight (Opus 78), Third Concerto for Orchestra (Opus 80) 1994, Clarinet Concerto (Opus 82) 1996, Peer Gynt (Opus 84) 1984–97, Scenes from Antwerp (Opus 85) 1997, Gilded Goldberg for two pianos 1999, Symphony 1999, Missa Caiensis 2001, Cello Sonata 2001, Spring Music (Opus 96) 2002, String Quartet No. 1 2003, String Quartet No. 2 2004. *Recordings:* Fantasy Pieces (Opus 16) 1971, Sea Surface Full of Clouds chamber cantata, Romanza for violin and small orchestra (Opus 28) 1974–75, Second Concerto for Orchestra (Opus 40) 1978–79, Horn Concerto (Opus 43) 1979–80, Third Concerto for orchestra (Opus 80) 1981–90, Violin Concerto (Opus 70) 1990, Gilded Goldberg (Opus 86) 1992–97, Missa Caiensis, Organ Fantasy 1993–2001, Woefully Arrayed 1999, Fourth Concerto for Orchestra 2003–05, Reliquary – Scenes from the life of Mary Queen of Scots enclosing an instrumentation of Robert Schumann's 'Gedichte der Königin Maria Stuart' 2009–10, Andante and Variations 2010, Fifth Concerto for Orchestra (Opus 107) 2011, Trio for Oboe, Violin, Piano 2011, String Quartet No. 4 2011, C'est l'extase (after Debussy) for soprano and orchestra 2012, Europa and the Bull for tuba and orchestra 2013. *Publications include:* Debussy and Wagner 1978, On Music: Essays and Diversions 1963–2003 2004; numerous articles and reviews. *Address:* Finella, Queen's Road, Cambridge, CB3 9AH, England (home). *Telephone:* (1223) 335424. *E-mail:* rgh@robinholloway.info. *Website:* www.robinholloway.info.

HOLLOWAY, Stephen, MA (Cantab.), LGSM; British singer (bass); b. 1951, England. *Education:* Christ's Coll., Cambridge, Guildhall School of Music and Drama, London and private tuition and coaching. *Career:* appearances with Scottish Opera as Don Fernando in Fidelio, Commendatore in Don Giovanni, Private Willis in Iolanthe, Doctor Grenvil in La Traviata, Thanatos/The Oracle in Alceste, Old Hebrew in Samson et Delila, Harapha in Samson, Basilio in Il Barbiere di Siviglia; Sarastro in Die Zauberflote, Alidoro in La Cenerentola, Ferrando in Il Trovatore, Sparafucile in Rigoletto, Sacristan in Tosca, Bartolo in Le Nozze di Figaro for European Chamber Opera; The Speaker in The Magic Flute under Jane Glover at the Covent Garden Festival, Chub in Tchaikovsky's Cherevichki and The Chamberlain in Stravinsky's Nightingale for Chelsea Opera Group; Tom in Un Ballo in Maschera for Holland Park Opera; numerous concert engagements. *Address:* 8 St Catherines, Lincoln, LN5 8LY, England (home). *Telephone:* (1502) 520014 (home). *E-mail:* stephen@stephenholloway.co.uk (office). *Website:* www .stephenholloway-bass.co.uk.

HOLM, Peder; Danish composer and educator; b. 30 Sept. 1926, Copenhagen. *Education:* Royal Danish Conservatorium. *Career:* Dir, Western Jutland Conservatorium; Dir, West Jutland Symphony Orchestrs; mem. of programme cttee, Danish Radio 1963–67; mem. of music cttee, State Cultural Foundation 1965–68. *Compositions include:* Pezzo Concertante for orchestra 1964, VYL for orchestra 1967, Khebeb for two pianos and orchestra 1968, two pieces for wind quintet 1968, Music for brass band 1969, Ole Wivel children's song for children's choir 1970, Concertino for clarinet and chamber orchestra 1970, Legend, Erik Knudsen for children's choir 1971, Ene Mene, Inscription, Mobile, September Evening, Regards to Borge (five choral songs) for mixed choir, Pikkutikka for children's choir and orchestra 1973; arrangements of works by Schumann, Grieg, Couperin and Mozart; pieces for the Musica Ensemble series; works for solo voice, orchestra, symphonic works, concertos and chamber music; The Wandering Prince and the Poor Maiden (drama) 1984, Ode for the Year 1988, Voices of Funen for mixed chorus and ensemble 1995.

HOLM, Renate; singer (soprano); b. 10 Aug. 1931, Berlin, Germany. *Education:* studied with Marie Ivogun in Vienna. *Career:* sang in films and entertainment programmes from 1953; Vienna Volksoper from 1957, debut as Gretchen in Der Wildschütz by Lortzing; appearances at the Vienna Staatsoper, Bolshoi Theatre, Moscow, Covent Garden, London, and the Teatro Colón, Buenos Aires in the soubrette repertory, including Despina, Norina, Sophie, Zerlina and Marzelline; Salzburg Festival from 1961, as Blondchen in Die Entführung, Papagena and Musetta 1975. *Recordings:* Die Fledermaus, Der Vogelhändler, Das Land des Lächelns; Die Zauberflöte; Die Entführung.

HOLMAN, Peter Kenneth, MBE, DMus; British harpsichordist, chamber organist, conductor, musicologist and academic; b. 19 Oct. 1946, London, England. *Education:* King's Coll., London with Thurston Dart. *Career:* as a student, directed the pioneering early music group Ars Nova; Co-founder, with violinist Roy Goodman, The Parley of Instruments 1979, The Parley later recognised as one of the leading exponents of Renaissance and Baroque string consort music; Musical Dir and Co-founder Opera Restor'd (specialised in authentic productions of 18th-century English operas and masques) 1985; Prof., RAM, London for 10 years and has taught at many conservatories, univs and summer schools in UK and abroad; Artistic Dir Suffolk Village Festival; Jt Artistic Dir Boston Early Music Festival 1995; Reader in Historical Musicology, Univ. of Leeds; regular broadcaster on BBC Radio 3; writer and researcher, with special interest in early history of the violin family, in European instrumental ensemble music of the Renaissance and Baroque, and in English 17th- and 18th-century music; edn of Arne's Artaxerxes performed London 1995; directed Opera Restor'd in Lampe's The Dragon of Wantley 1996, and double bill of Scarlatti's La Dirindina and Haydn's La Canterina 1998. *Recordings include:* many of the extensive series of recordings of lesser-known English baroque music for Hyperion Records' English Orpheus series 1980–2010. *Publications:* numerous edns of early music; Four and Twenty Fiddlers, The Violin at the English Court 1540–1690 1993, London: Commonwealth and Restoration in the Early Baroque Era (ed.) 1993, paper on Monteverdi's string writing (Early Music, Nov. 1993 issue), Four and Twenty Fiddlers: The Violin at the English Court, 1540–1690 1996, Henry Purcell: A General Survey of Purcell's Music 1994, Dowland: Lachrimae (1604) 1999, From Renaissance to Baroque: Change in Instruments (co-author) 2005, Music in the British Provinces, 1690–1914 (co-author) 2007, Life After Death: The Viola Da Gamba in Britain 2010, Purcell – 23 Articles (ed.) 2011; contrib. of various articles and reviews to a range of newspapers and journals. *Honours:* Hon. ARAM 1979. *Website:* www.parley.org.uk.

HOLOMAN, D(allas) Kern, BA, MFA, PhD; musicologist, conductor and music educator; b. 8 Sept. 1947, Raleigh, North Carolina, USA; m. Elizabeth R Holoman, 1 s., 1 d. *Education:* North Carolina School of the Arts, Accademia Musicale Chigiana, Siena, Italy, Duke Univ., Princeton Univ. *Career:* founding Dir, Early Music Ensemble 1973–77, 1979; Conductor, Symphony Orchestra 1978–, Chair of Music Dept, Univ. of California at Davis 1980–88; founding Co-Ed., 19th-Century Music Journal 1977; Gen. Ed., Recent Researches in the Music of the Nineteenth and Early Twentieth Centuries 1989; guest lecturer, various professional organizations; mem. American Musicological Soc., Music Library Asscn, Asscn Nat. Hector Berlioz. *Publications:* The Creative Process in the Autograph Musical Documents of Hector Berlioz c. 1818–1840 1980, Musicology in the 1980s (ed. with C. Palisca) 1982,

Dr Holoman's Handy Guide to Concert-Going 1983, Catalogue of the Works of Hector Berlioz 1987, Writing About Music: A Style-Sheet from the Editors of the 19th-Century Music 1988, Berlioz 1989, Berlioz's Roméo et Juliette (New Berlioz Edition, ed.); contrib. numerous articles and reviews to journals and other publications.

HOLSZKY, Adriana; composer; b. 30 June 1953, Bucharest, Romania. *Education:* Bucharest Conservatory with Milko Kelemen, studied in Germany and with Franco Donatoni in Italy. *Career:* teacher, Stuttgart Hochschule 1980–89. *Compositions include:* Space for four orchestras 1980, Erewhon for 14 instruments 1984, Bremer Freiheit (opera) 1987, Lichtflug for violin, flute and orchestra 1990, Gemalde Eines Erschlagenen for 74 voices 1993, The Rise of the Titanic (music theatre) 1998, also vocal and chamber music. *Honours:* prizewinner in competitions in Rome, Paris, Mannheim and Heidelberg.

HOLT, Olivier; French conductor; b. 1960, Paris. *Education:* Vienna Hochschule für Musik. *Career:* Asst at Opéra de Nancy and Opéra de Paris; conducted performances at the Paris Châtelet, Opéra-Comique and at Marseille Opéra; Music Dir, Orchestre Symphonique d'Europe 1987–91, with tours to Vienna, Salzburg and Madrid; guest with the Orchestre National de Lille, Marseille Philharmonique and Colonne Concerts; season 1999–2000 with the Orchestre de Picardie (Haydn/Bach/Webern) and at Lille (Franck/ Liszt/Saint-Saëns); Conductor, Conservatoire de Rouen 1997–; season 2001 with concerts in Miami and throughout France. *Recordings include:* albums with Nathalie Dessay, Françoise Pollet and Isabelle Vernet; Stabat Mater by Gouvy.

HOLT, Simon, FRNCM, FBU; British composer; b. 21 Feb. 1958, Bolton, Lancs., England. *Education:* Bolton Coll. of Art, Royal Northern Coll. of Music. *Career:* commissions from London Sinfonietta: Kites, Ballad of the Black Sorrow, eco-pavan; from Nash Ensemble: Shadow Realm, Era madrugada, Canciones, Sparrow Night, all fall down, the other side of silence, Four Quarters and String Sextet: the torturer's horse; from BBC Proms: Syrensong 1987, walking with the river's roar 1992, The Coroner's Report 2004, Troubled Light 2008; featured composer at Bath Festival 1985; also featured at Music in London Now, Festival of Japan 1986 and at Huddersfield Festival 1998; Composer in Association, BBC Nat. Orchestra of Wales 2008–12, portrait concert 2009. *Compositions include:* Lunas Zauberschein, The Ruin, Palace at 4am, Maiastra, Kites, Shadow Realm, Era madrugada, Black Lanterns, Burlesca Oscura, Tauromaquia, Canciones, Syrensong, Ballad of the Black Sorrow, Capriccio Spettrale, String Quartet: Danger of the disappearance of things, Sparrow Night, a song of crocuses and lightning, Lilith, walking with the river's roar, Icarus Lamentations, Minotaur Games, a book of colours, all fall down, Banshee, Nigredo, Daedalus Remembers, The Nightingale's to Blame, Six Caprices, eco-pavan, Sunrise' Yellow Noise (Prince Pierre de Monaco Medal 2001), Sphinx, Clandestiny, Two Movements for string quartet (Royal Philharmonic Award), startled Grass, Boots of Lead (Ivor Novello Award for Classical Music 2002), Odradek, Who Put Bella in the Wych Elm? (British Composer Award for Best Stage Work 2004), feet of clay, brief candles, the other side of silence, The Coroner's Report, Klop's last bite, the sharp end of night, Migas, 5 settings of E.D., witness to a snow miracle (British Composer Award for Best Orchestral Work 2006), disparate, 4 Quarters, mantis, Sueños, a second box of brief candles, Piano Trio: Los Ojos, a table of noises (British Composer Award for Best Orchestral Composition 2009), Troubled Light, St Vitus in the Kettle, a knot of time, amapolas, disparate dos, Centauromachy, String Sextet: the torturer's horse, Telarañas, a farewell, everything turns away, bagatelarañas, The Wasp Queen, Morpheus Wakes, The Yellow Wallpaper, escaramuza, Ellsworth 2. *Recordings:* Era Madrugada, Canciones, Shadow Realm, Sparrow Night with Nash Ensemble; eco-pavan, feet of Clay, Lilith, Boots of Lead, Kites with BCMG; piano pieces with Rolf Hind. *Address:* c/o Chester Music Ltd, 14–15 Berners Street, London, W1T 3LJ, England. *Telephone:* (20) 7612-7475. *E-mail:* jenny .wegg@musicsales.co.uk.

HOLTEN, Bo, PhD; Danish composer and conductor; b. 22 Oct. 1948, Rudkøbing; four d. *Education:* Univ. of Copenhagen, Royal Danish Music Conservatory. *Career:* f. Ars Nova vocal group, Copenhagen 1979, Artistic Dir 1979–96; founder and Artistic Dir, Musica Ficta vocal ensemble 1996–; regularly conducts Danish Symphony Orchestra; Prin. Guest Conductor, The BBC Singers 1990–2006; Chief Conductor, Flemish Radio Choir, Brussels 2008–12; guest conductor of numerous European choirs; has conducted around 200 world premieres, over 1500 concerts and operas. *Compositions include:* operas: The Bond 1979, The Celestial Dog 1983, Operation Orfeo 1992, Maria Paradies 1999, Gesualdo 2003, The Visit of the Royal Physician 2007–08; concertos for cello, clarinet, bassoon, oboe; two symphonies 1982, 1986; various orchestral pieces and chamber music, five large song-cycles for voice and instruments, 10 film scores, 35 a cappella works. *Address:* W. Marstrandsgrade 28, 2100 Copenhagen, Denmark (office). *E-mail:* bo.holten@ ficta.dk (office). *Website:* boholten.dk.

HOLTEN, Kasper Bech; Danish theatre, opera and film director; *Director of Opera, The Royal Opera;* b. 24 March 1973, Copenhagen. *Education:* Univ. of Copenhagen. *Career:* worked as an Asst Dir to John Cox, David Pountney and Harry Kupfer; mem. Danish Music Council 1995–99, Danish Radio and TV Council 2000–08; Artistic Dir Århus Sommeropera Festival 1997–2000; Artistic Dir Royal Danish Opera 2000–11, led move into Copenhagen's new opera house 2005; Assoc. Prof., Copenhagen Business School 2007–; Dir of Opera, The Royal Opera, Covent Garden 2011–; has staged more than 60 productions of opera, drama, operetta and musical theatre in Denmark, Sweden, Norway, Finland, Iceland, France, Austria, Latvia, USA and Russia; production of Wagner's Ring in Copenhagen 2003–06, other key productions include Le nozze di Figaro, Theater an der Wien, Tannhäuser, Copenhagen, A Clockwork Orange, Stockholm, My Fair Lady, Copenhagen and Die Tote Stadt, Helsinki, Don Giovanni, Covent Garden 2014; mem. Bd European Acad. of Music Theatre. *Film:* Juan (writer and dir) 2010. *Address:* c/o Ian Stones, Harrison/Parrott Ltd, 5–6 Albion Court, London, W6 0QT, England. *Telephone:* (20) 7313-3504. *Fax:* (20) 7221-5042. *E-mail:* ian.stones@ harrisonparrott.co.uk. *Website:* www.harrisonparrott.com. *Address:* Royal Opera House, Bow Street, Covent Garden, London, WC2E 9DD, England (office). *Telephone:* (20) 7240-1200 (office). *Website:* www.roh.org.uk (office); www.holten.com.

HOLTENAU, Rudolf; singer (baritone); b. 1937, Salzburg, Austria. *Education:* studied in Linz and in Vienna with Alfred Jerger. *Career:* sang in concert 1959–61; opera engagements at Klagenfurt 1961–62, Regensburg 1962–65, Bielefeld 1965–67, Essen 1967–75; further appearances at Cologne 1972–73, Vienna Staatsoper 1973–75, Graz 1977–79; guest throughout the 1970s at Stockholm, Lyon, Brussels, Barcelona, Monte Carlo, Lisbon, Marseille and Bologna; performances of Der Ring des Nibelungen at Seattle 1978–79; sang such roles as Wagner's Dutchman, Sachs, Wotan, Gunther, Kurwenal and Amfortas, Strauss's Mandryka and Verdi's Amonasro at Hamburg, Berlin (Deutsche Oper), Buenos Aires, Venice, San Francisco and Rio de Janeiro; sang at Cape Town 1982, 1985. *Recordings include:* Ballads by Carle Loewe.

HOLTHAM, Ian, BA, BMus, DipEd, PhD; Australian pianist and educator; b. 1 Feb. 1955, Melbourne, Vic. *Education:* Melbourne Univ., Durham Univ., studied with Peter Feuchtwanger, Geza Anda and Geoffrey Parsons. *Career:* debut in Purcell Room and Wigmore Hall 1977; appearances in the UK, Switzerland, France, Austria, Italy, Thailand, Hong Kong and Australia; concerto soloist and recitalist; numerous radio and television broadcasts, including frequently for Australian Broadcasting Corporation; Head of Keyboard and Practical Studies in the Faculty of Music, Univ. of Melbourne. *Recordings:* Chopin: 24 Etudes, Op 10 and Op 25; Godowsky: Selection of transcriptions of Chopin Etudes; Imo pectore-music by Beethoven, Schubert, Schumann and Rachmaninov; Acts of Homage–Music by Brahms and Schubert. *Publications:* The Essentials of Piano Technique 1992; contrib. various articles in the Oxford Companion to Australian Music. *Address:* Heavitree, PO Box 412, Canterbury, Vic. 3126, Australia.

HOLTMANN, Heidrun; German pianist; b. 18 Oct. 1961, Munster, Westphalia. *Education:* studied with Eleonore Jäger in Münster, with Prof. Renate Kretschmar-Fischer at Musikhochschule Detmold/Westphalia, with Nikata Magaloff in Geneva, Switzerland, with Vladimir Ashkenazy in Lucerne, Switzerland. *Career:* concerts in England, France, Germany, Israel, Italy, Japan, Yugoslavia, North Africa, Austria, Poland, Hungary, Switzerland, USA; concerts at festivals in Bordeaux, France; Brescia and Bergamo, Italy; Salzburg; Lockenhaus, Austria; Lucerne, Switzerland; Berlin, West Germany; concerts with Detroit Symphony Orchestra (Ivan Fischer), Royal Philharmonic Orchestra, London (Antal Dorati), Mozarteum Orchestra/ Salzburg, Tonhalle Orchestra/Zürich (Gerd Albrecht, Ferdinand Leitner, David Zinman), ARD/NDR-ZDF, West Germany; DRS-TV, Zürich, Switzerland; RTV Skopje, Yugoslavia; television recordings at ARD and ZDF, West Germany; radio broadcasts with radio stations in Germany. *Recordings:* Gidon Kremer Chamber Music Festival, 1983; Anneliese Rothenberger Presents, 1984; Bach, Goldberg Variations, 1986; Schumann, Carnaval and Kreisleriana, 1987. *Address:* c/o MIX / Detlev Roth, Zossener Str. 55, 10961 Berlin, Germany. *E-mail:* info@heidrun-holtmann.de (office). *Website:* www.heidrun-holtmann.de.

HOLTON, Ruth; singer (soprano); b. 1961, England. *Education:* choral exhibitioner Clare Coll., Cambridge, studied with Elizabeth Lane, Nancy Long and Julie Kennard. *Career:* appearances from 1985 in Baroque music at Bruges, Turku (Finland), Berlin, Amsterdam, Rome, Vienna, Paris; recitals in Cambridge, Oxford, London, Glasgow and at the Three Choirs Festival in Gloucester; Fauré's Requiem at the Théâtre du Châtelet, Paris, and Ilia in Idomeneo 1991; radio broadcasts, BBC Recital, Radio 3 1992, 1994, 1995, 1996, 1997; WDR Recital 1992; worldwide broadcast of Bach's St John Passion with choir of St Thomas', Leipzig 1997; concert work with Fretwork, Orchestra of the Age of Enlightenment, Ton Koopman, John Eliot Gardiner, Gustav Leonhardt, Taverner Consort. *Recordings:* Bach's St John Passion and Cantatas, Jephtha by Handel and Carissimi, Dido and Aeneas, Handel's Messiah, Mozart's Salzburg Masses, works by Schütz and Buxtehude; Angel in Schütz's Christmas Story with the King's Consort; Grand Pianola Music by John Adams, also music by Steve Reich.

HOLZAPFEL, Marcela; singer (soprano); b. 1960, Chile. *Education:* studied in Chile. *Career:* sang at Santiago Opera 1985–88, as Clorinda in La Cenerentola, Mozart's Constanze, Strauss's Zerbinetta and Verdi's Nannetta; Rio de Janeiro 1988, as Zerbinetta; Stuttgart Staatsoper from 1990, as Sophie in Werther, Antonoe in Henze's Bassarids, Puccini's Musetta and Oscar in Un Ballo in Maschera; Berlin Staatsoper 1991, as Constanze in Die Entführung; Santiago from 1992, notably as Gilda and as Micaela in Carmen; many concert engagements.

HOLZMAIR, Wolfgang; Austrian singer (baritone); b. 24 April 1952, Vöcklabruck. *Education:* Vienna Acad. of Music and Dramatic Arts with Hilde Rössel-Majdan and Erik Werba. *Career:* appearances in opera and concert halls throughout Germany, Austria and Switzerland; premiered Berio's orchestration of Mahler Lieder 1992; has sung with leading European and American orchestras, including the Israel Philharmonic, Berlin Philharmonic, Vienna Symphony, Leipzig Gewandhaus, Cleveland and Concertgebouw Orchestras, and the Orchestra of the Age of Enlightenment; Covent Garden debut, as Papageno 1993; other opera roles include Rossini's Figaro and Valentin, Gluck's Orpheus and Eugene Onegin, Udo Zimmermann's Die Weisse Rose, Ireo in Cesti's Semiramide, Serezha in Nigel Osborne's The Electrification of the Soviet Union, Peri's Orfeo, Creonte in Haydn's Orfeo and Enrico in Haydn's Isola disabitata in Lyon, Pelléas, the Count in Capriccio in Cagliari, Speaker of the Temple in Die Zauberflöte, the title role in Daniel Schnyder's Casanova; season 2003–04 included appearances in London, Lisbon, New York, Ottawa, Graz, Vienna and at the Risör and Bregenz festivals, and sang Lieder eines fahrenden Gesellen with the Minnesota Orchestra, Schubert songs with the Orchestra of St Luke's, Carnegie Hall, and Mahler's Das Lied von der Erde at the Vienna Festival; season 2004–05 included recitals in New York, Washington, Dublin, London, Vienna and at the Bath, Menuhin and Carinthian Summer Festivals; teacher of lied and oratorio, Mozarteum, Salzburg 1998–. *Recordings:* Lieder by Clara and Robert Schumann, Eichendorff songs, recordings of Schubert, Pelléas et Mélisande (with Haitink and the Orchestre National de France), Brahms' Ein deutsches Requiem (with Herbert Blomstedt) (Grammy Award). *Current Management:* c/o Owen/White Management, Flat 6, 22 Brunswick Terrace, Hove, East Sussex BN3 1HJ, England. *Telephone:* (1273) 727127. *Fax:* (1273) 527038. *E-mail:* info@owenwhitemanagement.com. *Website:* www .owenwhitemanagement.com.

HOMOKI, Andreas; German opera director; *Director and Intendant, Zurich Opera House;* b. 16 Feb. 1960, Marl. *Education:* Bremen Hochschule, Acad. of Fine Arts, Berlin. *Career:* Asst at Deutsche Oper Berlin, Theater des Westens and Komische Oper, Berlin; Asst to Harry Kupfer at Salzburg Festival, Stuttgart State Opera and Cologne Opera 1986–87; Asst to Michael Hampe, Willy Decker and Harry Kupfer, at Cologne Opera 1987; Asst to Michael Hampe at Salzburg Festival; opera productions have included Mozart's Bastien und Bastienne in Oslo, Le nozze di Figaro for Kammeroper Herdecke 1988, Fidelio and Jakob Lenz by Wolfgang Rihm for the Cologne Music Acad. 1989–90; Dir, Michael Hampe Australian Opera production of Die Meistersinger 1990, for New Zealand Int. Festival of the Arts; Il Trovatore for Wellington City Opera 1991; Instructor in Drama Opera Dept, Cologne Music Acad. 1988–93; freelance director 1993–; Chief Dir, Komische Oper, Berlin 2002–, Intendant 2003–12; Dir and Intendant, Zurich Opera House 2012–; opera productions have included L'Enfant et les Sortilèges for Cologne Music Acad. 1992, Die Frau ohne Schatten, Grand Théâtre de Genève 1992 and Le Châtelet, Paris (French Theatre Critics' Award for Best Opera) 1993, Cav and Pag in State Theatre, Mainz 1993, Madama Butterfly, Essen 1993, Das Schloss by Reimann, Hannover 1994, Frau ohne Schatten, Paris 1994, Wildschütz, Cologne 1994, Rigoletto, Hamburg 1994, Tristan und Isolde, Wiesbaden 1994, Idomeneo at the Nationaltheater, Munich 1996, Falstaff 1996, L'Amour pour les trois oranges 1998, The Merry Widow 2000, Arabella, Nationaltheater Munich 2001, The Bartered Bride 2002, Eine Florentinische Tragödie/Der Zwerg by Zemlinsky 2002, Manon Lescaut, Nationaltheater Munich 2002, The Gypsy Princess, Komische Oper Berlin 2003. *Honours:* French Theatre Critics Award for Best Opera 1994. *Address:* Letzer 3, Zollikon 8702, Switzerland (home). *Address:* Opernhaus Zürich, Falkenstrasse 1, 8008 Zürich, Switzerland (office). *Telephone:* (44) 2686400 (office). *Fax:* (44) 2686401 (office). *E-mail:* info@opernhaus.ch (office). *Website:* www .komische-oper-berlin.de (office).

HONECK, Manfred Maria; Austrian conductor; *Music Director, Pittsburgh Symphony Orchestra;* b. 17 Sept. 1958, Nenzing; m. Christiane Honeck; six c. *Career:* Co-founder and Conductor Vienna's Jeunesse Orchestra; Asst to Claudio Abbado at Gustav Mahler Youth Orchestra, Vienna; Kapellmeister, Zurich Opera House 1991; one of three main conductors of MDR Symphony Orchestra Leipzig 1996–99; Music Dir Norwegian Nat. Opera, Oslo 1997; Prin. Guest Conductor Oslo Philharmonic for several years; Music Dir Swedish Radio Symphony Orchestra Stockholm 2000–06; Music Dir Staatsoper Stuttgart 2007–11, premieres include Berlioz's Les Troyens, Mozart's Idomeneo, Verdi's Aida, Strauss's Rosenkavalier and Wagner's Lohengrin and Parsifal; Prin. Guest Conductor Czech Philharmonic Orchestra 2008–11, 2013–(16); Music Dir Pittsburgh Symphony Orchestra 2008–; operatic guest appearances include Semperoper Dresden, Komische Oper Berlin, Théâtre de la Monnaie in Brussels, Royal Opera of Copenhagen, White Nights Festival, St Petersburg, Salzburg Festival, Verbier Festival; guest conductor of major orchestras including Bavarian Radio Symphony Orchestra, Deutsches Symphonie-Orchester, Berlin, Gewandhausorchester, Leipzig, Sächsische Staatskapelle, Dresden, Royal Concertgebouw Orchestra, London Philharmonic Orchestra, Orchestre Philharmonique de Radio France, Vienna Philharmonic, Chicago Symphony Orchestra, Los Angeles Philharmonic, Nat. Symphony Orchestra, Washington, Boston Symphony Orchestra. *Recordings include:* Mahler Symphony No. 4 (Int. Classical Music Award for Best Symphonic Recording 2012) 2011, Dvorak: Symphony No. 8 and Janacek: Jenufa Suite (with Pittsburgh Symphony Orchestra) 2014, Bruckner: Symphony No. 4 (with Pittsburgh Symphony Orchestra) 2015, Beethoven: Symphony Nos. 5 & 7 (with Pittsburgh Symphony Orchestra) 2015. *Honours:* Dr hc (St Vincent Coll., Latrobe, Pa) 2010; European Prize for Conducting 1993. *Current Management:* c/o Künstlersekretariat am Gasteig, Rosenheimerstrasse 52, 81669 Munich, Germany. *Telephone:* (89) 444-8879-0. *Fax:* (89) 4489522. *E-mail:* team@ks-gasteig.de. *Website:* www.ks-gasteig.de.

HONG, Haeran, BM, MM; South Korean singer (soprano); b. Kwangwon. *Education:* Korean Nat. Univ. of Arts, Juilliard School, masterclasses with Edith Bers. *Career:* professional debut as Pamina in Die Zauberflöte with Daejeon Art Center Opera; Young American Artist at Glimmerglass Opera 2011. *Opera roles include:* Poppea in L'Incoronazione di Poppea, Sœur Constance in Dialogues des Carmélites, Dalinda in Ariodante, Susanna in Le Nozze di Figaro, Papagena in Die Zauberflöte (all Juilliard Opera Theater), Susanna in Le Nozze di Figaro, Adina in L'Elisir d'amore (Korean Nat. Univ. of Arts Opera Theater), Gilda in Rigoletto (Guang-Gin Gu Opera), Barbarina in Le Nozze di Figaro (Glimmerglass Opera). *Honours:* First Place, Daegu and Georgia Christian Univ. competitions, Korean Ministry of Culture Award, winner Career Bridges Competition, New York 2010, First Prize (Singing), Queen Elisabeth Music Competition, Belgium 2011. *Address:* c/o The Juilliard School, 60 Lincoln Center Plaza, New York, NY 10023, USA. *Website:* www.julliard.edu.

HONG, Hei-kyung; South Korean singer (soprano); b. 1958, Seoul. *Education:* Juilliard School, New York. *Career:* debut as Gilda in Rigoletto, Houston 1983; sang Musetta at Chicago 1983; debut at Metropolitan Opera as Servilia in La Clemenza di Tito 1985; repertoire includes Ilia in Idomeneo, Pamina in Die Zauberflöte, Mimi in Die Zauberflöte, Zerlina in Don Giovanni, the Countess in Le Nozze di Figaro, Susanna in Le Nozze di Figaro, Despina, in Cosi fan Tutte, Cleopatra in Giulio Cesare, Liu in Turandot, Lauretta in Gianni Schicchi, Gilda in Rigoletto, Gounod's Juliette, Rosina in The Ghosts of Versailles, Eva in Die Meistersinger von Nürnberg, Violetta in La Traviata, Freia in Das Rheingold, Leila in Les Pêcheurs de Perles, Tatyana in Eugene Onegin, Bellini's Giulietta; sang in premiere of Giuseppe Sinopoli's Lou Salome Suite; has appeared with New York Philharmonic, Boston Symphony, Cleveland Orchestra, Chicago Symphony, Philadelphia Orchestra. *Recordings include:* Rheingold and Götterdämmerung, I Capuletti e i Montecchi, Bellezze Vocale, Carmina Burana. *Current Management:* IMG Artists, Carnegie Hall Tower, 152 West 57th Street, 5th Floor, New York, NY 10019, USA. *Telephone:* (212) 994-3500. *Fax:* (212) 994-3550. *E-mail:* mhorner@imgartists.com. *Website:* www.imgartists.com.

HONG, Sung Jin; South Korean composer and conductor; *Artistic Director, One World Symphony*; m. Adrienne Metzinger-Hong. *Education:* Illinois Wesleyan Univ., Vienna Conservatory, Bard Coll. *Career:* fmrly Principal Conductor, IES Singverein, Vienna, Music Dir and Conductor, Peoria Sinfonietta, apprentice conductor, The Bard Music Festival, Asst Conductor, Twin Cities Ballet Company; f. and Artistic Dir, One World Symphony, championing new music by living composers 2001–; has conducted works by composers including John Corigliano, George Crumb, Michael Daugherty, George Perle, Steve Reich, and Joan Tower; guest conductor with orchestras in France, Austria, UK and USA. *Address:* One World Symphony, 209 Argyle Road, Brooklyn, NY 11218, USA (office). *Telephone:* (718) 462-7270 (office). *E-mail:* staff@oneworldsymphony.org (office). *Website:* www.oneworldsymphony.org (office).

HONNA, Tetsuji; Japanese conductor; *Music Director and Principal Conductor, Vietnam National Symphony Orchestra*; b. 19 Jan. 1957, Koriyama City, Fukushima Pref.; s. of Zembei Honna and Mariko Honna. *Education:* Tokyo Univ. of Fine Arts and Music, Royal Amsterdam Concertgebouworkest, studied with Carl Anton Buente, Inoue, Michiyoshi and Yamada Kazuo. *Career:* debut in Tokyo, Japan Philharmonic Orchestra 1986; European performances include Scala Filharmonia Milano, Orchestra dell'Emilia Romagna Arturo Toscanini, Hungarian State Symphony Orchestra, Carinthischer Sommer 1994, Netherlands Philharmonic Orchestra, Salzburg Mozarteum Orchestra, Philharmonia Orchestra, Brno Philharmonic; Perm. Conductor, Osaka Symphony Orchestra 1994–2001; Guest Perm. Conductor, Nagoya Philharmonic Orchestra 1998–2001; Conductor, Shirakawa Symphonia 2000–03; currently Music Dir and Prin. Conductor, Vietnam Nat. Symphony Orchestra, also Music Dir Orchestra Nipponica. *Recordings include:* Akutagawa Works (with Japan Philharmonic Orchestra), Dvořák and Schumann (with New Japan Philharmonic Orchestra), numerous Japanese orchestral works. *Honours:* Muramatsu Award 1994, Nippon Steel Award 1995, Japanese Cultural Affairs Award, Osaka Stage Arts Award 1997, Japanese Amb. in Vietnam Award 2009, Cultural Award of Vietnam, Foreign Minister's Award of Japan 2011, Cultural Medal, Ministry of Culture, Sports and Tourism of Vietnam. *E-mail:* tetsuji.honna@yahoo.com (office).

HOOKS, Bridgett; singer (soprano); b. 1967, New York, USA. *Education:* Manhattan School of Music, Curtis Inst., Philadelphia. *Career:* sang at the Ghent Opera from 1990 as Mozart's Countess, and Madame Cortese in Rossini's Viaggio a Reims; Philadelphia Opera 1990–92, in Argento's Postcard from Morocco, Copland's The Tender Land and Don Giovanni, as Donna Anna; concerts include Alice Tully Hall, New York 1994, Aspen Festival (Verdi Requiem), Spoleto Festival 1995, and Mahler's 8th Symphony (Cologne 1995); further repertory includes Spirituals (at the Vatican), Beethoven's Ninth and Shostakovich's 14th Symphonies, and Poulenc's Stabat Mater; many lieder recitals.

HOOPER, Adrian John; Australian conductor and mandolinist; *Teacher in Performance, Sydney University*; b. 6 May 1953, Sydney, NSW; s. of John Hooper and Ailsa Hooper; m. Barbara Michele Jackson 1975; two s. one d. *Education:* Sydney Conservatorium of Music. *Career:* founder and conductor of Australia's foremost mandolin orchestra, The Sydney Mandolins 1975–; regular player with Australian Opera and Ballet Orchestra which accompanies Australian Opera, and performed in such works as Otello and The Merry Widow; worked with Sydney Symphony Orchestra in such works as Agon by Stravinsky; regularly takes part in radio and concert performances as mandolin soloist and conductor for Australian Broadcasting Comm. (ABC); performs classical music from all periods and has commissioned, often with the help of Australia Council and NSW Ministry of the Arts, more than 200 works from contemporary composers including Larry Sitsky, Eric Gross, Michael Smetanin, Dolcie Holland, Ann Carr-Boyd, John Peterson, Caroline Szeto and Ian Shanahan; soloist, Australian Chamber Orchestra; Mandolin Teacher, Sydney Conservatorium of Music 1983–; Teacher-in-Performance, Sydney Univ. 1996–. *Recordings include:* more than 115 CDs, including The Acolyte, Places in Time, Twilight Pieces, Cremorne Pastoral, Music from Saint Michaels, Vaucluse and Saint Andrews Cathedral, Sydney, Earth Spirit, Times Remembered, Album Leaves, Ossia, Splendour of The Past, Betty Beath, River Songs, Portrait of Australian Composers, Home Thoughts from Abroad, Poetic Nostalgia, Where No Shadows Fall, Shade of Summer, Sydney Mandolins, Music for a Late Afternoon, Music from The Fellowship of Australian Composers, Symphony, Concerto, Phoenix and The Turtle, Music for a Champagne Breakfast, Watercolours, Colin Brumby Live, Masques, In This Garden, Barely Spring, Tales from Nowhere, Sonata, Music for a Festive Occasion, Baroque Angels, Arc of Light, Grass Tree Hill, Study in Green, Northbridge Sketches, Artisans of Australia, Twin Towers, Best of Jade Classics, The Glasshouse Suite, Music for a Candlelight Dinner, Autumn Pastorale, Classics of Australian Music, Romantic Australian Classics, Voodoo Fire, Songs of Henry Lawson and Best of Australian Classics, Remembering Alan Spence, Australian Landscape, Aubade, Australian Fanfare, Penshurst Sounds, Sydney Twilight, Remembering Adrian Braun, Eden in Atlantis, Music for a Champagne Breakfast Vol. 2, Afternoon Light, Fandango, Solar Dust, Sanctus, Music of Colin Brumby, Concerto Grosso, The Original Music for a Champagne Breakfast New Digital Master, Fray, Shoalhaven Suite, Echoes Fantasies, Dulcie Holland and Friends, American Dream, Lines of Light, Auburn Splendour, Concerto – Australia Suite, An Australian Festival, Music for All Seasons, When The World Was Green, Morning by an Ocean, Processional, Dangerous by Moonlight, Fading Light, Séance on a Wet Afternoon, Winter Solstice, Bradgate Park, Reflections through a Stained Glass Window, Sonata Piccola, The Colin Sapsford Years, Arias and Interludes, Vision of Mary, Forever Sunset, Rhapsody in Green, Jazz Waves, Jade 20th Anniversary Celebration, Music for an Imaginary Italian Film, Fiji Moon, Thoughts out of Season, Johnson – Serenades and Divertimenti Decaying Splendour, Last Look at Bronte, Sydney Mandolins. *Publications:* published and edited several early mandolin works. *Address:* 24 Kitchener Street, Oatley, NSW 2223, Australia (home). *E-mail:* adrian@sydneymandolins.com (office). *Website:* www.sydneymandolins.com (office).

HOOVER, Katherine, MM; American composer and flautist; *Partner, Papagena Press*; b. 2 Dec. 1937, Elkins, W Va; m. Richard V. Goodman. *Education:* Eastmann School and the Manhattan School of Music. *Career:* Lecturer, Manhattan School and Juilliard School; organizer, Women's Interart Center music festivals, New York 1978–81; guest teacher, Teacher's Coll. 1984–88, Sarah Lawrence Coll. 1988-89; masterclasses and performances nationwide; mem. Nat. Flute Asscn Bd 2002–05; Pnr, Papagena Press. *Compositions include:* Homage to Bartók, for wind quintet 1975, Trio, for violin, cello and piano 1978, Piano Book 1977–82, Lyric Trio, for flute, cello and piano 1983, Medieval Suite for flute and piano 1984, Clarinet Concerto 1987, Wind Quintet 1987, Eleni: a Greek Tragedy, for orchestra 1987, Double Concerto for 2 violins and strings 1989, Da pacem, for piano and string quintet 1989, Kokopeli for flute 1990, Canyon Echoes for flute and guitar 1991, Night Skies, for orchestra 1992, Sonata for oboe and piano 1993, Central American Songs, for voice, flute, percussion and piano 1995, Dances and Variations for flute and harp 1996, Winter Spirits, for flute 1997, Kyrie, for 12 flutes 1997, The Heart Speaks, for soprano and piano 1998, String quartet 1998, Masks, for flute and piano 1998, Requiem for SATB soloists, chorus, brass, organ 2002, String Quartet 2 2003, Sketches, for piccolo and piano 2004, Preludes, for piano 2005, To Greet the Sun, for flute 2005, St Qt #2 2006, Line Drawings, for piano 2007, Concertante for flute orchestra 2007, Turner Impressions, for orchestra 2007, Suite for two pianos 2008, Dream Dances for piano 2008. *Recordings:* 26 CDs. *Honours:* Acad. of Arts and Letters Award in Composition 1994, Nat. Endowment for the Arts Composers' Fellowship, Nat. Flute Asscn Newly Published Music Award (five times). *Address:* c/o Papagena Press, PO Box 20484, Park West Station, New York, NY 10025 (office); 160 West 95th Street, #5, New York, NY 10025, USA (home). *Telephone:* (212) 749-3012 (office); (212) 666-4745 (home). *Fax:* (212) 749-3012 (office). *E-mail:* khoover@papagenapress.com (office). *Website:* www.papagenapress.com (office).

HOPE, Daniel; Irish violinist; *Artistic Director, Festival Mecklenburg-Vorpommern*; b. 1973, South Africa. *Education:* Royal Acad. of Music, studied with Zakhar Bron. *Career:* work involves standard repertory, new music, raga, and jazz; int. debut with the Jyväskylä Symphony Orchestra of Finland, playing the Mendelssohn Concerto; numerous concerts with Yehudi Menuhin, including his final performance 1999; has performed with orchestras including Boston Symphony, Chicago Symphony, Toronto Symphony, Atlanta Symphony, major orchestras in Berlin, Birmingham, Dallas, Detroit, Dresden, Israel, London, Moscow, Oslo, Paris, Stockholm, and Vienna; performed world premieres including Stewart Copeland's Celeste for Violin and Percussion 2008, Alban Berg's Violin Concerto 2008, Sir Peter Maxwell

Davies' Concerto, Leipzig and BBC Proms 2009; festivals include Lucerne, Ravinia, Salzburg, Schleswig-Holstein; mem. Beaux Arts Trio 2002–08; Assoc. Artistic Dir, Savannah Music Festival, USA 2003–; Artistic Dir, Festival Mecklenburg-Vorpommern, Germany 2009–. *Recordings include:* Bach concerti, Mendelssohn concerti, Vivaldi concerti, Air: A Baroque Journey 2010. *Publications:* Familienstücke 2007, Wann darf ich klatschen? 2009. *Honours:* Winner, Hugh Bean Violin Competition 1986, Peter Morrison Concerto Competition 1989, Classical BRIT Award for Young British Classical Performer 2004, ECHO Klassik Prize 2004, 2005, 2006, 2008, 2009. *Current Management:* c/o Meyer Arts Management, Dolderstrasse 18, 8032 Zurich, Switzerland. *Telephone:* (44) 7962277. *Fax:* (44) 7962276. *E-mail:* contact@ meyerartsmanagement.ch. *Website:* meyerartsmanagement.ch. *E-mail:* office@danielhope.com (office). *Website:* www.festspiele-mv.de; www .savannahmusicfestival.org; www.danielhope.com.

HOPKINS, Sarah; New Zealand composer; b. 1958, Lower Hutt. *Education:* New South Wales Conservatorium of Music High School, Victorian Coll. of the Arts Music School. *Career:* toured extensively throughout Australia, the UK, Europe and the USA; musician-in-residence, GIAE, Gippsland, Victoria, Australia 1978, CIT, Caulfield, Victoria 1979; Composer-in-Residence, Arts Victoria Music 1981; musician-in-residence, Brown's Mart Community Art Project 1981, guest artist-in-residence 1983; Let's Make Music, Northern Territory 1982; New Music ACTION Residency, Victorian Coll. of the Arts, Melbourne 1982; Composer/Performer-in-Residence, Darwin Theatre Group 1984; Artist in Schools 1985, 1986; Composer/Performer, Sky Song Project, Brown's Mart, Darwin, and major tour 1987, 1988; Performer-in-Residence, The Exploration San Francisco 1988; Composer-in-Residence, Northern Territory Arts Council, Darwin 1989. *Compositions:* ensemble works: Cello Timbre 1976, Seasons II 1978, Cellovoice 1982, Whirlies 1983, Sunrise/Sunset 1983, Interweave 1984, Deep Whirly Duo 1984, Aura Swirl 1986, Eclipse 1986, Bougainvillea Bells 1986, Cello Chi 1986, Flight of the Wild Goose 1987, Ring 1987, Songs of the Wind 1989, Circle Bell Mantra 1989, Spiral Bells 1989, Soul Song 1989, Transformation 1989, Heart Songs 1989. *Recordings:* Soundworks 1: Collaborative Works; Soundworks 2: Solo and Duo Works; Soundworks 3: Whirliworks Performance; Interweave; Soundworks Performance.

HOPKINS, Tim; British stage director; b. 1963, London, England. *Education:* Queen's Coll., Cambridge. *Career:* productions at Musica nel Chiostro, Battignano 1989–91; Peter Grimes for Dublin Grand Opera 1990; The Gondoliers for New Doyle Carte 1991, Falstaff for English Touring Opera 1992, Mario and the Magician for Almeida Opera 1992, Così fan tutte for WNO 1992; Zampa at the 1993 Wexford Festival; staged the premiere of Judith Weir's Blond Eckbert for ENO 1994 and Berio's Vera Storia at the Festival Hall; Yeomen of the Guard for WNO 1995 (also seen at Covent Garden and in the USA), Così fan tutte, also for WNO and Rimsky's Golden Cockerel for Rome Opera; Iphigénie en Aulide for Opera North 1996; season 1997–98 with Il Trovatore at Graz Oper, Maria Stuarda at Basel Opera and at the Royal Opera with a new production of The Golden Cockerel; season 1999–2000, Radamisto for Opera North, A-ronne for Almeida Opera and Eugen Onegin for Basel Opera; season 2001–02, Forest Murmurs for Opera North, Kantan/ Damask Drum by Goehr for Almeida Opera; Only the Names Have Been Changed for the Munich Festival; Mare Nostrum for Theatre Basel; The Rake's Progress in Hanover. *Honours:* NESTA Fellowship 2002.

HORIGOME, Yuzuko; Japanese violinist; b. 1960, Tokyo. *Education:* Toho Gakuen School of Music, Tokyo with Toshiya Eto. *Career:* London debut 1983, concerts with London Symphony Orchestra under Claudio Abbado and André Previn; US debut 1982, at Tanglewood with Boston Symphony; later appearances in Pittsburgh, Chicago, Los Angeles and Montréal; 1988–89 season included concerts in Europe and Japan with the Salzburg Camerata, Royal Liverpool Philharmonic and Scottish National Orchestras, and at the Prague Spring Festival; USA tour with the Chamber Music Players of Marlboro 1995; featured in film, Testimony, on the life of Shostakovich. *Recordings:* Bach Concerti with the English Chamber Orchestra with A. Litton; Bach's Solo Violin Sonatas; Sibelius and Mendelssohn Concertos with the Concertgebouw Orchestra and Ivan Fischer, music by Bruch (Tring, 1996); Mozart Concerti, Camerata Academic Salzburg with Sándor Végh; Takemitsu by Denon, 1999; Beethoven, Kakadu Variations with Rudolph Serkin and Peter Willey. *Honours:* winner Queen Elisabeth of the Belgians Int. Competition 1980.

HORNE, David; British pianist and composer; b. 12 Dec. 1970, Tillicoultry, Stirling, Scotland. *Education:* St Mary's Music School, Edinburgh, Curtis Inst., Philadelphia and Harvard Univs. *Career:* soloist with BBC Philharmonic and Symphony, Welsh and Scottish Orchestras, City of Birmingham Symphony Orchestra, Scottish Nat. and London Sinfonietta; festival engagements at Edinburgh, Aldeburgh, Almeida and London; BBC Promenade Concert debut in 1990 with Prokofiev's Third Concerto; other repertory includes Ravel G major, Gershwin Concerto, Brahms Concerto in D minor, Beethoven 1st Concerto and Choral Fantasia, Iain Hamilton 2nd Concerto (world premiere), Mozart K271, Frank Symphonic Variations and Tchaikovsky 1st Concerto. *Compositions:* String Quartet 1988, Splintered Unisons for clarinet, violin, cello and piano 1988, Towards Dharma for 6 instruments 1989, Light Emerging for symphony orchestra 1989, Out of the Air 1990, Contraries and Progressions for ensemble 1991, Northscape for chamber orchestra 1992, Piano Concerto 1992, Pensive, for mezzo, voices and chamber orchestra 1998, Spike, for ensemble 1998, Broken Instruments 1999, Zip, for cello and piano 1999, The Year's Midnight for tenor, chorus and orchestra

2000, Blunt Instruments for large ensemble 2000, Ignition for solo percussion and orchestra 2002, Concerto for Orchestra 2003, Disembodied Instruments for large ensemble 2003, Double Violin Concerto for 2 violins and strings 2003, Flight from the Labyrinth for string quartet 2004, Gossamer for saxophone quartet 2004, Splintered Instruments for harp ensemble 2004, Double Concerto for piano quintet 2005; vocal music: Jason Field (ENO Opera Studio), Travellers, cantata The Lie, Opera, Friend of the People (Scottish Opera 1999). *Honours:* 1st Prize, Nat. Mozart Competition 1987, 1st Place for Piano, BBC Young Musician of The Year 1988, Winner, Huddersfield Contemporary Music Festival Composers Competition 1988. *Address:* c/o Boosey and Hawkes, 1st Floor, Aldwych House, 71–91 Aldwych, London, WC2B 4HN, England. *Website:* www.boosey.com/horne.

HORNE, Marilyn; American singer (mezzo-soprano); b. 16 Jan. 1934, Bradford, Pa; d. of Bentz Horne and Berneice Horne; m. 1st Henry Lewis (divorced); one d. *Education:* Univ. of Southern California with William Vennard. *Career:* debut as Hata in The Bartered Bride, Guild Opera Co. 1954; performed with several German opera cos in Europe 1956; has since appeared at Covent Garden, London, San Francisco Opera, Chicago Lyric Opera, La Scala, Milan, Metropolitan Opera, New York; repertoire includes Eboli in Don Carlo, Marie in Wozzeck, Adalgisa in Norma, Jane Seymour in Anna Bolena, Amneris in Aida, Carmen, Rosina in Il Barbiere di Siviglia, Fides in Le Prophète, Mignon, Isabella in L'Italiana in Algeri, Romeo in I Capuletti ed i Montecchi, Tancredi in Tancredi, Orlando in Orlando Furioso, Malcolm in La Donna del Lago, Calbo in Maometto II; retd from singing 1999, with galas in New York and San Francisco 1998; f. Marilyn Horne Foundation to coach and encourage young singers 1993 (now part of Weill Music Inst. at Carnegie Hall); mem. Faculty, Music Acad. of the West 1995–, Dir Voice Program 1997–; Fellow, American Acad. of Arts and Sciences 2009–. *Publications:* My Life (autobiography with Jane Scovell), The Song Continues (autobiography with Jane Scovell) 2005. *Honours:* Commdr, Ordre des Arts et des Lettres; numerous hon. doctorates, including Hon. DMus (Univ. of Pittsburgh) 2005; Nat. Medal of Arts 1992, Kennedy Center Honor 1995, Musical American Musician of the Year 1995, Classic FM Gramophone Award for Lifetime Achievement 2005, Opera News Award 2008, Nat. Endowment for the Arts Opera Award 2009. *Address:* Voice Program, Music Academy of the West, 1070 Fairway Road, Santa Barbara, CA 93108, USA (office). *E-mail:* info@ musicacademy.org (office). *Website:* www.musicacademy.org (office).

HORNER, Ronald, BSc, DMus; American musician (percussion) and academic; *Senior Lecturer and Director of Percussion Studies, Frostburg State University.* *Education:* Indiana Univ. of Pennsylvania, Duquesne Univ., West Virginia Univ., studied Indonesian music under Ki Mantle Hood and African music with Paschal Yao Younge. *Career:* mem. Westmoreland Percussion Trio 1987–93; percussionist, Israel Philharmonic Orchestra 1978–80 and regular performer with Pittsburgh Symphony Orchestra 1989–96; has accompanied numerous soloists including Yefim Bronfman, Dietrich Fischer-Dieskau, Luciano Pavarotti, Isaac Stern, Itzhak Perlman, Leontyne Price, Yo-Yo Ma, Jean Pierre Rampal, Nathan Milstein, Bernadette Peters, Frank Sinatra, Jr; premiere performances of works composed for him, including Toccata for Timpani by Emma Lou Diemer; Prin. Timpanist, Johnstown Symphony Orchestra 1990–, Westmoreland Symphony Orchestra 2001–; Music Dir and Conductor, Arion Band of Frostburg, Md 1995–; timpanist, Keystone Wind Ensemble 1997–; Asst Prof., Indiana Univ. of Pennsylvania 1996–; also currently Sr Lecturer and Dir of Percussion Studies, Frostburg State Univ.; guest lecturer, master-classes at Pennsylvania State Univ., James Madison Univ., Univ. of Maryland, Tel-Aviv Univ., Curtis Inst. of Music, among others; adjudicator for solo and ensemble competitions throughout NE USA; mem. ASCAP, Nat. Conf. on Percussion Pedagogy, Percussive Arts Soc. *Recordings include:* numerous recordings, especially of Leonard Bernstein with Israel Philharmonic. *Publications include:* The Tuneful Timpanist 2000, What Do Drummers Really Want: A Survey of American University Percussion Instructors 2009. *Honours:* Governor's Citation (Md) 2002, Int. Mozart Award for Musical Achievement 2009. *Address:* 209 Performing Arts Center, Department of Music, Frostburg State University, 101 Braddock Road, Frostburg, MD 21532-2303 (office); 163 Gilmour Road, Somerset, PA 15501-7011, USA (home). *Telephone:* (301) 687-7453 (office); (814) 445-6465 (home). *Fax:* (301) 687-4784 (office). *E-mail:* rhorner@frostburg.edu (office). *Website:* www.frostburg.edu/dept/music (office).

HORNIK, Gottfried; singer (baritone); b. 5 Aug. 1940, Vienna, Austria. *Education:* studied in Vienna. *Career:* sang at Klagenfurt as Papageno and as Silvio in Pagliacci; Graz Opera as Mozart's Figaro, Don Giovanni and Alberich; Deutsche Oper Berlin and San Francisco as Beckmesser in Die Meistersinger; Salzburg Easter Festival as Kurwenal in Tristan und Isolde, under Karajan; sang Alberich and other Wagner roles at the Vienna Staatsoper; sang at Leipzig Opera as the Villains in Les Contes d'Hoffmann, Cologne Opera 1983 as Klingsor in Parsifal, Covent Garden 1987 as Faninal in Der Rosenkavalier, Deutsche Oper Berlin 1988 as Alberich in The Ring and sang Wozzeck at the Metropolitan 1990; sang Orestes in Elektra at Athens 1992; Vienna Staatsoper 1995, in the premiere of Schnittke's Gesualdo; Emperor in Turandot 2001. *Recordings:* Die Zauberflöte, Tosca, and Die Meistersinger conducted by Karajan; Der Wildschütz by Lortzing.

HOROVITZ, Joseph, MA, BMus, FRCM; British composer and conductor; *Professor of Composition, Royal College of Music;* b. 26 May 1926, Vienna, Austria. *Education:* New Coll., Oxford and Royal Coll. of Music (RCM), London and studied with Nadia Boulanger, Paris. *Career:* resident in UK

1938–; Music Dir Bristol Old Vic 1949–51; Conductor Festival Gardens Orchestra and open-air ballet, London 1951; Co-Conductor Ballets Russes, English season 1951–52; Assoc. Dir Intimate Opera Co. 1952–63; Asst Conductor Glyndebourne Opera 1956; Prof. of Composition, RCM 1961–; mem. Council, Composers' Guild 1970–, Performing Right Soc. 1969–96; Pres. Int. Council of Composers and Lyricists, Int. Fed. of Socs of Authors and Composers 1981–89. *Compositions:* 12 ballets including Alice in Wonderland, Les Femmes d'Alger, Miss Carter Wore Pink, Concerto for Dancers; opera: Ninotchka; one-act operas: The Dumb Wife, Gentlemen's Island; concertos for violin, trumpet, jazz-piano (harpsichord), oboe, clarinet, bassoon, percussion, tuba; other orchestral works include Horizon Overture, Jubilee Serenade, Sinfonietta for Light Orchestra, Fantasia on a Theme of Couperin, Toy Symphony; brass band music includes a euphonium concerto, Sinfonietta, Ballet for Band, Concertino Classico, Theme and Co-operation, The Dong with a Luminous Nose; music for wind band includes a divertimento Bacchus on Blue Ridge, Windharp, Fête Galante, Commedia dell'Arte, Dance Suite and Ad Astra in commemoration of the Battle of Britain; choral music includes Samson, Captain Noah and his Floating Zoo (Ivor Novello Award for Best British Music for Children 1976), Summer Sunday, Endymion, Sing Unto the Lord a New Song, three choral songs from As You Like It; vocal music includes Lady Macbeth (mezzo-soprano and piano) and works for the King's Singers (e.g. Romance); chamber music includes five string quartets, oboe sonatina, oboe quartet and clarinet sonatina; contribs to Hoffnung Concerts: Metamorphoses on a Bed-Time Theme and Horrortorio for chorus, orchestra and soloists; numerous scores for theatre productions, films and TV series (Ivor Novello Award for Best TV Theme of 1978 for the series Lillie); productions of Son et Lumière include St Paul's Cathedral, Canterbury Cathedral, Brighton Pavilion, English Harbour, Antigua, Bodiam Castle, Chartwell. *Honours:* Cross of Honour for Science and Art, First Class (Austria) 2007; Commonwealth Medal Composition 1959, Leverhulme Music Research Award 1961, Gold Order of Merit of Vienna 1996, Nino Rota Prize (Italy) 2002, Cobbett Medal for services to chamber music, Worshipful Co. of Musicians 2008. *Address:* Royal College of Music, Prince Consort Road, London, SW7 2BS, England (office). *Website:* www.rcm.ac.uk (office).

HORTON, Peter Bernard, MA, DPhil, DipLib; British music librarian and musicologist; *Deputy Librarian, Royal College of Music;* b. 19 June 1953, Ashford, Kent, England; m. Elaine Wood; two s. one d. *Education:* Sir Roger Manwood's Grammar School, Sandwich, Magdalen Coll., Oxford, Univ. Coll., London. *Career:* Asst Reference Librarian, Royal Coll. of Music, London 1984–95, Reference Librarian and Research Co-ordinator 1995–2005, Deputy Librarian 2005–; mem. Musica Britannica Editorial Cttee; mem. Royal Musical Asscn, Hymn Soc., Church Music Soc. *Publications:* edns: Samuel Sebastian Wesley: Anthems 1 Musica Britannica 57 1990, Anthems 2 Musica Britannica 63 1992, Vaughan Williams: Symphony No. 5 2008, Samuel Sebastian Wesley: Anthems 3 Musica Britannica 89 2010; books: Samuel Sebastian Wesley: A Life 2004. *Honours:* Hon. RCM . *Address:* Royal College of Music, Prince Consort Road, London, SW7 2BS (office); 13 Spencer Gardens, London, SE9 6LX, England (home). *Telephone:* (20) 7591-4324 (office); (20) 8850-3791 (home). *Fax:* (20) 7589-7740 (office). *E-mail:* phorton@rcm.ac.uk (office).

HORVATH, László, MMus; Hungarian clarinettist; b. 14 July 1945, Koszeg; m. (divorced); one s. one d. *Education:* Music Gymnasium, Gyor, studied with Prof. György Balassa, Ferenc Liszt Acad. of Music, Budapest, Conservatoire de Musique, Paris, studied with Prof. Ulysse Delecluse. *Career:* debut at Competition in Budapest 1965; clarinettist 1965–68, soloist and leading clarinettist 1968–, Hungarian State Symphony Orchestra, Budapest; Prof., Conservatory of Music Debrecen 1974–79, Béla Bartók Conservatory of Music, Budapest 1980–; toured as soloist, Buffet-Crampon Company, Japan 1981, 1986; many solo recitals worldwide and appearances as clarinet duo with Klara Kormendi, and chamber music with Philharmonic Wind Quintet in Europe, USA, Canada, Australia and Japan 1983–; recitals at Claude Champagne Hall, Montréal 1991, 1993; radio broadcasts in Budapest, Paris, London and Tokyo and television appearances in Hungary; masterclasses at Montréal 1991, 1993; jury mem. Int. Competition for Musical Performers, Geneva 1990. *Recordings:* works by Leo Weiner 1970, Attila Bozay 1976, 1979, Carl and Johann Stamitz 1979, Johann Molter 1979, 1991, Mozart 1981; 20th-Century Clarinet Music 1991, Clarinetto all'Ungherese 1992. *Address:* 6 Jászai Mari Tér V-44, 1137 Budapest, Hungary.

HORWOOD, Michael Stephen, BA, MA; American/Canadian composer; b. 24 May 1947, Buffalo, NY; m. Celia M. Roberts 1974; two s. *Education:* State Univ. of New York (SUNY), Buffalo. *Career:* debut, performance of his works at Baird Hall, SUNY, Buffalo 1966; Prof. of Music and Humanities, Humber Coll. of Applied Arts and Tech., Ont. 1972–2003; Assoc. Composer, Canadian Music Centre 1979; Featured Composer, Saskatoon Symphony, Saskatchewan 1991–92; Featured Composer, Composers and Orchestras – What's the Score? Conf., Kitchener, Ont. 1995; retrospective concerts of his works Toronto 1982, 1990; mem. Canadian League of Composers 1979, Assoc. Composer Canadian Music Centre 1979, Edmonton Composers' Concert Soc. 2005; comms include Ontario Arts Council 1978, 1979, 1980, 1981, 1984, 1985, 1997, Canada Council 1991, 1995, Piccolo Soc. 1979, Norbert Kraft 1981, Cameron Walter 1979, Yvar Mikhashoff 1987, Mary Kenedi 1997, 2006, Alberta Foundation for the Arts (2) 2006, CBC 1990, Laidlaw Foundation 1995, 1996, 1999, the McLean Foundation of Toronto 1986, Jene LaRue 1966, Theatre Passe Muraille (2) 1972, Toronto Dance Theatre Workshops 1978,

Ardeleana Trio 1988, Staten Island Chamber Music Players 1988; Composer Residency Program, SOCAN Foundation 1997, 1998, 1999; performing arts affiliations include SOCAN (Canada), BMI (USA). *Compositions include:* Durations for 1–4 Keyboards 1965, Pièce Percussionique No. 1 for six percussionists and piano 1965, revised 1979, Women Of Trachis, incidental music for chamber orchestra 1966, Concerto for double bass and string orchestra 1967, revised 2002, Double Quintet for 2 wind quintets 1968, Asteroids for brass quartet 1969, 8 Microduets 1969–83, Pièce Percussionique No. 5 for two percussionists and Tape 1970, Little Bow Piece for percussion octet 1972, 5, 3, 4 for jazz orchestra and percussion ensemble 1973, Facets for augmented chamber group 1974, Talos IV for solo accordion 1975, Andromeda for wind ensemble 1976, revised 1980, Bipolarity for accordion and string trio 1979, Birds for piccolo, piano and optional visual program 1979, Io for double bass and violin 1979, Splinters for chamber sextet 1981, Residue for tuba and vibraphone 1981, Three Cadenzas for guitar and harpsichord 1981, Exit To Your Left for wind quintet 1982, Brass-Fast for brass quintet 1984, Three Landscapes for solo piano 1984, Amusement Park Suite for orchestra 1986, Nervous Disorder for chamber trio 1988, Broken Chords for solo piano 1990, National Park Suite for orchestra 1991, Psalm 121 for SSA choir 1991, Symphony No. 2, Visions of a Wounded Earth, for chorus and orchestra 1995, Do You Live For Weekends? for chamber orchestra 1996, Symphony No. 3, Andromeda, for tenor saxophone and orchestra 1996, Intravariations for piano and orchestra 1997, Quartzite Dialogues for narrator and wind quintet 1999, T + I = Ewigkeit, for solo piano 2000, Fragments, for two treble instruments 2006, Pièce Percussionique No. 6 (Requiem) for percussion quartet 2008. *Film:* Dynamite (soundtrack) 1968. *Recordings include:* CDs: Overture for Piano Player and Two Assistants 1977, Pièce Percussionique No. 5 1982, Birds 1982, Dynamite 1983, Six Pieces for piano, Broken Chords 1998, A Long Time Ago into the Future 1998, Brass Feast: Asteroids and Brass-Fast 1999, Tantrum IV 2000, For the Birds: Birds 2000, Motility: Motility, Fugue for Sam and Tantrum IV 2000, Tango Diablo!: Horizontal Tango 2003, Masterworks of the New Era, Vol. 3: Six Chromosomes for Orchestra 2004, Masterworks of the New Era, Vol. 10: Three Interludes for Orchestra 2007, Suite and Serious: Amusement Park Suite, National Park Suite, Intravariations and Symphony No. 1 2007, Cult Figures: Monday Afternoon 2008, Devil's Dance: Microduet No. 8. 2009, Percussionique: Dynamite, Fragments, Little Bow Piece, Mathematics, Pièce Percussionique No. 1, Pièce Percussionique No. 3, Pièce Percussionique No. 4, Pièce Percussionique No. 5, Pièce Percussionique No. 6 (Requiem) and The Shadow of Your Drum 2009; LP: Convergence: Six Free Improvisation works (live recording) 2012, Two Electronic Music settings of poems by Robert Creeley from his collection Words. *Publications:* Birds 1982, Residue 1982, Music as History, The Representation of the Individual in Western Music (co-author) 1996, That Pioneering Spirit (co-ed.) 1998. *Address:* PO Box 69, Cowley, Alberta, T0K 0P0, Canada (home). *E-mail:* michael@horwoodcomposer.com. *Website:* www.horwoodcomposer.com.

HORYSA, Inghild; singer (mezzo-soprano); b. 2 Jan. 1944, Bielitz, Germany. *Education:* studied with Helena Braun in Munich. *Career:* debut at Munich Staatsoper 1966 in Hansel and Gretel; Munich 1969 in the premiere of The Play of Love and Death by Cikker; sang at Nuremberg, the Vienna Volksoper, Düsseldorf, Frankfurt, Mannheim, Hamburg and Stuttgart; other roles include Dorabella, Amneris, Eboli, Venus, Brangaene, Marina in Boris Godunov, Orsini in Lucrezia Borgia, Fricka in Walküre, Clytemnestra in Elektra, Baba the Turk in The Rake's Progress and Octavian; frequent concert appearances.

HOSE, Anthony Paul, ARCM; British conductor and pianist; *Principal Conductor, Welsh Chamber Orchestra;* b. 24 May 1944, London, England; s. of Stanley Karl Hose and Edith Annie Hose; m. Moira Griffiths 1977; two d. *Education:* Latymer Upper School, London, Royal Coll. of Music, London. *Career:* Glyndebourne Festival 1966–68; Bremen Opera, Germany 1968–69; Welsh Nat. Opera 1969–83; Music Dir Buxton Festival 1979–87; Artistic Dir Welsh Chamber Orchestra 1986–, Beaumaris Festival 1986–, Buxton Festival 1988–91, Rhyl Easter Festival 1994–95, Llandudno October Festival 1994–2000, Mount Dora Spring Festival, Fla 1998–2005; Prof., Royal Coll. of Music 1991–; Prof., RAM 1992–98; Dir of Orchestras, Stetson Univ., Fla 2000–; currently Prin. Conductor Welsh Chamber Orchestra. *Television:* series The Story and the Song, New York Film Festival, The Madrigal Players, Prague Film Festival. *Radio:* various opera and concert broadcasts. *Recordings:* works by William Mathias and Alun Hoddinott. *Publications include:* trans of Le Huron (Grétry), Elektra (Strauss), Ariodante (Handel), Don Quixote (Conti). *Honours:* Burgher of Beaumaris; Percy Buck Award, Countess of Munster Award. *Current Management:* c/o 421 N Woodland Blvd, DeLand, FL 32723, USA. *Telephone:* (386) 822-8960. *Fax:* (386) 822-8948. *Address:* 6 Lôn-y-Celyn, Cardiff, CF14 7BW, Wales (home). *Telephone:* (29) 2062-3602 (home). *E-mail:* ahose@stetson.edu (office).

HOSEK, Jiri; Czech cellist; b. 20 Aug. 1955, Prague; m. Marie Kaplanova 1977; two d. *Education:* Prague Conservatory, Academy of Music, Prague, Conservatory National, Paris, and courses at Nice and Szombately. *Career:* debut in Tchaikovsky's Rococco Variations, 1974; Tours to Russia, Germany, France, Italy and Poland; Many television and radio appearances including Anton Kraft Concertos. *Recordings:* Elgar Concerto, 1985; Anton Kraft Concertos; Radio recordings of Vivaldi Concerto, D Popper Konzertstücke, Dvořák's Rondo, Tchaikovsky's Rococco Variations, Prokofiev Symphony Concerto and Elgar Concerto. *Address:* Sudomerska 29, 13000 Prague 3, Czech Republic.

HOSFORD, Richard, ARCM; British clarinettist; *Professor of Clarinet, Royal College of Music, London*; b. Dorset. *Education:* RCM, studied with John McCaw and Thea King in London. *Career:* fmr mem. Nat. Youth Orchestra; featured in the Park Lane Group Young Artists Series 1984; founder mem. and Principal Clarinet, Chamber Orchestra of Europe; fmr Principal Clarinet, London Philharmonic; Principal Clarinet, BBC Symphony Orchestra 1994–; mem. The Gaudier Ensemble; has performed as soloist in USA, Japan, Hong Kong, Italy, Germany, Switzerland, UK; has performed with leading conductors, including Claudio Abbado, Sir Colin Davis, Michael Tilson Thomas, Oscar Shumsky, Roger Norrington, Gerard Korsten, Paavo Berglund; performed the Nielsen Concerto with Paavo Berglund, Ferrara and Cologne 1997; frequent performances with The Nash Ensemble; world premiere broadcast performance of Robin Holloway's Clarinet Concerto with BBC SO 1999; currently Prof. of Clarinet, RCM, London. *Recordings include:* Mozart, Three Wind Concertos 1993, Brahms, Complete Trios 1998, The Music of Aaron Copland 1999, Poulenc, Complete Chamber Works (with The Nash Ensemble) 1999, Holbrooke, Chamber Works 2002, Mozart/Copland, Clarinet Concertos 2006. *Honours:* Tillett Trust Award 1984. *Address:* Royal College of Music, Woodwind Department, Prince Consort Road, London, SW7 2BS, England (office). *Telephone:* (20) 7589-3643 (office). *Fax:* (20) 7589-7740 (office). *E-mail:* info@rcm.ac.uk (office). *Website:* www.rcm.ac.uk (office).

HOSKINS, (William) Donald, MBE, BMus, MA, PhD; British pianist, conductor, teacher and university lecturer; *Artistic Director and Conductor, Aminta Chamber and Concert Orchestra (of London)*; b. 9 June 1932, Abertillery, Wales; s. of William Charles Hoskins and Olive Hoskins; m. Dinah Patricia Stanton 1972. *Education:* Abertillery Grammar School, Univ. of Wales, Cardiff. *Career:* Nat. Service 1954–56; directed choral groups, gave lectures and piano recitals; music teacher, Tudor Grange Grammar School, Solihull 1956–60; presented piano recitals; adjudicated at school festivals; f. local arts orchestra; performed piano concertos with the Birmingham Philharmonic Orchestra and was guest conductor on a visit to S Wales 1962; Dir of Music, Hayes Grammar School, Middx 1960–64; f. and conducted local chamber orchestras and ensembles; solo recital, Paris 1963; Lecturer, Eastbourne Coll. of Educ. 1964–67; soloist, Hillingdon Festival 1964; conducted professional chamber ensembles at notable London venues; apptd Sr Lecturer, Dept of Educ., Barking Regional Coll. of Tech. 1967; song recital accompanist, Purcell Room, South Bank 1972; Head of North East London Polytechnic Music Centre 1978; est. annual East London concert band festival 1980; Guest Conductor, London Mozart Players 1983; piano recital, Athens 1984; Founder, Artistic Dir and Conductor Aminta Chamber Concert Orchestra (of London) 1985; soloist with combined Desford Dowty, Fodens and Coventry brass bands conducted by Harry Mortimer 1989; soloist at inaugural concert, Univ. of Zweibrucken, Germany 1994; presented concert band performances, Witten, Germany 1995, Univ. of Kaiserslautern 1997, Royal Star and Garter Home, Richmond 1998–2002; conducted concerts with London Philharmonic Choir and Aminta Concert Orchestra at Queen Elizabeth Hall (QEH), London 2000; performed 75th birthday orchestral concert at QEH 2007; conducted Cantus Firmus Chamber Orchestra, Bulgarian Cultural Centre, Moscow 2004, 2007; presented 27th annual performance by Univ. of East London Concert Band and 22nd annual concert by Aminta Chamber Orchestra in Church of St Martin-in-the-Fields, London 2006; performed in chamber music concert at Moscow Conservatoire 2007; has regularly organized and directed mayoral concerts, charity concerts, children's concerts and open-air symphony concerts; conducted Handel's Messiah 2009 and Haydn's The Creation with Aminta Singers 2010; Visiting Prof., Univ. of Provo, USA 1994, Music Conservatorium, Univ. of Cincinnati, USA 1994; Pres. Redbridge Music Soc. 1996; Consultant and Dir of Concerts, Univ. of East London 1996; Guest Conductor, Royal Philharmonic Concert Orchestra 1995, 1996, BBC Concert Orchestra 1997, 1998, London Philharmonic Choir 1999, 2002, 2004; conducted 15th annual open-air concert at Barking Abbey in celebration of Queen's Jubilee and at St James's Church, Piccadilly 2010 and 80th birthday concert 2012. *Honours:* Freedom of London Borough of Barking and Dagenham 2005; Hon. DMus (Univ. of East London) 2003. *Address:* 'Aminta', 12 Hurst Park, Midhurst, West Sussex, GU29 0BP, England (home). *Telephone:* (1730) 810220 (home). *E-mail:* donaldhoskins@ btinternet.com. *Website:* www.amintaorchestra.com (office).

HOSOKAWA, Toshio; Japanese composer and conductor; b. 23 Oct. 1955, Hiroshima. *Education:* studied in Berlin with Isang Yun, in Freiburg with Klaus Huber and Brian Ferneyhough. *Career:* composer-in-residence at festivals in Geneva, London, Darmstadt, Seattle and Warsaw; Guest Prof. Tokyo Coll. of Music 2004, Kunitachi Coll. of Music 2013. *Compositions include:* Manifestation for violin and piano 1981, In Tal der Zeit for string quartet and piano 1986, Ferne Landschaft I for orchestra 1987, Flute Concerto 1988, Ave Maria 1991, Hiroshima Requiem for voices and orchestra 1988–92, Fragmente for wind quintet 1989, Landscape for string quartet 1992, Landscape II for harp and string quartet 1993, Landscape III for orchestra 1993, Super Flumina Babylonis for soloists and orchestra 1995, String Trio 1996, Cello Concerto 1997, Seascapes-Night for chorus and ensemble 1997, Voyage I–III for ensemble 1997, Cloudscapes-Moon Night for sho and accordion 1998, Memory of the Sea, Hiroshima Symphony 1998, Seascapes-Oita for orchestra 1998, Piano Concerto Ans Meer 1999, Silent Flowers for string quartet 1999, Voiceless Voice in Hiroshima for chorus and orchestra 2000, Hanjo (opera) 2004, Circulating Ocean for orchestra 2005, Woven Dreams (for orchestra, premiered at Lucerne Festival) (British Composer Awards Int. Award 2013) 2010, Matsukaze (opera) 2011. *Honours:* Berlin

Philharmonic Centenary Prize 1982. *Current Management:* c/o Schott Music GmbH & Co KG, Weihergarten 5, 55116, Mainz, Germany. *Telephone:* (61) 312460. *Fax:* (61) 31246211. *E-mail:* info@schott-music.com. *Website:* www .schott-music.com.

HOSSFELD, Christiane; German singer (soprano); b. 2 March 1961, Schwerin. *Education:* Hanns-Eisler Musikhochschule, Berlin. *Career:* sang at Halberstadt from 1983, Dresden Staatsoper from 1986, notably as Zerbinetta, Gilda, Nannetta (Falstaff), Gretel, and Olympia in Les contes d'Hoffmann; Premiere of Meyer's Der goldene Topf, 1989, and Zemlinsky's Der Zwerg, 1993; guest engagements at the Berlin Staatsoper and elsewhere; Bayreuth Festival, 1989–95, in Parsifal and Tannhäuser; sang Zerlina and Papagena at Dresden, 2000; many radio and television engagements. *Recordings include:* Die Lockende Flamme by Künneke. *Current Management:* Agentur Sigrid Rostock, Eugen-Schönhaar-Strasse 1, 10407 Berlin, Germany. *Telephone:* (30) 4257514. *Fax:* (30) 4239136. *E-mail:* sigridrostock@ web.de.

HOTEEV, Andrei; Russian pianist; b. 2 Dec. 1946, St Petersburg. *Education:* St Petersburg Conservatoire, Moscow Conservatoire with Lev Naumov. *Career:* debut, Moscow 1983, Rotterdam 1990; recitals include Shostakovich in Concertgebouw, Amsterdam 1990, Prokofiev in Musikhalle, Hamburg 1991, Hommage a Schnittke, Hamburg 1992, manuscript version of Mussorgsky's Pictures at an exhibition, first British performance in Purcell Room, London 1993, the original versions of Tchaikovsky's four piano concertos, Moscow 1996, numerous television broadcasts. *Recordings:* Tchaikovsky Piano Concerto No. 3; All the Works of Tchaikovsky for Piano and Orchestra; Mussorgsky Pictures at an Exhibition–manuscript version; Boris Godunov Suite. *Publications:* contrib. to Fono Forum 1998, Klassik Heute 1998, Frankfurter Allgemein 1999, Fanfare 1999.

HOU, Runyu; Chinese orchestral conductor; b. 6 Jan. 1945, Kunming; s. of Hou Zhu and Zhu Bangying; m. Su Jia 1971; one s. one d. *Education:* Music Middle School of Shanghai Conservatory, Shanghai Conservatory, Musikhochschule, Cologne, Germany and Mozarteum, Salzburg, Austria. *Career:* started playing piano aged seven, debut, Kunming 1954; Prin. Conductor, Shanghai Symphony Orchestra 1990; Headmaster, Xiamen Music School 2002–; debut Carnegie Hall, New York 1990; currently Conductor, East China Normal Univ. Orchestra and Chair. Music Dept. *Honours:* Hon. mem. Richard Wagner Asscn, Cologne. *Address:* 105 Hunan Road, Shanghai (office); RD. 1601 No. 12 Lane 125, Cao Xi Road, Shanghai, People's Republic of China. *Telephone:* (21) 64690942 (office); (21) 315234747 (home). *E-mail:* rhou@gmx .net (home).

HOUGH, Stephen Andrew Gill, CBE, MMus, GMus, FRNCM, PPRNCM; British pianist, composer and writer; b. 22 Nov. 1961, Heswall, Cheshire, England. *Education:* Chetham's School of Music, Royal Northern Coll. of Music, Juilliard School, USA. *Career:* guest performer with Berlin Philharmonic, London Symphony, New York Philharmonic, Cleveland, Philadelphia, Los Angeles Philharmonic, Boston Symphony, NHK Symphony, Chicago Symphony, Philharmonia, Royal Philharmonic and London Philharmonic Orchestras; Visiting Prof., Juilliard School and RAM; Int. Chair of Piano, RNCM; regular appearances with other orchestras and as recitalist in USA, Europe, Australia, Far East and at int. music festivals including Verbier, Salzburg, Aldeburgh, Edinburgh, BBC Proms, Mostly Mozart, Ravinia, Blossom, Tanglewood, Hollywood Bowl, La Roque d'Anthéron; regular blog for The Telegraph website. *Exhibition:* 'Appassionato' solo show, Broadbent Gallery, London 2012. *Compositions:* Transcriptions, Suite R-B and Other Enigmas, Piano Album, songs and choral works 2005, Viola Sonata 2000, Piano Pieces, The Loneliest Wilderness: Elegy for Cello and Orchestra 2005, Mass of Innocence and Experience 2006, Missa Mirabilis 2007, The Bible as Prayer 2007, Un Piccolo Sonatina, Threnody for Guitar, Three Grave Songs, Was mit den Tranen Geschieht: trio for flute or piccolo, bassoon or contrabassoon and piano, Herbstlieder for baritone and piano, Requiem Aeternum (after Victoria) for string sextet, Other Love Songs for SATB solo voices and piano duet, Sonata for piano (Broken Branches) 2011, Piano Sonata No. 2 (Notturno Luminoso), Bridgewater for bassoon and piano, Missa Mirabilis (orchestral version) 2012, Sonata for cello and piano (Les Adieux) 2013, Piano Sonata III (Trinitas) 2015. *Recordings include:* complete Beethoven violin sonatas (with Robert Mann), Hummel piano concertos, recitals of Liszt and Schumann, Brahms concerto Nos 1 and 2, The Piano Album Vols I, II, Britten Music for One and Two Pianos, Scharwenka and Sauer concertos, Grieg, Liszt, Rubinstein cello sonatas (with Steven Isserlis), Brahms violin sonatas (with Robert Mann), York Bowen piano music, Franck piano music, Mompou piano music, Liebermann piano concertos, Mendelssohn piano and orchestral works, Schubert sonatas and New York Variations, Brahms clarinet trio, The New Piano Album, Liszt sonata, Mozart piano and wind quintet, Brahms F minor sonata, Saint-Saëns Complete Music for Piano and Orchestra (Gramophone Gold Disc Award and CD of the Year), English Piano Album, Hummel piano sonatas, Chopin ballades and scherzos, Rachmaninov and Franck cello sonatas (with Steven Isserlis), Rachmaninov piano concertos (with Dallas Symphony and A. Litton) (Classical BRIT Critics' Award 2005, Classic FM Gramophone Editor's Choice Award 2005) 2004, Brahms, Dvořák and Suk 2005, Liszt Années de Pèlerinage (Suisse), Brahms cello sonatas with Stephen Isserlis, Children's Cello with Steven Isserlis, Beethoven and Mozart piano and wind quintets with the Berlin Philharmonic Wind Quintet, Stephen Hough's Spanish Album, Tsontakis Man of Sorrows, Brahms piano quintet with the Takacs Quartet, complete Tchaikovsky works for piano and orchestra with Minnesota Orchestra and Osmo Vanska, Stephen Hough in Recital, Chopin: Late Masterpieces, Chopin Complete Waltzes (Diapason d'Or de l'Année 2011) , Liszt and Grieg Concertos 2011, Broken Branches (compositions by Stephen Hough) 2011, Stephen Hough's French Album 2012, Two Brahms Piano Concertos 2013, In the Night recital 2014, Grieg, Mendelssohn and Hough Cello Sonatas (with Steven Isserlis) 2014, Grieg Lyric Pieces 2015, Scriabin and Janacek recital 2015. *Honours:* Hon. RAM; Hon. DMus; Dayas Gold Medal, RNCM, Terence Judd Award 1982, Naumburg Int. Piano Competition 1983, Gramophone Record of the Year 1996, 2002, MacArthur Foundation Fellowship 2001, Jean Gimbel Lane Prize 2007, Gramophone Gold Disc 2008, Royal Philharmonic Soc. Award for Best Instrumentalist 2010. *Current Management:* c/o Harrison Parrott, 5–6 Albion Court, London, W6 0QT, England. *Telephone:* (20) 7229-9166. *Fax:* (20) 7221-5042. *E-mail:* info@harrisonparrott.co.uk. *Website:* www.harrisonparrott.co.uk. *E-mail:* houghwebsite@gmail.com (office). *Website:* www.stephenhough.com; blogs .telegraph.co.uk/culture/author/stephenhough.

HOWARD, Brian Robert, BMus, DMus; Australian composer and conductor; b. 3 Jan. 1951, Sydney, NSW. *Education:* Univ. of Sydney, Univ. of Melbourne, studied with Peter Sculthorpe, Bernard Rands, Richard Meale, Maxwell Davies, Neville Marriner and Michael Gielen. *Career:* resident, Royal Danish Ballet 1980–81, State Opera of South Australia 1989; Musical Dir, Western Australia Ballet 1983–85; Dean, WA Conservatory 1992–95; commissions from Festivals of Sydney and Perth, and from Opera Factory Zürich 1991, among others. *Compositions include:* A Fringe of Leaves for chorus and orchestra 1982, Metamorphosis (opera) for six voices and chamber ensemble 1983, The Rainbow Serpent for ensemble 1984, Fly Away Peter for wind quintet 1984, Sun and Steel for string orchestra 1986, The Celestial Mirror for orchestra 1987, Whitsunday (opera) for ten voices and chamber ensemble 1988, Wildbird Dreaming for orchestra 1988, The Enchanted Rainforest (musical) 1989, Masquerade (ballet) 1994, Wide Sargasso Sea (opera) 1996.

HOWARD, Emily, MA, MMus, PhD; British composer and academic; b. 23 Feb. 1979, Liverpool. *Education:* Lincoln Coll., Oxford, Royal Northern Coll. of Music, Univ. of Manchester. *Career:* works performed and broadcast internationally by orchestras and ensembles including BBC Philharmonic, The Black Dyke Band, Cantus Ansambl, City of Birmingham Symphony Orchestra, Dortmund Philharmonic, Endymion Ensemble 10/10, London Symphony Orchestra, Musica Vitae, Royal Liverpool Philharmonic, Tonkünstler-Orchester Niederösterreich, Vienna Radio Symphony Orchestra; works featured at festivals including Cantiere Internazionale d'Arte, Montepulciano, Italy 2003, Sounds New, Canterbury 2006, 2008, 2010, Liverpool European Capital of Culture 2008, Soundings VI (Austrian Cultural Forum and British Council), London and Vienna 2009, WASBE, Cincinnati, USA 2009, Båstad Chamber Music Festival, Sweden 2009, eu-art-network 2010, Wien Modern (Composer Focus) 2011, BBC Proms 2012; one of 20 composers commissioned as part of New Music 20x12 for London Cultural Olympiad; works performed at venues including Musikverein and Konzerthaus, Vienna, Royal Albert Hall, Barbican and Southbank Centre, London, Gran Teatro La Fenice, Venice and Bridgewater Hall, Manchester by conductors including Vasily Petrenko, Andris Nelsons, James MacMillan, Juanjo Mena; mem. composition faculty, Royal Northern Coll. of Music; Hon. Research Fellow in Composition, Liverpool Hope Univ. 2010–. *Compositions include:* orchestral: Symphony Magnetite 2007–09, Solar 2010, Calculus of the Nervous System 2011, Axon 2013; other: Wild Clematis in Winter for mezzo soprano and piano 2008, Obsidian for brass band 2010, Ada Sketches for mezzo soprano, flute, clarinet and percussion 2011, Mesmerism for piano and chamber orchestra (British Composer Awards Making Music Award 2012) 2011, Zátopek! (opera, for 2012 Olympiad) 2012. *Recordings include:* Zátopek! 2012; works included on John McCabe Farewell Recital, Mark Simpson Prism, The NMC Songbook (winner, Classic FM Gramophone Award for Best Contemporary Recording 2009). *Honours:* Paul Hamlyn Foundation Award 2008. *Address:* c/o Royal Northern College of Music, 124 Oxford Road, Manchester, M13 9RD, England (office). *Website:* www.emilyhoward.com (office). *Current Management:* Cathy Nelson Artists and Projects, The Court House, Dorstone, HR3 6AW, England. *Telephone:* (1981) 551903. *E-mail:* cathy@cathynelson.co.uk. *Website:* www .cathynelson.co.uk.

HOWARD, Jason; British singer (baritone); b. 1960, Merthyr Tydfil, S Wales. *Education:* Trinity Coll. of Music, Royal Coll. of Music with Norman Bailey. *Career:* has sung a wide repertoire from Mozart through Puccini to contemporary music; now focuses on the Verdi repertoire, noted for his portrayals of Rigoletto and Macbeth, in particular; has worked extensively with Welsh Nat. Opera and with all the UK regional cos as well as the ENO and Covent Garden; has sung with many of the major houses in France, including Opera Nat. de Paris, and in N America with the leading US and Canadian cos; concert work has included collaborations with such conductors as Sir Colin Davis, Mark Elder and Mstislav Rostropovich; concert work also includes musical theatre. *Recordings include:* Student Prince, Song of Norway, A Little Night Music, Make Believe (collection of classic American show tunes). *Honours:* Ricordi Prize, Rowland Jones Award and Singing Faculty Award, TCM. *Current Management:* c/o Simon Goldstone, Intermusica Artists Management Ltd, 36 Graham Street, Crystal Wharf, London, N1 8GJ, England. *E-mail:* sgoldstone@intermusica.co.uk. *Website:* www .jasonhoward.net.

HOWARD, Jeffrey John, BMus; British vocal coach, organist, pianist, conductor and arranger and singer; *Vocal Coach, Royal Welsh College of Music and Drama;* b. 19 March 1969, Cardiff, Wales; s. of Graham John Howard and Valerie Ann Mayne; m. Rachael Jones 1997; two s. one d. *Education:* Fitzalan High School, Cardiff, Univ. of Wales Coll., Cardiff, Royal Acad. of Music, London. *Career:* accompanist to numerous male voice and mixed choirs; solo organist and pianist in recital and concert; appeared as accompanist on several recordings and TV and radio work; foreign tours; Voice Coach at Welsh Coll. of Music and Drama; has worked extensively with Swansea Bach Choir, BBC Welsh Chorus, South Glamorgan Youth Choir and early music performances including Orchestra of the Age of Enlightenment; performer on Live Music Now scheme; Guest Artist-in-Residence at First United Methodist Church, Lubbock, Texas, USA, 1996–97; Visiting Prof. of Organ, Texas Tech Univ. 1996–97; repetiteur, Welsh Nat. Opera (WNO) 1999–; coach and accompanist at Cardiff Int. Acad. of Voice; accompanist for solo singers in recital, cabaret and music theatre performances, including Bryn Terfel, Sir Willard White, Dennis O'Neil, Rebecca Evans, Alfie Boe, Wynne Evans, Shan Coth and others; repetiteur work on opera and music theatre; Royal Albert Hall solo debut in Shostakovich's Piano Concerto No. 2 2002; accompanist, arranger and singer with Only Men Aloud! (winners of BBC choir competition Last Choir Standing 2008); organist, harpsichordist and conductor for choral works, oratorios, masses and recordings; arranger for orchestras, bands and various ensembles; accompanist at Royal Nat. Eisteddfod of Wales; currently Conductor of Cambrensis, the South Wales Baptist Choir and St David's Praise Choir and Orchestra, Cardiff. *Recordings:* several Christian recordings with Cambrensis (South Wales Baptist Choir) including Hymns 1995; recording as Organist with Cor Meibion de Cymru 1995; Bryn Terfel, organist with male voice choir and orchestra of WNO; arranger for solo vocal albums with Royal Philharmonic Orchestra 2000 and Budapest Symphony Orchestra 2002; arranger, pianist and singer on two albums with Only Men Aloud; organist with Serendipity (mixed choir); live DVD and CD recordings of London Welsh Festival of Male Choirs (the Thousand Voices) at Royal Albert Hall, London; Band of Brothers (Classical Brit Award). *Radio:* Sunday Half Hour, Morning Worship (BBC). *Television:* Songs of Praise, Children in Need and various others for BBC and ITV, Dechrau Canu, Dechrau Canmol, The Shan Cothi show and various others for S4C (Welsh language). *Publications:* Kevin Mayhew – Welsh Folk Song Arrangements for flute and harp. *Honours:* Glynne Jones Prize for Organ 1990, Michael Head Accompaniment Prize 1991, Prizewinner, San Antonio Organ Competition 1997. *Address:* 9 Clos Alyn, Pontprennau, Cardiff, CF23 8LB, Wales.

HOWARD, John Stuart, BA, PhD; composer, academic, writer and conductor; b. 22 Dec. 1950, Glasgow, Scotland; m. Ellen Jane Howard 1974, one s. one d. *Education:* Ilford County High School, Royal Coll. of Music, Univ. of Durham. *Career:* teacher in various posts; Sr Lecturer and Principal Lecturer, Kingston Polytechnic/Univ. 1979–92, Hon. Sr Research Fellow 1993–95; Assoc. Prof. and Head of Music, Nanyang Technological Univ., Singapore 1993–; mem. PRS, ISME. *Compositions:* Dunstable Cantus for piano 1974, The Two Regions for brass band 1976, Bubbles for Ever? for flute, clarinet, violin and cello 1981, Games/End Game for Chinese orchestra 1983, Sonata for brass quintet 1983, Fantasia and Dance for Chinese orchestra 1985. *Publications:* Learning to Compose 1990, Performing and Responding 1995; contrib. to Schools Council Magazine, Pears Encyclopedia, Music File (four articles) 1991–93, IJME (reviewer), Proceedings of British-Swedish Ethnomusicology Conference 1991.

HOWARD, Jonathan; British singer (bass); b. 23 Jan. 1987, London. *Education:* Christ's Hospital School, Sussex, New Coll., Univ. of Oxford. *Career:* Founder mem. Oxford Clerks vocal group; mem. The King's Singers 2010–. *Current Management:* Claire Long, General Manager, The King's Singers, Music Productions Limited, Unit 14, 21 Wadsworth Road, Perivale, UB6 7JD, England; Alec C. Treuhaft or Stephanie Reiss, IMG Artists, Carnegie Hall Tower, 152 West 57th Street, 5th Floor, New York, NY 10019, USA. *Telephone:* (1753) 646100; (212) 994-3500; (212) 994-3521. *Fax:* (1753) 437134; (212) 994-3550. *E-mail:* Claire@kingssingers.com; Claire@ musicprods.co.uk; atreuhaft@imgartists.com; sreiss@imgartists.com. *Website:* www.imgartists.com. *E-mail:* jonathan@kingssingers.com. *Website:* www .kingssingers.com.

HOWARD, Leslie John, AMusA, LMus, BA, MA, AM, DMus; British/Australian pianist, composer, conductor and musicologist; b. 29 April 1948, Melbourne, Vic., Australia. *Education:* Monash Univ., studied with June McLean, Donald Britton, Michael Brimer, Guido Agosti and Noretta Conci. *Career:* debut in Melbourne 1967; mem. staff, Monash Univ. 1970–73, Guildhall School of Music and Drama, London 1987–92; concertos with various orchestras in Australia, England, Europe, N and S America, Asia; regular broadcasts as pianist, chamber musician and musicologist for BBC, ABC, RAI and various US networks; telecasts in the Americas, Australia and SE Asia; mem. Council, Royal Philharmonic Soc.; Pres. Liszt Soc., Alkan Soc., Grainger Soc., Prokofiev Foundation; Trustee, Geoffrey Parsons Memorial Trust. *Compositions:* Fruits of the Earth, ballet, Hreidar the Fool, opera, Prague Spring, opera, Sonatas for violin, clarinet, percussion, double bass horn, cello and piano, Trios, String Quartets, Piano Quartet, Piano Quintet, Piano Solos, Canzona for brass ensemble, Missa Sancti Petri 1993, Songs, Motets. *Recordings:* more than 130 recordings, including the complete solo piano music of Liszt, music by Tchaikovsky, Rakhmaninov, Rubinstein, Glazunov, Stravinsky, Grainger. *Publications:* Edition of complete works of Liszt for cello and piano 1992, and Piano Trio 1993 and Violin and Piano 2003, A Liszt Catalogue, with Michael

Short 1993, volumes of piano and Choral Music and Songs 1999–; contrib. to Liszt Society Journal, on Liszt, Music and Musicians, on Grainger, Musical Opinion, on Liszt, Viking Opera Guide, on Liszt and Rachmaninov, Dubal's Horowitz Symposium. *Honours:* Hon. FZAM; Medal of St Stephen (Hungary) 2004; Diploma d'Onore, Siena 1972, Naples 1976, Ferenc Liszt Medal of Honour 1986, Liszt Grand Prix du Disque, Liszt Acad., Budapest six times, Ferenc Liszt Medal of Honour (Hungarian Repub.) 1989, Pro Cultura Hungarica Award 2000, Alumnus of the Year, Monash Univ. 1994. *Current Management:* c/o Margaret Murphy Management, 7 Grove Park, Wanstead, London, E11 2DN, England. *Telephone:* (20) 8530-1305. *E-mail:* info@margaretmurphy.com. *Website:* www.margaretmurphy.com; www.lesliehowardpianist.com.

HOWARD, Patricia, MA, PhD; British writer and lecturer; *Visiting Research Fellow in Music, Open University;* b. 18 Oct. 1937, Birmingham; m. David Louis Howard 1960; two d. *Education:* Lady Margaret Hall, Oxford and Univ. of Surrey. *Career:* Lecturer and Tutor of Music, Open Univ. 1976–2003, Visiting Research Fellow in Music 2008–; many broadcasts both on network and for Open Univ. *Publications:* Gluck and the Birth of Modern Opera 1963, The Operas of Benjamin Britten: An Introduction 1969, Haydn in London 1980, Mozart's Marriage of Figaro 1980, C. W. Gluck: Orfeo 1981, Haydn's String Quartets 1984, Beethoven's Eroica Symphony 1984, Benjamin Britten: The Turn of the Screw 1985, Christoph Willibald Gluck: A Guide to Research 1987, Music in Vienna, 1790–1800 1988, Beethoven's Fidelio 1988, Music and the Enlightenment 1992, Gluck: An Eighteenth-Century Portrait 1995, Gluck's Orpheus Operas 1997, From Composition to Performance: The String Family 1998, The Solo Voice: Evidence for a Historical Investigation 1998, In Defence of Modern Music and its Celebrated Performers, translation and critical edition of Vincenzo Manfredini, Difesa della musica moderna (1788) 2002, An introduction to gender studies: Mozart's operas and sonatas 2002, Beethoven's Eighth Symphony; reception studies 2002, The Turn of the Screw: analysis and interpretation 2002, The Modern Castrato: Gaetano Guadagni and the coming of a new operatic age 2014, Gluck 2015; contrib. to Musical Times, Music and Letters, The Consort, The Listener, The Gramophone, Opera, ENO and Friends, Acta musicologica, Eighteenth-Century Fiction, Il Saggiatore musicale, Notes, Cambridge Opera Journal, The Opera Journal, programme books for Covent Garden Opera, Glyndebourne Opera, The Barbican Centre and La Monnaie, Brussels. *Honours:* Susette Taylor Travelling Fellowship 1971, Leverhulme Research Award 1976, British Acad. Research Award 1988. *Address:* Stepping Stones, Gomshall, Surrey, GU5 9NZ, England (home).

HOWARD, Yvonne; British singer (mezzo-soprano); b. 1950, Staffordshire, England. *Education:* Royal Northern College of Music. *Career:* operatic appearances as Mozart's Marcellina with Glyndebourne Touring Opera, Cenerentola for English Touring Opera and Suzuki for Birmingham Music Theatre; sang Fricka and Waltraute in The Ring of the Nibelungen, City of Birmingham Touring Opera; season 1990–91 sang Mercedes at Covent Garden, and Meg Page in Falstaff for ENO; sang Amastris in Xerxes, Meg Page and Maddalena in Rigoletto for ENO in 1992; Glyndebourne 1994, as Mrs Sedley in Peter Grimes; Royal Opera 1998, as Marcellina; sang Meg Page for Opera North and in Rinaldo at Garsington 2000; concert engagements include Mozart's Requiem under Menuhin at Gstaad, Messiah with the Tokyo Philharmonic, Vivaldi's Gloria with the English Chamber Orchestra, Messiah with the Hallé Orchestra and Liverpool Philharmonic, De Falla's Three Cornered Hat at Festival Hall and with Ulster Orchestra; Song recitals include Wigmore Hall debut in 1989. *Honours:* RNCM Curtis Gold Medal.

HOWARTH, Elgar, ARAM, DMus, FRCM, FRNCM; British musician (trumpet), conductor and composer; b. 4 Nov. 1935, Cannock, Staffs.; s. of Oliver Howarth and Emma Wall; m. Mary Bridget Neary 1958; one s. two d. *Education:* Eccles Grammar School and Manchester Univ./Royal Northern Coll. of Music (jt course). *Career:* orchestral player 1958–70; Chair. Royal Philharmonic Orchestra 1968–70; Prin. Guest Conductor Opera North 1985–88; freelance orchestral conductor 1970–; Musical Adviser and Conductor, Grimethorpe Colliery Brass Band 1972–; Dir of Brass Ensembles, Royal Acad. of Music; Fellow, Welsh Coll. of Music and Drama. *Compositions include:* Trombone Concerto 1962, Trumpet Concerto 1968, Music for Spielberg 1984, Songs for BL for brass band. *Honours:* Hon. FRNCM 1999; Hon. FRCM 2001, Univ. Coll. Salford; Hon. DUniv (Cen. England, York); Hon. DMus (Keele) 1996, (York) 2000; Hon. DLitt (Salford) 2003; Eddison Award 1977, Olivier Award for Outstanding Achievement in Opera 1997. *Address:* Brass Department, Royal Academy of Music, Marylebone Road, London, NW1 5HT, England (office). *Website:* www.ram.ac.uk (office).

HOWARTH, Judith; British singer (soprano); b. 11 Sept. 1962, Ipswich; m. 1986. *Education:* Royal Scottish Acad. of Music and Drama and studies with Patricia Macmahon. *Career:* recipient of special bursary to join Royal Opera House, Covent Garden as prin. soprano in 1985–86 season; maj. roles with Royal Opera include Musetta, Ännchen in Der Freischütz, Gilda, Adela, Marguerite de Valois in Les Huguenots, Liu, Norina, Marzelline and Morgana in Alcina 1989–96; now freelance; numerous concert and recital engagements in UK, USA, Far East, Australia and NZ; debut at Salzburg Festival in Mozart's Der Schauspieldirektor 1991; has also appeared with Florida Grand Opera, Drottningholm Festival, Opera North and Glyndebourne Touring Opera; debut with Deutsche Staatsoper, Berlin in Cavalli's La Didone 1996. *Address:* c/o Hazard Chase, 48-49 Russell Square, London, WC1B 4JP, England.

HOWELL, Gwynne Richard, CBE, BSc, DipTP, MRTPI; British singer (bass); b. 13 June 1938, Gorseinon, Wales; m. Mary Edwina Morris 1968; two s. *Education:* Univ. of Wales, Univ. of Manchester, Manchester Royal Coll. of Music with Gwilym Jones, studied with Otakar Kraus. *Career:* principal bass at Sadler's Wells, singing roles including Monterone and the Commendatore; sang at Glyndebourne and Covent Garden in debut as First Nazarene in Salome, 1969–70; Metropolitan House debut in 1985 as Lodovico in Otello and Pogner in Die Meistersinger; sang Gurnemanz in a new production of Parsifal at London Coliseum in 1986; sang the Parson and the Badger in a new production of The Cunning Little Vixen in 1990 and sang the Fliedermonolog at the Reginald Goodall Memorial Concert in London, 1991; sang at London Coliseum in 1992 as King Philip in a new production of Don Carlos, Daland at Covent Garden and Mozart's Bartolo on tour with the company to Japan; sang Dikoy in Katya Kabanova at Covent Garden 1997, Seneca in Poppea for WNO, Arkel in Pelléas et Mélisande at Glyndebourne and the London Proms 1999; sang in Martinů's Greek Passion, Covent Garden 2000, premiere of Turnage's The Silver Tassie for ENO and the Commendatore at Glyndebourne 2000; sings in Europe and USA and records for BBC and major recording cos. *Repertory includes:* Verdi and Mozart Requiems and Missa Solemnis; other roles include the King in Aida, Mephisto in Damnation of Faust, High Priest in Nabucco, Hobson in Peter Grimes and Sparafucile in Rigoletto. *Address:* 197 Fox Lane, London, N13 4BB, England (home).

HOWELLS, Anne Elizabeth, ARMCM; British singer (mezzo-soprano); b. 12 Jan. 1941, Southport, Lancs.; d. of Trevor Howells and Mona Howells; m. 1st Ryland Davies (q.v.) 1966 (divorced 1981); m. 2nd Stafford Dean 1981 (divorced 1998); one s. one d. *Education:* Sale Co. Grammar School, Royal Northern Coll. of Music. *Career:* three seasons in Chorus with Glyndebourne Festival Opera 1964–66, took leading role at short notice in L'Ormindo (Cavalli) 1967; subsequent roles include Dorabella in Così fan tutte, Cathleen in world premiere Rising of the Moon (Nicholas Maw), Composer in Ariadne, Diana in Calisto; with Royal Opera House, Covent Garden 1969–71, appearing as Lena in world premiere of Victory (Richard Rodney Bennett), Rosina in The Barber of Seville, Cherubino in The Marriage of Figaro; Guest Artist with Royal Opera House 1973–; has also appeared with Welsh Nat. Opera, Scottish Opera, ENO, Chicago Opera, Geneva Opera, Metropolitan Opera, New York, Lyon Opera, Marseille Opera, Nantes Opera, Netherlands Opera and in Naples, San Francisco, Hamburg, Berlin, La Scala, Milan, in Belgium and at the Salzburg Festival 1976 and 1980 (Tales of Hoffmann and film version of Clemenza di Tito); Prof. of Singing, RAM 1997–. *Honours:* Hon. FRNCM. *Address:* c/o Vocal Department, Royal Academy of Music, Marylebone Road, London, NW1 5HT, England.

HOWIE, Alan Crawford, BMus, PhD; British academic; b. 6 Nov. 1942, Stornoway, Scotland; m.; three c. *Education:* Coatbridge High School, Scotland, Royal Scottish Acad. of Music and Drama (jr student), Univ. of Edinburgh, Acad. of Music, Vienna, Austria, Univ. of Manchester. *Career:* Lecturer in Music, Univ. of Manchester, especially on the 19th century and research in the music of Schubert and Bruckner; Assoc. Ed. Bruckner Journal 1997–; Chair. Schubert Inst. (UK) 2008–; Ed. The Schubertian 2002–; mem. Royal Musical Asscn, Inc. Soc. of Musicians, Internationale Bruckner Gesellschaft. *Publications include:* Perspectives on Anton Bruckner (co-ed. with Paul Hawkshaw and Timothy Jackson) 2001, Anton Bruckner: A Documentary Biography (two vols) 2002; contrib. to Music and Letters, Music Quarterly; papers at int. 19th-century music confs early 1980s–. *Address:* 11 Brookhill Street, , Nottinghamshire, NG9 7BQ, Stapleford, Notts., NG9 7BQ, England (home). *Telephone:* (115) 875 9738 (home). *E-mail:* acrhowie@blueyonder.co.uk (home).

HOWLETT, Neil Baillie, MA; singer (baritone); b. 24 July 1934, Mitcham, Surrey, England; m. Elizabeth Robson; two d. *Education:* St Paul's Cathedral Choir School, King's Coll., Cambridge, Hochschule für Musik, Stuttgart. *Career:* debut in the world premiere of Britten's Curlew River at Aldeburgh 1964; roles with Sadler's Wells, English Opera Group, Royal Opera House Covent Garden, Hamburg, Bremen, Nantes, Bordeaux, Toulouse, Nice and Marseille; Principal Baritone, ENO, London; has sung most major baritone roles; sang title roles in the premieres of Blake's Toussaint and Crosse's The Story of Vasco; appearances at most major festivals; sang Hector in King Priam with the Royal Opera at Athens 1985 and Amfortas in Buenos Aires 1986; sang Scarpia in Tosca with ENO 1987–90; Holland Festival 1990 as Ruprecht in Prokofiev's The Fiery Angel; Faninal in Der Rosenkavalier at Catania 1992; Wotan in Das Rheingold and Die Walküre at Leicester 1998–99; other roles include Golaud in Pelléas, King Fisher in The Midsummer Marriage and Wagner's Dutchman; recitalist, teacher and regular broadcaster; Prof., Guildhall School of Music. *Honours:* Kathleen Ferrier Memorial Prize.

HOYLAND, Vic, DPhil; British composer; b. 11 Dec. 1945, Wombwell, Yorkshire, England. *Education:* Univ. of Hull, York Univ. with Robert Sherlaw Johnson and Bernard Rands. *Career:* Hayward Fellow in Music, Univ. of Birmingham 1980–83; Visiting Lecturer, York Univ. 1984; Lecturer, Barber Inst. for Fine Arts, Univ. of Birmingham 1985–93, Sr Lecturer 1993–98, Reader in Composition 1998–, Prof. in Composition 2000–11, now retired; founder mem. and Co-Dir, Northern Music Theatre; compositions have been featured at the Aldeburgh, Bath, Holland and California Contemporary Music Festivals; survey of works at the 1985 Musica Concert Series in London; commissions from the Northern Music Theatre, the Essex Youth Orchestra, New MacNaghten Concerts, Musica, the Barber Institute, BBC

Promenade series, BCMG, Southbank Summerscope, Huddersfield Festival, Almeida Festival, York and Cheltenham Festivals. *Compositions include:* Em for 24 voices 1970, Jeux-Theme for mezzo and ensemble 1972, Esem for double-bass and ensemble 1975, Xingu (music theatre) 1979, Reel for double-reed instruments 1980, Michelagniolo for male voices and large ensemble 1980, Quartet Movement 1982, Head and Two Tails (three pieces) for voice(s) and ensemble 1984, String Quartet 1985, Seneca/Medea for voices and ensemble 1985, In Transit for orchestra 1987, Work-Out for trombone 1987, Work-Out for marimba 1988, Trio 1990, The Other Side of the Air for Rolf Hind for piano solo 1991, In Memoriam P.P.P. 1992, Piano Quintet 1992, Concerto for pianoforte ensemble 1993, String Quartet No. 3: Bagatelles 1994, Vixen (large-scale work) for full orchestra 1997, QIBTI for full orchestra 2002, Phoenix for full orchestra 2003, The Attraction of Opposites for 2 pianos 2005, Sicilian Vespas for flute and piano 2006, Pierrot (for Boulez) amplified solo flute and 14 instruments 2008, Hey Presto for 3 woodwind, 3 brass, 2 percussion and pianoforte 2009, Omer for solo oboist and percussion 2012, WULF for 24 voices and 24 instruments 2012. *Address:* c/o University of York Music Press Ltd, Department of Music, University of York, Heslington, York, YO1 5DD, England.

HOYLE, Ted, BMus, MMus, DMA; American cellist; b. 17 Aug. 1942, Huntsville, Ala. *Education:* Eastman School of Music, Yale Univ., Manhattan School of Music, studied with André Navarra, Ecole Normale de Musique, Paris, France. *Career:* cellist, Kohon Quartet; Prof. Emer. of Music, Kean Univ., NJ; cellist, Performing Arts Trio, New Jersey; Co-Dir Hear America First, Manhattan concert series, 1978–81; mem. Violoncello Soc., American String Teachers' Asscn. *Compositions:* ed works by Bach, Schumann, Scriabin for Boosey and Hawkes. *Recordings:* several with the Kohon Quartet, including: String quartets by Walter Piston, Peter Mennin, Charles Ives, William Schuman, Aaron Copland, Julia Smith, Roger Sessions and Penderecki; Quartet of Joseph Fennimore, Quintet of Robert Baksa, Trio Sonatas of J.S. Bach, G.F. Handel, G. Telemann. *Address:* 340 West 28th Street 15D, New York, NY 10001, USA (home). *E-mail:* tedhoy@aol.com (home).

HRACHYA, Avanesyan; Armenian violinist; b. 1986, Gumri. *Education:* Tchaikovsky School, Yerevan, Brussels Royal Conservatoire, Queen Elisabeth College of Music. *Career:* mem. Young Virtuosos of Armenia, performed as soloist in several cities in Europe, in Iran, Lebanon, USA, Canada, Russia, Australia and China; moved to Belgium 2003; worked with Wallonie Royal Chamber Orchestra with Christopher Warren-Green, Nat. Orchestra of Lille under Joji Hattori, Armenian Nat. Orchestra with Loris Tjegnavorian, Odense Symphony Orchestra, Denmark and Gulbenkian Orchestra, Portugal with Joana Carneiro; recital tours in Denmark and Sweden 2008–09. *Honours:* first prize, Henry Vieuxtemps Competition, Belgium 2004, Gold Medal, European Competition for Young Soloists, Luxembourg 2005, first prize, Menuhin Int. Violin Competition 2006, Special Prize, European Union of Music Competitions for Youth 2006, first prize, Carl Nielsen Int. Violin Competition 2008. *Current Management:* c/o Copenhagen Artists, Christian IX's gade 2, 1111 Copenhagen, Denmark. *Telephone:* 44492900. *E-mail:* office@copenhagenartists.com. *Website:* www.copenhagenartists.com.

HRUBA-FREIBERGER, Venceslava; Czech singer (soprano); b. 28 Sept. 1945, Dublocive. *Education:* studied in Prague. *Career:* debut with Prague National Theatre 1969, in Wranitsky's Oberon; sang at Pilzen Opera, 1970–72, Leipzig Opera, 1972–88; roles have included Verdi's Gilda, Mozart's Constanze and Queen of Night, Lucia di Lammermoor, Janáček's Vixen, Violetta, and Glinka's Lyudmila; Guest appearances at the Aix Festival, 1982, Nice and Prague; Staatsoper Berlin from 1987; concerts in Austria, Spain, England, Poland and Japan. *Recordings include:* Bach's The Choice of Hercules; C. P. Bach's Magnificat, Handel's L'Allegro ed il Pensieroso and Mozart's Apollo et Hyacinthus.

HRŮŠA, Jakub; Czech conductor; *Music Director and Chief Conductor, Prague Philharmonia*; b. 23 Aug. 1981, Brno; s. of Petr Hrůša; m. Klára Hrůšová. *Education:* Acad. of Performing Arts, Prague, studied with Jiri Belohlavek. *Career:* Prin. Conductor, Prague Philharmonia 2005–08, Music Dir and Chief Conductor 2009–; Music Dir, Glyndebourne on Tour 2010–12; Prin. Guest Conductor, Tokyo Metropolitan Symphony Orchestra; appears regularly with Philharmonia Orchestra, Czech Philharmonic, Leipzig Gewandhaus Orchestra, Orchestre Philharmonique de Radio France, Finnish Radio Symphony, SWR Symphony Stuttgart, WDR Symphony Cologne, BBC Symphony, Melbourne and Sydney Symphony Orchestras, Hong Kong Philharmonic, Seoul Philharmonic; opera appearances include Glyndebourne Festival Opera 2008, 2010, 2011, Finnish Nat. Opera 2014, Royal Danish Opera and Prague Nat. Theatre; debuts in 2013–14 season included Los Angeles Philharmonic, Vienna Radio Symphony Orchestra, Russian Nat. Orchestra, Baltimore Symphony Orchestra, Montreal Symphony Orchestra, Netherlands Radio Philharmonic and Oslo Philharmonic Orchestra; became the youngest conductor since 1949 to lead the opening concert of the Prague Spring Festival 2010; Pres. Int. Martinů Circle. *Recordings include:* Smetana 'Ma Vlast' (Live from Prague Spring Festival) 2010, Tchaikovsky and Bruch Violin Concertos (with Nicola Benedetti) 2010, Berlioz 'Symphonie fantastique' (Live with Tokyo Metrolpoitan Symphony Orchestra) 2013. *Current Management:* c/o Alexander Monsey, IMG Artists, The Light Box, 111 Power Road, London W4 5PY, England. *Telephone:* (20) 7957-5800. *Fax:* (20) 7957-5801. *E-mail:* amonsey@imgartists.com. *Website:* www.imgartists.com.

HSU, John T., BMus, MMus; American (b. Chinese) academic, cellist, viola da gamba player, barytonist and conductor; b. 21 April 1931, Swatow (Shantou), China; m. Martha Russell 1968. *Education:* New England Conservatory of Music. *Career:* Instructor, Cornell Univ. 1955–58, Faculty mem. 1955–2005, Chair. Dept of Music 1966–71, Old Dominion Prof. of Music and Humanities 1976–2005, Prof. Emer. 2005–; Fellow, Cornell Soc. for the Humanities 1971–72; artist-faculty, Aston Magna Foundation for Music and the Humanities 1973–90, Artistic Dir 1987–90; barytonist, Haydn Baryton Trio 1982–; Artist-in-Residence, Univ. of California, Davis 1983; Regents Lecturer in Music, Univ. of California, Santa Cruz 1985; viola da gamba recitalist, including radio broadcasts in N America and Europe; Dir, Aston Magna Performance Practice Inst. 1986–90; Music Dir and Conductor, Apollo Ensemble 1991–2005; Artistic Dir and Conductor, Atlanta Baroque Orchestra 2006–09. *Recordings include:* Pièces de Viole by Louis de Caix d'Hervelois and Antoine Forqueray 1966, Three Gamba Sonatas by J. S. Bach 1971, complete recording of the five suites for viola da gamba by Antoine Forqueray 1972, Pièces de viole by Maria Marais 1973–76, Pièces de viole by Charles Dollé and Jacques Morel 1978, two vols of Baryton Trios by Joseph Haydn 1988–89, Apollo Ensemble and John Hsu, three volumes of Symphonies by Joseph Haydn 1993–99, Baryton Trios by Haydn 1996, Apollo Ensemble and John Hsu: Symphonies by Joseph Haydn, Vivaldi Project Ensemble and John Hsu, Sinfonias for Strings by Carl Philipp Emanuel Bach, W. 182. *Publications include:* A Handbook of French Baroque Viol Technique 1981; editor: The Instrumental Works, by Marin Marais (1656–1728) Vol. I 1980, Vol. II 1987, Vol. III 1995, Vol. IV 1998, Vol. V 2000, Vol. VI 2001, Vol. VII 2002; contrib. to Early Music 1978. *Honours:* Hon. DMus (New England Conservatory of Music) 1971; Hon. DArts (Ramapo Coll. of New Jersey) 1986; Chevalier des Arts et des Lettres 2000. *Address:* Department of Music, Cornell University, 256 East Avenue, 101 Lincoln Hall, Ithaca, NY 14853, USA (office). *Telephone:* (919) 918-3523 (home). *E-mail:* jth12@cornell.edu (office). *Website:* www .music.cornell.edu (office).

HSU, Ya-Ming, DipMus, MA, DMus; Taiwanese composer; b. 5 Feb. 1963; m. Wen-Chi Lin 1994; one s. one d. *Education:* National Taipei Teachers' College, Tunghi University, Boston University, USA. *Career:* debut aged 17, received First Prize in Taiwan Composition Competition, Taiwan Educational Ministry; Lecturer, Chinese Culture University; Head of Chinese Music Talent Development Association; mem, ASCAP; Asian Composer League; National Association of Composers, USA. *Compositions:* Two Romantic Suites, Arts Trio commission, 1994; The Joyful News from Heaven, 1995; Bright be the Place of Thy Soul, 1997; Wind-Color, China Found Music Ensemble commission, 1998; A Tone Poem for Baritone, Chorus and String Quartet, Chinese Choral Society of Rochester commission, 1998; Four Choral Music, 1998; Snowing in June, 1999; Taiwan Mass, Taipei Philharmonic Chorus commission, 2000; Elegy, Arts Trio Taipei commission, 2000; Elegy for cello and piano, 2003; Twelve preludes for piano, 2003. *Recordings:* Snowing in June, Taipei Philharmonic Chamber Choir, 1999. *Publications:* Four Choral Music, 1998. *Honours:* Several Prizes, Taiwan Educational Ministry, Provincial Music Association, Chung Hwa Rotary Educational Association, National Taipei Teachers' College, Taipei International Community Cultural Association; Best Composition, The Golden Melody Award, 2000. *Address:* 2F, Nr 10 51st Alleyway, 102 Lane, Shei-fu Road, Tamshui, Taipei County, Taiwan. *Telephone:* (2) 26263274. *Fax:* (2) 26215713. *E-mail:* taiwanmass@yahoo.com.

HU, Kun; French/Chinese conductor, violinist and academic; *Professor of Violin, Royal Academy of Music*; b. 22 Feb. 1963, Chengdu, Sichuan Prov., China; s. of Hu Wei Min and Peng Shi Jun. *Education:* Cen. Conservatory of Music, Beijing, Menuhin Int. Music Acad., Switzerland, pvt. studies with the late Lord Yehudi Menuhin, London. *Career:* began studying violin and piano with his parents at age six; soloist, China Cen. Radio Symphony Orchestra and China Nat. Defence Cttee Artists Co. 1976; debut with Helsinki Radio Symphony and Helsinki Philharmonic Orchestras 1980; debuts in London and Paris 1985, in Berlin and Vienna 1986, in Leipzig 1991, in New York 2001, in Dresden 2003, in Chicago 2006; followed by concerts with Philharmonia Orchestra at the Barbican; performed with major orchestras world-wide, now also conducts major orchestras in China and abroad; f. own orchestra Hu Kun and Friends 2005; Prof. of Violin, Royal Acad. of Music; Guest Conductor, London Schubert Players; Guest Prof. at Beijing, Sichuan and Guangzhou conservatories; jury mem. major int. violin competitions. *Television:* The First Winner (Beijing TV) 1981, The Story of HU Kun (Phoenix CNE) 2003. *Recordings include:* Bach Triple Concerto in D major, Vivaldi Concerto for Four Violins in D major, Prokofiev First Concerto No. 1 with the English String Orchestra, Sibelius and Khachaturian Concertos all conducted by Yehudi Menuhin, Barber Concerto and Bernstein Serenade conducted by William Boughton, Alun Hoddinott's Heaventree of Stars conducted by Tadaaki Otaka, Two Virtuosi Live, Chinese Violin Music, Telemann Concerto for Four Violins, Cadenza from the Paganini Concerto in D major, Wieniawski Polonaise in D major. *Honours:* Hon. RAM; Exceptional Solo Performer Prize, Nat. Mil. Artists Co. 1977, prizewinner, Sibelius Violin Competition 1980, winner, City of Paris Menuhin Competition 1984, Queen Elisabeth Violin Competition 1985, Francescatti Competition 1987, Lipizer Violin Competition (Italy) 1988, Great Palm Beach Annual Invitation Violin Competition (USA) 1989. *Current Management:* c/o Robert Gilder & Co., 91 Great Russell Street, London, WC1B 3PS, England. *Telephone:* (20) 7580-7758. *Fax:* (20) 7580-7739. *E-mail:* cathycarson@blueyonder.co.uk. *Website:* www.robert-gilder.com. *Address:* Strings Department, Royal Academy of Music, Marylebone Road, London, NW1 5HT, England (office). *Telephone:* (20) 8947-3252 (office). *Fax:*

(20) 8947-3252 (office). *E-mail:* hukun@hukun.net (home); hukun63@hotmail .com (home). *Website:* hukun.net.

HUA, Lin; Chinese composer and academic; b. 8 Aug. 1942, Shanghai. *Education:* Shanghai Conservatory of Music, studied with Sang Tong, Wang Jianzhong and Chen Mingzhi. *Career:* composer for Shanghai Wind Band 1967–76, Shanghai Opera and Ballet House 1976–79; Assoc. Prof., Counterpoint, Fugue, Shanghai Conservatory of Music 1979–; consultant, Shanghai Philharmonic Asscn 1982–. *Compositions include:* Bright Mountain Flowers in Full Bloom, ballet, 1976; Fantasy for piano and accordion, 1978; Love of The Great Wall for piano and accordion, 1978; Farewell Refrains At Yang Gate Pass for piano quartet, 1978; Beauty of Peking Opera for string quartet, 1979; Album of Woodcuts for piano quintet, 1979; Amid Flowers Beside a River Under the Spring Moon for 4 harps, 1979; Flower and Song, concertino for soprano and orchestra, 1980; Suite Tragedy for chamber symphony, 1988; 24 Preludes and fugues on reading Sikong Tu's Shipin (Personalities of Poetry in Tang Dynasty), 1990; Album of World Folk Songs for piano, 1991; stage, film and television music. *Publications:* Guide the Teaching of Polyphony by Using Creative Psychology 1980, Stravinsky Techniques in Polyphonic Writing 1987, The Sense of Ugliness and its Application in Western Music 1988, Abstraction of Art and Abstractionism 1989, Course of Polyphone 1994, The Pilgrimage to Music 1995, Talk on Music 1998, 101 World Folk Songs 1998. *Address:* 20 Fenyang Road, Shanghai, People's Republic of China.

HUANG, An-Lun, MM, FTCL; Canadian (b. Chinese) composer; b. 15 March 1949, Guangzhou City, Guangdong Prov.; s. of Huang Fei-Li and Zhao Fang-Xing; m. Ouyang Rui-Li 1974; one s. *Education:* Central Conservatory of Music, Beijing, Univ. of Toronto, Trinity Coll. of Music, UK, Yale Univ., USA. *Career:* started piano aged five; studied with Shaw Yuan-Xin and Chen Zi; works have been widely performed in China, Hong Kong, Philippines, northern Africa, Australia, Europe, USA and Canada; apptd Resident Composer and Asst Conductor, Cen. Opera House of China 1976; arrived in Canada 1980; Founder and Pres. Canadian Chinese Music Soc., Ont. 1987–96; Fellowship in Composition, Trinity Coll. of Music, London 1983. *Compositions include:* operas: Flower Guardian Op. 26 1979, Yeu Fei Op. 37 1986 and 6 others; symphonic, chamber, vocal, choral and film music, including: Symphonic Concert Op. 25, Symphonic Overture, The Consecration of the Spring in 1976 Op. 25a 1977, Piano Concerto in G Op. 25b 1982, Symphony in C Op. 25c 1984, The Sword (symphonic poem) Op. 33 1982, Easter Cantata (text by Semuel Tang) Op. 38 1986; Psalm 22-A Cantata in Baroque Style Op. 43c 1988, Piano Concerto in G; ballets: The Little Match Girl Op. 24 1978, A Dream of Dun Huang Op. 29 1980, The Special Orchestra Album 1997. *Honours:* Yale Alumni Asscn Prize, Yale Univ. 1986, Skills for Change New Pioneer Award, Ontario 2004.

HUANG, Zhun; Chinese composer; b. 25 June 1926, Huang Yan County, Zhe Jang Province. *Education:* studied with Xian Xinghai and others. *Career:* singer (mezzo-soprano) 1941–42; composer, Peking Film Studio, 1949–51; composer and music director at Shanghai Film Studio, 1951–87; mem. standing cttee of Chinese Musicians' Association; Vice-Chairman of China Film Music Society; Committee of Shanghai Artists Association; Standing Committee of Chinese Music Copyright Society. *Compositions:* over 40 film scores which include Old Man and Nymph, 1956; Red Women Soldiers, 1960; Sisters on Stage, 1964; Horsekeeper, 1982; numerous television music and songs. *Publications:* Selected songs of Huang Zhun; Life and Melodies; Music and My Life. *Honours:* theme song for Red Women Soldiers, chosen as one of the 20th-century masterpieces of Chinese Music, 1989; winner, 50th anniversary of Chinese television and films music prize, 1999. *Address:* Apmt 9C, 34 Fu Xing Xi Lu, Shanghai 200031, People's Republic of China.

HUANGLONG, Pan; Taiwanese composer; b. 9 Sept. 1945, Puli. *Education:* National Taiwan University, studied with Ulrich Lehmann in Zürich, Helmut Lachenmann in Hannover, Berlin Hochschule der Kunste with Isang Yun. *Career:* Prof., National Institute of Arts in Taipei 1981–; founded Modern Music Centre 1984; co-founded Taiwan branch of ISCM 1989. *Compositions:* Night-Mooring near a Maple Bridge for orchestra 1974, Bird's Eye View for marimba and vibraphone 1977, Metempsychose for five solo strings and orchestra 1977, String Quartet 1977, Paradise for orchestra 1978, Enlightenment for ensemble 1979, Clarinet Quartet 1980, String Quartet No. 2 1981, Cello Concerto 1997, Concerto for cello and three instruments 1997, Totem and Taboo for six percussion 1997, East and West for ensemble 1998, Solo I for harpsichord 1998; series: Expelling Yearnings 1975–76, Elements of Change 1979–86, Kaleidoscope 1986–95, Formosa Landscape 1987–95, Labyrinth Promenade 1988–98, Ying-Yong 1992–95. *Address:* c/o CHA, Second Floor, No. 7 Ching Dao East Road, Taipei, Taiwan.

HUBER, Gerold; German pianist; b. 1961, Straubing, Bavaria. *Education:* Munich Hochschule für Musik. *Career:* lied accompanist, has appeared at many festivals including Schubertiades, Schwarzenberg, Austria and Vilabertran, Spain, Rheingau Musikfestival, Schleswig-Holstein Festival; also featured in festivals in Cheltenham, England and Saintes, France; has performed at Cologne Philharmonic Hall, Frankfurt's Alte Oper, Leipzig Gewandhaus, Vienna Konzerthaus, Konzertgebouw Amsterdam, Wigmore Hall, London and Frick Collection, New York; solo performances of Bach, Beethoven, Schubert and Brahms. *Recordings include:* Schubert's Winterreise (Echo Klassik Award) 2002, Schubert's Die schöne Müllerin (Echo Klassik Award) 2004. *Honours:* Prix Int. Pro Musicis, Paris 1998, prizewinner, Johann Sebastian Bach Int. Piano Competition, Saarbrücken. *Address:*

Gumstrasse 19, 82152 Planegg, Germany (office). *Telephone:* (89) 47099433 (office). *E-mail:* ger.huber@web.de (office). *Website:* www.gerold-huber.de.

HUBER, Klaus; Swiss composer; b. 30 Nov. 1924, Berne. *Education:* Zürich Conservatory with Stefi Geyer and Willy Burkhard, studied with Boris Blacher in Berlin. *Career:* taught violin, Zürich Conservatory from 1950, Lucerne Conservatory 1960–63, Basle Music Acad. from 1961. *Compositions:* orchestral: Invention und Choral 1956, Litania instrumentalis 1957, Terzen-Studie 1958, Alveare vernat 1967, James Joyce Chamber Music 1967, Tenebrae 1967, Tempora for violin and orchestra 1970, Turna 1974, Zwischenspiel 1986, Lamentationes 1994; choral: Quem terra 1955, Das Te Deum Laudamus Deutsch 1956, Antiphonische Kantate 1956, Soliloquia 1959–64, Cuius legibus rotantur poli 1960, Musik zu eines Johannes-der-Taufer Gottesdienst 1965, Kleine Deutsche Messe 1969, ...inwendig voller figur... after the Apocalypse and Durer 1971, Hiob xix 1971; vocal: Abendkantate 1952, Kleine Tauf Kantate für Christof 1952, six Kleine Vokalisen 1955, Der Abend ist mein Buch 1955, Oratorio Mechtildis 1957, Des Engls Anredung an der Seele 1957, Auf die ruhige Nacht-Zeit 1958, Askese 1966, Psalm of Christ 1967, Grabschrift 1967, Der Mensch 1968, Traumgesicht 1968, ...ausgespant... 1972, Jot oder Wann kommt der Herr zuruck (opera) 1973, Im Pardies (opera pieces) 1975, A Prayer on a Prayer for women's voices and ensemble 1996, Umkehr–im Licht Sein for mezzo, chorus and ensemble 1997; instrumental: Ciacona for organ 1954, Concerto per la camerata 1955, In Memoriam Willy Burkhard for organ 1955, Partita 1955, Noctes intelligibis lucis for oboe and harpsichord 1961, Moteti-Cantiones for string quartet 1963, six Miniaturen 1963, In te Domine spervai for organ 1964, Sabeth 1967, Ascensus for flute, cello and piano 1969, three Kleine Meditationen for string trio and harp 1969, Ein Hauch von Unzeit I–III 1972, Chamber Concerto for piano and ensemble 1994, Ecce homines for string quintet 1998, L'ombre de notre âge for ensemble 1999. *Honours:* first prize ISCM Competition, Rome (for Die Engels Anredung an die Seele) 1959, Arnold Bax Soc. Medal 1962, Beethoven Prize of Bonn (for Tenebrae) 1970.

HUBER, Nicolaus A.; German composer; b. 15 Dec. 1939, Passau. *Education:* studied in Munich with Gunter Bialas, at Darmstadt with Stockhausen and in Venice with Luigi Nono. *Career:* Professor at the Folkwanghochschule, Essen from 1974. *Compositions include:* Spärenmusik, for orchestra, 1981; 6 Bagatellen, for 10 instruments and tape, 1981; Nocturnes, for orchestra, 1984; La force du vestige, for ensemble, 1985; Vier Stücke, for orchestra and tape, 1986; Doubles, mit einem beweglichhen ton, for string quartet, 1987; Clash Music, for cymbals, 1988; Tote Metren, for baritone and ensemble, 1989; Off enes Fragment, for soprano and ensemble, 1991; First Play Mozart, for flute, 1993; En face d'en face, for orchestra and tape, 1994; Disappearances, for piano, 1995; Sein als Einspruch, for 8 solo voices, 1997;... in die Stille, for cello, 1998; Covered with Music, for soprano and ensemble, 1998; Ach, des Erhabene... beträubte Fragmente, for double chorus, 1999; Mixed Media works, including Eröffnung und Zertrümmerung, for ensemble and tape, 1992.

HUBER-HERING, Vita, DPhil; Austrian opera director; b. 27 Sept. 1938, Salzburg. *Education:* Univ. of Vienna. *Career:* Asst, Landestheater Darmstadt, Germany 1963–71; Producer, Staatstheater Wiesbaden, Germany 1972–75, Staatstheater Darmstadt 1976–81; Chief Producer, Städtische Bühnen Augsburg, Germany 1981–82, Staatstheater Darmstadt 1982–84, Staatsoper Hamburg, Germany 1984–86, Deutsche Oper am Rhein, Düsseldorf-Duisburg, Germany 1986–. *Publications:* Ein großer Herr, Fürst Pückler (co-author) 1968, Flirt und Flitter, Lebensbilder aus der Bühnenwelt 1970, Applaus für den Souffleur, Teather-Anekdoten 1973; trans of operas and plays. *Address:* Deutsche Oper am Rhein, Heinrich-Heine-Allee 16A, 4000 Düsseldorf, Germany (office).

HUBERMAN, Lina; violinist; b. 1955, Moscow, Russia. *Education:* Moscow Conservatoire with Yanketevich. *Career:* mem., Prokofiev Quartet, founded at the Moscow Festival of World Youth and the International Quartet Competition at Budapest; many concerts in the former Soviet Union and on tour to Czechoslovakia, Germany, Australia, the USA, Canada, Spain, Japan and Italy; repertoire includes works by Haydn, Mozart, Beethoven, Schubert, Debussy, Ravel, Tchaikovsky, Bartók and Shostakovich.

HUDEČEK, Václav; Czech violinist; b. 7 June 1952, Rozmital pod Třemšínem; m. Eva Trejtnarova 1977. *Education:* Acad. of Performing Arts, Prague, studied with David Oistrakh in Moscow. *Career:* debut with Royal Philharmonic Orchestra in London 1967; soloist with Czech Philharmonic Orchestra 1984–90, Royal Philharmonic Orchestra, London, Berlin Philharmonic, Leipzig Gewandhaus Orchestra, NHK Orchestra of Tokyo; concert tours in Europe, Japan and USA since London debut, and tours in Europe, USA, Japan and Australia; f. School for Talented Young Violinists in Czech Repub.; mem. Central Cttee, Union of Czech Composers and Concert Artists; mem. Asscn of Czech Musicians. *Recordings include:* Bach: Concertos, Bravo Vivaldi, Czech Christmas – Eva Urbanová, Drdla/Sarasate/Hubay/Lehár/ Ravel, Dvorák: Compositions for Violin and Piano, Dvorák: Concerto for Violin and Orchestra in A minor, Op. 53, Guitar: Prague Guitar Concertos, Haydn: Sitkovetsky, Davidovich, Hudeček play Haydn, Mendelssohn-Bartholdy/ Sibelius: Violin Concertos, Mozart: The Famous Violin Concertos, Music for Weddings, P.I. Tchaikovsky, J. Sibelius: Violin Concertos, Paganini: Hudeček and Brabec play Paganini, Prokofjev/Tchaikovsky, Souvenir, Václav Hudeček – Violin Recital, Supraphon Stars 2000, Tartini/Paganini/Gragnani/Giuliani, Triny – Gipsy Streams, Trojan: Suites from the Films, Violin: Hudeček II

Giardino di Musica, Vivaldi: Concertos for Various Instruments, Vivaldi: Le Quattro Stagioni (Record of the Year 1992). *Honours:* Award for Outstanding Labour 1978, Artist of Merit of Czechoslovakia 1980, Supraphon Gold Record Prize 1994, recognized by Pres. Vaclav Klaus through the Nat. Award for Achievement in the Area of Culture and the Arts 2007, Award of the City of Prague 2012. *Address:* Londynskà 25, 120 00 Prague 2, Czech Republic. *Telephone:* (323) 640225 (home). *E-mail:* violin@vaclav-hudecek.cz. *Website:* www.vaclav-hudecek.cz.

HUDSON, Benjamin; violinist; b. 14 June 1950, Decatur, IL, USA. *Education:* studied in New York. *Career:* co-founder, Schoenberg String Quartet 1977, renamed Columbia String Quartet 1978; has performed many modern works, including the premieres of Charles Wuorinen's Archangel 1978 with trombonist, David Taylor, and 2nd String Quartet 1980, Berg's Lyric Suite in its version with soprano, Bethany Beardslee, New York 1979, and Roussakis' Ephemeris 1979; further premieres include quartets by Morton Feldman 1980, Wayne Peterson 1984 and Larry Bell 1985. *Recordings include:* String Quartet No. 3 by Lukas Foss and Ned Rorem's Mourning Song with baritone, William Parker. *Honours:* NEA grants 1979–81.

HUDSON, John; British singer (tenor); b. 1967, Barnsley, Yorkshire, England. *Education:* Guildhall School with Laura Sarti, studied with Josephine Veasey. *Career:* debut with ENO as Verdi's Macduff, 1993; season 1993–94 with ENO as Rodolfo, Nadir in The Pearl Fishers and Don Ottavio; Alfredo in La Traviata for WNO and for Auckland Opera, New Zealand; concerts include Beethoven's Ninth at the Barbican and in Paris, Messiah in Ottawa with Trevor Pinnock and Mozart's Requiem with the English Chamber Orchestra; 50th-anniversary concert with ENO and television appearance with Lesley Garrett in Viva la Diva, on BBC 2; season 1996–97 as Alfredo and Nadir with ENO; season 1998 as Des Grieux in Manon and Robert Dudley in Mary Stuart, for ENO. *Current Management:* Ingpen & Williams Ltd, 7 St George's Court, 131 Putney Bridge Road, London, SW15 2PA, England.

HUDSON, Paul; singer (bass); b. 24 June 1946, Barnsley, England. *Education:* Royal Coll. of Music and the London Opera Centre. *Career:* debut at Sadler's Wells Opera 1969, in the premiere of Williamson's Lucky Peter's Journey; many appearances with ENO and the WNO, in works by Puccini, Britten and Wagner; Opera North 1979, in Der fliegende Holländer and Peter Grimes; guest appearances elsewhere in Baroque and contemporary music; frequent concert engagements; season 1998 as Rocco in Fidelio for English Touring Opera and Cacique in Il Guarany by Gomes for Chelsea Opera. *Recordings include:* Music by Stravinsky and La fanciulla del West; Laertes in Hamlet by Thomas; Scenes from Gilbert and Sullivan.

HUDSON, Richard, RDI; British stage designer; b. 9 June 1954, Rhodesia (now Zimbabwe). *Education:* Wimbledon School of Art. *Career:* designs for ENO include The Force of Destiny, The Marriage of Figaro; premieres of Judith Weir's A Night at the Chinese Opera (Kent Opera) and The Vanishing Bridegroom (Scottish Opera); Glyndebourne debut 1992, The Queen of Spades, followed by Eugene Onegin, the British stage premiere of Rossini's Ermione, and Manon Lescaut 1997; Die Meistersinger von Nürnberg at Covent Garden 1993; further engagements with I Puritani at La Fenice, Venice, The Rake's Progress for the Lyric Opera Chicago, Lucia di Lammermoor at Zürich and Munich, Rossini's L'Inganno felice at the Pesaro Festival; Samson et Dalila at the Metropolitan Opera, New York; The Rake's Progress at the Saito Kinen Festival, Japan; Ernani and Guillaume Tell at the Vienna Staatsoper season 1997–98; other designs for Manon (Opera North), Mary Stuart (Scottish Opera), Les Contes d'Hoffmann (Staatsoper, Vienna); Così fan tutte, (Glyndebourne) 1998; season 2001–02 with Carlisle Floyd's Of Mice and Men at Bregenz, Houston and Washington; The Cunning Little Vixen for Opera North; Les Vêpres Siciliennes and Khovanshchina in Paris; Tamerlano and Idomeneo in Florence; Benvenuto Cellini in Zürich; Peter Grimes in Amsterdam; Rhinegold, Valkyrie, Siegfried and Twilight of the Gods for ENO 2004–05; The Fall of the House of Usher at Bregenz 2006, The Makropulos Case at Copenhagen 2006; costumes for Death in Venice at Aldeburgh and Bregenz festivals and La Bohème, Athens 2007, for La Forza del Destino, Vienna and Rushes, Royal Ballet, London 2008; Rigoletto for Wiener Volksoper 2009, Pictures from an Exhibition, Kafka's Monkey, Young Vic 2009, Goldberg Variations, Linbury Studio 2009, Ruddigore, Opera North 2010, Armida, Metropolitan Opera 2010, The Nutcracker, American Ballet Theater 2010, Die Entführung aus dem Serail, Rome, Romeo and Juliet, Nat. Ballet of Canada, Le Coq d'Or and La Bayadère for Royal Danish Ballet; British Scenography Commr to Org. Internationale des Scénographes, Techniciens et Architectes de Théâtre; Fellow, Royal Welsh Coll. of Music and Drama 2010. *Honours:* Dr hc (Surrey) 2005; Royal Designer for Industry, Laurence Olivier Award 1988, Tony Award 1998, Prague Quadreniale Gold Medal for set design 2003, Companion, Liverpool Inst. for Performing Arts 2009. *Current Management:* c/o Judy Daish Associates, 2 St Charles Place, London, W10 6EG, England.

HUFFSTODT, Karen; singer (soprano); b. 31 Dec. 1954, Peru, Illinois, USA. *Education:* Illinois Wesleyan and Northwestern Universities. *Career:* sang with the New York City Opera from 1982 as Lehar's Merry Widow, Micaela, Violetta and Donna Anna; Santa Fe Opera in 1984 as the Soldier's Wife in the US premiere of Henze's We Come to The River, returning in 1989 as L'Ensoleillad in Massenet's Chérubin; other engagements with Chicago Opera as Magda in La Rondine and Fiordiligi, Illinois Opera in title role in Mary,

Queen of Scots by Thea Musgrave, Washington Opera in the premiere of Menotti's Goya in 1986, Cologne Opera as Constanze, Agrippina, Donna Anna and Mozart's Countess, and Metropolitan Opera as Violetta and Rosalinda in season 1989–90; other roles include Musetta at Los Angeles and Hamburg, Thais at Paris Opéra, Nancy and Toulouse, Amalia in I Masnadieri by Verdi for Australian Opera, Salome at Lyon, Agathe and Arabella at Catania, and Odabella in Attila for Opera North in 1990 and Covent Garden in 1991; season 1992 as Tosca at Antwerp, Turandot at Lyon, and Chrysothemis at the Opéra Bastille Paris; opened season at La Scala in 1993 as Spontini's Vestale; sang Strauss's Ariadne at the Opéra Comique, Salome at the Bastille Opéra and Alice Ford at Antwerp in 1994; Season 1996–97 as Sieglinde at Covent Garden and Salome at San Francisco; season 1998 as Elisabeth at Palermo, Isolde at Monte Carlo and Katerina Izmailova at Florence; season 1999–2000 as Katerina Izmailova at Dresden, the Walküre Brünnhilde for Geneva Opera and Kundry in Washington; Klementina in Sancta Susanna, Montpellier Opera 2009. *Recordings include:* Salomé in a French language version of Strauss's opera. *Current Management:* Theateragentur Heidi Steinhaus, Auerfeldstr. 26, 81541 Munich, Germany. *E-mail:* Steinhaus@heidi-steinhaus .de. *Website:* www.heidi-steinhaus.de.

HUFSCHMIDT, Wolfgang; German composer; b. 15 March 1934, Mülheim. *Education:* studied church music and composition at Essen. *Career:* church organist at Essen 1954–68; Lecturer in Composition 1971–88, Folkwang Hochschule; Rektor 1988–96. *Compositions include:* Mass, for soprano and chorus, 1961; Easter Story, 1964; Meissner Te Deum, 1968; Verwandlungen, for string quartet, 1969; Stephanus, mixed media, 1972; Solo, for violin, 1972; Agende for 4 choruses and ensemble, 1973; Trio, I–IV, 1970–95; We Shall Overcome for speaker, low voice, chorus and 9 instruments, 1984; Lieder ohne Worte, 24 Klavierstücke, with tape, 1986; Double Woodwind quintet 1989; an E for low voice and piano, 1995. *Honours:* Ruhr Prize, Mülheim 1973.

HUGGETT, Monica; British violinist; *Artistic Director, Historical Performance Graduate Program, Juilliard School;* b. 16 May 1953, London. *Education:* Royal Acad. of Music with Manoug Parikian, studied with Sigiswald Kuijken, Gustav Leonhardt and Ton Koopman. *Career:* co-founder, Amsterdam Baroque Orchestra 1980, leader until 1987; many performances on authentic gut-string violins with such ensembles as the Hanover Band, Acad. of Ancient Music, Raglan Baroque Players and Hausmusik; worldwide tours as soloist, dir and chamber musician in a repertoire extending from the late Renaissance to the Romantic with performances and recordings of Mozart, Beethoven, Schubert, Mendelssohn and the concertos of Vivaldi and Bach; mem. Sonnerie ensemble, currently Dir 1982–; played the Beethoven Concerto with the Orchestra of the Age of Enlightenment under Ivan Fischer at the QEH 1991; the Mendelssohn Concerto under Charles Mackerras 1992; Prof. of Baroque and Classical Violin, Hochschule für Kunste in Bremen; Artistic Dir of the Portland Baroque Orchestra, USA, Irish Baroque Orchestra, Dublin; founded The Greate Consort 1995; Artistic Dir, Historical Performance Graduate Program, Juilliard School 2008–. *Recordings include:* Symphonies by Beethoven with the Hanover Band (as director), Vivaldi La Stravaganza and Schubert Octet with the Academy of Ancient Music, Vivaldi La Cetra and Schubert Trout Quintet with the Raglan Baroque Players and Hausmusik, Rameau Pièces de Clavécin en Concerts and Corelli Violin Sonatas op 5 with Trio Sonnerie and Vivaldi Four Seasons, Mozart Violin Concertos, Bach Violin Concertos with the Amsterdam Baroque Orchestra, Beethoven Concerto and Mendelssohn Concerto with the Orchestra of the Age of Enlightenment, Bach Sonatas and Partitas for solo violin (Gramophone Editor's Choice Award 1997), Biber Violin Sonatas (Gramophone Award for Best Instrumental Recording 2002). *Honours:* Hon. Fellow, RAM; Vantaa Baroque Energy Prize, Finland 2005. *Address:* Music Division, Juilliard School, 60 Lincoln Center Plaza, New York, NY 10023-6588, USA (office). *Telephone:* (212) 799-5000 (office). *Website:* www.juilliard.edu/college/music/historical_performance .html (office); www.sonnerie.org.uk.

HUGH, Tim; British cellist; b. 1965, England. *Education:* Yale Univ., studied with William Pleeth and Jacqueline du Pré. *Career:* fmr solo cellist with the BBC Symphony Orchestra and joint principal with the London Symphony Orchestra; many concerts with the Liverpool Philharmonic Orchestra, the Royal and BBC Philharmonics, Bournemouth Symphony Orchestra and Sinfonietta, and London Mozart Players; appearances at the Leipzig Gewandhaus, La Scala Milan and Amsterdam Concertgebouw; solo cello suites by Bach and Britten at 1994 Glasgow Mayfest, tour of the UK with the Polish State Philharmonic and engagements at Aldeburgh and the London Proms; chamber music by Fauré and others with Domus and the Solomon Trio. *Recordings include:* Britten's Suites; Sonatas by Beethoven and Grieg with Yonty Solomon; C.P. Bach and Boccherini Concertos. *Honours:* prizewinner Tchaikovsky International Competition, Moscow 1990. *Website:* www.timhugh.com.

HUGHES, Martin Glyn; pianist; b. 23 March 1950, Hemel Hempstead, England; one s. one d. *Education:* Salisbury Cathedral Choir School, Bryanston School, Paris Conservatoire, France, Moscow Conservatory, Russia, studied with Yvonne Lefebure, Wilhelm Kempff. *Career:* debut at Wigmore Hall, London, England 1972; Proms 1972; French radio and television 1972; Cheltenham Festival 1973; Making a Name, BBC television 1974; tour of USSR 1974; RPO and London Symphony Orchestra debuts 1975; Chichester and Llandaff Festivals 1975; recital and concerto debut at QEH 1977; tours and radio recitals in Portugal and Germany 1977; Beethoven Sonata cycle 1979; regular Radio 3 broadcasts, solo appearances including:

Royal Festival Hall, European tours 1980–; founder 1984, Artistic Dir of Music, Fens Festival and summer school 1984, 1986; Fengate Music trust; Dir, Annual Summer School, Val de Saire, France 1988, 1989; Bath Festival 1983, 1985, 1986; mem., Kreutzer Piano Trio 1985; tours of USA, Israel 1987–88; Prof., Hochschule für der Kunste, Berlin, Germany 1991–; tour of Japan 1993; guest teacher, Acad. of Music, Bucharest 1993–95. *Publications:* Russian School of Piano Playing (ed. and translator) 1976, contrib. chapter to Performing Beethoven 1994. *Honours:* bronze medal Marguerite Long Competition 1969, British Council Scholar 1970–71, Arts Council of Great Britain Award 1975, Hon. MMus (Univ. of Surrey) 1991.

HUGHES, Owain Arwel, CBE; British conductor; *Music Director, National Youth Orchestra of Wales and Camerata Wales*; b. 21 March 1942, Cardiff, Wales; m. Jean Bowen Lewis 1966; one s. one d. *Education:* Univ. Coll., Cardiff, Royal Coll. of Music with Adrian Boult and Harvey Philips 1964–66, and with Kempe in London and Haitink in Amsterdam. *Career:* guest conductor with all UK orchestras and choirs esp. Hallé Orchestra; Assoc. Conductor BBC Nat. Orchestra of Wales 1980–86, Philharmonic Orchestra 1984–90; Music Dir Huddersfield Choral Soc. 1980–86; Principal Conductor Aalborg Symphony Orchestra 1994–99; Guest Conductor throughout Scandinavia esp. Danish Radio Symphony Orchestra, Helsinki Philharmonic Orchestra, Århus Symphony Orchestra; Founder and Artistic Dir Welsh Proms 1986–; Principal Assoc. Conductor Royal Philharmonic Orchestra 2004–08; Music Dir Nat. Youth Orchestra of Wales 2003–, Camerata Wales 2005–; Principal Guest Conductor, Cape Town Philharmonic Orchestra 2007–; TV Presenter Conductor Music for the Masses and Much Loved Music Show (BBC) television; 50th anniversary VE Day, 60th anniversary Holocaust Memorial Palace of Westminster; on radio Royal Albert Hall concert series (Classic FM). *Television:* performances of Mahler 8, Verdi Requiem, Handel Messiah, Mendelssohn Elijah, Walton Belshazzar's Feat, Rossini Stabat Mater, Cherubini Requiem, Sibelius Kullervo Symphony. *Recordings include:* Music of Delius and Vaughan-Williams London Symphony (Philharmonia Orchestra), 14 Symphonies, orchestral works and concertos by Holmboe (Aalborg Symphony Orchestra), Rachmaninov Symphonies (Royal Scottish Nat. Orchestra), Rachmaninov Piano Concertos (Malmö Symphony Orchestra), Holst Planets, Choral Classics, Opera Classics, Verdi Requiem and Messiah (Royal Philharmonic Orchestra), Carols Album and Hymns Album (Huddersfield Choral, both gold discs), Vaughan-Williams Hymns Album and Vaughan-Williams Carols Album (Cardiff Festival Choir), Sibelius Symphony No. 1 and Sullivan Irish Symphony (BBC Concert Orchestra), Ludwig Nielsen Oratorio Moses and Hermann D. Kottel Oratorio Tower of Babel (Danish Radio Symphony Orchestra and Chorus), Tchaikovsky Piano Concertos, Borressen Symphonies and Norby Orchestral Works (Aalborg Symphony Orchestra). *Honours:* Hon. DMus (Univ. of Wales, Council for National Academic Awards, London); Fellowships (Univ. Coll., Cardiff, Univ. of Wales Trinity Coll., Royal Welsh Coll. of Music and Drama, Univ. Coll., Lampeter, Univ. Coll., Bangor). *Current Management:* c/o Sinead O'Carroll. *Telephone:* (1753) 855432. *Fax:* (1753) 855432. *E-mail:* sinead.ocarroll@btinternet.com. *Website:* www.sineadocarroll.co.uk; www.owainarwelhughes.co.uk.

HUI, He; Chinese singer (soprano); b. 1972, Shanghai. *Career:* debuted as mezzo-soprano as Dorabella in Cosí fan tutte, Shanghai 1995; debuted as soprano as Cio-Cio-San in Madama Butterfly 1996; Prin. Soloist, Grand Theatre, Shanghai; operatic appearances include: Mascagni, Cavalleria Rusticana 1999, Verdi, Aida, Los Angeles Opera 2001, Arena di Verona 2007, 2009, Puccini, Turandot, Washington Opera 2001, Arena di Verona 2009, Puccini, Tosca, Teatro Regio, Parma 2002, Verdi, Alzira, Parma 2002, Verdi, Un Ballo in maschera, Teatro Filarmonico, Verona 2002. *Honours:* 42nd Int. Voci Verdiane Competition First Prize, Bussetto 2001. *Current Management:* Zemsky Green Artists Management, 104 West 73rd Street, Suite 1, New York, NY 10023, USA. *Telephone:* (212) 579-6700. *Fax:* (212) 579-4723. *E-mail:* bzemsky@zemskygreen.com; agreen@zemskygreen.com; jmitchell@zemskygreen.com. *Website:* www.zemskygreen.com.

HULA, Pavel; Czech violinist and conductor; *Artistic Director, Praha Camerata*; b. 23 Jan. 1952, Prague; m. Helena Sirlova 1976, one d. *Education:* Acad. of Music Arts, Prague. *Career:* debut at Prague Spring Festival 1976; First Violin, Kocian Quartet 1975–2010, with performances at over 3,200 concerts in 33 countries; First Violin, Prazak Quartet 2010–15; broadcasts on radio and TV; Wigmore Hall debut 1992; Artistic Dir Praha Camerata (String Orchestra) 2001–; Prof., Acad. of Performing Arts, Prague 2006–. *Recordings include:* Virtuoso Violin Duets, Mozart's String Quartets, Dvořák's String Quartets, Haydn: Quartets, Hindemith's String Quartets, over 50 CDs for Praga Digitals. *Honours:* First Prize, Kocian Violin Competition 1963, 1964, Second Prize, Concertino Praga, Radio Competition 1969, Prize, Soc. of Chamber Music of Czech Philharmonic 1981, Grand Prix du Disque, Acad. Charles Cros, Paris 1997. *Address:* Secská 1875/11, 100 00 Prague 10, Czech Republic (home). *Website:* www.concerts-prague.cz/Kocian (office); www.prazakquartet.com (office); www.pragacamerata.com (office).

HULL, Eric; Canadian conductor; b. 1963. *Education:* Vienna Hochschüle für Musik. *Career:* asst at La Scala, Toronto Symphony, Florence and Salzburg Festivals; conductor of opera and concerts with the Berlin Radio, Naples (Teatro San Carlo), Rome, Lisbon, Moscow, Venice (La Fenice), Verona, Genoa, Toronto, Monte-Carlo, Madrid (Teatro Real), Las Palmas, Bilbao, Oviedo, Lausanne, Vienna; La Scala Milan from 1988, with the premiere of Donatoni's Il Velo Dissotto, La Clemenza di Tito, Iphigénie en Tauride and Pergolesi's Lo Frate 'nnamorato; Edition of Salieri's L'Europa Riconoscuita and Adam's Giselle for La Scala, Piccinni's L'Americano published by Ricordi; Belcanto Gala in Moscow, and engagements with the Milan Symphony and Orchestre Philharmonique de Monte Carlo; modern premiere of Piccinni's L'Americano at Martina Franca 1996 and Cimarosa's Armida Immaginaria 1997. *Recordings include:* L'Americano Incivilito. *Telephone:* 99-408052 (Malta, mobile) (office). *E-mail:* erichull@onvol.net (office). *Current Management:* c/o Opera-Connection Alste & Mödersheim, Leibnizstrasse 94, 10625 Berlin, Germay. *Telephone:* (30) 31996688. *Fax:* (30) 31809739. *E-mail:* info@opera-connection.com. *Website:* www.opera-connection.com. *E-mail:* info@erichullconductor.com (office). *Website:* www.erichullconductor.com (office).

HULMANOVA, Stefania; singer (soprano); b. 20 Jan. 1920, Dolné Dubové, Czechoslovakia; m. Cyril Hulman 1943, two s. *Education:* State Conservatory, Bratislava. *Career:* debut as Rusalka in Dvořák's Rusalka, State Theatre, Kosice 1948; soloist, Opera of the State Theatre, Kosice 1948–51; soloist, Opera of the Slovak National Theatre, Bratislava 1952–79; core repertoire includes Julia in Jakobin by A. Dvořák, Marenka in The Bartered Bride, Vendulka in The Kiss by Smetana, Halka in Halka by Moniuszko, Santuzza in Cavalleria Rusticana by Mascagni, Countess in The Marriage of Figaro, Aida, Nella in Gianni Schicchi; numerous other roles performed include Leonora in Trovatore, Elisabeth de Valois in Don Carlos, Desdemona in Otello, all by Verdi; Tosca; guest performances include The Whirlpool by Suchon at Dresden; Tosca, Moscow; Svätopluk, Perugia, Italy; concerts in Peking, China, Hanoi, Viet Nam; The Whirlpool, Budapest, Hungary; hon. mem. Opera of the Slovak National Theatre.

HUMBLET, Ans; Dutch singer (soprano); b. 17 Sept. 1957, Maastricht. *Education:* studied with Elisabeth Ksoll and at Amsterdam. *Career:* appearances with Netherlands Opera from 1983 and Wuppertal Opera 1986–90, in such roles as the Queen of Night, Blondchen, Marie in Zar und Zimmermann, Woglinde, Despina and Musetta; sang Kunigunde in the German premiere of Bernstein's Candide at Wuppertal 1990; Enschede Holland 1990 as Ninetta in Mozart's La Finta Giardiniera; guest appearances at Düsseldorf and Aachen as the Queen of Night, and at Mönchengladbach as Frasquita in Carmen; concert engagements in Beethoven's 9th, Mendelssohn's St Paul, Bruckner's Te Deum, Carmina Burana and Masses by Haydn and Mozart; broadcasts in The Netherlands, Germany and Belgium; engaged at Maastricht from 1990.

HUNKA, Pavlo, DipMus; British singer (bass); b. 7 April 1959, England. *Education:* Royal Northern College of Music with Joseph Ward. *Career:* has performed in concerts throughout the UK as soloist and conductor; Royal Albert Hall in London, 1988 in a concert celebrating 1000 years of Christianity in the Ukraine; opera debut as Melisso in a 1989 production of Handel's Alcina at the RNCM; has also sung Theseus in A Midsummer Night's Dream and Philip II in Don Carlos with the RNCM; professional opera debut as Basilio in Il Barbiere di Siviglia with Welsh National Opera, 1990; engagements as Rangoni in Boris Godunov for Basle Opera and Dulcamara in L'Elisir d'amore; other roles include Colline in La Bohème and Prince Gremin in Eugene Onegin; on contract to Basel Stadttheater, Switzerland; Salzburg 1994–95, in Boris Godunov and Elektra, Bregenz Festival, 1995 as Pizarro; Bonn 1995–96, as Leporello and Tomsky in The Queen of Spades; Basle Opera 1996, as Rigoletto; season 2000–01 as Verdi's Renato at Bregenz, Telramund in Munich, Wozzeck for Dallas Opera and Creon in Oedipus Rex at Naples; Weber's Euryanthe at the London Proms, 2002. *Honours:* Ricordi Opera Prize, Peter Moores Foundation and Wolfson Foundation Scholarships. *Current Management:* Artists Management Zurich, Rütistrasse 52, 8044 Zürich-Gockhausen, Switzerland. *Telephone:* (1) 8218957. *Fax:* (1) 8210127. *Website:* www.artistsman.com.

HUNT, Alexandra, BA, BS; American singer (soprano), librettist and libretto translator; b. 1940. *Education:* Vassar College, Juilliard School of Music, Sorbonne University, Paris, France. *Career:* debut as Marie in La Scala's first production of Wozzeck in German, 1971, conducted by Claudio Abbado; sang title role of Lulu at Metropolitan Opera and Katya Kabanova sung in Czech, Janáček Festival, Brno; Jenůfa at Lincoln Center, NY; soprano soloist in Penderecki Passion According to St Luke, Philadelphia Orchestra; Amelia in Ballo in Maschera, Providence, RI, and Bucharest; Title role of Tosca in Bulgaria, Romania and Czechoslovakia; sang Marie in Wozzeck at Hamburg Staatsoper; Lady Macbeth in Macbeth at Florentine Opera and Kentucky Opera; soprano soloist in Mahler's Fourth Symphony, Bogotá Filarmonica; in Beethoven's Ninth Symphony, Omaha and Des Moines Symphonies; many other roles. *Recordings:* Songs of John Alden Carpenter, Charles T. Griffes and Edward MacDowell. *Publications:* New English Translation of Mozart's Don Giovanni and Cosi fan tutte. *Address:* 170 West 74th Street, Apt 1106, New York, NY 10023, USA.

HUNT, Fionnuala; Irish violinist; b. 1960, Belfast, Northern Ireland; m. Raymond Blake. *Education:* Ulster Coll. of Music, Royal Coll. of Music, Vienna Hochschule für Musik with Wolfgang Schneiderhan. *Career:* leader and soloist with the Vienna Chamber; former mem., Bavarian State Opera Orchestra in Munich; co-leader of the RTE Symphony Orchestra in Dublin; guest leader, Ulster Orchestra; duo recitals with pianist sister, Una Hunt, performing throughout Ireland, Austria, Germany, Czechoslovakia, Italy, UK; mem., Dublin Piano Trio; solo appearances with the Nat. Symphony Orchestra of Ireland, RTE Concert Orchestra, Ulster Orchestra; played Lutoslawski's Partita at Maltings Concert Hall, Snape; Artistic Dir and Leader, Irish Chamber Orchestra 1995–2002. *Honours:* Hon. DMus (Queen's Univ., Belfast) 2007. *Current Management:* c/o Owen/White Management,

Flat 6, 22 Brunswick Terrace, Hove, East Sussex BN3 1HJ, England. *Telephone:* (1273) 727127 (office). *Fax:* (1273) 527038 (office). *E-mail:* info@ owenwhitemanagement.com (office). *Website:* www.owenwhitemanagement .com (office); www.fionnualahunt.com (home).

HUNT, Gordon; British oboist and conductor; *Professor of Oboe, Guildhall School of Music and Drama;* b. 20 Nov. 1950, London, England. *Education:* Royal Coll. of Music, London with Terence MacDonagh. *Career:* fmr Prin., BBC Nat. Orchestra of Wales and London Philharmonic Orchestra; Prin. Oboist, Philharmonia Orchestra and London Chamber Orchestra; solo and chamber music appearances throughout Europe, USA, the Far East, S America, Australia and NZ; Music Dir, Swedish Chamber Winds 1991–97; Artistic Dir, Danish Chamber Players 2001–04; has often conducted the Danish Radio Sinfonietta; Prof. of Oboe, Dept of Wind, Brass and Percussion, Guildhall School of Music and Drama; Consultant Prof., RAM, London; mem. of jury, triennial Int. Oboe Competition, Japan; numerous radio and TV broadcasts; conducts and directs many orchestras and ensembles; gives masterclasses on six continents. *Recordings include:* all of Mozart's solo music, including Mozart Concerto, Mozart Sinfonia Concertante, Mozart Quartet and Quintets; Britten, Bax, Bliss 1997, Soliloquy 1998, 'elevazione' 2002, Richard Stauss Concerto (named finest version by Penguin CD Guide), Vivaldi Concerto in C Major, Saeverud Concerto, Sally Beamish – Tam Lin. *Honours:* Hon. ARAM. *Address:* Department of Wind, Brass and Percussion, Guildhall School of Music and Drama, Silk Street, Barbican, London, EC2Y 8DT, England (office). *E-mail:* gordonhunt@oboist.co.uk (office). *Website:* www .oboist.co.uk.

HUNT, Michael; British stage director; b. 1957, London, England. *Education:* Liverpool Univ. *Career:* debut with Gounod's Mireille for Liverpool Grand Opera; Artistic Dir, Cheltenham Arts Centre from 1980, staging a number of plays and Così fan tutte; directed the British premiere of Berwald's Queen of Golconda at Nottingham and The Rake's Progress at Cambridge; staff dir at ENO, directing Aida and Orpheus in the Underworld, also Madama Butterfly for the Education Unit; Oedipus Rex for Opera North; Rossini's Tancredi at Las Palmas; Der Freischütz in an outdoor touring production; Oedipus Rex and Iolanthe for Scottish Opera; La Traviata for Dublin; Figaro for British Youth Opera; world premieres of Giles Swayne's Le nozze di Cherubino and Harmonies of Hell; Artistic Dir, Bloomsbury Festival; Dir of Performing Arts, Riverside Studios in London; teacher, Royal Acad., Birmingham School of Music and various drama schools; in 1996 directed Puccini's La Bohème at the Royal Albert Hall; Dir Theatre Royal, Waterford 2004–06; CEO Wexford Festival Opera 2006–07; currently Instructor of Theatre, History and Performance Studies, Univ. of Virginia's College at Wise. *Current Management:* c/o Proscenium KG, Rudolfsplatz 12, 1010 Vienna, Austria. *E-mail:* nader@proscenium.at; berger@proscenium.at. *Website:* www.proscenium.at. *E-mail:* m_hunt@uvawise.edu (office). *Website:* www.wise.virginia.edu/arts/theater/faculty (office); www.michael-hunt.eu.

HUNZIKER, Bernhard, MA, PhD; Swiss singer (tenor), conductor, musicologist and academic; *University Professor, Universität für Musik und darstellende Kunst Wien;* b. 27 Aug. 1957, Thun. *Education:* studied with Paul Lohmann in Frankfurt and Wiesbaden, in Zürich with Irwin Gage, Munich with Ernst Haefliger and with Heather Harper and Peter Pears at Aldeburgh and London, studies in Church Music and Musicology in Zürich, postgraduate studies at Vienna Univ. of Music and Performing Arts. *Career:* Zürich Opera Studio 1987–88, Augsburg Opera, Athens Megaron, Lucerne, St Gallen, including solo appearances; has worked with conductors including Jesus Lopes-Cobos, Marc Soustrot, K.A. Rickenbacher, Helmut Rilling, Yehudi Menuhin; concert engagements in Switzerland, Austria, Italy, Germany and France, and several performances at the Israel Festival, Lucerne Festival, Opera Festival, Bad Hersfeld, Germany and Aldeburgh Festival; repertory includes works from Monteverdi, Bach, Mozart, Schubert to Britten, masses and oratorios; Evangelist and Arias in Bach's St Matthew Passion, conducted by M. Corboz 2004, F. Martin: In Terra Pax with Liverpool Philharmonic 2004, tour (Europe) with La petite bande under Sigiswald Kuijken, Bach St John Passion 2006, High Mass in B Minor 2008, St Matthew Passion 2009; Univ. Prof., Hochschule der Künste, Zürich, Universität für Musik und darstellende Kunst Wien, Vienna; Pres. European Voice Teachers Asscn (Swiss Section) 2001–08. *Recordings include:* Musikalische Exequien by H. Schütz; CD, Swiss Lieder by Schoeck, Huber and others 2001; Lieder Quartets by Swiss composers, Zürich Vocal Quartet; J.S. Bach's St John Passion, B Minor Mass, St Matthew Passion. *Honours:* Promotion Prize, Migros Company, Zurich 1983, Kiefer-Hablitzel-Prize 1985, Prize, Swiss Musicians Association 1987. *Address:* c/o Kirchgasse 15, 8001 Zürich, Switzerland (office); Universität für Musik und Darstellende Kunst Wien, Institut Antonio Salieri, Rennweg 8, 1030 Vienna, Austria (office). *Telephone:* (44) 2525802 (Zürich) (office); (1) 71155-4701 (Vienna) (office). *Fax:* (1) 71155-4799 (Vienna) (office). *E-mail:* bernhard-hunziker@bluewin.ch (home); bernhard.hunziker@zhdk.ch (office); hunziker@mdw.ac.at (office). *Website:* www.mdw.ac.at; operissimo.com.

HUREL, Philippe; composer; b. 24 July 1955, Domfront, France. *Education:* Paris Conservatoire with Betsy Jolas, studied with Tristan Murail, and at IRCAM electronic music studios, Paris. *Compositions include:* Eolia for flute 1982, Trames for strings 1982, Memento pour Marc for orchestra 1983, Diamants imaginaire, diamant lunaire for ensemble and electronics 1986, Pour l'image for 14 instruments 1987, Fragment de lune 1987, Mémoire vive for orchestra 1989, Remanences for 14 instruments 1992, La Celebration des invisibles (shadow theatre) 1992, Leçon des choses 1993, Pour Luigi for ensemble 1994, Kits for six percussion instruments and double bass 1996, ...a mèsure for flute and ensemble 1997. *Honours:* Siemens Prize, Munich 1995.

HURFORD, Peter John, OBE, MusB, MA, FRCO; British organist; b. 22 Nov. 1930, Minehead, Somerset, England; s. of Hubert John Hurford and Gladys Winifred James; m. Patricia Mary Matthews 1955; two s. one d. *Education:* Blundell's School, Royal Coll. of Music (Open Foundation Scholar), Jesus Coll., Cambridge (Organ Scholar) and pvt. studies with André Marchal, Paris. *Career:* commissioned into Royal Signals 1954–56; debut, Royal Festival Hall, London 1956; Organist and Choirmaster, Holy Trinity Church, Leamington Spa 1956–57; Dir of Music, Bablake School, Coventry 1956–57; Master of the Music, Cathedral and Abbey Church of St Alban 1958–78; freelance concert and recording organist 1978–98; Visiting Prof., Coll. Conservatory of Music, Cincinnati, USA 1967–68, Univ. of Western Ontario, Canada 1976–77; Acting Organist, St John's Coll. Cambridge 1979–80; Visiting Artist-in-Residence, Sydney Opera House 1980–82; Prof., RAM 1982–88; John Betts Fellow, Univ. of Oxford 1992–93; Decca recording artist 1977–; concerts in USA, Canada, Australia, NZ, Japan, Far East, Eastern and Western Europe 1958–98; f. St Albans Int. Organ Festival 1963, Artistic Dir 1963–78, Hon. Pres. 1978–; Pres. Inc. Asscn of Organists 1995–97; mem. Council Royal Coll. of Organists 1964–2003, Pres. 1980–82; Fellow, Royal School of Church Music 1977. *Compositions include:* organ music; Suite – Laudate Dominum, Chorale Preludes; choral music: The Communion Service, Series III, The Holy Eucharist, Rite 2 (for American Episcopal Church), music for the Daily Office, miscellaneous anthems, songs, carols, etc. *Recordings include:* complete organ works of J.S. Bach, Handel, F. Couperin, P. Hindemith, music of Franck, Mendelssohn; numerous recitals for BBC, including 34 commentated programmes of J.S. Bach's complete organ works 1980–82, Bach organ music cycle (Herald Angel Critics Award), 50th Edin. Int. Festival 1997. *Publications:* Making Music on the Organ 1988; contrib. to journals, numerous forewords. *Honours:* Hon. FRCM 1987; Hon. Fellow in Organ Studies, Univ. of Bristol 1997–98; Hon. Jesus Coll. Cambridge 2006; Hon. RAM 1982; Hon. DMus (Baldwin-Wallace Coll., Ohio, USA) 1981, (Bristol) 1992; Hon. DArts (Univ. of Hertfordshire) 2007; Gramophone Award 1979, Royal Coll. of Organists Medal 2013. *Address:* Broom House, St Bernard's Road, St Albans, Herts., AL3 5RA, England.

HURLEY, David, BA; British singer (countertenor); b. 1962; m. Sarah Hurley. *Education:* Winchester Coll., New Coll., Oxford. *Career:* chorister, Winchester Cathedral; freelance singer –1990; mem., The King's Singers 1990–2016. *Recordings include:* with The King's Singers: Good Vibrations 1991, Chanson d'Amour 1992, English Renaissance 1994, Street Songs 1997, Fire-water 2000, Gesualdo 2004, 1605: Treason and Dischord 2005, Sacred Bridges 2005, Six 2005, Sermons and Devotions 2005, Thomas Tallis Spem in Alium 2006, Landscape & Time 2006, The Triumphs of Oriana 20006, The Quiet Heart 2007, Live at the Proms 2008, The Golden Age 2008, Simple Gifts (Grammy Award) 2008, Reflections 2008, Romance du Soir 2009, Swimming over London 2010; with Eric Whitacre, the Eric Whitacre Singers, Christopher Glynn, Laudibus and the Pavão Quartet : Light and Gold (Grammy Award for Best Choral Performance 2012) 2010. *Current Management:* c/o Music Productions Ltd., Pinewood Studios Pinewood Road, Iver Heath, SL0 0NH, England. *Telephone:* (1753) 783739. *E-mail:* Claire@kingssingers.com. *Website:* www.kingssingers.com.

HURLEY, Laurel; American singer (soprano); b. 14 Feb. 1927, Allentown, PA. *Education:* studied with her mother. *Career:* debut in the Student Prince at New York 1943; New York City Opera debut as Zerlina 1952; sang at the Metropolitan Opera from 1955 as Oscar, Musetta, Mimi, Adele, Susanna, Olympia, Papagena, Zerlina and Perichole; also sang in I Capuleti e i Montecchi by Bellini; many concert appearances in North America.

HURST, John; American singer (tenor); b. 1958, Norfolk, WV. *Education:* studied in the USA, Vienna, and at the Salzburg Mozarteum. *Career:* sang at the Vienna Volksoper from 1987, notably as Mozart's Idomeneo, Max in Der Freischütz, Erik in Der fliegende Holländer and Lenski in Eugene Onegin 1990; Alwa in Berg's Lulu; guest appearances at the Schwetzingen Festival, Hamburg Staatsoper, Cologne (as Eisenstein in Die Fledermaus), Strasbourg and Tokyo. *Honours:* winner Belvedere Competition, Vienna 1982. *Current Management:* Ariën Arts & Music Management, De Boeystraat 6, 2018 Antwerp, Belgium. *Telephone:* (3) 285-96-80. *Fax:* (3) 230-35-23. *E-mail:* arien@pandora.be.

HURT, Leopold; German composer and zither player; b. 12 Feb. 1979, Regensburg. *Education:* Richard Strauss Conservatory of Music, Munich, Hamburg Acad. for Music and Theatre. *Career:* has been commissioned by several orchestras, ensembles and soloists, including Regensburg Philharmonic Orchestra, Ensemble Modern, Frankfurt, Munich Chamber Orchestra; compositions include two chamber operas, orchestral and vocal works, chamber music and solo pieces, also with electronics. *Compositions include:* ALPenmusik 1999, Treibgut 1999, Stele 2000, Anna Livia Plurabelle 2001, Muspilli 2002, Aggregat 2005, Hiatus 2006, Erratischer Block 1 2007, August Frommers Dinge 2008, MEDEA 2008, Tunnel 2008, Flex 2009, Seisographien 2009. *Honours:* Rauhe Preis für Neue Kammermusik, Gustav Mahler Prize, Klagenfurt 2008, Cité Internationale des Arts, Villa Concordia, Stuttgart Kompositionspreis 2010. *Address:* Bernstorffstrasse 159, 22767 Hamburg, Germany (office). *E-mail:* info@leopoldhurt.de (office). *Website:* www .leopoldhurt.de.

HUS, Walter; composer and pianist; b. 2 July 1959, Mol, Belgium. *Education:* Brussels Royal Conservatory. *Career:* recitals as classical pianist since early childhood, Italy, Germany, Poland; performances as improviser/interpreter of own compositions 1982–; concerts throughout Europe with group Maximalist, own compositions 1984–; mem., Belgisch Pianokwartet, Simpletones, etc.; various radio and television broadcasts; film with Marie André and Walter Verdin; composer, several works for ballet, full-sized opera. *Compositions include:* Huit etudes on improvisation for piano solo, music for fashion show in Yamamoto, Brussels, Muurwerk (music for choreography, Roxane Huilmand), Die Nacht (two-act opera, libretto by Wolfgang Klob), Compositie (video film by Marie André about W. Hus), Hus/Verdin (video tape by Walter Verdin), Liefde for four pianists at two pianos, La Theorie (for Belgisch Pianokwartet), Nox aeterna for piano 1994, Kopnaad (incidental music) 1995. *Recordings:* Huit etudes on improvisation 1984, Maximalist 1985, Muurwerk 1986, Die Nacht 1987. *Honours:* Brussels Royal Conservatory first prize for piano 1981, for harmony 1981, for practical harmony 1983.

HUSA, Karel; American (b. (Czech) composer and conductor; b. 7 Aug. 1921, Prague, Czech Repub.; s. of the late Karel Husa and Bozena Husova; m. Simone Husa (née Perault); four d. *Education:* Prague Conservatory of Music, Prague Acad. of Music, Paris Conservatory of Music, Ecole normale de musique de Paris, France. *Career:* composer, conductor in Paris, guest conductor with European orchestras , Kappa Alpha Prof. of Music, Cornell Univ. 1954, Asst Prof. 1954, Assoc. Prof. 1957, Prof. 1961; conductor of the univ. orchestras, teacher of composition (retd 1992), guest conductor with American orchestras and lecturer; Prof., School of Music, Ithaca Coll. 1967–86; mem. Belgian Royal Acad. of Arts and Sciences 1974–, American Acad. of Arts and Letters 1994–. *Dance:* Monodrama (ballet) for Butler Ballet, Indiana 1976, The Steadfast Tin Soldier for Boulder Philharmonic, Colorado 1974, The Trojan Women for Louisville Ballet, Kentucky 1980. *Film:* Young Generation 1946, Gen, Prague 2001, Karel Husa Comes Home 2002. *Music:* Music for Prague 1968, Apotheosis of this Earth 1972, four string quartets; concertos for piano, brass quintet, organ, viola, violin, cello, saxophone, percussion, trumpet, orchestra; symphonies (Mosaiques, Fantasies); chamber music includes quintets for wind, brass, works for piano, sonatas for violin, music for band. *Publications:* Music for Prague; Apotheosis of this Earth; Concerto for Orchestra; The Trojan Women; An American Te Deum; Concerto for Sax and Winds; Concerto for Wind Ensemble; Les couleurs fauves, Cayuga Lake; Four Quartets; Twelve Moravian Songs; Sonata a Tre; Symphony No. 1; Evocation de Slovaquie; Serenade. *Honours:* Dr hc (Coe Coll.) 1976, (Cleveland Inst. of Music) 1985, (Ithaca Coll.) 1986, (Baldwin-Wallace Coll.) 1991, (St Vincent Coll.) 1995, (Hartwick Coll.) 1997, (New England Conservatory) 1998, (Masaryk Univ., Brno) 2000, (Acad. of Musical Arts, Prague) 2000, (Univ. of Louisville) 2012; Pulitzer Prize 1969, Sudler Prize 1984, Friedheim Award 1985, Grawemeyer Award 1993, Guggenheim Award 1964, 1965, Sousa Order of Merit 1985, Czech Repub. Medal of Merit (First Class) 1995, Medal of Honor of the City of Prague 1998. *Current Management:* c/o Stanton Management, 25 Cimarron Road, Putnam Valley, NY 10579, USA. *Telephone:* (620) 563-7312. *E-mail:* TDStanton@StantonMgt.com. *Website:* www.stantonmgt.com.

HUSSAIN, Leo; British conductor. *Education:* Eton Coll., St John's Coll., Cambridge, Royal Acad. of Music. *Career:* Founding Musical Dir Kettle's Yard Ensemble; Musical Dir Ashover Festival 2003, 2004; Prin. Conductor Univ. of London Symphony Orchestra 2003–06; Musical Dir and Prin. Conductor Newbury Choral Soc. 2004–; conducted British Youth Opera's Le Nozze di Figaro in Queen Elizabeth Hall, London, Prokofiev's Peter and the Wolf and Britten's Serenade at Royal Acad. of Music; conducted English Touring Opera in Figaro 2004, The Magic Flute, Cosí fan Tutte and Donizetti's Mary Queen of Scots 2005; also at Batignano and Aberdeen Festivals, Opera North and Glyndebourne on Tour; season 2005–06: conducted opera Gentle Giant for ROH2, Clore Studio, Royal Opera House, London, Pelléas et Mélisande (as Sir Simon Rattle's asst) with Berliner Philharmoniker at Salzburg Easter Festival, Cosi fan Tutte for Opera Holland Park, London. *Current Management:* c/o Intermusica Artists Management Ltd, 36 Graham Street, Crystal Wharf , London, N1 8GJ, England.

HUSSON, Suzanne; Argentine/French pianist; b. 4 April 1943, Buenos Aires. *Education:* studied with Mrs E. Westerkamp, Conservatoire M. de Falla, Buenos Aires, Conservatory of Geneva with Prof. Hilbrandt, Staatliche Hochschule für Musik, Cologne with Prof. B. Seidlhofer, studied with Arturo Benedetti Michelangeli in Italy and Switzerland. *Career:* debut public recital aged eight, Buenos Aires; various int. performances in recitals and as soloist with conductors such as Marc Andreae, W. Sawallisch, C. Dutoit, and Orchestre Philarmonique de Lyon, Stuttgart Philharmonic, Orchestre de la Radio Suisse Italienne and Orchestra de la Suisse Romande; TV and radio appearances in Germany and Switzerland; radio appearances in Argentina, Poland and France. *Recordings include:* Stravinsky, Les Noces, directed by Charles Dutoit 1973, R. Vuataz, Concert for Piano and Orchestra, Opus 112, Orchestre de la Suisse Romande, directed by Wolfgang Sawallisch 1981, Scarlatti-Ginastera-Debussy-Ravel 1987, Latin American Classics, Guatemala, Mañuel Martinez-Sobral piano music, Vols 3 and 5, 1999, 2003, Radio Suisse Romande CD live Bach, Rachmaninov, Ravel, Ginastera, Albeniz, Scriabin 2005, CD (violin-piano) Miniatures Kreisler 2008, CD (violin-piano) R. Strauss, Ravel, Chausson, Ponce-Heifetz, Elgar 2010, CD Zipoli/Ginastera, Piazzolla, Ginastera, Scriabin, Rachmaninov, Albeniz 2010, CD Szymanowski, Francoeur/Kreisler, Prokofiev, Paganini/Kreisler 2010, CD (violin piano). *Current Management:* c/o Achille Rizza, 24 rue de la Dôle, 1203 Geneva, Switzerland. *E-mail:* arizza@bluewin.ch. *E-mail:* shusson@bluemail.ch (office). *Website:* www.suzannehusson.com.

HUSZÁR, Lajos; Hungarian composer; b. 26 Sept. 1948, Szeged; m. Éva Papp Huszár. *Education:* Secondary Music School, Szeged, with Istvan Vantus, Acad. of Music, Budapest, with Endre Szervanszky and Zsolt Durko, Acad. of St Cecilia, Rome, Italy, with Goffredo Petrassi. *Career:* Prof. of Music Theory, Univ. of Szeged 1990–2008; mem. Asscn of Hungarian Composers, Hungarian Soc. of Music. *Compositions include:* Musica concertante for 13 players 1975, 69th Psalm for tenor and piano 1976, 5 Pieces for piano 1977, Scherzo and Adagio for chamber orchestra 1979, Sonata for harpsichord 1979–85, Brass Quintet 1980, Songs of Solitude for soprano and percussion 1983, Notturno for piano 1984, Concerto Rustico for chamber orchestra 1985, Chamber Concerto for cello and 17 strings 1987, Libera me for organ 1993, The Silence, opera in 2 acts 1994–98, Trittico estivo for oboe and piano 1998, Icons to the memory of János Pilinszky for soprano and chamber orchestra 2000–01, Passio for soloists, choir, organ and percussion 2003–04. *Honours:* Erkel Prize 1994, Bartók-Pásztory Prize 2003. *Address:* Vörösmarty u. 53. fsz. 10. 1064 Budapest, Hungary (home). *E-mail:* huszarla@hotmail.com (home).

HUTCHESON, Jere Trent, BMus, MMus, PhD; American composer and academic; *Professor of Music, Michigan State University*; b. 16 Sept. 1938, Marietta, Georgia; m. 1st Virginia Bagby; one d.; m. 2nd Mary Ellen Gayley Cleland 1982; one s. one d. *Education:* Stetson Univ., Louisiana State Univ., Michigan State Univ., Berkshire Music Center. *Career:* Prof., Michigan State Univ. 1965–. *Compositions include:* Passacaglia for band, three Things for Dr Seuss, Shadows of Floating Life, Wonder Music I, II, III, IV, V, Sensations, Transitions, Construction Set, Colossus, three Pictures of Satan, Electrons, Fantaisie-Impromptu, Nocturnes of the Inferno, Passing, Passing, Passing, Patterns, Cosmic Suite, Earth Gods Symphony, Chromophonic Images for symphonic band, Will-o-the-Wisps for solo violin, The Song Book for tenor and flute, Duo Sonata for clarinet and percussion, Concerto for piano and wind orchestra, Metaphors for orchestra, Interplay for alto saxophone and mallet percussion, Ritual and Dance for female chorus, Five French Portraits for wind orchestra, Duo Concertante in memoria di Margot Evans for violin and piano, Concerto for violin and small orchestra, Long Live the Composer (chamber opera), Dance of Time Symphony 1995, Caricatures for wind symphony 1997, Portfolio for cello and chamber ensemble 1997, More Caricatures for wind symphony 1999, Glosses, Annotations and an Exegesis for cello and piano (also violin and piano) 1999, Mrs Dalloway's Party for mezzo-soprano and piano 1999, More Caricatures for wind symphony 1999, Glosses, Annotations and an Exegesis for cello and piano (also for violin and piano) 1999, Mrs Dalloway's Party for mezzo-soprano and piano 1999, Caricatures III for wind symphony 2000, Three Notions for saxophone quartet 2000, Three Visions for full orchestra 2001, Quirky Etudes for piano, Sonata for piano, Concerto for solo percussion and wind symphony, Divertimento for flute solo, winds and percussion, Three Pieces for tuba and piano, Gradus ad Parnassum – Caricatures IV for wind symphony, Petals Over Time for mezzo-soprano and piano, Variations and Excursions for string trio, Concerto for saxophone and wind symphony, hist whist for mixed chorus and arranged for children's chorus SA, Lament for mixed chorus and arranged for women's chorus SSA, Taj Mahal for small orchestra, Desert Flower for wind symphony, Mist of Tears for mixed chorus and piano, Reflections-Caricatures V for wind symphony, Nuclear Conversation for percussion solo, 12 Introspections for oboe solo, A Good Old-Fashioned Trio (piano trio), Concertino for orchestra, The Ride for women's chorus and small orchestra, Sunrise, Sunset for wind symphony, Games Concerto for solo clarinet and wind symphony, Earth Song Concerto for oboe and wind symphony, Place Your Bets for woodwind quintet. *Recordings:* Déjà View contains Caricatures for wind symphony 1997, Caricatures by Rutgers Univ. Wind Ensemble contains Caricature Suite 2004. *Publication:* Musical Form and Analysis 1995. *Honours:* Music Teachers' Nat. Asscn Composer of the Year 1976. *Address:* 6064 Abbott Road, East Lansing, MI 48823, USA (home). *Telephone:* (517) 355-7664 (office); (517) 337-0295 (home). *E-mail:* hutcheson@msu.edu (office). *Website:* www.music.msu.edu/faculty (office).

HUTCHINSON, Nigel; pianist; b. 1963, England. *Education:* Univ. of Glasgow, Guildhall School with Craig Sheppard and Juilliard with Earl Wild. *Career:* debut at Wigmore Hall 1988; concerts in France, Germany, Italy, Czechoslovakia and elsewhere in Europe; concerto debut with the London Mozart Players under Jane Glover; festival engagements at Harrogate and Glasgow, and recitals at the Salle Pleyel Paris, Barbican Centre and Festival Hall, London and Symphony Hall Birmingham; broadcasts for BBC and Italian radio; Purcell Room recital 1993, with Schubert (D664), Liszt and Debussy. *Recordings:* Rachmaninov music for six hands, with John Ogdon and Brenda Lucas, and Carnival of the Animals with the London Symphony Orchestra under Barry Wordsworth.

HUTCHINSON, Stuart, BMus, LRAM, ARAM; British conductor and accompanist; *Vocal Tutor, University of Chichester*; b. 3 March 1956, London, England. *Education:* Royal Acad. of Music, London, Univ. of Cambridge, studied with Bernstein and Pritchard. *Career:* opera, ballet and music-theatre conductor; productions for ENO, Scottish Opera, Theater des Westens Berlin, New Sadler's Wells Opera Co., Sadler's Wells Theatre/ROH, London Int. Opera Festival, Royal Acad. of Music; Conductor, Scottish Ballet 1991; Chorus Master, Dublin Grand Opera and Wexford Festival Opera; music staff, ENO, Opera North; Dir of Music and organist, Univ. of London Chaplaincy 1976–89; Music Dir, Northcott Theatre, Exeter 1982–84; Music Dir and Artistic Dir,

Morley Opera, London 1986–90; Music Dir, Jonathan Miller's Co./Old Vic Theatre 1988–89; currently Vocal Tutor, Univ. of Chichester; world premiere, Alice in Wonderland (Carl Davis), Lyric Theatre, Hammersmith 1986; British premiere, Postcard from Morocco (Dominick Argento) LIOF 1988; world premiere, Tables Meet (Stephen Oliver), Royal Festival Hall 1990; also productions for RSC, London, On Your Toes, with Makarova, West End 1984; mem. PRS, Musicians' Union. *Compositions:* incidental theatre music, including King Lear (Miller/Old Vic), frequent arranger and orchestrator. *Recordings include:* National Philharmonic Orchestra with James Galway, Philharmonia Orchestra with Michie Nakamaru; several recordings for BBC Radio 3 and 4, many for BBC Radio Drama, BBC and ITV. *Honours:* Young Artist Award, Incorporated Soc. of Musicians 1981. *Address:* University of Chichester, College Lane, Chichester, PO19 6PE, England (office). *Telephone:* (1243) 816000 (office). *E-mail:* s.hutchinson@chi.ac.uk (office); mail@StuartHutchinson.org. *Website:* www.chi.ac.uk/staff/stuart-hutchinson (office); www.stuarthutchinson.org.

HUTTENLOCHER, Philippe; singer (baritone); b. 29 Nov. 1942, Neuchâtel, Switzerland. *Education:* studied with Juliette Bise in Fribourg. *Career:* sang with the Ensemble Vocal de Lausanne and with the Choeurs de la Foundation Gulbenkian, Lisbon; festival appearances in Montreux, Lausanne, Strasbourg and Ansbach in the Baroque repertory; tour of Japan 1974; Zürich Opera 1975, as the title role in Monteverdi's Orfeo, produced by Jean-Pierre Ponnelle; London Bach Festival 1978; guest appearances in Vienna, Berlin, Hamburg, Milan and Edinburgh; Genoa 1987, in Dido and Aeneas and Les Malheurs d'Orphée by Milhaud. *Recordings include:* Bach Cantatas and operas by Monteverdi including Il Ritorno d'Ulisse and L'Orfeo (video); St Matthew Passion; Le Devin du Village by Rousseau; Die Jahreszeiten by Haydn, Bach B Minor Mass; Les Indes Galantes by Rameau, Così fan tutte, Il Maestro di Capella, Pénélope, St John Pasion, Handel Dettingen Te Deum and works by Carissimi, M.A. Charpentier and Gabrieli.

HUYBRECHTS, Francois; conductor; b. 15 June 1946, Antwerp, Belgium. *Education:* Antwerp Conservatory, studied with Daniel Sternefeld, Bruno Maderna and Hans Swarowsky. *Career:* debut as cellist 1960; conducting 1963 The Fairy Queen by Purcell, Royal Flemish Opera; conducted the Netherlands Chamber Opera 1966–67; concerts at the Salzburg Mozarteum 1967; assisted Bernstein at the New York Philharmonic and conducted the Los Angeles Philharmonic and the Berlin Philharmonic; Musical Dir, Wichita Symphony 1972–79, San Antonio Symphony 1979–80. *Recordings include:* Janáček's Taras Bulba and Lachian Dances (London Philharmonic), Nielsen's 3rd Symphony (London Symphony Orchestra). *Honours:* winner Dimitri Mitropoulos Competition, New York 1968, prizewinner Herbert von Karajan Foundation Competition 1969.

HVOROSTOVSKY, Dmitri Alexandrovich; Russian opera singer (baritone); b. 16 Oct. 1962, Krasnoyarsk; m. 1st (divorced), two c.; m. 2nd Florence Illi Hvorostovsky; one s. one d. *Education:* Krasnoyarsk Inst. of Arts. *Career:* debut as opera singer 1985; soloist, Krasnoyarsk Opera Theatre 1985–90; performances in La Scala, Covent Garden, Metropolitan Opera and Paris Opéra; roles include The Queen of Spades (Opéra de Nice) 1989, (Metropolitan Opera, New York) 1999, Eugene Onegin (La Fenice) 1991, (Châtelet, Paris) 1992, (Covent Garden) 1993, 2005, (Vienna) 2010, Il Barbiere di Siviglia (Berlin State Opera) 1994, (San Francisco Opera) 1996, I Puritani (Covent Garden) 1992, La Traviata (Chicago Lyric Opera) 1993, (Covent Garden) 1996, 2012, (Metropolitan Opera, New York) 2003, 2012, (Cagliari) 2004, (San Francisco Opera) 2004, (La Fenice) 2004, (San Carlo, Naples) 2007, I Masnadieri (Covent Garden) 1998, 2002, Rigoletto (Novaya Opera, Moscow) 2000, (Covent Garden) 2005, 2010, Don Giovanni (Geneva and Salzburg) 1999, (Metropolitan Opera, New York) 2002, Don Carlos (Teatro Real, Madrid) 2001, (Zürich Oper) 2003, (Vienna) 2005, (Tokyo and Nagoya) 2012, Don Giovanni and Leporello in the film Don Giovanni Unmasked 2003, Pikovaya Dama (Metropolitan Opera, New York) 1995, (La Scala, Milan) 2005, (Vienna State Opera), War and Peace (Metropolitan Opera) 2003, (Salzburg Festival) 2004, Il Trovatore (Covent Garden) 2003, (Bastille Opera, Paris) 2004, (Metropolitan Opera) 2009, 2011, 2012, (Arena Verona) 2012, Faust (Metropolitan Opera, New York) 2005, Un Ballo in Maschera (Chicago Lyric Opera) 2003, (Covent Garden) 2006, (Metropolitan Opera) 2008; Count di Luna in Il trovatore, (Metropolitan Opera, New York) 2015. *Honours:* First Prize, USSR Nat. Glinka Competition 1987, Toulouse Int. Competition 1988, BBC Cardiff Singer of the World Competition 1989, State Prize of Russia 1991, People's Artist of Russia 1995, Opera News Award for invaluable contrib. to opera 2011. *Address:* c/o Diane Blackman, President, BR Public Relations, 144 East 84th Street, Suite 7G, New York, NY 10028, USA (office). *Telephone:* (212) 249-5125 (office). *E-mail:* dblackman@brpublicrelations.com (office). *Website:* www.brpublicrelations.com (office); www.hvorostovsky.com/en.

HWANG, Der-Shin, BA, MFA, ARCM; Taiwanese singer (mezzo-soprano) and teacher; b. 8 Feb. 1958. *Education:* Taiwan Normal Univ., Univ. of California, Los Angeles, Royal Coll. of Music and RCM Opera School, London. *Career:* debut, Suzuki, Holland Park; debut of Ian Venables' Millennium Hymn, Cheltenham Town Hall; Serenade to Music with Hanley/RPO in Festival Hall and with Charles Groves/Philharmonia in the Barbican 1989; Anitra in Peer Gynt with Neeme Järvi/Gothenburg Symphony Orchestra, Barbican 1992–93; Haydn and Handel solo contatas with Tallis Chamber Orchestra 1993; Mozart arias in Sandwich Festival 1993; Christmas Magnificat with English Baroque Orchestra in Queen Elizabeth Hall 1993; Judas Maccabaeus in Handel's Canon Park Church with London Mozart Players 1994; performed Paul

Hindemith's song cycle Das Marienleben (to mark 50th anniversary of composer's death) at Three Choirs Festival, and in univs in Taiwan 2013; many other oratorio concerts with choral societies in UK including works such as Elgar's The Music Makers, Rossini's Stabat Mater, Petite Messe Solennelle, Mozart's C Minor Mass; operas include Suzuki with many companies including Singapore Lyric Theatre, Crystal Clear and in Festival Mozart at Roubaix, France; other operatic roles including Idamante, Madame de Croissy, Isolier, Prince Orlofsky, Siebel, Pitti-sing, Cherubino, Baba the Turk, Olga; worked with companies such as Clonter Opera for All, Holland Park Opera, Wexford Festival, Kentish Opera, Wessex Opera, London City Opera, Taipei Theatre, City of Birmingham Touring Opera, Opera Factory and English National Opera; solo recitals in Switzerland, Germany, France, Malaysia, Singapore, Taiwan, USA and UK. *Address:* Flat 2, 19 Woodstock Road, London, NW11 8ES, England (home). *Telephone:* (20) 8731-9784 (home).

HWANG, Sin-nyung; South Korean singer (soprano). *Career:* opera roles include Barbarina in Le Nozze di Figaro, Geneva, First Dame in Die Zauberflöte Opéra de Marseille 2003, Deuxième Dame in Dido and Aeneas, Opéra de Marseille 2005, Norina in Don Pasquale, Pescia, Italy 2005; performed a Haydn mass, Besançon, France 2005, Violetta in La Traviata, Festival Musiques au coeur at Antibes Festival Lacoste, France 2006; performed Carmina Burana at Nantes 2006, Gilda in Rigoletto Opéra de Marseille 2006, Queen of the Night in Die Zauberflöte, Vancouver Opera, Canada 2007. *Honours:* Julian Gayarre Int. Singing Competition Orfeon Pamplones Prize, Pamplona 2002, first prize Arles Singing Competition 2003, Winner, Montréal Int. Singing Competition 2005.

HYDE-SMITH, Christopher; British flautist and teacher; b. 11 March 1935, Cairo, Egypt; one s. one d. *Education:* Royal College of Music, London. *Career:* debut at Royal Festival Hall 1962; mem., Camden Wind Quintet, London Mozart Players; many flute and piano and/or harpsichord concerts with Jane Dodd; appearances in Netherlands, Switzerland, Italy, France, Germany, Spain, Portugal, Scandinavia, Russia, North and South America; Prof., Royal Coll. of Music; dedicatee of works by Alwyn, Dodgson, Horovitz, Mathias and Rawsthorne; judge at Leeds, Mozart and Tunbridge Wells Competitions; mem. Haydn Mozart Soc., British Flute Soc. (fmr chair.).

HYKES, David Bond; composer; b. 2 March 1953, Taos, NM, USA. *Education:* studied with Zevulon Avshalomov, S. Dhar. *Career:* founded the Harmonic Choir 1975; resident at the Cathedral of St John the Divine, New York from 1979; tours of the USA and Europe from 1980. *Compositions:* Harmonic Tissues for electronics 1971, Shadow Frequencies for piano and electronics 1975, Looking for Gold/Life in the Sun for children's voices and ensemble 1975, Well-struck Strings for dulcimer 1975–83, Special Delivery/Rainbow Voice for low voice 1975–84, Test Studies for Harmonica Orchestra for ensemble 1975–85, Hearing Solar Winds for voices 1977–83, Outside of Being There for voices 1981, Turkestan for synthesizer 1979, Current Circulation for voices 1984, Subject to Change for low voice and drones 1983, Desert Hymns 1984. *Honours:* NEA grants 1978, 1983, Rockefeller Foundation grants 1980–83, UNESCO grant 1983.

HYNES, Rachel, BA, MMus; British singer (soprano); b. (Rachel Chapman), 1 June 1971, Newport, Gwent, S Wales; d. of Garnet Chapman and Christine Chapman; m. Matthew Hynes 1994. *Education:* Univ. of Leeds and Royal Scottish Acad. of Music. *Career:* appearances from 1997 with Scottish Opera in Rigoletto (Page), The Queen of Spades (Masha), Aida (High-Priestess) and Macbeth (also at Vienna Festival); Company Prin. 2000–04, with Freia in Das Rheingold, Helmwige in Die Walküre and Third Nom in Götterdämmerung 2000–03, Essential Scottish Opera Tours 2001, 2002, Giannetta in L'Elisir d'amore, Ines in Il Trovatore, Fiordiligi in Così fan tutte, Euridice in Orfeo ed Euridice, First Lady in The Magic Flute and Mimi in La Bohème; sang Anna Kennedy in Donizetti's Maria Stuarda in concert debut at Edinburgh Int. Festival with Sir Charles Mackerras 2002; sang role of Denise in three productions of Tippett's The Knot Garden at Scottish Opera, concert performance with BBC Symphony Orchestra and Sir Andrew Davis at Barbican Centre, London (broadcast live on BBC Radio 3) and at Cantiere Internazionale D'Arte di Montepulciano (broadcast live on RAI 3) 2005; sang Cara in world premier of David Bruce's opera Push!, with Tête-à-Tête 2005, 4th Maid in Strauss's Elektra at opening of Edinburgh Int. Festival 2006; Ellen Orford in Peter Grimes, Opera North 2008; broadcasts also on Radio Scotland, Classic FM, BBC TV, RAI; currently freelance opera singer. *Honours:* Alexander Peden Fyfe Scholarship, Barcapel Foundation Award, The Charitable Trust Award, Trades House (Glasgow) Scholarship, Ye Cronies Award, Hobart Trust Award. *Current Management:* c/o Michael Letchford Artists, Goar Lodge, Smith's Green, Takeley, Bishop's Stortford, Herts., CM22 6NS, England. *Telephone:* (1279) 871114; (7815) 871766 (mobile). *Fax:* (1279) 871114. *E-mail:* mlartists@gmail.com. *Website:* michaelletchfordartists.co.uk. *Address:* Flat 1/2 Kelvingate, 143 Yorkhill Street, Glasgow, G3 8NS, Scotland (home). *Telephone:* (7771) 601820 (home). *E-mail:* rachel.hynes@virgin.net (home).

HYNNINEN, Jorma; Finnish singer (baritone); b. 3 April 1941, Leppävirta; m. Reetta Salo 1961; one s. two d. *Education:* Sibelius Acad., Helsinki. *Career:* debut as Silvio in Pagliacci, Finnish Nat. Opera 1969; Staatsoper Vienna 1977; La Scala, Milan 1977; Paris Opéra 1979; Bavarian State Opera, Munich 1979; Metropolitan Opera, New York 1984 as Posa; San Francisco Opera 1988; Lyric Opera of Chicago 1989; Deutsche Oper Berlin 1991 as Hindemith's

Mathis der Maler; lieder recitals, New York, London, Europe and Beijing; soloist with Vienna Symphony, Boston Symphony and Israel Philharmonic; sang Amfortas in Parsifal at Antwerp 1996; Savonlinna Festival 1998, as Wagner's Wolfram; premieres include The Red Line and The King Goes Forth to France by Sallinen 1978, 1984, Thomas, and Vincent by Rautavaara 1985, 1990, and Sallinen's Kullervo 1992; season 2000 at Helsinki as Simon Boccanegra, Papageno, and Gloucester in the premiere of Lear by Aulis Sallinen; Tsar Nicholas in the premiere of Rautavaara's Rasputin, Helsinki 2003; Artistic Dir Finnish Nat. Opera 1984–90, Savonlinna Opera Festival 1991; Prof. of Arts, Finland 1990–; Prof. of Singing, Sibelius Acad. 1997–2003. *Recordings:* Le nozze di Figaro with Riccardo Muti, Orestes in Elektra with Seiji Ozawa, Brahms' Requiem and Mahler's Eighth with Klaus Tennstedt, Winterreise, Die schöne Müllerin, Dichterliebe, Songs of Sibelius, Die schöne Magelone, Lieder eines Fahrenden Gesellen, Evergreen Love Songs. *Honours:* Prix Caecilia 1996. *Address:* Frederikinkatu 71A 23, 00100 Helsinki, Finland (home). *Telephone:* (40) 5212100 (home).

HYPOLITE, Andrée-Louise, BMus; British singer (mezzo-soprano); b. 1975, London, England. *Education:* Royal Scottish Acad. with Patricia McMahon, Nat. Opera Studio, London. *Career:* early roles include Clarice in Rossini's La Pietra del Paragone, Mrs Herring, and Bizet's Mercedes; other roles include Dorabella and Mrs Grose in The Turn of the Screw; concerts include Ravel's Chansons madécasses, Elgar's Sea Pictures, Vier ernste Gesänge by Brahms and Berio's Folk Songs; sang Mahler's Rückert Lieder for Scottish Ballet. *Address:* c/o National Opera Studio, The Clore Building, 2 Chapel Yard, Wandsworth High Street, London, SW18 4HZ, England.

HYTNER, Sir Nicholas Robert, Kt, MA; British theatre director; b. 7 May 1956, Manchester; s. of Benet A. Hytner and Joyce Myers. *Education:* Manchester Grammar School and Trinity Hall, Cambridge. *Career:* staff producer, ENO 1978–80; Assoc. Dir Royal Exchange Theatre, Manchester 1985–89; Assoc. Dir Royal Nat. Theatre 1989–97, Artistic Dir 2003–15. *Theatre and opera productions include:* Wagner's Rienzi (ENO) 1983, Tippett's King Priam (Kent Opera) 1984, Handel's Xerxes (ENO) (Olivier Award) 1985, The Scarlet Pimpernel (Chichester Festival) 1985, As You Like It, Edward II, The Country Wife, Schiller's Don Carlos (Royal Exchange) 1986, Handel's Giulio Cesare (Paris Opera), Measure for Measure (RSC) 1987, Tippett's The Knot Garden (Royal Opera), The Magic Flute (ENO), The Tempest (RSC) 1988, The Marriage of Figaro (Geneva Opera), Joshua Sobol's Ghetto (Nat. Theatre), Miss Saigon (Theatre Royal, Drury Lane) 1989, King Lear (RSC) 1990, The Wind in the Willows (Nat. Theatre) 1990, Volpone (Almeida) 1990, The Madness of George III (Nat. Theatre) 1991, The Recruiting Officer (Nat. Theatre) 1992, Carousel (Nat. Theatre) (Tony Award for Best Dir of a Musical 1994) 1992, The Importance of Being Earnest (Aldwych) 1993, Don Giovanni (Bavarian State Opera) 1994, The Cunning Little Vixen (Paris) 1995, The Cripple of Inishmaan 1997, The Crucible 1997, The Lady in the Van 1999, Cressida 2000, Orpheus Descending 2000, The Winter's Tale (Nat. Theatre) 2001, Mother Clap's Molly House (Nat. Theatre) 2001, Sweet Smell of Success (Broadway) 2002, The History Boys (Nat. Theatre) (Olivier Award for Best Director 2004, Tony Award for Best Director 2006) 2004, Così fan tutte (Glyndebourne) 2006, The Man of Mode (Nat. Theatre) 2007, The Rose Tattoo (Nat. Theatre) 2007, England People Very Nice (Nat. Theatre) 2009, Phèdre (Nat. Theatre) 2009, One Man, Two Guvnors (Nat. Theatre and touring) (Best Play, Evening Standard Theatre Awards) 2011, Travelling Light (Nat. Theatre) 2012, Timon of Athens (Nat. Theatre) 2012, Othello (Nat. Theatre) 2013, Great Britain (Nat. Theatre) 2014, The Hard Problem (Nat. Theatre) 2015. *Films:* The Madness of King George 1994, The Crucible 1996, The Object of My Affection 1998, Twelfth Night, or What You Will (TV) 1998, Center Stage 2000, The History Boys 2006, Phèdre 2009. *Honours:* Evening Standard Opera Award 1985, Evening Standard Best Dir Award 1989. *Current Management:* c/o Tim Menah, Askonas Holt, Lincoln House, 300 High Holborn, London, WC1V 7JH, England. *E-mail:* tim.menah@askonasholt.co.uk. *Address:* c/o Royal National Theatre, South Bank, London, SE1 9PX, England (office). *Telephone:* (20) 7452-3333 (office). *E-mail:* info@nationaltheatre.org.uk (office). *Website:* www.nationaltheatre.org.uk (office).

I

IANNACCONE, Anthony, BMus, MMus, PhD; American composer, conductor and teacher; b. 14 Oct. 1943, New York; m. Judith Trostle; one s. one d. *Education:* Manhattan School of Music, Eastman School of Music. *Career:* conducted orchestras, choruses, wind ensembles and chamber groups throughout the USA, including Lincoln Center, New York; many university appearances as guest conductor and composer; teacher, Manhattan School of Music 1967–68; Prof. of Composition 1971, Dir of Collegium Musicum 1973; record debut as conductor of Cornell Wind Ensemble 1983. *Compositions include:* three Symphonies 1965, 1966, 1992, Octet 1985, Chautauqua Psalms 1987, Concertante for clarinet and orchestra 1994, Crossings for orchestra 1996, Piano Quintet 1995, two string quartets 1965, 1997, West End Express for orchestra 1997. *Recordings include:* Partita for piano 1967, Rituals for violin and piano 1973, Aria Concertante for cello and piano 1976, Walt Whitman Song for chorus, soloists and winds 1981, No. 2 Terpsichore 1981, Images of Song and Dance No. 1 Orpheus 1982, Divertimento for orchestra 1983, Two Piano Inventions 1985, Night Rivers Symphony No. 3 1992, Sea Drift 1993, String Quartet No. 3 1999, Waiting for Sunrise 2002.

IBRAGIMOVA, Alina Rinatovna, MBE; British (b. Russian) violinist; b. 28 Sept. 1985, Polevskoy, Russian SFSR, USSR. *Education:* Gnessin State Musical Coll., Moscow, Yehudi Menuhin School, Surrey, Royal Coll. of Music, London, studied with Christian Tetzlaff, Gordan Nikolic, Kronberg Acad. Masters. *Career:* engagements have included Philharmonia, HR Sinfonieorchester Frankfurt, BBC Symphony, La Fenice, Orchestra of the Age of Enlightenment, Seattle Symphony, Deutsche Kammerphilharmonie Bremen with conductors including Valery Gergiev, Sir John Eliot Gardiner, Vladimir Jurowski, Sir Charles Mackerras; debut as soloist/director with the Kremerata Baltica during Salzburg Mozartwoche 2005; BBC Proms debut with London Symphony Orchestra 2009; solo and duo recitals and chamber music at the Wigmore Hall London, Carnegie Hall, New York, Musée du Louvre, Paris, Palais des Beaux Arts, Brussels and at festivals including Salzburg, Verbier, City of London, Lockenhaus, Aldeburgh and Edinburgh; mem. BBC New Generation Artists Scheme 2005–07; directed The Academy of Ancient Music 2012. *Recordings include:* Complete Violin Works of K.A. Hartmann, Violin Concertos of Roslavets (Preis der Deutschen Schallplattenkritik 2009), Complete Violin Works of Karol Szymanowski (with Cédric Tiberghien) (Diapason d'Or 2009), Bach Sonatas & Partitas for solo violin, Complete Beethoven Violin Sonatas (with Cédric Tiberghien), Felix Mendelssohn: Violin Concerto (Mendelssohn) in E minor, Op 64, Violin Concerto in D minor with Orchestra of the Age of Enlightenment, Vladimir Jurowski 2012, Eugène Ysaÿe: Sonatas for solo violin 2015, Johann Sebastian Bach: Violin Concertos with Arcangelo & Jonathan Cohen (conductor) 2015. *Honours:* Borletti-Buitoni Trust Award, Best Young British Performer, Classical BRIT Awards 2009, Royal Philharmonic Soc. Young Artist Award 2011. *Current Management:* c/o Matt Fretton, Ferus Management. *Telephone:* (20) 7253-1353. *E-mail:* matt@ferus.co.uk. *Website:* www.ferus.co.uk. *E-mail:* info@ alinaibragimova.com (office). *Website:* www.alinaibragimova.com.

ICHIHARA, Taro; Japanese singer (tenor); b. 2 Jan. 1950, Yamagata. *Education:* Juilliard School, New York, studied in Italy. *Career:* debut in Tokyo 1980, as Gounod's Faust; sang at the Teatro San Carlos, Lisbon from 1982, notably as Calaf; Paris Opéra from 1983, as Verdi's Macduff, Don Carlos, Riccardo and Duke of Mantua; Salzburg Festival 1984–85, as Malcolm in Macbeth; further engagements at Nice, Turin, Naples, Buenos Aires (Verdi Requiem), Orange Festival (Ismaele in Nabucco) and Tokyo; Metropolitan Opera, New York 1986–89, as the Italian Singer in Der Rosenkavalier and the Duke of Mantua; La Scala 1989, as Gabriele Adorno; Cologne Opera 1992; other roles include Alfredo, Enzo in La Gioconda and Edgardo.

ICONOMOU, Panajotis; Greek singer (bass); b. 1971, Munich, Germany. *Education:* Guildhall School of Music, National Opera Studio, London. *Career:* concert choir of the Tolzer Knabenchor, 1982–86, with the tours of Europe and solos under leading conductors; Bass with the Tolzer concert choir, 1988–92, with Mozart's Vespers at Versailles; Bach's Christmas Oratorio at the First Israel Bach Festival, under Peter Schreier; Further concerts at Munich, Hamburg, Milan and Vienna; Season 1997–98 with Bach and Telemann cantatas at the York Early Music Festival; Beethoven's Missa Solemnis at the Barbican; Christmas Oratorio in Munich; Mozart Sarastro at Holland Park and Osmin at Saar; Season 1999–2000 with Sparafucile for Welsh National Opera and Masetto for Scottish Opera. *Current Management:* c/o Aria's di Novella Partacini & Alexandra Plaickner, Via Josef Weingartner 4, 39022 Lagundo, Italy. *Telephone:* (473) 200200. *Fax:* (473) 222424. *E-mail:* info@ arias.it. *Website:* www.arias.it.

IDANE, Yasuhiko; Japanese singer (tenor); b. 1962. *Career:* frequent appearances in the Far East and Europe, in operas by Puccini (Il Tabarro), Leoncavallo (La Bohème) and Mascagni (Cavalleria Rusticana); also songs by Japanese composers, including Kobayashi; contestant at the 1995 Cardiff Singer of the World Competition.

IGOSHINA, Valentina; pianist; b. 1972, Bryansk, Russia. *Education:* Moscow Conservatory Central Music School. *Career:* recitals and concerts throughout Russia and Western Europe 1993–, with repertory including Bach, Chopin, Brahms and Schumann; performed Rachmaninov Preludes in

Tony Palmer's film biography, The Harvest, and appeared as Delfina Potocka in The Mystery of Chopin; season 2000–01 with Hallé Orchestra and BBC Scottish Symphony Orchestra; London debut 2002, at South Bank Harrods Int. Piano Series concert; season 2002–03 with Hallé Orchestra concerts, debut with London Philharmonic and tours of Channel Islands and Yugoslavia. *Honours:* winner Arthur Rubinstein Int. Piano Competition 1993, Rachmaninov Int. Competition, Moscow 1997.

IHLE, Andrea; German singer (soprano); b. 17 April 1953, Dresden. *Education:* Musikhochschule Dresden. *Career:* debut at Dresden Staatsoper 1976, as Giannetta in L'Elisir d'amore; appearances in Dresden have included Aennchen and Marianne, in the productions of Freischütz and Rosenkavalier which opened the rebuilt Semperoper 1985; other roles in Dresden and elsewhere in Germany, including Mozart's Papagena and Despina, Euridice, Gretel, Sophie (Der Rosenkavalier), Carolina (Il Matrimonio Segreto) and Marie in La Fille du Régiment; concert and oratorio engagements; season 1999–2000 at Dresden in Lady Macbeth of the Mtsensk District and Der Rosenkavalier. *Recordings:* Freischütz and Rosenkavalier, Bach's Christmas Oratorio, Missa Brevis by Carl Friedrich Fasch.

IHLOFF, Jutta-Renate; German singer (soprano); b. 1 Nov. 1944, Winteberg. *Education:* studied with Marja Stein in Hamburg, with Giorgio Favaretto in Rome and Siena. *Career:* debut at Staatsoper Hamburg 1973, as Zerlina in Don Giovanni; has sung in Munich, Berlin, Vienna and Salzburg; Frequent guest appearances elsewhere in Europe; Other roles include Mozart's Despina, Susanna, Blondchen and Pamina; Marzelline in Fidelio; Monteverdi's Poppea; Sophie and Zdenka; Mimi, Marie in Die Soldaten by Zimmermann, Adele in Die Fledermaus and Nannetta in Falstaff. *Recordings include:* Serpetta in La Finta Giardiniera by Mozart.

IKAIA-PURDY, Keith; American singer (tenor); b. 1956, Hawaii. *Education:* studied with Tito Gobbi, and with Carlo Bergonzi in Busetto. *Career:* sang in opera throughout the USA from 1983, notably as Turiddu, the Duke of Mantua, Gustavo in Un Ballo in Maschera, Cavaradossi in Tosca, Don José in Carmen, Rodolfo in La Bohéme, Roberto in Le Villi, Duca in Rigoletto, Ernesto in Don Pasquale, Aroldo; Florestan in the original version of Fidelio at Berkeley 1987; European debut as Corrado in Il Corsaro at Bussetto 1989; ensemble mem., Vienna Staatsoper 1992–; other roles includes Tebalo in Capuleti; Arnold in Guillaume Tell, Ismaele, Macduff in Macbeth, Don Carlos, Gaston in Jérusalem, Faust, Rodolfo in Luisa Miller, Alfredo in La Traviata, Edgardo in Lucia di Lammermoor, Stiffelio, Hoffmann, Des Grieux in Manon, Faust in Mefistofele, Fernand in La Favorite, Nemorino in L'Elisir d'Amore. *Current Management:* c/o Ingrid Krause, Hilbert Artists Management, Maximilianstrasse 22, 80539 Munich, Germany. *Telephone:* (89) 2907470. *Fax:* (89) 29074790. *E-mail:* krause@hilbertartists.de. *Website:* www.hilbert .de; www.ikaia-purdy.com.

IKEDA, Kikuei; Japanese violinist; b. 31 Aug. 1947, Yokosuka; Juilliard School with Dorothy DeLay and mems of the Juilliard Quartet. *Career:* second violin, Tokyo Quartet 1974–; regular concerts in the USA and abroad; first cycle of the complete quartets of Beethoven at the Yale at Norfolk Chamber Music Festival 1986; performances at Ravinia and Israel Festivals, Alice Tully Hall, the Metropolitan Museum of Art, New York, Boston, Washington, DC, Los Angeles, Cleveland, Detroit, Chicago, Miami, Seattle, San Francisco, Toronto; tours of South America, Paris, Amsterdam, Bonn, Milan, Munich, Dublin, London, Berlin; quartet-in-residence, Yale Univ. and at the Univ. of Cincinnati Coll.-Conservatory of Music. *Recordings include:* Schubert's Major Quartets. Mozart Flute Quartets with James Galway and Clarinet Quintet with Richard Stoltzman. Quartets by Bartók, Brahms, Debussy, Haydn, Mozart and Ravel. Beethoven Middle Period Quartets. *Honours:* Grand Prix du Disque du Montreux, Stereo Review Best Chamber Music Recording of the Year, Gramophone Best Chamber Music Recording of the Year. *Current Management:* c/o Patricia Winter, Opus 3 Artists, 470 Park Avenue South, 9th Floor North, New York, NY 10016, USA. *Telephone:* (212) 584-7525. *Fax:* (656) 300-8225. *E-mail:* pwinter@opus3artists.com. *Website:* www.opus3artists .com; www.tokyoquartet.com.

IKONOMOU, Katharine; singer (soprano); b. 1957, Tashkent, Uzbekistan. *Education:* studied in Tashkent and at the Cologne Musikhochschule with Joseph Metternich. *Career:* debut in Würzburg 1984, as Salome; after further study in Italy sang Salome at Zürich 1986, and Jenůfa at the 1988 Spoleto Festival (Chrysothemis 1990); sang Beethoven's Leonore at Trieste 1990, and Fevronia in Rimsky's Invisible City of Kitezh (Florence 1990) Rome 1991, as Ariadne, Amelia in Ballo in Maschera at Genoa and Wagner's Senta at Catania 1992. *Recordings include:* songs by Russian composers.

IM, Sunhae; South Korean singer (soprano); b. 15 Jan. 1976, Seoul. *Education:* Coll. of Music, Seoul Nat. Univ.; studied at Hochschule für Musik in Karlsruhe, Germany with Roland Hermann. *Career:* European stage debut as Barbarina in Mozart's Le Nozze di Figaro, Frankfurt Opera 2000; mem. Hannover Opera 2001–04; has worked with conductors including Philippe Herreweghe, William Christie, Fabio Biondi, Thomas Hengelbrock, Sigiswald Kuijken, Manfred Honeck, Frans Brüggen, Kent Nagano, Riccardo Chailly, Sylvain Cambreling, Ton Koopman and Marek Janowski; concert repertoire centred on Handel, Bach, Mozart and Haydn; recitals include Brahms'

Requiem, Bach's Saint Matthew Passion and Mass in B Minor, Mozart's Exsultate, jubilate and Mass in C Minor, Haydn's The Seasons. *Opera repertoire includes:* Blondchen in Die Entführung aus dem Serail, Barbarina in Le Nozze di Figaro, Papagena in Die Zauberflöte, Adele in Die Fledermaus, Cupid in Orpheus in the Underworld, Yniold in Pelleas et Mélisande, Valetto and Amor in L'Incoronazione di Poppea. *Recordings include:* Haydn: Creation 2005, La Clemenza di Tito 2006, Die Zauberflöte (BBC Music Magazine Award, Opera Category 2011) 2010, Mahler Symphony No. 4 (Int. Classical Music Award for Best Symphonic Recording 2012) 2011). *Honours:* First Prize at Korean Schubert Soc. Competition 1997, Grand Prix, 10th Korean Youth and Music Competition 1997. *Address:* c/o Harmonia Mundi, Mas de Vert, BP 20150, 13631 Arles, France (office).

IMAI, Nobuko; Japanese violist and academic; b. 18 March 1943, Tokyo; m. Aart van Bochove 1981; one s. one d. *Education:* Toho School of Music, Juilliard School and Yale Univ., USA. *Career:* mem. Vermeer Quartet 1974–79, now mem. Michelangelo String Quartet; soloist with Berlin Philharmonic, London Symphony Orchestra, Royal Philharmonic, BBC orchestras, Detroit Symphony, Chicago Symphony, Concertgebouw, Montréal Symphony, Boston Symphony, Vienna Symphony, Orchestre de Paris, Stockholm Philharmonic; festival performances include Marlborough, Salzburg, Lockenhaus, Casals, South Bank, Summer Music, Aldeburgh, BBC Proms, Int. Viola Congress (Houston), New York Y', Festival d'Automne, Paris; chamber music partners include Gidon Kremer, Yo-Yo Ma, Itzhak Perlman, András Schiff, Isaac Stern and Pinchas Zukerman; conceived Int. Hindemith Viola Festival (London, New York, Tokyo) 1995; Prof., High School of Music, Detmold, Germany 1985–2003; currently teaches at Amsterdam School of the Arts, Conservatory in Geneva, Kronberg Acad.; Artistic Adviser, Casals Hall, Tokyo. *Honours:* First Prize Munich, Second Prize Geneva Int. Viola Competitions; Avon Arts Award 1993, Japanese Educ. Minister's Art Prize for Music 1993, Mobil Japan Art Prize 1995, Suntory Hall Prize 1996. *Current Management:* c/o Tivoli & Crescendi Artists, Læderstræde 9, 4, 1202 Copenhagen K, Denmark. *Address:* Kronberg Academy, Friedrich-Ebert-Str. 6, 61476 Kronberg, Germany; Amsterdam School of the Arts, Oosterdokskade 151, Postbus 78022, 1070 LP Amsterdam, Netherlands. *Website:* www .kronbergacademy.de; www.ahk.nl.

IMMELMAN, Niel, FRCM; British pianist; *Professor of Piano, Royal College of Music;* b. 13 Aug. 1944, Bloemfontein, South Africa. *Education:* Royal Coll. of Music, London with Cyril Smith, studied with Maria Curcio. *Career:* debut, Rachmaninov, London Philharmonic Orchestra 1969; has given concerts at the Royal Festival Hall, London and Amsterdam Concertgebouw with major orchestras and leading conductors; concert tours of all continents; teaching positions: Prof. of Piano, Royal Coll. of Music 1980–; master-classes at Chopin Acad., Warsaw, Hong Kong Acad. for Performing Arts, Moscow Conservatoire, Sibelius Acad., Helsinki, Toronto Royal Conservatory and Univs of Berlin and Vienna; mem. Royal Soc. of Musicians of GB, European Piano Teachers' Asscn. *Recordings include:* Complete Piano music of Suk, Works by Beethoven, Schubert, Schumann, Dale and Bloch, featured in Classic CD Magazine's Pick of the Year. *Publications:* contrib. to International Piano Quarterly, Musicus, The Independent. *Honours:* Chappell Gold Medal 1969. *Address:* 41 Ashen Grove, London, SW19 8BL, England. *Telephone:* (20) 8947-7201. *Fax:* (20) 8946-8846. *E-mail:* immelman@lineone.net.

INBAL, Eliahu; British/Israeli conductor; b. 16 Feb. 1936, Jerusalem, Israel; s. of Jehuda Joseph Inbal and Leah Museri Inbal; m. Helga Fritzsche 1968; two s. one d. *Education:* Acad. of Music, Jerusalem, Conservatoire Nat. Supérieur, Paris, courses with Franco Ferrara, Hilversum and Sergiu Celebidache, Siena. *Career:* guest conductor with numerous orchestras including Milan, Rome, Berlin, Munich, Hamburg, Stockholm, Copenhagen, Vienna, Budapest, Amsterdam, London, Paris, Tel-Aviv, New York, Chicago, Toronto and Tokyo from 1963; Chief Conductor HR Radio Symphony Orchestra, Frankfurt 1974–90, Hon. Conductor 1995–; Chief Conductor Teatro La Fenice 1984–87, Music Dir 2007–11; regularly conducted Konzerthaus Berlin Symphony Orchestra 1992–, Chief Conductor 2001–06, Hon. mem. 2006–; Chief Conductor Tokyo Metropolitan Symphony Orchestra 2008–14, Hon. Conductor 2014–; Music Dir Czech Philharmonic Orchestra 2009–12. *Recordings:* numerous recordings, particularly of Mahler, Bruckner, Berlioz and Shostakovich. *Honours:* Hon. Conductor, HR-Sinfonieorchester Frankfurt 1990–, Orchestra Nazionale della RAI, Turin 1995–2001; Officier des Arts et des Lettres 1990, Goldenes Ehrenzeichen, Vienna 2001, Order of Merit (FRG) 2006; First Prize, Int. Conductors' Competition 'G. Cantelli' 1963, Golden Medal for Merit, City of Vienna 2001, Goethe Badge of Honour, City of Frankfurt 2006, numerous prizes for recordings, including Deutschen Schallplattenpreis, Grand Prix du Disque, Prix Caecilia, Symphony Prize of 50th Record Academy Award (Japan) 2012. *Current Management:* c/o Karsten Witt Music Management, Leuschnerdamm 13, 10999 Berlin, Germany. *Telephone:* (30) 214594-0. *E-mail:* info@karstenwitt.com. *Website:* www .karstenwitt.com.

INCE, Kamran, DMus; American/Turkish composer, pianist and academic; *Professor of Composition, University of Memphis;* b. 1960, Glendive, Mont. *Education:* Ankara Conservatory, İzmir Univ., Oberlin Coll., Ohio, Eastman School of Music. *Career:* moved to Turkey aged six; returned to USA in 1978; Visiting Prof., Univ. of Michigan 1988–92; mem. faculty Univ. of Memphis 1992–, now Prof. of Composition; Founding Co-Dir MIAM (Center for Advanced Research in Music), Istanbul Tech. Univ. 1999; Visiting Artist-in-Residence, N Central Coll., Naperville 2007; his music has been performed at

concerts and festivals throughout Europe; concerts have included Holland Festival, CBC Encounter Series, Toronto, Istanbul Int. Festival, Estoril Festival, Lisbon,TurkFest, London; one of five composers commissioned to write the mass And On Earth, Peace for Chanticleer Ensemble 2007. *Film scores:* Love Under Siege 1997, Aphrodisiac 1998, Sarkici 2001. *Selected compositions include:* FEST for orchestra and new music ensemble (written for the orchestras of Milwaukee, Dayton, Albany and Present Music) 1998, Flight Box (commissioned by Present Music for opening of new building for Milwaukee Art Museum) 1999, Symphony No. 4: Sardis (commissioned by U.C. Berkeley archeologist Crawford Greenewalt) 2000, Concerto for orchestra, Turkish instruments and voices (commissioned by Turkish Ministry of Culture) 2002, Istathenople for bozouki, mandolin, clarinet and new music ensemble (commissioned by Present Music) 2003, Strange Stone (commissioned by Relache of Philadelphia and the Commissioning USA Fund) 2003, Symphony No. 5: Galatasaray 2005, Requiem Without Words 2005, Gloria: Everywhere (commissioned as part of a new mass And On Earth, Peace for Chanticleer Ensemble) 2006. *Recordings include:* Kamran Ince, In White, Symphony No. 2 (Fall of Constantinople), Remembering Lycia, Arches, Ince: Symphonies No. 3 & 4 2005, And on Earth, Peace (with others) 2007; chamber music: Kamran Ince, Kamran Ince & Friends, Sheherazade Alive, Gates, Recitative and Frenzy (with others) 2003. *Honours:* Prix de Rome 1987, Guggenheim Fellowship, Lili Boulanger Prize. *Address:* Rudi E. Scheidt School of Music, The University of Memphis, Music Building, Room 235, 3775 Central Avenue, Memphis, TN 38152-3160, USA (office); c/o Schott Music International, KG Weihergarten 5, 55116 Mainz, Germany (office). *Telephone:* (901) 678-4339 (office); (6131) 2460 (Schott) (office). *Fax:* (6131) 246211 (Schott) (office). *E-mail:* knince@memphis.edu (office); kamranince@ kamranince.com (office). *Website:* music.memphis.edu/ince (office); www .kamranince.com.

INCIHARA, Taro; singer (tenor); b. 2 Jan. 1950, Yamagata, Japan. *Education:* studied in Japan and at the Juilliard School, New York. *Career:* debut in Tokyo 1980, as Gounod's Faust; European debut 1982, as Calaf at the Teatro San Carlo, Naples; Paris Opéra from 1983 as Macduff, Riccardo, Don Carlos and the Duke of Mantua; guest appearances at Nice, Turin, Naples, Santiago and Buenos Aires, Verdi's Requiem 1987; Macerata Festival 1987, Orange 1989, as Isamaele in Nabucco; Metropolitan Opera 1987–89, as the Italian Singer and the Duke of Mantua; further European engagements at Turin and Genoa; sang Riccardo in Un Ballo in Maschera for Opera Pacific at Costa Mesa, California 1991; other roles include Gabriele Adorno, La Scala 1989; Verdi's Rodolfo and Alfredo, Enzo in La Gioconda and Edgardo in Lucia di Lammermoor.

INCONTRERA, Roxana; singer (soprano); b. 1966, Ploiesti, Romania. *Education:* studied in Bucharest. *Career:* sang at the Rudolstadt Opera, then at the Dresden Staatsoper as Queen of Night in The Magic Flute 1989; guest appearances at Barcelona, in La Cenerentola 1992, Salle Pleyel (Paris), Berlin, Essen, Düsseldorf, Hannover, Chemnitz, Leipzig, Hallé; other roles include Rossini's Rosina, Mozart's Sandrina in La Finta giardiniera and Constanze, Violetta, Zerbinetta, Fiakermilli in Arabella, Italian Singer in Capriccio, Olympia and Oscar; sang Elvira in L'Italiana in Algeri at Dresden 1998; sang the Queen of Night and Verdi's Oscar at Dresden 2000; frequent concert engagements.

INGLE, William; singer (tenor); b. 17 Dec. 1934, Texhoma, TX, USA. *Education:* Acad. of Vocal Arts in Philadelphia with Dorothy di Scala, studied with Sidney Dietsch in New York and Luigi Ricci in Rome. *Career:* debut at Flensburg 1965, as Tamino; sang at the Linz Opera, Düsseldorf, Kassel, Frankfurt, Graz, Leipzig, Montréal, Hanover, Wellington and Vienna; other roles include Ernesto, Don Ottavio, Manrico, Lohengrin, Parsifal, Walther, Canio, Erik, Radames, Ferrando, Rodolfo, Almaviva, Flamand in Capriccio, the Duke of Mantua and Alfredo; sang at Linz 1976, in the premiere of Der Aufstand by Nikolaus Eder; Masaniello in La Muette de Portici by Auber 1989; television appearances as Herod (Salome) in Canada, and Tom Rakewell (The Rake's Progress) in Austria.

INGOLFSSON, Atli, DipMus, BM, BA; Icelandic composer; b. 21 Aug. 1962, Keflavik; m. Thuridur Jonsdottir 1990. *Education:* Reykjavík School of Music, Univ. of Iceland, Milan Conservatory with D. Anzaghi, studied with G. Grisey. *Career:* Auditor, CNSMP, Paris 1988–90; performances at Young Nordic Music festivals, other Nordic music festivals and various occasions in Iceland 1981–; his Due Bagatelle for clarinet premiered in Milan 1986 and widely performed; various performances in Europe 1990–, including Montreuil 1991, Varèse 1991; Amsterdam 1991, Milan 1991; commissioned by IRCAM, Paris to write for computer piano and ensemble 1993. *Compositions:* Due Bagettelle for clarinet, Et Toi Pale Soleil for four voices and instruments, A Verso for piano, O Versa for piano and 12 instruments, OPNA for bass clarinet and marimba, Le Pas les Pentes for eight instruments.

INGRAM JAÉN, Jaime Ricardo, DipMus; Panamanian pianist and diplomat; b. 13 Feb. 1928, Panama City, Panama; m. Nelly Hirsch 1950; two s. one d. *Education:* Juilliard School of Music, New York, USA with Olga Samaroff and Joseph Bloch, Conservatoire National de Paris, France with Yves Nat, studied with Alberto Sciarretti in Panama and Bruno Seidlhofer in Vienna, Austria. *Career:* Prof. of Piano, National Conservatory of Music, Panama 1952–56; Escuela Paulista de Música, São Paulo, Brazil 1958–60; Escuela Profesional, Panama 1962–64; Conservatorio Jaime Ingram 1964–69; Univ. of Panama 1972–74; Dir of Culture 1969–73; Gen. Dir of Culture 1974–78;

Ambassador to Spain 1978–82, to the Holy See 1982–87; concert tours as soloist and piano duo with Nelly Hirsch; concerts in South and Central America, Spain, Italy, Germany, Bulgaria, Poland, Switzerland, England, The Netherlands, USSR, Israel; retired from stage 1996; co-f. Fundación Concursos Internacionales, Panama; performed comeback concert with wife 2008. *Publications:* Hector Villa-Lobos, Muzio Clementi: the Father of the Pianoforte, Antonio de Cabezón: Tientos y Diferencias, Orientacion Musical 1974, Historia, Compositores y Repertorio del Piano 1978. *Honours:* Gran Cruz, Orden Manuel Amador Guererro (Panama) 2008. *E-mail:* concursoint@ cwpanama.net (office). *Website:* www.concursopanama.com.

INKINEN, Pietari; Finnish conductor and violinist; *Music Director, New Zealand Symphony Orchestra;* b. 1980, Kouvola. *Education:* Cologne Music Acad., Sibelius Acad. *Career:* Music Dir, New Zealand Symphony Orchestra 2008–; Principal Guest Conductor, Japan Philharmonic Orchestra 2009–; has worked with orchestras including Dresden Staatskapelle, Deutsche Symphony Orchestra Berlin, Leipzig Gewandhaus, Bayerische Rundfunk, WDR Cologne, Maggio Musicale, La Scala, Vienna Radio Symphony Orchestra, Rotterdam, Oslo and Helsinki Philharmonics, BBC Symphony, RAI Torino, CBSO, Israel Philharmonic, Orchestre Philharmonique de Radio France, Paris; collab. with soloists such as Vadim Repin, Hilary Hahn, Pinchas Zukerman; conducted three opera productions at Finnish Nat. Opera; also performed as solo violinist, and appeared with Inkinen Trio at Wigmore Hall 2007 and St John's Smith Square, London. *Current Management:* c/o Sara Hunt, IMG Artists, The Light Box, 111 Power Road, London, W4 5PY, England. *Telephone:* (20) 7957-5800. *Fax:* (20) 7957-5801. *E-mail:* shunt@imgartists.com. *Website:* www.imgartists.com; www.pietariinkinen .com.

INOUE, Michiyoshi; Japanese conductor; *Principal Conductor, Osaka Philharmonic Orchestra;* b. 23 Dec. 1946, Tokyo. *Education:* Toho Gakuen Acad. of Music with Prof. Saitoh. *Career:* Assoc. Conductor, Tokyo Metropolitan Symphony Orchestra 1970; conducted at La Scala 1971; conducted orchestras in Paris, Vienna, Geneva, Berlin, Brussels, Hamburg, Munich, Stuttgart, Madrid, Naples, Turin, Florence, Lisbon, London, Helsinki, Leipzig, Copenhagen; tours of Israel, Eastern Europe, Russia; conducted the East Berlin Orchestra on tour to Japan; concerts in Australia, New Zealand and USA; conducted numerous operas in Japan; Music Dir, New Japan Philharmonic Orchestra 1983–88, Kyoto Symphony Orchestra 1990; Music Dir, Orchestra Ensemble Kanazawa and Artistic Adviser of Ishikawa Ongakudo 2007–; Pres. D. Shostakovich Soc., Japan; Prin. Conductor, Osaka Philharmonic Orchestra 2014–. *Recordings include:* Mahler's 6th, 5th and 4th Symphonies with the Royal Philharmonic, Shostakovich Symphonies. *Honours:* Chevalier, Ordre des Arts et des Lettres; first prize Guido Cantelli Competition, Milan 1971. *Current Management:* Kajimoto Concert Management Co. Ltd., Kahoku Building, 8-6-25 Ginza, Chuo-ku, Tokyo 104-0061, Japan. *E-mail:* yuji.arai@kajimotomusic.com. *Address:* Shibuyaku Uehara 2-28-8, Tokyo, Japan (home). *Telephone:* (3) 3466-5911 (home). *E-mail:* maestro@sc4.so-net.ne.jp (home). *Website:* www.michiyoshi-inoue .com.

INVERNIZZI, Roberta; Italian singer (soprano); b. 1966, Milan. *Education:* vocal tuition with Margaret Heyward. *Career:* originally studied piano and double bass before turning to singing; specializes in baroque and classical repertoire; has performed in many well-known concert halls in Europe and USA, with conductors such as Giovanni Antonini, Rinaldo Alessandrini, Fabio Biondi, Ivor Bolton, Franz Brüggen, Alan Curtis, Ottavio Danton, Antonio Florio, Nikolaus Harnoncourt, Ton Koopman, Gustav Leonhardt and Jordi Savall; teaches singing at Centro di Musica Antica, Naples. *Opera roles include:* Armida in Handel's Rinaldo, Euridice in L'Orfeo, Minerva in Il Ritorno d'Ulisse (all Teatro alla Scala, Milan), Nerone in Handel's Agrippina (Teatro Real, Madrid), title role in La Statira (Teatro San Carlo, Naples), Galuppi's Olimpiade, Vivaldi's Ercole sul Termodonte and Cavalli's Virtu degli Strali d'Amore (all Teatro La Fenice, Venice), Ottavia in L'Incoronazione di Poppea. *Recordings:* over 70 recordings including Handel's Cantate per il Cardinal Pamphili (Stanley Sadie Handel Recording Prize 2007) 2006, Handel Italian Cantatas (Stanley Sadie Handel Recording Prize 2010) 2009, Dolcissimo Sospiro (Midem Classical Award, Stanley Sadie Handel Recording Prize) 2010, Handel Apollo e Dafne (Gramophone Award for Baroque Vocal Disc, Stanley Sadie Handel Recording Prize 2011) 2011. *Address:* Allegorica Opera Management, 36 rue de la Roquette, 75011 Paris, France (office). *Telephone:* 1-43-73-09-32 (office). *E-mail:* info@robertainvernizzi.it (office). *Website:* www.robertainvernizzi.it (office).

IOACHIMESCU, Calin; Romanian composer; b. 29 March 1949, Bucharest; m. Anca Vartolomei-Ioachimescu; one s. one d. *Education:* Bucharest High School, Bucharest Music Coll., Acad. of Music, IRCAM, Paris, studied with Stefan Niculescu, International New Music holiday courses at Darmstadt. *Career:* debut concert, Bucharest Radio Symphonic Orchestra 1978; symphonic, chamber and electronic works played throughout Romania and over the world; compositions broadcast in Bucharest, France and Brussels; sound engineer, Romanian Broadcasting; Head Computer Music Studio, Bucharest. *Compositions include:* Magic Spell for female voices, strings and percussion 1974, String Quartet No. 1 1974, Tempo 80 1979, Oratio II 1981, Hierophonies 1984, String Quartet No. 2 1984, Spectral Music for saxophones and tape 1985, Concerto for trombone, double bass and orchestra 1986, Celliphonia for cello and tape 1988, Palindrom/7 1992, Concerto for saxophones and orchestra 1994, Les Eclats de l'Abîme for double bass, saxophone and tape 1995,

Heptagrama for saxophones and tape 1998, Concerto for violin, cello and orchestra 2002; also film music. *E-mail:* ucmr@itcnet.ro.

IONESCU-VOVU, Constantin, PhD; Romanian pianist and academic (retd); b. 27 May 1932, Floresti; s. of Ion Ionescu and Virginia Vovu; m. Margareta Gabriel 1961 (died 1983). *Education:* Bucharest Superior Music Conservatory (now Nat. Univ. of Music). *Career:* concerts as soloist with symphony orchestras, piano recitals and chamber music in Romania, France, Germany, UK, Poland, Hungary, fmr Czechoslovakia, Russia, Ukraine, Norway, Sweden, Denmark, Belgium, Netherlands, Switzerland, Austria, Portugal, USA, Korea, Japan, Warsaw Autumn Festival 1967, Evian Festival 1977; Prof. (Piano, Concert Class) and Head of Piano Section, Nat. Univ. of Music, Bucharest; Visiting Prof., Musikhochschule Trossingen, Germany, Nagoya Coll. of Music, Japan and Keimyung Univ., Taegu, Repub. of Korea; master-classes in Romania, Germany, Netherlands, Portugal, USA, Korea, Japan; mem. int. juries for piano competitions in Romania, France, Germany, Italy, Portugal, Serbia, Croatia; Pres. European Piano Teachers' Asscn, Romania. *Television:* TV recordings in Romania. *Recordings include:* radio recordings and albums in Romania, Germany, the Netherlands, Austria. *Publications include:* Music Ed.: Aurel Stroé – Concert Music for piano, percussion and brass (dedicated to Constantin Ionescu-Vovu), C. Silvestri – Piano Works, Vols I and II, Woodwind Quartet, Sonata for Flute and Piano, Dinu Lipatti – Fantaisie for Piano Solo Op. 8, Romanian Piano Music Vol. 1; book: Musical Performance – The Specific Thinking; essays on technique, aesthetics and style of musical interpretation, music critic in musical periodicals. *Address:* 020492 Bucharest, Str. Vasile Lascar 35, Romania. *Telephone:* (21) 2111263; 72-3979861 (mobile). *E-mail:* cionvovu@ yahoo.com; cionvovu@gmail.com.

IRANYI, Gabriel; composer, pianist and lecturer; b. 6 June 1946, Cluj, Romania; m. Elena Nistor 1969; one s. *Education:* Special School of Music, Cluj, George Dima High School of Music, Cluj with Prof. D. Sigismund Todutza. *Career:* teaching asst, George Enesco High School of Music, Jassy 1971–76; Lecturer, Cfar Saba Conservatoire 1982–86; Prof., Leo Borchara Musikschule, Berlin, Germany 1988. *Compositions:* Segments de Profundis, Bird of Wonder, Until the Day Breaks, Portraits of J.S. Bach, Laudae for two pianos, Song of Degrees for chamber ensemble, Alternances for percussion, Alef for soprano voice, clarinet, cello and piano, Realm for solo cello and electric amplification, Solstice for violin, cello and clarinet, Electric Amplication, Shir Hamaalot for organ, Tempora for string quartet, Meditation and Prayer for violin and 15 strings, Laudae for two pianos, or with chamber orchestra.

IRELAND, Helen Dorcas, BMus (Hons), MMus; British musician; *Musical Director, Pianist, Coach and Teacher, Guildhall School of Music and Drama and Italia Conti Academy of Theatre Arts;* b. 2 Nov. 1952, Co. Durham, England; d. of Frank E. Ireland and Edna C. Meredith; m. Gregory Rose; one s. *Education:* Purcell School, London, Univ. of Birmingham, Royal Northern Coll. of Music, Peabody Conservatory, Baltimore, USA. *Career:* accompanist and ensemble player 1976–84; theatre musical dir in many English repertory theatres and the Royal Nat. Theatre; extensive work in Germany; educ. work in drama schools and summer schools; pvt. coaching, on staff of Guildhall School of Music and Drama 1999–, Italia Conti Acad. of Theatre and Arts 2004–; mem. Musicians' Union, Inc. Soc. of Musicians. *Honours:* Rotary Foundation Fellowship for study in USA 1975–76. *Address:* 57 Whitehorse Road, Stepney, London, E1 0ND, England (home). *Telephone:* (20) 7790-5883 (home); 7825-563032 (mobile). *Fax:* (20) 7265-9170 (home). *E-mail:* helen .ireland1@virgin.net (home).

IRELAND, (William) Patrick, ARCM; British violist; b. 20 Nov. 1923, Helston, Cornwall; m. Peggy Gray; four c. *Education:* chorister at St Paul's Cathedral, Wellington Coll., Worcester Coll., Oxford. *Career:* viola, Allegri String Quartet 1953–77, 1988; has taken part in the premieres of quartets by Martin Dalby 1972, Nicola LeFanu, Peter Sculthorpe, Elizabeth Maconchy, Robert Sherlaw-Johnson and Sebastian Forbes; two clarinet quintets by Jennifer Fowler and Nicola LeFanu 1971; four quartets by Barry Guy, Jonathan Harvey, Alison Bauld, Edward Cowie 1973; complete Beethoven Quartets at the 1974 Cheltenham Festival; taught and coached chamber music at the Menuhin School of Music in the 1960s; Asst Head of Strings, Royal Northern Coll. of Music 1977–80. *Recordings include:* with Allegri String Quartet; Bach Brandenburg Concertos with Menuhin and Bath Festival Orchestra; two recordings with Lindsay Quartet, as 2nd viola: Dvořák and Mozart Quintets. *Honours:* Hon. DMus (Southampton) 1975; Hon. MMus (Hull) 1995. *Address:* Ashgate, West End, Frome, Somerset, BA11 3AD, England (home). *Telephone:* (1373) 229318 (home). *E-mail:* patrick .ireland23@virgin.net.

IRMAN, Regina; Swiss composer and percussionist; *Lecturer, Thurgau University of Education;* b. 22 March 1957, Winterthur. *Education:* Winterthur Conservatory (guitar and percussion). *Career:* Lecturer, Thurgau Univ. of Educ. 2003–. *Compositions include:* Hügel bei Céret for two violas and double bass (also possible for other types of string ensemble) 1983, Ein vatter ländischer Gesang (based on texts by Adolf Wölfli) for mezzo and partly prepared grand piano 1985–86, Ein Trauermarsch (A Funeral March, based on texts by Adolf Wölfli) for spoken voice and percussion trio 1987, Requiem 'An den Tod' (To Death, based on a poem by Anna Achmatova) for 25 female and at least three male voices 1991–93, Wörter (Words) for saxophone ensemble and percussion 1994–95, '...wie eine Heuschrecke über die Meere...' (Like a Grasshopper over the Seas, based on text, pictures and an object by Meret Oppenheim) for large mixed choir and backing tape 1995–96, Drei Tänze (Three Dances, based on a text by Anna Achmatova) for soprano, female speaker/piano, clarinet and accordion 1996–97, Sculptures (for Bruce Nauman) for quarter-tone gamba quartet 1997, Surdina for altus solo 2000, Poem ohne Held (Poem without a Hero, opera based on a text by Anna Achmatova, libretto Peter Schweiger) 1997–2002, Landschaften (Landscapes) five pieces for percussion sextet 2003, Vier Kommentare zu den Sprechstücken von Carl Orff for speaking voices and drums 2003, Vögel und andere fliegende Tiere for four speaking voices, three pairs of glasses and playback CD, based on a text by Hildegard von Bingen 2004, Zehn kurze Stücke nach Motiven von Bach und Biber for (Baroque) violin solo 2004, Schilfbilder for alto flute, bass clarinet, violin, cello and piano 2005, Lautfelder und Linien, Musik zu Hildegard von Bingen, Lautfelder: for eight women's speaking voices, small percussion and small light sources, Linien: for two-train trumpet (soprano trombone) and two alto trombones 2006–07, Sieben Szenen für recorder/shawm, zinc, Renaissance/Baroque guitar, harpsichord/chamber organ, drums, Baroque violin, Baroque cello/bass viol, violone, Contribution to Community Music Dance Theatre Project Lambranzis curieuse Tantz-Schul on an idea by Regina Irman 2007–08, Songs for soprano, bass clarinet, cello and piano, to texts by William Blake and a Nursery Rhyme 2009, Follia/Schattenvariationen for two recorders, Baroque cello, theorbo and harpsichord, with percussion 2009–10, Im Park, short opera with a libretto by Ilma Rakusa, for soprano, mezzo-soprano, alto, tenor, baritone, clarinet, violin, double bass, accordion and percussion 2010–11, Locus solus, electronic sound images to the novel by Raymond Roussel Ab 2012 (in progress), L'Espagnole (Petite Entrée) for five-course Baroque guitar, six-course Baroque guitar, Baroque violin, Baroque cello and percussion 2013. *Recording:* Portrait 2001. *Address:* Wasserfurristrasse 48, 8406 Winterthur, Switzerland (home). *E-mail:* mail@regina-irman.ch (office). *Website:* www.regina-irman.ch.

IROSCH, Mirjana; singer (soprano); b. 24 Oct. 1939, Zagreb, Yugoslavia. *Education:* Zagreb Conservatory with Fritz Lunzer. *Career:* debut at Linz 1962, as Mercedes in Carmen; sang for many years at the Vienna Volksoper; took part in the 1968 premiere of the revised version of Der Zerrissene by Von Einem; Tour of Japan 1982; guest appearances in Graz, Frankfurt, Basle, Brussels and Munich; other roles include Micaela, Marenka in The Bartered Bride, Fiordiligi, Donna Elvira, Judith in Duke Bluebeard's Castle, Concepcion in L'Heure Espagnole, Rosina and Rosalinde. *Recordings include:* Die Lustige Witwe.

IRVINE, Robert, DipRCM, ARCM; British cellist; b. 11 May 1963, Glasgow, Scotland. *Education:* Royal Coll. of Music, London, studied with Christopher Bunting, Amaryllis Fleming. *Career:* mem., Brindisi String Quartet 1984–, Philharmonia Orchestra 1986–; various television and radio broadcasts; Principal Cello, London Soloists Chamber Orchestra, Britten-Pears Orchestra 1985–86; founder mem., Da Vinci Piano Trio, appearances at Cheltenham Music Festival, Sound Festival Aberdeen, broadcasts on BBC Radio 3; mem. Musicians' Union. *Recordings:* Britten 2nd Quartet; Berg Op 3 Quartet, Mozart/Schumann/Brahms, Clarinet Trios, Sally Beamish, Bridging the Day. *Honours:* RCM Foundation Scholar, Ivor James Cello Prize, Stern Award for Diploma Recital. *Current Management:* c/o Bows Art Classical Music Management, 10 Broom Road, Glasgow G77 5DP, Scotland. *Telephone:* (141) 616-2333. *E-mail:* info@bowsart.co.uk. *Website:* www.bowsart.co.uk.

IRWIN, Jane; British singer (mezzo-soprano); b. 1968, England. *Education:* Lancaster University and Royal Northern College of Music. *Career:* early appearances in Mahler's 3rd Symphony, under Kent Nagano, and Des Knaben Wunderhorn; Tchaikovsky's Maid of Orleans at the RNCM, 1994; recitals at the Paris Châtelet, Bienne, Poland, Japan and Geneva; Elgar's Sea Pictures in Scotland, Beethoven's Ninth and Missa Solemnis at the Edinburgh Festival, 1996–97; Rossini's Stabat Mater under Semyon Bychkov, Penderecki's Te Deum with the composer and The Dream of Gerontius conducted by David Willcocks; Covent Garden 1995–96, in Götterdämmerung and Die Walküre; Season 1997 in Die Zauberflöte and Ariadne auf Naxos at Aix, concert tour with the English Concert to Italy and Vienna and Hallé Orchestra concert. *Honours:* Decca Kathleen Ferrier Prize, 1991; Frederic Cox Award, 1992; Winner, 1993 Singers' Competition at the Geneva International Competition; Richard Tauber Prize, 1995. *Current Management:* Ingpen & Williams Ltd, 7 St George's Court, 131 Putney Bridge Road, London, SW15 2PA, England.

ISAACS, Mark, MMus; Australian composer and pianist; b. 22 June 1958, London, England; m.; one d. *Education:* New South Wales Conservatorium of Music, Eastman School of Music, USA, studied with Peter Sculthorpe, Josef Tal and Samuel Adler. *Career:* mem. Mark Isaacs Jazz Trio; commissions from Musica Viva, Australia Ensemble, Sydney String Quartet and Seymour Group, among others; conductor and producer of various projects; toured Russia, 1994, 1995, 1996; established GraceMusic record label, 1997; mem. cello/piano duo Tapas with Trish O'Brien 2003–; curator, Brisbane Jazz Festival 2005–10; mem. APRA. *Compositions:* more than 100 works composed including: Three Excursions for woodwind 1971, Reverie for piano and orchestra 1972, Reflections for piano and orchestra 1973, Three to Go for big band 1974, Interlude for flute and piano 1975, Ballade for big band 1976, D'Urbeville House for big band 1976, Mad Jean: A Musical 1977, Ode to Peace for big band 1977, Footsteps for big band 1977, Sad Girl for big band 1977,

Lamente for oboe and piano 1978, Fantasy for violin and piano 1979, Four Lyric Pieces for string trio 1980, Liturgy for string orchestra 1980, Ha Laitsun for two pianos 1981, Quintet for Brass 1981, Moving Pictures for piano and orchestra 1982, Four Glimpses for orchestra 1982, Diversion for six players 1983, I Am for mixed chorus a cappella 1984, Three Scherzi for winds and cello 1984, String Quartet 1984, So It Does for six players 1985, Ballade for Orchestra 1985, Three Songs for soprano and piano 1985, Character References for violin and piano 1985, Memoirs for percussion and piano 1986, Preludes for piano 1986, Visitation for solo piano 1986, Four Comments for winds 1986, Cantilena for bass clarinet and piano 1987, Piece for flute and strings 1987, Elegy for cello and piano 1987, Variations for flute, clarinet and cello 1988, Debekuth for violin and orchestra 1988, Burlesque Miniatures for String Quartet 1988, Drums of Thunder 1988, Purple Prayer for jazz quartet and strings 1989, Beach Dreaming (one-act opera for young people) 1990, Litany for piano and orchestra 1991, Threnody for violin and cello 1992, Lyric Caprice for cello and piano 1993, Songs of the Universal for viola, cello, clarinet and piano 1994, Scherzo for small orchestra 1995, Voices: The Passion of St Jeanne 1996, The Burning Thread for mixed chorus a cappella 1997, Scherzo for wind quintet 1998, Three Excursions for concert band and strings 1999, Chaconne/Salsa for cor anglais and orchestra 2001, Three Days of Rain 2001, Kensington Rags 2002, Ave Maria for cello and piano 2003, Canticle for trumpet and orchestra 2003, Autumnal Dances for guitar quartet 2003, Night Songs for viola and piano 2004, String Quartet No. 3 2004, Over the Rainbow 2005, Side-Wise Suite for jazz sextet 2005, Preludes for piano 2005, I Carry Your Heart for Me 2006, Divertimento 2006, Chinkon for bass koto solo 2006, Pange Lingua: Fantasia on a Hymn of St Thomas Aquinas 2007, Nacht und Tag for piano solo 2007, Between the Shores 2007, Songs at First Light 2008, Cantus Firmus 2009, Five Bagatelles 2009, Sonatine for violin and piano 2010, Serenade for orchestra 2011, Anniversary Fanfare 2011, Duende for solo piano 2012, The Quieter Path 2013, Barcarolle 2014, Berceuse 2015; various television and film themes. *Recordings:* Originals 1981, Preludes 1987, Encounters 1990, For Sure 1993, The Elements (four vols, Earth, Air, Water and Fire) 1996, Elders Suite (with Kenny Wheeler) 1997, On Reflection 1998, Closer 2000, Keeping the Standards 2004, Visions 2005, Resurgence 2007. *Honours:* Fellowship Australia Council for the Arts 1996–98, Miriam Hyde Composer-Pianist Award 1996, winner, Albert H Maggs Composition Prize, Univ. of Melbourne 2007. *E-mail:* markisaacs@optusnet.com.au (office). *Website:* www.markisaacs.com.

ISAKADZE, Liana; Georgian violinist and conductor; b. 2 Aug. 1946, Tbilisi. *Education:* Tchaikovsky Conservatory, Moscow. *Career:* debut at International Festival Congregation, Moscow 1956; concerts all over the world and for Russian, Georgian and German television; Art Dir and Conductor, Georgia State Chamber Orchestra 1980–; Leader of David Oistrakh School, Lenting bei Ingolstadt, Germany; opened D. Oistrakh Akademie Ingolstadt 1993. *Compositions:* many arranged for string orchestra, Sextets of Brahms, Tchaikovsky, Boccherini, Gershwin, Haydn, Bernstein, Dvořák, Mendelssohn and others. *Recordings include:* Firma Melodia, Firma Orfeusm Munich. *Honours:* Folk Artist of USSR 1988, Georgia State Prize 1982, Rustaveli Prize, Taliashvili Prize, first prize Tchaikovsky international violin competition 1970, Paris international violin competition 1965, Sibelius international violin competition 1970.

ISAKOVIĆ, Smiljka, MMus, PhD; Serbian harpsichordist and pianist; b. 23 March 1953, Belgrade. *Education:* music secondary school, Belgrade, American Community Schools, Athens, Belgrade Music Acad., Tchaikovsky Conservatory, Moscow, Royal Conservatory of Music, Madrid, Spain. *Career:* debut in Belgrade 1972; performances throughout fmr Yugoslavia, including festivals at Dubrovnik, Ljubljana, Ohrid, Belgrade, East and West Europe, the UK, USSR, USA, Cuba, Colombia and Iceland; harpsichord masterclasses, int. Centre des Jeunesses Musicales, Groznjan, fmr Yugoslavia; harpsichord lectures and recitals; music reviews for several publs and Radio Belgrade; Pres. Asscn of Serbian Musicians 1985–92. *Recordings:* Lady Plays–Keyboards, 1998; radio and TV appearances, fmr Yugoslavia, Spain, Colombia. *Honours:* First Lady of the Harpsichord; Masaryk's Prize, artistic activities, Masaryk Acad. of Arts, Prague 1997; Title Queen of the Harpsichord 1997. *E-mail:* info@smiljkaisakovic.com. *Website:* www.smiljkaisakovic.com.

ISBIN, Sharon, BA, MMus; American guitarist; *Chair of Guitar Department, The Juilliard School;* b. 7 Aug. 1956, Minneapolis, Minn. *Education:* Yale Univ., Yale School of Music, studied with Andrès Segovia, Oscar Ghiglia, Rosalyn Tureck. *Career:* has appeared as soloist with over 160 orchestras, including New York Philharmonic, Orchestre Nat. de France, London Symphony Orchestra, BBC Scottish Symphony Orchestra, Milan Verdi Orchestra, Tonkünstler Orchestra, Tokyo, Jerusalem, Houston, National, Dallas, Baltimore, St Louis, Minnesota, Milwaukee Symphonies, St Paul, Los Angeles, Zürich, and Scottish Chamber Orchestras; has performed at festivals, including Mostly Mozart, Aspen, Ravinia, Interlochen, Santa Fe, Mexico City, Bermuda, Hong Kong, Montreux, Strasbourg, Paris, Athens, Istanbul, Prague Spring, Budapest; as chamber musician has collaborated with Joan Baez, Steve Vai, Laurindo Almeida, Nigel Kennedy, Susanne Mentzer, Emerson String Quartet, Chamber Music Soc. of the Lincoln Center; performances include Ground Zero memorial concert, New York 11 Sept. 2002, world premiere of John Duarte's Joan Baez Suite 2003, Concierto de Aranjuez with New York Philharmonic 2004, world premiere of Steve Vai's Blossom Suite (with the composer), Paris 2005; Chair of Guitar Dept The

Juilliard School 1989–; Dir Guitar Dept, Aspen Music Festival; Dir Carnegie Hall Guitarstream Festival, New York 92nd Street Y series, Nat. Public Radio Guitarjam. *Recordings:* J. S. Bach, Complete Lute Suites 1989, Love Songs and Lullabies 1991, Road to the Sun 1992, American Landscapes 1995, Journey to the Amazon 1997, Dreams of a World (Grammy Award for Best Instrumental Soloist Performance without orchestra 2001) 1999, Rodrigo and Latin Romances 2000, Rouse, Concert de Gaudi/Tan Dun Yi2 (Echo Klassik Best Concert Recording 2002, Grammy Award 2002) 2001, Baroque Favourites for Guitar 2003, Sharon Isbin 2004, Concierto de Aranjuez with NY Philharmonic 2005, The Departed Score Soundtrack 2006, Journey to the New World (with Joan Baez and Mark O'Connor) (Grammy Award for Best Instrumental Soloist Performance (without orchestra) 2010) 2009. *Publication:* Classical Guitar Answer Book. *Honours:* First Prize, Toronto Competition 1975, Winner, Munich Competition 1976, Prize Winner Reina Sofia Madrid 1979. *Current Management:* c/o Jay K. Hoffman & Associates, 136 E 57th Street, Suite 801, New York, NY 10022, USA. *Telephone:* (212) 371-6690. *Fax:* (212) 754-0192. *E-mail:* info@jaykhoffman.com. *Address:* The Juilliard School, 60 Lincoln Center Plaza, New York, NY 10023-6588, USA (office). *Telephone:* (212) 799-5000 (office). *Website:* www.juilliard.edu (office); www .sharonisbin.com.

ISHIKAWA, Shizuka, DipMus; Japanese violinist; b. 2 Oct. 1954, Tokyo; m. Jiri Schultz 1978. *Education:* Prague Music Acad., studied with Prof. Shinichi Suzuki and Saburo Sumi. *Career:* performances at the Prague Spring Festival; Belgrade Music Festival; Warsaw Autumn Festival; Hungarian Music Week; Helsinki Music Festival; Czechoslovak Music Festival in Japan; performances in Tokyo, Copenhagen, Prague, Vienna, Brussels, Bonn; numerous radio and television broadcasts; soloist with many major orchestras. *Recordings:* Concertos by Bartók, Bruch, Mozart, Myslivecek and Paganini. *Honours:* second prize Wieniawski International Violin Competition 1972, silver medal Queen Elisabeth in Brussels 1976, third prize F. Kreisler International Violin Competition 1979.

ISHIZAKA, Danjulo; German/Japanese musician (cello); b. 14 May 1979, Bonn; s. of Junkichi Ishizaka and Ruth Nathrath. *Education:* studied with Boris Pergamenschikow at Hanns Eisler Conservatory Berlin, also with Tabea Zimmermann. *Career:* began cello lessons aged four; BBC Radio 3 New Generation Artist 2007–08; int. debut with Vienna Symphony in Vienna Musikverein under Krzysztof Penderecki 2003; Carnegie Hall debut 2006; performed as soloist with numerous orchestras including NHK Symphony, London Philharmonic and Acad. of St Martin-in-the-Fields, Tokyo and Singapore symphonies, Orchestre de l'Opéra Nat. de Paris, Mariinsky Theatre Orchestra, Baltimore Symphony, Radio Symphony Orchestra Vienna, Yomiuri Nippon Symphony Orchestra and Bavarian Radio Symphony under conductors including Krzysztof Penderecki, Gerd Albrecht, Andrew Davis, Christoph Eschenbach, Lawrence Foster, Michail and Vladimir Jurowski, Sir Roger Norrington, Mstislav Rostropovich, and Leonard Slatkin; regular performer at festivals such as Bachwoche Ansbach, Cellofestival Kronberg, Schleswig-Holstein, Penderecki, Rheingau, Kissinger Sommer, Kammermusikfest Lockenhaus, BBC Proms, Verbier, Luzern, City of London, Manchester Cello Festival, Hong Kong Arts Festival and Salzburg Easter Festival; chamber music with artists including Gidon Kremer, Lisa Batiashvili, Viviane Hagner, Tabea Zimmermann, Julia Fischer, Baiba Skride, Antje Weithaas, Veronika Eberle, Martin Helmchen and Ray Chen; Prof., Hochschule für Musik Carl Maria von Weber, Dresden 2011–. *Recordings include:* Cello Sonatas: Britten/Franck/Mendelssohn-Bartholdy (Echo Klassik Award) 2006, Schubert's String Quartet in D minor/Cello Quintet (with Pavel Haas Quartet, Gramophone Award for Best Chamber Music Recording 2014), Grieg/Janácek/ Kodály 2014. *Honours:* First Prize, Int. Gaspar Cassado Competition, Spain 1998, Lutosławski Competition, Warsaw 1999, ARD Int. Music Competition 2001, Grand Prix Emanuel Feuermann, Kronberg Acad./Universität der Künste Berlin 2002, Hideo Saito Memorial Fund Award, Sony Music Foundation, Tokyo 2012. *E-mail:* office@ishizaka.de. *Website:* www.ishizaka .de.

ISOIR, André; French organist; b. 1935, Saint-Dizier. *Education:* Conservatoire de Paris, studied with Rolande Falcinelli. *Career:* organist, Église St Médard 1952–57, Église St Séverin 1967–73, Eglise St-Germain-des-Prés 1973–, currently Hon. Organist; recitals, especially works of J. S. Bach; mem. Trio Alborada 1987–2007; Prof. École Nat. de Musique d'Orsay 1978–83, Conservatoire Nat. Régionale de Boulogne-Billancourt 1983–94. *Compositions include:* Variations sur un psaume Huguenot (Prix de Composition des Amis de l'Orgue). *Recordings:* over 60 albums and CDs. *Honours:* Chevalier, Ordre des Arts et des Lettres, Ordre Nat. du Mérite; First Prize, St Albans Competition 1965, Haarlem Competition 1966, 1967, 1968, Prix du Président de la République, Instrumental Soloist of the Year, Victoires de la Musique Classique 2000, Choc de l'Année du Monde de la Musique 2000. *Website:* ladolcevolta.com (office).

ISOKOSKI, Soile; Finnish singer (soprano); b. 14 Feb. 1957, Posio. *Education:* Sibelius Acad., Kuopio and studied with Dorothy Irving in Sweden. *Career:* fmr church organist; concert debut as singer at Helsinki 1986; appearances at concert halls in Europe, Japan, USA; performances at La Scala, Milan, Paris Bastille, Covent Garden, London, state opera houses in Hamburg, Berlin, Munich, Vienna, also at Salzburger Festspiele, Tanglewood, Orange Festival, Savonlinna Opera Festival; season 1993 with Salzburg Festival debut, as First Lady in Die Zauberflöte, and Mozart's Countess at Hamburg; Covent Garden debut as Fiordiligi in Così fan tutte 1997; Strauss's

Four Last Songs with Bavarian State Orchestra under Zubin Mehta at BBC Proms, London 1999; season 2000–01 as Amelia Grimaldi at Helsinki, Wagner's Eva at Covent Garden, Liu in Turandot and Desdemona at Vienna Staatsoper; New York Met debut as the Countess in Figaro 2002; Mahler's Symphony of a Thousand at BBC Proms 2002; Mozart and Sibelius with New York Philharmonic 2006, Tatyana in Helsinki 2006, Ellen Orford in Dresden 2007, Rosenkavalier in San Francisco 2007, Lohengrin in Geneva 2008, Les dialogues des Carmelites in Munich 2010, Lohengrin in Los Angeles 2010, Falstaff in Toulouse 2011, Don Giovanni in Los Angeles 2012, Ariadne auf Naxos in Glyndebourne 2013 and Vienna 2014; numerous recitals and recordings. *Recordings:* Schumann, Frauenliebe und Leben, Liederkreis; Sibelius, Luonnotar, conducted by Neeme Järvi; Zemlinsky, Der Zwerg, conducted by James Conlon; Mozart, Donna Elvira in Don Giovanni conducted by Claudio Abbado; Beethoven, Fidelio conducted by Barenboim, Strauss: Four Last Songs (Gramophone Magazine Ed.'s Choice Award) 2002, Mozart Arias 2004, Sibelius: Songs (BBC Music Magazine Award for Disc of the Year 2007) 2006, Scene d'amore 2008, Kullervo 2008, Das Marienleben 2009, Strauss Lieder 2011, Strauss Hymnen and Opera Arias 2012. *Honours:* Pro Finlandia Medal 2002, Kammersängerin (Austria) 2008; Dr hc (Helsinki) 2011; Winner Lappeenranta Singing Competition 1987, Second Prize, Cardiff Singer of the World Competition 1987, Winner Elly Ameling and Tokyo Int. Competitions, BBC Music Magazine Vocal Award 2007, MIDEM Classical Award 2007, Sibelius Medal 2007, Diapason d'Or de l'année 2008. *Current Management:* c/o Allegro Artist Management, Tapiolan keskustorni 4.krs, 02100 Espoo, Finland. *Telephone:* (9) 4123012. *E-mail:* allegro@allegroartist .com. *Website:* www.allegroartist.com.

ISOMURA, Kazuhide; Japanese violinist; b. 27 Dec. 1945, Tokyohashi. *Education:* Juilliard School, New York. *Career:* violist of the Tokyo Quartet from 1969; regular concerts in the USA and abroad; first cycle of the complete quartets of Beethoven at the Yale at Norfolk Chamber Music Festival 1986; repeated cycles at the 92nd Street Y, New York, Ravinia and Israel Festivals, Yale, Princeton Univs; season 1990–91 at Alice Tully Hall, Metropolitan Museum of Art, New York, Boston, Washington, DC, Los Angeles, Cleveland, Detroit, Chicago, Miami, Seattle, San Francisco, Toronto; tour of South America and two tours of Europe, including Paris, Amsterdam, Bonn, Milan, Munich, Dublin, London, Berlin; quartet-in-residence, Yale Univ.; Univ. of Cincinnati Coll.-Conservatory of Music. *Recordings:* Schubert's major Quartets; Mozart Flute Quartets with James Galway and Clarinet Quintet with Richard Stoltzman; Quartets by Bartók, Brahms, Debussy, Haydn, Mozart and Ravel; Beethoven Middle Period Quartets. *Honours:* Grand Prix du Disque du Montreux, Stereo Review Best Chamber Music Recording of the Year, Gramophone Best Chamber Music Recording of the Year. *Website:* www .tokyoquartet.com.

ISRAEL, Robert, DipEd, DipMus; Israeli violist and teacher (retd) and composer; b. 12 June 1918, Berlin, Germany; m. Tamar Amrami 1951; one s. one d. *Education:* Rubin Acad., Jerusalem and Tel-Aviv, studied violin with Rudolph Bergmann, viola with Oedeon Partos, theory and harmony counterpoint composition with Yitshak Edel, Rosowsky and Mordecai Seter. *Career:* debut, Elegie for Viola with string orchestra by Mordecai Seter 1969; violist and tubist, Opera Orchestra, Tel-Aviv; violin teacher at various Kibbuzim 1946–48; Teacher of Violin, Viola and Theory, Conservatory Hadera 1952–; mem. Bass, Rinat Choir 1957–58; Prin. Violist, Haifa Symphony Orchestra 1962–83; performed with many chamber music groups. *Compositions include:* Five verses from Song of Songs for two-voice choir 1955, six pieces for violin and piano 1988, Arrangement of Rosamunde, the Trout, Marche militaire (Schubert) for three violins or two violins and viola 1989, 14 songs, arrangement for popular orchestra 1990, Saraband, Bourrée, Polonais (J. S. Bach) Sonatine (Beethoven), arranged for two violas or viola and violoncello 1993, Diatonic three-octave scales with special fingering for violin 1997, and for viola 2000, Music for four violas, accompaniment parts for Mazas op. 36 Etudes, Four Basic Fingerings of One-Octave Scales for violin, the same for viola, Canons for four violins from J. S. Bach Choral verses, the same for viola and violoncello 1999, Sonatine (Telemann) adapted for two violas or viola and violoncello 1998, V for string quartet Marcia I, Marcia II Meditation, Dance 2004, arranged G. J. Gershwin, Soon for string quintet, S. Joplin, The Entertainer for string quartet 2005, Schubert Sonatine III (op. 137), Telemann Concerto for Viola, arranged for four violas 2005. *Honours:* Haifa Symphony Orchestra Award 1999. *Address:* Ytsiat-Europa st 11, Beth Eliezer PO Box 10772, Hadera 38484, Israel (home). *Telephone:* (4) 6201370 (home).

ISSERLIS, Steven John, CBE; British cellist; b. 19 Dec. 1958, London, England; s. of George Isserlis and the late Cynthia Isserlis; m. Pauline Mara (died 2010); one s. *Education:* City of London School, Int. Cello Centre, Scotland, Oberlin Coll., Ohio, USA. *Career:* concerts and recitals world-wide 1977–; exponent of contemporary music as well as authentic period performance; chamber concerts include own 'Shadow of War' series at Wigmore Hall, London 2013; series of recitals with Olli Mustonen and Stephen Hough, and appearances at Verbier and Salzburg Festivals, 92nd Street Y, New York; gives regular children's concerts; Artistic Dir IMS Prussia Cove, Cornwall; writer of children's books about the lives of great composers; extensive and award-winning discography. *Recordings include:* Brahms Sonatas 2005, Bach Solo Cello Suites (Gramophone Award for Best Instrumental Recording) 2007, Schumann Music for Cello and Piano 2009, Revisions 2010, Lieux Retrouves with Thomas Adès 2012, Dvorak Cello Concertos 2013, Beethoven Cello Sonatas with Robert Levin 2014, Prokofiev & Shostakovich Cello Concertos

2015, Bach, Handel & Scarlatti Gamba Sonatas 2015, Mendelssohn, Grieg & Hough Cello Sonatas 2015, Elgar & Walton Cello Concertos 2015. *Publications:* transcription of Beethoven Variations in D arranged for violin or cello and piano or harpsichord, Edn of Saint-Saëns pieces for cello and piano, Steven Isserlis's Cello World, Unbeaten Tracks, Why Beethoven Threw the Stew 2001, Why Handel Waggled His Wig 2006. *Honours:* Hon. mem. RAM; Piatigorsky Award 1993, Royal Philharmonic Soc. Award 1993, Schumann Prize, Zwickau 2000, Time Out Classical Musician of the Year 2002, Gramophone Hall of Fame 2013. *Current Management:* c/o Alexander Monsey, IMG Artists, The Light Box, 111 Power Road, London, W4 5PY, England. *Telephone:* (20) 7957-5800. *Fax:* (20) 7957-5801. *E-mail:* amonsey@imgartists .com. *Website:* www.imgartists.com; www.stevenisserlis.com.

ITAMI, Naomi; singer (soprano); b. 1961, USA. *Education:* Guildhall School, London, Manhattan School, New York and Columbia Univ., New York. *Career:* debut as Zerlina in Don Giovanni under Charles Mackerras, Estates Theatre, Prague 1991; engagements at the Bach Festival, California; tours of the USA and Far East with the Gregg Smith Singers; Covent Garden Young Artists' Recital Series; Mozart's Blondchen with Scottish Opera; Lincoln Center Out-of-Doors Festival, New York; Divas' Tour of Europe; Despina at the Ludlow Festival, England; Susanna for Neath Opera, Wales and the European Centre of Vocal Arts, Belgium; Snape Maltings with the Borodin String Quartet; Buxton Festival; Maria in West Side Story, Dublin; Lady Thiang in The King and I, Broadway tour; four Lehar operettas under Richard Bonynge. *Honours:* Maggie Teyte Prize 1991, Prix de Maurice Ravel, France 1991.

ITIN, Ilya; Russian pianist; b. 1970. *Education:* Sverdlovsk Music School for Gifted Children with Natalia Litvinova, Tchaikovsky State Conservatoire, Moscow with Lev Naumov. *Career:* appearances with leading orchestras, including the Cleveland under Dohnányi, and National Symphony under Skrowaczewski from 1991; recitals at Washington Kennedy Center and Lincoln Center, New York; further concerts with European orchestras; season 1997–98 debut at the London Proms with the BBC Philharmonic under Sinaisky, engagements associated with the Leeds Piano Competition, and European tour with the City of Birmingham Symphony under Simon Rattle. *Honours:* first prize and Chopin Prize Robert Casadesus Competition, Cleveland, first prize and Contemporary Music Prize Leeds Int. Piano Competition 1996. *Current Management:* c/o Jonathan Wentworth Associates Ltd, 10 Fiske Place, Suite 530, Mount Vernon, NY 10550, USA. *Telephone:* (914) 667-0707. *Fax:* (914) 667-0784. *E-mail:* office@jwentworth.com. *Website:* www.jwentworth.com.

IVALDI, Jean-Marc; French singer (baritone); b. 6 May 1953, Toulon. *Education:* Conservatoire National and the School of the Grand Opera, Paris. *Career:* debut at Paris Opéra 1983 as Yamadori in Butterfly; Sang Rossini's Figaro at Liège, 1983, and appeared at Bordeaux, Toulouse, Nancy, Metz, Dijon, and Tours; As Bretigny in Manon and Ramiro in L'Heure Espagnole at Paris; Philadelphia in 1986 as Morales in Carmen, and Heidenheim 1989 as Escamillo; Other roles include Alfonso in La Favorite, Belcore, Albert in Werther, Ourrias in Mireille, Manuel in La Vida Breve, Germont, Paquiro in Goyescas, Frederic in Lakmé and Jarno in Mignon; Sang Valentin in Faust at St Etienne in 1990; Concert engagements include Carmina Burana at St Etienne and Joseph in L'Enfance du Christ at Nancy; Sang Escamillo at St Etienne, 1995. *Recordings:* La Favorite; Sonora in La Fanciulla del West, conducted by Leonard Slatkin. *Current Management:* c/o Agence Artistique Thérèse Cédelle, Boulevard Malesherbes 78, 75008 Paris, France. *Telephone:* 1-49-53-00-02. *Fax:* 1-45-63-70-23. *E-mail:* Agence.Cedelle@wanadoo.fr.

IVAN, Monica; Swedish singer (soprano); b. 1940, Stockholm. *Education:* studied in Stockholm and in Siena with Luigi Ricci. *Career:* debut at Stora Theater, Gothenburg 1964, as the Queen of Night; sang at the Hanover Opera 1966–68, Zürich 1968–69, Gothenburg from 1970; sang the Queen of Night at the 1974 Savonlinna Festival; guest appearances in Moscow and elsewhere in Russia from 1976, as Violetta, Gilda and Marguerite in Faust; other roles have included Santuzza, Butterfly, the Trovatore Leonora and Amelia (Un Ballo in Maschera).

IVANOV, Emil; singer (tenor); b. 1960, Rome, Italy. *Education:* Sofia, Bulgaria. *Career:* sang first at the National Opera, Sofia, then appeared as Don Carlos at Essen, 1987; St Gallen, 1988–89, as Ernani and Pollione in Norma; Macerata Festival as Manrico; guest engagements as Cavaradossi and Radames at Frankfurt, Zamoro in Verdi's Alzira at Fidenza, as the Prince in Rusalka at Houston and Don José at the Bregenz Festival, 1991; Vienna Staatsoper, 1992, as Dvořák's Dimitri, Radames and in Carmen; Il Tabarro at Volksoper; Attila at Nice; Cavaradossi in Tosca at Metropolitan New York, 1993–94; 1994–95 season: Carmen, La Traviata, Hérodiade, Madama Butterfly at Vienna-Staatsoper; Alfredo, Pinkerton, Don José, Carmen at Cologne, Il Tabarro at Birmingham and Don José at Pretoria; I Lombardi at St Gallen; Otello at Nancy; season 1999–2000 as Smetana's Dalibor at Cagliari, Alim in Le Roi de Lahore by Massenet at Bordeaux, Radames in Karlsruhe and Henri in Les Vêpres Siciliennes at St Gallen; Covent Garden debut 2002, as Carlo in I Masnadieri. *Current Management:* Atelier Musicale, Via Caselle 76, San Lazzaro di Savena 40068, Italy. *Telephone:* (051) 19984444. *Fax:* (051) 19984420. *E-mail:* info@ateliermusicale.com. *Website:* www.ateliermusicale .com.

IVANOV, Yossif; Belgian violinist; b. 1986, Antwerp; s. of Dmitri Ivanov. *Education:* studied with Zakhar Bron in Lübeck, Igor and Valery Oistrakh at Brussels Royal Conservatory, Augustin Dumay at Chapelle Musicale Reine Elisabeth. *Career:* has performed in venues in Europe, USA, Canada and S America, including Carnegie Hall New York, Musikverein, Vienna, Concertgebouw Amsterdam, Palais des Beaux-Arts Brussels, Cité de la Musique, Paris, Wigmore Hall, London; as concert soloist has worked with London Philharmonic Orchestra (debut 2007), Montreal Symphony Orchestra, Orchestra Sinfonica della RAI, Vancouver Symphony, Residentie Orchestra, The Hague, English Chamber Orchestra, Orchestre de la Suisse Romande, Rotterdam Philharmonic, Konzerthausorchester, Berlin, Lucerne Symphony, Sinfonia Varsovia, Milano Verdi Orchestra, Orchestre de Chambre de Lausanne, Luxembourg Philharmonic, Orchestre Nat. de Lille, Ensemble Orchestral de Paris, as well as all major Belgian orchestras; youngest violin teacher at Royal Conservatory of Brussels 2008–. *Recordings include:* Bartók, Violin Concerto No. 2, Shostakovich, Violin Concerto No. 1 with Royal Flemish Philharmonic conducted by Pinchas Steinberg 2008, Con Passione: Works for violin and piano of Tchaikovsky, Ravel, Chausson, Kreisler, Sarasate, Shchedrin and Waxman, with Itamar Golan, piano 2008, Violin Sonatas of Franck, Ysaye and D'Haene (Diapason d'Or de l'Année) 2006, Concertos of Dutilleux & D'Haene with Orchestre de l'Opéra National de Lyon conducted by Kazushi Ono 2010. *Honours:* First Prize Herman-Krebbers Competition, Maastricht (Holland), First Prize Charles-de-Bériot Competition, Brussels, First Prize Wieniawski Competition, Lublin (Poland), First Prize Tenuto Competition, Brussels, First Prize Int. Yehudi-Menuhin Violin Competition (England), First Prize Jeunesses Musicales Int. Montreal Music Competition 2003, Midem Awards Outstanding Young Artist 2006. *Current Management:* c/o CLB Management Ltd, 44a Floral Street, London, W6 9JG, England. *Telephone:* (20) 8563-7997. *E-mail:* kate@clbmanagement.co.uk. *Website:* www.yossifivanov.com.

IVERSEN, Audun; Norwegian singer (baritone); b. 1977, Harstad. *Education:* Toneheim Folkehøgskole, Norwegian State Acad. of Music, Hochschule für Musik und Theater, Leipzig. *Career:* began singing aged 22; singer/actor in Jesus Christ Superstar, State Theatre of Cen. Norway 1999–2000; performed with Royal Danish Opera, Copenhagen 2007–08; fmr soloist with Norwegian Soloist Choir; performed Eumete in Il Ritorno D'Ulisse in Patria, Oslo Chamber Music Festival 2005; sang at Grand Opening Gala of new Norwegian Nat. Opera House, Oslo 2008, Nobel Peace Prize Award Ceremony 2008, Bergen Int. Festival 2008; Prin. Artist, Royal Danish Opera 2008–09; Covent Garden debut , title role in Eugene Onegin 2011; debut with San Francisco Opera as Figaro 2013; roles with Norwegian Nat. Opera include title role in Eugene Onegin 2015, Germont in La Traviata 2015–16. *Honours:* winner Queen Sonja Int. Singing Competition, Oslo 2007, Reumert Talent Award, Denmark 2009. *Current Management:* c/o Artefact Artists Management, St.. Olavs Plass 3, 0165 Oslo, Norway. *Telephone:* 22-46-46-10. *E-mail:* me@ artefact.no. *Website:* www.artefact.no. *Address:* Ægirsgade 60, 3 t.v., 2200 Copenhagen N, Denmark (office). *Telephone:* 41-28-16-70 (office). *E-mail:* auduni@gmail.com (office). *Website:* www.auduniversen.com.

IWASAKI, Ko; Japanese cellist; *Professor, Graduate School, Toho Conservatory, Tokyo;* b. 16 Aug. 1944, Tokyo; m. Yurie Ishio 1979; two s. *Education:* Toho Conservatory, Tokyo, Juilliard School of Music, USA, studied with Leonard Rose, Harvey Shapiro, Pablo Casals in Puerto Rico. *Career:* debut recital at Carnegie Recital Hall, New York 1966; recital at Wigmore Hall, London, England 1968; performed with London Symphony 1972; participant, Summer Festivals, including Marlboro, Portland (Oregon), Kuhmo (Finland), Lockenhaus (Austria); performances in USA, Europe, Russia and the Orient; Dir, Moonbeach Music Camp, Okinawa, Japan 1979–; Dir, Cello Masterclass, Southern Methodist Univ., USA; Prof., Toho Conservatory Graduate School, Tokyo. *Recordings:* Ko Iwasaki Plays Schubert Arpeggione Sonata; Beethoven Sonatas; Shostakovich Sonata; Japanese Contemporary Works for Cello; Ko Iwasaki and Staffan Scheja Play Sonatas by Rachmaninov and Grieg; Iwasaki, Requibros; 19 Short Pieces, Compact Disc; Beethoven: 2 Trios; Dvořák, Tchaikovsky with Polish National Radio Symphony; Haydn Cello Concerto No. 1 and No. 2, with Polish Chamber Orchestra. *Honours:* 3rd Prizes: Vienna International Cello Competition, 1967; Munich International Competition, 1967, Budapest International Cello Competition, 1968, Tchaikovsky International Competition; 2nd Prize, Cadao International Cello Competition. *Address:* 5732 Still Forest Drive, Dallas, TX 75252, USA.

IZAMBARD, Sébastien; French singer (tenor) and musician (guitar, piano); b. 7 March 1973. *Career:* mem., Il Divo 2003–. *Recordings include:* albums: Il Divo 2004, Ancora 2005, The Christmas Collection 2005, Siempre 2006, The Promise 2008. *Current Management:* c/o Becca Barr Management, 5th Floor, Dorland House, 14-16 Regent Street, London, SW1Y 4PH, England. *Website:* www.ildivo.com.

IZQUIERDO, Juan Pablo; Chilean musician and conductor; *Principal Conductor, Chamber Orchestra of Chile;* b. 21 July 1935, Santiago; m. Trinidad Jiménez 1973; one s. one d. *Education:* Univ. of Chile, studied with Prof. Hermann Scherchen in Gravesano, Switzerland. *Career:* debut with Nat. Symphony of Chile 1961; Dir Music Dept, Catholic Univ. of Santiago; Prin. Conductor, Gulbenkian Orchestra, Lisbon, Philharmonic Orchestra of Chile, Nat. Symphony of Chile; guest conductor in Berlin, Frankfurt, Hamburg, Vienna, Paris, Madrid, Jerusalem, Munich and elsewhere; Dir of Orchestral Studies, Carnegie-Mellon Univ., Pittsburgh, USA 1989–2009; Music Dir Nat. Symphony of Chile 2000–01; Prin. Conductor, Chamber Orchestra of Chile. *Recordings include:* Bach: The Art of Fugue, Mozart: Requiem, Beethoven:

Symphonies, Brahms: German Requiem, Mahler: Symphonies, Britten: War Requiem, Stravinsky: Rite of Spring, Firebird; Schoenberg: Transfigured Night, Complete Chamber Arrangements; Messiaen: Turangalîla Symphony, Varèse: Amériques, George Crumb: Black Angels and Makrokosmos III (Diapason d'Or 2007), Xenakis, Kagel, Scelsi, other contemporary composers. *Honours:* Critics Award, Santiago 1963, 1999, First Prize, Dimitri Mitropoulos Competition, New York 1966, Premio Nacional de Musica (Chile) 2012. *Address:* San Crescente 280, Apt 902, Santiago, Chile (home). *Telephone:* 205-0659 (home). *Fax:* 343-5453 (home). *E-mail:* juanpabloizquierdo@gmail.com (office). *Website:* www.juanpabloizquierdo.com.

IZZO D'AMICO, Fiamma; singer (soprano); b. 1964, Rome, Italy. *Education:* Santa Cecilia Conservatory, Rome. *Career:* debut as Mimi in La Bohème at the Teatro Regio, Turin 1984; sang Violetta at Treviso 1985; sang Elisabeth de Valois at the 1986 Salzburg Festival, followed by Micaela in Carmen; US debut Philadelphia 1986 in La Bohème, with Luciano Pavarotti, celebrated his 15th anniversary with him at Modena 1986; Bologna 1986 in La Traviata, conducted by Riccardo Chailly; season 1987–88 with appearances in Bohème at Vienna, Metropolitan, New York; Manon in Genoa, Tosca and the Verdi Requiem at Salzburg; further engagements at the Paris Opéra, London, Chicago, Monte Carlo, Monaco and Hamburg.

J

JABLONSKI, Krzysztof; Polish pianist; b. 2 March 1965, Wrocław. *Education:* Karol Szymanowski Acad. of Music, Katowice, studied with Prof. Andrzej Jasinki. *Career:* numerous concert engagements in Poland and worldwide. *Recordings include:* Chopin: 24 Preludes Op 28, Haydn: Sonata in C Minor No. 33, Beethoven: Sonata in C Minor Op 13, Pathetique, Mozart: Piano Concerto in F Major K 459 (Orchester der Ludwigsburger Festspiele), Chopin: 24 Preludes Op 28, Polonaise in A flat Major, Op 43, Heroique, Study in G flat Major Op 10-5 Black Keys, Study in C Minor Op 10-12, Revolutionary, Chopin: Sonata in B Minor Op 58, Barcarolle in F sharp Major Op 60, Polonaises in A flat Major Op 53, Heroique in G Minor in B flat Major, in A flat Major, Nocturnes, in B flat Major Op 9-3 in F sharp Major Op 15, 2, Mussorgsky: Piano solo, Pictures at an Exhibition, Schumann: Kinderszenen Op. 15, Debussy: Children's Corner 1993.

JABLONSKI, Peter; Swedish pianist; b. 1971, Lyckeby. *Education:* Malmö Music College, Royal College of Music, London. *Career:* started as a percussionist; performed jazz with Thad Jones and Buddy Rich at Village Vanguard, New York, 1980; has appeared with such orchestras as the Royal and Moscow Philharmonics, Philharmonia, Philadelphia, Cleveland and the Los Angeles and Japan Philharmonics in Berlin and Milan; annual concert tours to Japan and Far East and America since 1992; visits to Australia and New Zealand; engagements include Deutsche Symphonie Orchestra, Philharmonia, Royal Stockholm Philharmonic, Swedish Radio, Hong Kong Philharmonic, Orchestre National de France and Czech Philharmonic under Ashkenazy; world premiere of Kilar's Piano Concerto, 1997. *Recordings include:* Concertos by Gershwin, Rachmaninov, Lutosławski and Tchaikovsky; Chopin Waltzes and solo music by Liszt; Grieg recital, 1997. *Honours:* Edison Award, 1993; Årets Svensk I Varlden, 1996; Orpheus Award at Warsaw Autumn Festival, 1998. *Current Management:* Harrison Parrott, 5–6 Albion Court, London, W6 0QT, England. *Telephone:* (20) 7229-9166. *Fax:* (20) 7221-5042. *E-mail:* info@harrisonparrott.co.uk. *Website:* www .harrisonparrott.com.

JACKIW, Stefan; American violinist; b. 1985. *Education:* New England Conservatory with Zinaida Gilels, Michèle Auclair. *Career:* season 1997 with the Wieniawski Second Concerto at the Boston Pops, and with the Minnesota Orchestra and Pittsburgh Symphony; further engagements with the Boston Symphony Orchestra's Youth Concert, conducted by Keith Lockhart; European debut with the Philharmonia, London, in Mendelssohn's Concerto, conducted by Benjamin Zander 2000; season 2000–01 with the Strasbourg Philharmonic conducted by Yoel Levi. *Current Management:* Opus 3 Artists, 470 Park Avenue South, 9th Floor North, New York, NY 10016, USA. *Telephone:* (212) 584-7500. *Fax:* (646) 300-8200. *E-mail:* info@opus3artists .com. *Website:* www.opus3artists.com.

JACKMAN, Jeremy S., BMus; British conductor, composer and arranger; b. 22 April 1952, London; m. Angela; one s. one d. *Education:* Jr Exhibitioner Royal Coll. of Music, Hull Univ. *Career:* mem. of King's Singers 1980–90; Chorus Master, Belfast Philharmonic choir 1991–97, London Philharmonic Choir 1992–94; f. OSJ Voices in 1994 for the Orchestra of St John's Smith Square; Dir of Music, English Baroque Choir 2000–; mem. Asscn of British Choral Dirs, Incorporated Soc. of Musicians. *Compositions:* 22 compositions, arrangements and edns for Harmonia; Veni Emanuel, Who Shall Hold the Heart of Man? for Maecenas, Music of the World for Novello. *Recordings:* many recordings for The King's Singers. *Publications:* contrib. to Meistersinger, Church Music Quarterly, Music Journal. *Address:* Palace Music, 64 Park Avenue North, London, N8 7RT, England (office). *Telephone:* (20) 8341-3408 (office). *Fax:* (20) 8341-3408 (office). *E-mail:* jeremyjackman@btinternet .com (office). *Website:* www.jeremyjackman.co.uk (office).

JACKSON, Francis Alan, CBE, DMus, FRCO; British organist and composer; *Organist Emeritus, York Minster;* b. 2 Oct. 1917, Malton, Yorks., England; s. of William Altham Jackson and Eveline May (née Suddaby); m. Priscilla Procter 1950 (died 2013); two s. one d. *Education:* York Minster Choir School and with Sir Edward Bairstow, Durham Univ. *Career:* Organist, Malton Parish Church 1933–40; war service with 9th Lancers in N Africa and Italy 1940–46; Asst Organist, York Minster 1946, Master of the Music 1946–82, Organist Emer. 1988–; Conductor York Musical Soc. 1947–82, York Symphony Orchestra 1947–80; now freelance organist and composer; Patron, Whitlock Trust; Fellow, Guild of Musicians and Singers. *Music:* published works include Symphony in D minor 1957, Organ Concerto 1985, Eclogue for piano and organ 1987, Recitative and Allegro for trombone and organ 1989, organ music including six sonatas, three duets, church music, songs and monodramas, Sonatina Pastorale for recorder and piano 1999, Sonata for trumpet and organ 2003, Fantasy-Duo for two organs 2014. *Publications:* Blessed City: The Life and Works of Edward C. Bairstow 1996, Music for a Long While (autobiog.) 2013. *Honours:* Hon. Fellow, Royal School of Church Music, Westminster Choir Coll., Princeton, NJ, USA 1970, Royal Northern Coll. of Music 1982, Guild of Church Musicians 2005, Royal Coll. of Organists 2012; Order of St William of York 1983; Hon. DUniv (York) 1983, Hon. DMus (Lambeth) 2012. *Address:* Nether Garth, East Acklam, Malton, North Yorks., YO17 9RG, England (home). *Telephone:* (1653) 658395 (home).

JACKSON, Garfield; British violist; b. 1955, England. *Career:* founder-mem. and violist, Endellion Quartet 1979–; many concerts in Munich, Frankfurt, Amsterdam, Paris, Salzburg and Rome; South Bank Haydn Festival 1990 and Quartet Plus series 1994; Wigmore Hall Beethoven series 1991; Quartet in Residence, Univ. of Cambridge from 1992; residency at MIT, USA 1995, 2005, RNCM and The Venue, Leeds. *Recordings include:* works by Haydn, Bartók, Dvořák, Walton, Smetana, Beethoven, Tchaikovsky, Schubert, Britten, Vaughan Williams, Barber. *Current Management:* Hazard Chase Ltd, 25 City Road, Cambridge, CB1 1DP, England. *Telephone:* (1223) 312400. *Fax:* (1223) 460827. *E-mail:* info@hazardchase.co.uk. *Website:* www.hazardchase .co.uk. *E-mail:* info@endellionquartet.com (office). *Website:* www .endellionquartet.com.

JACKSON, Isaiah, BA, MA, MS, DMA; American musician and conductor; *Associate Professor of Composition, Berklee College of Music;* b. 22 Jan. 1945, Va; m. Helen Tuntland 1977; one s. two d. *Education:* Harvard Coll., Stanford Univ., Juilliard School of Music. *Career:* Asst Dir, American Symphony 1970–71; Assoc. Conductor, Rochester Philharmonic 1973–87; Music Dir, Royal Ballet, Covent Garden, London, UK 1987–90; Music Dir, Dayton Philharmonic 1987–95; Prin. Guest Conductor, Queensland Symphony 1993–; Music Dir, Youngstown Symphony 1996–2006; guest conducting, New York Philharmonic, Cleveland Orchestra, Boston Pops, San Francisco Symphony, Orchestre de la Suisse Romande, BBC Concert Orchestra, Berlin Symphony, Royal Liverpool Philharmonic, Houston Symphony. *Film:* Still Life at the Penguin Cafe/Galanteries, Sadler's Wells Royal Ballet. *Recordings:* string orchestra compositions of Herrmann, Waxman, Rozsa, Berlin Symphony; Dance music of William Grant Still, Berlin Symphony; Gospel at the Symphony, Louisville Orchestra; Harp concerti of Ginastera and Mathias, English Chamber Orchestra. *Publications:* As We Forgive Those, Know the Music! Show the Music!, Vols 1 and 2. *Honours:* Gov.'s Award for Arts, Va 1979, Signet Soc. Medal for the Arts, Harvard Univ. 1991. *Address:* Berklee College of Music, 1140 Boylston Street, Boston, MA 02215, USA (office). *Telephone:* (617) 747-8841 (office). *E-mail:* ijackson@berklee.edu (office). *Website:* www.berklee.edu (office).

JACKSON, Laurence, DipRAM; British violinist; *Leader, City of Birmingham Symphony Orchestra;* b. 1967, Lancashire, England. *Education:* Chetham's School of Music, Manchester, Royal Acad. of Music, London with Emanuel Hurwitz, Maurice Hasson and Anne-Sophie Mutter. *Career:* concerto repertoire includes works by Bruch, Mendelssohn, Vaughan Williams and Tchaikovsky; Aldeburgh Festival in Concerto Grosso by Schnittke 1988; soloist at Royal Festival Hall in Vivaldi's The Four Seasons 1990; recitals at Fairfield Halls, Queen's Hall, Edinburgh, Brangwyn Hall and Turner Sims Hall; solo concert tour of Chile and Argentina; concerto and recital performances in Spain 1992; Leader, Maggini Quartet 1994–2006; Leader, City of Birmingham Symphony Orchestra (CBSO) 2006–, appeared as soloist in Dvorak, Bruch and Brahms double concertos; Violin Tutor, Birmingham Conservatoire. *Recordings include:* works for violin and piano by Sir Arnold Bax with Ashley Wass (piano), solo recording with ensemble Laureate 1991, Violin Solo in Strauss's Ein Heldenleben with CBSO 2009. *Honours:* Hon. Fellow, Brunel Univ., London, Christ Church Univ. Coll., Canterbury; David Martin Concerto Prize 1987, and Principal's Prize 1988, Royal English Heritage Award 1983, 1985, 1986, First Prize, Vina del Mar (Chile) 1990, Third Prize, first Pablo Sarasate Int. Violin Competition, Pamplona (Spain) 1991, Gramophone Award for Chamber Music with Maggini Quartet 2001. *Address:* City of Birmingham Symphony Orchestra, CBSO Centre, Berkley Street, Birmingham, B1 2LF, England (office). *Telephone:* (121) 616-6500 (office). *Fax:* (121) 616-6518 (office). *E-mail:* information@cbso.co.uk (office). *Website:* www.cbso.co.uk (office).

JACKSON, Sir Nicholas Fane St George (Bart), Kt, LRAM, ARCM; British organist, harpsichordist and composer; *Director, Concertante of London;* b. 4 Sept. 1934, London, England; s. of Sir Hugh Jackson and Lady Jackson (née St George); m. Nadia Michard 1971; one s. *Education:* Radley Coll., Wadham Coll., Oxford, Royal Acad. of Music with C. H. Trevor, George Malcolm, Gustav Leonhardt. *Career:* Wigmore Hall debut 1964; Organist at St James's, London 1971–74, St Lawrence Jewry next Guildhall 1974–77; Organist and Master of Choristers of St David's Cathedral 1977–84; organ recital at Royal Festival Hall 1984; Dir Concertante of London 1987–, annual performances at The Banqueting House, Whitehall 2004–11; masterclasses in Segovia, Spain 1989; Dir of Festival Bach, Santes Creus, Spain; tours of Croatia 2002–13; solo performances at South Bank, London and at Notre Dame, Paris, Teatro Real, Madrid and New York; world premiere of his opera The Reluntant Highwayman at Broomhill 1995; first performance of Four Temperaments at Split 2009; The Rose & The Ring Opera 2013 (premiered at The Charterhouse, London 2016). *Compositions include:* Mass for a Saint's Day 1964, 20th Century Merbecke 1966, Four Images 1971, Magnificat & Nunc Dimittis 'The Short Service' 1971, Benedicite 1972, Organ Mass 1975, Magnificat & Nunc Dimittis 'St Davids Service' 1977, Magnificat & Nunc Dimittis 'Phrygian Mode' 1979, Two Short Introits 1980, I Will Give Thanks (Psalm 111) 1980, Jubilate 1980, Missa Brevis 1980, Missa cum Jubilo 1980, Divertissement for Organ 1983, Psalm 23 1983, Mass for Organ 1984, Organ Sonata 1986, Salve Regina 1986, Suite 1987, Brass Quintet 1990, The

Reluctant Highwayman 1992, Organ Sonata 1995, Wedding Suite 1996, Concert Variations 'Praise to the Lord' 1999, 16 Hymn Tune Reharmonisations 2000, Rhapsody on 'This Joyful Eastertide' 2000, Two Short Anthems 2000, Behold a Great Priest 2000, Tantum Ergo 2000, The Rood 2000, Four Pieces for trumpet & organ 2000, Purcell's Rondo from Abdelaaza 2000, Sonata da Chiesa for 2 Trumpets & Organ 2000, Carillon 'O Praise Ye the Lord' 2002, Five Variations on Good King Wenceslas 2002, Orgelbuchlein Vol. 1 – Advent/Christmas 2002, Orgelbuchlein Vol. 2 – Lent/Easter 2002, Orgelbuchlein Vol. 3 – Miscellanous 2002, Office Hymn 2002, Seis Piezas Espanolas 2002, Hommage a Langlais 2003, Variations on Victimae Pascali 2003, Responses 2003, 6 Elizabethan Songs 2009, Venetian Seranade (Sextet) 2009, Four Temperaments (Piano Concertino) 2009, 5 Pièces pour un orgue classique Français 2009. *Recordings include:* The Organ of St David's Cathedral, Bach's Christmas Organ Music, Music for Trumpet and Organ, two albums with Maurice Murphy, Complete Organ Works of Richard Arnell, Bach's 2- and 3-part Inventions, François Couperin, Harpsichord Concertos, Mass for a Saint's Day, Own Organ Works and Works for Trumpet and Organ, played at Chartres Cathedral 2000, Spanish Organ Music, Segovia Cathedral Priory 2001, Herald 2004, Organ of Rab Cathedral, Croatia 2009, two Naxos recordings of own works, also recordings on Priory, Herald and Somm, including Bach's Musical Offering 2009, Instrumental Music 2013. *Publication:* 'Recollections' of Sir T. G. Jackson RA (ed. and arranger). *Honours:* Master of the Worshipful Co. of Drapers 1994–95; Liveryman of the Worshipful Co. of Musicans; Hon. Fellow, Hertford Coll., Oxford 1995, Hon. Patron, Hertford Coll. Music Soc. *Address:* 42A Hereford Road, London, W2 5AJ, England (home). *E-mail:* nicholas@jacksonmusic.co.uk (office). *Website:* www.jacksonmusic.co.uk.

JACOBS, Paul Abraham, MM, AD; American organist; *Chair, Organ Department, Juilliard School*; b. 1 Feb. 1977, Washington, Pa. *Education:* Curtis Inst. of Music, Phila, Yale Inst. of Sacred Music. *Career:* organist, Washington Memorial Chapel, Nat. Shrine at Valley Forge 1995–2000; organist and choirmaster, Christ and St Stephen's Episcopal Church 2001–03, Artist-in-Residence 2003–; mem. faculty, Juilliard School 2003–04, Chair, Organ Dept 2004–, William Schuman Scholars Chair 2007–; debut, Grand Teton Music Festival; recent performances include with Philadelphia Orchestra conducted by Michael Tilson Thomas, San Francisco Symphony led by Yan Pascal Tortelier, Phoenix Symphony conducted by Michael Christie; concerts throughout N and S America, Europe, Australia and Asia; mem. bd, Yale School of Music. *Recordings include:* Messiaen's Livre du Saint-Sacrement (Grammy Award for Best Instrumental Soloist Performance) 2011. *Honours:* Arthur W. Foote Award, Harvard Musical Asscn 2004, Distinguished Alumni Award, Yale School of Music 2005. *Current Management:* c/o Phillip Truckenbrod, Concert Artists, PO Box 331060, West Hartford, CT 06103-1060, USA. *Telephone:* (860) 236-2288. *E-mail:* email@concertartists.com. *Website:* www.concertartists.com.

JACOBS, René, BPhil; Belgian singer (countertenor) and conductor; b. 30 Oct. 1946, Ghent; m. Roubina Saidkhanian. *Education:* Univ. of Ghent, studied singing with Louis Devos in Brussels, Lucie Frateur in The Hague. *Career:* recitals in Europe, Canada, USA, Japan, Mexico and the Philippines; performances with madrigal ensembles and with early music groups, including Leonhardt Consort, Il Complesso Barocco, La Petite Bande and groups led by Alan Curtis and Nikolaus Harnoncourt; sings Baroque music and directs own ensemble, Concerto Vocale; best known in operas by Monteverdi, Cesti, Handel, Gluck and Cavalli; sacred music by Charpentier and Couperin; regularly invited as conductor by Brussels La Monnaie, Berlin Staatsoper Unter den Linden and Theater an der Wien; conducted Cavalli's Giasone, La Calisto, Eliogabalo, Gassmann's Opera seria, Handel's Flavio, Agrippina, Rinaldo, Semele, Giulio Cesare, Monteverdi's L'Incoronazione de Poppea, L'Orfeo, Il ritorno d'Ulisse in patria, Madrigals, Graun's Cleopatra e Cesare, Scarlatti's Griselda, Haydn's Il mondo della luna, Orlando Paladino, Conti's Don Chisciotte, Telemann's Orpheus, Der geduldige Sokrates, Keiser's Croesus, Mozart's Nozze di Figaro, Così fan tutte, Don Giovanni, La Clemenza di Tito, Idomeneo, Die Zauberflöte, La Finta Giardiniera; Rossini's Tancredi; Artistic Dir Innsbrucker Festwochen der alten Musik 1991–2009; teacher of performing practice in Baroque singing, Schola Cantorum, Basle; appointments at Int. Summer School for Early Music, Innsbruck, and Aston Magna Acad. for Baroque Music, USA. *Recordings include:* Cesti's L'Orontea (from the 1982 Holland Festival), Arias by Monteverdi and Benedetto Ferrari, Motets by Charpentier, Bach's St Matthew Passion, Handel's Admeto and Partenope, Lully's Bourgeois Gentilhomme, Gluck's Orfeo ed Euridice and Echo et Narcisse, Giasone and La Calisto by Cavalli, Handel's Alessandro and Tamerlano, Charpentier's David et Jonathas, Handel's Flavio (Deutsche Schallplattenkritik Jahrespreis 1991), Telemann's Orpheus (Deutsche Schaalplattenkritik Jahrespreis 1998), Scarlatti's Il primo omicidio, Keiser's Croesus, Handel's Giulio Cesare, Handel's Rinaldo (Cannes Classical Award 2004), Mozart's Così fan tutte, Mozart's Le nozze di Figaro (Echo Klassik 2005, MIDEM Classical Music Award for Recording of the Year 2005, Grammy Award for Best Opera 2007) 2004, Handel's Saul (MIDEM Classical Music Award Baroque category 2006, Gramophone Award for Best Baroque Vocal Recording 2006, Echo Klassik 2006) 2005, Haydn's Symphonies Nos 91 & 92 2005, Handel's Messiah 2006, La Clemenza di Tito (Deutsche Schallplattenkritik Jahrespreis 2006, Abendzeitung Stern des Jahres 2006, Classical BRIT Award Critics' Award 2007, Echo Klassik 2007, Opernwelt 2007), Mozart's Don Giovanni, Idomeneo 2009, Mozart's The Magic Flute 2010, Handel's Agrippina (BBC Music Magazine Opera Award 2012). *Honours:* Dr hc (Univ. of Ghent) 2008; Acad. Charles Cros Prix in Honorem 2001, Deutsche Schallplattenpreis Ehrenurkunde 2004, MIDEM Classical Award for Artist of the Year 2005, Gramophone Award for Musical Personality of the Year 2006, Partituren Dirigent des Jahres 2007, Telemmann Prize 2008. *Current Management:* c/o Double Bande, 2 passage Philippe Auguste, 75011 Paris, France. *E-mail:* doublebande@aol.com (office).

JACOBSON, Bernard Isaac, BA, MA; British writer on music; b. 2 March 1936, London, England; m. 1st Bonnie Brodsky 1968 (divorced 1982); one s. one d.; m. 2nd Dr Laura Dale Belcove 1983. *Education:* City of London School, Corpus Christi Coll., Oxford. *Career:* music critic, Chicago Daily News 1967–73; Dir, Southern Arts Asscn, Winchester 1973–76; Deputy Dir of Publications, Boosey & Hawkes Music Publishers Ltd, London 1979–81, Dir of Promotion 1982–84; Man. of Publications and Educational Programmes, Philadelphia Orchestra 1984–88, Programme Annotater and Musicologist 1988–91; Artistic Dir, Residentie Orkest, Hague Philharmonic 1992–94; Independent Assoc., Joy Mebus Artists' Management 1993–94; Artistic Adviser, North Netherlands Orchestra 1994–. *Publications include:* The Music of Johannes Brahms 1977, Conductors on Conducting 1979; many translations; libretti; contrib. to Dictionary of 20th-Century Music 1974, The New Grove 1980.

JACOBSON, Julian; British pianist; b. 1947, Scotland. *Education:* Royal College of Music, Univ. of Oxford, studied with Lamar Crowson, Louis Kentner, Arthur Benjamin, Humphrey Searle. *Career:* debut in London, Purcell Room, 1974; appearances in over 30 countries including concerto engagements with London Symphony, BBC Symphony, City of Birmingham Orchestra, English Chamber Orchestra, London Mozart Players, Bournemouth Sinfonietta; chamber music recitals with: Nigel Kennedy, Lydia Mordkovitch, Zara Nelsova, Steven Isserlis, Colin Carr, Christian Lindberg, Ivry Gitlis, Brodsky and Arditti Quartets; Artistic Director, Paxos Festival, Greece; teacher and performer, Dartington International Summer School; Head of Keyboard Studies, Welsh College of Music and Drama, 1992–96; solo recitals include five cycles of the complete Beethoven Sonatas; concerts; masterclasses in France, Germany, Malta, Hungary and China, 1994–95; Conductor, European Union Chamber Orchestra, 1999; Sec., Beethoven Piano Society of Europe. *Compositions:* songs, piano works, chamber music, film scores. *Recordings include:* complete piano sonatas of Weber. *Telephone:* (20) 8694-9525. *E-mail:* julian.jacobson@onetel.net. *Website:* www.julianjacobson.co.uk.

JAFFE, Monte; American singer (baritone); b. 5 June 1940, Chattanooga, TN. *Education:* Curtis Inst. and studied with Giorgio Tozzi. *Career:* appearances with Krefeld Opera as Wotan, Kaspar (Der Freischütz), Dr Schön (Lulu), Reimann's Lear, the Dutchman, and in Cerhaa's Baal and the premiere of Judith by Matthus; appearances at the Metropolitan Opera in Death of Venice, Lear with ENO, the Hoffmann villains for Israel Opera and Bluebeard (Bartók) for Scottish Opera; returned to ENO for the title role in the premiere of Timon of Athens by Stephen Oliver 1991; has also sung at Karlsruhe (Graf Mirabeau by Matthus), Berne (Nekrotaz in Le Grand Macabre), Tel-Aviv (Mephistopheles in Faust), Bonn (Gianni Schicchi) 1993, Turin (Walküre Wotan), Antwerp (Klingsor) and Bielefeld (Barak in Die Frau ohne Schatten); other roles include Scarpia, Konchak (Prince Igor), Zaccaria (Nabucco) and Old Sam in Bernstein's A Quiet Place; sang the Rheingold Wotan at Braunschweig and Osmin for New York City Opera 1999; Nekrotzar in Ligeti's Le Grand Macabre for Flemish Opera 2001.

JAFFE, Stephen, AB, AM; American composer and musician; *Mary D.B.T. and James H. Semans Professor of Music, Duke University*; b. 30 Dec. 1954, Washington, DC; m. Mindy Oshrain 1988; two d. *Education:* Univ. of Pennsylvania with George Crumb, George Rochberg and Richard Wernick, Univ. of Massachusetts, Conservatoire de Musique, Geneva. *Career:* Dir Encounters with the Music of Our Time, and teacher, Duke Univ. 1981–, currently Mary D.B.T. and James H. Semans Prof. of Music; performances and commissions include Nat. Symphony under Leonard Slatkin, Tanglewood and Oregon Bach Festivals, North Carolina Symphony under G. Llewellyn, San Francisco Symphony under S. Mosko, New Jersey Symphony under Hugo Wolff, New York New Music Ensemble, Spectrum concerts, Berlin, Aurora and Ciompi Quartets. *Compositions include:* Singing Figures Chamber Concerto for solo oboe, violin, viola, piano, harpsichord, celesta (two players), Rega Raga for jazz ensemble 1975, Three Yiddish Songs for soprano and orchestra 1978, Three Images for chorus and chamber orchestra 1979, Partita for cello, piano and percussion 1981, Quartet from Arch for violin, cello, clarinet and piano 1981, Four Images for orchestra 1983, Autumnal for orchestra 1986, Three Figures and a Ground for flute and piano 1987, The Rhythm of the Running Plough for chamber orchestra 1988, Four Songs with Ensemble for mezzo-soprano and ensemble 1988, Double Sonata for two pianos 1989, Fort Juniper Songs for soprano, mezzo-soprano and piano 1989, First Quartet for string quartet 1991, Pedal Point for baritone, low strings, harp and timpani 1992, Triptych for piano and woodwind quintet 1993, The Reassurance for high voice and piano 1995, Offering for flute, harp and viola 1996, Songs of Turning for chorus and orchestra 1996, Spinoff for guitar 1998, Concerto for violin and orchestra 1999, Homage to the Breath: Instrumental and Vocal Meditations for mezzo-soprano and ten instruments 2001, Crazy Quilt for flute, oboe and cello 2001, Designs for flute, guitar and percussion 2002, Concerto for violoncello and orchestra 2003, Cut Time for orchestra 2004, Adagio con Sordino for violin and piano 2005, String Quartet No. 2: Sylvan and Aeolian Figures 2006, Four Pieces Quasi Sonata for viola and piano 2006, Poetry of the Piedmont for orchestra 2006, Sonata in four parts for cello and piano 2007, Cíthera mea (Evocations): Spanish Music Notebook for orchestra 2008. *Honours:* Joseph H. Bearns Prize 1976, Tanglewood Crofts Fellowship 1979, Rome Prize 1980, NEA Composer Fellowship 1981, Guggenheim Foundation Fellowship 1984, Brandeis Univ. Creative Arts Citation 1989, Kennedy Center Friedheim Award 1991, North Carolina Arts Council Artist Fellowship 1991, Nat. Flute Asscn Best Newly Published Music Citation 1991, American Acad. Inst. of Arts and Letters Lifetime Achievement Award 1993, Brown Univ. Eliza Gardner Howard Foundation Award 1996, Aaron Copland Foundation for Music Award 2002, Classical Recording Foundation Composer of the Year 2005, Koussevitsky International Recording Award (KIRA) 2006. *Current Management:* Theodore Presser Company, 588 North Gulph Road, King of Prussia, PA 19406, USA. *Telephone:* (610) 592-1222. *Fax:* (610) 592-1229. *Website:* music.duke.edu/jaffe.htm.

JAFFEE, Kay, BA, MA, PhD; American musician and musicologist; b. 31 Dec. 1937, Mich.; m. Michael Jaffee 1961. *Education:* Univ. of Michigan, New York Univ. *Career:* debut at Carnegie Recital Hall 1966; Founder-mem. and Assoc. Dir The Waverly Consort 1964–; performer on renaissance wind and keyboard instruments, harps, psalteries and percussion; appearances in major concert halls, New York 1965–; annual tours of N America since 1967; also tours to UK and Latin America; festival appearances include Casals Festival, Madeira Bach Festival, Hong Kong Festival and Caramoor Festival; TV appearances in USA; mem. American Musicological Soc. *Recordings:* 13 albums with The Waverly Consort. *Publications:* contrib. of articles and reviews to the Journal of Musicology, The American Recorder and The Brass Quarterly. *Honours:* Distinguished Alumna Award, New York Univ. 1990, Howard Mayer Brown Lifetime Achievement Award for Excellence in Early Music Performance, Early Music America 2000, American Eagle Award, Nat. Music Council 2003. *Address:* PO Box 386, Patterson, NY 12563, USA (home). *E-mail:* kjaffee@verizon.net (office).

JÄGGI, Andreas; singer (tenor); b. 30 March 1952, Basle, Switzerland. *Education:* studied with Maria Stader in Zürich. *Career:* singer and designer with the Companie Alain Germain in Europe and the USA from 1976; sang at Kiel Opera from 1985, Paris from 1987 (Weill's Mahagonny at the Opéra Bastille 1995); guest appearances at Covent Garden, Cologne (from 1988), Paris Opéra-Comique (Handel's Theodora) and Strasbourg (Narraboth in Salome 1994); other roles include Mozart's Pedrillo, Wagner's David, Andreas in Wozzeck and Flute in A Midsummer Night's Dream; further engagements at the Athens, Orange and Granada Festivals; sang Sylvester in Turnage's The Silver Tassie at Dublin 2001.

JAHN, Gertrude; Croatian singer (mezzo-soprano); b. 13 Aug. 1940, Zagreb. *Education:* Vienna Music Acad. with Elisabeth Rado and Lily Kolar, studied with Erik Werba and Josef Witt. *Career:* debut in Basle 1963, as Gluck's Orpheus; appearances at the State Operas of Vienna, Hamburg, Munich and Stuttgart; Glyndebourne 1968, as Olga in Eugene Onegin; Salzburg Festival from 1967, as Feodor in Boris Godunov, Mozart's Ascanio, Margret in Wozzeck and Countess Laura in the premiere of Penderecki's Die schwarze Maske 1986; Munich and Madrid 1988, as Adelaide in Arabella and the Countess Geschwitz in Lulu; further engagements in Düsseldorf, Salzburg, Moscow, Trieste and Montréal; other roles include Carmen, Giulietta in Les Contes d'Hoffmann, Octavian, Eboli, Preziosilla in La Forza del Destino, Fatima in Oberon and Magdalene in Die Meistersinger; frequent concert appearances. *Recordings include:* Masses by Haydn and Schubert; Missa Choralis by Liszt; Wozzeck. *Current Management:* Helmut Fischer Artists International, Obere Donaustrasse 45A/14, 1020 Vienna, Austria. *Telephone:* (1) 925-09-16. *E-mail:* fischerartists@yahoo.co.uk. *Website:* www.fischerartists.com.

JAHNS, Annette; German singer (mezzo-soprano); b. 1958, Dresden. *Education:* Dresden Musikhochschule, studied with Judith Beckmann in Hamburg and Ute Niss in Berlin. *Career:* sang with the Dresden Opera 1982–99, as Mozart's Ramiro in La Finta giardiniera, Dorabella and Cherubino, Nicklausse, Mistress Quickly, and Maddalena in Rigoletto; Carmen, Orpheus, Hansel and Olga; has also performed in the Brecht/Weill Sieben Todsunden; season 2000–01 as Sarah in Thomas Chatterton by Matthias Pintscher at the Vienna Volksoper and in the premiere of Celan by Peter Ruzicka. *Honours:* Berlin Reviewers' Award, 1987; Dresden Art Award, 1995. *Current Management:* Künstleragentur, Tobias Kade, Ammonstraße 72, 01067 Dresden, Germany. *Telephone:* (351) 490-6794. *Fax:* (351) 490-6793. *E-mail:* mail@kuenstleragentur-kade.de. *Website:* www.kuenstleragentur-kade.de.

JAHREN, Helen Mai Aase, MFA; Swedish oboist; b. 2 May 1959, Malmö. *Education:* Malmö Coll. of Music, Staatliche Hochschule für Musik, Freiburg, Konservatorium für Musik, Berne, studied with Heinz Holliger. *Career:* debut solo appearance with orchestra, age 17; tours France, Italy, Spain, Germany, Switzerland, Poland, Denmark, Norway, Finland, Iceland, Japan, 1980–; Belgian tour with Orchestre National de Belgique, 1982; Vienna debut, Grosses Konzerthaus, 1983; toured Colombia, Ecuador, Peru, Argentina, Uruguay, Brazil, Venezuela, Costa Rica, Mexico 1984; debut with Stockholm Philharmonic Orchestra 1987; invited to represent Scandinavia at Louisville Symphony Orchestra's 50th Anniversary, USA 1987; Pan Music Festival, Seoul 1988; gala Opening Concert, with Hong Kong Philharmonic Orchestra, World Music Days, Hong Kong 1988; debut with Swedish Radio Orchestra 1988; many television and radio appearances world-wide; teacher Malmö Coll. of Music 1984–87, Ingesund College of Music 1991–93, Stockholm Royal Coll.

of Music 1993–95; masterclasses; Initiator and Artistic Director of Båstad Chamber Music Festival; many pieces dedicated to her by composrers such as Erik Bergman, Poul Ruders, Daniel Börtz; Jouni Kaipainen, Per-Henrik Nordgren, Sven-David Sandström and many others; life mem. Royal Swedish Acad. of Music 1998–. *Recordings include:* Swedish music for oboe and organ with Hans-Ola Ericsson 1986, Schnittke Double Concerto for oboe and harp, with Stockholm Chamber Orchestra 1987, J H Roman, Oboe Concerto 1988, E Larsson, Oboe Concertino 1990, J Kaipainen, Oboe Concerto 1995, Mozart, Oboe Concerto in C major, J C Bach: Oboe Concertos, Ferlendis: Oboe Concerto 2000, Börtz: Oboe Concerto, Kithairon for Oboe Solo, Ekström: Oboe Concerto, The Accelerating Ice-cube, Gamstorp: Oboe Concerto, Pulse II for oboe solo 2000. *Honours:* winner, Jeunesses Musicales International Oboe Competition 1981, Biennial for Nordic Soloists 1986, Swedish Composers' Soc. Interpretation Award 1986, Swedish Phonogram Award 1986, 1987, Crystal Prixe 1995, City of Stockholm Artist Award 2001. *Current Management:* Svensk Konsertdirektion, Gunilla Lodding Ruijsenaars, Danska Vägen 25B, 412 74, Göteborg, Sweden. *Telephone:* (31) 83-00-95. *Fax:* (31) 40-80-11. *E-mail:* info@loddingkonsert.se. *Website:* www.loddingkonsert.se. *E-mail:* info@jahren.se (office). *Website:* www.jahren.se.

JAMES, Buddug Verona; British singer (mezzo-soprano); b. 1963, Cardigan, Wales. *Education:* Guildhall School of Music and Drama; Nat. Opera Studio. *Career:* 50 operatic roles include Gluck's Orfeo in America and Canada; Dardano in Handel's Amadigi in New York and Europe; Cherubino in Mozart's Marriage of Figaro in Tokyo and Toronto; has worked in Netherlands Opera, Cleveland Opera (USA), Glyndebourne; Almedia Opera; Opera Theatre Co.; Opera Northern Ireland; Opera North; Opera Atelier; Opera Circus; English Pocket Opera; Opera 80; Operavox Cartoons, Siobhan Davies Dance Co.; Music Theatre Wales and Mid Wales Opera; premieres in operas by Gerald Barry, Jonathan Dove, Deirdre Gribbin, Wolfgang Rihm and John Woolrich; Concert repertoire includes Mozart's Ch'io mi scordi di te with BBC Welsh Symphony Orchestra and Jane Glover; Matthaus Passion with Paul Steinitz; Johannes Passion with Thomas Dausgaard; Theodora with Paul McCreesh; Bach Cantatas with John Georgiadis; Elijah with Owain Arwel Hughes. *Recordings include:* Thomas Chilcot Songs; Arias by Handel and Gluck; The James Sisters Sing Gospel. *Website:* www.buddug.co.uk.

JAMES, Carolyn; American singer (soprano); b. 1963. *Education:* Arizona State Univ. and the Juilliard School. *Career:* sang Mozart's Countess at Miami and the New York Metropolitan 1991–92; Vienna Volksoper 1990, as Donna Anna, Fiordiligi at Cologne 1993; Vienna Staatsoper 1993–94, Metropolitan 1995, as Ellen Orford in Peter Grimes; Verdi's Elisabeth de Valois at Seattle and Elettra in Idomeneo at the Paris Opéra Bastille 1996; other roles include Berlioz's Beatrice and Purcell's Dido; concerts include the Mozart and Verdi Requiems, Messiah, Elijah, and Mahler's 8th Symphony.

JAMES, David; singer (countertenor); b. 1949, England. *Education:* Magdalen Coll., Oxford. *Career:* From 1978 has sung with the Hilliard Ensemble and other early music groups; Tours of Russia and Mexico, Schütz's Psalms of David and Cesti's Orontea in Innsbruck and at the Holland Festival; Handel's Orlando in Spain and Portugal with the Amsterdam Baroque Orchestra; Messiah in Finland and with The Sixteen (tours include visit to Utrecht 1990); Concerts with the Collegium Vocale Gent and La Chapelle Royale; Bach's St John Passion in London and Salzburg, the B minor Mass at Bruges and Cantatas in Finland 1991; Promenade Concerts 1990, in the cantata Herz und Mund und Tat und Leben; Contemporary Music Network tour with the Hilliard Ensemble in Pärt's St John Passion; Has sung at the Aldeburgh Festival, for Handel Opera in London, English National Opera and at Covent Garden; Frantz in the premiere of Dr Ox's Experiment, by Bryars, ENO 1998; Gen. Dir, New Sussex Opera, mid-scale touring opera with emphasis on new or lesser known works. *Recordings:* Orlando; Messiah; Pärt St John Passion (ECM), Bach St John Passion. *Honours:* Winner, 's-Hertogenbosch Competition, Netherlands 1978. *Current Management:* Hazard Chase Ltd, 25 City Road, Cambridge, CB1 1DP, England. *Telephone:* (1223) 312400 (office). *Fax:* (1223) 460827 (office). *Website:* www.hazardchase.co.uk; www.newsussexopera.com (office).

JAMES, Eirian; British singer (mezzo-soprano); b. 1952, Cardigan, Wales. *Education:* Royal College of Music with Ruth Packer. *Career:* debut at Kent Opera, 1977, as Olga in Eugene Onegin; returned as Cherubino, Poppea, Rosina, and Meg Page in Falstaff; English National Opera in The Makropulos Case, War and Peace, Rigoletto and Rusalka; Buxton Festival in Handel's Ariodante; Lyon Opéra as Fatima (Oberon) and Rossini's Isolier; Genera Opera as Hansel; Houston Opera as Siebel in Faust and Sesto in Handel's Giulio Cesare; Aix-en-Provence as Dorabella (Così fan tutte); Covent Garden debut 1987 as Annina in Der Rosenkavalier, returned as Smeton in Anna Bolena, 1988 and Nancy in Albert Herring, 1989; Sang Dorabella at Aix-en-Provence, 1989, second Lady in Die Zauberflöte at the 1990 Prom Concerts; Ascanio in Benvenuto Cellini for Netherlands Opera, Cherubino at Houston; Concert Appearances at the BBC Promenades, Aldeburgh Festival, the Barbican and with the BBC National Orchestra of Wales; repertoire includes the Lieder eines fahrenden Gesellen (Lyon), Beethoven's Mass in C (London), Mozart's C Minor Mass (Edinburgh and Paris); Haydn's Harmoniemesse; Mendelssohn's Elijah; Gluck's La Corona (City of London Festival); Hermia, Midsummer Night's Dream, Aix-en-Provence, 1991; Orlofsky, Fledermaus, 1991, English National Opera; Rosina (Barber of Seville), 1992; Scottish Opera, Sextus (Julius Caesar), 1992; Sang Cyrus in Handel's Belshazzar at the 1996 Göttingen Festival; Sang Falsirena inMazzochi's La Catena d'Adone at Innsbruck and Britten's Hermia at Rome, 1999. *Recordings include:* Zerlina in Don Giovanni, conducted by John Eliot Gardiner, (Deutsche Grammophon); Sextus (Julius Caesar by Handel) conducted by Jean-Claude Malgoire. *Current Management:* c/o Neil Dalrymple, Music International, 13 Ardilaun Road, London, N5 2QR, England. *Telephone:* (20) 7359-5183. *Fax:* (20) 7226-9792. *E-mail:* music@musicint.co.uk.

JAMES, Kevin G. G.; Canadian modern and baroque violist, violinist, researcher and writer; b. 30 July 1961, Toronto. *Education:* summer sessions University of Toronto, Carleton University, University of Ottawa, Oberlin College, McGill University. *Career:* freelance orchestral and chamber player, recitalist; staff writer, Encyclopedia of Music in Canada 1989–92; occasional contributor on Canadian topics to The Strad, Early Music, Musick, Performing Arts in Canada, Continuo, Newsletter of the American Musical Instrument Society, Canadian Viola Society Newsletter. performed premieres of : Jan Jarvlepp's Encounter 1991, Alyssa Ryvers' Two Songs for Viola and Voice 1990, and Synergy for nine violas 1994, Gilles Leclerc's Suite for Viola and Organ 1997, Michael Spassov's Fantasy for Solo Viola 1997, Brian Pantekoek's The Letter, for viola and percussion 1998, Deirdre Piper's Fantasy for Solo Viola 1999, Eldon Rathburn's Soliloquy for Solo Viola 1999, Andrew Ager's Garden Shadows, for viola and chamber choir 2000, Jan Jarvlepp's Street Scene, for viola and electric guitar 2000, Peter Amsel's Poème pour Alto, for solo viola 2000, Jan Jarvlepp's Suite for Viola and Strings 2001, Peter Willsha's Intermezzo for Viola and Strings 2002; mem. Asscn of Canadian Orchestras 1985–, Canadian Viola Society 1991–. *Recordings:* John Playford, The English Dancing Master, 1983; Jan Jarvlepp, Encounter, 1994, and Trio No. 2, 2000; The Mystical Music of Andalucia, with Barbara Solís, piano, 2003; Chamber and recital performances for Radio-Canada. *Address:* 455 Lisgar Street, No. 505, Ottawa, Ont. K1R 5G9, Canada (home). *Telephone:* (613) 230-2299 (home). *Fax:* (613) 230-1486 (home). *E-mail:* kggjames@canada.com (home).

JAMES, Peter Haydn, BMus, PhD, CertEd; Australian music editor; b. 17 Oct. 1940, Melbourne, Vic.; m. A. Heather; one s. one d. *Education:* Univ. of Wales, Cardiff and Univ. of Bristol. *Career:* Lecturer then Dir of Studies, Birmingham School of Music (now Birmingham Conservatoire) 1970–83; Vice-Prin. RAM 1983–95; Series Ed., Cathedral Press Ltd 1997–2010; part-time Lecturer, Open Univ. 1973–81; Vicar Choral, Lichfield Cathedral 1969–74; Chorus Master, City of Birmingham Symphony Orchestra Chorus 1974–76; mem. Royal Musical Asscn. *Recordings:* Chorus Master for City of Birmingham Symphony Orchestra Chorus recordings 1975–77. *Publications:* more than 50 edns of early sacred music; contrib. to Music & Letters 1983, Annual Byrd Newsletter 1999, 2000, Johnson Society 1981, Thomas Tomkins: The Last Elizabethan by Anthony Boden and others 2005. *Honours:* Fellow, Birmingham School of Music 1984; Hon. mem. RAM 1984, Royal Coll. of Music 1985. *Address:* Alltycham House, Pontardawe, Swansea, SA8 4JT, Wales (home). *Telephone:* (1792) 865197 (home). *E-mail:* james@cathpress.fsnet.co.uk (office).

JAMET-LARDÉ, Marie-Claire Thérèse Odile; French harpist; b. 27 Nov. 1933, Reims; d. of the late Pierre Jamet and Renée Jamet (née Hanson); m. Christian Lardé 1955; two s. *Education:* Conservatoire Nat. Supérieur de Musique, Paris. *Career:* has given over 2,000 concerts world-wide as soloist and with Christian Lardé; specializes in contemporary music; Soloist, Ensemble Inter Contemporain 1976–; Prof., Conservatoire Nat. Supérieur de Musique, Lyon 1981–95, Paris 1984–95, Ecole Normale de Musique de Paris 1984–95. *Recordings include:* Concerto pour flûte et harpe (Mozart), Les danses et sonate (Debussy), Introduction et allegro (Ravel), Musique du XVIIIème siècle 1978, La harpe au XXème siècle 1980, Harpe en élégance (jtly), Récital flute et harpe. *Honours:* Chevalier de l'Ordre nat. du Mérite 1983, Chevalier des Arts et Lettres 1992, Chevalier de la Légion d'honneur 1995; First Prize for Harp, Conservatoire Nat Supérieur de Musique 1948, First Prize for Chamber Music 1951, several prizes from Acad. Charles Cros, numerous int. prizes for recordings. *Address:* 844 Route du Peyron, 83780 Flayosc, France. *E-mail:* marieclaire.jamet@club-internet.fr.

JAMIESON, Peter; British music executive; m. Jane Jamieson; three c. *Career:* fmr management trainee, EMI; fmr Man. Dir EMI Greece; fmr sr exec. EMI and BMG; worked extensively in Europe, Australasia and Far East; helped establish BMG Asia Pacific and MTV Asia; Founding Pres. MTV Asia 1995–97; Exec. Chair. British Phonographic Industry (BPI) 2002–07. *Address:* c/o British Phonographic Industry, Riverside Building, County Hall, Westminster Bridge Road, London, SE1 7JA, England.

JANARCEKOVA, Viera; Czech composer; b. 23 Sept. 1944, Svit. *Education:* Bratislava Conservatory, Prague Acad. *Career:* keyboard performer and composer in Germany from 1981. *Compositions include:* Biomasse (for radio drama) 1984, four string quartets 1983–89, Pausenfabrik for two clarinets and ensemble 1987, Donna Laura for mezzo and 15 instruments 1989, Der Gehemnisvolle Nachen for mezzo cello 1989, Beschattungtheater for four cellos 1990, Piano Concerto 1991.

JANES, Fiona; Australian opera singer (mezzo-soprano); b. 28 Dec. 1964, Sydney, NSW. *Education:* Killara High School, Pittwater High School, New South Wales Conservatorium of Music. *Career:* mem., Australian Opera 1988–, notably as Adalgisa, Komponist, Rossini's Cenerentola, Rosina, Isabella, Mozart's Donna Elvira, Sesto, Annio, Dorabella, Zerlina, Cherubino, Mercedes, Siebel in Faust for Victoria State Opera, Siebel, Margherite and Rosina for the Lyric Opera of Queensland; Margherite, and Beethoven's Missa

Solemnis for Royal Scottish Nat. Orchestra; Scitalce in Semiramide with Richard Bonynge for Rossini Festival Wildbad; Int. debut at Buxton Festival 1992 as Nero in Handel's Agrippina, then Rosina with ENO, Netherlands Opera and Welsh Nat. Opera; season 1993–94 at the Edinburgh Festival, as Sesto in La Clemenza di Tito for the Glyndebourne Tour, Cenerentola for Semperoper Dresden and New Zealand , Les Troyans with London Symphony Orchestra; season 1995–96 at the Semperoper Dresden, Mozart's Idamantes with the Flanders Philharmonic Orchestra and Rossini's Isabella in Australia under Richard Bonynge; sang Lucia di Lammermoor at Auckland 1998; concerts include Mozart's Requiem, Beethoven's Missa Solemnis, Dream of Gerontius, Mahler 2, Schubert Mass in A, Coronation Mass, Messiah, Rossini's Stabat Mater, Pulcinella and L'Allegro il Penseroso; worked under numerous renowned conductors including Richard Bonynge, Sir Charles Mackerras, Sir Colin Davis, Simone Young, Walter Weller; performances with Royal Opera House Covent Garden, Scottish Opera, Sydney, Melbourne, Adelaide, West Australian and Brisbane Symphony's, Sydney Philharmonia, Madrid Orchestra, Nottingham Philharmonic. *Recordings include:* Meyerbeer's Semiramide (Naxos), Parisina (Opera Rara), Pulcinella (Naxos), Bicentennial CD ABC/TAO. *Television:* Cosi fan Tutte, Don Giovanni and 50th Anniversary Opera Gala, Opera Australia. *Honours:* Joan Sutherland Scholarship 1983, Marianne Mathy Scholarship 1986, Remy Martin Scholarship 1991, Vienna State Opera Award 1995, two Green Room Awards for Best Performer in a Lead Role. *Current Management:* Arts Management Pty Ltd, Level 1, 405 Elizabeth Street, Surry Hills, NSW 2010, Australia. *Telephone:* (2) 9211-9422. *Fax:* (2) 9211-9466. *E-mail:* enquiries@artsmanagement.com .au. *Website:* www.artsmanagement.com.au.

JANEVA-IVELIC, Veneta; Bulgarian singer (soprano); b. 1950. *Education:* Sofia Conservatory. *Career:* sang at the Sofia Opera from 1973, Nat. Opera Zagreb from 1980; guest appearances in Salzburg (with Zagreb company as Norma 1985), Berlin Staatsoper, Paris Opéra (Abigaille in Nabucco), Luxembourg and Karlsruhe; other roles have included Maddalena (Andrea Chénier), the Forza and Trovatore Leonoras, Violetta, Desdemona, Lady Macbeth, Butterfly and Elvira in I Puritani. *Honours:* prizewinner Rio Int. Competition 1980.

JANICKE, Heike, DipMus; German violinist; b. 20 Dec. 1962, Dresden. *Education:* Musikhochschule Dresden, Musikhochschule Freiburg. *Career:* violin soloist with Philharmonic Dresden, Berliner Sinfonie Orchestra, Rundfunksinfonie Orchestra Berlin, Radio Sinfonieorchestra Stuttgart, Gewandhaus Orchestra, Leipzig, Odense Sinfonie Orchestra, Bucharest Philharmonic; solo and chamber music concerts throughout Europe, Middle East, Japan, Middle and South America; television and radio productions; mem., Berlin Philharmonic Orchestra 1991–93; mem., London Symphony Orchestra 1993–; Concertmaster, Dresden Philharmonic Orchestra 1995–. *Honours:* Mendelssohn Scholarship 1988, Int Violin Competition, Geneva 1985, Fritz Kreisler, France 1987, Georg Kulenkampff, Cologne 1988, Carl Nielsen, Odense 1988, Zino Francescatti, Marseille 1989.

JANIS, Byron; American pianist; b. 24 March 1924, McKeesport, PA; m. 1st June Dickson-Wright; one s.; m. 2nd Maria Veronica Cooper. *Education:* studied with Josef and Rosina Lhevinne in New York, with Adele Marcus and Horowitz. *Career:* made debut performance playing Rachmaninov's 2nd Concerto with Pittsburgh Symphony Orchestra 1944; made Carnegie Hall debut 1948; European debut with Concertgebouw Orchestra 1952; toured Russia 1960, 1962, appearing with Moscow Philharmonic Orchestra; further engagements with Boston Symphony, Philadelphia Orchestra and Indianapolis Symphony; Liszt concerts in Boston and New York 1962; discovered manuscripts of two Chopin waltzes in France 1967; career interrupted by psoriatic arthritis 1970s; honored by Pres. Reagan at White House concert 1988; repertoire also includes Chopin, Prokofiev and Gottschalk; Nat. Arthritis Foundation Ambassador for the Arts 1985. *Recordings include:* Concertos by Liszt and Rachmaninov. *Publication:* Chopin and Beyond: My Extraordinary Life in Music and the Paranormal (with Maria Cooper Janis) 2010. *Honours:* Commdr, Ordre des Arts et des Lettres 1965; Dr hc (Trinity Coll.); Harriet Cohen Award, Grand Prix du Disque, France, Stanford Fellowship, Distinguished Pennsylvania Artists Award, Gold Medal, Soc. for the Encouragement of Progress. *Current Management:* c/o Bettina L. Klinger, Klinger Partners, 694 Third Avenue, New York, NY 10017-4005, USA. *Telephone:* (212) 953-9280. *E-mail:* bklinger@klingerpartners.com. *Website:* www.klingerpartners.com; byronjanis.com.

JANK, Helena; Brazilian harpsichordist; b. 1955, Salvador, Bahia; m. Eduardo Ostergren 1992, one d. *Education:* Staatliche Hochschule für Musik, Germany. *Career:* debut in Munich 1967; Prof., Campinas State Univ.; harpsichordist, Münchener Bach-Orchester; performances as soloist and in chamber music ensembles in Germany, USA and Brazil; mem. Int. Bach Soc. *Recordings:* Helena Jank Plays Bach, Scarlatti, Ligeti; The Finest Baroque Sonatas, Erich; Mozart Sonatas; J. S. Bach Goldberg Variations: A Guide for the Complete Person. *Honours:* Academic Recognition for Excellence in Teaching.

JANKOVIC, Eleonora; Italian singer (mezzo-soprano); b. 18 Feb. 1941, Trieste. *Education:* studied in Trieste and Milan. *Career:* mem., Opera at Zagreb, then made Italian debut at Trieste 1972, in Smareglia's Nozze Istriane; appearances at La Scala from 1974, Bologna 1975, Florence 1976, Teatro Lirico Milan 1975, in the premiere of Al gran sole carico d'Amore by Luigi Nono; guest engagements at Turin, Venice, Naples and Catania; Verona

Arena 1975–78, 1983, 1987; Rio de Janeiro and Buenos Aires 1982–83; sang Enrichetta in I Puritani at Rome 1990, and appeared in Luisa Miller at Trieste 1990; sang in Wolf-Ferrari's I Quattro Rusteghi, for Geneva Opera 1992; has also sung the Countess in The Queen of Spades, Ulrica, Amneris, Leonora in La Favorita, Carmen, Charlotte, Marina in Boris Godunov and Mother Goose in The Rake's Progress; many concert appearances.

JANOVICKY, Karel, MMus; Czech/British composer and broadcaster; b. 18 Feb. 1930, Plzeň; m. Sylva Šimsová 1950; one s. one d. *Education:* Realné Gymnasium, Plzeň, Surrey Coll. of Music, England, studied with Jan Šedivka (chamber music) and Matyas Seiber (composition). *Career:* debut at Wigmore Hall, London 1956; numerous scores in manuscript; language coach. *Compositions include:* Passages of Flight song cycle, Sonata for bass clarinet and piano, Three Cambridge Songs, Terzina for violin and piano 1988, four string quartets 1992, 1995, 1997, 2006, Saxophone Quartet 1996, Sonata for alto saxophone and piano 1999, Clarinet Quartet 2000, Harp Sonata 2000, In Praise of Rossini for flute and piano 2001, Concerto for strings 2002, Symphony 2004, Sonata for Clarinet and Piano 2007, Piano Sonatas, Sonatas for Violin and Piano, Ballads, Laments and Reels for violin, cello and Percussion 2008, Impromptus on Old Scottish Airs for treble recorder and harpsichord 2008. *Publications include:* contrib. to new edn of Leoš Janáček: A Biography by Jaroslav Vogel 1981, Introducing Mr Brouček 1978; contrib. to New Music Journal of Dvořák Society of Great Britain. *Honours:* Gratias agit 2011; First Prize, Shakespeare Competition, Bournemouth Symphony Orchestra (for Variations on a Theme of Robert Johnson Op. 17) 1957. *Address:* 18 Muswell Avenue, London, N10 2EG, England (home). *E-mail:* simsova@simsova.demon.co.uk. *Website:* www.karel-janovicky.co.uk.

JANOWITZ, Gundula; Austrian singer (soprano); b. 2 Aug. 1937, Berlin, Germany; d. of Theodor Janowitz and Else Janowitz (née Neumann); m.; one d. *Education:* Acad. of Music and Performing Arts, Graz. *Career:* debut with Vienna State Opera 1960; perm. mem. Deutsche Oper, Berlin 1966; sang with Metropolitan Opera, New York 1967, Salzburg Festival 1968–81, Teatro Colón, Buenos Aires 1970, Munich State Opera 1971, Grand Opera, Paris 73, Covent Garden Opera 1976, La Scala 1978; concerts in cities throughout the world, appearances at Bayreuth, Aix-en-Provence, Glyndebourne, Spoleto, Salzburg, Munich Festivals; Opera Dir at Graz 1990–91; mem. Vienna State Opera, Deutsche Oper, Berlin; mem. Main Prize Jury, BBC Cardiff Singer of the World Competition 2003, 2005, 2007. *Honours:* Hon. Mem. Vienna State Opera, Acad. of Music, Graz, RAM, London.

JANOWSKI, Marek; German conductor; *Chief Conductor and Artistic Director, Rundfunk Sinfonieorchester Berlin*; b. 18 Feb. 1939, Warsaw, Poland. *Education:* Cologne Musikhochschule and studied in Siena, Italy. *Career:* fmrly Asst Conductor in Aachen, Cologne and Düsseldorf opera houses; Music Dir, Freiburg and Dortmund Operas 1973–79; Artistic Adviser and Conductor Royal Liverpool Philharmonic Orchestra 1983–86; Music Dir and Chief Conductor Orchestre Philharmonique de Radio France 1984–2000; Chief Conductor Gurzenich-Orchester, Cologne 1986–90; Artistic Dir Monte Carlo Philharmonic Orchestra 1999, Music Dir and Chief Conductor 2000–05; Prin. Conductor and Artistic Dir Dresden Philharmonic Orchestra 2001–03; Chief Conductor and Artistic Dir Rundfunk Sinfonieorchester Berlin 2002–; Artistic and Music Dir Orchestre de la Suisse-Romande, Geneva 2005–12; Endowed Guest Conductor Chair, Pittsburgh Symphony Orchestra 2005–; regular guest conductor in Paris, Berlin, Hamburg, Cologne and Munich opera houses; has also conducted at Metropolitan Opera (New York), Chicago, San Francisco (American opera debut 1983), Dresden and Vienna State Operas, Teatro Colón (Buenos Aires), Orange Festival (France) and Théâtre du Châtelet (Paris); has conducted concerts with Berlin Philharmonic, Chicago Symphony, London Symphony Orchestra, Philharmonia, NHK (Tokyo), Dresden Staatskapelle, Boston Symphony Orchestra, Stockholm Philharmonic and BBC Symphony Orchestra. *Recordings include:* Wagner's Der Ring des Nibelungen (with the Dresden Staatskapelle), Weber's Euryanthe, Strauss's Die Schweigsame Frau, Penderecki's The Devils of Loudun, Korngold's Violanta, Hindemith's Die Harmonie der Welt, Bruckner Symphonies No. 4 and No. 6 (with Orchestre Philharmonique de Radio France), Roussel four symphonies (with Orchestre Philharmonique de Radio France) (Diapason D'Or 1996), Weber's Oberon 1997, Strauss's Four Last Songs (Gramophone magazine Editor's Choice Award 2002). *Current Management:* c/o Jessica Ford, Intermusica Artists' Management Ltd, 36 Graham Street, Crystal Wharf, London, N1 8GJ, England. *Telephone:* (20) 7608-9000. *Fax:* (20) 7490-3263. *E-mail:* mail@intermusica.co.uk. *Website:* www .intermusica.co.uk. *Address:* Rundfunk Sinfonieorchester Berlin, Charlottenstr. 56, 10117 Berlin, Germany. *Website:* www.rsb-online.de.

JANSEN, Janine; Dutch violinist; b. 1978, Utrecht. *Education:* Conservatory of Utrecht, studied with Coosje Wijzenbeek, Philipp Hirshhorn, Boris Belkin. *Career:* debut at Amsterdam Concertgebouw 1997; has performed with leading orchestras, including Royal Concertgebouw, Gewandhausorchester Leipzig, Gothenburg Symphony, Radio Symphony Orchestra, Berlin, City of Birmingham Symphony, Kirov Orchestra, NHK Symphony Orchestra, Tokyo, Melbourne Symphony, BBC Orchestras, Acad. of St Martin-in-the-Fields, Philharmonia, RPO, Philadelphia Orchestra, Nat. Symphony Orchestra, Washington, Israel Philharmonic, Nat. Orchestra of Spain; fmr BBC New Generation Artist; several performances at BBC Proms 2003–; as chamber musician performs with Yuri Bashmet, Itamar Golan, Mischa Maisky, Paul Meyer, Emmanuel Pahud, Christian Poltéra, Julian Rachlin, Menahem Pressler, Heinrich Schiff, Kathryn Stott; Curator, Utrecht Chamber Music

Festival; mem., Spectrum Concerts Berlin chamber music series 1998–. *Recordings:* Janine Jansen (Khachaturian/Ravel et al) 2004, Vivaldi, The Four Seasons 2005, Mendelssohn/Bruch, Concertos and Romance 2006, Bach: Inventions and Partitia 2007, Tchaikovsky: Violin Concerto 2008, Britten & Beethoven Violin Concertos 2009, Beau Soir 2010. *Honours:* Ministry of Culture Dutch Music Prize 2003, Edison Classic Public Award 2004, 2005, Dutch Theatres' and Concert Halls' Classical Artist of the Year 2008, Royal Philharmonic Soc. Award for Best Instrumentalist 2009. *Current Management:* c/o Linda Marks, HarrisonParrott Ltd, 5–6 Albion Court, London, W6 0QT, England. *Telephone:* (20) 7229-9166. *Fax:* (20) 7221-5042. *E-mail:* info@ harrisonparrott.co.uk. *Website:* www.harrisonparrott.co.uk; www .janinejansen.com.

JANSEN, Rudolf; Dutch pianist; b. 19 Jan. 1940, Arnhem; s. of Simon C. Jansen; m. 1st Margreet Honig; two c.; m. 2nd Christa Pfeiler; two c. *Education:* Amsterdam Conservatory, studied piano with Nelly Wagenaar, organ with Simon C. Jansen and harpsichord with Gustav Leonhardt. *Career:* soloist; accompanist for numerous leading singers and other artists throughout the world, including Elly Ameling, Robert Holl, Han de Vries, Andreas Schmidt, Olaf Bär, Barbara Bonney, Tom Krause and Hans-Peter Blochwitz; conducts masterclasses for singers and accompanists in Europe, N America and the Orient; gave a masterclass at the Juilliard School, New York 1996; guest teacher, Conservatorium van Amsterdam, Netherlands, Hochschule für Musik, Nuremberg/Augsburg, Germany, Franz Schubert Institut, Baden, Austria. *Recordings:* more than 120 recordings as Lieder accompanist or chamber music player. *Honours:* Kt, Order of Orange-Nassau 1998; Prix d'Excellence for Organ 1964, Toonkunst Jubileum Prize 1965, Prix d'Excellence for Piano 1966, Zilveren Vriendenkrans, Friends of Amsterdam Concertgebouw 1966, Edison Prize (for recording of the Complete Webern Songs with Dorothy Dorow) 1987, Deutschen Schallplattenpreis (for recording made with Dietrich Fischer Dieskau/Netherlands Chamber Choir) 1992. *Address:* Schepenenlaan 2, 1181 BB Amstelveen, Netherlands. *Telephone:* (20) 641-6344. *E-mail:* rudolfjansen.piano@planet.nl.

JANSONS, Mariss; Latvian conductor; b. 14 Jan. 1943, Riga; s. of Arvid Jansons and Erhaida Jansons; m. Irina Jansons 1967; one d. *Education:* studied with father, Leningrad Conservatory with N. Rabinovich, Vienna Conservatory with Hans Swarovsky, Salzburg with von Karajan. *Career:* Prin. Guest Conductor, Leningrad (now St Petersburg) Philharmonic Orchestra; Chief Conductor, Oslo Philharmonic 1979–2002; Guest Conductor, Welsh Symphony Orchestra 1985–88; Salzburg debut with the Vienna Philharmonic 1994; Prin. Guest Conductor, London Philharmonic Orchestra 1992–97; Prof. of Conducting, St Petersburg Conservatory 1995–; Music Dir Pittsburgh Symphony Orchestra 1995, Chief Conductor 1997–2002; Chief Conductor, Symphonieorchester des Bayerischen Rundfunks and Bavarian Radio Choir 2003–; Chief Conductor, Royal Concertgebouw Orchestra 2004–15; has appeared with Baltimore Symphony Orchestra, Berlin Philharmonic, Boston Symphony Orchestra, Chicago Symphony Orchestra, Cleveland Orchestra, London Philharmonia Orchestra, New York Philharmonic, Philadelphia Orchestra, among others. *Recordings include:* Shostakovich Symphony No. 7 (BBC Music Magazine Orchestral Award 2007) 2006. *Honours:* Commdr with Star, Royal Norwegian Order of Merit 1994, Austrian Cross of Honor for Scholarship and Art 2008, Bavarian Order of Maximilian 2010; winner, Herbert von Karajan Competition 1971, Anders Jahre Cultural Prize (Norway), RSFSR People's Artist 1986, Hans von Bülow Medal, Berlin Philharmonic 2003, Royal Philharmonic Soc. Conductor of the Year Award 2004, Classical Music Award for Artist of the Year, MIDEM, Cannes 2006, ECHO-Klassik Conductor of the Year 2007, Ernst von Siemens Music Prize 2013. *Current Management:* Opus 3 Artists, 470 Park Avenue South, 9th Floor North, New York, NY 10016, USA. *Telephone:* (212) 584-7500. *Fax:* (646) 300-8200. *E-mail:* info@opus3artists.com. *Website:* www.opus3artists.com.

JANULAKO, Vassilio; singer (baritone); b. 14 Sept. 1933, Athens, Greece. *Education:* Athens Conservatory. *Career:* debut in Athens 1961, as the High Priest in Alceste; engagements at opera houses in Stuttgart, Berlin, Düsseldorf, Hamburg, Munich, Vienna, Frankfurt, Nuremberg, Zürich, Toulouse and San Francisco; roles include Pizarro, the Dutchman, Telramund, Amfortas, Don Giovanni, Mozart's Count, Gerard, Scarpia, Escamillo, Mandryka, Milhaud's Christopher Columbus and parts in operas by Verdi; Cologne 1986, as Pandolfe in Cendrillon by Massenet; Spoleto and Philadelphia 1988, in Jenůfa and Rusalka; sang Paolo in Simon Boccanegra at Cologne 1990.

JAPE, Mijndert; Dutch lutenist, classical guitarist, writer and music historian; b. 11 July 1932, Geleen, Limburg; m. Marie-Hélène Habets 1960 (died 1987). *Education:* Muzieklyceum Heerlen, Conservatory of Maastricht, Schola Cantorum, Paris, Royal Conservatory of the Hague; studied with Hans-Lutz Niessen, Ida Presti, Alexandre Lagoya, Toyohiki Satoh, Eugen Dombois, Thomas Binkley, Anthony Bailes. *Career:* soloist, accompanist on lute instruments, baroque operas, vocal groups, Belgium, Netherlands, France; Director, Delitiae Musicae, specialising in 1550–1650 music and poetry concerts, Netherlands, Belgium, France; guest lecturer; teacher of Lute and Guitar 1955–92, Musical director 1986–92, Sittard Musical School, 1955–92; Teaching Lute and Guitar, Music Academy, Maasmechelen and Tongeren, Belgium. *Recordings:* 4 (solo, ensemble), Belgium, Netherlands. *Publications:* Fernando Sor–Opera Omnia for the Guitar; On Lute Tuition, 1987; Classical Guitar Music in Print, bibliography, 12 vols (with Marie-Hélène Habets), vols 5, 8 and 9, 1980–1989; Louys de Moy–le Petit Boucquet,

1990; Elementa Pro Arte, lute tutor, in progress; The 'Wilhelmus van Nassouwe', Dutch National Anthem, development and relationship to the lute music, 1994.

JAR, Valentin; Dutch (b. Romanian) singer (tenor); b. 1950, Bucharest. *Education:* Bucharest and Hague Conservatories. *Career:* sang at Gelsenkirchen Opera 1981–83; Frankfurt 1983–96; roles have included Mozart's Monostatos and Pedrillo, Verdi's Macduff and Cassio, Apollo in Monteverdi's Orfeo, Mime in Siegfried and Janáček's Mr Brouček, Vitek and Luka for Opéra du Rhin Strasbourg; Iro in Monteverdi's Ulisse at Antwerp, Avignon and Lausanne; Strauss's Valzacchi at Toulouse; Weill's Fatty, Wexford; season 1998–99 with Monostatos at Liège; Iro for Opera North and Lisbon. *Current Management:* TACT International Art Management, Tefelenstraat 120, 1107 SN Amsterdam, The Netherlands. *Telephone:* (20) 6977091. *Fax:* (20) 6977831. *E-mail:* info@tact4art.com. *Website:* www.tact4art.com. *Address:* Nieuwstraat 71, 70G1DE Dinxperlo, The Netherlands (home). *E-mail:* zangjar@zonnet.nl (home).

JARMAN, Douglas, BA, PhD; British academic and writer; b. 21 Nov. 1942, Dewsbury, Yorks.; m. Angela Elizabeth Brown 1970; two d. *Education:* Univ. of Hull, Durham Univ., Univ. of Liverpool. *Career:* Lecturer in Music, Univ. of Leeds 1970–71; Lecturer, Royal Northern Coll. of Music, Manchester 1974–86, Prin. Lecturer in Academic Studies 1986–2008, Prof. Emer. 2008–; Visiting Distinguished Scholar, Univ. of Manchester 2010; Artistic Dir, Young Musicians' Chamber Music Festival; Chair. Psappha (new music ensemble). *Recording:* Talk, Lulu, The Historical Background (recording of The Complete Lulu). *Publications:* The Music of Alban Berg 1979, Kurt Weill 1982, Wozzeck 1989, The Berg Companion 1989, Alban Berg, Lulu 1991, Expressionism Reassessed 1993, Alban Berg: Violin Concerto (critical edn) 1998, Hans Werner Henze at the RNCM (Vols 1–3) 1999, The Twentieth-Century String Quartet 2002, Alban Berg: Chamber Concerto (critical edn) 2004; contribs to Perspectives of New Music, Musical Quarterly, Musical Times, Music Review, Journal of Royal Musical Association, Newsletter of International Alban Berg Society, Alban Berg Studien Vols 2 and 6. *Honours:* Hon. FRNCM 1986; Hon. Prof. of Music, Univ. of Manchester 2002. *Address:* 1 Birch Villas, Birchcliffe Road, Hebden Bridge, HX7 8DA, England (home). *E-mail:* douglas.jarman@rncm.ac.uk (office).

JAROUSSKY, Philippe; French singer (counter tenor); b. 13 Feb. 1978, Maisons Laffite. *Education:* Conservatoire de Paris; studied singing with Nicole Fallien. *Career:* debut performance, Royaumont Festival 1999; large baroque repertoire, from Italian Seicento with Monteverdi, Sances and Rossi to Handel and Vivaldi; has explored both modern and contemporary repertoire with pianist Jerôme Ducros, performing melodies composed by Marc André Dalbavie from poems of Louise Labbé and French melodies of late 19th and early 20th centuries; has worked with leading baroque orchestras, including Ensemble Matheus, Les Arts Florissants, Les Musiciens du Louvre, Le Concert d'Astrée, L'Arpeggiata, Le Cercle de l'Harmonie and Europa Galante, with conductors including Jean-Christophe Spinosi, Marc Minkowski, René Jacobs, Christina Pluhar, Jérémie Rhorer, Emmanuel Haïm, Jean-Claude Malgoire and Fabio Biondi; frequently performs in major French concert halls, including Théâtre des Champs-Elysées, Théâtre du Châtelet, Salle Pleyel, Salle Gaveau, Opéra de Lyon, Opéra de Montpellier, Opéra de Nancy, Arsenal de Metz, Théâtre de Caen, and abroad, including the Barbican Centre and Southbank Centre, London, Palais des Beaux Arts, Brussels, Grand Théâtre du Luxembourg, Konzerthaus, Vienna, Staatsoper and Philharmonia, Berlin, Teatro Real, Madrid, Lincoln Center, New York; f. l'Ensemble Artaserse 2002, performed in Madrid, Carnegie Hall and Lincoln Center in New York; recently joined Cecilia Bartoli in Salzburg as Sesto for stage performances of Handel's Giulio Cesare; returned to the int. stage with the Farinelli tour with Venice Baroque Orchestra and Andrea Marcon, performed in Paris Théâtre des Champs Elysées, Ambronay Festival, Svetlanov Hall, Moscow, Berlin Philharmonie, Dortmund, Alte oper of Frankfurt, Liederhalle, Stuttgart, Prinzregentheater, Munich, Luxembourg Philharmonie, Brussels Bozar, Madrid Auditorio Nacional and Teatro de Liceu of Barcelona and touring in Asia and USA; season 2013–14, debut with ensemble Orfeo 55, conducted by Nathalie Stutzmann; performing with I Barocchisti and Diego Fasolis for a tour of Pergolesi Stabat Mater with soprano Julia Lezhneva. *Recordings include:* Vivaldi Opera Arias, Lamenti, Un concert pour Mazarin 2004, Vivaldi: Virtuoso Cantatas 2005, Beata Vergine 2006, Carestini: The Story of a Castrato (Midem Classical Award for Baroque Music Recording 2009) 2007, numerous Vivaldi albums with Jean-Christophe Spinosi and Matheus, Heroes – Vivaldi's Opera Arias (Disque d'Or 2007, Diapason d'Or, awarded a 10 by Classica-Repertoire, a Choc by Magazine Monde de la Musique, Gramophone Award, Timbre de Platine by Opera International), Carestini (CD of the Year, Victoires de la Musique 2008, Midem Classical Awards 2009), Lamenti (Victoires de la Musique 2009), Teatro d'Amore with L'Arpeggiata and Christina Pluhar (ECHO Klassik Award) 2009, Opium – French Melodies 2009, album dedicated to Johann Christian Bach with Le Cercle de l'Harmonie 2009, Stabat Mater 2010, Caldara in Wien 2010, Duetti with Max Emanuel Cencic and Les Arts Florissants (ECHO Klassik Award for Opera Recording of the Year/Arias & Duets 2012), Fauré Requiem/Cantique de Jean Racine (with Matthias Goerne) (Int. Classical Music Award for Best Choral Recording 2012) 2011, The Best of La voix des Anges 2012, Farinelli, Arias of Porpora 2013, Pergolesi Stabat Mater (with J. Lezhneva) 2013, La Dolce Fiamma (castrato arias by Johann Christian Bach) with Le Cercle de l'Harmonie and Jérémie Rhorer 2013, Via Crucis 2014, Pietà - Sacred Works

2014, Steffani: Niobe, Regina Di Tebe 2015. *Honours:* Chevalier, Ordre des Arts et des Lettres 2009; Victoires de la Musique (Révélation Artiste Lyrique) 2004, (Artiste lyrique) 2007, 2010, ECHO Klassik Award for Male Singer of the Year 2008, Midem Classical Award for Vocal Artist of the Year 2009. *Current Management:* c/o Les Concerts Parisiens, 21 rue Bergère, 75009 Paris, France. *Telephone:* 1-48-24-16-97. *Fax:* 1-48-24-16-29. *E-mail:* virginie@concertsparisiens.fr. *Website:* www.concertsparisiens.fr.

JARRETT, Keith; American pianist and composer; b. 8 May 1945, Allentown, Pa. *Education:* Berklee School of Music. *Career:* gave first solo concert aged 7, followed by professional appearances; two-hour solo concert of own compositions 1962; led own trio in Boston; worked with Roland Kirk, Tony Scott and others in New York; joined Art Blakey 1965; toured Europe with Charles Lloyd 1966, with Miles Davis 1970–71; soloist and leader of own groups 1969–; Guggenheim Fellowship 1972. *Recordings include:* albums: Bach's Well-Tempered Klavier, Personal Mountains 1974, Luminessence 1974, Mysteries 1975, Changeless 1987, Nude Ants, The Cure 1990, Bye Bye Black 1991, At the Dear Head Inn 1992, Bridge of Light 1993, At the Blue Note 1994, La Scala 1995, Tokyo '96 1998, The Melody at Night With You 1999, Whisper Not 2000, Inside Out 2001, Always Let Me Go 2002, Selected Recordings 2002, Radiance 2005, The Carnegie Hall Concert 2006, Dmitri Shostakovich: 24 Preludes and Fugues 2006, Jasmine (with Charlie Haden) 2010. *Honours:* Prix du Prés. de la République 1991, Polar Prize, Royal Swedish Acad. of Music 2003, Léonie Sonning Music Prize 2004, Jazz Masters Award 2014; Officier, Ordre des Arts et des Lettres. *Current Management:* c/o Vincent Ryan, 135 West 16th Street, New York, NY 10011, USA.

JARŮŠEK, Peter; Slovak musician (cello); b. 23 Sept. 1976, Bratislava; m. Veronika Jarúskova. *Education:* Acad. of Performing Arts, Prague, studied with Daniel Veis and later with Milan Škampa. *Career:* mem. Skampa Quartet 1999–2003; Guest Prof. RAM, London 2001–03; mem. Pavel Haas Quartet 2003–, performed in numerous venues including London's Wigmore Hall, Concertgebouw Amsterdam, Palais des Beaux-Arts Brussels, Auditorio Nacional Madrid, Zurich Tonhalle, Munich Herkulessaal, Luxembourg Philharmonie and at Aldeburgh, Edinburgh, Verbier and Zeist festivals; BBC New Generation Artists scheme 2007–09; Artists-in-Residence, Cologne Philharmonie, Birmingham Town Hall, Prague Spring Festival 2014, Bodensee Festival 2015; tours of Australia, Japan and Korea 2015; led master-classes at Concertgebouw Amsterdam, Univ. of Tasmania, Univ. of Mexico City, Acad. of Performing Arts Bratislava. *Recordings include:* with Pavel Haas Quartet: Janáček's Quartet No. 2 (Intimate Letters) and Haas' Quartet No. 2 (From the Monkey Mountains) (Gramophone Award for Best Chamber Recording 2007), Janacek's Quartet No. 1 (Kreutzer Sonata) and Haas' Quartets Nos. 1 and 3 2007, Prokofiev's String Quartets (Diapason d'or de l'année) 2010, Dvořák's String Quartets (Gramophone Award for Recording of the Year 2011), Franz Schubert works (Gramophone Award for Best Chamber Recording 2014) 2013, Smetana string quartets (Gramophone Award for Best Chamber Recording 2015). *Honours:* (with Pavel Haas Quartet) First Prize, Paolo Borciani competition 2005, ECHO Rising Stars Award 2007, Special Ensemble Scholarship, Borletti-Buitoni Trust 2010. *Current Management:* Intermusica Artists' Management, 36 Graham Street, Crystal Wharf, London, N1 8GJ, England. *Telephone:* (20) 7608-9918. *E-mail:* nfriemel@intermusica.co.uk. *Website:* www.intermusica.co.uk; www .pavelhaasquartet.com.

JARŮŠKOVÁ, Veronika; Slovak musician (violin); m. Peter Jarůšek. *Education:* Acad. of Performing Arts, Prague, studied with Milan Skampa. *Career:* f. Pavel Haas Quartet 2002–, performed in numerous venues including London's Wigmore Hall, Concertgebouw Amsterdam, Palais des Beaux-Arts Brussels, Auditorio Nacional Madrid, Zurich Tonhalle, Munich Herkulessaal, Luxembourg Philharmonie and at Aldeburgh, Edinburgh, Verbier and Zeist festivals; BBC New Generation Artists scheme 2007–09; Artists-in-Residence, Cologne Philharmonie, Birmingham Town Hall, Prague Spring Festival 2014, Bodensee Festival 2015; tours of Australia, Japan and Korea 2015. *Recordings include:* with Pavel Haas Quartet: Janáček's Quartet No. 2 (Intimate Letters) and Haas' Quartet No. 2 (From the Monkey Mountains) (Gramophone Award for Best Chamber Recording 2007), Janacek's Quartet No. 1 (Kreutzer Sonata) and Haas' Quartets Nos. 1 and 3 2007, Prokofiev's String Quartets (Diapason d'or de l'année) 2010, Dvořák's String Quartets (Gramophone Award for Recording of the Year 2011), Franz Schubert works (Gramophone Award for Best Chamber Recording 2014) 2013, Smetana string quartets (Gramophone Award for Best Chamber Recording 2015). *Honours:* with Pavel Haas Quartet: First Prize, Paolo Borciani competition 2005, ECHO Rising Stars Award 2007, Special Ensemble Scholarship, Borletti-Buitoni Trust 2010. *Current Management:* Intermusica Artists' Management, 36 Graham Street, Crystal Wharf, London, N1 8GJ, England. *Telephone:* (20) 7608-9918. *E-mail:* nfriemel@intermusica.co.uk. *Website:* www.intermusica.co.uk; www.pavelhaasquartet.com.

JÄRVI, Kristjan; Estonian/American conductor; *Music Director, MDR Leipzig Radio Symphony Orchestra*; b. 13 June 1972, Tallinn; s. of Neeme Järvi; brother of Paavo Järvi and Maarika Järvi; m. 1st Leila Josefowicz; one s.; m. 2nd Hayley Melitta; three c. *Education:* Manhattan School of Music, Univ. of Michigan. *Career:* aged seven, emigrated with family to New York; Asst Conductor to Esa-Pekka Salonen, Los Angeles Philharmonic 1998–2000, debut at Hollywood Bowl 1999; Chief Conductor, Norrlands Opera and Symphony Orchestra of Umeå, Sweden 2000–04; Chief Conductor and Music Dir, Tonkünstler Orchestra, Vienna, Austria 2004–09; Music Dir, MDR

Leipzig Radio Symphony Orchestra 2012–; Chief Conductor, Gstaad Festival Orchestra; Founder and Music Dir, new music group Absolute Ensemble 1993–, concerts/tours worldwide; Founding Conductor, Baltic Youth Philharmonic, tours throughout Europe; Artistic Advisor, Basel Chamber Orchestra; Artist-in-Residence, Festspiele Mecklenburg-Vorpommern and Danish Nat. Symphony Orchestra 2012–13; regular Guest Conductor, London Symphony Orchestra, also with Staatskapelle Dresden, Bayerische Rundfunk Symphony Orchestra, NDR Hamburg, Frankfurt Radio Symphony Orchestra, Orchestre Nat. de France, Orchestre de Paris, Accademia Naz. di Santa Cecilia Rome, Nat. Symphony Orchestra (Washington, DC), Minnesota Orchestra, Sydney Symphony and NHK Symphony, Japan; commissioned and collaborated with musicians including Arvo Pärt, Tan Dun, John Adams, Esa-Pekka Salonen, H. K. Gruber, Renée Fleming, Joe Zawinul, Goran Bregovic, Paquito d'Rivera, Eitetsu Hayashi, Marcel Khalife and Benny Anderson; f. Absolute Acad. at Bremen Univ. for Music and Arts; f. Muusikaselts Music (music education project in Estonian orphanages); judge, first Beijing Int. Composers Competition 2011. *Recordings include:* more than 30 CDs including Hilding Rosenberg: Isle of Bliss (Swedish Grammi Award for Best Opera Performance), Pärt: Cantique 2010, Orff: Carmina Burana 2012, Cloud Atlas Symphony 2013. *Honours:* German Record Critics Prize for Best Album (for Absolute Mix) 2000, Deutsche Bank Prize for Outstanding Artistic Achievement (with Absolute Ensemble) 2007. *Current Management:* c/o Libby Abrahams, IMG Artists, The Light Box, 111 Power Road, London, W4 5PY, England. *Telephone:* (20) 7957-5823. *Fax:* (20) 7957-5801. *E-mail:* labrahams@imgartists.com. *Website:* www.imgartists.com.

JÄRVI, Neeme; Estonian conductor; *Music Director, Orchestre de la Suisse Romande*; b. 7 June 1937, Tallinn; s. of August Järvi and Elss Järvi; m. Liilia Järvi 1961; two s. one d. *Education:* Tallinn Music School, Leningrad Conservatorium and Leningrad Postgraduate Studium, studied with N. Rabinovich and Y. Mravinsky. *Career:* Conductor Estonian Radio Symphony Orchestra –1963; Chief Conductor Estonian State Opera House 1963–76; Chief Conductor, Estonian Nat. Symphony Orchestra 1976–80 now Prin. Conductor; emigrated to USA 1980; Prin. Guest Conductor, City of Birmingham Symphony Orchestra, UK 1981–83; Chief Conductor Royal Scottish Nat. Orchestra 1984–88, Conductor Laureate 1990–; Prin. Conductor Gothenburg Orchestra, Sweden 1982–2004; Music Dir Detroit Symphony Orchestra, USA 1990–2005, Music Dir Emer. 2006–; Music Dir Emer. New Jersey Symphony Orchestra, USA 2005–09, Conductor Laureate and Artistic Advisor 2009–; Chief Conductor Residentie Orchestra, The Hague 2005–11, Chief Conductor Emer. 2012–; Artistic Dir Estonian Nat. Symphony Orchestra 2011–; Music Dir Orchestre de la Suisse Romande 2012–; guest conductor of many int. symphony orchestras, including New York Philharmonic, Boston, Chicago, Royal Concertgebouw, Philharmonia, London Symphony, London Philharmonic; conducted Eugene Onegin 1979, 1984, Samson and Delilah 1982 and Khovanshchina 1985 at Metropolitan Opera House, New York; Head of Conducting, Gstaad Conducting Acad.; has held int. master-classes in summer resort town of Pärnu, Estonia 2000–. *Recordings include:* more than 450 CDs since 1983, including all Prokoviev, Sibelius, Grieg, Nielsen, Dvorak, Shostakovich, Franz Berwald and Stenhammar symphonies as well as recordings of Pärt and Tubin. *Honours:* Hon. mem. Royal Swedish Acad. of Music, Estonian Composers Union 1989; Hon. Citizen, City of Gothenburg 1987, State of Michigan 1992; Kt Commdr, Order of the North Star (Sweden) 1990, Sash, Order of Nat. Coat of Arms 1996, Insignia, Coat of Arms, Tallinn 1997; Dr hc (Royal Swedish Acad. of Music) 1988, 1990, (Estonian Music Acad.) 1989, (Aberdeen) 1990, (Gothenburg) 1985, 1991, (Tallinn Music Conservatory), Wayne State Univ., USA) 1994, (Michigan) 1999; First Prize, Young Conductors' Competition, Leningrad 1957, Estonian Soviet Socialist Repub. (ESSR) Honoured Artist 1965, First Prize, Accademia Nazionale di Santa Cecilia Conductors' Competition 1971, ESSR People's Artist 1971, USSR State Prize 1978, Sibelius Soc. Medal 1986, Gramophone Magazine's Artist of the Year 1990, Gold Record, Chandos recording co. 1992, Toblach's Mahler Prize (for recording of Mahler's Third Symphony) 1993, Grand Prix du Disque, Charles Cros Recording Acad. of Paris (for CD of Stravinski's Symphony of Psalms) 1993, Toblach's Mahler Prize (for recording of Mahler's Seventh Symphony with the Hague Orchestra) 2010. *Current Management:* c/o Harrison Parrott, 5–6 Albion Court, Albion Place, London, W6 0QT, England. *Telephone:* (20) 7229-9166. *Fax:* (20) 7221-5042. *E-mail:* info@harrisonparrott.co.uk. *Website:* www.harrisonparrott.com. *E-mail:* nmjarvi@gmail.com. *Website:* www.neemejarvi.ee.

JÄRVI, Paavo; Estonian/American conductor; *Chief Conductor, NHK Symphony Orchestra*; b. 1962, Tallinn; s. of Neeme Järvi; brother of Kristjan Järvi. *Education:* studied in Tallinn, at the Juilliard School, New York, in Los Angeles with Bernstein, at the Curtis Inst and also with Max Rudolf. *Career:* Guest Conductor, Chicago, Los Angeles, New York Philharmonics, Boston, Philharmonia, Orchestre de Paris, Orchestre Philharmonique de Radio France, Bayerische Rundfunk, Amsterdam Concertgebouw, Dresden Statskapelle, La Scala and NHK Symphony; debut with Vienna Philharmonic 2006; subscription series debut with the Cleveland Orchestra 2007; debut with the Philadelphia Orchestra 2007–08; return invitations to Cleveland and Philharmonia Orchestras, Chicago Symphony Orchestra and Orchestre Nat. de Paris 2007–08; Music Dir, Cincinnati Symphony Orchestra 2001–11, hr-Sinfonieorchester (Frankfurt Radio Symphony Orchestra) 2006–; Artistic Dir, Deutsche Kammerphilharmonie Bremen 2004–; Artistic Adviser, Estonian Nat. Orchestra; Music Dir, Orchestre de Paris 2010–16; Chief Conductor, NHK Symphony Orchestra 2015–. *Recordings:* Sibelius Cantatas (Grammy Award); Best Orchestral Recording, BBC Music Magazine Awards 2006: Grieg's Peer Gynt, The Maiden in the Tower and two albums by Arvo Pärt with Estonian Nat. Symphony Orchestra; Beethoven: Symphony Nos 3 (Eroica) and 8 with Die Deutsche Kammerphilharmonie; albums of music by Rachmaninov, Britten, Elgar, Lutoslawski, Bartok, Dvorak, Martinu, Debussy, Ravel, Berlioz, Sibelius, Tubin, Stravinsky and Prokofiev (Romeo and Juliet), with the Cincinnati Symphony Orchestra; album of Schumann, Bloch and Bruch with Orchestre Nat. de Paris, Sibelius album with the Royal Stockholm Philharmonic Orchestra, Sibelius Kullervo 1997, Britten and Shostakovich with the City of Birmingham Symphony Orchestra, Fauré Requiem/Cantique de Jean Racine with Choeur de l'Orchestre de Paris (Int. Classical Music Award for Best Choral Recording 2012) 2011. *Honours:* Order of the White Star 2013; Gramophone Award for Artist of the Year 2015. *Current Management:* Harrison Parrott, 5–6 Albion Court, London, W6 0QT, England. *Telephone:* (20) 7229-9166. *Fax:* (20) 7221-5042. *E-mail:* jennifer.spencer@harrisonparrott.co.uk. *Website:* www.harrisonparrott.com; www.paavojarvi.com.

JARVIS, Robert; British composer, musician (trombone) and music producer; b. 1963. *Career:* work lies between composition and creative research; has collaborated with experts from numerous disciplines, including outside of the arts; involved in the creation of temporary and permanent sound pieces; began professional music career as a trombonist playing in a wide range of spaces, from busking outside to performances in schools, residential home and hosps 1985; grew into project work focused on the creation of a music composition and often involving collaboration with other art forms; has composed pieces for various ensembles and continued his teenage experiments with manipulating raw sound using tape, etc.; developed own brand of socially interactive composition projects, cr. works such as Sparks & Waves 1998, Mossley Mill 1999 and Lambourn Voices 2011; concentrated on compositions for gallery spaces in order to bring forth a new understanding in harmony with the sounds of the area and the lives of the people living there, and to encourage his listeners to reconsider their environments and question how they related to their surroundings; compositions during this period include Disappear 2005 and Magic Stones 2006 (both winning works in New Media Category of British Composer Awards); current work is installation based and often inspired by scientific data collected from natural processes; has also moved outdoors to be directly in contact with nature, pieces such as Grow 2007 for the Hannah Peschar Sculpture Garden, Surrey, Echolocation 2008, and aroundNorth 2014 (now permanently installed at Armagh Observatory); continues to play trombone, working internationally as an improviser, and performing with the London Improvisers' Orchestra. *Sound installations include:* community-based: Landscapes 1994, Locomotion 1995, Pathways 1998, Sparks & Waves 1998, Jeg Gik Mig Over Sø Og Land 2000, What We Make of It 2000, Sonic Mapping 2002, Europhonix 2003, Slow 2009, Lambourn Voices 2011, Cross Currents 2012. *Recordings include:* Global Village, Mossley Mill, Celtic Connection, Sonic Mapping, Sparks and Waves, Carving Up Time, Magic Stones 2006. *Radio:* Sounds of Oxfordshire 2009. *E-mail:* robertjarvis@usa.net (office). *Website:* www.robertjarvis.co.uk.

JARVLEPP, Jan Eric, BMus, MMus, PhD; Canadian/Finnish composer, teacher, cellist and recording technician; *Member, Ottawa Symphony Orchestra*; b. 3 Jan. 1953, Ottawa, Ont.; s. of Eric Jarvlepp and Leena Jarvlepp (née Hirvonen); m. Kuniko Soda (separated); one d. one step-s. *Education:* Univ. of Ottawa, McGill Univ., Montréal, Univ. of California, San Diego, USA. *Career:* CBC Chamber Music Broadcasts; mem. Ottawa Symphony Orchestra 1981–, Nepean Symphony Orchestra 1981–91; electronic compositions performed on several different Canadian and US univ. campuses and radio stations; Music Dir Espace Musique Concert Soc. 1993–99; mem. SOCAN, Canadian Music Centre, SODRAC; numerous composition comms. *Compositions:* Lento 1975, Ice 1976, Aurora Borealis 1976, Buoyancy 1977, Flotation 1978, Transparency and Density 1978, Trumpet Piece 1979, Cello Concerto 1980, Time Zones 1981, Night Music 1982, Harpsichord Piece 1984, Evening Music for Carillon 1984, Cadenza for Solo Cello 1985, Guitar Piece 1985, Morning Music for Carillon 1986, Afternoon Music for Carillon 1986, Sunrise 1987, Sunset 1987, Trio 1987, Liquid Crystals 1988, Camerata Music 1989, Dream 1990, Life in The Fast Lane 1990, Encounter 1991, Underwater 1992, Music from Mars 1993, Moonscape 1993, Robot Dance 1994, Pierrot Solaire 1994, Garbage Concerto 1995, Tarantella 1996, Bassoon Quartet 1996, Saxophone Quartet 1996, Trio No. 2 1997, Earth Song 1998, Five-Way Crossover 1998, Overture 1999, Dilemma 1999, Concerto 2000, Quintet 2000, Street Scene 2000, Quintet 2001, Suite for Viola and Strings 2001, Shinkausen 2001, Quintet 2002, Comet 2002, The Lord's Prayer 2002, Quintet 2003, Quintet 2004, Procession and Auction 2004, Quintet 2005, Three Cello Duets 2005, Pre-Concert Announcement 2005, Three Stories by Hans Christian Andersen 2006, Quintet 2007, Double Concerto 2008, Suite for Strings 2009, String Quartet No. 1 2010, Music for Young Violinists 2010–11, Symphony for Brass and Percussion 2011, String Quartet No. 2 2012, Follow the Leader 2013, Seagulls 2013, Trio No. 2 2013. *Recordings:* Chronogrammes, Soundtracks of The Imagination, Flights of Fancy, Garbage Concerto. *Publications:* Compositional Aspects of Berio's Tempi Concertati, Interface, Vol. II, No. 4 1982, Pitch and Texture Analysis of Ligeti's Lux Aeterna, ex tempore, Vol. 2-1 1982, Alchemy in the Nineties 1997. *Address:* PO Box 2684, Station D, Ottawa, ON K1P 5W7, Canada (office). *Telephone:* (613) 729-7766 (home). *E-mail:* jarvlepp@magma.ca (home). *Website:* www.janjarvlepp.com.

JASIŃSKA-JĘDROSZ, Elżbieta Maria; Polish musicologist; b. 11 Jan. 1949, Katowice; d. of Edward Jasiński and Wanda Jasińska; m. Janusz Jędrosz 1970; one s. *Education:* Univ. of Warsaw. *Career:* engaged in bibliographic documentation of Polish musical works and in other tasks at Archive of Polish Composers, Polish Composers Archive, Warsaw Univ. Library Music Collection 1973–, currently Head of Polish Composers Archives; mem. Polish Composers' Union, Karol Szymanowski Music Asscn, Zakopane, Polish Librarians' Asscn, Polish Musicians Asscn. *Publications:* Music and Polish Musicians in French 1925–1950 1977, Karol Szymanowski 1882–1937 1983, The Manuscripts of Karol Szymanowski's Musical Works (catalogue) 1983, Karol Szymanowski in the Polish Collections (guide-book, co-author) 1989, Karol Szymanowski: Writer-Poet-Thinker 1997, The Manuscripts of Poland's Young Composers (catalogue) 1997, Collection of the 20th Century Polish Composers' Archives 1999, Four Seasons: Selected Poetry 2004; contrib. to Muzyka 1981, Ruch Muzyczny 1980, 1981, 1983, 1988–89, 1998–99, 2002–12, Pagine 1989, Przeglad Biblioteczny 1989, 2002, Polski Rocznik Muzykologiczny 2004, Biblioteke Muzycka 2007, 2009, 2010, Musica Sacra Nova 2010. *Honours:* Medal of Honour, Ministry of Culture and the Arts for popularization of Karol Szymanowski's compositions 1998, Hon. Medal for contribution to the Polish librarianship. *Address:* ul Janinówka 11 m 122, 03-562 Warsaw, Poland (office). *E-mail:* e.m.jasinska@uw.edu.pl (office).

JEDLICKA, Dalibor; Czech singer (bass-baritone); b. 23 May 1929, Svoyanov. *Education:* studied in Ostrava with Rudolf Vasek. *Career:* debut in Opava 1953, as Mumlala in The Two Widows by Smetana; sang at the Nat. Theatre, Prague 1957–77, also guest appearances with the company in Brno, Amsterdam, Zürich and Edinburgh (1970 in the British premiere of The Excursions of Mr Brouček by Janáček); engagements at Belgrade, Zagreb, Warsaw, Venice and Bologna; repertoire included buffo roles and German, French and Czech operas; Mozart's Figaro and Papageno, Don Pasquale and Kaspar in Der Freischütz; Opéra Comique, Paris 1988, in From the House of the Dead. *Recordings include:* Janáček's Katya Kabanova, The Cunning Little Vixen and From the House of the Dead, conducted by Charles Mackerras; Pauer's Suzanna Vojirva and Don Giovanni.

JEFFERS, Gweneth-Ann; British singer (soprano); b. 1975. *Education:* Univ. of Exeter, Goldsmiths Coll. and Guildhall School, London. *Career:* appearances with major London orchestras; concert repertoire includes Schubert, Schumann, Ravel, Barber, Messiaen (Harawi at the Cheltenham Festival 2000) and Cage; Verdi Requiem at Truro Cathedral, Brahms Requiem and Strauss's Vier Letzte Lieder in Canterbury Cathedral; season 2000–01 as Massenet's Navarraise at the Guildhall, Strauss's Ariadne with the Orchestre de Picardie and the original version of Berg's Lyric Suite with the Endellion Quartet at Aldeburgh; performed Verdi Requiem with York Musical Soc. 2014. *Current Management:* c/o Steven Swales Artist Management, 46 Twinwood Road, Clapham, Bedford, MK41 6HL, England. *Telephone:* (7742) 882167. *Fax:* (1753) 882378. *E-mail:* mail@ssartists.co.uk. *Website:* www.ssartists.co.uk.

JEFFERS, Ronald Harrison; American composer and conductor; b. 25 March 1942, Springfield, IL. *Education:* University of Michigan with Ross Lee Finney, University of California at San Diego with Pauline Oliveros, Kenneth Gaburo and Robert Erickson, Occidental College, Los Angeles. *Career:* Dir of Choral Activities, Stony Brook, New York, Oregon State Univ.; tours of Europe 1978, 1982. *Compositions include:* Missa concrete for three choruses 1969, revised 1973, In Memoriam for chamber ensemble 1973, Time Passes for mezzo, tape and ensemble 1974–81, Transitory for chorus and tape 1980, Arise My Love for 12 voices, chimes and gongs 1981, Crabs for tape 1981, This We Know for chorus 1987, Songs of the Sea 1991, Salut au Monde! for chamber ensemble 1993.

JEFFERY, Darren; British singer (bass-baritone); b. 1976, England. *Education:* Royal Northern Coll. of Music, Vilar Young Artists Programme, Covent Garden. *Career:* sang Falstaff and Der Sprecher in Die Zauberflote with Royal Northern Coll. of Music; sang Antinöus in Monteverdi's Il ritorno d'Ulisse at the Creakes Festival and Solino in Gli Equivoci for the Batignano Festival, Italy; Glyndebourne Festival 2001, covering Don Fernando in Fidelio and Matthew in The Last Supper; sang Masetto in Don Giovanni at Covent Garden 2002; other roles with the Royal Opera, Covent Garden are Rambaldo, Mandarin in Turandot 2002, Monterone in Rigoletto 2002, Tutor in Elektra, Baron Douphol in La Traviata 2002, Masetto in Don Giovanni 2003, Bonzo in Madama Butterfly 2003, Der Sprecher in Die Zauberflote 2003, Gravedigger in Hamlet 2003, Bartender in Sophie's Choice (world premiere) 2003; roles elsewhere include Cadmus in Handel's Semele, Donner in The Rheingold (ENO), Figaro in Le Nozze di Figaro (Savoy Opera Theatre). *Current Management:* Harlequin Agency Ltd, 203 Fidlas Road, Llanishen, Cardiff CF14 5NA, Wales. *Telephone:* (29) 2075-0821. *Fax:* (29) 2075-5971. *E-mail:* info@harlequin-agency.co.uk. *Website:* www.harlequin-agency.co.uk.

JEFFERY, Peter, MFA, PhD; American academic; b. 19 Oct. 1953, New York, NY; m. Margot Fassler 1983, two s. *Education:* Princeton Univ. *Career:* Hill Monastic Manuscript Library 1980–82; Mellon Faculty Fellow, Harvard Univ. 1982–83; Prof. of Music, Univ. of Delaware 1984–92, Boston Coll. 1992–93, Princeton Univ. 1993–; mem. American Musicological Soc., Medieval Acad. of America, North American Acad. of Liturgy, Societas Liturgica. *Publications:* A Bibliography for Medieval and Renaissance Musical Manuscript Research 1980, Re-Envisioning Past Musical Cultures; contrib. to Journal of the American Musicological Society, Studia Liturgica, Archiv für Liturgiewis-

senschaft, Gregorian Chant website. *Honours:* Alfred Einstein Award 1985, Nat. Endowment for the Humanities grant 1986–88, John D. MacArthur Fellowship 1987–82.

JEFFES, Peter; British singer (tenor); b. 1951, London, England. *Education:* Royal Coll. of Music, London, studied in Rome with Paolo Silveri. *Career:* Italian debut in Rome Opera in Spontini's Agnese di Hohenstaufen; Paris Opéra in Doktor Faust; with English Bach Festival at Covent Garden in Rameau's Castor et Pollux; Nero in L'Incoronazione di Poppea for Swiss television; European engagements as Lohengrin, Tamino and Lensky; sang Mozart in Rimsky's Mozart and Salieri at Barcelona 1987; festival appearances at Aix-en-Provence, Orange, Monte Carlo, Athens and in the USA; engagement with British cos in Roméo et Juliette, Les Contes d'Hoffmann, Die Zauberflöte, The Rake's Progress and A Midsummer Night's Dream; Opera North in the British premiere of Strauss's Daphne 1987; season 1988–89 in The Love for Three Oranges for Opera North; since 1988 roles in Cavalleria Rusticana, Pagliacci, Idomeneo, Faust, Werther, Salome, Fliegende Holländer, Macbeth, Attila and Eisenstein in Die Fledermaus; sings extensively in Europe and regularly in Israel; sang the Prince in The Love for Three Oranges 1992; sang Wagner's Rienzi for Chelsea Opera Group (concert) and the High Priest in Idomeneo at Lyon 1999.

JEFFREYS, Celia, ARCM; British singer (soprano); b. 20 Jan. 1948, Southampton, England. *Education:* Royal Coll. of Music. *Career:* debut with WNO 1970, as Adele in Die Fledermaus; sang at various regional opera houses in the UK; aang at Kassel and Darmstadt, Germany, Theater am Gärtnerplatz, Munich from 1976, Stadtheater Basel 1978–81; appeared as guest artist in Bern, Berlin Koblenz, Salzburg, Theater an der Wien, Schlosspiele Heidelberg, Festspiele, Bregenz 1981–88; engagements in Linz, Austria 1988–91; appeared regularly in Salzburg and Linz from 1997; opera roles include Donna Elvira in Don Giovanni, Mimi in La Bohème, the Marschallin in Rosenkavalier, Agathe in Der Freischütz, Nedda in Pagliacci, Leonore in Fidelio; operetta roles include Hanna Glawari in The Merry Widow, Rosalinde in Die Fledermaus; Teacher, Bayerische Theaterakademie, Munich. *Recordings:* Student Prince, Brahms German Requiem. *Address:* Grasmeierstrasse 12 B, 80805 Munich, Germany.

JEHLICKOVA, Zora, DiS; Czech singer (soprano); b. 10 April 1950, Brno. *Education:* Prague Conservatory. *Career:* sang at the Prague Nat. Theatre from 1974, notably as Natasha in War and Peace, Marenka in The Bartered Bride, Rusalka, Pamina, Donna Elvira, Tatiana in Eugene Onegin, and Mimi; title role in Dvořák's Armida 1987; Smetana Theatre, Prague 1992, as the Princess in Der Zwerg by Zemlinsky; guest appearances in Dresden, Komische Oper, Berlin, La Scala, Milan, and Nationaltheater, Mannheim; numerous concert appearances; currently soloist with Prague State Opera. *Address:* Prague State Opera, Legerova 75, 11 000 Prague 1 (office); Hradištko-Brunšov, 389, 25 209 Prague, Czech Republic (home). *Telephone:* 604-428116 (mobile) (home). *E-mail:* jeelly@seznam.cz (home). *Website:* www.jehlickova .cz.

JELEZNOV, Irina; pianist; b. 4 Oct. 1958, Astrakhan, Russia; m. Maxim Jeleznov 1980; one s. *Education:* Tchaikovsky Conservatoire, Moscow. *Career:* debut in Tashkent Conservatoire Hall 1984; annual recitals and orchestra performances, Tashkent 1984–93; appearances in Moscow at The Maly Hall, Moscow Conservatoire 1986, 1987, Rachmaninov Hall and Shuvalova's Home 1991; piano duo festivals at Sverdlovsk 1989, Leningrad 1990, Nizny Novgorod 1991, Novosibirsk 1992; int. piano duo competitions in Belgrade, Yugoslavia 1989, Caltanissetta, Italy 1990, Hartford, CT 1990, Miami, FL 1991; television and radio appearances; Docent, Chair of Chamber Music, Tashkent Conservatoire; mem. Int. Piano Duo Asscn, Tokyo, Japan. *Address:* Prospekt Kosmonavtov d 12-106, 700015 Tashkent, Uzbekistan.

JELEZNOV, Maxim; Russian duo pianist; b. 19 May 1958, Moscow; m. 1980, one s. *Education:* Tchaikovsky Conservatoire, Moscow. *Career:* debut at Tashkent Conservatoire Hall, 1984; performances: Tashkent, yearly 1984–93; Maly Hall, Moscow Conservatoire, 1986, 1987; Sverdlovsk Piano Duo Festival, 1989; Belgrade, Yugoslavia, 1989; International Piano Duo Festival Leningrad, 1990; Hartford, USA, 1990; Caltanissetta, Italy, 1990; Rachmaninov Hall, Moscow, 1991; Shuvalova's Home, Moscow, 1991; Nizny Novgorod Piano Duo Festival, 1991; International Piano Duo Festival, Ekaterinburg, 1991–93; Piano Duo Festival, The Masters of Piano Duo, Novosibirsk, 1992; television and radio broadcasts. *Address:* Prospekt Kosmonavtov d 12-106, 700015 Tashkent, Uzbekistan.

JELINEK, Ladislav; Czech concert pianist; b. 21 Feb. 1947, Brno; m.; two s. *Education:* State Conservatory, Brno, Janáček Univ. of Musical Arts, Brno, majoring in solo piano under Prof. Frantisek Schäfer. *Career:* debut: Besedni Dum, Brno 1966; appearances as soloist with orchestra, solo pianist and chamber musician in fmr Czechoslovakia and majority of Eastern European countries; radio and TV appearances in Eastern Europe 1968–81; numerous appearances (including radio and TV) in nearly all European countries, America, S Korea and Japan 1981–; Univ. Teacher, Frankfurter Hochschule für Musik and Darstellende Kunst 1984–; mem. Artistic Advisory Bd, Janáček Univ. of Musical Arts, Brno; recordings on CD and DVD. *Recordings include:* Beethoven, Brahms, Chopin, Dvořák, Haydn, Janáček, Liszt-Verdi, Liszt-Wagner, Mozart, Jan Novák, V. Novák, Prokofiev, Rachmaninov, Smetana and others. *Honours:* piano competitions: Acad. of Music, Czechoslovakia 1961, Hradec Kralove 1963. *Address:* Lerchenweg 2, 61350 Bad Homburg,

Germany (home). *E-mail:* contact@classicalpiano.de (home). *Website:* www .classicalpiano.de (home).

JENISOVA, Eva; Slovak singer (soprano); b. 1963, Presov. *Education:* Bratislava Conservatory. *Career:* soloist with the National Theatre Bratislava from 1986; further appearances (from 1988) with the Deutsche Oper Berlin, Bolshoi Moscow, Budapest State Opera, National Theatre Prague and the Israel and Edinburgh Festivals; Vienna Staatsoper from 1990, as Marguerite in Faust, Donna Elvira, Katya Kabanova and Rusalka; Elvira under Harnoncourt at Amsterdam, Pamina and Violetta at Trieste, and Janáček's Vixen at the Paris Châtelet; Covent Garden debut 1997, as Katya Kabanova; season 1997–98 as the Duchess of Parma in Busoni's Faust at Lyon, the Vixen in Madrid and Paris, and Mozart's Vitellia at Nancy; concerts include Mareiken in Martinů's Legends of Mary, with the Vienna Symphony Orchestra, the Missa Solemnis at Madrid, the German Requiem in Bologna, Carmina Burana in Munich, and Dvořák's Stabat Mater at Salzburg; Mahler's Second Symphony in Graz, and Rusalka at the Salle Pleyel, Paris; Teatro Regio Turin 1997, as Mélisande.

JENKINS, Carol; violinist; b. 1965, Toronto, Canada. *Education:* Univ. of Toronto with Rodney Friend and Victor Danchenki. *Career:* Assoc. Leader, Denver Symphony Orchestra and other orchestras; Second Violinist, Da Vinci Quartet from 1988, founded 1980 under the sponsorship of the Fine Arts Quartet; many concerts in USA and elsewhere, in a repertoire including works by Mozart, Beethoven, Brahms, Dvořák, Shostakovich and Bartók; Artist-in-Residence, Univ. of Colorado. *Honours:* awards and grants from the NEA, Western States Arts Foundation and the Colorado Council for the Humanities (with Da Vinci Quartet).

JENKINS, Graeme James Ewers; British conductor; *Music Director, Dallas Opera;* b. 1958, England; m. Joanna, two d. *Education:* Dulwich Coll., Univ. of Cambridge, Royal Coll. of Music with Norman del Mar and David Willcocks. *Career:* debut conducting Albert Herring and the Turn of the Screw at coll.; The Beggar's Opera, Die Entführung and Le nozze di Figaro for Kent Opera; Andrea Chénier, Brighton Festival; Cesti's La Dori (Spitalfields); Il Trovatore, Le nozze di Figaro and Così fan tutte with Scottish Opera; Così fan tutte with ENO (debut) 1988; European debut 1987, Hansel and Gretel and Ravel double bill with Geneva Opera; Simon Boccanegra, Netherlands Opera 1989; Music Dir Glyndebourne Touring Opera 1986–91, conducting A Midsummer Night's Dream, Albert Herring, Simon Boccanegra and Così fan tutte; La Traviata and Death in Venice (on BBC television) 1989; Glyndebourne Festival debut 1987, with Carmen and Capriccio; returned for Ravel double bill and Falstaff; Arabella 1989; Oedipus Rex and Petrushka with Scottish Opera 1989; further engagements include Carmen and La Rondine with Canadian Opera in Toronto, La Bohème with Australian Opera 1990; concert appearances with the Hallé Orchestra, BBC Scottish, BBC Philharmonic, BBC Symphony, Royal Philharmonic, Kraków Radio Symphony and Scottish Chamber Orchestras; Fidelio (Glyndebourne tour); Iphigénie en Tauride (Netherlands Opera); La Bohème (Australian Opera) 1990; Idomeneo (Glyndebourne Festival) 1991; appearance at Hong Kong Festival 1991; conducted the world premiere of Stephen Oliver's Timon of Athens, London Coliseum 1991; Residente Orkest The Hague, Netherlands Chamber Orchestra 1991; Così fan tutte, US opera debut, Dallas; Elektra, Dallas Opera 1994; Death in Venice at the 1992 Glyndebourne Festival, Cologne Opera 1996, Handel's Serse; Meistersinger, Australian Opera 1993; Music Dir Dallas Opera 1994–(2013); Chief Dir Cologne Opera 1997–2002; season 1997–98, numerous opera performances including Billy Budd, Katya Kabanova (with David Alden), Dallas; Macbeth (with Robert Carsen), Cologne; appearances with Finnish Radio Symphony Orchestra; debut with Utah and Dallas Symphony Orchestras; work as orchestral conductor with major orchestras in the UK and with broadcasts on radio; conducted London Philharmonic Orchestra at Royal Festival Hall 1998; Artistic Dir Arundel Festival 1992–1998; has worked with many leading European orchestras; season 1998–99 with a new production of Parsifal in Cologne and the Ring Cycle in Dallas; since 1999 Clemenza di Tito for Glyndebourne Festival; Makropolos Case and Love of three Oranges for Cologne Opera; Wozzeck, Simon Boccanegra and Acis and Galatea in Dallas; Cunning Little Vixen for Deutsche Oper Berlin 2001; Ballo in Maschera 2002; Paris concert debut 2001; Orchestra Philharmonique de Radio France; Houston Symphony debut 2001; Perth and Melbourne Symphony debuts 2002. *Current Management:* Dallas Opera, Winspear Opera House, 2403 Flora Street, Suite 500, Dallas, TX 75201, USA. *Telephone:* (214) 443-1000 (office). *Website:* www.dallasopera.org (office).

JENKINS, Sir Karl William Pamp, Kt, CBE, DMus, ARAM, LRAM, FRAM; British composer, pianist and oboist; b. 17 Feb. 1944, Penclawdd, Wales. *Education:* Gowerton Grammar School, Univ. of Wales, Cardiff and Royal Acad. of Music, London. *Career:* initially resident jazz oboist at Ronnie Scott's; Co-founder Nucleus, then played in Soft Machine; currently composer and conductor; Pres. Friends of the Nat. Youth Orchestra of Wales, Penclawdd Brass Band; Patron Nat. Youth Choir of GB; Fellow, Royal Welsh Coll. of Music and Drama, Trinity Coll., Carmarthen, Swansea Inst. *Compositions include:* Palladio 1992–95, Adiemus I: Songs of Sanctuary 1994, Adiemus II: Cantata Mundi 1996, Eloise 1997, Adiemus III: Dances of Time 1998, The Armed Man: A Mass for Peace 1999, Y Celtiaid (film score) (BAFTA Cymru Award for Best Original Music Soundtrack) 2000, Dying to Dance (TV score) 2001, Over the Stone 2002, Pwy Ysgrifennodd Y Testament Newydd? (film score) (BAFTA Cymru Award for Best Original Music Soundtrack) 2003, In

These Stones Horizons Sing 2003, Quirk 2005, River Queen (film score) 2005, The Peacemakers 2012, The Healer - A Cantata For St Luke 2014. *Recordings include:* Adiemus (Songs of the Sanctuary), Palladio (with Smith Quartet and London Philharmonic Orchestra) 1996, Imagined Oceans 1998, The Armed Man: A Mass for Peace (with Nat. Youth Choir of GB and London Philharmonic Orchestra) 2000, Requiem 2005, Quirk 2005, Kiri Sings Karl (with Kiri Te Kanawa) 2006, This Land of Ours 2007, Stella Natalis 2009, The Very Best of Karl Jenkins 2011, The Peacemakers 2012, Adiemus Colores 2013, Motets 2014, Still With The Music 2015. *Publication:* Still With The Music (autobiography) 2015. *Honours:* First Prize, Montreal Jazz Festival (with Nucleus), two D&AD awards for best advertising music, Classic FM Red F Award for outstanding service to classical music. *Address:* Karl Jenkins Music Ltd, 46 Poland Street, London, W1F 7NA, England (office). *Telephone:* (20) 7434-2225 (office). *Fax:* (20) 7494-4998 (office). *E-mail:* info@karljenkins .com (office). *Website:* www.karljenkins.com (office).

JENKINS, Katherine, OBE; Welsh singer (mezzo soprano); m. Andrew Levitas; one d. *Education:* Royal Acad. of Music, London. *Career:* fmr school teacher; fmr mem. Nat. Youth Choir of Wales; mem. Royal School of Church Music Cathedral Singers 1990–96; numerous public performances, including singing the Welsh nat. anthem at int. rugby matches, FA Cup Final at the Millennium Stadium, Cardiff 2005, VE Day celebration Trafalgar Square, London 2005; in Viva La Diva touring production (with Darcey Bussell) 2007. *Recordings include:* albums: Première 2004, Second Nature (Classical BRIT Award for Album of the Year 2005) 2004, Living a Dream (Classical BRIT Award for Album of the Year 2006) 2005, Serenade 2006, You Raise Me Up 2006, Rejoice 2007, Sacred Arias 2008, Believe 2009, Daydream 2011, This is Christmas 2012, Home Sweet Home 2014. *Honours:* awarded Pelenna Valley Male Voice Choir scholarship, BBC Radio Two Welsh Choirgirl of the Year (twice), BET Welsh Choirgirl of the Year. *Current Management:* c/o Tara Joseph, Nettwerk Management, 59–65 Worship Street, London, EC2A 2DU, England. *Telephone:* (20) 7456-9500. *Fax:* (20) 7456-9591. *E-mail:* kjrequests@ nettwerk.com. *Website:* www.nettwerk.com; www.katherinejenkins.co.uk; www.kj.tv.

JENKINS, Neil, MA; British singer (tenor) and music editor; *Artistic Director, AIMS International Music School;* b. 9 April 1945, Sussex; m. 1st Sandra Anne 1969; m. 2nd Penelope Anne 1982; four s. one d. *Education:* Westminster Abbey Choir, Dean Close School Cheltenham, King's Coll., Cambridge, Royal Coll. of Music, London. *Career:* debut in Purcell Room, London, song recital with Roger Vignoles 1967; guest soloist, Israel Chamber Orchestra 1968–69, London Bach Soc., USA tours 1971, 1973; mem. Deller Consort 1967–76; mem. Kent Opera 1971–89; appearances at festivals in Israel, Paris, London and Spain; performances with Welsh Nat. Opera, Scottish Opera, Opera North, Glyndebourne, Edinburgh, Paris Opera, Tours, Venice and Frankfurt; new productions of Le nozze di Figaro and the Ravel double bill in Geneva; sang Don Jerome in Prokofiev's The Duenna, Wexford 1989, Bernstein's Candide, 1989; also heard in oratorio and concert, in premiere of orchestral version of Tippett's The Heart's Assurance, Canterbury 1990; debut at ENO in Monteverdi's Orfeo and Il Ritorno d'Ulisse 1992; sang Tchekalinsky in The Queen of Spades, Glyndebourne Festival 1995, Marquis in Lulu 1996, General Wingrave in Owen Wingrave 1997, Vitek in The Makropolos Case, Brooklyn Acad. of Music, New York, and Glyndebourne Festival 2001; Guest Artist, Deutsche Oper Berlin and Opéra de Lyon 2004–05; Musical Dir Sussex Chorus 2002–14; Cummins Harvey Visiting Fellow Commoner, Girton Coll. Cambridge 2002; currently Artistic Dir, AIMS Int. Music School; Pres. Grange Choral Soc., Shoreham Oratorio Choir, Basildon Choral Soc., Haywards Heath Music Soc., Kent Chorus; mem. and Warden of PCS, Inc. Soc. of Musicians 1998–99; Patron Goldsmiths Choral Union. *Compositions include:* Christmas Carols for unaccompanied SATB singers in Christmas is Coming 1993. *Recordings include:* Bernstein's Candide and White House Cantata, Bach's St Matthew Passion, Tippett's King Priam, Mozart's Le nozze di Figaro, Henze's Kammermusik 1958, Britten's Serenade for tenor, horn and strings, with Oriol Ensemble, Britten's Peter Grimes conducted by Bernard Haitink; three tenor and guitar recital records. *Publications:* The Carol Singer's Handbook (ed.) 1993, O Praise God, O Holy Night (ed.) 1994; Ed. Bach choral works: St Matthew Passion 1997, St John Passion 1999, Christmas Oratorio 1999, Magnificat 2000, Mass in B Minor 2002, Easter Oratorio 2003, Ascension Oratorio 2007; Sing Solo Sacred 1997, Schütz Christmas Story 2000, Haydn The Seasons 2005, Haydn The Creation 2005; article on Haydn's Oratorio texts in Haydn Society Journal 2005, article on John Beard in Göttinger Händel-Beiträge 2008, and in Handel (ed.) David Vickers 2011, John Beard, Handel and Garrick's Favourite Tenor 2012. *Honours:* Nat. Fed. of Music Socs Vocal Award 1972, The Worshipful Co. of Musicians Sir Charles Santley Memorial Award 2004. *Current Management:* c/o Music International, 13 Ardilaun Road, London, N5 2QR, England. *Telephone:* (20) 7359-5183. *E-mail:* music@musicint.co.uk. *Address:* Barn End, Castle Lane, Bramber, West Sussex, BN44 3FB, England. *Telephone:* (1903) 879591. *E-mail:* neil@neiljenkins.com. *Website:* www.neiljenkins.com; www.neiljenkins.info.

JENKINS, Speight; American administrator; *General Director, Seattle Opera;* b. 31 Jan. 1937, Dallas, TX. *Education:* Univ. of Texas and Columbia Univ. Law School. *Career:* Ed. Opera News 1967–73; music critic New York Post 1973–81; host for the 'Live from the Met' broadcasts 1981–83; Gen. Dir, Seattle Opera 1983–; has presided over such productions as The Ring Cycle 1986–87, 1991, 1995, War and Peace, Die Meistersinger, and Werther in the version for baritone 1989, the US premiere of Gluck's Orphée et Eurydice, Les Dialogues des Carmelites 1990, Glass Artist Dale Chihuly's scenic debut in Pelléas et Mélisande 1993, Norma 1994, Der Rosenkavalier 1997, Tristan und Isolde 1998. *Honours:* Dr hc (Seattle) 1992, (Univ. of Puget Sound) 1992; Artsfund Outstanding Achievement in Arts Award 2006, Mayor of Seattle's Arts Award 2009. *Address:* Seattle Opera, PO Box 9248, Seattle, WA 98109-0248, USA (office). *E-mail:* mary.brazeau@seattleopera.org (office). *Website:* www.seattleopera.org (office).

JENKINS, Terry, BSc; British singer (tenor); b. 9 Oct. 1941, Hertford, Herts., England; m. Pamela Ann Jackson 1965; one s. one d. *Education:* Univ. Coll., London, Guildhall School of Music, London Opera Centre. *Career:* debut with Opera for All 1966–67, Nemorino in L'Elisir d'amore; Basilic Opera 1968–71; Glyndebourne Touring Opera 1969–71; Malcolm in Macbeth, M Triquet in Eugene Onegin, Schmidt in Werther, Scarramuccio in Ariadne auf Naxos; Glyndebourne Festival Opera 1971, Major Domo in Queen of Spades, Officer in Ariadne auf Naxos; Glyndebourne Festival Opera 1972, Scarramuccio; Sadler's Wells Opera 1972–74; ENO 1974–, roles include Basilio in Marriage of Figaro, Pedrillo in Entführung, Remendado in Carmen, Goro in Madama Butterfly, Gaston in La Traviata, Vanya in Katya Kabanova, Spoletta in Tosca, Schmidt in Werther, Fenney in Mines of Sulphur, Tchekalinsky in Queen of Spades, Loge in Rheingold, Borsa in Rigoletto, Duke in Patience, Orpheus in Orpheus in the Underworld; various roles Pacific Overtures, Hauk Sendorf in The Makropulos Case, Schoolmaster in Cunning Little Vixen, Dr Caius in Falstaff; ENO tour, USA 1984; New Opera Co. 1976, 1979, 1980; Royal Opera, Covent Garden 1976, 1977, 1981; English Bach Festival 1983, Versailles and Sadler's Wells; City of London Festival 1978; Barbican Hall 1984–88; Seattle Opera 1983, Loge-Rheingold; Vienna Festival with ENO 1985; Chelsea Opera Group 1986; Boston Concert Opera, USA 1986, Guillot-Manon; Aix-en-Provence Festival 1991, 1992, Snout, A Midsummer Night's Dream, Britten; sang Dr Caius at Garsington 1998, Rome Opera, Snout in A Midsummer Night's Dream 1999; Bregenz Festival, Schoolmaster in Greek Passion 1999, Dubai, Amahl & the Night Visitors 1999; Curzio in Marriage of Figaro 2000, Greek Passion, Brno 2005; Dir and Trustee, Harrow Young Musicians 1997–. *Recordings:* Justice Shallow in Sir John in Love, Vaughan Williams; Borsa in Rigoletto; Pacific Overtures, Street Scene. *Publications:* The Life of Lady Henrietta Herbert née Waldegrave (Montgomeryshire Collections, Vol. 94) 2006, The Will of John Rich – Probate and Problems (Theatre Notebook, Vol. 64, No. 1) 2010, Sir Ernest Lemon – A Biography 2011, Christopher Rich – From Puritan to Theatre Manager (Theatre Notebook, Vol. 66, No. 2) 2012, A Portrait of John Rich (British Art Journal, Vol. 13, No. 1) 2012. *Address:* 9 West End Avenue, Pinner, Middx, England.

JENNINGS, Diane; singer (soprano); b. 1959, California, USA. *Education:* San Diego Opera School. *Career:* sang small roles in opera at San Diego, then studied further in Munich 1984–86; sang at the Landestheater Salzburg 1986–87, as Marzelline in Fidelio, Susanna, Pamina and Marenka in The Bartered Bride; Aachen Opera 1988–91, as Mimi; Mainz 1990, as Donna Anna; concert engagements in Vienna, Graz, Munich and Verona. *Recordings include:* Suor Angelica and Brixi's Missa pastoralis.

JENSEN, Julian; British singer (tenor); b. 1968, Fowey, Cornwall. *Education:* Royal Acad. of Music, London. *Career:* Principal with D'Oyly Carte Opera 1992; opera roles include: Mozart's Tamino, Basilio and Ferrando, Theatre Kernow 1999; Verdi's Alfredo, Holland Park 1999; Duke in Rigoletto; Wexford Festival 1998, in Pavel Haas's Sarlatan and Zandonai's I Cavalieri di Ekebu; Laerte in Mignon, Univ. Coll. Opera; Bardolph in Falstaff, Palace Opera; concerts include Puccini's Messa di Gloria, Haydn's Creation, Pärt's St John Passion.

JENSON, Dylana Ruth Lockington; violinist; b. 14 May 1961, Los Angeles, CA, USA. *Education:* studied with Manuel Compinsky, Jascha Heifetz and Josef Gingold, masterclasses with Nathan Milstein in Zürich. *Career:* first public appearance as soloist in the Bach A Minor Concerto aged seven; professional debut as soloist in the Mendelssohn Concerto with the New York Philharmonic Orchestra 1973; European debut as soloist with the Zürich Tonhalle Orchestra 1974; regular tours worldwide as a soloist with leading orchestras, as a recitalist and as a chamber music player. *Honours:* second prize Tchaikovsky Int. Competition, Moscow 1978.

JEON, Minje; South Korean composer; b. 1987, Incheon, South Korea. *Education:* Korea Nat. Univ. of Arts. *Career:* studied with Hans-Jürgen von Bose in Munich; compositions and arrangements performed at many festivals including Tongyoung Int. Music Festival 2003, Int. Contemporary Music Festival, Seoul; f. Sum group of composers 2008. *Compositions:* numerous pieces for piano 1995–2005, Soak, for five percussionists and orchestra 2002, Symphony No. 1 for orchestra 2003, Particle Beam, for seven musicians 2005, Altertumklang, for clarinet and harp 2007, Affine, for violin and contrabass clarinet 2008, Kettenspektra, for piano, Le Tombeau d'Anglebert, for harpsichord 2009. *Honours:* Winner, Queen Elisabeth Int. Music Competition 2009. *Current Management:* Konzertdirektion Lee e. K, Potsdamer Platz 11, 10785 Berlin, Germany. *Telephone:* (30) 25-89-40-74. *Fax:* (30) 25-89-41-00. *E-mail:* mail@Konzertdirektion-Lee.de. *Website:* www.Konzertdirektion-Lee.de.

JEPPSSON, Kerstin Maria, DipMus, BA, MFA; Swedish composer; b. 29 Oct. 1948, Nyköping. *Education:* Social Univ. of Stockholm, Stockholm Conservatory of Music, Kraków Conservatory of Music, Poland with Krzysztof Meyer and Krzysztof Penderecki, studied with Maurice Karkoff in Stockholm,

California Inst. of the Arts with Melvin Powell. *Compositions include:* three Sentenzi for orchestra 1970, Tre visor (choral) 1972, Blomstret i Saron (choral) 1972, Tre ryska poem for soprano and clarinet 1973, five Japanese Images (choral) 1973, Hindemith in memoriam for clarinet and piano 1974, Crisis for string orchestra and percussion 1976–77, Vocazione for guitar solo 1982, Prometheus for percussion 1983, Tendenze for strings and piano 1986, Kvinnosånger (female songs).

JEPSON, Kristine; American singer (mezzo-soprano); b. 1965, USA. *Education:* Indiana Univ. *Career:* Season 1997–98 as Stephano in Roméo et Juliette at the Metropolitan, Hansel with the Canadian Opera Co. and Schoolboy in Berg's Lulu at San Francisco; other roles include Bartók's Judith for Vancouver Opera, Strauss's Composer for Santa Fe Opera, Rosina with New York City Opera and Cherubino at the Met; Season 1999–2000 as Mozart's Annio in Dallas and Dorabella with Florida Grand Opera; Season 2000–01 as Octavian and Cherubino at the Met, Sister Helen in premiere of Jake Heggie's Dead Man Walking at San Francisco and Siebel in Faust at Paris Opéra; Octavian at the Monnaie, Brussels, Mozart's Sesto for Netherlands Opera and Nicklausse in Paris; concerts include Falla's El Amor Brujo at Alice Tully Hall and Bernstein's Jeremiah Symphony with the American Symphony Orchestra. *Current Management:* Zemsky/Green Artists Management, 104 West 73rd Street, Suite #1, New York, NY 10023, USA. *Telephone:* (212) 579-6700. *Fax:* (212) 579-4723. *E-mail:* agreen@zemskygreen.com. *Website:* www.zemskygreen.com.

JERUSALEM, Siegfried; German singer (tenor), academic and university administrator; b. 17 April 1940, Oberhausen; m. 1980; one s. one d. *Education:* studied violin and piano at Folkwang Hochschule, Essen, studied singing with Hertha Kalcher, Stuttgart. *Career:* played bassoon in German orchestras, including Stuttgart Radio Symphony Orchestra 1961–77; made singing debut in Zigeunerbaron 1975; debut Bayreuth Festival 1977, Metropolitan Opera, New York 1980, La Scala 1981, Vienna State Opera 1979; sang Loge and Siegfried, Wagner's Ring Cycle, Metropolitan New York 1990, Tristan, Bayreuth 1993, Wagner's Ring Cycle, Vienna 1994, Wagner's Rienzi, Vienna 1997, Tristana, Berlin Staatsoper 2000; Prof., Hochschule für Musik Nürnberg-Augsburg 2000, Rector 2001–09. *Honours:* Bundesverdienstkreuz (1st Class) 1996; Grammy Award (for Wagner's Ring Cycle) 1982, (for Rheingold) 1991, Bambi Award 1996. *Current Management:* Hilbert Artists Management, Maximilianstrasse 22, 80539 Munich, Germany. *E-mail:* agentur@hilbert.de. *Website:* www.hilbert.de.

JEURISSEN, Herman G. A., DipMus; Dutch horn player and arranger; *Professor of Horn, Amsterdam Conservatory, Royal Conservatoire, The Hague, Fontys Conservatory, Tilburg*; b. 27 Dec. 1952, Wijchen. *Education:* Brabants Conservatorium, Tilburg. *Career:* Co-first Horn, Utrecht Symphony Orchestra 1975–78; Solo Horn, The Hague Philharmonic Orchestra 1978–; solo and concerto, radio and TV appearances with orchestras in Netherlands, Austria, Germany, France and USA; Prof. of Horn, Amsterdam Conservatory, Royal Conservatoire, The Hague, Fontys Conservatory, Tilburg. *Recordings:* Mozart's Complete Horn Concertos, Complete Horn Music, by Leopold Mozart, Chamber Music, Franz and Richard Strauss, compositions for horn and organ; compositions for brass and carillon, Wagneriana for horn ensemble, Wagner for Brass, Paraphrases for Horn Ensemble. *Publications:* reconstruction and completion of Mozart's unfinished Horn Concertos K370b and K371, K 494a, compositions and arrangements for horns, Mozart and the Horn 1978, Basic Principles of Horn Playing (three vols) 1997; contrib. to Mens en Melodie, Praeludium, Horn Call Brass Bulletin, Historic Brass Society Journal, Timbres, Orgelpark Research Reports. *Honours:* Prix d'excellence 1978, Silver Laurel of the Concertgebouw Friends 1979. *Address:* Jacob Mosselstraat 58, 2595 RJ The Hague, Netherlands. *Website:* www .hermanjeurissen.nl.

JEWEL, Ian, ARAM; British violist; b. 1950, England; m. Carol Slater. *Education:* Royal College of Music with Cecil Aronowitz, studied in Italy with Bruno Giuranna. *Career:* solo performances of the Walton and Rubbra Concertos, Harold in Italy by Berlioz and the Mozart Concertante; Prof., Royal Academy of Music and Head of Strings, Purcell School; co-founder, Gabrieli Quartet 1967, toured with them to Europe, North America, the Far East and Australia; mem. Zivoni Quartet; festival engagements in the United Kingdom, including the Aldeburgh, City of London and Cheltenham; concerts every season in London in the Barbican's Mostly Mozart Festival; Resident Artist, University of Essex from 1971; co-premiered works by William Alwyn, Britten, Alan Bush, Daniel Jones and Gordon Crosse, two Quartets of Nicholas Maw and Panufnik 1980, 1983, and the 3rd Quartet of John MacCabe 1979; British premiere of the Piano Quintet by Sibelius 1990. *Recordings include:* early pieces by Britten, Dohnányi's Piano Quintet with Wolfgang Manz, Walton's Quartets and the Sibelius Quartet and Quintet, with Anthony Goldstone. *Honours:* Dr hc (Essex). *Address:* The Garden Flat, 8a Belsize Park Gardens, London, NW3 4LD, England. *E-mail:* ian.jewel@hotmail.co.uk.

JIRIKOVSKY, Petr; Czech pianist; b. 24 June 1971, Prague. *Education:* Prague Conservatory with Emil Leichner, Acad. of Performing Arts, Prague with Ivan Klansky, Conservatoire de Paris with Theodor Paraschivesco, Itamar Golan, Hochschule für Musik, Vienna with Michael Schnitzler, masterclasses with Eugen Indjic. *Career:* concerts in the Czech Republic, Europe, Japan; Prague-Rudolfinum, Munich-Gasteig, Paris, London, Warsaw, Kyoto Concert Hall; Prague Spring Festival, Orlando Festival, Ohrid

Summer Festival; mem., Academia Trio. *Recordings:* B. Smetana: Czech Dances 1994, B. Smetana: My Country (piano four hands) 1995, B. Smetana: Polkas 1997, A. Dvořák: Piano Trios (Academia Trio) 1997, Dvořák, Brahms: Gypsy Songs (with Bernarda Fink, mezzo-soprano) 1997, B. Martinů: Concerto Grosso for two pianos and chamber orchestra (with Josef Hala, Prague Chamber Orchestra) 1997, B. Smetana: Works for two and four pianos (live recording from Prague Spring Festival) 1998, Beethoven: Geister Trio, Shostakovich Trio No. 2, Academia Trio 1999. *Honours:* first prize Beethoven Piano Competition 1986, first prize Chopin Competition 1987, third prize Smetana Piano Competition 1988, first prize North London Festival 1992, first prize Heerlen (Netherlands, with Academia Trio) 1995.

JO, Sumi; South Korean singer (soprano); b. 22 Nov. 1962, Seoul. *Education:* studied in Seoul and at the Accademia di Santa Cecilia, Rome, 1983–86. *Career:* debut as Gilda at Teatro Verdi, Trieste 1986; sang at Lyon, Nice and Marseille 1987–88; appeared in Jomelli's Fetonte at La Scala 1988; discovered by Karajan and sang Barbarina at the 1988 Salzburg Festival; Oscar in Un Ballo in Maschera 1989–90, conducted by Solti; guest appearances at Munich from 1988, Vienna from 1989, and Paris; La Scala Milan in Ravel's L'Enfant et les Sortilèges, conducted by Lorin Maazel, and as Zerlina in Auber's Fra Diavolo 1992; Metropolitan Opera as Gilda 1988 and 1990; Royal Opera, Covent Garden, as Olympia in Tales of Hoffmann and as Elvira in I Puritani 1991 and 1991; Chicago Lyric Opera as Queen of Night in 1990 and as Queen of Night with Danish Philharmonic conducted by Zubin Mehta in 1991; season 1992 as Matilde in Rossini's Elisabetta at Naples, Olympia and Adina at Covent Garden; sang Zerbinetta at Lisbon 1996; season 1997–98 with L'Enfant et les Sortilèges at Boston, Zerbinetta at Lisbon and Turin, and in Mozart's Lucio Silla at Mozart Festival, New York; Zerline in Fra Diavolo, Opéra Comique, Paris 2009; Donna Fiorilla in Il turco in Italia, Hamburg 2020–11; Marie in La fille du régiment, Hamburg 2012; Madame Mao in Nixon in China, Châtelet, Paris 2012. *Recordings:* 50 recordings including: Arias; Adèle in Le Comte Ory; Un Ballo in Maschera; Queen of Night in Die Zauberflöte, conducted by Armin Jordan and by Solti; Fiorilla in Rossini's Il Turco in Italia, conducted by Neville Marriner; Soprano soloist in Mahler Symphony No. 8, conducted by Sinopoli; Soprano soloist in Rossini's Messa di Gloria, conducted by Neville Marriner; Angèle d'Olivarès in Auber's Le Domino Noir, conducted by Richard Bonynge, Only Bach 2014. *Television:* sang operatic arias for Mildred Pierce, HBO 2011. *Current Management:* c/o SMI Entertainment Inc., Suite 601, Union Center Building, 837-11 Yeoksam 1-Dong, Gangnam-Gu, Seoul, 135-734, South Korea. *Telephone:* (2) 34610976; (10) 89460374. *E-mail:* smi@josumi.com; facundo@josumi.com. *E-mail:* youngjoon_jo@hotmail.com (office). *Website:* www.josumi.com.

JOBIN, André; singer (tenor); b. 20 Jan. 1933, Québec, Canada. *Education:* studied in Paris and worked with Jean-Louis Barrault. *Career:* sang at first as a baritone in Paris musicals; operatic roles as tenor from 1962, notably Pélleas at Marseilles, Nice, Paris, Madrid and San Francisco 1965; Glyndebourne Festival 1976, New York City Opera from 1970; other roles have been Romeo, Don José, Massenet's Des Grieux, Rodrigo and John the Baptist, Julien (Louise) and Hoffmann; many appearances at Québec, Lyon, Brussels, Berlin and Madrid; Liège Opera 1982–87, as Rodrigo in Le Cid, John the Baptist (Hérodiade) and Des Grieux; Cologne Opera 1987, as Werther; engaged in musicals and operettas in Chicago, London and Detroit; sang in Bernstein's Candide at Turin 1997.

JOCHUM, Veronica, MA; pianist; b. 6 Dec. 1932, Berlin, Germany; m. Wilhelm Viggo von Moltke 1961. *Education:* Staatliche Musikhochschule, Munich, studied with Edwin Fischer, Josef Benvenuti, Rudolf Serkin. *Career:* debut in Germany 1954; numerous appearances as soloist with orchestras in Europe, North and South America 1961–; appeared with Boston Symphony, London Symphony Orchestra, London Philharmonic Orchestra, Berlin, Hamburg and Munich Philharmonics, Vienna Symphony and Concertgebouw Orchestra, among others; radio and television broadcasts; recitals in over 50 countries in Europe, North and South America, Africa and Asia; featured in a German film, Self-Attempt (based on a novel by Christa Wolf). *Honours:* Cross of Order of Merit by German President (Bundesverdienstkreuz) 1994, Bunting Fellowship, Harvard-Radliff 1996.

JOEL, Nicolas Rodolphe; French stage and opera director; b. 6 Feb. 1953, Paris. *Career:* Opéra du Rhin, Strasbourg from 1973, with Der Ring des Nibelungen 1979; stagings of Samson et Dalila at Chicago and San Francisco, Aida in Vienna, Lohengrin at Copenhagen and Eugene Onegin in Amsterdam; Rigoletto and La Traviata for Zurich Opera, Parsifal in San Francisco and Roméo et Juliette at Covent Garden, London; Dir Théâtre du Capitole, Toulouse 1990–2009; Dir-Gen. Opéra Nat. de Paris 2009–14; further engagements for La Scala, Milan (Manon and La Rondine), New York Metropolitan (Andrea Chénier and Lucia di Lammermoor); other stagings include Boris Godunov, Cavalleria Rusticana and Pagliacci double bill and Salome (at Essen). *Honours:* Chevalier, Légion d'honneur; Critics Award (twice), Victoire de la Musique (Best Opera Production) for Dialogues of the Carmelites 1996. *Address:* c/o Opéra National de Paris, 120 rue de Lyon, 75012 Paris, France (office). *Telephone:* 1-40-01-16-06 (office). *Fax:* 1-40-01-20 59 (office). *E-mail:* njoel@operadeparis.fr (office). *Website:* www.operadeparis.fr (office).

JOEL-HORNAK, Emmanuel; French conductor; b. 1958, Paris. *Education:* Paris Conservatoire. *Career:* early engagements with Opéra de Lyon and at the Aix-en-Provence Festival; Paris Opéra debut with Offenbach's Les Brigands 1993; Semele and Les Pêcheurs de Perles in Melbourne and regular appearances with the Opéra de Nantes; Boildieu's La Dame Blanche at the Wexford Festival and Don Quichotte for English National Opera 1996; La Belle Hélène for Scottish Opera, Carmen and Werther in Israel; season 1996–97 with Chausson's Le Roi Arthus in Montpellier, Samson et Dalila in Sydney and Israel, Butterfly in Rouen, La Bohème for ENO and Eugene Onegin in Toulouse; US opera debut in San Francisco Opera's production of Carmen 1996; conducted Pearl Fishers at Sydney Opera House 2008 and Lakme 2011; Les contes d'Hoffmann in Hong Kong 2013; several appearances with Scottish Opera 2014. *Current Management:* Pinnacle Arts Management, 889 Ninth Avenue, 2nd Floor, New York, NY 10019, USA. *Telephone:* (212) 397-7915. *Fax:* (212) 397-7920. *Website:* www.pinnaclearts.com.

JOERES, Dirk; German conductor and pianist; b. 13 Aug. 1947, Bonn. *Education:* studied in Berlin, Cologne, London and Paris. *Career:* engagements with renowned orchestras; repeat appearances at festivals in Berlin, London, Prague, Klavierfestival Ruhr and Schleswig-Holstein; Artistic Dir, Westdeutsche Sinfonia, 1987; recordings and television productions; worldwide orchestral tours; guest conductor, London Royal Philharmonic; Associate Conductor, Royal Philharmonic Orchestra. *Recordings:* solo recording, Brahms and his Friends; Two Brahms Serenades, with Westdeutsche Sinfonia. *Honours:* first prize International piano competition, Vercello, 1972; Critic's Choice, two Brahms Serenades, Gramaphone Magazine, London. *Address:* Humboldstr 17, 51379 Leverkusen, Germany.

JOHANNSEN, Kay; German organist and church musician; b. 1 Oct. 1961, Giengen; m. Andrea Ermer 1987; one s. one d. *Education:* studied at Freiburg and NEC, Boston with William Porter. *Career:* concerts in major German cities and in foreign countries, broadcast concerts with almost all German stations, several concerts with orchestras such as the Nurnberg Symphonic, Radio Symphony Orchestra Prague, Radio Symphony Orchestra Hannover, Staatsphilharmonic Rheinland-Pfalz, Philharmonic Orchestra Gelsenkirchen, Berlin Philharmonic Orchestra and Stuttgart Philharmonic Orchestra; guest teacher, Freiburg Conservatory 1992–93; teacher, Karlsruhe Conservatory 1994–2000; organist of the Stiftskirche Stuttgart 1994–; masterclasses in Frankfurt, Sofia, Kiev and Seoul. *Recordings:* albums: Bach, Reger, Fortig 1990, Christian Hommel, Bach, Mozart, Huber, ars musici 1993, French organ music from the 19th century 1993, Brahms, Complete Organ Works 1996, Bach, Trio Sonatas 1997, Bach Masterworks of Weimar 1998, Bach III Part of Clavierübung 1999, The Young Bach–a Virtuoso 1999, Bach, Neumeister–Chorales 1999, Bach, Sonatas for violin and harpsichord 2003. *Honours:* various prizes in music competitions, German Nat. Foundation Scholarship. *Address:* c/o Stiftsmusik Stuttgart, Altes Schloss, Schillerplatz 6, 70173 Stuttgart, Germany.

JÓHANNSSON, Jóhann; Icelandic composer and producer; b. 19 Sept. 1969, Reykjavík. *Career:* compositions combine classical orchestration with electronic music; co-f. Reykjavik Kitchen Motors recording label/think tank/art collective and Apparat Organ Quartet (four organists, one drummer); performed worldwide with this ensemble, at festivals and in venues including Centre Pompidou, Paris, Barbican Hall, London, Palais des Beaux Arts, Brussels, Prague Rudolfinum, Roskilde and Spot Festivals in Denmark, ICA London, Batofar in Paris, New York Central Park Summer Stage, Stockholm's Kulturhuset, Lowlands Festival, Holland and Pukkelpop Festival, Belgium, also in St Petersburg and Helsinki; also composes for theatre, film and dance. *Music for film:* nine soundtracks to documentaries including Free the Mind, Varmints, Copenhagen Dreams, The Miners' Hymns, The Good Life, The Theory of Everything (Golden Globe Award for Best Original Score – Motion Picture 2015) 2014. *Recordings include:* solo: Englabörn 2004, Virðulegu Forsetar 2004, IBM 1401, A User's Manual 2006, Fordlândia 2008, And In The Endless Pause There Came The Sound Of Bees 2009, The Miners' Hymns 2011; other: Kitchen Motors: Nart Nibbles 2001, Apparat Organ Quartet 2004. *Honours:* awards for film music at Rhode Island and Sapporo Int. Film Festivals. *E-mail:* tim.husom@spectrevision.com. *E-mail:* staffofntov@gmail.com. *Website:* johannjohannsson.com.

JÓHANNSSON, Kristján; Icelandic singer (tenor); b. 1950, Akureyi Du. *Education:* Nicolini Conservatory, Piacenza, studied with Campogalliani and Tagliavini. *Career:* debut at Nat. Theatre of Iceland, Reykjavík, as Rodolfo 1961; sang Pinkerton in a production of Madama Butterfly, by Ken Russell at Spoleto 1983; engagements as guest artist at the Chicago Lyric Opera in Faust 1991, Metropolitan New York, Vienna, Staatsoper and La Scala Milan; roles have included Radames, Alvaro in La Forza del Destino, Cavaradossi and Dick Johnson; sang Turiddu in Cavalleria Rusticana at Naples and Florence, season 1990–91; Calaf at the Verona Arena 1991; sang Manrico in the opening production at the New Teatro Carol Felice, Genoa 1991; Andrea Chénier at Florence, Calaf at Chicago, Cavaradossi at Rome and Manrico at Turin 1992; Calaf at Torre del Lago 1996; Dick Johnson at Zürich 1998; season 2000 as Otello at Budapest and Enzo in La Gioconda at the Deutsche Oper Berlin.

JOHANSSON, Eva; Danish singer (soprano); b. 25 Feb. 1958, Copenhagen. *Education:* Copenhagen Conservatory, Opera School of the Royal Opera, Copenhagen, studied in New York with Oren Brown. *Career:* sang at the Royal Opera, Copenhagen, 1982–88, as the Countess in Figaro (debut), Tatiana, Pamina, Marie in Wozzeck and Chrysothemis (Elektra); guest appearances in Oslo as Marie and Donna Anna (1985, 1987); Marie at the Paris Opéra, 1986; sang in productions of Der Ring des Nibelungen at Berlin and Bayreuth, 1988, as Gutrune and as Freia and Gerhilde; sang Freia in a concert performance of Das Rheingold at Paris, 1988, conducted by Daniel Baremboim; Vienna

Staatsoper, 1989, as Fiordiligi; Tel-Aviv, 1990, as Donna Anna in Don Giovanni, conducted by Claudio Abbado; since 1990 Elsa in Lohengrin at Bayreuth; guest appearances in Barcelona, Munich, Dresden, Japan, Paris, Seville, Nice, Madrid, Stuttgart, Cologne and Hamburg; debut as Donna Anna, at Covent Garden, 1992; sang Elsa at the Accademia di Santa Cecilia, Rome, 1996; Chrysothemis in Elektra at Århus, 1998; season 2000–01 at the Deutsche Oper Berlin as Sieglinde, Elsa, Tatiana, Eva, Liu, Senta, and Elisabeth in Tannhäuser. *Recordings:* Das Rheingold conducted by Bernard Haitink; Es War Einmal, by Zemlinsky. *Current Management:* Hilbert Artists Management, Maximilianstrasse 22, 80539 Munich, Germany. *Telephone:* (89) 2907470. *Fax:* (89) 29074790. *E-mail:* agentur@hilbert.de. *Website:* www.hilbert.de.

JOHNS, William; American singer (tenor); b. 2 Oct. 1936, Tulsa, OK. *Education:* studied in New York. *Career:* debut at Lake George 1967, as Rodolfo in La Bohème; sang with the Bremen Opera as the Prince in The Love of Three Oranges and the Duke of Mantua; WNO 1970–72, as Radames and Calaf; further appearances in Cologne, Düsseldorf, Dallas, Hamburg, Bregenz, Houston, Vienna, Aix-en-Provence, Rome and New York (Metropolitan Opera); Covent Garden debut 1987, as Bacchus in Ariadne auf Naxos; Philadelphia Opera 1988, as Florestan in Fidelio; Holland Festival 1989, as Siegfried in a concert performance of Götterdämmerung; other roles include Wagner's Lohengrin, Tannhäuser, Siegmund and Tristan, Huon (Oberon), the Emperor in Die Frau ohne Schatten, Jason in Medea in Corinto by Mayr, Hoffmann and Verdi's Otello; sang Tristan at San Francisco 1991.

JOHNSON, Anne Pemberton; American singer (soprano); b. 3 Sept. 1958, New York, NY. *Education:* New England Conservatory, Peabody Inst. *Career:* sang in Heinz Holliger's Not I at Frankfurt, Paris and Almeida Festival, London; appearances at Munich in George Crumb's Star Child conducted by Paul Daniel and at Salzburg Festival with the Ensemble Modern under Hans Zender; premieres of works at Library of Congress and Kennedy Center, Washington, DC; engagements of Pli selon Pli by Boulez and Berg's Altenberg Lieder with RAI Milan and BBC Philharmonic Orchestras; season 1992–93 with Stravinsky's Rossignol in The Hague, conducted by Edward Downes, and opening concert of Luigi Nono Festival of the Venice Biennale 1993.

JOHNSON, Ben; British singer (tenor); b. 1984. *Education:* Royal Coll. of Music, pvt. study with Tim Evans-Jones. *Career:* opera roles with Opera de Baugé, France 2005, 2006, British Youth Opera 2007, Scottish Opera, Benjamin Britten Int. Opera School 2008; debut in Elgar's The Dream of Gerontius with Nat. Philharmonic of Lithuania 2007; has worked with leading conductors including Sir Charles Mackerras, Peter Schreier, Andrew Parrott and Neil Thompson; regular appearances with London Mozart Players; mem. Nat. Opera Studio 2008–; Assoc. Artist, Classical Opera Co. 2008–; roles include Albert Herring, Don Ottavio in Don Giovanni, Tam Rakewell in The Rake's Progress, Tonik in the Two Widows; recitals repertoire includes Bach, Schubert, Mozart, Poulenc, Stravinsky; mem. BBC Radio 3 New Generation Artists 2011. *Honours:* winner Wigmore Hall Int. Song Competition, 2007, First Prize, Kathleen Ferrier Awards 2008. *Current Management:* Intermusica Artists Management, 16 Duncan Terrace, London N1 8BZ, England. *Telephone:* (20) 7278-5455. *Fax:* (20) 7278-8434. *E-mail:* mail@intermusica.co.uk. *Website:* www.intermusica.co.uk.

JOHNSON, David Carl; American composer and flautist; b. 30 Jan. 1940, Batavia, NY. *Education:* Antioch Coll. with Donald Keats and David Epstein, Harvard Univ. with Leon Kirchner, studied with Nadia Boulanger in Paris, further study in Cologne. *Career:* teacher, Rheinische Musikschule Cologne 1966–67; worked with Stockhausen in the creation of Hymnen at the studios of West German Radio; mem., Stockhausen ensemble at the Osaka World Fair 1970; co-founder, Feedback Studio, Cologne 1970; Dir electronic music studio, Basle Music Acad. 1975. *Compositions:* Five movements for flute 1962, Bells for flute, guitar and cello 1964, Thesis for string quartet 1964, three pieces for string quartet 1964, three pieces for string quartet 1966, Tonantiton for tape 1968, Process of Music for tape and instruments 1970, Sound-environment pieces Music Makers, Gyromes mit und für Elise, Cybernet, Gehlhaar, Organica I'IV and Klangkoffer 1969–74, Proganica for speaker and two electric organs 1973, Audioliven for flute and electronics 1976, In Memoriam Uschi for tape and three instruments 1977, Jadermann incidental music to play by Hoffmansthal 1980, Bach: Encounter of the Third Kind (stage piece) 1981, Calls in Search for tape 1981. *Address:* c/o ASCAP, ASCAP Building, 1 Lincoln Plaza, New York, NY 10023, USA.

JOHNSON, Douglas; American singer (tenor); b. 1958, California. *Education:* University of Los Angeles. *Career:* appearances in Les Dialogues des Carmélites, La Fille du Régiment and La Clemenza di Tito while a student; sang at Aachen, 1984–87, notably as Don Ottavio, Handel's Serse, Jacquino, Count Almaviva, Rinuccio in Gianni Schicchi, Belmonte and the Steuermann; Hanover, 1988–89, Frankfurt am Mainz, from 1989 notably as Tamino, 1991; Salzburg Festival, 1987, 1991 in Moses und Aron and as Arbace in Idomeneo; guest appearances at Hamburg, Chateauneuf in Zar und Zimmermann, Deutsche Oper Berlin, Nicolai's Fenton, Vienna Staatsoper, Tamino, Cologne, Nemorino, 1987 and Ludwigshafen, Gualterio in Vivaldi's Griselda, 1989; sang Rossini's Almaviva at Seattle, 1992. *Recordings include:* L'Oca del Cairo by Mozart.

JOHNSON, Emma, MBE; British clarinettist and conductor; b. 20 May 1966, Barnet, Herts. *Education:* Pembroke Coll., Cambridge, studied with John Brightwell, Sidney Fell and Jack Brymer. *Career:* debut, Barbican, London

1985; appearances with ECO, London Symphony Orchestra, Ulster Orchestra, Royal Liverpool Philharmonic Orchestra, Hallé Orchestra, City of London Sinfonia and Royal Philharmonic Orchestra; debut in Vienna at the Musikverein 1985; French debut with Polish Chamber Orchestra 1986; performances in Netherlands, Finland and Monte Carlo; radio and TV appearances in UK; Japanese debut, Tokyo 1990; New York debut 1992; Schumann Weekend concerts at Blackheath 1997; Visiting Prof., Royal Coll. of Music 1997–; conducting debut with London Mozart Players 2001; conducting debut with Royal Philharmonic Orchestra 2004; Guest Artistic Dir Leeds Int. Chamber Series 2009. *Recordings:* Mozart Clarinet Concerto 1984, Crusell Clarinet Concerto No. 2 1985, Bottesini Duo for clarinet and double bass (with Tom Martin) 1986, Weber Clarinet Concerto No. 1 1987, Recital Disc La Clarinette Française (with Gordon Back) 1988, The Romantic Clarinet (concertos by Weber, Spohr and Crusell), Finzi and Stanford Concertos (with Royal Philharmonic Orchestra) 1992, Recital of Encores 1992, Michael Berkeley Concerto 1993, British Recital Disc 1994, Encores II 1994, Malcolm Arnold: Complete Clarinet Works 1995, Mozart and Weber Clarinet Quintets 2000, Voyage 2004, The Mozart Album 2005, Dankworth, Copland and Bernstein 2009, Brahms Sonatas 2012. *Honours:* Hon. Fellow, Pembroke Coll. Cambridge 1999; BBC TV Young Musician of the Year 1984, Bronze Award, European Young Musician of the Year Competition, Geneva 1984, voted Young Professional All Music Musician, Wavendon All Music Awards 1986. *Current Management:* c/o Nick Curry, Clarion/Seven Muses, 47 Whitehall Park, London, N19 3TW, England. *Telephone:* (20) 7272-8448. *E-mail:* Nick@c7m.co.uk. *Website:* www.emmajohnson.co.uk.

JOHNSON, Graham Rhodes, OBE, FRAM, FGSM; British pianist; b. 10 July 1950, Bulawayo, Rhodesia (now Zimbabwe); s. of the late John Edward Donald Johnson and of Violet May Johnson. *Education:* Hamilton High School, Bulawayo, Rhodesia, Royal Acad. of Music. *Career:* Artistic Adviser, accompanist Alte Oper Festival, Frankfurt 1981–82; Prof. of Accompaniment, Guildhall School of Music 1986–; Song Adviser, Wigmore Hall 1992–; Artistic Dir The Songmakers' Almanac; writer and presenter of BBC Radio 3 series on Poulenc, BBC TV series on Schubert 1978, Liszt 1986; concert debut, Wigmore Hall 1972; has accompanied numerous singers including Dame Elisabeth Schwarzkopf, Jessye Norman, Victoria de los Angeles, Dame Janet Baker, Sir Peter Pears, Dame Felicity Lott, Ann Murray, Matthias Goerne, Christine Schäfer, Dorothea Roeschmann, François Le Roux; has appeared at festivals in Edinburgh, Munich, Hohenems, Salzburg, Bath, Hong Kong, Bermuda; Chair. Jury Wigmore Hall Int. Singing Competition 1997, 1999, 2001; Sr Prof. of Accompaniment, Guildhall School of Music and Drama 1985–; mem. Royal Swedish Acad. of Music 2000; numerous recordings. *Publications:* contrib. to The Britten Companion 1984, Gerald Moore: The Unashamed Accompanist, The Spanish Song Companion 1992, The Songmakers' Almanac Reflections and Commentaries 1996, A French Song Companion 2000, Gabriel Fauré: The Songs and Their Poets 2009, Franz Schubert: The Complete Songs 2013, articles and reviews. *Honours:* Chevalier, Ordre des Arts et des Lettres 2002; Gramophone Award 1989, 1996, 1997, Royal Philharmonic Prize for Instrumentalist 1998, Wigmore Hall Medal 2013. *Address:* Guildhall School of Music and Drama, Silk Street, Barbican, London, EC2Y 8DT (office); 83 Fordwych Road, London, NW2 3TL, England. *Telephone:* (20) 8452-5193. *Fax:* (20) 8452-5081 (home).

JOHNSON, Marc; cellist; b. 1945, USA. *Education:* Eastman School of Music and Indiana Univ. *Career:* played with the Rochester Philharmonic while a student; solo appearances in Rochester and with the Denver Philharmonic; recital and chamber concerts in Washington, DC, St Louis and Baltimore; founder mem., Vermeer Quartet at the Marlboro Festival 1970; performances in all major US centres, Europe, Israel and Australia; festival engagements at Tanglewood, Aspen, Spoleto, Edinburgh, Mostly Mozart (New York), Aldeburgh, South Bank, Santa Fe, Chamber Music West, and the Casals Festival; resident quartet for Chamber Music Chicago; annual masterclasses at the Royal Northern Coll. of Music, Manchester; mem. resident artists' faculty, Northern Illinois Univ. *Recordings:* Quartets by Beethoven, Dvořák, Verdi and Schubert; Brahms Clarinet Quintet with Karl Leister. *Honours:* Denver Symphony and Washington Int. Competitions, Kammersänger 1960s.

JOHNSON, Mary Jane; American singer (soprano); b. 22 March 1950, Pampa, TX; m. David; two c. *Education:* West Texas Univ. *Career:* debut, New York Lyric Opera as Agathe in Der Freischütz 1981; Philadelphia and Santa Fe 1982, as Musetta and Rosalinde; sang at the San Francisco Opera from 1983, as Freia in Das Rheingold, Jenifer in the US premiere of The Midsummer Marriage 1983, Marguerite, and the Empress in Die Frau ohne Schatten, Washington Opera from 1984, Boston and Cincinnati from 1986; European engagements with Opera North at Leeds, Torre del Lago (Puccini Festival), Bologna, Geneva and the Baths of Caraccala at Rome (Minnie in La Fanciulla del West); sang Salome at Santiago 1990, Desdemona at Pittsburgh and Minnie at the 1991 Santa Fe Festival; Helen of Troy in Mefistofele at Chicago 1991; La Scala and Opéra Bastille, Paris 1992, in the title role of Lady Macbeth of Mtsensk; Teatro Municipal Santiago as Senta in Der fliegende Holländer 1992; other roles include Mozart's Countess, Leonore, Alice in Falstaff, Tosca, Giulietta, the Duchess of Parma in Busoni's Faust, and Mrs Jessel in The Turn of the Screw; sang Janáček's Emilia Marty at Vancouver 1996, and Salome there in 1998; sang Elektra at Santa Fe 2000; Artist Prof., Amarillo Coll. 2000–; staff vocal coach, Santa Fe Opera 2001–05. *Recordings include:* Scenes and Arias. *Current Management:* Pinnacle Arts Management, Miller Divison, 889 Ninth Avenue, 2nd Floor, New York, NY 10019, USA.

Telephone: (212) 397-7911. *Fax:* (212) 397-7920. *E-mail:* jmiller@pinnaclearts .com. *Website:* www.pinnaclearts.com.

JOHNSON, Nancy; American singer (soprano); b. 1954, California. *Education:* California State University, Hayward. *Career:* sang at the Landestheater Detmold, 1980–81, Wiesbaden, 1981–82, Mannheim, 1982–87; engaged at the Stuttgart Staatsoper from 1987 and has made guest appearances at Düsseldorf, the Vienna Staatsoper, San Francisco (Eva in Die Meistersinger, 1988); other roles have included Manon Lescaut, and the Empress in Die Frau ohne Schatten (Mannheim, 1984). *Current Management:* Theateragentur Heidi Schäfer, Glauburgstrasse 83, 60318 Frankfurt am Main, Germany. *Telephone:* 69283347; (171) 2884544 (mobile). *E-mail:* hs@santuzza.de.

JOHNSON, Robert; American singer (tenor); b. 10 Dec. 1940, Moline, IL. *Education:* Northwestern Univ., Evanston, studied in New York. *Career:* debut with New York City Opera 1971, as Count Almaviva; sang in New York, Chicago, Baltimore, Houston, New Orleans and Washington as Mozart's Ferrando, Belmonte and Tamino; Ernesto, Beppo in Donizetti's Rita, Alfredo, Fenton in Falstaff, Hoffmann, Rodolfo, Sali in A Village Romeo and Juliet, and Tom Rakewell; frequent concert appearances.

JOHNSON, Tom, BA, MMus; American composer; b. 18 Nov. 1939, Greeley, CO. *Education:* Yale Univ., studied with Morton Feldman. *Career:* music critic, Village Voice, New York 1971–82; freelance composer 1982–. *Compositions include:* Spaces 1969, An Hour for piano 1971, The Four Note Opera 1972, Septapede 1973, Verses for alto flute, horn and harp 1974, Trinity for SATB 1978, Dragons in A 1979, Movements for wind quintet 1980, Harpiano 1982, Predictables 1984, Voicings for four pianos 1984, Tango 1984, Choral Catalogue 1985, Pascal's Triangle 1987, Riemannoper 1988, Bonhoeffer Oratorium 1988–92, Narayana's Cows 1989, Formulas for string quartet 1995, Self-Similar Melodies 1996, Organ and Silence 2000, Tilework 2003, Kirkman's Ladies 2005. *Publications:* Imaginary Music 1974, Private Pieces 1976, Symmetries 1981, Rational Melodies 1982. *Address:* c/o Editions 75, 75 rue de la Roquette, 75011 Paris, France. *E-mail:* tom@johnson.org. *Website:* www.tom.johnson.org.

JOHNSSON, Catrin, BA, Dip RAM, LRAM; Swedish singer (mezzo-soprano); b. 1973. *Education:* Royal Univ. Coll. of Music, Stockholm, Royal Acad. of Music, London with Anne Howells. *Career:* opera singer and recitalist. *Honours:* Christine Nilsson Prize, Royal Acad. of Music, Stockholm 1997, Elena Gerhardt Lieder Prize, RAM, London. *E-mail:* catrinjohnsson@ntlworld.com (home).

JOHNSTON, Benjamin (Ben) Burwell, AB, MM, MA; American composer and teacher; b. 15 March 1926, Macon, GA. *Education:* College of William and Mary, Cincinnati Conservatory of Music, Mills College. *Career:* faculty mem., University of Illinois 1951–83. *Compositions:* Concerto for brass, 1951; St Joan, ballet, 1955; Passacaglia and Epilogue for orchestra, 1955–60; Septet for wind quintet, cello and bass, 1956–58; Gambit, ballet, 1959; Knocking Piece for 2 percussionists and piano, 1962; Gertrude, or Would She Be Pleased to Receive It?, opera, 1965; Quintet for groups, 1966; Carmilla, opera, 1970; Trio for clarinet, violin and cello, 1982; The Demon Lover's Doubles for trumpet and microtonal piano, 1985; Symphony in A, 1988; 10 string quartets, 1959–96; Piano pieces; Choruses; Songs; Sleep and Waking for percussion ensemble, 1994; Quietness, for speaking bass and string quartet, 1996. *Publications:* Maximum Clarity and Other Writings 2006. *Honours:* Guggenheim Fellowship 1959–60. *Address:* 120 Charlotte Street, Rocky Mount, NC 27804-3706, USA. *E-mail:* benbetjo@yahoo.com.

JOHNSTONE, Harry (Diack), BMus, MA, DPhil, FRCO, FTCL, ARCM, FSA; Canadian academic (retd); *Fellow Emeritus, St Anne's College, Oxford;* b. 29 April 1935, Vancouver, BC; m. Jill Margaret Saunders 1960 (died 1989); one s. one d. *Education:* Royal Coll. of Music, London and Balliol Coll., Oxford, UK. *Career:* Asst Organist, New Coll. Oxford 1960–61; Asst Lecturer in Music, Univ. of Reading, UK 1963; Lecturer, St Anne's Coll., Oxford 1965, Sr Lecturer 1970, Tutorial Fellow in Music 1980–2000, Fellow Emer. 2000–; Lecturer in Music, St John's Coll. Oxford 1980–2000; Reader in Music, Univ. of Oxford 1998–2000; Visiting Prof. of Music, Memorial Univ., St John's, Newfoundland 1983; Gen. Ed. Musica Britannica 2002–. *Publications:* Blackwell History of Music in Britain IV (ed. and co-author), The Eighteenth Century 1990, Maurice Greene: Cambridge Ode and Anthem (ed. Musica Britannica 58) 1991, Greene: Phoebe, a Pastoral Opera (ed. Musica Britannica 82) 2004, Thomas Roseingrave: Complete Keyboard Music (co-ed. with R. Platt) (Musica Britannica 84) 2006, William Croft: Complete Chamber Music (ed. Musica Britannica 88) 2009; numerous edns of 18th-century music, mainly English; articles and reviews in the Journal of the Royal Musical Association, Notes, RMA Research Chronicle, The Musical Times, Music and Letters, Proceedings of the Royal Musical Association, The Galpin Society Journal, Journal for Eighteenth-Century Studies, Studies in Bibliography, Early Music, Early Music History, The New Grove, The New Oxford Dictionary of National Biography. *Address:* St Anne's College, University of Oxford, Woodstock Road, Oxford, OX2 6HS, England (office). *E-mail:* harry .johnstone@st-annes.ox.ac.uk (office).

JOLAS, Betsy, BA; French/American composer and academic; *Professor, Conservatoire National Supérieur de Musique;* b. 5 Aug. 1926, Paris, France; d. of Eugène Jolas and Maria Jolas; m. Gabriel Illouz 1949; two s. one d. *Education:* Bennington Coll., Vt and Conservatoire Nat. Supérieur de Musique, Paris. *Career:* pianist, organist and chorister, Dessoff Choirs,

USA; Prof., Conservatoire Nat. Supérieur de Musique, Paris 1971–; has taught in USA at Yale Univ., Univ. of California, Berkeley, Univ. of Southern California, Harvard Univ., Univ. of Michigan; Darius Milhaud Chair., Mills Coll., Calif.; compositions have been performed by Boston Symphony Chamber Players, London Sinfonietta, Lincoln Center Chamber Music Soc., Ensemble Intercomtemporain, Groupe Vocal de France, etc; mem. American Acad. of Arts and Letters 1983, American Acad. of Arts and Sciences 1995. *Recordings:* appearances on D'un opéra de voyage, Episode quatrième, JDE, Points d'Aube, Quatuor II, Quatuor III, Sonate A 12, Stances, Episode huitième, Musique de jour, EA (petite suite variée), Répertoires Polychromes, Clavecin d'aujourd'hui 1977, Joelle Léandre 1988, Mady Mesplé 1989, L'Orgue Contemporain 1990, Musique Française pour Trompette et Percussion 1990, Betsy Jolas 1990, Recital 1995, Oeuvres françaises de XXe siècle 1999, Ventosum Vocant 2006. *Operas:* Le Pavillon au bord de la Rivière 1976, Le Cyclope 1986, Schliemann; numerous compositions for choirs, solo voices, orchestra, piano, etc. *Publication:* Molto Expressivo 1999. *Honours:* Chevalier, Ordre nat. du Mérite, Commdr des Arts et des Lettres, Chevalier, Légion d'honneur 1997; Laureate Int. Orchestra Conducting Competition, Besançon 1953, Copley Foundation Prize, Chicago 1954, American Acad. of Arts Prize 1973, Fondation Koussevitzky Prize 1974, Grand Prix Nat. de la Musique 1974, Grand Prix de la Ville de Paris 1981, Maurice Ravel Prix Int. 1992, Prix Soc. des auteurs, compositeurs & éditeurs de musique (SACEM) 1994, Prix Arthur Honegger 2000, Prix du Pres. de la République, Acad. Charles Cros 2012. *Address:* 12 rue Meynadier, 75019 Paris, France. *E-mail:* betsyjolas@ noos.fr. *Website:* www.betsyjolas.com.

JOLL, Philip; British singer (baritone); b. 14 March 1954, Merthyr Tydfil, Wales. *Education:* Royal Northern College of Music with Nicholas Powell and Frederick Cox, National Opera Studio in London. *Career:* sang with ENO from 1979, as Donner and The Dutchman; Welsh National opera as Wotan (also with the company at Covent Garden, 1986), Kurwenal, Amfortas, Chorebus in The Trojans, The Forester (Cunning Little Vixen), Onegin, Orestes, Don Fernando in Fidelio, Jochanaan in Salome and Barak in Die Frau ohne Schatten; Covent Garden debut, 1982, in Salome, returning in Der Freischütz, Das Rheingold and Die Frau ohne Schatten; German debut, Frankfurt, 1983, as Amfortas, returning for The Dutchman; Guest appearances in Düsseldorf, 1985–86, Berlin and Wiesbaden (with the Welsh National Company in The Midsummer Marriage, 1986); Metropolitan Opera debut, 1988, as Donner in Das Rheingold; Australian debut as Jochanaan, for the Lyric Opera of Queensland, 1988; Bregenz Festival, 1989, in Der fliegende Holländer; Lyric Opera of Queensland, 1989–90, as Jochanaan in Salome and Marcello; Sang Orestes in Elektra and Rigoletto for Welsh National Opera, 1992–97; Season 2000 as Gurlitt's Wozzeck at Turin, Wotan for Seattle Opera and Britten's Balstrode at Amsterdam; Engaged as Wotan in The Ring, Seattle 2000–01. *Recordings include:* The Greek Passion by Martinů; Amfortas in Parsifal; Kurwenal in Tristan and Isolde, conducted by Reginald Goodall. *Current Management:* c/o Musica Management, Neubauerstrasse 4, 65193 Wiesbaden, Germany. *Telephone:* (611) 2386811. *Fax:* (611) 2386810. *E-mail:* marcus .carl@opernagent.de.

JOLLY, James; British writer; *Editor-in-Chief, Gramophone Magazine.* *Education:* Univ. of Bristol, Univ. of Reading. *Career:* producer, Record Review (BBC Radio 3); Asst Ed. Gramophone Magazine –1989, Ed. 1990–2005, Ed.-in-Chief 2006–; Co-presenter The Classical Collection (BBC Radio 3) 2007. *Publications include:* Ed.: The Greatest Classical Recordings of All Time 1995, The Gramophone Opera 75: The 75 Best Opera Recordings of All Time 1997, The Gramophone Opera Good CD Guide 1998, The Gramophone Classical Good CD Guide 2001 (co-ed) 2002, The Gramophone Classical Music Guide 2012 2011. *Address:* Gramophone, Teddington Studios, Broom Road, Teddington, TW11 9BE, England (office). *E-mail:* gramophone@ haymarket.com (office). *Website:* www.gramophone.co.uk (office).

JOLY, Simon, BA, MA, ARCO; British conductor and repetiteur; b. 14 Oct. 1952, Exmouth, Devon, England. *Education:* Corpus Christi Coll., Cambridge. *Career:* music staff, WNO 1974–78; Assoc. Chorus Master, ENO 1978–80; Asst, then Principal Conductor, BBC Singers 1980–95; conducted opera at ENO, BBC, Wexford Festival, Dublin, Berlin; conducted the Dutch, Irish, Finnish and French Radio Choirs; concerts with the BBC Singers include the Proms; many festivals including Warsaw 2001; numerous programmes and concerts emphasising 20th-century music; orchestral work includes concerts and BBC programmes with the BBC Symphony, Philharmonic and Concert Orchestras, Nat. Orchestra of Wales, London Sinfonietta and Endymion Ensemble. *Recordings include:* Choral Works of Peter Maxwell Davies, Granville Bantock. *Address:* 49b Disraeli Road, Putney, London, SW15 2DR, England. *Telephone:* (20) 8785-9617. *Fax:* (20) 8785-2568. *E-mail:* simonjoly@ toadflax1.demon.co.uk.

JONAS, Sir Peter, Kt, CBE, BA (Hons), LRAM, FRCM, FRNCM, FRSA; British arts administrator, opera company director and academic; b. 14 Oct. 1946, London; s. of Walter Adolf Jonas and Hilda May Jonas; m. 1st Lucy Hull 1989 (divorced 2000); m. 2nd Barbara Burgdorf 2012. *Education:* Worth School, Univ. of Sussex, Royal Northern Coll. of Music, Royal Coll. of Music, Eastman School of Music, Univ. of Rochester, USA. *Career:* Asst to Music Dir, Chicago Symphony Orchestra 1974–76, Artistic Admin. 1976–85; Dir of Artistic Admin., The Orchestral Asscn, Chicago 1977–85; Gen. Dir ENO 1985–93; Staatsintendant (Gen. and Artistic Dir) Bavarian State Opera, Munich 1993–2006 (retd); mem. Bd of Man., Nat. Opera Studio 1985–93, Council, Royal Coll. of Music 1988–95, Council of Man., London Lighthouse 1990–92, Kuratorium Richard

Strauss Gesellschaft 1993–, Advisory Bd, Bayerische Vereinsbank 1994–2004, Rundfunkrat (Bd Govs), Bayerische Rundfunk 1999–2006, Supervisory Bd, Berlin State Opera Trust 2004–12, Advisory Bd, Tech. Univ., Munich 2006–12, Governing Bd, Netherlands Opera Amsterdam 2009–, Univ. Council, Univ. of Lucerne 2008–; Visiting Lecturer, St Gallen Univ. 2003–; Lecturer, Univ. of Zurich 2004–, Bavarian Theatre Acad., Univ. of Munich; mem. Kuratorium and Governing Bd, Wissenschaftszentrum für Sozialforschung (Social Science Research Centre), Berlin 2015–; workshop organizer, Wissenschaftzentrum Berlin and Univ. of Zurich; mem. Bavarian Acad. of Fine Arts 2004; Fellow, Univ. of Sussex 2012. *Publications:* Powerhouse (with M. Elder and D. Pountney) 1993, Eliten und Demokratie 1999. *Honours:* Bayerische Verdienstorden (Germany) 2003, Maximiliansorden (Germany) 2007; Hon. DMus (Sussex) 1993; Queen's Lecturer, Berlin 2001, Bavarian Constitutional Medal 2003, City of Munich Kulturellen Ehrenpreis 2004, Karl Valentin Orden (Germany) 2006. *Address:* Scheuchzerstrasse 36, 8006 Zurich, Switzerland (home). *Telephone:* (43) 4779871 (office). *Fax:* (43) 4779872 (office). *E-mail:* sirpeterjonas@gmail.com (home).

JONÁŠOVÁ, Jana; Czech singer; b. 28 April 1943, Plzeň; d. of Václav Růžek and Anna Růžková; m. Petr Jonáš 1964; one d. *Education:* Acad. of Performing Arts, Prague. *Career:* soloist, Prague Nat. Theatre 1970–; also tutor Acad. of Performing Arts, Prague; has performed at opera houses throughout Europe and at numerous int. festivals including Prague Spring Festival, Edinburgh Festival, UK, and in Madrid, Moscow, Strasbourg, France and Paris, Hamburg, Germany, Salzburg, Austria; currently teaching at Music Faculty, Acad. of Performing Arts, Prague. *Operas include:* Hoffmann's Tales, Don Pasquale, Fidelio, Orpheus, Jenufa, Excursions of Mr Brouček, From the House of the Dead, Così fan tutte, The Magic Flute, Titus, Don Giovanni, Boris Godunov, Beautiful Helene, The Lady's Maid, The Kiss, Orlando, Lancelot, The Barber of Seville, Rigoletto, La Bohème, Ariadne auf Naxos, Two Widows, Cunning Little Vixen, La Traviata. *Recordings:* Mozart Arias for Soprano 1970, Bach Kantate 1978, Italian opera arias 1986, concert coloraturas 1990, Love Songs 1994. *Honours:* UNESCO Prize 1970, Wiener Flotenuhr Prize 1974, Artist of Merit 1981, Czech Nat. Artist 1985. *Address:* c/o Academy of Performing Arts, Malostranské nám. 12, 118 00 Prague 1, Czech Republic.

JONES, Aled, MBE; Welsh singer and broadcaster; b. 29 Dec. 1970, Llandegfan. *Education:* Royal Acad. of Music, London, Bristol Old Vic Theatre School. *Career:* joined Bangor Cathedral Choir aged nine, won numerous nat. singing competitions and Eisteddfodau; gained int. success as a child soprano, making three programmes for BBC TV, recording numerous singles and albums; recording of Walking in the Air featured in BBC film The Snowman 1985; performed with BBC Welsh Symphony Orchestra and Neville Mariner, Leonard Bernstein, Los Angeles Philharmonic; worked briefly in musical theatre, performed in Joseph and the Amazing Technicolour Dreamcoat; numerous concerts and tours in UK and world-wide. *Television and radio:* presenter Songs of Praise (BBC TV), Good Morning Sunday (BBC Radio 2), The Choir (BBC Radio 3), and programmes on Classic FM, BBC Radio Wales, S4C. *Recordings include:* albums: Diolch a Chan 1983, Ave Maria 1984, Voices from the Holy Land 1985, All Through the Night 1985, Carols for Christmas (with BBC Welsh Chorus) 1985, Where E'er You Walk 1986, Pie Jesu 1986, An Album of Hymns 1986, Aled 2002, Higher 2003, The Christmas Album 2004, A Journey with Aled Jones 2005, New Horizons 2005, Reason to Believe 2007, Aled's Christmas Gift 2010, Forever 2011. *Honours:* Andrew Cross Religious Broadcaster of the Year. *Current Management:* c/o Tony Clayman, Vicarage House, 60 Kensington Church Street, London, W8 4DB, England. *Telephone:* (20) 7368-3336. *Fax:* (20) 7368-3338. *E-mail:* tony@tonyclayman.com. *Website:* www.tonyclayman.com; aledjones.co.uk.

JONES, Bryn Terfel (see TERFEL, Bryn)

JONES, Della; British singer (mezzo-soprano); b. 13 April 1946, Neath, Wales. *Education:* Royal Coll. of Music, London and Centre Lyrique Music School, Geneva. *Career:* sang first at Grand Théâtre, Geneva; mem. of English Nat. Opera 1977–82, in La Gazza Ladra, Il Barbiere di Siviglia, La Cenerentola, Le Comte Ory, Figaro, Giulio Cesare, Orfeo, Carmen, L'Incoronazione di Poppea and La Forza del Destino; appearances with Welsh Nat. Opera in Les Troyens, Salome, Barbiere di Siviglia and Tristan und Isolde; Scottish Opera in L'Egisto, Hansel and Gretel and Don Giovanni; Opera North as Rosina and in La Cenerentola, Le Comte Ory, Die Meistersinger, Oedipus Rex and Salome; other engagements with English Music Theatre (world premiere of Tom Jones by Stephen Oliver and The Threepenny Opera), Dublin Opera and Handel Opera Soc.; Baba the Turk in The Rake's Progress in Geneva and Venice; Ruggiero in Alcina for Los Angeles Opera; sang Cecilio in Lucio Silla, also La Finta Giardiniera for Mostly Mozart Festival, New York; other festivals in London (English Bach), Cheltenham, Aldeburgh, Chester, Salisbury, Edinburgh, Athens, Switzerland and throughout France; sang Preziosilla in Forza del Destino for Scottish Opera 1990; Ruggiero in Alcina at Geneva and Théâtre du Châtelet, Paris; Mrs Noye in Noyes Fludde at 1990 Promenade Concerts, Hermia in Midsummer Night's Dream at Sadler's Wells, many other Prom appearances including Last Night 1993; Marchesa Melibea at Covent Garden 1992 (Il Viaggio a Reims); sang Gluck's Armide at the Baroque Festival Versailles 1992 and Clytemnestra in Iphigénie en Aulide for Opera North 1996; Welsh Nat. Opera 1994, as Ariodante; sang Rossini's Isabella for English Nat. Opera 1997; Aunt Hermance in the premiere of Dr Ox's Experiment, ENO 1998; sang Mozart's Marcellina at the Opéra Bastille, Paris 2002; concerts and recitals in USSR, USA, Europe and Japan. *Recordings include:* Haydn L'Incontro Improvviso and Il Ritorno di Tobia, conductor Dorati, Alcina, conductor Hickox, Marcellina in Figaro and Elvira in Don Giovanni, conductor Arnold Östmann, Donizetti L'Assedio di Calais, L'Incoronazione di Poppea, Rossini Stabat Mater and Arias, Bliss Pastoral, conductor Hickox, Recital of French Songs with Malcolm Martineau, The Bear by Walton, Dido in Dido and Aeneas, Giulio Cesare (video of ENO production). *Address:* Westhall Copse, , 61 Westhall Road, Warlingham, CR6 9BG, England (home).

JONES, Gareth; Welsh conductor; *Musical Director, Sinfonia Cymru;* b. 1959, Port Talbot. *Education:* Royal Northern Coll. of Music with Timothy Reynish. *Career:* Assoc. Music Dir, D'Oyly Carte Opera 1988–90; Welsh Nat. Opera 1990–2006, with Nabucco, The Barber of Seville, Ernani, Faust, Fidelio and Un Ballo in Maschera, The Carmelites, Billy Budd, Jenůfa, Carmen; Musical Dir, Sinfonia Cymru 1996–; concerts with the Scottish Chamber Orchestra at Edinburgh Festivals, including Handel's L'Allegro and Purcell's Dido; Australian Chamber Orchestra at the Adelaide Festival; BBC Proms debut 2002, with Bryn Terfel, Renee Fleming and the Orchestra of Welsh Nat. Opera; debut at ENO, conducting The Mikado 2003. *Current Management:* Harlequin Agency Ltd, 203 Fidlas Road, Cardiff, CF14 5NA, Wales.

JONES, Gordon; British singer (bass-baritone); b. 1960, Northampton, England. *Education:* York Univ., choral scholarship to York Minster. *Career:* concert engagements include visits to the Lincoln Center in New York, the Royal Palace in The Hague, Hallé Orchestra, Martin's Le Vin Herbé at the Siena Festival and The Fairy Queen on tour in Italy; performances of Berio's Sinfonia conducted by the composer, Simon Rattle and Esa-Pekka Salonen; Bach's St John and St Matthew Passions with the Choir of King's Coll., Cambridge; sang in Arvo Pärt's St John Passion at the 1986 Almeida Festival and on tour of the UK 1988; further engagements in Bristol and Aberdeen and at the Malvern and Aix-en-Provence Festivals; Bach's St John Passion with The Sixteen on tour in Spain. *Recordings:* Vièrne's Les Angelus; Lully's Idylle pour la Paix, BBC; Schütz Schwanengesang and Bach Motets with the Hilliard Ensemble; Pärt St John Passion.

JONES, Gwyn Hughes; British singer (tenor); b. 1968, Llanbedrgoch, Wales. *Education:* Guildhall School of Music, National Opera Studio, London. *Career:* engagements with WNO as Ismaele in Nabucco, 1995; The Duke of Mantua, Don Ottavio, Rodolfo in La Bohème; Rinuccio in Gianni Schicchi for English National Opera; season 1999–2000 with Fenton in Falstaff at Brussels and Chicago, Ismaele for San Francisco Opera; concerts include Mozart's C Minor Mass with the London Symphony Orchestra; Verdi Requiem; Mendelssohn's Elijah; West Coast of USA tour with orchestra of Royal Opera House, 1999; sang Elektra at the Deutsche Oper Berlin, 1999. *Honours:* winner Neue Stimmen Competition, Gutersloh, 1995. *Current Management:* Harlequin Agency Ltd, 203 Fidlas Road, Llanishen, Cardiff, CF14 5NA, Wales. *Telephone:* (29) 2075-0821. *Fax:* (29) 2075-5971. *E-mail:* peter@harlequin-agency.co.uk. *Website:* www.harlequin-agency.co.uk.

JONES, Dame Gwyneth, DBE, FRCM, ARCM; British/Swiss singer (soprano); b. 7 Nov. 1936, Pontnewynydd, Mon., Wales; d. of the late Edward George Jones and Violet Webster; one d. *Education:* Royal Coll. of Music, Accad. Chigiana, Italy, Zurich Int. Opera Centre, Switzerland. *Career:* with Zürich Opera House 1962–63; a Prin. Dramatic Soprano, Royal Opera House, Covent Garden 1963–; with Vienna State Opera House 1966–, Deutsche Oper Berlin 1966–, Bavarian State Opera 1967–; guest performances in numerous opera houses throughout the world including La Scala, Milan, Rome Opera, Berlin State Opera, Munich State Opera, Hamburg, Paris, Metropolitan Opera, New York, San Francisco, Los Angeles, Zürich, Geneva, Dallas, Chicago, Teatro Colón, Buenos Aires, Tokyo, Beijing, Hong Kong, Seoul, Bayreuth Festival, Salzburg Festival, Arena di Verona, Edin. Festival and Welsh Nat. Opera; known for many opera roles including title roles in Aida, Madame Butterfly, Norma, Tosca, Elektra, Salome, and Medea, Leonora in Il Trovatore, Desdemona in Otello, Leonore in Fidelio, Senta in The Flying Dutchman, Sieglinde in Die Walküre, Lady Macbeth in Macbeth, Elizabeth in Don Carlos, Donna Anna in Don Giovanni, Eva in Die Meistersinger, Kundry in Parsifal, Isolde in Tristan und Isolde, Helena in Aegyptische Helena (R. Strauss), Färberin in Frau ohne Schatten, Elisabeth/Venus in Tannhäuser, Marschallin and Octavian in Der Rosenkavalier, Brünnhilde in Der Ring des Nibelungen, Ortrud in Lohengrin, Minnie in Fanciulla del West, Erwartung (Schoenberg), La voix humaine (Poulenc), Kabanicha in Katia Kabanowa (Janacek), Kostelnicka Küsterin in Jenůfa (Janacek), Herodias in Salome (Richard Strauss), Klytämnestra in Elektra (Richard Strauss), Queen of Hearts in Alice in Wonderland (Unsuk Chin), Begbick in Mahagonny (Kurt Weill); Pres. Richard Wagner Soc., London 1990; masterclasses in UK, Germany, France, Netherlands, Canada and Switzerland; debut as Stage Dir with new production of Der Fliegende Holländer by Richard Wagner at Deutsches Nat. Theater, Weimar; recordings for Decca, DGG, Philips, Chandos, EMI, CBS, Claves, Orfeo; Fellow, Royal Welsh Coll. of Music and Drama 1992. *Film:* Quartet (Anne Langley), directed by Dustin Hoffman. *Television films:* Fidelio, Aida, Flying Dutchman, Leonore, Beethoven 9th Symphony, Elisabeth and Venus in Tannhäuser, Poppea (Monteverdi), Rosenkavalier (R. Strauss), Die Walküre, Siegfried, Götterdämmerung, Die lustige Witwe, Don Carlos, Tristan und Isolde, La voix humaine (Mahagonny), Begbick (Mahagonny), Turandot, Senta (Der fliegende Holländer), Queen of Hearts (Alice in Wonderland). *Honours:* Kammersängerin in Austria and Bavaria; Hon. mem. RAM 1980, Vienna State Opera 1989; Bundesverdienstkreuz (Germany) 1988, Commdr des Arts et des Lettres 1993, Österreichisches

Ehrenkreuz für Wissenschaft und Kunst, 1. Klasse 1998; Hon. DMus (Glamorgan) 1995, (Wales) 1998; Shakespeare Prize, Hamburg 1987, Golden Medal of Honour, Vienna 1991, Premio Puccini Award Torre del Lago 2003, Cymry for the World Honour, Wales Millennium Centre, Cardiff 2004. *Address:* PO Box 2000, 8700 Küsnacht, Switzerland.

JONES, Ieuan, ARCM, Dip RCM, FRCM; British harpist; *Professor of Harp, Royal College of Music*; b. 24 Jan. 1963, Wales; s. of David Edward Humphreys Jones and Beryl Elizabeth Mary Jones. *Education:* Royal Coll. of Music, London with Marisa Robles. *Career:* appearances on UK, Dutch and Italian TV; soloist, London Rodrigo Festival 1986; soloist, Mozart Concerto for Flute and Harp, Bournemouth Sinfonietta 1986; invited performer, World Harp Congress, Vienna 1987; recitals in Spain, North America; featured in premiere of Alan Hoddinott's Tarantella for Harp and Orchestra, St David's Day Concert, Cardiff 1988; Mozart and Daniel Jones Concertos for Flute and Harp, Swansea, Aberystwyth 1988; played Mozart Flute and Harp Concerto, Debussy's Danses Sacrées et Profanes, Margam Festival, Swansea 1988; US Miami recital, North Wales tour; premiere, Rodrigo Concerto, Wales 1991; guest soloist of Enrique Batiz and the State Orchestra of Mexico 1992; soloist, Rodrigo Homage Concert, Seville EXPO celebrations 1992; Welsh premiere of Sonata for Harp by William Mathias (dedicated to Ieuan Jones) at Machynlleth Festival 1993; further recitals in Hong Kong, The Philippines, Brunei, Australia, Buenos Aires etc. *Recordings:* The Uncommon Harp 1987, Two Sides of Ieuan Jones 1988, In the French Style 1990, Mozart in Paris 1990, All Through the Night (with Huw Rhys-Evans, tenor) 1991, The Liszt of the Harp – The Music of Franz Liszt and Elias Parish-Alvars 1999, Schubert for the Harp 2016. *Honours:* Tagore Gold Medal, Royal Coll. of Music Award, Gold Medal, Royal Overseas League Music Competition, Runner-Up, Israel Int. Harp Contest 1985. *E-mail:* ieuanj@googlemail.com. *Website:* www .ieuanjones.co.uk.

JONES, Isola, BA; American musician and singer (mezzo-soprano); b. 27 Dec. 1949, Chicago, IL; m. Russell Thomas Cormier 1984. *Education:* Northwestern Univ. *Career:* debut as Olga in Eugene Onegin, Metropolitan Opera 1977; Live from the Met (television series); Maddalena in Rigoletto 1977, 1981; Lola in Cavalleria Rusticana 1978; Girl in Mahagonny 1979; Madrigal in Manon Lescaut 1980; recital with Placido Domingo 1982; The Met Centennial Gala 1983; Preziosilla in La Forza del Destino 1984; Smaragdi in Francesca da Rimini; Spoleto Festival 1989, as Giulietta in Les Contes d'Hoffmann. *Recordings:* Porgy and Bess, with Cleveland Orchestra conducted by Lorin Maazel; Flying Dutchman, with Chicago Symphony conducted by Georg Solti; Les Noces, with Chicago Symphony conducted by James Levine; Cavalleria Rusticana, with New Philharmonic Orchestra conducted by James Levine. *Honours:* merit award Northwestern Univ. 1984.

JONES, Jonathan Hellyer, MA, FRCO, ARCM; British teacher, organist, harpsichordist and conductor; *Director of College Music, Precentor and College Organist, Magdalene College Cambridge*; b. 1 June 1951, Warwicks., England. *Education:* Oakham School, Rutland, Royal Coll. of Music, London, St John's Coll., Cambridge. *Career:* taught at Perse School for Boys, Cambridge 1974–82, Anglia Polytechnic Univ. 1979–2004, Univ. of Cambridge 1995–, Guildhall School of Music and Drama 1979, St John's Coll. School, Cambridge 1974–80; Fellow, Hughes Hall Cambridge 2000–02; Fellow, Precentor, Coll. Organist and Dir of Coll. Music, Magdalene Coll. Cambridge 2002–. *Recordings:* The Muse Delight'd 1981, The Organ in the Age of Reason 1983, Principia Musica 1988, Rare Baroque Flute Concertos 1991, Brandenburg Concertos 1998, Bach's St Mark Passion 1999. *Honours:* Brian Runnett Prize (organ playing), Univ. of Cambridge 1973, John Stewart of Rannoch Scholarship in Sacred Music, Univ. of Cambridge 1972. *Address:* Magdalene College, Cambridge, CB3 0AG, England (office).

JONES, Julia; British conductor; *Chief Conductor, Orquestra Sinfónica Portuguesa*; b. 28 April 1961, Droitwich Spa, Worcestershire. *Education:* Chetham's School of Music, Univ. of Bristol, Guildhall School of Music and Drama, Nat. Opera Studio. *Career:* Repetiteur, Cologne Opera 1980s, Stastsoper Stuttgart –1991; Music Dir, Ulm Municipal Theatre 1991–95; Music Dir, Staatstheater Darmstadt 1995–97; Prin. Conductor, Basel Theatre and Basel Opera 1998–2002; Prin. Conductor, Orquestra Sinfónica Portuguesa 2008–. *Address:* Orquestra Sinfónica Portuguesa, Teatro Nacional de São Carlos, Rua de Serpa Pinto n°9, 1200-442 Lisbon, Portugal (office). *Telephone:* 213-253-000 (office). *Fax:* 213-253-083 (office). *E-mail:* geral@ saocarlos.pt (office). *Website:* www.saocarlos.pt (office).

JONES, Karen, AGSMD; British flautist; *Principal Flute, City of London Sinfonia and London Chamber Orchestra*; b. 8 July 1965, Hampton, Middlesex, England. *Education:* Guildhall School, studied in Vienna with Wolfgang Schulz and in New York with Thomas Nyfenger. *Career:* played the Ibert Concerto with the London Symphony Orchestra 1985; concerto performances with Neville Marriner at the QEH, Andrew Litton at the Festival Hall and George Malcolm at the Snape Concert Hall; further engagements with the Ulster Orchestra, the Philharmonia, the Wren Orchestra and London Musici; solo recitals at the Purcell Room and Wigmore Hall; mem., Pears-Britten Ensemble, with performances in the UK and USA; guest principal with the Australian Chamber Orchestra at the 1992 Promenade Concerts; Principal Flute, City of London Sinfonia and London Chamber Orchestra; faculty mem., Royal Acad. of Music; consultant, Birmingham Conservatoire of Music. *Films:* principal flute for Harry Potter, Bridget Jones, A Week with Marilyn and Iron Lady. *Recordings include:* Arnold's Concerto No. 1 and Panufnik's Hommage à Chopin, Malcolm Arnold Flute Concerto No. 2, The Flute Album. *Honours:* Hon. ARAM 2009; winner woodwind section BBC TV Young Musician of the Year 1982, Gold Medal, Shell/London Symphony Orchestra Scholarship 1985, Fulbright Scholarship 1987, Harkness Fellowship 1987. *Address:* Royal Academy of Music, Marylebone Road, London NW1 5HT, England (office). *Telephone:* (20) 7873-7320 (office). *E-mail:* woodwind@ ram.ac.uk (office); karenjonesflute@me.com. *Website:* www.ram.ac.uk (office).

JONES, Leah-Marian; British singer (mezzo-soprano); b. 1964, Wales. *Education:* Royal Northern College of Music and the National Opera Studio. *Career:* appearances with the Royal Opera at Covent Garden as Mercédès in Carmen, Zulma in L'Italiana in Algeri, Flosshilde in Rheingold, Second Lady in Die Zauberflöte, Emilia in Otello, Rosette in Manon, Flora in La Traviata, Annina in Der Rosenkavalier, Dorotea in Stiffelio, Elena in Aroldo, Flosshilde in Götterdämmerung; season 1995–96 with WNO as Lola in Cavalleria Rusticana; other roles include Maddalena, Carmen, Siebel, Isolier in Le Comte Ory, Adalgisa in Norma; season 1996 with Royal Opera as Fenena in Nabucco and Dorabella and Carmen for English National Opera; sang Laura in Luisa Miller for the Royal Opera at Edinburgh 1998; season 2000–01 as Tisbe in La Cenerentola and Emilia in Otello, at Covent Garden; Flowermaiden in Parsifal at Covent Garden 2002. *Recordings include:* solo album: Intermezzo. *Current Management:* c/o Harlequin Agency Ltd, 203 Fidlas Road, Llanishen, Cardiff CF14 5NA, Wales. *Telephone:* (29) 2075-0821. *Fax:* (29) 2075-5971. *E-mail:* peter@harlequin-agency.co.uk. *Website:* www .harlequin-agency.co.uk.

JONES, Martin; British pianist; b. 4 Feb. 1940, England. *Education:* studied in London. *Career:* debut at the QEH, London, and Carnegie Hall 1968; regular appearances with major British orchestras at the Festival Hall, the Barbican and other venues; tour of Canada with the BBC National Orchestra of Wales and recitals in Florida, Tennessee and California; broadcasts in the UK, Ireland and the USA; Pianist-in-Residence at University College, Cardiff 1971–88; Brahms recital at the Wigmore Hall 1993; repertoire includes many standard concertos and also those by Busoni, Benjamin, Barber, Mathias, McCabe, Lambert and Scharwenka; played Grainger's Bridal Lullaby and Mock Morris on the soundtrack of the film Howard's End. *Current Management:* c/o Owen/White Management, Flat 6, 22 Brunswick Terrace, Hove, East Sussex BN3 1HJ, England. *Telephone:* (1273) 727127. *Fax:* (1273) 527038. *E-mail:* info@owenwhitemanagement.com. *Website:* www .owenwhitemanagement.com.

JONES, Maureen; Australian pianist; b. 1940. *Education:* New South Wales Conservatorium, Sydney. *Career:* formed trio with Breton Langbein and Barry Tuckwell and gave the premiere of the Horn Trio by Don Banks at the 1962 Edinburgh Festival; regular tours of Australia and Europe, including appearances in Dublin, Siena, Innsbruck, Paris, Sydney and Melbourne; duo recitals with Barry Tuckwell; concert debut playing Beethoven's 1st Concerto with the Sydney Symphony; appearances at the Edinburgh Festival include concerts with the Berlin Philharmonic.

JONES, Nerys; British singer (mezzo-soprano); b. 1965, Wales; d. of Alun Jones and Enid Jones; m. Matt Stermer; two d. *Education:* Royal Scottish Acad., Guildhall School, studied with Pat MacMahon, David Pollard. *Career:* debut as Karolka in Jenůfa for Scottish Opera; appearances with Scottish Opera as Marzelline in Fidelio and WNO as Norina in Don Pasquale; ENO debut as Melissa in Ken Russell's production of Princess Ida 1992; further roles with ENO (Principal from 1994) include Cherubino, Despina, Zerlina, Proserpina in Orfeo, Mercédès in Carmen, Rosette in Manon, Flora in La Traviata, Hansel, Flower Maiden in Parsifal, Sister Mathilde in Dialogues des Carmélites; sang in the premiere of Blond Eckbert by Judith Weir 1994, Cherubino at Grange Park Opera, and Kitchen Boy in Rusalka for ENO 1998, sang Rosina for Grange Park Opera 1999, Lisette in Haydn's Il mondo della luna, Garsington Opera 2000; Dorabella in Così fan tutte, Grange Park Opera 2001; other roles include Flight (Jonathan Dove) for Reis Opera 2001, Antwerp 2002; Adelaide Festival 2006; Amelia, Seattle Opera 2008; many concert engagements. *Recordings include:* album: Blond Eckbert, The Thieving Magpie. *Honours:* Royal Scottish Acad. Peter Morrison Prize, John Noble bursary.

JONES, Paul Carey; British singer (baritone); b. 1965, Cardiff, Wales. *Education:* Queen's College, Oxford, Royal Academy of Music with Mark Wildman and Julius Drake. *Career:* appearances as Mozart's Figaro, Marcello and Schaunard in La Bohème, Enby in Purcell's The Indian Queen and Ariodates in Handel's Xerxes; Eleven baritone roles in Stephen Oliver's A Man of Feeling; Concerts recitals and broadcasts throughout the United Kingdom; Season 2001–2002 with Purcell's The Fairy Queen at the Linbury Theatre, Covent Garden, National Eisteddfod in Wales and St David's Hall, Cardiff. *Honours:* Royal Academy Hubert Kiver Prize. *Website:* www.paulcareyjones .com.

JONES, Richard, CBE; British opera and theatre director and producer; b. 7 June 1953, Lambeth, London, England. *Education:* Univs of Hull and London. *Career:* working as a jazz musician; debut, A Water Bird Talk by Dominick Argento for Scottish Opera 1982; has directed for theatre and for opera cos; Musica nel Chiostro, Battignano (Mozart's Apollo et Hyacinthus 1984); Salieri's La Grotta di Trofonio and Paisiello's Il re Teodoro in Venice 1985; Opera Northern Ireland (Don Pasquale 1985); Wexford Festival (Mignon 1986); Cambridge Univ. Opera (The Magic Flute 1986); Opera 80 (The Rake's Progress 1986, Rigoletto 1987); Opera North (Manon 1987, Carmen and The

Love for Three Oranges 1987); Scottish Opera-Go-Round (Macbeth and Die Entführung 1987); Scottish Opera (Das Rheingold 1989); Kent Opera (Le Comte Ory and A Night at the Chinese Opera 1988); The Love for Three Oranges and David Blake's The Plumber's Gift, world premiere for ENO 1989; Bregenz Festival, Austria (Mazeppa 1991); Netherlands Opera (The Flying Dutchman 1993); Bavarian State Opera (Julius Caesar 1994); Royal Opera House (Das Rheingold and Die Walküre 1994, Siegfried and Götterdämmerung 1995); Netherlands Opera (Mazeppa 1991); ENO (Die Fledermaus 1991); Scottish Opera (Die Walküre 1991); The Midsummer Marriage at Munich 1998; ENO (Les Troyens 2003, Lady Macbeth of Mtsensk (Olivier Award for Best New Opera Production 2005) 2004, 2006, The Bitter Tears of Petra von Kant 2005); Sun Kingdom Opera 2003–08; Royal Opera (Gianni Schicchi, L'Heure Espagnole) 2007; Bavarian State Opera in Munich (Les Contes d'Hoffmann) 2011; Royal Opera House (Britten's Gloriana) 2013; New York City Opera (US premiere of Anna Nicole) 2013. *Theatre includes:* Too Clever By Half (Olivier Award), The Illusion (Evening Standard Award), A Flea in Her Ear (Old Vic Theatre); Six Characters Looking for an Author, Hobson's Choice, The Good Soul of Szechuan, Annie Get Your Gun, The Government Inspector, Public Enemy – a version of The Enemy of the People (Young Vic Theatre), Into The Woods (Phoenix Theatre West End) (Olivier Award, Evening Standard Award); Black Snow (American Repertory Theatre); All's Well that Ends Well (Public Theater), David Hirson's La Bête and Wrong Mountain (Eugene O'Neill Theater); Titanic (Lunt Fontaine Theater); Holy Mothers (Ambassadors Theatre/Royal Court Theatre, London); Le Bourgeois Gentilhomme, Tales from the Vienna Woods (Royal Nat. Theatre, London); A Midsummer Night's Dream (RSC, Yale and Salamanca Festival); David Sawer's Rumpelstiltskin (Birmingham Contemporary Music Group, Spitalfields Festival London); David Harrower's Government Inspector (after Gogol's Revisor of 1836) (Warwick Arts Centre and Young Vic Theatre, London) 2011. *Honours:* Laurence Olivier Award for Best Newcomer in Theatre 1988, Evening Standard Drama Award for Best Dir 1990, Evening Standard Award for Outstanding Artistic Achievement for Der Ring des Nibelungen, Olivier Award for The Trojans, Olivier Award and TMA Award for Hansel and Gretel, TMA Award for Wozzeck, The Queen of Spades and Die Meistersinger von Nuremburg, South Bank Show Award for Die Meistersinger von Nuremburg, Opernwelt Designer of the Year (with Antony MacDonald) for Un ballo in maschera, Opernwelt Production of the Year for Julius Caesar. *Current Management:* c/o Tracey Elliston, Judy Daish Associates Ltd, 2 St Charles Place, London, W10 6EG, England. *Telephone:* (20) 8964-8811. *E-mail:* tracey@judydaish.com. *Website:* www.richardjonesdirector.co.uk.

JONES, Samuel, BA, MA, PhD; American composer, conductor and educator; b. 2 June 1935, Inverness, Miss.; m. 1st; two d.; m. 2nd Kristin Barbara Schutte 1975. *Education:* Millsaps Coll., Eastman School of Music, Univ. of Rochester, NY. *Career:* Dir of Instrumental Music, Alma Coll., Mich. 1960–62; Music Dir Saginaw Symphony 1962–65; Conductor Rochester Philharmonic 1965–73; Founding Dean, Shepherd School of Music 1973–79; Prof. of Conducting and Composition, Rice Univ. 1973–97, Prof. Emer. 1997–; Composer-in-Residence, Seattle Symphony Orchestra 1997–2011, Dir Composers' Workshop 2011–13; guest conductor, Buffalo Philharmonic, Symphonies of Detroit, Pittsburgh, Houston, Prague and Iceland; Music Alive Composer-in-Residence, Meridian Symphony (Meet the Composer and American Symphony Orchestra League); Past Pres. Conductors' Guild. *Compositions include:* In Retrospect 1959, Chaconne and Burlesque 1959–60, Symphony No. 1 1959–60, Piano Sonata 1961–62, Four Haiku 1962, Elegy for string orchestra 1963, Festival Fanfare 1964, Overture for a City 1964, Let Us Now Praise Famous Men 1972, Contours of Time 1974, Fanfare and Celebration 1980, A Christmas Memory 1981, A Symphonic Requiem 1983 (revised 2002), Listen Now, My Children 1985, The Trumpet of the Swan 1985, Two Movements for Harpsichord 1989, Symphony No. 2: Canticles of Time 1990, Symphony No. 3: Palo Duro Canyon 1992, The Seas of God 1992, The Temptation of Jesus (oratorio) 1995, Sonata for Cello and Piano 1996, Janus 1998, Reunion Benediction 1999, Roundings: Musings on Texas New Deal Murals 2000, Machines (Roundings Suite No. 2) 2000, The Open Range (Roundings Suite No. 3) 2000, Hymn to the Earth 2000, Aurum Aurorae 2001, Eudora's Fable (The Shoe Bird) 2002, Mount Rainier Overture (Chorale Overture for organ and orchestra) 2003, Tuba Concerto 2006, Benediction 2006, Horn Concerto 2008, Trombone Concerto 2009, Cello Concerto 2010, Organ Benediction 2010, Meditations for a cappella choir 2011, Reflections (Songs of Fathers and Daughters) 2011, Hear the Music 2011, Suite from A Christmas Memory 2012, Violin Concerto 2013, Four Haiku (chamber version) 2014, String Quartet 2015. *Honours:* Dr hc (Millsaps Coll.); Mississippi Inst. of Arts and Letters Award 1986, 1991, 2003, 2007, 2011, Ford Foundation Recording/Publication Award, numerous ASCAP Awards, Int. Angel Award, Martha Baird Rockefeller Grant, Houston Symphony Distinguished Service Award, Seattle Symphony Artistic Recognition Award, Inaugural Class, Mississippi Musicians' Hall of Fame. *Address:* 35247 34th Avenue South, Auburn, WA 98001, USA (home). *Telephone:* (253) 874-0767 (home). *Fax:* (253) 517-5698 (office). *E-mail:* sj@samueljones.net. *Website:* www.samueljones.net.

JONES, Warren, BM, MM; American vocal coach and accompanist; b. 11 Dec. 1951, Washington, DC. *Education:* New England Conservatory of Music, San Francisco Conservatory of Music. *Career:* has accompanied artists including Luciano Pavarotti, Marilyn Horne, Frederica von Stade, Judith Blegen, Håkan Hagegård, Elisabeth Söderström, Martti Talvela, Carol Vaness, Lynn Harrell, Thomas Allen, Roberta Peters, Robert Alexander, Samuel Ramey, Barbara Bonney, Ruth Swenson, Dame Kiri te Kanawa, Denyce Graves, Stephanie Blythe, Bo Skovhus, Juilliard String Quartet; appearances at Tanglewood, Ravinia, Caramoor and Salzburg Festivals; fmr Asst Conductor, Metropolitan Opera, San Francisco Opera; classes at Harvard, San Francisco Conservatory of Music, Hartt School of Music, California State Univ., Manhattan School of Music; Principal Pianist, Camerate Pacifica. *Honours:* Musical America Award for Collaborative Pianist of the Year 2010. *E-mail:* warren@warrenjones.com (office). *Website:* www.warrenjones.com.

JOOS, Martina; Swiss recorder player; b. 15 Feb. 1972, Glarus. *Education:* Hochschule für Musik und Theater in Zürich with Kees Boeke and Matthias Weilenmann. *Career:* mem., Trio O'Henry (with Claudia Gerauer and Barbara Nägele); appearances include Bludenzer Tage für Zeitgemässe Musik, Austria 1997, Festival of Ancient Music, Stary Sacz, Poland 2000, Festival Musica Nova, Sofia, Bulgaria 2001, Festival Bohemia-Saxony, Czech Republic 2001; cycle of premieres with works of Swiss composers, Zürich 2000–01; radio broadcasts include St Peter's Church, Zürich 1996, Great Hall of the HFMT, Zürich; premieres of Kees Boeke's The Unfolding 1997, Martin Derungs's A Set of Pieces 2000, Thomas Müller's Erste Etappe in Richtung farbiger Eindrücke 2000, Giorgio Tedde's Medio Aevo 2000, Andreas Nick's Trio pour flûtes à bec 2000.

JORDAN, Irene; American singer (soprano); b. 25 April 1919, Birmingham, AL. *Education:* Judson Coll., studied with Clyrie Mundy in New York. *Career:* sang first as mezzo-soprano (Mallika in Lakmé at the Metropolitan 1946), and after further study sang Donna Anna and Micaela at the Chicago Lyric Theatre 1954; appeared at the New York City Opera and the Metropolitan (the Queen of Night) 1957; elsewhere in America sang Verdi's Aida and Lady Macbeth, Madama Butterfly, Weber's Euryanthe, Mozart's Vitellia (La Clemenza di Tito) and Leonore in Fidelio. *Recordings include:* Stravinsky's Pulcinella, conducted by the composer, and songs by Schoenberg.

JORDAN, Philippe Dominique; Swiss/Irish conductor; *Music Director, Opéra National de Paris;* b. 18 Oct. 1974, Zürich, Switzerland. *Education:* Konservatorium, Zürich with Boris Mersson, Karl Engel and Hans Ulrich Lehmann. *Career:* Asst to Jeffrey Tate, Théâtre du Châtelet in Paris and Festival of Aix-en-Provence; Theatre in Ulm; Opera Ireland, Dublin; Aalto-Theater Essen; Théâtre de la Monnie, Brussels; Kapellmeister and Asst to Daniel Barenboim 1999–2001, Staatsoper Unter den Linden in Berlin, opening with D. Milhaud's Christophe Colomb with Peter Greenaway; Teatro dell'Opera in Rome; Grand Théâtre Genève; Wiener Staatsoper; Théâtre du Châtelet Paris; Semperoper Dresden; Opéra National de Lyon; Festival d'Aixen Provence; Salzburger Festspiele; Houston Grand Opera; Glyndebourne Festival; Metropolitan Opera NY; Royal Opera House, Covent Garden; Opera Bastille; Bavarian State Opera; Zurich Opera; Berlin Philharmonic Orchestra; Philharmonia Orchestra, London; Orchestre Philharmonique de Radio France; Vienna Philharmonie; Vienna Symphony; NDR Hamburg; Montreal Symphony Orchestra; Chamber Orchestra of Europe, New York Philharmonic, Philadelphia Orchestra, Cleveland Symphony Orchestra, Chicago Symphony Orchestra, Gustav Mahler Youth Orchestra; Gen. Music Dir, Oper Graz 2001–04; Prin. Guest Conductor, Staatsoper Unter den Linden, Berlin 2006–; Music Dir, Opéra National de Paris 2009–. *Current Management:* c/o Peter Wiggins, IMG Artists, 31 rue du Temple, 75004 Paris, France. *Telephone:* 1-44-31-00-10. *Fax:* 1-44-31-44-01. *E-mail:* pwiggins@imgartists.com. *Website:* www.imgartists.com. *Address:* c/o Opéra National de Paris, Palais Garnier, 8 rue Scribe, 75009 Paris, France (office); Bamberger Strasse 44, 10779 Berlin, Germany (home). *E-mail:* info@philippe-jordan.com (office). *Website:* www.operadeparis.fr (office); www.philippe-jordan.com.

JORGENSEN, Jerilyn; American violinist; b. 1960, New York. *Education:* Juilliard School with Joseph Fuchs. *Career:* soloist with several orchestras in the Brahms and Tchaikovsky Concertos; further study with members of the Juilliard Quartet and co-founder of the Da Vinci Quartet 1980–, under the sponsorship of the Fine Arts Quartet; many concerts in the USA and elsewhere, with the repertoire including works by Mozart, Beethoven, Brahms, Dvořák, Shostakovich and Bartók; Artist-in-Residence, Univ. of Colorado. *Honours:* awards and grants from the NEA, the Western States Arts Foundation and the Colorado Council for the Humanities (with the Da Vinci Quartet).

JOSEFOWICZ, Leila, BMus; Canadian violinist; b. 20 Oct. 1977. *Education:* Curtis Inst. of Music. *Career:* engagements with the Chicago Symphony Orchestra (Tchaikovsky Concerto), Philadelphia Orchestra under Sawallisch, Los Angeles Philharmonic and London Philharmonic with Franz Welser-Möst; Carnegie Hall debut with the Acad. of St Martin in the Fields under Neville Marriner 1994; returned to New York, with the Boston Symphony and Seiji Ozawa 1996; season 1996–97 with the Bamberg Symphony, the Rotterdam Philharmonic under Gergiev, the Danish Radio Symphony Orchestra, Monte Carlo Orchestra, Dallas Symphony Orchestra; tour of USA with Neville Marriner and Mendelssohn's Concerto at the London Proms 1997; season 1997–98 with Sydney Symphony Orchestra, Swedish RSO, tour of Germany with Neville Marriner and ASMF, Orchestre Nat. de France/Dutoit, Budapest Festival Orchestra, Finnish RSO; season 2003–04 soloist at Last Night of the Proms, London 2003; concerts with Hessischer Rundfunk, 2003, with the Oslo Philharmonic for Norwegian premiere of Knussen Violin Concerto 2004; premieres with Steven Mackey, Colin Matthews; collaborations with John Adams, Oliver Knussen. *Recordings include:* Tchaikovsky and

Sibelius Concertos with the Academy of St Martin in the Fields, Bartók's Solo Sonata and pieces by Pagnanini, Ysaÿe, Kriesler and Ernst, Bohemian Rhapsodies with Marriner/ASMF, Shostakovich's Violin Concerto No. 1 2006, Knussen, Ades, Adams, Matthews, Mackey concerti. *Honours:* MacArthur Fellowship 2008. *Current Management:* Harrison Parrott, 5–6 Albion Court, London, W6 0QT, England. *Telephone:* (20) 7229-9166. *Fax:* (20) 7221-5042. *E-mail:* info@harrisonparrott.co.uk. *Website:* www.harrisonparrott.com.

JOSELSON, Rachel; singer (mezzo-soprano); b. 16 Sept. 1955, Englewood, NJ, USA. *Education:* Florida State and Indiana Univs, studied with Mario del Monaco at Treviso. *Career:* sang at Darmstadt Opera 1982–84, Hamburg from 1984; roles have included Mozart's Idamante, Cherubino and Dorabella, Gluck's Orpheus, and Siebel in Faust; soprano roles include Mimi, Micaela, Eva in Die Meistersinger, Elisabeth de Valois and Gounod's Mireille; Debussy's Mélisande at Essen 1990; guest appearances at Berlin, Brussels, Barcelona and Atlanta; frequent concert appearances.

JOSEPH, David Robin, BMus; Australian composer; b. 27 Jan. 1954, Melbourne, Vic. *Education:* Univ. of Melbourne. *Career:* Adelaide Chamber Orchestra 1986–87; Tutor, Univ. of Melbourne 1993–95; commissions from Kammermusiker Zürich, Adelaide CO, Queensland Ballet and others. *Compositions include:* Images for orchestra 1983, The Dream for orchestra 1986, Clarinet Concerto 1987, Horn Concerto 1988, two String Trios 1988, 1990, Symphony 1989, The Haunting for orchestra 1990, Chamber Concerto for strings 1992, Dialogues for violin and strings 1992, Pelléas and Mélisande (ballet) 1994, The Memory for orchestra 1994, From Endymion for two sopranos, alto, tenor, baritone and bass 1995. *Honours:* Alex Burnard Scholarship 1980, AC Int. and AC Composers Fellowships 1982, 1992.

JOSEPHSON, Kim Alan; American singer (baritone); b. 1954, Akron, OH. *Career:* debut in Strauss's Salome at Houston 1977; Spoleto Festival, USA 1991, in Menotti's Maria Golovin and Sarasota Festival 1992, as Simon Boccanegra (both versions); Vancouver Opera as Rigoletto; Metropolitan Opera, New York from 1991, as Sonora in La Fanciulla del West, Enrico in Lucia di Lammermoor, Germont in Traviata, Sharpless in Madama Butterfly, Silvio in Pagliacci, Count in Capriccio, the title role in Rigoletto and Marcello in La Bohème; Vienna Staatsoper debut 1994, as Marcello in La Bohème followed by roles as Count di Luna in Il Trovatore, Germont in Traviata, Enrico in Lucia and Belcore in L'Elisir d'amore; Chicago debut as Marcello in La Bohème and sang Eddie Carbone in the world premiere of A View from the Bridge by Bolcom 1999; many concert performances. *Honours:* Richard Tucker Foundation grant, William Sullivan/George London Award, Puccini Foundation Award, Baltimore Opera Competition.

JOSHUA, Rosemary; British singer (soprano); b. 16 Oct. 1964, Cardiff, Wales. *Education:* Royal College of Music, London, masterclasses with Thomas Allen, Graziella Sciutti and Claudio Desderi. *Career:* debut at the Aix-en-Provence festival as Angelica in Orlando; engagements with Opera Northern Ireland as Pamina, and at the 1992 Buxton Festival as Blondchen in Die Entführung; ENO as Adele in Die Fledermaus, Yum-Yum in The Mikado, Princess Ida, Norina, Sophie in Der Rosenkavalier and Susanna; Covent Garden Festival as Pamina 1993; Royal Opera debut as Pousette in Manon 1994; Angelica in Orlando at Aix-en-Provence Festival, Poppea in Agrippina and Susanna, Cologne Opera 1994; sang Sophie with ENO 1997; season 1999 as Handel's Semele for ENO and in Fauré's Requiem at the London Proms; sang Poppea in Agrippina at Brussels, Sophie at the Deutsche Oper, Berlin; title role of La Calisto at the Deutsche Staatsoper, Berlin, and in Brussels; Juliette in Romeo and Juliette and Ginevra in Ariodante in San Diego; title role in The Cunning Little Vixen at the Flanders Opera and at the Theatre des Champs Elysées in Le nozze di Figaro, the Glyndebourne Festival as Cleopatra in Giulio Cesare and to the Royal Opera House as Oscar in Un ballo in Maschera, Anne Trulove at Glyndebourne and Handel's Cleopatra for Florida Opera 2000; Janáček's Vixen for Netherlands Opera 2001 and at La Scala; Mahler's Symphony of a Thousand at the London Proms 2002; season 2002–03 in Die Fledermaus at the Met and in Handel's Saul and Der Rosenkavalier at Munich; concert appearances include Bach's B Minor Mass with the London Philharmonic Orchestra under Mark Elder at the Royal Festival Hall, Beethoven's Symphony No. 9 with Sir Simon Rattle and the Orchestra of the Age of Enlightenment, Jephtha with René Jacobs and the Orchestra of the Age of Enlightenment in London, Brussels and New York, Mahler's Symphony No. 8 with Sir Simon Rattle and the Nat. Youth Orchestra of Great Britain at the BBC Proms, Handel's Messiah with Daniel Harding and the Deutsche Kammerphilharmonie Bremen, Bach Cantatas with Nikolaus Harnoncourt and the Concentus Musicus Wien and Bach's B Minor Mass with Sir Roger Norrington and the Orchestra of the Age of Enlightenment, Cleopatra in Guilio Cesare at Théatre des Champs Elysées and Netherlands Opera, Janacek's Cunning Little Vixen at Opernhaus Zürich, Acis and Galatea with the Gabriel Consort, Semele with the Early Opera Company, Handel's Orlando at the Bayerische Staatsoper and the Royal Opera House, Rossini's Tancredi with Orchestre des Champs Elysées and René Jacobs. *Recordings:* Orlando with Les Arts Florissants and William Christie, Venus and Adonis and Dido and Aeneas with René Jacobs, Sophie in Der Rosenkavalier, The Sandman in Hansel und Gretel. *Honours:* Royal Philharmonic Award in debut category. *Address:* c/o Academy of Ancient Music, 32 Newnham Road, Cambridge, CB3 9EY, England (office). *Telephone:* (1223) 301509 (office). *Fax:* (1223) 323202 (office). *E-mail:* info@aam.co.uk (office). *Website:* www.aam.co.uk (office).

JOSIPOVIĆ, Ivo, MA, PhD; Croatian composer, lawyer, academic, politician and fmr head of state; b. 28 Aug. 1957, Zagreb; m. Tatjana Klepac; one d. *Education:* Univ. of Zagreb, Music Acad., Zagreb. *Career:* co-f. Hrvatski pravni centar (Croatian Law Centre) 1994–; musical debut with two children's songs 1978; compositions performed in nearly all European countries, USA, Canada and Japan (European Broadcasting Union concert transmitted over 30 stations world-wide); recordings for radio and TV stations; performances at European festivals; Dir of Music, Zagreb Biennale 1981–; Docent, Music Acad., Univ. of Zagreb 1992–; Prof. for Criminal Procedure Law, Univ. of Zagreb; has represented Croatia at Int. Court of Justice (ICJ) and Int. Criminal Tribunal for fmr Yugoslavia (ICTY); mem. Savez Komunista Hrvatske (SKH—League of Communists of Croatia) 1980 (later renamed Socijaldemokratska Partija Hrvatske (SDP—Social Democratic Party of Croatia); mem. Sabor (Parl.) 2003–10; SDP presidential cand. 2009; Pres. of Croatia 2010–15. *Compositions include:* Variations for piano, Play of the Golden Pearls for piano, Enypion for harp solo, Quartetto rusticano for string quartet, Per fiati for wind quintet, Passacaglia for string orchestra, Samba da camera for 13 strings, Diptych for large orchestra, Epicurus' Garden for symphony orchestra, Man and Death for soloists, choir and orchestra, Pro musica for accordion orchestra, The Most Beautiful Flower for voice and instrumental ensemble, Drmeš for Penderecki for folk orchestra, Thousands of Lotuses for choir and instrumental ensemble, Jubilus for piano solo, Elegaic Song for violin and piano, Dreams for voice and string orchestra. *Address:* c/o Office of the President, 10000 Pantovčak 241, Zagreb, Croatia.

JOUBERT, John Pierre Herman, FRAM, BMus; British composer and academic; b. 20 March 1927, Cape Town, South Africa; m. Florence Mary Litherland 1951; one s. one d. *Education:* Diocesan Coll., Cape Town, Royal Acad. of Music, London. *Career:* Lecturer in Music, Univ. of Hull, England 1950–62; Lecturer (later Reader) in Music, Univ. of Birmingham 1962–86, currently Sr Research Fellow. *Compositions:* four String Quartets 1950, 1977, 1987, 1988, Concertos for violin 1954, piano 1957, bassoon 1973, two Symphonies 1955, 1969, three Sonatas for piano 1957, 1972, Pro Pace Motets for unaccompanied choir 1959, String Trio 1960, Octet 1961, Silas Marner (opera) 1961, Under Western Eyes (opera) 1969, six Poems of Emily Brontë for soprano and piano 1969, Déploration for orchestra 1978, The Turning Wheel for soprano and piano 1979, Herefordshire Canticles for choir and orchestra 1979, Gong-Tormented Sea for choir and orchestra 1981, Temps Perdu for string orchestra 1984, Rorate Coeli for unaccompanied choir 1985, Piano Trio 1987, Jane Eyre (opera) 1998, Wings of Faith (oratorio) 2000, Concerto for oboe and string orchestra 2006, An English Requiem 2010, Concerto for cello and chamber orchestra 2012, That Time of Year (song cycle to words by Shakespeare) for baritone and piano 2013. *Honours:* Hon. DMus (Durham) 1991, (Birmingham) 2007, Fellowship Birmingham Conservatoire 2014; Royal Philharmonic Soc. Prize 1949. *E-mail:* johnjoubert27@aol.com (home). *Website:* www.johnjoubert.org.uk.

JUDD, James; British conductor; *Music Director Emeritus, New Zealand Symphony Orchestra;* b. 30 Oct. 1949, Hertford, England. *Education:* Trinity Coll. of Music, London. *Career:* Asst Conductor to Lorin Maazel, Cleveland Orchestra 1973–75; Assoc. Conductor, European Community Youth Orchestra 1978–90, Hon. Artistic Dir 1990–; founder and Dir, Chamber Orchestra of Europe; Music Dir, Florida Philharmonic Orchestra 1987–2001; Artistic Dir, European Communities Youth Orchestra 1990; Artistic Dir, Greater Miami Opera 1993–96; Music Dir, New Zealand Symphony Orchestra 1999–2007, Music Dir Emer. 2007–; performances with New Zealand Symphony include Summer Sydney Olympic Arts Festival 2000, the New Zealand International Arts Festivals, the Osaka Festival of International Orchestras, Millennium Concert with Kiri Te Kanawa; guest conductor with the Vienna Symphony, Prague Symphony, Berlin Philharmonic, Orchestre Nat. de France, Zürich Tonhalle, Orchestre de la Suisse Romande, Leipzig Gewandhaus Orchestra, ENO, Hallé Orchestra, English Chamber Orchestra, London Symphony Orchestra, Royal Philharmonic, London Philharmonic, Royal Scottish Nat. Orchestra, Cincinnati Symphony, Indianapolis Symphony; Orchestra of the Mozarteum, Salzburg, NHK Symphony, Tokyo, CBC Vancouver Symphony Orchestra, Pittsburgh Symphony, Israel Philharmonic, at Glyndebourne Festival, Salzburg Festival. *Recordings:* with Chamber Orchestra of Europe, English Chamber Orchestra, Philharmonia Orchestra. *Current Management:* c/o Ron Merlino, Musicvine, 2576 Broadway, Suite 239, New York, NY 10025, USA. *Telephone:* (646) 825-9585. *E-mail:* musicvine@gmail.com (office). *Website:* www.jamesjudd.net.

JUDD, Wilfred; British opera director and opera translator; b. 1952, Hertford, Hertfordshire, England. *Education:* Oxford and London Opera Centre. *Career:* began as freelance director 1979; has been prod. with Royal Opera 1984–, for which has staged Die Zauberflöte, Tosca, and La Fanciulla del West; notable production Finnissy's Thérèse Raquin for The Garden Venture; Artistic Dir, Royal Opera House Garden Venture 1988–93; wrote and dir, The Inner Ear, a concert drama premiered by Florida Philharmonic Orchestra 2002; Dir of Productions, Opera 80 1988–91. *Address:* Apt A007, The Jam Factory, 27 Green Walk, London SE1 4TT, England (home). *Telephone:* (20) 8894-2277 (home). *Fax:* (20) 8894-7952 (home).

JUDGE, Ian, GSMD; British theatre and opera director; b. 21 July 1946, Southport, Merseyside, England; s. of John Judge and Marjorie Judge; partner Efthymios Peppas. *Education:* Guildhall School of Music and Drama, London. *Career:* joined the RSC 1975, productions there include: The Wizard of Oz, The Comedy of Errors, Love's Labour's Lost, The Relapse, Twelfth

Night, A Christmas Carol, Troilus and Cressida and The Merry Wives of Windsor; theatre productions include The Rivals and King Lear, Old Vic, Henry VIII, Chichester; opera productions include Faust, The Merry Widow, Cavalleria Rusticana, Pagliacci, Don Quixote, La Belle Vivette, Mephistopheles and Sir John in Love for ENO, Macbeth, Tosca, Acis and Galatea, Boris Godunov, Attila for Opera North, The Flying Dutchman and Simon Boccanegra for Covent Garden; has staged operas regularly in Europe, Australia and USA, Macbeth in Cologne, Faust in Sydney, Les Contes d'Hoffmann in Houston, Tosca, Madama Butterfly, Roméo et Juliette, Le Nozze di Figaro, Don Carlo, Tannhäuser and Die Gezeichneten in Los Angeles, Simon Boccanegra in Washington, DC; directed the original 1857 version of Verdi's Simon Boccanegra at Covent Garden 1997; staged Falstaff for the BBC Proms 1998, Mephistopheles by Boito at Teatro Colon, Buenos Aires 1999, Falstaff for Théâtre du Châtelet, Paris 2001, La Bohème and Der Fliegende Holländer for Mariinsky Opera, St Petersburg 2001, 2008, Ernani for Reisoper, Netherlands 2002; credits include numerous plays and musicals, Oh Kay!, Chichester, Merrily We Roll Along, London, A Little Night Music, Piccadilly Theatre, Show Boat, London Palladium, The Roar of the Greasepaint – The Smell of the Crowd and West Side Story in Australia. *Honours:* Gold Medal (Directing), three Green Room Awards (Australia). *Address:* 16 Brookfield Road, Bedford Park, London, W4 1DQ, England. *Telephone:* (20) 8995-5187. *E-mail:* ijudge1@mac.com. *Website:* www.ianjudge.com.

JUDSON, Colin; British singer (tenor); b. 20 Sept. 1968, England. *Education:* Guildhall School of Music. *Career:* made debut in The Magic Flute with ENO; regular appearances with De Vlaamse Opera, Scottish Opera, Covent Garden, Glyndebourne Festival Opera, Opera Bordeaux, Théâtre du Capitole de Toulouse, Opera du Rhin, Strasbourg, Opéra de Limoges, Opera North, Opéra de Nantes, Netherlands Opera; roles have included Remendado in Carmen, L'Indredibile in Andrea Chenier, Isaac in La Gazza Ladra, Rossini's Almaviva, Purcell's Aeneas, Monostatos in Die Zauberflöte, Coryphée in Le Comte Ory, Mime in Das Rheingold, Dr Caius in Falstaff, Novice in Billy Budd, Jacquino in Fidelio, Tichon in Katja Kabanova, Janek in The Macropoulos Case, Truffaldino in L'amour de Trois Oranges, Third Jew in Salome, Pang in Turandot, Trout in A Midsummer Night's Dream, Novice and Squeak in Billy Budd; concerts include Schumann's Dichterliebe, Haydn's Nelson Mass, Bach's Christmas Oratorio, The Dream of Gerontius, Verdi's Requiem, Puccini's Messa di Gloria and Stravinsky's Pulcinella. *Current Management:* Athole Still Opera Ltd, Forresters Hall, 25–27 Westow Street, London, SE19 3RY, England. *Telephone:* (20) 8771-5271. *Fax:* (20) 8771-8172. *E-mail:* enquiries@atholestill.co.uk. *Website:* www.atholestill.com; www.colinjudson.co.uk.

JUNG, Doris; American singer (dramatic soprano) and teacher; b. 5 Jan. 1924, Centralia, Ill.; d. of John Crittenden and May Crittenden (née Middleton); m. Felix Popper 1951; one s. *Education:* Univ. of Illinois, Mannes Coll. of Music, Vienna Acad. of Performing Arts, Austria and under Julius Cohen, Emma Zador, Luise Helletsgruber and Winifred Cecil. *Career:* professional debut as Vitellia in Clemenza di Tito, Zurich Opera, Switzerland 1955; appearances with Hamburg State Opera and Munich State Opera, Germany, Vienna State Opera, Copenhagen Royal Opera, Stockholm Royal Opera, New York City Opera and Metropolitan Opera, New York, opera cos in Marseille and Strasbourg, France, Naples and Catania, Italy and with Syracuse Symphony 1981; teacher, New York 1970–. *Publication:* trans.: La Nilsson (autobiog. of Birgit Nilsson) 2007. *Address:* 40 West 84th Street, New York, NY 10024, USA (home). *Telephone:* (212) 873-3147 (home). *E-mail:* dorispopper@gmail.com (home).

JUNG, Manfred; German singer (tenor); b. 9 July 1940, Oberhausen. *Education:* studied in Essen with Hilde Wesselmann. *Career:* Bayreuth Youth Festival 1967, as Arindal in Die Feen by Wagner; sang in the Bayreuth Festival Chorus 1970–73; sang in Dortmund and Kaiserslautern from 1971; mem., Deutsche Oper am Rhein Düsseldorf from 1977; Bayreuth Festival from 1977, as Tristan, Parsifal and Siegfried (production of Der Ring des Nibelungen 1983, by John Bury and Peter Hall); sang in Wagner operas at the Salzburg Easter Festival, under Karajan (Tristan and Parsifal 1980); Metropolitan Opera debut 1981; guest appearances in Zürich, Chicago, Toronto, Vienna; Hamburg, Munich, Barcelona, Cologne, Frankfurt, Lisbon, Rome and Montréal; other roles include Walther, Florestan, Loge and Siegmund; sang Herod in Salome at Munich 1990, Aegisthus in Elektra at the Spoleto Festival; season 1991–92 as Herod at Barcelona and Valzacchi in Rosenkavalier at Catania; season 1997–98 as Mime in The Ring, at Kassel. *Recordings include:* Siegfried in The Ring from Bayreuth.

JUNG, Seung-Gi, MMus; South Korean singer (baritone); *Soloist, Badisches Staatstheater Karlsruhe*; b. 9 Sept. 1979. *Education:* Chung-Ang Univ., Hochschule für Musik, Karlsruhe. *Career:* operatic debut in Korea singing Figaro in Le nozze di Figaro and Germont in La Traviata; season 2006–07 engaged as Le chat in Ravel's L'Enfant et les Sortilèges as well as Golaud in Pelléas et Mélisande in Karlsruhe; other engagements include Renato in Un Ballo in Maschero at the Theatre in Bern, Switzerland, Yeletsky in Konzerthaus, Karlsruhe and Tonio in I Pagliacci at Menuhin Festival, Gstaad with Noëmi Nadelmann and Giuseppe Giacomini; member of ensemble at Augsburg Theatre, Germany 2009–, roles include Ping in Turandot, Enrico in Lucia di Lammermoor and Marchese di Posa in Don Carlos; sang Marcello in La Bohème in Théâtre du Capitole, Toulouse and Teatro La Fenice, Venice 2011; soloist, Badisches Staatstheater, Karlsruhe 2011–; collaborations with La Fenice include Germont in La Traviata 2011 and title role in Rigoletto 2012; season 2012 also included Marcello, Wolfram in Tannhäuser and title role in Rigoletto (all Karlsruhe); sang Donner in Das Rheingold 2013. *Honours:* prizewinner at several int. competitions, including First Prize, Int. Singing Competition, Toulouse 2008, First Prize, Int. Singing Competition Ernst Haefliger, Bern 2008, Second Prize, Int. Singing Competition Luciano Pavarotti, Modena 2008, First Prize, Int. Queen Sonja Competition, Oslo 2009. *Current Management:* c/o Opera-Connection Alste & Mödersheim, PO Box 121233, 10606 Berlin, Germany. *Telephone:* (30) 31996688. *Fax:* (30) 31809739. *E-mail:* info@opera-connection.com. *Website:* www.opera-connection.com. *E-mail:* opernsaenger@gmail.com (office).

JUNGHÄNEL, Konrad; German lutenist and music director; *Professor, Hochschule für Musik, Cologne*; b. 1953; two s. two d. *Career:* appearances as soloist and member of early music ensembles throughout Europe, in the USA, Japan, South America and Africa; collaborations with René Jacobs as soloist and continuo player in opera performances from the Baroque era and concerts with La Petite Bande, Musica Antiqua Köln, Les Arts Florissants and Tafelmusik; founded Cantus Cölln 1987, with festival performances at Berne, Stuttgart, Utrecht, Innsbruck and Breslau; conducted Francesco Cavalli's La Calisto in Cologne and Domenico Mazocchi's La Catena d'Adone in Innsbruck and Antwerp and a scenic production of Monteverdi's Madgrigals throughout Europe; directed the production of Heinrich Schütz's Was liegt die Stadt so wüste at the Theater Basel, 2000 and at the Sächsische Staaatsoper Dresden, 2004–06, Henry Purcell's Evening Hymn, Staatsoper Hannover, 2004 and Rameau's Les Paladins, Basel, 2004; conducted staged production of Bach cantatas at the Hamburg Opera, 2000; Directed Handel's Israel in Egypt at Basle, 2002; Handel's Semele and Monteverdi's L'Incoronazione di poppea, 2003; repertory centres on Italian and German Renaissance and Baroque music. *Recordings include:* lute solos by Silvius Leopold Weiss, Schein's Diletti Pastorali, Rosenmuller's Vespro della beata Vergine, J. S. Bach: Lute Works, J. S. Bach: Motets, H Schütz: Psalmen Davids, Monteverdi: Vespro della beata Vergine. *Honours:* German Critics' Prize, for Weiss lute solos; Numerous Diapason d'Or Awards, 1991–98; Grand Prix du Disque, Académie Charles Cros, 1993; Editors Choice, Gramophone, 1999; Diapason d'Or and Lux du Monde de la Musique for CD Artus tragicus, 2000; Gramophone Award, Cecilia Award, Preis der deutschen Schallplattenkritik (CD, Monteverdi: Selva morale e spirituale), 2002, Preis der deutschen Schallplattenkritik, Echo Klassik (CD, Altbachisches Archiv) 2004. *Address:* Cantus Cölln, Mittelstrasse 6a, 50321 Brühl, Germany (office). *Telephone:* (2232) 34433 (office); (2232) 370754 (home). *Fax:* (2232) 35113 (office). *E-mail:* cautus_coellu@t-online.de (office); k.junghaenel@web.de (home). *Website:* www.cantuscoelln.com (office).

JUON, Julia; Swiss singer (mezzo-soprano); b. 28 Nov. 1943, St Gallen. *Education:* Zürich Conservatory. *Career:* sang in opera at St Gallen, 1975–80, Karlsruhe, 1980–83, and Kassel from 1984, notably as Ortrud and as Tina in the European premiere of The Aspern Papers by Dominick Argento; guest appearances as Fricks at Amsterdam and at the Hamburg Staatsoper as the Nurse in Die Frau ohne Schatten, 1989; other roles include Waltraute, Carmen, Agrippina, Donizetti's Leonora, Verdi's Ulrica, Eboli, Amneris and Azucena, Wagner's Kundry, Venus and Brangaene; modern repertoire includes Bartók's Judith, the Priestess in Schoeck's Penthesilea and Catherine in Jeanne d'Arc au Bûcher by Honegger; sang Kabanicha in Katya Kabanova at Basel in 1991 and Kundry at Essen in 1992; Countess Geschwitz in Lulu at Opéra Bastille, Paris, 1998; sang Waltraute and Azucena for Bonn Opera, 2000; Brangaene at Hamburg and Antwerp, 2000–01; concert engagements in Switzerland and Germany, at the Bregenz Festival and in Vienna. *Address:* Staatstheater, Friedrichplatz 15, 34117 Kassel, Germany.

JUROWSKI, Dmitri; Russian conductor and fmr cellist; *Music Director, Vlaamse Opera*; b. 1979, Moscow; s. of Mikhail Jurowski. *Education:* Tchaikovsky Conservatory, Moscow, Musikschule C. Ph.E., Berlin, Rostock Acad. of Music and Drama, Hanns Eisler Acad. of Music, Berlin. *Career:* Asst Conductor for Berlin Radio Orchestra recording of Prokofiev's Boris Godunov 2003; Asst Conductor for Parsifal, Teatro Carlo Felice, Genoa, Italy 2004; conductor for Palau de les Arts Reina Sofia, Valencia, Spain, Filarmonica Toscanini, Parma, Italy, Al Bustan Festival, Beirut, Lebanon 2007–08 season; debuted at Wexford Opera Festival, Ireland 2008; debuted with Dresden Philharmonic, Liège Opera of Belgium, Orquestra Sinfónica Portuguesa, Lisbon, New Israeli Opera, Mihailovsky Theatre, St Petersburg 2008; debuted at Vlaamse Opera, Antwerp, Monte Carlo Opera, Deutsche Oper Berlin, Teatro Municipal de Santiago 2009; Music Dir, Vlaamse Opera 2011–; other appearances include: Teatro Nazionale di Roma, Teatro Massimo di Palermo, Residence Orchestra of the Hague, Orchestra Sinfonica del Lazio, Orchestra of Teatro Filarmonico di Verona, Shanghai Philharmonic Orchestra. *Current Management:* c/o Ronald Wilford, Columbia Artists Management, 1790 Broadway, New York, NY 10019-1412, USA; c/o Mafara Artist Promotions, Kirchengasse 191 14, 1070 Vienna, Austria. *Telephone:* (212) 841-9501; (1) 4782649. *E-mail:* office@mafara.com. *Website:* www.cami.com; www.mafara.com. *Address:* Vlaamse Opera, Van Ertbrornstraat 8, 2018 Antwerp, Belgium (office). *Telephone:* (3) 202-10-11 (office). *Fax:* (3) 231-07-85 (office). *E-mail:* info@vlaamseopera.be (office). *Website:* www.vlaamseopera.be (office); www.dmitri-jurowski.com.

JUROWSKI, Vladimir; Russian conductor; *Principal Conductor, London Philharmonic Orchestra*; b. 4 April 1972, Moscow. *Education:* Music Acad., Berlin and Dresden, Germany. *Career:* Chief Conductor, Sibelius Orchestra, Berlin 1993–96; Founder and Conductor, United Berlin ensemble, performing modern music; int. debut conducting May Night by Rimsky-Korsakov, Wexford Festival 1995; fmr Prin. Guest Conductor, Orchestra Sinfonica Verdi, Milan; First Kapellmeister, Komische Oper Berlin 1997–2001; Prin. Guest Conductor, Teatro Comunale, Bologna 2000–03; Music Dir, Glyndebourne Festival Opera 2001–07, Glyndebourne Opera 2001–13; Prin. Guest Conductor, London Philharmonic Orchestra 2003–06, Prin. Conductor 2007–; Prin. Guest Conductor, Russian Nat. Orchestra 2006–09; Prin. Artist, Orchestra of the Age of Enlightenment; Artistic Dir, Russian State Academic Symphony Orchestra 2011–; has conducted in venues world-wide, including Metropolitan Opera (New York), Opera Bastille (Paris), Komische Oper (Berlin), Teatro Comunale (Bologna), Teatro Real (Madrid), Royal Opera House (London), and with Chicago Symphony, Philadelphia, Berlin Philharmonic, Mahler Chamber Orchestras, Chamber Orchestra of Europe, Tonhalle-orchester Zurich, Gewandhausorchester Leipzig and Staatskapelle Dresden. *Recordings include:* Stravinsky's The Rake's Progress (with London Philharmonic Orchestra and Glyndebourne Chorus), Complete Symphonies of Brahms (with London Philharmonic Orchestra); DVD releases: La Cerentola, Gianni Schicchi, Die Fledermaus, Don Giovanni (Glyndebourne Festival Opera), Hansel und Gretel (Metropolitan Opera of New York). *Honours:* Royal Philharmonic Soc. Conductor Award 2007. *Current Management:* c/o IMG Artists, The Light Box, 111 Power Road, London, W4 5PY, England. *Telephone:* (20) 7957-5800. *Fax:* (20) 7957-5801. *E-mail:* nmathias@imgartists.com. *Website:* www.imgartists.com. *Address:* London Philharmonic Orchestra, 89 Albert Embankment, London, SE1 7TP, England (office). *Website:* www.lpo.co.uk (office); www.vladimirjurowski .com.

K

KAAL, Anu; Estonian singer and singing teacher; b. 4 Nov. 1940, Tallinn; m. Hillar-Kalev Kaal 1961; one d. *Education:* Music Coll. and Music Conservatory, Tallinn and Scuola di Canto alla Scala, Milan, Italy. *Career:* opera singer, Tallinn Opera House 1963–96; Prof., Tallinn Music Acad. from 1984; Assoc. Prof., Voice Dept, Estonian Acad. of Music and Theatre –2007. *Operas include:* The Magic Flute, Porgy and Bess, Rigoletto, The Mighty Magician, The Warriors, Der Rosenkavalier, Don Carlos, The Telephone, Die Fledermaus, La Traviata, Don Giovanni, Cyrano de Bergerac, La Bohème, La Serva Padrona, The Bartered Bride, Un Ballo in Maschera, Boris Godunov, Mefistofele, Manon. *Honours:* Folk Artist of Estonia 1977, Folk Artist of USSR 1981. *Address:* c/o Estonian Academy of Music and Theatre, Rävala pst 16, Tallinn 10143, Estonia.

KAAPPOLA, Anna Kristiina, MMus; Finnish singer (soprano); b. 17 Feb. 1965, Oulu. *Education:* Sibelius Acad., Helsinki. *Career:* ensemble mem. Finnish Nat. Opera; has performed with opera cos throughout Europe, including Paris, Toulouse, Aix-en-Provence, Salzburg, Italy (La Scala) and London (Covent Garden); Metropolitan opera debut as Queen of the Night (her signature role until 2009) in Die Zauberflöte 2007; debut at Weill Hall/Carnegie Hall, New Year 2009; has sung under conductors Riccardo Muti (La Scala and Salzburg Festival), Jos van Immerseel (Anima enterna), Jean Christophe Spinosi (Ensemble Matheus), Esa-Pekka Salonen (Helsinki Festival), Hans-Christoph Rademann (Rias Kammerchor), René Jacobs (Akademie für Alte Musik); regular appearances at Savonlinna Opera Festival 1992–; opera repertoire includes Micaëla in Carmen, Miss Wordsworth in Albert Herring, Juliette in Roméo et Juliette, Marguerite in Faust, Galatea in Acis and Galatea, Liù in Turandot, Alice Ford in Falstaff, Violetta in La Traviata, Woglinde in Der Ring. *Recordings include:* Nielson Symphony Expansiva 2000, Rautavaara The House of the Sun 2004, Beethoven Symphony No. 9 2010, Mozart Die Zauberflöte (BBC Music Magazine Award, Opera Category 2011) 2010. *Current Management:* c/o Allegro Artist Management, Tapiolan Keskustorni, Tapiontori 1, 02100 Espoo, Finland. *Telephone:* (9) 4123012. *E-mail:* allegro@allegroartist.com. *Website:* www.allegroartist.com; www.kaappola.eu.

KAASCH, Donald; singer (tenor); b. 19 Dec. 1968, Denver, CO, USA. *Education:* Colorado and Northwestern Univs. *Career:* sang at the Chicago Lyric Opera 1985–88; European engagements at Florence 1989 in Idomeneo and at Geneva; Metropolitan Opera 1989 in the character roles in Les Contes d'Hoffmann and returned for Jacquino in Fidelio and Mozart's Titus; Opéra Bastille 1991 as Idamante in Idomeneo, Salzburg 1992 as Argirio in Rossini's Tancredi; other roles include Mozart's Tamino, Ferrando and Don Ottavio, Count Almaviva, the Prince in Lulu, Rinuccio and Argento's The Voyage of Edgar Allan Poe; frequent concert performances, including Leukippos in Strauss's Daphne at Antwerp 1998; sang the Priest in Stravinsky's Persephone at the Royal Festival Hall, London 1997; Royal Opera debut 1998, in The Golden Cockerel; sang Gluck's Admète at Amsterdam 1999; season 2000–01 as Britten's Male Chorus at Lausanne and Mozart's Mitridate in Sydney; season 2002–03 in Thais at Chicago and in Der fliegende Holländer at Los Angeles.

KABAIVANSKA, Raina; Bulgarian singer (soprano); b. 15 Dec. 1934, Burgas; d. of Joachin and Staika Kabaivanska; m. Franco Guandalini 1972; one d. *Education:* pvt. singing tuition and Sofia Conservatory. *Career:* debut in Puccini's Tabarro in Milan 1959; sang with Joan Sutherland and under direction of Maria Callas; has since performed with all major directors including Von Karajan in theatres world-wide; Prof. Chigiana Acad. of Music, Italy; est. Raina Kabaivanska fund, New Bulgarian Univ. 2002. *Films include:* Tosca, I Pagliacci, Falstaff, Il Trovatore, Madame Butterfly. *Records include:* Beatrice di Tenda, Mefistofele, Adirana Lecouvreur, Faust, Manon, Madama Butterfly, Manon Lescaut, Tosca, Don Carlo, Ernani, Falstaff, Otello, Il Trovatore, Rienzi, Francesca di Rimini, Omaggio a Puccini, Raina Kabaivanska in Concerto, Arie da Opere, Raina Kabaivanska canta Puccini, Raina Kabaivanska canta Verdi, Magic Kabaivanska, Raina Kabaivanska Today, Omaggio da Carriera. *Honours:* Order of Stara Planina (Bulgaria) 1994, Order of Italy for outstanding contribution to the arts; Dr hc (New Bulgarian Univ.) 2000; Premio Bellini 1965, Premio Viotti d'Oro 1974, Premio Puccini 1978, Premio Illica 1979, Premio Monteverdi 1980, Academia Medici Award 1990. *Address:* Accademia Musicale Chigiana, Via di Città 89, 53100 Siena, Italy (office). *Telephone:* (0577) 22091 (office). *Fax:* (0577) 288124 (office). *E-mail:* accademia.chigiana@chigiana.it (office). *Website:* www.chigiana.it (office); www.rainakabaivanska.net (home).

KACZANOWSKI, Andrzej, DipMus, MA; Polish double bassist; b. 22 April 1955, Białystok; m. 1974; two s. one d. *Education:* Chopin Acad. of Music, Warsaw. *Career:* debut with Domenico Dragonetti Concerto with Białystok Philharmonic Orchestra 1975; regular appearances as soloist or chamber player with numerous orchestras; Warsaw Chamber Orchestra under J. Kasprzyk 1978–84; Chamber Ensemble of the Nat. Philharmonic under K. Teutsch, including concerts in Salle Pleyel (Paris), Santa Cecilia (Rome), Musikverein (Vienna), Tivoli (Copenhagen), Carnegie Hall (New York), among others; Polish Chamber Orchestra under Jerzy Maksymiuk 1984–85; numerous recordings and concerts; also collaboration with Warsaw Sinfonietta and Collegium Musicum; Co-founder Camerata Vistula Ensemble 1986;

teacher, Josef Elsner First Music School in Warsaw 1991–96; co-producer, opening concert at Boguslawski Concer Hall, Warsaw 1997; S Korean tour 1997; solo recitals, concerts and recordings 1998; first performance of Concerto by Emil Tabakov (with Sofia Philharmonic Orchestra) 1999; performances at festivals, including Glasgow 1986, Berlin 1990, 1992, Warsaw Autumn 1985, 1986, 1988, 1989, Białystok (Poland) 2000–03; organized series of chamber concerts 'Interpretations' and 'Portrait with Music'; gave recitals in Poland and other European countries in cooperation with Polish Cultural Insts 2004; participated in Third World Bass Festival performing recital programme and leading masterclasses 2008; during career, has played with musicians and conductors, including Claudio Abbado, Marek Drewnowski, Ruggiero Gerlin, Jacek Kspszyk, Konstanty Andrzej Kulka, Jerzy Maksymiuk, Janusz Olejniczak, Henryk Szeryng. *Recordings:* Polish Chamber Orchestra, Warsaw, Chamber Philharmonic Orchestra, Bach Keyboard Concerts, Ruggero Gerlin 1980, Lutoslawski, Prokofiev and Gorecki 1990, Schubert's Quintet op 114, Trout, Dvořák op 77 for Polish Radio SA, Fantasia Contrabasso 2004, Fantasia Con tra Basso (album) 2004. *Current Management:* Agencja Filharmonia s.c Izabella Dargiel, Kacper Czechowski-Salzman, ul. Kazimierzowska 71/75 lok. 63, 02-518 Warsaw, Poland. *Telephone:* (22) 6467291. *Fax:* (22) 6464628. *E-mail:* agfilhar@medianet.pl. *Website:* www.agencjafilharmonia.pl. *Address:* Pradzynskistr 20a 109, 05-200 Wotomin, Poland (office). *E-mail:* akaczan@poczta.onet.pl (home).

KADOUCH, David; French pianist; b. Dec. 1985. *Education:* Nice Conservatoire, Conservatoire nat. supérieur de musique et de danse de Paris, Reina Sofia School, Madrid with Dimitri Bashkirov. *Career:* played under Itzhak Perlman at Metropolitan Hall and Carnegie Hall, New York 1999; invited to play at Bolshoi Hall of Tchaikovski Conservatory, Moscow 2000; played at first Sommets Musicaux (Gstaad) 2001 under Artistic Dir Caroline Murat; chosen by Daniel Barenboim to take part in 'Barenboim on Beethoven' DVD at Symphony Centre of Chicago 2005; play at Verbier Festival 2010; solo and chamber music recitals world-wide. *Honours:* Young Talents Competition, Milan 1999, Premier Prix, CNSM, Paris 2003, Best Pianist Prize, Int. Summer Acad. Mozarteum, Salzburg 2005, Third Prize, Int. Beethoven Competition, Bonn 2005, Grand Prix, Verbier Acad. 2009, Young Artist of the Year, Int. Classical Music Awards 2011. *Address:* Escuela Superior de Música Reina Sofía, Plaza de Oriente s/n, 28013 Madrid, Spain. *Telephone:* (915) 230419. *Fax:* (915) 329661. *E-mail:* info@escuelasuperiordemusicareinasofia.es. *Website:* www.escuelasuperiordemusicareinasofia.es.

KAEGI, Dieter; Swiss stage director; b. 1950, Zurich. *Education:* Musicology and German Literature in Zurich and Paris. *Career:* Asst Dir, ENO 1980; Dir of Productions at Aix-en-Provence Festival, 1989; Artistic Dir Opera Ireland; Der Rosenkavalier and Der Freischütz for Seattle Opera; stagings of Tristan und Isolde at Monte Carlo, Idomeneo and Figaro at Copenhagen, Roméo et Juliette in Geneva and Anna Bolena by Donizetti at Metz; Bartók's Bluebeard's Castle at Strasbourg; Fidelio in Liège and Lady Macbeth of Mtsensk for Opera Ireland; season 2001–02 with Der Freischütz at Ulm, Don Carlos in Ireland and Die Entführung in Nancy; Asst at Zurich Opera 1980–82; Asst to Jean-Pierre Ponnelle for opera and opera films in Europe and USA 1982–86; Asst Dir, Deutsche Oper am Rhein 1986–89; Production and Personal Asst to Dir-Gen. of Opéra de Monte-Carlo 1989–90; Production Man., Music Festival in Aix-en-Provence 1990–98; Artistic Dir Opera Ireland, Dublin 1998–2010; mem. Bd Opera Europa 2001–; mem. Chambre des directeurs d'opéra 2002–; mem. jury at various singing competitions in Europe and USA; Founding Dir Lismore Music Festival (Ireland) 2010–; Gen. Man. of theatres in Biel and Solothurn (Switzerland) and their orchestra 2012–. *Honours:* Cavaliere, Order of Merit (Italy) 2010. *Current Management:* c/o APA Artists' Management, Studio 1, 79 Bedford Gardens, London, W8 7EG, England. *Telephone:* (20) 7794-7633. *Fax:* (20) 7431-4344. *E-mail:* alexandra@mercer.uk.com. *Website:* www.apaartistsmanagement.com; www.dieterkaegi.com.

KAHANE, Jeffrey Alan, BMus; American pianist and conductor; *Music Director, Colorado Symphony Orchestra;* b. 12 Sept. 1956, Los Angeles, CA; m. Martha Philips 1979; one s. one d. *Education:* San Francisco Conservatory of Music. *Career:* debut as pianist, San Francisco, California 1973; soloist, New York and Los Angeles Philharmonics, Pittsburgh, San Francisco and Israel Symphonies; appearances with Cleveland Orchestra, New York, Los Angeles, Rotterdam and Israel Philharmonics, Boston, Chicago, Pittsburgh, San Francisco, Atlanta Symphonies; soloist in Bernstein's Age of Anxiety at the 1991 Promenade Concerts, London; Music Dir, Santa Rosa Symphony 1996–2006, Los Angeles Chamber Orchestra 1997–, Green Music Festival, Colorado Symphony Orchestra 2004–; mem. Piano Faculty, New England Conservatory of Music, Boston, Eastman School of Music, Rochester, NY. *Recordings:* Works of Gershwin and Bernstein with Yo-Yo Ma; Paul Schoenfield's Four Parables; Strauss' Burleske with the Cincinnati Symphony; Brandenburg Concerti (on harpsichord) with the Oregon Bach Festival Orchestra; Schubert's complete works for violin and piano with Joseph Swensen; Bach's Sinfonias and Partita No. 4 in D Major; Bernstein's Age of Anxiety. *Honours:* Grand Prize Arthur Rubinstein Int. Piano Competition, Tel-Aviv, Israel 1983, fourth prize Van Cliburn Int. Piano Competition 1981. *Current Management:* IMG Artists, Carnegie Hall Tower, 152 West 57th

Street, 5th Floor, New York, NY 10019, USA. *Telephone:* (212) 994-3539. *Fax:* (212) 995-3550. *E-mail:* eyim@imgartists.com. *Website:* www.imgartists.com.

KAHLER, Lia; singer (mezzo-soprano); b. 1952, USA. *Education:* studied in Los Angeles, New York and Milan, Italy. *Career:* sang at the Holland Festival 1982, Detmold 1983–85, notably as Eboli and Brangaene; sang at Gelsenkirchen 1985–89, as Laura in La Gioconda, Monteverdi's Ottavia, the Witch and Mother in Hansel und Gretel, and in the premiere of Deinen Kopf, Holofernes by Blumenthaler 1989; other roles at Gelsenkirchen and elsewhere in Germany have included Ortrud, Maddalena, Marina in Boris Godunov, Dalila and Baba the Turk in The Rake's Progress; many concert appearances.

KAHMANN, Sieglinde; German singer (soprano); b. 28 Nov. 1937, Dresden; m. Sigurdur Bjornsson. *Education:* studied in Stuttgart. *Career:* debut at Stuttgart Staatsoper 1959, as Aennchen in Der Freischütz; engaged at the Theater am Gärtnerplatz, Munich, and sang at Hamburg, Vienna, Stuttgart, Leipzig, Karlsruhe and Kassel; roles have included Mozart's Pamina, Donna Elvira, Countess and Cherubino, Lortzing's Gretchen and Mair, Martha and Musetta; guest appearances at Lisbon, Strasbourg, Bucharest, Salzburg and Edinburgh, as Micaela, Lisa (Queen of Spades), Marenka (Bartered Bride) and Adele in Fledermaus.

KAIN, Timothy, DipMus; Australian classical guitarist; b. 25 Jan. 1951, Braidwood, NSW. *Education:* Canberra School of Music, Royal Northern College of Music, Manchester, and in Alicante, Spain. *Career:* debut, Purcell Room 1982; played all over the world for 20 years; major tours of the United Kingdom and Australia with John Williams' ensemble Attacca in 1992 and 1996, also Australia in 1996; leader of Guitar Trek, a quartet playing a family of different sized guitars; Head of the Guitar Department at Canberra School of Music, Australian National University 1982–; mem. Australian Music Centre. *Compositions:* has commissioned close to 30 new works for guitar, solo, chamber and concerto from Australian composers. *Recordings include:* The Mantis and The Moon with John Wiliams 1996, Guitar Trek, music for a guitar family, Guitar Trek II, the family continues, Music for Flute and Guitar, Music of the Americas with flautist Virginia Taylor, Classic Williams - Romance of the Guitar 2000. *Publications:* Three Preludes by Richard Vella is the first of a series, published 1998; Black Wattle Caprices, by Ross Edwards, 1999. *Honours:* winner, Int Guitar Competition, Spain 1977, RNCM Bach Prize 1979. *Address:* School of Music, Building 100, The Australian National University, Canberra, ACT 0200, Australia (office). *Telephone:* (2) 6125-5760 (office). *Fax:* (2) 6248-0997 (office). *E-mail:* timothy.kain@anu.edu.au (office). *Website:* www.anu.edu.au/music/study/staff/tkain.php (office).

KAISER, Barbara; German conductor; b. 1 June 1947, Bremen. *Education:* Hochschule für Musik, Freiburg/Breisgau, Hochschule der Künste, Berlin. *Career:* debut as guest conductor, Philharmonisches Staatsorchester, Bremen 1986; founder mem., Musikfrauen Berlin 1978; man. of several projects with contemporary music of women composers; man. of series of concerts with contemporary music at Hochschule der Künste Berlin 1984–96; Neue Musik Berlin in co-operation 1986; Lecturer, Hochschule der Künste, Berlin 1986–96; guest conductor, Philharmonisches Staatsorchester Bremen, Filharmonia Pomorska, Poland and Orchester der Stadt Heidelberg; mem. International Arbeitskreis Frau und Musik, Kulturinstitut Komponistinnen gestern-heute, Heidleberg. *Recordings:* Instrumental und Vocal, Musik von Komponistinnen, 1985; Komponistinnen in Berlin, 1987.

KAJIMA, Fusao, MA; Japanese conductor; *Principal Conductor, National Taiwan Symphony Orchestra;* b. 1963, Tokyo. *Education:* New England Conservatory, Boston, Univ. of Michigan, USA, Mozarteum, Salzburg, Austria. *Career:* moved to USA at age of 16; held academic positions at Northern Illinois Univ., Georgia State Univ.; fmr Music Dir Fox Valley Symphony Orchestra, Aurora, Illinois; fmr Music Dir Georgia State Univ. Symphony Orchestra; Music Dir Bellevue Philharmonic Orchestra 1998–2008, Resident Conductor 2008–10; Music Dir Fort Collins Symphony Orchestra 1999–2001; Prin. Conductor, Nat. Taiwan Symphony Orchestra 2010–; also conducted Papagena Opera Co., Mich.; fmrly Asst Conductor, Greater Lansing Symphony Orchestra, Mich., Freiburger Theater, Staatstheater Darmstadt, Germany, Opera Co. of Mid-Michigan. *Honours:* Winner, Austrian Broadcasting Corpn Young Conductor's Prize Competition 1985, Masterplayers Conducting Competition 1988, Antonio Pedrotti Conducting Competition 1995. *Address:* National Taiwan Symphony Orchestra, No. 738-2, Zhongzheng Road, Wufeng Township, Taichung County 413, Taiwan (office). *Telephone:* (4) 2339-1141 (office). *Fax:* (4) 2339-9072 (office). *E-mail:* chief@ntso.gov.tw (office). *Website:* www.ntso.gov.tw/eng (office).

KALE, Stuart; British singer (tenor); b. 27 Oct. 1944, Neath, Glamorgan, Wales; m. Deborah Kale. *Education:* Guildhall School of Music and Drama, London Opera Centre. *Career:* made debut as the Prince in the first production by a British company of Berg's Lulu with Welsh Nat. Opera 1971; repertoire includes Lepreux in St François d'Assise, Aumonier in Les Dialogues des Carmélites, Reverend Adams in Peter Grimes, Hauptmann in Wozzeck, Dr Caius in Falstaff, Goro in Madama Butterfly, Pirelli in Sweeney Todd, Bob Boles in Peter Grimes, Schoolmaster in The Cunning Little Vixen, Curzio and Don Basilio in The Marriage of Figaro, Barclay de Tolly and Karataev in War and Peace, Shuisky in Boris Godunov, Aegisthe in Elektra, Distiller in May Night, Justice Shallow in Sir John in Love, Nilsky in The Gambler; has sung at La Scala, Milan, Royal Opera House, London, Grand Théâtre de Genève, with ENO, Opera North, Hallé Orchestra, Orchestre Symphonique de Montréal, New Israeli Opera, Garsington Opera, Opera di Roma, Mahler

Chamber Orchestra, Opera de Nantes. *Recordings include:* Idomeneo (title role, video from Drottningholm). *Current Management:* c/o Athole Still Opera Ltd, Foresters Hall, 25–27 Westow Street, London, SE19 3RY, England. *Telephone:* (20) 8771-5271. *Fax:* (20) 8771-8172. *E-mail:* enquiries@atholestill .co.uk. *Website:* www.atholestill.co.uk.

KALES, Elisabeth; Austrian singer (soprano); b. 1952, Graz. *Education:* Graz Conservatory. *Career:* sang at the Graz Opera 1975–79, Vienna Volksoper from 1979; sang Papagena in Die Zauberflöte at Salzburg 1980, 1986; Bregenz Festival 1984, as Christel in Zeller's Der Vogelhändler; other roles have included Millöcker's Laura, and the Fox in The Cunning Little Vixen; Dir, Baden Opera from 1996; further guest engagements at the Vienna Staatsoper.

KALHOR, Kayhan, BMus; Iranian musician (kamancheh) and composer; b. 23 Nov. 1963, Tehran. *Education:* Carleton Univ., Canada. *Career:* virtuoso performer on, and teacher of, the kamancheh (Persian spiked fiddle); raised in Kermanshah in Kurdish region of Iran; began musical studies on santur (zither) aged five with Ostad Ahmed Mohajer; later studied with Ostad Mehdi Kamalian, M. R. Lotfi and Ali Pour Nazeri; invited aged 13 to work with Nat. Orchestra of Radio and Television of Iran, where he performed for five years; began working with Shayda Ensemble of the Chavosh Cultural Centre 1980; left Iran during the revolution and studied music in Italy; learned the Persian classical repertoire (radif) in the traditional manner; has travelled extensively throughout Iran, studying the music of Khorasan and Kurdestan, in particular; has toured world-wide as a soloist with various ensembles and orchestras, including the New York Philharmonic, Orchestre Nat. de Lyon and Dresdner Philharmonie; invited by US composer John Adams to give a solo recital at Zankel Hall as part of Carnegie Hall's Perspectives 2004; appeared on a double bill at Lincoln Center's Mostly Mozart Festival 2004; has composed music for TV and film; also teaches the santur (zither) and setar (lute); Co-founder of ensembles Dastan, Ghazal: Persian & Indian Improvisations, Masters of Persian Music with Mohammad Reza Shajarian and Hossein Alizadeh and his own ensemble; has composed works for Iranian vocalists Mohammad Reza Shajarian and Shahram Nazeri; has performed and recorded with Iran instrumentalists; original mem. Yo-Yo Ma's Silk Road Project with whom he continues to tour; compositions appear on all of the ensemble's albums; numerous projects include collaborations and recordings with Kurdish lute virtuoso Ali Akbar Moradi, Turkish lute maestro Erdal Erzincan, Kurdish vocalist Aynur, String Quartet Brooklyn Rider and composer Osvaldo Golijov; worked with an Australian instrument-maker to create new instrument called the shah kaman, with a range similar to the cello. *Compositions include:* Night Silence Desert (for Mohammad Reza Shajarian) 1995, Gallop of a Thousand Horses (commissioned by the Kronos Quartet) 1999, Blue as the Turquoise Night of Neyshabur (commissioned by The Silk Road Project) 2000, Mountains Are Far Away (commissioned by the Silk Road Project/NHK TV for ten-part series on the Silk Road) 2004, score for Youth Without Youth (film by Francis Ford Coppola) 2007, I Was There (commissioned by Maya Beiser for 'Provenance') 2008, Silent City (commissioned by The Silk Road Project) 2010, Cinema Jenin – A Symphony (commissioned by Dresdner Sinfoniker) 2011, Layers of Loneliness (film) 2015. *Recordings include:* Eastern Apertures 1995, Lost Songs of the Silk Road: Ghazal Ensemble 1997, As Night Falls on the Silk Road: Ghazal Ensemble 1998, Scattering Stars Like Dust 1998, Through Eternity: Dastan Ensemble 1998, Night Silence Desert 1998, Moonrise Over the Silk Road: Ghazal Ensemble 2000, Night Silence Desert 2000, Caravan: Kronos Quartet 2000, Silk Road Journey: Yo-Yo Ma and the Silk Road Ensemble 2001, Without You: Masters of Persian Music 2002, Rain, Ghazal Ensemble 2003, In the Mirror of the Sky: Persian and Kurdish Improvisations 2004, Enchantment: Yo-Yo Ma and the Silk Road Ensemble 2004, Faryad: Masters of Persian Music 2005, The Wind: Persian and Turkish Improvisations 2006, New Impossibilities, Silk Road Ensemble 2007, Silent City: Kayhan Kalhor & Brooklyn Rider 2008, Off the Map, Silk Road Ensemble 2009, I Will Not Stand Alone 2011. *Current Management:* c/o Live Sounds, New York, USA. *Telephone:* (917) 292-6812. *Fax:* . *E-mail:* isoffer@gmail.com; info@ livesounds.org. *Website:* livesounds.org. *E-mail:* isArtsNY@gmail.com (office). *Website:* kayhankalhor.net (office).

KALICHSTEIN, Joseph, MSc; American/Israeli pianist; b. 15 Jan. 1946, Tel-Aviv; s. of Isaac Kalichstein and Mali Kalichstein; m. Rowain Kalichstein (née Schultz); two c. *Education:* Juilliard School, studies with Edward Steuermann and Ilona Kabos, summer studies with Vladimir Ashkenazy. *Career:* New York debut 1967; European debut 1970; appearances with numerous orchestras worldwide; engagements include Nat. Symphony Orchestra, Washington, DC, Cincinnati Symphony, US tour with Jerusalem Symphony and Lawrence Foster, and return tours to Japan and Scandinavia; mem. Piano Faculty, Juilliard School 1983–; Edwin S. and Nancy A. Marks Chair in Chamber Music Studies 2003–; Founding mem. Kalichstein-Laredo-Robinson Trio 1977; Chamber music consultant, Kennedy Center 1997–, Artistic Dir Fortas Chamber Music Concerts. *Honours:* First Prize, Leventritt Int. Competition 1969, Edward Stevermann Memorial Prize 1969. *Current Management:* Opus 3 Artists, 470 Park Avenue South, 9th Floor North, New York, NY 10016, USA. *Address:* The Juilliard School, 60 Lincoln Center Plaza, New York, NY 10023, USA (office). *E-mail:* jkalichstein@juilliard.edu (office). *Website:* www .juilliard.edu/degrees-programs/music/piano (office); kalichstein-laredo -robinsontrio.com.

KALININA, Galina; singer (soprano); b. 1951, Russia. *Education:* studied in Moscow. *Career:* mem., Bolshoi Opera, Moscow from 1977, notably as Donna Anna, Verdi's Trovatore Leonora, Elisabetta, Desdemona and Amelia (Ballo in Maschera); Tchaikovsky's Tatiana and Lisa and Madama Butterfly; guest appearances in the West from 1982, notably as Tosca at Stuttgart 1988, and with Scottish Opera, Yaroslavna in Prince Igor at Wiesbaden and Zemfira in a concert performance of Rachmaninov's Aleko at Rome; season 1987–88, as Tatiana at Buenos Aires, Butterfly in Oslo and Yaroslavna at Verona; Covent Garden 1991, as Tosca; Aida at Buenos Aires 1996; Turandot at Toronto 1997; season 2000 as Lady Macbeth for Oslo Opera and Abigaille at St Margareth. *Recordings:* Fevronia in The Legend of the Invisible City of Kitezh by Rimsky Korsakov.

KALISH, Gilbert, BA; American pianist and teacher; b. 2 July 1935, New York. *Education:* Columbia Coll., Columbia University Graduate School of Arts and Sciences, studied with Isabelle Vengerova, Leonard Schure and Julius Herford. *Career:* New York Recital debut, 1962; European debut, London, 1962; subsequent tours of the USA, Europe and Australia; pianist with the Contemporary Chamber Ensemble and the Boston Symphony Chamber Players; regular accompanist to Jan DeGaetani until 1989; Artist-in-Residence, Rutgers, The State University of New Jersey, 1965–67, Swarthmore College, 1966–72; Head of Keyboard Activities, Chair. of Faculty, 1985–, Tanglewood Music Center, Tanglewood, Massachusetts; faculty mem., Head of Performance Faculty, State University of New York at Stony Brook, 1970–. *Recordings:* as a soloist chamber player, and accompanist. *Honours:* Paul Fromm Award, University of Chicago for Distinguished Service to the music of our time, 1995. *Address:* c/o Music Department, State University of New York, Stony Brook, NY 11794, USA.

KALJUSTE, Tonu; Estonian choral director and conductor; b. 1953, Tallinn. *Education:* Tallinn and Leningrad Conservatories. *Career:* Lecturer, Tallinn Conservatory 1978–81; conducted works by Mozart, Britten and Weber with Estonian Opera; founder, Estonian Philharmonic Chamber Choir 1981; Artistic Dir of choral festivals Tallinn '88 and Tallinn '91; founder, Tallinn Chamber Choir 1992; founder, Tallinn Chamber Orchestra 1993; Principal Conductor, Swedish Radio Choir from 1994; guest conductor with choir and orchestras in Europe, Australia and North America; has featured contemporary Estonian composers and concert series of Bach and other Baroque composers; Principal Conductor, The Netherlands Chamber Choir 1998–, Estonian Philharmonic Chamber Choir, Tallinn Chamber Orchestra. *Recordings:* Forgotten People by Veljo Tormis 1992, Te Deum by Arvo Pärte 1993, Vespers Op 37 by Sergei Rachmaninov 1995, Requiem by Alfred Schnittke and Miserere by Henryk Gorecki 1995, Crystallisatio by Erkki-Sven Tüür 1996, Casting a Spell by Veljo Tormis 1996, Arvo Pärt's Litany 1997, Beatus 1997, Kanon Pokajanen 1998, Psalms of Repentance by Alfred Schnittke 1999. *Honours:* State Award of the Republic of Estonia 1997, Best Musician of Estonia 1998, ABC Music Award (with Swedish Radio Choir) 1998.

KALLISCH, Cornelia; German singer (mezzo-soprano); b. 1955, Marbach am Neckar. *Education:* studied in Stuttgart and Munich, with Josef Metternich in Cologne and with Siglind Bruhn and Anna Reynolds. *Career:* began musical career as an instrumentalist (violin and piano) before concentrating on singing; graduated at opera studio of Bavarian State Opera; focused at first on oratorios of Bach, Handel and Mozart as well as on lied singing; perm. mem. Zurich Opera, increasingly devoted to operatic repertoire; repertoire includes all breeches parts from Mozart to Strauss, dramatic roles including Wagner's Brangäne, Kundry, Fricka and Waltraute, as well as roles in rare works including Zemlinsky's Der Kreidekreis (Yü Pei) and Glinka's Aus dem Leben des Zaren Susanin (Wanja) and Mussorgsky's Chowanschtschina (Marfa); favourite roles include Judith in Bartok's Duke Bluebeard's Castle; appeared as Queen in world premieres of Heinz Holliger's opera Schneewittchen and H. K. Gruber's opera Der Herr Nordwind, both in Zurich, as well as Boesmann's A Winter's Tale in Brussels and Barcelona; more recent highlights have included new staging of Arabella at Royal Opera House, Covent Garden as well as Lulu, Pelléas and Mélisande, Peter Grimes, Gianni Schicchi, Eugen Onegin, Genoveva, Andrea Chénier, Der Ring des Nibelungen and Parsifal at Zurich Opera; appeared in role of Waltraute in Budapest's Ring production under Adam Fischer 2010; sang in Eugen Onegin in Zurich, amongst others 2011; has appeared with leading conductors including Blomstedt, von Dohnányi, Ivan and Adam Fischer, Gielen, Harnoncourt, Maazel, Marriner, Nagano, Norrington, Rilling, Sawallisch and Welser-Moest, and with orchestras including Munich and Berlin Philharmonic, all German radio orchestras, Vienna Philharmonic, Tonhalle Orchestra Zurich, New York Philharmonic, Orchestre de Paris, London Symphony Orchestra and Royal Concertgebouw Orchestra; soloist in Hartmann's 1st Symphony at opening of Kunstfest Weimar 2005; as a concert singer, focuses on romantic orchestral lied repertoire and contemporary music (Reger, Wagner, Schoenberg, Holliger); especially devoted to works of Mahler; teaches and gives masterclasses. *Recordings include:* songs of Dvorak, Mahler, Liszt and Brahms together with pianist Gabriel Dobner, Le Roi David by Honegger, Bach's Christmas Oratorio, Mozart's Requiem, F. Schmidt, Das Buch mit sieben Siegeln, Klavierlieder by O Schoek, César Franck's Les Béatitudes, Duke Bluebeard's Castle with SWR Radio-Sinfonieorchester Stuttgart under Peter Eötvös, Mahler's 2nd and 3rd Symphonies, with SWF Sinfonieorchester Baden-Baden under Michael Gielen and with Orchestre de la Suisse Romande under Armin Jordan, respectively, Franck's Les Béatitudes and Zemlinsky's Maeterlinck with Lieder Orchestre de la Suisse Romande under Armin

Jordan, Hartmann's Symphony No. 1 with Bamberg Symphony under Ingo Metzmacher, Wagner's Die Meistersinger von Nürnberg with Wolfgang Sawallisch, Mendelssohn's Elijah with the Bach Collegium Stuttgart and the Gächinger Kantorei under Helmuth Rilling, Beethoven's Missa Solemnis under Roger Norrington. *Current Management:* c/o KünstlerSekretariat am Gasteig, Rosenheimer Strasse 52, 81669 Munich, Germany. *Telephone:* (89) 44488790. *Fax:* (89) 4489522. *E-mail:* team@ks-gasteig.de. *Website:* www.ks-gasteig.de.

KALLWEIT, Georg; German musician (baroque violin) and concertmaster; *Member, Concertmaster and Soloist, Akademie für Alte Musik Berlin;* b. 1966, Greifswald. *Education:* Musikhochschule Hanns Eisler, Berlin. *Career:* specialist in solo repertoire of the Baroque violin and leadership of ensembles; joined Akademie für Alte Musik Berlin 1989, now Mem., Concertmaster and Soloist; guest concertmaster and soloist with historical and modern chamber orchestras including Ensemble Resonanz Hamburg, Finnish Baroque Orchestra, Deutsche Kammervirtuosen Berlin, Deutsches Sinfonie Orchester, Lautten Compagney Berlin; formed duo Ombra e Luce with lutenist Björn Colell, specialising in early Italian Baroque music; has performed across Europe, in N and S America and Asia; teaches at music schools in Leipzig, Weimar and Helsinki; coach, youth Baroque orchestra Bach's Erben. *Recordings include:* numerous recordings, including with Akademie für Alte Musik Berlin: Venice: The Golden Age 2014, and numerous violin concertos; other: chamber music with the Berlin Barock Compagney and Ombra e Luce. *Address:* Akademie für Alte Musik Berlin, Lübeckerstraße 22, 10559 Berlin, Germany (office). *Telephone:* (30) 32304440 (office). *Fax:* (30) 32304442 (office). *E-mail:* info@akamus.de (office). *Website:* www.akamus.de (office).

KALMAR, Carlos; Uruguayan conductor; *Chief Conductor and Artistic Director, RTVE Symphony Orchestra and Chorus;* b. 26 Feb. 1958, Montevideo. *Education:* Vienna Acad. of Music, Austria. *Career:* began violin studies at age of six; studied conducting with Karl Österreicher; made conducting debut with NDR Symphony Orchestra, Hamburg, Germany 1985; Music Dir Hamburg Symphony Ochestra 1989–91; Music Dir Stuttgart Philharmonic Orchestra 1991–95; Music Dir Anhaltisches Theater, Dessau, Germany 1996–2000; Prin. Conductor, Torkünstlerochester, Vienna 2000–03; Prin. Dir Grant Park Music Festival, Chicago 2000–; Music Dir Oregon Symphony Orchestra 2003–13; Chief Conductor and Artistic Dir RTVE Symphony Orchestra and Chorus, Madrid 2010–. *Recordings:* albums: as conductor: American Works for Organ and Orchestra (with David Schrader and Grant Park Orchestra) 2002, Joachim/Brahms, Violin Concertos (with Rachel Barton and Chicago Symphony Orchestra) 2003, Szymanowski/Martinů/Bartók, Violin Concertos (with Jennifer Koh and Grant Park Orchestra) 2006, Jennifer Larmore, Royal Mezzo 2008, Aaron Jay Kernis, Symphony in Waves 2008, Robert Kurka, Symphony No. 2 2009, Oregon Symphony with Pink Martini 2010, Spirit Of The American Range (with Oregon Symphony) 2015. *Honours:* Hans Swarowsky Conducting Competition First Prize, Vienna 1984. *Current Management:* Seldy Cramer Artists, 3436 Springhill Road, Lafayette, CA 94549, USA. *Telephone:* (925) 299-0623. *Fax:* (925) 299-0624. *E-mail:* Seldy@aol.com. *Website:* www.seldycramerartists.com. *Address:* Orquesta y Coro de RTVE, Avenida Radio Televisión 4, Edificio Prado del Rey, Planta 2a, despacho 2/072, 28223 Pozuelo de Alarcón, Madrid, Spain (office); Oregon Symphony Orchestra, 921 SW Washington, Suite 200, Portland, OR 97205, USA (office). *Telephone:* (503) 228-4294 (office). *Fax:* (503) 228-4150 (office). *E-mail:* symphony@orsymphony.org (office). *Website:* www.rtve.es/rtve/orquesta-coro (office); www.orsymphony.org (office).

KALMAR, Magda; Hungarian singer (soprano); b. 4 March 1944, Budapest. *Education:* Béla Bartók Conservatory, Budapest. *Career:* Budapest State Opera 1969–; frequent performer in Hungary's concert halls and on Hungarian radio and television; guest performer at numerous operas, including Austria, Belgium, Cuba, Czechoslovakia, Teatro la Fenice, Italy, Berlin, Leningrad, Stockholm and Paris; roles include Mozart's Blondchen, Despina and Cherubino, Verdi's Oscar, Adele in Die Fledermaus, Don Pasquale and Norina by Donizetti, Adina in L'Elisir d'amore, Mozart's Pamina, Rossini's Rosina, Alban Berg's Lulu, Sophie in Der Rosenkavalier and Gilda in Rigoletto; sang at Budapest 1987, in the premiere of Szokolay's Ecce Homo. *Recordings include:* Haydn's Il Ritorno di Tobia, Rossini's Mosè in Egitto, Dittersdorf's oratorio Esther, Motets. *Honours:* Grand Prix du Disque 1975, 1977, first prize Int. Rostrum for Young Performing Artists, Bratislava 1972, Budapest State Opera scholarship 1967.

KALT, Frederic; singer (tenor); b. 1963, Utah, USA. *Education:* studied in Anchorage, Alaska. *Career:* debut with New York City Opera 1987, as Faust in Mefistofele; Puerto Rico 1987, as Don José; sang in Europe from 1991, notably Bacchus at Karlsruhe; Des Grieux in Manon Lescaut at La Scala and Otello at Cologne 1996; Vienna Staatsoper from 1992, as Calaf, Cavaradossi and Verdi's Manrico; other roles include Samson, Paolo in Francesca da Rimini (Bregenz 1995), Pinkerton and Erik in Der fliegende Holländer (Los Angeles 1995); Apollo in Daphne by Strauss at Santa Fe 1996; concerts include Verdi Requiem at Carnegie Hall.

KALUDOV, Kaludy; Bulgarian singer (tenor); b. 1953, Varna. *Education:* Sofia Conservatory with Jablenska. *Career:* mem., Sofia Opera from 1978; guest engagements in Europe and North America, including Dimitri in Boris Godunov at Houston and Chicago, conducted by Abbado; sang Faust in Mefistofele at Lisbon 1990, Alvaro in La Forza del Destino at Poznan, 1991;

Riccardo in Un Ballo in Maschera at Genoa 1991, Puccini's Des Grieux at Trieste and Radames at Tel-Aviv, 1992; Manrico in Trovatore at Salzburg 1992, Deutsche Oper Berlin 1992, 1993, Wiener Staatsoper, 1994; Puccini's Des Grieux at La Scala, Milan, 1992 and at Palermo, 1993; Foresto in Attila at Wiener Staatsoper, 1984 and at La Scala 1991 (conducted by Riccardo Muti) and RAI Video; singer in Rosenkavalier at Wiener Staatsoper, 1990 and at Deutsche Oper Berlin 1993, Staatsoper Berlin, 1992; Don Carlo at Bayerische Staatsoper, Munich 1993, National Opera, Sofia 1988, Madrid 1986; Requiem, G. Verdi at London 1983 at Houston 1992, Tel-Aviv with Israel Philharmonic Orchestra conducted by Zubin Mehta; Radames in Aida at Staatsoper Berlin 1993, Finland 1994 and Philadelphia, 1996; sang Alvaro at Savonlinna, 1998. *Recordings:* Golitsin in Khovanschchina and Vladimir in Prince Igor, with forces of the Sofia Opera conducted by Emil Tchakarov; Janáček's Glagolitic Mass with Charles Dutoit, Montréal, 1991; Rachmaninov's The Bells with Charles Dutoit, Philadelphia, 1992; Puccini's Des Grieux (Manon Lescaut) with BRT Philharmonic Orchestra, Brussels (conducted by Alexander Rahbari) 1992.

KALUZA, Stefania; Polish/Austrian opera singer (mezzo-soprano); b. 15 April 1951, Katowice, Poland; two c. *Education:* studied in Wrocław and Vienna with Hans Hotter and Anton Dermota. *Career:* debut at Opera Wrocław; sang in Warsaw and Poznań, also at the Landestheater Salzburg from 1984, and made guest appearances at the Vienna Staatsoper, Bregenz Festival and Brussels (in The Cunning Little Vixen); Versailles Festival as Bersi in Andrea Chénier 1989, in Düsseldorf as Amneris 1989; appearances with Zürich Opera 1988–, roles include Marcellina in The Marriage of Figaro, Martha in Mefistofele, Pamela in Fra Diavalo and Larina in Eugene Onegin, Preziosilla, Dorabella, Frau Fluth, Ulrica, Rosina, Wagner's Venus, Enrichetta in I Puritani, Verdi's Maddalena; concert engagements in Poland, Hungary, Italy and Russia. *Recordings include:* Frau Litumlei in Zemlinsky's Kleider Machen Leute. *Honours:* Winner, Belvedere Int. Competition, Vienna 1983. *Current Management:* c/o Artists Management Verena Keller, Lohwisstrasse 52, 8123 Ebmatingen, Switzerland. *Telephone:* (44) 9801513. *Fax:* (44) 9803686. *E-mail:* keller.verena@bluewin.ch. *Website:* keller -artistsmanagement.ch.

KAM, Sharon; Israeli musician (clarinet); b. 11 Aug. 1971, d. of Rachel Kam; m. Gregor Bühl. *Education:* studied with Eli Eban and Chaim Taub in Israel and with Charles Neidich at Juilliard School, USA. *Career:* orchestral debut aged 16 with Israel Philharmonic Orchestra and Zubin Mehta (Mozart Clarinet Concerto); US debut (Mozart Clarinet Quintet) with Guarneri String Quartet, Carnegie Hall, New York; performance of Mozart's concerto for Mozart's 250th birthday celebrations at Nat. Theatre, Prague (televised live in 33 countries); as chamber musician, regularly works with artists such as Lars Vogt, Christian Tetzlaff, Enrico Pace, Daniel Müller-Schott, Martin Helmchen and the Jerusalem Quartet; frequent guest at festivals in Schleswig-Holstein, Heimbach, Rheingau, Risør, Cork, Verbier, Delft and at Schubertiade festival; has premiered works by Penderecki (Clarinet Concerto and Clarinet Quartet), Herbert Willi (Clarinet Concerto, at Salzburg Festival), Iván Erőd and Peter Ruzicka (at Donaueschingen); tour as soloist with Israel Philharmonic Orchestra 2014. *Recordings include:* Weber Clarinet Concerto with the Gewandhaus Orchestra Leipzig/Kurt Masur (Echo Klassik Award for Instrumentalist of the Year) 1998, American Classics with the London Symphony Orchestra/Gregor Bühl (Deutschen Schallplattenkritik Prize) 2002, works by Spohr, Weber, Rossini and Mendelssohn with Leipzig Radio Orchestra (Echo Klassik Award for Instrumentalist of the Year 2006) 2005, Mozart Concerto and Clarinet Quintet using the basset clarinet (Diapason d'Or) 2009, Opera! arias arranged for clarinet and chamber orchestra 2013, Reger/Brahms clarinet quintets 2015. *Honours:* Winner, ARD Int. Music Competition 1992. *Address:* c/o Sonia Simmenauer, Impresariat Simmenauer GmbH, Kurfürstendamm 211, 10719 Berlin, Germany. *Telephone:* (30) 414781710. *Fax:* (30) 414781713. *E-mail:* oda.caspar@impresariat-simmenauer.de. *Website:* www .impresariat-simmenauer.de.

KAMBASKOVIC, Rastislav, DipMus, MA; Serbian academic; b. 20 June 1939, Prokuplje; m. (divorced); one s. one d. *Education:* Acad. of Music, Belgrade. *Career:* debut, Serious Variation for Violins, Belgrade, 1965; Ed., Ed.-in-Chief, Chamber and Vocal, Symphonic Music, 1964–88; Chief Admin., Belgrade Radio-Television Symphony Orchestra, 1970–76; Prof. of Theory and Music Analysis, Theory Dept, Faculty of Music, Belgrade, 1988–, Head, Theory Dept, 1992–. *Compositions:* solo instrumental music: Violin and Piano Sonata in G, 1964; Sonata for Two Violins, 1975; Six Piano Preludes, 1991; chamber music: Serious Variations for Flute and String Orchestra, 1966; Wood Wind Quintet, 1967; Piano Trio, 1975; Kumb Brass Wind Quintet, 1980; Pester Sketches for 14 Flutes, 1988; Four Harp Sonata, 1991; Jefimia Lamentoso for Cello and String Orchestra, 1993. *Publication:* Interaction: Diatonic and Chromatic in Prokofiev's Symphonies 1992. *Honours:* Belgrade Music Festival Award, 1974; Serbian Asscn of Composers Awards, 1974, 1975, 1982, 1983; Belgrade Radio-Television Award, 1982. *Address:* 109 Nova 22, 11060 Belgrade, Serbia.

KAMENSEK, Karen; American conductor; *Music Director, Staatstheater Hannover;* b. 2 Jan. 1970, Chicago, Ill. *Education:* Indiana Univ. Music School. *Career:* fmr Conductor, Houston Grand Opera; fmrly toured with New York City Opera; fmr Conductor, Orchesta Sinfonica Nacional de Honduras, Louisville Orchestra, Bochumer Symphoniker; Music Dir Vienna Volksoper 2000–02; Conductor, Opera Australia 2003; Music Dir Freiburg Opera House 2003–06; Guest Conductor, Deutsche Oper 2004; Chief Conductor, Slovenian Nat. Theatre, Maribor 2007–08; Deputy Music Dir Hamburg State Opera

2008–09, Proxy Music Dir 2009–10; Music Dir Staatstheater Hannover 2011–12; guest conductor of many other orchestras including: Malaysian Philharmonic Orchestra, Odense Symphony Orchestra, Duisburger Philharmoniker, Hamburg Philharmoniker; several collaborations with Philip Glass including: Orphée, New York, Les Enfants Terribles, Spoleto Festival, USA 1996, Wozzeck, New York Shakespeare Festival. *Current Management:* c/o Michael Lewin Artists' Management International, c/o Euro Artists Künstlermanagement GmbH, Bastiengasse 27/1, 1180 Vienna, Austria. *Telephone:* (676) 375-19-63. *E-mail:* office@lewin-management.com. *Website:* www.lewin -management.com. *Address:* Staatstheater Hannover, Kramerstrasse 21, 30159 Hanover, Germany (office). *Telephone:* (511) 1692278 (office). *Website:* www.staatstheater-hannover.de (office).

KAMINKOVSKY, Rimma; Russian violinist; b. 1940. *Education:* studied in Odessa, Warsaw, Tel-Aviv and in the USA with Samuel Ashkenazi. *Career:* teacher, Rubin Academy of Music in Jerusalem, former co-leader of the Jerusalem Symphony Orchestra; mem., Israel Philharmonic, with appearances as soloist; co-founder, Jerusalem String Trio 1977–; repertoire includes string trios by Beethoven, Dohnányi, Mozart, Reger, Schubert and Taneyev, piano quartets by Beethoven, Brahms, Dvořák, Mozart and Schumann; concerts with Radu Lupu and Daniel Adni. *E-mail:* alperin@netvision.net.il.

KAMINSKY, Laura, BA, MMus; American composer, arts administrator and academic; *Composer-in-Residence, American Opera Projects;* b. 28 Sept. 1956, New York, NY; d. of Leonard Kaminsky and Eva Sarna; m. Rebecca Allan. *Education:* Oberlin Coll. and City Coll. of New York. *Career:* Co-founder Musicians Accord ensemble 1980; Assoc. Dir for the Humanities, 92nd Street, New York 1984–88; Artistic Dir New York Town Hall 1988–92; artistic consultant/educator, Nat. Acad. of Music, Winneba, Ghana 1992–93; Dir Music and Theatre Programs, The New School Univ., New York 1993–96; Dir European Mozart Acad., Poland 1996–97; Vice-Pres. for Programs, Meet the Composer, New York 1997–98; Chair. Music Dept, Cornish Coll. of the Arts, Seattle, Wash. 1999–2004; Dean, Conservatory of Music, Purchase Coll., State Univ. of New York 2004–08, Prof. of Music 2008–; Artistic Dir Symphony Space, New York 2007–14; Composer-in-Residence, American Opera Projects 2014–. *Compositions include:* Proverbs of Hell for soprano, marimba and piano 1989, Triftmusik for piano 1991, Whitman Songs for baritone and piano 1992, Vukovar Trio for violin, cello and piano 1999, River Music for flute, piano and percussion 2000, Transformations for string quartet 2000, The Full Range of Blue 2001, Libra for chorus 2002, Danza Piccola for solo piano 2002, Transformations II for string quartet 2002, Duo for cello and piano 2003, Runaway Anemone for mandolin and guitar 2003, Until a Name for solo flute 2003, The Seasons for women's chorus 2003, Piano Quartet 2003–04, Cadenza Variations for woodwind quintet 2004, Monotypes 2005, Music for Thelma for violin and piano 2005, L'arcipelago delle delizie for solo cello 2005, Duo for flute and piano 2006, Music for Artur for piano 2006, Spiritlines for string orchestra 2007, Duo for violin and piano 2007, Piano Trio 2007, Terra Terribilis: Concerto for percussion and orchestra 2008, Calendar Music for piano 2008, American Nocturne for string quartet 2009, Wave Hill for violin and piano 2009, Cadmium Yellow for string quartet 2010, Fantasy for piano 2010, The Great Unconformity 2010, Horizon Lines for oboe, bassoon and piano 2010, Piano Concerto 2011, Catastrophe for flute, oboe, two guitars, violin and cello 2012, Rising Tide for string quartet 2012, Homage to Havel for flute, oboe, 2 guitars, violin and cello 2013, Five Songs 2013, Oboe Concerto 2014, Deception for clarinet, violin, cello, piano 2014, AS ONE (opera) 2014, Dreaming Absinthe for flute, oboe, 2 guitars, violin and cello 2015, undercurrent for violin and piano 2015, Some Light Emerges (opera) 2015. *Honours:* Nat. Endowment for the Arts Grants and Fellowships, Koussevitzky Foundation Fellowship, Opera America, Chamber Music American, ArtsLink Int. Fellowship, Likhachev Foundation Fellowship, numerous other comms, fellowships and awards. *Current Management:* c/o Bill Holab Music, 377 Sterling Place, No. 4, Brooklyn, NY 11238, USA. *Telephone:* (718) 499-3946. *Fax:* (718) 310-6190. *E-mail:* bill@holabmusic.com. *Website:* www .billholabmusic.com. *Address:* 2500 Johnson Avenue, #16np, Bronx, NY 10463, USA (office). *Telephone:* (718) 825-7528 (office). *E-mail:* laurakaminsky928@gmail.com (office). *Website:* www.laurakaminsky.com.

KAMIO, Mayuko; Japanese violinist; b. 12 June 1986, Osaka. *Education:* Toho Gakuen School of Music, study with Zakhar Bron at Hochschule Musik und Theater, Zürich, Switzerland. *Career:* began to play violin aged four, TV concerto debut aged 10; New York concerto debut, Orchestra of St Luke's 2003; has appeared with many leading orchestras including Russian Nat. Orchestra, BBC Philharmonic, Zürcher Kammerorchester, Bavarian Staatsoper, Orchestre Nat. d'Ile de France, NHK Symphony, Tokyo Symphony, Hyogo Performing Arts Cen. Orchestra, Tonhalle Orchestra Zurich, Israel Philharmonic, Prague Philharmonic, Orchestre Nat. de Lille, Orchestre Philharmonique de Monte Carlo. *Honours:* winner, Menuhin Int. Violin Competition 1998, Monte Carlo Violin Masters Competition 2004, First Prize and Gold Medal at Int. David Oistrakh Violin Competition, Ukraine 2004, Gold Medal Int. Tchaikovsky Competition, Moscow 2007, Idemitsu Music Award. *Current Management:* Aspen Incorporated, 20-16 Nishi-Azabu, 2 chome Minato-ku, Tokyo 106-0031, Japan. *Telephone:* (3) 5467-0081 (office). *Fax:* (3) 5468-0066 (office). *E-mail:* yamane@aspen.jp (office). *Website:* www.aspen.jp (office).

KAMMERLOHER, Katharina; German singer (mezzo-soprano); b. 16 Nov. 1968, Munich. *Education:* studied with Mechthild Böhme in Detmold, with Vera Rozsa in London. *Career:* mem., Staatsoper, Berlin from 1993, as Rosina, Costanza in Haydn's L'isola disabitata, Suzuki, as Meg Page under Claudio

Abaddo, Mélisande under Michael Gielen, Octavian under Philippe Jordan; under Daniel Barenboim she sang Magdalene, Wellgunde, Zerlina and Dorabelle in the Doris Dörrie-Production of Così fan tutte; Salzburg debut, Lulu 1995; Schwetzingen Festival 1997, Anna in Cavalli's Didone 1997; concerts include Ravel's Shéhérazade, Kantscheli's Lamento (with Gidon Kremer, violin) and Beethoven's Ninth Symphony with Daniel Barenboim, Bach Cantatas under René Jacobs, Elijah with Wolfgang Sawallisch, Berlioz's Romeo with Luisi, Orchesterlieder by Schönberg in Munich and Vienna 2001 and Le Visage Nuptial by Boulez (Proms, London and Edinburgh 2001) both with Boulez; tour of Japan with the Berlin State 2002; Second Lady in Magic Flute and Mozart Requiem at Salzburg 2002; Anita in West Side Story with Kent Nagano 2003; debut as Komponist in Ariadne auf Naxos with Fabia Luisi in Berlin 2003. *Recordings include:* Elektra, Haydn's L'Isola disabitata, Bach Cantatas, Così fan tutte (DVD), Otello (DVD). *Address:* c/o Deutsche Staatsoper Berlin, Unter den Linden 9–11, 10117 Berlin, Germany.

KAMMINGA, Martin; Dutch organist and conductor; b. 23 Dec. 1933, Muiden; m. Renske van der Hauw 1957; two s. one d. *Education:* Amsterdam Conservatory with Piet Kee, Frans Moonen, Anton Kersjes. *Career:* organist, live and on radio, in major churches and cathedrals in Netherlands and France; Conductor Royal Christian Choral Soc., Amsterdam 1967–2007; Conductor of numerous major works for large orchestra, choir and soloists, Concertgebouw Amsterdam; Dir Hilversum Conservatory of Music 1979–98; Conductor, annual Festival of Nine Lessons and Carols, Grote of Laurenskerk, Weesp; jury mem. organ and choral conducting examinations, Conservatorium van Amsterdam 1999–2005; mem. Royal Netherlands Soc. of Organists. *Honours:* Hon. Conductor, Royal Christian Choral Soc., Amsterdam; Ridder in de Orde van Oranje Nassau, on 40th anniversary as a musician, Concertgebouw Amsterdam 1999; Conductor of the Year, City of Amsterdam 1981, Choir of the Year, City of Amsterdam 1983, Culture Award, City of Weesp 2003. *Address:* Prinses Beatrixlaan 12, 1381 Weesp, The Netherlands (home). *Telephone:* (294) 412907 (home). *E-mail:* martinkamminga@xs4all.nl.

KAMPE, Anja; singer (soprano); b. 1968, Germany. *Career:* many appearances in opera throughout Germany and elsewhere in Europe, notably in Rossini's Il Turco in Italia and as Fiordiligi in Così fan tutte; also sings songs by Bizet and Wolf (Spanisches Liederbuch); contestant in the Cardiff Singer of the World Competition 1995.

KAMU, Okko; Finnish conductor and violinist; b. 7 March 1946, Helsinki; m. Anna Aminoff. *Education:* Sibelius Acad. *Career:* leader, Suhonen Quartet 1964; began professional career with Helsinki Philharmonic Orchestra 1965; subsequently appointed leader, Finnish Nat. Opera Orchestra 1966–69, Third Conductor 1967; Guest Conductor, Swedish Royal Opera, Stockholm 1969; Chief Conductor, Finnish Radio Symphony Orchestra 1971–77; Music Dir Oslo Philharmonic 1975–79, Helsinki Philharmonic 1981–89; Prin. Conductor, Netherlands Radio Symphony 1983–86; Prin. Guest Conductor, City of Birmingham Symphony Orchestra 1985–88; Prin. Conductor, Sjaelland Symphony Orchestra, Copenhagen 1988–94; Music Dir Stockholm Sinfonietta 1989–93; Prin. Conductor Helsingborg Symphony Orchestra 1991–2000; First Guest Conductor, Singapore Symphony Orchestra 1995–2001, now Prin. Guest Conductor; Music Dir Finnish Nat. Opera, Helsinki 1996–2000; Prin. Guest Conductor Lausanne Chamber Orchestra 1999–2002; Prin. Conductor, Lahti Symphony Orchestra 2011–; Artistic Dir Int. Sibelius Festival 2011–; conducted world premières of Sallinen's operas The Red Line, The King Goes Forth to France, Palace and King Lear; numerous engagements with orchestras and opera houses world-wide; mem. Royal Swedish Acad. of Music 1994–. *Recordings include:* Sibelius: La Tempête, Le Barde, Tapiola, with Orchestre symphonique de Lahti (Diapason d'Or de l'année 2011). *Honours:* First Prize, First Int. Karajan Conductor Competition, Berlin 1969. *Current Management:* Patrick Garvey Management, 40 North Parade, York, YO30 7AB, England. *E-mail:* patrick@patrickgarvey.com. *Address:* Lahti Symphony Orchestra, Sibelius Hall, Ankkurikatu 7, 15140 Lahti, Finland (office). *Telephone:* (3) 8144451 (office). *Fax:* (3) 8144451 (office). *Website:* www.sinfonialahti.fi (office).

KANAWA, Dame Kiri Te (see TE KANAWA, Dame Kiri)

KANCHELI, Giya (Georgy); Georgian composer; b. 10 Aug. 1935, Tbilisi; s. of Alexander Kancheli and Agnessa Kancheli; m. Valentina Djikia; one s. one d. *Education:* Tbilisi State Conservatory, studied composition with I. Tuskiya. *Career:* worked as freelance composer following graduation from 1963; mem. of 'Soviet avant-garde' during 1960s, subsequently dedicated himself to developing a personal musical style based on simple formulas occurring in the music of different epochs, ancient folk songs and in popular music; later collaborated with dir Robert Sturua who inspired him to write music for films and several plays; Prof., Tbilisi Conservatory 1970–90; Dir of Music, Rustaveli Theatre, Tbilisi 1971–91, wrote incidental music for many of Sturua's productions, including his opera 'Music for the Living' 1984 (re-staged for Deutsches Nat. Theater, Weimar 1999), for Brecht's The Caucasian Chalk Circle, Shakespeare's Richard III, Hamlet and King Lear, Sophocles' Oedipus and Beckett's Waiting for Godot; best known as a composer of symphonic and other large-scale works; Fourth Symphony, 'In Memoria di Michelangelo', received its US premiere with the Philadelphia Orchestra, Yury Temirkanov conducting 1978; left Georgia with his family 1991, first went to Berlin and received a grant from German Academic Exchange Service; commissions and frequent performances in Europe and USA with Jansug Kakhidze, Dennis

Russell Davies, Kim Kashkashian, Gidon Kremer, Yuri Bashmet, Mstislav Rostropovich and the Kronos Quartet; Composer-in-Residence, Royal Flemish Philharmonic Orchestra, Antwerp 1995–96. *Compositions include:* symphonies: First 1967, Second 1970, Third 1973, Fourth (In Memoria di Michelangelo) 1975, Fifth 1977, Sixth (In Memory of Parents) 1980, Seventh (Epilogue) 1986; other symphonic works: Mourned by the Wind for orchestra and viola 1989, Lament (in memory of Luigi Nono), for violin, soprano and orchestra 1995; opera: Music for the Living 1984; chamber works: Life Without Christmas 1989–90 (cycle of four works for chamber ensembles), Magnum Ignotum, for wind ensemble and tape 1994, Exil, for soprano, small ensemble and tape 1994, Dixi for mixed choir and symphony orchestra 2009, Chiaroscuro for soloist (violin/viola) and orchestra 2010, Lingering for symphony orchestra 2012, Angels of Sorrow 2013. *Honours:* USSR State Prize 1976, USSR People's Artist 1988, State Prize of Georgia 1982, Nika Prize for film music 1987, Triumph Prize Moscow 1998, Wolf Foundation Prize in the Arts (Music) 2008, Lifetime Achievement Award, Istanbul 2012. *Address:* Tovstonogov str. 6, 0162 Tbilisi, Georgia (home). *E-mail:* mail@kancheli.de (office).

KANG, Clara-Jumi, BMus; German/South Korean violinist; b. 10 June 1987, Mannheim, Germany. *Education:* Staatliche Hochschule für Musik und Darstellende Kunst, Mannheim, Musikhoschule, Lübeck, Juilliard School, New York, Hochschule für Musik Hanns Eisler, Berlin with Christopher Poppen, Korean Nat. Univ. of Arts with Nam Yun Kim. *Career:* began playing violin and piano aged three; debut with Hamburg Symphony Orchestra aged five; debut concert in Korea aged eight with Korean Chamber Ensemble performing the Mozart Concerto No. 5 at Seoul Arts Center; numerous performances in USA, Europe and Asia; first recording for Teldec, performing Beethoven Triple Concerto with her sibling, aged nine; auditioned for Daniel Barenboim 1998. *Honours:* Third Prize, Tibor Varga Competition 2007, Winner, Seoul Int. Violin Competition 2009, Second Prize, Hanover Int. Violin Competition 2009, Winner, Sendai Int. Violin Competition 2010, First Prize and Gold Medal, Int. Violin Competition of Indianapolis 2010. *Address:* Korea National University of Arts, Seokgwan-dong Campus, 146-37 Hwarang-ro 32-gil, Seongbuk-gu, Seoul, South Korea. *Telephone:* (2) 746-9073; (2) 746-9075. *Fax:* (2) 746-9079. *Website:* karts.ac.kr.

KANG, Dong-suk; South Korean violinist; b. 28 April 1954, Seoul; m. Martine Schittenhelm; one s. one d. *Education:* Juilliard School, Curtis Inst. with Ivan Galamian. *Career:* went to New York to study 1967; won San Francisco Symphony Foundation Competition and Merriweather Post Competition, Washington, DC 1971; winner at other competitions including Queen Elisabeth, Brussels, Montréal, and Carl Flesch, London; has appeared with orchestras throughout USA, UK, Europe and Far East and at music festivals around the world including BBC Promenade concerts (debut 1987); Prof., Yonsei Univ.; Artistic Dir MusicAlp Festival, France, Seoul Spring Festival, South Korea. *Recordings include:* complete repertoire for violin and orchestra by Sibelius, Nielsen Violin Concerto, Elgar Violin Concerto, Bruch Violin Concerto, Walton Violin Concerto. *Honours:* Chevalier, Ordre des Arts et Lettres 2012. *Website:* www.yonsei.ac.kr/eng/academics/colleges/music; www.festivalmusicalp.com; www.seoulspringnew.org.

KANG, Philip; South Korean singer (bass); b. 10 April 1948, Seoul. *Education:* Seoul Nat. Univ., also studied in Milan and Berlin. *Career:* sang small roles at the Deutsche Oper Berlin from 1976; engagements at Wuppertal, Kiel and Nuremberg, Nationaltheater Mannheim 1986–93; roles have included Sarastro, Rocco, Kaspar, Verdi's Sparafucile, Ramphis, Philip II, Ferrando and Padre Guardiano, Wagner's Daland, Pogner, Mark, King Henry and Gurnemanz; Sang in Italy from 1982, Rodolfo in Sonnambula at Toulouse 1983, Lisbon 1984, as Attila, Sarastro at the Théâtre des Champs Elysées, 1987; American engagements at New York and Philadelphia, European at Madrid, Rome, Frankfurt (as Rocco) and Cologne, as Rossini's Basilio; Théâtre de la Monnaie Brussels as Pimen in Boris Godunov and as Antonios in Stephen Climax by Hans Zender, 1990; Bayreuth Festival 1987–92, as Fafner, Hagen and Hunding; Season 1999–2000 as Verdi's King Philip at the Komische Oper, Berlin, and as Fafner and Hunding at Bayreuth; consultant, Seoul Opera; Prof. of Voice, Seoul Nat. Univ. 1995–. *Honours:* winner, Mario del Monaco Competition 1979, Toti dal Monte Competition 1979, 1981. *Current Management:* Hilbert Artists Management, Maximilianstr. 22, 80539 Munich, Germany. *Telephone:* (89) 2907470. *Fax:* (89) 29074790. *E-mail:* agentur@hilbert.de. *Website:* www.hilbert.de.

KANGA, Skaila, LRAM, ARAM, FRAM; harpist; b. 8 Jan. 1946, Bombay, India; m. (divorced); two s. two d. *Education:* Royal Acad. of Music, studied with Prof. Vivian Langrish and Prof. Tina Bonifacio. *Career:* BBC Concert Orchestra and freelance with regional and major London orchestras; solo career includes concerts and broadcasts, as well as numerous commercial recordings; performed the Ravel Introduction and Allegro at the Proms 1994; Michael Tippett's 90th Birthday Celebrations, Barbican Hall 1994; Fauré and the French Connection, festival in Manchester 1995; Head of Harp, Royal Acad. of Music; mem. PRS, BAC&S, MCPS. *Compositions include:* Les saisons de la harpe for solo harp, British Folk Songs Vol. I for flute and harp, Miniatures Bks I and II harp duets for flute and harp, American Sketches for clarinet (or flute) and harp, Cadenzas for Mozart Concerto for flute and harp. *Recordings include:* three chamber works of Arnold Bax, French Chamber Music with Academy of St Martins, two solo albums (with Tommy Reilly), Mozart Flute and Harp Concerto (with City of London Sinfonia), Bax Chamber Music (with Nash Ensemble).

KANI, Wasfi, OBE, MA; British opera producer; *Chief Executive, Grange Park Opera*; b. 7 March 1956, London, England. *Education:* Univ. of Oxford. *Career:* played violin in Nat. Youth Orchestra; fmr programmer and designer financial computer systems, London; studied conducting 1980s; est. computer consultancy 1986–93; f. Pimlico Opera (touring co.) 1989, productions staged in banks, hosps, country houses, prisons (performance of Sweeney Todd was inspiration for BBC TV film Tomorrow La Scala! 2002); Chief Exec. Garsington Opera 1992–97; f. Grange Park rural opera festival, Hants. 1997, Chief Exec. 1997–, productions of Rinaldo, I Capuleti e I Montecchi, Enchantress, Maria Stuarda, Le Roi Malgré Lui, Thaïs, Gambler, Rusalka, La Fanciulla del West, Norma, The Cunning Little Vixen, Eliogabalo; mem. Bd Royal Court Theatre; Trustee, The Mayor's Fund for London. *Honours:* Hon. DMus; Walpole Award for British Cultural Excellence 2004, Asian Woman of Achievement, Lloyds TSB Award 2008. *Address:* General Administration, Grange Park Opera, 24 Broad Street, Alresford, Hants., SO24 9AQ, England (office). *Telephone:* (1962) 737360 (office). *E-mail:* info@grangeparkopera.co.uk (office). *Website:* www.grangeparkopera.co.uk (office).

KANKA, Michal; Czech cellist; b. 23 May 1960, Prague; m. 1982; two d. *Education:* Prague Conservatory and Academy of Performing Arts, University of Southern California. *Career:* debut with Dvořák Concerto with Czech Philharmonic Orchestra 1983; regular appearances with Czech Orchestras 1982–; tours to Europe, America, Japan and Australasia 1982–; mem., Prazak Quartet 1986–; Berlin debut with RIAS 1987; regular concerts in Salzburg, Munich, London, Amsterdam, Milan, Tokyo and Sydney; official soloist, Prague Radio Orchestra 2003–. *Recordings include:* Beethoven, Mozart and Janáček works with Prazak Quartet 1989–; also Chopin, Sonata, Stravinsky's Italian Suite 1984, Schubert's Sonata in C 1989, Franck's Sonata 1989, Mozart's Concertone with S Accardo 1990, Martinů, three sonatas 1991, Vivaldi, seven Cello Concertos 1993, complete works for cello and orchestra by B Martinů 1995, Boccherini, seven Sonatas 1998, Myslivecek, six Sonatas 1999, Rubinstein: Complete set for cello/piano; Haydn Cello Concertos. *Honours:* laureate, Tchaikovsky Competition in Moscow 1982, first prize, Prague Spring Competition 1983, winner, Cello International Competition, ARD Munich 1986, soloist of the State Philharmony Brno 1995, Diapason D'or, Chock de la Musique, Télérama 1995. *Current Management:* c/o Světlana Jahodová, Jahoda Artists Management. *Telephone:* 603293985. *E-mail:* info@jahoda-arts.cz. *Website:* www.jahoda-arts.cz. *Address:* Peckova 17, Karlin, 18600 Prague 8, Czech Republic (home). *Website:* www.prazakquartet.com.

KANTA, Ludovit; Slovak cellist; *Solo Cellist, Orchestra Ensemble, Kanazawa, Japan*; b. 9 July 1957, Bratislava; m. 1977; two s. one d. *Education:* Bratislava Conservatorium with G. Vecerny, Academy of Music, Prague with A. Vectomov. *Career:* debut in Strauss' Don Quixote, with Slovak Philharmonic, International Music Festival, Bratislava, Oct 1982; 1st Solo Cello, Slovak Philharmonic, Bratislava, 1983; Concert tours and international festivals as Soloist with Slovak Philharmonic, Bulgaria, 1984, USSR and Poland, 1985, Japan, 1987, Spain, 1988; Other foreign tours, Germany, 1980, 1983, 1986, Italy, 1981, Bulgaria, 1983, 1985, Yugoslavia, 1985, Romania, 1985, 1987, Sweden, 1985; Solo Cellist, Orchestra Ensemble, Kanazawa, Japan, 1990–; Associate Professor, Aichi Prefectural University of Arts, Nagoya, 1995–. *Recordings:* Dvořák-Cello Concerto, Haydn-Concerto in D Major, with Large Orchestra of Bratislava Radio, conducted by Kurt Hortnagel and Ondrej Lenárd; Igor Dibak-premiere recording of Cello Concerto, with Slovak Philharmonic, conductor Bystrik Rezucha; Haydn-Boccherini Concertos, Capella Istropolitana, conductor Peter Breiner; Cello Recital, 1997; Ludovit Kanta Cello Recital, with Heller on piano; Kodaly: Cello Solo Sonata op. 8; Dvořàk: Concerto h-mol op.104 with Orchestra Ensemble Kanazawa, conductor Jan Latham Koenig. *Honours:* 1st Prize, Beethoven Competition, OPAVA, 1977; 2nd Prize, Prague Spring International Competition, 1980; Concert Imagine; Concert Service Company. *Address:* Midorigaoka 1-2, 929-0322 Tsubata, Ishikawa, Japan (home). *Telephone:* (76) 288-7677 (home). *Fax:* (76) 288-7677 (home). *E-mail:* hanka@naa.att.ne.jp (home).

KANTCHEFF, Slava; German pianist; b. 15 July 1959, Wiesbaden; d. of Kantcho Kantcheff and Mathilde Kantcheff; m. Peter Horton 1986. *Education:* Conservatoire Nat. Supérieur de Musique et de Danse and Sorbonne (Music History), Paris. *Career:* first TV appearance aged seven; performed Beethoven and Mozart piano concertos with orchestra aged ten; recorded first album aged 23; co-presenter, TV series with Peter Horton 1989–91; has performed at more than 2,000 concerts. *Recordings include:* seven solo albums (Beethoven, Brahms, Schumann, Scriabin, Rachmaninov and Chopin), six albums with Peter Horton and one with Symphonic Trio (Slava Kantcheff, Peter Horton, Andreas Keller). *Address:* Hererostr. 12, 81827 Munich, Germany (office). *Telephone:* (89) 6259189 (office). *Fax:* (89) 6259189 (office). *E-mail:* ph@peter-horton.de (office).

KAPELLMANN, Franz-Josef; German singer (baritone); b. 23 Sept. 1945, Cologne. *Education:* studied in Cologne. *Career:* sang at the Deutsche Oper Berlin, 1973–75, Dortmund from 1975, notably as Verdi's Luna, Posa, Germont, Iago and Amonasro, Scarpia, Gianni Schicchi, Wolfram, Beckmesser and Kurwenal; Alberich in a new production of Das Rheingold, 1990; Guest appearances at Düsseldorf, Wiesbaden, Karlsruhe, Klagenfurt, Lubeck and Paris (Alberich in Götterdämmerung); Other roles have included Riccardo in Puritani, Guglielmo, Papageno, Toby in The Red Line by Sallinen, Escamillo (at Regensburg), Mozart's Figaro (Gelsenkirchen) and Don Fernando in Fidelio (Granada Festival); Gala concert at the Alte Oper Frankfurt, 1989; Sang Alberich in Siegfried at Brussels, 1991, Beckmesser at Trieste, 1992; Pizarro in a concert of Fidelio, Edinburgh, 1996; Season 1998 at La Scala, Milan and Catania as Weber's Kaspar and Pizarro in Fidelio; Season 2000–01 as Alberich for Bonn Opera, Pizarro at La Scala and Kaspar in Der Freischütz at the Staatsoper Berlin. *Recordings:* Handel's L'Allegro, il Penseroso ed il Moderato. *Current Management:* Theateragentur Dr Germinal Hilbert, Maximilianstrasse 22, 80539 Munich, Germany. *Telephone:* (89) 290 747-0. *Fax:* (89) 290 747-90. *Website:* www.hilbert.de.

KAPLAN, Abraham; conductor; b. 5 May 1931, Tel-Aviv, Israel. *Education:* Israel Acad., Jerusalem, Juilliard School, New York, USA and studied with William Steinberg, Frederick Prausnitz, Darius Milhaud. *Career:* Dir, Kol Israel Chorus 1953–54, 1958–59; Conductor, Haifa Oratorio Soc. 1958–59; founder, Camerata Singers, USA 1960; Dir of Choral Music, Juilliard School 1961–77, Symphonic Choral Soc. of New York 1968–77; founder, Camerata Symphony Orchestra 1968; appeared as guest conductor with leading orchestras in the USA and Israel; teacher, Berkshire Music Center and at Union Theological Seminary, New York 1961–73; Dir of Choral Studies, Chautauqua, New York 1976; Prof. of Music, Univ. of Washington, Seattle 1977; many choral engagements and recordings with the New York Philharmonic.

KAPLAN, Lewis, BMus, MMus; American violinist; b. 10 Nov. 1933, Passaic, NJ; m. Adria Goodkin 1961; one s. one d. *Education:* Juilliard School. *Career:* debut at the Town Hall, New York 1961; solo concerts, USA, Europe and Far East 1953–; violinist-founder, Aeolian Chamber Players 1961–; mem. Violin and Chamber Music Faculties, Juilliard School 1964–; Artistic Dir and co-founder, Bowdoin Summer Music Festival 1964–; mem. Violin Faculty, Summer Acad. Mozarteum, Salzburg, Austria 1987; mem. Violin Faculty, Mannes Coll. of Music 1987–; numerous conducting appearances in USA and Europe. *Publications:* Caprice Variations for Unaccompanied Violin by George Rochberg (ed.) 1973.

KAPLAN, Lisa S.; American musician (piano); b. Detroit, Mich. *Education:* Oberlin Conservatory, Cincinnati Coll.-Conservatory and Northwestern Univ. *Career:* has collaborated with artists including Mario Batali, Bryce Dessner, Glenn Kotche, Robert Spano and Dawn Upshaw; Co-founder and mem. contemporary music ensemble eighth blackbird 1996–, ensemble has commissioned and performed new works by composers such as Steve Reich, Frederic Rzewski, Jennifer Higdon, Stephen Hartke and Steven Mackey and performed with orchestras including Cleveland Orchestra, Toronto Symphony and Atlanta Symphony at venues including Carnegie Hall, Barbican, Sydney Opera House and Kennedy Center; residencies at univs and conservatories worldwide, including Univs of Richmond and Chicago, Oberlin Conservatory, Queensland Conservatorium, Southern Methodist Univ., Colburn School and Curtis Inst. of Music. *Composition:* whirligig for piano four hands 2013. *Recordings:* thirteen ways 2003, beginnings 2004, fred 2005, strange imaginary animals (Grammy Award for Best Chamber Music Performance 2007) 2006, Paul Moravec: The Time Gallery 2006, Steve Reich: Double Sextet 2010, Jennifer Higdon: On a Wire 2011, Steven Mackey: Lonely Motel: Music from Slide (Grammy Award for Best Small Ensemble Performance) 2011, meanwhile (Grammy Award for Best Chamber Music/Small Ensemble Performance) 2012. *Honours:* winner (with eighth blackbird) Fischoff Chamber Music Competition 1996 and numerous awards including Naumburg Chamber Music Award 2000, ASCAP Award for Adventurous Programming 1998, 2000, American Music Center Trailblazer Award 2007, Meet the Composer Award 2007. *Current Management:* 3Arts, 180 North Michigan Avenue, #305, Chicago, IL 60601; David Lieberman Artists, PO Box 10368, Newport Beach, CA 92658, USA. *Telephone:* (312) 443-9621 (3Arts); (714) 979-4700 (DLA). *Fax:* (312) 443-9622 (3Arts); (714) 979-4740 (DLA). *E-mail:* mark@3arts.org; info@dlartists.com. *Website:* www.dlartists.com. *Address:* c/o eighth blackbird, 5315 North Clark Street, #104, Chicago, IL 60640-2113, USA (office). *Telephone:* (773) 484-8811 (office). *Fax:* (773) 961-7328 (office). *E-mail:* kap@eighthblackbird.org (office). *Website:* www.eighthblackbird.org (office).

KAPLAN, Mark, BMus; American violinist; *Professor of Violin, Jacobs School of Music*; b. 30 Dec. 1953, Boston, Mass. *Education:* studied with Dorothy DeLay at Juilliard School, New York. *Career:* US engagements 1973–; performances with Cleveland, Philadelphia, Los Angeles, New York, St Louis, Pittsburgh, Baltimore Orchestras etc.; Summer Festivals of Seattle Chamber Music, Aspen, Blossom, Ambler, Grant Park and Santa Fe; European career 1975–; concerts with Berlin Philharmonic and Klaus Tennstedt; engagements in England and Israel with Rudolf Barshai, and thereafter with all major European Orchestras; gave European premiere of Marc Neikrug's Violin Concerto with Hallé Orchestra; BBC Promenade Concerts and Concerts with Royal Philharmonic in London and Italy; played with Queensland Orchestra, Brisbane 2009, also Perth, Sydney, Melbourne, Auckland, Malaysian Philharmonic, Singapore Symphony Orchestra; associations with conductors Lawrence Foster, Marek Janowski, Michael Gielen and Charles Dutoit; piano recitals in Europe and America; recitals with with Golub/Kaplan/Carr Trio, with Weiss-Kaplan-Newman Trio since 2001 playing each season in USA and Europe; trio toured Italy and UK 1994–95, appearing at St John's Smith Square; fmr Prof., UCLA; Prof. of Violin, Indiana Univ. Jacobs School of Music 2005–. *Recordings:* Bach Sonatas and Partitas (twice), concertos of Paganini, Wieniawski, Berg, Bartok, Stravinsky, Lalo, Nono, Viotti; trios of Brahms, Schubert, Smetana, Tchaikowsky, Dvorak, Mendelssohn, contemporary works; violin/piano works of Sarasate, Schumann, Bartok, Schubert. *Honours:* Fritz Kreisler Memorial Award, Award of Special Distinction, Leventritt Competition 1973. *Address:* Indiana University Jacobs School of Music, 1201

East Third Street, Bloomington, IN 47405, USA (office). *Telephone:* (812) 855-3139 (office). *E-mail:* mkmk@indiana.edu (office). *Current Management:* c/o Sulivan Sweetland, 1 Hillgate Place, Balham Hill, London, SW12 9ER, England. *Telephone:* (20) 8772-3470. *Fax:* (20) 8673-8959. *E-mail:* info@sulivansweetland.co.uk. *Website:* www.sulivansweetland.co.uk.

KARABITS, Kirill; Ukrainian conductor; *Principal Conductor,* ; b. Dec. 1976, Kiev; s. of Ivan Karabits. *Education:* Lysenko Music School, Nat. Tchaikovsky Music Acad., Int. Bach Acad., Stuttgart, Musikhochschule, Vienna. *Career:* conducting debut with Kiev Camerata, becoming Prin. Conductor 1995–99; Asst Conductor, Budapest Festival Orchestra 1998–2000; Assoc. Conductor, Orchestre Philharmonique de Radio France 2002–05; Prin. Guest Conductor, Orchestre Philharmonique de Strasbourg 2004; Prin. Guest Conductor, Ukraine Nat. Opera; Musical Dir, Kiev Int. Music Festival; debut with Bournemouth Symphony Orchestra 2006, Prin. Conductor 2009–; Artistic Dir I,CULTURE Orchestra of Poland 2014–; also noted for conducting opera, with companies including Opéra Nat. du Rhin, Glyndebourne Festival Opera, Geneva Opera, Opéra National de Lorraine, Opéra de Lyon. *Honours:* Nikolai Malko Prize (Denmark), Prix de la Fondation Européenne, Maria Gusella Prize (Italy). *Current Management:* Harrison Parrott, 5–6 Albion Court, London, W6 0QT, England. *Telephone:* (20) 7229-9166. *Fax:* (20) 7221-5042. *E-mail:* info@harrisonparrott.co.uk. *Website:* www.harrisonparrott.com. *Address:* Bournemouth Symphony Orchestra, 2 Seldown Lane, Poole, Dorset BH15 1UF, England (office). *Website:* www.bsolive.com (office).

KARADAGLIĆ, Miloš, BMus (Hons), MMus; Montenegrin guitarist; b. 1983. *Education:* Royal Acad. of Music, London with Michael Lewin. *Career:* began playing the guitar aged eight; has performed in concerts with London Philharmonic Orchestra; recitals at Lucerne Festival and in London, Windsor and other venues in UK 2008, concerts with London Philharmonic Orchestra (Concierto de Aranjuez) 2009; recitals in Amsterdam, Rome, Switzerland and London's Spitalfields Festival 2009; concerto engagements in London, Leeds and Singapore 2010; recitals at Wigmore Hall, London, Vienna Konzerthaus with Rolando Villazón, Schloss Elmau (Germany), Gstaad (Menuhin), Cheltenham, Spitalfields, iTunes (London) and Norwich festivals, as well as St Martin-in-the-Fields and Southampton, Bristol and Scotland 2011; recital appearances at the Wigmore Hall, in Munich, at Schloss Elmau and at the Brighton and Boca Raton (Florida) festivals 2011; Meaker Junior Fellow, RAM (first guitarist). *Recordings include:* Miloš Karadaglić Live at the iTunes Festival 2010, The Guitar 2011, Mediterráneo (ECHO Klassik Award for Newcomer of the Year/Guitar 2012) 2011. *Honours:* Julian Bream Prize 2005, Winner, Maisie Lewis Young Artist Platform 2006, Prince's Prize (presented by HRH Prince Charles) 2007, Silver Medal, Worshipful Company of Musicians, London 2007, Gramophone Award for Specialist Classical Chart (The Guitar) 2011, Gramophone Award for Young Artist of the Year 2011, Classic BRIT Award – MasterCard's Breakthrough Artist of the Year 2012. *Current Management:* c/o IMG Artists, Carnegie Hall Tower, 152 West 57th Street, 5th floor, New York, NY 10019, USA. *Telephone:* (212) 994-3500. *Fax:* (212) 994-3550. *E-mail:* rjaroff@imgartists.com. *Website:* www.imgartists.com; www.milosguitar.com.

KARAMÜRSEL, Arin, MA; Turkish pianist; b. 19 Oct. 1936, Istanbul; d. of Abdülkadir Karamürsel and Azade Karamürsel. *Education:* Conservatory, Istanbul, Acad. Marguerita Long, Paris and Tchaikovsky Conservatory, Moscow. *Career:* began playing the piano aged eight 1944; first performance Istanbul 1948; has performed in many countries including Turkey, France, UK, Luxembourg, Switzerland, Finland, Poland, Mexico, Cuba, Japan, People's Republic of China, Kuwait, Bahrain, Qatar, UAE; has played with orchestras including Orchestre Lamoureux 1966; soloist State Symphony Orchestra, Istanbul 1988–. *Honours:* First Prize Tchaikovsky Conservatory 1980, Bright Interpretation Award, Cervantino Festival, Mexico 1983. *Address:* Ihlamur Yolu, Güney Apt 83/7, Tešvikiye, Istanbul, Turkey. *Telephone:* (1) 2300532.

KARASEV, Grigory; Russian singer (bass); b. 1960. *Career:* concert and opera performances throughout Russia; appearances at the Kirov Opera, St Petersburg, from 1987 as Ferrando in Il Trovatore, Mozart's Antonio (Figaro), Raimondo in Lucia di Lammermoor and Rossini's Don Basilio; Other roles include Don Pasquale, Orlik in Mazeppa, Nikitich in Boris Godunov and Storm Wind in Rimsky-Korsakov's Kashchei the Immortal; Guest appearances with New Israel Opera and La Fenice, Venice; sang with the Kirov Opera in Summer Season at Covent Garden, 2000.

KARASIK, Gita; American pianist; b. 14 Dec. 1952, San Francisco, CA; m. Lee Caplin 1975. *Education:* Juilliard School with Rosina Lhevinne, San Francisco Conservatory of Music, studied with Karl Ulrich Schnabel, Lev Schorr. *Career:* debut, San Francisco/SF Symphony 1958; NYC/Carnegie Hall 1969; guest soloist, The Bell Telephone Hour, NBC 1963; guest soloist, San Francisco Symphony 1958, 1969, 1972, 1974; Los Angeles Philharmonic 1971; St Louis Symphony 1974–75; Boston Pops Orchestra with Arthur Fiedler 1975; Indianapolis Symphony 1972, 1976; Atlanta Symphony 1972; Singapore Symphony 1980–81; Hong Kong Philharmonic 1980–82; tours of Latin America, Far East, Europe, USA; film scores for Andy Warhol: Made in China 1986, The Serpent and the Rainbow 1988, To Die For 1989, Son of Darkness 1992. *Compositions:* Concerto for Gita Karasik No. 2 by Andrew Imbrie, as first prize Ford Foundation Artists Award, World Premiere with Indianapolis Symphony for Bicentennial 1976.

KARAYANIS, Plato Steven; American opera administrator, singer and consultant; b. 26 Dec. 1928, Pittsburgh, Pa; s. of Theodore Karayanis and Thalia Karayanis; m. Dorothy Krebill Karayanis. *Education:* Carnegie Mellon Univ., Curtis Inst. of Music, Hamburg State Opera, Germany. *Career:* six years as a leading baritone in European houses; Dir of Rehearsal Dept, San Francisco Opera; Asst Stage Dir and Admin., Metropolitan Opera Nat. Co. 1965–67; Exec. Vice-Pres. of Affiliate Artists Inc. 1967–77; Gen. Dir Dallas Opera 1977–2000, presiding over a complete Ring cycle, world premiere of Argento's The Aspern Papers 1988, US premieres of operatic works by Vivaldi and Falla, co-commissioned Argento's Dream of Valentino and Mark-Anthony Turnage's The Silver Tassie; Chair. Opera America 1993–97; consultant, Palm Beach Opera 2002–08, Opera San Antonio 2013; Past Chair. of Alumni Council, Bd of Overseers, Curtis Inst. of Music. *Honours:* Hon. mem. Bd of Dirs, Santa Fe Opera; Award for Excellence in the Creative Arts, Dallas Historical Soc. 1993, TACA Award for Excellence in the Performing Arts 1998, Alumni Award, Curtis Inst. of Music 2012. *Address:* 46 Camino Espejo, Santa Fe, NM 87507, USA (home). *Telephone:* (505) 424-8174 (office). *Fax:* (505) 424-8174 (home). *E-mail:* skarayan@swbell.net (home).

KARCHIN, Louis, BMus, PhD; American composer and conductor; *Professor of Music, New York University*; b. 8 Sept. 1951, Pa; m. Julie Sirota 1987; two d. *Education:* Eastman School of Music, Harvard Univ. *Career:* comms from Fromm Foundation at Harvard 1994, 2003, Serge Koussevitzky Music Foundation 1998; Prof. of Music, New York Univ.; Music Dir, Orchestra of the League of Composers. *Compositions:* Capriccio for violin and seven instruments 1979, Duo for violin and cello 1981, Viola Variations 1982, Songs of John Keats 1984, Songs of Distance and Light 1988, Sonata for cello and piano 1989, String Quartet 1990, Galactic Folds for chamber ensemble 1992, String Quartet No. 2 1994, Sonata da Camera for violin and piano 1995, Rustic Dances 1995, Rhapsody for orchestra 1996, Cascades 1997, American Visions: Two Songs on Poems of Yevgeny Yevtushenko 1998, Romulus (one-act opera) 1990, Quartet for percussion 2000, Deux Poèmes de Mallarmé 2001, Songs – Meditation, Interlude, Echoes, Memory, Carmen de Bohème, To the Sun 2001–03, Voyages for alto saxophone and piano 2001, Orpheus, a Masque for baritone, chamber ensemble and dancers 2003, Roethke Songs 2004, Rhapsody for violin and piano 2005, The Gods of Winter for baritone and chamber ensemble 2006, Chesapeake Festival Overture 2006, Three Epigrams for piano 2008, Chamber Symphony 2009, Evocations for clarinet and piano 2010, Two Lyrics for solo cello 2012. *Honours:* Nat. Endowment for the Arts Award 1983, 1985, 2009, Hinrichsen Award, American Acad. of Arts and Letters 1985, Koussevitzky-Tanglewood Award 1971, Hecksher Foundation Prize 1999, Goddard Lieberson Award, American Acad. of Arts and Letters 2001, Barlow Endowment Comm. 2001, Guggenheim Foundation Fellowship 2011, Andrew Imbrie Award, American Acad. of Arts and Letters 2012. *Current Management:* c/o Howard Stokar, 870 West End Avenue, New York, NY 10025, USA. *Telephone:* (212) 866-5798. *E-mail:* hstokar@stokar.com. *Address:* 24 Waverly Place, Room 268, New York, NY 10003, USA (office). *Telephone:* (212) 998-8303 (office). *E-mail:* LSK1@nyu.edu (office). *Website:* louiskarchin.com.

KARCZYKOWSKI, Ryszard; singer (tenor); b. 6 April 1942, Tczew, Poland. *Education:* studied in Gdansk with Halina Mickiewiczowna. *Career:* sang in Gdansk and Stettin, then at the Landestheater Dessau (debut as Beppe in Pagliacci 1969); other roles included Tamino, Ferrando, Fenton and Rodolfo; sang in Leipzig from 1974, then in Berlin, Dresden (Tamino and Lensky), Moscow, Zürich, Vienna, New York, Rome, Prague and Aix-en-Provence; Covent Garden debut 1977, as Alfred in Die Fledermaus, returned as the Duke of Mantua, Ferrando and Alwa in the first local production of Berg's Lulu 1981; sang in the 1981 stage premiere of Prokofiev's Maddalena (Graz) and the same year sang in Haydn's Orlando Paladino, at the Vienna Festival; other roles include Ernesto, Nemorino, Rinuccio, Lionel (Martha), Jenik (Bartered Bride), Belmonte, Macduff and Elemer in Arabella; further appearances in Boston (Duke of Mantua 1981), Washington, Leningrad, Los Angeles, Zagreb and Lisbon; sang in Rigoletto with the company of the Deutsche Oper Berlin at the Wiesbaden Festival 1989; Star Guest at the Vienna Opernball 1998. *Recordings include:* Szymanowski's 3rd Symphony, The Bells by Rachmaninov, Shostakovich 13th Symphony; Die Lustige Witwe and Die Fledermaus; Arias and Duets From Celebrated Operas, 1991; Laudate Dominum Omnes Gentes, 1992; A. Schoenberg–Von Heute auf Morgen, 1997; A. Berg–Lulu, 1998; F. Lehar–Gold and Silver, 1999.

KARIS, Aleck, BM; pianist; b. 21 Jan. 1945, Washington DC, USA. *Education:* Manhattan School with Charles Wuorinen, Juilliard School with Beveridge Webster, studied with Artur Balsam and William Daghlian. *Career:* Latin American debut 1981 at São Paulo; New York debut 1984, playing Chopin, Schumann, Stravinsky and Elliott Carter; has premiered works by Mario Davidovsky, Milton Babbitt and Morton Subotnick; mem., Speculum Musicae from 1983 and has performed with the Contemporary Chamber Ensemble, New York, St Luke's Chamber Ensemble and the Group Contemporary Music; Assoc. in Music Performance, Columbia Univ. from 1983. *Honours:* prizewinner Rockefeller Foundation Int. Competition 1978, Fromm Foundation grant 1983.

KÄRKKÄINEN, Paivi, Lic.Phil; Finnish media industry executive and opera company director; *General Director, Finnish National Opera*; b. 1955. *Education:* Univ. of Tampere, Ohio State Univ., USA, Helsinki School of Econs and Business Admin. *Career:* early career as Lecturer, Univ. of Tampere, also journalist, TV host, elocution teacher; Head of Programming and Deputy Programme Dir for TV2, YLE Finnish Broadcasting Co. 1994–2001, Dir of Programming for TV2 and mem. TV Man. Group 2002–06, Deputy to the Dir and Head of Programming for Fact and Culture YLE 2006–07; Gen. Dir Finnish Nat. Opera 2007–. *Address:* Finnish National Opera, Helsinginkatu 58, POB 176, 00251, Helsinki, Finland (office). *Telephone:* (9) 40302200 (office). *Fax:* (9) 40302202 (office). *E-mail:* paivi .karkainen@opera.fi (office). *Website:* www.operafin.fi (office).

KARLSEN, Turid; singer (soprano); b. 1961, Oslo, Norway. *Education:* Maastricht Conservatory, The Netherlands. *Career:* prizewinner at the 1984 Francisco Vinas Competition, Barcelona and sang at the Weikersheim Festival 1985 as Romilda in Xerxes and Gluck's Euridice; Karlsruhe Opera from 1986 in Wiener Blut and as Donna Elvira, which she has also sung in Stuttgart, Wiesbaden and Düsseldorf; sang in the premiere of Graf Mirabeau by Matthus at Stuttgart 1989; guest at Dresden 1989 as Isotta in Schweigsame Frau and Luxembourg 1991 as Butterfly; other roles include Mozart's Countess and Pamina, Mimi, Natasha in War and Peace and Violetta; concert engagements include Bach's St Matthew Passion at Bogotá.

KARLSSON, Erik Mikael; Swedish composer; b. 10 Dec. 1967, Nynäshamn. *Education:* studied with Tamas Ungvary, Anders Blomquist and others. *Career:* Composer, EMS, Stockholm, Swedish Broadcasting Corporation, Danish Inst. for Electro-acoustic Music, Århus, also in Berlin and France; appearances at festivals and concerts for electro-acoustic music in Europe and elsewhere and many int. radio appearances. *Compositions:* Threads and Cords 1990, Anchorings, Arrows 1992, La Disparition de L'Azur 1993, Interiors and Interplays 1994, Épitaphe pour Iqbal Masih 1995. *Publications:* Circle Almost Closing, and Fylkingen–60 Years of Experimental Art 1994; contrib. various articles on contemporary music in Nutida Musik.

KARLSSON, Lars Olof, DipMus; Finnish composer; b. 24 Jan. 1953, Jomala, Åland; m. Helena Hartikainen 1994; one s. one d. *Education:* Sibelius Acad., Hochschule der Künste, Berlin. *Career:* critic, Hufvudstadsbladet 1982–89; Lecturer, Sibelius Acad. 1983–; co-founder, Åland Culture Festival 1983; mem. Soc. of Finnish Composers; bd mem., Scandinavian Guitar Festival 1986–. *Compositions:* Five Aphorisms for piano 1973, Med Havet (song cycle) for baritone and piano 1976, Canto Drammatico for solo violin 1980, Concerto for violin and orchestra 1993, Suite for Helena for wind quintet 1994, Toccata, Variations and Fugue on the Chorale Den Blomstertid Nu Kommer for organ 1994, Ludus Latrunculorum (oratorio) 1996, String Quartet 1997, Two Love Scenes and a Daydream for voice, soprano saxophone and big band 1997. *Honours:* Svenska Kulturfonden grant 1986, State Artists grant 1995.

KARNÉUS, Katarina; Swedish singer (mezzo-soprano); b. 1965, Stockholm. *Education:* Trinity Coll. of Music, London, Nat. Opera Studio. *Career:* varied concert repertoire including Beethoven's Ninth with Frans Brüggen and the Hallé Orchestra, Mozart's C Minor Mass in the Salzburg Festival with Roger Norrington, Les Nuits d'Eté and a Sylvester Concert with the Filharmonisch Orkest and Grant Llewellyn, Rossini-Mozart programme with Nicholas McGegan and the Hanover Band, Pergolesi Stabat Mater with the Netherlands Chamber Orchestra and Hartmut Haenchen and a concert at Buckingham Palace with Franz Welser-Möst; BBC Prom debut with Rafael Frühbeck de Burgos and Edinburgh Festival debut with Charles Mackerras; appearances at Royal Albert Hall with David Willcocks and at Royal Festival Hall with the Bach Choir; broadcast of Lieder eines fahrenden Gesellen with Grant Llewellyn and the Ulster Orchestra; two concerts with Scottish Chamber Orchestra; South Bank debut in Purcell Room with a programme of Spanish and Scandinavian songs; Wigmore Hall recital as part of the Voices series; for Welsh Nat. Opera (WNO): Angelina in La Cenerentola, Cherubino in Le nozze di Figaro and Rosina in Il Barbiere di Siviglia; Sesto in La Clemenza di Tito, Mercédès in Carmen for ENO and Opéra de Paris; Rosina and the title role in Carmen for Opéra Comique, Paris; The Page in Salome for Lyric Opera of Chicago; Tamiri in Il Re Pastore for Netherlands Opera; further engagements include Sesto in La Clemenza di Tito for WNO; debut with Glyndebourne Festival Opera as Dorabella; Cherubino at La Monnaie; Varvara in Katya Kabanova for Metropolitan Opera; returned to the Bastille in 1999 to sing Dorabella, to the Opéra-Comique for Carmen and as Annio in La Clemenza di Tito at Bayerische Staatsoper; returned to WNO as Octavian in Der Rosenkavalier in 2000; Season 2000–01 as Gluck's Orpheus for WNO, as Dorabella at Munich and engaged as Olga in Eugene Onegin, New York Met; also sang La Belle Hélène, Châtelet, Paris 2001, Annio in La Clemenza di Tito at Covent Garden 2002, Sesto in Giulio Cesare for Glyndebourne 2006, Brangöne in Tristan und Isolde for Glyndebourne 2007, Composer in Ariadne auf Naxos, Geneva 2007, Elisabetta in Maria Stuarda for Staatsoper Berlin 2007 and title role of Arianne et Barbe-Blue, Frankfurt 2008. *Recordings:* R. Strauss, Mahler, Marx, Lieder, Sibelius Songs, Szymanowski Love Songs of Hafiz with CBSO and Sir Simon Raffle, Grieg Songs. *Honours:* Christine Nilsson Award 1994, Winner, Cardiff Singer of the World Competition 1995. *Current Management:* Ingpen & Williams, 7 St George's Court, 131 Putney Bridge Road, London, SW15 2PA, England. *Telephone:* (20) 8874-3222. *Fax:* (20) 8877-3113. *E-mail:* info@ingpen.co.uk. *Website:* www.ingpen.co.uk.

KAROLYI, Sandor, DipMus; Hungarian violinist and academic; b. 24 Sept. 1931, Budapest; m. 1st Suzanne Godefroid 1954; two s. one d.; m. 2nd Regina Bauer 1998; one s. *Education:* Franz Liszt Music Acad., Budapest, Music Conservatory of Brussels, studied with Ede Zathureczky, Leo Weiner, Antal Molnar and André Gertler. *Career:* debut at Franz Liszt Acad. 1941; violin solo, Opera House in Frankfurt 1956; Prof., Musikhochschule, Frankfurt am Main, Akad. für Tonkunst Darmstadt; currently First Solo Violin, Frankfurter Opernhaus und Museuumsorchester; concerts for the BBC and broadcasting cos in Europe; TV appearances in Germany, Japan, the Philippines and Australia; mem. Deutsche Bachsolisten. *Recordings:* Paul Hindemith: four Violin Sonatas with Werner Hoppstock, piano, and Károlyi String Quartet recorded Quartets Nos 2 and 6 plus the Clarinet-Quartet of Paul Hindemith; Max Reger: Violin Sonatas A and C major with Suzanne Godefroid, piano; Prelude and Fugas for violin solo; Giuseppe Tartini Devil's Trill. *Publications:* Gustav Mahler Orchestra studies for 10 symphonies 1989. *Honours:* Diploma Contests in Geneva 1947, Budapest 1948, London 1953, Contemporary Contest, Darmstadt 1952, Vieuxtemps Prize, Belgium 1959, Médaille Eugène Ysaye, Brussels 1967. *Address:* Dehnhardtstrasse 30, 60433 Frankfurt am Main, Germany (home). *E-mail:* sandor.karolyi@t-online.de.

KARPATI, Janos, PhD, DSc; Hungarian musicologist and academic (retd); b. 11 July 1932, Budapest. *Education:* Ferenc Liszt Acad., Budapest. *Career:* folk music research in Morocco 1957–58, in Japan 1988; recording production, Hungaroton 1959–61; apptd Head Librarian and Lecturer, Ferenc Liszt Acad. of Music, Budapest 1961, Prof. of Musicology 1983–; Vice Pres. Int. Asscn of Music Libraries 1980–86; Chair. Hungarian Musicological Soc. 1998–2005. *Recording:* Kagura: Japanese Shinto Ritual Music. *Publications:* A. Schoenberg 1963, Muzsikalo zenetortenet vol. II 1965, vol. IV 1973, Bartók String Quartets 1975, Music of the East 1981, Bartók's Chamber Music 1994, Music and Myth in the Japanese Ritual Tradition 1998, Bartók Analysis 2003, Képes Magyar Zenetörténet 2004, Music in Hungary: An Illustrated History 2011. *Honours:* Erkel Prize 1971, Grand Prize Hungarian Artist 1995, Medal of the American Liszt Soc. 1996, Széchenyi Prize 2005. *Address:* Egressy út 178/D, Budapest 1149, Hungary (office). *Telephone:* 20-4921807 (mobile) (office); (1) 325-5747 (home). *E-mail:* janos.karpati@t-online.hu (office).

KARR, Gary; American double bass player; b. 20 Nov. 1941, Los Angeles, CA. *Education:* studied with Herman Reinshagen, Warren Benfield and Stuart Sankey. *Career:* debut in New York 1962 in concert with Leonard Bernstein, and at New York Town Hall; European tour 1964, playing at Wigmore Hall London; founder, Int. Inst. for the String Bass 1967; teaching appointments at Juilliard School, Yale School of Music, Indiana Univ., New England Conservatory and Hartt School of Music, Hartford 1976; formed duo with keyboard player, Harmon Lewis 1972, tours of Europe, the Far East, USA and Canada; appearances as soloist with the Chicago Symphony, New York Philharmonic, English Chamber Orchestra, London Symphony and Toronto Symphony; composers who have written for him include Vittorio Giannini, Henze, Wilfred Josephs, Lalo Schifrin, John Downey and Gunther Schuller; debut tour of Australia 1987–88; formed Karr Doublebass Foundation Inc. 1983, to provide valuable instruments for talented players. *Television includes:* Gary Karr and Friends (CBC, Canada), Bass is Beautiful (Channel 4, UK). *Recordings:* Transcriptions of Paganini's Moses Fantasy and Dvořák Cello Concerto, Concerto by Lalo Schifrin.

KARSKI, Dominik, BA, MMus; Australian/Polish composer; b. 24 June 1972, Szczebrzeszyn, Poland. *Education:* West Australian Conservatorium of Music, Queensland Conservatorium, Brisbane. *Career:* freelance composer; lived in Australia 1991–2006; instrumental works from solo to orchestra commissioned and performed in Australia, N America, Asia and Europe; radio broadcasts in Australia and Europe; participant in World New Music Days 'Trans-it', Switzerland 2004. *Compositions:* instrumental works from solo to orchestra include: La Musique (aprés Henri Matisse) 1995, The Seventh Star 1996, Aphrodite 1996, Floating on the River of Time 1997, Where Once Narcissus Died... 1998, The Luminous Chariot 1998, Along the Edge of Darkness 1999, The Secret Mirror 1999, Les Éruptions du Rêve 2000, Streams of Consciousness 2000, Wildchild 2000, Flexible Strings 2000, Matter of Perspective 2000, Streaming Voices 2000, Threads of Fate 2001, Glimmer 2002, Inner Stream II 2002, Galileo's Idea 2002, Beginnings To No End 2003, Streamforms 2003, Streams Within 2003, Open cluster M45 2003, Motion+-form 2003, The Impulse Within 2004, Inward 2004, Streamforms II 2004, (E)motion of forms 2005, To Remain in Change 2005, The Source Within 2006, The Outward Impulse 2007, Gates of the Irrational 2007. *Recordings:* Floating on the River of Time, West Australian Symphony Orchestra 20th Century Ensemble; Les Eruptions du Rêve, Le Nouvel Ensemble Moderne. *Honours:* ABC Young Composers' Award 1998, Ian Potter Music Commissions, Melbourne 1999, Le Nouvel Ensemble Moderne, Forum 2000, First Prize, Panufnik Int. Young Composers Competition, Kraków 2001, Albert H. Maggs Composition Award 2003. *E-mail:* dominikkarski@yahoo.pl (office). *Website:* dominikkarski.com.

KARTTUNEN, Anssi Ville; cellist; b. 30 Sept. 1960, Helsinki, Finland; m. Muriel Von Braun 1985, one d. *Education:* Sibelius Acad., Helsinki, studied with Vili Pullinen, Erkki Rautio, William Pleeth, Jacqueline du Pré, Tibor de Machula. *Career:* soloist with major Scandanavian Orchestras, also Los Angeles Philharmonic, Philharmonia Orchestra, BBC Symphony, BBC Scottish, Orchestre de Paris, Dutch Radio Orchestra, London Sinfonietta, Ensemble Modern, among others; appearances in festivals, including: Edinburgh, Lockenhaus, Salzburg, Berlin, Vienna, Venice, Strasbourg, Montpellier, Helsinki; Artistic Dir, Avanti! Chamber Orchestra 1994–98, Helsinki Biennale 1995. *Recordings include:* complete Beethoven works for cello, 20th Century Solo Cello, Concertos by Zimmermann, Hindemith, Lindberg and Saariaho with London Sinfonietta, the Los Angeles Philharmonia and Avanti!, Dutilleux: Correspondances/Cello Concerto Tout un monde lointain (Gramophone Award for Best Contemporary Recording 2013).

Honours: first prize Young Concert Artist Competition, Tunbridge Wells, England 1981, first prize and gold medal Festival des Jeunes Solistes, Bordeaux 1982.

KASAROVA, Vesselina; Bulgarian singer (mezzo-soprano); b. 1963, Stara Zagora. *Education:* Sofia Conservatory. *Career:* appearances at the Sofia National Opera as Fenena, Rosina, Preziosilla and Dorabella; mem. of the Zürich Opera, 1988–91 as Annio in Clemenza di Tito, Stephano in Roméo et Juliette, and Anna in Les Troyens; Salzburg Festival 1991–92 as Annio and Rossini's Tancredi; further appearances as Rosina at the Vienna Staatsoper in 1991 and the Geneva Opera, and as Pippo in La Gazza Ladra at Barcelona in 1992; Season 1996 with Mozart's Zerlina at the Salzburg Festival and Idamante at Florence; season 1998 as Cenerentola at Pesaro and Charlotte in a concert performance of Werther at the Deutsche Oper Berlin; Octavian at New York Met, 2000; season 2000–01 as Mozart's Idamante at Salzburg and Sesto at Covent Garden (returned, 2002); Giovanna Seymour in Anna Bolena at Zürich and Rosina for Chicago Lyric Opera; concert repertory includes Mozart's Requiem in Milan, and Agnese in Bellini's Beatrice di Tenda in Vienna. *Recordings include:* Romeo in Bellini's I Capuleti 1998. *Current Management:* c/o Hilbert Artists Management, Maximilianstrasse 22, 80539 Munich, Germany; c/o Opéra et Concert, 37 rue de la Chaussée d'Antin, 75009 Paris, France. *Telephone:* (89) 2907470 (Hilbert); (1) 42-96-18-18 (O&C). *Fax:* (89) 29074790 (Hilbert); (1) 42-96-18-00 (O&C). *E-mail:* agentur@hilbert.de; agence@opera-concert.com. *Website:* www.hilbert.de; www.opera-concert.com; www.kasarova.com.

KASHKASHIAN, Kim; American violist and teacher; b. 31 Aug. 1952, Detroit. *Education:* Peabody Conservatory of Music, Baltimore with Walter Trampler and Karen Tuttle. *Career:* various engagements as a soloist with leading orchestras in North America and Europe; recitals, chamber music appearances notably with the Tokyo and Guarneri Quartets and the Beaux Arts Trio; faculty mem. New School of Music, Philadelphia 1981–86, Mannes Coll. of Music, New York 1983–86, Indiana Univ. School of Music, Bloomington 1985–87, Staatliche Hochschule für Musik, Freiburg 1989–2000, New England Conservatory of Music 2000–; has prepared transcriptions and commissioned various works for viola including music by Betsy Jolas, Schnittke and Sofia Gubaidulina. *Recordings include:* as a soloist and chamber music artist, Mozart's Sinfonia Concertante and Divertimento, Hindemith's Viola Sonatas, Shostakovich's Sonata op. 147, Britten, Penderecki, Kancheli and Schnittke, Bartók, Eötvös, Kurtág concerti, works by Linda Bouchard and Paul Chihara, Bach Sonatas for viola, Brahms' Sonatas, Voci 2002, Hayren 2003, Monodia 2004, Asturiana 2007, Neharot, Neharot 2009, Thomas Larcher: Madhares 2010, Kurtág & Ligeti: Music For Viola (Grammy Award for Best Classical Instrumental Solo 2013) 2012. *Honours:* Cannes Classical Award 2001. *Address:* New England Conservatory, 290 Huntington Avenue, Boston, MA 02115, USA (office). *Telephone:* (617) 585-1101 (office). *Fax:* (617) 585-1115 (office). *Website:* necmusic.edu/faculty (office).

KASPSZYK, Jacek; Polish conductor; *Music and Artistic Director, Warsaw Philharmonic Orchestra*; b. 10 Aug. 1952. *Education:* Acad. of Music, Warsaw. *Career:* debut Warsaw Nat. Opera 1975; Prin. Guest Conductor Deutsche Oper am Rhein, Düsseldorf 1976–77; debut Berlin Philharmonic and New York 1978; Prin. Conductor Polish Nat. Radio Symphony Orchestra, Katowice 1978–80, Music Dir 1980–82, 2009–12; Prin. Conductor and Artistic Adviser, North Netherlands Orchestra 1991–95; Prin. Guest Conductor Polish Philharmonic 1996–; Artistic and Musical Dir Polish National Opera, Warsaw 1998–2005, Artistic and Gen. Dir 2002–05; Artistic Dir Witold Lutosławski Philharmonic Symphony Orchestra, Wrocław 2006–; Music and Artistic Dir Warsaw Philharmonic Orchestra 2013–; has conducted French Nat., Stockholm Philharmonic, Bavarian Radio Symphony, Rotterdam, Czech Philharmonic Orchestras; conducted Detroit Opera and San Diego Symphony Orchestra 1982; Prin. Guest Conductor English Sinfonia 1992–; has toured with the Yomiuri Nippon Symphony and performed with Tokyo and Hong Kong Philarmonics, New Zealand, San Diego, Cincinnati, Winnipeg, Calgary Symphonies, and Detroit Opera. *Music includes:* operas conducted include: Queen of Spades (Düsseldorf) 1977, Haunted Manor (Detroit) 1982, A Midsummer Night's Dream (Lyon) 1983, Eugene Onegin (Bordeaux) 1985, The Magic Flute (Opéra Comique, Paris and Stockholm) 1986, Seven Deadly Sins (Lyon) 1987, Die Fledermaus (Scottish Opera), Flying Dutchman (Opera North, UK) 1988, Barber of Seville (English Nat. Opera) 1992, Der Rosenkavalier (Warsaw) 1997, Don Giovanni (Warsaw) 1999, The Nutcracker (Zürich) 2000; numerous productions and recordings with Teatr Wielki, Warsaw, including performances in Luxembourg, Lvov, Beijing, Paphos, Japan (tour) and Bolshoi Theatre in Moscow; recordings with London Symphony Orchestra, London Philharmonic Orchestra, Royal Philharmonic, Philharmonic Orchestras, Warsaw Symphony Orchestra; several other recordings. *Honours:* III Prize, Karajan Competition 1977, 2011 Elgar Soc. Medal 2011. *Current Management:* International Classical Artists, Dunstan House, 14a St Cross Street, London, EC1N 8XA, England. *E-mail:* info@icartists.co.uk. *Address:* Warsaw Philharmonic, Jasna 5 Street, 00-950 Warsaw, Poland (office). *E-mail:* sekretariat@filharmonia.pl (office). *Website:* filharmonia.pl/strona-glowna_en (office).

KASRASHVILI, Makvala; Georgian singer (soprano); *Artistic Director, Bolshoi Theatre Opera*; b. 13 March 1948, Kutaisi; d. of Nina Nanikashvili and Filimon Kasrashvili; m. (divorced). *Education:* Tbilisi Conservatory. *Career:* joined Bolshoi Co., Moscow 1968, Artistic Dir Bolshoi Theatre Opera Dept 2000–; has performed internationally, including Covent Garden, London,

Metropolitan Opera, New York, Verona, Vienna State Opera. *Roles include:* Lisa, Tatyana, Maria, Tosca, Lauretta, Donna Anna, Leonora, Aïda, Turandot, Amelia. *Honours:* Order For Services to the Fatherland 2001; First Prize, Transcaucasian Contest for Musicians and Singers, Tbilisi 1964, Grand Prix, Montreal Vocal Competition 1973, Merited Artist of Russian Fed. 1975, People's Artist of Georgian SSR 1980, Zakhar Paliashvili Georgian SSR State Prize 1983, People's Artist of the USSR 1986, State Prize of Russia 1998. *Address:* Bolshoi Theatre, Moscow 125009, Teatralnaya Pl. 1, Russia. *Telephone:* (495) 200-58-00 (home). *Website:* www.bolshoi.ru (office).

KASSEL, Wolfgang; singer (tenor); b. 1930, Germany. *Career:* sang at the Flensburg Opera 1954–57; engagements at Mainz 1957–58, Wuppertal 1958–60, Krefeld 1960–66, Bielefeld 1967–74; sang at Nuremberg 1974–80 and made guest appearances at Munich 1973–76; appeared as Tannhäuser at Covent Garden 1973, Siegmund at Rouen 1975; other roles have included Lohengrin, Walther, Siegfried, Florestan, Max, Herod in Salome and Bacchus (Ariadne auf Naxos); further engagements at Toulouse, Oslo, Würzburg and elsewhere in Europe.

KASTON, Motti; Israeli singer (baritone); b. 1965, Tel-Aviv. *Education:* Tel-Aviv Conservatory, Mannes College of Music, New York. *Career:* sang Schaunard in La Bohème at Tel-Aviv, 1987; Germont and other roles at the Metropolitan, New York; Philadelphia, 1991, as Malatesta in Don Pasquale: Staatsoper Stuttgart from 1991, as Sharpless in Madama Butterfly, Dandini in La Cenerentola, Wolfram in Tannhäuser and Rossini's Figaro; Opéra-Comique, Paris, 1991, as Alphonse in La Favorite; Tel-Aviv, 1994, as Valentin in Faust and Stuttgart, 1996, as Roderick in La Chute de la Maison Usher, by Debussy; Season 1998 as Dandini in La Cenerentola at Tel-Aviv. *Website:* www.mottikaston.com.

KASYAN, Anna; Georgian singer (soprano); b. 7 Oct. 1981. *Education:* State Conservatory, Tbilisi, Conservatoire Nat. Supérieur de Musique et de Danse, Paris. *Career:* began musical studies on piano and violin; performed concerts and recitals in Paris, at the Ile de France, Opéra de Montpellier, in San Remo, Festival de l'Orangerie de Sceaux, Festival d'Été de Draguignan, in Canada, Olympus Music Festival, St Petersburg, Brescia Festival, Italy; opera repertoire includes Cleopatra in Julius Caesar, Susanna in Le Nozze di Figaro, Zerlina in Don Giovanni, Despina in Così fan tutte, Juliette in Romeo et Juliette, Ännchen in Der Freischütz, Adina in L'Elisir d'Amore. *Honours:* First Prize Int. Autumn Symphony Competition 2004, First Prize and Teresa Berganza Special Prize Julian Gayarre Int. Singing Contest, Pamplona, Spain 2006, W A Mozart Prize for best in opera category Unisa Int. Voice Competition, S Africa 2006. *Current Management:* c/o Ariën Arts & Music Management, Groot-Brittanniëlaan 27, 9000 Ghent, Belgium. *Telephone:* (9) 3303990. *Fax:* (9) 2303523. *E-mail:* arien@pandora.be.

KASZA, Katalin; Hungarian singer (soprano); b. 1942, Szeged. *Education:* Ferenc Liszt Acad., Budapest. *Career:* debut as Abigail in Nabucco, Budapest State Opera 1967; Judith in film of Duke Bluebeard's Castle and guest performer as Judith in the Edinburgh Festval 1973 and at many other int. venues; Brünnhilde in Wagner's Ring at Covent Garden Opera House, London 1974–76, and at Geneva and several German cities 1977–78; US debut in Duke Bluebeard's Castle, Los Angeles, CA 1980; sang Eudossia in Respighi's La Fiamma at Erkel Theatre, Budapest 1989; other roles include Octavia in L'Incoronazione di Poppea, Leonore in Fidelio, Lady Macbeth, title roles of Salome and Elektra, Senta in Der fliegende Holländer, Ortrud in Lohengrin, Fricka in Rheingold, Isolde in Tristan und Isolde and Kundry in Parsifal. *Recordings:* radio and television film recording of Fidelio 1969, Judith in Duke Bluebeard's Castle 1970, in television film and the same role for the complete Bartók edition, Kundry in Parsifal 1983. *Honours:* Sofia Int. Singing Competition Best Dramatic Performer Diploma 1968, Liszt Prize 1974, Béla Bartók–Ditta Pasztory Prize 1992.

KATS-CHERNIN, Elena; Australian/Uzbek composer and lecturer; b. 4 Nov. 1957, Tashkent, Uzbekistan. *Education:* State Conservatorium of Music, NSW, Hanover Musikhochschule with Helmut Lachenmann. *Career:* resident in Australia from 1975; composer of incidental music for dance theatre in Germany 1985–93; Lecturer, New South Wales Conservatory 1995; commissions from ZKM Karlsruhe 1993, Munchener Biennale 1994, Sydney Alpha Ensemble 1995, among others; Sehrayahn Resident, Ministry for the Arts Lower Saxony 1984–85; Iphis premiered by Music Theatre Sydney 1997. *Compositions include:* Piano Concerto 1979, Bienie for orchestra 1979, In Tension for six instruments 1982, Reductions for two pianos 1983, Duo I for violin and piano 1984, Stairs for orchestra 1984, Transfer for orchestra 1990, Tast-en for piano 1991, Totschki: Dots for oboe and clarinet 1992, Clocks for 20 musicians and tape 1993, Retonica for orchestra 1993, Clip for percussion 1994, Concertino for violin and 11 players 1994, Coco's Last Collection (dance theatre) for two pianos 1994, Cadences, Deviations and Scarlatti for 14 instruments 1996, Wild Rice for cello 1996, The Schubert Blues for piano 1996, Charleston Noir for double bass quartet 1996, Purple Prelude for six instruments 1996, Russian Rad for ensemble 1996, Zoom and Zip for string orchestra 1997, Iphis (opera, after Ovid's Metamorphoses) 1997, Champagne in a Teapot for horn and 13 instruments 1997, Matricide, the musical 1998, Umcha for percussion ensemble 1998, Sonata Lost and Found for piano 1998, Stur in Dur for piano 1999, Heaven is Closed for orchestra 2000, Displaced Dances for piano and orchestra 2000, Piano Concerto No. 2 2001, Mr Barbeque (12 cabaret songs) 2002, Garden Symphony for solo voices and orchestra 2002, Wild Swans (ballet) 2002, Undertow (chamber dance-opera) 2004. *Honours:*

Sounds Australian 1996. *Address:* c/o Boosey & Hawkes, First Floor, Aldwych House, 71–91 Aldwych, London, WC2B 4HN, England (office). *Website:* www.boosey.com/katschernin.

KATZ, Martin; American pianist and academic; b. 27 Nov. 1945, Los Angeles, CA. *Education:* Univ. of Southern California at Los Angeles, studied with Gwendolyn Koldovsky. *Career:* pianist for the US Army chorus in Washington 1966–69; accompanist to singers, including José Carreras, Kiri Te Kanawa, Teresa Berganza, Katia Ricciarelli and Nicolai Gedda; concert tours of North and South America, Australia, Europe and Asia, notably with Marilyn Horne; editions of Rossini operas performed by Houston Grand Opera and at the Rossini Festival, New York 1982–83; edition of Handel's Rinaldo performed at the Ottawa Festival 1982, Metropolitan Opera 1984; Assoc. Prof., Westminster Choir Coll. 1976; Prof., Univ. of Michigan 1983.

KATZ, Paul; American cellist; b. 1941. *Career:* mem., Cleveland Quartet 1969–94; regular tours of the USA, Canada, Europe, Japan, Russia, South America, Australia, New Zealand and the Middle East; faculty mem., Eastman School, Rochester; in residence at the Aspen Music Festival, co-founding the Center for Advanced Quartet Studies; tour of the Soviet Union and five European countries 1988; season 1988–89 with appearances at the Metropolitan Museum and Alice Tully Hall, New York; concerts in Paris, London, Bonn, Prague, Lisbon and Brussels; festivals of Salzburg, Edinburgh and Lucerne; many complete Beethoven cycles and annual appearances at Lincoln Center's Mostly Mozart Festival; in addition to standard repertory, has commissioned works by John Harbison, Sergei Slonimsky, Samuel Adler, George Perle, Christopher Rouse, Toru Takemitsu, Stephen Paulus, Libby Larsen, John Corigliano and Oswaldo Golyov. *Recordings:* repertoire from Mozart to Ravel, collaborations with Alfred Brendel (Schubert Trout Quintet), Pinchas Zukerman and Bernard Greenhouse (Brahms Sextets), Emanuel Ax, Yo-Yo Ma and Richard Stoltzman, Complete Beethoven Quartets 1982. *Publication:* Interpretation problems of the Beethoven Quartets (RCA) 1982. *Address:* c/o Eastman School of Music, 26 Gibbs Street, Rochester, NY 14604, USA.

KATZ, Shelley, BMus, MMus, PhD; Canadian pianist, composer and conductor; b. 1960, Montréal. *Education:* Montréal Conservatoire, Juilliard School, New York, USA. *Career:* solo repetiteur at the Deutsche Oper am Rhein from 1987, Studienleiter in Koblenz from 1989, Kappelmeister and Asst to the Gen. Music Dir at Mainz Opera; accompanist to such singers as Nicolai Gedda, Gwyneth Jones and Jochen Kowalski; Musician-in-Residence, Int. Study Centre, Queen's Univ. *Compositions:* Drei Jüdische Lieder 1988, Eyshes Chayil 1998, Kaddish 2000. *Recordings:* Songs by Canadian Composers with D. Gilchrist, Solo Piano Works by Canadian Composers, Of Fire and Dew, 21 Baritone Songs by John Jeffreys with J. Veira, Lieder: Mozart Beethoven Schumann with J. Kowalski. *Publication:* A Description of Research into Electronically Generated Expressivity (with F. Rumsey) 1994.

KATZARAVA, Maria; Mexican singer (soprano); b. 1985, Mexico City; d. of Artchil Katzarav and Velia Hernández. *Career:* performed with Ramón Vargas, Jorge Lagunes, Rolando Villazón, Anna Netrebko, Fernando De La Mora; sang Musetta in La Bohème at Palacio de Bellas Artes, Liú in Turandot at Festival Internacional Tamaulipas; debut at Royal Opera House, Covent Garden as Juliette in Roméo et Juliette 2010; mem., Los Angeles Opera's Domingo-Thornton Young Artists Program. *Honours:* first prize, Concurso Maritza Alemán 2004, first prize and Zarzuela Prize, Plácido Domingo's Operalia Competition 2008.

KATZER, Georg; German composer; b. 10 Jan. 1935, Habelschwerdt; m. Angelika Szostak 1975, three s. *Education:* Hochschule für Musik, Berlin, AMU, Prague and Akademie der Künste. *Career:* freelance composer 1960; Prof. of Composition, Acad. of Fine Arts, Berlin. *Compositions:* chamber music, more than 10 symphonic works, solo concertos (with orchestra) for flute, oboe, piano, cello, harp and cello, electro-acoustic works, multimedia works, two ballets, three operas, Offene Landschaft for orchestra, Landschaft mit steigender flut for orchestra, Sound House (after F. Bacon's The New Atlantis) for three orchestras, organ and tape, Kommen und Gehen for woodwind quintet and piano, Aide-Memoirem (tape composition), Harpsichord Concerto, Concerto for orchestra No. 1, Baukasten for orchestra, Empfindsame Musik, Streichermusik 1.

KAUFMAN, Frederick, MMus; American composer; b. 24 March 1936, Brooklyn, NY. *Education:* Manhattan School with Vittorio Giannini, Juilliard School with Vencent Persichetti. *Career:* played trumpet in the New York City Ballet Orchestra and for various New York bands; Composer-in-Residence, Univ. of Wisconsin 1969; Dir of Music, city of Haifa, Israel 1971–72; music performed by major Israeli orchestras and dance companies; Chair of the Music Dept, Eastern Montane Coll. 1977–82; Prof. of Composition, Philadelphia Coll. of the Performing Arts 1982. *Compositions:* A Children's Opera 1967, The Nothing Ballet 1975, three Symphonies 1966, 1971, 1978, Concerto for violin and strings 1967, Interiors for violin and piano 1970, Violin Sonata 1970, And the World Goes On for percussion and ensemble 1971, three Cantatas for chorus and organ 1975, Triple Concerto 1975, Five Moods for oboe 1975, Percussion Trio 1977, Echoes for chorus, clarinet and percussion 1978, Five Fragrances for clarinet, harp and percussion 1980, When the Twain Meet for orchestra 1981, Metamorphosis for piano 1981, Southeast Fantasy for wind ensemble 1982, Mobile for string quartet 1982, Stars and Distances for spoken sounds and chorus 1981, Meditation for a Lonely Flute 1983, Kiddish Concerto for cello and strings 1984, A/V Slide Show for

trombone 1984, Masada for chorus, clarinet and percussion 1985. *Publication:* The African Roots of Jazz 1979.

KAUFMANN, Jonas; German singer (tenor); b. 10 July 1969, Munich; m. Margarete Joswig (separated); three c. *Education:* Munich Hochschule für Musik, master-classes with Hans Hotter and James King. *Career:* first engagement, Saarbrücken Opera 1994–96; Così fan tutte in Milan (last production of Giorgio Strehler) 1997; Salzburg Festival debut as Dr Faust (Busoni) 1999; debut at Zurich Opera in Mozart's Die Zauberflöte 2000; US debut at Lyric Opera in Chicago 2001; debut at Royal Opera House, Covent Garden, London in Puccini's La Rondine 2004; debut at the Metropolitan Opera, New York in Verdi's La Traviata 2006; La Traviata in Zürich, Paris and at La Scala, Milan 2007; Tosca in London, Manon in Chicago, Fidelio in Paris 2008; Lohengrin in Munich, Don Carlo in London 2009; Werther in Paris and Bayreuth Festival debut in Lohengrin 2010; role debut as Siegmund in Die Walküre at the Met 2011; Don Carlo in Munich, Carmen and Ariadne auf Naxos at the Salzburg Festival, Lohengrin at La Scala 2012; Parsifal at the Met and Wiener Staatsoper 2013; Manon Lescaut at Royal Opera House and Bayerische Staatsoper 2014; Carmen, Royal Opera House 2015; numerous recital performances at leading int. venues including the Met 2011 (first solo recital at the Met since Pavarotti 1994), La Scala 2014, Last Night of the Proms, Royal Albert Hall, London 2015; best known for playing Don José in Carmen, Cavaradossi in Tosca, title role in Don Carlos and Siegmund in Die Walküre. *Recordings include:* Strauss Lieder (Gramophone Award for Best Solo Vocal Recording) 2007, Romantic Arias by Mozart, Schubert, Beethoven and Wagner (Grand Prix du Disque, Diapason d'or, Qobus/Classica: Le meilleur disque) 2008, Madame Butterfly (Gramophone Award) 2009, Sehnsucht (Prix Caecilia, Echo Klassik Award for Best Vocalist of the Year 2010, Orphée d'or 'Wolfgang Wagner' 2010) 2009, Die schöne Müllerin (Diapason d'or) 2010, Verismo Arias (Diapason d'or 2010, Gramophone Award for Best Recital Recording) 2011, Werther (DVD) (Diapason d'or) 2011, Fidelio (Echo Klassik for Best Opera Recording of the Year) 2012, Tosca (Puccini) (BBC Music Magazine DVD Performance Award 2014), Der Ring des Nibelungen (DVD) (Grammy Award for Best Opera Recording) 2013, The Verdi Album 2013, Wagner Arias (Gramophone Award for Best Vocal Recording, BBC Music Magazine Vocal Award 2014) 2013, Schubert: Winterreise (Gramophone Award for Best Solo Vocal Recording 2014) 2014, Sehnsucht 2014, Du Bist die Welt für Mich (Echo Klassik Singer of the Year 2015) 2014, Nessun Dorma - The Puccini Album 2015. *Film:* An Evening with Puccini 2015. *Honours:* Bayerische Europamedaille 2012; prizewinner, Meistersinger Competition, Nuremberg 1993, Musical American Vocalist of the Year 2012, Int. Opera Awards Foundation Best Male Singer and Readers' Award 2013, European Culture Award 2015. *Current Management:* c/o Zemsky/Green Artists Management, 104 West 73rd Street, New York, NY 10023, USA . *Telephone:* (212) 579-6700. *Fax:* (212) 579-4723. *E-mail:* bzemsky@zemskygreen.com. *Website:* www.zemskygreen.com; www.jonaskaufmann.com.

KAUFMANN, Julie; American singer (soprano); *Professor, Universität der Künste Berlin;* b. 25 May 1955, Iowa. *Education:* Iowa Univ., Zürich Opera Studio, Musikhochschule, Hamburg. *Career:* first engagement at Hagen, then at Frankfurt (Oscar, Blondchen, Norina), Bayerische Staatsoper Munich 1983–96, (Despina, Sophie, Zdenka, Marzelline, Zerbinetta, Aminta/Schweigsame Frau, Atalanta/Serse, Dalinda/Ariodante, Zerlina, Susanna, Ännchen, Musetta Rosina/Barbiere di Sevilla, Woglinde; appearances in Hamburg (Blondchen, Oscar), Bonn (Norina), Stuttgart (Zerlina), Berlin (Susanna, Zdenka) and Covent Garden debut 1984 (Zerlina/ Don Giovanni), Salzburg debut (Blondchen) 1987 and Wiesbaden Festivals (Despina) 1987, Ludwigsburg Festival Despina 1984 und Susanna 1989; Munich Opera 1988 (tour of Japan 1988 and at La Scala, Milan 1988), Aminta/Schweigsame Frau, Zdenka 1992, Ludwigsburg Festival 1989, Woglinde in Wagner's Ring at Paris Châtelet 1994; world premiere of Udo Zimmermann's Gib Licht meiner Augen 1986; world premiere of Manfred Trojahn's Frammenti di Michelangelo 1995; Opera Cologne 96-2004 (Pamina, Susanna, Musetta, Sancta Susanna; world premiere Trojahn's Limonen aus Sizilien, Blanche/Dialogue des Carmelites); Maria in the premiere of Trojahn's Was ihr Wollt (Twelfth Night), Munich 1998; world premiere Peter Eötvös' Die Tragödie des Teufels, Munich 2010; sang St Matthew Passion with Chicago Symphony 1997; Brahms Requiem with NHK Orchestra, Tokyo 1997; Mahler's 8th Symphony, San Francisco 1998; recital tours and radio broadcasts Wolf's Italienisches Liederbuch in Italy, USA, France and Germany; Hindemith's Marienleben in Germany; Prof. of Voice, Universität der Künste, Berlin 1999–; mem. NATS, (USA), BDG (Germany); Paul Hindemith Gesellschaft, Berlin; Hans Pfitzner Gesellschaft. *Recordings:* Despina in Così fan tutte, Amor in Orfeo ed Euridice, Walther in La Wally, Woglinde in Das Rheingold (conducted by Haitink), Echo in Ariadne and Naxos, Schumann's Mignon Requiem and Mendelssohn's Lobgesang, Rezia in Pilgrims from Mecca, Nannetta in Falstaff (with Colin Davis), solo recital album with Schoenberg, Debussy, Strauss (with Irwin Gage) 1993, Brahms Duette and Lieder (with Marilyn Schmiege and Donald Sulzen), Beethoven Welsh, Scottish, Irish Songs (with Neues Münchener Klavietrio), Hans Pfitzner Lieder (with Donald Sulzen) 1999, Carl Loewe Lieder und Balladen (with Cord Garben) 1999, Lieder Sigfrid Karg Elert (with Bernhard Kastner) 2006, Haydn Songs and Scottish Trios (with Münchener Klaviertrio) 2009, Lieder Henri Marteau (with string quartet) 2012. *Honours:* Bayrischer Kammersängerin 1991, Bayerischer Verdienstorden 2000. *Address:* Universität der Künste, Fasanenstrasse 1b, 10623 Berlin, Germany (office). *Telephone:* (30) 31852322 (office). *Website:* www.julie-kaufmann.de.

KAUPOVA, Helena; Czech singer (soprano); b. 1965. *Education:* Brno Conservatory, Bratislava Academy. *Career:* Slovak National Theatre, Bratislava, 1990, as Pamina and Micaela; soloist, National Theatre, Prague 1992–; as Mozart's Donna Anna; Donna Elvira; Pamina and Countess; Mimi, Jenůfa, Nedda and Tatiana; guest appearances as Mimi at Toronto; Countess, Vancouver; Jenůfa in Santiago; Smetana's Marenka at Monte Carlo; Edinburgh Festival, 1993 as Janáček's Sarka and Krasava in Libuše, 1998. *Recordings include:* Libuše and highlights from Don Giovanni and Die Zauberflöte. *Address:* Prague National Theatre (Národní divadlo v Praze), Ostrovní 1, 11230 Prague 1, Czech Republic (office). *Telephone:* 224901111 (office). *Fax:* 224913528 (office). *Website:* www.nationaltheatre.cz (office).

KAVAFIAN, Ani; American violinist and teacher; *Adjunct Professor of Violin, Yale University;* b. 10 May 1948, Istanbul, Turkey; sister of Ida Kavafian; m. Bernard Mindich; one s. *Education:* studied with Ara Zerounian, Mischa Mischakoff in Detroit, Juilliard School with Ivan Galamian and Felix Galimir. *Career:* debut at Carnegie Recital Hall, New York 1969; European debut, Salle Gaveau, Paris 1973; soloist with many major orchestras; recitalist; duo recitals with sister, Ida Kavafian; artist mem. Chamber Music Soc., Lincoln Center, New York 1980–; teacher, Mannes Coll. of Music, New York 1982, Manhattan School of Music, New York 1983, Queens Coll. CUNY 1983–2002, State Univ. of New York, Stony Brook 2002–, Yale Univ. 2002–, Adjunct Prof. of Violin 2006–; Concertmaster, Seattle Symphony Orchestra 2007–, New Haven Symphony Orchestra 2008–; mem. Trio da Salo, Kavafian-Schub-Shifrin trio. *Recordings:* as a recitalist and chamber music artist. *Honours:* Avery Fisher Prize 1976. *Current Management:* Herbert Barrett Management, 505 Eight Avenue, Suite 601, New York, NY 10018, USA. *Telephone:* (212) 245-3530. *Fax:* (212) 397-5860. *Website:* www.herbertbarrett .com. *Address:* Yale School of Music, PO Box 208246, New Haven, CT 06520-8246, USA (office). *Telephone:* (203) 432-1965 (office). *E-mail:* anikv@aol.com (home). *Website:* www.yale.edu/music (office).

KAVAFIAN, Ida; American violinist; b. 29 Oct. 1952, Istanbul, Turkey; sister of Ani Kavafian; m. Steven Tenenbom. *Education:* studied with Ara Zerounian and Mischa Mischakoff, Detroit and with Oscar Shumsky and Ivan Galamian, Juilliard School. *Career:* founding mem. chamber group, Tashi 1973–; New York recital debut 1978; European debut, London 1982; appearances in duo recitals with sister, Ani Kavafian; mem., Beaux Arts Trio 1992–98; Artistic Dir, Music from Angel Fire festival 1984–; f. Opus One ensemble; founder and Artistic Dir Bravo!Colorado festival; faculty mem. Bard Coll. Conservatory of Music, Curtis Inst. of Music 1998–; artist mem. Chamber Music Soc., Lincoln Center. *Recordings:* as a chamber music artist. *Honours:* winner Vienna da Motta Int. Violin Competition, Lisbon 1973, silver medal Int. Violin Competition of Indianapolis 1982, Avery Fisher career grant 1988. *Current Management:* Herbert Barrett Management, 508 Eigth Avenue, Suite 601, New York, NY 10018, USA. *Telephone:* (212) 245-3530. *Fax:* (212) 397-5860. *Website:* www.herbertbarrett.com. *Address:* The Curtis Institute of Music, 1726 Locust Street, Philadelphia, PA 19103, USA (office). *Telephone:* (215) 893-5252 (office). *Fax:* (215) 893-9065 (office). *E-mail:* info@curtis.edu (office). *Website:* www.curtis.edu (office).

KAVAKOS, Leonidas; Greek violinist; b. 1967, Athens. *Education:* Greek Conservatory with Stelios Kafantaris, studied with Joseph Gingold at the University of Indiana, USA. *Career:* debut at Athens Festival, 1984; Cannes Festival, 1985; US debut with the Santa Barbara Symphony, 1986; Athens Festival 1988, conducted by Rostropovich, leading to concerts with the National Symphony Orchestra in Washington, DC; concerts at the Helsinki Festival and with the Swedish Radio Symphony conducted by Esa-Pekka Salonen; European tour with the Helsinki Philharmonic conducted by Okku Kamu, 1989; further appearances in Italy, Spain, France, Cyprus, Turkey, Hungary and Japan; television and radio recordings in Greece, France, Germany, Spain and England; Dvořák's Concerto at the 1999 London Proms; London Proms, 2002; Artistic Dir Camerata Salzburg 2007–09. *Honours:* winner Sibelius Violin Competition, Indianapolis 1985, International Competition 1986, Naumburg Competition, New York 1988, Paganini Competition, Genoa 1988. *Current Management:* Opus 3 Artists, 470 Park Avenue South, 9th Floor North, New York, NY 10016, USA. *Telephone:* (212) 584-7500. *Fax:* (646) 300-8200. *E-mail:* info@opus3artists.com. *Website:* www .opus3artists.com. *Current Management:* Intermusica Artists Management Ltd, 16 Duncan Terrace, London, N1 8BZ, England. *Telephone:* (20) 7278-5455. *Fax:* (20) 7278-8434. *E-mail:* mail@intermusica.co.uk. *Website:* www .intermusica.co.uk.

KAVRAKOS, Dimitri; Greek singer (bass); b. 26 Feb. 1946, Athens. *Education:* Athens Conservatory of Music. *Career:* debut with Athens Opera 1970, as Zaccaria in Nabucco; Athens Opera until 1978; US debut at Carnegie Hall, in Refice's Cecilia; Metropolitan Opera debut 1979, as the Grand Inquisitor in Don Carlos, returned to New York as Silva (Ernani), Walter (Luisa Miller), Ferrando (Il Trovatore), Capulet (Roméo et Juliette) and in I Vespri Siciliani; Chicago Lyric Opera in Aida, Lakmé, Les Contes d'Hoffmann and Fidelio; San Francisco Opera in La Gioconda; Guest engagements at La Scala, Paris Opéra, Aix-en-Provence, Spoleto, Lyon and Avignon; British debut Glyndebourne 1982, as the Commendatore in Don Giovanni; London debut at the Barbican Hall in Cherubini's Medée; Covent Garden debut 1984, as Pimen in Boris Godunov, returned in new productions of La Donna del Lago (Douglas 1985), Le nozze di Figaro (Bartolo) and Anna Bolena (Enrico VIII 1988); Rome Opera 1989, as Silva in Ernani, Bellini's Giorgio in Florence; Sang Fiesco in Simon Boccanegra at Cologne, 1990 and Prince Gremin in

Eugene Onegin in Chicago; Maggio Musicale Florence, 1990 as Ernesto in Donizetti's Parisina; Season 1992–93 as Timur in Turandot at Chicago, Rossini's Mosè with the Israel Philharmonic, Banquo at Cologne and the Commendatore at Aix-en-Provence; Don Giovanni (Commendatore) and Le nozze di Figaro (Bartolo, Salzburg); I Puritani, Bregenz, 1985; Il Barbiere di Siviglia, Florence, 1994; Paris Opéra: Don Carlos and Puritani, 1987; Lucia, 1995; Lucrezia Borgia, Teatro San Carlo Naples, 1992; La Vestale, La Scala, 1993; Sang Banquo at Florence, 1995; La Scala 1997, in Lucia di Lammermoor; Season 1998–99 at Paris Opéra with Lucia di Lammermoor and I Capuleti e i Montecchi; Sang Arkel in Pelléas at Toronto, 2000. *Recordings include:* Don Giovanni; La Vestale, La Scala, 1993; Rigoletto, La Scala, 1994; Ravenna, Norma, 1994.

KAWAHARA, Yoko; singer (soprano); b. 3 Sept. 1939, Tokyo, Japan. *Education:* studied with Toishiko Toda in Tokyo and with Ellen Bosenius at the Cologne Musikhochschule. *Career:* debut with Niki Kai Opera Tokyo 1958, as Fiordilgi; sang in Bonn as Pamina 1969; Bayreuth Festival 1972–77, as the Woodbird in Siegfried; mem., Cologne Opera from 1975; guest appearances in Frankfurt, Hamburg and Tokyo; Staatsoper Hamburg 1986, in La Clemenza di Tito; other roles include Euridice, Sophie in Der Rosenkavalier, Desdemona, Freia and Liu; many concert appearances. *Recordings include:* Reger's Requiem.

KAWALLA, Szymon Piotr; Polish conductor and composer; b. 2 June 1949, Kraków; m. Hanna Kiepuszewska 1973, one d. *Education:* Chopin Acad. of Music, Warsaw. *Career:* debut with Philharmonic, Kraków 1964; Conductor, Philharmonic Poherien 1974–78; Conductor and Dir, Torun Chamber Orchestra 1978–80; Conductor and Dir, Philharmonic and Opera Zielona Gora 1980–86; Symphonic Orchestra and Chorus, RTV Kraków 1985–; concerts in Austria, Bulgaria, Canada, Cuba, England, Germany, The Netherlands, France, Italy, Poland, Romania, Spain, Czechoslovakia, Russia, Vatican; radio, television and film recordings; Prof., Chopin Acad. of Music, Warsaw. *Compositions:* Divertimento, Capriccio for violin solo, Oratorio, Pater Kolbe, Cantata, Wit Stwosz, Stabat Mater, Quartet for Strings.

KAWASAKI, Masaru, DipMus; Japanese composer and conductor; *Professor Emeritus, Tokoha Gakuen University;* b. 19 April 1924, Tokyo; m. Taeko Koide 1953; two s. *Education:* Tokyo Acad. of Music. *Career:* first performance of Compos at Festliche Musiktage Uster, Switzerland 1971, 1974, 1977, 1981; Dir, Int. Youth Musicale, Shizuoka 1979, 1982 and 1985; Prof. Emer., Tokoha Gakuen Univ.; mem. Japanese Soc. Rights Authors and Composers, Nat. Band Asscn. *Compositions:* March Ray of Hope, 1963; March Forward for Peace, 1966; Essay on a Day for flute and piano, 1969; March Progress and Harmony, 1969; Warabe-Uta for symphony band, 1970; Prayer Music Number 1, Dirge, commissioned by Hiroshima City, 1975; Poem for symphony band, 1976; Prayer Music Number 2, Elegy, 1977; Romantic Episode, 1979; Romance for trumpet and symphony band, 1982; March Dedicated to Cupid, 1983; In the Depth of Night for flute and cello, 1993; La improvvisazione, for string trio 2004. *Publications:* Instrumentation and Arrangement for Wind Ensemble 1972, New Band Method 1979; contrib. to Band Journal, Tokyo. *Honours:* hon. mem. Int. Soc. of Contemporary Music, UNESCO Creative Artists Fellow 1966–67; Ministry of Education and President of NHK Composition Prize 1956. *Address:* 4-2-38 Hamatake, Chigasaki-shi 2530021, Japan (home). *Telephone:* (467) 866020 (home). *Fax:* (467) 866020 (home). *E-mail:* masaruk@ jcom.home.ne.jp (home).

KAY, Donald Henry, AM, BMus; composer; b. 25 Jan. 1933, Smithton, Tasmania. *Education:* Univ. of Melbourne, studied with Malcolm Williamson. *Career:* faculty mem., Tasmanian Conservatorium 1967–; commissions from APRA, Lyrian String Quartet, Tasmanian Symphony Chamber Players and others. *Compositions include:* Dance Movement for small orchestra 1968, Four Australian Folk Songs for women's or young voices 1971, The Quest for string quartet 1971, There is an Island for children's choir and orchestra 1977, The Golden Crane opera for children and adults 1984, Dance Cameos for mandolin and wind quintet 1986, Hastings Triptych for flute and piano 1986, Northward the Strait for chorus, soprano, baritone and wind band 1988, Tasmania Symphony: The Legend of Moinee for cello and orchestra 1988, Dance Concertante for string orchestra 1989, Haiku for women's voices, piano and string quartet 1990, Night Spaces for flute, string trio and piano 1990, Piano Concerto 1992, Moonlight Ridge for string quintet or string orchestra 1994, AEstivernal for mandolin, wind quintet or orchestra 1994, River Views for trombone and string orchestra 1995, The Edge of Remoteness for piano trio 1996, Symphony–The South Land 1997, Sonata for cello and piano 1999, Sonata for piano 1998, Different Worlds for piano 1999, Bird Chants for piano 1999, Blue Sky Through Still Trees for flute and piano 1999, String Quartet No. 5: A Tragic Life 2002, The Death of Ben Hall for SATB chorus and concert band 2002. *Honours:* Sounds Australian Award 1989, 1990.

KAY, Serena; British singer (mezzo-soprano); b. 1973, England; d. of Norman Kay and Janice Kay. *Education:* Univ. of London, Royal Coll. of Music Opera School, currently studies with Philip Doghan. *Career:* opera roles include Hermia in A Midsummer Night's Dream, English Touring Opera, Second Lady in The Magic Flute, Opera North, Cenerentola, Mid Wales Opera and Garden Opera, Rosina in Il Barbiere, Clonter Opera, Grange Park Young Artists and Pimlico Opera, Guido in Flavio, London Handel Soc., Dorabella in Così fan tutte, Mananan Opera, Sara in Tobias and the Angel, Young Vic/ English Touring Opera, Nancy T'Ang in Nixon in China, ENO, Tisbe in Cenerentola, Welsh Nat. Opera, Composer in The Jewel Box, Sandrina in

L'Infedelta delusa and Rosina in La Vera costanza, Hansel in Hansel and Gretel Opera Theatre Co., Ireland; concerts include Messiah (Handel), Huddersfield Choral Soc., Les Nuits d'ete (Berlioz), Oxford Sinfonia, Kew Sinfonia and Berlioz Society, Lieder eines fahrenden gesellen (Mahler), Barber of Seville highlights (with Gerald Finlay), Hansel (Hansel and Gretel highlights) BBC Concert Orchestra, Wesendonk Lieder (Wagner), OML-Portugal, Stravinsky and Respighi with LPO, Dream of Gerontius (Elgar). *Honours:* Jr Fellowship, Royal Coll. of Music 2002–03. *Current Management:* c/o Ingpen and Williams Ltd, St George's Court, 131 Putney Bridge Road, London, SW15 2PA, England. *Telephone:* (20) 8874-3222. *Fax:* (20) 8877-3113. *E-mail:* info@ingpen.co.uk. *Website:* www.ingpen.co.uk. *Fax:* (20) 8940-5270 (office). *E-mail:* serena@serenakay.org (office). *Website:* www.serenakay.org (office).

KAZARAS, Peter; American singer (tenor); b. 1956, New York. *Career:* debut in New York 1981 in a concert performance of Khovanshchina; Houston 1983 as Francois in the premiere of Bernstein's A Quiet Place; Santa Fe and Seattle 1985 in Henze's English Cat and as Števa in Jenůfa; returned to Seattle as Wagner's Froh and Erik, Hoffmann, Lensky and Pierre in War and Peace; New York City Opera debut 1988 as Quint in The Turn of The Screw; sang with Metropolitan Opera from 1990 as Narraboth in Salome, Shuisky in Boris Godunov and Almaviva in the premiere of Corigliano's The Ghosts of Versailles; other modern repertory includes Udo Zimmermann's Die Weisse Rose, at Omaha 1986, Pelegrin in the premiere of Tippett's New Year, at Houston 1989, and Busoni's Die Brautwahl at Berlin Staatsoper 1991; sang Boris in the New Zealand premiere of Katya Kabanova, 1996; Captain Vere in Billy Budd at Dallas, 1997. *Current Management:* Columbia Artists Management, 1790 Broadway, New York, NY 10019-1412; Pinnacle Arts: Uzan Division, 889 Ninth Avenue, Second Floor, New York, NY 10019, USA. *Telephone:* (212) 841-9500 (CAMI); (212) 397-7926 (Pinnacle). *Fax:* (212) 841 9744 (CAMI); (212) 397-7920 (Pinnacle). *E-mail:* info@cami.com; vuzan@ pinnaclearts.com. *Website:* www.cami.com; www.pinnaclearts.com.

KAZARNOVSKAYA, Ljuba (Lubov); Russian singer (soprano); b. 18 July 1960, Moscow; m.; one c. *Education:* Moscow Conservatory with Irina Arkhipova and Elena Shumilova, N. Malysheva. *Career:* debut, La Scala Milan 1989 in Verdi's Requiem under R. Muti; has sung at the Bolshoi, Moscow as Nedda, Mimi and Lida in La Battaglia di Legnano; tour of Italy with the Maily Theatre, Leningrad 1984; Kirov Theatre, Leningrad from 1986 as Leonora (La Forza del Destino and Trovatore), Marina, Violetta, Marguerite, Donna Anna and Tchaikovsky's Iolanta; Paris Opéra and Covent Garden 1987, as Tatiana with the Kirov Co.; Salzburg Festival 1989, in the Verdi Requiem, conducted by Karajan; Zürich Opera 1989–90, as Amelia Boccanegra and the Trovatore Leonora; Cologne Opera 1989–90, as Manon Lescaut and Amelia; Covent Garden 1990, as Desdemona; Metropolitan Opera as Tatjana in Eugene Onegin under Levine, Desdemona in Otello, Nedda in Pagliacci 1991–95; debut in Strauss' Salome 1995; new productions of Clemenza di Tito and Il Trovatore at San Francisco Opera and at Lyric Chicago, Tosca in Houston, Berlin and Vienna; recitals at the major music festivals; sang Pauline in Prokofiev's The Gambler at La Scala and in Paris 1996–97; Aithra in Strauss' Aegyptische Helena under Thielemann with the Royal Opera at the Festival Hall 1998; Massenet and Puccini premiere at the Bolshoi Theatre, Moscow and afterwards at opera festivals in Italy, Sweden, Germany and USA; personal television music show 'Glimpse of Love' 2000; concert and oratorio appearances, song recitals with works by Brahms, Wolf, de Falla, Dvořák and Rachmaninov; film and opera projects; recital tours in Europe and Asia; mem. Russian Opera Forum; Chair. Russian Music Soc. (RMPO); Pres. Ljuba Kazarnovskaya Foundation; Chair. and Artistic Dir Nat. Verdi Museum, Busetto, Italy; Founder and Artistic Dir Summer Acad. of Music, Slovenia; master-classes in Russia and Europe and at Chengdu Conservatory, China; Jury Chair., Renato Bruson Int. Vocal Competition. *Radio:* weekly programme Vocalissimo, Radio Orpheus. *Recordings include:* Shostakovich's 12th Symphony, Prokofiev's The Gambler, Tchaikovsky's The Complete Songs Op 103 (five vols), The Great Singers of Russia (video) 1901–99, Gypsy Love (recital programme), Glimpse of Love (DVD). *Honours:* The Voice of the Year (Russia) 2001. *Address:* Arbat 35, Moscow 121002, Russia (home). *Telephone:* (495) 248-09-44 (home). *Fax:* (495) 248-09-44 (home). *E-mail:* fond_kl@mail.ru (home).

KEATING, Roderic Maurice, MA, MMus, DMus, ARCO, ARCM; British singer (tenor) and teacher (retd); b. 14 Dec. 1941, Maidenhead, Berks., England; s. of Maurice Keating and Suzanne Judith Keating (née Mills); m. Martha Kathryn Post 1968; one d. *Education:* Gonville and Caius Coll., Cambridge, Yale Univ. and Univ. of Texas, USA. *Career:* debut at Houston Grand Opera in Tales of Hoffmann 1970; Glyndebourne Touring and Festival Opera 1971–73; Theater an der Wien, Freddy in My Fair Lady 1971; perm. contracts in Lübeck 1972–74, Saarbrücken 1974–80, Wuppertal 1980–86, Bonn 1986–89, Stuttgart 1989–2010; more than 80 roles as lyric and character tenor; guest throughout Germany; guest appearances at Interlaken Festspiel 1975, Tbilisi, Georgia 1976, Wiesbaden 1977, Paris Opera 1981, London Coliseum 1982, Warsaw 1983, Cologne 1985, Salzburg Festival 1986, Covent Garden 1988, Moscow 1989, Vienna and Schwetzingen Festivals 1990, Edinburgh Festival 2001; sang Tiresias in Henze's The Bassarids at Stuttgart 1989, Der Rosenkavalier, Théâtre Châtelet, Paris 1993 and Bologna 1995, Weill's Seven Deadly Sins, Tel-Aviv 1997; sang the Doctor in Three Sisters by Eötvös at Freiburg 2000; concerts and radio recordings for BBC, Bavarian Radio and SWF, WDR, SDR in Germany; oratorio and church concerts in Italy, France,

Spain, Belgium, The Netherlands, Germany; Voice Teacher, Musikhochschule Stuttgart –2011. *Publications:* The Songs of Frank Bridge 1970; contrib. to Musical Times, Musical Opinion. *Honours:* Kammersänger, Stuttgart Opera 2007. *Address:* Lehenbühlstrasse 36, 71272 Renningen, Germany. *Telephone:* (7159) 18156. *E-mail:* roderickeating@aol.com; roderickeating0@gmail.com.

KEATS, Donald Howard, BMus, MA, PhD; American composer and academic (retd); b. 27 May 1929, New York, NY; m. Eleanor Steinholz 1953 (died 2004); two s. two d. *Education:* Yale Univ. School of Music, Columbia Univ., Staatliche Hochschule für Musik, Hamburg, Univ. of Minnesota. *Career:* Prof. of Music, Antioch Coll. Ohio; Visiting Prof. of Music, Univ. of Washington, Seattle; Prof. of Music, Univ. of Denver, Colorado 1975–99, Prof. Emeritus 1999–, Lawrence C Phipps Prof. in the Humanities 1982–85; Composer, Pianist, at concerts devoted solely to his music in USA, England and Israel. *Compositions include:* Symphonies No. 1 and No. 2 (An Elegiac Symphony), String Quartets No. 1, No. 2 and No. 3 2001, Piano Sonata, The Hollow Men (T. S. Eliot) for chorus and instruments, Anyone Lived in a Pretty How Town (Cummings) for a cappella chorus, The Naming of Cats (T. S. Eliot) for chorus and piano, Tierras del Alma (Poemas de amor, song cycle) for soprano, flute and guitar, Theme and Variations for piano, Concerto for piano and orchestra, Diptych for cello and piano, Polarities for violin and piano, A Love Triptych (W. B. Yeats, song cycle), Musica Instrumentalis for nine instruments, Elegy for full or chamber orchestra, Branchings for orchestra, Revisitations for violin, cello and piano. *Honours:* Fulbright Scholar 1954–56, Guggenheim Fellowships 1964–65, 1972–73, ASCAP Awards annually from 1964, Rockefeller Foundation Awards 1965, 1966, Ford Foundation 1968, NEA Fellowship grant 1975. *Address:* 12854 West Buckhorn Road, Littleton, CO 80127, USA (home). *Telephone:* (303) 948-3033 (home). *E-mail:* dkeats@du.edu (home).

KEBERLE, David Scott, BM, MMus; composer, clarinettist and academic; b. 6 June 1952, Wausau, Wisconsin, USA. *Education:* Indiana Univ., New England Conservatory of Music, Boston, Accademia di S. Cecilia, Rome, studied with Bernhard Heiden, Donald Martino, Earl Bates, Joe Allard and W. O. Smith. *Career:* Instructor of Music, Univ. of Wisconsin, Baraboo 1977–81; co-founder, Electravox Ensemble, Rome 1983; Instructor of Music, Loyola Univ., Chicago, Rome Centre 1984–88; as clarinet soloist, performed in Brazil, Uruguay, Argentina, France, Italy, Israel, Austria and USA; performed on nat. Italian radio 1987, 1988; Instructor of Music, St Mary's Coll., Rome Programme 1991–; mem. American Music Center, New York. *Compositions:* Incantation for clarinet and live electronics 1986, Galoppando Attraverso il Vuoto for solo clarinet 1986, Concerto for trumpet and chamber ensemble 1980, Murmurs for solo flute 1989. *Recordings:* ElectraVox Ensemble Incantation for Clarinet and Live Electronics 1986, Musicisti Contemporanei Clarinet and Piano 1989. *Honours:* Fulbright Scholarship in Composition 1979.

KECHABIAN, Rafael, DipMus; Armenian violinist and academic; b. 14 Feb. 1949, Yerevan; m. Irene Kechabian 1978, two s. *Education:* Special Musical School and Musical Secondary School, Sukhumi, State Yerevan Conservatory, Armenia. *Career:* Prof. of Violin, Yerevan Music School, Armenia 1970–83; Concertino, Nat. Symphony Orchestra, Nicaragua 1983–87; Prof. of Violin, Nat. Conservatory, Nicaragua 1983–87; soloist, State Chamber Ensemble of Armenia 1987–93; Prof. of Chamber Music, State Yerevan Conservatory, Armenia 1987–93; principal of the second violins, Symphony Orchestra of the Murcia Region, Spain 1993–94; Prof. of Violin, Musical Acad., Murcia, Spain 1995; violin maker, Murcia, Spain 1995. *Honours:* Ministry of Culture of the Republic of Nicaragua diploma 1987.

KEE, Piet; Dutch organist and composer; *Town Organist Emeritus, St Bavo Church, Haarlem;* b. (Pieter William Kee), 30 Aug. 1927, Zaandam; m. E.L.S. Hendrikse; two c. *Education:* studied with father, Cor Kee, with Anthon van der Horst, Ernest W. Mulder, Willem Andriessen at the Amsterdam Conservatoire. *Career:* debut at Zaandam 1941; organist of Schnitger Organ, St Laurens Church, Alkmaar 1952–87; Town Organist, St Bavo Church, Haarlem 1956–89, now Emer.; Prof. of Organ, Conservatoire of the Soc. Muzieklyceum, Sweelinck Conservatoire, Amsterdam –1987; Prof., Int. Summer Acad., Haarlem; many concert tours worldwide; TV films of compositions, Confrontation and Integration. *Compositions include:* Two Songs (text Edgard Lemaire) for mezzo soprano and string quartet, Variations on a Carol 1954, Triptych on Psalm 86 1960, Two Organ Works 1962, Four Manual Pieces 1966, Music and Space for two organs and five brasswinds 1969, Intrada for two organs, Valerius Gedenck-Clanck 1976, Confrontation for three street organs and church organ 1979, Integration for mixed choir, flageolet, mechanical birds, barrel organs and church organ 1980, Frans Hals Suite for Carillon 1990, Flight for flute solo 1992, Bios for organ 1994, Network for two organs, electronic keyboard, alto saxophone and descant recorder 1996, Op-streek for violin and piano 1997, The World (text by Henry Vaughan) mini oratorio for mixed choir and continuo instrument 1999, Winds for reed winds quintet 2000, The Organ (homage to Pieter Saenredam) for organ 2000, Festival Spirit for five organs (for the Int. Organ Festival of St Albans) 2001, Heaven (text by George Herbert) echo-fantasy for mixed choir and two solo sopranos, Bios II for organ, tuned percussion, one violin and more percussion 2002, The Distant Choral for solo trumpet or alto saxophone 2004, Haarlem Concerto for organ solo, orchestra and harmonium 2005, Cervus for harmonium 2006, Seventy chords for organ 2007, Voluntary on HSAE 2008, 'Performance' for alto saxophone and organ 2009, Kampanella for carillon 2011, Magic Pipes for panpipes and organ 2012. *Television includes:*

Confrontation for organ and three street organs, Integration. *Recordings include:* baroque music, romantic and modern music, numerous recordings for HMV, Telefunken, Philips, series of albums for Chandos, including Bach organ works (four vols), Franck organ works (San Sebastian), Piet Kee at Weingarten, Piet Kee at the Concertgebouw, Piet Kee plays Sweelinck and Buxtehude, Piet Kee plays Bruhns, Piet Kee plays Hindemith and Reger. *Publications include:* The Secrets of Bach's Passacaglia 1982, Astronomy in Buxtehude's Passacaglia, The Diapason, Ars Organi 1984, Numbers and Symbolism in the Passacaglia and Ciacona 1986, Musik und Kirche 1987; contrib. to Musical Times 2006, Organist's Review 2007. *Honours:* Hon. FRCO; Hon. mem. Koninklijke Nederlandse Organisatie van Verloskundig; Prix d'excellence, Conservatoire Amsterdam, Winner, Int. Improvisation Concours, Haarlem 1953, 1954, 1955, Harriet Cohen Bach Medal 1958. *Address:* Nieuwe Gracht 41, 2011 Haarlem, The Netherlands. *Telephone:* (23) 531-45-10. *E-mail:* piet.kee@wxs.nl.

KEEFFE, Bernard, BA; British conductor, broadcaster and academic; b. 1 April 1925, London; s. of Joseph Keeffe and Theresa Keeffe (née Quinn); m. Denise Walker 1954; one s. one d. *Education:* St Olave's Grammar School and Clare Coll., Cambridge. *Career:* served in Intelligence Corps 1943–47; mem. Glyndebourne Opera Co. 1951–52; BBC Music Staff 1954–60; Asst Music Dir Royal Opera House 1960–62; Conductor BBC Scottish Orchestra 1962–64; Prof., Trinity Coll. of Music 1966–89; freelance conductor and broadcaster on radio and TV, concerts with leading orchestras 1966–; mem. int. juries, competitions in Sofia, Liège, Vienna and London; Warden solo performers section, Inc. Soc. of Musicians 1971; Chair. Anglo-Austrian Music Soc. *Radio:* Music in Japan (BBC World Service). *Television:* Elgar and the Orchestra (Best Music Programme of the Year) (BBC) 1979. *Publications:* Harrap's Dictionary of Music and Musicians (Ed.), ENO Guide to Tosca. *Honours:* Hon. Fellow, Trinity Coll. of Music 1968. *Address:* 153 Honor Oak Road, London, SE23 3RN, England. *Telephone:* (20) 8699-3672.

KEEGAN, Liane; Australian singer (mezzo-soprano); b. 1963. *Education:* Melba Conservatorium, Melbourne, Nat. Opera Studio, London and Graz Summer School. *Career:* appearances as Suzuki in Butterfly for Opera North 1996, Barbara in Korngold's Violanta at the London Proms 1997, Waltraute in Act III of Die Walküre at the Edinburgh Festival 1997; other roles include Fricka, Dalila, Ulrica in Un Ballo in Maschera, Mistress Quickly, Dorabella, Rosina, Azucena, Erda, First Norn and Waltraute in Der Ring des Nibelungen, Gaea in Daphne, Offred's Mother in The Handmaid's Tale, Dritte Dame in Die Zauberflöte, Mary in Die Fliegende Holländer, Mama Lucia in Cavalleria Rusticana; recitals throughout Australia, the UK, in France, Austria and Germany; concerts include Mahler's Lieder eines fahrenden Gesellen, Das Lied von der Erde, Symphonies 2 and 3; Elijah, The Dream of Gerontius, Verdi Requiem, the Wesendonck lieder and Elgar's Sea Pictures. *Current Management:* Arts Management Pty Ltd, Level 1, 405 Elizabeth Street, Surry Hills, NSW 2010, Australia. *Telephone:* (2) 9211 9422. *Fax:* (2) 9211 9466. *E-mail:* enquiries@artsmanagement.com.au. *Website:* www.artsmanagement.com.au.

KEEN, Catherine; singer (mezzo-soprano); b. 1970, California, USA. *Education:* Adler Fellow, San Francisco Opera. *Career:* appearances as Dalila at the Deutsche Oper Berlin and with Netherlands Opera as Federica in Luisa Miller, Verdi's Emilia and Suzuki in Butterfly; Wagner's Flosshilde 1999–2000; San Francisco Opera as Britten's Hermia, Magdelene, Venus in Tannhäuser, Fricka and Offenbach's Giulietta; Verdi's Amneris and Fenena at the 1998 Verona Arena and Brangaene in Tristan with the Cincinnati Symphony Orchestra; season 1999–2000 with Waltraute and Fricka at Catania, Amneris in Houston and Kundry and Handel's Cornelia in Giulio Cesare at Washington; Concerts include Das Lied von der Erde in Paris, Mahler 8 at the Edinburgh Festival, Beethoven 9 and Schubert's Rosamunde.

KEENER, Andrew David, BMus; British classical producer; b. 23 March 1954, Barry, S Wales; s. of Mr & Mrs Philip Keener; civil partner Peter Avis. *Education:* Barry Boys' Comprehensive School, Univ. of Edinburgh. *Career:* worked at EMG Handmade Gramophones record shop, London; first orchestral recording assignments for Classics for Pleasure and Hyperion, these and many ind. and major labels/clients since; has worked on more than 1,000 recordings with artists including Joshua Bell, Boris Berezovsky, Paavo Berglund, Sir Andrew Davis, Sir Colin Davis, Christoph Eschenbach, Stephen Hough, Steven Isserlis, Mariss Jansons, Nigel Kennedy, Andrew Litton, Julian Lloyd-Webber, Sir Neville Marriner, Sir Peter Maxwell Davies, Sir Yehudi Menuhin, Kent Nagano, Steven Osborne, Leif Ove Andsnes, André Previn, Sir Simon Rattle, Leonard Slatkin, Bryn Terfel, Jean-Yves Thibaudet, Michael Tilson Thomas, Sir Michael Tippett, Anne Sofie von Otter, Diana Yukawa, and with the Acad. of St Martin-in-the-Fields, BBC Scottish Symphony Orchestra, Chamber Orchestra of Europe, City of Birmingham Symphony Orchestra, Dallas Symphony Orchestra, Florestan Trio, Leopold String Trio, Manchester Camerata, Swedish Chamber Orchestra, The Takács Quartet, Hallé Orchestra's own label. *Honours:* various Gramophone Awards, Grammies, Diapason d'Or, etc.. *Address:* 91 Cambridge Road, New Malden, Surrey, KT3 3QP, England (home). *Telephone:* (7767) 685179 (mobile). *E-mail:* andrewkeener@btinternet.com (home). *Website:* www.keener.org.uk (office).

KEENLYSIDE, Simon, CBE; British singer (baritone); b. 3 Aug. 1959, London; s. of Raymond and Ann Keenlyside; m. Zenaida Yanowsky; one s. one d. *Education:* Cambridge Univ., Royal Northern Coll. of Music. *Career:* gave concert performances before joining Scottish Opera 1989–94; debut at Royal

Opera House Covent Garden 1989, at Glyndebourne 1993, at Metropolitan Opera, New York 1996; numerous leading roles in all the major int. opera houses including Vienna State Opera, La Scala, Milan, Welsh Nat. Opera, San Francisco Opera, Deutsche Oper, Berlin, Grand Théâtre de Genève, Théâtre de la Monnaie, Brussels, etc; wide recital repertoire including Britten's War Requiem and Schubert Lieder. *Repertoire includes:* title roles in Billy Budd, Don Giovanni, Hamlet, Wozzeck, Orfeo, Macbeth, Eugene Onegin, Rigoletto; Papageno in Die Zauberflöte, Guglielmo in Così fan tutte, Figaro and Fiorello in The Barber of Seville, Ping in Turandot, Steersman in Tristan und Isolde and many more. *Recordings include:* Tales of Opera (Gramophone Award for Best Recital Recording) 2007, Schumann Dichterliebe and Brahms Lieder 2009, Adès, The Tempest 2009, Songs of War (Gramophone Award for Best Solo Vocal Recording 2012) 2011. *Honours:* winner Richard Tauber Competition 1986, Musical America Award for Vocalist of the Year 2011, Opera News Award for invaluable contribution to opera 2012. *Current Management:* Askonas Holt Ltd, Lincoln House, 300 High Holborn, London, WC1V 7JH, England. *Telephone:* (20) 7400-1700 (office). *Website:* www.askonasholt.co.uk (office).

KEHL, Sigrid; German singer (soprano, mezzo-soprano); b. 23 Nov. 1932, Berlin. *Education:* studied in Erfurt, Berlin Musikhochschule and with Dagmar Freiwald-Lange. *Career:* debut at Berlin Staatsoper 1956, in Prince Igor; Member of the Leipzig Opera from 1957, notably as Brünnhilde in Der Ring des Nibelungen, 1974; Engagements at the Berlin Staatsoper from 1971, Vienna Staatsoper from 1975; Further appearances at the Komische Oper Berlin and in Prague, Bucharest, Rome, Bologna, Geneva, Warsaw and Basle; Lausanne Festival 1983, as Isolde.

KEINONEN, Heiki; Finnish singer (baritone); b. 1951. *Education:* studied in Helsinki. *Career:* sang in concert from 1976, and at the Savonlinna Festival; Finnish Nat. Opera at Helsinki from 1981, notably as Germont in La Traviata 1993, and the premiere of Insect Life by Kalevi Aho 1996; Vasa Opera 1994, in the premiere of Miss Julie by Ilkka Kuusisto; sang Pontto in the premiere of The Key, by Aho at Helsinki 1995; title role in Sweeney Todd 1998. *Recordings include:* Kung Karls Jakt by Pacius.

KEITH, Gillian, Dip RAM, ARAM; Canadian singer (soprano); b. Toronto, Ont. *Education:* McGill Univ., Montréal, Royal Acad., London with Ian Partridge. *Career:* Royal Opera debut as Tytania in A Midsummer Night's Dream under Hickox, Royal Opera Main Stage debut as Zerbinetta in Ariadne auf Naxos under Sir Mark Elder; Zerbinetta for Welsh Nat. Opera and Opera de Oviedo; Pretty Polly in Birtwistle's Punch and Judy; St John Passion, King Arthur, Tytania in Midsummer Night's Dream and Nanneta in Falstaff for ENO, Woodbird in Siegfried, Amor in Gluck's Orfeo and Papagena for Scottish Opera, Poppea for Theater Basel and for Boston Early Music Festival, Sylvia in La Colombe, Tullia in Ottone in Villa, Philine in Mignon, Iole in Hercules and Sylvia in Ascanio in Alba for Buxton Festival, Diana in The Assassin Tree for Edinburgh Festival and Linbury Theatre, Elmira in Croesus at Opera North, Ginevra in Ariodante in Halle, Tiny in Paul Bunyan for Bregenz Festival; soloist for Sir John Eliot Gardiner in Bach Cantatas 2000; concerts include Oliver Knussen Second Symphony at BBC Proms with Gianandrea Noseda and BBC Philharmonic, Handel Silete Venti with The Sixteen in Hong Kong, Sydney Opera House and Wellington Int. Festival, Mahler 8 with Gatti and Royal Philharmonic Orchestra, Mozart Requiem with Colin Davis and The Creation with Paul McCreesh; regular appearances with The Sixteen, Tafelmusik Baroque Orchestra, Royal Philharmonic Orchestra, City of Birmingham Symphony Orchestra, Toronto Symphony Orchestra, Liverpool Philharmonic, Royal Scottish Nat. Orchestra, Calgary Philharmonic and Retrospective Ensemble. *Recordings include:* Handel Nine German Arias, Handel Messiah (Handel & Haydn Society), Handel's Gloria (Gardiner), Debussy: Early Songs, Debussy Songs Vol. 2 (with Simon Lepper), Strauss Lieder (Simon Lepper), Bach Cantatas (Gardiner), Schubert Lieder (Aldeburgh Connection, Canada), Mozart Mass in C Minor (Harry Christophers), Dallapiccola Orchestral Works (BBC Philharmonic, Noseda), Purcell's The Tempest, Hasse's Il Cantico de' tre fanciulli. *Honours:* Hon. ARAM; Royal Overseas League prize 1998, Kathleen Ferrier Award 2000. *Current Management:* c/o Musicall Ltd, Oast House, Hollow Lane, East Hoathly, East Sussex, BN8 7QX, England. *Telephone:* (1825) 840437. *E-mail:* info@musicall.uk.com. *Website:* www.musicall.uk.com.

KEKULA, Josef; Czech violinist; b. 1952. *Education:* studied with Václav Snítil and members of Smetana Quartet, Kostecky and Kohout. *Career:* co-founder and 2nd Violinist, Stamic Quartet of Prague, 1977; Performances at Prague Young Artists and Bratislava Music Festivals; Tours to: Spain, Austria, France, Switzerland, Germany, Eastern Europe; USA tour, 1980; Debut concerts in the United Kingdom at London and Birmingham, 1983; British tours, 1985, 1987, 1988 at Warwick Arts Festival, 20 concerts in 1989; Season 1991–92: Channel Islands, Netherlands, Finland, Austria, France, Edinburgh Festival, Debut tours of Canada, Japan and Indonesia; In 1994 visited Korea and Japan; In 1995 visited USA. *Recordings:* Shostakovich No. 13; Schnittke No. 4 Panton; Mozart K589 and K370, Lyrinx; Dvořák; Martinů; Janáček complete quartets, Cadenza; Complete Dvořák String Quartets; Complete Martinů String Quartets; 1 CD, Clarinet Quintets by Mozart and Krommer. *Publications:* Complete Works of Smetana and Janáček String Quartet. *Honours:* with members of Stamic Quartet: Winner, International Festival of Young Soloists, Bordeaux, 1977, Winner, EBU International String Quartet Competition, 1986, Academie Charles Cros Grand Prix du Disque,

1989 for Dvořák Quartets, 1991 for Martinů Quartets; Diapason d'Or, 1994 for Dvořák Quintets.

KELANI, Reem Yousef, BSc; Palestinian singer, musicologist, broadcaster and teacher; b. 7 Aug. 1963, Manchester, England; d. of Yousef Zaid Kelani and of the late Yusra Sharif Zu'bi; m. Christopher Somes-Charlton. *Education:* Kuwait Univ. *Career:* raised in Kuwait; fmr marine biologist; returned to UK 1989; est. The Miktab Ltd with Chris Somes-Charlton 2005; performer and researcher of Arabic music, has carried out research into traditional music in Palestine and in Lebanese refugee camps; workshops and lectures on Arabic and Palestinian music; performed jt concert with Kardes Turkuler, TIM Maslak, Istanbul 2014. *Radio:* Distant Chords (writer and presenter, BBC Radio 4) 2001–02, In Praise of God (presenter, BBC World Service), The Dance of the Seven Veils (writer and presenter, BBC Radio 4) 2007, Lullabies in the Arab World (contrib. in interview and songs) 2012. *Films:* The Unholy Land (series assoc. producer) 1998, Les Chebabs de Yarmouk (wrote and performed title music) 2013, The Brick 2013. *Recordings include:* Exile (BBC Jazz Award for Best CD) 2003, Sprinting Gazelle: Palestinian Songs from the Motherland and the Diaspora 2006, Celebrating Subversion – The Anti-Capitalist Roadshow 2012. *Address:* The Miktab Ltd, PO Box 31652, London, W11 2YF, England (office). *Telephone:* (7092) 811747 (office). *E-mail:* miktab@reemkelani.com (office). *Website:* www.reemkelani.com.

KELEMEN, Barnabás; Hungarian violinist; b. 12 June 1978, Budapest. *Education:* Franz Liszt Academy, Budapest. *Career:* appeared at Brabant Festival, Netherlands, and Cambridge Festival, England, 1992; performances in Italy, 1995, Spain, 1996, on 3SAT television, Saarbrücken, Germany, 1997, and at Wigmore Hall, London, 1998. *Recordings:* F. Liszt: Works for Violin and Piano, with Sergely Bogányi, Bartók Violin Sonatas Nos 1 & 2/Sonata for Solo Violin (Gramophone Award for Best Chamber Recording 2013). *Honours:* 2nd Prize, Szigeti Competition, Budapest, 1997; 1st Prize, Mozart Competition, Salzburg, 1999. *Current Management:* Clemens Concerts Ltd, Attila út 61, 1013 Budapest, Hungary; Béla Simon Artist Management, 29 Goldhurst Terrace, London NW6 3HB, England. *E-mail:* bs@zene91.freeserve.co.uk.

KELEMEN, Milko; composer; b. 30 March 1924, Slatina, Croatia. *Education:* Zagreb Academy of Music, studied with Messiaen and Aubin in Paris, with Wolfgang Fortner in Freiburg, at Siemens Electronic Music Studio, Munich. *Career:* taught composition, Zagreb Conservatory, 1955–58, 1960–65; founder, Zagreb Biennial Festival, President, 1961; taught at Schumann Conservatory, Düsseldorf, 1972; Professor of Composition, Hochschule für Musik, Stuttgart, 1973; Professor of Composition, Hochschule Hans Eisler, Berlin, 1999. *Compositions include:* The Abandoned, ballet, 1964; O Primavera, tenor, strings, 1965; Words, cantata, 1966; Composé, 2 pianos, orchestra, 1967; Changeant, cello, orchestra, 1968; Motion, string quartet, 1969; The Siege, opera after Camus, 1970; Floreal, orchestra, 1970; Varia Melodia, string quartet, 1972; Gasho, 4 choir groups, 1974; Seven Agonies, mezzo, 1975; Mageia, orchestra, 1978; Apocalypse, ballet opera, 1979; Grand Jeu Classique, violin, orchestra, 1982; Love Song, strings, 1984; Dramatico, cello, orchestra, 1985; Fantasmus, viola, orchestra, 1986; Archetypon, orchestra, 1986; Landscapes, mezzo, string quartet, 1986; Memories, string trio, 1987; Sonnets, string quartet, 1987; Nonet, 1988; Requiem, speaker, ensemble, 1994; Salut au Monde, oratorio, soloists, two choruses, orchestra, projections, light actions, text Walt Whitman, 1995; Concerto for Oboe, English Horn, Oboe D'Amore and chamber orchestra; Good Bye My Fancy for violin and piano; Fantastic Animals for chorus, 1996; For Anton (Bruckner) for orchestra, 1996; Delicate Clusters for orchestra, 1999; Concerto 2000 for five singers and orchestra, 1999; Horn and Strings, 1999; Glissade, concerto for clarinet and orchestra, 2001; Tromberia, concerto for trumpet and orchestra, 2001; Aural, trio for violin, cello and piano, 2002; Orion, Venus, Andromeda, chorus for children; Inferno di Dante for bass solo; Intonazioni Poetiche for chamber orchestra; Pas de Deux, duo for violin and cello; Incanto for solo violin. *Address:* Bergstrasse 62/II, 70186 Stuttgart, Germany.

KELÉN, Peter; Hungarian singer (tenor); b. 27 July 1950, Budapest. *Career:* sang at the Nat. Opera, Budapest from 1974, notably as Werther, Edgardo in Lucia di Lammermoor, Alfredo, Don Carlos, the Duke of Mantua, Don Ottavio and Don José; guest appearances at La Scala, Milan, as Fenton in Falstaff 1983, Ernesto in Don Pasquale at the Vienna Staatsoper, Des Grieux in Rio de Janeiro and Riccardo at Milwaukee 1990; Earl's Court, London 1991, as Cavaradossi in Tosca; Budapest 1995, in the premiere of Karl and Anna by Balassa.

KELESSIDI, Elena; Kazakhstani singer (soprano); b. 1970. *Education:* Alma-Ata Conservatory. *Career:* season 1991 at the Alma-Ata Opera as Bizet's Leila, Zerlina in Auber's Fra Diavalo, Wolf-Ferrari's Serafina and Amor in Orfeo ed Euridice; Mozart's Mme Herz and Constanze at the Athens State Opera, 1992; Donna Anna for Latvian Opera, under Gustav Kuhn; Royal Opera, Covent Garden from 1996, as Voice from Heaven in Don Carlos, Violetta and Handel's Cleopatra 1997; season 1998–99 as Violetta for the Bavarian State Opera; Sang the Queen of Shemakha in The Golden Cockerel with the Royal Opera at Sadler's Wells 1991 and Giulietta in I Capuleti e i Montecchi at Covent Garden 2001; further engagements as Violetta in Monte Carlo and Hamburg, Tatiana (Eugene Onegin) at Montpellier and Gilda in Rio; season 2001–02 as Mimi at the Opéra Bastille and the New York Met, Susanna for Dallas Opera and Liu in Turandot for Netherlands Opera. *Current Management:* Zemsky/Green Artists Management, 730 Fifth Avenue,

Suite 1802, New York, NY 10019, USA. *Telephone:* (212) 300-8003. *Fax:* (212) 300-8001. *E-mail:* zgartists@aol.com. *Website:* www.zemskygreen.com.

KELLER, András; Hungarian violinist; *Chief Conductor, Hungarian Symphony Orchestra;* b. 1960. *Education:* Franz Liszt Acad., Budapest and with Sandor Devich, György Kurtág and András Mihaly. *Career:* member of the Keller String Quartet 1986–, debut concert at Budapest March 1987; Played Beethoven's Grosse Fuge and Schubert's Death and the Maiden Quartet at Interforum 87; series of concerts in Budapest with Zoltan Kocsis and Deszö Ranki (Piano) and Kalman Berkes (Clarinet); Further appearances in Nuremberg, at the Chamber Music Festival La Baule and tours of Bulgaria, Austria, Switzerland, Italy (Ateforum 88 Ferrara), Belgium and Ireland; Artistic Dir Arcus Temporum Festival, Budapest 2005–; Chief Conductor, Hungarian Symphony Orchestra 2007–. *Recordings:* albums for Hungaroton (from 1989). *Honours:* MIDEM Classical Award, Grand Prix, l'Academie Charles Cros, Caecilia Prize, Belgium, Deutsche Schallplattenpreis. *Address:* Vitorla U.3, 1031 Budapest, Hungary.

KELLER, Heinrich; Swiss flautist and composer; b. 14 Nov. 1940, Winterthur; m. 1968; three s. *Education:* Conservatory, Zürich. *Career:* debut, 1965; Philharmony, Bremen, 1965–66; Orchestra of St Gallen, 1967–72; Musikkollegium Winterthur, solo Flautist, 1972–; mem, Schweizerischer Tonkunstlerverein; Musikkollegium Winterthur, solo Flautist, 1972–1990; Musikhochschule Winterthur, Professor of Flute, 1972–2003. *Compositions:* Aleph, 1966; Blaserquintett, 1972; Puzzle, 1973; Streichquartett, 1973–74; Reduktion, 1974; Refrains, 1975; Ritual, 1979; Rencontre, flute and harpsichord, 1985; Verlorene Spur for piano, 1986; Rand for flute solo, 2002. *Recordings:* Flotenmusik aus Frankreich and Italien; Schubert, ihr Blumlein; Baroque and Rokoko, Flute music; 'Wie Risse im Schatten' by Mathias Steinauer; Sonata for Flute by Philipp Jarnach. *Honours:* Prize for composing String Quartet, Tonhalle, Zürich, 1974; Carl-Heinrich-Ernst Prize, 1998; Cultural Award of the City of Winterthur, 2000. *Address:* Grüzenstrasse 14, 8400 Winterthur, Switzerland.

KELLER, Helen; singer (soprano); b. 5 March 1945, Horgen, Zürich, Switzerland. *Education:* studied in Zürich and with Agnes Giebel in Cologne. *Career:* concert performances in Switzerland and elsewhere from 1971, with a repertoire including Rossini's Stabat Mater, L'Enfance du Christ, Schöpfung and Jahreszeiten, Elijah and St Paul, works by Bach and Handel and Honegger's Roi David; appearances at Amsterdam, Antwerp, Paris, Milan, Annsbach, Karlsruhe and the USA, in Britten, Brahms, Schubert, Monteverdi, Pergolesi, Vivaldi and Schumann; stage engagements as Salome in San Giovanni Battista by Stradella at St Gallen and in Le Convenzione Teatrali by Donizetti at Zürich. *Recordings:* Messiah, Schubert's Mass in G and San Giovanni Battista.

KELLER, Peter; Swiss singer (tenor); b. 16 March 1945, Thurgau; m. Helen Keller. *Education:* studied in Zürich, with Ernst Haefliger in Berlin and Agnes Giebel in Cologne. *Career:* has sung at the Zürich Opera from 1973, notably in the Monteverdi series and as Pedrillo, Monostatos, Jacquino, Wagner's David and Steuermann, Valzacchi in Rosenkavalier and M. Triquet in Eugene Onegin 1991; guest engagements at Munich, Hamburg, Düsseldorf (Edgar in Reimann's Lear), Milan, Edinburgh, Berlin and Vienna; concert singer in Europe and on tour with Helen Keller in the USA; sang in Puccini's Trittico at Zürich, 1996; season 2000–01 at Zürich in Lulu, Carmen, The Queen of Spades and Die Zauberflöte (Priest). *Recordings include:* Die Zauberflöte, Il Ritorno d'Ulisse and Monteverdi's Orfeo; Diary of One who Disappeared by Janáček; Handel's Israel in Egypt and Mendelssohn's Christus; Zemlinsky's Kleider Machen Leute. *Current Management:* Aria's di Novella Partacini & Alexandra Plaickner, Via Josef Weingartner 4, 39022 Lagundo, Italy. *Telephone:* (473) 200200. *Fax:* (473) 222424. *E-mail:* info@arias.it. *Website:* www.arias.it.

KELLER, Verena; German singer (mezzo-soprano); b. 8 Sept. 1942, Schwerin. *Education:* studied in Vienna with Hans Hotter and in Berlin, lieder with Erik Werba. *Career:* engaged at Hanover 1963–66, Bonn 1979–88, Mainz 1983–86; guest appearances at Cologne, Geneva, Naples, Herrenhausen and Göttingen; roles have included Mozart's Ramiro, Carmen, Santuzza, Ortrud, Brangaene, Kundry, Venus, Fricka; Verdi's Amneris, Azucena and Ulrica, Strauss's Clytemnestra and Herodias, Janáček's Kabanicha and the Witch in Hansel and Gretel; concert engagements in Baroque music throughout Germany and in Paris, Rome, Los Angles and Vancouver. *Recordings include:* Dvořák's Mass in D.

KELLERMAN, Julia Eleanor Margaret, BA; British music book editor (retd); b. 10 March 1937, London, England; m.; one s. *Education:* Univ. of Bristol and Birkbeck Coll., London. *Career:* House Ed., Master Musicians Series, J. M. Dent & Sons Ltd 1972–94; freelance ed., Oxford Univ. Press 1994–99; Man. Music & Letters Trust 1996–2005; mem. Royal Musical Assocn. *Address:* 87 Hampstead Way, London, NW11 7LG, England (home). *Telephone:* (20) 8458-6113 (home).

KELLOGG, Cal Stewart, DipMus; American conductor and composer; *Music Director, Symphony of the Southwest;* b. 26 July 1947, Long Beach, CA. *Education:* Conservatorio di Musica Santa Cecilia, Rome. *Career:* symphonic debut at Monte Carlo 1975; opera debut with Rome Opera 1976; debut as bassoonist, toured with Renato Fasano's Piccola Teatro Musicale di Roma 1967–72; soloist, RAI Orchestra of Rome 1972; Music Dir, Virginia Chamber Orchestra 1993–98; Music Dir, Arizona Opera 1999–2005; Music Dir, Symphony of the Southwest 2005–; conductor of symphonic concerts with

Baltimore Symphony, New World Symphony, Monte Carlo, Accademia Nazionale di Santa Cecilia, Maggio Fiorentino, La Fenice, San Carlo, RAI Orchestras of Rome, Torino and Naples, Antwerp Philharmonic, Spoleto Festival Orchestra, Orchestra of Illinois, Seattle Symphony, Israel Sinfonietta of Beersheva; Dir of Opera, Rome Opera, Teatro Communale di Firenze, San Francisco Opera, San Carlo, Teatro Regio di Parma, NYC Opera, Santa Fe, Washington Opera, St Louis, Houston Grand Opera, Canadian Opera Company, Opera Montréal, Seattle Opera, Edinburgh Opera Festival, Israel Festival, Spoleto Festival, Chautauqua Festival PBS television live from Lincoln Center, New York City Opera production of Menotti's The Saint of Bleecker Street; radio broadcasts of Tosca 1978, Houston Grand Opera, Ballo in Maschera 1981, Canadian Opera Company, Il Trovatore 1984 and Macbeth 1986; conducted Andrea Chénier at Philadelphia 1997. *Compositions:* Sullivan Ballou's Letter to his Wife for bass baritone and orchestra (a setting of a Civil War letter) 1990. *Recordings:* Thomas Pasatieri: Three Sisters (two-act opera) 1986. *Current Management:* Pinnacle Arts Management, 889 Ninth Avenue, 2nd Floor, New York, NY 10019, USA. *Telephone:* (212) 397-7915. *Fax:* (212) 397-7920. *Website:* www.pinnaclearts.com. *Address:* Symphony of the Southwest, 122 North Macdonald Street, Mesa, AZ 85201, USA (office). *Telephone:* (480) 827-2143 (office). *E-mail:* symphonyofthesouthwest@gmail.com (office). *Website:* symphonyofthesouthwest.org (office).

KELLOGG, Paul, BA; American opera company director; b. 1947, Hollywood, Calif. *Education:* Univ. of Texas, Univ. of Nancy. *Career:* taught French at Allen-Stevenson School, Asst Head 1967–75; Gen. Dir Glimmerglass Opera, Cooperstown, NY 1979–96, Artistic Dir 1996–2006; Gen. Dir and Artistic Dir New York City Opera 1996–2007 (retd); fmr mem. Bd of Dirs Opera America. *Honours:* Hon. DFA (Hartwick Coll.), (Syracuse Univ.), (Hamilton Coll.). *Address:* c/o New York City Opera, New York State Theater at Lincoln Center, New York, NY 10023, USA.

KELLY, Bryan; British composer, pianist and conductor; b. 3 Jan. 1934, Oxford, England. *Education:* Royal Coll. of Music with Gordon Jacob and Herbert Howells, studied in Paris with Boulanger. *Career:* taught at the Royal Scottish Acad. of Music; Prof. of Composition, Royal Coll. of Music 1962–84; resident at Castiglione del Lago, Italy 1984–. *Compositions:* orchestral: The Tempest Suite for strings 1964, Cookham Concertino 1969, Divertimento for brass band 1969, Oboe Concerto 1972, Edinburgh Dances for Brass Band 1973, Guitar Concerto 1978, Andalucia and Concertante Music or Brass 1976, 1979, two Symphonies 1983, 1986; vocal: Tenebrare Nocturnes for tenor, chorus and orchestra 1965, Magnificat and Nunc Dimittis for chorus and organ 1965, The Shield of Achilles for tenor and orchestra 1966, Sleep Little Baby (carol) 1968, Stabat Mater 1970, At the Round Earth's Imagin'd Corners for tenor, chorus and strings 1972, Abingdon Carols 1973, Let There Be Light for soprano, narrator, chorus and orchestra 1973, Latin Magnificat 1979, Te Deum and Jubilate for chorus and organ 1979, Dover Beach for chorus 1995, Piano Sonata 1971, Prelude and Fugue for organ 1960, Pastorale and Paen for organ 1973; chamber music; for children: Herod do your Worst (nativity opera) 1968, On Christmas Eve (suite of carols) 1968, The Spider Monkey Uncle King (opera pantomime) 1971. *Recordings include:* The Choral Music of Bryan Kelly.

KELLY, Declan; singer (tenor); b. 1965, Ireland. *Education:* Royal Irish Acad. of Music, Nat. Opera Studio, London. *Career:* debut in Mozart's The Magic Flute, Opéra du Rhin, A Midsummer Night's Dream 1998; mem., National Chamber Choir, Dublin; mem., St Patrick's Cathedral Choir, Dublin, Tamino, Mid-Wales Opera, Wexford Festival Opera, Holland Park Opera, European Chamber Opera, Opera Theatre Company, Dublin; Ferrando, Young Dublin Opera; Camille, Clonter Opera; Borsa, Pimlico Opera and Holland Park Opera; Frederic, Carl Rosa Productions, and both La Chericia and the Villager, Wexford Arithmetic/Teapot/Frog in L'Enfant et les Sortilèges, National Concert Hall, Dublin; Spirit, and understudy of Pylade, English Bach Festival, Covent Garden and Athens; regular soloist, National Symphony and RTE Concert Orchestra; concerts, television and radio; solo recitals in Ireland, the UK and USA; charity concerts for Irish Youth Fund, New Jersey 1991; Mozart Requiem, Ulster Orchestra 1998–99, performances in Belfast, Wexford and at the NCH, Dublin; festival company tenor, Buxton Festival 1998; Tamino, Mid-Wales Opera on tour; Messiah, Fairfield Halls, London Mozart Players; Mozart Requiem with Vladimir Spivakov and Moscow Virtuosi, Madrid; Rossini Petite Messe Solennelle, Gower Chorale; Carmina Burana, Hastings; The Creation, Dublin; Scaramuccio, Opéra National du Rhin; Almaviva, The Barber of Seville, Mid-Wales Opera. *Recordings:* Te Deum with Myung-Whun Chung and L'Accademia di Santa Cecilia. *Address:* 9 The Court, Dalcassian Downs, Glasnevin, Dublin 9, Republic of Ireland.

KELLY, Frances; British harpist; b. 1955. *Career:* regular performances with the New London Consort in medieval and renaissance music; has toured in Europe and the Far East; Early Music Network tours in the UK 1986 and 1988; freelance engagements with the Consort of Musicke and the Gabrieli Consort and Players Recitals with soprano Evelyn Tubb; on modern harp was mem. of the Ondine Ensemble, giving performances in the UK and USA; partnership with the flautist Ingrid Culliford from 1977; BBC recital with tenor Ian Partridge; concerto soloist in the premieres of Edward Cowie's Concerto in Newcastle and London and for Tyne Tees Television; season 1988 included Debussy and Ravel with the Lindsay Quartet, chamber music by Bruch for the BBC and concerts in London, Denmark, Bruges and Utrecht as continuo player with the Consort of Musicke; South Bank Summer Music

Festival with the New London Consort; played in Oswald von Wolkenstein concert 1997. *Recordings include:* Debussy's Trio Sonata with the Athena Ensemble, Britten's A Ceremony of Carols with the Choir of Christ Church Cathedral, Oxford, Mozart's Concerto K299 with the Academy of Ancient Music, Harp collection (solo, Amon Ra). *Address:* Trinity Laban Conservatoire of Music and Dance, Faculty of Music, King Charles Court, Old Royal Naval College, Greenwich, London, SE10 9JF, England (office). *Telephone:* (20) 8305-4444 (office). *E-mail:* f.kelly@trinitylaban.ac.uk (office). *Website:* www.trinitylaban.ac.uk (office).

KELLY, Janis; singer (soprano); b. 1954, Glasgow, Scotland. *Education:* Royal Scottish Acad. of Music, Royal Coll. of Music, studied in Paris. *Career:* represented Britain at the UNESCO Young Musicians' Rostrum at Bratislava 1981; operatic roles include Serpetta in La Finta Giardiniera (Glyndebourne 1991); Flora in The Knot Garden and Mozart's Despina, Zerlina and Susanna 1991, for Opera Factory; ENO as Amor in L'Incoronazione di Poppea, Flora in The Turn of the Screw, Kitty in Anna Karenina by Iain Hamilton, Barbarina, Bekhetaten in Akhnaten, Woman/Fury in The Mask of Orpheus, Papagena, Yum-Yum, and Rose in Street Scene; Magnolia in Show Boat for Opera North; concert appearances in the USA, Canada, Paris and fmr Czechoslovakia; season 1992 as Ottavia in The Coronation of Poppea, and Countess in Marriage of Figaro for Opera Factory, Governess in Turn of the Screw, Bath City Opera, Tatyana in Eugene Onegin for Kentish Opera; sang the Countess in Figaro for ENO, Amaranta in La fedeltà Premiata (Garsington), and Fairy in Purcell's Fairy Queen for ENO 1995; Dorabella at Garsington and Romilda in Xerxes and the Countess in Figaro for ENO 1997; Rosalinda in Die Fledermaus for Scottish Opera and Opera Ireland 1998; Violetta in La Traviata with Opera North 1998; Wigmore Hall Soirée Fauré 1999; King Arthur in Concert in Portugal and St John Passion in Madrid; La Rondine with Opera North 1999; Mrs Nixon in Nixon in China with ENO; The Cunning Little Vixen with Opera North 2001; directed Così fan tutte, Grange Park 2001; Marschallin in Der Rosenkavalier with Opera North 2002; Despina in Così fan tutte with ENO 2002; Miss Jessel, Grange Park; Elettra in Mozart's Idomeneo with Opera North 2003; directed Iolanthe, Grange Park; appeared as Elizabeth in Maria Stuarda, Grange Park 2005, Magda in La Rondine for Opera North; Royal Opera House debut Gianni Schicchi 2009; title role in premiere of Rufus Wainwright's Prima Donna, Manchester Int. Festival 2009; Met Opera debut as Pat Nixon in Nixon in China 2011; Lady Billows in Albert Herring, Los Angeles Opera 2012. *Films:* sang on soundtrack for The Talented Mr. Ripley; appeared as Liu in The Life of David Gale (directed by Alan Park), as Violetta in Matchpoint (directed by Woody Allen). *Television:* BBC Comedy music series, appears in Question Time, Panorama Special, Applicants (music by Richard Thomas). *Recordings:* Magnolia, Showboat; Rose, Street Scene; Mozart, Gluck, Puccini, Massenet Arias on Inspector Morse soundtrack albums. *Honours:* Royal Coll. of Music Anna Instone Award, Countess of Munster, Caird and Royal Soc. of Arts scholarships. *Current Management:* c/o Musichall Ltd, Vicarage Way, Ringmer, East Sussex, BN8 5LA, England. *Telephone:* (1273) 814240. *Fax:* (1273) 813637. *E-mail:* info@musichall.uk.com. *Website:* www.musichall.uk.com.

KELLY, Judith (Jude) Pamela, CBE, OBE, BA; British theatre director; Artistic Director, Southbank Centre; b. 24 March 1954, Liverpool, England; d. of John Kelly and Ida Kelly; m. Michael Bird 1983; two s. (one deceased) one d. *Education:* Calder High School, Liverpool and Univ. of Birmingham. *Career:* freelance folk and jazz singer 1970–75; actress, Leicester Phoenix Theatre 1975–76; Founder Solent People's Theatre, Dir 1976–80; Artistic Dir Battersea Arts Centre (BAC) 1980–85; Dir of Plays Nat. Theatre of Brent 1982–85; freelance dir 1985–88; Festival Dir York Festival and Mystery Plays 1988; Artistic Dir West Yorkshire Playhouse 1988–2002, Chief Exec. 1993–2002; Founder and Artistic Dir Metal community arts lab., London, Liverpool, Bogotá, Colombia 2002–; Visiting Prof. of Drama, Leeds and Kingston Univs; British Rep. on Culture for UNESCO 1997–; Chair. Common Purpose Charitable Trust 1997–, Qualifications and Curriculum Authority Advisory Group on the Arts 2001–03, Culture, Arts and Educ. Cttee, London 2012 Olympics; Artistic Dir Southbank Centre, London 2005–; Vice-Chair. Nat. Advisory Cttee on Creative and Cultural Educ. 1998; mem. Council RSA 1998–, Ind. TV Comm. 1999–. *Productions include:* at West Yorkshire Playhouse: The Merchant of Venice 1994, Beautification of Area Boy 1996, The Seagull 1998, The Tempest 1998, Singin' in the Rain (Olivier Award for Outstanding Musical Production 2001) 1999, 2000, Half A Sixpence 2000; elsewhere: Sarcophagus (RSC) 1987, When We Were Married (Chichester Festival Theatre, transferred to Savoy Theatre) 1996, Othello (Shakespeare Theatre), Washington, DC 1997, The Elixir of Love (ENO) 1997, Johnson Over Jordan, On the Town (ENO) 2005, The Importance of Being Earnest (Sydney Opera House, Barbican London) 2005–06. *Honours:* Hon. Fellow, Dartington Coll. of Arts, Cen. School of Speech and Drama; Hon. DLitt (Leeds Metropolitan) 1995, (Bradford) 1996, (Leeds) 2000, (York) 2001, (Open Univ.) 2001; Woman of the Year, Yorks. 1996, 2002, Yorkshire TV Personality of the Year 2002, Dream Time Fellowship, NESTA 2003, named by The Independent newspaper No. 8 in "Theatreland's top 100 players" 2006, assessed by Woman's Hour (BBC Radio 4) as one of the 100 most powerful women in the UK 2013. *Address:* Southbank Centre, Belvedere Road, London, SE1 8XX (office); Metal, 198A Broadhurst Gardens, London, NW6 3AY, England. *Telephone:* (20) 7921-0636 (office). *E-mail:* jude.kelly@southbankcentre.co.uk (office). *Website:* www.southbankcentre.co.uk (office).

KELLY, Paul Austin; American singer (tenor); b. 1964. *Career:* debut at New York City Opera, as Tamino in Mozart's Die Zauberflöte; roles in Rossini's Barbiere di Siviglia at Royal Opera, Rome Opera, Pesaro and New York Metropolitan Opera 2000; in Zelmira at Pesaro, Opéra de Lyon and Paris; in Ermione at Glyndebourne; in Comte Ory at Canadian Opera and Glimmerglass; Cenerentola at Die Vlaamse Opera and Philadelphia; Turco in Italia at La Scala; Donizetti roles include Tonio at La Scala, Rome Opera, Opéra de Monte Carlo, Ernesto at Bologna and Austin Lyric Opera; Mozart roles include Tamino at La Scala, City Opera and Opera Pacific; Belmonte at Catania and Hawaii Opera; Don Ottavio at Dublin, Santiago and New York City Opera; Alessandro in Il Re Pastore at Opéra de Nice and Mostly Mozart Festival; season 1999–2000 with Don Ottavio at New Israeli Opera; Ferrando at Glyndebourne; Bach B Minor Mass in Paris; other repertory includes roles in Bellini's La Sonnambula, Donizetti's Lucrezia Borgia, Offenbach's La Belle Hélène, and Rossini's Pietra del Paragone and Otello; concerts include Rossini's Stabat Mater in Paris and Wexford, Mozart Requiem in Rome and Lisbon, Messiah, St Matthew Passion, Magnificat and Missa Solemnis. *Recordings include:* Three Rossini Tenors; Zoraide di Granata; La Romanzesco; Rossini Cantatas; Der Stein der Weise; The Holy Sonnets of John Donne by Britten. *Current Management:* Herbert Barrett Management, 266 West 37th Street, 20th Floor, New York, NY 10018, USA. *Telephone:* (212) 245-3530. *Fax:* (212) 397-5860. *Website:* www.herbertbarrett.com; www.paulaustinkelly.com.

KELM, Linda; American singer (soprano); b. 11 Dec. 1944, Utah. *Education:* studied with Jennie Tourel at the Aspen School of Music and in New York. *Career:* debut in Seattle 1977, as Helmwige and Third Norn in the Ring; sang Turandot with Wilmington, 1979, followed by performances at Seattle, New York City Opera 1983, Chicago, San Francisco and Amsterdam; sang Salome at St Louis and Princess in Rusalka at Carnegie Hall; Perugia 1983, as Dirce in Cherubini's Demofoonte; Seattle Opera, 1985; as Brünnhilde; further guest appearances include Helmwige in the Ring.

KELTERBORN, Rudolf, DipMus; Swiss composer, conductor and academic; b. 3 Sept. 1931, Basel; m. Erika Kelterborn Salathe 1957; one s. *Education:* Music Acad., Basel, studied composition with Blacher and Fortner, Salzburg and Detmold, conducting with Markevitch. *Career:* teacher, conductor, Basel 1956–60; Prof. of Composition, North-West German Music Acad., Detmold 1960–68, Hochschule, Zürich 1968–75; Ed. Swiss Music Review 1968–75; Head of Music Dept, Swiss Radio 1975–80; Prof. of Composition, Hochschule, Karlsruhe 1980–83; Dir Music Acad., Basel 1983–94; Guest Prof. in USA 1970, 1980, Japan 1986, 1990, China 1993, St Petersburg 2001; mem. Akad. der Freien Künste Mannheim 1994–. *Compositions include:* chamber music including seven string quartets 1954–2001; five symphonies; five operas: Kaiser Jovian 1967, Ein Engel Kommt nach Babylon 1977, Der Kirschgarten 1984, Ophelia 1984, Julia 1990; Namenlos for ensemble and electronics 1996; various works for orchestra including 4 Movements for Classical Orchestra 1996, Herbstmusik, 7 pieces for orchestra 2002, Grosses Relief for orchestra 2002; concertos for various solo instruments; a ballet, cantatas, piano and organ works. *Recordings:* several under various labels. *Publications:* Ensemble-Bücher 1–5 for different ensembles 1990–2014, Komponist, Musikdenker, Vermittler (various authors) 1993, Analyse und Interpretation 1993, Suche nach Wörtern, Suche nach Musik-Kompositorischer Umgang mit Texten 2009. *Honours:* Bernhard Sprengel Prize of the German Industry 1962, Arts Prize City of Basel 1984, Composition Prize, Swiss Musicians' Asscn. *Address:* Delsbergerallee 61, 4053 Basel, Switzerland (home). *Telephone:* (61) 2618319 (home). *E-mail:* rudolf.kelterborn@bluewin.ch (home). *Website:* www.kelterborn.ch.

KEMENY, Alexander; violinist; b. 22 April 1943, Solna, Sweden; m. (divorced); one d. *Education:* Bratislava Conservatory, Czechslovakia, Music Acad. in Prague with Prof. A. Plocek. *Career:* debut in 1970; Concertmaster, Innsbruck Symphonic Orchestra 1973–75; violinist, Prague Symphonic Orchestra, Norrkoping Symphony Orchestra, Sweden; freelance concert violinist 1978–; soloist with orchestra playing works by Myslivecek, Mozart, Beethoven, Brixi, Mendelssohn, Wieniawski, Eklund, and chamber music player of both classical and modern music concerts in Czechoslovakia, Sweden, Denmark and Poland; performed in Piano Trio and in Duo with guitarist Vladimir Vectomov; radio performances in Czechoslovakia, Sweden and Austria; performed at Bornholm Music Festival, Denmark 1987. *Recordings:* Paganini, Giuliani, and Kowalski, Radio Prague and Bratislava; Smetana, Johansson and Telemann, Radio Sweden; Suk, Smetana, Foerster, and Suchoñ, Radio Austria.

KEMMER, Mariette; Luxembourg singer (soprano); b. 1960. *Education:* Luxembourg Conservatoire, Rheinland National College of Music in Düsseldorf. *Career:* sang at the Théâtre de la Monnaie, Brussels, as Mélisande, Sophie, Pamina, Micaela and Mozart's Countess; guest appearances at the Vienna Staatsoper, Munich, Berlin, Hamburg, Frankfurt, Dresden, Stuttgart, Zürich, Geneva, Basle, Berne, Lausanne, Verona, Dublin, Karlsruhe, Mannheim, Nürnberg, Strasbourg, Marseille, Nancy, Montpellier, Nantes, Avignon, Metz and Liège; has appeared at the festivals of Aix-en-Provence, Wexford and Bregenz; Other roles include Mozart's Ilia, Fiordiligi and Donna Elvira, Marguerite, Antonia, Tatiana and the Countess in Capriccio; Has appeared in concert, with major orchestras in Vienna, Paris Prague, Zürich, Brussels, Luxembourg, Monte-Carlo, Antwerp, Liège, Bregenz, Bonn, Nürnberg, Bamberg, Stuttgart, Heidelberg, Metz, Nancy, Nantes, Montpellier and the festival at Round Top, Texas. *Current Management:* Living Art

Impresariat – Paris, 21 rue Foucher-Lepelletier, 92130 Issy les Moulineaux, France. *Telephone:* (1) 40-93-05-28. *Fax:* (1) 46-38-65-54. *E-mail:* angelika.belamaric@wanadoo.fr.

KEMP, Nicola-Jane; British singer (coloratura soprano); b. 1965, England. *Education:* Chetham's School of Music, Girton Coll., Cambridge, Royal Coll. of Music, RSAMD, Glasgow, studied with Margaret Hyde. *Career:* appearances with British Youth Opera, Music Theatre Wales, London Opera Players, Central Festival Opera, Music Theatre Kernow, Aix-en-Province Festival, Covent Garden; roles have included Verdi's Oscar; Mozart's Constanze and Queen of Night; Birtwistle's Pretty Polly in Punch and Judy; season 1998, Covent Garden Festival; Jauchzet Gott (Bach) at the Purcell Room; Barbican with the London Soloists Chamber Orchestra and at Crans Montana Festival; season 1999 with Strauss's Zerbinetta, St John's Smith Square, and the Académie Européenne de Musique at Aix-en-Provence; A Mind of Winter (Benjamin) with Orchestre de Rouen 2001; Lakmé (Belcanto Opera) 2001; Queen of Night and Papagena at Covent Garden 2002; Jubilee Concert at Chatsworth House 2002; UK tour with Vienna Galan 2002–03; concerts throughout the UK. *Current Management:* c/o Foxroe Artist Management, 103 Nottingham Road, New Basford, Nottingham, NG7 7AJ, England. *Telephone:* (115) 847-8719. *Fax:* (115) 847-8719. *E-mail:* info@foxroe.com. *Website:* www.foxroe.com; www.nicolajanekemp.co.uk.

KEMPF, Frederick; British pianist; b. 14 Oct. 1977, England. *Education:* Royal Acad. of Music with Ronald Smith, studied with Christopher Elton. *Career:* debut with Mozart's Piano Concerto No. 12 in A major, K414 with Royal Philharmonic Orchestra 1985; has worked with world's leading orchestras and conductors, including Philharmonia Orchestra under Sir Andrew Davis and Kurt Sanderling, Royal Philharmonic Orchestra under Daniele Gatti and Matthias Bamert, City of Birmingham Symphony (CBSO)/Oramo, La Scala Philharmonic/Chailly, St Petersburg Philharmonic/Temirkanov, Russian State Symphony/Sinaisky, Dresden Symphony/Herbig, Seattle Symphony/Schwarz, San Francisco Symphony/Tortelier, Philadelphia Orchestra/Sawallisch, NHK Symphony/Simonov, European Union Youth Orchestra/Ashkenazy, Prague Philharmonia/Belohlavek, Rotterdam Philharmonic/Viotti, Residentie Orkest/Jaarvi, Vancouver Symphony/Tovey, Luxembourg Philharmonic/Krivine and São Paulo State Symphony/Kalmar; recent and forthcoming highlights include engagements with Royal Philharmonic in Europe, at London's Cadogan Hall and Royal Festival Hall, CBSO, Royal Liverpool Philharmonic, RTÉ Symphony Orchestra, English Chamber Orchestra, projects with European Union Chamber Orchestra, Brabants Orkest, Salzburg Mozarteum, Orchestra della Toscana, Bergen Philharmonic, St Petersburg Philharmonic, major UK tour with Moscow Philharmonic, Prague Philharmonia, Staatstheater Stuttgart, Westdeutsche Sinfonia, Oregon Symphony, Hong Kong Sinfonietta, KBS Symphony and New Zealand Symphony, concerts with Tasmania, Adelaide and Queensland Orchestras, tour of Japan with Royal Philharmonic Orchestra 2009; has appeared as recitalist at Barbican Centre and Cadogan Hall, London, Symphony Hall, Birmingham, Herkulessaal, Munich, Musikhalle, Hamburg, Suntory Hall, Tokyo, Symphony Hall, Osaka, Grande Teatro di Verona, Milan Conservatorio's Sala Verdi, Tonhalle, Zurich, Great Hall of the Conservatoire, Moscow and Philharmonic Hall, St Petersburg; return visits to Moscow Grand Conservatory, St Petersburg Philharmonia, Conservatorio G. Verdi, Milan and UK recital tour with programme featuring Bach's Goldberg Variations in leading concert halls including Cadogan Hall, London, Bridgewater Hall, Manchester, Sage Gateshead, Newcastle, St David's Hall, Cardiff and Nat. Concert Hall, Dublin 2009. *Recordings include:* piano music by Mussorgsky, Ravel, Balakirev, Bach, Beethoven, Chopin, Liszt, Prokofiev and Schumann. *Honours:* Jt Winner, Nat. Mozart Competition 1987, Winner, BBC Young Musician of the Year 1992, Best Young British Classical Performer, Classical Brit Awards 2001. *Current Management:* c/o IMG Artists, The Light Box, 111 Power Road, London, W4 5PY, England. *Telephone:* (20) 7957-5800. *Fax:* (20) 7957-5801. *E-mail:* arance@imgartists.com. *Website:* www.imgartists.com.

KEMPSTER, David; British singer (baritone); b. 1969, Chirk, North Wales; m. Charlotte Kinder; one s. *Education:* Royal Northern Coll. of Music. *Career:* engagements with English Nat. Opera in Tosca, House of the Dead 1997–98; Otello, La Traviata, Carmen, Salome and Dialogue of the Carmelites 1998–99; Lescaut in Manon Lescaut; Schaunard in La Bohème, Toddy Foran in the world premiere of the Silver Tassie, Chouen Lai in the London premiere of Nixon in China 1999–2000; Di luna in Il Trovatore, Poacher in A Cunning Little Vixen 2000–01; Marcello in La Bohème, Pilate in St John Passion and Renato in Ballo in Maschera 2001–02; roles for Glyndebourne: Escamillo in Carmen, Germont in La Traviata; for Welsh Nat. Opera: Belcore in L'Elisir d'Amore, Marcello in La Bohème; other roles include Rigoletto, Barber's Figaro, Don Giovanni, and Mozart's Count Almaviva; concert repertoire includes Handel's Messiah, Saul and Judas Maccabaeus, Elgar's The Dream of Gerontius, Fauré's Requiem, Mendelssohn's Elijah, Orff's Carmina Burana, Mozart's Requiem, Puccini's Messa di Gloria, Vaughan Williams' A Sea Symphony and Walton's Belshazzar's Feast. *Honours:* BBC Music Magazine Opera Award (for Britten: Peter Grimes) 2014. *Address:* c/o Sue Nicholls, Hazard Chase, 25 City Road, Cambridge, CB1 1DP, England. *Telephone:* (1223) 312400. *Fax:* (1223) 460827. *E-mail:* sue.nicholls@hazardchase.co.uk. *Website:* www.hazardchase.co.uk.

KENDALL, Christopher Wolff, BA, MM; American conductor, lutenist and artistic director; b. 9 Sept. 1949, Zanesville, OH. *Education:* Antioch Coll., Univ. of Cincinnati Conservatory, Dalcroze School of Music, New York.

Career: Dir of 20th-Century Consort, in residence at the Smithsonian Institution, Washington 1976–; Assoc. Conductor, Seattle Symphony 1987–; founder and lutenist, Folger Consort, Ensemble-in-Residence at Folger Shakespeare Library in Washington, DC 1977–; Artistic Dir, Millennium Inc. 1980–; guest conductor, Seattle Symphony, Chamber Music Soc. of Lincoln Center, Eastman Musica Nova, Da Capo Chamber Players, Washington Sinfonia. *Recordings:* 20th-Century Consort Vols I and II, Into Eclipse (Stephen Albert) 20th-Century Consort, Shakespeare's Music (Folger Consort), A Distant Mirror: Carmina Burana (Folger Consort). *Honours:* Houston Film Festival for the Millennium 10 Centuries of Music Gold Award 1986, Emmy Award (for 20th-Century Consort PBS programme on Aaron Copland) 1984.

KENDALL, William; British singer (tenor); b. 1960, London, England. *Education:* King's School, Canterbury, University of Cambridge, studied with Robert Tear and Peter Pears. *Career:* concert appearances under such conductors as Hogwood, Harnoncourt, Gardiner, Mackerras and Boulez; works by Tippett and Tavener conducted by the composers; sang in the world premiere of Penderecki's Polish Requiem; tour of Germany, 1989 with the Monteverdi Choir and Orchestra in the Missa Solemnis and Beethoven's Mass in C; further appearances in season 1990–91 as the Evangelist in the St John Passion, in The Dream of Gerontius and Britten's Serenade in Australia; Mozart Requiems in Oxford and Cambridge and Bach's B Minor Mass with The Sixteen at St John's Smith Square; London Promanade concert appearances and showings at the Holland Festival, Festival Berlin, 1987, and the 1989 Salzburg Festival. *Recordings:* Beethoven Missa Solemnis and Mass in C; Bach and Schütz with the Stuttgart Kammerchor; sacred music by Haydn. *Current Management:* Bureau de Concerts de Valmalète, 7 rue Hoche, 92300 Levallois Perret, France. *Telephone:* 1-47-59-87-59. *Fax:* 1-47-59-87-50. *Website:* www.valmalete.com.

KENGEN, Knud-Erik, DipMus; Danish organist, pianist and composer; b. 17 July 1947, Copenhagen; m. Gerlinde Maria Pagel 1969, one s. one d. *Education:* Univ. of Copenhagen, Royal Danish Acad. of Music, studied with Prof. Aksel Andersen, Leif Kayser. *Career:* Asst Organist, Dome of Copenhagen 1974; Organist, Gladsaxe Church, Copenhagen 1979–; concert organist at numerous concerts in Denmark, Germany, England and Sweden; also played as soloist at first performance of Musica Autumnalis by Axel Borup Jorgensen in The Danish Broadcasting Corpn; as pianist, rehearser and chorus master; accompanist at lieder recitals; organ and choir-music composition style somewhat indebted to modern French church music since Langlais, Duruflé and early Messiaen. *Compositions:* for organ: Toccata (opus 5), Choral Preludes (opus 14 and 26), seven Chorales for the concert (op 43) 1993, Rhapsody, Surrexit Dominus (opus 22), Organ Fantasy, Victimae Paschali (opus 24), Missa Fons Bonitatis (opus 26), Proprium for Hallo-Mass (opus 28), Choral Fantasy, Veni Creator Spiritus (opus 40); for choir: Psalm 12 (opus 21), Cantatas with instruments (opus 35), Stabat Mater 1992, Psalm 23 1999. *Publication:* contributed to The History of Music in Denmark 1978. *Address:* Tranegardsvej 69, 1 TV, 2900 Hellerup, Denmark (home). *Telephone:* 396298 (home). *E-mail:* knudderrik@mobilixnet.dk (home).

KENNEDY, Andrew James, MA; British singer (tenor); b. 1977, England; s. of Thomas Kennedy and Julia Kennedy; m. Kate Kennedy; one s. *Education:* choral scholar King's Coll., Cambridge, Royal Coll. of Music with Neil Mackie. *Career:* concerts include Jaquino in Fidelio, Francesco in Benvenuto Cellini, Mozart's Requiem, London Symphony Orchestra and Sir Colin Davis; Novice in Billy Budd, London Symphony Orchestra and Daniel Harding; Junger Seeman and Hirt in Tristan und Isolde, Shepherd in Oedipus Rex at Edinburgh Int. Festival; Mozart's Requiem and Young Man in Korngold, Das Wunder der Heliane, London Philharmonic Orchestra and Jurowski; Mozart's Mass in C Minor, Hallé Orchestra and Berlioz's Grande Messe de Morts, London Symphony Orchestra, Tortelier and Elgar's Spirit of England Last Night of the BBC Proms 2007; orchestral performances of Britten include Nocturne, BBC National Orchestra of Wales, Serenade for Tenor, Horn and Strings, CBSO, BBC Scottish Symphony Orchestra and BBC National Orchestra of Wales, Les Illuminations, the Scottish Ensemble at the Edinburgh Int. Festival; recitals include Wigmore Hall with Julius Drake, LSO St Luke's with Stephen Osborne, Leeds Lieder Festival with Iain Burnside, Cadogan Hall 2007 BBC Proms with the Nash Ensemble and Edward Gardner, opening recital for the 2005/6 Concertgebouw recital series, Amsterdam, numerous studio recordings for BBC Radio 3; roles include Tamino in The Magic Flute; Flute in A Midsummer Night's Dream, Jaquino in Fidelio, Ferrando in Cosi fan tutte, Nemorino in L'elisir d'amore, Tom Rakewell in The Rake's Progress, Captain Vere in Billy Budd. *Honours:* winner, London Handel Competition 2002, Lieder Prize, Richard Tauber Competition 2003, BBC Cardiff Singer of the World Rosenblatt Recital Prize 2005, Royal Philharmonic Soc. Award for Young Artist 2006, Borletti-Buitoni Trust Award 2007. *Current Management:* Intermusica Artists Ltd, 16 Duncan Terrace, London N1 8BZ, England. *Telephone:* (20) 7239-0191. *Fax:* (20) 7278-8434. *E-mail:* jmaynard@intermusica.co.uk. *Website:* www.intermusica.co.uk.

KENNEDY, John, OBE; British music industry executive; b. 10 Feb. 1953, London. *Education:* Univ. of Leicester. *Career:* mem. Business Affairs Dept, Phonogram 1978, Dir of Business Affairs 1979; then Dir of Business Affairs, CBS Records UK –1984; founding partner entertainment law firm, J. P. Kennedy & Co. 1984–96; CEO PolyGram UK 1996–98 (merged with Universal Music 1998), Chair. and CEO Universal Music UK 1998–2001, Pres. and COO Universal Music Int. 2001–04; bd mem. Int. Fed. for Phonographic Industry (IFPI) 2002–04, and Chair. European Regional Bd 2002–04, Chair. and CEO IFPI 2005–10; co-produced 10 Live 8 concerts worldwide 2005. *Honours:* Chevalier, Ordre des Arts et des Lettres.

KENNEDY, Nicki, BA, RSAMD, ARCM; British singer (soprano) and teacher; *Head of Singing, Repton School;* b. (b. Nicola Jones), 5 Sept. 1966, England; m. John Bowley; two c. *Education:* Univ. of Bristol, Royal Scottish Acad. of Music and Drama, Royal Coll. of Music, London. *Career:* specialist in baroque and classical music; appearances with Philharmonia, Royal Philharmonic Orchestro, Orchestre des Champs Élysées, Academy of Ancient Music, Les Musiciens du Louvre, London Handel Festival, Concertgebow Amsterdam, Wigmore Hall, Snape Maltings, Three Choirs Festival, Aix-en-Provence Festival and festivals of Hallé, Bayreuth, Chaise Dieu, Brighton, Potsdam, Santiago de Compostela; appearances throughout Europe, Japan, Egypt, Dubai, numerous operatic roles by Handel, Monteverdi, Vivaldi and Mozart; broadcasts for EMI, WDR, CPO and others in recordings with Les Musiciens du Louvre, Modo Antiquo, Koelner Akademie, Brook Street Band; performances in Mexico (Festival Cervantino), Turin, Florence, St John's Smith Square, Wigmore Hall 2015; teacher on courses in Czech Repub., France, Spain, UK; Head of Singing, Repton School; teacher for Nat. Youth Choirs of GB, Eton Choral Courses. *Recordings:* Vivaldi Operas and Cantatas; Spanish Lute Songs; Les Musiciens du Louvre; The Musicians of the Globe; Modo Antiquo; Charivari Agreable; Brook Street Band. *E-mail:* nickikennedy@me .com. *Website:* www.nickikennedy.com.

KENNEDY, Nigel Paul, ARCM; British violinist; b. 28 Dec. 1956, Brighton; s. of John Kennedy and Scylla Stoner; m. Agnieska Kennedy; one s. *Education:* Yehudi Menuhin School, Juilliard School of Performing Arts, USA. *Career:* debut playing Mendelssohn's Violin Concerto at Royal Festival Hall with London Philharmonic Orchestra under Riccardo Muti 1977; subsequently chosen by BBC as subject of a five-year documentary on the devt of a soloist; other important debuts include with Berlin Philharmonic 1980, New York 1987; has made appearances at all leading UK festivals and in Europe at Stresa, Lucerne, Gstaad, Berlin and Lockenhaus; tours to Australia, Austria, Canada, Denmark, Germany, Hong Kong, India, Ireland, Italy, Japan, Republic of Korea, New Zealand, Norway, Poland, Spain, Switzerland, Turkey and USA; has given jazz concerts with Stephane Grappelli, including at Edinburgh Festival and Carnegie Hall; performs with his own jazz group; five-year sabbatical 1992–97; Artistic Dir Polish Chamber Orchestra 2002–; apptd Sr Vice-Pres. Aston Villa Football Club 1990. *Television:* Coming Along Nicely (BBC documentary on his early career) 1973–78. *Recordings include:* Strad Jazz 1984, Elgar Sonata with Peter Pettinger 1985, Elgar's Violin Concerto with the London Philharmonic and Vernon Handley (Gramophone magazine Record of the Year, BPI Award for Best Classical Album of the Year) 1985, Vivaldi's Four Seasons, Bartók Solo Sonata and Mainly Black (arrangement of Ellington's Black Brown and Beige Suite), Sibelius Violin Concerto with the City of Birmingham Symphony Orchestra conducted by Sir Simon Rattle, Walton's Violin Concerto with the Royal Philharmonic Orchestra and André Previn, Bruch and Mendelssohn concertos with the English Chamber Orchestra conducted by Jeffrey Tate, Kafka (Kennedy's compositions), Tchaikovsky's Chausson Poème with the London Philharmonic Orchestra 1988, Brahms Violin Concerto with the London Philharmonic under Klaus Tennstedt 1991, Beethoven Violin Concerto with the NDR-Sinfonieorchester and Klaus Tennstedt 1992, chamber works by Debussy and Ravel, Berg's Violin Concerto, Vaughan Williams' The Lark Ascending with Sir Simon Rattle and the CBSO, works by Fritz Kreisler 1998, The Kennedy Experience, chamber works by Bach, Ravel and Kodaly (with Lynn Harrell) 1999, Classic Kennedy with the English Chamber Orchestra 1999, Bach's Concerto for Two Violins in D Minor, Concerto for Oboe and Violin in D Minor and the A Minor and E Major violin concertos the Berlin Philharmonic 2000, Nigel Kennedy Plays Bach 2006, Inner Thoughts 2006, Blue Note Sessions 2006, Polish Spirit 2007, Beethoven and Mozart Violin Concertos 2008, A Very Nice Album 2008, Shhh! 2010. *Publication:* Always Playing 1991. *Honours:* Hon. DLitt (Bath) 1991; Golden Rose of Montreux 1990, Variety Club Showbusiness Personality of the Year 1991, BRIT Award for Outstanding Contribution to British Music 2000, Male Artist of the Year 2001, Echo Klassik Award for Instrumentalist of the Year 2008. *Address:* c/o John Stanley, Kennedy, 90–96 Brewery Road, London, N7 9NT, England. *Website:* www.nigel-kennedy.net.

KENNEDY, Roderick; British singer (bass-baritone); *General Director, Dorset Opera Festival;* b. 7 May 1951, Birmingham, England; m. Jane Randall (deceased); two s. three d. *Education:* Guildhall School, studied with Otakar Kraus. *Career:* debut at Covent Garden 1975; more than 500 performances with the Royal Opera; cr. Lt of Police in The Ice Break by Tippett 1977; appeared with Royal Opera on visits to La Scala 1976, S Korea and Japan 1979, 1986; sang The Doctor in Wozzeck at Edinburgh and San Francisco 1980–81, with further engagements at opera houses throughout Europe and USA; Glyndebourne debut as Don Fernando in Fidelio 1981, followed by Alidoro, Rocco, Seneca in Poppea, and Britten's Theseus; further festival appearances at Aldeburgh, Aix-en-Provence, Montpellier, Strasbourg and Florence; regular performances with ENO, Welsh Nat. Opera and Scottish Opera; repertoire includes the coloratura works of Handel and Rossini; roles include Don Alfonso, King Philip, Pogner, Bottom, as well as many 20th-century works; regular Promenade and concert appearances in UK and abroad; has worked and recorded with conductors including Muti, Kleiber, Colin Davis, Ozawa, Harnoncourt, Solti, Haitink, Mehta, Prêtre, Mackerras and Thieleman; appeared with Carreras, Domingo, Pavarotti, Caballé; sang Britten's Bottom for ENO 1995, 1996, 2004; sang and recorded the Animal Trainer/Athlete in Lulu at Palermo 2001; Gen. Dir, Dorset Opera Festival 2004–. *Recordings include:* Messiah, La Traviata, Hérodiade, La Forza del Destino, Maria Padilla, Die Sieben Todessunden, Offenbach's Robinson Crusoe, Tosca, The Immortal Hour and Le Comte Ory; television films of Lucrezia Borgia, Giulio Cesare, Idomeneo, L'Egisto, Hérodiade, Otello, L'Incoronazione di Poppea, La Cenerentola, Tosca and A Midsummer Night's Dream; The Complete Vocal and Piano Works of Lord Berners (one of Gramophone magazine's Records of the Year 1998), Berg's Lulu 2001. *Address:* Cheselbourne, Dorset, DT2 7NP, England (home). *Telephone:* (1258) 840000 (office). *E-mail:* info@dorsetopera.com. *Website:* www.dorsetopera.com.

KENNER, Kevin Park, BMus, MMus, Artist Dipl., Konzertexam; American/British concert pianist and academic; *Professor, Royal College of Music;* b. 19 May 1963, Calif., USA. *Education:* Peabody Conservatory, Baltimore, Hochschüle für Musik, Hannover, studied with Leon Fleisher and Karl-Heinz Kaemmerling. *Career:* has appeared in Europe, N and Cen. America, the Orient and the fmr Soviet Union since 1989, performing with St Paul Chamber Orchestra, Rochester Philharmonic and ensembles in San Diego, San Francisco, Kansas City and Baltimore; recitals at the Salle Pleyel in Paris, the Châtelet, Queen Elizabeth Hall, London (Int. Piano Series) Carnegie Hall, Avery Fisher Hall and at Kennedy Center, Washington, DC; broadcasts in Japan, Australia, Poland, Germany and Costa Rica; numerous recordings of Chopin, Ravel, Schumann and Piazzolla. *Honours:* First Prize, Kosciuszko Foundation Nat. Competition, New York 1983, New York Chopin Competition 1987, Fifth Prize, Gina Bachauer Int. Competition, Salt Lake City 1988, Three Special Prizes, Van Cliburn Int. Piano Competition, Fort Worth 1989, Int. Terence Judd Award, Manchester 1990, Top Prize (first not awarded), Int. Chopin Piano Competition 1990, Third Prize, Tchaikovsky Int. Piano Competition, Moscow 1990, Fryderyk Award for Best Chamber Music CD of the Year (for recording Piazzoforte) Warsaw 2007. *Current Management:* c/o Künstlersekretariat Rolf Sudbrack, Gösselkoppel 54A, 22339 Hamburg, Germany. *Telephone:* (40) 5382165. *Fax:* (40) 5387720. *E-mail:* rolf.sudbrack@t-online.de. *Website:* www.sudbrackmusik.de. *Telephone:* (20) 7193-1239 (office). *E-mail:* musicunlimiteduk@yahoo.co.uk (office). *Website:* www.kevinkenner.com.

KENNY, Courtney Arthur Lloyd; Irish pianist, repetiteur, accompanist and cabaret singer; b. 8 Nov. 1933, Dublin; s. of Stanhope Lloyd Kenny and Maeve French; m. Caroline Anne Florence Arthur 1972; one s. *Education:* Wellington Coll., Berks., Royal Coll. of Music, London. *Career:* Musical Dir, Bristol Old Vic 1954–57; solo pianist, Western Theatre Ballet 1950s, Royal Ballet 1957; mem. Glyndebourne Festival Opera music staff; Founder Western Opera, Ireland 1963; Wexford Festival Opera staff 1963–96, Head of Music Staff 1974, Sr Repetiteur 1982; Repetiteur for BBC operas La Vida Breve, The Merry Widow, The Count of Luxemburg, The Mikado, Die Fledermaus; Head of Music Staff, New Sadler's Wells Opera 1983–89; Assoc. Music Dir, Ohio Light Opera 1983; mem. of various ensembles, including Bureau Piano Trio, Barbican Ensemble, Peter Lloyd Baroque Trio; Faculty mem., Blossom Festival School of Cleveland Orchestra and Kent State Univ. 1972–80; numerous concert appearances as soloist and accompanist in Europe, USA, Middle East; conducting debut, John Curry Theatre of Skating, then Ohio Light Opera, New Sadler's Wells Opera; cabaret songs at the piano; appearances in USA, Canada, Middle East, England, Scotland and Ireland. *Television:* Reflections in Song (BBC). *Recordings:* with Glyndebourne Festival Opera, recitals with Ian Wallace, two solo recitals (cabaret songs). *Publications:* contrib. to Opera, Musical Theatre. *Address:* Russets, Straight Mile, Etchingham, East Sussex, TN19 7BA, England. *Telephone:* (1580) 819125. *E-mail:* courtney@courtneykenny.co.uk.

KENNY, Jonathan Peter; British singer (countertenor) and conductor; b. 1960, Liverpool. *Education:* Exeter Univ. and Guildhall School of Music. *Career:* appearances with ENO, Opera Theatre Co., Dublin, Opera Factory Zürich, Musica nel Chiostro and at Karlsruhe; roles have included Bertarido in Rodelinda, Arsamenes in Xerxes, Guido in Flavio, Medoro in Orlando and Britten's Oberon; other engagements as Andronico in Tamerlano for Glimmerglass Opera (US debut 1995), Amadigi at Prague and Monteverdi's Ottone at the Brooklyn Acad.; Royal Opera debut as Nireno in Giulio Cesare 1997; season 1998–99 as Handel's Amadigi at Lisbon, Hamor in Jephtha with the Netherlands Bach Soc. and Arsamenes in Handel's Serse with the Gabrieli Consort in France; other roles include Gluck's Orfeo; concerts throughout Europe including St Matthew Passion, in Jonathan Miller's dramatisation and Handel's Theodora in Berlin. *Recordings include:* albums with John Eliot Gardiner and Andrew Parrott.

KENNY, Yvonne Denise, AM, BSc; Australian singer (soprano); b. 25 Nov. 1950, d. of the late Arthur Raymond Kenny and of Doris Jean Kenny. *Education:* Sydney Univ. *Career:* debut at Queen Elizabeth Hall, London 1975; prin. soprano, Royal Opera House, London 1976; appearances with Berlin Staatsoper, Vienna State Opera, Australian Opera and at La Scala (Milan, Italy), La Fenice (Venice, Italy), Paris, Hamburg (Germany) and Zürich (Switzerland); performer Closing Ceremony Sydney Olympic Games 2000; numerous recordings. *Operas include:* Die Zauberflöte, Idomeneo, Fidelio, Le Nozze di Figaro, L'Elisir d'Amore, Turandot, Mitridate, Alcina, Semele, Giulio Cesare, Don Giovanni, The Fairy Queen, Capriccio, Der Rosenkavalier, Falstaff. *Current Management:* Helmut Fischer Artists Inter-

national, Obere Donaustrasse 45A/14, 1020 Vienna, Austria; Jenifer Eddy Artists' Management, Suite 11, The Clivedon, 596 St Kilda Road, Melbourne, Vic. 3004, Australia. *Telephone:* (699) 1925-0916 (Vienna); (3) 9525-2700 (Melbourne). *Fax:* (3) 9529-5410 (Melbourne). *E-mail:* fischerartists@yahoo.co.uk; jenifereddy@jeam.com.au. *Website:* www.fischerartists.com; www.jeam.com.au; www.yvonnekenny.com.

KENT, Christopher John, BMus, MMus, PhD, FRCO, FSA, ARMCM; British musicologist, organist and organ adviser; b. 12 Aug. 1949, London, England; m. 1st Angela Thomas 1973 (deceased); m. 2nd Susan Langston 2004. *Education:* Univ. of Manchester and King's Coll., London. *Career:* Asst Music Master, City of London School for Girls, 1975–80; Sr Lecturer in Music, Univ. of Reading 1980–2002, Hon. Fellow 2002–; mem. Editorial Bd Elgar Complete Edn 1979–; mem. Asscn of Ind. Organ Advisors; Trustee Councillor, Royal Coll. of Organists 2014–. *Recordings include:* Pachelbel's Hexachordum Apollinis, The Organ of Bowood Chapel 2005, organ music by John Blow. *Publications:* Elgar Complete Edition: Symphony No. 1 (co-ed., five vols) 1981, The Dream of Gerontius 1982, The Apostles 1983, The Kingdom 1984, Music for Organ 1987, The Music of Edward Elgar: A Guide to Research 1993; contrib. to Musical Times, The Listener: Journal of British Institute of Organ Studies, The Organ Year Book, Music and Letters: Journal of the Royal College of Organists, Proceedings of the Royal Music Association, Cambridge Companion to the Organ 1998, Die bemalten Orgelflügel in Europa 2001, Cambridge Companion to Elgar 2004, Early Keyboard Journal 2005, Händel-Jahrbuch 2007, Music in the British Provinces 1690–1914 2007, Edward Elgar – A Thematic Catalogue and Guide to Research 2013. *Honours:* Liveryman, Worshipful Co. of Musicians 2007; Hilda Margaret Watts Prize for Musicology, King's Coll. London 1973, Louise Dyer Award, Editorial Cttee of Musica Britannica 1976, C.B. Oldman Prize, Int. Asscn of Music Libraries, Archives & Documentation Centres 2014. *Address:* The Laurels, Tytherton Lucas, Wilts., SN15 3RJ, England. *Telephone:* (1249) 740294. *E-mail:* christopherkent9680@btinternet.com.

KENYON, Sir Nicholas Roger, Kt, CBE, BA; British arts administrator; *Managing Director, Barbican Centre;* b. 23 Feb. 1951, Altrincham, Cheshire; s. of Thomas Kenyon and Kathleen Holmes; m. Marie-Ghislaine Latham-Koenig 1976; three s. one d. *Education:* Balliol Coll., Oxford. *Career:* music critic, The New Yorker 1979–82, The Times 1982–85, The Observer 1985–92; Music Ed. The Listener 1982–87; Ed. Early Music 1983–92; programme adviser, Mozart Now Festival, South Bank, London 1991; Controller, BBC Radio 3 1992–98, Dir BBC Proms 1996–2007, Controller BBC Millennium Programmes 1998–2000, BBC Live Events and TV Classical Music 2000–07; Man. Dir Barbican Centre, London 2007–; mem. Bd Sage Gateshead, ENO 2005–; mem. Arts Council England; Trustee, Dartington Hall Trust; Gov. Wellington School. *Publications:* The BBC Symphony Orchestra 1930–80 1981, Simon Rattle: The Making of a Conductor (revised edn as Simon Rattle: From Birmingham to Berlin 2001), Authenticity and Early Music (ed.) 1988, The Viking Opera Guide (ed.) 1993, The Penguin Opera Guide (co-ed.) 1995, Musical Lives (ed.) 2001, The BBC Proms Guide to Great Concertos (ed.) 2003, The BBC Proms Pocket Guide to Great Symphonies (ed.) 2003, The Faber Pocket Guide to Mozart 2005, The Faber Pocket Guide to Bach 2011. *Honours:* Royal Philharmonic Soc. Awards for Fairest Isle (BBC Radio 3) 1996 and Sounding the Century 2000, President's Medal, British Acad. 2011. *Address:* Barbican Centre, Silk Street, London, EC2Y 8DS, England (office). *Telephone:* (20) 7382-7005 (office). *Website:* www.barbican.org.uk (office).

KERMES, Simone; German singer (soprano); b. 1970, Leipzig. *Education:* studied at Felix-Mendelssohn Bartholdy Univ. of Music and Theatre, Leipzig, under Helga Forner; master classes with Elisabeth Schwarzkopf and Dietrich Fischer Dieskau. *Career:* specializes in virtuoso baroque works by Handel and Vivaldi as well as arias and concert music by Mozart, Haydn and Beethoven; has performed with opera cos throughout Germany and worldwide including New York, Paris, Moscow, Lisbon and Copenhagen. *Opera repertoire includes:* Konstanze in Die Entführung aus dem Serail, Queen of the Night in Die Zauberflöte, Rosalinde in Die Fledermaus, Gilda in Rigoletto, Fiordiligi in Così fan tutte, Donna Anna in Don Giovanni, title role in Euridice; numerous Händel heroines including Adelaide in Lotario, Asteria in Tamerlano, Laodice in Mitridate, Merab in Saul, title roles in Alcina, Deidamia and Rodelinda. *Recordings include:* Händel's Deidamia (Jahrespreis der Deutschen Schallplattenkritik) 2003, Amor Sacro 2007, Lava: Opera Arias from 18th Century Naples 2009, Colori d'amore 2010, Best of 2011. *Honours:* First Prize, Felix-Mendelssohn Bartholdy Competition, Berlin 1993, Bach Prize, Int. Johann Sebastian Bach Competition, Leipzig 1996, Female Singer of the Year Award, ECHO Klassik Awards 2011. *Address:* Andreas Dommenz Artist Management, Kirchhohl 39a, 56179 Vallendar, Germany (office). *Telephone:* (261) 96-39-682 (office). *E-mail:* dommenzartists@aol.com (office). *Website:* www.simone-kermes.de (office).

KERNIS, Aaron Jay; American composer; b. 15 Jan. 1960, Philadelphia, Pa. *Education:* San Francisco Conservatory of Music, Manhattan School of Music, Yale Univ., studied under John Adams, Jacob Druckman, Morton Subotnick and Charles Wuorinen. *Career:* commissions from leading ensembles and soloists world-wide; works premiered by orchestras including New York Philharmonic, Baltimore Symphony, San Francisco Symphony, Birmingham Contemporary Music Group, Los Angeles Chamber Orchestra, Renée Fleming, Dawn Upshaw and Joshua Bell; New Music Adviser, Minnesota Orchestra 2003–13, now Dir Composers Inst.; Composer-in-Residence, Northwestern Univ. 2013–15; Adjunct Prof. of Composition, Yale School of Music

2003–; mem. American Acad. of Arts and Letters. *Compositions include:* orchestral: Dream of the Morning Sky 1983, Symphony in Waves 1989, Musica Celestis for string orchestra 1990, Symphony No. 2 1991, New Era Dance 1992, Goblin Market, a setting of a Christina Rossetti poem for narrator and large ensemble 1995, Air for Violin and Orchestra 1995, Lament and Prayer violin concerto 1995, String Quartets 1 & 2 (Pulitzer Prize) 1998, Color Wheel 2001, Colored Field for English horn and orchestra 2002, Newly Drawn Sky 2005, Symphony of Meditations/Symphony No. 3 with solo voices and chorus 2009, Garden of Light choral symphony (commissioned by Disney for its millennium celebrations); chamber, solo and vocal: Quattro Stagioni dalla Cucina Futurisimo 1991, 101 Greatest Dance Hits for guitar and string quartet 1993, Still Movement with Hymn piano quartet 1993, Valentines song cycle 1999, Two Movements (with Bells) 2007, A Voice, a Messenger concerto for trumpet solo 2009, L'Arte della Dansa for soprano flute, viola, harp and percussion 2010, Perpetual Chaconne quintet 2012. *Recordings include:* 100 Greatest Dance Hits 1993, Colored Field/Still Movement with Hymn 1996, Lament & Prayer 1999, Second Symphony/Musica Celestis 2005, Symphony in Waves 2008, String Quartets 2009. *Honours:* grants from ASCAP, BMI, Nat. Endowment for the Arts, Guggenheim Foundation and New York Foundation of Arts; Rome Prize 1984, Grawemeyer Award for Music Composition 2002, Nemmers Prize in Music Competition 2012. *Address:* Yale School of Music, PO Box 208246, New Haven, CT 06520-8246, USA (office). *Website:* yalemusic.yale.edu (office).

KERR, Virginia; Irish singer (soprano) and opera administrator; *Chairperson, Opera Theatre Company*; b. 1964. *Education:* Royal Irish Academy and the Guildhall School, London. *Career:* appearances with Dublin Grand Opera as Leila, Liu (Turandot), Musetta, Micaela and Elvira in L'Italiana in Algeri (1996); Other roles include Fiordiligi for City of Birmingham Touring Opera, Anita in Krenek's Jonny Spielt Auf (at Leipzig), Mozart's Countess (Malta), and Grete in Schreker's Der ferne Klang (Opera North); Appearances with Scottish Opera as Jenůfa, Salome, Julia in Dvořák's Jacobin and the soprano lead in Judith Weir's The Vanishing Bridgegroom; Ariadne for Castleward Opera, Tchaikovsky's Enchantress for New Sussex Opera and Donna Elvira at Leipzig (season 1996–97); Ortlinde in Die Walküre and Jenifer in The Midsummer Marriage at Covent Garden; Concerts include Stravinsky's Pulcinella, Schreker's Von Ewigen Leben (BBC Philharmonic Orchestra), Missa solemnis and Verdi Requiem (Mississippi Symphony Orchestra) and Carmina Burana at the Festival Hall; Beethoven's Ninth and Mahler's 2nd Symphony in Mexico; mem. Bd of Dirs, Opera Theatre Co. 2003– (Chair. 2004–). *Address:* Opera Theatre Company, Temple Bar Music Centre, Curved Street, Dublin 2, Ireland (office). *Telephone:* (1) 67949628 (office). *Fax:* (1) 6794963 (office). *E-mail:* info@opera.ie (office). *Website:* www.opera.ie (office).

KERRY, Gordon, BA; Australian composer, writer and critic; b. 21 Jan. 1961, Melbourne, Vic. *Education:* Univ. of Melbourne, studied with Barry Conyngham, Virginia Center for the Creative Arts, USA. *Career:* freelance composer; music critic for the Sydney Morning Herald 1996–; commissions from Musica Viva, ABC, Adelaide Chamber Orchestra and others. *Compositions include:* Winter Through Glass, for piano 1980, Canticles for Evening Prayer, for choir 1983, Siderius Nuncius for organ 1985, Obsessions, for mezzo and piano 1985, Phaselus, for ensemble 1986, Ongaku, for mandolin 1987, Dream for violin and piano 1987, Paradi, for viola and piano 1988, Perpetual angelus for piano 1988, Cantata for chorus and chamber orchestra 1989, Cipangu for choir and orchestra 1990, Highwires for flute, guitar & cello 1990, Cipangu 1990, Sonata for flute, percussion, piano and cello 1990, Sonata da camera 1991, Torquing Points, for string quartet 1991, Serious music 1991, Viola Concerto 1992, Medea, chamber opera in 3 scenes 1992, Sinfonietta: Like Meteors from Elysium 1992, Quadrivial Pursuits, for clarinet, piano, viola and cello 1993, Harvesting the Solstice Thunders 1993, Sinfonia for viola, cello and strings 1993, No Orphean Lute, piano trio 1994, Splenderà 1994, No atmosphere for solo harp 1995, Harmonie for wind quintet 1996, Concerto for cello, percussion and strings 1996, Variations for orchestra 1996, Bright Meniscus for orchestra 1997, Seven improvisations for cello and percussion 1998, Cantata Davidica 1998, Breathtaking for soprano and ensemble 1999, Such Sweet Thunder for orchestra 1999, Blue latitudes 1999, Breathtaking 1999, Antiphon for viola 1999, Etude for solo viola 1999, He wishes for the cloths of heaven 1999, Mass of Christ the King 1999, Vigil for two pianos 1999, Etude for solo horn 2000, Fioritura for solo clarinet in B flat 2000, Im Winde 2000, Rasa 2000, Kindled Skies 2000, Seraphim for four flutes 2000, Caritas for viola and piano 2000, Sennet for solo trumpet in C 2000, Concerto for clarinet and orchestra 2001, Aria for tenor trombone 2001, Prelude for solo guitar 2001, This Insubstantial Pageant 2002, A kind of radiant darkness 2002, Cold Pastoral 2002, Upon Empty Air 2003, Through the Fire 2003, Ricercare 2004, Fronting Eternity 2005, For those in peril on the sea 2005. *Honours:* Sounds Australian Award 1990, Australian Music Centre Award for Orchestral Work of the Year 2004. *E-mail:* gkerry@bigpond.com (home). *Website:* www.gordonkerry.com.

KERSTENS, Tom; Dutch classical guitarist; *Artistic Director, International Guitar Foundation and Festivals. Education:* Univ. of Utrecht, Guildhall School of Music and Drama, UK. *Career:* European debuts at Amsterdam and Paris 1996, UK debut Greenwich Festival 1997; as soloist, has performed most of major repertoire as well as new works, including world premiere of Barrington's Pheloung's Double Guitar Concerto and Giles Swayne's Mancanza for guitar and orchestra; has toured UK and Europe and performed at most festivals; collaborations include City of London Sinfonia, the Composers Ensemble, Emperor and Brodsky Quartets; Artistic Dir Int. Guitar Foundation and Festivals 1995–; est. major int. guitar competitions for young players. *Recordings:* ¡Fandango!, Serenade, Walton's Five Bagatelles, The Sanctity of Trees, Black Venus: New Music for Guitar Vol. 1, ¡Zapateado!: Homage to Rodrigo, Standing Wave: New Music for Guitar Vol. 2. *Honours:* Joaquin Rodrigo Medal for Outstanding Contrib. to the Dissemination of Rodrigo's Work. *Current Management:* c/o Phil Castang, 3M Music Marketing and Management, 22 Grosvenor Place, Bath, BA1 6AX, England. *Address:* International Guitar Foundation, Bath Spa University, Newton Park, Newton St Loe, Bath, BA2 9BN, England (office). *Telephone:* (1225) 875522 (office). *Fax:* (1225) 875495 (office). *E-mail:* tom@igf.org.uk (office). *Website:* www.igf.org.uk (office); www.tomkerstens.com.

KERTESI, Ingrid; singer (soprano); b. 1961, Budapest, Hungary. *Education:* Franz Liszt Acad., Budapest and studied in Bayreuth. *Career:* debut in Budapest 1985, as Oscar in Un Ballo in Maschera; sang Olympia at the Vienna Volksoper 1987, Sophie in Budapest and Frasquita in Carmen at the 1991 Bregenz Festival; other roles include Blondchen, Despina, Susanna and Mozart's Zerlina, Donizetti's Norina, Lucia and Adina, Amina in La Sonnambula, Gilda, Nannetta and Aennchen in Der Freischütz; sang Adina at Budapest 1996; concert repertory includes works by Handel, Haydn, Mozart, Bach and Vivaldi.

KERTESZ, Otto; cellist; b. 1960, Hungary. *Education:* Franz Liszt Acad., Budapest, studied with Sandor Devich, György Kurtàg and András Mihaly. *Career:* mem., Keller String Quartet from 1986, debut concert at Budapest 1987; played Beethoven's Grosse Fuge and Schubert's Death and the Maiden Quartet at Interforum 87; series of concerts in Budapest with Zoltán Kocsis and Deszö Ranki (piano) and Kalman Berkes (clarinet); further appearances in Nuremberg, at the Chamber Music Festival La Baule and tours of Bulgaria, Austria, Switzerland, Italy (Ateforum 88 Ferrara), Belgium and Ireland; concerts for Hungarian radio and television. *Honours:* second prize Evian Int. String Quartet Competition 1988.

KETILSSON, Jon; Icelandic singer (tenor); b. 1970, Reykjavík. *Education:* studied in Vienna. *Career:* debut in Offenbach's Barbe-bleue at Schönbrunn; sang Alfredo and Florestan at Prague State Opera, Max in Der Freischütz, Cavaradossi, Wagner's Erik and Candide at Dortmund; Strauss's Bacchus at Lausanne and Enée in Les Troyens at Lisbon; Cologne Opera as Tamino, Cavaradossi, Macduff, Don José, and Herr M. in Hindemith's Neues vom Tage; Other roles include Hoffmann, Pinkerton, Rodolfo and Sergei in Lady Macbeth of Mtsensk; Season 2001–2002 as Don José at Brussels and Geneva, Max in Lausanne and Enée at the Salzburg Festival; Concerts include Beethoven's Ninth, Carmina Burana, Messiah and Dvořák's Requiem. *Current Management:* Aria's di Novella Partacini & Alexandra Plaickner, Via Josef Weingartner 4, 39022 Lagundo, Italy. *Telephone:* (0473) 200200. *Fax:* (0473) 222424. *E-mail:* info@arias.it. *Website:* www.arias.it.

KEYES, John; American singer (tenor); b. 1964, Illinois. *Education:* studied in Chicago. *Career:* based with the Chicago Lyric Opera –1991; season 1991–92 with Siegmund in Die Walküre for Scottish Opera, Radames at Mexico City and Parsifal in Robert Wilson's production of Wagner's opera for Houston Grand Opera; concert performances of Otello (as Roderigo) in Chicago an New York under Solti, 1991; season 1992–93 as Siegmund at Hamburg and Nantes, Erik in Fliegende Holländer at Toulouse and Parsifal at Antwerp and Hamburg; other roles include Walther von der Vogelweide and Eisenstein (Houston), Samson, Don Carlos, Don José and Dick Johnson; sang Lohengrin in a new production of Wagner's opera for ENO 1993; season 1996–98 with Parsifal at Munich; Jean in Massenet's Hérodiade at San Francisco and Turiddu and Canio for Israel Opera; Florestan at Buenos Aires and Siegmund in Amsterdam; sang Parsifal in Munich, Lohengrin in San Diego and Strauss's Emperor at the Deutsche Oper, Berlin; concert repertoire includes Beethoven's Ninth. *Recordings include:* Otello. *Honours:* winner San Antonio Competition 1990, Richard Tucker Competition Ruth Richards grant 1990. *Current Management:* Alferink Artists Management, Herengracht 340, 1016 CG Amsterdam, The Netherlands; Pinnacle Arts: Deutsch Division, Thierschstrasse 11/5 OG, 80802 Munich, Germany. *Telephone:* (20) 6643151 (Alferink); (89) 34086300 (Pinnacle). *Fax:* (20) 6752426 (Alferink); (89) 34086310 (Pinnacle). *E-mail:* info@alferink.org; jdietsch@pinnaclearts.com. *Website:* www.alferink.org; www.pinnaclearts.com.

KEYLIN, Misha; American concert violinist; b. 5 March 1970, St Petersburg, Russia. *Education:* Juilliard School, New York. *Career:* emigrated to USA aged nine; debut at Carnegie Hall, New York 1981 (aged 11); performed both in recital and as soloist in concert halls in more than 45 countries on five continents; mem. Hermitage Piano Trio. *Recordings:* complete cycle of the seven Henri Vieuxtemps violin concertos. *Honours:* winner, Hannover, Paganini, Sarasate and Sigall int. violin competitions. *E-mail:* misha@keylin.com (office). *Website:* www.keylin.com; www.hermitagepianotrio.com.

KEYTE, Christopher Charles; British singer (bass-baritone); b. 11 Sept. 1935, Shorne, Kent, England; m. June Matthews. *Education:* Choral Scholar, King's Coll., Cambridge. *Career:* oratorio, opera, concert and recital appearances; Founder-mem. Purcell Consort of Voices 1963–75; opera with The Fires of London; Prof. of Singing, RAM 1982–87; Royal Opera House, Covent Garden 1989–2000. *Recordings:* Monteverdi Songs, Sacred Concertos; Purcell Anthems, Indian Queen; Haydn and Schubert Masses; Vaughan Williams Serenade to Music and Pilgrim's Progress; Songs by Quilter, Gurney and Glazunov; Mass of the Sea by Paul Patterson; The Lighthouse by Peter Maxwell Davies, Billy Budd by Benjamin Britten. *Honours:* Hon. RAM 1983;

Dr hc (Anglia Ruskin) 2006. *Address:* 20 Brycedale Crescent, Southgate, London, N14 7EY, England (home).

KHACHATRYAN, Sergey; Armenian violinist; b. 1985, Yerevan. *Education:* Taunus Music School, Eschborn, Germany, Würzburg and Karlsruhe Music Acads, masterclasses in Keshet Eilon, Israel with Shlomo Mintz. *Career:* participation in music competitions in Rome, Krakow, Germany and Spain from 1995; appearances with symphony and chamber orchestras throughout Europe, including Bruch Concerto with English CO at Fairfields Hall, Croydon 2001; concerts throughout Finland, notably with the Sibelius Concerto, and in Israel, Ecuador, Brazil and Armenia; season 2001–02 with Music at Oxford recital, concerts with Bournemouth SO, Royal Philharmonic, Frankfurt Radio SO and Bochum Symphony; season 2006–07 performed with New York Philharmonic Orchestra, Cleveland Orchestra and Boston Symphony Orchestra; also toured with sister Lusine Khachatryan on piano 2007. *Recordings include:* Sibelius/Khachaturian Violin Concertos 2003, Shostakovich Violin Concertos 2006, Shostakovich/Franck Violin Sonatas 2008, Bach, Sonatas and Partitas 2010. *Honours:* winner Louis Spohr Competition, Freiburg, Int. Team Sibelius Competition, Helsinki, first prize Queen Elisabeth Competition, Belgium 2005. *Address:* c/o Naive Classique, 148 rue du Faubourg Poissonniere, 75010 Paris, France (office). *Telephone:* (1) 44-91-64-00 (office). *Fax:* (1) 44-91-64-02 (office). *E-mail:* contact@naive.fr (office). *Website:* en.naive.fr (office); www.sergeykhachatryan.net (home).

KHADEM-MISSAGH, Bijan; Iranian violinist, conductor and composer; *President, GLOBArt and Artistic Director Allegro Vivo*; b. 26 Oct. 1948, Tehran, Iran. *Education:* Univ. of Vienna, Austria, Acad. of Music, Vienna. *Career:* debut, as soloist with orchestra aged 13; int. concert tours, including radio and television appearances and festivals; founder, Eurasia Quartet 1969–75; founder, The Dawnbreakers, Austrian Baha'i singing group 1970; founder, conductor and soloist, Tonkuenstler Chamber Orchestra, Vienna 1977–2001; Artistic Dir Allegro Vivo, International Chamber Music Festival, Austria 1979–, conductor and soloist Academia Allegro Vivo 2001–; Artistic Dir Midsummer Music Festival, Sweden 1981–90, Badener Beethoventage 1980–86; Prof., J. M. Hauer Konservatory, Wiener Neustadt 1988–; masterclasses for violin; Pres., GLOBArt, 1997–; Musical Dir, Music Forum Landegg, Switzerland 1991–2000. *Compositions:* instrumental and vocal works. *Recordings:* works by Beethoven, Schubert, Schoenberg, Weigl, Vivaldi, Mendelssohn, Vitali, Paganini, Debussy, Szymanowski, Bach, Tchaikovsky, Haydn, Handel, Dvořák, Respighi, Bartók, Strauss, Kreisler; albums: Dawnbreakers 1976, The Child 1979, To A Friend 1982, Vision 1986, Call of the Beloved, Phoenix, Glad Tidings, Wie Sterne, Dawnbreakers – Collections 2005. *Publications:* Lieder – Book of Songs 1976, Das Musische als Lebensweise, Ein Credo 1998. *Honours:* Austrian Cross for Arts and Sciences 1998; Silbernes Ehrenzeichen Niederösterreich 1993, Kulturpreis der stadt Baden 1994. *Address:* Allegro Vivo International Chamber Music Festival Austria, Wiener Strasse 2, 3580 Horn, Austria (office). *Telephone:* 2982-4319 (office). *E-mail:* office@allegro-vivo.at (office). *Website:* www.allegro-vivo.at (office).

KHALEMSKAIA, Marianna; singer (soprano); b. 1960, St Petersburg, Russia. *Education:* St Petersburg State Conservatory, studied with soloists of the Mariinsky Theatre. *Career:* concerts from 1992, including Mozart's Requiem and Kurt Weill songs; opera debut in V. Plesak's opera, Tale of a Dead Princess 1996; Paris Opéra-Comique as Elisetta in Il Matrimonio Segreto; seasons 1996–98 as Annina in A Night in Venice, Rosina in Mozart's La Finta Semplice and Musetta in La Bohème. *Honours:* prizewinner Barcelona and Toulouse Competitions.

KHANER, Jeffrey, BM; Canadian flautist; *Principal Flautist, Philadelphia Orchestra*. *Education:* Juilliard School, with Julius Baker. *Career:* Prin. Flautist Cleveland Orchestra 1982–90, Philadelphia Orchestra 1990–; also served as Prin., New York Mostly Mozart Festival, Atlantic Symphony in Halifax, NS and Co-Prin. Pittsburgh Symphony; chosen by Sir Georg Solti as Prin. Flute World Orchestra for Peace, celebrating 50th anniversary of the UN 1995; co-f. Syrinx Trio, debut 2001; has performed as concerto soloist in USA, Canada and Asia under conductors including Christoph von Dohnanyi, Charles Dutoit, Christoph Eschenbach, Claus-Peter Flor, Hans Werner Henze, Kurt Masur, Yutaka Sado, Wolfgang Sawallisch, Gerard Schwartz, David Zinman; also recitals, festivals, seminars and masterclasses; Prof. of Flute, Juillard School 2004–; mem. faculty Curtis Inst. of Music, Philadelphia 1985–. *Recordings include:* Jeffrey Khaner Plays Romantic Flute Music, British Flute Music 2004, American Flute Music 2004, French Flute Music 2004, Brahms Sonatas/Schumann Romances 2005, David Chesky – Area 31 2005. *Current Management:* Music Company (London), 103 Churston Drive, Morden, Surrey, SM4 4JE, England. *Telephone:* (20) 8540-7357. *Fax:* (20) 8542-4854. *E-mail:* melanne@musicco.force9.co.uk. *Address:* Syrinx PFC, 240 Central Park South #6M, New York, NY 10019, USA (office). *E-mail:* admin@iflute.com (office). *Website:* www.iflute.com.

KHANUM, Farida; Pakistani singer; b. Kolkata, India; five d. one s. *Career:* moved to Pakistan 1947; first public performance 1950; performs in the Ghazal tradition and known as 'Malika-e-Ghazal' (Queen of the Ghazal); has performed in fmr Soviet Union, People's Republic of China, UK, Afghanistan. *Recordings:* Excellence of Farida Khanum, Farida Khanum in Concert, Ghazal Paikar, Greatest Hits of Farida Khanum, Gulistan Vol. I and II, Hits of Farida Khanum, Khwaab Vols 1–3, Aaj Jaane Ki Zid Na Karo, Great Ghazals: Sur ki koi Seem nahin, Tum Lakh Mujh Se. *Honours:* Hilal-e-Imtiaz 2005. *Address:* c/o Sony Music Entertainment India Pvt Ltd, Span Centre, South Avenue, Santacruz, Mumbai 400054, India (office). *Website:* www.sonymusic.co.in (office).

KHANZADIAN, Vahan Avedis, BEd; American singer (tenor) (retd); b. 23 Jan. 1939, Syracuse, NY; s. of Avedis Sarkis Khanzadian and Araxey Youghian. *Education:* Univ. of Buffalo, Curtis Inst. of Music. *Career:* debut at San Francisco Spring Opera as Ruggero in Puccini's La Rondine 1968; roles in numerous productions, including Wozzeck, Fra Diavolo, Madama Butterfly, Lucia di Lammermoor; appearances with opera cos throughout USA and Canada, including New York City Center, Baltimore, Houston, Memphis, New Orleans, St Paul, Providence, Birmingham, Kentucky, Kansas City, Dayton, Toledo, Portland, Honolulu, Montréal, Edmonton, Vancouver; guest soloist with major orchestras, including Boston, Chicago, Philadelphia, Baltimore, Boston Pops; numerous recital tours; masterclasses; radio and TV broadcasts; tenor soloist in world premiere of Menotti's Landscapes and Remembrances at Milwaukee 1976; European debuts include Cavaradossi in Tosca at Aachen 1992, title role in Don Carlo at Basel 1992, Metropolitan Opera debut as Riccardo in Ballo in Maschera 1993, Lyric Opera, Chicago debut as Riccardo 1993; Bavarian State Opera, Munich as Calaf in Turandot 1995; Cincinnati Opera, USA as Radames in Aida 1995. *Television:* role of Gherman in Tchaikovsky's The Queen of Spades (PBS TV) 1971. *Recording:* Follies (Broadway cast recording) 1998. *Address:* 47 Finnish Lane, Jewett, NY 12444, USA (home). *Fax:* (518) 734-4016 (office). *E-mail:* vahan@optonline.net (home).

KHARITONOV, Dimitri; singer (baritone); b. 18 Oct. 1958, Kuibyshev, Russia. *Education:* Rimsky-Korsakov College of Music, Leningrad Nezhdanova State Conservatory, Odessa. *Career:* recital singer, Odessa Philharmonic Soc.; Prin. Baritone, Odessa State Opera, 1984; sang 55 times at the Bolshoi Opera, Kremlin Hall, roles included: Prince Yeletsky, Queen of Spades, Duke Robert, Iolanta (Tchaikovsky), Duenna (Prokofiev); also sang in Moussorgsky's Khovanshchina and Boris Godunov, Rimsky-Korsakov's Tzar Saltan, Germont in La Traviata and Conte di Luna, Il Trovatore (Verdi), Figaro, Il Barbiere di Siviglia (Rossini), Silvio in Pagliacci; sang in main opera houses and concert halls, Moscow, Leningrad, Kiev, Minsk; appeared regularly on Russian television; settled in England 1989; British debut as Jokanaan in Salome, Edinburgh Festival 1989, returning for Tchaikovsky's Cantata Moskow; season 1989–90 as Germont in Liège, Opera de Wallonie; in America sang at the Chicago Lyric Opera with Placido Domingo in La Fanciulla del West (Puccini) amongst others; recital, Palais des Beaux Arts, Brussels 1992; title role in Nabucco, Genoa 1994; also Rachmaninov lieder recitals, Oslo and Lillehammer; sang Sharpless in Madama Butterfly, Teatro Colón, Buenos Aires; Prince Yeletsky in The Queen of Spades, Glyndebourne Festival Opera 1993, also three recitals at the Risor Festival, Norway. *Recordings include:* Shostakovich's romances on Pushkin's poems with the City of Birmingham Symphony Orchestra; Tchaikovsky's Ode to Joy; Eugene Onegin; Khovanshchina; Prince Yeletsky in Queen of Spades, Glyndebourne production video. *Honours:* Winner All-Ukrainian Lysenko Competition for Opera Singers, Kiel 1983, Odessa 1984; All-USSR M. I. Glinka Competition with special prize for best interpretation of Rimsky-Korsakov works, 1984; Grand Prix, Verviers Int. Opera Competition, Belgium, 1987; Gold Medal, Bastianini Int. Competition, Siena, 1988; Voci Verdiane Competition, Brusseto 1988; Carlo Alberto Cappelli Competition, Arena di Verona, for International Competition Winners. *Address:* Landshuter Allee 55, 80637 Munich, Germany.

KHARITONOVA, Yelena; Russian violinist; b. 1960, Moscow. *Education:* Moscow Conservatoire with Andrei Shislov. *Career:* co-founder, Glazunov Quartet 1985; many concerts in the former Soviet Union and appearances in Greece, Poland, Belgium, Germany and Italy; works by Beethoven and Schumann at the Beethoven Haus in Bonn; further engagements in Canada and The Netherlands; teacher at the Moscow State Conservatoire and resident at the Tchaikovsky Conservatoire; repertoire includes works by Borodin, Shostakovich and Tchaikovsky, in addition to the standard works. *Recordings include:* the six quartets of Glazunov. *Honours:* prizewinner Borodin Quartet Competition, Shostakovich Chamber Music Competition (with the Glazunov Quartet).

KHERSONSKAJA, Natalya Mikhailovna; Ukrainian musicologist, pianist and organist; b. 1 Nov. 1961, Poltava; m. Sergei Zagny 1986; one s. *Education:* Poltava Music Coll., Moscow State M. Lomonosov Univ., studied with Prof. L.I. Roizman at Moscow State Conservatory. *Career:* Ed. chief edn of Ostankino, Television-Radio co. musical broadcasting, Moscow 1990–94; Chief Scientific Collaborator, Database Section (electronic musical encyclopaedia), Computer Centre, Moscow State Conservatory 1995–98; Instructor of Computer Courses by cathedra geofisique, Moscow State M. Lomonosov Univ. 1997. *Recordings include:* many broadcasts as author and interviewer including cycles, Music of 20th Century including Webern, Berg, Schoenberg, Scriabin, Mosolov and Boulez, Sviatoslav Richter plays Franz Schubert, Rondo; Masters of Antique Music including English virginalists and S. Scheidt and Schütz; 9 Hours of French Music from Perotin to Messiaen. *Publications include:* author of musicologic works including separate studies of the organ and klavier music of Samuel Scheidt (first in Russia) entitled, Word and Number as a Structural Idea of Organ Composition of S. Scheidt 1987, Tabulatura Nova of S. Scheidt (new concept) 1990, Word For Windows As Possible Cover for Database 1995, Notation and Forming Word and Number as a Structural Idea of Klavier Composition 1994, Unfinished Works by Franz Schubert and His Unfinished Sonatas Performed by Sviatoslav Richter 1997, Eclipses and the Tungussky Meter (and Meteors) 2000, Proportional Canon as a Basis of Movement of the Planets Around the Sun 2000. *Address:* Ul. Vagonoremontnaja 5 korpus 1, kv 23, 127411 Moscow, Russia.

KHOLMINOV, Alexander; Russian composer; b. 8 Sept. 1925, Moscow. *Education:* Moscow Conservatory with Golubev. *Career:* stage works have been widely performed in Moscow and Elsewhere in Russia. *Compositions:* operas: An Optimistic Tragedy Frunze, 1965; Anna Snegina, Gorky, 1967; The Overcoat, after Gogol, 1975; The Carriage, after Gogol, Moscow, 1975; Chapayev, Moscow Radio, 1977; The Twelfth Series, Moscow, 1977; The Wedding, after Chekhov, Moscow, 1984; Vanka, Monodrama after Chekhov, Moscow, 1984; The Brothers Karamazov, after Dostoyevsky, Moscow, 1985; Hot Snow, 1985; The Fruits of Enlightenment, after Tolstoy, 1990; 5 Symphonies, 1973, 1975, 1977, 1990, 1995; Viola Concerto, 1989; 3 string quartets, 1980, 1985, 1994; 24 Preludes for piano, 1994. *Honours:* USSR State Prize, 1978; People's Artist of the USSR, 1984.

KHOLODENKO, Vadym; Ukrainian pianist; b. 4 Sept. 1986, Kiev. *Education:* Mykola Lysenko Music School, Kiev, Moscow State Tchaikovsky Conservatoire with Vera Gornostaeva. *Career:* regularly performs with New Russia orchestra 2004–; regularly appears at music festivals in Russia and abroad; toured throughout Russia, Czech Repub., USA, Austria, Italy, Switzerland, Israel, Hungary, Croatia and China; has collaborated with numerous conductors, including Yuri Bashmet, Vladimir Spivakov, Mark Gorenstein, Dmitry Liss, Eugeny Bushkov, Alexander Sladkovskiy; chamber concerts and a CD recording with violinist Alena Baeva in Japan; co-f. (with Andrey Gugnin) piano duet 2007, subsequently named iDuo. *Recordings include:* solo: works by Schubert, Chopin, Rachmaninoff and Medtner; with iDuo: works by Debussy, Ravel and Rachmanino. *Honours:* Third Prize, V. Krainev Competition, Kharkov 1999, Second Prize, V. Horowitz Int. Competition, Kiev 2000, Third Prize, Liszt Int. Competition, Budapest 2001, Triumph Youth Prize 2004, Winner, Int. Maria Callas Grand Prix Piano Competition, Athens 2004, Third Prize, Gina Bachauer Int. Competition 2006, Winner, Sendai Int. Music Competition (Japan) 2010. *Address:* Moscow P. I. Tchaikovsky Conservatory, 125009 Moscow, Bolshaya Nikitskaya street 13/6, Russia. *Telephone:* (495) 629-94-01. *Website:* www.mosconsv.ru.

KHOMA, Natalia, BM, DipMus, MM, DMA; Ukrainian cellist; b. 5 Dec. 1963, Lviv; m. Suren Bagratuni 1986, one d. *Education:* Lviv Music School, Tchaikovsky Moscow Conservatory, Boston University. *Career:* debut as soloist with Lviv Philharmonia Orchestra 1975; performances and recitals at Weill Recital Hall, Carnegie Hall, New York, Merkin Hall, New York, Jordan Hall, Boston, Rachmaninov Hall, Moscow, Moscow Conservatory Small Hall, Academy of Music Big Hall, Oslo, Norway, Palais des Beaux Arts, Brussels, Belgium, Schauspielhaus, Berlin, Germany, Grand Hall of Academy of Music, Budapest; performed throughout the Soviet Union, East Europe, Spain, Germany, Belgium, Italy, Norway, Canada, USA. *Honours:* first prize All-Ukrainian Competition, 1981; Max Reger Special Prize, 1985; 2nd Prize, Markneukirchen International Competition, Germany, 1987; 1st Prize, Belgrade International Competition, 1990; 4th Prize, Tchaikovsky Competition, Moscow, 1990. *Address:* c/o Tchaikovsky Moscow Conservatory, Ul Gertzena 13, 103009 Moscow, Russia.

KIBERG, Tina; Danish singer (soprano); b. 30 Dec. 1958, Copenhagen. *Education:* studied in Copenhagen. *Career:* debut at Royal Opera Copenhagen 1983, as Leonora in Nielsen's Maskarade; sang Elsa in Lohengrin at Copenhagen 1984, the Marschallin 1988, Mozart's Countess and Purcell's Dido 1990, Hélène in Les Vepres Siciliennes 1991; guest appearances at Geneva and Frankfurt 1988, as Agathe and the Countess, at Ärhus as Mimi, Vienna Staatsoper 1990, as Elsa and Opéra Bastille Paris 1991 as Lisa in The Queen of Spades; lieder recitals in England, Germany and Italy from 1984; sang Strauss's Ariadne at Copenhagen and Elisabeth in Tannhäuser at Bayreuth 1992; sang Wagner's Eva with the Royal Danish Opera 1996; other roles in opera have included Donna Elvira, Pamina, Desdemona, and Tatiana in Eugene Onegin; sang Chrysothemis in Elektra at Catania 1998; concert repertoire includes Schmidt's Das buch mit Sieben Siegeln (Copenhagen), Beethoven's Mass in C (Lausanne), Haydn's Lord Nelson Mass (Vienna) and Elijah in Berlin; tour of Moscow, Dresden, Berlin and London with Missa Solemnis conducted by Antal Dorati; season 1999–2000 as Salome and Lisa in The Queen of Spades at Copenhagen, Sieglinde for Geneva Opera and Chrysothemis in Elektra for New Israeli Opera at Savonlinna. *Recordings include:* Lulu by Kuhlau.

KIERNAN, Patrick; violinist; b. 1962, England. *Career:* debut at Wigmore Hall 1984 with Peter Pears; co-founder, Brindisi String Quartet, Aldeburgh 1984; concerts in a wide repertory throughout the UK and in France, Germany, Spain, Italy and Switzerland; festival engagements at Aldeburgh (residency 1990), Arundel, Bath, Brighton, Huddersfield, Norwich, Warwick and Prague Spring Festival; first London performance of Colin Matthews' 2nd Quartet 1990, premiere of David Matthews' 6th Quartet 1991; Quartet by Mark Anthony Turnage 1992; world premiere of Colin Matthews' 3rd Quartet, Aldeburgh 1994; many BBC recitals and resident artist with the Univ. of Ulster. *Recordings include:* Quartets by Britten, Bridge and Imogen Holst; Works by Pierné, Lekeu, Schoenberg, Berg and Webern. *Honours:* prizewinner Banff Int. String Quartet Competition, Canada (with Brindisi Quartet) 1989.

KIKUCHI, Yoshinori; Japanese conductor; b. 16 Sept. 1938, Yawatahama. *Education:* Tokyo Nat. Univ. of Fine Arts and Music, studied with Kasei Yamada in Japan, Peter Maag at the Accademia Chigiana at Siena, and with

Franco Ferrara in Rome. *Career:* Chief Asst, Nikikai Opera, Tokyo 1961–64; engagements at Palermo (Teatro Lirico and Teatro Massimo) 1973–77; Hessisches Staatstheater Wiesbaden 1978–84; guest conductor in Japan, Italy, Germany, France, Spain and Belgium; La Scala, Milan 1985–86; Verona Arena 1987.

KILDEA, Paul Francis, BMus, MMus, DPhil; Australian conductor; b. 10 Feb. 1968, Canberra. *Education:* Univ. of Melbourne, Univ. of Oxford. *Career:* conductor on Young Artist Programme, Opera Australia 1997; Asst to Simone Young 1999–2002; Head of Music, Aldeburgh Productions 1999–2003; Artistic Dir, Wigmore Hall, London 2003–05; opera and concert performances throughout Europe and Australia. *Publications:* Selling Britten: Music and the Market Place 2002, Britten on Music 2003, Benjamin Britten: A Life in the Twentieth Century 2013; contrib. to The Cambridge Companion to Britten 1999, The Proms: A New History 2007. *Current Management:* c/o Music International, 13 Ardilaun Road, London, N5 2QR, England. *Telephone:* (20) 7359-5183. *Fax:* (20) 7226-9792. *E-mail:* music@musicint.demon.co.uk.

KILDUFF, Barbara Jane, BM, MM; American singer (soprano); b. 31 May 1959, Huntington, NY. *Education:* State Univ. Coll., New York at Fredonia, Univ. of Connecticut, Storrs, Vale Univ. *Career:* debut at Washington Opera, Blonde; performances include Blonde with Metropolitan Opera, conductor James Levine 1990; with Baltimore Symphony, David Zinman 1990; with Zürich Opera 1990, Barenreiter–Carlos Kalmar; sang Zerbinetta in Munich 1987, 1988; conductors Bender, Sawallisch, Köhler in Vienna 1987, 1991; conductor Theodor Guschlbauer, Metropolitan Opera 1987; James Levine, Hamburg 1988; Julius Rudel, Basel 1988; Vancouver 1989 (Martin André); in Vienna 1991 with Horst Stein; Olympia, Bregenz 1987, 1988; Marc Soustrot in Geneva 1990; sang Adele at Metropolitan Opera 1987, 1988, 1990, 1991; Julius Rudel; Cleopatra, Metropolitan 1988; Trevor Pinnock; Sophie in Der Rosenkavalier, Munich 1989, 1990, 1991; Dir, Brigitte Fassbaender, Heinrich Hollreiser; Metropolitan Opera 1991, Jiri Kout; Queen of Night, Oviedo, Spain 1991; many concert appearances and television and radio performances; season 1993 as the Countess in Capriccio at Vienna; appeared as Papagena in Met video of Die Zauberflöte; sang Mozart's Blondchen at Bonn 2000.

KILLEBREW, Gwendolyn; singer (mezzo-soprano); b. 26 Aug. 1939, Philadelphia, USA. *Education:* Templeton Univ., Juilliard School, Metropolitan Opera Studio. *Career:* debut with Metropolitan Opera 1967, in Die Walküre; 1968–69 sang Carmen in Munich and at the New York City Opera; 1970 Copenhagen, Geneva and Prague in Handel's Tamerlano; 1972–73 Salzburg Festival, as Amneris and in the premiere of Orff's De Temporum fine Comedia; 1973 Washington Opera as Baba the Turk (The Rake's Progress) and San Francisco as Marina (Boris Godunov); Deutsche Oper am Rhein, Düsseldorf from 1976, as Gluck's Orfeo, Verdi's Preziosilla and Azucena and Rossini's Isabella; Bayreuth debut 1978, as Waltraute in Götterdämmerung; Zürich 1981, as Mistress Quickly in Falstaff; sang Frau Leimgruber in Klebe's Der Jüngste Tag, Duisburg 1989; season 1991–92 as the Nurse in Rimsky's Golden Cockerel and Strauss's Herodias at Duisburg; also sings in concert. *Recordings:* Tamerlano, Orlando Paladino by Haydn, Edgar (Puccini), Schvanda the Bagpiper, De Temporum fine Comedia (Orff), Mahler's 3rd Symphony. *Honours:* Temple Univ. Outstanding Musician 1971.

KILLMAYER, Wilhelm; German composer; b. 21 Aug. 1927, Alunich. *Education:* studied with Carl Orff and others. *Career:* ballet conductor, Bavarian State Opera 1961–64; Prof., Munich Hochschule für Musik 1973–91. *Compositions:* operas: La Tragedie di Orfeo 1961, Yolimba 1963, 1970, Un Leçon de français 1964, Der Weisse Hut 1967, Ballets Encores 1969, Paradies 1974; instrumental: two string quartets 1969, 1975, three symphonies 1968, 1969, 1973, Encore for orchestra 1970, Kammermusik 1–3 1970–73, The Broken Farewell for trumpet and chamber orchestra 1977, Brahms-bildnis for piano trio 1977, French Songbook for soprano, baritone and ensemble 1980, Im Freien (symphonic poem) 1980, Sostenuto for cello and strings 1984, four songs in four European languages 1993, Die Schönheit des Morgens for viola and piano 1994, eight Poesies for soprano and ensemble 1995, La Joie de vivre for small orchestra 1996, Neue Heine-Lieder for tenor and piano 1999, Pindar Odes for mixed chorus and organ 1999.

KIM, Ettore; South Korean singer (baritone); b. 14 Nov. 1965. *Education:* studied in South Korea and Italy. *Career:* debut at Teatro Delle Erbe, Milan, in Salieri's Arlecchinata, 1990; sang in Henze's We Come to the River at La Scala and in the premiere of Ferroro's La Figlia del Mago at the Teatro San Carlo, 1992; Concert performances of Otello, as Iago, at Bordeaux, 1992; Engaged as Germont at Covent Garden, 1993, Chorebus in concerts of Les Troyens with the London Symphony Orchestra and on stage at La Scala, 1993–94, Belcore at Strasbourg, Antonio in Linda di Chamounix at Stockholm and Riccardo in Puritani for Bavarian Radio; Other roles include Scarpia, and Gerard in Andrea Chénier; Sang Camoëns in Donizetti's Don Sébastien at Aachen, 1998. *Recordings include:* Linda di Chamounix and I Puritani, both with Edita Gruberova. *Honours:* Gold Medal, International Giuseppe Verdi Competition at Bussetto, 1989.

KIM, Hae-jung, BM, MM; American pianist; b. 18 May 1965, New York. *Education:* Juilliard School of Music, Peabody Conservatory, Moscow Conservatory. *Career:* debut with Vienna Tonkunstler Orchestra, Vienna 1985; Pittsburgh Symphony, St Louis; Royal Philharmonic, London Philharmonic, Moscow State Symphony, Barcelona Philharmonic, NHK Symphony, Lausanne Chamber, English Chamber, Monte Carlo Philharmonic. *Recordings:* Rachmaninov concertos no. 2 and 3, Prokofiev Concerto no. 1, Tchaikovsky

Concerto no.1 (with St Petersburg Symphony), Rachmaninov no. 4 and Rhapsody. *Honours:* first prize Cologne Int. Competition 1998, D'Angelo Young Artist Competition, medal from Republic of Korea Govt. *Current Management:* IMG Artists, Carnegie Hall Tower, 152 W 57th Street, Fifth Floor, New York, NY 10019, USA. *Telephone:* (212) 994-3500. *Fax:* (212) 994-3550. *E-mail:* artistsny@imgartists.com.

KIM, Kathleen, MMus; Korean/American singer (soprano); b. Seoul, S Korea. *Education:* Manhattan School of Music. *Career:* graduate of Ryan Opera Center, Lyric Opera of Chicago; Metropolitan Opera debut 2007; European debut as Marie (La Fille du régiment) for Asociación Bilbaína de Amigos de la Ópera, followed by Olympia in Richard Jones staging of Les contes d'Hoffmann for Bayerische Staatsoper and Madame Mao in John Adams' Nixon in China, with BBC Symphony Orchestra conducted by the composer at BBC Proms 2012; has performed in numerous opera houses and concert halls including Oper Frankfurt, San Diego Opera, Sarasota Opera, Opéra de Lille, Glyndebourne (in Laurent Pelly's production of L'enfant et les sortilèges), Gran Teatre del Liceu, Barcelona, under conductors including James Conlon, James Levine, Fabio Luisi, Manfred Honeck and Stéphane Denève; guest soloist at 2010 Korean Independence Day Celebration Concert with Seoul Philharmonic Orchestra, rejoining them for performances of Mahler's Symphony No. 2 and Beethoven's Symphony No. 9; guest appearance at Seoul Arts Center's New Year's Eve Gala Concert 2014. *Recordings include:* Mahler Symphony No. 2 2012, Ravel L'heure espagnole/L'enfant et les Sortilèges (Gramophone Award for Best Opera Recording 2014) 2013, Beethoven Symphony No. 9 2014. *Current Management:* c/o Shirley Thomson, Harrison/Parrott Ltd, 5-6 Albion Court, Albion Place, London, W6 0QT, England. *Telephone:* (20) 7229-9166. *Fax:* (20) 7221-5042. *E-mail:* shirley.thomson@harrisonparrott.co.uk. *Website:* www.harrisonparrott.co.uk.

KIM, Michael Injae, BMus, MM, DMA; Canadian academic and pianist; b. 13 Feb. 1968, Québec. *Education:* Univ. of Calgary and Juilliard School, New York. *Career:* debut with Calgary Philharmonic Orchestra, Canada aged 15; performances with orchestras of Canada and USA, including Boston, Milwaukee, Cincinnati, Oklahoma City, Toronto, Vancouver, National Arts Centre, Calgary, Edmonton, Regina, Saskatoon, Winnipeg, London; toured Scotland with the Royal Scottish Nat. Orchestra; appearances in Glasgow, Edinburgh, Dundee, Aberdeen 1994; BBC Scottish Symphony, Glasgow 1992; recitals throughout Canada and USA, including appearances in virtually every series in Canada; recital tour, Scotland 1994; recitals broadcast regularly by CBC, BBC, National Public Radio; as chamber musician, appeared throughout Canada and USA with sister violinist, Helen Hwaya Kim (The Kim Duo), including appearances at Carnegie Hall, New York 1992. *Recordings:* Chamber Works of Saint-Saëns; Ballades of Chopin and Grieg; Works of Stravinsky, Rachmaninov, Mussorgsky. *Honours:* laureate of Scottish (Glasgow) Competition 1992, Leeds Competition 1993, Ivo Pogorelich (Pasadena, CA) Int. Piano Competition 1993, grand prizewinner Canadian Music Competitions in Montréal and Québec 1988, Canadian Broadcasting Corporation Competition for Young Performers, Toronto 1989.

KIM, Re-yang; South Korean singer (mezzo-soprano); b. 1953. *Education:* studied in Seoul, Vienna and Augsburg. *Career:* sang at the Berne Opera 1977–78, Karlsruhe Staatstheater from 1978; Deutsche Oper am Rhein, Düsseldorf 1982–87; sang the Nurse in Die Frau ohne Schatten at Bonn 1992, and Ulrica in Un Ballo in Maschera at Cologne 1993; other roles include Azucena in Il Trovatore, Eboli in Don Carlos, Carmen, Brangaene in Tristan und Isolde, Ortrud in Lohengrin and Herodias in Salome.

KIM, Seikyo; Japanese conductor; *Principal Conductor, Kanagawa Philharmonic Orchestra, Yokohama;* b. Osaka. *Education:* Univ. of Boston, New England Conservatory of Boston. *Career:* studied violin and piano from childhood; moved to USA aged 14; participated in Tanglewood Music Festival Conducting Seminar 1995; Conductor, Szeged Orchestra, Hungary 1996; Conductor, Lisbon Metropolitan Orchestra 1996, 1997; Guest Conductor, Osaka Symphoniker 1997; Asst to Takashi Asahina and Mstislav Rostropovich, 10th Affinis Summer Music Festival, Tokyo 1998; participated in Pacific Music Festival, Sapporo, Japan 1998, 1999, 2000; conducted subscription concert, Danish Nat. Radio Symphony Orchestra 2000; Conductor, Korea Nat. Theater 2001; Conductor, Orchestra Lamoureux, Paris 2003–04; Artistic Pnr, Orchestra Ensemble Kanazawa 2003–; Prin. Conductor, Kanagawa Philharmonic Orchestra, Yokohama 2009–; Prin. Conductor, Flanders Symphony Orchestra, Bruges, Belgium 2010–; has conducted many other Japanese orchestras including NHK Symphony Orchestra, Tokyo Metropolitan Symphony, Japan Philharmonic, New Japan Philharmonic, Tokyo Symphony, Tokyo Philharmonic, Osaka Philharmonic, Kyoto Symphony. *Recordings include:* albums: as conductor: with Orchestra Ensemble Kanazawa: Beethoven, Symphony Nos. 2 & 7 2003, Beethoven, Symphony No. 3 2003, Beethoven, Symphony No. 5 2004, Beethoven, Symphony No. 6 2006, Brahms, Symphony Nos. 1 & 2 2007, Brahms, Symphony No. 3 2008; with Flanders Symphony and Pieter Wispelwey: Britten, Cello Symphony 2010. *Honours:* First Prize, Nikolai-Malko Int. Conductor's Competition, Copenhagen 1998. *Address:* Onyx Classics, 43 Blenheim Grove, London, SE15 4QS, England (office). *E-mail:* info@onyxclassics.com (office). *Website:* www.onyxclassics .com (office); www.seikyokim.com.

KIM, Sun-joo, BMus; South Korean conductor and educator; b. 5 Oct. 1929, Sun Cheh Pyung an Buk-Do; m. Hye Sook-lee 1955; one c. *Education:* Kyung Hee Univ. *Career:* Principal Associate Conductor, Korean Broadcasting Symphony, Seoul, 1963–; Instructor, Yung-Hee University, Seoul, 1965; Principal Associate Conductor, Seoul Philharmonic, 1965–69; Principal Conductor, National Symphony Korea, 1969–70; Professor, Kyung Hee University; Conductor, Korean Symphony Orchestra, Seoul; mem, Board of Executives, 1975–82, Korean Musicians Union. *Address:* Kyung-Hee University, School of Music, Whoe Ki Dong, Seoul, Republic of Korea.

KIM, Young-mi, BA, MA; South Korean singer (soprano); b. 6 Nov. 1954, Seoul; m. Kim Sung-ha 1984. *Education:* Seoul Art School, Conservatory of Santa Cecilia, Rome, Academy of Santa Cecilia, Rome. *Career:* debut at Alice Tully Hall, New York Lincoln Center, 1980; Appearances with New York City Opera, Los Angeles Music Center Opera, Houston Grand Opera, Opera Company of Philadelphia, Opéra de Paris, Bastille Orchestra, National Symphony, Seattle Symphony, San Diego Symphony, Minnesota Orchestra, Colorado Symphony. *Recordings:* Sung-Eum Gramophone. *Honours:* Verona International Contest, 1977; Giacomo Contest, 1979; Maria Callas International Voice Competition, 1980; Luciano Pavarotti International Voice Competition, 1981. *Address:* c/o Seoul Arts Center, 700 Seocho-dong, Seocho-gu, Seoul 137-718, Republic of Korea (office).

KIM, Young-uck; South Korean violinist; *Dean of College of Music, Seoul National University;* b. 1 Sept. 1947, Seoul. *Education:* Curtis Inst. of Music, Philadelphia with Ivan Galamian. *Career:* solo debut, Philadelphia Orchestra conducted by Ormandy 1963; mem. Beaux Arts Trio 1998–2002; currently mem. Ax-Kim-Ma Trio; currently Prof. of Violin, Seoul Nat. Univ.; appearances in USA with the St Paul Chamber Orchestra, St Louis Symphony, Cleveland Orchestra, Pittsburgh Symphony, New York Philharmonic, Philadelphia Orchestra, Chicago Symphony, Los Angeles Philharmonic, Washington Nat. Symphony, at Tanglewood, Ravinia, Mostly Mozart and Blossom Festivals, in Europe with the Berlin Philharmonic, Concertgebouw Orchestra, Vienna Philharmonic, London Symphony, St Petersburg Philharmonic, at Salzburg and Edinburgh festivals and the Proms; concerto repertoire includes works by Bach, Berg, Mozart, Prokofiev, Sibelius, Stravinsky and Vivaldi; performed premieres of Gunther Schuller's Violin Concerto, André Previn's Sonata for Violin and Piano, Tobias Picker's Sonata for Violin and Piano, Hans Vogt's Violin Concerto. *Recordings include:* Complete Mozart Concertos with the London Philharmonic under Christoph Eschenbach, Dvořák Trios with Ax/Kim/Ma Trio (Sony Classical Record of the Year Award 1988), Mozart Piano Quartets with Previn, Heichiro and Gary Hoffman, Bach Partita in B Minor, Beethoven Violin Sonata in E Major, Mendelssohn and Bruch Violin Concertos. *Address:* Department of Instrumental Music, College of Music, Seoul National University, San 56–1, Sillim-Dong, Gwanak-Gu, Seoul 151-742, South Korea. *E-mail:* kimyounguck@snu .ac.kr (office). *Website:* music.snu.ac.kr (office).

KIMBELL, David Rodney Bertram, MA, DPhil, LRAM; British academic; *Professor Emeritus of Music, University of Edinburgh;* b. 26 June 1939, Gillingham, Kent; m.; one s. two d. *Education:* Worcester Coll., Oxford. *Career:* Lecturer, Univ. of Edinburgh 1965–78, Prof. of Music 1987–2001, Prof. Emer. 2001–; Prof. of Music, St Andrews Univ. 1979–1987. *Publications:* Verdi in the Age of Italian Romanticism 1981, Italian Opera 1991, Vincenzo Bellini: Norma 1998; contrib. to Hallische Händel-Ausgabe, New Oxford History of Music, Cambridge Companion to Verdi, Cambridge History of Italian Literature, Viking Opera Guide, The Classics of Music by D. F. Tovey (editorial contrib.). *Address:* 3 Bellevue Crescent, Edinburgh, EH3 6ND, Scotland (home). *E-mail:* d.kimbell@virgin.net (home).

KIMBROUGH, Steven, PhD; American singer (baritone); b. 17 Dec. 1936, Athens, AL. *Education:* Birmingham Southern Coll., Duke Univ., Princeton Theological Seminary and studied in Italy. *Career:* debut in Mantua 1968, as Marcel in La Bohème; appearances in Mannheim, Frankfurt, London, San Francisco, New York and Philadelphia; mem., Bonn Opera 1971–; sang in the premiere of Christophorus by Schreker, Freiburg 1978; Essen 1989 as Mirabeau by Siegfried Matthus; concert tours of the USA, Germany, Italy and Austria; guest appearances at the opera houses of Vancouver, Cincinnati, Rio de Janeiro, Barcelona, London, Vienna; repertoire includes roles in operettas and musicals; German premiere op 20 Zemlinsky 1994; mem. American Guild of Musical Artists, Actors' Equity. *Recordings include:* Schreker, Zemlinsky, Korngold, Schönberg, Weigl, Kienzl, Bach, American Art Song, Songs of the Wild West, Korngold's Hollywood Songbook, Sacred and Secular Songs of Charles Wesley. *Publications:* Piano Vocal: Sweet Singer 1984, Global Praise 1996, Global Praise 2 2000, Global Praise 3 2004, God Be in My Heart 2006, Steal Away to Jesus 2006. *Honours:* Rita Hoernle Vocal Award, Liederkranz Vocal Award, New York, winner American Opera Auditions. *Address:* 128 Bridge Avenue, Bay Head, NJ 08742, USA. *Website:* www.stkimbrough.com.

KIMM, Fiona; British singer (mezzo-soprano); b. 24 May 1952, Ipswich, Suffolk. *Education:* Royal Coll. of Music, London. *Career:* performed at Glyndebourne Festival in Die Zauberflöte, The Love for Three Oranges, Titus and L'Enfant et les Sortilèges; appearances with Opera North as Hansel, Mercédès, Rosalind in The Mines of Sulphur, Hermia in A Midsummer Night's Dream and Baba the Turk; sang in the premiere of Edward Cowie's Kate Kelly's Road Show, Chester 1983; with English Nat. Opera has sung Orlofsky, Lola and Fyodor in Boris Godunov, and in Orpheus in the Underworld and Rusalka; Covent Garden debut in Boris Godunov; Berlioz Festival at Lyon in Dido and Aeneas; sang in the premiere of Greek by Mark Anthony Turnage (Munich 1988) and again in the Edinburgh Festival; Scottish Opera in Lulu,

Die Zauberflöte, Eugene Onegin and Das Rheingold; Bath Festival in El Rey de Harlem by Henze, with Ensemble Modern; sang Smeraldina in The Love for Three Oranges, ENO 1989, Siebel in Faust 1990; Opera North/RSC at Stratford as Julie in Showboat; Glyndebourne Festival 1990, as Third Lady in Die Zauberflöte; Michael Berkeley, Baa Baa Black Sheep, world premiere 1993; concert performances with the London Symphony, English Chamber Orchestra, City of Birmingham Symphony and London Sinfonietta; conductors include Abbado, Haitink, Elder, Hickox, Andrew Davis, and Roger Norrington; sang in Param Vir's Snatched by the Gods, for Almeida Opera 1996; Mistress Quickly for Garsington Opera and Rosa Mamai in Cilea's L'Arlesiana for Opera Holland Park 1998; Mrs Sedley in Peter Grimes for Frankfurt Opera; Markolfa in Simon Holt's The Nightingale's to Blame and in L'Enfant et les Sortilèges for Opera North and Larina in Onegin for Glyndebourne Touring Opera; television appearances in The Gondoliers, L'Enfance du Christ and Man and Music series on Channel 4; repertoire includes Rosa Mamai (L'Arlesiana), Orfeo (Orfeo ed Euridice), Julie (Showboat), Sextus (La Clemenza di Tito), Marcellina (Le nozze di Figaro), Dido (Dido and Aeneas), Clairon (Capriccio), Baba the Turk (The Rake's Progress), Madame Larina (Eugene Onegin), Wife/Sphinx/Doreen (Greek), Mlle Arvidson (Un Ballo in Maschera), Mistress Quickly (Falstaff), Azucena (Il Trovatore), Fricka (Der Ring des Nibelungen); recent engagements include Jezibaba (Rusalka), Kabanicha (Katya Kabanova) (English Touring Opera), Jane's Mother (Snow White) (Nationale Reisopera), The Old Crone /Mrs Chin (A Night at the Chinese Opera) (Scottish Opera), Beethoven Choral Symphony (Milton Keynes City Orchestra), The Music Makers, The Songs and Dances of Death and Alexander Nevsky (The Anvil, Basingstoke) and Verdi Requiem (Albert Hall, Nottingham). Brangwyn Hall, Swansea), Katharina Schratt (Mayerling) for The Royal Ballet on tour in Japan and Agnes the Digger (Fantastic Mr Fox) (ETO). *Current Management:* James Black Management Ltd, Old Grammar School, High Street, Rye, TN31 7JF, England. *Telephone:* (17) 9722-4668. *Fax:* (20) 7738-0909 (home). *E-mail:* james@jamesblackmanagement.com. *Website:* www.jamesblackmanagement.com.

KINCSES, Veronika; Hungarian singer (soprano); d. of György Kincses and Etelka Angyal; m. József Vajda; one s. *Education:* Liszt Ferenc Music Acad. Budapest and Accademia Santa Cecilia, Italy. *Career:* soloist, State Opera, Budapest; song-recitals, also oratorio performances; guest performances in USA, Argentina, Venezuela, Hong Kong, Singapore etc. 1997–98; operatic roles include Madame Butterfly, Mimi in La Bohème, Manon Lescaut, Liu in Turandot, Le Villi (Puccini), Contessa in Le Nozze di Figaro, Fiordiligi in Così fan Tutte, Vitellia in La Clemenza di Tito, Elvira in Don Giovanni, Amelia in Simone Boccanegra, Leonora in La Forza del destino, Micaela in Carmen, Marguerita in Faust, Silvana in Fiamma–Respighi, Eva in Meistersinger von Nürnberg, Adriana in Adriana Lecouvreur, Tosca, Judit in Bluebeard's Castle; Prof., Univ. of Pécs 2002–. *Recordings include:* Die Königin von Saba, Haydn's Der Apotheker and La Fedeltà Premiata, Songs by Bellini, Liszt's Hungarian Coronation Mass, Madame Butterfly, Orfeo ed Euridice, La Bohème (also DVD), Suor Angelica, Le Nozze di Figaro, etc. *Honours:* winner, Dvořák Int. Singing Competition, Prague 1971, Liszt Prize, Kossuth Prize (Hungary), Prix de l' Acad. du Disque, Paris (four times). *Current Management:* International Management of the Hungarian State Opera, Andrássy ut 22, 1061 Budapest, Hungary; Robert Lombardo Associates, 61 West 62nd Street, New York, NY 10023, USA.

KING, Andrew Graham, BA (Hons), PGCE, ARCM; British singer (tenor), music director, conductor and record producer; *Tutor, Historical Vocal Programme, Birmingham Conservatoire, Birmingham City University;* b. 8 May 1953, Bury St Edmunds, England; s. of Joseph William King and Joan Mary King (née Clinton). *Education:* St John's Coll., Durham, King's Coll., Cambridge, vocal studies with Graham Watts, Ivor Davies, David Johnston, Eric Vietheer, Iris dell'Acqua. *Career:* Durham Cathedral Choir 1972–75, King's Coll. Choir 1975–76; debut, Wigmore Hall 1977; Proms, Baroque Cantatas, BBC Singers 1978; Lay Clerk, Guildford Cathedral 1976–77; BBC Singers 1977–80; sang with many emerging early music groups, including Tallis Scholars, Clerkes of Oxenford, The Sixteen, Medieval Ensemble of London, Landini Consort, Gothic Voices, Taverner Consort, King's Consort, New London Consort; mem. Consort of Musicke 1978–; also performs with Ex Cathedra, I Fagiolini and Pro Cantione Antiqua; performed contemporary works with the song group, English Echoes and Singcircle; noted as an interpreter of Renaissance and Baroque music and is in particular demand as Evangelist in the Bach Passions; performances throughout Europe, also USA, Canada, Middle East, Japan and Australia; festival appearances include Bruges, Edinburgh, Prague, Salzburg, Utrecht, York and numerous appearances at BBC Proms; performances of early operas and masques in Austria, Belgium, China, Germany, The Netherlands, Italy, Norway, Spain, Sweden, Switzerland and UK; professional tenor, Noblemen and Gentlemen's Catch Club 2001–; several world premieres, most notably Leaving by Mark-Anthony Turnage with CBSO; conducted several operatic performances for Birmingham Conservatoire, including The Fairy Queen (Purcell), Psyche (Locke), L'Incoronazione di Poppea (Monteverdi), Dido and Aeneas (Purcell), Acis and Galatea (Handel); masterclasses in Czech Repub., England, Israel, Italy, Poland, Spain and Sweden; Musical Dir The Renaissance Ensemble 1997–; Visiting Tutor, Historical Vocal Programme, Birmingham Conservatoire, Birmingham City Univ. *Film:* Banquet of the Senses – madrigali erotici e spirituali, Monteverdi (Consort of Musicke). *Television:* BBC Proms, Madrid concerts: Messiah, Judas Maccabaeus (Handel), Requiem (Mozart), RTVE. *Recordings include:* Monteverdi Vespers (New London Consort, Taverner Consort), Apollo and

other roles in Monteverdi's Orfeo (NLC), many Monteverdi madrigal recordings (Consort of Musicke), Handel's Esther (Academy of Ancient Music), Purcell's Ode for St Cecilia's Day (Taverner Consort), Purcell Late Songs (Mantle of Orpheus—Consort of Musicke); Bach's Christmas Oratorio (New London Consort), live recording of Mendelssohn's version of Bach's St Matthew Passion (with Choir and Orchestra of Swiss Italian Radio TV), numerous recordings of medieval and Renaissance music. *Honours:* Choral Scholarship, Durham Cathedral 1972–75. *Current Management:* c/o Davies Music, 23 Church Street, Tewkesbury, Glos., GL20 5PD, England. *Telephone:* 7721-317030 (mobile). *E-mail:* daviesmusic@btinternet.com. *Website:* www.daviesmusic.org.uk. *Address:* 49 Dalmeny Avenue, London, SW16 4RS, England (home). *Telephone:* (20) 8764-5563 (home); 7930-558548 (mobile). *Fax:* (20) 8679-8300 (home). *E-mail:* kingag@btinternet.com (home).

KING, Mary, BA, PGCE, DipMus; British singer (mezzo-soprano); b. 16 June 1952, Tonbridge Wells, England. *Education:* Birmingham Univ., St Anne's Coll., Oxford, Guildhall School of Music. *Career:* sang in opera at Glyndebourne 1980, US debut 1985, Covent Garden 1990; regular appearances with major British orchestras; Spanish tour with BBC Symphony Orchestra 1991; Proms 1991; new music a speciality with many first performances, including The Undivine Comedy by Finnissy in Paris and London, Valis by Machover in Paris, Boston and Tokyo; teacher, Guildhall School of Music, London 1990–; Artistic Dir, Live Culture, a youth group of English National Opera, Baylis Programme; founder, Green Light Music Theatre 1990; has sung Marcellina and Baba the Turk at Glyndebourne, The Cockerel in The Cunning Little Vixen at Covent Garden; sang Florence Pike in Albert Herring at Garsington 1996, Meg Page in Falstaff 1998; Knussen's Where the Wild Things Are and Higglety, Pigglety, Pop! at the London Proms 2002; mem. Equity, Asscn of Teachers of Singing. *Recordings:* Where the Wild Things Are, by Knussen; The Cunning Little Vixen; Britten's Praise We Great Men; Machover's Valis; Birtwistle's Meridian; Stilgoe's Brilliant the Dinosaur. *Address:* 34a Garthorne Road, Honor Oak, London SE23 1EW, England.

KING, Robert John Stephen, MA; British conductor, harpsichordist and editor; *Artistic Director, The King's Consort;* b. 27 June 1960, Wombourne, Staffs., England; m. Viola Scheffel; one s. one d. *Education:* St John's Coll., Cambridge. *Career:* Artistic Dir The King's Consort 1980–; Guest Conductor, Netherlands Chamber Orchestra, NDR Symphony Orchestra, WDR Symphony Orchestra, Atlanta Symphony Orchestra, Minnesota Symphony, Nat. Symphony Orchestra of Washington, Houston Symphony Orchestra, Detroit Symphony Orchestra, New World Symphony, Seattle Symphony, Baltimore Symphony, Calgary Philharmonic Orchestra, OBC Orchestra Barcelona, Navarra Symphony Orchestra, Royal Galicia Philharmonic Orchestra, Royal Symphony Orchestra of Seville, Norrköping Symphony Orchestra, Israel Camerata, Swiss Radio Choir, Netherlands Chamber Choir, Danish Radio Choir, RAI Nat. Symphony Orchestra; Artistic Dir Purcell Tercentenary Festival, Wigmore Hall, London 1995, Nordic Baroque Festival 2002–04, ION Festival Nürnberg 2003–07; Artistic Dir VIVAT CD label 2012–. *Recordings:* 105 CDs with The King's Consort. *Publications:* Henry Purcell 1994, English Church Music Vol. 1 2010, Vol. 2 2011; many edns of Baroque and classical music. *Address:* The Old Rectory, Alpheton, Suffolk, CO10 9BT, England (home). *E-mail:* info@tkcworld.com (office). *Website:* www.tkcworld.org (office).

KING, Terry B., BM; American cellist, conductor and teacher; b. 20 Aug. 1947, Santa Monica, CA; m. Leslie Morgan 1976. *Education:* Mt St Mary's College, Los Angeles, Claremont Graduate School, University of Northern Iowa. *Career:* debut at Carnegie Recital Hall, New York, 1975; Asst to Piatigorsky, University of Southern California, 1971–72; Instructor, San Francisco Conservatory, 1972; Lecturer, California University, Fullerton, 1972–75; Artist-in-Residence, Grinnell College, 1975–; Vienna Chamber Orchestra, 1978; St Paul Sunday Morning, 1984–87; Asst Professor, University of Northern Iowa, 1990–; Voice of America, America in Concert, Music from the Frick Museum, New York, Austrian Radio, NPR, PBS, several documentaries; Piatigorsky, McPhee, Harrison. *Compositions:* Arrangements, Trio music by Anderson, Enesco, de Falla, Fauré, Glinka; Voice and Instruments, Mozart, Bachelet, Godard; Cello Ensembles, Sibelius, Prokofiev, Shostakovich. *Recordings include:* cello music by Cowell, Barber, Cooper, Harris; Concertos by Harrison, Reale, Beethoven, Haydn; Trios with Mirecourt Trio, Beethoven to present day composers. *E-mail:* Tkingcello@aol.com. *Website:* www.kingcello.com.

KINGDON, Elizabeth; singer (soprano); b. 25 Jan. 1928, Schenectady, NY, USA. *Career:* sang in opera at Bielefeld 1958–63, notably in the 1962 German premiere of Scarlatti's Griselda, at Nuremberg 1962–68, also Hostess in the 1980 premiere of Zemlinsky's Der Traumgörge; guest appearances at Cologne 1964, Oslo 1970, Graz 1982, and London 1988; other roles have included Mozart's Donna Anna and Fiordiligi, Verdi's Elisabetta, Forza Leonora and Aida, Elisabeth in Tannhäuser, Giulietta and Myrtocle in Die Toten Augen by d'Albert. *Recordings include:* Don Giovanni.

KINGSLEY, Colin, BMus, DMus, ARCM; British academic and pianist; b. 15 April 1925, London, England; m. 1955, two s. two d. *Education:* King's Scholar, Westminster School, Gonville and Caius College, Cambridge, studied in Edinburgh and at RCM. *Career:* debut in 1947; freelance keyboard playing, broadcasting, 1948–; solo pianist, Royal Ballet, 1957–59; several performances of contemporary music in the USA, Japan, Poland, France and the UK; mem., MacNaghten Cttee, 1957–63; Associated Bd Examiner, 1959–93; pianist,

University College of Wales, Aberystwyth, 1963–64; principal radio, concertos 1955–; Lecturer, University of Edinburgh 1964, Sr Lecturer 1968–92 (retd); series, Piano Music of P. R. Fricker 1974, followed by premiere of his Anniversary for piano, Cheltenham International Festival, 1978; series, The English Musical Renaissance, Piano Music, 1977; mem. Incorporated Society of Musicians. *Recordings include:* Lyrita, Sonatas for Piano by John White.

KINGSLEY, Margaret, FRCM, LRAM, ARCM; British singer (soprano, mezzo-soprano) and fmr academic; b. 20 Feb. 1939, Pool, Cornwall, England; m. W. A. Newcombe. *Education:* Royal Coll. of Music, London. *Career:* debut with Opera for All; Glyndebourne debut 1966, in Die Zauberflöte; regular appearances, Royal Opera House, Covent Garden, ENO, Scottish Opera, Opera North, State Operas of Hamburg, Munich, Stuttgart and Vienna, Stockholm Royal Opera, Paris Opéra, Naples, Miami, Washington, Metropolitan Opera, New York; roles include Wagner's Brunnhilde, Beethoven's Leonore, Waltraute, Eboli, Elvira, Verdi's Amelia and Lady Macbeth, Mozart's Fiordiligi, Donna Anna, Donna Elvira and Elektra, Cassandre in Les Troyens, Reiza in Oberon, title role in Ariadne auf Naxos, Azucena, Amneris, Marina in Boris Godunov, Akhrosimova in War and Peace, Mrs Grose in The Turn of the Screw; concert appearances with leading British orchestras and on TV; Prof. of Singing, Royal Coll. of Music 1977–2007; vocal consultant, Centre de Formation Lyrique at the Opéra Bastille; currently semi-retd, giving master-classes and teaching privately in Europe and Cornwall. *Address:* 20 Belvedere, Truro, Cornwall, TR1 1UU, England (home). *Telephone:* (1872) 272074 (home); 7769-608773 (mobile). *E-mail:* kingsley@wnewcombe.fsnet.co.uk.

KIRBY, James Nicholas Joseph, ARAM, LRAM, GRSM (Hons); British pianist; *Visiting Teacher of Piano, Royal Holloway, University of London*; b. 15 April 1965, Hull. *Education:* Royal Acad. of Music, Moscow Tchaikovsky Conservatoire. *Career:* debut at Wigmore Hall, London 1991; performances as recitalist, chamber musician and concerto soloist throughout the UK including Royal Opera House Covent Garden, Wigmore Hall, South Bank Centre, Royal Albert Hall, London, and Europe; performed with English Chamber Orchestra, Scottish Chamber Orchestra and Moscow Symphony Orchestra; mem. Barbican Piano Trio, performing on four continents; currently Visiting Teacher of Piano, Royal Welsh Coll. of Music and Drama and Royal Holloway, Univ. of London. *Recordings:* Lalo: Complete piano trios, and Trios by Rachmaninov, Tchaikovsky and Schnittke with Barbican Piano Trio, Appassionato, pieces for violin and piano with Lydia Mordkovitch, Taneyev Piano Trio and Piano Quartet, chamber works by composer Margaret Hubicki. *Honours:* Hon. Prof., Rachmaninov Inst., Tambov, Russia; semi-finals, Int. Tchaikovsky Competition 1990, First Prize, Città di Marsala Int. Competition, Sicily 1992. *Address:* 3 Campbell Road, Bow, London, E3 4DS, England (home). *Telephone:* (20) 8980-5711 (home); (07967) 990860 (mobile). *E-mail:* jnjkirby@btinternet.com (home). *Website:* www.barbicanpianotrio.com.

KIRCHHOF, Lutz; lutenist; b. 15 May 1953, Frankfurt-am-Main, Germany. *Education:* Frankfurt Univ., studied with Lother Fuchs. *Career:* appearances throughout Germany and Europe from 1964; Studio der Frühen Musik, Frankfurt 1973–80; founded own ensemble 1976, for performances of early music; repertoire from Renaissance to contemporary music; recitals with Max von Egmond (bass) and Derek Lee Ragin (countertenor); Festival of Lute Music, Frankfurt from 1988, as founder and Dir, later International Festival of Lute Music; founder, Research Soc. 1990, to assemble lute manuscript music from 16th–17th centuries. *Honours:* winner Jugend Musiziert Competition 1972.

KIRCHNER, Volker David; German composer; b. 25 June 1942, Mainz. *Education:* studied with Gunther Kehr and Gunter Raphael at Peter Cornelius Conservatory, Mainz, Cologne Musikhochschule with B. A. Zimmermann, studied in Detmold with Tibor Varga. *Career:* violinist with the Kehr String Trio 1964–67, Frankfurt Radio Symphony Orchestra 1966–88; freelance composer 1989–. *Compositions include:* Music theatre: Riten für kleines klangtheater, 1971; Die Traung, 1975; Die funf Minuten des Isaak Babel, 1980; Belshazar, 1986; Das Kalte Herz 'Ein Deutsches Märchen', 1988; Erinys Threnos, 1990; Inferno d'amore 'Shakespearion I', 1995; Other works include Fragmente for orchestra, 1961–67; Chorale Variations for 15 solo strings, 1968, rev. 1990; Nachtmusik for ensemble, 1970; Nachtstück for viola and orchestra, 1980; Piano Trio, 1980; Bildnisse I–III for orchestra, 1981–1991; 2 Symphonies, 1980, 1992; String Quartet, 1982; Violin Concerto, 1982; Mysterion, for ensemble, 1985; Piano Sonata, 1986. Requiem, 1988; Saitenspiel for violin and viola, 1993; Missa Moguntina, 1993; Hortus Magicus for orchestra, 1994; Horn concerto, 1996; Ahasver, Scenic Oratorio, 2000. *Current Management:* Schott & Co Ltd, Promotion Department, 48 Great Marlborough Street, London, W1 F7BB, England.

KIRCHSCHLAGER, Angelika; Austrian singer (mezzo-soprano); b. 1965, Salzburg; m.; one s. *Education:* Musisches Gymnasium, Salzburg and Vienna Music Acad. *Career:* studied with Walter Berry in Vienna 1984; first performance in Die Zauberflöte, Vienna Kammeroper; concert performances in Austria, France, Germany, Italy, Czech Repub., Denmark, USA and Japan; recitals in London, Edinburgh, Amsterdam, Cologne, Frankfurt, Hohenems, Graz, Bilbao and in Scandinavia; role of Composer in Jonathan Miller production of Ariadne auf Naxos, Lausanne Opera 1998–99; sang with London Symphony Orchestra, New York Chamber Orchestra and Vienna Symphony Orchestra 1999–2000; feature broadcasts on Austrian Nat. Radio and TV (ORF); participated in film production about Hugo Wolf in role of Frieda Zerny

1992; operatic roles include appearances in Le nozze de Figaro (Schloss Schönbrunn, Vienna), Der Rosenkavalier (Geneva), Hänsel und Gretel (Graz), The Merry Widow (Vienna), Palestrina (Vienna), Don Giovanni (Ravenna and Milan), Les Contes d'Hoffmann (Paris), Ariadne auf Naxos (London), Die Dreigroschenoper (London and Paris) 2009, Die Fledermaus (Vienna) 2010–11, Pelléas et Mélisande (Helsinki) 2012; currently Prof., Mozarteum in Salzburg, Univ. of Graz. *Recordings include:* album of Lieder by Alma Mahler, Gustav Mahler and Erich Wolfgang Korngold (solo debut) 1997; featured on recording of Mendelssohn with Claudio Abbado and Berlin Philharmonic; When Night Falls (solo recital) 1999, Handel Arias 2006, Bach Arias 2008, Hugo Wolf Songs 2009, Schumann Songs 2010, Brahms Songs Vol. 1 2010, Liszt Songs Vol. 1, Vol. 2 (BBC Music Magazine Vocal Award 2013). *Honours:* awarded the title Kammersängerin (Govt of Austria) 2007; three prizes, Int. Belvedere Competition, Vienna 1991. *Website:* www.askonasholt.co.uk/artists/singers/mezzo-soprano/angelika-kirchschlager.

KIRK, Vernon; British singer (tenor); b. 1966, England. *Education:* Royal Academy of Music and Actors' Centre, London and Britten-Pears School, Aldeburgh. *Career:* concerts include tour of Germany and Netherlands in Monteverdi's Christmas Vespers with the Academy of Ancient Music; Bach St Matthew Passion with the London Baroque Soloists, St John Passion in Norway; Messiah and The Creation under David Willcocks; Berlioz L'Enfance du Christ and Brahms Lieder at the London Proms; Schumann's Manfred at the Festival Hall, Die schöne Müllerin at St Martin in the Fields; Lutoslawski Paroles Tissées at the Barbican Hall; opera roles include Mozart's Tamino, Ferrando and Don Ottavio, Donizetti's Ernesto and Nemorino; Lensky, and Gonslave in L'Heure Espagnole (season 1996–97). *Current Management:* Grant Rogers Musical Artists' Management, 8 Wren Crescent, Bushey Heath, Hertfordshire WD23 1AN, England. *Telephone:* (20) 8950-2220. *Fax:* (20) 8950-3570. *E-mail:* info@ngrartists.com. *Website:* www.ngrartists.com.

KIRKBRIDE, Simon; British singer (bass-baritone); b. 1970, Northamptonshire, England. *Education:* Peterborough Cathedral, Guildhall School of Music and Drama and Royal Coll. of Music. *Career:* debut, Jankel in Arabella at Glyndebourne 1996; appearances as Publio in La Clemenza di Tito for Welsh National Opera, Masetto, and Morales in Carmen for Scottish Opera; Mozart's Figaro and Thaddeus in Birtwistle's The Last Supper (2001) at Glyndebourne; roles include Lycomedes in Deidamia, Masetto in Don Giovanni, God in In Sera, Sylvan in Diocletian, Mr Redburn in Billy Budd, Second Elder in Susanna and Cappadocian in Salome, High Priest of Jupiter in Hercules, Starveling and Theseus in A Midsummer Night's Dream, The Voice of Neptune in Idomeneo and Hobson in Peter Grimes; concerts include the Requiems of Brahms, Mozart, Fauré and Duruflé, The Dream of Gerontius, Mozart's C Minor Mass, Bach's Passions and B Minor Mass, Belshazzar's Feast and Mendelssohn's Elijah; Soloist with the Britten Sinfonia, London and Calgary Philharmonics, London Handel Orchestra, Florileguim, Montreal SO, London Baroque and London Mozart Players. *E-mail:* simonkirkbride@hotmail.com.

KIRKBY, Dame (Carolyn) Emma, DBE, OBE, MA; British singer (soprano); b. 26 Feb. 1949, Camberley, Surrey; d. of the late Capt. Geoffrey Kirkby and of Beatrice Daphne Kirkby; one s. with Anthony Rooley; m. Howard Williams. 2015. *Education:* Sherborne School for Girls and Somerville Coll., Oxford and pvt singing lessons with Jessica Cash. *Career:* specialist singer of renaissance, baroque and classical repertoire; debut London concert 1974; full-time professional singer 1975–; since mid-1970s involved in revival of performances with period instruments and the attempt to recreate the sounds the composers would have heard; performances at the Proms from 1977; freelance work with many groups and orchestras in the UK and Germany, including Consort of Musicke, Taverner Players, Acad. of Ancient Music, London Baroque, Florilegium, Freiburger Barockorchester, Fretwork, Orchestra of the Age of Enlightenment, Concerto Copenhagen, Purcell Quartet; appearances at festivals, including Bruges, Utrecht, Luzern, Mosel, Rheingau, Passau, Schleswig-Holstein, Saintes, Beaune, Ottawa, Elora, Tanglewood, Mostly Mozart (New York) and many others. *Television:* subject of South Bank Show (ITV) 2008. *Recordings include:* Complete songs of John Dowland 1976–77, Messiah (Handel) 1979, 1988, Madrigals by Monteverdi, Wert, Scarlatti and other Italians, Schütz, Grabbe, Wilbye, Ward and other English composers, Monteverdi Vespers, Mass in B Minor (Bach), Handel's Athalia, Joshua, Judas Maccabaeus, Sequences by Hildegarde of Bingen (Hyperion), Arie Antiche and Songs of Maurice Greene, Dido and Aeneas, Handel's German Arias, Italian Cantatas, Songs by Arne and Handel, Stabat Mater (Pergolesi), Haydn's Creation, Mozart Motets, Mozart Concert Arias, Vivaldi Opera Arias, Handel Opera Arias, Christmas Music with Westminster Abbey Choir, Christmas Music with London Baroque, with Bell'Arte Salzburg, Bach Cantatas with Freiburger Barockorchester and with Purcell Quartet, Byrd Consort Songs with Fretwork, Handel: Sacred Contatas, Handel Gloria 2001, Lute song recitals with Anthony Rooley and with Jakob Lindberg, Bingen: A Feather On The Breath Of God 2010, Emma Kirkby - A Portrait 2011. *Honours:* Hon. DLitt (Salford) 1985; Hon. DMus (Bath) 1994, (Sheffield) 2000, (Oxford) 2008, (Newcastle) 2010; Hon. FGSM; Hon. FRAM; Hon. Fellow, Royal Coll. of Music, Trinity Coll. of Music; Handel Prize, Halle, Germany 1997, Classic FM Artist of the Year 1999, Queen's Medal for Music 2011. *Website:* www.emmakirkby.com.

KIRKENDALE, Warren, BA, DrPhil; Canadian music historian; *Professor Emeritus of Music History, University of Regensburg*; b. 14 Aug. 1932, Toronto, Ont.; m. Ursula Schöttler 1959; three d. *Education:* Univ. of Toronto,

Univ. of Vienna, Austria. *Career:* began career as editorial asst, Knud Jeppesen, Florence, Italy; reference librarian, Library of Congress 1963; Asst Prof., Univ. of Southern California 1963–67; Assoc. Prof., Duke Univ. 1967–75, Prof. 1975–82; Prof. Ordinarius, Univ. of Regensburg, Germany 1983–92, Prof. Emer. of Music History 1992–; Visiting Prof., Harvard Univ. Center for Italian Renaissance Studies, Florence, Univ. of Pavia, Moscow State Univ., Hungarian Acad. of Sciences; mem. Italian and American Musicological Socs; Fellow, Deutscher Akademischer Austauschdienst (twice), Nat. Endowment for the Humanities (twice), American Council of Learned Socs, Volkswagen-Stiftung; elected mem. Gesellschaft zur Herausgabe von Denkmälern der Tonkunst in Österreich. *Publications:* Fuge und Fugato in der Kammermusik des Rokoko und der Klassik 1967 (revised English edn 1979), L'Aria di Fiorenza 1972, Madrigali a diversi Linguaggi 1975, The Court Musicians in Florence during the Principate of the Medici 1993, Emilio dei Cavalieri 2001, Music and Meaning: Studies in Music History and the Neighbouring Disciplines (with Ursula Kirkendale) 2007, trans. and revision of Ursula Kirkendale, Antonio Caldara 2007; contrib. to Journal of the American Musicological Society, Acta Musicologica, Musical Quarterly, Mozart-Jahrbuch, Quadrivium, Dizionario Biografico degli Italiani, Rivista italiana di musicologica, Studi musicali. *Honours:* Dr hc (Univ. of Pavia 1986), Accademico Filarmonico hc (Univ. of Bologna) 1987; Medal, Collège de France 1994, Medal, Univ. of Pavia, Festschrift: Musicologia Humana (with bibliography) 1994. *Address:* Via dei Riari 86, 00165 Rome, Italy. *Telephone:* (06) 6861697. *E-mail:* wkirkendale@gmail.com.

KIRSCHSTEIN, Leonore; singer (soprano); b. 29 March 1933, Stettin, Germany. *Education:* Robert Schumann Conservatory, Düsseldorf with Franziska Martiensen-Lohman. *Career:* sang first with the Städtische Opera Berlin from 1958; Kiel 1960–63, Augsburg 1963–65, Cologne 1965–68; sang with the Bayerische Staatsoper Munich from 1968; Salzburg Festival 1961, 1970, Edinburgh Festival 1965, 1971; Montreux Festival 1965; guest appearances in Hamburg, Stuttgart, Zürich and Vienna; concert tours of USA, Argentina, England, Italy and Turkey. *Recordings include:* Die Zauberflöte and Cardillac; Bach Cantatas; Beethoven's Missa solemnis.

KIRSHBAUM, Ralph, FRNCM; cellist; b. 4 March 1946, Denton, TX, USA; s. of Joseph Kirshbaum. *Education:* studied with his father, with Lev Aronson in Dallas and with Aldo Parisot at Yale Univ. *Career:* debut with the Dallas Symphony 1959; from 1970 performed with most leading orchestras including those in London, Berlin, Amsterdam and Paris; US engagements with many American orchestras, including the Boston Symphony, Chicago Symphony and the Los Angeles Philharmonic; tours of Germany, Hungary, Switzerland, Israel, Scandinavia, New Zealand, Australia and Japan; debut with the Orchestre de Paris 1990; festival appearances include Edinburgh, London's South Bank and the Mostly Mozart Festival in NY; Promenade concerts in London include premiere of Tippett's Triple Concerto 1980; premiered the Cello Concerto by Peter Maxwell Davies with Cleveland Orchestra under Christoph von Dohnànyi 1989; has appeared with many renowned conductors, including Georg Solti, Yuri Temirkanov, Simon Rattle, André Previn and Colin Davis; founder and Artistic Dir, RNCM Manchester Int. Cello Festival; Tutor, RNCM; frequent guest of the violinist and conductor Pinchas Zukerman, playing Brahms' Double Concerto in London, Edinburgh, Tokyo and Chicago; Elgar's Concerto with the BBC Philharmonic Orchestra at the 1999 London Proms; played the Schumann Concerto with Israel Philharmonic 2004; mem. Pres.'s Cttee on the Arts and Humanities. *Recordings include:* Barber Concerto, Elgar Concerto, Tippett Triple Concerto, Bach Suites, Haydn Concertos, Brahms Double Concerto, Beethoven Triple Concerto, Shostakovich and Prokofiev Sonatas. *Honours:* Hon. Pres. Violincello Soc. of London; winner Int. Tchaikovsky Competition, Moscow 1970. *Current Management:* c/o Ingpen & Williams, 7 St George's Court, 131 Putney Bridge Road, London, SW15 2PA, England. *Telephone:* (20) 8874-3222. *Fax:* (20) 8877-3113. *E-mail:* info@ingpen.co.uk.

KISER, Wiesław Maria; Polish conductor, critic and composer; b. 20 July 1937, Poznań. *Education:* High School of Music, Poznań. *Career:* debut as composer, Poznań 1965; as Conductor, Poznań 1963; over 750 concerts in Poland, Bulgaria, Finland, France, Germany, USSR and Czechoslovakia; Artistic Manager, The Boys Choir of Gniezno, Poland, 1989; Music Lecturer and Promotor of Music Life, 1990–; The Thrushes; Television and Radio broadcasts in Poland, Finland, France, USSR and Germany; several concerts in Belgium as Conductor of The Starlings (men's choir). *Compositions:* From the Years 1989–1990; Scherzo for the violin and string orchestra; Aria to J. S. Bach's chorale for the violin and string orchestra; Trio for the viola, violoncello and contrabass; Impromptu for the viola, violoncello and contrabass; Six Children compositions for the piano Sonata for the piano; Over 70 choral compositions; Sonatina for string quartet, 1995; 12 Preludes for piano, 1996–98; 30 one choirs song, 1995–98. *Publications:* Organisation and Education of Children's Choirs, 1971; Aerials of Poznan, 1975; The Selected Problems of Music History, 1969; Watchword, The Music, in Encyklopedia Wielkopolska, The Great Poland Encyclopaedie; Watchword, The Music, in Dzieje Poznania, The Aets of Poznan, 1989–90; Mr Jerzy Kurczewski: The Man and the Artist, 1994; The Poznan Inhabitants on the records, 1994. *Address:* u Szelagowska 12, 61-626 Poznań, Poland.

KISSIN, Evgeny Igorevich; Russian pianist; b. 10 Oct. 1971, Moscow; s. of Igor Kissin and Emilia Kissin. *Education:* Moscow Gnessin Music School, studied piano with Anna Kantor. *Career:* debut playing Mozart's D-minor concerto aged 10; appeared with Moscow Philharmonic, playing Chopin concertos 1984; tour of Japan with the Moscow Virtuosi; debut in Western Europe with the Berlin Radio orchestra 1987; British debut at the Lichfield Festival with the BBC Philharmonic 1987; London Symphony Orchestra concert 1988; concerts with the Royal Philharmonic and Yuri Temirkanov 1990; promenade concert debut with the BBC Symphony, playing Tchaikovsky's First Concerto 1990; US debut with the New York Philharmonic and a solo recital at Carnegie Hall 1990, subsequent US tour included Tanglewood 1991; Grammy Award ceremony and performances with the Chicago Symphony and Philadelphia Orchestra 1991–92; performed with the Boston Symphony; London recital debut and concert with the Philharmonia 1992–93; Prokofiev Concertos with the Berlin Philharmonic 1992–93; played Chopin and Schumann at the Royal Festival Hall, London 1997; first pianist to perform a recital at the London Proms 1997; Chopin's First Concerto at the London Proms with the Bavarian State Orchestra 1999; first concerto soloist to play in the Proms Opening concert 2000; 10th anniversary tour of recitals in the USA, including Carnegie Hall 2000–01; appearances with the Warsaw Philharmonic, Philharmonia Orchestra, Bavarian Staatskapelle, Chicago Symphony, Boston Symphony, Metropolitan Opera, Bayerische Rundfunk, and the Leipzig Gewandhaus 1999–2001; Brahms' Concerto No. 2 in B flat major at the London Proms 2002. *Recordings include:* Tchaikovsky Concerto No.1 with Berlin Philharmonic conducted by Herbert von Karajan; live recording of Chopin Conertos with Moscow Philharmonic conducted by Dmitri Kitaenko 1984, Rachmaninov 2nd Concerto and Etudes Tableaux with the London Symphony conducted by Gergiev, Rachmaninov Concerto No. 3, Chopin Vols I and II live recital from Carnegie Hall, Prokofiev Piano Concertos 1 and 3 with Berlin Philharmonic conducted by Claudio Abbado, Haydn and Schubert Sonatas 1995, Beethoven: Moonlight Sonata, Franck: Prelude, Choral et Fugue, Brahms: Paganini Variations 1998, Chopin: 4 Ballades, Berceuse op 57, Barcarolle op 60, Scherzo No. 4 op 54 1999, Chopin recital including 24 Preludes Op. 28, Sonata No, 2 and Polonaise in A-flat, Brahms 2003, Scriabin, Medtner, Stravinsky (Grammy Award for Best Instrumental Soloist Performance, without orchestra 2006) 2005, Schubert: Piano Music for Four Hands (with James Levine) 2006, Schumann's Piano Concerto and Mozart's Piano Concerto No. 24 2007, Beethoven's Complete Piano Concertos 2008, Prokofiev Piano Concertos Nos. 2 and 3 (Grammy Award for Best Instrumental Soloist Performance with Orchestra 2010) 2009, Mozart Piano Concertos Nos. 20 and 27 2010,. *Honours:* Hon. mem. Royal Acad. of Music; Hon. DMus (Manhattan School of Music) 2001, Dr hc (Hebrew Univ. of Jerusalem) 2010; Diapason d'Or (France), Grand Prix Nobel Academie de Disque (France), Edison Klassiek Award (Netherlands) 1990, Chigiana Acad. Musician of the Year (Sienna) 1991, Musical America's Instrumentalist of the Year 1995, Triumph Award for outstanding contribution to Russia's culture 1997, Echo Award (Germany) 2002, Shostakovich Award (Moscow) 2003, Herbert von Karajan Award 2005, Arturo Benedetti Michelangeli Award 2007, Distinguished Artistic Leadership Award, Atlantic Council 2008. *Current Management:* IMG Artists, 7 West 54th Street, New York, NY 10019, USA. *E-mail:* lpetrikova@imgartists.com. *Website:* www .kissin.dk.

KIT, Mikhail; Russian singer (bass); b. 1950, Russia. *Education:* Odessa Conservatoire. *Career:* sang first with the Perm Opera, then joined the Kirov Opera, 1966, singing Pimen, Boris, Prince Igor, Dosifei, Ivan Susanin, Gremin, Basilio, Leporello, Mephistopheles, Iago and Sarastro; visited Edinburgh and the Metropolitan with the Kirov, 1991–92, Japan, 1993; sang Dosifei in Khovanshchina with the Kirov Opera at Tel-Aviv, 1996; Engaged as Gremin at the Opéra Bastille, Paris, 1997; season 1998 in Mazeppa with the Kirov Opera at the Metropolitan, as Mussorgsky's Dosifey at La Scala. *Recordings include:* The Fiery Angel and the title role in Prince Igor; Shostakovich songs with Larissa Gergieva for the BBC. *Address:* Mariinsky Theatre, 190000 St Petersburg, 1, Teatralnaya Square, Russia (office). *Telephone:* (812) 326-41-41 (office). *Fax:* (812) 314-17-44 (office). *E-mail:* post@mariinsky.ru (office). *Website:* www.mariinsky.ru (office).

KITAJENKO, Dmitriy Georgievich; Russian conductor; b. 18 Aug. 1940, Leningrad. *Education:* Glinka School of Music, Rimsky-Korsakov Conservatory before leaving to study with Leo Ginzburg in Moscow and Hans Swarowsky and Karl Österreicher in Vienna. *Career:* teacher at Moscow Conservatory 1969, Prof. 1986–90; Conductor, Nemirovich-Danchenko Theatre 1969, Prin. Conductor 1970–76; Chief Conductor, Moscow Philharmonic 1976–89; Principal Conductor, Frankfurt Radio Orchestra 1990–95, Bergen Philharmonic Orchestra 1990–98; Conductor, Bern Symphony Orchestra 1994–2004; Prin. Conductor, KBS Symphony Orchestra, Seoul 1999–2004; Prin. Guest Conductor Berlin Konzerthaus Orchestra 2012–, Danish Nat. Radio Symphony Orchestra; has conducted orchestras from Europe, America and Asia including Berlin Philharmonic, Leipzig Gewandhaus, Vienna Symphony, London Symphony, Gothenburg Symphony, Radio Symphony Orchestra Hamburg, Stuttgart Radio Symphony, Dresden Philharmonic, Qatar Philharmonic (Brahms cycle). *Recordings:* numerous recordings, including with Moscow Philharmonic, Frankfurt RSO, Bergen Philharmonic Orchestra, Danish National Radio Symphony Orchestra, Cologne Gürzenich Orchestra; complete recordings of symphonies of Scriabin, Rachmaninov, Stravinsky, Rimsky-Korsakov, Prokofiev, Tchaikovsky and Shostakovich; also recorded works by Chopin, Gade, Grieg, Richard Strauss, Siegfried Wagner and contemporary music. *Honours:* Hon. Conductor, Cologne Gürzenich Orchestra 2009–; USSR People's Artist 1984, RSFSR State Prize 1988, Pizzicato Excellentia and Supersonic awards, Midem Classical Award 2006, Echo Klassik Award 2006, Lifetime Achievement

Award, International Classical Music Awards 2015. *Current Management:* Vera van Hazebrouck, Chrysanthemenstraße 5, 41466 Neuss, Germany. *E-mail:* office@kitajenko.com. *Address:* Chalet Kalimor, 1652 Botterens, Switzerland (home). *Website:* www.kitajenko.com.

KITCHEN, Linda; British singer (soprano); b. 1960, Morecambe, Lancs., England. *Education:* Royal Northern Coll. of Music with Nicholas Powell, Nat. Opera Studio, studied with David Keren and Audrey Langford. *Career:* sang Blonde in Mozart's Die Entführung 1983 and Monteverdi's Amor at Glyndebourne Festival 1984; later sang Flora in The Knot Garden at Covent Garden and Barbarina in The Marriage of Figaro at London Coliseum; other roles include Mozart's Susanna, Papagena and Zerlina, and Adele; concert repertory includes Rossini's Stabat Mater, Mozart's Requiem, Poulenc's Gloria and Schoenberg's Pierrot Lunaire; sang Iris in Handel's Semele, at Covent Garden 1988; sang Oscar in Ballo in Maschera, Flora in The Knot Garden, Sophie in Werther, Jemmy in Guillaume Tell, Pamina, Magic Flute, Dublin, Cherubino, Zerlina, Serpetta in Finta Gardiniera and Magnolia in Showboat for Opera North; sang Eurydice in new production of Orpheus in the Underworld for Opera North 1992, followed by Susanna in The Marriage of Figaro, Despina and Martinů's Julietta for Opera North and Drusilla in Poppea for WNO 1997–98, Xenia in Boris Gounov at Brighton and Celia in Mozart's Lucio Silla for Garsington Opera 1998. *Recording:* Vaughan Williams: Serenade to Music 1990. *Honours:* Heinz bursary.

KITCHINER, John; British singer (tenor); b. 2 Dec. 1933, England. *Education:* London Opera Centre with Joan Cross. *Career:* debut at Glyndebourne 1965, as Count Almaviva; appearances with ENO, Scottish Opera and WNO; roles include Guglielmo, Don Alfonso, Don Giovanni, Renato in Un Ballo in Maschera, Count di Luna, Figaro and Bartolo in Il Barbiere di Siviglia, Robert in Le Comte Ory, Marcello, Escamillo, and Count Eberbach in Der Wildschütz by Lortzing; also sang in the British stage premieres of Prokofiev's War and Peace and The Bassarids by Henze, at the London Coliseum 1972, 1974; frequent concert engagements.

KITSENKO, Dmitry; composer; b. 24 July 1950, Belay Tserkov, Kiev province, Moldavia. *Education:* Kishinyov Inst. of Arts, Bucharest Music Acad. *Career:* Lecturer, Kishinyov Inst. 1977–82, Musicescu Acad. 1990–. *Compositions include:* Concerto for bayan 1977, oboe 1977, organ 1982, trombone 1990, 1991, cello 1992, four Symphonies 1986, 1992, 1995, 1998, The Seasons for children's chorus and orchestra 1980, Stabat Mater for mezzo and chamber orchestra 1989, Mariengebet for women's chorus 1989, Tinitatea Iupului for contralto and chamber orchestra 1995, Ave Maria for soprano, clarinet and organ 1993, Alleluja for soprano and trumpet 1999, two String Quartets 1975, 1983, In Memoriam Oscar for 13 solo strings 1988, Pastoral Games for ensemble 1988, The Field for brass quintet 1991, Transfiguration for ensemble 1991, Exodus for ensemble 1994, Kyrie 1997, Concerto for Ars Poetica Ensemble 1999, Exodus II for ensemble 1999, Strikhira for four cellos 1999, also keyboard and incidental music.

KITTS, Christopher Martin; British conductor, violinist and educator; b. 7 April 1943, London, England; m. 1982. *Education:* Trinity Coll. of Music, London, studied with Dr Boyd Neel in Toronto, Dr Hans Lert in Virginia, Bernard Robbins at New York Philharmonic, Clifford Evans in Toronto. *Career:* Conductor, Royal Conservatory Orchestra, Toronto 1967, 1968, 1969, Scarborough Coll. Choir and Band 1970; Concertmaster, North York Symphony Orchestra 1971, 1972; freelance violinist, Toronto 1972–85; conducted tours with Birchmount Park Collegiate, in England, France, Germany, The Netherlands 1980, 1983, 1987, 1991; Adjudicator, Toronto Int. Music Festival 1986, 1987; Music Dir and Conductor, Scarborough Philharmonic Orchestra 1985–93; guest conductor, Brampton Symphony, Mississauga Symphony, Scarborough Philharmonic 1994–95.

KLAES, Armin; German conductor; b. 17 Sept. 1958, Koblenz; m. Monika Hachmoller 1982, one s. one d. *Education:* Folkwang-Musikhochschulen Essen with Reinhard Peters, Musikhochschule, Cologne, Univ. of Cologne, studied with Gunter Kehr. *Career:* debut at Bedford Springs Festival for the Performing Arts, Pennsylvania, USA; guest conductor with several orchestras since 1978; founder and regular Leader, Kolner Konzertgemeinschaft 1978–85; Music Dir, Mannesmann-Sinfonieorchester Duisburg 1985–92; founder and Conductor, Amadeus Kammerorchester 1991; Artist Leader of symphonic orchestra and oratorio chorus, Musikgemeinschaft Marl 1992–. *Recordings:* Bach, Concert for organ with H. Schauerte, Le Carnaval des Animaux. *Honours:* Folkwang–Forderpries 1987.

KLANSKA, Vladimira; Czech horn player; *Professor of Horn Class, Jan Neruda Gymnasium, Prague;* b. 9 Sept. 1947, Ceské Budejovice; m. Ivan Klansky 1973; two s. *Education:* Conservatory of Music, Prague, Academy of Music, Prague, masterclasses with Hermann Baumann. *Career:* debut, Mozart II, Rudolfinum Hall, Prague 1966; Co-Principal, Prague Symphony Orchestra 1968–74; concert tours throughout Europe in Duo Recitals with pianist Ivan Klansky, Mozarteum Salzburg 1972, Concertgebouw, Amsterdam 1974; mem., Prague Wind Quintet 1980; mem., Czech Nonet 1982; Artistic Leader, PWQ and CN 1991–, concert tours with both ensembles in Europe, USA and Japan, including festivals in Salzburg, Edinburgh, Stresa, Sorrento; radio recordings in Prague, Stockholm, Brussels, Bremen, Genève, Montreux; President, Stich Punto Horn Society 1989–; Prof. of Horn Class, Jan Neruda Gymnasium, Prague 1988–; masterclasses in the Czech Republic, Austria, France, USA, Brazil and Japan; practitioner in therapeutic One Brain System and SRT System. *Recordings:* albums of both solo and chamber

music. *Honours:* prizewinner, International ARD Music Competition, Munich 1973, juror, International Horn Competitions. *Address:* Cajkovského 26, 13000 Prague 3, Czech Republic (home). *Telephone:* 220807634 (home); 606474570 (mobile). *E-mail:* vladimira.klanska@tiscali.cz (home).

KLAPER, Michael; German musicologist and academic; *Professor of Musicology, Institut für Musikwissenschaft Weimar-Jena;* b. 25 Dec. 1970, Bietigheim-Bissingen. *Career:* Asst, Institut für Musikwissenschaft, Univ. of Erlangen-Nürnberg 2002–07; Head of microfilm archive of medieval musical manuscripts (Bruno Stäblein-Archiv) and Ed.-in-Chief Monumenta monodica medii aevi 2007–10; Prof. of Musicology, Institut für Musikwissenschaft Weimar-Jena 2010–. *Publications:* Hildegard von Bingen: Lieder, Facsimile Riesencodex (HS. 2) der Hessischen Landesbibliotek Wiesbaden 1998, Die Musikgeschichte der Abtei Reichenau im 10. und 11. Jahrhundert: ein Versuch 2003, Introitus-Tropen II: Introitus-Tropen in Quellen ober-und mittelitalienischer Herkunft (with Raffaella Camilot-Oswald). *Honours:* Promotions Prize, Philosophy Faculty, Univ. of Erlangen 2002. *Address:* Institut für Musikwissenschaft Weimar-Jena, Postfach 2552, 99406 Weimar (office); Blumenstr 5, 07743 Jena, Germany (home). *Telephone:* (9131) 944990 (office); (3641) 6382745 (home). *Fax:* (9131) 944992 (office). *E-mail:* michael.klaper@hfm-weimar.de (office).

KLAS, Eri; Estonian conductor; *Artistic Director, Tallinn Philharmonic Society;* b. 7 June 1939, Tallinn; s. of Eduard Klas and Anna Klas; m.; one d. *Education:* Tallinn State Conservatory, studied at Leningrad State Conservatory with Nikolai Rabinovich. *Career:* percussionist, Estonian State Symphony Orchestra 1959–65; Asst Conductor to Boris Khaikin, Bolshoi Theatre, Moscow 1969–72; Conductor Orchestra of Estonian Radio 1964–70; Conductor Nat. Opera Theatre Estonia 1965–94, Music Dir 1975–94, Conductor Laureate 1994–; Music Dir Royal Opera, Stockholm 1985–89; Prin. Guest Conductor Finnish Nat. Opera 1990–; Chief Conductor Århus Symphony Orchestra, Denmark 1991–96;; Music Dir Orchestra of Netherlands Radio Symphony Orchestra 1996–2003; Artistic Dir and Prin. Conductor Tampere Philharmonic Orchestra 1998–2006, Conductor Laureate 2006–; Musical Adviser, Israel Sinfonietta 1999–2002; Chief Conductor, Kolobov Novaya Opera Theatre, Moscow 2006–11; Artistic Dir Tallinn Philharmonic Soc.; Prin. Guest Conductor Holland Kammerphilharmonie; Prof., Sibelius Acad. Helsinki 1993–97; currently Guest Prof., Estonian Acad. of Music and Theatre; conducted at Nobel Prize Ceremonial Concert in Stockholm 1989; Chair. Estonian Cultural Foundation 1991–; Goodwill Amb. for UNICEF; mem. Estonian International Olympic Cttee. *Repertoire includes:* more than 50 operas, operettas, musicals and ballets. *Achievements include:* fmr Estonian lightweight junior boxing champion. *Honours:* Order of Nordstjernen (Sweden), Order of the Finnish Lion, Order of the White Star (Estonia); Dr hc (Estonian Acad. of Music and Theatre) 1994. *Address:* Tallinna Filharmoonia, Mustpeade maja, Pikk 26, 10133 Tallinn, Estonia (office). *E-mail:* fila@filharmoonia.ee (office). *Website:* www.filharmoonia.ee (office); tko.ee/en/eri-klas.

KLASS, Myleene; British singer, pianist and television presenter; b. 6 April 1978, Norfolk; m. Graham Quinn 2011 (divorced 2013); two d. *Education:* Guildhall School of Music and Drama, Royal Acad. of Music. *Career:* made stage debut in Miss Saigon, London; winning participant on ITV series Popstars with band Hear'Say 2001; solo artist 2002–; owner of several fashion businesses and brands; Amb. for Save The Children 2012, Nat. Foundation for Youth Music. *Recordings include:* albums: with Hear'Say: Popstars 2001, Everybody 2001; solo: Moving On 2003, Myleene's Music for Romance 2007, Myleene's Music for Mothers 2008. *Radio:* presenter: Classic FM Weekend Breakfast Show, Friday Night is Music Night (BBC Radio 2) 2008. *Television:* presenter: cd:uk (ITV) 2005, Heaven and Earth Show (BBC 1) 2006, The Proms (BBC 1) 2006, The All Star Talent Show (Channel 5) 2006, The People's Quiz (BBC 1) 2007, The One Show (BBC 1) 2007, The Screening Room (CNN International) 2007, Saturday Night Divas (ITV1) 2007, The Classical Brits (ITV1) 2008–, Popstar to Operastar 2010–11, Loose Women (ITV) 2014–. *Film:* Igor (voice) 2008. *Publication:* My Bump and Me 2008. *Website:* www.myleeneklass.co.uk.

KLATZOW, Peter; South African composer; b. 14 July 1945, Springs. *Education:* studied in Johannesburg, RCM, London with Bernard Stevens, Nadia Boulanger in Paris. *Career:* producer, Rhodesian Broadcasting Corporation; faculty, Univ. of Cape Town from 1973, Assoc. Prof. 1979–; founder, Univ. of Cape Town Contemporary Music Soc. 1974–. *Compositions include:* Piano Sonata 1969, In Memoriam for soprano and strings 1970, Interactions I for piano, percussion and ensemble 1971, Phoenix Symphony 1972, The Temptations of St Anthony for cello and orchestra 1972, Time Structure I for piano 1973, Time Structure II for organ and orchestra 1974, Still Life with Moonbeams for orchestra 1975, Gardens of Memories and Discoveries for soprano and tape 1975, two String Quartets 1977, 1997, Concerto for organ 1986, for marimba 1985, for clarinet 1989, for piano with eight instruments 1995, Hamlet (ballet) 1992, A Mass for Africa 1994, Prayers and Dances from Africa for chorus and brass quintet 1996. *Publications include:* Composers in South Africa Today (ed.) 1987.

KLAVA, Sigvards; Latvian choral conductor; *Chief Conductor and Artistic Director, Latvian Radio Choir;* b. 29 Nov. 1962. *Education:* Jāzeps Vītols Latvian Acad. of Music (JVLMA), Stuttgart Bach Acad., Germany, masterclasses at Oregon Bach Festival, USA. *Career:* began working with Latvian Radio Choir 1987, Chief Conductor and Artistic Dir 1992–; has collaborated with main choirs and orchestras in Latvia, including premieres of new choral works by Latvian composers; as guest conductor, has led leading European choirs; chief conductor at several Nordic and Latvian song festivals; Assoc. Prof., Jāzeps Vītols Latvian Acad. of Music. *Recordings including:* with Latvian Radio Choir: Pēteris Vasks: Māte Saule 2001, Pēteris Vasks: Pater Noster 2007, Rachmaninov: Liturgy of St John Chrysostom 2010, Bernat Vivancos: Blanc/Choral Works 2011, Pēteris Vasks: Plainscapes 2012, Rachmaninov: All-Night Vigil, Op. 37 2012, Rautavaara: Missa a cappella 2013. *Honours:* Latvian Great Music Award, Latvian Cabinet of Ministers Award. *Address:* Latvian Radio Choir, Maskavas Street 4/1 (Spīkeri), Riga 1050, Latvia (office). *Telephone:* 67206671 (office). *Fax:* 67213488 (office). *E-mail:* sigvards.klava@radiokoris.lv (office). *Website:* www.radiokoris.lv (office).

KLEE, Bernhard; German conductor; b. 19 April 1936, Schleiz. *Education:* Cologne Conservatoire. *Career:* asst to Otto Ackermann and Wolfgang Sawallisch at Cologne Opera House; debut at Cologne 1960, Die Zauberflöte; early appointments in Salzburg, Oberhausen and Hannover; Music Dir in Lubeck 1966–73; British debut with the Hamburg Opera at the 1969 Edinburgh Festival, Der fliegende Holländer; Chief Conductor North German Radio in Hannover 1976–79; General Music Dir in Düsseldorf from 1977; Chief Guest Conductor BBC Philharmonic Orchestra 1985–89, conducted orchestra at 1989 Promenade Concerts, with Berg's Three Pieces from Wozzeck and Mahler's 6th Symphony; has conducted numerous orchestras, including English Chamber Orchestra, Stockholm and Rotterdam Philharmonics, Zürich Tonhalle, RAI Rome, Vienna Symphony, and NHK Tokyo; US debut 1974, with the New York Philharmonic; has since conducted in San Francisco, Chicago, Detroit and Washington; regular guest conductor at opera houses in Hamburg, Munich, Berlin, Covent Garden and Geneva; festival engagements at Edinburgh, Salzburg, Netherlands, Hong Kong and Dubrovnik; Promenade Concerts, London 1991, Mozart's Clarinet Concerto and Bruckner's 9th Symphony (BBC Philharmonic). *Current Management:* c/o Tennant Artists, Unit 2, 39 Tadema Road, London, SW10 0PZ, England. *Telephone:* (20) 7376-3758. *Fax:* (20) 7351-0679. *E-mail:* christopher@tennantartists.com. *Website:* www.tennantartists.com.

KLEIBERG, Ståle, BMus, DipMus; Norwegian composer and academic; b. 8 March 1958, Stavanger; m. Åsta Ovregaard 1982; one d. *Education:* Univ. of Oslo, State Acad. of Music, Oslo. *Career:* Assoc. Prof., Univ. of Trondheim; mem. Norwegian Soc. of Composers. *Compositions include:* String Quartet 1985, Stilla for orchestra and soprano/tenor 1986, Two Poems by Montale 1986, Symphony No. 1: The Bell Reef 1991, The Rose Window 1992, Sonetto di Tasso 1992, Dopo for cello and strings 1993, Symphony No. 2: Chamber Symphony 1996, Sonanza e Cadenza 1998, Concerto for double bass and orchestra 1999. *Publications:* Form in Impressionism 1985, The Music of Hans Abrahamsen 1986, C.P.E. Bach and the Individual Expression 1989, Sturm und Drang as Style and Period Designation in Music History 1991, Grieg's Slåtter, Op. 72: Change of Musical Style or New Concept of Nationality (in Journal of the Royal Musical Association) 1996, A National Music by French Means 1999, Following Grieg 1999.

KLEIN, Judy, BA, MA; American composer; b. (Judith Ann Klein), 14 April 1943, Chicago, Ill. *Education:* studied in Berkeley, Calif., Basel Conservatory, Switzerland, New York Univ., studied with Charles Dodge and Ruth Anderson. *Career:* Dir Computer Music Studio and Instructor in Computer Music Composition, New York Univ.; Consultant for Electro-Acoustic Music, New York Public Library for the Performing Arts; Guest Lecturer, Cincinnati Coll. Conservatory, Studio for Electronic Music, Basel; Guest Composer, Brooklyn Coll. Center for Computer Music; Founder Electro-Acoustic Music Archives, New York Library for the Performing Arts; Guest and Artist-in-Residence, Dartmouth Coll. and Studio for Electronic Music, Basel; Guest Composer, Computer Music Center, Columbia Univ. 2000–; Residency, Institut Int. de Musique Electroacoustique de Bourges (IMEB) 2007. *Compositions include:* Little Piece 1979, Dead End 1979, Dream/Song 1980, Journeys, art installation collaboration 1982, The Mines of Falum, Part 1 1983, God Bites 1983, The Tell-Tale Heart, film music, after Edgar Allan Poe 1983, From the Journals of Felix Bosonnet 1987, 88" for Nick 1992, Elements 1 and 2, sound installation 1993, The Wolves of Bays Mountain 1998, Railcar 2008; music for radio plays and theatre productions: Family Play 1981, Unheile Dreifaltigkeit 1983, Sound installations in collaboration with visual artists include Journeys 1982 and Elements 1.2 1984, Railcar comm. from IMEB 2007, Image miniature for Gutenberg Galaxia exhibit visual artist Jana Kluge 2010. *Honours:* Honours at IMEB Music Competition 1988, for Journals. *Current Management:* c/o ASCAP, ASCAP Building, One Lincoln Place, New York, NY 10023, USA. *Address:* 130 West 17th Street, Apt 7-S, New York, NY 10011, USA. *E-mail:* jakmail@earthlink.net.

KLEIN, Kenneth; American music director and conductor; b. 5 Sept. 1939, Los Angeles, CA. *Education:* Univ. of Southern California, Stanford Univ. *Career:* debut in Europe 1970, Paris 1974, Moscow 1974, Vienna 1975; Conductor, Stuttgart Ballet in Stuttgart, then Metropolitan Opera in many US cities; toured fmr USSR, Romania and Sweden 1971, 1972; conducted four concerts in Puerto Rico 1974; conducted Suisse Romande Orchestra, Lamoureux Orchestra, Paris, France, Vienna Symphony, Montreux Festival; debut with American Symphony Orchestra at Carnegie Hall, New York; Bruckner Orchestra, Austria 1978; debut at Rome Festival 1979; debut with Philharmonia Orchestra, Royal Albert Hall, London 1979; Florida Philharmonic, Miami, FL 1980–81; Edmonton Symphony; Louisville Orchestra;

North Carolina Symphony; Kansas City Philharmonic; San Francisco Chamber Orchestra; Music Dir (conducting over 60 concerts per season), Guadalajara, Mexico; Music Dir, New York Virtuosi, South Dakota Symphony and the Waterville Valley Festival; has made numerous guest appearances worldwide.

KLEINDIENST, Stella; German singer (soprano); b. 1957; m. Johannes Schaaf. *Education:* Studied at the Cologne Opera Studio. *Career:* Sang at the Bremen Opera, 1981–88, Deutsche Oper Berlin, 1988–89 and the Vienna Staatsoper from 1990; Sang in Musgrave's Voice of Ariadne at the 1981 Edinburgh Festival and in Zemlinsky's Der Kreidekreis at Amsterdam in 1986; Covent Garden in 1987 and 1989 as Cherubino in a production of Figaro by her husband; Further guest appearances at Stuttgart as Ariadne and at Geneva and Antwerp; Other roles include Mila in Janáček's Osud, Anne Trulove, Belinda in Dido and Aeneas and Weber's Agathe; Sang Boulotte in Offenbach's Barbe-bleue at Stuttgart, 1996; Marzelline in Fidelio, 1998.

KLEMENS, Adam; Czech composer and conductor; b. 14 Jan. 1967, Prague. *Education:* Conservatoire, Prague, Acad. of Performing Arts, Prague. *Career:* debut as composer, Sinfonia Lacrimosa, Piano Concerto 1989; Conductor, Prague Conservatoire Symphony Orchestra 1994; Conductor, Amy (with Lynn Barber, percussionist), Night of the Four Moons (with George Crumb) 1994; Suk Chamber Orchestra 1997; Bambini di Praga 1997; teacher of musical theory, Prague Conservatoire 1996–; mem. Asscn of Musical Artists, Jeunesses Musicales of the Czech Republic. *Compositions:* Clarinet Sonata 1987, Sinfonia Lacrimosa 1989, Perspectives for oboe solo 1992, Music for four players 1993, Piano Concerto 1994, Windy Music for wind orchestra 1995, Fantasy for wind quintet and harp 1997, also film and theatre music. *Honours:* first prize Composers Competition, Generace 1989, 1990, third prize Czech Ministry of Culture Composers Competition 1990.

KLIMOV, Valery Alexandrovich; violinist; b. 16 Oct. 1931, Kiev, USSR. *Education:* studied with Mordkovich in Odessa, Moscow Conservatory with David Oistrakh. *Career:* Soloist, Moscow Philharmonic 1957; British debut with BBC Symphony Orchestra at the Royal Festival Hall 1967; regular visits to USA, Canada, Australia, Italy, Germany, Switzerland, Sweden; other than the standard repertoire, plays music by Prokofiev, Khachaturian, Hindemith and Schnittke; Head of Violin Studies, Moscow Conservatory 1975–. *Recordings include:* album: Khachaturian Concerto. *Honours:* prizewinner at competitions in Paris and Prague 1956, gold medal Tchaikovsky Competition, Moscow 1958, National Artist of the RSFSR 1972.

KLOS, Wolfgang; Austrian violist and academic; *Vice-President, Universität für Musik und Darstellende Kunst, Vienna;* b. 15 July 1953, Vienna; m. Olga Sommer 1982. *Education:* Univ. of Vienna, Musikhochschule, Vienna, masterclasses with M. Rostal, U. Koch, B. Giuranna. *Career:* leader, Viola Sections, Tonhalle Orchestra, Zürich, Switzerland 1977–81, Vienna Symphony Orchestra 1981–89; teacher, viola, chamber music and orchestra, Vorarlberg State Conservatory of Music, Feldkirch, Austria 1977–89; Prof., viola and chamber music and masterclasses, Vienna Musikhochschule 1988–91, Head of String Dept 1991–2007; Vice-Pres., Universität für Musik und Darstellende Kunst (University of Music and Performing Arts), Vienna 2002–; masterclasses, various locations world-wide; soloist worldwide 1975–; mem. Vienna String Trio, numerous concerts, radio, television recordings world-wide. *Recordings include:* gradually recording entire string trio repertory; numerous recordings with various orchestras and chamber music groups. *Honours:* Das Große Ehrenzeichen für Verdienste um die Republik Österreich (Austria) 2003. *Address:* c/o Universität für Musik und Darstellende Kunst, Anton-von-Webern-Platz 1, 1030 Vienna (office); Hainbugerstrasse 35, 1030, Vienna, Austria (home). *Telephone:* (1) 711-55-60-30 (office); (1) 712-93-77 (home). *Fax:* (1) 711-55-60-39 (office); (1) 712-93-77 (home). *E-mail:* klos@mdw.ac.at (office). *Website:* www.mdw.ac.at (office).

KLOSINSKA, Izabella; Polish singer (soprano); b. 1959. *Education:* Warsaw Acad. *Career:* appearances with Warsaw Nat. Opera as Roxana in King Roger, Micaela, Pamina, Mozart's Countess, and Mimi; season 1989 in Moniuszko's Haunted Castle at Vienna and Cassandra in Les Troyens at Amsterdam; season 1993–94 as Roxana at Cincinnati and Buffalo, New York; Mozart Gala at Vienna; Carnegie Hall and Cologne concerts 1995; lieder recitals and further concerts at many venues; sang in Penderecki's Polish Requiem at the Viva il Canto Festival, Cieszyn 1997.

KLOUBOVA, Zdena; Czech singer (soprano); b. 1963. *Education:* Prague Academy, studied in Zwickau. *Career:* sang at the Smetana Theatre, Prague, from 1992, National Theatre from 1993; roles have included Mozart's Blondchen, Susanna, Servilia, Queen of Night and Despina, Verdi's Gilda; Strauss's Zerbinetta and Sophie and the title role in The Cunning Little Vixen; guest appearances in Denmark, Russia, Israel and Japan; many concert appearances, in repertory from baroque to contemporary. *Recordings include:* Carmina Burana; Schnittke's Requiem; Bach Mass in B minor; Kitchen Boy in Rusalka, conducted by Charles Mackerras, 1998. *Current Management:* c/o Neil Dalrymple, Music International, 13 Ardilaun Road, London, N5 2QR, England. *Telephone:* (20) 7226-9792. *E-mail:* music@musicint.co.uk.

KLÜGL, Michael, DMus; German music administrator; *Intendant, Staatsoper Hannover;* b. 1954, Offenbach am Main. *Education:* Univ. of Marburg, Technische Universität Berlin. *Career:* fmr music and theatre critic, Frankfurter Allgemeine Zeitung; Asst Dir Oper Frankfurt 1985–86; stage dir Theater Oberhausen, Bremer Theater 1988–94; Deputy Dir Nationaltheater

Mannheim 1994–98; Intendant Landestheater Linz, Austria 1998–2006; Intendant, Staatsoper Hannover 2006–. *Address:* Staatsoper Hannover, Opernplatz 1, Hannover 30159, Germany (office). *Telephone:* (511) 999-900 (office). *Website:* www.staatstheater-hannover.de (office).

KLUSAK, Jan-Filip; Czech composer; b. 18 April 1934, Prague; m. Milena Kaizrova 1979; one s. *Education:* Acad. of Music and Dramatic Arts, Prague, studied with Jaroslav Ridky and Pavel Borkovec. *Compositions include:* published: Four Small Vocal Exercises, 1–11, for flute 1965, Rondo for piano 1967; published and recorded: Proverbs for Deep Voice and Wind Instruments 1959, Pictures for 12 wind instruments 1960, Variation on a Theme by Gustav Mahler for orchestra 1960–62, 1st Invention for chamber orchestra 1961, 2nd String Quartet 1961–62, Sonata for violin and wind instruments 1965–66, Czech Ordinarium Missae 1966, 6th Invention for Nonet 1969, Invenzionetta for flute solo 1971, Monody in Memoriam Igor Stravinsky 1972, 7th Invention for orchestra 1973, 3rd String Quartet 1975, Variations for two harps 1982, Fantasia on Adam Michna of Otradovice for brass quintet and harp 1983, Six Small Preludes for orchestra, Vor deinen Thron Tret ich Hiermit 1984, What You Want, opera in 2 acts 1984–85, Hero and Leandros, ballet 1988, Dämmerklarheit, Songs on Friedrich Rückert 1988, The King with the Golden Mask, ballet 1990, 4th String Quartet, Mozart-Sickness, Fancy for chamber orchestra 1991, Concerto for oboe and small orchestra 1991, Tetragrammaton sive Nomina Eius for orchestra 1992, Die Kunst des guten Zusammenspiels for wind 1992, Ein Bericht für eine Akademie, opera in 1 act 1993–97, 5th String Quartet 1994, It is a Paradise to Look At, symphonic poem 1999, Bertram and Mescalinda, opera pasticcio in 1 act 2002, GaDe, Fancy for violin 2002, 6th String Quartet 2003, Axis temporum for orchestra 2003, Scherzo capriccioso, symphonic poem No. 2 2005, The Lost Happiness, symphonic poem no. 3 2006–08, In Autumn – 9th Invention for contralto, male chorus and orchestra (1992/2011), Filoktétés, opera 2012–14, Bitterness, cycle of songs for baritone and orchestra 2015. *Recordings:* Inventions Nos 1–10, Perished Happiness. *Honours:* State Decoration for Merit in Art and Culture 2006. *Address:* Navrátilova 11, 110 00 Prague 1, Czech Republic (home). *Website:* www.musica.cz/skladatele/klusak-jan.htm.

KLUSON, Josef; Czech violist; b. 1953. *Education:* Prague Conservatory, Acad. of Fine Arts. *Career:* founder mem., Prazak String Quartet 1972–; tour of Finland 1973, followed by appearances at competitions in Prague and Evian; concerts in Salzburg, Munich, Paris, Rome, Berlin, Cologne and Amsterdam; tour of the UK 1985, including Wigmore Hall debut; tours of Japan, the USA, Australia and New Zealand; tour of the UK 1988, and concert at the Huddersfield Contemporary Music Festival 1989; recitals for the BBC, Radio France, Dutch Radio, the WDR in Cologne and Radio Prague; appearances with the Smetana and LaSalle Quartets in Mendelssohn's Octet. *Honours:* winner, Nat. Violin Competiton, Pisek 1973, Chamber Music Competition of the Prague Conservatory 1974, Grand Prix, International String Quartet Competition, Evian Music Festival 1978, National Competition of String Quartets in Czechoslovakia 1978, Best String Quartet of the Prague Spring Festival 1978. *Current Management:* c/o Světlana Jahodová, Jahoda Artists Management. *Telephone:* 603293985. *E-mail:* info@jahoda-arts.cz. *Website:* www.jahoda-arts.cz; www.prazakquartet.com.

KNAIFEL, Alexander Aronovich; Russian composer; b. 28 Nov. 1943, Tashkent; s. of Aron Iosifovich Knaifel and Muza Veniaminovna Shapiro-Knaifel; m. Tatiana Ivanovna Melentieva 1965; one d. *Education:* Moscow and Leningrad Conservatoires. *Career:* mem. Composers' Union 1968–, Cinematographers' Union 1987–. *Compositions include:* Sonata on a Fairy Tale 1961, A Sling 1962, Diada 1962, Burlesca 1963, Non stop 1963, Marching and Dancing Two-voice Textures 1963, A Toast by Robert Burns 1963, Ostinati 1964, An Angel and Five Poems by Mikhail Lermontov 1964, Piano: musique militaire 1964, A Plain-air-fugue, a Fugue-interior 1964, An Anthem to Foolishness 1964, Turno a turno 1964, In via 1964, In Memory of Samuil Marshak 1964, Those Seeking the City to Come 1964–65, Passacaglia 1965, The Canterville Ghost 1965, Canterville 1965–66, Disarmament 1966, 150 000 000 1966, Lamento 1967, Salve! 1967, Petrograd Sparrows 1967, A Little White One and a Little Black One 1968, Monodia 1968, Medea 1968, Argumentum de jure 1969, Jeanne 1970–78, Baby Songs in Sleep 1972, A prima vista 1972, Appelli 1972, Status nascendi 1973–75, Two Times Two 1975, Vampampet 1975, Ainana 1978, FFPh 1978–2004, Rafferty Jazz Chorus 1980, Vera (Faith) 1980, A Call 1980, Solaris 1980, Da (Yes) 1980, A Silly Horse 1981, Accidental 1982, Nika 1983–84, Churiki 1984, Epitaphs 1984, God 1985, Agnus Dei 1985, A Kholop's Wings (A Serf's Wings) 1986, Through the Rainbow of Involuntary Tears 1987–88, Litania 1988, Notturno 1988, Shramy Marsha (Scars of Marching) 1988, Voznosheniye (The Holy Oblation) 1991, Svete Tikhiy (O Gladsome Light) 1991, Once Again on the Hypothesis 1992, Ionus – postludia 1992, Scalae Iacobis 1992, Chapter Eight 1992–93, Cantus 1993, Maranatha 1993, Butterfly 1993, In Air Clear and Unseen 1994, Alice in Wonderland 1994–2002, Amicta sole 1995, Blazhenstva 1996, Bliss 1997, With the White on the White 1997–98, Lux aeterna 1997, This Child 1997, The Tabernacle 1998, A Snowflake on a Spiderthread 1998, A Day 1999, Small Blue Feathers 2001, Petia i Dolg (Folk) 2001, A Fairy Tale of a Fisherman and a Little Fish 2002, Lukomoriye 2002–03, Confession 2003, Birth 2003, The Cherubimic Hymn 2004, Gee! 2004, Chalice 2004, Old Photos 2004, The Little Beads for Njua 2004, Of the Pope and of His Workman Balda 2004, O Spirit of Truth 2005, Tzarevna (A Tzar's Daughter) 2005, Bridge 2006–08, O Master of My Days 2007, A Mad Tea-Party 2007, For Tatianka and Annushka 2007, E.F. 2008, The Spire of Bujan 2010; incidental music for 40

films. *Publications:* Musique militaire 1974, Diada (Two Pieces) 1975, Classical Suite 1976, The Canterville Ghost 1977, Five Poems by Mikhail Lermontov 1978, Lamento 1979, The Petrograd Sparrows 1981, A Silly Horse 1985, Medea 1989, Vera (Faith) 1990, Passacaglia 1990, Da (Yes) 1991, O Comforter 1997, Bliss 1997. *Honours:* Order of Friendship 2004; DAAD Honoured Grant-Aided Composer, Berlin 1993, Honoured Art Worker of Russia 1996. *Address:* Skobelevski pr. 5, Apt 130, 194214 St Petersburg, Russia. *Telephone:* (812) 293-82-68. *Fax:* (812) 293-53-97. *E-mail:* knaifel@hotmail.com (office); knaifel@mail.ru (home). *Website:* www.ceo.spb.ru/rus/music/knaifel.a.a.

KNAPP, Peter; British singer (baritone) and opera director; b. 4 Aug. 1947, St Albans, England; m. Mary Anne Tennyson 1984, one s. *Education:* St Albans School and St John's Coll., Cambridge. *Career:* debut with Glyndebourne Touring Co.; Kent Opera appearances include Monteverdi's Orfeo (televised on BBC), Eugene Onegin, Don Giovanni, La Traviata; ENO appearances include Don Giovanni, La Traviata, The Marriage of Figaro; performances abroad in Sofia, Zürich, Frankfurt, Venice, Florence, tour of Australia; Dir of own opera company 1978–; La Périchole filmed for BBC television; two-week season at Sadler's Wells Theatre, London 1989; sang Mozart's Figaro 1989; Zelta in The Merry Widow for Scottish Opera; sang Wolfram in Tannhäuser for New Sussex Opera 1990; made version of Carmen for Travelling Opera 1992. *Recordings:* Monteverdi Vespers, De Falla Master Peter's Puppet Show. *Publications:* translations of Così fan tutte, The Marriage of Figaro, La Périochole, Orpheus in the Underworld, La Bohème, The Barber of Seville. *Honours:* Benson and Hedges Gold Award 1977.

KNEZKOVA-HUSSEY, Ludmila, DMus; Ukrainian pianist, composer, choral conductor and clinician; b. 22 April 1956, Mukacevo; m. Bernard Hussey 1990, one d. *Education:* Lvov Central Music School, Moscow Music School, Tchaikovsky Conservatory, Moscow, Acad. of Music, Prague, studied in France, Germany, Banff Centre School of Fine Arts, Canada. *Career:* many recitals and concert engagements with leading orchestras in the USA, Canada, Germany, Italy, Russia, Czech Republic, Slovakia, Austria, Hungary, Poland, Ukraine, Switzerland; television and radio broadcasts in Canada, USA, Czech Republic, Russia, Latvia, Austria, Germany, Italy, Ukraine; established the Ludmilla Knezkova-Hussey Int. Piano Competition, held every two years 1993–. *Compositions include:* Symphonic Fantasy for orchestra 1985, Sonata for piano and flute 1986, Compositions for chorus 1986, Symphonic Ballad for orchestra 1988, Fantaisie for piano and orchestra 1991, Moods of Mustique 2000, If This Be Love for piano, soprano and violin 2000, St Andrews Anthology for piano, soprano and orchestra 2001.

KNIAZEV, Alexander A.; Russian cellist and organist; b. 21 April 1961, Moscow; s. of Alexandre S. Schwarzmann and Ludmila P. Kniazeva; m. (deceased). *Education:* Moscow State Conservatory, Nyzhny-Novgorod State Conservatory. *Career:* Prof., Moscow State Conservatory 1995–2004; masterclasses in France, Spain, South Korea, Philippines; concerts in Russia, UK, France, Germany, Italy, Spain, Belgium, Austria, USA, South Africa, South America, South Korea, Japan; currently mem. Orchestra Co. Mariinsky Theatre, St Petersburg; performed with partners V. Afanasyev, S. Milstein, E. Leonskaya, B. Engerer, Kun Woo Oark, V. Spivakov, V. Tretyakov, M. Brunello, Yuri Bashmet, Yuri Milkis. *Honours:* First Prize, Nat. Competition, Vilnius, Lithuania 1977, Third Prize, G. Cassado Int. Competition, Florence, Italy 1979, First Prize, Int. Chamber Music Competition, Trapani, Italy 1987, Second Prize, Tchaikovsky Int. Competition, Moscow, Russia 1990, First Prize, Unisa Int. Competition, Pretoria, South Africa, Russian Musician of the Year 1999, Honoured Artist of Russia. *Address:* Mariinsky Theatre, St Petersburg 190000, Theatre Square, 1, Russia (office); Moscow 107078, Skornyzhny per. 1, apt 58, Russia (home). *Website:* www.mariinsky.ru/en (office); kniazev.homestead.com.

KNIE, Roberta; singer (soprano); b. 13 May 1938, Cordell, OK, USA. *Education:* Oklahoma Univ. with Elisabeth Parham, Judy Bounds-Coleman and Eva Turner. *Career:* debut in Hagen, Germany 1964, as Elisabeth in Tannhäuser; sang at Freiburg 1966–69; Graz Opera 1969, as Salome, Tosca and Leonore; Zürich and Nice 1972–73, as Brünnhilde; Metropolitan Opera from 1975; guest appearances in Kassel, Mannheim, Montréal, Buenos Aires, Brussels, Barcelona, Hamburg, Berlin, Munich and Stuttgart; other roles include Isolde, Senta, Elsa, Sieglinde, Donna Anna, Elektra, the Marschallin, Lisa in The Queen of Spades, Electra in Idomeneo and both Leonoras of Verdi. *Recordings include:* Isolde in Tristan und Isolde.

KNIGHT, Gillian, BA, FRAM; British singer (mezzo-soprano); b. 1 Nov. 1939, Redditch, Worcestershire, England. *Education:* Royal Academy of Music, London, Open University. *Career:* D'Oyly Carte Opera 1959–64 as Buttercup in HMS Pinafore, Dame Hannah in Ruddigore, Fairy Queen, Iolanthe, Duchess in The Gondoliers, Dame Carruthers in Yeoman of the Guard; also in contralto roles as Katisha in Mikado, Ruth in Pirates of Penzance, and Lady Jane in Patience; Sadler's Wells/English National Opera as Suzuki in Butterfly, Ragonde in Comte Ory, Juno in Semele and Carmen; debut as Carmen, Covent Garden 1970–, premiere of Maxwell Davies' Taverner, 1972, Der Ring des Nibelungen, Rigoletto, Eugene Onegin and Semele, 1988; Paris Opéra debut, 1978, in Die Zauberflöte; US debut, 1979, as Olga in Eugene Onegin at Tanglewood: Tours of USA singing Gilbert and Sullivan; Season 1986/87 Gertrude in Hamlet for Pittsburgh Opera; Nurse in Die Frau ohne Schatten for Welsh National Opera, 1989; Sang the Forester's Wife in The Cunning Little Vixen at Covent Garden; France: Rouen, Lile, Nantes,

Avignon, Tours, Paris, Toulouse (Carmen, Don Quixote, Werther); Germany; Frankfurt, Ulrica in Ballo in Maschera; Spain: Carmen with Domingo in Valencia and Zaragoza; Switzerland: Rigoletto, Geneva; Sang Marguérite in La Dame Blanche at the 1990 Wexford Festival; Sang the title role in the British premiere of Gerhard's The Duenna, Opera North, 1992; Third Maid in Elektra at the First Night of the 1993 London Proms; Sang Annina in La Traviata at Covent Garden, 1996; Roméo et Juliette, 2000; Concert engagements with conductors such as Bertini, Boulez, Colin Davis, Charles Groves and Solti. *Films:* video: Salome, La Traviata, Cavalleria Rusticana. *Recordings:* Six Gilbert and Sullivan roles; Messiah, Damnation of Faust and Mozart Masses with Colin Davis; Schoenberg's Moses und Aron with Boulez; Suor Angelica, Il Tabarro and Madama Butterfly with Maazel; La Forza del Destino with Levine. *Address:* c/o Royal Opera House (Contracts), Covent Garden, London, WC2E 9DD, England. *E-mail:* gknighthq@aol.com (home).

KNIGHT, Katherine; cellist; b. 1960, USA. *Education:* Johns Hopkins Univ., New England Conservatory. *Career:* co-founder, Da Vinci Quartet 1980, under the sponsorship of the Fine Arts Quartet; many concerts in the USA and elsewhere, in a repertoire including works by Mozart, Beethoven, Brahms, Dvořák, Shostakovich and Bartók; Artist-in-Residence, Univ. of Colorado. *Honours:* NEA, Western States Arts Foundation and Colorado Council for the Humanities grants.

KNIGHT, Mark Anthony, AGSM; British academic; *Professor of Violin, Viola and Chamber Music, Guildhall School of Music, Royal Northern College of Music;* b. 24 April 1941, Worcestershire, England; m. Patricia Noall 1965; one s. one d. *Education:* Guildhall School of Music and Drama, London, Tanglewood International Summer School, Massachusetts, USA. *Career:* debut in Brighton 1962; freelance violinist 1965–69, including London Philharmonic Orchestra; Leader, New Cantata Orchestra of London 1966–69; Senior String Tutor, Wells Cathedral School, Wells, Somerset 1975–88; Professor of Violin, Viola and Chamber Music, Guildhall School of Music and Drama, London 1976–, Royal Northern Coll. of Music 2003–; several radio and television broadcasts. *Compositions:* cadenzas: for Mozart's Violin Concertos No. 1 in B flat, K207, and No. 2 in D, K211, for Karl Stamitz's Viola Concerto in D, for Hoffmeister's Viola Concerto in D, for Haydn's Cello Concerto in C, for Mozart's Horn Concerto in E flat K495 for both valve and natural horn; transcriptions for viola of Haydn's Cello Concerto in C with cadenzas, Geoffrey Burgon's Six Studies for solo cello. *Recordings:* A Boy Is Born, as Conductor of Wells Cathedral School Chamber Orchestra 1977. *Publications:* editor: Violin Sonatas Op 5 by Archangelo Corelli 1991, 42 Violin Studies by Rodolphe Kreutzer 1992. *Current Management:* Strings Attached Ltd, Great Skewes Cottage, St Wenn, Bodmin, Cornwall PL30 5PS, England. *Telephone:* (7968) 503971. *Fax:* (1208) 815029. *Telephone:* (1726) 890639 (home). *Fax:* (1726) 890639 (home). *Website:* www.cadenzas.net.

KNIPLOVA, Nadezda; singer (soprano); b. 18 April 1932, Ostrava, Czechoslovakia. *Education:* Prague Conservatory with Jarmila Vavrdova, Acad. of Musical Arts with K. Ungrova and Zdenek Otava. *Career:* sang at Usti nad Labem 1956–59, Janáček Opera Brno 1959–64, notably as Renata in The Fiery Angel, Katerina in The Greek Passion and Katerina Izmailova; Principal, Prague Nat. Theatre from 1965; roles include the Kostelnicka in Jenůfa, Brünnhilde, Leonore, Milada (Dalibor), Libuše, Emilia Marty, Isolde, Tosca, Aida and Senta; guest appearances in Salzburg (Brünnhilde 1967), Barcelona (as Isolde), Turin (in Götterdämmerung) Berlin, Hamburg, New York and San Francisco (Die Walküre); sang with the Berlin Staatsoper on tour in Japan; Janáček's Glagolitic Mass at the 1971 Salzburg Festival. *Recordings:* Jenůfa, Libuše, Dalibor, Orfeo ed Euridice, Katya Kabanova, Der Ring des Nibelungen. *Honours:* prizewinner at competitions in Geneva 1958, Vienna 1959, Toulouse 1959, Czech Artist of Merit 1970.

KNITTEL, Krzysztof; Polish composer; b. 1 May 1947, Warsaw. *Education:* Warsaw Acad. of Music with Tadeusz Baird. *Career:* experimental studio of Polish radio 1973–; co-founder of various electro-acoustic and improvised music groups in Poland; Dir, Warsaw Autumn Festival 1995–98; Pres., Union of Polish Composers 1999. *Compositions include:* String Quartet 1976, Woman's Voice (ballet) 1980, Low Sounds Nos 1–5 1979–91, Norcet 1 and 2 for tape 1980, Black Water, White Water, Old Stream for instruments and tape 1983, String Quartet with tape and percussion 1985, 14 Variations on 14 Words by John Cage 1986–92, Three Songs Without Words for soprano and tape 1987, Nibiru for strings and harpsichord 1987, Histoire I–III 1988–90, Borders of Nothing for computers 1990, Instant Reactions for ensemble and computer 1992, Satan in Goray (ballet) 1993, Legs (sound installation) 1993, Sonata da Camera 1–3 1994–95, Radio Sculpture 1994, Der Erwählte (ballet after Thoman Mann) 1995. *Honours:* Solidarity Prize 1985.

KNIZIA, Martin; organist and harpsichordist; b. 1960, England. *Education:* studied in Lübeck, at the Royal Acad. of Music, London, and with David Titterington and Martin Haselböck. *Career:* organ and harpsichord soloist, continuo playing with London Sinfonia, London Mozart Players and other orchestras; founder, Sweelink Ensemble, performing at St Martin-in-the-Fields, St James's Church, Brompton Oratory, and at the London Bach Festival; Asst Dir, English Bach Festival, Lully/Molière Bourgeois Gentilhomme, Linbury Theatre Covent Garden 2001; teacher of figured bass and baroque organ improvisation, Royal Acad. of Music; Foundation Fellowship RAM. *Publications include:* editions of organ works by Orlando Gibbons.

KNOBEL, Marita; singer (mezzo-soprano); b. 1947, Johannesburg, South Africa. *Education:* studied in Pretoria and at the London Opera Centre.

Career: sang at Cologne Opera 1973–85, notably as Auntie in Peter Grimes, Magdalene in Meistersinger and Mother Goose in The Rake's Progress; guest appearances in Düsseldorf, Dresden, Basle, Barcelona and Edinburgh; sang at the Munich Staatsoper 1990–91 and at the Vienna Staatsoper from 1992, in such roles as Suzuki, Fidalma (Matrimonio Segreto) and the Witch in Hansel and Gretel. *Publication:* Singing Opera in Germany: A Practical Guide (co-author) 2008.

KNODT, Erich; German singer (bass); b. 1945. *Education:* studied in Koblenz. *Career:* sang at the Stadttheater Koblenz, 1970–72; Wuppertal, 1972–76, Mannheim, 1976–87; guest appearances at Düsseldorf, Hamburg, Stuttgrt, Brussels, 1989, Paris, Barcelona, Strasbourg and Madrid; Bregenz and Aix-en-Provence Festivals, 1985, 1989, as Sarastro; Wagner repertoire includes King Mark, Lisbon 1985, King Henry in Lohengrin, 1986, Hunding, Lisbon 1989, Pogner and Hagen; also sang Mozart's Commendatore, Rocco, King Philip, Boris Godunov, Banquo and Ramphis (Bordeaux 1989); Sang Peneois in a concert performance of Daphne at Rome, 1991; Sarastro at Bordeaux, Pogner at Trieste and Roldano in Franchetti's Christoforo Colombo at the Montpellier Festival, 1992; Sang King Mark in Tristan und Isolde at Trieste, 1996. Many further concert engagements.

KNOX, Garth Alexander, ARCM; violist; b. 8 Oct. 1956, Dublin, Ireland. *Education:* Royal Coll. of Music, London, studied with Frederick Riddle, masterclasses with Paul Doktor and Peter Schidloff. *Career:* mem., English Chamber Orchestra 1979–81, and of London Sinfonietta; dedicatee and first performance of Henze's Viola Sonata, Witten 1981; first performance of James Dillon's Timelag Zero, Brighton 1981; guest principal viola, Opera La Fenice, Venice 1981–83; performances of Harold in Italy and Jonathon Lloyd's Viola Concerto with Danish Radio Symphony Orchestra, Copenhagen 1982; mem., Pierre Boulez's Ensemble Intercontemporain, Paris 1983–90; concertos by Luciano Berio and Marc-Andre Dalbavie conducted by Pierre Boulez in Bordeaux, Lisbon, Paris and New York; concerto by Karl-Amadeus Hartmann, Théâtre du Rond-Point, Paris 1987; tour of USSR with Jan Latham Koenig playing Shostakovich Viola Sonata 1987; first performance of Donatoni's La Souris sans Sourire with Quator Ensemble Intercontemporain, Paris 1989; mem., Arditti String Quartet 1990–98, premiering quartets by Ferneyhough (No. 4), Goehr (No. 4), Xenakis' Tetora and Feldman's Quintet; first performance of Ligeti's Loop for solo viola 1991; solo career 1998–; Prof. of Viola, Musikene School of Music, San Sebastiàn, Spain. *Recordings:* Henze's Viola Sonata 1981, Schoenberg's Verklärte Nacht (supervised by Boulez), Embellie for solo viola (by Iannis Xenakis), Bruno Maderna, D'Amore. *E-mail:* garthknox@googlemail.com (home). *Website:* www1.uni-hamburg.de/rz3a035/gknox.html.

KNUSSEN, (Stuart) Oliver, CBE; British composer and conductor; b. 12 June 1952, Glasgow, Scotland; s. of Stuart Knussen and Ethelyn Jane Alexander; m. Susan Freedman 1972; one d. *Education:* Watford Field School, Watford Boys Grammar School, Purcell School, pvt. composition study with John Lambert 1963–68;. *Career:* conducted first performance of his First Symphony with London Symphony Orchestra 1968; fellowships to Berkshire Music Center, Tanglewood, USA 1970, 1971, 1973; Caird Travelling Scholarship 1971; Head of Contemporary Music Activities, Tanglewood Music Center 1986–93; Co-Artistic Dir, Aldeburgh Festival 1983–98; Music Dir, London Sinfonietta 1998–2002, Conductor Laureate 2002–; Artist in Association, BBC Symphony Orchestra 2009–, Artist in Association, Birmingham Contemporary Music Group. *Compositions include:* operas: Where the Wild Things Are 1979–81, Higglety Pigglety Pop! 1984–85; symphonies: Symphony in one movement 1969, No. 2 (soprano and small orchestra) (Margaret Grant Composition Prize, Tanglewood 1971) 1970–71, No. 3 1973–79; concertos: Horn Concerto 1994, Violin Concerto 2002; other: Requiem (Songs for Sue) for soprano and ensemble 2005–06; other works for chamber ensemble and for voice and ensemble, for orchestra and for piano. *Honours:* Hon. mem. American Acad. of Arts and Letters 1994, Royal Philharmonic Soc. 2002; Dr hc (Royal Scottish Acad. of Music and Drama) 2002; Countess of Munster Awards 1964, 1965, 1967; Peter Stuyvesant Foundation Award 1965; Watney-Sargent Award for Young Conductors 1969; Arts Council Bursaries 1979, 1981; winner, first Park Lane Group Composer Award 1982, Michael Ludwig Nemmers Prize in Musical Composition 2006, Royal Philharmonic Soc. Award for Best Conductor 2010. *Current Management:* Harrison Parrott, 5–6 Albion Court, London, W6 0QT, England. *Telephone:* (20) 7229-9166. *Fax:* (20) 7221-5042. *E-mail:* info@harrisonparrott.co.uk. *Website:* www.harrisonparrott.com.

KNUTSON, David; singer (tenor); b. 19 March 1946, Wisconsin, USA. *Education:* studied in Wisconsin. *Career:* has sung in Germany from 1971; sang lyric roles at the Deutsche Oper Berlin from 1972; guest appearances in Hamburg; Munich 1978, in the premiere of Lear by Reimann; Berlin 1975, 1980, in the local premieres of La Calisto by Cavalli and Hippolyte et Aricie by Rameau; Spoleto Festival 1986, as the Witch in Hansel and Gretel; sang Bishop Abdisu in Pfitzner's Palestrina, Berlin 1996. *Recordings include:* Lear.

KOBAYASHI, Junko; Japanese pianist; b. Sept. 1960, Kobe. *Education:* Osaka College of Music, Essen Musik Hochschule, Germany, studied with Maria Curcio and Louis Kentner. *Career:* debut at the Royal Festival Hall, London, 1988; The Purcell Room Recitals, 1983–93; St John's, Smith Square concerts 1995–2001; appearances in England, Germany, France, Denmark, Bulgaria, Poland, Thailand, Canada, USA, Venezuela, Zambia and Japan; Played with orchestras such as the London Philharmonic Orchestra, the

Osaka Philharmonic Orchestra, the New Philharmonic Orchestra, The Academy of St Nicholas, Polish Baltic Symphony Orchestra; broadcasts on BBC Radio 3, WKAR Televion, USA, ZDF Television, Germany; founder-Chair., Takemitsu Society, 1997–. *Recording include:* Nocturnes. *Publications:* contrib. essays to Kansei Music newspaper, monthly music column for Pelican Club Europe. *Website:* www.junkokobayashi.com.

KOBAYASHI, Ken-Ichiro; Japanese conductor; b. 9 April 1940, Fukushima. *Education:* Univ. of Fine Arts and Music, Tokyo with Akeo Watanabe. *Career:* debut with Tokyo Symphony Orchestra 1972; Music Dir of the Metropolitan Symphony Orchestra, Tokyo, then Symphony Orchestra of Kyoto 1985–90; Principal Guest with the Tokyo Symphony and Prof. at the Tokyo College of Music; many appearances with European orchestras, notably the Amsterdam Philharmonic and other Dutch ensembles; Permanent Conductor, Hungarian State Symphony (later renamed National Philharmonic Orchestra) from 1984; fmr Principal Conductor, Japan Philharmonic Orchestra; currently Permanent Conductor, Arnhem Philharmonic Orchestra 2006–. *Honours:* Prizewinner, International Competition Min-On, Tokyo, 1970; Budapest International Competition, 1974. *Address:* Kantoor Het Gelders Orkest, Velperbuitensingel 12, Postbus 1180, 6801 BD Arnhem, The Netherlands (office). *Website:* www.hetgeldersorkest.nl.

KOBAYASHI, Marie; Japanese singer (mezzo-soprano); b. 31 Aug. 1955, Kamakura, Japan. *Education:* Arts and Music Nat. Univ., Tokyo and Nat. Conservatory of Music, Paris. *Career:* debut with 2E2M, Int. Contemporary Music Festival, Strasbourg 1983; appearances with C. R. Alsina's Prima Sinfonia, Radio France concert with Nat. Orchestra of France 1985; Satie's La Mort de Socrate, Radio France concert with Nouvel Orchestre Philharmonique 1989; Smeton in Donizetti's Anna Bolena, Nimes 1989; Birtwistle's Meridian with Pierre Boulez, Châtelet Theatre 1990; J. Fontyn's Roses des Sable, Radio Brussels (RTBF) 1991; has sung in many concerts of oratorios by Bach, Handel, Rossini, Mozart. *Recordings:* Les Madrigaux of G. Arrgo 1990, Motets of Vivaldi 1990, Mozart's Requiem 1991.

KOBEKIN, Vladimir; Russian composer; b. 22 July 1947, Sverdlovsk. *Education:* Leningrad Conservatory with Sergei Slonimsky. *Career:* teacher, Urals Conservatory, 1971–80. *Compositions include:* Swan Song, chamber opera after Chekhov, Moscow, 1980; Dairy of a Madman, mono-opera, Moscow 1980; The Boots, chamber opera, 1981; Pugachyov, musical tragedy, Leningrad, 1983; The Prophet, a Pushkin Triptych, Sverdlovsk 1984; Play about Maximilian, Eleanor and Ivan, Moscow, 1989; The Jester and the King, chamber opera, 1991; The Happy Prince, chamber opera after Wilde, 1991; A Tale of Witchcraft, opera, 1992; N.F.B., after The Idiot by Dostoyevsky, 1995; The Young David, opera, 1997; Moses, monodrama, 1999; Instrumental, choral and chamber music including Cello Concerto, 1997; Fantasia for piano and orchestra, 1999; The Seventh of September: Demons, symphonic poem, 1999. *Honours:* USSR State Prize, 1987, Honoured Artist of the RSFSR. *Address:* c/o RAO, Bolchaia Bronnai 6-a, Moscow 103670, Russia.

KOBEL, Benedikt; Austrian singer (tenor); b. 1960, Vienna. *Education:* Vienna Musikhochschule and the Studio of the Staatsoper. *Career:* sang in concert performances of Gurlitt's Wozzeck and Reimann's Gespenstersonate, Vienna 1985; appearances throughout Austria and the Theater am Gärtnerplatz, Munich, in operettas by Lehar, Zeller, Oscar Straus and Johann Strauss; Vienna Volksoper 1991–92, as Don Ottavio, Camille in Dantons Tod, Tamino, Belmonte, Ferrando, Almaviva and Rinuccio; Vienna Staatsoper 1992, as Cassio in Otello and Narraboth, Flamand (Capriccio), Steuermann (Flying Dutchman).

KOBILZA, Siegfried; Austrian classical guitarist; b. 24 Aug. 1954, Villach, Carinthia; m. Vera Kobilza-Schweder 1983. *Education:* Musisch-Padagogisches Realgymnasium, Hermagor, Academy of Music, Vienna, studied with Karl Scheit. *Career:* first concert tour, Austrian cities including Vienna, 1979; Recitals in main Austrian venues including Wiener Musikverein, Wiener Konzerthaus, Grosses Festspeilhaus Salzburg, Mozarteum Salzburg, Brucknerhaus Linz; Soloist with orchestras including Vienna Symphony, Mozarteumorchester Salzburg, Vienna Chamber Orchestra; Television and radio recordings; Teaching master classes, various European countries and China; Debuts in London, Paris, New York, 1982; Concert tours, Germany, Switzerland, the United Kingdom, France, Netherlands, Iceland, Yugoslavia, Hungary, USA, USSR, Czechoslovakia, Turkey, Tunisia, China. *Address:* Servitengasse 7/16, 1090 Vienna, Austria.

KOBLER, Linda, BM, MM; American harpsichordist; b. 1952, New York, NY; m. Albert Glinsky 1979. *Education:* Peabody Conservatory of Music, Juilliard School. *Career:* debut at Carnegie Recital Hall 1984; concerto soloist with Zürich Chamber Orchestra, New York Chamber Orchestra, Broadway Bach Ensemble, American Baroque Ensemble, Bach Gesellchaft, Seabrook Chamber Players, Cathedral Orchestra, New York Chamber Symphony, Toronto Symphony; fmr mem., Ensemble Tafelmusik Quartet; performances in New York, Ohio, New Jersey, California, Washington (DC), South Carolina, Louisiana, including Philips Collection, Cleveland Inst., Univ. of California, Carnegie Recital Hall, Merkin Concert Hall, Spoleto Festival, Town Hall, New York, Metropolitan Museum of Art, Indianapolis, Early Music Festival, Smithsonian Inst.; performances in Switzerland and Germany; radio appearances in USA; world premiere of works by Zwillich and Persichetti; faculty mem., Juilliard School 1989–96; commentator, Nat. Public Radio programme, Performance Today 1997. *Recordings:* Musical Heritage Society; Works of

Christophe Moyreau and Pancrace Royer; Classic Masters; Works of Frescobaldi, Strozzi.

KOBRIN, Alexander; Russian pianist; b. 1980, Moscow. *Education:* Gnessin State Music Coll., Moscow, Moscow Conservatoire. *Career:* has performed with New York Philharmonic, Dallas Symphony Orchestra, Royal Liverpool Philharmonic Orchestra, Ulster Orchestra, City of Birmingham Symphony, Deutsches Symphonie Orchester Berlin, Wroclaw Philharmonic; recitals at the Louvre, Paris, Wigmore Hall, London, Esplanade Concert Hall, Sheung Wan Civic Centre, Hong Kong; tours of USA, Japan and Italy; festivals include Ravinia Festival, Beethoven Easter Festival, Hannover Prize winners Series, Turner Sims, Klavier-Festival Ruhr, Ruidoso Chamber Music Festival and Bolzano Busoni Festival; BBC Proms debut 2008; teaches at Gnessin State Music Coll., Moscow. *Honours:* first prize and A. Benedetti Michelangeli Special Prize, Busoni Int. Piano Competition, Bolzano, Italy 1999, Nancy Lee and Perry R. Bass Gold Medal, Van Cliburn Int. Piano Competition 2005. *Current Management:* c/o Gershunoff Artists, 2533 NW 9th Terrace, Wilton Manors, FL 33311-23236, USA. *Telephone:* (954) 267-0550. *Website:* www.gershunoff.com; www.alexkobrinpianist.com.

KOC, Jozik; singer (baritone); b. 1968, Oxford, England. *Education:* York Univ. and Guildhall School, London. *Career:* concerts and recitals throughout the UK 1991–92, leading to Wigmore Hall debut 1993; opera debut as Fiorello in Il Barbiere di Siviglia, and Guide in Death in Venice, for Glyndebourne Touring Opera; Spirit in Monteverdi's Orfeo for ENO, Purcell's Aeneas for Opera Factory and Prince Lindoro in Haydn's Pescatrici (Garsington Festival Opera 1997); other roles include Mozart's Don Giovanni, Count and Guglielmo, Sancho in Massenet's Don Quichotte, and Schaunard (La Bohème); concert repertoire includes Bach's B minor Mass, Messiah, Rossini's Petite Messe and the Fauré Requiem; appearances with the London and Royal Philharmonics, the English Chamber Orchestra. *Recordings include:* Baroque Anthems.

KOCH, Sophie; singer (mezzo-soprano); b. 19 Feb. 1969, Versailles, France. *Education:* Paris Conservatoire with Jane Berbié. *Career:* appearances throughout France, notably in Marseille, Strasbourg, and Théâtre du Châtelet, Paris; season 1998–99 as Rossini's Rosina and Mozart's Dorabella with the Royal Opera in London; Zerlina at the Schwetzingen Festival, in Monteverdi's Orfeo at the Vienna Festival, the Prince in Massenet's Cendrillon at Geneva, and Mercédès (Carmen) at the Opéra Bastille, Paris; Composer in Ariadne auf Naxos at Dresden and Zerlina in Munich, season 1999–2000 with Cherubino and Octavian at the Vienna Staatsoper and the Composer at La Scala; other roles include Sextus in La Clemenza di Tito, Silla in Pfitzner's Palestrina and Cenerentola, all with the Royal Opera at Covent Garden 2000–01; Mozart's Cherubino in Brussels and Paris, and on tour with the Bavarian State Opera to Japan; engagements in 2005 included Siebel and the Composer at Covent Garden, and Octavian on tour with the Vienna State to Israel; concerts include Beethoven's Missa Solemnis and Elgar's Sea Pictures.

KOCMIEROSKI, Matthew; American percussionist, historian and educator; *Principal Percussionist, Pacific Northwest Ballet Orchestra;* b. 18 Aug. 1953, Roslyn, NY; m. Elaine S. Schmidt 1974. *Education:* Nassau Community Coll., Mannes Coll. of Music. *Career:* active in chamber music, performances include Seattle Chamber Players, New Music America, Seattle Chamber Music Festival, Auburn Symphony Chamber Music Series, Bergen Int. Festival, Goodwill Arts Festival, Seattle Spring Festival of Contemporary Music, Moscow Autumn Festival, Moscow Alternativa Festival, Warsaw Autumn Festival, Orcas Island Festival, Icicle Creek Festival, Icebreaker Festivals I–VII, Methow Valley Festival, Aeolian Chamber Players; numerous recital and concerto appearances in Pacific Northwest; freelance orchestral performances include Martha Graham Dance Co., New York City Ballet, Washington Square Music Festival, Queens Symphony, Seattle Symphony, Seattle Opera, Bolshoi Ballet, Joffrey Ballet, Mariinsky Orchestra, Northwest Chamber Orchestra, Britt Festival, Bellingham Music Festival; Instructor of Percussion, Cornish Coll. of the Arts, Seattle; mem. New Performance Group, Seattle 1981–96, Artistic Dir 1984–96; Prin. Percussionist, Pacific Northwest Ballet Orchestra 1990–; Founder-mem. Pacific Rims Percussion Quartet 1995–; Pres. Int. Guild of Symphony, Opera and Ballet Musicians 2004–11. *Films:* performed on numerous film and video game soundtracks, including Die Hard with a Vengeance, Valkyrie, Lord of Illusion, Rabbit in the Moon, Halo, World of Warcraft. *Recordings include:* Paul Dresher's Night Songs 1984, Atlas Eclipticalis (John Cage conducting) 1986, Malcolm Goldstein qerneraq 1986, Four Beckett Songs 1987, Janice Giteck Breathing Songs 1988, Janice Giteck Home 1992, Reza Vali Chant and Dance 2006, Edge (Paul Taub) 2011, All Spring (Emily Doolittle) 2015, Ispirare (Melia Watras) 2015. *Address:* 12724 19th Avenue NE, Seattle, WA 98125, USA (home). *Telephone:* (206) 365-8925 (office).

KOCSAR, Miklós; Hungarian composer; b. 21 Dec. 1933, Debrecen. *Education:* Budapest Acad. of Music with Farkas. *Career:* teacher, Béla Bartók Conservatory, Budapest 1972–; Deputy Head of Music, Hungarian Radio 1983–. *Compositions include:* Horn Concerto 1957, Capriccio for orchestra 1961, Solitary Song for soprano and chamber ensemble 1969, Variations for orchestra 1977, Capricorn Concerto for flute and chamber orchestra 1978, Metamophoses for orchestra 1979, Sequenze for strings 1980, Elegia for bassoon and chamber ensemble 1985, Formazioni for orchestra 1986, Visions of the Night oratorio for mezzo-soprano solo, mixed choir and orchestra 1987,

The Fire of St Anthony for orchestra 1992, Concerto for violoncello and orchestra 1994, Salve Regina for voices and orchestra 1995, Notturno for piano 1996, Magnificat 1996, Missa Seconde 1997; choral music: I Will Invoke You, Demon 1985, Missa in A for equal voices 1991; chamber: Wind Quintet 1959, Brass Trio 1959, Variziioni for woodwind quintet 1968, Sestetto d'ottoni 1972, seven Variations for viola 1983, Wind Quintet No. 3 1984, Quintetto d'ottoni 1986, Rhapsody for trombone, piano and percussion 1989, Trio for strings 1990, Music for four trombones and percussion 1991; also songs and piano pieces. *Honours:* Erkel Prize 1973, 1980, Merited Artist of the Hungarian People's Republic 1987, Bartók-Pasztory Award 1992.

KOCSIS, Zoltán; Hungarian pianist, conductor and composer; *General Music Director, Hungarian National Philharmonic Orchestra*; b. 30 May 1952, Budapest; s. of Ottó Kocsis and Mária Mátyás; m. 1st Adrienne Hauser 1986; one s. one d.; m. 2nd Erika Tóth 1997; one s. one d. *Education:* Budapest Music Acad. (under Pál Kadosa). *Career:* appeared with Berlin Philharmonic Orchestra and performed in Germany, USSR, Austria and Czechoslovakia 1971; toured USA with Dezsö Ranki and Budapest Symphony Orchestra under George Lehel 1971; recitals in Netherlands, Paris, London and Ireland 1972; concerts in Norway, with Svyatoslav Richter in France and Austria, with Claudio Abbado and London Symphony Orchestra and at BBC Promenade Concerts in London and Festival Estival, Paris 1977, Edinburgh Festival 1978, Verbier Festival, Ferrara Festival, La Roque d'Anthéron Festival, with New York Philharmonic, Chicago Symphony, Atlanta Symphony and Minnesota orchestras; Asst Prof., Music Acad. Budapest 1976–79, Prof. 1979–; Producer of Archive Section of Hungaroton (record co.); Co-founder and Artistic Co-Dir Budapest Festival Orchestra 1983–96; Gen. Music Dir Hungarian Nat. Philharmonic Orchestra 1997–. *Compositions include:* completion of Schoenberg's Moses & Aron (Third Act) 2008, Little Christmas – Variations on a Hungarian Folk Song for choir and orchestra 2010. *Recordings include:* Debussy Solo Piano Works (Gramophone Award for Best Instrumental Recording 1990), Bartók Violin Sonatas Nos 1& 2 (as pianist) (Gramophone Award for Best Chamber Recording 2013). *Publications:* Miscellaneous Publications, Arrangements for Piano and 2 Pianos, Violoncello, Clarinet etc.; orchestrations from the originals of Liszt, Debussy, Rachmaninov, Bartók, Kodály; completion of Ravel's Le Tombeau de Couperin (Fugue, Toccata) and Bartók's Village Scenes. *Honours:* Chevalier, Ordre des Arts et des Lettres 2002; First Prize, Beethoven Piano Competition, Hungarian Radio and Television 1970, Liszt Prize 1973, Kossuth Prize 1978, 2005, Cæcilia Award (Belgium) 1981, Merited Artist's Title 1984, Mumm Award, Ovation magazine (USA) 1988, Bartók-Pásztory Award 1988, 2004, Lifetime Achievement Award, MIDEM, Cannes 2004, Classical Internet Award 2004, Prima Primissima Award 2007. *Address:* Hungarian National Philharmonic Orchestra, Komor Marcell u. 1, 1095 Budapest, Hungary (office). *Telephone:* (1) 4116620 (office). *Fax:* (1) 4116624 (office). *E-mail:* kocsis.z@filharmonikusok.hu (office). *Website:* www.filharmonikusok.hu (office).

KODALLI, Yelda; Turkish singer (soprano); b. 20 Oct. 1968; m. *Education:* Hacettepe Univ., Ankara State Conservatory with Prof. Mustafa Yurdakul. *Career:* debut, ORF Austrian television 1991; Vienna State Opera 1992; Zauberflöte, Reykjavík 1991; performed in Vienna at Staatsoper and at Volksoper, Mannheim, Essen, Düsseldorf; Opéra Bastille, Paris; Munich Staatsoper; Strasbourg Festival; Schönbrunn Festival; La Scala; Hamburg and Wiener Staatsoper; Lyric Opera of Chicago; in Vienna in Hansel and Gretel, Arabella, Capriccio, Zauberflöte and Siegfried; new production of Zauberflöte, Teatro Regio, Turin 1994; Lucia di Lammermoor, Teatro Carlo Falice, Genoa; sang in Japan, Tel-Aviv and Haifa; opened La Zarzuela Theatre of Madrid in Stravinsky's Le Rossignol 1995; sang Gilda in Rigoletto in Japan, RAI orchestra of Turin; sang in concerts in Ankara and Istanbul, Zürich and Basel; on tour with the Orchestra della Toscana; performed Luciano Berio's Outis, La Scala; I Puritani, Tenerife; Christmas concert, ABAO, Bilbao; Zauberflöte, Vienna. *Recordings:* Constanze in Mozart's Die Entführung aus dem Serail with the Scottish Chamber Orchestra conducted by Charles Mackerras, Mozart in Turkey at the Topkapi Palace in Istanbul (film, dir by Elijah Moshinsky). *Publications:* Musica Viva, Lucia, Franca Cella 1994; contrib. to La Stampa 1994, Opera International Herald Tribune 1996, Readers Sun Times 1996, L'Opera TAA The Best Vocal of the Year 1996.

KODAMA, Momo; Japanese concert pianist; b. 1972, Osaka. *Education:* Conservatoire de Paris. *Career:* concerts with Seiji Ozawa with the new Japanese Philharmonic, and with Boston Symphony Orchestra, 2000; further concerts with Kent Nagano, Eliahu Inbal, Bernard Klee, Gerard Schwarz, Charles Dutoit, Lawrence Foster, Sir Roger Norrington and Valery Gergiev; Orchestras include Berlin Radio, Bayerische Rundfunk, Strasbourg Philharmonic, RSO Stuttgart, RAI Turin, DSO Berlin, Orchestre de la Fondation Gulbenkian, NDR Hamburg; all major Japanese orchestras; Wigmore Hall recital debut, 1999, wth Chopin, Ravel and Messiaen; festival engagements at Davos, 1999–2000, Berlin, Lucerne; Mostly Mozart and Marlboro, USA, Enescu Festival, Schleswig Holstein, La Roque d'Antheron Int. Piano Festival 2005; further recitals at the Paris Châtelet and Tonhalle, Zürich; wide repertoire from Bach to Takemitsu, including Messiaen's Vingt Regards sur l'Enfant Jesus. *Recording:* Messiaen's Vingt Regards sur l'Enfant Jesus 2005. *Address:* c/o Kajimoto Concert Management, 30 boulevard Pasteur, 75015 Paris, France. *Telephone:* 1-42-19-32-65 (office). *Fax:* 1-442-19-92-12 (office). *E-mail:* paris@kajimotomusic.com (office). *Website:* www.kajimotomusic.com (office).

KOEHNE, Graeme John, BMus, MMus; Australian composer and academic; b. 1956, Adelaide, SA. *Education:* Univ. of Adelaide, Yale Univ. School of Music, USA with Virgil Thomson and Louis Andriessen, and studied with Richard Meale, Tristam Cary and Bernard Rands. *Career:* Tutor in Piano and Composition, Univ. of New England, Armidale, NSW 1978; collaborated with choreographer Graeme Murphy and Sydney Dance Orchestra; commissions for Australian Bicentenary, West Australian Ballet Co., Queensland Ballet Co., Australian Chamber Orchestra, Seymour Group (Sydney), Australian Ballet; Lecturer in Composition, Univ. of Adelaide. *Compositions:* orchestral: The Iridian Plateau 1977, First Blue Hours 1979, Toccata 1981, Fanfare 1981, Rain Forest 1981, riverrun... 1982, Once Around the Sun 1988, Unchained Melody 1991, Powerhouse 1993, Elevator Music 1997, Ballet Suite from The Selfish Giant 1985, Capriccio for piano and strings 1987; for ensemble: Sextet 1975, Cantilene 1978, Crystal Islands 1982, Divertissement Trois Pièces Bourgeoises for string quartet 1983, Ricecare and Burletta for string trio 1984, Miniature 1985, String Quartet No. 2, Shaker Dances 1995; for voice and ensemble: Cancion (text by F. Garcia Lorca) 1975, Fourth Sonnet (suite, text by S. Mallarmé) 1984, Nearly Beloved 1986, Nocturnes 1987; keyboard music: Piano Sonata 1976, Harmonies in Silver and Blue for piano 1977, Twilight Rain for piano 1979, Gothic Toccata (aka Toccata Aurora) 1984.

KOENIGS, Lothar; German pianist and conductor; *Music Director, Welsh National Opera*; b. 1965, Aachen. *Education:* Cologne Conservatory. *Career:* Music Dir, Städtische Bühnen, Osnabrück 1999–2003; guest engagements since 2003 have included the Vienna State Opera, Metropolitan Opera New York, Munich, Dresden, La Scala, Hamburg, Brussels and Lyon in a wide repertoire ranging from Mozart to Berg, especially the operas of Wagner, Strauss and Janáček; initial engagement with Orchestra of Welsh Nat. Opera (WNO) 2005, Music Dir 2009–, conducted new production of Die Meistersinger and in televised concert at BBC Proms 2010, appears annually with Orchestra of WNO in concert at St David's Hall, Cardiff; symphonic engagements include the Hallé, Beethoven Orchester, Bonn, Orchestre Philharmonique de Luxembourg, Yomiuri Nippon Symphony Orchestra, Tokyo, Deutsche Kammerphilharmonie, Bremen, Radio Orchestra, Saarbrücken, RAI Orchestra, Turin, DSO, Berlin, Orchestra dell' Accad. di Santa Cecilia, Rome, Rotterdam Philharmonic, Orchestra Sinfonica de São Paulo, RAI Orchestra, Turin, Radio Symphony Orchestra, Berlin, Wiener Symphoniker, Dresden Philharmoniker in Verona, and concerts at the Tanglewood Festival; recent and future engagements include Tristan und Isolde, Don Giovanni, Katya Kabanova, Fidelio, Ariadne auf Naxos, Turandot (WNO), Wozzeck, Ariadne and Lohengrin for the Bavarian State Opera in Munich, Elektra in La Monnaie, Mahagonny in Cologne as well as concert performances in UK and Europe; conducted concert performance of Tristan und Isolde at Edinburgh Int. Festival 2012, Act 3 of Die Walküre with Boston Symphony Orchestra and Bryn Terfel at the Tanglewood Festival 2013. *Address:* Welsh National Opera, Millennium Centre, Bute Place, Cardiff, CF10 5AL, Wales (office). *Telephone:* (29) 2063-5000 (office). *Fax:* (29) 2063-5099 (office). *E-mail:* enquiries@wno.org.uk (office). *Website:* www.wno.org.uk (office); www.lothar-koenigs.de.

KOERPPEN, Alfred; German composer; b. 16 Dec. 1926, Wiesbaden. *Education:* studied with Kurt Thomas in Frankfurt. *Career:* Professor, Staatliche Hochschule für Musik und Theater, Hannover 1964–91. *Compositions include:* Virgilius der Magier von Rome, opera 1951, Der Turmbauzu Babel, oratorio 1951, Das Feuer des Prometheus, oratorio 1956, 17 Choralfantasien und Partiten, for organ 1948–90, Wassermarken for soprano, tenor and string quartet 1961, Joseph und seine Brüder, for female chorus and speakers 1967, Arachne, ballet 1968, Parabel vom Dornbusch, for mixed chorus and ensemble 1969, Das Stadtwappen for solo voices, chorus and orchestra 1973, Konzert im Dreieck 1974, Donum Kinguarum, for 3 solo voices and chorus 1976, Ein Abenteuer auf dem Friedhof, chamber opera 1980, Symphony 1985, ECHO for solo voices and three chourses 1985, Trio in zwei Sätzen for violin, cello and piano 1986, Jona for chorus and organ 1995, Abgesang for violin and orchestra 1995, Concerto for bass tuba and orchestra 1998, Streichquartett 1 2006, Streichquartett 2 2007, Konzert f. VI. u. Orchester 2008. *Publications:* Melodielehre, Möseler–Verlag, Anleitungen f. Musikalische, Erfindungsübungen, Diesterweg. *Honours:* Low Saxony Prize for culture 1983. *Telephone:* (49) 51363434 (home); (39) 0773887132 (home). *Fax:* (49) 51366242 (home); (39) 0773887132 (home). *E-mail:* koerppen@alfred-koerppen.de (office). *Website:* www.alfred-koerppen.de.

KOFRON, Petr; composer; b. 15 Aug. 1955, Prague, Czechoslovakia. *Education:* Janacek Acad., Brno. *Career:* founder and Dir, Agon Orchestra 1983–; co-founder, Czech Soc. for New Music; Ed. of music journal, Konzerva/Na Hudbu 1989–. *Compositions include:* In Memoira I.O. Dunayevsky for speaker and brass quintet 1975, Farewell Waltz for orchestra 1977, The Bow for orchestra 1979–81, String Quartet 1982, For Soprano and Orchestra (after Georg Trakl) 1982, E.S.T. concerto for piano and ensemble 1988, Liber LXXII for two orchestras and tape 1988, Alpha and Centaur for violin and ensemble 1989, Spira for clarinet and ensemble 1990, Enhexe for ensemble 1991, The Golden Fern (opera) 1991, The Fire is Mine for ensemble and electronics 1993, Abram for eight instruments 1994, Tworl for string quartet 1994, Big Dipper for ensemble 1996. *Publications include:* Graphic Scores and Concepts 1996.

KOGAN, Pavel; Russian violinist and conductor; *Music Director and Chief Conductor, Moscow State Symphony Orchestra*; b. 6 June 1952, Moscow; s. of Leonid Kogan and Elizaveta Gilels; m. (divorced); one s. *Education:* Moscow Conservatory, studied conducting in Leningrad with I. Mussin and in Moscow with Leo Ginzburg. *Career:* has performed as soloist and conductor in major concert halls of Europe, USA and Asia with leading orchestras; Conductor Bolshoi Theatre 1986–87; Music Dir Zagreb Philharmonic Orchestra 1987–90; Music Dir and Chief Conductor Moscow State Symphony Orchestra 1989–; Prin. Guest Conductor, Utah Symphony Orchestra, USA 1997–2005; mem. Russian Acad. of Arts. *Recordings:* numerous works with the Moscow State Symphony Orchestra and other ensembles. *Honours:* Peoples' Artist of Russia 1994, Order of Friendship of the Russian Fed. 2002, Order of Merit of Russia 2007; First Prize, Jean Sibelius Int. Violin Competition 1970, State Prize of the Russian Fed. 1997. *Address:* 105082 Moscow, Spartakovskaya sq., 1/2 (office); 125009 Moscow, Brusov per. 8-10, Apt 8, Russia (home). *Telephone:* (499) 763-35-36 (office); (495) 692-13-95 (home). *Fax:* (499) 763-35-37 (office). *E-mail:* a.mizikaeva@msso-kogan.ru (office); info@msso-kogan.ru (office). *Website:* www.msso-kogan.ru (office).

KOGAN, Semjon; Ukrainian conductor; b. 24 April 1928, Bobruisk. *Education:* St Petersburg Conservatoire. *Career:* founder, State Symphony Orchestra at Omsk; Artistic Dir, Rostov State Symphony Orchestra 1976, participating in the 1990 Tchaikovsky Int. Competition, Moscow; guest appearances with the USSR State Symphony, Moscow Philharmonic, Moscow Radio and St Petersburg Philharmonic Orchestras, and invitations to conduct in Poland, Czechoslovakia and Germany; repertoire includes Stravinsky and Shostakovich in addition to the standard repertoire; has given the premieres of works by Denisov, Shchedrin and Khrennikov; Prof., Rostov on Don Conservatoire; founder, Rostov Conservatoire Orchestra 1993.

KOHN, Karl George, BA, MA; American pianist, conductor and composer; *William M. Keck Distinguished Service Professor Emeritus, Pomona College*; b. 1 Aug. 1926, Vienna, Austria; m. Margaret Case Sherman 1950; two d. *Education:* New York College of Music, Harvard Univ., studied piano with Werschinger, conducting with Prüwer and composition with Piston, Ballantine, Fine and Thompson. *Career:* Instructor in Music, Pomona Coll., Claremont, California 1950–54, Asst Prof. 1954–59, Assoc. Prof. 1959–65, Prof. 1965–85, William M. Keck Distinguished Service Prof. 1985–95, Prof. Emer. 1995–; Teaching Fellow, Harvard Univ. 1954–55; Teacher, Berkshire Music Center, Tanglewood, summers 1954, 1955, 1957; appearances as pianist and conductor. *Compositions include:* Sinfonia concertante for Piano and Orchestra 1951, Castles and Kings, suite 1958, Concerto mutabile for Piano and Orchestra 1962, Episodes for Piano and Orchestra 1966, Interlude ll for Piano and String Orchestra 1969, Centone for Orchestra 1973, The Prophet Bird 1 1976, Time Irretrievable 1983, Lions on a Banner, Seven Sufi Texts for Soprano Solo, Chorus and Orchestra 1988, Ode for String Orchestra 1991, Concert Music for String Orchestra 1993, End Piece for Chamber Ensemble 1993, Ternaries for Flute and Piano 1993, Middle Piece for Chamber Ensemble 1994, Encounters I–VI for various instrumental combinations, Reconnaissance for large chamber ensemble 1995, Memory and Hope: Essay for Orchestra 1996, Sax for 4, for saxophone quartet 1996, More Reflections for clarinet and piano 1997, Tripartita for vihuela and guitar 1998, Number Play for two pianos 1999, Trio, 2K for violin, cello and piano 1999, Again, Again, for two pianos 2000, Prelude for organ 2000, Night Music for six guitars 2000, Violaria for viola and piano 2000, Night Music 2 for six guitars 2000, After 09/11/01 for piano, November Piece for piano 2001, Return – Symphonic Essay, transcribed for two pianos 2001, Grand Fantasy for organ 2002, Fourth Rhapsody for piano 2003, Three Proverbs for chorus of mixed voices a cappella 2003, Sonata for cello and piano 2003, Three Pieces for string quartet 2004, Fortyseven for Graydon – Essay for Concert Band 2005, Three Diversions for piano, four hands 2008, Triple Set for Concert Band 2009, Concords 3.5 for mandolin and guitar 2009, Trialogue II for two cellos and piano 2010, Four More Bagatelles for piano 2010, Notes for cello solo 2010, Cantilena III for marimba and piano 2011, Rhapsodic Music for string quartet 2011, A Piece for Julia for three violins 2011, More Recreations for two pianos 2011, Meditation for accordion 2012. *Publications:* End Piece 1994, Ternaries 1995, Set of Three 1996, Reconnaissance 1997. *Address:* 890 East Harrison Avenue #19, Pomona, CA 91767-2003, USA (home). *Telephone:* (909) 607-4568 (home). *E-mail:* kkohn@pomona.edu (home).

KOHONEN, Jyrrki; Finnish singer (bass); b. 11 Oct. 1964, Helskinki. *Education:* Sibelius Acad., Helsinki with Tom Krause, Opera Studio of Zurich Opera. *Career:* appearances with Finnish Nat. Opera from 1994, as Mozart's Bartolo, Colline in La Bohème and Fafner in The Ring; Savonlinna Festival 1994, as Gremin and Banquo; Darmstadt Opera as Mozart's Osmin, Lord Plunkett in Martha, Raimondo, Sarastro and the Landgrave in Tannhäuser; engagements at Cagliari in Wagner's Die Feen and at Bayreuth in Die Meistersinger; season 2000–2001 in Beethoven's 9th and Mahler's 8th Symphonies under Riccardo Chailly, Rocco in Fidelio at Pisa and Truffaldino in Ariadne auf Naxos under Simon Rattle; Bayreuth 2001, in Lohengrin.

KOITO, Kei; Japanese organist, composer and academic; b. 4 Jan. 1950, Kyoto. *Education:* Tokyo School of Fine Arts, Geneva Conservatory with Pierre Segond and Eric Gaudibert, studied with L. F. Tagliavani, Xavier Darasse and Reinhard Goebel. *Career:* debut as solo recitalist at Victoria Hall, Geneva, Maurice Ravel Auditorium, Lyon; soloist with symphonic and chamber orchestras, regularly performing at festivals and on radio and TV; since 1978 has performed over 80 new works for organ, premiering a large number written especially for her; Prof. of Organ, Conservatoire in Lausanne; adjudicator, guest lecturer and master classes in USA, Europe and Asia. *Compositions include:* Les Tours du Silence for narrator and chamber ensemble, Labryrinthe Dynamique for brass ensemble, Orestes-Stasimon for choir, Esquisse Alpha for two pianos, Wenn aus der Ferne for organ, Splendid Rotation for two amplified harpsichords, In Step for string quartet, Poème Pulvérisé for voice and percussion, Meta-Matic No. 22 for tape. *Recordings:* six trio sonatas, five concertos, Canonic Variations of J.S. Bach, sonatas of C.P.E. Bach, contemporary organ music.

KOIZUMI, Kazuhiro; Japanese conductor and music director; *Resident Conductor, Tokyo Metropolitan Symphony Orchestra*; b. 16 Oct. 1949; m. Masami. *Education:* Univ. of the Arts, Tokyo, Hochschule für Musik, Berlin. *Career:* worked with Seiji Ozawa for two years; Asst Conductor, Japan Philharmonic 1970–72; Music Dir, New Japan Philharmonic 1975–79, Winnipeg Symphony Orchestra, Canada 1983–84; Prin. Guest Conductor, Tokyo Metropolitan Orchestra 1998–, Sendai Philharmonic Orchestra 2006–; Prin. Conductor, Century Orchestra Osaka 2003–; Resident Conductor, Tokyo Metropolitan Symphony Orchestra 2008–; Music Dir, Century Orchestra, Osaka 2008–; guest conductor, Berlin Philharmonic, Chicago Symphony, Nat. Orchestra of France, Royal Philharmonic, Vienna Philharmonic, Toronto Symphony, Tokyo Metropolitan, Kyoto Symphony, Nagoyo Symphony, Montréal Symphony, RAI in Naples and Munich Philharmonic; adviser, Manitoba Conservatory of Music and Arts. *Recordings:* Lalo Concerto Russe/ Concerto in F with Radio France, Tchaikovsky, Kodály, Dvořák. *Honours:* first prize Int. Conductors Competition (MIN-ONO 1970), first prize Von Karajan Competition 1972, Grand Prix du Disque. *Current Management:* Kajimoto Concert Management Co. Ltd, Kahoku Building, 8-6-25 Ginza, Chuo-ku, Tokyo 104-0061, Japan. *Telephone:* (3) 3574-0969. *Fax:* (3) 3574-0980. *Website:* www.kajimotomusic.com.

KOK, Nicholas; British conductor; b. 1962, England. *Education:* New Coll., Oxford, Royal Coll. of Music. *Career:* music staff of ENO 1989–93; Music Adviser to Contemporary Opera Studio; has conducted for ENO, The Return of Ulysses, The Marriage of Figaro, Così fan tutte and King Priam; The Fairy Queen, (Purcell) and Così fan tutte in 1995 and Orfeo in 1996; for ENO Bayliss Programmes he conducted Arion and the Dolphin, a new commission by Alec Roth; for Almeida Opera, Mario and The Magician by Stephen Oliver and A Family Affair, a new commission by Julian Grant; conducted Così fan tutte, The Coronation of Poppea, Reimann's The Ghost Sonata, Xenakis's The Bacchae and Nigel Osborne's Sarajevo for Opera Factory, London; for Opera Factory Zürich, Marschner's Der Vampyr in his own version for chamber orchestra and Cavalli's La Calisto; further engagements with Opera Factory London include Dido and Aeneas and Britten's Curlew River; other operatic engagements have included Don Giovanni for English Touring Opera, The Barber of Seville for Dublin Grand Opera, Gerald Barry's The Intelligence Park for the Almeida Festival/Opera Factory and Trois Operas Minutes by Milhaud and The Judgement of Paris by Eccles for Trinity Coll. of Music; has also worked with Scottish Opera; Philharmonia, Ulster Orchestra, London Sinfonietta; Scottish Chamber Orchestra; Royal Scottish Nat. Orchestra; Bournemouth Sinfonietta; Endymion Ensemble; Almeida Ensemble; Cambridge Univ. Chamber Orchestra; London Pro Arte Orchestra and the Philippines Philharmonic Orchestra; a number of choral societies; BBC engagements include The Soldier's Tale, The Carnival of the Animals, Reginald Smith Brindle's Journey Towards Infinity, Mondrial by Erollyn Wallen and several television and radio plays; The Marriage of Figaro for ENO 1997. *Honours:* Countess of Munster Award, Lofthouse Memorial Prize. *Address:* Kauzenhecke 3, 70597 Stuttgart, Germany.

KOKKOS, Yannis; French (b. Greek) stage director and stage designer; b. 1944, Athens. *Education:* Nat. Theatre of Strasbourg. *Career:* has created designs for sets and costumes for productions of Macbeth, Lohengrin and Reimann's Lear at Paris Opéra Garnier, Pelléas et Mélisande at La Scala and the Vienna Staatsoper, Don Carlos at Bologna and Elektra at Geneva and San Francisco; directed the Oresteia by Xenakis in Sicily; directed and designed Boris Godunov in Bologna and Opéra Bastille, Paris, Ariane et Barbe Bleue in Geneva, La Damnation de Faust at the Théâtre du Châtelet, Paris, Nancy Opéra with Death in Venice, Festival d'Orange with Carmen, Tosca and Don Giovanni, Welsh Nat. Opera and Scottish Opera with Tristan und Isolde 1993, and Opéra de Bordeaux with Salome; Pelléas et Mélisande and Tristan, Covent Garden 1993; Norma, Opéra Bastille, Paris 1996; Alceste, Scottish Opera 1996; Tristes Tropiques by Aperghis, world premiere with Opéra Strasbourg 1996; Elektra, Opéra de Lyon 1997; Clemenza di Tito, Welsh Nat. Opera 1997; Hänsel and Gretel, Châtelet, Paris 1997; Queen of Spades for Scottish Opera and Götterdämmerung, Teatro alla Scala, Milan 1998; Outis, Luciano Berio, Châtelet, Paris 1999; Pelléas et Mélisande, Bordeaux 2000; Der Fliegende Holländer, Bologna 2000 and La Scala 2004; L'Orestie, Epidaure 2001; Iphigénie en Aulide, La Scala 2002; Phaedra, Dido and Aeneas, Opéra de Nancy 2003; Les Troyens, Châtelet, Paris 2003, Fenelon's Les Rois (world premiere), Opéra Bordeaux 2004, H. W. Henze's The Bassarids, Châtelet, Paris 2005, Cherubini's Medea, Opéra Toulouse, Châtelet 2005, Scymanowski's King Roger, Teatro Massimo, Palermo 2005, Gluck's Iphigénie en Tauride, Opéra Nancy 2005, Philippe Manoury's On Iron, Cité de la Musique, Paris 2005, Tristan und Isolde, La Monnaie, Brussels 2006, Giulio Cesare, Opéra de Nancy 2007, Boris Godounov, Vienna 2007, Medea, Epidaurus Greek Festival 2007, Les Troyens, Geneva 2007, Tancredi, Teatro Real, Madrid 2007, Nabucco, Munich 2008, The Excursions of Mr Bzovček, Geneva 2008, Idomeneo, Opéra Nat. de Bordeaux 2008, Giulio Cesare in Egitto, Opéra de Marseille 2008, Die Frau ohne Schatten, Maggio Musicale Fiorentino 2010. *Publications:* Yannis Kokkos, Le Hèron et le Scénographe 1989, 10 Rendezvous en Compagnie de Yannis Kokkos (co-author) 2005. *Honours:* Commdr, Ordre des Arts et des Lettres, France,

Médaille d'or, Quadriennale of Prague 1987; Laurence Olivier Award 1997, Prix de la Critique for best opera production (for Les Troyens) 2003. *Address:* 7 rue Bourdaloue, 75009 Paris, France (home). *Telephone:* 1-49-70-06-69 (home). *E-mail:* anneyannis@hotmail.fr (home).

KOLB, Barbara, MM; American composer; b. 10 Feb. 1939, Hartford, CT. *Education:* Hartt Coll. of Music, Berkshire Music Center with Lukas Foss and Gunther Schuller. *Career:* played clarinet in the Hartford Symphony Orchestra 1960–66; composer-in-residence, Marlboro Music Festival 1973, American Acad. in Rome 1975; teacher of theory and composition, Brooklyn Coll. and Temple Univ.; Artistic Dir of Music New to New York, Third Street Music School Settlement 1979. *Compositions:* Rebuttal for two clarinets 1964, Chanson bas for voice, harp and percussion 1965, Three Place Settings for narrator and ensemble 1968, Trobar clus for 13 instruments 1970, Soundings for 11 instruments and tape 1972 (version for orchestra 1975 and 1977), Frailities for tenor, tape and orchestra 1971, Spring, River, Flowers, Moon, Night for two pianos and tape 1975, Appello for piano 1976, Musique pour un vernissage for ensemble 1977 (concert version 1979), Songs before an Adieu for flute, guitar and voice 1979, Chromatic Fantasy for narrator and ensemble 1979, Three Lullabies for guitar 1980, Related Characters for viola and piano 1980, Related Characters for viola and piano 1980, The Point that Divides the Wind for organ and four percussionists 1981, Cantico (film score) 1982, Millefoglie for ensemble and computer-generated sound 1985, Time... and Again for oboe, string quartet and tape 1985, Umbrian Colours for violin and guitar 1986, Yet That Things go Round for chamber orchestra 1986–88, Molto Allegra for guitar 1988, The Enchanted Loom for orchestra 1988–89, Extremes for flute and cello 1989, Voyants for piano and chamber orchestra 1991, Clouds for organ and piano, recorded tape 1992, All in Good Time for orchestra 1993, In Memory of David Huntley for string quartet 1994, New York Moonglow for ensemble 1995, Sidebars for bassoon and piano 1996, Criss Cross for percussion and orchestra 2000. *Honours:* Rome Prize 1969–71, Fulbright Scholarship 1966–67, MacDowell Colony and Guggenheim Fellowships, grants from the Ford Foundation and the NEA 1972–79. *Address:* Boosey & Hawkes Ltd, First Floor, 71–91 Aldwych, London, WC2B 4HN, England. *Website:* www.boosey.com/kolb.

KOLLO, René; German singer (tenor); b. (René Kollodzieyski), 20 Nov. 1937, Berlin; s. of the late Willi Kollodzieyski and of Marie-Louise Kollodzieyski; m. 1st Dorthe Larsen 1967; one d.; m. 2nd Beatrice Bouquet 1982. *Career:* began career with Staatstheater, Brunswick 1965; First Tenor, Deutsche Oper am Rhein 1967–71; Dir Metropol Theater, Berlin 1996–97; guest appearances with numerous leading opera cos and at annual Bayreuth Wagner Festival. *Performances include:* The Flying Dutchman 1969, 1970, Lohengrin 1971, Die Meistersinger von Nürnberg 1973, 1974, Parsifal 1975, Siegfried 1976, 1977, Tristan (Zürich) 1980, (Bayreuth) 1981. *Publication:* Imre Fabian im Gespräch mit René Kollo 1982, René Kollo: Die Kunst, das Leben und alles andre 2004. *Honours:* Bundesverdienstkreuz; Goldene Kamera Award, Hörzu 2000. *Website:* www.kollo.com.

KOLLY, Karl-Andreas; Swiss pianist; b. 26 May 1965. *Education:* Music Academy, Zürich, studied with Karl Engel and Mieczyslaw Horszowski. *Career:* debut with Grieg Piano Concerto at Zürich 1982; concerto as soloist and chamber musician all over Europe, USA, Japan and Australia; several radio and television programmes in Switzerland, Germany, Spain and Czech Republic 1991; Professor, Hochschule für Musik, Zürich 1991–. *Recordings:* albums of Schumann piano works including Symphonic Etudes; Brahms, the Piano Trios, with Trio Novanta; The Piano Concertos of Skriabin, Glazunov, d'Albert, Wellesz, Schmidt; Liszt/Bach: The Complete Piano Transcription; Chopin: Complete Etudes, Ballades, Nocturnes, Impromptus, Pollonaises; Bach: Well-tempered Clavier I and II, Goldberg Variations, Partitas. *Honours:* First Prize, Jecklin Competition 1975, University Competition of Zürich 1988, Young Musicians Competition, Union of Swiss Banks 1990, Tschumi prize for best soloist diploma of the year 1991, Prix Maurice Sandoz 1990. *Address:* Rosenrain 12, 8400 Winterthur, Switzerland (office). *Telephone:* 522133220 (office). *Fax:* 522133220 (office). *E-mail:* karl-andreas.kolly@zhdk.ch.

KOLOMYJEC, Joanne; Canadian singer (soprano); b. 1955. *Career:* appearances in concert and opera throughout Canada, the USA and UK 1983–; opera roles include the Countess and Susanna in Le Nozze di Figaro, Donna Elvira and Donna Anna in Don Giovanni, Fiordiligi in Cosi fan Tutti, Tatiana in Eugene Onegin, the title roles in Tosca and Jenůfa, Marguerite in Faust, Magda Sorel in The Consul, Violetta in La Traviata, Mimi in La Bohème, Agathe in Der Freischutz, Micaela in Carmen, Madame Lidoine and Blanche in Les Dialogues des Carmelites, Lia in L'Enfant Prodigue, Rosalinda in Die Fledermaus and Anna Glawari in The Merry Widow; concert engagements with Toronto Symphony and Calgary Philharmonic Orchestra; repertoire includes the Mozart and Verdi Requiems, Messiah, Rossini's Stabat Mater, Bruckner's Te Deum, Beethoven's Ninth and Shostakovich's 14th Symphony; sang David Del Tredici's Alice for the National Ballet of Canada at the London Coliseum, 1987, followed by Zemlinsky's Lyric Symphony. *Recordings include:* None But the Lonely Heart (with Janina Fialkowska), Song to the Moon (with Mario Bernardi and the Calgary Philharmonic Orchestra), A Night in Vienna, Raffi Armenian. *Current Management:* Dean Artists Management, 204 St George Street, Toronto, ON M5R 2N5, Canada.

KOLTAI, Ralph, CBE FRSA; British stage designer; b. 31 July 1924, Berlin, Germany; s. of Alfred Koltai and Charlotte Koltai (née Weinstein); m. Annena Stubbs 1954 (divorced 1976). *Education:* Cen. School of Art and Design, UK.

Career: served in Royal Army Service Corps and with British Intelligence 1945–47; Assoc. Designer, RSC 1963–66, 1976–; Head, Dept of Theatre Design, Cen. School of Art and Design 1965–72; elected Royal Designer for Industry, Royal Soc. of the Arts 1984; Opera Dir The Flying Dutchman, Hong Kong Arts Festival 1987 and La Traviata 1990; over 200 productions of opera, drama and dance throughout Europe, the USA, Canada and Australia; Fellow, Acad. of Performing Arts, Hong Kong 1994, London Inst., Rose Bruford Coll. Art 1999. *Exhibition:* retrospective exhbn London 1997, touring Asia, Europe 1998–99. *Designs include:* musical Metropolis 1989 (London), The Planets (Royal Ballet) 1990, The Makropulos Affair (Norwegian Opera) 1992, My Fair Lady (New York) 1993, La Traviata (Stockholm) 1993, Hair (London) 1993, Othello (Essen) 1994, (Tokyo) 1995, Madame Butterfly (Tokyo) 1995, Twelfth Night (Copenhagen) 1996, Carmen (Royal Albert Hall, London) 1997, Simon Boccanegra (Wales) 1997, Timon of Athens (Chicago) 1997, Nabucco (Festival Orange, France) 1998, Suddenly Last Summer (also Dir, Nottingham Playhouse) 1998, Dalibor (Edin. Festival) 1998, A Midsummer Night's Dream (Copenhagen 1998), Don Giovanni (St Petersburg) 1999, Genoveva (Edin. Festival) 2000, Katya Kabanova (La Fenice, Venice) 2003. *Publication:* Ralph Koltai: Designer for the Stage 1997. *Honours:* Hon. Fellow, London Inst. 1996; Dr hc (Liverpool Inst. for Performing Arts) 2007; Royal Design for Industry, London Drama Critics' Award (for As You Like It) 1967, Gold Medal (Prague Quadriennale) 1975, Soc. of West End Theatres Designer of the Year (for Brand) 1978, Golden Triga (Prague) 1979, 1991, 2003, London Drama Critics' Award (for The Love Girl and The Innocent) 1981, Designer of the Year Award (for Cyrano de Bergerac) 1989, Silver Medal, Prague (for Othello) 1987, Distinguished Service to Theater, US Inst. of Theater Tech. 1993. *Address:* c/o Rachel Daniels, Berlin Associates, 7 Tyers Gate, London SE1 3HX; Suite 118, 78 Marylebone High Street, London, W1U 5AP, England. *Telephone:* (20) 7836-1112. *Fax:* (20) 7836-1112. *Website:* www.ralphkoltai.com.

KOMATSU, Chosei; Japanese conductor; *Artistic Director, National Symphony Orchestra of Costa Rica;* b. 1 March 1958, Fukui; ; m. Christine Walters Komatsu 1990. *Education:* Tokyo Univ., Eastman School of Music. *Career:* Assoc. Conductor, Buffalo Symphony Orchestra 1986–88; Assoc. Conductor, Baltimore Symphony Orchestra 1988–; Music Dir Kitchener-Waterloo Symphony Orchestra 1993–99; Music Dir Canadian Chamber Ensemble 1993–99; Prin. Conductor, Tokyo Philharmonic Orchestra 2000–04; Prin. Conductor, Nat. Symphony Orchestra of Costa Rica 2004–; Music Dir Cen. Aichi Symphony Orchestra, Japan 2004–, currently Conductor Laureate; fmrly Music Dir Takefu Int. Music Festival; frequent engagements as guest conductor, New Japan Philharmonic Orchestra. *Recordings:* albums: as conductor: gala concert with Tokyo Philharmonic Orchestra, Renato Bruson and Stefania Bonfadelli 2003, Akira Senju, Piano Concerto Shukumei (with the Japan Philharmonic Orchestra and Kentaro Haneda) 2004, two CDs with Orchestra Ensemble Kanazawa 2006. *Honours:* Winner, Exxon Competition for Conductors 1986. *Current Management:* Parker Artists, 382 Central Park West, 9G, New York, NY 10025, USA. *Telephone:* (212) 864-7928. *Fax:* (212) 864-8189. *E-mail:* tom@parkerartists.com. *Website:* www.parkerartists.com. *Address:* Orquesta Sinfonica Nacional de Costa Rica, Ministerio de Cultural y Juventud, San José, Costa Rica (office). *Telephone:* 2240-03-33 (office). *Website:* www.osn.go.cr (office); www.c-komatsu.com.

KOMLÓS, Péter; Hungarian violinist and academic; *Professor of Violin, Liszt Ferenc Academy of Music;* b. 25 Oct. 1935, Budapest; s. of László Komlós and Franciska Graf; m. 1st Edit Fehér 1960, two s.; m. 2nd Zsuzsa Árki 1984, one s. *Education:* Budapest Music Acad. *Career:* f. Komlós String Quartet 1957; First Violinist, Budapest Opera Orchestra 1960; Leader, Bartók String Quartet 1963–; Prof. of Violin, Liszt Ferenc Acad. of Music, Budapest 1981–. *Performances:* extensive concert tours to USSR, Scandinavia, Italy, Austria, German Democratic Repub. Czechoslovakia 1958–64, USA, Canada, NZ and Australia 1970, including Human Rights Day concert, UN HQ New York, Japan, Spain and Portugal 1971, Far East, USA and Europe 1973; performed at music festivals of Ascona, Edin., Adelaide, Spoleto, Menton, Schwetzingen, Lucerne, Aix-en-Provence. *Recordings:* recordings of Beethoven's string quartets for Hungaroton, Budapest and of Bartók's string quartets for Erato, Paris. *Honours:* first prize Int. String Quartet Competition, Liège 1964, Liszt Prize 1965, Gramophone Record Prize of Germany 1969, Kossuth Prize 1970, 1997, Eminent Artist Title 1980, UNESCO Music Council Plaque 1981; Order of Merit, Middle Cross of Repub. of Hungary 1995. *Address:* 2083 Solymár, Sport-u. 6, Hungary. *Telephone:* (6) 26-360-697. *Fax:* (6) 26-360-772. *E-mail:* stradivari@axelero.hu (office). *Website:* www.lfze.hu (office).

KOMLOSI, Ildiko; singer (mezzo-soprano); b. 1959, Békésszentandra's, Hungary. *Education:* Szeged Music Acad. with Valeria Berdal, Franz Liszt Acad., Budapest with András Miko, Guildhall School with Vera Rozsa, Studio of La Scala with Giulietta Simionato. *Career:* concert appearances include the Verdi Requiem in Philadelphia, conducted by Lorin Maazel; concerts with the BBC Symphony, the Royal Philharmonic with Antal Dorati and the Hungarian Radio and State Television Co.; engagements with the Hungarian State Opera Co., Budapest and the State Operas of Berlin, Vienna, La Scala and in America in San Francisco, Portland, Houston, Columbus, Ohio; roles include Carmen, Sextus, Leonora in Favorita, Laura, Octavian, Giovanna Seymour (Anna Bolena) and Purcell's Dido; sang Judit in a concert performance of Duke Bluebeard's Castle with the BBC Philharmonic conducted by András Ligeti 1991, and at the 1992 Prom Concerts London; Giovanna Seymour at Santiago; sang Octavian at Palermo 1998.

KOMOROUS, Rudolf; Czech/Canadian composer and bassoonist; b. 8 Dec. 1931, Prague. *Education:* Conservatory of Music; Academy of Musical Arts, Prague with Pavel Borkovec. *Career:* teacher, Central Conservatory of Peking, China, 1959–61; co-founder, Musica Viva Pragensis, Czechoslovakia; emigrated to Canada 1969; Assoc. Prof. of Composition and Theory, University of Victoria, later Prof. and Dir, School of Music 1971–89; Dir School for the Contemporary Arts, Simon Fraser Univ. 1989–94. *Compositions include:* Mignon for string quartet 1965, Gone for tape 1969, Bare and Dainty for Orchestra 1970, Lady Whiterose for Chamber opera 1971, Anatomy of melancholy for tape 1974, 4 Sinfonies 1988, 1990, 1995, 1997, No, no, Miya, chamber opera 1988, Hermione Dreaming for ensemble 1992, The Seven Sides of Maxines' Silver Die for ensemble 1998. *Honours:* First Prize, Concours International d'Exécution Musicale, Geneva, 1957. *Address:* 978 Carolwood, Victoria, BC V8X 2V1, Canada (home). *Telephone:* (250) 658-8776 (home).

KONG, Joanne, BMus, MMus, DMA; American pianist and harpsichordist; b. 2 March 1957, Suffern, NY; m. Paul Hanson 1981. *Education:* University of Southern California, University of Oregon. *Career:* solo and chamber pianist and harpsichordist; special expertise in music of J. S. Bach, including performances of Goldberg Variations and complete Well-Tempered Klavier; artist faculty, University of Richmond, VA. *Honours:* Ruth Lorraine Close Fellowship Winner, Harpsichord, 1979, Piano, 1980, 1981; Laureate, Beethoven Foundation Fellowship Auditions, 1981; Fellowships to Bach Aria Festival and Institute, SUNY Stony Brook, 1982, 1984; 4th Place, J. S. Bach International Piano Competition, 1983. *Address:* 1211 Claremont Avenue, Richmond, Virginia 23227-4008, USA.

KONGSTED, Ole Dan; Danish musicologist, composer, church musician and jazz musician; *Senior Research Fellow, The Royal Library;* b. 22 Sept. 1943, Copenhagen; m. Ida Wieth-Knudsen 1967; one s. two d. *Education:* Univ. of Copenhagen. *Career:* holder of scholarship, Danish State 1976–80; freelance collaborator, Danish Radio 1976–; Conductor, Choir of the Jeunesses Musicales 1978–86; Asst Dir, Musikhistorisk Museum and Carl Claudius Samling, Copenhagen 1980–2000; Choirmaster and Organist, Church of the Sacred Heart, Copenhagen 1982–; Founder and Leader, Capella Hafniensis 1990–; holder of scholarship, Danish State/Royal Library 1994–2000; Sr Research Fellow, The Royal Library 2000–. *Compositions:* 71 opus numbers. *Recordings:* several recordings with Choir of the Jeunesses Musicales, with Ben Webster and Arnved Meyer Band, and Capella Hafniensis. *Publications:* E turri tibiis canere – Traek af taarnblaesningens historie, in Festskrift Johannes Simons (ed.) 1974, Census as Source Material for the History of Music 1976, Nils Schioerring: Musikkens Historie i Danmark (ed.) 1977–78, Music in Denmark at the Time of Christian IV 1988, Heinrich Schütz und die Musik in Dänemark zur Zeit Christians IV (co-ed.) 1989, Kronborg-Motetterne Tilegnet Frederik II og Dronning Sophie 1582, 1990, Kronborg-Brunnen und Kronborg-Motetten, Ein Notenfund des späten 16 Jahrhunderts aus Flensburg und seine Vorgeschichte 1991, Liber cantionum, I 1993, Royal Danish Water Music 1582 1994, Liber cantionum, II 1994, Liber cantionum, III 1996, Liber cantionum, IV 1996, Liber cantionum, V 1996, Liber cantionum, VI 1998, Liber cantionum, VII 1998, Gregorius Trehou in the Vatican Library 1998, Liber cantionum, VIII 1999, Liber cantionum, IX 2000, 10 Maria motetter, 10 Maria motets, Bernard Lewkovitch 2000, Dansk musik i 1000 år – syngespil og opera 2000, Motetter, Motets, Motetten, af Ludwig Senfl 2001, Liber cantionum, X 2001, Opusculum cantionum, 1571, Johannes Flamingus (floruit 1565–1573) 2002, Ps. 23: Herren er min hyrde, 14 kompositioner af danske komponister 2005, Motectorum quinque vocum Liber secundus (1591), Jan Tollius 2005, Lejlighedsværker, Gelegenheitswerke, Occasional works 2004, Jan Tollius 2005, 10 Maria motetter, 10 Maria motets, Bernard Lewkovitch 2005, Sacrarum cantionum (1601), Vincentius Bertholusius 2005, Liber primus motettorum (1581), Rinaldo del Mel 2005, Moduli trium vocum (1597), Jan Tollius 2005, Liber primus motectorum quinque vocum (1591), Jan Tollius 2005, Indspilning Musica nuptialis, Bartholomaeus Stockmann (co-ed.) 2005, Ars Baltica musicalis 2007, 12 korsatser 2008, 14 liturgiske kompositioner 2008, A due, musical essays in honour of John D. Bergsagel and Heinrich W. Schwab (co-ed. with assistance of Lisbeth Larsen, musikalische Aufsätze zu Ehren von John D. Bergsagel und Heinrich W. Schwab) 2008, Missa super doulce mémoire, necnon varii cantus, Mattheus le Maistre 2009. *Honours:* Organist and Kantor Otto Koebkes Mindelegat 1992. *Address:* The Royal Library, PO Box 2149, 1016 Copenhagen K, Denmark (office). *Telephone:* 40-31-93-23 (office). *E-mail:* ok@kb.dk (office).

KÖNIG, Christoph; German conductor; b. Dresden. *Education:* Hochschule für Musik, Dresden. *Career:* fmrly boy soprano, Dresdner Kreuzchor; fmrly Asst to Sir Colin Davis with Sächsische Staatskapelle, Dresden; Conductor, Malmö Symphony Orchestra 2003–06; fmrly Prin. Guest Conductor, Orquesta Filarmónica de Gran Canaria; Prin. Conductor, Orquestra Sinfónica do Porto Casa da Música 2008–14; Prin. Guest Conductor, Solistes Européens, Luxembourg 2010–; Guest Conductor for several orchestras during 2009–10 season including Mozarteum Orchestra, Tonkünstler Orchester/Vienna, Real Filharmoniá de Galicia, BBC Scottish Symphony Orchestra, Orquesta Sinfónica y Coro de RTVE and the Vilabertan Schubertiada; worked with London Mozart Players and Bournemouth Symphony Orchestra; Guest Conductor, BBC Philharmonic Orchestra, BBC Scottish Symphony Orchestra. *Recordings include:* albums: as conductor: Henryk Melcer, Piano Concertos Nos. 1 and 2 2008, Orquesta Filarmónica de Gran Canaria 2008, Trumpet Concertos: apres le nuit... 2011, Gösta Nystroem: Symphonien Nr. 1

& 2011, Brahms Piano Concerto No. 1 2014. *Current Management:* Sulivan Sweetland Management, 1 Hillgate Place, Balham Hill, London, SW12 9ER, England; Schmidt Artists International, Inc., 59 East 54th Street, Suite 83, New York, NY 10022, USA. *Telephone:* (20) 8772-3470 (London); (212) 421-8500 (NY). *Fax:* (20) 8673-8959 (London); (212) 421-8583 (NY). *E-mail:* info@sulivansweetland.co.uk; info@schmidtart.com. *Website:* www.sulivansweetland.co.uk; www.schmidtart.com; www.christophkoenig.at.

KÖNIG, Hans-Peter; German singer (bass). *Education:* Detmold Acad. of Music and with Gladys Kuchta in Düsseldorf. *Career:* mem. Zürich Opera Studio; in early career, engaged at Niedersächsischen Staatstheater Hannover; specialises in bass roles of Wagner and Verdi including Gurnemanz in Parsifal, King Marke in Tristan und Isolde, Landgrave Hermann in Tannhäuser, Fasolt, Fafner, Hunding and Hagen in the Ring, Pogner in Die Meistersinger von Nürnberg, Daland in Der fliegende Holländer, Zaccaria in Nabucco, Grossinquisitor in Don Carlos and Fiesco in Simon Boccanegra; mem. Deutsche Oper am Rhein 2001–; guest appearances at opera houses including Berlin, Hamburg, Dresden, Munich, Stockholm, Bilbao, Marseille, Bordeaux, Paris, Milan, Barcelona, Helsinki, Taipei, Tokyo, São Paulo, New York (Met debut 2010); festivals include Baden-Baden and Bayreuth. *Honours:* Kammersänger 2009. *Address:* Deutsche Oper Berlin, Bismarckstrasse 35, 10627 Berlin, Germany (office). *Telephone:* (30) 3438401 (office). *Fax:* (30) 34384232 (office). *E-mail:* info@deutscheoperberlin.de (office). *Website:* www.deutscheoperberlin.de (office).

KÖNIG, Klaus; German singer (tenor); b. 26 May 1936, Beuthen. *Education:* studied with Johannes Kemter in Dresden. *Career:* sang in Cottbus 1970; Dessau from 1973, as Max, Don Carlos, and Erik in Der fliegende Holländer; sang at Leipzig 1978–82, Staatsoper Dresden from 1982; guest appearances in Karlsruhe 1983–85 (Tristan and Tannhäuser), at La Scala and Covent Garden 1984 (as Tannhäuser) and the Théâtre de la Monnaie Brussels 1985, as Tristan; sang Max in Der Freischütz, at the opening of the restored Semper Opera House, Dresden 1985; guest appearances in Paris, Parma, Strasbourg, Madrid, Venice and Barcelona; other roles include Lensky, Florestan, Radames, Don José, Alvaro in La Forza del Destino, Lohengrin, Walther, Parsifal and Bacchus; Lisbon 1986, as Florestan; sang Tannhäuser at Cologne and London 1987; Munich Opera 1988, as Menelaos in Die Aegyptische Helena by Strauss; Buenos Aires and Vienna Staatsoper 1988, as Florestan and Bacchus; sang the Mayor in Friedenstag by Strauss, Dresden 1998; many engagements in concerts and oratorios. *Recordings:* Tannhäuser, Der Rosenkavalier, Choral Symphony.

KONSTANTINOV, Julian; Bulgarian singer (bass); b. 1966, Sofia. *Education:* Sofia Acad. *Career:* sang in The Rake's Progress and Il Barbiere di Siviglia while a student and represented Bulgaria at the 1992 Cardiff Singer of the World Competition; Appearances with the Sofia National Opera in Lucia di Lammermoor, Aida, Rigoletto, Luisa Miller and Turandot (as Timur); Season 1998 with the Royal Opera at Savonlinna and elsewhere as Massimiliano in Verdi's Masnadieri; Further engagements include Fiesco in Simon Boccanegra with the Berlin Philharmonic and Salzburg Festival conducted by Claudio Abbado, Padre Guardino in La Forza del Destino at the Savonlinna Festival and Cardinal Brogni in La Juive at the New Israeli Opera, 1999–2000. *Current Management:* Opéra et Concert, 37 rue de la Chaussée d'Antin, 75009 Paris, France. *Telephone:* 1-42-96-18-18. *Fax:* 1-42-96-18-00. *E-mail:* agence@opera-concert.com. *Website:* www.opera-concert.com.

KONSULOV, Ivan; singer (baritone); b. 29 May 1946, Varna, Bulgaria. *Education:* studied with Jossifov in Sofia and with Aldo Protti in Italy. *Career:* debut at Opera National Russe, Bulgaria 1972; sang in Berne from 1977, as Simon Boccanegra, Marcello (La Bohème), Scarpia, Don Giovanni, Mandryka, Tonio, Pizarro, Don Carlos (La Forza del Destino), Alfio and Iago; Bologna 1980, Zurga in Les Pêcheurs de Perles; Philadelphia Opera 1982, Marcello; Bratislava 1984, as Eugene Onegin; Stuttgart and Berlin 1985, Don Giovanni; at the Monte Carlo opera 1986 sang Gryaznoy in The Tsar's Bride by Rimsky-Korsakov; engagements at Graz, Barcelona, Madrid and Karlsruhe; sang Amfortas in Parsifal at Berne 1989; season 1992 as the Major-domo in Zemlinsky's Der Zwerg at Trieste. *Recordings include:* La Bohème-Marcello Opus-Bratislava Stereo with P Dvorsky and television film 1980; The Queen of Spades (Tomsky), Musik Mundial-Sofia with International Stars, 1988; Don Carlo-Posa, Balkanton Sofia, 1988; Opera Recital Arias Balkanton, 1988.

KONTARSKY, Alois; German pianist; b. 14 May 1931, Iserlohn; brother of Alfons Kontarsky. *Education:* studied in Cologne with Else Schmitz-Gohr and Maurits Frank in Hamburg with Eduard Erdmann. *Career:* int. performances with his brother from 1955 in modern repertoire, including Michael Gielen, de Grandis, Henri Pousseur, Berio and Zimmermann; gave premiere of Stockhausen's Klavierstücke I–XI, Darmstadt 1966; concerts with the Stockhausen ensemble and duo with the cellist Siegfried Palm; masterclass at the Cologne Musikhochschule from 1969; premieres of music by Kagel, Stockhausen (Mantra), Berio and Bussotti. *Recordings include:* Bartók's Sonata for two pianos and percussion, Klavierstücke I–XI by Stockhausen. *Honours:* first prize for piano duo Munich Radio Int. Festival 1955.

KONTARSKY, Bernhard; German conductor; b. 1940. *Education:* Musikhochschule, Cologne. *Career:* engagements at Bonn Opera and throughout Europe; Berg's Lulu for Flanders Opera and Wozzeck at the Deutsche Oper am Rhein; Adriana Hölszky's Die Wände and Henze's Boulevard Solitude for Frankfurt Opera; Henze's Der Prinz von Homburg at Antwerp and

Schoenberg's Moses und Aron for the Deutsche Oper, Berlin; productions for the Staatstheater Stuttgart include Zender's Don Quixote, Intolleranza by Nono, Bluebeard's Castle, and Zimmermann's Die Soldaten; Boulevard Solitude at Covent Garden, London 2001; Prof., Acad. of Frankfurt 1981–. *Honours:* Mendelssohn Award, Cologne, Int. German Press Disc Award 1992.

KOOPMAN, Antonius (Ton) Gerhardus Michael; Dutch musician, academic and conductor; b. 2 Oct. 1944, Zwolle; m. Christine H. H. Mathot 1975; three d. *Education:* Amsterdam Conservatory and Univ. of Amsterdam. *Career:* Prof. of Harpsichord, Royal Conservatory, The Hague; f. Amsterdam Baroque Orchestra 1979, Amsterdam Baroque Choir 1992; has made over 200 recordings of harpsichord and organ works by Bach, Handel, others; fmr Prin. Conductor Netherland Radio Chamber Orchestra; f. Antoine Marchand record label (sub-label of Challenge Classics); Artist-in-Residence, Cleveland Orchestra 2011–14; Prof., Univ. of Leiden; Artistic Dir French Festival Itinéraire Baroque. *Publications include:* Interpretation of Baroque Music 1985 and a small book about J. S. Bach 1985; The Harpischord in Dutch Paintings (co-), The World of the Bach Cantatas (co-ed with Christoph Wolff) 1996. *Honours:* Hon. mem. RAM, London; Dr hc (Utrecht) 2000; Deutsche Schallplattenpreis "Echo Klassik and Prix Hector Berlioz for conducting and recording all existing Cantatas by Johann Sebastian Bach 1994–2004, Bach-Medaille, City of Leipzig 2006. *Address:* Meerweg 23, 1405 BC Bussum, Netherlands. *Telephone:* (35) 6913676. *Fax:* (35) 6939752. *E-mail:* ton.koopman@wxs.nl (office). *Website:* www.tonkoopman.nl (office); www.amsterdambaroque.com.

KOPATCHINSKAJA, Patricia; Moldovan musician (violin); b. 1977, Chişinău. *Education:* Vienna Acad. of Music, Austria. *Career:* emigrated with family to Austria as a teenager; European tour with London Philharmonic (LPO) and Vladimir Jurowski 2013; debuts in 2014 included Edinburgh Festival with LPO, Berliner Philharmoniker performing Peter Eötvös' DoReMi conducted by composer at Musikfest Berlin, Tonhalle-Orchester Zürich/Michael Sanderling and performances with Rotterdam Philharmonic Orchestra, Radio-Sinfonieorchester Stuttgart des SWR/Sir Roger Norrington and Philharmonia Orchestra/Vladimir Ashkenazy; Artist-in-Residence, hr-sinfonieorchester 2014–15; Artistic Partner, St Paul Chamber Orchestra 2014–; mem. ensemble Quartet-lab, with Pekka Kuusisto, Lilli Maijala and Pieter Wispelwey; regular chamber recital partners include Sol Gabetta, Markus Hinterhäuser and Polina Leschenko, as well as members of her family; Goodwill Amb., Terre des Hommes. *Recordings include:* Kühr/Resch/Zykan: Violin Concertos 2007, Beethoven/Ravel/Bártok/Say Sonatas (Echo Klassik Award 2009) 2008, Say: 1001 Nights in the Harem 2009, Beethoven: Complete works for violin 2009, Rapsodia: The music of my life 2010, Bartók Violin Concerto No 2/Ligeti Violin Concerto/Eötvös seven (Gramophone Award for Recording of the Year 2013, ICMA Award 2013, Echo Klassik Award 2013) 2012, Prokofiev/Stravinsky Violin Concertos 2013, Take Two! rare duets 2014, Tigran Mansurian: Quasi parlando 2014, Galina Ustvolskaya 2014. *Honours:* Royal Philharmonic Soc. Instrumentalist of the Year Award 2014. *Current Management:* c/o Ariane Lévy-Künstler, Harrison Parrott Ltd, 5-6 Albion Court, Albion Place, London, W6 0QT, England. *Telephone:* (20) 7313-3538. *E-mail:* alk@harrisonparrott.co.uk. *Website:* www.harrisonparrott.com; patriciakopatchinskaja.com.

KOPCAK, Sergei; singer (bass); b. 23 April 1948, Dacov, Carpathia. *Education:* studied in Leipzig, Vienna and Milan. *Career:* Slovak Nat. Opera at Bratislava from 1974 in the Slav, French and German repertory; Metropolitan Opera, New York from 1983, as Ivan Khovansky, Wurm in Luisa Miller and Sparafucile in Rigoletto; The Commendatore, and Pimen in Boris Godunov; Salzburg Festival 1986–87 in Moses und Aron; Edinburgh Festival 1989 as Konchak in Prince Igor and Marseille 1994, as Boito's Mephistopheles; Shostakovich's Boris at Florence, Maggio Musicale 1998. *Recordings:* Janáček's Glagolitic Mass.

KOPP, Miroslav; Czech singer (tenor); b. 23 Feb. 1955, Plzeň. *Education:* Prague Conservatory. *Career:* Prague National Theatre from 1981 as Alfredo, Ernesto, Don Pasquale, Pelléas, 1986 and the Prince in Rusalka, 1991; Vienna Staatsoper, 1986, in The Bartered Bride and Paris Opéra Comique in From the House of the Dead, 1988, (also at the Salzburg Festival); Geneva, 1992 as Boris in Katya Kabanova and Florence, 1993 as Steva in Jenůfa; Basle Opera as Don Carlos; Other roles include Wenzel in The Bartered Bride and Vitek in Smetana's Dalibor. *Recordings:* Dvořák's The Cunning Peasant; Smetana's Dalibor and Martinů's Ariane; Tikhon in Katya Kabanova, under Charles Mackerras.

KOPPEL, Anders; Danish composer and musician (organ, piano); b. 17 July 1947, Copenhagen; s. of the late Herman D. Koppel and Edel Vibeke Koppel; brother of Lone Koppel; m. Ulla Lemvigh-Müller 1969; one s. two d. *Career:* played the piano as a child and later clarinet, several TV and concert appearances; sang in Copenhagen Boys Choir; began playing the organ 1966; Co-founder rock group Savage Rose 1967, toured Europe and USA, performed at Newport Jazz Festival 1971; mem. trio Bazaar 1976–; active as a producer and studio musician 1974–80; since then has concentrated on composition and touring as a musician; also plays with his son, saxophone player Benjamin Koppel and musicians including Kenny Werner, Miroslav Vituos, Brian Blade; has hosted workshops in Salzburg, Vienna and Linz, Austria; mem. Danish Composers Asscn, Danish Artists Asscn. *Compositions:* music for 10 ballets, 200 films and plays, three musicals, one opera (Rebus), Piano Concerto, Percussion Concerto, four marimba concertos, two saxophone concertos, Bass Trombone Concerto, Flute/Harp Concerto, Saxophone and Piano Concerto, Violin and Saxophone Concerto, Tuba Concerto, Cello Concerto, Sinfonia Concertante for violin, viola, clarinet and bassoon, Doublebass Concerto, Concerto for violin and accordion, Viola Concerto, Bassoon Concerto, Concerto Piccolo for accordion, Concerto for recorder and saxophone, Triple Concerto for saxophone, cello and harp, Trio for saxophone, cello, piano, Trio for violin, cello, piano, Toccata for vibes, marimba and orchestra, three string quartets, Partita for chamber ensemble, Concertino for chamber ensemble, Passacaglia for chamber ensemble, Trio for violin, horn, piano, four pieces for two guitars, Sonata for recorder and guitar, Portrait for sextet, String Trio, Wind Quintet, Brass Quintet, Piano pieces, Piano Quintet, Mezzo Sax Quintet, Cello Quartet (Le Balajo); solo pieces for piano, clarinet and pipe organ. *Recordings:* nine albums with Bazaar; The Poetic Principle with Miroslav Vitous and Benjamin Koppel 2007, Everything is Subject to Change (with Benjamin Koppel and Kenny Werner) 2012, Breaking Borders (duo with Kenny Werner) 2013; own compositions: Works for saxophone and orchestra, Double Concertos, Concertos, String Quartets, Marimba Concertos, Double Triple Koppel. *Honours:* several awards and prizes, including Danish Prize for Best Film Score 1994, 1996, Wilhelm Hansen Prize, Danish State Art Foundation Lifetime Award. *Current Management:* c/o Edition Wilhelm Hansen AS, Bornholmsgade 1A, 1266 Copenhagen K, Denmark. *Telephone:* 33-11-78-88. *Fax:* 33-14-81-78. *E-mail:* ewh@ewh.dk. *Website:* www.ewh.dk. *Address:* Cæciliavej 70, 2500 Valby, Copenhagen, Denmark. *E-mail:* anders.h.koppel@gmail.com.

KOPPEL, Lone Herman; Danish opera singer (soprano); b. 20 May 1938, Copenhagen; d. of the late Herman D. Koppel and Edel Vibeke Koppel; sister of Anders Koppel; m. Björn Asker 1983; one d. two s. *Education:* Royal Danish Acad. of Music, Danish Opera Acad. *Career:* debut as Musetta in La Bohème, Royal Danish Opera, Copenhagen 1962; sang at Kiel Opera 1964–65, Royal Opera Copenhagen 1962–95; mem. Australian Opera, Sydney 1973–78 and later as a guest; guest appearances at Århus from 1972 as Leonore in Fidelio and the Trovatore Leonora; sang Salome at Bonn and Oslo 1973–74, Lady Macbeth in Macbeth at Stockholm 1981, Tosca at Stockholm 1991; at Copenhagen as Judith in Bluebeard's Castle and Shostakovich's Katerina Izmailova; other roles included Puccini's Tosca, Mikal in Saul and David, Santuzza in Cavalleria Rusticana, Wagner's Elisabeth, Venus, Kundry, Ortrud and Senta, Elektra, Salome, Octavian in Rosenkavalier, Jenůfa, Donna Anna and Donna Elvira, Giorgetta in Il Tabarro, Abigaille in Nabucco, Amelia in Un Ballo in Maschera, Amelia in Simon Boccanegra, Elisabetta and Eboli in Don Carlo, Leonora in Trovatore, Amneris in Aida, Lady Macbeth in Macbeth, Tatjana in Eugene Onegin, Lisa in The Queen of Spades, Jenůfa and Kostelnicka in Jenůfa, Katya in Katya Kabanowa, Leonore in Fidelio, Marie in Wozzeck, Tosca, Manon in Manon Lescaut, Kundry in Parsifal, Senta in Der Fliegende Holländer, Ortrud in Lohengrin, Elisabeth and Venus in Tannhäuser and Ariadne and Composer in Ariadne auf Naxos; sang Mme de Croissy in Poulenc's Carmélites at Copenhagen 1997; season 2002 as The Old Countess in The Queen of Spades and Herodias in Salome; directed Peter Heise's opera Drot og Marsk (King and Marshal), Royal Danish Theatre 1993, Verdi's Nabucco, Värmland Opera, Sweden 2003; teacher, Danish Opera Acad. *Films:* Tosca (TV) 1964, Katya Kabanova 1971, Dialogues des Carmelites 1990. *Recordings:* Cavalleria Rusticana from Royal Theatre, Copenhagen 1967, Richard Wagner, Faust Lieder, Lone Koppel: Live and Studio Recordings 1963–86 2004, and others. *Honours:* Royal Operasinger; Kt of the Dannebrog (R1). *Address:* Åboulevard 50, 5, 2200 Copenhagen N, Denmark. *Telephone:* 61-46-02-46. *E-mail:* lonekoppel@mail.dk.

KOPTAGEL, Yüksel; Turkish pianist and composer; b. 27 Oct. 1931, Istanbul; m. Danyal Kerven 1964. *Education:* Real Conservatorio de Música, Madrid, Ecole Superieure de Musique, Paris, studied with Djemal Rechid and in Santiago. *Career:* debut concert, Istanbul aged five; concerts in Europe (Spain, France, Italy, Switzerland, Czechoslovakia, Germany) USA, India, Pakistan, Russia; compositions published by Max Eschig, Paris and Bote and Bock, Berlin; int. concerts with European orchestras 1953–; mem. of jury, Schola Cantorum, Paris; participant in numerous music festivals.

KORD, Kazimierz; Polish conductor; b. 18 Nov. 1930, Pogórze nr. Cieszyn; m. *Education:* Leningrad Conservatory with Wladimir Nilsen, Acad. of Music, Kraków, State Higher School of Music in Kraków with Artur Malawski. *Career:* Artistic Man. Music Theatre, Kraków 1962–69; Man. and Music Man. Great Symphonic Orchestra of Polish Radio and TV, Katowice 1969–73; Artistic Dir and Prin. Conductor Warsaw Philharmonic 1977–2001; Chief Conductor Südwestfunk Orchestra, Baden Baden 1980–86; six years' co-operation with Metropolitan Opera, New York; Music Dir Teatr Wielki, Warsaw 2005–06 (resgnd), Acting Gen. Dir 2006. *Recordings:* complete Beethoven symphonies, Górecki's Symphony No. 3 and works by J.S. Bach, Chopin, Lutoslawski, Penderecki, Panufnik, Schumann, Richard Strauss, Szymanowski and Szymański. *Honours:* Critics' Award at Music Biennale Berlin 1971, Gold Orpheus Prize of Polish Musicians' Union 1972, Star of the Year, Munich 1975, Minister of Culture and Arts Prize (1st Class) 1977, 1998. *Address:* ul. Nadarzyńska 37A, 05-805 Kanie-Otrebusy, Poland.

KORDES, Heidrun; German singer (soprano); b. 1960. *Education:* Freiburg Musikhochschule. *Career:* debut at Gelsenkirchen Opera; engagement at the Hessichen Staatstheater, Wiesbaden from 1986; roles have included Mozart's Pamina and Susanna, Nedda in Pagliacci, Gilda in Rigoletto and parts in operas by Handel; guest engagements at Leipzig, Dresden, Mannheim, Frankfurt and the Deutsche Oper am Rhein, Düsseldorf; frequent concert appearances. *Recordings include:* Oreste and Xerxes by Handel, albums of lieder.

KOREVAAR, David, BMus, MMus, DMA; American pianist and composer; b. 25 July 1962, Madison, WI; m.; one s. one d. *Education:* Juilliard School. *Career:* debut at Town Hall, New York 1985; recitals throughout USA, Japan; chamber music appearances in USA, Japan, Australia, Europe; founding mem. of piano and wind ensemble, Hexagon; Prometheus Piano Quartet; mem. Chamber Music America, Coll. Music Soc., American Liszt Soc. *Compositions:* Piano Concerto, two Piano Sonatas, works for piano trio, violin and piano, string trio, clarinet and piano. *Recordings:* Bach, Well-Tempered Klavier, musicians' showcase; Brahms, later piano music; Liszt, orchestral music transcribed for piano; Dohnànyi Etudes; Ruralia Hungarica. *Honours:* first prize William Kapell Int. competition 1988, Peabody Mason Music Foundation award 1985, French music award Robert Casadesus Int. Competition 1989. *Address:* 3 Sasqua Pond Road, Norwalk, CT 06855, USA.

KORF, Anthony, BA, MA; American composer and conductor; b. 14 Dec. 1951, New York, NY. *Education:* Manhattan School of Music. *Career:* Artistic Dir, Conductor, Parnassus 1975–; guest conductor, Group for Contemporary Music; League ISCM; co-founder and Artistic Dir, The Riverside Symphony; commissioned by San Francisco Symphony, American Composers Orchestra and others. *Compositions:* Symphony No. 2, Symphony in the Twilight, Oriole, A Farewell, Cantata, Double Take, Brass Quintet, Symphonia, Requiem three movements for clarinet solo. *Publications:* Stefan Wolpe Chamber Piece No. 2 (ed.). *Honours:* Koussevitzky Commission 1992, American Acad. of Arts and Letters Lieberson Fellowship 1988.

KORHONEN, Erkki; Finnish pianist; b. 1956. *Career:* Gen. Dir Finnish Nat. Opera 2001–07; jury mem. Polytech Choir 100th Anniversary Composition Contest 2003, Mirjam Helin Song Competition 2004, The Klaudia Taev Int. Competition for Young Singers 2005. *Recordings:* Tauno Marttinen, Vox Angelica 2002. *Address:* Antreantie 4, 13600 Hämeenlinna, Finland; Gislifluhweg 10, 5022 Rombach, Switzerland. *E-mail:* erkki.korhonen@aina.net (office). *Website:* www.erkki-korhonen.com.

KORHONEN, Ritva-Liisa; Finnish singer (soprano); b. 1959. *Education:* studied in Helsinki and Zürich, Sibelius Academy. *Career:* debut in Helsinki 1984 as Gilda; sang Musetta and Adina in Helsinki, Fiordiligi at Tampere, Traviata at Oulu and Adele in Die Fledermaus at Lahti; further appearances at the Savonlinna Festival and in concert; sang Pamina at Helsinki, 1998.

KORN, Artur; singer (bass); b. 4 Dec. 1937, Wuppertal, Germany; m. Sabine Hass. *Education:* studied in Cologne, Munich and Vienna with Clemens Glettenberg and Schuch-Tovini. *Career:* debut at Cologne Opera Studio 1963, in Un Ballo in Maschera; sang in Graz 1965–68, Vienna Volksoper and Staatsoper from 1968; Glyndebourne Festival 1980–84, as Baron Ochs, Bartolo in Le Nozze di Figaro and Waldner in Arabella; Metropolitan Opera from 1984, as Osmin, Bartolo and Ochs; engagements in Chicago (debut 1984), San Francisco, Detroit, London and Toronto and in Germany, Italy, South Africa and Switzerland; Salzburg Festival 1987, in Schoenberg's Moses and Aron; Sarastro in Magic Flute, Buenos Aires; Ochs in Rosenkavalier, Santiago de Chile; Met Tour, Japan 1988; State Opera Munich Tour, Japan 1988; Vienna Festival State Opera Vienna with Harnoncourt (Osmin-Entführung) 1988; sang 1991/92 as Hagen at Brussels and Mozart's Bartolo at the Salzburg Festival; often heard in oratorios and lieder. *Recordings include:* Alfonso und Estrella by Schubert, Le nozze di Figaro with Haitink, Vespro della Beata Vergine with Harnoncourt, Ariadne auf Naxos (video), Arabella (video), Le nozze de Figaro (video), Die Entführung (video).

KORNIENKO, Alexei; Russian conductor and pianist; *Chief Conductor, International Danube Philharmonic;* b. Moscow; m. Elena Denisova. *Education:* music schools in Kharkov and Kiev, Moscow P.I. Tchaikovsky Conservatory. *Career:* fmrly piano teacher, Kharkiv Conservatory and P.I. Tchaikovsky Conservatory, Moscow; Prof. of Piano, Carinthian State Conservatory, Austria 1999–2004, Dir, Chamber Music Dept 2005–; Music Dir, chamber orchestra Collegium Musicum Carinthia 2005–; Chief Conductor, Sofia Philharmonic Orchestra 2009–12; Chief Conductor, Int. Danube Philharmonic 2012–; co-f. Classic et Cetera Asscn, Gustav Mahler Ensemble; Artistic Dir, Wöthersee Classic Festival 2000–; mem. Bösendorfer Artistic Club; has conducted operas by Hummel, Mozart, Dargomyszky, Stingl, Prestele, Wold, Hazod, Glass and others; plays regularly with Collegium Musicum Carinthia; concerts in Austria, Germany, Slovenia, Italy, Hungary, Holland, with orchestras including Royal Philharmonic Orchestra London, Moscow Philharmonic Orchestra, Georgian Chamber Orchestra, Munich Symphony Orchestra, George Enescu Philharmonic Orchestra Bucharest, symphony orchestras of Zagreb, Volgograd, Carinthia and Ukraine, Slovakian Youth Symphony Orchestra, and chamber orchestra Solisti Italiani; festivals include Salzburg, Ljubljana, Carinthian Summer Music Festival, Wörthersee Classics Festival, Vienna, Bodensee, Frankfurt, Riedenburg, Chopin Festival, Flanders, Russian Winter Festival, Concerti dai Primavera, Normandy; mem. jury, int. competitions. *Recordings include:* as conductor: Gegenwert Gegenwart, Franz Hummel, Liszt, Dvorak Saint-Saens Franck, Sauschlachten, Helmut Neumann: Neue Violinmusik aus Österreich, Max Reger, Musica Concertante, Vivaldi Kaufmann, Beethoven, Fheodoroff; as pianist: Schnittke Brahms Prokofiev, Wien um 1900, Jascha Heifetz, Bernhard Paumgartner, Mendelssohn, Danzmayr, Tartini, Grieg, Prokofiev, Tschaikovsky, Jo Sporck, Franz Schubert, Solisten im Trio. *Honours:* winner, Sergey Rachmaninov Int. Piano Competition, Moscow. *Current Management:* c/o Herbert Waltl, Media Hyperium Inc, 111 Calle De Andalucia, Redondo Beach, CA 90277-6702, USA. *Telephone:* (310) 378-1078. *E-mail:* herbert.waltl@mediahyperium.com.

E-mail: office@alexei-kornienko.com. *Website:* www.donauphilharmonie.at; www.alexei-kornienko.com.

KORONDI, Anna; Hungarian singer (soprano); b. 1967, Budapest; d. of György Korondi. *Education:* studied in Budapest, Bartók Conservatory and Vienna. *Career:* concerts from 1991, notably at Styriarte and Prague Spring Festivals; Komische Oper Berlin 1993–97, as Mozart's Susanna and Zerlina, Lauretta in Gianni Schicchi; Sophie in Werther and Nannetta in Falstaff; concerts include Bach's Christmas Oratorio, Vienna 1994, Mendelssohn's St Paul, Carmina Burana, and appearances at the Leipzig Gewandhaus 1996; mem. Komische Oper Berlin 1993–97, Bonn Opera 1997–99; world premiere of opera Bernarda Albas Haus by Aribet Reiman, Bayerische Staatsoper 2000; Adele in Die Fledermaus, Salzburg Festival 2001; sang Lied at the Kissinger Sommer; has worked with orchestras across Europe, under Hans Neuenfels, Marc Minkowski, Howard Arman, Frans Brügen, Adam Fischer, Nikolaus Harnoncourt and Helmuth Rilling; repertoire from baroque to modern, including Lieder; season 2002–2003 included Mendelssohn's Athalia, Mozart's Requiem, Bach Cantatas and Brahms's Requiem; season 2003–2004 included debut as Sophie in Der Rosenkavalier and Parsifal under Pierre Boulez; collaborated with Enoch zu Guttenbert and Philipp Herrewoghe with orchestras in Belgium, Germany and Scandinavia; sang Zdenka in R. Strauss's Arabella at Bayerische Staatsoper, Munich 2005–06; voice teacher, Hochschule für Musik Hanns Eisler, Berlin 2013–. *Recordings* Mendelssohn's Athalia (Cappricio), Arnold Schoenberg, Brahms: Secular Choruses, Mozart. *Honours:* Prize winner, Schubert and Pavarotti International Competitions 1991, won ARD Competition, Munich 1993. *Current Management:* Boris Orlob Management, Jägerstrasse 70, 10117 Berlin, Germany. *Telephone:* 49 (30) 20450839. *Fax:* 49 (30) 20450849. *E-mail:* info@orlob.net. *Website:* www.orlob.net.

KOROVINA, Tatjana; Russian singer (soprano); b. 1967, Kursk. *Education:* Tchaikovsky Conservatory, Moscow. *Career:* sang the Queen of Night in Die Zauberflöte at Staatsoper Vienna, 1990; concert arias and Exultate Jubilate by Mozart, La Scala, Milan, Prague and Tokyo Suntory Hall, 1990–91; Komische Oper Berlin as Princess in The Legend of Tsar Saltan by Rimsky-Korsakov, 1994–2002; Blondchen in Die Entführung aus dem Serail, 1995; Adele in Fledermaus, 1996; Ninetta Prokofiev's Love for Three Oranges, 1998; Scolatella in Henze's König Hirsch, 1998; Zerbinetta in R Strauss's Ariadne auf Naxos, 1999; Sang at Rossini Festival in Wildbad with Cerere in Le Nozze di Teti e di Peleo, 1994; Aldimira in Sigismondo, 1995; Zenobia in Aureliano in Palmira, 1996; Argene in Un vero omaggio, 1997; Sang in Rossini's Stabat Mater at Philharmonic Berlin, 1996; Gabrielle and Eve in Die Schöpfung in Closter Chorin, 1998; Jauchzet Gott in allen Landen by J.S.Bach at Konzerthaus and Philharmonic (KMS) Berlin 1999; Fiorilla in Il Turco in Italia (premiere) Stadttheater Schwerin 2000–01; Gilda in Rigoletto, Komische Oper Berlin 2002; Angelo in La Resurrezione G.F.Handel Festival Autunno Musicale, Como, Italy 2003; Laudate Pueri Dominum, Psalmus per Soprano, G.F.Handel Festival Autunno Musicale, Como 2004; Adele in Die Fledermaus at Philharmonic Berlin (KMS) 2008. *Recordings:* Abramo ed Isaaco by Myslivecek; Boccherini, Stabat Mater; Mozart's Concert Arias and Exultate jubilate; Rossini's Sigismondo; Aureliano in Palmira; Le nozze di Teti e di Peleo, Sacred Music (DVD). *Honours:* first prize Int. Mozart Competition 1990. *Current Management:* TS Opera Singers Agency, Ruhlsdorfer Str. 12, Berlin 10963, Germany. *Telephone:* (30) 25796842. *Fax:* (30) 25796841. *E-mail:* info@tsoperagency.de. *Website:* www.tsoperagency.de. *E-mail:* tatjana@korovina.com. *Website:* www.korovina.com.

KORSAKOVA, Natasha; violinist; b. 29 Jan. 1973, Moscow, Russia. *Education:* Central Music School, Moscow. *Career:* debut concert with Moscow Chamber Orchestra at the Conservatoire; has given concerts in Bulgaria, Germany, Greece, Yugoslavia, China, Italy, Belgium and Japan 1989–; played at the Panatei Festival, Italy 1991, and the Bruch Second Concerto with the Russian State Symphony Orchestra 1991; repertoire also includes works by Vivaldi, Bach, Mendelssohn, Mozart, Tchaikovsky and Lalo; chamber recitals in Japan 1991 with her mother, Iolanthe Miroshnikova as accompanist, in works by Brahms, Saint-Saëns, Beethoven and Prokofiev; based in Germany from 1993. *Honours:* awards at Wieniawski and Lipinski Competitions, Poland 1988, Young Violinists Int. Competition, Kloster Schontal, Germany 1989.

KORSTEN, Gérard; South African conductor and violinist; *Music Director, London Mozart Players;* b. 1960, Pretoria. *Education:* Curtis Inst. of Music, USA, Salzburg Mozarteum, studied with Sándor Végh. *Career:* began career as Concertmaster and Asst Music Dir, Camerata Salzburg; Concertmaster, Chamber Orchestra of Europe 1987–96; Prin. Conductor State Theatre of Pretoria, Uppsala Chamber Orchestra 1996–99; Music Dir Orchestra del Teatro Lirico di Cagliari 1999–2005; has conducted first Italian performances of Strauss' Die ägyptische Helena, Weber's Euryanthe, Schubert's Alfonso und Estrella; Prin. Conductor Symphonieorchester Vorarlberg, Bregenz 2005–; Music Dir London Mozart Players 2010–; guest conductor, Teatro alla Scala, Maggio Musicale Florence, Teatro Reggio di Parma, Teatro Lirico Verdi Trieste, Opéra National de Lyon, Royal Swedish Opera, Netherlands Opera, English Nat. Opera, Glyndebourne Festival Opera, Salzburg Mozarteum Orchestra, Hallé Orchestra, Stockholm Chamber Orchestra, Nieuw Sinfonietta Amsterdam, Deutsche Kammerphilharmonie. *Current Management:* c/o Monika Wiktorowicz, International Classical Artists, Dunstan House, 14A St Cross Street, London, EC1N 8XA, England. *Telephone:* (20) 7902-0520. *Fax:* (20) 7404-0150. *E-mail:* info@icartists.co.uk. *Website:* www.icartists.co.uk.

KORTE, Karl Richard, BS, MS; American composer; *Professor Emeritus of Music, University of Texas at Austin*; b. (Carl Richard Korte), 23 June 1928, Ossining, NY; s. of Carl Richard Korte and Dorothy McCoull; m. 1st Elizabeth Brown; m. 2nd Freda Chalcraft; one s. one d. *Education:* Juilliard School with Peter Mennin, Vincent Persichetti, Otto Luening, Goffredo Petrassi and Aaron Copland. *Career:* teacher, Arizona State Univ. 1963–64, State Univ. of New York at Binghamton 1964–70; Prof. of Composition, Univ. of Texas at Austin 1971–96, Prof. Emer. of Music 1996–; Visiting Prof., Williams Coll. 1996–99. *Compositions:* music in many categories, including chamber music, symphonic music, choral and piano; orchestral: Concertino on a Choral Theme 1955, For a Young Audience 1959, 2 Symphonies 1961, 1968, Southwest, dance overture 1963, Concerto for piano and winds 1977, Fibers 1977; chamber: 2 string quartets 1948, 1965, Fantasy for violin and piano 1958, Quintet for oboe and strings 1960, Matrix 1968, Facets 1969, Remembrances for flute and tape 1971, Symmetrics 1973, Trio for violin, cello and piano 1976, Piano Trio 1977, Concertino for bass trombone, wind and percussion 1978, The Whistling Wind for mezzo and tape 1982, Double Concerto for flute, double bass and tape 1983, Voci 1984, Te Maori 1985, Texarkana for band 1991, The Freda Variations 1997, Makam for violin and guitar 2004, Revisitation 2004, Viola Dance 2006; band music and works for chorus: Mass for Youth 1963, Aspects of Love 1968, Pale is this Good Prince, oratorio 1973, Of Time and Seasons 1975; solo piano: Three Miniatures 1958, Songs of Wen I-To 1968, Five New Zealand Songs 1988, Epigrams 1989, Three Bake Songs 2001; choral music: Aspects of Love 1968, Sappho Says 1968, Carols New Fashioned 1969, Music for a New Easter 1982, Music for a New Christmas 1982, Four Songs of Experience 2001, Holy Thursday 2001, Three Psalm Settings 2001, Shiki 2002, Virtual Voices for guitar, violin and digital tape 2009. *Honours:* two Guggenheim Fellowships, Fulbright Fellowships to Italy 1953, to New Zealand 1985, Gold Medal, Queen Elizabeth Int. 1969. *Address:* 545 Stage Road, Kuskirk, NY 12028-2605, USA (home). *Telephone:* (518) 677-3976 (office). *E-mail:* kkorte@aol.com (home). *Website:* www.kkorte.com.

KORTEKANGAS, Jaakko; Finnish singer (baritone); b. 1961. *Education:* Sibelius Acad., Helsinki, studied in Zurich, Switzerland. *Career:* sang at Freiburg Opera 1989–2001, notably as Posa in Don Carlos, Belcore, Rossini's Figaro, Billy Budd and Wolfram in Tannhäuser; guest appearances in Berne, Zürich, Paris, Genoa, Hanover, Karlsruhe, Chemnitz, Copenhagen, Stockholm and as concert singer in Europe, Far East and North America including New York 1990, Savonlinna Opera Festival and Finnish Nat. Opera 1996–; roles include Oppenheimer in Dr Atomic by John Adams, Rossini's Figaro, Ping in Turandot, Marcello in La Bohème, Posa in Don Carlo, Jaufré Rudel in L'amour de loin by Kaija Saariaho, Athanael in Massenet's Thaïs 2013, and Sibelius' Kullervo with Cincinnati Symphony Orchestra and Singapore Symphony Orchestra; several radio broadcasts. *Recordings:* opera: Madetoja: Pohjalaisia, Puccini: Edgar, Rautavaara: Kaivos; TV opera (DVD): Rantavaara: Tietäjien lahja; solo: Me kiitämme sinua, Sibelius's Cantata for the Conferment Ceremony, Nuori Psyyke (Songs of Erkki Melartin), Schumann's Faust-Szenen. *Honours:* First Prize, Lappeenranta Competition 1989. *E-mail:* jaakko.kortekangas@gmail.com.

KORTEKANGAS, Olli; Finnish composer; b. 16 May 1955, Turku. *Education:* Sibelius Acad. and studied in Berlin, Germany. *Career:* Choral Conductor and Pedagogue, Sibelius Acad., Nat. Theatre Acad.; founding mem. Korvat auki Soc. (for promotion of new music); bd mem. Soc. of Finnish Composers; mem. Finnish Composers' Copyright Bureau TEOSTO. *Compositions include:* Grand Hotel (TV opera) 1984–85; orchestral: Okologie1-Vorspiel 1983, Okologie 2, Konzert 1986–87, Alba 1988, Amores 1989, Organ Concerto 1997, Ark 1998, Instrumental Threnody 1977, Sonata for organ 1979, Emotion 1988, Imaggio a M. C. Escher 1990, Iscrizione 1990, Choral MAA 1984–85, Verbum 1987, A 1987–88, Movement Echoing 1997, Electronic Memoria 1988–89. *Honours:* Salzburg Opera Prize 1989, Gianfranco Zaffrani Prize 1989.

KOSENDIAK, Andrzej; Polish musical administrator; *General Manager, Wrocław Philharmonic Orchestra*; b. 1955, Wrocław; m. Dorota Kosendiak; four c. *Education:* Faculty of Composition, Conducting and Music Theory, Acad. of Music, Wrocław. *Career:* Founder and Artistic Dir Collegio di Musica Sacra early music ensemble 1985–; Artistic School Inspector, Lower Silesia region 1990–2000; devised and developed Pedagogical Courses, Acad. of Music, Wrocław 1992–2004; Co-founder, Man. and Co-owner Wrocław School of Jazz and Popular Music 1998–2000; Dir Artistic School Programming and Supervision Dept, Ministry of Culture 2000–01; Head of Interfaculty Early Music, Acad. of Music in Wrocław 2002–; Cultural Advisor and Proxy to Mayor of Wrocław 2002–; Chair. Concert Hall Construction Programming Team 2003–; f. Wrocław Music Acad. Student Baroque Orchestra 2003; Gen. Dir Wrocław Philharmonic Orchestra 2006–; currently Gen. Dir Wratislavia Cantans Int. Festival. *Address:* Filharmonia im. Witolda Lutoslawskiego, ul. Marszalka Józefa Pilsudskiego 19, 50-044 Wrocław (office); Wratislavia Cantans International Festival, Rynek 7, Pasaż pod Błękitnym Słońcem, 50-106 Wrocław, Poland (office). *Telephone:* (71) 342-20-01 (office); (71) 330-52-10 (office). *Fax:* (71) 342-20-02 (office); (71) 330-52-12 (office). *E-mail:* office@wratislavia.art.pl (office). *Website:* www.filharmonia.wroclaw.pl/en (office); www.wratislaviacantans.pl (office).

KOSKY, Barrie; Australian theatre and opera director; *Artistic Director Designate, Komische Oper, Berlin*; b. 1967, Melbourne. *Education:* Melbourne Grammar School, Univ. of Melbourne. *Career:* f. Gilgul Theatre 1990; numerous theatre and opera productions for cos including Victorian State Opera 1991, Opera Australia 1993, Melbourne Theatre Co. 1993, Sydney Theatre Co. 1997–, Wiener Staatsoper 2005, Aalto-Musiktheater, Essen 2006, Edinburgh Festival 2007; Artistic Dir Adelaide Festival of the Arts 1996; Co-Dir Schauspielhaus, Vienna 2001–05; several productions for Komische Oper Berlin 2003, 2005, 2007, apptd Artistic Dir Desig. (2012–). *Productions include:* The Knot Garden 1989, The Marriage of Figaro 1991, 2005, The Barber of Seville 1991, The Golem 1993, Faust I and II 1993, The Exile Trilogy 1993, Oedipus Rex 1993, Nabucco 1996, Tartuffe 1997, Mourning Becomes Electra 1998, King Lear 1998, Medea 2001, The Tales of Hoffmann 2002, Macbeth 2002, Le Grand Macabre 2003, Lohengrin 2005, Orfeo 2005, The Lost Echo (Sydney Theatre Award for Best Dir) 2006, The Flying Dutchman 2006, The Tell-Tale Heart 2007, L'Incoronazione di Poppea 2007, Iphigénie en Tauride 2007, Kiss Me, Kate 2007, The Women of Troy 2008. *Publications:* On Ecstasy (essay) (jt author) 2008. *Address:* Komische Oper, Behrenstrasse 55-57, 10117 Berlin, Germany (office). *Telephone:* (30) 47997400 (office). *Fax:* (30) 20260405 (office). *E-mail:* info@komische-oper-berlin.de (office). *Website:* www.komische-oper-berlin.de (office).

KOSMO, Ingebjørg; Danish singer (mezzo-soprano); b. 1967. *Career:* frequent concert and opera engagements throughout Scandinavia and Europe; repertoire includes L'Enfant Prodigue by Debussy, the Composer in Ariadne auf Naxos, with songs by Schubert, Strauss and Stravinsky; contestant in the Cardiff Singer of the World Competition 1995. *Address:* Den Norske Opera, Postboks 8800, Youngstorget, 0028 Oslo, Norway (office). *E-mail:* ingebjorg.kosmo@chello.no (office). *Website:* www.operaen.no/sw3050.asp (office).

KOSTAS, Rudolf; singer (baritone); b. 1950, Vienna, Austria. *Education:* studied in Vienna with Waldemar Kmentt. *Career:* sang at the Vienna Kammeroper and Staatsoper from 1975; Salzburg Festival 1981 in the premiere of Cerha's Baal; Stadttheater Freiburg 1984–89; season 1995–96 at Schwerin as Hans Sachs in Die Meistersinger and Westmoreland in Sly by Wolf-Ferrari; other roles include Wagner's Amfortas and Wolfram; Mozart's Don Giovanni and Count; Berg's Wozzeck; Verdi's Luna; Rigoletto and Iago; Mozart's Figaro; further appearances in Tel-Aviv, Munich and throughout Germany; many concerts and lieder recitals.

KOSTLINGER, Josef; singer (tenor); b. 24 Oct. 1946, Braunau am Inn, Austria. *Education:* studied in Salzburg and Stockholm. *Career:* sang in the 1973 Stockholm premiere of Tintomora by Werle; Tamino in the Ingmar Bergman version of Die Zauberflöte; Salzburg Landestheater from 1974, in the premieres of König Ubu by F. Hummel 1994; roles have included Mozart's Ferrando, Tamino and Belmonte; Ernesto in Don Pasquale; many concert appearances. *Recordings include:* The Magic Flute.

KOSZUT, Urszula; singer (soprano); b. 13 Dec. 1940, Psyczszyna, Poland; m. Gerhard Geist. *Education:* studied with Maria Eichler-Cholewa in Katowice and with Bogdan Ruskiewicz in Warsaw. *Career:* debut at Stuttgart 1967 as Lucia di Lammermoor; guest appearances in Germany, Warsaw, Geneva, Zürich, Lisbon, Chicago and Toronto; roles include Regina in Mathis der Maler, Norma, Gounod's Juliette, Mozart's Donna Anna and Fiordiligi and parts in operas by Strauss, Verdi and Puccini; concert engagements in works by Beethoven, Bach, Brahms, Handel, Haydn, Mozart and Mahler; Glyndebourne 1970 as the Queen of Night; mem., Vienna Staatsoper from 1971; Hamburg Staatsoper in the premieres of Ein Stern geht auf aus Jakob by Burkhard, Staatstheater by Kagel and Under Milkwood by Steffens; further engagements at Cologne and Stuttgart. *Recordings:* Beethoven's 9th Symphony, conducted by Kempe; Roles in Don Giovanni, Mathis der Maler, Sutermeister's Romeo and Juliet and Paer's Leonora; Countess de la Roche in Zimmermann's Die Soldaten.

KOTCHERGA, Anatoly; Ukrainian singer (bass); b. 1947. *Education:* Vinitza Conservatory, Tchaikovsky Conservatory, Kiev, studied with Marguerita Corosio and Giulio Cassaletta. *Career:* soloist, Kiev Opera from 1972, notably as Basilio, Mephistopheles, Pimen and Arkel; guest appearances at La Scala Milan, and in Canada, Spain, France, Bulgaria, Czechoslovakia, Germany and Australia; has sung Boris Godunov with the company of Warsaw Opera (also televised 1986); Vienna Staatsoper 1988–91, as Shaklovity in Khovanshchina and in Don Carlos; Theater an der Wien, Vienna, as the Commendatore in Don Giovanni 1990; season 1992 as Boris and The Sergeant in Lady Macbeth of the Mtsensk District at the Opéra Bastille, Paris and La Scala Milan; concert appearances include Rimsky's Mozart and Salieri at the Vienna Konzerthaus and a recital of Russian songs in Lyon; sang Boris Godunov at Montpellier 1996; Pimen in Boris at Toulouse 1998. *Recordings:* Khovanshchina by Mussorgsky, conducted by Abbado. *Honours:* Winner, Ukrainian Ministry of Culture Glinka Competition 1971, prizewinner at int. competitions in Berlin 1973, Tchaikovsky Competition, Moscow 1974.

KOTCHINIAN, Arutjun; Armenian singer (bass); b. 1965. *Education:* Tchaikovsky Conservatory, Moscow with Yevgeny Nesterenko, and studied with Helmuth Rilling. *Career:* Prin., Deutsche Oper Berlin 1996–, as Wurm in Luisa Miller, Zaccaria in Nabucco, Gounod's Mephistopheles and Henry VIII in Anna Bolena; Guest artist in Munich, Dresden, Barcelona and Bregenz as Don Giovanni, Leporello, Banquo, Sparafucile, Philip II and the Grand Inquisitor; season 2001–02 as Lodovico in Otello at Covent Garden, Verdi Requiem in Berlin, Zaccaria at Bilbao and Fiesco in Simon Boccanegra at San Diego; season 2008–09 included Aida, La Bohème, and Turandot at Deutsche Oper, Berlin; season 2010–11 Turandot, Rigoletto and Ilbarbiere di Siviglia at

Deutsche Oper, Lucia di Lammermoor at La Fenice, Venice and Wurm in Luisa Miller at Opéra de Paris. *Honours:* Winner Belvedere Competition, Vienna 1995, ARD Competition, Munich 1996, BBC Cardiff Singer of the World 1997, Placido Domingo Operalia 1997, Maria Callas Competition, Athens 1999. *Current Management:* c/o Alexandra Mercer, APA Artists' Management, Studio 1, 79 Bedford Gardens, London, W8 7EG, England. *Telephone:* (20) 7794-7633. *Fax:* (20) 7431-4344. *E-mail:* Alexandra@mercer .uk.com. *Website:* www.apaartistsmanagement.com.

KOTIK, Petr; Czech composer, conductor and flautist; *Artistic Director, Orchestra of the SEM Ensemble;* b. 27 Jan. 1942, Prague; m. 1966; three s. *Education:* Prague Conservatory, Music Academy, Vienna and Prague. *Career:* f. Musica Viva Pragensis, later became QUaX Ensemble 1961; performed with John Cage and Merce Cunningham Dance Company in Vienna, Prague and Warsaw 1964; moved to USA 1969; f. SEM Ensemble, group dedicated to new music with annual concerts USA and Europe 1970–; group became Orchestra of the SEM Ensemble 1992; conducted the SEM Orchestra in concerts at Carnegie Hall, Konzerthaus Berlin, Alice Tully Hall at Lincoln Center, Prague Spring Festival and Oji Hall, Tokyo; conducted operas New York and Berlin, Manhattan Book of the Dead, by David First, Der Kaiser von Atlantis by Victor Ullman and Gilgamesh by Stephen Dickman; frequently conducts Janáček Philharmonic in Czech Repub. and on tours including Warsaw Autumn Festival, Berliner Festspiele MaerzMusik and other European orchestras; founder and Artistic Dir biennial Ostrava Days Summer Inst., Festival Ostrava, Czech Repub. and Ostrava Center for New Music 2001–. *Compositions include:* Music for Three 1964, Kontrabandt, electronic music commissioned by WDR Cologne 1967, There is Singularly Nothing (text Gertrude Stein) 1971–73, Many Many Women (text Gertrude Stein) 1975–78, Explorations in the Geometry of Thinking (text R. Buckminster Fuller) 1978–80, Solos and Instrumental Harmonies 1981–83, Letters to Olga (text Václav Havel) 1989–91, Quiescent Form for orchestra 1994–95, Music in Two Movements 1998–2003, Variations for 3 Orchestras 2003/05, Děvín (text Vladislav Vančura 2000/04, The Plains at Gordium 2004, Spheres & Attraction (text R. Buckminster Fuller) 1981/2005, String Quartet No. 1 2007–08, In Four Parts for three percussionists 2009. *Recordings include:* Many Many Women, Music by Marcel Duchamp, Feldman: Turfan Fragments, Feldman: For Philip Guston, Cage: Atlas Eclipticalis (with David Tudor) and 103, Somei Satoh: Works for Orchestra. *Address:* SEM Ensemble, 25 Columbia Place, Brooklyn, NY 11201, USA (office). *Telephone:* (718) 488-7659 (office). *E-mail:* pksem@semensemble.org (office). *Website:* www .semensemble.org (office).

KOTILAINEN, Juha; singer (baritone); b. 1954, Finland. *Education:* Kuopio Acad., Sibelius Acad., Helsinki. *Career:* sang at first in concert, then made opera debut at Helsinki 1986 as Dandini in La Cenerentola; has made many appearances as Mozart's Figaro and sang in the premieres of Rautavaara's Vincent at Helsinki 1990 and Sallinen's Kullervo at Los Angeles 1992; engaged at the Aalto Theatre in Essen where roles have included Besenbinder in Humperdinck's Hansel and Gretel, Krushina in Smetana's The Bartered Bride and Pantalon in Prokofiev's The Love for Three Oranges; recently he has appeared in title roles of Tchaikovsky's Eugene Onegin, Bartók's Duke Bluebeard's Castle and Guglielmo in Così fan tutte; has also performed in Paul Dessau's opera Die Verurteilung des Lukullus and appeared as Paolo in Verdi's Simon Boccanegra; title role of Mozart's Don Giovanni at the Aalto Theatre 1995; sang the Priest in Dallapiccola's Prigioniero, for Tampere Opera 1996; season 2000–01 with Puccini's Sharpless and Marcello at Helskinki and Leontes in the premiere of Boesmans's Wintermärchen, at Brussels and the Paris Châtelet; repertoire also includes solo songs and bass and baritone parts in great church music works; has appeared in Bach's St Matthew Passion and the B minor Mass; has given recitals in Finland, Scandinavia, Germany, Greece and Russia.

KOTKOVA, Hana; Czech violinist; b. 3 May 1967, Olomouc; m. Osvaldo Tritten; two d. *Education:* Conservatory Ostrava, Music Acad., Prague, Int. Menuhin Music Acad., Gstaad, masterclasses with W. Marschner, J. Gingold, P. Amoyal. *Career:* debut at Opava with Opava Chamber Orchestra 1977; recitals and solos with orchestras in Czech Republic, Switzerland, Sweden, Italy and France 1985–; plays with Camerata Lysy, Yehudi Menuhin and A. Lysy in Europe and USA 1990–93; chamber music with N. Magaloff, Jeremy Menuhin, P. Coker; recital in Prague, Rudolfinum (Dvořáks Hall) for Y. Menuhin's 80 1996; duo with pianist, S. Mulligan 1996–; mem. Smetana trio 2000–03. *Recordings:* albums: with Enescu and Janáček, Sonatas, with Martinů, three Sonatas, Ysaye solo sonatas. *Honours:* Laureat Kocian Int. Competition 1977, first prize Beethoven Int. Competition 1985, winner Prague Spring Competition 1997, Gideon Klein Foundation Prize 1997, City of Prague Prize 1997. *Address:* Casa di Sopra, 6935 Bosco Luganese, Switzerland (home).

KOTOSKI, Dawn; singer (soprano); b. 1967, Maryland, USA. *Education:* studied in New York. *Career:* sang in the YCA concert series in Washington and New York 1990–91; further concerts at Carnegie Hall, Avery Fisher Hall, with the Atlanta, Baltimore and Chicago Symphony Orchestras and at the Metropolitan Opera; sang Mozart's Susanna with the Canadian Opera Company at Calgary, in Handel's Partenope at Omaha and as Massenet's Sophie at St Louis; European engagements as Pamina, Oscar and Musetta at the Vienna Staatsoper, Susanna at Munich, Gilda in Strasbourg and Oscar at the Opéra Bastille, Paris; Gilda, Adele in Die Fledermaus, Sophie and Musetta, Zürich Opera season 1996–97; engaged as Jemmy in a new

production of Guillaume Tell in Vienna and as Zdenka in Arabella at Santa Fe; concert repertory includes Die Schöpfung, by Haydn. *Recordings include:* Handel's Acis and Galtaea, and Giustino; Lisa in La Sonnambula, with Edita Gruberova.

KOUBA, Maria; singer (soprano); b. 1924, Altenmarkt, Austria. *Education:* Graz Conservatory. *Career:* debut at Graz 1957, as Salome; sang at Graz 1957–61, Frankfurt from 1961; roles included Madama Butterfly, Salome, both Leonoras of Verdi, Alice Ford, Jenůfa, Senta, Eva, Tosca and Octavian; guest appearances in Paris 1962, London 1963 as Salome; Metropolitan Opera 1964–65; Brussels, Vancouver, Santa Fe, Naples, Vienna, Hamburg and Berlin; other roles include Donna Anna, Liu, and Marenka in The Bartered Bride.

KOUKL, George, DipMus; Swiss/Czech pianist, harpsichordist and composer; b. 23 March 1953, Prague, fmr Czechoslovakia; m. Chiara Solari. *Education:* Milan Conservatory, Zürich Conservatory, masterclasses. *Career:* debut in 1972; radio recordings and TV appearances across Europe; concerts in Europe, USA, Japan, S America; festival appearances; master classes. *Compositions include:* ballet: Pandora's Box; orchestral: Te Deum, Contest Piece for clarinet and orchestra, Dream, Ceremony after a Fire Raid, Ideogrammi, Contra-variations, Diamond Head, Tre Canti Disperati; chamber music: Imaginor for two pianos, The Messenger for solo piano, Four Pieces for piano, Fantasia for two pianos, Five Miniatures for harpsichord, Fylgjur for solo flute, Divertimento for wind quintet, Narcisse for string quartet, Maschera for saxophone, Zappabis for cello and piano, Tango de la muerte for accordion and piano, Piccola Rapsodia for flute and harp, Trioplay for oboe, clarinet and bassoon, Ritournelles for oboe and bassoon, Musica for piano and string quartet, Potato Polca for contrabassoon and piano, SEMA: a dance for Mevlana, Variations over Hospodine for organ. *Recordings include:* complete piano music of Bohuslav Martinu (seven CDs), complete piano concertos of Bohuslav Martinů (two CDs), complete piano solo music of Alexandre Tcherepnin (seven CDs), complete music for violin and piano of Alexandre Tansman, complete piano music of Paul LeFlem, complete piano music of Vitezslava Kapralova, complete piano music of Arthur Louriè. *Honours:* Alienor Award, Washington, DC (USA) 1986, CD of the Month (three times), Gramophone (UK) 2009–12, CD of the Year (twice), Musicweb 2015. *Current Management:* c/o Lux Nova Press, 2107 North Decatur Road #458, Decatur, GA 30033, USA. *Telephone:* (404) 664-0759. *E-mail:* luxnova@luxnova.com. *Website:* www.luxnova.com. *Address:* Via Cantonale 28, 6945 Origlio, Switzerland (home). *E-mail:* musicplay@sunrise.ch (office). *Website:* www .koukl.com.

KOUKOS, Periklis; Greek composer and opera director; b. 3 Jan. 1960, Athens. *Education:* studied with Yannis Papaionnou and Dimitris Dragatakis in Athens, with Hans Werner Henze and Paul Patterson in London. *Career:* Prof. of Piano, Advanced Theory and Composition, Nat. and the Athens Conservatories 1990–; Artistic Dir, Greek Nat. Opera 1997–99; Artistic Dir and Supervisor of Millennium Advent, Acropolis 1999–2000; Pres., Hellenic Festival SA 2000–. *Compositions include:* Merlin the Magician (children's opera) 1987–89, Conroy's Other Selves (one-act opera) 1990, The Manuscript of Manuel Salinas (three-act opera), A Midsummer Night's Dream (opera-ballet) 1982.

KOUT, Jiri; Czech conductor; *Chief Conductor, Prague Symphony Orchestra;* b. 26 Dec. 1937, Novedvory. *Education:* Prague Conservatory, Nat. Acad. of Music, Prague. *Career:* first engagement as resident conductor, Pilsen Opera and Symphony Orchestra; Principal Conductor of the Nat. Opera in Prague 1972, also appearing with the Prague Symphony Orchestra and the Nat. Radio Orchestra; Principal Conductor, Deutsche Oper am Rhein, Düsseldorf 1978–84; Musical Dir, Saarbruck 1985–90; Principal Conductir, Deutsche Oper Berlin 1990–99; Music Dir Leipzig Opera 1993–99; Music Dir, St Gallen Theater and Chief Conductor, St Gallen Symphony Orchestra 1998–; Chief Conductor, Prague Symphony Orchestra 2006–; conducted Der Rosenkavalier at Munich 1985, leading to engagements in Stuttgart, Berlin and Vienna; debut with the Berlin Philharmonic 1987; regular appearances in Saar-brucken, Venice, Naples, Florence, Cincinnati and Birmingham; conducted Katya Kabanova in Paris and Los Angeles 1988; Principal Resident Conductor, Deutsche Oper Berlin 1990, with Lady Macbeth, Tristan und Isolde and Mathis der Maler; Bluebeard's Castle at the Vienna Staatsoper; returned to Los Angeles with Boris Godunov and Parsifal; Metropolitan Opera debut 1991 (Der Rosenkavalier); season 1992 with Tannhäuser at the Deutsche Oper Berlin and The Makropulos Case at Los Angeles; Covent Garden debut 1993, with Jenůfa; Musical Dir, Leipzig Opera 1993; Wagner's Ring at the Deutsche Oper 1997; Elektra at San Francisco 1997–98; Der Rosenkavalier at the Met 2000; conducts leading orchestras, including Berliner Philharmonie, Gewandhausorchester Leipzig, München Philharmoniker, Gürzenichochester Köln, Orchestre Nat. de France, Orchestre de Paris, Orchestre Nat. du Capitole de Toulouse, Orchestre Nat. de Bordeaux Aquitaine, Los Angeles Philharmonic Orchestra, Birmingham Symphony Orchestra, NHK Sympho-nie Orchestra of Tokyo, Orchestra Sinfonica Nationale della RAI Torino, Orchestra Filarmonica della Scala Milano, Orchestra dell'Accademia di Santa Cecilia Roma, and Orquesta Nacional de España, Madrid. *Honours:* President's Medal for Services to the State in the field of culture and art 2007; winner of conducting competitions at Besançon and Brussels 1965, 1969, Ministry of Culture Prize 2007. *Current Management:* Nachtigall Artists Management, Čerchovská 6/1981, 120 00 Prague, Czech Republic. *Telephone:* 602219611. *E-mail:* a.nachtigalova@nachtigallartists.cz. *Website:*

www.nachtigallartists.cz. *Address:* Prague Symphony Orchestra, nám. Republiky 5, 110 00 Prague, Czech Republic (office). *Website:* www.fok.cz (office).

KOVACEVICH, Stephen; American pianist; b. 17 Oct. 1940, Los Angeles, Calif.; s. of Nicholas Kovacevich and Loreta Kovacevich (née Zuban). *Education:* Berkeley High School, Calif., studied under Lev Shorr and Dame Myra Hess. *Career:* concert debut as a pianist aged 11; moved to UK to study with Dame Myra Hess 1959; has appeared with leading world orchestras and conductors, including Colin Davis, Hans Graf, Bernard Haitink, Kurt Masur, Simon Rattle and Georg Solti; chamber music collaborations with Jacqueline du Pré, Steven Isserlis, Gautier Capuçon, Renaud Capuçon, Kyung-wha Chung, Truls Mørk, Emmanuel Pahud, Anna Larsson, Khatia Buniatishvili, Belcea Quartet, Philippe Graffin, Alina Ibragimova and Martha Argerich. *Recordings include:* Beethoven's Diabelli Variations 1968, Beethoven's Sonatas No. 3 and No. 5 with Jacqueline du Pré, Brahms' Piano Concerto No. 1 (Gramophone Award) 1993, series of Schubert Sonatas, set of the 32 Beethoven Sonatas 2003, Piano Concertos of Beethoven and Brahms and Bartok's Piano Concerto No. 2 (Edison Award) with Sir Colin Davis, Beethoven's Diabelli Variations (Classic FM Gramophone Ed.'s Choice Award 2009) 2008. *Publication:* Schubert Anthology. *Honours:* Kimber Award, Calif. 1959, Mozart Prize, London 1962. *Current Management:* c/o Claire Parker-Paphitis, International Classical Artists, Dunstan House, 14A St Cross Street, London, EC1N 8XA, England. *Telephone:* (20) 7902-0520. *Fax:* (20) 7404-0150. *E-mail:* info@icartists.co.uk. *Website:* www.icartists.co.uk.

KOVACIC, Ernst; Austrian violinist and conductor; *Artistic Director, Leopoldinum Orchestra Wrocław;* b. 12 April 1943, Kapfenberg; m. Traude Holzer; four s. *Education:* Acad. of Music, Univ. of Music, Vienna. *Career:* teacher, Univ. of Music, Vienna 1975–; Artistic Dir Vienna Chamber Orchestra 1996–98, Leopoldinum Orchestra Wrocław, Poland 2007–; has directed Scottish Chamber Orchestra, Ulster Orchestra, Northern Sinfonia, Camerata Salzburg, Deutsche Kammerphilharmonie, Klangforum, Ensemble Modern, Stuttgart Chamber Orchestra, Camerata Bern, Camerata Nordica, Zagreb Philharmonic, Taipei Symphony Orchestra; mem. Zebra String Trio; has appeared at numerous many festivals including Salzburg, Berlin, Vienna, Bath, Edin., Aldeburgh and London Proms; first performances of works by composers including H. K. Gruber, K. Schwertsik, E. Krenek, F. Cerhe, I. Erod, R. Holloway, B. Furrer, G. F. Haas, N. Osbourne, K. H. Essl, H. Eder; Pres. Ernst Krenek Privatstiftung. *Recordings include:* Friedrich Cerha's violin concerto with Radio Symphonieorchester Wien, works by Beethoven and Schoenberg with Wrocław Chamber Orchestra, Krenek's 2nd Violin Concerto with RSO Wien and Symphonic Elegy with Leopoldinium Orchestra, Sir Michael Tippett's Triple Concerto with the composer conducting the BBC Philharmonic, Mozart's complete works for violin and orchestra with Scottish Chamber Orchestra, Robin Holloway's Concerto, HK Gruber's Nebelsteinmusik with Camerata Salzburg and Franz Welser-Möst. *Honours:* prizewinner, int. competitions, Geneva 1970, Barcelona 1971, Munich 1972;. *Current Management:* Ikon Arts Management Ltd, 114 Business Design Centre, 52 Upper Street, London, N1 0QH, England. *E-mail:* info@ikonarts.com. *Address:* Kriehuberpasse 29/5, 1050 Vienna, Austria (home).

KOVÁCS, Eszter; Hungarian singer (soprano); b. 18 May 1939, Tiszanana. *Education:* Franz Liszt Acad., Budapest. *Career:* debut at Budapest Nat. Opera 1965, as Mercédès in Carmen; sang in the dramatic repertory throughout Hungary, and as a guest in Prague, Warsaw, Moscow, Berlin and Washington; Metropolitan Opera, New York 1982–84, notably as Brünnhilde in Die Walküre; other roles include Leonore in Fidelio; Wagner's Elisabeth, Elsa, Eva and Sieglinde; frequent concert appearances.

KOVÁCS, János; Hungarian conductor; b. 1951, Budapest. *Education:* Ferenc Liszt Acad. of Music, Budapest with Prof. Andràs Korodi. *Career:* coach and Conductor, Budapest State Opera; Musical Asst, Bayreuth Festival 1978, 1979; frequent conductor of Hungarian symphony orchestras; has conducted several guest performances given by the Budapest State Opera at the Dresden Festival and in the Berlin State Opera House; two guest performances with Hungarian State Symphony Orchestra and festive concert series marking the opening of Berlin's reconstructed Neues Konzerthaus 1984; conductor of several performances at Vienna Chamber Opera 1984; Suisse Romande Orchestra, Geneva, Switzerland 1985; conducted Le nozze di Figaro at Budapest 1998. *Honours:* Liszt Prize 1985.

KOVACZ, Peter; singer (baritone); b. 1952, Budapest, Hungary. *Education:* studied in Budapest, Dortmund and Munich. *Career:* sang in opera at Munich and Pforzheim, followed by Gelsenkirchen and Dortmund; appearances throughout Germany in operas by Mozart, Verdi and Wagner, notably as Gunther in Götterdämmerung 1994, Dortmund. *Honours:* Treviso Singers Competition (winner for performances as Silvio in Pagliacci) 1978.

KOVATS, Kolos; singer (bass); b. 1948, Hungary. *Education:* Ferenc Liszt Acad. of Music, Budapest. *Career:* debut with Budapest State Opera; numerous appearances, including operas The Magic Flute, Eugene Onegin, Boris Godunov, Don Carlos, La Forza del Destino, Ernani, Simon Boccanegra, Norma and title role in Rossini's Moses, in concert halls and opera houses around the world; title role in Bartók's Duke Bluebeard's Castle; sang Zaccaria in Nabucco at Brussels 1987; Bluebeard at Turin 1989; sang Catalani's La Wally at the 1990 Bregenz Festival; other roles include Verdi's Philip, Banquo, Sparafucile, Fiesco, Padre Guardiano, Pagno (Lombardi), Fernando, Silva and Ramphis; also Mozart's Sarastro and Commendatore;

Mephistopheles, Creon, Oroveso, Pimen, Gremin and Henry VIII in Anna Bolena; sang Bluebeard at the Théâtre du Châtelet, Paris 1996; has appeared in television and films; oratorios. *Recordings include:* Medea, Ernani, Don Carlos, Lombardi, Macbeth, Liszt's St Elizabeth, Masses by Mozart and Schubert, Guillaume Tell, Bluebeard's Castle (video). *Honours:* first prize Erkel Int. Voice Contest 1973, first prize Rio de Janeiro Int. Vocal Competition 1973, second prize Moscow Tchaikovsky Int. Vocal Concours 1974, Liszt Prize, Kossuth Prize 1992.

KOWALKE, Kim H., BA, MA, MPhil, PhD; American academic and musicologist; *Richard L. Turner Professor of Humanities, University of Rochester;* b. 25 June 1948, Monticello, Minnesota, USA; m. Elizabeth Keagy, 19 Aug 1978, 1 s. *Education:* Macalester Coll., Yale Univ. *Career:* Asst Prof. of Music 1977–82, Assoc. Prof. 1982–86, Occidental Coll., Los Angeles, CA; Prof. of Music and Musicology, Eastman School of Music, Univ. of Rochester, NY 1986–, Richard L. Turner Prof. of Humanities 2004–; Pres., Kurt Weill Foundation for Music Inc.; mem. Editorial Bd, Kurt Weill Edition 1992–; mem. Advisory Bd Yale Broadway Masters Series 1999–, Studies in Musical Theatre 2005–. *Publications:* Kurt Weill in Europe 1979, A New Orpheus: Essays on Kurt Weill (ed.) 1986, Accounting for Success: Misunderstanding Die Dreigroschenoper 1990, A Stranger Here Myself: Kurt Weill Studien (ed.) 1993, Speak Low: The Letters of Kurt Weill and Lotte Lenya (ed.) 1995, For Those We Love: Hindemith, Whitman and An American Requiem 1997, Seven Degrees of Separation: Weill, Brecht and the Deadly Sins 2005. *Honours:* five times winner ASCAP-Deems Taylor Award for Excellence in Writing about Music, Theatre Library Asscn Friedley Award, two times winner of Sonneck Soc. for American Music Irving Lowens Prize for best article on American Music, Univ. of Rochester Goergen Award for Distinguished Achievment and Artistry in undergraduate education. *Address:* 888 Quaker Road, Scottsville, NY 14546-9757, USA (home). *Telephone:* (585) 889-3615 (home); (585) 275-8340 (office). *Fax:* (585) 889-3615 (home); (585) 273-5337 (office). *E-mail:* kkwk@ mail.rochester.edu (office).

KOWALSKI, David Leon, BA, MM, PhD; American composer; b. 29 March 1956, New Haven, CT; m. Michelle Disco 1983 (died 1994). *Education:* Univ. of Pennsylvania, New England Conservatory of Music, Princeton Univ., studied with Donald Martino, Arthur Berger, Milton Babbitt. *Career:* freelance composer 1978–. *Compositions include:* Quintus Obscurus for bass flute, viola, celeste and two percussion 1977, Metamorphosis for jazz trio and orchestra 1978, Dichotomies for solo viola 1979, revised 1983, Come Sopra for oboe and cello 1979, Les Voyageurs for horn and three celli 1979, revised 1991, Quintetino for string quartet and piano 1980, Concertino for flute/piccolo, clarinet, horn, violin, cello, bass, harp, piano and two percussion 1980, Double Helix for orchestra 1980, revised 1991, Alle Tode for soprano and piano 1981, String Quartet No. 2 1982, Chamber Concerto 1982, revised 1984, Toccata for organ 1982, Circonspection for soprano and clarinet 1983, Four Frames for percussion quartet 1983, Clarinet Quartet for clarinet, violin, cello and piano 1983, Variations for wind quartet 1983, revised 1991, Premonitions for piano solo 1983, Skid Row for computer-generated tape 1983, Masques for oboe 1984, Echoes for soprano and computer-generated tape 1984, Windhover for soprano and piano 1985, Masques II for solo flute 1986, Masques III for solo clarinet 1987, Two Sonnets for soprano and piano 1988, A Memory of Evening for mezzo and piano 1989.

KOWALSKI, Jochen; German singer (countertenor); b. 30 Jan. 1954, Wachow, Brandenburg. *Education:* Berlin Musikhochschule with Heinz Reeh, studied with Marianne Fischer-Kupfer. *Career:* sang at the Handel Festival Halle 1982, in the pasticcio Muzio Scevola; Has appeared with the Komische Oper Berlin from 1983, debut as Feodor in Boris Godunov; Guest appearances at the State Operas of Munich and Hamburg; Paris Opéra 1987 as Ptolomeo in Giulio Cesare; Vienna Staatsoper 1987 as Orlofsky in Die Fledermaus; Vienna Volksoper in Giustinio by Handel; Has also sung in Düsseldorf, 1989, Amsterdam and Minneapolis; Sang Gluck's Orpheus with the Komische Oper at Covent Garden 1989, returned as Orlofsky 1990, in performances which also featured Joan Sutherland's retirement; Other roles include Daniel in Handel's Belshazzar, and Annio in La Clemenza di Tito; Sang Farnace in Mozart's Mitridate, Covent Garden 1991, Amsterdam 1992; Ottone in L'Incoronazione di Poppea at the 1993 Salzburg Festival; Sang Britten's Oberon at the Met, 1996–97 and at the Vienna Volksoper, 1998. *Recordings include:* Baroque Arias by Prussian composers; Handel and Mozart Arias; Gluck's Orfeo and Euridice; Symphoniae Sacrae by Schütz (Capriccio). *Current Management:* Mitglied im Verband der Deutschen Konzertdirektionen e.V., Hans Reimann, Geschäftsführer Cm Reimann GmbH, Adlershofer Str. 6, 12557 Berlin, Germany. *Telephone:* (30) 6780112. *Fax:* (30) 6780110. *E-mail:* info@cm-reimann.com. *Website:* www.cm-reimann .com; www.jochen-kowalski.de.

KOX, Hans; Dutch composer; b. 19 May 1930, Arnhem. *Education:* Utrecht Conservatory, studied with Henk Badings. *Career:* Dir, Doetinchem Music School 1957–71; teacher, Utrecht Conservatory 1971–. *Compositions include:* Dorian Gray (opera) 1974, Lord Rochester (opera) 1978, three Symphonies 1959, 1966, 1985, Le Songe du Vergier for cello and orchestra 1986, Magnificat I and II for vocal ensemble 1989–90, Das Grune Gesicht (opera) 1981–91, Sonate for violoncello and piano (revised) 1991, Face to Face concerto for alto saxophone and strings 1992, Cyclophony XIV, The Birds of Aengus for violin and harp 1992, Oratorium Sjoah 1993, Violin Concerto No. 3 1993, Orkester Suite Aus der Oper Das Grune Gesicht 1994, Ballet Suite for orchestra (revised) 1994, Das Credo Quia Absurdum for soprano solo, bass solo, choir and orchestra 1995. *Honours:* Visser Neerlandia Prize (for Symphony No. 1) 1959, Prix Italia (for In Those Days) 1970, first prize Rostrum of Composers (for L'Allegria) 1974.

KOZAR, John, BMus, MMus; American pianist and conductor; b. 12 June 1946, Indiana. *Education:* Acad. of Music, Zagreb, Croatia, Indiana Univ., USA. *Career:* debut in New York 1978; British concerto debut 1981; teacher, Univ. of Kansas, Indiana Univ., New England Coll., State Univ. of New York, Ball State Univ.; recitals in New York, London, Chicago, Munich, Vienna, Zagreb, Hong Kong, Johannesburg, Paris, Vancouver, Sydney; television and radio broadcasts worldwide; Music Dir, Kentish Opera Group, England, Opera Program of State Univ. of New York, Potsdam; Program Dir, The Beethoven Foundation, Indiana; freelance conductor of opera, ballet; founder, Piano Productions 1989; Music Dir and Conductor, Grand Piano Orchestra, including three tours of People's Republic of China.

KOŽELUHOVA, Jitka; Czech composer, pianist and singer; b. 19 Nov. 1966, Prague; m. Marcus Gerhardts 1996; one s. *Education:* Conservatory of Prague, Acad. of Performing Arts, Prague. *Compositions:* Sonatine for pianoforte, 1986; Touzeni (Longing) cycle of songs for soprano and pianoforte, 1987; Obrazy (Images), string quartet, 1990–91; Six Songs On The Texts Of The Poems Of Emily Dickinson, cycle for soprano and pianoforte, 1991–92; Three Sentences About The Story Of Christmas, quartet for oboe, clarinet, bassoon and pianoforte, 1992–93; further compositions: Pierres (Stones) (cycle of women's choirs), 1992; Aus Der Tiefe (de Profundis) for mixed choir with soprano solo, 2 narrators and organ, 1994; Secret Dolour, Fantasy on themes from Schubert's Rondo Op 84, for 4 piano hands, 1994; The Inner Voice, viola solo and symphony orchestra, 1994–95; All You Are Thirsty, Come To The Waters, small cantata for alto and baritone solo, English horn, piano and percussions, 1995; For Angels, for 2 flutes, 2 clarinets, string quartet and piano, 1996; Yet, Still, the Hallelujah is Sounding, for piano and cello, 1998. *Address:* Na Roktyce 30, 18000 Prague 8, Czech Republic.

KOŽENÁ, Magdalena; Czech singer (mezzo-soprano); b. 26 May 1973, Brno; m. Sir Simon Rattle 2008; two s. one d. *Education:* Conservatoire, Brno, Coll. of Performing Arts, Bratislava. *Career:* guest singer, Janáček Opera, Brno 1991–; debut as soloist, Vienna Volksoper 1996–97; appearances include Bach's B Minor Mass at the Queen Elizabeth Hall, London 2000, Salzburg Festival debut as Zerlina in Don Giovanni 2002, charity concerts following floods in Czech Repub. 2002, Idamante in Idomeneo at Glyndebourne 2003 and Salzburg Festival, Cherubino for Bavarian State Opera, Metropolitan Opera, Dorabella at Salzburg Easter Festival, Berlin, Varvara, Dorabella, Zerlina at Metropolitan Opera, Theatre des Champs Elysees, Covent Garden debut in La Cenerentola 2007; regular broadcasts for Czech radio and TV; tours in Europe, USA, Japan, Venezuela, Taiwan, Hong Kong, S Korea, Canada; roles include Dorabella in Così fan tutte, Isabella in Italiana in Algeri (Rossini), Venus in Dardanus (Rameau), Mercedes in Carmen, Annius in La Clemenza di Tito, Paris in Paride ed Elena, lead in Orfeo ed Eurydice (both Gluck), lead in Hermia (Britten), Poppea in L'Incoronazione di Poppea (Monteverdi), Mélisande (Debussy). *Recordings include:* Bach Arias (Harmony Magazine Award 1998), Johann Sebastian Bach Cantatas 2000, G.F. Handel Italian Cantatas 2000, G.F. Handel Messiah 2001, Magdalena Kožená – Le belle imagini (Echo Klassik Award 2002, Gold Record of Universal 2003) 2002, Johann Sebastian Bach Arias (Gold Record of Universal 2003, Platinum Record of Universal 2003) 2003, G.F. Handel – Giulio Cesare 2003, Magdalena Kožená – French Arias (Gramophone Award 2003) 2003, Magdalena Kožená – Songs 2004, Magdalena Kožená – Lamento 2005, Paride ed Elena 2005, La Clemenza di Tito 2006, Enchantment 2006, Mozart Arias 2006, Ah! Mio Cor 2007, Songs My Mother Taught Me 2008, Martinů's Julietta Fragments (Gramophone Award for Best Recital Recording 2009, Echo Klassik Award for Recording of the Year 2010) 2009, Ryba: Czech Christmas Mass 2009, Vivaldi Arias 2009, Des Knaben Wunderhorn 2010, Letter Amorose 2010. *Honours:* Chevalier, Ordre des Arts et des Lettres 2003; First Place in Int. Scheider Competition 1992, First Place in Int. Mozart Competition, Salzburg 1995, Georg Solti Award (France), Youngster of Arts, Europe 1996, Orphée d'Or, L'Académie du Disque Lyrique (France) 1999, Diapason d'Or (France) 2000, Echo Klassik Best New Artist (Germany) 2000, Gramophone Award (London) 2001, Gramophone Artist of the Year 2004, Person of the Year in Culture (Czech Repub.) 2002, 2003. *Current Management:* Central European Music Agency, Polní 6, 639 00 Brno, Czech Republic. *Telephone:* (5) 42213053. *Fax:* (5) 42213056. *E-mail:* david@cema-music.com. *Website:* www.cema-music.com; www.kozena.cz.

KOZHUKHIN, Denis; Russian pianist; b. 1986, Nizhny Novgorod. *Education:* Escuela Superior de Música Reina Sofia, Madrid, Int. Piano Acad., Lake Como, Staatliche Hochschule für Musik und Darstellende Kunst, Stuttgart. *Career:* formed Cervantes Trio at coll.; appearances at numerous festivals including Verbier Festival, Klavier-Festival Ruhr, Rheingau Music Festival, Jerusalem Int. Chamber Music Festival, Santander Int. Festival; chamber musician with Radovan Vlatkovic, Dora Schwarzberg, Ailsa Weilerstein, Jacob Koranyi, Alissa Margulis. *Honours:* Prix d'Honneur, Verbier Festival 2003, Winner, Vendôme Prize, Lisbon 2009, Queen Elisabeth Int. Music Competition 2010, Solti Foundation Award 2010. *Current Management:* Arcadia Musica, Aurélie Moron, 22 Passage Dauphiné, 75006 Paris, France; Bridget Emmerson, Intermusica Artists' Management Limited, 36 Graham Street, Crystal Wharf, London, N1 8GJ, England. *Telephone:* (9) 81-02-02-91; (20) 7608-9900. *Fax:* (20) 7490-3263. *E-mail:* contact@arcadiamusica.com;

bemmerson@intermusica.co.uk. *Website:* www.arcadiamusica.com; www.intermusica.co.uk; www.cmireb.be/en.

KOZMA, Lajos; Hungarian singer (tenor); b. 1938, Lepesny. *Education:* Franz Liszt Acad., Budapest, Accademia di Santa Cecilia, Rome with Giorgio Favaretto and Franco Capuana. *Career:* debut as Debussy's Pelléas, Budapest 1962; appearances from 1964 in Florence, Venice, Rome, Milan, London, Philadelphia, New York and Copenhagen; Amsterdam 1982, as Monteverdi's Orfeo; Teatro San Carlo Naples in Rossellini's La Reine Morte; further engagements in Paris, Brussels, Aix-en-Provence and Strasbourg; many concerts in oratorio and lieder. *Recordings include:* Lucia di Lammermoor, Monteverdi Orfeo, Orlando Furioso by Vivaldi.

KRAEMER, Nicholas, BMus, ARCM; British conductor and harpsichordist; b. 7 March 1945, Edinburgh, Scotland; s. of the late William Kraemer and Helen Bartrum; m. Elizabeth Andreson; three s. (one deceased) two d. *Education:* Lancing Coll., Dartington Coll. of Arts, Univ. of Nottingham, Guildhall School of Music and Drama, Schola Cantorum Basiliensis. *Career:* harpsichordist with Acad. of St Martin-in-the-Fields and English Baroque Soloists; f. Raglan Baroque Players 1978–2001, concerts, numerous radio and TV broadcasts; first Musical Dir, Opera 80 (now English Touring Opera); conducted Unicorn Opera, Abingdon 1971–75 (all Handel), Mozart at Glyndebourne 1980–83, Netherlands Opera, Orlando 1985, Geneva Opera, Ariodante 1986, Poppea 1989, ENO, Magic Flute 1992, 2004, Jephtha 2005, Marseille Opera, Poppea 1993, Den Nye Opera, Bergen, Figaro 2010, Grange Park, Idomeneo 2012, Buxton Festival, La Finta Giardinera 2013; Assoc. Conductor, BBC Scottish Symphony Orchestra 1983–85; Artistic Dir Irish Chamber Orchestra 1986–92, London Bach Orchestra 1985–93; Perm. Guest Conductor, Manchester Camerata 1992–2014; Prin. Guest Conductor, Music of the Baroque, Chicago, USA 2002–, Kristiansand Symphony Orchestra; Guest Conductor with Israel Chamber Orchestra, Birmingham Contemporary Music Group, North Netherlands Orkest, Australian Chamber Orchestra, Orchestra of the Age of Enlightenment, Scottish Chamber Orchestra, Nat. Youth Orchestra of Scotland, London Classical Players, City of Birmingham Symphony Orchestra, Northern Sinfonia; led Raglan Baroque Players in Rodelinda (dir Jonathan Miller) and Tolomeo (dir Charles Sturridge) for Broomhill Opera; recent guest appearances with Berlin Philharmonic, Chicago Symphony, Bergen Philharmonic, Rotterdam Philharmonic, Gothenberg Symphony, Kristiansand Symphony, Auckland Philharmonia, Lapland Chamber Orchestra, BBC Philharmonic, BBC Nat. Orchestra of Wales, Musikkollegium Winterthur, Orchestra Ensemble, Kanazawa, Detroit Symphony, Iceland Symphony, Toronto Symphony, Phiharmonia Baroque, St Paul Chamber Orchestra, Western Australia Symphony, Hallé, London Mozart Players, Aalborg Symphony, Ulster Orchestra; worked with El Sistema, Venezuela 2007–08, Colorado Symphony, Sonderjullands Orchestra, Denmark; regular work with Chicago Civic Orchestra, Trinity Laban Conservatoire, Opera Neo, San Diego; further engagements include Scottish Opera (Ariodante), Orquesta Metropolitana Lisboa, Chicago Symphony, Gothenburg Symphony, Houston Symphony; mem. Royal Soc. of Musicians. *Film:* The Madness of King George (Baroque conductor) 1994. *Recordings:* Vivaldi Violin Concertos Op. 9 with Monica Huggett, Op. 8 including The Four Seasons with Raglan Baroque Players; complete harpsichord concertos of Bach; complete cello concertos of Vivaldi with Raphael Wallfisch; Music from Versailles, Locatelli Op. 1, Op. 3, Tartini Op. 1 and Neapolitans with Elizabeth Wallfisch and Raglan Baroque Players; Vivaldi Wind Concertos, La Stravaganza Op. 4 Cello Concertos with City of London Sinfonia, Scottish Chamber Orchestra (Thea Musgrave). *Current Management:* c/o Caroline Phillips Management, 11 Pound Pill, Corsham, Wilts., SN13 9HZ, England. *Telephone:* (1249) 716716. *Fax:* (1249) 404123. *E-mail:* info@caroline-phillips.co.uk. *Website:* www.caroline-phillips.co.uk.

KRAFT, Jean; American singer (mezzo-soprano); b. 9 Jan. 1940, Menasha, WI. *Education:* Curtis Institute with Giannini Gregory, studied with Theodore Harrison in Chicago, William Ernst Vedal in Munich and Povla Frijsch in New York. *Career:* debut at New York City Opera 1960, in Six Characters in Search of an Author by Weisgall; sang in Houston, Boston, New Orleans, Philadelphia, Santa Fe, Chicago and Dallas; Metropolitan Opera from 1970, as Flora in La Traviata, Emilia (Otello) 1987, Herodias, Ulrica and Suzuki; Maggio Musicale Florence 1988, as Mrs Sedley in Peter Grimes. *Recordings include:* Andrea Chénier and Cavalleria Rusticana.

KRAFT, William, BA, MA; American composer; b. 6 Sept. 1923, Chicago, IL; m.; two s. one d. *Education:* Columbia Univ., studied with Jack Beeson, Henry Brant, Henry Cowell, Paul Henry Lang, Otto Luening, Vladimir Ussachevsky. *Career:* organized and directed Los Angeles Percussion Ensemble; as percussion soloist performed American premiere of Stockhausen's Zyklus and Boulez's Le Marteau sans Maitre; also recorded Histoire du Soldât under Stravinsky's direction; conductor of contemporary and other music; Asst Conductor, Los Angeles Philharmonic for three years; Musical Dir and Chief Adviser, Young Musicians' Foundation Debut Orchestra, Los Angeles; appeared frequently at Monday evening concerts; Visiting Prof. in Composition, USC; guest lecturer in composition, California Inst. of Arts, Faculty of Banff Center for Performing Arts; similar residences at Univ. of Western Ontario, Royal Northern Coll. of Music, Manchester, UK, among others; frequent lecturer at festivals and concert series, including Percussive Arts Soc. Int. Conference, California State Univ., Sacramento Festival of New American Music, Res Musica Baltimore concert series; has given numerous seminars and masterclasses at univs and music festivals; Composer-in-

Residence, Los Angeles Philharmonic; founder and Dir, Los Angeles Philharmonic New Music Group 1981–85; Composer-in-Residence, Cheltenham Int. Music Festival, Cheltenham, England 1986; Visiting Prof. in Composition, UCLA 1988–89. *Compositions include:* Dialogues and Entertainments for soprano solo and wind ensemble 1980, Double Play for violin, piano and chamber orchestra 1982, Gallery 83 1983, Timpani Concerto 1983, Contextures II: The Final Beast 1984, Interplay 1984, Weavings for string quartet 1984, Gallery 4–5 1985, Quintessence 1985, Mélange 1986, Of Ceremonies, Pageants and Celebrations 1986, Quartet for the Love of Time 1987, Interplay 1984, Episodes 1987, Horn Concerto 1988, Kennedy Portrait 1988, Vintage Rennaissance for orchestra 1989, Songs of Flowers, Bells and Death 1991, Concerto for percussion and chamber ensemble 1993, Music for string quartet and percussion 1993, Symphony of Sorrows 1995, Encounters IX for English horn and percussion 1999.

KRAJNY, Boris; pianist; b. 28 Nov. 1945, Kromeriz, Czechoslovakia. *Education:* Conservatory Kromeriz, Acad. of Prague. *Career:* soloist, Prague Chamber Orchestra 1972–80, Czech Philharmonic 1982–. *Recordings:* Bach's Complete Organ Works, Busoni's Complete Organ Works, works by Beethoven, Chopin, Ravel, Debussy, Prokofiev, Bartók, Honegger, Roussel, Poulenc, Martinů. *Honours:* first prize Piano Competition, Senigallia 1976, Grand Prix du Disque Charles Gros, Paris 1982.

KRAKAUER, David, MMus; American clarinettist; *Founder, Klezmer Madness!*; b. 1956, New York. *Education:* Juilliard School. *Career:* performances of classical chamber music, Eastern European Jewish klezmer music, and avant-garde improvisation; genre includes world music and jazz, rock, funk and hip-hop; began career as classical musician, veered towards klezmer 1980s; f. Klezmer Madness! ensemble 1990s; regular European tours, performances at festivals and jazz clubs and at Library of Congress, Stanford Lively Arts, San Francisco Performances, Hancher Auditorium, Symphony Space in New York; venues in Europe have included Venice Biennale, Krakow Jewish Culture Festival, BBC Proms, Saalfelden Jazz Festival, La Cigale, WOMEX, New Morning, Paris; has also appeared as guest soloist with ensembles including Tokyo String Quartet, Kronos Quartet, Emerson String Quartet, Orion String Quartet, Lark Quartet, Eiko and Koma, Orquesta Sinfonica de Barcelona, Brooklyn Philharmonic Orchestra; nine years with Aspen Wind Quintet; faculty mem. New School Univ.'s Mannes Coll. of Music, Manhattan School of Music, Bard Conservatory of Music. *Recordings:* klezmer albums: Klezmer Madness! 1995, Klezmer NY 1998, A New Hot One 2000, The Twelve Tribes (Preis der Deutschen Schallplattenkritik in jazz category) 2001, David Krakauer Live in Krakow (with hip-hop artist Socalled) 2003, Bubbameises: Lies My Gramma Told Me (with Socalled) 2005; classical albums: The Dreams and Prayers of Isaac the Blind 1997, Klezmer Concertos and Encores 2003. *Current Management:* c/o Steven Saporta, Invasion Group, 34 E 32nd Street, Suite 100, New York, NY 10016, USA. *Telephone:* (212) 414-0505. *E-mail:* steven@invasiongroup.com. *Website:* www.davidkrakauer.com.

KRÄMER, Gunter; stage director; b. 2 Dec. 1940, Neustadt an der Weinstrasse, Germany. *Education:* Heidelberg and Freiburg Univs. *Career:* debut opera production, Krenek's Karl V at Darmstadt 1979; Head of Drama, Bremen and produced Nono's Intelleranza 60 at Hamburg Staatsoper 1985; Deutsche Oper am Rhein, Düsseldorf 1986–87, with Die Tote Stadt and Schreker's Die Gezeichneten; productions at Deutsche Oper Berlin have included The Makropulos Case (seen at Los Angeles 1992); Die Entführung and Die Zauberflöte 1991; Intendant, Theatre Co. of Cologne 1990, producing Weill's Die Dreigroschenoper with it at the Spoleto Festival 1991; Les Contes d'Hoffmann at Cologne 1998.

KRÄMER, Toni; German singer (tenor); b. 14 Sept. 1935, Malsch. *Education:* Karlsruhe Musikhochschule. *Career:* debut at Stuttgart 1965, in Les Contes d'Hoffmann; sang in Stuttgart as Pinkerton and Alvaro, and other roles in operas by Puccini and Verdi; sang Florestan and Erik in Klagenfurt, Parsifal and Lohengrin in Saarbrucken; Stuttgart Staatsoper as Walther in Die Meistersinger, Siegfried, and König Hirsch in the opera by Henze; Munich Staatsoper as Dimitri in Boris Godunov; Bayreuth Festival 1985–86, as Siegfried in Der Ring des Nibelungen; Deutsche Oper Berlin 1987, as Siegfried and Froh in the Ring; Metropolitan 1988, as Siegfried in Götterdämmerung; sang Aegisthus in Elektra at Stuttgart 1989; Stuttgart Staatsoper 1992, as Bacchus in Ariadne auf Naxos. *Recordings include:* Lohengrin, Der Freischütz (video).

KRANZLE, Johannes Martin; German singer (baritone); b. 1962, Augsburg. *Education:* Frankfurt Musikhochschule. *Career:* sang in opera at Dortmund, from 1987; Hanover Staatstheater from 1991, notably as Papageno, Guglielmo, Rossini's Figaro and Dandini, 1996; Sang in the premiere of Draussen vor der Tur by F X Thoma, 1994; Guest appearances at the State Operas of Hamburg and Munich, in Henze's Junge Lord, 1994; In Leipzig, as Eisenstein, 1995; Festival engagements at Spoleto and Schleswig Holstein; Season 1998 as Lescaut in Henze's Boulevard Solitude, Frankfurt. *Honours:* Prizewinner at Vercelli, Paris, Perpignan and Rio de Janeiro Competitions.

KRAPP, Edgar, PhD; German organist, harpsichordist and academic; *Professor of Music, Hochschule für Musik und Theater, Munich*; b. 3 June 1947, Bamberg; m. Dr Maria-Christine Behrens 1978; two s. *Education:* Regensburg Cathedral Church Choir, Coll. of Music, Munich, studied with Franz Lehrndorfer in Munich and Marie Claire Alain in Paris. *Career:* concerts in Europe, N and S America, Japan; radio and TV programmes in

Germany and Japan; Prof. of Organ, Hochschule für Musik, Frankfurt 1974; Visiting Prof., Salzburg Mozarteum 1982–91; Prof. of Organ, Hochschule für Musik, Munich 1993–2012; mem. jury of Int. Organ Competitions in Berlin, Munich, Nuremberg, Linz, Tokyo, Chartres; mem. Bd of Dirs Neue Bachgesellschaft, Leipzig 1993–2012; Artistic Dir Organ Series at New Concert Hall, Bamberg; mem. Bayerische Akad. der Schönen Künste. *Recordings:* Handel: all organ and harpsichord works; organ recordings in Haarlem (St Bavo Church), Berlin (St Hedwig's Cathedral), Passau Cathedral, historical instruments in Germany (Brandenburg Cathedral and Benediktbeuern, Ottobeuren Basilica), Bamberg Concert Hall: recordings with Bamberg Symphony Orchestra (Guilmant, 2 Organ Symphonies). *Honours:* First Prize, ARD Competition, Munich 1971, Mendelssohn Prize, Berlin 1971, German Recording Prizes for Organ 1981, Harpsichord 1983, Grand Prix du Disque 1983, Frankfurt Music Prize 1983, E.T.A. Hoffmann Prize, Bamberg. *Telephone:* (89) 81041484 (office). *Fax:* (89) 81042298 (office). *E-mail:* ekrapp@t-online.de (home).

KRAUKLIS, Georgij; Russian musicologist; b. 12 May 1922, Moscow; m. Irina Shklaeva 1946, one d. *Education:* Musical College, Conservatory of Moscow. *Career:* consultant to Moscow Philharmonic, 1952–60; teacher, Choral College, Moscow, 1955–62; teacher, 1956–67, Docent, 1967–80, Dean, 1978–89, Prof., 1980–, Conservatory of Moscow; Dir of Stage, France's Violinists, Sarla, France, 1982; Assoc. Ed., JALS, USA 1987–92. *Publications:* Piano Sonatas of Schubert, 1963; Operatic overtures of R. Wagner, 1964; Symphonic Poems of R. Strauss, 1970; Symphonic Poems of F. Liszt, 1974; Conceptions of Orchestral Program Music in the Age of Romanticism, 1999; contrib. to Bayreuth Music Festival after 116 years, in Musical Academy, 1993. *Honours:* Ministry of Culture prize for article 1979; hon. title of Merited Man (representative) of Russian Art 1994. *Address:* Kostiakova Street 6/5, Ap 81, 125422 Moscow, Russia.

KRAUS, Anthony Charles, BA (Hons); British conductor, chorus master, accompanist and organist; *Member of Music Staff, Opera North*; b. 24 Oct. 1974, London. *Education:* St Paul's School, Univ. of Bristol, GSMD, Nat. Opera Studio, London. *Career:* fmrly Univ. Organ Scholar and conductor, Univ. Chamber Choir and Orchestra, Univ. of Bristol; held positions with English Touring Opera, New Youth Opera; attended Rossini Opera Festival Academia 1999; resident coach on young singers' programme, Opéra du Rhin, Strasbourg 2000; trainee répétiteur, ENO 2000, later full-time music staff mem.; prin. accompanist, London Concert Choir –2003; Chorus Master, Opera North 2003–06, mem. Music Staff 2006–; coach at music summer schools, including Royal School of Church Music, Finchley Children's Music Group; has performed as pianist and organist throughout UK and Europe. *Honours:* Ricordi Prize for conducting. *Address:* Opera North, Grand Theatre, 46 New Briggate, Leeds, LS1 6NU, England (office). *Telephone:* (7970) 396081 (office). *E-mail:* anthony.kraus@operanorth.co.uk (office). *Website:* www.operanorth .co.uk (office).

KRAUS, Michael; Austrian singer (baritone); b. 17 Jan. 1957, Vienna. *Education:* studied in Vienna with Otto Edelmann and Josef Greindl. *Career:* sang at Aachen Opera 1981–84, Ulm 1984–87, Vienna Volksoper 1988–91, notably as Papageno; US debut 1991 at San Francisco Opera; guest appearances in France, Hungary, The Netherlands, Greece and Israel, as Mozart's Leporello, Guglielmo and Count, Puccini's Marcello and Lescaut, Janáček's Forester, Monteverdi's Ottone and the Count in Lortzing's Wildschütz. *Recordings include:* Die Zauberflöte; Jonny Spielt auf by Krenek; Der Rosenkavalier; Turandot by Busoni; Krasa's Verlobung im Traum. *Honours:* winner of various competitions, including the Hugo Wolf Competition, Vienna. *Current Management:* Aria's di Novella Partacini & Alexandra Plaickner, Rappresentanza Artisti, Via Josef Weingartner, 4, 39022 Lagundo, Italy. *Telephone:* (0473) 200200. *Fax:* (0473) 222424. *E-mail:* info@arias.it. *Website:* www.arias.it.

KRAUZE, Zygmunt, MA; composer, pianist and academic; *Professor, Academy of Music, Łódź and Frederic Chopin University of Music*; b. 19 Sept. 1938, Warsaw. *Education:* studied with Kazimierz Sikorski and Maria Wilkomirska at the Warsaw Conservatory, with Nadia Boulanger in Paris. *Career:* soloist in recitals of new music in Europe and USA; f. Warsaw Music Workshop 1967, group consisting of clarinet, trombone, cello and piano, for which 100 composers have written works; taught piano at Cleveland State Univ., USA 1970–71; lectures at Int. Course for New Music at Darmstadt, in Stockholm, Basle and at US univs, Tokyo Coll. of Music, Acad. for Performing Arts, Hong Kong, Jerusalem Music Center and Hebrew Univ., Jerusalem, Central Conservatory of Music, China; Visiting Prof., Yale Univ., USA 1982; Eminent Corresp. Prof., Keyimiung Univ., Chengdu, S Korea; Pres. Polish Section of Int. Soc. for Contemporary Music (ISCM) 1980–95, Pres. ISCM 1987–90, Hon. mem. ISCM 1999, Hon. mem. Polish Section of ISCM 2010; has worked for IRCAM (Electronic Music Centre) with Boulez; Prof., Acad. of Music, Łódź, Frederic Chopin Univ. of Music; Artistic Dir Garden Festival, Warsaw; resident in Paris 1982–. *Compositions:* opera: The Star, one-act opera (commissioned and produced by the Nat. Theatre, Mannheim, Germany 1981, other productions: Wroclaw Opera House, Grand Opera Theatre, Warsaw, International Music Festival, Lille, France, Hamburg City Opera, Germany, Theatre Nat. de la Colline, Paris), Balthasar (two-act opera, commissioned and produced by The Warsaw Chamber Opera) 2001, Ivonne, Princess of Burgundy, four-act opera commissioned by the City of Warsaw, premiered in Theatre Sylvie Monfort, Paris 2004, Polyeucte, five-act opera 2010, The Letters 2010, Voyage de Chopin 2010; orchestral: Piece for

Orchestra No. 1 1969, Folk Music for orchestra 1972, Fête Galante et Pastorale for four soloists and orchestra (commissioned by Austrian Radio, Graz) 1975, Suite de Dances et de Chansons for harpsichord and orchestra (commissioned by Westdeutscher Rundfunk, Cologne) 1977, Piece for Orchestra No. 3 (commissioned by French Ministry of Culture) 1982, Arabesque for piano and chamber orchestra (commissioned by French Radio) 1983, Symphonie Parisienne for chamber orchestra (commissioned by Ensemble Intercontemporaine and IRCAM, Paris) 1986, La Terre for soprano and orchestra (commissioned by French Radio) 1995, Rhapsod for string orchestra (commissioned by F. Chopin Acad. of Music, Warsaw) 1995, Piano Concerto No. 2 (commissioned by Suntory Ltd, Tokyo) 1996, Serenade for orchestra (commissioned by Polish Radio) 1998, Emille Bell for string orchestra (commissioned by The Korean Chamber Ensemble) 2000, Adieu for orchestra (commissioned by musica viva, Munchen) 2001; instrumental: Five Piano Pieces 1957–58, Prelude, Intermezzo, Postlude for piano 1958, Seven Interludes for piano 1958, Malay Pantuns for female voice and three flutes 1961, Polychromie for clarinet, trombone, cello and piano 1968, Voices for 15 instruments 1968–72, String Quartet No. 2 1970, Aus Aller Welt Stammende for ten string instruments (commissioned by Int. Music Workshop, Innsbruck) 1973, Idyll for 32 folk instruments and tape 1974, Soundscape for amplified instruments and tape (commissioned by Stericher Herbst Int. Music Festival, Graz) 1975, Music Box Waltz for piano 1977, String Quartet No. 3 (commissioned by French Radio, Paris) 1983, Quatuor pour la Naissance for clarinet, violin, cello and piano (commissioned by the French Govt) 1984, Rivière Souterraine for seven amplified instruments and eight track tape (commissioned by the French Govt) 1987, Nightmare Tango for piano (commissioned by Ivar Mikhashoff) 1987, La Chanson du Mal Aimé for piano 1990, For Alfred Schlee for string quartet 1991, Piano Quintet (commissioned by the Museum of Art, Łódź) 1993, Refrain for piano 1993, Terra Incognita for ten strings and piano (commissioned by Kunst und Ausstellungshalle der Bundesrepublik Deutschland, Bonn) 1994, P-53 (collective improvised composition with Chris Cutler, Lutz Glandien, Marie Goyette, Otomo Yoshihide, commissioned by Hessischer Rundfunk, Frankfurt) 1994, Pastorale for wind quintet (commissioned by Hungarian Radio, Budapest) 1995, Trois Chansons (commissioned by Rendez-vous Musique Nouvelle, Forbach, France) 1996, Five Songs for baritone and piano (commissioned by Culture Foundation, Warsaw) 2000. *Honours:* Silver Cross of Merit 1975, Chevalier, Ordre des Arts et des Lettres 1984, Golden Cross of Merit 2004, Officer, Legion d'honneur 2008; Medal of Distinction, Jeunesses Musicales in Poland 1979, Prize of Ministry of Culture 1989, 2005 UNESCO Heritage of the Humanity Award 2005, Gold Medal Merit for Culture, Gloria Artis 2010. *Address:* c/o Society of Authors ZAiKS, 2 Hipoteczna Street, 00 092 Warsaw, Poland. *Telephone:* (4822) 8281705. *Fax:* (4822) 8281347. *E-mail:* sekretariat@zaiks.org.pl. *Website:* www.zaiks.org.pl.

KRAVITZ, Ellen King, BA, MM, PhD; American fmr musicologist and educator; b. 25 May 1929, Fords, NJ; m. Hilard L. Kravitz 1972; two d. three step-s. *Education:* Georgian Court College, Lakewood, NJ, Univ. of Southern California. *Career:* Full Prof. of Music History, California State Univ., Los Angeles 1967; researcher in musicology and related arts; Dir exhbn of Schoenberg's art and music during Schoenberg Centennial Celebration, Univ. of Southern California 1974; Founder Friends of Music 1976, Chair. 1978–82; participant in Faculty Vocal Extravaganza, California State Univ. 1981, 1983, 1985, 1987, 1989, 1991, 1993, 1995, 1997; mem. Pacific Southwest Chapter, American Musicological Soc., Historical Assoc., Music Center, Los Angeles. *Publications:* A Correlation of Concepts Found in German Expressionist Art, Music and Literature 1970; Ed.: Journal of the Arnold Schoenberg Institute, Vol. I, No. 3 1977, Vol. II, No. 3 1978 (article with Laurence Schoenberg), Catalogue of Schoenberg's Paintings, Drawings and Sketches 1978, Music in Our Culture 1996, three CDs edn 1997, Arnold Schoenberg as Artist: Another Look (paper for Musicology Meeting) 1995. *Honours:* Departmental Award for Master's Thesis, Univ. of Southern California School of Music 1966, Dean's Award for Excellence in Teaching 1983. *Address:* 317 South Canon Drive, Beverly Hills, CA 90212-4515, USA (home). *Telephone:* (310) 270-3333 (home). *E-mail:* ellenkravitz@gmail.com (home).

KREBBERS, Herman Albertus; Dutch violinist; b. 18 June 1923, Hengelo; m. A. Torlau; one s. one d. *Education:* Amsterdam Conservatory with Oskar Back. *Career:* debut concert 1932; soloist with Concertgebouw Orchestra 1935; Leader, Gelderland Orchestra, then Hague Residentie Orchestra 1950–62; Leader, Concertgebouw Orchestra 1962–79; many tours of Europe and USA as soloist; f. Guarneri Trio 1963, played in violin duo with Theo Olof; Prof., Robert Schumann Inst., Düsseldorf; teacher, Amsterdam Conservatory, masterclasses in Brussels, Vienna, Pretoria, Poznan, Tokyo, Montréal, Madrid etc. *Recordings:* Bach and Badings Concertos for Two Violins, with Theo Olof and the Hague Philharmonic; Beethoven Concerto with the Hague Philharmonic; Brahms and Bruch Concertos with the Brabant Orchestra; Paganini 1st Concerto with the Vienna Symphony; Haydn Concertos with the Amsterdam Chamber Orchestra, Beethoven and Brahms violin concertos, Tzigane and Rondo Capricioso (Ravel), Heldenleben and Zarathustra (R. Strauss), Sheherazade (Rimsky-Korsakov) with Royal Concertgebouw Orchestra. *Honours:* Officer, Order of Orange Nassau; Amsterdam Conservatory Prix d'Excellence 1940, many int. competition awards. *Address:* Prof Cobbenhagenlaan 724, 5037 DW Tilburg, The Netherlands (home). *Telephone:* (13) 4688780 (home). *E-mail:* okrebbers@hotmail.com (office).

KREJCI, Jiri; Czech oboist; b. 11 Dec. 1935, Dolni Hbity; two s. one d. *Education:* Military Music School, Kosice and Conservatory of Music, Prague. *Career:* debut as soloist, Haydn Concerto, Radio Symphony Orchestra, Prague 1960; solo oboist of the Theatre Orchestra, Vinohrady, Prague 1953–56, Karlin, Prague 1957–59; Principal Oboe, Radio Symphony Orchestra, Prague 1959–64; solo oboist, Prague Chamber Orchestra 1965–77; Artistic Leader, Collegium Musicum Pragense 1965–90; mem., Czech Nonet 1977–; mem., Prague Wind Quintet 1982–93; live recordings for the BBC in London. *Honours:* Composers' Soc. Prize 1984, Hon. Ministry of Culture Prize, Czech Republic.

KREMER, Gidon; Russian/German violinist; *Artistic Director, Kremerata Baltica*; b. 27 Feb. 1947, Riga, Latvia. *Education:* Riga School of Music, Moscow Conservatory with David Oistrakh. *Career:* recitalist and orchestral soloist worldwide 1965–; has played in most major int. festivals including Berlin, Dubrovnik, Helsinki, London, Moscow, Prague, Salzburg, Tokyo and Zürich; has played with most major int. orchestras including Berlin Philharmonic, Boston Symphony, Concertgebouw, LA Philharmonic, New York Philharmonic, Philadelphia, San Francisco Symphony, Vienna Philharmonic, London Philharmonic, Royal Philharmonic, Philharmonia, NHK Symphony of Japan and all main Soviet orchestras; has worked with Bernstein, von Karajan, Giulini, Jochum, Previn, Abbado, Levine, Maazel, Muti, Harnoncourt, Mehta and Marriner; f. Kremerata Baltica (chamber orchestra) 1977, Artistic Dir 1977–; Founder Lockenhaus Chamber Music Festival 1981–2011. *Recordings:* has made more than 120 albums. *Performances:* first performances include Henze, Stockhausen, Schnittke, Pärt, Astor Piazzola. *Honours:* prizewinner, Queen Elisabeth Competition, Brussels, Montreal Competition and Fourth Int. Tchaikovsky Competition (First Prize) 1970, Paganini Prize, Genoa, Grand Prix du Disque and Deutsche Schallplattenpreis, Ernst-von-Siemens Musikpreis, Bundesverdienstkreuz, Premio dell' Accademia Musicale Chigiana, Triumph Prize 2000, Unesco Prize 2001, Saeculum-Glashütte Original-Musikfestspielpreis 2007, Rolf-Schock Prize 2008, Life Achievement Prize, Istanbul Music Festival 2010, Una Vita Nella Musica – Artur Rubinstein Prize 2011. *Current Management:* Opus 3 Artists, 470 Park Avenue South, 9th Floor North, New York, NY 10016, USA. *E-mail:* info@opus3artists.com. *Address:* Kremerata Baltica, R. Vagnera iela 4, 1050 Riga, Latvia. *Telephone:* 6722-4055. *Fax:* 6721-3072. *E-mail:* kristijonas@gidonkremer.net. *Website:* www.gidonkremer.net; www.kremerata-baltica.com.

KRENZ, Jan; Polish conductor and composer; b. 14 July 1926, Włocławek; s. of Otton Krenz and Eleonora Krenz; m. Alina Krenz 1958; one s. *Education:* Higher School of Music. *Career:* conducting debut, Łódź Philharmonic Orchestra 1946; Chief Conductor, State Poznań Philharmonic Orchestra 1947–49; Chief Conductor Polish Nat. Radio Symphony Orchestra of Katowice 1953–67; Chief Conductor Danish Radio Orchestra, Copenhagen 1960s; Leader, Grand Opera House Orchestra (Teatr Wielki), Warsaw 1968–73; conducted Berlin Philharmonic, Staatskapelle Dresden, Leningrad Philharmonic and all the major London orchestras; Gen. Dir of Music, Bonn Orchestra 1979–82; frequent collaboration with Yomiuri Nippon Symphony Orchestra; performing only as guest conductor 1983–; Diploma of Ministry of Foreign Affairs 1980. *Compositions include:* chamber, vocal and symphonic music, orchestral transcriptions of Polish classics, J.S. Bach (including Polyphonic suite on four fragments from Bach's Die Kunst der Fuge) and Szymanowski, film and stage music. *Honours:* Hon. mem. Asscn of Polish Composers; Hon. Conductor Polish Nat. Radio Symphony Orchestra of Katowice; decorations include Order of Banner of Labour (First Class), Commdr's Cross with Star of Polonia Restituta Order; State Prize 1955, 1972, Prize of Asscn of Polish Composers 1968, Grand Prix du Disque, France 1972, Prize of Polish Artists' and Musicians' Asscn (SPAM) Orfeusz 1974. *Address:* al. J. Ch. Szucha 16, 00-582 Warsaw, Poland.

KREPPEIN, Ulrich Alexander, PhD; German composer and musician (piano, organ); b. 9 Feb. 1979, Leverkusen. *Education:* Musikhochschule R. Schumann, Düsseldorf, Harvard Univ., also studied with Tristan Murail at Columbia Univ., New York. *Career:* music performed in Europe and USA including Berlin Philarmonie and Carnegie Hall, New York and in Moscow, Düsseldorf, Munich, Seoul, London and Cambridge, Mass; commissions include ROC-Gmbh Berlin, Callithumpian Consort, Boston, Britten Sinfonia, UK, SWR Stuttgart, Kammerakademie Potsdam and Heidelberger Frühling Festival. *Compositions include:* Drei Gesänge nach Ingeborg Bachmann, three songs 2002, String Quartet for strings and soprano solo 2003, Rain, keep on falling... for 2 violins, saxophone, trombone, and piano, Der Herr Gevatter, opera 2005, Agnus Dei for 12 part choir a capella 2005, String Quartet No. 2 2006, Paysage nocturne for orchestra 2006, Sine Nomine for 7 instruments 2007, Fabel for ensemble 2009, Konstruktionen der Dämmerung for percussion quartet 2010, Windinnres for string trio 2010, Die Versuchung des heiligen Antonius 2012. *Honours:* scholarships and fellowships from Studienstiftung des Deutschen Volkes, DAAD, Acad. for Contemporary Music Theatre/Deutsche Bank Foundation, Acad. of Fine Arts, Berlin, Künstlerhof Schreyahn, Harvard Univ.; Jury and Audience Prizes, Heidelberger Frühling Festival 2012, Ernst von Siemens Foundation Composers Award 2012. *Address:* Nollendorfstrasse 18, 10777 Berlin, Germany (home). *Telephone:* (151) 61021959 (home). *E-mail:* uakreppein@gmx.de (home). *Website:* www.ulrich-kreppein.de (home).

KRETH, Wolfgang, DipMus; German lutenist; b. 29 May 1946, Cologne. *Education:* Musikhochschule, Köln, Musikhochschule, Düsseldorf, Musikhochschule, Frankfurt, Musikhochschule, Aachen. *Career:* several concerts in Europe (Schwetzinger Festspiele, Musica Bayreuth, Dubrovnik-Festival,

Wiener Festwochen, Brühler Barock-Fest); radio broadcasts; mem. Lute Soc. of England, Lute Soc. of America, Soc. Nova Giulianiad, Freiburg, EGTA. *Recordings:* Lute Music of Anthony Holborne and Nicolas Vallet, Lute Concerto of Antonio Vivaldi. *Publications:* contrib. several articles to Gitarre und Laute, Köln.

KRETSCHMAR, Helmut; German singer (tenor); b. 3 Feb. 1928, Kleve; m. Renate Fischer. *Education:* studied in Frankfurt with Kurt Thomas and Hans Emge. *Career:* sang first in concerts and oratorios from 1953; at Hamburg 1954 sang in the first performance (concert) of Schoenberg's Moses und Aron; sacred music by Bach at the Berliner Festwochen and the Bach Festivals at Luneberg and Heidelberg 1960–62; further appearances at the Handel Festival at Göttingen, in Düsseldorf, and in Japan, Republic of Korea, France, Spain, India and the UK; lieder recitals with Renate Fischer, piano; repertoire includes sacred music by Handel, Haydn and Mendelssohn; songs by Wolf, Debussy, Schubert and Schumann; Prof., Detmold Musikhochschule from 1963. *Recordings include:* Fidelio; Moses and Aron, conducted by Hans Rosbaud; St Matthew Passion, Christmas Oratorio and B Minor Mass by Bach; Beethoven's Missa solemnis; Schubert's Mass in A flat; Die Jahreszeiten by Haydn. *Honours:* first prize German Music High Schools 1953, Kunstpreis of Nordrhein-Westfalen 1958.

KREUTER, Melanie; German singer (soprano); b. 24 Feb. 1963, Braunschweig. *Education:* studied in Hanover and with Ileana Cotrubas. *Career:* sang at Stuttgart Opera 1989–91, as Mozart's Susanna, Zerlina and Papagena; Aennchen in Der Freischütz and Lucilla in La Scala di Seta; Komische Oper Berlin from 1989, with guest appearances at Wiesbaden and Hannover; Dortmund Opera from 1992, as Mozart's Susanna, Pamina and Despina; Sophie in Der Rosenkavalier; sang in local premieres of Argento's The Voyage of Edgar Allan Poe and Casken's The Golem; many concert and lieder programmes.

KRIIKKU, Kari; Finnish clarinettist and teacher; *Artistic Director, Avanti! Chamber Orchestra. Education:* Sibelius Acad., Helsinki, and with Alan Hacker in England and Charles Neidich and Leon Russianoff in USA. *Career:* solo engagements with New York Philharmonic, Los Angeles Philharmonic, Leipzig Gewandhaus Orchestra, London Sinfonietta, Ensemble Intercontemporain, BBC Symphony Orchestra, Stockholm and Oslo Philharmonics, City of Birmingham Symphony Orchestra, Frankfurt Radio Symphony Orchestra and Toronto Symphony Orchestra; performed at Carnegie Hall with New York Philharmonic under Alan Gilbert, BBC Proms under Semyon Bychkov; chamber music with Arditti, New Helsinki, Avanti!, Borodin and Jean Sibelius Quartets; Artistic Dir Crusell Week, Uusikaupunki 1994–99; Artistic Dir Avanti! Chamber Orchestra 1998–; concertos written for him by Unsuk Chin, Kimmo Hakola, Magnus Lindberg, Jukka Tiensuu, Kaija Saariaho and Jouni Kaipainen; Prof. in Arts. *Recordings include:* A Due: Contemporary Duos for Clarinet and Cello, Molter and Mozart, Weber's Clarinet Concertos, Kimmo Hakola Clarinet Concerto (Janne Prize 2000), Crusell Clarinet Concertos, Mozart Jubilee, Kaija Saariaho Clarinet Concerto, Magnus Lindberg's Clarinet Concerto (BBC Music Magazine Award, Gramophone Awards Record of the Year for Contemporary Music 2006), Michel van der Aa: Hysteresis. *Honours:* Nordic Council Music Prize. *Address:* Avanti! Chamber Orchestra, Tallberginkatu 1 B 80, 00180 Helsinki, Finland (office). *Fax:* (9) 694-2208 (office). *E-mail:* kari.kriikku@uniarts.fi (office). *Website:* www .karikriikku.com.

KRIKORIAN, Mari; Bulgarian singer (soprano); b. 25 May 1946, Varna. *Education:* Secondary School of Music, Varna, Bulgarian State Conservatoire, Sofia, studied with James King in Vienna. *Career:* debut as Adalgisa in Norma, Varna Nat. Opera 1976; first soprano, Varna Nat. Opera, in La Bohème, Simon Boccanegra, Fliegende Holländer, Otello, Don Carlo and Tosca; first soprano, Sofia Nat. Opera 1983–; permanent repertoire includes Norman, Attila, Aida, Il Trovatore, La Forza del Destino, Don Carlos, Otello, La Bohème, Madama Butterfly, Tosca, Liu, Senta, Adriana Lecouvreur, Tatiana in Eugene Onegin, Lisa in Queen of Spades, Yaroslavna in Prince Igor, Verdi's Requiem, Donizetti's Requiem, Bruckner's Requiem, Brahms Deutsches Requiem, Liszt's Christus Oratorio, Rossini's Stabat Mater, Pergolesi's Stabat Mater; foreign tours to Czech Republic, Hungary, Russia, Armenia, Germany, Italy, France, Spain, Austria, Greece, Egypt, Cyprus, India, Mexico, USA. *Television:* film portrait for Bulgarian television 1989. *Recordings:* opera recital, airs from Bellini, Verdi and Puccini, with Sofia Opera Orchestra, conductor Ivan Marinov, State Recording Company Balkanton, 1984; Attila, by Verdi, with Sofia Philharmonic Orchestra, conductor Vladimir Ghiaurov, and with Nicola Guzelev; Chants Liturgiques Armeniens 1992; live and studio recordings for Bulgarian radio and television. *Honours:* first prize Opera Belcanto Competition, Ostende, Belgium 1980, Honoured Artist of Bulgaria 1984. *Address:* Druzba 2 bl 213 A, Ap 11, Sofia 1582, Bulgaria.

KRILOVICI, Marina; Romanian singer (soprano); b. 11 June 1942, Bucharest. *Education:* studied with Mme Vrabiescu-Varianu in Bucharest and with Matia Caniglia and Luigi Ricci in Rome. *Career:* debut at Nat. Opera Bucharest 1966, as Donna Anna; sang major roles in the Italian repertory with the Bucharest Opera; Covent Garden debut 1971, as Aida; Chicago Lyric Opera 1972, as Mimi; further appearances in Vienna, Berlin, Munich, Montréal, Lisbon, San Francisco and Strasbourg; Hamburg Staatsoper 1968–76; sang Adriana Lecouvreur at Athens 1998. *Recordings include:* Cavelleria Rusticana, Donizetti's Il Duca d'Alba.

KRINGELBORN, Solveig; Norwegian singer (soprano); b. 4 June 1963, Drøbak. *Education:* Stockholm Royal Acad. *Career:* regularly sought after opera and concert performer; particularly famed for her concert interpretation of Scandinavian music, especially works of Norwegian and Finnish composers; regularly works with conductors such as Mariss Jansons, Zubin Mehta, Sir Simon Rattle, Herbert Blomstedt, Neeme Järvi, Esa-Pekka Salonen, Claudio Abbado, Sir Neville Marriner and Sir Colin Davis; appearances have included the San Francisco Opera, La Monnaie in Brussels, the Liceu in Barcelona, Covent Garden, numerous performances at Metropolitan Opera, New York, Salzburg, Aix-en-Provence and Glyndebourne Festivals and with orchestras such as the Sydney Symphony Orchestra, Leipzig Gewandhaus and Israel Philharmonic; opera roles include Marschallin in Der Rosenkavalier for Norwegian Opera, Capriccio at Opera Nat. de Paris, Elsa in Lohengrin at La Scala, Milan 2007, Marschallin in Der Rosenkavalier, Bolshoi Theatre, Moscow 2013. *Recordings:* numerous recordings, including Grieg Songs conducted by Rozhdestvensky, a Grieg Solo Song and Tavener Choral Music conducted by David Hill. *Current Management:* c/o Simon Goldstone, Intermusica Artists Management Ltd, 36 Graham Street, Crystal Wharf, London, N1 8GJ, England. *E-mail:* sgoldstone@intermusica.co.uk.

KRISCAK, Manuela; Italian singer (soprano); b. 1965, Trieste. *Education:* G. Tartini Conservatoire, Trieste. *Career:* debut as Musetta in La Bohème at the Teatro Nuovo, Spoleto 1990; appearances as Tisbe in Cenerentola at Spoleto and Rome, Bianca in La Rondine and Zerlina at Catania; Gianetta in L'Elisir d'amore for French television, Un Plaisir in Gluck's Armide at La Scala 1996; sang Kristina in The Makropulos Case at Glyndebourne 1995–97, and at Strasbourg and Lisbon; season 1997–98 as Papagena (Die Zauberflöte) and in Paisiello's Il Barbiere di Siviglia at Trieste.

KRIVINE, Emmanuel; French violinist and conductor; *Music Director, Orchestre Philharmonique du Luxembourg;* b. 7 May 1947, Grenoble; s. of Henri Krivine and Rejla Krivine (née Weisbrod); one d. *Education:* Conservatoire Nat. Supérieur de Musique et de Danse, Conservatoire Royal de Bruxelles, pupil of Henryk Szeryng and Yehudi Menuhin;. *Career:* solo violinist, Paris 1964, Brussels 1965–68; Perm. Guest Conductor Radio-France 1976–83; Dir Lorraine-Metz Regional Orchestra 1981–83; Prin. Guest Conductor Orchestra of Lyon 1983; Music Dir Orchestre Français des Jeunes 1984–2004; Music Dir Nat. Orchestra of Lyon 1987–2000; Conductor French Nat. Orchestra 2001–; Co-founder and Prin. Conductor, La Chambre Philharmonique 2004–; Music Dir Orchestre Philharmonique du Luxembourg 2006–; Principal Guest Conductor, Barcelona Symphony Orchestra 2013–, Scottish Chamber Orchestra 2015–; guest conductor to various int. orchestras including Berlin Philharmonic, Philadelphia Orchestra, Nat. Symphony Orchestra, Washington, London Philharmonic, Mahler Chamber Orchestra, Concertgebouw and Chamber Orchestra of Europe 1977–. *Honours:* Chevalier, Ordre nat. du Mérite, Officier des Arts et Lettres; Ginette-Neveu Medal 1971 and numerous other awards. *Current Management:* Intermusica Artists Management Ltd, 36 Graham Street, Crystal Wharf, London, N1 8GJ, England. *Website:* www.opl.lu; www.lachambrephilharmonique.com; www .sco.org.uk.

KROLL, Mark, BA, MMus; American harpsichordist and academic; b. 13 Sept. 1946, Brooklyn, NY; m. Carol Lieberman 1975, one s. *Education:* Brooklyn Coll., CUNY, Yale Univ. School of Music. *Career:* debut at Carnegie Hall, New York 1975; performance in solo recitals, chamber music ensembles and as concerto soloist throughout Europe, South America, USA and Canada; radio and television broadcasts; numerous television shows for PBS and BBC; Prof. of Harpsichord and Theory and Chair of the Dept of Historical Performance, Boston Univ.; Conductor, orchestral works of Rameau, C.P.E. Bach, Vivaldi; Artist-in-Residence, Lafayette Coll.; Conductor and Artistic Dir, Opera New England; Visiting Prof., Würzburg Conservatory, Zagreb Music Acad. and Belgrade Music Acad.; Visiting Prof., Acads of Music at Warsaw, Kracow and Athens. *Recordings include:* J. S. Bach, complete sonatas for violin and harpsichord; Handel and Scarlatti, harpsichord works; G. F. Handel, complete works for recorder and harpsichord; Vivaldi's The Seasons, with Boston Symphony Orchestra; Solo Harpsichord works of J. S. Bach; Harpsichord works of J.N.P. Royer; Franz Schubert, three Sonatinas for violin and fortepiano; M. de Falla, El Retablo de Maese Pedro, with Montréal Symphony; Contemporary American Harpsichord Music; H. von Biber Sonatas of 1681. *Publications:* French Harpsichord Music 1994, 17th-Century Keyboard Music 1997, Beethoven Violin Sonatas 2002, Hummel Transcriptions 2001, 2002, Hummel's Piano Method 2003: contrib. to Early Music America Magazine 2001, 2002, articles for Bostonia magazine. *Honours:* NEA grant 1984, CIES grant 1989, Whiting Foundation grant 1993, DAAD grant 1996, 2002, IREX grant 1996, NEH grant 2002, Copland Fund grant 2001, 2002. *Address:* c/o Boston University School of Music, 855 Commonwealth Avenue, Boston, MA 02215, USA.

KROLOPP, Wojciech Aleksander; musician, artist manager and journalist; b. 12 April 1945, Poznań, Poland. *Education:* Academy of Music, Poznań. *Career:* debut as soloist soprano 1957; soloist baritone 1964; soloist from 1957 (soprano, bass from 1964); Teacher and Conductor, Polish Choir School, Poznan, 1968–; Managing Director, 1969–, Poznań Boys' Choir, and Director of International Boys' Choir Festival, Poznań, 1980–; 3000 concerts with the Poznań Boys' Choir, 400 conducted concerts in 24 countries; solo parts in major vocal-instrumental works and songs; Camerata, chamber orchestra, 1980–83; Premiere of Mozart opera, Bastien und Bastienne at the Great Theatre in Poznan also in Taiwan and Hong Kong; manager and artistic director of the Polish Nightingales. *Recordings:* Mozart's Coronation Mass and Szymanowski's Stabat Mater, 1991. *Publications include:* The Poznan Choir School, monography, 1989. *Address:* Torenstraat 13, 9160 Lokeren, Belgium.

KROSNICK, Aaron Burton, BA, MS; American violinist; b. 28 June 1937, New Haven, CT; m. Mary Lou Wesley 1961; one s. *Education:* Yale Coll., Juilliard School of Music, Royal Conservatory of Music, Brussels, Belgium, studied with Howard Boatwright, Joseph Fuchs, Ivan Galamian, Arthur Grumiaux. *Career:* Concertmaster (and soloist with orchestras), Springfield, Ohio, Symphony Orchestra 1962–67, Jacksonville Symphony Orchestra 1969–80, Sewanee Festival Orchestra 1969–82, Florida Bicentennial Chamber Orchestra 1976; faculty mem., Wittenberg Univ. 1962–67, Jacksonville Univ. 1967–, summers at Syracuse Univ., Kneisel Hall Summer School of Ensemble Playing, Sewanee Summer Music Centre; soloist with extensive concerto repertoire; appearances with Rome Festival Orchestra, Florida Symphony Chamber Orchestra, Jacksonville Univ. Orchestra and many others; summers of 1985–86, concertmaster and featured artist, Rome Festival, Italy. *Recordings:* Music of Frederick Delius, Musical Heritage Society. *Honours:* semi-finalist Paganini Int. Competition, Genoa 1970. *Address:* 13734 Bermuda Cay Court, Jacksonville, FL 32225-5426, USA. *E-mail:* abkmlk@hotmail.com.

KROSNICK, Joel, BA; American cellist; b. 3 April 1941, New Haven, CT. *Education:* Columbia Univ. and studied with William d'Amato, Luigi Silva and Claus Adam. *Career:* co-founder and Dir, Group for Contemporary Music, Columbia Univ. 1962; Prof., Univ. of Iowa 1963–66, cellist in Univ. String Quartet; Prof., Univ. of Massachusetts 1966–70, performed with New York Chamber Soloists and made solo tours to Belgrade, Hamburg, Berlin, London and Amsterdam; performances as sonata duo with Gilbert Kalish 1976–; solo debut, New York 1970; has given first performances of works by Babbitt, Subotnick and Ligeti; teacher, California Inst. of Arts 1970–74; Cellist, Juilliard String Quartet 1974–; faculty mem., Juilliard School 1974–, Chair., Cello Dept 1994–; worldwide tours in the standard repertoire and contemporary works; performances in London 1990, of works by Mozart. *Recordings include:* with Juilliard String Quartetcomplete quartets of Beethoven, Bartók, Schoenberg, Janacek, Hindemith, Brahms, ten Mozart quartets, four Elliott Carter quartets, works of Haydn, Debussy, Ravel, Duttilleux, Berg, Smetana, Franck, Mendelssohn, Shostakovich, Verdi, Sibelius, Bach, Roger Session, Donald Martino, Stefan Wolpe; with Gilbert Kalish: In the Shadow of World War I, In the Shadow of World War II, Brahms' Sonatas; solo: Artur Schnabel's Sonata for Solo Cello, Roger Sessions' Six Pieces for Solo Cello. *Honours:* Dr hc (Michigan State Univ.), (Jacksonville Univ.), (San Francisco Conservatory of Music); Chevalier du Violoncelle Award, Eva Janzer Memorial Cello Center, Indiana Univ., two Grammy Awards (with Juilliard String Quartet). *Address:* Music Division, The Juilliard School, 60 Lincoln Center Plaza, New York, NY 10023-6588, USA (office). *Website:* www.juilliard.edu (office); www.juilliardstringquartet.org.

KRUGER, Anna; American violist; b. 1965. *Education:* Manhattan School of Music, Indiana Univ. with James Buswell. *Career:* fmr principal, New Jersey Symphony; co-founder, Lark String Quartet, New York; concert tours to Australia, Taiwan, Hong Kong, People's Republic of China, Germany and The Netherlands; US appearances at the Lincoln Center, New York, Kennedy Center, Washington, DC and in Boston, Los Angeles, Philadelphia, St Louis and San Francisco; repertoire includes quartets by Haydn, Mozart, Beethoven, Schubert, Dvořák, Brahms, Borodin, Bartók, Debussy and Shostakovich; concerts at the Wigmore Hall, London 1994. *Honours:* gold medal Naumberg Competition (with Lark Quartet) 1990, Premio Paulio Borciani 1990, Reggio Emilia Competition 1990, Karl Klinger Competition, Munich 1990, Shostakovich Competition (with Lark Quartet) 1991, prizewinner London Int. String Quartet Competition 1991, Melbourne Chamber Music Competition 1991.

KRUGLOV, Jurij; singer (bass); b. 1960, Sevastopol, Ukraine. *Education:* Tchaikovsky Acad., Kiev. *Career:* appearances at the Sevtchenko Opera Theatre, Kiev; Nat. Theatre, Prague and Estates Theatre 1989, notably as Masetto and the Commendatore in Don Giovanni, conducted by Charles Mackerras; guest appearances at Odessa, St Petersburg and Ostrava; festivals of Savonlinna, Wexford and Macerata; concerts in France, Germany, Russia, the Czech Republic and Slovakia.

KRUMM, Philip Edwin; American composer and writer; b. 7 April 1941, Baltimore, Md. *Education:* studied orchestration and composition with Raymond Moses, at St Mary's Univ. with Frank Sturchio, Univ. of Michigan with Ross Lee Finney, Univ. of California, Davis with Karlheinz Stockhausen. *Career:* produced early concert series of major modern works at McNay Art Inst., San Antonio 1960–61; performer and composer at ONCE Festival, Ann Arbor, Mich. 1962–64; concert producer, HemisFair 1968; managed own production co. and two rock bands 1967–69; miscellaneous works for dance productions; f. Clipper Ship Book Store, San Antonio 1982–. *Exhibition:* month-long show of scores, astrological art, assemblages at San Antonio Museum of Modern Art 1979. *Radio:* presenter, Musica Nova, Texas Public Radio 1986–96. *Television includes:* Music Hour (with Jerry Hunt) 1964, Sampler (with Robert Wilson) 1964. *Compositions include:* Into the Pines for electronic instruments, The Gabrieli Thing for electronic instruments, Axis, Mumma Mix, Paragenesis for two violins and piano 1959, Music for Clocks 1962, Formations 1962, Concerto for saxophone 1964, Sound Machine 1966, Concerto for bass clarinet 1972, Farewell to LA (electronic theatre) 1975,

Secret Pleasures (dance suite) 1988–89, No Time At All for electronic instruments 1989, Banshee Fantasia (commissioned by Bay Area Pianists for 100th anniversary of Henry Cowell's birth) 1997. *Film soundtrack:* Angel of God (short film). *Publication:* Music Without Notes 1962. *Honours:* Pres.'s Award Fund Grant, Univ. of Michigan 1962. *Address:* 103 Erskine Place, San Antonio, TX 78201-2638, USA (home). *Telephone:* (210) 733-1008 (home). *E-mail:* clippershipbooks@worldshare.net (office).

KRUMMACHER, Friedhelm Gustav-Adolf, DPhil; German academic; b. 22 Jan. 1936, Berlin; m. Aina Maria Landfeldt 1964; one s. one d. *Education:* studied in Berlin, Marburg and Uppsala, Sweden, Free Univ. of Berlin. *Career:* Asst 1965, Private Docent 1973, Erlangen-Nurnberg Univ.; Prof., Musikhochschule Detmold 1975; Prof., Dir, Musicological Inst., Univ. of Kiel 1976–2001, in charge of Brahms Gesamtausgabe, Buxtehude Collected Works; Leipziger Mendelssohnausgabe; mem. Vetenskapssocietet Lund, Sweden, Akad. der Wissenschaften, Hamburg, Norwegian Acad., Royal Swedish Acad. of Music; corresponding mem. American Musicological Soc. 2007–. *Publications:* Die Überlieferung... 1965, Mendelssohn der Komponist 1978, Die Choralbearbeitung... 1978, Mahlers III Symphonie 1991, Bachs Jahrgang der Choralkantaten 1995, Musik im Norden 1996, Bachs Weg in der Arbeit am Werk 2001, Das Streichquartett Vol.I 2001, Vol. II 2003, Festschrift: Rezeption als Innovation (ed. S. Oechsle et al) 2001, Geschichte des Streichquartetts Vol. I–III 2005, Kieler Schriften zur Musikwissenschaft Vols 22–50 (ed.) 1978–2004, Schütz-Jahrbuch (co-ed); contrib. On Mendelssohn's Oratorios in, The Mendelssohn Companion 2001; contrib. about 200 articles in Archiv für Musikwissenschaft, Die Musikforschung, Kongressberichte, Festschriften. *Honours:* Hon. mem. Humboldt Universität, Berlin 1994–, Gesellschaft für Musikforschung 2008–; Dr hc (Uppsala) 2001. *Address:* Wippen 1, 24107 Kiel 1, Germany (home).

KRUSE, Tone; Norwegian singer (contralto); b. 1958, Oslo. *Education:* Oslo Music High School. *Career:* sang at Oslo Opera 1982–85, then at Cologne Opera; roles have included Gluck's Orpheus, Magdalene in Die Meistersinger, Margaret in Wozzeck, Suzuki in Madama Butterfly, Zulma in L'Italiana in Algeri, Mother Goose in The Rake's Progress; sang Erda in Das Rheingold 1996, and again at Norwich, on tour with the Norwegian Nat. Opera 1998; frequent guest appearances in opera and concert throughout Germany. *Recordings:* The Maiden in the Tower, Sibelius.

KRUTIKOV, Mikhail; Russian singer (bass); b. 23 Aug. 1958, Moscow. *Education:* Moscow State Conservatory and the Opera Studio of Bolshoi Opera, 1982–85; further studies with Evgeni Nesterenko. *Career:* appearances with Bolshoi Opera, 1985–, as Boris Godunov, Pimen, Mephistopheles, Basilio, Mendosa in Prokofiev's The Duenna and Dunua in The Maid of Orleans by Tchaikovsky; Sang in La Straniera and La cena delle Beffe at Wexford Festival, and with the Bolshoi Company on tour to England, 1990; Season 1991–92 as the Inquisitor in Prokofiev's The Fiery Angel at the Prom Concerts, London, The Love for Three Oranges at Florence, the Commendatore in Dargomizhsky's Stone Guest at Salzburg and as King Philip in Don Carlos at the Deutsche Oper Berlin; Concert engagements at Queen Elizabeth Hall, London, Shostakovich's 14th Symphony in Vancouver and Lausanne, the Verdi Requiem and Tchaikovsky's Moscow Cantata at the Salle Pleyel, Prokofiev's Ivan the Terrible in Rome and Elijah at Düsseldorf. *Recordings include:* Holofernes in Serov's Judith, Saison Russe; The Gamblers by Shostakovich. *Address:* c/o Bolshoi Opera, Bolshoi Theatre, 1 Teatraknaya Square, 125009 Moscow, Russia.

KRYSA, Oleh; Ukrainian/American violinist; b. 1 June 1942, Lublin, Poland; m. Tatiana Tchekina 1966, three s. *Education:* Lviv Musical School, Ukraine and Moscow Conservatory with David Oistrakh. *Career:* debut in Lviv, Ukraine, 1958; Professor of Violin, Kiev Conservatory, Moscow Conservatory, Manhattan School of Music; Eastman School of Music; Solo Recital Tours in USSR, Europe, North America, Far East, Australia, New Zealand; First Violin, Beethoven String Quartet, Moscow; Soloist with Symphony Orchestras of Moscow, Leningrad, Kiev, Berlin, Leipzig, Dresden, Stuttgart, Warsaw, Prague, Budapest, Bucharest, Belgrade, Torino, London, Stockholm, Bergen, New York, Chicago, Washington, Wellington, Cape Town. *Recordings:* Mozart Concertos Nos 3 and 5; Bruch Scottish Fantasy; Viotti No. 22; Tchaikovsky; Wieniawski No. 1; Schnittke Nos 3 and 4; Shostakovich No. 1; Prokofiev No. 1; Works for Violin and Piano by Beethoven, Brahms, Paganini, Wieniawski, Ravel, Debussy, Poulenc, Franck, Dvořák, Elgar, Delius, Walton, Szymanowski, Prokofiev, Bartók, Schulhoff, Berio, Schnittke; String quartets by Beethoven, Brahms, Arensky; Shostakovich, Berg, Schnittke, String Sextet, Souvenirs de Florence, by Tchaikovsky; Beethoven Violin Concerto; Tchaikovsky Piano Trio. *Honours:* Wieniawski Competition 2nd Prize, 1962; Paganini Competition 1st Prize, 1963; Tchaikovsky Competition 3rd Prize, 1966; Montreal Competition 2nd Prize, 1969; Outstanding Artist of Ukrainian Republic, 1970. *Address:* c/o Christa Damestoy, 291 Rolling Oaks Street, Augustin, FL 32086, USA (office). *E-mail:* cdamestoy@aol.com. *Website:* www .olehkrysa.com.

KRYSTEVA, Neva; Bulgarian composer, organist and academic; *Professor of Music, National Academy of Music;* b. 2 Aug. 1946, Sofia; d. of Venelin Krystev and Luba Obretenova. *Education:* Moscow Conservatory, studied in Prague and Zürich. *Career:* Lecturer, Sofia State Acad. 1974–; Founder of Bulgaria's organ school; organ teacher, New Bulgarian Univ.; Prof. of Music, Nat. Acad. of Music. *Compositions include:* Mythological Songs for Soprano and Ensemble 1976, The Old Icon for Low Voice and Organ 1987, Apokriff, cantata 1989,

Quantus Tremor, cantata for mezzo-soprano, trumpet, organ and cello 1989, Missa Angelus for female chorus 1991, Oboe Sonatina 1991, Reflections, for low voice and piano 1994, Obretenov's Requiem for contralto, chorus and organ 1995, Sonata da chiesa for flute and organ 1996, Tebe odeyushagosia for male choir and organ 1998, In Memorias Exire for piano, organ and percussion 1998, The Summit for 12-voice choir and organ 1998, Hussite choral on the Stake for organ and eurhythmist 2002. *Publications:* Contrapunctus et Compositio (Aspects of Polyphonic Composition) 2001, Music Theory Research (three vols) 2001. *Honours:* Bulgarian Composers Union Citation 1986, 1996. *Address:* National Academy of Music, Sofia 1505, 94 Evlogy & Hristo Georgiev Blvd, Bulgaria (office). *E-mail:* nevakryst@yahoo.com (office).

KRZANOWSKA, Grażyna; Polish composer; b. 1 March 1952, Legnica. *Education:* studied in Wrocław. *Career:* teacher at the Bielsko-Biala Music School. *Compositions include:* Melodies, cantata, 1975; Passacaglia for Orchestra, 1976; Drumroll Symphony, 1978; Bonfires for 2 Voices and Chamber Ensemble, 1979; String Quartet No. 2, 1980; The Little Choral Symphony, 1985; Silver Line for 15 Strings, 1991. *Honours:* prizewinner Karol Szymanowski Competition 1988. *Address:* c/o Society of Authors ZAiKS, 2 Hipoteczna Street, 00 092 Warsaw, Poland. *Telephone:* (4822) 828 17 05. *Fax:* (4822) 828 13 47. *E-mail:* sekretariat@zaiks.org.pl. *Website:* www.zaiks.org.pl.

KUBIAK, Teresa, BA, MA; Polish singer (soprano); b. 26 Dec. 1937, Łódź. *Education:* Łódź Music Acad. with Olga Olgina. *Career:* debut at Music Festival in Łódź, Amelia in Amelia al Ballo; Grand Opera Theatre Łódź as Michaela in Carmen 1967; appeared in the 1969 world premiere of The Story of St John and Herod by Twardowski; other roles at Łódź, Aida, Tosca, Lohengrin 1970; US debut at Carnegie Hall 1970 as Shulamith in Goldmark's Die Königin von Saba; Glyndebourne Festival 1971 as Lisa in The Queen of Spades and Juno in La Calisto by Cavalli-Leppard; Covent Garden 1972 as Madama Butterfly and Metropolitan Opera from 1973 as Lisa, Jenůfa, Giorgietta in Il Tabarro, Tosca, Elsa in Lohengrin, Eva in Meistersinger and Elisabeth in Tannhäuser; appearances in San Francisco, Chicago, Houston, Seattle, Miami, Leipzig, Prague, Warsaw, Venice, Barcelona, Madrid, Lisbon, Munich, Vienna, Paris Opéra, Rome, Canada, Bulgaria, United Arab Emirates, People's Republic of China, The Philippines, Georgia; other roles include Ariadne, Euryanthe, Halka, Senta, Tatiana, Chrysothemis in Elektra, Leonore in Fidelio and Ellen Orford; many recitals and orchestra appearances; Prof. of Music/Voice, Indiana Univ. School of Music, Bloomington, Indiana 1990–; judging nat. and int. vocal competitions. *Recordings include:* Operatic Arias–Muza, 14 Symphonies-Shostakovich, Glagolitic Mass, La Calisto, Eugene Onegin, Euryanthe Elektra, Strauss, Fidelio, Beethoven. *Honours:* Cross of Knight, Polish Govt 1975; Nat. Opera Competition, Katowice 1960, Int. Music Competition, Toulouse, France 1963, Int. Music Competition, Munich, Germany 1965. *Address:* 2912 Dale Court, Bloomington, IN 47401, USA.

KUBICKA, Vitazoslav; Slovak composer, music broadcasting editor and dramaturg; b. 11 Oct. 1953, Bratislava, Czechoslovakia; m. Gabriela Jurolekova 1988; one s. one d. *Education:* Univ. of Music, Bratislava. *Career:* debut, Rostrum of Composers, UNESCO, Paris 1982; mem. Union of Slovak Composers. *Compositions include:* orchestral: Dramatic Overture for Large Orchestra 1980, Concerto for Piano and Orchestra 1984, Maturing, Overture for Orchestra 1984, Fantasy for Violoncello and Large Orchestra 1985; chamber opuses: Fantasy for Flute and Piano 1979, Quintet for Clarinet, Violin, Viola, Violoncello and Piano 1982, Winter, Sonata for Piano 1986; choral: Fugue for Children's Choir 1982; electro-acoustic: Dedicated to Mussorgsky 1981, Satyr and Nymph 1985; for children and youth: Five Stories for Piano 1982, 1985, Harpsichord Concerto 1986, Bass Clarinet Concerto 1989, Autumn Music for violin and strings 1990, Hedge By the Danube for accordion 1990, Way, electro-acoustic 1991, 30 Biblical Songs and Choirs 1990–2003, Gospel according to St Luke, opera to the Biblical text 2000, Born Again, opera to the Biblical text 2003, Danube Requiem for soprano, bass, mixed choir, three trombone, timpani 2004; incidental music for radio (130 pieces), television (20 pieces), film (12 pieces), theatre and video. *Honours:* Slovak Music Fund of Bratislava Jan Levoslav Bella Prize 1988, Prix Critique Radiomagazin Bratislava 1989. *Address:* Drotarska 9, 81102 Bratislava, Slovakia.

KUBIK, Ladislav, PhD; Czech composer; b. 26 Aug. 1946, Prague; m. Natalie Bartosevicova 1974; one s. one d. *Education:* Prague Acad. of Music. *Career:* Music Dir, Czechoslovak Radio Prague 1979–83; Gen. Sec., Union of Czech Composers and Concert Artists 1983–. *Compositions:* symphonic works: Symphony 1970, Drammatic Toccata 1972, Concerto for piano and orchestra 1974, Hommage a Majakowski 1976, Concerto for violin and orchestra 1980; choral works: Songs of Hope 1982: chamber-cantat: Lament of a Warrior's Wife 1974; radio opera: Solaris 1975; ballet: Song of Man 1984; vocal symphony works: February 1973, Wolkeriana 1982, To the Earth of Future 1985; songs with orchestra: Words; chamber music: two String Quartets 1981, 1986, Trio Concertante 1983, Duo Concertante, Concerto Grosso 1987, Divertimento for eight wind instruments 1988, Symphony No. 2 1993, Harpsichord Concerto 1995, The River in Spring for mezzo and percussion 1997, In Night for baritone and ensemble 1997, Piano Concerto 1999, Sinfonietta 1999. *Address:* Na Brezince 6, 150 00 Prague 5, Czech Republic.

KUBIK, Reinhold, PhD; Austrian musicologist, pianist, composer and choirmaster; b. 22 March 1942, Vienna; one s. one d. *Education:* Humanistic Coll., Vienna II, Univ. Erlangen-Nuremberg, Germany, Hochschule für Musik, Vienna with Hans Swarowsky. *Career:* Conductor Deutsche Oper am Rhein, Düsseldorf/Duisburg and many European cities, including Lille, Barcelona, Ljubljana 1966–74; Lecturer 1980; Proprietor, Hänssler Musik Verlag, Kirchheim, Germany 1980–90; Visiting Prof., Yale Univ., USA 1987; Production Man., Universal Edition, Vienna 1992–97; Chief Ed. Gustav Mahler Gesamtausgabe, Wiener Urtext Edn; teacher of period acting techniques in Vienna, London, Karlsruhe and Michaelstein; Ed. all Bach Cantatas for John Eliot Gardiner's project Bach Cantata Pilgrimage; Vice-Pres. Int. Gustav Mahler Soc., Vienna –2012. *Exhibitions:* curator of three major Mahler exhbns: Jewish Museum, Vienna 2005, Austrian Theatre Museum, Vienna 2010, German Theatre Museum, Munich 2011. *Publications:* Handel's Rinaldo 1980, some 120 edns, including 80 cantatas by J. S. Bach (Hänssler), EdM 96, 106 and 110, Schubert, Lazarus (Neue Schubert Ausgabe II/10); Handel, Arianna in Creta; Mahler, 5th, 6th and 7th Symphonies and Das Klagende Lied (three-movement version); contrib. to Festschrift Arnold Feil 1985, K. B. Stuttgart 1985, Festschrift Martin Ruhnke 1986, Veröffentlichungen der International, Handel-Akademie Karlsruhe (Vols 2–4, 7), Handel-Symposium Halle 1989, Musikinstrumente und Musizierpraxis zur Zeit Gustav Mahlers 2007, Mahlers Welt. Die Orte seines Lebens 2011; catalogues for the Mahler Exhbns in Vienna 2005, 2010 and Munich 2011. *Address:* Liechtensteinstrasse 39/6, 1090 Vienna, Austria. *E-mail:* reinhold.kubik@chello.at.

KUBO, Yoko, BA, MA; composer, pianist and academic; b. 5 Dec. 1956, Nishinomiya, Japan. *Education:* Osaka Coll. of Music, Univ. of Paris, France. *Career:* debut in 1979; many concerts of her compositions in Japan and France 1979–; Lecturer, Osaka Coll. of Music 1981–; Assoc., Institute de Recherche Co-ordination Acoustique/Musique, Paris, France 1984–. *Compositions:* La Sensation de Vingtième Siecle for 12 percussionists 1977, Collage for orchestra 1978, Objet for two pianos and percussions 1979, Play for violin, violoncello and piano 1979, Crossword for piano 1980, Mon parc for string orchestra 1980, Quatuor à Cordes No. 2 1980, Concerto pour violon No. 1 1981, Puzzle for three marimbas 1981, On the Tree for soprano, eight voices and piano 1981, Chikya ni hajimete yuki ga futta hi no koto for soprano, eight voices and piano 1981, Quatuor à Cordes No. 3 1981, Concerto pour orgue, quatre cuivres et percussions 1981, Livre Illustré des chats for string orchestra 1982, ...SONG... for five voices and piano 1982, Quatuor à Cordes No. 4 1982, Paysage for flute, percussion and piano 1983, Quatuor pour flute, hautbois, violon et violoncelle 1983, Quintette pour piano No. 1 1983, Marche du roi (extract from Le Roi Nu) for string orchestra 1984, Espace for 11 players 1985, Vision for piano 1987, Concerto pour sept interprètes 1987.

KUČERA, Václav, PhDr, CSc; Czech composer and musicologist; *Professor of Composition and New Music Technology, Academy of Performing Arts, Prague;* b. 29 April 1929, Prague; m. Marie Jerieová 1951; two s. *Education:* Charles Univ. Prague, Tchaikovsky Conservatory in Moscow with Vissarion Shebalin, L. Mazel, V. Zuckerman, N. Tumanina. *Career:* Music Dept of Radio Prague 1956–59; Cabinet for New Music Studies, 1959–62; Inst. of Musicology 1962–69; Gen. Sec. Union of Czech Composers and Concert Artists 1969–83; Teacher of Composition, Music Faculty, Acad. for Performing Arts, Prague 1972–, Professor 1988–; mem. Union of Czech Composers 1957–69, Union of Czech Composers and Concert Artists 1969–89, Soc. of Czech Composers 1990–; Pres. Int. Prague Spring Festival 1988–92; mem. Exec. Cttee Int. Soc. for Contemporary Music 1978–1982, European Asscn of Conservatoires, Acads de Musique et Musikhochschulen 1992–98; mem. Supervisor Bd Soc. for Performance and Mechanical Rights of Composers, Authors and Publrs 1994–. *Compositions include:* Dramas for 9 Instruments 1961, Symphony for large Orchestra 1962, Protests 1963, Blue Planet, male chorus on M. Červanka 1964, The Pied Piper 1964, Hic Sunt Homines, a cycle for Piano quartet 1965, Genesis 1965, Spectra, for dulcimer 1965, Diptychon 1966, Duodrama 1967, "To be" 1968, Panta rhei 1969, Invariant 1969, Tableau 1970, Scenario 1970, Argot 1970, Diario 1971, Taboo a Due Boemi 1972, Salut 1975, Orbis Pictus 1975, Amoroso 1975, Consciousness of Continuities 1976, Aphorisms 1978, Horizons 1978, Epigrams 1978, Catharsis 1979, Science Fiction 1980, Rosen für Rosa 1980, Aquarelles 1981, Capriccios 1983, Cardiograms 1983, Bird 1983, Nouvelles 1984, Ballad and Romance 1984, Eruptions 1984, Gogh's Self Portrtait 1985, Bitter and Other Songs 1985, A Serious Hour 1986, Prague Ritornelles 1986, Duettinos 1988, Consonanza 1990, Celebrations of Phantasy 1991, Oraculum 1992, Tuning 1994, Concierto Imaginativo 1994, Guitariana 1996, Invocation of Joy 1996, Criterion for orchestra 1997, Intimate Conversations 1998, Mimesis, for dulcimer and harp 1998, Metathesis 1998, Satiricon De Creatione 1999, Mysterious Players 2000, Pax imago vitae 2000, Cryptoblues 2000, Two Sonnets on Shakespeare 2000, When We Two Parted 2001, Drei Frauenchöre mit Epitaf auf Gedichte von R.M.Rilke 2002, Cum Grano Lorca 2001, Saxonata 2002, Esta noche 2002, Imagination 2003, O Lebent, Wunderliche Zeit, Liederzylclus on Rilke 2004, When: a Melodrama on Shakespeare 2004, Elegiaco Appassionato for viola 2005, Romanetto for harp and cello 2005, Burlesca for violin and piano 2006, Vibration, chamber melodrama on V.Holan 2006, Touches, suite for dulcimer 2006, Hidden Light for bass clarinet 2007, Whirlwind-Pseudowaltz for bass clarinet and piano 2007, Sketch for clarinet and piano 2009; electro-acoustic compositions: Kinetic Ballet 1968, Kinechromia 1969, Lidice 1972, Spartacus 1976. *Publications:* M. P. Mussorgsky – Music of Life 1959, Talent, Mastery, World Outlook 1962, New Trends in Soviet Music 1967, S. Volkov, Testimony: Memoires of Shostakovich (trans.) 2005; musicological studies, radio and TV lectures. *Honours:* Prize of Queen Marie-José, Geneva 1970, Prix d'Italia, Rome 1972, Prize of Czech Radio Prague 1977, Prize of Czech Trade Unions,

Prague 1977, Prize of Union of Czech Composers and Concert Artists, Prague 1983, Trentino International Prize 1994, Prize of Canary Islands 2002, Int. Valašské Meziříčí Prize 2006. *Address:* Jizni II, 778, 141 00 Prague 4, Czech Republic (home). *Telephone:* 272766326 (home). *Fax:* 272766326 (home). *E-mail:* vac.kuc@tiscali.cz (home). *Website:* www.musica.cz/comp/kucera.htm (home).

KUDELA, Irene; French pianist; b. 1965. *Education:* studied in Prague and at Paris Conservatoire. *Career:* vocal coach at Glyndebourne Festival from 1997 (The Makropulos Case 2001); other engagements at Philadelphia, New York, Rome, Washington, Helsinki, Budapest, Orange, Salzburg and Paris (Châtelet and Opéra Bastille); Assistant to Mstislav Rostropovich 1985–88, in Europe and USA; Associate Chorus Master at Opéra National de Paris 1999; Season 2001–02 with Dialogues des Carmélites at Gothenberg. *Recordings:* Albums for Erato, Hungaroton and Teldec. *Address:* c/o Göteborgs Operan, Christina Nilssons Gata, 411 04 Göteborg, Sweden.

KUDRIASCHOV, Vladimir; Russian singer (tenor); b. 1947. *Education:* Gnessin Conservatory, Moscow. *Career:* sang at the Stanislavsky Theatre in Moscow, 1971–83, then at the Bolshoi Theatre; roles have included Sobinin in Glinka's Life for the Tsar, Shuisky in Boris Godunov, Count Almaviva, Rodolfo and Sergei in Lady Macbeth of Mtsensk; guest at Edinburgh in 1991 as Diak in Christmas Eve by Rimsky-Korsakov.

KUDRIAVCHENKO, Katerina; Russian singer (soprano); b. 2 March 1958, Karpnsk, Sverdlovskaya; m. Paolo Kudriavchenko. *Education:* Tchaikovsky Conservatoire, Moscow. *Career:* member of Bolshoi Opera, 1986–, as Iolanta, Tatiana, Agnes Sorell in The Maid of Orleans, Marfa in The Tsar's Bride, Gilda, Antonida in A Life for the Tsar, Lisa in The Queen of Spades, Prokofiev's The Duenna, Rachmaninov's Francesca, Violetta, Mimi, Liu and Oxsana in Rimsky's Christmas Eve; Western debut as Iolanta at La Scala, 1989; Season 1990–91 with Bolshoi Opera on tour to Spain, Italy, USA (Metropolitan), Japan and Glasgow, Scotland; Freelance Artist debut as Tatiana for New Israel Opera Company at Tel-Aviv, 1992; Season 1992–93 as Mimi with Scottish Opera, Liu and Titania at the Bolshoi; Sang Butterfly at Bologna, 1996. *Honours:* Gold Medallist, Madama Butterfly Competition, Miami, 1990. *Address:* c/o Bolshoi Opera, Bolshoi Theatre, 1 Teatraknaya Square, 125009 Moscow, Russia.

KUDRIAVCHENKO, Paolo; Russian singer (tenor); b. 12 Aug. 1952, Odessa, Crimea; m. Katerina Kudriavchenko. *Education:* Tchaikovsky Conservatory, Odessa. *Career:* sang first with Odessa Opera, then Kiev Opera; Bolshoi Opera, Moscow, 1984–, in Rimsky's Invisible City of Kitezh and as Canio, Turiddu, Dimitri in Boris Godunov, Don José and Jéromir in Mlada; Sang Sobinin in A Life for the Tsar with the Bolshoi Company at La Scala and made US debut, 1989, as Manrico for Greater Miami Opera (repeated for Omaha Opera, 1991), as Turiddu and Dimitri; Season 1991–92 as Turiddu at Munich Staatsoper and as Ernani for Welsh National Opera, followed by Manrico for Scottish Opera, Ishmaele in Nabucco at Bregenz Festival, 1993, and Canio at Rouen; season 1993–94 as Calaf and Radames at the Bolshoi; Many concert appearances. *Address:* c/o Bolshoi Opera, Bolshoi Theatre, 1 Teatraknaya Square, 125009 Moscow, Russia.

KUDRYA, Alexey; Russian singer (tenor) and musician (flute); b. 1982, s. of Vladimir Leonidovich Kudrya. *Education:* Russian Acad. of Music. *Career:* appearances include: Neue Stimmen 2005, Galina Vishnevskaya Int. Opera Singers Competition 2006; performances include Count Almaviva in The Barber of Seville, State Theatre of Bern, Switzerland 2008, Ferrando in Così fan tutte, Vlaamse Opera House, Netherlands 2009; current engagement at Stanislavsky Opera. *Honours:* as flautist: First Prize and Potential of the Nation Award, Romance 2003 Competition, Moscow 2003, as tenor: Iris Adami Corradetti Int. Competition of Opera Singing 2007, Special Prize from Hungarian State Opera and First Prize Winner, Operalia Plácido Domingo World Opera Competition, Hungary 2009. *Address:* Stanislavsky and Nemirovich-Danchenko Moscow Music Theatre, 17 Moscow, B. Dmitrovka, Russia (office). *Website:* www.stanmus.com (office).

KUEBLER, David; American singer (tenor); b. 23 July 1947, Detroit, MI. *Education:* Elmhurst Coll.; studied with Thomas Peck in Chicago. *Career:* sang in the chorus of the Chicago Opera; solo career with the Santa Fe Opera from 1972; European debut as Tamino in The Magic Flute, Berne Opera 1974; sang Mozart and bel canto roles with Cologne Opera; repertoire includes Ferrando in Così fan tutte, the Steersman in Der fliegende Holländer, Don Ottavio in Don Giovanni, Rodolfo in La Bohème, Pinkerton in Madama Butterfly, Lionel in Martha, Jacquino in Fidelio, Paolino in Il Matrimonio Segreto, Giannetto in La Gazza Ladra, Ernesto in Don Pasquale, Nemorino in L'Elisir d'Amore, Flamand in Capriccio, Almaviva in La Cambiale di Matrimonio, Doric in La Scala di Seta, in Dvořák's The Spectre's Bride, Boris in Katya Kabanova, Alwa in Lulu, Andres in Wozzeck, Stefa in Jenůfa, Albert Gregor in Vec Makropoulos, Henri in Les Vêpres Siciliennes, Matteo in Arabella, title roles in Lucio Silla, Il Cambiale di Matrimonio, Il Signor Bruschino, Der Zwerg, Faust; has made appearances at Seattle Opera, Santa Fe Opera, Opera Company of Philadelphia, Washington Opera, Lyric Opera of Chicago, Metropolitan Opera, also in Sydney, Bern, Rome, Parma, La Scala Milan, Venice, Frankfurt, Hamburg, Cologne, Zürich, Munich, Paris, Vienna, Bayreuth Festival, Glyndebourne Festival, Salzburg Festival, Edinburgh Festival, International Rossini Festival of Pesaro, Bregenz Festival. *Recordings include:* Mitridate re di Ponto by Mozart, Fidelio, La Scala di Seta (video), Zeminsky's Vocal and Orchestral Works 2008, Idomeneo (video, as Idamante)

2009. *Honours:* Hon. DMus (Elmhurst Coll.) 1987. *Address:* c/o EMI Classics, 27 Wrights Lane, London, W8 5SW, England (office). *Telephone:* (20) 7795-7000 (office). *Website:* www.emiclassics.com (office).

KUENTZ, Paul; French conductor; b. 4 May 1930, Mulhouse; m. Monique Frasca-Colombier 1956. *Education:* Paris Conservatoire with Noel Gallon, Georges Hugon and Eugene Bigot. *Career:* founder, Paul Kuentz Chamber Orchestra 1951, with many tours of Europe and the USA, including the orchestral works of Bach at Saint-Severin and concert at Carnegie Hall 1968; frequent performances of French music, including premieres of works by P. M. Dubois, J. Casterede and J. Charpentier; founder, Paul Kuentz Chorus 1972. *Recordings include:* Bach's Orchestral Suites, Mass in B Minor and Musikalisches Opfer; Vivaldi's Four Seasons, and other concertos; Flute Concertos by Haydn, Blavet, Mozart, Leclair and Pergolesi; Music by Delalande, Mouret, Gabrieli and Gluck; Mozart's Concerto K299, Requiem, Bastien und Bastienne and Church Sonatas; Harp concertos by Handel, Albrechtsberger, Boieldieu, Wagenseil and Dittersdorf; Haydn Symphonies Nos 85 and 101.

KUERTI, Anton Emil, BM, DipMus, OC; Canadian pianist and composer; b. 21 July 1938, Vienna, Austria; s. of Gustav Kuerti and Rosa Jahoda; m. Kristine Bogyo 1973; two s. *Education:* Cleveland Inst. of Music, Curtis Inst. of Music. *Career:* soloist, New York Philharmonic, Cleveland Orchestra, Detroit Symphony, Philadelphia Orchestra, St Louis Symphony, San Francisco Symphony, Denver Symphony, 41 appearances with Toronto Symphony, National Arts Centre Orchestra (Ottawa), Dresden Staatskapelle, Leipzig Gewandhaus, London Symphony; tours worldwide, including Soviet Union, Far East, Australia, New Zealand, Latin America; numerous television appearances, radio broadcasts; founder, Festival of Sound, Parry Sound, Ontario; Prof., Univ. of Toronto, McGill Univ., Univ. of Ottawa. *Compositions:* Magog for cello and piano 1968, Linden Suite for piano 1970, String Quartet 1972, Violin Sonata and Symphony Epomeo 1975, Piano Man Suite and Piano Concerto 1985, Clarinet Trio 1989, Concertino, Jupiter Concerto 1996, Solo Sonatas for flute and violin 2000, Reconstruction of Beethoven's Concerto No 4 2005, Duo for two violas 2008. *Recordings include:* complete cycle of Beethoven Sonatas and Concerti, Brahms and Schumann Concerti, Complete Schubert Sonatas. *Publications:* contribs to Globe and Mail, Piano, Literary Review of Canada. *Honours:* Hon. Fellow, Royal Conservatory, Toronto 2009; Dr hc (Laurentian Univ.) 1985, (York Univ.) 1985, (Cleveland Inst. of Music) 1996, (McGill Univ.) 2004, (Univ. of Western Ontario) 2006, (Wilfrid Laurier Univ.) 2006, (Dalhousie Univ.), (Memorial Univ.); Schumann Prize, Gov. General's Lifetime Achievement Award, Banff Centre Nat. Arts Award, Leventritt Award 1957, Toronto Arts Award 1997. *Current Management:* Concertmasters Inc., 22 Linden Street, Toronto, M4Y 1V6, Canada. *E-mail:* concertmasters@sympatico.ca. *Address:* 20 Linden Street, Toronto, ON M4Y 1V6, Canada (home). *Website:* www.jwentworth.com/kuerti/.

KUHLMANN, Kathleen Mary; American singer (mezzo-soprano) (retd); b. 7 Dec. 1950, San Francisco; d. of Hugo S. Kuhlmann and Elvira L. Kuhlmann; m. 1983 (divorced 1998). *Education:* Mercy High School, San Francisco and Univ. of San Francisco. *Career:* student, Chicago Lyric Opera School 1976–79; resident mezzo-soprano, Cologne Opera 1980–82; freelance 1982–; int. débuts: Teatro alla Scala, Milan 1980, San Francisco Opera 1982, Royal Opera House, Covent Garden 1982, Teatro Regio Parma 1983, Glyndebourne Festival Opera 1983, Wiener Staatsoper 1983, Teatro Communale Pisa 1983, Chicago Lyric Opera 1984, Salzburger Festspiele 1985, Stuttgart Opera 1985, Hamburg State Opera 1985, Lausanne/Geneva 1986, Australian Opera 1986, Napoli 1987, Tel-Aviv 1988, Capitôle de Toulouse 1988, Metropolitan Opera, New York 1989, Théâtre Châtelet, Paris 1989, Semperoper Dresden 1992, Bayerische Staatsoper, Munich 1994, Staatsoper Unter den Linden, Berlin 1995, Deutsche Oper, Berlin 1995, Aix-en-Provence 1996, Opéra de Paris 1997, Opera di Roma 1998, Opéra de Bordeaux 1998; specialized in Rossini roles, also Monteverdi and Handel; final performances, Semperoper, Dresden 2004; retd 2004. *Current Management:* c/o IMG Paris (Vocal Division), 54 Avenue Marceau, 75008 Paris, France.

KUHN, Alfred; German singer (bass); b. 2 Nov. 1938, Ober-Roden. *Education:* Frankfurt Musikhochschule. *Career:* debut as Trulove in The Rake's Progress, Darmstadt 1963; guest appearances throughout Germany, notably as Wagner's Daland and Landgrave, Rocco in Fidelio, Mozart's Osmin and Sarastro, King Philip in Don Carlos, Donizetti's Dulcamara; Kaspar in Der Freischütz; Düsseldorf 1986, in the premiere of Belshazzar by Kirchner; Mozart's Antonio at the 1991 Salzburg Festival; La Scala 1992 as Waldner in Arabella; sang Varlaam in Boris Godunov at Munich 1995.

KUHN, Gustav, DPhil; Austrian conductor, director, producer and composer; *Artistic Director, Tyrolean Festival Erl;* b. 28 Aug. 1945, Turrach, Styria; s. of Friedrich Kuhn and Hilde Kuhn; m. Andrea Kuhn 1971; one s. one d. *Education:* studied conducting with Hans Swarowsky, Bruno Maderna and Herbert von Karajan at conservatories in Vienna and Salzburg; Univ. of Salzburg. *Career:* advanced conducting studies under Bruno Maderna and Herbert von Karajan; professional conductor in Istanbul (three years), Enschede (Netherlands), Dortmund (prin. conductor) and Vienna; debut at Vienna State Opera (Elektra) 1977, Munich Nat. Theatre (Così fan tutte) 1978, Covent Garden, London 1979, Glyndebourne, Munich Opera Festival and Salzburg Festival 1980, Chicago (Fidelio) 1981, Paris Opéra 1982, La Scala, Milan 1984, Arena di Verona (Masked Ball) 1986, Rossini Opera Festival, Pesaro 1987; Gen. Music Dir in Berne, Bonn and Rome; production debut in Trieste (Fliegender Holländer) 1986; other projects include Parsifal, Naples 1988, Salome, Rome 1988, Don Carlos (French version) and Don Carlo (Italian) for 250th anniversary of Teatro Reggio, Turin 1990; Artistic Dir Neue Stimmen (New Voices) competition, Bertelsmann Foundation 1987–, Macerata Festival, Italy (productions of Così fan tutte and Don Giovanni) 1990–94, Filarmonica Marchigiana 1997–2002, Haydn Orchestra of Bolzano and Trento 2003–12, Conservatorio di Milano Philharmonic Orchestra 2004; Founder and Pres. Accad. di Montegral 1992–, Tyrolean Festival, Erl, Austria 1997–; Producer and Conductor Complete Ring Cycle of Richard Wagner, Tyrolean Festival Erl 2003, 2004, 2005, 2007, took the production on tour to Santander 2005, produced 24-hour Ring, performance of Lohengrin 2012, Winter Festival 2012–; performed series of classical concerts entitled Delirium in Salzburg 2007–11; conducted two performances of Wagner's Parsifal in Beijing (first ever in China) 2013; compositions include orchestral works, masses and solo pieces. *Publications:* Aus Liebe zur Musik 1993, instrumentation of Janáček's Diary of One Who Disappeared, Opéra Nat. de Paris (released by Edition Peters). *Honours:* First Prize, Int. Conducting Contest of Austrian TV and Broadcasting Corpn (ORF) 1969, Lilly Lehmann Medal (Mozarteum Foundation), Max Reinhardt Medal (Salzburg), Senator of Honour Award 'Lorenzo il Magnifico' (Florence) 1988. *Address:* Tiroler Festspiele Erl, Betriebsgesm.b.H., Mühlgraben 56A, 6343 Erl, Austria. *Telephone:* (5373) 8181. *Website:* www.tiroler-festspiele.at; www.gustavkuhn.at.

KUHN, Pamela, BMus, MMus; American singer (soprano); b. 1960, Oregon. *Education:* Univ. of Oregon, Univ. of Southern California with Gwendolyn Koldofsky and Margaret Schaper. *Career:* debut in London, Wigmore Hall with Graham Johnson 1984; recitals at the Purcell Room with Stephen Wilder, Stephen Coombs and Geoffrey Parsons; Isle of Man Festival with Roger Steptoe; oratorio includes Rossini Petite Messe Solennelle at QEH, Verdi Requiem at Fairfield Halls, Dartington (Diego Masson), Oregon Bach Festival (Helmut Rilling), Penderecki Polish Requiem at Oregon Bach Festival (Penderecki), Brahms Requiem at the Royal Festival Hall and in the USA, Beethoven Missa Solemnis in Lugano, Switzerland, Janáček Glagolitic Mass at Salisbury Cathedral; opera includes Ariadne at Dartington, Aida with Florentine Opera in Milwaukee, Rezia with Scottish Opera at La Fenice, Venice, Soloist in Oberon conducted by Seiji Ozawa at Tanglewood, Edinburgh Festival and Frankfurt Alte Oper, High Priestess with Scottish Opera; other roles include Micaela, Tosca, Amelia and Sieglinde; further concert repertory includes operatic evenings with City of Birmingham Symphony Orchestra, Southampton Symphony and Ernest Read Symphony at the Barbican, Shostakovich Symphony 14 with Mark Wigglesworth at St John's Smith Square and Four Last Songs in Nottingham.

KUIJKEN, Barthold, PhD; Belgian flautist, recorder player and conductor; b. 8 March 1949, Dilbeek, Brussels; brother of Sigiswald Kuijken and Wieland Kuijken. *Education:* Conservatoires of Bruges, Brussels and the Hague with Frans Vester and Frans Brueggen; Brussels Univ., self-taught on the Baroque flute. *Career:* concerts in Europe, North and South America, Japan, Australia, New Zealand, Korea and Israel with his brothers, Sigiswald and Wieland, with Lucy van Dael, René Jacobs, Frans Brueggen, Gustav Leonhardt, Bob van Asperen, Luc Devos, Ewald Demeyere. the Parnassus Ensemble, La Petite Bande and the Collegium Aureum; Teacher of Baroque flute at the Hague and Brussels Conservatories; Repertoire includes music by Couperin, Telemann, Handel, Haydn, Bach, Mozart, Schubert and Debussy; Took part in the Towards Bach concert series on the South Bank, London, August 1989. *Recordings:* Solos by J. S. and C. P. E. Bach, Boismortier, Debussy, Fischer, Hotteterre, Telemann, Vivaldi, Weiss; Duos by Boismortier, Hotteterre and W.F. Bach; Suites by Couperin, Hotteterre and Montéclair; Sonatas by Albinoni, J. S. and C. P. E. Bach, Benda, Blavet, Boismortier, Corelli, Friedrich der Grosse, Geminiani, C.H. and J.G. Graun, Guignon, Händel, Kirnberger, Leclair, Locatelli, Müthel, Platti, Quantz, Telemann, Veracini, Vivaldi; A recital of 19th century works for flute and fortepiano (Hummel, F.X. Mozart, Mendelssohn, Schubert); Chamber music by J. S., C. P. E. and J. C. Bach, Boismortier, Couperin, Debussy, Devienne, Dornel, Galuppi, Geminiani, Händel, Haydn, Hotteterre, Janitsch, Mozart, Rameau, Telemann; Concertos by J. S. Bach, Haydn, Mozart, Richter, J. and C. Stamitz, Telemann, and Vivaldi; as a conductor: Mozart's Gran Partita and a program of suites concertantes from the German baroque (J. L. and J. S. Bach, Telemann, Handel). *Publications:* J. S. Bach's flute compositions (ed.). *Current Management:* c/o Allied Artists, 42 Montpelier Square, London SW7 1JZ, England. *Telephone:* (20) 7589-6243. *Fax:* (20) 7581-5269. *E-mail:* info@alliedartists.co .uk. *Website:* www.alliedartists.co.uk. *Address:* Zwartschaapstraat 38, 1755 Gooik, Belgium (home). *Website:* bartholdkuijken.be.

KUIJKEN, Sigiswald; Belgian violinist and conductor; *Artistic Director, La Petite Bande*; b. 16 Feb. 1944, nr Brussels; brother of Barthold Kuijken and Wieland Kuijken; m. Marleen Thiers; one s. four d. *Education:* Bruges Conservatory, Conservatoire Royal de Bruxelles with M. Raskin. *Career:* began to re-establish old technique of violin playing, resting the instrument on the shoulder not under the chin, in 1969, adopted by many players in early 1970s; played in the Alarius Ensemble (with brother Wieland Kuijken, Robert Kohnen and Janine Rubinlicht) 1964–72, performances throughout Europe and USA; Founder and Artistic Dir La Petite Bande (Baroque orchestra) 1972–; tours of Europe, Australia, S America, China and Japan with La Petite Bande and in chamber music and solo programmes; Founder Kuijken String Quartet (with François Fernandez, Marleen Thiers and Wieland Kuijken), specialising in quartets and quintets (with Ryo Terakado, First Viola) of the Classical period 1986–; re-introduced the violoncello da spalla (shoulder cello) for the music of Vivaldi and Bach (cello suites) 2004; occasional conductor of modern symphonic orchestras such as Royal Philharmonic Orchestra of Flanders, Cappella Colonienses (WDR Köln), Orchestre Nat. de Bordeaux & Aquitaine, in Romantic programmes (Beethoven, Schumann, Brahms, Mendelssohn) 1998–; teacher of Baroque violin, Koninklijk Conservatorium, The Hague 1971–96, Koninklijk Muziekconservatorium, Brussels 1993–2009; guest teacher at numerous insts, including Royal Coll. of Music, London, Salamanca Univ., Accad. Chigiana, Siena, Schola Cantorum Basiliensis. *Recordings include:* numerous with La Petite Bande including: Music by Lully, Muffat, Gluck, Haydn's Creation and Symphonies, Mozart's Requiem and Davidde Penitente, Così fan tutte, 1992, J. S. Bach's Passions and Brandenburg Concertos 1994, Bach Sonatas with Gustav Leonhardt, 20 Haydn Symphonies, Mozart Concert Arias, German Chamber Music, Don Giovanni 1997, Le nozze di Figaro 1998, Die Zauberflöte 2004, 17 CD series of Bach Cantatas 2005–12, Vivaldi. *Honours:* Dr hc (Catholic Univ. of Leuven) 2007; Deutsche Schallplattenpreis several times, Grand Prix du Disque, France several times, Deutsche Handel Preis 1994, Choc de l'année for recording Debussy chamber music 2000, Lifetime Achievement Award, York Early Music Festival 2006, Life Achievement Award, Flemish Community (Belgium) 2009, Golden Medal, Royal Flemish Acad. for Arts and Sciences 2015. *Current Management:* c/o Allied Artists, 42 Montpelier Square, London SW7 1JZ, England. *Telephone:* (20) 7589-6243. *Fax:* (20) 7581-5269. *E-mail:* info@alliedartists.co.uk. *Website:* www.alliedartists.co.uk. *Address:* La Petite Bande, Geert Robberechts, Vital Decosterstraat 72, 3000 Leuven, Belgium (office). *Telephone:* (16) 23-08-30 (office). *Fax:* (16) 22-76-10 (office). *E-mail:* info@lapetitebande.be (office). *Website:* www.lapetitebande.be (office).

KUIJKEN, Wieland; Belgian viola da gamba player, cellist and conductor; b. 31 Aug. 1938, Dilbeek, Brussels; brother of Barthold Kuijken and Sigiswald Kuijken. *Education:* Bruges Conservatory, Brussels Conservatoire Royale. *Career:* played with the Alarius Ensemble 1959–72; played in the avant-garde group Musiques Nouvelles 1962–72; teacher at Brussels Conservatoire Royal de Bruxelles and Koninklijk Conservatorium, he Hague 1971–; mem. Kuijken Early Music Group 1972–; masterclasses in the United Kingdom, Innsbruck and the USA; festival appearances at Flanders, Saintes and the English Bach Festival; cellist with the Kuijken String Quartet 1987–, made London debut 1990; collaborations with his brothers, Sigiswald Kuijken and Barthold Kuijken, also with Frans Brueggen, Alfred Deller, Robert Kohnen and René Jacobs; repertoire includes music by French, English, Italian and German composers. *Recordings include:* Leclair Flute Sonatas, Marais Pièces de Viole du Cinquieme Livre and German Chamber Music. *Current Management:* Allied Artists, 42 Montpelier Square, London SW7 1JZ, England. *Telephone:* (20) 7589-6243. *Fax:* (20) 7581-5269. *E-mail:* info@alliedartists.co.uk. *Website:* www.alliedartists.co.uk.

KUJAWINSKA, Krystyna; Polish singer (soprano); b. 4 April 1938, Kalisz. *Education:* Poznán Acad. *Career:* debut at Bytom 1967 as Arabella; sang at the Poznán Opera from 1970, notably as Elisabeth de Valois, Aida, Desdemona, Micaela, Butterfly, Gioconda and Santuzza; later roles included Tosca, the Forza Leonora and Turandot; guest appearances in France as Electra in Idomeneo, Hamburg as Aida, Parma as Halka, Dresden in Verdi Requiem and Leonora in La Forza del Destino, in The Netherlands as Tosca and Santuzza and in Germany and Belgium as Abigaile in Nabucco; has also appeared at the Nat. Theatre Warsaw as Fidelio, Aida and the Trovatore Leonora.

KULENTY, Hanna, BMus; Polish composer; b. 18 March 1961, Białystok. *Education:* F. Chopin Acad. of Music, Warsaw, Royal Conservatory of Music, The Hague, the Netherlands, studied under Włodzimierz, Kotoński and Louis Andriessen. *Career:* guest performer, Deutscher Akademischer Austauschdienst in Berliner Künstler Programm 1990–91; performances of works by many orchestras in countries including Poland, the Netherlands, Latvia, UK, Denmark, Germany; Lecturer, F. Chopin Acad. of Music 1992; Composer-in-Residence, Het Gelders Orkest, Netherlands 1999–2000; Guest Prof., Conservatory of Music, Arnhem/Zwolle 2005, ESMUC Music Acad., Barcelona, Spain 2007. *Compositions include:* opera/stage: Przypowieść o ziarnie 1985; opera: The Mother of Back-Winged Dreams 1995, Hoffmanniana 2003, Lost & Found – twenty five 2008; for orchestra: Ad Unum 1985, Quatro 1986, Symphony No. 1 1986, Symphony No. 2 1987, Breathe 1987, Perpetuus 1989, Trignon 1989, Piano Concerto No. 1 1990, Piano Concerto No. 2 1991, Air 1991, Violin Concerto No. 1 1992, A Few Minutes for Eerprijs 1992, Passacaglia 1992, Violin Concerto No. 1 1993, Sinequan Forte A 1994, Sinequan Forte B 1994, Going Up 2 1995, Violin Concerto No. 2 1996, Certus 1997, Elfen 1997, Part One 1998, Symphony No. 3 2000, Flute Concerto No. 1 2001, Trumpet Concerto 2002, Piano Concerto No. 3 2003, Mezzo Tango 2004, Postcard from Europe 2004, Mezzo Tango 2 2005, GG Concerto 2009; chamber music: String Quartet No. 1 1984, Quinto 1986, Ride 1987, Arcus 1988, aaa TRE 1988, Cannon 1988, String Quartet No. 2 1990, A Cradle Song 1993, A Fourth Cradle 1994, Lysanxia 1994, A Sixth Cradle 1995, Going Up 1 1995, Rapidus 1996, Sierra 1996, Waiting For ... 1997, Stretto 1998, MM-blues 1999, Decimo 2000, Blattinus 2001, Asjaawaa 2001, Crossing Line 2001, Rainbow 3 2003, Sun 2004, Brass No. 2 2005, Kisses and Crosses 2007, Preludium, Postludium and Psalm 2007, String Quartet No. 3 – Tell Me About It 2006, String Quartet No. 4 – A Cradle Song 2007, Walc z Lost & Found 2008, Sugar-Fela Tango 2009; solo instruments: Three Minutes for a Double Bass 1983, Sesto for piano 1985, Still Life with a Violin 1985, One by One for marimba 1988, E for E for harpsichord 1991, Cadenza for violin 1992, Still Life with a Cello 1993, Fifth Circle for alto flute 1994, A Third Circle for piano 1996, Harmonium 1999, Drive Blues for piano 2000, Brass No. 1 for trumpet 2004, Brass No. 3 for horn 2005, Brass No. 4 for tuba 2007, Preludium and Psalm for harmonium 2007, Walc in A for piano 2009, G for G for harpsichord 2009. *Recordings include:* 12½ Musis Sacrum, Chronicles from Warsaw Autumn Festivals, Hanna Kulenty: Ad Unum, Sesto, Arci, Piano Concerto No. 1, Violin Concerto No. 1, Arcs and Circles: Portrait of Hanna Kulenty. *Honours:* Stanisław Wyspiański Award 1987, first prize Composers' Competition, Polish Composers' Union 1986, 1987, first prize Int. Rostrum of Composers Competition 2003, other awards in music competitions. *Current Management:* c/o Donemus, Music Center The Netherlands, Rokin 111, 1012 KN Amsterdam, The Netherlands. *Telephone:* (20) 344-60-60. *Fax:* (20) 673-35-88. *E-mail:* info@mcn.nl. *Website:* www.muziekcentrumnederland.nl. *E-mail:* martin.majoor@planet.nl. *Website:* www.hannakulenty.com.

KULESHA, Gary Alan, LMus, FTCL; Canadian composer, conductor and pianist; b. 22 Aug. 1954, Toronto; m. Larysa Kuzmenko 1983. *Education:* Royal Conservatory of Music, Toronto, studied with John McCabe in London, England and John Corigliano in New York, USA, Trinity Coll., London, England. *Career:* composer-in-residence, Kitchener-Waterloo Symphony 1989–92, Candia Opera Co. 1993–95; composer and adviser, Toronto Symphony Orchestra 1995–; guest conducting throughout Canada; Principal Conductor, Festival Theatre, Stratford Festival, Canada; Artistic Dir and Principal Conductor, Canadian Contemporary Music Workshops and the Composers' Orchestra; works performed throughout North America, Europe, Iceland, Australia and Latin America. *Compositions:* Essay for orchestra, Second Essay for orchestra, Chamber Concertos 1–5, Duo for bass clarinet and piano, Second Sonata for piano, Lifesongs for alto and string orchestra (text by composer), Nocturne for chamber orchestra, Angels for marimba and tape 1986, Shama Songs 1991, Concerto for recorder 1990, three Essays for orchestra, Pico Sonata Nos 2–3, Concerto for viola 1992, Red Emma (opera) 1995, Symphony 1998, Partita for piano and strings 1999, Violin Concerto 1999. *Compositions for theatre:* scores for several Shakespearean plays, including All's Well That Ends Well, Nimrod, Sydney, Australia 1986, Henry VIII, Stratford 1986. *Recordings:* Recorder Concerto, Michela Petri and ECO conducted by Kamn; Political Implications, Indiana Clarinet Quartet.

KULHAN, Jaroslav; Czech cellist; b. 7 Dec. 1950, Ceske Budejovice; m. Stepanka Kazilova 1978; one s. two d. *Education:* Prague Conservatory, Acad. of Music and Arts, Prague. *Career:* mem., Panocha Quartet 1968–; teacher, Prague Conservatory 1990–. *Recordings:* Haydn Op 51, Op 33, Op 55, Op 76; Smetana Quartets 1 and 2; Dvořák's Chamber Music, Martinů's Quartets; Janáček Quartets No. 1, Schubert Op 29, 125, 161, 163; Fibich Op 8, Quartet A major, Op 11, Op 42; Schumann Op 47; solo recordings for radio: Reger, 2nd Suite Op 131e/2, Boccherini, Sonata in C major No. 17, Beethoven, Variatonen, P. Hejny, Metal Sonata for solo cello. *Honours:* Grand Prix Acad. Charles Cros (Martinů's Quartet Nos 4, 6) 1983, Midem Cannes Classical Award 1994. *Address:* c/o Prague Conservatory, Na Rejdisti 1, 11000 Prague, Czech Republic (office).

KULINSKY, Bohumil; Czech conductor; b. 5 May 1959, Prague. *Education:* Prague Conservatory, Prague Music Acad., Music Acad. of Janáček-Brno. *Career:* Conductor, Czechoslovak Children's Choir Bambini di Praga 1976–; concert tours to France, Italy, Germany, Mongolia, Finland, UK, Japan; appeared on radio and television; Conductor, Prague Symphony Orchestra, appearing at concerts and festivals 1984; Conductor, Czech Chamber Philharmonic Orchestra; concert tours to Spain and Germany.

KULJUNTAUSTA, Petri, MA, PhD; Finnish composer and musician; b. 28 Feb. 1961, Tampere. *Education:* Univ. of Jyväskylä. *Career:* electronic compositions and performances as improviser 1980s; music for Petri Kuljuntausta Project 1989–94; music for Petri Kuljuntausta Ensemble, string quartet, piano, synthesiser, saxophone, guitar and percussion 1993–94; sound/media works and installations in galleries, museums and halls 1993–; founder and Chair., Charm of Sound 1995–; founder and bd mem., Finnish Soc. for Acoustic Ecology 1999–; Vice-Chair., Muu 1997–98; co-Dir, Charm of Sound concert series 1997–; Ed., Charmed Sounds radio programme, Finnish Radio, YLE 1997–2004; Curator, Sound Box webcast project, Museum of Contemporary Art, Finland 1998–99; mem. Soc. of Finnish Composers, Charm of Sound, Muu, WFAE, FSAE. *Films:* Texas Scramble 1996, The Blow 1997, Video Surveillance 1998, Days 2000, Tomato One/Navigator 2006, Eight Rooms 2008, Whistles, Trills and Clicks 2008, Grooves 2009, Water Cities 2009. *Compositions:* various works for improvisers 1980s; chamber music: Kuun arvet 1988, Chain 1994, Ancient Dream 1994, Pro 1994, Time 1994, Enigma 1994; Storm… for big band 1993; sound/media installations: Soundscapes I 1994, Lux in tenebris 1995, The Good and Evil 1995, Birdscape Music 1997, Free Zone 1998, Transitions 1998, Formation 2002, Mixer 2002, Music for Three Bazookas and 12 Steel Sheets 2002, SoundHappens 2003, Yokomono #3 (Staalplaat Soundsystem) 2005, Wave Motion 2005, SoundscapePGH 2005, Patterns and Waves 2006, Document Project Tampere 2006–07, Musique et Jardin 2007; electronic music: Violin Tone Orchestra 1996, Momentum 1998, Idea of Proof 1999, The Waiting Room 1999, Hysteria 1999, St Virus City 2000, Vroom! 2000, Aurora Borealis 1 2002, Four Notes 2002, Departs/Arrivals 2002, Canvas 2002, Deep Blue 2002, Northern Lights Live 2004, Navigator 2004, Zoomusicological 1-2 2003–05, Nordic Prince 2005, Noise City 2005, Water City 2005, Heavy Feather 2008, Whistles, Trills and Clicks 2008, Irresistible District 2009, Heureka!! (fanfare for 20th anniversary of Heureka Finnish Science Centre) 2009, Mexican Cars 2009. *Publications:*

On/Off 2002, Äänen eXtreme 2006, First Wave 2008. *Honours:* Farao Horn Competition Prize 1995, Finnish Cultural Foundation grant 1998, 2008, State art grant 2000, Finnish State Prize for Art 2005. *Address:* c/o Aureobel, Terveystie 12 B 7, 00730 Helsinki, Finland (office). *E-mail:* petriear@gmail .com (home); aureobel@gmail.com (office). *Website:* www.aureobel.com/ petrikuljuntausta.

KULKA, Konstanty Andrzej; Polish violinist and academic; *Professor, Fryderyk Chopin University of Music;* b. 5 March 1947, Gdańsk; m.; two d. *Education:* Higher State School of Music (now the Stanisław Moniuszko Acad. of Music), Gdańsk. *Career:* Prof., Acad. of Music, Warsaw (now the Fryderyk Chopin Univ. of Music) 1994–, Head of Inst. of String Instruments; numerous gramophone, radio and TV recordings; soloist with Nat. Philharmonic Orchestra, Warsaw 1984–; more than 1,500 concerts world-wide since 1967; participates in numerous int. festivals, including Lucerne, Prague, Bordeaux, Berlin, Granada, Barcelona, Brighton; concerts with Berlin Philharmonic Orchestra, Chicago Symphony Orchestra, Minneapolis Orchestra, London Symphony Orchestra, Concertgebouw Orchestra, English Chamber Orchestra, St Petersburg Philharmonic Orchestra and others. *Recordings include:* Antonio Vivaldi Cztery pory roku (The Four Seasons), Szymanowski: Violin Concertos Nos 1 & 2 1997, Mozart: Best Of 2000, Karlowicz: Tone Poems/ Violin Concerto 2002, Paderewski: Violin & Piano Works 2003, Penderecki: Violin Concertos Nos 1 & 2 2003, F. Mendelssohn and A. Glazunov's Violin Concertos with the National Philharmonic Orchestra under Jerzy Katlewicz; Brahms's Violin Concerto with National Philharmonic Orchestra under Witold Rowicki; J. S. Bach's Sonatas for Solo Violin. *Honours:* Hon. Citizen of the City of Wolbromia; Gold Cross of Merit, Commdr's Cross, Order of Polonia Restituta 2001; Diploma and Special Prize, Paganini Competition, Genoa 1964, firsts prize, Music Competition, Munich 1966, Minister of Culture and Arts Prize 1969, 1973, Minister of Foreign Affairs Prize 1977, Pres. of Radio and TV Cttee Prize 1978, prize winner, 33rd Grand Prix du Disque, Int. Sound Festival, Paris 1981. *Address:* Uniwersytet Muzyczny Fryderyka Chopina, ul. Okólnik 2, 00-368 Warsaw, Poland. *Telephone:* (22) 8277241. *Fax:* (22) 8278305. *E-mail:* konstanty.kulka@wp.pl. *Website:* www .chopin.edu.pl/en/people/konstanty-andrzej-kulka.

KULLBERG, Jakob; Danish musician (cello); b. Aarhus. *Education:* Royal Danish Acad. of Music, Amsterdam Conservatoire (Netherlands), Zagreb Acad. of Music (Croatia), Royal Acad. of Music, London, studied with Dmitri Ferschtman, Valter Despalj, Mats Lidström, Colin Carr, Reinhard Latzko and Morten Zeuthen. *Career:* has performed at festivals including Aldeburgh, Warsaw Autumn and Huddersfield; concerto debut, Bergen Int. Festival (Norway) and with Royal Philharmonic Orchestra, London; solo and chamber music performances across Europe and in USA and Canada; composers who have written works for him include Bent Sørensen, Kaija Saariaho and Per Nørgård; has collaborated closely with Nørgård, whose works he has performed, often as premieres, and who dedicated his 2nd Cello Concerto and 4th Cello Sonata to him; Artist-in-Residence, Copenhagen's Round Tower 2007, Tivoli Garden Concert Hall 2008, Copenhagen Royal Library's Black Diamond 2009, New Music Orchestra (Poland) 2013; has given masterclasses in Europe and USA; Artistic Dir, Open Strings Cello Acad.; has taught at Royal Danish Acad. of Music 2005–. *Recordings include:* Per Nørgård: String Quartets (with Kroger Quartet) (Danish Radio Lyt til Nyt Prize 2009) 2008, Momentum: Nordic Cello Concertos (Danish Radio P2 Prize) 2012. *Honours:* Gladsaxe Music Prize, Copenhagen Philharmonic 2011. *Telephone:* 27149819. *E-mail:* info@jakobkullberg.com. *Website:* www.jakobkullberg.com.

KUNDE, Gregory, PhD; American singer (tenor) and conductor; *Founder and Leader, Gregory Kunde Chorale;* b. 24 Feb. 1954, Kankakee, Ill. *Education:* Illinois State Univ. and the Opera School of Chicago Lyric Opera. *Career:* sang at Chicago from 1979, Washington Opera 1983, Dallas 1986, Seattle 1987; Metropolitan Opera debut 1987, as Des Grieux in Manon; European engagements in Guillaume Tell at Nice, Théâtre des Champs Elysées, Paris 1989, Geneva 1995, Pesaro 1995, Vienna 2001; as Raoul in Les Huguenots, Montpellier 1990; as Gounod's Roméo, Detroit 1989; other roles have included Mozart's Belmonte and Tamino, Ernesto, Alfredo; Montreal 1987, Berlin 1991, San Francisco 1993, Carnegie Hall 1995, Philadelphia 1995, Bologna 1997, Vienna 1997, Munich 2001, Metropolitan Opera 2006–07; sang Arturo in Bellini's Puritani; other roles include Edgardo in Lucia, Turin 1993, Leicester in Maria Stuarda, Bologna 1994, Carnegie Hall 2001, Baltimore 2007, Ernesto in Don Pasquale, La Scala 1994, Don Ottavio in Don Giovanni, Geneva 1992, La Scala 1993, Rodrigo in Donna del Lago, La Scala 1993, Montpellier 2002, San Sebastian, 2004, Edinburgh, 2006, Berlin 2007, Rinaldo in Armida, Pesaro 1993, Carnegie Hall 1997, Tonio in La Fille du Régiment and Nadir in Les Pêcheurs de Perles, as Des Grieux, and Laertes in Hamlet by Thomas, Montpellier and Chicago 1989; sang Lindoro in L'Italiana in Algeri at Berlin 1992, Idreno in Semiramide, Pesaro Festival 1992, 2003, Geneva 1998; Danish Knight in Gluck's Armide to open the 1996–97 season at La Scala, Rossini's Ermione in Santa Fe 2000, New York City Opera 2005, Pesaro 2008, Berlioz' Benvenuto Cellini 2002 in Zurich, Paris 2004, London 2007, Enée in Les Troyens, Paris 2003, Doctor Faust of Busoni, Zurich 2006, Otello, Pesaro 2007, Tokyo 2008, La Damnation du Faust of Berlioz, London 2003, Sydney 2004, Atlanta 2005, Cardiff 2006, Dallas and San Francisco 2007, Berlin, Chicago and Glasgow 2008; founder and leader, Gregory Kunde Chorale 1999–. *Recordings:* Bianca e Fernando 1991, Semiramide 1992, Armida 1993, Hamlet 1993, Lakme 1997, Benvenuto Cellini (Gramophone Award for Opera Recording of the Year) 2005, Les Troyens (Gramophone Award for DVD of the Year) 2005, Great Tenor Scenes 2006, La Donna del Lago 2007, Doktor Faust 2007, Don Pasquale 2007. *Address:* Gregory Kunde Chorale, PO Box 51, Penfield, New York, NY 14526, USA (office). *Telephone:* (585) 377-7568 (office). *E-mail:* gregory@gregorykundechorale.org (office). *Website:* www .gregorykunde.com; www.gregorykundechorale.org.

KUNDLAK, Josef; singer (tenor); b. 1956, Bratislava, Czechoslovakia. *Education:* studied in Bratislava and the European Opera Centre in Belgium. *Career:* sang with Bratislava State Opera 1983–, in works by Janáček and Smetana, in addition to standard repertory; sang Nemorino in L'Elisir d'amore at Teatro Comunale, Bologna 1987; Ferrando in Così fan tutte at La Scala Milan 1989, returning in Die Meistersinger 1990; sang at Donizetti Festival at Bergamo 1991 in Elisabetta al Castello di Kenilworth; further engagements at Teatro San Carlo, Naples and Bayerische Staatsoper, Munich; appeared as Belmonte in a new production of Die Entführung at Deutsche Oper Berlin 1991; sang Rossini's Almaviva at Genoa 1992. *Recordings include:* Kudryash in Katya Kabanova, under Charles Mackerras 1997. *Honours:* winner Luciano Pavarotti Competition in Philadelphia 1985.

KUNKEL, Renata; Polish composer; b. 1 Sept. 1954, Gdańsk. *Education:* Warsaw Acad. of Music. *Career:* Lecturer, Warsaw Acad.; performances of her music in Europe, the USA and Central America. *Compositions include:* orchestral works: Shadows for four instrumental groups 1981, Symphony for symphony orchestra 1983, Inner Landscapes for chamber orchestra 1984, Music for Sirius B for woodwind chamber orchestra 1985, Where Worlds are Naught for string chamber orchestra 1987, The Stream for symphony orchestra 1990; chamber works: three String Quartets 1979–91, Penetrations for flute and percussion 1980, Events for violin and percussion 1980, Idiochrome II for oboe and violin 1986, In A Lit-Up Streak Of Sounds for Ensemble 1989; solo works: Mimesis for violin 1981, Phrases for Piano 1984, Eidos I for flute 1986, Promethidion for violin 1986, Eidos II for clarinet 1987, Intensity for piano 1988, for organ 1990, Ánodos for violin 1990; vocal works: Apogéios for vocal group and orchestra 1984, Idiochromie I for two sopranos and ensemble 1985, Elegy for mixed choir and symphony orchestra 1988, And Give Us Silence to Drink for female choir 1990; other: In Memoriam for magnetic tape 1982. *Honours:* Special Prize, Int. Competition for Women Composers, Mannheim 1989, Prizewinner at the First Lutoslawski International Composers' Competition, 1990. *Address:* c/o Society of Authors ZAiKS, 2 Hipoteczna Street, 00 092 Warsaw, Poland. *Telephone:* (4822) 828 17 05. *Fax:* (4822) 828 13 47. *E-mail:* sekretariat@zaiks.org.pl. *Website:* www .zaiks.org.pl.

KUNTZSCH, Matthias; German conductor and academic; b. 22 Sept. 1935, Karlsruhe; s. of Alfred Kuntzsch and Nora Kuntzsch; m. Sylvia Anderson 1966; one s. one d. *Education:* Hochschule für Musik und Theatre, Hanover, Mozarteum, Salzburg with Lovro von Matacic, Hermann Scherchen, Herbert von Karajan, Zermatt with Pablo Casals, Karl Engel. *Career:* debut conducting Don Pasquale, State Theatre, Brunswick 1960; Conductor, Jeunesses Musicales Orchestra, Brunswick 1957; Musical Asst, Hannover Opera 1958; Kapellmeister, Opera Braunschweig 1959; Asst to Wolfgang and Wieland Wagner, Bayreuth Festival 1959–64; Principal Conductor, Bonn Opera 1962–64, Mannheim Opera 1964–66, Hamburg State Opera 1966–69, Staatskapellmeister, Munich State Opera 1969–73; Music Dir, Lübeck Opera and Symphony 1973–77; Music Dir and Opera Dir, Saarbrücken State Opera and Symphony 1977–85; Conductor, Int. Youth Festival Orchestra, Bayreuth 1981–86; Prin. Guest Conductor and Artistic Adviser, Basque Nat. Symphony, San Sebastian, Spain 1986–89; Music Dir, Bay Area Summer Opera Theater Inst. (BASOTI) 1992–2009; conducted world premieres of operas, Humphrey Searle's Hamlet, Hamburg 1968 and Gian Carlo Menotti's Help, Help, the Globolinks!, Hamburg 1968; Günther Bialas's Aucassin et Nicolette, Munich 1969; Detlev Mueller-Siemens's Genoveva, Germany TV ZDF; guest conductor with Utah Opera and Symphony, Colorado Symphony and Vancouver Opera. *Recordings include:* with soloists Ruggiero Ricci, Eugene List and others; Conrad Susa's The Blue House with the Colorado Symphony 2002. *Fax:* (415) 457-0580 (office). *E-mail:* mkuntzsch@aol.com. *Website:* www .matthiaskuntzsch.com.

KUPFER, Harry; German opera producer; b. 12 Aug. 1935, Berlin. *Career:* worked at theatres in Halle, Stralsund and Karl-Marx-Stadt (now Chemnitz); Dir, Deutsches Nationaltheater, Weimar 1963–72; Chief Producer, Staatsoper Dresden 1972–81; Chief Producer, Komische Oper Berlin from 1981, Dir from 1994; has produced for Bayreuth Der fliegende Holländer 1978, Der Ring des Nibelungen 1988; opera productions for WNO at Cardiff, Covent Garden London, Staatsoper and Volksoper Vienna, Amsterdam, San Francisco, Paris, Hamburg, Cologne, Stuttgart and Frankfurt; important productions include Orfeo ed Euridice by Gluck, Mozart Cycle, La Damnation de Faust, Pelléas et Mélisande, Moses und Aron, Lear by A. Reimann, premiere production of Die Schwarze Maske by Penderecki at Salzburg 1991, Die Soldaten by B.A. Zimmermann; shortened version of The Invisible City of Kitezh by Rimsky-Korsakov at the 1995 Bregenz Festival; staged Wagner's Parsifal and the Ring at Berlin Staatsoper 1995–96; Boris Godunov at the Vienna Volksoper 1998.

KUPIEC, Ewa; Polish/German pianist; *Professor of Piano, Hochschule für Musik, Theater und Medien Hannover;* b. 2 Nov. 1964, Duszniki, Poland; m. Randall Meyers. *Education:* Chopin Acad., Warsaw and Royal Acad. of Music, London. *Career:* has performed with numerous orchestras, including Netherlands Philharmonic, Royal Stockholm Philharmonic, Royal Liverpool Philharmonic, Munich Philharmonic, Berlin Radio Symphony, Flemish Radio

Orchestra, Leipzig Gewandhaus, Gulbenkian Orchestra, Warsaw Philharmonic, Orchestre de Paris, Yomiuri Nippon Symphony, Nagoya Philharmonic, BBC Scottish Orchestra, Iceland Symphony, Royal Danish Orchestra, Tasmanian Symphony; US debut with the Milwaukee Symphony 2002, Japanese debut, Tokyo 2002, Australian debut with Melbourne Symphony 2005; as chamber musician has worked with cellists Mørk, Vogler, Cohen, Pergamenscsikov and Gerhardt, violinists Oleg and Faust, flautist Piccinini, pianist Duchâble and with the Petersen, Prazak and Keller Quartets; festival appearances include Schleswig-Holstein, Rheingau, Jersey Arts Festival, Bad Kissinger Sommer, Casals Festival, Kuhmo, MDR Musiksommer; has performed at Int. Piano Series, South Bank Centre, London; regularly performs works by contemporary composers and Polish composers; Prof. of Piano, Hochschule für Musik, Theater und Medien Hannover. *Recordings:* Carl Loewe, Symphony In D Minor/Concerto for Piano and Orchestra in A Major 1995, Shostakovich/Prokofiev/Stravinsky, Works for Cello and Piano 1996, Paderewski, Piano Works 1996, Bartók, Violin Sonatas 1997, Chopin, Nocturnes, Vol. 1 1998, Vol. 2 1998, Chopin, Preludes Op28/Szymanowski, Preludes Op1 1999, Paderewski, Piano Concerto, Op. 12/Fantaisie Polonaise, Op. 19 1999, Lutosławski, Concerto for piano/Szymanowski, Symphony No. 4 1999, Graztna Bacewicz, Solo Works 2001, Janáček, Sonate pour violon et piano/Lutosławski, Partita/Szymanowski, Mythes 2003, Chopin, Piano Concertos Nos 1 and 2 2004, Meyers and Bibalo, Conception 2005, Children's Corner 2005, Shostakovich, Piano Quintet/String Quartets 1 and 4 2005, Grazyna Bacewicz, Sonatas for Violin and Piano 2006, Szpilman, Works for Piano and Orchestra, Janáček, Solo Works 2007, Schnittke, Piano concerti 2008, Chopin/Schubert solo works 2010, Schnittke, Piano Quintet 2011, Chopin Nocturnes/Concerti 2012, Lutosławski solo works 2013. *Honours:* Winner ARD Competition, Munich 1992, ECHO Klassik Award 1997. *Current Management:* c/o Peter Szesny, PR2 Classic, Kreuznacherstrasse 63, 50968 Cologne, Germany. *Telephone:* (221) 381063 (home). *Fax:* (221) 383955 (home). *E-mail:* office@pr2classic.de. *Website:* www.pr2classic.de; www.ewakupiec .com.

KUROSAKI, Hiro; Japanese violinist; b. 1949, Tokyo. *Education:* Vienna Musikhochschule, Austria. *Career:* solo engagements with the Royal Philharmonic, Dresden Staatskapelle, Salzburg Mozarteum and Vienna Symphony Orchestras; Leader, Les Arts Florissants (under William Christie), and has also played in Baroque and early music ensembles with the Clemencic Consort of Vienna and London Baroque; teacher, Univ. of Vienna, Salzburg Mozarteum. *Recordings include:* Mozart's violin sonatas (with Linda Nicholson). *Honours:* prizewinner Wieniawski Competition 1977, Kreisler Competition 1979.

KURTÁG, György; Hungarian composer; b. 19 Feb. 1926, Lugos (Lugoj, Romania). *Education:* Franz Liszt Music Acad., Budapest and in Paris with Marianne Stein. *Career:* Repetiteur, Bela Bartok Music Secondary School, Budapest 1958–63, Nat. Philharmonic 1960–68; Asst to Pal Kadosa, Franz Liszt Acad. of Music, Budapest 1967, Prof. of Chamber Music 1967–86; Composer-in-Residence, Wissenschaftskolleg zu Berlin 1993–95, Wiener Konzerthaus, Vienna 1995–96; mem. Bayerische Akad. der Schönen Künste, Munich 1987, Akad. der Künste, Berlin 1987. *Compositions include:* Viola Concerto 1954, String Quartet, Op. 1 1959, Wind Quintet 1959, The Sayings of Péter Bornemissza 1963–68, Hommage à Mihály András 1977, Bagatelles 1981, Scenes from a Novel 1981–82, Three Old Inscriptions 1967–86, Kafka-Fragmente 1985–87, Requiem for the Beloved 1982–87, Officium breve in memoriam Andreae Szervánszky 1988–89, Ligatura–Message to Frances-Marie 1989, Hommage à R. Sch. 1990, Transcriptions from Machaut to Bach 1974–91, Attila József Fragments 1981, Three in memoriam 1988–90, Games, two series, Beads 1994, Omaggio a Luigi Nono 1979, eight Choruses 1981–82, Songs of Despondency and Grief 1980–94, Inscriptions on a Grave in Cornwall 1994, Rückblick (Altes und Neues für vier Spieler, Hommage à Stockhausen) 1986, Three Songs to poems by János Pilinszky 1986, Mémoire de Laïka 1990, Curriculum Vitae 1992, Messages of the late Miss R. V. Troussova, Grabstein für Stephan for guitar and Instrumentengruppen, Op. 15c (Prix de Composition Musicale, Fondation Prince Pierre de Monaco 1993) 1989, . . . quasi una fantasia. . ., Double Concerto for piano, cello and 2 chamber ensembles Op. 27.2 (Prix de Composition Musicale, Fondation Prince Pierre de Monaco 1993) 1989–90, Ligature e Versetti for organ 1990, Layka- Emlèk for synthesizer and real sounds (co-composition with his son) 1990, Samuel Beckett: What is the Word for solo voice, voices and chamber ensemble Op. 30b 1991. *Honours:* Hon. mem. American Acad. of Arts and Letters 2001; Merited Artist of Hungarian People's Repub. 1980, Outstanding Artist 1984, Officier des Arts et Lettres 1985; Erkel Prize 1954, 1956, 1969, Kossuth Prize 1973, Bartok-Pasztory Award 1984, Herder Prize, Freiherr vom Stein, Hamburg 1993, Feltrinelli Prize, Accad. dei Lincei, Italy 1993, Austrian State Award for European Composers 1994, Denis de Rougemont Prize 1994, Kossuth Prize 1996, Ernst von Siemens Music Prize, Munich 1998, Grawemeyer Award (for his composition . . .concertante. . . op. 42 for violin, viola and orchestra) 2006, Gold Medal, Royal Philharmonic Soc. of London 2013, BBVA Foundation Frontiers of Knowledge Award in the category of Contemporary Music 2014. *Address:* Liszt Ferenc tér 9.I.6, 1061 Budapest, Hungary.

KURTAKOV, Krassimir; singer (bass-baritone); b. 1953, Sofia, Bulgaria. *Education:* studied in Sofia. *Career:* sang at the Bulgarian Nat. Opera from 1979; guest tours of Russia, Cuba, France and Austria 1980–82; Vienna Kammeroper 1987–88, as Nicolai's Falstaff and Don Alfonso; Bremerhaven 1988–90 and Gelsenkirchen Opera from 1990, including Denisov's L'Ecume des jours 1992; Vienna Staatsoper and elsewhere as Rocco in Fidelio, Mozart's Bartolo, Verdi's Fiesco, King Philip and Ramphis; Colline in La Bohème; Boris, Varlaam and Pimen, in Boris Godunov; Bonn Opera 1992 in Jakob Lenz by Rihm.

KURZ, Ivan; Czech composer; b. 29 Nov. 1947, Prague; m. Zdeňka Sklenářová 1951; two s. one d. *Education:* studied music theory with Karel Risinger, composition with Emil Hlobil, Acad. of Arts and Music, Prague with Václav Dobiáš. *Career:* dramaturgist for Prague TV 1972–74; teacher of Music Theory, Acad. of Performing Arts, Prague 1976–91, teacher of Composition 1991–, Head of Composition 2004–10. *Compositions include:* orchestral: Concertino for piano, flute, percussion and strings 1974, Inclined Plane symphonic picture 1979, Emergence symphonic picture 1981, Parable symphonic picture 1982, Symphony No. 3 1986, The Gospel's Folly symphonic picture 1987–89, I Come to Thee symphonic picture 1988, Magnifikace for orchestra 2003, Garden of Life symphonic picture 2004, Living Soul symphonic picture 2005; chamber: Sonata for Piano 1976, Circle of Notes for string quartet 1979, The Touch for piano trio 1982, Litanie for organ and percussion 1984, Expectatio for French horn and piano 1985, Rosae Eglanteriae for string quartet 1999, Song from Bretagne quartet for flute, clarinet, cello and piano 2003, The Last Supper for violin and 12 string instruments 2006, I Hear the Angels Singing (3rd string quartet) 2008, Singing Alphabet for piano 2011; vocal: Missa Bohemica for children's choir and orchestra 2001, Ave Maria for soprano and orchestra 2001, Song of Divine Lamb for soprano and orchestra 2004, Angelic Landscapes for baritone and symphonic orchestra 2009; oratorio: At the End of Times cycle of four oratorios for mezzo-soprano, baritone, narrator, mixed choir and orchestra 1992–96; opera: Evening Meeting 1989–90. *Publications:* Expressionism in Music 2002, Teaching of Composition in Middle Europe, Int. Seminar of Middle-European Composition Schools 2002. *Honours:* Ministry of Culture Generation 74 Award 1975, Asscn of Czech Composers Award 1980, 1989, Premium of Czech Music Fund 1990. *Address:* Department of Composition, Malostranské náměstí 13, 118 01 Prague 1 (office); Drtinova 26, 150 00 Prague 5, Czech Republic (home). *Telephone:* (2) 34244141 (office). *Fax:* (2) 57532081 (office). *E-mail:* ivan.kurz@seznam.cz (home). *Website:* katedraskladby.hamu.cz (office).

KURZAK, Aleksandra; Polish singer (soprano); b. 7 Aug. 1977, Brzeg Dolny; m. Jacek Jaskula. *Education:* Acad. of Music, Wroclaw, Hochschule für Musik und Theater, Hamburg. *Career:* began career as soloist with Staatsoper Hamburg 2001–07; debut at Metropolitan Opera, New York as Olympia in Hoffmann's Erzählungen 2004, and at Royal Opera House, Covent Garden as Aspasia in Mitridate, Re di Ponto 2005; debut at Teatro alla Scala, Milan as Gilda in Rigoletto 2010; has also appeared regularly at Bayerische Staatsoper, Munich, Vienna Staatsoper, Salzburg Festival, Theater an der Wien. *Opera repertoire includes:* Cleopatra in Julius Caesar, Norina in Don Pasquale, Adina in L'Elisir d'Amore, Gilda in Rigoletto, Ännchen in Der Freischütz, Blondchen in Die Entführung aus dem Serail, Maria in La fille du régiment, Susanna in Le nozze di Figaro, Gretel in Hänsel and Gretel, Olympia in The Tales of Hoffman, Rosina in Il barbiere di Siviglia, Donna Anna in Don Giovanni, Kate Pinkerton in Madame Butterfly, Queen of the Night and Papagena in Die Zauberflöte, Oberto in Alcina, Nannetta in Falstaff, Sophie in Der Rosenkavalier, Zerbinetta in Ariadne auf Naxos, Adele in Die Fledermaus. *Current Management:* IMG Artists Italia, Viale C.Castracani, Trav.IV 335, 55100 Lucca, Italy. *Telephone:* (0583) 955540 (office). *Fax:* (0583) 474685 (office). *E-mail:* gmacheda@imgartists.com (office). *Website:* www .aleksandrakurzak.com (office).

KUSIEWICZ, Piotr, DipMus; Polish pianist and singer; b. 30 June 1953, Gdańsk. *Education:* Acad. of Music, Gdańsk and studied with Prof. Zbigniew Sliwinski, Prof. Jerzy Szymanski. *Career:* singer, Kraków State Opera 1981–, Teatr STU 1983–, Warsaw State Opera House 1984–, Wroclaw State Opera 1986–; guest performances in operas in Germany, Switzerland, Austria, The Netherlands, Luxembourg and Italy; co-operation with philharmonic societies, chamber ensembles; mem. of vocal ensemble of ancient music, Bornus Consort; as pianist, performances with leading Polish singers as accompanist in Poland and abroad, and accompanist in Geneva Int. Singer Competition 1978; as singer and pianist, at Festival of Contemporary Music, Warsaw Autumn 1981, 1983, 1984, 1987, Krzysztof Penderecki's Festival in Lusawice, Poland on invitation from the composer 1983, and recordings for Polish radio; vocal teacher, Acad. of Music in Gdańsk 1986. *Recording:* G.F. Handel's Sosarme, opera seria in three acts. *Publication:* Gdańsk Composers (co-author) 1980.

KUSNJER, Ivan; singer (baritone); b. 10 Nov. 1951, Rokytancy, Czechoslovakia. *Career:* sang in operas at Ostrava and Brno from 1977; National Theatre Prague from 1982; Roles have included Mozart's Count, Verdi's Macbeth and Rigoletto, Marcello, Bohus in Dvořák's Jacobin, 1995, and Constantin in Martinů's Greek Passion; Vienna Staatsoper as Germont in La Traviata; Further guest appearances in Paris, Janáček's From the House of the Dead; Berlin, Brussels and Milan; Concerts include Carmina Burana, Zemlinsky's Lyric Symphony and the Spectre's Bride by Dvořák; Season 1998 as Tausendmark in Smetana's Brandenburgers in Bohemia at Prague and Premoyl in Libuše at the Edinburgh Festival. *Recordings:* Dimitri by Dvořák, Smetana's Dalibor and Janáček's Osud. *Current Management:* c/o Neil Dalrymple, Music International, 13 Ardilaun Road, London, N5 2QR, England. *Telephone:* (20) 7359-5183. *Fax:* (20) 7226-9792. *E-mail:* music@ musicint.co.uk.

KÜTHEN, Hans-Werner, MA, PhD; German musicologist and editor; b. 26 Aug. 1938, Cologne; m. Annette Magdalena Leinen; one s. *Education:* Bonn Univ., studied in Bologna. *Career:* Ed., Beethoven Archives; mem. Gesellschaft für Musikforschung, VG Musikedition; Patron of the Verein Beethoven-Haus Bonn. *Film:* Beethoven's Hair 2005. *Publications include:* On Beethoven: Article Beethoven Herder, Das Grosse Lexikon der Musik 1978, Complete edn, Henle, München: Ouverturen und Wellingtons Sieg 1974, Critical Report, separately 1991, Klavierkonzerte I (nos 1–3) 1984, Klavierkonzerte II (nos 4–5) 1996, Klavierkonzerte III (WoO 4, WoO 6, op. 61a) 2004, each with Critical Report; contrib. to int. professional publications, including Beethoven yearbooks, congress reports, scholarly periodicals; journal contribs include: Gradus ad partituram: Erscheinungsbild und Funktionen der Solostimme in Beethovens Klavierkonzerten, Hudební věda 1, Prague 1999; Gradus ad Partituram: Appearance and Essence in the Solo Part of Beethoven's Piano Concertos, Beethoven Forum Vol. 9 No. 2, Urbana-Champaign, Ill. 2002; Ein unbekanntes Notierungsblatt Beethovens aus der Entstehungszeit der Mondscheinsonate, Prague 1996; Rediscovery and reconstruction of an authentic version of Beethoven's Fourth Piano Concerto for pianoforte and 5 strings (1807), in Beethoven Journal Vol. 13 No. 1, San José 1998 and Bonner Beethoven-Studien Vol. 1, Bonn 1999; On Viadana: Article V in Herder-Lex 1982, id in Lexikon für Theologie und Kirche, Herder 2000; Co-Ed., Beethoven im Herzen Europas. Leben und Nachleben in den Böhmischen Ländern, Prague 2000; Ed., Beethoven und die Rezeption der Alten Musik, Die hohe Schule der Überlieferung, Report of the Int. Symposium, Bonn 2000; A Lost Sonority: Beethoven's imitation of the Aeolian Harp, Arietta Vol. 4, London 2004; Ein verlorener Registerklang Beethovens Imitation der Aeolsharfe, Musik & Ästhetik 34 2005; Wer schrieb den Endtext des Violinkonzerts op. 61 von Beethoven? Franz Alexander Pössinger als letzte Instanz für den Komponisten, Bonner Beethoven-Studien Vol. 4, Bonn 2005; Coriolanus Overture, conducting score with Preface, Wiesbaden 2005, Piano Concerto Op. 19 and Rondo WoO 6, Munich 2012, Rondo WoO 6 for two pianos with Preface, Wiesbaden and Munich 2012, Piano Concerto WoO 4 (1784) with Preface, Munich 2013. *Address:* Am Hofgarten 7, 53113 Bonn, Germany. *E-mail:* hans-werner@kuethen.de. *Website:* kuethen.de.

KUTTENBAUM, Annette; German singer (mezzo-soprano); b. 15 July 1957. *Career:* debut at Opernhaus, Zürich 1981; sang at Hannover from 1983 and throughout Germany as guest, notably in The Ring and Parsifal at Bayreuth 1988–92; Dorabella at Nuremberg; Adriano in Rienzi at Berlin and Brangäne in Tristan und Isolde at Weimar 1996; Octavian in Der Rosenkavalier at Bologna 1995; further appearances as Hansel at Amsterdam and Fricka in Walküre at Trieste 1998; Ortrud in Lohengrin, Braugüne in Tristan, Fricka in Walküre and Kundry in Parsifal, all at Weimar; concert engagements in Vienna and elsewhere. *Recordings:* Das Rheingold, Götterdämmerung.

KUUSISTO, Ilkka Taneli, DipMus; Finnish composer; b. 26 April 1933, Helsinki; m. Marja-Lisa Hanninen 1972; two s. two d. *Education:* Sibelius Acad. with Aarre Merikanto and Nils-Eric Fougstedt, School of Sacred Music and Union Theological Seminary, New York with Seth Bingham, studied in Germany, Vienna. *Career:* debut as conductor 1955, composer 1956; Asst Head of Music Section, Finnish Broadcasting Corpn; Choral Dir, Finnish Nat. Opera, Gen. Dir 1984–92; Artistic Dir, Fazer Music Corpn 1982–84; Pres. Finnish Copyright Asscn 1990–94; Musical Dir, Helsinki City Theatre; Conductor, Radio Symphony Chorus; mem. Composers of Finland, Finnish Light and Film Music Composers. *Compositions:* operas: The Moomin Opera 1974, The Rib of a Man 1978, The War for the Light 1981, Jaeger Stahl 1982, Pierrot or the Secrets of the Night 1991, Mail Maiden 1992, Miss Julia 1994, The Daughters of the Fatherland 1998, Gabriel Come Back 1998, Aino Kallas 2000, Kings Ring 2001, The Shortage 2002, Matilde and Nikolai 2004, Towards Home 2005, The Prison of Freedom 2007, Taipale-River 2009, Aino Ackté 2010; ballets: Snow Queen 1978, Robin Hood 1986, Concerto Improvvisando for violin and chamber orchestra 2006; other: Raps by Lapps for orchestra 1994, Symphony No. 1 2000, Tapiola Today for orchestra 2003, Symphony No. 2 2004. *Recordings:* Christmas Carols from Finland with Soile Isokoski (soprano). *Honours:* Hon. Prof. 1992; World Council of Churches Scholarship 1958, Finnish State Scholarship 1968, Pro Finlandia Medal 1990, Finnish State Music Price 2007. *Address:* Apollonkatu 7 A9, 00100 Helsinki, Finland (home). *Telephone:* (9) 446232 (office); 500-253273 (mobile). *E-mail:* ile.tane@kolumbus.fi (home).

KUUSISTO, Jaakko; Finnish conductor, composer and violinist; b. 1974, Helsinki; s. of Ilkka Kuusisto; brother of Pekka Kuusisto; m. Lotta Nykäsenoja; one d. *Education:* Sibelius Acad. with Géza Szilvay and Tuomas Haapanen, Ind. Univ. with Miriam Fred and Paul Biss, studied composition with Eero Hämeenniemi and David Dzubay. *Career:* Concertmaster Lahti Symphony Orchestra 1999–2012, began conducting with the orchestra 2002; has conducted Finnish Radio Symphony, Tapiola Sinfonietta, Minnesota Orchestra, Savonlinna Festival Opera, BBC Concert Orchestra; Prin. Guest Conductor Oulu Symphony Orchestra 2005–09; Jt Artistic Dir (with his brother) Tuusula Lake Chamber Music Festival 1999–2007; Artistic Dir Oulu Music Festival and Oulu Festivo student orchestra 2013–; compositions have been performed in Scandinavia, UK and USA; first opera The Princess and the Wild Swans premiered Espoo, Finland 2003; has performed as soloist and chamber musician in China, Japan, USA and throughout Europe. *Compositions include:* chamber: String Quartet No. 1 1993, Trio 1994, Fantasia 1995, String Quartet No. 2 'Dancez' 1997, Play 1998, Loisto 2000, Play II 2006, Play III 2008, Valo 2009; orchestral: Välivuodenajat (Between Seasons) 1996; solo:

Violin Concerto 2012; vocal: Tänä aamuna 1995, Leaving 1994, Musiikki 1996, Kolme vuodenaikaa (Three Seasons) 1996; opera: The Princess and the Wild Swans 2002, The Canine Kalevala 2003, Makuukamariooppera 2009, Leirintäalueooppera 2012; for film: Täällä Pohjantähden alla 2009. *Recordings include:* Sibelius, Complete Works for Violin and Orchestra, Sibelius, Rarities, Olli Mustonen, Triple Concerto, Johann Sebastian Bach, Violin Concertos, Tango for Four Vols 1 and 2, Music! 2002, Mussorgsky, Kalevi Aho 2003, Sibelius Soundtrack 2003, Sibelius, Complete Piano Trios Vol. 1 2003, Einojuhani Rautavaara, The Journey 2004, Sibelius, Complete Piano Trios Vol. 2 2004, Sibelius, Complete Piano Quartets 2005. *Current Management:* c/o Sublime Music Agency Ltd, Sanna Nyyssölä, Ruusulankatu 14, 00250 Helsinki, Finland. *Telephone:* 45-3278222 (mobile). *E-mail:* sanna.nyyssola@sublime.fi. *Website:* www.sublime.fi; www.jaakkokuusisto.fi.

KUUSISTO, Pekka Taneli; Finnish concert violinist; b. 1976, Espoo; s. of Ilkka Kuusisto; brother of Jaakko Kuusisto. *Education:* East Helsinki Music Inst. with Geza Szilvay, Sibelius Acad. with Tuomas Haapanaen, Indiana Univ. School of Music, Bloomington with Miriam Fried and Paul Bliss, Steans Inst. for Young Artists at the Ravinia Festival. *Career:* many concerts with leading Finnish orchestras, including the Finnish Radio Orchestra and the Helsinki Philharmonic Orchestra; tour of Japan season 1996–97; festival engagements at Helsinki, Turku, Ravinia and Schleswig-Holstein; season 1998–99 Australian tour; season 1999–2000 tours to the USA and Japan with the Lahti Symphony and Osmo Vänskä, a tour to S America with Ashkenazy and the Czech Philharmonic and a tour to Germany with the Sibelius Acad. and Lief Segerstam; season 2002–03 Henze's Violin Concerto No. 3 with Orchestra della Toscana, the Beethoven concerto with Beethoven Academie Antwerp, visits to Malaysian Philharmonic, Singapore Symphony, Deutsche Kammerphilharmonie and Australian Chamber Orchestras; season 2003–04 concerts with Zürich Tonhalle Orchestra, Royal Stockholm Philharmonic, Swedish and Australian Chamber Orchestras; season 2013–14 with Britten Sinfonia, Cincinnati Symphony, Royal Stockholm Philharmonic, Singapore Symphony, City of Birmingham Symphony and Philharmonia orchestras; Artistic Partner Tapiola Sinfonietta 2006–13. *Recordings include:* Sibelius Concerto (with the Helsinki Philharmonic Orchestra under Segerstram) 1996, Strings Attached (recital album) 1997, Vivaldi's Four Seasons (with the virtuosi di Kuhmo) 1999, Bach Violin Concertos (with Tapiola Sinfonietta and Jaako Kuusisto), album of Olli Mustonen's works conducted by the composer, Folk Trip (Finnish Folk Music with the Luomu Players) 2002, Rautavaara: Works for violin and piano 2011, Kiestinki 2011, Magnus Lindberg Violin Concerto. *Honours:* winner Int. Jean Sibelius Violin Competition, Helsinki, winner Kuopio Violin Competition 1995, Nordic Council Music Prize 2013. *Current Management:* Harrison Parrott, 5–6 Albion Court, London, W6 0QT, England. *Telephone:* (20) 7229-9166. *Fax:* (20) 7221-5042. *E-mail:* info@harrisonparrott.co.uk. *Website:* www.harrisonparrott.com.

KUZMENKO, Vladimir; Ukrainian singer (tenor); b. 1960, Kiev. *Education:* studied in Kiev. *Career:* from 1988 sang with the Nat. Opera Co. of Kiev as Lensky, Rodolfo, Don José, Faust, Dimitri and Count Almaviva; guest appearances in France, Finland, Austria, Switzerland and Spain; Warsaw Opera in season 1994–95; British debut with the Kiev Opera as Alfredo in La Traviata, on tour 1995; Hermann in The Queen of Spades for Scottish Opera 1998.

KUZNETSOV, Fyodor; Russian singer (bass); b. 1960, Sverdlovsk, Ekaterinburg. *Career:* many appearances in concerts throughout Russia: Repertoire includes Mahler No.8, Beethoven No.9 and Shostakovich no.14 symphonies, Rossini's Stabat Mater, Bruckner's Missa Solemnis and Handel's Hercules and Samson; Engagements with the Kirov Opera, St Petersburg, from 1994 as Verdi's Philip II, Ferrando, Grand Inquisitor and Sparafucile; Mozart's Figaro and Commendatore, Boris, Pimen and Varlaam in Boris Godunov, Dosifei in Khovanshchina, Prince Gremin and Rimsky-Korsakov's Tsar Saltan; Sang Nikolai Bolkonsky in War and Peace with the Kirov at Covent Garden, 2000; Other roles include Khan Konchak in Prince Igor, Maliuta in The Tsar's Bride and Salieri in Rimsky-Korsakov's Mozart and Salieri; Mussorgsky's Boris Godunov at the London Proms, 2002. *Honours:* winner All-Russia Competition, 1987; Laureate Prize of the Mayor of St Petersburg, 1994.

KUZUMI, Karina; Japanese violinist; b. 29 April 1973, Tokyo. *Education:* Toho Gakuen, Tokyo, Univ. of Music and Arts, Tokyo, Escuela Superior de Musica Reina Sofia, Madrid, Spain, Musikhochschule, Lübeck and Hochschule für Musik, Cologne. *Career:* debut with Tokyo City Philharmonic Orchestra, Tokyo 1986; concert, Nara 1992; NHK-FM, Japan 1992; Radio II Clásica, Spain 1994; recitals at Auditorio Nacional, Madrid and Tokyo 1994, Burgos, Melilla, Malaga, Valencia and Santander 1995; concert at Tokyo, Gronau and Rheine 1997; tour of Japan 1998; La Radio Suisse Romande 1998; recital at Tokyo Opera City Recital Hall 1999; concert at Alte Oper in Frankfurt 1999; concerts with Budapest Symphony Orchestra, Klassiche Philharmonie Bonn 1999–2000; Leader (Concertmaster), Stuttgart Philharmonic, Germany 2001–. *Honours:* first prize All-Japan Student Music Competition 1988, Foundation Isaac Albeniz Scholarship 1994, Culture Dept Scholarship, Japan 1997, third prize Szigeti Int. Competition 1997, third prize Brahms Int. Competition 1998. *E-mail:* kkuzumi@gmx.de.

KVAPIL, Jan; Czech violinist; b. 4 Feb. 1943, Mladá Boleslav; s. of Jan Kvapil and Jarmila Kvapil; m. 1963; one d. *Education:* Prague Conservatory, Prague Acad. of Arts. *Career:* mem. Talich String Quartet 1962–94; tours to most European countries and to Egypt, Iraq, North America, Japan and Indonesia;

mem. Radio Symphony Orchestra, Prague 1994–97, Czech Philharmonic Orchestra 1997–2007; Trio Mysterium Musicum Prague (sacred music); with Talich Quartet annual visits to France from 1976 and tours of UK 1990–91 with concerts at Wigmore Hall, London, appearances at Bath and Bournemouth Festivals, QEH, London and on BBC 2's Late Show, with Janáček's 2nd Quartet; played Beethoven's Quartet Op. 74, Brahms A minor Quartet, Smetana D minor Quartet and works by Mozart, UK 1991; festival appearances in Vienna, Besançon, Lucerne, Helsinki, Amsterdam, Prague and Salzburg; repertoire also includes works by Debussy, Bartók (complete quartets recorded), Shostakovich, Ravel and Dvořák. *Recordings include:* complete quartets of Beethoven, Mozart and Bartók. *Honours:* Grand Prix du Disque Acad. Charles Cros 1977, Diapason d'Or, Supraphon Award. *Address:* Hrádková 2169, Újezd Nad Lesy, 19016 Prague 9, Czech Republic (home). *Telephone:* (732) 641268.

KVAPIL, Radoslav; Czech pianist; b. 15 March 1934, Brno; s. of Karel Kvapil and Marie Kvapilová; m. Eva Mašlaňová 1960 (died 1993); one s. *Education:* Gymnasium Dr Kudely, Brno and Janáček Acad. of Musical Arts with Ludvík Kundera. *Career:* first piano recital Brno 1950; Prof. of Piano, Prague Conservatory 1963–73; concerts throughout Europe, USA and Japan 1963–; gives master classes; performed world premiere of Dvořák's Cypresses 1983; Founder and Dir South Bohemia Music Festival 1991–; f. Int. Dvorák Soc. 1999; Pres. Yehudi Menuhin Soc., Prague 1990–, Dvořák Soc., Prague 1997–, Czech Soc. for Music and Arts 1990–; Founder and Chair. Czech branch of European Piano Teachers Asscn (EPTA), European Pres. EPTA 2008–09. *Recordings include:* complete piano works of Dvořák and Martinů, complete piano and chamber music of Janáček, complete piano works of Jan Hugo Voříšek 1973–74, complete polka cycles of Smetana, Czech contemporary piano music, Piano Concerto by A. Rejcha (first ever recording), Anthology of Czech piano music (for Unicorn-Kanchana label), eight vols, works of Dvořák performed on the composer's piano 1999, Ullman's Sonatas 5–7 2002, Vorísek: Piano Works 2003, Dvořák: Piano Works Played on Dvořák's Own Bösendorfer Piano 2004, Dvorák: Theme & Variations; Poetic Tone Pictures 2013, Beethoven: Piano Sonatas 2013. *Honours:* Hon. Vice-Pres. Dvořák Soc., London; Chevalier des Arts et des Lettres 2002; First Prize, Janáček Competition 1958, Int. Competition, Czechoslovak Radio 1968, Janáček Medal (Cultural Ministry). *Address:* Hradecká 5, 13000 Prague 3, Czech Republic. *Telephone:* (2) 67312430. *Fax:* (2) 67312430 (home). *E-mail:* r.kvapil@ecn.cz (office).

KVARAN, Gunnar; Icelandic cellist; b. 1960, Reykjavík. *Education:* Reykjavík Coll. of Music, Copenhagen Conservatory, studied in Basle and Paris. *Career:* solo concerts, recitals and chamber music throughout Scandinavia, France, Germany, The Netherlands and North America; appearances with the Icelandic Symphony, the Tivoli Orchestra and the Jutland Philharmonic; Prof., Reykjavík Coll. of Music; mem., Reykjavík Piano Trio.

KVECH, Otomar; Czech composer and academic; *Conservatory, Acad. of Music Arts, Prague;* b. 25 May 1950; m. 1st Miluska Wagnerová 1972 (died 2000); two d.; m. 2nd Dr Jana Smékalová 2003. *Education:* studied composition and organ at Music Conservatory, Prague, and composition with Prof. Pauer at Acad. of Music Arts, Prague. *Career:* debut, Symphony for Organ and Orchestra, Dvořák's Hall, Prague; pianist, Nat. Theatre, Prague 1974–77; Music Producer, Radio Prague 1977–80; Prof., Music Conservatory, Prague 1990–, Head of Composition Dept 1996–; Prof., Acad. of Music Arts, Prague 2002–; dramaturg, Czech Radio Symphony Orchestra, Prague 2010–; numerous recordings on Czech Radio, also in UK, Germany and France. *Compositions include:* five symphonies: Organ 1974, E flat Major 1982, D Major 1984, E Minor with String Quartet 1987, A Major – Four seasons for Organ and Orchestra 2001; Methamorfosis for violin solo and strings 1977, The Waltz Across the Room, cantata 1979, The World Carnival 1983, RUR 1986, Requiem 1991, Serenata notturna for strings 1996, Nocturnalie for woodwind 1997, Missa con viola obligata 1998, Crescendo, songs for baritone and orchestra 2002, Capriccio concerto for piano trio and orchestra, Recitatives and arias for cor anglais and orchestra 2004, Serenade for orchestra (based on Czech Christmas carols) 2004, nine string quartets 1972–2007, three violin sonatas 1974–82, Cello Sonata 1985, four Organ Sonatas 1986–2005, Piano Quintet 1990, Viola Sonata 1990, Oboe Sonata 1995, Sextet for string quartet, oboe and harp 1999, numerous chamber song cycles. *Recordings:* numerous works on Supraphon and Panton. *Publications:* Fundamentals of Classical Musical Composition 2013; contrib. to Hudebni Rozhledy (Prague), Opus Musicum (Brno). *Address:* Mraćnická 2, 10200 Prague 10, Czech Republic (home). *E-mail:* otomar.kvech@rozhlas.cz (home); info@kvech.cz (home). *Website:* www.kvech.cz.

KWELLA, Patrizia, GRSM, ARCM; British singer (soprano); b. 26 April 1953, Mansfield, Notts.; d. of Josef Piotr Kwella and Valeria Mies; m. Robin Cooke-Hurle. *Education:* Royal Coll. of Music, London. *Career:* Promenade Concert debut in 1979 with John Eliot Gardiner; concerts and festivals include Ansbach, Bergen, Innsbruck, Aldeburgh, Bologna, Warsaw, Bath, City of London, Edinburgh and Salzburg; US debut in 1983 with the San Diego Symphony; further concerts with the San Francisco, Houston and Washington Symphony Orchestras; sang in many of the Bach, Handel and Scarlatti tercentenary concerts of 1985; premiere of Night's Mask by Colin Matthews at the 1985 Aldeburgh Festival; Sang Handel's Alcina at the 1985 Spitalfields and Cheltenham Festivals; Repertoire includes Haydn, Mozart, Brahms, Mahler, Stravinsky and Britten; television includes many 'Man and Music' appearances (Channel 4). *Recordings include:* Handel's L'Allegro, Alcina, Alceste, Resurrezione and Esther, Monteverdi's Orfeo 2000 and Il Combattimento, Bach's B minor Mass, Magnificat and St John Passion, Mozart's Coronation Mass 2000, Missa Solemnis and Regina Coeli, Handel's Messiah (Highlights) 2010, Monteverdi Lamento D'Arianna 2014. *E-mail:* patrizia@ kwella.co.uk. *Website:* www.kwella.co.uk.

KWIECIEŃ, Mariusz; Polish singer (baritone); b. 1965, Kraków. *Career:* debut, Kraków Opera 1993 as Purcell's Aeneas; appearances as Mozart's Figaro in Luxembourg and Poznań and Papageno at Warsaw; sang in premiere of Zemlinsky's König Kandaules at Hamburg 1996; mem., Metropolitan Opera Lindemann Young Artist Program 1998; frequently appears with Metropolitan Opera; best known for title role in Don Giovanni (over 100 performances in 16 different productions including Royal Opera, Bayerische Staatsoper, Metropolitan Opera, Vienna State Opera, San Francisco Opera etc); other roles include Eugene Onegin, Marcello in La Bohème, Silvio in I Pagliacci, Malatesta in Don Pasquale, Almaviva in Le Nozze di Figaro, Guglielmo in Così fan Tutte, Escamillo in Carmen, Belcore in L'elisir d'amore, Ottokar in Der Freischütz, Count Robinson in Il Matrimonio Segreto, Enrico in Lucia di Lammermoor, Germont in La Traviata, Ricardo in I Puritani; has performed with Boston Symphony Orchestra, Vienna State Opera, Bilbao Opera, Houston Grand Opera, San Francisco Opera, Santa Fe Opera, Seattle Opera, Warsaw Opera, Veroza Japan Company, San Diego Opera, Los Angeles Opera, Lyric Opera of Chicago, Paris Opera, Netherlands Opera, La Scala, Bolshoi Opera, Graz Opera, Hamburg State Opera. *Recordings include:* Slavic Heroes 2012, Eugene Onegin (DVD) 2014, Don Giovanni (DVD) 2014, Szymanowski Król Roger (DVD) 2015. *Honours:* winner, Duszniki-Zdroj Int. Competition 1994, Hans Gabor/Belvedere Competition, Vienna 1996, Mozart Interpretation Prize and Audience Choice Award, Francisco Viñas Competition, Barcelona 1998, represented Poland at 1999 Cardiff Singer of the World Competition, Polish Ministry of Culture Gloria Artis Silver Medal 2009, City of Krakow Award 2011. *Current Management:* c/o William Guerri, Columbia Artists Management, 1790 Broadway, New York, NY 10019-1412, USA. *Telephone:* (212) 841-9680. *E-mail:* guerri@cami.com. *Website:* www.cami .com; www.mariuszkwiecien.com.

KWON, Hellen; singer (soprano); b. 11 Jan. 1961, Seoul, Republic of Korea. *Education:* studied in Cologne. *Career:* debut in Wiesbaden 1984, as the Queen of Night; has sung at Mannheim 1985–, Paris Opéra 1986 in Die Zauberflöte, and Hamburg 1987; created the role of Alexis de Lechebot in Liebermann's La Forêt at Geneva 1987; sang at Bayreuth Festival 1988 as a Flower Maiden, Glyndebourne Festival 1990 as the Queen of Night, followed by performances at Bonn and Vienna 1991; sang Susanna at Hamburg 1990, Wellgunde in a concert performance of Götterdämmerung at Rome 1991 and Blondchen in Die Entführung at Salzburg Festival 1991; other roles include Strauss's Sophie and Zerbinetta, Rosina, Norina and Musetta; sang Susanna at the 1992 Israel Festival, Adele in Die Fledermaus at Hamburg 1996; Constanze in Die Entführung at the Vienna Kammeroper 1998; concert tours of USA, France, Italy, Belgium and the The Netherlands, notably in the B minor Mass and St Matthew Passion of Bach. *Recordings include:* Nightingale in Die Vögel by Braunfels 1997.

KWUN, Hyuk Joo; South Korean violinist; b. 1985, Seoul. *Education:* P. I. Tschaikovsky Conservatory, Moscow, Hochschule für Musik und Theater, Hannover. *Career:* moved to Russia 1995; debut with Moscow Nat. Orchestra, aged 11; concerts in the halls of Moscow and other Russian cities and also in South Korea, Israel, Germany, Lithuania, Ukraine; solo performances with Moscow Nat. Orchestra, Moscow Chamber Orchestra, Murcia Symphony Orchestra, Kiev Symphony Orchestra, Moravian Philharmonic, Nuremberg Philharmonic Orchestra, Odense Symphony Orchestra, Sinfonia Toronto; also recitals. *Honours:* first prize, EMCY Prize for Outstanding Performance, and Special Prize for Best Interpretation, Kulturstiftung Hohenlohe Int. Violin Competition, Kloster-Schontal 2001, first prize, Yampolsky Violin Competition, Moscow 2002, first prize, Prize for the Best Performance of Danish Composition and Young Performer Prize, Carl Nielsen Violin Competition 2004, first prize, Paganini Moscow Int. Violin Competition 2004.

KYHLE, Magnus; Swedish singer (tenor); b. 1959. *Education:* Stockholm Coll. of Music, State Opera School in Stockholm. *Career:* debut at Vadstena Acad. 1983; engaged at the Royal Opera, Stockholm 1986–89, Stadttheater Darmstadt 1989–90 and Landestheater Salzburg 1990–92; roles include Mozart's Don Ottavio, Tamino, Monostatos and Ferrando, Pelléas, and Paris in La Belle Hélène; guest appearances at Tenerife and Tokyo; season 1990–92 as Tamino and Don Ottavio with the Royal Opera Stockholm, Tamino at Salzburg Landestheater and Ferrando at Semperoper Dresden; season 1992–93 as Beppe in a new production of Pagliacci at Stockholm, and in a new production of Traviata; Stockholm production of The Phantom of the Opera 1994–.

KYLLÖNEN, Timo-Juhani, MA; Finnish composer, accordion player and conductor; b. 1 Dec. 1955, Saloinen; m. Catharina Kyllönen; three d. *Education:* Tchaikovsky Conservatoire and Gnesin Music Inst., Moscow. *Career:* debut concert of works at Tchaikovsky Conservatory, Moscow 1986; Finnish debut, Helsinki 1986; biographical programmes, Finnish TV 1982, 1988; several concerts and radio and TV programmes in Finland, Sweden, Norway, Germany, Russia, USA, Peru, Ecuador; composer-portrait on Netherlands Radio 1990, also on Argentinian, Brazilian, Cuban, Israeli and Peruvian radio; mem. Finnish Composer's Union. *Compositions include:* Symphony No. 1 Op. 8 1985–86, Symphony No. 2 Op. 29 1991–95, Suite for string orchestra Op. 27 1991, Awakening Op. 23b for string orchestra, two Kalevala Songs for chorus and piano 1996, Accordion Concerto Op. 60 2001, Concerto grosso Op. 65 for orchestra, Licthtenthal Op. 43 symphonic poem for orchestra 1999, The Opera Roope Op. 76, Amor Vivus for orchestra and bariton Op. 2007, Dies Irae Op. 74 for string orchestra, The Book of the Kings (opera) Op. 30/79, Missa Festiva Op. 78 for orchestra, choir and organ. *Recordings include:* Compositions by Timo-Juhani Kyllönen, Elegia quasi una sonata Op. 15 1987, Trio No. 1 Op. 9 1986, Trilogy for two pianos Op. 4 1984, String Quartet No. 1 Op. 3 1984, Ciclo para coro mixto Op. 5, Concerto Grosso Op. 65, Accordion Concerto Op. 60, Lichtenthal Op. 43, Trio No. 5 Op. 74. *Honours:* Pro Musica Award 1988, Espoo City Arts prize 1989, Finnish Ministry of Educ. three-year scholarship 1991–93, 1996–98, Finnish Culture Foundation one-year stipendium 2001, 2004, Wihuri Foundation one-year scholarship 2007, Swedish Culture Foundation Grant 2008. *Current Management:* c/o Finnish Music Information Centre, Lauttasaarentie 1, 00200 Helsinki, Finland. *Telephone:* (9) 681011. *Fax:* (9) 677134. *Address:* Vanha Muuralantic 29B, 02770 Espoo, Finland (home). *Telephone:* (9) 805-3003 (home); (400) 953426 (mobile). *Fax:* (9) 805-3003 (home). *E-mail:* tjkyllonen@ gmail.com (home). *Website:* www.timo-juhanikyllonen.com.

KYNASTON, Nicolas, ARCM, FRCO; British concert organist; b. 10 Dec. 1941, Morebath, Devon; s. of the late Roger Tewkesbury Kynaston and of Jessie Dearn Caecilia Kynaston (née Parkes); m. 1st Judith Felicity Heron 1961 (divorced 1989); two s. two d.; m. 2nd Susan Harwood Styles 1989. *Education:* Westminster Cathedral Choir School, Downside, Accademia Musicale Chigiana, Siena, Conservatorio Santa Cecilia, Rome, Royal Coll. of Music. *Career:* Westminster Cathedral Organist 1961–71; debut recital, Royal Festival Hall 1966; recording debut 1968; concert career 1971–, travelling throughout Europe, N America, Asia and Africa; Artistic Dir J. W. Walker & Sons Ltd 1978–82, Consultant 1982–83; organist, Athens Concert Hall 1995–2010; Organ Prof., RAM 2002–14; Jury mem. Grand Prix de Chartres 1971, St Albans Int. Organ Festival 1975; Pres. Inc. Asscn of Organists 1983–85; Chair. Nat. Organ Teachers Encouragement Scheme 1993–96; mem. Westminster Abbey Fabric Comm. 2000–05; consultant for various new organ projects; recordings. *Publication:* Transcriptions for Organ 1997. *Honours:* Hon. FRCO 1976, Hon. RAM 2010; EMI/CFP Sales Award 1974; Deutscher Schallplattenpreis 1978. *Address:* 28 High Park Road, Kew, Richmond-upon-Thames, Surrey, TW9 4BH, England (home). *Telephone:* (20) 8878-4455 (home).

KYR, Robert Harry, BA, MA, PhD; American composer and teacher; b. 20 April 1952, Cleveland, OH. *Education:* Yale Univ., Royal Coll. of Music, London, Univ. of Pennsylvania, Harvard Univ. *Career:* Composer-in-Residence, New England Philharmonic 1985–89; resident composer of extension works, Composers' and Performers' Consortium, Boston, MA 1985–; teaching Fellow of composition and theory, Harvard Univ. 1985–89; Dir of Compositional Studies, Longy School of Music 1986–; Visiting Lecturer, Hartt School of Music 1988. *Compositions include:* Maelstrom 1981, There is a River for soprano, women's chorus and orchestra 1985, Images from Stillness for string trio 1986, The Greater Changing, Symphony No. 2 1986, Images of Reminiscence for piano 1987, A Signal in the Land 1987, The Fifth Season, Symphony No. 3 1988, Book of the Hours, Symphony No. 1 1988, Toward Eternity 1988, Symphony No. 4 1989, Symphony No. 5 1990.

L

LA BARBARA, Joan Lotz, BS; American composer, singer and writer; b. 8 June 1947, Philadelphia, PA; m. Morton Subotnick 1979; one s. *Education:* Syracuse Univ. School of Music, Berkshire Music Center, Tanglewood, New York Univ. *Career:* debut with Steve Reich and musicians, Town Hall, New York 1971; with Steve Reich 1971–74, Philip Glass 1973–76, John Cage, premiering Solo for Voice 45 with Atlas Eclipticlis, Winter Music with Orchestra of the Hague 1976; in Avignon premiere, Einstein on the Beach (Philip Glass) 1976; premiered Subotnick's Double Life of Amphibians, Los Angeles Olympics Arts Festival 1984; own work, Houston and San Francisco Symphonies 1982, Los Angeles Philharmonic 1983, New York Philharmonic 1984; premiered Subotnick's chamber opera Jacob's Room, American Music Theater Festival and MANCA Festival, Nice 1993–94, quartet of operas Now Eleanor's Idea (R. Ashley), Brooklyn Acad. of Music and Avignon Festival 1994; Balseros (Ashley) for Miami Grand Opera 1997; Dust (Ashley) Yokohama, Japan 1998; Celestial Excursions (Ashley), Berliner Fest Spiele 2003; Messa di Voce (own interactive media work), with Jaap Blonk, Golan Levin and Zachary Lieberman, Ars Electronica, Linz, Austria 2003; vocal soloist on sound score by John Frizzell for the film, I Still Know What You Did Last Summer 1998; film scores include Signing Alphabet 1977, Anima 1991, Immersion 1998, Endless Songs: Artemesia, Egon Schiele, Eva Hesse 2002, Triptych: Buffalo and Maine 2003; many commissions; newborn vocals for film Alien Resurrection 1997; Series Dir and performer, When Morty Met John…, a three-year series focussing on the New York School of Composers (John Cage, Morton Feldman, Earle Brown, Christian Wolff) at Carnegie Hall 2001–03; Artistic Dir and Host, Insights, a series of encounters with distinguished composers for The American Music Center 2003–; Curator, EMF@Chelsea Art Museum 2003; mem. ASCAP, The American Music Center, SAG, AFTRA, AEA. *Compositions include:* Angel Voice (for film, Date with an Angel) 1987, To hear the wind roar (choral) 1989–91, In the Dreamtime (self portrait, sound painting) 1989, L'albero dalle foglie azzurre for solo oboe with tape 1989, Awakenings for chamber ensemble 1991, Klangbild Köln 1991, Anima (film score) 1991, A Trail of Indeterminate Light for solo cello 1991, 73 Poems to poems by Kenneth Goldsmith 1994, Calligraphy II/Shadows for voice, dizi, erhu, yangqi, Chinese percussion 1995, In the shadow and act of the haunting place for voice and chamber ensemble 1995, de profundis: out of the depths, a sign 1996, A Different Train 1996, Snowbird's Dance, Into the Light for voice, flute and string quartet 2000, Dragons on the Wall, Tianji for voices, instruments and tape collage 2001, Snowbird's Dance: Into the Light and Beyond for voice, flute and string quartet 2004, Woolf Song (an opera in progress) 2004–, Landscape over Zero for voice, string quartet, piano, trombone and sonic atmospheres 2005. *Recordings include:* The Art of Joan La Barbara, Sound Paintings, Joan La Barbara Singing through John Cage, Three Voices for Joan La Barbara (Morton Feldman), Jacob's Room (M. Subotnick), 73 Poems 1994, Awakenings, L'albero dalle Foglie azzurre, Only: Works for Voice and Instruments (Feldman) 1996, ShamanSong 1998, Voice is the Original Instrument 2003. *Exhibition:* 73 Poems, a collaborative work with text artist Kenneth Goldsmith, included in The American Century Part II: Soundworks, The Whitney Museum of American Art. *Publications:* contrib. to Grove's Dictionary, Contemporary Music Journal, Los Angeles Times, Musical America/High Fidelity magazine, Schwann/Opus. *Honours:* DAAD Artist-in-Residency, Berlin, seven NEA Fellowships, Guggenheim Fellowship in Music Composition 2004; ISCM Int. Jury Award, Akustische Int. Competition Award, ASCAP awards. *Address:* 25 Minetta Lane (4B), New York, NY 10012-1253, USA. *Website:* www.joanlabarbara.com.

LA PIERRE, John; singer (tenor); b. 1961, USA. *Education:* studied in Purchase, New York and at St Louis Conservatoire. *Career:* appearances in opera at Atlanta, St Louis, Omaha, Nevada, Mobile, Cologne Opera as Mozart's Tamino, Ferrando, Ottavio, Belmonte, Belfiore; Glyndebourne as Idamante in Idomeneo; Opéra Comique in La Cambiale di Matrimonio and Il Signor Bruschino by Rossini; Netherlands Opera as Andres in Wozzeck and in Die Meistersinger; concerts include Bach's B Minor Mass, Washington; Mozart's Requiem, St Louis Symphony Orchestra; Messiah, St Matthew Passion; Haydn's Seasons, Cologne. *Honours:* finalist Met Opera National Auditions 1985.

LAAKMAN, Willem; singer (bass-baritone); b. 7 Oct. 1940, Aachen, Germany. *Education:* studied in Maastricht and Cologne. *Career:* debut as Lord Tristan in Martha, Amsterdam 1969; sang in The Netherlands until 1975; then Krefeld and from 1984 at Coburg; roles have included Boris Godunov 1987; Don Giovanni, Macbeth and Papageno; Altenburg from 1992 as Amonasro and Jochanaan in Salome; Dessau Opera from 1995; other roles elsewhere in Germany have been Strauss's Faninal and Dandini in La Cenerentola; concerts include Beethoven's Ninth.

LABADIE, Bernard, OC; Canadian conductor; *Music Director, Les Violons du Roy and La Chapelle de Québec;* b. 27 March 1963, Quebec City. *Education:* Collège Saint-Charles-Garnier, Univ. of Laval, studied with Pierre Dervaux, John Eliot Gardiner and Simon Streatfeild. *Career:* expert on 17th-century and 18th-century repertoire; f. Les Violons du Roy 1984 and La Chapelle de Québec 1985, Music Dir, conducting regular seasons in Quebec City and Montreal and tours throughout the Americas and Europe; guest conductor with numerous N American orchestras including New York and Los Angeles Philharmonic, Chicago, Boston, San Francisco, Saint Louis, Houston and Toronto Symphony, Cleveland Orchestra and Metropolitan Opera Orchestra; has also conducted Concertgebouw Amsterdam, Bavarian Radio Symphony, Orchestre philharmonique de Radio-France, orchestra of Gran Teatre del Liceu Barcelona and Melbourne Symphony Orchestra; regular guest conductor, Acad. of Ancient Music, also worked with other period instrument ensembles including Orchestra of the Age of Enlightenment, The English Concert, Collegium Vocale Gent Orchestra. *Recordings include:* with Les Violons du Roy/La Chapelle du Québec: J.S. Bach Psalm 51. *Honours:* mem. Académie des Grands Québécois for contrib. to society 2007; Chevalier, Ordre national du Québec 2006; Dr hc (Laval) 2007; Conseil québécois de la musique Special Opus Award 2006, Univ. of Laval La Gloire de l'Escolle award 2006, two Prix d'excellence de la culture awards 1998, Banff Centre Nat. Arts Award for contribution to the arts in Canada 2008, Le Soleil—Radio Canada Grand Lauréat 2009, Fondation de l'Orchestre symphonique de Québec Prix d'excellence des arts et de la culture 2009. *Address:* Les Violons du Roy, 995 place d'Youville, Quebec City, PQ G1R 3P1, Canada (office). *Telephone:* (418) 692-3026 (office). *Fax:* (418) 692-2078 (office). *E-mail:* info@violonsduroy.com (office). *Website:* www.violonsduroy.com (office).

LABELLE, Dominique; Canadian singer (soprano); b. 1960, Montréal; m.; two c. *Education:* Boston Univ. and with Phyllis Curtin. *Career:* first major performance as Donna Anna in Don Giovanni, New York; concert appearances with Symphony Orchestras of Dallas, Montréal and Boston; Messiah with Pittsburgh Symphony, Mahler's 2nd Symphony in St Louis and Vaughan Williams's Antarctica Symphony at Indianapolis; other repertory includes the Verdi Quattro Pezzi Sacri, the Requiems of Mozart and Frank Martin, Mahler's Fourth, Les Nuits d'Eté and Mozart's Exsultate Jubilate; opera roles include Elizabeth Zimmer in Elegy for Young Lovers, Mimi in La Bohème, the Countess and Susanna in Le nozze di Figaro, Giulietta in I Capuleti e i Montecchi; Handel's Rodelinda, Sigismondo in Arminio, Arianna in Vivaldi's Giustino. *Recordings include:* Elektra, with Boston Symphony; Don Giovanni, Masha and Chloe in The Queen of Spades, Handel's Arminio (Handel Prize 2002). *Honours:* winner, Metropolitan Opera Nat. Council Auditions 1989. *Current Management:* c/o Carrie Sykes, Schwalbe and Partners, 170 East 61st Street, Suite 5N, New York, NY 10021, USA. *Telephone:* (212) 935-5650. *Fax:* (212) 935-4754. *E-mail:* carrie@schwalbeandpartners.com. *Website:* www.schwalbeandpartners.com. *E-mail:* dominique@dominiquelabelle.com (office). *Website:* www.dominiquelabelle.com.

LABÈQUE, Katia; French pianist; b. 3 March 1950, Bayonne; sister of Marielle Labèque. *Education:* Paris Conservatoire. *Career:* performs worldwide with sister, Marielle Labèque; appearances with the Berlin Philharmonic, Bayerischer Rundfunk, Boston Symphony, Chicago Symphony, Cleveland Orchestra, Leipzig Gewandhaus, London Symphony, London Philharmonia, Los Angeles Philharmonic, Filarmonia della Scala, Philadelphia Orchestra, Dresden Staatskapelle and Vienna Philharmonic; has played under direction of Bychkov, Davis, Dutoit, Mehta, Ozawa, Pappano, Rattle, Salonen, Slatkin and Tilson Thomas; festival performances at Berlin, Blossom, Hollywood Bowl, Lucerne, Ludwigsburg, Mostly Mozart New York, BBC Proms, Ravinia, Rheingau, Ruhr, Schleswig Holstein, Tanglewood, Schubertiade in Schwarzenberg and Salzburg Easter Festival; formed new duo with Viktoria Mullova 2001, regular performances throughout Europe at Musikverein, Vienna, Musikhalle Hamburg, Philharmonie Munich, Schwetzinger Festspiele amongst numerous others; performances in 2005 season included recitals at Carnegie Hall, New York, Lucerne, Belgrade, Athens, Essen, throughout Italy as well as at Schubertiade Festival, Schwarzenberg; joined French saxophonist François Jeanneau's Paris Big Band Pandemonium; jazz collaborations with guitarist John McLaughlin; founder, Katia Labèque Band 2001–; first European tour with special guest Gonzalo Rubalcaba 2001; further concerts at Piano Festival Ruhr, Lucerne Festival, Easter Festival Salzburg and during opening ceremony of the new Konzerthaus in Dortmund; Katia Labèque Band and Orchestre Philharmonique de Montpellier performed première of a five-movt concerto (Spellbound by Dave Maric) for piano, keyboards, percussion and orchestra entitled 2004. *Recordings include:* Gershwin's Rhapsody in Blue and Concerto in F, recitals of Brahms, Liszt, Debussy, Ravel and Stravinsky, Rossini's Petite Messe (with the choir of King's College Cambridge), Bartók's Concerto for two pianos and orchestra, Symphonic Dances from West Side Story, España, Encores, Love of Colours, Visions de l'Amen (jtly), Little Girl Blue, Unspoken (with Katia Labèque Band) 2003, Ravel 2006, B for Bang 2007, Schubert/Mozart 2007, Stravinsky/Debussy 2007, De Fuego y De Agua 2008, Shape of My Heart 2009. *Current Management:* Abeille Musique, Usine Springcourt, 5 Passage Piver, 75011 Paris, France. *Telephone:* 1-49-26-97-77. *Fax:* 1-49-26-95-78. *E-mail:* benoitbuttner@abeillemusique.com *Website:* www.abeillemusique.com. *E-mail:* info@labeque.com (office). *Website:* www.katialabeque.com; www.labeque.com.

LABÈQUE, Marielle; French pianist; b. 6 March 1952, Bayonne; sister of Katia Labèque; pnr Semyon Bychkov. *Education:* Paris Conservatoire. *Career:* performs worldwide with sister, Katia Labèque; appearances with the Berlin Philharmonic, Bayerischer Rundfunk, Boston Symphony, Chicago Symphony, Cleveland Orchestra, Leipzig Gewandhaus, London Symphony,

London Philharmonia, Los Angeles Philharmonic, Filarmonia della Scala, Philadelphia Orchestra, Dresden Staatskapelle and Vienna Philharmonic; has played under direction of Bychkov, Davis, Dutoit, Mehta, Ozawa, Pappano, Rattle, Salonen, Slatkin and Tilson Thomas; festival performances at Berlin, Blossom, Hollywood Bowl, Lucerne, Ludwigsburg, Mostly Mozart New York, BBC Proms, Ravinia, Rheingau, Ruhr, Schleswig Holstein, Tanglewood, Schubertiade in Schwarzenberg and Salzburg Easter Festival; jazz collaborations with guitarist John McLaughlin. *Recordings include:* Gershwin's Rhapsody in Blue and Concerto in F, recitals of Brahms, Liszt, Debussy, Ravel and Stravinsky, Rossini's Petite Messe (with the choir of King's College Cambridge), Bartók's Concerto for two pianos and orchestra, Symphonic Dances from West Side Story, España, Encores, Love of Colours, Visions de l'Amen (jtly), Little Girl Blue, Unspoken (with Katia Labèque Band) 2003, Ravel 2006, B for Bang 2007, Schubert/Mozart 2007, Stravinsky/ Debussy 2007, De Fuego y De Agua 2008. *Current Management:* Abeille Musique, Usine Springcourt, 5 Passage Piver, 75011 Paris, France. *Telephone:* 1-49-26-97-77. *Fax:* 1-49-26-95-78. *E-mail:* benoitbuttner@ abeillemusique.com. *Website:* www.abeillemusique.com. *E-mail:* info@labeque .com (office). *Website:* www.labeque.com.

LABUDA, Izabela; singer (soprano); b. 1961, Poland. *Career:* sang Adina in L'Elisir d'amore and other roles in Poland from 1982; moved to Germany 1990, singing at the Essen Opera as Frau Fluth, Janáček's Vixen, and Hanna Glawari in Die Lustige Witwe; guest at Mannheim Opera, the Vienna Volksoper and the State Opera of Vienna as First Lady in Die Zauberflöte 1992; Antonia in Hoffmann at Cologne 1998; other repertory includes Lucille in Dantons Tod at Volksoper.

LACHENMANN, Helmut; German composer; b. 27 Nov. 1935, Stuttgart. *Education:* studied at Stuttgart with Jurgen Uhde and Johann Nepomuk David, in Venice with Luigi Nono. *Career:* teacher of music theory, Stuttgart Hochschule für Musik 1966–70, Ludwigsburg Hochschule 1970–76, Hanover Hochschule für Musik 1976–81, Musikhochschule Stuttgart 1981–99; masterclasses in composition at Basle Music Acad.; Instructor at the Ferienkurse in Darmstadt 1978, 1982, 1998, Cursos Latinamericanos de Musica Contemporanea in Brazil 1978, and Dominican Republic 1980; composition seminars in Blonay 1988, Oslo and Paris 1989, St Petersburg 1992, Barcelona and Chicago 1997, Viitasaari adn Akiyoshidai 1998; mem., Akademie der Künste, Berlin, Akademie der Schönen Künste, Munich, Freie Akademie der Künste, Hamburg, Leipzig, Mannheim and Academie voor Wetenschapen, Letteren in Schone Kunsten van Belgie, Brussels. *Compositions include:* Souvenir for 41 instruments 1959, String Trio 1966, Consolation I and II for voices and percussion 1967–68, Les Consolations 1977–78, TemA for flute, voice and cello 1968, Air for percussion and orchestra 1968–69, Pression for cello 1969, Dal Niente for clarinet 1970, Klangschatten mein Seitenspiel for 48 strings and three pianos 1972, Kontrakadenz for orchestra 1971, Gran Torso String Quartet 1972, Fassade for large orchestra 1973, Accanto for clarinet and orchestra 1975, Tanzsuite mit Deutschlandlied for string quartet and orchestra 1979–80, Harmonica for tuba and orchestra 1981–83, Mouvement - vor der Erstarrung for ensemble 1983–84, Ausklang for piano and orchestra 1984–85, Allegro Sostenuto for clarinet, cello and piano 1986–88, Reigen Seliger Geister String Quartet 1989, Zwei Gefühle, Musik mit Leonardo for ensemble 1992, Das Mädchen mit den Schwefelhölzern (opera) 1990–96, Serynade for piano 1998, Nun for flute, trombone and orchestra 1999, Grido String Quartet 2002, Schreiben for orchestra 2004, Concertini for ensemble 2005. *Honours:* Cultural Prize of Music, City of Munich 1965, Composition Prize, City of Stuttgart 1968, Bach Prize, Hamburg 1972, Siemens Prize 1997. *Address:* c/o Breitkopf and Hartel, Walkmuhlstr. 52, Wiesbaden 65195, Germany (office). *E-mail:* info@breitkopf.com (office). *Website:* www.breitkopf .com (office).

LACHMANN, Elisabeth; singer (soprano); b. 20 April 1940, Vienna, Austria. *Education:* studied in Vienna. *Career:* debut in Berne 1961 as Despina, and Cagliari in Wiener Blut; sang at Karlsruhe 1962–64 as Micaela, Marenka, Cherubino and Regina in Mathis der Maler, and Graz 1964–68 as Pamina, Susanna, Frau Fluth and Zdenka in Arabella; engaged at Dortmund from 1968 as Mimi, Sophie, Sieglinde, Desdemona, Donna Anna, the Trovatore Leonora, Wagner's Elisabeth, Venus and Brünnhilde, Tosca, Amelia in Un Ballo in Maschera, Aida, Senta, Ariadne, Abigaille, Marschallin, Leonore (Fidelio) and Elektra, (R. Strauss); these and other roles in guest appearances at Vienna State Opera, Hamburg, Stuttgart, Frankfurt, Cologne, Zürich and Antwerp; concert and opera tours to The Netherlands, France, Far East, Africa, South America and Switzerland; Prof., Detmold Musikhochschule 1984–. *Honours:* Kammersängerin 1994.

LACHOUT, Karel, MusD; Czech composer, musicologist, writer, pianist and teacher; b. 30 April 1929, Prague; s. of Ing. Karel Lachout and Marie Lachoutová; m. (divorced). *Education:* Charles Univ., Acad. of Musical Arts, Prague. *Career:* teacher of music and English (approbation for grammar schools) 1952; Ed. Music Dept. Radio Prague 1953–79; freelance artist, composer and musicologist with specialization in Spanish and Latin American folk music 1979–. *Compositions include:* Such is Cuba orchestral suite 1962, Symphonietta for grand orchestra, America Latina orchestral suite (including 'Mar del Plata'), two string quartets, piano pieces. *Radio:* scripts for music programmes on Radio Prague of authentic music from Latin America, Spain and other countries, including Music From Cristóbal Colón's Land series 1974. *Publications:* The Problem of Composer's Creation (dissertation) 1953, The World Sings (Czech Music Fund Prize) 1957, Music of Chile 1976, Music of

Cuba (honoured by invitation from UNEAC to Music Festival, Havana 1986) 1979, Folk Music of Latin America (edn to commemorate 500th anniversary of discovery of S America, with two LPs and booklet) 1992, Folk Music of Spain (double LP and booklet) 1993. *Honours:* recognition from Queen Sofía of Spain for promotion of Spanish music 1995, from Pres. Eduardo Frei of Chile for promotion of Chilean music in Prague 1999. *Address:* Viklefova 11, 130 00 Prague 3, Czech Republic (home). *Telephone:* (2) 71770347 (home).

LACKNER, Christopher, DipMus; New Zealand singer (baritone); *Chorister, Royal Opera House*; b. 29 Oct. 1951. *Education:* Auckland Univ., London Opera Centre, and privately with Otakar Kraus. *Career:* Chorus mem. Opera North, then prin. roles with Kent Opera, Pavilion Opera and Opera 80; appearances with Royal Opera from 1990, in Turandot (Mandarin), Die Zauberflöte (Man in Armour), Les Huguenots, Die Frau ohne Schatten, Rigoletto, Paul Bunyan, Der Freischütz (Kilian), Palestrina, La Bohème (Benoit), Andrea Chenier, Otello (Herald), Arabella (Welko), Tosca (Sciarrone), Barber of Seville (Officer), Madame Butterfly (Imperial Commissioner), Lady Macbeth of Mtsensk (Mill Worker), Baron Douphol (Traviata). *Honours:* Winner, New Zealand Mobil Song Contest 1974, Prize, Friends of ENO 1978. *Address:* Royal Opera House (contracts), Bow Street, Covent Garden, London, WC2E 9DD, England. *Telephone:* (20) 7240-1200. *Website:* www.roh.org.uk.

LACOMBE, Jacques, CQ; Canadian conductor; *Chief Conductor, Bonn Opera*; b. 14 July 1963, Cap-de-la-Madeleine, Québec. *Education:* Conservatoire de Musique, Montréal, Hochschule für Musik, Vienna. *Career:* Head of Orchestra and Music Dir, Grands Ballets Canadiens 1990–2003; Asst to Charles Dutoit, Montréal Symphony Orchestra 1994–98; Music Dir Philharmonie de Lorraine, France 1998–2001; Prin. Guest Conductor, Montréal Symphony Orchestra 2002–06; Artistic Dir and Prin. Conductor, Orchestre Symphonique de Trois-Rivières 2006–; Music Dir New Jersey Symphony Orchestra 2010–16; Chief Conductor, Bonn Opera 2016–; Guest Conductor with Edmonton Symphony Orchestra, Québec Symphony Orchestra, Royal Opera, Bavarian State Opera, Opéra de Monte Carlo, Deutsche Oper Berlin, Metropolitan Opera. *Current Management:* c/o Chris Putnam, Colbert Artists Management, 111 West 57th Street, New York, NY 10019, USA. *Telephone:* (212) 757-0782. *Fax:* (212) 541-5179. *E-mail:* putnam@colbertartists.com. *Website:* www.colbertartists.com; www.jacqueslacombe.com.

LAFITTE, Florence; pianist; b. 10 July 1961, France. *Education:* Conservatoire National Supérieur de Musique, Lyon, Liszt Acad., Budapest, Hungary, Manhattan School of Music, New York, USA. *Career:* piano duettist with twin sister Isabelle Lafitte; numerous concert appearances in France, Germany, Hungary, USA and Sweden; tours of Australia, New Caledonia, Indonesia, Brazil, Argentina and Chile; radio and television broadcasts. *Recordings:* Concerto for two pianos and orchestra by Poulenc (Orchestre Symphonique Français, conductor Laurent Petitgirard), two-piano recital of Mozart, Liszt, Mendelssohn. *Honours:* International Music Video Competition, Fuji television Network, Tokyo 1987, hon. award Murray Dranoff Two Piano Competition, Miami 1990. *Address:* Rue Langeveld 69, 1180 Brussels, Belgium.

LAFITTE, Isabelle; pianist; b. 10 July 1961, France. *Education:* Conservatoire National Supérieur de Musique, Lyon, Liszt Acad., Budapest, Hungary, Manhattan School of Music, New York, USA. *Career:* piano duettist with twin sister Florence Lafitte; numerous concert appearances in Germany, Hungary, USA, Sweden; tours of Australia, New Caledonia, Indonesia, Brazil, Argentina and Chile; several radio and television broadcasts. *Recordings:* Concerto for two pianos and orchestra by Poulenc (Orchestre Symphonique Français, conductor Laurent Petitgirard), two-piano recital of Mozart, Liszt, Mendelssohn. *Honours:* International Music Video Competition, Fuji television Network, Tokyo 1987, hon. award Murray Dranoff Two-Piano Competition, Miami 1990. *Address:* Rue Langeveld 69, 1180 Brussels, Belgium.

LAFONT, Jean-Philippe; French singer (bass-baritone); b. 11 Feb. 1951, Toulouse; m.; two d. *Education:* Opéra Studio de Paris; studied with Denise Dupleix in Toulouse and Paris. *Career:* debut at Toulouse 1974 as Papageno; sang at Paris Opéra 1977 as Nick Shadow in The Rake's Progress, Albi from 1977 as Mozart's Guglielmo and in Grétry's Les Femmes Vengées and Tom Jones, and Paris from 1978 in operas by Gounod, Offenbach, Gluck and Cherubini; sang in Berlin in the European premiere of Debussy's La Chute de la Maison Usher, at Lyon 1980 as Choroebus in the French premiere of Les Troyens, and at Aix-en-Provence 1982 as Boréas in the stage premiere of Rameau's Les Boréades; guest appearances in Strasbourg, Geneva, Lille, Hamburg, Hanover and Nimes; New York debut 1983 as Fieramosca in Benvenuto Cellini at Carnegie Hall; Perugia 1983 in Salieri's Les Danaides, Paris Opéra 1983 as Rossini's Moise, Brussels and Barcelona 1984 as Mozart's Count, Rome 1985 in Cherubini's Demophoon, Aix 1986 as Leporello in Don Giovanni and sang Amonasro at Bonn 1989, Debussy's Golaud at Marseilles 1990, and Alcide in Lully's Alceste at the Théâtre des Champs Elysées 1991–92; Rigoletto for New Israeli Opera 1997; season 1998 with Amfortas at Brussels and Falstaff at the London Prom concerts; season 2000–01 as Gerard in Nice, Macbeth at Montpellier and Scarpia for Chicago Lyric Opera; other roles include Thaos in Iphigènie en Tauride and Astor in Cheubini's Démophon. *Recordings include:* Vive Offenbach, Messe de Sainte Cécile, Orphée aux Enfers, Les Mamelles de Tirésias, Samson et Dalila, Leonore, Les Boréades, Gounod's Messe Solennelle, La Belle Hélène, Le Postillon de Lonjumeau by Adam, Verdi's Falstaff (conducted by John Eliot Gardiner) 2001. *Honours:* Chevalier, Ordre National de la Légion d'honneur, Officier,

Ordre National du Mérite, Officier, Ordre des Artes et des Lettres. *Address:* 83 Avenue Bosquet, Paris 75007, France (home); Agentur Hilbert, Maximilianstr. 22, Munich 80539, Germany (office). *Telephone:* 1-45-56-00-98 (home); 1-42-71-20-08 (office); (89) 290747-0 (office). *Fax:* 1-44-18-04-12 (home). *E-mail:* jphlafont@gmail.com (home). *Website:* www.hilbert.de (office).

LAGRANGE, Michèle; French singer (soprano); b. 29 May 1947, Conches, Saone-et-Loire. *Education:* studied in Paris. *Career:* engaged at Lyon Opéra from 1978; sang at Paris Opéra 1984–85 in Jerusalem by Verdi and as Alice in Robert le Diable by Meyerbeer; Opéra Comique 1987 as Donna Anna, at the Teato Colón in Buenos Aires 1982 as Teresa in Benvenuto Cellini, at the Aix-en-Provence Festival 1989 as Fata Morgana in The Love for Three Oranges; sang Marguerite in Faust at Avignon and St Etienne season 1990–91; Montpellier Festival in 1991 in Bizet's Ivan IV, concert performance; sang Fiorella in Offenbach's Les Brigands at Amsterdam and Isabella in Franchetti's Christoforo Colombo at Montpellier in 1992; other roles include Musette and Elisabeth de Valois. *Recordings include:* Poulenc Salve Regina and Stabat Mater, Guercoeur by Magnard, The Love for Three Oranges. *Address:* c/o François Rousseau, Le Bureau, 26 rue Duperré, 75009 Paris, France. *Telephone:* 1-45-26-79-36. *E-mail:* frousseau@fr-lebureau.com.

LAGZDINA, Vineta, BMus; Australian/Latvian composer; b. 11 Nov. 1945, Oldenberg, Germany; one d. *Education:* Univ. of Adelaide and Conservatory. *Career:* sound works included in exhibitions in Australia, New Zealand and Japan; film music includes electronic, computer generated and instrumental 1978–; video art music; grants for experimental music and movement performances 1981–82; composer's grant for radio 1983; Curated Audio-Eyes, exhibition 1983; Lecturer, Sydney Coll. of the Arts, Music Across the Arts 1984–; ABC Radio 1987; The White Bird Music Theatre 1987; Shock of the New, video soundtrack 1987; Speaking Out, film soundtrack 1987. *Compositions:* Obstruction (computer sound tape for dance) 1981, Noh-Work for quadrophonic percussion tape 1982, The Black Snake tape piece for voice and electronics 1983, Double-Dream, Triple Fate (video soundtracks) 1984–85, Media Massage spoken song 1986. *Publications:* 22 Contemporary Australian Composers; contrib. articles in Art Network 1983 , New Music Australia 4 1985.

LAHO, Marc; Belgian singer (tenor); b. 1964, Seraing. *Education:* Liège Conservatory, studied with Gabriel Bacquier and Luigi Alva. *Career:* appearances at Rennes as Mylio in Le Roi d'Ys, at Marseilles in Thais, I Puritani, L'Africaine, Die Meistersinger and Montségur by Landowski, 1993; Zürich 1994–95 in La Périchole by Offenbach and at Strasbourg as Alfredo in La Traviata; Further appearances in Italy and the USA, Orlando, Florida; Dijon Opera as Don Ottavio, Des Grieux in Manon Lescaut and Paris in La Belle Hélène; Sang Rossini's Comte Ory at Glyndebourne, 1998; Sang Laërte in Hamlet by Thomas in Toulouse and Donizett's Tonio at St Gallen, 2000;. *Honours:* Prizewinner, Pavarotti Competition, Philadelphia, 1992. *Address:* Opéra de Lausanne, Avenue du Théâtre 12, CP 7543, 1002 Lausanne, Switzerland (office). *Telephone:* 213101616 (office). *Fax:* 213101620 (office). *E-mail:* opera@lausanne.ch (office). *Website:* www.opera-lausanne.ch (office).

LAKATOS, Roby; Hungarian violinist; b. 1965, Budapest. *Education:* Béla Bartók Conservatory, Budapest. *Career:* made public debut on violin aged nine; resident with his ensemble at Restaurant Les Atéliers de La Grande Ille, Brussels 1986–1996; performances at Schleswig-Holstein, Ludwigsburg and Helsinki festivals, at Acads Musicales de Saintes in New York Cen. Park, with Orchestre Nat. de Radio France and Dresden Philharmonic 1996, at Autumn Strings Music Festival, Prague 2003, at Genius of the Violin Festival, London Symphony Orchestra 2004; 'homecoming' concerts, Thalia Theatre, Budapest 1999; concerts with The Lakatos Sextet 2004–, included in cultural programme of Ireland's presidency of EU. *Recordings:* In Gypsy Style 1991, Alouette: König der Zigeunergeiger 1998, Lakatos Gold 1998–99, Post Phrasing: Lakatos Best 1998–99, Lakatos: Live from Budapest 1999, With Musical Friends 2001, Kinoshita Meets Lakatos 2002, As Time Goes By (film score from Le Grand Blonde) 2002, The Legend of the Toad 2004, Prokofiev 2004, Firedance 2005, Klezmer Karma 2006, Roby Lakatos with Musical Friends 2008. *Honours:* First Prize for Classical Violin, Béla Bartók Conservatory 1984. *Address:* Lakatos Productions, c/o Eric Sterckx, Bergstraat 127/2, 2220 Heist-op-den-Berg, Belgium (office). *Telephone:* (1) 524-88-96 (office). *Fax:* (1) 525-17-08 (office). *E-mail:* robylakatos@telenet.be (office). *Website:* www.robylakatos.com (office).

LAKES, Gary; American singer (tenor); b. 26 Sept. 1950, Dallas, TX. *Education:* studied with William Eddy at Seattle Opera. *Career:* debut in Seattle 1981 as Froh in Das Rheingold; sang at Mexico City 1983 as Florestan in Fidelio and Charlotte Opera 1984 as Samson in Samson et Dalila; Metropolitan Opera debut 1986 as the High Priest in Idomeneo, returning as Tannhäuser and as Siegmund in a new production of Die Walküre; sang the Emperor in Die Frau ohne Schatten at the Metropolitan 1989, Radames at New Orleans, Erik in Der fliegende Holländer at the Metropolitan 1990 followed by Siegmund in New York (also televised) and San Francisco; sang in Das Lied Von der Erde at the 1991 Promenade Concerts, London; season 1991–92 as Lohengrin at Buenos Aires and Erik at the Metropolitan; sang the Berlioz Faust at the Festival Hall, London, 1994; Florestan at the Lincoln Center Festival, 1996. *Recordings include:* Die Walküre conducted by James Levine. *Current Management:* Pinnacle Arts, 889 Ninth Avenue, Second Floor, New York, NY 10019, USA. *Telephone:* (212) 397-7911. *Fax:* (212) 397-7920. *E-mail:* jmiller@pinnaclearts.com. *Website:* www.pinnaclearts.com.

LAKI, Krisztina; singer (soprano); b. 14 Sept. 1944, Budapest, Hungary. *Education:* Budapest Conservatory. *Career:* debut in Berne 1976 as Gilda in Rigoletto; sang with the Deutsche Oper am Rhein, Düsseldorf, in Cologne, and at Bregenz and Edinburgh Festivals; Glyndebourne 1979–80 as Aminta in Die schweigsame Frau and Sophie in Der Rosenkavalier; Salzburg 1980 as Lucille in Von Einem's Dantons Tod; tour of Germany 1984, notably in cantatas by Bach; Paris Opéra 1984 as Sophie; other roles include Zdenka in Arabella, Mozart's Queen of Night, Zerlina and Susanna, Carolina in Il Matrimonio Segreto and Nannetta in Falstaff; sang Marzelline in Fidelio at Hamburg 1988 and Zdenka at Barcelona 1989; sang Marzelline with the company of the Cologne Opera at Hong Hong; also widely heard in oratorio. *Recordings:* St Matthew Passion by Bach; Handel's Partenope; Masses by Haydn; Dantons Tod; Concert Arias by Mozart; Bach's Christmas Oratorio; Mozart's C minor Mass; Paisiello's Il Barbiere di Siviglia; Mozart's Schauspieldirektor and Myslivecek's Il Bellerofonte.

LALE, Peter; violist; b. 1960, England. *Career:* founder mem., Britten Quartet with debut concert at Wigmore Hall 1987; quartet-in-residence, Dartington Summer School 1987 with quartets by Schnittke; season 1988–89 includes BBC Lunchtime Series at St John's Smith Square, concerts with the Hermann Prey Schubertiade and collaborations with the Alban Berg Quartet in the Beethoven Plus Series; season 1989–90 includes debut tours of The Netherlands, Germany, Spain, Austria and Finland, festival appearances at Brighton, City of London, Greenwich, Canterbury, Harrogate, Chester, Spitalfields and Aldeburgh; formerly resident quartet at Liverpool Univ.; teaching role at Lake District Summer Music 1989 and Univs of Bristol and Hong Kong 1990. *Recordings:* Beethoven Op 130 and Schnittke Quartet No. 3; Vaughan Williams On Wenlock Edge and Ravel Quartet; Britten, Prokofiev, Tippett, Elgar and Walton Quartets.

LALLOUETTE, Olivier; French singer (baritone); b. 1960, Paris. *Career:* appearances with Glyndebourne Festival and Tour, as Dancaïre in Carmen, and Mozart's Guglielmo; Don Giovanni at Rennes, Count Almaviva for Flanders Opera, Simone in La finta Semplice at Versailles and Papageno for Opéra d'Avignon; Geneva Opera as Puccini's Sharpless, La Monnaie Brussels as Giove in Cavalli's La Calisto and Berlin Staatsoper as Passagallo in L'Opera seria, by Gassmann; Further Baroque opera roles with René Jacobs, William Christie, Christophe Rousset and Phillipe Hereweghe; Season 2000–01 as Tusenach in Three sisters by Peter Eövös, at Hamburg, Edinburgh and Vienna; Concerts with Pierre Boulez, Webern Cantata, and Kent Nagano, Carter's opera What Next?; Season 2001–2002 with Massenet's Lescaut at Lyon, Don Giovanni in Avignon, Guglielmo at Liège and Merlin in Chausson's Le Roi Arthus at La Monnaie, Brussels. *Recordings:* Giulio Cesare; Il Ritorno d'Ulisse; Handel's Scipione and Riccardo Primo, Les Fêtes de Paphos by Mondonville; Carmen. *Current Management:* c/o Musicaglotz, 11 rue le Verrier, 75006 Paris, France. *Telephone:* (1) 42-34-53-40. *Fax:* (1) 40-46-93-77. *E-mail:* general@musicaglotz.com. *Website:* www.musicaglotz.com.

LALOR, Stephen, MMus; Australian composer and music director; b. 11 Jan. 1962, Sydney, NSW. *Education:* Univ. of New South Wales, Tchaikovsky Conservatory, Moscow. *Career:* freelance composer and music education writer; Dir and Arranger, Sydney Domra Ensemble 1978–85; commissions from Macquarie Univ. 1994, among others. *Compositions include:* Alice: A Musical for Children 1986, Prelude and Dance for violin and piano 1988, Six Angels song cycle for baritone and piano, Three Pieces for piano 1989, Three Pieces for solo violin 1989, Damascus (opera) 1990, At the Edhe for orchestra 1991, String Quartet 1991, Maroubra Song Cycle for soprano 1991, Capricornia for string orchestra 1993, Way Home for soprano or treble, narrator and tape 1994. *Honours:* USSR Government Ukrainian Soc. Scholarship 1988.

LAM, Yvonne Yun-Won; American musician (violin, viola); b. 1981, Los Angeles, Calif. *Education:* Colburn School, Curtis Inst. of Music with Victor Danchenko, Juilliard School with Robert Mann; also studied with Alexander Treger, Laura Schmieder, Alice Shoenfeld and Linda Rose. *Career:* mem. contemporary music ensemble eighth blackbird 2011–, ensemble has commissioned and performed new works by composers such as Steve Reich, Jennifer Higdon, Brett Dean, Nico Muhly and Steven Mackey, and performed with orchestras including Cleveland Orchestra, Toronto Symphony and Atlanta Symphony at venues including Carnegie Hall, Barbican, Sydney Opera House and Kennedy Center; residencies at univs and conservatories, including Univs of Richmond and Chicago, Oberlin Conservatory, Queensland Conservatorium, Colburn School and Curtis Inst. of Music; as soloist, has appeared worldwide with orchestras including Los Angeles Philharmonic, Los Angeles Chamber Orchestra, Pacific Symphony and Auckland Philharmonia; as chamber musician, performed with artists such as Paul Katz, Roger Tapping and Anthony Marwood; toured with SONYC (String Orchestra of New York City) and performed with ACME (American Contemporary Music Ensemble); toured Israel with her own group, Colburn Quartet; festivals include Marlboro, Music from Angel Fire and Ravinia; Asst Concertmaster, Washington Nat. Opera Orchestra 2008–11. *Recordings include:* meanwhile (Grammy Award for Best Chamber Music/Small Ensemble Performance) 2012. *Honours:* Silver Medal, Michael Hill World Violin Competition 2005, Grand Prize, Pasadena Instrumental Competition, Prize for Best Performance of a Commissioned Work, Irving M. Klein Int. String Competition. *Current Management:* David Lieberman Artists, PO Box 10368, Newport Beach, CA 92658, USA. *Address:* c/o eighth blackbird, 5315 North Clark Street, #104, Chicago, IL 60640-2113, USA (office). *Telephone:* (773) 484-8811 (office). *Fax:*

(773) 961-7328 (office). *E-mail:* yvonne@yvonnelam.com (office); yvonne@eighthblackbird.org (office). *Website:* www.eighthblackbird.org (office).

LAMB, Anthony Stuart, ARCM; British clarinettist; b. 4 Jan. 1947, Woodford, England; m. Philippa Carpenter-Jacobs, one s. two d. *Education:* Royal Coll. of Music. *Career:* debut with Chamber Ensemble Capricorn at Wigmore Hall, London 1974; Principal Clarinet, Royal Ballet Orchestra 1969–71; founder mem., Capricorn (violin, clarinet, cello and piano) 1973, with many concerts and broadcasts; co-Principal, ENO Orchestra 1976–; several BBC broadcasts; freelance clarinettist with most major British orchestras; mem. Musicians' Union. *Recordings:* with Capricorn: Rimsky-Korsakov's Quintet in B flat for Piano and Wind, Glinka's Grand Sextet in E flat for Piano and Strings 1985. *Address:* c/o English National Opera, London Coliseum, St Martin's Lane, London, WC2N 4ES, England.

LAMB, Christopher S.; American percussionist; *Principal Percussionist, New York Philharmonic;* b. Sandusky, Ohio; m. Virginia Perry Lamb; two s. *Education:* Eastman School of Music, Rochester, NY. *Career:* fmr mem. Metropolitan Opera Orchestra and Buffalo Philharmonic; Principal Percussionist, New York Philharmonic 1985–, solo debut in world premiere of Joseph Schwantner's Percussion Concerto, celebrating Philharmonic's 150th anniversary; other works commissioned for him by New York Philharmonic include Tan Dun's Concerto for Water Percussion and Susan Botti's EchoTempo for Soprano, Percussion, and Orchestra; mem. Faculty, Manhattan School of Music 1989–; RSAMD Int. Fellow, Royal Conservatoire of Scotland. *Recordings include:* Chasing Light: Joseph Schwanter's Concerto for Percussion and Orchestra (with Nashville Symphony) (Grammy Award for Best Classical Instrumental Solo 2012). *Honours:* Fulbright Scholar Award 1999. *Address:* New York Philharmonic, Avery Fisher Hall, 10 Lincoln Center Plaza, New York, NY 10023-6970, USA (office). *Website:* nyphil.org (office).

LAMBERTI, Giorgio; singer (tenor); b. 9 July 1938, Adria, Rovigo, Italy. *Education:* studied in Mantua. *Career:* debut in Rome 1964 as Arrigo in I Vespri Siciliani; US debut at Chicago 1965 as Radames; Rome 1965 in the premiere of Wallenstein by Zafred; Metropolitan Opera from 1974 as Enzo, Cavaradossi, Radames and Turiddu; engagements in Paris, Brussels, Budapest, Baltimore, Amsterdam, Helsinki, Florence and Venice; Covent Garden debut, Don Carlos 1979; other roles include Pollione, Don José, Jason in Médée, Verdi's Ernani, Alvaro, Manrico and Riccardo, Wagner's Tannhäuser and Lohengrin, Edgardo in Lucia di Lammermoor; sang Radames at Berlin and Luxor 1987 and Caracalla Festival, Rome 1989; Andrea Chénier at Stuttgart 1988 and appeared as Stiffelio in the first Covent Garden production of Verdi's opera 1993. *Recordings include:* Ernani, I Lombardi, Il Corsaro, Gemma di Vergy by Donizetti, Bellini's Zaira.

LAMBERTINI, Marta; composer; b. 13 Nov. 1937, San Isidri, Buenos Aires, Argentina. *Education:* Catholic Univ. and studied in Buenos Aires. *Compositions include:* chamber operas: Alice in Wonderland 1989, Oh, Eternidad... Ossia SMR Bach 1990, Concertino Serenata 1981, Galileo Descubre las Cuatro Lunas de Jupiter for orchestra 1985; instrumental pieces: Assorted Kochels 1991; vocal music: Escena de la Falsa Tortuga 1993, Reunión for string quartet and piano 1994, La Ribera for speaker and string quartet 1996, Pathfinder for string trio 1997.

LAMBRO, Phillip; American composer, conductor, pianist and writer; b. 2 Sept. 1934, Wellesley, MA. *Education:* studied in Boston, Miami, FL, Music Acad. of the West, CA, studied with Donald Pond and György Sandor. *Career:* debut, Pianists' Fair, Symphony Hall, Boston 1952; composed and conducted music for several motion pictures, including documentaries; major performances in Israel, Europe, S America, Australia, Africa and the Orient; compositions performed by Leopold Stokowski, Philippe Entremont, Santiago Rodriguez, Roman Rudnytsky, the Philadelphia Orchestra, the Rochester Philharmonic, Baltimore, Indianapolis, Miami, Denver, Oklahoma and New Orleans Symphonies. *Compositions include:* Miraflores for string orchestra, Dance Barbaro for percussion, Two Pictures for solo percussionist and orchestra, Four Songs for soprano and orchestra, Toccata for piano, Toccata for guitar, Parallelograms for flute quartet and jazz ensemble, Music for wind, brass and percussion, Obelisk for oboist and percussionist, Structures for string orchestra, Fanfare and Tower Music for brass quintet, Night Pieces for piano, Biospheres for six percussionists, Trumpet Voluntary, Eight Little Trigrams for piano. *Recordings:* Crypt of the Living Dead 2006, Murph the Surf 2006, The Film Music of Phillip Lambro 2008. *Publication:* Close Encounters of the Worst Kind (memoirs) 2007. *Honours:* Nat. Bd of Review Award for Best Music for a Documentary (for music to Mineral King) 1972, ASCAP Standard Award 2007. *Address:* 1801 Century Park E, Suite 2400, Los Angeles, CA 90067-2326, USA (home). *Telephone:* (310) 556-9683 (home). *E-mail:* phillip.lambro@yahoo.com (home).

LAMOREAUX, Rosa Lea, BMus, MMus, ARCM; American musician and singer (soprano); b. 19 Oct. 1955, Farmington, NM; m. James L. McHugh 1991. *Education:* Univ. of Redlands, CA and Royal Coll. of Music, London, England. *Career:* debut at Kennedy Center; numerous performances at Kennedy Center, Mozart-Requiem, Exultate Jubilate, Bach-B-minor Mass and Magnificat, Coffee Cantata and Peasant Cantata both staged; Carmel Bach Festival in California: Mozart, Bastien Bastienne, Handel, Xerxes, role of Romilda, Bach, B minor Mass, Haydn, Paukenmasse, Lord Nelson Mass, St John Passion, Lieder Recitals; Bach, St Matthew Passion; St Theresa Mass, Pergolesi, La Serva Padrona, Purcell, Dido and Aeneas (the role of Belinda); Bethlehem Bach Festival: B minor Mass, St John Passion and Coffee Cantata,

Atlanta Symphony with Robert Shaw, B minor Mass, La demoiselle Elue by Debussy, Cincinnati May Festival; Mozart C minor Mass, Rheingau Music Festival, Germany; BBC Proms concert, Royal Albert Hall with Bethlehem Bach Festival; Shostakovich's 14th Symphony with Northwest Chamber Orchestra, Benaroya Hall, Seattle; Magic Flute and Messiah with Nat. Chamber Orchestra; Handel's Gloria, Grace Cathedral, San Francisco; mem. Cosmos Club. *Recordings:* Four Centuries of Song, Spain in the New World, Masters in this Hall, Luminous Spirit (Hildegard von Bingen, chants), I Love Lucette (15th- and 16th-century French theatre music), Berlioz's Messe Solennelle, Gentle Annie (Stephen Foster and Charles Ives), Bach Mass in B minor, Dancing Day (16th–18th Century Christmas, Classical Cabaret: Gershwin, Porter, Arlen, Poulenc, Montmartre Cabaret: Music from Toulouse Lautrec's Time. *Address:* 4112 Fessenden Street NW, Washington, DC 20016, USA. *Telephone:* (202) 363-5004 (office). *E-mail:* rlsings@earthlink.net. *Website:* www.jwentworth.com.

LANCELOT, James Bennett, MA, FRCO (CHM), ARCM; British choirmaster and organist; *Master of the Choristers and Organist, Durham Cathedral;* b. 2 Dec. 1952, Kent, England; s. of the Rev. Roland Lancelot and Margaret Lancelot; m.; two d. *Education:* St Paul's Cathedral School, Ardingly Coll., Royal Coll. of Music (RCM), London, King's Coll., Cambridge. *Career:* Dr Mann Organ Student, King's Coll., Cambridge 1971–74; sub-organist, Winchester Cathedral 1975–85; Master of the Choristers and Organist, Durham Cathedral 1985–; Conductor Durham Univ. Choral Soc. 1987–2013; Lay Canon, Durham Cathedral 2002–; Pres. Inc. Asscn of Organists 2013–15; mem. Council, Royal Coll. of Organists (RCO) 1988–2000, 2001–06, Cathedral Organists' Asscn (Pres. 2001–03). *Recordings:* numerous with King's College Choir, Winchester Cathedral Choir, Durham Cathedral Choir; solo including Complete Organ Works of Hubert Parry, Mendelssohn Organ Sonatas, Elgar Organ Sonata (DVD). *Publications:* Durham Cathedral Organs (with Richard Hird); contrib. to The Sense of the Sacramental. *Honours:* Hon. FGCM, Hon. FRSCM 2008; Hon. DMus (Durham) 2014; RCO Turpin Prize 1969, RCM Stuart Prize 1971. *Address:* 6 The College, Durham, Co. Durham, DH1 3EQ, England (home). *Telephone:* (191) 386-4766 (home). *E-mail:* organist@durhamcathedral.co.uk (office). *Website:* www.durhamcathedral.co.uk (office).

LANCERON, Alain; French record company executive. *Career:* Man. Dir EMI Classics France 1978–, Pres. Virgin Classics 1996–, Vice-Pres. EMI Classics A&R 2007–. *Honours:* Chevalier, Ordre Nat. du Mérite 1993.

LANDER, Thomas; Swedish singer (baritone); b. 1961. *Education:* Stockholm Coll. of Music and the State Opera School. *Career:* sang with Norrlandsoperan 1982–83; engaged at Hamburg Staatsoper 1986–87, and Vienna Volksoper 1987–89 as Mozart's Count and Guglielmo; guest appearances at Aix-en-Provence, Opéra de Lyon and in Italy, Iceland and Israel; engaged at Hanover 1990–; other roles include Mozart's Don Giovanni and Papageno, Malatesta, and Harlequin in Ariadne auf Naxos; sang Christus in Bach's St John Passion at Lucerne Easter Festival 1993.

LANDESMAN, Rocco, DLit; American arts organization executive, business executive and fmr theatre producer; *Chair, National Endowment for the Arts;* b. 20 July 1947, St Louis, Mo.; m. Debby Landesman; three s. *Education:* Colby Coll., Univ. of Wisconsin, Madison, Yale School of Drama. *Career:* Asst Prof., Yale School of Drama 1973–77; f. private investment fund 1977; Pres., Jujamcyn, which owns and operates five Broadway theatres 1987–2009, owner 2005–; Chair, Nat. Endowment for the Arts 2009–; mem. numerous Bds, including Municipal Arts Soc., Times Square Alliance, The Actor's Fund, Educational Foundation of America. *Theatre includes:* as producer: Big River (Tony Award for Best Musical 1985), Angels in America: Millennium Approaches (Tony Award for Best Play 1993), Angels in America: Perestroika (Tony Award for Best Play 1994), and The Producers (Tony Award for Best Musical 2001). *Address:* National Endowment for the Arts, 1100 Pennsylvania Avenue NW, Washington, DC 20506, USA (office). *Telephone:* (202) 682-5414 (office). *Fax:* (202) 682-5639 (office). *E-mail:* chairman@arts.gov (office). *Website:* www.arts.gov (office).

LANDSMAN, Vladimir, DMus; violinist; b. 1941, Dushambe, Russia. *Education:* Moscow School of Music, Moscow State Conservatory. *Career:* soloist, Moscow Philharmonic Soc.; toured Soviet Union; Hollywood Bowl, Los Angeles; concert tours throughout the world; guest soloist; Bolshoi Hall, Moscow Conservatory; Artistic Dir, Seasons Orchestra, Moscow 1994–95; teacher in music faculty, Université de Montréal; Assoc. Prof.; teacher at acads worldwide; teacher, Orford Arts Centre, Québec; masterclasses; served on examination juries. *Honours:* third prize Jaques Thibaud Int. Violin Competition, Paris 1963, first prize Montréal Int. Competition 1966.

LANE, (Alan) Piers, AO, BMus, ARCM, LMusA, AMusA; British/Australian pianist, artistic director and broadcaster; b. 8 Jan. 1958, London, England; s. of Peter Alan Lane and Enid Muriel Hitchcock. *Education:* Queensland Conservatorium of Music, Royal Coll. of Music, London. *Career:* broadcaster for BBC Radio 3; critic CD Review; has appeared with numerous orchestras, including London Philharmonic, Philharmonia, Royal Philharmonic, all BBC orchestras, City of Birmingham Symphony, Halle, Australian Chamber Orchestra, all ABC orchestras, New Zealand Symphony Orchestra, Auckland Philharmonic, Christchurch Symphony, Southern Sinfonia, Orchestra Ensemble Kanazawa (Japan), Orchestre National de France, Orchestre Philharmonique de Montpellier, American Symphony Orchestra, Czech Philharmonic, Warsaw Philharmonic, Gothenberg Symphony; has toured extensively in Australia, Africa, Europe, India, Japan, NZ, Russia, Scandinavia, S America, USA; has appeared at festivals including Aldeburgh, Bard, BBC Promenade Concerts, Huntington, Husum Festival of Piano Rarities (Germany), Blair Atholl, Speedside, Toronto, Singapore Piano Festival, Newport Festival, Rhode Island, Duznicki Chopin Festival, Poland, Ruhr Piano Festival, Bergen Festival, Bridgewater Piano Festival, Manchester 2003, Bagatelles Chopin Festival, Paris; La Roque d'Anthéron, Storioni Festival (Netherlands), El Paso Promusica, Sitka Summer Music Festival, Alaska; Int. Adjudicator Tbilisi and Sydney Int. Piano Competitions; Prof., RAM 1989–2011; Dir Myra Hess Day Nat. Gallery 2006–, Australian Festival of Chamber Music 2007–; Dir and Trustee The Hattori Foundation; Patron, European Piano Teachers' Asscn (UK), The Old Granary Studio, Queensland Music Teachers' Asscn, Accompanists' Guild of Queensland, Youth Music Foundation of Australia, Tait Memorial Trust; Vice-Pres. Putney Music Club. *Recordings include:* Moskowski, Paderewski Concertos 1990, Complete Etudes of Scriabin 1992, Piano Quintet by Brahms (New Budapest Quartet) 1992, Violin Virtuoso (with Tasmin Little) 1992, Cello Sonatas (with Alexander Baillie) by Shostakovich, Prokofiev, Schnittke and Rachmaninoff, d'Albert Concertos 1994, Vaughan-Williams and Delius Concertos plus Finzi Eclogue 1994, Elgar Piano Quintet (with Vellinger String Quartet) 1994, Delius Violin Sonatas (with Tasmin Little) (Diapason d'Or) 1997, d'Albert Solo Piano Works 1997, Saint-Saëns Complete Etudes 1998, Kullak & Dreyschock Concertos (with Niklas Willen) 1999, Complete Scriabin Preludes 2000, Grainger Piano Transcriptions 2001, Bach Transcriptions 2002, Moscheles Etudes 2003, Henselt Etudes 2004, Stanford Quintet (with Vanburgh Quartet) 2004, Delius and Ireland Piano Concertos 2005, Alnaes and Sinding Concertos 2005, Bloch Piano Quintets (with Goldner String Quartet) 2008, Bridge Piano Quintet (with Goldner String Quartet) 2008, Dvořák Piano Quintets (with Goldner String Quartet) 2009, Bach/d'Albert organ transcriptions 2010, Elgar Piano Quintet (with Goldner String Quartet) 2010, Virtuoso Clarinet (with Michael Collins) 2012, Harty Piano Quintet (with Goldner String Quartet) 2011, Strauss and Respighi Violin Sonatas (with Tasmin Little) 2012, Piers Lane Goes to Town 2013, Mozart Piano Concertos K482 and K491 (with Queensland Symphony) 2013, Walton and Ferguson Violin Sonatas (with Tasmin Little) 2013, Liszt/Berlioz Harold in Italy and Roger Viola Sonata (with Philip Dukes) 2013, Taneyev and Arensky Piano Quintets (with Goldner String Quartet) 2013. *Honours:* Hon. ARAM 1994; Hon. DUniv (Griffith Univ.) 2007; Bartók Special Prize, Liszt Int. Competition, Budapest 1976, Best Australian Pianist, Sydney Int. Piano Competition 1977, winner, Royal Overseas League Competition 1982. *Current Management:* c/o Hazard Chase, 25 City Road, Cambridge, CB1 1DP, England. *Telephone:* (1223) 312400. *Fax:* (1223) 460827. *E-mail:* sibylle.jackson@hazardchase.co.uk. *Website:* www.hazardchase.co.uk; www.pierslane.com.

LANE, Gloria; American singer (mezzo-soprano, soprano); b. 6 June 1930, Trenton, NJ; m. Samuel Krachmalnick. *Education:* studied with Elisabeth Westmoreland in Philadelphia. *Career:* debut in Philadelphia 1950 in the premiere of Menotti's The Consul; Broadway 1954 in the premiere of Menotti's The Saint of Bleecker Street; British debut 1958 as Baba the Turk in The Rake's Progress, returning 1972 as Dorabella in Così fan tutte, Strauss's Ariadne and Lady Macbeth; Covent Garden debut 1960 as Carmen and sang at Florence 1966 as Federica in Verdi's Luisa Miller; guest appearances in Vienna, Paris, Venice, Rome, Palermo, Boston, Chicago and San Francisco; New York City Opera 1971 as Santuzza in Cavalleria Rusticana. *Recordings:* The Consul, Rossini's Mosè in Egitto, The Saint of Bleecker Street.

LANE, Jennifer Ruth, BMus, MA; American singer (mezzo-soprano); b. 25 Nov. 1954, Berwyn, IL; m. James H. Carr, 1987. *Education:* Chicago Musical College, Roosevelt University, City University of New York. *Career:* debut as Elsbeth in Strauss's Feuersnot, Santa Fe Opera in 1988; Performances with Santa Fe Opera, New York City Opera, Opera Monte Carlo, L'Opéra Français de New York, Opera Omaha, US stage premiere of Handel's Partenope, Milwaukee's Skylight Opera, Opera Ensemble of New York; Prior to operatic career, toured North and South America with the Waverly Consort; Also tours of the Far East with the Gregg Smith Singers; Many concert performances including appearances with the Atlanta Symphony under Robert Shaw, San Francisco Symphony, The National Symphony, St Louis Symphony, and Harrisburg Symphony in Mahler's 2nd and 3rd Symphonies; Many radio broadcasts including Mahler's 3rd Symphony, personal interviews and Radio Canada recital with countertenor, Alan Fast; Sang Alessandro in Handel's Tolomeo at Halle, 1996; Handel's Serse with New York City Opera, 1997. *Recordings include:* JS Bach's St John Passion, Smithsonian Collection of Recordings; Handel's Theodora with Nicholas McGegan conducting; Bach's Solo Cantata for Alto; John Adams, Grand Pianola Music with composer conducting. *Current Management:* c/o Guy Barzilay Artists, 360 West 28th Street #6B, New York, NY 10001, USA. *Telephone:* (212) 741-6118. *Fax:* (212) 741-2558. *E-mail:* guybar@aol.com. *Website:* guybarzilayartists.com. *Address:* 514 West 110th Street, Apt 92, New York, NY 10025, USA. *Website:* www .stanford.edu/~jlane.

LANG, Aidan; British stage director and artistic director; *General Director, New Zealand Opera;* b. 9 Oct. 1957, England; m. Linda Kitchen; one d. *Education:* Tiffin School, Univ. of Birmingham. *Career:* Glyndebourne from 1984, becoming Dir of Productions for the Tour 1991, Prin. Assoc. Dir for the Festival; productions with Glyndebourne Touring Opera have included his debut, La Bohème 1991, Matthus's Song of Love and Death and Il Barbiere di Siviglia; premiere of Hamilton's Lancelot at the Arundel Festival, Tamerlano at Göttingen, Carmen for Canadian Opera and La Traviata, Die Zauberflöte

(Barcelona) 1990–97; Artistic Dir, Opera Zuid, Netherlands, with productions of Werther, Ariadne, The Cunning Little Vixen and Don Giovanni; further engagements include Le Comte Ory for Welsh Nat. Opera, Hansel and Gretel in Belfast, Così fan tutte at Cologne, Tosca at Nice, Die Entführung for Istanbul Festival, Il Ritorno d'Ulisse in Lisbon, Mozart's La Finta Semplice at Buxton 1998, Lucio Silla at Garsington; season 1999 directed Magic Fountain by Delius (Scottish Opera) and Don Giovanni (Brazil); season 2000 directed Fierrebras (Buxton) and Cav and Pag (São Páolo); fmr Artistic Dir Maastricht Festival, Netherlands eight years; Artistic Dir, Buxton Festival 2000–06; Gen. Dir New Zealand Opera 2006–; other recent productions include La Sonnambula (Rio de Janeiro) and Un Giorno di Regno, La Périchole, Maria Padilla, Hercules, Merry Wives of Windsor, Armide (Buxton); directed a new Wagner's Der Ring des Nibelungen at Amazonas Opera Festival, Brazil 2005, Le nozze di Figaro 2010 and Acis & Galatea (New Zealand Opera) 2013. *Address:* New Zealand Opera, PO Box 6478, Wellesley Street, Auckland 1141, New Zealand (office). *Telephone:* (9) 379-4020 (office). *Website:* www.nzopera .com (office).

LANG, David, PhD; American composer; b. 1 Aug. 1957, Los Angeles, Calif.; m.; three c. *Education:* Stanford Univ., Univ. of Iowa, Yale School of Music, studied with Jacob Druckman, Hans Werner Henze and Martin Bresnick. *Career:* Jr Composer-in-Residence, Horizons Summer Festival 1980s; commissioned by Boston Symphony Orchestra, Cleveland Orchestra, St Paul Chamber Orchestra, BBC Singers, American Composers Orchestra and Santa Fe Opera and Settembre Musica Festival, Turin; co-f. (with Michael Gordon and Julia Wolfe) New York annual music festival Bang on a Can 1987–; composed album Brian Eno: Music for Airports 1998 for group Bang on a Can All-Stars; Carnegie Hall's Debs Composer's Chair for 2013–14; Composer-in-Residence, de Doelen centre, Rotterdam 2014–15, Carlsbad Music Festival Sept. 2014. *Recordings include:* The Little Match Girl Passion (Grammy Award for Best Small Ensemble Performance 2010) 2009, The Woodmans 2011, Love Fail 2012, Death Speaks 2013. *Compositions include:* chamber music: Frag 1984, Dance/Drop 1987, Burn Notice 1989, Music for Gracious Living 1992, Cheating, Lying, Stealing 1993, Face so Pale 1992, Wreck/Wed 1995, Slip 1996, Follow 1996, Little Eye 1999, My Very Empty Mouth 1999, Sweet Air 1999, Short Fall 2000, Birds of Minnesota 2000, Darker 2010, Man Made 2013; for chorus: By Fire 1984, Hecuba 1995, This Condition 2000, I Lie 2001, Again (After Ecclesiastes) 2005, Evening Morning Day 2007, The Little Match Girl Passion (Pulitzer Prize for Music 2008) 2007; opera: Judith and Holofernes 1989, Music for Gracious Living 1992, Modern Painters 1995, The Carbon Copy Building 1999, The Difficulty of Crossing a Field 2000, Lost Objects 2001; orchestral and large ensemble: Hammer Amour 1978, Eating Living Monkeys 1985, Spud 1986, Are You Experienced? 1987–89, Bonehead 1990, International Business Machine 1990, Fire and Forget 1992, My Evil Twin 1992, Slow Movement 1993, Under Orpheus 1994, Grind to a Halt 1996, The Passing Measures 1998, I Fought the Law 1998, Ariel's Version 1998, Haircut 2000, How to Pray 2002, Fur 2004, Loud Love Songs 2004, Pierced 2007, Every Ounce of Strength 2007, Mountain 2014. *Honours:* Rome Prize, American Acad., Rome; BMW Prize, Munich Biennale for New Music Theatre; Friedheim Award, Kennedy Center; Revson Fellowship with New York Philharmonic, Musical America's Composer of the Year 2013; grants from Guggenheim Foundation, New York Foundation of Arts and Nat. Endowment for the Arts. *Current Management:* c/o Amanda Ameer, First Chair Promotion, 331 West 57th Street, Suite 132, New York, NY 10019, USA. *E-mail:* info@ davidlangmusic.com. *Website:* davidlangmusic.com.

LANG, Istvan; Hungarian composer and academic (retd); b. 1 March 1933, Budapest; m. Csilla Fülöp 1966; one s. *Education:* Acad. of Music, Budapest. *Career:* freelance composer 1958–66; Musical Adviser, State Puppet Theatre 1966–84; Prof. of Chamber Music, Acad. of Music, Budapest 1973–2006; Sec.-Gen. Asscn of Hungarian Musicians 1978–90; mem. Int. Soc. for Contemporary Music (Cttee mem. 1984–87), Int. Music Council (Cttee mem. 1990–94), Hungarian Composers' Union. *Compositions:* Dream about the Theatre, Rounded up television operas, In memoriam NN, Symphonies Nos 2, 3, 4, 5, 6 and 7, Violin Concerto, Double Concerto for clarinet and harp, Concerto Bucolico, Pezzo Lirico Ad nominem Mahler, Rhymes, Constellations, Affetti, Intarsia around a Bartók theme, Music 2-4-3, Sempre in tensione, solo pieces for various instruments, String Quartets Nos 2 and 3, Wind Quintets Nos 1, 2 and 3, Sonata for violin and piano 1990, Cimbiosis 1991, Sonata for cello and piano 1992–93, Off and On for harp and live electronics, Budapest Liszt Ferenc Square, Vibrating Object on Parabola Line, Knotes on the Line (chamber music) 1993, Viviofa (chamber music) 1995, The Coward (opera in one act) 1998, Night-fall for trumpet and live electronic music, Meeting a Young Man (electroacoustic radio play), Concertino for soprano and live electro-acoustic 1999, No Man is an Island (John Donne), Chamber Cantata No. 3, Diamont in Durst of Earth (cantata) 2004, Sinfonietta 2008–09, Exclamations (chamber music) 2011, Cimbiofonia 2011, Close Connections 2011–12. *Honours:* several decorations; Erkel Prize 1968, 1975, Merit Artist 1985, Bartók Pásztori Prize 1994, Artisius Prize 2005. *Address:* Frankel Leo Ut 24, 1027 Budapest, Hungary (home). *Telephone:* (1) 3164253 (home); 20-2284158 (mobile) (home). *E-mail:* langistvan@chello.hu.

LANG, Klaus; Austrian composer, concert organist and academic; *Professor, Universität für Musik, Graz;* b. 26 April 1971, Graz. *Education:* Universität für Musik und Darstellende Kunst, Graz with H. M. Pressl and B. Furrer, studied with Y. Pagh-Paan at Hochschule der Künste, Bremen. *Career:* performances at Steirischer Herbst, Wien Modern, MaerzMusik, Berlin,

Wittener Tage für neue Kammermusik, Donaueschinger Musiktage, Klangspuren Schwaz, Huddersfield Contemporary Music Festival, Münchener Biennale, Eclat Stuttgart, Lucerne Festival, Monday evening concerts, Takefu Festival, Dresdener Tage für Neue Musik and others; compositions performed by Klangforum Wien, Arditti Quartet, ICE-New York, Musikfabrik-NRW, Ensemble Intercontemporain, Ensemble die Reihe, SWR Chorus, WDR Choir, Studio Percussion Graz, HR-Orchestra Frankfurt, RSB-Berlin, RSO-Vienna, Tehran Symphony Orchestra, etc.; operatic works performed at Opera Bonn, Hebbeltheater Berlin, Volksbühne Berlin, Gasteig Munich, Theater Aachen, Staatstheater Braunschweig, Landestheater Linz, Landestheater Innsbruck, etc.; Prof. of Music, Universität für Musik und Darstellende Kunst, Graz 2006–. *Recordings:* Trauermusiken die Überwinterung der Mollusken, Lichtgeschwindigkeit (Duoimprovisationen mit Werner Dafeldecker) (grob) sei Jaku für Streichquartet (Arditti Quartet), Missa beati pauperes spiritu (col legno), The Book of Serenity. *Publications:* Auf Wohlklangswellen durch der Töne Meer 1999; contrib. to New Grove Dictionary. *Honours:* Musikförderungspreis der Stadt Graz 1992, Würdigungspreis des Bundesministeriums 1993, Preis der Kompositionswettbewerbes der Musikprotokolls in steirischeherbst 1993, Komponistenseminar des Klangforum 1998, Andrzej Dobrowolski Preis 2011. *Address:* Universität für Musik und Darstellende Kunst Graz, Leonhardstr. 15, PO Box 208, Palais Meran, 8010 Graz, Austria (office). *Telephone:* (316) 389-0 (office). *Fax:* (316) 389-1101 (office). *E-mail:* klaus.lang@mur.at (office). *Website:* www.klang.mur.at; www.zeitvertrieb.mur.at.

LANG, Petra; German singer (mezzo-soprano); b. 29 Nov. 1962, Frankfurt. *Education:* studied in Darmstadt and Mainz. *Career:* sang at Basle Opera 1990–91, Karlsruhe 1991–92, Dortmund 1992–95; Brunswick 1995–96: Judith in Bluebeard's Castle, Brangaene in Tristan and Marie in Wozzeck; Salzburg Festival 1993: Virtu in Monteverdi's Poppea; Bregenz 1994: Fenena in Nabucco; La Scala 1995: Die Zauberflöte; other roles include Mozart's Dorabella and Cherubino, Strauss's Octavian and Composer, Suzuki in Butterfly and Gluck's Orpheus; Lieder recitals throughout Germany and at Théâtre du Châtelet, Paris; sang Waltraute in Götterdämmerung with Royal Opera, Birmingham 1998; Brangaene in Tristan und Isolde 2000; Schoenberg's Gurrelieder, London Proms 2002; season 2002–03 as Ariadne at Covent Garden and Brangaene for the Vienna Staatsoper;. *Recordings include:* Le nozze di Figaro, Bach Cantatas, Bruckner's Te Deum. *E-mail:* petra@petralang.org. *Website:* www.petralang.org.

LANG, Rosemarie; German singer (mezzo-soprano); b. 1955, Grünstädtel, Schwarzenberg. *Education:* studied in Leipzig. *Career:* sang in opera at Altenburg, then Leipzig; Guest engagements at Dresden as Venus by Wagner, 1988; Berlin Staatsoper as Gluck's Clytemnestra and Wagner's Brangäne, and in premiere of Graf Mirabeau by Siegfried Matthus, 1989 (also televised), and as Azucena by Verdi, 1989; other roles include Mozart's Dorabella, Cherubino and Sextus, Bellini's Romeo, Rossini's Cenerentola and Rosina, Strauss's Octavian and Composer in Ariadne; Sang Countess Geschwitz in Lulu, 1997; Many concert appearances. *Recordings include:* Mendelssohn's St Paul; Larina in Eugene Onegin; Schoenberg's Gurre-Lieder; Mozart's Masses; Songs by Schumann and Brahms; Pfitzner's Palestrina as Silla; 8th Symphony by Mahler under Abbado; Rheingold and Walküre (Fricka) by Wagner; Götterdämmerung by Wagner under Barenboim, Frau von Kirchstallen (Elegie), Kenze; Guest appearances in Oslo, Washington, Tokyo. *Address:* c/o Staatsoper Berlin, Unter den Linden 7, 10117 Berlin (office); Küfferstr. 51, 04229 Leipzig, Germany (home).

LANG LANG; Chinese pianist; b. 14 June 1982, Shenyang; s. of Lang Guoren and Zhou Xiulan. *Education:* Central Music Conservatory, Beijing, Curtis Inst. of Music, Philadelphia, USA. *Career:* played the complete Chopin Études, Beijing Concert Hall 1995; performed as one of the soloists at the inaugural concert of the China Nat. Symphony 1996; US debut with Baltimore Symphony Orchestra 1998; last-minute substitution at the Ravinia Festival Gala of the Century, playing the Tchaikovsky Concerto with the Chicago Symphony Orchestra 1999; Carnegie Hall debut playing the Grieg Concerto with Baltimore Symphony under Yuri Temirkanov, April 2001; joined Philadelphia Orchestra and Wolfgang Sawallisch for the orchestra's 100th anniversary tour, including a performance in the Great Hall of the People, Beijing, June 2001; BBC Proms debut, playing Rachmaninov's Third Concerto, Aug. 2001; 2001/02 season included recital debuts at London's Wigmore Hall, Washington's Kennedy Center and the Paris Louvre, tour of Europe with the NDR Symphony Orchestra of Hamburg, and performance with the NHK Symphony Orchestra under Charles Dutoit; performed in five concerts at the Ravinia Festival 2002; season 2002/03 included performances with New York Philharmonic and Lorin Maazel in New York and a tour of Asia, concerts with the Cleveland Orchestra at Severance Hall, a tour of the Midwest with Franz Welser-Möst, appearances with Los Angeles Philharmonic, San Francisco Symphony, Pittsburgh Symphony, Philadelphia Orchestra; tour of China 2003; festival appearances 2003 included opening concert of BBC Proms, London, Mostly Mozart, Aspen, Tanglewood, Ravinia, Saratoga, Blossom, Verbier, Schleswig-Holstein and Ruhr Piano Festival; Carnegie Hall recital debut Nov. 2003; orchestral appearances with the Philadelphia, Los Angeles Philharmonic, London Philharmonic, Orchestre de Paris, Israel Philharmonic, Staatskapelle Berlin, Berliner Philharmoniker; guest soloist at Nobel Prize concert, Stockholm 2007; performed at opening ceremony for Summer Olympics, Beijing 2008; appeared at Carnegie Hall China Festival 2010, Queen's Diamond Jubilee Concert, London 2012, Latitude Festival, UK 2012; played with Korean artist PSY for opening ceremony of Asian Games in Incheon, South Korea 2014; performed 'Rhapsody in Blue' for US Independence Day televised celebration, Washington, DC 2015; UNICEF Int. Goodwill Amb. 2004–; Vice-Pres. All-China Youth Fed.; f. Lang Lang Int. Music Foundation, New York 2008; Global Amb. Leeds Int. Piano Competition 2013. *Recordings include:* Peter Tchaikovsky Piano Concerto No. 1 and Mendelssohn Piano Concerto No. 1, with Chicago Symphony Orchestra under Daniel Barenboim, Haydn, Rachmaninov, Brahms, recorded Live at Seiji Ozawa Hall, Tanglewood 2001, Rachmaninov Piano Concerto No. 3 and Scriabin Etudes, with St Petersburg Philharmonic under Yuri Temirkanov 2003, Lang Lang live at Carnegie Hall 2004, Lang Lang Memory 2005, Rachmaninov Piano Concerto No. 2 2005, Dragon Songs 2006, The Art of Lang Lang 2007, Chopin Piano Concerto No. 1 and No. 2 2008, Tchaikovsky and Rachmaninov Piano Trios 2009, Lang Lang Live 2010, Liszt: My Piano Hero 2015, The Chopin Album 2015, The Mozart Album 2016, Chopin Etudes 2016. *Publication:* Journey of a Thousand Miles: My Story (with David Ritz) 2008. *Honours:* Hon. DMus (Royal Coll. of Music) 2011; First Prize, Shenyang Piano Competition 1987, First Prize, Fifth Xing Hai Cup Piano Competition, Beijing, First Prize and Outstanding Artistic Performance, Fourth Int. Young Pianists Competition, Germany, First Prize, Second Tchaikovsky Int. Young Musicians' Competition, Japan 1995, Leonard Bernstein Award 2002, 2007, Presidential Merit Award, Recording Acad. 2010, Crystal Award, World Econ. Forum 2010, Echo Klassik Award 2010. *Current Management:* c/o CAMI Music LLC, 1790 Broadway, New York, NY 10019-1412, USA. *Telephone:* (212) 841-9500. *Fax:* (212) 841-9719. *E-mail:* LangLang@columbia-artists.net. *Website:* www.camimusic.com; www.LangLang.com (office).

LANG-LESSING, Sebastian; German conductor; *Chief Conductor and Artistic Director, Tasmanian Symphony Orchestra*; b. 1966, Gelsenkirchen. *Career:* fmrly Asst Conductor, Hamburg State Opera; Resident Conductor Deutsche Oper Berlin 1993–2001; apptd Chief Conductor and Artistic Dir Orchestre Symphonique et Lyrique de Nancy; Music Dir Opéra Nat. de Lorraine 1999–2006; Chief Conductor and Artistic Dir Tasmanian Symphony Orchestra 2004–; Music Dir San Antonio Symphony Orchestra 2010–; engagements at Los Angeles Opera, San Francisco Opera, Houston Grand Opera, Washington Nat. Opera, Opéra de Bordeaux, Royal Theatres in Oslo and Stockholm, West Australian Opera, Opera Colorado Denver and Capetown Opera; guest appearances with Tokyo Philharmonic, Leipzig Gewandhaus, Frankfurt Radio, Hamburg Symphony, Orchestre de Paris, Orchestre Philharmonique de Radio France, Orchestre de Toulouse and major orchestras in Australia. *Recordings include:* Joseph-Guy Ropartz: Symphonies No.2 & 5 and No.1 & 4, Schumann Complete Symphonies, Mozart Arias (with Sara Macliver), Romantic Overtures, Brett Dean: Testament, works by Mendelssohn, Bruch and Ravel (with Niki Vasilakis), and Franck, D'Indy and Saint-Saëns (with Duncan Gifford). *Honours:* Ferenc Fricsay Prize, Berlin. *Current Management:* c/o Beatrice Hörtnagel, Konzertdirektion Hörtnagel Berlin, Oranienburger Strasse 50, D–10117 Berlin, Germany. *Telephone:* (30) 30887730. *Fax:* (30) 30887733. *E-mail:* beatrice@hoertnagel.com. *Address:* Tasmanian Symphony Orchestra, POB 1450, Hobart, TAS 7001, Australia (office). *E-mail:* info@lang-lessing.com (office). *Website:* www.lang-lessing.com.

LANGAN, Kevin, BM, MM; American singer (bass); b. 1 April 1955, New York, NY; m. Sally Wolf 1983. *Education:* New England Conservatory of Music, Indiana Univ., studied with Margaret Harshaw. *Career:* debut with New Jersey State Opera in Don Carlos 1979; Prin. Bass with San Francisco Opera for 30 years; appeared with New York City Opera, Houston Grand Opera, Philadelphia Opera, Canadian Opera, Miami, Detroit and Dallas Opera, Geneva, Lyon, Winnipeg and St Louis Opera, Colorado, Santa Fe, Edmonton, Vancouver, Seattle, Tulsa, Pittsburgh, San Diego and Washington, DC Opera; appeared with Chicago Lyric and Metropolitan Opera, Maggio Musicale Firenze, and Saito Kinen Festival in Japan; sang Colline (Boheme) and Basilio (Barbiere) at Metropolitan Opera, Friar Laurent (Romeo), Sparafucile (Rigoletto), Ferrando (Trovatore), Ariodate (Xerses), Pirate King (Pirates of Penzance) and Sprecher (Zauberflote) with Lyric Opera of Chicago, Leporello (Giovanni), Sarastro (Zauberflöte), Timur (Turandot) and Swallow (Peter Grimes) with Santa Fe Opera, Pimen (Boris) with Seattle and Miami Opera; also sang Sparafucile in San Francisco Opera's Rigoletto, Daland (Dutchman) in San Diego, New York, Portland and Atlanta, Timur in Turandot with Dallas Opera and Flemish Opera, Antwerp, Sobakin in The Tsar's Bride (Rimsky-Korsakov) at San Fransciso, as well as Sarastro in San Diego, San Francisco, Dallas, Houston, Austin, St Louis, Omaha, Toronto, Winnipeg and Washington, DC. *Achievement:* first artist to achieve 300 career performances as a leading artist with San Francisco Opera in their 87-year history 2010. *Recordings:* Nozze di Figaro conducted by with Nicklaus Harnoncourt 1994; DVDs; as Timur (Turandot), Old Hebrew (Samson), Astolfo (Orlando Furioso) and King (Aida) in San Francisco Opera productions, as Badger/Parson (Cunning Little Vixen) in Saito Kinen production. *Honours:* Finalist, Nat. Metropolitan Opera 1980 Second Place, San Francisco Opera Auditions 1980, Richard Tucker Foundation Award for Advanced Studies 1984. *Current Management:* c/o Columbia Artists Management, 1790 Broadway, New York, NY 10019-1412, USA. *Telephone:* (212) 841-9500. *Fax:* (212) 841 9744. *E-mail:* info@cami.com. *Website:* www.cami.com.

LANGDON, Sophie Catherine, ARAM; British violinist and academic; b. 26 Aug. 1958, Hemel Hempstead, Hertfordshire, England. *Education:* Royal Acad. of Music and Guildhall School of Music and Drama, London, Juilliard School, New York and Curtis Inst., Philadelphia (both USA). *Career:* debut as soloist 1981 Spitalfields Festival, London in Kurt Weill's Violin Concerto; violinist, Trio Zingara 1980–83, winning Munich International Competition 1981; recitals, concertos, leading, directing and chamber music performances and broadcasts in England at festivals and all London's major venues and throughout Europe and North America; teacher, Guildhall School of Music and Drama 1981–86, Central Ostrabothnian Conservatoire, Finland 1986–87, Trinity Coll. of Music 1987–, Menuhin School 1991–92, Chetham's School, Manchester 1988–90, Royal Acad. of Music 1990–, Prof. of Violin, TCM and RAM; concerto performances and recordings with the Royal Philharmonic Orchestra, Philharmonia, BBC Symphony Orchestra, BBC Nat. Orchestra of Wales, BBC Scottish Symphony Orchestra, BBC Philharmonic and Berlin Radio Orchestra; chamber music performances and recordings with Lontano, Jeux, Aquarius, Music Projects, Langdon Chamber Players and London Sinfonietta; Leader and Dir, London Chamber Symphony, Ambache Chamber Orchestra and Acad. of London; guest leader of City of London Sinfonia, London Mozart Players and Orchestra of St John's Smith Square. *Recordings:* Dame Ethel Smyth Double Concerto for violin and horn, Mozart Chamber Music with Ambache Chamber Ensemble.

LANGER, Elena, PhD; composer; b. 1974, Moscow, Russia. *Education:* Gnessin Music School, Moscow, Moscow Conservatoire, Royal Coll. of Music, London with Julian Anderson, Royal Acad. with Simon Bainbridge, studied with Yuri Vorontsov. *Career:* commissions from Moscow Variety Theatre and Almeida Theatre (first Jerwood Composer in Asscn). *Compositions:* The Crying for four clarinets 1994, Transformations for violin and piano 1998, Reflection for piano 1999, Ariadne for voice and ensemble 2002, music theatre commission from the Almeida 2003.

LANGFORD, Roger; British singer (baritone); b. 1965, England. *Education:* Royal College of Music and Royal Academy of Music. *Career:* soloist with Yorkshire Bach Choir in the St John Passion, Christmas Oratorio, Bach B minor Mass and Monteverdi Vespers; Concerts in France and Germany including Purcell's Aeneas for Cologne Radio; Music theatre includes Eight Songs For A Mad King by Maxwell Davies, Master Peter's Puppet Show and Monteverdi's Combattimento; Visits to Europe with Nigel Rogers's group, Chiaroscuro, performing English and Italian Baroque music; Sang Elijah at Lincoln Cathedral and The Apostles by Elgar at St Albans Abbey; Season 1989–90 as Papageno for British Youth Opera and in Trouble in Tahiti at Edinburgh Festival; Sang title role of Nicolson's Cat Man's Tale at BOC Covent Garden Festival, 1998.

LANGHURST, Rebecca; American singer (soprano); b. 1965. *Education:* Yale Opera Program, Princeton. *Career:* roles at Yale included Olympia in Les Contes d'Hoffmann, Zdenka in Arabella and Mozart's Despina; professional debut as Pamina, for Minnesota Opera, followed by appearances in Ariadne auf Naxos at St Louis and Il Trittico for Spoleto Festival, USA; Corinna in Il Viaggio a Reims and Verdi's Nannetta for Wolf Trap Opera; Hero in Béatrice et Bénedict at Alice Tully Hall, New York, and Rossini's Elvria at Kansas City; Other roles include Alexandra in Blitzstein's Regina and Angel More in Thomson's The Mother of us All, for New York City Opera; Staatstheater Mannheim, from 2000, as Mozart's Ilia and Sandrina, Gretel, and Helena in A Midsummer Night's Dream.

LANGLAMET, Marie-Pierre; French musician (harp); *Principal Harpist, Berlin Philharmonic Orchestra*; b. 1967, Grenoble. *Education:* Nice Conservatoire, studied with Elizabeth Fontan-Binoche, Curtis Inst. of Music, USA. *Career:* soloist with Orchestre Philharmonique de Nice aged 17; moved to USA to study aged 18; regular performances with Metropolitan Opera Symphony Orchestra under James Levine 1988–93; soloist and Prin. Harpist with Berliner Philharmoniker under Sir Simon Rattle 1993–; appearances with Rundfunk Sinfonie Orchester Berlin, Israel Philharmonic Orchestra, Orchestre de la Suisse Romande, Orchestre de la Radio Suisse, Orchestre Nat. de Lille, under conductors including Claudio Abbado, Marek Janowski, Donald Runnicles, Hugh Wolf, François-Xavier Roth, Ilan Volkov, Horst Stein; chamber musician partners have included Emmanuel Pahud, François Leleux, Paul Meyer, Renaud and Gautier Capuçon, Tabea Zimmermann, Jean-Guihen Queyras, Marc Coppey; collaborations with and commissions from US composer Sebastian Currier, performed his harp concerto with Berliner Philharmoniker 2009; teacher, Herbert von Karajan Acad. 1995–; Prof., Berlin Univ. of the Arts 2010–. *Honours:* Chevalier, Ordre des Arts et des Lettres 2009; First Prize, Int. Louise Charpentier Competition, Paris 1984, Int. Concert Artists Guild Competition, New York 1989, Int. Harpists Competition, Israel 1992, European Council's Juventus Prize, Cino Del Duca Prize, Acad. des Beaux Arts 2003. *Address:* Berliner Philharmonie, Herbert-von-Karajan-Str. 1, 10785 Berlin, Germany (office). *Telephone:* (30) 254880 (office). *Website:* www.berliner-philharmoniker.de (office).

LANGMAN, Krzysztof Maria; Polish flautist; b. 22 July 1948, Kraków. *Education:* Acad. of Music, Kraków and Santa Cecilia Academy of Music, Rome with S. Gazzeloni. *Career:* principal flautist, State Opera House and Philharmonic Soc., Wroclaw; principal solo flute, Baltic Philharmonic Orchestra, Gdansk 1974–; Asst Prof. of Flute, Acad. of Music, Gdansk; co-operates with Ensemble MW2 Vanguard Group; concerts in various countries, including Austria, Germany, Greece, Norway, Sweden, Denmark, The Netherlands, Belgium, the UK, Italy, Mexico, Spain, Luxembourg, Switzerland and France. *Address:* ul Pawla Gdanca 4a-42, 80-336 Gdańsk, Poland.

LANGRÉE, Louis; French conductor; *Music Director, Mostly Mozart Festival, New York*; b. 1961, Mulhouse. *Career:* Music Dir, Orchestre de Picardie 1993–98; Music Dir, Glyndebourne Touring Opera, with Don Giovanni 1993, La Bohème 1995, 2000, Così fan tutte 1998, Pelléas et Mélisande 1999, Fidelio, Le Nozze di Figaro 2001, Carmen 2002; Dir Opéra National de Lyon 1998–2000; Music Dir, Orchestre Philharmonique de Liège 2001–06; Music Dir, Mostly Mozart Festival, New York 2002–; Prin. Conductor, Camerata Salzburg 2011–; Music Dir, Cincinnati Symphony Orchestra 2013–; London Proms debut 2000, with the Orchestra of the Age of Enlightenment (OAE), in Haydn's 44th Symphony and Beethoven's 8th; opera includes Glyndebourne Festival Opera, Royal Opera House, Dresden Staatsoper, Grand Théâtre Genève, Opéra Bastille, Théâtre des Champs Elysées, Netherlands Opera; season 2006–07 included Baltimore, Dallas, and Finnish Radio Symphony Orchestras, Lyric Opera of Chicago (Gluck's Iphigénie en Aulide); season 2007–08 included Metropolitan Opera (Iphigénie en Tauride). *Recordings include:* Berlioz songs (with Véronique Gens) 2001, Mozart Arias (with Natalie Dessay and the OAE) 2001, Mozart C minor Mass (with Le Concert d'Astrée) 2006, Mozart Violin Concertos 1 and 3 2009. *Honours:* Chevalier des Arts et des Lettres; Best Musical Achievement in Opera (Glyndebourne, with Sir Simon Rattle) 2001. *Address:* c/o Mostly Mozart Festival, Lincoln Center for the Performing Arts Inc., 70 Lincoln Center Plaza, New York, NY 10023, USA (office); Camerata Salzburg, Bergstrasse 12, 5020 Salzburg, Austria (office). *Telephone:* (212) 875-5000 (New York) (office); (662) 873104 (Salzburg) (office). *Fax:* (662) 8731045 (Salzburg) (office). *E-mail:* info@camerata.at (office). *Website:* www.mostlymozart.org (office); www.camerata.at (office).

LANKESTER, Michael, ARCM, GRSM; conductor, music director and academic; b. 12 Nov. 1944, London, England. *Education:* Royal Coll. of Music. *Career:* Musical Dir, National Theatre 1969–75, composing and conducting numerous items to accompany productions; Conductor, Surrey Philharmonic Orchestra 1972–, and English Chamber Orchestra; founder of Contrapuncti; radio and television broadcasts for BBC; collaborator with Young Vic Theatre in various productions; Conductor, Cheltenham Festival, Sadler's Wells Theatre and at opening of Royal Northern Coll. of Music 1973; made orchestral suite of Britten's The Prince of the Pagodas, and conducted it at the 1979 Promenade Concerts; mem. Noise Abatement Soc. *Recordings include:* Gordon Crosse, Purgatory, Ariadne. *Honours:* Watney/Sargent Conducting Scholarship 1967.

LANO, Stefan, PhD; American conductor and composer; *Music Director, Teatro Colón, Buenos Aires. Education:* Harvard Univ., Oberlin Conservatory of Music, studied with Richard Hoffmann in Oberlin and Isang Yun in Berlin. *Career:* repetiteur, Graz Opera; mem. music staff, Vienna State Opera 1982–88; Assoc. Conductor, Pittsburgh Symphony Orchestra and Music Dir, Pittsburgh Youth Symphony Orchestra 1988–91; as conductor has worked with Pittsburgh Symphony Orchestra, Montréal Symphony Orchestra, Yomiuri Nippon Symphony, Basler Symphoniker, Nürnberger Philharmoniker, Nürnberger Symphoniker, Staatskapelle Wiesbaden, Orquestra de la Ciudad de Rio de Janeiro, Sinfonica Nacional de Chile, Orquesta Filarmónica de Santiago de Chile, Slovak Sinfonietta, Nat. Philharmonic of Lithuania, State Orchestra of Greece, Singapore Symphony, Buenos Aires Philharmonic; works conducted include Turandot (Hamburg State Opera, Nat. Theatre of Lithuania, Teatro Argentino), Wolfgang Rihm's Jakob Lenz (Bonn) and Die Eroberung von Mexiko (Nürnberg), Mayako Kubo's Rashomon (world premiere, Graz), Le Nozze di Figaro (Basel, Munich, St Louis), La Bohème (Basel, Munich), The Rake's Progress (Basel, New York Met), Elektra (Basel) Jenůfa (Basel), Moses und Aron (New York Met), Lulu (San Francisco), Salome (Cincinnati), Douglas Moore's The Ballad of Baby Doe (San Francisco), Wozzeck (Montréal), Jake Heggie's Dead Man Walking (Cincinnati), Bluebeard's Castle (Montréal), Roussel's Bacchus et Ariane (Montréal), Mark Adamo's Lysistrata (world premiere, Houston) 2005, Richard Danielpour's Margaret Garner (world premiere, Michigan) 2005, Porgy and Bess (Atlanta) 2005; as guest at Teatro Colón, Buenos Aires has conducted Lulu 1993, Wozzeck 1995, Bluebeard's Castle 1995, L'Amour des trois oranges 1998, Die Tote Stadt 1999, Salome 1999, The Rake's Progress 2001, La Damnation de Faust 2002, Ginastera's Bomarzo 2004, Capriccio 2005; Music Dir, Teatro Colón, Buenos Aires 2005–; conducted his own Sinfonie No. 1, Newport Festival 1976, Sinfonie No. 3, with Lithuanian Nat. Philharmonic Orchestra 2004. *Compositions:* Sinfonie No. 1 1976, Sinfonie No. 2, Sinfonie No. 3 – EIKASIA 2004. *Honours:* Asscn of Argentine Music Critics Best Foreign Conductor Award 1999. *Current Management:* Pinnacle Arts Management, 889 Ninth Avenue, Second Floor, New York, NY 10019, USA. *Telephone:* (212) 397-7926 (office). *Fax:* (212) 397-7920 (office). *E-mail:* buzan@pinnaclearts .com (office). *Website:* www.pinnaclearts.com (office). *Address:* Teatro Colón, Cerrito 618, C 1010 ANN, Buenos Aires, Argentina (office). *Website:* www .teatrocolon.org.ar (office).

LANSKY, Paul, BA, PhD; American composer; b. 18 June 1944, New York. *Education:* Queens Coll., New York with George Perle and Hugo Weisgall, Princeton Univ. with Milton Babbitt and Earl Kim. *Career:* teacher, Princeton Univ. from 1969; Assoc. Ed., Perspectives of New Music 1972. *Compositions:* Modal Fantasy for piano 1969, String Quartet 1972–77, Mild und Leise for tape 1974, Crossworks for piano and ensemble 1975, Artifice on Ferdinand's Reflections for tape 1976, Folk Images for tape 1981, As If for string trio and electronics 1982, Folk Images and As it Grew Dark for tape 1980–83; electro-acoustic music: Night Traffic 1990, Now and Then 1991, Word Color 1992, Memory Pages 1993, Thinking Back 1996, For the Moment 1997, Shadows 1998. *Honours:* League of Composers ISCM electronic music award 1975, Koussevitsky Foundation Award 1981.

LANTOS, Istvan; Hungarian pianist; b. 1949, Budapest. *Education:* Bela Bartók Conservatory, Budapest with Mme Erzsebet Tusa, Ferenc Liszt Acad. of Music. *Career:* played solo part in Messiaen's Turangalîla Symphonie, Bayreuth International Youth Festival 1970, Hitzacker Festival, Germany, and Bratislava International Rostrum of Young Artists; numerous appearances in Hungarian concert halls and worldwide; guest performances in Eastern Europe and Cuba, Austria, the UK, Canada, Germany, The Netherlands, Ireland, Italy and Switzerland; has twice toured and held masterclasses in Japan; soloist with Hungarian State Symphony Orchestra during US tour; has toured the major cities in Germany with Hungarian State Symphony Orchestra 1972–; also renowned organist; Asst Prof., Budapest Liszt Acad. of Music 1974–.

LANZA, Alcides Emigdio; Canadian (b. Argentine) composer, pianist, conductor and academic (retd); b. 2 June 1929, Rosario, Argentina; two s. two d. *Education:* Centro Latinoamericano de Altos Estudios Musicales Instituto Di Tella, Buenos Aires, studied with Julián Bautista, Alberto Ginastera, Ruwin Erlich, Roberto Kinsky, Columbia Univ., USA, studied with Vladimir Ussachevsky. *Career:* concert tours of Europe, N and S America; artistic staff, Teatro Colón, Buenos Aires 1959–65; pianist, lecturer and conductor, Composers/Performers Group, touring Europe; composer and teacher, Columbia-Princeton Electronic Music Centre; Dir Emer. of Electronic Music Studio and Prof. of Composition, McGill Univ., Montreal 1971–; Artistic Dir Group of the Electronic Music Studio. *Radio:* CBC Radio 2 Concerts on Demand: ...backwards and forwards, A Retrospective Concert (works: Preludio and Tocatta, Diastemas, Ontem, Sensors VI, Ektenes III and Vôo) 2008. *Compositions include:* Módulos II 1982, Módulos III 1983, Sensors III for organ and two percussionists 1982, Eidesis VI for string orchestra with piano 1983, Interferences III for chamber ensemble and electronic sounds 1983, Acúfenos V for trumpet, piano and electronic computer tape 1980, Ekphonesis VI for actress-singer tape 1988, There is a way to sing it... for solo tape 1988, Un mundo imaginario for choir and computer tape 1989, Vôo for voice, electroacoustic music and digital signal processing 1992, Ontem for voices, tabla, tape and digital signal processing 1999, aXents for chamber orchestra and tape 2003, Diastemas for marimba and tape 2005, Seimos for piano and tape 2009, aXenia for toy piano, piano and percussion 2009. *Recordings include:* double CD: Alcides Lanza: Portrait (CD1: interview with Meg Sheppard and Alcides Lanza, prepared by Eitan Corfield, CD2: compositions: eidesis II, penetrations II, un mundo imaginario, ontem, ektenes III and aXents). *Publications:* Compositional Crossroads (articles by and on Alcides Lanza). *Honours:* Hon. Diploma (High Distinction) (OAS and Int. Centre for Music Educ.) 1996; Victor Martin Lynch-Staunton Award for exceptional talent and achievements as a composer 2003, Distinguished Artist, City of Rosario, Argentina 2007. *Address:* 6351 Trans Island Avenue, Montreal, QC H3W 3B7, Canada (home). *Telephone:* (514) 733-7216 (home). *Fax:* (514) 398-1540 (office). *E-mail:* alcides.lanza@mcgill.ca (office). *Website:* www.music .mcgill.ca/~alcides (office); alcideslanza.blogspot.com.

LAPERRIERE, Gaétan; Canadian singer (baritone); b. 1959, Verdun, Montréal; m.; two s. *Education:* St Laurent Coll., studied with Robert Savoie. *Career:* sang in opera at Montréal from 1981, Canadian Opera at Toronto from 1986 as Gounod's Mercutio, Donizetti's Enrico, Mozart's Count 1991, and Raimbaud in Le Comte Ory 1994; performed the title role of Rigoletto at the Calgary Opera, Opéra de Quebec, Opéra-Théâtre de Metz, Opéra-Théâtre de Rennes, Kentucky Opera, New York City Opera; appeared as Renato in Verdi's Un Ballo Maschera at l'Opéra-Bastille de Paris, Opéra d'Avignon, Hong Kong Arts Festival, Opera Lyra at The Nat. Arts Center, Canada; Rodrigo in Don Carlos at Toronto, Montréal, Metz, Boston; US appearances at Washington as Bizet's Zurga, Miami as Hamlet, Boston as Enrico in Lucia di Lamermoor, and Houston (Marcello 1991); San Francisco and New York City 1991, as Germont; Toronto 1995, as Ford in Falstaff, and Montréal 1995, as de Siriex in Fedora; Mercutio at Dallas and Escamillo in Carmen at Metz 1996; sang Debussy's Golo at Bologna; Picariello in Estacio and Murrell's Filumena (world premiere) at Calgary Opera 2002; many concert performances. *Recordings include:* Great Baritone Arias, Les Septs Paroles du Christ, Grandes Voix du Québec, La Bohème (DVD). *Radio:* broadcasts of Romeo and Juliet, Les Dialogues des Carmélites. *Honours:* first prize Nat. Mozart Competition. *Current Management:* Pinnacle Arts Management, Uzan Division, 889 Ninth Avenue, 2nd Floor, New York, NY 10019, USA. *Telephone:* (212) 397-7926. *Fax:* (212) 397-7920. *E-mail:* vuzan@pinnaclearts.com. *Website:* www.pinnaclearts.com. *E-mail:* laperriere@distributel.net.

LAPINSKAS, Darius, BA; Lithuanian composer and conductor; b. 9 March 1934, Kaunas; m. Laima Rastenis 1970; one s. *Education:* South Boston High School, New England Conservatory, Boston, Akademie für Musik und Darstellende Kunst, Vienna, Musik Hochschule, Stuttgart. *Career:* Musikdirektor, Tuebingen Landestheatre 1960–65; Kapelmeister, Staatsoper Stuttgart 1961–65; Schiedsgericht, Composer-Conductor, Mainz television; guest conductor with Stuttgart Symphony Orchestra, Stuttgart Philharmonic, South German Radio Orchestra, Mannheim Opera Orchestra, National Symphony Orchestra of Bogotà and Symphony Orchestra of Antioquia; Artistic Dir, New Opera Company of Chicago. *Compositions:* operas: Lokys, Maras, Amadar, Dux Magnus, Rex Amos; ballet: Laima; instrumental: Concerto for piano, strings and percussion, Concerto for violin and orchestra, Haiku song cycle, Balyvera song cycle for mezzo-soprano and orchestra, Les Sept Solitudes aria for mezzo-soprano and orchestra, Ainiu Dainos song cycle for voice and chamber orchestra. *Honours:* BML Prize for Composition, Boston 1955,

Wurttemberg Prize for Composition 1961, Illinois Arts Council grants for composition 1985, 1986.

LAPLANTE, Bruno; singer; b. 1 Aug. 1938, Beauharnois, QC, Canada; two s. *Education:* Conservatoire de Musique du Québec, Montréal. *Career:* debut in Cimarosa's The Secret Marriage in Germany; worked first in Germany, in Paris, France under the direction of Pierre Bernac and in Montréal with Lina Narducci; numerous radio and television appearances, including Susanna's Secret, Gounod's Romeo and Juliette, and Lehar's Merry Widow; engagements with major Canadian symphony orchestras; Les Noces and Carmina Burana with Grands Ballets Canadiens; 30 concerts in Canada for Les Jeunesses Musicales du Canada; film dealing with his career in the series, Les Nouveaux Interprètes; stage appearances include Carmen, Il Trittico, Manon, Don Giovanni and many others; regular tours throughout Europe for concerts and festivals, including Festival du Marais, Paris 1979 and two recitals at Festival International de Musique et d'Art Lyrique, Aix-en-Provence; mem. Union des Artistes de Montréal. *Recordings include:* Integrale des 15 Mélodies de Duparc; Mélodies de Lalo et de Bizet; Mélodies de Berlioz; Works by Offenbach, Jules Massenet, Reynaldo Hahn, Charles Gounod, and César Franck among others. *Honours:* Concours International de Genève 1966, de Barcelona 1966, de Montréal 1967, Grand Prix du Disque 1977, scholarships from Canada Arts Council, Govt of Québec, private foundations and from Goethe Inst., Munich.

LAPORTE, André; Belgian composer; b. 12 July 1931, Oplinter. *Education:* Catholic Univ. of Louvain, studied with Flor Peeters and Marinus de Jong. *Career:* Prod. for Belgian Radio 1963; Brussels Conservatory from 1968; Artistic Dir, Belgian Radio Philharmonic Orchestra 1989–96. *Compositions:* Piano Sonata 1954, Psalm for six voices and brass 1956, Jubilus for 12 brass instruments and three percussionists 1966, Story for string trio and harpsichord 1967, Ascension for piano 1967, De Profundis for mixed choir 1968, Le Morte Chitarre for tenor, flute and 14 strings 1969, Night Music for orchestra 1970, La Vita Non e Sogno for vocalists, chorus and orchestra 1972, Peripetie for brass sextet, Chamber Music for soprano and ensemble 1975, Transit for 48 strings 1978, Das Schloss (three-act opera after Kafka) 1986, Fantasia-Rondino for violin and orchestra 1988, The Magpie on the Gallows 1989. *Honours:* Lemmens-Tinel Award 1958, Belgian Ministry of Culture Koopal Award 1971, 1976, Prix Italia 1976.

LAPPALAINEN, Kimmo; Finnish singer (tenor); b. 1944, Helsinki, Finland. *Education:* Sibelius Acad., studied with Fred Hustler in Lugano and Luigi Rici in Rome. *Career:* Finnish Nat. Opera, Helsinki 1968–72 and Stuttgart Opera from 1972; sang at Glyndebourne Festival 1972–74 as Pedrillo in Die Entführung and Idamantes in Idomeneo; many performances at the Savonlinna Festival in Finland; sang at Stuttgart 1983 as Britten's Albert Herring; also heard in concert.

LAPTEV, Yuri; Russian singer (baritone) and stage director; b. 1955. *Education:* St Petersburg Conservatoire. *Career:* stage director at Kirov Opera, St Petersburg, from 1988; Head of Planning, 1991–; Director of the Welcome Back St Petersburg Gala at the Royal Opera House, 1992; Co-productions with the Kirov of Otello, Boris Godunov, The Fiery Angel, Le nozze di Figaro and War and Peace, Opera roles include Mozart's Almariva, Valentin in Faust, Mathias in The Fiery Angel and Don Carlos in Prokofiev's Betrothal in a Monastery; Sang Captain Jacqueau in War and Peace with the Kirov at Covent Garden, 2000. *Recordings include:* The Maid of Pskov, The Fiery Angel, War and Peace, Khovanshchina. *Address:* c/o Kirov Opera, Mariinsky Theatre, Theatre Square, St Petersburg, Russia.

LARA, Christian; French singer (tenor); b. 15 Aug. 1946, Mérignac. *Education:* studied in Bordeaux. *Career:* sang at Lille Opéra 1976–79 and studied further with Michel Sénéchal in Paris; sang Juan in Don Quichotte at Venice 1982, Rodolfo at Nantes, Cavaradossi at Avignon, Faust at Ghent and Antwerp; Theater des Westens, Berlin 1987 as Sou-Chong in Das Land des Lächelns; sang Faust at Cologne 1989 and appeared in La Rondine at Tours 1991; concert repertoire includes Mendelssohn's 2nd Symphony; sang Faust at Vienna 1991, Ismaele in Nabucco at Karlsruhe, Samson at Besançon, Ruggero in La Rondine at Tours, Cavaradossi in Tosca at Angers, Don José in Carmen at Bregenz and Liège, and Florestan in Fidelio at Tours, all 1991; in 1992 sang Oedipe Roi by Paul Bastide at Strasbourg, Andrei Khovansky at Strasbourg, Ismaele at Karlsruhe, Florestan at Angers, Don José at the Festival of Bregenz, Jean in Hérodiade at Liège, and in Vestale at Nantes; in 1993 sang Luigi in Il Tabarro at Tours, Jean at Toulon; in 1994 sang Des Grieux in Manon and Don José at Bordeaux.

LARCHER, Thomas; Austrian composer and pianist; b. 1963, Innsbruck. *Education:* Musikhochschule Wien. *Career:* f. Klangspuren Contemporary Music Festival 1994, Dir 1994–2003; compositions performed by artists including Mark Padmore, Leif Ove Andsnes, Viktoria Mullova, Kim Kashkashian, Thomas Demenga, Heinrich Schiff, Till Fellner, Natalie Clein, Christian Teztlaff, Juliane Banse and Martin Fröst; commissions from musicians including Artemis Quartet, Radio Symphony Orchestra of Vienna, Matthias Goerne and London Sinfonietta, Isabelle Faust, San Francisco Symphony, BBC Proms; as pianist, performed under conductors including Claudio Abbado, Pierre Boulez, Dennis Russell Davies and Franz Welser-Möst; piano teacher, Musikhochschule Basel 2001–04. *Compositions include:* orchestral: Still for viola and chamber orchestra 2002, Hier, heute for violin, orchestra and CD 2005, Böse Zellen for piano and orchestra 2007, Concerto for violin and orchestra 2008/09, Red and Green for large orchestra 2010,

Concerto for violin, cello and orchestra (British Composer Award 2012) 2011; for ensemble/chamber: Naunz for piano 1989, IXXU for string quartet 1998–2004, Uchafu for trumpet and piano 2003, Smart Dust for piano 2005, Cello Sonata 2006, Madhares for string quartet 2006/07, Nocturne –Insomnia 2008, Die Nacht der Verlorenen for baritone and ensemble 2008, Das Speil ist aus for 24 voices 2012. *Recordings include:* as pianist: Heinz Holliger: lieder ohne Worte 1997, Schonberg/Schubert Piano Works (solo) 1999, Michelle Makarski: Elogio per un'ombra 2000, Thomas Demenga: Hhosokawa/Bach/Yun 2002, Chonguri 2006, Schubert's Schwanengesang, as composer: Naunz (Preis der Deutschen Schallplattenkritik) 2001, IXXU 2005, Madhares 2010. *Current Management:* c/o Cathy Nelson Artists, The Court House, Dorstone, Herefords., HR3 6AW, England. *Telephone:* (1981) 551903. *E-mail:* cathy@cathynelson.co.uk. *Website:* www.cathynelson.co.uk. *Telephone:* (20) 7543-0710. *Website:* www.thomas-larcher.com; www.schottmusic.co.uk.

LAREDO, Jaime; Bolivian violinist and conductor; *Conductor and Music Director, Vermont Symphony Orchestra;* b. 7 June 1941, Cochabamba; m. Sharon Robinson. *Education:* studied violin with Antonio de Grassi and Frank Hauser in San Francisco, Josef Gingold and George Szell in Cleveland, and Ivan Galamian at the Curtis Inst., Philadelphia, USA. *Career:* orchestral debut San Francisco 1952; won Queen Elisabeth of the Belgians Competition 1959 and subsequently appeared with most major orchestras in Europe and America; New York debut Carnegie Hall 1960; London debut Albert Hall 1961; frequent visitor to summer festivals at Spoleto, Tanglewood, Hollywood Bowl, Ravinia, Marlboro and Edinburgh; repertoire ranges from Baroque to contemporary works; gave the premiere of Ned Rorem's Concerto; Dir, soloist, works with St Pauls and Scottish Chamber Orchestras; Dir Chamber Music at the 92nd Street NY series in New York; piano concerts worldwide with Joseph Kalichstein and Sharon Robinson as Kalichstein, Laredo, Robinson Trio 1977–; Conductor and Music Dir Vermont Symphony Orchestra 1999–. *Recordings include:* Trios by Mendelssohn, Brahms and Beethoven, Brahms Piano Quartets with Emanuel Ax, Isaac Stern, Yo-Yo Ma (Grammy Award). *Honours:* New York City Handel Medallion 1960; Stadium in La Paz named after him, Bolivian stamps with his portrait issued in his honour, Deutsche Schallplatten Prize. *Address:* Vermont Symphony Orchestra, 2 Church Street, Suite 3B, Burlington, VT 05401, USA (office). *Telephone:* (802) 864-5741 (office). *Fax:* (802) 864-5109 (office). *Website:* www.vso.org (office).

LARGE, Brian; British musicologist, pianist, writer and television producer; b. 1937, London, England. *Education:* Royal Acad. of Music and London Univ. *Career:* producer of opera on BBC television with many other opera television engagements in Europe and the USA, including La Cenerentola (Houston Opera); TV Dir, La Bohème (Bregenz Festival) (Grand Prix Goldenes Prag Hauptpreis for live performance of opera 2003) 2002. *Film:* Le nozze di Figaro (Best Performing Arts Programme award for opera, 44th Golden Prague Festival 2007). *Publications:* books on Smetana, Martinů and Czech Opera; contrib. entry on Martinů to The New Grove Dictionary of Music and Musicians 1980.

LARMORE, Jennifer May, BMus; American singer (mezzo-soprano); b. 21 June 1958, Atlanta, Ga; d. of William C. Larmore and Eloise O. Larmore; m. William Powers 1980. *Education:* Sprayberry High School, Marietta, Ga, Westminster Choir Coll., Princeton, NJ. *Career:* operatic debut with L'Opéra de Nice, France 1985, debut with Metropolitan Opera, New York 1995, Salzburg Festival debut 1993, Tanglewood Festival debut 1998; specializes in music of the Bel Canto and Baroque periods; Spokesperson and Fundraiser, US Fund for UNICEF 1998–. *Music:* over 40 recordings of operatic and solo repertoire; operatic appearances with most of the world's leading cos; recital appearances include Carnegie Hall, New York, Wigmore Hall, London, Musik Verein, Vienna, Concertgebauw, Amsterdam, Palais Garnier, Paris, L.& G Arts Center, Seoul, Teatro Colón, Buenos Aires, Teatro Liceo, Barcelona, Teatro Monnaie, Brussels, Arts Centre, Melbourne, etc. *Television:* appearances include Star Trek 30th Anniversary broadcast, live Christmas Eve service from St Patrick's Cathedral, numerous live broadcasts from the Metropolitan Opera, etc. *Achievements:* selected by the US Olympic Cttee to sing the Olympic Hymn for the closing of the Atlanta Olympic Summer Games 1996. *Honours:* Chevalier, Ordre des Artes et des Lettres 2002; William M. Sullivan Fellowship 1983, Maria Callas Vocal Competition, Barcelona 1984, McAllister Vocal Competition, Indianapolis 1986, Alumni Merit Award, Westminster Choir Coll. 1991, Gramophone Award for Best Baroque Album 1992, Richard Tucker Foundation Award, New York 1994. *Current Management:* IMG Artists, Carnegie Hall Tower, 152 West 57th Street, 5th Floor, New York, NY 10019, USA. *Telephone:* (212) 994-3500. *Fax:* (212) 994-3550. *E-mail:* salmansi@imgartists.com. *Website:* www.imgartists.com. *E-mail:* jenniferlarmore@aol.com (home). *Website:* www.jenniferlarmoremezzo.com.

LARNER, Gerald, BA; British music critic; b. 9 March 1936, Leeds, England; m. Celia Ruth Mary White, two d. *Education:* New Coll., Oxford. *Career:* Asst Lecturer, Univ. of Manchester 1960–62; staff mem., The Guardian, London from 1962, chief northern music critic from 1965; translated Wolf's Der Corregidor into English; wrote libretto for John McCabe's The Lion, the Witch and the Wardrobe 1971; Artistic Dir, Bowden Festival 1980–84; mem. Critics' Circle. *Publications:* contrib. to Musical Times, The Listener.

LARSEN, Libby Brown; American composer; b. 24 Dec. 1950, Wilmington, DE. *Education:* Univ. of Minnesota with Dominick Argento. *Career:* co-founded Minnesota (American) Composers' Forum 1973; resident composer with the Minnesota Orchestra 1983–87; Artistic Dir, Hot Notes series 1993; many commissions from leading orchestras and organizations; has appeared widely as speaker and teacher. *Compositions include:* operas: Frankenstein, The Modern Prometheus (music drama) 1990, A Wrinkle in Time 1992, Mrs Dalloway 1993, Water Music Symphony 1985, Piano Concerto Since Armstrong 1990, Ghosts of an Old Ceremony for orchestra 1991, Sonnets from the Portuguese for soprano and chamber orchestra 1989, String Quartet Schoenberg, Schenker and Schillinger 1991, The Atmosphere as a Fluid System for flute, strings and percussion 1992, Mary Cassatt for mezzo, trombone and orchestra 1994, Eric Hermannson's Soul (opera) 1997, String Symphony 1998, Songs of Light and Love for soprano and chamber orchestra 1998, Solo Symphony 1999. *Recordings:* Missa Gaia 1994, Dancing Solo 1997, Water Music, London Symphony Orchestra 1997. *Honours:* Grammy Award 1994. *E-mail:* info@libbylarsen.com. *Website:* www.libbylarsen.com.

LARSON, Sophia; Austrian singer (soprano); b. 1954, Linz; m. Hans Sisa. *Education:* Salzburg Mozarteum with Seywald-Baumgartner, studied with Ettore Campogalliani. *Career:* sang at St Gallen from 1976 as Verdi's Amelia Boccanegra, Mozart's Ilia, and Silvia in Mascagni's Zanetto; sang at Ulm, 1979–80 as Fiordiligi, the Marschallin, Beethoven's Leonore and Katya Kabanova; Bremen, 1980–83, and guest at Hamburg, Stuttgart, Trieste and Rome; sang at Bologna in 1985 as the Duchess of Parma in Busoni's Doktor Faust, and Turin in 1986 as Puccini's Turandot and in Ghedini's Maria d'Alessandria; Further appearances in South America, Berlin, Berne, Wiesbaden and Bratislava; Bayreuth Festival, 1984–85 as Gutrune in The Ring, and Festival of Verona in 1986 as Minnie in La Fanciulla del West; Studio recordings for French and Italian Radio; Sang Venus in Tannhäuser at Bayreuth Festival in 1987, Gutrune in The Ring at Staatsoper Munich in 1987, Tosca at Turin in 1987, Isolde at Toronto in 1987, War Requiem at Carnegie Hall in 1988, Fedra by Pizzetti at Palermo in 1988, Renata in The Fiery Angel at Grand Théâtre Genève in 1988, Turandot at Zürich in 1988, Senta at Nice and San Francisco in 1988, Sieglinde in Die Walküre at Bayreuth Festival in 1989, Renata at Amsterdam in 1989, Lyrische Symphonie by Zemlinsky at Amsterdam in 1989, Brünnhilde at Linz Brucknerfestival in 1989, Fidelio at Catania in 1989 and Turandot and Tosca at Turin and Zürich in 1990; British debut as Turandot at the London Coliseum, 1995; Sang Leonore in Fidelio at Toronto, 1998.

LARSSON, Anders; Swedish singer (baritone); b. 24 April 1969, Östersund. *Education:* Royal Acad. of Music, Stockholm (postgraduate diploma). *Career:* opera performances at Glyndebourne Festival Opera, Frankfurt Opera, La Monnaie, Brussels, Teatro Real, Madrid, Gran Teatre del Liceu, Barcelona, Spoleto Festival (Italy), Staatsoper, Berlin and Royal Danish Opera; frequent guest at Royal Swedish Opera, roles have included the Four Villains in Les Contes d'Hoffmann, the Count in Le Nozze di Figaro, Germont in La Traviata, Belcore in L'elisir d'amore, Lescaut in Manon Lescaut, the Count in Capriccio, Ford in Falstaff, title role of Eugene Onegin and Falke in Die Fledermaus; repertoire also includes Mandryka in Arabella, Posa in Don Carlo, Silvio in Pagliacci, Escamillo in Carmen, Marcello in La Bohème, Fernando in Fidelio, Harlekin in Ariadne auf Naxos, Pelléas in Pelléas et Mélisande, Papageno in Die Zauberflöte, Giuglielmo in Così fan tutte, Don Alvaro in Il viaggio a Reims, Young Mariner in Ballata (Francesconi), title role in Der Kaiser von Atlantis, Macduff in Macbeth (Bloch) and Creonte in Orfeo ed Euridice (Haydn); recent roles have included Wotan in Das Rheingold at Dalhalla Festival, Der Heerufer in Lohengrin at Teatro Real, Amfortas in Parsifal at Malmö Opera, Donner and Gunther in Wagner's Ring with Wermland Opera, Valentin in Faust and Sharpless in Madama Butterfly at the Folkoperan in Stockholm and the title role in Daniel Börtz's opera Goya at the world premiere at Gothenburg Opera; concert performances include Mahler's Des Knaben Wunderhorn, Beethoven's Symphony No. 9 and Mahler's Symphony No. 8, Daniel Börtz's Hans namn var Orestes with the Royal Stockholm Philharmonic Orchestra and Alan Gilbert, Lawrence Renes and Sakari Oramo; has appeared with Gothenburg Symphony Orchestra in Mahler's Sechs frühe Lieder with Carlo Rizzi and as Donner in a concert performance of Das Rheingold with Kent Nagano, and with Swedish Radio Symphony Orchestra as Joseph in L'Enfance du Christ with Charles Dutoit, Die Schöpfung with Manfred Honeck, as well as Bach's Christmas Oratorio with the San Francisco Symphony Orchestra. *Honours:* Christina Nilsson and Birgit Nilsson Awards. *Current Management:* c/o Ann Braathen Artist Management AB, Folkskolegatan 5, 117 35 Stockholm, Sweden. *Telephone:* (8) 556-908-50. *Fax:* (8) 556-908-51. *E-mail:* info@braathenmanagement.com. *Website:* www.braathenmanagement.com. *Telephone:* 73-0692766 (mobile) (office). *E-mail:* operasingeranders@telia.com (office). *Website:* www.ingeback-larsson.com.

LARSSON, Anna; Swedish singer (contralto). *Education:* Opera Acad., Stockholm. *Career:* made int. debut in Mahler's Second Symphony with Berlin Philharmonic Orchestra 1997; operatic debut as Erda in Wagner's Das Rheingold with Berliner Staatsoper; repertoire includes Kundry in Parsifal, Waltraute in Götterdämmerung, Orphée, Fricka in Die Walküre, Delilah in Samson and Delilah; has performed with Teatro alla Scala Milan, Bayerisches Staatsoper München, Festspiele Salzburg, Festival Aix-en-Provence, Teatro Maggio Musicale Firenze, Palau des Arts Valencia, Royal Opera Copenhagen, Finnish National Opera, Royal Opera Stockholm, Berliner Philharmoniker, Lucerne Festival Orchestra, New York Philharmonic, Wiener Philharmoniker, Chicago Symphony Orchestra, Los Angeles Philharmonic Orchestra, London Symphony Orchestra and London Philharmonic Orchestra; frequently performs Mahler concert works and song cycles, also Handel's Messiah, Elgar's Sea Pictures, Verdi's Requiem; mem. Royal Swedish Acad. of

Music 2010. *Recordings:* Brahms, Alto Rhapsodie 1999, 2004, Unander-Scharin, Tokfursten 2000, Mahler, Symphony No. 8 2001, Beethoven, Missa Solemnis 2002, Mahler, Des Knaben Wunderhorn 2002, Mahler, Second Symphony 2004, 2007, Mahler, Third Symphony 1998, 2002, 2008, Handel, Messiah 2005, Strauss, Daphne 2005, Daniel Börtz, Hans namn var Orestes 2007, Zivkovic and Staern, Unheard of Again 2008. *Honours:* apptd Court Singer by King Carl XVI Gustaf of Sweden 2010; Int. Prize, Royal Swedish Acad. of Music. *Current Management:* c/o Eliasson Artists Stockholm, Skeppargatan 86, 114 59 Stockholm, Sweden. *Telephone:* (8) 667-24-03. *Fax:* (8) 667-24-13. *E-mail:* info@eliassonartists.com. *Website:* www.eliassonartists.com; www.annalarsson.nu.

LARSSON, Charlotte; Swedish singer (soprano); b. 1966. *Education:* State Opera School in Stockholm. *Career:* debut with Norrlandsoperan as Signe in Stenhammar's Gillet pa Solhaug; concert appearances including opening of Århus Festival, 1991; sang at Karlstad Opera Festival in 1992 and as Liu in Turandot for Stockholm Folkoperan in 1993; other roles include Mozart's Pamina and Sandrina, Rosalinda and Dvořák's Rusalka; engaged at Stockholm Royal Opera, 1994. *Current Management:* Svenska Konsertbyrån, Jungfrugatan 45, 11444 Stockholm, Sweden. *Telephone:* (8) 665-8088. *Fax:* (8) 665-8066. *E-mail:* info@svenskakonsertbyran.se. *Website:* www.svenskakonsertbyran.se.

LARSSON, Lisa; Swedish singer (soprano); b. 1967. *Education:* studied singing in Basel, Switzerland. *Career:* fmr flautist; operatic debut at Zurich Opera House in performances under Nikolaus Harnoncourt, Franz Welser-Möst and other conductors; first engagement outside Switzerland was Papagena in The Magic Flute at Teatro alla Scala in Milan under Riccardo Muti; est. herself as a leading Mozart singer performing Zerlina, Susanna, Pamina, Zaide, Servilia, Ilia, Fortuna and Ismene under batons of Claudio Abbado, Adam Fischer, Daniel Harding, Ivor Bolton, Massimo Zanetti and others; other roles have included Marzelline, Anne Trulove, Ännchen, Eurydice, Adele, Adina, Oscar, Xenia, Tytania, Polissena and Morgana; appeared at Royal Opera House, Covent Garden, Bayerische Staatsoper, Teatro La Fenice, Opéra de Monte Carlo, Oper Leipzig, Opernhaus Zürich, Grand Théâtre de Genève, Theater Basel, Royal Swedish and Danish Opera; invited by major festivals, including Salzburg Festival, Lucerne Festival, Glyndebourne Festival and Festival d'Aix-en-Provence; concert performances with Claudio Abbado, Mikhail Pletnev, Daniel Harding, Sir Colin Davis, Antonello Manacorda, Adam Fischer, Lawrence Renes, Massimo Zanetti, Louis Langrée, Vassily Sinaisky and orchestras including Berlin Philharmonic Orchestra, Vienna Symphony Orchestra, Zurich Tonhalle Orchestra, HR Symphony Orchestra, Frankfurt, Camerata Salzburg, NHK Symphony Orchestra, Mahler Chamber Orchestra and many others; has worked with many leading period instrumental ensembles and their conductors, including Ton Koopman, Sir John Eliot Gardiner, Emmanuelle Haïm, Nicholas McGegan, Paul Goodwin, Martin Haselböck, Gottfried von der Goltz, Trevor Pinnock and David Stern; season 2009–10, collaborations with orchestras including Mahler Chamber Orchestra, Deutsche Kammerphilharmonie Bremen, La Risonanza, Monte Carlo Philharmonic Orchestra, Munich Bach Collegium, I pomeriggi musicali, Hague Philharmonic, Hong Kong Philharmonic Orchestra, Milwaukee Philharmonic Orchestra and Nathalie Stutzmann's newly formed orchestra Orfeo 55, conductors include Thomas Hengelbrock, Antonello Manacorda, Edo de Waart, among others. *Recordings include:* Mozart's Don Giovanni (Daniel Harding), Mitridate (Adam Fischer) and Il sogno di Scipione (Gottfried von der Goltz), Handel's Jephta (David Stern) as well as Bach cantatas with Sir John Eliot Gardiner, Christmas and Easter Oratorios, Magnificat and numerous cantatas conducted by Ton Koopman, Mahler's Symphony No. 8 (Mater gloriosa) under David Zinman with Zurich Tonhalle Orchestra. *Current Management:* c/o Impulse Art Management, Oudezijds Voorburgwal 74, 1012 GE Amsterdam; PO Box 15401, 1001 MK Amsterdam, The Netherlands. *Telephone:* (20) 626-6944 (office). *Fax:* (20) 622-7118 (office). *E-mail:* info@impulseartmanagement.nl (office). *Website:* www.impulseartmanagement.nl (office); www.lisalarsson.info.

LASCARRO, Juanita; Colombian singer (soprano); b. 1971, Bogotá. *Education:* studied biology and music at Universidad de los Andes, Bogotá, singing at Cologne Musikhochschule with Klesie Kelly-Moog, Lied with Hartmut Holl and Mitsuko Shirai, further voice lessons with Patricia McCaffrey in New York. *Career:* notable operatic roles to date include Lulu, Manon, Donna Elvira, Violetta, Fiordiligi, Suor Angelica, and Agrippina for the Opera in Frankfurt (a prin. soloist); has performed Juliette (Roméo et Juliette) at Vienna and Bavarian State Operas, Poppea at Opera in Zurich, Daphne at Deutsche Oper Berlin and De Nederlandse Opera, Manon (Boulevard Solitude), Nuri (Tiefland) and Zerlina at Gran Teatre del Liceu, and Susanna (Le nozze di Figaro) at Opéra Nat. de Paris; performed Liù (Turandot), Mimì (La Bohème) and The Cunning Little Vixen at Welsh Nat. Opera; sang title role in Pelléas et Mélisande and Fiorilla in Il turco in Italia at La Monnaie; Season 2009/10 opera highlights included Zdenka, Fiordiligi, Pamina, Juliette, Emma (Fierrabras) and Musetta in Frankfurt, Poppea and Adele in Die Fledermaus at the Theater an der Wien and Princess Laoula in Chabrier's L'Étoile under Sir Simon Rattle at Berlin State Opera; performed in Armida with the Ensemble L'arte del mondo as well as Josef Mysliveceks Medonte; collaboration with Academy of Ancient Music and Rodolfo Richter, Wigmore Hall and West Road Concert Hall, Cambridge; regular guest at Teatro Colón, Bogotá in roles including Adina (L'elisir d'amore), Micaëla

(Carmen), Susanna, Violetta and Juliette; sang Daphne, Adele (Le Comte Ory) and Mirandolina (Martinů) at Garsington; performances in concert include appearances with Leipzig Gewandhaus under Lothar Zagrosek, Deutsches Symphonie-Orchester Berlin under Vladimir Ashkenazy, Israel Philharmonic Orchestra under Antonio Pappano, Finnish Radio Symphony Orchestra under Sakari Oramo, Danish Radio Sinfonietta under Adam Fischer and the Gürzenich Orchestra under James Conlon; BBC Proms debut in Weill's Der Silbersee, conducted by Markus Stenz, and performed Villa Lobos' Bachiana brasileira No. 5 with the 12 Cellists of the Berlin Philharmonic Orchestra at the Proms and the Salzburg Easter Festival; Season 2011/12 sings role of Farzana in Wagner's Die Feen at Frankfurt Opera, Daphne by Richard Strauss (previously performed under Christian Thielemann and Ingo Metzmacher), Antonia from Hoffmanns Erzählungen as well as Gräfin Almaviva from Le nozze di Figaro; sings role of Rosina from Haydns La vera costanza with WDR Rundfunkorchester under Maestro Manuel Hernández-Silva at the broadcasting centre Cologne; recital appearances at the Bath Int. Festival, Steensgard Festival, West Cork Music Festival and at Wigmore Hall, London. *Recordings include:* Les contes d'Hoffmann, Alcina, Der Silbersee, Die Verlobung im Traum, Der Zwerg, La senna festeggiante, Arcadian Duets by Handel, a selection of Spanish songs, and a CD of music by de Falla, with the Katona Twins guitar duo. *Honours:* Winner, Leipzig Opera, Mendelssohn and Münchner Konzertgesellschaft Competitions 1992–93. *Current Management:* c/o Harrison Parrott, 5–6 Albion Court, London, W6 0QT, England. *Telephone:* (20) 7229-9166. *Fax:* (20) 7221-5042. *E-mail:* info@harrisonparrott.co.uk. *Website:* www.harrisonparrott.com; www.juanita-lascarro.de.

LASH, Hannah, BMus, PS, PhD, AD; American composer and harpist; *Guest Professor, Yale School of Music;* b. 22 Nov. 1981. *Education:* Eastman School of Music, Cleveland Inst. of Music, Harvard Univ., Yale School of Music; studied with Martin Bresnick, Bernard Rands, Julian Anderson and Robert Morris. *Career:* works performed at The Times Center, The Stone, Chicago Art Inst., Tanglewood Music Center, Harvard Univ. and on American Opera Project's stage in New York City; collab. with American Opera Projects on opera Shutter 2006; participated in festivals as composer fellow at Tanglewood Music Center 2003, Greenlake Summer Music Festival 2005, and as harpist at Round Top Summer Festival Inst. 2007; Adjunct Prof. of Composition, Alfred Univ.; Guest Prof. Yale School of Music 2012–. *Compositions include:* chamber music, opera, orchestral and solo works, including Blood Rose (chamber opera) presented by NYC Opera's VOX 2011, God Music Bug Music performed by Minnesota Orchestra 2012. *Honours:* Bernard and Rose Sernoffsky Prize in Composition 2002, Barnard Rogers Prize in Composition 2003, Harvard Univ. Composers Orchestral Competition Winner 2006, BMI Women's Music Comm. Hon. Mention 2006, Howard Hanson Grant 2007, Dissertation Completion Fellowship, Harvard Univ. 2009, Helen L. and Benjamin J. Buttenweiser Scholarship Fund, Harvard Univ. 2009, John Knowles Paine Traveling Fellowship, Harvard Univ. 2009, William Mitch Fund, Harvard Univ. 2009, Naumburg Prize, ASCAP Morton Gould Young Composer Award, American Acad. of Arts and Letters Charles Ives Scholarship, Fromm Foundation Commission. *Address:* 5544 Maple Crest, Alfred Station, NY 14803, USA (office). *E-mail:* HMLash@gmail.com (office). *Website:* www.hannahlash.com.

LASKE, Otto, BMus, MMus, PhD, EdD; composer, poet and musicologist; b. 23 April 1936, Olesnica, Oels, Silesia, Poland. *Education:* Akademie für Tonkunst, Darmstadt, New England Conservatory of Music, Boston, USA, Goethe University, Frankfurt am Main, Germany, Harvard University, USA, Institute of Sonology, Utrecht, Netherlands. *Career:* debut, Composers' Forum, New York 1969; freelance composer; Prof. of Music; Artistic Dir, Newcomp Inc 1981–91. *Compositions:* 65 works for instrumental, vocal and electro-acoustic music including: Kyrie Eleison, a cappella, 1969, Distances and Proximities for tape, 1973, Perturbations for chamber orchestra, 1979, Terpsichore for tape, 1980, Soliloquy for double bBass, 1984, Furies And Voices, 1989, Treelink for tape, 1992. *Publications:* Music, Memory and Thought 1977, Understanding Music with AI (co-ed.) 1992. *Address:* 83 Appleton Street, Arlington, MA 02174, USA.

LASSEN, Morten Ernst, DipMus; Danish singer (baritone); b. 1969. *Education:* Royal Danish Acad. of Music with Prof. Kirsten Buhl-Miller. *Career:* debut as Papageno with The Young Operacompagnie 1993; sang Bach's B minor Mass, St John and St Matthew Passions, as Jesus and the bass arias; Fauré's Requiem, Handel's Messiah, Mahler's Des Knaben Wunderhorn; concerts with MDR-Sinfonieorchester, Berliner Symfoniker, Deutsches Symfonie Orchester Berlin, Danish Radio Orchestras; several radio and television productions; appearances in festivals of modern music, including Davos Musikfestival with works by Kurt Weill and Ernst Krenek; season 1996–97, sang Masetto at Confidencen in Stockholm, and sang at Tiroler Landestheater at Innsbruck as Dandini in Cenerentola and in Willi's Schlafes Bruder; season 1999–2000 at Deutsche Oper Berlin, Papageno in Die Zauberflöte, Sharpless in Madama Butterfly, Schaunard in La Bohème, Masetto in Don Giovanni, Dancairo in Carmen and Bill in Mahagonny; concert engagements include appearances with the Danish symphony orchestras and bass part in B minor Mass with Danish Radio Symfony Orchestra conducted by Herbert Blomstedt; several recitals in Denmark and abroad; retd from professional stage 2004. *Honours:* Carl Nielsen Travel Scholarship 1996, EBU Competition Winner 1997, prize winner VII International Hugo Wolf Lieder Competition, Stuttgart, Aksel Schiotz Prize 1997. *Website:* www.mortenernstlassen.com.

LASSMANN, Peep, DipMus; Estonian pianist; *Rector, Estonian Academy of Music and Theatre*; b. 19 March 1948, Tartu; m. Kadri Lassmann; two s. *Education:* Tallinn Conservatory, Moscow Conservatory. *Career:* teacher, Tallinn Conservatory 1973, Assoc. Prof. 1985, Head of Piano Dept 1987, Prof. and Pro-Rector 1991, Rector 1992; Rector, Estonian Acad. of Music 1993, Estonian Acad. of Music and Theatre; many concert tours world-wide; recitals include the complete piano works of Messiaen; mem. Estonian Piano Teachers' Asscn (Pres.), Music Council of Estonia (Pres.). *Publications:* contrib. of numerous articles to various Estonian newspapers and magazines. *Honours:* Orders of Estonia and Belgium; prizes in piano competitions in USSR, Estonian Radio Merited Artist of Estonia 1987, Musician of the Year 1989, music prizes of Estonian Cultural Foundation 1999, 2008. *Address:* Estonian Academy of Music and Theatre, Rävala pst 16, Tallinn 10143, Estonia (office). *Telephone:* 6675700 (office). *Fax:* 6675800 (office). *E-mail:* peep@ema.edu.ee (office).

LATARCHE, Vanessa Jayne, FTCL, LRAM, ARCM; British concert pianist and professor of piano; *Head of Keyboard, Royal College of Music*; b. 3 April 1959, Isleworth, Middx. *Education:* studied with Kendall Taylor, Royal Coll. of Music, and privately with Alexander Kelly, Vlado Perlemuter and Claude Frank in Aspen Music school. *Career:* solo career; broadcasts for Radio 3, BBC television and cable TV in USA; has played with major orchestras, including Royal Liverpool Philharmonic, BBC Concert Orchestra, BBC National Orchestra of Wales; performed the complete '48' at Lichfield Int. Festival; Prof. of Piano, Royal Acad. of Music 1992–2005, Head of Keyboard, Royal Coll. of Music, London 2005–; moderator, lecturer, examiner for the ABRSM and int. adjudicator and juror; contrib. to ABRSM Teaching Notes and CDs. *Recordings:* solo piano works of Mendelssohn, Bach and Chopin. *Honours:* Hon. ARAM . *Address:* Royal College of Music, Prince Consort Road, London, SW7 2BS, England (office). *Telephone:* (7831) 656827 (office). *E-mail:* vanessalatarche@aol.com (home). *Website:* www.rcm.ac.uk (office).

LATCHEM, Malcolm, ARCM; British violinist; b. 28 Jan. 1931, Salisbury; m. 1964; one s. three d. *Education:* Royal Coll. of Music. *Career:* mem. Philharmonia Orchestra 1960–65; Sub-Leader, London Philharmonic Orchestra 1965–69; mem. Dartington String Quartet 1969–80; founder mem., Acad. of St Martin-in-the-Fields 1959–2007; leader, Ten Tors orchestra, Devon 1998–. *Recordings:* Chamber music with Acad. of St Martin-in-the-Fields Chamber Ensemble, Handel Trio Sonatas, Mozart's Divertimenti, Spohr's Double Quartets; other chamber music. *Honours:* Hon. MMus (Bristol Univ. 1980). *Address:* Station House, Staverton, Totnes, Devon, TQ9 6AG, England (home). *Telephone:* (1803) 762670 (home).

LATHAM, Alison Mary, BMus; British editor and writer; b. (Alison Mary Goodall), 13 July 1948, Southsea, Hants., England; m. Richard Latham; three s. *Education:* The Maynard School, Exeter, Univ. of Birmingham. *Career:* Sr Copy Ed., The New Grove Dictionary of Music and Musicians 1971–77, Asst Ed., The Grove Concise Dictionary of Music 1986–88; Co-Ed., The Musical Times 1977–88; Publs Ed., Royal Opera House, Covent Garden 1989–2000; Ed. Edinburgh Int. Festival programmes 2003–; mem. Royal Soc. of Arts, Royal Musical Asscn, Soc. of Authors, Critics' Circle. *Publications:* The Cambridge Music Guide (with Stanley Sadie) 1985, Verdi in Performance (co-ed. with Roger Parker) 2001, The Oxford Companion to Music (ed.) 2002, Sing Ariel: Essays and Thoughts for Alexander Goehr's Seventieth Birthday (ed.) 2003, The Oxford Dictionary of Musical Terms 2004, The Oxford Dictionary of Musical Works 2004. *Address:* c/o Joanna Harris, Oxford University Press, Walton Street, Oxford, OX2 6DP, England. *Telephone:* (1865) 556767. *Fax:* (1865) 354635. *E-mail:* joanna.harris@oup.com.

LATHAM, Catherine; British oboe d'amore player; b. 1965, England. *Education:* Guildhall School of Music, London. *Career:* concerts with the European Baroque Orchestra 1985–86, under Ton Koopman, William Christie and Roger Norrington: regular appearances with the London Handel Orchestra (Flavio and Muzio Scevola 2001); The King's Consort, and the Orchestra of the Age of Enlightenment; concerto performances in Edinburgh, Dublin, Utrecht and the Wigmore Hall, London; tour of Europe in John Eliot Gardiner's Bach Cantata Pilgrimage 2000; Handel's Amadigi with The New Chamber Opera at New Coll., Oxford 2001. *Recordings include:* Bach Brandenburg Concertos, Concertos for two oboes by Vivaldi and Albinoni.

LATHAM-KOENIG, Jan; British pianist and conductor; *Chief Conductor and Head of the Artistic Board, Novaya Opera Theatre*; b. 15 Dec. 1953, London, England. *Education:* Royal Coll. of Music with Norman del Mar, Kendall Taylor and Lamar Crowson. *Career:* f. Koenig Ensemble 1976; concert pianist until 1981 then turned to conducting; Music Dir Orchestra of Porto (which he est. at the request of Portuguese govt) 1989–92; Perm. Guest Conductor Vienna State Opera 1991–; Music Dir Orchestre Philharmonique de Strasbourg, Opéra national du Rhin 1997–2002; fmr Music Dir Teatro Massimo, Palermo, Teatro Municipal, Santiago, Wrocław Symphony Orchestra, Poland, Wratislavia Cantans International Festival, Cantiere Internazionale d'Arte di Montepulciano, Young Janáček Philharmonic; Artistic Dir Orquesta Filarmónica de la UNAM, Mexico City 2012–; Artistic Dir Flanders Symphony Orchestra, Bruges 2013–; Chief Conductor Novaya Opera Theatre 2011–, Head of the Artistic Bd 2013–; regular appearances as conductor with Royal Philharmonic, Philharmonia, London Philharmonic, BBC Symphony, BBC Philharmonic Orchestra and BBC Nat. Orchestra of Wales; Guest

Conductor, Los Angeles Philharmonic and St Paul Chamber Orchestras, Danish and Swedish Radio Orchestras, Stockholm Philharmonic, Maggio Musicale Orchestras, RAI, Italy, Zürich Tonhalle and Gulbenkian Orchestra, Lisbon. *Recordings include:* Weill's Mahagonny with Anja Silja, Der Zar Lässt sich Photographieren, Walton Concertos with London Philharmonic Orchestra. *Honours:* Golden Mask Prize for Opera/Best Conductor for Wagner's Tristan und Isolde 2014. *Current Management:* Athole Still Limited, Foresters Hall, 25-27 Westow Street, London, SE19 3RY, England. *E-mail:* enquiries@ atholestill.co.uk. *Address:* Novaya Opera Theatre, 127006 Moscow, 3/2 Karetny Ryad (Hermitage Garden), Russia (office). *Website:* www .novayaopera.ru/en (office).

LATRY, Olivier; French organist; *Organiste Titulaire du Grand Orgue, Cathédrale Notre-Dame de Paris*; b. 22 Feb. 1962, Boulogne-sur-Mer; m. Marie-Thérèse; three c. *Education:* Saint Maur-des-Fossés Conservatoire with Gaston Litaize, Paris Conservatoire with Jean-Claude Raynaud. *Career:* organiste titulaire, Meaux Cathedral 1981–85; Organiste Titulaire du Grand Orgue, Cathédrale Notre-Dame de Paris 1985–; teacher of organ, Conservatoire at St Maur-des-Fossés 1990–95; Organ Prof., Paris Conservatoire 1995–; recitals in Europe, Russia, N and S America, Japan, China and Australia, concentrating on 17th- to 20th-century French organ music; renowned for improvisation. *Composition:* Salve Regina for voice and organ Op. 1. *Recordings include:* music of J. S. Bach, the complete organ works of Maurice Duruflé, Louis Vierne's Symphonies 2 and 3, Widor's Symphonies 5 and 6, Boëllmann's Suite Gothique, works by Litaize, the complete organ works of Olivier Messiaen, transcriptions for the organ ('Midnight at Notre-Dame'), organ works of César Franck. *Publication:* L'oeuvre d'orgue d'Olivier Messiaen 2008. *Honours:* Hon. Fellowship, North and Midland School of Music, UK 2006, Royal Coll. of Organists, UK 2007; Prix de la Fondation Cino et Simone del Duca 2000, Int. Performer of the Year, American Guild of Organists 2009. *Address:* Cathédrale Notre-Dame de Paris, 6 Place du Parvis, 75004 Paris, France (office).

LAUBENTHAL, Horst; German singer (tenor); b. 8 March 1939, Duderstadt, Germany; m. Marga Schiml. *Education:* studied in Munich with Rudolf Laubenthal. *Career:* debut in Würzburg 1967, as Mozart's Don Ottavio; Staatsoper Stuttgart from 1968, in operas by Wagner, Mozart and Beethoven; guest appearances in Vienna, Hamburg and Barcelona; Bayreuth Festival 1970, as the Steersman in Der fliegende Holländer; Deutsche Oper Berlin, as Lensky in Eugene Onegin and Pfitzner's Palestrina; Glyndebourne 1972, as Belmonte in Die Entführung; Paris Opéra 1977; Turin 1985, as Tamino in Die Zauberflöte (returned 1987 as Don Ottavio); often heard as the Evangelist in the Passions of Bach. *Recordings:* Tannhäuser, Fidelio, Die Meistersinger; Wozzeck and Lulu; Bach Cantatas and Christmas Oratorio; Trionfi by Orff; Konrgold's Violanta; Schubert's Lazarus.

LAUBER, Anne Marianne; composer and conductor; b. 28 July 1943, Zürich, Switzerland. *Education:* Lausanne Conservatory, Univ. of Montréal, studied with André Prevost. *Career:* teacher at French-language univs in Canada and pres. of the Canadian Music Centre from 1987; commissions from leading orchestras and soloists. *Compositions include:* Au-Dela Du Mur Du Son, (symphonic tale) 1983, Concertos for string quartet 1983, violin 1986, piano 1988, Le Songe for flute and string quartet 1985, Jesus Christus (oratorio) 1986, Piano Quintet 1989, Requiem 1989, Canadian Overture for strings 1989, vocal music. *Address:* c/o Canadian Music Centre, 20 St Joseph Street, Toronto, ON M4Y 1J9, Canada.

LAUFER, Beatrice; American composer; b. 27 April 1923, New York, NY. *Education:* Juilliard School with Roger Sessions, Marion Bauer and Vittorio Giannini. *Career:* performances of her music in Germany, Stockholm, People's Republic of China and USA. *Compositions include:* two Symphonies 1944, 1961, Opera Ile (after O'Neill's Long Voyage Home) 1958, Violin Concerto, Concerto for flute, oboe trumpet and strings 1962, Lyric for string trio 1966, The Great God Brown (ballet) 1966, My Brother's Keeper (biblical opera) 1968, Adam's Rib for soloists, chorus and orchestra, Concertante for violin, viola and orchestra 1986, choral music.

LAUGHLIN, Roy; Northern Irish conductor and pianist; *Head of Music, National Opera Studio*; b. 1954, Belfast. *Education:* Edinburgh and Durham Univs. *Career:* conducted Haydn's L'Infedeltà Delusa at Durham; Head of Music with Opera North conducting The Magic Flute, Orpheus in The Underworld, La Cenerentola and Der Freischütz 1989–95; Twice Chorus Master at Wexford Festival and conducted Die Schöpfung in 1989; Asst Conductor of Halifax Choral Society; engagements with Opera North include Fidelio, The Pearl Fishers, Peter Grimes and the British premiere production of Verdi's Jérusalem in 1990, also La Traviata, Attila and Faust; season 1992–93 with Falstaff for English Touring Opera and Cimarosa's Secret Marriage for the Cheltenham and Buxton Festivals; Head of Music, Nat. Opera Studio 1995–; led British Youth Opera in La Bohème 1998. *Address:* National Opera Studio, The Clore Building, 2 Chapel Yard, Wandsworth High Street, London, SW18 4HZ, England (office). *Telephone:* (20) 8874-8811 (office). *Fax:* (20) 8875-0404 (office). *E-mail:* r.laughlin@nationaloperastudio .org.uk (office). *Website:* www.nationaloperastudio.org.uk (office).

LAUKKA, Raimo; Finnish singer (baritone); b. 1954. *Education:* studied in Helsinki. *Career:* sang with Finnish Nat. Opera from 1989, as Mozart's Figaro, Count, Don Giovanni, Guglielmo and Papageno; Posa in Don Carlos 1995–96, Germont, Eugene Onegin, Gounod's Valentin in Faust, Donner in Das Rheingold 1996, Escamillo and Marcello; title role of Dallapiccola's Il

Prigioniero, Tampere 1996; as Wolfram in Tannhäuser, Savonlinna Festival 1996, Carlo in La Forza del Destino 1998; concert tours include USA with Neeme Järvi 1988, London Proms 2002. *Recordings include:* Kullervo by Sibelius. *Current Management:* c/o Anne-Kathrin Seibel, Allegro Artist Management, Yorckstrasse 81, 10965 Berlin, Germany. *Telephone:* (30) 78896635. *Fax:* (30) 78896711. *E-mail:* allegro@allegroartist.com. *Website:* www.allegroartist.com.

LAUKVIK, Jon; Norwegian organist, harpsichordist and composer; *Professor of Organ and Historical Keyboard Instruments, University of Music and Performing Arts, Stuttgart;* b. 16 Dec. 1952, Oslo. *Education:* Acad. of Oslo, Musikhochschule, Cologne with Prof. M. Schneider and Prof. H. Ruf, private studies with Marie-Claire Alain, Paris. *Career:* debut in Oslo 1973; recitals in Western and Eastern Europe, Canada, Israel, Japan, Korea and USA; Prof. of Organ and Historical Keyboard Instruments, Univ. of Music, Stuttgart 1980–; Prof. of Organ, Norwegian Acad. of Music, Oslo 2001–; recordings for several European radio stations; masterclasses; jury mem. for int. competitions. *Compositions:* Via Crucis, Triptychon, Suite for organ, Anrufung for two organs, tape and brass, Euphonie I for organ and five percussionists, Euphonie III for cello and organ, Contre-danse for orchestra, Lamento for trumpet and organ, Sonata for piano and organ, Arabesque for trombone and organ, Variations on a Relation for marimba and piano, Passacaglia for organ, Aria, Fugue & Final for organ, Three Poems (George Herbert) for choir and organ, Concerto for organ and string orchestra. *Recordings:* Neresheim Monastery (works by J.S. and C.P.E. Bach, Raison, Kittel), Motette-Ursina. *Publications:* Orgelschule zur historischen Aufführungspraxis, Part 1 (translated as Historical Performance Practice in Organ Playing) 1990, Part 2: Orgel und Orgelmusik in der Romantik 2000 (translated as The Romantic Period 2010)), Part 3: Die Moderne, G. F. Handel: Organ Concertos Op. 7 and Nos 13–16 (with W. Jacob) 1990, Complete organ works of Louis Vierne (with David Sanger) 2008. *Honours:* First Prize and Bach Prize, Int. Organ Week, Nuremberg 1977. *Address:* Alte Weinsteige 20, 70180 Stuttgart, Germany (home). *E-mail:* jon.laukvik@t-online.de (office). *Website:* www.laukvik.de.

LAURENCE, Elizabeth, ATCL, LTCL; British/French singer (mezzo-soprano); b. (Elizabeth Scott), 22 Nov. 1949, Harrogate, Yorks., England; d. of John Lawrence Scott and Nancy Parkinson. *Education:* Princess Helena Coll., Herts., Colchester School of Art and Trinity Coll. of Music, London. *Career:* Vienna in Le Marteau sans Maître under Boulez 1983; further concerts with Barenboim, Casadesus, Downes, Myrat, Jordan and Zender; recording for French TV, L'Heure Espagnole by Ravel 1985–86; sang at Madrid Opera as Jocasta in Oedipus Rex 1986, also in Buffalo, USA with M. Valdes 1991, Paris Opéra as Erda in Siegfried and Fricka in Rheingold, as Blumenmädchen in Parsifal 1987–88 and as Cherubino in Le nozze di Figaro, returning for the 1989 world premiere of Der Meister und Margarita by Höller, conducted by L. Zagrosek; sang in the world premiere of The Electrification of the Soviet Union by Nigel Osborne, conducted by E. Howarth, Glyndebourne Festival 1987; tour of Italy and Germany with Ensemble Intercontemporain 1987, in Le Marteau sans maître/Pierrot Lunaire, conducted by Pierre Boulez, and Matchavarian ballet music; Gurrelieder with Boulez, Proms 1987; sang in the premiere of Boulez's revised version of Le Visage Nuptial, La Scala, Milan 1988, Schoenberg's Op. 22 songs and Mahler's 3rd Symphony in Turin under Lothar Zagrosek and Rudolf Barshai; Covent Garden debut in the British premiere of Berio's Un Re in Ascolto 1989, La Bastille Opéra, Paris 1991; appeared as Judith in a BBC TV production of Bartók's Duke Bluebeard's Castle 1989; contemporary recital of Berio, Bartók, Britten, Reger and Schoenberg at Festival of Montreux; Gurrelieder at Leeds Town Hall 1989; sang Erda in Rheingold at Bonn Opera 1990, Ligeti's Requiem in Belgium and Germany 1991; sang and recorded Le Rossignol, Stravinsky, for the Proms with Boulez; sang Lady de Hautdesert in premiere of Birtwistle's Gawain at Covent Garden 1991; season 1991–92 as Ravel's Concepcion at Turin and the Duchess of Alba in the premiere of Osborne's Terrible Mouth at the Almeida Theatre; Verdi Requiem, London 1992; season 1993, Die Wuste hat zwolf Ding, Zender, Berlin Opera (concert), Folksongs by Berio, Ulisse by Dallapiccola, Salzburg Festival; season 1994, The Page in Salome, Opéra de Marseille, toured Germany in Pulcinella by Stravinsky, Orchestre de Paris, conductor S. Bychkov; season 1996, toured France in Pelléas et Mélisande by Debussy, conductor Du Closel, Flora in La Traviata, Marseille Opera, conductor N. Santi, Salzburg Festival with Ravel's Trois Poèmes de S. Mallarmé, L'Enfance du Christ by Berlioz in Malaga, Spain; French premiere of Gurlitt's Wozzeck in Rouen and Caen Opéras, conductor B. Ferrandis; Schoenberg recital, Academia S. Caecilia, Rome; Japanese premiere of Duke Bluebeard's Castle in Tokyo conducted by Peter Eötvös; debut at Théâtre Champs Elysées, Paris, with Les Nuits d'été by Berlioz; Stabat Mater by Rossini in Imola; season 1997, Drei Lieder by Stockhausen at Concertgebouw, Amsterdam conducted by Peter Eötvös; Sechs Gesänge by Zemlinsky with Vienna Philharmonic conducted by Heinz Holliger; Second Symphony by Leonard Bernstein conducted by D. Shalon; Das Lied von der Erde Kindertotenlieder; concert of symphonic music 1998, Die Mutter in Lulu, Paris Bastille Opéra; La madre in Nono's Al gran sole carico d'amore, Hamburg Staatsoper conducted by I. Metzmacher; Ommou in Hölszky's Die Wände, Frankfurt Staatsoper; debut as Mère Marie in Les Dialogues des Carmelites at La Scala, Milan; Leucade: L. Martin Toulouse/Nice; premiered Duke Bluebeard's Castle in Tbilisi, Georgia; also Phaedra: Britten; sang Rückert Lieder conducted by V. Matchavariani; sang Grimmgerde in Act 3 of Die Walküre conducted by D. Runnicles in BBC Proms, London 2000; Rihm: Die Eröberung von Mexico under M. Stentz at Frankfurt Staatsoper 2001–02;

Geneviève in Pelléas et Mélisande conducted by M. Zanetti, De Vlaamse Opera, Antwerp 2001; Gertrude in A. Thomas' Hamlet for Chelsea Opera Group; Duke Bluebeard's Castle for Graz Opera 2001; regular recitals in Europe; season 2002, Erwartung SWF Saarbrücken; Rihm's Dies; Henze's The Bassarids, Amsterdam; Henze's We Come to the River, Hamburg Staatsoper conducted by I. Metzmacher; Monleone's Cavelleria Rusticana conducted by F. Layer, Schmidt's Mascagni and Notre Dame at Festival Montpellier conducted by A. Jordan; Frau ohne Schatten conducted by U. Schirmer, Der Rosenkavalier (Annina) conducted by J. Conlon and Lulu at Opéra Bastille; concert of Berio in Milan; recital of Schoenberg with Jay Gottlieb; Falstaff with NSO conducted by B. Cinquegrani, UK 2004, Sir John in Love by R. Vaughn Williams for ENO (doubling), Henze Elegy for Young Lovers conducted by L. Koenigs, Ancona; has given master-classes in France and the UK. *Television:* numerous TV recordings, including educational programmes on 20th-century music, P. Boulez, D. Masson. *Recordings include:* Le Marteau sans Maître, Le Visage Nuptial, Bartók's Bluebeard's Castle, Gurlitt's Wozzeck, L'Heure Espagnole, Stravinsky's Le Rossignol. *Honours:* Diapason d'or, Prix d'Italia 1988, Grand Prix du Syndicat de la Presse 1997–98. *Current Management:* Robert Gilder & Co., 91 Great Russell Street, London, WC1B 3PS, England. *Telephone:* (20) 7580-7758. *Fax:* (20) 7580-7739. *E-mail:* rgilder57@hotmail.com; iarlaith@robert-gilder.com. *Website:* www.robert-gilder.com. *Address:* 26/28 rue du Buisson, St Louis, 75010 Paris, France (home). *E-mail:* elizabethlaurence@yahoo.co.uk (home).

LAURENS, Guillemette; French singer (mezzo-soprano); b. 1950, Fontainebleau. *Education:* Toulouse Conservatoire and Paris Opéra Studio. *Career:* debut at Paris Salle Favart as Anne Trulove in The Rake's Progress; Has performed throughout Europe, the USA and South America; sang Cybele in Lully's Atys at the Paris Opéra with Les Arts Florissants; repertoire includes German Lieder, French and Italian Baroque chamber music, Pierrot Lunaire by Schoenberg, La Clemenza di Tito, Giulio Cesare, and I Puritani (Paris Opéra); appeared with Capriccio Stravagante in America in 1989; Engagements with the Ensemble Sequentia in 12th Century Liturgical Drama; sang at the Festival of Aix-en-Provence in Iphigénie en Aulide, with John Eliot Gardiner, and Towards Bach concert series on London's South Bank in 1989; Monteverdi's Penelope at the 1998 Vienna Festival. *Recordings:* Monteverdi's Vespers with Philippe Herreweghe; Atys and Il Ballo dell'Ingrate, conducted by William Christie; Bach's B minor Mass with Gustav Leonhardt; Charpentier's Le Malade Imaginaire under Marc Minkowski; Diana in Iphigénie en Aulide under John Eliot Gardiner. *Current Management:* c/o Ariën Arts & Music Management, De Boeystraat 6, 2018 Antwerp, Belgium. *Telephone:* (3) 285-96-80. *Fax:* (3) 230-35-23. *E-mail:* arien@pandora.be.

LAURIDSEN, Morten Johannes, DMA; American composer; *Professor of Composition, Thornton School of Music, University of Southern California;* b. 27 Feb. 1943, Colfax, Wash. *Education:* Whitman Coll., Univ. of Southern California. *Career:* Prof. of Composition, Thornton School of Music, Univ. of Southern California 1967–, Chair. Composition Dept 1990–2002; Composer-in-Residence, Los Angeles Master Chorale 1994–2001; Visiting Prof. at over 40 univs. *Film:* Shining Night: A Portrait of Composer Morten Lauridsen by Michael Stillwater (Winner, Best Documentary, DC Ind. Film Festival, Eugene Film Festival) 2012. *Compositions include:* vocal cycles: Les Chansons des Roses, Mid-Winter Songs, Cuatro Canciones, A Winter Come, Madrigali: Six 'FireSongs' on Renaissance Italian Poems, Nocturnes, Lux Aeterna, O Magnum Mysterium, Ave Maria, O Nata Lux, Ubi Caritas et Amor, Ave Dulcissima Maria. *Honours:* Thornton School of Music Outstanding Alumnus Award, named American Choral Master, Nat. Endowment for the Arts 2006, Nat. Medal of Arts 2007. *Address:* Department of Composition, USC Thornton School of Music, Los Angeles, CA 90089-0851, USA (office). *Telephone:* (213) 740-7416 (office). *Fax:* (213) 740-3217 (office). *E-mail:* lauridse@usc.edu (office). *Website:* www.usc.edu/schools/music (office).

LAURIE, Alison Margaret, MA, BMus, PhD, ARCM; British music librarian and musicologist; b. 5 Jan. 1935, Glossop. *Education:* Beacon School, Bridge of Allan, Stirlingshire, Glasgow Univ., Univ. of Cambridge. *Career:* Sr Asst Librarian, Glasgow Univ. Library 1961–63; Music Librarian, Reading Univ. Library 1963–99; mem. Purcell Soc. Cttee (sec. 1983–88, chair. 1989–2006), Royal Musical Asscn. *Publications:* Purcell: Dioclesian 1961, Dido and Aeneas (with Thurston Dart) 1961, King Arthur 1971, Secular Songs for Solo Voice 1985, The Indian Queen 1994, The Gresham Autograph (facsimile edn introduction with Robert Thompson) 1995, Dramatic Music, Part 1 2007, Dramatic Music, Part 3 2010, Services (with Bruce Woods) 2013; contrib. to Musik in Geschichte und Gegenwart 1973, New Grove Dictionary of Music and Musicians 1980, Music and Bibliography: Essays in Honour of Alec Hyatt King 1980, Source Material and the Interpretation of Music: a Memorial Volume to Thurston Dart 1981, Music in Britain: The Seventeenth Century 1992, Henry Purcell, Dido and Aeneas: an Opera 1986, Purcell Studies 1995, contrib. to periodicals, including Brio, Fontes Artis Musicae, Irish Musical Studies, Musical Times, Proceedings of the Royal Musical Asscn. *Address:* 123 Nightingale Road, Woodley, Reading, RG5 3LZ, England (home).

LAUS, Michael; Maltese conductor and pianist; *Music Director, Malta Philharmonic Orchestra;* b. 30 Nov. 1960; one d. *Education:* Conservatorio Giuseppe Verdi, Milan. *Career:* Music Dir, Malta Philharmonic Orchestra 1991–; Assoc. Prof. of Music, Univ. of Malta 1994–; f. Malta Nat. Youth Orchestra 2004; guest conductor with Bournemouth Symphony Orchestra, Slovak Philharmonic Orchestra, Slovak Radio Symphony Orchestra, Berne Symphony Orchestra; several CD albums. *Address:* Malta Philharmonic

Orchestra, 88 Old Mint Street, Valletta, VLT 1112, Malta (office). *Telephone:* 21244473 (office). *Fax:* 21244473 (office). *E-mail:* michael.laus@ maltaorchestra.com (office). *Website:* www.maltaorchestra.com (office).

LAVENDER, Justin; British singer (tenor), conductor and teacher; *Professor of Vocal Studies, Royal College of Music;* b. 4 June 1951, Bedford. *Career:* debut as Nadir in Les Pêcheurs de Perles at Sydney Opera House 1982; has sung Tamino and Medoro in Haydn's Orlando Paladino at St Gallen, Tamino in Die Zauberflöte with Vienna Staatsoper and Volksoper, Cassio and Pilade in Rossini's Ermione, Madrid, Le Comte Ory at La Scala, Don Ottavio with Rome Opera, Royal Danish Opera, Prague Spring Festival; Faust, Arnold in Guillaume Tell and Almaviva at Covent Garden; Belmonte in Vienna, Berlin, La Monnaie; appearances in premieres of Il Ritorno di Casanova by Arrigo at the Grand Théâtre Geneva and La Noche Triste by Prodomidès at Théâtre des Champs Elysées, Paris; other engagements include Fernande in La Favorite at Vichy, Almaviva at Pittsburgh (US debut), Ferrando in Così fan tutte, Venice and Essen, Lindoro at Buxton Festival, Neocles in Le Siège de Corinthe in Madrid and the Festival Hall, London, Il Pirata in Lausanne, Marzio in Mitridate and Aronne in Mosè in Egitto at Covent Garden, Don José in Royal Opera House production in Taipei and in Raymond Gubbay's Carmen, Royal Albert Hall, Gluck's Admeto at Drottningholm, Maurizio in Adriana Lecouvreur, Florestan in Leonore, Don José in Carmen, Pinkerton in Madama Butterfly, Faust at Covent Garden; concert performances include Bartók's Cantata Profana with Georg Solti, Schubert's Mass in E flat with Giulini and Berlin Philharmonic, Schnittke's Faust Cantata under Claudio Abbado and Oedipus Rex under Bernard Haitink, Mahler's 8th Symphony at Royal Albert Hall; other conductors have included John Lubbock (Dream of Gerontius), John Pritchard, Yehudi Menuhin, Alberto Zedda and Leonard Slatkin; Artistic and Musical Dir, Opera at Bearwood, Berkshire 2013–15; Prin. Conductor and Artistic Dir Opera at Arcadian Opera; Vocal Consultant to Choir of King's Coll. Chapel, Cambridge; currently Prof. of Vocal Studies, Royal Coll. of Music. *Recordings include:* Elgar, Dream of Gerontius (with Oramo), City of Birmingham Symphony. *Publications include:* contrib. to The Singer, Irish Examiner. *E-mail:* justinlavender53@gmail.com (office). *Website:* www.justinlavender.co.uk.

LAVIRGEN, Pedro; singer (tenor); b. 31 July 1930, Bujalance, Andalusia, Spain. *Education:* studied with Miguel Barrosa in Madrid. *Career:* debut in Mexico City 1964 as Radames; European debut at the Teatro del Liceo, Barcelona as Don José; sang at Metropolitan 1969 as Cavaradossi in Tosca, Verona Arena 1974, 1976 as Radames, Covent Garden 1975, 1978 as Don José and Pollione in Norma, La Scala Milan 1975 as Don José, repeating the role at the 1978 Edinburgh Festival; other appearances in Hamburg, Munich, Prague, Budapest and Madrid. *Recordings include:* Il Retablo de Maese Pedro by De Falla.

LAVISTA, Mario; Mexican composer; b. 3 April 1943, Mexico City. *Education:* Nat. Conservatory of Mexico with Carlos Chávez and Rodolfo Halffter, studied in Paris with Jean Etienne Marie, in Cologne with K. Stockhausen and Henry Pousseaur. *Career:* Prof. of Theory and Composition, Nat. Conservatory of Mexico 1970–; founder of group, Quanta 1970–73; Ed., Pauta, Journal of Music 1982–; mem. Int. Soc. of Contemporary Music, Mexican Editions of Music, Nat. Coll. of Mexico, Mexican Acad. of Arts. *Compositions include:* Canto del Alba in C for flute, Nocturno in G for flute, Lamento for bass flute, Ofrenda for alto recorder, Dusk for contrabass, Cante for two guitars, Marsias for oboe and crystal cups, Ficciones for orchestra, Simurg for piano, Lacrymosa for orchestra, Missa ad Consolationis Dominam Nostram for choir a capella, Clepsidra for orchestra, Reflections of the Night for string quartet, Hacia el Comienzo for mezzo-soprano and orchestra (poems by Octavio Paz), Ciucani in B flat for flute and clarinet, Madrigal in B flat for clarinet, Three Nocturnes for mezzo-soprano and orchestra (poems by Alvaro Mutis), Aura (one-act opera based on Aura, a short story by Carlos Fuentes), Music for My Neighbor for string quartet, Danza isorrítmica for four percussionists, Lacrymosa for orchestra 1994.

LAWLESS, Stephen; British stage director; b. 1958, England. *Career:* Dir of Productions, Glyndebourne Touring Opera 1986–91; Death in Venice televised and staged at the 1992 Festival; Dir The Pearl Fishers for Scottish Opera, Falstaff at Glyndebourne and Rameau's Les Boréades at the Royal Acad. 1985; Kirov Opera debut with Boris Godunov 1990, also directed Boris Godunov at the Vienna Staatsoper and La Fenice, Venice 1994; Figaro and Rosenkavalier for Canadian Opera, Ariadne and Ballo in Maschera in Los Angeles, Capriccio in San Francisco and Così fan tutte in Chicago; Hamlet by Thomas at the Vienna Volksoper and a Baroque double bill at Innsbruck: Venus and Adonis, with Dido and Aeneas; season 1996–97 with Wozzeck in Braunschweig, Carmen for New Israeli Opera, Il Trovatore in Los Angeles, The Rake's Progress in Pisa and Mozart's Finta Semplice at Potsdam; L'Elisir d'amore at Madrid 1998; has directed opera worldwide, including Covent Garden, Glyndebourne, Vienna State Opera, Berlin Staatsoper, Nürnberg Opera, Metropolitan Opera (New York), Chicago, New York City Opera, Los Angeles, San Francisco, Washington, and the Hong Kong and New Zealand Festivals; Dir the complete Der Ring des Nibelungen for Beijing Music Festival 2005; Dir numerous LA Opera productions including Albert Herring, Ariadne auf Naxos, Un Ballo in Maschera, Il Trovatore, Don Pasquale, Falstaff and L'Elisir d'Amore. *Honours:* New York City Opera Award for Artistic Excellence 2007. *Address:* Los Angeles Opera, Dorothy Chandler Pavilion, 135 North Grand Avenue, Los Angeles, CA 90012, USA (office).

Telephone: (213) 972-7219 (office). *Fax:* (213) 687-3490 (office). *E-mail:* wehelpyou@laopera.com (office). *Website:* www.laopera.com (office).

LAWLOR, Thomas, BA; singer (bass-baritone); b. 1938, Dublin, Ireland. *Education:* Nat. Univ. of Ireland, Dublin Coll. of Music, Guildhall School of Music. *Career:* sang with D'Oyly Carte Co. 1963–71 with tours of North America; Glyndebourne 1971–, in Eugene Onegin, Ariadne, Così fan tutte, Die Entführung, La Bohème, Le nozze di Figaro, Capriccio, Intermezzo, and The Cunning Little Vixen; engagements with Opera North in A Village Romeo and Juliet, Tosca, Der Rosenkavalier, Der Freischütz, A Midsummer Night's Dream, Manon Lescaut, the premiere of Rebecca by Wilfred Josephs 1983, Werther, La Cenerentola, Beatrice and Benedict, Jonny Spielt Auf, Die Meistersinger, The Golden Cockerel and Intermezzo; further appearances with Kent Opera, English Music Theatre, New Sadler's Wells Opera and Opera Northern Ireland, Royal Opera, Dublin Grand Opera; sang in Rising of the Moon at Wexford Festival 1990 and Prokofiev's The Duenna; regular broadcaster on Radio Telefis Eireann and on BBC radio and television; faculty mem., Summer Conservatory of Music, Bay View, MI, USA.

LAWRENCE, Amy; American singer (soprano); b. 1962, Philadelphia. *Education:* Florida State University, New England Conservatory and Zürich Opera. *Career:* sang in La Forza del Destino and Albert Herring at Zürich, Der Schauspieldirektor by Mozart at Basle; Kiel Opera from 1994, as Dianora in Mona Lisa by Schillings, Adele (Fledermaus), Constanze, Susanna, and Speranza in L'Orfeo in Monteverdi's Orfeo; Concerts include Messiah, Die Schöpfung, and Mozart's C minor Mass; Carmina Burana and Barber's Knoxville Summer of 1915 with the Louisiana Philharmonic Orchestra; Season 1997 with the Mozart's Queen of Night for the Norwegian Opera, Oslo, and at Oper Frankfurt in 1998; Constanze with Opera Memphis, 1999; In concert with Brahms Requiem in Basel and Zürich and Bernstein's Symphony No. 3, Kaddish, with London Philharmonic Orchestra. *Recordings:* Beethoven Volkslieder, Weltliche Vokalwerke; Mona Lisa, opera by Max Schillings. *Honours:* National Finalist, Metropolitan Opera Competition; Semi-finalist, Belvedere Opera Competition, New York.

LAWRENCE, Helen Ruth, LRAM, ARAM; British singer (soprano/mezzo-soprano); b. 22 July 1942, London, England; m. Abraham Marcus 1969; two c. *Education:* Royal Acad. of Music, London. *Career:* guest artist, Covent Garden, ENO, Handel Opera, Chelsea Opera, Phoenix Opera, Germany, Far East; concerts and recitals with UK music clubs and choral socs, Wigmore Hall, South Bank, Barbican, and in Germany, Italy, Netherlands, Israel; Songmakers' Almanac, SPNM, Lontano, Hallé Orchestra; roles as soprano include Donna Anna, Constanze, Fiordiligi, Médée (Cherubini), Lucrezia Borgia, Lady Macbeth, Violetta, Leonora, Amelia, Abigaille, Tosca, Santuzza, Carmen; mezzo-soprano roles from 1989 include Carmen, Fidalma, Marcellina, Azucena and Mistress Quickly; Artistic Dir and Admin., New Shakespeare Co. opera season, Regent's Park Open Air Theatre 1983; London masterclasses 1989–92; Chair. Hampstead & Highgate Festival 2003–08; mem Equity, Incorporated Soc. of Musicians. *Recordings include:* title roles Giordano's Fedora, Berthold Goldschmidt's Beatrice Cenci; Amme Meme in Goldschmidt's Der Gewaltige Hahnrei, Berlin 1992, Ornamente by A. Krein 1997, Portrait of an Artist 1999. *Publications:* Life of Mozart (trans. from Italian), A History of the Camden Festival 2004. *Address:* 121 Anson Road, London, NW2 4AH, England (home). *Telephone:* (20) 8450-8864 (office). *E-mail:* helen@helenlawrence.co.uk (home). *Website:* www.helenlawrence.co .uk.

LAWRENCE-KING, Andrew, MA, DMus, LRAM; British opera, choral and orchestral director and musician (early harps, baroque gesture); *Director, The Harp Consort;* b. (Andrew King), 3 Sept. 1959, Guernsey, Channel Islands; s. of Gerald Robert King and Sylvia Lawrence; m. Katerina Antonenko. *Education:* Univs of Cambridge and Sheffield, London Early Music Centre. *Career:* Founder-mem. and Dir The Harp Consort; Founder-mem. and Co-Dir Tragicomedia 1987–93; Dir Il Corago; soloist and Dir, appearances with Hilliard Ensemble, Hesperion XX 1988–, The King's Singers, Jordi Savall, Paul Hiller; concerts in Europe, Scandanavia, USA, Canada, Japan, Australia, NZ, S America, Russia; directed Monteverdi's Ulisse at 1992 Swedish Baroque Festival, Malmö; Handel's Almira at Bremen Goethetheater 1994, Purcell's Dido and Aeneas in Helsinki 1995, Ribayaz's Luz y Norte at Sydney Opera House, Madrid Nat. Auditorium, Berlin and Warsaw Philharmonics, Wigmore Hall, London 1997–99, Florentine 1589 Intermedi 2000, Peri's Euridice in Los Angeles 2000, Padilla's Missa Mexicana at La Scala, Milan 2001 and Queen Elizabeth Hall, London 2001, first UK performance of La Púrpura de la Rosa, Sheffield 2003, Orgambide's Oratorio del Nacimiento, Sheffield 2005, first UK performance of Celos aun del Aire Matan, Sheffield 2008; solo recital to open 1992 Utrecht Festival, three concerts within 1995 Boston Early Music Festival, tours of USA and Japan; Dir Amherst Early Music Festival Opera 2002–06; AHRC Research Fellow, Univ. of Sheffield 2005–08; directed Ludus Danielis at Southwark Cathedral, London and King's Coll., Cambridge 2007, in York Minster Cathedral 2009; Bach Brandenburg concerto series with Kymi Sinfonietta, Finland 2009–14; staged production of Monteverdi's Combattimento with historical swordsmanship for the Wallace Collection, London 2012; directed music and historical staging of Purcell's Dido & Aeneas with Concerto Copenhagen for the Copenhagen Opera Festival 2012; directed opening production for new hall at Natalya Satz Theatre, Moscow 2012; directed first performance in Spain in modern times of the earliest surviving Spanish Christmas Oratorio at Festival Portico del Paraíso (stage and music) 2013, first staged production in modern times of Landi's La Morte d'Orfeo at St Petersburg Philharmonia 2013; currently Prin. Guest Conductor, Concerto Copenhagen; teacher, Helsinki Stadia and Sibelius Acad., Finland 2005–08; Prof. of Early Harp and Continuo, Akad. für Alte Musik, Bremen –1996; Prof., Escuela Superior de Música de Catalunya, Barcelona 1996–2007; currently Prof. of Early Harp and Continuo, Guildhall School of Music and Drama, London; Dir of Int. Baroque Opera Studio; Tutor in Early Harps and Continuo, Royal Danish Acad. of Music, Copenhagen; Sr Research Fellow, Univ. of Western Australia, Perth. *Achievement:* Royal Yachting Asscn Yachtmaster (Ocean). *Recordings include:* Les Travailleurs de la Mer (traditional music from Guernsey), Chorégraphie (music for Louis XIV's dancing masters), The Harp of Luduvico & The Secret of the Semitones (solo harp music), Luz y Norte (Spanish 17th century dances with guitar band), Almira (Handel's first opera), La Púrpura de la Rosa (first New World opera) (Noah Greenberg Award), The Italian Concerto (concerto soloist and dir, Bach, Handel, Vivaldi) (ECHO Klassik Prize for Best Baroque CD), Carolan's Harp (baroque Irish), Missa Mexicana (17th century polyphony and dances from Puebla Cathedral), The Play of Daniel and Miracles (medieval); concert programmes include: Luz y Norte (with Spanish Dance), Missa Mexicana (vocal and instrumental ensemble), Miracles (medieval lyrics), His Majesty's Harper (solo recital) as well as orchestral repertoire and operas from medieval to 21st century; appears as dir, concerto soloist and harp continuo player on more than 600 CDs (most recorded harpist of all time). *Publications:* Der Harpfenschlaeger (Historical harp technique); Luz y Norte (Spanish harp music); article in Companion to Medieval and Renaissance Music 1992, two chapters in La Púrpura de la Rosa (Hispanic Baroque opera), Durham Modern Languages Series 2008; numerous articles in specialist music journals. *Honours:* Dr hc (Sheffield); first Winner, Int. Award from Cambridge Early Music Soc. 1992, Winner, Gramophone Award 1992, Noah Greenberg Award 1996, Best Recording, American Handel Soc. 1996, Winner, German Phonographic Soc., Best Early Music CD, ECHO Klassik Prize 1998, Edison Award for Best Medieval CD 2004, Erwin Bodky Award for Outstanding Achievement in Early Music, Grammy Award for Best Small Ensemble directed by Jordi Savall 2011, Golden Mask (Russia), Jury's Special Prize for all categories of Music-Theatre) 2013, Helpmann Award (Australia) for Chamber Music for duo with Savall 2013. *Address:* c/o The Harp Consort, 9 Cliff Street, St Peter Port, Guernsey, GY1 1LH, Channel Islands (office). *Telephone:* (1481) 713037 (office). *E-mail:* info@theharpconsort.com (office). *Website:* www.theharpconsort.com (office); www.andrewlawrenceking.com.

LAWSON, Colin James, BA, MA, PhD, DMus, ARCM, FRCM, FRNCM, FLCM; British clarinettist, musicologist and broadcaster; *Director, Royal College of Music*; b. 24 July 1949, Saltburn-by-the-Sea, North Yorks., England; m. Hilary Birch 1982; one s. *Education:* Keble Coll., Oxford, Univs of Birmingham, Aberdeen and London. *Career:* Lecturer in Music, Univ. of Aberdeen 1973–77; Lecturer, Sr Lecturer and Reader in Music, Univ. of Sheffield 1978–97; Guest Prin. Clarinet, Orchestra of the Age of Enlightenment 1987–; Prof. of Classical Studies and Early Clarinet, Guildhall School of Music, London 1988–91; Prin. Clarinet, Hanover Band 1987–2006, London Classical Players 1989–92, English Concert 1991–2006; Visiting Lecturer, Royal Northern Coll. of Music, Manchester, RAM, London 1992; Prof. of Music, Goldsmiths Coll. 1998–2001; Pro-Vice-Chancellor/Dean, Thames Valley Univ. 2001–05; Dir Royal Coll. of Music, London 2005–; current specialisation in historical performance; mem. contemporary ensemble, Lysis; solo, chamber and orchestral appearances throughout the UK, Europe and USA; performed Mozart Concerto on a specially designed basset clarinet. *Recordings:* with Academy of Ancient Music, Albion Ensemble, Classical Winds, CM90, Cristofori, English Concert, The Parley of Instruments, La Petite Bande, L'Ecole d'Orphée, The King's Consort; concertos by Mahon, Hook, Weber, Spohr. *Publications:* The Chalumeau in Eighteenth-Century Music 1981, The Cambridge Companion to the Clarinet (ed.) 1995, Mozart Clarinet Concerto 1996, Brahms Clarinet Quintet 1998, The Historical Performance of Music: An Introduction (co-author) 1999, The Early Clarinet: A Practical Guide 2000, The Cambridge Companion to the Orchestra (ed.) 2003; contrib. of Beethoven and the development of wind instruments (in Beethoven and the Performer) 1994, Performing through history (in Musical Performance: A Guide to Understanding) 2002, The Cambridge History of Musical Performance (co-ed.) 2012. *Honours:* Hon. RAM . *Address:* Royal College of Music, Prince Consort Road, London, SW7 2BS, England (office). *Telephone:* (20) 7589-4363 (office). *Fax:* (20) 7589-4356 (office). *Website:* www.rcm.ac.uk (office).

LAWSON, Philip, BA (Hons); British composer, arranger and singer (baritone); b. 19 Feb. 1957, Crawley, Sussex. *Education:* Hazelwick Comprehensive School, Univ. of York (Choral Scholarship). *Career:* freelance singer 1979–82; Lay Clerk, Salisbury Cathedral Choir 1982–94; Dir of Music, Chafyn Grove Preparatory School 1988–94; with The King's Singers as first baritone 1993–2012; lecturer, European Seminar For Young Composers, Aosta, Italy 2014; has performed at venues including Concertgebouw, Amsterdam, Carnegie Hall, New York, Royal Albert Hall, London, Kennedy Center, Washington, DC, and Suntory Hall, Tokyo; music dealer (new and pre-owned) 1984–; now freelance composer, arranger, choral specialist, baritone. *Recordings:* with The King's Singers: numerous CDs and videos, including 1605: Treason and Dischord 2005, Sacred Bridges 2005, Six 2005, Thomas Tallis Spem in Alium 2006, Landscape & Time 2006, The Quiet Heart 2007, Live at the Proms 2008, The Golden Age 2008, Simple Gifts (Grammy Award 2009) 2008, Reflections 2008, Romance du Soir 2009, Swimming over London 2010. *Publications:* more than 100 published compositions. *E-mail:* philip@philiplawson.net (office). *Website:* www.philiplawson.net.

LAWTON, Jeffrey; British singer (tenor); b. 1941, Oldham, Lancashire, England. *Education:* studied with Patrick McGuigan. *Career:* with WNO has sung Tikhon in Katya Kabanova, also televised, various roles in The Greek Passion by Martinů, Florestan, Huon in Oberon, in Janáček's From the House of the Dead and Jenůfa as Laca, Otello, Aeneas in The Trojans and Don José; sang Siegfried in a new production of The Ring also seen at Covent Garden 1986, and the Emperor in Die Frau ohne Schatten; other operatic appearances for Opera North as Erik and Florestan, in Paris, Brussels and Nancy (Otello), and as Siegmund at Cologne, Prague State Opera; concert engagements include the Choral Symphony with the Royal Liverpool Philharmonic, Das Lied von der Erde with the BBC Symphony at the Brighton Festival and in Paris, and Mahler's 8th Symphony in Turin; sang Siegfried in Götterdämmerung in Cologne, Edmund in Lear for English National Opera, Edinburgh Festival 1990 in Martinů's Greek Passion, Laca in Jenůfa for WNO and Tristan, 1992–93, Shuisky in Boris for Opera North, 1993–94, Laca for New Israeli Opera and Tristan for Scottish National Opera; sang Herod in the final scene from Salome at Promenade Concerts in 1993; sang Pedro in the premiere of Macmillan's Inès de Castro, Edinburgh, 1996; Wagner concert with the Philhlarmonia, London, 1997; Tristan for WNO and at Buenos Aires, 1999–2000; Tristam for Chicago Lyric Opera 2000; President in Kurt Weill's Arms and the Cow for Opera North 2003; Der Meistersinger von Nürnburg, Edinburgh Festival 2006. *Recordings include:* The Greek Passion. *Current Management:* c/o Neil Dalrymple, Music International, 13 Ardilaun Road, London, N5 2QR, England. *Telephone:* (20) 7359-5183. *Fax:* (20) 7226-9792. *E-mail:* music@musicint.co.uk. *Website:* www.musicint.co.uk.

LAYTON, Richard; British violinist; b. 11 May 1940, Redditch, Worcs., England; m.; four c. *Education:* studied in London. *Career:* Assoc. Leader, Bournemouth Symphony Orchestra, worked regularly with conductors including Constantine Silvestri, George Hurst, Sir Charles Groves, Paavo Berglund; Leader Bournemouth Sinfonietta chamber orchestra; performed as soloist in concertos by composers including Haydn, Mozart, Beethoven, Prokofiev, Vaughan Williams, Bach's Brandenburg concertos; First Violin, Silvestri String Quartet, regular appearances at Dartmouth and Bath Music Festivals; Assoc. Leader, London Philharmonic Orchestra, worked regularly with conductors including Bernard Haitink, John Pritchard, Sir Simon Rattle, George Solti; Leader Park Lane Music Players, specializing in new works and those of neglected early composers; Assoc. Leader, Royal Philharmonic Orchestra working with conductors including Sir Charles Mackerras, Sir Yehudi Menuhin, Yuri Temirkanov, Vladimir Ashkenazy, Rudolf Barshai and Andre Previn; Guest Leader, Welsh Nat. Opera, BBC Wales Symphony Orchestra, ENO, BBC Concert Orchestra, Phiharmonia Orchestra of London; has also played with members of the Leipzig Gewandhaus Orchestra, English Chamber Orchestra, Polish Chamber Orchestra; has lived in France since 2003 and continues to play chamber music and lead orchestras. *Address:* Tessé, La Forêt de Tessé, 16240 Charente, France (home). *E-mail:* layton.richard@neuf.fr (home).

LAYTON, Robert; critic, producer and writer on music; b. 2 May 1930, London, England; m. Ingrid Nina Thompson. *Education:* Worcester Coll., Oxford, Univs of Uppsala and Stockholm, studied with Edmund Rubbra, Egon Wellesz and Prof. Carl-Allan Moberg. *Career:* Swedish film industry 1954–55; teacher in London 1956–59; BBC Music Division 1959–90 (music presentation 1959, music talks 1960); Gen. Ed., BBC Music Guides 1973–; Prod., BBC Lunchtime Concerts at St John's Smith Square 1984–88. *Publications:* Franz Berwald 1959, Jean Sibelius 1965, Sibelius and his World 1970, Dvořák Symphonies and Concertos 1977, Sibelius 1981, Companion to the Concerto 1988, responsible for Scandinavian music in The New Grove Dictionary of Music and Musicians 1980, translated Erik Tawaststjerna's Sibelius Vol. I 1976, Vol. II 1986, Vol. III 1997, Companion to the Symphony (ed.) 1993, Grieg: A Short Life 1997; contrib. to The Symphony 1966, The Gramophone, The Listener, The Times and professional journals in the UK and Sweden. *Honours:* Finnish State Literary Prize 1985, Sibelius Medal 1987, Knight of the Order of the White Rose of Finland 1988, Knight of the Order of the Polar Star, Sweden 2001.

LAYTON, Stephen; British choral director and organist; *Director of Music and Fellow, Trinity College, Cambridge*; b. 1962, England. *Education:* Chorister Winchester Cathedral, Music Scholar Eton Coll., Organ Scholar King's Coll., Cambridge. *Career:* appearances with King's Coll. Chapel Choir in Europe, USA and Japan; conducted Messiah and Gluck's Orfeo at Cambridge; founder and Dir of chamber choir, Polyphony, making London Proms debut 1995, with Pärt's Passio and Dido and Aeneas; Musical Dir, Holst Singers; organist and Dir of the Choir, Temple Church, London 1996–2006; engagements with the Philharmonic Chorus, London Philharmonic Choir and BBC Symphony Orchestra Chorus; tour of Brazil with Polyphony and Bournemouth Sinfonietta 1995; Bach's Christmas Oratorio and Messiah with the Brandenburg Concert in London 1996; further concerts in Estonia, Hong Kong, France, Spain and Copenhagen; directed Poulenc's Figure Humaine London Proms 1999; conducted BBC Singers London Proms Chamber Music 2002; Dir of Music and Fellow Trinity Coll., Cambridge 2006–; Artistic Dir and Principal Conductor, City of London Sinfonia 2010–. *Recordings include:* Macmillan's Seven Last Words from the Cross, Folksongs by Holst and Vaughan Williams, Howells Requiem (Gramophone Award for Best Choral Recording 2012). *Current Management:* Hazard Chase, 25 City

Road, Cambridge CB1 1DP, England. *Telephone:* (1223) 312400. *Fax:* (1223) 460827. *E-mail:* james.brown@hazardchase.co.uk. *Website:* www.hazardchase .co.uk.

LAZAR, Hans Jurgen; German singer (tenor); b. 1958, Bad Salzuflen. *Education:* studied in Detmold with Sandor Konya. *Career:* debut at Detmold 1982, as Mozart's Pedrillo; sang at the Hagen Opera 1985–87, Essen 1988–91, notably as Wagner's David, Janáček's Fox, Alfred in Fledermaus and Nicolai's Fenton; Frankfurt Opera 1988–91, notably as Britten's Flute; sang Mime at Trieste and Monteverdi's Arnalta in Frankfurt, 2000–01; many concert appearances, including Mozart masses, and Janáček's Diary of One Who Disappeared.

LAZAREV, Alexander Nikolayevich; Russian conductor; b. 5 July 1945; m. Tamara Lazarev; one d. *Education:* Leningrad and Moscow Conservatoires. *Career:* conducting debut at Bolshoi Theatre 1973, conducted numerous ballets and operas of the Bolshoi Theatre's European and Russian repertoires, Founder and conductor Ensemble of Soloists of the Bolshoi Theatre 1978–89, Chief Conductor, Artistic Dir, Bolshoi Theatre 1987–95; Chief Conductor Duisburg Symphony Orchestra 1988–93; has conducted numerous orchestras including Berlin Philharmonic, Munich Philharmonic, Orchestra Sinfonica del Teatro alla Scala di Milano, Orchestre Nat. de France and others; UK debut with Royal Liverpool Philharmonic Orchestra 1987; subsequently performed with City of Birmingham Symphony Orchestra, Royal Scottish Nat. Orchestra, etc.; Prin. Guest Conductor BBC Symphony Orchestra, 1992–95; Prin. Guest Conductor Royal Scottish Nat. Orchestra 1994–97, Prin. Conductor 1997–2005, Conductor Emer. 2005–; Prin. Conductor, Japan Philharmonic Orchestra 2008–11. *Honours:* Hon. Prof., Univ. of Glasgow 2005; First Prize USSR Nat. Competition 1971, First Prize and Gold Medal Karajan Competition (Berlin) 1972. *Current Management:* Tennant Artists, Unit 2, 39 Tadema Road, London, SW10 0PZ, England. *Telephone:* (20) 7376-3758. *Fax:* (20) 7351-0679 (office). *E-mail:* info@tennantartists.com (office). *Website:* www .tennantartists.com (office).

LAZARO, Francisco; singer (tenor); b. 13 March 1932, Barcelona, Spain. *Education:* Liceo Conservatory, Barcelona. *Career:* debut in Barcelona 1962 as Gaspare in Donizetti's La Favorita; sang in Macbeth and Der Rosenkavalier at the 1964 Salzburg Festival; guest appearances in Berlin, Düsseldorf and Frankfurt, San Francisco 1965 and Barcelona 1967, as Calaf in Turandot; frequent performances at the Munich Staatsoper from 1970; sang at Hamburg 1984 as Otello; other roles include Verdi's Manrico and Radames, Des Grieux in Manon Lescaut, Rodolfo and Don José.

LAZARTE, Julio Ricardo, BM; Argentine pianist and conductor; b. 12 July 1956, Tucumán. *Education:* Nat. Univ. of Tucumán, School of Musical Arts, Carnegie Mellon Univ., USA. *Career:* debut as pianist, integral version of sonatas and interludes by John Cage, US Embassy, Argentina 1985; conductor, complete version of church sonatas by Mozart, Santisimo Rosario Basilica, Tucumán 1990; as pianist has performed complete cycles of works for keyboard or chamber music with piano, by Pachelbel, Zipoli, Marcello, Handel, Haydn, Clementi, Mozart, Brahms, Weber, Debussy, Ravel, Satie, Cage, Ginastera and pioneers of Argentine and Latin American keyboard music; tours of USA, Spain, The Netherlands and Argentina; as conductor founder and Artistic Music Dir, Camerata Lazarte Chamber Orchestra, performing widely; has taught in many academic and cultural institutions. *Publication:* Lazarte Methodology. *Address:* c/o CESI, Marcos Paz 250, Tucumán 250, Argentina.

LE, Tuan Hung, BMus, Grad. Dip. Infor., DPhil; Australian (b. Vietnamese) composer and musicologist; *Program Director, Australia Asia Foundation;* b. 15 Oct. 1960, Viet Nam. *Education:* Royal Melbourne Inst. of Tech., Univ. of Melbourne, Monash Univ. *Career:* freelance composer, performer and musicologist 1987–; Program Man. of Music, Australia Asia Foundation 1994–, Program Dir 2000–. *Compositions:* Reflections 1990, Spring 1991, Prayer for Land 1991, Melorhythm 1993, Longing for Wind 1996, Calm Water 1996, Water Ways 1997, Scent of Memories 1998, Lotus Pond 1998, Scent of Time 2000, Echoes of an Old Festive Song 2003, A Song for Sky Bells 2004, Elegy 2004, On the Wings of a Butterfly 2004, From the Inner Space 2005, In the Shadows of the Wind 2006, Memories of Water 2006, Mantra for the Seeds of Love 2006, In the Shadows of the Wind 2006, Legend of the Light 2007, Journey to the Light 2007, A Time to Celebrate 2009, Soul of the Wind 2009, Celebration 2010, Melodia Guitarra 2012, Melody on a Broken String 2014. *Recordings:* Quivering String 1992, Musical Transfigurations 1993, Landscapes of Time 1996, Echoes of Ancestral Voices 1997, Scent of Time 2003, On the Wings of a Butterfly 2005. *Publications:* Dan Tranh Music of Vietnam: Traditions and Innovations 1998, Mindfulness of Hearing: Hearing Places from a Non-Western Perspective 2007; numerous articles in magazines, reviews and journals. *Honours:* Australian Acad. of Humanities Overseas Fellowship 1993. *Address:* PO Box 4136, Melbourne University, Parkville, Vic. 3052, Australia. *Website:* sonicgallery.org (office).

LE BRIS, Michele; singer (soprano); b. 1938, France. *Education:* Conservatoire Nat., Paris. *Career:* debut at Paris Opéra as Marguerite 1961; many appearances at such French opera centres as Marseilles, Nantes, Vichy, Strasbourg, Toulouse and Rouen; Strasbourg 1965 in local premiere of Mozart's La Finta Giardiniera, Amelia in Un Ballo in Maschera, Tokyo 1972; sang Halévy's Rachel in London 1973 and at Barcelona 1974; sang at Barcelona 1976 as Thais; other roles have included Rossini's Mathilde, Verdi's Desdemona and Trovatore Leonora, Manon Lescaut, Tosca, Mimi, Minnie and

Musetta, Massenet's Salome and Sapho, Regina in Mathis der Maler, Mozart's Countess and Donna, Lisa in The Queen of Spades and Janáček's Jenůfa. *Recordings include:* highlights from Un Ballo in Maschera and Il Trovatore.

LE BROCQ, Mark; British singer (tenor); b. 1966, England. *Education:* St Catharine's Coll., Cambridge, Royal Acad., Nat. Opera Studio. *Career:* fmr Principal with ENO, roles included Tamino in The Magic Flute, Paris in King Priam, Count Almaviva in The Barber of Seville, Narraboth in Salome, Cassio in Othello, The Schoolmaster in The Cunning Little Vixen, Don Ottavio in Don Giovanni, Cavalli's Egisto, Paolino in Il Matrimonio Segreto, Berlioz's Benedict, Spirit/Autumn in The Fairy Queen, Odoardo in Ariodante, Doctor Maxwell in The Silver Tassie (world premiere), Siward in A Better Place (world premiere); guest appearances include Idomeneo with Opera Northern Ireland, Belmonte in Die Entfuhrung Aus Dem Serail with Garsington Opera, Pinkerton in Madam Butterfly at Royal Albert Hall, Boggart in The Fairy Queen at the Liceu, Barcelona; appearances at Covent Garden and Aix-en-Provence festivals; concerts in the USA, throughout Europe and in the Middle East with Les Arts Florissants, The Gabrieli Consort and others; appeared at BBC Proms 2003. *Recordings include:* Il Trovatore, Carmen, Turandot, Hail Bright Cecilia, Utrecht Te Deum, I Was Glad. *Honours:* RAM Blyth Buesset Opera Prize, RAM Club Prize, Worshipful Co. of Musicians Medal. *Current Management:* Hazard Chase, 25 City Road, Cambridge, CB1 1DP, England. *Telephone:* (1223) 312400. *Fax:* (1223) 460827. *E-mail:* sue.nicholls@ hazardchase.co.uk. *Website:* www.hazardchase.co.uk.

LE DIZES, Maryvonne; French violinist and academic; b. 25 June 1940, Quimper; m. 1964, three s. one d. *Education:* National Conservatory of Music, Paris. *Career:* debut with Violin Concert; soloist with Ensemble Intercontemporain 1978–; also mem. Trio Quartett Capppa, Sextuor Schoenberg; Professor, Conservatory of Music, Boulogne Billancourt, France 1977–2007. *Recordings:* works by Berio, Messiaen, Xenakis, Machover, Carter, Brahms. *Honours:* Prize, International Thibaud Competition, Paris 1961, first prize, N Paganini Competition, Genoa 1962, International American Music Competition, New York 1983, SACEM Paris 1987. *Address:* c/o Conservatoire a Rayonnement Regional, 22, rue de la Belle-Feuille, 92100 Boulogne Billancourt, France (office).

LE FLEMING, Anthony Ralph, BA; British composer, organist and conductor; *Director of Music, Holy Trinity Clapham, London;* b. 16 March 1941, Wiltshire, England; m.; three c. *Education:* Salisbury Cathedral School and Queens' Coll., Cambridge. *Career:* organist Bedford School 1965–68; Dir of Music, Abingdon School 1968–73, Holy Trinity Clapham, London 1998–; Music Adviser, Birmingham LEA 1973–81, Devon County 1981–93; freelance composer, organist, conductor 1993–; mem. Incorporated Soc. of Musicians. *Compositions:* works for choir and orchestra, choir unaccompanied and with organ, songs with instrumental or piano accompaniment, instrumental pieces, arrangements in various styles. *Recordings:* Some Shadows of Eternity. *Honours:* first prize English Poetry and Song Soc. *Address:* 64 Park Hall Road, West Dulwich, London, SE21 8BW, England (home). *Telephone:* (20) 8761-4397 (home). *E-mail:* anthony.lefleming@gmail.com (home). *Website:* www .imple-music.co.uk/lefleming.htm.

LE MAGADURE, Gabriel; French violinist. *Education:* Boulogne-Billancourt Conservatory, Paris Conservatory with Ysaÿe Quartet, Geneva Conservatory with Gabor Takacs, Hochschule für Musik, Berlin with Eberhardt Feldz. *Career:* mem. Quatuor Ebène (chamber music ensemble) 1999–, joined BBC New Generation Artists Scheme 2006. *Recordings include:* Haydn: Quatuors à Cordes 2006, Bartók: Quatuors 1, 2, 3 2007, Ravel, Debussy and Fauré String Quartets (Echo Klassik Award for Recording of the Year 2009, Gramophone Award for Record of the Year 2009) 2008, Brahms: Piano Quintet No. 1 and String Quartet No. 1 2009, Fiction (Echo Award 2011) 2010, Mozart: KV 138, KV 421, KV 465 (Echo Award) 2012, Felix & Fanny Mendelssohn (BBC Music Magazine Chamber Award 2014) 2013. *Honours:* First Prize, ARD Int. Competition, Munich 2004, Karl Klinger Foundation Prize, Fondation Groupe Banque Populaire Award, Belmont Prize for Contemporary Music, Fondation Forberg-Schneider 2005, Borletti-Buitoni Trust Award 2007. *Current Management:* c/o Linda Uschinski, Impresariat Simmenauer, Kurfürstendamm 211, 10719 Berlin, Germany. *Telephone:* (30) 414781717. *E-mail:* linda.uschinski@impresariat-simmenauer.de. *Website:* www.impresariat-simmenauer.de; www.quatuorebene.com.

LE PAGE, David; British violinist; *Founder-member, Kreutzer Quartet;* b. 1965, England. *Education:* Yehudi Menuhin School. *Career:* co-founder and second violinist of the Kreutzer Quartet from 1988; South Bank debut in 1989 followed by Amsterdam Concertgebouw and recital at Palazzo Labia in Venice; formed groups Le Page Ensemble, The Harborough Collective and Mysterious Barricades; recital at Lancaster House for HRH Queen Elizabeth 1991; apptd leader, Orchestra of the Swan 1999; also Amb. European String Teachers Asscn; est. repertoire and new compositions with improvisations in The Chamber, featuring live film projection and static coloured images within a darkened set; teaches at Birmingham Conservatoire; appeared at many festivals across UK. *Recordings include:* The Reinvention of Harmony and Imagination. *Honours:* BBC Young Musician of the Year, winner Royal Overseas League Competition (with Kreutzer Quartet) 1991. *Address:* Orchestra of the Swan, Civic Hall, 14 Rother Street, Stratford-upon-Avon, CV37 6LU, England (office). *Telephone:* (1789) 267567 (office). *E-mail:* zoe@ orchestraoftheswan.org (office). *Website:* www.orchestraoftheswan.org/the -orchestra/the-players/david-le-page/ (office); www.davidlepage.co.uk.

LE ROUX, François; French singer (baritone); *Founder and Artistic Director, Académie Francis Poulenc Tours for the interpretation of French Art Song*; b. 30 Oct. 1955, Rennes; s. of Pierre Le Roux and Claudie Blanchard; m. François Lesens. *Education:* studied privately with François Loup, then Paris Opéra Studio with Vera Rozsa, then Elisabeth Grummer. *Career:* sang Mozart's Masetto, Papageno and Guglielmo, Opéra de Lyon 1980–85; appeared as Debussy's Pelléas, Paris Opéra, La Scala, Milan 1986, Vienna Staatsoper 1988, Barcelona, Helsinki 1989, Cologne 1992, Covent Garden 1994; debut at Glyndebourne Festival as Ramiro in L'Heure Espagnole 1987; appeared as Marcello in La Bohème, Hamburg 1987; debut as Don Giovanni, Paris Opéra-Comique 1987; debut at Covent Garden as Lescaut in Massenet's Manon 1988, returning as Papageno 1989; other roles include Hidraot in Armide, Orestes in Iphigénie, Ulisse in Il Ritorno, Valentin in Faust, Malatesta in Don Pasquale, Der Prinz von Homburg, Nick Shadow, Orpheus, Monsieur de in Madame de, Albert in Werther, Jupiter in Platée, Golaud in Pelléas, Peter Bel in Le Fou, Calchas in La Belle Hélène, Verlaine Paul, General Boum in Great Duchess of Gerolstein, Léandre in Love for Three Oranges, The Clock and the Cat in L'Enfant et les Sortilèges, Pandolphe in Massenet's Cendrillon, Golaud in Debussy's Pelléas et Mélisande, Paris (Opéra-Comique), Buenos Aires, Moscow (first ever staged version in Russia); cr. title role in world premiere of Birtwistle's Gawain at Covent Garden 1991. *Films:* Carmen (Francesco Rosi, part of Moralès), Beauty and the Beast (Disney, French soundtrack), Pelléas et Mélisande – Le Chant des aveugles (Béziat on the first ever staged production of Debussy's opera in Moscow). *Recordings include:* Pelléas et Mélisande under Claudio Abbado; L'Enfant et les sortilèges (Ravel) under Sir Simon Rattle; Poulenc Complete Songs with pianist Olivier Godin; Dutilleux songs with orchestra, Orchestre Nat. de Bordeaux, conductor Hans Graf. *Publication:* Le Chant intime 2004 (in Japanese 2009). *Honours:* Chevalier des Arts et des Lettres; First Prize, Int. Maria Canals Competition, Barcelona 1978, Int. Competition, Rio de Janeiro 1979, Winner, French Critics' Award, Révélation de l'année 1987, voted Musical Personality of the Season by French Critics 1997–98. *Current Management:* c/o Daniel Lombard, Musicaglotz, 29 rue Violet, 75015 Paris, France. *Telephone:* 1-42-34-53-47. *E-mail:* daniel.lombard@musicaglotz.com. *Website:* www.musicaglotz.com. *E-mail:* contact@francoisleroux.net (office). *Website:* www.francoisleroux.net.

LE SAGE, Eric; French pianist; b. 1964, Aix-en-Provence. *Education:* Conservatoire Nat. Supérieur de Paris. *Career:* recitals and chamber music concerts at numerous int. venues; has performed as soloist with Los Angeles Philharmonic, Toronto Philharmonic, St Louis Symphony Orchestra, Stuttgart SWR Symphony Orchestra, Bremen Philharmonic Orchestra, Royal Scottish Nat. Orchestra, Gothenburg Philharmonic, Rotterdam Philharmonic, NHK Symphony Orchestra, Dresden Philharmonic, Orchestre Nat. du Capitole de Toulouse, Zwickau Symphony Orchestra, Netherlands Radio Symphony Orchestra, Orchestre Philharmonique de Radio France, Orchestre Nat. d'Ile de France, Orchestre Philharmonique de Liège, Munich Chamber Orchestra, with conductors Armin Jordan, Edo de Waart, Stéphane Denève, Louis Langrée, Michel Plasson, Michael Stern and Sir Simon Rattle. *Recordings include:* complete solo piano and chamber music works of Schumann; works by Schumann, Fauré, Poulenc and others. *Honours:* First Prize, Porto Int. Piano Competition 1985, Robert Schumann Int. Piano Competition 1989, Grand Prix du Disque Acad. Charles Cros 2000, 2011, Prix Caecilia, Diapason d'Or de l'Année, Choc de l'Année Classica, Choc du Monde de la Musique, Grand Prix du Disque, Victoire de la Musique. *Current Management:* Solea Artist Management, 91 rue Lamarck, 75018 Paris, France. *Telephone:* 1-42-36-45-33. *E-mail:* rb@solea-management.com. *Website:* www.solea-management.com. *E-mail:* contact@ericlesage.org (office). *Website:* ericlesage.org (office).

LE TEXIER, Vincent; French singer (bass-baritone); b. 1957. *Education:* Grenoble Conservatory, studio of the Paris Opéra. *Career:* appearances at the Paris Opéra in Orphée aux Enfers and with the Opéra-Comique in From the House of the Dead; Sang Golaud in Pelléas et Mélisande and appeared at the 1989 Aix Festival, in The Love for Three Oranges; Lyon, as Schaunard in La Bohème, the four devils in Les Contes d'Hoffmann, the King in Debussy's Rodrigue et Chimène (word creation); In Bordeaux, as Leporello in Don Giovanni, Escamillo in Carmen, the Count in Le nozze di Figaro, Frère Laurent in Roméo et Juliette by Berlioz; In Rouen, as Basilio in Il Barbiere di Siviglia, Kaspar in Freischütz (French version by Berlioz), the Count in Capriccio, the Speaker in Zauberflöte, Mephisto in Faust, Sade in Teresa by Marius Constant, Wozzeck in Wozzeck by Gurlitt (French version); Appearances at the Paris Opéra in Madama Butterfly, and in Pelléas et Mélisande; Golaud in Impressions de Pelléas, by Peter Brook and Marius Constant, in Paris and on tour around Europe, 1991–92; Created the role of Ethnologist in Georges Aperghis's Tristes Tropiques, Strasbourg, 1996; season 2000–01 as the Berlioz Mephisto at Naples (concert), Eumée in Fauré's Pénélope at Lausanne and Golo for Leipzig Opera. *Recordings include:* The Love for Three Oranges; Alcyone by Marais; Salome, Strauss; Psalm 129, Guy Ropartz; Messa di Gloria, Donizetti; Platée by Rameau; L'Enfant et les Sortilèges by Ravel; Mélodies by Duparc, Ropartz and Fauré. *Honours:* Grand Critics' Prize 1997. *Current Management:* c/o Agence Artistique Thérèse Cédelle, Boulevard Malesherbes 78, 75008 Paris, France. *Telephone:* 1-49-53-00-02. *Fax:* 1-45-63-70-23. *E-mail:* Agence.Cedelle@wanadoo.fr.

LEA, Yvonne; singer (contralto); b. 1960, Cheshire, England. *Education:* Royal Northern Coll. of Music with Frederick Cox, National Opera Studio, London. *Career:* appearances with Glyndebourne Festival in Die Zauberflöte, Hippolyta in A Midsummer Night's Dream, Rosina in Il Barbiere di Siviglia and Linette in The Love for Three Oranges; Royal Opera House, Covent Garden, in Der Rosenkavalier and Third Lady in Die Zauberflöte; sang Suzuki with WNO and appeared at Batignano and Spitalfields Festivals in Cesti's La Dori; engagements in Graham Vick's version of The Ring for the City of Birmingham Touring Opera, as Hippolyta at the 1991–92 Aix Festivals and Grimgerde in Die Walküre for Scottish Opera; tour of France with A Midsummer Night's Dream 1994; sang Mother Goose in The Rake's Progress for WNO 1996; concert repertoire includes Messiah, Elgar's Sea Pictures, Elijah and Beethoven's Mass in C. *Recordings include:* Williamson's Six English Lyrics.

LEA-COX, Graham Russell, MA, ARCM, ARCO, MTC; British conductor, artistic director, lecturer and composer; b. 15 Feb. 1957, Bulawayo, Rhodesia. *Education:* Univ. of London, Royal Coll. of Music, London, Magdalen Coll., Oxford. *Career:* conducting debut, Carnegie Hall, New York 1983; Artistic Dir, Texas Boys' Choir, USA 1983–85; early career: UK conducting debut, Orchestra of St John's, Smith Square, London; Asst to Arnold Östman, Teatro Regio, Parma, Italy; Swedish Opera conducting debut, Goteborg Opera, Mozart: Le Nozze di Figaro; studentships: Prague, Czech Philharmonic, Sir Charles Makerras; Netherlands Opera, Amsterdam: Wagner, Die Walküre and later Asst to Chief Conductor, Hartmut Haenchen: Alban Berg, Wozzeck; freelance conductor, performer 1985–; tours of USA, Canada, Japan, Hong Kong; as freelance conductor: Europe, Scandinavia, North Africa, Mexico; Artistic Dir, English Performing Arts Ensemble 1988–98; Conductor and Artistic Dir, Elizabethan Singers of London 1987–97; Conductor, Hanover Band, London, including regular tours of Europe and Scandinavia; Warchild Festival Artistic Dir, South Bank, London 1993; Guest Conductor, WDR Symphony Orchestra, Köln, Germany, Cape Philharmonic Orchestra, South Africa, SA Chamber Orchestra and orchestras in Mexico; as scholar, noted for pioneering edns of works by 18th century British composers (autographs in UK, USA and Sweden (Gustavian manuscripts of the works of Gluck, Royal Drottningholm Theatre, Stockholm); Lecturer, univs in Mexico, USA and South Africa; Guest Lecturer in Film Music, AFDA (South African School of Motion Picture Science & Drama), Westminster School of Film, London; Speaker (The State of Film Music in the 21st century), Int. Congress of Film Schools, Cape Town 2012; Dir UK educational project 'Explorations' 1990–95, English Performing Arts Ensemble; Artistic Dir and Conductor, educational and performance events at Royal Festival and Queen Elizabeth Halls, London; f. English Performing Arts Educational Trust 1990–2000; British Council Artist in Residence to Sweden, Czech Repub. and Zimbabwe. *Compositions:* choral and instrumental music, incidental music for stage and recordings of poetical/literary compilations. *Recordings:* film and TV music; chamber music and song from The Court of Queen Victoria; Warchild Festival Highlights, Festival Hall, London; William Boyce Critical Edns and recording series, conducting the Hanover Band, New College Choir, Oxford, Soloists and others, 1998–; Secular Masque; Cantata: David's Lament on the Death of Saul and Jonathan; Odes to St Cecilia; Pindar's Ode, New Year's Ode 1774, The Symphony in Britain, Volume 1: Early British Symphonies 2001; operas and songs; performances of symphonies by Clementi, Wesley, William Sterndale and Bennett. *Publications include:* Gluck: The Swedish Opera Mss, Kungliga Teatra 1770–1815 (research for publication), William Boyce Masterworks (critical edn), British Symphonies of the 18th and 19th Centuries (critical edn), critical edns of symphonies by Clementi, Wesley, William Sterndale and Bennett. *Website:* www.grahamlea-cox.com.

LEACH, Mary Jane, BA; American composer; b. 12 June 1949, St Johnsbury, VT. *Education:* Univ. of Vermont, Columbia Univ. with Mark Zuckerman. *Career:* appeared at Experimental Intermedia Foundation, New York 1982, 1984, 1987, 1992; Relache, Philadelphia 1984, 1987; Music Gallery, Toronto, Metronome, Barcelona, Newband, New York 1985; Roulette, New York 1985, 1995; Charles Ives Center, Connecticut, Logos, Gent, Belgium 1986, 1987; BACA Downtown, Brooklyn, New Music America, Philadelphia, Palais des Beaux Art, Brussels, Sankt Peter, Cologne, Apollohuis, Eindhoven, The Netherlands 1987; Clock Tower, New York 1988; Real Ways, Hartford, CT, Franenzeichen Festival, Cologne, Ton Gegen Ton, Vienna, New Music America, New York 1989; Kunsthalle Bremen, Romanische Summer Festival, Cologne, Music Today, Tokyo 1990; Experimentelle Music, Munich 1991; Sound Symposium, Newfoundland, Ijsbreker, Amsterdam, Corn Palace, Minneapolis 1992; Bang on a Can Festival, New York 1992, 1993; Interpretations Series, New York, Walker Art Center 1993; Subtropics Festival, Miami 1994; radio and television broadcasts worldwide. *Compositions:* Note Passing Note 1981, Solar Spots 1983, 4BC, Held Held 1984, 8x4 1985, Bare Bones, Bruckstück, Pipe Dreams, Sephardic Fragments 1989, The Upper Room 1990, Kirchtraum 1991, Feu de Joie 1992, Ariadne's Lament, He Got Dictators, Xantippe's Rebuke 1993, Corrina Ocarina 1994, Tricky Pan, Windjammer 1995, Song of Sorrows 1995, Call of the Dance 1997, O Magna Vasti Creta 1997. *Recordings:* MJL 2 1986, Celestial Fires 1993, Aerial No. 6, Ariadne's Lament 1998.

LEADBETTER, Martin John, BA (Hons), DipMus, DipEurHum, AMusTCL, LMusTCL, FTCL, FFS, RFP; British fingerprint consultant, composer and arranger; b. 6 April 1945, London, England; s. of Albert Walter Leadbetter and Mildred Joan Leadbetter; m. Ivy G. 1969; two s. *Education:* Trinity Coll. of Music, London, Open Univ., studied with Dr Alan Bush and Eric Matthews. *Career:* mem. Performing Right Soc., Ralph Vaughan Williams Soc., The

Fingerprint Soc., Int. Asscn for Identification, British Acad. of Forensic Sciences, Council for the Registration of Forensic Practitioners; contracted by Alan Bush Music Trust to transcribe unpublished compositions by Dr Alan Bush. *Compositions include:* five symphonies, five string quartets, An English Requiem violin concerto 1972, songs, instrumental and choral works, Marche Tragique for orchestra 1991, Marche Ceremonielle, Laudate Dominium (performed Fontainebleau, France 1993) 1992, I Hear America Singing 1994, Clarinet Concerto 1999, English Music for strings 2004, Overture in the Classical Style 2004, Overture in the Style of Handel 2004, Jazz Toccata for piano 2004, Symphony in the Style of Mozart 2004, Train Music 2005, Tuba Concerto, Oradour-sur-Glane for orchestra, Celebration Serenade, Cassation for 18 wind instruments, Ronod Giocoso, Concertos for flute, oboe, clarinet, bassoon, horn, trumpet, tuba, violin (two), viola, cello and double bass; Three Violin Sonatas, Op. 265, Cello Sonata, Horn Sonata, Septet, Fantasy on an 18th Century Sea-Song, Toccata and Fugue for strings, Five Toccatas for organ, Two Fantasias and Sortie for Organ, Magnificat and Nunc Dimittis, Psalm 23, O Great Mystery!, Promenade (one-act opera), Every Eye Shall See, an oratorio. *Musical:* Becky. *Radio:* Radio Victory commission, Dorian Trio, Op. 50. *Publications include:* Soliloquy, Little Prelude and Fugue, Xylophonic Variations, Czech Suite, Czech Dances. *Honours:* Lewis Minshall Award. *Address:* 2 Priory Lane, Little Wymondley, Herts., SG4 7HE, England. *Telephone:* (1438) 359292. *E-mail:* leadzart@btopenworld.com.

LEAH, Phil, (J. P. Hale), GNSM, PGCE; British musician and teacher; *Sound Healing Researcher, Health and Wellness Professional, Resound;* b. (Alan Elliott), 23 Oct. 1948, Dulwich, London, England; divorced; two s. *Education:* Northern School of Music, Manchester, Padgate Coll. of Educ., Warrington, Lancs. *Career:* peripatetic music teacher, Glamorgan 1972–73, Birmingham 1973–90; Lecturer, North Worcestershire Coll. of Educ. 1977–80, Univ. of Wolverhampton 1982–90; Founder and Musical Dir, West Birmingham Schools Wind Band 1985–90, Halesowen Symphony Orchestra 1986–89; examiner, Guildhall School of Music and Drama 1988–; flute tutor, Univ. of Wales, Aberystwyth 2000–05; currently Sound Healing Researcher, Health and Wellness Professional, Resound; mem. Royal Soc. of Musicians of GB, Inc. Soc. of Musicians, Musicians' Union. *Compositions include:* Concertino for bass tuba and orchestra, Sinfonia for flute and strings, Acme, a suite for chamber orchestra, Sinfonia for chamber orchestra, Elegy for string sextet, Prelude and Scherzo for string quartet, Three Penny Bit for wind, Wind quintet, Fanfare (1969), Fanfare for a Golden Jubilee, Conversations for flute and piano, Chorale Prelude on Austria for organ, Wedding Suite for organ, In Annum for tenor solo, SATB choir and string quartet, Winter for SATB choir and string quartet, Song: Meditation for soprano and piano, Psychological Songs for bass voice and piano, various arrangements for woodwind instruments. *Honours:* First Prize, Horatio Albert Lumb Composition Competition 1992. *Address:* Resound, 15 Oak Tree Crescent, Lapal, Halesowen, B62 9DA, England (office). *Telephone:* 7816-488367 (mobile). *E-mail:* philresound@aol.com (office). *Website:* www.emupublishing.com (office); www.philresound.co.uk.

LEAPER, Adrian; British conductor; *Musical Director, RTVE Symphony Orchestra, Madrid;* b. 1953, England. *Education:* Royal Acad. of Music, studied with George Hurst. *Career:* Asst Conductor, Hallé Orchestra 1986–87, has subsequently worked with all leading British orchestras, the Vienna, Prague and Moscow Symphonies, the Belgian Nat. Orchestra; Music Dir, Orquesta Filarmonica de Gran Canaria 1994, currently guest conductor; Musical Dir, RTVE Symphony Orchestra, Madrid 2001–(11). *Recordings include:* albums of Sibelius, Elgar, Holst, Havergal Brian, Tchaikovsky and Nielsen. *Current Management:* Patrick Garvey Management, 40 North Parade, York YO30 7AB, England. *Telephone:* (1904) 621222. *Fax:* (1723) 330050. *E-mail:* patrick@patrickgarvey.com; andrea@patrickgarvey.com. *Website:* www.patrickgarvey.com.

LEATHERBY, Carol Ann; British singer (mezzo-contralto) and theatre director; b. 1948, Barking, London, England. *Education:* Morley College with Ilse Wolf, Guildhall School of Music and Drama, studied in Vienna with Eugenie Ludwig, in London with Lyndon Van der Pump. *Career:* debut in Purcell Room, London, 1973; WNO 1973–75; Covent Garden Opera, 1975–78; Glyndebourne Festival Opera, 1979–80; New Opera, 1981; Music in Camera, Southern Television, 1980; Delius Talk on Radio London, 1980; broadcasts for BBC, London and Cardiff; Recitals at Purcell Room, Wigmore Hall; Concerts at Festival Hall and QEH; memorial concert for Princess Grace of Monaco at QEH 1983; specialist in the songs of Frederick Delius; Athens Festival, 1985; Alte Oper, Frankfurt, 1985, 1986; Purcell Room concerts as mem. of Quintessence, founded 1984, presenting Victorian and Edwardian entertainment in costume and performing music by Gershwin and Cole Porter, 1984, 1985 and 1986; The Vampyr, soap opera for BBC 2 television, music by Heinrich Marschner, 1992; Street Singer (Dance to the Music of Time) BBC television, 1998; Dir, Victoriana (Victorian Musical Entertainment). *Recordings:* Czech songs by Foerster, Smetana and Dvořák, 1983; Songs of Praise, BBC television; Sita-Mother Earth-Holst recorded at St John's Smith Square in conjunction with the Holst Society. *E-mail:* carolann@leatherbyc.fsnet.co.uk.

LeBARON, (Alice) Anne, BA, MA, DMA; American composer and academic; *Professor, California Institute of the Arts;* b. 30 May 1953, Baton Rouge, La; d. of Gordon LeBaron and Gwendolyn LeBaron; m. Edward J. Eadon 1982; one d. *Education:* Univ. of Alabama, State Univ. of NY, Stony Brook; studied in Darmstadt, Köln Musikhochschule, Nat. Classical Music Inst., S Korea,

Columbia Univ. *Career:* Composer-in-Residence (Meet The Composer New Residencies), Washington, DC 1993–96; Asst Prof. of Music Composition and Theory, Univ. of Pittsburgh 1997–2001; Prof. of Music, California Inst. of the Arts 2001–; Darius Milhaud Visiting Prof., Mills Coll. 2005. *Compositions include:* opera: Crescent City, Sucktion, Wet, The E and O Line (electronic blues opera), Croak (The Last Frog) (chamber opera), Phantasmagoriettas from Crescent City; orchestral: Fleeting Shades, Strange Attractors, Southern Ephemera, Lasting Impressions, Mambo, American Icons, Traces of Mississippi 2000, Crescent City 2012; chamber music: four, Los Murmullos, The Left Side of Time, Transfiguration, Way of Light, Pope Joan, Sauger, Inner Voice, Telluris Theoria Sacra, The Sea and the Honeycomb, Noh Reflections, Metamorphosis, Rite of the Black Sea, Planxty Bowerbird, I Am An American... My Government Will Reward You, Lamentation-Invocation, Concerto for Active Frogs, Dish, Waltz for Quintet, Three Motion Atmospheres, Southern Ephemera, Devil in the Belfry, Sachamama, Solar Music, Sukey, Sukey and the Mermaid, Way of Light; choral: Light Breaks Where No Sun Shines, Story of My Angel, Nightmare. *Recordings include:* Rana, Ritual and Revelations; The Music of Anne LeBaron 1992, Phantom Orchestra: The Anne LeBaron Quintet 1992, The Musical Railism of Anne LeBaron 1995, Pope Joan/Transfiguration 20071, 2, 4, 3 2010. *Publications:* Reflections of Surrealism in Postmodern Musics, in Postmodern Music/Postmodern Thought (eds Judy Lochhead and Joseph Auner). *Honours:* Bearns Prize 1978, ASCAP Foundation Grant 1979, BMI Composition Award 1979, GEDOK Int. Prize, Mannheim 1982, McCollin Prize, Musical Fund Soc. of Philadelphia 1986, Nat. Endowment for the Arts Music Fellowship 1990, New York Foundation for the Arts Fellowship Award 1991, John Simon Guggenheim Memorial Foundation Fellowship 1991–91, Alumna in the Arts Award, Univ. of Alabama 1994, Cal Arts/Alpert Award in the Arts 1996–97, Fellowship in Music, Pennsylvania Council on the Arts 2000, 2002, City of Los Angeles Artist Award 2003, Aaron Copland Award 2005, Rockefeller Multi-Arts Production Fund 2007, CEC Arts Link Award 2008, Los Angeles Dept of Cultural Affairs Cultural Exchange Int. Grant 2009. *Address:* CalArts, School of Music, 24700 McBean Parkway, Valencia, CA 91355, USA (office). *Telephone:* (661) 312-9225 (office). *E-mail:* alebaron@calarts.edu (office). *Website:* www.annelebaron.com.

LEBHERZ, Louis; American singer (bass); b. 14 April 1948, Bethesda, MD. *Education:* Indiana University. *Career:* debut at Memphis Opera, as Padre Guardiano in La Forza del Destino, 1974; Many appearances at opera houses in North and South America (Caracas, 1981); European engagements at Frankfurt, 1981, Karlsruhe, 1984–85, Berne, 1985–86, Geneva, 1988; Sang Melothal in Guillaume Tell at Covent Garden and the Grand Inquisitor in Don Carlos at Los Angeles, 1990; Appeared in Massenet's La Navarraise with Long Beach Opera, 1990, as Basilio, the Commendatore in Don Giovanni at Los Angeles Music Center, 1991; Sang Rocco at New Orleans, 1992; Grech in Fedora at Los Angeles, 1997; other roles include Sarastro, King Mark, Fasolt, Baldassare in La Favorita, Verdi's Zaccaria, Nabucco and Fiesco, Colline, and Don Diego in L'Africaine. *Recordings include:* Verdi's Aroldo; Jone by Petrella. *Current Management:* c/o Pinnacle Arts: Miller Division, 889 Ninth Avenue, 2nd Floor, New York, NY 10019, USA. *Telephone:* (212) 397-7911. *Fax:* (212) 397-7920. *E-mail:* jmiller@pinnaclearts.com. *Website:* www.pinnaclearts.com.

LEBIČ, Lojze; Slovenian composer, conductor and academic; b. 23 Aug. 1934, Prevalje; m. Jelena Ukmar 1961; one d. *Education:* Univ. of Ljubljana, Acad. of Music, Ljubljana, studied in Darmstadt. *Career:* Conductor, RTV Ljubljana 1962–72; appeared at Musica Antiqua Europae Orientalis Festival, Bydgozscz, Poland 1968, Festival van Vlaanderen 1968, Ohrid Festival 1968, Jihlava Festival, Czechoslovakia 1969, Zagreb Biennale 1969, Dubrovnik Festival 1969, ISCM Festivals, Brussels 1981, Zürich 1991, Bucharest 1999, Yokohama 2001, Ljubljana 2003, Zagreb 2005, Växjö 2009; Prof. of Music Theory, Univ. of Ljubljana 1985–2012; mem. Slovenian Acad. of Arts and Sciences 1995–; Foreign mem. Royal Flemish Acad. of Arts and Sciences 2004–; Corresponding mem., Croatian Acad. of Sciences and Arts, Zagreb 2012–. *Compositions include:* orchestral works: Voices, Korant, Ouverture, Tangram, Cantico I, Nicina, Cantico II, Archiphonia for strings, Queensland Music, Intrada for brass and percussion, Za godala for string orchestra; solo instruments with orchestra: Sentences, Symphony with organ 1993, Musica concertata for horn and orchestra, Diaphonia – Piano Concerto, Music for Cello and Orchestra; voice with orchestra: Myth and Apocrypha, November Songs, Burnt Grass, Fables; chamber music: Kons a, Kons b, Expressions, String Quartet, Quartet for percussion, Illud tempus, Invisibilia, April vignettes, Chalumeau I–III, Meditation for two, Epicedion, From nearby and far away, Rubato per viola, A taste of time fleeting away, Rej, Events, Impromptus I–IV, Invocatio for clarinet and piano, Duettino for clarinet and guitar, Colour Circle for seven performers; vocal instrumental: Ajdna: Music About Time for choirs, recorders and percussion instruments, Fauvel 86-vocal instrumental scene, In the Silent Rustle of Time, Eulogy to the World, The Hope, Merry-go-Round. *Recordings:* various as conductor and composer. *Publications:* The Basis of Music Art 1982, Sound and Silence: Compositional Synthesis of the Eighties (Music Biennale Zagreb) 1985, From Near-by and Far Away 2000. *Honours:* First Prize, Let the People Sing, BBC 1972, Prešeren Prize 1994, Kozina Prize 2005. *Address:* Slovenian Academy of Sciences and Arts, Novi trg 1, 1000 Ljubljana (office); Bratov Včakar 134, 1000 Ljubljana, Slovenia (home). *Telephone:* (1) 4706429 (office); (1) 5183155 (home). *Website:* www2.arnes.si/~hlebic (office).

LEBRECHT, Norman; British writer; b. 11 July 1948, London; m. Elbie Spivack 1977; three d. *Education:* Bar Ilan Univ., Israel. *Career:* radio and TV producer 1969–78; writer 1978–; Asst Ed., Evening Standard, London 2002–09; presenter, Lebrecht.live, The Lebrecht Interview, BBC Radio 3 1999–; mem. Soc. of Authors. *Publications include:* Discord 1982, Hush! Handel's in a Passion 1985, The Book of Musical Anecdotes 1985, Mahler Remembered 1987, The Book of Musical Days 1987, The Maestro Myth 1991, Music in London 1991, The Companion to Twentieth-Century Music 1992, When the Music Stops 1996, Who Killed Classical Music? 1997, Covent Garden: Dispatches from the English Culture War, 1945–2000 2000, The Song of Names (Whitbread First Novel Award) 2002, Maestros, Masterpieces and Madness: The Secret Life and Shameful Death of the Classical Record Industry 2007, The Game of Opposites 2009, Why Mahler? 2010. *Address:* 3 Bolton Road, London, NW8 0RJ, England (home). *E-mail:* norman@ normanlebrecht.com. *Website:* www.normanlebrecht.com.

LECHNER, Gabriele Marianne Helene; Austrian singer (soprano); *Professor of Vocal Training and Interpretation, University of Music and Performing Arts, Vienna;* b. 8 March 1961, Vienna. *Education:* Hochschule für Musik und Darstellende Kunst, Vienna, diplomas in Vocal Training and Interpretation, Opera and Lied and Oratory. *Career:* debut as Sulamith in The Queen of Sheba with the Graz Opera, later in Don Giovanni (Elvira), Mefistofele (Margarita and Elena), La Forza del Destino (Leonora), Otello (Desdemona), Don Carlos (Elisabetta), Trovatore (Leonora), Elektra (Chrysothemis) and Cavalleria Rusticana (Santuzza); live TV broadcast of Un Ballo in Maschera (Amelia) at Vienna Staatsoper (with Pavarotti, Cappuccilli and Abbado), also Simon Boccanegra (Amelia), Trovatore, Otello, Zauberflöte, Rusalka, Elektra, Der Rosenkavalier (Marschallin), Capriccio (Gräfin), Contes d'Hoffmann (Giulietta) and Die Walküre (in Vienna); engagements with Zürich Opera as Elsa in Lohengrin, Der fliegender Holländer (Senta), Der Rosenkavalier (Marschallin), Capriccio (Gräfin), both Verdi Leonoras, Elektra (Chrysothemis), Don Carlos (Elisabetta), Tosca, Die Frau ohne Schatten (Kaiserin), Ariadne, Falstaff (Alice Ford), Aida, Un Ballo in Maschera (Amelia), Contes d'Hoffmann (Giulietta), Andrea Chénier (Maddalena); other roles include Valentine (Huguenots), Elettra (Idomeneo), Alceste in Amsterdam, Vitellia (Titus) in Amsterdam and Barcelona, Regan (Lear) in Germany, Carlotta in Die Gezeichneten by Schreker at Zürich and Paris; guest appearances in opera houses at Madrid, Barcelona, Paris, Berlin, Frankfurt, Hamburg, Cologne, Stuttgart, Munich, Amsterdam, Prague, Florence, Rome, Milan, Edinburgh and Glasgow; has worked with more than 120 conductors, including Abbado, Barenboim, Bernstein, Dohnányi, Luisi, Maazel, Mehta, Plasson, Sinopoli, Thielemann, Welser-Möst, Whun Chung; Prof. of Vocal Training and Interpretation, Univ. of Music and Performing Arts, Vienna 2001–, also Head of Vocal Dept; teacher of masterclasses, including AIMS, Graz, ISA-Int. Summer Acad. of Univs of Prague, Vienna and Budapest, Altenburg Music Acad., masterclasses in Gutenstein, Feldkirch and Achenkirch, Austria and Eggenfelden, Germany; jury mem. int. singing competitions, including Meistersinger Graz and Ljuba-Welitsch- competition, Vienna. *Recordings include:* Un Ballo in Maschera – Amelia with Pavarotti/Abbado (TV), Tosca with Neil Shicoff/Ruggiero Raimondi (TV), Beethoven's Ninth Symphony (album), Humperdinck's Hänsel und Gretel (DVD). *Honours:* several major competition awards, including Mario del Monaco (Italy), Opera en Belcanto (Belgium), Dr Luis Sigall (Chile). *Address:* Universität für Musik und Darstellende Kunst, Penzingerstrasse 7, 1140 Vienna, Austria (office). *Telephone:* (1) 71155-2765 (office). *E-mail:* lechner@mdw.ac.at (office). *Website:* www.mdw.ac.at/inst9 (office); www.gabriele-lechner.at; www.mdw.ac.at/inst9.

LEE, Chan Hae, BM, MM; South Korean composer and academic; *Professor, Yonsei University;* b. 8 Oct. 1945, Seoul. *Education:* Yonsei Univ., Catholic Univ. of America, Washington, DC, USA. *Career:* Lecturer, Prof., Yonsei Univ. 1977–; Visiting Prof. Wayne State Univ. 1984, Oakland Univ. 1985, Univ. of Calif., Berkeley 2004–05; Research Assoc., Nationale Conservatoire de Paris, France 1994; Pres., The Korean Soc. of 21st Century Music 1998–; Pres. Korean Women's Soc. of Composition 2001–; Vice-Pres. Korean Women's Asscn for Culture and Arts 2002–; Korean Liaison and mem. Admin. Cttee, Int. Alliance of Women in Music 2002–; mem. bd Korean Music Soc. 1996–; Gen. Sec. Asian Composers' League 1999–, Vice-Pres. (Korea) 2000–; mem. Int. Soc. of Contemporary Music 1990–. *Compositions include:* Hyesang and Chosaeng for voices and ensemble 1980–91, Galpiri for clarinet 1982, The Pilgrim's Progress for chamber ensemble 1990, Glorification for three percussion instruments 1990, The Martyr for string orchestra 1993, From the Point, From the Line for violin solo 1997, Transfiguration for string quartet 1998, Fire Flame for violin and orchestra 1999, Tabernacle for four percussion 1999, Musical He 1999, Be a Light in the Eastern Land for orchestra 2000, Sorickil for taeguem solo 2000, To The Hwangseung for pansori and chamber ensemble 2001, A Total Eclipse of the Sun for flute, clarinet, cello and percussion 2001, The Island under the Full Moon for solo trombone 2001, The Creation (musical) 2001, The Planet Earth for two drummers and orchestra 2001, Be a Light in the Eastern Land 2002, Celebration for wind orchestra 2002, A Beautiful Land for male chorus and orchestra 2002, Ave Maria Stella for mixed chorus 2002, Color in Color for clarinet, violin and cello 2003, Back to the Origin (opera) 2003, The King (musical) 2003, Sin Offering for solo haegeum 2003, Womb of Earth for daegeum, kayageum and traditional orchestra 2004, Pansori with Chamber Ensemble for Five repertoires 2005, Pansori series No. 1 JuckbyukGa 2006, Isudaeyup for Soprano and Four Percussion Players 2006, Pansori series No.2

SuGungGa 2007, WITH for String Quartet & Trombone 2007, Crane Dance for Violin, Cello and Piano 2007, Mittes Leben for Daegeum solo 2007, FurtherMore for Violin, Clar/Base clarinet and Piano 2007. *Recordings include:* Galpiri 1985, From the Point, From the Line 1998, Musical He 1999, Fire Flame 2000, Sorickil 2000, Back to the Origin 2003, Tabernacle 2003. *Publications:* Music Theory 1978, 16C Counterpoint 1985, Contemporary Music I and II 1991, New Approach to Sightsinging and Ear Training I and II 1995, Introduction to Contemporary Music 1998. *Honours:* Korean Nat. Composition Prize 1999, 2005, Int. Rome Choral Music Award 2002. *Address:* Itaewondong Chongwha, Apt 2-603, Yongsanku, Seoul, Republic of Korea (home). *Telephone:* (2) 2123-3080 (home). *Fax:* (2) 313-2821 (home). *E-mail:* chhlee@yonsei.ac.kr (home). *Website:* chanhaelee.pe.kr.

LEE, Colin; British singer (tenor); b. Cape Town, South Africa. *Education:* Drakensberg Boys' Choir School, Cape Town; private vocal studies with Jeffrey Talbot. *Career:* began career as chartered accountant for life assurance co., London 1994–2000; professional debut as Nanki Poo in The Mikado, D'Oyly Carte, West End Theatre, Savoy 2000; mem. ENO Young Singers Programme 2002–05; Royal Opera House debut as Tonio in La fille du régiment 2007; Paris Opera debut as Léopold in La Juive 2007; Metropolitan Opera debut as Arturo in Lucia di Lammermoor 2009; specializes in bel canto music by Rossini and Donizetti; has worked with conductors such as Pappano, Campanella, Rizzi, Minkowski, Hickox, Petrenko, Parry and Daniel; has performed with orchestras such as Accademia Nazionale di Santa Cecilia, Les Musiciens du Louvre – Grenoble, LPO, BBC Symphony, LSO and RLPO; Trustee, Concordia Foundation. *Opera repertoire includes:* numerous Rossini heroes including Almaviva in Barber of Seville, Don Ramiro in La Cenerentola , Uberto/Giacomo in La donna del lago, title role in Le Comte Ory, Narciso in Il Turco in Italia; also Marzio in Mitridate, Re di Ponto, Alphonse in Herold's Zampa, Elvino in La Sonnambula, Tonio in La fille du régiment, Alfredo in La Traviata. *Recordings include:* Entre nous: Celebrating Offenbach 2007, Mercadante's Maria Stuarda 2007, Rossini's Ermione (Gramophone Award for Best Opera Disc 2011) 2010. *E-mail:* info@colinleetenor.com (office). *Website:* www.colinleetenor.com (office).

LEE, Dennis (Ean Hooi), BMus (Hons), MMus; British (b. Malaysian) pianist; b. (Lee Ean Hooi), 2 Dec. 1946, Penang, Malaysia; b. to Chinese parents; m. Chee-Hung Toh 1990. *Education:* Univ. of London, Royal Coll. of Music, London with Angus Morrison, Vienna Hochschule with Josef Dichler, studied with Ilonka Deckers in Milan. *Career:* debut in Purcell Room, London and Kennedy Center, Washington, DC; concerts (recitals, chamber music and orchestral appearances), radio and TV recordings, UK, Europe, USA, Canada, S America, Hong Kong, Japan, China, SE Asia, Australia, NZ; festivals include Adelaide, Montreux, Spoleto, Cheltenham, Brighton, Lincoln, Newbury, Warwick, Mananan, Arundel, Singapore Piano Festival, Varna Summer Festival, Bulgaria; orchestral appearances include BBC Regional, Hallé, Wiener Symphoniker, London Mozart Players, RAI Milan, Polish and Slovak Chamber Orchestras, Warsaw Philharmonic Orchestra, Shanghai Symphony, Singapore Symphony, Malaysian Philharmonic; adjudicator at festivals and competitions; examiner for the Associated Bd of the Royal Schools of Music 1977–2008; Artist-in-Residence, Convention of Music Teachers of California 2006, Nanyang Acad. of Fine Arts, Singapore, Singapore Piano Festival, HSBC Piano Festival, Kuala Lumpur. *Radio:* frequent broadcasts on BBC Radio 3 and BBC World Service. *Recordings:* Szymanowski Piano Pieces, Ravel Duets with Philippe Entremont, Claude Debussy, Piano Works, Vol. 1 2016. *Honours:* BBC Competition Prize 1971, Casagrande Prize (Italy) 1975, 1977, Sydney Prize 1977, Busoni Prize (Italy) 1978. *Address:* Flat 5, 12 St Quintin Avenue, London, W10 6NU, England (home). *Telephone:* (20) 8969-7468 (home). *Fax:* (20) 8969-7468 (office). *E-mail:* dleepiano@btinternet.com (home).

LEE, Douglas Allen, BMus, MMus, PhD; American academic; *Professor Emeritus and Chair of Musicology, Vanderbilt University;* b. 3 Nov. 1932, Carmel, Ind.; s. of Ralph Henley and Flossie Chandler Lee; m. Beverly Haskell 1961. *Education:* DePauw Univ. (Rector Scholar), Univ. of Michigan, Nat. Endowment for the Humanities Seminar in Editing Early Music, studied piano with Theodore Lettvin and György Sandor. *Career:* Instructor, Mount Union Coll., Alliance, Ohio 1959–61; Rackham Fellow, Univ. of Michigan 1961–63; Prof. of Music, Wichita State Univ., Kan. 1964–86; Prof. of Musicology, Vanderbilt Univ., Nashville, Tenn. 1986–98, Prof. Emer. 1998–; mem. Faculty, Mount Union Coll., Univ. of Michigan, Int. Music Camp-Interlochen, Wichita State Univ., Vanderbilt Univ.; Ed. American Music Teacher 1968–70, Sonneck Soc. Newsletter 1988–90. *Publications include:* The Works of Christoph Nichelmann 1971, Christoph Nichelmann – Two Concertos 1977, Six Sonatas of Franz Benda, with Embellishments 1981, Franz Benda – A Thematic Catalogue 1984, Chapters in Great Lives in Music – Renaissance to 1800 1989, two chapters in Great Events in History, Arts and Culture 1993, A Musician at Court: An Autobiography of Franz Benda 1998, Masterworks of Twentieth Century Music 2002, C. P. E. Bach, Collected Works: Ser I/10.1 (Arrangements of Orchestral works) 2007, Ser III/8 (Sei concerti per il cembalo) 2005, Ser III/9.15 (Concertos of 1778) 2009, two essays in a reference encyclopedia on The Fifties in America (two vols) 2005; contrib. of 23 articles to New Grove Dictionary of Music and Musicians, The New Grove Dictionary of American Music; miscellaneous articles in professional journals; programme annotator, Nashville Symphony Orchestra 1988–2001. *Honours:* Outstanding Educators of America Award 1973, grants from American Philosophical Soc., Nat. Endowment for the Humanities, Packard

Humanities Inst. *Address:* Vanderbilt University, Blair School of Music, 2400 Blakemore Avenue, Nashville, TN 37212 (office); 119 Jackson Lake Drive, Franklin, TN 37069, USA (home). *Telephone:* (615) 599-2880 (office). *E-mail:* douglas.lee@vanderbilt.edu (office).

LEE, Lynda; singer (soprano); b. 1969, Ireland. *Education:* Dublin Coll. of Music. *Career:* opera engagements with Opera Northern Ireland, Wexford Festival, Musica nel Chiostro and at the Covent Garden Festival as Irene in Tamerlano; Karlsruhe Handelfestspiel, Halle Handelfestspiele; Théâtre de Caen; Expo '98 Lisbon; Covent Garden Festival; on contract with Opera Leipzig –2001; concerts with the Ulster Orchestra, at the Glasgow Mayfest, Bath Festival and in Jonathan Miller's production of the St Matthew Passion; RTE Symphony Orchestra; RIAS Kammerchor, Berlin; represented Ireland at the 1993 Cardiff Singer of the World Competition; sang Handel's Agrippina and Zenobia in Radamisto at Halle 2000–01. *Recordings include:* Bach's St Matthew Passion, Wallace's Maritana.

LEE, Mi-joo; South Korean pianist; b. 7 July 1959, Seoul; m. Klaus Hellwig. *Education:* Folkwanghochschule, Essen and Hochschule der Künste, Berlin, Germany, New England Conservatory, Boston, USA, Mozarteum, Salzburg, Austria. *Career:* stage appearances with orchestra and solo recitals at Berlin Philharmonic Hall, Schauspielhaus, Munich, Dresden, Paris, Milan, Brussels, Tokyo, Seoul, various European countries and many German cities; radio and TV appearances on WDR, NDR, RIAS Berlin, Deutschlandfunk, Deutschland Radio Berlin, Radio France, BRT Brussels, Czechoslovak broadcast, Korean broadcast, DeutscheWelle, Südwestfunk 3. *Recordings:* C. Saint-Saëns Op. 72, 52, 111, Humoresken (Schumann, Reger, Dohnany, Rachmaninov), Maurice Ravel Concerto G-Major, Robert and Clara Schumann Op. 105, 121, Op. 22, Beethoven Op. 13, Chopin, Liszt and six Paganini Études, Robert Schumann Op. 3, 10, 14. *Honours:* first prize Concorso Internazionale G. B. Viotti, Vercelli, Italy 1985, fourth prize Tokyo Int. Piano Competition 1986, sixth prize Brussels Queen Elizabeth Competition 1987. *Address:* Mommsenstrasse 58, 10629 Berlin, Germany (home). *E-mail:* hellwig-lee@gmx.de (home).

LEE, Michelle, MA, ARCM, FRSA; British flautist; b. 31 May 1952, London, England; d. of Eric Winters and Doreen Winters (née Gilchrist); one d. *Education:* Bartók Conservatory, Hungary, Royal Coll. of Music, London, Robert Schumann Inst., Germany, Franz Liszt Acad., Hungary. *Career:* regular solo performances world-wide; soloist for BBC Radio 3 and has given many first performances, including world premiere of György Kurtág's Seven Bagatelles, Op. 14b at her Wigmore Hall debut recital 1982; first broadcast performance of Fauré's Morceau de Concours for flute and piano on BBC Radio 3 1985; first British broadcast of György Kurtág's Seven Bagatelles, Op. 14b on BBC Radio 3 1987; first British broadcast of László Sáry's Pezzo Concerto on BBC Radio 3 1988; works composed for her by Francisco Estévez, Roland Freisitzer, Philip Grange, Raimund Jülich, György Kurtág and Geoffrey Winters; f. Festival de Musique Charles Cros, Fabrezan, France 2003; Examiner, Trinity Coll. London 1991–; mem. British Flute Soc. *Composition:* Scarlet Runner for flute, percussion, pre-recorded tape and five synthesizers. *Recordings include:* soloist, Record of Contemporary Music with Live Electronics (Germany), Morton Feldman Flute Concerto with Moscow Philharmonic Orchestra 1992, Günther Becker – Drei Inventionen 1999. *Publications include:* Trinity College London Woodwind World Flute Albums 4 and 5 (ed.). *Address:* 4 rue des Tonneliers, 11200 Fabrezan, France (home). *Website:* www.festivaldemusiquecharlescros.com.

LEE, Ming Cho, BA, LHD; Chinese stage designer; *Donald M. Oenslager Professor (Adjunct) of Design, Yale School of Drama*; b. 3 Oct. 1930, Shanghai; s. of Lee Tsu Fa. *Education:* Occidental Coll. and Univ. of California at Los Angeles. *Career:* theatre and ballet designs in New York, 1955–59; Peabody Arts Theater, Baltimore, 1959–63, with designs for Il Turco in Italia, Mahagonny, Werther, Hamlet and Les Pêcheurs de Perles; designed Tristan und Isolde for Baltimore Civic Opera and Butterfly for the Opera Company of Boston, 1962; Resident Designer at San Francisco Opera from 1961, Juilliard School, New York, 1964–70; Metropolitan Opera, 1965–, with Figaro, Boris Godunov, Lohengrin and Khovanshchina (1985); premiere of Ginastera's Bomarzo for the Opera Society of Washington, 1967, Giulio Cesare and Lucia di Lammermoor for Hamburg Staatsoper 1969, 1971; teacher of set design at Yale School of Drama School 1969–, currently Donald M. Oenslager Prof. (Adjunct) of Design. *Exhibition:* Stage Designs by Ming Cho Lee (retrospective) 2013–14. *Plays:* numerous as set designer on Broadway productions including: The Moon Besieged 1962, Mother Courage and Her Children, King Lear, The Glass Menagerie, The Shadow Box, For Colored Girls Who Have Considered Suicide When the Rainbow is Enuf, K2 (Tony Award for Best Scenic Design) 1983. *Honours:* five hon. degrees; Drama Desk Award for Outstanding Set Design, Helen Hayes Award, inducted into American Theatre Hall of Fame 1998, National Medal of Arts 2002, Rockefeller Award 2007, Tony Award for Lifetime Achievement in the Theatre 2013. *Address:* Yale School of Drama, PO Box 208325, New Haven, CT 06520-8325, USA (office). *Telephone:* (203) 432-1579 (office). *E-mail:* mingcho.lee@yale.edu (office). *Website:* yale.drama.edu (office).

LEE, Sung-sook; South Korean singer (soprano); b. 1948. *Education:* studied in Republic of Korea and at the Juilliard School, New York. *Career:* debut, Premiere of Menotti's Tamu Tamu, Chicago, 1973; sang at Spoleto Festival and San Francisco, 1974; La Scala and Covent Garden 1975; Frankfurt Opera 1976–77; Seattle Opera and Miami from 1978; New York City Opera 1975–76; Concert appearances with the Buffalo Philharmonic, Seattle, Dallas and Pittsburgh Symphonies; Repertoire has included music by Puccini and Rossini (Stabat Mater). *Address:* c/o New York City Opera, Lincoln Center, New York, NY 10023, USA.

LEE, Young-ja; South Korean composer; b. 4 June 1936, Wonju. *Education:* studied in Seoul, at the Paris and Brussels Conservatoires and the Manhattan School of Music. *Career:* performances of her work in Europe, Republic of Korea and Central America. *Compositions include:* Suite for orchestra, 1971; Movement symphonique for orchestra, 1972; Piano concerto, 1973; Piano sonata, 1985; Three Love Songs for soprano and harp, 1991; Gae-chun for orchestra, 1991; Quintet for flute, harp and string trio, 1992. *Address:* c/o KOMCA, 2,3/F Samjeon Building, 236-3 Nonhyeon-dong, Kangnam-gu, Seoul, Republic of Korea.

LEECH, Richard; American singer (tenor); b. 1956, Binghamton, CA. *Career:* sang first as baritone, then sang Offenbach's Hoffmann while a student; many concert and opera appearances from 1980, notably at Cincinnati, Pittsburgh, Baltimore, Houston and Chicago; European debut at the Deutsche Oper Berlin, 1987, as Raoul in Les Huguenots; Chicago Lyric Opera, 1987, and La Scala, 1991, as Rodolfo; has sung Gounod's Faust at San Diego, 1988, and at the Orange Festival and Metropolitan Opera, 1990; Pinkerton in Washington, DC and Florence and La Scala (debut 1990), 1987 and 1989; Donizetti's Edgardo and Nemorino at the Deutsche Oper Berlin, 1988–89, and the Duke of Mantua at the New York City Opera (1988) and Metropolitan Opera, 1990; season 1991–92 as Raoul in a new production of Les Huguenots at Covent Garden (debut), Pinkerton at Chicago and the Duke of Mantua at the Met; Rodolfo at the Met, 1994; sang Faust at the Met, 1997; season 1998 with Gounod's Roméo at San Diego, Werther for Netherlands Opera, 1999; season 2000–01 as Boito's Faust and Don José at the Met, Rodolfo in Luisa Miller for Palm Beach Opera and Verdi's Riccardo on debut at the Vienna Staatsoper; concert engagements include Beethoven's Ninth and Verdi Requiem. *Recordings:* Les Huguenots; Fledermaus; Salome; Faust; Rosenkavalier. *Current Management:* Wolf Piper Artists International, 13 East 69th Street, Suite 3R, New York, NY 10021, USA. *Telephone:* (212) 531-1514. *Fax:* (212) 861-6949. *E-mail:* info@wolfartists.com. *Website:* www.wolfartists.com; www.richardleech.com.

LEEDY, Douglas, BA, MA; American composer, conductor and educator; b. 3 March 1938, Portland, OR. *Education:* Pomona Coll., Univ. of California at Berkeley, studied karnatic vocal music with K. V. Narayanaswamy. *Career:* French horn, Oakland Symphony Orchestra, San Francisco Opera, Ballet Orchestras, Cabrillo Festival Orchestra, 1969–65; mem. music faculty, Univ. of California, Los Angeles 1967–70, Reed Coll. 1973–78; Prof. of Electronic Music, Centro Simon Bolivar, Caracas, Venezuela 1972; Music Dir, Portland Baroque Orchestra 1984–85; complete performances of Handel's Jephtha and Theodora, Portland Handel Festival 1985; mem. Music Library Asscn, Int. Heinrich Schütz Soc. *Compositions:* Usable Music I for Very Small Instruments with Holes, 1968; The Twenty-Fourth Psalm for chorus and orchestra, 1971; Fantasy on Wie schön leuchtet der Morgenstern for organ and voice; Canti/Music for contrabass and chamber ensemble; Music for Meantone Organ; Hymns from the Rig Veda for chorus and Javanese or American gamelan; Pastorale (Horace) for chorus and just-tuned piano, 4-hands, 1993; This is a Great Country, or What?, multimedia, 1995; 7 symphonies, No. 7 'Selene', 1997; 2 string quartets, 1975, 1995; No More Beethoven! for voices and electric guitar, 1997. *Recordings:* Entropical Paradise: 6 Sonic Environments, Seraphim. *Publications:* Harpsichord Book III (just tuning), Chansons from Petrucci in Original Notation 1983; contrib. to Interval, The Courant, MLA Notes, The New Grove Dictionary of American Music.

LEEF, Yinam Arie, BMus, MA, PhD; Israeli composer and professor of composition; *President, The Jerusalem Academy of Music and Dance*; b. 21 Dec. 1953, Jerusalem; m. Tanya Fonarev 1978; one s. one d. *Education:* Rubin Acad. of Music, Jerusalem, Univ. of Pennsylvania, and Tanglewood, USA. *Career:* Visiting Lecturer, Swarthmore Coll., USA 1982–84; Philadelphia Coll. of the Performing Arts 1984; teacher, Univ. of Pennsylvania 1984–85; Lecturer, Sr Lecturer, Assoc. Prof., Prof., The Jerusalem Acad. of Music and Dance 1985–, Chair., Dept of Composition 1995–97, 2003–05, Dean, Faculty of Composition, Conducting and Music Educ. 2008–11, Pres. of the Acad. 2012–; comms include Fromm Music Foundation at Harvard, Fels Fund, Philadelphia, Swarthmore Music and Dance Festival, Concerto Soloists Chamber Orchestra of Philadelphia, Penn Contemporary Players, Jerusalem Symphony Orchestra, Haifa Symphony Orchestra, Israel Sinfonietta Be'er Sheva, Israel Camerata, Chamber Orchestra of Hochschule für Musik, Karlsruhe, Jerusalem Dance Workshop, Rinat Choir, The Verdehr Trio, Meitar Ensemble, Ensemble Music Nova, Israel Contemporary Players, Philadelphia Chamber Music Soc., The Mannheim Soc. for Contemporary Music, Hambacher MusikFest, European Centre for the Arts, Dresden, Ensemble Plural, Madrid; mem. ACUM, League of Composers in Israel. *Compositions:* Gilgulim for woodwind trio 1976, for string trio 1980, Three Pieces for piano, Fireflies for soprano, flute, harpsichord 1977, String Quartet No. 1 1978, KO for solo oboe 1978, Ha'Bor 1978, Laments for chamber orchestra 1979, Flowers, Insects and a Very Thin Line for flute, oboe, piano trio 1979, Canaanit Fantasy for piano 1981, The Invisible Carmel for soprano and five players 1982, Violin Concerto 1983, Octet 1984, A Place of Fire for mezzo and 11 players 1985, Fanfares and Whispers for trumpet and string orchestra 1986, Sounds, Shadows for choir 1987, How Far East, How Further West? for piano 1988, Trio for oboe, violin, horn 1988, Scherzos and Serenades for orchestra 1989, Elegy for harpsichord 1990, Tribute for orchestra 1991, Elegy for string quartet 1991, Symphony No. 1 1992, Sea Songs for equal voice choir 1993, Cantilena for guitar 1994, Threads of Time and Distance for alto, oboe and string orchestra 1995, Visions of Stone City, Symphony No. 2 for orchestra 1995, Yizkor for flute 1995, Said his Lover for alto and clarinet 1996, Night Light for orchestra 1996, Triptych for clarinet, string trio and piano 1997, T'filah for three violins 1997, Viola Concerto 1998, Three Lyrical Songs for tenor and string trio 1999, Bagatelles for flute and piano 2000, String Quartet No. 2 2001, Offering for violin and piano 2001, Reminiscences of Tranquility for harp 2002, Hallel for cello, two horns and string orchestra 2002, Soliloquy for violin 2003, Serenity Lost for violin and chamber ensemble 2004, String Quartet No. 3 2005, Untitled for oboe and organ 2005, Trio for clarinet, violin and piano 2005, Fibers of Silence for soprano and chamber ensemble 2007, And Shadows Covered all the Paths for string quartet and piano four-hands 2007, Three Autumn Madrigals for cello and string orchestra 2009, Intermezzi for seven players 2009, Disruptive Reflective for flute and ensemble 2011, Intermezzi Book II for seven players 2012, Eloges des Choses Ephermes for tenor and piano 2012, Impro's Imprint for Ensemble 2014 (revised 2015), Nocturne for viola and piano 2014, Akalaton for 6 players 2015. *Recordings include:* Symphony No. 1, Jerusalem Symphony Orchestra; Violin Concerto, Bat-Sheba Savaldi-Kohlberg, violin, Jerusalem Symphony Orchestra; Yizkor for flute, Noam Buchman, flute; T'filah for Three Violins, 2001, How Far East, How Further West? 2003, Bagatelles, for flute and piano 2005, Elegy for Harpsichord 2008, Fibers of Silence, Thilah Nini-Goldstein, soprano, Meitar Ensemble 2010, Three Autumn Madrigals 2011, Trio for cello, violin and piano, Meitar Ensemble; Serenity Lost, Moshe Aharonov, Meitar Ensemble; Intermezzi for seven players, Said His Lover, Meitar Ensemble; The Invisible Carmel, Michal Shamir, soprano, Ensemble Musica Nova 2012, Reminiscences of Tranquility for harp, Eleanor Turner 2012; numerous from Israel Broadcasting Authority and radio stations in Germany, Spain, Czech Repub., Poland, Norway, South Korea and Hong Kong. *Honours:* ACUM Prize 1992, 1998, 2010, Israel Prime Minister Prize 1993, 2006. *Current Management:* c/o Israel Music Institute, 55 Begin, Tel-Aviv, Israel. *Telephone:* 3-6247095. *E-mail:* musicinst@bezeqint.net. *Website:* www.imi.org.il. *Address:* The Jerusalem Academy of Music and Dance, Givat-Ram Campus, Jerusalem 91904, Israel (office). *Telephone:* 2-6759903. *E-mail:* yleef@jamd.ac.il (home). *Website:* www.jamd.ac.il (office).

LEEK, Stephen, BA; Australian composer and conductor; b. 8 Oct. 1959, Sydney, NSW. *Education:* studied with Larry Sitsky, Canberra School of Music and ABC Young Composers Workshop. *Career:* Tasmanian Dance Co. 1982–85; Dir, Arts Now; Artistic Dir and Conductor, The Australian Voices; commissions from Seymour Group, Chamber Made Opera, Brisbane Biennial Festival, Opera Queensland, The Australian Voices, Gondwana Voices, Centenary of Federation Ceremony, among others; residencies with St Peters Lutheran Coll. 1988, 1989, 1996, and Tasmanian Dance Theatre 1993; part-time Lecturer in Composition and Improvisation, Queensland Conservatorium. *Compositions include:* At Times... Stillness for organ 1985, Thought for female chorus, flute and piano 1988, Once on a Mountain, and Songs of Space, Sea and Sky for choir 1988–89, Killcallow Catch (music theatre) 1990, Stroke (one-act music theatre) 1990, Voyage for chorus 1990, Five Songs for female chorus 1990, Five Songs of the Sun for orchestra 1991, As You Like It for piano 1992, Great Southern Spirits for chorus and vocal soloists 1993, Island Songs for chorus, female soloists and piano 1994, Ancient Cries 1999, Seeking True South (opera) 2001. *Recordings include:* Sea Children (The Australian Voices), One World (Chanticleer). *Honours:* Sounds Australian Award 1991, Churchill Fellowship 1997. *E-mail:* artsnow@thehub.com.au. *Website:* www.theaustralianvoices.com.au.

LEFANU, Nicola Frances, DMus, FRCM; British composer; *Professor Emerita, University of York*; b. 28 April 1947, Essex, England; d. of William Richard LeFanu and Elizabeth Violet Maconchy; m. David Newton Lumsdaine 1979; one s. *Education:* St Mary's School, Calne, St Hilda's Coll., Oxford and Royal Coll. of Music. *Career:* Dir of Music St Paul's Girls' School 1975–77; Composer-in-Residence New South Wales Conservatorium of Music, Sydney, Australia 1979; Del. to Moscow Int. New Music Festival 1984; Prof. of Music, Univ. of York 1994–2008, Prof. Emer. 2008–; Mendelssohn Scholar 1972; Harkness Fellow for Composition Study, Harvard Univ., Mass, USA 1973–74. *Compositions:* 100 pieces published by Novello and Edition Peters. *Honours:* Hon. Fellow, St Hilda's Coll., Oxford; Hon. DMus (Dunelm) 1995, (Aberdeen) 2006; Hon. DUniv (Open Univ.) 2004; Leverhulme Research Award 1989, Cobbett Prize for Chamber Music 1968, First Prize, BBC Composers Competition 1971, RPS Elgar Bursary 2015. *Address:* Department of Music, University of York, Heslington, York, North Yorks., YO10 5DD, England (office). *Telephone:* (1904) 651759 (home). *Fax:* (1904) 432450 (office). *E-mail:* n.lefanu@mac.com (home). *Website:* www.nicolalefanu.com.

LEFEBVRE, Pierre; Canadian singer (tenor); b. 1959, Drummondville, QC. *Education:* studied in Montréal and Italy. *Career:* sang at first in such roles as Edgardo and Rodolfo; guest appearances in Lucca, Rome and Montréal; La Scala Milan in Fidelio, Traviata and Don Carlos; Frankfurt Opera Franchetti's Cristoforo Colombo; further Giovanna d'Arco at Bologna, and in Don Zauberflöte at Turin; sang in Les Contes de Hoffmann at the Met 1998. *Recordings include:* Video of Giovanna d'Arco.

LEFKOWITZ, Mischa, MMus; American violinist; *Member, First Violin Section, Los Angeles Philharmonic*; b. 17 March 1954, Riga, Latvia; m. Irina Lefkowitz 1980. *Education:* Special School of Music, Riga, Moscow Conservatory of Music with Leonid Kogan, Wayne State Univ., Detroit, USA and Mozarteum Acad., Salzburg with Jean Fournier, studied with Nathan Milstein, Mischa Mischakoff, Roman Totenberg, Henri Temianka. *Career:* symphony debut aged 12; mem. first violin section, Los Angeles Philharmonic 1977–; soloist appearances with major orchestras worldwide, including the London Philharmonic, Detroit Symphony, English Chamber Orchestra, California Chamber Symphony, American Chamber Symphony, Academica Camerata and Victoria Symphony; recital appearances at Carnegie Hall, Merkin Hall (New York), Philips Collection (Washington, DC), Salle Playel (Paris), Wilshire Ebell (Los Angeles), California Palace of the Legion of Honor (San Francisco), and elsewhere; festival appearances include Meadow Brook, Aspen and Kneisel Hall; artist-in-residence, Chapman Univ. in Orange 1988–2006; founder and Music Dir of chamber orchestra and string ensemble, Masterpiece Virtuosi; Visiting Prof. of Violin, Univ. Coll. Irvine 2001; mem. Chamber Music America, Coll. Music Soc. *Recordings include:* works of Giardini, Michelet Violin Concertos, Rozsa Solo Violin Sonata, concertos by Bach, Haydn, Vaughan Williams with Masterpiece Virtuosi, concertos by Fauré, Sibelius, Diciedue with Polish Radio Symphony, Mozart and Giardini Concertos with English Chamber Orchestra, Bloch Concerto with London Philharmonic. *Honours:* third prize Carnegie Hall Int. American Music Prize 1983, Yehudi Menuhin Int. Violin Competition City of Paris 'Musique Française' Prize 1985, Rotary Int. Competition first prize, California, prizes at Paganini Int. Competition, Bach Festival, Young Artists Awards, All-State Contest for Violin Soloists, Concertino-Prague Radio Competition, NEA solo recitalist fellowship, California Council Touring grants 1985–. *Address:* c/o Los Angeles Philharmonic Orchestra, 151 South Grand Avenue, Los Angeles, CA 90012, USA (office). *Telephone:* (213) 972-7300 (office). *E-mail:* lirami@aol.com (home). *Website:* www.mischalefkowitz.com.

LEFTERESCU, Petre, DMus; Romanian violinist and academic; b. 1 May 1936, Bistrita; m. Ogneanca Tomici 1958. *Education:* Bucharest Music Acad. with I. Geanta, Moscow Conservatory, Russia and Bucharest Nat. Univ. of Music. *Career:* solo concerts and chamber music, tours as violinist, Romania 1958–; Violin Prof., Cluj Music Acad. 1958–69; Prof. of Chamber Music, Bucharest Acad. of Music 1960–; first violin, Forum String Quartet 1985–; Rector, Nat. Univ. of Music, Bucharest 1992–96, 1996–2000; Vice-Pres., Asscn Europeanne des Conservatoires (AEC), Paris 1992–2000; concert tours to Germany, Spain, Hungary, People's Republic of China, Singapore. *Recordings:* Romanian and universal music. *Publications:* contrib. to Muzica Contemporanul. *Address:* Calea Victoriei Nr 83, bl. 81, ap 37, Bucharest 010066, Romania (home). *Telephone:* (21) 3117167 (home). *E-mail:* oplefterescu@yahoo.com (home).

LEGA, Luigi; singer (tenor); b. 7 April 1940, Bordighera, Italy. *Education:* studied in Rome, Basle and Mannheim. *Career:* debut in Overhausen, as Pinkerton 1961; many appearancea at such German opera centres as Munich, Hamburg, Stuttgart, Mannheim, Berlin (Deutsche Oper) and Wuppertal; further engagements at Amsterdam, Palermo, Barcelona, Rio de Janeiro, Trieste and Vienna as Verdi's Radames, Duke of Mantua, Alvaro, Alfredo, Don Carlos, Manrico and Riccardo; also a noted interpreter of Don José, Edgardo, Florestan, Andrea Chénier, Turiddu, Rodolfo, Cavaradossi and Des Grieux in Manon Lescaut; teacher of singing in Wuppertal.

LEGANY, Denes, BM, MM, MD, DMA; Hungarian composer, pianist, conductor and academic; b. 14 May 1965, Budapest; m. Eva Toth 1990; three s. one d. *Education:* Bartók Conservatory of Music, Liszt Acad. of Music, Budapest Univ. *Career:* Prof., Budapest Univ. School of Music, 1987–94; Prof., Vice-Pres., Budapest Conservatory of Music, 1993–98; specialist, Hungarian Music Council, 1997–; Dir, László Lajtha School of Music and Arts, 1998–99; Artistic and Educational Adviser, Hungarian Music Council, 1999–; Liason Officer, Hungarian Music Information Centre, 1999–; Visiting Prof., several colls and univs; recitals in three continents; lectures on television and radio. *Recordings:* Hommage à Bartók, 1995; works recorded by Hungarian and foreign record companies; Werner Brüggemann series. *Publications:* Easy Piano Pieces for children; Festival Music, for band; Trios for French horn; Suite for trumpet; Trombone Quartets; Saxophone Quartet; Air, for saxophone and piano; Flute Duos; Three Children's Choruses; Fragments, for saxophone solo; Developing Contemporary Art Pedagogical Concepts, 1993.

LEGGATE, Robin, BA, MBA; British singer (tenor); b. (Roy Leighton Leggate), 18 April 1946, West Kirby, Cheshire; s. of James Leggate and Jean Leggate; partner Kenneth Cordeiro. *Education:* Queen's Coll., Oxford, Royal Northern Coll. of Music, Cranfield School of Man. *Career:* Royal Opera House, Covent Garden 1977–2003, as Cassio in Otello (conducted by Zubin Mehta, Christoph von Dohnányi and Sir Colin Davis); Elemer (Arabella), Narraboth (Salome), the Painter in Lulu and Tamino in a new production of Die Zauberflöte 1979; also sang in Prince Igor and Il Trovatore at Covent Garden; appearances with the Netherlands Opera and at the Hamburg Staatsoper from 1978; South Australian Opera 1982, as Ferrando in Così fan tutte; Théâtre du Châtelet, Paris, as Tamino 1983; other Mozart roles include Belmonte and Don Ottavio, which he sang with most of the regional British cos; engagements in Le nozze di Figaro in Madrid, Weber's Oberon with Scottish Opera, Eisenstein in a new production of Die Fledermaus for Scottish Opera, and the premiere of André Laporte's Das Schloss, in Brussels; appearances at the Festival Hall from 1976 (debut with the London Symphony in Pulcinella); sang in Mendelssohn's Elijah at Florence 1981, and appeared in Mozart's C minor Mass with the London Philharmonic, conducted by Solti; sang in the stage premiere of Gerhard's Duenna, Madrid 1992; sang in world premiere of Life with an Idiot by Schnittke at Netherlands Opera 1992; Opéra

Bastille (St François d'Assise) and at Salzburg Festival (Salome) 1993; sang in first production of Stiffelio (Verdi) at Royal Opera House 1993; Cassio at Covent Garden 1994; The Scribe (Khovanshchina) at La Monnaie, Brussels; Don Basilio in Figaro for the Royal Opera 1998; sang Dr Caius in Falstaff, which opened the new Royal Opera House and Pollux in Die Liebe der Danaë at Garsington 1999, Panait in The Greek Passion by Martinů at Covent Garden 2000, Peter Quint with Chicago Opera Theater 2003, Von Aschenbach with Chicago Opera Theater 2004, Captain Vere with Washington Nat. Opera 2004, Owen Wingrave with Chicago Opera Theater 2008, Goro (Butterfly) 2011 and Serano (Donna del Lago) for Royal Opera House 2013. *Recordings include:* La Fanciulla del West from Covent Garden, Haydn's Armida, The Light of Life by Elgar. *Address:* Rose Cottage, Low Road, Darsham, Suffolk, IP17 3PT, England (home). *Telephone:* (1728) 668461 (home). *E-mail:* rleg8@aol.com (home). *Website:* www.robinleggate.com.

LEGGE, Anthony; British conductor and chief coach; *Assistant Music Director, Opera Australia;* b. 1948, England. *Education:* Guildhall School London, Univ. of Oxford, London Opera Centre, studied piano accompaniment with Geoffrey Parsons and Paul Hamburger. *Career:* coach at Glyndebourne from 1993, with Béatrice et Bénédict, Eugene Onegin 1996 and Rodelinda 1998; song recitals with Janet Baker, Thomas Allen, Alan Opie and Robert Tear; Asst. Bayreuth for Die Meistersinger and Barenboim-Kupfer Ring cycle; Head of Music, ENO 1989–2003, part-time music adviser 2003–; Dir of Opera, RAM 2004–08, Sir Arthur Sullivan Visiting Prof. of Opera 2009–; Music Dir, Clonter Opera; Asst Music Dir, Opera Australia 2009–. *Recordings include:* recital albums with Linda Finnie. *Publication:* The Art of Auditioning. *Address:* Opera Australia, PO Box 291, Strawberry Hills, NSW 2012, Australia (office). *E-mail:* enquiries@opera-australia.org.au (office). *Website:* www.opera-australia.org.au (office).

LEHMANN, Charlotte; German singer (soprano) and academic; *Chair of Voice Emerita, Würzburg Academy of Music;* b. 16 Jan. 1938, Zweibrücken; m. Ernst Huber-Contwig 1965; one s. *Education:* Acad. of Music and Univ. of Saarland, Saarbrücken with Sibylle Ursula Fuchs, studied with Paul Lohmann, Wiesbaden. *Career:* sang at concerts in Europe and USA; broadcasts on all German radio stations, France Musique, Schweizerischer Rundfunk, RTB Brussels, NL Hilversum, Turkish Radio, others; TV performances on ARD and ZDF; began teaching at Hannover Music Acad. 1972; Chair of Voice Emer., Würzburg Acad. of Music 1988–; has taught winners of int. prizes, including Lioba Braun, Thomas Quasthoff and Maria Kowollik; has led int. masterclasses in Brazil, Chile, England, Bulgaria, Japan and Luxembourg; has regularly given courses at the Haus Marteau Music Centre, Lichtenberg-Bayreuth; Ed., Bach and Mozart arias for all voice parts, for publishers Bärenreiter-Verlag, and Von Schönberg bis Rihm, for Schott Int.; int. jury service; lectures. *Recordings:* Works of Bach, Mozart, Schumann, Wolf, Fauré, Debussy, Hindemith, Schoenberg, other composers. *Honours:* Hon. Pres. Bundesverband Deutscher Gesangspädagogen; prize winner L'Amour du Chant Int. Competition and UFAM, Paris, German Record Critics' Prize (for Debussy and Schoenberg recording) 1982. *Address:* Gellerstrasse 55, 30175 Hannover, Germany. *Telephone:* (511) 852437. *E-mail:* charlotte.lehmann@t-online.de.

LEHMANN, Hans Ulrich, BA, DipMus; Swiss composer and academic (retd); b. 4 May 1937, Biel; m. Ursula Lehmann (divorced). *Education:* Univs of Berne, Zürich and Basle, masterclasses in composition with Boulez and Stockhausen. *Career:* Lecturer, Zürich Univs 1969–90; Prof. of Theory and Composition 1972–98, Dir 1976–98, Musikhochschule, Zürich; Pres., SUISA (Swiss Authors' Assen) 1991–; mem. numerous professional orgs. *Compositions include:* Quanti, 1962; Mosaik, 1964; Noten, 1964–66; Spiele, 1965; Rondo, 1967; Instants, 1968; Konzert, 1969; Régions III, 1970; discantus I and II, 1970; Sonata da chiesa, 1971; Tractus, 1971; zu streichen, 1974; zu blasen, 1975; Tantris, 1976–77; Motetus Paraburi, 1977–78; Kammermusik I, 1978–79; Kammermusik II, 1979; Duette, 1980; Lege mich wie ein Siegel auf dein Herz, 1980–83; Canticum I and II, 1981; Stroking, 1982; Mirlitonnades, 1983; battuto a tre–tratto, 1983; Mon amour, 1983; Triplum, 1984; ludes, 1985; Alleluja, 1985; In Memoriam Nicolai de Flue, 1986–87; Fragmente, 1986–87; Streichquartett, 1987–88; Osculetur me, 1988–89; de profundis, 1988–89; Esercizi, 1989; Wandloser Raum, 1989; ad missam Prolationum, 1989–90; etwas Klang von meiner Oberfläche, 1989–90; Nocturnes, 1990–91; Ut signaculum, 1991–92; El mar, 1993; Prélude à une étendue, 1993–94; Battements, 1994–95; Book of Songs, 1999; Twi-Light, for soprano and ensemble, 1999; Vagues, 1999–2000; Inquiétudes, 2000; Instantanés, 2000; Ritenuto, 2000; Notturno, 2001; Dédales, 2001–02; Der rat der rose, 2002; Annäherungen an HH, 2002–03; Trajets, 2003; Viola in all moods and senses, 2003; Um-risse, 2003, Nachts ist der Himmel näher als am Tag 2004–05, Favole 2005–06, Apparition 2006–07, Contradictions 2008, Voyages aux îles des vestiges 2008–09, Nachtklänge 2009, Dans la nuit 2010, Lieder ohne Worte 2010–11. *Honours:* Swiss Musicians' Assen Composers Prize 1988, City of Zürich Music Prize 1993. *Address:* Haldenstrasse 35, 8615 Wermatswil, Switzerland (home). *Telephone:* (44) 9402747 (home). *E-mail:* h.u.lehmann@bluewin.ch (home). *Website:* www.hu-lehmann.ch (home).

LEHMANN, Wilfred; Australian composer, violinist and conductor; b. 1929, Melbourne, Vic. *Education:* studied in Australia and London. *Career:* violinist, Birmingham Orchestra 1958–60; Conductor, Tokyo Philharmonic Orchestra 1960–70; Asst Conductor, Queensland Symphony Orchestra 1972, Nashville Symphony, and Chamber Orchestra 1976–79, ABC Sinfonia, Australia 1982; mem., Sydney String Quartet. *Compositions include:* Song of Mululu 1977,

two String Quartets 1988, Bacchanals for orchestra 1988, Concerto for two pianos and percussion 1991. *Honours:* first prize Carl Flesch Int. Violin Competition, London 1958, Fellowship in Composition, Tennessee Arts Commission 1979.

LEHR, Edit; singer (soprano); b. 1954, Budapest, Hungary. *Education:* Budapest School of Music, Cologne Musikhochschule. *Career:* sang at Wuppertal Opera 1980–82, the Freiburg Opera 1982–86, then at Gelsenkirchen; guest appearances in Heidelberg, Vienna, Basel and Budapest; among roles are Gilda, Violetta, Musetta, Donna Anna, Lauretta, Rosina, Fiordiligi, Susanna, Gretel, the Princess in Der Zwerg by Zemlinsky; frequent concert appearances throughout Europe.

LEHRBAUMER, Robert, DipMus; Austrian pianist, conductor and organist; b. 20 July 1960, Vienna. *Education:* Vienna School of Music and Dramatic Art. *Career:* played with Vienna Philharmonic Orchestra, Vienna Symphonic Orchestra, Austrian Broadcasting Corporation Orchestra and other major orchestras; conductors: Claudio Abbado, Yehudi Menuhin, André Previn, Sándor Végh; appeared with Wolfgang Schneiderhan, Anton Dermota, Walter Berry, Philippe Entremont; concerts in most European countries, Korea, Japan, Thailand, Indonesia, Malaysia, Mexico, Argentina, USA (including Schubert Festival, Washington, and Carnegie Recital Hall, New York, Kenya, Uganda); int. festivals include Vienna, Salzburg, Lucerne, Nurnberg, Prague Spring Festival, Bruckner Festival, Linz Festival and Cervantino, Mexico; many radio and television performances; teaching, summer academies, Austria and abroad; world premieres of new works; specialist, Schubert piano works, Haydn, Mozart, Beethoven piano concertos, A. Berg, F. Schmidt, E. Schulhoff, K. Szymanowski; pres. of jury, Zagreb 2006 piano competition; mem. juries of numerous int. piano competitions. *Recordings:* Baroque, Romantic and contemporary piano and organ music (Liszt, Schumann, Tchaikovsky, Brahms, Schubert, Complete Piano Works by Gottfried von Einem, Albinoni, Pachelbel, Muffat, Kerll). *Current Management:* Freunde der Claviermusik, Penknergasse 21, 3150 Wilhelmsburg, Austria. *Fax:* (820) 555-769-6547 (office). *E-mail:* bueno@lehrbaumer.com. *Website:* www.lehrbaumer.com.

LEHRMAN, Leonard Jordan, BA, MFA, DMA, MSLS; American composer, conductor, pianist and organist, translator, editor, critic and teacher; *Organist/Music Director/Composer-in-Residence, Christ Church Lutheran, Rosedale, NY;* b. 20 Aug. 1949, Kansas; s. of Nathaniel S. Lehrman and Emily R. Lehrman; m. 1st Karen S. Campbell 1978 (divorced 1986); m. 2nd Helene R. Williams (Spierman) 2002; one step-s. *Education:* studied privately with Elie Siegmeister and with Nadia Boulanger at Fontainebleau Conservatoire and Ecole Normale de Musique, Paris, Harvard Coll., Salzburg Mozarteum, Indiana Univ., Cornell Univ., Long Island Univ. *Career:* Lecturer in Music, Cornell Univ. 1973; debut as pianist, Carnegie Recital Hall 1979, as conductor, Bremerhaven and Berlin 1981, 1983; Asst Chorus Master and Asst Conductor, Metropolitan Opera 1977–78; Asst Conductor, Heidelberg Festival 1979, Augsburg Städtische Bühne 1980, and Basler Theater 1980–81; Conductor, Schauspielhaus Wien 1981; Kapellmeister, Stadttheater Bremerhaven 1981–83; Chief Coach, Conductor, Theater des Westens 1983–84; Founder Jewish Music Theatre of Berlin 1983, Laureate Conductor 1986–; Artistic Admin., Prof. Edgar H. Lehrman Memorial Foundation for Ethics, Religion, Science & the Arts, Inc. 1986–; Founder and Dir Metropolitan Philharmonic Chorus 1988–; Pres. Long Island Composers Alliance 1991–98, Archivist Emer. 1999–; Co-founder Elie Siegmeister Soc. 1999–; Founder and Dir Long Island Composers Archive, Long Island Univ. 1994–; Reference Librarian, Oyster Bay-East Norwich Public Library 1995–; Co-Dir Court Street Music, Valley Stream, NY 2002–; Dir Oceanside Chorale 2003–05; Minister of Music, Christ Church Babylon 2003–06; Organist, Temple Isaiah of Great Neck 2003–05; Dir Workmen's Circle Chorus 2004; Music Dir/Composer-in-Residence, St George's Church, Hempstead, NY 2006–07; Interim Organist and Music Dir, United Methodist Church, Wayne NJ 2007; Music Dir/Composer-in-Residence, United Methodist Church, Huntington/Cold Spring Harbor, NY 2008–10; Interim Organist, New Dorp Moravian Church, Staten Island, NY 2010; Interim Organist/Music Dir, St Mary's Staten Island 2010; Interim Organist/Music Dir, Church of the Saviour, Denville NJ 2010–11; Dir Hanseaten Deern & Blaue Jung's German Chor, East Meadow, NY 2010–12; Organist, Community United Methodist Church of East Norwich, NY 2011–12; Organist/Music Dir, All Saints Church, Leonia NJ June–Nov. 2012; Organist/Music Dir, Church in the Garden, Garden City, NY 2013–14; Music Dir, Jericho Jewish Center 2013–; High Holidays Organist/Choir Dir, Metropolitan Synagogue, New York City 2013–; Organist/Music Dir/Composer-in-Residence, Christ Church Lutheran, Rosedale, NY 2014–; Adjunct Faculty, Hebrew Union Coll.-Jewish Inst. of Religion 2014; Ed. Opera Today 1999–2001; Copy Ed. and Critic-at-Large, The New Music Connoisseur 2006–09; Media Team, Nassau MoveOn 2012–; has appeared on numerous TV and radio stations, including WHRB (Chief Producer 1968–70), WQXR, WNYC and WBAI (Producer 1989–91); Co-Dir Nat. Cttee to Reopen the Rosenberg Case 2005–09; Founder Int. Cttee on the Arts for Social Justice 2010–. *Achievement:* completion of works begun by Marc Blitzstein: Tales of Malamud, Sacco and Vanzetti, Discourse, and 17 other works. *Dance:* nude pas de deux and pas de trois to Debussy's Clair de Lune and Chansons de Bilitis. *Plays:* adaptations: The Cradle Will Rock, I've Got the Tune, The Harpies, Barely Proper, Adam & Lilith & Eve; adaptation/translations: Days of the Commune, The Roundheads & The Pointedheads, A Life for the Tsar (opera), Dargomyzhsky's Rusalka, Musorgski's Zhenit'ba, Chabrier's L'étoile and L'éducation manquée. *Films:* more than 1,900 videos on www.youtube.-com. *Radio:* Barely Proper (WBAI) 1992, Bare Oaks, Sharon, Ontario (podcast) 2011. *Television:* interviews on German TV 1984; Artscene on Long Island with Shirley Romaine 1990, 2002, 2009, 2011–12, Russia Channel One 2015. *Compositions include:* Flute Concerto, Violin Concerto; seven musicals: Comic Tragedy of San Po Jo, Growing Up Woman, Let's Change the Woild!, E.G.: A Musical Portrait of Emma Goldman, Adam & Lilith & Eve, Superspy!: The S-e-c-r-e-t Musical, The Booby Trap or Off Our Chests; 11 operas: Idiots First (completion of work begun by Marc Blitzstein), Karla, Suppose a Wedding (all part of Tales of Malamud), Sima, Hannah, The Family Man, The Birthday of the Bank, New World: An Opera About What Columbus Did to the "Indians", Sacco and Vanzetti (completion of work begun by Marc Blitzstein), The Wooing, The Triangle Fire; 22 song cycles; 38 choral works; more than 400 individual vocal pieces; works for organ, piano solo, piano four hands. *Recordings include:* for Opus One, Capstone (four), Original Cast (four), Albany, Parma. *Publications:* The Marc Blitzstein Songbook, Vols 1–3 (ed.) 1999–2003, Marc Blitzstein: A Bio-Bibliography 2005, Elie Siegmeister, American Composer: A Bio-Bibliography (co-author) 2010. *Honours:* Harvard Coll. Scholarship, American Soc. of Composers, Authors and Publishers (ASCAP) awards annually since 1974–, 30 Meet the Composer Grants (including New England Foundation for the Arts) 1978–; winner, Brookhaven Arts Council Sunrise Sunset Composition Competition 2002. *Address:* 300 East Overlook, #444, Port Washington, NY 11050 (office); 33 Court Street, Valley Stream, NY 11580, USA (home). *Telephone:* (516) 825-2939 (office); (516) 256-4209 (after 10am) (home). *E-mail:* ljlehrman@gmail.com (home). *Website:* www.artists-in-residence.com/ljlehrman (office).

LEIB, Gunther; German singer (baritone) and academic; b. 12 April 1927, Gotha, Thuringen. *Education:* Weimar Conservatory. *Career:* first violin, Landeskapelle at Gotha from 1949; stage debut at Kothen 1952, as Bartolo in Il Barbiere di Siviglia; sang at Kothen, Meinigen and Nordhausen; Stadttheater Halle 1956–57; Staatsoper Dresden from 1957, Berlin from 1961; sang Christus in Bach's St John Passion in Italy 1957, conducted by Franz Konwitschny; annual appearances at the Handel Festivals, Halle; Salzburg Easter Festival 1974–75, as Beckmesser in Die Meistersinger, conducted by Karajan (also at the Met 1976); guest engagements at the Paris Opéra, Moscow Bolshoi, Hamburg Staatsoper, Nat. Operas of Warsaw, Prague and Budapest, Sofia, Stockholm and Helsinki; other roles were Guglielmo, Raimondo, Papageno, Don Pasquale and Germont; Prof., Carl Maria von Weber Hochschule, Dresden 1964–76; Prof., Musikhochschule Berlin. *Recordings:* Così fan tutte; Die Zauberflöte; Ein Deutsches Requiem; Lucia di Lammermoor; Don Pasquale; La Traviata; St Matthew Passion; Der Dorfjahrmarkt by Benda; La Bohème; Einstein by Dessau.

LEIFERKUS, Sergey Petrovich; Russian singer (baritone); b. 4 April 1946, Leningrad. *Education:* Leningrad Conservatory with Barsov and Shaposhnikov. *Career:* stage debut in Leningrad Theatre of Musical Comedy 1972; soloist Maly Theatre of Opera and Ballet 1972–78, sang in Eugene Onegin, Iolanta, Il Barbiere di Siviglia and Don Giovanni; Kirov (now Mariinsky) Theatre of Opera and Ballet 1977–85; has appeared frequently at Royal Opera House, Covent Garden, Vienna State Opera, Opera Bastille, La Scala, San Francisco Opera, Metropolitan Opera, Netherlands Opera, Teatro Colon; has also appeared with other orchestras including London Symphony, Boston Symphony, New York Philharmonic and Philadelphia Orchestra under numerous conductors including Claudio Abbado, Valery Gergiev, James Levine, Bernard Haitink, Zubin Mehta, Riccardo Muti, Seiji Ozawa and Sir Georg Solti. *Recordings include:* Songs of Borodin and Dargomizhsky 1996, Mahler's Symphony No. 8 1997, Mahler's Das klagende Lied 1997, Verdi, Tenor Arias 2001, Mussorgsky's Chansons 2003, Shostakovich's Songs and Waltzes 2006.

LEIGH, David Anthony, BA; British harpsichordist and fortepianist; b. 3 April 1953, London, England. *Education:* Reading Univ., Guildhall School of Music. *Career:* debut, Wigmore Hall 1975; recitals all over the UK, Canada, USA, the Netherlands, Belgium, Austria; lectures in USA and Austria; masterclasses in USA and the UK; radio broadcasts in the UK, Canada and USA; knowledge of early keyboard instruments and their restoration. *Recordings include:* Harpsichords Historic and Unique (five vols). *Publications:* encyclopaedia articles on harpsichord and clavichord; contrib. to Antique Collector. *Address:* Keppel Gate, Upton Road, Defford, Worcs., WR8 9BD, England (home). *Telephone:* (1451) 833693 (office); (1386) 751966 (home). *E-mail:* david@laurieleighantiques.com (home). *Website:* www.davidleigh.com.

LEISNER, David, BA; American classical guitarist, composer and teacher; *Co-Chairman, Guitar Department, Manhattan School of Music*; b. 22 Dec. 1953, Los Angeles, Calif.; s. of Elkan Leisner and Edith Leisner; m. Ralph Jackson. *Education:* Wesleyan Univ., studied privately with John Duarte, David Starobin, Richard Winslow, Virgil Thomson and David Del Tredici. *Career:* teacher of guitar, Amherst Coll. 1976–78, New England Conservatory 1980–2003; teacher of guitar, Manhattan School of Music 1993–, Co-Chair. Guitar Dept 2004–; New York debut at Merkin Hall 1979; solo and chamber music recitals in USA, Canada, Asia, Australia, NZ and Europe; concerto soloist with L'Orchestre de la Suisse Romande, Berlin Radio Symphony, Polish Nat. Radio Orchestra, Atlanta Symphony Orchestra, Brooklyn Philharmonic, Australian Chamber Orchestra, New York Chamber Ensemble and others; premiered and commissioned works by Del Tredici, Thompson, Glass, Rorem, Bennett, Sculthorpe and Golijov; compositions performed by Sanford Sylvan, Wolfgang Holzmair, Rufus Müller, Kurt Ollmann, William Ferguson, Patrick Mason, Eugenia Zukerman, Benjamin Verdery, David Starobin, Jon Klibonoff, Zuill Baile, St Lawrence, Enso, Avalon String Quartets, Cavatina Duo, Arc Duo, The Saturday Brass Quintet, Los Angeles Guitar Quartett, Eastman, Oberlin and New England Conservatory Percussion Ensembles. *Compositions include:* Dances in the Madhouse for violin (or flute) and guitar 1982 (orchestrated 1989), Passacaglia and Toccata for solo guitar 1982, Billy Boy Variations 1983, Confiding for voice and piano, voice and guitar 1985–86, Candles in Mecca for piano trio 1988, On Jazz Terrain for flute, clarinet, saxophone and piano 1990, Embrace of Peace for orchestra 1991, Ad Majorem Dei Gloriam for brass quintet 1992, Freedom Fantasies for solo guitar 1992, To Sleep for baritone and piano 1994, Battlefield Requiem for percussion quartet and solo cello 1995, Fidelity for tenor, baritone and piano 1996, Nel Mezzo sonata for solo guitar 1998, Vision of Orpheus for guitar and string quartet 2000, Acrobats 2002, Of Darkness and Light for tenor, oboe, violin and piano 2002, A Timeless Procession for baritone and string quartet 2004, Bloom for string quartet 2005, Labyrinths for solo guitar 2007, Three James Tate Songs for baritone and guitar 2007, Vapors for solo viola, 2007, Away for flute and guitar 2008, Labyrinths II for solo piano 2009, Das Wunderbare Wesen for baritone and cello 2011, West Wind for tenor and guitar 2011, Twilight Streams for cello and guitar 2012, Dreams of the Exile for flute, guitar and string quartet 2015, Eve's Diary for soprano and guitar 2015. *Publications:* several articles in Guitar Review, Classical Guitar and American String Teacher. *Honours:* Second Prize, Toronto Int. Guitar Competition 1976, Silver Medal, Geneva Int. Guitar Competition 1981. *Website:* www.davidleisner.com.

LEIXNER, Vladimir; Czech cellist; b. 1953. *Education:* studied in Prague with mems of the Smetana Quartet. *Career:* cellist in various Czech ensembles from 1970; co-founder and cellist of the Stamic Quartet, Prague, 1977; performances at the Prague Young Artists and the Bratislava Music Festivals; tours to Spain, Austria, France, Switzerland, Germany and Eastern Europe; tour of the USA 1980 with debut concerts in the UK at London and Birmingham in 1983; further British tours in 1985 and 1988 (Warwick Arts Festival) and 20 concerts 1989; gave the premiere of Helmut Eder's 3rd Quartet in 1986; season 1991–92 with visit to the Channel Islands with Festival of Czech Music, to Netherlands, Finland, Austria and France, Edinburgh Festival and debut tours of Canada, Japan and Indonesia. *Recordings:* Shostakovich No. 13; Schnittke No. 4; Mozart's K589 and K370; Dvořák, Martinů and Janáček's Quartets. *Honours:* with Stamic Quartet: prizewinner, International Festival of Young Soloists, Bordeaux, 1977, winner ORF Austria International String Quartet Competition, 1986, followed by live broadcast from Salzburg Mozarteum, Académie Charles Cros Grand Prix du Disque, 1991 for Dvořák Quartets.

LEJET, Edith; French composer and academic; *Professor of Composition, Ecole Normale de Musique de Paris Alfred Cortot*; b. 19 July 1941, Paris; d. of Donat Lejet and Frida Etheridge. *Education:* Conservatoire Nat. Supérieur de Musique de Paris. *Career:* Prof., Dept of Theoretical Studies, Conservatoire Nat. Supérieur de Musique de Paris 1988–2005, Prof. Emer. 2005–; Prof. of Composition, Ecole Normale de Musique de Paris Alfred Cortot 2004–. *Compositions:* Monodrame pour violon et orchestre 1969, Journal d'Anne Frank (oratorio) 1970, Quatuor de saxophones 1974, Harmonie du soir for 12 strings 1977, Espaces nocturnes for 7 instruments 1976, Gemeaux for guitar 1978, Triptyque for organ 1979, Volubilis for violoncello 1981, Balance for guitar 1982, Aube Marine 1982, L'Homme qui avait perdu sa voix (musical theatre) 1984, Ressac for orchestra 1986, Les Rois Mages (oratorio) 1989, Améthyste for 12 strings 1990, Trois eaux-fortes for piano 1992, Trois chants pour un Noël for children's chorus 1994, Océan pathétique for five instruments 1994, Almost a Song for guitar and viola 1995, Missa Brevis for choir and organ 1996, Des Fleurs en forme de diamants for guitar and seven instruments 1997, Psaume de joie for mixed chorus 1998, Parcours en duo for baritone saxophone and percussion 2001, Diptyque pour orgue et cordes 2003, L'Herbier de Colette for soprano and piano 2006, Lignes et résonances for 11 instruments 2008, Bruit de l'eau sur de l'eau for two violins 2009, Toute la Nature sort de l'or for 15 musicians 2009, La houle à l'assaut des récifs for cello solo 2010, De lumière et de cieux embrasés for harp solo 2010, Echos dans la vallée for violin, clarinet and piano 2011, Secret d'un paysage for violin solo and 17 musicians 2013, Fulgurances for harp solo 2015, Chemins croisés for celtic harp 2015. *Publications:* Pedagogic Books: La Précision Rythmique dans la Musique (three vols), Témoignage: enseigner la composition?. *Honours:* numerous first prizes at Paris Conservatory, Vocation Foundation 1967, Grand Prix de Rome 1968, Prix Florence Gould 1970, Prix Hervé Dugardin 1974, Grand Prix de la Musique de Chambre de la Soc. des auteurs, compositeurs et éditeurs de musique 1979, Prix Nadia et Lili Boulanger 2003. *Address:* 11–13 rue Cino del Duca, 75017 Paris, France. *E-mail:* e.lejet@free.fr. *Website:* www.edith-lejet.com.

LEKHINA, Ekaterina; Russian singer (soprano); b. Samara. *Education:* Music Coll. of Samara, Acad. of Choral Art, Moscow. *Career:* first engagement with Volksoper Vienna 2006; sang role of Madame Herz (Der Schauspieldirektor, Mozart), Briggita (Iolanta), Lisa (La Sonnambula), Giulietta (I Capuleti e I Montecchi); sang Les contes d'Hoffmann (Offenbach) at Summer Opera Festival in Klosterneuburg, Austria 2006, followed by Tel-Aviv 2007, Volksoper, Vienna 2007, Royal Opera House, Covent Garden, London 2008, role of Musetta at Teatro Municipal, Santiago de Chile 2008; debut in title role of Zaide (Mozart) at summer festival in Aix-en-Provence 2008; solo recital at St John's Smith Square, London in Rosenblatt recital series 2008; sang role of

Briggita from Iolanta (Tchaikovsky) in a concert version with London Philharmonic Orchestra under V. Jurovsky 2008; participated in concert with Nat. Philharmonic Orchestra of Russia at Grand Hall of Moscow Conservatory 2009; appeared at summer festival in Knowlton, Canada, singing role of Lisa (and covered Amina) from La Sonnambula, role of Giulietta from I Capuleti et I Montecchi 2009, title role in L'arbore di Diana by Martin y Soler in Teatro Liceu, Barcelona 2009 and Teatro Real, Madrid 2011, Olympia at Opera de Monte Carlo 2010, role of The Queen of Shemakha and Queen of the Night at Bolshoi Theatre, Moscow 2011, Queen of the Night at Munich Staatsoper and Tel-Aviv 2011, Gilda in Monte Carlo, Zerbinetta at Teatro Municipal, Santiago de Chile 2011; performances with conductors including Leopold Hager, Alfred Eschwe, David Stahl, Frederic Chaslin, Louis Langrée, Vladimir Jurowski, Harry Bicket, Jacques Lacombe, Ottavio Dantone, Kent Nagano, Antonio Pappano. Recordings include: L'amour de loin by Kaija Saariaho (Diapason d'Or 2011, Grammy Award for Best Opera Recording 2011) 2010. Honours: winner, All-Russia Competition, St Petersburg 2005, Plácido Domingo Operalia Competition, Paris 2007. Current Management: c/o Claudia Dickie Artist's Management, Josef Kollmann 35, 2500 Baden bei Wien, Austria. Telephone: (676) 5378953. E-mail: dickie .artists@kabsi.at. Website: ekaterina-lekhina.com (office).

LELEU, Romain; French trumpeter; b. 1983, Lille. Education: Paris Conservatoire, Karlsruhe Hochschule fur Musik, Germany. Career: numerous performances at music festivals and in concert halls world-wide; soloist with Orchestre Nat. de Lille, Orchestre Nat. d'Ile de France, Orchestre Nat. de Lorraine, Ensemble Orchestral de Paris, Orchestre de Bretagne, Orchestre Régional de Cannes PACA, Orchestre Philharmonique de l'Opéra de Marseille, Orchestre d'Auvergne, Orchestre des Concerts Colonne, Württembergisches Kammerorchester Heilbronn, Baltic Chamber Orchestra, Slovak Sinfonietta in France and abroad in Switzerland, Belgium, Spain, Portugal, Athenaeum Concert Hall, Romania, in Turkey, Algeria, Israel, Cuba, Egypt, Japan, USA; has collaborated with Karol Beffa (premiere of Subway and Nuit Etoilée), Philippe Hersant (premiere of Folk Tunes), Martin Matalon and others; f. Feeling Brass Quintet 2000; Laureate of the Fondation Meyer 2002–, of French Academie des Beaux Arts 2011, of French Victoires de la Musique Classique 2009–; currently trumpet teacher, Aubervilliers Regional National Conservatory; also Dir Trumpet Collection, Editions Billaudot, Paris; regularly invited to perform on radio and TV, including France 2, France 3, Direct 8 TV, France Musique, France Inter, Radio Suisse Romande, Radio Romania Muzical; gives numerous master-classes in France, Korea, Japan, USA and elsewhere. Recordings include: Famous Trumpet Sonatas 2008, Outrageously French – Wind Music from France 2008, L'école française des vents 2009, Classical Concertos with Baltic Chamber Orchestra (St Petersburg Philharmonic) 2011, Oeuvres de Bartok, Piazzolla, Tchaïkovky, Bellini, Michel Legrand, Nino Rota 2013. Honours: winner, Festival Musical d'Automne de Jeunes Interprètes, Special Interpretation Prize, Finnish Int. Competition, Lieksa Brass Week 1999, Adami's Classical Revelation, First Prize for Trumpet, Paris Conservatoire 2003, First Prize for Chamber Music 2003, Third Prize, Int. Competition of Chamber Music, Lyon 2005, Victoires de la Musique (category Revelation) 2009, Prix Del Duca, Acad. des Beaux Arts 2011. Current Management: c/o M. Jérémie Barret, Musicaglotz, 29 rue Violet, 75015 Paris, France. Telephone: 1-42-34-53-44. E-mail: jeremie.barret@ musicaglotz.com. Website: www.musicaglotz.com. E-mail: contact@ romainleleu.com. Website: www.romainleleu.com.

LELEUX, François; French oboist; b. 1971; m. Lisa Batiashvili. Education: Roubaix Conservatory, Conservatoire Nat. Supérieur de Musique, Paris. Career: fmr mem., European Community Youth Orchestra; early experience with French Nat. Opera; first oboe soloist, orchestra of the Paris Opera aged eighteen; currently Prin. Oboist, Chamber Music Orchestra of Europe; co-f., Paris-Bastille Wind Octet 1992; Musical Dir Orchestre de Neuburg 2002–; regularly performs with chamber music ensembles, including Mullova Ensemble, Emmanuel Strosser, Katia and Marielle Labèque; extensive int. appearances as soloist, including performances with Deutsche Symphony Orchestra, Tokyo Philharmonic, French Nat. Orchestra, Vienna Chamber Orchestra, Bratislava Chamber Orchestra, Hallé Orchestra, and at the Lincoln Center and Saratoga Chamber Music Festival, USA, Wigmore Hall, London, Tokyo Opera City Concert Hall; Prof. Hochschule für Musik, Berlin. Recordings: Poulenc, Trio/Britten, Metamorphoses Op49 1995, Beethoven, Octet for Winds/Mozart, Serenades 1996, Telemann, 12 Fantasias for Oboe 1996, Mozart, Concertos pour Hautbois 2000, Works for Oboe and Orchestra 2009, Strauss, Oboe Concerto, Serenade in E flat 2010. Honours: first prize Int. Competition of Toulon 1990, second prize Prague Spring Int. Music Competition 1991, second prize Int. Music Competition, Munich 1991, European Juventus Prize. Current Management: Künstleragentur Dr Raab und Dr Böhm GmbH, Plankengasse 7, Vienna 1010, Austria. Telephone: (1) 512-05-01. Fax: (1) 512-77-43. E-mail: office@rbartists.at. Website: www .rbartists.at.

LEMALU, Jonathan; New Zealand singer (bass-baritone); b. 1978; m. Sandra Martinović 2006. Education: Royal Coll. of Music, London. Career: concert appearances include the Serenade to Music at the London Proms, Stravinsky's Pulcinella and Symphony no. 14 by Shostakovich with the English CO at the Barbican; season 2001 in Les Troyens at Edinburgh and Messiah in Vienna; festival engagements at King's Lynn, Rávinia (Chicago SO) and Tanglewood (Boston SO) 2002; sang in Falla's Master Peter's Puppet Show at the 2002 London Proms, and as Talbot in Donizetti's Maria Stuarda at the Edinburgh Festival; season 2002–03 as Rossini's Basilio for ENO, Leporello at Sydney, in La Damnation de Faust under Colin Davis and as Neptune in Idomeneo at Glyndebourne; recitals include Schubert's Schwanengesang (Wigmore Hall) and Winterreise (Edinburgh) 2002; Zorastro in Handel's Orlando at Covent Garden 2003. Recordings: Songs: Brahms, Fauré, Finzi, Schubert 2002, Opera Arias 2004, Love Blows as the Wind Blows 2005, Britten: Billy Budd 2008. Address: c/o EMI Classics, 27 Wrights Lane, London, W8 5SW, England (office). Telephone: (20) 7795-7000 (office). Website: www.emiclassics.co.uk (office); www.jonathanlemalu.com (home).

LEMELIN, Stéphane, BMus, MMus, DMA; Canadian pianist and academic; b. 2 April 1960, Rimouski, Quebec. Education: Peabody Conservatory and Yale Univ., USA. Career: performs as soloist and chamber musician across Canada, the USA, Europe and Asia; frequent CBC and NPR broadcasts; piano faculty, Yale Univ. 1986–90, Univ. of Alberta 1990–2001; Prof. of Music, Univ. of Ottawa 2001–07, Dir 2007–; Visiting Prof., Université de Montréal 2001–. Recordings include: works by Schubert, Schumann, Fauré, Saint-Saëns, Roussel, Poulenc, Debussy, Samazeuilh, Ropartz, Complete Nocturnes by Fauré. Honours: prizewinner Casadesus Int. . Competition 1983. Address: Department of Music, University of Ottawa, Perez Hall, Room No. 103, 50 University Street, Ottawa, ON K1N 6N5 Canada (office). Telephone: (613) 562-5800 (office). Fax: (613) 562-5140 (office). E-mail: slemelin@uOttawa.ca (office). Website: www.music.uottawa.ca (office); www.stephanelemelin.net.

LEMMINGS, Christopher; British singer (tenor); b. 1965, Camberley, Surrey. Education: Guildhall School, London. Career: appearances with Glyndebourne Festival as Dancing Master in Manon Lesccaut, Servant in Capriccio, and Bartholomew in Birtwistle's The Last Supper 2001; Glyndebourne tour as Lechmere in Britten's Owen Wingrave and Mozart's Titus and Belmonte; further engagements as Don Ottavio at Cologne and Verona, as Ferrando and Rossini's Almaviva for Opera Holland Park and Molqui in The Death of Klinghoffer by John Adams, for Finnish National Opera 2001; concerts with the King's Consort, BBC Singers, Royal Liverpool PO, Monteverdi Choir and London PO under Riccardo Muti. Current Management: Robert Gilder & Company, 91 Great Russell Street, London, WC1B 3PS, England. Telephone: (20) 7580-7758. Fax: (20) 7580-7739. E-mail: iarlaith@ robert-gilder.com. Website: www.robert-gilder.com. E-mail: mail@ christopherlemmings.com (office). Website: www.christopherlemmings.com.

LEMPER, Ute; German singer, dancer and actress; b. 4 July 1963, Münster; pnr Todd Turkisher; three s. one d. Education: Dance Acad., Cologne, Max Reinhardt Seminary for Dramatic Art, Austria. Career: leading role in Viennese production of Cats 1983; appeared in Peter Pan, Berlin, Cabaret, Düsseldorf and Paris (recipient of Molière Award 1987), Chicago (Laurence Olivier Award) 1997–99 and in London and New York, Life's a Swindle tour 1999, Punishing Kiss tour 2000, The Last Tango in Berlin tour 2009; Die sieben Todsünden (Weill) at Covent Garden Festival, London 2000; collaborations with Michael Nyman, Paulo Coelho. Recordings include: Life is a Cabaret 1987, Ute Lemper Sings Kurt Weill 1988, (Vol. 2) 1993, The Threepenny Opera 1988, Mahagonny Songspiel 1989, Crimes of the Heart 1989, The Seven Deadly Sins 1990, Songbook (with Michael Nyman) 1992, Illusions 1992, Espace Indécent 1993, Portrait of Ute Lemper 1995, City of Strangers 1995, Berlin Cabaret Songs 1996, Nuits Étranges 1997, All that Jazz/The Best of Ute Lemper 1998, Punishing Kiss 2000, But One Day 2002, Blood and Feathers 2006, Between Yesterday and Tomorrow 2008, Paris Days/Berlin Nights (with Vogler String Quartet) 2012, Ute Lemper Sings Weill, Vol.2 2013, Punishing Kiss 2013, Forever: The Love Poems of Pablo Neruda 2013. Television appearances include: L'Affaire Dreyfus (Arte), Tales from the Crypt (HBO), Illusions (Granada) and The Look of Love (Gillian Lynne). Film appearances include: L'Autrichienne 1989, Moscou Parade 1992, Coupable d'Innocence 1993, Prêt à Porter 1995, Bogus 1996, Combat de Fauves, A River Made to Drown In, Appetite 1997. Honours: French Culture Prize 1993. Current Management: Dispeker Artists, 59 East 54th Street, Suite 81, New York, NY 10022, USA. Telephone: (212) 421-7678. E-mail: emmy@ dispeker.com. Website: www.utelemper.com.

LENDVAY, Jozsef; Hungarian musician (violin); b. 1974, Budapest; s. of Jozsef Lendvay, Sr. Education: Franz List Acad. of Music, Budapest. Career: began learning the violin aged five; worked with soloists and conductors including Yuri Bashmet, Giora Feidman, Andrea Bocelli, Sir Simon Rattle, Sir Yehudi Menuhin, Krzysztof Penderecki; long collaboration with Budapest Festival Orchestra/Iván Fischer; also performed with Royal Philharmonic Orchestra, Royal Concertgebouw Orchestra, Rotterdam Philharmonic, Los Angeles Philharmonic, Philharmonic of the Nations, Netherlands Radio Philharmonic Orchestra and Orchestre de la Suisse Romande; performed for Pope John Paul II at Castel Gandolfo, and for Mikhail Gorbachev, Angela Merkel, George Bush, Sr, Helmut Kohl and Reinhold Wurth; festivals haved included Schleswig Holstein and MDR Musiksommer (Germany), Salzburger Festspiele and Feldkirsch Festival (Austria), Brescia and Bergamo Festival (Italy), Edinburgh Int. Festival and BBC Proms; also plays folk music of Hungary, Romania, Moldova and Russia. Recordings include: Brahms's Hungarian Dances 1999, Lendvay (Echo Klassik ohne Grenzen Award) 2005, Dancing Paris (with Alliage Quintet) (Echo Klassik ohne Grenzen Award 2014). Honours: President's Gold Cross 1997; several awards and scholarships including Tibor Varga Int. Violin Competition 1997, Switzerland, Bela Bartók Award 2006. E-mail: kontakt@echomusic.pl. Website: jozseflendvay.com.

LENDVAY, Kamilló, DLA; Hungarian composer and academic; b. 28 Dec. 1928, Budapest; m. 1972; one d. *Education:* Ferenc Liszt Acad. of Music, Budapest. *Career:* Musical Leader, State Puppet Theatre 1960–66; Musical Dir Artistic Ensemble, Hungarian People's Army 1966–68; Conductor and Artistic Dir, Operetta Theatre, Budapest; Musical Lector, Hungarian Radio 1962–; Prof. and Head of Music Theory Dept, Ferenc Liszt Acad. of Music, Budapest 1973–; Pres. Artisjus: Bureau for the Protection of Authors' Rights, Asscn of Hungarian Composers. *Compositions include:* Orogenesis (oratorio) 1969–70, Requiem, Cantatas: Cart-Drive into the Night 1970, Scenes from Thomas Mann's Joseph and His Brothers 1978–81; orchestral works: Mauthausen (symphonic poem) 1958, Four Invocations 1966, Expressions for 11 strings, for chamber orchestra 1974, The Harmony of Silence 1980, Chaconne for orchestra 1988, Rhapsody for orchestra 1997, Jazz-Symphony 2010; concertos: Concertino 1959, Violin Concerto No. 1 1961–62, Pezzo Concerto 1975, Violin Concerto No. 2 1986, Concerto semplice 1986, Trumpet Concerto 1990, Concerto for violin, harpsichord and strings 1991, Concerto for piano 2000; chamber: String Quartet No. 2 2007; solo pieces: Sonata for violincello solo 2006; music for films and stage; Stabat Mater. *Honours:* Erkel Musical Prize 1962, 1964, 1978, Trieste Competition 1975, Title of Merited Artist 1981, Grand Prix Int. du Disque Lyrique (for opera The Respectable Street Walker) 1983, Kossuth Prize 1988, Bartók-Pasztory Prize 1989, 2005. *Address:* 1137 Budapest, Szent István Park 23, Hungary (office). *Telephone:* (1) 329-4884 (office). *Fax:* (1) 329-4884 (office). *E-mail:* klendvay@chello.hu (office). *Website:* www.lendvay.com; www.kamillolendvay.hu.

LENEHAN, John; British pianist, composer and arranger. *Career:* proms debut playing Harpsichord Concerto by Manuel De Falla 1996; has appeared as piano soloist with numerous orchestras including Ulster Orchestra, Manchester Camerata, BBC Nat. Orchestra of Wales, London Concert Orchestra, London Sinfonietta, London Philharmonic Orchestra, Royal Philharmonic, English Chamber Orchestra; has given recitals in major concert halls in Amsterdam, Vienna, Salzburg, New York, Washington, Toronto, Seoul, Tokyo and cities in Mexico, Sri Lanka and Kazakhstan; appearances abroad include Newport Music Festival, USA, Ephesus Festival with RPO, Enescu Festival with Britten Sinfonia, Kazakhstan, India, Georgia; performs regularly with Joachim Piano Trio and in duo with John Harle; recitals with many well-known musicians including Julian Lloyd Webber, Emma Johnson and Tasmin Little; has also arranged several film scores. *Compositions include:* String Fever 2000, Tchaikovskiana, Alice (for cello and piano), Christmas Variations, Little Gems (for flute and piano), Morning Song. *Recordings:* more than 60 CDs; solo recordings include Erik Satie, Ireland: Piano Works Vol 1 1998, Michael Nyman's Piano Concerto, Philip Glass: The Piano Music 2007, Ludovico Einaudi: The Piano Music 2007, Michael Nyman: The Piano Music 2007, Ireland Piano Works, Vol. 3 2008. *Current Management:* Upbeat Classical Management, PO Box 479, Uxbridge, UB8 2ZH, England. *Telephone:* (1895) 259441. *Fax:* (1895) 259341. *E-mail:* enquiry@upbeatclassical.co.uk. *Website:* www.upbeatclassical.co.uk; www.lenehan.dsl.pipex.com.

LENHART, Renate; singer (soprano); b. 1942, Austria. *Education:* Vienna Conservatory. *Career:* concert tour of South America 1966–67; subsequent engagement at Zürich Opera, with roles there including Micaela, Marzelline in Fidelio, Mozart's Pamina and Zerlina, Constanza in Henze's Il Re Cervo, Julia Farnese in Ginaster's Bomarzo, Miranda in The Tempest by Frank Martin and Lisa in The Queen of Spades; further roles at Zürich and as guest in Munich, Paris, Amsterdam and Vienna have included Alice Ford, Lyudmila, Glauce in Médée, Sophie, and Frau Fluth in Die Lustigen Weiber von Windsor; appearances in Monteverdi's Poppea and Ulisse at Bregenz and in the Jean-Pierre Ponnelle cycle at Zürich; most frequently heard as Pamina, also sang First Lady in the Ponnelle production of Die Zauberflöte.

LENTRODT, Ursula; German harpist; b. Berlin; d. of Wilhelm Lentrodt and Clara Lentrodt (née von Occolowitz); one d. *Education:* Hochschule für Musik, Berlin and in Paris. *Career:* solo harpist with orchestras, including Berliner Rundfunk and Bayerischer Rundfunkorchester 1953–74; numerous solo concerts in Germany and abroad; Prof., Musikhochschule, Munich. *Publications:* contribs to professional journals. *Honours:* Citoyen d'honneur, France; Bundesverdienstkreuz 1986, Bayerischer Verdienstorden 1991. *Address:* Wagnerstrasse 1A, 80802 Munich, Germany (home). *Telephone:* (89) 395826 (home).

LENTZ, Daniel Kirkland, BS, MFA; American composer; b. 10 March 1942, Latrobe, PA; m. Marlene Helen Wasco 1964, one d. *Education:* St Vincent Coll., Ohio Univ., Brandeis Univ., Tanglewood summer school, Stockholm Univ., Sweden. *Career:* founder and Dir, California Time Machine ensemble 1969–73, The San Andreas Fault ensemble 1974, 1976, The Daniel Lentz Ensemble 1978–80, Lentz ensemble 1983–85, Daniel Lentz and Group 1986–; European tours and major/premiere performances, including Gaudeamus Foundation 1972, New Music America Festivals 1983, 1986, LA Olympic Arts Festival 1984, Wild Turkeys at Carnegie Hall 1986, The Crack in the Bell, LAPhil New Music Group 1986. *Compositions include:* Canon and Fugle 1971, Loverise 1971, King Speech Song 1972, Song(s) of the Sirens 1973, Missa Umbrarum 1973, O-Ke-Wa 1974, Sun Tropes 1975, Requiem Songs 1976, Three Pretty Madrigals 1976, Composition in Contrary and Parallel Motion 1977, Elysian Nymph 1978, Wolf is Dead 1979, 1982, Uitoto 1980, Music By Candlelight 1980, Dancing on the Sun 1980, Point Conception 1981, Adieu 1983, On the Leopold Altar 1983, Lascaux 1984, Is it Love 1984, Bacchus 1985, Topanga Tango 1985, Time's Trick 1985, Wild Turkeys 1985, The Crack in the Bell 1986, Apache Wine for chamber orchestra 1989, Apologetica for soprano, mezzo chorus and ensemble 1996, Ze ghosts for ensemble 1997. *Recordings include:* Dinner Music 1999, Self Portrait 1999.

LEON, (Robert) Craig; American/British producer, composer and arranger; *Director, Atlas Realisations;* b. 7 Jan. 1952, Miami, Fla, USA; m. Cassell Webb 1984. *Career:* mem. British Record Producers' Guild, BRIT Awards Nominating Cttee, Nat. Acad. of Recording Arts and Sciences, Grammy.com; Dir, Atlas Realisations. *Compositions include:* Izzy, Libera Me album 1998, Izzy, Ascolta 2000, Izzy, New Dawn 2002, Joshua Bell/Academy of St-Martin-in-the-Fields: The Romance of the Violin 2003, Julia Thornton, Harpistry 2003, Andreas Scholl and the Orpheus Chamber Orchestra: Wayfaring Stranger 2003, James Galway/London Symphony Orchestra: Wings of Song 2004, C.T.Griffes-C.Leon: Roman Sketches for Orchestra, recorded with the London Symphony Orchestra 2005, Natasha Marsh, Amour Recital album 2007, L. Bernstein-C. Leon Symphonic Dances from West Side Story, jazz version premiere performance with Evelyn Glennie (percussion) and the London Symphony Orchestra 2007, Maestro (film-score) 2007, Orbit, La Luna (TV soundtrack) 2009, Ophelie Gaillard: Dreams 2010, Bell'aria (TV soundtrack and CD) 2010. *Recordings include:* three albums as featured artist: Nommos (ballet score) 1981, Visiting 1982, Klub Anima Theatre score (premiered Bristol Old Vic theatre) 1993; one album in collaboration with Arthur Brown: Tape From Atoya 1981; five albums in collaboration with Cassell Webb: Llano 1985, Thief of Sadness 1987, Songs of a Stranger 1989, Conversations At Dawn 1990, House of Dreams 1992; others as producer: Ramones 1976, Blondie 1977, Suicide 1977, Richard Hell 1977, Rodney Crowell 1980, Sir Douglas Quintet 1980, The Bangles 1983, The Roches 1983, Dr and the Medics 1986, The Pogues 1986, The Primitives 1986, Adult Net 1988, The Fall 1989–92, Jesus Jones 1990, New FADS 1992, Front 242 1993, Eugenius 1994, Angel Corpus Christi 1995, Martin Phillips and the Chills 1996, Mark Owen 1996, Cobalt 60 1996, Psyched Up Janis 1997, Blondie, No Exit 1998, Izzy 1998, Cinema Italiano, featuring Sting, Luciano Pavarotti, Lucio Dalla; James Galway's Wings Of Song (arranger) 2004, Charles T. Griffes' Roman Sketches (London Symphony Orchestra) (arranger) 2004, Midwinter (London Chamber Orchestra) (arranger) 2011, Early Electronic Works (composer and performer) 2014, The Anthology of Interplanetary Folk Music Vol. 1 (composer and performer) 2014, Bach to Moog (arranger, performer and conductor) 2015. *Radio:* numerous performances on BBC Radio 3 and Classic FM (UK), Radio Classique (France), Klassik Radio (Germany), NTS, Red Bull Radio, Boiler Room, etc. *Television:* Red Bull, Boiler Room in Concert, ARTE, and many others. *Honours:* Grammy Award 1976, Grammy Hall of Fame Award 2006. *Address:* Atlas Realisations Music, Trendalls Cottage, Beacons Bottom, Bucks., HP14 3XF, England. *Telephone:* (1494) 483121. *Fax:* (1494) 484303. *E-mail:* craig@craigleon.com (office). *Website:* www.craigleon.com; www.myspace.com/craigleon.

LEÓN, Tania Justina; American composer and conductor; b. 14 May 1943, Havana, Cuba. *Education:* studied in Havana and at New York Univ. *Career:* Founder-mem. and Music Dir Dance Theatre of Harlem 1969–; est. Brooklyn Philharmonic Community Concert Series 1978; New Music Adviser, New York Philharmonic Orchestra 1993–97; Co-founder American Composers Orchestra Sonidos de las Americas Festivals 1994; Claire and Leonard Tow Prof. of Music, Brooklyn Coll. 2000–04; Distinguished Prof., CUNY 2006–; has also taught at Harvard Univ., Univ. of Michigan, Univ. of Kansas, Hochschule für Musik, Hamburg, Germany; numerous conducting engagements include Savannah Symphony Orchestra, Charlotte Symphony Orchestra, Metropolitan Opera, Symphony Orchestra and Chorus of Marseille, Orchestre Symphonique de Nancy, France, Orquesta Sinfonica de Asturias, Spain, Orchestre de la Suisse Romande, Orquesta Santa Cecilia, Rome, Italy, Gewaundhausorchester, Leipzig, Germany, Orquesta de la Comunidad y Coro de Madrid, Spain. *Compositions include:* The Beloved (ballet) 1972, Haiku (ballet) 1973, Concerto Criolo for orchestra 1980, Bele (ballet) 1981, Batá for orchestra 1985, Kabiosile for orchestra 1988, Batey for vocal soloists and two percussion 1989, Carabali for orchestra 1991, Indigena for orchestra, Son sonore for flute and guitar 1992, Scourge of Hyacinths (opera) 1994, Para Viola y Orquesta 1994, Seven Spirituals for orchestra 1995, Drummin' 1997, Horizons for orchestra 1999, Desde for orchestra 2001, Duende 2003, Samarkand 2005, Didn't My Lord Deliver Daniel for orchestra 2005, Ácana for orchestra 2008, Inura (ballet) 2009. *Honours:* Dr hc (Colgate Univ.) 1999, (Oberlin Coll.) 2002, (Purchase Coll.); New York Gov.'s Lifetime Achievement Award 1998, Guggenheim Fellowship 2007, La Distinción de Honor de la Rosa Blanca, Patronato José Marti 2008, inducted to American Acad. of Arts and Letters 2010. *E-mail:* tlfpromo@gmail.com (office). *Current Management:* c/o Joanne Rile Artists Management, 93 Old York Road, Suite 222, Jenkintown Commons, Jenkintown, PA 19046-3925, USA. *Telephone:* (215) 885-6400. *Fax:* (215) 885-9929. *E-mail:* artists@rilearts.com. *Website:* rilearts.com. *E-mail:* tlfpromo@gmail.com (office). *Website:* www.tanialeon.com.

LEONARD, Edward, BMus, MusM; American conductor and pianist; *Music Director, Pittsburgh Philharmonic;* b. Charleston, S Carolina. *Education:* Coll. of Charleston with Enrique Graf, Carnegie Mellon Univ. with Juan Pablo Izquierdo. *Career:* began musical training on the violin with his parents, both players in Charleston Symphony Orchestra, aged four; performed in numerous venues at Coll. of Charleston, Candlelight Concert Series at Drayton Hall; appeared as soloist with College of Charleston Orchestra and Charleston Metropolitan Orchestra; composed several pieces premiered at annual Composers' Forum at Coll. of Charleston; has worked extensively with

Carnegie Mellon ensembles, including the Philharmonic, Contemporary Ensemble and Repertoire Orchestra; frequent guest conductor in the Pittsburgh area; conducted the Edgewood Symphony and Butler Symphony after winning the BCSO Young Conductors' Competition 2007; invited to be Asst Conductor, Opera Theater of Pittsburgh 2008; attended the Pierre Monteux School for Orchestral Conductors, Me, named an Orchestra Asst; fmr pianist for the Morningside Trio; Music Dir and Conductor, Pittsburgh Philharmonic 2011–. *Honours:* Winner, Butler County Symphony Orchestra Young Conductors Competition 2007. *Telephone:* (412) 223-7501 (office). *E-mail:* info@pghphil.org (office). *Website:* www.pghphil.org (office).

LEONARD, Lysiane; Belgian singer (soprano); b. 1957. *Education:* studied with Jules Bastin in Brussels, Juilliard School, and with Hans Hotter in Munich. *Career:* has sung at the Liège Opera from 1982, notably as Fenena in Nabucco, Elvira (Rossini) Norina, Siebel (Faust), Frasquita (Carmen) and Liu; guest appearances at Rouen in Les Indes Galantes, the Paris Opéra-Comique in La Belle Hélène and at Montpellier in Schumann's Faust 1985; concert repertory also includes Les Nuits d'été by Berlioz (Aix 1983); further concerts in music bv Vivaldi, Bach, Handel, Haydn and Telemann.

LEONARD, Sarah Jane, DipMus; British singer (soprano); b. 10 April 1953, Winchester, England; m. Michael Parkinson 1975 (divorced); one s. one d. *Education:* Winchester School of Art, Guildhall School of Music and Drama, London. *Career:* mem., BBC Singers 1976–81, London Sinfonietta Voices; broadcasts with BBC Singers, Endymion Ensemble and London Sinfonietta; television appearances include Alice (Channel 4), The Middle of the Road Hour (Channel 4); sang the Mad Boy in Goehr's Sonata about Jerusalem, Aldeburgh Festival, 1990; singer with Michael Nyman Band; guest appearances with Hilliard Ensemble; sang at La Scala, Milan, 1989 and 1992; int. soloist in 20th-century repertoire; sang in the premiere of Lachenmann's Das Mädchen, Hamburg, 1997; sang Queen Elizabeth in the premiere of Harle's Angel Magick, London Proms, 1998; mem. Incorporated Society of Musicians. *Recordings include:* Drusilla in L'Incoronazione di Poppea; Miserere by Arvo Pärt with Hilliard Ensemble; My Heart is Like a Singing Bird, English Song Company. *Honours:* Guildhall School of Music and Drama Susan Longfield Award 1976, winner Park Lane Group Young Artists and 20th-Century Music 1984. *Address:* 8 Woodbastwick Road, Sydenham, London, SE26 5LQ, England.

LEONSKAJA, Elisabeth; Russian pianist and teacher; b. 23 Nov. 1945, Tbilisi, USSR (now Georgia). *Education:* Moscow Conservatory. *Career:* gave first concert aged 11; left Soviet Union in 1978 and has since lived in Vienna; has appeared as soloist with numerous orchestras, including New York Philharmonic, Los Angeles Philharmonic, Cleveland Orchestra, London Philharmonic, London Symphony, Royal Philharmonic, BBC Symphony, Zurich Tonhalle, Berlin Philharmonic, Gewandhaus Leipzig, radio orchestras of Cologne, Hamburg and Munich, Czech Philharmonic under conductors including Kurt Masur, Sir Colin Davis, Christoph Eschenbach, Christoph von Dohnanyi, Kurt Sanderling, Maris Jansons, Yuri Temirkanov, Tugan Sokhiev; festivals include Salzburg (debut 1979), Vienna, Lucerne, Schleswig-Holstein, Schubertiade in Hohenems and Schwarzenberg; recitals in Paris, Madrid, Barcelona, London, Edinburgh, Munich, Zurich and Vienna; chamber music appearances with Emerson, Borodin and Artemis quartets; close collaboration with Sviatoslav Richter; teaches master-classes. *Recordings include:* Edvard Grieg's piano transcriptions of Mozart's piano sonatas K545 and K533/494, accompanied by Sviatoslav Richter 1996, Chopin: Nocturnes Nos. 1-11 2001, Shostakovich: Piano Concertos Nos. 1 & 2/Sonata No. 2 2001, Chopin: Piano Concertos Nos. 1 & 2 2002, Tchaikovsky: Symphony No. 4/Concert Fantasia 2003, Schubert: Piano Music 2003, Shostakovich: Piano Quintet/Piano Trio No. 2 2004, Schubert: Piano Sonatas Nos 19 & 21 2005, Schubert: Piano Sonatas D 958 & 960 2006, Schubert: Piano Sonatas Nos. 13 & 20 2006, Johannes Brahms: Piano Music, Op. 116-119 2006, Mendelssohn Bartholdy: Piano Concertos 1 & 2 2006, Chopin: Piano Works 2009, Paris: works by Ravel, Enescu, Debussy (Solo Artist of the Year, Int. Classical Music Awards 2014) 2013. *Honours:* Hon. mem. Konzerthaus of Vienna; Austrian Cross of Honour for Science and Art, 1st class 2005; prizes in Enescu, Marguerite Long–Jacques Thibaud and Queen Elisabeth int. piano competitions in Bucharest, Paris and Brussels. *Current Management:* IMG Artists, The Light Box, 111 Power Road, London, W4 5PY, England. *Telephone:* (20) 7957-5800. *Fax:* (20). *E-mail:* artistseurope@imgartists.com. *Website:* www.imgartists.com.

LEOSON, Markus; Swedish percussionist, timpanist and cimbalom player; *Professor, Hochschule für Musik Franz Liszt*; b. 16 Aug. 1970, Linköping. *Education:* Royal Conservatory of Music, Stockholm. *Career:* percussionist, Orchestra of the Royal Opera, Sweden 1993–; debut in Stockholm Concert Hall 1995; live radio concert, Stockholm and Reykjavík, Iceland 1995; Artist-in-Residence, P2 Swedish Radio 1996–97; also solo concerts, Norrtelje Festival, Stockholm, Linköping with wind orchestra; soloist with Tampere Philharmonic Orchestra; solo concert, Gothenburg; solo, Stockholm 1997, also soloist with Swedish Radio Symphony Orchestra, Kalmar; has performed with Gothenburg Symphony Orchestra, Helsingborg Symphony Orchestra, St Petersburg, Braunschweig, Norrköping Symphony Orchestra, Malmö Symphony Orchestra, Berlin Philharmonie etc.; Prof., Hochschule für Musik Franz Liszt, Weimar, Germany. *Television:* portrait on Nike Swedish TV, numerous appearances in different countries. *Recordings:* solo albums: Percussion 1996, Markussion 2002, Colludo 2006, Malletiana 2006. *Honours:* First Prize of the Soloist Prize (Sweden) 1995, Nordic Soloist Competition 1995, EBU IFYP Competition, Bratislava 1997. *Current Management:* c/o Helena Friberg Artists Management, Nibblevägen 25, 2 tr, 17736 Järfälla, Sweden; c/o Dagmar Körner Konzertagentur. *Telephone:* (8) 580-127-70. *Fax:* (8) 580-127-70. *E-mail:* hfam@swipnet.se; dkoerner@konzertagentur-koerner.de. *Website:* www.hfam.se; www.konzertagentur-koerner.de; www.norsk-percussion.no; www.markusleoson.com.

LEPPÄNIEMI, Olli; Finnish clarinettist; b. 1980. *Education:* Lappeenranta Music Inst., Sibelius-Academy. *Career:* studied with Jorma Lautanen, Reijo Koskinen, Hans-Christian Braein in Oslo, Yehuda Gilad in Los Angeles; fmr Prin. Clarinet, Bergen Philharmonic Orchestra; fmr Prin. Clarinet, Lahti Symphony Orchestra; currently Prin. Clarinet, Danish Nat. Symphony Orchestra; Guest Prin. Clarinet, Chicago Symphony Orchestra 2010; other appearances as soloist include with Bergen Philharmonic Orchestra, Odense Symphony Orchestra, Lappeenranta City Orchestra, Hyvinkää Orchestra, Sääksmäki Festival Orchestra, Pori Sinfonietta; appearances at chamber music festivals including Risör, Lyckeby, Tuusulanjärvi, Murten and Copenhagen festivals, and concerts in Washington and Sao Paulo; has premiered new works for clarinet by composers including Kimmo Hakola, Sampo Haapamäki and Aki Yli-Salomäki. *Honours:* Prize Winner, Int. Prague Spring Clarinet Competition 2008, Prize Winner, Int. Verdi Note Competition, Italy, Winner, Lahti Nat. Wind Instrument Competition, Winner, Carl Nielsen Int. Music Competition 2009. *Current Management:* Copenhagen Artists, Christian IX's gade 2, 5.th, 1111 Copenhagen, Denmark. *Telephone:* 4449-2900. *E-mail:* office@copenhagenartists.com. *Website:* www.copenhagenartists.com. *Telephone:* 278-44-284 (home); 50-588-6244 (home). *E-mail:* olli.leppaniemi@gmail.com (office). *Website:* www.ollileppaniemi.com.

LEPPARD, Raymond John, CBE, MA; British conductor and composer; b. 11 Aug. 1927, London; s. of A. V. Leppard and B. M. Beck. *Education:* Trinity Coll. Cambridge. *Career:* Fellow of Trinity Coll., Univ. Lecturer in Music 1958–68; Music Dir, BBC Philharmonic (fmrly BBC Northern Symphony) Orchestra 1973–80; Prin. Guest Conductor, St Louis Symphony Orchestra 1984–93; Music Dir Indianapolis Symphony Orchestra 1987–2001, Conductor Laureate 2001–; has also conducted New York Philharmonic, Chicago Symphony, Philadelphia and Pittsburgh Symphony Orchestras and Royal Opera, Covent Garden, English Nat. Opera, Metropolitan Opera, New York, New York City Opera and San Francisco Opera; realizations of Monteverdi's L'Incoronazione di Poppea, Il Ritorno d'Ulisse and L'Orfeo and Cavalli's L'Ormindo, L'Egisto, La Calisto and L'Orione. *Publication:* Authenticity in Music 1989. *Honours:* Commendatore della Republica Italiana; Dr hc (Purdue Univ.). *Current Management:* Schmidt Artists International, Inc., 59 East 54th Street, Suite 83, New York, NY 10022, USA. *Telephone:* (212) 421-8500. *Fax:* (212) 421-8583. *E-mail:* info@schmidtart.com. *Website:* www.schmidtart.com. *Address:* Orchard House, 5040 Buttonwood Crescent, Indianapolis, IN 46228-2323 (home). *Telephone:* (317) 259-0916 (home).

LERDAHL, Fred, BMus, MFA; American composer and music theorist; *Fritz Reiner Professor of Musical Composition, Columbia University*; b. 10 March 1943, Madison, WI; m. 1980, three d. *Education:* Lawrence Univ., Princeton Univ. *Career:* Prof. of Music, Univ. of California at Berkeley 1969–71, Harvard Univ. 1971–79, Columbia Univ. 1979–85, and Univ. of Michigan 1985–91; Prof. of Music, Columbia Univ. 1991–94, Fritz Reiner Prof. of Musical Composition 1994–; residency at IRCAM 1981, American Acad. in Rome 1987; works commissioned by the Fromm Music Foundation, the Koussevitzky Music Foundation, the Juilliard Quartet, the Pro Arte Quartet and the Spoleto Festival. *Compositions include:* Piano Fantasy 1964, String Trio 1966, Wake for soprano and chamber ensemble 1968, Aftermath for three singers and chamber ensemble 1973, Chords for orchestra 1974–83, Eros for mezzo-soprano and chamber ensemble 1975, Imitations for flute, viola and harp 1977, First String Quartet 1978, Waltzes for violin, viola, cello and bass 1981, Episodes and Refrains for wind quintet 1982, Second String Quartet 1982, Beyond the Realm of Bird for soprano and chamber orchestra 1984, Fantasy Etudes for chamber ensemble 1985, Cross-Currents for orchestra 1987, Waves for chamber orchestra 1988, Marches for clarinet, violin, cello and piano 1992, Without Fanfare for winds and percussion 1994, Quiet Music for orchestra 1994, Time after Time for chamber ensemble 2000, Imbrications for chamber ensemble 2001, Oboe Quartet 2002, Chasing Goldberg for piano 2004, Duo for Violin and Piano 2005, Spirals for chamber orchestra 2006, The First Voices for percussion ensemble and singers 2007, Third String Quartet 2008. *Publication:* A Generative Theory of Tonal Music (co-author) 1983, Tonal Pitch Space 2002. *Honours:* Hon. DFA (Lawrence Univ.) 1999; Koussevitsky Prize 1966, Composer Award, American Acad. of Arts and Letters 1971, 1988, Guggenheim Fellowship 1974. *Current Management:* c/o Becky Starobin, 200 Clinton Avenue, New Rochelle, NY 10801, USA. *Telephone:* (914) 654-9270. *E-mail:* bridgerec@aol.com. *Website:* www.bridgerecords.com. *Address:* Department of Music, Columbia University, 602 Dodge, M.C. 1824, Broadway at 116th Avenue, New York, NY 10027, USA (office). *Telephone:* (212) 854-1295 (office). *E-mail:* awl1@columbia.edu (office). *Website:* www.fredlerdahl.com.

LESCOVAR, Monika; cellist; b. 15 March 1981, Kreutztal, Germany. *Education:* Funktional Musical Pedagogie School, Zagreb, Musikhochschule Lubeck. *Career:* debut at Int. Tchaikovsky Competition for Young Musicians, Dendai 1995; Overseas Concert for Children Competition, Japan; solo performances, Hungarian State Symphony Orchestra, The Eurovision Festival, Budapest 1993; Philharmonia Hungarica, UNICEF Concert 1994; Moscow Philharmonic, Zagreb 1994; Sendai Philharmonic, Sendai 1995;

Slovenian Philharmonic, Slovenia 1996; Symphony Orchestra of Seville 1997; Zagreb Philharmonic, the Zagreb soloists, the Croatian Chamber Orchestra, the Dubrovnik Orchestra, Litvania Chamber Orchestra; recitals worldwide. *Recordings:* two albums. *Honours:* first prize Int. Tchaikovsky Competition for Young Musicians, Sendai 1995, second prize Janigro Competition, Zagreb 1996, third prize Rostropovich Competition, Paris 1997.

LESSER, Laurence, BA; American cellist; b. 28 Oct. 1938, Los Angeles, CA; m. Masuko Ushioda 1971; one s. one d. *Education:* Harvard Univ., Fulbright Scholar in Cologne with Gaspar Cassadò, studied with Gregor Piatigorsky in Los Angeles. *Career:* concert performances in USA, Europe, Japan and South America; appearances with Boston Symphony, Los Angeles Philharmonic, London Philharmonic and other major orchestras; asst to Piatigorsky, Univ. of Southern California, Los Angeles; teacher, Peabody Inst., Baltimore; Visiting Prof., Toho School of Music, Tokyo; teacher, New England Conservatory, Boston, MA, apptd Pres. 1983–96 (retd); full-time cello and chamber music faculty mem., NEC. *Recordings:* Schoenberg/Monn Concerto; Lazarof Concerto; Chamber Music in Heifetz-Piatigorsky Series.

LESSING, Kolja, DipMus; German violinist, pianist, composer and musicologist; *Professor of Violin, Hochschule für Musik, Stuttgart*; b. 15 Oct. 1961, Karlsruhe; m. Barbara Busch 2001; two s. one d. *Education:* studied violin in Basel, Switzerland, Hansheinz Schneeberger masterclasses, studied piano with Peter Efler, conducting with Berthold Goldschmidt. *Career:* debut violin recital at Ettlingen Castle 1981; world-wide performances in recital, chamber music and with orchestras as violinist and pianist; also performs as violin duo with Ingolf Turban, violin/piano duo with Anton Kuerti and duo violin/poetry with Elazar Benyoëtz; numerous premieres of solo violin pieces; has had violin pieces and concertos dedicated to him by Haim Alexander, Abel Ehrlich, Tzvi Avni, Jacqueline Fontyn, Berthold Goldschmidt, Dimitri Terzakis, Hans Vogt, Ursula Mamlok and others; Prof. of Violin, Hochschule für Musik, Stuttgart 2000–; regular masterclasses, Banff Centre for the Arts. *Compositions include:* various works for solo violin, solo clarinet, two clarinets and violin, Ravelesken for two violins. *Recordings include:* Westhoff: Complete Solo Violin Suites; Telemann: 12 Fantasias for solo violin; Székely/Veress/Bartók: Solo Violin Sonatas, Pioneers and Exiles, Solo Violin Music from Israel; Strasfogel: Piano Music, Hommage à Ysaÿe; Wladimir Vogel: Complete Piano Music; Reizenstein: Solo Sonatas, Reger: Complete Works for Violin and Orchestra. *Publications:* contribs to Dissonance, Neue Zeitschrift für Musik, various books on exiled composers and 20th century music. *Honours:* Preis der Deutschen Schallplattenkritik 1992, 2008, Johann-Wenzel-Stamitz Sonderpreis 1999, Deutscher Kritikerpreis für Musik 2008. *Address:* Steinbachtal 52, 97082 Würzburg, Germany (home). *Telephone:* (931) 67905 (home). *Website:* www.kolja-lessing.de.

LESTER, Richard; British cellist; *Professor of Cello, Guildhall School of Music and Drama* and *Royal College of Music*; b. 1959, England. *Education:* Royal Coll. of Music, London with Amaryllis Fleming, Düsseldorf Hochschule für Musik und Darstellende Kunst, Germany with Johannes Goritzki. *Career:* concerto and recital soloist and chamber musician; performs both on period and modern instruments; Prin. Cello, Chamber Orchestra of Europe and previously of Orchestra of the Age of Enlightenment; performed as concerto soloist with Chamber Orchestra of Europe under Claudio Abbado, Nikolaus Harnoncourt, Roger Norrington, Paavo Berglund and Myung Whun Chung; soloist with Sándor Végh and Salzburg Camerata, and in UK with Ulster Orchestra, Scottish Chamber Orchestra, BBC Scottish and Manchester Camerata; has also appeared as dir/soloist with Orchestra of the Age of Enlightenment, Acad. of St Martin-in-the-Fields, Irish Chamber Orchestra, and in Montréal and Québec with Les Violons du Roy; Founder-mem. Domus ensemble 1979–, toured world-wide and recorded most of piano quartet repertoire; Founder-mem. Florestan Trio 1995, performed Beethoven cycle at Wigmore Hall, London 2005, regular performances at South Bank, in Edinburgh, Aldeburgh, Cheltenham, at BBC Proms and at other major festivals, tours in Europe, USA, Japan, S America, Israel, Australia and NZ, own annual UK summer festival in Peasmarsh, E Sussex; mem. London Haydn Quartet; Prof. of Cello, Guildhall School of Music and Drama, London, Royal Coll. of Music, London, Birmingham Conservatoire; performs on a cello by G.B. Rogeri, Brescia, *c.* 1710. *Recordings include:* more than 40 albums, including Piano Quartets by Fauré (Gramophone Award for Best Chamber Music Record 1999) 1986, Dvořák, Brahms, Mozart and Mendelssohn, Schubert's Trout Quintet and Adagio and Rondo Concertante, works by Martinů, Suk, Kodály and Dohnányi, complete cello repertoire of Mendelssohn, complete works of Mendelssohn for cello and piano with Susan Tomes, Boccherini Cello Sonatas on period instruments, Schumann Trios (with the Florestan Trio) (Gramophone Award for Best Chamber Music Record) 1999, Haydn String Quartets with London Haydn Quartet. *Honours:* Deutsche Schallplattenpreis 1986, Gramophone Award 1986, prizewinner, Int. Scheveninges Cello Competition 1987, Royal Philharmonic Soc. Award for Chamber Ensemble (with Florestan Trio) 2000. *Current Management:* c/o Sulivan Sweetland, 1 Hillgate Place, Balham Hill, London, SW12 9ER, England. *Telephone:* (20) 8772-3470. *Fax:* (20) 8673-8959. *E-mail:* info@sulivansweetland.co.uk. *Website:* www.sulivansweetland.co.uk; www.florestantrio.com (home); www.londonhaydnquartet.co.uk (home); www.coeurope.com (home).

LETHIEC, Michel; French clarinettist; *Professor, Conservatoire de Paris*; b. 11 Dec. 1946, Poitiers; m. Françoise Lethiec; two d. *Education:* studied in Bordeaux and at the Paris Conservatoire. *Career:* concerto engagements with the Monte Carlo Philharmonic, Radio France Philharmonic, Ensemble Orchestre de Paris and the Lausanne Chamber Orchestra; British appearances with the English Chamber Orchestra, Acad. of St Martin-in-the-Fields and the Scottish Ensemble; recitals and chamber concerts with Leonard Rose, Aurèle Nicolet, Karl Engel, Joseph Suk, Elly Ameling, Philippe Entremont and the Talich, Vermeer, Takacs and Sibelius Quartets; has premiered works by Ballif, Boucourechliev, Marco, Corigliano and Scolari; festival engagements include Edinburgh and the Eastern Music Festival, USA; concert repertoire includes music by Copland, Crusell, Hindemith, Krommer, Mercadante, Mozart, Pleyel, Spohr, Stamitz and Weber; Boulez Domaines and Busoni Concertino; double concertos by Bruch with viola, Strauss with bassoon, Danzi with flute and Devienne with clarinet; with string quartets plays works by Mozart, Brahms, Weber, Reger, Reicha, Hindemith, Birtwistle, Yun and Bloch; Artistic Dir, Festival Pablo Casals, Prades; world premieres of works of Penderecki; masterclasses at Yale, Boston, Moscow, St Petersburg, Tel-Aviv and Shanghai; Prof. Conservatoire de Paris 1995–. *Recordings:* 25 CDs, including Larsson: 12 Concertinos, Op 45 1991, Kurtag/Ligeti/Pesson 1997, Mozart Clarinet Quintet 1999, Penderecki: Concertos pour clarinette 2000, Jean-Baptiste Vanhal: Concertos for clarinet, oboe and bassoon 2003, Penderecki: Sextet, Clarinet Quartet 2003, Eternal Penderecki 2008, Gershwin: Clarinet and Strings Music 2009, Golijov Klezmer Quintet, Bloch Jewish Life. *Honours:* Chevalier, Ordre nat. du Mérite, des Arts et des Lettres; Interpretation Prize, Int. Competition, Belgrade, Grand Prix du Disque (for Asceses by Jolivet) 1978. *Address:* Les Templiers, 06790 Aspremont, France (home). *Telephone:* (4) 68-96-33-07 (office). *E-mail:* festival.casals@wanadoo.fr (office).

LETNANOVA, Elena, PhD; Slovak concert pianist, author and music critic; b. 23 Oct. 1942, Bratislava; d. of Julius Letnan and Elena Letnanova; m. Andrej Mraz 1966 (divorced); one d. *Education:* Slovak Technical Univ., VSMU, Music Faculty, Bratislava, PWSM, Acad. of Chopin, Warsaw, Poland, Comenius Univ., Bratislava, Comenius Univ. *Career:* debut, solo pianist with Slovak Philharmonic Orchestra, 1969, recital, Carnegie Hall, New York, 1992; taught at univs of Comenius, Dayton, VSMU and STU, Academia Istropolitana; performed at festivals in Rome, Vienna, San Franciscso, Katowice, Ghent, Kromeriz, Munich, Prague, Bratislava and recitals in Madrid, Zaragosa, Zagreb, Berlin, London, Zürich, Baden, Bordeaux, Bologna, Ljubljana, Warsaw, Bruges, New York, Dallas, Denver, Dayton, Washington DC, Fairfax, Berkeley, Rochester, Cortland, Oxford and other cities in Canada, Israel, Netherlands, Croatia, Belgium, Slovakia, Austria, Italy, Japan; Dir, Festival of Flemish Music, Bratislava, 2000. *Recordings:* 30 recordings from Slovak radio, TV, Bratislava and Supraphon Prague: Scarlatti, Liszt, Chopin, Scriabin, Tchaikovsky, Szymanowski, F. Nietzsche to Bartók and J. Cage; Piano Concertos by J. S. Bach, J. Haydn, F. Chopin, H. Górecki, B. Buckinx, J. Hatrik, J. Farkas, G. Gershwin; two CDs with F. Nietzsche Music, Antwerp, 1997, and UNESCO Burgenland, Austria, 2000; performed in three television films (Three Women Artists, 1969, Jan Zelibsky, 1972, Paper's Heads (directed by Hanak) 1996. *Publications:* books: The Piano Interpretation in 17th, 18th, 19th Centuries 1991, The Presence of the Past 1996, Beginner's Slovak 2001; translations: Fundamentals of Musical Thinking by J. Kresanek, The Message from Exile, A. Soljenitsyn 1979, Scenario: Kandinsky-Mussorgsky: Pictures at an Exhibition, multi-media event premiered in Kennedy Union Boll Theatre, Dayton, Ohio 1990, The Sonate by Boris Pasternak 2006; more than 80 articles in journals in Northfield, Illinois, USA, London, Ghent, Delft, Moscow, Prague, Bratislava, Olomouc (Moravia), Brussels. *Honours:* Winner, Special Prize, Chopin Competition, Czech Repub. *Current Management:* Slovak Music Centre, Michalska 10, 81536 Bratislava, Slovakia. *Telephone:* (2) 5443-4003. *E-mail:* smetanova@hc.sk. *Address:* Mudronova 95, 81104 Bratislava, Slovakia (home). *Telephone:* (2) 6280-4323 (home). *E-mail:* letnanova@ba.telecom.sk (home). *Website:* elenaletnanova.slke.org.

LEVAILLANT, Denis, MPhil; French composer and pianist; *Owner, Denis Levaillant Music*; b. 3 Aug. 1952, Paris; m. Christine Rigaud 1972; one s. one d. *Education:* studied in Nancy and at Univ. of Paris Sorbonne and CNSMDP, Paris. *Career:* debut as concert pianist 1972; first composition recorded, Radio France 1975; many occupations as producer and artistic dir; Owner, Denis Levaillant Music; mem. SACEM, SACD, SPEDIDAM, ADAMI. *Compositions include:* representative works: Le Baigneur (opéra-bouffe) 1976, Douze Mouvements for piano 1980, Piano Transit for piano and tape 1983, Les Pierres Noires for chamber choir 1984, OPA MIA (opera) 1987–89, Les Couleurs de la Parole for orchestra 1990–91, Tombeau de Gesualdo for chamber choir 1994–95, Echo de Narcisse concerto for piano and orchestra 1995–96, Le Clair l'Obscur for string quartet No. 2 1996–97, Paysages de Conte for grand orchestra 1997–98, La Petite Danseuse (ballet) 2002, L'Opéra de la Lune for orchestra 2005, Images-Etudes for piano 2006–08, Trio 2008, Les Musiciens de Brême 2009, Music is The Film (for reeds quartet) 2011. *Recordings:* 22 albums. *Publications include:* L'Improvisation Musicale 1981, (revised edn) 1996, Le Piano 1986, (revised edn) 2009, Les Musiciens de Brême 2011, Eloge du musical 2012; contrib. to Le Monde de la Musique 1981–83. *Honours:* Villa Medici 1983, Italia Prize 1988. *Address:* 19 Paris-Forêt, 77760 Achères La Forêt, France (home). *Telephone:* 1-64-24-43-98 (office). *E-mail:* denis.levaillant@wanadoo.fr (home). *Website:* www.denislevaillant.net.

LEVI, Yoel, MA; Romanian/American conductor; b. 16 Aug. 1950, Romania; m. *Education:* Tel-Aviv and Jerusalem Acads of Music, Guildhall School of Music, UK, studied under Mendi Rodan, Franco Ferrara, Kiril Kondrashin.

Career: grew up in Israel; Asst to Lorin Maazel Cleveland Orchestra for six years, Resident Conductor 1980–84; Music Dir Atlanta Symphony Orchestra (ASO) 1988–2000, extensive European tour 1991, Music Dir Emer. 2000–; Prin. Conductor Brussels Philharmonic 2001–07; Prin. Guest Conductor Israel Philharmonic Orchestra, US tour 2004; Music Adviser to Flemish Radio Orchestra; Prin. Conductor Orchestre Nat. d'Ile de France 2005–12; frequent guest conductor of orchestras throughout N America, Europe and the Far East; conducted Stockholm Philharmonic at Nobel Prize Ceremony 1991; performed at Opening Ceremonies of Centennial Olympic Games 1996; apptd first Music Adviser to Israel Festival for 1997/98 seasons; opera conducting debut La Fanciulla del West at Teatro Comunale, Florence 1997; has also conducted Carmen at Lyric Opera of Chicago, Makropoulus Case by Janacek in Prague, Puccini's Edgar with Orchestra Nat. de France (released as live performance on CD by Radio France), with ASO: Mozart's Magic Flute, The Abduction from the Seraglio, Bartok's Bluebeard's Castle; Distinguished Visiting Prof., Univ. of Georgia School of Music. *Recordings:* more than 40 recordings on different labels with various orchestras, including Cleveland Orchestra, London Philharmonic, Philharmonia Orchestra, Atlanta Symphony Orchestra, of music by Barber, Beethoven, Brahms, Copland, Dohnanyi, Dvorak, Hindemith, Kodaly, Mahler, Mendelssohn, Mussorgsky, Nielsen, Prokofiev, Puccini, Ravel, Rossini, Saint-Saens, Schoenberg, Shostakovich, Sibelius, Stravinsky and Tchaikovsky. *Honours:* Chevalier des Arts et des Lettres 2001; Hon. DFA (Oglethorpe Univ., USA) 1997; won First Prize Conductors' Int. Competition Besançon, France 1978, Best Orchestra of the Year (awarded to ASO), Int. Classical Music Awards 1991–92. *Current Management:* Kaylor Management Inc., 130 West 57th Street, Suite 6A, New York NY 10019, USA. *Telephone:* (212) 977-6779. *E-mail:* hughkaylor@msn.com. *Website:* www.hughkaylor.com.

LEVI MINZI, Carlo, DipMus; pianist; b. 10 Dec. 1954, Milan, Italy. *Education:* Giuseppe Verdi Conservatory, Milan, Tchaikovsky Conservatory, Moscow, Curtis Inst. of Music, Philadelphia. *Career:* recitals and appearances with various orchestras in Europe and USA 1972–; television and radio broadcasts on national stations in Italy, Switzerland, France, Spain, Austria, Germany, Poland, Bulgaria, USA and Mexico; Vice-Pres. Classical Frontiers, New York, USA. *Composition:* completion of Schubert's F Sharp Minor Sonata (with Quirino Principe) 1983, (first performed Town Hall, New York 1984, recorded WDR, Cologne 1985).

LEVIN, Robert David; American pianist, conductor, musicologist, theorist and academic; b. 13 Oct. 1947, Brooklyn, NY; s. of Gerald Harold Levin and Beatrice Ann Spieler Levin; m. 1st Christine Noël Whittlesey 1974 (divorced 1991); m. 2nd Ya-Fei Chuang 1995. *Education:* Harvard Univ., studied with Stefan Wolpe, Louis Martin, Nadia Boulanger, Hans Swarowsky. *Career:* solo and chamber appearances, conducting appearances throughout Europe, USA, Australia and Asia 1970–; pianist, New York Philomusica 1971–2000; Head Theory Dept, Curtis Inst. of Music, Philadelphia 1968–73; Prof. of Music, School of the Arts, State Univ. of NY at Purchase 1972–86; Prof. of Piano, Staatliche Hochschule für Musik, Freiburg, Germany 1986–93; Dwight P. Robinson Jr Prof. of Music, Harvard Univ. 1993–2013; Visiting Prof., The Juilliard School, New York 2014–; Artistic Dir Sarasota Music Festival 2007–; Pres. Int. Johann Sebastian Bach Competition, Leipzig 2001–; mem. jury, numerous int. competitions. *Compositions:* Bach reconstructions (of missing obbligato lines in cantata arias), Flute Sonata in A BWV 1032; Mozart completions: Requiem, Mass in C minor, Concerto for piano, violin, orchestra in D, Rondo for clarinet and strings in A, Quintet for clarinet and strings in B flat, Symphonie Concertante for flute, oboe, horn, bassoon and orchestra in E flat, Larghetto and Allegro in E flat for two pianos, Oboe Concerto in F, Horn Concertos in E flat and in D, Sonata for piano four hands in G, various short piano pieces, Piano Sonata movements in G minor and B-flat major, Piano Trio in D minor (three movements), Violin Sonata in C, violin sonata movements in B-flat, G, A; Beethoven completions: Duo for violin and cello in E-flat, Cadenzas to Violin Concerto; Schubert completions: Piano Pieces D916B, 916C, Sonata in F-sharp minor D571/604/570; Cadenzas to Hoffmeister Viola Concerto, Lebrun flute concertos, Mozart Concertos for violin, flute, oboe, horn, harp and bassoon, Stamitz Viola Concerto, clarinet concertos. *Recordings:* Mozart Sonatas for piano four hands (with Malcolm Bilson), Music for two pianos (with Malcolm Bilson), Brahms and Hindemith: Complete Viola/ Piano Sonatas (with Kim Kashkashian), Complete Beethoven Piano Concertos (with ORR and John Eliot Gardiner), Mozart Concertos (with AAM and Christopher Hogwood), Haydn Four Piano Trios, Schubert Sonatas, Schubert four-hand works (with Malcolm Bilson), Complete Bach harpsichord concertos, English Suites, The Well-Tempered Clavier, Asturiana: Songs by Spanish and Argentine Composers (with Kim Kashkashian), Dutilleux: Complete Piano Music, Stanley Walden Five Similes for piano, Maquettes for two pianos (with Ya-Fei Chuang), Mendelssohn Capriccio brillant Op. 22, Double Concerto in A-flat (with Ya-Fei Chuang), Bochum Symphony Orchestra, Steven Sloane, Gershwin Preludes and Songbook, Beethoven works for cello and piano (with Steven Isserlis), Bernard Rands music for one and two pianos (with Ursula Oppens). *Publications:* Who Wrote the Mozart Four Wind Concertante? 1988, Sightsinging and Ear Training Through Literature (with Louis Martin) 1988; contrib. numerous articles to books and periodicals, texts in harmony and counterpoint published privately; contrib. to Mozart-Jahrbuch, Early Music, various musicological congress reports and Festschriften, Performance Practice, The New Grove, The Mozart Compendium, Eighteenth-Century Keyboard Music, The Cambridge Companion to Music. *Honours:* Hon. mem. American Acad. of Arts and Sciences; Dr hc (Eastman School of Music) 1996, (New England Conservatory) 2001, (Curtis Inst. of Music) 2009, ('Gheorghe Dima' Music Acad., Cluj, Romania) 2009; Copley Foundation grant for composition 1961, Lili Boulanger Memorial Fund Prize 1966, 1971. *Current Management:* c/o ARTRA Artists Management, Inc., 555 W Madison, Suite 2110, Chicago, IL 60661, USA. *Telephone:* (312) 648-4100. *Fax:* (312) 648-0600. *E-mail:* artra@aol.com. *Website:* www.artra.com. *Address:* Music Department, Harvard University, Cambridge, MA 02138, USA (office). *Telephone:* (617) 495-2791 (office). *Fax:* (617) 496-8081 (office).

LEVIN, Walter; violinist and academic; b. 6 Dec. 1924, Berlin, Germany. *Education:* Juilliard School, New York with Ivan Galamian. *Career:* co-founded the La Salle String Quartet at the Juilliard School 1949, with many concerts featuring modern composers and the quartets of Beethoven; European debut 1954; composers who have written for the ensemble include Hans Erich Apostel, Earle Brown, Henri Pousseur, Mauricio Kagel, György Ligeti, Penderecki and Witold Lutoslawski; quartet-in-residence, Colorado Coll. 1949–53, then Cincinnati Coll., Conservatory of Music, quartet disbanded 1988; jury mem. Int. String Quartet Competition, London 2000; Prof., Cincinnati Coll., Conservatory of Music. *Recordings include:* Works by Berg, Schoenberg, Webern and Zemlinsky; Beethoven's Late Quartets.

LEVINE, Gilbert, AB, MA; American conductor; b. (Gilbert Isidore Levine), 22 Jan. 1948, New York, NY; s. of Morris Levine and Sara Levine; m. Dr Vera Kalina-Levine. *Education:* Reed Coll., Juilliard School of Music, Princeton Univ., Yale Univ., studied with Manuel Zegler, Stephen Maxym, Sherman Walt, Arthur Mendel, Lewis Lockwood, Edward T. Cone, James Webster, Nadia Boulanger at Fontainbleau, Luise Vosgerchian at Dartmouth, Jacques-Louis Monod, Milton Babbitt, J. K. Randall, Claude Palisca, Gilbert Kalish, Franco Ferrara in Siena, Italy. *Career:* int. debut with Orchestre Philharmonique de Radio France, Paris 1973; guest conductor with various major N American and European orchestras, including debuts with NDR Symphony Orchestra, Hamburg 1977, Royal Philharmonic Orchestra, London 1978, Deutsches Symphonie-Orchester, Berlin 1980, Minnesota Orchestra 1984, Toronto Symphony 1986, Czech Nat. Orchestra, Prague 1986, New York Philharmonic Orchestra 1986, Dresden Staatskapelle 1986, San Francisco Symphony 1986, Philadelphia Orchestra 1986, RAI Symphony Orchestra, Rome 1988, Israel Chamber Orchestra 1990, Baltimore Symphony 1995, Bayerische Staatsorchester, Munich 1995, St Paul Chamber Orchestra 1995, Orchestre de la Bastille, Paris 1994, Montreal Symphony 2000, London Philharmonic 2000, Philharmonia Orchestra, London 2000, Orchestra of Saint Luke's, New York 2005, WDR Symphony Orchestra, Cologne 2007, Lyric Opera of Chicago Orchestra 2012, Chicago Symphony Chorus 2012; Music Dir Kraków Philharmonic Orchestra 1987–93; mem. Advisory Council, Princeton Univ. Music Dept; Assoc. Fellow, Trumbull Coll., Yale. *Televised concerts:* Reykjavik Arts Festival (Vladimir Ashkenazy, Founder) Closing Concert, 20 June 1982, Sinfóníuhljómsveitinn (Iceland Symphony Orchestra) and Iceland Symphony Choir, Glinka: A Life for the Tsar (excerpts), Mussorgsky: Boris Godunov (excerpts), soloist: Boris Christoff, RÚV – Icelandic Nat. Broadcasting 1982, A Musical Offering from the Vatican, Orchestra of RAI/Roma, Choirs of RAI, Kraków Philharmonic and Warsaw Philharmonic 1988, Brahms 'Ave Maria', Penderecki 'Stabat Mater, Dvořák Mass in D, RAI/Roma/European Broadcasting Union (EBU) 1988, PBS broadcast as 'A Musical Offering from the Vatican: A Papal Concert' 1992, Papal Concert to Commemorate the Shoah, Royal Philharmonic Orchestra, Coro della Filharmonia Romana. Bruch Kol Nidre, Beethoven Ninth Symphony (Third Movt), Schubert Psalm 92, Excerpt of the Bernstein Third Symphony ('Kaddish'), Bernstein Chichester Psalms (Movts 2 and 3), RAI/ EBU, PBS (WNET) 1994, Jubilee Creation, Philharmonia Orchestra and Chorus, Haydn: The Creation 2000, US broadcast by Maryland Public Broadcasting/PBS, Concert for the 80th Birthday of His Holiness Pope John Paul II, Haydn: The Creation. Philharmonia Orchestra and Chorus, RAI/EBU 2000, A Thousand Years of Music and Spirit, London Philharmonic Orchestra and Choir, Bogurodzica, Gorecki Third Symphony (Second Movt), Beethoven Ninth Symphony, Telewizja Polska 2000, US broadcast by WTTW, Concert in Commemoration of the 1st Anniversary of the Terror Attacks of Sept. 11, Sachsische Staatskapelle Dresden and Münchener Bach-Chor, Barber Agnus Dei, Gorecki Totus Tuus, Brahms Ein Deutsches Requiem, Telewizja Polska/ EBU 2002, Papal Concert of Reconciliation, Pittsburgh Symphony Orchestra, Mendelssohn Choir of Pittsburgh, London Philharmonic Choir, Kraków Philharmonic Choir, Ankara Polyphonic Choir, Harbison 'Abraham' (World Premiere), Mahler Second Symphony (First, Fourth, and Fifth Movts), RAI/ EBU 2004, US broadcast by WQED, Pittsburgh, Crossing the Bridge of Faiths: In Memoriam Pope John Paul II, Sachsische Staatskapelle Dresden and Munchener Bachchor, Gorecki Totus Tuus, Brahms Ein Deutsches Requiem, WQED (Pittsburgh)/PBS 2005, Missa Solemnis, Beethoven Missa Solemnis, Royal Philharmonic Orchestra, London Philharmonic Choir, WDR (Köln)/ 3SAT 2005, Bruckner Ninth Symphony, Bruckner Te Deum, WDR Sinfonieorchester (Köln), WDR Rundfunkchor (Köln), NDR Chor (Hamburg), WDR (Köln)/3SAT 2007, From Heart to Heart: Beethoven's Plea for Peace, Missa Solemnis from Cologne Cathedral, Royal Philharmonic Orchestra, London Philharmonic Choir, soloists: Bozena Harasimowicz, Monica Groop, Jerry Hadley, Franz-Josef Selig, co-production of WDR/Koln and Peter Rosen Productions, Inc., WQED Multimedia/Pittsburgh and American Public Television 2008, Music of Majestic Spirit, Anton Bruckner: Symphony 9 and 'Te Deum' from Cologne Cathedral, WDR Symphony Orchestra, WDR Radio Choir (Cologne), NDR Choir (Hamburg), soloists: Anja Harteros, Liliana Nikiteanu, Christian Elsner, Franz-Josef Selig, co-production of WDR/Koln and Peter Rosen Productions, Inc., WQED Multimedia/Pittsburgh 2010, Out of Many, One – a Musical Offering from Chicago – in the Spirit of John Paul, Bogurodzica, Edward. T. Cone: Psalm 91 (1948), J.S. Bach: Magnificat in D BWV 243, Beethoven: Symphony 3, 'Eroica', Lyric Opera of Chicago Orchestra, Chicago Symphony Chorus, soloists: Amanda Majeski, Sara Mingardo, Antonio Poli, John Relyea, co-production: Peter Rosen Productions, D2 Digital, WTTW/Chicago 2012, A Celebration of Peace Through Music: Copland, Fanfare for the Common Man; Verdi Sanctus (Messa da Requiem); Gorecki Totus Tuus; Bernstein Chichester Psalms; Brahms Symphony 1; Orchestra of Saint Luke's, Washington Choral Arts Society, Kraków Philharmonic Choir; Theodore Nesbitt, Boy Solo (Choir of St Paul's Cathedral, London); WETA (Washington, DC), European Broadcast Union 2015. *Recordings:* 16 broadcast concerts world-wide, ten concerts for US Public Television (WNET, WTTW, WQED, WETA). *Publication:* The Pope's Maestro (memoir) 2010 (Papieski Maestro 2012). *Honours:* Pontifical Kt Commdr, Equestrian Order of St Gregory the Great 1994, Silver Star of St Gregory 2005, Kt Grand Cross of St Gregory the Great 2015. *Address:* 1622 Locust Street, Philadelphia, PA 19103, USA.

LEVINE, James; American musician, conductor and pianist; *Music Director, Metropolitan Opera;* b. 23 June 1943, Cincinnati, Ohio; s. of Lawrence M. Levine and Helen Levine (née Goldstein). *Education:* Walnut Hills High School, Cincinnati, The Juilliard School. *Career:* Asst Conductor, Cleveland Orchestra 1964–70; Prin. Conductor, Metropolitan Opera, New York 1973–, Music Dir 1976–, Artistic Dir 1986–2004; Music Dir Ravinia Festival 1973–93, Cincinnati May Festival 1974–78; Chief Conductor, Munich Philharmonic 1999–2004; Music Dir UBS Verbier Festival Youth Orchestra 2000–04; Music Dir Boston Symphony Orchestra 2004–11; Guest Conductor, Philadelphia Orchestra 2015; regular appearances as conductor and pianist in Europe and the USA with orchestras including Vienna Philharmonic, Berlin Philharmonic, Chicago Symphony, Philadelphia Orchestra, Philharmonia, Dresden Staatskapelle, Boston Symphony, New York Philharmonic, Israel Philharmonic, Salzburg and Bayreuth Festivals; conducted Metropolitan Opera premieres of I Vespri Siciliani, Stiffelio, I Lombardi (Verdi), The Rise and Fall of the City of Mahagonny (Weill), Lulu (Berg), Porgy and Bess (Gershwin), Oedipus Rex (Stravinsky), Idomeneo, La Clemenza di Tito (Mozart), Erwartung, Moses und Aron (Schönberg), La Cenerentola (Rossini), Benvenuto Cellini (Berlioz), The Ghosts of Versailles (Corigliano) (world premiere), The Great Gatsby (Harbison) (world premiere); Conductor of Salzburg Festival premieres of Offenbach's Les contes d'Hoffmann 1980 and Schönberg's Moses und Aron 1987; conducted Munich Philharmonic Orchestra at the BBC Proms 2002, Boston Symphony 2007; led more than a dozen concerts on the Three Tenors World Tour 1996–2000. *Recordings include:* over 100 albums of symphonic works, chamber music, lieder and song recitals, solo piano music and 36 complete operas, including Wagner: Der Ring Des Nibelungen (Grammy Award for Best Opera Recording 2013). *Honours:* Dr hc (Univ. of Cincinnati, New England Conservatory, Northwestern Univ., State Univ. of New York, The Juilliard School); Grammy Awards for audio recordings of Orff's Carmina Burana, Mahler's Symphony No. 7, Brahms' A German Requiem, Verdi's La Traviata (film soundtrack), Wagner's Das Rheingold, Die Walküre, Götterdämmerung, Strauss' Ariadne auf Naxos, Ravel's Daphnis et Chloé; Cultural Award of New York City 1980, Smetana Medal 1987, Musical America's Musician of the Year Award, Gold Medal, Nat. Inst. of Social Sciences 1996, Nat. Medal of Arts 1997, Anton Seidl Award 1997, Lotus Award 1997, Kennedy Center Honors 2002, World Econ. Forum Crystal Award 2003, Metropolitan Opera Guild Opera News Award 2006, Nat. Endowment for the Arts Opera Award 2008, Award in the Vocal Arts, Bard Coll. 2009, Ditson Conductors Award, Columbia Univ. 2009, George Peabody Medal, Johns Hopkins's Peabody Conservatory 2010. *Address:* Metropolitan Opera, Lincoln Center, New York, NY 10023, USA (office). *Telephone:* (212) 799-3100 (office). *Website:* www.metopera.org (office).

LEVINSKY, Ilya; singer (tenor); b. 1965, Baku, Azerbaijan. *Education:* Baku Acad. of Music. *Career:* soloist with the Baku Opera 1987–; with Israel Philharmonic summer opera 1991–; mem. Komische Opera Berlin with leading roles in Falstaff, La Traviata, Don Giovanni, Così fan tutte and Die Zauberflöte –1998; season 1996–97 as Dimitri in Boris Gudunov with the Frankfurt Opera, in The Nose by Shostakovich for Netherlands Opera and as Sinodal in Rubinstein's The Demon at the Bregenz Festival; further engagements include Tamino in Die Zauberflöte at Salzburg Festival, Komische Oper and Frankfurt Opera; Lensky in Eugene Onegin at the Tivoli Festival and Števa in Jenůfa at the Salzburg Festival 2001. *Recordings include:* Rachmaninov Aleko and Francesca da Rimini 1997, Lady Macbeth of Mtsensk and Shostakovich Japanese Songs 2006, Tchaikovsky Songs; Kalman's Die Herzogin von Chicago, under Richard Bonynge. *E-mail:* ilyalevinsky@aol.com (office). *Website:* www.ilyalevinsky.com.

LEVIT, Igor; Russian pianist; b. 1987, Nizhny Novgorod. *Education:* Hochschule für Musik, Hannover, studied with Karl-Heinz Kämmerling, Matti Raekallio, Bernd Goetze, Lajos Rovatkay and Hans Leygraf. *Career:* moved with family to Hannover, Germany aged eight; has given recitals at Palais des Beaux Arts Brussels, Amsterdam Concertgebouw, Berlin Philharmonie, Queen Elizabeth Hall, London, Tonhalle Zürich, Stockholm Konserthus, Alte Oper Frankfurt, Prinzregententheater Munich, Laeiszhalle Hamburg, Konzerthaus Berlin, Copenhagen's Black Diamond, Birmingham Town Hall, Wigmore Hall, London (three solo recitals), also at Germany's summer festivals, Ludwigsburger Schlossfestspiele, Klavierfestival Ruhr,

Kissinger Sommer Festspiele (Artist-in-Residence), Mecklenburg-Vorpommern (Artist-in-Residence) and Schubertiade, Austria; New York City recital debut at Park Avenue Armory 2014; has appeared with numerous orchestras including Orchestre Philharmonique du Luxembourg, BBC Symphony Orchestra, WDR Sinfonieorchester, Danish Nat. Symphony Orchestra, London Philharmonic Orchestra, Staatskapelle Dresden (V. Jurowski), WDR Sinfonieorchester (Saraste), Deutsches Symphonie-Orchester Berlin, Konzerthausorchester Berlin, Vienna Symphonic Orchestra, NDR Radiophilharmonie Hannover and Royal Scottish Nat. Orchestra; debut Vienna Musikverein replacing Maurizio Pollini in recital and Helene Grimaud with City of Birmingham Symphony Orchestra and Andris Nelsons 2014; chamber music partners include Lisa Batiashvili, Simon Bode, Ning Feng, Julia Fischer, Sol Gabetta, Christiane Karg, Jörg Widmann, Maxim Vengerov and Tabea Zimmermann. *Recordings include:* The Late Beethoven Sonatas (BBC Music Magazine Newcomer of the Year Award 2014, Echo Klassik Award for Solo Recording of the Year (19th century)/Piano 2014) 2013, Bach Partitas 2014. *Honours:* First Prize, Int. Hamamatsu Piano Acad. Competition, Japan, Silver Prize, Best Performer of Chamber Music, Best Performer of Contemporary Music and Audience Prize, Arthur Rubinstein Competition, Tel Aviv, Royal Philharmonic Soc. Young Artist Prize 2014, scholarships to Studienstiftung des Deutschen Volkes and Deutsche Stiftung Musikleben. *Current Management:* c/o Kristin Schuster, IMG Artists, 152 West 57th Street, #5, New York, NY 10019, USA. *Telephone:* (212) 994-3530. *E-mail:* kschuster@imgartists.com. *Website:* www.imgartists.com; igor-levit.de.

LEWIS, Brenda; American singer (soprano); b. 2 March 1921, Harrisburg, PA. *Education:* studied in Philadelphia. *Career:* sang in The Bartered Bride with the Philadelphia Opera Company; sang with New York City Opera 1943–67, with debut as Santuzza in Cavalleria Rusticana, in San Francisco 1950 as Salome, at Metropolitan Opera from 1952 as Musetta in La Bohème, Marina in Boris Godunov, Barber's Vanessa and Rosalinde in Die Fledermaus, and at Chicago 1965 as Marie in Wozzeck; guest appearances in South America.

LEWIS, Daniel, BM; American conductor; b. 10 May 1925, Flagstaff, AZ. *Education:* San Diego State Coll., studied with Nino Marcelli in San Diego, with Eugen Jochum in Munich, Germany. *Career:* Leader, Honolulu Symphony (during war service); Asst Conductor, San Diego Symphony 1954–56, Leader and Assoc. Conductor 1956–59; Music Dir, Pasadena Symphony 1972–83, notably in neglected 18th-century and American music; guest conductor with the Los Angeles Philharmonic, Oakland Symphony, Atlanta Symphony, Minnesota Orchestra, Utah Symphony, Seattle Symphony, Los Angeles Chamber Orchestra and the Louisville Orchestra; Chair of Conducting Studies Dept, Univ. of Southern California.

LEWIS, Jeffrey, BMus, MMus, PhD, ARCM; British composer; b. 28 Nov. 1942, Port Talbot, South Wales; one s. one d. *Education:* Univ. Coll., Cardiff, Univ. of Wales, studied with Boguslaw Schaffer in Kraków, Poland, with Don Banks in London, with Stockhausen and Ligeti in Darmstadt, Germany. *Career:* pianist, Paris Chamber Ensemble 1967–68; Lecturer in 20th-Century Composition Techniques and Experimental Music, City of Leeds Coll. of Music, England 1969–72; Lecturer Dept of Music, Univ. Coll. of North Wales, Bangor 1973–87, Sr Lecturer 1987–93. *Compositions:* orchestral: Praeludium, Piano Concerto, Mutations I, Antiphony, Fanfares with Variations, Aurora, Memoria, Limina Lucis; instrumental: Mutations II, Esultante, Momentum for organ, Threnody for piano, Trilogy for piano, Tableau for piano, Fantasy for piano, two Cadenzas for piano, Night Fantasy for piano duet; chamber: Epitaph for Abelard and Heloise, Antiphon, Litania, Stratos, Ritornel, Mobile II, Time-Passage, Wind Quintet Sonante, Piano Trio, Cantus, Teneritas, Dead Leaves; choral: Carmen Paschale, Pro Pace, Hymnus Ante Somnum, Westminster Mass, Lux Perpetua, Sequentia de Sancto Michaele, Recordatis. *Recordings:* Sea of Glass, Dreams: Dances and Lullabies for harp, Jeffrey Lewis: Threnody, Cantus, Teneritas, Sonante, Trilogy. *Publications:* contrib. article 'The Current State of British Cathedral Music', to Choir and Organ 1993. *Address:* Crafnant, Park Crescent, Llanfairfechan, Gwynedd LL33 0AU, Wales. *Telephone:* (1248) 680776.

LEWIS, Keith; New Zealand singer (tenor); b. 6 Oct. 1950, Methven. *Education:* studied in New Zealand and in London. *Career:* sang in premiere of Tavener's Thérèse at Covent Garden returning as Rossini's Almaviva and as Bellini's Tebaldo and Tamino in Magic Flute; appearances worldwide in such operas as Don Giovanni, Armide, La Clemenza di Tito, Eugene Onegin, as Mozart's Ferrando, Belmonte, and Monteverdi's Giove; concert engagements in Damnation of Faust, Haydn's Creation, Schumann's Paradies und der Peri, The Dream of Gerontius, Bach B minor Mass, and Beethoven's 9th; further appearances include Mendelssohn's Elijah with Colin Davis, Verdi's Requiem, Mozart's Requiem and Bach Mass in B minor; sang in the opening concert of the 1991 Promenade Concerts, in Idomeneo at Glyndebourne 1991, in Britten's Serenade in London, and Haydn's Creation under Sinopoli; sang Alwa in Berg's Lulu at the Berlin Staatsoper 1997; Gregor in The Makropulos Case at Toulouse 1998; season 2000–01 as Bizet's Zurga and Verdi's Paolo in Sydney and Posa (Don Carlos) at Melbourne. *Recordings include:* Rossini's Tancredi, Otello and Moses; Gluck's Alceste; Don Giovanni conducted by Haitink; Messiah under Solti; Masses by Haydn under Marriner; Paradies und der Peri under Albrecht; Berlioz Lelio, Te Deum and Requiem under Inbal; Berlioz Requiem under Bertini; Mozart Requiem; Beethoven's 9th, Wand and Giulini; Salome under Mehta. *Current Management:* Aria's di Novella Partacini & Alexandra Plaickner, Via Josef Weingartner 4, 39022

Lagundo, Italy. *Telephone:* (0473) 200200. *Fax:* (0473) 222424. *E-mail:* info@arias.it. *Website:* www.arias.it.

LEWIS, Michael, AO; Australian singer (baritone); b. 1948, Adelaide, SA. *Education:* studied in Adelaide and at the London Opera Centre. *Career:* sang first at Wexford Festival, then with Glyndebourne Festival and Touring Operas, ENO, WNO, Opera North, Scottish Opera, Frankfurt Opera, Deutsche Oper Berlin, Netherlands Opera, La Fenice Venice, San Diego, Pittsburgh, Opera Australia, all other Australian companies and New Zealand Opera; repertoire includes 12 Verdi roles, notably Rigoletto (2010 season celebrating over 30 years with this role), also Puccini, Bizet, Mozart, Wagner, R.Strauss, Donizetti, Rossini, Massenet, Bellini, Britten, and more; notable world premieres as Jeronimus Cornelisz in Richard Mills' Batavia 2001, and The Major in John Haddock's Madeleine Lee 2004; 2011–12 performances include Macbeth, Capriccio, La Traviata, Marriage of Figaro, Madama Butterfly (Opera Australia); concert repertoire with orchestras worldwide includes Carmina Burana, Belshazzar's Feast, The Messiah, Elijah, Mahlers' 8th Symphony and song cycles, Dream of Gerontius, Brahms Requiem, War Requiem, Songs and Dances of Death, The Wound Dresser etc. *Recording:* Schubert Lieder Orchestrations with Adelaide Symphony Orchestra. *Honours:* Green Room Award (for Rigoletto). *Current Management:* Patrick Togher Artists Management, Suite 25, 450 Elizabeth Street, Surry Hills, 2010 NSW, Australia. *Telephone:* (2) 9319-6255. *Fax:* (2) 9319-7611. *E-mail:* pjtogher@ozemail.com.au. *Website:* members.ozemail.com.au/~pjtogher/index.htm.

LEWIS, Oliver; British violinist; b. 12 May 1966, London, England. *Education:* Purcell School of Music, London, Konservatorium für Musik, Bern, Switzerland, studied with Carl Pini, David Takeno, Sándor Végh, Aaron Rosand, Igor Ozim, Wen Xun Chen. *Career:* debut with National Children's Orchestra of Great Britain aged 12; solo concert tours, England, France, Spain, Portugal, Switzerland, Germany, Austria, Netherlands, Georgia; broadcasts worldwide; Swiss concerto debut with Bern Symphony Orchestra, Casino Berne 1990; Concertmaster and soloist, Heidelberg Chamber Orchestra 1991; masterclasses at Dartington Int. Summer School; concert performances with the Royal Philharmonic Orchestra 1999; Leader, Ceruti Ensemble, London. *Recordings include:* English Romanticism, music by Ferguson, Goossens and Ireland; English Romanticism II, music by Elgar and Goossens; solo violin music of Ennio Morricone (for film The Inverse Cannon) 1999; Malcolm Arnold String Quartets 2001. *Address:* 8 Colmans Wharf, 45 Morris Road, London, E14 6PA, England (home).

LEWIS, Paul, AGSM, FGSM; British pianist; b. 20 May 1972; m. Bjørg Vaernes Lewis; three c. *Education:* Chetham's School of Music with Ryszard Bakst, Guildhall School of Music and Drama with Joan Havill, studied with Alfred Brendel. *Career:* has performed with orchestras, including London Symphony, London Philharmonic, Royal Philharmonic, Philharmonia, Chicago Symphony, Los Angeles Philharmonic, Leipzig Gewandhaus, Swedish Radio Symphony, Vienna Symphony, Royal Liverpool Philharmonic, Bavarian Radio Symphony, Hong Kong Philharmonic, Hallé, Scottish Chamber Orchestra, BBC Symphony, Melbourne Symphony, Sydney Symphony, Bamberg Symhpony, Mahler Chamber Orchestra; has worked with leading conductors, including Sir Colin Davis, Bernard Haitink, Sir Andrew Davis, Christoph von Dohnanyi, Wolfgang Sawallisch, Sir Mark Elder, Marin Alsop, Daniel Harding, Richard Hickox, Emmanuel Krivine, Adam Fischer, Edo de Waart, Dimitri Kitajenko; concert appearances world-wide; regular appearances at BBC Proms and festivals, including Edinburgh Int., Schubertiade, Roque d'Antheron, Schleswig Holstein, Rheingau, Klavierfestival Ruhr; performed Schubert Piano Sonata Series at venues throughout the UK 2003; recorded and performed complete cycle of Beethoven Piano Sonatas at venues across Europe and N America 2005–07; first pianist in history of BBC Proms to play complete Beethoven concerto cycle in a single season 2010. *Recordings:* Schubert, Piano Sonatas in A minor D784 and C major D95 (Diapson d'Or de l'Année, France 2002), Schubert, Piano Sonatas D959 and D960 (Edison Instrumentalist Award, Holland 2004), Mozart, Piano Quartets (with Leopold String Trio), Schubert, Trout Quintet (with Leopold String Trio), Liszt, Sonata in B minor (Edison Instrumentalist Award 2005), Beethoven Complete Piano Sonatas (Gramophone Awards for Best Instrumental Recording and Record of the Year) 2008, Schubert, Winterreise (with Mark Padmore - Gramophone Best Solo Vocal recording 2010) 2009, Schubert Die Schöne Müllerin (with Mark Padmore), Beethoven Complete Piano Concertos (Preis der Deutschen Schallplattenkritik 2010), Schubert Piano Duets (with Steven Osborne) 2010. *Honours:* Hon. DMus (Southampton); Diapason d'Or de l'Année 2002, South Bank Show Classical Music Award 2003, Royal Philharmonic Soc. Instrumentalist of the Year Award 2003, Edison Award (Instrumental Category) 2004, 2005, Premio Accad. Chigiana Siena 2006, Gramophone Awards for Best Solo Vocal Recording 2010, Limelight Award Australia for Best Solo Performance 2010. *Current Management:* c/o Thomas Hull, Ingpen & Williams, 7 St George's Court, 131 Putney Bridge Road, London, SW15 2PA, England. *Telephone:* (20) 8874-3222. *Fax:* (20) 8877-3113. *E-mail:* th@ingpen.co.uk. *Website:* www.ingpen.co.uk; www.paullewispiano.co.uk.

LEWIS, Richard, MVO, MA, MSc, FRSA, FTCL, PGDip; British singer (tenor), educationalist, counsellor and psychotherapist; b. Trowbridge, Wilts., England. *Education:* Metropolitan Univ. of London, Trinity Coll. of Music with John Carol Case, Guildhall School of Music and Drama with Ellis Keeler, studied with Ilse Wolf, Metanoia Inst., Univ. of Wales, Newport. *Career:* debut, Wigmore Hall as tenor soloist with Praetorius Consort; sang with BBC Singers and other leading choirs; much work as oratorio soloist; Gentleman in Ordinary of HM's Chapel Royal, St James's Palace 1976–2002; Head of Counselling and Clinical Supervision Service, Trinity Laban Conservatoire of Music and Dance 2001–12; now an integrative psychotherapist and clinical supervisor in pvt. practice; soloist with Opera for All and in world premieres in St Paul's Cathedral and South Bank; mem. Royal Soc. of Musicians, Equity; Sr Accred mem. British Asscn for Counselling and Psychotherapy; Registered mem. UK Council for Psychotherapy. *Recordings include:* numerous as chorister, Music for the Christening of Prince William, Britten's Journey of the Magi (with James Bowman and Graham Trew), Royal Composers with Her Majesty's Chapel Royal Choir, St James's Palace. *Honours:* Queen's Silver Jubilee Medal 1977, Queen's Golden Jubilee Medal 2002, Oriana Madrigal Soc. Prize, Joseph Maas Prize for Tenors, Beryl Searle Scholarship, Vaughan Williams Scholarship, Mitchell City of London Scholarship, Alfred and Catherine Howard Scholarship, Corporation of London Scholarship, Max Hecht Scholarship. *Address:* Melin-y-Grogue, Llanfair Waterdine, Knighton, Powys, LD7 1TU, Wales.

LEWIS, William; American singer (tenor); *Professor of Voice and Opera, University of Texas, Austin*; b. 23 Nov. 1931, Tulsa, Okla. *Education:* Univ. of Colorado, Texas Christian Univ., New York Univ. *Career:* debut at Fort Worth in Gianni Schicchi 1953; early appearances in Cincinnati, San Francisco and Dallas; New York City Opera in Die Fledermaus 1957, Metropolitan Opera in Salome, Elektra, Boris Godunov, Jenůfa, The Queen of Spades, La Bohème and Francesca da Rimini from 1958; sang Aeneas in New York production of Les Troyens 1983 and at Spoleto in premiere of Barber's A Hand of Bridge 1959; sang at San Francisco as Loge in The Ring 1984–85, Wexford Festival and La Scala in Humperdinck's Königskinder 1986–87 and title role in premiere of Testi's Riccardo III; Spoleto Festival as Aegisthus in Elektra 1989; sang Arbace in Idomeneo at San Francisco 1989 and in premiere of Blimunda by Azio Corghi at Teatro Lirico Milan 1990; other roles include Pollione in Norma, the Emperor in Die Frau ohne Schatten, Don José, Offenbach's Hoffmann, Radames, Gabriele Adorno in Simon Boccanegra and Strauss's Guntram; sang Pollux in Die Liebe der Danaë at Avery Fisher Hall, New York 2000 (concert); currently Prof. of Voice and Opera, Univ. of Texas, Austin; Founder and Pres. Franco-American Vocal Acad. *Recordings include:* Adolar in Euryanthe. *Address:* Franco-American Vocal Academy, 16 Depot Street, Elgin, TX 78621, USA (office). *Telephone:* (512) 285-6604 (office). *E-mail:* fava.france@hotmail.com (office). *Website:* favaopera.org (office). *Current Management:* c/o Sardos Artists Management, 180 West End Avenue, Suite 22B, New York, NY 10023, USA. *Telephone:* (212) 874-2559. *Fax:* (212) 721-7815. *E-mail:* info@ritasardos.com. *Website:* www.ritasardos.com.

LEWKOVITCH, Bernhard; Danish composer and organist; b. 28 May 1927, Denmark. *Education:* Royal Danish Conservatory of Music, studied with Poul Schierbeck and Jorgen Jersild, and in France. *Career:* Organist, Sankt Ansgar Catholic Church, Copenhagen 1947–63, Cantor 1953–63; Organist and Cantor, Church of Holy Sacrament, Copenhagen 1973–; founder and Leader, Schola Gregoriana Men's Choir, Schola Cantorum Mixed Choir (both later named Schola Cantorum). *Compositions include:* vocal music and instrumental music for orchestra, ensemble, piano and organ, including: Mass for two corui and mixed choir, Songs of Solomon for tenor and clarinet, horn and bass trombone, Deprecations for tenor, horn and bass trombone, Preacher and Singer for tenor and piano, six Partitas for five brass instruments (vols I–II), Improperia Per Voce (Good Friday), three Tasso Madrigali for mixed choir, Responsoria for mixed choir (Good Friday), Helligandskoraler (Holy Ghost Chorales) for four brass players 1980, Il Cantico delle Creature for eight male voices, Alle meine Kinder (48 motets) 1996, five English Madrigals for tenor, clarinet, horn and bassoon 1997, Orgelchoräle: Notizen zu den Lübecher-Dialoguen, ten Songs for baritone and piano. *Honours:* Carl Nielsen Prize 1997.

LEZHNEVA, Julia, MMus; Russian singer (soprano); b. Dec. 1989, Sakhalin; d. of Mikhail and Alfiya Lezhnev. *Education:* Moscow State Conservatory Academic Music Coll., Cardiff Int. Acad. of Voice, studied with Dennis O'Neill, Guildhall School of Music with Yvonne Kenny. *Career:* at age 18, performed at opening of Rossini Festival with Juan Diego Flórez under Alberto Zedda 2008; debut at Salzburg Mozartwoche Festival in Mozart's Great Mass (2nd soprano) with Marc Minkowski 2010; sang at Classic BRIT Awards, Royal Albert Hall, London 2010 and Les Victoires 2012; opera roles have included Fiordiligi in Cosí fan tutte, Urbain in Les Huguenots at La Monnaie in Brussels and Asteria in Handel's Tamerlano with Plácido Domingo at Salzburg Festival 2011; has worked with singers including Anna Netrebko, Dame Kiri Te Kanawa, Philippe Jaroussky and Max Emmanuel Cencic and with conductors including J. C. Spinosi, Fabio Biondi, Diego Fasolis, Franz Welser-Möst, Louis Langrée, Vladimir Fedoseev, René Jacobs, Sir Roger Norrington and Giovanni Antonini at venues in Europe, USA and Asia including Barbican Hall in London, Lincoln Center Avery Fisher Hall in New York, Cleveland Severance Hall, Salle Pleyel, Théâtre des Champs Elysées and Salle Gaveau in Paris, Wiener Konzerthaus, Berlin Staatsoper, Théâtre Royal de la Monnaie in Brussels, Bolshoi Theatre, Theater an der Wien and Grand and Glinka Halls of St Petersburg Philharmonic and at Mostly Mozart, Verbier, Beaune, Torroella and Misteria Paschalia Festivals; toured with Il Giardino Armonico; recitals across Russian Fed. and in Europe. *Recordings:* solo: Rossini Arias 2011, Alleluia 2013; other: Bach's B-minor Mass 2008, Vivaldi: Ottone in villa 2010, Handel: Alessandro 2012, Pergolesi: Stabat

Mater 2013, Motets by Vivaldi, Handel, Porpora and Mozart 2013. *Honours:* Grand Prize, Elena Obraztsova Int. Opera Singing Competition 2007, Opernwelt Young Singer of the Year 2011. *Current Management:* c/o Bill Palant, IMG Artists, Carnegie Hall Tower, 152 West 57th Street, 5th floor, New York, NY 10019, USA. *Telephone:* (212) 994-3527. *E-mail:* bpalant@ imgartists.com. *Website:* www.imgartists.com; www.julialezhneva.com (office).

LI, Ao; Chinese singer (baritone); b. Dezhou. *Education:* Shangdong Normal Univ. *Career:* Merola Opera Program, San Francisco Opera 2010; debut, as Ascanio Petrucci in Lucrezia Borgia, San Francisco Opera 2011, Lorenzo in I Capuleti e i Montecchi, Sciarrone in Tosca and Ben Weatherstaff in The Secret Garden 2012–13; regular recitals in China. *Honours:* Youth of China Award, Adler Fellowship, First Prize, Plácido Domingo Operalia Competition 2013. *Address:* c/o San Francisco Opera, 301 Van Ness Avenue, San Francisco, CA 94102, USA (office). *Telephone:* (415) 861-4008 (office). *Website:* www.sfopera .com (office).

LI, Bo; Chinese composer; b. 1988, Jilin province. *Education:* Central Conservatory of Music, Beijing, studied with Tang Jian-Ping. *Compositions include:* for Chinese instruments: Dream for guzheng, Memory of Snow for sheng and Chinese orchestra, The Leaves for erhu and piano; other: Moonlight—City Wall—Prose Poem—Chamber Music for 11 instruments, Ten Facets, Encirclement. *Honours:* Paul Hindemith Prize, Schleswig-Holstein Music Festival 2012. *Address:* c/o China Central Conservatory of Music, Bao Street, Xicheng District, Beijing 100031, People's Republic of China.

LI, Hong-Shen; Chinese singer (tenor); b. 1960, Beijing. *Education:* Central Conservatory of Beijing and the Juilliard School with Ellen Faull. *Career:* joined the San Francisco Opera Merola Program, 1987, performing Rinuccio in Gianni Schicchi and Lindoro in L'Italiana in Algeri; further appearances as the Duke of Mantua, Aufidio in Mozart's Lucio Silla, the Italian Singer, Alfredo, Tebaldo, Pirro in Ermione and Leukippos in Daphne with the San Francisco Opera; Other roles include Rossini's Count Almaviva, Steuermann in Fliegende Holländer (debut with the Metropolitan Opera), Nadir, Macduff, Nemorino and Idreno in Semiramide; season 2000–01 as Zerlina at the Met, Handel's Cleopatra for Washington Opera and Manon for Dallas Opera; concert repertoire includes the Verdi Requiem and Mozart's Requiem, Beethoven's 9th Symphony and Rossini's Stabat Mater. *Honours:* Highest Fellowship Scholarship at Central Conservatory of Beijing; Winner, 1991 Metropolitan Opera Competition Nationals; George London Award; Adler Fellow with the San Francisco Opera, 1989–91. *Address:* c/o San Francisco Opera, War Memorial House, Van Ness Avenue, San Francisco, CA, USA.

LI, Ming Qiang; Chinese academic and pianist; b. 1936, Shanghai; m. Li Ben Wang, one d. *Education:* studied piano with Alfred Wittenberg and with Prof. Tatiana Petrovna Kravchenko, St Petersburg Conservatory of Music. *Career:* numerous concerts worldwide, performing with many major orchestras; lectures and masterclasses worldwide, including Carnegie Mellon Univ., Rutgers Univ., Univ. of California at Santa Barbara, Univ. of Illinois, Oberlin Coll. Conservatory of Music, Cincinnati Coll. Conservatory of Music, Yale Univ., School of Music, Acad. of Music in Bucharest and National Taiwan Normal Univ.; Vice-Pres., Shanghai Conservatory of Music 1984–89; Artist-in-Residence, Dept of Music and Fine Arts, Hong Kong Baptist Univ. 1993–97; piano masterclasses at other Hong Kong univs; judge in numerous international piano competitions, including Int. Chopin Piano Competition, China Int. Piano Competition, Hong Kong Int. Piano Competition, Santander Int. Piano Competition, Arthur Rubinstein Int. Piano Master Competition, Van Cliburn Int. Piano Competition, Sydney Int. Piano Competition, Montréal Int. Music Competition and Tchaikovsky Piano Competition; life mem. American Liszt Soc.; hon. mem. Trinity Coll. of Music, London. *Recordings:* repertoire of works by Bach, Beethoven, Brahms, Chopin, Handel, Liszt, Mozart, Rachmaninov and Schubert; piano music by Chinese composers He Luting, Ding Shande, Wan Jianzhong and Zhu Jainer. *Honours:* Hon. mem. Trinity Coll., London 2006; Third Prize, Third Int. Smetana Piano Competition, Prague Spring Festival 1957; First Prize, First George Enescu Int. Piano Competition, Bucharest 1958; Fourth Prize, Sixth Int. Chopin Piano Competition, Warsaw 1960, William Kopell Int. Piano Competition. *Address:* 11B Mansion Building, 846 King's Road, Quarry Bay, Hong Kong (home). *Telephone:* 2696-3763 (home). *Fax:* 2696-3114 (home).

LI, Xincao; Chinese conductor; *Principal Conductor, China National Symphony Orchestra;* b. 1971, Hebel Prov. *Education:* Cen. Conservatory of Music, Wiener Musikhochschule, Austria. *Career:* studied with Xu Xin; appearances with many domestic orchestras in China including Cen. Philharmonic Orchestra, Shanghai Symphony Orchestra; Prin. Conductor, Symphony Orchestra of Nat. Ballet of China from 1994; Asst Conductor, Wiener Staatsoper 1997; toured Japan with China Nat. Symphony Orchestra 1999, toured Japan, Australia and Europe 2002; frequent collaborations with Nat. Orchestra de Lille, Besançon Opera House, Copenhagen Philharmonic Orchestra, Tivoli Orchestra, Johannesburg Philharmonic Orchestra, Cape Town Philharmonic Orchestra, Chamber Orchestra of South Africa, Korean KBS Symphony Orchestra, Hong Kong Orchestra, Hong Kong Sinfonietta, Hong Kong Ballet; currently Prin. Conductor, China Nat. Symphony Orchestra; currently Prin. Conductor, Symphony Orchestra of Nat. Ballet Orchestra of China. *Honours:* First Prize, First Nat. Conducting Competition of China 1993, Winner, Carl Nielsen Int. Music Competition 2009. *Address:* China

National Symphony Orchestra, No. 1 Building Section 11, Heping Street, Dongcheng District, Beijing 100013, People's Republic of China (office). *Telephone:* 64211277 (office). *Fax:* 64213541 (office). *E-mail:* cnso@cnso.com .cn (office). *Website:* www.cnso.com.cn (office).

LI, Yundi; Chinese pianist; b. 1982, Chongqing; s. of Li Chuan. *Education:* Sichuan Music Acad. with Dan Zhao Yi, Shenzhen School of Arts, studied with Arie Vardi in Hanover, Germany. *Career:* originally learned to play accordion, started piano lesson aged seven; concert performances in the USA, Europe and Asia 2004, including New York recital debut, Metropolitan Museum. *Recordings include:* Chopin Recital 2002, Liszt Piano Sonata in B minor 2003, Liszt Klaviersonate h-moll 2003, Chopin Scherzi Impromptus 2004, Love Moods 2004, Chopin 4 Scherzi 3 Impromptus 2004. *Honours:* prize winner, Stravinsky Int. Youth Piano Competition 1995, South Missouri Int. Youth Piano Competition, USA 1998, Liszt Int. Piano Competition, Netherlands 1999, China Int. Piano Competition 1999; first prize at the Chopin Int. Piano Competition, Warsaw, Poland 2000. *Current Management:* Columbia Artists Management Inc., 1790 Broadway, New York, NY 10019-1412, USA. *Telephone:* (212) 841 9500. *Fax:* (212) 841 9744. *E-mail:* info@cami.com. *Website:* www.cami.com.

LIANG, Lei, BMus, PhD; American (b. Chinese) composer and academic; *Professor of Composition and Acting Chair of the Music Department, University of California, San Diego;* b. 28 Dec. 1972, Tianjin; m. Takae Ohnishi; one s. *Education:* New England Conservatory of Music, Harvard Univ., studied with Sir Harrison Birtwistle, Robert Cogan, Chaya Czernowin and Mario Davidovsky, also master-classes with Magnus Lindberg, James Tenney, and Chinary Ung at Harvard, and with Georg Friedrich Haas, Toshio Hosokawa and Wolfgang Mitterer at Internationale Ferienkurse für Neue Musik, Darmstadt, Germany. *Career:* first piano lessons aged four; moved to USA as a high school student 1990; Jr Fellow, Soc. of Fellows, Harvard Univ. 1998–2001, taught music theory at Harvard Univ. 2003–06; Visiting Asst Prof. of Music, Middlebury Coll. 2006–07; currently Prof. of Composition, Univ. of California, San Diego, also Acting Chair. Music Dept; Distinguished Visiting Prof., Shaanxi Normal Univ. Coll. of Arts, Xi'an 2004; numerous commissions, including by New York Philharmonic for inaugural concert of Contact! new music series; other commissions and performances from Taipei Chinese Orchestra, Boston Modern Orchestra Project, Berkeley Symphony Orchestra, Heidelberger Philharmonischer Orchester, Thailand Philharmonic, pipa virtuoso Wu Man, Koussevitzky Music Foundation, Fromm Music Foundation, Meet the Composer, Chamber Music America, Nat. Endowment for the Arts, MAP Fund, Mary Flagler Cary Charitable Trust, Manhattan Sinfonietta, Arditti Quartet, Shanghai Quartet, Scharoun Ensemble of the Berlin Philharmonic, San Francisco Contemporary Music Players, New York New Music Ensemble, Boston Musica Viva, among others; Chair. Boston chapter of Nat. Guild for Piano Teachers 2005–06. *Films include:* composed film music for The Giver, Shall We Sing? and incidental music for Der gute Mensch von Sezuan. *Compositions include:* orchestral: Brush-Stroke, for small orchestra 2004, Parallel Gardens, for saxophone orchestra 2006, Harp Concerto, for harp solo and chamber orchestra 2008, Xiaoxiang, concerto for alto saxophone and orchestra 2009/2014, Verge, for string orchestra 2009, Five Seasons, concerto for pipa and string orchestra 2010/ 2014, Tremors of a Memory Chord, for piano and grand Chinese orchestra 2011, Bamboo Lights for small orchestra 2013; also extensive chamber music, and vocal, keyboard, electro-acoustic works. *Recordings include:* March Cathedral 2000, Brush-Stroke 2009, Milou 2011, Verge 2012, Bamboo Lights 2014. *Publications include:* numerous articles about traditional and contemporary Asian music in US and Chinese journals. *Honours:* Hon. Prof. of Composition and Sound Design, Wuhan Conservatory of Music 2000; Derek Bok Distinguished Teaching Award, Harvard Univ., George Whitefield Chadwick Medal, New England Conservatory 1996, Tourjée Alumni Scholarship Award 1996, Aaron Copland Award 2008, ASCAPLUS Award 2008, Paul and Daisy Soros Fellowship 2002–04, Fondazione William Walton Residency Award 2008, named a Young Global Leader, World Economic Forum 2008, Guggenheim Fellowship 2009, Rome Prize, American Acad. in Rome 2011, Alpert/Ragdale Prize in Music Composition 2012, commissioning grant, Serge Koussevitzky Music Foundation 2015. *Address:* UCSD Department of Music, Conrad Prebys Music Center, 9500 Gilman Drive MC 0099, La Jolla, CA 92093-0099, USA (office). *Telephone:* (858) 822-1434 (office). *E-mail:* leiliang@ ucsd.edu (office); leiliang.music@gmail.com. *Website:* musicweb.ucsd.edu (office); www.lei-liang.com.

LIANG, Ning; Chinese singer (mezzo-soprano); b. 1957, Peking. *Education:* studied in Guangdong and Peking, Juilliard School and American Opera Center in New York. *Career:* debut at Central Conservatory Peking, 1983; sang at Peking and Shanghai as Carmen and Rosina, Cenerentola at the 1987 Aspen Festival; Philadelphia and Helsinki, 1988 as Dorabella and Carmen; sang Cherubino in London and Hamburg, 1989–91; La Scala, Milan 1990, as Suzuki in Butterfly; Sang Rosina at Toronto and at the Vienna Festiva, 1992; concert engagements include Beethoven's Ninth in Lisbon and Bellini's Il Pirata in New York; opera engagements include, Ottavia in L'Incoronazione di Poppea (Marseille and Amsterdam), Stephano in Roméo et Juliette (Hamburg), Octavian (Deutsche Oper Berlin and Hamburg) and Sesto in La Clemenza di Tito (Stuttgart). *Recordings include:* Carmen and Le nozze di Figaro. *Honours:* numerous prizes in American competitions: Metropolitan Opera National Council Competition, Rosa Ponselle International Vocal

Competition, Loren L Zachery Competition and the Luciano Pavarotti Competition.

LIAO, Chang-Yong; Chinese singer (baritone); b. 1969. *Career:* many engagements in the Far and East and Europe, notably in operas by Mozart (Le nozze di Figaro) and Massenet, with chansons by Duparc, Debussy and Ravel. *Address:* c/o Mr Wu Xun, Bureau of External Relations, Ministry of Culture, 2 Shatan Beijie, Beijing 100722, People's Republic of China.

LICARET, Nicolae; Romanian pianist, organist and harpsichordist; *Artistic Director, George Enescu Philharmonic Orchestra*; b. 24 Sept. 1943, Bucharest; s. of Valeriu Licaret and Elena Licaret; m. Rodica Licaret; one s. *Education:* Music School George Enescu, Bucharest, Music Acad., Bucharest. *Career:* debut at Dalles Hall, Bucharest 1959; piano teacher, Bucharest Music High School 1966–68; soloist, George Enescu Philharmonic Orchestra, Bucharest 1968–, Artistic Dir 1990–; mem. UNESCO, Union of Romanian Musicians, Rotary Club Old Court of Bucharest, German-Romanian Acad. *Recordings:* Bach's Sonatas, Concertino Ensemble, Concertino Quintet, George Enescu's Pieces, Italian Music, L. Alexandra Symphony, Pan Flute and Organ, Phonogram, Handel Organ Concertos, Mozart Piano Quartets, Aurel Stroe Orestia I, Ave Maria, Rameau Harpsichord Pieces, Nicolae Licaret piano, organ, harpsichord, Brahms Piano Quartets, Enescu cello and piano sonatas, Beethoven's Sonatas for piano and violin, Vox Celeste for organ, Piano Concertos, Poulenc's Concerts for harpsichord, two pianos and organ, Haydn's Trio Pro Arte. *Honours:* Commdr of Cultural Merit, Romania 1999, Commdr, Order of the Star of Solidarity, Italy 2005, Chevalier, Ordre des Arts et des Lettres 2008, Medal of King Mihai I for Loyalty. *Address:* George Enescu Philharmonic Orchestra, 10287 Bucharest, Str. Franklin 1, sect. 1 - Ateneul Român, Romania (office). *Telephone:* (21) 3152567 (office). *Fax:* (21) 3122983 (office). *E-mail:* filarmonicageorgeenescu@yahoo.com (office). *Website:* www .fge.org.ro (office).

LICHTENSTEIN, Romelia; Bulgarian singer (soprano); b. 1965, Sofia. *Education:* studied in Leipzig. *Career:* debut at Chemnitz, 1988, as Rossini's Rosina; appearances at Chemnitz Opera as Pamina, Sandrina in La finta giardiniera and the soprano roles in Les Contes d'Hoffmann; Leipzig Opera from 1992, notably as Mimi and Fiordiligi; Halle Opera from 1996, Tosca, Lucia di Lammermoor, Norma; Handel Festival at Halle, 1996, as Elisa in Tolomeo; Cleofide in Handel's Poro, 1998; Rodelina 2005; Alceste in Admeto 2006; guest appearances as concert singer in Berlin, Hamburg, Stuttgart, Duesseldorf, Madrid, Santander and Bratislava. *Honours:* winner Gera Int. Competition 1990, Barcelona Int. Competition 1990. *Current Management:* Theateragentur Heidi Schäfer, Glauburgstrasse 83, 60318 Frankfurt am Main, Germany. *Telephone:* (69) 283347. *E-mail:* hs@santuzza.de.

LIDDELL, Nona Patricia, MBE, FRAM; British musician; b. 9 June 1927, London; m. Ivor McMahon 1950 (deceased); one d. *Education:* Royal Acad. of Music. *Career:* Leader, English String Quartet 1957–73, Richards Piano Quintet 1964–79, London Sinfonietta 1970–94, London Piano Quartet 2000–04; mem. Schiller Trio 1972–90; Prof. of Violin, Royal Acad. of Music 1978–94; Prof. of Violin and Chamber Music, Trinity Coll. of Music 1994–2006; mem. Royal Soc. of Musicians, Incorporated Soc. of Musicians. *Recordings:* Violin Concerto, Kurt Weill; Phantasie by Schoenberg with John Constable; Gemini by Roberto Gerhard with John Constable; Chamber Music by Martinů, Chausson, Herbert Howells; Brahms' Horn Trio and Berkeley Horn Trio with Schiller Trio; Stravinsky's Soldier's Tale; Chamber Music by Schoenberg; Chamber Music by Cyril Scott; Chamber music by Alan Bush. *Honours:* Worshipful Company of Musicians Cobbett Medal 1993, Hon. FTCL 2006. *Address:* 28B Ravenscroft Park, Barnet, Hertfordshire, EN5 4NH, England (home).

LIDSTRÖM, Mats; Swedish cellist, teacher and composer; b. Stockholm. *Education:* Gothenburg Univ. with Maja Vogl, The Juilliard School, New York with Leonard Rose and Channing Robbins. *Career:* fmr Prin. Cellist Royal Swedish Opera, RPO, Norrköping Orchestra; has performed as soloist with orchestras, including LSO, Acad. of St Martin-in-the-Fields, Scottish SO, Royal Nat. Scottish Orchestra, Deutsche SO, Czech Philharmonic, Dallas Symphony, Los Angeles Philharmonic, Oslo Philharmonic; has appeared at festivals, including Aspen, Kinston, Tenerife, Edin., City of London; teacher Gothenburg Univ. 1992–93; Prof. of Cello, RAM 1993–; has given master-classes at Univ. of Oberlin, San Francisco Conservatory, Cleveland Inst. of Music; Artistic Dir, From Sweden festival 2004–05; transcriptions for cello include works by Stravinsky, Kreisler, Skryabin, J. Strauss, Gershwin, Oscar and Hammerstein. *Compositions:* The Sea of Flowers is Rising Higher for solo cello, Carnival of Venice for violin and two cellos, Christmas Cookies for mezzo-soprano and three cellos, Pastoral and Parody for cello and tuba, No Stopping Now for violin and piano, Maze of Love for voice, piano and symphony orchestra, Interlude for string quartet and orchestra, Suite Tintin for cello and piano. *Recordings:* Musica Sveciae (with Bengt Forsberg) 1994, Kabalevsky, Cello Concerto 1995, Godard and Boëllmann, Cello Sonatas (with Bengt Forsberg) 1996, Swedish Cello Sonatas (with Bengt Forsberg) 1996, Elgar, Cello Concerto (with LSO) 1997, Anne Sofie van Otter, Rendezvous with Korngold 1998, Nadja Salerno-Sonnenburg, Night and Day 1998, Gabriel Pierné/Charles Koechlin, Cello Sonatas 1998, Saint-Saëns, Music for Cello 1999, Schubert, The Trout Quintet 1999, French Cello Music 2001, Smörgasbord 2001, Gunnar de Frumerie, Cello Concerto 2001, Brahms, Clarinet Trio in A minor (with Kjell Fageus) 2003. *Honours:* Hon. ARAM; Palmaer Prize,

Sweden 1998. *Telephone:* (20) 8291-3090 (office). *Fax:* (20) 8291-3090 (office). *E-mail:* info@matslidstrom.com (office). *Website:* www.matslidstrom.com.

LIDTH DE JEUDE, Philip; Dutch singer (baritone, tenor); b. 17 June 1952, Voorburg. *Education:* Curtis Institute and Manhattan School. *Career:* sang at Pennsylvania Opera from 1974, Chicago from 1979; guest appearances elsewhere in USA as Marcello, Enrico (Lucia di Lammermoor), Germont and Gerard in Andrea Chénier; Studied further at Zürich and sang as tenor from 1988, notably at Krefeld Opera as Don José, Riccardo, Radames, Florestan, Bacchus, Peter Grimes and Dimitri in Boris Godunov; Engagements throughout Germany, including Otello at Detmold, 1996; Sang Samson in Netherlands, 1995. *Honours:* prizewinner at Geneva Competition 1981.

LIE, Tom Erik; Norwegian singer (baritone); b. 1965, Oslo. *Education:* Oslo Conservatory, Oslo Studio with Ingrid Bjoner, studied with Theo Adam, Berlin. *Career:* made debut in Düsseldorf 1991; sang at Gelsenkirchen Opera, as Malatesta in Don Pasquale, Silvio in I Pagliacci and Wagner's Wolfram 1993–98; ensemble mem., Oper Leipzig 1998–2001; sang at Deutsche Oper Berlin 2001–04; ensemble mem., Komische Oper Berlin 2004–; repertoire includes Morales in Carmen, Frère Leon in Messiaen's St François, Guglielmo in Così fan Tutte, Papageno in The Magic Flute, Siegfried in Schumann's Genoveva, Wolfram in Tannhäuser, Belcore in L'Elisir d'Amore, Robert Storch in Strauss's Intermezzo, Don Fernando in Fidelio, Conte Almaviva in Le Nozze di Figaro, Gabriel von Eisenstein in Die Fledermaus, Horatio in Hamlet, Don Giovanni in Don Giovanni, Conte Ceprano in Rigoletto, Siegfried in Genoveva, Edwin in The Gypsy Princess; concerts throughout Norway and Germany, also in the Czech Republic, Denmark and Spain. *Honours:* Ingrid Bjoner Scholarship 1995. *Current Management:* Theateragentur Kühnly, Wörthstrasse 31D, 70563 Stuttgart, Germany. *Telephone:* (711) 7802764. *Fax:* (711) 7804. *E-mail:* kuehnly@aol.com. *Website:* www.kuehnly.de.

LIEBECK, Jack; British violinist and academic; *Violin Professor, Royal Academy of Music*; b. 1980, London, England. *Education:* Purcell School of Music, Royal Acad. of Music. *Career:* first public appearance aged 10 as young Mozart for BBC TV; concertos and recitals since age 11; has performed with orchestras including the Hallé (concerto debut), Philharmonia, Moscow State Symphony, Nieuw Sinfonietta Amsterdam, Royal Liverpool Philharmonic, London Philharmonic, English Chamber, Bournemouth Symphony, Lausanne Chamber, Oslo Philharmonic, Royal Philharmonic, Royal Scottish Nat. and Royal Stockholm Philharmonic; toured in UK and abroad with Belgian Nat., English Chamber and Polish Nat. Radio Symphony Orchestras and appeared under conductors including Martyn Brabbins, Gunter Herbig, Alexander Lazarev, Sir Neville Marriner, Sakari Oramo, Libor Pesek, Jukka-Pekka Saraste, Yuri Simonov, Leonard Slatkin, Bramwell Tovey and Barry Wordsworth; also chamber music, and festivals including Australian Festival of Chamber Music, Bath, Bergen, Cheltenham, Harrogate, Kuhmo, Montpellier, Montreux, Reims, Rheingau and Spoleto. *Recordings:* Brahms: Complete Violin Sonatas 2010. *Honours:* Classical Brit Award 2010. *Current Management:* c/o Thomas Hull, Ingpen & Williams Ltd, 7 St George's Court, 131 Putney Bridge Road, London, SW15 2PA, England. *Telephone:* (20) 8874-3222. *E-mail:* th@ingpen.co.uk. *Website:* www.ingpen.co.uk. *E-mail:* direct_to_jack@jackliebeck.com (office). *Website:* www.jackliebeck.com.

LIEBERMAN, Carol, BA, MMus, DMA; American violinist; b. 18 Aug. 1943, New York, NY; m. Mark Kroll 1975; one s. *Education:* City Coll. of New York, Yale Univ. School of Music, studied with Raphael Bronstein and Broadus Erle. *Career:* debut at Carnegie Recital Hall, New York 1975; faculty mem., Boston Univ. School of Music 1979–; Concertmaster, Masterworks Chorale Orchestra 1980–; concerts throughout USA and in Rome, Italy, Antwerp, Caracas, Lisbon and Canada; broadcasts for WGBH Radio-TV and WBUR Radio, Boston, including six-part simulcast series for Maine Public Television; radio and television programmes for Canadian Broadcasting Corporation; fmr mem., Israel Philharmonic Orchestra and Toronto Symphony; Asst Prof., Coll. of Holy Cross 1985–88, Assoc. Prof. 1989–; Co-Dir, Holy Cross Chamber Players 1985–; broadcasts for Radio Nacional de España, Madrid 1985; soloist with Connecticut Early Music Festival 1985–; violinist with Early Music Ensemble of Boston; violinist of Lieberman/Kroll Duo. *Recordings:* albums: Schubert Sonatinas for Violin and Fortepiano, Dohnányi Sonata for Violin, Piano and Second Piano Quintet.

LIEBERMAN, Janis Joy, BMus, MA; American musician (French horn); b. 23 Aug. 1950. *Education:* studied with W. Erol Gomürgen in Ankara, Turkey, Boston Univ. School of the Arts with Harry Shapiro, American Univ., Washington, DC with Ted Thayer, San Francisco State Univ. *Career:* debut as soloist, Mozart Concerto No. 2 and No. 4; Schumann Konzertstück for four horns and orchestra, San Francisco Concerto Orchestra; Israel Sinfonietta Orchestra 1975–79, 1993–95, Principal Horn 1977–79; Jerusalem Symphony 1975–79; Israel Symphony 1994–95; Ensemble EnCor chamber music trio 2000–; mem. Sacramento Philharmonic Orchestra; mem. Int. Horn Soc. *Recordings:* with the Israel Sinfonietta and the Women's Philharmonic. *Honours:* Israel America Cultural Foundation grant 1977. *Address:* Sacramento Philharmonic Orchestra, 3418 Third Avenue, Sacramento, CA 95817, USA (office). *Telephone:* (916) 732-9045 (office). *E-mail:* office@sacphil.org (office). *Website:* www.sacphil.org/orchestra.php (office).

LIEBERMANN, Lowell, BM; American composer, conductor and pianist; b. 22 Feb. 1961, New York, NY. *Education:* Juilliard School, New York; studied composition with David Diamond and Vincent Persichetti; studied conducting with Laszlo Halasz; studied piano with Jacob Lateiner. *Career:* debut at

Carnegie Recital Hall, New York 1978; Composer-in-Residence, Dallas Symphony Orchestra 1999–2002; mem. ASCAP. *Compositions:* Symphony Op. 9, Piano Concerto Op. 11, 2 Piano Sonatas Op. 1, 10 and 82, Sechs Gesänge Nach Gedichten von Nelly Sachs for soprano and orchestra Op. 18, Sonata for viola and piano Op. 13, Missa Brevis for chorus and organ, Song Cycles, Chamber Music, Sonata for flute and piano Op. 24, Quintet for piano, clarinet and string trio Op. 26, Domain of Arnheim Op. 33, Quintet for piano and strings Op. 34, Nocturnes Op. 20, 31, 35, Gargoyles Op. 29, Piano Concerto No. 2 Op. 36 1992, Concerto for flute and orchestra Op. 39 1992, Songs and Piano Pieces, The Picture of Dorian Gray (opera) Op. 45 1995, Sonata for violin and piano Op. 46 1994, Album for the Young for piano Op. 43 1994, Revelry for orchestra, Op. 47 1995, Longfellow Songs Op. 57, Loss of Breath Op. 58, Flute and Harp Concerto Op. 48, Concerto for trumpet and orchestra Op. 64 1999, Nocturne No. 7 Op. 65 for piano 1999, Album Leaf Op. 66 for cello and piano, Symphony No. 2, Op. 67 1999, Three Impromptus Op. 68 for piano 2000, Nocturne Fantasy Op. 69 for two guitars 2000, Dorian Gray: A Symphonic Portrait Op. 70, suite from opera 2000, Pegasus Op. 71 for narrator and orchestra 2000, Rhapsody on a Theme by Paganini Op. 72 for piano and orchestra 2001, The Next Time Op. 73 for baritone and piano 2001, Concerto for violin and orchestra Op. 74 2001. *Recordings:* Piano Music of Lowell Liebermann, Koch International, James Galway plays Lowell Liebermann, BMG, 1998, Symphony No. 2 (Dallas Symphony Orchestra), 2000; numerous recordings on various labels. *Honours:* Grand Prize, Van Cliburn Int. Piano Competition Inaugural Composers' Invitational Competition. *Address:* c/o Theodore Presser Co., 588 North Gulph Road, King of Prussia, PA 19406, USA. *E-mail:* lowell@lowellliebermann.com (office). *Website:* www .lowellliebermann.com.

LIEBOLD, Angela; singer; b. 15 Aug. 1958, Dresden, Germany. *Education:* Dresden Musikhochschule. *Career:* appearances at the Dresden Opera from 1985 in the title role of the premiere of Weise Von Liebe und Tod Des Cornets Christopher Rilke by Siegfried Matthuss; lieder recitals in Russia, Hungary, France and Germany; engagements in opera elsewhere in Germany; teacher of singing, Dresden Musikhochschule from 1983. *Honours:* prizewinner Walter Gruner Lieder Competition, Bach Int., Maria Callas Competition, Athens, and Robert Schumann Competition.

LIEBREICH, Alexander; German conductor; *Artistic Director and Chief Conductor, Polish National Radio Symphony Orchestra;* b. 28 May 1968, Regensburg; m. Simone Geiger; one s. *Education:* Hochschule für Musik und Theater München, Salzburg Mozarteum. *Career:* early work with Claudio Abbado and Michael Gielen; fmr Asst to Edo de Waart, Netherlands Radio Philharmonic Orchestra; Artistic Dir and Prin. Conductor, Munich Chamber Orchestra 2006–; Artistic Dir Tongyeong Int. Music Festival, South Korea 2011–14; Artistic Dir and Chief Conductor, Polish Nat. Radio Symphony Orchestra 2012–; Artistic Dir Katowice Kultura Natura Festival 2015–; guest conductor with numerous orchestras including Concertgebouw Orchestra, Orchestre National de Belgique, BBC Symphony Orchestra, Auckland Philharmonia, Radio Symphony Orchestra Berlin, Munich Philharmonic, Bavarian Radio Symphony Orchestra, NDR Radio Philharmonic, Radio Symphony Orchestra Stuttgart, Dresden Philharmonic, Orchestre Philharmonique de Luxembourg, Osaka Philharmonic, NHK Symphony Orchestra; has performed with soloists such as Lisa Batiashvili, Claron McFadden, Frank Peter Zimmermann and Maxim Vengerov; has also conducted Deutsches Symphonie-Orchester Berlin, NHK Symphony Orchestra and Konzerthaus Orchestra Berlin; visited N and S Korea with Junge Deutsche Philharmonie, giving first Korean performances of Bruckner Symphony No. 8 2002; returned to N Korea as Guest Prof., in collaboration with Goethe Inst. and DAAD (German Academic Exchange Service) 2012; mem. Gen. Meeting of Goethe Inst. *Film:* Pyongyang Crescendo 2005 (documentary). *Recordings include:* with Munich Chamber Orchestra: works by Joseph Haydn and Isang Yun 2008, Bach Violin and Voice, with Hilary Hahn, Christine Schäfer and Matthias Goerne 2009, Rossini overtures 2011, Toshio Hosokawa 2011, Mozart's Requiem with Nuria Rial, Marie-Claude Chappuis, Christoph Prégardien, Franz-Josef Selig and the Bayerischen Rundfunks Chorus 2013. *Honours:* Kirill Kondraschin Conducting Competition Prize. *Current Management:* Janet Marsden, Dunstan House, 14a St Cross Street, London EC1N 8XA; c/o ICA Artists, 28 Queen Street, London, EC4R 1BB, England. *E-mail:* jmarsden@icartists.co.uk. *Website:* www.icartists.co.uk/artists/alexander -liebreich. *Address:* Polish National Radio Symphony Orchestra, plac Wojciecha Kilara 1, 40-202 Katowice, Poland (office). *E-mail:* nospr@nospr .org.pl (office). *Website:* www.nospr.org.pl (office); alexanderliebreich.de.

LIÉGEON, Samuel; French organist and pianist; *Organist, Saint Pierre de Chaillot, Paris;* b. 25 Oct. 1984, Besançon. *Education:* Conservatoire de Besançon, Conservatoire de St-Maur, Conservatoire Nat. Superieur de Musique, Paris. *Career:* has studied with Thierry Escaich, Eric Lebrun, Philippe Lefebvre, Jean François Zygel, Pierre Pincemaille; Organist, Saint Pierre de Chaillot, Paris 2009–. *Honours:* Winner, Concours Int. d'Improvisation, Leipzig 2008, First Prize, Boëllmann-Gigout Improvisation Competition, Strasbourg 2008, Winner, Int. Organ Improvisation Competition, Haarlem 2010. *Address:* Association des Grandes Orgues, 22 Cloître Notre-Dame, 28000 Chartres, (office); Saint Pierre de Chaillot, 28 rue de Chaillot, 75116 Paris, France (office). *Telephone:* (2) 37-36-67-48 (office); 1-47-20-12-33 (office). *Fax:* 1-47-23-87-84 (office). *E-mail:* orgues.chartres@yahoo.fr (office). *Website:* orgues.chartres.free.fr (office); www.chaillotgrandesorgues .com (office).

LIELMANE, Rasma; Latvian/Mexican violinist; b. 1958, Latvia. *Education:* Moscow Conservatoire with David Oistrakh. *Career:* appearances with the leading orchestras of Europe and North America; collaborations with the Munich Philharmonic, Berlin Symphony and the Dresden Philharmonic; appearances in London, Hamburg, Toronto, Montréal, Nice and Milan. *Honours:* first prize Int. Violin Competition, Sofia, prizewinner Vianna de Motta Competition, Portugal, Nicola Paganini Competition, Italy, Maria Canals Competition, Montréal, Tibor Varga Prize, Switzerland.

LIENBACHER, Edith; Austrian singer (soprano); b. 1959, St Andra, Kartnen. *Education:* Klagenfurt Conservatory, Vienna Musikhochschule. *Career:* mem. Vienna Volksoper 1985–; roles include Janáček's Vixen, Leila in Les Pêcheurs de perles and Lauretta in Gianni Schicchi; Bregenz, Aix and Salzburg Festivals 1985, 1989, 1993; sang Papagena in Die Zauberflöte; sang Mozart's Susanna at Cologne 1996; other roles include Fortuna in Handel's Giustino, Despina, Adele in Die Fledermaus and Christel in Der Vogelhändler; sang Mozart's Constanze at the Vienna Volksoper. *Honours:* winner Richard Tauber Competition, London 1984, Kammersängerin 1999. *Current Management:* c/o Benedikt Weingartner International Artists Management, Bösendorferstrasse 4/12, 1010 Vienna, Austria. *Telephone:* 1-4896154 (office). *Fax:* 1-4896154-44 (office). *E-mail:* office@bwartists.at (office). *Website:* www .bwartists.at (office).

LIFCHITZ, Max; American composer, conductor and pianist; *Professor of Music, State University of New York;* b. 11 Nov. 1948, Mexico City, Mexico. *Education:* Juilliard School of Music, New York, Harvard Univ., Berkshire Music Center. *Career:* debut in Mexico City 1955; pianist, Juilliard Ensemble; Lecturer, Nat. Music Camp, Michigan; Faculty mem. Manhattan School of Music; Asst Prof. of Music, Columbia Univ., New York; Exec. Dir and Conductor North South Consonance Inc.; Assoc. Prof. of Music, State Univ. of NY –2004, Prof. 2004–; Chair. Music Dept, State Univ. of NY at Albany 1995–98, Chair. Latin American Studies Dept 1996–99, 2010–14; Amos Eminent Scholar in Latin American Studies, Columbus State Univ. 2006. *Compositions include:* Intervencion for violin and orchestra, Night Voices #13 for cello and orchestra, Kaddish for choir and chamber ensemble, Tiempos, Tientos for accordion, Vignettes for woodwind quintet, Yellow Ribbons No. 40 for chamber orchestra, Mosaico Latinoamericano for flute and orchestra. *Recordings:* Affinities for solo piano, Transformation for Cello, Yellow Ribbons No. 2, Canto de Paz, Yellow Ribbons No. 21, Consorte, Winter Counterpoint for flute, oboe, bassoon, viola, Exceptional String Quartet, Of Bondage and Freedom; ten albums of American piano music. *Honours:* First Prize, Gaudeamus Competition 1976, Guggenheim Fellow 1982, Individual Artist Award, New York State Council on the Arts, Excellence in Research Award, State Univ. of NY at Albany 2005, ZETHUS Fund Lifetime Achievement Award 2009. *Address:* North/South Concerts, PO Box 5108, Albany, NY 12205-0108, USA (office). *Telephone:* (518) 442-4187 (office); ns.concerts@att.-net (office). *Website:* www.northsouthmusic.org (office).

LIFSCHITZ, Konstantin, ARAM, FRAM; Russian pianist, conductor and teacher; *Professor, Hochschule für Musik, Lucerne;* b. (Konstantin Yakovlevich Lifschitz), 10 Dec. 1976, Kharkov, Ukrainian SSR, USSR; s. of Yakov Lifschitz and Era Lifschitz; m. Galina Lifschitz. *Education:* Gnessin School Moscow, Int. Piano Foundation, Lago di Como, Royal Acad. of Music, UK. *Career:* concerts in the West from 1990; collaboration with violinist Vladimir Spivakov, including tour of Japan with the Moscow Virtuosi; further concerts with Monte Carlo Philharmonic, Moscow Philharmonic in Munich, Moscow State Symphony Orchestra (concerto debut) and St Petersburg Philharmonic on tour to Europe, with Yuri Temirkanov 1997; chamber music with Lynn Harrell, Gidon Kremer and Mischa Maisky; contracted to appear at Shostakovich Festival in Tokyo, performing Shostakovich Piano Concerto No. 1, and also for recital tour of Japan including performance with Tokyo Symphony Orchestra; debut with Chicago Symphony Orchestra 1999; Prof., Musik Hochschule, Lucerne 2008–. *Recordings include:* Bach, Schumann, Medtner, Scrjabin 1990, Beethoven, Chopin, Schumann, Liszt, Scrjabin 1990, Live in Milano 1993, Goldberg-Variationen 1994, Der Wanderer 1994, Scriabin and Rachmaninov 1995, Couperin, Brahms and Rachmaninov 1995, Schumann and Chopin 1997, En Concert à Montréal 1997, Tokyo Recital 1998, Joue 1999, Chopin, Schönberg, Webern, Messiaen 1999, Mozart's Concertos Nos 21 and 27 2001, Konstantin Lifschitz in Concert, Franz Schubert 2006, Beethoven's Bagatelles 2006, J. S. Bach's Musikalisches Opfer 2007, Bach Well-Tempered Clavier (DVD) 2008, Art of the Fugue 2009, Brahms Concerto No. 2 2010, Gottfried von Einem Concerto No. 1 2010, Schubert 2010, and others. *Honours:* St Sergius Order; Russian Cultural Foundation New Name Scholarship 1990, German ECHO Classic Record Prize 1995, Rowenna Award 2007. *Current Management:* c/o Gaby Schmidt, Concerto Winderstein GmbH, Leopoldstrasse 25, 80802 Munich, Germany. *Telephone:* (89) 38384610. *Fax:* (89) 337938. *E-mail:* schmidt@winderstein.de. *Website:* www.winderstein.de. *E-mail:* konstlifschitz@hotmail.com (office). *Website:* www.konstantinlifschitz.com.

LIGENDZA, Catarina; singer (soprano); b. 18 Oct. 1937, Stockholm, Sweden; m. Peter Ligendza. *Education:* studied in Vienna and Wuerzburg with Henriette Klink, Stuttgart with Trudi Eipperle and Saarbrücken with Josef Greindl. *Career:* debut in Linz 1963 as Mozart's Countess; sang in Brunswick and Saabrücken 1966–69 as Verdi's Elisabeth de Valois and Desdemona and Strauss' Arabella; sang at Hamburg Staatsoper from 1967, Deutsche Oper Berlin; Staatsoper Stuttgart from 1970, and Staatsoper Vienna from 1971 with Wagner's Ring, Isolde with Carlos Kleiber, Lisa in The

Queen of Spades, and Elsa in Lohengrin with Placido Domingo; sang at Staatsoper München in Fliegende Holländer, Lohengrin from 1978 and Götterdämmerung; sang Arabella at La Scala 1970 and at Salzburg Easter Festival under Karajan; Metropolitan Opera debut in 1971 as Beethoven's Leonore; Bayreuth Festival 1971–77 as Brünnhilde and Isolde 1986–87 as Elsa in Lohengrin and Isolde; Covent Garden debut 1972 as Senta in Der fliegende Holländer; sang in Wagner's Ring with Deutsche Oper Berlin 1987 in Japan; retired from the stage 1988. *Films and television productions:* Der fliegende Holländer, Lohengrin as Elsa, Freischütz as Agathe, and Elektra as Chrysothemis. *Recordings:* Third Norn in Götterdämmerung; Arias by Handel; Eva in Meistersinger von Nürnberg; Lars Erik Larsson, Förkläddgud; Three Songs, Rangström; Tristan und Isolde, conducted by Carlos Kleiber.

LIGETI, András, DipMus; Hungarian conductor; b. 1953. *Education:* Franz Liszt Academy, Budapest, studied with András Korodi. *Career:* Orchestra Leader, Hungarian State Opera House, 1976–80; Regular concerts as solo violinist in Europe and Canada; Associate Conductor, with György Lehel, the Budapest Symphony Orchestra, 1985, with tours of the UK, Europe and America; regular conductor at the Budapest Opera; British debut 1989 with the BBC Symphony Orchestra, returning to conduct the BBC Scottish Symphony Orchestra and BBC Philharmonic in 1991, with Bartók's Duke Bluebeard's Castle, Weber's 2nd Piano Concerto and Mahler's 5th Symphony. *Current Management:* The Music Partnership, New Broad Street House, New Broad Street, London, EC2M 1NH, England. *Telephone:* (20) 7840-9590. *E-mail:* office@musicpartnership.co.uk.

LIGI, Josella; singer (soprano); b. 10 Jan. 1948, Imperia, Italy. *Education:* studied in Milan. *Career:* debut at La Scala 1972, as a Priestess in Aida; sang in Milan and appeared as guest in Turin, Valencia and Toulouse 1974, as Mimi, Desdemona and Aida; Verona Arena 1983, and Ravenna Festival 1984, as Amelia in Un Ballo in Maschera; La Scala and Wexford Festival 1985, in Rossi's Orfeo and as Catalani's Wally; Turin 1986, as Alice Ford; US debut 1988, as the Trovatore Leonora for Newark Opera; concerts include Debussy's Le Martyre de St Sebastian, Salzburg Festival 1986. *Recordings include:* Sesto in Handel's Giulio Cesare.

LIIMOLA, Heikki Sakari, MMus; Finnish choir conductor and teacher; *Teacher in Choir Conducting, Sibelius Academy;* b. 24 March 1958, Tampere; m. 1st Katri Liimola 1983–2005; three d.; m. 2nd Päivi Liimola; two s. *Education:* Sibelius Acad., studied with Prof. Jorma Panula and Prof. Eric Erikson. *Career:* Asst Conductor and Singer, Finnish Radio Chamber Choir 1982–87; has been conductor with Chorus Cantorum Finlandie, EOL Chamber Choir, Helsinki, Savonlinna Opera Festival Chorus, Tampere Philharmonic Choir; currently conductor with Harju Chamber Choir, Tampere Opera Choir, Chamber Choir of Sibelius Acad., Klemetti Inst. Chamber Choir, and others; Artistic Dir Tampere Int. Choir Festival 1990–2004, mem. Artistic Bd 2004–; teacher of choir conducting, voice teacher, many courses in Finland and abroad; mem. Int. Fed. of Choral Music. *Recordings:* Harju Youth Choir, Christmas Music 1980, EOL Chamber Choir, Sacred and Profane 1990, Male Choir of Finnish Church Musicians 1990, Jaakko Ryhanen and Opera Festival Chorus 1993, Savonlinna Opera Festival Chorus and Helsinki Philharmonic Orchestra 1995, Tampere Philharmonic Choir and Tampere Philharmonic Orchestra 1998, 2000, Harju Chamber Choir, Church Music 2001, Chamber Choir of Sibelius Acad. 2009, Harju Chamber Choir 2009, Klemetti-Inst. Chamber Choir 2010, Chamber Choir of Sibelius Acad. Kuopio Dept 2012. *Publication:* contrib. to Companion of Singing (ed. John Potter). *Honours:* Conductor of the Year 1998. *Telephone:* 400-624714 (mobile). *E-mail:* heikki .liimola@uniarts.fi (office).

LIKA, Peter; German singer (bass-baritone); b. 1947, Augsburg. *Education:* Hochschule für Musik, Munich. *Career:* sang with the Augsburg Opera 1972–81, later joined the Bavarian Chamber Opera for performances of Baroque opera; interpreter of sacred music by Bach and Mozart; repertoire also includes works by Monteverdi, J.S. Bach, Mozart, Haydn, Beethoven, Felix Mendelssohn, Stravinsky, Blarr, Penderecki, Arnold Schoenberg and Heinze; has performed across Germany and Europe.

LIKIN, Jurij; oboist; b. 11 Nov. 1967, Minsk, Belarus; m. Anna Jermolowitch 1987, one d. *Education:* Music Lyceum, Belarusian State Music Acad., Minsk with Prof. Boris Nitchkov, studied in Paris with Maurice Bourgue, Prague Mozart Acad. *Career:* debut aged 16, stage of Belarusian Philharmonic, Minsk; Ekaterinburg, Moscow, Minsk, Kaliningrad, Prague, Berlin, Brunswick 1991–94; Trieste 1993; Stresa, Italy 1994; Paris Théâtre des Champs-Elysées 1994; Marseille 1995; Les Grands Heures de Saint-Emilion, France 1995; principal oboist, State Symphony Orchestra of Belarusian Philharmonic 1990–94; soloist of Prague Symphony Orchestra, Prague Chamber Philharmonic; mem., Prague Wind Quintet 1994–. *Recordings:* works by B. Martinů, A. Reicha, E. Bozza, Max Stern, F. Poulenc Sonata, Sextet. *Honours:* first prize nat. competitions of USSR 1986, 1987.

LILL, John Richard, CBE, FRCM; British pianist; b. 17 March 1944, London; s. of George Lill and the late Margery Lill (née Young); m. Jacqueline Clifton Smith. *Education:* Leyton County High School and Royal Coll. of Music. *Career:* London debut at Royal Festival Hall 1963; plays regularly throughout Europe, USA and Far East, as recitalist and as soloist with most prin. orchestras; Prof., Keyboard Faculty, Royal Coll. of Music. *Recordings include:* complete Beethoven piano sonatas, concertos and bagatelles, complete piano works of Rachmaninov (with BBC Nat. Orchestra of Wales/Otaka), Brahms piano concertos, Tchaikovsky Piano Concerto No. 1 (with London Symphony

Orchestra), complete Prokofiev sonatas 1991. *Honours:* Hon. DSc (Univ. of Aston); Hon. DMus (Exeter Univ.); Hon. FTCL, FLCM; First Prize, Royal Overseas League Competition 1963, Int. Tchaikovsky Competition, Moscow 1970, Dinu Lipatti Medal, Chappell Gold Medal. *Address:* Keyboard Faculty, Royal College of Music, Prince Consort Road, London, SW7 2BS, England (office). *Telephone:* (20) 7591-4300 (office). *Fax:* (20) 7591-4737 (office). *E-mail:* info@rcm.ac.uk (office). *Website:* www.rcm.ac.uk/keyboard (office).

LILTVED, Oystein; singer (bass); b. 20 Jan. 1934, Arendal, Norway; m. Virginia Oosthuizen. *Education:* studied with Maria Hittorf in Vienna, Luciano Donaggio in Trieste and Frederick Dalberg in Kapstad, South Africa. *Career:* debut in Basle 1959 as Konshak in Prince Igor; many appearances at the opera houses of Oslo, Stockholm, Helsinki, Düsseldorf, Kassel and Bordeaux; sang in South Africa at Cape Town and at Johannesburg; sang at Seattle Opera as Hagen in Götterdämmerung; other roles have been Wagner's Daland, Landgrave and Fafner, Verdi's King Philip and Fiesco, Mozart's Osmin and Sarastro, Mephistopheles, Varlaam in Boris Godunov, Oroveso, Rocco, Raimondo in Lucia di Lammermoor and Swallow in Peter Grimes; many appearances in concerts and oratorios.

LIM, Liza, BA, MMus; Australian composer and academic; b. 30 Aug. 1966, Perth, WA. *Education:* Victoria Coll. of the Arts, Univ. of Melbourne, studied with Ton de Leeuw. *Career:* Lecturer in Composition, Univ. of Melbourne 1991; commissions from Duo Contemporain, The Seymour Group, Inter-contemporain (Paris), ABC/BBC, Ensemble Modern 1995, and others. *Compositions include:* Blaze for mezzo and ensemble 1986, Pompes Funebres for string quartet 1987, Koan for alto saxophone and percussion 1987, Tarocchi for three guitars, double bass and percussion 1988, Voodoo Child for soprano and ensemble 1989, Constellations for violin and string orchestra 1989, Garden of Earthly Desire for ensemble 1989, Diabolical Birds for ensemble 1990, Amulet for viola 1992, Hell for string quartet 1992, The Oresteia (opera) for six voices, 11 instruments and one dancer 1993, Koto for ensemble 1993, Lin Shang Yin for coloratura soprano and 15 instruments 1993, Cathedral for orchestra 1994, Sri Vidya for chorus and orchestra 1994–95, Street of Crocodiles for ensemble 1995, Gothic for eight strings 1996, The Alchemical Wedding for orchestra 1996, The Cauldron: Fusion of the Five Elements for six voices and instruments 1996, The Heart's Ear for flute, clarinet and string quartet 1997. *Honours:* Sounds Australian Award 1990.

LIM, Soon-Lee, BM; Singaporean violist and conductor; b. 3 Aug. 1957; m. 1983. *Education:* Royal Schools of Music, Eastman School of Music, Univ. of Rochester. *Career:* debut, Paganini, Grand Viola Sonata, Kilburn Hall, Eastman School of Music; Sub-Principal, Singapore Symphony Orchestra; Asst Conductor, Singapore Youth Orchestra, 1991–97; conducted Singapore Symphony Orchestra for the opening and closing ceremonies of the 17th South East Asia Games, 1993; conducted the Singapore Symphony Orchestra for the World Trade Organisation First Ministerial Conference's Farewell Concert for 4,000 delegation, 1996; conducted the Asian Youth Orchestra for the National Day Celebration, 1997; Music Dir and Resident Conductor, National University of Singapore Symphony Orchestra; mem. American Conductors' Guild, American Viola Society, American String Teachers' Association. *Honours:* first prize, Viola/Cello Open, Singapore National Music Competition, 1981; Jean Frederic Petrenoud Prize with Certificate of Distinction in Orchestra Conducting, 4th Vienna International Music Competition, 1995. *Address:* 58 Toh Tuck Crescent, 596959 Singapore.

LIMA, Luis; singer (tenor); b. 12 Sept. 1948, Cordoba, Argentina. *Education:* studied voice with Carlos Guicchandut in Buenos Aires and with Gina Cigna in Italy. *Career:* debut in Lisbon in 1974 as Turiddu in Cavalleria Rusticana; Guest appearances in Mainz, Munich, Stuttgart and Hamburg; Sang at La Scala Milan in 1977 as Edgardo in Lucia di Lammermoor; Further appearances in Strasbourg and Spain as Rodolfo, Cavaradossi, and Faust in Mefistofele; US debut in 1976 in a concert performance of Donizetti's Gemma di Vergy at Carnegie Hall; Metropolitan Opera debut in 1978 as Alfredo in La Traviata; Sung at New York City Opera in 1979 in La Bohème and Rigoletto, Salzburg Festival in 1984 as Verdi's Macduff, Maggio Musicale Florence, 1985–86 as Don Carlos and as Riccardo in Un Ballo in Maschera, and Covent Garden in 1985 as Nemorino and Don Carlos, returning to London in 1988 as Edgardo; Salzburg Easter Festival in 1988 as Cavaradossi, and sang Faust at the opening of the season at the Teatro Colón Buenos Aires in 1990; Sang Don José in a new production of Carmen at Covent Garden in 1991 and Verdi's Don Carlos at San Francisco in 1992; Madrid in 1992 as Don José and New York Metropolitan in 1994 as Cilea's Maurizio; Season 1996 with Rodolfo at Covent Garden; Don Carlos at the New York Met, 1997; Season 2000–01 as Rodolfo at the Met, Turiddu for the Vienna Staatsoper, Don José at Zürich and Don Carlos in Madrid. *Recordings include:* Gemma di Vergy; Le Roi de Lahore; Video of Don Carlos and of Carmen, both from Covent Garden. *Current Management:* Stafford Law, Candleway, Broad Street, Sutton Valence, Kent ME17 3AT, England. *Website:* www.stafford-law.com.

LIMA, Paulo Costa, BM, MS, PhD; Brazilian composer and academic; b. 26 Sept. 1954, Salvador, Bahia; m. Ana Margarida Cerqueira Lima e Lima, two s. *Education:* Music School, Universidade Federal da Bahia, Univ. of Illinois, Urbana, USA. *Career:* Prof. of Music, Universidade Federal da Bahia 1979, Head of Music Dept 1986–88, Dir of Music School 1988–92, Asst Pres. 1996–98; participation as composer at many nat. and int. events, including at Dresden and Urbana; festivals include Campos de Jordao, São Paulo, UFRJ; Ed., Art (music periodical) 1981–91. *Compositions:* Bundle for solo flute 1977,

Ubaba, O Que Diria Bach 1983, Funarte for chamber orchestra, Atôtô-Balzare for percussion and piano, Cuncti-Serenata 1983, Funarte for piano solo, Fantasia 1984, Pega Essa Nega e Chera for piano solo 1993, Corrente de Xango for cello 1995, Ponteio for piano solo 1995, Atoto do l'homme armè for chamber orchestra 1996, Ibejis for flute and clarinet 1996, Frevo for piano solo 1997. *Recordings:* Compositores da Bahia vols 5, 7 and 8, Outros Ritmos 1997, Impressionem 1997. *Honours:* Max Feffer Composition Prize, São Paulo 1995, Vitae Foundation Fellowship in Composition 1995, Copene Prize 1996.

LIN, Chiu-Ling, LMus, BMus, MMus, DMus; Chinese pianist; b. 13 May 1948. *Education:* Royal School of Music, Singapore, New England Conservatory, Indiana Univ. *Career:* debut Carnegie recital, 1979; solo recitals in China, Hong Kong, Singapore, Malaysia, Peru, Argentina, Brazil, England, and Chicago, Minneapolis, Seattle, Atlanta, New York; soloist with Singapore Orchestra, Des Moines Symphony, Atlanta Symphony, Chicago Civic Orchestra; artist-in-residence, Indiana University at South Bend, 1975–76; Professor of Piano, Drake University, Des Moines, 1976–. *Recordings:* Kamran Ince's Cross Scintillation, with Sylvia Wang. *Publications:* Around the World on 88 Keys. *Address:* Music Department, Drake University, 2507 University Avenue, Des Moines, IA 50311, USA. *E-mail:* pianosecret@comcast.net.

LIN, Cho-Liang, BMus; American violinist; b. 29 Jan. 1960, Taiwan; s. of Kuo-Jing Lin and Kuo-Ling Yu; m. Deborah Lin. *Education:* Juilliard School, Sydney Conservatoire, Australia. *Career:* soloist with leading orchestras including London Symphony Orchestra, Philharmonia, Concertgebouw, Orchestre de Paris, Chicago Symphony Orchestra, Philadelphia Orchestra and Boston Symphony Orchestra; played Tchaikovsky's Concerto at London Proms 1999; Founder and Dir Taipei Int. Music Festival; Music Dir La Jolla Music Society's SummerFest 2001–; Artistic Dir Hong Kong Int. Chamber Music Festival, Nat. Taiwan Symphony Orchestra's Youth Music Summer Camp; mem. Faculty, Juilliard School 1991–; also Prof. of Violin, Shepherd School of Music, Rice Univ. *Recordings include:* standard violin concerti from Mozart to Stravinsky, chamber music from Brahms to Ravel and contemporary music from Chen Yi to Christopher Rouse. *Honours:* Gramophone Record Award 1989, Musical American's Instrumentalist of the Year 2000. *Current Management:* Opus 3 Artists, 470 Park Avenue South, 9th Floor North, New York, NY 10016, USA. *Address:* 2201 Alice Pratt Brown Hall, Shepherd School of Music, Rice University, Houston, TX 77005, USA (office). *E-mail:* cllin@rice .edu (office). *Website:* music.rice.edu (office); cholianglin.com.

LIN, Joseph; Taiwanese violinist; *First Violinist, Juilliard String Quartet;* b. 1978, USA. *Education:* Juilliard Pre-College, Harvard Coll. *Career:* studied with Mary Canberg, Shirley Givens, Lynn Chang; Fulbright Scholar of Chinese Music, Beijing 2004; f. Chamber Music Workshops, China Conservatory, Beijing 2005; Asst Prof. of Violin, Cornell Univ. 2007–11; devised Chinese Musicians Residency 2009; First Violinist, Juilliard String Quartet 2011–; Founder mem., Formosa Quartet; as soloist, has appeared with many orchestras including Santa Fe Symphony, New Japan Philharmonic, Sapporo Symphony, Taiwan Nat. Symphony, Kiev Chamber Orchestra, Moravian Philharmonic, Auckland Philharmonic; chamber music appearances include Ravinia and Marlboro Music Festivals, Seattle Chamber Music Soc.; tours with Musicians from Marlboro; collaborated with percussionist Svet Stoyanov at River to River Festival, New York. *Recordings:* albums: Violin Recital 2004, Busoni, Violin Sonatas Nos. 1 & 2/Four Bagatelles 2007. *Honours:* Concert Artists Guild Int. Competition First Prize 1996, Presidential Scholar in the Arts 1996, Pro Musicis Int. Award 1999, Hanover Int. Violin Competition 2000, Michael Hill World Violin Competition First Prize, New Zealand 2001, with Formosa Quartet: London Int. String Quartet Competition First Prize and Amadeus Prize 2006. *Current Management:* ASPEN Artists Inc., 20-16 Nishi-Azabu, 2 chome Minato-ku, Tokyo, 106-0031, Japan; Emily Motherwell, Publicity, Colbert Artists Management, 111 West 57th Street, New York, NY 10019, USA. *Telephone:* (3) 5467-0081; (212) 757-0782. *Fax:* (3) 5468-0066. *E-mail:* info@aspen.jp; publicity@colbertartists.com. *Website:* www.aspen.jp/ eng/index.html; www.colbertartists.com; www.juilliardstringquartet.org.

LIN, Richard, BMus; American/Taiwanese musician (violin); b. 6 July 1991, Phoenix, Ariz. *Education:* Taichung High School, Curtis Inst. of Music, Juilliard School, studied with Aaron Rosand and Lewis Kaplan. *Career:* grew up in Taiwan; Concertmaster, Taiwan Classical Student Orchestra 2001–04; performed as soloist with orchestras including Sendai Philharmonic, Auckland Philharmonia, Oklahoma City Philharmonic, Nat. Symphony Orchestra of Taiwan and Taipei Symphony. *Honours:* First Prize, Nat. Taiwan Violin Competition 2006, First Prize, Buttram String Competition 2008, Second Prize, NTDTV Int. Chinese Violin Competition 2009, Chi-Mei Artist Prize 2010, 2011, Second Prize, Michael Hill Int. Violin Competition, New Zealand 2011, First Prize and Audience Prize, Sendai Int. Violin Competition, Japan 2013.

LINCÉ, Janet Isabel, GGSM; British conductor; *Conductor and Chorusmaster, Choros, Encoro, Corona Strings, Newbury Spring Festival Chorus;* b. 4 Feb. 1951, London, England. *Education:* Guildhall School of Music and Drama. *Career:* Guest Chorus Master, BBC Symphony Chorus, London Symphony Chorus, Philharmonia Chorus; Musical Dir, Reading Festival Chorus, Oxford University Press Choir; performances in Germany and four tours of NZ; mem. Inc. Soc. of Musicians, Council Asscn of British Choral Dirs. *Recording:* album: He came all so stille 2004. *Address:* 6 Mill Lane, Upper Heyford, Oxon., OX25 5LH, England (office). *Telephone:* (1869) 232618 (office).

Fax: (1869) 232618 (office). *E-mail:* info@choros.org (office). *Website:* www .choros.org.

LINCOLN, Christopher; Australian singer (tenor); b. 1965, Canberra. *Education:* studied with Dame Joan Hammonds. *Career:* appearances throughout Australia as Tamino, Nadir, Fenton, Rossini's Almaviva, Ferrando (Opera Queensland) and Alfredo (in Perth); Donizetti's Edgardo and Gounod's Faust in Auckland; Cologne Opera from 1990, as Mozart's Pedrillo and Tamino; Rodolfo in Luisa Miller in Sofia and Dessau, Alwa in Lulu and Andrès in Wozzeck 1999, at San Francisco; Števa in Jenůfa for WNO; concerts include Handel's Saul, Samson and Solomon, Haydn's Creation and Seasons and the Verdi Requiem; solos in music by Bach; recital at Teatre del Liceu, Barcelona, 1999. *Current Management:* Harlequin Agency Ltd, 203 Fidlas Road, Llanishen, Cardiff, CF14 5NA, Wales. *Website:* www .christopherlincoln.com.

LIND, Eva; Austrian singer (soprano); b. 14 June 1966, Innsbruck. *Education:* studied in Vienna. *Career:* debut at Landestheater Innsbruck 1983, as a Flowermaiden in Parsifal; sang Lucia di Lammermoor at Basle 1985 and the Queen of Night at Vienna 1985, 1986 and Paris 1987; Salzburg Festival 1986, 1987, as the Italian Singer in Capriccio; Vienna Staatsoper from 1986, as Lucia in Lucia di Lammermoor, Adele in Die Fledermaus and Sophie in Werther; Stuttgart Staatsoper as Adele in Die Fledermaus; British debut as Nannetta in Falstaff, Glyndebourne 1988; Gounod's Juliette at Zürich 1990, followed by Sophie in Der Rosenkavalier at Vienna, Brussels and Berne Opera; concerts with Francisco Araiza at the Teatro Colón, Buenos Aires 1990; sang Mozart's Blonde at Catania 1996; season 2000–01 as Gounod's Juliette at Karlsruhe and Primadonna in Donizetti's La Convenienze Teatrali at Stuttgart; sang Marzelline, La Scala, Milan 2003; season 2004–05 as Konstanze at Stuttgart and Istanbul, Rosalinde at Karlsruhe and Stuttgart, Rosina in Barbiere di Siviglia, Shanghai 2006; debut at Carnegie Hall, New York 2007 and Washington Nat. Gallery of Arts 2008. *Recordings:* Die Fledermaus, conducted by Placido Domingo; Naiade in Ariadne auf Naxos, with the Leipzig Gewandhaus Orchestra conducted by Kurt Masur; Coloratura arias, including Elisabeth ou La Fille proscrit by Donizetti; Papagena in Die Zauberflöte, conducted by Marriner; Olympia in Tales of Hoffmann, with Jeffrey Tate; Operatic duets with Francisco Araiza; Aennchen in Der Freischütz, conductor, Colin Davis; Amina in La Sonnambula (conducted by G. Bellini), Ich bin verliebt (operetta arias) 1997, Lieder die zu Herzen geh'n 2000, Sentimento 2002, Wunder Gescheh'n 2004, Mozart rennt 2005, Stille Nacht 2006, Operetta Gala (with Placido Domingo, Thomas Hampson) 2007, Magic Moments 2008, Eva Lind: Best of Strasse der Lieder 2008, Haydn Nelson Mass (soprano solo) conducted by Michael Gielen 2009. *Honours:* European Music Award 1986, City of Basel honour 2000. *Address:* Konzertmanagement Georg Preisinger, Burgblick 8, 87671 Ronsberg, Germany (office). *Telephone:* 83-06-70-52 (office). *Fax:* 83-06-70-59 (office). *E-mail:* gpkonzerte@aol.com (office). *Website:* www.gp-konzerte.de (office); www.eva -lind.com (home).

LINDBERG, Christian; Swedish trombonist; b. 15 Feb. 1958, Danderyd, Stockholm; m.; four c. *Education:* studies in Stockholm, London, Los Angeles. *Career:* mem., Royal Stockholm Opera Orchestra 1977–78; Prof., Swedish Royal Acad. 1996–; gives over 100 concerts a year as trombone soloist with world's major symphony orchestras; solo programmes, including music theatre; appearances with Per Lundberg, piano, and with Hakan Hardenberger, trumpet; repertoire includes contemporary music, baroque music played on original instruments, classical and romantic music; works composed for him include concertos by Schnittke, Xenakis, Takemitsu and Arvo Pärt; played at several British festivals and Pitea Festival, North Sweden 1993; season 1993–94 with concerts in Germany, Switzerland, Iceland, Denmark, Sweden, Israel; tours to USA and with Scottish Chamber Orchestra; Schnittke's Dialogue with Nash Ensemble, London; performances with Prague Symphony Orchestra, Czech Republic, and Gothenburg Symphony Orchestra, Sweden; Carnegie Hall debut with Zwilich Trombone Concerto and world premiere of Trombone Concerto by Toru Takemitsu with St Paul Chamber Orchestra, USA; several German festivals and Japan tour 1994; 1994–95 season included performances of Trombone Concerto by Iannis Xenakis, new works by Kalevi Aho and Arvo Pärt, also tours to Australia, France, Japan; season 1998–99 participated at the Israel, Rheingau, Cadaquez and Stavanger Festivals and at the Chamber Unlimited Festival, Stockholm; played with the Singapore Symphony Orchestra and in Brussels and Helsinki; season 1999–2000 with concerts at the Gran Canaria Festival with the Norwegian Chamber Orchestra; premiere of new opera production by Luciano Berio at the Salzburg Festival; premiere of Trombone Concerto by Berio with the Tonnhalle Orchestra in Zürich, Australian premiere with the Sydney Symphony Orchestra; masterclasses; designs instruments and mouthpieces for CONN Instrument Co.; Prince Consort Prof., Royal Coll. of Music, London. *Recordings include:* British Trombone Concerti, American Concerti, Italian repertoire for Trombones, Voice and Chamber Organ, Gemeaux by Takemitsu, Frank Martin's Ballade with Concertgebouw Orchestra and Riccardo Chailly, Nordic Spell Flute Concertos (Midem Classical Music Award for Contemporary Music 2006). *Address:* c/o Edition Tarrodi, Valhallavägen 110, 114 41 Stockholm, Sweden (office). *E-mail:* info@ tarrodi.se (office). *Website:* www.tarrodi.se/cl.

LINDBERG, Magnus; Finnish composer, pianist and conductor; b. 27 June 1958, Helsinki. *Education:* Sibelius Acad., Helsinki and studied with Globokar in Paris, Donatoni in Siene and Ferneyhough at Darmstadt. *Career:* founder,

EArs Open Soc. 1980; Marie-Josée Kravis Composer-in-Residence, New York Philharmonic 2009–. *Compositions include:* Three Pieces for horn and string trio, Arabesques for wind quintet, Quintet for piano and wind, De Tartuffe je Croi for string quartet and piano, Drama for orchestra, Sculpture II for orchestra, Linea d'Ombra for flute and ensemble, Action Situation Signification for horn or clarinets and ensemble 1982, Ritratto for orchestra, Zona for ensemble, Metal Work for accordion and percussion, Kraft for orchestra (Nordic Music Prize) 1985, UR for five players and live electronics, Twine for piano, Trios Sculptures for orchestra, Etwas Zarter, Ohne Audruck, Faust (Prix Italia), Ensemble triptych Kinetics, Marea and Joy 1988–90, Corrente II 1991, Aura 1994, Arena 1995, Campana in Aria 1998, Cantigas 1998–99, Cello Concerto 1999, Grand Duo for orchestra 2000, Parada for orchestra 2001, Partia for cello 2001, Clarinet Concerto (Gramophone Award for Best Contemporary Recording 2006) 2001–02, Chorale for orchestra 2001–02, Jubilees for ensemble 2002, Bubo Bubo for ensemble 2002, Concerto for orchestra 2002–03, Tribute 2004, Ottoni for brass ensemble 2005, Violin Concerto 2006, Sculpture for orchestra 2005, GRAFFITI 2008–09, EXPO 2009. *Address:* c/o Boosey & Hawkes, First Floor, Aldwych House, 71–91 Aldwych, London, WC2B 4HN, England (office). *Website:* www.boosey.com/lindberg (office).

LINDE, Hans-Martin; German recorder player, flautist and conductor; b. 24 May 1930, Werne; m. Gudrun Olshausen; one s. two d. *Education:* Staatliche Hochschule für Musik, Freiburg with Konrad Lechner and Gustav Scheck. *Career:* solo flautist of the Cappella Coloniensis of West German Radio, Cologne; concert tours in Europe, USA, South America, Middle and Far East from 1955; teacher of baroque flute, recorder and conducting from 1957; conductor of vocal ensemble, 1965–; conductor of chamber orchestra, 1970–, of the Schola Cantorum Basiliensis, Basle; co-Ed., Zeitschrift für Spielmusik, 1966–; concert associations with August Wenzinger and Frans Brueggen; conducted with Basler-Linde Concert in Keiser's Tomyris and Vivaldi's La Griselda at Ludwigshafen, 1988, 1989. *Recordings include:* Flute Concertos by Leclair, Stamitz, Dittersdorf and Mozart; Recorder Concertos by Sammartini and Vivaldi; English Consort Music and Chamber Music by Bach, Handel, Haydn with the Linde-Consort; Conductor of the Linde-Consort and the Cappella Coloniensis; Guest Conductor of several orchestras and choirs in different European countries and in the USA; Recordings as a conductor include: Bach: Masses, Brandenburg Concertos, Orchestral Suites; Schütz: Exequien; Handel: Water-Music, Music for the Royal Fireworks, Concerti grossi op 6, Keiser's Der Grossmutige Tomyris. *Publications:* Kleine Anleitung zum Verrzieren alter Musik, 1958; Handbuch des Blockflötenspiels, 1962.

LINDEMANN, Jens; Canadian musician (trumpet); b. 1966; m. Jennifer Snow. *Education:* Juilliard School, USA. *Career:* has played in major concert venues world-wide, including Philharmonics of New York, Los Angeles, London and Berlin, also Suntory Hall, Tokyo and Great Wall of China; as orchestral soloist, performed at BBC Proms (Last Night) and gave solo command performance for HM Queen Elizabeth II; featured soloist with Edmonton Symphony Orchestra at Carnegie Hall, New York 2012; solo performances with orchestras including London Symphony, Philadelphia, Beijing, Bayersicher Rundfunk, Buenos Aires Chamber, Atlanta, Washington, Seattle, Dallas, Detroit, Houston, Montreal, Toronto, National Arts Centre, Vancouver, Warsaw, Welsh Chamber, I Musici de Montréal, St Louis and Mostly Mozart at Lincoln Center; has worked with musicians such as Sir Neville Marriner, Sir Angel Romero, Doc Severinsen, Charles Dutoit, Gerard Schwarz, Eiji Oue, Bramwell Tovey and Jukka Pekka Saraste; lead trumpet with ensemble Canadian Brass 1996–2001; taught at Dept of Musicology, UCLA Herb Alpert School of Music; Artistic Dir All Star Brass, live recordings and residencies at Banff Centre. *Recordings include:* with Canadian Brass: Goldberg Variations (Echo Klassik Award 2002) 2001; others: Rising Sun 2005, Flying Solo 2011, Dreaming of the Master 2011, The Classic Trumpet 2011, The Legend of King Arthur (with Foden's Band) 2012. *Honours:* Hon. Fellow, Royal Conservatory of Music; Dr hc (McMaster); prizewinner at numerous competitions including ARD Munich, First Prize, Prague Spring Festival and Ellsworth Smith (Florida) Int. Trumpet Competition 1992, Brass Herald's Int. Brass Personality of the Year 2006. *E-mail:* trumpetjens@gmail.com. *Website:* trumpetjens.com.

LINDÉN, Magnus; singer (baritone); b. 1 Nov. 1954, Sweden. *Education:* studied in Stockholm with Erik Saedén and in London with Vera Rozsa. *Career:* Royal Opera, Stockholm from 1980, notably as Papageno and Guglielmo and in the 1994 premiere of Sctschedrin's Lolita; Drottningholm Festival 1987, as Don Giovanni, and 1991 as Egisth in Haeffner's Electra; other roles include Tolomeo in Handel's Giulio Cesare, Zuniga in Carmen and Jovanin in the 1991 premiere of Don Juan Freestyle by Hillerud-Wannefors; many concert appearances. *Recordings include:* Così fan tutte, from Drottningholm.

LINDENSTRAND, Sylvia; Swedish singer (mezzo-soprano); b. 24 June 1942, Stockholm. *Education:* Opera School of the Royal Opera, Stockholm. *Career:* debut in Stockholm 1962, as Olga in Eugene Onegin; has sung at the Royal Opera, Stockholm as Dorabella, Cherubino, Marina in Boris Godunov, Octavian, Brangäne, Fricka in the Ring and Cenerentola; sang Tchaikovsky's Maid of Orleans 1986 and sang in Singoalla by Gunnar de Frumerie 1988; guest appearances at Bayreuth 1964, Copenhagen and the Moscow Bolshoi; Glyndebourne 1975, 1979, as Dorabella and Amaranta in La Fedelta Premiata; Aix-en-Provence 1976, Zerlina in Don Giovanni; sang Idamante in Idomeneo at Drottningholm; Royal Opera Stockholm 1991 as Dionysus in

the premiere of Backanterna by Daniel Börtz (production by Ingmar Bergman); many concert engagements. *Recordings include:* songs by Liszt. *Honours:* Swedish Court Singer 1982.

LINDHOLM, Berit Maria; Swedish singer (soprano); b. (Berit Maria Jonsson), 18 Oct. 1934, Stockholm; m. Hans Lindholm; two d. *Education:* Stockholm Opera School. *Career:* debut as Countess in Le nozze di Figaro, Stockholm 1963; performances all over the world including, New York Met, Carnegie Hall, San Francisco, Chicago, London, Paris, Hamburg, Berlin, Munich, Moscow, Naples, Madrid, Geneva, Zürich, Düsseldorf, Vienna, Barcelona, Bayreuth; repertoire includes Isolde, Brünnhilde, Kundry, Tosca, Salome, Elektra, Turandot, Fidelio, Dyer's Wife in Die Frau ohne Schatten; sang in the premiere of Backanterna by Daniel Börtz, Stockholm 1991; teaches singing; mem. Swedish Royal Acad. of Music. *Recordings include:* Les Troyens, Die Walküre, Songs by Swedish Composers. *Honours:* Opera Singer by Apptmt of the King of Sweden, Litteris et Artibus 1988.

LINDNER, Brigitte; singer (soprano); b. 1959, Munich, Germany. *Education:* studied in Munich. *Career:* debut at Gärtnerplatz-Theater, Munich as a Boy in Die Zauberflöte; sang Gretel in Humperdinck's opera (also televised) and in Mozart's Bastien and Bastienne; adult debut at the Ludwigsburg Festival 1980, as Barbarina in Le nozze di Figaro; Bayreuth Festival 1985, as the Shepherd boy in Tannhäuser; sang Despina in Così fan tutte for Kiel Opera 1990; other roles include Papagena and parts in operettas by Lehar and Johann Strauss; concert appearances in oratorios by Bach, Haydn and Mozart. *Recordings:* Hansel and Gretel, Die Zauberflöte.

LINDSEY, John Russell; American concert violinist and academic; *Concert Master, Orchestra of Northern New York, Eleva Chamber Players Orchestra;* b. 26 Aug. 1947, Chicago, Ill.; m. Amornrat P. Lindsey; two s. one d. *Career:* fmr Concertmaster, Dallas Chamber Players, Lexington Philharmonic Orchestra, The Warren (Ohio) Chamber Orchestra, The Castle Farm Summer Festival Orchestra (Michigan), Champlain Valley Symphony Orchestra, Hanover Chamber Orchestra; Chair. of Strings, Baylor Univ., The Governor's School of N Carolina, Univ. of Kentucky; Teacher of Strings, Dallas, Tex., Public Schools; performed and taught violin at Ithaca Chamber Music Inst. 1987–2007, Stage de Musique, Marcillat-en-Combraille, France 1988, Incontri di Canna Int. Chamber Music Festival, southern Italy 2000, Ameropa Festival, Prague 2004–10, Int. Festival, Bulgaria 2008; Concert Master, Orchestra of Northern New York and Eleva Chamber Players Orchestra; Violinist, Potsdam Baroque Players; First Violinist, Aurora Quintet; Distinguished Service Prof. of Violin, State Univ. of NY (SUNY) 2009; mem. Potsdam Piano Quartet and Potsdam Baroque Chamber Players, Crane School of Music 1981–; mem. Violin Faculties, Adult Chamber Music Conf. at Interlochen, Michigan 1983– and Mozart Festival, Woodstock, Vt 1996–; f. Thailand Chamber Music Festival 2010–12; took part in Saarburger Festival, Germany 2013; solo recitals at Carnegie Recital Hall, Museum of the City of New York, St Joseph's Church, Bruno Walter Auditorium, Lincoln Center, New York City; also in Boston, Montreal, Atlanta and Chicago; mem. Triple Nine Soc., American String Teachers' Asscn. *Honours:* Wilkes Coll. Mozart Award 1972, Winner, Second Annual Allegro Residency for the Arts, City of Dayton 1989, Pres.'s Award for Excellence in Teaching (Teacher of the Year Award), Potsdam Coll., SUNY 1993, Chancellor's Award for Excellence in Teaching, SUNY 2003. *Address:* Crane School of Music, SUNY Potsdam, Potsdam, NY 13676, USA (office). *Telephone:* (315) 267-2431 (office). *Fax:* (315) 267-2413 (office). *E-mail:* lindsejr@potsdam.edu (office). *Website:* www.johnrlindsey.com.

LINDSKOG, Par; Swedish singer (tenor); b. 1962, Kungelv. *Education:* studied in Gothenburg. *Career:* secondary roles at the Opera Studio and Theatre in Gothenburg; Berlin Staatsoper as Max in Der Freischütz, Narraboth (Salome), Števa (Jenůfa) and the Steersman in Der fliegende Holländer, from 1987; further engagements in Lisbon, Salzburg, Dresden and Leipzig; season 1995–96 as Young Man in Moses und Aron under Pierre Boulez at Amsterdam and Salzburg, and under Christoph von Dohnányi with the Philharmonia Orchestra at the Festival Hall, London; further roles include Tamino, Don Ottavio and Barinkay in Der Zigeunerbaron, Vienna, 1996. *Honours:* Bayreuth Scholarship 1993. *Current Management:* International Classical Artists, The Tower Building, 11 York Road, London, SE1 7NX, England; Agentur Sigrid Rostock, Eugen-Schönhaar-Strasse 1, 10407 Berlin, Germany. *Telephone:* (20) 7902 0520 (UK); (30) 4257514 (Germany). *Fax:* (20) 7902 0530 (UK); (30) 4239136 (Germany). *E-mail:* info@icartists.co.uk; sigridrostock@web.de. *Website:* www.icartists.co.uk.

LINDSLEY, Celina; American singer (soprano); b. 1953. *Education:* Eastman School of Music. *Career:* sang at Bielefeld, Kassel and Nuremberg; Queen of Night with New York City Opera 1977; with Düsseldorf Opera 1978–, including as Autonoe in The Bassarids 1991; Zerbinetta and in Zemlinsky's Der Zwerg, Vienna Staatsoper and Covent Garden 1985; premiere of Goehr's Behold the Sun, Duisburg 1985; Donna Anna, Komische Oper Berlin 1991; Violetta in La Traviata, Essen 1994; sang Marie in Gurlitt's Wozzeck at Florence 1998; many concerts and lieder recitals. *Recordings include:* Zemlinsky's Der Kreidekreis and Busoni's Turandot. *Current Management:* Konzert-Direktion Hans Adler, Auguste-Viktoria-Strasse 64, 14199 Berlin, Germany. *Telephone:* (30) 8959920. *Fax:* (30) 8263520. *E-mail:* info@musikadler.de. *Website:* www.musikadler.de.

LING, Jahja, MMus, DMusArts; American (b. Indonesia) conductor; *Music Director, San Diego Symphony;* b. 25 Oct. 1951, Jakarta, Indonesia; m. Jessie

Ling; two d. *Education:* Jakarta School of Music, Juilliard School (studied piano with Mieczyslaw Munz and conducting with John Nelson), New York, Yale School of Music, USA with Otto-Werner Mueller. *Career:* began playing the piano aged four; Founding Music Dir San Francisco Symphony Youth Orchestra 1981–84, Cleveland Orchestra Youth Orchestra 1986–93; debut as pianist with Cleveland Orchestra 1987; Resident Conductor, Cleveland Orchestra's Blossom Festival 1985–2002, Dir 2000–05; Artistic Dir Taiwan Nat. Symphony 1998–2001, Super World Orchestra, Tokyo 2001; conducted World Wide Chinese Festival Orchestra 2009; Music Dir San Diego Symphony 2007–; fmr Conducting Fellow, Los Angeles Philharmonic Inst.; appeared as guest conductor with Chamber Orchestra of Lausanne, China Philharmonic, Guangzhou Symphony, Hong Kong Philharmonic, Leipzig Gewandhaus Orchestra, Malaysia Philharmonic, MDR Symphony Orchestra, Netherlands Radio Philharmonic, NDR Radio-Philharmonie, NDR Symphony Orchestra, Orchestre Nationale du Capitole de Toulouse, Royal Philharmonic, London, Rundfunk-Sinfonieorchester, Berlin, Scottish Chamber Orchestra, Shanghai Symphony, Singapore Symphony, Sydney Symphony, Stockholm Philharmonic, Tokyo's Yomiuri Nippon Symphony; Vice-Pres. Stephen Tong Evangelistic Ministries International. *Recordings include:* Dupré Organ Symphony, Rheinberger Organ Concerto with Michael Murray and the Royal Philharmonic Orchestra, two albums of baroque works with Scottish Chamber Orchestra, Symphonic Dances (with Florida Orchestra), Stephen Montague's From the White Edge of Phrygia, American Celebrations (featuring world premiere of Ellen Taaffe Zwilich's Third Symphony with New York Philharmonic), Saint-Saëns' Symphony (with the Cleveland Orchestra). *Honours:* Dr hc (Wooster Coll.) 1993; Jakarta Piano Competition 1968, Rockefeller grant 1969, Bronze Medal, Arthur Rubinstein Int. Piano Master Competition (Israel) 1977, Certificate of Honour, Tchaikovsky Int. Piano Competition, Moscow 1978, Leonard Bernstein Conducting Fellowship, Tanglewood 1980, Conducting Fellow, Los Angeles Philharmonic Inst. 1982, Seaver/Nat. Endowment for the Arts Conductor's Award 1988. *Current Management:* c/o Opus 3 Artists, 470 Park Avenue South, 9th Floor North, New York, NY 10016, USA. *Telephone:* (212) 584-7500. *E-mail:* info@opus3artists.com. *Website:* www.opus3artists.com. *Address:* San Diego Symphony, 1245 Seventh Avenue, San Diego, CA 92101, USA (office). *Telephone:* (619) 235-0800 (office). *Fax:* (619) 235-0005 (office). *E-mail:* info@jahjaling.com; info@ sandiegosymphony.org (office). *Website:* www.sandiegosymphony.org (office); jahjaling.com.

LINJAMA, Jouko; Finnish composer; b. 4 Feb. 1934. *Education:* Sibelius Acad., Helsinki Univ., studied composition in Cologne, Staatliche Hochschule für Musik, Kölner Kurse für Neue Musik. *Career:* organist, St Henrik's Catholic Church, Helsinki 1958–60; Cantor-Organist, Parish of Tuusula 1964–97. *Play:* Jan Lehtola. *Compositions include:* opera: Finnish Tapir 1998–99; orchestra: two symphonies from oratorio Homage to Aleksis Kivi 1972, La Migration d'Oiseaux Sauvages 1977, Les Tapisseries for string orchestra 2004, 150 bars of music for flute, vibraphone and string orchestra 2008; choral works: How It Is oratorio 1968, Homage to Aleksis Kivi symphonic oratorio 1970, 1974, 1976, Missa De Angelis 1969, La Sapienza oratorio da camera 1980, Mailman Algusta ia Loomisesta oratorio 1983, Requiem 1998; chamber music: String Quartet No. 1 1978, No. 2 1979, Concerto for organ, marimba, vibraphone, two Wind Quartets 1981, Concerto for horn and organ 2001, Quartetto for cornetto, corno, trombone and organ 2002, Duo for piano and organ 2002, Trio for clarinet, horn and organ 2003; works for organ: Organum supra B-A-C-H 1967, Sonatina supra B-A-C-H 1968, Magnificat for organ 1970, Partitasonata Veni Creator Spiritus 1969, Missa Cum Jubilo for organ 1977, Toccata in D 1985, Reflections duet for organ 1991, Three Liturgical Stained-Glass Paintings 1993; a cappella choral works: Partita per coro 1979, On the Road to Splendour 1980, Kalevala Suite 1981, Toward the Future and Hope 1984; numerous solo songs. *Recordings include:* Works for Organ Vols 1–3. *Publication:* When My Father Composed the Olympic Hymn, Gummeus 2002. *Address:* Teosto, Lauttasaarentie 1, 00200 Helsinki 20 (office); Luomakuja 6, 04300 Tuusula, Finland (home). *E-mail:* jouko.linjama@gmail.com.

LINNENBANK, René; Dutch singer (bass); b. 1961, Abcoude. *Education:* Maastricht and Sweelinck Conservatories, Guildhall School, London. *Career:* Debut: Osmin in Die Entführung for Scottish Opera Go Round, 1992; Appearances with Opera-SKON, Netherlands, as Mozart's Sarastro, and Cols (Bastien and Basitienne); Bagheera the Panther in Berkeley's Baa-Baa-Black-Sheep for Opera North; Other roles include Mozart's Figaro, Harasta in The Cunning Little Vixen. Nicolai's Falstaff, and King Tartaglia in Jonathan Dove's The Little Green Bird; concerts and recitals throughout Europe with such conductors as William Christie, Paul Daniel and Mstislav Rostropovich; sang Un Turk in the Lully/Molière Bourgeois Gentilhomme, Linbury Theatre, 2001; season 2001–02 in Orfeo by Monteverdi at La Monnaie, Brussels, under René Jacobs. *Website:* www.renelinnenbank.com.

LINOS, Glenys; singer (mezzo-soprano); b. 29 Sept. 1941, Cairo, Egypt. *Education:* Athens Conservatory, London Opera Centre. *Career:* sang in Mainz, Ulm and Wiesbaden from 1970; guest appearances in most major German opera houses; Bayreuth and Salzburg Festivals; Toulouse 1983, as Carmen; Festival Hall, London 1983, in the Verdi Requiem; Ghent 1984, as Santuzza in Cavalleria Rusticana; Zürich 1984–85, as Pensithelia in the opera by Schoeck; Paris Opéra-Comique 1985, in The Stone Guest by Dargomyzhsky; Lausanne and La Scala Milan 1986, as the Sorceress in Dido and Aeneas and Geneviève in Pelléas et Mélisande; Rome Opera 1986, as

Ermengarda in Agnese di Hohenstaufen by Spontini; sang Clairon in Capriccio at Bologna 1987; Auntie in Peter Grimes at the Zürich Opera 1989; Clytemnestra in Elektra at the Teatro Nuovo, Spoleto 1990; television appearances include Adriano in Rienzi, Wiesbaden Opera. *Recordings include:* Monteverdi's Orfeo.

LINTU, Hannu Petteri; Finnish conductor; *Artistic Director and Chief Conductor, Finnish Radio Symphony Orchestra*; b. Rauma. *Education:* Sibelius Acad., Helsinki, Accademia Chigiana, Italy. *Career:* Artistic Dir Turku Philharmonic Orchestra 1998–2001; Artistic Dir Helsingborg Symphony Orchestra 2002–05; Artistic Dir and Chief Conductor, Tampere Philharmonic Orchestra 2009–13; regular Guest Conductor, Finnish Radio Symphony Orchestra, Chief Conductor 2013–; regular Guest Conductor, Avanti Chamber Orchestra, many other Finnish, European and int. orchestras; has conducted many opera productions with Finnish Nat. Opera. *Recordings:* albums: Rautavaara, Cantus Arcticus/Piano Concerto No. 1/ Symphony No. 3 (with Royal Scottish National Orchestra) 1998, Saariaho, From the Grammar of Dreams (with Anu Komsi, Piia Komsi and Avanti Chamber Orchestra) 2000, Rautavaara, A Requiem in Our Time (with Finnish Brass Symphony) 2000, Rasmussen, Symphony No. 1/Saxophone Concerto (with Jeanette Balland and Danish National Symphony Orchestra) (Nordic Council Music Prize 2002) 2002, The Sound of Shakespeare (with Helsingborg Symphony Orchestra) 2002, Shostakovich, Piano Concertos 1 & 2 (with Oleg Marshev and Helsingborg Symphony Orchestra) 2003, Grieg, Songs/Mahler, Lieder eines fahrenden Gesellen (with Herman Wallén and Helsingborg Symphony Orchestra) 2004, Kaipainen, Horn Concerto/Cello Concerto (with Esa Tapani, Marko Ylönen and Finnish Radio Symphony Orchestra) 2005, Pylkkänen, Mare and Her Son (with Estonian National Opera Chorus and Orchestra) 2005, Saariaho, Graal theatre/Solar/Lichtbogen (with John Storgårds and Avanti Chamber Orchestra) 2006, Virtuoso French Concertos for Harp and Orchestra (with Emmanuel Ceysson and Xavier de Maistre) 2006, Hämeenniemi, Viola Concerto (with Tommi Aalto and Finnish Radio Symphony Orchestra) 2007, Schumann/Volkmann/Gernsheim/Dietrich, Cello Concertos (with Alban Gerhardt and Rundfunk-Sinfonieorchester Berlin) 2007, Kaipainen, Symphony No. 3 (with Tampere Philharmonic Orchestra) 2007, Vieuxtemps/Wieniawski, Violin Concertos (with Corey Cerovsek and Orchestre de Chambre de Lausanne) 2008. *Honours:* Nordic Conducting Competition Winner, Bergen 1994. *Current Management:* c/o Linda Marks, Jane Brown or David Hooson, HarrisonParrott Ltd, 5–6 Albion Court, Albion Place, London, W6 0QT, England. *Telephone:* (20) 7229-9166; (20) 7313-3529; (20) 7313-3516. *E-mail:* linda.marks@harrisonparrott.co.uk; jane.brown@ harrisonparrott.co.uk; david.hooson@harrisonparrott.co.uk. *Website:* www .harrisonparrott.co.uk; yle.fi/aihe (office); www.hannulintu.fi.

LIPKIN, Malcolm Leyland, ARCM, LRAM, DMus; British composer and lecturer; b. 2 May 1932, Liverpool, England; m. Judith Frankel 1968; one s. *Education:* Liverpool Coll., Royal Coll. of Music, Univ. of London, studied privately with Mátyás Seiber. *Career:* debut at Gaudeamus Foundation, The Netherlands 1951; numerous broadcast and public performances of own compositions of orchestral, choral, vocal, chamber and instrumental music in many countries 1951–. *Compositions include:* Sinfonia di Roma (Symphony No. 1), The Pursuit (Symphony No. 2), Sun (Symphony No. 3), two violin concertos, Piano Concerto, Flute Concerto, Oboe Concerto, Psalm 96 for chorus and orchestra, Four Departures to poems of Herrick for soprano and violin, Five Shelley Songs for soprano and piano, Clifford's Tower for instrumental ensemble, String Trio, Harp Trio, six piano sonatas, two violin sonatas, Wind Quintet, Metamorphosis for harpsichord, Naboth's Vineyard for recorders, cello and harpsichord, Interplay for recorder, viola da gamba, harpsichord and percussion, Pastorale for horn and strings (also arranged for horn and string quintet), Piano Trio, Prelude and Dance for cello and piano, Nocturnes 1–8 for piano, Bartók Variations for string quartet, Dance Fantasy for solo violin, Five Bagatelles for oboe and piano, Duo for violin and cello, Pierrot Dances for viola and piano, From Across La Manche for string orchestra, Little Suite for flute and piano, Sonatine for solo clarinet, Festivo for string orchestra, Five Little Pieces for piano, Diversions for woodwind sextet, Invocation for double bass and piano. *Recordings include:* Clifford's Tower, Pastorale, String Trio recorded by the Nash Ensemble 1986, Piano Trio recorded by the English Piano Trio 1992, From Across La Manche recorded by Royal Ballet Sinfonia 2003, Symphony No. 1 recorded by the BBC Scottish Symphony Orchestra, Symphony No. 2 & Symphony No. 3 recorded by the BBC Philharmonic Orchestra 2015. *Publications:* contrib. to Musical Times, Musical Opinion, Classical Music. *E-mail:* mail@malcolmlipkin.co.uk. *Website:* www.malcolmlipkin.co.uk.

LIPMAN, Michael; American cellist and educator; *Cello, Pittsburgh Symphony Orchestra*; b. 15 March 1954, Meriden, Conn.; s. of Bruin Lipman and Rosalyn Lipman; m. Shirli Nikolsburg 1999; one d. *Education:* Hartt Coll. of Music with Paul Olefsky, Eastman School of Music with Ronald Leonard and Paul Katz, Blossom Music Festival with Leonard Rose. *Career:* debut recital in Pittsburgh 1985; soloist, Aspen Philharmonia Orchestra 1977; Cello, Rochester Philharmonic 1977–78; Prin. Cello, Aspen Chamber Symphony 1978–80; Assoc. Prin. Cello, New Haven Symphony 1978–79; Cello, Pittsburgh Symphony Orchestra 1979–, soloist 1985, 1993; recitals and chamber music concerts throughout USA; participant, Aspen Music Festival, New York String Seminar, Cleveland Chamber Seminar, Grand Teton Music Festival; cellist and founding mem. California Univ. of Pennsylvania String Quartet 1986; full-length radio broadcast of Pittsburgh debut recital, WQED 1986; solo and chamber music performances in Beijing, China and Moscow, Russia 1987, 1989; Faculty mem. Duquesne Univ. School of Music 1994–96, Chatham Univ. 2006–; Founding mem. The Dalihapa Ensemble 1995–; performed with Pittsburgh Chamber Music Project. *Recordings include:* albums with Pittsburgh Chamber Music Project 2002. *Honours:* First Prize, Aspen Concerto Competition 1977, Pittsburgh (Pa) Y Music Soc. Passamaneck Award 1985. *Address:* 4011 Blvd Drive, Pittsburgh, PA 15217, USA. *Telephone:* (412) 421-8852. *Fax:* (412) 421-8852. *E-mail:* niklip@comcast.net.

LIPOVETSKY, Leonidas, BMus, MMus; American pianist, lecturer and educator; b. 2 May 1937, Montevideo, Uruguay; m. Astrid Eir Jonsson 1973; one s. two d. *Education:* Juilliard School of Music, USA, Kolischer Conservatory, Montevideo, Uruguay with Wilhelm Kolischer, studied with Rosina Lhevinne and Martin Canin, School of Architecture, Nat. Univ. of Uruguay. *Career:* debut, Nat. Symphony, Montevideo 1959; New York debut 1967; recital, New York 1964; S American premiere of Britten's Piano Concerto in D at Montevideo 1959; concert tours in the UK, Europe, Russia, Scandinavia, USA, Canada, Central and S America, People's Repub. of China; soloist on tour with Czech Philharmonic, Leoš Janáček in Spain and Czechoslovakia and with English Chamber Orchestra in USA, Nat. Symphony Orchestra, Mexico, Nat. Orchestra Asscn, NY, Juilliard Orchestra, NY, Winnipeg Symphony, Canada, Royal Liverpool Philharmonic, Seville Philharmonic, Spain, Nat. Symphony of Iceland, Reykjavík, Chicago Chamber Orchestra, Cedar Rapids Symphony, IA, Nat. Symphony of Colombia, Bogotá, Ossodre, Montevideo, Mexico Nat. Conservatory; numerous broadcasts; Special Guest Artist, UN General Assembly; lectures at Trinity Coll. of Music and Dartington Coll., UK, Juilliard School of Music, New York, Moscow Conservatory, Russia, Shanghai Conservatory, Beijing Conservatory, Shenyang Conservatory, People's Repub. of China, Nat. Museum of Art of Puerto Rico, San Juan; inaugural piano recital, Mexico Nat. Piano Festival, Center for the Arts 2003; performance of 17 Mozart piano sonatas, Tampa, St Petersburg, Clearwater, Florida 2006; taught at Florida State Univ. 1969–2004. *Television:* three one-hour programmes for PBS Cincinnati on project 'Music and the Arts' 2003. *Honours:* Commemorative Gold Medal (150 years of Steinway & Sons) 2003. *Address:* Project Music and the Arts, 3523 Ballastone Drive, Land O'Lakes, FL 34638, USA (office). *Telephone:* (813) 242-2562 (office). *Fax:* (813) 388-6770 (office). *E-mail:* lipovetsky@tampabay.rr.com (home). *Website:* www .leonidaslipovetsky.com.

LIPOVŠEK, Marjana; Slovenian singer (contralto); b. 3 Dec. 1946, Ljubljana; d. of Marijan Lipovšek. *Education:* in Ljubljana and Graz Music Acad., Austria. *Career:* joined Vienna State Opera, then Hamburg State Opera, FRG; operatic roles include Oktavian in Der Rosenkavalier, Dorabella in Così fan tutte, Marina in Boris Godunov, Ulrica in Un ballo in maschera, Mistress Quickly in Falstaff, Orfeo, Azucena in Il trovatore, Amneris in Aida, Brangäne in Tristan und Isolde, Eboli in Don Carlo, Fricka, Marfa in Khovanshchina, Marina in Boris Godunov, Marie in Wozzeck, Klytemnestra in Elektra, and Amme in Die Frau ohne Schatten; has sung in the leading European opera houses including Berlin, Madrid, Frankfurt, La Scala, Vienna State Opera and Bavarian State Opera, Munich; int. debut as recitalist, Salzburg Festival 1985; gives master-classes in Austria and abroad; Artistic Dir Young Singers Project of Salzburg Festival 2010. *Recordings include:* the Bach Passions, Gluck's Orfeo, Handel's Messiah, Beethoven's Choral Symphony, Wagner's Das Rheingold, Johann Strauss's Die Fledermaus and Frank Martin's Cornet, Marina in Boris Godunov under Claudio Abbado, Mahler's Kindertotenlieder, recital discs of Brahms Lieder and Schumann Lieder. *Television includes:* various concerts and recitals, Carmen, Samson and Delila, Der Ring des Nibelungen, Die Frau ohne Schatten, Tristan und Isolde. *Honours:* Hon. Order of Merit in Gold, 1st Class (Austria) 2001; Grand Prix du Disque for Frank Martin's Cornet, Prix Spécial du Jury Nouvelle Académie du Disque Français; Gustav Mahler Gold Medal (Bavaria) 1993, (Vienna) 1996. *Current Management:* c/o Machreich Artists Management, Beatrixgasse 26/5/42, 1030 Vienna, Austria.

LIPP, Wilma; Austrian singer (soprano); b. 26 April 1925, Vienna. *Education:* studied in Vienna and with Toti dal Monte in Milan. *Career:* debut in Vienna 1943, as Rosina in Il Barbiere di Siviglia; mem., Vienna Staatsoper from 1945, notably as Mozart's Queen of Night; Salzburg Festival from 1948, as Mozart's Servilia, Blondchen, Donna Elvira and Queen of Night; Covent Garden 1951, as Gilda in Rigoletto; La Scala Milan 1950, and Glyndebourne 1957, as Constanze in Die Entführung; US debut at San Francisco 1962, as Nannetta in Falstaff; guest appearances in London, Hamburg, Munich, Berlin and Paris; returned to Salzburg 1983–84, as the Duenna in Der Rosenkavalier (also at Turin 1986). *Recordings:* Brahms Ein Deutsches Requiem; Die Zauberflöte; Die Entführung; Fra Diavolo; Die Fledermaus; Fidelio; Der Rosenkavalier.

LIPPERT, Herbert; German singer (tenor); b. 1963. *Career:* sang at the Lubeck Opera 1987–91, in such roles as Pedrillo and Albert Herring; Bregenz Festival 1989, as Ferrando in Così fan tutte, followed by Tamino in Vienna, Munich and Cologne; Salzburg Festival from 1990, in Fidelio, Die Zauberflöte and Die Frau ohne Schatten; Naples and Aix Festival 1992 as Wagner's Steersman and as Don Ottavio; further engagements at the Stuttgart and Leipzig Operas; sang Wagner's David at Covent Garden, 1997; sang Ferrando at Buenos Aires, 1999; concert repertory includes Bach's St Matthew Passion. *Recordings include:* Don Ottavio in Don Giovanni under Solti. *Current Management:* Italartist Austroconcert Kulturmanagement GmbH, Lothringerstrasse 14, 3400 Klosterneuburg, Austria. *Telephone:* (22) 4332614. *Fax:*

(22) 4325819. *E-mail:* italartist@ia-ac.com. *Website:* www.ia-ac.com; www .herbertlippert.com.

LIPS, Friedrich; Russian musician (accordion), teacher and arranger; *Professor of Accordion, Gnesins Institute for Music Education;* b. 18 Nov. 1948, Yemanzhelinsk, Urals. *Education:* Gnesins Inst. for Music Educ., Moscow. *Career:* gave first solo recital 1970; toured widely in Soviet Union and worldwide 1970–; performed in concert halls including Concertgebouw Amsterdam, Kennedy Center, Washington DC and Suntory Hall, Tokyo and at festivals including Boston, Huddersfield, Schleswig Holstein and Turin; worked with orchestras, chamber ensembles and soloists including Gideon Kremer, Yo-Yo Ma, Mark Pekarsky and Vladimir Tonkha; Prof. of Accordion, Gnesins Inst. for Music Educ. 1989–, Dir of Russian Music Acad. 1996–; Visiting Prof., RAM. *Publication:* The Art of Bayan Playing. *Honours:* Hon. ARAM; 1st Prize, Int. Musiktage, Klingenthal (Germany) 1969, Russian State award for Worthy Artist 1982 and Russian Folk Artist 1994, Merit Award, Confed. Int. des Accordéonistes 2012. *Address:* Gnesins Institute for Music Education, 121069 Moscow, Povarskaya st. 30/36 (office); 117208 Moscow, Sumskoj proezd 2/3–6, Russia (home). *Telephone:* (499) 7233824 (home). *E-mail:* friedrich_lips@hotmail.com (home).

LIPTAK, David, BM, MM, DMA; American composer, pianist and teacher; b. 18 Dec. 1949, Pittsburgh, PA; m. Catherine Tait; one d. *Education:* Duquesne Univ., Eastman School of Music. *Career:* composition and theory faculties, Michigan State Univ. 1976–80, Univ. of Illinois 1980–87; Eastman School of Music 1986–, including Chair of Composition Dept 1993–. *Compositions:* Duo 1979, 1992, Seven Songs 1984, Arcs 1986, Loner 1989, Trio 1990, Shadower 1991, Rhapsodies 1992, Ancient Songs 1992. *Recordings:* Seven Songs 1984, Illusions 1989.

LIPTON, Daniel B.; French/American/Canadian conductor and artistic director; *Artistic Director, Opera Ontario;* b. 1950, Paris, France; m. 1st Olga Lucia Gaviria 1983, divorced 1985; m. 2nd Sandra Belitz 2000; one s. one d. *Education:* High School of Music and Art, Manhattan School of Music, Juilliard School, Mannes Coll., Ecole Normale Supérieure, Accad. Chigiana. *Career:* conductor, Settimane Senese, American Ballet Theater, Denver Symphony, Holland Festival (Concertgebouw), Teatro Comunale Bologna, Maggio Musicale Fiorentino (Florence), Zürich Opera, Liceo Barcelona, Madrid Opera, Teatro La Fenice (Venice), Châtelet (Paris), Sadler's Wells (London), Houston Grand Opera, Utah Opera, San Antonio Festival, Hamburg Staatsoper, Opera Royal de Wallonie, Liege, Belgium 1987, Opera di San Carlo, Naples, Italy 1988, Opera de Montréal, Canada 1993, 2003, Teatro Regio di Parma, Italy 1988, 2000, Vlaamse Oper, Antwerp, Belgium, Teatro Real, Madrid, Spain 2001, London Philharmonia, London 2002, Macau Festival, China 2002; performances throughout North and South America, Paris Opéra Orchestra and Bayerische Staatsoper (Munich); opera and symphony concerts in Hanover, Hamburg, Dusseldorf, Nuremberg, Kassel, Berlin; gala operas in Mannheim and Karlsruhe; Artistic Dir Colombia Symphony Orchestra and Opera de Colombia, Bogotá 1975–83, Opera Ontario, Canada 1986–, San Antonio Festival, San Antonio, Tex. 1987–; conducted world premiere of Gian Carlo Menotti's The Wedding; season 2003 conducted Rigoletto in Montreal, Die Zauberflöte in Avenches, Carmina Burana in Mallorca; season 2004 conducted Rigoletto in Oviedo, Macbeth in Seville, Otello in Hamilton, Don Carlo in Zagreb; Artistic Dir EurOrchester, Ruhr Valley, Germany 2001–; Prin. Guest Conductor, Philharmonia Hungarica; Guest Conductor, Deutsche Oper, Berlin 1992–2001; Prof., McMaster Univ. 1988–; invited to conduct Verdi's Nabucco for opening of First Int. Opera Festival, Moscow, Carmen for Opera Ontario; conducted Montreal Symphony Orchestra for Int. Voice Competition of Jeunesses Musicales, Montreal; Macbeth in Spain with Carlos Alvarez; Artistic Dir European Classic Festival, Triennale, Germany; opera and symphony performances in Italy, Spain, Canada 1986–2010. *Recordings:* Tosca, Puccini; Recital of Montserrat Caballé and José Carreras at Gran Teatre del Liceo in Barcelona; on video: Donizetti, Don Pasquale; Giordano, Andrea Chénier; Leoncavallo, Pagliacci; Mascagni, Cavalleria Rusticana; Mozart, Nozze di Figaro; Ponchielli, Gioconda; Puccini, La Bohème, Tosca, Turandot; Verdi, Aida, Ballo, Forza, Rigoletto, Trovatore, Hommage à Bernstein, Ruy Blas – Machetti, La Belle Epoque; various recordings with Philharmonia Hungarica. *Honours:* Cross of Boyaca (Colombia); Dr hc (McMaster Univ.) 1999. *Current Management:* c/o Harwood Management Group Inc., 509 West 110 Street, New York, NY 10025, USA. *Telephone:* (212) 864-0773. *Fax:* (212) 663-1129. *E-mail:* jim@harwood -management.com. *Website:* www.harwood-management.com. *Address:* Bertha von Suttnertrasse 62, 14469 Potsdam, Germany (home). *Telephone:* (331) 200-565-25 (home). *Fax:* (331) 200-565-26 (home). *E-mail:* daniellipton@ hotmail.com (home).

LISICHENKO, Yuri; Russian pianist and academic; b. 1 Feb. 1954, Lvov; m. Irina Plotnikova 1974; one s. one d. *Education:* Lvov Special Music School, Moscow Conservatory. *Career:* debut with Philharmonic Orchestra, Hall of Lvov Philharmonia; Professor, Moscow Conservatory; Performed: The Great Hall, 1973, 1975, The Small Hall, 1988, 1989, Moscow Conservatory; Milan, Turin, Verona, Italy, 1991; Basel, Switzerland, with violinist Tatiana Grindenko, 1991; Many television and radio appearances including television film Avantgarde in Music (Company of Musical Programmes), 1989; mem, Union of Musicians, Moscow. *Recordings:* Chopin Sonata, Anton Rubinstein Sonata, Schumann; Melody; Baroque music with Chamber Orchestra under Tatiana Grindenki, 1990; Ondine, Finland. *Honours:* 3rd Prize, Marguerite Long and Jacques Thibaud Competition, Paris, 1975; Honorary Diploma,

Tchaikovsky Competitions, 1978. *Address:* Teply Satn styr 25 K1, Apt 244, Moscow 117133, Russia.

LISIECKI, Jan; Canadian pianist; b. 23 March 1995, Calgary. *Education:* Western Canada High School, Calgary, Glenn Gould School of Music, Toronto. *Career:* has performed with orchestras including New York Philharmonic under David Zinman, Orchestre de Paris under Paavo Järvi, Tonhalle Orchestra, Zürich and NHK Symphony, Tokyo, Philadelphia Orchestra under Yannick Nézet-Séguin 2013, Orchestra Filarmonica della Scala, Milan under Daniel Harding 2014; BBC Proms debut with Antonio Pappano and Orchestra dell' Accad. di Santa Cecilia 2013; festivals include Bravo Vail, Verbier, Roque d'Anthéron, Merano and Chopin and his Europe; radio broadcasts on CBC, BBC Radio and in Austria, France, Germany, Luxembourg and Poland; Nat. Youth Amb. for UNICEF Canada 2008–12, UNICEF Amb. to Canada 2012–. *Recordings:* Chopin Piano Concertos 2009, Mozart Piano Concertos 2012, Chopin Etudes 2013. *Honours:* Révélations Radio-Canada Musique 2010, Jeune Soliste des Radios Francophones 2011, Leonard Bernstein Award, Schleswig-Holstein Festival 2013, Gramophone Award for Young Artist of the Year 2013. *Current Management:* c/o Tanja Dorn, IMG Artists, Theaterstrasse 2, 30159 Hannover, Germany. *Telephone:* (511) 437-8134. *Fax:* (511) 437-8135. *E-mail:* tdorn@imgartists.com. *Website:* www.imgartists.com; www .janlisiecki.com (office).

LISITSA, Valentina; Ukrainian pianist; b. 1969, Kiev; m. Alexei Kuznetsoff 1992; one s. *Education:* Kiev Conservatoire. *Career:* performed Dutch premiere of Rachmaninoff's New 5th Concerto for her debut with Rotterdam Phiharmonic 2010; debut with Orchestra Sinfonica Brasileira under Lorin Maazel 2011; collaborated with orchestras including Chicago, Seattle, San Francisco and London Symphony; recitals and concerts worldwide including Carnegie Hall and Avery Fisher Hall, New York, Musikverein, Vienna and Wigmore Hall and Albert Hall, London; repertoire ranges from Bach and Mozart to Shostakovich and Bernstein with over 40 concerti; toured and recorded with violinist Hilary Hahn. *Recordings include:* Valentina Lisitsa: Live at the Royal Albert Hall 2012, Rachmaninov Concertos (with LSO) 2013; with Hilary Hahn: Charles Ives: Four Sonatas 2011. *Honours:* winner (with Alexei Kuznetsoff), Murray Dranoff Int. Two Piano Competition 1991. *Current Management:* c/o Tanja Dorn, IMG Artists, Bandelstrasse 35, 30171 Hannover, Germany. *Telephone:* (511) 4378134. *Fax:* (511) 4378135. *E-mail:* tdorn@ imgartists.com. *Website:* www.imgartists.com.

LISOWSKA, Hanna; Polish singer (soprano); b. 15 Sept. 1939, Warsaw. *Education:* Music High School and Warsaw Univ. *Career:* debut at Teatr Wielki, Warsaw, as Tatiana in Eugene Onegin 1967; Fidelio as Leonore at Staatsoper Berlin, Deutsche Oper Berlin, Deutsche Oper Düsseldorf, Staatsoper Hamburg, Munich, Stuttgart, Bonn, Zürich, Rome, Wiesbaden, Madrid, Frankfurt am Main, Tokyo, Hanover; Wagnerian repertoire includes Isolde at Leipzig, Senta, Sieglinde, Brünnhilde, Gutrune in Götterdämmerung, Eva in Meistersinger, Elisabeth and Venus from Tannhäuser, all at int. venues; Gutrune in Covent Garden; Gutrune und Sieglinde in Metropolitan Opera, New York; German repertoire includes Marschallin, Chrysothemis, Eglantine, Martha; Italian repertoire includes Elisabetta in Don Carlos, Tosca, Minnie, Tatiana, Lisa; sang Aida and Lady Macbeth and Turandot in Warsaw.

LISSITSIAN, Rouben; singer (tenor); b. 9 May 1945, Moscow, Russia. *Education:* Central Music School, Moscow, Russian Music Acad., Moscow. *Career:* debut at Great Hall of Conservatory, Moscow 1965; solo vocalist, cellist, flautist, Madrigal Ensemble 1965–69; part of Evangelist in Mattauspassion by Bach, Great Hall of Philharmonic, St Petersburg 1973; Samson in Oratorio Samson by Handel, Great Hall of Conservatory, Moscow 1974; War Requiem by Britten, Wrozlaw-Festival 1974; Ninth Symphony by Beethoven, Paris Congres de Palais 1974; Rubajat by Gubaidulina with Schoenberg Ensemble in Amsterdam 1996; tours of Germany, Israel, France, Finland, The Netherlands, Hungary, USA, Canada, Poland; Pres., German-Russian Cultural and Educational Acad.; Artistic Dir, Russian Dramatic Theatre, Cologne. *Recordings:* P. Cornelius, Weihnachtslieder; R. Schumann, Lieder; W. A. Mozart, Requiem; J. Brahms, Walzer; S. Gubaidulina, Perception; Pärt, Stabat Mater. *Honours:* gold medal Int. R. Schumann Competition, Germany 1969.

LISSNER, Stéphane Michel; French theatre director; *Director General, Opéra National de Paris;* b. 23 Jan. 1953, Paris; s. of Georges Lissner and Elisabeth Landenbaum; two s. one d. *Education:* Coll. Stanislas and Lycée Henri IV, Paris. *Career:* f. his first theatre, Théâtre Mécanique 1971; Sec.-Gen. Centre dramatique, Aubervilliers 1977–78; Co-Dir Centre dramatique, Nice 1978–83; Admin., Théâtre du Châtelet, Paris 1983–88, Gen. Man. 1988–98; Dir-Gen. Orchestre de Paris 1993–95; Artistic Dir Teatro Real de Paris 1996–97; Dir Aix-en-Provence Int. Festival 1998–2006; Co-Dir, with Peter Brook Théâtre des Bouffes du Nord, Paris 1998–; currently Dir Théâtre de la Madeleine, Paris, and Music Dir Vienna Festival; Supt and Artistic Dir Teatro alla Scala, Milan 2005–14; Musical Dir Wiener Festwochen 2005–; Dir-Gen.-designate Opéra Nat. de Paris 2012–14, Dir-Gen. 2014–. *Publication:* Métro Chapelle 2000. *Honours:* Chevalier, Légion d'honneur, Officier, Ordre nat. du Mérite, Ufficiale Ordine al Merito della Repubblica Italiana. *Address:* Opéra National de Paris, Palais Garnier, 8 rue Scribe, 75009 Paris; c/o Théâtre de la Madeleine, 19 rue de Surène, 75008 Paris, France. *Website:* www.operadeparis.fr; www.theatremadeleine.com; www.festwochen.at; www .bouffesdunord.com.

LISTER, Marquita, MMus; American singer (soprano); b. 24 April 1961, Washington, DC. *Education:* New England Conservatory of Music and Oklahoma City Univ. *Career:* has performed with opera cos in London, Houston, Mexico, Portland, Baltimore, Berlin, San Francisco, Utah, Pittsburgh, Japan, Milan, Paris; operas include Porgy and Bess, Carmen, La Clemenza di Tito, Aïda, Falstaff, Turandot, I Pagliacci; concerts with Plácido Domingo 1991, Sir Neville Marriner and the Acad. of St Martin in the Fields 1994, Keith Lockhart and the Boston Pops 1995–96, Leipzig Radio Orchestra 1995–96; Enid-Phillips Symphony Young Artist Award 1984; Wichita Symphony-Naftzger Young Artist Voice Award 1985; Stewart Awards-Eleanor Steber Music Foundation Award 1988; MacAllister Award 1989; Female Artist of the Year, Pittsburgh Opera 1995–96. *Current Management:* James W. Dietsch, Dietsch International Associates, 143 South Centre Street, South Orange, NJ 07079, USA. *Telephone:* (973) 763-8836. *Fax:* (973) 763-8837. *E-mail:* dietsch@dietschartists.com. *Website:* www.dietschartists.com. *E-mail:* marquita@marquitalister.com (office). *Website:* www.marquitalister .com.

LISTOVA, Irene; violinist; b. 1960, Moscow, Russia. *Education:* Moscow Conservatoire with Leonid Kogan. *Career:* mem., Prokofiev Quartet (founded at the Moscow Festival of World Youth and the Int. Quartet Competition at Budapest); many concerts in the former Soviet Union and on tour to Czechoslovakia, Germany, Austria, USA, Canada, Spain, Japan and Italy; repertoire includes works by Haydn, Mozart, Beethoven, Schubert, Debussy, Ravel, Tchaikovsky, Bartók and Shostakovich.

LITSCHAUER, Walburga, PhD; Austrian musicologist; b. 15 Oct. 1954, Klagenfurt. *Education:* Klagenfurt High School, Univ. of Vienna, Vienna Conservatory. *Career:* mem. editorial bd, Dir of Vienna Office, Neue Schubert Ausgabe (compendium of all Schubert's compositions); edited vols of Schubert's piano music; Dir, Austrian Soc. of Music 1998–; bd mem. several nat. and int. Schubert socs. *Publications include:* Neue Dokumente zum Schubert-Kreis, vol. 1 1986, vol. 2 1993, Schubert und das Tanzvergnügen (with Walter Deutsch) 1997, some 70 publications on Schubert, Bruckner and music history; contrib. to Reclams Musikfuehrer 1991, Anton Bruckner-Handbuch 1996, Schubert-Handbuch and Schubert-Lexikon 1997, Oesterreichisches Musiklexikon 2001. *Honours:* Franz Schubert Grand Prix for special achievements in Schubert research. *E-mail:* Walburga.Litschauer@oeaw.ac .at.

LITTLE, Tasmin E., OBE, ARCM, FGSM; British violinist; b. 13 May 1965, London, England; d. of George Little and Gillian Little; one s. one d. *Education:* Yehudi Menuhin School, Guildhall School of Music, studied privately with Lorand Fenyves in Canada. *Career:* has performed with New York Philharmonic, Berlin Philharmonic, Leipzig Gewandhaus, Cleveland Orchestra, Berlin Symphony, London Symphony, London Philharmonic, Philharmonia, Royal Philharmonic, New Japan Philharmonic, Royal Stockholm Philharmonic, Hong Kong Philharmonic, BBC Symphony, Royal Liverpool Philharmonic, European Community Chamber, Royal Danish and Stavanger Symphony Orchestras; has played with orchestras conducted by Gustavo Dudamel, Kurt Masur, Vladimir Ashkenazy, Leonard Slatkin, Tadaaki Otaka, Sir Charles Groves, Sir Andrew Davis, Vernon Handley, Yan Pascal Tortelier, Sir Edward Downes, Yehudi Menuhin and Sir Simon Rattle; played at the Proms since 1990; concerto and recital performances in UK, Europe, Scandinavia, S America, Hong Kong, Oman, Zimbabwe, Australia, NZ, USA and Japan; numerous TV appearances, including BBC Last Night of the Proms 1995, 1998, Wallace and Gromit Prom 2012. *Recordings include:* works by Bruch, Dvořák, Brahms, Sibelius, Delius, Rubbra, Saxton, George Lloyd, Ravel, Debussy, Poulenc, Delius, Elgar, Bax, Finzi; Dohnányi violin sonatas, Bruch Scottish Fantasy, Lalo Symphonie Espagnole, Pärt Spiegel im Spiegel and Fratres, The Naked Violin (Gramophone/Classic FM Award for Innovation 2008) 2007, Elgar Violin Concerto (Classic BRIT Award, Critic's Choice 2011) 2010, Strauss and Respighi sonatas, British Violin Sonatas 2013, Moeran Concerto, Lark Ascending 2013, Tasmin Little Plays Haydn Wood 2015, Beethoven: Complete Sonatas 2016. *Publication:* paper on Delius' violin concerto. *Honours:* Hon. DLitt (Bradford) 1996; Hon. DMus (Leicester) 2002; Hon. DArts (Hertfordshire) 2007, (City) 2008. *Address:* 67 Teignmouth Road, London, NW2 4EA, England (office). *Telephone:* (20) 8208-2480 (office). *Fax:* (20) 8208-2490 (office). *E-mail:* d.kantor.kcm@btinternet.com (office). *Website:* www.tasminlittle.net.

LITTON, Andrew, MM; American conductor and pianist; *Music Director, Bergen Philharmonic Orchestra;* b. 16 May 1959, New York. *Education:* Fieldston High School, New York, Mozarteum, Juilliard School. *Career:* Asst Conductor, La Scala, Milan 1980–81; Exxon/Arts Endowment Asst Conductor, then Assoc. Conductor, Nat. Symphony Orchestra, Washington, DC 1982–86; Prin. Guest Conductor, Bournemouth Symphony Orchestra 1986–88, Prin. Conductor and Artistic Adviser 1988–94, Conductor Laureate 1994–; Prin. Conductor and Music Dir Dallas Symphony Orchestra 1994–2006, Music Dir Emeritus 2006–; guest conductor with numerous orchestras world-wide, including Chicago Symphony, Philadelphia, Los Angeles Philharmonic, Pittsburgh Symphony, Toronto Symphony, Montréal Symphony, Vancouver Symphony, London Philharmonic, Royal Philharmonic, London Symphony, English Chamber Orchestra, Leipzig Gewandhaus, Moscow State Symphony, Stockholm Philharmonic, RSO Berlin, RAI Milan, Orchestre Nat. de France, Suisse Romande, Tokyo Philharmonic, Melbourne Symphony and Sydney Symphony orchestras; debut at Metropolitan Opera, New York with Eugene Onegin 1989; also conducted at St Louis Opera, LA Opera, Royal Opera

House, Covent Garden and ENO; Prin. Conductor, Bergen Philharmonic Orchestra 2002–, Music Dir 2005–; Artistic Dir Minnesota Orchestra's Sommerfest 2003–, Colorado Symphony Orchestra; music consultant to film The Chosen. *Recordings include:* Mahler Symphony No. 1 and Songs of a Wayfarer, Elgar Enigma Variations, complete Tchaikovsky symphony cycle, complete Rachmaninov symphony cycle, Shostakovich Symphony No. 10, Gershwin Rhapsody in Blue, Concerto in F and Ravel Concerto in G (as piano soloist and conductor), Bernstein Symphony No. 2, Brahms Symphony No. 1, Walton's Belshazzar's Feast (with Bryn Terfel and Bournemouth Symphony) (Grammy Award), Rachmaninov Piano Concertos (with Stephen Hough and Dallas Symphony Orchestra) (Classical BRIT Critics' Award 2005) 2004. *Honours:* Royal Order of Merit (Norway); Hon. DMus (Bournemouth) 1992; winner, Bruno Walter Conducting Fellowship 1981, William Kapell Memorial US Nat. Piano Competition 1978, BBC/Rupert Foundation Int. Conductors Competition 1982, Yale Univ. Sanford Medal, Elgar Soc. Medal. *Current Management:* c/o Ron Merlino, Musicvine, 2576 Broadway, Suite 239, New York, NY 10025, USA. *Telephone:* (646) 825-9585. *E-mail:* musicvine@gmail.com. *Website:* www.filharmonien.no; www.andrewlitton.com.

LITZ, Gisela; German singer (soprano); b. 14 Dec. 1922, Hamburg. *Education:* studied in Hamburg. *Career:* after singing in Wiesbaden joined the Hamburg State Opera; visited Edinburgh with the company 1952; sang in the 1954 stage premiere of Martinů's The Marriage; Bayreuth Festival 1953–54; often heard in operetta and in Bach's cantatas; guest engagements in Buenos Aires, Rome, Lisbon, Munich and Brussels; Prof., Hamburg Musikhochschule from 1969. *Recordings:* Lortzing's Der Waffenschmied and Die Opernprobe; Nicolai's Die Lustige Weiber von Windsor; Le nozze di Figaro; Hansel and Gretel; scenes from operettas.

LIU, Zhuang; Chinese composer; b. 24 Oct. 1932, Shanghai. *Education:* Shanghai Conservatory. *Career:* teacher at the Peking Central Conservatory and composer with the Central Philharmonic Society; collaborated with others in the 'Yellow River' piano concerto, 1971. *Compositions include:* Violin concerto, 1963; Plum Blossom Triptych for orchestra, 1979; Moon Night by the Spring River, woodwind quintet, 1978; Three Trios for flute, cello and harp, 1987; Impressions of Tashgul-Kan for orchestra, 1987. *Address:* c/o Music Copyright Society of China, 85 Dongsi Nan Jajie, Beijing 100703, People's Republic of China.

LIUBAVIN, Leonid; Russian singer (tenor); b. 1970, Krasnodar. *Education:* State Tchershakov Theatre and St Petersburg Conservatoire. *Career:* appearances with the Kirov Opera, St Petersburg, from 1996 as Narraboth in Salome, Tamino, the Prince in The Love for Three Oranges, Antonio in Prokofiev's Betrothal in a Monastery and the Simpleton in Boris Godunov; further engagements as Iskra in Tchaikovsky's Mazeppa, the Fisherman in Stravinsky's Nightingale and Erik in Der fliegende Holländer; Zinovy in Lady Macbeth of Mtsensk and Tchekalinsky in The Queen of Spades; sang the Master of Ceremonies in War and Peace with the Kirov Opera at Covent Garden, 2000.

LIVELY, David; American pianist; b. 27 June 1953, Ironton, Ohio. *Education:* Ecole Normale de Musique de Paris Licence de Concert 1970, studied privately with Wilhelm Kempff, Claudio Arrau. *Career:* debut with St Louis Symphony Orchestra 1968, soloist with: Cleveland Symphony Orchestra, Baltimore Symphony Orchestra, Kennedy Center, Washington, DC, English Chamber Orchestra, Royal Philharmonic Orchestra, Vienna Symphony Orchestra, Bavarian Radio Orchestra, Berlin Symphony Orchestra, Orchestre National de France, Orchestre National de Monte Carlo, La Scala, Orchestre de la Suisse Romande; Dir, St Lizier Festival, France; guest Prof., Univ. for Music and Performing Arts, Vienna; Analyse Musicale masterclasses at Royal Scottish Acad., Glasgow, Hochschule, Vienna. *Honours:* prizewinner, Queen Elisabeth Competition, Brussels 1972, Tchaikovsky, Moscow 1974, Geneva 1971, Marguérite Long 1971, Dino Ciani Award, La Scala 1977. *Current Management:* c/o Andrea Hampl, Konzertdirektion Hampl, Karl-Schrader Street 6, 10781 Berlin, Germany. *E-mail:* hampl@konzertdirektion.de. *Website:* www.konzertdirektion.de.

LIVENGOOD, Victoria, BM, MM; American singer (mezzo-soprano); b. 1961, Thomasville, NC. *Education:* Univ. of North Carolina at Chapel Hill, Boston Conservatory, Jacksonville Univ. *Career:* sang Gertrude in Hamlet for Miami Opera (1987) followed by Beauty in Beauty and the Beast by Oliver at St Louis; New York Academy of Music 1988, as Juno in Platée; Charlotte in Werther, Seattle Opera, 1989; Meg Page in Falstaff, Calgary Opera, 1991; European debut 1991, as Mozart's Idamante at Nice; Guest appearances as Dorabella for Hawaii Opera (1990) and Carmen at Cologne (1992); Metropolitan Opera debut 1991, as Laura in Luisa Miller; Isolier in Le Comte Ory, Spoleto Festival, Charleston, 1993; Maddalena in Rigoletto, Cologne and Edmonton, 1994; Lola, Cavalleria Rusticana, Metropolitan Opera, 1994; Girl in Mahagonny for Met Opera, 1995; Carmen, Edmonton Opera, 1995; Dalila, Baltimore Opera, 1995; Giulietta in Tales of Hoffmann, Santiago, Chile, 1995; Preziosilla in La Forza del Destino for Met Opera, 1996; Isabella in The Voyage and Maddalena in Rigoletto, for Met Opera, 1996; Hippolyta in A Midsummer Night's Dream, 1996; Waltraute in Die Walküre, 1997; Giulietta in Les Contes d'Hoffmann, 1998; Sonyetka, Lady Macbeth of Mtsensk; Recitalist, Kennedy Center, 1986; Carnegie Hall debut, 1986; Recitalist, Smithsonian Institute, Washington DC, 1986; New York City recital debut, 1987; Soloist with symphonies of Atlanta, Cologne, San Diego, Baltimore, Minnesota and Washington; Cincinnati May Festival, and Lincoln Center

Chamber Music Society, 1996; Season 1998–99 Verdi's Requiem Soloist, Carnegie Hall; Sang at the Spoleto Festival and at L'Opéra de Montréal Gala; Sang Marina in Boris Godunov for Washington Opera and Maddalena in Rigoletto at the Met, 2000; Sonyetka, Lady Macbeth of Mtsensk, Met Opera, 2000 as well as Myrtle Wilson in The Great Gatsby; Baba in The Rake's Progress for Vancouver, 2000; Dalila for Cleveland Opera, 2000; Meg Page in Falstaff for San Franscio Opera debut, 2001; Title role in the world premiere of La Señorita Cristina by Luis de Pablo in Madrid, 2001; Baba in The Rake's Progress in Buenos Aires, 2002; Madame Flora in The Medium for Spoleto Festival, Italy, 2002; Azucena in Il Trovatore for Portland Opera, 2002; 2002 Met Opera roles include title role of Carmen, Hippolyta in A Midsummer Night's Dream as well as Helene in War and Peace. *Recordings include:* Puck in Oberon; The Secretary in The Consul; Akrosimova in War and Peace; Abbie in Desire Under The Elms; Soloist on Aid's Requiem; Memento Mori as well as Piercing Eyes; Haydn Canzonettas; Also solo CD: The Secret of Christmas and on Holy Ground. *Honours:* Dr hc (Jacksonville Univ.). *Current Management:* c/o Guy Barzilay Artists International Artists Management, 420 West 25th Street, Suite 4F, New York, NY 10001, USA. *E-mail:* vickie@victorialivengood.com. *Website:* www.victorialivengood.com.

LIVINGSTONE, Laureen, DipMusEd, RSAM; Scottish singer (soprano) and teacher; *Professor of Singing, Trinity Laban Conservatoire of Music and Dance, London;* b. 3 Feb. 1946, Dumbarton, Scotland; one s. one d. *Education:* Royal Scottish Acad. of Music and Drama, London Opera Centre. *Career:* wide variety of operatic, concert and TV appearances in UK and abroad; BBC Proms; recitals including Wigmore Hall and first BBC Lunchtime recital 1976; guest appearances with London Symphony Orchestra, Hallé, English Sinfonia, Northern Sinfonia, London Philharmonic, Scottish Nat. and Scottish Chamber Orchestras; operatic roles include Zerlina, Pamina, Gretel, Lucia in Rape of Lucretia with Scottish Opera, Susanna, Sophie and Vrenchen in Delius's A Village Romeo and Juliet with Opera North, Gilda in Jonathan Miller's production of Rigoletto and Sophie in Der Rosenkavalier with Sir Charles Mackerras for ENO 1988; major roles with New Sadler's Wells Opera, Handel Opera and others; engagements abroad include Woglinde at Teatro di San Carlo, Naples 1980 and Gilda for Royal Flemish Opera in Antwerp 1985; Prof. of Singing, Trinity Coll. of Music (now Trinity Laban Conservatoire of Music and Dance), London 1993–. *Recordings include:* numerous recital programmes for the BBC, Lisa in Countess Maritza (NSWO), Gianetta in The Gondoliers (first colour production for BBC TV), Ninetta in L'Amour des Trois Oranges (BBC TV) 1980, Elsie in The Yeomen of the Guard (Channel 5 video), Amore in Il Ritorno d'Ulisse in Patria (Glyndebourne, video) 1973. *Honours:* Caird Scholarship 1967, Winner, Peter Stuyvesant Scholarship 1969. *Address:* 12 Pymmes Brook Drive, New Barnet, EN4 9RU, England (home). *Telephone:* (20) 8440-1513 (home). *E-mail:* laureen.livingstone@virgin.net (home).

LLEWELLYN, Grant; British conductor; *Music Director, North Carolina Symphony Orchestra;* b. 29 Dec. 1960, Tenby, Wales; m. Charlotte Imogen Rose 1984. *Education:* Chetham's School of Music, Manchester, Gonville and Caius Coll., Cambridge, Royal Coll. of Music, London and Tanglewood Music Center, USA. *Career:* conducted City of Birmingham Symphony Orchestra, English Chamber Orchestra, Scottish Nat. Orchestra, Royal Liverpool Philharmonic Orchestra, Northern Sinfonia, Scottish Chamber Orchestra, City of London Sinfonia and BBC Symphony, Philharmonic and Welsh Orchestras; took Stockholm Sinfonietta on British tour 1986 and conducted at Spoleto, Charleston and Jeunesses Musicales World Orchestra at Berlin Festival; BBC Proms, London debut with BBC Nat. Orchestra of Wales in Mendelssohn's Violin Concerto and Beethoven's Seventh Symphony 1993, now Assoc. Guest Conductor with the orchestra; conducted BBC Nat. Orchestra of Wales Opera Gala 1996; US premiere of Goehr's Arianna at Opera Theater of St Louis 1996; Music Dir, Handel and Haydn Soc., Boston 2001–08; Music Dir, North Carolina Symphony Orchestra 2004–. *Honours:* Tagore Gold Medal, Royal Coll. of Music 1984, Tanglewood Conducting Fellowship and English-Speaking Union Scholar 1985, First Prize, Leeds Conductors' Competition 1986. *Current Management:* c/o Hazard Chase, 25 City Road, Cambridge, CB1 1DP, England. *Telephone:* (1223) 312400. *Fax:* (1223) 460827. *E-mail:* info@hazardchase.co.uk. *Website:* www.hazardchase.co.uk.

LLEWELLYN, William Benjamin James, MBE, BMus, FRAM, FRSCM; British composer, conductor and music editor (retd); b. 6 May 1925, Farnworth, Widnes, Lancs., England; s. of William Basil Llewellyn and Ethel Lumb; m. Mildred Stott (died 2011); two s. one d. *Education:* Rydal School, Colwyn Bay, Emanuel Coll., Cambridge and Royal Acad. of Music; studied composition under William Alwyn and Eric Thiman. *Career:* Asst Music Master, Charterhouse 1950; f. The Linden Singers; Dir of Music, later Second Master, Charterhouse 1965–87; Music Adviser, Nat. Fed. of Women's Insts for six years; Pres. Inc. Soc. of Musicians 1984; Festival Conductor, Leith Hill Music Festival for 14 years, Petersfield Festival for six years; Conductor Bridgwater Choral Soc. 1995–2004; mem. Jury, Great Grimsby Int. Singing Competition 1992, Chair. of Cttee of Adjudicators 1995; adjudicated regularly at competitions and festivals, including Hong Kong; Chair., Royal School of Church Music in Devon for 12 years. *Compositions:* compiled and edited the Novello Book of Carols, Sing With All My Soul (52 Worship Songs for choirs) Royal School of Church Music followed by Worship in Song 1997, Lincolnshire Voices for the Grimsby Philharmonic Choir's 140th anniversary, Flying Colours for the Farnham Festival 1987, On Earth in Concert Sing a requiem, Cross and

Grave and Glory a passion sequence, The Figure on the Shore 2002. *Publications:* Music Ed.: A Calendar of Praise, High Days and Holy Days, The Voice of Faith, Above Every Name, Draw Near to God, A Mirror to the Soul. *Address:* Forecourt, Queen's Square, Colyton, Devon, EX24 6JX, England (home). *Telephone:* (1297) 552414 (home). *E-mail:* william .llewellyn@tiscali.co.uk (home).

LLOYD, Anthony Stuart; British singer (bass-baritone); b. 1970, Cardiff, Wales. *Education:* Welsh Coll. of Music and Drama. *Career:* Don Magnifico in Cenerentola at Ischia 1993; WNO as Mozart's Bartolo; Rossini's Basilio, the Commendatore and High Priest in Nabucco; Freiburg Opera from 1997, as Leporello, Lodovico in Otello; concerts include Les Troyens under Colin Davis in London and Michel Plasson in Toulouse; Eremit in Der Freischütz for Chelsea Opera; season 1998–99 as Mephistopheles in Faust and Selim in Il Turco in Italia. *Honours:* Geraint Evans Memorial Prize, Pontypridd. *Current Management:* c/o Parker Entertainments Ltd, 6 Chilham Close, Hemel Hempstead, HP2 4UG, England. *E-mail:* office@parker-entertainments.com. *Website:* www.parker-entertainments.com; www.anthonystuartlloyd.com.

LLOYD, David Bellamy; British piano accompanist; b. 22 Nov. 1937, Stockport, Cheshire. *Education:* ARMCM (Performance and Teaching). *Career:* debut recital with Heddle Nash, Wigmore Hall 1956; accompanist to Jan Peerce, Festival Hall, London and tour of France, Germany, Switzerland, Austria and Netherlands; concert and TV appearances with Jack Brymer, Adele Leigh and Charlotte Rimmer; fmr accompanist to Jack Brymer, Leon Goossens and Elizabeth Harwood in recitals and broadcasts in Singapore, Hong Kong, India, New Zealand, Spain, Canada and USA; Sr Lecturer, Royal Northern Coll. of Music 1967–93; professional accompanist and chamber musician 1967–; examiner, Associated Bd of Royal Schools of Music 1969–2002; mem. Inc. Soc. of Musicians. *Compositions:* Schubert Arpeggione Sonata (arranged by David Lloyd). *Recordings include:* Brahms Clarinet Sonata Op 120/1, Weber Duo Concertante; Brahms Clarinet Sonata Op 120/2; Schubert Arpeggione Sonata arranged for Clarinet; Schumann Phantasiestücke Op 73; Hurlstone Four Characteristic Pieces; Art of Leon Goossens. *Honours:* Royal Manchester Coll. of Music Hilary Haworth Prize 1958.

LLOYD, Jonathan; British composer; b. 30 Sept. 1948, London. *Education:* studied composition with Emile Spira, Royal Coll. of Music, London with Edwin Roxburgh and John Lambert, Electronic Music Studio with Tristram Cary. *Career:* Twentieth Century Ensemble 1968; awarded Mendelssohn Scholarship and lived in Paris 1969–70; occasional work as performer, street musician 1974–77; composer-in-residence, Dartington Coll. Theatre Dept 1978–79. *Compositions include:* orchestral: Cantique 1968, five Symphonies 1983–89, Rhapsody for cello and orchestra 1982, Viola Concerto 1979–80, Everything Returns for soprano and orchestra 1977–78, Mass for six solo voices 1983, Missa Brevis 1984, Toward the Whitening Dawn for chorus and chamber orchestra 1980, Revelation for eight voices 1990, Marching to a Different Song for soprano and chamber orchestra 1991, Ballad for the Evening of a Man for mixed quartet 1992; dramatic: The Adjudicator community opera 1985, Blackmail (music for Alfred Hitchcock's film) 1993, edn of the Beggar's Opera 1999, Tolerance for orchestra 1994, People Your Dreams for voice and ensemble 1994, Blessed Days of Blue for solo flute and strings 1995, Violin Concerto 1995, Piano Concerto 1995, And Beyond for chorus and ensemble 1996, A Dream of a Pass 1997, Shadows of Our Future Selves for ensemble 1998. *Recordings:* Mass, Second Symphony 1992, Largo. *Address:* c/o Boosey and Hawkes Ltd, First Floor, Aldwych House, 71–91 Aldwych, London, WC2B 4HN, England (office). *Website:* www.boosey.com/lloyd (office).

LLOYD, Phyllida, CBE, BA; British theatre director and film director; b. 17 June 1957, Bristol; d. of Patrick Lloyd and Margaret Lloyd (née Douglas-Pennent). *Education:* Lawnside School, Great Malvern, Univ. of Birmingham. *Career:* fmr Floor Asst, BBC TV for five years; awarded Arts Council of GB bursary to be Trainee Dir at Wolsey Theatre, Ipswich 1985; Assoc. Dir, Everyman Theatre, Cheltenham 1986–89, Bristol Old Vic 1989–91, Royal Exchange Theatre, Manchester 1991; Cameron Mackintosh Visiting Prof. of Contemporary Theatre, Univ. of Oxford 2006. *Theatre includes:* Six Degrees of Separation (Royal Court) 1992, Hysteria (Royal Court) 1993, Pericles 1993, The Threepenny Opera 1994, The Way of the World 1995, Dona Rosita (Almeida) 1997, The Prime of Miss Jean Brodie (Royal Nat. Theatre) 1998, Mamma Mia! (London and elsewhere) 1999–, Boston Marriage (Donmar) 2001. *Opera includes:* Gloriana 1993, La Bohème (Opera North at Sheffield Lyceum) 1993, Medea (Opera North) 1996, Carmen 1998, Dialogues of the Carmelites (ENO) 1999, Macbeth (Paris Opera) 1999, Verdi Requiem (ENO) 2000, The Handmaid's Tale (Copenhagen) 2000, Fidelio (Glyndebourne) (Royal Philharmonic Soc. Opera Award) 2001, The Valkyrie (Glastonbury Festival) 2004, Siegfried (ENO) 2004, Peter Grimes (Opera North) 2006. *Films:* Mamma Mia! 2008, The Iron Lady 2011. *Television film:* Gloriana (BBC 2) (Emmy Award 2000) 1999. *Honours:* hon. degree (Bristol) 2006; named one of the 100 most influential gay and lesbian people in Britain by the Independent 2006. *Current Management:* c/o Annette Stone Associates, Arthouse B7-3, 1 York Way, London, N1C 4AT, England. *Telephone:* (20) 3725-6893. *E-mail:* annette@annettestone.com. *Website:* www.annettestone .com.

LLOYD, Robert Andrew, CBE, MA; British singer (bass); b. 2 March 1940, Southend-on-Sea; s. of William Edward Lloyd and May Lloyd (née Waples); m. 1st Sandra D. Watkins 1964 (divorced 1990); one s. three d.; m. 2nd Lynda A.

Hazell (née Powell) 1992. *Education:* Southend High School for Boys, Keble Coll., Oxford, London Opera Centre. *Career:* served as Lt in Royal Navy 1963–66; Lecturer, Bramshill Police Coll. 1966–68; Prin. Bass, Sadler's Wells Opera 1969–72, Royal Opera House 1972–83, Sr Artist, Royal Opera House 2005–10; freelance singer with all maj. opera houses and orchestras worldwide, frequent broadcasts as presenter, BBC radio and TV 1983–; film appearances: Parsifal, Bluebeard's Castle; performed title role in Tarkovsky production of Boris Godunov at Kirov Opera, Leningrad 1990; created role of Tyrone in Tower by Alun Hoddinott; Visiting Prof., Royal Coll. of Music, London 1996–; Pres. British Youth Opera 1988–94, Southend Choral Soc. 1996–; mem. Exec. Cttee Musicians' Benevolent Fund 1989–92; mem. Conservatoires Advisory Group 1993–99; Pres. Inc. Soc. of Musicians 2006; Fellow, Royal Welsh Coll. of Music and Drama; Patron Carl Rosa Trust 1994–. *Radio:* regular presenter for BBC Radio 3. *Television:* wrote and presented documentary Six Foot Cinderella 1990, subject of BBC documentary Bob the Bass. *Publications:* numerous contribs to magazines. *Honours:* Hon. mem. Royal Acad. of Music; Hon. Fellow, Keble Coll. 1990; Artist of the Year, Teatro Colón, Buenos Aires 1996, Charles Santley Award 1997, Chaliapin Commemoration Medal (St Petersburg) 1998.

LLOYD DAVIES, John; British stage director and designer; b. 1950, Northampton, Northants., England. *Career:* Dir and designer of more than 100 productions, including Don Giovanni, Die Zauberflöte and Rigoletto for Vienna Kammeroper, Madama Butterfly for Royal Danish Opera, Die Zauberflöte, Un Ballo in Maschera in Klagenfurt, Tosca in Malmö; premieres of Death In Venice, Weisse Rose, Medea, Das Schloss in Vienna; Albert Herring in Aldeburgh, Les Contes d'Hoffmann in Nuremberg, Der Rosenkavalier and Don Giovanni in Dortmund, God's Liar at La Monnaie, Brussels and Almeida, London, Ariadne auf Naxos and Salome in Dallas, Maria de Buenos Aires in Los Angeles; Head of Opera Devt, ROH2 OperaGenesis programme, Royal Opera House 2005–12; plans include The Turn of the Screw at Teatro Sao Carlos, Lisbon, world premiere of Neil Hannon's opera Sevastopol at Royal Opera House and Reigen and Anna Karenina in Vienna. *Honours:* Josef Kainz Medal (Austria) 1998. *Website:* johnlloyddavies.com.

LLOYD-DAVIES, Mary; singer (soprano); b. 1965, Llanuwchllyn, Wales. *Education:* Royal Coll. of Music, studied in Paris with Pierre Bernac. *Career:* appearances with WNO as Elektra, Turandot, Tosca and Leonore in Fidelio; Isolde, Ortrud and Mrs Grose in The Turn of the Screw for ENO; Elisabeth in Tannhäuser and Wagner's Senta for Chelsea Opera Group; concerts in Germany, South America, USA and Canada; Beethoven's Ninth in Lisbon and Ravel's Schéhérazade in Toulouse; season 1998–99 with Amelia in Un Ballo in Maschera and Isolde for WNO.

LLOYD-HOWELLS, David, BMus, MMus, FTCL, FLCM; composer; b. 11 Jan. 1942, Cardiff, Wales. *Education:* Ealing Music Centre, London, Trinity Coll. of Music, Pontypridd Technical Coll., South Gwent Coll., Univ. of London, York Univ. *Career:* Tutor in Music, Gwent 1971–77; adult education 1980–83; community musician 1984; freelance composer, conductor, artistic dir and adjudicator; works mainly with electronic live media; music theatre, modern dance groups, Cedar Dance Theatre Company, London 1983; D.L.H. Productions, music for film, video and self-therapy 1990; Artistic Dir, Sonicity 2000, archive of scores, sonic art works, recordings, essays, poems letters at the Nat. Library of Wales 1993; Guild for the Promotion of Welsh Music Composers database, Arts Council of Wales. *Compositions include:* Bleak Sleaze, Dark Clowns, Nightcity Pulses, Canticles of Goth, Druidika, The Wrath Conference (Black Rain, Red Grass, Blue Snow, Green Sand), Digital Weave, Life Music, Surfing the Strobe, Sounds from the Noisebath, Dark Clowns, MEC, Legacy of the Icon Slave, The Insects' Convention, Fractosonic Graffiti, NOK, Requiem I-Spy, Youthworks, Rites of War, Mind Songs, Piani Melismata, Freakspeak, Edge of Shadows, Molecular Analysis, Ungrateful Utterance, Everything But Silence, Shadowself Connection, Miscreant Hues (sound opera in seven cadenzas). *Recording:* Piano Sonata 2 1978. *Publication:* Soundgazing: A personal view about the future of music.

LLOYD-JONES, David Mathias, BA; British musician and conductor; b. 19 Nov. 1934, London; s. of the late Sir Vincent Lloyd-Jones and Margaret Alwena Mathias; m. Anne Carolyn Whitehead 1964; two s. one d. *Education:* Westminster School, Magdalen Coll., Oxford. *Career:* Repetiteur, Royal Opera 1959–61; Chorus Master, New Opera Co. 1961–64; conducted at Bath Festival 1966, City of London Festival 1966, Wexford Festival 1967–70, Scottish Opera 1968, Welsh Nat. Opera 1968, Royal Opera, Covent Garden 1971, Sadler's Wells Opera Co. (now ENO) 1969; Asst Music Dir ENO 1972–78; Artistic Dir Opera North 1978–90; also conductor for TV operas (Eugene Onegin, The Flying Dutchman, Hansel and Gretel) and has appeared with most British symphony orchestras and conducted worldwide; Chair. Delius Trust 1997–, Gen. Ed. William Walton Edn 1996–. *Music includes:* many acclaimed recordings of British and Russian music; has edited works by composers, including Mussorgsky, Bizet, Walton, Berlioz, Elgar and Sullivan. *Publications include:* Boris Godunov–Translation, Vocal Score, Eugene Onegin–Translation, Vocal Score, Boris Godunov–Critical Edition of Original Full Score, numerous contribs to publs including Grove's Dictionary of Music and Musicians, Musik in Geschichte und Gegenwart, Music and Letters, The Listener. *Honours:* Hon. mem. Royal Philharmonic Soc. 2007; Hon. DMus (Leeds) 1986. *Address:* 94 Whitelands House, Cheltenham Terrace, London, SW3 4RA, England (home). *Telephone:* (20) 7730-8695.

LLOYD ROBERTS, Carys; singer (soprano); b. 1969, Wales. *Education:* Welsh Coll. of Music and Drama. *Career:* engagements with the WNO, Musica nel Chiostro and City of Birmingham Touring Opera as Papagena, First Lady, Barbarina and Hansel; Purcell's King Arthur with Les Arts Florissants at Covent Garden and The Fairy Queen with the Northern Sinfonia; concerts include the Jonathan Miller production of the St Matthew Passion and appearances at Llandaff Cathedral and St Martin-in-the-Fields, London; sang Lensky for Grange Park Opera 2000.

LLOYD-ROBERTS, Jeffrey; British singer (tenor); b. 1968, Wales. *Education:* Royal Northern College of Music with Barbara Robotham, Lancaster University. *Career:* appearances with WNO in The Makropulos Case, as Nemorino with English Touring Opera in Le Roi malgré Lui for Chelsea Opera and in Aroldo at the Buxton Festival; season 1995 as Lindoro in La fedeltà premiata for Garsington Opera and concerts of Korngold's Ring of Polycrates, the B Minor Mass, the Verdi Requiem, Mahler's 8th Symphony and The Dream of Gerontius.

LLOYD WEBBER, Baron (Life Peer), cr. 1997, of Sydmonton in the County of Hampshire; **Andrew Lloyd Webber,** FRCM; British composer; *Chairman, The Really Useful Group Ltd*; b. 22 March 1948, Kensington, London; s. of the late William Southcombe Lloyd Webber and Jean Hermione Johnstone; brother of Julian Lloyd Webber (q.v.); m. 1st Sarah Jane Tudor (née Hugill) 1971 (divorced 1983); one s. one d.; m. 2nd Sarah Brightman 1984 (divorced 1990); m. 3rd Madeleine Astrid Gurdon 1991; two s. one d. *Education:* Westminster School, Magdalen Coll. Oxford, Royal Coll. of Music. *Career:* Chair. The Really Useful Group Ltd; owner of six London theatres including Theatre Royal Drury Lane and The London Palladium. *Works:* musicals: Joseph and the Amazing Technicolor Dreamcoat (lyrics by Tim Rice) 1968 (revised 1973, 1991), Jesus Christ Superstar (lyrics by Tim Rice) 1970 (revised 1996, 2012), Jeeves (lyrics by Alan Ayckbourn) 1975 (revised as By Jeeves 1996), Evita (lyrics by Tim Rice) 1976 (stage version 1978), Tell Me on a Sunday (lyrics by Don Black) 1980 (revised 2003), Cats (based on T. S. Eliot's Old Possum's Book of Practical Cats) (Tony Awards for Best Score and Best Musical 1983) 1981, Song and Dance (lyrics by Don Black) 1982, Starlight Express (lyrics by Richard Stilgoe) 1984, The Phantom of the Opera (lyrics by Richard Stilgoe and Charles Hart) (Tony Award for Best Musical 1988) 1986, Aspects of Love (lyrics by Don Black and Charles Hart) 1989, Sunset Boulevard (lyrics by Christopher Hampton and Don Black) (Tony Award for Best Score and Best Musical 1995) 1993, Whistle Down the Wind (lyrics by Jim Steinman) 1996, The Beautiful Game (lyrics by Ben Elton) (London Critics' Circle Best Musical 2000) 2000, The Woman in White (lyrics by David Zippel) 2004, Love Never Dies (lyrics by Glenn Slater) 2010, Stephen Ward (lyrics by Christopher Hampton and Don Black) 2013, School of Rock 2015; other compositions: Variations (based on A minor Caprice No. 24 by Paganini) 1977 (symphonic version 1986), Requiem Mass 1985, Amigos Para Siempre (official theme for 1992 Olympic Games), UK Eurovision entry, It's My Time (co-written with Diane Warren), Moscow 2009; film scores: Gumshoe 1971, The Odessa File 1974. *Producer:* Joseph and the Amazing Technicolor Dreamcoat 1973, 1974, 1978, 1980, 1991, Jeeves Takes Charge 1975, Cats 1981, Song & Dance 1982, Daisy Pulls it Off 1983, The Hired Man 1984, Starlight Express 1984, On Your Toes 1984, The Phantom of the Opera 1986, Café Puccini 1986, The Resistible Rise of Arturo Ui 1987, Lend Me a Tenor 1988, Aspects of Love 1989, Shirley Valentine (Broadway) 1989, La Bête 1992, Sunset Boulevard 1993, By Jeeves 1996, Whistle Down the Wind 1996, 1998, Jesus Christ Superstar 1996, 1998, The Beautiful Game 2000, Bombay Dreams 2002, Tell Me On A Sunday, 2003, The Woman in White 2004, The Sound of Music 2006 and others. *Art collection:* Pre-Raphaelite and Other Masters: The Andrew Lloyd Webber Collection, Royal Acad., London 2003. *Film:* The Phantom of the Opera (dir Joel Schumacher) 2004. *Publications:* Evita (with Tim Rice) 1978, Cats: the book of the musical 1981, Joseph and the Amazing Technicolor Dreamcoat (with Tim Rice) 1982, The Complete Phantom of the Opera 1987, The Complete Aspects of Love 1989, Sunset Boulevard: from movie to musical 1993. *Honours:* seven Tony Awards, four Drama Desk Awards, seven Laurence Olivier Awards, 14 Ivor Novello Awards from British Acad. of Songwriters, Composers and Authors, Triple Play Award from ASCAP 1988, Star on the Hollywood Walk of Fame for live theatre 1993, Praemium Imperiale Award 1995, four Grammy Awards, Golden Globe Award, Academy Award 1996, Richard Rodgers Award for Excellence in Musical Theatre 1996, Kennedy Center Honor 2006, Woodrow Wilson Award for Public Service 2008, American Songwriters Hall of Fame; Commdr's Cross of the Order of Merit (Hungary) 2005. *Address:* c/o The Really Useful Group Ltd, 17 Slingsby Place, London, WC2E 9AB, England (office). *Telephone:* (20) 7240-0880 (office). *Fax:* (20) 7240-1204 (office). *Website:* www.reallyuseful.com (office); www.andrewlloydwebber.com.

LLOYD WEBBER, Julian, FRCM; British cellist, music educationist and writer; *Principal, Birmingham Conservatoire*; b. 14 April 1951, London; s. of the late William Southcombe Lloyd Webber and of Jean Hermione Johnstone; brother of Andrew Lloyd Webber (q.v.); m. 1st Celia M. Ballantyne 1974 (divorced 1989); m. 2nd Zohra Mahmoud Ghazi 1989 (divorced 1999); one s.; m. 3rd Kheira Bourahla 2001 (divorced 2007); m. 4th Jiaxin Cheng 2009; one d. *Education:* Univ. Coll. School, Royal Coll. of Music (scholar), studied with Pierre Fournier in Geneva. *Career:* debut with first London performance of Bliss Cello Concerto at Queen Elizabeth Hall 1972; debut, Lincoln Center, New York 1980; debut with Berlin Philharmonic Orchestra 1984; appears at major int. concert halls and on concert tours throughout Europe, N and S America, S Africa, Australasia, Singapore, Japan, China, Hong Kong and S Korea; numerous radio and TV appearances and broadcasts in UK, Netherlands, Africa, Germany, Scandinavia, France, Belgium, Spain, Australasia and USA; Patron Jacqueline du Pré Charity Concerts 2006–, BSO (Bournemouth Symphony Orchestra) Vibes 2012–; Chair. Sistema England charity 2008–; Prin. Birmingham Conservatoire 2015–; Pres. Elgar Soc. 2009. *Recordings include:* world premiere recordings of Britten's 3rd Suite for Solo Cello, Bridge's Oration, Rodrigo's Cello Concerto (Spanish Ministry of Culture Award for world premiere recording 1982), Holst's Invocation, Gavin Bryars' Cello Concerto, Michael Nyman's Cello and Saxophone Concerto, Sullivan's Cello Concerto, Vaughan Williams' Fantasia on Sussex Folk Tunes, Andrew Lloyd Webber's Variations (Gold disc 1978), Elgar's Cello Concerto (British Phonographic Industry Award for Best Classical Recording 1986), Dvořák Concerto, Saint-Saëns Concerto, Lalo Concerto, Walton Concerto, Britten Cello Symphony; Philip Glass Cello Concerto, And the Bridge is Love 2015. *Publications:* Classical Cello 1980, Romantic Cello 1981, French Cello 1981, Frank Bridge, Six Pieces 1982, Young Cellist's Repertoire (three vols) 1984, Holst's Invocation 1984, Travels with my Cello 1984, Song of the Birds 1985, Recital Repertoire for Cellists (four vols) 1986, Short Sharp Shocks 1990, The Great Cello Solos 1992, The Essential Cello 1997, Cello Moods 1999, String Quartets, 2003; Made in England 2003; columnist, Daily Telegraph 2003–; contrib. to: The Times, The Sunday Times, USA Today. *Honours:* Dr hc (Hull) 2003, (Thames Valley) 2004; Suggia Gift 1968, Brit Award for Elgar Cello Concerto recording 1987, Crystal Award, World Economic Forum (Switzerland) 1998, Classic FM Red Award for outstanding services to music 2005. *Current Management:* c/o IMG Artists Europe, The Light Box, 111 Power Road, London, W4 5PY, England. *Telephone:* (20) 7957-5800. *Fax:* (20) 7957-5801. *E-mail:* labrahams@imgartists.com (office). *Website:* www.imgartists.com; sistemaengland.org.uk; www.julianlloydwebber.com.

LOBANOV, Vassily; composer and pianist; b. 2 Jan. 1947, Moscow, USSR. *Education:* Tchaikovsky Conservatoire, Moscow with Leo Naumov, Sergei Balasanyan and Alfred Schnittke. *Career:* has accompanied Natalia Gutman and Oleg Kagan individually and as mem. of trio; interpreter of modern works at festivals in Moscow, Witten, Vienna and Kuhmo, Finland; premiered his Second Piano Sonata at the Moscow Autumn Festival 1980; has partnered Sviatoslav Richter in duets; December Nights concert in the Pushkin Museum Moscow 1981; soloist with the Moscow Philharmonic from 1982; Prof. of Piano, Cologne Hochschule 1997–. *Compositions include:* Oratorio Lieutenant Schmidt 1979, Opera Antigone 1985–88; orchestra: Symphony for chamber orchestra 1977, Piano Concerto 1981, Cello Concerto 1985, Sinfonietta 1986, Concerto for viola and strings 1989, Piano Concerto No. 2 1993, Double Concerto for violin and clarinet 1995, Trumpet Concerto 1998, Viola Concerto No. 2 1998; chamber: five string quartets 1966, 1968, 1978, 1987, 1988, Twelve Preludes for piano 1965, Partita for piano 1967, two Cello Sonatas 1971, 1989, two piano sonatas 1973, 1980, three Suites for piano, Seven Pieces for cello and piano 1978, Variations for two trumpets 1979, Seven Slow Pieces for piano 1978–80, Flute Sonata 1983, Clarinet Sonata 1985, Fantasia for solo cello 1987, Violin Sonata 1989, Viola Sonata 1990, Piano Quintet 1991, Piano Quartet 1996, String Trio 1996, Clarinet Quintet 1999; vocal: Three Haikus for low voice and piano 1963, Three Romances for bass 1965, Five Romances 1971, Four Poems to texts by Alexei Parin for bass 1984, Eight Poems for soprano 1984, Stravinsky's Italian Suite adapted for cello and chamber orchestra 1985. *Address:* c/o Boosey & Hawkes Music Publishers Ltd, Aldwych House, 71–91 Aldwych, London, WC2B 4HN, England (office).

LOCKHART, Beatriz; Uruguayan composer; b. 17 Jan. 1944, Montevideo; m. Antonio Mastrogiovanni 1969; one d. *Education:* Montevideo Conservatory, studied with Carlos Estrada and Héctor Tosar, Centro Latinoamericano de Altos Estudios Musicales, Buenos Aires, Argentina, studied with Alberto Ginastera, Accad. Musicale Chigiana, Siena, Italy, studied with Franco Donatoni. *Career:* teacher, Conservatorio de Caracas 1974–88, Prof., School of Music Universidad de Montevideo 1988–; f. Asociación Mujeres en Música 2001. *Compositions include:* Ecos for orchestra, Concerto Grosso, Masia muju for flute and orchestra 1987, Theme and variations for piano, Ejercio I for tape and other electronic music, Visión de los vencidos for voice and orchestra 1990, Homenaje a Astor Piazzola for piano 1994, Concertino for double bass and orchestra 1999, Concertino for violoncello and orchestra 2004, Concertino for trumpet, horn and trombone 2009, Cánticos Primigenios (string quartet) 2010. *Recordings include:* Música para la ciudad de Montevideo 2009. *Honours:* Premio Unico de Composición, Universidad Simón Bolívar, Venezuela, Premio Municipal de Música 1978, 1983, 1984, 1987, Premio Nacional de Música (Venezuela) 1980, 1984, Premio Trimalca (Argentina) 1997, named Woman of the Year, Asociación de Mujeres Periodistas y Escritoras (Uruguay) 2000, Premio 'Virgen del Pintado' (Uruguay) 2006, Premio Morosoli de Plata 2012. *Address:* c/o AGADU, Calle canelones 1122, 11100 Montevideo, Uruguay. *Website:* www.mujeresenmusica.org.

LOCKHART, James, BMus, FRCM, FRCO (CHM); British conductor and music director; b. 16 Oct. 1930, Edinburgh; s. of Archibald C. Lockhart and Mary B. Lawrence; m. Sheila Grogan 1954; two s. one d. *Education:* George Watson's Coll., Edin., Univ. of Edin. and Royal Coll. of Music. *Career:* Asst Conductor, Yorkshire Symphony Orchestra 1954–55; Repetiteur and Asst Conductor, Städtische Bühnen Münster 1955–56, Bayerische Staatsoper, Munich 1956–57, Glyndebourne Festival Opera 1957–59; Dir Opera Workshop, Univ. of Texas 1957–59; Repetiteur and Asst Conductor, Royal Opera House, Covent Garden 1959–60, Conductor 1962–68; Asst Conductor, BBC Scottish

Orchestra 1960–61; Conductor, Sadler's Wells Opera 1961–62; Prof. Royal Coll. of Music 1962–72; Musical Dir Welsh Nat. Opera 1968–73; General-musikdirektor, Staatstheater Kassel 1972–80, Koblenz and Theater der Stadt, Koblenz 1981–88, Rheinische Philharmonie 1981–91; Prin. Guest Conductor, BBC Concert Orchestra 1982–87; Dir of Opera, Royal Coll. of Music 1986–92, London Royal Schools' Vocal Faculty 1992–96, Opera Consultant 1996–98; Guest Prof. of Conducting, Tokyo Nat. Univ. of Fine Arts and Music (Tokyo Geidai) 1998–2001, Prof. Emer. 2001–; freelance conductor 2001–; Guest Prof. of Conducting, Sydney Conservatorium of Music 2005–. *Honours:* Hon. RAM 1993. *Address:* 5 The Coach House, Mill Street, Fontmell Magna, Shaftesbury, Dorset, SP7 0NU, England (home). *Telephone:* (1747) 811980 (home). *Fax:* (1747) 811980 (home). *E-mail:* lockgrog@zen.co.uk (home).

LOCKHART, Keith, BA, BMus, MFA; American conductor; *Principal Conductor, BBC Concert Orchestra*; b. 7 Nov. 1959, Poughkeepsie, NY; s. of Newton Frederick Lockhart and Marilyn Jean Woodyard Lockhart; m. 1st Ann Louise Hetherington 1981 (divorced 1983); m. 2nd Lucia Lin; one s.; m. 3rd Emiley Zalesky 2007; one s. *Education:* Furman Univ., Carnegie Mellon Univ., Brevard Music Center. *Career:* joined Gamma Eta chapter, Phi Mu Alpha Sinfonia 1978; Assoc. Conductor, Cincinnati Symphony Orchestra and Cincinnati Pops Orchestra 1990–95; Music Dir Cincinnati Chamber Orchestra 1992–99; Conductor, Boston Pops Orchestra 1995–; Music Dir Utah Symphony Orchestra 1998–2009, Conductor Laureate 2009–; Artistic Advisor and Prin. Conductor, Brevard Music Center 2007–; Prin. Conductor, BBC Concert Orchestra 2010–; fmr Conducting Fellow, Los Angeles Philharmonic Inst. *Recordings:* albums: with Boston Pops Orchestra: Runnin' Wild: The Boston Pops Play Glenn Miller 1996, American Visions 1997, The Celtic Album 1998, Holiday Pops 1998, A Splash of Pops 1999, Encore! 2000, The Latin Album 2000, My Favorite Things: A Richard Rodgers Celebration 2002, Sleigh Ride 2004, America 2005, American Visions, The Celtic Album. *Honours:* Dr hc (Muskingham Coll., New Concord), (Boston Conservatory), (Boston Univ.), (Centre Coll., Danville), (Furman Univ.), (Northeastern Univ.). *Current Management:* Tim Fox, Columbia Artist Management Inc., 1790 Broadway, New York, NY 10019-1412, USA. *Telephone:* (212) 841-9500. *Fax:* (212) 841-9744. *E-mail:* info@cami.com. *Website:* www.cami.com. *Address:* BBC Concert Orchestra, Room 220A, Drama Building, Wood Lane, London, W12 7RJ, England (office); KeithLockhart.com, Symphony Hall, 301 Massachusetts Avenue, Boston, MA 02115, USA (office). *Telephone:* (20) 8576-0333 (England) (office). *Fax:* (20) 8576-0356 (England) (office). *E-mail:* keith@keithlockhart.com. *Website:* www.bbc.co.uk/orchestras/concertorchestra (office); www.keithlockhart.com.

LOCKLEY, Michael Allen, BS, MM; American singer (tenor); b. 7 March 1960, Sodus, NY; m. Jennifer Bates 1989, one s. *Education:* Geneseo College, Binghamton University. *Career:* Artist-in-Residence, Tri-Cities Opera and European Mozart Acads; debut at Tri-Cities Opera, 1983; performances with New York City Opera, Baltimore Opera, Tulsa Opera, Ash Lawn-Highland Opera Festival and Maggio Musicale, Florence; has sung Rodolfo in La Bohème, Alfredo in La Traviata, Ferrando in Così fan tutte, Tamino in Die Zauberflöte, Romeo in Roméo et Juliette, and Don José in Carmen; mem. AGMA, Association of Film, Television and Radio Artists. *Recordings:* Arabesque, Greenhays Rivertown. *Honours:* Richard F. Gold grant, Ezio Pinza Council for American Singers. *Current Management:* William R. Hendrickson Artists Management, 47 Penny Lane, Ithaca, NY 14850, USA. *Website:* www.michaellockley.com.

LOCKWOOD, Annea Ferguson, BMus, LRAM, ARCM; New Zealand/American composer and academic; b. 29 July 1939, Christchurch, New Zealand. *Education:* Univ. of Canterbury, New Zealand, Royal Coll. of Music, London, Musikhochschule Cologne, Inst. for Sound and Vibration Research, Southampton Univ., England. *Career:* major performances of own compositions at Cheltenham Festival, UK 1965, 1969, Commonwealth Festival, UK 1965, Paris Biennale 1965, Fylkingen Festival, Stockholm 1970, QEH, London 1971, Lincoln Center Plaza, New York 1974, New Music America Festivals 1979, 1982, 1986, Autunno Musicale a Como, Italy 1979, Sydney Biennale 1982, Westdeutscher Rundfunk, Meet the USA Festival 1982, Asia Pacific Festival 1984, Westdeutscher Rundfunk, Ives & Co. 1988, New York-Cologne Festival 1989, Alice Tully Hall 1992, The Kitchen 1997, Engine 27 2000, Hudson River Museum 2003, Bang on a Can Marathon (all in New York) 2003, Los Angeles County Museum of Modern Art 1995, Summergarden Museum of Modern Art 1997, Whitney Museum of American Art 2000, Mystic und Maschine festival, Münster 2000, De Ijsbreker, New Music, New Zealand, Amsterdam 2001, Other Minds 8 Festival, San Francisco 2002; mem. BMI Inc., American Music Center. *Compositions include:* Red Mesa, Thousand Year Dreaming, Shapeshifter, I Give You Back, Ear-Walking Woman, Duende, Floating World, Piano Transplants, Immersion, Vortex, Ceci n'est pas un piano, A Sound Map of the Hudson River, Delta Run, Glass Concert, Humming, Malaman, Malolo, Monkey Trips, Nautilus, Night and Fog, Spirit Catchers, The Angle of Repose, Tiger Balm, World Rhythms, Wai Pounamu, A Sound Map of the Danube, Amazonia Dreaming, In Our Name, Jitterbug, A Sound Map of the Housatonic River, Thirst, Luminescence, Gone!. *Honours:* Hon. DFA (Clark Univ., Worcester, USA) 1999; NEA Composition Fellow, USA 1979, CAPS Composition Fellowship, USA 1979, Arts Council of Great Britain grant 1972, Gulbenkian Foundation grant 1972, Henry Cowell Award 2007. *Address:* 37 Baron de Hirsch Road, Crompond, NY 10517, USA. *Telephone:* (914) 528-3239. *Website:* www.annealockwood.com.

LOCKWOOD, Lewis Henry, BA, MFA, PhD; American musicologist, writer, editor and academic; *Professor Emeritus of Music, Harvard University*; b. 16 Dec. 1930, New York, NY; s. of Gerald Lockwood and Madeline Lockwood; m. 1st Doris Hoffmann Lockwood (deceased); m. 2nd Ava Bry Penman; one s. one d. *Education:* Queens Coll., City Univ. of New York, Princeton Univ. *Career:* Faculty, Princeton Univ. 1958–65, Assoc. Prof. 1965–68, Prof. 1968–80, Chair. Dept of Music 1970–73; Ed. Journal of the American Musicological Society 1963–66, Beethoven Forum 1991–2007; Prof. of Music, Harvard Univ. 1980–2002, Prof. Emer. 2002–, Chair. Dept of Music 1988–90; Distinguished Sr Scholar, Boston Univ.; Gen. Ed. Studies in Musical Genesis and Structure 1984–98; mem. American Acad. of Arts and Sciences, American Musicological Soc. (Pres. 1987–88, Hon. mem. 1993–). *Publications:* Music in Renaissance Ferrara, 1400–1505 1984, Beethoven Essays: Studies in Honor of Elliot Forbes (co-ed.) 1984, Essays in Musicology: A Tribute to Alvin Johnson (co-ed.) 1990, Beethoven: Studies in the Creative Process 1992, Beethoven: The Music and the Life 2003, Inside Beethoven's Quartets (co-authored with the Juilliard Quartet); contrib. to scholarly books and journals on studies in Renaissance musicology and on Beethoven. *Honours:* Dr hc (Università degli Studi, Ferrara) 1991, (New England Conservatory of Music) 1998, (Wake Forest Univ.) 2004; Nat. Endowment for the Humanities Sr Fellowships 1973–74, 1984–85, Guggenheim Fellowship 1977–78; Deems Taylor Award, The American Soc. of Composers, Authors and Publrs (ASCAP) 1993, Festschrift published in his honour 1997, Award in his name est. by American Musicological Soc. 2005, Lifetime Achievement Award, Renaissance Soc. of America 2008. *Address:* Department of Music, Harvard University, Cambridge, MA 02138, USA (office). *E-mail:* llockwood1216@gmail.com (office).

LOEBEL, David, BS, MMus; American conductor; *Associate Director of Orchestras, New England Conservatory of Music*; b. 7 March 1950, Cleveland, OH; m. Jane Cawthorn 1977. *Education:* Northwestern Univ. *Career:* Asst Conductor, Syracuse Symphony Orchestra 1974–76; Music Dir, Binghamton Symphony Orchestra 1977–82; Music Adviser, Anchorage Symphony Orchestra 1983–86; Asst 1982–86, Assoc. Conductor 1986–90, Cincinnati Symphony Orchestra; Assoc. Conductor 1990–94, Assoc. Principal Conductor, St Louis Symphony Orchestra 1994–2000; conductor-in-residence, New World Symphony 1997–99; Music Dir, Memphis Symphony Orchestra 1999–2010; Assoc. Dir of Orchestras, New England Conservatory of Music 2010–. *Honours:* third prize 1976, jt first prize 1978, Baltimore Symphony Orchestra Young Conductors' Competition, ASCAP Award for Adventuresome Programming 1981, 2001, 2002, 2005, Seaver NEA Conductors Award 1992, Northwestern Univ. Alumni Merit Award 2000. *Current Management:* William Reinert Associates, 163 Amsterdam Avenue, Suite 334, New York, NY 10023, USA. *Telephone:* (212) 799-5365. *Fax:* (775) 259-5585. *E-mail:* info@williamreinert.com. *Website:* www.williamreinert.com.

LOEVAAS-GERBER, Kari; singer (soprano); b. 13 May 1939, Oslo, Norway; m. Manfred Gerber 1968, one d. *Education:* Conservatory Oslo, Musikakademie Wien, studied with Erna Westenberger in Frankfurt. *Career:* debut in Nuri, Oslo 1959; opera houses in Dortmund and Mainz; festivals at Salzburg, Vienna, Lucerne, Bergen, Ludwigsburg, Schwetzingen, Athens, Flanders; television includes Fischer und seine Fru/Schoeck 1981 and Peer Gynt, W. Egk 1983; all major radio stations in Germany, Austria, Norway, Switzerland, France and Italy. *Recordings include:* Lieder (Grieg, Mussorgsky, Sibelius) with Erik Werba; Petite Messe Solennelle, Rossini; Die Feen, Wagner; War Requiem, Britten; more than 30 records. *Honours:* Deutsche Grammophon Sonderpreis, Vienna 1960. *Address:* Gugerhalde 10, 8207 Schaffhausen, Switzerland.

LOGIE, Nicholas, MA, PhD; British violist; *Viola Player, Orchestra of the Age of Enlightenment*; b. 12 May 1950, Hemel Hempstead, Herts., England; s. of Gordon Logie and Stephanie Logie; m. Marina Orlov 1972; two s. *Education:* Yehudi Menuhin School, Royal Coll. of Music, London, Northwest Deutsche Musikakademie, Detmold, Germany, Santa Cecilia, Rome, Italy, Open Univ. *Career:* debut at Wigmore Hall, London, 1984; mem. Vienna Symphony Orchestra. 1973–78; Chilingirian String Quartet, 1978–81; Orchestra Man., Glyndebourne Touring Opera 1990–2007; Baroque Viola, London Baroque, 1985–; Sr Lecturer, Dir of Early Music, Royal Northern Coll. of Music) 1989–2002; mem. Orchestra of the Age of Enlightenment, Co-Prin. Viola 1992–2008; researcher into role of leadership in conducting orchestras. *Recordings:* Schubert Cello Quintet, six Mozart Quartets with Chilingirian Quartet. *Publications:* five Sketches for solo viola by Elizabeth Maconchy; contrib. to Newsletter No. 24, The Viola Society, March 1985, The Role of Leadership in Conducting Orchestras 2013. *Honours:* Hon. Assoc., Open Univ. *Address:* Lott's End, Inkpen Lane, Forest Row, Sussex, RH18 5BQ, England (home). *Telephone:* (1342) 825661 (office). *E-mail:* research.logie@gmail.com (office).

LOH, Lisa, AGSM, LGSM, ARCM, LRAM; pianist; b. 6 Jan. 1967, Hong Kong. *Education:* Guildhall School of Music and Drama, Royal Acad. of Music, Royal College of Music. *Career:* debut in Purcell Room, South Bank, London 1993; appearances in concerts and recitals, Fairfield Halls, South Bank and Barbican Centre; broadcasts on TV and radio; Fellow Guild of Musicians and Singers. *Honours:* several prizes in British competitions.

LOJARRO, Daniela; Italian/Swiss opera singer (soprano); b. 24 June 1964, Rivoli, Turin, Italy. *Education:* studied with Carlo Bergonzi. *Career:* debut as Gilda in Busseto; performances at major opera houses in Naples, Parma, Trieste, Bari, Covent Garden London, Zurich, Monte Carlo, Turin, Pretoria,

Palm Beach, Liège and Opera Ireland; performed at Rossini Opera Festival, Pesaro and Martina Franca Festival; repertoire includes main roles in Bellini's La Sonnambula, Bizet's Les Pêcheurs de Perles, Delibes' Lakmé, Donizetti's Don Pasquale, l'Elisir d'amore, Lucia di Lammermoor, La Fille du Régiment, Handel's Alcina, Leoncavallo's Pagliacci, Mozart's Don Giovanni, Rossini's Barbiere di Siviglia, La Donna del Lago, Salieri's La Secchia rapita and Verdi's Rigoletto, Falstaff, Il Ballo in maschera and La Traviata; has worked with conductors including Allemandi, Brüggen, Carignani, Kuhn, Oestman, Oren, Paternostro, Rizzi, Viotti and Zedda and with directors including De Simone, del Monaco, Hampe, Kaegi, Pizzi and Zambello; concert and oratorio repertoire includes Bach's Cantata Jauchzet Gott, Corghi/ Rossini's Dodo Suite, Mozart's Concert Arias and Pergolesi's Stabat Mater. *Films:* sang Lucia and Gilda on soundtrack of Zeffirelli's Toscanini, Gilda for Harron's I shot Andy Warhol, Lucia for Martin Scorsese's The Departed. *Radio:* Handel's Alcina broadcast in Antwerp. *Television:* appeared in Ermione, La Sonnambula and Lakmé. *Recordings include:* Ermione by Rossini, Nina by Paisiello, Crispino e la Comare by Ricci and contribs to the Gala Concert recording with the Berlin Radio Orchestra (singing Gilda and Lucia). *Publication:* Il Suono Sacro di Arjiam (romance fantasy). *Honours:* Winner, Giuseppe Verdi Competition, Parma. *Address:* Gladbachstrasse 48, 8044 Zurich, Switzerland. *Telephone:* (44) 3620134. *E-mail:* daniela.lojarro@ bluewin.ch.

LOMAN, Judy; Canadian harpist; *Principal Harp Emerita, Toronto Symphony Orchestra;* b. 3 Nov. 1936, Goshen, Ind., USA; d. of Herschel Leatherman and Sabra Leatherman (née Waltz); m. Joseph Umbrico 1956; three d. one s. *Education:* Curtis Inst. of Music. *Career:* Principal Harpist, Toronto Symphony Orchestra 1960–2002, now Principal Harp Emer.; Prof. of Harp, Univ. of Toronto 1966–; Assoc. Prof. of Harp, McGill Univ.; Harp Instructor, Curtis Inst. of Music, Phila 1998–; Instructor Royal Conservatory of Music; est. Summer Harp School, Fenelon Falls, Ont.; tours in Europe, USA and Canada; numerous recordings. *Honours:* Grand Prix du Disque from Canada Council 1980, Juno Award for best classical recording. *Address:* c/o Faculty of Music, University of Toronto, Edward Johnson Building, 80 Queen's Park, Toronto, ON M5S 2C5 (office); 38 Burnside Drive, Toronto, ON M6G 2M8, Canada. *Telephone:* (416) 978-3750 (office). *Fax:* (416) 946-3353 (office). *E-mail:* judloman@sympatico.ca. *Website:* www.music.utoronto.ca (office).

LOMBARD, Alain; conductor; b. 4 Oct. 1940, Paris, France. *Education:* Paris Conservatoire with Line Talleul and Gaston Poulet. *Career:* debut at Salle Gaveau, Paris aged 11 with the Pasdeloup Orchestra; Asst to the Principal Conductor, Lyon Opéra 1961–65; American Opera Soc. 1963, with Massenet's Hérodiade; conducted New York Philharmonic and at Salzburg Festival 1966; Musical Dir, Miami Opera, Florida 1966–74; Metropolitan Opera 1967, Gounod's Faust; Dir, Strasbourg Philharmonic 1972–83, Opéra du Rhin 1974–80; guest conductor with Schveningen Festival, The Netherlands, Hamburg Opera, L'Orchestre de Paris and other leading orchestras; conducted Die Zauberflöte at Bordeaux 1992, Falstaff at Catania 1996 and Les Contes d'Hoffmann 1998. *Recordings include:* Mozart's Così fan tutte, with Strasbourg Ensemble; Berlioz Symphonie Fantastique, Harold in Italy and Roméo et Juliette; Verdi Requiem; Prokofiev Violin Concertos (Amoyal) and Ballet Suites; Bartók Concerto for Orchestra and Miraculous Mandarin; Ravel Piano Concerto, Queffelec, and Daphnis et Chloe No. 2; Gounod Roméo et Juliette. *Honours:* gold medal Dimitri Mitropoulos Competition 1966.

LOMBARDERO, Marcelo; singer (baritone) and artistic director; *Artistic Director, Teatro Colón, Buenos Aires. Education:* Instituto de Arte. *Career:* singer from 1992–, with leading roles including the protagonists of Berlioz's La Damnation de Faust, Korngold's Die tote Stadt, Menotti's The Consul, Dallapiccola's Il prigionero, Rigoletto (in Venezuela), Duke Bluebeard's Castle and Othello (in Colombia), Don Giovanni (in Teatro Argentino, La Plata); debut as Artistic Dir at Teatro Colón, with Duke Bluebeard's Castle 1994; currently mem. of staff, Instituto Superior de Arte, Teatro Colón; Artistic Dir, Teatro Colón 2005–. *Stage productions include:* La Fanciulla del West 2003, Les Dialogues des Carmélites 2003, Tosca (Teatro Brodway, Buenos Aires), The Soldier's Tale, Rigoletto (Teatro Heredia de Cartagena de Indias), Duke Bluebeard's Castle, La Clemenza di Tito (Buenos Aires Lírica), Der Kaiser von Atlantis (Teatro Colón) 2005, Der König Kandaules (Teatro Colón) 2006, Le Nozze di Figaro (Teatro Colón) 2006. *Honours:* Premio Asociación de Criticos del Espectáculo 1997, Clarín a la Música prize 2000. *Address:* Teatro Colón, Cerrito 618, 1010 ANN Buenos Aires, Argentina (office). *Telephone:* (11) 4378-7344 (office). *Fax:* (11) 4378-7305 (office). *E-mail:* boleteria@teatrocolon.org .ar. *Website:* www.teatrocolon.org.ar.

LOMBARDO, Bernard; singer (tenor); b. 15 Nov. 1960, Marseille, France. *Education:* studied in Marseille and Treviso. *Career:* sang widely in France, including Bruno in I Puritani at the Paris Opéra-Comique 1987; tour of Australia 1988–89, notably as Turiddu at Sydney and Melbourne; St Gallen 1988 as Edgardo and Opéra Bastille in France 1990 as Cassio in Otello; La Scala Milan debut 1991, as Floreski in Cherubini's Lodoiska; season 1992 as Hoffmann at Kaiserslautern and Roland in Esclarmonde at St Etienne; other roles include Jacopo in I Due Foscari, Tybalt in Roméo et Juliette at Zürich, Ismaele in Nabucco and Gabriele Adorno at Geneva. *Recordings include:* Lodoiska and Lucia di Lammermoor.

LOMON, Ruth; composer; b. 7 Nov. 1930, Montréal, Canada; m. Earle Lomon 1951; one s. two d. *Education:* McGill Univ., New England Conservatory.

Career: piano debut in Montréal, Canada; two-piano team with Iris Graffman Wenglin, with appearances on radio and television, performing and lecturing on works by women composers, playing contemporary and classical repertoire 1973–83; composer/resident scholar Women's Studies Research Center, Brandeis Univ., Waltham, MA 1998–. *Compositions include:* Esquisses for piano solo, Seven Portals of Vision for organ, five Songs on poems by William Blake for contralto and violin, Dust Devils for harp, Janus for string quartet, Diptych for woodwind quintet, Metamorphoses for cello and piano, Songs for a Requiem for soprano, piano or woodwinds, Equinox for brass quartet, Celebrations for two harps, Bassoon Concerto, Dialogue for harpsichord and vibraphone, Requiem Mass for full chorus and brass accompaniment, Butterfly Effect for string quartet 1990, Terra Incognita for orchestra 1993, Shadowing for piano quartet 1993, two piano quartets 1993, 1995, Songs of Remembrance (60-song cycle on poems of the Holocaust) for soprano, tenor, mezzo, bass, oboe, English horn and piano 1996, Odyssey Trumpet Concerto 1997, Nocturnal Songs for mezzo and harp 1997. *Recordings include:* Five Ceremonial Masks for Piano; Soundings and Triptych for two pianos, 1992; Terra Incognita with Warsaw Philharmonic Orchestra under Jerzy Swoboda, 1993; Bassoon Concerto in 3 movements, with bassoonist Grertzer under Gerard Schwarz with Prague Radio Symphony Orchestra; Songs of Remembrance.

LONGHI, Daniela; Italian singer (soprano); b. 1956. *Education:* studied in Verona and Mantua. *Career:* sang at the Verona Arena from 1981, as the Priestess in Aida and Liu in Turandot; guest appearances at Turin as Micaela and at Liège as Violetta and Thais; sang at Parma as Leonore in the French version of Il Trovatore 1990; Marseille and Madrid 1990–91 as Anna Bolena, Montpellier 1991 as Elizabeth I in Roberto Devereux by Donizetti; other roles include Manon and Mimi; sang Violetta at Detroit 1998.

LONSDALE, Michael James; Australian composer; b. 11 Oct. 1961, Newcastle, NSW. *Education:* New South Wales Conservatory, studied with Nigel Butterley and Bozidar Kos. *Career:* faculty mem., Barker Coll., Hornsby; commissions from David Forrest 1986, Warringah Council 1989–91. *Compositions include:* Calm Obstables, Mouna, and Pais all for piano 1985–86, Celeritas for string trio, piano and wind trio 1985, Fulgur Arbor for tenor trombone 1986, I See Past the River... for chorus and orchestra 1988, Lung Gompa for piano 1993, It Stirs Beneath for chorus 1994, Time is the Loser for string quartet 1994, Viper for contra bassoon 1995. *Honours:* ABC/Dept of Education Young Composer of the Year 1979.

LOOSLI, Arthur; singer (baritone); b. 23 Feb. 1926, La Chaux d'Abel, Berner, Jura, Switzerland; m. Theresia Rothlisberger; two s. *Education:* Conservatoire of Berne with Felix Loeffel, studied with Mariano Stabile in Venice, Italy, Arne Sunnergard in Stockholm, Sweden. *Career:* debut in Berne 1958; performances in Switzerland, Belgium, Sweden, The Netherlands, Germany and Italy; guest artist at Stadttheater, Berne; mem. Othmar Schoeck Asscn, Swiss Music Teachers' Asscn. *Recordings:* Elegie, Lieder (Othmar Schoeck); Winterreise (Schubert); Schwanengesang (Schubert); Johannes–Passion (Bach). *Publication:* Illustrations of Franz Hohler's Tschipo and Der Granitblock im Kino. *Honours:* first prize Int. Singers Competition, 's-Hertogenbosch, The Netherlands 1959.

LOOT, Jan Willem; Dutch orchestra director, cellist and lawyer; *Artistic Advisor, Tokyo Music Competition;* b. 15 Dec. 1943, Breda. *Education:* Univ. of Groningen, studied cello with René van Ast and Bertus van Lier. *Career:* fmr Gen. Dir of several Dutch orchestras, including Netherlands Philharmonic Orchestra; Gen. Dir Royal Concertgebouw Orchestra, Amsterdam 1998–2008; Artistic Dir, Orchestre Nat. de France 2009–13; Artistic Advisor, Tokyo Music Competition 2013–; fmr Pres. Delft Chamber Music Festival. *E-mail:* janwloot@xs4all.nl.

LOOTENS, Lena (Helena-Alice); Belgian singer (soprano); b. 14 April 1959, Genk; one d. *Education:* Royal Atheneum of Maasmechelen, Conservatories of Brussels and Gent, studied with Vera Rozsa in London, Margreet Honig and Kristina Deutekom in Amsterdam. *Career:* appearances with numerous orchestras; concert tours to Belgium, Netherlands, Germany, England, Switzerland, Israel and Poland; radio and television broadcasts on BRT, BBC, WDR, NDR, SDR; opera engagements in Innsbruck, Monte Carlo, Antwerp, Montpellier, Liège and Versailles; sang Fulvia in Handel's Ezio at Halle, 1998. *Recordings:* L'Infedeltà Delusa; Concert Arias; Flavio by Handel, Deutsche Schallplattenpreis; L'Incoronazia di Poppea by Monteverdi; Die Israeliten in der Wüste, C. P. E. Bach; Requiem/Mozart; La Guiditta/Almeida; Die Heirat Widerwillen/Humperdinck; Mahler's 4th Symphony. *Honours:* first prize for singing, National Competition for the Youth of Belgium; Alex Devries Scholarship, Roeping Foundation. *Address:* Platte-Lostr 341, 03010 Kessel-Lo, Belgium.

LOPARDO, Frank; American singer (tenor); b. 23 Dec. 1957, Brentwood, NY; m. Carolyn J. Montalbano 1982; two s. *Education:* Queen's Coll., City Univ. of New York and Juilliard School of Music, studied with Dr Robert White, Jr. *Career:* studied with Dr Robert White Jr; professional debut as Tamino in The Magic Flute, Opera Theater of St Louis 1984; European debut as Fenton at Teatro di San Carlo in Naples; debut at La Scala, Milan 1987, Glyndebourne Festival 1987, Metropolitan Opera as Almaviva in Il Barbiere di Siviglia 1989–90; has appeared as Tamino, Rodolfo in La bohème, Alfredo in La traviata, the Duke in Rigoletto, Edgardo in Lucia di Lammermoor, Tonio in La fille du régiment, Nemorino in L'elisir d'amore, Don Ottavio in Don Giovanni, Idreno in Semiramide, Ferrando in Così fan tutte, Fenton in

Falstaff; appearances with various North American opera cos, including Lyric Opera of Chicago, Los Angeles Opera, Houston Grand Opera, Dallas Opera, Canadian Opera Co., San Francisco Opera, Santa Fe Opera; In Europe, has sung as Edgardo, Rodolfo, the Duke, and Lenski in Eugene Onegin at Opéra Nat. de Paris; at Royal Opera House, Covent Garden, has sung as Lindoro in L'Italiana in Algeri; performances at other major European theatres include Vienna State Opera, Grand Théâtre de Genève, Teatro alla Scala, Milan, Teatro Comunale, Florence, Teatro Real, Madrid; has appeared at the Salzburg Festival, Glyndebourne Opera Festival, and Aix-en-Provence Festival, and has sung with De Nederlandse Opera; has sung with orchestras world-wide, including performances of Verdi's Requiem with London Symphony Orchestra and Montreal Symphony Orchestra, Mozart's Requiem with Berlin Philharmonic Orchestra at La Scala, Berlioz's Requiem and Orff's Carmina Burana with Boston Symphony Orchestra, Beethoven's Ninth Symphony with San Francisco Symphony Orchestra, Rossini's Stabat Mater with Philadelphia Orchestra and Dvořák's Requiem with Danish Radio Symphony Orchestra. *Recordings include:* Requiem (Mozart), with Riccardo Muti 1987, L'Italiania in Algeri (Rossini), with Claudio Abbado 1987, Don Giovanni (Mozart), with Riccardo Muti 1990, Great Mass in C minor (Mozart), with Leonard Bernstein 1991, Falstaff (Verdi), with Sir Colin Davis 1991, Il signor Bruschino (Rossini), with Ion Marin 1991, Il barbiere di Siviglia (Rossini), with Claudio Abbado 1992, Semiramide (Rossini), with Ion Marin 1992, Carmina Burana (Orff), with André Previn 1992, Don Pasquale (Donizetti), with Roberto Abbado 1993, Idomeneo (Mozart), with James Levine 1993, Così fan tutte (Mozart), with Sir George Solti 1993, La traviata (Verdi), with (Sir George Solti) 1994, Requiem (Berlioz), with Robert Spano 2003, Berlioz Requiem, with Atlanta Symphony Orchestra and Chorus, conducted by Robert Spano (Grammy Award for Best Choral Performance) 2005, Imelda de' Lambertazzi (Donizetti), with Mark Elder 2006, Ninth Symphony (Beethoven), with Franz Welser-Möst 2007. *Honours:* Hon. DMus (Aaron Copland School of Music) 1992; First Prize, Liederkranz Foundation competition 1983. *Current Management:* c/o Columbia Artists Management Inc., 1790 Broadway, New York, NY 10019-1412, USA. *Telephone:* (212) 841-9500. *Fax:* (212) 841-9744. *E-mail:* info@cami.com. *Website:* www.cami.com. *E-mail:* mail@franklopardo.com (office). *Website:* franklopardo.com.

LÓPEZ-COBOS, Jesús, DPhil; Spanish conductor; b. 25 Feb. 1940, Toro; s. of Lorenzo López and Gregoria Cobos. *Education:* Madrid Univ., Madrid Conservatory, Vienna Acad., Austria. *Career:* worked with major orchestras including London Symphony, Royal Philharmonic, Philharmonia, Concertgebouw, Vienna Philharmonic, Vienna Symphony, Berlin Philharmonic, Hamburg NDR, Munich Philharmonic, Cleveland, Chicago Symphony, New York Philharmonic, Philadelphia, Pittsburgh Symphony; conducted new opera productions at La Scala, Milan, Covent Garden, London and Metropolitan Opera, New York; Gen. Musikdirektor, Deutsche Oper, Berlin 1981–90; Prin. Guest Conductor London Philharmonic Orchestra 1981–86, Orquesta Sinfonica de Galicia 2010–; Prin. Conductor and Artistic Dir Spanish Nat. Orchestra 1984–89; Music Dir Cincinnati Symphony Orchestra 1986–2001 (now Music Dir Emer.), Music Dir Lausanne Chamber Orchestra 1990–2000, Orchestre Français des Jeunes 1998–2001, Teatro Real, Madrid 2002–10. *Recordings include:* Bruckner symphonies, Haydn symphonies, Donizetti's Lucia di Lammermoor, Rossini's Otello and recital discs with José Carreras; works by Mahler, Respighi, Franck, de Falla, Villa-Lobos and Richard Strauss; Rossini's Il Barbiere di Siviglia and L'Italiana in Algeri; Il Comte Ory, Manon, Les Contes d'Hoffmann, Il Viaggio a Reims. *Honours:* Cross of Merit (First Class) (FRG) 1989, Officier des Arts et des Lettres 2001; Dr hc (Arts Univ. Cincinatti); First Prize, Besançon Int. Conductors' Competition 1969, Prince of Asturias Award (Spanish Govt) 1981, Founders Award, American Soc. of Composers, Authors and Publrs 1988, Fine Arts Medal (Spain) 2001. *Address:* 8 Chemin de Bellerive, 1007 Lausanne, Switzerland. *Website:* jesuslopezcobos.com.

LOPEZ-YANEZ, Jorge; Mexican singer (tenor); b. 1963. *Education:* Univ. of Zacatecas, California State Univ., Univ. of Southern California. *Career:* debut, Long Beach Opera in 1986 as Rossillon in Die Lustige Witwe; European debut at Hannover in 1988 as the Duke of Mantua; Düsseldorf and Stuttgart 1988–89 as Ramiro in La Cenerentola; further engagements as Fenton at Los Angeles and Bordeaux, Oronte in Alcina at the Paris Châtelet, Rossini's Almaviva at Munich, Donizetti's Tonio at Zürich and Alfredo in La Traviata at the Vienna Staatsoper 1992; Glyndebourne debut in 1995 as Pyrrhus in the British stage premiere of Rossini's Ermione; sang Nemorino at Santiago and Ernesto at Turin 1998; sang Ramiro in Cenerentola at Monte Carlo 2000; Alfredo for Australian Opera 2001. *Recordings include:* Hamlet, Ermione, album of Mexican Mariachi music. *Honours:* winner, Loren Zachary Competition 1986.

LORAND, Colette; singer (soprano); b. 7 Jan. 1923, Zürich, Switzerland. *Education:* Musikhochschule Hanover, studied in Zürich with Frau Hirzel. *Career:* debut in Basle 1946, as Marguerite in Faust; Frankfurt Opera 1951–56, notably as the Queen of Night; Hamburg Opera from 1955, often in operas by Henze, Penderecki and Orff; Edinburgh Festival 1955; Lisbon 1961, as Constanze in Die Entführung; Deutsche Oper Berlin 1972, in the premiere of Fortner's Elisabeth Tudor; created roles in Orff's De Temporum fine Comoedia, Salzburg Festival 1973, and Reimann's Lear, Munich 1978 as Regan, repeated at the Paris Opéra 1982. *Recordings:* Lear and De Temporum fine Comoedia; Orff's Prometheus.

LORANGE, Nicole; singer (soprano); b. 28 Nov. 1942, Montréal, Canada. *Education:* studied with Pierrette Alarie and at the Vienna Music Acad. with Erik Werba. *Career:* sang at first in concert and made stage debut at the Linz Landestheater 1969 as Desdemona; further appearances with the Canadian Opera Co. as Musetta 1972, and Opéra Montréal as Tosca 1980; Metropolitan Opera 1982–84 as Butterfly, Adriana Lecouvreur and Francesca da Rimini; other roles include Donna Elvira and Offenbach's Giulietta; many concert appearances.

LORD, Bernadette; singer (soprano); b. 1965, Derby, England. *Education:* Guildhall School, European Arts Centre, studied with Suzanne Danco in Florence. *Career:* joined Opera Wallonie, Liège, and sang Helena in Schubert's Der Häusliche Krieg in Belgium, The Netherlands and France; Glyndebourne and Covent Garden debuts as Cis in Albert Herring; other roles include Despina for British Youth Opera at the Cheltenham Festival, Miss Wordsworth in Albert Herring, Lucia in The Rape of Lucretia, Gretel for Opera East, Susanna and Barbarina in Le nozze di Figaro; sang Jano in Jenůfa at Covent Garden 1993.

LORENTZEN, Bent; Danish composer; b. 11 Feb. 1935, Stenvad; m. Edith Kaerulf Moeller 1958; one s. three d. *Education:* Royal Acad. of Music, Copenhagen. *Career:* performances of his works throughout Europe, including Euridice, Die Music kommt mit äussert bekannt vor!, Eine Wundersame Liebesgeschichte, Stalten Mette, Toto, Fackeltanz, Samba, Piano Concerto, Saxophone Concerto, two choral songs to Enzensberger 1991, Bill and Julia (opera), The Magic Brilliant (with Danish Nat. Opera) 1993, The Scatterbrain (Royal Theatre) 1995, Pergolesi's Home Service, Circles, Der Steppenwolf, The Tinder Box, Contours, Cain and Abel (world premiere, Copenhagen) 2006. *Compositions include:* Purgatorio (choral), Granite, Quartz, Syncretism, Wunderblumen, Flamma, Zauberspiegel, Farbentiegel, Blütenweiss, Colori, Concerto for oboe, Cello Concerto, Hunting Concerto, Italian Concerto, Samba, Paradiesvogel, Graffiti, Purgatorio, three Madrigals, five Motets, Genesis, Stabat Mater, Canon I–V for two accordions, New Choral Dramatics, Ammen Dammen Des, Round, five easy Piano Pieces, Flood of Paradise, Olof Palme for mixed choir, Comics, three Latin Suites, Venezia, Tordenskiold, Der Steppenwolf (opera) 1999, Jeppe of the Hills (after Holberg), ACC, accordion concerto for accordion and symphonic orchestra 2006. *Recordings include:* The Bottomless Pit, Visions, Cloud-Drift, Mambo, Intersection, Puncti, Triplex, Groppo, Nimbus, Cruor, Goldranken, Abgrund, Die Musik kommt mir äusserst bekannt vor!, Syncretism, A Wonderous Love Story, Sol, Luna, Mars for organ 1985, Mercurius, Jupiter, Venus, Saturnus, Umbra, Paesaggio, Dunkelblau, Round, Cyclus I–IV, Piano and oboe concertos, Regenbogen, Comics, Lines, Tears, Orfeo Suite, Intrada, Alpha and Omega, Violin Concerto, Gewitter im Juni recorder concerto. *Publications:* Ej Sikkelej 1967, Recorder System 1962–64, Musikens AHC 1969, Mer om Musiken 1972, Introduction to Electronic Music 1969. *Honours:* Prix Italia 1970, first prize Serocki Competition 1984, Messiaen Prize 1988, Carl Nielsen Prize 1998. *Current Management:* Edition Wilhelm Hansen, Bornholmsgade 1, 1266 Copenhagen K, Denmark. *Website:* www.musicsalesclassical.com. *Address:* Søtoften 37, 2820 Gentofte, Denmark (home). *Telephone:* 39-65-76-01 (home). *Fax:* 39-65-76-71 (home). *E-mail:* eblorentzen@mail.tele.dk (home).

LORENZ, Andrew Bela, DSCM; Australian violinist; *Senior Lecturer in Violin and Viola, University of Southern Queensland;* b. 17 Oct. 1951, Melbourne, Vic.; m. Wendy Joy Lorenz, one s. *Education:* Sydney Conservatory of Music. *Career:* recitals; concerto, radio and TV performances; Deputy Leader, Melbourne Elizabethen Trust Orchestra 1972; led for D'Oyly Carte Opera Co., Sadler's Wells, England 1973–74; Leader, New England Ensemble (resident piano quartet) and Lecturer, Music Dept, Univ. of New England, Armidale, NSW, Australia 1975–82; founding mem. and Leader, New England Sinfonia; world tours with New England Ensemble; Assoc. Concertmaster, Adelaide Symphony Orchestra 1983–86; Leader, Australian Piano Trio 1983–87; Sr Lecturer in Violin and Viola, Univ. of Southern Queensland, Toowoomba, Queensland; Leader, Phoenix Ensemble; Dir, McGregor Chamber Music School; concerto soloist with many of Australia's leading orchestras and Slovak Radio Symphony; Australian premieres of Benjamin, McCabe and Myslivecek Concertos; world premiere performance of Alexander Negerevich Violin Concerto 2006. *Recordings:* works by Beethoven, Turina, Margaret Sutherland, Mozart, Fauré, John McCabe, Mendelssohn, Goossens, Mary Mageau, sundry chamber works. *Honours:* winner Victorian ABC Concerto Competition 1972. *Address:* 21 Merlin Court, M/S 852 Toowoomba Mail Servce, Queensland 4352, Australia. *Telephone:* (7) 4631-1113. *Fax:* (7) 4631-1133. *E-mail:* lorenza@usq.edu.au.

LORENZ, Gerlinde; singer (soprano); b. 1939, Chemnitz, Germany. *Education:* Vienna Music Acad. *Career:* sang at the Vienna Volksoper from 1967, Staatsoper from 1972; Cologne Opera 1971–86, with debut as Mimi; Bielefeld 1985, as Lola in Schreker's Irrelohe and Oldenburg 1992, as Ortrud in Lohengrin; other engagements at Zürich, the Munich Staatsoper, Deutsche Oper Berlin and Frankfurt; further roles include Mozart's Donna Elvira and Donna Anna, Wagner's Elsa, Eva and Sieglinde, Strauss's Elektra and Elisabeth de Valois; concerts in Vienna, Salzburg, Paris and elsewhere.

LORENZ, Ricardo, MM, PhD; Venezuelan composer; *Associate Professor of Composition and Chair of Music Composition, Michigan State University;* b. 24 May 1961, Maracaibo. *Education:* Olivares Conservatory, Landaeta Conservatory, Indiana Univ. and Univ. of Chicago. *Career:* Acting Dir, Indiana Univ. Latin American Music Center 1987–92, Visiting Assoc. Dir

2003–05; Assoc. Prof. of Composition, Michigan State Univ. 2005–, Chair of Music Composition 2014–; composer-in-residence, Chicago Symphony Orchestra 1998–2002, Billings Symphony Orchestra, Montana 1998–99. *Compositions include:* Sinfonietta concertante 1987, Concerto for Orchestra 1993, Cecilia en Azul y Verde 1998, En Tren Vá Changó 2001, Fantasía (del Equivocado Fritz) 2002, Rumba Sinfónica 2007, Canciones de Jara 2010, Habanera Science 2012. *Recordings:* Pataruco: Concerto for Venezuelan Maracas and Orchestra, Está Lloviendo Afuera y No Hay Agua. *Publications:* Scores and Recordings at Indiana Univ. Latin American Music Center 1995; Salsa Nueva. *Honours:* Meet the Composer Mid-west grant 1994; Barlow Endowment for Music Composition 1994; Cinitella Ramieri Foundation Fellowship 2004. *Address:* 206 MPB School of Music, Michigan State University, East Lansing, MI 48823, USA (office). *Telephone:* (517) 355-7658 (office). *E-mail:* lorenzri@msu.edu (office).

LORENZ, Siegfried; singer (baritone); b. 30 Aug. 1945, Berlin, Germany. *Education:* studied in Berlin. *Career:* debut at Komische Oper Berlin 1969, in The Love for Three Oranges; sang at the Komische Oper and Staatsoper Berlin, notably as Guglielmo, Wolfram, Mozart's Count, Germont, and Posa in Don Carlos; Agamemnon in Gluck's Iphigenia in Aulis 1987; soloist at the Leipzig Gewandhaus from 1974, in concert music by Bach, Brahms and Schubert; international appearances in lieder recitals. *Recordings include:* Winterreise, Die schöne Müllerin and the Brahms Requiem.

LORIMER, Heather; British singer (soprano); b. 1961, Wallasey, Cheshire; m. Gerard Quinn. *Education:* Royal Northern Coll. of Music, Manchester with Frederick Cox, studied with Iris Dell'Acqua. *Career:* Scottish Opera Go Round, Mimi in La Bohème 1987; Glyndebourne Festival and Touring Opera, Constanze, Die Entführung aus dem Serail 1988; Countess, Le nozze di Figaro 1989; Opera 80, Tatiana in Eugene Onegin 1989 and Hanna Glawari in The Merry Widow 1990; Travelling Opera, Mimi; Countess; Donna Elvira; Don Giovanni; Fiordiligi in Così fan tutte; Violetta in La Traviata and Micaela in Carmen; English Touring Opera, Mimi 1994; education tours for Glyndebourne, Opera 80 and ENO Lillian Bayliss Programme; other roles performed include Giorgetta, Il Tabarro; Liu, Turandot; Norina, Don Pasquale; Rosina, Il Barbiere di Siviglia; Rosalinde, Die Fledermaus; Rosario, Goyescas; Dirce, Medea; Leila, The Pearl Fishers; in 1993 created the title role in Michael Finnissy's Thérèse Raquin, for the Royal Opera's Garden Venture; concert repertoire includes Verdi Requiem, Rossini Stabat Mater, Dvořák Requiem, Elijah, Carmina Burana, Brahms Requiem, Fauré Requiem, Sea Symphony and The Kingdom. *Honours:* International Opera and Bel Canto Duet Competition, Antwerp, Gerard Quinn; Scottish Opera John Noble Competition.

LORTIE, Louis; Canadian pianist; b. 27 April 1959, Québec. *Education:* studied in Québec with Yvonne Hubert. *Career:* debut with Montréal Symphony Orchestra 1972; worldwide appearances from 1978, with concerts throughout Canada and tours to Europe, USA and Far East; founded the Lortié-Berick-Lysy Trio 1995–; engagements as soloist and conductor with Orchestra di Padova e del Veneto; Prokofiev's 1st Concerto at the London Prom Concerts 2001; Ravel's concerto for the Left Hand at the London Proms 2002. *Current Management:* Seldy Cramer Artists, 3436 Springhill Road, Lafayette, CA 94549, USA. *Telephone:* (925) 299-0623. *Fax:* (925) 299-0624. *E-mail:* seldy@aol.com. *E-mail:* info@louislortie.com (office). *Website:* www .louislortie.com.

LOSKUTOVA, Irina; Russian singer (soprano); b. 1965, Salavat, Bashkiria. *Education:* State Mussorgsky Conservatoire of Sverdlovsk. *Career:* appearances with Mussorgsky Opera and Ballet Theatre, St Petersburg, from 1989; Kirov Opera, Mariinsky Theatre, from 1995, as Tatiana, Yaroslavna in Prince Igor, Mimi, Elisabeth de Valois, Madama Butterfly and Paulina in The Gambler by Prokofiev; tours of Europe and North America with the Mussorgsky and the Kirov Opera companies; further roles include Tchaikovsky's Iolanta and Maria (Mazeppa) and Katerina Izmailova: Sang Lyubka in Semyon Kotko by Prokofiev with the Kirov at Covent Garden, 2000 (British premiere). *Recordings include:* Mazeppa. *Honours:* prizewinner Mussorgsky Vocal Competition 1989.

LOTHIAN, Helen; singer (mezzo-soprano); b. 1968, Scotland. *Education:* Royal Scottish Acad. and the Guildhall School, studied with Patricia Hay in Scotland. *Career:* concert appearances throughout the UK in music by Verdi, Bruckner, Beethoven, Mozart and Haydn; recitals at the Covent Garden Festival, Clonter Opera Farm and elsewhere; sang the Lady Artist in Berg's Lulu with the BBC Symphony Orchestra 1995; opera engagements include Christoph Rilke's Song of Love and Death by Matthus, for Glyndebourne Touring Opera; Dorabella, Carmen and Cherubino for British Youth Opera, Dardane in Haydn's L'Incontro Improvviso at Garsington and Mozart's Third Lady at the Covent Garden Festival; Romeo in Bellini's I Capuleti e i Montecchi for Castleward Opera 1995; Royal Opera and Scottish Opera debuts as Flora in La Traviata 1996.

LOTT, Dame Felicity Ann Emwhyla, CBE, DBE, BA, LRAM, FRAM; British singer (soprano); b. 8 May 1947, Cheltenham, Glos.; d. of John A. Lott and Whyla Lott (née Williams); m. 1st Robin Golding 1973 (divorced); m. 2nd Gabriel Woolf 1984; one d. *Education:* Pate's Grammar School for Girls, Cheltenham, Royal Holloway Coll., Univ. of London and Royal Acad. of Music. *Career:* debut with ENO as Pamina in Die Zauberflöte 1975; prin. roles at Glyndebourne, Covent Garden, ENO, WNO, New York Metropolitan Opera, Vienna, La Scala, Paris Opéra, Brussels, Hamburg, Munich, Chicago, San

Francisco, Dresden; wide recital repertoire; Founder-mem. Songmakers' Almanac; mem. Equity, Inc. Soc. of Musicians. *Roles include:* Countess in Le Nozze de Figaro, Ellen Orford in Peter Grimes, Fiordiligi in Così fan Tutti, Elvira in Don Giovanni, Xiphares in Mitridate, Marschallin in Der Rosenkavalier, Countess in Capriccio (Richard Strauss), many recitals with Graham Johnson and duets with Ann Murray, DVD of Offenbach's Hélène in La Belle Hélène and La Grande Duchesse. *Honours:* Hon. Fellow, Royal Holloway Coll., Hon. FRCM; Officier des Arts et des Lettres 2000, Chevalier, Légion d'honneur 2001; Dr hc (Sussex) 1990, Hon. DLitt (Loughborough) 1996, Hon. DMus (London) 1997, (Royal Scottish Acad. of Music and Drama) 1998, (Oxford) 2001, (Leicester) 2010, (Gloucester) 2010, (Paris Sorbonne) 2010; Kammersängerin, Bayerische Staatsoper, Munich 2003, Wigmore Medal 2010. *Address:* Monksdown House, Bishopstone, Seaford, BN25 2UD, England (home). *E-mail:* mail@felicitylott.de. *Website:* www.felicitylott.de.

LOTT, Maria-Elisabeth; German violinist; b. 1987. *Education:* studied with Josef Rissin at Karlsruhe. *Career:* concert engagements throughout Europe and the USA, including British debut performances 2000 with the Bournemouth Symphony Orchestra and Royal Liverpool Philharmonic Orchestra, playing Paganini's First concerto; further appearances with the Minnesota Orchestra and Malaysia Philharmonic in Kuala Lumpur; season 2000–01 with the London Philharmonic, Ensemble Orchestral de Paris, the Ulster Orchestra and NDR Hanover Orchestra. *Recordings include:* album of Mozart, played on violin used by the composer in 1760's.

LOTTI, Antonio; Italian singer (tenor); b. 1957, Lucca. *Education:* studied in São Paulo, Brazil. *Career:* debut in São Paulo, 1982, as Cavaradossi; sang in opera throughout South America, Europe from 1987; Verdi's Stiffelio in Amsterdam, Oslo and Copenhagen as Cavaradossi; Paolo in Francesca da Rimini at Bologna, Don Carlos at Catania; Bonn Opera from 1994, as Pery in Il Guaramento by Gomes, Turiddu in Cavalleria Rusticana, and Hoffmann; other roles include Rodolfo in Luisa Miller. *Current Management:* Agenzia l'Opera di Enrico Copedè, Viale Giusti 331, 55100 Lucca, Italy. *Telephone:* (583) 952546. *Fax:* (583) 952546. *E-mail:* enrico.copede@virgilio.it. *Website:* www.agenzialopera.it.

LOU, Qian-Gui; Chinese singer (tenor) (retd); b. 1923. *Education:* Aurora Univ. *Career:* sang roles in opera including Pinkerton in Madama Butterfly 1958, Lensky in Eugene Onegin 1962; soloist, concerts in USSR, Poland, Romania, Czechoslovakia, North Korea, 1953–54; solo recitals, Beijing, Shanghai, elsewhere in China 1978–97, and at Redlands Summer Music Festival, USA, 1990; appearances on Central TV programmes, MTV; documentary films for stage performances; Artistic Dir, Central Opera House of China, also Savonlinna Opera Festival, Finland 1988; fmr Prof. of Voice, Central Conservatory of Music, Beijing; mem., Jury for Nat. Vocal Competition, China. *Recordings:* albums released in Moscow 1954, Beijing 1956, 1980, Guangzhou 1983, The Treasurable Version of 100 Anthologies of Vocal Music performed by famous Chinese Musicians 1998. *Honours:* Lifetime Achievement Award, Golden Chime Award 2004. *Address:* 5-102 Building #50, Tian Tong Yuan, East District III, Chang Ping, Beijing 102218, People's Republic of China (home). *Telephone:* (10) 61764939 (home).

LOUGHRAN, James, CBE, FRNCM, FRSAMD; British conductor; b. 30 June 1931, Glasgow, Scotland; s. of James Loughran and Agnes Loughran (née Fox); m. 1st Nancy Coggon 1961 (divorced 1983); two s.; m. 2nd Ludmila Navratil 1985. *Education:* Glasgow, Bonn, Amsterdam and Milan. *Career:* Assoc. Conductor, Bournemouth Symphony Orchestra 1962–65; debut Royal Opera House, Covent Garden 1964; Prin. Conductor BBC Scottish Symphony Orchestra 1965–71; Prin. Conductor and Musical Adviser, Hallé Orchestra 1971–83, Conductor Laureate 1983–91; debut New York Philharmonic with Westminster Choir 1972; Prin. Conductor Bamberg Symphony Orchestra 1979–83; Chief Guest Conductor BBC Welsh Symphony Orchestra 1987–90; Guest Perm. Conductor, Japan Philharmonic Symphony Orchestra 1980, Hon. Conductor 2006–; Chief Conductor Århus Symphony Orchestra, Denmark 1996–2003, Chief Guest Conductor 2003–11; BBC Proms 1965–89 including The Last Night five times 1977–85. *Recordings include:* recorded complete Beethoven Symphonies with London Symphony Orchestra as contribution to European Broadcasting Union Beethoven Bicentenary Celebrations 1969–70; recordings with Hallé, London Philharmonic, Philharmonia, BBC Symphony, Århus Symphony, Scottish Chamber Orchestra, Japan Philharmonic. *Honours:* Liveryman, Worshipful Co. of Musicians 1992; Hon. DMus (Sheffield) 1983, (Royal Scottish Acad. of Music and Drama) 2005; First Prize, Philharmonia Orchestra Conducting Competition 1961, Mancunian of the Year 1981, Gold Disc, EMI 1983. *Address:* 18 Hatfield Drive, Glasgow, G12 0YA, Scotland (home). *Telephone:* (141) 337-2091 (home). *E-mail:* jamesloughran@btinternet.com (home).

LOUIE, Alexina Diane, OC, BMus, MA; Canadian composer; b. 30 July 1949, Vancouver, BC; m. Alex Pauk. *Education:* Univ. of British Columbia and Univ. of California, San Diego, USA. *Career:* professional solo pianist, Vancouver, BC 1966–71; music copyist 1970–73; Instructor of Music, Pasadena City Coll., Calif., USA 1974–80; Composer-in-Residence, Canadian Opera Co. 1996–2002; Nat. Arts Centre Award Composer 2002; mem. Canadian League of Composers; Assoc. Canadian Music Centre; Fellow, Royal Soc. of Canada 2006–. *Compositions include:* Molly 1972, O Magnum Mysterium: In Memoriam Glenn Gould 1982, Music for a Thousand Autumns for 12 performers 1983, Songs of Paradise, The Eternal Earth, Winter Music, Music for Heaven and Earth, Music From Night's Edge (piano quintet) 1988,

Love Songs for a Small Planet for chamber choir and ensemble 1989, Obsessions (Their Own Words) for baritone and orchestra 1993, Neon 1995, Shattered Night, Shivering Stars for orchestra 1997, The Scarlet Princess (mainstage opera for soloists, chorus, orchestra, clarinet, cello and piano) 2004, Imaginary Opera for 12 performers 2005. *Honours:* Dr hc (Calgary) 1997; Order of Ontario 1997; Composition Grantee Canada Council for the Arts 1974, 1980, 1981, Composer of the Year, Canada Music Council 1986, Juno Award 1988, Soc. of Composers, Authors and Music Publrs of Canada (SOCAN) Award 1990, 1992, Jules Léger Prize for Chamber Music 1999, Queen's Golden Jubilee Medal 2002. *Address:* c/o 41 Valleybrook Drive, Don Mills, ON M3B 2S6, Canada (office).

LOUKIANETS, Viktoria; Ukrainian singer (soprano); b. 1965, Kiev, Russia. *Education:* Kiev Music School and Kiev Conservatoire. *Career:* soloist with Ukrainian Opera, Kiev 1989; guest appearances in France, Portugal, Czech Republic, Italy and Switzerland; prinicipal with the Vienna Staatsoper, singing Adina in L'Elisir d'amore, Elvira in L'Italiana in Algeri, Rosina, the Queen of Night and Olympia in Les Contes d'Hoffman; other roles include Oscar in Ballo in Maschera, Donna Anna, Wagner's Woglinde; appearances include Violetta at the Salzburg Festival, New York Met debut 1996, Opéra Bastille, Paris 1998, La Scala Milan debut as the Queen of Night 1995, Gilda in Rigoletto at Covent Garden, London 1996–97, Berthe in Le Prophète at the Vienna Staatsoper 1998, Violetta at Covent Garden and the Vienna Volksoper 2000–01. *Honours:* Mozart Bicentennial Competition winner, Italy 1991, Maria Callas Competition winner, Athens 1991.

LOUP, François; Swiss/American/French singer (bass-baritone and basso-buffo); *Professor Emeritus of Voice, University of Maryland*; b. 4 March 1940, Estavayer-le-lac, Switzerland; m. Mary-Beth Parrotta; two d. one step-s. *Education:* Conservatoire de Fribourg, Geneva (voice and, piano teaching diplomas, organ certificate). *Career:* int. debut, Spoleto Festival 1974; more than 100 roles with Metropolitan Opera 1992–; repertoire includes Bartolo (Mozart and Rossini), Dulcamara in Elisir d'Amore, Sulpice in The Daughter of the Regiment, Sacristan in Tosca, Benoit and Alcindoro in La Bohème, Frank in Die Fledermaus, the Major d'Uomo in Strauss's Capriccio, Schigolch in A. Berg's Lulu; has performed with Florentine Opera, New Israeli Opera, Dallas Opera, Canadian Opera, San Francisco Opera, Houston Grand Opera, Lyric Opera of Chicago, Arizona Opera, Opera Company of Philadelphia, Santa Fe Opera, Washington Opera, Opéra de Paris, Opéra de la Bastille, Paris, Théâtre des Champs Elysées, Lyon, Metz, Nantes, Strasbourg, Rouen, Cannes, Nice, Toulouse, Madrid, Barcelona, Prague, Glyndebourne, Aix en Provence, Rome, Spoleto, Bologna, Rio de Janeiro, Buenos Aires, Ottawa, Toronto, Vancouver; has staged numerous operas world-wide; Assoc. Prof. of Voice, Univ. of Maryland 1996–2012, Prof. Emer. 2012–; Assoc. Prof. of Voice, Peabody Conservatory –2015, , Prof. Emer. 2015–; runs pvt. masterclasses at home called Solo Studio 2011–; now retd in Switzerland. *Films:* L'Heure Espagnole and L'Enfant et les Sortilèges (Ravel), Le Nozze di Figaro (Bartolo), Glyndebourne Productions, Il Turco In Italia (Rossini), Goldline Classics, Il Barbiere di Siviglia (Bartolo), Milwaukee Opera. *Recording:* new version of Schubert's Die Winterreise (with pianist Adam Mahonske and following poems' order of poet Willhelm Mueller) 2012. *Honours:* Premier Prix de virtuosité (Summa cum laude), Conservatoire de Fribourg, Artist of the Year, Washington Opera 1985. *Address:* Rue du Senet 5, 2024 Saint-Aubin-Sauges, Switzerland. *Telephone:* (32) 8351232; 79-9183790 (mobile). *E-mail:* loupbass@gmail.com. *Website:* www.solostudiobaltimore.com.

LOVE, Shirley; American singer (mezzo-soprano); b. 6 Jan. 1940, Detroit, MI. *Education:* studied with Avery Crew in Detroit, Margaret Harshaw in New York, Armen Bayajean in New York. *Career:* debut at Metropolitan Opera 1963 in Die Zauberflöte; remained in New York for 20 seasons, as Carmen, Dalila, Verdi's Maddalena, Amneris and Emilia, Rossini's Angelina and Rosina, Siebel in Faust, Pauline in The Queen of Spades and in operas by Ravel, Menotti and Bernstein; guest appearances in Cincinnati, Chicago, Miami and Philadelphia; sang at Baltimore 1962, in the premiere of Kagen's Hamlet; concert appearances in Amsterdam, Bologna and Florence; three recital tours of South Africa; three television performances in the Live from the Met series, Otello, Il Barbiere di Seviglia, Der Rosenkavalier; opera performances include Albert Herring, Cleveland Opera; Cavalleria Rusticana, Milwaukee Florentine Opera; festival appearances include Mostly Mozart, New York; Basically Bach, New York; Saratoga festival (Philadelphia Orchestra); Blossom Festival, Cleveland; Madeira Bach Festival, Portugal. *Recordings:* Diary of One Who Vanished, Janáček; The Rake's Progress, Stravinsky. *Honours:* Wayne State Univ. Arts Achievement Award 1990, Hon. DMus (Univ. of West Virginia) 1999.

LOVEDAY, Alan Raymond; British violinist; b. 29 Feb. 1928, Palmerston North, New Zealand; m. Ruth Stanfield 1952; one s. one d. *Education:* Royal Coll. of Music. *Career:* debut in England 1946; numerous concerts, broadcasts, TV appearances, the UK and abroad; played with leading conductors and orchestras; ranges from Bach, on unmodernised violin, to contemporary music; Prof., Royal Coll. of Music 1955–72; soloist, Acad. of St Martin-in-the-Fields.

LOWENTHAL, Jerome, BA, MS; American pianist; b. 11 Feb. 1932, Philadelphia, PA; m. Ronit Amir 1959, two d. *Education:* Univ. of Pennsylvania, Juilliard School of Music, Ecole Normale de Musique, studied with Olga Samaroff, William Kapell, Eduard Steuermann, Alfred Cortot. *Career:* debut with Philadelphia Orchestra 1945; appearances with orchestras of New York, Philadelphia, Boston, Cleveland, Israel Philharmonic, Stockholm, Chicago, Los Angeles, Detroit, Pittsburgh; tours of Southeast Asia, New Zealand, Latin America, Western Europe, USSR, Poland, Romania; mem. piano faculty, Juilliard School, New York 1990–. *Recordings:* Rorem Concerto No. 3, Louisville-Mester; Tchaikovsky Concerti 1, 2 and 3, London Symphony Orchestra Comissiona; Liszt Opera Paraphrases; Gershwin Concerto in F and Rhapsody in Blue, Utah Symphony Orchestra; Sinding, Sonata and short pieces for solo piano; Liszt Concerto No. 1, No. 3, Totentanz, Malediction: Vancouver Symphony, Commissiona. *Honours:* Laureat, Darmstadt Competition 1957, Busoni Competition 1957, Reine Elizabeth 1960.

LOY, Christof; stage director; b. 1950, Essen, Germany. *Education:* Folkwang Hochschule, Essen. *Career:* staged Falstaff at Maastricht, Die Entführung at Freiburg and La Damnation de Faust at Bremen; Mozart's La finta giardiniera at Mannheim, Le nozze di Figaro in Brussels and Idomeneo at Bonn; Manon, Lucia di Lammermoor, Orfeo and Don Carlos for the Deutsche Oper an Rhein, Dusseldorf; Don Giovanni at Graz, Alcina for Hamburg Opera and Carmen in Cologne; season 2002 with Gluck's Iphigénie en Aulide at Glyndebourne and Ariadne auf Naxos at Covent Garden, London; further productions include Der Rosekavalier and Eugene Onegin for the Théâtre de la Monnaie, Brussels, and The Queen of Spades at Bremen.

LOYOLA FERNÁNDEZ, José, PhD; Cuban composer, teacher and musician (flute); *Professor of Composition, Orchestration and Counterpoint, Instituto Superior de Arte de La Habana*; b. 12 March 1941, Cienfuegos; s. of Efraín Loyola. *Education:* School of Music of the Nat. School of the Arts, Havana, School for Advanced Studies in Music, Warsaw, Poland and Fryderyk Chopin Acad., Warsaw. *Career:* mem., Cienfuegos Nursery Musical Band 1950, Cienfuegos Firemen's Corps Band 1952–59, Loyola Orchestra 1959–62, Central Army Band 1959–60; flautist and composer, Youth and Students Orchestra of the Eighth Festival of Youth and Students, Helsinki, Finland 1962; teacher, Nat. School of the Arts, Havana 1973–75; Dir Amadeo Roldán Conservatory, Havana 1974–75; Nat. Co-ordinator, Gen. Office of Art Schools 1975–76; teacher of composition, Faculty of Music, Higher Inst. for the Arts 1976–, currently Prof. of Composition, Orchestration and Counterpoint, teaching Vice-Rector 1976–78, Dean 1977–78; Lecturer, Second Bambuco Festival, Mexico 1990; mem. Nat. Union of Writers and Artists of Cuba (pres. music bd 1976–77, sec. 1979, deputy pres. 1983–96, pres. 1996–), Cuban Fryderyk Chopin Soc. (pres. 1983–), Union of Writers and Artists of Cuba Golden Boleros Festival (pres. 1987). *Compositions:* Los piroperos 1960–69, Mi rico chachachá 1960–69, Lo sabe Isabel 1960–69, Sinfonietta 1965, Música para flauta y cuerdas 1968, Tres imágenes poéticas 1969, Antipoemas 1970, Música viva No. 1 for percussion 1971, Monzón y el Rey de Koré (opera) 1973, Poética del guerrillero for orchestra 1976, Música viva No. 2 1976, Música viva No. 3 1978, Música viva No. 4 1979, Canto negro 1979, Variaciones folklóricas 1982, Tres piezas cubanas for piano 1985, Tropicalia I 1987, Tropicalia II 1988, Canción del Soy Todo 1990. *Publications:* Música Cabana (ed.); contrib. numerous articles. *Honours:* Eighth Festival of Youth and Students Best Soloist of Popular Music, Helsinki 1962, 26 de Julio Musical Contest Chamber Music Prize, Centenary of Karol Symanowsky medal 1982, winner Union of Writers and Artists of Cuba Nat. Composition Contest 1985, Merit of Polish Culture 1985, winner Cuban Nat. Cultural Award 1988. *Address:* c/o Ana Margarita Cabrera, Instituto Superior de Arte, Calle 120, No. 1110 entre 9na y 13, Cubanacan Playa, Havana 12100, Cuba (office).

LU, Jia; Chinese conductor; *Music Director and Principal Conductor, Macao Orchestra*; b. 1964, Shanghai. *Education:* Central Conservatory of Music, Beijing, Universität der Künste Berlin, Germany. *Career:* Chief Conductor of the Nat. Youth Orchestra of China 1987; further engagements with the Leipzig Gewandhaus, Berlin Symphony and NDR Hamburg Symphony Orchestras; Chief Conductor and Music Dir, Trieste Opera 1991–95; Principal Conductor, Orchestra della Toscana, and Opera of Genova, Carlo Felice, Florence 1995–99; Chief Conductor and Artistic Adviser, Norrkoping Symphony Orchestra, Sweden 1999–2005; Principal Conductor, Lazlo Chamber Orchestra, Rome 2000–05; Music Dir, Fondazione Arena, Verona 2006–; Music Dir and Principal Conductor, Macao Orchestra 2008–; appearances with the Santa Cecilia Orchestra, Rome, and at the Bologna Opera; season 1995–96 included debuts with the Bamberg and Chicago Symphonies, English Chamber Orchestra, Deutsch Oper Berlin, Orchestre Nat. de Lyon and Chamber Orchestra of Europe; season 1996–97 debuts with the Oslo and St Petersburg Philharmonic Orchestras; Artistic Adviser and Principal Conductor, Norrkoping Symphony Orchestra; performed with the Stockholm Philharmonic, Hong Kong Philharmonic, Bournemouth Symphony Orchestra, Halle Orchestra and the Malaysian Philharmonic in Kuala Lumpur. *Honours:* winner Nat. Chinese Conducting Competition 1986, first prize Pedrotti Competition, Trento 1990. *Address:* Macao Orchestra, Avenida Conselheiro Ferreira de Almeida, 95A, Macao (office). *Telephone:* 28532000 (office). *E-mail:* om@icm.gov.mo (office). *Website:* www.icm.gov.mo/om (office).

LÜ, Shao-Chia; Taiwanese conductor; *Music Director, Philharmonia Taiwan, the National Symphony Orchestra*; b. Chutung Township, Hsinchu County; s. of Lu Yao-shu. *Education:* Nat. Taiwan Univ., Indiana Univ., USA, Vienna Hochschule für Musik, Austria, Accademia Musicale Chigiana, Italy. *Career:* Asst Conductor, Taipei Symphony Orchestra 1986–87; conducted Munich Philharmonic Orchestra, Taiwan 1994; Prin. Conductor, Komische Oper Berlin 1995–98; Music Dir Staatsorchester Rheinische Philharmonia and Koblenz Theatre 1998–2004; Music Dir Niedersächsische Staatstheater Hannover 2001–06; Music Dir Designate, Philharmonia Taiwan, Nat. Symphony Orchestra of Taiwan 2009–10, Music Dir 2010–. *Honours:* First Prize and Lyre d'Or Award, Int. Besançon Competition for Young Conductors, France 1988, Winner, Pedrotti Int. Competition for Orchestra Conductors 1991, Winner, Int. Kiril Kondrashin Competition for Conductors 1994, Peter Cornelius Plakette for Outstanding Contribution to Local Culture, Cultural Ministry of Rheinland 2004. *Address:* Miss Sarah Tu, Assistant Manager, International Affairs, Philharmonia Taiwan, National Symphony Orchestra, National Chiang Kai-Shek Cultural Center, Taipei, Taiwan (office). *Telephone:* (2) 3393-9623 (office). *Fax:* (2) 3393-9889 (office). *E-mail:* tuc@mail.ntch.edu.tw (office). *Website:* nso.ntch.edu.tw (office).

LUBAVIN, Leonid; Russian singer (tenor); b. 1962, Krasnodar. *Education:* State Academy of Theatre, Music and Cinema, Leningrad, State Rimsky-Korsakov Conservatory of St Petersburg. *Career:* debut as Narraboth in Salome at the Mariinsky Theatre, 1995; Principal Soloist of the Mariinsky Theatre (Kirov Opera), 1995–; appearances as Faust, Lohengrin, Tamino, Lensky, Fenton and Hermann in The Queen of Spades; Almaviva in Il Barbiere di Siviglia; tours with the Kirov to Japan, France, Italy and Germany; Iskra in Mazeppa and Yurodivity in Boris Godunov, New York Met, and tour of Latin America, 1998; with New Israel Opera, Tel-Aviv in Falstaff by Verdi as Fenton, 1998; performed Das Lied von der Erde by Mahler, Mikkeli Festival, Finland, 1997; other roles include Benvenuto Cellini by Berlioz at the St Petersburg Opera with the Mariinsky Orchestra, and with the Rotterdam Philharmonic, 1999.

LUBBOCK, John David Peter, OBE; British conductor; b. 18 March 1945, Herts., England. *Education:* Chorister at St George's Chapel, Windsor Castle, singing studies at Royal Acad. of Music, studied with Sergiu Celibidache. *Career:* sang with John Alldis Choir; Founder-mem. London Symphony Chorus; mem. Swingle Singers; Founder and Prin. Conductor, Camden Chamber Orchestra 1967, renamed the Orchestra of St John's Smith Square (now the Orchestra of St John's) 1972–; frequent concerts at St John's Church in Westminster and on tour in UK, Europe, USA and Canada; Guest Conductor with City of Birmingham Symphony, London Philharmonic, BBC Scottish Symphony, Bournemouth Symphony and Sinfonietta, London Mozart Players, Irish Chamber Orchestra, Stuttgart Symphony Orchestra and Netherlands Chamber Orchestra; works regularly with the Ulster Orchestra and as Prin. Conductor with Belfast Philharmonic Soc. and Oxford Univ. Orchestra; took part in premiere of Iain Hamilton's opera Lancelot 1985; conducted Berio's Sinfonia at Barbican Hall 1985 and premiere of Meirion Bowen's orchestration of Tippett's The Heart's Assurance; worked with the Hallé Orchestra 1992, 1995; Schumann's Requiem and Dvořák's Symphonic Variations at St John's 1997; conducted Orchestra of St John's at the BBC Proms, Royal Albert Hall, London 2002, 2006; f. Music for Autism (charity); has developed a series of concerts for people with dementia; Founder-Trustee, Thomley Activity Centre; Trustee, Music for Life Foundation, Clear Sky Foundation. *Recordings include:* Arnold Guitar Concerto and Rodrigo Concierto de Aranjuez; Haydn Symphonies Nos 44 and 49; Mendelssohn Symphonies Nos 3 and 4; Schubert Symphony No. 5; Stravinsky Apollon musagète and Orpheus; Tchaikovsky String Serenades; Mozart Overtures; Vivaldi Concerti Op. 10, all with the Orchestra of St John's Smith Square. *Honours:* Hon. FRAM 1999. *Address:* Orchestra of St John's, 7 Warborough Road, Shillingford, Wallingford, Oxon., OX10 7SA, England (office). *Telephone:* (1865) 858310; 7775-904626 (mobile; Admin). *E-mail:* orchestra@osj.org.uk (office); johnlubbock@calub.fsnet.co.uk. *Website:* www.osj.org.uk (office).

LUBIN, Steven, BA, MS, PhD; American pianist and academic; *Professor, Conservatory of Music, Purchase College, State University of New York;* b. 22 Feb. 1942, New York, NY; s. of Jack Lubin and Sophie Lubin; m. Wendy Lubin 1974; two s. *Education:* Harvard Univ., Juilliard School, New York Univ.; piano studies with Lisa Grad, Nadia Reisenberg, Seymour Lipkin, Rosina Lhevinne, Beveridge Webster. *Career:* recital and concert tours in USA, Canada, Mexico, UK, France, Netherlands, Spain, Italy, Germany, Austria, Finland, Australia, Taiwan, Japan and Ukraine; f. The Mozartean Players 1978–; mem. Faculty, Juilliard School 1964–65, Aspen Music School 1967, Vassar Coll. 1970–71, Cornell Univ. 1971–75; Prof., Conservatory of Music, Purchase Coll., State Univ. of New York (SUNY) 1975–. *Film:* soloist in Man and Music (British documentary) 1987. *Recordings include:* complete Beethoven Piano Concertos, Mozart and Schubert Trios, six Mozart Concertos as soloist and conductor and other solo and chamber music. *Publications:* articles in The New York Times, Keynote, Ovation, Keyboard Classics and Historical Performance, Brahms Soc. Newsletter 1999; contrib. to A Companion to Schubert's Schwanengesang 2000. *Honours:* Martha Baird Rockefeller Grant 1968, Stereo Review Recording of the Year Award 1988, Kempner Distinguished Professor Award, SUNY, Purchase 2001. *Current Management:* c/o John Gingrich Management, Inc., PO Box 1515, New York, NY 10023, USA. *Telephone:* (212) 799-5080. *E-mail:* gingarts@verizon.net. *Website:* www.gingarts.com. *Address:* Conservatory of Music, School of the Arts, State University of New York, Purchase, NY 10577, USA (office). *Telephone:* (914) 251-6715 (office). *E-mail:* steven.lubin@gmail.com (office). *Website:* www.stevenlubin.com.

LUBLIN, Eliane; singer (soprano); b. 10 April 1938, Paris, France. *Education:* studied in Paris, Verdi Conservatory in Paris. *Career:* debut at Aix-en-Provence as Debussy's Mélisande; Paris Opéra-Comique; Monte Carlo Opéra in Menotti's The Medium; Paris Opéra from 1969 in Les Dialogues des Carmélites, as Massenet's Manon, Marguerite in Faust, Ellen Orford in Peter Grimes and in the 1981 French premiere of Ligeti's Le Grande Macabre. *Recordings include:* Sapho by Gounod.

LUBOTSKY, Mark; violinist; b. 18 May 1931, Leningrad, Russia. *Education:* Moscow Conservatory with A. Yampolsky and D. Oistrakh. *Career:* debut in Bolshoi Hall of Moscow Conservatory 1950, Tchaikovsky Concerto; solo recitals and concerts with major orchestras in the UK, Scandinavia, Germany, The Netherlands, Italy, USA, Australia, Japan and Israel; many television and radio performances; teacher, Gnessin Inst., Moscow 1967–76; Prof., Sweelinck Conservatory, Amsterdam 1976–; Prof., Hochschule für Musik, Hamburg 1986–; British debut 1970, Britten's Concerto at the Promenade Concerts. *Recordings:* concertos from the Baroque by Mozart, Britten, Schnittke, Tubin; solo sonatas by Bach; sonatas by Brahms, Mozart, Shostakovich, Schnittke. *Honours:* Mozart Int. Competition, Salzburg 1956, Tchaikovsky Int. Competition, Moscow 1958. *Address:* Caversham Grange, The Warren, Mapledurham, Berkshire RG4 7TQ, England.

LUCAS OGDON, Brenda, FRSM; British pianist and piano teacher; b. 23 Nov. 1935, Cheshire, England; m. John Ogdon (died 1989); one s. one d. *Education:* Convent of the Nativity, Romiley, Cheshire, Royal Northern Coll. of Music, Manchester, Mozarteum, Salzburg, Austria. *Career:* solo career, including debut in Grieg Piano Concerto with Liverpool Philharmonic Orchestra 1956; duo piano career with John Ogdon; appearances in the 1960s included Edinburgh Festival 1962, 1963, 23rd Cheltenham Festival, Aldeburgh Festival, Sintra Festival, the Royal Concert at Royal Festival Hall with André Previn and Houston Symphony Orchestra 1969; toured USSR 1985; solo appearances in Hong Kong 1996; recital, Maine, USA 2003; est. The John Ogdon Foundation in memory of John Ogdon 1993; mem. Inc. Soc. of Musicians. *Recordings include:* Bartók: Sonata for two pianos 1968, Mendelssohn: Concerto for two pianos 1970, Rachmaninov: Suites Nos 1 and 2 1975, Saint-Saëns: Carnival of the Animals 1972, Schoenberg: Chamber Symphony 1974, Liszt: Concerto Pathétique, works by Schumann 1972, Brahms: Hungarian Dances, Arensky: Waltz, Bach, Milhaud, Stravinsky, Dvořák 1989, The Piano Music of John Ogdon 1991; many of these recordings re-released since 2000. *Publication includes:* 'Virtuoso' – The Story of John Ogdon 1981. *Honours:* Gold Medal of Associated Bd 1949, Harriet Cohen Silver Medal, Royal Northern Coll. of Music 1956, ARMCM Teacher's Distinction, ARMCM Performer's Distinction, LRSM Distinction, ATCL Distinction, FRSM Distinction. *Address:* 24 Shrewsbury House, 42 Cheyne Walk, London, SW3 5LN, England (home). *Telephone:* (20) 7823-3875 (home). *E-mail:* brenogdon@aol.com. *Website:* www.brendalucasogdon.com.

LUCIER, Alvin, BA, MFA; American composer; b. 14 May 1931, Nashua, NH; m. Wendy Wallbank Stokes 1979, one d. *Education:* The Portsmouth Abbey School, Yale Univ., Brandeis Univ. *Career:* Choral Dir, Brandeis Univ. 1962–70; Prof. of Music, Wesleyan Univ. 1970–, Chair of Dept 1979–84; co-founder, Sonic Arts Union 1966–77; Music Dir, Viola Farber Dance Co. 1972–77. *Compositions:* Action Music for piano 1962, Music for solo performer for enormously amplified brain waves and percussion 1965, Vespers 1967, Chambers 1968, I am Sitting in a Room 1970, Still and Moving Lines of Silence in Families of Hyperbolas 1972–, Bird and Person Dyning 1975, Music in a Long Thin Wire 1977, Crossings 1982–84, Seesaw 1984, Sound on Paper 1985, Fideliotrio for viola, cello and piano 1987, Navigations for string quartet 1992, Small Waves for piano, trombone and string quartet 1997, Cassiopeia for orchestra 1998, Diamonds for one, two or three orchestras 1999, Amplifier and Reflector (electro-acoustic work) 1991, Sound Installations, Empty Vessels, Resonant Objects and Sound on Glass (all electro-acoustic works) 1997. *Publications:* Chambers (with Douglas Simon) 1980; contrib. to professional publications. *Honours:* Fulbright Scholarship, Rome 1960–62.

LUCIUK, Juliusz Mieczyslaw; Polish composer; b. 1 Jan. 1927, Brzeznica; m. Domicela Dabrowska 1956; two d. *Education:* Acad. of Music, Kraków, studied with Nadia Boulanger and Max Deutsch in Paris, Jagiellonian Univ., Krákow. *Career:* debut performing three songs 1954; various works recorded for European radio. *Compositions include:* for piano: Maraton, Lirica di Timbri, Pacem in Terris, Passacaglia; three Passion Songs for soprano and organ, Image, Preludes and Tripticum Paschale for organ, Sonata for bassoon and piano, Variations for cello and piano, Fulfilment for violin, cello, double bass (5 strings), Monologues and Dialogues for soprano recorders; ballets: Niobe, Death of Euridice, Medea, L'Amour d'Orphée (opera-ballet), Demiurgos (chamber opera); works for solo voice and chamber ensemble: Floral dream, Le Souffle du Vent, Portraits Lyriques; works for solo voice and symphony orchestra: Tool of the Light; Poème de Loire, Wings and Hands; oratorios: St Francis of Assisi, Gesang am Brunnen, Sanctus Adalbertus flos purpureus, Christus Pantocrator, The Music Trilogy (Divine Stream 2004, Meditations on the Threshold of Sikstim Chapel 2006, The Hill in Moria Land, with text from Roman Triptych by Pope John Paul II 2011); S. Rafal Kalinowski 2007, Omaggio a L'Aquila 2013, Polish Litany, The Polish Mass for mezzo-soprano, mixed choir and wind orchestra; choral works include: four Antiphonae and vespera in Assumptione Beatae Mariae Virginis for men's choir, The Mass for men's choir and organ, The Mass, Hymnus de Caritate and Magnificat for mixed choir, Apocalypsis for four soloists and mixed choir; orchestral works: Four Symphonic Sketches, Symphonic Allegro, Composition for Four Orchestral Ensembles, Speranza Sinfonica, Lamentazioni in memoriam Grazyna Bacewicz, Warsaw Legend (Quasi Cradle Song), Osiers, 5 pieces for string chamber orchestra, Concertino for piano and small symphony orchestra, Concerto for double bass and symphony orchestra, Hommage for strings 1993. *Recordings:* albums include: Demiurgos, chamber opera, Sanctus Adalbertus flos purpureus oratorio, Polish Litany, Medea, ballet, Acte Prealable, Sonorous Piano Visions, Piano Concertino, Double bass concerto, Wings and Hands, Gesang an Brunnen, oratorio. *Honours:* Silver Medal Vercelli 1960, Netherlands Radio AVRO Prize, 1962, Winner Prince Pierre Competition, Monaco 1974, City of Krakow Award 1983, S. Alberts Award for sacred works 1983, Krakow Voivode Award 1992, Ministry of Culture Award 1995, Polish Composers' Asscn Award 1998, Medal Pro Ecclesia et Pontifice of Pope John Paul II 2001, Mayor of Krakow's Award 2006. *Address:* Os Kolorowe 6 m 10, 31-938 Krákow, Poland (office). *Telephone:* (12) 644-16-10 (office).

LUCKE, Hannfried; German organist and academic; *Professor, Mozarteum University, Salzburg;* b. 27 Feb. 1964, Freiburg. *Education:* Hochschule für Musik, Freiburg, Mozarteum Univ., Salzburg, Austria, Conservatoire de Musique, Geneva, Switzerland. *Career:* int. concert organist with concert performances and broadcasting recordings in numerous countries in Europe, USA, Canada, Japan, Hong Kong and Australia; Prof., Univ. Mozarteum Salzburg 2000–. *Recordings:* major organ works of J.S. Bach, organ works of the romantic period on instruments in Europe, USA and Japan. *Honours:* Prize of Honour, Austrian Minister for Cultural Affairs, Premier Prix at Conservatoire de Musique, Geneva. *Address:* Lawenastrasse 42, 9495 Triesen, Liechtenstein.

LUDWIG, Christa; Austrian/French singer (mezzo-soprano); b. 16 March 1928, Berlin, Germany; d. of Anton Ludwig and Eugenie Besalla-Ludwig; m. 1st Walter Berry 1957 (divorced 1970, died 2000); one s.; m. 2nd Paul-Emile Deiber 1972. *Career:* opera debut at 18, guest appearance at the Athens Festival in Epidauros 1965; joined Vienna State Opera 1955, Hon. mem. 1981; appearances at festivals in Salzburg, Bayreuth, Lucerne, Holland, Prague, Saratoga, Stockholm; guest appearances in season in Vienna, New York, Chicago, Buenos Aires, Milan, Berlin, Munich; numerous recitals and soloist in concerts. *Recordings include:* Lieder and complete operas including Norma (with Maria Callas), Lohengrin, Così fan tutte, Der Rosenkavalier, Carmen, Götterdämmerung, Die Walküre, Bluebeard's Castle, Don Giovanni, Die Zauberflöte, Le Nozze di Figaro, Capriccio, Fidelio. *Publication:* In My Own Voice (biog.) 1994. *Honours:* Hon. mem. Vienna Konzerthaus, Vienna Philharmonic; Hon. Prof.; Commdr des Arts et des Lettres 1989, Grosses Ehrenzeichen 1994, Commdr, Ordre pour le Mérite 1997, Commdr, Légion d'honneur 2010; winner, Bach-Concours, record award for Fricka in Walküre and Des Knaben Wunderhorn, awarded title of Kammersängerin by Austrian Govt 1962, Prix des Affaires Culturelles (for recording of Venus in Tannhäuser), Paris 1972, Silver Rose (Vienna Philharmonic) 1980, Golden Ring (Staatsoper, Vienna) 1980, Golden Gustav Mahler Medal 1980, Hugo Wolf Medal (Austria) 1980, Gold Medal (City of Vienna) 1988, Midem Classical Lifetime Achievement Award 2008, Hugo Wolf Medal (Germany) 2010. *Current Management:* c/o Ingpen & Williams, 7 St George's Court, 131 Putney Bridge Road, London, SW15 2PA, England. *Website:* www.ingpen.co .uk/artist/christa-ludwig.

LUFF, Enid, MA (Cantab.), MMus (Wales), LRAM; British composer; b. (Enid Meirion Roberts), 21 Feb. 1935, Ebbw Vale, Glamorgan, Wales; d. of Rev. R. Meirion Roberts and Daisy Jane Roberts; m. Alan Luff 1956; three s. one d. *Education:* Univ. of Wales, studied Advanced Composition with Elisabeth Lutyens and Franco Donatoni. *Career:* composer 1971–; runs Primavera self-publishing co. with Julia Usher 1980–; mem. British Acad. of Composers and Songwriters, Mechanical Copyright Protection Soc., Performing Right Soc., Women in Music, Cyfansoddwyr Cymru/Composers of Wales. *Compositions:* Four piano pieces, Tapestries for chamber group, Symphony No. 1, Mathematical Dream for solo harp, Wind Quintet: The Coastal Road, Sheila NaGig for soprano and pianoforte, Dream Time for Bells for chamber group, Sky Whispering for solo piano, Sonata: Storm Tide for piano, Come the Morning for chamber ensemble, Peregrinus, Trilogy for organ 1991, Listening for the Roar of the Sun for oboe, speaker, dance and slide projection 1992, Symphony 2 1994, The Glass Wall for solo cello, dancers and electronic tape 1996. *Recordings:* Hierusalem for chamber ensemble 2000, Heaven's Bird for chamber ensemble 2002, Taro Arian/Struck in Silver for sound sculptures and flute 2004; several works recorded on BBC and Danish Radio recordings. *Address:* 12 Heol Tyn y Cae, Cardiff, CF14 6DJ, Wales (home). *Telephone:* (29) 2061-6023 (office). *Fax:* (29) 2061-6023 (office). *E-mail:* enidluff@globalnet.co .uk (home). *Website:* www.primaveramusic.com (office).

LUGANSKY, Nikolai L.; Russian pianist; b. 26 April 1972, Moscow; s. of Lev Borisovich Lugansky and Anna Nikolayevna Luganskaya; m. Lada Borisovna Luganskaya; one s. one d. *Education:* Moscow State Conservatory. *Career:* repertoire includes more than 40 piano concertos and music from Bach to modern composers; ensemblist and interpreter of chamber music; performances in Russia and abroad in Australia, Austria, Belgium, Brazil, Canada, England, France, Germany, Italy, Japan and elsewhere, including at Royal Festival Hall and Wigmore Hall in London, Salle Gaveau and Louvre in Paris, Conservatoria Verdi in Milan, Gasteig in Munich, Concertgebouw in Amsterdam, Alte Oper in Frankfurt. *Recordings include:* numerous albums including Rachmaninov piano concertos, Tchaikovsky's Piano Concerto No. 1 2004, Liszt 2011, Prokofiev's Piano Concerto No. 3 and Grieg's Piano Concerto with Deutsches-Symphonie Orchester Berlin and Kent Nagano 2013, Chopin Piano Concertos with Sinfonia Varsovia and Alexander Vedernikov 2014. *Honours:* First Prize, All-Union student competition Tbilisi Georgia 1988, Silver Medal, Bach Int. Competition, Leipzig, Germany 1988, Second Prize, Rachmaninov Competition, Moscow 1990, First Prize, Tchaikovsky Int.

Competition, Moscow 1994, Terence Judd Award for the most promising pianist of a generation 1995, Honoured Artist of the Russian Fed. 2005, Echo Klassik Award 2005, 2007, 2013, BBC Music Magazine Award 2011, People's Artist of Russia 2013. *Current Management:* Harrison/Parrott Ltd, 5-6 Albion Court, Albion Place, London, W6 0QT, England. *E-mail:* lydia.connolly@ harrisonparrott.co.uk. *Website:* www.harrisonparrott.com/artist/profile/ nikolai-lugansky. *Address:* Moscow 119334, Kosygina str. 2, apt 2, Russia (home). *Telephone:* (495) 137-18-36 (home). *Website:* www.facebook.com/ NikolaiLugansky.

LUISI, Fabio; Italian conductor; b. 1959, Genoa; m. Barbara Luisi; three s. *Education:* Conservatorio Nicolò Paganini, Genoa, Graz Conservatoire of Music. *Career:* debut as conductor 1984; f. Graz Symphony Orchestra, Artistic Dir 1990–95; Artistic Dir and Chief Conductor, Tonkünstler Orchestra, Vienna 1995–2000; Artistic Dir and Music Dir, Orchestre de la Suisse Romande, Geneva 1997–2002; Artistic Dir, MDR Symphony Orchestra, Leipzig 1999–2007; Chief Conductor, Wiener Symphoniker 2005–; Gen. Music Dir, Sächsische Staatsoper Dresden 2007–10; Chief Conductor, Sächsische Staatskapelle Dresden 2007–10; Principal Guest Conductor, Metropolitan Opera, New York 2010–; Music Dir, Zurich Opera 2012–; appearances worldwide as guest conductor of symphonic works and opera. *Recordings include:* German Opera Arias 1995, Zandonai's Francesca Da Rimini 1997, Rossini's Guillaume Tell 1998, Mozart's Idomeneo, Beethoven's Missa Solemnis 2005, Mad Scenes 2006, Strauss' Rosenkavalier 2008, Wagner's Der Ring des Nibelungen (Grammy Award for Best Opera Recording 2013) 2012. *Publication:* Erst der halbe Weg (auto-biog.) 2008. *Honours:* Cross of Honour for Arts and Sciences (Austria), Cavaliere Ufficiale of the Italian Republic 2006. *Current Management:* c/o Tim Fox, Columbia Artists Management, 1790 Broadway, New York, NY 10019-1412, USA. *E-mail:* info@cami.com. *Website:* www.cami.com.

LUISOTTI, Nicola; Italian conductor; *Music Director, San Francisco Opera and Teatro di San Carlo;* b. 1961, Viareggio, Tuscany. *Education:* Musical Inst. Luigi Boccherini, Lucca. *Career:* int. debut with Stuttgart State Opera 2002; subsequent performances with most major opera cos world-wide, including Bavarian State Opera, Canadian Opera Co., Dresden Staatskapelle, Frankfurt Opera, La Scala, Los Angeles Opera, Metropolitan Opera, Paris Opera, Royal Opera House, Seattle Opera, Teatro Carlo Felice, Bologna's Teatro Comunale, Teatro La Fenice, Teatro Real, Teatro di San Carlo and Vienna State Opera; Prin. Conductor Tokyo Symphony Orchestra 2009–12; San Francisco Opera debut conducting La forza del destino 2005, subsequent performances of La bohème, Il trovatore, Salome, Otello, La fanciulla del West, Aïda, Le nozze di Figaro and Madama Butterfly with the co.; La Scala debut with Attila 2010; Puccini's La fanciulla del West, Metropolitan Opera 2010; operatic engagements for 2011–12 season included a return visit to La Scala for Tosca and appearances with Teatro di San Carlo in Verdi opera, I Masnadieri; orchestral conducting appearances with San Francisco Opera Orchestra, Berlin Philharmonic, Orchestra del Teatro di San Carlo, Orquesta Nacional de España and Cleveland and Philadelphia Orchestras; has also led numerous orchestral ensembles, including Accad. Nazionale di Santa Cecilia, Frankfurt's Alte Oper, Atlanta Symphony, Bavarian Radio Orchestra, Berlin Philharmonic, Budapest Radio Orchestra, Filarmonica della Scala, Hamburg Philharmonic, Hessischer Rundfunk Orchestra, London Philharmonia, NHK Symphony, Orchestra Sinfonica Nazionale della RAI, Russian Nat. Orchestra, Dresden Staatskapelle, San Francisco Symphony, Tokyo Symphony and Zagreb Philharmonic; led special concerts in Beijing in conjunction with the Olympic Games 2008; Music Dir San Francisco Opera 2009–; Music Dir Teatro di San Carlo, Naples 2012–. *Recordings include:* Stiffelio, Duets, La bohème with the Met (DVD). *Honours:* Seattle Opera Artist of the Year 2006, Premio Puccini Award 2010. *Current Management:* c/o Gianluca Macheda, IMG Artists, Viale C. Castracani, Traversa IV 335, 55100 Lucca, Italy. *Telephone:* (05) 83955540. *Fax:* (05) 83474685. *E-mail:* gmacheda@imgartists .com. *Website:* www.imgartists.com; www.nicolaluisotti.com.

LUITZ, Josef; Austrian cellist; b. 2 Aug. 1934, Vienna; m. Sonja Edelgard Mayerhofer 1962; one s. one d. *Education:* School for Musical Instrument Makers, Vienna, Konservatorium, Vienna with W. Kleinecke; masterclass with N. Hubner in Santiago de Compostella. *Career:* debut at Musikverein, Vienna 1957; first Cellist, Tonkuenstler Orchestra 1957–61; Solo Cellist 1962–; Member, Haydn Quartet 1965–72, Ensemble Kontrapunkta 1968–75, Philharmonia Quintet 1971–77, Concordia Trio 1979–; Professor of Cello, Konservatorium, Vienna 1972–; Chairman, Tonkuenstler Chamber Orchestra 1978–; Chairman, International Chamber Music Festival, Austria 1978–. *Recordings:* Chamber Music Series for Musical Heritage Society Inc, New York; Spohr Octet with Vienna Octet; With Tonkuenstler Chamber Orchestra; many Radio Productions as Soloist. *Honours:* Professor, Austrian Government, 1985. *Address:* Vienna Konservatorium, Stiegergasse 15-17, 1150 Vienna, Austria (office). *Telephone:* (1) 9858112 (office). *Fax:* (1) 8922813 (office). *E-mail:* office@viennaconservatory.at (office). *Website:* www .viennaconservatory.at (office).

LUKAS, Laslo; singer (baritone); b. 1964, Budapest, Hungary. *Education:* Franz Liszt Music Acad., Budapest. *Career:* sang with the Budapest State Opera four seasons, then with the Prague State Opera; Trier Opera from 1991, including Tcherikov in the first production this century of Zemlinsky's first opera, Sarema; guest appearances in Germany and elsewhere as Rigoletto, Scarpia, Jochanaan in Salome, Macbeth, Posa, Count Luna, Kaspar, Cardillac, and the Man in Hindemith's Mörder, Hoffnung der Frauen; Simone in Zemlinsky's Florentinische Tragödie, at the Prague State Opera. *Recordings include:* Sarema.

LUKHANIN, Viacheslav; Russian singer (bass); b. 1960, Maimi-Sai. *Education:* Frunze Conservatoire, Kirgizia. *Career:* sang at opera houses in Frunze, Novosibirsk and St Petersburg, 1985–94; Mariinsky Theatre, St Petersburg, from 1994 as Mozart's Figario, Verdi's Grand Inquisitor and King of Egypt, Storm Wind in Kshchei the Immortal by Rimsky-Korsakov and the Priest in Katerina Izmailova; European tours with the Mussorgsky Opera and Kirov Opera companies, St Petersburg; sang in the British premiere of Prokofiev's Semyon Kotko, with the Kirov at Covent Garden, 2000; other roles include Angelotti in Tosca and the Bonze in Madama Butterfly. *Honours:* Prizewinner, Glinka National vocal and Chaliapin International Competitions, 1987–89.

LUKOMSKA, Halina; singer (soprano); b. 29 May 1929, Suchedniow, Poland. *Education:* State Opera High School, Poznań, Warsaw State Music High School, studied with Toti dal Monte in Venice. *Career:* wide appearances as concert singer from 1960, notably in works by Webern, Serocki, Boulez, (Pli selon Pli), Maderna, Schoenberg, Nono and Lutoslawski; festival engagements at Edinburgh, Perugia, Vienna, Toulouse, and Warsaw; Holland Festival 1967, in Monteverdi's Orfeo; North American tour with Cleveland Orchestra 1973. *Recordings:* Works by Berg (Altenberglieder) and Webern; Pli Selon Pli; Confitebor Domine by J.C. Bach; Boris Godunov. *Honours:* winner 's-Hertogenbosch Competition 1956.

LUKOSZEVIEZE, Anton; British cellist, composer and artist; *Director, Apartment House;* b. 1965, Devon. *Education:* Royal Coll. of Music, London, with Michael Evans; master classes with William Pleeth; attended Oliver Knussen's contemporary music performance courses at Britten-Pears School, Snape. *Career:* performances have included premieres of avant garde, experimental and improvised music; concerti with City of Birmingham Symphony Orchestra at Aldeburgh Festival 2001 and with Netherlands Radio Symphony Orchestra; concerts and recitals in UK, Germany, France, Italy, Slovakia, USA and Canada; BBC Proms John Cage Evening 2012; collaborated with composers and performers including Jennifer Walshe, Christian Wolff, David Behrman, Alvin Lucier, Pierre Strauch, Christopher Fox and Alvin Curran; broadcasts on BBC Radio 3, Danish Radio, SR2, Sweden, Deutschland Rundfunk, WDR, Germany and ORT, Austria; Founding Dir, Apartment House contemporary ensemble 1995–; as artist, exhbns in UK and Europe; New Music Fellow, Kings Coll., Cambridge 2005–07. *Film soundtrack:* Aura Satz' Drone Rorschach. *Compositions include:* Each one is one for ensemble or solo 2004, Arborealmusik for ensemble 2005, For Fred Sandback for cellos 2005, Farewell organ for reed organ 2009, Dirty Angels for prepared piano, strings, clarinet and playback 2011, Chewing Gum Music for multi-track cello and recordings of locations in London (from photographs by Paulina Pukyte) 2011, H.Arp for harp, paper and electronics (commissioned by Rhodri Davies); also American Poets series, for organ/piano/cello and voices of poets including Lew Welch, William Carlos Williams and John Wieners 2010. *Recordings include:* solo: Zbigniew Karkowski's Nerve Cell-0, Christopher Fox: Complete Cello Music, Rebecca Saunders Portrait CD, Peter Eötvös: Intervalles Intérieurs; with Apartment House: Cornelius Cardew Chamber Music 1955–64 2001, Jennifer Walshe: XXX_Live_Nude_Girls (DVD) 2009, Peter Garland String Quartets 2009, John Lely: The Harmonics of Real Strings 2014. *Honours:* Royal Philharmonic Soc. Award for Outstanding Contrib. to Chamber Music and Song 2011 (Apartment House). *E-mail:* antonannex@googlemail.com (office); anton@apartmenthouse.fsnet.co.uk (office). *Website:* www.antonlukoszevieze.co.uk (office); www.apartmenthouse .co.uk (office).

LUKS, Václav; Czech conductor and musician (harpsichord, French horn); *Artistic Director, Collegium 1704;* b. 1970. *Education:* Acad. of Performing Arts, Prague and Schola Cantorum Basiliensis, Switzerland. *Career:* fmrly Principal horn, Akademie für Alte Musik Berlin; as soloist or chamber musician performed at European venues including Salzburg, Zürich, Davos, Barcelona, Paris, Warsaw, Berlin, Dresden, Prague, Istanbul and also Mexico City; transformed Collegium 1704 ensemble into full-time baroque orchestra, Artistic Dir 2005–; Founder and Artistic Dir, Collegium Vocale 1704 2005–; taught at Acad. of Performing Arts, Prague 1996–99, Univ. of Music and Theatre F. Mendelssohn-Bartholdy, Leipzig 2001–03. *Recordings include:* with Collegium 1704/Collegium Vocale 1704: several CDs of works of Jan Dismas Zelenka including Composizione per Orchestra 2005, Missa Votiva 2008, Officium defunctorum/Requiem in D (Gramophone Editor's Choice) 2011, Music for Funeral Rites of Augustus the Strong 2011, Responsoria pro hebdomada sancta 2012; also Reichenauer Concertos 2011, Bach Mass in B Minor. *Address:* c/o Collegium 1704, Mánesova 813/4, 120 00 Prague 2, Czech Republic (office). *Telephone:* (246) 052456 (office). *E-mail:* info@collegium1704 .com (office). *Website:* www.collegium1704.com (office).

LUMSDAINE, David, DMus; Australian composer; b. 31 Oct. 1931, Sydney, Australia; m. Nicola LeFanu, one s. two d. *Education:* NSW Conservatorium of Music, Sydney Univ., Royal Acad. of Music, London with Matyas Seiber. *Career:* composer, teacher of composition and music Ed. in London, England; Lecturer in Music, Durham Univ. 1970–77, Sr Lecturer 1977–81; Founder, Electronic Music Studio, Durham; Sr Lecturer, King's Coll., London 1981–93. *Compositions include:* orchestral: Episodes 1969, Looking Glass Music 1970, Sunflower for chamber orchestra 1975, Shoalhaven 1982, Mandela V for symphony orchestra 1988; vocal: The Ballad of Perse O'Reilly for tenor, male

chorus and two pianos 1953–81, Annotations of Auschwitz for soprano and ensemble 1964, 1970, Aria for Edward Eyre for soprano and double bass soloists, chamber ensemble, narrators, tape and electronics 1972, Tides for narrator, 12 voices and percussion 1972, Caliban Impromptu for piano trio, tape and electronica 1972, Empty Sky, Mootwingee for ensemble 1986, Round Dance for sitar, tabla, flute, cello and keyboard 1989; piano works: Canberra for piano solo 1980, Wild Ride to Heaven (with Nicola LeFanu) for electronics 1980, Garden of Earthly Delights 1992, Kalí Dances for ensemble 1994. *Current Management:* c/o University of York Music Press Ltd, Music Department, University of York, York, YO10 5DD, England. *Telephone:* (1904) 432434; (1904) 432450. *E-mail:* claire@uymp.co.uk. *Website:* www .uymp.co.uk. *E-mail:* d.lumsdaine@mac.com (home).

LUMSDEN, Sir David James, Kt, MusB, MA, DPhil; British musician (retd); b. 19 March 1928, Newcastle-upon-Tyne; s. of Albert Lumsden and Vera May Lumsden (née Tate); m. Sheila Daniels 1951; two s. two d. *Education:* Dame Allan's School, Newcastle-upon-Tyne, Selwyn Coll., Cambridge (Organ Scholar). *Career:* Asst Organist, St John's Coll. Cambridge 1951–53; Organist and Choirmaster St Mary's, Nottingham and Univ. Organist 1954–56; Founder and Conductor Nottingham Bach Soc. 1954–59; Rector Chori Southwell Minster 1956–59; Dir. of Music, Keele 1958–59; Prof. of Harmony, RAM 1959–61; Fellow and Organist, New Coll. Oxford and Lecturer, Faculty of Music, Univ. of Oxford 1959–76; Prin., Royal Scottish Acad. of Music and Drama, Glasgow 1976–82, RAM 1982–93; Conductor Oxford Harmonic Soc. 1961–63; Organist, Sheldonian Theatre 1964–76; Harpsichordist to the London Virtuosi 1972–75; Pres. Inc. Asscn of Organists 1966–68; Visiting Prof., Yale Univ., USA 1974–75; Conductor Oxford Sinfonia 1967–70; Choragus, Univ. of Oxford 1968–72; Pres. Inc. Soc. of Musicians 1984–85, Royal Coll. of Organists 1986–88; Chair. Nat. Youth Orchestra 1985–94, Nat. Early Music Asscn 1986–89; mem. Bd Scottish Opera 1978–83, ENO 1984–89. *Music includes:* recordings of organ, choral and chamber music; recitals worldwide. *Publications include:* An Anthology of English Lute Music 1954, Thomas Robinson's Schoole of Musicke 1603 1971, Music for the Lute (Gen. Ed.) 1965–82. *Honours:* Hon. Fellow, Selwyn Coll. Cambridge, New Coll. Oxford, King's Coll., London; Hon. RAM; Hon. FRCO; Hon. GSMD; Hon. FRCM; Hon. FRSAMD; Hon. FRNCM; Hon. FTCL; Hon. FLCM; Hon. FRSCM; Hon. FGCM 2005; Hon. DLitt (Reading) 1989. *Address:* 26 Wyke Mark, Dean Lane, Winchester, SO22 5DJ, England. *Telephone:* (1962) 877807. *E-mail:* lumsdendj@aol.com.

LUMSDEN, Ronald, ARCM, LRAM; pianist; b. 28 May 1938, Dundee, England; m. 1st Annon Lee Silver (deceased); one s.; m. 2nd Alison Paice Hill 1975; one s. one d. *Education:* Harris Acad., Dundee, Royal Coll. of Music, London. *Career:* pianist-in-residence, Univ. of Southampton 1965–68; Henry Wood Promenade Concerts 1973, 1974; soloist in Arts Council Contemporary Music Network 1974–76; visiting piano teacher 1976–; Hon. Dir of School of Music, Reading Univ. 1984–; frequent broadcasts and recitals in UK; mem. Soc. for Promotion of New Music (exec. cttee 1975–78), Incorporated Soc. of Music, European Piano Teachers' Asscn. *Recordings:* Messiaen's Canteyodjaya for Gaudeamus Foundation; Open University's Modern Music. *Publication:* contrib. article on Bartók, in Makers of Modern Culture 1981. *Honours:* first prize Int. Competiton for Interpreters of Contemporary Music, Utrecht 1968.

LUNA, Audrey; American singer (soprano); b. (Audrey Elizabeth Luna), 1979, Salem, Ore. *Education:* Portland State Univ., Cincinnati Conservatory of Music. *Career:* season 2010–11 included debut with the Metropolitan Opera as Queen of the Night and return to sing Najade; also sang title role in Lucia di Lammermoor with Opera Naples and Venus in Le Grand Macabre with New York Philharmonic conducted by Alan Gilbert; as soloist with Los Angeles Philharmonic in Unsuk Chin's Cantatrix Sopranica; as soloist in Messiah with the Nat. Philharmonic; as soloist in Mozart's Mass in C minor with Valdosta Symphony Orchestra; as Rosina in Il barbiere di Siviglia with Opera Memphis and Mississippi Opera; as Queen of the Night with Spoleto Festival USA and with Cincinnati Opera; season 2011–12 joined roster of Lyric Opera of Chicago for its production of Ariadne auf Naxos; debut with Lyric Opera as Queen of the Night; also sang Ariel in Thomas Adès' The Tempest with Orchestra dell'Accademia Nazionale di Santa Cecilia and with Festival Opéra de Québec, both conducted by the composer; as Madame Mao with Lyric Opera of Kansas City; as Queen of the Night with Teatro dell'Opera di Roma; as soloist in George Crumb's Star Child with the American Symphony Orchestra at Carnegie Hall; as Gretel with Intermountain Opera Festival; as soloist in Amy Beach's Grand Mass in E-flat Major and Debussy's Martyrdom of St Sebastien, both with the Nat. Philharmonic; season 2012–13 included a return to the Metropolitan Opera to sing Ariel in its production of The Tempest; Zerbinetta in debut with Fort Worth Opera, Queen of the Night with Utah Opera; La Santa Muerte in Sosa's Regina with American Lyric Theater; a return to the Nat. Philharmonic as soloist in Carmina Burana; season 2013–14 engagements include return to the Metropolitan Opera as Fiakermilli in Strauss' Arabella; Pittsburgh Opera as Queen of the Night in Die Zauberflöte; debuts with Opéra de Montréal in title role of Lakmé; San Francisco Symphony as Ariel in Scenes from The Tempest; with Virginia Opera as Zerbinetta in Ariadne auf Naxos; as soloist with The Williamsburg Symphonia in an Opera Gala Concert; Madame Mao in Adams' Nixon in China with Ireland's Wide Open Opera; Season 2014–15 engagements include a return to the Metropolitan Opera as Olympia in Les Contes d'Hoffmann, also with Den Norske Opera; Carmina Burana with the Minnesota Orchestra and debut with Wiener Staatsoper as Ariel in The Tempest; other highlights include Queen of the Night with Santa Fe Opera, Pittsburgh Opera and Opera Ontario; Zerbinetta with Tanglewood Music Festival; Cunegonde with Toledo Opera; Gilda in Rigoletto with San Antonio Opera; Rosina with Portland SummerFest and Gretel with Syracuse Opera; Blondchen, Juliette and Anne in Sondheim's A Little Night Music, all with Hawaii Opera Theatre; The Controller in Jonathan Dove's Flight, Adina in L'elisir d'amore, Giulietta in I Capuleti e i Montecchi, Erisbe in Cavalli's Ormindo, all with Pittsburgh Opera as a resident artist; the Accuser in Bright Sheng's world premiere of Madame Mao as an apprentice artist with Santa Fe Opera; Amor in Orfeo ed Euridice with Bel Canto Northwest Festival; has sung as soloist with the Nat. Philharmonic in Brahms' Requiem, Orff's Carmina Burana, Makris' Symphony for Soprano and Strings and Vivaldi's Gloria; has also appeared in recital, making her European debut at the Bach to Bartók Festival in Imola, Italy. *Recordings include:* The Tempest, with The Metropolitan Opera (DVD) (Diapason d'Or, Grammy Award for Best Opera Recording) 2014. *Honours:* Winner Elardo Int. Opera Voice Competition 2006, First Place, Eleanor Lieber Awards 2006, First Place, Altamura/Caruso Int. Voice Competition 2006, First Place, Altamura/Caruso Int. Voice Competition 2007, Winner Loren L. Zachary Vocal Competition 2008, Winner The Jensen Foundation Competition 2008, Second Place, Liederkranz Vocal Competition 2008, First Prize, Renata Tebaldi Int. Voice Competition 2009, First Place, Eleanor Lieber Awards 2009, First Place, The Loren L. Zachary Soc. Vocal Competition 2009, Winner and Audience Favorite Award, The Marguerite McCammon Voice Competition 2009, Third Place and The American Prize, José Iturbi Int. Vocal Competition 2009, Second Place, Spiros Argiris Int. Opera Competition 2011, Second Place, Renata Tebaldi Int. Voice Competition 2011, First Place, Alfredo Giacomotti Third Int. Opera Competition 2014; also prizes from Giulio Gari Foundation 2007, Licia Albanese-Puccini Foundation Competition 2008, Marquerite McCammon Voice Competition 2008, Elardo Int. Opera Competition, Irene Dalis Int. Voice Competition, Liederkranz Foundation, Jensen Foundation, Irma Cooper Int. Voice Competition, Lee Schaenen Foundation, Gerda Lissner Foundation, Metropolitan Opera Nat. Council Auditions. *Current Management:* c/o Barrett Vantage Artists, 505 Eighth Avenue, Suite 12A00, New York, NY 10018, USA. *Telephone:* (212) 245-3530. *Fax:* (212) 397-5860. *E-mail:* info@barrattvantage.com. *Website:* www.barrattvantage.com.

LUNDBERG, Gunnar; singer (baritone); b. 1958, Sweden. *Education:* State Opera School Stockholm, studied in Salzburg. *Career:* debut at Vadstena Acad. 1984; mem., Royal Opera Stockholm from 1988, notably as the Herald in Lohengrin, Escamillo, Valentin, Mozart's Count and Figaro, Don Giovanni and Rossini's Figaro; season 1991 as Barelli in the European premiere of The Aspern Papers by Argento; seasons 1992–94 as Silvio in Pagliacci and Marcello in La Bohème; sang in Carmina Burana at the Stockholm Royal Opera 1998; concert repertoire includes Ein Deutsches Requiem, the Bach Passions and B Minor Mass; St John Passion at the 1993 Lucerne Easter Festival.

LUNDBORG, Charles Erik, BM, MA, DMA; American composer; b. 31 Jan. 1948, Helena, MT; m. Zinta Bibelnieks 1981. *Education:* New England Conservatory of Music, Boston, Columbia Univ. *Career:* performances with and commissions from Houston Symphony Orchestra, American Composers Orchestra, Ursula Oppens, Piano, Speculum Musicae, Group for Contemporary Music, Parnassus, New Music Consort, Pittsburgh, New Music Ensemble, Light Fantastic Players, Composers Ensemble, Light Fantastic Players, New Jersey Percussion Ensemble, many others; mem. BMI, American Composers' Alliance (bd mem. 1980–82), ISCM, League of Composers (bd mem. 1975–78). *Compositions:* Passacaglia, two Symphonies, Piano Concerto No. 2, Soundsoup, Solotremolos. *Honours:* Guggenheim Fellowship 1976–77, NEA Fellowships 1975, 1981, 1983.

LUNDGREN, Stefan; Swedish lutenist and composer; b. 5 May 1949, Hogsby; m. Henrike Brose 1985. *Education:* Music School, Oskarshann, Sweden, Lund University, Schola Cantonum Basiliensis, Basel. *Career:* teacher, performer, composer and publisher; Ed., Lute Music 1979–; Dir, annual lute course, Ried im Zillertal, Austria 1983–; teacher of summer courses, Svenska Gitarr och lutasallskapets 1985. *Compositions:* over 30 compositions for lute. *Publications:* New School for the Renaissance Lute 1985, 50 English Duets (publisher, four vols), Charles Mouton, Suite in G Minor, J. A. Losy Two Suites, Little Book for Lute 1: Renaissance Lute, Little Book for Lute 2: Baroque Lute, J. S. Bach Complete Works for Lute. *E-mail:* slundgrenlaute@t-online.de (office). *Website:* www.luteonline.se.

LUNDSTEN, Ralph; Swedish composer, filmmaker, artist, author and diplomatist; *Owner, Andromeda*; b. 6 Oct. 1936, Ersnäs, northern Sweden; m. Diana Lundsten; one d. *Education:* self-taught. *Career:* Owner, Andromeda (Sweden's most famous picture and electronic music studio, including 'the Love Machine' and other invented synthesizers) since 1959, f. Andromeda Fan Soc. 1982; has worked for opera houses in Stockholm and Oslo, Modern Museum and Nat. Museum, Stockholm, the Louvre and Biennale, Paris, Triennale, Milan, Museum of Contemporary Crafts, New York, and others; more than 650 opus numbers, 122 recordings, 12 short films, as well as art exhbns, radio broadcasts; Cultural Amb. for Luleå 1999; mem. London Diplomatic Acad. 2000. *Exhibitions include:* electronic pictures, laser and sound sculptures; subject of several radio and TV portraits and special portrait exhbns at Music Museum, Stockholm 1991–92, 2000; Ralph Lundstengården, Ersnäs has hosted a perm. exhbn about him since 1998. *Compositions:* Nordic Nature Symphonies: No. 1 The Water Sprite, No. 2 Johannes and the Lady of the Woods, No. 3 A Midwinter Saga, No. 4 A Summer Saga, No. 5 Bewitched, No. 6 Landscape of Dreams, No. 7 The Seasons, No. 8 Pathways of the Soul, No. 9 In the Early Days of Summer, No. 10 Symphonia Linnæi, No. 11 In the Fairytale World; Erik XIV and Gustav III (two ballets about Swedish kings), Cosmic Love, Ourfather, Nightmare, Horrorscope, Shangri-La, Universe, Discophrenia, Alpha Ralpha Boulevard, Paradise Symphony, The New Age, Pop Age, Music for Relaxation and Meditation, Cosmic Phantazy, The Dream Master, The Gate of Time, The Ages of Man, Sea Symphony, Mindscape Music, Nordic Light, The Symphony of Joy (dedicated to the UN 50th anniversary), The Symphony of Light, The Symphony of Love, In Time and Space, Andromedian Tales, Happy Earthday, At the Fountain of Youth, A Vagabond of the Soul, Dreamlight, Suite Andromatique, Joy & Light, Prelude to the Future, Like the Wind my Longing, Out in the Wide World (Radio Sweden theme, chosen by Guinness World Records as "the most played musical composition" 2000), Lovetopia, Dance in the Endless Night, River of Time etc.; other: music for Herrskapstroll (children's opera) 1978 and for musical Glasblåsarens barn 2004. *Films include:* Främmande planet 1962–63, Komposition i tre satser 1965, EMS NR 1 1966, Hej natur 1966, Hjärtat brinner 1966–67, Reseminne 1968. *Recordings:* represented European music on EMI Classics series Inspiration 1996. *Publications:* Lustbarheter (with CD) 1992, Lustbarheter 1997, Happy Earthday (with CD) 2005, En själens vagabond 2006. *Honours:* more than 40 awards, including Grand Prix Biennale, Paris 1967, Swedish Film Inst. Prize 1964–67, Schwingungen Sonder-Preis (Oscar of electronic music) (Germany) 1997, Albert Schweitzer Medal for Science and Peace 2004, Gold Medal, Illis quorum meruere labores, given by Swedish Govt for musical and artistic works 2008. *Address:* Frankenburgs väg 1, 132 42 Saltsjö-Boo, Sweden (home). *Telephone:* (8) 715-14-37 (home). *E-mail:* ralph.lundsten@andromeda.se (office). *Website:* www.andromeda.se (office).

LUNELL, Hans, FilKand, FilDr; Swedish composer and computer scientist; b. 12 April 1944, Skellefteå. *Education:* Uppsala Univ., Linköping Univ., Royal Coll. of Music, Stockholm, studied with Greta Erikson. *Career:* Asst Prof., Linköping Univ. 1971–83; Assoc. Prof., KTH, Stockholm 1983–86; Dir, Inst. for Electro-Acoustic Music in Sweden 1989–93; mem. Soc. of Swedish Composers, Int. Confederation for Electro-Acoustic Music, STIM. *Compositions:* Intensità for piano trio 1981–82, La notte in Sicilia for soprano, bass clarinet and vibraphone 1984, Affinities I for piano solo 1985. *Publications:* contrib. numerous articles, many to Nutida Musik.

LUNETTA, Stanley, BA, MA; American composer and timpanist; b. 5 June 1937, Sacramento, CA; m. Sharon Lunetta; four c. *Education:* Sacramento State Coll., Univ. of CA at Davis with Jerome Rosen and Larry Austin, studied with John Cage, David Tudor and Karlheinz Stockhausen. *Career:* founded New Music Ensemble 1963; Ed., Source: Music of the Avant Garde 1971–77; percussionist and teacher in Sacramento. *Compositions:* Many Things for Orchestra 1966; Piano Music 1966; A Piece for Bandoneon and Strings 1966; Free Music 1967; Ta Ta for chorus and mailing tubes 1967; The Wringer, mixed media 1967; Funkart 1967; Twowomanshow, theatre piece 1968; Spider Song with Lartry Austin, 1968; Mr Machine for flute and tape 1969; A Day in the Life of the Mooscak Machines 1972; The Unseen Force theatre piece with dancers 1978; From 1970 much music from a series of self-playing electronic sound sculptures, e.g. Mooscak Machine, Sound Hat and Cosmic Cube. *E-mail:* sTANg@macnexus.org. *Website:* stang.donnerparty.net.

LUNN, Joanne; British singer (soprano); b. 1975, England. *Education:* Royal Coll. of Music, London, studied with Denise Mulholland. *Career:* operatic engagements have included ENO debut in Steven Pimlott's production of Monteverdi's L'Incoronazione di Poppea conducted by Harry Christophers, role of Helena in Britten's A Midsummer Night's Dream in Venice conducted by Sir John Eliot Gardiner, a tour of Purcell's Dido and Aeneas in Spain and semi-staged productions of Monteverdi's Orfeo in Paris and for the Beijing Int. Music Festival with Philip Pickett; concert perfomances include Bach's St Matthew Passion with the Orchestra of the Age of Enlightenment under Sir Roger Norrington, Musik Podium, Stuttgart under Frieder Bernius, Rotterdam Philharmonic Orchestra and with London Symphony Orchestra at the Barbican Hall; soloist in Messiah at Halle Handel Festival, St Mark's Venice, with Bach Collegium Japan (Suzuki) and with Mozarteum Orchester, Salzburg as well as in Handel's L'Allegro and Haydn's Heiligmesse, Harmoniemesse and Paukenmesse with the Monteverdi Choir under Sir John Eliot Gardiner; also sang Bach's Magnificat at BBC Proms with Academy of Ancient Music and with Bach Collegium Japan, Rutter's Requiem with Royal Liverpool Philharmonic Orchestra conducted by the composer, Haydn's The Seasons with Huddersfield Choral Soc., Fauré's Requiem in Toulouse directed by Marc Minkowski, Bach's B minor Mass with Bach Collegium Japan under Masaaki Suzuki, with Academy of Ancient Music in Alzenau and with Les Musiciens du Louvre and Minkowski, for the Akad. der alte Musik, and at the Sage, Gateshead; appeared in Mozart's Mass in C Minor for City of London Sinfonia and Melbourne Symphony Orchestra, Mozart Requiem in Moscow and at Mariinsky Concert Hall, St Petersburg, Purcell's The Blessed Virgin's Expostulation and The Fairy Queen in Salzburg, Easter Oratorio with BBC Nat. Orchestra and Chorus of Wales under Nicholas Kraemer, Nelson Mass for Ulster Orchestra, Rutter Mass of the Children at St Paul's Cathedral and Symphony Hall, Birmingham, Harmoniemesse for Scottish Chamber Orchestra, L'Allegro, Il Penseroso ed il Moderato at Handel Festival, Göttingen, The Creation at Cadogan Hall and Zelenka's Missa Votiva for Musik Podium Stuttgart, Mozart Exsultate Jubilate, Mahler 4th

Symphony at Tchaikovsky Concert Hall, Moscow; other concert performances have included Saul with Cappella Amsterdam and with Estonian Philharmonic Chamber Choir, first performances of J.C. Bach's Mailänder Vesperpsalmen with Concerto Köln at Frauenkirche, Dresden, Bach Cantatas with Le Concert Lorrain, Belinda Dido & Aeneas in Warsaw, Israel in Egypt with Düsseldorfer Symphoniker, St John Passion with Les Musiciens du Louvre (Minkowski) and Graun's Der Tod Jesu with Collegium Vocale; also appeared at Niedersächsische Musiktage with Bach Collegium Japan in programmes of Bach Cantatas, and also in Christmas Oratorio at Tonhalle, Zurich (Suzuki); soloist on numerous recordings; season 2012–13 included Bach Cantatas with Bach Collegium Japan in Tokyo and Utrecht, Bach Mass in B Minor with Ensemble Akamus, Messiah with Northern Sinfonia at the Sage and for Tafelmusik in Canada, Christmas Oratorio for Akad. für alte Musik, St Matthew Passion for the Academy of Ancient Music and for Musik Podium Stuttgart, St John Passion with Bach Collegium Japan in Tokyo and a C.P.E. Bach programme at the Ludwigsburger Schlossfestspiele; subsequent engagements include Christmas Oratorio with Musik Podium Stuttgart and further concerts with Bach Collegium Japan. *Recordings include:* Vivaldi's Laudate Pueri with The King's Consort; Haydn Masses with Sir John Eliot Gardiner and the Monteverdi Choir; John Rutter's Mass of the Children with the City of London Sinfonia conducted by the composer; Sir John Eliot Gardiner's Bach Cantatas cycle recorded during the Bach Pilgrimage in 2000, Bach's Easter Oratorio with Frieder Bernius and the Stuttgart Kammerchor; Bach Motets with The Hilliard Ensemble; Messiah with the Royal Philharmonic Orchestra and John Rutter. *Honours:* Tagore Gold Medal, Royal Coll. of Music. *Current Management:* c/o Hazard Chase Ltd, 25 City Road, Cambridge, CB1 1DP, England. *Telephone:* (1223) 312400. *Fax:* (1223) 460827. *E-mail:* info@ hazardchase.co.uk. *Website:* www.hazardchase.co.uk.

LUPERI, Mario; singer (bass); b. 1954, Sardinia, Italy. *Education:* studied in Calgliari, Verona and Siena. *Career:* debut in Perugia 1979, in Olympie by Spontini and in Cherubini's Requiem; Palermo and Florence 1981, as Publio in La Clemenza di Tito and as Thoas in Iphigénie en Tauride; La Scala from 1982, as the Emperor in The Nightingale, Simone in Gianni Schicchi and Pluto in the Monteverdi Orfeo; Macerata Festival 1984–86, as Colline and Timur, Salzburg Easter Festival 1986, as the Grand Inquisitor; Sang Ramphis in Aida at the Munich Staatsoper 1986, Luxor 1987; Season 1986–87 as Verdi's Pistol at Brussels, Oroe in Semiramide and Oroveso in Norma at Naples; North American debut 1988, as Timur at Pittsburgh; Sang Colline at Genoa, 1990, Giorgio in I Puritani in Marseilles, 1991; Mozart's Bartolo in Venice 1991 and in Fra Diavolo at La Scala, 1992; Sang Charon in Monteverdi's Orfeo at Milan, 1998; Season 2000 as the Cardinal in La Juive for New Israeli Opera, Mozart's Commendatore at La Coruña and Pistol in Falstaff in La Monnaie, Brussels; Many concert appearances; including the Commendatore in Don Giovanni at the Festival Hall, London, 1996. *Current Management:* Atelier Musicale, Via Caselle 76, San Lazzaro di Savena 40068, Italy. *Telephone:* (051) 19 98 44 44. *Fax:* (051) 19 98 44 20. *E-mail:* info@ ateliermusicale.com. *Website:* www.ateliermusicale.com.

LUPTACIK, Jozef; Slovak clarinettist; b. 10 Jan. 1947, Vysoka pri Morave; m. Eva 1972; one s. one d. *Education:* Musical Conservatory, Bratislava, Academy of Music, Bratislava, studied with Prof. V. Riha in Prague. *Career:* debut, A. Copland, Concerto, Music Festival, Bratislava, 1973; E. Suchon, Concertino (first performance), with Czech Philharmonic, Prague, 1978; Mozart, Weber, Krommer, Concertos with Slovak Philharmonic; mem., Slovak Philharmonic Orchestra, first clarinet Bratislava; Associate Professor, Academy of Music, Bratislava; mem. of international juries, international clarinet competitions. *Recordings:* E. Suchon, Concertino; Weber/Mozart, Quintets (B Major, A Major); Weber, Concerto in F Minor, E Major; Brahms/Beethoven, Trio; J. Brahms, Sonatas in E Major, F Minor; Mozart, Clarinet Concerto; J. Hummel, Clarinet Quartet. *Honours:* fourth Prize, Belgrade, 1971. *Address:* Hlavna 36, 900 66 Vysoka pri Morave, Slovakia.

LUPU, Radu, CBE, MA; Romanian pianist; b. 30 Nov. 1945, Galați; s. of Meyer Lupu and Ana Gabor. *Education:* High School, Brașov, Moscow Conservatoire, USSR. *Career:* first piano lessons 1951; won scholarship to Moscow 1961; entered Moscow Conservatoire 1963, graduated 1969; has toured Eastern Europe with London Symphony Orchestra; has appeared numerous times with Berlin Philharmonic since his debut with that orchestra at Salzburg Festival under Herbert von Karajan 1978; American debut 1972 with Cleveland Orchestra under Daniel Barenboim in New York and then with Chicago Symphony under Carlo Maria Giulini; frequent concerts with New York Philharmonic, Royal Concertgebouw Orchestra, Vienna Philharmonic; several tours of Japan; gave world première of André Tchaikowsky Piano Concerto, London 1975; Artist-in-Residence, Dresden Staatskapelle 2014; performances with Cleveland Orchestra at Teatro alla Scala, Milan and Gasteig, Munich 2015–16. *Recordings include:* complete Beethoven cycle (with Israel Philharmonic and Zubin Mehta), complete Mozart sonatas for violin and piano (with Szymon Goldberg), Brahms piano concerto No. 1 (with Edo de Waart and London Philharmonic Orchestra), Mozart piano concerto K467 (with Uri Segal and English Chamber Orchestra), various Beethoven and Schubert sonatas, Mozart and Beethoven wind quintets in E flat, Mozart concerto for 2 pianos and concerto for 3 pianos transcribed for 2 pianos (with Murray Perahia and English Chamber Orchestra), Schubert Fantasie in F minor and Mozart sonata in D for 2 pianos (with Murray Perahia), Schubert Lieder (with Barbara Hendricks), Schubert Piano Duets (with Daniel Barenboim); Schubert's Sonatas, D. 960 and 664 (Grammy Award 1995),

Schumann Kinderszenen, Kreisleriana and Humoresque (Edison Award 1995). *Honours:* First Prize, Van Cliburn Competition 1966, Enescu Int. Competition, Bucharest 1967, Leeds Int. Competition 1969, Abbiati Prize, Italian Critics' Assen 1989, 2006, Premio Internazionale Arturo Benedetti Michelangeli Award 2006. *Current Management:* c/o Opus 3 Artists, 470 Park Avenue South, 9th Floor North, New York, NY 10016, USA. *Telephone:* (212) 584-7500. *Fax:* (646) 300-8200. *E-mail:* info@opus3artists.com. *Website:* www .opus3artists.com/artists/radu-lupu.

LUTHER, Mark; singer (tenor); b. 14 Nov. 1961, Bristol, England. *Education:* National Opera Studio, Guildhall School with Noelle Barker. *Career:* debut at St John's Smith Square, 1989, in Elijah; concert appearances include Opera Gala Evening at Covent Garden, Vivaldi's Gloria with the Northern Symphonia and showings at the Purcell Room and the Queen Elizabeth Hall; Opera engagements include touring performances with British Youth Opera as Rodolfo; Other roles include: Idomeneo, Don Ottavio and Remendado (Carmen); Macduff and Arturo in Lucia di Lammermoor for Welsh National Opera, Don José at Rotterdam and the Verdi Requiem in Netherlands; Don Ottavio in Schönbrunn Vienna; Sang Lensky for Opera North at Norwich, 1998; Sang Tamino at Wellington, 1999.

LUTSIUK, Viktor; Ukrainian singer (tenor); b. 1965, Ivanitchi. *Education:* Kolliarevsky Conservatoire, Kharkov. *Career:* sang at the Dnypropetrov Opera until 1996; Mariinsky Theatre, St Petersburg, from 1996 as Lohengrin, Parsifal, Don Carlos, Lensky in Eugene Onegin, Herman (Queen of Spades), Vladimir in Prince Igor and Dmitiri in Boris Godunov; Andrei in Mazeppa at La Scala (1999), Parsifal at the Royal Albert Hall and Lohengrin in Baden-Baden; sang the title role in the British premiere of Prokofiev's Semyon Kotko, with the Kirov Opera at Covent Garden, 2000; Sofia Gubaidulina St John Passion at the London Proms, 2002; other roles include Alfredo, Radamès, the Duke of Mantua, Don José, Pinkerton, and Andrei in Khovanshchina. *Recordings include:* Mazeppa and Boris Godunov.

LUXON, Benjamin Matthew, CBE, FGSM; British singer (baritone); b. 24 March 1937, Redruth, Cornwall, England; s. of Maxwell Luxon and Lucille Grigg; m. Sheila Amit 1969; two s. one d. *Education:* Truro School, Westminster Training Coll., Guildhall School of Music and Drama. *Career:* sang with English Opera Group 1963–70; has sung with Royal Opera House, Covent Garden and Glyndebourne Festival Opera 1971–96, Boston Symphony Orchestra 1975–96, Netherlands Opera 1976–96, Frankfurt Opera House 1977–96, Paris Opéra 1980, La Scala, Milan 1986; roles include Monteverdi's Ulisse, Janáček's Forester, Mozart's Don Giovanni and Papageno, Tchaikovsky's Onegin, Verdi's Posa and Falstaff, Wagner's Wolfram, Alban Berg's Wozzeck, Count Almaviva and Sherasmin in Oberon; performed as recitalist with piano accompanist David Willison; folk-singing partnership with Bill Grofut 1976–96; retd from professional singing due to severe hearing loss 1996; vocal coach at Tanglewood, USA 1996. *Recordings include:* The Notebook of Anna Magdalena Bach 1981, Mahler: Symphony No. 8 'Symphony of a Thousand' 1983, Ralph Vaughan Williams: Songs of Travel; Four Poems of Fredegond Shove; House of Life 1986, Two Gentlemen Folk 1987, Warlock Songs 1988, Quilter Songs 1989, Beautiful Dreamer 1990, When I Was One-and-Twenty: Butterworth & Gurney Songs 1990, A Ticket to Heaven & Other Parlour Favorites, Vol. 2 1990, I Love My Love: A Collection of British Folk Songs 1992, Charles Villiers Stanford: Songs of the Sea; Songs of the Fleet; Frederick Delius: Sea Drift 1994, Down By the Salley Gardens 2001, Schubert: Schwanengesang 2003, Mussorgsky: Songs and Dances of Death; Sunless 2007, John Ireland: The Songs 2007, On Christmas Eve, Dance to Your Daddy, Walton: Henry the Fifth; Belshazzar's Feast. *Honours:* Hon. mem. RAM; Bard of Cornish Gorseth; Hon. DMus (Exeter), (Royal Scottish Acad. of Music and Drama) 1996, (Canterbury Christ Church Coll.) 1997.

LYONS, Gilda, PhD; American composer and singer (soprano); *Artistic Director, The Phoenix Concerts;* b. 11 Jan. 1975, Rhinebeck, NY; m. Daron Hagen; one s. *Education:* Bard Coll., Univ. of Pittsburgh, State Univ. of NY at Stony Brook. *Career:* debut as composer and vocalist with American Symphony Chamber Orchestra 1997; Artistic Dir and vocalist, The Phoenix Concerts series, New York; comms include works for American Opera Projects, Anonymous 4's Ruth Cunningham, Amy Pivar Dances, The American Soc. of Composers, Authors and Publrs (ASCAP) Foundation's Charles Kingsford Fund, Finisterra Piano Trio, Milwaukee Choral Artists, voice and piano duo Two Sides Sounding, Seasons Festival Chamber Orchestra, Sweet Plantain string quartet, tenor Paul Sperry and countertenor Daniel Gundlach, among others. *Compositions:* Feis, orchestral song cycle 1996, Candescence for brass quintet 2000, The Night Green Side of It for string trio 2000, Lampyridae for chamber ensemble 2001, Western Wind for concert band 2001, A Small Handful for solo voice 2002, Monarch for orchestra 2003, Silk Spinners for wind trio 2003, Three Robes for soprano and piano 2003, The Peasants' Congress for mixed chorus and recorder 2004, Owl Light for solo violin 2004, No Fame, No Trace for baritone and piano 2005, Chariot Wheel for soprano, tenor, violin, and piano 2005, Incantations: songs of blessing for two voices and cello 2005, The Walled-Up Wife, one-act opera for three voices & chamber ensemble 2005, Thy Lucifer for two countertenors and piano 2006, The Wallabout Martyrs for unaccompanied tenor 2006, Charms and Blessings for voice and viola 2006, A Blessing for bass and piano 2006, A Charm for the Night Fire for soprano and piano 2006, Come, Come, Arise! for tenor and piano 2006, A Rocking Hymn for mezzo and piano 2006, A Very Special Call, Just for Her 2006, Songs of Lament and Praise for high voice and piano 2007, Bone Needles for string quartet 2007, Phantoms and Visitations 2007, Nahuatl

Hymn to the All-Mother 2007. *E-mail:* info@burningsled.org. *Website:* www .burningsled.org. *Address:* The Phoenix Concerts, 26 West 84th Street, New York, NY 10024, USA (office). *Telephone:* (347) 684-1641 (office). *E-mail:* director@thephoenixconcerts.org (office); gilda@gildalyons.com (office). *Website:* www.thephoenixconcerts.org (office); www.gildalyons.com.

LYONS, Graham John, AGSM; British composer, music publisher and instrument manufacturer; *Director, Nuvo Instrumental Ltd;* b. 17 July 1936, London, England. *Education:* Univ. of Oxford, Guildhall School of Music and Drama, University Coll., London. *Career:* played saxophone, clarinet and piano in jazz groups and dance bands 1954–58; freelance as a woodwind doubler in many styles and orchestras 1962–80; arranger for BBC light orchestras 1970–80; arranger and session musician for New Zealand TV 1980–81; started own music publishing co. 1983; launched the Lyons C clarinet 1991 (design updated and renamed the Clarinéo 2009); Co-founder and Dir Nuvo Instrumental Ltd; mem. Inc. Soc. of Musicians, Musicians' Union, Nat. Secular Soc. *Compositions:* Mixed Bag: series of woodwind ensembles, Take up the Flute, Take up the Clarinet, 60 vols of solo and ensemble compositions for woodwind, Sonata for Clarinet and Piano 1986. *Publications:* numerous collections of short pieces for solo wind instrument and piano 1979–; The Russian Version of the Second World War (compiler and ed.) 1976, New York: Facts on File 1981. *Honours:* British Design Award for the Lyons C clarinet 1993. *Address:* 11 Tinley Garth, Kirkby Moorside, N Yorks., YO62 6AR, England (home). *Telephone:* (1751) 433379 (home). *E-mail:* usefulmusic@aol.com (home). *Website:* www.nuvo-instrumental.com (office).

LYSIGHT, Michel Thierry; Belgian composer, conductor, academic and publisher; *Professor of Contemporary Music and Musical Formation, Conservatoire Royal, Brussels;* b. 14 Oct. 1958, Brussels; m. Eriko Semba; one s. one d. *Education:* Free Univ. of Brussels, Acad. of Schaerbeek, Conservatoire Royal, Mons, Conservatoire Royal, Brussels. *Career:* Prof., Acad. of Schaerbeek 1979–2000, Acad. of Woluwe Saint-Pierre 1981–90; Prof. of Contemporary Music and Musical Formation, Conservatoire Royal, Brussels 1980–; Deputy Dir Acad. of Brussels 1990–94; Prof., Bilkent Univ. of Ankara, Turkey 2000–01; Founder Ensemble Nouvelles Consonances 1995, Fibonacci Publishing 1999; Artistic Dir Kalidisc 2000–12; Composer-in-Residence, Conservatoire Darius Milhaud 2008–09. *Compositions include:* Prélude et Toccata for piano 1982, Réflexion for clarinet or bassoon and piano 1982, Quatrain for wind quartet 1987, Soleil bleu for one wind instrument and piano 1989, Onirique for large orchestra 1989, Trois Croquis for one instrument and piano or one instrument and string orchestra or one instrument and string quartet or one instrument and clarinet choir (with saxophones ad lib.) or string orchestra or string quartet 1990, Monochrone for piano 1990, Chronographie I for wind quintet 1990, Sextuor for wind quintet and piano 1990, Oréades for violin or flute, percussion and piano 1991, Quadratura for two vibraphones and two marimbas 1991, 40 Études rythmiques à la pulsation 1986–92, Métaphores for marimba or accordion and piano or two pianos 1992, Chronographie II for string orchestra or piano quintet 1992, Samarkand for clarinet or viola and piano or clarinet or viola and string quartet 1992, D'après Stephen Hawking for three recorders 1993, Palimpsestes for piano 1994, Trois Instantanés for flute or recorder and piano or harp or harpsichord 1994, Thrène for high voice or instrument and piano 1995, De part et d'autre for two (groups of) performers 1995, Chronographie III for two instruments and piano or harp 1996, Chronographie IV for violin and piano 1996, Labyrinthes for flute or clarinet or bassoon or saxophone 1997, Épode for violin and piano or violin and string orchestra 1997, 25 Lectures rythmiques 1999, Ripple Marks for piano four-hands or four instruments or three performers 1999, Symboles for trumpet or flute 1999, Couleurs Noires for four cellos 1999, Hal got rhythm for wind ensemble 1999, A Tribute to Philip K. Dick for flute, clarinet, harp and string quartet 2001, Seven Koan for piano 2001, Chronographie V for piano 2001, Anamnèse for choir and string orchestra or choir and piano four-hands 2001, Élémentaires for three instruments 2001, Enigma for two instruments and piano or harp 2001, Alchemy for clarinet quartet or sax quartet or wind quartet or string quartet 2001, Random Walk for brass quintet or clarinet and string quartet 2002, Hexagramme for six instruments ad lib 2002, Concerto for clarinet and orchestra 2002, Cosmographic Mystery for horn 2002, An Awakening for string quartet or flute and string trio or two instruments and keyboard 2002, Perséides for recorder 2002, This is not a Bossa for piano or flute and marimba or harp or harpsichord or guitar or accordion 2003, Ritual for string quartet 2000–03, Sonata for clarinet and piano 2003, Initiation for flute and marimba 2003, Elegy to the memory of Lou Harrison for string orchestra 2004, Homage to Fibonacci for two clarinets or two violas or two saxophones or violin or flute and cello or bassoon 2004, Runes for violin, clarinet and piano 2004, Chronographie VI for guitar or marimba or accordion 2004, Chronographie VII for alto saxophone or clarinet and piano 2004, Chronographie VIII for cello or viola and piano 2004, Deux Esquisses for piano or four instruments 2004, Chronographie IX for alto saxophone or flute or bassoon or bass clarinet and piano 2005, Portrait for piano 2005, Septentrion for clarinet or viola and piano or clarinet or viola and string quartet or string orchestra 2005, Arcanes for flute quartet or three flutes and violin 2005, Concerto for bassoon or bass clarinet and string orchestra 2005, Lianes for piano 2006, Les Chants de Casanova for countertenor or baritone, choir and large orchestra 2006, Uchronie for symphonic band 2007, Le Principe d'incertitude for brass ensemble and percussion 2008, Le Théorème d'incomplétude for brass ensemble 2008, Heptagramme for two instruments and piano 2008, Trigramme for flute and two instruments 2008, Unsquare Quartet for guitar quartet 2008, Adagio for string quintet or string orchestra 2008, A While for Music for four viols or string quartet and three instruments 2009, Japanese Letters for viola da gamba 2008, Happy Birthday, Mr Darwin! for two trumpets, horn, trombone or sax quartet 2009, Axiom for clarinet and bassoon or clarinet and bass clarinet or 2 bass clarinets 2009, Pentagramme for wind quintet 2009, Méditation for flute or clarinet or violin or viola and guitar or marimba or harpsichord or harp or piano 2009, La Complainte des Esclaves for two voices, children's choir, two percussions and piano or two instruments 2009, Tétragramme for string quartet 2010, Concerto for alto saxophone and string orchestra or string quintet 2010, Oxymores for clarinet, cello and piano 2010, Chronographie X for flute, string trio and harp 2011, Chamber Symphony for wind quintet, harp and string orchestra or string quintet 2011, Hikari for flute and piano 2011, El Niño de Atocha for vocal quintet 2011, Gemini Sonata for violin and piano 2011, Énergie Noire for clarinet or saxophone and piano 2011, Minimal Harp for harp 2011, Langton's Ants for cello 2011, Seti for saxophone 2012, Sonata for alto saxophone and piano 2012, The Old Masters of Speyside for string orchestra 2012, Solve et Coagula for string quartet 2013, Remembering Steve for piano quartet 2013, Symphony No. 1 for orchestra 2013, Three Philosophers Songs for flute, violin, cello, baritone and piano 2013. *Recordings include:* XXth Century Belgian Works for Clarinet and Piano; Sit Down and Listen; Oréades; Discoveries; Belgian Sextets; Labyrinthes; Récital Joseph Grau; Serenata for 2000; XXth Century Belgian Works for Flute and Piano; Récital Damien Pardoen, violin and Stéphane De May, piano; Masterpieces for Horn and Piano; Couleurs XXème Siècle for Trumpet and Organ; Soledad; I Musici Brucellensis; Pièces pour la jeunesse; Ritual; Mendelssohn Ensemble; De l'Art d'Écouter (Orchestre Royal de Chambre de Wallonie); Music for Flute and Percussion 1 & 2; North, South, East, West; 4on1; Da Areia Também Se Vê O Mar; Septentrion; Equivoque; Pyrogravures; Enigma; Cosmographies; Belgian Chamber Music; Saxacorda; Road Movies; Le Monde Sonore de Michel Lysight (DVD). *Publication:* La Transposition 1982. *Honours:* Irène Fuérison Prize, Belgian Acad. of Fine Arts 1990, Silver Medal, Acad. of Lutèce, Paris 1992, Fuga Trophy, Belgian Composers' Union 1997. *Address:* 458 Avenue Georges Henri, 1200 Brussels, Belgium (home). *Telephone:* 479-33-44-03 (mobile). *Fax:* (2) 245-93-40 (home). *E-mail:* michel@michellysight.org (office). *Website:* www.michellysight.org.

LYSY, Antonio; Italian cellist; b. 1963, Rome; s. of Alberto Lysy. *Education:* studied with his father, Menuhin School with Maurice Gendron and William Pleeth, Menuhin Academy with Radu Aldulescu, Royal Northern College of Music with Ralph Kirshbaum. *Career:* concert engagements in Austria, Argentina, France, Germany, Israel, Italy and Spain; British venues include the Royal Festival Hall, Wigmore Hall, QEH and St John's Smith Square; chamber concerts with Radu Aldulescu, Gidon Kremer, Lamar Crowson and Yehudi and Jeremy Menuhin; Principal Cellist with the Chamber Orchestra of Europe and appearances with the Manchester-based Goldberg Ensemble; Camerata of Salzburg 1988, with Sándor Végh as conductor; solo performances of Tchaikovsky's Rococo Variations in Buenos Aires and Italy; further engagements with the Philharmonia Orchestra and at the Brighton Festival; Artistic Dir, Chamber Music Festival in Tuscany, Incontri Musicali in Terra di Siena from summer 1989. *Recordings:* Bloch's Prayer and Tchaikovsky's Souvenirs de Florence with the Camerata Lysy.

LYTTELTON, Richard; fmr record company executive. *Education:* Eton Coll. *Career:* joined EMI Music 1974, Pres. of Classics and Jazz 1988–2006, Trustee, EMI Archive Trust 2005–; Chair. English Touring Opera 2003–09; Pres. Royal Albert Hall 2010–11; Chair. Artis Education 2003–14; elected Chair. Help Musicians UK 2008; mem. Council, Royal Coll. of Music 2010–. *Address:* c/o English Touring Opera, 52–54 Rosebery Avenue, London, EC1R 4RP, England (office).

M

MA, Yo-Yo, BA; American cellist; b. 7 Oct. 1955, Paris, France; of Chinese parentage; m. Jill A. Hornor 1978; one s. one d. *Education:* Harvard Univ. and cello studies with his father, with Leonard Rose and at Juilliard School of Music, New York. *Career:* first public recital aged five; performed under numerous conductors with all major orchestras of the world, including Berlin Philharmonic, Boston Symphony, Chicago Symphony, Israel Philharmonic, London Symphony and New York Philharmonic; regularly participates in festivals of Tanglewood, Ravinia, Blossom, Salzburg and Edinburgh; also appears in chamber music ensembles with artists including Isaac Stern, Emanuel Ax, Leonard Rose, Pinchas Zukerman, Gidon Kremer and fmrly Yehudi Menuhin; premiered the Concerto by H. K. Gruber, Tanglewood 1989; recital tour with Emanuel Ax celebrating 20th anniversary of their partnership 1995–96; performed Bach's suites for solo cello at the Barbican Hall, London 1995; est. The Silk Road Project to promote study of cultural, artistic and intellectual traditions of the route 2001; Smithsonian Folklife Festival 2002; Judson and Joyce Green Creative Consultant, Chicago Symphony Orchestra 2010–; apptd Messenger of Peace by UN Sec.-Gen. 2006; mem. Pres.'s Cttee on the Arts and Humanities 2009–. *Recordings include:* Portrait of Yo-Yo Ma 1989, The Japanese Album 1989, A Cocktail Party 1990, Hush 1992, Made in America 1993, The New York Album 1994, King Gesar 1996, From Ordinary Things 1997, Seven Years in Tibet 1997, Liberty! 1997, Piazzolla: Soul of the Tango 1997, The Protecting Veil and Wake Up...and Die 1998, John Williams Greatest Hits 1969–1999 1999, My First 79 Years 1999, Solo 1999, Brahms: Piano Concerto No.2, Cello Sonata Op. 78 1999, Lulie the Iceberg 1999, Songs and Dances 1999, Franz Joseph Haydn 1999, Simply Baroque 1999, Crouching Tiger, Hidden Dragon (film soundtrack) 2000, Corigliano: Phantasmagoria 2000, Simply Baroque II 2000, Appalachian Journey 2000, Dvorak: Piano Quartet No. 2, Sonatina in G, Romantic Pieces 2000, Classic Yo-Yo 2001, Classical Hits 2001, Heartland: An Appalachian Anthology 2001, Yo-Yo Ma Plays Bach 2002, Isaac Stern: In Tribute and Celebration 2002, Mozart: Piano Quartets 2002, Naqoyqatsi (film soundtrack) 2002, Yo-Yo Ma Plays the Music of John Williams 2002, Silk Road Journeys—When Strangers Meet 2002, Obrigado Brazil 2003, Classics for a New Century 2003, Paris—La Belle Époque 2003, Vivaldi's Cello 2004, The Dvorák Album 2004, Silk Road Journeys—Beyond the Horizon 2005, Essential Yo-Yo Ma 2005, R. Strauss: Don Quixote 2005, Memoirs of a Geisha (film soundtrack) 2005, Yo-Yo Ma plays Ennio Morricone 2006, Bach: Unaccompanied Piano Suites 2006, Appassionato 2007, Songs of Joy and Peace (Grammy Award for Best Classical Crossover Album 2010) 2008, 'Cinema Paradiso' on Chris Botti in Boston 2009, The Goat Rodeo Sessions 2011, Songs Of Joy and Peace 2015, Hush (with Bobby McFerrin) 2015, Yo-Yo Ma Plays Ennio Morricone 2016. *Honours:* Dr hc (Northeastern Univ.) 1985 and from other colls and univs, including Harvard, Yale, Tufts and Juilliard, Chinese Univ. of Hong Kong; Hon. DMA (Princeton) 2005; Avery Fisher Prize 1978, Glenn Gould Prize 1999, Nat. Medal of the Arts 2001, Dan David Prize 2006, Sonning Prize 2006, Award of Distinction, Int. Cello Festival 2007, World Econ. Forum Crystal Prize 2008, Musical America Award for Musician of the Year 2009, Presidential Medal of Freedom 2010, 15 Grammy Awards, two Emmy Awards, 19 Canadian Gemini Awards, Honoree, Kennedy Center Honors 2011, Polar Music Prize (Sweden) 2012, Vilcek Prize in Contemporary Music 2013, Midwest Young Artists Golden Baton Award 2014, Fred Rogers Legacy Award 2014. *Current Management:* Opus 3 Artists, 470 Park Avenue South, 9th Floor North, New York, NY 10016, USA. *Telephone:* (212) 584-7500. *Fax:* (646) 300-8200. *E-mail:* info@opus3artists.com. *Website:* www.opus3artists.com; www.yo-yoma.com.

MAASS-GEIGER, Joachim; German singer (bass-baritone); b. 1957, Essen. *Education:* studied in Lubeck and Hamburg. *Career:* sang in opera at Kaiserslautern 1981–85, Essen from 1986; appearances at Eutin, Gelsenkirchen and elsewhere as Mozart's Figaro and Leporello, the Grand Inquisitor in Don Carlos, and Alberich in The Ring; Klingsor at Essen 1993, Don Giovanni and the Doctor in Wozzeck at Saarbrücken and Gelsenkirchen 1996; other roles include Curio in Giulio Cesare, Golaud in Pelléas et Mélisande, and Kecal in The Bartered Bride.

McADAMS, Ryan Bell; American conductor; *Music Director, New York Youth Symphony Orchestra;* b. 16 March 1982, St Louis, Mo. *Education:* Interlochen Center for the Arts, Clayton High School, Indiana Univ., Juilliard School. *Career:* Asst Conductor, Glimmerglass Opera 2007; Music Dir New York Youth Symphony Orchestra 2007–; Apprentice Conductor for Chateauville Foundation, Maazel Estate, Virginia 2007; Asst Conductor, Aspen Festival 2008; fmrly Apprentice Conductor, Royal Stockholm Philharmonic Orchestra; Conducting Fellow, Tanglewood Festival 2009; made subscription European debut with Maggio Musicale Orchestra, Florence 2010; made Eastern European debut with Acad. of St Martin in the Fields, London 2010. *Honours:* Recipient, Sir Georg Solti Emerging Conductor Award, Bruno Walter Memorial Scholarship; Recipient, Glimmerglass-Aspen Prize for Opera and Vocal Conducting 2007. *Current Management:* William Guerri, Columbia Artists LLC, 1790 Broadway, New York, NY 10019, USA. *Telephone:* (212) 841-9507. *Fax:* (212) 841-9516. *E-mail:* guerri@cami.com. *Website:* www.cami.com. *Address:* New York Youth Symphony Orchestra, 850 Seventh Avenue, Suite 505, New York, NY 10019-5230, USA (office).

Telephone: (212) 581-5933 (office). *Website:* www.nyyouthsymphony.org (office); www.ryan-mcadams.com.

MÁCAL, Zdeněk; Czech conductor; b. 8 Jan. 1936, Brno. *Education:* Brno Conservatory, Janáček Acad. *Career:* debut with Czech Philharmonic Orchestra 1966, at the Prague Spring Festival; British debut 1969, with the Bournemouth Symphony; US debut with the Chicago Symphony 1972; Conductor, Moravian Symphony Orchestra at Olomouc 1963–67; tours to Hungary, Bulgaria, Germany, Austria and Switzerland; Music Dir, Cologne Radio Symphony Orchestra 1970–74; Chief Conductor, Orchestra of Hanover Radio from 1980; Music Dir, Milwaukee Symphony from 1986, Sydney Symphony 1986–93; conducted Prince Igor at the Grant Park Concerts, Chicago 1990. *Recordings:* Dvořák's Cello and Piano Concertos; Brahms Alto Rhapsody, Soukupova; Mozart Piano Concertos K488 and K595; Schoeck's Penthesilea; Dvořák's 9th Symphony and Symphonic Variations, Classic for Pleasure. *Honours:* winner International Conductors' Competition at Bescançon 1965, Mitropoulos Competition, New York 1966.

McALISTER, Barbara; American singer (mezzo-soprano); b. 1944, Oklahoma. *Education:* Oklahoma University and in Los Angeles. *Career:* sang at Koblenz Opera from 1976, in The Medium, as Stravinskys Mother Goose ad Vercli's Uirica; sang at Passau 1980–81, Flensburg 1981–83 and Bremerhaven 1983–87; roles include Amneris in Aida, Madelon in Andrea Chenier, Carmen, Santuzza in Cavalleria Rusticana, Fricka and Rossweisse in Die Walkure, Eboli in Don Carlo, the Overseer in Elektra, Filipiewna in Eugen Onegin, Dame Quickly and Meg Page in Falstaff, Azucena in Il Trovatore, Preziosilla in La Forza del Destino, Marcellina in Le Nozze de Figaro, Ortud in Lohengrin, Fenena in Nabucco, Herodias in Salome, Principessa in Suor Angelica, The Mother and Vera Boronel in The Consul, Mother Goose in The Rake's Progress, Qualla in Mountain Windsong, Ulrica in Un Ballo in Maschera, Katisha in The Mikado, Erda in Das Rheingold, Mary in Der Fliegende Hollander; concert repertoire includes Messiah, Beethoven's Ninth, the Kindenotenlieder and the Alto Rhapsody. *Recordings include:* Soul Journey 1999. *Honours:* Loren Zacary Competition, Cherokee Medal of Honor 1999. *Address:* 666 W. End Avenue, New York, NY 10025, USA (home). *Telephone:* (212) 873-0316 (home). *Website:* www.barbaramcalister.com.

McANDREW, Fiona, BA (Hons); Irish/Australian singer (soprano); b. England. *Education:* Univ. of Western Australia and Guildhall School, London. *Career:* has sung major roles with Semper Oper, Dresden, Teatro Comunale, Bologna, Wexford Festival Opera, Lyric Opera, San Antonio, Texas, Opera Holland Park, London, Teatro Rossini, Lugo, Italy, Castleward Opera, Northern Ireland; roles include: Violetta (La Traviata), Lady Harriet (Martha), Fiordiligi (Così fan Tutte), Lucia (Lucia di Lammermoor), Konstanze (Die Entführung), Marie (La Fille du Regiment), Woglinde (Das Rheingold), Sr Rose (Dead Man Walking); Jackie in Jackie O (Daugherty) 2009. *Current Management:* Music International, 13 Ardilaun Road, London, N5 2QR, England. *Telephone:* (20) 7359-5183. *Fax:* (20) 7226-9792. *E-mail:* music@musicint.co.uk. *Website:* www.musicint.wd-uk.com.

MacANN, Rodney; singer (baritone); b. 1950, New Zealand. *Career:* European debut as The Speaker in The Magic Flute, with Welsh National Opera; Sang with New Zealand Opera before studying singing and theology in London; Appearances with Opera North as Don Alfonso, Sharpless and Jochanaan, and in La Cenerentola and Samson et Dalila; English National Opera as Tchaikovsky's Mazeppa, Ariodates in Xerxes by Handel, Don Alfonso, Klingsor in Parsifal; Scarpia and Escamillo; With the Royal Opera Covent Garden has sung in Andrea Chénier, King Priam, Les Contes d'Hoffmann and Tosca; Engagements in France, Norway and Italy, as Arthur in The Lighthouse by Peter Maxwell Davies; Adelaide Festival, South Australia as Ruprecht in The Fiery Angel; Sang Cuno in Der Freischütz at Covent Garden, 1989, the Music Master in Ariadne for ENO, 1990; Concerts with all the leading British orchestras and frequent performances of Christus in the Bach Passions; Further concerts in Bergen, Florence, NY, and Toulouse; Sang Mozart's Figaro at Wellington, New Zealand, 1995; Sang Sharpless in Butterfly at Wellington, 1999. *Recordings:* Video of Andrea Chénier, Covent Garden, 1984.

MACCAFERRI, Michael Jason; American musician (clarinet, bass clarinet); b. 25 Jan. 1973, Plymouth, Mass. *Education:* Oberlin Conservatory, Cincinnati Coll.-Conservatory and Northwestern Univ. *Career:* Co-founder and mem. contemporary music ensemble eighth blackbird 1996–, ensemble has commissioned and performed new works by composers such as Steve Reich, Frederic Rzewski, Jennifer Higdon, Stephen Hartke and Steven Mackey, and performed with orchestras including Cleveland Orchestra, Toronto Symphony and Atlanta Symphony at venues including Carnegie Hall, Barbican, Sydney Opera House and Kennedy Center; residencies at univs and conservatories, including Univs of Richmond and Chicago, Oberlin Conservatory, Queensland Conservatorium, Southern Methodist Univ., Colburn School and Curtis Inst. of Music; bass clarinet, Cabrillo Festival Orchestra. *Recordings:* thirteen ways 2003, beginnings 2004, fred 2005, strange imaginary animals (Grammy Award for Best Chamber Music Performance 2007) 2006, Paul Moravec: The Time Gallery 2006, Steve Reich: Double Sextet 2010, Jennifer Higdon: On a Wire 2011, Steven Mackey: Lonely Motel: Music from

Slide (Grammy Award for Best Small Ensemble Performance) 2011, meanwhile (Grammy Award for Best Chamber Music/Small Ensemble Performance) 2012. *Honours:* winner (with eighth blackbird) Fischoff Chamber Music Competition 1996 and numerous awards including Naumburg Chamber Music Award 2000, ASCAP Award for Adventurous Programming 1998, 2000, American Music Center Trailblazer Award 2007, Meet the Composer Award 2007. *Current Management:* David Lieberman Artists, PO Box 10368, Newport Beach, CA 92658, USA. *Address:* c/o eighth blackbird, 5315 North Clark Street, #104, Chicago, IL 60640-2113, USA (office). *Telephone:* (773) 484-8811 (office). *Fax:* (773) 961-7328 (office). *Website:* www.eighthblackbird .org (office).

McCAFFERTY, Frances Elizabeth, DRSAMD; British singer (mezzo-contralto); b. 26 April 1965, Edinburgh, Scotland. *Education:* Royal Scottish Acad. of Music and Drama, studied with Hans Hotter and Audrey Langford. *Career:* debut, sang in Il Barbiere di Siviglia and Manon Lescaut in Dublin; appearances as Verdi's Mistress Quickly, Mozart's Third Lady, Ericlea in Monteverdi's Ulisse, Genevieve in Pelléas et Mélisande, Palmist in Julietta, Public Opinion in Orpheus in the Underworld, Kedruta/Fanny Novakova in The Adventures of Mr Broucek for Opera North, Kabanicha in Katya Kabanova, Martinka in The Kiss, Baba and Mother Goose in Rake's Progress for Opera Theatre Co., Dublin, Ulrica in Ballo in Maschera, Neath Opera, First Maid in Elektra, Governess in Queen of Spades, Governess in Cyrano de Bergerac, Yeta Zimmerman in Sophie's Choice, the Nurse in Boris Godunov, the Mother in Lulu and Mother Goose in The Rake's Progress for the Royal Opera, Covent Garden, Mrs Trapes in The Beggar's Opera at the Linbury, Sister-in-law in May Night, Mrs Ott in Susannah and Madam Flora in the Medium for Wexford Festival, Verdi's Mistress Quickly for Stuttgart and Tel-Aviv; sang with ENO as Mistress Quickly, Katisha and Second Patient in A Dog's Heart, for Dorset Opera as Naina in Ruslan and Lyudmila and La Cieca in La Gioconda, Katisha in The Mikado for Palafenice, Katisha, Juno in Orpheus and Buttercup for the D'Oyly Carte, Madame Popova in The Bear in Singapore and Switzerland, Soloka in Cherevichki for Garsington Opera, Auntie in Peter Grimes, Gertrude in Hansel and Gretel, the Hostess in Boris and Katisha for the Nat. Reisopera in the Netherlands, Hata in The Bartered Bride, Mrs Herring for GTO and Glyndebourne Festival Opera, La Haine in Armide and Bostana in The Barber of Baghdad at Buxton, La Marieuse in Zhenitba for La Batie Festival, Geneva, Mrs Sedley in Peter Grimes for Den Norske Opera, Oslo, Mother Goose in The Rake's Progress for Opéra de Lille, Mrs Sedley in Peter Grimes at the Savonlinna Festival, Filipyevna in Eugene Onegin for English Touring Opera, Fairy Queen in Iolanthe and Lady Blanche in Princess Ida for the Int. Gilbert and Sullivan Festival; concerts with Scottish Chamber Orchestra, BBC Scottish Symphony Orchestra, BBC Concert Orchestra, Ulster Orchestra, Nat. Orchestra of Ireland, Singapore Symphony Orchestra, Royal Liverpool Philharmonic, Hallé and Grant Park Orchestral Asscn, Chicago. *Films:* DVDs: Sophie's Choice, Lulu. *Radio:* appearances on Friday Night is Music Night (BBC Radio 2). *Television:* cameo role in Whatever Happened to Radio 2 for BBC 4, Sophie's Choice/Yeta Zimmerman. *Recordings include:* The Marriage of Figaro/Marcellina, The Beggar's Opera/Mrs Trapes, Orpheus in the Underworld, HMS Pinafore, Cherevichki. *Current Management:* c/o Mark Kendall Artists Management Ltd, 56 St Anselm's Road, Worthing, West Sussex, BN14 7EN, England. *Telephone:* (1903) 233229; 7525-916598 (mobile). *E-mail:* markkendallartists@mac.com. *Website:* www.markkendallartists.com. *E-mail:* franmacdiva@sky.com.

McCALDIN, Denis James, BMus, BSc, PhD; British conductor, broadcaster and editor; *Professor Emeritus of Performance in Music, Lancaster University*; b. 28 May 1933, Nottingham, England; m. Margaret Anne Smith; one s. one d. *Education:* Univs of Birmingham and Nottingham, Mozarteum Salzburg, Austria. *Career:* Lecturer in Music, Univ. of Liverpool 1966–71; Prof. of Performance in Music, Lancaster Univ. 1971–98, Prof. Emer. 1998–; Guest Conductor, Royal Liverpool Philharmonic Orchestra, Manchester Camerata, London Mozart Players, Royal Philharmonic Orchestra, Hallé Orchestra; Vice-Chair. Lake District Summer Music 1998–; Dir Haydn Soc. of GB 1979–; Conductor Tyneside Chamber Orchestra 2010–; mem. Inc. Soc. of Musicians, Royal Musical Asscn; Trustee, Asscn of British Choral Dirs, Hexham Abbey Festival 2011–. *Compositions include:* Fanfare for a Celebration 1993. *Recordings include:* Schubert and Haydn: Church Music 1989, Haydn: Nelson Mass 1998, Haydn Scherzandi & Notturni 2009, 2013. *Publications include:* Stravinsky 1972, Berlioz: Te Deum (ed.) 1973, Mahler 1981, Haydn: Te Deum, Nelson Mass, Little Organ Mass (ed.) 1987–98, Haydn Mass in F 1993, editions of Haydn, Bach and Mozart 1998–; contribs to Beethoven Companion, Music Review, Music Times, Music and Letters, Music in Education, Times Higher Education Supplement, Soundings, Haydn Society Journal. *Honours:* Freeman, City of Lancaster 1990; Hon. Fellow, Lancaster Univ. 2006. *Address:* Haydn Society of Great Britain, 2 Hindley Hall, Stocksfield, Northumberland, NE43 7RY, England (office). *Telephone:* (1661) 842167 (home). *E-mail:* d.mccaldin@lancaster.ac.uk (office). *Website:* www .haydnsocietyofgb.co.uk (office).

McCALLA, Kathleen; American singer (soprano); b. 1957, Iowa, USA. *Education:* Wichita State Univ. and Manhattan School of Music, also studied with Tito Gobbi and Mario del Monaco in Italy. *Career:* debut, Treviso 1981 in Le nozze di Figaro; sang throughout Germany from 1983, notably as Traviata, and in the Mozart and Puccini repertory; Bonn Opera from 1992, as Desdemona, Suor Angelica and Leonore in Fidelio; guest engagements as Alice in Falstaff, Abigaille in Nabucco at Naples and Turandot in Rome 1996; other roles include Mozart's Vitelia, Constanze, Countess and Fiordiligi, Verdi's Aida, Amelia in Un Ballo in Maschera, Lucrezia in I Due Foscari, Elvira in Ernani, Leonora in Forza del Destino, Abigaille in Nabucco, Lady Macbeth, Amelia in Simon Boccanegra, Leonora in Il Trovatore, Puccini's Minnie in La Fanciulla del West, Madama Butterfly, Manot Lescaut, Suor Angelica, Georgetta in Il Tabarro, Tosca and Turandot. *Honours:* winner, Toti dal Monte Competition, Treviso, Viotti Competition, Vercelli, Puccini Competition, Lucca, Mario del Monaco at Villa Manin Competition, Francisco Vinas Competition, Barcelona. *Address:* via B. Salomoni 8a, 31100 Treviso, Italy (home). *Telephone:* (0422) 321520 (home). *Fax:* (0422) 321520 (home). *E-mail:* kathleen_mccalla@hotmail.com (home); kathleen@kathleenmccalla .com (office). *Website:* www.kathleenmccalla.com.

McCARTHY, Fionnuala; South African singer (soprano); b. 1963, Ireland. *Education:* studied in Johannesburg and at Detmold, Germany. *Career:* debut, Kaiserslautern 1987, as Mimi; Sang at the Mannheim Opera from 1988, debut as Wagner's Woglinde with further appearances as Lauretta, Euridice, Echo, Marzelline, Famine, Zerlina and Mozart's Countess; Sang Marguerite at Giessen (1990) and appeared with the Deutsche Oper am Rhein 1990–92; Sang Donna Elvira with Pimlico Opera at Tullnally, Ireland, 1996; Ighino in Pfitzner's Palestrina at the Deutsche Oper, Berlin, 1996, and Manon there 1998; season 2000–01 as Sophie, Janáček's Vixen, Pamina and Alice Ford at the Deutsche Oper. *Address:* c/o Deutsche Oper Berlin, Bismarckstraße 35, 10627 Berlin, Germany (office). *Website:* www.deutscheoperberlin.de (office).

McCARTNEY, Sir (James) Paul, Kt, MBE, FRCM; British singer, songwriter and musician (guitar, piano, organ); b. 18 June 1942, Liverpool; s. of James McCartney and Mary McCartney; m. 1st Linda Eastman 1969 (died 1998); one s. two d. one step-d.; m. 2nd Heather Mills 2002 (divorced 2008); one d.; m. 3rd Nancy Shevell 2011. *Education:* Stockton Wood Road Primary School, Speke, Joseph Williams Primary School, Gateacre and Liverpool Inst. *Career:* wrote first song 1956, wrote numerous songs with John Lennon; joined pop group The Quarrymen 1956; appeared under various titles until formation of The Beatles 1960; appeared with The Beatles for performances in Hamburg 1960, 1961, 1962, The Cavern, Liverpool 1960, 1961; worldwide tours 1963–66; attended Transcendental Meditation Course at Maharishi's Acad., Rishikesh, India Feb. 1968; formed Apple Ltd, parent org. of The Beatles Group of Cos 1968; left The Beatles after collapse of Apple Corpn Ltd 1970; formed MPL Group of Cos 1970; first solo album McCartney 1970; formed own pop group Wings 1971–81, tours of Britain and Europe 1972–73, UK and Australia 1975, Europe and USA 1976, UK 1979, World Tour 1989–90; also records as The Fireman, dance music duo with Youth 1994–; numerous collaborations including Elvis Costello, Dave Grohl and Krist Novoselic, Michael Jackson, Rihanna, Kanye West, Stevie Wonder; solo performances at Party at the Palace, Buckingham Palace 2002, Opening Ceremony, Summer Olympic Games, London 2012; Fellow, British Acad. of Composers and Songwriters 2000. *Recordings include:* albums: with The Beatles: Please Please Me 1963, A Hard Day's Night 1964, Beatles for Sale 1965, Help! 1965, Rubber Soul 1966, Revolver 1966, Sgt Pepper's Lonely Hearts Club Band 1967, Magical Mystery Tour 1967, The Beatles (White Album) 1968, Yellow Submarine 1969, Abbey Road 1969, Let It Be 1970, 1962–1966 (Red Album) 1973, 1967–1970 (Blue Album) 1973, Past Masters Vol. One 1988, Past Masters Vol. Two 1988, The Beatles Anthology: 1 1995, The Beatles Anthology: 2 1996, The Beatles Anthology: 3 1996, 1 2000; with Wings: Wild Life 1971, Red Rose Speedway 1973, Band On The Run (Grammy Award for Best Historical Album 2012) 1973, Venus and Mars 1975, Wings at the Speed of Sound 1976, Wings Over America 1976, London Town 1978, Wings Greatest 1978, Back To The Egg 1979, Wingspan 2001; solo: McCartney 1970, Ram 1971, McCartney II 1980, Tug of War 1982, Pipes of Peace 1983, Give My Regards to Broad Street 1984, Press To Play 1986, All the Best! 1987, CHOBA B CCCP 1988, Flowers in the Dirt 1989, Tripping the Live Fantastic 1990, Unplugged: The Official Bootleg 1991, Paul McCartney's Liverpool Oratorio (with Carl Davis) 1991, Off the Ground 1993, Paul is Live 1993, Flaming Pie 1997, Standing Stone (symphonic work) 1997, Run Devil Run 1999, Working Classical 1999, A Garland for Linda (with eight other composers for a cappella choir) 2000, Driving Rain 2001, Back in the US: Live 2002, Back in the World 2003, Chaos and Creation in the Back Yard 2005, Ecce Cor Meum (classical) (Classical BRIT Award for Best Album 2007) 2006, Memory Almost Full 2007, Kisses on the Bottom (Best Traditional Pop Vocal Album 2013) 2012, New 2013; with The Fireman: Strawberries Oceans Ships Forest 1994, Rushes 1998, Electric Arguments 2008; film soundtracks: The Family Way 1966, James Paul McCartney 1973, Live and Let Die 1973, The Zoo Gang (TV series) 1973. *Ballet:* Ocean's Kingdom (orchestral score, written for the New York City Ballet) 2011. *Films:* A Hard Day's Night 1964, Help! 1965, Magical Mystery Tour (TV film) 1967, Yellow Submarine (animated colour cartoon film) 1968, Let it Be 1970, Wings Over the World (TV) 1979, Rockshow 1981, Give My Regards to Broad Street (wrote and directed) 1984, Rupert and the Frog Song (wrote and produced) (BAFTA Award Best Animated Film) 1985, Press to Play 1986, Get Back (concert film) 1991, Live Kisses (concert film) (Grammy Award for Best Music Film 2014) 2012. *Radio:* (series) Routes of Rock (BBC) 1999. *Publications include:* Paintings 2000, The Beatles Anthology (with George Harrison and Ringo Starr) 2000, Sun Prints (with Linda McCartney) 2001, Many Years From Now (autobiography) 2001, Blackbird Singing: Poems and Lyrics 1965–1999 2001, High in the Clouds (juvenile, with Philip Ardagh and Geoff Dunbar) 2005. *Honours:* Freeman of the City of Liverpool 1984, Hon. Fellow, Liverpool John Moores Univ. 1998; Dr hc (Sussex) 1988, Hon. DMus

(Yale) 2008; two Grammy Awards for Band on the Run (including Best Pop Vocal Performance) 1975, Ivor Novello Award for Best Selling British Record 1977–78 for single Mull of Kintyre, for Int. Hit of the Year 1982 for single Ebony and Ivory, for Outstanding Services to British Music 1989, Guinness Book of Records Triple Superlative Award (43 songs each selling more than 1m copies, holder of 60 gold discs, estimated sales of 100m albums and 100m singles) 1979, Lifetime Achievement Award 1990, Polar Music Prize 1992, Lifetime Achievement Award People for the Ethical Treatment of Animals (with Linda McCartney) 1996, Radio Acad. Lifetime Achievement Award 2007, Q Icon Award 2007, BRIT Award for Outstanding Contribution to Music 2008, ASCAP Award for Songwriter of the Year 2009, Gershwin Prize for Popular Song, US Library of Congress 2010, Kennedy Center Honor 2010, Grammy Award for Best Rock Song (for Cut Me Some Slack, with Dave Grohl, Krist Novoselic and Pat Smear) 2014. *Current Management:* c/o MPL Communications Ltd, 1 Soho Square, London, W1D 3BQ, England. *Website:* www.paulmccartney.com.

McCARTY, Patricia, BMus; American violist, recitalist and chamber musician; b. 16 July 1954, Wichita, Kansas; m. Ronald Wilkison 1982. *Education:* Univ. of Michigan. *Career:* debut in New York 1978; Wigmore Hall, London, England 1986; Beethovenhalle, Bonn 1991; Japan tour 1993; performances throughout USA, Europe and Japan; appearances include Detroit, Houston, Brooklyn, Boston Pops, Beethovenhalle, Suisse Romande, Kyoto and Shinsei Nihon Tokyo orchestras; recitals in New York, San Francisco, Detroit, Boston and London; chamber music performances at Marlboro, Aspen, Tanglewood, Hokkaido and Sarasota festivals; Faculty mem. Meadowmount School of Music. *Recordings include:* Viola Works of Rebecca Clarke, Songs of Charles Martin Loeffler, Brahms Viola Quintets, Dvořák String Sextet, Keith Jarrett Concerto, Bach Suites, Schubert Arpeggione Sonata/Beethoven Notturno & Romances, Brahms Sonatas/Schumann Marchenbilder, Telemann Fantasias. *Publications include:* contrib. of graded repertoire lists, Playing & Teaching Viola 2005; numerous articles online. *Current Management:* c/o Anne Thomas, Ashmont Music, 25 Carruth Street, Boston, MA 02124, USA. *E-mail:* ashmontmus@aol.com. *Website:* www.ashmontmusic.com.

McCAULEY, John J., BS, BMus, MSc; American pianist, conductor and teacher; b. Des Moines, IA. *Education:* Univ. of Illinois at Urbana, Juilliard School of Music, piano with Claire Richards, Carlo Zecchi, Friedrich Wührer, conducting with Jorge Mester and Jean Morel, piano with Josef Raieff and Beveridge Webster, Tanglewood, Aspen, Mozarteum Summer Acad., Salzburg, Austria, masterclasses in conducting with Herbert von Karajan. *Career:* piano solo debut, Carnegie Recital Hall, New York 1975; Columbia Artists Management Community Concerts recital accompanist throughout USA 1980–84; piano recitals, chamber music concerts throughout USA and Europe, including Lincoln Center and Juilliard 1978–91; New York Radio, The Listening Room with Robert Sherman (WQXR) 1983, 1990; pianist in New York performance of The Night of the Murdered Poets, for narrator and chamber ensemble, by Morris Cotel 1985; American Cathedral's Arts George V recital series in Paris 2002, 2003; 92nd Street Y Tisch Center for the Performing Arts, Meet the Virtuoso Series of chamber music performances, spring 2003; solo piano recital Nov. 2004; conductor, Bel Canto Opera, New York; East Coast tours with Opera Northeast and Eastern Opera Theater 1978–85; Asst Conductor and musical coach, Des Moines Metro Opera 1984–94; Guest Conductor, Bronx Symphony Orchestra 1985, 1997; Asst Conductor, Arizona Opera at Tucson and Phoenix 1984; Music Dir, Nevada Opera Studio 1995; Assoc. Conductor, Brooklyn Philharmonic 1983; founder, Music Dir and Conductor, Chamber Orchestra of Science & Medicine (COSM), New York 2001–, with concerts at Rockefeller Univ., Music at St Paul's Series, Columbia Univ., Advent Lutheran Church, Good Shepherd Church at Lincoln Center; mem. piano faculty, Riverdale Country School and School of Music 1967–80; instructor, Lehman Coll., CUNY 1972–82; instructor in piano, vocal coaching, accompanist for student recitals and masterclasses, 92nd Street Y Music Dept 1997–; adjunct vocal coach, Manhattan School of Music 1997–. *Recording:* The Night of the Murdered Poets, for narrator and chamber ensemble, by Morris Cotel (pianist). *Publications:* contrib. reviews of new music in NOTES (journal of Music Library Asscn). *Honours:* scholarship, Univ. of Illinois, fellowships at Tanglewood, Aspen, graduate teaching fellowship, Juilliard. *Website:* www.cosmorchestra.org.

McCAWLEY, Leon, ARCM (Hons); British pianist; b. 12 July 1973, Culcheth, Warrington, England; m. Anna Hyunsook Paik. *Education:* Chetham's School of Music, Manchester, Curtis Inst. of Music, Philadelphia, USA. *Career:* debut, London Philharmonic Orchestra, Bryden Thomson, Royal Festival Hall 1990; works with top orchestras including London Philharmonic Orchestra, City of Birmingham Symphony Orchestra, BBC Nat. Orchestra of Wales, Royal Philharmonic Orchestra, Philharmonia, BBC Symphony, Royal Scottish Nat., Vienna Symphony, Vienna Chamber, Dallas Symphony, Philadelphia Orchestra; recital performances at Wigmore Hall, Queen Elizabeth Hall, Zürich Tonhalle, Vienna Musikverein, Berlin Philharmonie, Washington Kennedy Centre; performances at BBC Proms; frequent broadcasts on BBC Radio 3. *Recordings include:* Schumann Piano Music; Beethoven Sonatas and Variations, Complete Piano Works of Samuel Barber, Hans Gál Complete Works for Solo Piano, Mozart Complete Piano Sonatas, Chopin Piano Music, Brahms Piano Music. *Honours:* BBC Young Musician of the Year, piano section 1990, First Prize, Beethoven Int. Piano Competition, Vienna 1993, Second Prize, Leeds Int. Piano Competition 1993. *Current Management:* c/o Ikon Arts Management Ltd, Suite 114, Business Design Centre, 52 Upper Street,

London, N1 0QH, England. *Telephone:* (20) 7354-9199. *Fax:* (870) 130-9646. *E-mail:* office@ikonarts.com. *Website:* www.ikonarts.com; www.leonmccawley.com.

McCOLL, William Duncan; American clarinettist and basset hornist; b. 18 May 1933, Port Huron, MI; m. Sue McColl; one s. *Education:* Oberlin Coll., Manhattan School of Music, State Acad. of Music and Representational Arts, Vienna. *Career:* solo clarinettist with US Seventh Army Symphony Orchestra 1957–58 and Philharmonia Hungarica, Vienna 1959; clarinettist, Festival Casals; solo clarinettist with Puerto Rico Symphony Orchestra and clarinet instructor for Puerto Rico Conservatoire 1960–68; clarinettist, Soni Ventorum Wind Quartet 1963–; Prof., Univ. of Washington 1968–; bass clarinettist, Orquestra Filarmonica de las Americas, Mexico City, summer 1976–78. *Recordings:* Villa-Lobos, Trio for Bassoon, Clarinet, Oboe and quartet ditto with flute; Reicha Quintet in G major; Haydn Clock Organ pieces, arranged for wind quintet; Beethoven, Clock Organ pieces, arranged for wind quintet; Reicha Quintet in E minor; Danzi Quintet in F major; Poulenc Duo for Clarinet and Basson; Villa-Lobos Trio for Clarinet, Bassoon and Piano; Numerous other compositions and arrangements. *Address:* c/o School of Music, University of Washington, Seattle, WA 98195, USA.

McCORMACK, Elizabeth, BA; British singer (mezzo-soprano); b. 1964, Fife, Scotland; m. Douglas Vipond 1990. *Education:* Glasgow University; Royal Scottish Academy with Duncan Robertson and London Opera Studio. *Career:* Edinburgh Festival debut 1986 with Alan Ramsay's The Gentle Shepherd; Concert performances include Handel's Messiah, Samson and Coronation Anthem; Mozart Requiem, Beethoven Missa Solemnis and CPE Bach Magnificat; Stravinsky's Pulcinella with the English Chamber Orchestra at the Barbican; Sang De Nebra's Requiem and Handel's Dixit Dominus with La Chappelle Royale and Philippe Herreweghe 1989; Haydn's Theresian Mass with the Orchestra of the Age of Enlightenment at the Queen Elizabeth Hall; Has also sung in Elgar's The Music Makers, Vivaldi's Gloria and the Duruflé Requiem; English National Opera debut, 1989 in The Mikado; Scottish Opera 1990 in the premiere of Judith Weir's The Vanishing Bridegroom; Season 1994–95 as Cenerentola for Castleward Opera and Iolanthe for Scottish Opera; Season 1997 at the Opéra Bastille, Paris, in Parsifal and as Mozart's Annius. *Honours:* Scottish Opera John Noble Bursary, 1987; Decca-Kathleen Ferrier Prize, 1987; Isobel Baillie Performance Award, 1987; Scottish Opera John Noble Award, 1987; Royal Overseas League, 1987; English Speaking Union, 1988; Caird and Munster Scholarships, 1987–89.

McCRAY, James; American singer (tenor); b. 21 Feb. 1939, Warren, Ohio; m. Prizrenka Petkovic; one d. *Education:* Mannes School of Music, also studied with Raymond Buckingham. *Career:* debut, Stratford Festival, Canada, in Weill's Aufstieg und Fall der Stadt Mahagonny; appearances in Seattle, Kansas City, Miami, San Francisco and the New York City Opera, with Israeli Nat. Opera; engaged by Greater Miami Opera Asscn 1974–76; Principal Tenor, St Paul Minnesota Opera Festival 1974–76; guest with Tel-Aviv Opera, Israel; roles include Verdi's Ismaele, Radames and Manrico, Wagner's Siegmund and Siegfried, Don José, Samson, Ponchielli's Enzo and Puccini's Calaf, Dick Johnson and Cavaradossi, Florestan, in Carlyle Floyd's Of Mice and Men, La Fanciulla del West; Young Siegfried in the first modern Polish production of the Ring, Warsaw, 1989; Wuppertal 1989; began teaching 1994–. *Address:* Plaats 11A, 2315 The Hague, The Netherlands (home). *Telephone:* (70) 3622969 (home). *E-mail:* jamesjmccray@hotmail.com (home). *Website:* www.jamesjmccray-voicestudio.com.

McCREADY, Ivan; British cellist; b. 1963, England. *Education:* Royal Academy of Music with Derek Simpson. *Career:* member of the Borante Piano Trio from 1982; Concerts at the Wigmore Hall and in Dublin and Paris; Beethoven's Triple Concerto at the Festival Wien Klassik, 1989; Season 1990 at the Perth and Bath Festivals and tour of Scandinavia, Russia and the Baltic States; Cellist of the Duke String Quartet 1985–2001; Performances in the Wigmore Hall, Purcell Room, Conway Hall and throughout England; Tours of Germany, Italy, Austria and the Baltic States; South Bank series 1991, with Mozart's early quartets; Soundtracks for Ingmar Bergman documentary The Magic Lantern, Channel 4 1988; Features for French television 1990–91, playing Mozart, Mendelssohn, Britten and Tippett; Brahms Clarinet Quintet for Dutch Radio with Janet Hilton; Resident quartet of the Rydale Festival 1991; Residency at Trinity College, Oxford, tours to Scotland and Northern Ireland and concert at the Queen Elizabeth Hall 1991; Dir of Music, Bylaugh Hall, Norfolk; founding mem. Baker Piano Trio 2001–, Nelson Ensemble 2005–. *Recordings include:* Quartets by Tippett, Shostakovich and Britten (Third) for Factory Classics. *Honours:* Awards include the Harold Craxton at the RAM and the Leche Scholarship. *Address:* Bylaugh Hall, Bylaugh Park, Dereham, Norfolk, England (office). *Telephone:* (1362) 688121 (office). *E-mail:* info@bylaugh.com (office). *Website:* www.bylaugh.com (office).

McCREESH, Paul D.; British conductor; *Artistic Director, Gabrieli Consort & Players;* b. 24 May 1960, London, England; m. Susan Jones 1983. *Education:* Univ. of Manchester. *Career:* debut at St John Smith's Square 1981; Founder and Artistic Dir Gabrieli Consort & Players 1982–; Artistic Dir Brinkburn Music Festival 1994–; Wratislava Cantans Festival, Wroclaw, Poland 2006–; Principal Conductor and Artistic Adviser, Gulbenkian Orchestra, Lisbon 2013–; frequent performances and recordings of Baroque and Renaissance music in UK and abroad; guest conducting engagements include Netherlands Philharmonic Orchestra, Stockholm Philharmonic Orchestra, Gothenburg Symphony Orchestra, San Francisco Symphony Orchestra,

Orchestre Philharmonique de Radio France, Spanish Nat. Symphony, Danish Radio Symphony, Iceland Symphony, Budapest Festival Orchestra, Zurich Tonhalle, Orchestra dell' Accad. di Santa Cecilia, Basel Chamber Orchestra; f. Winged Lion label. *Recordings include:* Venetian Easter Mass and Venetian Vespers; Handel Solomon, Theodora and Messiah; Bach St Matthew Passion, Gluck Paride ed Elena, Mozart C Minor Mass, The Road to Paradise, A Spotless Rose, Haydn Creation, Monteverdi Vespro della Beata Vergine, Berlioz Grande Messe des Morts, Handel Arias with Gabrieli Players and Rolando Villazón, A New Venetian Coronation with Gabrieli Consort & Players (Gramophone Award for Best Early Music Recording 2013), Britten: War Requiem (BBC Music Magazine Choral Award 2014). *Honours:* Gramophone Awards 1990 (for A Venetian Coronation), 1993, ABC Record of the Year 1991, Dutch Edison Awards 1991, 1995, Diapason d'Or, France 1994, 1999, Echo Prize, Germany 1995, Gramophone Award for Best Choral Recording 2008. *Current Management:* c/o Leyla Güneş, Intermusica Artists Management Ltd, 36 Graham Street, Crystal Wharf, London, N1 8GJ, England. *Telephone:* (20) 7608-9900. *Fax:* (20) 7490-3263. *E-mail:* lgunes@intermusica.co.uk. *Website:* www.intermusica.co.uk. *Address:* Gabrieli Consort & Players, PO Box 68830, London, SE26 9BR, England (office). *Telephone:* (20) 7613-4574 (office). *E-mail:* susie@gabrieli.com (office). *Website:* www.gabrieli.com (office).

McCULLOCH, Jenifer Susan, ARCM; British singer (soprano) and voice teacher; *Professor of Singing, Guildhall School of Music and Drama*; b. 3 Aug. 1957, London, England. *Education:* Royal College of Music, National Opera Studio. *Career:* debut as Countess Almaviva in Mozart's Marriage of Figaro with ENO 1986; concerts at the major London venues and at festivals in Edinburgh, Cambridge, Henley and Manchester; appeared in oratorio all over the United Kingdom and Europe; has sung Brahms' Requiem with David Willcocks and Mendelssohn's Infelice with Solti; recorded Mozart's Exultate Jubilate and Strauss's Four Last Songs for BBC; American debut in the Four Last Songs, with San Jose Symphony Orchestra; Verdi's Requiem at the Three Choirs Festival and Usher Hall, Edinburgh; Beethoven's Ninth under Laszlo Heltay at 1992 Kenwood summer season opening; appearances in opera include Donna Anna in Don Giovanni for ENO; Glyndebourne festival debut as Vitellia in La Clemenza di Tito, followed by Musetta in La Bohème and Donna Anna for the Touring Opera; Tosca in Dublin, Mozart's Marcellina in Hong Kong, The Netherlands (Opera Zuid and Amsterdam), Lisbon, Paris, Ludwigsburg and London; various television broadcasts including two episodes of Inspector Morse; Prof. of Singing, Guildhall School of Music and Trinity College of Music, London; international adjudicator and course director; mem. BVA. *Recordings:* Marriage of Figaro; A Victorian Christmas; Gilbert and Sullivan. *Address:* Department of Vocal Studies, Guildhall School of Music and Drama, Silk Street, Barbican, London, EC2Y 8DT (office); Flat One, 80 Sunnyhill Road, Streatham, London, SW16 2UL, England (home). *Telephone:* (20) 7628-2571 (office). *Fax:* (20) 7256-9438 (office). *Website:* www.gsmd.ac.uk (office).

McDANIEL, Barry; American singer (baritone) (retd); b. 18 Oct. 1930, Lyndon, Kansas. *Education:* Juilliard School, New York; Stuttgart Musikhochschule with Alfred Paulus and Hermann Reutter. *Career:* debut sang in recital at Stuttgart in 1953; Mainz Opera, 1954–55; Stuttgart Opera, 1957–59; Karlsruhe, 1960–62; Deutsche Oper Berlin from 1962, notably in Baroque and contemporary works, also Mozart and Wagner; sang in the premieres of Henze's Der junge Lord, 1965, and Reimann's Melusine, 1971; Salzburg Festival, 1968; Metropolitan Opera, 1972 as Debussy's Pelléas; other roles include the Barber in Die schweigsame Frau and Olivier in Capriccio; guest appearances in Schubert Lieder and as Christus in the St Matthew Passion. *Recordings:* Bach, Christmas Oratorio; Ariadne auf Naxos, Dido and Aeneas, La Finta Giardiniera and Der junge Lord, Deutsche Grammophon; Orff's Trionfi, BASF.

MACDONALD, Hugh John, MA, PhD, FRCM; British musicologist and academic; b. 31 Jan. 1940, Newbury, Berks.; m. 1st Naomi Butterworth 1963; one s. three d.; m. 2nd Elizabeth Babb 1979; one s. *Education:* Pembroke Coll., Cambridge. *Career:* Lecturer in Music, Univ. of Cambridge 1966–71, Univ. of Oxford 1971–80; Visiting Prof., Indiana Univ., USA 1979; Gardiner Prof. of Music, Univ. of Glasgow 1980–87; Avis Blewett Prof. of Music, Washington Univ., St Louis, Mo., USA 1987–2011. *Publications include:* New Berlioz Edition (Gen. Ed., complete works) 1965–2006, Berlioz Orchestral Music 1969, Skryabin 1978, Berlioz 1982, Berlioz: Correspondance générale (ed.) Vol. 4 1984, Vol. 5 1989, Vol. 6 1995, Vol. 7 2001, Vol. 8 2002, Selected Letters of Berlioz 1995, Berlioz's Orchestration Treatise 2002, Beethoven's Century: Essays on Composers and Themes 2008; contrib. to The New Grove Dictionary of Music and Musicians, The New Grove Dictionary of Opera, many journals. *Honours:* Szymanowski Medal 1982, Grand Prix de Littérature Musicale Charles Cros 1985, 1996, Médaille de Rayonnement Culturel 2010. *Address:* 8514 Colonial Lane, St Louis, MO 63124, USA (home). *E-mail:* hjmacdon@wustl.edu.

McDONALD, John, BA, DMA; American composer and pianist; b. 27 Oct. 1959, Norfolk, VA; m.; two s. one d. *Education:* Yale University, Yale School of Music. *Career:* debut recital, Carnegie Hall, 1995; Associate Professor of Music, Tufts University, 1998–, Chair., Tufts Music Dept, 2000–03; Co-Director of Extension Works, Boston, 1990–2003; Artistic Ambassador, Cultural Specialist in Asia, 1994, 1995; Appearances on NPR, German radio; Premieres in Havana, Shanghai, St Petersburg; Commissions: Fleet Boston Celebrity Series, 1994, 2003; mem. Broadcast Music Inc. *Compositions*

include: nine piano sonatas, Duet for piano, Sonatina for soprano saxophone and piano, Sonatina for piccolo and piano 1997, two piano concertos, two string quartets, Ricercata for three bass viols 1998, 100 songs, works for piccolo, flute, early instruments, chamber ensembles, wind ensemble and orchestra, four film scores. *Recordings:* 20 piano albums, two solo piccolo albums 1995, 1998, as pianist featured in recordings of music by Donal Fox, John Harbison, Gardner Read, Gunther Schuller, George Walker. *Publications:* Essays, One Composer's Manifesto in the Form of a Wish List, Musings and Minor Writings. *Honours:* First prize, Leo M. Traynor Competition for New Viol Music, 1997; Mellon Fellowship, 1996; NEA grant 1995. *Address:* Music Department, Tufts University, 48 Professors Row, Medford, MA 02155, USA.

McDONALD, Margaret; British singer (mezzo-soprano); b. 1964, Grimsby, England. *Education:* Royal Northern College of Music and in Milan. *Career:* early experience with Glyndebourne Festival and Touring Opera; Engagements with Opera North as Carmen, and in Mason's Playing Away, Oberon (1985), Rebecca by Josephs and Gianni Schicchi; Eboli in Don Carlos for Scottish Opera Go Round, Ascanio in Benvenuto Cellini and Bizet's Djamileh for Chelsea Opera Group; Further appearances with English National Opera, English Bach Festival and Buxton Festival; concerts include the Three Choirs, Quimper, Spitalfields, Saintes and Dublin Contemporary Festivals; Extensive oratorio repertory at concert halls and cathedrals throughout the United Kingdom, including works by Henze and Boulez; has taught at Royal Scottish Acad. of Music and Drama and Royal Northern Coll. of Music. *Recordings include:* Isoletta in Bellini's La Straniera, with the Northern Sinfonia; She-Ancient in Tippett's Midsummer Marriage (Nimbus), Restoration. *Honours:* Curtis Gold Medal, RNCM. *E-mail:* rodith@onetel.net.uk. *Website:* www.margaret-mcdonald.cwc.net.

McDONALL, Lois; singer (soprano); b. 7 Feb. 1939, Larkspur, Alberta, Canada. *Education:* studied in Edmonton, Vancouver and Toronto and with Otakar Kraus in London. *Career:* debut, Toronto 1969 in Wolf-Ferrari's Il Segreto di Susanna; sang in Ottawa and Toronto, then Flensburg, Germany; Sadler's Wells/ENO from 1970, notably as Handel's Semele and in the title role of Hamilton's Anna Karenina 1981; other roles include Mozart's Countess, Constanze and Fiordiligi, Massenet's Manon and the Marschallin; sang the Comtesse de Coigny in Andrea Chénier at Toronto 1988; teacher, Univ. of Toronto –2001 (retd); freelance singing roles include Fedora, opera in concert, Anna in Anna Karenina as guest of ENO; appeared in concert and freelance opera, including at the Miami Festival in Don Sanche, Lizst, with Opera Barrie as the Witch in Hansel and Gretel, The Old Maid in The Old Maid and the Thief; continues to teach privately and adjudicate music festivals; many broadcasts for BBC Radio 2 and 3; mem. British Equity, ACTRA Canadian Soc. *Recordings include:* Freia in The Ring, Donizetti's Maria Padilla, Kurt Weill's Der Protagonist, Lizst's Don Sanche, Delius's Margot-la-rouge, Wagner's Rienzi. *Address:* c/o Canadian Opera Company, 227 Front Street E, Toronto, ON M5A 1EB, Canada.

McDONNELL, Thomas Anthony; Australian singer (baritone); b. 27 April 1940, Melbourne; m. Mary Jennifer Smith. *Education:* Melba Conservatorium, Melbourne with Lennox Brewer. *Career:* debut, Belcore in L'Elisir d'amore at Brisbane, 1965; Sadler's Wells/English National Opera from 1967, as Mozart's Figaro, Verdi's Germont, Escamillo and in the first British stage performance of Prokofiev's War and Peace (1972) and Henze's The Bassarids (1974); sang in War and Peace at the opening of the Sydney Opera House, 1973; created roles in Crosse's The Story of Vasco, 1974, Henze's We Come to the River and Tippett's The Ice Break (both at Covent Garden); Iain Hamilton's The Royal Hunt of the Sun and Nicola LeFanu's Dawnpath (both 1977); London Collegiate Theatre 1977 in the British premiere of Nielsen's Saul and David; well known as Mozart's Papageno and Tchaikovsky's Onegin; sang Mozart's Commendatore with Opera Factory, Queen Elizabeth Hall, 1990 and Silva in Ernani for Chelsea Opera Group; sang Lictor in The Coronation of Poppea for Opera Factory, 1992. *Recordings include:* Israel in Egypt; La Fanciulla del West; Tancredi; Donizetti rarities. *Honours:* Showcase Australia, 1965; Leverhulme Youth and Music Scholarship to Rome.

MacDOUGALL, James (Jamie) Sinclair, BA; British singer (tenor), broadcaster and presenter; b. 25 Jan. 1966, Glasgow, Scotland; s. of Robert Hamilton MacDougall and Amelia Isabella Sinclair MacDougall (née Lang); m. Susana Burciaga de MacDougall; two s. one d. *Education:* Royal Scottish Acad. of Music and Drama (RSAMD), Guildhall School of Music and Drama, Steans Inst. for Young Artists at Ravinia Festival, studied in Italy with Carlo Bergonzi. *Career:* has performed with many leading British opera cos, as well as in Europe and N America; concert performances with several major Baroque, chamber and symphony orchestras, including BBC Scottish Symphony, The Orchestra of the Age of Enlightenment, Scottish Chamber Orchestra, St Louis and Houston Symphony Orchestras; appearances with BBC Concert Orchestra on Friday Night is Music Night, BBC Radio 2; regularly appears as host and performer with the BBC Scottish Symphony Orchestra; helped form vocal group Caledon 2003, toured extensively in N America, Australia, NZ and Germany, group has also appeared with Scottish Opera Orchestra, BBC Concert Orchestra and given own Proms concert with Royal Scottish Nat. Orchestra; mem. Bd New Opera in Scotland Events (NOISE); masterclasses Muziekacademie, The Hague 2013, 2014. *Films:* The Gondoliers 1997, Purcell's Dido and Aeneas, Bach's St Matthew Passion; with Caledon: On a Beautiful Scottish Evening (DVD, broadcast in US 2004), Whirlin in Berlin. *Play:* Gentle Shepherd, Edinburgh Int. Festival. *Radio:*

Presenter, Grace Notes and Classics Unwrapped (BBC Radio Scotland) 2001–, MacAulay and Co (BBC Radio Scotland); Presenter on BBC Radio 3 including Edinburgh Int. Festival; various voice-overs for BBC Radio. *Television:* Proms in the Park (BBC Scotland) 2002–; various voice-overs for BBC Scotland. *Recordings:* more than 45 CDs recorded, including Baroque, Romantic, Scottish, English and German song as well as 20th and 21st century music; complete folk song arrangements of Joseph Haydn with Austrian chamber group, Haydn Trio Eisenstatt 2009, complete Britten Folksong arrangements with Malcolm Martineau, complete songs of Frank Bridge with Roger Vignoles; Inspirations (solo album) 2013. *Honours:* Jean Highgate Scholarship and Lieder Prize, RSAMD, finalist, Kathleen Ferrier Singing Competition 1986. *E-mail:* jamie.macdougall@bbc.co.uk (office); jamie.macdougall@me .com (office). *Website:* www.jamiemacdougall.tv.

McDOWELL, Kathryn, CBE; British music administrator; *Managing Director, London Symphony Orchestra*; b. 19 Dec. 1959, Belfast, Northern Ireland; m. Ian Ritchie 1997. *Education:* Univ. of Edinburgh. *Career:* began her career working with Welsh Nat. Opera; previous man. and devt positions with Scottish Chamber Orchestra and Ulster Orchestra; Opera and Music Theatre Officer, Arts Council of England 1992–94, apptd Music Dir 1994; fmr Chief Exec. Wales Millennium Centre; Dir City of London Festival 2001–05; Man. Dir London Symphony Orchestra (LSO) 2005–; mem. Bd Asscn of British Orchestras; mem. St Paul's Cathedral Council; Gov., Guildhall School of Music and Drama; DL of Greater London 2009–. *Honours:* Hon. FTCL 1996, Hon. RCM 1999. *Address:* London Symphony Orchestra, Sixth Floor, Barbican Centre, Silk Street, London, EC2Y 8DS, England (office). *Telephone:* (20) 7588-1116 (office). *Fax:* (20) 7374-0127 (office). *E-mail:* admin@lso.co.uk (office). *Website:* www.lso.co.uk (office).

McELROY, Sam; Irish singer (baritone); b. 1970, Cork. *Education:* Univ. of London, Guildhall School of Music and Drama, Centre de Formation Lyrique, Paris. *Career:* appearances with Opéra National de Paris in Katya Kabanova, Un Maris a la Porte, and Parsifaland as Dandini in Cenerentola for English Touring Opera, Nick Shadow in The Rake's Progress, Lockit in The Beggar's Opera and Blazes in Peter Maxwell Davies' The Lighthouse for Opera Theatre Company, Dublin, Rigoletto at Dartington; Concerts include Messiah with the Irish Chamber Orchestra and in Düsseldorf; Season 1999–2000 with Mozart's Count in Dublin; His opera roles for Opera Ireland include Figaro in Il Barbiere di Siviglia, Sharpless in Madame Butterfly, Harry Heegan in Silver Tassie and Cappadocian in Salome;; For Scottish Opera Go Round he has performed Malattesta in Don Pasquale; Japanese debut at the Pacific Music Festival, 1997; He has sung Lescaut in Manon for Opera Monte Carlo. *Honours:* Winner, Lombard and Ulster Music Awards 1992. *Current Management:* c/o Betina Brentano, Organisation International Artistique, 16 avenue Franklin Roosevelt, 75008 Paris, France. *Telephone:* 1-42-25-58-34. *Fax:* 1-42-25-64-97. *E-mail:* oia@oia-poilve.com. *Website:* www.oia-poilve.com; www.sammcelroy.com.

McFADDEN, Claron; American singer (soprano); b. 1961, Rochester, NY, USA. *Education:* Eastman School, Rochester. *Career:* has sung in concert, opera and oratorio from 1984; Opera debut 1985 in Hasse's L'Eroe Chinese conducted by Ton Koopman; Regular appearances with William Christie in Europe and North and South America, notably as Amour in Rameau's Anacréon at the Opéra Lyrique du Rhin; Netherlands Opera debut 1989, as Zerbinetta in Ariadne auf Naxos; Season 1991 included Mozart's Impresario at the Salzburg Festival and on South Bank, Acis and Galatea with the King's Consort and Rameau's Les Indes Galantes with Les Arts Florissants in Montpellier; Has also worked in concert with the Schoenberg Ensemble and composers Gunther Schuller, Louis Andriessen and Steve Reich; Carmina Burana conducted by Leopold Hager and L'Enfant et les Sortilèges under Sergiu Comissiona; Sang in Purcell's Fairy Queen with Les Arts Florissants at the Barbican Hall, 1992; King Arthur at Covent Garden, 1995; Sang in Bach's B Minor Mass at St John's London, 1997; Lulu at the 1996 Glyndebourne Festival and Controller in the premiere of Jonathan Dove's Flight, 1998; Tippett's The Mask of Time at the 1999 London Proms; Season 2000–01 as Britten's Tytania for Opera North, Musetta for Glyndebourne Touring Opera and Schoenberg's Pierrot Lunaire at the London Proms. *Recordings:* Acis and Galatea and Handel's Ottone with the King's Consort; Haydn's Orfeo with La Stagione Frankfurt; Vocal works by Glenn Gould (Sony Classical); Les Indes Galantes. *Honours:* Prize Winner at the 1988 International Competition, 's-Hertogenbosch. *Current Management:* Impulse Art Management, PO Box 15401, 1001 Amsterdam, Netherlands. *Telephone:* (20) 6266944. *Fax:* (20) 6227118. *E-mail:* info@impulseartmanagement.nl. *Website:* www .impulseartmanagement.nl.

McFARLAND, Robert; Canadian singer (baritone); *General Director, The Atlantic Coast Opera Festival*; b. 1958. *Education:* McMurry Univ. *Career:* season 1987 as Donner in Das Rheingold at the Metropolitan and Amonasro at Miami and Houston; European debut Nice 1988, as Jack Rance (repeated for Opera North at Leeds, 1990); Further guest appearances at Miami (Luna in Trovatore), Lisbon (Iago, 1990), Toronto (Escamillo, 1990) and Monte Carlo (Nottingham in Roberto Devereux); other roles include the villains in Les Contes d'Hoffmann; Renato at Antwerp, 1992 and Tonio (Miami, 1991); mem. Voice Faculty, Temple Univ. 1997–; Man. Dir McFarland Artists Management Int.; Gen. Dir The Atlantic Coast Opera Festival. *Address:* McFarland Artists Management International, 922 Daly Street, Philadelphia, PA 19148-3104, USA (office). *Telephone:* (312) 805-2600 (office). *Fax:* (215) 564-5893 (office).

E-mail: RobertM@McFarlandArtists.com (office). *Website:* www .mcfarlandartists.com (office).

McGEGAN, Nicholas, MA; British conductor; *Music Director, Philharmonia Baroque Orchestra*; b. 14 Jan. 1950, Sawbridgeworth, Hertfordshire. *Education:* Corpus Christi Coll., Cambridge, Magdalen Coll., Oxford. *Career:* Prof. of Baroque Flute 1973–79, Prof. of Music History 1975–79, Dir of Early Music 1976–80, Royal Coll. of Music; Artist-in-Residence, Washington Univ., St Louis, MO 1979–85; Music Dir, Philharmonia Baroque Orchestra, San Francisco 1985–; Music Dir, Ojai Music Festival, Ojai, CA 1988; Baroque Artistic Consultant, Santa Fe Chamber Music Festival 1990–92; Music Dir, Gottingen Handel Festival, Gottingen, Germany 1991–2011; founder and Artistic Dir, Arcadian Acad., San Francisco 1992–; Prin. Conductor, Drottningholm Court Theatre, Sweden 1993–96; Prin. Guest Conductor, Scottish Opera 1993–98 (new production of Così fan tutte 1998); Baroque Series Dir, St Paul Chamber Orchestra 1999–2004, Artistic Partner 2004–09; Music Dir, Irish Chamber Orchestra 2002–05; Artistic Dir, Killaloe Music Festival 2003–05; Artist-in-Residence, Milwaukee Symphony Orchestra 2003–06; appearances as guest conductor include San Francisco Symphony, Los Angeles Philharmonic, City of Birmingham Symphony Orchestra, Hallé Orchestra, Sydney Symphony, Melbourne Symphony, Houston Symphony, Nat. Symphony, Atlanta Symphony, Minnesota Orchestra, Orchestre de la Suisse Romand, St Louis Symphony, Detroit Symphony, Malaysian Philharmonic, Royal Concertgebouw Orchestra, Aspen Music Festival, Toronto Symphony, Philadelphia Orchestra, New York Philharmonic; mem. advisory bds Maryland Handel Festival and London's Handel House, Chicago Symphony Orchestra, Cleveland Orchestra, Boston Symphony Orchestra, Hollywood Bowl, Ravina Festival, Edinburgh Int. Festival, Mostly Mozart Festival, San Francisco Opera, Royal Opera, Covent Garden. *Recordings:* as a soloist: C.P.E. Bach's Quartets (flute), J.C. Bach's Sonatas Op1 18 (flute, with Christopher Hogwood), J.S. Bach's Anna Magdelena Notebook (harpsichord), Music for two flutes by the Bach family (with Stephen Preston), Haydn's London Trios (flute), Piano Trios (piano and flute), Vivaldi's Concertos for two flutes; as conductor: J.S. Bach's Cantatas and around 20 operas and oratorios by Handel, of which Susanna and Ariodante both won Gramophone Awards, and works by Arne, Corelli, P. Humfrey, Matteis, Monteverdi, Mozart, Purcell, Rameau (including three operas), A. Scarlatti, Telemann, Uccellini, Vivaldi. *Publications:* Editions, Philidor's Tom Jones 1978; contrib. articles, including on Handel to Musical Times 1994, on Handel as a practical opera composer (in the collected edn Die Gegenwart der musikalischen Vergangenheit: Meisterwerke der Musik in der Werkstatt des Dirigenten) 1999. *Honours:* Hon. RCM 1977, Hon. Prof., Georg-August Univ., Göttingen 2006; two Diapason d'Or Awards (for recordings with the Arcadian Acad.), Halle Handel Festival Handel Prize, Germany, Drottningholmsteaterns Vanners Hederstecken (hon. medal of the Friends of the Drottningholm Theatre). *Current Management:* Schwalbe and Partners, 170 E 61 Street #5N, New York, NY 10021, USA. *Telephone:* (212) 935-5650. *Fax:* (212) 935-4754. *E-mail:* info@schwalbeandpartners.com. *Website:* www.schwalbeandpartners .com; www.nicholasmcgegan.com (home).

McGIBBON, Roisin; Northern Irish singer (soprano); b. 1960. *Education:* Guildhall School of Music with Margaret Lensky, and at the National Opera Studio. *Career:* represented Northern Ireland in the Cardiff Singer of the World Competition, 1985; Appearances for Radio Telfis Eireann include Lieder by Schumann and Liszt; Wexford Festival 1986, in Humperdinck's Königskinder and Rossini's Tancredi; Has also sung the Composer in Ariadne auf Naxos; Concert engagements in Messiah at Armagh, Britten's War Requiem in Belfast, Savitri by Holst at Aix and Elgar's Apostles in Nottingham.

McGILLOWAY, Emer; Northern Irish singer (mezzo-soprano); b. 1967. *Education:* Medecine in Belfast and Dublin, Guildhall School with Laura Sarti. *Career:* Maddalena in Linda di Chamounix, Juno in La Calisto, Der Trommler in Der Kaiser von Atlantis and Veruna in Dvořák's Cunning Peasant at the GSM; Further study at the National Opera Studio, 1997–98; Studying with Robert Dean; Opera North from 1998 as Olga in Eugene Onegin, Lady Essex in Gloriana (also televised) and Mozart's Cherubino; Season 1998–99 in Rusalka and as Hope in Gluck's Orfeo for English National Opera. *Honours:* Herbert Morris Griffen Opera Award; Ann Price Mezzo-soprano Award; Finalist Grimsby International Singing Competition.

McGLYNN, Michael; Irish composer and singer; *Director, Anúna*; b. 1964, Dublin. *Career:* Founding Dir choral group Anúna 1987–; music commissioned and performed by Ulster Orchestra, Choir of St David's Cathedral, Wales, Rajaton, BBC Singers, Chanticleer; also solo singer specialising in early music; has worked with Elvis Costello, The Chieftains and Fretwork; has written country music songs with Rodney Crowell, Delbert McClinton and twin brother John McGlynn. *Music for plays:* Three Sisters (Gate Theatre, Dublin and Royal Court London), The Risen People (Gaiety Theatre, Dublin). *Film soundtrack:* The Work of Angels. *Compositions include:* Dúlamán for choir, Visions for saxophone and piano, Silver River for orchestra and oboe 2003, Behind the Closed Eye for choir and orchestra, Agnus Dei (commissioned by Chanticleer for mass And On Earth, Peace, premiered USA 2007) 2006. *Recordings include:* albums with Anúna: Anúna 1993, Omnis 1997, Deep Dead Blue 1996, Cynara 2000, Invocation 2003, Behind the Closed Eye 2003, Essential Anúna 2003, Sensations 2006, Winter Songs, The Best of Anúna. *E-mail:* info@anuna.ie (office). *Website:* www.anuna.ie/sheet_music/ mmcglynn.

McGREEVY, Geraldine, DipRAM, ARAM; British singer (soprano); b. 1968. *Education:* Univ. of Birmingham; Royal Acad. of Music, National Opera Studio. *Career:* operatic roles include Contessa Almaviva, Donna Anna, Vitellia, Rosalinde in Fledermaus, Micaela, First Lady and Miss Jessel (WNO); Ellen Orford (Oper Frankfurt); Alice Ford (Aix-en-Provence 2001, Paris 2002); Ghita Der Zwerg, La Monnaie; Fiordiligi (RAM conducted by Sir Colin Davis, 1997 and Opera Zuid, 1999); Female Chorus in Rape of Lucretia (Edinburgh Festival); Alcina, Cleopatra in Giulio Cesare, Angelica in Orlando and Poppea in Agrippina (Early Opera Co.); Galatea in Acis and Galatea; Laurette in Le Docteur Miracle; Donna Anna, First Lady, Mistress Page in Sir John in Love, Casilda in Gondoliers (British Youth Opera); concert repertoire includes: Schoenberg's Pierrot Lunaire; Villa Lobos' Bachianas Brasileiras No. 5; Berg's Orchestral Extracts from Wozzeck with Gennadi Rozhdestvensky; Britten's Les Illuminations; Strauss' Vier Letzte Lieder; Wigmore Hall debut, 1997, many appearances there since; Purcell Room debut, 1997; recitals at St John's Smith Square, Frankfurt Opera House, Klavier Festival Ruhr with Graham Johnson, Edinburgh Festival, and in Newcastle with Julius Drake; numerous broadcasts for the BBC and for European radio stations; concert engagements include The English Concert with Trevor Pinnock, Acad. of St Martin-in-the-Fields with Sir Neville Marriner, the Moscow Tchaikovsky Symphony Orchestra in Zurich with Jane Glover, the London Philharmonic Orchestra with Kurt Masur, the Sharoun Ensemble and Anne Manson in the Cologne Philharmonic and the Royal Liverpool Philharmonic Orchestra with Petr Altrichter and Libor Pesek. *Recordings:* Wolf Goethe Leider (with Graham Johnson); songs by Arthur Bliss (with the Nash Ensemble); contributions to Complete Schubert Edition; music by John Blow (with Red Byrd and the Parley of Instruments); Consort Songs by William Byrd (with Phantasm); Spanish Renaissance Music (with Music Antiqua of London). *Honours:* Worshipful Company of Musicians Silver Medal, 1995; RAM Shinn Fellowship, 1996; Kathleen Ferrier Award, 1996. *Website:* www.geraldinemcgreevy.com.

MacGREGOR, Joanna Clare, OBE, MA; British pianist, conductor, curator and academic; *Head of Piano, Royal Academy of Music*; b. 16 July 1959, London, England; d. of Alfred MacGregor and Angela Hughes; m. 1st Richard Williams 1986 (divorced 2002), remarried 2012; one d. (deceased). *Education:* South Hampstead High School for Girls, New Hall, Cambridge, Royal Acad. of Music, London. *Career:* Young Concert Artists Trust 1985–88; performances of classical, jazz and contemporary music in more than 80 countries at venues including Royal Albert Hall, Royal Festival Hall, Wigmore Hall, Lincoln Center and Carnegie Hall, New York, Sydney Opera House, Leipzig Gewandhaus, Opéra Bastille, Paris, Concertgebouw, Amsterdam; has performed with Rotterdam, Oslo and Netherlands Radio and Royal Philharmonic Orchestras, Sydney, Berlin, Chicago, BBC, RTÉ and London Symphony Orchestras, MDR Sinfonieorchester and Salzburg Camerata, New York and Hong Kong Philharmonics, Philharmonia, London Mozart Players, Manchester Camerata, Royal Scottish, Royal Liverpool, Hallé, English and Irish Chamber Orchestras; has worked with John Adams, Sir Harrison Birtwistle, Pierre Boulez, Sir Colin Davis, Sir Simon Rattle, Valery Gergiev, Lou Harrison, Arvo Pärt and numerous jazz artists, including Jason Yarde, Seb Rochford and Andy Sheppard; electronica artists and world music artists including Dhafer Youssef, Kuljit Bhamra, Brian Eno, Scanner, Bishi, Moses Molelekwa and Sibongile Khumalo; numerous radio and TV appearances, including Last Night of the Proms 1997, South Bank Show 2002, Messiaen's Turangalila (BBC 4) 2012, Mozart/Gershwin (BBC 2) 2012; est. own record label SoundCircus 1998; Prof. of Music, Gresham Coll. 1998–2002; Prof. of Performance, Liverpool Hope Univ.; Head of Piano, RAM 2011–; mem. Arts Council of England 1998–2002; conducting debut on UK tour with Britten Sinfonia 2000, Assoc. Artistic Dir 2002–05; cr. Cross Border, multimedia work touring China with Jin Xing's Dance Theatre of Shanghai 2003; Artistic Dir Bath Int. Music Festival 2005–12; created On the Edge of Life examining social issues through music/multimedia 2006–12; performed complete Chopin Mazurkas 2010; curated Deloitte Ignite at Royal Opera House, Covent Garden 2011, Aventure at Luxembourg Philharmonique 2012–13; currently performing complete cycle of Mozart piano concertos; Goldberg Variations at Royal Albert Hall 2013. *Play:* Memoirs of an Amnesiac (radio play about Erik Satie). *Compositions include:* Lute Songs (orchestra), Lullaby for M (percussion), arrangements of Piazzolla tangos, Lost Highway: Gospel and Spirituals of the Deep South (orchestral), new arrangement of The Magic Flute (ensemble), settings of Angela Carter poems (voice and ensemble), Sidewalk Dances and Art of Fugue (Bach and Moondog, orchestral). *Recordings include:* American contemporary music (Ives, Monk, Nancarrow, Copland, Barber, Cage, Lou Harrison), Britten Concerto, Satie, Gershwin recordings with LSO, and music by Bach (The Art of Fugue, French Suites, Goldberg Variations), Scarlatti, Bartók, Debussy, Ravel and Messaien (Vingt Regards, Harawi, Quartet for the End of Time), Deep River (music of the Deep South, with Andy Sheppard) 2006, orchestral arrangements of Moondog: Sidewalk Dances 2007, commissions and recordings of Harrison Birtwistle, Nitin Sawhney, Talvin Singh, Moses Molelekwa, Django Bates, Live in Buenos Aires (Piazzolla, Bach, Gismonti). *Publications:* wrote series of children's books for Faber Music 2001, Piano World (five vols) 2001, Art Not Chance 2001, Unbeaten Tracks 2006, Lowside Blues 2009. *Honours:* Hon. FRAM, Hon. Fellow, Trinity Coll. of Music, RSA, New Hall, Cambridge; Dr hc (Open Univ.) 2005, (Bath Univ.) 2008, (Bath Spa Univ.) 2011; European Encouragement Prize for Music 1995, NFMS Sir Charles Grove Award 1998, South Bank Show Award for Classical Music 2000, Royal Philharmonic Soc. Audience Development Award 2003. *Current Management:* c/o Ingpen & Williams, 7 St George's Court, 131 Putney Bridge Road, London, SW15 2PA, England. *Telephone:* (20) 8874-3222. *Fax:* (20) 8877-3113. *E-mail:* info@ingpen.co.uk. *Website:* www.ingpen.co.uk; www.warnerclassics.com/joanna-macgregor.

McGUIRE, Edward (Eddie), ARCM, ARAM; British composer; b. 15 Feb. 1948, Glasgow, Scotland. *Education:* Royal Acad. of Music with James Iliff, Royal Coll. of Music, Stockholm, Sweden with Ingvar Lidholm. *Career:* radio broadcasts on BBC Radio 3 include Symphonic Poem, Calgacus 1976, Symphonic Poem, Source 1979; Euphoria performed by The Fires of London 1980, Edinburgh Int. Festival; debut at London Proms 1982; BBC Radio 3 series featured trilogy, Rebirth, Interregnum, Liberation 1984; Wilde Festival commission (String Trio) for performance by The Nash Ensemble 1986; premiere of Guitar Concerto 1988; Peter Pan for Scottish Ballet 1989, Hong Kong Ballet 1996; mem. The Whistlebinkies 1973–, Harmony Ensemble 2004–; mem. Musicians' Union, Scottish Region Chair. 2001–. *Compositions include:* A Glasgow Symphony 1990, The Loving of Etain for Paragon Opera 1990, Trombone Concerto 1991, Viola Concerto 1998, Accordion Concerto 1999, Violin Concerto 2000, The Silent Traveller Returns for Edinburgh Quartet 2009, Encores en Suite for BBC Scottish Symphony Orchestra 2010, Work-In at UCS: A Celebration Suite for Alba Brass, Sax Ecosse and Whistlebinkies 2011, Symphonies of Galaxies (for School of Astronomy and Physics, Univ. of St Andrews) 2015. *Recordings include:* music has featured on albums, including Paragon Premieres 1993, Scotland's Music 1993, Viola Pieces 1994, The Voice of the Carnyx 1995, The Very Best of the BBC Orchestras 1997; Eddie McGuire: Music for Flute, Guitar and Piano (Ed.'s Choice, Gramophone Magazine Awards) 2006, The Albanach 2006, Embracing the Unknown 2009, Entangled Fortunes (Ed.'s Choice, Gramophone Magazine) 2015. *Honours:* RAM Hecht Prize 1968, Nat. Young Composers Competition, Univ. of Liverpool 1969, Competition for Test Piece for Carl Flesch Int. Violin Competition 1978, Competition for a String Quartet for performance at SPNM 40th Anniversary Gala Concert, Barbican 1983, Featured Composer, Park Lane Group Purcell Room series 1993, BBC Radio 3 Composer of the Week 1995, Featured Composer, Bath Int. Guitar Festival 1996, Int. Viola Congress 1998, Edinburgh Int. Harp Festival 2002, British Composers Award 2003, Creative Scotland Award 2004, Featured Composer, Passau Saiten Int. Guitar Festival 2015. *Current Management:* c/o Scottish Music Centre, City Hall, Candleriggs, Glasgow, G1 1NG, Scotland. *Website:* www.scottishmusiccentre.com/edward_mcguire.

MACHOVER, Tod, MM; American composer and cellist; *Professor of Music and Media, Media Lab, Massachusetts Institute of Technology*; b. 24 Nov. 1953, New York; m. June Kinoshita. *Education:* Juilliard School of Music, Univ. of California at Santa Cruz, Columbia Univ. *Career:* Composer-in-Residence, Institut de Recherche et Coordination Acoustique/Musique, Paris 1978–79; Dir, Musical Research 1979–85; faculty mem., Assoc. Prof. of Music and Media, later Prof., Dir of Experimental Media Facility, Media Laboratory, MIT 1985–, Co-Dir of research consortium 1994–; invented technology named hyperinstruments 1986, began instrument design for this technology 1991–; Brain Opera, first performance, Lincoln Center Festival 1996; tours with his repertoire in the USA, Europe and Asia; music performed by many prominent musicians, such as Yo-Yo Ma, and ensembles. *Compositions include:* Sun 1976, Ye Gentle Birds 1977, Fresh Spring 1977, With Dadaji in Paradise 1977–78, Two Songs 1978, Yoku Mireba 1978, Concerto for Guitar 1978, Déplacements 1979, Light 1979, Soft Morning City 1980, Winter Variations 1981, String Quartet No. 1 1981, Fusione Fugace 1981–82, Chansons d'Amour 1982, Electric Etudes 1983, Spectres Parisiens 1983–84, Hidden Sparks 1984, Nature's Breath 1984–85, VALIS 1986–87, Towards the Center 1988–89, Desires 1985–89, Flora 1989, Bug-Mudra 1989–90, Begin Again Again 1991, Hyperstring Trilogy 1991–93, Song of Penance 1992, Forever and Ever 1993, Spirit Quartet 1994, Wake-up Music 1995, Brain Opera 1995–96, He's Our Dad 1997, Hypermusic installations at Meteorite Museum, Essen 1998, Resurrection, premiered at Houston 1998–99, Trio for the Beginning of Time 1999, Sparkler 2001, Toy Symphony 2002–03, HyperEtudes 2004, I Dreamt a Dream 2004, Hyper Dim-Sums: Glade, Winding Line and Punchy 2004, Mixed Messiah 2004, Sea Soaring and Music Garden 2005, Jeux Deux 2005, ...but not simpler... 2005, Another Life 2006, Skellig, Death and the Powers (premiered by Boston Modern Opera Project, Mass 2011). *Publications include:* Hyperinstruments: A Progress Report 1992; contrib. book chapters, articles in learned musical journals. *Honours:* Chevalier, Ordre des Arts et des Lettres 1995; Gaudeamus Prize 1977, Gulbenkian Foundation Grant 1980, Nat. Endowment for the Arts Grants 1981, 1983, 1985, Prix de la Creation, French Culture Ministry 1984, Friedheim Award, Kennedy Centre 1987, Aaron Copland Fund for Music Grant 1994, DigiGlobe Prize, German Govt 1998. *Address:* MIT Media Laboratory, E15-444, 20 Ames Street, Cambridge, MA 02139, USA (office). *Telephone:* (617) 253-0394 (office). *Fax:* (617) 258-6264 (office). *E-mail:* tod@media.mit.edu (office). *Website:* www.media.mit.edu/people/bio_tod.htm (office).

MACIAS, Reinaldo; singer (tenor); b. 1 Sept. 1956, Cuba. *Education:* studied in the USA and at the Geneva Conservatory. *Career:* sang at first in concert, notably with Messiah, Haydn's Schöpfung and Jahreszeiten and the Requiems of Dvořák, Britten and Mozart; Verdi Requiem in Paris, 1989; Opera roles from 1989, with Almaviva in Vienna and Zürich, Don Ottavio and Ferrando in Netherlands, the Berlioz Iopas at Zürich and Gounod's Roméo in Liège (1993); other roles include the Duke of Mantua, Tamino and Lindoro (all in Zürich, 1991–92). *Current Management:* Stafford Law, Candleway, Broad

Street, Sutton Valence, Kent ME17 3AT, England. *Website:* www.stafford-law .com.

McINTOSH, Thomas Lee, MSc, FRSA; British conductor; b. 3 Dec. 1938; m. Miranda Harrison Vincent 1982. *Education:* Juilliard School of Music. *Career:* conductor and Music Dir London City Chamber Orchestra 1973–; Artistic Dir E Anglian Summer Music Festival 1978–, Penang Malaysia Music Festival 1986–87, Opera Anglia 1989–, Artanglia Ltd 1988; principal guest conductor Canton Symphony Orchestra 1994–. *Publications:* Eighteenth-Century Symphonic Music (contributing ed.), arrangements for orchestra of Valentine Waltzes (George Antheil), Rag Suite (various composers), Flower Rag Suite (Scott Joplin), Piano Concerto on Japanese Themes 2005. *Honours:* first prize Int. Kranichstein Competition, prize winner Busoni Competition, Bolanzo, three Sasakawa Foundation awards, UK. *Address:* Cath Anderson, The Old School, Bridge Street, Hadleigh, Suffolk IP7 6BY, England (office). *Telephone:* (1473) 822596 (office). *Fax:* (1473) 824175 (office). *E-mail:* thomas.mcintosh@ minstrelmusic.co.uk (office). *Website:* www.minstrelmusic.co.uk (office).

McINTYRE, Sir Donald Conroy, Kt, OBE, CBE; New Zealand singer (bass); b. 22 Oct. 1934, Auckland; s. of George Douglas and Hermyn McIntyre; m. Jill Redington 1961; three d. *Education:* Mt Albert Grammar School, Auckland, Auckland Teachers' Training Coll. and Guildhall School of Music, UK. *Career:* debut with Welsh National Opera 1959; Prin. Bass, Sadler's Wells Opera 1960–67; debut with Royal Opera House, Covent Garden 1967, numerous subsequent performances; annual appearances at Bayreuth Festival 1967–81; frequent int. guest appearances; fmr teacher, Univ. of Auckland. *Roles include:* Wotan and Wanderer in Der Ring, Dutchman in Der Fliegende Holländer, Telramund in Lohengrin, Barak in Die Frau ohne Schatten, Pizzaro in Fidelio, Golaud in Pelléas et Mélisande, Kurwenal and King Marke in Tristan and Isolde, Gurnemanz, Klingsor and Amfortas in Parsifal, Heyst in Victory, Jochanaan in Salome, Macbeth, Scarpia in Tosca, the Count in Marriage of Figaro, Nick Shadow in The Rake's Progress, Hans Sachs in Die Meistersinger, Dr. Schöne in Woyzeck, Cardillac in Cardillac by Hindemith, Rocco in Fidelio, The Doctor in Der Freischütz, Prospero in Un Re In Asloto, Sarastro in The Magic Flute, Balstrode in Peter Grimes, Telramund in Lohengrin, Prus in The Makropoulos Case, Rheingold, The Ring (video). *Recordings include:* Pelléas et Mélisande, Oedipus Rex, Il Trovatore. *Honours:* Hon. DMus (Auckland) 1992; Fidelio Medal, AIDO 1989, NZ Award for Outstanding Contribs, Festival of the Arts 1990, Arts Foundation Icon Award 2004. *Address:* Fox Hill Farm, Jackass Lane, Keston, Bromley, Kent, BR2 6AN, England (home). *Telephone:* (1689) 855368 (home). *Fax:* (1689) 860724 (home).

McINTYRE, Joy; American singer (soprano); *Professor Emerita of Music, Boston University;* b. 24 Sept. 1938, Kinsley, Kansas. *Education:* New England Conservatory, Salzburg Mozarteum. *Career:* sang at the Saarbrucken Opera 1964–66, Dortmund 1966–74 and Munich Staatsoper 1976–81; roles have included Suzuki, Brangaene, Leonore, Venus, Ortrud, the Dyer's Wife, Marie, Abigaille, Santuzza, Turandot, Judith in Bluebeard's Castle and Lady Macbeth; Guest appearances at the Vienna Staatsoper, Lyon, Strasbourg, Brussels, Hamburg and Glasgow (Scottish Opera); Prof. of Music, Boston Univ., now Emer. *Address:* c/o Boston University School of Music, 855 Commonwealth Avenue, Boston, MA 02215, USA (office). *E-mail:* cfamusic@ bu.edu (office). *Website:* www.bu.edu/cfa/music (office).

MacKAY, Charles; American opera administrator; *General Director, Santa Fe Opera;* b. Albuquerque. *Education:* Univ. of Minnesota. *Career:* began career as French horn player, Santa Fe Opera Orchestra 1969, later becoming Box Office Man. and Business Man. –1979, Gen. Dir 2008–; Dir of Devt and Finance, Spoleto Festival USA 1979–84; Exec. Dir Opera Theatre of St Louis 1984–85, Gen. Dir 1985–2008; Chair. OPERA America 2004–08. *Honours:* Hon. DMus (Missouri-St Louis); Missouri Arts Award, St Louis Arts & Educ. Council Excellence in the Arts Award. *Address:* Office of the General Director, The Santa Fe Opera, PO Box 2408, Santa Fe, NM 87504-2408, USA (office). *Telephone:* (505) 986-5908 (office). *E-mail:* director@santafeopera.org (office). *Website:* www.santafeopera.org (office).

McKAY, Elizabeth Norman, BSc, DPhil, LRAM; British musicologist, pianist and author; b. 21 Nov. 1931, London, England; d. of Sir Edward Norman and Lady Norman; one s. two d. *Education:* Bristol Univ., Somerville Coll., Oxford. *Career:* chamber musician, accompanist, coach, theatre work, teacher, lecturer, broadcaster, author; founder The Schubert Inst. (UK) 1992–. *Publications include:* Schubert's Music for the Theatre, in Proceedings of The Royal Musical Association 1966–67, Schubert as a Composer of Operas, in Schubert Studies 1982, The Impact of The New Pianofortes: Mozart, Beethoven and Schubert 1987, Franz Schubert's Music for the Theatre 1991, Schuberts Klaviersonaten von 1815 bis 1825, in Franz Schubert Reliquie-Sonate 1992, Franz Schubert: A Biography 1996, Proceedings of the Oxford Schubert Bicentenary Symposium (co-editor) 1997, Schubert's String and Piano Duos in Context, in Schubert Studies 1998, Schubert and the professional musicians with whom he associated in Schubert und seine Freunde 1999, New Light on Schubert's Music thrown by the Experiences of Britain's leading living composers, in Schubert-Jahrbuch III 1999, Schubert and the Year Without Summer 2001, Schubert: the Piano and Dark Keys 2009; contrib. to The New Grove Dictionary of Opera, Oxford University Press: Schubert's Music for the Theatre, Pipers Enzyklopädie des Musik Theaters 1994, Schubert Lexikon 1997, The Music Review, The Musical Times, Österreichische Musikzeitschrift, Music and Letters, The Beethoven

Newsletter, BBC Music Magazine, Journal of the IFSI, Schubert-Enzyklopädie 2004. *Honours:* Hon. bd mem. Int. Franz Schubert Inst. (IFSI) 1992–2005, Hon. mem. The Schubert Inst. (UK).

McKAY, Marjory Grieve, GRSM, ARMCM, FTCM, ARCM; British singer (soprano); b. 23 June 1951, Edinburgh, Scotland; m. Frederick Charles McKay 1981 (died 2007). *Education:* Trinity Acad., Edinburgh, Royal Manchester Coll. of Music, Royal Northern Coll. of Music. *Career:* debut as Esmeralda, Scottish Opera 1980; Scottish opera roles Esmeralda in Bartered Bride, Belleza in L'Egisto and Feklusa in Katya Kabanova; Scottish Opera Go Round, Violetta; WNO Workshop, Violetta in La Traviata; many concerts and recitals in Scotland and the north of England; joined Opera Australia 1984–, debut as Gerhilde in Die Walküre 1985 and Xenia in Boris Godonuv 1986; debut with Western Australian Opera as Madama Butterfly 1987; created the title role in Alan Holley's new opera, Dorothea; Les Huguenots Video (Joan Sutherland's Farewell) 1990.

MACKAY, Penelope Judith, AGSM; British singer (soprano); b. 6 April 1943, Bradford, Yorkshire. *Education:* secretarial coll., Lycée Français, London, Guildhall School of Music and Drama. *Career:* debut, Glyndebourne 1970; sang at Glyndebourne 1970–72, with English Opera Group 1973–75, English Music Theatre 1976–78, ENO 1980–83; freelance work in the UK, Europe and USA; over 20 leading roles; sang in premieres of Lutyens's Time Off 1971, Britten's Death in Venice 1973; British premieres of Hans Werner Henze's La Cubana in the title role 1978, Krenek's Jonny Spielt Auf (Anita) 1984, Ligeti, Le Grand Macabre (Miranda) 1982; Austrian premiere in modern times of Fux's Angelica, Vincitrice di Alcina (Angelica), Graz 1984, and British premiere in modern times of Handel's Rodrigo (Rodrigo) 1985; Prof. of Singing, Royal Acad. of Music, London and Guildhall School of Music and Drama, London; Pres., Hampstead Garden Opera 2007–; Tutor, AIMS Int. Music School; mem. Incorporated Soc. of Musicians, British Voice Asscn, Asscn of Teachers of Singing. *Honours:* Hon. ARAM . *Address:* 30 Fairfield Road, Saxmundham, Suffolk IP17 1BA, England (office). *E-mail:* pennymackay@gsmd.ac.uk (office).

MACKAY, Robert Andrew, BSc, MMus, PhD; British composer, actor, singer (baritone), musician (flute, classical guitar, bass) and academic; *Lecturer in Creative Music Technology, University of Hull;* b. 12 July 1973, London. *Education:* Univs of Keele and Bangor. *Career:* session musician in Wales 1997–; Composer-in-Residence, Radio Bratislava, Slovakia 1998–99, La Muse en Circuit, Paris 2007; bass player, Gyroscope 1998; flute, guitar and bass player, Tystion 1998–2002; flute player in Drymbago 2005–; collaborator with Pwyll ap Siôn on comm. for Nat. Youth Choir of Wales and Opera Heloise 1999; comms for Twisted I Theatre Company 2003, Rotunda Mapmaker project 2005–08; works performed throughout Europe, USA and NZ; several TV appearances and radio broadcasts; mem. PRS, MCPS, PRC, Equity, Soc. for the Promotion of New Music, BMIC, SAN. *Theatre:* Only Just 1997. *Film appearances:* Merlin, A Beautiful Mistake. *Television appearances:* I dot (S4C), Garej (S4C), 4-Track (S4C), Lois (S4C), Sesiwn Hwyr (S4C), Bandit (S4C). *Radio performances:* Late Junction (BBC Radio 3), Hear and Now (BBC Radio 3), two John Peel sessions (BBC Radio 1), various performances on BBC Radio Wales. *Compositions include:* Environs 1996, Sea Pictures 1997, Voicewind 1998, Postcards from the Summer 1999, Peiriant Gorllewinol, Meddwi Dros Gymru (BBC Radio Cymru Rap Award for Album of the Year 2000) 1999, Flute Melt 2000, Heloise 2001, Joyce's Vision 2002, Cain and Abel 2003, Phonemenon 2004, Altered Landscapes 2006, Song of Stones 2007. *Recordings:* ICMC98 1998, 1er Concurso Internacional de Miniaturas Electroacústicas 2003. *Publications:* ICMC98 1998, Shrug Off Ya Complex 1999, Mr Blaidd 2000, Hen Gelwydd Prydain Newydd 2000, Y Meistri 2001, Discontact! III 2003, Confluencias 2003, In Between 2004, Chops 2005, Costa Rita 2006, La Muse en Circuit 2007. *Honours:* Bourges Synthèse Festival Prix Résidence, France 1997, Hungarian Radio Special Prize (Ear 99) 1999, Winner, Concours Luc Ferrari 2006. *Address:* 57 Oak Road, Scarborough, North Yorkshire, YO12 4AP, England. *E-mail:* r.a.mackay@hull.ac.uk (office). *Website:* www.myspace.com/robflute.

McKELLAR FERGUSON, Kathleen; British singer (mezzo-soprano); b. 1959, Stirling. *Education:* Royal Scottish Acad., Royal Coll. of Music; studied with Margaret Hyde. *Career:* South Bank debut 1987, with London Bach Orchestra; Beethoven's Ninth at Gstaad Festival 1990 and with Ulster Orchestra; other repertoire includes Mozart's Requiem, Brahms Alto Rhapsody, Mahler's 8th, Songs of the Auvergne and A Child of our Time; season 1990–91 with Haydn's Nelson Mass and the English Chamber Orchestra, Messiah with Liverpool Philharmonic; also sings Elgar's Sea Pictures and Music Makers, St Matthew Passion (Fairfields Hall) and Elijah; concerts with Yehudi Menuhin at Festival Halls; opera repertoire includes Florence Pike in Albert Herring (Aldeburgh 1986), Maketaten in Aknaten by Philip Glass for ENO 1987, Mozart's Marcellina and Third Lady for Pavillion Opera, Cherubino, and Handel's Bradamante in Alcina for Flanders Opera 1991, Second Lady in The Magic Flute at Théâtre Royale de la Monnaie, Brussels, 1993, Suzuki in Madama Butterfly for Opera Forum in Nederlands, 1994, and Bradamante in Alcina with Nikolaus Harnoncourt at Zürich Opera; Second Lady at Festival of Aix en Provence; currently vocal studies teacher, Royal Scottish Acad. of Music and Drama. *Address:* c/o Department of Vocal Studies, Royal Scottish Academy of Music and Drama, 100 Renfrew Street, Glasgow G2 3DB, Scotland (office). *Website:* www.rsamd.ac.uk (office).

McKERRACHER, Colin; British singer (tenor); b. 1960, Falkirk. *Education:* Royal Northern College of Music with Joseph Ward, studied with Nicolai Gedda. *Career:* has sung with Glyndebourne Touring Opera and the Festival in Simon Boccanegra and Capriccio 1986–87; Appearances with Scottish Opera-Go-Round as Števa in Jenůfa, Beppe and Turiddu (Cav and Pag) and Don Carlos; Lensky in Eugene Onegin for Opera 80 followed by Monostatos in The Magic Flute and Ernesto in Don Pasquale; English National Opera and Covent Garden debuts season 1990–91, as Ferrando and in Così fan tutte. *Honours:* Prizewinner, Rio de Janeiro International Singing Competition 1989.

MACKEY, Steven; American composer, guitarist and academic; *Professor of Music and Chair of Music Department, Princeton University*; b. 14 Feb. 1956, Frankfurt, Germany; m. Sarah Kirkland Snider; one s., one d. *Education:* Univ. of California, Davis, Brandeis Univ. *Career:* compositions performed worldwide by orchestras including Los Angeles Philharmonic, San Francisco and Chicago Symphonies, BBC Philharmonic, Concertgebouw, Austrian Radio Symphony, Sydney Symphony and Tokyo Philharmonic; commissions from Los Angeles Philharmonic, St Louis and New Jersey Symphonies, Chamber Orchestra of Philadelphia, Carnegie Hall and Nasher Museum, Dallas, Nashville Symphony, New World Symphony, Swedish Chamber Orchestra, Irish Chamber Orchestra and Acad. of St Martin-in-the-Fields; as a guitarist, has performed with ensembles including Kronos Quartet, Arditti Quartet, London Sinfonietta, Nexttime Ensemble, Psappha and Joey Baron; Composer-in-Residence at major music festivals including Tanglewood, Aspen and the Holland Festival; joined Faculty Princeton Univ. 1985, currently Prof. of Music and Chair of Music Dept. *Compositions include:* for orchestra: Eating Greens 1994, Deal for improvising electric guitar soloist, optional drummer and small chamber orchestra 1995, Lost & Found 1996, Tuck and Roll, concerto for electric guitar and orchestra 1999, Pedal Tones for orchestra and pipe organ 2002, Dreamhouse 2003, Time Release, concerto for percussion and orchestra 2005, Turn the Key 2006, Beautiful Passing, concerto for violin and orchestra 2009, Four Iconoclastic Episodes, double concerto for violin, electric guitar and strings 2009, Learning Curve, concerto for piano and orchestra 2011; music theatre: Ravenshead 1998, Slide 2010; chamber music: Troubadour Songs for string quartet & electric guitar 1992, Physical Property for string quartet & electric guitar 1992, Feels So Baaad for violin, marimba, guitar, percussion 1994, Humble River for flute, violin, viola, cello 1997, String Theory for amplified string quartet and digital delay 1998, Micro-Concerto for percussion and five players 1999, Ars Moriendi 2000, Heavy Light for flute, cello, electric guitar, percussion and piano 2001, Gaggle and Flock, string octet 2001, Interior Design for solo violin 2003, Jango for classical guitar quartet and percussion 2003, Groundswell, concerto for viola and large chamber ensemble 2007; Lonely Motel. *Recordings include:* as composer: Ravenshead, Lost & Found (also performer) 1996, Tuck and Roll: The Music of Steven Mackey, String Theory (also performer) 2003, Heavy Light (also performer), Banana/Dump Truck (also performer) 2005, Interior Design 2006, Speak Like the People, Write Like the King 2008, Animal, Vegetable, Mineral 2009, Dreamhouse 2010, It Is Time 2011, Lonely Motel: Music From Slide (also performer) (Grammy Award for Best Small Ensemble Performance) 2011; as performer with Kronos Quartet: Physical Property 1992, Short Stories 1993. *Honours:* Guggenheim Fellowship, several awards from American Acad. of Arts and Letters, Chamber Music Soc. of Lincoln Center Stoeger Prize, Kennedy Center Friedheim Award, first recipient of Princeton Univ.'s Distinguished Teaching Award 1991. *Address:* Princeton University Department of Music, 316 Woolworth Center, Princeton, NJ 08544, USA (office). *Telephone:* (609) 258-4241 (office). *Fax:* (609) 258-6793 (office). *E-mail:* steve@princeton.edu (office); steve@stevenmackey.com (home). *Website:* www.stevenmackey.com (office).

MACKIE, David, MA, BMus, DipMusEd, ARCM; British accompanist, repetiteur and conductor; b. 25 Nov. 1943, Greenock, Scotland. *Education:* Greenock Acad., Royal Scottish Acad. of Music, Univs of Glasgow and Birmingham. *Career:* repetiteur, D'Oyly Carte Opera Co. 1975–76, Chorus Master and Assoc. Conductor 1976–82; freelance accompanist, repetiteur, conductor 1982–. *Publications include:* Reconstruction of Sullivan's Cello Concerto (with Sir Charles Mackerras) 1986, Arthur Sullivan and the Royal Soc. of Musicians of Great Britain 2005. *Address:* 16A Eglinton Gardens, Skelmorlie, North Ayrshire, PA17 5DW, Scotland (home). *Telephone:* (1475) 520494 (home). *E-mail:* david-mackie@tiscali.co.uk (home).

MACKIE, Neil, CBE, CStJ, FRSAMD, FRCM, FRSE; British singer (tenor); b. 11 Dec. 1946, Aberdeen, Scotland. *Career:* debut in London with the English Chamber Orchestra under Raymond Leppard; European engagements at the Flanders and Savonlinna Festivals, Concertgebouw Orchestra, in Rome for RAI and in Scandinavia; tours of Netherlands and Belgium with La Petite Bande conducted by Sigiswald Kuijken; association with Peter Maxwell Davies includes premieres of The Martyrdom of St Magnus, 1977, The Lighthouse 1980 and Into the Labyrinth 1983; sang Gomatz in Mozart's Zaide at Wexford, 1981; premiered Henze's Three Poems of W.H. Auden at Aldeburgh, 1984; appeared at Cheltenham and Aldeburgh Festivals; British engagements with the Hallé, Bournemouth Sinfonietta, BBC Symphony and Scottish Chamber Orchestras, and with the London Sinfonietta under Simon Rattle; 1988, Into the Labyrinth at the Ojai Festival in America; 1988–89 tour of USA with the Scottish Chamber Orchestra and appearances with the Orchestre National de Paris; Prof. of Singing, Royal College of Music, London 1985, Head of Vocal Studies 1993–. *Recordings include:* Mozart's Requiem and

Haydn's Die Schöpfung with La Petite Bande; Mozart Masses with the King's College Choir; Britten's Serenade, with premiere of Now Sleeps the Crimson Petal and unpublished songs. *Honours:* Hon. DMus (Aberdeen) 1993. *Current Management:* Svenska Konsertbyrån, Jungfrugatan 45, 11444 Stockholm, Sweden. *Telephone:* (8) 665-80-88. *Fax:* (8) 665-80-66. *E-mail:* info@svenskakonsertbyran.se. *Website:* www.svenskakonsertbyran.se.

MACKIE, William; British singer (bass); b. 16 Aug. 1954, Ayr, Scotland. *Education:* Royal Scottish Academy, Glasgow. *Career:* debut with Scottish Opera, 1980, as Antonio in Le nozze di Figaro; Welsh National Opera, 1982–83, in Cenerentola, A Midsummer Night's Dream and Butterfly; English National Opera, 1989, in Lear by Reimann; Season 1989–90 in Die Zauberflöte at Aix-en-Provence and Hansel and Gretel at Strasbourg; Pocket Opera Nuremberg, 1991, as Assur in Semiramide; Other roles include Rossini's Basilio, Fasolt in Das Rheingold and Lodovico in Otello. *Recordings include:* Parsifal.

McKINNEY, Thomas; American singer (baritone); b. 5 May 1946, Lufkin, TX. *Education:* studied in Houston, Hollywood and New York. *Career:* debut, Houston 1971 as Tchelkalov in Boris Godunov; Sang in opera in Cincinnati, Houston, San Diego and San Francisco; European engagements at the Wexford Festival (Thaïs), the Vienna Volksoper and the Théâtre Royale de la Monnaie, Brussels; Other roles have included Pelléas, Guglielmo, Don Giovanni, Mozart's Count, Papageno, Rossini's Figaro, Eugene Onegin, Hamlet, Belcore, Massenet's Hérode and Athanael (Thais), Verdi's Posa and Ford and Peachum in The Beggar's Opera; San Diego, 1972 in the premiere of Medea by Alva Henderson; Frequent concert appearances.

McKINNY, Ryan; American singer (bass-baritone); b. 1980. *Education:* Juilliard School of Music, Houston Grand Opera Studio. *Career:* early opera performances with Houston Grand Opera; has since performed opera roles with several cos including Los Angeles Opera, Deutsche Oper (debut as Escamillo in Carmen 2010), English Nat. Opera (debut as Tiridate in Radamisto 2010), Oper Leipzig, Metropolitan Opera (debut as Lieutenant Ratcliffe in Billy Budd 2011), Wolf Trap Opera; Carnegie Hall debut in Handel's Messiah 2004; mem. ensemble Deutsche Oper, Berlin 2011–. *Opera repertoire includes:* Masetto in Don Giovanni, Peter in Hänsel und Gretel, Figaro in Le Nozze di Figaro, Escamillo and Zuniga in Carmen, Nikitisch in Boris Godunov, Herald in Lohengrin, Ramfis in Aida, Pietro in Simon Boccanegra, Le Gouverneur in Le comte Ory, Sam in Un ballo in maschera, Flint and Lieutenant Ratcliffe in Billy Budd, Don Basilio in Il barbiere di Siviglia, Amfortas in Parsifal. *Honours:* Birgit Nilsson prize for singing at Plácido Domingo's Operalia Competition, Milan 2010. *Current Management:* Columbia Artists Management Inc., 1790 Broadway, New York, NY 10019, USA. *Telephone:* (212) 841-9685 (office). *Fax:* (212) 841-9557 (office). *E-mail:* djbristo@cami.com (office). *Website:* www.ryanmckinny.com (office).

MacKINTOSH, Catherine; British violinist; b. 1948, England. *Career:* debut concert at St John's Smith Square, London 1984; extensive tours and broadcasts in France, Belgium, Netherlands, Germany, Austria, Switzerland, Italy and Spain. Tours of the USA and Japan 1991–92; British appearances include four Purcell concerts at the Wigmore Hall 1987, later broadcast on Radio 3; repertoire includes music on the La Folia theme by Vivaldi, Corelli, CPE Bach, Marais, A Scarlatti, Vitali and Geminiani; Instrumental works and songs by Purcell, music by Matthew Locke, John Blow and Fantasias and Airs by William Lawes; 17th Century virtuoso Italian music by Marini, Buonamente, Gabrieli, Fontana and Stradella; J. S. Bach and his forerunners, Biber, Scheidt, Schenk, Reincken and Buxtehude; frequent engagements with other ensembles; member of the Purcell Quartet; Prof. of Baroque and Classical Violin and Viola, Royal Coll. of Music 1977–99, Fellow 1994; Fellow, Royal Scottish Acad. of Music.

McLACHLAN, Murray, KStJ, FRSA; British pianist, teacher, administrator and writer; b. 6 Jan. 1965, Dundee, Scotland; s. of Charles Thompson McLachlan and Edith Margaret Mitchell Chree; m. 1st Mary Russell 1993; m. 2nd Kathryn Page 2001; three c. 2 step-c. *Education:* Chetham's School, Magdalene Coll., Cambridge with Peter Katin and Norma Fisher, studied with Ryszard Bakst, Ronald Stevenson and David Hartigan. *Career:* debut, Free Trade Hall, Hallé Proms, Manchester, 1983; performed extensively throughout the UK as a recitalist and concerto soloist with Royal Philharmonic Orchestra, Scottish Chamber Orchestra, BBC Scottish Orchestra, Manchester Camerata; toured Belorussia 1991; has performed complete cycle of 32 Beethoven sonatas from memory in Glasgow, Dundee, Aberdeen and Manchester; Head of Keyboard, Chetham's School of Music, Manchester; Tutor, Royal Northern Coll. of Music; Chair. EPTA UK; Ed. Piano Professional Magazine; adjudicator, British Fed. of Festivals; repertoire also includes complete works of Brahms; Visiting Prof., Univ. of St Andrews; f. and Artistic Dir, Chetham's Int. Summer School and Festival for Pianists. *Recordings include:* Complete sonatas of Prokofiev, Myaskovsky, Beethoven and Kabalevsky and solo works of Khatchaturian; Piano concerto of Ronald Stevenson; Complete Piano Works of Camilleri; six Concertos of Alexander Tchereprin; 24 Preludes and Fugues of Shchedrin. *Publications:* contrib. numerous articles for International Piano, Piano, BBC Music, Piano Professional. *Honours:* Kt of the Order of St John of Jerusalem 1997; Chetham's Piano Prize, Cambridge Instrumental Exhibition, Penguin Rosette Award for album of music from Scotland. *Current Management:* c/o Chameleon Arts Management, 32 St Michael's Road, Sandhurst, Berks. GU47 8HE, England. *Telephone:* (845) 644-5530. *Fax:* (1252) 871517. *E-mail:* office@chameleon-arts

.co.uk. *Website:* www.chameleon-arts.co.uk. *Address:* c/o Chetham's School of Music, Long Millgate, Manchester, M3 1SB, England. *E-mail:* info@murraymclachlan.co.uk. *Website:* www.murraymclachlan.com.

McLAUGHLIN, Marie; British singer (soprano); b. 2 Nov. 1954, Hamilton, Lanarkshire, Scotland. *Education:* London Opera Centre, Nat. Opera Studio. *Career:* sang Susanna and Lauretta while a student; ENO from 1978, in The Consul, Dido and Aeneas, A Night in Venice and Rigoletto; Royal Opera Covent Garden from 1980 as Barbarina and Susanna in Le nozze di Figaro, Zerlina, Iris in Semele, Marzelline in Fidelio, Nannetta in Falstaff, Zdenka in Arabella and Tytania in A Midsummer Night's Dream; Glyndebourne Festivals as Micaela (Carmen) and Violetta 1985, 1987, Salzburg Festival as Susanna, conducted by James Levine; Scottish Opera in Orfeo ed Euridice and Le Nozze di Figaro; Deutsche Oper Berlin as Susanna and Marzelline; Hamburg, Susanna, Marzelline; Chicago Lyric, Zerlina, Despina; Washington, Susanna; Met New York as Marzelline; La Scala, Milan, Adina; Paris Opéra in Roméo et Juliette; sang Zdenka in Arabella at Covent Garden 1990; Marzelline in Fidelio at the 1990 Salzburg Festival, Zerlina at the Vienna Festival; Geneva Opera 1992, as Despina, and Jenny in Mahagonny; sang Jenny at the Opéra Bastille, Paris 1995; Donna Elvira at Lausanne 1996; concert appearances in London, Edinburgh, New York, Chicago, Berlin, Spain, France, Belgium and Germany; worked with conductors, including Maazel, Bernstein, Haitink, Barenboim, Davis, Leppard, Celibidache, Harnoncourt, Mehta and Levine; season 1992–93 as Blanche in the Carmélites at Geneva, Susanna on tour with the Royal Opera to Japan, Ilia in Idomeneo at Barcelona and Ivy in On the Town at the Barbican Hall; sang Anna Elisa in Lehar's Paganini at the Theater an der Wien, Vienna 1998; season 2000–01 as Katerina in Martinů's The Greek Passion at Covent Garden and Weill's Jenny in Geneva. *Recordings include:* Covent Garden Fidelio, Handel's L'Allegro, il Pensieroso ed Il Moderato, Die Zauberflöte and Dido and Aeneas, Così fan tutte, Mozart, Requiem (Bernstein), Rigoletto, Carmen, Traviata, Mozart's C Minor Mass and Haydn's Mass in Time of War.

McLEAN, Barton Keith, BS, MM, MusD; American composer; *Co-Director, McLean Mix Music/Media Duo*; b. 8 April 1938, Poughkeepsie, NY; m. Priscilla McLean 1967. *Education:* State Univ. of NY, Potsdam, Eastman School of Music, Indiana Univ. *Career:* teacher of music theory, editing, piano, double bass, State Univ. of NY, Potsdam 1960–66, Indiana Univ., South Bend 1969–76, Univ. of Texas, Austin 1976–83; Composer-Performer and Co-Dir McLean Mix music/media duo, giving over 400 events, full-time 1983–; teacher, iEar Studios, Rensselaer Polytechnic Inst. 1987–88, 1990–92, Co-Dir 1987–89; Head, Radio Series, Submissions, Exec. Cttee, Soc. of Composers, Inc. (SCI) 1974–79, Ind. Composer Rep., SCI 1995–99; Visiting Prof., Universiti Malaysia Sarawak 1996; mem. Artist Advisory Bd, New York Foundation for the Arts (NYFA) 2007–10. *Compositions include:* Dimensions I for violin and tape 1973, Dimensions II for piano and tape 1974, Metamorphosis for orchestra 1975, Dimensions III for saxophone and tape 1978, Dimensions IV for saxophone and tape 1979, Heavy Music for four crowbars, electronic 1979, Dimensions VIII for piano and tape 1982, Ixtlan for two pianos 1982, The Last Ten Minutes (computer generated) 1982, The Electric Sinfonia (Prize at Int. Bourges Electroacoustic Music Festival 1983) 1982, String Quartet from the Good Earth 1985, In the Place of Tears for chamber ensemble and voice 1985, In Wilderness is the Preservation of the World (environmental-electronic) 1986, Voices of the Wild – Primal Spirits for orchestra 1987, Visions of a Summer Night for computer tape 1989, Rainforest 1989, Rainforest Images for computer tape 1992, Rainforest Reflections for electronic processed soloist and orchestra 1993, Rainforest Images I and II (video) 1993, Forgotten Shadows for computer tape 1994, Jambori Rimba 1996, Desert Spring 1996, Dawn Chorus 1996, Forgotten Shadows 1996, The Ultimate Symphonius 2000 (audience interactive sound installation) 1999, Journey on a Long String for double bass and electronics 2001, Natural Energy 2008, Magic at Xanadu 2008, Concerto: States of Being 2010, Xanadu Revisited 2010. *Recordings include:* Mysteries from the Ancient Nahuatl—Excerpts, Dimensions III and IV for saxophone and tape, Heavy Music for four crowbars, The Sorcerer Revisited, Dimensions II for Piano and tape with David Burge, piano, Song of the Nahuatl, Dimensions I for Violin and tape, Genesis, The Sorcerer Revisited, Dimensions II, Spirals 1972–82, The Electric Sinfonia 1983, Dimensions VIII 1983, The Last Ten Minutes 1983, Etunytude 1983, In Wilderness is the Preservation of the World 1987, Visions of a Summer Night: (I, IV) 1990, Rainforest Images 1994, Himalayan Fantasy 1994, Dimensions III 1996, Visions of a Summer Night (III–V) 1995, Earth Music 1995, Dimensions II 1996, Dawn Chorus 1996, Song of the Nahuatl 1997, Etunytude 1997, Ritual of the Dawn 2000, Forgotten Shadows 2000, Happy Days 2000, 2007, Song of the Nahuatl 2007, Valley of Lost Dreams 2007, Ice Canyons 2009, Magic at Xanadu 2009, Demons of the Night 2009, Rainforest Images II 2009, Ritual of the Dawn 2009, Journey on a Long String, Concerto: States of Being 2009, Soundworlds 2009; DVDs: The McLeans Mix Three – Three Collaborations: Milling in the Ennium 2009, Jambori Rimba 2009, Natural Energy 2009 (all three in collaboration with Priscilla McLean), Mclean Mix Live: Happy Days 2009, Magic at Xanadu 2009, Symphony of Seasons 2009, Autumn Requiem (the last in collaboration with Priscilla McLean), Peter's People (video) 2012. *Publications:* numerous articles in professional journals; contrib. to The New Grove Dictionary of Twentieth Century Music. *Honours:* 55 Meet the Composer Grants from MTC New York, New England, Midwest, Mid-America, Texas, West and California 1975–95, Nat. Endowment for the Arts Media Arts Grant 1976, NYFA Composer Fellowship 1986, MacDowell Colony Fellowship 1979, 1981, 1983, Dimensions III chosen as US rep. at UNESCO-IMC-Rostrum Int. Festival 1981, Martha Baird Rockefeller grant to attend and perform in Zagreb Muzicki Biennale 1981, Nat. Endowment for the Arts Composer Fellowship 1976, 1982, 1985, Leighton Colony Banff Centre for the Arts Fellowship 1986, NYSCA Decentralization Grants for multimedia installations 1990, 1994, Virgil Thompson Foundation (for CRI recording), Universiti Malaysia Research Grant 1996, Asian Cultural Council (residency with Asian Composers League in Manila, Philippines) 1997, Virgil Thompson Foundation for CRI recording Forgotten Shadows 2000, Patricia and Jerry Mangione Fellow for MacDowell Colony Residency 2003, American Music Center Composer Award 2004, NYFA Fellows/Innova Award for complete CD production 2010. *Address:* 55 Coon Brook Road, Petersburgh, NY 12138, USA (home). *Telephone:* (518) 658-3595 (office). *Website:* www.fairpoint.net/~rainfor1/McLean_MAXMSP/Main_page.html.

McLEAN, Priscilla Taylor, BEd, BME, MM; American composer, performer, video artist, teacher and author and music reviewer; *Co-Director, The McLean Mix*; b. (Priscilla Ann Taylor), 27 May 1942, Fitchburg, Mass; d. of Conrad Jones Taylor and Grace Lesure Taylor; m. Barton Keith McLean 1967. *Education:* Fitchburg State Univ. and Lowell Univ., Mass, Indiana Univ. *Career:* concerts, The McLean Mix (husband-wife duo performing own electroacoustic music) in the Netherlands, Belgium, Zagreb Muzicki Biennale 1981; Amsterdam, Holland Radio, Oslo, Finland, Sweden 1983; Australia, NZ, Hawaii 1990, Tunugan Festival of Asian Music, the Philippines 1997, England 2004, Scotland 2007; tours, USA 1983–2013 annually, Canada 1986, 1999; Guest Composer, Kennedy Center for the Performing Arts 1977; Gaudeamus Musiekweek, the Netherlands 1979; Guest Composer, Nat. Orchestral Symposium, Indianapolis Symphony 1975, several metropolitan orchestras 1977–93; Guest Prof. and Composer/Performer, Univ. of Hawaii 1985; Guest Soprano Soloist, Cleveland Chamber Orchestra (Wilderness) 1989; Guest Composer/Performer (Research Residency), Univ. of Sarawak, Malaysia 1996; US Consortium comm. 2000; currently touring with music and original videos; classical music reviewer for the Albany, New York Times Union newspaper; mem. Broadcast Music, Inc. (BMI), American Music Center, Seamus, Soc. of Composers, Inc., Electronic Music Foundation. *Film:* Peter's People – Creating the Dream (documentary) (producer and co-dir) 2012. *Compositions include:* Variations and Mozaics on a Theme of Stravinsky (for orchestra), Interplanes (for two pianos), Dance of Dawn (electronic), Invisible Chariots (electroacoustic), The Inner Universe (for piano, taped sound and electron microscope slides), Fantasies for Adults and Other Children, eight songs for soprano and piano, Beneath the Horizon I, III (for tuba(s) and whale ensemble on recorded tape and optional slides-to-video), Night Images (electronic), Messages (for chorus and chamber ensemble), Fire and Ice (for trombone and piano), Elan! A Dance to all Rising Things from the Earth (for chamber ensemble), Three Pieces for In Wilderness is the Preservation of the World (soloist, chamber ensemble and recorded tape), In Celebration (chorus, percussion and recorded tape), Wilderness (soprano and recorded tape), A Magic Dwells (orchestra and tape) 1986, Voices of the Wild (orchestra, soloist and electronic music) 1988, The Dance of Shiva (electronic tape and multiple slides) 1990, Rainforest (coil with B. McLean) 1990, Everything Awakening Alert and Joyful (full orchestra and narrator) 1991, In the Beginning (for soprano, electronics and live video) 1995, Rainforest Images (with B. McLean) 1994, Where the Wild Geese Go (B flat clarinet and recorded sound) 1994, Desert Spring (with B. McLean) 1996, Jambori Rimba with (B. McLean) 1997, Desert Voices (for midi violin, tape and electronics) 1998, The Ultimate Symphonius 2000, with Barton McLean 1999, Angels of Delirium (electronic) 2001, Symphony of Seasons (music and video) 2001–03, Xaakalawe/Flowing 2004, Cyberlament 2005, Caverns of Darkness, Rings of Light (for solo tuba, recorded tubas and video) 2007, Natural Energy (live electroacoustic performance) 2008, Cries and Echoes for solo cello, recorded cellos and video 2009. *Recordings include:* Dance of Dawn, Interplanes, Variations and Mozaics on a Theme of Stravinsky, Invisible Chariots, Electronic Music from the Outside In, Beneath the Horizon III and Salt Canyons, In Wilderness is the Preservation of the World, Rainforest Images II, The Electric Performer, Gods, Demons and the Earth, McLean Mix and the Golden Age of Electronic Music, Fantasies for Adults and Other Children: The Vocal Music of Priscilla McLean, Electronic Landscapes, McLean Mix Live (DVD, The McLeans Mix Three (DVD), Symphony of Seasons (DVD). *Music videos include:* Milling in the Ennium 2001, Symphony of Seasons: Jewels of January 2001, The Eye of Spring 2002, July Dance 2003, Autumn Requiem (with Barton McLean) 2003, Xaakalawe/Flowing 2004, Caverns of Darkness, Rings of Light 2007, Natural Energy (with Barton McLean) 2008, Cries and Echoes 2009. *Radio:* Radiofest: New American Music, Series I and II (Co-Dir 13 half-hour programmes), Soc. of Composers, Inc. 1976–82. *Publication:* Hanging off the Edge – Revelations of a Modern Troubadour (memoir) 2006. *Honours:* Winner, 17th Sigvald Thompson Composition Award Competition 1988, winning composition IMC Rostrum 1990, numerous grants and commissions. *Address:* The McLean Mix/MLC Publications, 55 Coon Brook Road, Petersburgh, New York, NY 12138, USA (office). *Telephone:* (518) 658-3595 (office). *E-mail:* mclmix@cisbec.net (office). *Website:* www.fairpoint.net/~rainfor1/McLean_MAXMSP/Main_page.html (office).

MacLEAN, Susan; American singer (mezzo-soprano); b. 1962, California. *Education:* Minneapolis and Zürich Opera Studio. *Career:* sang at Bielefeld Opera from 1988, notably in Yerma by Villa Lobos and Der Sprung uber den Schatten by Krenek; Zürich, 1989, as Fenena in Nabucco; Wuppertal, 1991, in the premiere of Katharina Blum by Tilo Medek; Heidelberg Festival, 1994–95, as Mignon, by Thomas; Other roles include Carmen, Cenerentola, Strauss's Octavian and Composer, Selika in L'Africaine, and Honegger's Judith. *Recordings include:* Zulma in L'Italiana in Algeri.

McLEAN-MAIR, Kevin; British singer (tenor) and teacher; b. 7 Dec. 1962, St Albans; one s. *Education:* Royal Acad. of Music, Britten-Pears School, Aldeburgh, masterclasses with Tom Krause. *Career:* performed throughout the UK, including Barbican Hall, St James', Piccadilly, St John's, Smith Square, BBC Friday Night is Music Night and many choral socs; recitals in Lincoln, Bristol and Seattle; int. engagements in Canada, Germany, Netherlands (including Concertgebouw) and the USA; opera includes Attendant Spirit, Comus, Benslow Music Trust; Lucano and Nutrice, L'Incoronazione di Poppea, The Cavalli Baroque Ensemble; Ferrando, Così fan tutte, Dartington Hall; Chinese Man, The Fairy Queen, English Bach Festival at the Linbury Studio Theatre, Covent Garden 2001. *Recordings:* Dixit Dominus, The Songs of Ian Venables. *Honours:* Erna Spoorenberg Award for Oratorio, Netherlands 1996. *Address:* 50 Frederick Street, Hightown, Luton, Beds., LU2 7QS, England (home). *Telephone:* (7973) 393636 (home). *E-mail:* kevinmcleanmair@yahoo.co.uk (home).

McLEOD, John, FRAM, FTCL, LRAM, ARCM; Scottish composer, conductor, lecturer and publisher; *Artistic Director and CEO, Griffin Music*; b. 8 March 1934, Aberdeen, Scotland; m. Margaret Murray 1961; one s. one d. *Education:* Royal Acad. of Music, London, studied composition with Sir Lennox Berkeley, clarinet with Jack Brymer, Reginald Kell and Gervase de Peyer, conducting with Sir Adrian Boult, later influenced by Witold Lutoslawski who became a mentor. *Career:* Chief Conductor Perth Choral and Orchestral Socs 1965–72; Dir of Music, Merchiston Castle School, Edinburgh 1974–85; Conductor Edinburgh Royal Choral Union 1977–83; Visiting Lecturer, Royal Scottish Acad. of Music and Drama (now Royal Conservatoire of Scotland) 1985–89; Visiting Lecturer in Composition and Contemporary Music, Edinburgh Napier Univ. 1989–94; Visiting Composer, Edinburgh City Music School 1986–92; Ida Carroll Research Fellow, Royal Northern Coll. of Music 1988–89; Guest Conductor, Polish Radio and TV Symphony Orchestra of Krakow, as well as for various Scottish orchestras, including Royal Scottish Nat. Orchestra, BBC Scottish Symphony Orchestra and Nat. Youth Orchestra of Scotland; Dir of postgraduate course in composing for film and TV, Thames Valley Univ. and London Coll. of Music 1991–97; Visiting Prof., RAM, London 1993–97; freelance composer, conductor and lecturer 1997–; Artistic Dir and CEO Griffin Music; Dir, Performing Right Soc. 2000–04, British Acad. of Composers and Songwriters 2000–04; Council mem. Soc. for the Promotion of New Music 2000–02; Warden of Composers and Performers Section, Inc. Soc. of Musicians 2006–07; mem. Classical/Jazz Exec., British Acad. of Songwriters, Composers and Authors 2012–15. *Compositions include:* Lieder der Jugend for tenor and orchestra (Guinness Prize for British Composers) 1978, The Seasons of Dr Zhivago for baritone and orchestra (Royal Scottish Nat. Orchestra comm.) 1982, The Gokstad Ship for orchestra (Nat. Youth Orchestra of Scotland comm.) 1982, Stabat Mater for soloists, choirs and orchestra (Edinburgh Royal Choral Union comm.) 1986, Percussion Concerto (Evelyn Glennie soloist, Nat. Youth Orchestra of Scotland comm.) 1987, Piano Concerto (Peter Donohoe soloist, Perth Festival comm.) 1988, The Song of Dionysius (Evelyn Glennie comm., BBC Proms) 1989, The Seven Sacraments of Poussin for organ (Edinburgh Contemporary Arts comm.) 1991, The White Flame for baritone and piano (J.B. Priestley Estate comm.) 1994, The Chronicle of Saint Machar for baritone, choirs and orchestra (Aberdeen Bach Choir comm.) 1998, Thrashing the Sea God – a little Chinese opera for solo percussion (Colin Currie comm.) 1999, The Sun Dances for orchestra (Nat. Youth Orchestra of Scotland comm.) 2001, Symphonies of Stone and Water for solo piano and ensemble (Edinburgh Contemporary Arts comm.) 2001, Clarinet Concerto (Linda Merrick comm.) 2004, Chinese Whispers for brass ensemble (Fine Arts Brass comm.) 2005, Piano Sonata No. 4 (Sam Haywood comm.) 2006, Haflidi's Pictures for narrator and piano (Mark Tanner comm.) 2008, Guitar Concerto 2009, The Song of Leda for cello and piano (Edinburgh Contemporary Arts comm.) 2010, Fantasy on themes from Britten's 'Gloriana' for guitar (Ian Watt comm.) 2012, Fearful Tales for mezzo-soprano, viola and piano 2012, Piano Sonata No. 5 (Murray McLachlan comm.) 2013, Out of the Silence (Scottish Chamber Orchestra comm.) 2014, Songs from Above and Below (Live Music Now comm.) 2015); film scores for TV and cinema, including Michael Radford's Another Time, Another Place; works now commissioned, performed and recorded by leading artists, orchestras and at major int. festivals, including BBC Proms, Edinburgh, Aldeburgh, Canterbury, Perth, Aberdeen 'Sound' Festival and St Magnus, Orkney. *Honours:* Guinness Prize for British Composer 1979, British Music Educ. Award 1981, Gold Badge, British Acad. of Songwriters, Composers and Authors 2014. *Address:* Griffin Music, Hill House, 9 Redford Crescent, Edinburgh, EH13 0BS, Scotland (office). *Telephone:* (131) 441-3035 (office). *E-mail:* john.mcleod@btinternet.com. *Website:* www.johnmcleod.uk.com.

McLEOD, Linda; American singer (soprano); b. 29 Nov. 1952, Indiana. *Education:* Guildhall School, London. *Career:* sang with Opera for All, London, from 1978; English National Opera, as Sonia in War and Peace, as Donna Elvira, and Rusalka and in the premiere of Harvey's Inquest of Love, 1993; Brünnhilde in The Ring with Birmingham Touring Opera; Elisabeth de Valois and Tippett's Andromache for Opera North; Donna Anna for Scottish Opera; Washington Opera, 1992 as Wagne's Santa. *Recordings:* Video of Rusalka; Giovanna in Verdi's Ernani.

MacLEOD, Michael, BA; British/American music administrator; *General Director, Glimmerglass Opera*; b. Bogotá, Colombia. *Education:* Fettes Coll., Edinburgh, Scotland, Amherst Coll., Mass, USA. *Career:* Man. Dir John Eliot Gardiner's Monteverdi Choir, English Baroque Soloists, Orchestre Révolutionnaire et Romantique 1984–96; Exec. and Artistic Dir City of London Festival 1996–2001; Exec. Dir New Haven Symphony Orchestra 2001–05; Gen. and Artistic Dir Glimmerglass Opera 2005–(10). *Address:* Glimmerglass Opera, POB 191, Cooperstown, NY 13326, USA (office). *Telephone:* (607) 547-0700 (ext. 207) (office). *E-mail:* jscranton@glimmerglass.org (office). *Website:* www.glimmerglass.org (office).

McLIN, Lena Johnson, BMus; American composer, teacher, author and minister of religion; *Pastor, Holy Vessel Baptist Church*; b. 5 Sept. 1928, Chicago, Ill. *Education:* Booker T. Washington High School, Atlanta, Ga Spelman Coll., Atlanta, American Conservatory of Music, Chicago, Roosevelt Univ., Chicago and Chicago State Univ. *Career:* choral conductor for various community, school and church groups from 1951; accompanist Thomas Dorsey Choir, Pilgrim Baptist Church, Chicago 1952–53; founder and Dir, McLin Ensemble 1957–68; Minister of Music, Trinity Congregational Church, Chicago 1960s; Founder and Pastor, Holy Vessel Christian Center, Chicago 1980–; teacher, Julius H. Hess Upper Grade Center, Chicago 1959–60, Gurdon S. Hubbard High School, Chicago 1960–63, John Marshall Harlan Community Acad. High School, Chicago 1963–70; Head of Music Dept, Kenwood Acad., Chicago 1970–91; held choral workshops throughout USA; consultant, Westminster Choir Coll., Princeton, NJ. *Compositions include:* Impressions for piano 1957, And she Took a Ring and Placed it on his Finger 1963, A Summer Day for piano 1970, Free at Last: A Portrait of Martin Luther King Jr 1973, If I Could Give You All I Have 1986, Silence 1987, The Unlucky Apple 1987, My Love 1993, Christmas in Space 1997; choral music: All the Earth Sing Unto the Lord 1967, The Earth is the Lord's 1969, I Want Jesus to Walk With Me 1969, So Stands a College Tall of Higher Learning 1970, In This World 1970, The Colors of the Rainbow 1971, I am Somebody 1971, If They Ask You Why He Came 1971, If we Could Exchange Places 1971, I'm Moving Up 1971, We've Just Got to Have Peace All Over This World 1971, What Will You Put Under Your Christmas Tree? 1971, The Torch has been Passed 1971, For Jesus Christ is Born 1971, Psalm 100: Make a Joyful Noise 1971, Sanctus and Benedictus 1971, Psalm 117: Praise the Lord, All Ye Nations 1971, The Little Baby 1971, You and I Together 1971, Friendship 1972, Gwendolyn Brooks: A Musical Portrait 1972, New Born King 1972, Eucharist of the Soul 1972, Let the People Sing Praise Unto the Lord 1973, Winter, Spring, Summer, Autumn 1974, Memory 1976, Since He Came into my Life 1976, Challenge 1976, The Love of God 1976, Te Deum Laudamus 1976, This Land 1976, Christmas Time is Here Again 1978, Now that we are Leaving 1978, Two Introits 1978, Noel 1979, Reach Up! 1987, Introits and Responses for Worship 1990, Take Life's Challenge 1997, Makers of History 1998. *Publications:* Black Music in Church and School 1970, Pulse: A History of Music 1977; other published works include: Songs for Voice and Piano (collection of Art songs, Spirituals, and folk songs for solo voice and piano), The Christmas Cantata, The Church Cantata Songs: Don't Stop the World, When It's My Turn to Get On (light song), Follow Your First Mind, It's Usually Right Most of the Time (light song), I'm in Love, I'm Gonna Make it Anyway, I'll Be Your Friend, The Stoning of Stephen (cantata for male voices and male choirs only), Out of the Depths (anthem), Journey of Praise (instrumental march for orchestra). *Honours:* Nat. Black Music Caucus Outstanding Achievement Award 1980, Univ. of Chicago Outstanding Teacher Award 1983; scholarship American Conservatory of Music, Chicago 1951. *Address:* 6901 South Oglesby Street, Apartment 4A, Chicago, IL 60649-1827, USA (office). *Telephone:* (773) 493-3439 (office).

McMASTER, Sir Brian John, Kt, CBE, LLB; British arts administrator; b. 9 May 1943, Hitchin, Herts., England. *Education:* Wellington Coll., Univ. of Bristol. *Career:* with Int. Artists' Dept, EMI Ltd 1968–73; Controller of Opera Planning, ENO 1973–76; Gen. Admin., subsequently Man. Dir Welsh Nat. Opera 1976–91; Artistic Dir Vancouver Opera 1984–89; Festival Dir and CEO Edin. Int. Festival 1991–2006; mem. Bd Barbican Centre 2009–.

McMASTER, Zandra; British singer (mezzo-soprano); b. 26 May 1960, Ballymena, Northern Ireland. *Education:* Trinity Coll. of Music, London Opera Centre. *Career:* debut, Purcell Room, London 1983; sang Mahler's 4th Symphony in Madrid 1984; resident in Spain singing in concerts with most leading Spanish orchestras; Salzburg Mozarteum 1989–91, Concertgebouw Amsterdam 1990, US debut in Bernstein's 1st Symphony in Colorado 1991; Seville World Expo concert 1992 and Beethoven's Ninth in Berlin 1992; concerts in Europe, Asia and USA; regular recitals in Spain and UK; gala concerts with Edita Gruberova in Germany and Slovakia 2000–05; five gala concerts with Neil Schicoff in Switzerland 2003; concerts with BBC Symphony Orchestra, Lyon National, Berlin Symphony, Edmonton Symphony, NDR Hannover, Flemish Radio, Budapest Symphony, Israel Sinfonietta, Norway Radio, Aalborg Symphony, Prague Philharmonia, Gulbenkian Lisboa, etc under conductors including Jiri Belohlavek, Sir Colin Davis, Jun Märkl, Miguel Harth-Bedoya, Támas Vásáry, John Nelson, Adam Fischer, Josep Pons, Lawrence Foster, Juanjo Mena, Ari Rasilainen, Uri Segal, Yaron Traub and others. *Recordings include:* Lucia di Lammermoor by Donizetti with Edita Gruberova and Josep Bros conducted by Friedrich Haider, Beethoven's Ninth Symphony with Lyon Symphony Orchestra and Jun Märkl, Songs by Antón Garcia Abril with pianist Alessio Bax 2012, Mahler's 8th Symphony with the Spanish Nat. Orchestra and Josep Pons (DVD) 2013. *Current Management:* c/o Conciertos Augusto, Calle Viento No 15, 2B, Majadahonda, 28220 Madrid,

Spain. *Telephone:* (916) 340205. *E-mail:* info@conciertosaugusto.com. *Website:* www.conciertosaugusto.com. *E-mail:* info@zandramcmaster.com (office).

MacMILLAN, Sir James Loy, Kt, CBE; British composer, conductor and lecturer in music; *Principal Guest Conductor, Netherlands Radio Kamer Filharmonie;* b. 16 July 1959, Kilwinning, Ayrshire, Scotland; m. Lynne Frew; one s. two d. *Education:* Univs of Edinburgh and Durham. *Career:* fmr Lecturer, Music Dept, Univ. of Edinburgh, Univ. of Manchester; Lecturer, Royal Scottish Acad. of Music and Drama; performances of his music by the New Music Group of Scotland, Circle, Nomos, Lontano and Scottish Chamber Orchestra; comms from Edinburgh Contemporary Arts Trust, The Traverse Theatre, Scottish Chamber Orchestra, Paragon Ensemble, Cappela Nova, Scottish Chamber Choir; BBC Proms Comm., The Confession of Isobel Gowdie, BBC Scottish Symphony Orchestra; featured composer, Musica Nova Festival, Glasgow 1990; Seven Last Words from the Cross premiered on BBC TV, Easter 1994; Composer and Conductor, BBC Philharmonic Orchestra 2000–09; featured composer, BBC Weekend, The Barbican, London 2005; Prin. Guest Conductor, Netherlands Radio Kamer Filharmonie 2010–; Patron St Mary's Music School, Edinburgh, London Oratory School Schola Cantorum, The British Art Music Series. *Compositions include:* Study on Two Planes for cello and piano 1981, Three Dawn Rituals for ensemble 1983, Beatus Vir for chorus and organ 1983, The Road to Ardtalla for ensemble 1983, Songs of a Just War for soprano and ensemble 1984, Two Visions of Hoy for oboe and ensemble 1986, The Keening for orchestra 1986, Festival Fanfares for brass band 1986, Litanies of Iron and Stone for ensemble with tape 1987, Untold for ensemble 1987, Visions of a November Spring for string quartet 1988, Busqueda for eight actors, three sopranos, speaker and ensemble 1988, Into the Ferment for orchestra 1988, Cantos Sagrados for chorus and organ 1989, The Exorcism of Rio Sumpul for chamber ensemble 1989, As Mothers See Us for ensemble 1990, The Berserking piano concerto 1990, The Confession of Isobel Gowdie for orchestra 1990, Soweton Spring for wind band 1990, Catherine's Lullabies for chorus and ensemble 1990, Scots Song for soprano and ensemble 1991, Tuireadh for clarinet and string quartet 1991, Tourist Variations (one-act chamber opera) 1992, Visitatio Sepulchri for seven singers and chamber orchestra 1993, Vs for orchestra 1993, Seven Last Words from the Cross for choir and strings 1994, Inés de Castro (opera) 1996, Triduum (for London Symphony Orchestra) 1996–97, Symphony: Vigil, Raising Sparks for soprano and chamber ensemble 1997, 14 Little Pictures for piano trio 1997, Why is this Night Different? for string quartet 1997, Gaudeamus in loci pace for organ 1998, Quickening for soloists, chorus and orchestra 1998, Magnificat 1999, Mass 2000, Parthenogenesis, scena 2000, Birds of Rhiannon for orchestra 2001, Nunc Dimittis 2001, A Deep But Dazzling Darkness violin concerto 2001–02, Symphony No. 3: Silence (Classical BRIT Award for Contemporary Music 2006) 2002, Le Tombeau de Georges Rouault for organ 2003, A Scotch Bestiary organ concerto 2003–04, Lauda alla Vergine Maria for chorus 2004, Sun-Dogs for chorus a cappella 2006, The Sacrifice (opera) 2007, St John Passion 2008, Violin Concerto 2010, Clemency 2011, Woman of the Apocalypse 2012, St Luke Passion 2013, Percussion Concerto No. 2 2014, Symphony No. 4 2015. *Recordings include:* Confession of Isobel Gowdie, Veni Veni Emmanuel, Cello Concerto, Seven Last Words from the Cross. *Honours:* Hon. Fellow, Blackfriars Hall, Oxford; Hon. Patron London Chamber Orchestra's LCO New: Explore project 2008; Hon. Pres. Bearsden Choir; Hon. DUniv (Paisley) 1995; Hon. DLitt (Strathclyde) 1996; Gramophone Award 1993, Classic CD Award 1993, South Bank Show Award for Classical Music 1997, Evening Standard Classical Music Award for Outstanding Artistic Achievement, Ivor Novello Classical Music Award 2009, British Composer Award for Liturgical Music 2009. *Current Management:* c/o Catherine Gibbs, Intermusica, 36 Graham Street, London, N1 8GJ, England. *Telephone:* (20) 7608-9900. *Fax:* (20) 7490-3263. *E-mail:* mail@intermusica.co.uk. *Website:* www.intermusica.co.uk.

McNAIR, Sylvia; American singer (soprano); b. 23 June 1956, Mansfield, Ohio. *Education:* India University. *Career:* sang in Messiah at Indianapolis, 1980; Euroean debut in the premiere of Kelterborn's Ophelia, Schwetzingen, 1984; Concert appearances in Cleveland, Baltimore, San Francisco, Detroit, Montreal, Indianapolis, Atlanta, St Louis, Washington and Los Angeles; New York at the Carnegie, Avery Fisher and Alice Tully Halls; Season 1991–92 with the Chicago Symphony under Solti, Berlin Philharmonic under Haitink, City of Birmingham Symphony under Rattle, Concentus Musicus under Harnoncourt and London Philharmonic under Masur; Mozart's Ilia and Servilia with the Monteverdi Choir and Orchestra conducted by John Eliot Gardiner; US opera appearances as Pamina at Santa Fe, Ilia; Hero (Béatrice et Bénédict) and Morgana in Alcina at St Louis; Sang Ilia in Lyon and Strasbourg and Susana with Netherlands Opera; Pamina at the Deutsche Oper Berlin and the Vienna Staatsoper; Glyndebourne Festival 1989 as Anne Trulove; Covent Garden and Salzburg debuts as Ilia in Idomeneo; Season 1991–92 with Bastille Opéra (Paris) and Metropolitan Opera (as Marzelline in Fidelio) debuts; Covent Garden 1992, in Rossini's Il Viaggio a Reims; Sang Poppea at the 1993 Salzburg Festival and returned for Pamina in Die Zauberflöte, 1997; The Daughter in the US premiere of Lidholm's A Dream Play, Santa Fe, 1998; Sang Cleopatra in Handel's Giulio Cesare at the New York Met, 1999; Messiah at the 1999 Salzburg Festival. *Recordings:* Albums with Neville Marriner, Roger Norrington, John Eliot Gardiner, Colin Davis, Kurt Masur, James Levine and Bernard Haitink; Idomeneo with John Eliot Gardiner (Deutsche Grammophon). *Current Management:* JEJ Artists, 218 Wimbledon Place, Macon, GA 31211, USA. *Telephone:* (478) 742-1162. *Fax:*

(646) 304-1188. *E-mail:* janet@jejartists.com. *Website:* www.jejartists.com; www.sylviamcnair.com.

MacNEIL, Walter; American singer (tenor); b. 1957, New York; s. of Cornell MacNeil. *Career:* sang at the San Francisco Opera from 1983, as Froh, Rodrigo in Otello and Alfredo; Sang Alfredo at New Orleans 1984, with his father as Germont père; Carnegie Hall 1985, in Semele, and Don Ottavio at Milwaukee 1986; Glyndebourne 1987–88 and Metropolitan 1989, as Alfredo; Sang Aubry in Der Vampyr by Marschner at the 1992 Wexford Festival; Other roles include Tamino (Connecticut Opera, 1991), Ruggiero in La Rondine and Nadir in Les pêcheurs de Perles (Honolulu 1987).

McPHEE, George, MBE, BMus, DipMusEd, FRCO, FRSCM; British organist and composer; *Director of Music, Paisley Abbey;* b. 10 Nov. 1937, Glasgow, Scotland; m.; one s. two d. *Education:* Royal Scottish Acad. of Music and Drama (RSAMD), Univ. of Edinburgh, studied organ with Herrick Bunney and Fernando Germani. *Career:* Asst Organist, St Giles Cathedral, Edinburgh 1959–63; Dir of Music, Paisley Abbey 1963–; Sr Lecturer, RSAMD 1963–92; Visiting Prof. of Organ, St Andrew's Univ. 1992–2013; Conductor Scottish Chamber Choir 1971–75, Kilmarnock and Dist Choral Union 1975–84; has conducted and played organ with all major Scottish orchestras; numerous recital tours of USA, Canada and Europe; Pres. Glasgow Soc. of Organists 1971–72, Hon. Pres. 1995–; mem. Inc. Soc. of Musicians (Pres. 1999–2000), Royal Coll. of Organists (Vice-Pres. 2005). *Film:* Holiday Scotland 1964. *Compositions:* Magnificat and Nunc Dimittis (Paisley Service), Make We Joy, Whence is That Goodly Fragrance, The New Oxford Song Book (ed.), The Saltire Two-Part Song Book. *Honours:* Hon. Fellow, Guild of Church Musicians 2006; Hon. DUniv (Univ. of Paisley) 1997; Limpus Prize 1961. *Address:* 17 Main Road, Castlehead, Paisley, PA2 6AJ, Scotland (home). *Telephone:* (141) 889-3528 (home). *E-mail:* profmcphee@aol.com (home). *Website:* www.georgemcphee.co.uk.

McPHERSON, Gordon, DMus; Scottish composer and accordion player; *Head of Composition, Royal Scottish Academy of Music and Drama;* b. 27 Aug. 1965, Dundee. *Education:* Univ. of York, Royal Northern Coll. of Music. *Career:* composition teacher, Univ. of Edinburgh; composer-in-residence, Royal Scottish Acad. of Music and Drama; Lecturer in 20th-Century Music and Analysis, Univ. of St Andrews; Head of Composition, Royal Scottish Acad. of Music and Drama 1999–. *Compositions include:* Oh, why should I cry upon my wedding day? 1985, String Quartet No. 2 'Dead Roses' 1990, Maps and Diagrams of our Pain 1990, Handguns: a Suite 1995, The Baby Bear's Bed 1998, String Quartet No. 3 'The Original Soundtrack' 1999, Upbeat Destroyer (guitar concerto), Born of Funk and the Fear of Failing (guitar concerto) 2000–01, The Waterworks (multi-media), Morning Drunk and Buzzard, The New Black 2005. *Recordings include:* Detours (two-vol. collection). *Honours:* Creative Scotland Award 2003. *Address:* Royal Scottish Academy of Music and Drama, 100 Renfrew Street, Glasgow, G2 3DB, Scotland (office). *E-mail:* g.mcpherson@rsamd.ac.uk (office). *Website:* www.rsamd.ac.uk (office).

McTIER, Duncan Paul, BSc, ARCM; double bass player and teacher; b. 21 Nov. 1954, Stourbridge, Worcestershire, England; m. Yuko Inoue 1984. *Education:* King Edward VI Grammar School, Stourbridge, Bristol University. *Career:* Member, BBC Symphony Orchestra, 1975–77; Principal Bass, Netherlands Chamber Orchestra, 1977–84; Senior Double Bass Tutor, Royal Northern College of Music, 1984–; Professor of Double Bass, Royal College of Music, 1987–91; Double Bass Consultant, Royal Scottish Academy of Music and Drama, 1991–; Solo appearances with Netherlands Chamber Orchestra, Concertgebouw Chamber Orchestra, Bournemouth Sinfonietta, Netherlands Philharmonic Orchestra, Orchestre Regional d'Auvergne, Barcelona Municipal Orchestra, Northern Sinfonia Orchestre de Chambre Detmold, Nippon Telemann Ensemble of Osaka, Lausanne Chamber Orchestra, BBC Concert Orchestra, Scottish Chamber Orchestra, Bournemouth Symphony Orchestra; World Premieres of Concertos written by Peter Maxwell Davies, John Casken and Derek Bourgeois; Recitals and master classes throughout Europe and Japan. *Recordings:* Bottesini Grand Duo for Philips; Various pieces with Paganini Ensemble for Denon; Dutch television recordings of Bottesini Grand Duo and 2nd Concerto; Dvořák String Quintet and Waltzes with Chilingirian Quartet (Chandos); Extensive radio recordings. *Honours:* 1st Prize Winner, Isle of Man International Double Bass Competition, 1982.

MACURDY, John; American singer (bass); b. 18 March 1929, Detroit, Mich.; m. Justine Mae Votypka; one s. one d. *Education:* Wayne State Univ.; singing with Avery Crew, Detroit. *Career:* debut in New Orleans 1952, in Samson et Dalila; appearances in Baltimore, Houston, Philadelphia, San Francisco and Santa Fe; NYC Opera debut 1959, in Weill's Street Scene; Met Opera, New York from 1962 as the Commendatore, Crespel in Les Contes d'Hoffmann and Rocco in Fidelio; sang in the premieres of Antony and Cleopatra 1966 and Mourning Becomes Elektra 1967; first local performance of Les Troyens 1973; Paris Opéra 1973, as Arkel in Pelléas et Mélisande; La Scala Milan 1974, as Rocco in Fidelio; Salzburg Festival 1977–78, as the Commendatore in Don Giovanni; Milan 1984 as the Landgrave in Tannhäuser; Seattle Opera 1986, as Hagen and Hunding in the Ring; Met 1987, as Fasolt in Das Rheingold; Hunding at San Francisco 1990; appearances at Aix and Orange Festivals, Hollywood Bowl, Miami Opera and Scottish Opera; season 1992 in Billy Budd at the Met, as Trulove in The Rake's Progress at Aix-en-Provence, as Fiesco in Simon Boccanegra at Montpellier, The Flying Dutchman in Buenos Aires as Daland and L'Africaine in Marseille; sang Fafner in Das Rheingold at Marseille 1996; Hunding at the Met 1996; sang Death Scene from Boris

Godunov at 99th anniversary celebrations of the Ballets Russes 2008; 1,011 performances as leading bass, 1,780 operatic performances; mem. Bohemian Club. *Television:* role of Commendatore in Mozart's Don Giovanni (first colour broadcast of NBC Opera) 1961. *Recordings include:* Don Giovanni, Béatrice et Bénédict, Otello, The Rev. Hale in Ward's The Crucible, featured in album of 50 years of live recordings from the Archive of Teatro alla Scala. *Honours:* City of Detroit Medal 1969, Rockefeller Foundation Grant 1959, Wayne State Univ. Arts Achievement Award 2003. *Address:* 73 Tall Oaks Court, Stamford, CT 06903, USA. *Telephone:* (203) 322-8848. *Fax:* (203) 321-8535.

McVEAGH, Diana Mary, ARCM, GRSM; British writer on music; b. 6 Sept. 1926, Ipoh, Malaya; m. Dr C. W. Morley 1950 (died 1994). *Education:* Malvern Girls' Coll., Royal Coll. of Music, London. *Career:* Asst Ed. Musical Times 1965–67; Exec. Cttee of the New Grove 1970–76; contrib. to The Times 1947–69, also to Musical Times, The Listener, Records and Recordings; Exec. Cttee of the GKN English Song Award 1982–89; mem. Royal Musical Asscn Council 1961–76; Vice-Pres. Elgar Soc. *Publications:* Elgar (Dent) 1955, Gerald Finzi: His Life and Music 2005, 2010, Elgar the Music Maker 2007; contrib. to New Grove Dictionary of Music (articles on Elgar and Finzi) 1980 and 2000 edns, Twentieth-Century English Masters (MacMillan) 1986, The Oxford Dictionary of National Biography 2004. *Honours:* North American British Music Studies Asscn Diana McVeagh Prize est. in her honour for Best Book on British Music. *Address:* Ladygrove, The Lee, Great Missenden, Bucks., HP16 9NA, England. *E-mail:* dianamcveagh@waitrose.com.

McVICAR, Sir David, Kt, FRSAMD; British stage director; b. 1966, Glasgow, Scotland. *Education:* Williamwood High School, Royal Scottish Acad. of Music and Drama. *Career:* main productions: Le Nozze de Figaro, Faust, Die Zauberflöte, Rigoletto (Covent Garden), Cosi Fan Tutte (Strasbourg), Les Contes d'Hoffmann (Salzburg Festival), Giulio Cesare, Carmen, La Bohème (Glyndebourne), Billy Budd (Lyric Opera of Chicago), Macbeth (Kirov Opera, Covent Garden, Kennedy Center, Metropolitan Opera, New York), A Midsummer Night's Dream, Don Giovanni, Agrippina (La Monnaie, Brussels), La Clemenza di Tito, The Rape of Lucretia (Aldeburgh Festival/ENO), Alcina, Manon, Tosca (ENO), Der Rosenkavalier, Don Giovanni, Hamlet, Sweeney Todd, Il Re Pastore (Opera North), Idomeneo, Der Rosenkavalier, Madama Butterfly (Scottish Opera), Tamerlano (Düsseldorf), L'Incoronazione di Poppea, Semele (Paris), La Clemenza di Tito (Copenhagen), Agrippina (ENO), The Turn of the Screw (Maryinsky Theatre, Moscow) (Golden Mask Award for Best Opera Production 2007), La Traviata (Scottish Opera); season 2015 included productions of Die Entführung aus dem Serail and Carmen at Glyndebourne and Il Trovotore at the Met; 2016 productions included Roberto Devereux (Met), Manon (Dallas Opera) and Cosi fan tutte (Opera Australia). *Radio:* guest on Desert Island Discs (BBC Radio 4) 5 Oct. 2008. *Honours:* ranked by The Independent amongst the 100 most influential gay and lesbian people in Britain 2007. *Current Management:* c/o Tracey Elliston, Judy Daish Associates, 2 St Charles Place, London, W10 6EG, England. *Telephone:* (20) 8964-8811. *Fax:* (20) 8964-8966. *E-mail:* tracey@judydaish.com. *Website:* www.judydaish.com.

McWILLIAM, Fergus; British horn player; b. Loch Ness, Scotland. *Education:* studied in Canada with John Simonelli, Frederick Rizner and Eugene Rittich, in the Netherlands with Adriaan van Woudenberg and in Sweden with Wilhelm Lanzky-Otto. *Career:* solo debut aged 15 with Toronto Symphony Orchestra under Seiji Ozawa; mem. several Canadian orchestras and chamber music ensembles 1972–79; mem. Detroit Symphony Orchestra under Antal Dorati 1979–82; mem. Bavarian Radio Symphony 1982–85; mem. Berlin Philharmonic 1985–; mem. Berlin Philharmonic Wind Quintet 1988–; teaches at music schools including Berlin Philharmonic Orchestra Acad.; Trustee Berlin Philharmonic Foundation. *Recordings inlcude:* albums with Berlin Philarmonic Wind Quintet: Spiegel im Spiegel 2005, Franz Danzi Wind Quintets, Mozart – Music for Piano and Wind Quintet, 20th Century Hungarian Music, Romantic Music for Wind Quintet, Four Seasons Cycle, Mozart and Beethoven: Quintets for Piano and Winds. *Publications:* Blow Your Own Horn!: Horn Heresies 2011. *Address:* c/o Mosaic Press, 1252 Speers Rd, Units 1–2, Oakville, Ont. L6L 5N9, Canada (office). *Telephone:* (905) 825-2130 (office). *Fax:* (905) 825-2130 (office). *E-mail:* info@mosaic-press.com (office). *Website:* www.mosiac-press.com (office); www.windquintet.com/en/mcwilliam; www.fergusmcwilliam.com (home).

MADDALENA, James; American singer (baritone); b. 1954, Lynn, MA. *Education:* New England Conservatory of Music. *Career:* debut with Rogers and Hammerstein medley with the Boston Pops Orchestra, 1974; From 1974 has appeared in a complete cycle of Bach's cantatas at Emmanuel Church Boston, conducted by Craig Smith; Founder member of the Liederkreis Ensemble, Naumburg Awad, 1980; Association with director Peter Sellars from 1981 includes the title role in Don Giovanni and leading roles in Handel's Orlando, American Repertory Theatre, 1982; Così fan tutte, Castle Hill Festival, 1984; Haydn's Armida, New Hampshire Symphony, 1983; Giulio Cesare and the Brecht/Weill Kleine Mahagonny, Pepsico Summerfare, 1985; Soloist in Messiah at Carnegie Hall 1984, with Banchetto Musicale; Sang the title role in the world premiere of Nixon in China by John Adams, Houston, 1987, repeated at Edinburgh 1988 and The Captain in the premiere of Adams's The Death of Klinghoffer, Brussels 1991, and at Lyon, Vienna and New York; Has appeared as Mozart's Count in the Sellars version of Le nozze di Figaro, seen at Purchase, New York and Papageno at Glyndebourne, 1990; created Merlin in Tippett's New Year at Houston 1989 and in the British premiere at Glyndebourne; Season 1992 in Nixon in China at Adelaide and

Frankfurt, Don Alfonso at Glyndebourne; Sang in Susa's Transformations at St Louis, 1997; Frédéric in Lakmé at New Orleans, 1997. Recordings. Brahms Liebeslieder Waltzes, with Liederkreis; Nixon in China and The Death of Klinghoffer. *Current Management:* c/o Munro Artists Management, 786 Dartmouth Street, South Dartmouth, MA 02748, USA. *Telephone:* (508) 993-9011. *Fax:* (508) 993-9044. *E-mail:* Operamom@aol.com.

MADDISON, Dorothy, BMus; singer (lyric coloratura soprano); b. 12 Jan. 1956, Fergus Falls, MN, USA; m. Ian Maddison 1979. *Education:* St Olaf Coll., Minnesota, Guildhall School of Music and Drama, London, England, Britten-Pears School, Aldeburgh and studied with Audrey Langford and Andrew Feidld at Cantica Voice Studio, London. *Career:* debut in Purcell Room, London 1986 with Graham Johnson, piano; freelance concert and operatic singer; operatic roles include The Queen of Night in The Magic Flute; Zaide; Madames Herz and Silberklang in The Impressario, Mozart; Norina in Don Pasquale; Adina in Elixir of Love; Rita by Donizetti; Tytania in Midsummer Night's Dream, Britten; Mable, Pirates of Penzance; Zerbinetta, Ariadne auf Naxos, Strauss; The Nightingale, Stravinsky; oratorio repertoire: includes works by Bach, Handel, Haydn, Mozart, Mendelssohn, Orff; recital repertoire includes standard works by European composers, also songs from the American Midwest, a programme featuring works by Minnesota composers Argento, Dougherty, Franklin, Larsen, Paulus, first given 1988, Purcell Room, London with Robin Bowman, piano; appearances with English Bach Festival, New Sadler's Wells Opera Company, Opera Factory, London Opera Players; mem. Equity. *Honours:* Guildhall School Walter Hyde Memorial Prize.

MADER-TODOROVA, Marina; singer (soprano); b. 20 Aug. 1948, Silistra, Bulgaria. *Education:* studied in Varna, Sofia and Vienna. *Career:* sang at first in opera at Varna then Mainz and Bremen 1976–77 as Desdemona and Micaela; Gelsenkirchen 1977–80 as Elisabeth de Valois, Ariadne and Tosca; further appearances at Dortmund 1980–83, Hamburg, Stuttgart, Frankfurt and Basle; engaged at the Deutsche Oper am Rhein 1984–86, Graz, 1984–89, notably as Eva, Amelia in Un Ballo in Maschera, Leonara in Il Trovatore, Agathe and Ariadne; further appearances at the Deutsche Oper Berlin, Budapest, Mannheim, Palermo, Zürich, Copenhagen and Liège; other roles have included Butterfly, Elisabeth in Tannhäuser, Elsa, Mozart's Fiordiligi and Countess, Mimi and Arabella; many concert appearances.

MADGE, Geoffrey Douglas; Australian concert pianist and academic; *Professor of Classical and Contemporary Piano Repertoire, Royal Conservatorium of Music, The Hague;* b. 3 Oct. 1941, Adelaide; m.; one s. one d. *Education:* Elder Conservatorium Univ. of Adelaide with Clemens Leski, studied with Geza Anda (Lucerne), Peter Solymos (Budapest), Eduardo Del Pueyo (Brussels). *Career:* debuts, London, Amsterdam, Cologne 1969, Budapest 1970; toured Australia as a pianist in a piano trio 1959–63; Prof. of Classical and Contemporary Piano Repertoire and Head of Piano Dept, Royal Conservatorium of Music, The Hague –2005, Guest Prof. 2005–; Int. Soc. for Contemporary Music Festival, Athens 1979, first performance of 32 piano pieces by Skalkottas; annual Holland Festival, Utrecht 1982, second complete performance of Kaikhosru Sorabji's Opus Clavicembalisticum, first complete anthology of F. Busoni's music for solo piano 1988, complete piano concertos of Medther and Skalkottas; co-f. Camerata Busoni Ensemble 2005–. *Compositions:* Viola Sonata 1963, String Quartet 1965, Violin Sonatina 1966, Monkeys in a Cage (ballet, premiere Sydney Opera house 1977) 1976, Etude for two pianists 1977, Tendrils of the Rock (three movements for piano) 1979, Piano Concerto (premiere Amsterdam 1980) 1979. *Recordings:* first recording of Opus Clavicembalisticum by K. Sorabji 1983, first complete anthology of F. Busoni's music for solo piano 1988, first recording of Skalkottas 1st, 2nd and 3rd Piano Concertos 1999, 2005, 2004. *Honours:* Prix du Président de la République, France 1977, Edison Awards, Netherlands 1977, 1988, Schallplatten Preis, Germany 1984, 1988, 2002, 2004, Caecilia Prize, Belgium 1988, Gloria Artis Silver Medal for Merits to Culture, Poland 2005. *Address:* Van Beuningenstraat 77, 2582 KL Den Haag, Netherlands (office). *Telephone:* (70) 355-4374 (office). *E-mail:* madge@xs4all.nl (office). *Website:* www.xs4all.nl/~madge (office); www.cameratabusoni.com (office).

MADLALA, Njabulo; South African singer (baritone); b. 27 Jan. 1982, Inanda Township, Durban. *Education:* Guildhall School of Music and Drama, London, Cardiff Int. Acad. of Voice. *Career:* mem. of Glyndebourne on Tour Chorus 2009; many appearances including: Hawaii Performing Arts Festival, Sadler's Wells Theatre, Royal Opera House 2, Cheltenham Festival, Opera Holland Park, Montepulciano Festival, Oxford Lieder Festival, Scottish Opera, Queen Elizabeth Hall, London; supported by Oppenheimer Memorial Trust, South African Nat. Arts Council, Sir Peter Moores Foundation, Countess of Munster Trust, Music Benevolent Fund. *Honours:* Kathleen Ferrier Competition First Prize 2010; Britten Pears Young Artist, Samling Foundation Scholar, Kenneth Loveland Gift Prize. *Current Management:* James Black Management, The Old Grammar School, High Street, Rye, East Sussex, TN31 7JF, England; Williams-Ros Agency, 22 Wadley Road, Glenwood, Durban, 4001, South Africa. *Telephone:* (1797) 224668. *Fax:* (31) 2060432. *E-mail:* james@jamesblackmanagement.com; charon@wragency.co.za. *Website:* www.jamesblackmanagement.com; www.wragency.co.za.

MADRA, Barbara; singer (soprano); b. 1958, Koszian, Poznań, Poland. *Education:* studied in Poznań. *Career:* sang at first with the Poznań Opera then from 1980 at the Brussels Opera, notably as Mimi, Violetta, Fiordiligi, Elisabeth de Valois, Mozart's Vitellia and Arminda, the Trovatore Leonora and Amelia Grimaldi; guest appearances in Geneva, Lausanne, at the Holland

Festival, Buenos Aires, Barcelona and Toulouse (Donna Elvira, 1990); sang Tatiana at Zürich 1990 and at La Scala in Rimsky's Tale of Tsar Saltan, and as Eva in Die Meistersinger. *Address:* c/o Théâtre Royale, 4 Leopoldstrasse, 1000 Brussels, Belgium.

MADROSZKIEWICZ, Joanna Dorota, MA; Polish violinist; b. 22 March 1956, Szczecin; one s. two d. *Education:* Akademia Muzyczna Gdansk and Hochschule für Musik, Vienna. *Career:* engagements in Geneva, Prague, Lublin, Naples; concerts with Vienna Symphony Orchestra, Polish National Philharmonie, London Mozart Players, Residentre Orkest, Austria Radio Orchestra, Deutsche Kammerakad; numerous recitals; debut at Salzburg Festival as a violin soloist in Weill's Violin Concerto with Vienna Philharmonic Orchestra. *Recordings:* Schubert, Haydn, Beethoven, Wieniawski. *Honours:* Best Young Artist of Poland Award 1977, Commander of the Order of Polonia Restituta 1994.

MADZAR, Aleksandar; Serbian pianist; b. 1968, Belgrade, Yugoslavia. *Education:* Belgrade Academy of Music, studied with Eliso Virsaladze in Moscow, at the Strasbourg Conservatory and with Daniel Blumenthal in Brussels. *Career:* frequent appearances from 1985 with leading orchestras in France, Germany, Italy, Spain, Scandinavia and the UK; Berlin Philharmonic debut 1990 and further engagements with the Chamber Orchestra of Europe, Royal Philharmonic, Leipzig Gewandhaus, Bremen Philharmonic Orchestra and Czech Philharmonic 1996; further engagements include visits to the Scottish Chamber Orchestra and the Aldeburgh festival; chamber Concerts in Munich and Italy; recitals at Salzburg, Davos, Bad Kissingen and Ivo Pogorelich Festivals and at the Théâtre de la Ville in Paris; Chamber music collaborations in Boston, New York (Carnegie Hall), Milan, Amsterdam Concertgebouw, Vienna Musikverein, and South Africa. *Recordings include:* Prokoviev Violin Sonatas with Kyoko Takezawa, Chopin Concertos and solo works by Ravel, Two concertos by Erwin Schulhoff, Chabrier's music for two pianos. *Honours:* winner, Barenreiter Prize at the International Mozart Competition, Salzburg 1985, winner, Ferruccio Busoni Competition 1989, prizewinner, Leeds International Piano Competition 1996.

MAE, Vanessa; British violinist; b. (Vanessa-Mae Vanakorn Nicholson), 27 Oct. 1978, Singapore. *Education:* Cen. Conservatoire, Beijing, People's Repub. of China, Royal Coll. of Music, UK, studied with Lin Yao Ji and Felix Andrievsky. *Career:* concerto debut aged ten, Philharmonic Orchestra 1989; first nat. tour of UK with Tchaikovsky Concerto 1990; first int. tour with London Mozart Players 1990; released three classical recordings with orchestra (youngest artist to record both Tchaikovsky and Beethoven Violin Concertos) 1990–92; over 400 live performances in the Middle East, South Africa, China, SE Asia, Russia, Europe, Baltic States, Cen. Asia, USA, Cen. and S America; The Classical Tour 1997, Int. Red Hot Tour 1995, Storm on World Tour 1998; performed at Hong Kong to China Reunification Ceremony 1996, exclusively for HM The Queen, Buckingham Palace 1998, at 50th Anniversary of Geneva Conventions 1999; opened Classical Brit Awards, Royal Albert Hall 2000; collaborated on soundtrack for Walt Disney film Mulan; catwalk debut with Jean-Paul Gaultier; frequent TV appearances and participant in crossover concerts; involved in work with ICRC, participated in TV Campaign Even Wars Have Limits. *Recordings include:* Tchaikovsky and Beethoven Concertos 1990, The Violin Player (quadruple platinum) 1994, The Classical Album I 1996, China Girl: The Classical Album II 1997, Storm 1997, The Original Four Seasons 2000, Vanessa Mae: The Classical Collection Part I 2000, Subject to Change 2001, Choreography 2004. *Film:* Arabian Nights 2000. *Achievements include:* competed for Thailand in Giant Slalom at 2014 Sochi Winter Olympics. *Honours:* BAMBI Top Int. Classical Artist Award, Echo Klassik Award for Bestselling Album of the Year 1995, World Music Award for Best Selling Classical Artist 1996. *Current Management:* Agency Group Ltd, 361-373 City Road, London, EC1V 1PQ, England.

MAFFEO, Gianni; singer (baritone); b. 30 March 1939, Vigevano, Milan, Italy. *Education:* Liceo Musiale di Vercelli. *Career:* debut singing Tonion in Pagliacci with the Associazione Lirico Compagnia, 1961; many appearances at such opera centres as La Scala Milan, Genoa, Palermo, Turin and Verona, 1973; sang Schaunard in the Zeffirelli/Karajan Bohème at La Scala, 1963; guest engagements at Vienna, Prague, Rouen, Monte Carlo, Brno, Lisbon, Munich and the NYC Opera; further appearances at Toulouse, Nice, Bordeaux and Frankfurt as Marcello, Sharpless, Germont, Count Luna and Rigoletto. *Recordings:* Madama Butterfly, La Bohème.

MÁGA, Othmar; Czech conductor; b. 30 June 1929, Brno. *Education:* Stuttgart Hochschule für Musik, Tubingen Univ., Accademia Chigiana at Siena with Paul van Kempen, studied with Sergiu Celibidache. *Career:* conducted the Göttingen Symphony Orchestra 1963–67, Nuremberg Symphony 1968–70; Gen. Music Dir, Bochum 1971–82; Artistic Dir, Odense Symphony Orchestra, Denmark; Permanent Conductor, Orchestra of the Pomeriggi Musicali de Milano 1987–90; Prof., Folkswangschule at Essen; Chief Conductor, KBS-Symphony Orchestra in Seoul, Republic of Korea 1992–96; guest conductor with leading orchestras in Europe, Japan and America. *Current Management:* Musicontact Egbert Zinner, Kirchenallee 22, 20099 Hamburg, Germany. *E-mail:* service@musicontact.de. *Website:* www.musicontact.de. *E-mail:* contact@othmar-maga.de. *Website:* www.othmar-maga.de.

MAGEAU, Mary, BMus, MMus; composer and harpsichordist; b. 4 Sept. 1934, Milwaukee, WI, USA. *Education:* DePaul Univ., Chicago, Univ. of Michigan. *Career:* faculty mem., Queensland Conservatory 1987–91; Queensland Univ.

of Technology 1992–95; founder mem., Brisbane Baroque Trio. *Compositions include:* Concerto for harpsichord and strings 1978, Australia's Animals for piano 1978, Concert Pieces for violin, cello and piano 1984, Indian Summer for youth orchestra 1986, Concerto Grosso 1987, Australis 1788 (music drama) 1987, Triple Concerto for violin, cello, piano and orchestra 1990, Suite for strings 1991, An Early Autumn's Dreaming for orchestra 1993, Dialogues for clarinet, viola, cello and piano 1994, The Furies for piano and orchestra 1995. *Honours:* Alienor Harpsichord Composition Award 1994.

MAGEE, Emily; American singer (soprano); b. 1968, New York. *Education:* University of Indiana with Margaret Harshaw. *Career:* debut as Fiordiligi in Cosi fan Tutte, Chicago 1994; European debut as Fiordiligi, Paris Opéra 1996; sang Elsa in Lohengrin, Berlin Staatsoper 1996, Châtelet, Paris, and Bayreuth Festival 1997; Covent Garden debut as Jenůfa 2001; further engagements at Portland and San Diego Operas, La Scala, Opéra Bastille, Vienna Staatsoper and Florence; other roles include Countess in The Marriage of Figaro, and Donna Elvira, Marguerite in Faust, Poppea, Agathe, Desdemona and Arabella, Liu in Turandot, Ellen Orford in Peter Grimes, Marietta in Die Tote Stadt, Rosalinde in Die Fledermaus, Lina in Stiffellio, Katerina in The Greek Passion. *Recordings:* Lohengrin and Die Meistersinger von Nürnberg under Barenboim. *Honours:* MacAllister Award, Richard F. Gold career grant. *Current Management:* Hilbert Artists Management, Maximilianstrasse 22, 80539 Munich, Germany. *Telephone:* (89) 2907470. *E-mail:* agentur@hilbert.de. *Website:* www.hilbert.de; www.emilymagee.com.

MAGEE, Garry; British singer (baritone); b. 1968, England. *Education:* Guildhall School, Nat. Opera Studio. *Career:* debuts with La Monnaie as Malatesta in Don Pasquale and Dandini in La Cenerentola, with Vlaamse Opera as Yeletsky in Pique Dame, with Glyndebourne Festival Opera as the Steward in Flight, and title-roles in Don Giovanni for Opera North and Pelléas and Mélisande for English Nat. Opera; recent notable roles include Jean in Julie at La Monnaie, title-roles in Pelléas et Mélisande with Bayerische Staatsoper, Wozzeck with Komische Oper Berlin, Don Giovanni and Eugene Onegin for WNO; concerts include Brahms Requiem with the New Jersey Symphony Orchestra, Mahler's Des Knaben Wunderhorn with the Halle Orchestra, Wozzeck with the Philharmonia; has performed at Wigmore Hall, Théâtre du Châtelet, Stavanger Chamber Music Festival. *Recordings include:* Valentin in Faust and Donizetti Scenes and Overtures, Don Giovanni, Flight, The Wound Dresser, The Maiden and the Tower (with Estonian Nat. Symphony Orchestra). *Honours:* prizewinner Kathleen Ferrier Awards 1995, Int. Belvedere Competition, Vienna 1996. *Current Management:* Harrison Parrott, 5–6 Albion Court, London, W6 0QT, England. *Telephone:* (20) 7229-9166. *Fax:* (20) 7221-5042. *E-mail:* info@harrisonparrott.co.uk. *Website:* www.harrisonparrott.com.

MAGNUSON, Elizabeth; American singer (soprano); b. 1968, Chicago. *Education:* studied in Chicago and with Lucille and Robert Evans in Salzburg. *Career:* appearances with the Zürich Opera as the Queen of Night, Amanda in Ligeti's Le Grand Macabre, Genio in Haydn's Orfeo and Euridice and Marzelline in Fidelio, from 1992. Concert engagements in the Missa Solemnis, Carmina Burana, Henze's Being Beauteous and Bach's Christmas Oratorio; Concert tours to St Petersburg and South America, with further opera appearances at the Würzburg Festival, the Deutsche Oper Berlin (Queen of Night, 1996), and Zürich, Oberto in Alcina and Mozart's Constanze, season 1996–97; Conductors include Christoph Eschenbach, Rolf Beck, Jesus Lopez Cobos (Messiah in Lausanne) and Ingo Metzmacher (Strauss's Burger als Edelmann, in Stuttgart); season 1999–2000 as Constanze in the Deutsche Oper Berlin, Marcelina in Paêr's Leonora at Winterthur, and Woglinde for Zürich Opera. *Honours:* winner Chicago Belcanto Competition 1991. *Current Management:* Mariedi Anders Artists Management, 535 El Camino del Mar, San Francisco, CA 94121-1099, USA. *Telephone:* 415-752-4404. *Fax:* 415-752-7451. *E-mail:* maaminc@aol.com. *Website:* www.andersmanagement.com.

MAGNUSSON, Lars; Swedish singer (tenor); b. 10 March 1955, Gothenburg. *Education:* University of Gothenburg and the Opera School in Stockholm. *Career:* Principal tenor at the Royal Opera, Stockholm, from 1982; Roles have included, the Italian Tenor in Der Rosenkavalier, Lensky, the Duke of Mantua, Alfredo, David in Die Meistersinger and Rodolfo in La Bohème; Sang Pedrillo in a new production of Die Entführung at Covent Garden in 1987; Further performances in Monte Carlo, Nice, Strasbourg, Vienna, Staatsoper, and San Francisco, 1990; Metropolitan Opera debut 1990 as Pedrillo, returning as David, 1992; Royal Opera Stockholm, Gabriele in Verdi's Simon Boccanegra, 1991; Further engagements as David in Paris, Vienna and Marseilles, and the Steersman in Der fliegende Holländer in Geneva; Sang David in a new production of Die Meistersinger at the Metropolitan, 1993, also San Francisco; Season 1997–98 as the Swan in Carmina Burana at Stockholm, Royal Opera.

MAGOMEDOVA, Ludmilla; singer (soprano); b. 23 May 1961, Ukraine. *Education:* studied in Moscow. *Career:* made concert tour of Siberia 1986–87, stage debut 1987, as the Trovatore Leonara at Kuibishev; Verdi birthday concert in Moscow 1988 and Staatsoper Berlin from 1989, as Tosca and Leonora; sang Norma at Graz 1989, Aida at the Split Festival 1990; other roles include Violetta, Lisa in The Queen of Spades and Amelia (Un ballo in maschera); Turandot with the Latvian National Opera at the Albert Hall 1998; season 2000–01 as Lady Macbeth at the Macerata Festival and Abigaille at the Bolshoi, Moscow.

MAHLER, Hellgart, ARCM; Australian composer, writer and music teacher (retd); b. 7 May 1931, Vienna, Austria; d. of Hillel Mahler; great-niece of Gustav Mahler; m. Robert Flitney 1951 (died 1995); two s. one d. *Education:* Saffron Walden Friends' School, Essex, England, Bucks School of Music, High Wycombe. *Career:* freelance composer; music teacher 1954–. *Compositions include:* Three Galactic Fragments for piano 1966, 1980, Mira Ceti for violin and orchestra 1973, Albedo 0.43 for symphony orchestra 1965, 1973, Glasscapes 1976, Equations for trumpet and percussion 1980, And the Desert Shall Blossom for small orchestra 1980, The Icknield Quartett II for string quartet and flute 1978, Zero-G for winds, brass, six percussion, harp, piano and violin 1982, Skyscapes for Five Players for percussion orchestra, piano and solo horn 1989, Scherzo and Quatro for violin 1989, Divertimento for guitar 1989, How Beautiful Are Thy Dwelling Places for flute, Quintet 1991, Sonnets for strings (vol. 1) for cello 1991, Isochasm for violin, cello and piano 1991, Sound Sculptures for clarinet, bass clarinet and bassoon 1994, Scherzos for the whole piano 1994, 1995, The Moon and the Lamp 2 for soprano and clarinet 2000, In Hungarian Mode for violin, tubular bells and piano 2003, Duet for One for piano and tape, Sonnet for Strings Vol. V, for string trio, percussion and double bass, Sonnet for Strings, Vol. VI for four harps, Skywave, Fluorescence, Seven Peaceful Things, songs for a cappella choir 2009, piano pieces for concert pianists Ambre Hammond and Rhodri Clarke 2013–14; commissions from Silver Harris 1977, Geoffrey Tozer 1988, Jan Sedivka 1989, John Bussey 1994, Gabriella Smart 1994–95, among others. *Publications:* Three Galactic Fragments, Photons for solo piano, The 1991 Quintet, Sonnets for Strings (vol. 1), Scherzo and Quatro, Divertimenti, Five Caprices and Isochasms 91, Aspects of Truth (poetry and art) 2011; contrib. of several articles to The String Teacher and a large contribution to Sitzky's book on the piano and its role. *Address:* 108 Stoney Rise Road, Devonport, Tasmania 7310, Australia (home). *Telephone:* (3) 6423-2313 (home).

MAISENBERG, Oleg; Austrian pianist and academic; *Professor of Piano, Instituts für Tasteninstrumente, Universität für Musik und darstellende Kunst Wien;* b. 29 April 1945, Odessa, USSR (now Ukraine); s. of Adel Maisenberg and Josef Maisenberg; two c. *Education:* Moscow Gnessin Inst. of Music (pupil of A. Yokheles). *Career:* performed Rachmaninov's 1st Piano Concerto with Nat. Orchestra of Moldavia; performed regularly with Moscow Philharmonic and other major Soviet orchestras 1971–80; emigrated to Austria 1981; recordings of Schubert, Schuman, Liszt, Scriabin, Berg, Stravinsky, R. Strauss, Dvořák, Milhaud, Weber, Schönberg, Bartok, Rachmaninov and Prokofiev; Prof., Stuttgart Conservatory 1985–98; Prof. of Piano, Instituts für Tasteninstrumente, Universität für Musik und darstellende Kunst Wien (Inst. for Keyboard Studies, Univ. of Music and the Performing Arts, Vienna) 1998–; jury mem. at various int. competitions including Clara Haskil, Vevey, Géza Anda, Zurich, ARD, Munich, Sviatoslav Richter, Moscow. *Honours:* Hon. mem. Konzerthaus Gesellschaft, Vienna 1995; Österreichisches Ehrenkreuz für Wissenschaft und Kunst I. Klasse 2005; winner, Franz Schubert Competition in Vienna 1967, 20th Century Music Competition, Vienna 1967. *Current Management:* Künstleragentur Dr Raab und Dr Bohm, Paniglgasse 18-20 / 14, 1040 Vienna, Austria. *Telephone:* (1) 5120501. *Fax:* (1) 5127743. *E-mail:* studer@rbartists.at. *Website:* www .rbartists.at; www.mdw.ac.at/inst4.

MAISKY, Mischa (Michael); Belgian cellist; b. 10 Jan. 1948, Riga, Latvia (b. USSR); m. Maryanne Kay Lipman 1983; one s. one d. *Education:* Moscow Conservatory, studied with Mstislav Rostropovich and Gregor Piatigorsky, Univ. of Southern California, USA. *Career:* debut with Leningrad Philharmonic Orchestra 1965; imprisoned in labour camp near Gorky for 18 months 1970; emigrated from USSR to Israel 1972; debut with Pittsburgh Symphony Orchestra at Carnegie Hall 1973; London concerto debut with Royal Philharmonic Orchestra 1976, London recital debut with pianist Radu Lupu 1977; debut at Berlin Philharmonic Hall 1978; returned to Moscow for the first time in 23 years to give a concert and to record works by Prokofiev and Miaskovsky with Mikhail Pletnev and Russian National Orchestra 1995. *Recordings include:* Six Suites for Solo Cello (Bach), Three Sonatas for Cello and Piano (Bach), Concerto in A minor Op. 102 for Violin, Cello and Orchestra (Brahms), Concerto for Cello and Orchestra in A Minor (Schumann), Morgen 2009, ¡España! Songs and Dances from Spain (with Lily Maisky) 2011. *Honours:* All-Soviet prizewinner 1965, Int. Tchaikovsky Competition 1966, winner of Cassada Competition, Florence 1973 and Rostropovich Competition, Paris 1981, Grand Prix du Disque, Paris 1985, Record Acad. Prize, Tokyo 1985. *Current Management:* Weinstadt Artists Management, Populierenlaan 3, bus 26, 2020 Antwerp, Belgium. *E-mail:* info@concerts-weinstadt.be. *Current Management:* Columbia Artists Music, LLC, 1790 Broadway, 16 Floor, New York, NY 10019, USA. *E-mail:* ab@camimusic.com. *Website:* www .mischamaisky.com.

MAISURADZE, Badry; singer (tenor); b. 1967, Georgia, Russia. *Career:* frequent recitals, concerts and opera appearances throughout Europe and in Russia; contestant at the 1995 Cardiff Singer of the World Competition; repertory includes Donizetti's Il Duca d'Alba, Carmen, Tosca, Verdi's Il Corsaro and songs by Rachmaninov; sang Cavaradossi at Covent Garden 2000.

MAIXNEROVA, Martina, MMus; Singapore pianist and academic; b. 20 Sept. 1947, Prague, Czechoslovakia; m. Pavel Pranti 1972; two s. *Education:* Conservatory of Music, Prague, Academy of Musical Arts, Prague. *Career:* Professor of Piano in Singapore, 1980; Assistant Professor of Piano at the Academy of Musical Arts, Prague, 1975–80; Professor of Piano at the Music

School for Especially Gifted Children in Prague, 1970–73; Adjudicator at the First Rolex Piano Competition in Singapore, 1987; Festival appearances in England, Germany, Czechoslovakia, Austria, Poland, USA and Korea; Solo appearances with orchestras including: Guest soloist with the Prague Chamber Orchestra without a Conductor, 1980; Guest soloist with the Singapore Symphony Orchestra, 1981, England, Sweden, Czechoslovakia and Japan; mem, ARS Cameralis Ensemble, 1976–80; Prague Baroque Ensemble, 1973–80. *Address:* 110 Wishart Road, 03-07 Pender Court, 0409 Singapore.

MAJOR, Dame Malvina Lorraine, ONZ, GNZM, DBE; New Zealand operatic soprano; *Senior Fellow, Conservatorium of Music Faculty of Arts and Social Sciences, University of Waikato;* b. 28 Jan. 1943, Hamilton; d. of Vincent Major and Eva Major; m. Winston William Richard Fleming 1965 (died 1990); one s. two d. *Education:* Hamilton Tech. Coll. and London Opera Centre. *Career:* debut as Rosina in The Barber of Seville, Salzburg Festival 1968; performances in Europe, UK, USA, Australia, Japan, Jordan, Egypt and NZ; concerts, opera and recording with NZ Symphony Orchestra, Auckland Philharmonia and Southern Symphony Orchestra; Founder Dame Malvina Major Foundation (for excellence in the performing arts) 1991; Amb. for NZ Year of the Family 1994; fmr Prof. of Vocal Studies, Univ. of Canterbury; currently Sr Fellow, Conservatorium of Music Faculty of Arts and Social Sciences, Univ. of Waikato; fmr Chair. Diana, Princess of Wales Trust; Patron, Christchurch City Choir, Canterbury Opera, Nelson School of Music, Waikato Multiple Sclerosis. *Honours:* Hon. Life mem. NZ Horticultural Soc.; Dame Grand Companion, NZ Order of Merit 2007; Hon. DLitt (Massey Univ.); Dr hc (Waikato); NZ Winner, Mobil Song Quest 1963, Kathleen Ferrier Competition winner 1966, Outstanding Achievements in Music Award 1988, NZ Medal 1990, Entertainer and Int. Performer of the Year 1992, NZ Music Award— Classical Disc 1993, 1994, Benny Award, Variety Club of NZ 1998 and numerous other awards for services to music. *Address:* c/o James Bennett MNZM JP, 3 Featherstone Drive, Flagstaff, Hamilton 3210, New Zealand (office). *Telephone:* (7) 8543255 (office). *E-mail:* jimbennett@xtra.co.nz (office). *Website:* www.damemalvinamajor.co.nz; www.damemalvinamajorfoundation .co.nz.

MAJOR, Margaret, FRCM; violist; b. 1932, Coventry, England. *Education:* Royal Coll. of Music. *Career:* debut at Wigmore Hall, London 1955 with Gerald Moore; Principal Viola, Netherlands Chamber Orchestra 1955–59, Oromonte Trio 1958–65, Philomusica of London 1960–65; Viola, Aeolian String Quartet 1965–81; Prof. of Viola, Royal Coll. of Music, London 1969–97. *Recordings:* Complete String Quartets of Haydn, Late Beethoven Quartets, Ravel and Debussy Quartets, Complete Mozart Viola Quintets. *Honours:* Lionel Tertis Prize 1951, International Music Asscn Concert Award 1955, Hon. MA (Univ. of Newcastle upon Tyne) 1970.

MAKRIS, Cynthia; American singer (soprano) and opera coach; b. 1956, Sterling, Colo. *Education:* Univ. of Colorado and Adams State Coll. *Career:* sang Alice Ford, Donna Elvira and Tosca while a student; European debut at Graz as Violetta; Stadttheater Freiburg as Constanze, Pamina 1980–82, Violetta and Saffi in Zigeunerbaron; sang at Bielefeld 1982–, as Donna Anna, Agathe, Marenka, Lucia di Lammermoor and Manon Lescaut and in revivals of Schreker's Irrelohe and Max Brand's Maschinist Hopkins; mem. Dortmund Opera 1986–, as Desdemona, Leonora in Il Trovatore, Amelia in Un Ballo in Maschera, and Arabella; other roles include Marietta in Die Tote Stadt at Düsseldorf and at Antwerp 1995, Marie in Wozzeck at Karlsruhe, Mozart's Countess, Wagner's Eva and Freia and the Empress in Die Frau ohne Schatten; has sung title role in Salome, at Dortmund, Berlin Staatsoper and Deutsche Oper, Tokyo and Scottish Opera at Glasgow 1990; Covent Garden debut as Abigaille 1996; debut as Lady Macbeth in Verdi's Macbeth at La Scala and the Teatro Colón, Buenos Aires; Norma at Philadelphia; season 2000 as Forza Leonora at Savonlinna, Leonora in Trovatore and Beethoven's Leonore in Helsinki; Salome at Wiesbaden Festival, Marie in Wozzeck at Santiago and Zandonai's Francesca in Buenos Aires; Venus and Elizabeth in Tannhäuser, Savolinna Opera Festival 2006; title role in Turandot, Brisbane 2008; currently working as opera coach. *Current Management:* c/o Athole Still Opera Ltd, Foresters Hall, 25–27 Westow Street, London, SE19 3RY, England. *Telephone:* (20) 8771-5271. *Fax:* (20) 8771-8172. *E-mail:* enquiries@atholestill.co.uk. *Website:* www.atholestill.co.uk; www .cynthiamakris.com.

MAKSYMIUK, Jerzy; Polish conductor, composer and pianist; *Conductor Laureate, BBC Scottish Symphony Orchestra;* b. 9 April 1936, Grodno, Byelorussia (now Belarus); s. of Roman Maksymiuk and Bronisława Maksymiuk; m. Irena Kirjacka. *Education:* Acad. of Music, Poland. *Career:* Conductor, Great Theatre, Warsaw 1970–72; f. Polish Chamber Orchestra 1972–84; Prin. Conductor Polish Nat. Radio Symphony Orchestra, Katowice 1975–77; Prin. Conductor BBC Scottish Symphony Orchestra, Glasgow 1984–93, tours of Greece, Canada and Germany, Conductor Laureate 1993–; Guest Conductor Calgary Symphony, Nat. Arts Centre (Ottawa), BBC Welsh and Philharmonic Orchestras, English Chamber Orchestra, Scottish Chamber Orchestra, City of Birmingham Symphony, London Symphony, London Philharmonic, Philharmonia, Orchestre National de France, Rotterdam Philharmonic, Luxembourg Philharmonic, Hong Kong Philharmonic, Royal Liverpool Philharmonic, Bournemouth Sinfonietta, Ulster Orchestra, Tokyo Metropolitan Symphony, Israeli Chamber Orchestra, Los Angeles Chamber Orchestra, Staatskapelle, Sinfonia Varsovia and other orchestras; has toured Europe, USA, Canada, Japan, Israel and Australia with Polish Chamber Orchestra; collaborated with ENO (Mozart's Don Giovanni) 1990, (Johann

Strauss' Die Fledermaus) 1993; regularly performs works of Penderecki, Lutoslawski, Gorecki, Szymanowski, as well as British composers including Peter Maxwell Davies and James MacMillan. *Recordings include:* Paderewski: Symphony 'Polonia', The Romantic Piano Concerto, (Vols 1–4), Vivaldi Violin Concertos, Grieg: Pier Gynt Suites Nos. 1 & 2. *Honours:* Commdr's Cross, Order of Merit; Hon. DLitt (Strathclyde) 1990; First Prize, Paderewski Piano Competition 1964, Gold Medal, Elgar Society 1999, Gloria Artis Gold Medal. *Address:* Gdańska 2 m. 14, 01-633 Warsaw, Poland (home). *Telephone:* (22) 8323021 (home). *Website:* jerzymaksymiuk.pl/en.

MALACHOVSKY, Martin; singer (bass); b. 23 Jan. 1968, Bratislava, Czechoslovakia; m. Iveta Pasková; one d. *Education:* Acad. of Arts, Bratislava, Hochschule für Musik und darstellende Kunst in Vienna, masterclasses with E. Nesterenko, Conservatoire National Superieur de Paris with Prof. Gottlieb. *Career:* debut at Slovak National Theatre 1991; J. Massenet, Don Quixote; Rossini, Il Barbiere di Siviglia (Don Basilio); La Bohème (Colline), Slovak National Theatre, Bratislava; J. Offenbach, Les Contes d'Hoffmann (Luther and Crespel), Opéra Comique, Paris 1996; W. A. Mozart, Le nozze di Figaro, Bartolo 1995; Mozart Festival, Madrid 1992; May Festival, Wiesbaden 1996; Gounod, Faust (Wagner), National Theatre Prague 1996; tour of Japan as Sagristano in Puccini's Tosca with Sherrill Milnes as Scarpia, Peter Dvorsky as Cavaradossi and Shinobu Satoh as Tosca 1997; mem. Slovak Music Union. *Honours:* third place International A. Dvořák Singing Competition, Carlsbad 1988. *Address:* Gorkého 13, 811 01 Bratislava, Slovakia.

MALAGNINI, Mario; Italian singer (tenor); b. 1959, Salo. *Education:* Brescia Conservatory, Giuseppe Verdi Conservatory, Milan with Piermirando Ferraro, studied with Tito Gobbi and Giuseppe di Stefano. *Career:* sang in Frankfurt and Milan, La Scala, 1985, as Radames, and in Il Corsaro; returned to La Scala 1986–87, as Alfredo and Ismaele in Nabucco; Verona Arena from 1987, as Foresto in Attila, Pinkerton, Riccardo and Radames; appeared as Don José at Glyndebourne 1987, and in a concert performance of La Battaglia di Legnano at Carnegie Hall, as Arrigo; further engagements at Florence, as Pinkerton and Gabriele Adorno, Nîmes and Monte Carlo, Pollione in Norma, Vienna, Berlin, Houston, Budapest and Seoul, 1988; Teatro La Fenice Venice, 1990 as Rodolfo in Leoncavallo's Bohème; sang Radames at Verona and Pinkerton for the Munich Staatsoper, 2000. *Recordings:* Emilia di Liverpool, with the Philharmonia Orchestra, Opera Rara; Norma conducted by Emil Tchakarov. *Honours:* winner Tito Gobbi Competition 1983, Concorso Enrico Caruso and Belvedere Competition, Vienna 1984. *Current Management:* Il Trittico - Opera Management Company di Giorgio Benati, Viale della Repubblica 19, 37126 Verona, Italy. *Telephone:* (045) 8347953. *Fax:* (045) 8389873. *E-mail:* info@iltrittico.net. *Website:* www.iltrittico.net; www.mariomalagnini.com.

MALAS, Spiro; American singer (bass-baritone); b. 28 Jan. 1933, Baltimore, MD; m. Marlene Kleinman. *Education:* Peabody Conservatory of Music, Baltimore with E. Nagy, studied with E. Baklor and D. Ferro in New York, and with I. Chicagov. *Career:* debut as Marco, Gianni Schicchi, Baltimore Civic Opera 1959; New York City Opera debut, Spinellocchio in Gianni Schicchi 1961; toured Australia with Sutherland-Williamson International Grand Opera Co. 1965; Covent Garden debut, London as Sulpice in La fille du Régiment 1966; Pluto in Haydn's Orfeo ed Euridice, Edinburgh Festival 1967; Chicago Lyric Opera debut as Assur in Semiramide 1971; Metropolitan Opera debut in New York as Sulpice 1983; other roles have been the Sacristan in Tosca, Zuniga, Mozart's Bartolo and Frank in Die Fledermaus; sang Frank Maurrant in the British premiere of Weill's Street Scene, Glasgow 1989; Don Isaac in Prokofiev's Duenna at the 1989 Wexford Festival; Vancouver 1990, as Baron Zeta in The Merry Widow; many concert engagements; teacher, Peabody Conservatory of Music. *Honours:* winner Metropolitan Opera Auditions 1961.

MALAS-GODLOEWSKA, Ewa; singer (coloratura soprano); b. 1955, Warsaw, Poland. *Education:* studied in Warsaw. *Career:* sang at the Warsaw Opera from 1978 as Zerbinetta, the Queen of Night, Rosina, Norina, and Constanze in Die Entführung; leading roles at the Vienna Volksoper, Paris Opéra-Comique, Nantes, Olympia, Basle, Berne, Wiesbaden and Dresden; sang Celia in Mozart's Lucio Silla, at Nanterre and Brussels 1986; sang Madeleine in Le Postillon de Longjumeau at the Grand Theatre Geneva 1990; Queen of Night in new productions of Die Zauberflöte at Houston and Paris, Opéra Bastille 1991; Théâtre du Châtelet Paris in L'Enfant et les Sortilèges; concert performances in the UK, Switzerland, Poland, Germany, The Netherlands, Belgium and France; Gstaad Festival 1987 in Beethoven's Ninth, conducted by Yehudi Menuhin. *Honours:* winner Toulouse International Competition 1978.

MALASPINA, Massimiliano; Italian singer (bass); b. 17 May 1925, Fara Novarese; m. Rita Orlandi-Malaspina. *Education:* studied with Lina Pagliughi. *Career:* appearances from 1959 at such Italian Opera centres as La Scala Milan, Teatro San Carlo Naples, Teatro Fenice Venice and the Teatro Regio Parma; further engagements at Genoa, Turin, Brussels, Munich Staatsoper, Montréal, Toulouse, Frankfurt, Rio de Janeiro, Paris, Barcelona and Miami; roles have included Colline in La Bohème, Oroveso in Norma; Ptolomey in Giulio Cesare; Sarastro and Verdi's Padre Guardiano; Banquo and Ramphis; teacher of singing in Milan after retiring from stage.

MALCOLM, Carlos Edmond; composer and pianist; b. 24 Nov. 1945, Havana City, Cuba; one s. one d. *Education:* Vedado Inst., Havana, Amadeo Roldan Conservatory, Inst. Superior de Arte, Havana, Univ. of Music F.

Chopin, Warsaw, Poland. *Career:* pianist in Havana's night clubs 1961–62; composer and pianist, Nat. Modern Dance Ensemble 1964–68, Cuban Inst. of Radio and TV, occasionally Cuban Inst. of Film 1968–70; performed at festivals 1969–85; mem. Staff of Composers, Ministry of Culture of Cuba 1970–90; toured throughout Mexico, Jamaica, Ecuador, playing own works, teaching and lecturing with choreographer Lorna Burdsal 1979–82; guest artist, New Music Concerts 1986; performed own piano compositions at Royal Conservatory of Toronto, Canada; freelance composer and pianist, living in Poland 1990–; accompanied flautist Robert Aitken during a special presentation of Quetzalcoatl for flute and piano (also recorded this piece for Cuban label EGREM with flautist Luis Bayard); recorded own music for Polish TV and Radio; works have been played in New Music Concerts, Warsaw Autumn Festival, Berlin's Biennale, Foros mexicanos de la Música Contemporanea, Japan, Argentina, Hungary, Spain; mem. Soc. of Cuban Composers and Authors. *Compositions:* Quetzalcoatl (Song of the Feathered Serpent) for flute and piano, Beny More redivivo, for string quartet, Adagio for piano (4 hands), Eclosion, Articulaciones for piano, 13 studies for piano, Sonatina (1 movement) for piano, Marionetas for orchestra (commissioned by Nat. Modern Dance Ensemble), Montaje for wind orchestra and percussion, Songs set to texts by Caribbean poets, Rumores for violin, cello and piano, Allegro en Son for wind quintet 1963–90, Autografo for piano 1998, 4 Escenas breves for piano 2005, Sonata for violin and piano 2007, Sonata Divertimento No. 1 (for piano) 2009, Sonata Divertimento No. 2 (for piano) 2012. *Honours:* several awards including UNEAC Music Awards. *Address:* ul Piękna 16 m 2, 00-539 Warsaw, Poland. *Telephone:* (22) 6290431. *E-mail:* cmalcolmw@gmail.com.

MALEFANE, Pauline; South African singer (soprano), actress, writer and director; b. 1976, Khayelitsha Township, Cape Town; m. Mark Dornford-May; three c. *Education:* Masiyile High School, Univ. of Cape Town, Coll. of Music. *Career:* joined Simon Estes Choir (now Heavenly Voices) 1993; joined Lyric Theatre Co. Dimpho Di Kopane; Co-founder Isango Portobello Theatre Co. 2006. *Films:* U-Carmen eKhayelitsha (Carmen from Khayelitsha) (Berlin Film Festival's Golden Bear Award 2005, Best Feature at the LA Pan African Film Festival), Son of Man (as actor, co-writer and translator) (Best Feature, LA Pan African Film Festival, Los Angeles 2006, Best Actress at South African TV and Film Awards 2007) 2006. *Plays:* operatic roles include Carmen in Xhosa-language version of Bizet's Carmen, Queen of the Night in Mozart's The Magic Flute – Impempe Yomlingo (transferred to London 2008, won Olivier Award for Best Musical Revival 2008), Mary in The Mysteries – Yimimangaliso, Garrick Theatre, London 2009; other stage work includes: Bess in Porgy and Bess, Cape Town and Sweden 2006; as composer: Aesop's Fables, Fugard Theatre 2010. *Address:* Isango Portobello, Portobello Pictures, 12 Addison Avenue, Holland Park, London, W11 4QR, England (office). *Telephone:* (20) 7605-1396 (office). *Fax:* (20) 7605-1391 (office). *E-mail:* mail@portobellopictures.com (office). *Website:* www.portobellopictures.com (office); www.magicflutethemusical.com (office).

MALFITANO, Catherine; American singer (soprano) and stage director; b. 18 April 1948, New York City; d. of Maria Maslova and Joseph Malfitano; one d. *Education:* Manhattan School of Music. *Career:* debut at Central City Opera 1972; has appeared at the world's leading opera houses, including the Metropolitan Opera, Lyric Opera of Chicago, Vienna State Opera, La Scala, Bavarian State Opera, Paris Opera, Royal Opera Covent Garden, Berlin's Deutsche Opera and State Opera, Teatro Comunale Florence, San Francisco Opera, Netherlands Opera, Los Angeles Opera, Houston Grand Opera, Théâtre du Chatelet Paris, Grand Théâtre du Genève, Liceu Barcelona, Hamburg State Opera and Théâtre Royal de la Monnaie Brussels; numerous recitals worldwide, orchestral concerts and cabaret performances; private voice teacher and gives masterclasses world-wide; debut as Stage Dir with Madama Butterfly at Central City Opera 2005, followed by Poulenc's La Voix humaine at Theatre Royal de la Monnaie, Brussels 2006; mem. Faculty, Depts of Voice and Chamber Music and Ensembles, Vocal, Manhattan School of Music 2008–. *Opera roles include:* Ottavia in L'incoronazione di Poppea, La Femme in La Voix humaine, Kostelnicka in Jenůfa, Lulu, Marie in Wozzeck, Madama Butterfly, Herodias in Salome, Eugene Onegin, Jenny in Mahagonny, Erisbe in L'Ormindo, Annina in Saint of Bleecker Street, Euridice, Polly Peachum in The Threepenny Opera, Lucia di Lammermoor, Gretel, Marzelline and Leonore in Fidelio, Thérèse in Les Mamelles de Tirésias, Konstanze in Die Entführung aus dem Serail, Susanna in Le nozze di Figaro, Zerlina and Donna Elvira in Don Giovanni, Cleopatra in Antony and Cleopatra, Fiorilla in Il Turco in Italia, Emilia Marty in The Makropulos Case, the three heroines in Les Contes d'Hoffmann, the three heroines in Il Trittico, Violetta in La Traviata, Lady Macbeth of Mtsensk, Rose and Anna Maurrant in Street Scene, Manon, Tosca, Carmen, Regina, La Fanciulla del West, Kundry in Parsifal, Senta in Der Fliegende Holländer, Kat'a Kabanova, Stiffelio; sang in the world premieres of Carlisle Floyd's Bilby's Doll, Thomas Pasatieri's Washington Square and The Seagull, Conrad Susa's Transformations, William Bolcom's Beatrice in A View from the Bridge, McTeague, Medusa and Victoria in A Wedding. *Operas directed include:* Madama Butterfly, Central City Opera 2005, La Voix Humaine, La Monnaie 2006, The Saint of Bleecker Street, Central City Opera 2007, Tosca, Florida Grand Opera 2008, Rigoletto, Washington National Opera 2008, Don Giovanni, San Francisco Opera/Merola 2008. *Honours:* Hon. PhD (De Paul Univ.); Emmy Award (for Tosca). *Address:* Manhattan School of Music, 120 Claremont Avenue, New York, NY 10027, USA (office). *Telephone:* (917) 304-8079 (home). *E-mail:* Divamomcat@aol.com (office). *Website:* www.msmnyc.edu/voice (office).

MALGOIRE, Jean-Claude; French conductor and oboist; b. 25 Nov. 1940, Avignon. *Education:* studied in Avignon and at Paris Conservatoire. *Career:* founded La Grande Ecurie et la Chambre du Roy, for the performance of Baroque music 1966; founded Florilegium Musicum de Paris; concerts of medieval and Renaissance Music; Handel's Rinaldo at the Festival Hall, London; Rameau's Hippolyte et Aricie for the English Bach Festival at Covent Garden; Campra's Tancrède for the Copenhagen Royal Opera and at the Aix-en-Provence Festival 1986; L'Incoronazione di Poppea at the Stockholm Opera; Rameau's Les Indes Galantes at the Versailles Opéra Royal; conducted Cephale et Procris by Elisabeth Jacquet de la Guerre at St Etienne 1989, Kreutzer's Paul et Virginie at Tourcoing; season 1992 with Lully's Alceste at the Théâtre des Champs-Elysées, Paris, a Vivaldi pastiche, Montezuma, at Monte Carlo and Gnecco's Prova di un'opera seria at Montpellier; conducted Salieri's Falstaff at Tourcoing 1996; Polish premiere of Lully's Alceste with the Warsaw Chamber Orchestra 1998. *Recordings:* Rinaldo; Handel's Xerxes; Hippolyte et Aricie and Les Indes Galantes; Tancrède; Cavalli's Ercole Amante; Handel Concerti Grossi op 3 and 6, Water and Fireworks Music; Lully Alceste, Psyché and Le Bourgeois gentilhomme; Vivaldi Beatus Vir, Gloria and flute concertos; Charpentier Messe de Minuit; Renaissance music with the Florilegium Musicum de Paris. *Honours:* Prix Internationale de Geneve (oboe) 1968.

MALIPONTE, Adriana; singer (soprano); b. 26 Dec. 1938, Brescia, Italy. *Education:* Conservatoire de Mulhouse with Suzanne Stappen Bergmann, studied with Carmen Melis in Milan, Rosa Ponselle in Baltimore. *Career:* debut at Paris Opéra as Micaela in Carmen 1962–63; Gran Teatro Liceo, Barcelona with Massenet's Manon 1964; sang in San Carlo Naples, Lisbon, Milan, Marseille, Tokyo and in all major operas of the world; has wide repertoire of some 60 roles; British debut 1967, at Glyndebourne Festival in Elisir d'amore; La Scala debut in Manon with Pavarotti 1970, returning in I Masnadieri 1978, and La Bohème, Elisir d'amore, Carmen, Turandot (Liu), Luisa Miller; Metropolitan Opera debut in La Bohème 1971; Japan in La Bohème (Mimi), Traviata and Carmen 1975, returning in La Bohème 1981; Pagliacci, Covent Garden 1976; La Bohème and Traviata, Vienna Staatsoper and at Mozart Festival 1977; Iris at Newark Symphony Hall; La Traviata, Pretoria 1983; Maria Stuarda and Guglielmo Tell, Zürich 1986–87, 1990; debut in Adriana Lecouvreur, Tenerife 1989–90; concerts in Taipei, also Carmen, Turandot and Liu 1994; recital at Salle Gaveau, Paris 1994. *Recordings include:* Micaela in Carmen 1973, Le Villi (Puccini), Les Pêcheurs des Perles, Pagliacci (video). *Honours:* winner Génève International d'Execution Musicale 1960, Prix Villabella, Grand Prix du Disque 1965, Grammy Award, USA 1973, Maschera d'Argento, Campione d'Italia 1976, Premio Illica 1983, Rosa d'Oro 1984, Vittoria Alata, Brescia 1985, Chevalier, Ordre des Arts et des Lettres, France.

MALIS, David; American singer (baritone); b. 1961. *Career:* many appearances in concert and opera in North America and Europe from 1985; season 1995 with performances in Athens, Buenos Aires from Pittsburgh; Metropolitan Opera in Peter Grimes and La Bohème; sang Belcore at San Diego 1996; Wolfram in Tannhäuser at Palermo 1998. *Honours:* winner Cardiff Singer of the World Competition 1985.

MÄLKKI, Susanna, MMus, Dip RAM; Finnish conductor; *Principal Guest Conductor, The Gulbenkian Orchestra;* b. 1969, Helsinki. *Education:* Sibelius Acad., Helsinki, studied conducting with Jorma Panula and Leif Segerstam, cello studies at Sibelius Acad., Royal Acad. of Music, London and Edsberg Inst. of Music, Stockholm. *Career:* Co-Prin. Cellist, Gothenburg Symphony Orchestra, Sweden 1995–98; Artistic Dir Stavanger Symphony Orchestra, Norway 2002–05; Music Dir Ensemble Intercontemporain, Paris 2006–13; Prin. Guest Conductor, The Gulbenkian Orchestra, Lisbon, Portugal 2013–; Guest Conductor, Philharmonia Orchestra, Boston Symphony, Chicago Symphony, Berlin Philharmonic, Bavarian Radio Symphony Orchestra, Royal Concertgebouw Orchestra, Swedish and Finnish Radio Symphony Orchestras, Teatro della Scala, L'Opéra de Paris; mem. Royal Swedish Acad. of Music. *Recordings include:* world premiere recordings for BIS, Alba and Kairos. *Honours:* Pro Finlandia Medal, Order of the Lion of Finland 2011; Suomi Award, Ministry of Culture 2005. *Current Management:* c/o Rose Hooks, Harrison Parrott Ltd, Artist and Project Management, 5–6 Albion Court, Albion Place, London, W6 0QT, England. *Telephone:* (20) 3725-9177. *Fax:* (20) 7229-9166. *E-mail:* rose .hooks@harrisonparrott.co.uk (office). *Website:* www.harrisonparrott.com/ artist/profile/susanna-malkki.

MALMBERG, Urban; Swedish singer (baritone); b. 29 March 1962, Stockholm. *Education:* studied in Stockholm with Helge Brilioth and Erik Saeden. *Career:* sang in the Boy's Choir of the Stockholm Opera and appeared as First Boy in the 1974 Bergman film version of Die Zauberflöte; sang at Stockholm in works by Peter Maxwell Davies and Janake Hillerud; Hamburg Staatsoper from 1983, as Malatesta, Don Pasquale, Masetto, Papageno, Schaunard in La Bohème, Harlequin in Ariadne and in Nono's Intolleranza and Die Gespenstersonate by Reimann; Guest appearances in Düsseldorf, Las Palmas, London, Moscow, San Francisco and Tokyo; Other roles have included Guglielmo and Donner, Brussels and Bonn, 1990, Belcore, Marcello and Lescaut; Season 1992 with Malatesta at Vancouver and Frère Leon in Messiaen's St François d'Assise at the Salzburg Festival; Concert repertoire includes the St Matthew Passion, Beethoven's Ninth, Ein Deutsches Requiem and Peer Gynt; Sang title role in premiere of Matthias Pintscher's Thomas Chatterton, Dresden 1998. *Recordings:* Ariadne auf Naxos and Les Contes d'Hoffmann; The Count in Schreker's Der Schatzgräber, with Hamburg

forces. *Current Management:* Aria's di Novella Partacini & Alexandra Plaickner, Rappresentanza Artisti, Via Josef Weingartner, 4, 39022 Lagundo, Italy. *Telephone:* (0473) 200200. *Fax:* (0473) 222424. *E-mail:* info@arias.it. *Website:* www.arias.it.

MALONE, Carol; singer (soprano); b. 16 July 1943, Grayson, KY, USA. *Education:* Univ. of Indiana at Bloomington, Hamburg Musikhochschule, studied with Joseph Metternich in Cologne. *Career:* debut at Cologne 1966, as Aennchen in Der Freischütz; many appearances at such German opera centres as the State Operas of Hamburg, Munich and Stuttgart, Deutsche Oper am Rhein Düsseldorf, Nationaltheater Mannheim and Frankfurt; further engagements at Brussels, Vienna Volksoper, Salzburg, San Francisco, Amsterdam, Venice and the Edinburgh Festival; sang with the Deutsche Oper Berlin in the premiere of Love's Labours Lost by Nabokov, Brussels 1973 and as Zerlina in Don Giovanni, Berlin 1988; other roles have included Marzelline, Nannetta, Despina, Susanna, Blondchen, Sophie, Adele in Die Fledermaus and Adelaide in Blacher's Preussiches Märchen; many concert appearances. *Recordings:* Trionfo d'Afrodite by Orff.

MALOV, Sergey; Russian violinist and violist; b. 1983, St Petersburg. *Education:* Universität Mozarteum, Salzburg, Hochschule für Musik Hanns Eisler, Berlin. *Career:* has performed with orchestras including Bavarian Radio Symphony Orchestra, London Philharmonic Orchestra, Camerata Salzburg, Moscow, St Petersburg Philharmonics; chamber music partners include Austrian Ensemble for New Music Salzburg, Ensemble Capriccioso, Nicolas Altstedt, Julian Arp, Paul Badura-Skoda, Jérôme Ducros, Ilya Gringolts, Jérôme Pernoo, Antoine Tamestit, Antje Weithaas, Tabea Zimmermann; collaborations with composers including Guillaume Connesson and Christoph Ehrenfellner (dedicated his solo double concerto for violin and viola, Hommage à St Petersburg, to him); asst teacher, studio of Prof. Weithaas, Berlin 2010. *Honours:* Laureate of Paganini Competitions (both in Genoa and Moscow) 2008, Winner, ARD Viola Competition, Munich 2008, Winner, Jasha Heifetz Competition, Vilnius 2009, Winner, Int. Tokyo Viola Competition 2009, Winner, Michael Hill Int. Violin Competition, New Zealand 2011, Winner, Int. Mozart Competition, Salzburg 2011. *Current Management:* c/o Laurent Delage Artists Management, Siebensterngasse 46/1/44, 1070 Vienna, Austria. *Telephone:* (403) 634-9. *Fax:* (403) 63-49-90. *E-mail:* office@delage.at. *Website:* www.delage.at. *E-mail:* sergeymalov@gmx.at. *Website:* sergeymalov .com.

MALSBURY, Angela Mary, ARCM, LRAM; British clarinettist; b. 5 May 1945, Preston, Lancs., England; m. David Pettit 1965; one s. *Education:* Beauchamp School, Kibworth, Leicester, Royal Coll. of Music, London. *Career:* concert debut, Royal Festival Hall, with London Mozart Players (LMP) 1976; concerto soloist with major orchestras world-wide; chamber music artist and freelance orchestral player; clarinet quintets, including classical and contemporary repertoire; mem. De Saram Trio, Albion Ensemble, London Winds; Prof. of Clarinet, RAM; Buffet Crampon Artist Worldwide. *Recordings include:* Richard Baker's Musical Menagerie, Cameristi of London, Mozart Serenade for 13 Wind Instruments (Academy of St Martin-in-the-Fields, Albion and LMP); Mozart, Clarinet Quintet with the Coull String Quartet; Mozart, Clarinet Concerto, London Mozart Players and Jane Glover; Mississippi Five with Albion Quintet; A Trio of French Styles with De Saran Trio. *Honours:* Hon. RAM 1991; Hon. Fellow, Birmingham Conservatoire; Philip Cardew Memorial Prize 1963, Marjorie Whyte Prize 1964, Mozart Memorial Prize 1974. *Current Management:* c/o Stephannie Williams Artists, 16 Swanfold, Stratford-upon-Avon, Warwicks., CV37 9XH, England. *Telephone:* (1789) 266272. *E-mail:* enquiries@swartists.co.uk. *Address:* 40 Greenford Avenue, Hanwell, London, W7 3QP, England (home). *Telephone:* (20) 8579-0420 (office). *E-mail:* angelam@drpettit.eclipse.co.uk (office).

MALTA, Alexander; Swiss singer (bass); b. 28 Sept. 1942, Visp, Wallis Canton. *Education:* studied with Desider Kovacz in Zürich, Barra-Carracciolo in Milan and Enzo Mascherini in Florence. *Career:* debut at Stuttgart 1962, as the Monk in Don Carlos. US 1976, with the San Francisco Opera; Sang in Brunswick, Munich, Berlin, Vienna, Frankfurt, Geneva, Paris and Venice from 1966; Chicago Lyric Opera in Ariadne auf Naxos; Seattle Opera as Osmin in Die Entfuhrung; Brussels Opera from 1979, notably in Wozzeck, Lulu and Schubert's Fierrabras; Rome Opera as Orestes in Elektra; Maggio Musicale Florence as Wagner's Fasolt and Landgrave; La Scala Milan in Handel's Ariodante; Hamburg Opera as Golaud in Pelléas et Mélisande, Colline in La Bohème, Die Fledermaus, Munich State Opera, Hoffmann, Adriana Lecouvreur, Deutsche Oper Berlin as Nicolai's Falstaff, Gounod's Mefistophélès and Rocco in Fidelio; Salzburg Festival in Carmen and Don Giovanni, conducted by Karajan; Covent Garden 1985, in Tippett's King Priam, title role; Sang the Voice of Neptune in Idomeneo at the 1990 Salzburg Festival. *Recordings:* Lady Macbeth of the Mtsenk District; Carmen, Don Giovanni and the Bruckner Te Deum; Rigoletto; Zar und Zimmermann; Wozzeck.

MALTA, Alvaro; singer (bass); b. 19 May 1931, Lisbon, Portugal. *Education:* studied in Lisbon. *Career:* has sung at the Teatro San Carlos Lisbon, as Figaro, Papageno, Mephistophélès and Klingsor further appearances until 1984 as the Commendatore, Wurm in Luisa Miller, Ramphis and Trulove in The Rake's Progress; guest engagements in Italy and France and at the Wexford Festival 1977–79 in Herodiade, Tiefland and L'Amore dei tre Re; other roles have included Monterone, Colline and Des Grieux.

MALTMAN, Christopher; British singer (baritone); b. 1970, England. *Education:* Univ. of Warwick, Royal Acad. of Music, London, studied with

Sesto Bruscantini and Thomas Hampson. *Career:* has sung the role of Don Giovanni at the Salzburg Festival, in Berlin, Munich, Cologne and at the Royal Opera House, Covent Garden, where he has also sung Papageno, Guglielmo, Lescaut, Forester, Marcello, Ramiro; roles at Vienna State Opera include Siskov (Aus einem Totenhaus), Onegin, Figaro and Prospero (The Tempest); Verdi roles include Simon Boccanegra in Frankfurt, Post (Don Carlos) in Amsterdam and Frankfurt, Conte di Luna (Il trovatore) at Covent Garden 2015–16; other operatic appearances include Il Conte in Paris, Alfonso in Munich, Friedrich (Das Liebesverbot) in Madrid and Figaro (Il barbiere di Siviglia), Papageno and Silvio at Metropolitan Opera, New York; concert engagements have included the LSO with Sir Colin Davis, Sir Simon Rattle, Gergiev and Ticciati, Dresden Staatskapelle with Thielemann, Rotterdam Philharmonic with Nézet-Séguin, Filarmonica della Scala with Harding, Los Angeles Philharmonic with Salonen and Dudamel, New York Philharmonic Orchestra with Masur and Boston Symphony Orchestra with Conlon and Davis; recital appearances include the Aldeburgh, Edinburgh, Salzburg, Schwetzingen and Schwarzenberg Festivals, Vienna Konzerthaus, Amsterdam Concertgebouw, Cologne Philharmonie, Alte Oper Frankfurt and Carnegie Hall, New York; regular guest at Wigmore Hall, London. *Recordings include:* Paris in Roméo et Juliette, Serenade to Music, Beethoven Folk Songs, Warlock Songs, Ireland Songs, Schubert Song Cycles 2011–12, Britten: War Requiem (BBC Music Magazine Choral Award 2014). *Honours:* Queen's Commendation for Excellence at the RAM, Cardiff Singer of the World Competition Lieder Prize 1997. *Current Management:* c/o Henry Lindsay, Askonas Holt, Lincoln House, 296–302 High Holborn, London, WC1V 7JH, England. *Telephone:* (20) 7400-1700. *E-mail:* henry.lindsay@askonasholt.co.uk. *Website:* www.askonasholt.co.uk.

MALZEW, Stefan; German pianist, conductor and composer; *Principal Conductor, Neubrandenburger Philharmonie;* b. 1964, Berlin. *Education:* Hanns Eisler School of Music. *Career:* fmr Asst to George Solti and Yehudi Menuhin at Schleswig Holstein Music Festival; Dir Mecklenburgischen Staatstheater Schwerin 1987–2000; Chief Conductor, Stadttheater Giessen 2000–02; Principal Conductor, Neubrandenberger Philharmonie 2001–; Dir Landestheater Neustrelitz 2003–08; has conducted many German orchestras and choirs at halls including Berlin Philharmonie and Konzerthaus Berlin, Leipziger Gewandhaus, Dresdner Kulturpalast, Kölner Philharmonie and in Warsaw, Palermo, Brussels, China and S Korea; has worked with artists including Andrei Gavrilov, Vladimir Stoupel, Alexander Zintchenko, Pietro Massa, Caroline Anne Widmann and Matthias Schorn. *Compositions include:* opera: Opernpupp 1996, Libuschas Tod 2001; other: five concertos, chamber music. *Recordings include:* as conductor: Busoni: Concerto for Piano & Orchestra with Male Choir (with Pietro Massa) 2008, Martucci: Piano Concerto No. 2 2011, Castelnuovo-Tedesco: Piano Concertos Nos. 1 &2 (with Pietro Massa) 2013; as performer/arranger: Paris Days, Berlin Nights (with Ute Lemper and Vogler Quartett) 2012. *Honours:* Federal President's Prize (for Unterwegs zum Olymp). *Current Management:* Victoria Artists. *E-mail:* info@victoria-artists.com. *Website:* www.victoria-artists.com. *Address:* c/o Schauspielhaus Neubrandenburg, Pfaffenstrasse 22, 17033 Neubrandenburg, Germany. *Telephone:* (395) 5699832. *Fax:* (395) 5826350. *E-mail:* stefan.malzew@web.de (office).

MAMLOK, Ursula; American composer; b. 1 Feb. 1923, Berlin, Germany. *Education:* studied in Berlin and Ecuador, at Mannes Coll., New York with Szell, and at Manhattan School of Music with Vittorio Viannini, studied with Wolpe, Steuermann, Shapey and Sessions. *Career:* Prof. of Composition, Manhattan School of Music 1957–2003; teacher, NYU 1967–76, Kingsborough Community Coll. 1972–75, Manhattan School 1976–; represented USA at the 1984 Int. Rostrum of Composers. *Compositions:* Concerto for strings 1950, Woodwind Quintet 1956, Grasshoppers: six Humoresques 1957, two String Quartets 1962, 1997, Stray Birds for soprano, flute and cello 1963, Haiku Settings for soprano and flute 1967, Capriccios for oboe and piano 1968, Variations and Interlude for percussion quartet 1971, Oboe Concerto 1974, Sextet 1978, String Quintet 1981, From My Garden for violin or viola 1983, Akarina for flute and ensemble 1985, Concertino for wind quartet, two percussion and string orchestra 1987, Der Andreas Garten for mezzo, flutes and harp 1987, Bagatelles for clarinet, violin and cello 1988, Rhapsody for clarinet, viola and piano 1989, Sunflowers for ensemble 1990, five Intermezzi for guitar 1992, piano music and pieces for tape, Constellations for orchestra 1993. *Honours:* American Acad. and Inst. of Arts and Letters Walter Hinrischen Award 1989, Guggenheim Fellowship 1995. *Address:* c/o ASCAP, ASCAP Building, 1 Lincoln Plaza, New York, NY 10023, USA (office). *Telephone:* (212) 427-9411 (home). *E-mail:* hummelmors@earthlink.net (home).

MAMMOSER, Carmen; German singer (mezzo-soprano); b. 1953, Stuttgart; m. Ulrich Walddörfer, one s. *Education:* studied in Stuttgart with Hildegard Dietz and Konrad Richter. *Career:* sang at Hagen Opera from 1980, Stuttgart Staatsoper from 1985; roles have included Mozart's Cherubino and Annio, Offenbach's Nicklausse, Eboli in Don Carlos, Suzuki in Butterfly, Adalgisa in Norma, Emilia in Othello (with Plaido Domingo), Carmen; premiere of Hans Zender's Don Quichote, 1993; concert tour of South America with the Verdi Requiem; 1999 concert tour of Australia with Wagner Wesendonck-Lieder; other concert repertory includes the Passions of J. S. Bach, Bruch's Achilleus and Orchestral Songs by Manfred Trojahn. *Recording:* Rêve d'Amour, French Songs by Fauré and Duparc.

MANAGER, Richetta, BMus; singer (soprano); b. 1952, USA. *Education:* Washburn Univ. of Topeka, Kansas. *Career:* leading artist with Gelsenkirchen Opera from 1982, appeared in the roles of Violetta in La Traviata, Amelia in Un Ballo in Maschera, Alice Ford in Falstaff, Elena in I Vespri Siciliani, Leonora in La Forza del Destino, Nella in Gianni Schicchi, Mimi in La Bohème, Leonore in Fidelio, Tosca, Elsa in Lohengrin, Venus and Elisabeth in Tannhäuser, Agathe in Der Freischütz, The Countess in Le nozze di Figaro, Donna Anna in Don Giovanni, First Lady in Die Zauberflöte, Cleopatra in Handel's Giulio Cesare, and title role in Alcina, Giulietta in Les Contes d'Hoffmann, Marenka in The Bartered Bride, Rosalinde in Die Fledermaus, Saffi in Der Zigeunerbaron, The Duchess of Parma in Busoni's Dr Faustus, Ariadne, Arabella, the Countess in Capriccio, Denise in Tippett's The Knot Garden; sang in the premiere of Tippett's New Year, Houston and Glyndebourne 1989–90; season 1996 as Elisabeth de Valois at Wuppertal and Isolde at Würzburg; season 1999–2000 in Leonore at Eutin, and Salome and Alice Ford at Wuppertal; performed at numerous festivals with several professional orchestras. *Honours:* first prize Metropolitan Opera Guild Auditions, first prize Federated Music Clubs Competition, Gelsenkirchen Alfred Weber Prize of Excellence.

MANASSEN, Alex Jacques; Dutch composer; b. 6 Sept. 1950, Tiel. *Education:* Sweelinck Conservatory, Amsterdam with Ton de Leeuw. *Career:* performances live, on radio and TV in the Netherlands; performances in Italy, France, England, Germany, Israel, Sweden, USA, Poland; commissions for important Dutch funds; teacher of contemporary and electronic music, Sweelinck Conservatory, Amsterdam 1991; Co-founder, composer, Man., Delta Ensemble; teacher of music and informatica, Utrecht Conservatory 1990; Dean, Dir, teacher of composition, Swolle Conservatory 1991–. *Compositions:* Katarsis-Arsis for organ 1973, Prelude for strings and harpsichord 1973, 1995, Mei for flute and string quartet 1974, Citius, Altius, Fortius for variable instrumentation 1979, Pandarus Sings for mezzo-soprano, flute, clarinet and piano 1980, Pandarus Sings, Higher for soprano, flute, clarinet and piano 1980, De Waal for one or more instruments, especially for beginners 1980, Interlude 1 Sextet for oboe, bassoon, french horn and string trio 1980, Bass Clarinet Concerto for bass clarinet and orchestra 1982, Helix for marimba 1983, Denkmal an der Grenze des Fruchtlandes for soprano and chamber ensemble 1983, Air for orchestra 1985, Air for electronic music 1986, Air-Facilmente for clarinet, violin, cello and piano 1986, Songs and Interludes for soprano and chamber ensemble 1979–88, A Call to La Source Possible for soprano and chamber ensemble 1988, Air Conditioned for computer-controlled player piano 1988, Lamento for a Landscape electronic music 1988, Moordunkel for soprano, accordion, bass clarinet and percussion 1990, Two Ears to Hear Two Eyes to See for contralto, tenor and piano 1990, for soprano, clarinet and piano (arranged by Paul van Ostaijen) 1993, Hallo, Hallo for computer-controlled sound-generating object (on request of the Art Foundation Neerijnen, commissioned by Amsterdam Fund for the Arts and the Province of Gelderland) 1991, Evening Beach Piano 1991, Farewell to a Landscape for high voice and clarinet 1994, Lamento for the Hanze Towns 1994, Requiem for a Landscape (based on The Tree Bible by William van Toorn, Gerrit Noordzij and others), Elegy in Memoriam Chris Walraven for eight celli (commissioned by the Fund for the Creation of Music) 1996. *Address:* Ankummerdijk 6, 7722 XJ Dalfsen, The Netherlands.

MANCA DI NISSA, Bernadette; Italian singer (mezzo-soprano); b. 27 Sept. 1954, Cagliari, Sardinia. *Education:* studied at the Salzburg Mozarteum. *Career:* debut at Pesaro Festival 1982 as Isaura in Rossini's Tancredi; La Scala 1983, 1988, as Bradamante in Alcina and Libya in Jommelli's Fetonte; Gluck's Orpheus 1989; Venice Teatro Fenice 1991–92, as Farnace in Mitridate and Isabella in L'Italiana in Algeri; Palermo and Chicago 1996, as Orpheus and the Princess in Suor Angelica by Puccini; other roles include Otho in Handel's Agrippina; Tolomeo in Giulio Cesare and Meg Page in Falstaff; sang Gluck's Orfeo at Naples 1988; and La Scala, Milan 1989; Covent Garden debut 1999 as Mistress Quickly in Falstaff. *Recordings include:* Tancredi (video).

MANCINELLI, Aldo; American pianist and academic; b. 1929, Steubenville, OH; m. 1st; one s. one d.; m. 2nd Judith Elaine Young 1971; one s. one d. *Education:* Oberlin Conservatory of Music, Accademia Nazionale di Santa Cecilia, Rome, Italy, studied with Claudio Arrau, Rudolf Firkusny and Carlo Zecchi. *Career:* debut with Beethoven 1st Piano Concerto, with Wheeling (West Virginia) Symphony 1941; recitals throughout Europe, North Africa, Middle East, North America; appeared as soloist with symphony orchestras throughout Europe and USA, including Cleveland Symphony, San Antonio Symphony, La Scala (Milan), Royal Liverpool Philharmonic, Santa Cecilia Orchestra (Rome), NDR Orchestra (Hamburg). *Recordings:* Piano Music of Charles Griffes (Musical Heritage Soc.), Beethoven's Concerto No. 5 (Emperor); many recordings for Radiotelevisione Italiana, French North Africa Radio, Tunis, Romanian Radio, Bucharest, Beethoven 4th Concerto with the Czech National Symphony Orchestra. *Publication:* contrib. 'Charles Griffes: An American Enigma', in Clavier 1985. *Honours:* first prize Ferruccio Busoni Int. Piano Competition, Bolzano, Italy 1954, laureate Liverpool Int. Piano Concerto Competition 1959, laureate Casella Int. Piano Competition, Naples 1953.

MANDAC, Evelyn; singer (soprano); b. 16 Aug. 1945, Malaybalay, Mindanao, The Philippines. *Education:* Oberlin Coll. Conservatory and Juilliard School, New York. *Career:* debut in Mobile, AL 1968 in Orff's Carmina Burana; Santa Fe 1968, in the US premiere of Henze's The Bassarids; Washington, DC 1969, as Mimi in La Bohème; toured with Juilliard Quartet

1969, in Schoenberg's 2nd Quartet; Seattle Opera 1972, in the premiere of Pasatieri's The Black Widow; sang in the US premiere of Berio's Passaggio; San Francisco 1972, as Inez in L'Africaine; Glyndebourne 1974–75, as Susanna and Despina; Houston Opera 1975, as Lauretta in Gianni Schicchi; Baltimore Opera 1976, in the premiere of Pasatieri's Inez de Castro; Lisa in The Queen of Spades for US television 1977; guest appearances in Toulouse, Turin, Rome, Salzburg Festival and Geneva. *Recordings include:* Carmina Burana (conducted by Ozawa).

MANDANICI, Marcella, DipMus; Italian composer; b. 15 April 1958, Genoa; m. Giuseppe Venturini 1978. *Education:* studied in Brescia, Milan and Santa Cecilia Acad., Rome. *Career:* Autumn Musicale, Como 1984; Aspekte, Salzburg 1986; Nuove Musica Italiana, Rome 1987–88; Settimana di Musica Contemporanea Desenzano 1987–88; Musica Rave, Milan 1985; Spazio Musica, Cagliari 1988; founded Nuovi Spazi Sonori, Italian Asscn for Contemporary Music, Artistic Dir 1987–. *Compositions include:* for solo instruments, chamber ensemble and orchestra, including: Invenzione a Cinque for flute, clarinet, viola, cello and piano 1982, Edipan Steps for piano 1983, Rugginenti, Senza Testo for voice 1987. *Honours:* Steirischer Herbst Selection, Graz 1986, IGNM Selection, Cologne 1987, Antologia Radiotre Selection, Rome 1988, with Double Path.

MANDEL, Alan Roger, BS, MS, DipMus; American pianist, composer, academic and artistic director; *Professor Emeritus of Music, American University*; b. 17 July 1935, New York, USA; m. Nancy Siegmeister 1963 (divorced 1989), remarried 1996. *Education:* Juilliard School of Music, Akademie Mozarteum, Salzburg, Austria, Accademia Monteverdi, Bolzano, Italy. *Career:* debut, Town Hall, New York 1948; numerous int. concert tours worldwide; repertoire of esoteric and seldom-played pieces; Prof. of Music, American Univ., Washington, DC and Chair., Music Div. 1992–2004, Prof. Emer. 2004–; Artistic Dir, (Washing)ton Music Ensemble; commissions from institutions including US Nat. Portrait Gallery (in honour of bicentennial of birth of Pres. Abraham Lincoln), Library of Congress (Croft Memorial Fund), Nat. Museum of African American History and Culture. *Compositions include:* several large symphonic works, piano concerti, choral works, piano compositions, over 130 songs. *Recordings include:* The Complete Piano Works of Charles Ives, Louis Moreau Gottschalk, Forty Works for the Piano, Anthology of American Piano Music 1790–1970, Three Sides of George Rochberg, Carnival Music, Elie Siegmeister, Sonata No. 4 for Violin and Piano, American Piano, Rags and Riches 1992. *Address:* 3113 Northampton Street NW, Washington DC 20015, USA (home). *Telephone:* (202) 244-8484 (home); (202) 885-3063 (office).

MANDELBAUM, Joel, BA, MFA, PhD; American composer; *Professor Emeritus, Queens College, City University of New York*; b. 12 Oct. 1932, New York, NY; m. Ellen Mandelbaum. *Education:* Harvard Univ., Brandeis Univ. and Indiana Univ., studied with Walter Piston, Irving Fine, Harold Shapero and Bernhard Heiden. *Career:* Prof., Queens Coll., CUNY, New York 1961–2016, Prof. Emer. 2016–; Dir Aaron Copland School of Music 1981–84; Fellow, MacDowell Colony 1968; mem. American Festival of Microtonal Music, American Soc. for Jewish Music, Long Island Composers' Alliance. *Compositions:* operas: The Man in the Man-Made Moon 1955, The Four Chaplains 1957, The Dybbuk 1971, The Village 1995; orchestral: Concovation Overture 1951, Piano Concerto 1953, Sursum Corda 1960, Sinfonia Concertante for oboe, horn, violin, cello and chamber orchestra 1962, Memorial for string orchestra 1965, Trumpet Concerto 1970, Concertino for cello and chamber orchestra 1984, In Sainte Chapelle for orchestra 2002, In Marian Woods 2007; chamber: two wind quintets 1957, 1991, two string quartets 1959, 1979, Sonatas with piano for flute 1951, Sonatas with piano for recorder 1972, Sonatas with piano for second piano 1980, Sonatas with piano for oboe 1981, Sonatas with piano for clarinet 1983, Sonatas with piano for cello 1986, Duo Sonata for violin and cello 1989, Trio for piano, violin and cello 2012; works for special microtonal instruments 1961, 1963, 1967, 1977, 1991; choruses, 15 song cycles, musicals and incidental music. *Publication:* Multiple Division of the Octave and the Tonal Resources of 19-tone Equal Temperament 1961. *Address:* 39–49 46th Street, Sunnyside, Queens, NY 11104, USA (home). *Telephone:* (718) 361-8154 (home). *E-mail:* mjoelm@gmail.com (office).

MANDUELL, Sir John, Kt, CBE, FRAM, FRNCM, FRCM, FRSAMD, FWCMD; British composer and music director; b. 2 March 1928, Johannesburg, South Africa; m. Renna Kellaway 1955; three s. one d. *Education:* Haileybury Coll., Jesus Coll., Cambridge, Univ. of Strasbourg, France, Royal Acad. of Music. *Career:* BBC Music Producer 1956–61; Gov. Nat. Youth Orchestra 1964–73, 1978–; Chief Planner, The Music Programme 1964–68; Dir of Music, Univ. of Lancaster 1968–71; Associated Bd of Royal Schools of Music 1971–96; Gov. Chetham's School 1971–; Prin. Royal Northern Coll. of Music 1971–96; Programme Dir Cheltenham Festival 1969–94; Dir Young Concert Artists' Trust 1983–95, Lake District Summer Music Festival 1984–; Pres. European Asscn of Music Acads 1988–96, Opera Bd 1988–95, Bd Royal Opera House 1989–95, Bd Manchester Arts 1991–97; engagements and tours as composer, conductor and lecturer in Canada, Europe, Hong Kong, South Africa and USA; chair. numerous cttees; Chair. or mem. of many int. musical competition juries; European Opera Centre opened with Tosca at Manchester 1998; Mozart's Lucio Silla in London and elsewhere 1999. *Compositions:* Sunderland Point (overture) 1969, Diversions for orchestra 1970, String Quartet 1976, Prayers from the Ark 1981, Double Concerto 1985, Vistas for orchestra 1997, Into the Ark (song cycle) 1997, Flutes Concerto 2003, Nonet 2005. *Recordings:* several albums of own music issued. *Publication:* The Symphony 1966. *Honours:* Hon. Lecturer in Music, Univ. of Manchester 1976–96; Hon. FTCL 1973; Hon. GSM 1986; Chevalier, Ordre des Arts et des Lettres 1990; Hon. DMus (Lancaster) 1990, (Manchester) 1992, (RSA) 1996; Royal Philharmonic Soc. and PRS Leslie Boosey Award 1980, 1990. *Address:* Chesham, High Bentham, via Lancaster, LA2 7JY, England. *Telephone:* (1524) 261702. *Fax:* (1524) 261702.

MANN, Robert; American violinist, composer, conductor and teacher; b. 19 July 1920, Portland, OR; m. Lucy Rowan; one s. one d. *Education:* Juilliard School, with Edouard Dethier, Adolfo Beti, Felix Salmond, Edgar Schenkman, Bernard Wagenar and Stefan Wolpe. *Career:* debut violin recital in New York 1941; faculty mem., Juilliard School after wartime service 1946–; Founder and First Violinist, Juilliard String Quartet 1946–97; many concert engagements in Europe and USA; established Quartet-in-Residence under the Whittall Foundation at the Library of Congress, Washington, DC 1962; Quartet-in-Residence at Michigan State Univ. 1977; first performances of quartets by Carter, Kirchner, Schuman, Sessions, Piston, Babbitt, Copland and Foss; first US Quartet to visit USSR 1961; repertory of 600 works; conductor of contemporary music; has performed and lectured at the Aspen Music Festival; Pres., Walter W. Naumburg Foundation 1971–; Chair. of chamber music panel 1980; coach to Concord, Tokyo, LaSalle and Emerson String Quartets; formed duo with son, Nicholas Mann 1980; faculty mem., Manhattan School of Music 2006–; Fellow, American Acad. of Arts and Sciences 1996–. *Compositions:* over 30 works for narrator and music. *Recordings include:* solo: Bartók's Solo Violin Sonata, Sonata No. 1 for violin and piano, Contrasts, Beethoven's and Brahms's complete violin sonatas (with pianist Stephen Hough), numerous Mozart violin sonatas (with pianist Yefim Bronfmann), Elliott Carter's Duo for Violin and Piano. *Honours:* winner, Naumberg Competition 1941, three Grammy Awards (with Juilliard String Quartet), Artist-Teacher of the Year, American String Teachers' Asscn 2000. *Address:* Manhattan School of Music, 120 Claremont Avenue, New York, NY 10027, USA (office). *Telephone:* (212) 749-2802 (office). *Website:* www.msmnyc.edu (office).

MANN, Werner; German singer (bass); b. 25 June 1935, Berlin. *Education:* studied in Munich and Berne. *Career:* sang at Aachen Opera 1980–84; Trier 1985–90; Pforzheim from 1993; roles have included Mozart's Osmin and Sarastro, Pizarro, Don Pasquale, Falstaff, Verdi's Attlia, King Philip and Padre Guardiano; Rossini's Basilio, Wagner's Daland and King Mark; Ochs in Der Rosenkavalier and Trulove in The Rake's Progress; guest appearances in Geneva, Glasgow and Salzburg; frequent concert engagements throughout Europe. *Recordings:* Schoenberg's Moses und Aron.

MANNING, Jane, OBE, LRAM, FRAM, ARCM, FRCM, GRSM; British singer (soprano), lecturer and writer; *Visiting Professor, Royal College of Music*; b. 20 Sept. 1938, Norwich, Norfolk, England; d. of the late Gerald Manning and Lily Thompson; m. Anthony Payne 1966. *Education:* Norwich High School for Girls, Royal Acad. of Music, Scuola di Canto, Switzerland. *Career:* London debut concert 1964; since then active world-wide as freelance soprano soloist with special expertise in contemporary music; more than 350 BBC broadcasts; regular tours of USA since 1981 and of Australia since 1978; appearances at most leading European festivals and concert halls; New York debut 1983; more than 300 world premières including several operas; Founder/Artistic Dir Jane's Minstrels (ensemble) 1988; many recordings including complete vocal works of Messiaen and Satie; Vice-Pres. Soc. for Promotion of New Music 1996–2008; Visiting Prof., Mills Coll., Oakland, Calif. 1981, 1982, 1983, 1986, Royal Coll. of Music 1995–; Arts and Humanities Research Council Creative Arts Research Fellow, Kingston Univ. 2003–07, Visiting Prof. 2007–10; frequent visiting lecturer at univs in UK, USA, Canada, Australia, NZ and Scandinavia; Chair. Eye Music Trust; Trustee, Musicians' Benevolent Fund. *Publications include:* New Vocal Repertory (Vol. I) 1986, (Vol. II) 1998; contrib. to A Messiaen Companion 1995, Voicing Pierrot (A Practical Guide) 2011; contrib. to History of Musical Performance; numerous articles in Tempo, etc. *Honours:* Hon. Prof., Keele Univ. 1996–2002; Hon. DUniv (York) 1988; Hon. DMus (Keele) 2004, (Dunelm) 2007; Special Award for Services to British Music, Composers' Guild of GB 1973. *Address:* 2 Wilton Square, London, N1 3DL, England. *Telephone:* (20) 7359-1593. *E-mail:* janetone@gmail.com. *Website:* www.classical-artists/janemanning.com.

MANNING, Peter; violinist; b. 17 July 1956, Manchester, England. *Education:* Chetham's School, Royal Northern Coll. of Music, Indiana Univ., USA. *Career:* debut concert at Wigmore Hall 1987; solo appearances with Philharmonia Orchestra, Hallé Orchestre, City of Birmingham Symphony; co-leader, London Philharmonic Orchestra; Prof., Royal Northern Coll. of Music; quartet-in-residence at the Dartington Summer School, with quartets by Schnittke; season 1988–89 in the Genius of Prokofiev series at Blackheath and BBC Lunchtime Series at St John's Smith Square; South Bank Concerto conducted by Neville Marriner concerts with the Hermann Prey Schubertiade and collaborations with the Alban Berg Quartet in the Beethoven Plus series; tour of South America 1988, followed by Scandinavian debut; season 1989–90 with debut tours of The Netherlands, Germany, Spain, Austria and Finland; tours from 1990 to the Far East, Malta, Sweden and Norway; Schoenberg-Handel Concerto with the Gothenburg Symphony; festival appearances at Brighton, the City of London, Greenwich, Canterbury, Harrogate, Chester, Spitalfields and Aldeburgh; collaborations with John Ogdon, Imogen Cooper, Thea King and Lynn Harrell; formerly resident quartet at Liverpool Univ.; teaching role at Lake District Summer Music 1989, Univs of Bristol, Hong Kong 1990. *Recordings:* Beethoven Op 130 and Schnittke Quartet No. 3;

Vaughan Williams On Wenlock Edge and Ravel Quartet; Britten, Prokofiev, Tippett, Elgar and Walton Quartets.

MANNION, Rosa; British singer (soprano); b. 1962, Liverpool, England; one c. *Education:* Royal Scottish Acad. of Music. *Career:* fmr singer with Scottish Opera; Prin. Soprano English Nat. Opera, London 1989–92; appearances in Lisbon, Amsterdam (Netherlands), Berlin, Paris, Salzburg (Austria), Aix-en-Provence (France), Glyndebourne, Royal Opera House, Covent Garden (London); visiting vocal coach, Bath Spa Univ.; Trustee, Jackdaws Educational Trust. *Operas include:* L'Elisir d'amore, Rigoletto, Der Rosenkavalier, La Traviata, Manon, Show Book, Die Zauberflöte, Le Roi malgré lui, Werther, A Masked Ball, Xerxes, Figaro's Wedding.

MANNOV, Johannes; Danish singer (baritone); b. 1965, Copenhagen. *Education:* Conservatoires of Freiburg and Karlsruhe. *Career:* sang with the boys' choir Kobenhauns-Drengekor before adult study; Has sung with the Kassel Opera from 1987 as Mozart's Papageno, Masetto and Figaro; Concert performances under such conductors as Helmuth Rilling, Luigi Nono, George Malcolm, Frans Brüggen, Leif Segerstram and Hans Martin Schneidt; Has performed Mozart's Requiem in Bremen, the Christmas Oratorio in Cologne and Frankfurt and an Italian tour with Bach's St John Passion, 1991–92; Britten's War Requiem in Frankfurt; Sang Mozart's Figaro for Opera Northern Ireland 1991; Season 2000–01 as Christus in the St Matthew Passion, in Berlin, Siegfried in Schumann's Genoveva at Garsington and Papageno for San Diego Opera. *Recordings include:* Keresmin in Holger Danske by Kunzen 1996. *Honours:* Prizewinner, 's-Hertogenbosch Competition, 1986; Helsinki Competition, 1989. *Current Management:* Robert Gilder and Co., 91 Great Russell Street, London, WC1B 3PS, England. *Telephone:* (20) 7580-7758. *Fax:* (20) 7580-7739. *E-mail:* rgilder@robert-gilder.com. *Website:* www.robert-gilder.com.

MANOURY, Philippe; French composer; *Lecturer in Composition, University of California;* b. 19 June 1952, Tulle. *Education:* Conservatoire Nat. de Musique de Paris. *Career:* Music Researcher, Inst. de Recherche et Coordination Acoustique/Musique (IRCAM) 1981–; Prof. of Composition and Electronic Music, Conservatoire Nat. Supérieur Musique et Danse de Lyon 1987–97; Dir Acad. Européenne de Musique du Festival d'Aix-en-Provence 1998–2000; Composer-in-Residence Orchestre de Paris 1995–2001, Scène Nat. d'Orléans 2001–03; Lecturer in Composition, Univ. of Calif. 2004–. *Compositions include:* opera: 60e Parallèle 1995–96, K… (Grand prix de la SACD, Prix de la critique musicale, Prix Pierre Ier de Monaco 2002) 2001, La Frontière 2003; chamber music: Focus 1973, Puzzle 1975, Le Tempérament variable 1978, Quatuor à cordes op. 6 1978, Musique I 1986, Musique II op. 14 1986, Le Livre des claviers 1987, Deux mélodies 1988, Neptune op. 21 1991, Michigan Trio 1992, Gestes 1992, Métal 1995, Ultima 1996, Slova 2001–02, Fragments d'Héraclite; symphonic works: Numéro huit op. 8 1980, Aleph 1985–87, Pentaphone op. 24 1993, Chronophonies I and II 1994, Prelude and Wait 1995, Douze moments 1998, Sound and Fury 1999, Noon 2003, Abgrund 2007, Terra Ignota 2007. *Honours:* Grand prix de composition de la Ville de Paris 1998, SACEM Prix de la musique de chambre 1976, SACEM Grand prix de la musique symphonique 1999, Prix Victoires Composer Award 2012. *Address:* Music Department, Mandeville RM 111 9500, Gilman Dr., MC 0326, La Jolla, CA 92093-0326, USA (office). *Telephone:* (858) 822-6724 (office). *Fax:* (858) 534-8502 (office). *E-mail:* pmanoury@ucsd.edu (office). *Website:* music .ucsd.edu (office).

MANSON, Anne; American conductor; b. 1961. *Education:* Harvard Univ., King's Coll. London, Royal Coll. of Music with Norman del Mar and James Lockhart, Royal Northern Coll. of Music. *Career:* Music Dir, Mecklenburgh Opera, conducting a wide range of 20th-century and contemporary chamber operas; conductor at the Salzburg Festival 1994; conducted English Touring Opera in Don Pasquale and Don Giovanni; The Rise and Fall of the City of Mahagonny for Netherlands Touring Opera 1996; Seven Deadly Sins at the Proms 1997; Asst to Claudio Abbado at 1992 Salzburg Festival in From the House of the Dead and in Boris Godunov at Vienna Staatsoper; conducted at La Monnaie Brussels 1993 in a triple bill of works by Monteverdi and Judith Weir; conducted Boris Godunov with the Vienna Philharmonic and Sam Ramey 1994; US debut at Washington Opera with Samuel Barber's Vanessa 1995, returned with Dangerous Liaisons 1998; conducted Royal Scottish National Orchestra, BBC Scottish, Los Angeles Philharmonic, St Pauls Chamber Orchestra, Scharoun Ensemble; regular guest of Ensemble Intercontempoain and Iceland Symphony; Music Dir, Kansas City Symphony 1999–; conducted Susannah, by Carlisle Floyd, Théâtre de Genève 2000; conducted Houston Symphony 2001. *Recordings:* Tristan Keuris with Residentie Orchestra, Jon Leifs with Iceland Symphony Orchestra. *Honours:* Fellow in Conducting Royal Northern Coll. of Music, Marshall Scholarship, RCM and RNCM prizes. *Current Management:* ICM Artists, 40 West 57th Street, New York, NY 10019, USA.

MANSUR, Cem, BSc; Turkish conductor; b. 4 Sept. 1957, Istanbul; m. Lale Mansur 1984. *Education:* The City Univ., London, England, studied conducting at the Guildhall School, London and with Leonard Bernstein at the Los Angeles Philharmonic Inst. *Career:* Conductor, Istanbul State Opera 1981–89, also giving orchestral concerts; London debut with English Chamber Orchestra 1985; conducted first performance of Elgar, The Spanish Lady, London 1986; further engagements with orchestras and opera cos in the Netherlands, France, Italy, Czech Repub., Romania, Hungary, Germany, Sweden, Spain, Mexico, Israel, South Africa, Finland and Russia; regular appearances at

Holland Park Opera and Mid Wales Opera; several operas with Kirov Opera at St Petersburg 1993 and 1994; Prin. Conductor, City of Oxford Orchestra 1989–96, including tours to Vienna, Zürich, Prague and Budapest; led Debussy's Le Martyre de Saint Sebastian at St John's Smith Square; further concerts with Britten Sinfonia, Royal Philharmonic Orchestra, English Chamber Orchestra, London Mozart Players, City of London Sinfonia, BBC Concert Orchestra, George Enescu Philharmonic Orchestra (Bucharest), Concerto Grosso Frankfurt, Mexico City Philharmonic Orchestra; Artistic Dir Conductor, Akbank Chamber Orchestra, Istanbul, Turkey 1998–2011; first performance since its creation of Offenbach's Whittington at the City of London Festival 2000; Pres., Ipswich Choral Soc. 1999–; Founding Musical Dir, Turkish Nat. Youth Orchestra; mem. Conductors' Guild (USA). *Recordings:* works by Turkish composers with the Hungarian State Orchestra. *Honours:* Guildhall School Ricordi Conducting Prize 1981. *Address:* 31 Carlingford Road, London, NW3 1RY, England (home). *Telephone:* (20) 7431-2973 (home). *E-mail:* cemmansur@aol.com (home).

MANTLE, Neil Christopher, MBE; British conductor; *Conductor, Scottish Sinfonia;* b. 16 March 1951, Essex; m. Inga Wellesley 1980; one s. one d. *Education:* Royal Acad. of Music, London, Royal Scottish Acad. of Music. *Career:* founder and conductor, Scottish Sinfonia 1970–; conductor Edinburgh Opera Co. 1975–81, Sinfonia Opera 1983–84; guest conductor, Scottish National Orchestra 1984, BBC Scottish Symphony Orchestra 1986–94, Scottish Chamber Orchestra 1994–; mem. Elgar Soc. *Honours:* Royal Scottish Acad. of Music Hugh S. Robertson Conducting Prize 1973, second prize Leeds Conductors' Competition 1986. *E-mail:* webmaster@scottishsinfonia.org.uk. *Website:* www.scottishsinfonia.org.uk.

MÄNTYNEN, Jaana; Finnish singer (soprano); b. 1964. *Education:* Sibelius Acad., Helsinki. *Career:* represented Finland at 1992 Cardiff Singer of the World Competition; appearances at Helsinki in Die Zauberflöte, in the title role of Suor Angelica, Gabriel Come Back by Ilkka Kuusisto, The Telephone by Menotti, La Vida Breve, Eugene Onegin (as Tatiana) and The Maiden in the Tower by Sibelius; Savonlinna Festival 1995, in the premiere of The Palace by Sallinen. *Honours:* prizewinner Timo Mustakallio and Lappeenranta Competitions 1991–92.

MANZ, André, DipMus, MMus; Swiss organist, pianist, harpsichordist and teacher (retd); b. (Andrea-Otto Manz), 15 Dec. 1942, Chur; m. Irene Pomey. *Education:* Music Acad., Zurich, Conservatory, Winterthur, Hochschule für Musik, Cologne, Germany. *Career:* debut 1964; organ recitals in Switzerland, Germany, Italy, Denmark, Japan, Poland, USA, Canada, Spain and Austria; Organist, Protestant City Church of Amriswil 1971–2005; various radio series; piano duo with Irene Manz-Pomey; mem. Schweizer Tonkünstlerverein (STV), Schweizer Musikpädagogischer Verband (SMPV), Thurgau Organists' Asscn (Pres. 1973–93), Rotary Club. *Compositions include:* Play B-A-C-H for six organists and assistants 1971. *Recordings include:* Swiss Baroque Soloists, several organ solo recordings, including complete organ works by Franz Liszt, Variations on National Anthems, Battles and Thunderstorms for Organ, and Four Hands Organ-Playing Throughout Five Centuries, Festive organ music of the 19th and 20th century 2003, Romantic Music for violin and organ 2005. *Publications include:* contrib. to various musical journals. *Honours:* Hon. Citizen of the City of Amriswil 2004; numerous musical prizes and scholarships, Eastern Swiss Radio and Television Asscn Annual Prize 1994, Canton Thurgau Government Annual Cultural Prize 1996. *Address:* Brunnenfeldstrasse 11, 8580 Amriswil, Switzerland (home). *Telephone:* (71) 4112425 (home). *Fax:* (71) 4113978 (home). *E-mail:* i.manz-pomey@bluewin .ch.

MANZ, Sebastian; German clarinettist; b. 1986, Hannover; grandson of Boris Goldstein. *Career:* solo debut (Mozart clarinet concerto with Nordwestdeutsche Philharmonie and Eugene Tzigane), Tonhalle Zürich 2010; performances with orchestras including Dresden Philharmonic, Nürnberg Symphony, Lisbon Metropolitan, Sapporo and Hiroshima Symphony Orchestras; festivals at Salzburg, Lisbon, Heidelberg and Bad Kissingen; appeared in chamber groups in Berlin, Hamburg, Dortmund, Stuttgart, Essen, Tilburg, Nijmegen, Tokyo and Osaka; mem. Junge Wilde concert series, Dortmund Konzerthaus 2012–; worked with Lars Vogt's Rhapsody in School music outreach project. *Recordings include:* Duo Riul 2011, Mozart/Beethoven: Quintette für Bläser und Klavier (ECHO Klassik Awards Deutscher Musikpreis for Chamber Music Recording of the Year/Wind – 17th/18th Century) 2012, Christian Wilhelm Westerhoff 2012, Gottfried Hendrik Mann 2012. *Honours:* Audience Prize and First Prize, Clarinet category, ARD Int. Music Competition, Munich 2008, ECHO Klassik Awards Deutscher Musikpreis for Newcomer of the Year 2011. *Current Management:* c/o Daniela Wiehen, Espellohweg 65, 22607 Hamburg, Germany. *E-mail:* daniela@wiehen.de. *Website:* www.wiehen.de; www.sebastianmanz.com.

MANZ, Wolfgang; German pianist and academic; *Professor of Piano, Nürnberg University of Music;* b. 6 Aug. 1960, Düsseldorf; m. Julia Goldstein 1985; two s. one d. *Education:* Univ. of Music, Hannover, studied with Drahomir Toman, Prague and Karlheinz Kämmerling, Hanover. *Career:* teacher, High School of Music, Karlsruhe 1994–98; concert tours of UK, Germany, Belgium and Japan; performed Promenade Concerts, London 1984, Gilels Memorial Concert, Düsseldorf 1986, Karajan Foundation, Paris 1987; currently Prof. of Piano, Nürnberg Univ. of Music. *Recordings include:* Chopin Studies, Beethoven Triple Concerto, with English Chamber Orchestra, solo recital Liszt, Schumann and Debussy, Dohnanyi Piano Quintet, Russian

Music for Two Pianos (with Rolf Plagge). *Honours:* First Prize Mendelssohn Competition, Berlin 1981, Second Prize, Leeds Piano Competition 1981, Second Prize Brussels Queen Elizabeth Competition 1983, Van Cliburn Int. Piano Competition Award, Texas 1989. *Address:* Altdorfer Kirchenweg 5, 90518 Altdorf, Germany. *Fax:* (9817) 808183. *E-mail:* info@wolfgangmanz.de; wolfgangmanz@t-online.de (home). *Website:* www.wolfgangmanz.de.

MANZE, Andrew Mark, FRAM; British conductor; *Principal Conductor, NDR Radio Philharmonic Orchestra;* b. 14 Jan. 1965, Beckenham, Kent, England. *Education:* Univ. of Cambridge, Royal Acad., London, studied with Marie Leonhardt in Amsterdam. *Career:* as guest conductor, regular performances with several leading int. orchestras, including the Deutsches Symphonie-Orchester Berlin, Munich Philharmonic, Royal Stockholm Philharmonic, Finnish Radio Symphony Orchestra, Gothenburg Symphony, Oslo Philharmonic, City of Birmingham Symphony, Hallé, Royal Liverpool Philharmonic, Mahler Chamber Orchestra and the Scottish and Swedish Chamber Orchestras; future orchestral debuts include the New York Philharmonic, Los Angeles Philharmonic, Leipzig Gewandhaus, London Philharmonic, Frankfurt Radio Symphony and Orquestra Sinfônica do Estado de São Paulo. *Radio:* co-presenter, Early Music Show (BBC Radio 3) 2003–. *Recordings include:* Brahms Symphonies Nos 1, 2, 3 and 4, Haydn Variations, Tragic Overture, Academic Festival Overture (Helsingborg Symphony Orchestra), Britten Symphony for cello and orchestra (Alban Gerhardt/BBC Scottish Symphony Orchestra. *Honours:* Rolf Schock Prize 2011. *Current Management:* c/o Bridget Emmerson, Intermusica Artists Management Ltd, 36 Graham Street, Crystal Wharf, London, N1 8GJ, England. *Telephone:* (20) 7608-9900. *Fax:* (20) 7490-3263. *E-mail:* bemmerson@intermusica.co.uk. *Website:* www.intermusica.co.uk.

MANZINO, Leonardo, MMus, PhD; Uruguayan pianist and musicologist; *Professor of the History of Music, Escuela Municipal de Música de Montevideo;* b. 24 Feb. 1962, Montevideo; s. of Raúl Manzino and Myrtha Rebuffo de Manzino; m. Mercedes Xavier de Mello 2003; one s. *Education:* Kolischer Conservatory, Montevideo, Univ. of Uruguay, Catholic Univ. of America, USA. *Career:* debut, Sala Martins Pena, Brasilia 1983; int. summer music festivals of Brasilia 1983–84; Uruguayan Music Students' Asscn 1983; Jeunesses Musicales of Uruguay Series 1984–85; Argentine Music Foundation Series 1986; Adjunct Prof., School of Music, Univ. of Uruguay 1993–94, 1995–; Dir Musicanga Classics 1995; Prof. of the History of Music, Escuela Municipal de Música de Montevideo 1997–. *Publications include:* Composers of the Americas, Vol. 20 (ed.) 1993, Uruguayan Music in the 1892 Celebrations for the IV Centenary of the Encounter of Two Worlds, Latin American Music Review 1993, León Ribeiro: 150th Anniversary of the Romantic Uruguayan Composer 2004, Uruguayan Opera in the 19th-Century: Premières by Tomás Giribaldi in the Teatro Solís 2010, Musicology in Uruguay: Contributions to its Field of Study (ed.) 2014. *Honours:* winner, Uruguayan Music Students' Piano Competition 1983, Jeunesses Musicales of Uruguay Piano Competition 1984, Research Fund from Uruguayan nat. endowment Fondos Concursables para la Cultura 2008. *Address:* Brito del Pino 1423, Montevideo 11600, Uruguay (home).

MANZONE, Jacques Francis; violinist and academic; b. 4 June 1944, Cannes, France. *Education:* Nice Conservatoire with Henri Mazioux, Paris Conservatoire with Roland Charmy and Jacques Fevrier, studied with Eugène Bigot and Henryk Szeryng. *Career:* soloist with the French Radio Orchestra and Société des Concerts du Conservatoire; co-founder, Ensemble Instrumental de France, Paris 1966; soloist with Orchestra of Paris 1967; Prof., Nice Conservatoire 1977; soloist, Nice Philharmonic Orchestra; Prof. of Chamber Music, Nice Int. Summer Acad.; Musical Dir, Chamber Orchestra of Nice 1984, Chamber Opera of France; plays a Maggini violin. *Recordings:* as soloist or conductor.

MANZONI, Giacomo, MusM; Italian composer; b. 26 Sept. 1932, Milan; m. Eugenia Tretti 1960; one s. *Education:* Bocconi Univ., Univ. of Tübingen, Germany, Conservatorio Verdi. *Career:* Ed. Il Diapason (music review) 1956; music critic, l'Unità 1958–66; music ed. Prisma 1968; mem. editorial staff, Musica/Realtà 1980–; Prof., Conservatorio Verdi 1962–64, 1974–91, Conservatorio Martini, Bologna 1965–68, 1969–74, Scuola di Musica Fiesole 1988–2004, Accad. Musicale Pescarese 1993–96; mem. Accad. Nazionale di Santa Cecilia, Rome 1994–; has given master-classes in composition in Buenos Aires, Granada, Tokyo, Santiago, Beijing, etc. *Compositions include:* music theatre: La Sentenza 1960, Atomtod 1965, Per M. Robespierre 1975, Dr. Faustus—Scene dal romanzo di T. Mann 1989; with orchestra: Insiemi 1967, Ombre (alla memoria di Che Guevara) for chorus and orchestra 1968, Parole da Beckett 1971 for 2 choruses and orchestra, Masse: omaggio a E. Varèse, for piano and orch. 1977, Ode 1982, Scene Sinfoniche per il Dr Faustus 1984, Dedica (text by B. Maderna) 1985, 10 versi di E. Dickinson 1989, Malinamusik 1991, Finale e aria (I. Bachmann) 1991, Il deserto cresce (F. Nietzsche) 1992, Moi, Antonin A. (Artaud) 1997, Trame d'Ombre (da Zeami) 1998, O Europa! (A. József) 1999; Sul passaggio del tempo (R. Sanesi) 2001, Sembianti 2003, Studio da concerto for violin, winds and percussion 2005, Mercurio transita davanti al sole 2006, KOKIN b for two voices and orchestra 2008, Progetto Eliogabalo for narrator and orchestra 2009, Studio 2012 etc.; chamber music: Musica notturna 1966, Una voce chiama, for voice, viola and live electronics (F. Fortini) 1994, Quanto oscura selva trovai (Dante), for trombone, chorus and live electronics 1995, Oltre la soglia, for voice and string quartet 2000, Pensiero XX di G. Leopardi for narrator and string quartet 2001, Vergers for choir 2006, 6 Canti dal Kokin shū 2007, Il rumore del tempo for soprano and

instruments 2010, 4° Rivolto for string sextet 2012, Per questo, for soprano and trumpet 2012; film and incidental music. *Publications include:* A. Schoenberg 1975, Scritti 1991, Tradizione e Utopia 1994, Parole per musica 2007, Écrits 2007, Musica e progetto civile 2009; trans of Adorno and Schönberg. *Honours:* Dr hc (Udine) and others; Premio Abbiati 1989, Golden Lion for musical career, Biennale Musica, Venice 2007, Premio Principe Gesualdo 2012. *Address:* Viale Papiniano 31, 20123 Milan, Italy. *Telephone:* (02) 4817955. *E-mail:* gmanz-@libero.it.

MARANGONI, Bruno; Italian singer (bass); b. 13 April 1935, Rovigo. *Education:* studied with Campogalliani and in Venice. *Career:* debut in Venice 1960, as Anselmo in La Molinarelli by Piccinni; many appearances at the Teatro Fenice Venice, Teatro San Carlo Naples, Teatro Massimo Palermo and in Turin, Triste and the Caracalla Baths, Rome; Verona Reana 1973, 1978, 1983–84; guest engagements at Aix-en-Provence, Lisbon, Barcelona and Chicago; other roles have included Geronimo in Il Matrimonio Segreto, Mozart's Leporello, Osmin and Sarastro, Marcel in Les Huguenots, Bartolo in Paisiello's Il Barbiere di Siviglia, Uberto in Pergolesi's La Serva Padrona, Alvise in La Gioconda and Wagner's Daland, Pogner and Hunding; television appearances in La Pietra del Paragone, as Asdrubal, L'Elisir d'amore, Don Carlos, Il Trovatore, Guillaume Tell and Aida.

MARATKA, Kryštof; Czech composer; b. 1972, Prague; m. *Education:* Acad. of Performing Arts Řehoř, Eben, IRCAM. *Career:* based in Paris from 1994; has received commissions from festivals including Festival Présences, Dresdener Musiktage, Korsholm Music Festival, Caramoor Int. Music Festival; commissioned to write an opera and a symphonic piece for Prague Nat. Opera, the latter was performed at a ceremony to mark Czech entry to EC; works have been performed by musicians including Patrick Gallois, Michel Lethiec, Franz Helmersohn, Gustavo Romero, Raphaël Oleg, Vladimir Mendelssohn, by ensembles including Talich Quartet, Quatuor Ysaye, Quatuor Kandinsky, Mozart Piano Quartet, Ensemble Fa, Grieg Trio, and by orchestras including Orchestre de Radio France, St Petersburg Camerata, Brno State Philharmonic, FOK Prague Symphony Orchestra; composer-in-residence Festival Pablo Casals 2002, Czech Centre, Paris 1993, Caramoor Int. Music Festival 1994; world premieres of his work at Festival Int. de Sully-sur-Loire, Wigmore Hall, Konzerthaus Berlin, Louvre Museum, Prague Spring Festival, Novossibirsk; Czech premiere of his viola concerto performed by the Berg Chamber Orchestra, Dvorák Concert Hall, Prague 2004; world premiere of orchestral work Otisk, Caramoor Int. Music Festival 1994. *Compositions include:* Astrophonia for viola and orchestra, Luminarium for clarinet and orchestra, Exaltum for piano quartet, Otisk for symphony orchestra. *Address:* Editions Jobert, 27 boulevard Beaumarchais, Paris 75004, France (office). *Telephone:* 1-56-68-86-60 (office). *Fax:* 1-56-68-90-66 (office). *E-mail:* info@jobert.fr (office). *Website:* www.jobert.fr (office).

MARC, Alessandra; American singer (soprano); b. 29 July 1957, Berlin, Germany. *Career:* debut at Waterloo Festival 1983, as Mariana in Wagner's Das Liebesverbot; sang Gluck's Iphigénie (en Aulide) 1984, Tosca at the Connecticut Opera 1987; Wexford Festival 1987, as Lisabetta in La cena delle beffe; Santa Fe 1988, as Maria in Strauss's Friedenstag, followed by Adriadne 1990; Chicago and San Francisco as Aida, which she also sang on her Metropolitan Opera debut; other roles include the Empress in Die Frau ohne Schatten (Holland Festival, 1990), Sieglinde, and Silvana in La Fiamma by Respighi; Turandot at Philadelphia and Covent Garden (1994); sang Turandot at the 1996 Macerata Festival and at Turin, 1998 and La Scala, 2001; sang Königin der Erdgeister in Hans Heiling by Marschner at the Deutsche Oper, 2001; Concert repertoire includes the Verdi Requiem and Beethoven's Ninth; also a noted recitalist (Wigmore Hall, London, 1990). *Recordings include:* Two versions of Elektra; as Chrysothemis under Barenboim, 1996, and the title role under Sinopoli, 1997. *Website:* www.alessandramarc.com.

MARCELLINO, Raffaele, BMus, GradDip, PhD; Australian composer, educator and administrator; *Chief Academic Officer, SAE Institute, Navitas;* b. 22 April 1964, Sydney, NSW; m. Geraldine Therese Joseph; two s. *Education:* New South Wales Conservatory, Sydney Coll. of Advanced Educ., Univs of Sydney and Tasmania. *Career:* teaching staff, Sydney Conservatorium 1984–86 2001–03; Faculty mem. St Vincent's Coll., Potts Point 1990–94; Univ. of Tasmania 1995–2000; Resident Composer, Sydney Youth Orchestra 1992; Dir, Tasmanian Conservatorium 1996–98; Dean, Australian Inst. of Music 2003–09; Founding Dean, Australian Coll. of the Arts 2009–13; Dir of Academic and Student Services for SAE Australia 2013–15; Chief Academic Officer, SAE Inst. Global, part of Navitas 2015–; mem. Australian Music Centre (full representation), Bd of inaugural 10 Days on the Island Festival Tasmania, Bd of Dirs, The Song Co. *Compositions include:* Woodwind Quintet 1983, Cathedrale for seven brass instruments 1984, Five Bells for string quartet and percussion 1984, Five Bells for string quartet and percussion 1984, Incunabula for orchestra 1985, Responsorio for chorus 1987, Antipodes for orchestra 1987, Suite Etuis for orchestra 1988, Whispers of Fauvel for clarinet and percussion 1988, The Remedy (one-act opera) 1989, Nona for violin 1991, Prester John for ensemble 1991, Don Juan (dance theatre) 1992, Corbaccio for trombone and orchestra 1993, Leviathan for trombone 1994, Fish Tale (song cycle) 1995, The Lottery in Babylon (chamber work) 1995, On the Passing of Time triple concerto 1996, Art of Resonance tuba concerto 1998, Maze for ensemble 1998, Terror Australis for ensemble 1998, Musica Viva 1999, Heart of Fire 2000, The Flight of Les Darcy (opera) 2001, The Art of Memory 2001, Mrs Macquarie's Cello 2003. *Recordings include:* Ein Psalm Davids 2005, Dinner Fanfare (for brass ensemble) 2007, Going Postal (for trumpet and percussion) 2007, Hekuba's Lament (for voice and chamber ensemble) 2008, Companion of the Heart & Caro m'e'l sonno – 2 a cappella settings written and performed by the Song Company 2012, A Strange Kind of Paradise 2013, Turbulent Passions Calm 2014. *Honours:* Australian Composers' Nat. Opera Award 1988, Paul Lowin Prize (highly commended) 1997, Music Fellowship, Music Board of the Australia Council 2003. *Address:* SAE Institute, Littlemore Park, Armstrong Road, Oxford, OX4 FY4, England (office). *Telephone:* 7715-493563 (mobile) (office). *E-mail:* rafmarcellino@gmail .com (home). *Website:* sae.edu (office); rafmarcellino.com.

MARCHADIER, Ludmila; French singer (soprano); b. 1970, Paris. *Education:* Geneva Conservatoire and Royal Acad. of Music, London. *Career:* appearances in Rigoletto at the Grand Théâtre, Geneva, and King Arthur at the Teatro Arriaga, Bilbao; Despina in Così fan tutte with Garden Opera and Adele in Die Fledermaus for European Chamber Opera; sang in Purcell's Fairy Queen and the Lully/Molière Bourgeois Gentilhomme for the English Bach Festival at the Linbury Theatre, Covent Garden 2001; other roles include Niece in Peter Grimes; mem. of chorus, Glyndebourne Festival Opera.

MARCHAND, Jacques, BAC; composer; b. 1 Dec. 1948, Quebec, Canada. *Education:* McGill University, Montréal, Vincent D'Indy Music School, Montréal. *Career:* Nearer the Stars, Ballet for violin solo (Colorado Ballet Company) 1981; Founder, Orchestre Symphonique Regional d'Abitibi-Temiscamingue, 1986; mem. SOCAN; SODRAC; AOC. *Compositions:* Nearer the Stars, 1981; Suite Pour Orchestre, 1987; Fantaisie Pour Orchestre, 1989; Impromptu Pour Piano et Orchestre, 1993; Un Dimanche A Poznań (Poème Symphonique), 1993. *Recordings include:* Jacques Marchand Compositeur 1988. *Honours:* Citoyen d'Honneur de la Societe Nationale des Quebecois, 1992; Hommage de la Chambre de Commerce de Rouyn-Noranda, 1993. *Address:* 22, 8 Rue Rouyn-Noranda, Quebec J9X 2A4, Canada.

MARCHI, Claudia; Italian singer (mezzo-soprano); b. 1967, Bologna. *Education:* studied with Elvina Ramella. *Career:* appearances at Savona from 1992 as Isabella (L'Italiana in Algeri), Verdi's Maddalena and as Sigismonda in the opera by Rossini, under Richard Bonynge 1992; Australian tour, with Luciano Pavarotti in Verdi's Requiem, 1994; season 1995 as Fenena in Nabucco and Azucena in Trovatore, at Marseilles; season 1996–97 as Isabella in Genoa and Isaura in Rossini's Tancredi at the Zürich Opera; further engagements as Rosina and in works by Jommelli, Bach, Mozart and Pergolesi. *Honours:* Prizewinner at the Verdi Competition in Parma and the Luciano Pavarotti International Voice Competition. *Current Management:* c/o Miguel Pons and Daniel Aragall, 2wise artist management, Ronda Sant Pere 29 2º- 3ª, 08010 Barcelona, Spain; c/o Giovanni Montanari, Dimensione Opera, Via Rocca Brancaleone 92, 48100 Ravenna, Italy. *Telephone:* (93) 3041168 (Spain); (544) 456873 (Italy). *Fax:* (544) 456532 (Italy). *E-mail:* miguelpons@ 2wiseartist.com; dimensione.opera@tin.it. *Website:* www.2wiseartist.com; www.dimensioneopera.com; www.claudiamarchi.cjb.net.

MARCINGER, Ludovit; pianist and educator; b. 21 Dec. 1932, Malacky, Czechoslovakia; m. Maria Marcingerova 1977; two d. *Education:* State Conservatoire, Bratislava, Acad. of Music and Drama, Bratislava, Ferencz Liszt Acad. of Music, Budapest. *Career:* debut recital, Dresden 1958; recitals in Prague 1965, Havana 1980, with orchestra, Prague 1964, J. Cikker, Concertino for piano and orchestra, Carlsbad 1966, Grieg, Concerto in A Minor, Bratislava 1967, A. Rubinstein, Concerto No. 5 in D Minor; piano accompaniment for singers, including Peter Dvorsky (tenor) song recitals, Oper der Stadt, Bonn 1983; Grosser Musikvereinssaal, Vienna, Teatro alla Scala, Milan, Brucknerhaus Linz, Slovak Nat. Theatre, Bratislava 1984; Deutsche Oper Berlin, Théâtre de L'Athénée Paris 1986; Suntory Hall Tokyo 1989; Peter Mikulas (bass) song recitals, Mexico City, Caracas, Managua, San José 1992, Bratislava Music Festival 1994, Prague 1996; and with other singers in Peking 1987, Buenos Aires 1996; mem. Slovak Music Union, Asscn of Concert Artists of Bratislava. *Recordings include:* A. Dvořák: Biblical Songs (Op 99), Tchaikovsky: Songs (with Peter Mikulas, bass) 1990, R. Schumann: Frauenliebe und Leben, A. Dvořák: Four Songs (Op 2 V narodnim tonu), F. Schubert: Lieder (with Peter Mikulas, bass) 1997. *Honours:* several prizes in music competitions.

MARCO-BUHRMESTER, Alexander; singer (baritone); b. 1963, Basle, Switzerland. *Education:* studied in Basle and Berne. *Career:* debut in Berne 1985, as Weber's Abu Hassan; toured Switzerland as Dandini in La Cenerentola and sang at the Biel Opera 1986 as Marcello in La Bohème; Essen Opera 1989–92, Dortmund from 1992, notably in the premiere of Caspar Hauser by Reinhard Febel; season 2000–01 in Moses und Aron at the Deutsche Oper Berlin and as Count Luna in Bielefeld. *Current Management:* c/o Boris Orlob Management, Jägerstrasse 70, 10117 Berlin, Germany. *Telephone:* (30) 20450839. *Fax:* (30) 20450849. *E-mail:* info@orlob.net. *Website:* www.orlob.net; www.marco-buhrmester.de.

MARCUS, Marshall, MA, Cert. Ed., ARCM; British arts industry executive and violinist; *Chief Executive, European Union Youth Orchestra*; b. 29 Jan. 1955; m. Annia Casagrande 1984; two d. *Education:* The Queen's Coll., Oxford, Trinity Coll., Cambridge, Royal Coll. of Music, London. *Career:* designed and taught music educ. at primary, secondary and univ. level; as a chamber musician, soloist and orchestral violinist performed in more than 60 countries; fmr mem. BBC Symphony Orchestra; Prof., Simon Bolivar Youth Orchestra of Venezuela 1979–80; Concert Master, Orquesta Philarmonica de Caracas 1979–81; Leader, Orchestra of St Johns 1988–94; Prin. Amsterdam Baroque 1994–97; Exec. Dir Endymion Ensemble 1997–2000; Founding mem. The

Orchestra of the Age of Enlightenment 1985, Chair. 1994–2003, CEO 2003–07; Head of Music, Southbank Centre, London 2006–11, Leader Southbank Centre Venezuelan Sistema Partnership 2011–12; Chief Exec. European Union Youth Orchestra 2012–; Founder and Pres. Sistema Europe; Founder Sistema Africa; Founder and Dir SERA (Sistema Evaluation and Research Archive); Trustee and Dir Sistema England; mem. Sistema Global Advisory Bd; Adviser, London Music Masters, Nat. Orchestra For All; mem. British Council Arts, Creative Economy Advisory Council; Vice-Patron Kampala Music School Appeal; fmr Dir Fundacion Musical Simon Bolivar Baroque Youth Orchestra of Venezuela; fmr Advisor and Tutor I, Culture Orchestra, teaching students from Poland, Belarus, Moldova, Ukraine, Azerbaijan, Armenia and Georgia; fmr mem. Bd Sphinx UK, Asscn of British Orchestras, Kings Place Music Foundation, Music Preserved; judge, RPS Awards, London Music Masters Awards, Leverhulme Trust; Guest on BBC 4's Proms Series, Classic FM podcasts; occasional writer for The Guardian and Chameleonworld; writer and thinker on El Sistema. *Recordings include:* award winning recordings of Rossini String Sonatas, Globokar String Quartet. *Honours:* Hon. Fellow, Worshipful Co. of Musicians. *Address:* European Union Youth Orchestra, 6A Pont Street, London, SW1X 9EL, England (office). *Telephone:* (20) 7235-7671 (office). *Fax:* (20) 7235-7370 (office). *E-mail:* marshall@euyo.eu (office). *Website:* www.euyo.eu (office); marshallmarcus.wordpress.com.

MARCUSSEN, Kjell, DipMus; Norwegian composer; b. 19 May 1952, Arendal. *Education:* Agder Music Conservatorium, Guildhall School of Music, London with Robert Saxton. *Career:* debut at Cardiff Festival of Music 1982; mem. Norwegian Soc. of Composers. *Compositions include:* cantatas, orchestral works, guitar concerto, solo and chamber works; Woodcut for violin, flute and cello 1988, Guitar Sonata No. 1 1988, Partita Jubilante for brass 1993, Festival Overture for symphonic band 1994, Tordenskjold Kantate, Early Part of Summer for flute and harp, Introduction and Allegro for guitar duo. *Address:* c/o Music Information Centre Norway, PO Box 2674, Solli, 0203 Oslo, Norway (office).

MARESTIN, Valérie; singer (mezzo-soprano); b. 1962, Pau, France. *Education:* studied in Lyon with Eric Tappy and in Paris. *Career:* debut at Théâtre de Paris 1987, as La Belle Hélène; guest appearances throughout France, including Carmen at Angers 1988; sang Debussy's Geneviève at Moscow 1987 and Mistress Quickly at Limoges; other roles include Maddalena, Rossweise, Marcellina in Figaro, Rossini's Isabella (at Rheims and Tours), Massenet's Dulcinée and Fenena in Nabucco; Bregenz Festival 1991, as Carmen; frequent concert appearances.

MARGGRAF, Wolfgang, PhD; German musicologist; b. 2 Dec. 1933, Leipzig; m. Anne-Marie Lorz 1975; two s. *Education:* Univs of Leipzig and Jena. *Career:* Prof., Musikhochschule Weimar 1987, Rector 1990–93; mem. Liszt Soc., Weimar 1984–; Gesellschaft für Musikforschung 1991–. *Publications:* Franz Schubert 1967, Giacomo Puccini 1977, Franz Liszt, Schriften zur Tonkunst 1980, Giuseppe Verdi 1982, Franz Liszt in Weimar 1985, Bach in Leipzig 1985.

MARGIONO, Charlotte; Dutch singer (soprano); b. 24 March 1955, Amsterdam. *Education:* Netherlands Opera Studio. *Career:* appearances with Netherlands Opera from 1983, as Kate Pinkerton, Fiordiligi, Pamina, Liu and Amelia Grimaldi; Komische Oper Berlin 1985 as Marenka in The Bartered Bride; Berne and the Aix Festival 1988, as Mozart's Countess and Vitellia; Fiordiligi in Così fan tutte at Amsterdam, 1990; repeated Vitellia at Salzburg 1991 and sang Pamina at Bordeaux, 1992; Strauss's Four Last Songs at the 1995 Prom Concerts, London; Beethoven concert with Roger Norrington at Bremen, 1995 (also televised); season 1995–96, as Agathe at Florence and Desdemona in Amsterdam; sang Leonore in Fidelio at Glybdebourne, 2001. *Recordings include:* Die Zauberflöte, as First Lady (Erato); Beethoven's Mass in C and Missa Solemnis; Ein Deutsches Requiem; Così fan tutte and La Finta giardiniera; Countess in Le nozze di Figaro, conducted by Harnoncourt; Donna Elvira in Don Giovanni, under John Eliot Gardiner. *Current Management:* Alferink Artists Management, Herengracht 340, 1016 CG Amsterdam, The Netherlands. *Telephone:* (20) 6643151. *Fax:* (20) 6752426. *E-mail:* info@ alferink.org. *Website:* www.alferink.org.

MARGISON, Richard Charles, OC; Canadian singer (tenor); b. 16 July 1953, Victoria, BC; m. Valerie Mary Kuinka 1989; one d. *Education:* Univ. of Victoria, Victoria Conservatory of Music, Banff School of Fine Arts, studied singing with Selena James, Leopold Simoneau, Frances Adaskin. *Career:* debut in The Bartered Bride with the Pacific Opera Co., Victoria, BC; has performed with many orchestras, including Vancouver 1989, Toronto 1989, Montréal 1990, London Philharmonic 1991, Chicago 1991, Victoria 1991; regular appearances with opera cos, including ENO 1989 and 1991 as Verdi's Riccardo and as Vakula in Rimsky's Christmas Eve, Montréal Opera 1991, Canadian Opera Co. 1991, Santiago Opera (Teatro Municipal) 1991, Den Norske Opera (Norway) 1991, Calgary Opera 1991 as Nadir in Les Pêcheurs de Perles; other roles include Mozart's Ferrando (Ottawa) and Tito, Pinkerton (Edmonton), Fenton in Falstaff, Faust (at Houston), Don Carlos (San Francisco 1992), Nemorino, Edgardo, Alfredo, Rodolfo and Lensky; season 1992–93 as Riccardo at Antwerp, Don José at Brussels, Don Carlos at Melbourne and Cavaradossi at Covent Garden; many appearances on radio and TV in opera, oratorio and concert; Cavaradossi in Tosca at the reopening of the San Francisco Opera 1997 and at Amsterdam 1998; Boito's Faust at the New York Met 2000, and Manrico in Il Trovatore 2000. *Recordings:* Les Grand

Duos D'Amour from French Operas, Quebec Symphony, Simon Streatfield conducting 1988, Beethoven 9th with London Philharmonic Orchestra, Yehudi Menuhin conducting 1991. *Honours:* Hon. DMus (Univ. of Victoria) 1996; Hon. DLitt (McMaster Univ.) 2002, (Univ. of British Columbia) 2006; Golden Jubilee Medal 2002. *Current Management:* Zemsky/Green Artists Management, 104 West 73rd Street, Suite 1, New York, NY 10023, USA. *Telephone:* (212) 300-8005. *E-mail:* agreen@zemskygreen.com. *Website:* www .zemskygreen.com. *E-mail:* andante@richardmargison.com (office). *Website:* www.richardmargison.com.

MARGITA, Stefan; Slovak singer (tenor); b. 3 Aug. 1956, Košice. *Education:* studied in Košice. *Career:* mem., National Theatre Prague 1986–91, notably as Hoffmann; guest appearances in Moscow, Genoa, Stuttgart, Paris and Budapest; Wexford Festival 1991, as Lucentio in The Taming of the Shrew by Goetz; season 1991–92 as Don Ottavio at the Savonlinna Festival and Bellini's Tebaldo at Budapest; sang Lensky at Trieste, 1996; and in Smetana's Libuše at Edinburgh, 1998; season 2000–01 as Laca in Jenůfa at Glynde-bourne, Lensky at Montpellier and Anatol in War and Peace for the Opéra Bastille, Paris. *Recordings include:* Bellerofonte by Myslivecek and Mahler's Das klagende Lied. *Current Management:* Living Art Impresariat - Paris, 21 rue Foucher-Lepelletier, 92130 Issy les Moulineaux, France; Caecilia Lyric Department, Rennweg 15, 8001 Zürich, Switzerland. *Telephone:* (1) 40-93-05-28 (France); 2213388 (Switzerland). *Fax:* (1) 46-38-65-54 (France); 2117182 (Switzerland). *E-mail:* angelika.belamaric@wanadoo.fr; caecilia@caecilia -lyric.ch. *Website:* www.caecilia.ch.

MARGOLINA, Yelena; pianist; b. 1964, Lviv, Ukraine. *Education:* studied in Lvov and at the St Petersburg State Conservatoire. *Career:* debut with Beethoven's Second Concerto, Lvov 1974; notable performances at Moscow, Kiev, Khabarovsk, Lvov and Dnepropetrovsk; western debut playing Prokofiev's Third Concerto, Berlin Schauspielhaus 1985; concerts at the Prokofiev Centenary Festival in Scotland 1991; performs in chamber concerts and as solo recitalist in a repertoire including works by Haydn, Mozart, Liszt, Beethoven, Debussy and Shostakovich; concerto repertoire includes Beethoven 1–4, Schumann, Chopin, Tchaikovsky, Ravel and Prokofiev. *Honours:* winner Scottish Int. Piano Competition 1990, Casals Monferrato in Italy 1990.

MARIANELLI, Dario; Italian composer; b. Pisa. *Education:* studied piano and composition in Florence and Guildhall School of Music and Drama, London, Bretton Univ. Coll., Nat. Film and Television School. *Career:* classical composer and composer of film soundtracks. *Compositions:* Canti di Uqbar 1991, Rondo for piano and orchestra 1991, Quintet for Winds No. 1 1992, Six Variations on a theme by S. Prokofief for chamber group 1993, One Movement for string quartet 1993, Fantasia for oboe and piano 1993, Four Songs for piano and tenor 1993, I Think I Do Remember Him for cello solo 1994, Pagine Di Sinfonie Perdute 1994, Variations on nought for voice, orchestra and live electronics 1994, 3 Madrigals 1994, Two Digressions for violin and piano 1995, String Quartet No. 1 1995, The Art Of Road Crossing 1996, Seeing Things (for text by Seamus Heaney) 1996, No Hot Ashes for violin solo 1996, Sohini and Mahival (cantata in Urdu, in collaboration with B.Shrivastav) 1997, Quintet for Winds No. 2 1998, Small and Neglectable Discrepancies 1998; for dance: Falling Facades 1994, Lock, Stock and Barrel 1995, Shame 1996, Amongst Shadows 1996, Sketches to Portraits 1996, Seeing Things 1996, Spool of Threads 1997, The Brutality of Fact 1998; for theatre: Molecatcher's Daughter (Production Village, London) 1992, Romeo and Juliet (Pentameters Theatre, London) 1993, Doña Rosita the Spinster (Pentameters Theatre, London) 1993, Antonio's Revenge (Chelsea Centre Theatre, London) 1994, Dr Faustus (RSC) 1997. *Compositions for film:* Models Required 1994, Ailsa 1994, The Sheep Thief 1997, Streetwise, The Long Way Home, The Key, The Man Who Held His Breath, The Stick (TV), I Don't, The Star, Meter Running, Citizen Locke (TV), I Went Down 1997, Preserve (TV) 1999, The Funeral of the Last Gypsy King 1999, Southpaw: The Francis Barrett Story 1999, Being Considered 2000, Pandaemonium 2000, The Warrior 2001, Happy Now?, The Visitor 2002, Blood Strangers (TV) 2002, In This World 2002, I Capture the Castle 2003, This Little Life (TV) 2003, September 2003, The Bypass 2003, Cheeky 2003, Burnt Out, Passer By (TV) 2004, The Brothers Grimm 2005, Shooting Dogs 2005, Opal Dream, Pride & Prejudice (Classical BRIT Award for Soundtrack/ Musical Theatre Composer 2006) 2005, Pobby and Dingan 2005, V for Vendetta 2006, The Return 2006, Goodbye Bafana, Atonement 2007, We Are Together 2007, The Brave One, Far North 2007, Anna Karenina 2012; also for numerous film and TV documentaries. *Honours:* Gulbenkian Foundation scholarship; Benjamin Britten Int. Composition Prize 1997, ASCAP Award 2006. *Current Management:* Air-Edel Associates Ltd, 18 Rodmarton Street, London, W1U 8BJ, England. *Telephone:* (20) 7486-6466. *Fax:* (20) 7224-0344. *E-mail:* air-edel@air-edel.co.uk. *Website:* www.air-edel.co.uk.

MARIANI, Lorenzo; stage director; *Artistic Director, Teatro Massimo, Palermo;* b. 1950, New York, USA. *Education:* Harvard Univ., Univ. of Florence, Italy. *Career:* debut, Maggio Musicale Florence 1982, Bluebeard's Castle; directed L'Heure Espagnole at Florence, La Traviata, Luisa Miller and Offenbach's Barbe-Bleue 1994 at Bologna; Montepulciano Festival with the Henze-Paisiello Don Chisciotte, Greek by Mark Anthony Turnage and Puccini's Edgar; other productions include La Forza del Destino at Florence, Massenet's Esclarmonde in Turin, I Quattro Rusteghi in Geneva, La Bohème in Chicago and Don Giovanni in Tel-Aviv; revived Antoine Vitez's production of Pelléas et Mélisande for Covent Garden 1993; Aida at Florence 1996; Artistic Dir, Teatro Massimo, Palermo 2005–. *Address:* Teatro Massimo, Piazza G. Verdi, 90138 Palermo, Italy (office). *Telephone:* (091) 6053111

(office). *E-mail:* direzioneartistica@teatromassimo.it (office). *Website:* www .teatromassimo.it (office).

MARIATEGUI, Suso; Spanish singer (tenor); b. 1947, Las Palmas. *Education:* studied in Spain, Austria and Italy. *Career:* sang Tamino at the Salzburg Landestheater 1971; Wexford Festival 1973, in Donizetti's L'ajo nell'imbar-azzo; Teatro Liceo, Barcelona 1987, in the local premiere of Mozart's Lucio Silla; guest engagements in Spain, Italy, Vienna and Tehran; Madrid concerts in Bach's St Matthew Passion and Haydn's Creation. *Recordings include:* L'ajo nell'imbarazzo.

MARIMPIETRI, Lydia; singer (soprano); b. 1932, Italy. *Education:* studied in Italy. *Career:* sang at La Scala, Milan 1959, at first as Nella in Gianni Schicchi, and as Micaela; further appearances in Rome, Venice, Parma (Pamina 1974) and Covent Garden (Nedda and Nannetta 1973–75); Glyndebourne Festival 1962–65, as Drusilla in Poppea and Susanna; other roles have included Mimi (at the Vienna Staatsoper), Marguerite, Manon, Bizet's Leila, Donna Elvira, Butterfly (Dallas 1966) and Rossini's Elvira; sang Mimi at Rome 1976. *Recordings include:* L'Incoronazione di Poppea.

MARÍN, Carlos; Spanish singer (baritone); b. 13 Oct. 1968, Rüsselsheim, Germany; m. Geraldine Larrosa 2006. *Education:* Madrid Conservatoire, studied with Montserrat Caballé and Jaime Aragall. *Career:* roles include Figaro in Il Barbiere di Siviglia, Sulpice in La Fille du Régiment, Silvio in Pagliacci, Ostasio in Francesca da Rimini, Taddeo in L'Italiana in Algeri, Ford in Falstaff, Valentin in Faust, Riccardo in I Puritani, Posa in Don Carlos, Marcello in La Bohème, Enrico in Lucia di Lammermoor, Mercutio in Campoamor, Don Giglio in La Capricciosa Corretta, and roles in Madama Butterfly and La Traviata; performances in Spanish zarzuela include La Gran Vía, La Revoltosa, La Verbena de la Paloma; mem., Il Divo 2003–. *Films:* sang in The Nightmare Before Christmas 1993, sang the part of the Prince in Walt Disney's Cinderella (Spanish version) 2000. *Musical theatre roles:* Marius in Les Misérables 1993, The Beauty and the Beast, Vince Fontaine in Grease, Peter Pan. *Recordings include:* albums: solo: The Little Caruso, Mijn Lieve Mama; with Il Divo: Il Divo 2004, Ancora 2005, The Christmas Collection 2005, Siempre 2006, The Promise 2008, Wicked Game 2011. *Honours:* winner Jacinto Guerrero Competition, Francisco Alonso Competition, Julián Gayarre Competition 1996. *Website:* www.ildivo.com.

MARIN, Ion; Romanian conductor; b. 8 July 1960, Bucharest. *Education:* George Enescu Music School, Bucharest, Mozarteum, Salzburg, Accademia Chigiana, Siena and Int. Acad., Nice. *Career:* Music Dir, Transylvania Philharmonic, 1981, appearing in Romania, East Germany, Czechoslovakia, Greece, Italy and France; Resident Conductor, Vienna Staatsoper 1987–91, with repertoire from Mozart to Berg; season 1991–92, in Japan for concerts with Margaret Price and Ruggiero Raimondi, Gala Concert in Prague and Le nozze di Figaro at the Teatro la Fenice, Venice; London debut with the London Symphony Orchestra 1991, English Chamber Orchestra with Yo-Yo Ma as soloist 1992; US debut conducting L'Elisir at Dallas 1991, San Francisco 1992, with Il Barbiere di Siviglia, led Roman Polanski's production of Les Contes d'Hoffmann at the Opéra Bastille, Paris 1992; Metropolitan Opera, 1992–93, Semiramide and Ariadne auf Naxos, Magic Flute; further engagements in L'Italiana in Algeri at Venice 1992, and with Houston Grand Opera; concerts with the City of Birmingham Symphony, Philadelphia Orchestra, Santa Cecilia, Rome, BBC Symphony, Rotterdam Philharmonic and Montreal Symphony 1993; season 1997 with Scottish Chamber Orchestra, Orchestre Nat. de France and the Yomiuri Nippon Symphony Orchestra, Japan; tour of Australia with the ABC; season 1998–99 with Così fan tutte for Nuovo Piccolo Teatro di Milano, and concerts with the Leipzig, Gewandhaus Orchestra, Dresden Staatskapelle and Swedish Radio Symphony Orchestra; season 1999–2000 with Orchestre Nat. d'Ile de France, Orchestre Philharmonique de Monte-Carlo and the BBC Scottish Orchestra; conducted the BBC Scottish Symphony Orchestra, London Proms 2002; season 2008–09 conducted Czech Philharmonic, Munich Philharmonic, Budapest Festival Orchestra, London Symphony Orchestra and Vienna Symphony Orchestra; season 2009–10 conducted St. Petersburg Philharmonic and Berliner Philharmoniker. *Recordings:* Lucia di Lammermoor, with Studer and Domingo, series of Rossini one-acters starting with Il Signor Bruschino; Semiramide, and sacred music for DGG; Various for other major labels including Mozart arias with Barbara Hendricks and the ECO, 1997; Rodrigo and Khachaturian flute concertos with the Philharmonia Orchestra and Patrick Gallois; Opera Arias with the London Symphony Orchestra and Cheryl Studer. *Honours:* Deutsche Schallplatten Awards, Critics Award, 1992, 1994. *Website:* www.ionmarin .com (home).

MARINOV, Swetoslav; violinist; b. 21 Sept. 1945, Lom, Bulgaria; m. Elena Maeva 1967; two s. *Education:* Music School of Sofia, Bulgaria, Bulgarian State Conservatoire, Sofia, studied with Vilmoš Tatrai in Budapest, with Mischa Geler in Moscow Conservatoire, with Yfrah Neaman at the Guildhall School of Music and Drama. *Career:* debut as violinist, Orpheus String Quartet, 1969; Performed with the Tilev String Quartet from 1973, and the Bulgarian RT String Quartet, 1975; Leader of Sofia Soloist Chamber Orchestra, 1981 and Leader of Bremerhaven Opera, Germany, 1988; Other concert activity includes violinist and violist of Bulgarian RT String Quartet and Sofia Chamber Orchestra; Concert tours in Europe, Asia, Australia, South America; In duo violin and piano, concerts with Katia Evrova in France, Cycle of Mozart 16 sonatas, 1990, 1991; Cycle of Beethoven 10 sonatas, 1997; In solo viola concert tour with G Tilev, violin, in Sinfonia Concertante by Mozart with

Niederrheinischen Sinfoniker, Mönchengladbach. *Recordings:* with Radio Sofia, Warsaw, Moscow and Paris. *Honours:* Prizewinner of competition for string quartets in Colmar, 1978 and Evian, France, 1980.

MARK, Peter, BA, MS; American conductor; b. 31 Oct. 1940, New York, NY; m. Thea Musgrave 1971. *Education:* Columbia Univ., Juilliard School of Music with Jean Morel, Joseph Fuchs, Walter Trampler. *Career:* boy soprano soloist, Children's Chorus, New York City Opera and Metropolitan Opera 1953–55; principal freelance and string quartet violist, Juilliard Orchestra, Princeton Symphony, Trenton Symphony, Tiemann String Quartet, Beaux Arts and Los Angeles String Quartet, Santa Barbara Symphony, Lyric Opera Chicago 1960–68; Asst Principal Violist, Los Angeles Philharmonic Orchestra 1968–69; solo violist, Europe, South America and US tours 1965–77; Artistic Dir and Conductor, Virginia Opera 1975–2010; Conductor, Chamber Players, Santa Barbara Chamber Orchestra 1976–77; Guest Conductor, Wolf Trap Orchestra 1979, New York City Opera 1981, Los Angeles Opera Repertory Theater 1981, Royal Opera House, London 1982, Hong Kong Philharmonic Orchestra 1984; Jerusalem Symphony Orchestra 1988; Tulsa Opera 1988; Conductor, local premiere of Porgy and Bess, Buenos Aires and São Paulo 1992; Guest Conductor, Opera Nacional de México 1989, 1992; New York Pops, Carnegie Hall 1991; Orlando Opera Co. 1993; Richmond Symphony 1993; conducted La Bohème at the 1996 Torre del Lago Festival; mem. Musicians' Union. *Recordings:* as conductor: Mary, Queen of Scots 1979, A Christmas Carol 1980, Handel's Julius Caesar 1997; numerous recordings as violist. *Honours:* Juilliard School of Music Elias Lifchey Viola Award 1963, Rosa Ponselle Gold Medal 1997. *Address:* c/o Virginia Opera, Harrison Opera House, 160 East Virginia Beach Boulevard, Norfolk, VA 23510, USA (office).

MARKAUSKAS, Arvydas; singer (baritone); b. 25 Sept. 1951, Kaunas, Lithuania. *Education:* Vilnius Conservatory. *Career:* sang at the Vilnius Opera from 1979, making his debut as the Count in Lortzing's Der Wildschütz; guest appearances throughout Russia and Eastern Europe and with the Lithuanian Opera in the USA (notably in Chicago); other roles include Belcore, Posa, Eugene Onegin, Amonasro, Iago, Nabucco and Marcello; concert repertoire includes Handel's Samson, the War Requiem, Carmina Burana and Kabalevsky's Requiem.

MARKERT, Annette; German singer (mezzo-soprano); b. 1957, Kaltensundheim. *Education:* studied in Leipzig with Helga Forner and with Hannelore Kuhse and Eleanore Elstermann. *Career:* British debut in the Alto Rhapsody with BBC Philharmonic under Kurt Sanderling 1989; has sung with Landestheater Halle as Handel's Floridante, Rinaldo and Tamerlano, Gluck's Orpheus and Carmen; Bach oratorios on German radio and oratorio performances and Lieder recitals throughout Germany. *Honours:* Second Prize, Maria Canals Competition, Barcelona 1985, Handel Prize 1989. *Current Management:* c/o Balmer & Dixon Management, Kreuzstrasse 82, 8032 Zurich, Switzerland. *Telephone:* (43) 2448644. *Fax:* (43) 2448649. *E-mail:* mail@badix.ch. *Website:* www.badix.ch.

MARKHAM, Ralph; Canadian pianist; b. 1949. *Education:* Royal Toronto Conservatory of Music, Cleveland Institute of Music with Vronsky and Babin. *Career:* formed Piano Duo partnership with Kenneth Broadway and has given many recitals and concerts in North America and Europe; BBC debut recital 1979 and further broadcasts on CBC television, Radio France Musique, the Bavarian Radio Hilversum in Netherlands; Stravinsky's Three Dances from Petrushka at the Théâtre des Champs Elysées, Paris, 1984; season 1987–88, included 40 North American recitals; concert with the Vancouver Symphony and New York debut on WQXR Radio; season 1988–89 included the concertos for Two Pianos by Mozart and Bruch in Canada and a recital tour of England and Germany; performances of the Bartók Sonata for two pianos and percussion, with Evelyn Glennie and a 1990–91 tour of North America, Europe and the Far East; festival appearances include Newport USA 1988. *Recordings:* Duos by Anton Rubinstein; Vaughan Williams Concerto for Two Pianos; Saint-Saëns Carnival of the Animals. *Honours:* Young Artist of the Year, Musical America Magazine, 1980, with Kenneth Broadway.

MARKHAM, Richard, ARAM, DipRAM, LRAM, ARCM, FISM; British concert pianist; b. 23 June 1952, Grimsby, Lincs., England; s. of Charles Robert Markham and Marion Edna Markham. *Education:* Wintringham Grammar School, Grimsby, piano privately with Shirley Kemp, at RAM, London with Max Pirani. *Career:* debut, Queen Elizabeth Hall 1974; recitals and concerto performances throughout the UK and abroad; several London appearances at Royal Festival Hall, Royal Albert Hall, Queen Elizabeth Hall, Wigmore Hall, Barbican Hall and Purcell Room; The BBC Henry Wood Promenade Concerts; appearances at festivals in Aldeburgh, Bath, Berlin, Cheltenham, Harrogate, City of London, Schleswig-Holstein and York; regular broadcasts of recitals and concerts for BBC and numerous television and radio stations abroad; has performed with the Philharmonia Orchestra, London Symphony Orchestra, Royal Philharmonic Orchestra, London Philharmonic Orchestra, English Chamber Orchestra, Scottish Nat. Orchestra, London Mozart Players, Bournemouth Sinfonietta, Hallé, Ulster and BBC Philharmonic and Scottish Symphony Orchestras; frequent appearances and tours with piano duo partner David Nettle in Europe, N America, Australia, Japan, Far East and Middle East. *Recordings include:* Kabalevsky, Stravinsky and Rachmaninov with Raphael Wallfisch (cello), Bernstein (arr. Nettle and Markham), Bennett and Grainger (two pianos), Holst, The Planets (two pianos) and Stravinsky, Petrushka and Le Sacre du Printemps (piano duet) with David Nettle, Elgar, Holst, Grainger and Rossini with CBSO Chorus, Saint-Saëns Carnival of the

Animals with Jeremy Nicholas, South of the Border, a Latin American Collection with Jill Gomez, Nettle and Markham in England; Nettle and Markham in France, Arnold, Concerto for Two Pianos and Concerto for Piano Duet, Complete Two-Piano Works of Brahms; Piano Trio Serenade with Rebecca Hirsch (violin) and Jonathan Williams (cello). *Honours:* Frederick Shinn Fellowship 1975, Gulbenkian Foundation Music Fellowships 1976–78; Silver Medal, Geneva Int. Piano Competition 1972, RAM Chappell Gold Medal 1973, Countess of Munster Musical Trust Award 1973–74, Music Retailers' Asscn Award for Excellence 1985. *E-mail:* richardpianouk@gmail.com (office). *Website:* www.nettleandmarkham.com.

MÄRKL, Jun; German conductor, opera director and music director; *Principal Conductor and Artistic Director, MDR Leipzig Radio Symphony Orchestra;* b. 1959, Munich. *Education:* Music Acad., Hannover, Univ. of Michigan, Ann Arbor, USA with Kees Bakels, Sergiu Celibidache and Gustav Meier. *Career:* mem., Junge Deutsche Philharmonie 1980–84; Principal Conductor and Music Dir, Saarland State Theatre 1991–94; Opera and Music Dir, National Theater Mannheim 1994–2000; conducted performances of Tosca, Marriage of Figaro, and Dvořák's Dmitrij; conducted premiere of Detlev Glanert's Der Spiegel des grossen Kaisers 1995; season 1995–96, London debut at Royal Opera House, Covent Garden, with Götterdämmerung; season 1996–97, with Bavarian State Opera in Munich, included new production of Smetana's Bartered Bride, Aida, Madama Butterfly, La Traviata, Peter Grimes; with Berlin State Opera, productions of Lohengrin, Salome, The Flying Dutchman 1996–97; also engagements in the same season with La Clemenza di Tito in Stuttgart and Falstaff in Bern, Madama Butterfly, Manon, Tales of Hoffmann, Tosca, Turandot and Hindemith's Cardillac; premiere of Babylon by Detlef Heusinger, Schwetzinger Festspiele 1997; tours to Japan and Australia 1998 and debut at the Metropolitan Opera, New York; led Berg's Lulu at Mannheim 1998, also concerts with the Orchestre de Paris and the RSO Copenhagen; season 1999 debut at the Metropolitan Opera, New York and the Dallas Symphony Orchestra; Permanent Conductor, Bavarian State Opera 2000–06; Music Dir Orchestra National de Lyon 2004–11; Principal Conductor and Artistic Dir MDR Leipzig Radio Symphony Orchestra 2006–. *Honours:* Conducting Competition winner, German Music Council 1986, Scholarship for study at Tanglewood with Leonard Bernstein and Seiji Ozawa, with the Boston Symphony Orchestra. *Current Management:* Intermusica Artists' Management, 36 Graham Street, Crystal Wharf, London N1 8GJ, England. *Telephone:* (20) 7608-9900. *Fax:* (20) 7490-3263. *E-mail:* mail@intermusica.co.uk. *Website:* www.intermusica.co.uk.

MARKOV, Albert, DMus; American (b. Ukrainian) violinist, composer and writer; *Professor, Manhattan School of Music and Long Island Conservatory;* b. 8 May 1933, Kharkov, USSR; s. of Alexander Markov and Raisa Averbakh; one s. *Education:* Kharkov Music School, Moscow Gnessin Conservatory. *Career:* concert tours in USSR, Europe, USA, Asia; solo performances with Leningrad Philharmonic, Moscow Philharmonic, major orchestras in Belgium, USA, Netherlands, Sweden, UK, Denmark, Portugal, Poland, Germany, Yugoslavia and other countries 1957–; emigrated to USA 1975; debut with Houston Symphony Orchestra 1976; Prof., Manhattan School of Music, USA 1981–, also Long Island Conservatory; Artistic Dir, Rondo Bennington Music Festival, Vt 1999–2006; Founder and Musical Dir Albert Markov Summer Music Festival, NS 1995–99; mem. Rondo Music Soc. (also Pres.), Nat. Acad. of Recording Arts and Sciences. *Compositions:* operas: Queen Esther, Tamara, Checkmate; Symphony 'Kinnor David', Violin Concerto, Formosa, suite for violin and orchestra, Six Violin Rhapsodies, Two Sonatas for violin solo, Duo-sonata for two violins, Two Violin Caprices, Popular Pieces for violin and piano, Paganini Ostinato, variations for solo violin, Cadenzas for violin concerti by Mozart, Viotti, Beethoven, Paganini, Brahms, Cantata 'Bach and Bacchus', Tamara orchestral suite, System of Violin Playing (method), The Little Violinist (method), Vocal Cycle on A. S. Pushkin Words. *Recordings:* Paganini Concerto No. 2; other recordings with orchestras and solo compositions by Bach, Veracini, Schubert, Paganini, Prokofiev, Shostakovich. *Publications:* Six Violin Rhapsodies, Two Sonatas for solo violin, Duo-sonata for Two Violins, System of Violin Playing, Violin Technique, The Little Violinist (method), Violin Caprices, Cadenzas, Edition of the Tchaikovsky Violin Concerto; contrib. to Sovetskaya Musica (USSR), Novoye Russkoe Slovo (Russian daily, USA) Short Stories (Mir Collection). *Honours:* Gold Medals, nat. and int. competitions, Moscow 1957, Gold Medal, Queen Elisabeth Violin Competition, Brussels 1959, Ysaye Medal, Belgium. *Address:* 3 Farm Creek Road, Rowayton, CT 06853, USA. *Website:* www.albertmarkov.com.

MARKOV, Alexander; Russian violinist; b. 24 Jan. 1963, Moscow. *Education:* Central Music School, Moscow; Gnessin School; Manhattan School of Music. *Career:* debut at Carnegie Hall, New York, 1979 (recital debut 1983); many tours in USA and Europe in virtuoso repertoire, notably concertos and Caprices by Paganini; British debut with BBC Philharmonic, 1993; Wigmore Hall, London, 1997, with Paganini's 24 Caprices. *Recordings include:* Paganini's Concertos Nos 1 and 2, 24 Caprices. *Honours:* Gold Medal Paganini Int. Competition 1982, First Prize (jtly) Elena Obraztsova Competition, St Petersburg 2005. *Current Management:* c/o Transart UK, Cedar House, 10 Rutland Street, Filey, N Yorks. YO14 9JB, England. *Telephone:* (1723) 515819. *E-mail:* transartuk@transartuk.com.

MARKOVA, Jirina; Czech singer (soprano); b. 9 Sept. 1957, Prague. *Education:* Prague Conservatory. *Career:* with Prague Nat. Theatre 1979–, notably in operas by Mozart, Donizetti, Smetana, Weber and Janáček; guest appearances in Germany, Austria, New York (Carnegie Hall 1984), Philadelphia 1984, Japan 1985; sang Zerlina in the bicentenary performance of Mozart's Don Giovanni, Prague, 1987; Nat. Theatre, 1991, as Rusalka in Dvořák's opera, 1991 and in Puccini's Tabarro; Mozart Festivals Loudr 1992, Remes 1993, Crest 1994; Kata Kabanova at Opernhaus Zurich 1994; Countess in Marriage of Figaro, Japan 1995, 1997; Abigail in Nabucco, 2001 (also at Castle Loket festival, 2002–03); Amneris in Aida, at State Opera Prague 2003; Princess Strange, Prague Nat. Theatre 2004; Dimitrij, State Opera, Prague 2004; Jenufa and Queen, Ostrava Nat. Theatre 2004; Man and Boy: Dada, Prague Nat. Theatre 2005; Tosca, Opava Theatre 2005; Milada, Opava Theatre 2006; Old Lady in Candide, States Opera Prague 2006; Dir, Childern oper Prag, 1999–. *Recordings include:* Arie Songs 1999. *Publication:* Opera nás baví (co-author) 2005. *Honours:* Czechoslovakia Music Fund 1978, Prize for Partes Barca and Chytracka 1982, Prague Spring Festival Prize 1997. *Current Management:* A.CATS Agency, Zderaská 779/10, Prague 5 153 00, Czech Republic. *Telephone:* (604) 716-552 (office). *E-mail:* a.cats@seznam.cz (office).

MARKOVA, Juliana; pianist; b. 8 July 1945, Sofia, Bulgaria; m. Michael Roll; one s. *Education:* Sofia Conservatory; Verdi Conservatory Milan with Ilonka Deckers. *Career:* after success in Enescu and Marguérite Long Competitions she performed on both sides of the Atlantic; Berlin Festival, Boston Symphony Orchestra and Andrew Davis and the Los Angeles Philharmonic under Zubin Mehta; concerto engagements with all major orchestras in the USA and recitals at Lincoln Center NY and in Los Angeles; recent performances in Atlanta, Cleveland, Chicago, Philadelphia, Detroit, Dallas, Montréal, Toronto and Milwaukee; European tours have included Berlin, Florence and Milan; London concerts with the London Symphony Orchestra, Royal Philharmonic and the Philharmonia, with Claudio Abbado and Simon Rattle; regional engagements with the City of Birmingham Symphony and Royal Scottish Orchestra; British tour with the Sofia Philharmonic; season 1991–92 with tour of Japan and debut with the San Francisco Symphony; repertoire includes concertos by Beethoven, Haydn, Mozart, Prokofiev and Saint-Saëns.

MARKOVA-MIKHAILENKO, Olga; Russian singer (mezzo-soprano); b. 1950. *Career:* many appearances throughout Russia in concert and opera; Kirov Opera, St Petersburg, from 1990 as the Mother Superior in The Fiery Angel, Death in Stravinsky's Nightingale, Valsyevna in the Maid of Pskov by Rimsky-Korsakov and Alkonost in Rimsky's Invisible City of Kitezh; Appearances at San Francisco Opera in Boris Godunov and War and Peace; Sang Khivrya in the British premiere of Prokofiev's Semyon Kotko, with the Kirov at Covent Garden, 2000; Other roles include Fillipyevna in Eugene Onegin, Nezhata in Rimsky's Sadko, Vanya in Ivan Susanin, the Duenna in Prokofiev's Betrothal in a Monastery and Naina in Ruslan and Lyudmila.

MARKOVIC, Aleksandar; Austrian conductor; *Chief Conductor, Brno State Philharmonic Orchestra*; b. 1975, Vienna. *Education:* Univ. for Music and Performing Arts, Vienna, Accademia Musicale Chigiana, Siena, Italy. *Career:* Music Dir Stanislaw Moniuszko Philharmonic Koszalin 2004; Chief Conductor, Tiroler Landestheater, Innsbruck 2005–08; Chief Conductor, Brno State Philharmonic Orchestra 2009–; collaborations include: Scottish Chamber Orchestra 2008, Deutsche Staatsphilharmonie Rheinland-Pfalz 2008, Wuerttemberg Philharmonic Orchestra 2008, Qatar Philharmonic Orchestra 2008, Slovak Philharmonic Orchestra 2011; other guest appearances as conductor include: Mozarteum Orchestra Salzburg, Prague Symphony Orchestra, Wiener Symphoniker, Slovakian and Slovenian Philharmonic Orchestras, Szymanowski Philharmonic Orchestra, Krakow, Janáček Philharmonie, Wiener Kammerorchester, Wiener Konzertverein, Symphonieorchester St. Gallen, Rheinische Philharmonie Koblenz, Dresdner Philharmonic Orchestra; awarded scholarship by Herbert von Karajan Trust, Berlin. *Honours:* First Prize, Int. Grzegorz Fitelberg Conducting Competition, Katowice, Poland 2004. *Current Management:* ItalArtist AustroConcert, Gluckgasse 1, 1010 Vienna, Austria. *Telephone:* (1) 513-2657. *Fax:* (1) 512-6154. *E-mail:* austroconcert@ia-ac.com. *Website:* www.ia-ac.com. *Address:* Robert Hanč, General Manager, Filharmonie Brno, Komenského náměstí 534/8, 602 00 Brno, Czech Republic (office). *Telephone:* (539) 092-842 (office). *E-mail:* robert.hanc@filharmonie-brno.cz (office). *Website:* www.filharmonie-brno.cz (office).

MARKSON, Gerhard; German conductor; b. Bensheim an der Bergstrasse. *Education:* Frankfurt Acad. of Music, conducting with Igor Markevitch in Monte Carlo, Franco Ferrara in Rome. *Career:* worked as opera and symphony conductor at opera houses in Augsburg, Oldenburg and Freiburg; Music Dir, Hagen Theatre 1991–98; Principal Conductor, Radio Telefis Éireann (RTÉ) Nat. Symphony Orchestra 2001–09; has conducted world-wide, including Bavarian State Opera, Hamburg State Opera, Norwegian State Opera, St Cecilia Orchestra, Rome, RAI, Turin, Monte Carlo Philharmonic, Bournemouth Symphony Orchestra, Norwegian Radio Symphony Orchestra, Swiss Radio Symphony Orchestra, Polish Radio Symphony Orchestra. *Current Management:* c/o Leor Segal, Anglo-Swiss Artists' Management, 31 Betterton Street, London WC2H 9BQ, England. *Telephone:* (7964) 195246. *Fax:* (20) 7240-0429. *E-mail:* angloswissartists@gmail.com. *Website:* gerhardmarkson.com.

MARKUS, Urs; Swiss singer (baritone); b. 29 Sept. 1941, Villmergen, Aargau. *Education:* studied in Zürich, Milan and Fribourg. *Career:* sang as a bass at the Biel-Solothurn Opera, 1979–81, baritone roles at Trier, 1983–86;

Engaged at Brunswick 1986–88, Nationaltheater Mannheim from 1988; Guest engagements at Geneva, Nancy and Metz; Roles have included Pizarro and Gluck's Agamemnon, Mozart's Count and Alfonso, Verdi's Amonasro and Iago, Telramund, the Dutchman and Hans Sachs, Escamillo and Gerster's Enoch Arden; Concert appearances throughout Switzerland in Berlin, Venice and Copenhagen. *Current Management:* c/o Agentur Klein, Possartstrasse 8, 81679 Munich, Germany. *Telephone:* (89) 45579931. *Fax:* (89) 45579942. *E-mail:* aklein@agenturklein.de. *Website:* www.agenturklein.de.

MARKVART, Jan; singer (tenor); b. 30 Aug. 1948, Brno, Czechoslovakia. *Career:* sang at the Janáček Theatre, Brno, as the Prince in Rusalka, Ismael in Nabucco and Fernando in La Favorita; Turin 1985, in The Bartered Bride; Buenos Aires 1986, as Gregor in The Makropulos Case; Prague National Theatre from 1986, notably as Florestan 1989; Amsterdam 1988–90, in operas by Janáček; Don José at Bratislava; Theater Luxemburg 1986–95, as Smetana's Dalibor, Ladislav in The Two Widows and the Prince in Rusalka; Nerone (Nerone, A Boito), State Opera, Prague 1998; Pinkerton in Madama Butterfly at Tchai-Pei, Taiwan 1999. *Recordings include:* Stahlav in Smetana's Libuše.

MARLEYN, Paul; British cellist; b. 1965, England. *Education:* Royal Academy of Music with David Strange, studied with Lawrence Lesser in Boston and Aldo Parisot at Yale University. *Career:* recital and solo appearances from 1988 throughout Europe, Canada and the USA, Jordan Hall Boston, Merkin Hall, New York, Chamber Music East and Cape and Island's Music Festivals; Wigmore Hall, London; tour of Europe 1985 as solo cellist with the European Community Youth Orchestra under Claudio Abbado; radio and television engagements in the UK, the USA and Switzerland; tours of Japan, South Korea and Switzerland, 1991. *Honours:* Suggia Scholarship, Dove Prize and Thomas Igloi Trust Prize at the RAM; First Prize, Hudson Valley National String Competition, New York 1988.

MARLTON, Hilton; singer (tenor); b. 1970, South Africa. *Education:* Guildhall School, London. *Career:* appearances as Mozart's Tamino and Ottavio, the Mad Woman in Curlew River, Bardolph in Falstaff, Triquet in Eugene Onegin, Alfredo at the Covent Garden Festival, the Serenade to Music at the Festival Hall and The Seven Deadly Sins for the BBC; further roles include Mozart's Basilio, Rossini's Ramiro, Tonio in La Fille du Régiment, parts in Monteverdi's Ulisse, Ferrando and Don Ottavio for the State Theatre, Pretoria; recitals at St George's, Bristol (songs by Mendelssohn) and elsewhere; Lechmere in Owen Wingrave for Channel 4 TV, Simon the Canaan in Birtwistle's The Last Supper at Glyndebourne 2001.

MAROS, Miklós; Swedish composer, teacher and chamber orchestra leader; b. 14 Nov. 1943, Pécs, Hungary; m. Ilona Maros. *Education:* Acad. of Music, Budapest, State Coll. of Music, Stockholm. *Career:* compositions frequently performed in Europe and USA; Leader, Maros Ensemble; mem. Royal Swedish Acad. of Music, Soc. of Swedish Composers, Int. Soc. for Contemporary Music (Swedish Section), Soc. for Experimental Music and Arts. *Compositions include:* Castratos (opera), Symphonies Nos 1–4, Sinfonietta, Oolit for chamber orchestra, Divertimento for chamber orchestra, Concerto for harpsichord and chamber orchestra, Concerto for trombone and orchestra, Concerto for alto saxophone and orchestra, Concerto for clarinet and orchestra, Concerto for piano and strings, Concerto for flute and strings, Gran sestetto concertante for harpsichord and ensemble, Sonata for piano, String Quartet No. 2 and No. 3, Pentafoglio for guitar and string quartet; chamber music; electroacoustic music. *Recordings:* Descort for soprano flute and double bass, Quartet for saxophones, Oolit for chamber orchestra, Divertimento for chamber orchestra, Circulation for strings, Dimensions for percussion, Symphony No. 1, Stora grusharpan (radio opera), Four songs from Gitanjali for soprano and chamber ensemble, Concerto for trombone and orchestra, Capriccio for guitar, Marimbacapriccio for marimba, Gioco di rincorrersi for marimba and percussion, Undulations for alto saxophone and piano, Passacaglia for soprano and organ, Duo for two celli, Burattinata for alto saxophone and piano, Lyria for trumpet and harp, Ricamo for flute and organ, Feinschnitten for flute and percussion, Gorg for marimba and organ, Schattierungen for cello, Praefatio for organ, Rabescatura for alto saxophone, Concerto for alto saxophone and orchestra, Sinfonia concertante (Symphony No. 3), Trifoglio for harp, Aurora for double wind quintet and windband, Concerto Grosso for saxophone quartet and orchestra, Turba for choir, Concerto for piano and strings. *Honours:* Guest of Berliner Kunstlerprogramm/DAAD in West Berlin (Berlin Artist's Program) 1980–81, Lifetime Artists' Award, Swedish Govt 1990, Christ Johnson Music Prize 2004, Rosenberg Prize 2013. *Address:* Krukmakargatan 18, 118 51 Stockholm, Sweden. *Telephone:* (8) 669-4862. *E-mail:* miklos98@yahoo.com. *Website:* www.mmaros.com.

MÁROVÁ, Libuše; Czech singer (mezzo-soprano); b. 24 Dec. 1943, Sušice; d. of František and Libuše Mára; m. 1st Norbert Snitil 1968 (divorced 1976); m. 2nd Tomáš Šimerda 1980 (divorced 1986). *Education:* Music Acad. (Prague). *Career:* soloist Plzeň Theatre 1965–66, Nat. Theatre, Prague 1966–; has performed in Germany, Netherlands, Austria, Italy, Belgium, France, Spain, Yugoslavia, Norway, Turkey; has recorded recitals and oratorios, and made TV films of Czech and Slovak operas. *Address:* c/o National Theatre Prague, Ostrovní 1, PO Box 865, 112 30 Prague 1, Czech Republic.

MARQUEZ, Marta; German singer (mezzo-soprano); b. 1955, San Juan, Puerto Rico. *Education:* Juilliard School, New York, studies with Tito Gobbi in Florence. *Career:* debut as Oscar in Un Ballo in Maschera, New York City

Opera; sang at Saarbrucken from 1979, notably as Constanze, Frau Fluth, Mimi, Violetta, Susanna and Zdenka in Arabella; Spoleto Festival 1982, as Sylvie in Gounod's La Colombe; sang with Deutsche Oper am Rhein, Düsseldorf 1984–, with notable roles including Poppea, Hänsel, Cherubino, Idamantes, Cenerentola and Rosina (Barbiere), and further engagements throughout Germany; Puerto Rico at the Pablo Casals Festival and appearances in Moscow with the Düsseldorf co.; other roles include Nedda and Musetta; frequent concert appearances; guest appearances at Royal Opera House, Covent Garden and Bavarian State Opera, Munich; sang title role in premiere of Klebe's Gervaise Macquart, Düsseldorf 1996, Mascha in Three Sisters by Eötvös at Düsseldorf 1999, Rossini's Isabella 2001, Penelope in Il Ritorno d'Ulisse 2003, Ottavia in L'Incoronazione di Poppea 2004, Dido in Les Troyens 2005, Mélisande in Pelléas et Mélisande 2009. Address: c/o Opernhaus Düsseldorf, Theatergemeinschaft Düsseldorf-Duisburg, Heinrich-Heine-Allee 16A, 40213 Düsseldorf, Germany (office). Website: www.rheinoper.de (office).

MARRINER, Andrew Stephen; British clarinettist; Principal Clarinet, London Symphony Orchestra; b. 25 Feb. 1954, London, England; s. of Sir Neville Marriner and Lady Elizabeth Marriner; m. Elizabeth Ann Sparke 1988; one s. Education: King's Coll. Choir School, Cambridge, King's School, Canterbury, Univ. of Oxford, Musichochschule, Hannover, Germany. Career: debut, solo chamber and orchestral work 1977–; Principal Clarinet, London Symphony Orchestra 1986–, Acad. of St-Martin-in-the-Fields 1987–2007; first performances of pieces written for him by John Tavener 1997, Robin Holloway 1997, Dominic Muldowney 1997; mem. Lords Taverner. Recordings: Mozart Quintet and Concerto, Weber Concerto, Finzi Concerto, Tavener. Publications: Clarinet Cantilena 2014, Rossini: Quoniam, arranged for clarinet and piano 2014. Honours: Hon. RAM 1995. Current Management: c/o Ingpen & Williams, 7 St George's Court, 131 Putney Bridge Road, London, SW15 2PA, England. Telephone: (20) 8874-3222. Fax: (20) 8877-3113. E-mail: info@ingpen.co.uk. Website: www.ingpen.co.uk; andrewmarrinerclarinet.com.

MARRINER, Sir Neville, Kt, CH, CBE, FRCM, FRAM; British music director and conductor; Life President, Academy of St Martin in the Fields; b. 15 April 1924, Lincoln, Lincs., England; s. of Herbert H. Marriner and Ethel M. Marriner; m. Elizabeth M. Sims 1955; one s. (Andrew Stephen Marriner) one d. Education: Lincoln School, Royal Coll. of Music, London. Career: Founder and Dir Acad. of St Martin-in-the-Fields, London 1956–, now Life Pres.; Musical Dir Los Angeles Chamber Orchestra 1969–78; Dir South Bank Festival of Music 1975–78, Dir Meadowbrook Festival, Detroit, Mich., USA 1979–84; Music Dir Minnesota Orchestra 1979–86, Stuttgart Radio Symphony Orchestra 1984–89, Barbican Summer Festival 1985–87; Fellow, Trinity Coll. of Music, Hong Kong Acad. for Performing Arts. Recordings include: Dvořák Serenades, Haydn Violin Concerto in C, Mozart Serenade K361, Il Barbiere di Siviglia, all Schubert's Symphonies, The English Connection (Vaughan Williams' The Lark Ascending, Elgar Serenade and Tippett Corelli Fantasia), Trumpet Concertos (with Hakan Hardenberger), Mendelssohn Piano Works (with Murray Perahia), Mozart Haffner Serenade, Bach Concertos, Suites and Die Kunst der Fuge, Vivaldi's The Four Seasons, Concerti Grossi by Corelli, Geminiani, Torelli, Locatelli and Manfredini, Mozart Symphonies, Concertos, Serenades and Divertimenti, Handel Messiah, Opera overtures and Water and Fireworks music, Die Zauberflöte 1980, Handel Arias (with Kathleen Battle), Il Turco in Italia and Don Giovanni, Verdi's Oberto 1997, Sylvia McNair: Love's Sweet Surrender 1998, Brahms Symphonies 1–4 1998, Schumann Symphonies 1–4 1998, complete Symphonies of Beethoven, Tchaikovsky, Weber, Gounod, Cantatas of Bach (with Fischer-Dieskau, Janet Baker), Haydn Symphonies. Honours: Hon. Conductor, I, Culture Orchestra 2011–; Kt of the Polar Star (Sweden) 1984, Officier, Ordre des Arts et Lettres 1995; Hon. DMus (Hull) 1998, (Royal Scottish Acad.) 1999; Tagore Gold Medal, six Edison Awards (Netherlands), two Mozart Gemeinde Awards (Austria), three Grand Prix du Disque (France), two Grammy Awards (USA), Shakespeare Prize, Gramophone Award for Outstanding Achievement 2014. Address: Academy of St Martin in the Fields, Fourth Floor, 8 Baltic Street East, London, EC1Y 0UP, England (office). Telephone: (20) 7702-1377 (office). Fax: (20) 7481-0228 (office). E-mail: info@asmf.org (office). Website: www.asmf.org (office).

MARSALIS, Wynton; American musician (trumpet), music administrator and composer; b. 18 Oct. 1961, New Orleans, La; s. of Ellis Marsalis and Dolores Marsalis; three c. Education: Berkshire Music Center, Tanglewood, Juilliard School. Career: played with New Orleans Philharmonic age 14; joined Art Blakey and the Jazz Messengers 1980; toured with Herbie Hancock 1981; formed own group with brother Branford Marsalis 1982; leader Wynton Marsalis Septet; in addition to regular appearances in many countries with his own jazz quintet, follows a classical career and has performed with the world's top orchestras; regularly conducts master classes in schools and holds private tuition; Artistic Dir Lincoln Center Jazz Dept, New York 1990–; apptd UN Messenger of Peace 2001. Compositions include: Soul Gestures in Southern Blues 1988, Citi Movement 1992, Blood on the Fields (oratorio) (Pulitzer Prize for Music 1997) 1994, Jazz/Syncopated Movements 1997, Abyssinian 200: A Celebration 2008. Recordings include: All American Hero 1980, Wynton 1980, Wynton Marsalis 1981, Think of One 1983, Trumpet Concertos: Haydn, Hummel, Mozart 1983, English Chamber Orchestra 1984, Hot House Flowers 1984, Baroque Music: Wynton Marsalis, Edita Gruberova, Raymond Leppard and the English Chamber 1985, Black Codes (From the Underground) 1985, J Mood 1985, Live at Blues Alley 1986, Tomasi/Jolivet:

Trumpet Concertos 1986, Carnaval 1987, Baroque Music for Trumpets 1988, The Majesty of the Blues 1989, Crescent City Christmas Card 1989, Tune in Tomorrow (soundtrack) 1991, Quiet City 1989, 24 1990, Trumpet Concertos 1990, Blue Interlude 1992, Citi Movement 1992, In This House, On This Morning 1992, Hot Licks: Gypsy 1993, On the Twentieth Century 1993, Joe Cool's Blues 1994, Live in Swing Town 1994, In Gabriel's Garden 1996, Jump Start and Jazz 1996, Live at Bubba's 1996, One By One 1998, The Marcial Suite 1998, At the Octoroon Ball: String Quartet No. 1 1999, Big Train 1999, Fiddler's Tale 1999, Reeltime 1999, Sweet Release and Ghost Story 1999, Listen To The Storyteller 1999, Goin' Down Home 2000, Immortal Concerts: Jody 2000, The London Concert 2000, All Rise 2002, Angel Eyes 2002, The Magic Hour 2004, Two Men with the Blues (with Willie Nelson) 2008, He and She 2009. Television includes: consultant on documentary series Jazz 1999. Publications include: Sweet Swing Blues on the Road 1994, Marsalis on Music 1995, Requiem 1999. Honours: Hon. RAM 1996; Chevalier, Légion d'honneur 2009; numerous hon. doctorates; Edison Award, Netherlands, Grand Prix du Disque, numerous Grammy Awards in both jazz and classical categories, Algur H. Meadows Award, Southern Methodist Univ. 1997, National Medal of Arts 2005, Ronnie Scott Award for Int. Trumpeter 2007, Gold Medal (Vitoria, Spain) 2009, Nat. Endowment of the Arts Jazz Masters Award 2011. Current Management: c/o James Ziefert, Kurland Agency, 173 Brighton Avenue, Boston, MA 02134-2003, USA. Website: www.thekurlandagency.com/artists/wynton-marsalis. E-mail: info@wyntonmarsalis.org. Website: www.wyntonmarsalis.org.

MARSCHNER, Wolfgang; violinist; b. 23 May 1926, Dresden, Germany. Education: Conservatory Dresden and Mozarteum Salzburg. Career: debut aged nine with Tartini's Devil's Trill sonata; Prof., Folkwang-School, Essexn 1956, Music Conservatory, Cologne 1958, Music Conservatory, Freiburg 1963–; regular masterclasses in Warsaw and Weimar; Dir of Pfluger-Foundation for Young Violinists, Freiburg; int. soloist career, concerts in Edinburgh Festival and with Berlin Philharmonic and Royal Philharmonic, London; Premiere, Schoenberg's Violin Concerto in many cities, including London, Vienna and Zürich; founder, Int. Ludwig Spohr Violin Competition, Jacobus Stainer Violin Maker's Competition, Int. Youth Violin Competition, German Spohr Acad., Festival Wolfgang Marschner, Hinterzarten. Compositions: various works for orchestra, two concerti for violin and orchestra, Sonata for solo violin, Canto notturno for violin and organ, Rhapsody for viola solo. Honours: Kranichsteiner Prize for contemporary music 1954, English record prize for interpretation of Schoenberg's Violin Concerto, Bundesverdienstkreuz 1986.

MARSH, David; British singer (bass); b. 29 May 1947, Middlesbrough; s. of Alfred Marsh and Dorothy Thompson; m. Susan; two s. Education: Royal Northern Coll. of Music, studied with Otakar Kraus. Career: sang with ENO, Scottish Opera, Glyndebourne Touring Opera, City of Birmingham Touring Opera, English Touring Opera, Opéra de Lyon, Pfalzbau Theatre Ludwigshafen, Singapore Lyric Theatre, Wexford Festival; roles include Amonasro, Macbeth, Gérard in Andrea Chénier, Don Magnifico, Banquo, Masetto and Commendatore in Don Giovanni, Ramfis, Ferrando in Trovatore, Pantheus in Les Troyens, Dr Grenvil, Pistola in Falstaff, Nourabad in Les Pêcheurs de perles, Abimelech in Samson et Dalila, Trulove in The Rake's Progress, Quince in A Midsummer Night's Dream, Luther/Crespel in Les Contes d'Hoffmann, Sempronius in Timon of Athens, by Stephen Oliver, The King in Pavel Haas's Sarlatan, Tyrone in Alun Hoddinott's Tower; also works as commissioned portrait artist. Address: Cherrybank, Lands of Loyal, Alyth, Perthshire, PH11 8JQ, Scotland (home).

MARSH, Jane, BM; American singer (soprano); Lecturer, Metropolitan Opera, New York; b. 25 July 1946, California. Education: Oberlin College with Ellen Repp, studied with Lili Wexburg and Otto Guth in New York, Gladys Kuchta, Germany, Luigi Ricci, Rome. Career: debut as Desdemona, Spoleto Festival 1965; international singing performer 1966–; roles include Fiordiligi in Cosi fan Tutte, the Countess in The Marriage of Figaro, Donna Elvira and Donna Anna in Don Giovanni, Elettra in Idomeneo, Vitelia in La Clemenza di Tito, Konstanze in Entführung aus dem Serail, Violetta in La Traviata, Elisabetta in Don Carlo, Amelia and Desdemona in Simon Boccanegra and Otello, Leonora in Il Trovatore and La Forza del Destino, Abigaile, Lady Macbeth, Sieglinde in Die Walküre, Elizabeth in Tannhäuser, Daphne, Liebe der Danae, Tatyana in Eugene Onegin, Norma in Bellini, Leonora in Paer's Leonora, Leonore in Beethoven's Leonore, title role in Traetta's Sofonisba, Lisa in Pique Dame, Joanna in Maid of Orleans, Fevoronia in Invisible City of Kitisk; performed at Le Fenice, Venice, San Carlo, Naples, Trieste, Parma, Palermo, Turin, Rome, Florence, Milan, Munich, Dresden, Amsterdam, Madrid, Moscow, Prague, Barcelona, San Antonio, San Francisco, Covent Garden, Deutsche Oper am Rhein, Deutsche Oper Berlin, Berlin Staatsoper unter den Linden, Hamburg Staatsoper, Bayerische Staatsoper, Vienna Staatsoper, New York, Los Angeles, Japan; has performed at many festivals including Verona, Salzburg, Carinthischer Sommer, Sagra Umbra, London Proms, Lincoln Center, Seoul Verdi Fest; held Int. Master Classes, Europe and USA 2006–; Como Opera/Vocal Series Consultant 2006–; Lecturer, Metropolitan Opera and Metropolitan Opera Guild, NY 2007–, Consultant, Metropolitan Opera Guild Masterly Singing Series 2008–; Perguia Bel Canto Voci Consultant, Italy 2008–;. Television: appearances including: Johnny Carson Show 1966–75, Merv Griffin Show 1966–70, Mike Douglas Show 1968–80, Art Buchwald Show 1966–78, BBC Television 1967, Shakespeare in Opera, British Folk Songs, Marcel Prawy in

Vienna and New York 1981–95. *Recordings:* Here She Is 1966, Mendelssohn's Elijah 1968, Beethoven's Ninth Symphony 1969, Orff's De Temporum fine comoedia 1974, Rimsky Korsakov's Invisible City of Kitish 1978, Schubert's Alfonso und Estrella 1978, Traetta's La Sofonista 1978, Verdi's Requiem 1980, Marschner's Der Vampir 1981, Rameau's Zais 1981, Schoek's Penthesilea 1984, Hindemith's Marienleben 1984, Bruckner's Te Deum 1985, Handel's Deidamia 1987, 1999, Strauss's Vier Letzte Lieder 1992, Verdi's Requiem 1995, Beethoven's Missa Solemnis 1999, Verdi's Scenes and Arias 2001, Hindemith's Motets 2002, Hindemith's Life of Maria 2004, Marsh Sings Einem and Rorem 2005, Wolf Spanish Song Book Religious/Worldly Songs 2005, Marx Italian Songbook 2006, Goethe und Gott 2006, Berg Seven Early Songs 2007, Advent and Christmas Recital Songs 2008, Gifts Recital 2010, Treasures Recital 2011. *Publications:* Diva Party Recipes 2006, Jane Talks Anecdotes 2006, Spirit be Joyful: Advent and Christmas Recital Songs 2008. *Honours:* New York Handel Medaille 1966, First Time Gold Medalist, Int. Tchaikovsky Competition in Voice 1966, Presidential Award 1966, Time/Life Merit Award 1966, Key to New York City 1966, Key to San Francisco 1966, US World Report Award 1966, Nat. 4-H Horsemanship Award 1966. *Address:* c/o Metropolitan Opera Guild, 70 Lincoln Center Plaza, New York, NY 10023-6593, USA. *Telephone:* (212) 787-4388. *Fax:* (212) 787-4388. *E-mail:* jmparade@gmail.com. *Website:* www.janemarsh.com.

MARSH, Peter Randall; violinist, violist and conductor; b. 15 June 1931, Glen Ridge, NJ, USA; Juilliard School with Hans Letz, American Conservatory with Scott Willits, Univ. of Washington with Emanuel Zetlin. *Career:* teacher, California Inst. of the Arts 1985–87; Artist-in-Residence and Lecturer, California State Univ. at Fullerton 1987–90; Violin Forum Ed., American String Teachers Magazine 1988–90; Prof., Western Washington Univ., Bellingham 1990–97; Lecturer, Univ. of Southern California 1996–; Dir of String Chamber Music, Univ. of Southern California Thornton School of Music; chamber music includes First Violin, Lenox Quartet 1957–81, Philadelphia Quartet 1981–82, Berkshire Quartet 1983–85, Sequoia Quartet 1985–87, Southwest Chamber Music Soc. 1988–96; Violin/Viola, Picasso Trio 1992–95; First Violin, Pacific Quartet 1993–96; orchestra includes First Violin, Seattle Symphony 1955–57; Viola/First Violin, Pittsburgh Symphony 1957–61; Concertmaster, Seattle Symphony, Seattle Opera, Pacific Northwest Ballet 1982–83; California Chamber Symphony, Colorado Festival Orchestra 1987–89; mem. The Bohemians (New York). *Recordings include:* as first violinist with Lenox Quartet and Southwest Chamber Music Society: Milton Babbitt, Composition for four instruments, 1948; Beethoven, Sextet for string quartet and two horns; Beethoven Violin Sonatas 1–10 2001; Beethoven String Quartet Op.18 No.1 and Op.59 No.3; Berger, String Quartet; Haydn, String Quartets op 20, Nos 1–6; L. Kirchner String Quartet No. 2; Krenek, op 231 for violin and organ, op 237 for string trio; Prokofiev, Quintet op 39 and Overture on Hebrew Themes; Schoenberg, Concerto for string quartet and orchestra, with the London Symphony, and String Trio.

MARSH, Roger, BA, DPhil; British composer and academic; *Professor of Music, University of York*; b. 10 Dec. 1949, Bournemouth, Dorset, England; m. 1st Christina Rhys 1976; two s. one d.; m. 2nd Anna Myatt 1992; one s. two d. *Education:* Univ. of York, studied with Bernard Rands. *Career:* Harkness Fellow, Univ. of California, San Diego, USA 1976–78; Lecturer, Keele Univ. 1978–88; Lecturer, then Sr Lecturer, then Prof., Univ. of York; mem. Midland Music Theatre; Dir Black Hair contemporary music ensemble. *Compositions:* Not a Soul but Ourselves for four amplified voices 1977, The Big Bang (music theatre) 1989, Stepping Out for piano and orchestra 1990, Kagura 1991, Love on the Rocks (music theatre) 1988, Espace for orchestra 1994, Heathcote's Inferno for wind orchestra 1996, Spin for piano and ensemble 1997, Canto I for string orchestra 1999, Chaconne for violin 1999, Sukeruko for percussion quartet 2000, Pierrot Lunaire - 50 Rondels Bergamesques for mixed voices 2002, Il Cor Tristo for the Hilliard Ensemble 2008, What Charlie Did Next for ensemble 2009, Rising for Black Hair 2010. *Radio:* Incidental Music for Goethe's Faust (BBC Radio 3). *Recording:* Pierrot Lunaire 2007. *Honours:* Arts Council Composition Bursary 1993. *Address:* The New Rectory, Everingham, York, North Yorks., YO42 4JA, England (home).

MARSHALL, Ingram Douglass, BA, MFA; American composer; *Visiting Lecturer in Composition, Yale School of Music*; b. 10 May 1942, New York, NY; s. of Harry R. Marshall and Bernice Douglass; m. Veronica Tomasic 1985; one s. *Education:* Lake Forest Coll., Columbia Univ. with Ussachevsky, with Morton Subotnick in New York and California, and traditional Indonesian music at California Inst. of the Arts. *Career:* taught at Inst. of the Arts –1974; performances in USA and Europe; Visiting Lecturer in Composition, Yale School of Music 2005–. *Compositions include:* Transmogrification for tape 1966, Three Buchla Studies for synthesizer 1969, Cortez (text-sound piece) 1973, Vibrosuperball for four amplified percussion 1975, Non Confundar for string sextet, alto flute, clarinet and electronics 1977, Spiritus for six strings, four flutes, harpsichord and vibraphone 1981, Fog Tropes for brass sextet and tape 1982, Voces resonae for string quartet 1984, Three Penitential Visions 1987, Sinfonia Dolce far Niente 1990, Peaceable Kingdom for orchestra and tape 1991, Evensongs for string quartet and tape 1993, Raving in the Wind (dance) 1997, Dark Waters for English horn, tape and electronics 1995, Kingdom Come for orchestra and tape 1997, SOE-PA for guitar with digital delay 1999, Authentic Presence 2001, Muddy Waters for choral ensemble 2002, September Canons 2003, Five Easy Pieces 2003, Bright Kingdoms for orchestra 2004, Dark Florescence 2004, Orphic Memories 2006, Sea Tropes 2006, Baghdad Blues 2006, Seven Sentimental Songs 2007, Florescence Soledad 2007, Psalmbook 2010, New Haven Psalter 2012. *Honours:* AAAL Acad. Award 1999, Guggenheim Fellow 2000; Hon. DFA (Lake Forest Coll.) 2000. *Address:* 17 Rolfe Road, Hamden, CT 06517, USA (home). *E-mail:* ingrammarshall@sbcglobal.net (home). *Website:* www.ingrammarshall.com (home).

MARSHALL, Margaret Anne, OBE; British singer (soprano); b. 4 Jan. 1949, Stirling, Scotland; d. of Robert Marshall and Margaret Marshall; m. Dr Graeme G. K. Davidson 1970; two d. *Education:* High School of Stirling and Royal Scottish Acad. of Music and Drama. *Career:* first opera appearance in Orfeo ed Euridice, Florence 1977; has since sung at La Scala, Covent Garden, Glyndebourne, Scottish Opera, Barcelona, Hamburg, Cologne and Salzburg; concert performances in maj. European and US cities and festivals with maj. orchestras; numerous recordings. *Honours:* Hon. DMus (Univ. of St Andrew) 2009; First Prize, Munich Int. Competition 1974, James Gulliver Award for Performing Arts in Scotland.

MARSHALL, Nicholas, MA; British composer, pianist, conductor and teacher; b. 2 June 1942, Plymouth, Devon, England; s. of Benjamin Haigh Marshall and Dulce Marshall (nee Rapaport); m. Angela Marshall 1982; one s. one d. *Education:* Univ. of Cambridge, Royal Coll. of Music, London. *Career:* Chair. and Artistic Dir Ashburton Festival 1980–84; Artistic Dir Budleigh Music Festival 2006–. *Compositions include:* Partita for Guitar; Three Japanese Fragments for guitar; Seven Folk Songs for voice, recorder and piano; Inscriptions for A Peal of Eight Bells for SATB; Suite for guitar, flute, clarinet, violin and cello; Four Haiku for solo recorder; Trio for recorders; Sonatina for solo flute; Five West Country Folk Songs for SATB; A Country Garland for SATB; Six Elizabethan Love Songs for male voices; Five Country Dances for orchestra; Cool Winds for cello and guitar; The Willow Pattern Story (children's opera); The Young King (children's opera); The Falling of the Leaves (song-cycle for high voice, recorder, cello and harpsichord); Cat and Mouse (song-cycle for counter-tenor, recorder and harpsichord); The Birds (song-cycle for mezzo soprano, recorder and piano); Carousel (seven children's songs for voice, recorder and piano); Music in the Wood (song-cycle for high voice and piano); Three Short Songs for high voice and piano; A Playford Garland for recorder and guitar; Sonata for recorder and piano; The Garden of Eden for recorder, guitar and harpsichord; Concerto for recorder and string quartet; The Nightingale for recorder and string quartet. *Recordings include:* Here we come a-piping (Forsyth), Sonata for recorder and piano (Metier), Cat and Mouse (Guild). *Telephone:* (1395) 568802. *E-mail:* nicholas@marshall21.eclipse.co.uk.

MARSHALL, Robert Lewis, AB, MA, PhD; American musicologist and academic; b. 12 Oct. 1939, New York, NY; m. Traute Maass 1966; one s. one d. *Education:* Columbia Univ., Princeton Univ.; French Horn with Gunther Schuller, High School of Music and Art, New York. *Career:* mem. Music Faculty, Univ. of Chicago 1966–83, Chair. 1972–78; Visiting Prof., Princeton Univ. 1971–72, Columbia Univ. 1977; mem. Music Faculty, Brandeis Univ. 1983–2000, Louis, Frances and Jeffrey Sachar Prof. (Incumbent Endowed Chair) and Chair. 1985–2000; mem. American Bach Soc., Neue Bach-Gesellschaft. *Publications:* The Compositional Process of J. S. Bach 1972, Studies in Renaissance and Baroque Music in Honour of Arthur Mendel 1974, J. S. Bach: Cantatas for 9th and 10th Sundays after Trinity (critical edn) 1985, J. S. Bach Cantata Autographs in American Collections 1985, The Music of J. S. Bach: The Sources, The Style, The Significance 1989, Mozart Speaks: Views on Music, Musicians and The World 1991, Eighteenth Century Keyboard Music 1994, Dennis Brain on Record: A Comprehensive Discography 1996, Bach and Mozart's Artistic Maturity 1998, Variations on the Canon: Essays on Music from Bach to Boulez in Honor of Charles Rosen 2008, Exploring the World of J. S. Bach: A Traveler's Guide 2016; contrib. to Musical Quarterly, Journal of American Musicological Society. *Honours:* Hon. mem. American Musicological Soc. 2003; Otto Kinkeldey Award, American Musicological Soc. 1974, first incumbent Harold Spivacke Consultant to Music Div., Library of Congress 1985, ASCAP-Deems Taylor Award 1990. *Address:* 100 Chestnut Street, West Newton, MA 02465, USA (home). *E-mail:* rmarshal@brandeis.edu (office).

MARSHALL, Wayne, ARCM, FRCO, FRCM; British organist, conductor and pianist; *Principal Guest Conductor, Orchestra Sinfonica di Milano Giuseppe Verdi*; b. 13 Jan. 1961, Oldham, Lancs., England. *Education:* Chetham's School, Manchester, Royal Coll. of Music, Vienna Hochschule. *Career:* organ scholar at Manchester Cathedral and St George's Chapel Windsor; Organist-in-Residence, Bridgewater Hall, Manchester; recitals at St Paul's Cathedral, Westminster Abbey, Suntory Hall, Notre Dame, Festival Hall, Leeds and Birmingham Town Halls, and King's Coll. Cambridge; tours of the USA and Yugoslavia; Windsor and Hong Kong Festivals; worked as repetiteur for Glyndebourne production of Porgy and Bess 1986, appeared as Jasbo Brown the jazz pianist; Asst Chorus Master, Glyndebourne 1987; season 1988–89 included BBC Promenade Concert debut with the Poulenc Concerto and appearances with City of Birmingham Symphony under Simon Rattle and BBC Symphony under Paul Daniel; Carmen Jones in West End, London 1991; regular performer at BBC Proms, including three organ recitals, UK première of A Scotch Bestiary, Last Night of the Proms 1997, First Night of the Proms 2008; conducted Porgy and Bess to celebrate Gershwin centenary and four Proms in the Park; solo pianist appearances include recitals world-wide, Abu Dhabi Festival with London Symphony Orchestra 2010; duo partnership with Kim Criswell; as guest conductor, highlights include Vienna Symphony and Radio, RAI Turin, Hallé, Santa Cecilia, BBC, London, Strasbourg, Dresden,

Royal Stockholm and Monte Carlo Philharmonic orchestras, Orchestre Nat. de Lille, Luxembourg Philharmonic, Orchestre Nat. d'Île de France, Tonkunstlerorchester, Leipzig Gewandhausorchester and Brabant Philharmonic, Porgy and Bess with Washington Nat. Opera, Orchestra Sinfonica di Milano Giuseppe Verdi (Principal Guest Conductor 2007–), Royal Stockholm Philharmonic and Iceland Symphony Orchestra and Candide at Deutsche Staatsoper Berlin 2011. *Recordings include:* I Got Rhythm, Gershwin Song Book (ECHO (Deutscher Schallplattenpreis) Award), Rhapsody in Blue, Saint-Saëns Third (Organ) Symphony with Olso Symphony Orchestra and Mariss Jansons. *Honours:* Dr hc (Bournemouth) 2004. *Address:* c/o Fondazione Orchestra Sinfonica e Coro Sinfonico di Milano Giuseppe Verdi, c.so San Gottardo 39, 20136 Milan, Italy (office). *Telephone:* (2) 4950153 (office). *E-mail:* dirart@laverdi.org (office); info@waynemarshall.com (office). *Website:* www.laverdi.org/english/index.php (office); www.waynemarshall.com (home).

MARSONER, Ingrid; Austrian pianist; b. 1970, Leoben. *Education:* Hochschule für Musik und Kunst, Graz and Universität für Musik und Darstellende Kunst, Vienna. *Career:* teacher, Universität für Musik, Graz 1996–; has performed concerts worldwide, including Musikverein, Vienna, Vienna Festweeks, Grafenegg Castle, Steinway Festival, Arhus, Downers Grove Music Festival, Merkin Hall, New York, Dame Myra Hess Memorial Concert Series, Chicago, Beijing; repertoire includes J. S. Bach, Goldberg Variations, B. Furrer, Drei Klavierstücke, Beethoven, Sonata op. 111, Schubert, Sonata in B Major, piano concertos by Haydn, Mozart, Beethoven, Mendelssohn, Schumann, Bartók, Shostakovich, Messiaen. *Recordings:* Schumann, Kreisleriana op. 16, Schubert Sonatas, works by Schubert and Janáček. *Honours:* Bosendorfer Scholarship 1984, Martha Debelli Scholarship 1985, first prize Steinway Competition 1988, Int. YAPMF Kawai Prize, Los Angeles 1995, first prize Jeunesse Competition, Vienna 1996. *Telephone:* (1) 8248581 (office). *Fax:* (1) 8248581 (office). *E-mail:* ingrid.marsoner@chello.at (office). *Website:* www.ingridmarsoner.at (office).

MARSTON, Nicholas John, MA, PhD, ARCM, ARCO; British academic and musicologist; *Reader in Music Theory and Analysis, and Fellow, King's College, University of Cambridge*; b. 27 Dec. 1958, Penzance, England. *Education:* Humphry Davy Grammar School, Corpus Christi Coll., Cambridge. *Career:* Jr Research Fellow, Selwyn Coll., Cambridge 1984–86; British Acad. Post-doctoral Research Fellow, King's Coll. London 1986–89; Lecturer, Exeter Univ. 1989–94, Bristol Univ. 1994–95; Reader, Univ. of Oxford 1995–2001; Reader in Music Theory and Analysis, Univ. of Cambridge, and Fellow, King's Coll. 2001–; Ed.-in-Chief, Beethoven Forum 2006–08; mem. Soc. for Music Analysis, Vice-Pres. 2000–04, chair. editorial bd 2001–07, Royal Musical Asscn, American Musicological Soc. *Publications:* Schumann: Fantasie Op. 17, Beethoven's Piano Sonata in E Op. 109, The Beethoven Compendium (co-author); contrib. to The Cambridge Companion to Beethoven, The Cambridge Companion to Schumann, 19th Century Music, Music Analysis, Journal of the American Musicological Association, Beethoven Forum, Journal of the Royal Musical Asscn. *Address:* King's College, Cambridge, CB2 1ST, England (office). *Telephone:* (1223) 331331 (office). *Fax:* (1223) 331115 (office). *E-mail:* njm45@cam.ac.uk (office). *Website:* www.mus.cam.ac.uk (office).

MARTA, Istvan, DipMus; Hungarian composer; b. 14 June 1952, Budapest; two d. *Education:* studied in Yugoslavia with W. Lutoslawski, Ferenc Liszt Academy of Music, Budapest. *Career:* folk music collecting tour in Moldavia, Romania, 1973; over 30 pieces of stage and film music composed; teacher of history of classical music and analysis of 20th-century music, Jazz Dept, Bela Bartók School of Music, Budapest, 1981–83; organizer of Planum and Rendezvous, festivals of international contemporary music, 1982 and 1984; Music Dir, National Theater, New Theater, Budapest, 1990–95; Dir, Art Valley Multicultural Festival, 1995. *Compositions:* Text and Music, stage performance based on Samuel Beckett's radioplay, 1978; King of the Dead, cantata 1979; Christmas Day–24th Lesson, Music for Chamber ensemble, 1980; Our Heats, movements for chamber choir and chamber orchestra, 1983; Visions, ballet performed by the ballet corps of the Hungarian State Opera, 1984; Dolls House Story, composition for percussion instruments, 1985; Workers' Operetta, musical 1985; per quattro tromboni, 1986; Kapolcs Alarm, a videoclip, 1987; Slips and Streams, a ballet for tape, 1989; Doom, A Sigh, string auartet, 1989; The Glassblower's Dream, string quartet, 1990; Anatomy of a Scream, ballet for tape, 1990; Blasting in the Bird Cage for tape, 1990; The Temptation of St Anthony, ballet for tape, 1992; Don't Look Back, ballet for tape, 1995; Faust, ballet for tape, 1995; Liliomfi, musical play, 1997. *Address:* Ferenciektere 7–8, 1053 Budapest, Hungary.

MARTIN, Andrea; German singer (baritone); b. 9 March 1949, Klagenfurt. *Education:* studied in Vienna, Santa Cecilia Academy in Rome, studied with Anton Dermota, Hans Hotter, Ettore Campogallian, Mario del Monaco and Giuseppe Taddei. *Career:* debut in Treviso 1979, as Malatesta in Don Pasquale; sang with the Wiener Kammeroper and in Klagenfurt, Salzburg, Graz and Munich; Further Italian engagements at Rome, Palermo, Bologna, Venice, Naples and Verona; Ravenna Festival as Michonnet in Adriana Lecouvreur; Has sung in Maria di Rudenz by Donizetti at Venice and Wiesbaden, as Luna in Trovatore at the Dresden Staatsoper; Guest appearances at the Théâtre des Champs-Elysées, Paris, Liège, Barcelona, Lisbon and Vienna; Concert tours of Japan, Korea, the USA and Brazil. *Recordings:* Imelda de Lambertazzi and Alina, Regina di Golconda by Donizetti, Salieri's Axur, and Così fan tutte. *Current Management:* c/o Opera Vladarski,

Döblinger Hauptstraße 57/18, 1190 Vienna, Austria. *Telephone:* (1) 368-6960/6961. *Fax:* (1) 368-6962. *E-mail:* opera.vladarski@utanet.at.

MARTIN, George Whitney, BA, LLB; American writer; b. 25 Jan. 1926, New York, NY. *Education:* Harvard Coll., Trinity Coll., Cambridge, UK, Univ. of Virginia Law School. *Career:* practised law 1955–59; writer 1959–. *Publications:* The Damrosch Dynasty, America's First Family of Music 1983, Verdi, His Music, Life and Times (fourth edn) 1992, Aspects of Verdi (second edn) 1993, Verdi at The Golden Gate, Opera and San Francisco in the Gold Rush Years 1993, The Opera Companion (sixth edn) 2008, Twentieth Century Opera, A Guide 1999, CCB: The Life and Century of Charles C. Burlingham, New York's First Citizen 1858–1959 (US Supreme Court Historical Soc. Erwin N. Griswold Award 2006) 2005, Verdi in America, Oberto through Rigoletto 2011, The Battle of the Frogs and the Mice, A Homeric Fable (third edn) 2013, Opera at the Bandstand, Then and Now 2014; numerous articles on Verdi and his operas in The Opera Quarterly. *Address:* 53 Crosslands Drive, Kennett Square, PA 19348, USA. *Telephone:* (610) 388-0529. *E-mail:* gwmverdi@verizon.net. *Website:* www.georgewmartin.com.

MARTIN, Kathleen; singer (soprano); b. 28 Feb. 1948, TX, USA. *Education:* UCLA, California State Univ., Long Beach. *Career:* debut with San Francisco Opera as Madama Butterfly; England at the Lubeck Opera 1974–80, as Fiordiligi, Donna Elvira, Nedda, Mimi, Desdemona, the Trovatore Leonora, Elsa, Tatiana and Katya Kabanova; sang at the Frankfurt Opera 1980–83, guest engagements at the Theater am Gärtnerplatz, Munich; sang at Toulouse as Jordane in the 1985 premiere of Landowski's Montségur and appeared at the Paris Opéra 1987.

MARTIN, Marvis; American singer (soprano); b. 1956, Tallahassee, FL. *Education:* Univ. of Miami and Manhattan School. *Career:* sang the Princess in L'Enfant et les Sortilèges, Metropolitan Opera 1983; further New York appearances in Boris Godunov, Ariadne auf Naxos, Porgy and Bess, as Clara; Tchaikovsky's Maid of Orleans; Savonlinna Festival 1992 as Clara and appearances elsewhere as Pamina and Liu in Turandot; many concert engagements.

MARTIN, Matthew, MA, DipRAM, ARAM; British composer, organist and conductor; *Director of Music, Keble College, University of Oxford*; b. 5 July 1976, Birmingham; s. of Richard Martin and Sylvia Hayman. *Education:* Magdalen Coll., Oxford, RAM, studied in Paris with Marie-Claire Alain. *Career:* regular commissions for ensembles including BBC Singers, The Cardinall's Musick, choirs of Westminster Abbey, St Paul's Cathedral, Chester Cathedral and St John's Coll., Cambridge, The Sixteen, Gabrieli Consort, The Tallis Scholars, Help Musicians UK, St David's Cathedral Festival, Bergen Festival, Norway and American Guild of Organists; as recitalist, has performed at UK festivals including Cheltenham, Spitalfields and Southbank and played at Royal Coll. of Organists diploma presentation ceremony 2010; Asst Master of Music, Westminster Cathedral 2004–10; held positions at New Coll., Oxford 2000–02 and Canterbury Cathedral 2002–04; Organist, The London Oratory 2011–15; currently Dir of Music, Keble Coll., Oxford; fmrly Organist, Edington Festival of Music within the Liturgy, Music Dir, Nave Choir 2006–. *Compositions include:* Ecce Concipies 2001, Iustorum animae 2004, O Magnum Mysterium 2005, Westminster Mass 2006, Adam Lay Ybounden 2006, Novo profusi gaudio 2010, The St John's College Service 2011, When David Heard 2011, O Rex Gentium 2011, Preces and Responses 2011, A Song of the New Jerusalem 2011, Festival Anthem: I Saw the Lord 2012, Mass of St Dominic 2012, O Oriens 2012, The Westminster Service 2012, Te Lucis ante terminum 2013, A Hymn of St Ambrose 2013, A Hymn to St Etheldreda 2013, Chester Missa Brevis 2013, Stabat Mater 2014, Jubilate Deo 2014, Laudate Dominum 2014, Nowell Sing We 2014, Ut unum sint 2015, Invocation 2015, Haec Dies 2015, Behold Now Praise the Lord 2015, Lamentations 2016, Petrarch Sonnets 2016. *Honours:* British Composer Award, Liturgical category 2013. *Address:* Keble College, Oxford, OX1 3PG, England (office). *E-mail:* matthew.martin@keble.ox.ac.uk (office). *Website:* www.matthewmartincomposer.co.uk.

MARTIN, Philip James; pianist and composer; b. 27 Oct. 1947, Dublin, Ireland; m. 1970, one s. one d. *Education:* St Mary's Coll., Rathmines, Dublin, Patricia Read Pianoforte School, Dublin, Royal Acad. of Music, London, studied with Mabel Swainson in Dublin, with Louis Kentner in London, Yvonne Lefèbure in Paris. *Career:* debut at Wigmore Hall, London 1970; regular performances with major British orchestras; Royal Festival Hall and Royal Albert Hall debut 1977; BBC Prom concerts 1985, 1987, recorded live on Omnibus at the Proms, BBC television. *Compositions:* two Piano Concertos, Harp Concerto, Beato Angelico for large orchestra, three Piano Trios, chamber music and over 150 songs, Symphony 1999, two large choral works.

MARTIN, Will; New Zealand singer (tenor); b. 31 Aug. 1984, Wellington. *Career:* began career singing on cruise ships; fmr mem. band Rikoche; f. Will Martin Trio; sang NZ Nat. Anthem at three All Blacks rugby matches 2005. *Recordings:* A New World 2008. *Address:* c/o Universal Music Classics and Jazz, 364-366 Kensington High Street, London, W14 8NS, England (office). *E-mail:* info@classicsandjazz.co.uk (office). *Website:* www.universalclassics.com (office); willmartin.net.

MARTINCEK, Dusan; composer; b. 13 June 1936, Presov, Slovakia; m. Magdalena Kockova 1961, one s. *Education:* Bratislava Conservatory, Bratislava Acad. of Music and Drama. *Career:* Asst of Music Theory 1961–72; Assoc. Prof of Theory 1973–86; freelance artist 1987–92; Univ.

Prof. of Composition, Bratislava Acad. of Music and Drama, Bratislava 1993; mem. of numerous musical institutions. *Compositions include:* Dialogues in the Form of Variations for piano and orchestra 1961, Simple overture for small orchestra 1961, eight Piano Sonatas 1967–81, String Quartet 1982–84, Animation for 35 solo strings 1983–86, Continuities for large orchestra 1987–88, Communications for violin and piano 1988, Interrupted Silence for large orchestra 1989–90, Coexistences for string quintet 1993, ten Movements for piano 1992, New Nocturnes for piano 1993–94, Dedications for piano 1997, Verso fine...? for violin solo 1998, compositions for flute and piano, for solo guitar. *Honours:* J. L. Bella Prize 1981, Certificate of Merit 1993, Award Certificate, Switzerland 2002.

MARTINEAU, Malcolm, OBE; British pianist; b. 3 Feb. 1960, Edinburgh, Scotland. *Education:* St Catharine's Coll., Cambridge, Royal Acad. of Music with Kendall Taylor and Geoffrey Parsons, studied with Joyce Rathbone. *Career:* has presented own series (complete songs of Debussy and Poulenc), St John's, Smith Square; Britten series broadcast Wolf, Wigmore Hall; complete lieder of Hugo Wolf, Edinburgh Festival; has appeared throughout Europe, N America and Australia and at festivals in Aix-en-Provence, Vienna, Edinburgh, Schubertiade, Munich, Salzburg. *Recordings:* Schubert, Schumann and English song recitals with Bryn Terfel; Schubert, Strauss, Brahms and Schumann recitals with Simon Keenlyside; recital records with Angela Gheorghiu and Barbara Bonney, Magdalena Kožená and Della Jones; the complete Fauré songs with Sarah Walker and Tom Krause; the complete Britten Folk Songs; the complete Beethoven Folk Songs; accompaniments for Dame Janet Baker, Sarah Walker, Frederica von Stade, Anne Sofie von Otter, Thomas Hampson, Olaf Bär, Karita Mattila, Solveig Kringelborn, Michael Schade, Ian Bostridge, Amanda Roocroft, Joan Rodgers, Sir Thomas Allen, Ann Murray, Susan Graham, Dame Felicity Lott, Christopher Maltman and Jonathan Lemalu; as accompanist (with Simon Keenlyside): Songs of War (Gramophone Award for Best Solo Vocal Recording 2012) 2011. *Honours:* Walter Gruener Int. Lieder Competition 1984. *Website:* www.martineau.info.

MARTÍNEZ, Ana María, BMus, MMus; singer (soprano). *Education:* Juilliard School. *Career:* fmr mem., Houston Grand Opera; operatic roles include Fiordiligi in Così fan tutte, Donna Elvira in Don Giovanni, Micaëla in Carmen, Amelia in Simon Boccanegra, Nedda in I Pagliacci, Violetta in La Traviata, the Contessa in Le Nozze di Figaro, Mimi in La Bohème, Rosina in Il Barbiere di Siviglia, Pamina in the Die Zauberflöte, Liù in Turandot, Blanche in Poulenc's Dialogues des Carmélites, Adina in L'Elisir d'amore, Mélisande in Pelléas et Mélisande; created role of Lucero in world premiere of Daniel Catán's Salsipuedes; performances with opera cos worldwide, including Deutsche Oper Berlin, Hamburg Opera, Vienna Staatsoper, Dresden Semper Oper, Paris Opéra Bastille, Netherlands Opera, Met, Los Angeles Opera, Santa Fe Opera, San Francisco Opera, ROH London; festival appearances include Casals Festival, Puerto Rico, Maggio Musicale Festival, Florence; featured in worldwide tours with Plácido Domingo and Andrea Bocelli. *Recordings:* Glass, La Belle et la Bête 1995, Sheng, The Song of Majnun 1997, Bacalov, Misa Tango 2000, Glass, Symphony No. 5 2000, Albeniz, Merlin (Latin Grammy Award for Classical Album 2001) 2000, Catan, Florencia en el Amazonas 2002, Rodrigo, 100 Años – La Obra Vocal I–IV 2002, Albeniz, Henry Clifford 2003, Spanish Night from the Berlin Waldbuhne (DVD) 2003, Caltelnuovo – Tedesco: Naomi and Ruth 2003, Introducing the World of American Jewish Music 2003, Levy, Masada (Canto de Los Marranos) 2004, Weisgall, T'Kiatot Rituals 2004, Beveridge/Marriner, American Classics 2005, Soprano Songs and Arias 2005. *Honours:* regional prizewinner Metropolitan Opera Nat. Council Auditions 1993, first prize Houston Grand Opera Eleanor McCollum Auditions and Awards 1994, Pepita Embil Award, Operalia II 1995. *Current Management:* c/o Alison Pybus, IMG Artists LLC, Carnegie Hall Tower, 152 West 57th Street, Fifth Floor, New York, NY 10019, USA. *Telephone:* (212) 994-3500 (office). *Fax:* (212) 994-3550 (office). *Website:* www.imgartists.com (office); www.anamariamartinez.info.

MARTINEZ, Odaline de la, BFA, MMus, FRAM; American composer and conductor; *Artistic Director, Lontano Records Limited and Lontano Ensemble*; b. (Odaline de la Caridad Martinez Mijares), 31 Oct. 1949, Matanzas, Cuba; d. of Julian J. Martinez and Odaline M. Martinez. *Education:* Tulane Univ., Royal Acad. of Music and Univ. of Surrey, UK. *Career:* Founder and Music Dir Lontano and London Chamber Symphony, Artistic Dir Lontano 1976–, Lontano Records Ltd 1992–; first woman to conduct a BBC Promenade Concert, Royal Albert Hall, London 1984; Founder and Dir European Women's Orchestra (EWO) 1990–; Founder London Festival of American Music 2006; performances at the Queen Elizabeth Hall and Purcell Room, Barbican, Royal Albert Hall, and St John's Smith Square, London; Bath Festival, Huddersfield Festival, Glamorgan Festival, Chard Festival of Women in Music; tours for Contemporary Music Network; tours abroad in Mexico, USA, NZ, Canada, Colombia, Argentina; conductor with EWO of works by female composers, including Clara Schumann, Grazyna Bacewicz, Eleanor Alberga, Minna Keal, etc.; freelance conductor in N, Cen. and S America, Australia, NZ, Africa, and Europe; composer of three operas and numerous chamber and choral works. *Operas:* Sister Aimée: An American Legend 1984 (premiered in New Orleans 1984, London 1987, California 1990), Imoinda and The Crossing (two parts of a slavery opera trilogy) (premiered in New Orleans, La 2013, London 2015). *Compositions include:* First String Quartet, Litanies, Canciones, Cantos de Amor, orchestral and other chamber music. *Publication:* first edited edn of Ethel Smyth's Symphonic Serenade. *Honours:* Marshall Scholar, Guggenheim Fellowship, Nat. Endowment for the Arts, Danforth Fellowship, Watson Fellowship, Outstanding Alumna Tulane Univ., Villa-Lobos Medal from Brazilian Govt . *Address:* Lontano Trust, Office 44, 219 Walworth Road, London, SE17 1RL, England (office). *Telephone:* 7948-099298 (mobile) (office). *E-mail:* odaline@lontano.co.uk (office); admin@lorelt.co.uk (office). *Website:* www.lontano.co.uk (office); www.lorelt.co.uk (office).

MARTINEZ, Ruben; singer (tenor); b. 1962, Argentina. *Career:* many opera engagements in S America and Europe, notably in Donizetti's L'Elisir d'amore and Gounod's Roméo et Juliette; also sings chansons by Fauré; Contestant at the 1995 Cardiff Singer of the World Competition; Mozart's Lucio Silla with Opera for Europe in London and elsewhere 1998.

MARTINEZ-IZQUIERDO, Ernest; Spanish conductor and composer; b. 11 June 1962, Barcelona. *Education:* diplomas in composition and orchestral conducting. *Career:* debut, Barcelona 1985 with his Ensemble 'Barcelona 216'; Principal Conductor, Ensemble Barcelona 216; Asst Conductor, JONDE (Youth Spanish Orchestra) 1985–87; Asst Conductor, ONE (Spanish Nat. Orchestra) 1988; Asst Conductor, Ensemble Intercontemporain 1988–90; concerts with foreign orchestras, including Philharmonic Orchestra of Minsk, Ensemble Contemporain de Montréal, Orchestra of Teatro Comunale di Bolonia or Avanti Orchestra of Helsinki; concerts with the mainly Spanish orchestras as Symphonic Orchestra of Barcelona, ONE, Cadaqués Orchestra, Symphonic Orchestra of Tenerife, Symphonic Orchestra of Granada; as guest conductor or with his own ensemble, conducted in Europe, including Paris, Prague, Bordeaux, Amsterdam, Palermo, Luxembourg, Madrid, Rome and in festivals, including Festival Internacional de Alicante, Festival de Torroella de Montgri, Zagreb's Biennal, Festival Castell de Perelada, Festival de Cadaqués, Holland Festival, Helsinki's Biennal, Barcelona's Festival de Musica del Segle XX, Festival Aujourd'hui Musiques of Perpignan; mem. Associacio Catalena de Compositors. *Compositions:* Música para orquesta de cuerdas 1986, Música para 10 vcl y orquesta 1991, Música per a un festival 1992, Norte-Sur 1993, Alternanqa 1995, Fanfare for chamber ensemble 1995. *Recordings include:* Album de Colien, Spanish and Portuguese Contemporary Piano Music, 1995; Music for the film Metropolis by Martin Matalon, 1995; Composers of Cercle Manuel de Falla, 1995; Xavier Benguerel: 7 Fables de La Fontaine, 1995.

MARTINIS, Carla; singer (soprano); b. 1921, Danculovice, Yugoslavia. *Education:* Zagreb Conservatory. *Career:* sang first in Zagreb and Prague; New York City Opera, 1950–53, debut as Turandot; Vienna Staatsoper 1951–, debut as Aida, conducted by Karajan; Salzburg Festival, 1951, as Desdemona, conducted by Furtwängler; Paris Opéra, 1951, as Amelia in Un Ballo in Maschera; La Scala Milan, Aix-en-Provence, Naples and Florence, 1952; San Francisco Opera, 1954; sang La Gioconda at Trieste, 1956. *Recordings:* Otello from Salzburg; Donna Anna in Don Giovanni; La Forza del Destino; Tosca.

MARTINOVIĆ, Boris; Croatian singer (bass-baritone); b. 1953. *Education:* Juilliard School, New York. *Career:* made debut at Avery Fisher Hall, New York in Refice's Cecilia; appeared in The Queen of Spades and Menotti's The Consul 1977; made European debut at Spoleto Festival 1981; other European appearances at Trieste, Rome, Naples, Paris, Milan and Croatia; mem. Opernhaus Zurich 1991–; other roles include Il Conte Rodolfo in Sonambula, Frere Laurent in Romeo et Julietta, De Capitaine in Lelio, Mephistopheles in La Damnation de Faust, Escamillo in Carmen, Creon in Medea, Arnoldo in Adelia, Raimondo in Lucia di Lammermoor, Don Alfonso in Lucrezia Borgia, Ivan Susanin in Une Vie Pour le Tsar, Banquo in Macbeth, Roger in Jerusalem, Pagano in Il Lombardi, Zaccaria in Nabucco, Silva in Ernani, Amonasro in Aida, Conte Almaviva in Le Nozze di Figaro, Don Alfonso in Cosi fan Tutte, Lindorf in Les Contes d'Hoffman, Colline in La Bohème, Jake Wallace in La Fanciulla del West, Timur in Turandot, Assur in Semiramide, Le Turc Selim in Il Turco in Italia, Orbazzano in Tancredi, Don Basilio in Il Barbiere di Siviglia, Le Conte Tomsky in La Dame de Pique, Le Roi Rene in Iolanta, Fernando in Il Travatore, lead roles in Prince Igor, Don Carlo, Don Quixote, Don Giovanni, Boris Godunov, Eugene Onegin, Attila; concert repertory Mozart, Fauré and Verdi Requiems. *Honours:* Grand Prix Acad. Charles Cros. *Current Management:* c/o Dr Giuseppe De Spitiro, 5 ruelle du Lycee, 1700 Fribourg, Switzerland. *Telephone:* 263232664. *E-mail:* sisto3@hotmail.com. *Address:* 23271 Kukljica, Villa Piccolo, Kukljica 38/7, Croatia (home). *E-mail:* boris@boris-martinovich.com (home). *Website:* www.boris-martinovich.com.

MARTINOVIĆ, Sandra; Croatian singer (mezzo-soprano); b. Doboj, Bosnia and Herzegovina; m. Jonathon Lemalu 2006. *Education:* Acad. of Music, Zagreb and RCM. *Career:* fmr soloist with the Croatian Nat. Radio Chorus, touring throughout Europe; operatic roles include Nella in Gianni Schicchi, Tonina in Prima la Musica poi le Parole, Mrs Gobineau in Medium, Marianna in Il Signor Bruschino, Genevieve in Suor Angelica; has performed in opera choruses with Savoy Opera, Holland Park Opera; numerous concert recitals include Schumann's Frauenliebe und Leben; performed charity concert for Adopt-a-Minefield, Wigmore Hall, London 2005; Social and Cultural Events Sec., Croatian Students and Young Professionals Network. *E-mail:* sandramartinovic@yahoo.co.uk (office).

MARTINPELTO, Hillevi; Swedish singer (soprano); b. 9 Jan. 1958, Älvalden. *Education:* Stockholm Opera School. *Career:* sang Pamina in Die Zauberflöte with the Folksopera in Stockholm and at the Edinburgh Festival; Norrlands Opera from 1987 in Ivar Hallström's Den Bergtagno, also on Swedish television and at the York Festival; Tatiana in Eugene Onegin and Marguerite; Royal Opera Stockholm debut 1987, as Madama Butterfly; Sang the title roles in Gluck's Iphigénie operas at the Drottningholm Festival, 1989–90; Théâtre de la Monnaie, Brussels, from 1990 as Fiordiligi and the Countess in Le nozze di Figaro; Season 1991–92 with Fiordiligi at the Hamburg Staatsoper, Wagner's Eva at Nice, Donna Anna at Aix-en-Provence; Season 1992–93 included: Don Giovanni, Aix-en-Provence Festival, France; Così fan tutte, Hamburg State Opera, Germany; Das Rheingold, Lyric Opera of Chicago, USA; Le nozze di Figaro, Toulouse Opera, France; Châtelet, Monteverdi and Wagner's Eva in Tokyo with Deutsche Oper Berlin; Further engagements include Verdi's Desdemona in Helsinki; Concert engagements with Dvořák's Requiem, Scottish National Orchestra, 1987; Residentie Orchestra of The Hague in Mozart; Belgian Radio Orchestra; Philharmonia of London in The Creation, conducted by Claus Peter Flor; Sang Donna Anna in Don Giovanni, at Glyndebourne, 1994–; Agathe in Der Freischütz for the Royal Danish Opera at Copenhagen, 1997; Further engagements include: Don Giovanni and Clemenza di Tito (Munich) and Idomeneo (Lausanne); Concert appearances with the National Orchestra of Wales, City of Birmingham Symphony Orchestra, the Gesellschaft der Musikfreunde in Vienna and the Vienna Symphony Orchestra amongst others; Alice Page in Falstaff at the 1998 Proms; London Proms 1999, as The Virgin in The Kingdom by Elgar and Schumann's Scenes from Faust; Elsa in Lohengrin at Gothenburg, 2000; season 2000–01 as Elsa at Gothenburg, Alice Ford at the Paris Châtelet and Agathe for the Berlin Staatsoper; recital at the 2001 Edinburgh Festival. *Recordings:* Elettra in Idomeneo, conducted by John Eliot Gardiner; Countess in Figaro with Gardiner; Così fan tutte under Simon Rattle; Alice and Oberon in Falstaff. *Honours:* named Court Singer by King Carl XVI Gustaf of Sweden 2006. *Current Management:* Artists Sekretariat Ulf Tornqvist, Sankt Eriksgatan 100, 2 tr, 113 31 Stockholm, Sweden.

MARTINSEN, Tom; Norwegian singer (tenor); b. 1957. *Education:* studied in Stockholm with Nicolai Gedda. *Career:* sang in lyric repertory at Royal Opera, Stockholm, Koblenz Opera, 1985–88; Gelsenkirchen from 1988; sang Tamino at Dresden, 1992 followed by Hoffmann, 1993; guest appearances throughout Germany as Mozart's Ferrando; Rossini's Lindoro and Almaviva; Nemorino and Fenton in Falstaff; modern repertory includes Werle's Drommen om Thérèse; The Two Fiddlers by Maxwell Davies and Norgaard's Siddharta; sang Hoffmann at Kiel, 1999, Strauss's Narraboth at Dresden, 2001. *Website:* www.tommartinsen.de.

MARTINUCCI, Nicola; singer (tenor); b. 28 March 1941, Tarent, Italy. *Education:* studied with Sara Sforni in Milan. *Career:* debut, Teatro Nuovo Milan 1966, as Manrico; sang at La Scala and at the Teatro La Fenice, Venice; Deutsche Oper am Rhein Düsseldorf from 1973; Florence 1974 as Filippo in a revival of Spontini's Agnese di Hohenstaufen; Verona Arena 1982–86, as Radames, Calaf and Andrea Chénier; Covent Garden debut 1985, as Dick Johnson in La Fanciulla del West; appearances in Dublin, Tehran, Budapest and Salzburg; Rome Opera 1989, as Poliuto; sang Calaf in London 1990; Pollione at Catania, Manrico at Parma; Season 1992 as Enzo in La Gioconda at Rome and Calaf at the Festival of Caracalla; sang Andrea Chénier there 1996; Calaf at Turin 1998; Season 2000–01 as Calaf in Taiwan and Radames at the Macerata Festival. *Recordings:* Turandot, from Verona (video); Donizetti's Poliuto.

MARTON, Eva Erzsebet; Hungarian/German singer (soprano) and academic; *Professor, Ferenc Liszt Academy of Music;* b. (Eva Heinrich), 18 June 1943, Budapest; d. of Bela Heinrich and Ilona Heinrich (née Krammer); m. Zoltan Marton 1965; one s. one d. *Education:* Franz Liszt Acad., Budapest. *Career:* debut at Budapest State Opera, singing there 1968–72; has sung with various opera companies, including Frankfurt Opera 1972–77, Hamburg State Opera 1977–80, Maggio Musicale Fiorentino, Italy, Vienna State Opera, La Scala Milan, Rome Opera, Metropolitan Opera, Lyric Opera of Chicago, Grand Opera Houston and San Francisco Opera, Bayreuth and Salzburg Festivals, Teatro Liceo, Barcelona, Teatro Colón, Buenos Aires, Royal Opera House, Covent Garden, Vienna State Opera, Washington Opera; roles include: Empress in Die Frau ohne Schatten, Salome, all three Brünnhildes in Ring Cycle, Elisabeth and Venus in Tannhäuser, Elsa and Ortrud in Lohengrin, Senta in Der fliegende Holländer, title roles of Turandot, Tosca, Manon Lescaut, Fedora, Gioconda, Aida, Amelia in Ballo in Maschera, Leonora in Il Trovatore, Lady Macbeth in Macbeth, Elisabetta in Don Carlo, Leonore in Fidelio, Maddalena in Andrea Chénier, Leonora in La Forza del Destino; Prof., Ferenc Liszt Acad. of Music 2005–; mem. Hungarian Nat. Volleyball team. *Films include:* Turandot, Il Trovatore, Lohengrin, Tannhäuser, Elektra, La Gioconda, Tosca. *Recordings include:* Turandot, Andrea Chenier, Fedora, Bluebeard's Castle, Violanta, Tiefland, Mefistofele, Die Walküre, La Wally, Semirama, Götterdämmerung, Siegfried, Tosca, La Gioconda. *Honours:* numerous awards including Gold Star, Repub. of Hungary 1989, Bartók Award 1990, Kossuth Award 1997, Köztarsáság Polonia Restituta Stars Award 2003, Pro Cultura Hungarica Award 2009, Gold Medal, Teatro Liceu 2009. *Address:* Department of Vocal and Opera Studies, Ferenc Liszt Academy of Music, 1391 Budapest, PO Box 206, Hungary (office). *E-mail:* mez@floria1974.hu (office). *Website:* www.martoneva.hu.

MARTURET, Eduardo; Venezuelan conductor and composer; *Music Director and Conductor, Miami Symphony Orchestra;* b. (Eduardo Antonio Marturet Machado), 19 Sept. 1953, Caracas; m. Athina Klioumi. *Education:* studied in Cambridge, UK, degree in Piano, Percussion, Conducting and Composition. *Career:* following his studies, returned to Venezuela 1979, permanent position as Assoc. Conductor with Orquesta Filarmónica de Caracas and later as Artistic Dir to Orquesta Sinfónica Venezuela until 1995;

maintains close contact with Venezuelan Nat. Youth Orchestra movement; first Music Dir Teresa Carreño Theatre, Caracas 1984–87; int. conducting career in Italy, Greece, France, Spain, UK, Denmark, Netherlands, Korea, Norway, Sweden, Germany, Czechoslovakia, Belgium, Canada and USA since 1987; led Berlin Symphony on a 12-concert tour of major South American cities including Caracas, São Paulo, Cordoba, Montevideo and Buenos Aires 2001; Asian debut with Seoul Philharmonic 2003; opened Chorin Summer Festival, Berlin 2003; debut with Buenos Aires Philharmonic in Argentina and Florida Philharmonic in Miami 2003; guest conductor in Europe, including Berlin Symphony, European Community Chamber Orchestra, Staatsphilharmonie Rheinland-Pfalz, RAI Symphony Orchestra, Danish Radio Symphony, Royal Flemish Philarmonique, Nordwestdeutsche Philharmonie, Gelders Orkest, Bohemian Chamber Philharmonic, Budapest Radio Symphony, Brabant Orkest and Concertgebouw Chamber Orchestra, Amsterdam; currently Music Dir and Conductor Miami Symphony Orchestra. *Compositions include:* Chamber works: Mi Marioneta tiene Tres Caras 1974, Tres Tiempos 1990, La Hamaca 1998, Paramythia 2002; Symphonic works: Notturno 1981, Sol por Occidente 1982, Music for the ballet "Secretos" 1986, XXXIII Variations on a German Theme 1989, Siglos de Luz 1995, Capricho Criollo 1996, Mantra 1997, Memorias de Un Bravo Pueblo 2002, Latidos del Tíbet 2011; soundtracks for films Oriana 1984, Manuela Saenz 2000, Miranda 2006. *Recordings:* more than 40 CDs ranging from a Brahms orchestral cycle to surveys of Latin America's most important orchestral composers. *Honours:* Orden Diego de Losada 1992, Orden Andres Bello 1992; Best Conductor 1992, Best Classical Record 1992, Medal of Merit of US Congress 2012. *Address:* PO Box 2912, Caracas, Venezuela. *E-mail:* eduardo@marturet.net (office). *Website:* www.marturet.com.

MARUZIN, Yuri; Russian singer (tenor); b. 8 Dec. 1947, Perm. *Education:* studied in Leningrad. *Career:* debut at Maly Theatre, Leningrad, 1972; appearances with the Kirov Opera Leningrad, St Petersburg from 1978 notably as Hermann in The Queen of Spades and Dimitri in Boris Godunov and touring to Covent Garden, 1987 as Lensky; sang the Tsarevich in Rimsky's The Tale of Tsar Saltan at La Scala and Reggio Emilia, 1988; Galitsin in Khovanshchina at the Vienna Staatsoper, 1989; San Francisco Opera as Anatol in War and Peace, Andrei Khovansky in Khovanshchina at Edinburgh, 1991; Bayan in Ruslan and Lyudmila at San Francisco and Palermo, 1995; other guest engagements at Turin, Nice, Madrid and Toronto; other roles include Faust, Pinkerton, Rodolfo, Don Carlos, Don Alvaro, Alfredo and the Duke of Mantua; sang Hermann at Glyndebourne, 1992, 1995; New Israeli Opera, 1997 in Lady Macbeth of the Mtsensk District; season 2000–01 as Lensky at Miami and Grischa in Rimsky's Invisible City of Kitezh at St Petersburg.

MARVIN, Frederick; American pianist and musicologist; b. 11 June 1920, California; s. of Harry and Ann Marvin; m. Ernst Schuh 2011. *Education:* Curtis Inst. of Music, Philadelphia, Southern California Conservatory, Los Angeles Coll. *Career:* first major concert, Los Angeles 1936; debut at Carnegie Hall 1948; toured USA 1949–54; concerts in every major capital of Europe from 1954, also in India and Mexico, solo recitals, concert lectures and masterclasses; Head of Piano Dept and Prof. of Piano, Syracuse Univ. 1968–90, Prof. Emeritus and Artist-in-Residence 1990–; special 90th birthday concert, Vienna, Austria 2010. *Recordings include:* George Antheil Sonata No. 4, Grosses Konzertsolo by Liszt and Sonatas by Moscheles and L. Berger, Schubert, Sonatas by J.L. Dussek (three CDs), Sonatas and Fandango by Antonio Soler (eight CDs), Four Villancicos by A. Soler and his Lamentación, Stabat Mater and Salve Regina, pianist on Martha Moedl's Lieder. *Publications:* 63 sonatas by Soler, four vols of Villancicos and Salve, Lamentation, Stabat Mater by Soler, edited eight vols of Sonatas, and seven vols of choral works by Padre Antonio Soler, two sonatas by J. L. Dussek, Liederabende with Martha Mödl, seven vols of Sonatas and Fandango by Padre Antonio Soler 1957; contrib. to music magazines, article on Padre Antonio Soler, New Grove Dictionary of Music and Musicians 2000. *Honours:* Hon. Fellow, Hispanic Soc. of America 2000; Comendador, Orden del Mérito Civil (Spain) 1966, Croix de Commandeur, Médaille de Vermeil, Arts-Sciences, Lettres (France) 1974; Carnegie Hall Award for Most Outstanding Debut in New York City 1948, Schnabel Gold Medal, London 1955, Cervantes Medal, Hispanic Soc. of America 2000. *Address:* 246 Houston Avenue, Syracuse, NY 13224, USA (home); Rienösslgasse 9/15A, 1040 Vienna, Austria (home). *Telephone:* (315) 472-6066 (USA) (home); (1) 5484938 (Austria) (home). *Fax:* (315) 472-6066 (USA) (home).

MARVIN, Roberta Montemorra, BM, MA, PhD; musicologist; b. 29 July 1953, Massachusetts, USA; m. Conrad A. Marvin 1973. *Education:* Boston Conservatory of Music, Tufts Univ., Brandeis Univ. *Career:* Lecturer, Tufts Univ. 1991–92; Visiting Asst Prof., Boston Univ. 1992–93; Asst Prof., Univ. of Alabama 1993–97; Assoc. Prof., Univ. of Iowa 1997–; mem. American Musicological Soc., Royal Musical Asscn; mem. advisory bd American Inst. of Verdi Studies. *Publications:* Artistic Concerns and Practical Considerations in the Composition of I masnadieri, in Studi Verdiani 7 1992, A Verdi Autograph and the Problem of Authenticity, in Studi Verdiani 9 1993, Shakespeare and Primo Ottocento Opera: The Case of Rossini's Otello, in The Opera and Shakespeare 1994, Aspects of Tempo in Verdi's Early and Middle Period Italian Operas, in Verdi's Middle Period: Source Studies, Analysis and Performance Practice (1849–59) 1997, Giuseppe Verdi's I Masnadieri (ed., critical edn), The Censorship of Verdi's Operas in Victorian London, in Music and Letters 2001, Verdi's Sinfonia in Re maggiore (ed.); contrib. to The New

Grove Dictionary of Opera 1992, The New Grove Dictionary of Music and Musicians (revised edn), Music Quarterly 2000. *Honours:* Premio Internazionale Giuseppe Verdi 1991, Fulbright Research Fellowships 1988, 1993, American Philosophical Soc. Prize 1992, NEH Summer Stipend 1993.

MARWOOD, Anthony; British violinist; b. London. *Education:* RAM Jr Dept, Guildhall School of Music and Drama. *Career:* solo debut, BBC Proms, London 1993; mem. Florestan Trio 1995–; numerous solo engagements with orchestras worldwide including Chamber Orchestra of Europe, Los Angeles Philharmonic, London Philharmonic, Orchestra of the Mariinsky Theatre, Australian Chamber Orchestra; frequent collaborations with Acad. of St Martin in the Fields; important premieres include Thomas Ades's violin concerto, written for him in 2005; Artistic Dir, Irish Chamber Orchestra 2006–11. *Recordings:* Schumann Trios (with the Florestan Trio) (Gramophone Award for Best Chamber Music Record) 1999, Schumann Sonatas (with Susan Tomes), concerto recordings include Stanford, Coleridge Taylor, Somervell, Peteris Vasks and Kurt Weill, also Vivaldi's Four Seasons, Thomas Ades concerto, Haydn Piano Trios, Beethoven Trios, Dvořák Trios, Mendelssohn Trios, Mozart Trios. *Honours:* first prize Shell-LSO competition 1982, Royal Philharmonic Soc. Award (with Florestan Trio) 1999, Gramophone Award (with Florestan Trio) 1999, Royal Philharmonic Soc. Award for Best Instrumentalist 2005. *Current Management:* c/o Sibylle Jackson, Hazard Chase, 25 City Road, Cambridge, CB1 1DP, England. *Telephone:* (1223) 312400. *Fax:* (1223) 460827. *E-mail:* sibylle.jackson@hazardchase.co.uk. *Website:* www.hazardchase.co.uk; www.anthonymarwood.com; www.florestantrio.com.

MASAOKA, Miya, BA, MA; American composer and koto (zither) player; *Professor, Milton Avery School, Bard College;* b. 1958, Washington, DC; m. George Lewis; one c. *Education:* San Francisco State Univ., Mills Coll. *Career:* performs on 17-string Japanese koto zither; compositions represent a blend of Western and Eastern music, incorporating many styles including Gagaku (Japanese court orchestral music), jazz, avant-garde, new improvised and electronic music; f. and Dir San Francisco Gagaku Soc.; work has been presented in Japan, Canada, Western and Eastern Europe and India; venues include V2, Rotterdam, Cybertheater, Brussels, Elektronisch Festival, Groningen, Cleveland Performance Art Festival, Electronik Body Festival, Bratislava, Slovakia, Radio Bremen, Germany, Festival of Lights, Hyderabad, India, London Musicians Collective; fmr lecturer in Japanese American Art and Aesthetics, San Francisco State Univ.; fmr lecturer in Music Composition and Jazz Theory, San Francisco Community Music Center; founding mem., San Francisco Electronic Music Festival; currently Prof. Milton Avery School, Bard Coll. *Compositions include:* Pieces for Plants, Thinking Sounds, Bang On a Can, Engine 27, Harvestworks, Bee Project #1 1996, What is the Difference Between Stripping & Playing the Violin? *Recordings include* Compositions/Improvisations 1996, Trio: Masaoka, Nunn, Robair, Innocent Eyes and Lenses, Duets: George Lewis and Miya Masaoka, Tribute to Sun Ra. *Honours:* CalArts Alpert Award in the Arts 2004. *Address:* 455 Central Park West 7-C, New York, NY 10025, USA (office). *E-mail:* miyamasaoka@mindspring.com (office). *Website:* www.miyamasaoka.com.

MASHAYEKHI, Nader; Iranian composer and conductor; b. 25 Oct. 1958, Tehran; m. Gisela Beer 1990. *Education:* Hochschule für Musik, Vienna. *Career:* debut at Konzerthaus Festival, Vienna 1992; opera performance, Malakut, Vienna Modern 1997; Pentimento for full orchestra, in Festival Steierische Herbst 1998; Mise en scène for ensemble in Berlin Philharmonie; mem., Ensemble Wien 2001; Chief Conductor, Tehran Symphony Orchestra 2006–08. *Compositions include:* Malakut (opera), Pentimentos for orchestra, Sonne for orchestra, Mahler: Das Lied von der Erde (adaptation for ensemble). *Recordings:* Duell for two flutes (on Tomio and Mari Duo album), Malakut, Music for flute in the 20th Century, Flute Music (with Gisela Mashayekhi-Beer). *Publications:* contrib. articles to music journals. *E-mail:* info@nadermashayekhi.com (office). *Website:* nadermashayekhi.com.

MASHEK, Michal; Czech pianist; b. 17 Sept. 1980, Usti Nad Labem. *Education:* Music Conservatory, Teplice, Music Conservatory in Prague. *Career:* various television and radio broadcasts and recordings. *Recordings:* Fantaisie and Toccata by B. Martinů, Goldberg Variations by J. S. Bach. *Honours:* first prize Int. Piano Competition 'Virtuosi Per Musica di Pianoforte', first prize Int. Beethoven Piano Competition.

MASLANKA, David Henry, BMus, MM, PhD; American composer; b. 30 Aug. 1943, Mass; m. Alison Matthews; two s. one d. *Education:* New England Conservatory, Oberlin Coll., Michigan State Univ. *Career:* teacher, State Univ. of New York at Geneseo 1970–74, Sarah Lawrence Coll. 1974–80, Kingsborough Coll., CUNY 1981–90; freelance composer 1990–. *Compositions:* eight symphonies, 12 concertos, a mass, numerous concert pieces for wind ensemble and orchestra and numerous chamber, choral, and percussion works. *Recordings:* more than 60 recordings. *Honours:* MacDowell Colony Fellowships, grants from Nat. Endowment for the Arts, Martha Baird Rockefeller, The American Soc. of Composers, Authors and Publrs (ASCAP), Nat. Symphony Orchestra. *Address:* 2625 Strand Avenue, Missoula, MT 59804, USA. *Telephone:* (406) 721-3453. *E-mail:* david@davidmaslanka.com. *Website:* www.davidmaslanka.com.

MASON, Andrew, BMus; British clarinettist; b. 30 Sept. 1977, Kent, England. *Education:* Royal Coll. of Music (Foundation Scholar), studied with Colin Bradbury, Janet Hilton, Robert Hill, Michael Harris. *Career:* solo performances for Park Lane Group at Purcell Room and Wigmore Hall; solo broadcasts for BBC Radio 3; mem. of Aurora Ensemble 1997–; performances St David's

Hall, Cardiff, Bridgewater Hall, Manchester, Purcell Room (Park Lane Group), St Martin in the Fields, Cheltenham and Chelmsford Festivals; 'Sounds Exciting' education project 2000–; performs for Live Music Now! with London Clarinet Quartet and the Aurora Ensemble; freelance orchestral musician. *Honours:* prizewinner with Aurora Ensemble, Music d'Ensemble, Paris Conservatoire 2001, Royal Coll. of Music Thurston Clarinet Prize, Royal Coll. of Music Roger Fallows Memorial Prize. *Address:* 40 Westgate Road, Faversham, Kent ME13 8HF, England. *E-mail:* arm1977@btinternet.com. *Website:* www.auroraensemble.com.

MASON, Anne, ARAM; British singer (mezzo-soprano); b. 1954, Lincolnshire, England. *Education:* Royal Academy of Music with Marjorie Thomas, National Opera Studio. *Career:* WNO Chorus, 1977–79; Opera North from 1982 as Fenena in Nabucco, and in Madama Butterfly; ENO 1983, as a Valkyrie in a new production of Die Walküre; Innsbruch Early Music Festival 1983, in Cesti's Il Tito, conducted by Alan Curtis; Kent Opera and Scottish Opera 1984, in new productions of King Priam by Tippett and Edward Harper's Hedda Gabler; Covent Garden appearances in Carmen, as Mercedes; Otello, Emilia; Das Rheingold, Madama Butterfly, Die Walküre, La Clemenza di Tito, Cenerentola, Rosenkavalier, Traviata and Götterdämmerung; Glyndebourne Tour 1987, as Dorabella in Così fan tutte; engagements as Annius in La Clemenza di Tito at Aix, Casoi fan tutte with WNO and as Marcellina in Le nozze di Figaro in Madrid; season 1992 as Donna Clara in the stage premiere of Gerhard's The Duenna, at Madrid, as Henrietta Maria in I Puritani at Covent Garden and Cornelia in Julius Caesar for Scottish Opera; Second Maid in Elektra at the First Night at the 1993 London Proms; sang Gertrude in Hansel and Gretel for Scottish Opera, 1996; Minsk Woman in the premiere of Jonathan Dove's Flight, Glyndebourne, 1998; season 2000–01 as Fricka in Das Rheingold at Edinburgh, Verdi's Fenena for ENO and Mozart's Marcellina for WNO; concerts in the UK, Germany, France, Austria and Belgium, notably in The Dream of Gerontius and Verdi's Requiem. *Recordings:* Video of HMS Pinafore; Helen in King Priam; Second Bridesmaid in Le nozze di Figaro, conducted by Solti; Marcellina, Figaro, with Haitink; Emilia di Liverpool, Opera Rara. *Honours:* Gerhardt Lieder Prize, Royal Academy of Music Recital Diploma and the Countess of Munster Award, Finalist in the 1983 Benson and Hedges Gold Award.

MASON, Barry; British lutenist, classical guitarist and music director; b. 6 Sept. 1947, Cottingham, Yorkshire, England; m. Glenda Simpson 1983. *Education:* Hull College of Technology, Royal Academy of Music with Anthony Rooley and David Munrow, Royal College of Music with Dian Poulton. *Career:* debut, Purcell Room, 1973; Director, Camerata of London, 1974; Director, 1st Early Music Centre Festival, London, 1977; Director, Progress Instruments Tours, Japan, Europe and USA, 1978; The Wicked Lady film, BBC Shakespeare Films: Director, The Guitarist's Companion, 1986; mem, Council Member, Early Music Centre. *Recordings:* Popular Music From The Time of Elizabeth I; The Muses Garden of Delights; Music For Kings and Courtiers'; The Queens Men; Thomas Companion; Elizabethan Ayres and Duets. *Publications:* contrib. to Guitar International; Early Music News; Early Music Magazine; Music in Education. *Honours:* Peter Latham Award for Musicology, Royal Academy of Music, 1971; 1996 Britten Award for Composition. *Current Management:* Francesca McManus, 71 Priory Road, Kew Gardens, Richmond, Surrey TW9 3PH, England. *E-mail:* info@spanishguitarcentre.com.

MASON, Benedict; British composer; b. 21 June 1955, Budleigh, Salterton. *Education:* King's Coll., Cambridge, studied with Peter Maxwell Davies, and with Henri Pousseur in Liège. *Compositions include:* Hinterstoisser Traverse for 12 players 1986, Lighthouses of England and Wales for orchestra 1987, Oil and Petrol Marks on a Wet Road are Sometimes Held to be Spots where a Rainbow Stood for 16 voices 1987, Concerto for the viola section 1990, Self-Referential Songs and Realistic Virelais for soprano and 16 players 1990, Six Rilke Songs 1991, Animals and the Origins of Dance for 21 players 1992, Music for Concert Halls Nos 1–10 1993–97, two String Quartets 1987, 1993, Schumann Auftrag: Live Hörspiel ohne Worte 1994, Playing Away (opera) 1994, Szene for female voices, orchestra and sampler 1998. *Honours:* winner Benjamin Britten Composers Competition 1998, Siemens Stiftungspreis 1992. *Website:* www.benedictmason.com.

MASON, Christian, PhD; British composer; b. 1984. *Education:* Univ. of York, King's Coll. London, studied with George Benjamin, Frank Denyer, also with Sinan Savaskan, Nicola LeFanu, Thomas Simaku and Julian Anderson. *Career:* Resident Composer, Takefu Int. Festival, Japan 2008; residency at Lucerne Festival Acad. under guidance of Pierre Boulez Sept. 2013; Composer-in-Residence, Eton Coll.; Composition Asst to Sir Harrison Birtwistle; Composition Support Tutor for London Symphony Orchestra Panufnik Young Composers Project; Founding Artistic Dir Octandre Ensemble; commissions for numerous orgs including Radio-France/Orchestre Nat. de France, Klangforum Wien/Tokyo Sinfonietta, Auditorium du Louvre, Paris/Wigmore Hall, London/CDMC, Madrid, also a piece for Pierre Boulez's 90th birthday performed by Ensemble Intercontemporain at Lucerne Festival 2015, and a work for percussion ensemble for opening of Asian Arts Theatre in Gwangju, S Korea 2015–16; works presented in London at Spitalfields Festival 2014, by Tokyo Philharmonic Chorus at the Shizuoka Concert Hall, at Tanglewood Festival of Contemporary Music under the direction of Pierre-Laurent Aimard 2013, Venice Biennale 2013, and at BBC Proms 2015, by musicians and ensembles including Midori, Jean-Guihen Queyras, Carolin Widmann, Gergely Mardaras, Elgar Howarth, Francois-Xavier Roth, Baldur

Bronnimann, James MacMillan, Pavel Kotla, Stilian Kirov, Ligeti Quartet, Elysian Quartet, London Sinfonietta, Britten Sinfonia, London Symphony Orchestra, BBC Philharmonics. *Compositions include:* ...from bursting suns escaping..., for orchestra 2006, In Space Enlaced, trio 2008/2012, In Time Entwined, trio 2008, Learning Self-Modulation (British Composer Award, solo/duo category) 2011, Remembered Resonance, for solo piano with Japanese wind chimes 2012, Isolarion: Rituals of Resonance 2012–13, The Years of Light, for two sopranos and ensemble 2013, Equinoxes of the Infinite, for two pianos and two percussion 2013, Unseen Seasons, for choir 2013, Somewhere Between Us... for amplified vocal quartet 2014, Triptych (three operas) 2014, Sympathetic Resonance, for orchestra 2015, Open to Infinity: a Grain of Sand, for large ensemble 2015, and many other orchestra, large ensemble, chamber, solo/duo, choral, vocal, theatre and dance works. *Honours:* Mendelssohn Scholarship 2012, Ernst von Siemens Foundation Composer's Award 2015. *Current Management:* c/o Catherine Le Bris, CLB Management, 5 passage Piver, 75011 Paris, France. *Telephone:* 1-48-06-46-94. *E-mail:* catherine@clbmanagement.co.uk. *Website:* www.clbmanagement.co.uk. *E-mail:* christianmason.net@gmail.com.

MASON, Marilyn; organist; b. 29 June 1925, Oklahoma, USA. *Education:* Oklahoma State Univ., Univ. of Michigan, Union Theological Seminary, New York, studied with Nadia Boulanger, Maurice Duruflé and Arnold Schoenberg. *Career:* teacher, Univ. of Michigan 1947, Chair. of Organ Dept 1962, Prof. 1965; recital tours of North America, Europe, Australia, Africa and South America; concerts with the Detroit and Philadelphia Orchestras; 60 commissions for such composers as Krenek, Cowell, Albright, Ulysses Kay, Sowerby and Ross Lee Finney. *Recordings:* albums of music by Sessions, Satie, Schoenberg and Virgil Thomson.

MASQUELIN, Martine; singer (soprano); b. 1957, Paris, France. *Education:* Paris Conservatoire. *Career:* debut at Montpellier 1982 as Lakmé; Düsseldorf 1983, as Strauss's Sophie and Rossini's Rosina; Liège 1988–89 as Julietta and Edvige in Offenbach's Robinson Crusoe; appearances throughout France as Massenet's Thais and Violetta; Saint Care Festival; concerts in Paris and elsewhere. *Recordings:* Monteverdi's Poppea, Grétry's Zémire et Azor.

MASSARD, Robert; singer (baritone); b. 15 Aug. 1925, Pau, France. *Education:* Conservatories of Pau and Bayonne. *Career:* sang the High Priest in Samson et Dalila at the Paris Opéra 1952; Thoas in Iphigénie en Tauride at Aix 1952; sang Ashton in Lucia di Lammermoor at the Paris Opéra 1957; Glyndebourne 1958, in Alceste; Orestes in Iphigénie en Tauride with the Covent Garden Co. at Edinburgh 1961; sang Fieramosca in Benvenuto Cellini with the Royal Opera in London; Bolshoi Theatre Moscow 1962, as Rigoletto; La Scala Milan 1967, as Valentin in Faust; Paris 1974, as Sancho Panza in Massenet's Don Quichotte; other roles include Nero in L'Incoronazione di Poppea, the Count in Capriccio, Milhaud's Orpheus, Escamillo and Ravel's Ramiro. *Recordings:* Iphigénie en Tauride, Mireille, Thais, Rigoletto, Benvenuto Cellini, Raimbaud in Le Comte Ory, Chant du Monde.

MASSET, Françoise; singer (soprano); b. 1970, France. *Education:* Douai Conservatoire, Opera Studio of the Baroque Music Centre, Versailles. *Career:* appearances throughout France in Chabrier's Une Education manquée, Purcell's Dido and Aeneas and Mozart's Bastien und Bastienne; chanteuse and comedienne. *Recordings:* title role La Diane de Fontainebleau by Desmarets, Lully's Acis et Galatée, Rameau's Dardanus, Melisse in Gluck's Armide.

MASSEY, Andrew John, BA, MA; American (b. British) conductor; *Music Director, Racine Symphony Orchestra;* b. 1 May 1946, Nottingham, England; s. of Harry Massey and Margaret Massey; m. Sabra A. Todd 1982; one s. one d. *Education:* Merton Coll., Oxford, Nottingham Univ., Dartington Summer School with Hans Keller, Witold Lutoslawski and Luciano Berio, Canford Summer School. *Career:* debut, Cleveland 1978; Asst Conductor Cleveland Orchestra, USA 1978–80; Assoc. Conductor New Orleans Symphony Orchestra 1980–86, San Francisco Symphony Orchestra 1986–; Music Dir Rhode Island Philharmonic 1986–1991, Fresno Philharmonic 1986–93, Music Dir 1987–1992; Music Dir Toledo Symphony, Ohio 1990–2002; currently Music Dir, Racine Symphony Orchestra; guest appearances with Nat. Symphony, Pittsburgh, Vancounver Symphony, Milwaukee Symphony, San Diego Symphony and others; mem. American Fed. of Musicians; Dreyfus Fellow, Millay Colony for the Arts 2004. *Compositions:* Marina for soprano and chamber ensemble 1973, Cadenza for Winter (solo violin) 2002, Early Morning for orchestra 2003, Another Spring, violin concerto 2007. *Current Management:* John Gingrich Management, PO Box 1515, New York, NY 10023, USA. *Telephone:* (802) 598-7710. *E-mail:* dom9th@yahoo.com (office). *Website:* www.andrewmassey.com.

MASSEY, Roy Cyril, MBE, BMus, FRCO (chm), ADCM, ARCM; British organist and choral conductor; *Organist Emeritus, Hereford Cathedral;* b. 9 May 1934, England; s. of Cyril Charles Massey and Beatrice May Massey; m. Ruth Carol Craddock Grove 1975. *Education:* Univ. of Birmingham, studied with David Willcocks. *Career:* Organist, St Alban's, Conybere Street, Birmingham 1953–60, St Augustine's, Edgbaston 1960–65, Croydon Parish Church 1965–68; Conductor, Croydon Bach Soc. 1966–68; Special Commr, Royal School of Church Music 1964–; Organist to the City of Birmingham Choir 1954–2004; Organist and Master of Choristers, Birmingham Cathedral 1968–74; Dir of Music, King Edward's School, Birmingham 1968–74; Conductor, Hereford Choral Soc. 1974–2001; Organist and Master of Choristers, Hereford Cathedral 1974–2001, Organist Emer. 2001–; Conductor-in-Chief, alternate years Assoc. Conductor, Three Choirs Festival 1975–2001; adviser on organs to Dioceses of Birmingham and Hereford 1974–; led the premieres of Geoffrey Burgon's Requiem, Lux Aeterna by William Mathias, Veni Sancte Spiritus by William Mathias and Te Deum by Paul Patterson; Pres. Royal Coll. of Organists 2003–05, Gwent Bach Soc., Hereford Organists' Soc.; mem. Royal Soc. of Musicians 1991. *Honours:* Hon. FRSCM 1971; Hon. Fellow, Guild of Church Musicians 2000; Hon. DMus (Cantuar) 1991. *Address:* 2 King John's Court, Tewkesbury, Glos., GL20 6EG, England. *Telephone:* (1684) 290019. *E-mail:* drroymassey@talktalk.net.

MASSIS, Annick; singer (soprano); b. 1960, France. *Education:* Francis Poulenc Conservatoire, Paris. *Career:* debut in Toulouse 1991; engagements include Ophélie in Hamlet and Philène in Mignon by Thomas at Compiègne; Rosina, Micaela and Anna in The Merry Wives of Windsor at the Opéra-Comique, Paris; Carolina in Il Matrimonio Segreto at Nantes and Aricie (Hippolyte et Aricie by Rameau) at the Paris Opéra Garnier and the Brooklyn Acad. of Music; Lucia di Lammermoor at Rouen and as Countess Adèle in Le Comte Ory at the 1997 Glyndebourne Festival; season 1997–98 as Gluck's Eurydice and Marie in La Fille du Régiment at Geneva; Bizet's Leila at Toulouse and Countess Adèle at Florence and Montpellier; season 1998 as Ophelia in Hamlet at Washington and Lucia di Lammermoor at the New York Met; Ophelia's Mad Scene from Hamlet by Thomas at the 1999 London Prom concerts; season 2000–01 as Lucia di Lammermoor at Barcelona, Amina in Madrid and Philine in Mignon at Toulouse; title role in first modern performance of Meyerbeer's Margherita d'Anjou (concert), Festival Hall 2002; Lucia di Lammermoor at the Met 2002; engaged as the Queen of Shemakha in The Golden Cockerel, San Francisco 2003.

MASSIS, René; singer (baritone); b. 1946, Lyon, France. *Education:* studied in Lyon and Milan. *Career:* debut in Marseille 1976, as Silvio in Pagliacci; sang in L'Heure Espagnole at La Scala 1978 and has appeared throughout France and Italy; Lucca 1985 in Dejanice by Catalani, Paris Opéra 1988, as Valentin in Faust; Paris Opéra-Comique 1990, in Auber's Manon Lescaut and at Nice Opéra 1990–91, in Wozzeck and as Guglielmo; other roles include Rossini's Figaro (Glyndebourne Touring Opera 1989), Mozart's Count, Belcore, Verdi's Ford and Posa, Fieramosca in Benvenuto Cellini, Eugene Onegin and the Marquis in Massenet's Grisélidis; sang the title role in the premiere of Goya by Prodromidès, Montpellier 1996; season 1999–2000 as Tonio in Pagliacci at Nice, Albert in Werther at Lille and Donizetti's Sulpice for Opéra du Rhin, Strasbourg. *Recordings include:* Chausson's Le Roi Arthus, Iphigénie en Aulide and La Juive.

MASSON, Askell; Icelandic composer and musician; b. 21 Nov. 1953, Reykjavík. *Education:* Reykjavík Children's School of Music, Reykjavík Coll. of Music, studied with Patrick Savill in London, percussion with James Blades. *Career:* debut, Icelandic TV playing own music 1969; composer 1967–; composer, instrumentalist, Nat. Theatre of Iceland 1973–75; producer, Icelandic State Radio 1978–83; Gen. Sec. Icelandic League of Composers 1983–85; Chair. STEF (Performing Rights Soc. of Iceland) 1989–99; working solely on composition. *Dance works:* The Elements 1974, Black and White Pieces 1974, The Fire Troll 1974, To Life 2001, White Shadows 2011. *Plays:* Macbeth, The Bell of Iceland, Death of a Salesman, Salka Valka and several others. *Films:* The Outlaw, Sesselja, The Dance of Horses 2009, The Track of the Drop 2010. *Compositions include:* The Ice Palace (opera) 1995, Sinfonia Trilogia 1992, Piano Concerto 1985, Konzertstück for snare drum and orchestra 1982, Prim for snare drum 1984, Sonata for violin and piano 1993, Woodwind Quintet 1991, Trio for piano trio 1995, Meditation for organ 1992, Sindur for percussion quartet 1989, Okto November for strings 1982, Run for orchestra 1994, Chamber Symphony 1997, Boreas for tuba 1999, Kim for snare drum 2001. *Radio:* Loftur the Sorcerer, Hamlet, The Song of Songs and others. *Television:* Time Has Left Me (Jonas Hallgrimsson, Blood and Ink (Gunnar Gunnarsson) and others. *Recordings include:* Marimba Concerto, Clarinet Concerto, Trio, Sonata, Partita, Hrim, Snow, Helfro, Violin Concerto, Percussion Concerto, Crossings, ORA and others. *Honours:* Iceland Music Prize 2006, 2008. *Address:* Leifsgata 20, 101 Reykjavík, Iceland (office); Editions BIM, PO Box 300, 1674 Vuarmarens, Switzerland (office). *Telephone:* 551-9902 (office). *E-mail:* askellmasson@hotmail.com; askell@askellmasson .com (office). *Website:* www.editions-bim.com (office); www.askellmasson.com.

MASSON, Diego; Spanish conductor; b. 21 June 1935, Tossa. *Education:* Paris Conservatoire, studied with Leibowitz, Maderna and Boulez. *Career:* worked as percussionist in Paris with the ensemble Domaine Musicale; founded Musique Vivante, 1966; conducted premieres of Stockhausen's Stop and Setz die Segel zur Sonne; early performances of works by Boulez including Domaines and... explosante fixe... and Berio; Musical Dir, Marseilles Opéra and Ballet-Theatre Contemporian, Angers; guest engagements as orchestral conductor in France, Europe, Australia and New Zealand; conducted La Bohème for Opera North, 1989, premiere of Caritas by Robert Saxton, 1991; premiere of Il giudizio Universidade by Claudio Ambrosini at Citti dilastelle, 1996; conducted Turnage's Greek at the QEH, London, 1998; premiere of Sally Beamish's Monster, Scottish Opera at Glasgow, 2002. *Recordings:* Boulez, Domaine; Globoka, Fluide and Ausstrahlungen; John Woolrich; Stockhausen Aus den sieben tagen, and Liaison; Keuris Alto saxophone concerto. *Current Management:* Ingpen & Williams Ltd, 7 St George's Court, 131 Putney Bridge Road, London, SW15 2PA, England. *Telephone:* (20) 8874-3222. *Fax:* (20) 8877-3113. *E-mail:* info@ingpen.co.uk.

MASTERS, Rachel, ARCM; harpist; b. 9 Sept. 1958, Purley, Surrey, England. *Education:* Guildhall School of Music and Drama, Royal Coll. of Music. *Career:* mem., Nat. Youth Orchestra 1972–76; debut at Wigmore Hall 1982; Principal Harp, London Philharmonic Orchestra 1989–; Prof., Royal Coll. of Music. *Recordings:* Mozart Flute and Harp Concerto (with Phillipa Davies, City of London Sinfonia and Richard Hickox), harp pieces by Debussy, Ravel, Glière, Ginastera and Alwyn, Britten: Ceremony of Carols (with King's College, Cambridge). *Honours:* jt winner SE Arts Young Concert Artists Award 1979, jt second prize Mobil Oil Harp Competition 1980, Incorporated Soc. of Musicians Young Concert Artist 1981, RCM Jack Morrison Harp Prize, RCM Elisabeth Coates Harp Prize.

MASTERSON, (Margaret) Valerie, CBE; British singer (soprano); b. Birkenhead; d. of Edward Masterson and Rita McGrath; m. Andrew March; one s. one d. *Career:* Prof. of Singing, RAM, London 1992–97; Pres. British Youth Opera 1994–99, Vice-Pres. 2000–; has sung with D'Oyly Carte Opera, Glyndebourne, Royal Opera House, Covent Garden and English Nat. Opera and on TV and radio; also in major opera houses abroad including Paris, Aix-en-Provence, Toulouse, Munich, Geneva, Milan, San Francisco and Chicago. *Opera roles include:* La Traviata, Manon, Semele, Merry Widow, Louise, Lucia di Lammermoor, Mireille; other leading roles in Faust, Alcina, Die Entführung aus dem Serail, Le Nozze di Figaro, Così fan Tutte, La Bohème, Magic Flute, Julius Caesar, Rigoletto, Orlando, Der Rosenkavalier, Xerxes, The Pearl Fishers, Die Fledermaus. *Recordings include:* Julius Caesar, La Traviata, Elisabetta Regina d'Inghilterra, Bitter Sweet, Ring Cycle, recitals and various Gilbert and Sullivan discs. *Honours:* Hon. FRCM 1992; Hon. FRAM 1993; Hon. DLitt (South Bank Univ.) 1999; Award for Outstanding Individual Performance of the Year in a New Opera, Soc. of West End Theatre 1983. *Current Management:* c/o Music International, 13 Ardilaun Road, London, N5 2QR, England. *Telephone:* (20) 7359-5183. *Fax:* (20) 7226-9792. *E-mail:* music@musicint.co.uk. *Website:* www.musicint.co.uk.

MASTILOVIC, Daniza; singer (soprano); b. 7 Nov. 1933, Negotin, Serbia. *Education:* Belgrade Conservatory with Nikola Cvejic. *Career:* sang operetta in Belgrade 1955–57; minor roles at Bayreuth from 1956; joined Georg Solti at Frankfurt Opera 1959, debut as Tosca; guest appearances in Hamburg, Düsseldorf, Zagreb, Vienna and Munich; Teatro Colón Buenos Aires 1972, as Abigaille in Nabucco; Zürich 1973, as Ortrud in Lehengrin; Covent Garden 1973–75, as Elektra; Metropolitan Opera 1975, as Elektra; commemorated the 50th anniversary of Puccini's death with a performance of Turandot at Torre del Lago 1974; Landestheater Salzburg 1987, as Clytemnestra in Elektra.

MASTROMEI, Giampietro; singer (baritone); b. 1 Nov. 1932, Camoire, Tuscany, Italy. *Education:* studied in Buenos Aires with Apollo Granforte, Mario Melani and Hilda Spani. *Career:* sang at the Teatro Colón, Buenos Aires for 13 seasons from 1952; European debut 1962, appearing in France and Italy, and at the Covent Garden 1973, as Renato, Un Ballo in Maschera and Amonasro; Verona Arena 1971–86, as Amonasro and Scarpia; further appearances in Caracas, Bilbao, Tokyo, Barcelona, Hamburg, Madrid, San Francisco, Dallas and Philadelphia; also sang Verdi's Iago and Rigoletto and roles in operas by Pergolesi, Scarlatti and Dallapiccola. *Recordings:* Simon Boccanegra, Il Corsaro, Aida.

MASUROK, Yuri; Ukrainian singer (baritone); b. 18 July 1931, Krasnik, Poland. *Education:* Lvov Institute and Moscow Conservatoire. *Career:* sang at the Bolshoi, Moscow from 1963, debut as Eugene Onegin; Vienna Staatsoper as Scarpia, Luna and Escamilio; Aix-en-Provence 1976, as Germont in La Traviata; Covent Garden debut 1975, as Renato in Un Ballo in Maschera; returned to London as Posa in Don Carlos, Eugene Onegin and Count di Luna; US debut at Metropolitan Opera 1975, with Bolshoi Company; San Francisco, 1977, as Renato; Metropolitan debut as Germont, 1978; Covent Garden 1983 and 1986, as Luna and Germont; Sang at Wiesbaden 1987 as Scarpia, Budapest as Robert in Iolanta, with the company of the Bolshoi Theatre; Gran Teatre del Liceu Barcelona 1989, as Eugene Onegin; Concerts in the United Kingdom have included Wigmore Hall recitals and Festival Hall concert conducted by Svetlanov; Song repertory includes music by Ravel, Debussy, Schumann and Henze; Other operatic roles include Andrei Bolkonsky in War and Peace, Mazeppa, Rossini's Figaro and Yeletsky in The Queen of Spades; Sang Onegin at Milwaukee, 1992; Scarpia at Metropolitan, New York, 1993 and at Moscow, 1996. *Recordings:* Eugene Onegin, Tosca, The Queen of Spades and Iolanta on Russian labels; Tosca, Il Trovatore and Boris Godunov. *Address:* c/o Bolshoi Theatre, Ochotnyj Rjad 812, 103009 Moscow, Russia.

MATAEVA, Irina; Russian singer (soprano); b. 1972, Tumen. *Education:* St Petersburg Conservatoire. *Career:* young singer, Acad. of the Mariinsky Theatre, St Petersburg 1998–, Prin. Soloist 2007–; roles have included Mozart's Susanna and Barbarina, Tatiana in Eugene Onegin, Natasha in War and Peace, Lisa in la Sonnambula, Zerlina and Sofya in Semyon Kotko by Prokofiev; appeared with the Kirov Opera in summer season at Covent Garden 2000; London Proms 2002. *Honours:* prizewinner, Gumelev Vocal Competition 1997. *Address:* Mariinsky Theatre, 1 Theatre Square, 190000 St Petersburg, Russia (office). *Telephone:* (812) 326-41-41 (office). *Fax:* (812) 326-41-44 (office). *Website:* www.mariinsky.ru/en (office).

MATEJ, Daniel, (DanoM); Slovak composer, performer and lecturer; *Lecturer in 20th and 21st-Century Music History, Music Theory, Composition and Performance Strategy, Bratislava Academy of Music and Drama*; b. 9 March 1963, Bratislava; m. Renáta Matej; one s. one d. *Education:* Bratislava Acad. of Music and Drama, Conservatoire Nat. Supérieur de Musique, Paris, France, Koninklijk Conservatorium, The Hague, Netherlands, Dartington Summer Music School. *Career:* Founder and Artistic Dir contemporary music ensembles, Veni ensemble 1987, Vapori del Cuore 1994, Over4tea 2004, don@u.com 2004; Composer-in-Residence, Deutscher Akademischer Austauschdienst, Berlin, Germany 1995–96; Lecturer in 20th and 21st-Century Music History, Music Theory, Composition and Performance Strategy, Bratislava Acad. of Music and Drama 1996–2014, Faculty of Pedagogy, Comenius Univ., Bratislava 2011; Founder and Artistic Dir Evenings of New Music int. festival 1990–2009, (New) Music at Home concert series 2003–09; mem. Programme Cttee Melos Ethos int. contemporary music festival 2005, 2009 (Artistic Dir 2009); Veni Acad. 2010; Mi-65 2011; Pres. Slovak Section, Int. Soc. for Contemporary Music 2003–10. *Compositions include:* Musica aeterna 1989, Gloria 1992, Nikabrik or Trumpkin? 1992, Memories of You 1 1993, Schneller, weiter, höher 1996, Wenn wir in höchsten Nöten sein 1999, Vingt Regards (sound installation) 2000, John King (ballad opera) 2001, CAravenGE (sound installation) 2002, NICE 2005, Cave Songs (remixed) 2005, 3m für WAM 2008, Stormy Monday 2010, Structures, Pages (Improvisations) 2010, 2012, Save Our Souls 2015. *Recordings include:* Schneller, weiter, höher 2006, Lieder ohne Worte 2007, Bratislava 2008, Possible Stories 2011, Unpredictable Standards 2014, Memories of You 2015, Crippled Symmetry (in broken patterns) 2016. *Address:* Music Centre Slovakia, Michalská 10, 815 36 Bratislava 1, Slovakia (office). *Telephone:* (908) 728970 (home). *E-mail:* evenings.matej@gmail.com (office). *Website:* www.hc.sk (office).

MATHE, Ulrike-Anima; German violinist; b. 5 March 1964, Freiburg. *Education:* studied in Basel, Juilliard School, Konzertexamen Detmold with Tibor Varga, masterclasses. *Career:* debut in New York 1992; extensive chamber music and solo career, Berlin, Cologne, Munich, USA, Australia, Spain, Italy, Switzerland, Prague, Salzburg, Belgium, Netherlands; Repertory: from Vivaldi to Penderecki, with the whole violin concerto repertoire. *Recordings:* Reger Solo sonatas, Korngold violin concerto, Kreisler Pieces. *Publications:* contrib. to coverage of Strad magazine, Fono Forum, NMZ, Stereoplay. *Honours:* first prize, German Music Competition 1986, first prize, European Youth Competition 1985, Young Concert Artists Award 1988. *Current Management:* SKS Russ, Erwin Russ GmbH, Charlottenplatz 17, 70173 Stuttgart, Germany. *Telephone:* (711) 1635311. *Fax:* (711) 1635330. *E-mail:* info@sks-russ.de. *Website:* www.sks-russ.de.

MATHER, Bruce, PhD; composer and pianist; b. 9 May 1939, Toronto, Canada; m. Pierrette LePage. *Education:* Royal Conservatory of Music, Toronto, studied in Paris with Roy Harris, Boulez, Milhaud and Messiaen, Univs of Stanford and Toronto. *Career:* teacher, McGill Univ., Montréal from 1966; solo piano recitals and piano duet performances with Pierrette LePage. *Compositions:* Five Madrigals for soprano and ensemble 1967–73, Music for Vancouver 1969, Musique pour Rouen for string orchestra 1971, Music for organ, horn and gongs 1973, Eine Kleine Blassermusik 1975, Au Chateau de Pompariain for mezzo and orchestra 1977, Musique pour Champigny for vocal soloists and ensemble 1976, Ausone for 11 instruments 1979, Musigny for orchestra 1980, Barbaresco for viola, cello and double bass 1984, Scherzo for orchestra 1987, Dialogue pour trio basso et orchestre 1988, Travauz de Nuit for baritone and chamber orchestra 1990, Princesse Blanche (opera) 1994, Tallbrem Variations for five percussion and orchestra 1995, also songs.

MATHES, Rachel Clarke, BA, MM, DMA; singer (soprano) and academic; b. 14 March 1941, Atlanta, GA, USA. *Education:* Birmingham-Southern Coll., Univ. of South Carolina, Akademie für Musik und Darstellende Kunst, Vienna, Austria. *Career:* debut in Aida at Basel, Switzerland 1965; Deutsche Oper am Rhein, Düsseldorf, Germany 1965–71; freelance throughout Europe 1971–74; Metropolitan Opera, New York 1974–77, debut as Donna Anna; New York City Opera 1975, debut in Turandot; Wolf Trap Festival, Verdi's Requiem 1975; Glasgow Opera, as Donna Anna 1975. *Recordings include:* highlights from Mozart's Don Giovanni (with the Glasgow Opera) 1975.

MATHESON, James; American composer; *Director, Composer Fellowship Program, Los Angeles Philharmonic Orchestra*; b. 1970, Des Moines, Ia. *Career:* commissions include Chicago Symphony Orchestra, Los Angeles Philharmonic, New York Philharmonic, Albany Symphony, Carnegie Hall, Borromeo String Quartet, Sequitur; works performed by ensembles including American Composers Orchestra, Chamber Music Soc. of Lincoln Center, Orchestra 2001, San Francisco Contemporary Music Players, and at festivals including Ravinia, Aspen, Spoleto and Sante Fe; Exec. Dir MATA Festival of New Music, New York; Dir Los Angeles Philharmonic Composer Fellowship Program 2009–; fmr Fellow, Aspen Music Festival and Norfolk Chamber Music Festival. *Compositions include:* for orchestra: Gliss 1999, Burn for wind ensemble 2001, River, River, River 2001, Umbras and Illuminations 2004, True South 2010, Four Fanfares 2011; for chamber orchestra: Sleep for violin and chamber orchestra 1997, Colonnade 2003, The Paces for piano and chamber orchestra 2003; for chamber ensemble and vocal: Pull, Spin, Falling, Songs of Desire, Love and Loss for soprano and mixed chamber ensemble 2004, Buzz for clarinet, violin, cello and piano, La Seine for English horn 2007, Violin Sonata 2007, The Anatomy of Melancholy for B flat clarinet, violin, cello and piano 2008, Violin Concerto 2011, Borromean Rings for piano 2010, Bagatelle for 3 pianos, 6 hands 2012. *Honours:* residencies at Yaddo and Luguria Study Center, fellowships from Guggenheim, Bogliasco and Sage Foundations, ASCAP, American Acad. of Arts and Letters Hinrichsen Award 2002, Robbins Prize, American Acad. of Arts and Letters Goddard Lieberson Fellowship 2008, American Acad. of Arts and Letters Charles Ives Living

2011. *E-mail:* james@jamesmatheson.com (office). *Website:* www.jamesmatheson.com (office).

MATHIESEN, Thomas James, MMus, DMA; American musicologist and academic; *Distinguished Professor Emeritus, Indiana University*; b. 30 April 1947, Roslyn Heights, NY; m. Penelope Jay Price 1971. *Education:* Willamette Univ., Univ. of Southern California, Los Angeles. *Career:* Lecturer in Musicology, Univ. of Southern California 1971–72; Prof. of Music and Head of Musicology Area, Brigham Young Univ., Provo, UT 1972–86, Assoc. Dean, Honours and General Educ. 1986–88; Prof. of Music, Indiana Univ. 1988–96, Distinguished Prof. 1996–2010, Distinguished Prof. Emer. 2010–, Dir Center for History of Music Theory and Literature 1998–2009, David H. Jacobs Chair in Music 1998–2010; Fellow, American Acad. of Arts and Sciences 2001. *Publications:* Thesaurus Musicarum Latinarum (project dir 1990–2009), Doctoral Dissertations in Musicology (project dir 1996–2009), A Bibliography of Sources for the Study of Ancient Greek Music 1974, Aristides Quintilianus on Music in Three Books (trans., commentary and annotations) 1983, Ancient Greek Music Theory: A Catalogue Raisonné of Manuscripts (Duckles Award 1989) 1988, Festa Musicologica: Essays in Honor of George J. Buelow (ed.) 1995, Greek Views of Music 1997, Apollo's Lyre: Greek Music and Music Theory in Antiquity and the Middle Ages (Kinkeldey Award, Berry Award, ASCAP-Deems Taylor Award 2000) 1999, Music in the Mirror: Reflections on the History of Music Theory and Literature for the 21st Century (ASCAP-Deems Taylor Award 2003) 2002, Greek and Latin Music Theory (ten vols, Gen. Ed.) 1982–2004, Studies in the History of Music Theory and Literature (five vols, Gen. Ed.) 2005–; contrib. to New Grove Dictionary of Music and Musicians (second edn), Die Musik in Geschichte und Gegenwart (second edn), Encyclopedia of Ancient Natural Scientists, Routledge Companion to Philosophy and Music, various journals and Festschriften. *Honours:* American Council of Learned Socs grant 1977, Nat. Endowment for the Humanities (NEH) Fellowship 1985–86, Guggenheim Fellowship 1990–91, NEH grant 1992–96. *Address:* 1800 Valley View Drive, Ellettsville, IN 47429-9487, USA.

MATHIS, Edith; Swiss singer (soprano); b. 11 Feb. 1938, Lucerne; m. Bernhard Klee. *Education:* Lucerne Conservatoire. *Career:* début Lucerne (in The Magic Flute) 1956; sang with Cologne Opera 1959–62; appeared Salzburg Festival 1960, Deutsche Oper, W Berlin 1963; début Glyndebourne (Cherubino in Le Nozze di Figaro) 1962, Covent Garden (Susanna in Le Nozze di Figaro) 1970, Metropolitan Opera House, New York (Pamina in The Magic Flute) 1970, Berne City Opera 1990; sang to Mendelssohn, Brahms and Schubert, Wigmore Hall, London 1997; mem. Hamburg State Opera 1960–75. *Current Management:* Bureau de Concerts de Valmalete, 7 rue Hoche, 92300 Paris, France. *Telephone:* 1-47-59-78-59. *Fax:* 1-47-59-87-50. *Website:* www.valmalete.com.

MATORIN, Vladimir Anatolievich; Russian singer (bass); b. 2 May 1948, Moscow; s. of Anatoly Ivanovich Matorin and Maria Tarasovna Matorina; m. Svetlana Sergeyevna Matorina; one s. *Education:* Gnessin Pedagogical Inst. (now Acad.) of Music. *Career:* soloist, Moscow Stanislavsky and Nemirovich-Danchenko Music Theatre 1974–91, Bolshoi Theatre 1991–; teacher at Russian Acad. of Theatre Art 1991–, Prof. and Head of Faculty of Solo Singing 1994–; numerous int. tours. *Opera roles include:* Boris Godunov, Ivan Susanin, King René (Iolanthe), Gremin (Eugene Onegin), Dosifei (Khovanshchina), Count Galitsky (Prince Igor), Don Basilio (Barber of Seville), Count (Invisible City of Kitezh) and more than 65 others. *Recordings include:* Modest Mussorgsky's Sorochintsy Fair 1983, Sergei Rachmaninov's Ale 1990, Rachmaninov's Francesca da Rimini 1992, Nikolai Rimsky-Korsakov's May Night 1997, Rimsky-Korsakov's Kashchey the Immortal, Vissarion Shebalin's The Taming of the Shrew. *Honours:* winner, All-Union Glinka Competition of vocalists and Int. Competition of Singers in Geneva, Merited Artist of Russia, People's Artist of Russia. *Current Management:* Robert Gilder & Co., N102, Westminster Business Square, 1–45 Durham Street, London, SE11 5JH, England. *Address:* Bolshoi Theatre of Russia, 103009 Moscow, Teatralnaya pl. 1 (office); 129090 Moscow, Periy Koptelskiy Pereulok 9/29; 103045 Moscow, Ulansky per. 21, korp. 1 Apt. 53, Russia (home). *Telephone:* (495) 692-38-86 (office); (495) 680-44-17 (home). *Fax:* (495) 680-44-17 (home). *Website:* www.bolshoi.ru (office).

MATOUŠEK, Bohuslav, MgA; Czech violinist; *Professor, Akademie Múzických Umění (HAMU), Prague*; , *Janaček Akademia (JAMU), Brno*; b. 26 Sept. 1949, Havlickuv Brod. *Education:* Acad. of Music, Prague with Jaroslav Pekelsky and Vaclav Snitil, further study with Arthur Grumiaux, Nathan Milstein and Wolfgang Schneiderhan. *Career:* soloist with Tokyo Yomiuri Nippon Symphony Orchestra, 1977–78; Co-founder and leader of Stamic Quartet of Prague 1980–95; solo artist 1995–; mem. Antonin Dvořák Trio; performances at Prague Young Artists and Bratislava Music Festivals; tours to Spain, Austria, France, Switzerland, Germany, Eastern Europe, USA 1980, debut concerts in UK at London and Birmingham 1983; Prof., Music Faculty, Akad. Múzických Umění (HAMU), Prague 2007–, Janaček Akademia (JAMU), Brno 2007–. *Recordings include:* Haydn Violin Concertos 1972–76, Dubble Concerto 1973, Schubert: Grand Duo 1978, Smetana, Dvořák, Suk: Violin Works 1982, Duo Concertant 1990, Czech music for violin and piano 1993, Vivaldi's Le Quatro Stagioni 1995, Antonin Dvořák: The Complete Work for Violin and Piano 1995, Brahms/Bruch: Konzert für Violine und Orchester 1995, Wenceslaus Wodizka: The European Music of 18th Century 1996, Antonin Dvořák: Die Werke für Violine und Orchester, Complete Works for Violin and Piano by A. Dvořák, Complete Works for Violin and Piano Vol. 1 and Vol. 2 by B. Martinů (Midem Classical Award 2001), Ludvig van Beethoven: Works for violin and orchestra (Concerto for violin in D major Op. 61, Romance in F major/G major Op. 50/Op. 40) 1999, Complete Works for Concertante Violin and Orchestra (Czech Philharmonic Orchestra with Christopher Hogwood). *Honours:* with mems of Stamic Quartet: Prizewinner, Winner, ORF, Austrian Radio 1986, Int. String Quartet Competition followed by live broadcast from Salzburg Mozarteum, Acad. Charles Cros Grand Prix du Disque, for Dvořák quartets 1991, Winner, Prix Int. Violin Competition Prague, as soloist 1972. *Current Management:* c/o Lubomír Herza, Art Production Slámová 667, 251 68 Struhařov, Czech Republic. *Telephone:* (2) 22936651; 72-4034356 (mobile). *E-mail:* lherza@iol.cz; Margita.Losova@seznam.cz. *Address:* Dvořákova 311, 252 64 Velké Prilepy, Czech Republic (home). *Telephone:* (2) 20930468 (home); 602-373600 (mobile). *E-mail:* bmatousek@volny.cz (home). *Website:* www.bohuslavmatousek.cz.

MATOUŠEK, Lukáš; Czech composer, clarinettist and performer of medieval instruments; *Teacher of Music Theory, Academy of Performing Arts, Prague*; b. 29 May 1943, Prague; m. 1st Zuzana Matouškova 1966 (deceased); two d.; m. 2nd Zdenka Kratka 2002. *Education:* Prague Conservatory of Music, Janáček Acad. of Performing Arts, Brno, studied with Miloslav Kabeláč. *Career:* Artistic Dir Ars Cameralis Ensemble; many concerts and recordings for radio and TV throughout Europe; recordings as performer with Ars Cameralis, and of own works; Music Dir Record Label Studio Matous; Programme Dir Prague Symphony Orchestra; currently Teacher of Music Theory, Acad. of Performing Arts, Prague. *Compositions include:* for orchestra: Radices Temporum, Stories, Concerto for percussion and winds, In memoriam J.F.K., Metamorphoses of Silence for strings, Fanfare of 17th November for 12 brass, Memory of Prague's Palace, Viderunt omnes fines millennii, Sonnet Sequence for cello and orchestra; chamber music: Sonata for violin and piano (version for violin and orchestra), Sonata for double-bass and chamber ensemble, Wind Quintet, Aztecs for percussion, Intimate Music for viola or cello, Recollection of Mr Sudek for brass sextet, Sonatina for clarinet and piano, Sonnet Sequence for cello and piano, Shadows and Reflections for chamber ensemble, Min-Kaleidoscope for chamber ensemble, Trio for clarinet, violin and piano, Solo for clarinet, Czech Sonatina for clarinet or saxophone and piano, Sonata for organ, Biblical Sonata for harp; vocal: Three Cantatas, Colours and Thoughts, Flower of Paradise, Not a Sorrow We Will Not Live to the End; several children's choir pieces. *Recordings:* Gothic Music in Bohemia, Music of Charles University, Machaut-Chansons, Gothic Christmas in Bohemia, L. Matousek: Chamber Music, L. Matousek: Sonnet Sequence; single compositions on other CDs. *Address:* Hačálka 247, 25101 Tehov u Říča, Czech Republic. *Telephone:* (3) 23601851; 77-7029518 (mobile). *E-mail:* cameralis@volny.cz. *Website:* www.musica.cz/skladatele/matousek-lukas.html; www.volny.cz/cameralis.

MATSUEV, Denis Leonidovich; Russian musician (piano); b. 11 June 1975, Irkutsk, Siberia; s. of Leonid Matsuev and Irina Gomelskaya. *Education:* Central Music School, Moscow, studied with Aleksey Nasedkin and Sergei Dorensky. *Career:* moved to Moscow 1991, concerts 1993–; regular engagements with Russian orchestras such as St Petersburg Philharmonic, Mariinsky Orchestra and Russian Nat. Orchestra; performs world-wide with orchestras such as New York Philharmonic, Chicago Symphony Orchestra, Philadelphia Orchestra, Los Angeles Philharmonic Orchestra, Pittsburgh Symphony Orchestra, Berlin Philharmonic Orchestra, Leipzig Gewandhaus Orchestra, Bavarian Radio Symphony Orchestra, London Symphony, London Philharmonic, Royal Philharmonic Orchestra, Royal Concertgebouw Orchestra, Rotterdam Philharmonic, Orchestra Filarmonica della Scala, Orchestre de Paris, Orchestre Nat. du Capitole de Toulouse, European Chamber Orchestra, Helsinki Philharmonic, among numerous others; has appeared with conductors including Valery Gergiev, Yuri Temirkanov, Yevgeny Svetlanov, Mariss Jansons, Lorin Maazel, Zubin Mehta, Kurt Masur, Paavo Jarvi, Antonio Pappano, Charles Dutoit, Alain Gilbert, Leonard Slatkin, Myung-Whun Chung, Semyon Bychkov, Iván Fischer, Adam Fisher, Gianandrea Noseda, Jukka-Pekka Saraste, James Conlon, Vladimir Spivakov, Mikhail Pletnev, Vladimir Fedoseyev, Yury Bashmet, Claudio Abbado; recitals at Carnegie Hall, New York, Lincoln Center, Washington, DC, Salle Gaveau and Théâtre des Champs-Elysées, Paris, Concertgebouw, Amsterdam, Mozarteum Salzburg, Musikverein Vienna, Royal Festival Hall, London, Great Hall of Philharmonie, St Petersburg, La Scala, Milan, Suntory Hall, Tokyo, Mariinsky Theatre Concert Hall; has performed at numerous festivals including BBC Proms, Edinburgh, Ravinia, Chicago, Schleswig-Holstein, Chopin Festival, Poland, Maggio Musicale Fiorentino, La Roque d'Anthéron, France, Montreux, Budapest Spring, Russian Winter in Moscow, Stars of the White Nights in St Petersburg, Shanghai; soloist at New York Philharmonic's 15,000th concert in Avery Fisher Hall conducted by Valery Gergiev; torchbearer Winter Olympics, Sochi 2014, performed at opening and closing ceremonies; Founder and Artistic Dir Crescendo music festival (classical and jazz), held annually in cities such as Moscow, St Petersburg, Yekaterinburg, Tel-Aviv, Kaliningrad, Paris and New York 2005–; Artistic Dir Annecy Music Festival, France 2010–, Int. Astana Piano Passion Festival and Competition 2012–, Int. Sberbank Debut Festival and Competition, Kiev 2013–; organiser, Stars on Baikal, Irkutsk, Siberia 2004–; Pres. New Names charity discovering and supporting talented children and developing music education in regions of Russia 2008–; has collaborated for many years with Sergei Rachmaninov Foundation, and was chosen to perform and record Rachmaninov's unknown pieces on the composer's own piano at Rachmaninov's house Villa Senar in Lucerne, later Artistic Dir; mem. Presidential Council for Culture and Arts 2006–; UNESCO

Goodwill Amb. 2014–. *Recordings include:* Unknown Rachmaninoff 2007, Denis Matsuev – Concert at Carnegie Hall 2009, Rachmaninoff Concerto No. 3 2009, Shostakovich Concertos No. 1, No. 2 and Schedrin's Fifth (Mariinsky Orchestra/Gergiev) 2011, Rachmaninoff Piano Concerto No. 2 and Gershwin Rhapsody in Blue (New York Philharmonic/Gilbert) 2013, Szymanowski Symphonia Concertante (LSO/Gergiev) 2013, Tchaikovsky Concerti Nos. 1 & 2 2014. *Honours:* Hon. Citizen of Irkutsk 2009, Hon. Prof., Moscow State Univ.; winner, 11th Int. Tchaikovsky Competition 1998, Shostakovich Music Prize, State Prize in Literature and Arts, People's Artist of Russia, Honoured Artist of Russia. *Current Management:* c/o Douglas Sheldon, Columbia Artists Management, 5 Columbus Circle @ 1790 Broadway, New York, NY 10019-1412, USA. *Telephone:* (212) 841 9500. *Fax:* (212) 841 9744. *E-mail:* info@cami .com. *Website:* www.cami.com. *E-mail:* alexeypilyugin@gmail.com. *Website:* matsuev.com.

MATSUZAWA, Yuki; Japanese pianist; b. 1960, Tokyo. *Education:* Tokyo Univ. of Fine Arts, studied with Akiko Iguchi and Hiroshi Tamura, further study with Vladimir Ashkenazy in Europe. *Career:* concert engagements in Europe, Asia and USA; radio and television engagements in the UK, Ireland, The Netherlands, Greece, USA, Japan; Irish debut with the Berlin Radio Symphony Orchestra 1990; London debut at Wigmore Hall 1990; London appearances at Wigmore Hall, Barbican Hall, St John's Smith Square; concerto appearances with Royal Philharmonic Orchestra, BBC Symphony Orchestra, Montréal Symphony Orchestra, Athens Radio Symphony Orchestra, Berlin Radio Symphony Orchestra, NHK Symphony Orchestra, New London Orchestra; chamber music appearances with Suk Quartet in the UK and Czechoslovakia and with Martinů Quartet in the UK; tours of the UK and Europe; concerts with: English Chamber Orchestra, Brno Philharmonic and Bournemouth Sinfonietta. *Honours:* prizewinner at such competitions as Queen Elizabeth, Brussels, Maria Canals, Barcelona, and Montréal International, Canada. *Current Management:* c/o Alex Durston Management, 43 Haven Lane, London, W5 2HZ, England. *Telephone:* (20) 8998-3533. *E-mail:* ad@admus.demon.co.uk.

MATTEI, Peter; Swedish singer (baritone); b. 1965, Piteå. *Education:* Royal Swedish Acad. of Music and Univ. Coll. of Opera, Stockholm. *Career:* debut in Drottningholm 1990 as Nardo in Mozart's La Finta Giardiniera; debut at Royal Opera Stockholm 1991 in the premiere of Backanterna by Daniel Bortz; Drottningholm 1992–93 in Salieri's Falstaff and Haeffner's Electra; int. debut with Scottish Opera 1995 as Don Giovanni; Salzburg Festival 1996 as Minister in Fidelio; season 1998 as Mozart's Guglielmo for Scottish Opera and Don Giovanni at Aix; sang Posa in Don Carlos at Stockholm 1999; season 2000–01 as Mozart's Figaro at Glyndebourne, Chorèbe in Les Troyens at the Barbican Hall and as Eugene Onegin in Brussels; Mahler's Symphony of a Thousand at the London Proms 2002; since 2008 has sung at Metropolitan Opera (Don Giovanni, Šiškov in From the House of the Dead, Marcello in La Bohème, Prince Yeletsky in The Queen of Spades, Figaro in Il barbiere di Siviglia, Amfortas in Parsifal), Royal Opera House, Covent Garden (Count Almaviva in Le Nozze di Figaro), Teatro alla Scala (Don Giovanni, Šiškov in From the House of the Dead), Opera Nat. de Paris (Don Giovanni), Vienna State Opera (Eugene Onegin, Don Giovanni), Oper Frankfurt (Billy Budd), Opernhaus Zürich (Don Giovanni), Bolshoi Theatre (Don Giovanni), Den Norske Opera (Rodrigo in Don Carlo), Salzburg and Lucerne Festivals (Don Pizzaro and Don Fernando in Fidelio); has performed in concert with Mahler Chamber Orchestra, Gewandhaus Orchestra, Concertgebouw Orchestra, Berlin Philharmonic, London Symphony Orchestra, Boston Symphony Orchestra, Chicago Symphony Orchestra and leading orchestras in Sweden and Scandinavia; repertoire includes Brahms Ein deutsches Requiem, Sibelius's Kullervo, Mahler's Lieder eines fahrenden Gesellen and Des Knaben Wunderhorn, Bach's St Matthew Passion and St John Passion, and Zemlinsky's Lyrische Sinfonie; has worked with conductors including Sir Georg Solti, Claudio Abbado, Riccardo Muti, Daniel Barenboim, Sir Colin Davis, Esa-Pekka Salonen, Herbert Blomstedt, Daniel Harding, Jeffrey Tate, Riccardo Chailly, Antonio Pappano, Sir Andrew Davis, John Eliot Gardiner and Gustavo Dudamel. *Recordings:* Electra, Carmina Burana. *Honours:* Opera News Award for invaluable contrib. to opera 2011. *Current Management:* c/o Ann Braathen Artist Management, Folkskolegatan 5, 117 35 Stockholm, Sweden. *Telephone:* (8) 55690850. *Fax:* (8) 55690851. *E-mail:* info@braathenmanagement.com. *Website:* www.braathenmanagement.com.

MATTEUZZI, William; singer (tenor); b. 1957, Bologna, Italy. *Education:* studied with Paride Venturi. *Career:* debut singing Massenet's Des Grieux in Milan; season 1987 sang Rossini's Ramiro at Bologna, Nemorino at Bergamo and Evander in Alceste at La Scala; Rossini's Comte Ory at Venice, 1988, La Scala, 1991; Pesaro Festival, 1988, in La Scala di Seta, as Roderigo in Rossini's Otello, 1991; Count Almaviva on Metropolitan Opera debut 1988 and at Barcelona, 1991; Sang Lindoro in L'Italiana in Algeri, at Monte Carlo, 1989; Medoro in Orlando Furioso by Vivaldi at San Francisco; Other roles include Flamand in Capriccio and Ernesto in Don Pasquale. *Recordings:* Francesca da Rimini; Borsa in Rigoletto; Edmondo in Manon Lescaut and in Barbiere di Siviglia; Rossini's Zelmira; Tonio in La Fille du Régiment, Carlo and Goffredo in Rossini's Armida; sang Lindoro in L'Italiana in Algeri at Parma, 1998. *Honours:* winner Caruso International Competition, Milan.

MATTHEW-WALKER, Robert; composer and writer on music; b. 23 July 1939, Lewisham, London, England; m. Lynn Sharon Andrews 1969, one s. *Education:* London Coll. of Printing, Goldsmiths' Coll., London Coll. of Music, studied with Darius Milhaud in Paris. *Career:* Ed., Music and Musicians

1984–88; mem. PRS, Critics' Circle. *Compositions:* Symphonies 1–6 1955, 1958, 1959, 1964, 1968 (two), Violin Concerto 1962, Piano Sonatas 1–4 1976 (two), 1980, 1982, Piano Trio 1978, Horn Concerto 1980, Cello Sonata 1980, String Quartet 1980, Sinfonia Solemnis 1981. *Recordings:* Le Tombeau de Milhaud, Divertimento on a Theme of Mozart. *Publications:* Rachmaninov: his Life and Times 1980, Madonna: The Biography 1989, Havergal Brian 1995, Heartbreak Hotel: The Life and Music of Elvis Presley 1995, The Keller Column (ed.) 1990, The Symphonies of Robert Simpson 1991; contrib. to National Dictionary of Biography, Musical Times.

MATTHEWS, Andrea, AB; American singer (soprano); b. 6 Nov. 1956, Needham, MA. *Education:* Princeton Univ. *Career:* debut in Marriage of Figaro as Susanna at Virginia Opera, 1984; Semele in Semele; Gretel in Hansel and Gretel, Virginia Opera; Gilda in Rigoletto, Piedmont Opera; Zerlina in Don Giovanni, Greensboro Opera; Euridice in Orfeo ed Euridice, Violetta in La Traviata, Susanna in Marriage of Figaro, Marie in Bartered Bride and Ilia in Idomeneo at The Stadttheater Aachen, Germany; other roles include Musetta, Mimi in La Bohème, Pamina in Magic Flute, Lauretta in Gianni Schicchi, Marzelline in Fidelio, Lucy in The Telephone, Marguerite in Faust, Nannetta in Falstaff; soloist with many orchestras and companies, including St Louis Symphony; Houston Symphony; Baltimore Symphony; Atlanta Symphony; Stuttgart Philharmonic, Prague Autumn Festival, Philadelphia Orchestra, Puerto Rico Symphony, Honolulu Symphony, National Symphony at Wolf Trap, Los Angeles Master Chorale, Dessoff Choirs, Oratorio Society of New York, Mostly Mozart Festival, New Mexico Symphony, Kalamazoo Symphony, Utah Symphony, St Paul Chamber Orchestra, American Ballet Theater, American Symphony, Raleigh Symphony and Cincinnati Symphony; art-song recitals in many US states. *Recordings:* Vaughan Williams's Serenade to Music; Handel's Siroe, Muzio, Berenice, Tolomeo; Christmas Album; Victor Herbert's Thine Alone (songs); Ned Rorem's Three Sisters. *Current Management:* Thea Dispeker Inc., 59 East 54th Street, Suite 81, New York NY 10022, USA. *Telephone:* (212) 421-7676. *Fax:* (212) 935-3279. *E-mail:* info@dispeker.com. *Website:* www.dispeker.com.

MATTHEWS, Colin, OBE, BA, MPhil, DPhil, FRCM, FRNCM; British composer; *Prince Consort Professor of Composition, Royal College of Music;* b. 13 Feb. 1946, London. *Education:* Univ. of Nottingham, studied with Arnold Whittall and Nicholas Maw. *Career:* collaborated with Deryck Cooke on performing version of Mahler's 10th Symphony; Cortège premiered under Bernard Haitink at Covent Garden 1989, Machines and Dreams by the London Symphony Orchestra 1991; taught at Univ. of Sussex 1972–73, 1976–77; Visiting Composer and Teacher at Tanglewood, NY, USA 1991; Admin. Holst Foundation 1983–; Trustee, Britten-Pears Foundation 1983; Asst to Benjamin Britten in last years; Founder NMC Recordings 1989; Assoc. Composer, London Symphony Orchestra 1992–99, Hallé Orchestra 2001–11, Composer Emer. 2011–; Chair. Britten Estate 2000; Gov., Royal Northern Coll. of Music, Manchester 2001–08; Prince Consort Prof. of Composition, Royal Coll. of Music, London 2001–; Special Prof., Univ. of Nottingham 2005–; Distinguished Visiting Fellow in Composition, Univ. of Manchester; mem. Council Royal Philharmonic Soc. 2005–, mem. Exec. Cttee. *Compositions:* Ceres for nonet 1972, Sonata No. 4 for orchestra 1975, Partita for violin 1975, Five Sonnets to Orpheus for tenor and harp 1976, Specula for quartet 1976, Night Music for small orchestra 1977, Piano Suite 1979, Rainbow Studies for quintet 1978, Shadows in the Water for tenor and piano 1979, String Quartet No. 1 1979, Sonata No. 5 Landscape for orchestra 1977–81, Oboe Quartet 1981, Secondhand Flames for five voices 1982, Divertimento for double string quartet and string orchestra 1982, The Great Journey for baritone and ensemble 1981–86, Toccata Meccanica for orchestra 1984, Triptych for piano quintet 1984, Cello Concerto 1994, Three Enigmas for cello and piano 1985, String Quartet No. 2 1985, Suns Dance for ten players 1985, Monody for orchestra 1987, Two-Part Invention for chamber orchestra 1987–88, Pursuit for 16 players 1987, Fuga for eight players 1988, Cortège for orchestra 1989, Oboe Quartet No. 2 1989, Hidden Variable for 15 players 1989, Quatrain for wind, brass and percussion 1989, Chiaroscuro for orchestra 1990, Machines and Dreams for full or small orchestra and children 1990, Broken Symmetry for orchestra 1992, Contraflow for 14 players 1992, Memorial for orchestra 1993, String Quartet No. 3 1994, Cello Concerto No. 2 1996, Renewal for chorus and orchestra 1996, Elegaic Chaconne for ensemble 1997, Elegia for 14 players 1998, Aftertones for chorus and orchestra 1999, Pluto for orchestra 1999, Continuum for soprano and ensemble 2000, Horn Concerto 2001, Orchestration of seven Debussy Préludes 2001–03, Estrangements for chorus 2002, Vivo for orchestra 2002, Flourish with Fireflies 2002, Reflected Images 2003, Berceuse for Dresden for cello 2005, Turning Point 2006, Postlude 2006, Chaconne 2006, project involving the orchestration of all 24 of Debussy's Preludes 2007, Alphabicycle Order for children's chorus, narrator and orchestra to poems by Christopher Reid 2007, Violin Concerto 2008, Crossing the Alps for chorus and organ, on a text by William Wordsworth (The Prelude, Book VI) 2010, No Man's Land (vocal) (British Composer Award 2012). *Honours:* Hon. mem. RAM 2010; Dr hc (Nottingam) 1999; BBC Chamber Music Prize 1970, Ian Whyte Award 1975, Park Lane Group Composer Award 1983, Royal Philharmonic Soc. Prize 1997, Royal Philharmonic Soc./Performing Right Soc. Leslie Boosey Award 2005. *Address:* Royal College of Music, Prince Consort Road, London, SW7 2BS (office); c/o The Hallé Concerts Society, The Bridgewater Hall, Manchester, M1 5HA, England. *Telephone:* (20) 7591-4300 (London) (office); (161) 237-7000 (Manchester). *Fax:* (20) 7591-4737 (London) (office). *E-mail:* composition@rcm.ac.uk (office); info@halle.co .uk. *Website:* www.rcm.ac.uk (office); www.halle.co.uk.

MATTHEWS, David John, BA; British composer and writer; b. 9 March 1943, Walthamstow, London, England; m. Jenifer Wakelyn. *Education:* Univ. of Nottingham, studied with Anthony Milner, Nicholas Maw and Peter Sculthorpe. *Career:* worked with Deryck Cooke on completion of Mahler's 10th Symphony; Asst to Britten 1966–70; Artistic Dir Deal Festival 1989–2003; Artistic Adviser to English Chamber Orchestra; Fifth Symphony premiered at BBC Promenade Concerts, London 1999, Sixth Symphony premiered at BBC Proms 2007, A Vision and a Journey premiered at BBC Proms 2013. *Compositions include:* eight symphonies 1975, 1978, 1983, 1990, 1999, 2007, 2009, 2015, two violin concertos 1982, 1999, 13 string quartets 1970, 1976, 1978, 1981, 1984, 1990, 1994, 1998, 2000, 2001, 2008, 2010, 2015, three piano trios 1983, 1993, 2005, two string trios 1989, 2003, The Book of Hours for voice and piano 1975, Four Hymns for chorus 1978, The Company of Lovers for small chorus 1980, Introit for two trumpets and strings 1981, Serenade for small orchestra 1982, Duet Variations for flute and piano 1982, The Golden Kingdom for voice and piano 1983, Winter Journey for solo violin 1983, Clarinet Quartet 1984, Three Studies for solo violin 1985, In the Dark Time for orchestra 1985, Variations for strings 1986, Chaconne for orchestra 1987, The Flaying of Marsyas for oboe quintet 1987, Cantiga for soprano and orchestra 1988, Marina for baritone, basset horn, viola and piano 1988, Piano Sonata 1989, The Ship of Death for chorus 1989, Romanza for cello and small orchestra 1990, The Music of Dawn for orchestra 1990, Capriccio for two horns and strings 1991, From Coastal Stations for voice and piano 1991, Oboe Concerto 1992, From Sea to Sky for small orchestra 1992, The Sleeping Lord for soprano, flute, clarinet, harp and string quartet 1992, A Little Threnody for cor anglais 1993, A Vision and a Journey for orchestra 1993, A Congress of Passions for voice, oboe and piano 1994, Vespers for mezzo-soprano and tenor solo, chorus and orchestra 1996, Variations for piano 1997, Hurrahing in Harvest for chorus 1997, The Doorway of the Dawn for chorus 1999, Winter Passions for baritone and ensemble 1999, Two Pieces for strings 2000, Aubade for chamber orchestra 2000, A Congress of Passions for medium voice, oboe and strings 2000, Three Roman Miniatures for clarinet 2000, Band of Angels for organ 2001, After Sunrise for chamber orchestra 2001, Winter Remembered for solo viola and strings 2001, Eight Duos for two violins 2001, Concerto in Azzurro for cello and orchestra 2002, 15 Fugues for solo violin 2002, Aequam Memento for chorus 2004, Piano Quintet 2004, Darkness Draws In for solo viola 2005, Fanfares and Flowers for symphonic wind band 2006, Terrible Beauty for voice and ensemble 2007, Two Dionysus Dithyrambs for piano 2007, Adonis for violin and piano 2007, The Key of the Kingdom for chorus 2007, One Foot in Eden for voice and piano quintet 2008, Journeying Songs for solo cello 2008, Piano Concerto 2009, Horn Quintet 2010, Toward the Sunrise for orchestra 2011, Lebensregeln for voice and piano 2011, Romanza for solo violin and strings 2011, Fortune's Wheel for chorus and strings 2011–12, A Blackbird Sang for flute and string trio 2011–12, Double Concerto for violin, viola and strings 2011–12, Duo Sonata for violin and cello 2012, Four Portraits for piano 2012, A Vision of the Sea for orchestra 2012–13, To What God Shall We Chant Our Songs of Battle? for chorus 2014, 15 Preludes for solo violin 2014, Nachtgesang for orchestra 2015, Norfolk March for orchestra 2015. *Publications include:* Michael Tippett 1980, Landscape into Sound 1992, Britten 2003; contrib. to Tempo, TLS, London Review of Books, Musical Times. *Honours:* Hon. DMus 1998. *Address:* c/o Faber Music Ltd, 74–77 Great Russell Street, London, WC1B 3DU, England. *Telephone:* (20) 7908-5310. *E-mail:* information@fabermusic.com (office). *Website:* www.fabermusic.com (office); www.david-matthews.co.uk.

MATTHEWS, Emma; Australian singer (soprano); *Principal Artist, Opera Australia.* *Career:* debut as Damigella in Monteverdi's L'incoronazione di Poppea with Opera Australia 1993, later becoming Prin. Artist; performs regularly with all Australian symphony orchestras, Sydney Philharmonia Choirs, New Zealand Chamber Orchestra; Welsh Nat. Opera debut as Aspasia in Mitridate under Sir Charles Mackerras 2009, Royal Opera debut in The Cunning Little Vixen (2010); roles include: Lakmé, Lulu, Lucia di Lammermoor, Papagena and Pamina in The Magic Flute, Juliette in Roméo et Juliette, Almirena in Rinaldo, Ilia in Idomeneo, Sophie in Der Rosenkavalier, Vixen in The Cunning Little Vixen, Konstanze/Blonde in Abduction from the Seraglio, Morgana in Alcina, Marie in La fille du régiment, Sofia in Il Signor Bruschino, Cherubino in Marriage of Figaro, Hero in Beatrice and Benedict, Zwanntie in Batavia, Oscar in Un ballo in maschera, Cleopatra in Giulio Cesare, Rosina in Il barbiere di Siviglia, Zdenka in Arabella, Yum-Yum in Mikado, Stasi in The Gypsy Princess, Genovieffa in Suor Angelica, Olympia in The Tales of Hoffmann, Servilia in La Clemenza di Tito, Sky/Aunt Olive/Tour Guide in The Eighth Wonder, Nannetta in Falstaff, Sophie in Werther, Adele in Die Fledermaus, the Four Heroines in The Tales of Hoffmann, Philomele in The Love of the Nightingale, Zdenka in Arabella, Angelica in Orlando. *Recordings include:* Handel Arias 2002. *Honours:* Remy Martin Opera Award 1999, Green Room Awards 1999, 2000, 2001, Best Female Singer, Lulu 2003, Sofia 2005, Helpmann Award for Best Female Performer in an Opera 2007. *Address:* The Opera Centre – Sydney, 480 Elizabeth Street, Surry Hills, NSW 2010, Australia (office). *Telephone:* (2) 9699-1099 (office). *Fax:* (2) 9699-3184 (office). *E-mail:* enquiries@opera-australia.org.au (office). *Website:* www.opera-australia.org.au (office).

MATTHEWS, Sally; British singer (soprano); b. 1975, England. *Education:* Guildhall School, London, Young Artist Programme, Covent Garden. *Career:* debut as Nannetta in Falstaff, Covent Garden 2000; season 2000–01 as Mozart's Fiordiligi for Grange Park Opera and Elisa in Il Re Pastore for the Classical Opera Co.; concerts with the Orchestra of St John's, Philharmonia,

English Chamber Orchestra and Royal Liverpool Philharmonic Orchestra; first night of 2001 London Proms in Serenade to Music, by Vaughan Williams; season 2001–02 with Debussy's Le Martyre de St Sebastien, with the LSO under Pierre Boulez, and Messiah with the London Philharmonic. *Honours:* Kathleen Ferrier Award 1999. *Current Management:* Van Walsum Management Deutschland GmbH, Königstrasse 36, 30175 Hannover, Germany. *Telephone:* 511 366 07 23. *Fax:* 511 366 07 24. *E-mail:* vwm@kdschmid.de.

MATTHUS, Siegfried; German composer; b. 13 April 1934, Mallenuppen, E Prussia; s. of the late Franz Matthus and of Luise Perrey; m. Helga Spitzer 1958; one s. *Education:* Hochschule für Musik, Berlin, Acad. of Arts and Music, Berlin, master-class with Hanns Eisler. *Career:* composer and consultant, Komische Oper, Berlin 1964–2002; Prof. 1985–; Artistic Dir Chamber Opera Festival, Rheinsberg 1991; mem. Acad. of Arts of GDR, Acad. of Arts of W Berlin, Acad. of Arts, Munich. *Compositions include:* Te Deum, 10 operas, one oratorio, concertos, orchestral and chamber music, etc. *Honours:* Bundesverdienstkreuz (First Class) 2000; Nat. Prize 1972, 1984. *Address:* Elisabethweg 10, 13187 Berlin (home); Seepromenade 15, 16348 Stolzenhagen, Germany (home). *Telephone:* (30) 4857362 (Berlin) (home); (33397) 21736 (Stolzenhagen) (home). *Fax:* (30) 48096604 (Berlin) (home); (33397) 71400 (Stolzenhagen) (home). *E-mail:* smatthus@t-online.de (home). *Website:* www.siegfried-matthus.de.

MATTILA, Karita Marjatta; Finnish singer (soprano); b. Somero; d. of Arja Mattila and Erkki Mattila (née Somerikko); m. Tapio Kuneinen. *Education:* Sibelius Acad., and studied with Liisa Linko-Malmio, and Vera Rozsa in London. *Career:* performs in all major opera houses and festivals world-wide and regularly with conductors including Levine, Abbado, Davis, Dohnanyi, Haitink, Pappano, Rattle, Salonen and Sawallisch; operatic repertoire encompasses works by Beethoven, Strauss, Tchaikovsky, Verdi, Puccini, Wagner and Janáček; has worked with prominent stage dirs, including Luc Bondy in his Don Carlos at Paris, London and Edinburgh Festival; collaborations with Lev Dodin in productions of Elektra for Salzburg Easter Festival and Pique Dame and Salome at Opéra Bastille, Peter Stein's productions of Simon Boccanegra in Salzburg and Don Giovanni in Chicago, and Jürgen Flimm's Fidelio in New York; regularly collaborates with contemporary composers in debut performances of modern works, including world premiere of Mirage by Kaija Saariaho with Orchestre de Paris led by Christoph Eschenbach in Paris. *Recordings include:* numerous solo and opera recordings, including 40th birthday concert, Helsinki (CD); other recordings include Strauss's Four Last Songs with Claudio Abbado, Arias & Scenes from the operas of Puccini, Verdi, Janacek, Tchaikovsky, Wagner and R. Strauss, German Romantic Arias by Beethoven, Mendelssohn and Weber with Sir Colin Davis, Grieg and Sibelius Songs with Sakari Oramo; complete recordings of Die Meistersinger von Nürnberg with the late Sir Georg Solti (Grammy Award for Opera 1998), Jenufa with Bernard Haitink (Grammy Award for Opera 2004), Schoenberg's Gurrelieder, Shostakovich's Symphony No. 14 with Sir Simon Rattle. *Honours:* Chevalier des Arts et des Lettres 2003; First Prize, Finnish Nat. Singing Competition 1981, First Prize, BBC Singer of the World, Cardiff 1983, François Reichenbach Prize Orphée du Lyrique, Acad. du Disque Lyrique, Paris, Evening Standard Ballet, Opera and Classical Music Award for Outstanding Performance of the Year 1997, Acad. du Disque Lyrique Award 1997, Grammy Award for Best Opera 1998, chosen by the New York Times as the Best Singer of the Year for her performance in Fidelio at the Metropolitan Opera 2001, Pro Finlandia 2001, Musical America Musician of the Year 2005, Opera News Award for invaluable contrib. to opera 2011. *Current Management:* c/o Bill Palant, IMG Artists, 7 West 54th Street, New York, NY 10019, USA. *Telephone:* (212) 994-3527. *E-mail:* bpalant@imgartists.com. *Website:* imgartists.com/artist/karita_mattila.

MATTINSON, David; singer (bass-baritone); b. 1964, England. *Education:* choral scholar Trinity Coll., Cambridge, Guildhall School of Music with Thomas Hemsley, studied with Rudolf Pierney. *Career:* concert repertoire includes the B minor Mass, Messiah, The Creation, Requiems of Brahms, Verdi and Fauré, The Dream of Gerontius and A Child of Our Time; appearances with the City of London Sinfonia, the Bournemouth Symphony and the London Philharmonic Orchestras; further concerts include Elijah at the Albert Hall, Christus in the St Matthew Passion at the Festival Hall, Mozart's Requiem, and Beethoven's Ninth in Koblenz; song recitals with the accompanist Clare Toomer in Winterreise, Dichterliebe, La Bonne Chanson and the Songs of Travel by Vaughan Williams; appearances with the New Songmakers and the Mistry String Quartet and at the Buxton, Malvern and Warwick Festivals; operatic roles include Gualtiero in Musgrave's The Voice of Ariadne, Mozart's Figaro, Germont, and Glover in La Jollie Fille de Perth; Scottish Opera debut 1991, as Zuniga in Carmen; debut as Mozart's Figaro, Opera North 1992; season 1992 as Villotto in Haydn's La Vera Costanza for Garsington Opera and in Billy Budd for Scottish Opera; sang Mozart's Figaro for Central Festival Opera 1996. *Recordings include:* Bach St John Passion. *Honours:* GSM Gold Medal Rosebowl, Worshipful Co. of Musicians' Silver Medal, gold medal Royal Overseas League Music Competition 1988, prizewinner Walter Gruner Int. Lieder Competition, Elly Ameling Int. Lied Concours, first prize BP Peter Pears Award 1990.

MATTIOTTO, Claudia; Italian pianist and teacher; b. 21 Jan. 1959, Turin; m. Guido Scano 1985; one s. *Education:* High School for Training of Primary Teachers, Verdi High Conservatory, Turin, Ecole Internationale de Piano, Lausanne, Switzerland, Mozarteum, Salzburg, Austria, Manhattan School of Music, New York, USA, Instituto Liongueres, Barcelona, Spain, Juilliard

School, New York, Longy School, Boston, USA. *Career:* solo debut 1981, piano duo debut 1985, with orchestra 1988; formed duo with Guido Scano 1985–; concerts in all Italy and in France, Germany, Egypt, India, Slovenia, Romania, Andorra, Greece and Poland; conductor and special teacher in musical courses and seminars; many European broadcasting appearances; collaborator in Caleidoscopio Project 1996–; concert series A Suon Di Musica 2000–; currently teacher, piano improvisation, Cuneo Music Conservatory; Pres. Int. Centre for Musical Research. *Recordings:* 4 Steps in 4 Hands, series of 15 weekly programmes, Radiokoper, Monte Carlo, Bucharest, Marseille, Trieste radio and TV broadcasts; album: Documents (rarities) 2001. *Publications:* In Musica, piano teaching methodology text 1986, Concerto in Famiglia, A Guide for Younger Musicians 2003. *Honours:* Dalcroze Teaching Certificate, Manhattan School of Music 1991, First Prize, Genova Competition 1986. *Address:* Corso Rosselli 105/10A, 10129 Turin, Italy (office). *E-mail:* info@cirmonline.it (office). *Website:* www.cirmonline.it (office).

MATTSSON, Jack; composer and musician; b. 12 Dec. 1954, Åland, Finland. *Education:* Sibelius Acad. *Career:* debut with Alandskt Requiem for soloists, chorus and orchestra 1990; composer, arranger, conductor 1980–; Finnish radio and television, recordings for various record companies 1986–; Conductor, Swedish Theatre, Helsinki. *Compositions:* Ålandskt Requiem 1991, Serenade for basson and strings 1990, Carating for violin and piano 1990, Four Bagatelles for flute, violin and viola 1986, Joy and Thoughts for organ 1992, Katrina for solo voices chorus and orchestra (for music theatre) 1998. *Honours:* Åland Culture Prize 1990, Finnish Swedish Culture Foundation Prize 1987.

MATUSZCZAK, Bernadetta; Polish composer; b. 10 March 1931, Thorn; d. of the late Józef Matuszczak and Helena Glowacka. *Education:* Queen Jadwiga Polish Secondary School, Karol Szymanowski Fundamental and Secondary School of Music, studied with Szeligowski and Sitowski at the Poznań Higher Musical School and Warsaw Conservatories, studied in Paris with Nadia Boulanger. *Career:* mem. Asscn of Polish Composers (ZKP), Asscn of Artists and Composers of Polish Stages (ZAiKS). *Compositions include:* Septem Tubae for mixed choir and symphony orchestra 1965, Julia i Romeo, chamber opera, Warsaw 1970, Humanae Voces, radio oratorio 1972, Mysterium Heloizy, opera 1973–74, Elegy about a Polish Boy, symphony composition 1975, The Diary of a Madman, monodrama after Gogol, Warsaw 1978, Apocalypsis, radio oratorio 1979, Prometheus, chamber opera after Aeschylus 1981–83, In the Night on the Old Market, symphony for soloists, choir and orchestra 1988, Wild Swans, ballet fairy-tale 1991, Quo Vadis, opera after H. Sienkiewicz 1993–94, Canto funebre, for strings 1995, Crime and Punishment, drama after Dostoyevsky 2008. *Honours:* prize winner Young Polish Composers' Competition 1965, prize winner Grzegorz Fitelberg Composers' Competition for Septem Tubae 1966, prize winner competition organized by Jeunesses Musicales for Musica da camera 1967. *Address:* c/o Society of Authors ZAiKS, 2 Hipoteczna Street, 00 092 Warsaw, Poland (office). *Telephone:* (4822) 828 17 05 (office). *Fax:* (4822) 828 13 47 (office). *E-mail:* sekretariat@zaiks.org.pl (office). *Website:* www.zaiks.org.pl (office).

MATYS, Jiří, MgA; Czech composer; b. 27 Oct. 1927, Bakov, Nachod area. *Education:* Brno Conservatory, Janáček Acad. of Music, Brno with Kvapil. *Career:* teacher, Janáček Acad. 1953–57; Head of the School of Music, Kralove Pole in Brno 1957–60; Prof. of the Conservatory, Brno; mem. Asscn of Czech Musicians and Scientists (Prague), Moravian Composers Club (Brno). *Compositions:* Viola Sonata 1954, 5 String Quartets 1957–90, Variations on Death for narrator, horn and string quartet on a poem by Milan Kundera 1959, Morning Music 1962, Solo viola sonata 1963, Music for string quartet and orchestra 1971, Suite for viola and bass clarinet 1973, Symphonic Overture 1974, Dialogue for cello and piano 1976, Sonata for Violin Solo No. 1 1977, Divertimento for Four Horns 1981, Suite for flute and guitar 1981, Music for strings 1982, Suite for Wind Quintet 1984, Music for Piano 1985, I Wish You Knew…, for mezzo, cello, piano 1985–86, The Urgency of Time, symphonic picture for viola, orchestra and reciter 1986–87, Poetic Movements V, four compositions for four guitars 1988, Tuning, five compositions for guitar solo 1990, Sonata for Violin Solo No. 2 1991, No. 3 1993, No. 4 1994, No. 5 1995, No. 6 1996, Night Thoughts, a cycle of piano compositions in five parts 1992, Dedicated to a poet, a fantasy for baritone and string quartet 1995, String Trio for violin, viola and violoncello 1996–97, Friendly Sketches for piano 1998, Duo for violin and cello 1999–2000, Music for contrabass solo 2001, Suite for two contrabass 2002, Leaving…, for flute, violin, cello, piano 2002, String Quartet No. 6 2003, Music for violoncello solo II 2004, While of the Standstill, melodramas for reciter, flute and viola of a poem by Jiří Wolker 2004, Impromptu for flute solo 2004–05, Call, vocal cycle for baryton and piano 2004–05, Music for violoncello solo III 2006, Suite for solo violin 2007, String quartet No. 7 2007–08, Epizody for solo violin 2008. *Recordings:* albums: Tuning In for Guitar Solo 1990, Music for string quartet and orchestra 1998, String Quartet No. 3 1999, 5 Impromptus for violin and piano 1999, Suite for viola and bass clarinet 2000, Music for Strings 2001, Written by grief into silence…, vocal cycle for mezzo and orchestra 2001, String trio for violin, viola and violoncello 2004, Lyrical Melodramas of a poem by Josef Kainar for reciter and piano, Leaving... for flute, violin, cello and piano 2006, Music for solo cello 2007, Call, vocal cycle for baritone and piano 2008. *Honours:* Int. Award at the Festival of Choral Art, Jihlava 1993, Czech Radio Sacred Music Competition award 1994. *Address:* Milénova 2, 638 00 Brno 38, Czech Republic (home). *Telephone:* 548529482 (home). *Website:* www.musica.cz/comp/matys.htm.

MAUCERI, John F., MPhil, BA; American conductor, music director and teacher; *Chancellor, University of North Carolina School of the Arts*; b. 12 Sept. 1945, New York; m. Betty Weiss 1968; one s. *Education:* Yale Univ., Tanglewood (Berkshire Music Center). *Career:* Music Dir, Yale Symphony Orchestra 1968–74; Assoc. Prof., Yale Univ. 1968–84; Music Dir, Washington Opera 1979–82; Music Dir of Orchestras, Kennedy Center 1979–91, Consultant, Music Theater 1982–91; Music Dir, American Symphony Orchestra 1985–87; Music Dir, Scottish Opera 1987–93; Dir, Hollywood Bowl Orchestra 1991–06, founding Dir 2006–; Direttore Stabile, Teatro Regio, Turin, Italy 1995–98; Visiting Prof., Yale Coll. 2000–01; Music Dir, Pittsburgh Opera 2001–06; Music Producer, all versions of Bernstein's Candide –1973; Co-Producer, On Your Toes, Broadway and London's West End 1982; San Francisco Opera debut 1976; Metropolitan Opera debut in Fidelio 1977; Lyric Opera of Chicago debut, La Bohème 1987; conducted the Metropolitan Opera Orchestra Brass and Empire Brass, reopening of Carnegie Hall 1987; British premiere of Weill's Street Scene 1989; Les Troyens in Glasgow and Covent Garden; conducted own edition of Blitzstein's Regina at Glasgow, British Premiere 1991; premiere of original version of Weill's Der Weg der Verheissung, Chemnitz, 1999; Chancellor NC School of the Arts 2006–; principal conductor, Entartete Musik series, Decca Records 2008; conducts official commemorative concert celebrating Erich Wolfgang Korngold 2008; mem. Advisory Bd, Nat. Endowment for the Arts 1973–76, American Inst. of Verdi Studies 1986–; Dir Charles Ives Soc. 1986–91; Trustee, Nat. Inst. for Music Theater 1986–91. *Recordings:* over 50 CDs including Original Cast: Candide 1973 (Best Opera Recording), On Your Toes, 1983, New York City Opera, Candide 1985, Original Cast, Song and Dance 1985, My Fair Lady, with Kiri Te Kanawa and Jerry Hadley. *Publications:* contrib. to Opera Magazine 1985. *Honours:* numerous awards including Antoinette Perry 1983, Outer Critics Circle 1983, Drama Desk Awards 1983, Grammy Award 1986, Olivier Award 1988, Wavendon Award Conductor of the Year 1990, Edison Klassiek Award 1991, Emmy Award 1994, 1998, Cannes Classical Music Award 2003, four Deutsche Schallplatten awards, two Diapason d'Or awards, American Acad. in Berlin Fellowship Prize 1999, Magic Baton Award 2005. *Current Management:* c/o Jean-Jacques Cesbron, Columbia Artists Management, 1790 Broadway, NY 10019-1412, USA. *Telephone:* (212) 841-9500. *Fax:* (212) 841-9744. *E-mail:* info@cami.com. *Website:* www.cami.com.

MAULTSBY, Nancy; American singer (mezzo-soprano); b. 1970. *Career:* appearances with Seattle Opera as Charlotte in Werther, Carmen at San Francisco and Erda in Siegfried at Buenos Aires; further engagements as Carmen for Pittsburgh Opera, Anmeris in Minnesota and Ursula (Béatrice et Benedict) at Santa Fe; sang The Omniscient Sea-Shell in Die Aegyptische Helena by Strauss for the Royal Opera at the Festival Hall, London, 1998; concerts include Das Lied von der Erde, the Brahms Alto Rhapsody, Mahler's 2nd symphony (Cleveland Orchestra) and Schoenberg's Gurrelieder, with the Minnesota Orchestra. *Honours:* Marian Anderson Award, Martin E. Segal Award 1993. *Current Management:* IMG Artists, Carnegie Hall Tower, 152 West 57th Street, 4th Floor, New York, NY 10019, USA. *Telephone:* (212) 994-3500. *Fax:* (212) 994-3550. *E-mail:* artistsny@imgartists.com. *Website:* www.imgartists.com.

MAUNDER, Charles Richard Francis, MA, PhD; British academic, musicologist and early music practitioner; b. 23 Nov. 1937, Portsmouth, England; m.; three s. *Education:* Jesus Coll., Cambridge. *Career:* Fellow, Christ's Coll., Cambridge 1964–; Lecturer, Univs of Cambridge, London, Reading, Leeds, and in the USA in Philadelphia, Chicago, Northwestern, Northern Illinois, and at musicological conferences, Int. Mozart Congress, Salzburg 1991; performer on the bass viol, Cambridge Consort of Viols, baroque, classical viola, Cambridge Early Music; violone, concerts in Cambridge and elsewhere include Messiah, St John Passion, Brandenburg Concertos, Bach Christmas Oratorio and Monteverdi Vespers; restored early keyboard instruments, including square piano by Johannes Zumpe, London 1766, for Emmanuel Coll., Cambridge; instruments built include copies of two manual harpsichord by Thomas Hitchcock and Mozart's forepiano; founder, Cambridge Classical Orchestra 1990. *Publications:* Mozart's Requiem: On Preparing a New Edition 1988, numerous editions of 17th- and 18th-century music, including 13 of the 48 vols of J.C. Bach's Collected Works, Mozart's Requiem K626, C minor Mass K 427 and Vesperae; contrib. to Galpin Society Journal, Musical Times, Early Music, Journal of the Royal Musical Association, Music and Letters, Notes, Mozart-Janrbuch.

MAUNDER, Stuart, AM; Australian stage director and administrator; *General Director, New Zealand Opera*; b. 29 Oct. 1957, Sydney, NSW; m. Ann-Maree McDonald; one d. *Career:* Resident Dir Opera Australia 1981–87, Artistic Admin. 1999–2003, Exec. Producer 2004–09; Staff Dir Royal Opera House, Covent Garden 1991–97; Opera Australia productions include Nabucco, Die Fledermaus, Don Pasquale, Roméo et Juliette, Manon, The Tales of Hoffman; directed for all Australian state cos; directed music theatre pieces by Bernstein, Sondheim and Sullivan throughout Australia, NZ, France, UK, USA, Hong Kong; Opera Australia productions of Trial by Jury, HMS Pinafore, The Pirates of Penzance have been televised nationally on ABC TV; Artistic Dir APEC Cultural Performance, Sydney Opera House 2007, Australia's Nat. Day at Expo Shanghai 2010; directed the nat. tour of Dusty – The Original Pop Diva and 2008 production of Shout! Legend of the Wild One, 'Little Women' for Kookaburra, My Fair Lady, A Little Night Music for Opera Australia and Music of Andrew Lloyd Webber (Australian, NZ and Asian tour), Sunday in the Park with George (Victorian Opera); currently Gen. Dir

New Zealand Opera. *Address:* PO Box 2620, Strawberry Hills, NSW 2012, Australia.

MAURER, Elsie; singer (mezzo-soprano); b. 1938, Germany. *Career:* sang at the Aachen Opera from 1963, Pforzheim 1964–67, Frankfurt Opera from 1968; among her best roles have been Meg Page, Olga in Eugene Onegin and Mary in Fliegender Holländer; guest appearances at Brunswick, Oldenburg and elsewhere as Ortrud, Amneris, Herodias and Preziosilla; sang Countess Geschwitz in Lulu for Essen Opera as guest at Barcelona 1969 and Trieste 1971); also guested at the Vienna State Opera. *Recordings include:* Die Soldaten by Zimmermann.

MAURO, Ermanno; singer (tenor); b. 20 Jan. 1939, Trieste, Italy. *Education:* Toronto Conservatory with Herman Geiger-Torel. *Career:* debut with Canadian Opera Co. 1962, as Tamino in Die Zauberflöte; sang Manrico in Toronto 1965; Covent Garden from 1967, debut in Manon Lescaut; guest appearances with WNO, Scottish Opera and at Glyndebourne; New York City Opera 1975 as Calaf in Turandot; BBC television as Paco in La Vida Breve; Metropolitan Opera from 1978, as Canio, Manrico, Ernani, Pinkerton, Paolo in Zandonai's Francesca da Rimini and Des Grieux; La Scala and Rome 1978; San Francisco 1982; Vienna 1983; Brussels 1984, as Manrico; Dallas Opera 1985, as Otello; other roles include Male Chorus in The Rape of Lucretia, Donizetti's Edgardo, Gounod's Faust, Verdi's Radames, Riccardo, Alfredo and Gabriele Adorno, Don José, Cavaradossi, Dick Johnson and Enzo in La Gioconda; sang Cavaradossi at the Met 1986, Turiddu 1989; Calaf at the Deutsche Oper Berlin 1987; San Francisco and Barcelona 1989, as Otello and Enzo; sang Manrico with Zürich Opera 1990, Maurizio in Adriana Lecouvreur at Montréal; season 1992 at Radames at Dallas, Puccini's Des Grieux in Miami, Calaf at Philadelphia and Turiddu at the Teatro Colón, Buenos Aires; sang Loris in Fedora at Montréal 1995.

MAURUS, Elsa; French singer (mezzo-soprano); b. 1968. *Education:* studied with Eugénia Besala-Ludwig, and in Geneva. *Career:* sang in Le Roi l'a Dit by Delibes at Nantes, then Rossini's Rosina at Rouen, 1994; Opéra d'Aran by Bécaud at the Vienna Konzerthaus, 1994; concerts include Debussy's Le Martyre, in Rome, Cesar Franck's Les Béatitudes with the Orchesra of Ile de France, Mendelssohn's Erstes Walpurgisnacht at the Théâtre de Champs Elysées and Mozart's Requiem in colmar (1998); Mahler's 2nd and 3rd Symphonies in Japan (1999–2000), the Berlioz Roméo et Juliette in Paris and Poulenc's Carmélites in Italy; season 2002 in Ravel's Sheherazade with the Utah symphony, Les Nuites d'été at Lille, as Carmen at Nantes, Nicklausse in Trieste, and Dulcinée in Massenet's Don Quichotte at Marseille. *Current Management:* c/o Musicaglotz, 11 rue le Verrier, 75006 Paris, France. *Telephone:* (1) 42-34-53-40. *Fax:* (1) 40-46-93-77. *E-mail:* general@musicaglotz.com. *Website:* www.musicaglotz.com.

MAUS, Peter; singer (tenor); b. 1948, Germany. *Career:* debut at Bayreuth Youth Festival 1972, in Wagner's Das Liebesverbot; Deutsche Oper Berlin from 1974, in such character roles as Wenzel in The Bartered Bridge, Sparlich in Lustigen Weiber, Peter Ivanov in Zar und Zimmermann, Pong, the Count in Zimmermann's Die Soldaten, Fatty in Mahagonny and Eljeya in From the House of the Dead; sang in the 1981 premiere of Kagel's Aus Deutschland; Bayreuth Festival from 1982, with minor roles in Parsifal and Die Meistersinger; Shepherd in Tristan 1993; teacher of singing, Hochschule für Kunste, Berlin from 1987; sang M. Triquet in Eugene Onegin and Mozart's Don Curzio at the Deutsche Oper Berlin 2000. *Recordings:* Das Liebesverbot, Die Meistersinger, Masses by Schubert, Donizetti Mass and Wolf's Der Corregidor, Esquire in Parsifal (conducted by Barenboim).

MAUTI, Nunziata; singer (soprano); b. 28 Aug. 1946, Palma Campania, Italy. *Education:* studied in Naples and with Gina Cigna. *Career:* debut in Palermo 1965 aas Liu in Turandot; appearances throughout Italy, including La Scala and the Verona Arena 1975–85; US debut in Dallas 1973, as Elvira in I Puritana; Chicago 1978, as Butterfly and Gilda; Metropolitan Opera 1977–80 in Traviata and Pagliacci; Wiesbaden 1986, in Zandonai's Giulietta e Romeo; Turin 1991, as Sulamith in Goldmark's Königin von Sheba; other roles include Manon and Mozart's Fiordiligi and Donna Elvira, Verdi's Desdemona and Trovatore Leonora.

MAVEL, Regina; singer (contralto); b. 1958, Cologne, Germany. *Education:* Cologne Musikhochschule. *Career:* sang in Die Zauberflöte and Tannhäuser at Dortmund 1983–84; Essen 1988 and Munster from 1989 in operas by Bizet, Cornelius and Millöcker; Wiesbaden 1992–93, in Wagner's Ring; Cologne Opera from 1995; premiere of Patmos by Schweinitz at Munich 1990; other roles include Mary in Der fliegende Holländer and Geneviève in Pelléas et Mélisande; concerts include Beethoven's Ninth at Bonn 1994.

MAX, Robert, GRSM, LRAM, ARAM; British cellist, conductor, chamber music coach and cello teacher; *Musical Director, Oxford Symphony Orchestra;* b. 7 Feb. 1968, London, England; m. Zoë Solomon 1993; two s. one d. *Education:* Royal Acad. of Music, Royal Northern Coll. of Music, Juilliard School, New York. *Career:* concerts throughout the UK, Europe, North and South America, Russia and the Far East; string finalist, BBC Young Musician of the Year 1984; Music Dir, Nonesuch Orchestra 1993–96, Zemel Choir 1994–98, Pro Corda 1998–2000, Oxford Symphony Orchestra 2005–; Conductor, Royal Holloway, Univ. of London Symphony Orchestra 2001–13; cellist with Barbican Piano Trio 1987–; Prin. Cellist, London Chamber Orchestra; MusicWorks chamber music courses; mem. Jr Dept, RAM, London 1993–; Pres. North London Festival of Music, Drama and Dance 2013–; mem. Int. Bd

of Govs, Jerusalem Acad. of Music and Dance 2013–; Artistic Dir, Frinton Festival. *Recordings include:* Barbican Piano Trio: recordings of Mendelssohn, Alan Bush, John Ireland, Lalo, Tchaikovsky, Rachmaninov, Schnittke, Taneyev; The Zemel Choir: Liturgical Music of Louis Lewandowski, The English Tradition of Jewish Choral Music; Cello music by Hubicki; MusicWorks: Saint Saens. *Honours:* Hon. Prof., Rachmaninov Inst., Russia. *E-mail:* robertmax3@gmail.com (office). *Website:* www.barbicanpianotrio.com (office); www.frintonfestival.com (office).

MAXWELL, Donald, MA, FRWCMD, FLCM; British singer (baritone); *Head of Opera Studies, Royal Welsh College of Music and Drama;* b. 12 Dec. 1948, Perth, Scotland; m. Alison Jayne Norman; one d. *Education:* Univ. of Edinburgh. *Career:* debut with Scottish Opera in Musgrave's Mary Queen of Scots 1977; Covent Garden debut in Sallinen's The King Goes Forth to France; performances at La Scala, Paris Opéra, Vienna Staatsoper, Covent Garden, Teatro Colón, Buenos Aires, Edinburgh Festival, Glyndebourne and BBC Proms; major roles include Falstaff, Iago, Wozzeck, Golaud, Baron Zeta (all for television), Flying Dutchman, Scarpia, Rigoletto, Gunther, Don Alfonso, Bottom in A Midsummer Night's Dream, Tarquinnius in Lucretia, in Fille du Regiment, in Beatrice and Benedict; world premieres by Berio, Manoury, Harle, Holt, Eötvos; sang Swallow in Peter Grimes in Amsterdam and at Salzburg Festival; sings regularly at Covent Garden; Dir Nat. Opera Studio 2001–08; currently Head of Opera Studies, Royal Welsh Coll. of Music and Drama. *Address:* Department of Vocal and Opera Studies, Royal Welsh College of Music and Drama, Castle Grounds, Cathays Park, Cardiff CF10 3ER, Wales (office). *Website:* www.rwcmd.ac.uk (office).

MAXWELL DAVIES, Sir Peter, Kt, CH, CBE, MusB, FRCM, FRSAMD, FRNCM; British composer and conductor; b. 8 Sept. 1934, Manchester, England; s. of Thomas Davies and Hilda Davies (née Howard). *Education:* Leigh Grammar School, Royal Manchester Coll. of Music, Univ. of Manchester; studied with Goffredo Petrassi, Rome 1957 and with Roger Sessions, Milton Babbitt, Earl Kim, Princeton Univ., NJ, USA (Harkness Fellow) 1962–64. *Career:* Dir of Music, Cirencester Grammar School 1959–62; Harkness Fellowship, Grad. School, Princeton Univ. 1962–64; lecture tours in Europe, Australia, USA, Canada, Brazil; Visiting Composer, Univ. of Adelaide 1966; Prof. of Composition, Royal Northern Coll. of Music, Manchester 1965–80 (Fellow 1978); Pres. Schools Music Asscn 1983–, Composers' Guild of GB 1986–, Nat. Fed. of Music Socs 1989–, Cheltenham Arts Festival 1994–96, Soc. for Promotion of New Music 1995–; Visiting Fromm Prof. of Composition, Harvard Univ. 1985; Founder and Co-Dir (with Harrison Birtwistle) Pierrot Players 1967–71; f. and Artistic Dir The Fires of London 1971–87; f. and Artistic Dir St Magnus Festival, Orkney Islands 1977–86, Pres. 1986–; Artistic Dir Dartington Summer School of Music 1979–84; Assoc. Conductor and Composer Scottish Chamber Orchestra 1985–94, Composer Laureate 1994–; Conductor and Composer, BBC Philharmonic Orchestra (Manchester) 1992–2001; Assoc. Conductor and Composer Royal Philharmonic Orchestra 1992–2001; Master of the Queen's Music 2004–14; Fellowship British Acad. of Composers and Songwriters 2005; mem. Accad. Filarmonica Romana 1979, Royal Swedish Acad. of Music 1993, Bayerische Akad. der Schönen Künste 1998, British Acad. of Songwriters, Composers and Authors. *Compositions include:* Sonata for trumpet and piano 1955, Alma redemptoris mater for ensemble 1957, St Michael sonata for 17 wind instruments 1957, Prolation for orchestra 1958, Five Klee Pictures for percussion, piano and strings 1959, Five Motets for soli, chorus and ensemble 1959, O Magnum Mysterium for chorus, instruments and organ 1960, Te Lucis ante Terminum 1961, String Quartet 1961, Frammenti di Leopardi for soprano, contralto and chamber ensemble 1962, First Fantasia on John Taverner's In Nomine for orchestra 1962, Veni Sancte Spiritus for soli, chorus and orchestra 1963, Second Fantasia on John Taverner's In Nomine 1964, Ecce Manus Tradentis for mixed chorus and instruments 1964, Shepherd's Calendar for young singers and instrumentalists 1965, Notre Dame des Fleurs 1966, Revelation and Fall for soprano and instrumental ensemble 1966, Antechrist for chamber ensemble 1967, Missa super L'Homme Armé for speaker and ensemble 1968, Stedman Caters for instruments 1968, Nocturnal Dances (ballet) 1969, St Thomas Wake-Foxtrot for orchestra 1969, Worldes Blis 1969, Eram quasi Agnus (instrumental motet) 1969, Eight Songs for a Mad King for male singer and ensemble 1969, Vesalii Icones for dancer and ensemble 1969, Taverner (opera) 1970, From Stone to Thorn for mezzo-soprano and instrumental ensemble 1971, Blind Man's Buff (masque) 1972, Hymn to Saint Magnus for chamber ensemble and mezzo-soprano 1972, Renaissance Scottish Dances 1973, Stone Litany for mezzo-soprano and orchestra 1973, Fiddlers at the Wedding 1974, Miss Donnithorne's Maggot for mezzo-soprano and chamber ensemble 1974, The Kestrel Paced Round the Sun 1975, Ave Maris Stella for chamber ensemble 1975, Three Studies for Percussion 1975, The Blind Fiddler for soprano and chamber ensemble 1975, Stevie's Ferry to Hoy (beginner's piano solo) 1975, Three Organ Voluntaries 1976, Kinloche His Fantassie (with Kinloch) 1976, Anakreontika (Greek songs for mezzo-soprano) 1976, Orchestral Symphony No. 1 1976, The Martyrdom of St Magnus (chamber opera) 1976, Runes from a Holy Island 1977, Westerlings (unaccompanied part songs) 1977, A Mirror of Whitening Light for chamber ensemble 1977, Le Jongleur de Notre Dame (Masque) 1978, The Two Fiddlers 1978, Salome (ballet) 1978, Black Pentecost (for voices and orchestra) 1979, Solstice of Light (for Tenor, Chorus and Organ) 1979, The Lighthouse (chamber opera) 1979, Cinderella (pantomime opera for young performers) 1979, A Welcome to Orkney (chamber ensemble) 1980, Orchestral Symphony No. 2 1980, Little Quartet (string quartet) 1980, The Yellow Cake Revue (for voice and piano) 1980, The Medium 1981, The

Bairns of Brugh 1981, Piano Sonata 1981, Little Quartet No. 2 (for string quartet) 1981, Lullabye for Lucy 1981, Brass Quintet 1981, Songs of Hoy (Masque for children's voices and instruments) 1981, The Pole Star 1982, Sea Eagle (for horn solo) 1982, Image, Reflection, Shadow (for chamber ensemble) 1982, Sinfonia Concertante (for chamber orchestra) 1982, Into the Labyrinth (tenor and chamber orchestra) 1983, Sinfonietta Accademica (chamber orchestra) 1983, Unbroken Circle 1984, Guitar Sonata 1984, The No. 11 Bus 1984, One Star, At Last (carol) 1984, Orchestral Symphony No. 3 1984, The Peat Cutters 1985, Violin Concerto 1985, First Ferry to Hoy 1985, An Orkney Wedding, with Sunrise 1985, Sea Runes (vocal sextet) 1986, Jimmack the Postie (overture) 1986, Excuse Me 1986, House of Winter 1986, Trumpet Concerto 1987, Resurrection (opera in one act with prologue) 1987, Oboe Concerto 1988, Cello Concerto 1988, Mishkenot (chamber ensemble) 1988, The Great Bank Robbery 1989, Orchestral Symphony No. 4 1989, Hymn to the Word of God (for tenor and chorus) 1990, Concerto No. 4 for clarinet 1990, Caroline Mathilde (ballet) 1990, Tractus 1990, Dangerous Errand (for tenor soli and chorus) 1990, The Spiders' Revenge 1991, First Grace of Light 1991, Strathclyde Concerto No. 5 for violin and viola, No. 6 for flute 1991, Ojai Festival Overture 1991, A Selkie Tale (music-theatre work for performance by children) 1992, The Turn of the Tide (for orchestra and children's chorus and instrumental groups) 1992, Strathclyde Concerto No. 7 for double bass 1992, Sir Charles his Pavan 1992, Strathclyde Concerto No. 8 for bassoon 1993, A Spell for Green Corn: The MacDonald Dances 1993, Orchestral Symphony No. 5 (Royal Philharmonic Soc. Award for Large-Scale Composition 1995) 1994, Cross Lane Fair (for orchestra) 1994, Strathclyde Concerto No. 9 for six woodwind instruments 1994, The Three Kings (for chorus, orchestra and soloists) 1995, The Beltane Fire (choreographic poem) 1995, The Doctor of Myddfai (opera) 1995, Orchestral Symphony No. 6 1996, Strathclyde Concerto No. 10 for orchestra 1996, Piccolo Concerto 1996, Job (oratorio for chorus, orchestra and soloists) 1997, Mavis in Las Vegas–Theme and Variations 1997, Orkney Saga I: Fifteen keels laid in Norway for Jerusalem-farers 1997, The Jacobite Rising (for chorus, orchestra and soloists) 1997, Piano Concerto 1997, Orkney Saga II: In Kirkwall, the first red Saint Magnus stones 1997, Sails in St Magnus I–III 1998, A Reel of Seven Fishermen 1998, Sea Elegy (for chorus, orchestra and soloists) 1998, Roma Amor Labyrinthus 1998, Reel with Northern Lights 1998, Swinton Jig 1998, Temenos with Mermaids and Angels (for flute and orchestra) 1998, Spinning Jenny 1999, Sails in Orkney Saga III: An Orkney Wintering (for alto saxophone and orchestra) 1999, Trumpet quintet (for string quartet and trumpet) 1999, Mr Emmet Takes a Walk 1999, Horn Concerto 1999, Orkney Saga IV: Westerly Gale in Biscay, Salt in the Bread Broken 2000, Orchestral Symphony No. 7 2000, Orchestral Symphony No. 8 (Antarctic Symphony) 2000, Canticum Canticorum 2001, De Assumtione Beatae Mariae Virginis 2001, Crossing Kings Reach 2001, Mass 2002, Missa Parvula 2002, Naxos Quartet No. 1 2002, Piano Trio 2002, Naxos Quartet No. 2 2003, No. 3 2003, No. 4 2004, No. 5 2004, Children's Games 2004, Judas Mercator for trombone solo 2004, Fanfare for Carinthia for four trumpets 2004, Tecum Principium for flute and marimba 2004, The Fall of the Leafe for string orchestra 2004, Lullay, my child and weep no more for SATB chorus 2004, Naxos Quartets No. 6 and No. 7 2005, O Verbum Patris for SATB chorus & organ 2005, The Golden Rule (anthem with lyrics by Andrew Motion, for the 80th birthday of HM Queen Elizabeth II) 2006, A Little Birthday Music (for the 80th birthday of HM Queen Elizabeth II) 2006, Liber Pulsationis Fabulatoris for chorus (dedicated to Sir Paul McCartney) 2008, A Birthday Card for Prince Charles (for the 60th birthday of HRH the Prince of Wales) 2008, The Sorcerer's Mirror (for 800th anniversary of Univ. of Cambridge) 2009, Violin Concerto No. 2 2009, The Last Island for string sextet 2009, Sea Orpheus 2010, Blake Dreaming for baritone and string quartet 2010, Homerton (for the choir of Homerton Coll., Cambridge) 2010, Kommilitonen! (opera) 2011, Symphony No. 9 2012, Symphony No. 10 2014; has written music for films: The Devils, The Boyfriend and many piano pieces, works for choir, instrumental works and realisations of 15th and 16th-century composers. *Recordings:* Naxos Quartets – Maggini Quartet (five-CD set); Missa parvula, two organ pieces, two motets; Magnificat and Nunc Dimittis and O Sacrum Convivium; Symphonies 1–6 (BBC Philharmonic, Scottish Chamber Orchestra, Philharmonia, Royal Philharmonic/composer); Ave Maris Stella, Image, Reflection, Shadow, Runes from a Holy Island – Fires of London/composer. *Honours:* Hon. RAM 1979; Hon. mem. Guildhall School of Music and Drama 1981, Royal Philharmonic Soc. 1987, Royal Scottish Acad. 2001; Hon. Fellow, Royal Incorporation of Architects in Scotland 1994, Univ. of Highlands and Islands 2004; Freeman of the City of Salford; Officier des Arts et des Lettres 1988; several hon. degrees, including Hon. DMus (Edin.) 1979, (Manchester) 1981, (Bristol) 1984, (Open Univ.) 1986, (Glasgow) 1993, (Durham) 1994, (Hull) 2001, (Kingston) 2005; Hon. DLitt (Warwick) 1986, (Salford) 1999; Hon. DUniv (Heriot-Watt) 2002; Olivetti Prize 1959, Koussevitsky Award 1964, Koussevitsky Recording Award 1966, Cobbett Medal for services to chamber music 1989, First Award of Assn of British Orchestras, for contribs to orchestras and orchestral life in UK 1991, Gulliver Award for Performing Arts in Scotland 1991, Nat. Fed. of Music Socs Charles Groves Award for outstanding contrib. to British Music 1995, Royal Philharmonic Soc. Award for Large-scale Composition (for Symphony No. 5) 1995, Inc. Soc. of Musicians Distinguished Musicians Award 2001, Ivor Novello Classical Music Award 2010. *Current Management:* c/o Intermusica, Crystal Wharf, 36 Graham Street, London, N1 8GJ, England. *Telephone:* (20) 7608-9900. *Fax:* (20) 7490-3263. *E-mail:* mail@intermusica.co.uk. *Website:* www.intermusica.co.uk; www.maxopus.com.

MAY, Marius; cellist; b. 1950, England. *Education:* studied with Andre Navarra in Paris and with Pierre Fournier in Geneva. *Career:* debut at Wigmore Hall 1973, followed by recital and concerto appearances throughout the UK; Festival Hall 1976, with the Schumann Concerto and the Philharmonia Orchestra; played in public from age ten, giving a recital at the Royal Coll. of Music, London, and playing the Saint-Saëns A minor Concerto in Edinburgh; Edinburgh and Bath Festivals 1976; soloist with leading orchestras in Europe; several tours of Germany have included Berlin Philharmonic concert 1980; concerts with Yehudi Menuhin at the Gstaad Festival, Switzerland; played the Elgar Concerto with the London Philharmonic and the Finzi Concerto at the Three Choirs Festival with the Royal Philharmonic; teacher, Univ. of California in Los Angeles; BBC television concerts include the Tchaikovsky Rococo Variations and a Gala from the Edinburgh Festival.

MAYER, Albrecht; German oboist. *Education:* studied with Gerhard Scheuer, Georg Meerwein, Maurice Bourgue, Ingo Goritzki. *Career:* mem. Bamberg Cathedral Choir as a child; Principal Oboist, Bamberg Symphony Orchestra 1990–92, Berlin Philharmonic 1992–; mem. Sabine Meyer Wind Ensemble; numerous int. performances as soloist; has performed with conductors, including Claudio Abbado, Sir Simon Rattle, Nikolaus Harnoncourt; performs frequently with Berlin Baroque Soloists, Thomas Quasthoff, Matthias Goerne, Leif Ove Andsnes, Hélène Grimaud. *Recordings:* with Sabine Meyer Wind Ensemble: Dvorák Serenade/Myslivecek, Octetts 1995, Mozart, Serenades 1997, Beethoven, Octets 1999, Sabine Meyer plays Mozart (two vols); other: Bach Cantatas (with Matthias Goerne, baritone) 1996, G. Müller, Oboen-Quintett (with Bamberger Streichquartett) 1997, Bach, Brandenburg Concert No. 2 (with Michala Petri), Passion Flight (with Kaori Fujii), Kennedy Plays Bach (with Nigel Kennedy) 2000, Telemann, Concerto for Oboe d'Amore 2001, Bach, Reconstructed Concertos 2002, Fauré, Clair de Lune 2002, Romantic Oboe-Concertos in the 20th Century, Schumann/Daelli/Nielsen/Cossart/Yvon/Koechlin 2003, Bach, Lieder ohne Worte 2003, In Search of Mozart (with Claudio Abbado and Mahler Chamber Orchestra) 2004, Albrecht Mayer: New Seasons 2006, In Venice 2008, Voices of Bach: works for oboe, choir and orchestra 2010. *Honours:* Instrumentalist of the Year, ECHO-Klassik Prize, E.T.A. Hoffmann Prize, Bamberg 2006. *E-mail:* mail@albrechtmayer.com (office). *Website:* www.albrechtmayer.com.

MAYER, Richard, PhD; Czech composer; b. 9 June 1948, Brno. *Education:* Univ. of Brno, Conservatory of Brno. *Career:* debut in Brno 1969, Zlin 1980; recordings of compositions on Czech television and radio; premiere of Iceland Piano Fantasy, USA 1990; mem. Nordic Soc. of Prague, Bohemian Music Assn, Club of Moravian Composers. *Compositions include:* Sonata for violin and piano, Concerto for two pianos and tromba, Quartet for clarinet, violin, viola and cello, Variation for clarinet and piano, Reykjavík Sonata for viola and cello, Variation for tromba and piano, Iceland Fantasy for piano solo, Saga of Northern Night, Cycle of Compositions for alto and bassoon, Drama Musicum Sine Verbis–Chronikon Mundi: First Symphony for chamber orchestra, Magna Missa Millennia Islandica: Great Magnificent Mass for large orchestra, organ, narrator, solos and choir, Symphony No. 2: Icelandic for large orchestra. *Address:* Cihlarska 14, 602 00 Brno, Czech Republic.

MAYER, William Robert, BA; composer; b. 18 Nov. 1925, New York, USA. *Education:* Yale Univ., Juilliard School with Roger Sessions, Mannes Coll. of Music. *Career:* Sec., Nat. Music Council 1980. *Compositions:* stage: The Greatest Sound Around (children's opera) 1954, Hell World (children's opera) 1956, One Christmas Long Ago (one-act opera) 1964, Brief Candle (micro-opera) 1964, A Death in the Family (opera) 1983, The Snow Queen (ballet) 1963; orchestral: Andante for strings 1955, Hebraic Portrait 1957, Overture for an American 1958, Two Pastels 1960, Octagon for piano and orchestra 1971, Inner and Outer Strings for string quartet and string orchestra 1982, Of Rivers and Trains 1988, String Quartet and other chamber music, Piano Sonata, choruses and songs. *Honours:* Guggenheim Fellowship 1966, Nat. Inst. for Musical Theater Award 1983.

MAYFORTH, Robin; violinist; b. 1965, USA. *Education:* Juilliard School, New York. *Career:* appearances with I Solisti Veneti, under Claudio Scimone; co-founder, Lark Quartet, USA; concert tours to Australia, Taiwan, Hong Kong, People's Republic of China, Germany, The Netherlands; US appearances at the Lincoln Center, New York, Kennedy Center, Washington, DC and in Boston, Los Angeles, Phildelphia, St Louis and San Francisco; repertoire includes quartets by Haydn, Mozart, Beethoven, Schubert, Dvořák, Brahms, Borodin, Bartók, Debussy and Shostakovich. *Honours:* with Lark Quartet: gold medals at the Naumberg Competition 1990 and Shostakovich Competition 1991, prizewinner London Int. String Quartet Competition 1991, Melbourne Chamber Music Competition 1991, Premio Paulio Borciani (Reggio Emilia) 1990, Karl Klinger (Munich) Competition 1990.

MAYNOR, Kevin Elliott, DipMus, BME, MM, MV, DM; American singer (bass); b. 24 July 1954, Mt Vernon, NY. *Education:* Manhattan School of Music, Bradley University, Northwestern University, Moscow Conservatory, Indiana University. *Career:* debut at Carnegie Hall, 1983 in a concert of Strauss's Die Liebe der Danaë; Avery Fisher Hall as Nocco in Fidelio, 1985; New York City Opera, Akhnaten, 1985; Chicago Lyric Opera; Santa Fe Opera; Virginia Opera; Nashville Opera; Long Beach Opera; Chicago Opera Theater; Mobile Opera Theater; Mobile Opera; apprenticeship, 1st from the West, Bolshoi Opera, 1979–80; Scottish Opera 1987 and Opera Pacific 1994 as Hunding in Die Walküre. *Current Management:* c/o Herbert Barrett Management, 266

West 37th Street, 20th Floor, New York, NY 10018, USA. *Telephone:* (212) 245-3530. *Fax:* (212) 397-5860. *Website:* www.herbertbarrett.com; www .kevinmaynor.com.

MAZURA, Franz; Austrian singer (bass-baritone); b. 22 April 1924, Salzburg. *Education:* studied with Fred Husler in Detmold. *Career:* debut in Kassel 1955; sang at Mainz and Brunswick until 1964; Mannheim 1964–89; Salzburg 1960, in La Finta Semplice; Pizarro in Fidelio, 1970; mem., Deutsche Oper Berlin 1963; Paris Opéra from 1973, as Wagner's Wotan, Alberich and Gurnemanz; sang Dr Schön in the 1979 premiere of the three-act version of Berg's Lulu; Bayreuth Festival from 1971, as Biterolf, Alberich, Gunther, Gurnemanz, Klingsor and the Wanderer in the 1988 Ring Cycle directed by Harry Kupfer; Hamburg Opera from 1973; Israel Festival, Caeserea, as Moses in Schoenberg's Moses und Aron; Guest appearances in Vienna, Buenos Aires, San Francisco, Nice and Strasbourg; Metropolitan Opera debut 1980, as Dr Schön, returned to New York as Klingsor, Alberich, Gurnemanz, Creon in Oedipus Rex, Pizarro, Doctor in Wozzeck, Frank in Die Fledermaus, Rangoni in Boris Godunov and the Messenger in Die Frau ohne Schatten, 1989; Bayreuth Festival, 1988–89 as Klingsor and the Wanderer; Season 1991–92 as Voland (the Devil), in Höller's Meister und Margarita at Cologne and Klingsor at the Met and the Bayreuth Festival; Narrated Henze's Raft of the Medusa, Festival Hall, London, 1997; Schigolch in Lulu at San Francisco, 1998; sang Schigolch at Bielefeld and the New York Met, 2001. *Recordings include:* Dr Schön, Jack the Ripper in Lulu (Grammy Award 1980), Gunther in Götterdämmerung, Schoenberg's Moses.

MAZURKEVICH, Yuri Nicholas, DipArt; academic and violinist; b. 6 May 1941, Lvov, USSR; m. Dana Mazurkevich 1963, one d. *Education:* School of Gifted Children, Lvov, Moscow State Conservatoire with D. Oistrakh. *Career:* concert violinist, with appearances worldwide; recorded for Radio Moscow, France, BBC, ABC (Australia), CBC (Canada), Sender Freies (West Berlin), WGBH (Boston) and many others; Asst Prof. of Violin, Kiev State Conservatory 1967–73; Assoc. Prof. of Violin, Univ. of Western Ontario 1975–85; Prof. of Violin and Chair of String Dept, Boston Univ. 1985–; mem., Quartet Canada 1980–; mem. Music Council of Canada. *Recordings:* works by Beethoven, Paganini, Tartini, Handel, Spohr, Leclair, Prokofiev, Sarasate, Honegger, Telemann and others. *Honours:* prizewinner Helsinki Int. Violin Competition 1962, Munich Int. Violin Competition 1966, Montréal Int. Violin Competition 1969.

MAZZAMUTO, Alessandro; Italian pianist; b. 1988, Catania. *Education:* Istituto Musicale di Catania, Accad. Pianistica Siciliana with Epifanio Comis. *Career:* first recital aged nine; performed Mozart's Concerto K414 aged 10, Schumann's Concerto in A minor aged 11, Brahms' Concerto in D minor aged 13; played Rachmaninov Concerto No. 2 and No. 3 in USA 2002, 2004; has performed in halls including Salle Cortot, Paris and La Fenice Venice and worked in several European countries with orchestras including Rias Jugendorchester Berlin, Kiev Chamber Orchestra and Bacau Philharmonic Orchestra; invited by Martha Argerich to perform at her annual Lugano project 2013. *Recordings include:* Rachmaninoff: Sonata No. 2 2012. *Honours:* Gianandrea Lodovici Special Prize, Busoni Competition 2011, Int. Classical Music Awards Young Artist of the Year 2013. *E-mail:* alessandro_mazzamuto@hotmail.it (office). *Website:* www .alessandromazzamuto.com (office).

MAZZARIA, Lucia; singer (soprano); b. 1964, Gorizia, Poland. *Education:* studied in Trieste and Rome. *Career:* debut in Venice 1987, as Mimi; Hamburg Opera 1987, as Mimi, Liu and Micaela; La Scala Milan debut 1988, as Lauretta in Gianni Schicchi, returning as Liu, Euridice and Violetta; Cologne Opera 1991, as Amelia Boccanegra; Further appearances at Monte Carlo, Covent Garden (London), Houston and Vienna; Venice 1990, as Mimi in Leoncavallo's Bohème; Further tours of Russia, Japan and Korea; sang Desdemona at the 1996 Holland Festival and Micaela in Carmen at Macerata, 1998; season 2000–01 as Amelia Grimaldi at Macereta, Suor Angelica in Verona and Desdemona in Venice. *Recordings include:* Leoncavallo's Bohème. *Current Management:* Walter Beloch Artists Management, via Melzi d'Eril 26, 20154 Milan, Italy. *Telephone:* (2) 33101922. *Fax:* (2) 3313643. *E-mail:* lirica@ walterbeloch.com. *Website:* www.walterbeloch.com.

MAZZOLA, Denia; singer (soprano); b. 1956, Bergamo, Italy. *Education:* studied with Corinna Malatrasi. *Career:* sang Amina in La Sonnambula at Brescia, then Lucia di Lammermoor, and Adina at Florence and Milan; Landestheatre Salzburg 1984, as Gilda, St Gallen 1985 as Violetta; Sang at the Zürich Opera 1985–87, notably as Elvira in I Puritani; Appearances as Lucia at Naples, 1988–89, New York City Opera; La Scala Milan, 1987, Sole in Fetonte by Jommelli; Further engagements at Houston, Alice Ford, San Francisco, in Maria Stuarda, Bergamo, Amelia in Elisabetta al Castello di Kenilworth by Donizetti, 1989, Reggio Emilia, Violetta, Barcelona, Elvira, 1990 and the 1990 Montpellier Festival, Palmide in a concert performance of Meyerbeer's Il Crociato in Egitto; Sang Mimi at the 1996 Torre del Lago Festival; Season 2000–01 as Manon Lescaut at Catania, Cherubini's Médée for the Macerata Festival and Hélène in Les Vêpres Siciliennes at Schwerin (concert). *Recordings include:* Lucia di Lammermoor, with forces of the San Carlo, Naples (Nuova Era).

MAZZOLA, Enrique; Italian (b. Spanish) conductor; *Music Director, Orchestra National d'Ile de France. Education:* Giuseppe Verdi Conservatory, Milan, Italy. *Career:* bel canto specialist, performances at opera houses worldwide; opera engagements have included Glyndebourne Festival (L'elisir

d'amore, Don Pasquale, Poliuto), Teatro del Maggio Musicale Fiorentino (L'italiana in Algeri), New Nat. Theatre Tokyo (Don Giovanni), Opéra du Rhin (Macbeth, La cenerentola), Théâtre des Champs-Elysées (Don Pasquale, Tancredi), Deutsche Oper Berlin (Barbiere di Siviglia, Falstaff, Le Vaisseau fantôme and Dinorah), Bolshoi Thetre (La sonnambula) and Teatro alla Scala (Don Pasquale); has conducted at major European festivals, including Aix-en-Provence, München Opernfestspiele, Festival de Radio France, Rossini Opera Festival, Venice Biennale, George Enescu Festival, Dvořák Prague Festival, Les Chorégies d'Orange; Artistic and Music Dir, Cantiere Internazionale d'Arte, Montepulciano 1999–2003; debut at Metropolitan Opera (L'elisir d'amore) 2015; Music Dir Orchestre Nat. d'Ile de France 2012–, performs regularly at Salle Pleyel, Paris and at new Philharmonie in Paris (Orchestre Associée 2015–). *E-mail:* rona.eastwood@askonasholt.co.uk. *Website:* www .askonasholt.co.uk/artists/conductors/enrique-mazzola. *Address:* Orchestre National de l'Ile de France, 19 rue des Écoles, 94140 Alfortville, France (office). *Telephone:* 1-41-79-03-40 (office). *Fax:* 1-41-79-03-50 (office). *E-mail:* courrier@orchestre-ile.com (office). *Website:* www.orchestre-ile.com (office); www.enriquemazzola.com.

MAZZUCATO, Daniela; Italian singer (soprano); b. 1 Dec. 1946, Venice. *Education:* Venice Conservatory. *Career:* made debut as Gilda in Rigoletto, Teatro Fenice, Venice 1966; repertoire includes Gasparina in Il Campaiello, Felice in I Quatro Rusteghi, Ocasr in Un Ballo in Maschera, Euridice in Orphée aux Enfers, Adina in L'Elisir d'Amore, Gretel in Hänsel und Gretel, Lisa in Il Paese del Sorriso, Euridice in Orfeo ed Euridice, Susanna in Le Nozze di Figaro, Musetta in La Bohème, Elisabetta in L'Incoronazione di Poppea, Miss Jessel in The Turn of the Screw, in La Vedova Scaltra, Cosi fan Tutte, Die Entführung aus dem Serail, Il Matromonio Segreto, Sogno di un Valzer, La Cecchina, Barbablù, Dido and Aeneas, L'intrigo della lettera, Trittico, Cin-Ci-La, La scugnizza, Al cavallino bianco, Offenbach's Croquefer, I due ciechi and Il Signor Choufleury; has performed at Teatro alla Scala, Teatro dell'Opera di Roma, Teatro di San Carlo, Naples, Arena di Verona, Teatro Comunale, Bologna, Teatro Massimo di Palermo, Festival dei Due Mondi di Spoleto, Covent Garden, London, Opéra National, Paris, New Israeli Opera, Tel Aviv, Glyndebourne Opera Festival, Hamburgische Staatsoper, Frankfurt, Bordeaux, Ottawa and Marseilles. *Recordings:* Vivaldi's Serenata a tre; Medea by Cherubini. *Current Management:* Stage Door, Via San Giorgio 4, 40121 Bologna, Italy. *Telephone:* (051) 262126. *Fax:* (051) 271452. *E-mail:* info@stagedoor.it. *Website:* www.stagedoor.it.

MEAD, Philip John, ARCM, FTCL, LRAM, GRSM; British pianist; *Professor, London College of Music and Media;* b. 8 Sept. 1947, Chadwell St Mary, Essex, England; m. Gillian Mead 1969; three d. *Education:* Royal Acad. of Music, London Coll. of Music and Media. *Career:* debut, Purcell Room 1973; performances at major festivals, England and overseas; specialist in 20th-century piano music; commissioned works include works for piano and electronics by Dennis Smalley, Jonathan Harvey, Tim Souster and others; featured soloist at London South Bank Electric Weekend 1987; soloist, BBC Symphony Orchestra Ives Festival 1996; founder and Artistic Dir, British Contemporary Piano Competition, Cambridge 1988; Prof. and Head of Dept of Contemporary Piano, London Coll. of Music and Media 1998–; repertoire includes Messiaen, Tippett, Stockhausen and George Crumb; commissioned works for brass and piano, Sackman, Poole, Burrell, Ellerby, Wilkins and Emmerson 1999–2003; mem. Sonic Arts, Soc. for the Promotion of New Music (dir), EPTA. *Recordings:* Southern Lament; eight albums of electronic music, complete solo piano works of Charles Ives, George Crumb; works for piano and brass. *Publications:* contrib. to Electro Acoustic Music, Classical Piano, International Piano, Contemporary Music Review. *Honours:* Hon. ARAM 1993, Hon. FLCM 1997; research awards, prizewinner Gaudeamus Int. Competition for Interpreters of Contemporary Music 1978. *Address:* 31 Lingholme Close, Cambridge, CB4 3HW, England (home). *Telephone:* (1223) 357431 (home). *E-mail:* meadpj@hotmail.com (home). *Website:* www .philipmead.com.

MEADE, Angela; American singer (soprano); b. Washington, DC. *Career:* operatic debut singing Verdi's Elvira in Ernani for Metropolitan Opera 2008 (repeated 2012); performed role of Elisabetta in Roberto Devereux, Dallas Opera, title roles of Anna Bolena and Lucia di Lammermoor, Acad. of Vocal Arts, title role of Rossini's challenging Semiramide, Caramoor Festival; operatic credits include Agathe in Der Freischütz, title role in Handel's Agrippina, Fiordiligi in Così fan tutte, Mme Herz in Der Schauspieldirektor, The Queen of the Night and First Lady in Die Zauberflöte, Rosalinde in Die Fledermaus; European operatic debut at Wexford Festival in title role of Mercadante's Virginia 2010; debut with Deutsche Oper as Lucrezia Contarini in I due Foscari 2012; concert debut with Pittsburgh Symphony in Verdi's Requiem conducted by Manfred Honeck; performed the Mendelssohn Lobgesang at San Antonio Symphony under Sebastian Lang-Lessing; other highlights include Dvořák Stabat Mater with New York Choral Soc. at Carnegie Hall, Brahms Requiem with Choralis Foundation at Strathmore Hall and recitals with Sarasota Artists Series. *Honours:* Winner, Met Nat. Council Auditions 2007, Concours Musical Int. de Montréal 2008, Richard Tucker Award 2011, Beverly Sills Artist Award 2012, Winner, Belvedere Competition, Vienna, Int. Press Prize, La Scala Prize, Winner, Jose Iturbi Competition, Gerda Lissner Competition, Licia Albanese-Puccini Foundation Competition, George London Competition, Liederkranz Foundation Competition, Nat. Opera Asscn Competition, Opera Index Competition, Marguerite McCammon Competition, Giargiari Bel Canto Competition, Eleanor Lieber

Award. *Current Management:* c/o IMG Artists, Carnegie Hall Tower, 152 West 57th Street, 5th Floor, New York, NY 10019, USA. *Telephone:* (212) 994-3500. *E-mail:* mhorner@imgartists.com. *Website:* www.imgartists.com; www .angelameade.com.

MEDCALF, Stephen, BA (Hons), FGSM; British stage director; b. 1958; m. Susan Gritton; two c. *Education:* Univ. of Nottingham, London Drama Studio (Diploma). *Career:* Assoc. Dir Glyndebourne 1988, working with Peter Sellars, Peter Hall and Trevor Nunn; has directed in many major int. opera houses in France, Portugal, Italy (including La Scala), Austria and Australia as well as for Glyndebourne Festival, Opera North, Opera Northern Ireland, Wexford Festival, English Touring Opera (Dir of Productions 1992–97), Garsington, Mid-Wales Opera and numerous festivals; Resident Producer of opera course, Guildhall School of Music and Drama 1991–2003; has directed more than 100 opera productions; recent credits include Death in Venice, Salzburg; The Saint of Bleeker Street, Marseille; Le Disgrazie d'Amore, Pisa; Luisa Miller, Buxton Festival; Capriccio, Eugene Onegin, Grange Park Opera; Carmen, Sao Carlos Lisbon; Falstaff, Teatro Farnese, Parma; Aïda, Royal Albert Hall; Our Town, Guildhall School of Music and Drama; Village Romeo and Juliet, Cristina, Regina di Svezia, Wexford Festival; La Finta Giadiniera, Passau; Die Zauberflöte, Manon Lescaut, Valencia; Burning Fiery Furnace, Salzburg; Orfeo, Buxton Festival; La Bohème, Grange Park Opera. *Recordings:* videos: Zauberflöte, Così fan tutte, with John Eliot Gardiner; Le nozze di Figaro, Glyndebourne Festival Opera and Channel 4; Aida, Sky Arts. *Honours:* Assoc. Naz. Critici Musicali Premio Abbiati Prize for Director 2006, Manchester Evening News Opera Award 2007, 2009. *Current Management:* c/o Athole Still Opera Ltd, Foresters Hall, 25–27 Westow Street, London, SE19 3RY, England. *Telephone:* (20) 8771-5271. *Fax:* (20) 8771-8172. *E-mail:* enquiries@atholestill.co.uk. *Website:* www.atholestill.co.uk.

MEDEK, Ivo, DipEng, MMus, PhD; Czech composer; b. 20 July 1956, Brno; m. Zuzana Medková 1986, two s. *Education:* Technical Univ., Janáček Acad. of Music and Dramatic Art, Brno. *Career:* television broadcasts and festivals in the Czech Republic, Europe and USA; Docent of Darmstadt courses, lectures in Brno, Austria, Poland, The Netherlands, Portugal; Prof., Janáček Acad. of Music, Brno; mem. Camerata Brno 'Q' Soc., Czech Music Council. *Compositions include:* Adledaivan 1988, Pangea 1989, Triads 1989, Cepheidy 1991, Flow 1992, Postludio 1994, Persofonie 1995, 11 Gestalten des Mondscheins 1997, Enlargement for flute, clarinet, piano, violin and cello 1999, Crossings for multimedia 1999, Ancient Stories 1999, Triax 2001, Adai, Fests, Wandering in Well-known Landscape. *Publications:* Basic General Composing Principles 1989, Processuality as a Complex Composing Method 1996; contrib. some 100 articles to journals, including Opus Musicum, Czech Music, The Silence. *Honours:* Czech Music Fund Prize 1993.

MEDEK, Tilo; German composer; b. (Tilo Müller-Medek), 22 Jan. 1940, Jena, Thuringia; s. of Willy Müller-Medek and Rosa Gewehr; m. 2nd Dorothea Medek; three d. one s. *Education:* Humboldt Univ., Berlin with W. Vetter, E. H. Meyer and G. Knepler, German Acad. of Music, East Berlin with R. Wagner-Régeny. *Career:* moved to West Germany 1977; established music publishing house Edition Tilo Medek 1982; founder mem. Freie Akademie der Künste (Ind. Acad. of Arts), Mannheim. *Compositions include:* opera: Einzug 1969, Icke und die Hexe Yu 1970–71, Appetit auf Frükirschen 1971, Katharina Blum 1984–86, Gritzko und der Pan 1987, Ballet David and Goliath 1972, Der Überfall 2003; orchestral: Triade 1964, Das zögernde Lied 1970, Flute Concerto 1973, Piccolo Concerto 1975, König Johann oder Der Ausstieg for orchestra and organ 1976, Marimba Concerto 1977, Cello Concertos 1978, 1982, 1984, 1992, Organ Concerto 1979–80, Violin Concerto 1980–83, I Sinfonie (Eisenblatter for organ and orchestra) 1983, II Sinfonie (Rheinische) 1986–88, III Sinfonie (Sorbische) 1994–96; chamber: Flute Sonata 1963, six Wind Quintets 1965–99, String Trio 1965, Divertissement for wind quintet and harpsichord 1967, Stadtpfeifer, Schwanengesang for clarinet, trombone, cello and piano 1973, two Nonett 1974, 1996, Tagtraum for seven instruments 1976, Giebichenstein for eight instruments 1976, Reliquienschrein for organ and percussion 1980; vocal: Altägyptische Liebeslieder for two voices and orchestra 1963, Sintflutbestanden for tenor, horn and piano 1967, Gethsemane (cantata) 1980, Der Frieden wird immer gefährlicher for tenor, chorus and orchestra 1996–98; also music for guitar, piano, organ and for other solo instruments. *Publications:* Das Volksliederbuch 1993. *Honours:* Int. Composers' Competition, Gaudeamus Foundation, Netherlands 1967, State Univ. of New York 1968, Opera Competition, GDR 1969, Friedrich-Kuhlau Competition, Uelzen 1970, 22ème Tribune Internationale des Compositeurs, UNESCO, Paris 1975, Prix Folklorique de Radio Bratislava 1975, Prix Danube Bratislava 1977, Ernst-Reuter-Preis (with Dorothea Medek) 1982. *Address:* Edition Tilo Medek, Rheinhöhe, Westerwaldweg 22, 53424 Remagen-Oberwinter, Germany (office). *Telephone:* 02228-8175 (office). *Fax:* 02228-8176 (office). *E-mail:* tilo@medek.net (office). *Website:* www.medek .net.

MEDJIMOREC, Heinz; pianist; b. 1940, Vienna, Austria. *Education:* studied in Vienna. *Career:* performances of Haydn and other composers in Vienna and elsewhere from 1968; co-founder, Haydn Trio of Vienna 1968–, with performances in Brussels, Munich, Berlin, Zürich, London, Paris and Rome; New York debut 1979 and has made frequent N American appearances with concerts in 25 states; debut tour of Japan 1984, with further travels to the Near East, Russia, Africa, Central and South America; series at the Vienna Konzerthaus Soc. from 1976, with performances of more than 100 works; summer festivals at Vienna, Salzburg, Aix-en-Provence, Flanders and

Montreux; masterclasses, Royal Coll. and Royal Acad., London, and in Stockholm, Bloomington, Tokyo and the Salzburg Mozarteum. *Recordings include:* complete piano trios of Beethoven and Schubert, Mendelssohn D minor, Brahms B major, Tchaikovsky A minor, Schubert Trout Quintet, works by Haydn, Schumann, Dvořák and Smetana.

MEDLAM, Charles; British cellist and bass viol player; b. 10 Sept. 1949, Port of Spain, Trinidad. *Education:* studied the cello in London, Paris (with Maurice Gendron at the Conservatoire), Vienna and Salzburg (performance practice with Nikolaus Harnoncourt). *Career:* lectured and played in resident string quartet at Chinese Univ. of Hong Kong; Founder (with Ingrid Seifert), London Baroque 1978; 2,700 concerts world-wide. *Recordings include:* 80 CDs with the group: Marais La Gamme, Theile Matthew Passion, Bach Trio Sonatas, Charpentier Theatre Music, Handel Aci, Galatea e Polifemo, Venus and Adonis, Purcell Chamber Music; Purcell Fantasias, Bach Violin Sonatas, Monteverdi Orfeo, Handel German Arias; A Vauxhall Gardens Entertainment; English Music of the 18th Century; François Couperin Chamber Music; The complete trio sonatas of Corelli, Handel, Purcell, Lawes; Gamba sonatas by CPE Bach, harpsichord concertos by J.C. Bach/W.A. Mozart; Vivaldi, Trio sonatas Op. 1, Christmas Music and Handel Latin Motets with Emma Kirkby, Purcell Fantasias, Couperin's Apothéoses, Rameau Pièces de Clavecin en Concert, eight CDs of Trio sonatas, Handel: Sacred Cantatas (with Emma Kirkby) 2001, Corelli & Purcell: Trios, Sonatas & Fantasias (with London Baroque) 2005, Fleur de Lys 2010, CPE Bach: Trio Sonatas for viola da gamba and continuo 2012. *Address:* Brick Kiln Cottage, Hollington, nr Newbury, Berks., RG20 9XX, England (home). *Telephone:* (1635) 254331 (office).

MEDVECZKY, Adam; conductor and timpanist; b. 1941, Budapest, Hungary. *Education:* Bela Bartók Conservatory, Liszt Acad. of Music, Budapest, masterclass with Franco Ferrara in Italy. *Career:* Timpanist, Hungarian State Symphony Orchestra for nine years; Conductor, Budapest State Opera from 1974; numerous guest appearances in Bulgaria, Germany, Greece, The Netherlands, Poland, Italy, Romania, Russia and USA; Prof., Ferenc Liszt Acad., Budapest 1981–. *Honours:* Liszt Prize 1976, second prize Hungarian Television Int. Competition for Young Conductors 1974.

MEE, Anthony; British singer (tenor); b. 9 Sept. 1951, Lancs., England; m. Heather Mee; one d. *Education:* Royal Northern Coll. of Music, Manchester. *Career:* debut with Welsh Nat. Opera as Ernani 1984; Street Scene for Decca and for Lyric Opera, Chicago 2001; Gabriele Adorno, Cavaradossi, Nadir and Calaf for ENO; Bardolfo in Falstaff at Berlin Staatsoper, Bayerische Staatsoper, Munich; concerts include Verdi's Giovanna d'Arco, Boito's Mephistopheles and Verdi's Aroldo in London; season 1999–2000 with Bardolfo at Ferrara Musica, Italy and in Munich with Claudio Abbado and Zubin Mehta. *Recordings include:* Weill's Street Scene and Falstaff, conducted by Abbado. *Current Management:* c/o Neil Dalrymple, Music International, 13 Ardilaun Road, Highbury, London, N5 2QR, England. *Telephone:* (20) 7359-5183 (office). *Fax:* (20) 7226-9792 (office). *E-mail:* music@musicint.co.uk (office). *Website:* www.musicint.co.uk (office). *E-mail:* info@anthonymee.com (office). *Website:* www.anthonymee.com.

MEEK, Clarissa; British singer (mezzo-soprano); b. 1970, England. *Education:* Guildhall School of Music and Drama. *Career:* appearances with Scottish Opera in The Merry Widow, Street Scene, Figaro, The Magic Flute, Death in Venice, Jenůfa and Salome; Iolanthe in the opera by Sullivan (also broadcast); Glyndebourne Festival as Madame Larina in Eugene Onegin, Pauline (The Queen of Spades), Glasha (Katya Kabanova) and two roles in the premiere production of Birtwistle's Second Mrs Kong (1994); season 1996–97 with Haydn's Stabat Mater at Aldeburgh, Thisbe (Cenerentola) in Japan and Maddalena in Rigoletto at Guernsey; Maurya in Hart's Riders to the Sea at Cambridge 1998; concerts include Messiah in Hanover and The Dream of Gerontius; other operas include Les Boréades by Rameau, Tchaikovsky's The Enchantress and Monteverdi's Ulisse (as Penelope). *Honours:* Erich Vietheer Memorial Award at Glyndebourne 1995.

MEEK, James; British singer (baritone); b. 29 July 1957, Winchester, England. *Education:* Guildhall School of Music. *Career:* sang for three seasons at the Buxton Festival and appeared as Owen Wingrave at Aldeburgh; Other roles include Escamillo, Rossini's Figaro, Mozart's Count and Guglielmo, Valentin in Faust and the Doctor in Debussy's posthumous Fall of the House of Usher (Queen Elizabeth Hall 1989); Sang in Haydn's La Vera Costanza in Germany; Concert repertoire includes Elijah, the Petite Messe Solennelle, Handel's Judas Maccabaeus (Flanders Festival) Israel in Egypt and Dixit Dominus; Bach's Christmas Oratorio at the Snape Maltings, St John and St Matthew Passions; Britten's War Requiem in Germany and Yugoslavia and the Requiems of Mozart, Fauré and Brahms; Sang Messiah at the National Concert Hall Dublin, Pulcinella at the Barbican and the Missa Solemnis at Guilford Cathedral; Songs by Henri Dutilleux at Aldeburgh and concerts with the Songmakers' Almanac at the Bath, Nottingham, Buxton and Derby Festivals; Recitals on South Bank in the Schoenberg Reluctant Revolutionary Series, 1989 and Schubert directed by Hermann Prey, accompanied by Iain Burnside; sang Starveling in A Midsummer Night's Dream at Aix-en-Provence, 1992.

MEHNERT, Thomas; singer (bass); b. 1966, Chemitz, Germany. *Education:* Richard Strauss Conservatory, Munich and the Munich Singschule. *Career:* concert performances at the 1995 Rheingau Music Festival, and the Mozart Festival at Würzburg; engagements at the Cottbus Opera as Colline, Colas in Mozart's Bastien und Bastienne, the Hermit in Der Freischütz Figaro and

Banquo from 1995; guest appearances with Netherlands Opera as Pluto in Monteverdi's Orfeo and Fifth Solo Voice in Moses und Aron, under Pierre Boulez (also at the Salzburg Festival); Royal Festival Hall, London, in Moses und Aron with the Philharmonia Orchestra under Christoph von Dohnányi 1996. *Honours:* Deutsche Buhnvereins grant 1993.

MEHTA, Bejun; American singer (countertenor); b. 29 June 1968, Laurinburg, N Carolina; s. of Dady Mehta and Martha Ritchey Mehta. *Education:* studied cello at Yale Univ. with Aldo Parisot; vocal tuition at Boston Univ. with Phyllis Curtin (baritone) and at Manhattan School of Music and Curtis Inst. with Joan Patenaude-Yarnell (countertenor). *Career:* performed as solo boy soprano in concerts and recordings between ages of nine and 15; several years as cellist, both soloist and orchestral player; returned to singing professionally 1998, initially as baritone before focusing on countertenor voice; operatic debut as Armindo in Partenope, New York City Opera 1998; has appeared with many leading int. opera cos including ROH Covent Garden, Bayerische Staatsoper, Opéra Nat. and Théatre an der Wien, Berliner Staatsoper, Théatre du Châtelet Paris, Theater an der Wien, Berliner Staatsoper, Théatre de la Monnaie, Netherlands Opera, Liceu Barcelona, Teatro Real Madrid, Metropolitan Opera, Chicago Lyric, Los Angeles, San Francisco and New York City Operas, Salzburg Festival, Glyndebourne, Edinburgh, Aix-en-Provence, Verbier and BBC Proms, London. *Opera repertoire includes:* title roles in Orlando, Tamerlano, Giulio Cesare, Telemaco, Radamisto; also Bertarido in Rodelinda, Orfeo in Orfeo ed Euridice, Oberon in A Midsummer Night's Dream, Farnace in Mitridate, Didymus in Theodora, Hamor in Jeptha, Cyrus in Belshazzar, Arsamenes in Xerxes, Andronico in Tamerlano, Arsace in Partenope, Masha in Eötvös' Three Sisters, Ottone in Agrippina, Emone in Antigone, George Benjamin: Written on Skin (BBC Music Magazine Premiere Award, Gramophone Award for Best Contemporary Recording 2014). *Recordings include:* Bejun: Songs and Arias of Handel, Schubert, Brahms, Britten 1992, Ombra Cara (Echo Klassik Prize for Opera Recording of the Year 2011) 2010, Agrippina 2011, Down by the Salley Gardens 2011, Che puro ciel: The Rise of Classical Opera 2013, Handel Orlando 2014. *Current Management:* c/o Centre Stage Artist Management, Universal Music Group International, Stralauer Allee 1, 10245 Berlin, Germany. *Telephone:* (30) 520071762. *E-mail:* judith.neuhoff@umusic.com. *Website:* www.centrestagemanagement.com; bejunmehta.com.

MEHTA, Zarin, FCA; Indian arts administrator; *Co-Executive Director, Green Music Center, Sonoma State University;* b. 28 Oct. 1938, Bombay; s. of the late Mehli Mehta and of Tehmina Daruvala Mehta; brother of Zubin Mehta (q.v.); m. Carmen Lasky 1966; one s. one d. *Career:* Chartered Accountant in London 1957, accountant, Frederic B. Smart & Co., London 1957–62, Coopers & Lybrand, Montreal, Canada 1962–81; Dir Orchestre Symphonique de Montréal 1973–81, Man. Dir 1981–90; Exec. Dir and COO Ravinia Festival, Ill. 1990–99, CEO 1999–2000; Exec. Dir New York Philharmonic 2000–12, Pres. 2004–12; Co-Exec. Dir Green Music Center, Sonoma State Univ. 2013–; mem. Ordre de Comptables Agréés du Québec; Treas. Barenboim-Said Foundation; mem. Bd of Dirs WNYC Radio. *Honours:* Dr hc (Roosevelt Univ., Chicago) 1998; Bravo Award, Dominican Univ. 1996, Arts Entrepreneurship Award, Columbia Coll., Chicago, 1997, Dushkin Award, Music Inst. of Chicago 1998, Theodore L. Kesselman Award for Arts Educ., New York Youth Symphony 2007. *Address:* Sonoma State University, Green Music Center, 1801 East Cotati Avenue, Rohnert Park, CA 94928, USA (office). *E-mail:* greenmusiccenter@sonoma.edu (office). *Website:* gmc.sonoma.edu (office).

MEHTA, Zubin; Indian conductor; b. 29 April 1936, Bombay; s. of the late Mehli Mehta and of Tehmina Daruvala Mehta; m. 1st Carmen Lasky 1958 (divorced 1964); one s. one d.; m. 2nd Nancy Diane Kovack 1969. *Education:* St Xavier's Coll., Mumbai, Vienna Acad. of Music, Austria, studied under Hans Swarowsky. *Career:* first professional conducting in Belgium, Yugoslavia and UK (Liverpool); Music Dir Montreal Symphony 1961–67, Los Angeles Philharmonic Orchestra 1962–78, New York Philharmonic Orchestra 1978–91; Music Dir Israel Philharmonic 1969–, apptd Dir for Life 1981; Music Dir Maggio Musicale, Florence 1969, 1986–, Chief Conductor 1985–; Gen. Music Dir Bavarian State Opera 1998–2006; conductor at festivals of Holland, Prague, Vienna, Salzburg and Spoleto; debut at La Scala, Milan 1969; conducts regularly with Vienna and Berlin Orchestras; conducted Vienna New Year's Concert 1990, 1995, 1998, 2007 and 2015; Pres. Annual Festival del Mediterrani in Valencia 2006–; co-f. Mehli Mehta Music Foundation, Mumbai. *Publication:* Zubin Mehta: The Score of My Life 2009. *Honours:* Hon. mem. Vienna State Opera 1997, Hon. Conductor, Vienna Philharmonic Orchestra 2001, Hon. Conductor, Munich Philharmonic Orchestra 2004, Hon. Conductor, Los Angeles Philharmonic 2006, Hon. Conductor, Teatro del Maggio Musicale Fiorentino 2006, Hon. Conductor, Bavarian State Opera 2006, Hon. mem. Bavarian State Opera 2006, Hon. mem., Gesellschaft der Musikfreunde Wien 2007, Hon. citizenship Florence and Tel-Aviv; Commendatore (Italy), Médaille d'Or Vermeil (City of Paris), Commdr, Ordre des Arts et des Lettres, Great Silver Medal of Service (Austria) 1997, Commander's Cross of Order of Merit (Germany) 2012; Dr hc (Tel-Aviv Univ., Weizmann Inst. of Science, The Hebrew Univ. of Jerusalem, Jewish Theological Seminary, Westminster Choir Coll., Princeton, Brooklyn Coll., Colgate Univ.); winner of Liverpool Int. Conducting Competition 1958, Padma Bhushan 1966, co-winner Wolf Prize 1996, Lifetime Achievement Peace and Tolerance Award, UN 1999, Padma Vibhushan 2001, Kennedy Center Honor 2006, Bridgebuilder Award 2007, Dan David Prize 2007, Praemium Imperiale Award for Music, Tokyo 2008, Tagore Award for cultural

harmony 2013. *Address:* c/o Natalia Ritzkowsky, Assistant to Zubin Mehta, Traubingerstr. 10 D, 82327 Tutzing, Germany (office). *Telephone:* (49) 8158906791 (office). *Fax:* (49) 8158906794 (office). *E-mail:* info@zubinmehta .net. *Website:* www.zubinmehta.net.

MEI, Eva; Italian singer (soprano); b. 3 March 1967, Fabriano. *Education:* Luigi Cherubini Conservatory, Florence. *Career:* debut as Aspasia in Salieri's Axur, re d'Ormus, Siena, 1989; sang Mozart's Constanze at the Vienna Staatsoper, 1990; engaged at Zürich as Donna Anna, Alcina, Mozart's Countess and Luitgarde in Schubert's Des Teufels Lustschloss; Covent Garden debut as the Queen of Night, 1993, Berlin Staatsoper as Violetta; La Scala debut as Amenaide in Tancredi, 1993; Rossini Festival at Pesaro as Fanny in La Cambiale di Matrimonio and Berenice in L'Occasione fa il ladro, 1995–96; Vienna Festival as Genio in Haydn's Orfeo ed Euridice, 1995; Norina in Don Pasquale at Genoa, 1998; Season 2000–01 as Violetta for Zürich Opera, Meyerbeer's Dinorah at Parma, Bellini's Amina at Palermo and Giulietta in Verdi's Un giorno di regno at Bologna; Concert engagements at the Amsterdam Concertgebouw, Queen Elizabeth Hall (London), Academia di Santa Cecilia (Rome) and halls in Buenos Aires, Vienna, St Petersburg and Moscow. *Recordings include:* A. Mezzanote, songs by Bellini, Rossini and Donizetti; Rossini's Tancredi and Mozart's Il re Pastore. *Honours:* Mozart Competition Caterina Cavalieri Prize, Vienna 1990. *Current Management:* Atelier Musicale, Via Caselle 76, San Lazzaro di Savena 40068, Italy. *Telephone:* (51) 19984444. *Fax:* (51) 19984420. *E-mail:* info@ateliermusicale .com. *Website:* www.ateliermusicale.com.

MEIER, Jaroslav; Czech composer; b. 7 Dec. 1923, Hronov; m. Marta Kurbelova 1950, two s. *Education:* Acad. of Music, Prague, Acad. of Music, Bratislava. *Career:* Head of Music Dept, Radio Bratislava 1949–56, Czechoslovakia Television, Bratislava 1956–; Music Designer (television and radio plays, films); mem. Union of Czechoslovak Composers, IMZ. *Compositions include:* Erindo (rewriting of opera by J. S. Kusser), The Night Before Immortality (TV opera, libretto after A. Arbuzov), The Wooden Shoes (opera, libretto after Guy de Maupassant); orchestral: Dances from my Country, Songs from my Country, What a Smell (song cycle based on Stefan Zary's poems), Concerto da Camera for organ and orchestra 1982. *Recordings:* Trois Impromptus (chamber music), Prelude and Double Fugue, Divine Love, The Cycle Nocturnal Songs, Toccata et fuga, Fantasia concertante. *Publications:* Obrazovka pina hudby (The Screen Full of Music) 1970, Johann Sigismund Kusser 1986; contrib. to Slovenska hudba (Slovak Music), Hudebni zivot (Music Life), Czeskoslovenska televize (television weekly paper). *Honours:* Golden Prague Int. Television Festival Critics' Prize (for television opera The Night Before Immortality) 1976.

MEIER, Johanna; singer (soprano); b. 13 Feb. 1938, Chicago, USA; m. Guido Della Vecchia. *Education:* Univ. of Miami with Arturo di Filippi, Manhattan School with John Brownlee. *Career:* debut with New York City Opera 1969, as the Countess in Capriccio; sang with the City Opera as Donna Anna, Senta, Louise and Tosca; Metropolitan Opera from 1976, as Marguerite, Ariadne, the Marschallin, Ellen Orford, Chrysothemis, Elisabeth, Brünnhilde in Die Walküre and Kaiserin; guest engagements in Seattle, Washington, Philadelphia, San Diego, Ottawa and Chicago; other roles include Sieglinde, Musetta, Mozart's Countess, Amelia (Un ballo in Maschera), Agathe and Eva; Bayreuth Festival debut 1981, as Isolde; Vienna Staatsoper from 1983, Fidelio and Senta; tour of Japan 1986, as Isolde and the Marschallin; Barcelona and Buenos Aires 1987, as Elisabeth in Tannhäuser and Chrysothemis; sang Turandot at Dallas and New Orleans 1987–88; Ariadne at Trieste 1988; Pittsburgh Opera 1989, as Chrysothemis; The Dyer's Wife in Die Frau ohne Schatten at the 1990 Holland Festival; world premiere Les Liaisons Dangereuses at San Francisco Opera 1994; retired 1994; Dir and Prod., Black Hills Passion Play.

MEIER, Jost; composer and conductor; b. 15 March 1939, Solothurn, Switzerland. *Education:* Berne Conservatory, studied with Frank Martin in The Netherlands. *Career:* conducted at the Biel Opera 1968–79, Basle 1980–83. *Compositions include:* Sennentuntschi, dramatic legend 1983, Der Drache (two-act opera) 1985, Der Zoobar (opera in four scenes) 1987, Augustin (opera in four scenes) 1988, Dreyfus (opera) 1994, Glarus for strings 1980, Musique for trombone and orchestra 1986, Musique Concertante 1989, Esquisses for piano and percussion 1993, Variations for viola and chamber orchestra 1996, String Quartet 1988, two Clarinet Trios 1969, 1999, Franz von Assisi for soloists, women's chorus and orchestra 1996, Galgenlieder for soprano, clarinet, cello and piano 1996, Music for the Fêtes des Vignerons for soloists, choruses, orchestra and brass bands 1999.

MEIER, Waltraud; German singer (mezzo-soprano); b. 9 Jan. 1956, Würzburg. *Education:* studied with Anton Theisen in Würzburg and Dietger Jacob in Cologne. *Career:* sang in Würzburg from 1976 as Cherubino, Dorabella, Nicklaus in Les Contes d'Hoffmann and Concepcion in L'Heure Espagnole, Mannheim 1978–80, as Carmen, Fricka, Waltraute and Octavian; Dortmund 1980–83, as Kundry in Parsifal, Eboli in Don Carlos and as Santuzza in Cavalleria Rusticana; guest appearances in Cologne, Hamburg, Buenos Aires, Opéra de Paris, Staatsoper Wien, Scala di Milano, San Francisco Opera, Munich, Bayreuth from 1983; sang Kundry in Götz Friedrich's production of Parsifal, Brangäne in Jean-Pierre Ponelle's Tristan und Isolde, and Waltraute in Harry Kupfer's 1988 production of The Ring; Covent Garden debut 1985, as Eboli, returned to London 1988 as Kundry; made her Metropolitan Opera debut 1987 as Fricka in Rheingold and

Walküre; other roles include Azucena (Il Trovatore), Venus (Tannhäuser), the Composer (Ariadne auf Naxos); sang Venus at Hamburg 1990; debut at the Teatro San Carlos, Lisbon 1990 as Ortrud in Lohengrin; Théâtre du Châtelet, Paris 1990 as Marguerite in La Damnation de Faust; sang Waltraute at the Bayreuth Festival 1988–92, Tchaikovsky's Maid of Orleans at Munich; season 1992–93 as Kundry at La Scala and the Metropolitan, Berg's Marie at the Théâtre du Châtelet, Paris and 1993–97 and 1999 as Isolde at Bayreuth; sang Sieglinde at the Vienna Staatsoper and La Scala, Milan 1994; Carmen at the Metropolitan 1997; Isolde at Munich 1998; sang Leonore at Munich and La Scala, Milan 1999; season 2000–01 as Marie in Wozzeck at La Scala, in Salzburg and Vienna as Isolde, Sieglinde at Bayreuth, Amneris at the Berlin Staatsoper and Les Troyens at Munich 2001; Wagner's Ortrud at Covent Garden 2003; slso a concert singer, in Beethoven, Brahms, Mahler and Verdi; new production of Les Contes d'Hoffmann/Giulietta at the Salzburg Festival 2003; season 2003–04 concentrated on lieder and concert singing. *Recordings include:* opera: Dittersdorf's Doktor und Apotheker, Venus and Kundry, Brahms Alto Rhapsody, Fricka in Bernard Haitink's Die Walküre, Wesendonk and Kindertotenlieder, Missa Solemnis, Mozart Requiem, Wagner recital with the Symphonieorchester des Bayerischen Rundfunks under Lorin Maazel 1997, Isolde with Barenboim, Leonore with Barenboim, Ortrud with Claudio Abbado, Mahler-Lieder with Maazel 1998, Tristan und Isolde at Munich (DVD) 1998, Walküre with Zubin Mehta at Munich (also DVD) 2002. *Honours:* titles of Bayerische Kammersängerin at the Bavarian State Opera, Kammersängerin at the Vienna State Opera. *Current Management:* Opéra et Concert, 37 rue de la Chausée d'Antin, 75009 Paris, France. *Telephone:* (1) 42-96-18-18. *Fax:* (1) 42-96-18-00. *E-mail:* agence@opera-concert.com. *Website:* www.opera-concert.com; www.waltraud-meier.com.

MEIRON, Rhys; British singer (tenor); b. 1970, Wales. *Education:* Guildhall School, London 1997–99. *Career:* Glyndebourne Festival Chorus from 1998; sang Edmondo in Manon Lescaut at Glyndebourne, 1999; concert engagements in London, Guilford, Bournemouth, Toronto and Barbados; ENO from 1999, as Major Domo in Der Rosenkavalier, First Armed Man in The Magic Flute and Nadir in The Pearl Fishers. *Honours:* prizewinner National Eisteddfod, Wales 1996–97. *Current Management:* Harlequin Agency Ltd, 203 Fidlas Road, Llanishen, Cardiff, CF14 5NA, Wales. *Telephone:* (29) 2075-0821. *Fax:* (29) 2075-5971. *E-mail:* peter@harlequin-agency.co.uk. *Website:* www.harlequin-agency.co.uk.

MEISTER, Cornelius; German conductor; *Chief Conductor and Artistic Director, Vienna Radio Symphony Orchestra*; b. 23 Feb. 1980, Hannover. *Education:* Hannover Conservatory, Salzburg Mozarteum, Austria. *Career:* made opera debut as conductor, Hamburg Opera 2001, New Nat. Theatre Tokyo 2006, San Francisco Opera 2006, Deutsche Oper Berlin 2009; Music Dir Heidelberg Philharmonic Orchestra and Opera 2005–; Chief Conductor and Artistic Dir Vienna Radio Symphony Orchestra 2010–; Conductor, Tristan und Isolde, Royal Opera House, Copenhagen 2010, Conductor, Riga, Latvian Nat. Opera 2011; guest conductor with many orchestras including Bamberg Symphony Orchestra, NDR Symphony Orchestra Hamburg, Munich Radio Orchestra, BBC Philharmonic Orchestra, Orchestre de l'Opéra National de Paris, Indianapolis Symphony Orchestra, Deutsche Symphonie-Orchester Berlin, City of Birmingham Symphony Orchestra, Swedish Radio Symphony Orchestra, Baltimore Symphony Orchestra. *Honours:* Prize Winner, Deutsche Musikwettbewerb, Prize Winner, Schleswig-Holstein Musik Festival. *Current Management:* Cornelia Schmid or Alice Moser, Konzertdirektion Schmid, Postfach 34 09, 30034 Hannover, Germany. *Telephone:* (511) 366-07-39/86. *Fax:* (511) 366-07-34. *E-mail:* cornelia.schmid@kdschmid.de; alice.moser@kdschmid.de; mail@kdschmid.de. *Website:* www.kdschmid.de. *Address:* ORF Radio-Symphonieorchester Wien (Vienna Radio Symphony Orchestra), Argentinierstrasse 30a, 1040, Vienna Austria (office). *Telephone:* (1) 501-01-18420 (office). *Fax:* (1) 501-01-18358 (office). *E-mail:* rso-wien@orf.at (office). *Website:* rso.orf.at (office).

MEKLER, Mani; singer (soprano); b. 1951, Haifa, Israel. *Education:* studied in Italy. *Career:* sang Leonora in Il Trovatore at Stockholm and with WNO 1976, 1977; Glyndebourne debut 1978, as First Lady in Die Zauberflöte; Wexford Festival 1979, as Giulia in Spontini's La Vestale; Deutsche Oper am Rhein, Düsseldorf from 1979 as Janáček's Jenůfa and Mila (Osud) and Chrysothemis; further appearances at Drottningholm, Zürich and Milan, La Scala (premiere of Testi's Riccardo III 1987); other roles include Puccini's Manon Lescaut, Tosca and Butterfly, Strauss's Salome and Ariadne, and Goneril in Reimann's Lear.

MELBY, John B., DipMus, BMus, MA, MFA, PhD; American composer; b. 3 Oct. 1941, Wisconsin; m. Jane H. Thompson 1978, two s. one d. *Education:* Curtis Institute of Music, University of Pennsylvania, Princeton University. *Career:* Professor of Music, University of Illinois, Urbana. *Compositions include:* ...Of Quiet Desperation for computer-synthesized tape, 1976; Concerto No. 1 for violin and computer-synthesized tape, 1979, No. 2, 1986; Layers for computer-synthesized tape, 1981; Wind, Sand, and Stars for 8 instruments and computer-synthesized tape, 1983; Concerto for violin, English horn and computer-synthesized tape, 1984; Concerto for computer-synthesized tape and orchestra, 1987; Symphony No. 1, 1993; The rest is silence... for organ, 1994; Other concerti, songs and keyboard works. *Recordings include:* 91 Plus 5 for brass quintet and computer-synthesized tape; Forandre: 7 variations for digital computer; Two Stevens Songs for soprano and computer-synthesized tape; Concerto for violin, English horn and computer-synthesized tape; Concerto No. 1 for violin and computer-synthesized tape; Concerto Nos 1 and 2 for flute and computer-synthesized tape; Chor der Steine; Chor der Waisen. *Publications:* Some recent developments in computer-synthesized music, 1973; Proceedings of the 1975 Music Computation Conference (edited with James Beauchamp), 1976; 'Layers': An approach to composition for computer based upon the concept of structural levels, 1983; 'Computer' Music or Computer 'Music', 1989. *Address:* School of Music, 2136 Music Building, 1114 West Nevada, University of Illinois, Urbana, IL 61801, USA.

MELBYE, Mikael; Danish singer (baritone), stage director and designer; b. 15 March 1955, Frederiksberg; s. of Erik Melbye and Birgitte Skak Melbye (née Olufsen); m. Jan Lund 2001. *Education:* Royal Danish Conservatory and Royal Danish Opera Acad., Copenhagen. *Career:* operatic debut as Guglielmo in Così fan tutte, Royal Danish Opera 1976; vast repertoire of mainly lyric baritone roles including Mozart, Rossini, Donizetti, Verdi and Puccini; int. debut as Danilo in The Merry Widow at Spoleto Festival 1981; has since appeared in opera houses world-wide, including La Scala di Milano, The Paris Opéra, Royal Opera House, Covent Garden, Staatsoper, Munich, Hamburgische Staatsoper, Metropolitan Opera, New York; debut as Stage Dir and Designer at Royal Danish Opera in Così fan tutte 1995, was thereafter engaged as Prin. Dir and Designer for this house; directed and designed premiere performance of Turandot at the Royal Danish Opera 1996; Dir Arabella 1997 (Houston 1998), Magic Flute 1998 (Boston Lyric 2000), La Bohème, Royal Danish Opera 1999, Rigoletto at Santa Fe Opera 2000; sets and Costumes for Giselle at San Francisco Ballet 1999, La Sylphide for Royal Swedish Ballet 1999, and for Nat. Ballet of China 1999; directed Salome for Jutland Opera 1999, Royal Danish Opera 2001, and also Capriccio for Royal Danish Opera 2001; designed sets and costumes and directed Nutcracker at Tivoli Gardens 2001; costumes and sets for Symphony in C (Balanchine) at Royal Danish Ballet 2000, and Royal Norwegian Ballet 2001; Rigoletto for Royal Danish Opera 2002; Das Rheingold for Den ny Opera, Esbjerg 2003; Il Trovatore for Royal Danish Opera 2003, Norwegian Opera 2004; Pelléas et Mélisande for Jutland Opera 2004; opening of new Royal Opera House in Copenhagen with Aida 2005; Turn of the Screw for Royal Danish Opera 2006; set and costumes for Anna Karenina, Royal Danish Ballet 2004, Lithuanian State Ballet 2005 and Finnish Nat. Ballet 2006; sets and costumes for La Sylphide, Estonian State Ballet 2006; singer is a descendant of 19th century painter Anton Melbye, began his training as a painter with his mother (a watercolorist) in early childhood and since then has studied with several Danish and American painters, including Kay Christensen, Richard Schmid and Francis Cunningham; paintings in public and pvt. collections in Europe, USA and Australia. *Selected commissions:* Royal Opera singer, Royal Commdr, Sir Ib Hansen for the Royal Danish Opera, Dame Susse Wold, actress Dame, Royal Commdr, Ghita Noerby for Christianborg Museum Collection, Copenhagen, Joergen Faerch, Pres. Scandinavian Tobacco Co., John O. Crosby, Founder and Pres. Santa Fe Opera, Vagn Egeberg, Pres. Young & Rubicam Scandinavia. *Exhibitions include:* Susanne Hoejriis Gallery, Copenhagen 2001, 2002, Scandinavian Art Fair in The Forum, Copenhagen 2003, Gimsinghoved Kulturcenter, Struer 2004, Henrik Kampmann Gallery, Copenhagen 2005, Galleria Il Ponte Contemporanea, Rome 2005, Kirsten Kjaer Museum 2006. *Recordings include:* Carmen (Karajan), Die Zauberflöte (Colin Davis). *Honours:* Kt's Cross of the Dannebrog 1995, peerage bestowed by Queen Margrethe 2006; Oberdörfer Preis (Germany), Golden Pegasus Award (Italy), Gladsaxe Music Award (Denmark), OV Award for Best Production – Turandot (Denmark), Torben Anton Petersens Memorial Award. *Current Management:* c/o Michael Moore, LTM Artists, 5290 West Washington Blvd, Los Angeles, CA 90016, USA. *Telephone:* (310) 652-1464) ext. 103. *Fax:* (310) 362-8803. *Website:* www.ltmartists.com. *Address:* Hejreskovhus, Hejreskovvej 11, 4173, Fjenneslev, Denmark (home). *Telephone:* 35550384 (studio); 57608040 (home). *E-mail:* mmelbye@attglobal.net (home). *Website:* www.mikael-melbye.com.

MELCHER, Wilhelm; violinist; b. 5 April 1940, Hamburg, Germany. *Education:* studied in Hamburg and Rome. *Career:* Leader, Hamburg Symphony Orchestra 1963; fmr mem., Karl Munchinger's Stuttgart Chamber Orchestra, Heilbronn; co-founder, Melos Quartet of Stuttgart 1965; represented West Germany at the Jeunesse Musicales in Paris 1966; int concert tours from 1967; bicentenary concerts in the Beethoven Haus at Bonn 1970; British concerts and festival appearances from 1974; cycle of Beethoven quartets at Edinburgh Festival 1987; Wigmore Hall, St John's Smith Square and Bath Festival 1990; associations with Rostropovich in the Schubert Quintet and the Cleveland Quartet in works by Spohr and Mendelssohn; teacher, Stuttgart Musikhochschule. *Recordings include:* complete quartets of Beethoven, Schubert, Mozart and Brahms, quintets by Boccherini with Narciso Ypes, and by Mozart with Frank Beyer. *Honours:* Academie du Disque Grand Prix du Disque, Brussels (with Melos Quartet), Academie du Disque Prix Caecilia, Brussels (with Melos Quartet).

MELKUS, Eduard; violinist; b. 1 Sept. 1928, Baden, Austria; m. Marlis Melkus-Selzer, four c. *Education:* Vienna Univ. with Erich Schenk, studied with Ernst Moravec, Firmin Touche, Alexander Schaizhet and Peter Rybar. *Career:* debut in Vienna 1944; founder, Eduard Melkus Ensemble and Capella Academia 1965, playing mainly on original instruments of the 18th century; Prof. of Violin and Viola, Vienna Hochschule für Musik from 1958; premiered Concerto by Egon Wellesz 1962; concerts in Europe, USA, Australia, Japan, S. America; Visiting Prof., Univ. of Georgia, USA 1973–74, Univ. of Illinois and others; lectures and masterclasses in many univs all over the world; mem. Austria ESTA (fmr pres.). *Recordings:* concertos by Bach, Tartini, Vivaldi,

Haydn, sonatas by Biber, Corelli, Bach, Mozart and Handel, solo violin music by Bach, Haydn's La Vera Costanza at the Schönbrunn Palace, Vienna 1984. *Publications:* Die Violine, Schott, many articles on interpretation. *Honours:* Kornerpreis 1967, Prix Academia Charles C. Gros Edison Prize, Great Cross of Honour of the Republic of Austria.

MELLON, Agnès; French singer (soprano); b. 17 Jan. 1958, Epinay-sur-Seine; m. Dominique Visse. *Education:* studied in Paris and San Francisco. *Career:* sang with the Paris Opéra and the Opéra-Comique; later appearances in the Baroque repertoire, notably as Tibrino in Cesti's Orontea at the 1986 Innsbruck Early Music Festival, Eryxene in Hasse's Cleofide, 1987 and Telaire in Rameau's Castor et Pollux at the 1991 Aix-en-Provence Festival; sang the title role in Rossi's Orfeo at the Queen Elizabeth Hall, London, with Les Arts Florissants, 1990; sang in Mondonville's Les Fêtes de Paphos at Versailles, 1996. *Recordings include:* Rossi's Orfeo, Cavalli's Xerxes, Lully's Atys, Charpentier's Médée and David et Jonathas, Hasse's Cleofide, Rameau's Anacréon and Zoroastre; Labels include Erato and Harmonia Mundi. *Current Management:* Pelléas Artists, 169 rue Jules Besme, 1081 Brussels, Belgium. *Telephone:* (2) 241-59-88; (496) 403516 (mobile). *Fax:* (2) 241-59-88. *E-mail:* cdrijck@pelleas-artists.com. *Website:* www.pelleas-artists.com.

MELLOR, Alwyn; singer (soprano); b. 1968, Rawtenstall, Lancashire, England. *Education:* Royal Northern Coll. of Music, studied in Italy and St Petersburg. *Career:* roles with WNO from 1992 have included Tatiana, Ginevra in Ariodante, Liu, Fiordiligi, Marguerite, Anne Trulove and Micaela; Donna Elvira for WNO and Glyndebourne Touring Opera, Fiordiligi at Sante Fe 1997; concerts include Edinburgh Festival with the Scottish Chamber Orchestra; Die Schöpfung in Amsterdam with the Bach Soloists under Marc Minkowski 1993; US debut with the Kansas City Camerata 1996; season 1997 with Britten's Spring Symphony (Rotterdam Philharmonic Orchestra under Donald Runnicles); sang Marenka in new production of The Bartered Bride for Opera North 1998. *Recordings include:* Elsie in Yeomen of the Guard (with WNO). *Honours:* awards from the Peter Moores Foundation.

MELNIKOV, Alexander; Russian concert pianist; b. 1973, Moscow. *Education:* Moscow Central Music School, Moscow Tchaikovsky Conservatory with Lev Naumov, Fondazione per il Pianoforte, Como, Italy. *Career:* greatly influenced by early encounter with Sviatoslav Richter who regularly invited him to festivals in Russia and France; discovered a career-long interest in historical performance practice at an early age; major influences include Andreas Staier and Alexei Lubimov, with whom he collaborated on numerous projects; performs regularly with period ensembles including Concerto Köln and Akademie für Alte Musik Berlin; together with Andreas Staier (harpsichord), developed a programme that sets excerpts from Bach's Well-Tempered Clavier in musical dialogue with Shostakovich's 24 Preludes and Fugues, as well as a unique all-Schubert programme of four-hand pieces they have recorded and performed in concert; chamber music collaborations with cellists Alexander Rudin and Jean-Guihen Queyras, and the baritone Georg Nigl; regular recital partner, violinist Isabelle Faust, numerous acclaimed recordings; has performed as soloist with orchestras including the Royal Concertgebouw Orchestra, Gewandhausorchester Leipzig, Philadelphia Orchestra, NDR Sinfonieorchester, HR-Sinfonieorchester, Russian Nat. Orchestra, Munich Philharmonic, Rotterdam Philharmonic, BBC Philharmonic, NHK Symphony, under conductors including Mikhail Pletnev, Teodor Currentzis, Charles Dutoit, Paavo Järvi and Valery Gergiev; Artist-in-Residence, Muziekgebouw, Amsterdam 2013–14; season 2013–14: debut at BBC Proms with Warsaw Philharmonic under Antoni Wit; Artistic Partner of Tapiola Sinfonietta; season 2015–16: launch of The Man with the Many Pianos programme (solo recital on three different instruments reflecting the periods in which the works were written); continuous collaboration with Mahler Chamber Orchestra and Freiburger Barockorchester; concerts with Camerata Salzburg and Louis Langrée at the Mozartwoche, Salzburg, Seattle Symphony Orchestra and Vancouver Symphony Orchestra, engagements in Wigmore Hall, London, Muziekgebouw aan't Ij, Amsterdam, De Singel, Antwerp, Opéra, Dijon, Palau de la Música Catalana, Barcelona. *Recordings:* solo works by Brahms, Rachmaninov and Scriabin; chamber music recordings with Isabelle Faust, Jean-Guihen Queyras and Teunis van der Zwart; Shostakovich 24 Preludes and Fugues for Piano (Choc de Classica for the Best Recording of 2010, Deutschen Schallplattenkritik Prize 2010, BBC Music Magazine Award—instrumental category 2011, one of the "50 greatest recordings of all time", BBC Music Magazine 2011); Beethoven Sonatas for Piano and Violin (with Isabelle Faust) (Echo Klassik Prize 2010, Gramophone Award for Best Chamber Music Recording 2010) 2009; Shostakovich Piano Concerti with the Mahler Chamber Orchestra and Teodor Currentzis 2012, Chamber Works of Weber 2013, Beethoven Trios with Isabelle Faust and Jean-Guihen Queyras 2014. *Publications:* contrib. of illuminating notes to the booklets accompanying his CDs. *Honours:* Laureate, Robert Schumann Competition, Zwickau 1989, Concours Musical Reine Elisabeth, Brussels 1991. *Current Management:* c/o Impresariat Simmenauer, Kurfürstendamm 211, 10719 Berlin, Germany. *Telephone:* (30) 414781710. *Fax:* (30) 414781713. *E-mail:* elaine.yeung@impresariat-simmenauer.de. *Website:* www.impresariat-simmenauer.de.

MELROSE, Leigh; singer (baritone); b. 1972, New York, USA. *Education:* St John's Coll., Cambridge, Royal Acad. of Music. *Career:* debut as Dancairo in Carmen, for ENO; other roles with ENO Mozart's Count, Papageno, Ned Keene, Junius and Leoncavallo's Rodolfo; roles elsewhere include Rossini's Figaro for New York City Opera; Silvio for WNO; Birtwistle's Punch in Porto;

Rambo in John Adam's The Death of Klinghoffer (Channel 4 film); concerts include various BBC Proms; Carmina Burana; Belshazzar's Feast; Friar Lawrence in Berlioz's Romeo et Juliette.

MENA, Juanjo; Spanish conductor; *Chief Conductor, BBC Philharmonic Orchestra;* b. 21 Sept. 1965, Vitoria-Gasteiz; m. Noemi Mena; two c. *Education:* Vitoria-Gasteiz Conservatory, Madrid Royal Conservatory. *Career:* studied with Carmelo Bernaola, Enrique Garcia Asensio, Sergiu Celibidache; formed Youth Orchestra of Euskal Herria 1997; fmr Assoc. Conductor, Euskadi Symphony Orchestra; Artistic Dir and Principal Conductor, Bilbao Symphony Orchestra 1999–2008; Principal Guest Conductor, Teatro Carlo Felice, Genoa, Italy 2007–10; Principal Guest Conductor, Bergen Philharmonic Orchestra 2007–; Chief Conductor, BBC Philharmonic Orchestra 2011–; other engagements include: Oslo Philharmonic Orchestra, Orchestre National de France, Orchestra Filarmonica della Scala, BBC Scottish Symphony Orchestra, Baltimore Symphony Orchestra, Philadelphia Orchestra, Boston Symphony Orchestra. *Recordings:* albums: as conductor: Haydn/Hummel/Mozart/Neruda, Trumpet Concertos (with Bamberg Symphony Orchestra and Karl-Heinz Steffens) 2010, Pierne, Bavouzet (with BBC Philharmonic Orchestra and Jean-Efflam Bavouzet) 2011; with Bilbao Symphony Orchestra: Arriaga, Sinfonia en Re, Sarasate, Aires Bohemios (with Siging Lu), Guridi, Diez melodias Vascas 2003, Arambarri, Ocho Canciones Vascas 2003, Isasi, Sinfonia No. 2 2004, Usandizaga, Mendi mendiyan 2005, Guridi, Sinfonia Pirenaica 2005, Escudero, Illeta 2005, Guridi, El Caserio 2006. *Honours:* Guridi-Bernaola Scholarship, Munich. *Current Management:* Schmidt Artists International Inc., East 54th Street, Suite 83, New York, NY 10022, USA. *Telephone:* (212) 421-8500. *Fax:* (212) 421-8583. *E-mail:* info@schmidtart.com. *Website:* www.schmidtart.com. *Address:* BBC Philharmonic Orchestra, New Broadcasting House, Oxford Road, Manchester, M60 1SJ, England (office); Servicios Artísticos Alain, Apartado de correos 10, Legutiano, Álava, 01170, Spain (office). *Telephone:* (161) 244-4001 (office). *Fax:* (161) 244-4010 (office). *E-mail:* philharmonic@bbc.co.uk (office). *Website:* www.bbc.co.uk/orchestras/philharmonic (office); www.juanjomena.com.

MENARD, Pierre; violinist; b. 1945, Québec, Canada. *Education:* Québec Conservatory, Juilliard School with Dorothy DeLay, Ivan Galamian and the Juilliard Quartet. *Career:* solo appearances in Canada and the USA; fmr Concertmaster, Aspen Festival Orchestra and the Nashville Symphony; co-founder and Second Violinist, Vermeer Quartet from 1970; performances in most North American centres, Europe, Israel and Australia; festival engagements at Tanglewood, Aspen, Spoleto, Berlin, Edinburgh, mostly Mozart (New York), Aldeburgh, South Bank, Santa Fe Chamber Music West, and the Casals Festival; Resident Quartet for Chamber Music Chicago; masterclasses at the Royal Northern Coll. of Music, Manchester; mem. Resident Artists Faculty, Northern Illinois Univ. *Recordings:* quartets by Beethoven, Dvořák, Verdi and Schubert, Brahms Clarinet Quintet (with Karl Leister). *Honours:* first prize in chamber music Québec Conservatory, winner Nat. Festival of Music Competition, Prix d'Europe from the Québec Govt.

MENESES, Antonio; cellist; b. 23 Aug. 1957, Recife, Brazil. *Education:* studied with Antonio Janigro in Düsseldorf and Stuttgart. *Career:* appeared widely in Europe and America from 1977; appearances with the Berlin Philharmonic conducted by Karajan, with the London Symphony Orchestra in London and the USA, and with the Israel Philharmonic, Vienna Philharmonic and Concertgebouw Orchestras; other conductors include Abbado, Previn, Maazel and Muti; tours of Australia 1984, 1987; engagements at the Lucerne and the Salzburg Easter Festivals, with the Berlin Philharmonic; mem., Beaux Arts Trio 1998–2008. *Recordings include:* Brahms Double Concerto (with Anne-Sophie Mutter), Strauss Don Quixote (conducted by Karajan). *Honours:* second prize int. competitions in Barcelona and Rio de Janeiro, first prize ARD Competition, Munich 1977, gold medal Tchaikovsky Int. Competition, Moscow 1982. *Telephone:* (812) 320-4389. *E-mail:* info@encoreartsmanagement.com. *Website:* www.encoreartsmanagement.com; www.beauxartstrio.org.

MENKOVA, Irina; Russian violinist; b. 1960, Moscow. *Career:* co-founder, Glazunov Quartet 1985; concerts in the former Soviet Union and in Greece, Belgium, Poland, Germany and Italy; works by Beethoven and Schumann at the Beethoven Haus in Bonn; further engagements in Canada and The Netherlands; teacher, Moscow State Conservatoire; resident at the Tchaikovsky Conservatoire; repertoire includes works by Borodin, Shostakovich and Tchaikovsky, in addition to the standard works. *Recordings include:* works by Tchaikovsky. *Honours:* prizewinner Borodin Quartet and Shostakovich Chamber Music Competitions (with the Glazunov Quartet).

MENTZER, Susanne; singer (mezzo-soprano); b. 21 Jan. 1957, Philadelphia, USA. *Education:* Juilliard School, New York, studied with Norma Newton. *Career:* debut at Houston Opera 1981, as Albina in La Donna del Lago; appeared with Dallas Opera 1982, in Gianni Schicchi and Das Rheingold; Washington Opera as Cherubino; Chicago Lyric Opera, Phladelphia Opera and New York City Opera as Rosina in Il Barbiere di Siviglia; Houston Opera as Rossini's Isolier, and at Rossini Festival Pesaro, Italy, the Composer in Ariadne auf Naxos and Giovanna Seymour in Anna Bolena; European debut with Cologne Opera 1983, as Cherubino, later Massenet's Cendrillon; La Scala Milan as Zerlina in Don Giovanni; Vienna Staatsoper as Cherubino; Covent Garden debut 1985, as Rosina, returned as Giovanna Seymour 1988, and Dorabella in Così fan tutte 1989; Metropolitan Opera debut 1989, as

Cherubino; Monte Carlo 1988, as Adalgisa in Norma; sang Octavian at the Théâtre des Champs-Elysées, Paris 1989; Annius in La Clemenza di Tito at La Scala 1990 and Sesto in the Chicago premiere of Mozart's opera 1991; Salzburg Festival, Cherubino and Zerlina, Metropolitan Opera, Idamante 1991; In Les Contes d'Hoffmann as Nicklausse, Octavian in Der Rosenkavalier, Composer in Ariadne auf Naxos, Metropolitan Opera 1992–93; Geneviève in Pelléas et Mélisande at the Palais Garnier, Paris 1997; Roméo at the Opéra Bastille; Nicklausse at the Met 1998; season 2000–01 as Octavian and Mélisande at the Met, Adalgisa at Covent Garden and Mozart's Idamante at the Dresden Staatsoper. *Recordings include:* Anna Bolena with Sutherland and Bonynge and Bruckner Te Deum, Mozart Masses with King's College Choir, Barber of Seville (Rosina), Idomeneo (Idamante), Don Giovanni (Zerlina).

MENUHIN, Jeremy; American pianist; b. 2 Nov. 1951, San Francisco, Calif. *Education:* studied in Paris with Nadia Boulanger, Israel with Mindru Katz (piano), Vienna with Hans Swarowsky (conducting). *Career:* public performances from 1965; New York recital debut 1984; Berlin Philharmonic 1984; Dame Myra Hess series, Chicago 1985; regular recitals, Kennedy Center (Washington, DC), Berlin Philharmonie, Amsterdam Concertgebouw, La Salle Pleyel; US tours with Czech Philharmonic and Prague Chamber Orchestra 1989; guest appearances, San Francisco and Houston Symphonies; European orchestras include BBC, Royal and Amsterdam Philharmonics, Salzburg Mozarteum, Orchestre Nat. de France; season 1987–88 included Windsor Festival concert with English Chamber Orchestra; Beethoven's 1st Piano Concerto with Leningrad Philharmonic conducted by Yehudi Menuhin; 1989 European concert tour with Toulouse Chamber Orchestra; chamber music with cellists Colin Carr, Steven Isserlis, Marius May; recitals with sopranos Edith Mahis and Arleen Auger, Aldeburgh 1987; with Hallé Orchestra, Zürich Tonhalle Orchestra, Sinfonia Varsovia 1994; tour of Germany, Czech Repub. and Poland with Philharmonia Hungarica (Schumann, Bartók's 3rd Piano Concerto); Bath Festival with English Symphony Orchestra; Beethoven's 5th Piano Concerto with Orchestra of St John's Smith Square; tour of Russia and further concerts throughout Europe 1995; St Nazaire Festival, Wigmore Hall, and other festivals; season 1998–99 toured Germany, Lithuania, the Netherlands and France; solo recitals at Ubeda Festival, Spain and Ravello Festival (Italy); other performances include concerts in Brazil and Mexico and recitals in the Netherlands, Switzerland and UK and tours with Sinfonia Varsovia in Germany. *Recordings include:* works by Schubert, Mozart, Debussy, Beethoven; Bartók's two violin sonatas with father, Yehudi Menuhin; Dvořák Quartets and Quintet with Chilingirian Quartet; Schubert's Late Piano Works 1998. *Honours:* Grand Prix de Disque 1981. *Current Management:* c/o Upbeat Classical Management, PO Box 479, Uxbridge, UB8 2ZH, England. *Telephone:* (1895) 259441. *Fax:* (1895) 259341. *E-mail:* admin@upbeatclassical.co.uk. *Website:* www.upbeatclassical.co.uk; www.jeremymenuhin.com.

MENZEL, Peter; singer (tenor); b. 31 Jan. 1943, Dresden, Germany. *Education:* Dresden Muskihochschule. *Career:* sang with the Dresden Opera from 1968; Berlin Staatsoper from 1977, notably in the 1979 premiere of Leonce und Lena by Dessau; other roles have included Monostatos, Oronte in Alcina, Jacquino, Mime, Pang in Turandot, the Captain in Wozzeck, and Bardolph; many concert appearances, notably with the Thomas Choir Leipzig on tour to Switzerland, Italy and Japan.

MERCER, Alexandra; British singer (mezzo-soprano) and artists' manager; *Owner, APA Artists' Management;* b. (Alexandra Dawson), 12 May 1944, Gravesend, Kent, England; m. Philip Mercer 1965; twin d. *Education:* studied with Maestro Antonio and Lina Riccaboni Narducci in Milan, Royal Scottish Acad. of Music. *Career:* debut, Barga Festival 1970; has appeared in opera throughout UK and Europe, with companies such as English Bach Festival Trust, Kent Opera, Royal Opera House Covent Garden, Opera Rara, and Barber Inst.; roles include Poppea, Despina, Dorabella, Rosina, Hansel, Ascanius, Smeton, Isabella, Mrs Sedley, The Sorceress and Samson; festival appearances include Barga 1970, Edinburgh 1978, 1979, Bath 1981, Wexford 1984; regular appearances in concert, oratorio and recital; BBC soloist for Radio 2 and 3, BBC debut 1984; Founder and Owner APA Artists' Management, London 2005–. *Recordings:* Opera Rara, 100 Years of Italian Opera 1800–1910. *Honours:* Vaughan Williams Trust Award 1972, 1973. *Address:* APA Artists' Management, Studio 1, 79 Bedford Gardens, London, W8 7EG, England (office). *Telephone:* (20) 7794-7633 (office). *E-mail:* alexandra@mercer.uk.com (office). *Website:* www.apaartistsmanagement.com (office).

MERCER, Gregory; American singer (tenor); b. 1960. *Career:* opera appearances at the Metropolitan, New York, Chicago, Sarasota Opera and Dalls; Lawrenceville, NJ, 1988 as Ferrando in Così fan tutte; Monadnock Festival, New York, from 1987; Graz Opera, from 1992, notably as Raffaele in Stiffelio by Verdi, 1994; concert and broadcast appearances. *Recordings include:* Lord Byron by Virgil Thomson. *Current Management:* Thea Dispeker Inc., 59 East 54th Street, Suite 81, New York NY 10022, USA. *Telephone:* (212) 421-7676. *Fax:* (212) 935-3279. *E-mail:* info@dispeker.com. *Website:* www.dispeker.com.

MERCHANT, Jan; singer (mezzo-soprano); b. 1960, South Carolina, USA. *Education:* Metropolitan Opera Studio, Univ. of South Carolina. *Career:* opera engagements in Switzerland, Germany, The Netherlands and USA; 1989 with Hannover Opera, Venus in Offenbach's Orpheus in the Underworld; independent productions include Mephisto in Hervé's Le Petit Faust in Hamburg,

Fildama in Cimarosa's Matrimonio Segreto, Countess in Le nozze di Figaro, Maddelena in Rigoletto, Second Dame in Zauberflöte; concert soloist with Nord Deutsche Rundfunk in Hamburg, most notably Stabat Mater (Dvořák), Requiem (Mozart); Elijah in Maryland; Dir of Choral Music and mem. of vocal staff, Vienna Musical School 1995–98.

MERIGHI, Giorgio; Italian singer (tenor); b. 20 Feb. 1939, Ferrara. *Education:* Conservatorio Rossini di Pesaro. *Career:* made debut as Riccardo in Un Ballo in Maschera, Spoleto Festival 1962; made debut at La Scala as Pinkerton in Madama Butterfly 1963; many appearances on Italian stages, including the Verona Arena and at the Florence Festival; made debut at Metropolitan Opera as Manrico in Il Trovatore 1978; guest engagements in Berlin, Monte Carlo, Barcelona, Marseilles, Brussels, Geneva, London; repertoire includes Pollione in Norma, the Duke of Mantua, Maurizio in Adriana Lecouvreur, Luigi in Il Tabarro, Don José, Andrea Chénier, Ismaele in Nabucco, Gabriele Adorno in Simon Boccanegro, Loris in Fedora; Artistic Dir Teatro Pergolesi di Jesi 1992–94. *Honours:* Premio Illica 2004, Premio Casa Sonzogno 2004. *Website:* www.giorgiomerighi.it.

MERKA, Ivan; cellist and musicologist; b. 15 May 1926, Kosice, Czechoslovakia; m., one s. one d. *Education:* Masaryk Inst. of Music and Singing, Ostrava, Masaryk Univ., Brno, Janáček Acad. of Musical Arts, Brno. *Career:* Deputy Lead Cello, Radio Orchestra, Ostrava 1945–47; Lead Violoncello, Opera Orchestra of the Nat. Moravian-Silesian Theatre, Ostrava 1953–60; Lead Violoncello, Janáček Philharmonic Orchestra, Ostrava 1960–68; teacher of violoncello, Janáček Conservatory, Ostrava 1953–, Conservatory Dir 1990–92; Lecturer, Janáček Acad. of Musical Arts, Brno 1970–80, Asst Prof. 1992–; soloist in concerts, broadcasts; mem., Brno Quartet 1948–50, Silesia Piano Trio 1946–56, Ostrava String Quartet 1953–88, State Ensemble of Janáček Philharmonic Orchestra 1960–; mem. Beethoven Soc. of the Czech Republic, Leoš Janáček Foundation (mem. of bd of dirs). *Publications:* contrib. articles, studies, papers, TV scripts on music, annual reports; Violoncello: History, Literature, Personalities (monograph) 1995. *Honours:* Ostrava String Quartet Haydn Prize, Budapest 1959, Zdenka Podhajská Foundation Award 1997, Sr Prix 2000, European Union of the Arts Gustav Mahler Prize 2001.

MERLIN, Raphaël; French cellist, composer and pianist; b. 1982, Clermont-Ferrand. *Education:* Clermont-Ferrand Conservatory, Boulogne-Billancourt Conservatory, Paris Conservatory. *Career:* pianist, Wildflower Quartet 1997–2002; mem. Quatuor Ebène (chamber music ensemble) 2002–, joined BBC New Generation Artists Scheme 2006; performs as soloist with Tchaikovsky Conservatory Orchestra, Moscow. *Recordings include:* with Quatuor Ebène: Haydn: Quatuors à Cordes 2006, Bartók: Quatuors 1, 2, 3 2007, Ravel, Debussy and Fauré String Quartets (Echo Klassik Award for Recording of the Year 2009, Gramophone Award for Record of the Year 2009) 2008, Brahms: Piano Quintet No. 1 and String Quartet No. 1 2009, 'Fiction' (Echo Klassik Award 2011) 2010, Mozart: KV 138, KV 421, KV 465 2011, Mozart: Dissonances 2011, Fauré: Quintettes avec Piano, Opp. 89 & 115 2011, Felix & Fanny Mendelssohn (BBC Music Magazine Chamber Award 2014) 2013, Brazil 2014, Menahem Pressler: 90th Birthday Celebration Live in Paris 2014, Green: Mélodies françaises o Poems by Paul Verlaine 2015. *Honours:* First Prize, ARD Int. Competition, Munich 2004, Karl Klinger Foundation Prize, Fondation Groupe Banque Populaire Award, Belmont Prize for Contemporary Music, Fondation Forberg-Schneider 2005, Borletti-Buitoni Trust Award 2007. *Current Management:* c/o Linda Uschinski, Impresariat Simmenauer, Kurfürstendamm 211, 10719 Berlin, Germany. *Telephone:* (30) 414781717. *Fax:* (30) 414781713. *E-mail:* linda.uschinski@impresariat -simmenauer.de. *Website:* www.impresariat-simmenauer.de; www .quatuorebene.com.

MERRITT, Chris; American singer (tenor); b. 27 Sept. 1952, Oklahoma City. *Education:* Oklahoma City Univ., apprentice artist with Santa Fe Opera. *Career:* sang in Augsburg as Idomeneo, Rossini's Otello, Rodolfo and Julien in Louise; New York City Opera debut as Arturo in I Puritani 1981; appeared in Rossini's Tancredi at Carnegie Hall, Il Viaggio a Reims at the Vienna Staatsoper, Ermione in Naples and Maometto II at San Francisco Opera; Paris Opéra debut in Rossini's Moise 1983; sang Uberto in La Donna del Lago at Covent Garden; season 1985–86 in Il Viaggio a Reims at La Scala, as Rodrigo (La Donna del Lago) in Paris, Idreno in a concert performance of Semiramide at Covent Garden; Leukippos in Daphne at Carnegie Hall; Benvenuto Cellini, Maggio Musicale Florence 1986; Aeneas in Les Troyens in Amsterdam; Nemorino in L'Elisir d'amore at Orlando, Florida; opened 1988–89 season at La Scala in Guillaume Tell by Rossini; title role in Robert le Diable at Carnegie Hall; sang in I Puritani, Rome Opera 1990; Arnold in a new production of Guillaume Tell at Covent Garden 1990; Admète in Alceste, Chicago 1990–91; Benvenuto Cellini at Geneva 1992; season 1992–93 as Leicester in Rossini's Elisabetta at Naples, Arnold at Covent Garden and San Francisco, Rodrigo in La Donna del Lago at La Scala and Conte di Libenskof in Il Viaggio a Reims at Pesaro; season 1996–97 as Schoenberg's Aron in Amsterdam and Paris and premiere of Henze's Venus and Adonis at Munich; concert engagements in Verdi's Requiem, Haydn's Creation and the Choral Symphony in Israel; Rossini's Petite Messe Solennelle in Amsterdam; Benvenuto Cellini by Berlioz, Festival Hall, London under Valery Gergiev 1999; sang Lilaque in Henze's Boulevard Solitude at Covent Garden 2001. *Recordings:* Rossini's Stabat Mater, Ermione and Il Viaggio a Reims; Donizetti's Emilia di Liverpool; I Puritani; Faust, conducted by Michel Plasson. *Address:* Wexstrasse 26, 20355 Hamburg, Germany.

MERTENS, Klaus, DipMus; German singer (bass-baritone); b. 25 March 1949, Kleve; m. Ingrid Mertens 1986, one s. three d. *Career:* numerous radio recordings and television productions; oratorio work and song recitals 1976–; sang the title role in Handel's Riccardo Primo at Magdeburg 1996; mem. Bach-Gesellschaft. *Recordings include:* Renaissance to 20th-century composers, including Bach complete recordings of all Cantatas, St Matthew Passion, St John Passion and all other major vocal works. *Current Management:* Ariën Arts & Music Management, Groot-Brittannieëlaan 27, 9000 Gent, Belgium. *Telephone:* (9) 330-39-90. *E-mail:* arien@telenet.be. *Website:* www.arien-artists.com.

MESHIBOVSKY, Alexander; violinist and academic; b. 15 April 1949, Kharkov, Russia. *Education:* Special School of Music for Gifted Children, Kharkov, Kharkov Conservatory, masterclasses with Boris Goldstein in Moscow. *Career:* Concertmaster, soloist, Moscow Chamber Orchestra, Russian Concert Agency 1971–72; soloist, Moscow Concert Agency 1972–74; Docent, Innsbruck Conservatory 1975–76; concerts in many European countries, USA; Assoc. Prof., East Tennessee State Univ. 1984–; Assoc. Prof., West Virginia Univ. 1988. *Compositions:* Paganini Variations, transcriptions of works by Debussy, Gershwin, Rachmaninov and many others. *Address:* 82-46 Lefferts Blvd, Apt 2D, Kew Gardens, NY 11415, USA.

MESPLÉ, Magdeleine (Mady); French singer (coloratura soprano) and teacher; b. 7 March 1931, Toulouse; d. of Pierre and Yvonne (née Sesquière) Mesplé; m. 1st René Guedon 1957; one d.; m. 2nd Raymond Dawalibi 1983 (divorced). *Education:* Institut Sainte-Elisabeth and Conservatoire Nat. de Musique, Toulouse. *Career:* made debut Liège, Belgium 1952; has appeared at major opera houses including Théâtre de la Monnaie, Brussels 1954, Opéra de Paris 1956–, Bolshoi Theatre, Moscow, USSR (now Russian Fed.), Palais Royal 1972, Metropolitan Opera, New York, USA 1973, Aix en Provence festival; teacher Conservatoire Nat. de Région de St-Maur-des-Fossés, Bordeaux, Lyon, Conservatoire Européen, Paris; has taught masterclasses in Toronto, Beijing, Shanghai, Taipei, Hong Kong, La Réunion etc.; mem. jury for numerous int. competitions including Washington, Bucharest, Paris, Cologne, Bilbao, Toronto; has had works written for her by Betsy Jolas, Maurice Ohana, Charles Chaynes. *Performances include:* Lakmé 1952, Lucia di Lammermoor 1960, Il était une fois l'opérette 1972, 1974, Les Dialogues des Carmélites, Guillaume Tell, Il Barbiere di Siviglia, Rigoletto, Les Contes d'Hoffman, Elégie pour jeunes amants, Cloches de Corneville, Vie Parisienne, Les Saltimbanques. *Recordings include:* Lakmé, Werther, Véronique, Valses de Vienne, Le maître de chapelle, Les Saltimbanques, Art de la coloratura (No 1 Airs français, No 2 Airs italiens). *TV includes:* Château des Carpathes. *Honours:* Officier de la Légion d'honneur, Grand Officier, Ordre nat. du Mérite; Commdr, Ordre des Arts et Lettres. *E-mail:* mady.mesple@orange.fr (home).

MESSINA, Patrick; French clarinettist; *Principal Clarinet, Orchestre National de France;* b. Nice. *Education:* Conservatoire Nat. de Musique, Paris, Cleveland Inst. of Music, USA. *Career:* New York recital debut at Weill Recital Hall, Carnegie Hall 1996; worked regularly with Metropolitan Opera Orchestra, New York under Levine, Rizzi, Slatkin and Gergiev 1996–2002; Prin. Clarinet, Orchestre Nat. de France 2003–, debut as soloist, conducted by Riccardo Muti, Théâtre des Champs-Elysées 2007; frequent soloist with many orchestras, performed with Houston Symphony Orchestra, Orchestre Nat. de France, Orchestre de Cannes, Philharmonie of the Nations, Orchestre Nat. d'Ile de France and Orchestre Nat. de Chambre de Toulouse, under conductors including Menuhin, Mercier, Frantz, Axelrod and van Zweden; as chamber musician, collaborated with Jean-Yves Thibaudet, Katia and Marielle Labèque, Daniel Hope, Matt Haimowitz, Jean-Marc Luisada, Gautier Capuçon, Elysée and Debussy String Quartets and Beaux Arts Trio; festivals include Les Flâneries Musicales de Reims, Pablo Casals in Prades, Yehudi Menuhin in Gstaad, Savannah Music Festival (USA) and Mecklenburg and Spoleto Festivals; Visiting Prof. of Clarinet, RAM, London. *Recordings include:* Mozart Clarinet Concerto 2012. *Current Management:* c/o Hilda Woolf Arts Management, 12 rue Christiani, 75018 Paris, France. *Telephone:* 3-86-33-36-21. *E-mail:* hildawoolf@orange.fr. *Website:* hildawoolfarts.com. *Address:* c/o Royal Academy of Music, Marylebone Road, London, NW1 5HT, England (office).

MESSITER, Malcolm, ARCM; oboist; b. 1 April 1944, Kingston, Surrey, England; m. Christine Messiter. *Education:* Paris Conservatoire, Royal Coll. of Music, London. *Career:* debut at Purcell Room, London 1971; Principal Oboe, BBC Concert Orchestra 1972–77; solo concert engagements; many appearances as chamber music player. *Honours:* RCM Oboe Prize 1970.

MESTER, Jorge, MA; Mexican conductor; *Music Director, Louisville Orchestra;* b. 10 April 1935, Mexico City, Mexico. *Education:* Juilliard School of Music, New York, Berkshire Music Center, Tanglewood with Leonard Bernstein, studied with Albert Wolff in The Netherlands. *Career:* teacher of conducting, Juilliard School of Music 1955–67; Music Dir, Louisville Orchestra 1967–79, 2006–, Aspen (Colorado) Music Festival 1970–91; Musical Adviser and Principal Conductor, Kansas City (Missouri) Philharmonic Orchestra 1971–74; Music Dir, Casals Festival, Puerto Rico 1979–86; teacher of conducting, conductor of school ensembles 1980–; Chair. of Conducting Dept, Juilliard School 1984–87; Music Dir, Pasadena (California) Symphony Orchestra 1984–2010; Artistic Dir Nat. Orchestra Assocn's New Orchestra Music Project 1988–92; Artistic Dir Orquesta Filarmonica de la Ciudad de Mexico 1998–2002; guest conductor in N America and overseas. *Recordings*

include: Dallapiccola Piccola musica notturna, Hindemith Concert Music for viola and Kammermusik No. 2, Bruch's 2nd Symphony, Penderecki de Natura Sonoris, Shostakovich Hamlet Music, Strauss's Six Songs Op 68, Milhaud Symphony No. 6, Martin Cello Concerto. *Honours:* Naumburg Award 1968, Ditson Conductor's Award, Columbia Univ. 1985. *Address:* Louisville Orchestra, 323 West Broadway, Suite 700, Louisville, KY 40202, USA (office). *Telephone:* (502) 587-8681 (office). *E-mail:* jmester@louisvilleorchestra.org (office). *Website:* www.louisvilleorchestra.org (office).

MESZOLY, Katalin; singer (contralto); b. 1950, Hungary. *Education:* studied with Prof. Jenö Sipos in Budapest, Prof. Paula Lindberg in Salzburg, Austria. *Career:* Budapest State Opera 1976–, from debut, leading contralto of Budapest Opera; performed title role of Carmen 129 times in Budapest and overseas; Azucena, Il Trovatore; Amneris, Aida; Ulrica, Un Ballo in Maschera; Preziosilla, La Forza del Destino, Marfa in Khovanshchina; Judith, Bluebeard's Castle, at La Scala 1981; sang Britten's Mrs Herring at Budapest 1988, Herodias in Salome 1989; Ulrica (Un Ballo in Maschera) for Opéra de Montréal 1990; sang in Kodály's Spinning Room at Budapest 1998; has appeared in oratorios, including Verdi's Requiem, Mozart's Requiem; song recitals; guest performer in numerous countries, including Italy, Austria, Germany, Spain, France, Mexico and Egypt. *Honours:* Liszt Prize.

METCALF, John Philip, MBE, BMus; British composer; *Artistic Director, Vale of Glamorgan Festival;* b. 13 Aug. 1946, Swansea, Wales; m. Gillian Alexander 1972 (divorced); two s. one d. *Education:* Univ. of Cardiff. *Career:* commissions from festivals of Cardiff, Swansea and North Wales, Bath and Cheltenham, England and Frankfurt, Germany, also from BBC, Gulbenkian Foundation, London Sinfonietta and Welsh Nat. Opera; opera, Kafka's Chimp, premiered at Banff 1996, Chair in Love, premiered in Swansea 2005, Montreal 2006; Artistic Dir, Vale of Glamorgan Festival 1969–; Assoc. Artistic Dir, then Artistic Dir, Music Theatre, Banff, Canada 1986–96; Artistic Dir, Swansea Festival 1996–2007. *Compositions:* opera/music theatre: PTOC 1973, The Journey 1979, The Crossing 1984, Tornrak 1986-1990, Kafka's Chimp 1992-1996, A Chair in Love 2002–05; for ensemble: Flute Quartet 1982 (revised 1995), Brass Quintet 1983, Dance from Kafka's Chimp 1994, Never Odd or Even 1995, Sky High Cloud Light 1995, Vanish in the Heavens Blue 1995, Pull Up If I Pull Up 1997, Light Music 1997; for solo instrument: Llyfr Lloffion y Delyn – Harp Scrapbook 1992, Inner Landscapes 1994, Endless Song 1999; chamber music: Piano Trio 1988, Rest in Reason, Move in Passion 1994, Paradise Haunts... 1995, Mountains Blue Like Sea 1996, Airstream 1997, Not the Stillness... 1998, Transports 2000, Mapping Wales 2000, Three Mobiles 2001/06, Unbroken Fragments 2001, Continuous Study 2002; for orchestra: Paradise Haunts... 1999, Passus 2000/05, Cello Symphony the singing...' 2002–04; for chamber orchestra: Dyad 1976, Marimba Concerto 1991, Dances from Forgotten Places 1999, Mapping Wales 2001, Three Mobiles 2001/06, Line Dance 2006; for voice and piano: Auden Songs 1973 (revised 1992), The Great Question Mark 1983, Five Poems by or About Wagner Caneuon y Gerddi – Songs of the Gardens 1999; for voice and orchestra: The Great Question Mark 1983, Morris Museum of the Air 1997, To Poems by Gwyneth Lewis in Time of Daffodils 2006; choral: Two Mediaeval Carols 1981 (revised 1992), Ave Maria 1978, Two Settings of Ceiriog 1998, Gardd Cymru – The Garden of Wales 1999, Agoriad – to words by Menna Elfyn 2000, Plainchants 2001. *Honours:* Gulbenkian Dance Fellow 1973, UK-USA Bicentennial Arts Fellow 1977–78, Univ. of Wales Creative Arts Fellow 1984, Fellowships, Univ. of Wales, Lampeter, Royal Welsh Coll. of Music and Drama, Univ. Coll., Cardiff. *Current Management:* c/o Deborah Keyser, 20 Orchard Street, Llandovery, SA20 0DG, Wales. *Telephone:* (1550) 721565. *E-mail:* deborah.keyser@virgin.net. *E-mail:* john@metcalf.demon.co.uk (office). *Website:* www.johnmetcalf.co.uk.

METCALFE, John; British violist; b. 1964, England. *Education:* Royal Northern College of Music with Simon Rowland-Jones, Guildhall School of Music, studied with Bruno Giuranna at Berlin Hochschule. *Career:* concerts, Europe, USA, Japan, also on Channel 4 and Canadian television; principal viola with the Kreisler String Orchestra; mem., Durutti Column, 1984–88; violist with Duke String Quartet from 1985; performances in the Wigmore Hall, Purcell Room, Conway Hall and throughout the UK; with Duke Quartet, tours with Rosas throughout Europe and to Brazil; South Bank series, 1991, with Mozart's early quartets; soundtrack for Ingmar Bergman documentary The Magic Lantern, Channel 4, 1988; BBC debut feature; features for French television, 1990–91, playing Mozart, Mendelssohn, Britten and Tippett; Brahms Clarinet Quintet for Dutch Radio with Janet Hilton; Live Music Now series with concerts for disadvantaged people; the Duke Quartet invites... at the Derngate, Northampton, 1991, with Duncan Prescott and Rohan O'Hara; resident quartet, Rydale Festival, 1991; residency, Trinity College, Oxford, tours to Scotland and Northern Ireland and concert at the QEH 1991; season 1993–94 with Duke Quartet at Casa Manilva Festival, Spain, and tour of the UK; founder Factory Classical label 1988. *Compositions:* arranger for Pretenders, Blur, Cranberries, Morrissey, Lloyd Cole; compositions for television; with Duke Quartet, composing music for Union Dance Co. *Recordings include:* Quartets by Tippett, Shostakovich and Britten (Third), music by Dvořák, Barber and Glass, three world premieres by Kevin Volans. *Honours:* Martin Musical Trust Award; South East Arts Scholarships. *Address:* 81b Sarsfield Road, London, SW12, England.

METTERS, Colin Raynor, ARCM; British conductor; b. 22 Jan. 1948, Plymouth, Devon, England; m. Susan Furlong 1980, two d. *Education:* Royal College of Music, studied with Vernon Handley and George Hurst, Liverpool

Seminar under Charles Groves, masterclasses with Nadia Boulanger. *Career:* Musical Dir, Ballet Rambert, 1972–74; Conductor, Sadler's Wells Royal Ballet, 1974–82; teacher of conducting, Canford Summer School of Music, 1973–83; Musical Dir, East Sussex Youth Orchestra, 1979–; guest conductor with London Schools Symphony Orchestra, British Youth Symphony Orchestra, National Centre for Orchestral Studies; freelance conductor, 1982–; Dir of Conducting, Royal Academy of Music, 1983–; conducted major British, provincial and BBC orchestras; conducted extensively abroad. *Honours:* Hon. RAM 1995. *Current Management:* Donald Scrimgeour Artists Agent, 49 Springcroft Avenue, London, N2 9JH, England. *Telephone:* (20) 8444-6248. *Fax:* (20) 8883-9751. *E-mail:* vwest@dircon.co.uk. *Website:* www.donaldscrimgeour.com.

METTRAUX, Laurent; Swiss composer; b. 27 May 1970, Fribourg. *Education:* St Michael's Coll., Conservatoire de Fribourg with Prof. René Oberson, studied composition with Prof. Eric Gaudibert, conducting with Prof. S.-L. Chen, Geneva, other studies in piano, violin, Ancient Music, Musicology, Music History. *Career:* first compositions aged 12; Symphonie pour orchestre de chambre first performed by Orchestre de Chambre de Lausanne, conductor Jesus Lopez-Cobos; first performance of Concerto for 15 solo strings under Tibor Varga at opening concert, Tibor Varga Festival 1994; first German performance of Organ Concerto, together with world premiere of the Choral Variations for choir and orchestra (commissioned by the Gewandhaus Orchestra Leipzig), conducted by Riccardo Chailly 2010; numerous comms; mem. Swiss Musicians' Asscn 1995–, mem. Bd 2007–. *Compositions include:* Symphonie pour orchestre de chambre (first prize and public prize Competition for Young Composers) 1993, Concerto for 15 solo strings 1994, Vers le Soleil Couchant (oratorio) 1995–96, Trio No. 2 for piano, violin and cello 1995–96, three Concertos for violin 1996, 1998, 1999, Elògio della Nòtte (after Michelangelo) for bass voice and piano 1997, Ombre for orchestra 1995–98, String Trio 1998, Crucifixion for mixed choir 1998, Le Cocyte for orchestra 1999, String Quartet (first performed by Talich Quartet) 1998–99, La Plus belle des Lumières for a cappella mixed choir 2000, Wind Quintet 2000, String Quintet 2001–02, Le Nom Caché (oratorio for the Nat. Swiss Exposition of 2002) 2001–02, Concerto for organ and orchestra (for inauguration of new great organ, Lausanne Cathedral) 2002–03, Complainte for solo violin (written at request of Shlomo Mintz as set piece for Int. Violin Competition of Sion) 2003, Double-Concerto for violin, pipa and orchestra 2002–05, Trio for clarinet, cello and piano 2003, Plus près de toi que tu ne l'es toi-même for vocal ensemble 2006, Emergences for violin and accordion 2006, Le Tombeau de Ravel for ensemble 2006, La Mort sur un Cheval Pâle for orchestra 2007, Quintet for clarinet and strings 2008, Stèles for piano 2008, Choral Variations on the Christmas Carol 'Vom Himmel hoch, da komm' ich her' for choir and orchestra 2008–09, Traces gravées dans le Sable for piano 2009, Offrande funèbre en hommage à Bach for ensemble 2010, Symphonie de chambre for 13 instruments 2012–13, Concerto for improvising trombonist and ensemble 2013, Recitatives on the gospel texts to complete the St Mark Passion by Bach for soloists, choir and baroque instrumental ensemble 2013–14, Quartet for flute and strings 2014–15. *Honours:* Donaueschinger Musiktage Prize 1998, UBS Kulturstiftung Award ad personam 2000, numerous other distinctions. *Address:* Route Principale 160, 1791 Courtaman, Switzerland (office). *E-mail:* laurent.mettraux@bluewin.ch (office). *Website:* www.laurentmettraux.com.

METZ, Catherine; violinist; b. 1965, USA. *Education:* studied in New York. *Career:* recitalist, Lincoln Center's Alice Tully Hall, 92nd Street 'Y' and appearances with major orchestras; chamber musician at the Santa Fe Festival, Spoleto Festival and Lockenhaus Kammermusikfest and the Int. Musicians' Seminar in Prussia Cove; co-founder, Orion Quartet; has given concerts at Washington, DC 's Kennedy Center, at Boston Gardner Museum and throughout the USA; Carnegie Hall recital 1991 and as part of the Centenial Celebration tribute; concerts as Turku Festival in Finland.

METZMACHER, Ingo; German conductor; b. 10 Nov. 1957, Hanover. *Education:* studied piano, theory and conducting in Hanover, Salzburg and Cologne. *Career:* joined Ensemble Modern contemporary music ensemble as pianist 1981, began conducting the ensemble 1985; apptd solo répétiteur at Frankfurt Opera 1985, made conducting debut at Frankfurt with The Marriage of Figaro 1987; apptd Music Dir, Musiktheater im Revier, Gelsenkirchen 1987; debut at Brussels Opera with Franz Schreker's Der Ferne Klang 1988; Prin. Guest Conductor, Bamberger Symphony Orchestra 1995–99; Gen. Music Dir, Hamburg State Opera, Hamburg Philharmonic Orchestra and Hamburg Music Festival 1997–2005; works conducted in Hamburg include Richard Strauss's Der Rosenkavalier, Verdi's Macbeth and Don Carlos, Wagner's Lohengrin, Von Weber's Der Freischütz, Debussy's Pelléas et Mélisande, Berg's Wozzeck and Lulu, Poulenc's Dialogue des Carmélites, Beethoven's Fidelio, Maderna's Hyperion, Nono's Al Gran Sole Carico d'Amore; tours with Hamburg Philharmonic include Lucerne Festival and BBC Proms; performances as guest conductor include opera houses throughout Germany, Vienna Philharmonic, with London Philharmonic, Berlin Philharmonic, Munich Philharmonic, Boston Symphony, Orchestre Nat. de France, Vienna Symphony, San Francisco Symphony, Los Angeles Symphony, Montréal Symphony, Russian Nat. Orchestra, Accad. Nazionale di Santa Cecilia, New Japan Philharmonic, St Petersburg Philharmonic, Dresden Philharmonic, Salzburg Festival; toured Europe with Gustav Mahler Jugendorchester 2004, 2005, 2009; Music Dir, Chief Conductor Netherlands Opera, Amsterdam 2005–08; works conducted in Amsterdam include Korngold's Die Tote Stadt, Henze's The Bassarids, Verdi's Simon Boccanegra, Janáček's The Cunning Little Vixen, Richard Strauss's Elektra, Mozart's Da Ponte Operas and Messiaen's Saint François d'Assise; Chief Conductor and Artistic Dir, Deutsches Symphonie-Orchester (DSO), Berlin 2007–10; thematic concert cycles during this time entitled From The German Soul, Breakthrough 1909 and Temptation; Casual Concerts moderated by himself; tours with DSO to Hamburg, Cologne, Bonn, Baden-Baden, Paris, Brussels, Edinburgh, London, Vienna, Rimini, Meran, Madrid, Zagreb, Riga, Vilnius, Warsaw, Kuala Lumpur, Hong Kong, Tokyo and Beijing; appearances at Salzburg Festival: Al gran sole carico d'amore 2009, world premiere of Wolfgang Rihm's opera fantasy Dionysos 2010, Prometeo 2011; highlights 2007–11: The Rake's Progress and Die tote Stadt for Royal Opera, Covent Garden, series of new productions for Zurich Opera House (Königskinder, Tristan und Isolde, Der ferne Klang, Tannhäuser, From the House of the Dead), The Rake's Progress for Berlin Staatsoper, Lady Macbeth of the Mtsensk District and Parsifal for Vienna Staatsoper; concerts with orchestras including Vienna Philharmonic in subscription concerts, Russian Nat. Orchestra, Bamberg Symphony Orchestra, Orchestre de Paris, Orchestra of the Accad. Nazionale di Santa Cecilia, Gustav Mahler Jugendorchester, Czech Philharmonic, New Japan Philharmonic, Staatskapelle Berlin, Vienna Symphony Orchestra, ORF Radio Symphony Orchestra, Vienna, Dresden Philharmonic and St Petersburg Philharmonic; season 2011–12 returns to Zurich Opera House for new productions of The Nose by Shostakovich and Palestrina by Pfitzner and Vienna State Opera for Weill's Rise and Fall of the City of Mahagonny; debut at Grand Théâtre de Genève in new production of Verdi's Macbeth directed by Christof Loy; revivals of his Salzburg productions of Nono's Al gran sole carico d'amore and Rihm's Dionysos scheduled at Berlin's Staatsoper; guest conductor, Deutsches Symphonie-Orchester Berlin, New Japan Philharmonic, Vienna Symphony Orchestra, Czech Philharmonic, Orchestre de Paris and Gustav Mahler Jugendorchester; season 2012–13 new production of Die Soldaten at Salzburg Festival, Il prigioniero and Suor Angelica at Teatro Real, Madrid, Das Rheingold at Grand Théâtre de Genève, Gawain at Salzburg Festival; concerts with Berlin Philharmonic, Czech Philharmonic, ORF Radio Symphony Orchestra, Vienna, New Japan Philharmonic, Munich Philharmonic, Orchestre de Paris, Radio Filharmonisch Orkest, Filarmonica della Scala, Vienna Symphony Orchestra, BBC Symphony Orchestra; season 2013–14 Die Walküre, Siegfried and Götterdämmerung at Grand Théâtre de Genève, Fierrabras at Salzburg Festival; concerts with New Japan Philharmonic, Bamberg Symphony Orchestra, Czech Philharmonic, Vienna Symphony Orchestra, Orchestre de Paris, New Japan Philharmonic; Luigi Nono Trilogy for Holland Festival 2014, Prometeo in Zurich. *Recordings:* A Portrait of Charles Ives (with Ensemble Modern) (Académie Charles Cros Grand Prix) 1992, Conlon Nancarrow, Studies (with Ensemble Modern) 1993, Hans Werner Henze, Requiem (with Ensemble Modern) 1994, A Tribute to Benny Goodman 1998, Henze, Symphony No. 9 (with Berlin PO) 1998, Britten, Serenade (with Bamberger SO) 1999, Karl Amadeus Hartmann Symphonies Nos 1–8 (with Bamberger SO) (Preis der Deutschen Schallplattenkritik) 2000, Who is Afraid of 20th Century Music? (with Hamburg Philharmonic) 2001–05, Pfizner, Von deutscher Seele, Messiaen, Eclairs sur l'Au-delà…, Messiaen, Saint François d'Assise (on DVD with Nederlandse Opera), Schubert recital (as pianist with Matthias Goerne). *Publications:* Keine Angst vor Neuen Tönen (Opernwelt Book of the Year) 2005, Vorhang Auf! Oper entdecken und erleben 2009. *Honours:* Echo Preis Conductor of the Year 1998, Opernwelt magazine Opera Conductor of the Year 1998, Opernwelt Opera House of the Year 2005, Opernwelt Conductor of the Year 2010. *Current Management:* c/o Christoph Boller, Ingo Metzmacher Office, Magnolienstrasse 3, 8008 Zurich, Switzerland. *Telephone:* (44) 4226683. *Fax:* (44) 4226673. *E-mail:* mail@ingometzmacher.com. *Website:* www.ingometzmacher.com.

MEUNIER, Lionel; French singer (bass) and conductor; *Artistic Director, Vox Luminis*; b. 12 May 1981, Clamecy. *Education:* Institut Supérieur de Musique, Namur, Belgium and vocal studies at Royal Conservatoire of The Hague, Netherlands with Rita Dams and Peter Kooij. *Career:* sang with ensembles including P. Herreweghe's Collegium Vocale Gent, T. Koopman's Amsterdam Baroque Choir, Namur Chamber Choir, Ex Tempore, and with soloist ensembles including J. Tubéry's I Favoriti de la Fenice and Capella Pratensis; Co-founder, mem. and Artistic Dir, early music ensemble Vox Luminis 2004–; performances at venues and festivals in Belgium, France, Germany, Netherlands, Portugal and Croatia; as soloist, performances included Schubert A Minor Mass, Bach St John Passion and cantatas, Haydn Stabat Mater and Nelson Mass, Kronung Mass, Mozart C Minor Mass. *Recordings include:* with Vox Luminis: vocal works by Domenico Scarlatti (Preis der Deutschen Schallplatten Kritik) 2007, Samuel Scheidt: Sacrae Cantiones 2010, Schütz Musicalische Exequien (Gramophone Award for Recording of the Year and Best Baroque Vocal Recording 2012, Int. Classical Music Award for Best Baroque Vocal Recording 2012) 2011, Purcell, Morley, Tomkins: English Royal Funeral Music 2013, Reinhard Keiser: Brockes-Passion 2014. *Current Management:* c/o Lucy Rice, Hazard Chase, 25 City Road, Cambridge, CB1 1DP, England. *Telephone:* (1223) 706029. *E-mail:* lucy.rice@hazardchase.co.uk. *Website:* www.hazardchase.co.uk. *Address:* Vox Luminis, Chaussée de Dinant 698, 5100 Wépion, Belgium (office). *Telephone:* (491) 366689 (office). *E-mail:* info@voxluminis.com (office). *Website:* voxluminis.com (office).

MEWES, Karsten; German singer (baritone); b. 18 March 1959, Pirna, Saxony. *Education:* Hanns Eisler Musikhochschule Berlin. *Career:* sang at Potsdam Opera and Komische Oper Berlin 1985–88; Berlin Staatsoper from

1985, notably in premiere of Graf Mirabeau by Siegfried Matthus 1989; Season 2000–01 as Iago at Halle and as Schtschelkalov in Boris Godunov at Komische Oper, Berlin; guest appearances in Dresden and elsewhere as Mozart's Count, Masetto, Guglielmo and Papageno, Lortzing's Zar, Silvio, Escamillo and Hans Scholl in Udo Zimmermann's Die weisse Rose; at Nat. Opera of Mannheim, sang Wotan and Wanderer in Wagner's Ring, Hans Sachs in Meistersinger, Macbeth in Verdi's Macbeth and Scarpia in Puccini's Tosca; concert repertoire includes works by Bach, Handel, Brahms and Fauré; lieder recitals in Germany, Finland, Norway, Czechoslovakia, Poland and France. Honours: Competition First Prize Winner and Gold Medal, Zwickau, Verona, Hamburg, Rio de Janeiro 1985–87. Current Management: c/o Konzert-Direktion Hans Adler, Auguste-Viktoria-Strasse 64, 14199 Berlin, Germany. Telephone: (30) 8959920. Fax: (30) 8263520. E-mail: info@musikadler.de. Website: www.musikadler.de.

MEYER, Dominique; French opera house director; General Director, Vienna Staatsoper; b. 8 Aug. 1955, Alsace. Education: studied econs and business. Career: began career at Ministry of Culture 1984–93; worked as an adviser in French Ministry of Culture under Jack Lang 1984–86; consultant and Pres. Admin. Council, Opéra de Paris 1986–89, Gen. Dir 1989–90; Dir Opéra de Lausanne 1994–99; Dir Théâtre des Champs-Elysées, Paris 1999–2010; Gen. Dir Vienna Staatsoper 2010–. Address: Wiener Staatsoper, Opernring 2, Vienna 1010, Austria (office). Telephone: (1) 51444-2303 (office). Website: www.staatsoper.at (office).

MEYER, Edgar, BMus; American composer and double bassist; b. 24 Nov. 1960, Tulsa, Okla; s. of Edgar A. Meyer and Anna Mary Metzel; m. Cornelia (Connie) Heard 1988; one s. Education: Georgia Inst. of Tech., Indiana Univ. School of Music. Career: began playing bass aged five under tutelage of father; began composing pop songs and classical pieces as a child; studied with Stuart Stanley at univ.; formed bluegrass band Strength in Numbers, Nashville, Tenn. 1984; regular bass player, Santa Fe Chamber Music Festival 1985–93; appeared with concert artists Emanuel Ax (piano) and Yo-Yo Ma (cello); premiere of Concerto for Bass 1993; joined Chamber Music Soc., Lincoln Center, New York 1994; formed band Quintet for Bass and String Quartet, soloist debut performance 1995; premiere of Double Concerto for Bass and Cello 1995; premiere of Violin Concerto 2000; frequent collaborations with Chris Thile, Amy Dorfman, Bela Fleck, Mike Marshall; performed at Aspen, Caramoor and Marlboro Festivals; debuted with Boston Symphony Orchestra, Tanglewood, Mass 2000; Visiting Prof. of Double Bass, Curtis Inst. of Music, Visiting Prof., RAM, UK. Recordings include: albums Unfolding 1986, The Telluride Sessions (Strength in Numbers) 1989, Dreams of Flight 1987, Love of a Lifetime 1988, Appalachia Waltz (with Yo-Yo Ma and Mark O'Connor) 1996, Uncommon Ritual 1997, Short Trip Record 1999, Bach Unaccompanied Cello Suites Performed on a Double Bass 1999, Appalachian Journey (with Yo-Yo Ma and Mark O'Connor) (Grammy Award 2001) 2000, Perpetual Motion 2000, Edgar Meyer 2006, The Goat Rodeo Sessions (with Yo-Yo Ma, Chris Thile, Stuart Duncan) (Grammy Award for Best Folk Album 2012) 2011, Bass and Mandolin (with Chris Thile) (Grammy Award for Best Contemporary Instrumental Album 2015) 2014; collaborated with Katty Mattea on album Where Have You Been (Grammy Award, Country Music Award, Acad. of Country Music Asscn Award) 1990. Honours: winner, Zimmerman-Mingus Competition, Int. Soc. of Bassists 1981, Avery Fisher Prize 2000, Grammy Award for the Best Crossover Album 2001, MacArthur Award 2002. Current Management: c/o Dean Shultz IMG Artists, 7 West 54th Street, New York, NY 10019, USA. Telephone: (212) 994-3533. E-mail: dshultz@imgartists.com. Website: edgarmeyer.com.

MEYER, Felix, PhD; Swiss musicologist; Director, Paul Sacher Foundation; b. 24 May 1957, St Gallen; m. Rosmarie Anzenberger 1986; one s. one d. Education: Univ. of Zurich, studied violin in St Gallen, piano with Hans Steinbrecher in St Gallen, Werner Bärtschi in Zurich, Ian Lake in London. Career: Sec. Swiss Youth Music Competition 1984–85; Curator of Music Manuscripts, Paul Sacher Foundation, Basel 1986, duties including curator of concert series Klassizistische Moderne, Basel 1996, and curator of exhbn of music manuscripts at Pierpont Morgan Library, New York 1998; Dir Paul Sacher Foundation 1999–; mem. Swiss Musicological Soc., German Musicological Soc., American Musicological Soc. Publications: A Study of Charles Ives's Concord Sonata 1991, Quellenstudien II: Zwölf Komponisten des 20. Jahrhunderts (ed., contrib.) 1993, Klassizistische Moderne (ed., contrib.) 1996, Settling New Scores (ed., contrib.) 1998, Béla Bartók's Music for Strings (facsimile edn, ed.) 2000, Edgard Varèse: Composer, Sound Sculptor, Visionary (co-ed., contrib.) 2006, Elliott Carter: A Centennial Portrait in Letters and Documents (co-author) 2008; co-ed. and contrib. two facsimile edns of works by Igor Stravinsky; contrib. to journals, including Music Analysis, Archiv für Musikwissenschaft, Revista de musicología, Neue Zürcher Zeitung. Address: Paul Sacher Foundation, Auf Burg. Münsterplatz 4, 4051 Basel, Switzerland (office). Telephone: (61) 2696644 (office). E-mail: johanna.blask@unibas.ch (office). Website: www.paul-sacher-stiftung.ch (office).

MEYER, Kerstin, CBE; Swedish singer (mezzo-soprano) and rector emerita; b. 3 April 1928, Stockholm; m. Björn G. Bexelius 1974 (died 1997). Education: Royal Swedish Conservatory, Stockholm, Swedish University College of Opera, Accademia Chigiana, Italy, Mozarteum, Austria. Career: debut, Royal Opera, Stockholm 1952, as Azucena in Il Trovatore; orchestra appearances with the Hallé Orchestra, London Philharmonic, Berlin and Vienna Philharmonics, Suisse Romande, Santa Cecilia, Chicago, ABC, BBC, NZBC television; leading roles in most of the important houses and festivals in

Europe, North and South America, Far East, such as Royal Opera House Covent Garden, Welsh and Scottish Operas, Glyndebourne and Edinburgh Festivals, La Scala, Milan, La Fenice and Santa Cecilia, Italy, Vienna and Salzburg, Austria, Munich, Berlin, Cologne and Hamburg, Germany, Paris, Marseilles, France, Moscow, Tashkent, Tallinn, Riga, Russia, Metropolitan Opera House, San Francisco, Santa Fe, Tulsa, USA, Teatro Colón, Argentina, Mexico City, Tokyo, Hong Kong; sang in first British performances of operas by Henze and Einem at Glyndebourne and in the world premieres of operas by Goehr and Searle (Hamburg), Henze's The Bassarids at Salzburg 1966, and Ligeti's Le Grand Macabre at Stockholm 1978; President, Swedish University College of Opera 1984–94; Advisory Director, European Mozart Academy, Kraków and New York 1994–98; since retirement teaching vocal interpretation; giving Masterclasses at the Summer school of Music, Mozarteum, Salzburg; mem. Board Member, STIM; Assessor, HEFCE, London 1994–95. Recordings: Operas, recitals with von Karajan, Barbirolli, Solti, Hans Schmidt-Isserstedt and Sixten Ehrling. Honours: Swedish Vasa Order, Italian Order of Merit, German Cross of Honour, 1st Class; Royal Swedish Court Singer 1963, Swedish Litteris et Arbitus, Swedish Illis Quorum 1994. Address: Porsvägen 48, 16570 Hässelby, Sweden (office).

MEYER, Krzysztof; composer, music theorist and pianist; b. 11 Aug. 1943, Kraków, Poland; one s. one d. Education: High School of Music, Kraków and American Conservatory, Fontainebleau. Career: debut in Warsaw 1965; Prof., High School of Music, Kraków 1966–87, High School of Music, Cologne 1987–; Pres., Union of Polish Composers 1985–89. Compositions include: stage works: Cyberiada (opera) 1986, The Gamblers (completion of Shostakovich's opera) 1983, The Maple Brothers (children's opera) 1990; orchestral: four Symphonies, Hommage à Johannes Brahms, Musica Incrostate, Concertos for piano, violin, violoncello, two for oboe, trumpet, saxophone, two for flute, Double concerto for harp and cello, Symphony in Mozartean Style, Caro Luigi for four cellos and orchestra; for choir and orchestra: Epitaphium Stanislaw Wiechowicz in memoriam (Symphony No. 2), Symphonie d'Orphée (Symphony No. 3), Farewell Music for orchestra 1997, Lyric Triptych for tenor and chamber orchestra, Mass for choir and organ; chamber works: Clarinet Quintet, Piano Quintet, ten String Quartets 1963–94, Piano Trio, String Trio; for ensemble: Concerto Retro, Hommage à Nadia Boulanger, Capriccio, Canzona, Sonata for cello and piano; for piano: five Sonatas, 24 Preludes; solo sonatas for cello, cembalo, violin, flute, Fantasy for organ. Publications: Dimitri Shostakovich 1973, Shostakovich 1995; contrib. to various journals. Honours: Grand Prix Prince Pierre de Monaco 1970, Minister of Culture and Art Award, Poland 1973, 1976, Govt of Brazil medal 1975, Gottfried von Herder Preis, Vienna 1984, Union of Polish Composers Prize 1992, Jurzykowski Foundation award, New York 1993.

MEYER, Paul André; French clarinettist and conductor; Principal Conductor, Tokyo Kosei Wind Orchestra; b. 5 March 1965, Mulhouse. Education: Paris Conservatoire, Basle Musikhochschule. Career: debut with Orchestre Symphonique du Rhin 1978; concerts in New York 1984; formed association with Benny Goodman; engagements with the Orchestre National de France, BBC Symphony Orchestra, Royal Philharmonic, Tokyo Symphony Orchestra, Salzburg Mozarteum, Suisse Romade, Zürich Tonhalle and ABC Australia; modern repertory includes works by Boulez (Domains), Gould and Henze; premiere of Concerto by Gerd Kuhr at the Sinfonia Varsovia 1994; premiered Penderecki's arrangement of Viola Concerto 1996, and the Concerto by Berio, with the Concertgebouw Orchestra 1997; tour of the USA with Yo-Yo Ma, Emmanuel Ax and Pamela Frank, playing Brahms and Schoenberg 1995; further partnerships with Eric Le Sage, Barbara Hendricks, Gidon Kremer, Maria João Pires, Jean-Pierre Rampal, Rostropovich, Heinrich Schiff and Isaac Stern; quintet with the Carmina, Cleveland, Emerson and Takacs String Quartets; concerts as conductor with the Seoul Philharmonic, Copenhagen Philharmonic, Ensemble Orchestral de Paris, Orchestre Philharmonique de Nice, Orchestre Philharmonique de Strasbourg, Munich Chamber Orchestra, Stuttgart Chamber Orchestra, English Chamber Orchestra, Scottish Chamber Orchestra, Geneva Chamber Orchestra, Orchestra Sinfonica di Milano G.Verdi, Orchestra di Padova e del Veneto, Sinfonia Varsovia, Belgrade Philharmonic, Bilbao Symphony, Taipei Symphony Orchestra, Prague Chamber Orchestra, Archi Italiana, Orchestre Philharmonique de Radio France. Recordings include: Concertos by Mozart, Copland and Busoni, with the English CO; Weber and Fuchs wth the Carmina Quartet; Mendelssohn and Reinecke, with Eric Le Sage. Honours: Officier des Arts et des Lettres; Winner French Young Artists Competition 1982, US Young Artists Competition 1984. Current Management: c/o Romain Blondel, Solea Artists Management, 56 rue des Trois Frères, 75018 Paris, France. Telephone: 1-42-36-45-33. Fax: 1-42-36-45-33. E-mail: rb@solea-management.com. Website: www.solea-management.com. E-mail: mail@paulmeyer.fr (office). Website: www.paulmeyer.fr.

MEYER, Sabine; German clarinettist; b. Crailsheim; d. of Karl Meyer; m. Reiner Wehle. Education: studied with Otto Hermann in Stuttgart and Hans Deinzer in Hanover. Career: embarked on career as an orchestral musician with Bavarian Radio Symphony Orchestra; engaged as solo clarinettist by Berlin Philharmonic, abandoned this to concentrate on solo career; numerous concerts and broadcast engagements in Europe as well as Brazil, Israel, Canada, Africa, Australia, Japan and USA; guest performances with all the main orchestras in Germany and with Vienna Philharmonic, Chicago Symphony Orchestra, London Philharmonic Orchestra, NHK Symphony Orchestra, Orchestra of the Suisse Romande, Berlin Philharmonic Orchestra,

Broadcast Orchestras of Vienna, Basel, Warsaw, Prague and Budapest as well as numerous additional ensembles; chamber music collaborations with Heinrich Schiff, Gidon Kremer, Oleg Maisenberg, Leif Ove Andsnes, Fazil Say, Martin Helmchen, Juliane Banse, Hagen Quartet, Tokyo String and Modigliani Quartet; co-f., with husband Reiner Wehle and brother Wolfgang Meyer, Trio di Clarone 1983, repertoire includes some nearly forgotten compositions by Mozart and many contemporary works; trio has appeared with the jazz clarinet soloist Michael Riessler; other repertoire includes crossover project Bach 2000 (recorded by EMI) and 'Paris mecanique' featuring music from 1920s Paris; f. Bläserensemble Sabine Meyer to host leading wind players from around the world 1988, regular concerts in Germany and abroad with repertoire ranging from classic to avant-garde; prominent champion of contemporary music, including works by Jean Françaix, Edison Denisov, Harald Genzmer, Toshio Hosokawa, Niccolo Castiglioni, Manfred Trojahn, Aribert Reimann and others; performed with Wolfgang Meyer the world premiere of Concerto for two Clarinets by Peter Eötvös 2008; mem. Akad. der Künste Hamburg; Prof., Hochschule für Musik, Lübeck 1993–. *Recordings include:* pre-classical to contemporary compositions, all important solo concerti and chamber music pieces for clarinet, including Clarinet Concerti of Johann and Carl Stamitz (Echo Award), new recording of the Mozart Concerto with Berlin Philharmonic under Claudio Abbado (Echo Award), works of Weber, Mendelssohn and Baermann with the Academy of St Martin-in-the-Fields (Echo Award), Clarinet Concertos 2014. *Honours:* Chevalier des Arts et des Lettres 2010, Bundesverdienstkreuz 2013; Winner, ARD Competition at Munich, eight Echo Klassik Awards, Niedersachsen Prize and Brahms Prize, Brahms-Gesellschaft Schleswig-Holstein 2001, Praetorius Music Prize Niedersachsen 2007. *Current Management:* c/o Konzertdirektion Hans Ulrich Schmid, Postfach 3409, 30034 Hanover, Germany. *Telephone:* (511) 3660769. *Fax:* (511) 3660774. *E-mail:* erdmuthe .pirlich@kdschmid.de. *Website:* www.kdschmid.de; www.sabine-meyer.com.

MEYER-TOPSØE, Elisabeth, MA; Danish opera singer (soprano) and teacher; *Professor of Voice, University of Trondheim*; b. (Anna Elisabeth Meyer), 7 Sept. 1953, Copenhagen; d. of Anna Ingeborg Topsøe and Tine Elisabeth Topsøe; m. Vilhelm Topsøe; two d. *Education:* studied in Copenhagen with Else Brems, Vagn Thordal and Sten Høgel; in Sweden with Birgit Nilsson. *Career:* lyric dramatic soprano; debut at Augsburg 1989 as Oxana in Tchaikovsky's Cherevichki; sang the Trovatore Leonora and Arabella at Augsburg; Nuremburg Opera from 1990, as Wagner's Elisabeth and Senta; Weber's Euryanthe, also at Aix en Provence 1993; Copenhagen from 1992 as Ariadne, the Marschallin, Desdemona and Senta; Vienna Staatsoper debut 1995 as Third Norn in Götterdämmerung; US debut 1996 in Strauss's Vier Letzte Lieder at Monterey; sang Ariadne at Maggio Musicale, Firenze, Vienna Staatsoper, Toulouse, Lausanne, Nancy, Modena and Ferrara; sang Senta in Vienna Staatsoper, Zürich, Mannheim, Stockholm, Savonlinna, Staatsoper, Berlin, Copenhagen, Verona, Wiesbaden Mai-Festspiele, Santiago de Compostella, Bonn, Malaga; sang Marschallin at the Teatro Colón, Buenos Aires, Trieste, Leipzig, Unter den Linden, Berlin and Sevilla; sang Ingeborg in Heise's Drot og Maske at Århus 2000; sang Elsa at Torino, Essen; sang Chrysothemis at Rome, Verona, Paris in concert; sang Senta in Rome 2004; Freischütz and Madama Butterfly in Århus; Ellen Orford in Peter Grimes, Trieste; Prof. of Voice, Univ. of Trondheim, Norway 2010–; master classes at Operschool, Stockholm, Sibelius Acad., Helsinki and in Denmark, Norway and Iceland; numerous lectures on singing, opera life, Birgit Nilsson's singing technique. *Recordings:* Strauss: Vier Letzte Lieder & Wagner: Wesendonk Lieder; Wagner-Strauss: Opera Arias; Danish Hymns; Rangström & Sibelius Songs; Danish Songs, Vols 1 & 2, Paul Hindemith: Das Marienleben (1948 version) 2007; To Our Lady 2009. *Honours:* Musikanmelderringens .Kunstnerpris, Birgit Nilsson Prisen, Slott-Møller Prisen, Elisabeth Dons Prisen, Christina Nilsson Prisen, Noilly Prat Prisen, Tagea Brandts Rejselegat and others. *Address:* Rosenvangets Sideallé 3, 2100 Copenhagen, Denmark (home); Dronningens Gate 27, 7012 Trondheim, Norway (home). *Telephone:* 26-36-44-41 (Copenhagen) (office); 91-38-47-14 (Trondheim) (office). *E-mail:* meyertop@youmail.dk (office); elisabeth.meyer-topsoe@ntnu.no (office). *Website:* www.elisabethmeyer-topsoe.dk.

MEYER-WOLFF, Frido, singer (bass-baritone); b. 22 April 1934, Potsdam, Germany. *Education:* studied in Berlin, Paris and Hamburg. *Career:* debut in Stralsund 1955, as Mozart's Figaro; appearances at Trier, Hamburg, Kassel, Kiel and the Deutsche Oper Berlin; Opéra Comique Paris 1963, in the premiere of Menotti's The Last Savage; Spoleto Festival 1964, as Ochs in Der Rosenkavalier; Aix en Provence Festival 1963, 1964, Marseilles from 1961, Brussels 1965, Monte Carlo 1967–94, Nice 1962–89, Lausanne 1987; direction of open-air theatre Jean Cocteau Cap d'All near Monaco, created and conducted a new chamber orchestra from 1989; other roles include parts in operas by Verdi, Wagner, Puccini, Strauss, Rossini, Smetana and Moussorgsky; sang in Wozzeck, Samson et Dalila, and Das Schloss by Reimann, first performance 1992 at Deutsche Oper Berlin; frequent concert appearances. *Honours:* Chevalier, Ordre des Arts et des Lettres 1985, Chevalier, Ordre des Palmes Academiques 1997. *Address:* c/o Boris Orlob, Jägerstr. 70, 10117 Berlin, Germany.

MEYERS, Anne Akiko; American violinist; b. 1970, San Diego, CA. *Education:* Indiana University with Josef Gingold, Colburn School of Performing Arts with Alice and Eleanor Schoenfeld, Juilliard School, New York with Dorothy DeLay and Masao Kawasaki. *Career:* debut as concerto soloist aged seven; later appeared with Los Angeles Philharmonic, New York Philharmonic conducted by Mehta and New York String Orchestra at Carnegie Hall; Far East engagements with Japan Philharmonic and NHK Symphony Orchestra; summer festivals include Aspen, Ravinia, Tanglewood, Hollywood Bowl; tours of St Louis Symphony with Leonard Slatkin, Australian Chamber Orchestra, Baltimore Symphony with David Zinman, Moscow Philharmonic; appeared on television with John Williams and Boston Pops; played with Minnesota Orchestra, Prague Symphony Orchestra, Hallé Orchestra, Orchestre de Paris and Jerusalem Symphony; appearances in Montreal Symphony, Boston Symphony, St Louis Symphony, Philadelphia Orchestra, Toronto Symphony, Swedish Radio Orchestra, Moscow Philharmonic, Belgian Radio Orchestra, Berlin Radio Symphony; currently Regent's Lecturer, UCLA. *Recordings include:* Barber and Bruch Concertos 1988, Fauré/Saint Saens Sonatas 1989, Bruch/Lalo Album 1992, Franck/Strauss Sonatas 1993, Mendelssohn and Romances 1993, Salût d'Amour 1994, French Orchestral Works 1995, Classical Ecstasy 1996, American Album 1996, Schubert 1997, Prokofiev Album 1997, UltraSound 1999, Violin for Relaxation 2000, Romantic Violin 2003, Smooth Classics 2003, East Meets West 2004, Kisetsu 2004, Angelfire 2006, OEK/Iwaki/AAM/Bruch 2006, American Classics 2006, Smile 2009. *Honours:* youngest to sign with Young Concert Artists, Avery Fisher Career Grant 1993. *Current Management:* c/o Charlotte Schroeder, Colbert Artists Management, 111 West 57th Street, New York, NY 10019, USA. *Telephone:* (212) 757-0782. *Fax:* (212) 541-5179. *E-mail:* schroeder@colbertartists.com. *Website:* www.colbertartists.com. *E-mail:* anne@anneakikomeyers.com (office). *Website:* www.anneakikomeyers.com.

MEYERSON, Janice, BA, MMus; American singer (mezzo-soprano); b. 12 March 1951, Omaha, Neb.; m. Raymond Scheindlin 1986. *Education:* Washington Univ., St Louis, Mo., New England Conservatory. *Career:* Fellowship, Berkshire Music Center, Tanglewood; Carmen (title role), New York City Opera and Théâtre Royal de la Monnaie, Brussels; Amneris in Aida, Teatro Colón, Buenos Aires and Frankfurt Opera; Santuzza in Cavalleria Rusticana, New York City Opera; Judith in Bluebeard's Castle, New York Philharmonic and Palacio de Bellas Artes, Mexico City; Brangaene in Tristan and Isolde, Leonard Bernstein conducting Philadelphia Orchestra; soloist, Mahler's 3rd Symphony, American Symphony, Carnegie Hall; soloist, Boston Symphony, Milwaukee Symphony, Minnesota Orchestra, New Orleans Symphony, Nat. Symphony, Dallas Symphony, Houston Grand Opera, Montreal Opera, Opera Co. of Philadelphia, Aspen Festival, Spoleto USA, Marlboro, Tanglewood, Wolf Trap, Schleswig-Holstein Music Festival, Deutsche Oper Berlin, Moscow State Symphony Orchestra; Teatro São Carlo, Lisbon and Vlaamse Opera, Antwerp; Adriano in Rienzi in London 1999; Kabanicha in Katia Kabanova in Dublin 2000; Herodias in Salome, Florida Grand Opera 2003, Barcelona Liceu 2004, Washington Nat. Opera 2007–08; Elektra, New York Philharmonic 2008–09, San Diego Opera 2009; Lyric Opera of Chicago 2009–10. *Recordings include:* For the Night to Wear (with Boston Musica Viva) 1994. *Honours:* grants from Sullivan Foundation and Martha Baird Rockefeller Fund. *Address:* 420 Riverside Drive, Apt GC, New York, NY 10025, USA. *E-mail:* janicemeyerson@gmail.com. *Website:* www .janicemeyerson.com.

MEYFARTH, Jutta; singer (soprano); b. 1933, Germany. *Career:* sang at Basle 1955; Aachen Opera 1956–59; mem., Frankfurt Opera from 1959; La Scala Milan debut 1960; Maggio Musicale Florence 1961, as Elsa in Lohengrin; Bayreuth Festival 1962–64, as Freia, Gutrune and Sieglinde; Munich Opera 1965, as Donna Anna; guest appearances in Buenos Aires, Brussels, Rome, London, Lisbon, Athens, Lyon and Antwerp; other roles included Wagner's Isolde, The Empress in Die Frau ohne Schatten, Aida, and Martha in Tiefland.

MEYLAN, Raymond, DLitt; Swiss flautist and musicologist; b. 22 Sept. 1924, Geneva; m. Anne-Marie Bersot 1959; one d. *Education:* Univ. of Lausanne, Univ. of Zürich, Conservatoire of Geneva, studied in Paris with Marcel Moyse, Accademia Chigiana, Siena, with Ruggero Gerlin. *Career:* debut in 1944; solo flute, Orchestra Alessandro Scarlatti, Naples 1951–54; Pomeriggi Musicali, Milan 1954–58; Orchestra of Radio Beromünster, Zürich 1958–70; Basler Orchester Gesellschaft, Basel 1971–89; Lecturer in Musicology, Univ. of Zürich 1969–77; Conductor, Orchestre Académique de Zürich 1969–77, Orchesterverein Liestal 1977–91; studies in archaeology of flutes 1972–; mem. Swiss Asscn of Musicians, Swiss Musicological Soc., French Soc. of Musicology. *Compositions:* Le Choix for voice, choir, flute, vibraphone and marimba 1979, Notre Dame de Lausanne for wind 1986, Bourrasque for large orchestra in ampitheatre 1987, Cinq Miniatures for flute and guitar 1987, Assonances for scattered orchestra 1988. *Recordings:* Flute Concertos by Danzi, Widor and Reinecke; Salieri, in Virtuoso Oboe; Bernard Reichel, VDE Gallo; Beethoven, 10 themes and variations, op 107; Telemann, triple concerto, with Zagreber Solisten, A. Janigro, Amadeo and the Bach Guild. *Publications:* L'Énigme de la musique des basses danses du quinzième siècle 1969, Réparation de la roue de Cordier 1972, La Flûte 1974, Neues zum Musikaliennachlass von Hans Georg Nägeli 1996, studies on Cordier, Attaingnant, Mazzocchi, A. and D. Scarlatti, Sarri, Bach, Nardini, Fischer, Schwindl, Kozeluh, Bellini, Donizetti, Cimarosa, complete works of Theobald Böhm, Stuntz; contrib. to musical and scholarly journals, musical dictionaries. *Address:* Pumpwerkstrasse 3, 4142 Münchenstein, Switzerland (home). *Telephone:* 614115633 (home).

MEZÖ, László; Hungarian cellist; b. 1940. *Education:* Franz Liszt Acad., Budapest. *Career:* cellist, Bartók Quartet 1977–; performances in nearly every European country and tours of Australia, Canada, Japan, New Zealand and the USA; festival appearances at Adelaide, Ascona, Aix, Venice, Dubrovnik, Edinburgh, Helsinki, Lucerne, Menton, Prague, Vienna, Spoleto and Schwetzingen; tours of the UK, including concerts at Cheltenham, Dartington, Philharmonic Hall, Liverpool, RNCM, Manchester, Wigmore Hall, Sheldonian Theatre, Oxford, Harewood House and Birmingham; repertoire includes standard classics and Hungarian works by Bartók, Durkö, Bozay, Kadosa, Soproni, Farkas, Szabo and Lang. *Recordings include:* complete quartets of Mozart, Beethoven and Brahms, major works of Haydn and Schubert, complete quartets of Bartók. *Honours:* with mems of Bartók Quartet, Kossuth Prize, Outstanding Artists of the Hungarian People's Republic 1981; UNESCO/IMC Prize 1981. *Address:* Nippon Artists Management Inc., 5-4-10-3F Koishikawa Bunkyo, Tokyo 112-0002, Japan.

MICHAEL, Audrey; singer (soprano); b. 11 Nov. 1949, Geneva, Switzerland; d. of Jean-Marie Auberson. *Education:* studied with father, and in Milan and Hamburg. *Career:* sang with the Hamburg Staatsoper 1976–81, Deutsche Oper am Rhein Düsseldorf 1981–86; guest appearances throughout Europe; roles have included Gluck's Amor in Orpheus, Ilia (Idomeneo), Mozart's Pamina, Susanna, Countess and Papagena, Elvira (L'Italiana in Algeri), Adina, Lauretta, Zdenka, Mélisande and Elisabeth Zimmer in Elegy for Young Lovers by Henze; sang at Hamburg in the premieres of Kommen und gehen by Heinz Holliger 1978, William Ratcliff by Ostendorf 1982 and Jakob Lenz by Wolfgang Rihm 1979; Théâtre Municipal Lausanne 1991 as Sextus in Gluck's La Clemenza di Tito; sang Sextus at the Théâtre des Champs Elysées, Paris 1996; concert engagements in the Baroque and modern repertory throughout Switzerland and in Berlin, Stuttgart, Paris, Lisbon and Buenos Aires. *Recordings include:* Monteverdi Orfeo, L'Enfant et les Sortilèges, Masses by Schubert and Beethoven, Rigoletto, Luisa Miller and Parsifal, Monteverdi Ballo delle Ingrate and Vespers of 1610.

MICHAEL, Beth; singer (soprano); b. 1962, Gwent, Wales. *Education:* Welsh Coll. of Music and Drama, RAM, London. *Career:* debut as Pheadra in Cavalli's L'Egisto for Scottish Opera 1982; roles with Opera 80/English Touring Opera include Cenerentola, Carmen, Gretel, Frasquita, the Merry Widow and Lucia; further engagements as Manon Lescaut, Butterfly (Surrey Opera), Tosca (Regency Opera) and at Wexford, Bayreuth and London (ENO); appearances with the Royal Opera, Covent Garden, in Death in Venice, The Cunning Little Vixen, Turandot, Der Rosenkavalier, La Traviata and Die Walküre; Countess Ceprano in Rigoletto 1997; many concert appearances and engagements on radio and television.

MICHAEL, Nadja; German singer (soprano); b. 1969, Leipzig. *Education:* studied in Stuttgart and in the USA with Carlos Montane. *Career:* debut, Ludiwgsburg Festival 1993, as Third Lady in Die Zauberflöte; appearances at Wiesbaden as Amastris (Xerxes) and Eustazio (Rinaldo), Dulcinée in Don Quixote at St Gallen and Tchaikovsky's Olga at Glyndebourne; Strauss's Dryad at the Dresden Semper Oper and Handel at the Berlin Staatsoper; season 1997–98 as Varvara in Katya Kabanova at Covent Garden (debut), Ottavia in Poppea at Munich, Wagner's Venus at Naples and Mahler's Rückert Lieder and Second Symphony; further concerts include Elijah, Messiah, Berio's Folk Songs and Mahler's Das Lied von der Erde (Swiss television); appearances in Carmen in Italy and at St Gallen and Tokyo; sang in Tippett's Midsummer Marriage at Munich 1998; sang Hansel in Hansel and Gretel at the Staatsoper in Berlin; engaged to sing Charlotte in Werther and Carmen at the New Nat. Theatre in Tokyo and at La Monnaie in Brussels; Delilah in Samson and Delilah in Venice; Venus in Tannhäuser in Toulouse and at the Bavarian Staatsoper, Munich 2000; season 2000–01 as Carmen in Vienna, Naples and Berlin (Deutsche Oper), Eboli in Don Carlos at Munich and Amneris in Verona. *Current Management:* c/o Elizabeth Gottmann, Arts und Promotion GmbH, Düsseldorfer Street 40A, 65760, Eschborn-Frankfurt, Germany. *Telephone:* 6196768520 (office). *Fax:* 61967685220 (office). *E-mail:* gottmann@artsundpromotion.de (office). *Website:* www.nadja-michael.de.

MICHAELS-MOORE, Anthony, BA; British singer (baritone); b. (Anthony Michael Frederick Moore), 8 April 1957, Grays, Essex, England; s. of John Frederick Moore and Isabel Shephard; m. 1st Ewa Bozena Migocki 1980; one d.; m. 2nd Emily Doyle Schluter 2010. *Education:* Gravesend School for Boys, Univ. of Newcastle, Royal Scottish Acad. of Music and Drama, Fenham Teacher Training Coll. *Career:* Prin. Baritone, Royal Opera House, Covent Garden 1987–97; roles in all British opera cos; debut La Scala, Milan (Licinius in La Vestale) 1993, Paris Bastille (Sharpless in Madama Butterfly) 1995, New York Metropolitan Opera (Marcello in La Bohème) 1996, Teatro Colón Buenos Aires (Andrea Chénier) 1996, Vienna Staatsoper (Lescaut in Manon) 1997, San Francisco Opera (Eugene Onegin) 1997, Santa Fe Opera (title role in Simon Boccanegra) 2004, Paris Théâtre des Champs-Elysées (title role in Falstaff) 2010, Opéra de Montréal (title role in Rigoletto) 2010, Opernhaus Zurich (title role in Falstaff) 2011, Seoul, Korea (Scarpia in Tosca) 2012, Oper Köln (Scarpia in Tosca) 2012; specialises in 19th-century baritone repertoire and English song. *Television appearances include:* BBC Proms (Beethoven's Missa Solemnis, Mahler's Symphony No. 8), Carmina Burana recorded at La Scala, Milan 1996. *Recordings include:* Carmina Burana, Lucia di Lammermoor, La Vestale, La Favorite, Falstaff and Il Tabarro, Aroldo. *Radio:* regular BBC Radio 3 broadcasts, Verdi operas from Royal Opera House, Met Opera relays from New York. *Honours:* winner, Luciano Pavarotti/Opera Co. of Philadelphia Prize 1985, Royal Philharmonic Soc. Award Winner 1997. *Current Management:* c/o Julia Maynard, Intermusica Artists Management Ltd, 36 Graham Street, Crystal Wharf, London, N1 8GJ, England. *Telephone:*

(20) 7608-9902. *E-mail:* jmaynard@intermusica.co.uk. *Website:* www.intermusica.co.uk/michaels-moore; www.anthonymichaelsmoore.com.

MICHAILIDIS, Myron, LLB; Greek conductor; *Artistic Director, Thessaloniki State Symphony Orchestra;* b. Heraklion, Crete. *Education:* Music Acad., Berlin, Univ. of Athens. *Career:* Perm. Conductor, Opera of Eastern Saxonia, Germany 1999–2004; regular collaborator with Greek Nat. Opera 2001–; Artistic Dir Thessaloniki State Symphony Orchestra 2004–; guest conductor with many other orchestras in Greece and internationally including Berlin Symphony Orchestra, Rome Symphonic Orchestra, Slovak Philharmonic Orchestra, George Enescu Philharmonic Orchestra, Prague Radio Symphony Orchestra, Jerusalem Symphony Orchestra, Mexico State Orchestra; collaborations with many solo artists including Paul Badura-Skoda, Salvatore Accardo, Aldo Ciccolini, Cyprien Katsaris, Lars Vogt, Shlomo Mintz, Misha Maisky, Martino Tirimo, June Anderson, Cheryl Studer, Fazil Say. *Recordings:* albums: with Thessaloniki State Symphony Orchestra: Impressions for Saxophone and Orchestra (also with Theodore Kerkezos) (Pizzicato Classics Supersonic Award, Luxembourg 2007) 2006; Pizzetti, Concerto dell'estate 2009. *Current Management:* IUMA Management Worldwide, Via Montecassiano 157, A/7, 00156 Rome, Italy. *Telephone:* (6) 04508732. *Fax:* (6) 04115308. *E-mail:* info@iumamanagement.com. *Website:* www.iumamanagement.com. *Address:* Thessaloniki State Symphony Orchestra, Kolokotroni 21, Thessaloniki, 56430, Greece (office). *Telephone:* 2310589163 (office); 2310589165 (office). *Fax:* 2310604854 (office). *E-mail:* info@tsso.gr (office); myrmich@otenet.gr (office); myrmich@gmx.de (office). *Website:* www.tsso.gr (office); www.myronmichailidis.net.

MICHAILOV, Maxim; Russian singer (bass); b. 1961, Moscow. *Education:* Gnessin Conservatory, Moscow. *Career:* sang with the Bolshoi company, Moscow from 1987 as Sarastro, Ivan Khovansky in Khovanshchina, Tsar Dodon in The Golden Cockerel and Zaccaria in Nabucco; Edinburgh Festival 1991 on tour with the Bolshoi in Eugene Onegin and Rimsky's Christmas Eve; guest appearances in opera and concert throughout Russia; Sang Sarastro at Schönbrunn, Vienna, 1996.

MICHALOWSKA, Krystyna; singer (mezzo-soprano); b. 13 July 1946, Vilnius, Poland. *Education:* studied in Gdansk. *Career:* debut in Bydgoszcz 1970, as Azucena; engagements in Szczecin, Poznań and Gdansk; guest appearances in Germany, Bulgaria, Romania, Russia and Czechoslovakia. Appearances at Bielfeld and elsewhere in Germany from 1980, as Leonora in La Favorita, Carmen, Eboli, Lady Macbeth, Ulrica, Fides, Rosina, Konchakovna, Olga and Larina in Eugene Onegin, Dalila, Laura in La Gioconda, Sara in Roberto Devereux and the Nurse in Die Frau ohne Schatten; Bielefeld 1991, in Yerma by Villa-Lobos, as Ortrud and in the premiere of Katharin Blum by Tilo Medek; frequent concert appearances. *Address:* c/o Stadtisches Buhnen, Brunnenstrasse 3, 4800 Bielefeld 1, Germany.

MICHELI, Lorenzo; Italian classical guitarist and theorbist; *Guitar Professor, Hochschule of the Conservatorio della Svizzera Italiana;* b. 13 June 1975, Milan; m. Giulia Ichino 2002. *Education:* Univ. of Milan, Conservatory of Trieste, Musik Akad. der Stadt Basel, studied with Paola Coppi in Milan, F. Zigante in Lausanne and O. Ghiglia in Basel. *Career:* has played more than 600 concerts all over Europe, in hundreds of US and Canadian cities, in Africa, Asia and Latin America; has performed world-wide in duo with Matteo Mela under the name SoloDuo in venues including New York's Carnegie Hall, Seoul's Sejong Hall, Kiev's Hall of Columns, Moscow's Tchaikovsky Hall and Vienna's Konzerthaus; Guitar Prof., Hochschule of the Conservatorio della Svizzera Italiana, Lugano; Dir SoloDuo Collection for Canadian publr Editions d'OZ. *Recordings:* 20 CDs of classical, modern and Baroque music. *Publications:* Mauro Giuliani's Guitar Technique and Early Nineteenth-Century Pedagogy (essay, Guitar Forum II) 2004, Miguel Llobet, a cura di Lorenzo Micheli (book) 2004; articles in musical journals; some 20 sheet music publications of works by Castelnuovo-Tedesco, Rebay, Scarlatti, Beethoven, Mozart, Couperin. *Honours:* First Prize, Alessandria Competition 1997, First Prize, Guitar Foundation of America Competition 1999. *E-mail:* lor.micheli@gmail.com. *Website:* www.soloduo.it; www.lorenzomicheli.com.

MICHELS, Maria; singer (soprano); b. 1931, Germany. *Career:* sang at the Städtische Oper Berlin from 1955 and appeared further in opera at Kiel, Mannheim and Frankfurt; Essen 1963–66, Munich Staatsoper 1966–69, then the Hanover Opera; roles have included Cherubini's Médée, the Queen of Night, Strauss's Sophie and Zerbinetta, Lulu, Lucia di Lammermoor, Musetta and Olympia; guest appearances at the Vienna and Stuttgart State Operas, Florence and Brussels (in Arabella), Paris Opéra and Barcelona (as Lulu) 1969).

MICHIELS, Jan Prosper; Belgian pianist; *Professor of Piano, Koninklijk Conservatorium, Brussels;* b. 10 Oct. 1966, Izegem; m. Inge Spinette 1991. *Education:* Koninklijk Conservatorium, Brussels, Hochschule der Künste, Berlin with Hans Leygraf. *Career:* Prof. of Piano, Koninklijk Conservatorium, Brussels; worked with conductors as Peter Eötvös, Hans Zender, Serge Baudo, Lothar Zagrosek. *Recordings:* Several CDs with works of Brahms, Beethoven, Mendelssohn, Debussy, Ligeti, Huybrechts, Poulenc, Weber, Benjamin, Bartók and Liszt, Ligeti: Etudes I–XIV, Brahms, op 116–119, Debussy: Préludes, Images; Schönberg, Berg, Webern: Complete piano music. *Honours:* Prizewinner, several competitions including Queen Elizabeth Competition, Brussels 1991. *Address:* Achterstraat 22B, 9310 Meldert (Aalst), Belgium (home). *E-mail:* janinge@scarlet.be (home). *Website:* www.michielsjan.be.

MICHNIEWSKI, Wojciech; conductor and composer; b. 4 April 1947, Łódź, Poland. *Education:* Warsaw Academy of Music. *Career:* Assistant Conductor 1973–76, Conductor 1976–79, Warsaw National Philharmonic Orchestra; Artistic Director, The Grand Opera Theatre, Łódź, 1979–81; Musical Director, Modern Stage, Warsaw Chamber Opera, 1979–83; Principal Guest Conductor, Polish Chamber Orchestra and Sinfonia Varsovia, 1984–; Conductor, concerts in most European countries, South America, Asia; appeared West Berlin Philharmonic Hall, La Scala, Milan, Teatro Colón in Buenos Aires; participant in numerous international festivals, including Steyrischer Herbst, Graz, Austria; International May Festival, Barcelona, Spain; Recontres Musicales, Metz, France; International May Festival, Wiesbaden, Germany; Bemus Festival, Belgrade, Yugoslavia; Dimitria Festival, Thessaloniki, Greece; Warsaw Autumn Festival; Wratisalvia Cantans Music Festival; International Biennale, East Berlin; Polish Chamber Orchestra and Sinfonia Varsovia, 1984–86; General and Artistic Director, Poznań Philharmonic Orchestra, 1987–. *Address:* ul Braci Zauskich 3/77, 01 773 Warsaw, Poland.

MICHNO, Alexander; double bass player; b. 29 Nov. 1947, Moscow, Russia; m. Elena Stoliarenko 1991, two d. *Education:* Gnessin School of Music, Moscow. *Career:* debut in Moscow 1969; teacher, Gnessin Coll. of Music 1966–, Gnessin Inst. of Music (Acad. of Music 1991–) 1977–; bassist in Moscow Philharmonic Symphonic Orchestra under K. Kondrashin 1973–80; Co-Principal Bassist, State Acad. Symphony Orchestra under E. Svetlanov 1980–94; Principal Double Bass, Asturias Symphony Orchestra, Spain 1994–; performed as soloist on Moscow radio and television, giving many recitals and concerts with symphony and chamber orchestras and appearing at Int. Bass Week, Michaelstein 1996–99, Bass Festival 1998 in Reading, England, and Dresden, Germany 1999; served on jury for bass competitions in USSR 1980, 1984, Russia 1988, Kishinev (as jury chair.) 1989, Munich 1991, Kromeriz 1997; has given courses in Spain and Germany; mem. British Double Bass Soc. *Composition:* Study for double bass (ed.) 1983, 1998. *Recordings include:* Bottesini: Grand Duo for violin and double bass 1975, Ivanov: Concerto in the Romantic Style 1977, Respighi: Concerto a Cinque 1988, Eccles, Bottesini, Glier and others (with Galina Schastnaja, piano) 1997. *Publications include:* Development of Playing Skills 1988, History of the Art of Playing the Double Bass 1988, Musical Heritage of G. Bottesini 1989, Giovanni Bottesini 1997; contrib. 'Italian Influences in St Petersburg', in The BIBF Journal 1999. *Honours:* first prize Int. Markneukirchen Double Bass Competition 1975.

MICKELTHWATE, Alexander; German conductor; *Music Director, Winnipeg Symphony Orchestra*; b. 2 June 1970, Frankfurt; m. Abigail Camp; two s. *Education:* Hochschule für Musik, Karlsruhe, Peabody Inst. of Music, USA. *Career:* Asst Conductor, Atlanta Symphony Orchestra 2003–04; Assoc. Conductor, Los Angeles Philharmonic Orchestra 2004–06; Music Dir, Winnipeg Symphony Orchestra 2006–; guest conductor, Nat. Arts Centre Orchestra, Ottawa, NDR Sinfonieorchester, Royal Scottish Nat. Orchestra, Nurnberg Symphony, Milwaukee Symphony, Rochester Philharmonic, Vancouver Symphony, Houston Symphony, Heidelberg Philharmonic, Edmonton Symphony, Orchestre Philharmonique de Monte Carlo, Stuttgart Radio Symphony Orchestra, Deutsche Kammerphilharmonie. *Current Management:* Opus 3 Artists, 470 Park Avenue South, Ninth Floor North, New York, NY 10016, USA. *Telephone:* (212) 584-7500. *E-mail:* info@opus3artists.com. *Website:* www.opus3artists.com. *Address:* Winnipeg Symphony Orchestra, 1020-555 Main Street, Winnipeg, MB R3B 1C3, Canada (office). *E-mail:* lmarks@wso.mb.ca (office). *Website:* www.wso.ca (office).

MIDDENWAY, Ralph, BA; Australian composer, writer and editor; b. 9 Sept. 1932, Sydney, NSW; m., three d. *Education:* Univ. of Sydney, NSW Conservatory. *Career:* music and drama teacher Tudor House School, Moss Vale 1958–64; theatre consultant, Sec., Warden Adelaide Univ. Union 1965–77; theatre consultant, Gen. Man. The Parks Community Centre 1977–82; mem. Faculty of Music, University of Adelaide 1977–82; music and opera critic 1970–86; freelance writer 1970–; editor 1982–; horticulturist 1989–; Founding Chair. Richard Wagner Soc. of S Australia 1988–2002; Pres. Town and Country Planning Asscn 1973–74; Vice-Pres. S Australian Flowergrowers Asscn 1999–2000, Pres. 2000–01; mem. Adelaide Univ. Union, Australian Music Centre, Australasian Performing Right Asscn, Soc. of Editors, Australian Arts Media Alliance, Richard Wagner Soc. of S Australia. *Compositions include:* Missa Omnibus Sanctis, for chorus 1960, Mosaics for 13 brass and two percussion 1970, The Child of Heaven, for chorus, brass sextet and two percussion 1971; Two arias for The Tempest, baritone and orchestra 1980, Stone River, for medium voice and 4 percussion 1984; Stream of Time, for bass clarinet and piano 1984; Sinfonia Concertante for brass quintet and orchestra 1985; Sonata Capricciosa, for piano 1986; Mosaics for orchestra and saxophone ensemble 1986; The Letters of Amalie Dietrich, 1 act opera 1986; Barossa, Singspiel in 2 acts 1988; Stone River, for mezzo-soprano and piano 1989, The Lamentations of Jeremiah, for chorus 1990; The Eye of Heaven, for baritone and string quartet 1991; East River, sonata for piano 1995, The Eye of Heaven, for chorus 2000, Sång Sångars, for 7 solo voices, flute, cello and organ 2002, music for Sure and Certain Hope, epic theatre piece (with playwright Chris Tugwell) 2003, The Enchanted Island for soprano, baritone and orchestra 2005, The Tempest, opera in two acts 2006; commissions from Univ. of Adelaide Foundation and Adelaide Chamber Orchestra, among others. *Publications:* The Enigma of Parsifal, essays (co-ed. and contrib.) 2001, What is Love? (3 one-act plays for young actors) 2004; contrib. to journals, magazines and newspapers in Australia, Canada, UK and USA. *Address:* POB 753, Victor Harbor, S Australia 5211, Australia (home). *Telephone:* (8) 8558-8325 (home). *E-mail:* venteman@comstech.com (home). *Website:* www.comstech.com/~venteman/.

MIDORI, MSc; Japanese violinist; *Jascha Heifetz Chair in Violin, Thornton School of Music, University of Southern California*; b. (Midori Goto), 25 Oct. 1971, Osaka; d. of Setsu Goto. *Education:* Professional Children's School, Juilliard School of Music, New York Univ. *Career:* began violin studies with mother aged four; moved to USA 1982; debut with New York Philharmonic 1982; recording debut 1986 aged 14; now makes worldwide concert appearances; Founder and Pres. Midori and Friends (foundation) 1992–; mem. Faculty, Manhattan School of Music 2001–06; Jascha Heifetz Chair in Violin, Thornton School of Music, Univ. of Southern California 2006–, also Distinguished Prof. and Chair. Strings Dept. *Recordings include:* Paganini: Caprices, Op.1 1989, Bach & Vivaldi - Double & Violin Concertos 1990, Encore 1992, Tchaikovsky and Shostakovich: Violin Concertos 1999, Mendelssohn & Bruch: Violin Concertos 2003, Partitas for Solo Violin I-III 2011, J.S. Bach: Partitas & Sonatas for Violin Solo 2015, The Art Of Midori 2016. *Honours:* Dorothy B. Chandler Performing Arts Award, New York State Asian-American Heritage Month Award, Crystal Award (Japan), Suntory Award 1994, Kennedy Center Gold Medal in the Arts 2010, Award of Merit for Achievement in Performing Arts, Association of Performing Arts Presenters 2015. *Current Management:* c/o Intermusica Artists Management Ltd, Crystal Wharf, 36 Graham Street, London, N1 8GJ, England. *Website:* www.intermusica.co.uk/artists/violin-viola/midori/biography. *Address:* c/o Midori and Friends, 352 Seventh Avenue, Suite 301, New York, NY 10009, USA (office). *E-mail:* mgoto@usc.edu; violin@gotomidori.com (office). *Website:* www.midoriandfriends.org; www.gotomidori.com; music.usc.edu/midori-goto.

MIELDS, Dorothee; German singer (soprano); b. 1971, Gelsenkirchen. *Education:* studied at Hochschule für Künste Bremen with Elke Holzmann and in Stuttgart with Julia Hamari and Harry van der Kamp. *Career:* learned violin and piano as child; fmr teacher, Hochschule für Musik Franz Liszt, Weimar; specializes in baroque music, especially Bach, Monteverdi and Purcell, as well as Lieder and contemporary music; regular recital and opera performances in Germany and abroad, including numerous int. festivals, including Bachwoche Ansbach, Bach Festival of Köthen, Bachfest Leipzig, Halle and Göttingen Händel Festivals, Suntory Music Foundation Festival, Boston Early Music Festival, Tanglewood Festival, and others; works regularly with Ludger Rémy, le Collegium Vocale de Gand, Bach Collegium Japan, Nederlandse Bachvereniging, Tafelmusik Baroque Orchestra, Freiburger Barockorchester; has worked with conductors such as Ivor Bolton, Beat Furrer, Martin Haselböck, Wolfgang Helbich, Philippe Herreweghe, Gustav Leonhardt, Kenneth Montgomery, Helmut Müller-Brühl, Hans-Christoph Rademann, Stephen Stubbs, Masaaki Suzuki and Jos van Veldhoven. *Recordings include:* Die Liebe Gottes ist ausgegossen 2008, Loves Alchymie (17th/18th Century Chamber Music Recording of the Year, ECHO Klassik Awards 2011), Purcell Love Songs 2010. *Address:* c/o Hochschule für Musik Franz Liszt, Postfach 2552 99406 Weimar, Germany (office).

MIGENES, Julia; American singer (soprano) and actress; b. 1948, New York; m. 4th Peter Medak. *Education:* Juilliard School of Music, New York. *Career:* opera debut at $3\frac{1}{2}$ years; has appeared in operas, on Broadway, on TV and in films; performances include on Broadway in Zero Mostel production of Fiddler on the Roof 1964, Royal Opera House, Covent Garden, London 1987, Earl's Court, London, UK 1991. *Operas include:* Madam Butterfly, Manon Lescaut 1987, Tosca 1991, Angels in America 2004. *Films include:* Eine Nacht in Venedig 1974, Carmen 1984, L'unique 1986, Berlín Blues 1988, Mack the Knife 1989, La voix humaine 1990,. *TV includes:* Madame Pompadour 1974, Together We Stand (series) 1987, Angels in America 2004. *Theatre includes:* West Side Story. *Recordings include:* Carmen, Kismet, Rags. *Address:* Les Visiteurs du Soir, 40 rue de la Folie Régnault, 75011 Paris, France. *E-mail:* OGluzman@visiteursdusoir.com. *Website:* www.juliamigenes.com.

MIHALIČ, Alexander, PhD; Slovak composer; b. 7 Aug. 1963, Medzilaborce. *Education:* Košice Conservatory, Bratislava Acad. of Music and Drama, Ecole Normale de Musique, Paris, Conservatoire Nat. de Région, Boulogne, Université de Paris VIII and Ecole de Sciences Sociales, Paris. *Career:* fmr mem. of teaching staff, Institut de Recherche et Coordination Acoustique/Musique, Paris; later Manager, Computer Music Dept, Nat. Centre for Electroacoustic Music, Bourges. *Compositions include:* six prelúdii 1982–83, Forlana 1983, Hudba 1986, Skladba 1987, Music for String Quartet 1988, Kompozicia 1990, Encyclopaedia musicalis (multiple work in progress) 1991–. *Honours:* Prix de Résidence int. electro-acoustic competition, Bourges 1988. *E-mail:* mihalic@club-internet.fr (home).

MIHELCIC, Pavel, DipMus; composer; b. 8 Nov. 1937, Novo Mesto, Yugoslavia; m. Majda Lovse 1965, two d. *Education:* Academy of Music, Ljubljana. *Career:* Prof., Conservatory of Music, 1982–; Man. of Dept of Smyphonic Music, Ljubljana Broadcasting Corporation, 1982–; Pres., Slovenian Composers' Society 1984–. *Compositions include:* orchestral works: Bridge for strings; Asphalt ballet; Concerto for horn and orchestra; Sinfonietta; Musique Funèbre for violin and orchestra; Chamber works: Limite; Blow Up; Take-off for piano; Sonatine; Sonata 80; Chorus, 1, 2, 3, 4, 5, 10, 13; Games and Reflections; Double Break; Published by Edition DSS, Ljubljana and Edition Peters, Leipzig; Recorded: Quinta Essentia for brass quintet; Timber-line for chamber orchestra; Exposition and Reflections for 9 horns; Stop-time for horn and chamber orchestra; Team for woodwind quintet; Introduction and Sequences for orchestra; Scenes From Bela Krajina; Fading

Pictures; Snow of First Youth for orchestra; Glittering Dusk for Orchestra, 1993; Return to Silence, for Orchestra, 1995; Concerto Grosso, 1997. *Publications:* contrib. to Standing Music Critic, Delo, Ljubljana; Zvuk, Sarajevo. *Honours:* Preseren Prize, 1979; Zupancic Prize, 1984. *Address:* Melikova ul 10, 61108 Ljubljana, Slovenia.

MIHEVC, Marko, MusM; Slovenian university professor and composer; *Head of Department of Music Theory, University of Ljubljana, Academy of Music;* b. 30 April 1957, Ljubljana; m. Marija Mihevc; one s. one d. *Education:* Univ. of Ljubljana Acad. of Music; Hochschüle für Musik, Vienna. *Career:* since 1989 works performed by Zagreb Philharmonic Orchestra, Ljubljana, Slovene Philharmonic Orchestra, Ljubljana, Symphonic Orchestra and Choir of RTV, Slovenia, Orchestra of Camerata Labacensis, Ljubljana Opera orchestra, Amadeus String Orchestra, I Palpiti Orchestra, Kammersymphonie Berlin, Brandenburgisches Staatsorchester Frankfurt; apptd tenured Prof. of Composition and Head of Composition Dept, Univ. of Ljubljana Acad. of Music 1994, Head of Music Theory Dept 2004–; Initiator and Organiser of the Night of Slovene Composers 1991–; Ed. in Chief Editions of Soc. of Slovene Composers 2002–; Artistic Dir KOS Orchestra of Soc. of Slovene Composers 2004–. *Compositions:* Children's Opera Aladdin and his Wonder Lamp 1981, Equi, symphonic poem for orchestra 1990, In signo tauri, symphonic poem for orchestra 1992, Miracula, symphonic poem for orchestra 1993, Proverbia, cantata for two soloists, choir and orchestra 1995, Alibaba, symphonic poem for orchestra 1996, The Planets, symphonic poem for orchestra 1998, Enigmata, cantata for mixed choir, flute and string orchestra 1998, Pizziquattro-Quattroarci, Pizzicato Verlag Helvetia PVH 710 1998, Mar Saba, symphonic poem for orchestra 1999, Biconcentus, concerto for two pianos and string orchestra 1999, Concerto for two violins and orchestra 2000, Eppur si muove, concerto for oboe, viola, violoncello and orchestra 2000, Lesson Hour, concerto for oboe, viola, violoncello and orchestra 2001, Tadu, concerto for clarinet, piano and string orchestra 2001, Tango for flute and piano 2000, Tempus est iucundum for choir and string orchestra 2001, Gipsy flute, concerto for flute and string orchestra 2002, Karneval for symphonic orchestra 2002, Fidfadl for violin solo, violoncello solo and string orchestra 2003, Halleluyah for mixed choir, brass quintet, flute and clarinet 2003, Romance for violin solo, violoncello solo and string orchestra 2003, Jamal symphonic poem 2004, Cingalini for string orchestra 2005, Lautari for orchestra 2006, Brelka concert for clarinet and orchestra 2006, Poppy's Dances for orchestra 2006, Flossg'schichten for string orchestra 2007, Romantic Concertino for piano and string orchestra 2008. *Honours:* acknowledgment of Fritz Kreisler Gesellschaft for works for solo string instruments and orchestra, Vienna 2000; Marjan Kozina Award for eight symphonic poems, Soc. of Slovene Composers, Ljubljana 2003. *Address:* Groharjeva 18, 1000 Ljubljana, Slovenia. *E-mail:* music.mihevc@siol.net. *Website:* www.markomihevc.com.

MIKHAILOV, Maxim; Russian singer (bass-baritone); b. 1956, Moscow. *Education:* Gnessin Institute, Moscow. *Career:* soloist at the Bolshoi Theatre from 1987; recitalist and guest opera appearances in Italy, Germany, Denmark, Hungary and elsewhere; has performed in Rossini's La Scala di Seta and Massenet's Chérubin at the Wiener Kammeroper, in the Mozart Festival at Schönbrunn and in Rachmaninov's Miserly Knight at the Bolshoi, as Orlik in Mazeppa at Amsterdam, as Prince Khovansky in Khovanshchina at Nantes, in Mozart's Masetto at Covent Garden, as Giove in Cavalli's Calisto in Vienna, as Banquo in Oslo, the Mayor in Rimsky's May Night, at Bologna; concert performance of Prokoviev's War and Peace at the Vienna Konzerthaus, and Rimsky's May Night at the Wexford Festival.

MIKLOSA, Erika; singer (soprano); b. 1970, Hungary. *Education:* studied in Budapest, Philadelphia, USA and Milan, Italy. *Career:* sang Papagena and Adele in Die Fledermaus and Donizetti's Lucia di Lammermoor at the Opera House, Budapest; Mozart's Queen of Night at Vienna, Berlin, Stuttgart, Cologne, Leipzig and Wiesbaden 1993–; other roles include Donizetti's Linda di Chamounix, Stravinsky's Le Rossignol and Oscar in Verdi's Un Ballo in Mascera; sang the Fiakermilli in Arabella at Zürich 2000. *Honours:* winner Int. Mozart Competition, Budapest 1993, European Culture Prize, Zürich 1995.

MIKULAS, Peter; Slovak singer (bass); b. 1954. *Education:* University of Music and Drama, Bratislava with Viktoria Stracenská. *Career:* soloist with the Slovak National Theatre in Bratislava, 1978–; Roles have included Kecal, Dulcamara, Gremin, Raimondo, Fiesco, Don Alfonso, Sarastro, Lodovico, Lindorf, Coppelius, Dr Miracle and Dapertutto, Mephisto, Don Pasquale, Banquo, Philip, Don Quichotte, Zaccaria and Golaud; Extensive concert repertoire. Guest appearances in leading European theatres, National Theatre Prague, Berlin Staatsoper, De Nederlandse Opera in Amsterdam; Has sung in Vienna, Salzburg, Paris, London, Liverpool, Birmingham, Madrid, Barcelona, Granada, Rome, Milan, Genoa, Frankfurt, Stuttgart, Hamburg, Copenhagen, Ankara, Budapest, Tokyo, Dallas, Ottawa, Buenos Aires, Rio de Janeiro and at the Prague Spring, Carinthian Summer and Edinburgh Festivals; Sang Lutobor in Smetana's Libuše at Edinburgh, 1998; Season 2000–01 as Dulcamara at Bratislava and Kolenati in The Makropulos Case at the Met; Collaborated with conductors Ceccato, Bychkov, Pesek, Belohlavek, Solti, Mackerras, Giulini and Altrichter. *Current Management:* c/o Baron & Weingartner International Artists Management, Bösendorferstrasse 4 / 12, 1010 Vienna; c/o Primusic Konzert- und Musiktheaterproduktionen, Herrengasse 6, 1010 Vienna, Austria. *Telephone:* 1-489-61-54 (B&W); 1-532-71-24 (Primusic). *Fax:* 1-485-67-11 (B&W); 1-532-71-40 (Primusic).

E-mail: office@baronartists.com. *Website:* www.baronartists.com; www.primusic.at.

MILAN, Susan, ARCM (Hons), PGdip GSMD, FRCM; British flautist; *Professor of Flute, Royal College of Music;* b. 3 Sept. 1947, London, England; d. of John Milan and Daisy Milan; m.; two s. *Education:* Jr Exhibitioner, Royal Coll. of Music, London, studied with John Francis, studied with Geoffrey Gilbert at Guildhall School of Music, attended Marcel Moyse masterclasses in Switzerland. *Career:* Prin. Flute, Bournemouth Sinfonietta 1968–72; Prin. Flute and first woman mem. Royal Philharmonic Orchestra 1974–82; developed solo career; numerous comms/first performances from composers including Nareshe Sohal 1967, Peter Lamb 1970, Robert Saxton 1973, David Morgan 1974, Jindrich Feld 1975, Antal Dorati 1980, Richard Rodney Bennett 1981, 1982, Ole Schmidt 1984, Robert Walker 1987, Carl Davis 1989, Robert Simpson 1991, Roger Steptoe 1995, Edward Cowie 1997, Edwin Roxburgh 2000, Jean Sichler 2001, Cecilia McDowall 2003, Brian Lock 2005; tours world-wide as soloist, chamber musician, recitalist and teacher; Lady Chair. British Flute Soc. 1990–94; Prof. of Flute, Royal Coll. of Music 1984–; Adjunct Prof., Henen Univ. (China) 2008; ensembles: Instrumental Quintet of London (Susan Milan flute, Nicholas Ward violin, Matthew Jones viola, John Heley cello, Ieuan Jones harp), Debussy Ensemble (Susan Milan flute, Matthew Jones viola, Ieuan Jones harp), Milan Trio (Susan Milan flute, Christopher Jepson cello, Andrew Ball piano), Milan/Ball Duo (Susan Milan flute, Andrew Ball piano); Dir Charterhouse Int. Music Festival 2007–. *Recordings include:* Flute Concerto by Ole Schmidt, Saint-Saëns Tarantella, Mozart Flute Concertos K313/314 with the English Chamber Orchestra conducted by Raymond Leppard, Mozart Flute and Harp Concerto K299, Salieri Flute and Oboe Concerto with the City of London Sinfonia conducted by Richard Hickox, La Flute Enchantée, French Pieces for Flute and Orchestra, City of London Sinfonia conducted by Richard Hickox, Beethoven Trios with Sergio Azzolini, Ian Brown, Levon Chilingirian and Louise Williams, Saint-Saëns Romance and Prokofiev Sonata in D with Clifford Benson, The Chamber Music of Eugene Goossens, London Chamber Music Group 2004, Contemporary British Flute Repertoire, with Andrew Ball (piano) 2008, researched and released Historic Flute Recordings CD Series. *Publications:* Flute Technique: Quadruplets, Cadenzas for Mozart Concertos in D/G, and Andante in C, Cadenzas for Salieri Concerto for Flute and Oboe, Flute Technique 2: Triples and Sextuplets 2006. *Current Management:* c/o John S. Cronin, Music and Media Consulting Ltd, Doddington, Cambs., PE15 0LE, England. *Telephone:* (1354) 740847. *Fax:* (1354) 740847. *E-mail:* john@musicandmediaconsulting.com. *Website:* www.musicandmediaconsulting.com. *Address:* Oakcombe, Marley Common, Haslemere, Surrey, GU27 3PP, England. *Telephone:* (1428) 641457. *E-mail:* smilan3805@aol.com. *Website:* www.susanmilan.com.

MILANOV, Michail; singer (bass); b. 1949, Sofia, Bulgaria. *Education:* studied in Sofia. *Career:* sang in Bulgaria from 1974; throughout Germany from 1977, notably at the Theater am Gärtnerplatz, Munich, from 1988 (Dosifey in Khovanshchina 1992); other roles have included Mefistofele, King Philip, Rocco, Hagen, King Mark, and Colline in La Bohème (Verona Arena 1982); season 1993 as Sparafucile at Macerata and Dosifey in Munich; sang the Duc d'Arco in Salvator Rosa for Dorset Opera 2000; many concert appearances and lieder recitals.

MILANOVA, Stoika; Bulgarian concert violinist; b. 5 Aug. 1945, Plovdiv. *Education:* studied with father Trendafil Milanova and with David Oistrakh at the Moscow Conservatory. *Career:* appearances with principal British orchestras from 1970; engagements in most European countries, as well as Yomiuri Nippon Symphony Orchestra, Japan 1975; concerts with the Hallé Orchestra and at the Hong Kong Festival; tour for Australian Broadcasting Commission 1976; US and Canadian debuts 1978; tours of Eastern Europe 1985–86; Duo recitals with Radu Lupu and Malcolm Frager; currently Prof., Pančo Vladigerov State Acad. of Music. *Recordings:* Balkanton (Bulgaria), including the complete Brandenburg Concertos with Karl Munchinger and Prokofiev's Violin Concertos; Sonatas with Malcolm Frager. *Honours:* second prize, Queen Elisabeth Competition, Belgium 1967, first prize, City of London Int. Competition (Carl Flesch) 1970, Grand Prix du Disque 1972. *Address:* Pančo Vladigerov State Academy of Music, 1505 Sofia, E. Georgiev 94, Bulgaria (office). *Telephone:* (2) 943-34-00 (office). *Fax:* (2) 944-14-54 (office). *Website:* www.art.acad.bg/music/index-e.html (office).

MILASHKINA, Tamara Andreyevna; Russian singer (soprano); b. 13 Sept. 1934, Astrakhan. *Education:* Moscow Conservatory with Elena Katul'skaya. *Career:* debut at the Bolshoi Theatre 1957, as Titania in Eugene Onegin; has sung Lisa in The Queen of Spades, Zarina in The Legend of Tsar Saltan, Yaroslavna in Prince Igor and Natasha (War and Peace) with the Bolshoi Company; guest appearances at La Scala (Lida in La battaglia di Legnano, 1962), Helsinki, Paris, Wuppertal and in North America; Vienna Staatsoper 1971, as Lisa; Deutsche Oper Berlin 1974, as Tosca; other roles include Fevronia (The Invisible City of Kitezh), Maria (Tchaikovsky's Mazeppa) and Lyuba (Prokofiev's Semyon Kotko) and Verdi's Elisabeth de Valois and Leonora (Il Trovatore). *Recordings include:* Mazeppa, Tosca, The Queen of Spades and The Stone Guest.

MILCHEVA-NONOVA, Alexandrina; singer (mezzo-soprano); b. 27 Nov. 1936, Shoumen, Bulgaria. *Education:* Sofia Conservatory with G. Cherkin. *Career:* debut at Warna 1961, as Dorabella in Così fan tutte; sang at the Bulgarian Nat. Opera in Sofia from 1968; guest appearances in Vienna, Brussels, Paris, Amsterdam, Berlin (Komische Oper), London and Zürich;

Munich 1979, 1984; Verona Arena 1980, 1984; Maggio Musicale Florence 1983, in Suor Angelica, Teatro Liceo Barcelona 1983, as Preziosilla in La Forza del Destino; La Scala Milan as Marfa in Khovanshchina, repeated at the Paris Opéra 1984; Geneva 1984, as Adalgisa in Norma; other roles include Azucena, the Princess in Adriana Lecouvreur, Dalila, Carmen and Cenerentola. *Recordings include:* Carmen, Boris Godunov, Khovanshchina, Aida, songs by Mussorgsky, Leoncavallo's La Bohème.

MILES, Alastair; British singer (bass); b. 1961, England. *Education:* Guildhall School and National Opera Studio. *Career:* debut as Trulove, in The Rake's Progress, for Opera 80, 1985; appearances from 1986 with Glyndebourne Festival and Touring Opera in Capriccio, Katya Kabanova, The Rake's Progress and Die Zauberflöte; WNO as Basilio, Sparafucile, Raimondo and Silva, in Ernani; Royal Opera, Covent Garden in Parsifal, Viaggio a Reims, I Capuleti, Fidelio, Rigoletto, La Cenerentola and La Bohème; other engagements in Vancouver, Amsterdam, San Francisco, Lyon and Deutsche Oper Berlin; concert appearances under Gardiner in Beethoven's Missa Solemnis, Mozart's Requiem, Handel's Saul and Agrippina and Verdi Requiem; under Harnoncourt in Handel's Samson and Bach Cantatas; with Kurt Masur in Elijah and the St Matthew Passion; Berlioz, La Damnation de Faust and Romeo and Juliette under Colin Davis; Bartolo in Figaro with Simon Rattle and the CBSO; Messiah under Helmut Rilling; Damnation of Faust with Myung Whun Chung; Season 1993 in the Choral Symphony under Giulini and title role in Le nozze di Figaro under Harnoncourt for Netherlands Opera; sang Sir George Walton in I Puritani, Met, 1997; sang Philip II in Don Carlos for Opera North 1998; Season 2000 as Gounod's Frère Laurent at Covent Garden, Bellini's Giorgio in Munich, Alvise in La Gioconda for ENO (concert) and in Beethoven's Ninth at the Ravenna Festival; Mendelssohn's Elijah at the London Proms, 2002. *Recordings include:* Lucia di Lammermoor; Saul and Agrippina; Elijah; La Traviata; Rigoletto; Verdi Requiem; Die Zauberflöte; Don Giovanni; Berlioz Roméo et Juliette; Le nozze di Figaro; La Cenerentola. *Current Management:* AOR Management Inc., 6910 Roosevelt Way NE, PMB 221, Seattle, WA 98115, USA.

MILES-JOHNSON, Deborah; British singer (mezzo-soprano); b. 1965, England. *Career:* concerts include: Handel's Israel in Egypt on tour to Spain, Elijah in Toronto, St Matthew Passion under Andrew Parrott, Mozart's C Minor Mass at the Barbican and Elgar's Music Makers at Peterborough Cathedral; Opera roles include: Bianca in The Rape of Lucretia, Mrs Peachum in The Beggar's Opera, Madame Popova in Walton's Bear (Thaxted Festival), Orlofsky in Fledermaus (Haddo House) and Mrs Sedley in Peter Grimes; Royal Opera Covent Garden in Birtwistle's Gawain; Dido and Aeneas with the English Bach Festival; Season 1997 with Schubert and Haydn in Switzerland, Handel's Il Parnasso in Festa and Stravinsky's Requiem Canticles with the CBSO under Simon Rattle; Further concerts with Klangforum at the Vienna Konzerthaus (Barraqué's au dela du hasard...) and at the Wigmore Hall with Fretwork: debut there in Upon Silence by George Benjamin. *Recordings include:* Resurrection by Peter Maxwell Davies; Rutti's Magnificat; Pärt's Stabat Mater, with Fretwork, under Parrott. *Current Management:* c/o Grant Rogers Musical Artists' Management, 8 Wren Crescent, Bushey Heath, Hertfordshire, WD23 1AN, England. *Telephone:* (20) 8950-2220. *Fax:* (20) 8950-3570. *E-mail:* info@ngrartists.com. *Website:* www.ngrartists.com.

MILJAKOVIĆ, Olivera; Serbian singer; b. 26 April 1939, Belgrade; one d. *Education:* Belgrade. *Career:* singer at Belgrade Opera House 1960; soloist Vienna State Opera 1962–; guest appearances in Europe, USA, Japan, S America, etc; has performed at numerous festivals in Germany, Austria and Yugoslavia; Kammersängerin 1984. *Address:* Neulinggasse 37, 1030 Vienna, Austria.

MILLER, David; American singer (tenor); b. 14 April 1973, San Diego, Calif. *Education:* Oberlin Conservatory, Ohio. *Career:* performed in various operas, including Baz Luhrmann's version of La Bohème; mem., Il Divo 2003–. *Recordings include:* albums: Il Divo 2004, Ancora 2005, The Christmas Collection 2005, Siempre 2006, The Promise 2008, Wicked Game 2011. *Website:* www.ildivo.com.

MILLER, David Alan, MM; American conductor; *Music Director, Albany Symphony Orchestra;* b. 1961, Los Angeles, Calif.; m.; three c. *Education:* Univ. of California, Berkeley, Juilliard School. *Career:* Music Dir New York Youth Symphony 1982–88; Asst Conductor to André Previn at Los Angeles Philharmonic 1987–89, Assoc. Conductor 1990–92; Music Dir Albany Symphony Orchestra 1992–; has performed as guest conductor with most major US orchestras, including Minnesota Orchestra, Chicago Symphony Orchestra, and orchestras of Baltimore, Detroit, Houston, Indianapolis, Los Angeles, New York, Philadelphia, Pittsburgh and San Francisco, and New World Symphony, New York City Ballet, Grand Teton Music Festival, Nat. Arts Center Orchestra and the Edmonton Symphony in Canada; has appeared with Melbourne Symphony in Australia, leading performances of John Adams' El Niño at Sydney Opera House; int. debut with RAI Orchestra, Turin, Italy 1999; has since conducted European orchestras in Berlin, Barcelona, Prague, Dresden, Hannover, Halle and Mainz; appeared with Adelaide Symphony, Hong Kong Philharmonic and Singapore Symphony; led Australian Youth Orchestra on its European tour and conducted Asian Youth Orchestra on Far East tour; Artistic Dir New Paths in Music Festival, New York City. *Recordings include:* with the Albany Symphony: Kamran Ince: Fall of Constantinople 1997, Roy Harris 2002, Morton Gould 2003, Peter Mennin 1997, Michael Torke's Strawberry Fields (opera, world premiere) 2005, major

works by George Tsontakis 2008, Corigliano: Conjurer: Concerto/Vocalise (Grammy Award for Best Instrumental Solo) 2013; with London Symphony Orchestra: works of Todd Levin; with Los Angeles Philharmonic: Mel Powell: Duplicates: Concerto for Two Pianos (Pulitzer Prize for Music) 1992, Luís Tinoco with Gulbenkian Orchestra 2013, Seeing - Kabir Padavali (with Albany Symphony) 2015. *Honours:* first-ever ASCAP Leonard Bernstein Award for Outstanding Educational Programming 1999, ASCAP Morton Gould Award for Innovative Programming 2001, Columbia Univ. Ditson Conductor's Award 2003. *Current Management:* c/o Opus 3 Artists, 470 Park Avenue South, 9th Floor North, New York, NY 10016, USA. *E-mail:* info@opus3artists.com. *Address:* Albany Symphony Orchestra, 19 Clinton Avenue, Albany, NY 12207, USA (office). *Telephone:* (518) 465-4755 (office). *Fax:* (518) 465-3711 (office). *Website:* www.albanysymphony.com (office).

MILLER, Sir Jonathan Wolfe, Kt, CBE, MB, BCh, FRCP; British stage director, film director, physician and writer; b. 21 July 1934, London; s. of the late Emanuel Miller; m. Helen Rachel Collet 1956; two s. one d. *Education:* St Paul's School, St John's Coll., Cambridge and Univ. Coll. Hosp. Medical School, London. *Career:* co-author of and appeared in Beyond the Fringe 1961–64; Dir John Osborne's Under Plain Cover, Royal Court Theatre 1962, Robert Lowell's The Old Glory, New York 1964 and Prometheus Bound, Yale Drama School 1967; Dir at Nottingham Playhouse 1968–69; Dir Oxford and Cambridge Shakespeare Co. production of Twelfth Night on tour in USA 1969; Research Fellow in the History of Medicine, Univ. Coll., London 1970–73; Assoc. Dir Nat. Theatre 1973–75; mem. Arts Council 1975–76; Visiting Prof. in Drama, Westfield Coll., Univ. of London 1977–; Exec. Producer Shakespeare TV series 1979–81; Artistic Dir Old Vic 1988–90; Research Fellow in Neuropsychology, Univ. of Sussex; Pres. Rationalist Soc. 2006–; Fellow, Univ. Coll. London 1981–, Royal Coll. of Physicians; mem. American Acad. of Arts and Sciences. *Productions include:* for Nat. Theatre, London: The Merchant of Venice 1970, Danton's Death 1971, The School for Scandal 1972, The Marriage of Figaro 1974; other productions The Tempest, London 1970, Prometheus Bound, London 1971, The Taming of the Shrew, Chichester 1972, The Seagull, Chichester 1973, The Malcontent, Nottingham 1973, Arden Must Die (opera) 1973, The Family in Love, Greenwich Season 1974, The Importance of Being Earnest 1975, The Cunning Little Vixen (opera) 1975, All's Well That Ends Well, Measure For Measure, Greenwich Season 1975, Three Sisters 1977, The Marriage of Figaro (ENO) 1978, Arabella (opera) 1980, Falstaff (opera) 1980, 1981, Otello (opera) 1982, Rigoletto (opera) 1982, 1984, Fidelio (opera) 1982, 1983, Don Giovanni (opera) 1985, The Mikado (opera) 1986, Tosca (opera) 1986, Long Day's Journey into Night 1986, Taming of the Shrew 1987, The Tempest 1988, Turn of the Screw 1989, King Lear 1989, The Liar 1989, La Fanciulla del West (opera) 1991, Marriage of Figaro (opera), Manon Lescaut (opera), Die Gezeichneten (opera) 1992, Maria Stuarda (opera), Capriccio (opera), Fedora (opera), Bach's St Matthew Passion 1993, Der Rosenkavalier (opera), Anna Bolena (opera), Falstaff (opera), L'Incoronazione di Poppea (opera), La Bohème (opera) 1994, Così fan tutte (opera) 1995, Carmen (opera) 1995, Pelléas et Mélisande (opera) 1995, She Stoops to Conquer, London 1995, A Midsummer Night's Dream, London 1996, The Rake's Progress, New York 1997, Ariadne auf Naxos, Maggio Musicale, Florence 1997, Falstaff, Berlin State Opera 1998, The Beggar's Opera 1999, Tamerlano, Sadler's Wells, Paris and Halle 2001, Jenůfa, Glimmerglass Opera 2006, The Cherry Orchard, Sheffield Crucible 2007, La Bohème, ENO, London 2009, La Traviata, Vancouver 2011, Così fan tutte, Washington 2012. *Films include:* Alice in Wonderland 1966, Take a Girl Like You 1969 and several films for television including Whistle and I'll Come to You 1967, The Body in Question (series) 1978, States of Mind (series) 1983, The Emperor 1987, Jonathan Miller's Opera Works (series) 1997, Brief History of Disbelief (series) 2005. *Art exhibition:* Mirror Image, National Gallery, London 1998. *Publications include:* McLuhan 1971, Freud: The Man, his World, his Influence (ed.) 1972, The Body in Question 1978, Subsequent Performances 1986, The Don Giovanni Book: Myths of Seduction and Betrayal (ed.) 1990, On Reflection 1998, Nowhere in Particular 2001. *Honours:* Hon. Fellow, St John's Coll. Cambridge, Royal Coll. of Physicians (Edin.) 1998; Hon. Assoc., British Humanist Asscn, Nat. Secular Soc.; Dr hc (Open Univ.) 1983, Hon. DLitt (Leicester) 1981, (Kent) 1985, (Leeds) 1996, (Cambridge) 1996, (London) 2015; Royal Television Soc. Silver Medal 1981, Royal Soc. of Arts Albert Medal 1992.

MILLER, Kevin; singer (tenor); b. 1929, Adelaide, Australia. *Education:* Elder Conservatory, Adelaide, studied in London, and in Rome with Dino Borgiloi. *Career:* sang with the Australian Nat. Theatre Co., Melbourne in operas by Mozart, Rossini and Vaughan Williams; toured with Australian Opera 1955; Glyndebourne Festival 1955–57, as Pedrillo, Monostatos and Scaramuccio in Ariadne auf Naxos; WNO from 1958, notably as Rossini's Ramiro, Vanja in Katya Kabanova, Sellem in The Rake's Progress and Offenbach's Orpheus; toured Germany and Australia 1962 with Orpheus in the Underworld and The Rake's Progress. *Recording:* The Rake's Progress (conducted by the composer).

MILLER, Lajos; Hungarian singer (baritone); b. 23 Jan. 1940, Szombathely; s. of Lajos Miller and Teréz Sebestyén; m. Zsuzsa Dobránszky; one s. *Education:* studied at Music Acad. of Budapest under Jenö Sipos. *Career:* mem. Hungarian State Opera 1968–; roles include Verdi's Renato, Rodrigo, Simon Boccanegra, Don Carlos, Rolando in Battaglia di Legnano, Iago, Nabucco, Conte di Luna, Miller, Germont, Gluck's Orpheus, Orestes, Mozart's Don Giovanni, Guglielmo, Giordano's Carlo Gérard, Leoncavallo's Silvio, Rossini's Figaro, Guglielmo Tell, Tchaikovsky's Eugene Onegin, Yeletsky,

Puccini's Scarpia, Bizet's Escamillo, Berio's Commandante Ivo, Donizetti's Enrico, Rimsky-Korsakov's Grasnoi, Puccini's Sharplesshas; sang with major cos in France, Germany, Italy, Monaco, Switzerland, Austria, UK, USA, Belgium, Venezuela, Canada, Chile, Japan, Argentina, Russia. *TV films:* Orfeusz Es Eurydike (Rainieri de Calzabigi and Christoph Willibald Gluck) 1985, Enrico (Lucia di Lammermoor), Marcello (Tabarro), Silvio (Pagliacci), Loth (Madarasz Loth), two portrait films 1995, Angelica (Ibert), L'elisir d'amore (Donizetti), Rigoletto (Verdi), Bank Ban 2002. *Honours:* A Magyar Köztársasági Érdemrend középkeresztje 2008; Grand Prix, Fauré singing contest, Paris 1974, First Prize, Toti del Monte singing contest, Treviso, Italy 1975, Liszt Prize 1975, Kossuth Prize 1980, A Nemzet Művésze 2014. *E-mail:* info@millerlajos.hu. *Website:* millerlajos.hu.

MILLER, Leta Ellen, BA, PhD, MM; American musicologist, flautist and academic; b. 30 Sept. 1947, Burbank, CA; m. Alan K. Miller 1969, one s. one d. *Education:* Stanford Univ., Hartt Coll. of Music. *Career:* Prof., Univ. of Calif., Santa Cruz; Recitalist of baroque and modern flute. *Recordings:* Modern Flute: The Prismatic Flute, by Lou Harrison, David Cope and Gordon Mumma, with Ensemble Nova 1988, Solstice, Canticle No. 3 Ariadne by Lou Harrison, with A Summerfield Set 1990, Music of Germaine Tailleferre 1993, Birthday Celebration by Lou Harrison 1994, Chansons de Bilitis and other French Chamber Works, by Debussy 1995, Lou Harrison: Rapunzel and other Works 1997, La Musique de Germaine Tailleferre 1999, Baroque Flute: 6 Sonatas for Flute and Continuo and Flute Unaccompanied by CPE Bach 1988, 6 Sonatas for Flute and Continuo, The Earlier Sonatas 1990, 4 Sonatas for Flute and Keyboard 1992, New Music for Early Instruments 1995, Josef Bodin de Boismortier, Music for 1–4 Flutes 1996, Antonio Vivaldi: Soprano Cantatas 1997, Renaissance Flute: Les Plaisirs d'amour – Sixteenth Century Chansons from the French Provinces 1993, Instant Breath for Solo Flute, Music by Hi Kyung Kim 2000, Dancing with Henry: New Discoveries in the Music of Henry Cowell 2001, Drums Along the Pacific 2003, Lou Harrison: works: 1939–2000 2003. *Publications:* Music in the Paris Academy of Sciences 1666–1793 (with A Cohen) 1979, Music in the Royal Society of London 1660–1806 (with A Cohen) 1987, Lou Harrison: Composing a World 1998, Lou Harrison 2006; Editor: Chansons from The French Provinces 1530–1550, vol. 1 1980, vol. 2 1983, Thirty Six Chansons by French Provincial Composers 1529–1550 1981, Giuseppe Caimo: Madrigali and Canzoni for Four and Five Voices 1990, Lou Harrison: Selected Keyboard and Chamber Music 1937–1994 (editor) 1998, Lou Harrison in New Grove Dictionary 2001, Lou Harrison in Musik in Geschichte und Gregenwart 2002; contrib. to Music and Letters 1985, Journal of The Royal Musical Association 1990, Studies in the History of Music 1992, Journal of Musicology 1993, Early Music 1995, Current Musicology 1995, American Music 1999, Opera Journal 1999, Musical Quarterly 2001, John Cage: Music, Intention and Philosophy 2002, American Music 2002, Cambridge Companion to John Cage 2002, Journal of Musicology 2002, American Music 2005, Twentieth-Century Music 2005, Journal of the American Musicological Society 2006, Journal of the Society for American Music 2007, California History 2009, Music, American Made 2010; Journal of Black Music Research 2010. *Address:* Music Center, University of California, Santa Cruz, CA 95064, USA (office).

MILLER, Margaret; violist; b. 1960, Indiana, USA. *Education:* Indiana and Wisconsin Univs. *Career:* Principal Violist, Colorado Springs Orchestra; co-founder, Da Vinci Quartet 1980, under the sponsorship of the Fine Arts Quartet; many concerts in the USA and elsewhere in a repertoire including works by Mozart, Beethoven, Brahms, Dvořák, Shostakovich and Bartók; Artist-in-Residence, Univ. of Colorado. *Honours:* with the Da Vinci Quartet: awards and grants from the NEA, the Western States Arts Foundation and the Colorado Council for the Humanities.

MILLER, Mildred, BMus; American singer and academic; b. 16 Dec. 1924, Cleveland, OH; m. Wesley W. Posvar 1950; one s. two d. *Education:* Cleveland Inst. of Music, New England Conservatory. *Career:* debut with Metropolitan Opera 1951; Metropolitan Opera 1951–74 as Cherubino, Marriage of Figaro; Octavian, Der Rosenkavalier; Siebel, Faust; Nicklausse, Les Contes d'Hoffman; Suzuki, Butterfly; radio debut 1952, Telephone Hour; television debut 1952, Voice of Firestone; appearances with all major US opera companies and in Vienna, Berlin, Munich, Stuttgart, Frankfurt 1959–73; film of The Merry Wives of Windsor; musical comedy with Pittsburgh Civic Light Opera; founder, Opera Theater of Pittsburgh 1978; faculty mem., Carnegie Mellon Univ. 1990–. *Honours:* four hon. degrees; Distinguished Daughter of Pennsylvania, Grand Prix du Disque.

MILLER, Rebecca; American conductor; *Resident Conductor, Louisiana Philharmonic Orchestra;* b. 1975, California; m. Danny Driver 1999; one d. *Education:* Oberlin Conservatory, Northwestern Univ. *Career:* Paul Wood-house Junior Fellow in Conducting, Royal Coll. of Music 1999–2001; fmrly Asst Conductor, Benjamin Britten Int. Opera School; Conducting Fellow, Houston Symphony 2005–07; Resident Conductor, Louisiana Philharmonic Orchestra 2007–; Music Dir, The New Professionals Orchestra, London 1999–; guest conductor, London Sinfonietta and The Orchestra of the Swan, Houston Symphony, Musiqa Houston, Royal Acad. of Music's Manson Ensemble at Sounds New Festival, New Asiana Ensemble at Seoul Arts Centre, Bard Festival Chamber Players, Jerusalem Symphony Orchestra, BBC Proms. *Recordings:* with The New Professionals: Harrison's Pipa Concerto (with Wu Man) 2004, Music by Aaron Kernis 2009. *Honours:* first prize, Eduardo Mata Int. Conducting Competition 2009. *Current Management:* c/o William Reinert Associates, 163 Amsterdam Avenue #334, New York, NY 10023, USA.

Telephone: (212) 799-5365. *Website:* www.williamreinert.com. *Address:* Louisiana Philharmonic Orchestra, 1010 Common Street, Suite 2120, New Orleans, LA 70112, USA (office). *Telephone:* (504) 523-6530 (office). *Fax:* (504) 595-8468 (office). *E-mail:* info@lpomusic.com (office). *Website:* www.lpomusic .com (office); www.rebeccamiller.net.

MILLER, Tania, BMus, MMus, DMA; Canadian conductor; *Music Director, Victoria Symphony, Canada;* b. 28 Aug. 1969, Foam Lake, Saskatchewan. *Education:* Univ. of Saskatchewan, Univ. of Michigan, USA. *Career:* Co-founder and Dir Michigan Opera Works 1997–2000; Asst Conductor, Carmel Bach Festival 1997–2001; Asst Conductor, Vancouver Symphony Orchestra 2000–03, Assoc. Conductor 2003–04; Music Dir and Principal Conductor, Victoria Symphony 2003–; guest conductor, McGill Symphony Orchestra, Opera McGill, Royal Conservatory Orchestra, Banff Festival of the Arts, Toronto Symphony, Vancouver Symphony, Calgary Philharmonic, Orchestre Métropolitain du Grand Montréal, Winnipeg Symphony. *Honours:* Canada Council Fellowship. *Current Management:* Kaylor Management, 130 West 57th Street, Suite 6A, New York, NY 10019, USA. *Telephone:* (212) 977-6779. *Fax:* (212) 977-6856. *E-mail:* hughkaylor@msn.com. *Website:* www .hughkaylor.com. *Address:* Victoria Symphony Society, 620 View Street, Suite 610, Victoria, BC V8W 1J6, Canada (office). *Website:* www.victoriasymphony .ca (office).

MILLET, Gilles; violinist; b. 1965, England. *Education:* studied in London and with Feodor Droujinin. *Career:* many concerts throughout the UK, in works by Shostakovich, Fauré and English composers; venues include Aldeburgh Festival (Quartet-in-Residence), Middle Temple (London), Huddersfield and Andover. *Honours:* (with the Danel Quartet) prizewinner in competitions at Florence, St Petersburg, Evian and London 1991–94.

MILLGRAMM, Wolfgang; German singer (tenor); b. 16 April 1954, Ostseebad Kuhlungsborn. *Education:* Musikhochschule, Berlin and studied with Gunter Leib. *Career:* debut at Semperoper in Dresden 1992 as Graf Elemer in Arabella; Deutsche Staatsoper, Berlin, singing the Steersman in Fliegender Holländer, Walther in Tannhäuser and Alfred in Die Fledermaus; Visited Japan, Hungary and Switzerland with Deutsche Staatsoper; Solo appearances in Yugoslavia, Romania and the former Soviet Union; Chamber Singer in 1988; Sang the Steersman at Bregenz Festival, 1988, 1989, and in concert for Radio France, 1990; Season 1992–93 was engaged at the City of Nuremberg Theatre where he made guest appearance in 1991 as Adolar in Euryanthe; Other roles include: Erik in Holländer, José in Carmen; During that period also sang the Drum Major in Wozzeck and Max in Freischütz; Further appearances: Frankfurt am Main as Alfred in Fledermaus; Parsifal in Nuremberg and Hoffmann at Gärtnerplatz in Munich, 1995; Eleazar in La Juive, Aegisth in Elektra, Florestan in Fidelio at Dortmund in season 1995–96; season 1998 with Max in Jonny Spielt auf by Krenek at Karlsruhe and Assad in Goldmark's Die Königin von Saba at Dortmund; season 2000–01 as Manrico at Dortmund, Tristan in Prague and Bacchus at the Theater am Gärtnerplatz, Munich. *Recordings include:* Ariadne auf Naxos and First Prisoner in Fidelio, conducted by Haitink. *Address:* Eugen-Schonhaar-Strasse 1, 10407 Berlin, Germany.

MILLING, Stephen; Danish singer (bass); b. 1965. *Career:* many appearances with the Royal Danish Opera, Copenhagen, and elsewhere in Scandinavia; repertory includes Die Zauberflöte (Sarastro) and Don Carlos (King Philip); Also sings Lieder by Brahms; Contestant in the 1995 Cardiff Singer of the World Competition; Guest at Covent Garden, London, with the Royal Danish Opera in Prokofiev's Love for Three Oranges; season 2000–01 as Fasolt and Hunding in The Ring, for Seattle Opera, Landgrave in Tannhäuser at the Deutsche Oper Berlin and as soloist in The Dream of Gerontius with the London SO. *Current Management:* c/o Tivoli Artists Management, 3 Vesterbrogade, PO Box 233, 1630 Copenhagen, Denmark. *Telephone:* 33-75-04-00. *Fax:* 33-75-03-75. *E-mail:* artistsmanagement@tivoli.dk. *Website:* www .tam.dk.

MILLINGTON, Barry John, BA; British music journalist and writer; b. 1 Nov. 1951, Hadleigh, Suffolk, England; m. Deborah Jane Calland 1996. *Education:* Clare Coll., Cambridge. *Career:* editorial staff mem. The New Grove Dictionary of Music and Musicians 1975–76; criticism for Musical Times and newspapers, notably The Times 1977–82, 1988–2001; Reviews Ed. for BBC Music Magazine 1992–2002; Chief Music Critic, Evening Standard 2002–; Founder and Artistic Dir Hampstead and Highgate Festival 1999–2003; dramaturgical adviser on various productions at int. venues, including Bayreuth Festival; Ed. The Wagner Journal 2007–; Exec. Dir Counterpoise ensemble 2008–; mem. Royal Musical Asscn, Critics Circle. *Publications:* Wagner 1984, Selected Letters of Richard Wagner (trans. and co-ed.) 1987, The Wagner Compendium: A Guide to Wagner's Life and Music (ed.) 1992, Wagner in Performance (co-ed.) 1992, Wagner's Ring of the Nibelung: A Companion (co-ed.) 1993, The New Grove Wagner 2002; contrib. to Oxford Illustrated History of Opera 1994, The New Grove Dictionary of Opera 1992, The New Grove Dictionary of Music and Musicians (revised edn) 2001, The New Grove Guide to Wagner and his Operas 2006, Richard Wagner: The Sorcerer of Bayreuth 2012; numerous other publs in newspapers and periodicals. *E-mail:* milcal@btinternet.com (office). *Website:* www .thewagnerjournal.co.uk (office).

MILLIOT, Sylvette, DMus; French cellist and musicologist; b. 6 June 1927, Paris. *Education:* Nat. Conservatory of Music, Paris. *Career:* Research Asst, Museum of the Nat. Conservatory of Music, Paris; soloist, Radio France;

various concert tours; Head of Research, CNRS, French Nat. Centre for Scientific Research in Musicology and Musical Iconography; mem. French Musicology Soc., French Soc. of 18th-Century Studies. *Publications include:* Documents inédits sur les Luthiers parisiens du XVIIIe siécle 1970, La Sonate 1978, Le Violoncelle en France au XVIIIe Siècle 1981, Le Quatuor 1986, Marin Marais 1991, Entretiens avec André Navarra 1991, Catalogue descriptif des instruments de Stradivarius et de Guarnerius del Gesù de Charles-Eugène Gand 1994, History of Parisian Violin Making from the XVIIIth Century to 1960: Vol. I The Family Chanot-Chardon 1994, Vol. II: The Violin Makers of the XVIIIth Century 1997, Vol. III: The Vuillaume Family 2005; contrib. to Revue Française de Musicologie, Recherches sur la Musique française classique, The Strad, articles on Lutherie Française 1992, 1993, 1995, 1998, The Grove Dictionary of Music and Musicians, Die Musik in Geschichte und Gegenwart. *Honours:* first prize for cello Nat. Conservatory of Music, Hélène Victor Lyon Prize, Solo Artist's Guild Prize. *Address:* 6 Villa de la Réunion, 75016 Paris, France (home). *E-mail:* sylvette.milliot@orange.fr (home).

MILLISCHER, Fabrice; French musician (trombone, sackbut); b. 1985, Toulouse. *Education:* studied cello and trombone at Conservatoire of Toulouse and CNSMD de Lyon, master-classes on trombone with Michel Becquet and on sackbut with Daniel Lassalle, and cello at CNSMD de Paris, with Roland Pidoux and Xavier Philips. *Career:* solo trombonist, German Radio Philharmonic Orchestra Saarbrücken/Kaiserslautern 2008–; tours with Baroque groups including Le Concert des Nations under Jordi Savall, Les Sacqueboutiers conducted by Daniel Lassalle and Jean-Pierre Canihac; as soloist has played with Vienna Chamber Orchestra, Stuttgart Radio Symphony Orchestra, State Hermitage Orchestra in St Petersburg, Orchestra Nat. du Capitole Toulouse, Orchestre Symphonique Cannes and Ukrainian Nat. Orchestra; recitals in Washington, DC, Beijing, Basel, Tokyo, Seoul, Munich, Geneva and Paris; performed at brass festivals including Eastern Trombone Workshop, Epsival, Cuivres en Dombes and Limoux Cuivrée Spéciale; co-f. quartet Quartbone 2006; several works created for him including Trombone Concerto for Trombone and Brass Ensemble by Jean Guillou, Trombone Concerto for Trombone and Orchestra (La chute de Lucifer) by Patrick Burgan, Libretto by Etienne Perruchon and L'appel sauvage by Alain Celo; taught at Conservatoire Paul Dukas, Paris 2008; Prof. of Trombone, Hochschule für Musik Saar 2009–, Prof. of Trombone, Hochschule für Musik Freiburg 2013–; gives regular master-classes in France and elsewhere in Europe and in Washington, DC, Beijing and Quebec. *Recordings include:* French Trombone Concertos (Echo Klassik Award for Concerto Recording of the Year 2014), Peregrinations, Trombone All Styles. *Honours:* First Prize, ARD Int. Music Competition 2007, Silver Medal Acad. of Arts and Letters 2007, Best Newcomer (Instrumental Soloist) Victoires de la Musique Classique 2011, Grand Prix Académie Charles Cros 2011, among other awards. *Current Management:* c/o Eugénie Guibert, Sartory Artists, 140 Avenue Victor Hugo, 75116 Paris, France. *Telephone:* 1-45-05-31-69. *Address:* fabricemillischer@yahoo.fr (home). *Website:* www.fabricemillischer.com.

MILLO, Aprile; American singer (soprano); b. 14 April 1958, New York. *Education:* studied with her parents and with Rita Patané. *Career:* debut in Salt Lake City 1980, as Aida; Gave concert performances in Los Angeles and made La Scala Milan and Welsh National Opera debuts at Elvira in Ernani; Metropolitan Opera debut 1984, as Amelia Boccanegra; returned to New York as Elvira, Elisabeth de Valois and Aida; Guest appearances in Hamburg and Vienna; Other roles include Leonara in Il Trovatore and La Forza del Destino; Sang Aida and Liu at the Metropolitan 1987, followed by Elvira in Ernani, Elisabeth de Valois and Imogene in Il Pirata; Carnegie Hall 1987, Il Battaglia di Legnano, as Lida, Verona Arena and Caracalla festival 1988–90; sang Aida at Washington 1990, Luisa Miller at Rome; Season 1991–92, as Marguerite at Chicago, debut, Elisabeth de Valois at the Met and Verona and Aida at the Festival of Caracalla; Sang Maddalena in Andrea Chénier at Rome, 1996; Amelia (Ballo in Maschera) at Palma de Mallorca, 1998 and for Palm Beach Opera, 2001. *Recordings:* Luisa Miller and Don Carlos conducted by James Levine, Met production of Aida, Un Ballo in Maschera. *Current Management:* Columbia Artists Management, 1790 Broadway, New York, NY 10019-1412, USA. *Telephone:* (212) 841-9500. *Fax:* (212) 841 9744. *E-mail:* info@cami.com. *Website:* www.cami.com.

MILLOT, Valérie; French singer (soprano); b. 1963. *Education:* Paris Conservatoire. *Career:* Lyon Opéra 1990–91 in The Three Wishes by Martinů and as Puccini's Musetta; season 1992 as Gounod's Mireille at Avignon and Sacchini's Antigone at Montpellier; Nancy Opéra 1994, as Elsa in Lohengrin; Montpellier 1993–94, as Offenbach's Giulietta and Brunehild in Reyer's Sigurd; Mme Lidone in Poulenc's Carmélites, Nantes, 1996; Poulenc's La Voix Humaine at Nancy, 1998; sang Elisabeth de Valois at Dusseldorf, 2000; frequent concert engagements. *Recordings include:* Les Brigands by Offenbach. *Current Management:* Organisation Internationale Artistique, 16 avenue Franklin D. Roosevelt, 75008 Paris, France. *Telephone:* 1-42-25-58-34. *Fax:* 1-42-25-64-97. *E-mail:* oia@oia-poilve.com. *Website:* www.oia-poilve.com.

MILLS, Alan, MA; British composer and pianist; b. 21 July 1964, Belfast, Northern Ireland. *Education:* Ulster Coll. of Music, Churchill Coll., Cambridge, Guildhall School of Music and Drama, London. *Career:* pianist and accompanist for BBC Radio Ulster, Dutch TV and Radio France 1987–; Dir of Music, Anna Scher Theatre 1989–; Lecturer, Birkbeck Coll., London 1993–2008; staff pianist, City Literary Inst. 2002–; Tutor, Univ. of Middlesex 2010–. *Compositions include:* 35 songs for voice and piano 1986–, A Wedding Postlude for organ 1981, Daybreak over Newgrange for large orchestra and chorus 1987, Night-music for piano 1987, Three Irish Poems for baritone and small orchestra 1991, Incantation for trombone and piano 1993, Hymn to the Aten for chamber choir and harp 1993, Capriccio for harpsichord 1993, Romanza for horn and piano 1994, Epitaph for a cappella double choir 1995, Psalm 137 for a cappella choir 1996, Ave Maria for female voices 1997, Memorial for cello and piano 1998, Nocturne for piano 1998, Hymn to Inana for a cappella choir 2000, Three Studies for piano solo 2001, In Nomine for string trio 2002, Marsyas for solo flute 2002, Reproduction (sets I and II) for piano 2002–07, The Lord at First did Adam make for a cappella choir 2003, The Birth of Orpheus for string quartet and voice 2003, Sapphic Verses for soprano and flute 2004, White-Black Blues for piano 2007, Celtic Minuet for piano 2008, Interlude and Burlesque for clarinet and piano 2009. *Recordings:* Hymn to the Aten, by Concert de L'Hostel-Dieu, Lyon. *Publications:* Incantation 1993, Hymn to the Aten 1994, A Wedding Postlude 2006, The Lord at First did Adam make 2007, White-Black Blues 2008, The Birth of Orpheus 2009, Celtic Minuet 2009, Invention 2010, Two Seasonal Carols 2011, Consolation and Fugue 2012, Narcissus 2012. *Honours:* Special Youth Prize, Lloyd's Bank Composers' Award 1988, Lower Machen Festival Prize 1993. *Address:* 87 Palmerston Road, Wood Green, London, N22 4QS, England. *Telephone:* (20) 8888-8214. *E-mail:* alanmills@musichaven.co.uk.

MILLS, Beverly; singer (mezzo-soprano); b. 1957, Kent, England. *Education:* Trinity Coll., London Opera Studio with Nancy Evans. *Career:* debut at Batignano Festival 1980, as Alessandro in Handel's Tolomeo; Aldeburgh from 1981, as Britten's Nancy and Lucretia; Glyndebourne Touring Opera 1981, as Cherubino; sang in Cavalli's L'Egisto for Scottish Opera 1982, and on tour to Venice and Schwetzingen; further appearances with WNO and City of Birmingham Touring Opera (Smetana's Two Widows 1999 and as Debussy's Geneviève 2000); other roles include Dorabella, Suzuki in Butterfly, Rosina, Siebel and Cenerentola; Operetta and concert engagements.

MILLS, Bronwen; singer (soprano); b. 1960, England. *Education:* Univ. of London, Guildhall School of Music, studied with Joy Mammon. *Career:* opera engagements include Dido and Aeneas with Opera Restor'd at the 1986 Edinburgh Festival; QEH 1989 in The Death of Dido by Pepusch and Dibdin's Ephesian Matron; season 1989–90, with Traviata for New Israeli Opera and Dublin Grand Opera; Elizabeth Zimmer in Henze's Elegy for Young Lovers in London; Norina in Don Pasquale and Madeline in Fall of the House of Usher by Glass in Wales; Donna Anna in Don Giovanni for Opera North 1992; Man Who Mistook his Wife for a Hat, Michael Nyman, for Music Theatre Wales 1992–93; other roles include Mozart's Countess and Fiordiligi, Opera 80, the Governess and Miss Jessel in the Turn of the Screw, and Micaela; Opera North as the Queen of Shemakah in The Golden Cockerel, Strauss's Daphne and Blondchen in Die Entführung; concert engagements with the Scottish Chamber Orchestra in Handel's Dixit Dominus and Bach's B minor Mass; St Matthew Passion in Stratford and Haydn's Stabat Mater at St John's Smith Square; Mozart's C minor Mass with the Northern Sinfonia, Beethoven's Missa Solemnis at Canterbury Cathedral and the Christmas Oratorio in Belgium; Wexford Festival 1990, in Handel's L'Allegro, il Penseroso ed il Moderato; tour of English cathedrals with London Festival Orchestra 1991, Messiahs in Germany, Norway 1992 also Messiahs in Lithuania and Moscow, Kremlin, with Yehudi Menuhin; further appearances at the Malvern, Music at Oxford, Cambridge and Sully-sur-Loire Festivals. *Recordings:* Solomon by John Blow, Beggar's Opera, Polly Peachum, Dibdin Operas, 100 years of Italian Opera, Emilia di Liverpool.

MILLS, Erie, BMus, MA; American singer (soprano); b. 22 June 1953, Granite City, IL. *Education:* National Music Camp, Interlochen, MI, University of Illinois, studied with Karl Trump, Grace Wilson and Elena Nikolai. *Career:* debut in St Louis 1978, in the US premiere of Martin y Soler's L'Arbore di Diana; Ninette in Love for Three Oranges, Chicago Lyric Opera, 1979; Sang New York City Opera debut as Cunegonde, Candide, 1982; Metropolitan Opera debut, New York as Blondchen, Die Entführung aus dem Serail, 1987; New York recital debut, 1989; Guest appearances with Cincinnati Opera; Cleveland Opera; San Francisco Opera; Minnesota Opera; Opera Society of Washington, DC; Santa Fe Opera; Houston Grand Opera; Hamburg State Opera; Teatro alla Scala, Milan; Vienna State Opera; sang Marie in La Fille du Régiment at New Orleans, 1989, Blondchen in Die Entführung for Opéra de Montréal, 1990; sang Zerlina at Milwaukee, 1996 and the Queen of Night at New Orleans, 1997; soloist with many leading orchestras; numerous recitals; television appearances; roles include Rossini's Rosina; Offenbach's Olympia; Donizetti's Lucia; J. Strauss's Adele; R. Strauss's Zerbinetta.

MILLS, John, ARCM, ARAM, FCLCM; British classical guitarist; *Head of Guitar, Royal Welsh College of Music and Drama*; b. 13 Sept. 1947, Kingston-upon-Thames; m. Jacoba Cornelia; one s. one d. *Education:* Royal Coll. of Music. *Career:* recitalist throughout British Isles 1965–; international debut, Canada 1972; has performed widely overseas, including USA, Australia, New Zealand, Japan, Singapore, Scandinavia, Holland, France, Greece, Italy; work in the chamber music field; specialist teaching areas early guitar (particularly 19th century) and postural difficulties; Prof. at the Royal Acad. of Music; Head of Guitar, Royal Welsh Coll. of Music and Drama 1991–; mem. Musicians' Union, Incorporated Soc. of Musicians, Delius Soc. *Compositions:* Hommage to Frederick Delius, Suite for Five Guitars, Idyll for Violin and Guitar. *Recordings:* Guitar Music of Five Centuries 1972, Music from the Student Repertoire 1973, 20th Century Guitar Music 1977, John Mills and Raymond Burley 1983, The John Mills Guitar Trio 1981. *Publications:* John Mills Guitar

Tutor; contrib. to Classical Guitar Magazine. *Current Management:* Sympathetic Developments, 5 Greenclose Lane, Wimborne, BH21 2AL, England. *Telephone:* (1202) 880331 (office). *Fax:* (1202) 888037 (office). *E-mail:* graham@symdev.co.uk (office). *Website:* www.symdev.co.uk; www.pitchperfect.org/johnmills.

MILLS, Sir Jonathan Edward Harland, Kt, FRSE, FRSA; Australian composer and arts administrator; *Director and Chief Executive, Edinburgh International Festival;* b. 21 March 1963, Sydney, NSW. *Education:* Univ. of Sydney. *Career:* Artistic Dir, Blue Mountains Festival 1988–90, Melbourne Millennium Eve celebrations 1999, Melbourne Int. Arts Festival 2000–01, Melbourne Federation Festival, Brisbane Biennial Int. Music Festival; Composer-in-Residence and Research Fellow in Environmental Acoustics, RMIT Univ. 1992–97, Adjunct Prof. in Environmental Acoustics 1998–2003; Composer-in-Residence, Bundanon Trust 2002, Adjunct Prof., La Trobe Univ. 2004–07; Vice-Chancellor's (Professorial) Fellow 2006, Dir Alfred Deakin Lectures and Artistic Adviser to the new Melbourne Recital Centre and Elisabeth Murdoch Hall, Univ. of Melbourne 2003–06; Dir and Chief Exec., Edinburgh Int. Festival 2007–; mem. Australia Council New Media Arts Bd; Artistic Adviser, Brisbane Biennial Int. Music Festival 1995–97, Melbourne Recital Centre and Elisabeth Murdoch Hall 2005–; Visiting Prof., Edinburgh Napier Univ., Univ. of Edinburgh; Commr Australian Heritage Comm. 2002–04; Chair. Review into the Australian Youth Orchestra & the Australian Nat. Acad. of Music, Commonwealth Govt 2004–05, Review of Opera, Victorian Govt 2005; mem. Australian Int. Cultural Council 1998–2003, Bd Synergy Percussion 2001–06, New Media Arts Bd, Australia Council 2003–05, Bd Melbourne Recital Hall 2004–05, Australian Heritage Council 2004–06, Major Performing Arts Bd, Australia Council 2005–, Bd Arts Exhibitions Australia 2005–; Artistic Dir Seaborne Broughton & Walford Foundation 1988–; mem. Jury, Pratt Prize for Musical Theatre 2002–, Ian Potter Foundation Music Comms 2003–05; Patron Leigh Warren & Dancers 2001–. *Compositions:* various works and performances for radio, film, theatre and concert, including Ethereal Eye electro-acoustic dance opera 1996, The Ghost Wife chamber opera 1999–2002, Sandakan Threnody for solo tenor, chorus and orchestra 2001, touring 2004–06 (Prix Italia 2005), The Eternity Man chamber opera 2003. *Honours:* Centenary Medal Australia 2002; Hon. DUniv (Stirling) 2009, (Queen Margaret Univ. 2009); Hon. DLitt (St Andrews) 2013; Genesis Prize Comm. for Opera 2003. *E-mail:* director@eif.co.uk (office). *Website:* www.eif.co.uk (office).

MILLS, Richard John; Australian composer and conductor; *Artistic Director, West Australian Opera;* b. 14 Nov. 1949, Toowoomba, Queensland. *Education:* Univ. of Queensland, Queensland Conservatorium, Guildhall School of Music, London, England. *Career:* regular guest conductor of all major Australian orchestras; Artist-in-Residence, Australian Ballet 1987–88, Australian Broadcasting Corporation 1989–90; Artistic Dir, Adelaide Chamber Orchestra 1991–97; Artistic Adviser, Queensland Symphony Orchestra 1991–94, Brisbane Biennial Int. Music Festivals 1995–97; Artistic Dir, West Australian Opera 1997–, Artistic Dir Victorian Opera 2012–. *Compositions include:* Music for Strings, Concerti for trumpet and percussion, Bamaga Diptych, Fantastic Pantomines, Flute Concerto (written for James Galway), Concerto for violoncello and orchestra, Violin Concerto (for Carl Pini) 1992, Summer of the Seventeenth Doll (opera) 1994, Requiem Diptych for brass quintet 1997, The Code of Tupsichore for orchestra 1997, A Symphony 1998, Batavia (opera) 2001, The Love of the Nightingale (opera) 2007. *Honours:* Nat. Critics Awards 1988, 1991, Sir Bernard Heinze Award 1997, Best Music Direction (for The Love of the Nightingale), Helpmann Awards, Australia 2007. *Current Management:* Arts Management Pty Ltd, Level 1, 405 Elizabeth Street, Surry Hills, NSW 2010, Australia. *Telephone:* (2) 9211 9422. *Fax:* (2) 9211 9466. *E-mail:* enquiries@artsmanagement.com.au. *Website:* www.artsmanagement.com.au.

MILNE, Hamish, FRAM; British pianist; b. 27 April 1939, Salisbury, England; m. Margot Gray, one s. two d. *Education:* Royal Academy of Music, London, studied with Guido Agosti in Rome, Siena. *Career:* debut in 1963; Concerto, Recital, Chamber Music in the UK, Europe, USA and USSR; over 100 BBC broadcasts; Proms debut 1978; Prof. of Piano, Royal Academy of Music, London. *Recordings:* Piano works by Chopin, Liszt, Haydn, Medtner, Mozart, Reubke, Schumann, Weber, Busoni's Fantasia Contrappuntistica. *Publications:* Bartók 1981, Medtner-Centenary Appraisal (contrib.) 1981, Heritage of Music (contrib.) 1982. *Honours:* Collard Fellowship 1977. *Website:* www.hamishmilne.com.

MILNE, Lisa, MBE; British singer (soprano); b. 1971, Scotland. *Education:* Royal Scottish Acad. of Music. *Career:* from 1994 appearances throughout Scotland in concert and recital; mem. of Scottish Opera from 1994, as Gianetta in L'Elisir d'amore (debut role), Mozart's Susanna, Zerlina and Ilia, the Dew Fairy in Hansel and Gretel and Coryphée in Alceste; season 1996 in recitals at Covent Garden and Aix en Provence and City of London Festivals; concerts with the Nat. Youth Orchestra of Scotland, Scottish Chamber, Royal Philharmonic, London Philharmonic and Royal Liverpool Philharmonic Orchestras; season 1997–98 as Servilia in La Clemenza di Tito for WNO, Atalanta in Xerxes at Göttingen and Handel's Rodelinda at Glyndebourne; Nielsen's Springtime on Funen at the 1999 London Proms; with ENO as Aennchen in Der Freischütz and Morgana in Alcina 1999; season 2000–01 with Marzelline in Fidelio at Glyndebourne and Stravinsky's Anne Trulove for ENO; Handel's Samson at the London Proms 2002; Micaela in Carmen for GTO and Marzelline in Fidelio at Dallas Opera; season 2007–08 as Sian in

James MacMillan's The Sacrifice for Welsh National Opera; season 2010–11 as Leonore in Beethoven's Fidelio for Welsh National Opera; numerous other engagements and recitals. *Recordings include:* Handel and Vivaldi with the King's Consort, Vaughan Williams Serenade to Music, Songs of John Ireland 1999, Mozart's Idomeneo (role of Ilia) 2002, Songs of Roger Quilter 2003, Land of Heart's Desire 2005, Moonstruck: Songs of F.G. Scott 2007, Beethoven's Fidelio 2009, Thea Musgrave's Turbulent Landscapes 2009. *Honours:* Maggie Teyte Prize 1993, John Christie Award 1996, Royal Philharmonic Soc. Young Artist Award 1998.

MILNES, Sherrill, MMusEd; American singer (baritone); b. 10 Jan. 1935, Hinsdale, Ill.; s. of James Knowlton Milnes and Thelma Roe Milnes; m. 2nd Nancy Stokes 1969; one s. one d. by first marriage; m. 3rd Maria Zouves 1996. *Education:* Drake Univ., Northwestern Univ., studied with Boris Goldovsky, Rosa Ponselle, Andrew White, Hermanes Baer. *Career:* with Goldovsky Opera Co. 1960–65, New York City Opera Co. 1964–67, debut with Metropolitan Opera Co., New York 1965, leading baritone 1965–; has performed with all American city opera cos and major American orchestras 1962–73; performed in Don Giovanni, Vespri Siciliani and all standard Italian repertory baritone roles, Metropolitan Opera and at San Francisco Opera, Hamburg Opera, Frankfurt Opera, La Scala, Milan, Covent Garden, London, Teatro Colón, Buenos Aires, Vienna State Opera, Paris Opera and Chicago Lyric Opera; Founder and Artistic Dir VOICE (Vocal and Operatic Intensive Creative Experience) 2001–; Chair. of Bd Affiliate Artists Inc. *Recordings:* over 60 albums. *Publication:* American Aria: From Farm Boy to Opera Star 2000. *Honours:* Order of Merit (Italy) 1984, Chevalier, Ordre des Arts et des Lettres 1996; three hon. degrees; three Grammy Awards, Sanford Medal, named mem. Lincoln Acad. 2003, Yale Univ., Opera News Award 2008. *Current Management:* Barrett Vantage Artists, 505 8th Avenue, Suite 12A00 New York, NY 10018, USA. *Address:* The VOICExperience Foundation, PO Box 1576, Plain Harbor, FL 34682-1576, USA (office). *E-mail:* voicexp@aol.com (office). *Website:* www.voicexperiencefoundation.com (office).

MILTON, Nicholas, DMus; Australian conductor and violinist; *Chief Conductor and Artistic Director, Canberra Symphony Orchestra. Education:* Sydney Conservatorium of Music, Michigan State Univ., Boston Univ., Mannes Coll. of Music, Juilliard School, City Univ. of New York, USA. *Career:* as violinist, Concertmaster, Adelaide Symphony Orchestra 1996–2002; mem. Macquarie Trio Australia 1998–2005; Chief Conductor and Artistic Dir, Dubrovnik Symphony Orchestra 2000–04; Chief Conductor, Willoughby Symphony Orchestra, Sydney 2001–; Gen. Music Dir and Chief Conductor, Jena Philharmonic Orchestra 2003–; made USA debut with Phoenix Symphony Orchestra 2005; Chief Conductor and Artistic Dir, Canberra Symphony Orchestra 2007–; guest conductor, Melbourne Symphony Orchestra, Adelaide Symphony Orchestra, Tasmanian Symphony Orchestra, Royal Philharmonic Orchestra, Tonkünstler Orchestra, Orchestra della Svizzera Italiana, Berlin Konzerthausorchester, SWR-Stuttgart, NDR-Hannover. *Honours:* Symphony Australia Young Conductor of the Year 1999, Australian Centenary Medal 2003. *Address:* Canberra Symphony Orchestra, GPO Box 1919, Canberra, ACT 2601, Australia (office). *Telephone:* (2) 6247-9191 (office). *Website:* www.cso.org.au (office).

MILYAEVA, Olga; Russian violist; b. 1967, Moscow. *Education:* Central Music School, Moscow. *Career:* Co-founder Quartet Veronique 1989; many concerts in the former Soviet Union and Russia, notably in the Russian Chamber Music Series and the 150th Birthday Celebrations for Tchaikovsky 1990; masterclasses at the Aldeburgh Festival 1991; concert tour of the UK 1992–93; repertoire includes works by Beethoven, Brahms, Tchaikovsky, Bartók, Shostakovich and Schnittke; resident quartet, Wilwaukee Univ., USA. *Honours:* with Quartet Veronique: winner All-Union String Quartet Competition, St Petersburg 1990–91, third place Int. Shostakovich Competition, St Petersburg 1991.

MIMS, Marilyn; singer (soprano); b. 1962, USA. *Education:* Indiana Univ. with Virginia Zeani. *Career:* sang at Kentucky Opera from 1987 as Lucia and Violetta, New Orleans Opera from 1990 and at the Metropolitan Opera 1990 as Donna Anna and Fiordiligi; guest appearances with Hawaii Opera as Constanze 1988, and Fiordiligi at Santa Fe; sang at San Francisco Opera 1990–92 as Donna Anna and Anna Bolena. *Recordings include:* Ortlinde in Die Walküre (conducted by James Levine).

MIN, Lee Huei; violinist; b. 1982, Singapore. *Education:* Univ. of Michigan, Yale Univ. School of Music with Erick Friedman. *Career:* appearances with Washington Symphony and Prague Chamber Orchestras; inaugurated Singapore Symphony young audience programmes 2000; Wigmore Hall, London debut 2001; season 2001–02 with tours of People's Republic of China and elsewhere in Asia; plays Giuseppe Guarneri violin 1704. *Honours:* winner Singapore Nat. Music Competition 1990, Kocian Int. Violin Competition 1993.

MINCH, John, MBA; British music publishing executive; *CEO, Boosey & Hawkes Group. Career:* began career in advertising industry; fmr Man. Dir Boosey & Hawkes publishing div., formed Regent Street Music Ltd, purchasing Boosey & Hawkes 2003, currently CEO, also CEO Imagem Music UK (part of parent co. Imagem Music Group) 2009–. *Address:* Boosey & Hawkes Music Publishers Ltd, Aldwych House, 71–91 Aldwych, London, WC2B 4HN, England (office). *E-mail:* john.minch@boosey.com (office). *Website:* www.boosey.com (office).

MINCZUK, Roberto; Brazilian conductor and horn player; *Artistic Director and Principal Conductor, Orquestra Sinfónica Brasileira*; b. 1967, São Paulo; m. Valéria Minczuk; one s. three d. *Education:* Juilliard School, USA, also studied with Kurt Masur. *Career:* as horn player, Principal Hornist, Orquestra Sinfónica de São Paulo; as conductor, Assoc. Conductor, New York Philharmonic Orchestra 2002–03; Principal Guest Conductor, Orquestra Sinfónica de São Paulo –2005; Artistic Dir and Principal Conductor, Orquestra Sinfónica Brasileira, Rio de Janeiro; also Artistic Dir, Municipal Theatre, Rio de Janeiro and Int. Winter Festival, Campos do Jordão, São Paulo; Music Dir, Calgary Philharmonic Orchestra 2006–; led London Philharmonic Orchestra in tour of USA 2006; guest conductor, New York Philharmonic, Los Angeles Philharmonic, San Francisco Symphony, St Louis Symphony, Atlanta Symphony, Orchestra Symphonique de Montreal, Ottawa Symphony, Israel Philharmonic, BBC Symphony Orchestra, Hallé Orchestra, Royal Liverpool Philharmonic. *Recordings:* Hector Villa-Lobos' Bachianas Brasileiras, Antonio Carlos Jobim's Complete Symphonic Works (Latin Grammy Award 2004). *Honours:* Prêmio Moinho Santista 1991, Martin E. Segal Award 2000, Prêmio Carlos Gomes 2006, Prêmio Carioca do Ano, Veja magazine 2007, Medalha Pedro Ernesto 2009. *Address:* Orquestra Sinfónica Brasileira, Avenida Rio Branco 135, Salas 915 a 920, Rio de Janeiro, RJ 20040-006, Brazil (office). *Telephone:* (21) 2142-5800 (office). *Fax:* (21) 2142-5844 (office). *Website:* www.osb.com.br (office); www.robertominczuk.com.

MINDEL, Meir; composer; b. 25 Dec. 1946, Lvov, Russia; m. Tzippi Bozian 1968; four d. *Education:* Rubin Music Acad., Tel-Aviv, studied with Itzhak Saday, Abel Ehrlich. *Career:* debut concert in Rubin Acad., Agony for Flute, 1974; radio broadcasts, Israeli Young Composer, The Blue and the White, 1982, Circle, A Maya Prophecy, 1987, Together with... Meir Mindel, An Hour of M. M. Compositions, 1988, Israel Broadcasting Authority; represented Israel at World Festival of Jewish Music, Montréal, Canada, 1983; Genesis with Morli Consort, Israel Defence Forces Army Broadcasting, 1984; attempted to develop a new musical 'language' for recorders; music performed in Israel and abroad; mem., Kibbutz Composers' Organisation (Gen. Dir, Sec.), Israel Composers' League (Sec. of Management and board mem.), Open-Air Museum Project, Kibbutz Negba (founder). *Compositions include:* The Tie, strings, 1980; Grotesque, piano, 1983, recorders, 1985; Genesis, recorders, 1983; A Maya Prophecy, mixed choir a cappella, 1985; Agony, flute, 1986; The Courting Muse, trombone, 1986; Tamar, flute, horn, piano, 1988; Poem, horn, 1988; My City, 2 choirs; The Family Tree, singers ensemble, 1989; Iri, 2 choirs, 1989; Koli, songs, 1989; The Shadow, children's choir, 1989; Murmurs, trumpet, flugelhorn, 1989; Between Rosh Pina and Safed, song; Music for Michal Gretz-Mindel's poem A White Lie, for children's choir, 1994; Symbiosis, for clarinet, bass clarinet and magnetic tape; Circles; The Catch; Where Are You All?; SugiHara, for shakuhachi Japanese bamboo flute, eastern percussion instruments and orchestra, 1995; Sounds of Strings, 18 arrangements for string quartet, 1996. *Recordings:* Negba 40; Bereshit (Genesis), 1987; Song of Songs 85-Duo Beersheba; A Maya Prophecy, Tel-Aviv Philharmonic Choir; Murmurs, A Courting Muse, in Composers in search of their roots; Iri (Acum Prize), 1989; Tamar; Israeli Sounds of Strings, 18 arrangements of folk songs, 1998. *Address:* The Open-Air Museum, Negba, Kibbutz Negba, D.N. Lachish 79408, Israel.

MINEVA, Stefka; singer (mezzo-soprano); b. 1949, Stara Zagora, Bulgaria. *Education:* studied in Sofia. *Career:* debut at Staga Zora 1972, as Berta in Il Barbiere di Siviglia; sang Suzuki, Olga and Amneris at Stara at Zagora; Sofia Opera from 1977, notably as Marfa in Khovanshchina; guest appearances throughout Europe; Metropolitan Opera 1986–88, as Marfa; sang Konchakovna in Prince Igor at Perugia 1987, Liubasha in The Tsar's Bridge at Rome and Kabanicha in Katya Kabanova at Florence 1989; other roles include Marina in Boris Godunov, Eboli, Adalgisa and Leonora in La Favorita; sang Fenena in Nabucco at the 1991 Verona Arena. *Recordings:* Rimsky-Korsakov's Vera Sheloga and Prokofiev's War and Peace, Madama Butterfly. *Honours:* prizewinner Sofia Int. Competition 1976, Osten Int. Competitions 1977.

MINGARDO, Sara; Italian singer (contralto); b. 1970, Venice. *Education:* Academia Chigiana of Siena. *Career:* many performances at leading Italian opera houses, including Teatro Comunale of Bologna, La Scala Milan, Teatro Comunale Florence, Teatro Regio Turin and Teatro San Carlo, Naples; further engagements in Puccini's Trittico under Riccardo Chailly, as Emilia in Otello under Claudio Abbado in Berlin and Salzburg 1996; sang title role in revival of Handel's Riccardo Primo with Les Talens Lyriques under Christophe Rousset at Fontevraud, France, 1995. *Recordings include:* Riccardo Primo.

MINKOWSKI, Marc; French conductor; *Music Director, Sinfonia Varsovia*; b. 4 Oct. 1962, Paris. *Education:* Hague Conservatory, Pierre Monteux Memorial School, USA. *Career:* founder (and performed with), Les Musiciens du Louvre 1982; conducted works by Handel, including Riccardo Primo 1991, for the English Bach Festival and Gluck's Iphigénie en Tauride at Covent Garden; French repertoire includes Charpentier's Malade Imaginaire, Alcyone by Marin Marais, Mouret's Les Amours de Ragonde and Titon et l'Aurore by Mondonville, Rameau's Hippolyte et Aricie, Gluck's Armide; Lully's Phaëton, Opéra de Lyon 1993; Ariodante by Handel, Welsh NO 1994; Agrippina by Handel, Semper Oper, Dresden 1994; Dido and Aeneas by Purcell, Houston Grand Opera 1995; Orchestre de Chambre de Genève 1995; Amsterdamse Bach Solisten 1995; Rotterdam Philharmonic 1995; Idomeneo by Mozart, Opéra de Paris-Bastille 1996; Orfeo ed Euridice by Gluck, Nat. Opera, The Netherlands 1996; Armide by Gluck, Opéra de Nice 1996; L'Inganno Felice by Rossini, Poissy, France 1996; Acis et Galatée, summer tour 1996; Die Entführung at the 1998 Salzburg Festival; Music Dir, Flanders Opera from 1997; Le nozze di Figaro at Aix 2000; Music Dir, Sinfonia Varsovia 2008–. *Recordings:* Les Amours de Ragonde by Mouret; Mondonville's Titon et l'Aurore; Stradella's San Giovannia Battista; Grétry's La Caravane du Caire; Alcyone by Marin Marais; Le Malade Imaginaire by Charpentier; Platée by Rameau; Rebel's Les Elemens; Handel's Amadigi; Handel's Teseo; Il Trionfo del Tempo by Handel; Concerti Grossi op 3, by Handel; Rameau's Hippolyte et Aricie, 1994; La Resurrezione by Handel, 1995; Gluck's Armide, 1999. *Honours:* first prize Int. Concert of Ancient Music, Bruges 1984; Chevalier, Ordre du Mérite. *Address:* Orkiestra Sinfonia Varsovia, 00-901 Warsaw, Palac Kultury i Nauki, Pl. Defilad 1, Poland (office). *Telephone:* (22) 6566419 (office). *E-mail:* imp@sinfoniavarsovia.org (office). *Website:* www.sinfoniavarsovia.org (office).

MINTER, Drew; singer (countertenor); b. 11 Jan. 1955, Washington, DC, USA. *Education:* Indiana Univ., studied with Rita Streich, Erik Werba and Marcy Lindheimer. *Career:* performed in concert with various early music ensembles, including the Waverly Consort of New York; stage debut as Handel's Orlando at the St Paul's Baroque Festival 1983; further appearances in early opera at Boston, Brussels and Los Angeles; Omaha and Milwaukee 1988, as Arsace in Handel's Partenope and Otho in L'Incoronazione di Poppea; Santa Fe 1989, in the US premiere of Judith Weir's A Night at the Chinese Opera and as Endimione in La Calisto by Cavalli; television appearances include Ptolemeo in Handel's Giulio Cesare, directed by Peter Sellars; sang the title role in Handel's Ottone, Göttingen 1992; Endymion in Cavalli's Calisto at Glimmerglass 1996. *Recordings include:* Ottone in Handel's Agrippina and the title role in Floridante, conducted by Nicholas McGegan.

MINTON, Yvonne Fay, CBE; Australian singer (mezzo-soprano); b. 4 Dec. 1938, Sydney; d. of R. T. Minton; m. William Barclay 1965; one s. one d. *Education:* Sydney Conservatorium of Music, studied in London with H. Cummings and Joan Cross. *Career:* sang with several opera groups in London; debut at Covent Garden 1965, prin. mezzo-soprano 1965–71; US debut at Lyric Opera, Chicago (Octavian in Der Rosenkavalier) 1972; guest artist, Cologne Opera 1969–, Australian Opera 1972–73, also with Hamburg State Opera and at Bayreuth, Paris, Salzburg, Metropolitan Opera, New York, Munich and San Francisco; many concert appearances; created role of Thea in Tippett's The Knot Garden 1970. *Recordings include:* Der Rosenkavalier, Figaro, La Clemenza di Tito, Mozart's Requiem, Elgar's The Kingdom. *Honours:* Hon. ARAM.

MINTZ, Shlomo; Israeli violinist, conductor and academic; b. 30 Oct. 1957, Moscow, USSR; s. of Abraham Mintz and Eve Mintz (née Labko); m. Corina Ciacci; two s. *Education:* Juilliard School of Music, USA, studied with Dorothy DeLay, also studied with Ilona Feher. *Career:* moved to Israel aged two; Premio Accad. Musicale Chigiana, Siena, Italy 1984; Music Dir, Conductor and Soloist, Israel Chamber Orchestra 1989–93; Artistic Adviser, Limburg Symphony Orchestra, The Netherlands 1994; Artistic Adviser and Prin. Guest Conductor, Maastricht Symphony Orchestra 1994–98; Prin. Guest Conductor, Arena di Verona 1999–2000, Zagreb Philharmonic Orchestra 2008–10; Artistic Dir, Int. Music Festival, Sion Valais 2012–; Artistic Dir, Crans Montana Classics (masterclass), Switzerland 2012–; Mentor and Pres. of the Jury, Int. Violin Competition, Buenos Aires; presides over Munetsugu Angel Violin Competition, Japan; Pres. of the Jury, Sion Valais Int. Violin Competition, Switzerland 2002–11; Co-founder and Patron, Keshet Eilon Int. Violin Mastercourse, Israel 1992–2010; guest conductor and soloist for numerous orchestras world-wide. *Recordings include:* Violin Concertos by Mendelssohn and Bruch (Grand Prix du Disque, Diapason d'Or) 1981, J.S. Bach Complete Sonatas and Partitas for Solo Violin, The Miraculous Mandarin by Bartok (with Chicago Symphony Orchestra, conducted by Abbado), Compositions and Arrangements by Kreisler (with Clifford Benson, piano), Twenty-four Caprices by Paganini, Two Violin Concertos by Prokofiev (with London Symphony Orchestra, conducted by Abbado), The Four Seasons by Vivaldi (with Stern, Perlman, Mehta). *Honours:* Dr hc (Ben-Gurion Univ.) 2006; Diapason d'Or 1981, Premio Accademia Musicale Chigiana 1984, Edison Award 1985, 2001, 2007, Grand Prix du Disque 1992, 1997, 1998, Gramophone Award 1994. *Telephone:* 6-07249734 (mobile). *E-mail:* b.alonsomonedero@gmail.com. *Website:* www.belenalonsomanagement.com; www .shlomomintzviolin.com.

MINUTILLO, Hana; singer (mezzo-soprano); b. 1963, Jihlava, Czechoslovakia. *Education:* Pardubice Conservatory, studied in Belgium and with Svatava Subrtova. *Career:* sang at Liberec in Nabucco, Manon and Rusalka; Opera Studio of the National Theatre Prague from 1989, as Carmen, Rosina and Arsamene in Handel's Serse; Mozart's Clemenza di Tito in Darmstadt (1993–94 season) and concert performances of Les Troyens under Michel Plasson in Toulouse and Arhens; Bregenz Festival in Francesca da Rimini and Nabucco; season 1994–95 as Carmen and The Fox in The Cunning Little Vixen, under Mackerras, at the Théâtre du Châtelet, Paris; further engagements as the Witch in Rusalka at Essen, The Diary of One who Disappeared, by Janáček, with Peter Schreier in Leipzig, Olga in Eugene Onegin at Amsterdam and Mozart's Annio (Clemenza di Tito) at Wiesbaden; Flowermaiden at Zürich, 1997. *Recordings include:* Rusalka, conducted by Charles Mackerras. *Current Management:* c/o Aliopera, Via Carlo Poma 9, 20129 Milan Italy. *Telephone:* (02) 89866690. *E-mail:* aliopera@aliopera.it. *Website:* www.aliopera.it; www.minu-vi.de.

MIRABASSI, Gabriele; Italian musician (clarinet); b. 16 Sept. 1967, Perugia. *Education:* Morlacchi Conservatory. *Career:* mem. various jazz groups. *Recordings include:* albums: Fiabe 1995, Como una Volta 1996, Cambaluc 1997, Velho Retrato 1999, Lo Stortino 2000, Luna Park 2000, Una a Zero 2001, Fuori le Mura 2003, Latkia Blend 2004, Graffiando Vento 2007, Canto di Ebano 2008. *E-mail:* info@gabrielemirabassi.com. *Website:* www .gabrielemirabassi.com.

MIRAGEAS, Evans, BA; American artistic director and casting director; *Artistic Director, Cincinnati Opera;* b. Ann Arbor, MI. *Education:* Univ. of Michigan. *Career:* joined WFMT radio station, Chicago 1982, became prod. of classical music programmes; produced radio broadcasts for Lyric Opera of Chicago 1983–89; Artistic Admin. Boston Symphony Orchestra, worked with Seiji Ozawa 1989–94; Sr Vice-Pres. of A&R, Decca Record Co., London 1994–2000; ind. consultant and casting dir to institutions, including Brooklyn Philharmonic, Brooklyn Acad. of Music, Handel and Haydn Soc. of Boston, Milwaukee Symphony Orchestra, WDR Symphony Orchestra of Cologne, Pasadena Pops, Los Angeles Opera, Lincoln Center Festival 2000–; Artistic Dir Cincinnati Opera 2005–; Dir of Artistic Planning, Atlanta Symphony 2007–. *Address:* Cincinnati Opera, Music Hall, 1243 Elm Street, Cincinnati, OH 45202, USA (office). *Telephone:* (513) 768-5500 (office). *Fax:* (513) 768-5552 (office). *E-mail:* EMirageas@cincinnatiopera.org (office). *Website:* www .cincinnatiopera.org (office); www.evansmirageas.com.

MIREA, Marina; Romanian singer (soprano); b. 1941, Bucharest; m. *Education:* Bucharest Conservatory. *Career:* sang at the Bucharest National Opera, 1969–, notably as Violetta, Constanze, Pamina, Lucia di Lammermoor, Olympia, Lakmé, Gilda, Norina, Rosina, Rosalinde, Anchen, Caroline, Miss Wordswoord (A. Hering); guest engagements at the Berlin and Budapest State Operas, at Tel-Aviv and in France, Russia, Germany, Greece, Czechoslovakia and Yugoslavia; teacher, Bucharest Music Univ., 1992–, Constanta Ovidius Univ., 1997–. *Address:* Garoafei str., bl. 6, Bucharest, Romania.

MIRFIN, Timothy (Tim), MA, DipRAM, LRAM; British singer (bass); b. 1974. *Education:* Gonville & Caius Coll., Cambridge, Royal Acad. of Music, Nat. Opera Studio, London. *Career:* early roles included Mozart's Figaro (RAM) and Clodomiro in Lotario, for the London Handel Festival; other roles include Argante in Rinaldo, for Grange Park Opera, Britten's Bottom, and Don Pedro in Beatrice and Benedict; Wigmore Hall debut 2000, singing Russian songs; with Welsh National Opera 2001–03, as Colline in La Bohème, Publio in La Clemenza di Tito, Angelotti in Tosca, Fernando in Beethoven's Leonore, and Parson in The Cunning Little Vixen; performances each year for Edinburgh Int. Festival 2001–07; Seasons 2003–05 played Sarastro in Magic Flute for Scottish Opera, Rodolpho in La Sonnambula for Holland Park, Truffaldino in Ariande auf Naxos and First Apprentice in Wozzeck for WNO, Selim in Turco in Italia for Buxton Festival, Collatinus in Rape of Lucretia for Opera East; bass with Hamburg Staasoper 2005–08, roles included Leporello, Selim in Turco in Italia, Sarastro, Colline, Sparafucile, Sagrestano in Tosca, Pistola, Publio, Peter Quince in A Midsummer Night's Dream, Titurel in Parsifal, Farasmane in Radamisto, Doctor in La Traviata, Tom in Un Ballo in Maschera; played Sarastro, Holland Park Opera 2008; Commendatore in Don Giovanni, Berbiguiere Festival 2008; Don Basilio in The Barber of Seville 2008; Medecin in Pelléas, Theater an der Wien 2009. *Recordings include:* Robert Saxton, The Wandering Jew 2011. *Honours:* Friends of Covent Garden and Countess of Munster Trust Award, Winner, Royal Overseas League Competition, Nat. Mozart Singing Competition, Wagner Prize.

MIRICIOIU, Nelly, Diploma of Bacalaureat (Piano) and Degree (Voice); Romanian/ British singer (soprano); b. 31 March 1952, Adjud; d. of Voicu Miricioiu and Maria Miricioiu; m. Barry J Kirk; one s. *Education:* Octav Bancila Music School, Iasi, George Enescu Conservatoire. *Career:* professional debut as Queen of the Night in The Magic Flute in Romania 1970; West European debut as Violetta in Scottish Opera production of La Traviata 1981; debut at Covent Garden as Nedda in I Pagliacci 1982, at La Scala as Lucia in Lucia di Lammermoor 1983; has since appeared at all major opera houses of the world and in int. recitals and concerts (Salzburg Festival, Concertgebouw, Royal Festival Hall); repertoire includes Mimi (La Bohème), Julietta (I Capuleti e I Montecchi), Gilda (Rigoletto), Elvira (Ernani), Marguerite and Elena (Mefistofele), Michaela (Carmen), Marguerite (Faust), Violetta (La Traviata), Roberto Devereux, Lucrezia Borgia and Maria Stuarda (Donizetti), Tancredi (Rossini), Elisabeth (Don Carlos), Il Pirata and Norma (Bellini), Emma d'Antiochia (Mercadante), Helena in I Vespri Siciliani (Verdi), Jerusalem (Verdi), Semiramide (Rossini), Desdemona in Othello, title roles in Giovanna d'Arco, Tosca, Luisa Miller, Manon Lescaut, Anna Bolena, Lucia di Lammermoor and many more; has worked with many leading conductors and dirs, singing leading roles such as Tosca with José Carreras, José Cura, Neil Schicoff, Mimi in La Bohème with Plácido Domingo, Violetta in La Traviata with Franco Bonisolli, with Roberto Alagna, Renato Bruson, Alfredo Kraus, and many other leading artists; began 20-year series of Vara Matinee Concerts at Amsterdam Concertgebouw 1986; first recording, recital at Wigmore Hall, London 1986; master-classes at numerous venues; jury mem. Maria Callas Grand Prix 2003, London Int. Music Festival 2003, Athens 2003, Dutch IVC 2004, 2010, 2012; Guest Prof., Acad. of Music, Maastricht 2010–. *Recordings include:* Puccini's Tosca, Mercadante's Orazi e Curiazi, Donizetti's Rosamunda d'Inghilterra (with Renée Fleming and Bruce Ford) and Maria de Rudenz (Maria), Rossini's Riccardo e Zoraide, Pacini's Maria Regina d'Inghilterra (Maria) 1998, Mascagni's Cavalleria Rusticana (Santuzza), a live recording in Rome of Respighi's La Fiamma (Silvana) and Nelly Miricioiu

Live at the Concertgebouw, Nelly Miricioiu – A Rossini Gala 2000, Nelly Miricioiu – Bel Canto Portrait 2001, Roberto Devereux (Elisabetta) at Covent Garden 2003, Mercadante's Emma d'Antiochia 2005, Donizetti's Maria Padilla 2012. *Honours:* Cross Royal House of Romania, Comandor Meritul Cultural; winner of 10 int. competitions, including Second Prize, Francisco Viñas (First Prize not awarded) 1974, First Prize, Maria Callas Competition, Athens 1974, Second Prize, Paris 1975, Second Prize, Geneva 1976, Gold Medal, Katia Popova Competition 1977, First Prize, 's-Hertogenbosch Competition 1978, First Prize, Ostende 1980, American Biographical Insts Award 1994, Romanian Medal of Cultural Merit 2004. *Current Management:* c/o Zemsky/Green Artists Management, 104 West 73rd Street, New York, NY 10023, USA. *Telephone:* (212) 579-6700. *Fax:* (212) 579-4723. *E-mail:* agreen@ zemskygreen.com; bzemsky@zemskygreen.com. *Website:* www.zemskygreen .com; www.nellymiricioiu.com.

MIROGLIO, Thierry Jean-Michael; French percussionist; b. 1 Sept. 1963, Paris. *Education:* Paris University, Sorbonne with Iannis Xenakis, National Conservatory, Versailles with J. P. Drouet and Sylvie Gualda, National Conservatory of Boulogne, Billancourt. *Career:* researcher and soloist with ensembles, including Musique Vivante, Atelier Ville d'Avray, Orchestra Opera de Paris, Orchestre Radio France, Musica Insieme; soloist, concerts in festivals of Radio France, Angers, Besancon, Orleans, Nice, Salzburg, Athens, Paris, Würzburg, Venice, Bamberg, Rouen, Munich, Trento, Cremona also in South America; Artistic Dir, percussion season of the French Soc. of Contemporary Music; radio broadcasts; masterclasses, lectures, seminars on the volution of percussion style from the origin until our time, numerous countries; masterclasses, South America 1990; world or grand premieres of works of Cage, Ohana, Boucourechiev, Ballif, Pousseur, Denisov, Donatoni, Kelemen, Henze; Prof., Darius Milhaud Conservatory, Paris; premiered work of Xenakis for solo percussion and ensemble and the percussion concerti of Marlos Nobre; tours have taken him throughout Europe, Asia, South America ant the USA. *Recordings include:* album of Saariaho's pieces. *Honours:* first prize in percussion National Conservatory, Versailles, prize for chamber music National Conservatory of Boulogne. *Address:* 215 ave Henri Ravera, 92220 Bagneux, France. *Telephone:* 1-46-56-61-00. *Fax:* 1-46-56-61-00. *E-mail:* miroglio@club-internet.fr. *Website:* www.thierrymiroglio-percussion .com.

MIRSHAKAR, Zarrina; Tajikistani composer and teacher; b. 19 March 1947, Dushanbe. *Education:* Moscow State Conservatory. *Career:* mem. Union of Composers of Tajikstan, 1992; Union of Soviet Composers, 1974–92. *Compositions include:* String Quartet; 24 music pieces for piano; Three Frescos of Pamir for violin and piano, published 1979; Sonata for clarinet solo, published 1982; Sonata for oboe solo; Respiro for violin, chamber orchestra and timpani; Six pieces for piano, published 1987; Music for documentary film, Our Baki; Colours of Sunny Pamir, symphonic poem, published 1989; Sonata for oboe solo; Symphonietta for string orchestra; Symphony for chamber orchestra; Three Inventions for piano quintet. *Recordings include:* 24 music pieces for piano; Sonata for clarinet solo; Sonata for oboe solo; Cycle of songs for children on M. Mirshaker's poems; Six Pieces for flute and clarinet, 1995. *Honours:* Lenin Komsomol Prize Laureate 1985. *Address:* Pionersky St proezd I 12, 734003 Dushanbe, Tajikstan.

MIRTOVA, Elena; Russian singer (soprano); b. 1962, South West Siberia. *Education:* Leningrad Conservatory. *Career:* debut, sang at the Musical Academy and Philharmonic Hall in Prague while a student; Sang Maria in Rimsky-Korsakov's The Tsar's Bride in Moscow and Leningrad; Series of concerts in Moscow and Leningrad, 1984; Principal soloist at the Kirov Theatre in Leningrad, St Petersburg, from 1988; Rimsky's Olga and Maria, Tchaikovsky's Tatiana and Iolanta and Violetta; Sang in the 14th Symphony of Shostakovich with the Chamber Orchestra of the Lithuanian Philharmonia at the Berliner Philharmonie, 1989; sang Iolanta at Frankfurt 1990 and Leonora in Il Trovatore with Omaha Opera 1991. *Honours:* Winner, Glinka Competition, 1984; First prize, Dvořák Voice Competition, Karlovi Vari, 1987; Winner, Fidenza, Parma Verdi Competition, 1990. *Address:* c/o Marinksky Theatre, 1 Teatralnaya Square, St Petersburg, 190000, Russia. *Website:* www .mariinsky.ru.

MISHENKINE, Arkadij; Russian singer (tenor); b. 1961. *Education:* studied in Kazan, Moscow Conservatory and the Bolshoi Opera Studio. *Career:* sang at the Bolshoi Theatre, Moscow, from 1989, Tchaikovsky's Lenski and Jaromir, Rossini's Almaviva, Paolo in Francesca de Rimini by Rachmaninov, Vladimir in Prince Igor, Lykov in The Tsar's Bride by Rimsky, Alfredo, and Antonio in Prokofiev's Betrothal in a Monastery; guest appearances in France, North America and Japan; many concert engagements.

MISHURA, Irina; Russian singer (mezzo-soprano); b. 1965, Krasnodar. *Education:* Gnessin Institute, Moscow. *Career:* appearances with the Moldovan State Opera as Carmen, Amneris, Azucena, Adalgisa in Norma, Ulrica and Princess Eboli (Don Carlos); Mussorgsky's Marina and Marfa, Olga (Eugene Onegin) and Lyubasha in The Tsar's Bride, by Rimsky-Korsakov; European engagements 1998–99, as Carmen and Amneris at the Vienna Staatsoper, and appearances in Munich, Brussels and Tel-Aviv (New Israeli Opera); Rimsky's The Snow Maiden with the Detroit Symphony, Carmen for San Francisco Opera, Dalila at Michigan and Adalgisa for Baltimore Opera; Concerts include Los Angeles Philharmonic under Valery Gergiev and Verdi Gala in Israel; Season 1999–2000 with Carmen in Vienna and Munich, Fricka in Die Walküre for Dallas Opera and Principessa in Adriana Lecouvreur at

Trieste; Season 2001–2002 with Carmen, Dalila, Azucena and Amneris at the New York Met, and for Opera Pacific, Washington Opera and Cologne Opera. *Current Management:* c/o Opera Art, Via Isolalta Forette 11, 37068 Vigasio (VR), Italy. *Telephone:* (45) 6649911. *Fax:* (45) 6649912. *E-mail:* info@operaart .it. *Website:* www.operaart.it.

MISKELL, Austin, LRAM; singer (tenor) and academic; b. 14 Oct. 1925, Shawnee, OK, USA; m.; two s. *Education:* Oklahoma City Univ., Hochschule für Musik, Zürich, Mozarteum of Salzburg, Royal Acad. of Music, London. *Career:* featured soloist with Elizabethan Consort of Viols, London, Anglian Chamber Soloists London, Ricecare, Ensemble for Ancient Music, Zürich, Arte Antica Zürich; Musinger Players, New York 1986–; sang in 25 countries 1950–86; performances with Tonhalle Orchestra, Zürich, Orchestra de la Academia Santa Cecilia Rome, London Symphony Orchestra, Pro Arte, London, Stuttgarter Synfoniker and others; participant at music festivals, including Sagra Musicale (Perugia, Italy), Settimane Musicali (Ascona, Switzerland), Salzburger Festspiel, Britten, Purcell Festival (Buenos Aires), Mozart Festival (Munich), Bergen Festival (Norway) 1970–80; Asst Prof. of Voice, Nat. Univ. of Columbia, Bogotá 1976–82; Head of Voice, Conservatory of Tolima, Ibague, Colombia 1978–82; Teacher of Voice, Italian Opera, Teatro Colón, Nat. Opera Co., Bogotá 1978–82; Lecturer in Voice, Univ. of New Mexico 1982–84; Prof. of Voice, Coll. of Santa Fe 1982–96.

MISKIMMON, Annilese, MA (Cantab.), MA; Northern Irish artistic director, opera and stage director and arts consultant; *Artistic Director/General Manager, Danish National Opera. Education:* Christ's Coll., Cambridge, City Univ., London. *Career:* Assoc. Dir and Tour Consultant, Glyndebourne Festival 2002–04; Artistic Dir, Opera Theatre Co., Dublin 2004–12; Artistic Dir/Gen. Man. Danish Nat. Opera 2012–; has also worked extensively with ENO and BBC orchestras and at the Proms; Guest Dir Opera Ireland, Salzburg Landestheater, Garsington Opera and other major int. houses. *Productions include:* for Opera Theatre Company: Pelléas, Fidelio, Orlando and Poppea, Apollo and Hyacinthus, La Bohème, Vera of Las Vegas, Cinderella; also Il Re Pastore at Garsington Festival, Barbe-Bleu at Buxton Festival, Shadowtracks for W11 Opera, The Vanishing Bridegroom, The Protagonist, Vanessa, John Cage's Songbooks for BBC Symphony Orchestra, Iolanta, Così fan tutte, L'elisir d'amore, L'Amico Fritz and Falstaff for Holland Park Opera, London, Semele for British Youth Opera, The Queen Who Didn't Come to Tea for Scottish Chamber Orchestra, Arianna, Endimion for Cambridge Classical Opera, La vida breve for BBC Proms, On the Town for BBC Concert Orchestra, Figaro for Beijing Music Conservatory, Der Freischütz for Salzburg Landestheater, Romeo and Juliet for Opera Ireland, Katya and Don Quichotte for Danish Nat. Opera. *Current Management:* c/o Tracey Elliston, Judy Daish Associates, 2 St Charles Place, London, W10 6EG, England. *Telephone:* (20) 8964-8811. *E-mail:* tracey@judydaish.com. *E-mail:* info@jyske-opera.dk (office). *Website:* www.jyske-opera.dk (office).

MISSENHARDT, Gunter; German singer (bass); b. 29 March 1938, Augsburg; m. Agnes Baltsa 1974. *Education:* Augsburg Conservatory, studied with Helge Roswaenge. *Career:* sang at the Bayerische Staatsoper Munich, 1965–68; Frankfurt, 1968–72; Berne, 1973–78; appearances from 1978 at Aachen, Bremen and Brussels, 1986; Since 1984, State Opera Vienna (Ochs, Osmin, Varlaam, Colline); 1984, Grand Opéra Paris (Ochs); Covent Garden, London, since 1985, Bartolo, Varlaam, Ochs, Rocco; 1994 Scala di Milano (Osmin); Düsseldorf, 1988; Théâtre des Champs Elysées Paris, 1989, as Ochs in Der Rosenkavalier; Season 1987–88 as the Doctor in Wozzeck at Strasbourg and Schigolch in Lulu at Brussels; Other roles have included Kecal, Osmin, Bett in Zar und Zimmerman, Masetto, Mozart's Figaro and Varlaam in Boris Godunov; Sang Osmin in Die Entführung at Geneva, 1996; Simon in Lortzing's Regina at Karsruhe, 1998; Season 2000 as Osmin at Dresden and Baron Ochs for the Teatre Real, Madrid. *Current Management:* c/o Gerstel International Opera Management, Stockerstrasse 10, 8002 Zurich, Switzerland. *Telephone:* (76) 3918801. *Fax:* (44) 2531453. *E-mail:* gerstel@swissonline .ch.

MITCHELL, Clare; British costume designer and stage designer; b. 1960, England. *Education:* Bristol Old Vic Theatre School. *Career:* Asst Costume Designer, RSC, Stratford; costumes for premiere of Rebecca by Wilfred Josephs at Leeds 1983, ENO for Madama Butterfly, Scottish Opera Don Giovanni, Jenůfa at Zürich and Covent Garden 1986–93; costumes and sets for Ulisse by Monteverdi and Handel's Flavio at the Batignano Festival, Rigoletto for Opera 80 and Donizetti's Tudor trilogy for Monte Carlo Opera; costumes for La Traviata at ENO 1996; Donizetti's Anna Bolena for Bavarian State Opera 2003, King Lear on Broadway 2004, Pelléas and Mélisande for Met Opera 2010, Don Giovanni for Palau de les Arts, Valencia 2012. *Current Management:* Dennis Lyne Agency, 108 Leonard Street, London EC2A 4RH, England. *Telephone:* (20) 7739-6200. *E-mail:* info@dennislyne.com. *Website:* www.dennislyne1.com.

MITCHELL, Donald Charles Peter, PhD, CBE, FRCM; British writer on music and critic; *Life President, Britten Estate Ltd;* b. 6 Feb. 1925, London; m. Kathleen Livingston; two foster s. *Education:* Durham Univ., with Arthur Hutchings and A. E. F. Dickinson, Southampton Univ. *Career:* founder, Music Survey 1947; Ed. (with Hans Keller), Music Survey series 1949–52; music critic, The Musical Times 1953–57; Ed., Tempo 1958–62; Head of Music Dept, Faber and Faber 1958, Man. Dir. Faber Music 1965–76, Vice-Chair. 1976–77, Chair. 1977–88, Pres. 1988–95; music staff, Daily Telegraph 1959–64; founding Prof. of Music, Sussex Univ. 1971–76, Visiting Prof. 1977–; Chair.,

Britten Estate Ltd 1986–2000, Life Pres. 2000–; Trustee, Britten-Pears Foundation 1986–2000, Trustee Emer. 2000–; Gov., Royal Acad. of Music 1988–, Council of Honour 2000–; Chair., Performing Right Soc. 1989–92; Vice-Pres., CISAC 1992–94; Dir. of study courses, Britten-Pears School, Snape; Visiting Prof., York Univ. 1991, King's Coll., London 1995–99. *Television:* music adviser for film, Owen Wingrave (Channel 4) 2001. *Publications include:* Benjamin Britten (ed. with Hans Keller) 1952, The Mozart Companion (ed. with H. C. Robbins Landon) 1956, The Life and Music of Mahler 1958–2008 (four vols), The Language of Modern Music 1963, Benjamin Britten 1913–76: Pictures from a Life (with John Evans) 1978, Britten and Auden in the Thirties 1981, Benjamin Britten: Death in Venice 1987, Letters from a Life: Selected Letters and Diaries of Benjamin Britten Vols 1–2 1923–45 (ed. with Philip Reed) 1991, Vol. 3 1946–51 (ed. with Philip Reed and Mervyn Cooke) 2004, Vol. 4 1952–57, Cradles of the New: Writings on Music 1951–1991 1995, The Mahler Companion (with Andrew Nicholson) 1999, Discovering Mahler: Writings on Mahler 1995–2005 2007; contrib. to magazines and journals, including Music Survey, The Chesterian, Tempo, TLS, Musical Times, Music and Letters, Nexus Institute (Tilburg), Opera; contrib. articles and broadcasts on Berg, Britten, Hindemith, Mahler, Malcolm Arnold, Mozart, Prokofiev, Reger, Schoenberg, Stravinsky and Weill. *Honours:* Hon. MA (Sussex), Hon. DUniv (York), Hon. DMus (Srinakharinwirot Univ., Bangkok) 2001;Hon. RAM 1992, Hon. Research Fellow Royal Coll. of Music 2000; Royal Philharmonic Soc. Award 1992, Gustav Mahler Soc. Mahler Medal of Honour, Vienna 1987, Univ. of Toronto Dist. Visitor Award 1999, Charles Flint Kellogg Award 2002. *Address:* 83 Ridgmount Gardens, London, WC1E 7AY, England (home). *Fax:* (20) 7436-7964 (office). *E-mail:* mahler@ mitchelld.demon.co.uk.

MITCHELL, Geoffrey Roger; British singer (countertenor), conductor and choir manager; *Director, Geoffrey Mitchell Choir;* b. 6 June 1936, Upminster, Essex, England; s. of Horace Stanley Mitchell and Madge Amy Mitchell. *Education:* studied with Alfred Deller and Lucy Manen. *Career:* countertenor, lay clerk, Ely Cathedral 1957–60, Westminster Cathedral 1960–61; Vicar-choral, St Paul's Cathedral 1961–66; Founder and Conductor Surrey Univ. Choir 1966; Man. John Alldis Choir 1966–, Cantores in Ecclesia 1967–77; Conductor, New London Singers 1970–86; Prof., RAM 1974–95; Singing Teacher, King's Coll. and St John's Coll., Cambridge 1975–85; Conductor, Geoffrey Mitchell Choir 1976–, London Festival Singers 1987–; BBC Choral Man. 1977–92; Guest Conductor, Camerata Antigua of Curitiba, Brazil. *Recordings:* various with John Alldis Choir, Cantores in Ecclesia, Pro Cantione Antigua; 70 recordings with Opera Rara/Geoffrey Mitchell Choir, 23 complete operas for Chandos Opera in English Series. *Honours:* Hon. ARAM 1975, Hon. FTCL 1990. *Address:* 49 Chelmsford Road, Woodford, London, E18 2PW, England. *Telephone:* (20) 8491-0962. *E-mail:* geoffrey -mitchell@ntlworld.com.

MITCHELL, Ian, BMus, GRSM; British clarinettist and academic; *Head, Faculty of Wind, Brass & Percussion, Trinity Laban Conservatoire of Music and Dance, London;* b. 14 Feb. 1948, S Yorks., England; m. Vanessa Noel-Tod 1970; one s. one d. *Education:* Royal Acad. of Music, London, Goldsmiths Coll. *Career:* debut in Purcell Room, London 1971; solo appearances throughout UK, Europe, Middle East, USA, Australia, Democratic People's Repub. of Korea and Taiwan; chamber concert performances in Europe, Middle East, Ear East, Australia; solo broadcasts on BBC and for Swedish, American, Belgian, Austrian and German radio stations; soloist on British TV and in films of composers Cornelius Cardew and John Cage; numerous first performances, many works written for him; Dir Gemini chamber ensemble; mem. Dreamtiger, Eisler Ensemble of London, Entertainers Clarinet Quartet, AMM, Critical Band, Mitchell Ryan Duo; part-time Sr Lecturer in Performance, Univ. of Exeter, Univ. Dir of Music 1996–2007, Warden, Inc. Soc. of Musicians (ISM) Performers and Composers Section 2005–06; currently Head of Faculty of Wind, Brass & Percussion, Trinity Laban Conservatoire of Music and Dance, London; mem. ISM, Clarinet and Saxophone Soc. of GB (Chair. 2000–02), Inst. for Learning and Teaching in Higher Educ. *Recordings:* works of Nicola LeFanu (with Gemini), works of Oliver Knussen (with London Sinfonietta), Draughtman's Contract, The Masterwork and others (with Michael Nyman Band), Eisler (with Dagmar Krauze), works by Maxwell Davies, David Lumsdaine, John White, Lindsay Cooper, Philip Grange, Geoffrey Poole, Xenakis, Janáček, solo album of music for bass clarinet, duo album with mezzo-soprano Alison Wells, numerous chamber ensemble recordings, featured soloist for film My Friends Told Me About You (music by Carlos Dengler). *Publications:* Structure and Content of Lessons, Preparing for Performance, two chapters in The Versatile Clarinet, contrib. to Musical Times, Clarinet and Saxophone, Contact, New Grove Dictionary of Music and Musicians, Music Teacher, Musical Performance. *Honours:* Hon. ARAM 1997, Hon. TCL 2006. *Address:* 137 Upland Road, East Dulwich, London, SE22 0DF, England (home). *Telephone:* (20) 8693-4694 (office). *E-mail:* i.mitchell@trinitylaban.ac.uk (office); ianmitchell1@btinternet.com (home). *Website:* www.trinitylaban.ac.uk (office); www.gemini-ensemble.org .uk (office).

MITCHELL, Lee, BMus, PhD; composer, pianist and educator; b. 27 April 1951, Wilmington, DE, USA. *Education:* Peabody Inst., Johns Hopkins Univ., Univ. of California, Santa Barbara, Univ. of Berne, Switzerland. *Career:* debut at Wilmington, DE; Prof. of Music Theory and History, Acad. of Music, Biel, Switzerland 1973–76; Prof. of Music Theory and History, Peabody Inst., Johns Hopkins Univ., Baltimore 1976–86; Chair of Theory 1984–86, Prof. of Music,

School of Continuing Studies 1986–; Adjunct Prof. of Music, Goucher Coll., Towson, MD 1980–83; Lecturer, Univ. of Esztergom, Hungary 1980, 1981, 1983; television appearances, radio broadcasts; piano concerts in the USA, Switzerland, Germany, The Netherlands, Greece, Hungary; compositions performed in the USA, Peru, Europe; mem. Sonneck Soc., American Musicological Soc. *Compositions include:* Baltimore Reflections for flute and piano 1989, Variations and Toccata for organ, Fantasy Allegro for flute and organ 1993, Ballade for violin, viola and piano 1994, Four Jewish Melodies for clarinet and piano 1995. *Honours:* Rockefeller grant in composition 1965, Dame Myra Hess Memorial Concert Series Award, Chicago 1987, Artist Fellow in Musical Composition, State of Delaware 1991, Meet the Composer grants 1992–94, 1996.

MITCHELL, Leona; singer (soprano); b. 13 Oct. 1949, Enid, OK, USA. *Education:* Univ. of Oklahoma, studied in Santa Fe and San Francisco, and with Ernest St John Metz in Los Angeles. *Career:* debut in San Francisco 1972, as Micaela in Carmen; Metropolitan Opera from 1975, as Micaela, Pamina, Puccini's Manon, Liu and Mini, Elvira in Ernani and Leonora in La Forza del Destino; Barcelona 1975, as Mathilde in Guillaume Tell; guest appearances in Houston, Washington, Stuttgart and Geneva; Covent Garden debut 1980, as Liu in Turandot; Sydney Opera 1985, as Leonora in Il Trovatore; Nice Opera 1987 as Salome in Massenet's Hérodiade; Paris Opéra-Comique in Puccini's Trittico (all three soprano leads); Verona 1988, Aida; sang Elvira in Ernani at Parma 1990, the Trovatore Leonora at the Teatro Colón Buenos Aires; season 1992 as Aida for New Israeli Opera; sang Strauss's Ariadne at the Sydney Opera House 1997 and Aida at Santiago; season 1999–2000 as Turandot at Sydney and Elisabeth de Valois in Melbourne. *Recordings include:* Gershwin's Bess.

MITCHELL, Madeleine Louise, MMus, GRSM, ARCM, FRSA; British concert violinist, academic and director; *Professor of Violin, Royal College of Music;* one d. *Education:* Royal Coll. of Music Foundation Scholar, Eastman and Juilliard Schools, New York. *Career:* BBC TV Music Time 1979; debut recital, South Bank, London 1984; South Bank recitals include awards by Worshipful Co. of Musicians, Kirckman Soc., Park Lane Group; numerous solo tours in concertos and recitals in the UK, Germany, Czechoslovakia, Spain, Italy, USA, Canada; world tour, British Council 1989, 1990; Violinist Fires of London 1985–87; numerous int. festival appearances, including Aspen, Athens, Belfast, BBC Proms, Brazil – Articulacouns, Curitiba, Cardiff, Cheltenham, Dartington, ISCM Masters of 20th Century Music Warsaw, Huddersfield, Kiev, Lincoln Center, Malta, Malvern, St Magnus, Schwetzingen, Toronto, Warwick, York; soloist on tour with Wurttemberg, Munich Chamber Orchestras, Ulster, Czech Radio Symphony (Plzen), Malaga Symphony, Karlovarsky Symphony, London Festival Orchestra; Wigmore Hall debut recital 1989; solo tour, S America 1991; concertos with City of London Orchestra, Queen Elizabeth Hall, London 1992, Royal Philharmonic Orchestra, London 1993 under Sir Alexander Gibson, Polish Radio Symphony 1994, Kiev Radio/TV Orchestra 1994, Ulster Orchestra; Nyman Band tours and film 1992; tours also include Poland, Ukraine, South Bank recitals 1993, 1994, 1995, 1996, 2005; recitals in New York 1994, 1997, 2001; Wigmore Hall recitals 1995, 1997, 2001, 2003 (with Norbert Brainin); Prof. of Violin, Royal Coll. of Music 1994–; Faculty of Schlern Int. Festival, Italy 2004–; numerous master-classes world-wide; Artistic Dir London Chamber Ensemble 1994–, Red Violin Festival, Cardiff 1997, 2007, Music in Quiet Places 1993–97; US Embassy London concerts 2003–04; Artist-in-Residence, Canberra Int. Chamber Music Festival, Brazil 1999; soloist on tour with Welsh Chamber Orchestra 2000; Leader, Bridge String Quartet 2001–07; recital, Lincoln Center, New York, for UK in New York Festival 2001; concerto, Queen Elizabeth Hall, London 2004; festivals, France, Spain, Italy 2004, 2006, Croatia 2007; FiddleSticks collaboration with Ensemble Bash – Arts Council supported UK tours 2006–09, including Symphony Hall, Birmingham, Chelsea Festival; London recitals, St John's, Smith Square 2005, 2006, 2007; tours of Scotland, Malta; recitals at St David's Hall Cardiff, in Italy, Brazil, at UK Festivals: Cambridge, Hampstead and Highgate, Lake Dist, Vale of Glamorgan 2007; soloist, St Petersburg Philharmonic 2009; tours of UAE, Russia 2009, USA 2009, 2010; duo with pianist Noriko Ogawa-Buxton, North Aldborough festivals etc. 2010; works written for her and premiered by her by Brian Elias, Stuart Jones, Piers Hellawell, Anthony Powers, Vladimir Runshak, James MacMillan, John Woolrich, Michael Nyman, Jonathan Harvey, Thierry Pecou, Roxanna Panufnik, Stephen Montague, Nigel Osborne, Tarik O'Regan, Anne Dudley; mem. ISM, RSA, BFSA. *Radio:* BBC Radio 2, 3, 4, Classic FM, Bayerischer Rundfunk, ABC, SABC, CBC, nat. radio in Poland, Czech Repub., Spain, Bulgaria, Hong Kong, Singapore, Russia. *Television:* broadcasts in Poland, Ukraine, Hong Kong, Colombia, Australia (Channel 7), Germany, UK (including BBC TV, S4C), Singapore, Spain, Italy, Canada, Colombia, Czechoslovakia, Malta, Brazil. *Recordings:* Essential Michael Nyman 1993, Messiaen Quartet for the End of Time 1994, British Treasures (violin sonatas by Goossens, Hurlstone and Turnbull, with Andrew Ball) 2003, Hummel violin sonatas 2003, Bridge Chamber Music 2004, Quiet Music (with Joanna MacGregor) 2004, In Sunlight: Pieces for Madeleine Mitchell 2005, Alwyn Chamber Music 2007, Violin Songs (with Andrew Ball and Elizabeth Watts) 2007, Fiddlesticks 2008, Howard Blake Violin Works 2008. *Publications:* Tribute to Dorothy DeLay, in The Strad 2002, Perspectives in Muso Magazine and The Link 2004, 2007, Int. Record Review 2007. *Honours:* Fulbright/ITT Fellow, Tagore Medal, RCM 1978, Cosmopolitan Performance Arts Achievement Award (jtly with Darcey Bussell) 1991, Arts Council England Grant 2006–09. *E-mail:* info@redviolin.co.uk (office). *Cur-*

rent Management: c/o Margaret Murphy Management, 7 Grove Park London, E11 2DN, England. *Telephone:* (20) 8530-1305; (7717) 412358 (mobile). *Fax:* (20) 8530-1305. *E-mail:* margaret@margaretmurphy.com. *Website:* www.margaretmurphy.com. *Address:* The Loft House, 41 Queen's Gardens, London, W2 3AA, England (office). *E-mail:* info@redviolin.co.uk (office). *Website:* www.classical-artists.com/madeleinemitchell.

MITCHELL, Scott; British pianist; b. 1964, Perth, Scotland. *Education:* Royal Acad. of Music, London with Alexander Kelly and John Streets, studied with members of the Amadeus Quartet. *Career:* mem. Borante Piano Trio 1982–; London performances at the Purcell Room and Wigmore Hall in the trios of Beethoven; tours to Dublin, Paris and Vienna, Beethoven's Triple Concerto at Festival Wiener Klassik 1989; concerts in Tel-Aviv and Jerusalem and association with Israel Piano Trio at Dartington Summer School 1988; Season 1990 at the Perth and Bath Festivals, tour of Scandinavia, Russia and the Baltic States; TV appearances on Channel 4 and BSB; duo partnerships with Laurence Jackson (violin) and Duncan Prescott (clarinet); accompanist to Yvonne Howard (mezzo-soprano) and Barry Banks (tenor), including tour of France, Spain and Portugal 1989. *Recordings:* albums for Chandos with Duncan Prescott and Collins Classics with Jennifer Stinton (flute). *Honours:* Leverhulme Scholarship, English Speaking Union Scholarship, Lisa Fuchsova Prize, Royal Overseas League Competition 1990. *Address:* The Old Stable, Shudy Camps Park, Shudy Camps, Cambs., CB1 6RD, England. *Telephone:* (1382) 330883. *E-mail:* scott.piano@virgin.net.

MITCHINSON, John Leslie, ARMCM, FRMCM; British singer (tenor) and administrator; b. 31 March 1932, Blackrod, Lancashire, England; m. Maureen Guy 1958; two s. *Education:* Royal Manchester College of Music, singing with Frederick Cox, Heddle Nash and Boriska Gerab. *Career:* debut in TV series with Eric Robinson, Music for You; stage debut as Jupiter in Handel's Semele at Sadler's Wells Theatre, 1959; Senior Lecturer, Royal Northern = Coll. of Music, 1987–92; Head of Vocal Studies, Welsh Coll. of Music and Drama, 1992–; numerous radio, television, concert and opera appearances world-wide, including with ENO, WNO, Scottish Opera, Basle Opera, Prague Opera; Roles included: Idomeneo, Aegisthus, Luca in From the House of the Dead, Manolios in The Greek Passion; Dalibor, Florestan, Siegmund; Sang Svatopluk Cech in the first British production of Janáček's The Excursions of Mr Brouček, ENO, 1978; Wagner's Tristan and Peter Grimes for Welsh National Opera; Opera North and Buxton Festival, 1983 as Max in Der Freischütz and Gualtiero in Vivaldi's Griselda; Menelaus in Belle Hélène, Scottish Opera, 1995; Banff Arts Centre, Canada, performances of The Raven King (Opera in 2 Parts) by Mervyn Burtch, 1999. *Recordings:* Mahler 8th Symphony, Bernstein; Mahler 8th Symphony, Wyn Morris; Das Lied von der Erde, Alexander Gibson, Béatrice et Bénédict, Berlioz (Colin Davis); Lelio, Berlioz (Pierre Boulez); Tristan und Isolde, Wagner (Reginald Goodall); Glagolitic Mass, Janáček (Simon Rattle); Glagolitic Mass (Kurt Masur), Gewandhaus Orchestra, 1990; Das Lied von der Erde, Raymond Leppard; Das Lied von der Erde, Horenstein; Dream of Gerontius, Simon Rattle and CBSO. *Honours:* Queen's Prize and Royal Philharmonic Kathleen Ferrier Prize 1956–57, Curtis Gold Medal, RMCM, 1953, Ricordi Opera Prize 1952.

MITO, Motoko; Japanese violinist; b. 13 June 1957, Kyoto; m. Yoske Otawa 1989. *Education:* Toho School of Music, Tokyo, Hochschule Mozarteum, Salzburg, Austria. *Career:* debut in Salzburg; Concertmaster, Int. Music Art Soc. Orchestra, Tokyo 1980–81; soloist, Int. Mozart Week, Salzburg 1984; many recitals and appearances with Prof. Erika Frieser, piano, throughout Europe and Japan 1984–; mem., Salzburger Streichquartett 1987–. *Recordings:* two Salzburger Streichquartett albums. *Address:* Kamiyasumatsu 11, Tokorozawa, Japan.

MITTELMANN, Norman, DipMus; singer (baritone); b. 25 May 1932, Winnipeg, MB, Canada; m. 1979; two d. *Education:* Curtis Inst. of Music with Martial Singher and Ernzo Mascherini. *Career:* debut with Toronto Opera Co.; performances at opera houses in Germany, Italy, Austria, Puerto Rico, Canada, USA, Poland, Switzerland; roles include Amonasro in Aida at Zürich 1967, William Tell at the May Festival, Florence 1969, Rigoletto at Chicago Opera Theatre 1977, Scarpia in Tosca at Venice 1979, John Falstaff in Hamburg and Berlin 1979, Nelusko in L'Africaine at San Francisco Opera, Mandryka in Arabella at La Scala; sang at Zürich until 1982. *Recordings include:* La Gioconda (video, from San Francisco) 1979. *Honours:* Rockefeller Foundation Fellow 1956–59, Fischer Foundation Award 1959.

MIURA, Fumiaki; Japanese violinist; b. 1993. *Education:* Toho Gakuen School of Music, Tokyo, Vienna Conservatory, Austria. *Career:* studied with Tsugio Tokunaga in Tokyo and Prof. Pavel Vernikov in Vienna; has attended masterclasses with Jean-Jacques Kantorow, Zakhar Bron; performances with many orchestras including NDR Radiophilharmonie, Polish Amadeus Chamber Orchestra, Tokyo Symphony Orchestra, Tokyo Philharmonic, Osaka Philharmonic, Sapporo Symphony Orchestra, Nagoya Philharmonic Orchestra. *Honours:* Hannover Int. Violin Competition First Prize, Music Critics' Prize, Audience Prize 2009. *Current Management:* Benedikt Carlberg, Konzertdirektion Schmid, Postfach 34 09, 30034 Hannover, Germany; AMATI Inc., S201 1-14-5 Akasaka Minato-Ku, Tokyo 107-0052, Japan. *Telephone:* (511) 36607-77; (03) 3560-3007. *Fax:* (511) 36607-34; (03) 3560-3008. *E-mail:* benedikt.carlberg@kdschmid.de; haruko.araki@amati-tokyo.com. *Website:* www.kdschmid.de; www.amati-tokyo.com; www.fumiaki-miura.com.

MIZELLE, Dary John, PhD; American composer; b. 14 June 1940, Stillwater, OK; m.; five c. *Education:* California State Univ. and Univ. of California at Davis. *Career:* Prof., Univ. of South Florida 1973–75, Oberlin Coll. 1975–79, State Univ. at Purchase, New York 1990. *Compositions:* Polyphonies I–III 1975–78, Polytempus I for trumpet and tape 1976, Primavera-Heterphony for 24 celli 1977, Samadhi for quadrophonic tape 1978, Polytempus II for marimba and tape 1979, Quanta II and Hymn of the World for two choruses and ensemble 1979, Lake Mountain Thunder for cor anglais and percussion ensemble 1981, Thunderclap of Time (music for a planetarium) 1982, Requiem Mass for chorus, soloists and orchestra 1982–2002, Sonic Adventures 1982, Quintet for woodwinds 1983, Contrabass Quartet 1983, Indian Summer for string quartet and oboe 1983, Sounds for orchestra 1984, Concerto for contrabass and orchestra 1974–78, Genesis for orchestra 1985, Blue for orchestra 1986, Percussion Concerto 1987, Parameters for percussion solo and chamber orchestra 1974–87, Earth Mountain Fire 1987–, Fossy: A Passion Play (music theatre) 1987, Chance Gives Me What I Want (dance) 1988, SPANDA complex of 198 compositions lasting over 13 days, including Transmutations and Metamorphoses 1989, Silverwind for solo flute 1990, Polytempus IV Quartet for mallet instruments 1991, Metacontrasts for clarinet, violin and piano 1993, Transforms for piano 1995, Amore for two violins 1995, Summer Vision Concerto for violin and orchestra 1996, Endless Melody for orchestra 1996, Niagara for large orchestra 1999, Iguanas for brass, percussion and theatre 2001, Forbidden Colours for solo flute and chamber orchestra 2000, Illuminations for computer and chamber orchestra 2002, Dream of the Vacationers (chamber opera) 2002. *Address:* c/o ASCAP, ASCAP Building, 1 Lincoln Plaza, NY 10023, USA.

MIZUKOSHI, Satoshi, BMus, MMus; Japanese singer (tenor). *Education:* Tokyo Nat. Univ. of Fine Arts and Music, Royal Conservatory, The Hague with with Peter Kooij, Rita Dams and Michael Chance. *Career:* has sung regularly with Bach Collegium Japan 1997–; has performed as soloist in European festivals including Bachwoche Ansbach (Germany), Festival de Música de Canarias (Spain); mem. Collegium Vocale Gent (Philippe Herreweghe), Nederlands Kamerkoor, Capella Amsterdam (Daniel Reuss), Sette Voci (Peter Kooij), Vox Luminis; soloist, Europa Cantat XVII Utrech. *Recordings include:* J.S. Bach's Complete Motets (BBC Music Magazine Award, Choral Category) 2011; recordings with Sette Voci and Bach Collegium Japan. *Address:* Nederlands Kamerkoor, PO Box 10831, 1001 Amsterdam Netherlands (office). *Telephone:* (20) 5787978 (office). *Fax:* (20) 5787979 (office). *E-mail:* info@nederlandskamerkoor.nl (office). *Website:* www .nederlandskamerkoor.nl (office).

MIZZI, Alfred (Freddie) Paul; Maltese clarinettist; b. 12 Oct. 1934, Valletta; m. 1953, two d. *Education:* ALCM. *Career:* debut as soloist with the Malta Nat. Orchestra 1961; played at Belfast Arts Festival 1967; World Symphony Orchestra performances in New York, Washington and Florida 1971; soloist in concerts in Bucharest, Mannheim, Mozart Castle, Darmstadt, Wigmore Hall and Barbican Centre, London 1973–83; concerts in France and Greece as part of the Mediterranean Arts Festival 1985; concerts at the Czechoslovakia Arts Festival 1986; soloist with Stamitz Symphony Orchestra, Germany, Watford Chamber Orchestra, England, Zapadocesky Symphony Orchester, Czechoslovakia and others; soloist with string quartets, including The Brevis String Quartet, Malta, Salzburg String Quartet, Austria, Sinnhoffer String Quartet, Germany, Quartetto Academica, Romania, The Rasumovsky String Quartet, UK and others; television appearances and radio broadcasts; mem. PRS, London. *Honours:* Phoenicia Int. Culture Award 1985, Malta Soc. of Arts Award 1986. *Address:* c/o Il Klarinett, Ursuline Sisters Street, G'Mangia, Malta.

MOBBS, Kenneth William, MusB, MA, FRCO, LRAM; British keyboard player, music historian and tutor; b. 4 Aug. 1925, Higham Ferrers, Northants., England; s. of George William Mobbs and Grace Elsie Mobbs (née Pack); m. 1st Barbara Joyce Rosaline McNeill 1950; three d.; m. 2nd Mary Jeanette Randall 1979. *Education:* Kettering Grammar School, Clare Coll., Cambridge, Royal Coll. of Music, studied with Greville Cooke, M. P. Conway, Frank Merrick, Harold Darke, Richard Austin, John Dyer and Gordon Jacob. *Career:* debut organ recital, King's Coll., Cambridge 1949; Asst Lecturer, then Lecturer, then Sr Lecturer in Music, Univ. of Bristol 1950–83; Musical Dir Bristol Opera School 1954–64, Bristol Intimate Opera 1982–83; freelance keyboard performer, including harpsichord concerto, solo piano, violin and piano duo, fortepiano recitals and numerous accompaniments on BBC Nat. Radio; fmr Dir Mobbs Keyboard Collection. *Compositions include:* Engaged! (with George Rowell) (comic opera, adapted from Gilbert & Sullivan) 1963. *Recordings include:* Golden Age of the Clarinet (with Keith Puddy), Twenty Early Keyboard Instruments (Kensound 01), Four English Early Grands (Kensound 02), Die Schöne Müllerin, with Niall Hoskin (Kensound 03), Piano Recitals (Kensound 04), Organ Recitals (Kensound 05), Winter Journey (with Peter Allanson) (Kensound 06). *Radio:* numerous BBC performances as solo pianist and harpsichordist on modern and antique instruments; also accompanist and chamber music payer. *Television:* pianist for Network DVD: The Clifton House Mystery. *Publications:* contrib. to Encyclopaedia of Keyboard Instruments 1993; articles in Early Music, Galpin Society Journal, English Harpsichord Magazine, Harpsichord and Fortepiano Magazine. *Honours:* Organ Scholar and Hon. Scholar, Clare Coll. Cambridge, Turpin Prize in FRCO examination. *E-mail:* mobbsearlykeyboard@blueyonder.co.uk (office). *Website:* www .mobbsearlykeyboard.co.uk (office); earlykeyboards.co.nz.

MOE, Bjorn Kaare; Norwegian organist; b. 10 Aug. 1946, Hegra; m. Kristine Kaasa 1975. *Education:* Trondheim School of Music, Musik-Akad. der Stadt Basel Abteilung Konservatorium and Schola Cantorum Basiliensis, studied with Eduard Muller and Wolfgang Neininger, and with Gaston Litaize in Paris and Jiri Reinberger in Prague. *Career:* Prof., Trondelag Musikkonservatorium, Trondheim 1973–84; full-time concert organist 1985–; concerts with complete works of Olivier Messiaen, main works of Max Reger and other organ music from all periods, although mainly 20th century; world premiere of several new works from Switzerland, Iceland and Norway; cooperates with other arts such as theatre, dance and poetry; organ expert; counsellor arranged Te Deum by Ludvig Nielsen for choir, soloists, strings, brass, percussion and organ (premiere, Ratzenburg, Germany) 1971; transcribed among others Ferruccio Busoni's Fantasia Contrappuntistica for organ (premiere Trondheim, Norway) 1986 and George Gershwin's Rhapsody in Blue for organ (premiere Basle, Switzerland) 1988. *Recordings:* works of Torsten Nilsson 1999, works of Ludvig Nielsen 2005, works of Kjell Mørk Karlsen 2010. *Publication:* The Steinmeyer-organ, Trondheim Cathedral 1996, 2005. *Honours:* numerous scholarships and prizes from many countries, participant in the Norwegian Govt income guarantee programme for artists 1990–. *Address:* Postboks 16, 7221 Melhus, Norway. *E-mail:* k.k.moe@online .no.

MOENNE-LOCCOZ, Philippe; French musician and composer; *Artistic Director, Musiques Inventives d'Annecy;* b. 21 March 1953, Annecy; s. of André Moënne-Loccoz and Yvonne Quelvennec; m. Anne Courel; three s. *Education:* Conservatoire d'Annecy, Conservatoire de Genève, School of Mechanical systems. *Career:* debut aged ten; teaches aspects of music through animation at special children's centre; teacher of electro-acoustic music; Dir Musiques Inventives d'Annecy (studio for research, creative work and music educ.), Annecy; Artistic Dir Festival MIA en novembre, Annecy; int. career with Trio Collectif and The Sound Quartet ensembles in Canada, Hungary, the Netherlands, Sweden 2008–, Romania, Turkey, Finland, Estonia, Switzerland, Spain, Poland and USA for live electronic music; resident artist, Banff Centre, Canada, VICC, Sweden, EMS, Sweden; mem. Asscn for Electroacoustic Music, Geneva. *Compositions:* electro-acoustic works: Boucles, Rêves opaques, Oscillation, Petit musique du soir; mixed works, electro-acoustic and traditional instruments; Le cri des idées sur l'eau, Recontre, Mixage 4, Oscillation No. 1, 2, 6, Inventions 1991, Chaos for tape, Aspérites 1992, Fermez la porte 1992, Limites Extrêmes 1999, Mutations, Cloche, Oies, Cristal B, Harpe; music for theatre: Franz ou les changements profonds 1997, Les Cris 2004. *Radio:* Radio France, Radio Canada, Radio Roumania, Radio Suisse Romande. *Recordings:* Réves opaques, Le Cri des idées sur l'eau, Trola, Chutes 1989, Super Trio with Trio Collectif and Canadian Electronic Ensemble of Toronto, Limites 2000. *Honours:* Conservatoire Prize. *Address:* 24 bis avenue Marechal Leclerc, 38300 Bourgoin-Jallieu (home); 1 rue Jean Jaurès, 74000 Annecy, France (office). *Telephone:* (4) 50-45-09-76 (office). *Fax:* (4) 50-45-48-84 (office). *E-mail:* phil.moenne-loccoz@orange.fr (home); miannecydir@orange.fr (office). *Website:* www.miannecy.org (office); www .philippe-moenne-loccoz.fr.

MOFFAT, Anthony; British violinist; b. 1995, Hexham, Northumberland. *Education:* Royal Acad. of Music with Manoug Parikian. *Career:* founder mem., Borante Trio, with recitals throughout Europe and Beethoven's Triple Concerto in Vienna; London concerts at the Wigmore Hall and Purcell Room; solo performances for BBC radio; engagements as leader of the BBC Concert Orchestra, Royal Liverpool Philharmonic and National Symphony Orchestra of Ireland; former Assoc. Leader, Hallé Orchestra, Manchester; Leader, Orchestra of Scottish Opera 2000–. *Honours:* RAM Marjorie Hayward Prize.

MOFFAT, Julie; British singer (soprano); b. 1966, Leicester; m. Martyn Hill 2004. *Education:* Royal College of Music with Marion Studholme, studied with Pamela Cook and Paul Hamburger. *Career:* debut in London 1987, in Elliott Carter"s A Mirror on Which to Dwell; British premiere of Jonathan Harvey's From Silence, 1989; Appearances with such contemporary music groups as Klangforum Wien, Ensemble Inter Contemporain, Ensemble Modern of Frankfurt, London Sinfonietta and the BBC Singers; repertoire has included works by Zender, Barraqué, Webern, Zimmerman, Nono, Beat Furrer, Cerha and Varèse; Requiem for Reconciliation with Helmuth Rilling at the 1995 Stuttgart Music Festival; frequent engagements in oratorios by Bach, Beethoven, Haydn, Mozart, Rossini, Mendelssohn and Schubert; Season 1996–97 at the Vienna Konzerthaus, the Bregenz, Salzburg, Holland, Schleswig-Holstein Festivals, Venice Biennale and Brussels Ars Musica. *Recordings include:* albums with Klangforum Wien, Stuttgarter Bach Akademie and Ensemble Intercontemporain; music by Zimmermann, Dallapiccola and Zender. *Honours:* RCM Foundation Scholarship 1984. *Address:* Bromleys Farmhouse, 10 Weir Road, Kibworth Beauchamp, Leicestershire, LE8 0LP, England.

MOGENSEN, Mogens Eddie; Danish musician (bassoon); *Principal Bassoon, Royal Danish Orchestra;* b. 31 March 1948, Odense; m. Nora Andrea Mogensen 1972; two s. one d. *Education:* Det Fynske Musikkonservatorium, Odense, with Hagbard Knudsen. *Career:* Prin. Bassoon, Royal Danish Orchestra, Copenhagen 1972–; Teacher, Royal Danish Acad. of Music, RAM, London; mem. Int. Double Reed Soc. *Honours:* Kgl. Kapelmusicus. *Address:* Mikkelborg Park 7, 2970 Hørsholm, Denmark. *Telephone:* 43-73-41-89. *E-mail:* memogensen@gmail.com.

MOHR, Thomas; singer (baritone); b. 17 Oct. 1961, Neumunster, Holstein, Germany. *Education:* studied in Lubeck and Hamburg. *Career:* debut in Lubeck 1984, as Silvio in Pagliacci; sang at Lubeck and Detmold 1984–85, Bremen 1985–87, Nationaltheater, Mannheim from 1987; guest appearances at the Schleswig-Holstein Festival 1987, and at Cologne, Hamburg and Ludwigsburg; other roles include Mozart's Count and Papageno, Rossini's Figaro, Lortzing'z Zar and Count in Der Wildschütz, Wolfram and Billy Budd; many concerts and lieder recitals; season 2000–01 as Spohr's Faust for Cologne Opera, Moses in the US premiere of Weill's The Eternal Road (Brooklyn Acad., New York) and Mauregato in Schubert's Alfonso and Estrella, at Zürich. *Honours:* winner, Hertogenbosch Competition 1984, German Lied Competition, London 1985.

MOK, Warren; American singer (tenor); b. 1960, Hawaii. *Education:* University of Hawaii, Manhattan School of Music. *Career:* appearances at the Deutsche Oper, Berlin, 1988–, as the Duke of Mantuo, Alfredo, Rodolfo, Don Carlos, Ferrando, Count Almaviva, Nemorino and Prince Cou-Chong in Das Land des Lächelns; Premieres of Henze's Das verratene Meer and Reimann's Das Scholss; further engagements at the Vienna and Athens Festivals, Leipzig, Copenhagen and Lisbon Operas; many companies in the USA; season 1999–2000 with Calaf in Lithuania, Gabriele Adorno at Martina Franca, Don José in Hong Kong, Alfredo at Shanghai, Verdi's Alvaro at Copenhagen and Manrico for Opéra de Monte Carlo. *Current Management:* Music International, 13 Ardilaun Road, London, N5 2QR, England.

MOLDOVEANU, Eugenia; singer (soprano); b. 19 March 1944, Bursteni, Romania. *Education:* Ciprian Porumbescu Conservatory, studied in Bucharest with Arta Florescu. *Career:* debut in Bucharest 1968 as Donna Anna in Don Giovanni; guest appearances in Belgrade, Sofia, Athens, Amsterdam, Trieste, Stuttgart, Dresden and Berlin; repertoire includes roles in operas by Mozart, Verdi and Puccini; sang Mozart's Countess while on tour to Japan with Vienna Staatsoper 1986; season 1987 sang Mozart's Countess at La Scala Milan, Butterfly at Verona and Donna Anna at Turin, Countess 1989.

MOLDOVEANU, Nicolae, ARAM; conductor; b. 20 July 1962. *Education:* Musikhochschule in Zürich, Basel and Bern, Switzerland, Royal Academy of Music, London. *Career:* violinist 1982; repetiteur, conductor, Altmarkt Theatre, former E Germany; worked with orchestras in Switzerland, Germany, UK, South Africa and Romania; Resident Conductor, Bournemouth Orchestra 1996; Principal Conductor, English Sinfonia 1998–; Assoc. Guest Conductor, London Mozart Players 2002–. *Honours:* Edwin Samuel Dove Prize and Ricordi Conducting Prize, Royal Academy of Music, London, 1993. *Current Management:* Clarion/Seven Muses, 47 Whitehall Park, London, N19 3TW, England. *Telephone:* (20) 7272-4413. *Fax:* (20) 7281-9687. *E-mail:* admin@c7m.co.uk.

MOLDOVEANU, Vasile; singer (tenor); b. 6 Oct. 1935, Konstanza, Romania. *Education:* studied in Bucharest with Constantin Badescu. *Career:* debut in Bucharest 1966, as Rinuccio in Gianni Schicchi; Stuttgart debut 1972, as Donizetti's Edgardo; Munich Opera from 1976, as Rodolfo and the Duke of Mantua; Deutsche Oper Berlin and Chicago Lyric Oper 1977; Hamburg Opera 1978, as Don Carlos; Metropolitan Opera from 1979, as Pinkerton, Turiddu, Gabriele Adorno, Luigi in Il Tabarro and Henri in Les Vêpres Siciliennes; Covent Garden 1979, as Don Carlos; Zürich Opera 1980, in Verdi's Attila; Monte Carlo 1982, in Lucia di Lammermoor; guest appearances in Helsinki, Brussels, Barcelona, Dresden, Cologne, Frankfurt and Athens; other roles include Mozart's Don Ottavio, Pedrillo and Tamino; Stuttgart Staatsoper and Nice 1988, as Cavaradossi and as Puccini's Dick Johnson; sang Pinkerton at Rome 1990.

MOLEDA, Krzysztof; singer (tenor); b. 6 April 1955, Poznań, Poland. *Education:* Music High School, Lodz. *Career:* debut singing Wenzel in The Bartered Bride, Lodz, 1975; sang with Warsaw Chamber Opera, 1978–80, Stettin 1980–82 and Freiberg 1982–83; Dresden Staatsoper from 1983, as Nemorino, the Duke of Mantua, Alfredo, Cassio, Riccardo (Un ballo in Maschera), Fenton, Rodolfo, Pinkerton and Cavaradossi; guest engagements at Leipzig, Schwerin, Frankfurt an der Oder, Lille and Bratislava; Prague State Opera from 1990; other roles include Strauss's Elemer (Arabella), Italian Singer (Rosenkavalier) and Narraboth in Salome. *Recordings include:* Rossini's Il Signor Bruschino (Eterna). *Address:* c/o Prague State Opera, Legerova 75, CR-110 00 Prague 1, Czech Republic.

MOLINA, Arturo; Philippine conductor and violinist; *Principal Conductor and Music Director, Manila Symphony Orchestra.* *Education:* Moscow Conservatory, Kiev Conservatory, also studied with Basilio Manalo. *Career:* Concertmaster, Philippine Youth Orchestra 1979, Youth Artist Chamber Orchestra 1981, Philippine Philharmonic Orchestra 1987, Manila Chamber Orchestra 1991–93; taught violin through the Philippine Research for Developing Instrumental Soloists, St Scholastica's Coll.; Chair. of String Dept., Coll. of Music, Univ. of Philippines 1994–2003; co-f. Battig Trio 1999; Conducting Fellow, Conductor's Inst., Univ. of South Carolina, USA 2000; Prin. Conductor and Music Dir Manila Symphony Orchestra 2001–. *Address:* Manila Symphony Orchestra, c/o St Scholastica's College, 2560 Leon Guinto Street, Malate, Metro Manila 1004, Philippines (office). *Telephone:* (2) 985-6114. *E-mail:* manilasymphonyorchestra@gmail.com (office). *Website:* www.manilasymphony.com (office).

MOLINA, José Antonio; Dominican conductor and arranger; *Artistic Director, Orquesta Sinfónica Nacional de República Dominicana (National Symphony Orchestra of Dominica);* b. 1960, Santo Domingo. *Education:* Nat. Conservatory of Music, Dominican Republic, Manhattan School of Music, Juilliard School, New York. *Career:* Music Dir Greater Palm Beach Symphony Orchestra 1996–; Conductor and Principal Arranger, inauguration of Carnival Performing Arts Center, Miami 2006; Music Dir and Principal Conductor, Florida Symphony and Miami Pops Orchestra 2007–; Principal Guest Conductor, Nat. Symphony Orchestra of Dominican Republic 2008, Music Dir 2009–; guest conductor, Queens Symphony Orchestra, New York, Washington Chamber Symphony Orchestra; arranger and conductor for artists including Elton John, Gloria Estefan, George Michael, Luciano Pavarotti, Celine Dion; Prof. Emer., Autonomous Univ. of Santo Domingo. *Compositions:* Yaya Overture, Merengue Fantasia. *Recordings:* albums: as conductor and arranger: Jon Secada, The Gift 2001; as conductor: Yu Qiang Dai, Opera Arias 2004. *Honours:* Order of Duarte, Sanchez y Mella 2001; Dr hc (Pedro Urena Nat. Univ.) 2008; Soberano Award, Exxon Endowment for Conductors 1990. *Address:* National Symphony Orchestra of Dominica, Sinfonia Foundation, Eduardo Vicisoso No. 1, Santo Domingo, Dominican Republic (office). *Telephone:* 5326600 (office); 5358690 (office); 5358691 (office). *Fax:* 5331941 (office). *E-mail:* sinfoniaprensa@codetel.net.do (office). *Website:* www.sinfonia.org.do (office).

MOLINO, Pippo, BMus; Italian composer; b. 10 June 1947, Milan; m. Giovanna Stucchi 1972; one s. two d. *Education:* studied composition and choral music. *Career:* debut at Venezia Opera Prima Festival Competition 1981; mem. SIMC, Societa Italiana Musica Contemporanes. *Compositions:* Replay I and II for piano 1978, Tres for violin and viola 1978, Litanie for orchestra 1979, Il Canto Ritrovato for orchestra 1980, Il Cavalier Selvatico (oratorio) 1981, Cantabile for flute and piano 1983, Jeu for oboe 1984, Da Lontan for harp 1985, Per la Festa Della Dedicazione for organ 1986, Harmonien for wind quintet 1989, Radici for clarinet 1991, Ricordando for 12 instruments 1992, Quintetto for clarinet and string quartet 1993, Itinerari for string orchestra 1994, Angelus for soprano, alto and string orchestra 1997. *Recordings:* Il Pensiero Dominante, Nel Tempo. *Publications:* contrib. articles in La Musica, Musica e Realta, Reggio Emilia, Il Giornale della musica. *Honours:* Rimini Aterforum 1979, Venezia Opera Prima 1981, Roodeport Int. Eisteddfod of South Africa 1983. *Address:* Via Pistrucci 23, 20137 Milan, Italy.

MOLL, Kurt; German singer (bass); b. 11 April 1938, Buir, nr Cologne; m. Ursula Pade 1968; one s. two d. *Education:* Staatliche Hochschule für Musik, Cologne. *Career:* played cello and sang in school choir as a child; operatic debut in Cologne; subsequently sang operatic roles at Aachen, Mainz, Wuppertal, Hamburg; appeared at Bayreuth 1968, Salzburg 1970, La Scala, Milan 1972, San Francisco Opera (US debut) 1974, Covent Garden, London 1975, Metropolitan Opera, New York 1978; Prof., Staatliche Hochschule für Musik, Cologne 1991–; mem. Hamburg, Bavarian and Vienna State Operas; retd from the stage 2006; gave a master class at Carnegie Hall 2011; lives in Cologne with his family. *Recordings include:* numerous opera, sacred music and lieder recordings with many of the great conductors and piano-accompanists, winning several prestigious European record awards, including Grammy Award for his participation in James Levine's 1988 recording of Das Rheingold 1990; recorded as Ochs in no fewer than seven complete recordings of Der Rosenkavalier, as Sarastro in six recordings of Die Zauberflöte, as Marke in six sets of Tristan und Isolde, as the Archangel Raphael in three recordings of Haydn's Die Schöpfung; Schubert's Lieder für Bass. *Address:* Voigtelstr. 22, 50933 Cologne, Germany.

MOLLOVA, Milena; pianist and academic; b. 19 Feb. 1940, Razgrad, Bulgaria; one s. two d. *Education:* Bulgarian Music Acad. with Prof. Pelischeck, Moscow State Conservatory with Prof. Emil Gilels, studied with Pavla Jekova, Dimitar Nenov, Prof. Panka Pelisheck. *Career:* debut piano concert aged six; soloist in Sofia State Orchestra with the Beethoven third piano concerto, directed by Prof. Sasha Popov; during her education gave numerous concerts in Bulgaria and successful participation in int. competitions in Moscow, Paris and Munich; concert tours in USSR 1958, 1959, 1960, in Czechoslovakia, Poland, Belgium and Yugoslavia; apptd Asst to Prof. Pelischeck, Bulgarian Music Acad., Sofia 1963 and as a concert pianist to the Bulgarian Concert Agency; conducted own class of young piano students 1969–; tour of Japan and Cuba 1973; apptd Reader 1976 and Prof. 1989 in the Bulgarian Music Acad.; to celebrate 40 years on stage, played in Sofia and Varna the whole 32 Beethoven sonatas in nine concerts; conducted masterclasses in Essen, Germany and Manfredony, Foggia, Italy. *Recordings include:* piano works from Bach to modern composers.

MOLNAR, András; singer (tenor); b. 1948, Hungary. *Education:* Hungarian Radio Children's Choir. *Career:* mem., Choir of the Hungarian Radio and Television 1977–78; soloist at Budapest State Opera from 1979; appeared in title roles in Erkel's László Hunyadi, Mozart's Magic Flute, Verdi's Ernani and in La Forza del Destino, Don Johóe in Carmen 1981–82, title role in Lohengrin 1981–82; invited to sing title role in Theo Adam's new production of Wagner's Lohengrin at Berlin State Opera 1983; regular appearances with Budapest State Opera, including the premiere of Ecce Homo by Szokolay 1987; sang at Teatro Colón Buenos Aires 1987 as Donello in La Fiamma by Respighi; Budapest 1988–90, in Erkel's Hunyadi László and as Tannhäuser; frequently participates in oratorio performances; other performances in Florestan in Fidelio, Budapest 1984, Zürich and Graz 1994, Wagner's Meistersinger at Budapest 1985, Der fliegende Holländer at Bonn 1986, Zürich 1987 and Liège 1995, Tristan at Budapest 1988, Parsifal in Budapest 1982 and Antwerp 1987, Tannhäuser in Rouen 1992, Limoges 1994, Radames in Aida, Budapest 1994,

Die Walküre, Budapest with Yuri Simonow 1995; sang Siegfried in Götterdämmerung at Budapest 1998; Lohengrin at Trier 2001. *Honours:* first prize Treviso Toti dal Monte Int. Vocal Competition 1980, Kossuth Prize–First Hungarian Cultural Prize 1994.

MOLNAR, Nicolette; stage director; b. 1959, London, England. *Education:* Columbia Univ., New York, USA and Hochschüle für Musik, Hamburg, Germany with Götz Friedrich. *Career:* Staff Dir, ENO 1987–1994; directed for Stadttheater Luzern (Elisir d'Amore 1991), Dublin Grand Opera (Lakmé 1993), Castleward Opera, Belfast (I Capuleti e I Montecchi 1995, Ariadne auf Naxos 1996), Royal Acad./Royal Coll. of Music, London (A Midsummer Night's Dream 1996), Santa Fe Opera (Così fan tutte 1997), Orlando Opera (Tosca 1997, Turandot 1998, Fliegende Holländer 1999), Opera Ontario (Tosca 1998, Eugene Onegin 2001), Univ. of Michigan (Turn of the Screw 1998, Cenerentola 2002), Lyric Opera of Kansas City (Così fan tutte 1999), Wolf Trap Opera (Don Giovanni 2000), Atlanta Opera (Così fan tutte 2000, Fliegende Holländer 2002), Co-Opera/Opera Ireland (Madama Butterfly 2001), Lake George Opera (Entführung aus dem Serail 2002). *Current Management:* c/o Performing Arts, 6 Windmill Street, London W1T 2JB. *Telephone:* (20) 7255-1362. *Fax:* (20) 7631-4631. *E-mail:* info@performing-arts.co.uk. *Website:* www.performing-arts.co.uk.

MOLNAR-TALAJIC, Liljana; singer (soprano); b. 30 Dec. 1938, Bronsanski, Brod, Yugoslavia. *Education:* studied in Sarajevo. *Career:* debut in Sarajevo, 1959, as Mozart's Countess; Sang at Sarajevo and Zagreb, 1959–75; Guest appearances at the Vienna Staatsoper, Florence and San Francisco, 1969; Philadelphia from 1970, Naples 1971; Verona Arena, 1972–73, as Aida and the Forza Leonora; Sang at Covent Garden, 1975, 1977, Metropolitan Opera, 1976, Aida; Further appearandces at Barcelona, Nice and the Deutsche Oper Berlin, 1977–78, Milan, Rome and Marseilles; Other roles have included the Trovatore Leonora, Amelia in Ballo in Maschera, Desdemona and Norma. *Recordings include:* Verdi Requiem.

MONETTI, Mariaclara; Italian pianist; b. 1965. *Education:* studied in Turin, Salzburg Mozarteum and Conservatories of Venice and Lucerne, studied with Geza Anda and Vladimir Ashkenazy. *Career:* many appearances in 18th-century repertoire throughout Europe; British appearances with the London Symphony at the Barbican and London recitals in the Purcell Room and St John's, Smith Square. *Recordings include:* Mozart concertos K466 and K595, with the Royal Philharmonic; The complete Paisiello Piano Concertos, with the English Chamber Orchestra and a solo CD of the complete piano works of Dallapiccola. *Honours:* Gold Medal, Viotti International Competition. *Current Management:* c/o Manygate Management, Trees, Ockham Road South, East Horsley, Surrey KT24 6QE, England. *Telephone:* (1483) 281300. *Fax:* (1483) 281811. *E-mail:* manygate@easynet.co.uk.

MONK, Allan, OC; Canadian singer (bass-baritone); b. 19 Aug. 1942, Mission City, BC. *Education:* studied in Calgary with Elgar Higgin and in NY with Boris Goldovsky. *Career:* debut, Western Opera, San Francisco 1967 in Menotti's The Old Maid and The Thief; has sung in Portland, St Louis, Chicago, Hawaii and Vancouver; Canadian Nat. Opera, Toronto 1973 in premiere of Wilson's Abelard and Heloise; Metropolitan Opera from 1976 as Schaunard in La Bohème, The Speaker in Die Zauberflöte, Berg's Wozzeck, Wagner's Wolfram and Verdi's Posa and Ford; sang Macbeth at Toronto 1986, followed by Carlo in La Forza del Destino; Opéra de Montréal 1988 as Don Giovanni; sang Nick Shadow in The Rake's Progress for Vancouver Opera 1989; Wozzeck and Iago at Toronto in 1990; sang Simon Boccanegra for Long Beach Opera 1992; Visiting Prof. of Voice, Eastman School of Music 1997; owner of private singing studio in Calgary, Alberta. *Recordings include:* Andrea Chénier, La Traviata, Allan Monk with Calgary Philharmonic Orchestra. *Honours:* Artist of the Year 1983, Distinguished Visitor Award, Univ. of Toronto 1997. *Address:* 14415 Parkland Boulevard SE, Calgary, AB, Canada (home). *Telephone:* (403) 281-9640 (home).

MONK, Meredith Jane; American composer, singer, director and choreographer; b. 20 Nov. 1942, New York, NY; d. of Theodore G. Monk and Audrey Lois Monk (née Zellman). *Education:* Sarah Lawrence Coll. *Career:* Founder and Artistic Dir House Foundation for the Arts 1968–; formed Meredith Monk & Vocal Ensemble 1978–; Richard and Barbara Debs Composer's Chair, Carnegie Hall 2014–15; mem. American Acad. of Arts and Sciences 2006. *Films:* Book of Days, Ellis Island. *Compositions include:* Break 1964, 16 Millimeter Earrings 1966, Juice: A Theatre Cantata 1969, Key 1971, Vessel: An Opera Epic 1971, Paris 1972, Education of the Girlchild 1973, Quarry 1976, Songs from the Hill 1976, Dolmen Music 1979, Specimen Days: A Civil War Opera 1981, Ellis Island 1981, Turtle Dreams Cabaret 1983, The Games 1983, Acts from Under and Above 1986, Book of Days 1988, Facing North 1990, Three Heavens and Hells 1992, ATLAS: An Opera in Three Parts 1991, New York Requiem 1993, Volcano Songs 1994, American Archaeology 1994, The Politics of Quiet 1996, Steppe Music 1997, Magic Frequencies 1998, Micki Suite 2000, Eclipse Variations 2000, mercy 2001, Possible Sky 2003, impermanence 2004, Stringsongs 2005, Night 2005, Songs of Ascension 2008, Weave for two voices, chamber orchestra and chorus 2010, Realm Variations 2012, On Behalf of Nature 2013. *Honours:* Officer of the Order of Arts and Letters; Dr hc (Bard Coll.) 1988, (Univ. of the Arts) 1989, (Juilliard School of Music) 1998, (San Francisco Art Inst.) 1999, (Boston Conservatory) 2001; Golden Eagle Award 1981, Nat. Music Theatre Award 1986, German Critics' Award for Best Recording of the Year 1981, 1986, MacArthur Genius Award 1995, Samuel Scripps Award 1996, United States Artists Fellow 2006, Musical

America Composer of the Year 2012, Doris Duke Artist 2012, NPR's 50 Great Voices 2012. *Address:* The House Foundation, 260 West Broadway, Suite 2, New York, NY 10013, USA (office). *Telephone:* (212) 904-1330 (office). *Fax:* (212) 904-1305 (office). *E-mail:* monk@meredithmonk.org (office). *Website:* www.meredithmonk.org (office).

MONK FELDMAN, Barbara, PhD; Canadian composer and theorist; b. 18 Jan. 1953, Québec; m. Morton Feldman 1987. *Education:* McGill Univ., Montréal, studied with Bengt Hambraeus, State Univ. of New York, Buffalo. *Career:* compositions performed by the Arditti Quartet, clarinettist Roger Heaton, pianists Yvar Mikhashoff, Ursula Oppens, Frederic Rzewski, Aki Takahashi, percussionists Stven Schick, Robyn Schulkkowsky and Jan Williams, and cellist Frances-Marie Uitti; her music has been premiered at Darmstadt and festivals including Inventionen in Berlin, Nieuwe Muziek in Middelburg, Other Minds in San Francisco, Toronto New Music and in the Rotonda in Tokyo; faculty mem. Internationale Ferienkurse für Neue Musik, Darmstadt 1988, 1990; guest lectured at Hochschule der Künste in Berlin; Founder, Artistic Dir, Time Shards Music Series, Georgia O'Keefe Museum, Santa Fe, NM 2001–. *Compositions include:* orchestral: Design for String Orchestra 1980, The Northern Shore for Piano, Percussion and Orchestra or Chamber Orchestra 1997 (also version for violin, piano, percussion); chamber music: Movement for solo viola 1979, Trio for violin, cello and piano 1983, Variations for six string instruments 1986, Duo for piano and percussion 1988, The Immutable Silence for flute, clarinet, bass clarinet, violin, cello, piano (and celesta), two percussion 1990, Pure Difference for clarinet, bassoon, violin, piano, synthesizer and percussion 1990, Shadow for string quartet 1991, Three Clarinets and Percussion, for three clarinets, three percussion 1994 (also version for clarinet, percussion, tape), Verses for Metal, Wood and Drums, for percussion 1994, Verses for Five for flute, bass clarinet, French horn, piano (and celesta) and percussion 1996, The Northern Shore for violin, piano, percussion (version of orchestral work) 1997, Pour un nuage violet, for violin, cello 1998, Proche et lointaine... la femme for bass clarinet and accordion 2001, Glockenspiel for glockenspiel 2004, The Loons of Black Sturgeon Lake, for flute 2004, String Quartet No. 1 Desert Scape 2004, The Chaco Wilderness, for flute, clarinet, guitar, piano and vibraphone 2005, The Pale Blue Northern Sky, for two guitars and mandolin 2007, Landscape Near La Pocatière, Québec, for cello and percussion 2007; choral: Variations (text by Ludwig Wittgenstein) for string quartet and mixed chorus 1987, Infinite Other (text by Homer) for two sopranos, mixed chorus, flute, clarinet, string quartet, piano and film adlibitum (by Stan Brakhage) 1992; vocal: The Gentlest Chord (text by Rainer Maria Rilke), for mezzo-soprano 1991, Three Poems by Wallace Stevens, for speaker, clarinet, vibraphone 1997, The Love Shards of Sappho, for soprano, clarinet, violin, piano, two percussion 2001; piano: The I and Thou 1988, Two Pianos 1989, Clear Edge 1993, In the Small Time of a Desert Flower 2000, Piece for Prepared Piano (using the same preparations as Sonatas and Interludes by John Cage) 2007. *Publications:* articles include All Things Being Unmeasured (New Observations, 1989), Music and the Picture Plane, Res 32 1997 (Contemporary Music Review, vol 17 part 3 and part 4 1998). *Honours:* Edgard Varese Fellowship, SUNY Buffalo 1984–87. *Current Management:* Canadian Music Centre, 20 St. Joseph St, Toronto, Ont. M4Y 1J9, Canada; Frog Peak Music, PO Box 1052, Lebanon, NH 03766, USA (office). *Address:* SOCAN, 41 Valleybrook Drive, Don Mills, ON M3B 2S6, Canada (home).

MONNARD, Jean-François, LLM; Swiss artistic director; *Artistic Director, Deutsche Oper Berlin;* b. 4 Nov. 1941, Lausanne; m. Lia Rottier. *Education:* Univ. of Lausanne, Music Acad., Lausanne, Folkwang Hochschule, Essen, Germany. *Career:* resident conductor, Kaiserslautern, Graz, Austria, Trier, Aachen and Wuppertal; Music Dir in Osnabruck; orchestral and opera performances throughout Europe; Artistic Dir Deutsche Oper Berlin 1998–. *Publications:* contrib. articles to professional journals. *Address:* Richard-Wagner-Str. 10 10585 Berlin, Germany. *Telephone:* (30) 34384214. *Fax:* (30) 34384457. *E-mail:* straub@deutscheoperberlin.de (office).

MONOGAROVA, Tatyana Alexeyevna; Russian singer (soprano); b. 16 Feb. 1967, Moscow; d. of Alexey Alexeyevich Monogarov and Svetlana Pavlovna Monogarova; m.; two c. *Education:* Russian Acad. of Arts. *Career:* soloist Moscow Chamber Theatre Helicon Opera 1989–91; soloist Moscow Stanislavsky and Nemirovich-Danchenko Music Theatre 1991–2001; guest soloist in European countries including Opera houses of Bologna, Bern, Nantes, Venice, Vienna (Kammeroper) and Riga; has performed with many conductors including Vladimir Fedoseyev, Vladimir Spivakov and Peter Feranec. *Repertoire includes:* Micaela in Carmen, Lia in Prodigal Son, Violanta in La Finta Giardinera, Countess in The Marriage of Figaro, Pamina in Die Zauberflöte, Xenia in La Bohème, Manon in Manon Lescaut, Butterfly in Madame Butterfly, Liu in Turandot, Luisa in Luisa Miller, Violetta Valeri in La Traviata, Leonora in Il Trovatore, Elisabetta in Don Carlos, Desdemona in Othello, Amelia in Simon Boccanegra, Lida in La Batalia di Legnano, Tsaritsa in Immortal Kashchey, Swan Princess in The Tale of Tsar Saltan, Parasha in Mavra (Stravinsky), Tatyana in Eugene Onegin, Yolanta, Oksana in Cherevichki, Lisa in Pique Dame, Electra in Oresteya (Taneyev), Rosalinda in Die Fledermaus (Strauss); Solo parts in: Magnificat (Bach), An die Freunde Op 125 (Beethoven), Requiem (Verdi), Symphony No 4 (Mahler), Requiem (Mozart), Motet Exultate, Jubilate, Mass in G Major (Schubert). *Current Management:* Allied Artists, 42 Montpelier Square, London, SW7 1JZ, England. *Telephone:* (20) 7589-6243 (office). *Fax:* (20) 7581-5269 (office).

E-mail: info@alliedartists.co.uk (office). *Website:* www.alliedartists.co.uk (office).

MONOSOFF, Sonya; violinist and academic; b. 11 June 1927, Ohio, USA; m. Carl Eugene Pancaldo 1950, four d. *Education:* Juilliard School. *Career:* debut in New York; concerts and masterclasses in the USA, Canada, Europe, Israel, Australia and New Zealand; Prof. of Music, later Prof. Emerita, Cornell Univ.; mem. Early Music America (steering cttee), American Musical Instrument Soc. (editorial bd). *Recordings:* Heinrich Biber: Mystery Sonatas and 1681 Sonatas, J.S. Bach: Sonatas for Violin and Harpsichord, Mozart: Sonatas. *Publications:* contrib. to Early Music, The New Grove, The Musical Times. *Honours:* Stereo Review Record of the Year (for Bach) 1970, Fulbright Lectureship, New Zealand 1988, Bunting Inst. 1967–68, Smithsonian Inst. 1971.

MONOSZON, Boris; violinist and conductor; b. 1955, Kiev, Russia. *Education:* Moscow Conservatoire. *Career:* made several concert tours of European and Latin American countries as concertmaster, Prague Symphony; interpreted Concerto for violin and orchestra by Sibelius, Royal Festival Hall, London, England; soloist, Teplice State Philharmonic Orchestra 1982–. *Honours:* Laureate Tibor Varga Int. Competition, Switzerland 1981.

MONOT, Pierre-Alain, DipMus; Swiss musician (trumpet); b. 7 March 1961. *Career:* solo trumpet, Stadtorchester, Winterthur; Chief Conductor, Nouvel Ensemble Contemporain; Guest Conductor, Rousse Philharmonic; Bieler Sinfonieorchester; Orchester des Musikkollegium, Winterthur; mem., Novus Brass Quartet; mem. Asscn Suisse des Musiciens. *Compositions:* Stèles for strings 1998, Trois Airs de Cour for brass quartet and orchestra, Concertino for double bassoon, Concerto for bass trombone. *Honours:* first prize Competition of Union Bank of Switzerland 1987. *Address:* Weinbergstrasse 18, 8001 Zürich, Switzerland.

MONOYIOS, Ann, BA (Hons), MFA; American/Canadian singer (soprano); b. 28 Oct. 1949, Middletown, Conn.; d. of John Sease and Mary Sease; m. Glenn Hodgins; one d. *Education:* Putney School, Princeton Univ., USA. *Career:* concert performances in Baroque music with Baroque specialists including John Eliot Gardiner, Gustav Leonhardt, Christopher Hogwood, Frans Brueggen, Trevor Pinnock, William Christie, Rene Jacobs, Tafelmusik Baroque Orchestra and La Stagione Frankfurt; featured soloist with symphonies of Montreal, Houston, San Antonio, San Francisco and Rocheste; opera appearances with Paris Opera, Flemish Opera, and opera houses of Halle, Bremen and Basel; European debut at Göttingen Festival in Handel's Terpsichore with English Baroque Soloists conducted by John Eliot Gardiner 1986; Opéra Comique Paris and Aix-en-Provence Festival as Lully's Sangaride (Atys) and Psyché 1987; sang Elisa in Mozart's Il Re Pastore at Nakamichi Festival in Los Angeles 1990; season 1999 as Nice in J. C. Bach's Serenata Endimione at Duisburg, and Handel's Theodora at Göttingen; other opera roles include Handel's Almira (Almira), and Deidamia (Deidamia), Morgana (Alcina) and Hasse's Tisbe (Piramo e Tisbe). *Radio:* recordings on BBC, WDR Koln, NDR Hamburg, CBC Canada and Radio France. *Recordings:* numerous performances in concert, opera and recording world-wide. *Current Management:* c/o Carrie Sykes, Schwalbe and Partners, Inc., 170 East 61st Street, #5N, New York, NY 10065, USA. *Telephone:* (212) 935-5650. *Fax:* (212) 935-4754. *E-mail:* carrie@schwalbeandpartners.com. *Website:* www.schwalbeandpartners.com; www.annmonoyios.com (home).

MONTAGNIER, Jean-Paul C., MA, PhD (Duke), PhD (Sorbonne); French musicologist and academic; *Professor of Musicology, University of Lorraine (Nancy);* b. 28 Sept. 1965, Lyon; s. of Jacques Montagnier and Janine Prévost. *Education:* Univ. of Lyon, Conservatoire Nat. Supérieur de Musique, La Sorbonne, Paris, Duke Univ., USA. *Career:* Asst Prof., Music Dept, Université Nancy 2 (Univ. of Lorraine since 2012) 1992–96, Prof. of Musicology 2000–; Assoc. Prof., Music Dept, Metz Univ. 1996–2000, Dir of Grad. Studies 1996–2000, Chair. of Dept 1999–2000; Adjunct Prof., McGill Univ., Canada 2007–; Sec. to the Ed. Revue de Musicologie 1994–2004; mem. CNRS team 'Institut de Recherche sur le Patrimoine Musical en France' 2007–13; mem. Editorial Bd new critical edn of the works of Jean-Baptiste Lully 1997–; Sec. European Science Foundation research programme, 'Musical Life in Europe' 1600–1900: Circulation Institutions, 'Representations' 1998–2002; Sec. Lully Asscn 1998–2005; mem. Scientific Cttee, programme Musica Gallica 2001–, Advisory Panel, Eighteenth-Century Music 2002–; Artistic Dir Ensemble Vocal de la Chartreuse de Bonlieu; Guest Lecturer, Duke and Cornell Univs, USA 2004, Madison, Whitewater, Stanford and Berkeley Univs, USA 2005, McGill Univ. 2005, Canada, King's Coll. London and City Univ., London, UK 2006, Chicago, Pittsburgh, Columbia Univs, USA 2007, Université de Montréal, Canada 2007, 2008, 2009, Univ. of Maryland at College Park, USA 2008, Bishop's Univ., Canada 2008, Univ. of Oregon at Eugene, Wellesley Coll. and Brandeis Univ., USA 2014, Harvard Univ. and Wellesley Coll. 2015; mem. Soc. Française de Musicologie (mem. Bd 1994–99), Int. Musicological Soc., Royal Musical Soc., American Musicological Soc. *Publications:* La Vie l'œuvre de Louis-Claude Daquin 1694–1772, Un Mécène musicien. Philippe d'Orléans Régent 1674–1723, Charles-Hubert Gervais: Un Musicien au service du Régent et de Louis XV, Henry Madin 1698–1748: Un musicien lorrain au service de Louis XV; edns of Marcello's Le Théâtre à la mode, Charpentier's Te Deum, Charpentier's Messe de Minuit, de Mondonville's Jubilate Deo, Gervais' Super flumina Babilonis, Campra's Messe de mort, Du Mont's Magnificat, Madin's Les Messes, Madin and Marchand's Traités du contrepoint simple, Rameau's Cantatas and Motets, Bernier's Principes de Composition, Rousseau's Motets, Georges Montagnier's Collected Works, Debussy's Prélude à l'après-midi d'un faune, Dukas's Apprenti sorcier; contrib. of many articles to journals, conf. reviews and programme notes, New Grove Dictionary of Music and Musicians, Die Neue Musik in Geschichte und Gegenwart, Cambridge History of Music. *Honours:* Chevalier des Arts et des Lettres 2007, Officier 2012. *Address:* Université de Lorraine, 23 boulevard Albert 1er, 54000 Nancy, France (office). *E-mail:* jean-paul.montagnier@univ-lor.fr (office); jean-paul.montagnier@mcgill.ca (office). *Website:* www.iremus.cnrs.fr/fr/membres-associes/jean-paul-montagnier (office); www.music.mcgill.ca/staff/jean-paul.montagnier.html (office); jpmontagnier.monsite-orange.fr.

MONTAGUE, Diana, ARCM; British singer (mezzo-soprano); b. 8 April 1953, Winchester; d. of N. H. Montague; m. 1st Philip Doghan 1978; one s.; m. 2nd David Rendall 1990; one s. two d. *Education:* Testwood School, Totton, Hants., Winchester School of Art and Royal Northern Coll. of Music. *Career:* professional debut at Glyndebourne 1977; Prin. Mezzo-Soprano, Royal Opera House, Covent Garden 1978; freelance artist 1984–; has toured throughout Europe and USA appearing at Metropolitan Opera and Bayreuth, Aix-en-Provence, Salzburg and Glyndebourne festivals; sang at Promenade Concerts, London 1991; Ariadne auf Naxos for Opera North 1998. *Current Management:* Intermusica Artists Management, Crystal Wharf, 36 Graham Street, London, N1 8GJ, England. *Telephone:* (20) 7608-9900. *Fax:* (20) 7490-3263. *E-mail:* mail@intermusica.co.uk. *Website:* www.intermusica.co.uk.

MONTAGUE, Stephen Rowley, AA, BM, MM, DMA, IRCAM, CCRMA, FTCM, FLCM; British/American composer, conductor and pianist; *Professor of Composition, Trinity College of Music;* b. 10 March 1943, Syracuse, NY, USA; m. Patricia Mattin 1986 (divorced 2009); one s. two d. *Education:* St Petersburg Junior Coll., Fla, Florida State Univ., Stanford Univ., Ohio State Univ., Mozarteum, Salzburg, studied in Warsaw, Poland and at Institut de Recherche et Coordination Acoustique/Musique, Paris, France. *Career:* debut at Wigmore Hall, London 1975; Warsaw Autumn Festivals 1974, 1980, 1989, 1991, 1995; Metz Festival, 1976; New Music America, 1987, 1988, 1990; Montague/Mead Piano Plus first tour of USA, 1986; frequent European and N American tours to present; Chair. Sonic Arts Network, UK 1987–88, Almeida Festival, London, 1988; Guest Prof., Univ. of Texas at Austin 1992, 1995, 2000; Featured Composer, Speculum Festival, Norway 1992; world tours with Maurice Agis' inflatable sculpture, Dreamspace 1987–2005; Centre Pompidou premiere 1995; Composer-in-Asscn with Orchestra of St John's Smith Square, London 1995–97; Cheltenham Festival 1995, 1997, 2001; Ultima 95 Festival, Oslo; Featured Composer, Cambridge Festival 2000, Making New Waves Festival, Budapest 2001, 2002; Chair. Soc. for the Promotion of New Music 1993–98, Artistic Dir 1998–99; mem. British Acad. of Composers and Songwriters; Artistic Dir Open Score Project UK 2004–05; Artistic Consultant, BBC John Cage Uncaged Festival, London 2004; BBC Symphony Composer Portrait 2008; Composer Portrait Week, Univ. of Vienna 2009; Prof. of Composition, Trinity Coll. of Music, London 2004–, RAM, London 2006–08; Fellow, Leeds Coll. of Music 2004. *Compositions include:* Eyes of Ambush 1973, Sound Round 1973, Paramell Va 1981, At the White Edge of Phrygia 1983, String Quartet No. 1 1989–93, Behold a Pale Horse 1990, Wild Nights 1993, Silence: John, Yvar and Tim 1994, Varshavian Autumn 1995, Snakebite 1995, Dark Sun 1995, Piano Concerto 1997, Southern Lament 1997, A Toy Symphony 1999, Black 'n' Blues 2000, Bright Interiors III 2000, When Dreams Collide 2001, Disparate Dances 2002, The Hammer Hawk 2002, Intrada 1631 2003, Toccare Incandescent 2003, Autumn Leaves 2003, Five Easy Pieces 2003, Tam Linn 2004, Two Dirges–Three Dances 2004, Beyond the Stone Horizon 2006, Chorale for the Cauldrons of Hell 2005–06, Mephisto 2007, Apparitions 2008. *Recordings include:* CDs: Stephen Montague Orchestra and Chamber Works 1994, Snakebite 1997, Silence: John, Yvar and Tim 1997, Montague Piano Works 2005, Southern Lament (Int. Piano Award for Best Piano Music Recording) 2006. *Honours:* Hon. Fellow, Trinity Coll. of Music 2001; Ernst von Dohnányi Award 1995, First Prize, Bourges Electronic Music Competition 1994, runner up, British Acad. of Composers and Songwriters Award 2004, Int. Piano Award for Best New Music Piano Recording 2006. *Address:* 21 Stanley Crescent, London, W11 2NA (home); c/o United Music Publishers, 33A Lea Road, Waltham Abbey, Essex, EN9 1ES, England. *Telephone:* (20) 7229-1673 (home); (1992) 703110. *Fax:* (1992) 703189. *E-mail:* srmontague@aol.com (home); info@ump.co.uk. *Website:* www.ump.co.uk.

MONTAL, Andre; singer (tenor); b. 18 Nov. 1940, Baltimore, USA. *Education:* Eastman School, Music Acad. of the West at Santa Barbara, Curtis Inst. *Career:* debut with American Opera Soc., New York 1964, as Tebaldo in I Capuleti e i Montecchi; has sung at opera houses in Boston, Chicago, Philadelphia, San Francisco and Vancouver; Metropolitan Opera from 1974; further engagements with Australian Opera at Sydney; other roles have included Donizetti's Ernesto, Nemorino, Tonio and Edgardo, Oronte in Alcina, Gounod's Roméo, Rossini's Almaviva, Lindoro, and Idreno in Semiramide, Mozart's Ferrando, Belmonte and Don Ottavio; Mephistopheles in Prokofiev's Fiery Angel, Verdi's Duke, Pinkerton and the Italian Singer in Rosenkavalier.

MONTALVO, Marisol; American singer (soprano); b. 1970, Long Island. *Education:* Zürich Opera Studio, Mannes College of Music. *Career:* appearances with Dortmund Opera as Euridice, Flowermaiden in Parsifal and Sulamith in Goldmark's Königin von Saba; sang Rossini's Elvira at Chautauqua, Mozart's Barbarina at Sarasto and Musetta in La Bohème for Castel Vocal Arts, Bizet's Frasquita and Nannetta in Falstaff for Regina Opera, Echo in Ariadne auf Naxos and Mozart's Despina in Brooklyn,

Susanna for New Rochelle Opera, Esmeralda in The Bartered Bride at Glyndebourne, Marie in Lortzing's Zar, Zimmermann, Gretel, Micaela in Carmen, Suzel in Mascagni's L'Amico Fritz; has sung with Zurich Opera, Teatro Real, Cleveland Orchestra, Los Angeles Philharmonic Orchestra, San Francisco Symphony, Orchestre de Paris, Orchestra National de Capitole de Toulouse. *Honours:* winner, Philadelphia Concerto Soloists Competition. *Current Management:* Guy Barzilay Artists Management, 420 West 25th Street, Suite 4F, New York, NY 10001, USA. *Telephone:* (212) 741-6118. *Fax:* (212) 741-2558. *E-mail:* guy@guybarzilayartists.com. *Website:* guybarzilayartists.com.

MONTÉ, Ruth; harpsichordist, organist and pianist; b. 3 Dec. 1958, Galatzi, Romania; m. Noel Monté 1986. *Education:* Acad. of Music, Bucharest, Juilliard School of Music, New York, studied with Rozalyn Tureck, Trevor Pinnock, John Weaver, Peter Husford, Frederick Neemann, Peter Williams, Lukas Foss. *Career:* debut in Bucharest 1973; performances in Bucharest 1977, Weimar, Germany 1978; television and radio broadcasts in Romania; lecturer and performer of Bach on harpsichord, piano, organ in N America; performance, 50th anniversary of the UN, New York Acad. of Sciences; mem. Chamber Music America, Early Music and Gramophone. *Recordings include:* Integral of Bach's Keyboard Music on Harpsichord, Piano and Organ. *Honours:* Laureate, National Youth Music Festival, Romania 1973.

MONTEBELLO, Benedetto, BMus; conductor; b. 20 May 1964, Rome, Italy; m. Lorena Palumbo 1997. *Education:* La Sapienza Univ., Rome, S. Cecilia Musical Conservatory, Rome, studied with G. Kuhn and D. Gatti. *Career:* debut conducting Beethoven's 1st Piano Concerto and 2nd Symphony, Anzio Int. Festival 1989; has conducted major orchestras, including Radio Sofia Symphony Orchestra, Burgas Nat. Orchestra, Oradea Nat. Philharmonic Orchestra, Oltenia Philharmonic Orchestra, Craiova, S. Cecilia Nat. Acad. Symphonic Orchestra, in Italy and abroad; conducted premiere of G. Guaccero's Salmo Metropolitano for large orchestra, based on P. P. Pasolini's texts, on 20th anniversary of Pasolini's death; other performances include Stravinsky's Histoire du Soldât, Ibert's Flute Concerto, Brahms' 1st Symphony, Chopin's 1st and 2nd Piano Concertos, Mussorgsky's Pictures at an Exhibition; teacher of conducting, U. Giordano Conservatory of Music, Foggia. *Recordings:* complete works of G. Guaccero, Ennio Morricone's 3rd Concerto for Guitar, Marimba and Orchestra (with S. Cecilia Nat. Acad. Symphonic Orchestra). *Publications:* contrib. musical articles in national newspapers, encyclopaedic items on Treccani. *Honours:* Rinaldi Prize for Conductors 1995.

MONTENEGRO, Roberto; Uruguayan conductor; *Musical Director, Symphony Orchestra of Uruguay State Radio;* b. 18 Sept. 1956, Montevideo. *Education:* Hamburg Musikhochschule, studied with Guido Santorsola, Gerhard Markson, Aldo Ceccato and Sergiu Celibidache. *Career:* debut, Santa Barbara Festival Symphony Orchestra, California 1985; conducted the world premiere of Francisco Rodrico's Guitar Concerto with the Venezuelan Nat. Orchestra 1992, and world premiere of Cesar Cano's Piano Concerto with the Spanish Nat. Orchestra 1993; teacher of masterclasses in Uruguay and Argentina, Italy (European Community Music High School) and Spain (Santiago de Compostela's Int. Conducting Masterclasses); Asst to Aldo Ceccato in Hamburg and Hanover; jury mem., Young Concert Artists, New York, USA; Artistic and Musical Dir, SODRE, Uruguay 1991–95; guest conductor in Spain, France, Argentina, Venezuela, Czech Republic, USA, Canada, Israel; Shira Int. Symphony Orchestra in Jerusalem Classical Winter Festival; Musical Dir, OSSODRE (Symphony Orchestra of Uruguay State Radio) 2004–, performance at the Prague Spring Festival, centenary of Dvořák's death. *Honours:* Hon. mem. Young Concert Artists 1994, Baron, Royal Order of the Bohemian Crown 1995, Jerusalem Prize 2004. *Address:* Avenida del Libertador 1684, Apt 1202, Montevideo, Uruguay. *Telephone:* (2) 900-5725 (office). *Fax:* (2) 900-5725 (office). *E-mail:* rmontenegro@yahoo.com .ur (office).

MONTERO, Gabriela; Venezuelan pianist and composer; b. 10 May 1970, Caracas; m.; two d. *Education:* private studies in USA, Royal Acad. of Music, UK, studied with Hamish Milne. *Career:* gave first public performance aged five, concerto debut aged eight in Caracas; recitals at Avery Fisher Hall, Kennedy Center, Wigmore Hall, Vienna Konzerthaus, Berlin Philharmonie, Frankfurt Alte Oper, Cologne Philharmonie, Leipzig Gewandhaus, Munich Herkulessaal, Sydney Opera House, Amsterdam Concertgebouw, Luxembourg Philharmonie, Lisbon Gulbenkian Museum, Tokyo Orchard Hall, Manchester Bridgewater Hall, and at Edinburgh, Salzburg, Lucerne, Ravinia, Tanglewood, Saint-Denis, Aldeburgh, Cheltenham, Rheingau, Ruhr, Bergen, Istanbul, and Lugano festivals; has performed with numerous orchestras including Royal Liverpool, Rotterdam, Dresden, Oslo, Netherlands Radio and Malaysian Philharmonic orchestras, Chicago, Houston, Pittsburgh, Detroit, Atlanta, Toronto and RTÉ Nat. symphony orchestras, among others; debut as composer 2011; Hon. Consul, Amnesty Int. 2015, also nominated for outstanding work in human rights by Human Rights Foundation; featured performer at US Pres. Barack Obama's 2008 inauguration. *Compositions include:* Ex Patria, tone poem for piano and orchestra. *Recordings include:* Bach and Beyond (Echo Klassik Awards for Keyboard Instrumentalist of the Year 2006 and Classical Music without Borders 2007), Baroque 2008, Solatino 2010, Rachmaninov and own work Ex Patria (Latin Grammy Award) 2015. *Honours:* Rockefeller Award 2012. *Current Management:* c/o Derek Chandruang, IMG Artists, The Light Box, London, W4 5PY, England. *Telephone:* (20) 7957-5810. *E-mail:* dchandruang@imgartists.com. *Website:* www .imgartists.com; www.gabrielamontero.com.

MONTGOMERY, Kathryn; singer (soprano); b. 23 Sept. 1952, Canton, OH, USA. *Education:* Univ. of Bloomington, Indiana. *Career:* debut at Bloomington 1972, as Elvira in Ernani; sang at Norfolk from 1978 as Frasquita, and in the premiere of Musgrave's Christmas Carol; European debut at Cologne 1980, as Leonore in Fidelio; sang at Cologne and Zürich 1980–82, Mannheim 1981–85; guest engagements at Venice, Edinburgh, Barcelona and Brussels; Metropolitan Opera debut 1985, as Chrysothemis; Pretoria, South Africa, 1984 as Salome; other roles include Wagner's Elsa, Senta and Sieglinde, Tosca, Donna Anna, Berg's Marie, Donna Elvira and the Empress in Die Frau ohne Schatten; sang Aksinya in Lady Macbeth of Mtsensk at the Deutsche Oper Berlin 1988; frequent concert appearances.

MONTGOMERY, Kenneth, OBE; British conductor; b. 28 Oct. 1943, Belfast, Northern Ireland; m. Jan van Dooren 2002. *Education:* Royal Belfast Academical Inst., Royal Coll. of Music, London. *Career:* debut at Glyndebourne Festival 1967; staff conductor, Sadler's Wells, ENO 1967–70; Asst Conductor, Bournemouth Symphony Orchestra and Sinfonietta from 1970; conducted Weber's Oberon at Wexford 1972; Strauss's Ariadne and Capriccio for Netherlands Opera 1972, 1975; Dir Bournemouth Sinfonietta 1974–76; Covent Garden debut with Le nozze di Figaro 1975; Prin. Conductor Dutch Radio Orchestra 1976; Musical Dir, Glyndebourne Touring Opera 1975–76; guest appearances with Welsh Nat. Opera, Canadian Opera; concert performance of Donizetti's Anna Bolena at Amsterdam 1989; Hansel and Gretel for Netherlands Opera 1990; conducted Tosca and The Magic Flute for Opera Northern Ireland at Belfast 1990; season 1991 with Alcina for Vancouver Opera, Figaro in Belfast and The Passion of Jonathan Wade at San Diego Opera 1996; tour of Ireland, Netherlands & Belgium with Orchestra of the Eighteenth Century 2014; Gluck's Orfeo with Scottish Opera 2015; Prin. Conductor Ulster Orchestra 2007–10; Acting Music Dir, Santa Fe Opera 2007–08; Head of Opera Acad. 1991–, chair of opera studies cr. in his name after amalgamation of The Royal Conservatory, The Hague with Conservatory Amsterdam; conducting master-classes at Royal Conservatory, The Hague. *Honours:* Dr hc in Literature and Music (Queen's Univ., Belfast) 2010; Silver Medal, Worshipful Co. of Musicians 1963, Tagore Gold Medal, Royal Coll. of Music 1964. *E-mail:* janvdooren@gmail.com (office). *Website:* www .kennethmontgomery.net.

MONTVIDAS, Edgaras; Lithuanian singer (tenor); b. 1975, Vilnius. *Education:* Kaunas Music School, Conservatory of Juozas Gruodis, Lithuanian Music Acad., Young Artists' Programme, Covent Garden. *Career:* Alfredo and Donizetti's Arturo for Lithuanian Nat. Opera; Nemorino on tour to Chicago; concerts include Berlioz Te Deum, Mozart C Minor Mass and Liszt Coronation Mass; Covent Garden debut as Ruiz in Il Trovatore; sang in Falla's La Vida Breve, London Proms 2002 and as Alfredo at Covent Garden; sang Alfredo for GTO 2003. *Honours:* scholarships and awards in Lithuania and elsewhere. *Current Management:* Van Walsum Management Deutschland GmbH, Königstrasse 36, 30175 Hannover, Germany. *Telephone:* (511) 366 07 23. *Fax:* (511) 366 07 24. *E-mail:* vwm@kdschmid.de.

MOODY, Howard, MA, FRCO; British composer, conductor and pianist; b. 7 May 1964, Salisbury, Wilts., England; m. Emily Blows; one s. two d. *Education:* Salisbury Cathedral School, Canford School, New Coll., Oxford, Guildhall School of Music and Drama. *Career:* several comms as composer; Artistic Dir La Folia (fmrly Sarum Orchestra); has worked with many of the major British orchestras, including London Symphony Orchestra, Hallé Orchestra, Scottish Chamber Orchestra, Bournemouth Orchestras; has also worked with La Monnaie, Netherlands Radio Chorus, Opera Factory, Icelandic Opera, Orchestra della Toscana, Romanian State Chorus, Salisbury Festival Chorus and as a music dir in London's West End; as keyboard player established duo partnerships with cellist David Watkin using modern piano and fortepiano; plays harpsichord; organ continuo player with English Baroque Soloists for John Eliot Gardiner's Bach 2000 pilgrimage; collaborations with saxophonist John Surman, including recordings and appearances at European jazz festivals as improviser and conductor; Artistic Dir for devised opera projects with Norwich Theatre Royal, Chichester Festival Theatre. *Compositions:* comms include dramatic, instrumental and choral works for Station House Opera, Southern Cathedrals Festival 1997, stage works for Bangladesh Festival 1998, for ENO 2000, works for Children's Music Workshop (including oratorio Songs of the Forest 2005), Jack de Johnette, The Anvil, Moving Music and Border Lines for Scottish Chamber Orchestra 2008–11, six works for the London Symphony Orchestra 2009–14, The Brussels Requiem 2010 and Sinbad – A Journey through Living Flames for La Monnaie 2014, two for the Scottish Chamber Orchestra 2011, Where Two Worlds Touch for the Salisbury Int. Arts Festival 2011. *Recordings:* as pianist: Beethoven Cello Sonatas (with David Watkin, cello, recorded on original fortepianos) 1996, Francis Pott Cello Sonata (with David Watkin) 1997, Rain on the Window (duo album with John Surman) 2008; keyboard continuo for many of the Bach Cantata recordings from Bach Pilgrimage with John Eliot Gardiner 2000; as conductor: John Surman's Proverbs and Songs, numerous choral recordings for Dutch Radio, live recordings for the BBC. *Address:* The Song House, Ashdown Road, Forest Row, East Sussex, RH18 5BW, England (home). *Telephone:* 7803-900691 (mobile) (office). *E-mail:* howard.moody@lineone.net (office). *Website:* www.howardmoody.net.

MOODY, Very Rev. Ivan William George, BMus, PhD; British composer and conductor; *Researcher, Centro de Estudos de Sociologia e Estética Musical, Universidade Nova, Lisbon;* b. 11 June 1964, London, England; m. Susana Simoes Diniz 1989; one s., two d. *Education:* Royal Holloway Coll., Univ. of

London, Univ. of Joensuu, Finland, Univ. of York, and studied privately with John Tavener. *Career:* works performed and broadcast throughout Europe, N and S America and Japan; commissioned by Chanticleer, BBC, Norwegian Soloists' Choir, King's Singers, and others; has conducted choirs and ensembles in Europe and USA; lectures at univs, courses and music festivals in Europe and USA; Researcher, Centro de Estudos de Sociologia e Estética Musical, Universidade Nova, Lisbon –2012, 2015–; Prof. of Church Music, Dept of Orthodox Theology, Univ. of Eastern Finland 2012–14. *Compositions include:* Canticum Canticorum I 1985, Lament for Christ 1989, Angel of Light for violin & harpsichord 1991–92, Passion and Resurrection for STB soli, choir, tubular bells, 2 vl, viola, vcl, cb 1992, Epitaphios for solo cello & string orchestra 1993, Hymn to the Light 1994, Revelation for narrator, male chamber choir, 2 viols, 2 sackbuts and chamber organ 1995, Endechas y Canciones 1996, Lullaby for a Byzantine Princess for soprano and string quartet 1997, Pnevma for solo recorder and string orchestra 1998, Words of the Angel 1998, Akathistos Hymn for solo tenor and choir 1998, The Troparion of Kassiani 1999, Lamentations of the Myrrhbearer 2001, Lumière sans déclin 2002, A Lion's Sleep 2002, The Canon for Theophany 2002, The Morning Star for solo double bass and string orchestra 2003, The Dormition of the Virgin Texts from the Transitus Mariae, Matins of the Dormition and other liturgical sources for STB soloists, choir, 2 cornetti/trumpets and strings 2003, Linnunlaulu for solo piano and chamber orchestra 2003, Ossetian Requiem for chamber choir and 8 cellos 2004, Passione Popolare 2005, The Bird of Dawning for bass clarinet, violin, viola and cello 2005, Only the Bees Can Hear for string quartet 2006, Ravenna Sanctus 2006, Pipistrello for tuba & brass ensemble 2007, Led by the Light 2008, Stabat Mater 2008, Canti della Rosa 2008, Hymn to St Nicholas 2009, Birth of Leaves 2009, Nocturne of Light 2009, Angelus Domini Descendit 2010, Sub Tuum Praesidium 2010, Vespers (for children's voices) 2011, Pacific Canticles 2011, Simeron 2012, Baladilla de los Tres Rios 2012, Shoreline 2012, Keskiyö 2013, Dragonfly 2013, Fioriture 2013, Qohelet 2013, Aposticha for the Dormition 2013, Thy Fatherly Embrace 2014, The Land Which is Not 2014, Greek Liturgy 2014, Dante Trilogy 2014, O Isplendor 2014, The Descent of the Dove 2015, Uspomena 2015, . . .grace upon her heart. . . 2015. *Recordings:* as conductor: Ippolitov–Ivanov, Divine Liturgy, Ikon; Tavener, Ikon; Finnish Orthodox Music, Cappella Romana. *Publications:* Editions of Renaissance polyphony for Mapa Mundi 1989, 1991, Chester Music 1990–, Fundacão Calouste Gulbenkian 1991, Proceedings of the International Conference on Orthodox Church Music (Ed.) 2005, 2007, 2009, 2011; numerous published articles on contemporary and early music and music of the Orthodox Church. *Honours:* Hon. FACS . *Telephone:* (1851) 880216. *Address:* c/o Vanderbeek & Imrie Ltd, 15 Marvig, Lochs, Isle of Lewis, HS2 9QP, Scotland. *E-mail:* ivanmoody@gmail.com; vanderbeek@madasafish .com. *Website:* www.ivanmoody.co.uk.

MOOG, Joseph; German pianist; b. 1987, Ludwigshafen. *Education:* Acad. of Music Karlsruhe, Acad. of Music Würzburg with Bernd Glemser, Acad. for Music, Theatre and Media Hannover with Arie Vardi. *Career:* started playing piano aged four; since 2013, frequent guest performer at Stuttgart Liederhalle, Alte Oper Frankfurt, Munich Gasteig, Mariinsky Theatre Auditorium St Petersburg, De Doelen Rotterdam and Auditorium della Conciliazione in Rome, also at Royal Albert Hall, London, Louvre Auditorium and Salle Gaveau, Paris, Berlin Konzerthaus, Laeiszhalle Hamburg, La Roque d'Antéron and Ruhr Klavierfestival; performed with European orchestras including Helsinki, Stuttgart and Prague Philharmonics, BBC Nat. Orchestra of Wales, and with conductors including Andrey Boreyko, Karl-Heinz Steffens, John Axelrod, Fabrice Bollon, Theodor Guschlbauer, Philippe Entremont and Michael Sanderling; US debut with Colorado Symphony Orchestra 2011, appearances at Gilmore International Piano Series, Kalamazoo, Mich., Frick Collection, New York, Ravinia Festival, Washington Performing Arts Soc., Miami Int. Piano Festival; Wigmore Hall recital debut, London 2014; N American recital debut at Vancouver Recital Soc. 2015; opened Master Pianists Series at Concertgebouw Amsterdam 2015. *Recordings include:* nine CDs including Metamorphose(n) 2009, Divergences 2010, Franz Liszt Recital 2011, Rachmaninov/Rubinstein Piano Concertos 2012, Scarlatti Illuminated 2013, Tchaikovsky/Scharwenka Sonatas 2014, Grieg and Moszkoswki Piano Concertos 2015. *Honours:* ICMA Young Artist of the Year 2012, ICMA Solo Instrumentalist of the Year 2014, Gramophone Awards Young Artist of the Year 2015. *Website:* www.akonasholt.co.uk; www .josephmoog.com.

MOORE, Carman Leroy, BMus, MMus, MS; American composer, conductor, music critic and librettist; *Founder and Music Director, The Skymusic Ensemble;* b. 8 Oct. 1936, Lorain, Ohio; s. of Mr and Mrs Claude Moore; m. (divorced); two s. *Education:* Ohio State Univ., The Juilliard School, studied with Hall Overton, Luciano Berio, Stefan Wolpe and Vincent Persichetti. *Career:* commissioned performances by New York Philharmonic, San Francisco Symphony, Rochester Philharmonic, The Chamber Music Soc. of Lincoln Center, The Focus Ensemble; performances by Cleveland Orchestra, The American Composers Orchestra, Dayton Philharmonic, Orchestra of the Sorbonne, The American Symphony Orchestra, Nexus Ensemble, Aeolian Chamber Players, Continuum Ensemble; Founder, Composer, Conductor, Skymusic Ensemble 1978; taught at Yale School of Music, Queens and Brooklyn Colls, Manhattanville Coll.; music critic, columnist, The Village Voice 1966–76; Master Composer, Young Choreographers and Composers Project, American Dance Festival 1986–96. *Compositions include:* Madiba for orchestra and solo cello, Wildfires and Field Songs, Gospel Fuse, Girl of Diamond Mountain (intermedia song cycle), Hit: A Concerto for percussion

and orchestra, Mass for the 21st Century, Concertos, The Theme is Freedom (for Skymusic Ensemble), Wild Gardens of the Loup Garou, The Last Chance Planet (opera), Club Paradise (musical), Four Movements for a Five-Toed Dragon for orchestra and Chinese instruments, The Sorrow of Love for double choir and piano, Berenice Variations for clarinet, piano, violin and violoncello, Love Notes to Central Park (mixed media for Skymusic Ensemble) 1996, Gethsemane Park (gospel opera) 1998, Journey to Benares (musical) 1999, Night Angel (musical) 2000, The Mystery of Tao (chamber music) 2001, Rasur, God of Peace (Spanish language children's opera) 2002, The Sorcerer's Apprentice 2005, Blue. . .Red. . .Green for string trio 2007, Piano Sonata No. 2 (The Journey) 2008, Concerto for Ornette 2010, SHE (A Life) 2011, To High Heavens 2013, The Quiet Piece 2013, and numerous others. *Dance:* American Dance Fest Master Composer; numerous scores for New York City Ballet, Donald Byrd Dance, Elaine Summers, Ruby Shang Dance, etc.; Touch, Turn, Return for American Tap Dance Orchestra. *Plays include:* The Burial at Thebes (score/LaMama Theatre); librettist, Truth . . .life of Sojourner Truth (music by Alvin Singleton), Timon of Athens (Yale Rep score), The Second Shepherd's Play. *Publications include:* Somebody's Angel Child: The Story of Bessie Smith 1970, Rockit, Crossover: An American Bio (autobiography); frequent contrib. to New York Times, The Village Voice, Essence, Saturday Review of Literature, Vogue and others. *Honours:* numerous awards. *Address:* 152 Columbus Avenue, 4R, New York, NY 10023, USA (home). *Telephone:* (212) 580-0825 (home); (646) 238-7111 (office). *E-mail:* carman@carmanmoore .com; moorecarman@gmail.com. *Website:* www.carmanmoore.com; www .skymusicensemble.com.

MOORE, Diana; British singer (soprano); b. 1965, England. *Education:* Univ. of Birmingham, Royal Acad. of Music. *Career:* concert appearances in the Saint Matthew Passion and Rossini's Petite Messe at St John's Smith Square; Fauré's La naissance de Venus with The Sixteen, Bach's B minor Mass at the Brighton Festival and La Resurrezione by Handel at Oslo 2001; Psalm 4 by Alexander Goehr with the New London Chamber Choir and Still Life at the Penguin Café with the Royal Ballet; Janáček's The Diary of One Who Disappeared for English Nat. Opera and in the Netherlands; season 2001 with Armindo in Handel's Partenope at the Covent Garden Festival (Linbury Theatre) and Purcell's Dido under Trevor Pinnock; Bach's St Matthew Passion at the London Proms 2002. *Address:* The Cottage, Garrett Lee, Longhorsley, Morpeth, Northumberland, NE65 8RJ, England. *Website:* www.dianamoore .co.uk.

MOORE, Dorothy Rudd, BMus; American composer, teacher and singer; b. 4 June 1940, Wilmington, Del.; m. Kermit Moore. *Education:* Howard High School, Wilmington School of Music, Howard Univ., American Conservatory, France, private study with Chou Wen Chung 1965, private voice lessons with Lola Hayes 1972. *Career:* teacher, Harlem School of the Arts, New York 1965–66, New York Univ. 1969, Bronx Community Coll. 1971; private piano, voice, sight singing and ear training instructor, New York 1968–; founding mem., Soc. of Black Composers 1968–75; mem., New York State Council for the Arts 1988–90; Lucy Moten Fellowship 1963; American Music Center grant 1972; New York State Council on the Arts grant 1985; mem. Nat. Endowment for the Arts, Recording and Composers (panel mem. 1986–88), New York Women Composers, New York Singing Teachers' Asscn, American Composers' Alliance, BMI. *Compositions include:* Flight for piano 1956, Symphony No. 1 1962, Songs from the Rubaiyat 1962, Reflections for concert band 1962, Baroque Suite for unaccompanied violoncello 1964, Three Pieces for Violin and piano 1966, Modes for ensemble 1968, Moods for ensemble 1969, Lament for nine instruments 1969, Trio No. 1 1969, From the Dark Tower 1970, Dirge and Deliverance for cello 1970, Weary Blues 1972, Dream and Variations for piano 1974, Sonnets on Love, Rosebuds and Death 1975, In Celebration for chorus 1977, Night Fantasy for clarinet 1978, A Little Whimsy for piano 1978, Frederick Douglass (opera) 1981, Transcension (I Have Been to the Mountaintop) for chamber orchestra 1985, Flowers of Darkness 1988, Voices From The Light for chorus 1997. *Current Management:* c/o Gina Genova, American Composers Alliance, 802 West, 190th Street, Suite 1B, New York, NY 10040, USA. *Telephone:* (212) 925-0458. *E-mail:* info@composers.com. *Website:* composers.com/dorothy-rudd-moore.

MOORE, Gillian, CBE, MBE, BMus, MA, FRCM; British music administrator; *Head of Classical Music, Southbank Centre;* b. 20 Feb. 1959, Glasgow, Scotland; d. of Charles Moore and Sara Queen; pnr Bruce Nockles; one s. *Education:* Univ. of Glasgow, Royal Scottish Acad. of Music and Drama, Univ. of York, Harvard Univ., USA. *Career:* Educ. Dir London Sinfonietta 1983–93, Artistic Dir 1998–2006; Head of Educ., Southbank Centre, London 1993–98, also Music Audience Devt Man. 1996, Head of Contemporary Culture 2006–11, Head of Classical Music 2011–; Artistic Dir ISCM World Music Days, Manchester 1997–98; Visiting Prof., Royal Coll. of Music 1996–; Gov. Nat. Youth Orchestra of GB; mem. British Govt Nat. Curriculum Working Group on Music. *Honours:* Hon. Mem. Guildhall School of Music 1993; Dr hc (Brunel) 2006; Sir Charles Groves Award for Outstanding Contrib. to British Music 1992, Asscn of British Orchestras Award for Contrib. of Most Benefit to Orchestral Life in the UK 1999, Leslie Boosey Award 2008. *Address:* Southbank Centre, Belvedere Road, London, SE1 8XX, England (office). *Telephone:* (20) 7921-0897 (office). *Fax:* (20) 7639-6675 (home). *E-mail:* gillian .moore@southbankcentre.co.uk (office). *Website:* www.southbankcentre.co.uk (office).

MOORE, Jonathan; British actor, writer and stage director; b. 25 Nov. 1963; s. of Richard Moore and Nora Moore. *Education:* Croydon Art Coll. *Career:*

worked in the theatre and for television; co-librettist and director of Greek by Mark-Anthony Turnage, premiered at the 1988 Munich Biennale and seen later at the Edinburgh Festival, at the London Coliseum, 1990, directed the version on BBC television; directed Henze's Elegy for Young Lovers, La Fenice, Venice 1989; wrote the libretto for Horse Opera, a television film opera for Channel Four, music by Stewart Copeland; staged the premiere of Hans Jürgen von Bose's 63 Dream Palace at Munich 1990 and the premiere of Michael Berkeley's Baa Baa Black Sheep, Opera North 1993; British premiere of Schnitke's Life With an Idiot, ENO London Coliseum 1995; further projects: Cask of Amontillado, Holders, Barbados 1993; libretto and direction of premiere of East and West, by Ian McQueen, Almeida 1995; libretto and direction of premiere of Mottke the Thief by Bernd Franke, Bonn Opera 1998; The Nose (Shostakovich), ENO London Coliseum 1996; staged the premiere of Macmillan's Inès de Castro, Edinburgh 1996 and subsequent revivals including a filming by BBS TV and Porto Festival; directed world premieres of Die Versicherung by Jan Muller-Wieland, Darmstadt 1999, and Facing Goya by Michael Nyman, Santiago de Compostella and Valencia 2000; directed and translated The Magic Flute for Scottish Opera 2002–03; directed Sex, Chips and Rock 'n' Roll, Royal Exchange 2005; directed and acted in The Soldier's Tale, Savannah Festival, Georgia; The Ballad of Elizabeth Sulky Mouth, Greenwich 2006; Three Ways of Dying with Daniel Hope and Uri Caine at the Feldkirch Festival; Visiting Sr Lecturer, Royal Coll. of Music 2006; Visiting Lecturer, Drama Centre, London 2006. *Plays:* writer: Sea Change 1977, Obstruct the doors, cause delay and be Dangerous...1980, Street Captives (Edinburgh Festival, Royal Exchange) 1981, Treatment (Donmar, filmed for TV) 1982, The Hooligan Nights 1985, Behind Heaven (Royal Exchange, Donmar) 1986, Regeneration 1989, This Other Eden (Soho Theatre) 1990, Fall From Light 2002, The Bacchae (adaptation) 2003–05; actor: The Gorky Brigade (Royal Court) 1982, Venice Preserv'd (Almeida) 1985, Treatment, Gate (Donmar, Edinburgh Festival) 1986, Behind Heaven (Royal Exchange) Donmar 1986, The Art of Success (RSC) 1987, The Idiot (Barbican) 1990, Dead Funny (Salisbury Playhouse, Theatre Clwyd) 1998, Misalliance 1998, The School of Night (Chichester Festival Theatre) 1999, A Midsummer Night's Dream 2001, Macbeth 2002, Arcola; Round the Horne (West End and No 1 UK tour) 2004; 2Graves (one-man play, Edinburgh Festival, Arts Theatre) 2006, Holding Fire! (Shakespeare's Globe) 2007. *Television:* Inside Story 1986, Bleak House (series) 1986, Jack the Ripper (series) 1988, Roger Roger (two series) 1999, 2003, The People's Harry Enfield 2001, Foyle's War 2003. *Films include:* My Beautiful Laundrette 1985. *Publication:* Jonathon Moore: Three Plays 2002. *Honours:* Edinburgh Fringe Award 1982, Best Libretto Award, Munich (for Greek) 1988, Best Director Award (for 63 Dream Palace), Munich 1990, Royal Philharmonic Society Award and the Midem Award, Cannes 1991, BMW Award (for Die Vier Himmelsrichtungen), Munich 1994. *Current Management:* Performing Arts, 6 Windmill Street, London, W1T 2JB. *Telephone:* (20) 7255-1362. *Fax:* (20) 7631-4631. *E-mail:* info@performing-arts.co.uk. *Website:* www.performing-arts.co.uk; www.jonathanmooreuk.com.

MOORE, Latonia; American singer (soprano); b. Houston, Tex. *Education:* Univ. of North Tex., Acad. of Vocal Arts, Philadelphia, studied with Bill Schumann. *Career:* began professional career with performances for Acad. of Vocal Arts and the Opera Co. of Philadelphia; Royal Opera debut as Liu in Turandot 2009; debut at the Metropolitan Opera as Aida 2012; has also performed with Dallas Opera, Palm Beach Opera, Semperoper Dresden, Deutsche Oper Berlin; operatic roles include title role in Aida, Mimi in La Bohème, Donna Elvira in Don Giovanni, Despina in Così fan tutte, Marguerite in Faust, title role in Lucrezia Borgia, Countess in Le Nozze di Figaro, Fidelia in Edgar, Micaela in Carmen, Liu in Turandot; concert recitals include Mahler's Second Symphony with Nat. Symphony in Washington, Mahler's Fourth Symphony and Berg Lieder at Festival de Paques de Deauville, France, Mozart's Coronation Mass, Mendelssohn's Second Symphony, Verdi's Requiem. *Recording:* Mahler, Second Symphony 2002. *Honours:* winner Metropolitan Opera's Nat. Auditions 2000, first prize and public prize Competizione dell'Opera, Dresden 2002, first prize Licia Albanese Puccini Foundation Competition, New York 2002, first prize Palm Beach Opera Competition 2003, first prize Dallas Opera Competition 2003, first prize Marseilles Opera Competition 2003, second prize Int. Belvedere Competition, Vienna 2003, Dallas Opera Maria Callas Debut Artist of the Year 2005. *Current Management:* Askonas Holt Ltd, Lincoln House, 300 High Holborn, London, WC1V 7JH, England. *Telephone:* (20) 7400-1700 (office). *Fax:* (20) 7400-1799 (office). *E-mail:* info@askonasholt.co.uk (office). *Website:* www.askonasholt.co.uk (office).

MOORES, Sir Peter, Kt, CBE, DL, KB; British business executive; b. 9 April 1932, s. of Sir John Moores; m. Luciana Pinto 1960 (divorced 1984); one s. one d. *Education:* Eton Coll., Christ Church, Oxford, Wiener Akademie der Musik und darstellende Kunst. *Career:* worked in opera at Glyndebourne and Vienna State Opera; Dir The Littlewoods Org. 1965–93 (Chair. 1977–80); f. Peter Moores Foundation 1964; pioneered opera recordings in English trans. by EMI and Chandos; supported recordings by Opera Rara of rare 19th-Century Italian opera; annual Peter Moores Foundation Scholarships awarded to promising young opera singers, Royal Northern Coll. of Music; endowed Faculty Directorship and Chair of Man. Studies, Oxford Univ. 1992; est. Scotland Beef Project, Barbados (land conservation and self-supporting farming practice) 1993, Transatlantic Slave Trade Gallery, Merseyside Maritime Museum 1994; Benefactor, Chair of Tropical Horticulture, Univ. of W. Indies, Barbados 1995; f. Compton Verney House Trust 1993, Peter Moores Foundation 1998; Dir Singer & Friedlander 1978–92, Scottish Opera 1988–92; Trustee Tate Gallery 1978–85; Gov. BBC 1981–83. *Honours:* Hon. RNCM 1985, DL of Lancashire 1992; Hon. MA (Christ Church, Oxford) 1975; Gold Medal of Italian Repub. 1974, Gramophone Award for Special Achievement 2008. *Address:* Parbold Hall, Parbold, nr Wigan, Lancs., WN8 7TG, England (home).

MORA, Barry; New Zealand singer (baritone); b. 1944. *Education:* studied in London with Otakar Kraus and John Matheson. *Career:* sang at Gelsenkirchen 1977–79 as Verdi's Posa and Luna; Mozart's Speaker and Figaro; sang at Frankfurt from 1979 as Tamare, in Die Gezeichneten, and Ford, in Falstaff; Festival Hall debut 1979 as Schumann's Faust; Covent Garden debut 1980 as Donner, in Das Rheingold; Scottish Opera 1983 as the Traveller, in Death in Venice; WNO from 1986 as Donner, Gunther, The Forester in The Cunning Little Vixen and Frank in Die Fledermaus 1991; Netherlands Opera 1991; engagements at Deutsche Oper Berlin, Zürich Opera, Aachen, Düsseldorf, Barcelona, Wellington and Canterbury, New Zealand; also sang 1992 in Rosenkavalier, Sydney; La Traviata, Barcelona; Parsifal, Frankfurt; Così fan tutte, Wellington; Un Ballo in Maschera, Brussels; concert repertoire includes Puccini's Messa di Gloria, Bach's B minor Mass and St John Passion; Carmina Burana, Stravinsky's Canticum Sacrum, Lieder eines fahrenden Gesellen by Mahler, Lulu at Buenos Aires, Così fan tutte at Barcelona Opera, La Cenerentola, Australian Opera 1994 and for Opera New Zealand; roles with Australian Opera as Dr Schön in Lulu, Alidoro in La Cenerentola; Tales of Hoffmann 1995; with Wellington Opera, Ping in Turandot 1994; Balstrode in Peter Grimes 1995; Father in Hansel and Gretel 1995; season 1999 at Sydney as the Doctor in Wozzeck and in Auckland as Puccini's Sharpless. *Current Management:* Jenifer Eddy Management, Suite 11, The Clivedon, 596 St Kilda Road, Melbourne, Vic. 3004, Australia.

MORAGUÈS, Pascal; French clarinettist. *Career:* Principal Clarinet, Orchestre de Paris 1981–; mem., Quintette Moraguès, Ensemble Viktoria Mullova, Ensemble de Katia et Marielle Labèque; appearances include the Wigmore Hall, London, the Vienna and Berlin Concert Halls, Théâtre des Champs-Elysées, Théâtre du Châtelet (both in Paris), Carnegie Hall, New York, and concert series in Europe, the Middle East, the USA, Australia and Japan; teacher, Conservatoire National Supérieur de Musique, Paris 1995–. *Current Management:* Lorentz Concerts, 3 rue la Boétie, 75008 Paris, France. *Telephone:* 1-42-66-12-32. *Fax:* 1-42-68-08-87. *E-mail:* office@lorentzconcerts.com. *Website:* www.lorentzconcerts.com.

MORAL, Antonio; Spanish artistic director; *Artistic Director, Centro Nacional de Difusión Musical* and *Auditorio Nacional de Música de Madrid*; b. 30 Oct. 1956, Puebla de Almenara, Cuenca. *Career:* music critic for newspapers and other media 1984–91; f. Scherzo music magazine 1985, Dir –2001; f. and Dir Mozart Festival of Madrid 1988–97; Musical and Artistic Dir, Music Programme of the Foundation of the Caja Madrid Savings Bank 1990–2005; f. and Artistic Dir Liceo de Cámara, Madrid 1992–2005, f. and Artistic Dir Lied Cycle, Teatro de la Zarzuela 1994–; f. and Artistic Dir Mozart Festival of La Coruña 1998–2002; Artistic Dir Semana de Música Religiosa de Cuenca 2000–05; Artistic Dir Teatro Real, Madrid 2005–10; Artistic Dir Centro Nacional Difusion Musical 2010–; Artistic Dir Auditorio Nacional de Música de Madrid 2010–; Founding mem. Int. Jury, Cannes Classical Awards 1995–2001; mem. Int. Piano Competition Umberto Micheli, Milan (mem. Int. Cttee 1998). *Honours:* Gold Medal, Semana de Música Religiosa de Cuenca. *Address:* CNDM Auditorio Nacional de Música, C/ Príncipe de Vergara 146, Madrid 28002, Spain (office). *Telephone:* (91) 3370234 (office). *E-mail:* amoral@inaem.mcu.es (office). *Website:* www.cndm.inaem.mcu.es (office).

MORALES, Walter, MMus; American conductor; *Music Director, Edgewood Symphony Orchestra*. *Education:* School of Music, Univ. of Costa Rica, Coll. of Charleston, Mason Gross School of the Arts, Rutgers Univ., Carnegie Mellon's School of Music. *Career:* performed as guest conductor for Pittsburgh Symphony Orchestra, Nat. Symphony Orchestra of Costa Rica, Pittsburgh Youth Symphony Orchestra, Wheeling Symphony Orchestra, McKeesport Symphony Orchestra, Altoona Symphony Orchestra, Three Rivers Young People's Orchestra, Helix New Music Ensemble, Rutgers Chamber Orchestra, Rutgers Opera, Charleston TheatreWorks Co.; has collaborated with composers including John Adams, George Crumb, Richard Danielpour, Derek Bermel, Christopher Theofanidis, William Bolcom, Gary Schocker, Katherine Hoover, Mike Mower, Diefer Kieffer, Reza Vali, Nancy Galbraith, David Stock, Amy Williams, Roger Zahab, Eli Tamar, Leonardo Balada, Zulema de la Cruz, Eddie Mora, Alejandro Cardona; collaborations with artists including Lior Eitan, Wissam Boustany, Gary Schocker, Cuarteto Latinoamericano, Sarah Chang, Midori, Alexander Kerr, Walfrid Kujala, Jennifer Larmore, Julianne Baird, Herbert Perry, Anne Panagulias, Meir Rimon; has performed in solo and chamber music recitals in Md, Washington, DC, N and S Carolina, Pa, Mass, Weill Recital Hall, New York City, Steinway Hall, Lincoln Center; soloist with Nat. Symphony Orchestra of Costa Rica, Symphony Orchestra of Chile, Carnegie Mellon Philharmonic, Carnegie Mellon Virtuosi, Carnegie Mellon Contemporary Ensemble, Princeton Pro Musica, Charleston Symphony Orchestra, International Piano Series Orchestra, College of Charleston Orchestra, University of Costa Rica Chamber Orchestra; Music Dir and Conductor, Carnegie Mellon Contemporary Ensemble 2003–09; Head of Music, Opera Theater of Pittsburgh 2007–09; currently Music Dir Edgewood Symphony Orchestra; Prin. Guest Conductor, Pittsburgh Philharmonic 2011–. *Recordings include:* Sigel – Eight Works for Percussion 2006, Small Bear, Large Telescope 2006, George Crumb 2007, Seasons Within 2008, Nancy

Galbraith: Other Sun 2010, Ruidos...Voices...Canciones Lejanas 2010. *Address:* Edgewood Symphony Orchestra, PO BOX 82559, Edgewood, PA 15218-0559, USA (office). *Telephone:* (412) 473-8880 (office). *Website:* www.edgewoodsymphony.org (office); www.waltermoralesmusic.com.

MORAN, Robert; American composer; b. 8 Jan. 1937, Denver, CO. *Education:* studied with Hans Erich Apostel and Roman Haubenstock Ramati in Vienna, Luciano Berio and Darius Milhaud at Mills Coll. *Career:* founder and co-Dir, New Music Ensemble, San Francisco Conservatory; performances throughout USA and Europe as pianist; lecturer on contemporary music. *Compositions:* Silver and the Circle of Messages for chamber orchestra 1970, Emblems of Passage for two orchestras 1974, Angels of Silence for viola and chamber orchestra 1975, The Last Station of the Albatross for 1–8 instruments 1978, Survivor from Darmstadt 1984; mixed-media works and stage works: Let's Build a Nut House for chamber opera 1969, Erlösung dem Erlöser (music drama) 1982, Leipziger Kerzenspiel 1985, The Juniper Tree 1985, Desert of Roses 1992, From the Towers of the Moon 1992, Dracula Diary 1994, Night Passage (opera) 1995, Remember Him to Me: an Opera 1996, Entretien Mysterieux for orchestra 1996, four Partitions for violin and orchestra 1997, Voce della Fontana for soprano and ensemble 1998; numerous choral works for ensembles in USA, Europe, Canada, many recorded on the INNOVA label. *Address:* Box 54202, Philadelphia, PA 19105 (home); c/o BMI, 320 West 57th Street, New York, NY 10019, USA (office). *Telephone:* (215) 546-0582 (home). *E-mail:* rbtmoran@macconnect.com (home). *Website:* members.macconnect.com/users/r/rbtmoran/index.htm (office).

MORAVEC, Antonín; Czech violinist and composer; b. 29 April 1928, Brno; m. Karla Moravcova 15 July 1950. *Education:* Conservatory of Brno, Janáček Acad. of Musical Art, Brno, Moscow Tchaikovsky Conservatory. *Career:* Prof., Janáček Acad., Brno, Music Acad., Prague; mastercourses at Kunitachi Music Acad., Tokyo, Japan, Tchaikovsky Conservatory, Moscow, Mozarteum, Salzburg, Basel-Muttenz, Switzerland, courses of the Warsaw Acad. organized in Castle Lanzut, Castle of Pommersfelden, Germany; mem. 35 juries of int. violin competitions; has performed solo violin concertos world-wide; recitals on radio and TV. *Compositions:* several compositions for violin and piano including Snowdrop for Leni Bernstein, Violin Concerto 2003, Cadenzas for 18 Violin Concertos by Viotti, Haydn, Mozart, Paganini, Beethoven, Brahms, Slavik and Szymanowski, new rev. L. Janaček Violin Sonata. *Recordings:* Violin Sonatas by Martinů, Shostakovich, Prokofiev, Piano Trio by M. Istvan. *Honours:* Hon. Prof. Kumitachi Music Acad., Tokyo 1961; prizewinner, violin competitions in Brno 1940, 1958, Prague 1950, 1951, Berlin 1951, L. Janaček Medal, Ministry of Culture 1978, Merited Artist of Czech Repub. 1979, Prize, Union of Czech Composers 1982, Medal of Janaček Acad. of Music, Brno 1997, Sr Prize of Intergram and Foundation 'Life of Artist', Prague 1998. *Address:* Taussigova 1152, 182 00 Prague 8, Czech Republic.

MORAVEC, Paul, BA, MA, MMus, DMA; American composer, academic, electronic music synthesist and conductor; *University Professor of Music, Adelphi University*; b. 2 Nov. 1957, Buffalo, NY. *Education:* Harvard Univ., Cambridge, Columbia Univ., New York. *Career:* Asst Conductor, Harvard Collegium Musicum 1977–80; Teaching Asst Harvard Univ. 1980; Teaching Asst, Columbia Univ. 1980–84, Preceptor 1985–87; Asst Prof., Dartmouth Coll. 1987–93, Assoc. Prof., 1993–96; Univ. Prof. of Music, Adelphi Univ. 1996–; Visiting Assoc. Prof., Columbia Univ. 1996–98; Adjunct Assoc. Prof., Hunter Coll. 1997–98; Artist-in-Residence, Inst. for Advanced Study. *Compositions:* over 90 pieces including Missa Miserere 1981, Ave Verum Corpus 1981, Pater Noster 1981, Sacred Songs 1982, Three Anthems 1983, Songs for violin and piano 1983, Music for chamber ensemble 1983, Wings 1983, Spiritdance 1984, Innocent Dreamers 1985, Four Transcendent Love Songs 1986, Prayers and Praise 1986, Whispers 1986, The Kingdom Within 1987, three string quartets 1986, 1990, 1992, Aubade for strings 1990, Piano Concerto 1992, Violin Concerto 1994, Cello Concerto 1998, Mood Swings for piano trio 1998, Fire/Ice/Air dramatic cantata 1998, Tempest Fantasy for solo clarinet and piano trio (Pulitzer Prize in Music) 2004, Protean Fantasy 2005, Ariel Fantasy 2005, The Time Gallery 2005, The Blizzard Voices 2007, Brandenburg Gate 2008, The Letter 2009. *Honours:* Rome Prize Fellowship, Fellowship, Nat. Endowment for the Arts, Rockefeller Foundation Fellowship, Camargo Foundatioon Fellowship, two fellowships, American Acad. of Arts and Letters. *Address:* Department of Music, Adelphi University, Performing Arts Center, Room 211, PO Box 701, Garden City, NY 11530-0701, USA (office). *Telephone:* (516) 877-4285 (office). *Fax:* (516) 877-4286 (office). *E-mail:* moravec@adelphi.edu (office). *Website:* www.adelphi.edu (office); www.paulmoravec.com.

MORAWSKI, Jerzy, PhD; Polish musicologist; b. 9 Sept. 1932, Warsaw; m. Katarzyna Morawska. *Education:* Warsaw Conservatory, Inst. of Musicology, Warsaw Univ. *Career:* Asst Dept of Theory and History of Music, Polish Acad. of Sciences 1956–70, Head History of Music Section 1970–79, Vice-Dir Inst of Arts 1979–81 (retd 2005); Lecturer, Warsaw Univ. 1968–70, Acad. of Catholic Theology, Warsaw 1970–73, Jagiellonian Univ., Kraków 1971–82, 1999–2000; fmr Ed.-in-Chief of serial publications, Monumenta Musicae in Polonia and Musica Medii Aevi; mem. Polish Composers' Union, Musicological Section (fmr vice-sec. and pres.). *Publications include:* research papers: Liturgical Recitative in Poland 1973, 1986, 1992, 1995, The Problems of the Tropes Techniques 1976, 1979, Polish Hymns 1991, Sursum Corda: Presentation of a Motif 1999, Two Unfamiliar Tonaria from Silesian Antiphonaries dating from the Thirteenth and Fourteenth Centuries 2002, The Beginning of Polish Musical Culture: the Birth of the Traditions 2007, The Te Deum Laudamus in Polish Manuscripts from the Late Middle Ages 2008, Missa Jagellonica in the University Library of Vilnius 2009; books: Musical Lyric Poetry in Medieval Poland 1973, Theory of Music in the Middle Ages 1979, Liturgical Recitative in Medieval Poland 1996, The History of Music in Poland: Vol. I The Middle Ages 2003; editor: Musica Antiqua Polonica: Anthology of The Middle Ages 1972, The Rhymed History of St Jadwiga 1977, The Rhymed History of St Adalbert 1979, The Polish Cistercian Sequences 1984, Jan Stefani's Six Partitas for Wind Instruments 1993; contrib. to numerous professional publications. *Address:* ul Dluga 24 m 43, 00–238 Warsaw, Poland (home).

MORDLER, John; British opera house director. *Career:* Dir Opéra de Monte-Carlo 1984–2007; mem. Comité d'Honneur, Les Azuriales Opera Festival; mem. Bd Opera Europa. *Address:* c/o Opéra de Monte-Carlo, Casino de Monte-Carlo, Place du Casino, BP 139, Monte-Carlo 98007, Monaco (office). *Telephone:* 98-06-28-00 (office). *Fax:* 98-06-28-10 (office). *E-mail:* contact@opera.mc (office). *Website:* www.opera.mc (office).

MOREHEN, John Manley, JP, MA, PhD, DLitt, FRCO (Chm), FRCCO; British musicologist, organist and conductor; *Professor Emeritus of Music, University of Nottingham*; b. 3 Sept. 1941, Gloucester, England; s. of Harry Morehen and Gertrude (Rhoda) Morehen; m. Marie Catherine Jacobus 1969; one s. one d. *Education:* Clifton Coll., Bristol, Royal School of Church Music, Croydon, New Coll., Oxford, Coll. of Church Musicians, Washington, DC, USA and King's Coll., Cambridge. *Career:* Asst Dir of Music, St Clement Danes Church, Strand, Hampstead Parish Church, London; keyboard player, Hampstead Choral Soc., Martindale Sidwell Choir, London Bach Orchestra 1964–67; Lecturer, Coll. of Church Musicians, Washington Cathedral, American Univ., Washington, DC 1967–68; sub-organist, St George's Chapel, Windsor Castle 1968–72; Lecturer in Music, Univ. of Nottingham 1973–82, Sr Lecturer 1982–89, Prof. of Music 1989–2002, Head, School of Humanities 1998–2001, Prof. Emer. of Music 2002–; many broadcasts as organist, speaker and conductor 1964–; recital tours of Europe, N America and Australia; presentations on computer applications in music at confs in the UK, USA, Canada, France and the Netherlands; Pres. East Midlands Choirs Charitable Trust 1993–2000, Inc. Soc. of Musicians 2003–04; panel mem. Humanities Research Bd 1994–97; Subject Assessor (Music), Higher Educ. Funding Council for England 1994–95; Music Adviser, Commonwealth Scholarship Comm. 1996–2000; Gov. Chetham's School of Music 2007–12; Trustee, Good Vibrations 2012–14. *Recordings:* with choirs of New Coll. Oxford and Hampstead Parish Church. *Publications:* numerous critical edns of 16th and 17th-century English and Italian choral and instrumental music, including vols in the series Early English Church Music, The Byrd Edition, The English Madrigalists, Recent Researches in the Music of the Renaissance; contrib. to most major British and American musical journals and to New Grove Dictionary of Music 1980, 2002, Die Musik in Geschichte und Gegenwart, New Dictionary of National Biography 2004. *Honours:* Freeman of the City of London 1991; Liveryman, Worshipful Co. of Musicians 1991, Master 2012–13; Hon. FGCM. *Address:* Chestnut Barn, Syerston Hall Park, Newark, Notts., NG23 5NL, England (home). *Telephone:* (1636) 525068 (office). *E-mail:* john@morehen.fsworld.co.uk (home); john.morehen@nottingham.ac.uk (office). *Website:* www.morehen.com.

MOREL, François; composer; b. 14 March 1926, Montréal, Canada. *Education:* studied with Clude Champagne, Conservatoire de Muique, Montréal. *Career:* worked for Radio-Canada writing background music for theatre, radio and television 1956–81; Prof. of Composition, Orchestration and Analysis, Ecole de Musique, Université Laval, Québec City; Pres. of publishing firm, Les Editions Québec-Musique, Montréal; received commissions from Canadian Broadcasting Corporation, Int. Festival of Contemporary Music for Wind Symphony Orchestra, Edmonton Symphony Orchestra, McGill Chamber Orchestra, Société de Musique Contemporaine du Québec, Guitar Soc. of Toronto, Olympic Games Cttee, Montréal Int. Competition, among others. *Compositions:* orchestral: Antiphonie 1953, Boreal 1959, Departs 1968–69, Diptyque 1948, revised 1955–56, Esquisse 1947–47, L'Etoile noire 1961–62, Iikkii 1971, Jeux 1976, Litanies 1955–56, revised 1970, Melisma 1980, Le Mythe de la roche percee 1960–61, Neumes despace et reliefs 1967, Prismes-anamorphoses 1967, Radiance 1970–72, Requiem for winds 1962–63, Rituel de l'espace 1958–59, Sinfonia 1963, Spirale 1956, Trajectoire 1967; instrumental ensemble: Cassation 1954, Etude en forme de toccate 1965, Quatuor No. 1 1952, No. 2 1962–63, Quintette pour cuivres 1962, Rhythmologue 1970, Lumières sculptèes for wind and three percussion 1992, Les Éphemères for four horns and tuba 1995, Et le crepuscule se trouva libre for orchestra 1996, Metamporphoses for orchestra 1998, Symphonie pour cuivres 1956; also instrumental solo and vocal solos.

MORELLI, Adriana; Italian singer (soprano); b. 1954. *Education:* Regiio Calabria. *Career:* debut in Spoleto 1978, as Musetta; sang Sophie in Werther at Bergamo 1979, Lauretta in Gianni Schicchi at Lucca, 1981; further engagements as Butterfly and Mimi at Spoleto and Lille, Elisabeth de Valois at Dijon, Amsterdam, Amelia, Un Ballo in Maschera, at Trieste; sang Margherita in Mefistofele and Tosca at Genoa, 1987–88, Giorgetta in Il Tabarro at Florence 1988 and Maria Stuarda at Piacenza, 1990; La Scala debut, 1990, as Nedda in Pagliacci; sang Silvia in Mascagni's Zanetta at Florence, 1996; sang Puccini's Giorgetta at Verona, 2000; stage and concert appearances in South America. *Current Management:* Melos Konzerte Wien, Salesianergasse 12/11, 1030 Vienna, Austria. *Telephone:* (1) 714 91 96. *Fax:* (1) 714 91 91. *E-mail:* info@melos.at. *Website:* www.melos.at.

MORETTI, Isabelle Cécile Andrée; French harpist; b. 5 May 1964, Lyon. *Education:* studied with Germaine Lorenzini. *Career:* teacher, Conservatoire Nat. Supérieur de Paris 1995–; recital and masterclass tours of USA and Republic of Korea 2004, Estonia and Latvia 2005, Quebec 2006; premiere of two concertos, by Philippe Hersant with Ensemble Orchestral de Paris, and by Michele Reverdy with Orchestre Nat. de Lille, 2006. *Recordings include:* concertos by Boieldieu, , Rodrigo, and Ginastera, Debussy: Sonata for flute, viola and harp, Chansons de Bilitis; solo recitals: André Caplet, Le masque de la mort rouge; Ravel, Introduction and Allegro; Jean Gras, Double Concerto for Oboe and Harp (with François Leleux). *Honours:* Premier Prix, Conservatoire Nat. Supérieur de Paris 1983, Second Prize in Munich 1983, Bordeaux 1984, Geneva 1986, winner, Israel Harp Contest 1988, Grand Prix, Nouvelle Acad. du Disque 1995, Victoire de la Musique Classique 1996, Prix de l' Acad. Charles Cros 2000. *Address:* La Hillière, 44470 Thouaré sur Loire, France. *Telephone:* 2-40-77-58-46. *Fax:* 2-40-77-58-46. *E-mail:* isabelle.moretti@free.fr.

MORGAN, Arwel Huw; singer (bass); b. 1950, Ystalyfera, Swansea, Wales. *Career:* chorus mem., WNO 1978, solo roles included Don Fernando, Fidelio, Ladas in The Greek Passion, Angelotti in Tosca, Hobson, Peter Grimes, The Parson in The Cunning Little Vixen; created the role of Maskull for New Celtic Opera's Voyage to Arcturus; ENO from 1987 in Lady Macbeth of Mtsensk and The Cunning Little Vixen; toured the UK 1988, as Osmin in Opera 80s Die Entführung aus dem Serail; season 1992 as Leporello, and as Carl Olsen, in Weill's Street Scene for ENO; Fabrizio in The Thieving Magpie for Opera North; sang Leporello in a new production of Don Giovanni for WNO 1996; Zuniga in Carmen at the London Coliseum 1998; sang Britten's Snug at the Teatro Nazionale, Rome 1999. *Recordings:* Polonius in Hamlet by Ambroise Thomas, conducted by Richard Bonynge.

MORGAN, Beverly, BMus, MMus; singer (soprano); b. 17 March 1952, Hanover, NH, USA. *Education:* Mt Holyoke Coll., New England Conservatory of Music. *Career:* debut recital as winner of Concert Artists Guild Award 1978; operatic appearances with Wiener Staatsoper, San Francisco Opera, Netherlands Opera, Opera Company of Boston, Pittsburgh, Omaha and Philadelphia Operas, Kennedy Center in Washington and Scottish Nat. Opera; sang in the premiere of Glass's Satyagraha at Amsterdam 1980, and in the US premiere of Zimmermann's Die Soldaten, Boston 1982; other appearances in Bernstein's A Quiet Place at La Scala and in Vienna at Santa Fe in the US Premieres of Henze's English Cat and Penderecki's Die schwarze Maske 1985, 1988; Scottish Opera as Berg's Lulu 1987; other roles include Tatiana and Violetta at Seattle and Fusako in Henze's Das Verratene Meer, Berlin and Milan; concert appearances with Boston Symphony, San Francisco Symphony, Chamber Soc. of Lincoln Center, American String Quartet, Marlboro Music Festival, American Composers Orchestra; performances under Leonard Bernstein, Seiji Ozawa and Herbert Blomstedt. *Address:* c/o Columbia Artists Management Inc., 165 West 57th Street, New York, NY 10019, USA.

MORGAN, David S., BMus, ARCM; Australian composer, conductor and arranger; b. 18 May 1932, Ewell, Surrey, England; m. Crisetta Macleod (divorced), one s. two d.; m. 2nd Una Grimshaw. *Education:* Sydney Grammar School, Sydney Conservatorium, Univ. of Durham, studied in London with Norman del Mar and Matyas Seiber. *Career:* cor anglais player in the Sydney Symphony Orchestra; composer and arranger with the South Australian Dept of Education 1975–93; commissions from the Adelaide Chamber Orchestra and others. *Compositions include:* eight symphonies 1949–2012, concertos for flute, oboe, oboe d'amore, bassoon, horn, tuba, trumpet, violin, viola, piano, harpsichord, Concertante for Cor Anglais, Concerto Grosso No. 2 for string trio and string orchestra, Loss for four percussion, concerti grossi, wind octet, wind quintet, piano quartet, piano quintet, five piano trios, Trio for Clarinet, Violin and Piano, 18 string quartets, piano sonatas, works for choir, brass band, concert band, etc. *Address:* 31 Fourth Street, Nuriootpa, SA 5355, Australia (home). *Telephone:* (8) 8562-2566 (home).

MORGAN, Michael DeVard; American conductor; *Music Director, Oakland East Bay Symphony*; b. 17 Sept. 1957, Washington, DC. *Education:* Oberlin Coll. Conservatory of Music, Berkshire Music Centre, Tanglewood. *Career:* operatic debut with Vienna State Opera 1982, with Mozart's The Abduction from the Seraglio; apprentice Conductor, Buffalo Philharmonic 1979–80; Asst Conductor, St Louis Symphony 1980–81, Chicago Symphony Orchestra 1986–91; Music Dir, Oakland East Bay Symphony; Artistic Dir, Oakland Youth Orchestra; Music Dir, Sacramento Philharmonic; Artistic Dir, Festival Opera in Walnut Creek; teacher on graduate conducting course, San Francisco Conservatory of Music; Guest Conductor, New York and Warsaw Philharmonics, Vienna, Baltimore, Houston, New Orleans Symphony Orchestras, National Symphony, Washington, Deutsche Staatsoper, Berlin, Summer Opera Theater, Washington, DC, and orchestras in Italy, Denmark and the Netherlands. *Honours:* first prize Hans Swarowsky Int. Conductors' Competition, Vienna 1980, prizewinner in conducting competitions at Baltimore 1974, San Remo 1975, Copenhagen 1980, Recording Acad. San Francisco Chapter Governors Award for Community Service 2005, ASCAP Concert Music Award 2005. *Address:* c/o Oakland East Bay Symphony, 400 29th Street, Suite 501, Oakland, CA 94609, USA (office). *E-mail:* admin@oebs.org (office). *Website:* www.oebs.org.

MORGAN, Morris; singer (baritone); b. 26 Sept. 1940, Berlin, Germany. *Education:* studied in Düsseldorf, Cologne and Wiesbaden. *Career:* sang at Cologne in the 1965 premiere of Die Soldaten by Zimmermann; Kiel Opera 1965–68, notably in the 1965 premiere of Reimann's Traumspiel; Wiesbaden 1968–71, Bern 1971–79, Freiburg 1978–81; further engagements at Düsseldorf, Mannheim, Stuttgart, Bremen, Saarbrucken, Lubeck and Klagenfurt; returned to Berne 1985, as Marcello in La Bohème; concert appearances in baroque music and as lieder singer. *Recordings include:* Die Soldaten, Zemlinsky's Kleider Machen Leute, Israel in Egypt and Carmina Burana.

MORGNY, Bengt-Ola; Swedish opera singer (tenor); b. 1959, s. of Karl-Bertil Magnusson and Gerd Magnusson (née Pettersson). *Education:* studied in Gothenburg and Berlin. *Career:* soloist with the Deutsche Oper Berlin from 1986, including premiere of Das Schloss by Reimann, Deutsche Oper Berlin, 1992; Oper der Stadt Köln from 1993 as Mozart's Basilio and Curzio, Jacquino in Fidelio and Wenzel in The Bartered Bride; Royal Opera House, Copenhagen from 1996 as Mime (Rheingold and Siegfried), the Captain (Wozzek), Goro (Butterfly), Pong (Turandot), Brighella (Ariadne), Dr Cajus (Falstaff), Piet von Piels (Le Grand Macabre), Arbace (Idomeneo); Festival at Drottningholm from 1989, as Pedrillo in Die Entführung, Azor in Zémire et Azor by Grétry, and in Soliman II by J.M. Kraus; guest appearances in Oslo, Stockholm, Hamburg, Munich, Paris, Monte Carlo, Geneva as Pong (Turandot), Der Bucklige (Frau ohne Schatten), Brussels, Liège, Tel-Aviv and Sarajevo as Harlequin and Soldier (Der Kaiser von Atlantis); mem. soloist ensemble, Royal Danish Opera 1995–, roles include Valzacchi in Der Rosenkavalier and Monostatos in Die Zauberflöte 2014–15; sang Mozart's Pedrillo at Spoleto 1998, The Scourge of Hyacinth, production of Robert Wilson and Tania Leon, Geneva, Nancy, St Polten (Austria), Teatro Bellas Artes, Mexico City 2001, Latvian Nat. Opera, Riga (Rheingold and Sigfried) 2007–09, Festival of Bregenz (André Chénier) 2011, (Hoffman) 2015, Latvian Nat. Opera, Riga and Operafestival of Macao, People's Repub. of China (Rheingold and Siegfried) 2013, Bergen Nat. Opera and Grand Théâtre Genéve (A Midsummer Night's Dream) 2015. *Recordings include:* Zemlinsky's Der Kreidekreis; Mörder, Hoffnung der Frauen, Hindemith; Das Schloss, Reimann; video of Die Entführung; Turandot, as Pong, Copenhagen, G. Sinopoli; The Handmaid's Tale, P. Rouders, The Doctor, Wagner's Copenhagen Ring. *Address:* The Royal Danish Theatre, Postbox 2185, 1017 Copenhagen K, Denmark (office). *Telephone:* 33-69-69-33 (office). *E-mail:* morgny@gmail.com (home).

MORINO, Giuseppe; singer (tenor); b. 18 Aug. 1950, Assisi, Italy. *Career:* debut at Spoleto 1981, as Gounod's Faust; Festival of Martina Franca 1986, as Idreno in Semiramide; season 1987 as Admète in Gluck's Alceste at La Scala, Pylades in Rossini's Ermione at Pesaro and the Duke of Mantua at the Vienna Staatsoper; Donizetti's Edgardo at Naples 1989, Meyerbeer's Raoul at Novara 1993; Astrologer in Rimsky's Golden Cockerel at Rome 1995; other roles include Tebaldo in Bellini's Capuleti, Rossini's Almaviva, Donizetti's Gianni di Parigi and Gounod's Romeo.

MØRK, Truls; Norwegian cellist; b. 25 April 1961, Bergen; s. of John Mørk and Turid Otterbech; two s. one d. *Education:* studied under his father, with Frans Helmerson at Swedish Radio Music School, in Austria with Heinrich Schiff and in Moscow with Natalia Shakovskaya. *Career:* debut, BBC Promenade Concerts 1989; has since appeared with leading European, American and Australian orchestras, including the Berlin Philharmonic, New York Philharmonic, Philadelphia Symphony, Cincinnati Philharmonic, Rotterdam Philharmonic, London Philharmonic, Pittsburgh Symphony, City of Birmingham Symphony, Orchestre de Paris, NHK Symphony, Royal Concertgebouw and Cleveland, Los Angeles and Gewandhaus Symphony Orchestras; regular appearances at int. chamber music festivals; Founder Int. Chamber Music Festival in Stavanger, Artistic Dir –2003. *Recordings include:* Schumann, Elgar and Saint-Saëns concertos, Tchaikovsky Rococo Variations, recitals of cello works by Grieg, Sibelius, Brahms, Rachmaninov and Myaskovksy, Dvořák and Shostakovich cello concertos, Haydn cello concertos with Norwegian Chamber Orchestra, Britten Cello Symphony and Elgar Cello Concerto with Sir Simon Rattle and the City of Birmingham Symphony Orchestra, Britten Cello Suites (Grammy Award 2002), Schumann Cello Concerto with Paavo Jürvi and Orchestre Philharmonique de Radio France 2005, C.P.E. Bach Cello Concerti with Bernard Labadie and Les Violons du Roy (ECHO Klassik Award) 2011, Rautavaara Percussion Concerto/Cello Concerto No. 2 (Gramophone Award for Best Contemporary Recording 2012) 2011. *Honours:* prizewinner, Moscow Tchaikovsky Competititon 1982, First Prize, Cassado Cello Competition, Florence 1983, UNESCO Prize European Radio-Union Competition, Bratislava 1983, W. Naumburg Competition, New York 1986, Norwegian Critics' Prize 2011, Sibelius Prize 2011. *Current Management:* Harrison Parrott, 5–6 Albion Court, London, W6 0QT, England. *Telephone:* (20) 7229-9166. *Fax:* (20) 7221-5042. *E-mail:* info@harrisonparrott.co.uk. *Website:* www.harrisonparrott.com.

MORLOT, Ludovic, ARAM, FRAM; French conductor; *Music Director, Seattle Symphony Orchestra*; b. 1974, Lyon; m. Ghizlane Morlot; two d. *Education:* Royal Acad. of Music, London, Royal Coll. of Music, London, Pierre Monteux School for Conductors, USA. *Career:* trained as a violinist; Seiji Ozawa Fellowship Conductor, Tanglewood Music Center 2001; Conductor in Residence, Orchestre National de Lyon 2002–04; Asst Conductor, Boston Symphony Orchestra 2004–07; Music Dir, Seattle Symphony Orchestra 2011–; Chief Conductor, Orchestre de La Monnaie, Brussels 2012–14; toured with Netherlands Youth Orchestra 2010; Affiliate Prof. of Music, Univ. of Washington 2012–, Chair of orchestral conducting studies 2013–14; performances with Cleveland Orchestra, Dresden Staatskapelle, Tonhalle Orchestra, Royal Stockholm Philharmonic Orchestra, Tokyo Philharmonic Orchestra, Pittsburgh Symphony Orchestra, New York Philharmonic, Chicago Symphony Orchestra, Rotterdam Philharmonic, Royal Concertgebouw Orchestra,

Czech Philharmonic Orchestra, NDR Hamburg, Orchestre de la Monnaie, Opéra Nat. de Lyon, Opéra Comique, Paris, Rotterdam Philharmonic Orchestra, Ensemble Intercontemporain; collaborations with many soloists including Christian Tetzlaff, Gil Shaham, Renaud Capuçon, Lynn Harrell, Frank Peter Zimmermann, Emanuel Ax, Jessye Norman, Anne-Sophie Mutter. *Current Management:* c/o Opus 3 Artists, 470 Park Avenue South, 9th Floor North, New York, NY 10016, USA. *Telephone:* (212) 584-7503. *Fax:* (646) 300-8269. *E-mail:* cokaly@opus3artists.com. *Website:* www.opus3artists .com. *Address:* Seattle Symphony Orchestra, 200 University Street, PO Box 21906, Seattle, WA 98111-3669, USA (office). *Telephone:* (206) 215-4700 (office). *Fax:* (206) 215-4701 (office). *E-mail:* info@seattlesymphony.org (office). *Website:* www.seattlesymphony.org (office); www.ludovicmorlot.com.

MOROZ, Vladimir; Russian singer (baritone); b. 1974, Rechitsa, Ghornel District. *Education:* Minsk Academy of Music. *Career:* debut at Byelourussian National Opera, 1997, as Eugene Onegin; Young Singers Academy of the Mariinsky Theatre, St Petersburg, from 1999; Repertoire includes Robert in Tchaikovsky's Iolanta, Rossini's Figaro, Enrico (Lucia di Lammermoor), Yeletzky in The Queen of Spades and Andrei Bolkonsky in War and Peace; Sang Andrei, and Mizgir in The Snow Maiden by Rimsky-Korsakov, with the Kirov Opera at Covent Garden, 2000. *Honours:* prizewinner International Lysienko Competition 1997.

MOROZOV, Alexander; Russian singer (bass); b. 19 April 1953, Leningrad; s. of Viktor Morozov and Olga Morozova; m. Irina Soboleva; two d. *Education:* Leningrad State Conservatoire with Prof. Okhotnikov. *Career:* joined the Mariinsky Theatre 1984–, now soloist; repertoire includes Basilio in Il Barbiere di Siviglia, Mephistopheles in Faust, Padre Guardiano in La Forza del destino, Zaccaria in Nabucco, Inquisitore in Don Carlos, Jokanaan in Salome, Count Rodolfo in La Sonnambula, Escamillo in Carmen, Il Commendatore in Don Giovanni, Fasolt in Das Rheingold, Coppelius and Dr Miracle in Les Contes d'Hoffmann, Dosifei in Khovanshina, Prince Galitsky in Prince Igor, Kochubei in Mazepa, King Rene in Iolanta, Surin in The Queen of Spades, Prince Gremin in Eugene Onegin, Viking Merchant and Sea King in Sadko, The Storm Knight in Kashei the Immortal, Ruslan in Ruslan and Lyudmila, Tsar Ivan the Terrible in The Maid of Pskov, Burundai in The Legend of the Invisible City of Kitezh and the Maid Fevronia, Inquisitor in The Fiery Angel, Old Gypsy in Aleko, the Emperor of China in The Nightingale, Old Convict in Lady Macbeth of Mtsensk, and the title roles in Boris Godunov, Peter I; also Mozart's Requiem, Verdi's Requiem, Britten's War Requiem and Dmitry Shostakovich's Symphony No. 13; tours with the Mariinsky Theatre to Austria (Salzburg Festival), Finland (Savonlinna Festival and Mikkeli Music Festival), France, Germany (Berliner Philarmonischer), Israel, Italy (Maggio Musicale and Florence), Japan, Luxembourg, The Netherlands, Switzerland, the UK (Edinburgh Festival) and the USA; guest soloist at Amsterdam Opera, Arena di Verona, Metropolitan Opera, National Opera of Israel, Tel Aviv, Opéra Bastille, Öster und Sommer Festival Salzburg, Royal Opera House, London, San Diego Opera, San Francisco Opera, Seattle Opera, Teatro Colón. *Recordings include:* Boris Godunov, War and Peace, Kashei the Immortal, Love for Three Oranges (as Leander), Classical Russian Romances (solo) 1999. *Honours:* Honoured Artist of Russia 2002; All-Union Glinka Vocal Competition, Minsk 1981, Grand Prix Rio de Janeiro Int. Competition 1983, gold medal and first prize Int. Tchaikovsky Competition, Moscow 1986. *Current Management:* Allied Artists, 42 Montpelier Square, London, SW7 1JZ, England. *Address:* c/o Mariinsky Theatre, 1 Teatralnaya Square, St Petersburg 190000, Russia (office). *E-mail:* post@ mariinsky.ru (office). *Website:* www.mariinsky.ru/en/opera/soloist/morozov.

MOROZOV, Igor; Russian singer (baritone); b. 1948, Ukraine. *Education:* Moscow Conservatory. *Career:* first engagement at the Kirov Theatre Leningrad, then sang at the Bolshoi, Moscow, from 1976 as Eugene Onegin, Count Luna, Germont, Yeletzky, The Queen of Spades; Robert in Tchaikovsky's Iolanta; Sang in Shchedrin's Dead Souls at Boston, 1988; Guest engagements in Finland and Hungary as concert and opera atrist; British debut at Covent Garden, 1988; Season 2000–01 at the Deutsche Oper Berlin as Scarpia, Verdi's Miller and Renato, and Rochefort in Anna Bolena; Dubois in Tchaikovsky's Maid of Orleans and Kadoor in Si j'étais Roi at Wexford; Ferdinand in Prokofiev's Duenna at the Bolshoi, Moscow.

MORRICONE, Ennio; Italian composer; b. 10 Nov. 1928, Rome; s. of Mario Morricone and Libera Morricone; m. Maria Travia; three s. two d. *Education:* Accad. of Santa Cecilia. *Career:* began career in field of classical composition and arrangement; has composed and arranged scores for more than 500 film and TV productions; best known film scores include The Good, the Bad and the Ugly, Once Upon a Time in the West, The Mission, Le Professionnel. *Film scores include:* Il Federale 1961, La Voglia matta 1962, Diciottenni al sole 1962, La Cuccagna 1962, Il Successo 1963, Le Monachine 1963, I Basilischi 1963, Duello nel Texas (as Dan Savio) 1963, La Scoperta dell'America 1964, I Motorizzati 1964, ...e la donna creò l'uomo 1964, I Maniaci 1964, Prima della rivoluzione 1964, Per un pugno di dollari (For A Fistful of Dollars, as Leo Nichols) 1964, Le Pistole non discutono 1964, I Malamondo 1964, Thrilling 1965, Slalom 1965, Menage all'italiana 1965, Idoli controluce 1965, La Battaglia di Algeri 1965, Gli Amanti d'oltretomba 1965, Altissima pressione 1965, I Pugni in tasca 1965, Centomila dollari per Ringo 1965, Il Ritorno di Ringo 1965, Per qualche dollaro in più (For a Few Dollars More) 1965, La Ragazza del bersagliere 1966, Per Firenze 1966, Navajo Joe (as Leo Nichols) 1966, Mi vedrai tornare 1966, Matchless 1966, I Lunghi giorni della vendetta 1966, Un Fiume di dollari 1966, Uccellacci e uccellini 1966, El Greco 1966, Un Uomo a metà 1966, La Resa dei conti 1966, Il Buono, il brutto, il cattivo (The Good, the Bad and the Ugly) 1966, Sette donne per i MacGregor 1967, Pedro Páramo 1967, Il Giardino delle delizie 1967, Dalle Ardenne all'inferno 1967, L'Avventuriero 1967, Le Streghe 1967, OK Connery 1967, I Crudeli (as Leo Nichols) 1967, Per pochi dollari ancora (theme) 1967, Arabella 1967, Il Mercenario 1968, Italia vista dal cielo 1968, Grazie, zia 1968, Il Grande silenzio 1968, Ecce Homo 1968, Diabolik 1968, Da uomo a uomo 1968, La Bataille de San Sebastian 1968, Roma come Chicago 1968, C'era una volta il West (Once Upon a Time in the West) 1968, Vergogna schifosi 1969, Giotto 1969, La Donna invisibile 1969, L'Assoluto naturale 1969, Cuore di mamma 1969, L'Alibi 1969, Galileo 1969, Un Bellissimo novembre 1969, Ruba al prossimo tuo 1969, Un Tranquillo posto di campagna 1969, Una Breve stagione 1969, Le Clan des Siciliens 1969, Zenabel 1969, Uccidete il vitello grasso e arrostitelo 1970, Metello 1970, Giochi particolari 1970, La Califfa 1970, Two Mules for Sister Sara 1970, La Moglie più bella 1970, Indagine su un cittadino al di sopra di ogni sospetto 1970, Hornets' Nest 1970, Vamos a matar, compañeros 1970, Oceano 1971, Gli Occhi freddi della paura 1971, Incontro 1971, Forza 'G' 1971, Una Lucertola con la pelle di donna 1971, Veruschka 1971, Il Decameron 1971, La Tarantola dal ventre nero 1971, Giornata nera per l'ariete 1971, Il Giorno del giudizio 1971, Sacco e Vanzetti 1971, L'Istruttoria è chiusa: dimentichi 1971, Malastrana 1971, Giù la testa 1971, Maddalena 1971, ¡Viva la muerte... tua! 1971, La Violenza: Quinto potere 1972, Questa specie d'amore 1972, Quando la preda è l'uomo 1972, Perché? 1972, Il Maestro e Margherita 1972, Lui per lei 1972, Guttoso e il 'Marat morto' di David 1972, Les Deux saisons de la vie 1972, D'amore si muore 1972, Crescete e moltiplicatevi 1972, La Cosa buffa 1972, Chi l'ha vista morire? 1972, Bianchi bandinelli e la Colonna Traiana 1972, Anche se volessi lavorare, che faccio? 1972, Le Tueur 1972, Cosa avete fatto a Solange? 1972, Bluebeard 1972, J. and S. – storia criminale del far west 1972, L'Attentat 1972, Sbatti il mostro in prima pagina 1972, Un Uomo da rispettare 1972, Il Ritorno di Clint il solitario 1972, Quando le donne persero la coda 1972, La Vita, a volte, è molto dura, vero Provvidenza? 1972, Vaarwel 1973, Allonsanfan 1973, Le Serpent 1973, Le Moine 1973, La Proprietà non è più un furto 1973, Revolver 1973, Rappresaglia 1973, Il Mio nome è Nessuno 1973, Il Giro del mondo degli innamorati di Peynet 1974, Fatti di gente per bene 1974, La Cugina 1974, L'Anticristo 1974, Spasmo 1974, Mussolini: Ultimo atto 1974, Sesso in confessionale 1974, Le Trio infernal 1974, Le Secret 1974, Labbra di lurido blu 1975, Gente di rispetto 1975, Peur sur la ville 1975, Leonor 1975, Der Richter und sein Henker 1975, The Human Factor 1975, Una Vita venduta 1976, Todo modo 1976, René la canne 1976, Per amore 1976, Film 1976, Il Deserto dei Tartari 1976, L'Arriviste 1976, Ariel Limon 1976, L'Agnese va a morire 1976, Der Dritte Grad 1976, Divina creatura 1976, 1900 1976, L'Eredità Ferramonti 1976, Stato interessante 1977, Il Mostro 1977, The Dragon, the Odds 1977, Corleone 1977, Le Ricain 1977, Exorcist II: The Heretic 1977, Orca 1977, Holocaust 2000 1977, L'Immoralità 1978, Forza Italia! 1978, Il Gatto 1978, One, Two, Two: 122, rue de Provence 1978, Così come sei 1978, La Cage aux folles 1978, Ten to Survive 1979, Il Prato 1979, Il Ladrone 1979, Dedicato al mare Egeo 1979, L'Umanoide 1979, Bloodline 1979, La Luna 1979, I... comme Icare 1979, Uomini e no 1980, The Fantastic World of M.C. Escher 1980, Windows 1980, Un Sacco bello 1980, The Island 1980, L'Oeil 1980, La Banquière 1980, La Cage aux folles II 1980, La Dame aux camélias 1980, Il Pianeta azzurro 1981, Bianco, rosso e Verdone 1981, So Fine 1981, Le Professionnel 1981, La Tragedia di un uomo ridicolo 1981, Porca vacca 1982, Nana 1982, A Time to Die 1982, The Thing 1982, White Dog 1982, Blood Link 1982, Maja Plisetskaja 1982, Hundra 1983, Le Ruffian 1983, Le Marginal 1983, Sahara 1983, Pelota 1984, Once Upon a Time in America 1984, Les Voleurs de la nuit 1984, Code Name: Wild Geese 1984, Red Sonja 1985, Kommando Leopard 1985, Il Pentito 1985, La Cage aux folles 3 – 'Elles' se marient 1985, La Venexiana 1986, La Gabbia 1986, The Mission 1986, Quartiere 1987, Mosca addio 1987, Il Giorno prima 1987, The Untouchables 1987, Gli Occhiali d'oro 1987, Il Cuore di mamma 1988, Frantic 1988, A Time of Destiny 1988, Rampage 1988, Cinema Paradiso 1989, Casualties of War 1989, Fat Man and Little Boy 1989, Tre colonne in cronaca 1990, Tempo di uccidere 1990, ¡Átame! 1990, Stanno tutti bene 1990, The Big Man 1990, Tracce di vita amorosa 1990, State of Grace 1990, Hamlet 1990, Money 1991, La Domenica specialmente 1991, Bugsy 1991, A Csalás gyönyöre 1992, Beyond Justice 1992, City of Joy 1992, La Villa del venerdì 1992, Love Potion No. 9 1992, Roma imago urbis 1993, In the Line of Fire 1993, Il Lungo silenzio 1993, La Scorta 1993, Jona che visse nella balena 1994, Wolf 1994, Love Affair 1994, Disclosure 1994, The Night and the Moment 1995, Pasolini, un delitto italiano 1995, L'Uomo delle stelle 1995, I Magi randagi 1996, Vite strozzate 1996, La Lupa 1996, Cartoni animati 1997, Marianna Ucrìa 1997, U Turn 1997, Lolita 1997, Il Fantasma dell'opera 1998, Lucignolo 1999, In the Line of Fire: The Ultimate Sacrifice 2000, Canone inverso – making love 2000, Mission to Mars 2000, Malèna 2000, La Ragion pura 2001, Cowboys Don't Kiss in Public 2001, Threnody 2002, Senso '45 2002, Ripley's Game 2002, Il Diario di Matilde Manzoni 2002, L'Ultimo pistolero 2002, Arena Concerto 2003, La Luz prodigiosa 2003, The Wages of Sin 2003, 72 metra 2004, Kill Bill: Vol. 2 2004, Guardiani delle nuvole 2004, Sorstalanság 2005, Karol, un uomo diventato papa 2005, Libertas 2005, Fateless 2005, E ridendo l'uccise 2005, Adolfo Celi, un uomo per due culture 2006, A Crime 2006, La Sconosciuta 2006, The Weatherman 2007, Ultrasordine 2007, I demoni di San Pietroburgo 2008, Baaria – La porta del vento 2009, Spider Dance 2010, The Best Offer 2013, The Hateful Eight (Golden Globe Award for Best Original Score 2016, BAFTA for Best Original Music 2016) 2015, The Correspondence 2015. *Television scores include:* The Virginian (series theme) 1962, Lo Squarciagola

1966, 1943: un incontro 1969, La Sciantosa 1970, Nessuno deve sapere (series) 1971, Correva l'anno di grazia 1870 1971, L'Uomo e la magia 1972, L'Automobile 1972, Moses the Lawgiver 1975, Drammi gotichi 1976, Noi lazzaroni (series) 1978, Le Mani sporche 1978, Invito allo sport (series) 1978, Orient-Express (series) 1979, The Life and Times of David Lloyd George (series) 1981, Marco Polo (series) 1982, The Scarlet and the Black 1983, Wer war Edgar Allan? 1984, Die Försterbuben 1984, Via Mala (series) 1985, C.A.T. Squad 1986, I Promessi sposi (series) 1988, Gli Indifferenti (series) 1988, Camillo Castiglioni oder die Moral der Haifische 1988, Gli Angeli del potere 1988, C.A.T. Squad: Python Wolf 1988, Il Principe del deserto (series) 1989, The Endless Game 1990, Cacciatori di navi 1990, Una Storia italiana 1992, Piazza di Spagna (series) 1993, Missus 1993, La Piovra series 1–10 1984–99, Genesi: La creazione e il diluvio 1994, Abraham 1994, Jacob 1994, Joseph 1995, Moses (title music) 1996, Il Barone (series) 1996, Samson and Delilah 1996, In fondo al cuore 1997, Nostromo (series) 1997, David (theme) 1997, Ultimo 1998, I Guardiani del cielo 1998, Il Quarto re 1998, La Casa bruciata 1998, Ultimo 2 – La sfida 1999, Nanà 1999, Esther 1999, Padre Pio – Tra cielo e terra 2000, Un Difetto di famiglia 2002, Il Papa buono 2003, Musashi (series) 2003, Charlie Chaplin – Les années suisses 2003, Il Cuore nel pozzo 2005, Cefalonia 2005, Karol, un umono divetato Papa 2005, Lucia 2005, La Provinciale 2006, Giovanni Falcone, l'uomo che sfido Cosa Nostra 2006, L'ultimo de Corleonesi 2007, Résolution 819 2008, Pane e libertà 2009, Quatraro mysteriet 2009, Mi ricordo Anna Frank 2009. *Classical compositions:* more than 15 piano concertos, 30 symphonic pieces, choral music and one opera. *Honours:* Grand Official, Ordine al merito della Repubblica Italiana 2006, Chevalier, Légion d'honneur 2008; Dr hc (Cagliari) 2000, (Seconda Università, Rome) 2002, (New Bulgarian Univ.) 2013; numerous awards including Hon. Acad. Award 2007, Polar Music Prize 2010, Special Award for Career Achievement, Online Film Critics Soc. 2013. *Current Management:* c/o Gorfaine/Schwartz Agency Inc., 4111 West Alameda Avenue, Suite 509, Burbank, CA 91505, USA. *Telephone:* (818) 260-8500.

MORRIS, Colin, BA, PhD, ARCM; British singer (baritone); b. 17 Nov. 1952, Sheerness, Kent, England. *Education:* Univ. of Exeter, studied with Derek Hammond-Stroud. *Career:* debut at Edinburgh Festival with Kent Opera 1979; many concert and recital appearances in the UK and The Netherlands; lieder repertoire of over 300 songs; toured the UK and USA with Pavilion Opera, London Opera Players, Regency Opera, D'Oyly Carte, Crystal Clear Opera; Castleward Opera; Central Festival Opera, Holland Park; Penang Festival; overseas opera debut, as Bartolo (Rossini), Singapore 1992; main roles are Don Alfonso, Leporello, Magnifico, Bartolo, Pasquale, Dulcamara; Falstaff, Rigoletto, Sharpless, Scarpia, Tonio and Alberich; operetta, especially 'patter' roles in Gilbert and Sullivan. *Recordings:* several song recitals on BBC, Radio Kent.

MORRIS, James Peppler; American singer (bass-baritone); b. 10 Jan. 1947, s. of James Morris and Geraldine Peppler; m. 1st Joanne F. Vitali 1971; one d.; m. 2nd Susan Quittmeyer 1987; one s. one d. (twins). *Education:* Univ. of Maryland, Peabody Conservatory and Acad. of Vocal Arts. *Career:* debut at Metropolitan Opera, New York 1970; opera and concert appearances throughout USA, Canada, South America, Europe, Japan and Australia; repertoire including works by Wagner, Verdi, Puccini, Offenbach, Stravinsky, Mussorgsky, Mozart, Gounod and Britten; has performed in most int. opera houses and has appeared with major orchestras of Europe and USA; noted for his interpretation of the role of Wotan in Wagner's Der Ring des Nibelungen; has appeared in this role at Metropolitan Opera, Vienna State Opera, Bavarian State Opera, Munich, Deutsche Oper Berlin, Lyric Opera of Chicago, San Francisco Opera and many others; also noted interpreter of title role in Wagner's Der fliegende Holländer; has appeared as Hans Sachs in Die Meistersinger von Nürnberg in major houses of Europe and USA; debuted role of Oroveso in Norma at Metropolitan Opera 2013–14, also appeared as Hans Sachs in new production of Die Meistersinger von Nürnberg at Lyric Opera of Chicago and as the Four Villains in Les contes d'Hoffmann; concert performances of Die Meistersinger von Nürnberg at Tanglewood, Mahler's 8th Symphony with Michael Tilson Thomas and San Francisco Symphony and Orchestre National de France under Daniele Gatti, and Verdi's Simon Boccanegra with Boston Symphony Orchestra; sang Beethoven's Symphony No. 9 at Blossom Festival with Cleveland Orchestra under Franz Welser-Möst and appeared with Montreal Symphony under Kent Nagano in a programme of arias by Verdi and Wagner; concert performances of Berlioz's La Damnation de Faust in Madrid; other concert appearances have included performances with Berlin Philharmonic, London's BBC Proms, concerts with Zubin Mehta and New York Philharmonic, 'Pavarotti Plus' special at New York's Avery Fisher Hall, and several televised gala events at Metropolitan Opera; also appeared in La Damnation de Faust with Los Angeles Philharmonic at the Hollywood Bowl; concert of opera arias and Broadway songs with Chicago Symphony at Ravinia; Mendelssohn's Elijah with Boston Handel and Haydn Soc. under Christopher Hogwood as well as at Cincinnati May Festival under James Conlon; has also appeared frequently in recitals in cities including Minneapolis, Baltimore, Washington, DC and at Teatro Colon, Buenos Aires. *Recordings include:* two complete Ring cycles, one under James Levine and one under Bernard Haitink, and other operas of Wagner, Offenbach, Mozart, Massenet, Verdi and Gounod; operas by Donizetti, Puccini, Bellini and Thomas with Dame Joan Sutherland; orchestral recordings include Haydn's Creation, Beethoven's Symphony No. 9 'Choral' and Requiems by Mozart and Fauré, Thomas' Desire Under the Elms with George Manahan and London Symphony, Mahler's Symphony No. 8 with Michael Tilson Thomas and San Francisco Symphony (Grammy Award 2010),

Arias by Verdi and Wagner. *Current Management:* c/o Damon Bristo, Columbia Artists Management Inc., 5 Columbus Circle, @ 1790 Broadway, New York, NY 10019-1412, USA. *Telephone:* (212) 841-9500. *Fax:* (212) 841-9744. *E-mail:* info@cami.com. *Website:* www.cami.com.

MORRIS, Joan Clair; American singer and teacher; *Adjunct Associate Professor of Theatre (Cabaret), University of Michigan;* b. 10 Feb. 1943, Portland, Ore.; d. of Joseph Ellis Morris and Katherine Emma Fleck; m. William Bolcom 1975. *Education:* Gonzaga Univ., American Acad. of Dramatic Arts. *Career:* debut at Wigmore Hall 1993; performed at the Boston Pops 1976; Polly Peachum in The Beggar's Opera, Guthrie Theatre, Minneapolis 1979; soloist, world premiere of William Bolcom's Songs of Innocence and Experience, Stuttgart Opera 1984 and at New York premiere 1987; Weill Recital Hall, Carnegie Hall 1987; soloist, world premiere of William Bolcom's 4th Symphony with the St Louis Symphony 1987; played the Nurse in world premiere of William Bolcom's Casino Paradise 1990; Alice Tully Hall, Lincoln Center 1976, 1977, 1978, 1980, 1983, 1995; Ewart Hall, American Univ. in Cairo 1988; 20th anniversary concert with guest Max Morath at Hunter Coll. 1993; Church of Santo Spirito, Florence 1989; Adjunct Assoc. Prof. of Musical Theater, Univ. of Michigan 1981–, Azazels, Univ. of Michigan; wrote, produced, directed and starred in two original musical entertainments, The Police Gazette 2003 and Barnum's Nightingale 2005 for the Clements Library, Univ. of Michigan. *Plays:* The Police Gazette, a musical entertainment 2003 Barnum's Nightingale 2005. *Compositions include:* songs: Carol (with William Bolcom) 1981, Tears at the Happy Hour (with William Bolcom) 1983. *Recordings include:* 22 albums recorded to date, including After The Ball: A Treasury of Turn-of-the-Century Popular Songs 1974, Songs by Ira and George Gershwin 1978, Blue Skies 1985, Let's Do It: Bolcom and Morris Live at Aspen 1989, Orchids in the Moonlight, with tenor Robert White 1996, Songs of Rodgers and Hart, Jerome Kern, Cole Porter, Irving Berlin, George & Ira Gershwin and Leiber and Stoller; Cabaret Songs by Bolcom & Weinstein recorded live at the Flea Theater, New York 2003, Bolcom, Morris & Morath Sing Yip Harburg 2003, Bolcom, Morris, Morath & White Sing Gus Kahn 2004. *Publications:* contrib. to the New Grove Dictionary of American Music. *Honours:* Citation, Commonwealth of Mass House of Reps to Bolcom & Morris. *Current Management:* c/o ICM Artists, 40 West 57th Street, New York, NY 10019, USA. *Telephone:* (212) 556-6868. *Fax:* (212) 556-5677. *E-mail:* rkern@icmtalent.com. *Website:* www .icmtalent.com. *Address:* 3080 Whitmore Lake Road, Ann Arbor, MI 48105, USA (home). *Telephone:* (734) 769-1041 (office). *Fax:* (734) 769-1426 (office). *E-mail:* jcmorris@umich.edu (office). *Website:* www.bolcomandmorris.com.

MORRIS, Robert Daniel, BM, MM, DMA; composer, music theorist and academic; b. 19 Oct. 1943, Cheltenham, England; m. Ellen Koskoff 1979, one s. two d. *Education:* Eastman School of Music, Univ. of Michigan. *Career:* Instructor, Univ. of Hawaii 1968–69; Asst Prof., Yale Univ. 1969–75, Dir Yale Electronic Music Studio 1973–78, Assoc. Prof. 1975–78, Chair Composition Dept 1974–78; Assoc. Prof., Univ. of Pittsburgh 1977–80, Dir Electronic and Computer Music Studio 1977–80; Assoc. Prof., Eastman School of Music 1980–85, Prof. 1986–. *Compositions include:* Continua for orchestra 1969, Thunders of Spring Over Distant Mountains (electronic music) 1973, In Different Voices for five wind ensembles 1975–76, Plexus for woodwinds 1977, Passim 1982, Echanges for piano and computer-generated tape) 1983, Cuts for wind ensemble 1984, Concerto for piano and strings 1994, Phases for two-pianos and electronics, Motet On Doo-dah, Hamiltonian Cycle, Inter Alia, Karuna. *Publications:* Composition with Pitch-Classes: A Theory of Compositional Design 1986; contrib. reviews and articles in Journal of Music Theory, Perspectives of New Music, Musical Quarterly, JAMS, In Theory Only.

MORRIS, Stephen; violinist; b. 1970, Bridlington, Yorkshire, England. *Education:* studied with Yfrah Neaman in London, Royal Acad. of Music with Manoug Parikian and Maurice Hasson, studied with Howard Davis. *Career:* Leader of the RAM Symphony Orchestra 1988; Leader of the Pegasus and Thames Chamber Orchestra; as soloist plays Bruch, Bach, Mendelssohn and Lalo; 2nd violin of the Duke String Quartet from 1985; performances in the Wigmore Hall, Purcell Room, Conway Hall and throughout the UK; tours to Germany, Italy, Austria and the Baltic states; South Bank series 1991, with Mozart's early quartets; soundtrack from Ingmar Bergman documentary and The Magic Lantern (Channel 4) 1988; BBC debut feature; features for French television 1990–91, playing Mozart, Mendelssohn, Britten and Tippett; Brahms Clarinet Quintet for Dutch radio with Janet Hilton; Live Music Now series with concerts for disadvantaged people; The Duke Quartet invites... at the Derngate, Northampton 1991, with Duncan Prescott and Rohan O'Hara; resident quartet of the Rydale Festival 1991; residency at Trinity Coll., Oxford, tours of Scotland and Northern Ireland and concert at the QEH 1991. *Recordings:* quartets by Tippett, Shostakovich and Britten 3rd. *Honours:* RAM John Waterhouse Prize, London Orchestral Soc. Prize, Poulet Award, Inter-collegiate Quartet Prize.

MORRISON, Bryce, MA, MMus; British teacher, pianist, critic and lecturer; *Guest Professor, Royal Academy of Music;* b. 27 Nov. 1938, Leeds. *Education:* Music Scholar, King's School, Canterbury 1952; studied with Ronald Smith, Iso Elinson and Alexander Unisky. *Career:* has published interviews with most of the world's great pianists including Horowitz, Rubinstein and Clifford Curzon; adjudicator for over 40 int. piano competitions; Chair. First Terence Judd Int. Award 1982 and of Scottish Int. Piano Competition 1998; his students have been int. prizewinners including first prizes at Santander, Pozzoli and finalist status at Leeds; has lectured and given masterclasses world-wide with TV appearances in UK, USA, Canada and Australia; extensive broadcasts for

BBC, ABC and CBC; also in Poland, USA, and New Zealand; Guest Prof., Royal Acad. of Music, Birmingham Conservatoire, Chetham's School of Music, Manchester; Visiting Prof., Texas Conservatory for Artists; Trustee John Ogdon Foundation 2002. *Publications:* published extensively in The Times, The Times Literary Supplement, Observer, Telegraph, Independent, Gramophone and others; also in America and Australia; major contrib. to Phaidon Book of The Piano; two BBC Talks published by Oxford University Press; short biography of Liszt; over 300 annotations for Decca, EMI, Sony, DG and others; adviser for Testament Records for whom he has written tributes to Schnabel, Edwin Fisher, Solomon, Arrau and others. *Honours:* held Corina Frada Pick Chair of Advanced Piano Studies, Ravinia Festival, Chicago 1988; Hon. ARAM 1995. *Address:* Flat 19, 11 Hinde Street, London, W1M 5AQ, England (home). *Telephone:* (20) 9735-1440 (home). *Fax:* (20) 9735-1440 (home). *Website:* www.brycemorrison.net.

MORTENSEN, Lars Ulrik; Danish harpsichordist and conductor; *Musical Director, European Union Baroque Orchestra*; b. 9 Nov. 1955, Esbjerg. *Education:* Royal Danish Acad. of Music, studies with Trevor Pinnock in London. *Career:* performed as music dir, soloist and chamber musician in Europe, USA, Mexico, S America, Japan and Australia, with artists including Emma Kirkby, John Holloway and Jaap ter Linden; harpsichordist, London Baroque ensemble 1988–90, Collegium Musicum Copenhagen 1990–93; Artistic Dir, Concerto Copenhagen baroque orchestra 1999–; Musical Dir, European Union Baroque Orchestra 2004–; performances at concert halls including Royal Theatre, Copenhagen and Royal Albert Hall, London and tours in Europe, Japan and USA; as conductor, has worked with numerous orchestras; several productions at Royal Danish Opera, including Kunzen's Holger Danske, Handel's Giulio Cesare, Mozart's Marriage of Figaro and Monteverdi's Il Ritorno d'Ulisse in Patria; has worked exclusively with period instrument ensembles since 2003; Prof. of Harpsichord and Performance, Hochschule für Musik, Munich 1996–99; mem. Royal Swedish Acad. of Music. *Recordings include:* Bach Goldberg Variations (Diapason d'Or) 1989, Buxtehude Harpsichord Music (three vols) (Danish Musician of the Year 2000, Cannes Classical Award 2001) 1999, Buxtehude Chamber Music (Danish Grammy Award), Buxtehude Seven Sonatas 2005, Palschau/Schulz Concertos and Solo Works for Harpsichord 2007, Castello/Fontana Sonate concertate in stil moderno 2012; as conductor: Haydn Piano Concertos, Bach B Minor Mass, Bach Complete Harpsichord Concertos. *Honours:* Danish Music Critics' Award 1984, Léonie Sonning Music Prize 2007. *Current Management:* c/o Toccata Music Management, Gravesandelaan 10, 1222 Hilversum, The Netherlands. *Telephone:* (6) 81922722. *E-mail:* info@toccatamusic.nl. *Website:* www.toccatamusic.nl. *Address:* c/o Concerto Copenhagen, Esromgade 15, opg. 2, 4, 2401, 2200 Copenhagen N, Denmark (office). *E-mail:* info@coco.dk (office).

MORYL, Richard, MA; composer and conductor; b. 23 Feb. 1929, Newark, NJ, USA. *Education:* Montclair State Coll., New Jersey and Columbia Univ., studied with Boris Blacher and Arthur Berger. *Career:* teacher 1960–72; founder, New England Contemporary Music Ensemble 1970; Dir, Charles Ives Center for American Music 1979. *Compositions include:* Ballons for percussion, orchestra, radios and audience 1971, Volumes for piano, organ and orchestra 1971, Chroma 1972, Loops for large orchestra with any instruments 1974, Strobe for large orchestra with any instruments 1974, The Untuning of the Skies 1981, The Pond for flute and chamber orchestra 1984; instrumental music: Rainbows I and II 1982–83, The Golden Phoenix for string quartet and percussion 1984; vocal: Flourescents for two choruses, two percussion and organ 1970, Illuminations for soprano, 43 choruses and chamber orchestra 1970, De morte cantoris for soprano, mezzo and ensemble 1973, Das Lied for soprano and ensemble 1975, Stabat Mater 1982, Come, Sweet Death for chorus and piano 1983; mixed media works: Passio avium 1974, Atlantis 1976, Visiones mortis 1977, Music of the Spheres 1977, An Island on the Moon 1978, A Sunflower for Maggie 1979; music for tape, electronics.

MOSCA, Silvia; singer (soprano); b. 1958, Italy. *Education:* studied in Naples. *Career:* debut at Mantua Teatro Sociale as the Trovatore Leonara; has sung at opera houses throughout Italy and appeared as Luisa Miller at the Metropolitan 1988; Leonora at Liège and Miami 1988–89; sang Aida at Buenos Aires and the Savonlinna Festival 1989; Elvira in Ernani at Rome and Venice 1989–90.

MOSCATO, Jacques; conductor and clarinettist; b. 1945, France. *Career:* debut as clarinettist with Municipal Orchestra 1955; Dir, public concert, Switzerland 1962; Head of Music Dept, Int. Univ., Paris from 1968; Dir, Charleville Mezières Conservatorium from 1969; Guest Conductor, Australian Broadcasting Commission 1976, 1978; Conductor, Monte Carlo Symphony, Salle Garnier of Monte Carlo 1979–94; Guest Conductor, Istanbul Symphonic Orchestra, Symphony Orchestra, Pays Loire, France 1984, 1989. *Compositions:* score for film Symphonic Interdite 1983, score for ballet Resonances 1989. *Recordings:* albums: Symphony No. 2, eleven Viennese Dances (Beethoven) 1977, Les Musiciens Monegasquesm 1981.

MOSER, Edda; German singer (soprano); b. 27 Oct. 1942, Berlin; d. of the late Hans-Joachim and of Dorothea Moser. *Education:* Conservatory of Berlin. *Career:* has performed with numerous opera cos, including Vienna, Munich, Hamburg, Cologne and Metropolitan Opera, New York, USA; specializes in Mozart operas; own show on TV; title of Kammersängerin Wien conferred 1982; retd from professional singing; currently Prof. of Voice, Hochschule für Musik, Cologne. *Film:* Don Giovanni. *Publication:* Mehr als Worte (contrib). *Honours:* awarded Grand Prix du Disque three times. *Address:* Hochschule für Musik, Dagobertstrasse 38, 50668 Cologne, Germany (office). *Website:* www.mhs-koeln.de (office); www.eddamoser.com.

MOSER, Thomas; American singer (tenor); b. 27 May 1945, Richmond, VA. *Education:* Richmond Professional Institute, Curtis Institute Philadelphia, California with Martial Singher, Gerard Souzay and Lotte Lehmann. *Career:* after success at the 1974 Metropolitan Auditions sang in Graz from 1975; Munich Opera, 1976, as Mozart's Belmonte; Vienna State Opera from 1977, as Mozart's Tamino, Ottavio, Titus and Idomeneo, Strauss's Flamand and Henry; Achilles in Iphigénie en Aulide, conducted by Charles Mackerras; New York City Opera 1979, as Titus; Salzburg Festival 1983, in La Finta Semplice; La Scala Milan, 1985, as Tamino; Rome Opera, 1986, as Achilles; Paris Opéra Comique, 1987 as Mozart's Idomeneo and Tito; sang the Tenor in the premiere of Berio's un Re in Ascolto, Salzburg, 1984; Vienna Staatsoper, 1987, as Achilles in Iphigénie en Aulide, Schubert's Fierrabras at the Theater an der Wien, 1988; sang Florestan in Fidelio at La Scala and Salzburg, 1990; new production of Lucio Silla at Vienna, 1991, the Emperor in Die Frau ohne Schatten at Geneva, 1992; season 1992–93, with Florestan at Zürich and the Emporor at Salzburg; sang title role in Pfitzner's Palestrina at Covent Garden, 1997; as concert singer in Beethoven's Choral Symphony and Missa Solemnis, Britten's War Requiem, the Bach Passions, Schmidt's Das Buch mit Sieben Siegeln and Mozart's Requiem; Max in Der Freischütz with the Royal Opera at the Barbican, 1998; sang Nielsen's David at Ludwigsbug (concert) 1999; season 2000–01 as Strauss's Emperor at Barcelona and Florestan at the Teatro Real Madrid; Parsifal under Abbado at Edinburgh, 2002; sang Strauss's Emperor at the Opéra Bastille, 2002. *Recordings:* roles in Stiffelio, Verdi; Mozart and Salieri, Rimsky-Korsakov; Zaide; La Finta Giardiniera and Don Giovanni, Mozart; Die Freunde von Salamanka, Schubert; Genoveva, Schumann; Oedipus Rex, Stravinsky; Handel's Utrecht Te Deum and Dvořák's Requiem.

MOSES, Geoffrey; British singer (bass); b. 24 Sept. 1952, Abercynon, Wales. *Education:* Emmanuel College, Cambridge, Guildhall School of Music and with Otakar Kraus and Peter Harrison. *Career:* debut with Welsh National Opera 1977, as Basilio in Il Barbiere di Siviglia; other roles include Seneca, L'Incoronazione di Poppea, Sarastro and Padre Guardiano in La Forza del Destino; Covent Garden debut 1981, in Les Contes d'Hoffmann; returned in a new production of Otello; Glyndebourne Festival debut 1984; sang Fiesco in Simon Boccanegra 1986; Brussels Opera in Hoffmann and Boccanegra; Welsh National Opera in Peter Stein's production of Falstaff; season 1990–91, with WNO in Figaro, Carmen and Falstaff, also on tour to Japan; sang Professor Millar in the premiere of Friend of the People by David Horne, Glasgow 1999; created Petrus in The Last Supper, by Birtwistle, Berlin Staatsoper 2000; concert engagements include La Damnation de Faust in Frankfurt and the Choral Symphony with the Scottish National Orchestra; sang in Strauss's Die Liebe der Danaë for BBC Radio 3, conducted by Charles Mackerras. *Recordings:* Rigoletto. *Current Management:* Music International, 13 Ardilaun Road, Highbury, London N5 2QR, England. *Telephone:* (20) 7359-5183. *Fax:* (20) 7226-9792. *E-mail:* music@musicint.co.uk. *Website:* www.musicint.co.uk.

MOSHINSKY, Elijah, BA, PhD; British opera and theatre director; b. 8 Jan. 1946, Shanghai, China; s. of Abraham Moshinsky and Eva Moshinsky; m. Ruth Dyttman 1970; two s. *Education:* Univ. of Melbourne, Australia, St Antony's Coll., Oxford. *Career:* apptd to Royal Opera House 1973, Assoc. Producer 1979; work for Royal Opera includes original productions of Peter Grimes 1975, Lohengrin 1978, The Rake's Progress 1979, Un Ballo in Maschera 1980; Macbeth 1981, Samson et Dalila 1981, Tannhäuser 1984, Otello 1987, Die Entführung aus dem Serail 1987, Attila 1990, Simon Boccanegra 1991, Stiffelio 1993, Aida 1994, Otello 1994, The Makropoulos Case 1996, The Queen of Spades 1998; has also produced work for ENO, Australian Opera, Metropolitan Opera, New York, Holland Festival, Maggio Musicale, Florence etc. *Theatre productions include:* Troilus and Cressida (Nat. Theatre) 1976, The Force of Habit (Nat. Theatre) 1976, Three Sisters (Albery) 1987, Light Up the Sky (Globe) 1987, Ivanov (Strand) 1989, Much Ado About Nothing (Strand) 1989, Another Time (Wyndham's) 1989, Shadowlands (Queen's) 1989, Cyrano de Bergerac 1992, Genghis Cohn 1993, Danton 1994; Dir Matador (Queen's) 1991, Becket (Haymarket) 1991, Reflected Glory (Vaudeville) 1992, Shadowlands (Tony Award for Best Stage Director) 1992, Richard III 1998, The Female Odd Couple (Apollo) 2001; productions for BBC TV of works by Shakespeare, Ibsen and Sheridan. *Films include:* The Green Man 1990, Genghis Cohn 1993, Brazen Hussies 1996, Anorak of Fire 1998. *Honours:* . *E-mail:* sally@maestroarts.com. *Website:* www.maestroarts.com.

MOSLEY, George, AGSM; British singer (baritone); *Voice Teacher, St Catherine's College Cambridge*; b. 28 April 1959, England; m.; two s. *Education:* Guildhall School with Laura Sarti, Accad. Chigiana, Siena, Italy, Munich Hochschule für Musik, Germany, Nat. Opera Studio, London. *Career:* opera performances include Pallante in Agrippina, Vienna, Madrid, Paris (concerts), Karlsruhe Opera; Apollo in Alceste, Concertgebouw; Fléville/Fouquier in Andrea Chénier, Chelsea Opera Group; Bill in Aufstieg und Fall der Stadt Mahagonny, Teatro dell'Opera, Rome, Teatro Valli, Reggio Emilia, Teatro Piccinni, Bari; Father in Baa Baa Black Sheep, Opera North; Count Oscar in Bluebeard, Grange Park Opera; Count in Capriccio, City Opera, New York; Dancaire in Carmen, Royal Opera House, Arena di Napoli; Dancaire and Morales in Carmen, Beijing Festival; Morales in Carmen, Opéra de Nancy; Aubergiste in Chérubin, Teatro Lirico, Cagliari; Gulglielmo in Così fan tutte, Teatro Verdi, Pisa, Megaron, Athens; The Traveller in Curlew River, San Carlo, Napoli; Faninal (cover) in Der Rosenkavalier, ENO; Marquis (cover) in Dialogue Des Carmelites, ENO; Aeneas in Dido and Aeneas, Salerno Festival, Italy; Gabrieli Consort Concerts, Teatro Communale Bologna, Lugo; Orlovsky in Die Fledermaus, Scottish Opera; Falke in Die Fledermaus, Sha Tin Festival, Hong Kong; Prince de Condé in Die Teufel Von Loudun, Teatro Regio, Turin; Papageno in Die Zauberflöte, Scottish Opera; Don Giovanni in Don Giovanni, A. Toscanini, Milan, Holland Park Opera, Grange Park Opera; Don Giovanni (cover) in Don Giovanni, ENO; Malatesta in Don Pasquale, Teatro Verdi, Pisa; Sportsman (Cover for Neils Lyhne) in Fennimore & Gerda, ENO; Short Prisoner in From The House of the Dead, Opéra de Nice, France; Marco in Gianni Schicchi, ENO; Hamlet in Hamlet, Teatro Regio, Turin, Chelsea Opera Group; Architetto in Il Letto Della Storia, Teatro Communale, Florence; Josef K in Il Processo, La Scala, Milan, Teatro Valli, Reggio Emilia; Don Profundo in Il Viaggio a Reims, New Israeli Opera; Robineau in Il Volo Di Notte, Auditorium di Milano; Ottone in Incoronazione di Poppea, Teatro Verdi, Pisa; Patroclus in King Priam, Opera North, Flanders Opera; Fred Graham/Petrucchio in Kiss Me Kate, Teatro Regio, Turin, Teatro Massimo, Palermo; Schaunard in La Bohème, Scottish Opera; Hong Kong Festival, City of Birmingham Symphony Orchestra; Dandini in La Cenerentola, Teatro Verdi, Pisa; Rodolfo in La Sonnambula, Megaron, Athens; Germont in La Traviata, Castleward Opera, Grange Park Opera; Count in Le Nozze di Figaro (cover), ENO; Count in Le Nozze di Figaro, RAI Uno, Turin, Teatro Verdi, Pisa, Megaron, Athens; Duke of Albany in Lear, ENO, Teatro Regio, Torino; Dir Les Mamelles de Tirésias, Grange Park Opera; L'Horloge Comtoise/Le Chat in L'Enfant et les Sortilèges, Teatro delle Muse, Ancona, Verona, Reggio Emilia, Bari; Ramiro in L'Heure Espagnole, Grange Park Opera; Haly in L'Italiana in Algeri, New Israeli Opera, Seattle Opera; Yamadori in Madama Butterfly, ENO; Sharpless in Madama Butterfly, Hong Kong Festival; Don Pedro in Maria Padilla, Buxton Festival; Starveling in Midsummer Night's Dream, Teatro Petruzzelli, Bari, Teatro Valli, Reggio Emilia; Pasquale in Orlando Paladino, Downshire Players; Pelléas (cover) in Pelléas et Mélisande, Megaron, Athens; Golaud (cover) in Pelléas et Mélisande, Glyndebourne Festival; Berardo in Riccardo Primo, Göttingen Festival; Athanaël (cover) in Thaïs, ENO; Athanaël in Thaïs, Megaron, Athens; Picasso in The Banquet, Teatro Communale, Florence, Opera di Roma; Henry in The Fairy Queen, ENO; God in The Flood, Teatro delle Muse, Ancona, Verona, Reggio Emilia, Bari; Junius (cover) in The Rape of Lucretia, ENO; Junius in The Rape of Lucretia, Reggio Emilia, Parma, Modena; Albert in Werther, Beijing Festival; concert appearances have included Handel's Messiah with Nat. Symphony Orchestra, Washington, DC, Vaughan Williams's Five Mystical Songs, Sancta Civitas and Sea Symphony, Mahler's Symphony No. 8, Elgar's The Apostles, and Elijah, Bach's St John Passion and St Matthew Passion. *Recordings include:* Schumann's Dichterliebe and Liederkreis Op. 39, Aeneas in Dido and Aeneas conducted by John Eliot Gardiner, Agrippina, Tavener's Eternity's Sunrise 2000, Chérubin by Massenet Production from Cagliari 2006, NMC Songbook (Gramophone Award) 2009. *Honours:* First Place, Sir Frederick Painter Prize 1982, First Place, Mirsky Memorial Prize 1982, First Place, Schubert Prize 1984, Second Place, Sir Peter Pears Prize 1984, Finalist Kathleen Ferrier Competition 1985, First Prize, Int. Mozart Competition, Salzburg 1998. *Current Management:* c/o Robert Gilder & Co., N102 Vox Studios, 1–45 Durham Street, London, SE11 5JH, England; c/o Ornella Cogliolo, Via Valadier n. 1 interno 5, Rome 00193, Italy. *Telephone:* (20) 7580-7758 (London); (06) 320-7627 (Rome). *Fax:* (20) 7580-7739 (London). *E-mail:* rgilder@robert-gilder.com; cogliolo@cogliolo.it. *Website:* www.robert-gilder.com; www.cogliolo.it.

MOSUC, Elena, DMus; Romanian singer (soprano); b. 18 Jan. 1964, Iasi. *Education:* George Enescu Conservatory, Bucharest. *Career:* debut at Tasi Opera 1990, as Mozart's Queen of Night; further appearances as Lucia di Lammermoor, Gilda and Violetta; concerts with the Moldau Philharmonic and in Mozart masses at Bucharest; Theater am Gärtnerplatz Munich, Vienna Staatsoper and Deutsche am Rhein 1990; with Zürich Opera 1991–; roles include Lucia in Lucia di Lammermoor, Queen of the Night, Konstanze, Donna Anna, Linda di Chamounix, Gilda, Elvira, Violetta Valéry, Luisa Miller, Sophie, Zerbinetta, Aminta/Timidia, Musetta, Antonida, Micaëla, Olympia, Antonia, Giulietta. *Honours:* Officer of the Arts, Romania 2005, President's Medal, Italy 2009; Monte Carlo Competition 1991, Premio Bellini d'Oro 1995, Premio Zenatello di Verona 2002, Premio Verdi di Modena 2004, Premio Lina Pagliughi: Siola d'oro 2009. *Current Management:* Hilbert Artists Management, Maximilianstrasse 22, 80539 Munich, Germany. *Telephone:* (89) 2907470. *Fax:* (89) 29074790. *E-mail:* agentur@hilbert.de. *Website:* www.hilbert.de; www.mosuc.com.

MOTHERWAY, Fiona; singer (soprano); b. 1967, WA, Australia. *Education:* studied in Australia and at the Royal Acad. of Music, London. *Career:* performances with British Youth Opera and elsewhere as Fiordiligi; Cambridge Handel Opera Group as Melissa in Amadigi di Gaula; other Handel roles include Semele, Atalanta (Xerxes), Cleopatra and Ginevra (Ariodante); also sings Mozart's Countess, Susanna and Pamina, Musetta, Gilda and Purcell's Dido; season 1996–97 with Olympia in Contes d'Hoffman for Stowe Opera and Naiade in Ariadne for Castleward Opera; concerts include Strauss's Four Last Songs, Haydn's Creation and Nelson Mass, Messiah, Bach B minor Mass, Mozart's C minor Mass and Requiem; Mahler's 4th Symphony under Colin Davis.

MOTT, Louise, AGSM, ARCM (PG); British singer (mezzo-soprano); b. 1971, Barnet, Herts., England. *Education:* Guildhall School of Music and Drama (GSMD), Royal Coll. of Music (RCM), Nat. Opera Studio. *Career:* opera roles include Bradamante in Alcina, ENO; Annio in La Clemenza di Tito, Welsh Nat. Opera; Edith in Alfred, Agrippina, Ariodante, Sesto in Giulio Cesare, Orlando, Rosmira in Partenope, Serse and Dido in Dido and Aeneas, for The Early Opera Co.; Marlinchen in Roderick Watkins' The Juniper Tree at Munich Biennale; Marguerite in Deirdre Gribbin's Hey Persephone! for Almeida Opera; Emerald in Robin Holloway's Boys and Girls Come Out to Play, and Blind Mary in The Martyrdom of St Magnus, for The Opera Group, Oslo Kammermusikk Festival and Hebrides Ensemble; Wife/Sphinx/Doreen in Mark-Anthony Turnage's Greek, with the London Sinfonietta; concerts include Mozart's Requiem at the Albert Hall, Messiah at St John's, Smith Square, Elgar's Dream of Gerontius and The Music Makers, Dvořák Requiem, Elijah, and the Stabat Maters of Haydn and Rossini; Wigmore Hall debut 1996, with the Young Songmakers' Almanac series; Mozart's Requiem at Bath Abbey 1997; 2003–04 season as Fidalma in The Secret Marriage and Annina in Der Rosenkavalier for Opera North; Ariodante for English Touring Opera; Madame Larina in Eugene Onegin for Scottish Opera on tour; Vivaldi Gloria with the Bach Choir, Royal Festival Hall and Royal Albert Hall; Messiah at The Lighthouse, Poole with Bournemouth Symphony Orchestra; UK premiere of Caldara's Amarilli vezzosa with the Orchestra of St John's, Smith Square; performances of Mahler Kindertotenlieder and Mussorgsky Nursery Songs with Hebrides Ensemble; engagements for 2010 included Meg Page in Mayerling with Royal Ballet, Falstaff and Count Orlofsky in Die Fledermaus, Party Scene for Diva Opera in UK and on tour in Europe, Pergolesi Stabat Mater and Respighi Il Tramonto at Hampstead & Highgate Festival, Marcella in Tom Wiggall's Alban at St Alban the Martyr Church, Holborn; performances in 2011 included Fricka, Erda, Flosshilde and Gutrune in English Pocket Opera Co.'s Pocket Ring Cycle, Mozart's Requiem and Solemn Vespers for the Bach Choir and the Orchestra of the Age of Enlightment at the Royal Festival Hall, Meg Page in Falstaff for the Pfalztheater, Kaiserslautern, Germany, Praskowia in The Merry Widow for Opera Project, Marquise Berkenfield in La Fille du Régiment and Count Orlofsky in Die Fledermaus Party Scene for Diva Opera in UK and on tour in Europe; performances in 2012 included Helen in King Priam for Brighton Festival and 2nd Lady in Magic Flute for Diva Opera; performances in 2013 included Second Witch in Dido and Aeneas for Opera North, Flora Bervoix in La Traviata for Diva Opera, La Ciesca in Gianni Schicchi, La Frugola in Il Tabarro for Caledonian Opera, Mrs Grose in The Turn of the Screw for Seastar Opera Engagements; performances in 2014 included Elgar's The Kingdom, Bach's St Matthew Passion and Messiah (Mozart edn) at Truro Cathedral, Bach's B Minor Mass at Exeter Cathedral, Mrs Grose, The Turn of the Screw for Seastar Opera, a recital for the 100th Anniversary of the original Glastonbury Festivals, Mrs Segstrom, A Little Night Music for Opera Project and Ottavia (cover), The Coronation of Poppea for Opera North; performances in 2015 included Waltraute Die Walküre for Secret Opera, Alisa Lucia di Lammermoor & Marcellina, Le Nozze di Figaro for Diva Opera and Nicklausse/Muse, The Tales of Hoffmann for English Touring Opera. *Honours:* GSMD Susan Longfield Prize, RCM Lies Askonas Singing Prize, RCM Peter Pears Exhbn, RCM Keith Falkner Prize for Bach and Handel. *E-mail:* ladamemott@gmail.com. *Website:* www.louisemott.net.

MOTTADELLI, Marcello; Italian conductor; *Chief Conductor, Cairo Symphony Orchestra*; b. 1971, Torino. *Education:* Conservatorio di Musica Giuseppe Verdi di Milano, Musik Hochschule. *Career:* student and asst of Romano Gandolfi, Toscanini Asscn, Parma 1997–99; First Kappelmeister, Bern, Switzerland 1999–2001; debuted with Colorado Opera Co. 2001, Opera of Cape Town, South Africa 2001, Nat. Opera, Denmark 2007, Bialystok Philharmonic Orchestra, Poland 2007, Orchestra Teatro Carlo Coccia, Novara, Italy 2007; Principal Conductor, Cairo Symphony Orchestra 2008–. *Current Management:* Tivoli & Crescendi Artists, Læderstræde 9, 4, 1202 Copenhagen, Denmark. *Website:* www.crescendi.org. *Address:* Cairo Symphony Orchestra, Cairo Opera House, Gezira, 11211 Cairo, Egypt (office). *Telephone:* 27390157 (office). *Fax:* 27390186 (office). *E-mail:* maestro.it@fastwebnet.it (office). *Website:* www.cairo-symphony.com (office).

MOULDS, Christopher; conductor and keyboard player; b. 1967, Halifax, England. *Education:* City Univ., Guildhall School, Royal Coll. of Music. *Career:* conducted Figaro and The Rake's Progress at the RCM; mem. of music staff, ENO 1991–95, working on productions of Billy Rudd, Carmen, Wozzeck, Orfeo, Lohengrin and Street Scene; harpsichord continuo for ENO 's Xerxes and Ariodante; Chorusmaster, Glyndebourne Festival from 1995, conducting Figaro 1997; further engagements with British Youth Opera, Opera Co. Tunbridge Wells (Barber and Figaro), European Community Youth Orchestra and London Sinfonietta (as orchestral keyboard player); conducted The Magic Flute for ENO 1996–98.

MOULT, Daniel Adam Ashbrook, MA, FRCO; British organist; b. 13 Dec. 1973, Manchester, England; m. Melanie Evans 2004. *Education:* Manchester Grammar School, St John's Coll., Oxford, Amsterdam Conservatorium. *Career:* freelance concert organist and organ tutor throughout UK, Europe and Australia; Organist and Asst Dir of Music, Coventry Cathedral 1995–2002; Visiting Organ Tutor, Birmingham Conservatoire 2003–, Wells Cathedral School 2013–; organ tutor on UK, Amsterdam and Sydney courses; organ animateur, Bridgewater Hall, Manchester 2003–08; Examiner, Royal Coll. of Organists (RCO); tutor, RCO Acad. Organ School, London; mem. Editorial Panel, Organists' Review; mem. Royal Coll. of Organists (mem. Council), Inc. Soc. of Musicians, British Inst. of Organ Studies. *Recordings:* various recordings for BBC Radio 2, 3 and 4, BBC TV, Sony BMG, Fugue State Films, Regent Records and Dutch radio; organist for four albums from Coventry

Cathedral; producer for numerous albums. *Publications:* contrib. to Choir and Organ, Organists' Review, British Institute of Organ Studies Journal. *Honours:* Univ. of Oxford John Betts Organ Scholarship 1994, Durrant, Turpin and Dixon Prizes (FRCO) 1993. *Telephone:* 7866-699179 (mobile). *E-mail:* enquiries@danielmoult.com (office). *Website:* www.danielmoult.com.

MOUND, Vernon; British opera director; *Professor and Head of Music Theatre, University of Gothenburg*; b. 1954, England. *Education:* Univ. of London. *Career:* has worked with the Royal Opera, the Swan Theatre, Opera North and the Black Theatre of Prague as Stage Manager; Educ. Dir Scottish Ballet 1979–81; Assoc. Dir Opera North 1984–90, assisting on new productions and directing revivals; workshops for children and adults, including community piece Quest of the Hidden Moon; directed small-scale touring version of Carmen; The Gondoliers for New Sadler's Wells Opera, 1988; directed the Opera Informal and the Sondheim Workshop at the Royal College of Music, 1989–91; directed Handel's Ariodante for the Birmingham Conservatoire, 1990, and The Marriage Contract and Le Pauvre Matelot for Morley Opera; productions of Amahl and the Night Visitors at the Barbican Centre and Alice, the Musical at St Martin-in-the-Fields; La Finta Giardiniera for the Opera Hogskolan in Stockholm 1991, and Pedrotti's Tutti in Maschera at the Britten Theatre; La Fille du Régiment, 1992; produced Les Miserables, Rigoletto, La Cenerentola, 42nd Street 1996, Andrea Chenier, Falstaff, Macbeth, Les Miserables, My Fair Lady, Annie 1997, A Little Night Music, Kleine Mahagonny, Oliver, Alice, Andrea Chenier 1998, West Side Story, Martin Guerre Blitz, Me and My Girl 1999, Oliver, Les Miserables, Joseph and His Amazing Technicolour Dreamcoat, Showboat 2000, Hansel and Gretel, Crazy for You, Half a Sixpence 2001, Miss Saigon, Manon Lescaut, Nine, Les Pecheurs des Perles, Anything Goes, The Late Sleepers, Hansel and Gretel 2002, Guys and Dolls, Such Sweet Thunder, Oklahoma 2003, Redhunter, Miss Saigon 2004, Evita, A Little Night Music, Les Pecheurs des Perles 2005, Gianni Schicci, West Side Story, Sweeney Todd, Guys and Dolls, Pygmalion, Il Trovatore 2006, Carousel , City of Angels, Il Brigante delle Cese, Titanic, Hansel and Gretel, Candide 2007–08; Prof. and Head of Music Theatre, Univ. of Gothenburg 1999–; Artistic Dir MT4UTH 2003–. *Address:* Nordhemsgatan, 68, 41309 Gothenburg, Sweden (home). *Telephone:* (31) 24-05-56 (home). *E-mail:* vernon@vernonmound.com (home). *Website:* vernonmound.com.

MOUSSA, Samy; Canadian conductor and composer; b. 1984, Montréal. *Education:* Univ. de Montréal, studied with José Evangelista; conducting studies in Czech Repub. with Paolo Bellomia and composition in Finland with Magnus Lindberg and Kaija Saariaho; Hochschule für Musik Munich, studied with Matthias Pintscher and Pascal Dusapin; conducting masterclasses with Pierre Boulez and Peter Eötvös. *Career:* fmrly Asst Conductor, hr-Sinfonieorchester Frankfurt and Ensemble Modern; regular collaborations with several orchestras and ensembles including MDR Sinfonieorchester Leipzig, Frankfurt Radio Symphony Orchestra, Orchestre symphonique de Montréal, Vancouver CBC Radio Orchestra, Orchestre Nat. de Lorraine, Hamilton Phiharmonic Orchestra and Vancouver Symphony Orchestra; orchestral commissions from musicians including Kent Nagano and Orchestre symphonique de Montréal (three) and Pierre Boulez for Lucerne Festival; Music Dir, INDEX Ensemble, Munich 2010–. *Compositions include:* Étude no 4 Zodiakallicht 2009, Rondeau 2009, L'autre frère (opera, premiered at Munich Biennale 2010), Ruah 2010, A l'assaut des jardins 2011, Préludes 2012, Ahania's Lament 2012, A Globe Itself Infolding 2014, Vastation (opera, premiered at Munich Biennale 2014), Nocturne 2014, Crimson 2015. *Honours:* Bayerischen Kunstförderpreis 2012, winner, Siemens Foundation Composer Prize 2013, Québec Composer of the Year 2015. *Address:* c/o Patricia Alia, Editions musicales Durand, 16 rue des Fossées Saint Jacques, 75005 Paris, France (office). *Telephone:* 1-44-41-50-20 (office). *E-mail:* patricia.alia@umusic.com (office). *Website:* www.samymoussa.com (office).

MÖWES, Thomas; German singer (baritone); b. 7 Sept. 1951, Halle. *Education:* Weimar Hochschule. *Career:* sang as Bass-Baritone at the Magdeburg Opera from 1977, and Baritone roles at Halle from 1988, Leipzig and Dresden from 1990; Roles have included Busoni's Doktor Faust, Nekrotzar in Le Grand Macabre and Orestes in Elektra; Guest engagements as Basle as Verdi's Posa, and at Frankfurt as Faninal in Der Rosenkavalier; Other roles include Handel's Polyphemus, Don Alfonso, Ottokar in Der Freischütz, Luna, Nabucco, Rigoletto, Wolfram and Escamillo; Season 2000–01 as Kurwenal for Nederlandse Reisopera, Strauss's Faninal at Frankfurt and Reimann's Lear for Essen Opera; Many concert appearances. *Current Management:* c/o Opernagentur Inge Tennigkeit, Kempener Strasse 4, 40474 Düsseldorf; c/o Künstleragentur von Sohl, Mühlweg 34, 06114 Halle, Saale, Germany. *Telephone:* (211) 5160060 (Düsseldorf); (345) 68589960 (Halle). *Fax:* (211) 51600616 (Düsseldorf); (345) 68589961 (Halle). *E-mail:* opera@tennigkeit-ag.de; office@vonsohl.de. *Website:* www.tennigkeit-ag.de; www.vonsohl.de.

MOYER, Frederick, BMus; pianist; b. 1957. *Education:* Curtis Inst. of Music, Indiana Univ. *Career:* debut in New York 1982; performances across the USA, frequent tours of Europe, Asia and South America; solo appearances with orchestras, including Philadelphia, Houston, Milwaukee, Boston, Cleveland, Baltimore, Minnesota, St Louis, Dallas, Indianapolis, Pittsburgh, Utrecht, London, Rio di Janeiro, Montevideo, Singapore, Hong Kong, Tokyo and the major orchestras of Australia; participant of numerous music festivals.

MOYLAN, William David, BMus, MMus, DrArts; American composer, recording engineer, producer and academic; *Professor, Department of Music, University of Massachusetts, Lowell*; b. 23 April 1956, Virginia, Minn.; one s. *Education:* Peabody Conservatory, Johns Hopkins Univ., Univ. of Toronto, Canada, Ball State Univ. *Career:* Prof. and Chair. Dept of Music, Univ. of Massachusetts, Lowell 1983–. *Compositions include:* On Time – On Age for soprano, flute, trumpet, piano and four-channel tape 1978, Concerto for bass trombone and orchestra 1979, Brass Quintet for brass quintet and tape 1979, Two Movements for string orchestra 1980, Duo for flute and tape 1980, Seven Soliloquies for trumpet 1981, Trio in Twenty Miniatures for flute, horn and piano 1982, ACTS III: Askew Up the Amazon 1983, Metamorphic Variations for clarinet 1983, The Now for high voice, horn and piano, Trombone Trio for alto, tenor and bass trombones 1984, Three Interplays for trumpet duo 1984, Wind Quintet No. 2 1985, Stilled Moments for solo violin 1988, Evocations for guitar 1988, La Liberté for soprano and piano 1989, Eroica Piano Sonata 1989, Two Suspended Images for wind controller 1990, Ask Your Mama 1990, The Dream Deferred for two-channel tape 1990, Mother Earth: Her Whales 1993, Dawn 1993, The Stolen Child 1995, For a Sleeping Child 1996, Singing Bowl Suite: Coming Home 2013. *Publications:* The Art of Recording 1992, Understanding and Crafting the Mix 2002 (third edn 2013). *Honours:* Outstanding Alumni Award, Ball State Univ. School of Music. *Address:* Department of Music, University of Massachusetts, 35 Wilder Street, Suite 3, Lowell, MA 01854, USA (office). *Telephone:* (978) 934-3850 (office). *E-mail:* william_moylan@uml.edu (office).

MOYLE, Richard Michael, MA, PhD, LTCL; New Zealand ethnomusicologist; *Adjunct Professor, Queensland Conservatorium of Music Research Centre*; b. 23 Aug. 1944, Paeroa; m. Linden Averil Evelyn Duncan; one s. two d. *Education:* Trinity Coll., London, Univ. of Auckland. *Career:* Visiting Lecturer in Anthropology, Indiana Univ., USA 1971–72; Asst Prof. in Music, Univ. of Hawaii 1972–73; Research Fellow in Ethnomusicology, Australian Inst. of Aboriginal Studies 1974–77, Research Grantee 1977–82; Sr Research Fellow in Faculty of Arts, Univ. of Auckland 1983–86, Assoc. Prof. of Ethnomusicology and Dir of Archive of Maori and Pacific Music 1986–, Dir of Pacific Studies 2007–10, Hon. Res. Prof. 2011–; Adjunct Prof. Queensland Conservatorium of Music Research Centre, Griffith Univ. 2011–. *Recordings:* The Music of Samoa, Traditional Music of Tonga, Tonga Today (compiler), Songs from the Second Float. *Publications:* Fagogo: Fables from Samoa 1979, Songs of the Pintupi 1981, Alyawarra Music 1985, Tongan Music 1987, Traditional Samoan Music 1988, Sounds of Oceania 1989, Polynesian Song and Dance 1991, Fananga: Fables from Tonga in Tongan and English, Vol. I 1996, Vol. II 1998, Balgo: The Musical Life of an Aboriginal Community 1997, Na Kkai: Taku Musical Fables 2004, Songs from The Second Float: A Musical Ethnography of Taku Atoll, Papua New Guinea 2007. *Address:* Queensland Conservatorium Research Centre, South Bank campus, Griffith University, PO Box 3428, South Bank QLD 4101, Australia (office). *Telephone:* (7) 3735-6335 (office). *E-mail:* qcrc@griffith.edu.au (office). *Website:* www.griffith.edu.au/music/queensland-conservatorium-research-centre.

MOYSEOWICZ, Gabriela Maria, MA; Polish composer, pianist and choir director; b. 4 May 1944, Lwów; d. of Adolf Moyseowicz and Maria Moyseowicz. *Education:* Lyceum of Music, Kraków, Acads of Music, Kraków and Katowice. *Career:* debut playing own piano concerto, Kraków 1957; piano recitals; public performances of own compositions throughout Poland; radio appearances, discussions and interviews. *Compositions include:* Rhapsody for alto and orchestra 1968, Media vita for two violins, cello, soprano and bass recitativ, 9 Moments Musicaux for piano and strings, three Rhapsodies for piano 1983, 1984, 1989, Marche Funèbre for cello and piano, Deux Caprices for violin solo, Ave Maria for two mixed choirs a capella, Sonata No. 1 for cello and piano, two Canzonas for viola de gamba solo, Piano Sonata Nos 3–8, including the 6th Noumenon and 8th Concatenatio, Sonata Polska for violin and piano, four piano concertos 1957, 1960, 1965, 2002, Passacaglia for violin 1984, Alleluia for choir, Credo for four-voice choir 1991, Trio for piano, violin and violoncello 1992, 1993, Discours avec Madame H. Steingroever for flute and piano 1995, Shadow Symphony for large orchestra, Violin Sonata No. 2, Cello Sonata No. 2, Norwidiana for piano; church music: Media Vita, Dies irae, Ave Maria, Pater noster, Kyrie, Alleluia, Amen Credo, Memento Mori I and II, Chaconne for cello 2004, Stabat Mater, Piano Trio for violin and cello 2010. *Recordings:* piano recitals and chamber music, works for orchestra, choir and piano solo, sonatas for violin and piano, cello and piano, Piano Works by G. Moyseowicz. *Address:* Stallupöner Allee 37, 14055 Berlin, Germany (home). *Telephone:* (30) 3030-7191 (home). *Fax:* (30) 3030-7191 (home). *E-mail:* info@gabriela-moyseowicz.de (home). *Website:* www.gabriela-moyseowicz.de.

MOZES, Robert; Romanian violist; b. 1950. *Education:* Cluj Acad. of Music, Tel-Aviv Rubin Music Acad. *Career:* mem. and soloist, Israel Philharmonic; chamber music concerts in Israel, the USA, Canada and Japan; co-founder, Jerusalem String Trio 1977–; repertoire includes string trios by Beethoven, Dohnányi, Mozart, Reger, Schubert and Taneyev, piano quartets by Beethoven, Brahms, Dvořák, Mozart and Schumann. *E-mail:* alperin@netvision.net.il.

MOZHAYEV, Feodor; Russian singer (baritone); b. 1958, Lugansk, Ukraine. *Education:* Kharkov Conservatoire. *Career:* sang first at the Moldavian State Opera and at the Perm Opera 1982–93; Member of the Bolshoi Opera from 1994, with Mozart's Figaro, 1995; Guest engagements with the Kirov Opera, Kharkov Opera and in Kiev; has also sung widely in France and in Poland, Budapest and Malta; other roles include Verdi's Iago, Renato, Luna and Germont, Scarpia, Ruprecht in The Fiery Angel, Lionel in The Maid of Orleans, Escamillo and Rubinstein's Demon; sang Napoleon in War and Peace at La Scala, ROH, Met, and Donner in Das Rheingold at St Petersburg 2000; Alberich in Das Rheingold and Hollander in Fligende Hollander at Teatro Colón, Buenos Aires 2003–04; Poyarok at the Met, Onegin at Split Opera, Croatia, Escamillo in Carmen, Lisbon 2005; Shaklovity in Khovanshina, Theatre Liceu, Barcelona 2007; S. Gubaidulina's St John Passion, Warsaw 2007. *Recordings:* Rimsky-Korsakov's Sadko, Gubaidulina's St John Passion. *Honours:* Prizewinner at 1979 Riga Song Competition. *Current Management:* c/o Agentur Klein, Possartstrasse 8, 81679 Munich, Germany. *Telephone:* (89) 45579931. *Fax:* (89) 45579942. *E-mail:* aklein@agenturklein.de. *Website:* www .agenturklein.de. *Address:* Oktyabrskaya nab. 24\1-9, 193091 St Petersburg, Russia. *Telephone:* (812) 589-26-36 (also fax) (home). *E-mail:* mfn33@yandex .ru (home); mfn1@mail.ru (home). *Website:* www.mozhaev.com.

MUFF, Alfred; Swiss singer (bass-baritone); b. 31 May 1949, Lucerne. *Education:* studied with Werner Ernst in Lucerne, Elisabeth Grümmer and Irmgard Hartmann-Dressler in Berlin. *Career:* debut as Don Ferrando in Fidelio, Lucerne 1974; mem. opera companies in Lucerne, Linz, Mannheim and since 1986 Zürich; opera roles include, Philippo II and Grand Inquisitor, Don Carlo; Boris Godunov; Falstaff; Der fliegende Holländer; Barak in Die Frau ohne Schatten; Hans Sachs in Die Meistersinger von Nuernberg; King Marke and Kurwenal in Tristan und Isolde; appeared as Wotan and Wanderer in Ring des Nibelungen; King Heinrich in Lohengrin; Jochanaan in Salome; Orestes in Elektra; Musiklehrer in Ariadne auf Naxos; Ochs in Der Rosenkavalier; Morosus in Die scweigsame Frau; Waldner in Arabella; Osmin in Die Entführungl; Albert in Werther; Kezal in Die verkaufte Braut; Dr Schön in Lulu und Dokter in Wozzeck; Pizarro in Fidelio and Scarpia in Tosca at the Opernhaus Zürich from 1986; appearances also include Barak at Milan's La Scala, Munich Festival; title role of Der fliegende Holländer and Landgraf, Tannhäuser in Barcelona's Teatro del Liceu, Bruckner Festival, Linz, and at the Deutsche Oper Berlin and for recording; Philip II in the original (French) version of Don Carlo at the Paris Opéra, in the Italian version at the Théâtre de la Monnaie in Brussels and at the Munich State Opera; Stravinsky's Oedipus Rex under Erich Leinsdorf in Geneva; Beethoven's Ninth Symphony at Geneva, Vienna and Basel; Jochanaan, Salome at the Vienna State Opera, at the Semper Oper in Dresden, in Barcelona and at the Festival of Taormina (under Giuseppe Sinopoli); Dvořák's Te Deum, in Vienna and at the Prague Spring Festival; Beethoven's Missa Solemnis on a tour of Switzerland, in Turin, Cologne and Vienna; Mahler's Eighth Symphony in Bonn; Schoenberg's Gurrelieder in Barcelona and Torino; Schnittke's Faust Kantate under Claudio Abbado in Vienna; Haydn's Paukenmesse with the Israel Philharmonic Orchestra under Zubin Mehta; Wotan, Die Walküre at the Munich Opera Festival, at the Vienna State Opera and in a new production at the Cologne Opera; Gurnemanz in Parsifal at the Brucknerfest in Linz; Wanderer in a new production of Siegfried and Wotan in a revival of Rheingold at the Hamburg State Opera; Die Schöpfung under Wolfgang Sawallisch for a television concert and under Nikolaus Harnoncourt for a radio concert; Pizarro, Fidelio under Peter Schneider at the RAI Torino; Barak in a new production of Die Frau ohne Schatten and Morosus in Die schweigsame Frau at the Zürich Opera; opera roles in the 2003–04 season included Uraufführung L'Upupa by Hans Wwerner Nenze, Salzburger Festspiele; Musiklehrer, Ariadne; Grand Inquisitore; Landgraf; Osmin; Kezal (tschechisch); and Baron Ochs von Lerchenau in Zürich; under Wolfgang Sawallisch; Die Zauberflöte under Armin Jordan; Der fliegende Holländer under Pinchas Steinberg; Die Walküre under Christoph von Dohnanyi, Adorno in Schreker's Die Gezeichneten; Paul Dessau, Hagadah, Lulu Dr Schön for Television under Franz Welser Möst. *Recordings include:* first complete version of Die Frau ohne Schatten under Wolfgang Sawallisch; Die Zauberflöte under Armin Jordan; Der fliegende Holländer under Pinchas Steinberg; Die Walküre under Christoph von Dohnányi; Adorno in Schreker's Die Gezeichneten; Paul Dessau, Hagadah. *Honours:* Kunstpreis of the City of Lucerne. *Current Management:* Aria's di Novella Partacini & Alexandra Plaickner, Rappresentanza Artisti, Via Josef Weingartner, 4, 39022 Lagundo, Italy. *Telephone:* (0473) 200200. *Fax:* (0473) 222424. *E-mail:* info@arias.it. *Website:* www.arias.it. *Address:* Luzernerstr. 78, 6043 Adligenswil, Switzerland (office). *E-mail:* alfi1@bluewin.ch (office).

MUHLY, Nico, BA, MMus; American composer; b. 26 Aug. 1981, Vermont; s. of Frank Muhly and Bunny Harvey. *Education:* Columbia Univ., Juilliard School with Christopher Rouse and John Corigliano. *Career:* fmr boy chorister, Grace Episcopal Church, Providence, Rhode Island; composes extensively for choir and orchestra, as well as ballet, opera and film scores; has worked and recorded with classical and pop/rock composers and musicians including Philip Glass, folk-rock band Grizzly Bear, Björk, Antony and the Johnsons, librettist Craig Lucas, Valgeir Sigurðsson. *Film scores include:* Joshua 2007, The Reader 2008, Felicitas 2009, Margaret 2011, Kill Your Darlings 2013. *Recordings include:* Speaks Volumes 2006, Mothertongue 2008, So Far Around the Bend 2009, I Drink the Air Before Me 2010, Seeing is Believing 2011, Drones 2012, Cycles 2013. *Compositions include:* choral works: Set Me as a Seal 2003, A Good Understanding 2005, I Cannot Attain Unto It 2005, Pater Noster 2008, Grief is the Price We Pay for Love 2011; orchestral: Out of the Loop 2003, It Remains to be Seen 2006, Seeing is Believing 2007, The Only Tune 2009, Vocalise on Al lampo dell'armi 2009, Detailed Instructions 2010, Luminous Body 2011, So Far So Good 2012, Gait 2012, Bright Mass with Cannons 2013; opera: Dark Sisters 2010, Two Boys 2011; voice: Employment 2003, Wonders 2007, The Adulteress 2008, Impossible Things 2009. *Current Management:* c/o St Rose Music Publishing Co., Inc., 40 Exchange Place, Suite 1906, New York, NY 10005, USA. *Telephone:* (212) 979-2080. *E-mail:* fritz@dunvagen.com. *Website:* nicomuhly.com.

MUKERIA, Shalva; Georgian singer (tenor); b. 23 April 1964, Odessa, Ukraine. *Education:* Tbilisi Conservatory, Odessa Conservatory. *Career:* debut in Western Europe as Cassio in Otello at Las Palmas, Gran Canaria 1996–97 season; sang Rodolfo in La Bohème and Alfredo in La Traviata with the Ukraine Nat. Opera on tour in UK 1997–98 season; made debut in France debut as Rodolfo in La Bohème with Besançon Opera 1998; other roles include Elvino in La Sonnambula, the Italian singer in Der Rosenkavalier; has performed at Teatro Comunale, Florence, Santa Fe Opera, Copenhagen Royal Opera, also in Helsinki, Pavia, Como, Cremona, Leipzig; soloist, Wiener Staatsoper 2005–. *Honours:* winner, song competitions in Prague and Tbilisi. *Current Management:* c/o Operadomani S.r.l. Artists Management, Via San Vito 30, 95124 Catania, Italy. *Telephone:* (095) 310007. *Fax:* (095) 7461401. *E-mail:* info@operadomani.net. *Website:* www.operadomani.net.

MULA, Inva; singer (soprano); b. 1967, Albania. *Career:* sang in concert with Placido Domingo at Brussels, Munich and Olso, 1994; appearances at the Opéra Bastille as Frasquita in Carmen and as Donizetti's Adina and Norina at Los Angeles 1995; season 1995 as Offenbach's Antonia and Lisette in Puccini's La Rondine at Bonn; Dirce in Cherubini's Médée at Compiègne, 1996; sang Gilda in Rigoletto at the Verona Arena, 2001. *Honours:* winner Georg Enescu Competition, Bucharest, 1991; Grand Prix Madama Butterfly, Barcelona, 1992; Prizewinner, Concours International de Voix d'Opéra Placido Domingo, Paris, 1993. *Current Management:* Atelier Musicale, Via Caselle 76, San Lazzaro di Savena 40068, Italy; Organisation Internationale Artistique, 16 Avenue Franklin D. Roosevelt, 75008 Paris, France. *Telephone:* (51) 19984444 (Italy); 1-42-25-58-34 (France). *Fax:* (51) 19984420 (Italy); 1-42-25-64-97 (France). *E-mail:* info@ateliermusicale.com; oia@oia-poilve.com. *Website:* www.ateliermusicale.com; www.oia-poilve.com.

MULDOWNEY, Dominic John, BPhil; British composer; b. 19 July 1952, Southampton; s. of William Muldowney and Barbara Muldowney (née Lavender); m. Diane Ellen Trevis 1986; one d. *Education:* Taunton's Grammar School, Southampton and Univ. of York, studied with Jonathan Harvey, Bernard Rands, David Blake and Harrison Birtwistle. *Career:* Composer-in-Residence, Southern Arts Asscn 1974–76; Asst Music Dir Royal Nat. Theatre 1976–81, Music Dir 1981–97; Composer in Association, Orchestra of St John's Smith Square 1996–98; Prof. of Composition, RAM 1999–; has composed music for British and int. festivals, for many films and TV and over 50 scores for the theatre. *Compositions include:* Piano Concerto 1983, Saxophone Concerto 1984, Sinfonietta 1986, Ars Subtilior 1987, Lonely Hearts 1988, Violin Concerto 1989, Three Pieces for Orchestra 1990, Percussion Concerto 1991, Oboe Concerto 1992, Trumpet Concerto 1993, Concerto for 4 Violins 1994 The Brontës (ballet) 1995, Trombone Concerto 1996, Clarinet Concerto 1997, The Fall of Jerusalem (oratorio) 1998, God's Plenty (ballet) 1999, Red Razzmatazz (opera) 2005, War Oratorio 2007, The Last Confession 2007, Tsunami 2008. *Music for films and TV includes:* The Ploughman's Lunch 1983, The Ginger Tree 1989, Sharpe 1993, Bloody Sunday 2002, Copenhagen 2002. *Honours:* Prix Italia 1993, (for radio opera The Voluptuous Tango 1996) 1997, Sony Award (for The Voluptuous Tango 1996) 1997.

MÜLLEJANS, Petra; German violinist and conductor; *Professor of Baroque Violin, Hochschule für Musik und Darstellende Kunst. Education:* studied in Düsseldorf, New York and Freiburg (completed studies in performance with Rainer Kußmaul), studies with Helga Thoene in Düsseldorf and Nikolaus Harnoncourt in Salzburg. *Career:* Founder-mem. and Co-Artistic Dir Freiburger Barockorchester 1987–; teaches Baroque violin at Freiburg Conservatory; Prof. of Baroque Violin, Hochschule für Musik und Darstellende Kunst, Frankfurt-am-Main. *Recordings include:* Harmonia mundi (Gramophone Award for Baroque Instrumental Disc, CPE Bach Harpsichord Concertos) 2011. *Honours:* several Diapason d'Or Awards. *Address:* Hochschule für Musik und Darstellende Kunst, Escher Landstrasse 29–39, 60322 Frankfurt am Main, Germany (office). *Telephone:* (69) 154007 (office). *Fax:* (69) 154007108 (office). *Website:* www.hfmdk-frankfurt.de (office).

MÜLLER, Barbel; German singer (mezzo-soprano); b. 1968, Duisburg. *Education:* Frankfurt Musikhochschule and studied with Laura Sarti and Elsa Cavelti. *Career:* sang in concert from 1987 and made opera debut at Linz 1991, singing the Composer (Ariadne), Dorabella and Carmen; Further appearances as Sesto (Clemenza di Tito), Orlofsky, Charlotte and Octavian (Strasbourg, 1995); Concert repertoire includes Mozart's Requiem (at Stuttgart), the Christmas Oratorio (Ulm and Amsterdam), St Matthew Passion (Tubingen), Elijah (Zürich) and Bach's B Minor Mass (Frankfurt).

MÜLLER, Markus; singer (tenor); b. 1953, Saulgau, Germany. *Education:* studied in Stuttgart with Helmuth Rilling. *Career:* sang at Dortmund Opera from 1987, Deutsche Oper am Rhein at Düsseldorf from 1991; roles include Belmonde and Mozart's Arsace (Idomeneo), Nicolai's Fenton, Tamino, and the Astrologer in Rimsky's Golden Cockerel; guest appearances at Dresden from 1991, including Belmonte in Die Entführung and Rossini's Almaviva; premiere of Klebe's Gervaise Macquart at Düsseldorf 1995; sang Oronte in Alcina at Dusseldorf 1999; many concert appearances.

MÜLLER, Rufus, MA; British-German singer (tenor) and academic; *Assistant Professor of Music, Bard College*; b. 5 Feb. 1959, Kent. *Education:* New Coll., Oxford, studied with Thomas LoMonaco, New York. *Career:* has worked with many established conductors including Ivor Bolton, Richard Hickox, Joshua Rifkin, Andrew Parrott and Ivan Fischer; opera and concert appearances throughout Europe, Japan and the USA; roles performed include: Evangelist in Bach's St Matthew Passion (with CBSO), Bastien in Mozart's

Bastien und Bastienne, Aminta in Peri's Euridice, Tersandre in Lully's Roland, Giuliano in Handel's Rodrigo, Lurcanio in Handel's Ariodante, title role in Mozart's La Clemenza di Tito, Castor in Rameau's Castor et Pollux, Alessando in Handel's Poro, title role in Rameau's Pygmalian; Recitals include appearances at Wigmore Hall and Barbican, London, Musée d'Orsay, Paris, New York Festival of Song, Carnegie Hall, Schubert's Die schöne Müllerin, Munich, Schubert's Winterreise, Mendelssohn's St Paul with Leipzig Gewandhaus Choir, Beethoven's Ninth Symphony, Mendelssohn's Elijah in New York, Monteverdi's Il Ritorno d'Ulisse in Athens and Florence, performances in Munich, Tokyo, Madrid, Utrecht, Salzburg and New York; numerous performances of St Matthew Passion including in Sweden, Germany and Switzerland as well as Jonathan Miller production at Brooklyn Acad. of Music; many performances of Handel's Messiah including regular appearances at Carnegie Hall, New York, televised tour in Spain with Trevor Pinnock and the English Concert, as well as performances in Canada, Denmark, Norway, Sweden and UK; world première, Rorem's Song Cycle Evidence of Things Not Seen, Carnegie Hall, New York, and Washington, DC; US premiere of Handel's Giove in Argo, Avery Fisher Hall 2009; currently Asst Prof. . of Music, Bard Coll., New York. *Recordings include:* Bach's St John Passion, Bach Cantatas, Die Zauberflöte, Beethoven"s Choral Fantasia, Dowland's First Book of Airs, Haydn's O Tuneful Voice, 19th Century Songs, Bach's St Matthew Passion, Telemann's Admiraltätsmusik and Solo Cantatas, Rorem: Evidence of Things Not Seen, Haydn's Creation, Handel's Messiah, Ariodante and Rodrigo, songs by Franz Lachner. *Honours:* GKN English Song Award 1985, 2nd Prize, Oratorio Soc. of New York 1999. *Current Management:* c/o Nancy Knowles, Gossage Artists Management, 720 Bathurst Street, Suite 200, Toronto, ON, Canada. *Address:* Bard College, PO Box 5000, Annandale-on-Hudson, NY 12504-5000, USA (office). *Telephone:* (845) 758-6822. *E-mail:* rumu2000@earthlink.net; umu2000@earthlink.net. *Website:* www.bard.edu (office); www.rufusmuller.com.

MÜLLER-BRACHMANN, Hanno; German singer (bass-baritone) and teacher; *Professor of Song, University of Music, Karlsruhe*; b. 20 Aug. 1970, Cologne. *Education:* Knabenkantorei Basel, Basle Acad. of Music, Staatliche Hochschule für Musik Freiburg with Ingeborg Most, Hochschule der Künste, Berlin with Dietrich Fischer-Dieskau, Staatliche Hochschule für Musik Mannheim with Rudolf Piernay. *Career:* debut under Donald Runnicles, Theater Freiburg 1992; with Deutsche Staatsoper, Berlin 1996–, as Mozart's Figaro, Papageno, Leporello, Guglielmo; Orest, Kaspar, Golaud, Tomski, Escamillo, Amfortas, Wotan (Rheingold) under Daniel Barenboim, Sir Simon Rattle, Michael Gielen, Philippe Jordan, Sebastian Weigle, Gustavo Dudamel, Horst Stein; with Bayerische Staatsoper 1999–, as Fernando, Orest, Figaro, Guglielmo, Papageno under Zubin Mehta; with Vienna Staatsoper as Guglielmo, Leporello, Figaro under Adam Fischer; with Claudio Abbado in Modena as Papageno; with Elliott Carter's opera What Next? under Daniel Barenboim in Berlin, Chicago and New York (Carnegie Hall debut) 1999–2000; concert performances under conductors including Kurt Masur, Sir Neville Marriner, Christoph Eschenbach, Sir Charles Mackerras, Sir John Eliot Gardiner, Pierre Boulez, András Schiff, Christoph von Dohnányi, Philippe Herreweghe, Marcus Creed, René Jacobs, Fabio Luisi, Myung-Wun Chung, Riccardo Chailly, Vladimir Jurowsky, Herbert Blomstedt, Christian Thielemann, Franz Welser-Möst, Lorin Maazel, Daniel Harding, Michael Gielen and Nikolaus Harnoncourt; has performed with numerous int. orchestras including Berlin, Vienna, London and New York Philharmonics, Concertgebouw Amsterdam, Gewandhaus Leipzig, Academy of St Martin-in-the-Fields, Cleveland, Chicago and Boston Symphony Orchestras and Staatskapelle Berlin and Dresden; lieder recitals at Schubertiade Schwarzenberg, Edinburgh Festival, Berliner Festwochen, Beethovenfest, Bonn, Concertgebouw, Amsterdam, Wigmore Hall, London; Prof. of Song, Hochschule für Musik, Karlsruhe 2011–. *Films:* Beethoven's Symphony No. 9 with Michael Gielen, Così fan tutte with Daniel Barenboim 2003. *Television:* La Bohème 2002. *Recordings include:* Bach's bass solo cantatas (Müller-Brühl), Salieri's La Passione (Spehring), Schubert (Martineau, Eisenlohr) and Schumann (Johnson) recital, Bach's Mass in B minor (Herreweghe), Mozart's Requiem (Herreweghe), Rossini's Petite Messe Solonnelle (Creed), Schumann's Der Rose Pilgerfahrt (Creed), Telemann's Orpheus (Jacobs), Haydn's Creation (Spehring) and Seasons (Weil), Bach's Christmas Oratorio (Rilling), Brahms Requiem (Mehta), Schoenberg's Jakobsleiter (Gielen), Bach's Cantatas 213 and 214, Wagner's Tannhäuser (Barenboim), Bach's Matthäus-Passion (Chailly) and Johannes-Passion (Gardiner), Die Zauberflöte (Abbado) 2005, Mahler's Songs of Knaben Wunderhorn (Gielen) and Symphony No. 8 (Boulez and Gielen), Beethoven Symphony No. 9 (Chailly and Stenz), recital of Schoenberg, Gielen and Busoni (Kehring and Salemkour). *Honours:* First Prize, Bundeswettbewerb Gesang, Berlin 1992, 1994, Meistersingerwettbewerb Nürnberg 1995, Prix Davidoff 1995, Int. Brahms Soc. Schleswig-Holstein Brahms Prize 1995, int. competition prizes include ARD and Neue Stimmen 1996, Konzertexamen 2000. *Current Management:* c/o Askonas Holt Ltd, Lincoln House, 300 High Holborn, London, WC1V 7JH, England. *Telephone:* (20) 7400-1714. *Fax:* (20) 7400-1799. *E-mail:* jane.balmer@askonasholt.co.uk. *Website:* www.askonasholt.co.uk. *Current Management:* c/o Künstlersekretariat am Gasteig, Rosenheimer str. 52, 81669 Munich, Germany. *Telephone:* (89) 44488790. *E-mail:* elisabeth.ehlers@ks-gasteig.de. *Website:* www.ks-gasteig.de. *Address:* Hochschule für Musik Karlsruhe, Postfach 6040, 76040 Karlsruhe, Germany (office). *Telephone:* (721) 66290 (office). *Fax:* (721) 6629266 (office). *E-mail:* info@mueller-brachmann.com (office). *Website:* www.hfm-karsruhe.de (office); www.mueller-brachmann.com.

MÜLLER-LORENZ, Wolfgang; singer (tenor); b. 24 Nov. 1946, Cologne, Germany. *Education:* studied in Cologne, studied with Hans Hopf. *Career:* sang as baritone at the Mannheim Opera 1972; engagements at Munich, Nuremburg, Karlsruhe, Frankfurt and Mannheim as Papageno, Rossini's Figaro and Dvořák's Jacobin; sang at the Graz Opera from 1980 as Lohengrin, Cavardossi, Calaf and Loge; Siegmund and Siegfried in Ring Cycle 1989; sang with the Deutsche Oper Berlin on tour to Washington 1989, and as Bacchus in the original version of Ariadne auf Naxos at the Landestheater, Salzburg 1991; other roles have included Otello, Dimitri in Boris Godunov, Parsifal, The Marquis in Lulu, Erik, Herman and Fra Diavolo, Zürich Opera 1989; season 2000–01 as Tannhäuser at the Munich Staatsoper and Tristan at Covent Garden; frequent concert appearances, notably in contemporary works.

MÜLLER-MOLINARI, Helga; singer (mezzo-soprano); b. 28 March 1948, Pfaffenhofen, Bavaria, Germany. *Education:* studied with Felicie Huni-Mihaczek in Munich and with Giulietta Simionato in Rome. *Career:* sang at Saarbrucken 1972–73; La Scala, Milan 1975 in L'Enfant et Les Sortilèges, Piccola Scala 1979 in Vivaldi's Tito Manlio; further appearances at the Salzburg Festival, as Annina 1983, Barcelona, as Cherubino 1984, Turin as Carmen 1988 and Monte Carlo, Portrait de Manon by Massenet 1989; roles in operas by Rossini, Mozart and other composers at Nancy, Dublin, Pesaro and elsewhere; Trieste 1991 as Werther. *Recordings include:* Der Rosenkavalier, Ariadne auf Naxos, Mozart Requiem, Bruckner Te Deum, Oronte by Cesti, Monteverdi Madrigals; Handel Partenope; L'Arcadia in Brenta by Galuppi, Rossini's Aureliano in Palmira and La Gazza Ladra.

MÜLLER-SCHOTT, Daniel; German cellist; b. Nov. 1976, Munich. *Education:* studied with Walter Nothas, Heinrich Schiff, Steven Isserlis. *Career:* performed with orchestras, including New York Philharmonic, Philadelphia Orchestra, Baltimore Symphony, Boston Symphony, Chicago Symphony, Oslo Philharmonic, Rundfunk Sinfonieorchester Berlin, Hamburg Philharmonie, Munich Philharmonie, Orchestre National de France, Orchestre de Paris, Orchestra Philharmonique de Monte Carlo, Netherlands Philharmonic, BBC Philharmonic, London Philharmonic, City of Birmingham Symphony, New Japan Philharmonic, Spanish National Orchestra; chamber music pnrs have included Anne-Sophie Mutter, Sir André Previn, Lars Vogt, Steven Isserlis, Robert Kulek, Nicholas Angelich, Jonathan Bliss, Renaud Capuçon, Julia Fischer, Olli Mustonen, Christian Tetzlaff, Jonathan Gilad, Viviane Hagner, Daniel Hope, Jean-Yves Thibaudet, with Fauré Quartet, Quatuor Ebène, Vogler Quartet; festival appearances include Schleswig-Holstein, Rheingau, Schwetzingen and Mecklenburg-Vorpommern, Lucerne, Ravinia, Saratoga, Vancouver Chamber Music Festival, City of London Festival; world premiere performances include a piano trio by Matthias Pintscher (with Julia Fischer and Jean-Yves Thibaudet, Frankfurt), Olli Mustonen's Sonata for cello and piano (with Olli Mustonen, Hamburg), Sebastian Currier's Sonata for cello and piano (with Robert Kulek). *Recordings include:* Bach, Six Suites for Violoncello solo 2000, Debussy/Poulenc/Franck, Music for Cello and Piano (with Robert Kulek) 2002, Haydn, Concertos Nos 1 and 2/Beethoven Romances Nos 1 and 2 2003; Khachaturian, Concerto for Cello and Orchestra (with Arabella Steinbacher) 2004, Joseph Joachim Raff, Cello Concertos 2004, Schumann, Works for Cello and Piano (with Robert Kulek) 2005, Mozart, Klaviertrios (with Anne-Sophie Mutter, André Previn) 2006, Schubert, Streichquintett D956/D87 (with Vogler Quartett) 2006, Mendelssohn/Bartholdy, The Piano Trios 1 and 2 (with Julia Fischer, Jonathan Gilad) 2006, Elgar/Walton, Cello Concertos (with Oslo Philharmonic Orchestra, André Previn) 2006, Brahms Double Concerto for Violin and Cello 2007; Bach Gamba Sonatas (with Angela Hewitt) 2007, Schubert Der Hirt auf dem Felsen/Octet D 803 2007, Shostakovich Cello Concertos No. 1 & 2 2008; Beethoven Cello Sonatas Op.5 Nos 1&2 (with Angela Hewitt) 2008, Schumann/Volkmann Cello Concertos, Strauss Romance, Bruch Kol Nidrei 2009, Beethoven Cello Sonatas Vol.2 Op.102 No. 1 and No. 2 Variations op.66 (with Angela Hewitt) 2010, Britten The Cello Suites 2011, Prokofiev Britten The Cello Symphonies 2012. *Honours:* Anne-Sophie Mutter Foundation scholarship; first prize Int. Tchaikovsky Competition for Young Musicians, Moscow. *Current Management:* c/o Anke Kienitz-Kirk, Kulturmanagement, Schubertstr. 2, Vaterstetten 85591, Germany. *Telephone:* (8106) 899565. *Fax:* (8106) 899566. *E-mail:* anke@kienitz-kirk.de. *Website:* www.thecellist.com.

MULLIGAN, Brian; American singer (baritone). *Education:* Eastman School of Music, Juilliard School, Yale Univ. *Career:* debut Metropolitan Opera in Die Frau ohne Schatten season 2003–04, later as Fiorello in Il Barbiere di Siviglia; other roles include Malatesta in Don Pasquale at Palm Beach Opera, Gianni Schicchi at Oregon Lyric Opera, Marcello in La Bohème with Wolf Trap Opera, Silvio in I Pagliacci with New Zealand's Auckland Philharmonic, Don Giovanni with Wolf Trap Opera and Juilliard Opera Center, Masetto at New York City Opera, Prometheus in Die Vögel, Capulet in Roméo et Juliette at the Spoleto USA Festival, Ford in Falstaff at Japan's Saito Kinen Festival, Jake Wallace in La Fanciulla del West with New York City Opera, Count Almaviva in Le Nozze di Figaro and Der Kaiser von Atlantis at the Los Angeles Philharmonic, Ravinia Festival, and Juilliard Orchestra in New York; 2007–08 season: Marcello in La Bohème New York City Opera and Houston Grand Opera, Schaunard in La Bohème under Plácido Domingo and Melot in David Hockney's Tristan und Isolde for Los Angeles Opera, Sharpless in Madama Butterfly at the Metropolitan Opera and Eugene Onegin at Lyric Opera of Chicago; several roles with San Francisco opera 2014–15 including Sharpless in Madame Butterfly, Marcello in La Boheme, Ashton in Lucia di Lammermoor. *Honours:* Richard Tucker Career Grant, Sara Tucker Study

Grant, Winner Licia Albanese/ Puccini Foundation competition 2002, George London Prize 2003, Liederkranz competition 2004, Int. Hans Gabor Belvedere Vocal Competition 2006. *Current Management:* c/o Matthew Horner, IMG Artists, Carnegie Hall Tower, 152 West 57th Street, 5th Floor, New York, NY 10019, USA. *Telephone:* (212) 994-3500. *Fax:* (212) 994-3550. *E-mail:* mhorner@imgartists.com. *Website:* www.imgartists.com.

MULLOVA, Viktoria; Russian violinist; b. 27 Nov. 1959, Moscow; d. of Yuri Mullov and Raissa Mullova; one s. two d. *Education:* studied in Moscow at Cen. Music School and Moscow Conservatory under Leonid Kogan. *Career:* left USSR 1983; has appeared with most major orchestras and conductors and at int. festivals. *Recordings include:* Beethoven Violin Concerto, Mendelssohn Violin Concerto with the Orchestre Revolutionnaire et Romantique, John Eliot Gardiner, Mozart Violin Concertos Nos 1, 3 & 4, Orchestra of the Age of Enlightenment, Vivaldi Violin Concertos (Diapason D'Or of the Year 2005) 2005, Recital (with Katia Labèque) 2006, Bach's Six Solo Sonatas and Partitas 2009, The Peasant Girl 2011, Bach: Concertos 2013. *Honours:* First Prize, Sibelius Competition, Helsinki 1980, Gold Medal, Tchaikovsky Competition, Moscow 1982. *Website:* www.askonasholt.co.uk/artists/instrumentalists/violin/viktoria-mullova. *E-mail:* info@viktoriamullova.com (office). *Website:* www.viktoriamullova.com.

MUMELTER, Martin; Austrian violinist and academic; *Professor of Violin and Head of Institute for Contemporary Music, University Mozarteum, Salzburg;* b. 12 May 1948, Innsbruck, Austria; m. Magdalena Pattis; two s. two d. *Education:* Konservatorium Innsbruck, Philadelphia Coll. of Performing Arts, USA. *Career:* mainly with 20th century music and Wiener Symphoniker, Staatskapelle Berlin, Radio Symphony Orchestra Vienna, Symphony Orchestra des Bayerischen Rundfunks, Bamberger Symphoniker, RTL-Luxemburg, Mozarteum Orchestra Salzburg; appearances at Musikbiennale Berlin, Bregenzer Festspiele, Sagra Musicale Umbra, Edinburgh Fringe Festival, Festwochen der Alten Musik Innsbruck; recitals include New York at Merkin Hall and Carnegie Recital Hall 1983, 1987; Prof. of Violin and Dir of Orchestra, Konservatorium Innsbruck 1971–75; Prof. of Violin and Head, Inst. for Contemporary Music, Univ. Mozarteum, Salzburg 1986–. *Recordings:* 200 radio recordings; albums: complete Ives Sonatas (with Herbert Henck, piano), chamber music by Ives, Cage, Bartók; Violin Concertos by Schoenberg, Berg, B. A. Zimmermann, Schnittke, Duenser. *Publications:* Ums Leben spielen 1994, Proust for President! 2004, Standardfragen zum Violinunterricht 2009, several radio plays (for Austrian Radio and SRG Zürich). *Honours:* finalist, Gaudeamus Competition, Rotterdam 1971, Preis der Kritik Musikbiennale Berlin 1979, Berlanda Preis des Landes Tirol 1985. *Address:* Pizachw. 84D, 6073 Sistrans, Austria (office). *Website:* www.moz.ac.at (office).

MUMFORD, Jeffrey Carlton; American composer and academic; *Distinguished Professor, Lorain County Community College;* b. 22 June 1955, Washington; m.; one d. *Education:* Univ. of California at Irvine and San Diego, studied in Maryland with Lawrence Moss and in New York with Elliott Carter. *Career:* works extensively performed in USA and abroad, including performances at the Library of Congress, Aspen Music Festival, Bang on a Can Music Festival, Seattle Chamber Music Festival, Purcell Room, London, Helsinki Festival, Musica Nel Nostro Tempo Festival, Milan and the Musikverein, Vienna, and by Saint Paul Chamber Orchestra; Meet the Composer/Nat. Endowment for the Arts Commissioning US Program 1996; Sonia and Louis Rothschild for the Opus 3 Trio 1998; Contemporary Music Forum and Philip Berlin 1999; Artist-in-Residence, Bowling Green State Univ. 1999–2000; numerous comms, including those from Duo Harpverk, the Sphinx Consortium of 8 American Orchestras, Cincinnati Symphony Orchestra, Chicago Symphony, Nat. Symphony Orchestra (two) Cleveland Orchestra, Radio Station WCLV Cleveland (two), Argento Chamber Ensemble, Verge Ensemble/Nat. Gallery of Art; mem. Nat. Acad. of Recording Arts and Sciences. *Compositions include:* Fragments from the Surrounding Evening, A Flower in Folding Shadows for piano four hands, Linear Cycles VII for solo violin, Echoes in a Cloud Box for violin and cello, Jewels Beyond the Mist, Diamonds Suspended in a Galaxy of Clouds for soprano solo, Lullaby for soprano and piano, In Forests of Evaporating Dawns, A Pond Within the Drifting Dusk, As the Air Softens in Dusklight for orchestra 1994, Within a Cloudburst of Echoing Brightness for orchestra 1995, A Still Radiance Within Dark Air for piano solo, flute, clarinet, violin, violoncello 1996, A Layer of Vivid Stillness for cello solo and 12 cellos 1996, Ringing Fields Enveloping Blue for cello and piano, A Window of Resonant Light for cello, piano and percussion 1997, In Afternoons of Deep and Amplified Air for string quartet 1998, A Distance of Unfolding Light for orchestra 2000, Billowing Pockets Brightly Layered for cello and chamber orchestra 2000, As a Spray of Reflected Meadowlight Informs the Air for alto saxophone, violin and percussion 2000, Undiluted Days for piano trio 2000, A Precious Continuity is a Day Expanding 2001, Through the Filtering Dawn of Spreading Daybright 2001, Wending for solo viola 2001, A Landscape of Interior Resonances for solo piano 2001, Revisiting Variazioni Elegiaci for solo viola 2001, Amid the Light of Quickening Memory for orchestra 2002, The Promise of the Far Horizon for string quartet 2002, A Focused Expanse of Evolving Experience for flute, violin, viola, violoncello and piano 2003, Toward the Deepening Stillness Beyond Visible Light (piano quintet) 2004, An Evolving Romance for flute and piano 2005, Eight Musings… Revisiting memories for solo violin 2005, An Expanding Distance of Multiple Voices for solo violin 2005, Through Dancing Echoes Spreading Softly for orchestra 2005, The Comfort of his Voice 2006, In

the Community of Encompassing Hours for piano trio 2006, Two Haiku Settings: of Place and Love for violoncello and percussion 2006, . . . and symphonies of deepening light … expanding … ever cavernous, for orchestra 2008, in soft echoes … a world awaits, for string trio 2008, Three Rhapsodies for cello and strings 2009–10, Through a Stillness Brightening for violin and seven instruments 2011, A Dance into Reflected Daylight for orchestra 2012, Eight Aspects of Appreciation II for violin and cello 2012, Still Air for piano quartet 2013. *Publications:* contrib. to Quadrivium Music Press, Perspectives of New Music. *Honours:* Guggenheim Fellowship, Minnesota Composers' Forum Award, American Music Center Award, Alice M. Ditson Fund Award, Ohio Arts Council Individual Artist Fellowship 2002, American Acad. of Arts and Letters Award in Music 2003, Ohio Arts Council Individual Excellence Award 2006. *Address:* 22 King Street, Oberlin, OH (home); c/o Theodore Presser Co., 588 North Gulph Road, King of Prussia, PA 19406, USA (office). *Telephone:* (440) 774-1583 (home). *E-mail:* jmdc@oberlin.net (home). *Website:* www.jeffreymumford.com.

MUMMA, Gordon; American composer, writer and academic; b. 30 March 1935, Framingham, MA. *Career:* composer and performer of electro-acoustic and instrumental music with performances and recordings in North and South America, Europe and Japan; television and film performances, Germany and USA; visiting lecturer, various colls and univs; composer and musician, Sonic Arts Union, New York, and Merce Cunningham Dance Co. 1966–74; Prof. of Music, Univ. of California, Santa Cruz 1975–95, Prof. Emeritus 1995–; Visiting Prof. of Music, Univ. of California, San Diego 1985–87; mem. Soc. for Ethnomusicology, BMI. *Compositions include:* Music from the Venezia Space Theatre, Dresden Interleaf 1945, Mesa, Hornpipe, Schoolwork, Cybersonic Cantilevers, Pontpoint, Than Particle for percussion and digital computer 1985, Epifont for tape 1985, Begault Meadow Sketches for tape 1987, Songs Without Words 1995. *Publications:* contrib. to numerous books and journals, including James Klosty's Merce Cunningham, Appleton and Perera's Development and Practice of Electronic Music, Gilbert Chase's Roger Reynolds: A Portrait, Journal of Audio Engineering Society, Darmstadt Beitrage zur neue Musik, Neuland I, Sound Recording (article in The New Grove Dictionary of American Music) 1986. *Address:* c/o Porter College, University of California, Santa Cruz, CA 95064, USA.

MUNDT, Richard; singer (bass); b. 8 Sept. 1936, Illinois, USA. *Education:* studied in New York and Vienna. *Career:* debut at Saarbrucken 1962, as the Commendatore in Don Giovanni; appearances at Kiel, Dortmund, Darmstadt, Graz, Liège and the Spoleto Festival; American engagements at the New York City Opera, San Francisco, Portland, Chicago and Cincinnati; other roles have included Mozart's Osmin, Don Giovanni, Figaro and Sarastro, Rocco, Arkel in Pelléas et Mélisande, Ramphis, King Philip, Padre Guardiano and Wagner's Marke, Daland, Fasolt, Pogner, Hunding and Landgrave.

MUNI, Nicholas; American stage director; b. 1960. *Career:* Artistic Dir, Tulsa Opera, 1988–97; has directed over 150 opera productions with leading US companies; Season 1989–90, with Il Trovatore at Seattle, transferring to Houston, Toronto and Vancouver; French version of Verdi's opera at Tulsa, with new production of The Juniper Tree by Philip Glass and Robert Moran; New York City Opera debut with La Traviata, 1991; world premiere of Frankenstein the Modern Prometheus, by Libby Larsen, for Minnesota Opera; US premiere of Rossini's Armida at Tulsa, 1992; complete version of Lulu for Canadian Opera and Ariadne auf Naxos at Opera Theater of St Louis; world premiere of Moran's The Shining Princess at Minnesota, 1993; staging of Norma for Seattle and Houston, Los Angeles, 1996; Artistic Dir, Cincinnati Opera 1997–2005, produced Jenůfa there 1998; Distinguished Artist in Residence in Opera Univ. of Cincinnati Coll.-Conservatory of Music 2006. *Address:* c/o Cincinnati Opera, Music Hall, 1243 Elm Street, Cincinnati, OH 45202, USA.

MUNKITTRICK, Mark; singer (bass); b. 1951, Boston, MA, USA. *Education:* Fresno State Coll., California. *Career:* sang in Carnegie Hall concert performances of Donizetti's Gemma di Vergy and Puccini's Edgar 1976–77; New York City Opera 1977, as Daland and Pogner; guest appearances in Washington, Baltimore, Los Angeles and Atlanta, as Leporello, Alfonso, Raimondo and Monteverdi's Seneca; sang at Karlsruhe 1978–87, as Mephistopheles, Rocco, Basilio, Kecal, Banquo, King Philip, Ramphis, the Landgrave in Tannhäuser and Fafner; Madrid 1984, as Handel's Giulio Cesare; Dresden Staatsoper 1989 as Morosus in Die schweigsame Frau; Member of the Stuttgart Staatsoper from 1985; guest engagements throughout Germany and Europe; other roles include Arthur in The Lighthouse by Maxwell Davies, Kaspar and Henry VIII in Anna Bolena; sang Taddeo in L'Italiana in Algeri at Stuttgart 1996; sang Angelotti in Tosca at Stuttgart 1998; Poet in Donizetti's Le Convenienze Teatrali 2001; wide concert repertory including bass solo in the Missa Solemnis. *Recordings include:* Gemma di Vergy and Edgar.

MUNOZ, Daniel; singer (tenor); b. 1951, Buenos Aires, Argentina. *Education:* studied in Buenos Aires. *Career:* sang at the Teatro Colón Buenos Aires from 1979, Teatro de la Zarzuela Madrid from 1980; studied further in Milan and sang from 1982 at opera houses in Spain, Portugal and South America; Nancy Opera 1983, as Cavaradossi, Liège 1986 as Pinkerton and the Berne Stadttheater 1988; sang Cornil Schut in Pittore Fiamminghi at Trieste and Calaf at the Szeged Festival, Hungary 1991; other roles include Don José, Faust, Werther, Don Carlos and Des Grieux in Manon Lescaut; sang Andrea

Chénier at Buenos Aires 1996; Canio in Pagliacci at Cape Town 1998; sang Verdi's Riccardo at Budapest 2000; frequent concert appearances.

MUNRO, Timothy (Tim) Craig; Australian musician (flutes); b. 1978, Brisbane. *Education:* Univ. of Queensland School of Music, Queensland Conservatorium of Music, Oberlin Conservatory, USA. *Career:* mem. contemporary music ensemble eighth blackbird 2006–15, ensemble commissioned and performed new works by composers such as Steve Reich, Frederic Rzewski, Jennifer Higdon, Stephen Hartke and Steven Mackey, and performed with orchestras including Cleveland Orchestra, Toronto Symphony and Atlanta Symphony at venues including Carnegie Hall, Barbican in London, Sydney Opera House and Kennedy Center; residencies at univs and conservatories, including Univs of Richmond and Chicago, Oberlin Conservatory, Queensland Conservatorium, Southern Methodist Univ., Colburn School and Curtis Inst. of Music; Music Dir Sila by John Luther Adams, Brisbane Festival 2015; featured artist, Australian Flute Festival 2015. *Recordings:* Steve Reich: Double Sextet 2010, On a Wire 2011, Steven Mackey's Lonely Motel: Music from Slide (Grammy Award for Best Small Ensemble Performance) 2011, meanwhile (Grammy Award for Best Chamber Music/Small Ensemble Performance) 2012, one two three (solo album) 2014. *Honours:* winner (with eighth blackbird) American Music Center Trailblazer Award 2007, Meet the Composer Award 2007. *Current Management:* David Lieberman Artists, PO Box 10368, Newport Beach, CA 92658, USA. *Telephone:* 3124800853 (office). *E-mail:* timcmunro@gmail.com (office). *Website:* www.eighthblackbird.org (office).

MUNTEAN, Mihail; Moldovan singer (tenor); b. 15 Aug. 1943, Kriva, Briceni; s. of Ion Muntean and Elizaveta Muntean; m. Rosentul Galina Andrian 1969; one s. one d. *Education:* Kishinev Inst. of Arts, La Scala, Italy. *Career:* Prin. Tenor with Moldovan State Acad. Theatre of Opera and Ballet 1971–, Gen. Dir 1996–97; Prof. Chair of Vocal Arts, Music Acad. of Moldova 1993–; Provost Art Inst., Mil. Acad. Stefan Cel Mare 1996–; Pres. Centre for Devt and Support of Culture Mihai Munteanu 1998–. *Opera roles include:* Lensky in Eugene Onegin, Riccardo in Un Ballo in Maschera, Don Carlo in Don Carlo, Cavaradossi in Tosca, Calaf in Turandot, Hermann in The Queen of Spades, Radames in Aida, Turiddu in Cavalleria Rusticana, Otello in Otello, Canio in Pagliacci, Manrico in Il Trovatore, Samson in Samson et Dalila, Ismael in Nabucco, Don José in Carmen, Don Alvaro in La Forza del Destino, Pinkerton in Madame Butterfly; performances and concerts throughout the world. *Honours:* Hon. Prof., Modern Humanitarian Inst. Moscow 1997–; Dr hc (Univ. of Arts, Iasi, Romania), (Univ. Ovidius Constanţa, Romania); Verdi Award 1978, USSR People's Artist 1986, Moldovan State Award 1984, Award of the Republic 1993. *Address:* 16 N. Iorga str., Apt 13, 2012 Chişinău, Moldova (office). *Telephone:* 911-7577 (office); (2) 23-75-19. *Fax:* (2) 23-75-19. *E-mail:* mihai.muntean@mail.ru (home).

MURAIL, Tristan; French composer and academic; b. 11 March 1947, Le Havre. *Education:* Ecole Nat. des Langues Orientales Vivantes, Institut d'Etudes Politiques et Sciences Economiques, Paris, Conservatoire de Paris, studied with Olivier Messiaen. *Career:* pioneer in spectral music and computer-assisted composition; co-f. music collective L'Itinéraire 1973; Prof. of Composition, IRCAM, Paris 1990–97; Prof. of Composition, Columbia Univ., New York 1997–2011. *Compositions include:* orchestral: Gondwana 1980, Sillages 1985, Time and Again 1985, Le Partage des eaux 1995, Terre d'ombre 2004, Contes cruels for two electric guitars and orchestra 2007, Les Sept paroles for choir, orchestra and electronics 2010, Le Désenchantement du monde (piano concerto) 2012, Reflections/Reflets 2013; large ensemble: Couleur de Mer for 15 instruments 1969, Mémoire/Erosion for horn and nine instruments 1976, Ethers for flute and five instruments 1978, Désintégrations for 17 instruments and electronics 1982, Allégories for six instruments and electronics 1990, Serendib for 22 instruments 1992, L'Esprit des dunes for 11 instruments and electronics 1994, Le Lac for 19 instruments 2001, Pour adoucir le cours du temps for 18 instruments and electronics 2005, Légendes urbaines for 22 instruments 2006, Liber Fulguralis for nine instruments and electronics 2008, Lachrymae for six instruments 2011, Portulan cycle for eight instruments 1998–2011; chamber music: Treize couleurs du soleil couchant for five instruments 1978, Vues aériennes for four instruments 1988, Le Fou à pattes bleues for flute and piano 1990, La Barque mystique for five instruments 1993, Bois flotté for five instruments and electronics 1996, Feuilles à travers les cloches for four instruments 1998, Winter Fragments for five instruments and electronics 2000, Les Ruines circulaires for violin and clarinet 2005, Garrigue for four instruments 2008, Paludes for five instruments 2011; solo instruments: Territoires de l'oubli for piano 1977, Tellur for guitar 1977, Vampyr! for electric guitar 1984, Attracteurs étranges for cello 1992, La Mandragore for piano 1993, Unanswered Questions for flute 1995, Les Travaux et les jours for piano 2002; choir and electronics: Amaris et dulcibus aquis 1994. *Recordings include:* Tristan Murail: Treize Couleurs du soleil couchant, Mémoire/Erosion, Couleur de mer, Allégories/Vues aériennes/Territoires de l'oubli, Winter Fragments, Gondwana/Désintégrations/Time and again, Complete Piano Music, Serendib/L'Esprit des dunes/Désintégrations. *Publications:* numerous articles in professional journals. *Honours:* Prix de Rome 1971, Grand Prix du Disque, Acad. Charles Cros 1990, 1992, 2002, Best Contemporary Work of the Year, Soc. des auteurs, compositeurs & éditeurs de musique (SACEM) 2008, Grand Prix Del Duca, Acad. Beaux-Arts 2009. *Current Management:* c/o Editions Lemoine, 27 boulevard Beaumarchais, 75004 Paris, France. *Tele-*

phone: 1-56-68-86-74. *E-mail:* contemporain@editions-lemoine.fr. *Website:* www.henry-lemoine.com; www.tristanmurail.com; www.musicroom.com.

MURGATROYD, Andrew, BMus; British singer (tenor); b. 1955, Halifax, Yorks. *Education:* Lancaster Univ. *Career:* Lay-Clerk at Christ Church Cathedral, Oxford; currently Tenor with BBC Singers; notable concert engagements include Israel in Egypt for John Eliot Gardiner in Stuttgart, Milan, Paris, Rome, East Berlin and Turin; Handel's Esther for WDR in Cologne and Acis and Galatea for Swiss TV; Monteverdi Vespers and Alexander's Feast at Aix-en-Provence; performances of Bach's St Matthew Passion, Elgar's Coronation Ode and Mozart's Mass in C Minor with Sir David Willcocks and the Bach Choir, Royal Festival Hall; Beethoven's Missa Solemnis with the RTÉ in Dublin, Ninth Symphony with the Hanover Band, Elgar's Dream of Gerontius in Wells, Guildford and Ripon Cathedrals and York Minster; Verdi's Requiem in Salisbury and Canterbury Cathedrals, Barbican Hall and at Brighton and Flanders Festivals; Tavener's We Shall See Him As He Is with Richard Hickox and the Nat. Orchestra of Wales at the Proms; Andrea Chénier at the Concertgebouw; Tippett's Child of Our Time in Cologne; Britten's Paul Bunyan with BBC Concert Orchestra; several Christmas Gala Concerts at Royal Festival Hall, Barbican and Symphony Hall Birmingham. *Recordings include:* Beethoven's Missa Solemnis and Ninth Symphony; Monteverdi Vespers with The Sixteen and Rene Jacobs; Campra's Tancrède; Leclair Scylla et Glaucus; John Tavener, We Shall See Him As He Is; Antonio Teixeira, Te Deum, Britten's Death in Venice.

MURGU, Corneliu; Romanian singer (tenor); *Director-General, Opera Natională Timişoara;* b. 1948, Timişoara. *Education:* studied in Romania, in Florence and with Marcello del Monaco in Treviso. *Career:* debut, Wiener Staatsoper with Cavalleria Rusticana (Turiddu) 1978; other appearances include Deutsche Oper Berlin, Munich, Hamburg, Stuttgart, Düsseldorf, Zürich and Graz until 1982; Met debut with Ballo in Maschera (Riccardo) 1982; appearances in Naples, Rome and Andrea Chénier in Bonn 1982; Norma (Pollione) in Lyon, Carmen and Turandot in Caracalla, Rome 1983–85; La Scala debut with Aida (Radames) 1986; Andrea Chénier and Samson in Rio de Janeiro and Cavalleria Rusticana in Barcelona 1987–89; Otello at Opéra Bastille in Paris 1990; Cavalleria Rusticana/Pagliacci and Carmen in Rotterdam 1994–95; debut in Verona with Otello 1994; Covent Garden debut with Calaf in Turandot; retd from professional singing 2003; currently Dir-Gen., Opera Natională Timişoara. *Recordings include:* Otello with Renato Bruson, Fanciulla del West with Gwyneth Jones, Cavalleria Rusticana/Pagliacci, Carmen. *Address:* Opera Natională Timişoara, 300080 Timişoara, Marasesti str. nr. 2, Romania (office). *Telephone:* (256) 433020 (office). *Fax:* (256) 201283 (office). *E-mail:* murgule@hotmail.com (office). *Website:* www.ort .ro (office).

MURPHY, Aubrey, DipMus; violinist; b. May 1965, Dublin, Ireland. *Education:* Yehudi Menuhin School, Royal Irish Acad., Indiana Univ. at Bloomington. *Career:* guest leader with Scottish Chamber Orchestra and BBC Ulster Orchestra from 1992; Principal Violinist and guest leader, Orchestra of the Royal Opera House, Covent Garden eight years; Concertmaster, Opera Australia's Australian Opera and Ballet Orchestra, Sydney Opera House 2002–; founder mem., Utzon Ensemble; Guest Concertmaster, Eugene Onegin with ENO 2005. *Honours:* Centenary Medal of Australia for Services to Music 2002. *Address:* c/o Opera Centre, 480 Elizabeth Street, Sydney, NSW 2010, Australia (office). *E-mail:* roccaubs@aol.com (office). *Website:* www .aubreymurphy.com.

MURPHY, Emma, BMus, MMus, FTCL; British recorder player and singer (soprano). *Education:* Univ. of Birmingham, Trinity Coll. of Music, London and studied with Philip Thorby and Ashley Solomon. *Career:* founder mem., Da Camera period music ensemble; performed with The King's Consort, Ex Cathedra, Gabrieli Consort and Players, City of Birmingham Symphony Orchestra, New London Consort, New Trinity Baroque; performances of contemporary music, including with Park Lane Group and a duo with marimba; has performed at St Martin-in-the-Fields, Purcell Room, Greenwich Festival of Early Music 2006; Musical Dir, The City Carollers; tutor, Univ. of Surrey, Guildford, Dartington Int. Summer School. *Radio:* guest presenter Early Music Show (BBC Radio 3). *Recordings:* A Celtic Celebration (with Da Camera) 2006. *Publications:* Introduction to Ganassi's Fontegara and the Art of Divisions, Trouble at the Tudor Banquet. *Honours:* Countess of Munster Musical Trust Award. *Address:* Flat 4, 5 Prince Arthur Road, London, NW3 6AX, England (office). *Telephone:* (20) 7794-1684 (office). *Fax:* (20) 7794-1684 (office). *E-mail:* emma@emmamurphy.co.uk. *Website:* www.emmamurphy.co .uk.

MURPHY, Miriam, DipRAM; Irish singer (soprano); b. Tralee, Co. Kerry. *Education:* DIT Coll. of Music, Dublin, Royal Acad. of Music, Nat. Opera Studio. *Career:* started as mezzo-soprano (Dorabella) in Mozart's Così fan tutte under Sir Colin Davis and Frasquita in Bizet's Carmen; as soprano, has sung Overseer in Elektra at Edinburgh Festival, woman convict in Lady Macbeth of Mtsensk for the Royal Opera, Covent Garden, Lady Macbeth in Verdi's Macbeth, Santuzza in Cavalleria Rusticana with English Touring Opera, Elizabeth in excerpts from Verdi's Don Carlos at Royal Albert Hall and Anna Bolena at Queen Elizabeth Hall, London; engagements have included Abigaille in Nabucco (concert performance) and Santuzza in Cavalleria Rusticana for Haddo House Opera; covered and sang the role of Lady Macbeth at Royal Opera House, Covent Garden spring 2006; concert performances include Verdi's Requiem at the Barbican, London, Elijah for the Ulster

Orchestra, Beethoven's Mass in C at Nat. Concert Hall, Dublin, Mahler's Das Lied von der Erde under Sir John Eliot Gardiner for the BBC Proms and Beethoven 9th Symphony for RPO and at Barbican. *Honours:* Leverhulme Trust Award, Dame Eva Turner Award, Bayreuth Bursary, Rita Hunter Bursary, Silver Medal Int. Competition for Young Musicians, Antwerp, Winner Seattle Opera Int. Wagner Competition. *Current Management:* Hazard Chase, 25 City Road, Cambridge, CB1 1DP, England. *Telephone:* (1223) 312400. *Fax:* (1223) 460827. *E-mail:* sue.nicholls@hazardchase.co.uk. *Website:* www.hazardchase.co.uk.

MURPHY, Suzanne; Irish singer (soprano); b. 15 Oct. 1941, Limerick. *Education:* College of Music, Dublin with Veronica Dunne. *Career:* sang with WNO from 1976 as Constanze, Amelia in I Masnadieri and Un Ballo in Maschera, Elisabeth de Valois, Leonora in Il Trovatore, Elvira in Ernani and I Puritani, Violetta, Norma, Lucia di Lammermoor and Musetta; sang Constanze and Donna Anna for English National Opera; Donna Anna and the soprano roles in Les Contes d'Hoffmann for Opera North and Constanze for Scottish Opera; German debut 1985, as Norma in a concert performance of Bellini's opera in Munich; returned 1988 for Amelia in Un Ballo in Maschera; Vienna Staatsoper debut 1987, as Electra in Idomeneo; invited to return 1988–89 (Armenian Gala Benefit Concert); sang Reiza in Oberon at Lyon and Donna Anna at the Aix-en-Provence Festival; North American engagements include Norma at the New York City Opera, Amelia in Ballo, Elvira in I Puritani and Lucia in Vancouver, Fiordiligi, Ophelia in Hamlet and Violetta in Pittsburgh; sang Alice Ford in the Peter Stein production of Falstaff for Welsh National Opera (repeated in New York and Milan 1989); sang Norma for the Dublin Grand Opera Society 1989, Hanna Glawari in The Merry Widow for Scottish Opera; title role in La Fanciulla del West for Welsh National Opera, 1991; Electra in Idomeneo at the Albert Hall (Proms) and in Wales with WNO, 1991; season 1992 with Elvira in Ernani and Tosca, in new productions for WNO; concert appearances in Austria, Sweden, Denmark, Belgium and Portugal; sang Leonore in Fidelio on South Bank, London, 1989 and at Belfast, 1996; sang the Kostelnička in Jenůfa at Geneva, 2001. *Current Management:* Ingpen & Williams Ltd, 7 St George's Court, 131 Putney Bridge Road, London, SW15 2PA, England.

MURRAY, Ann; Irish singer (mezzo-soprano); *Professor of Singing, Royal Academy of Music;* b. 27 Aug. 1949, Dublin; m. Philip Langridge 1981; one s. *Education:* Royal Northern Coll. of Music, London Opera Centre with Frederick Cox. *Career:* debut at Aldeburgh with Scottish Opera as Alceste in the opera by Gluck 1974; US debut with the New York City Opera as Sextus in La Clemenza di Tito 1979; fmrly performed with ENO, Royal Opera; many concert appearances, including the London Proms, European recital tours, and has performed in festivals at Aldeburgh, Edin., Munich, Salzburg, Wexford, Glyndebourne, Vienna; recital at Song Fest (art song festival), Los Angeles 2015; roles in opera include Idamante, Octavian, Beatrice, Xerxes, Brangaene, Myrtale (Thaïs), Queen Laodicea (Eritrea), Siebel (Faust), Tebaldo (I Capuleti e i Montecchi), the Child (L'Enfant et les Sortilèges), Dorabella (Così fan tutte), Cecilio (Lucio Silla), the Composer (Ariadne auf Naxos), Sifare (Mitridate), Nicklausse (Les Contes d'Hoffmann), Minerva (Il Ritorno d'Ulisse), Ruggiero (Alcina), title role in Giulio Cesare, and roles in Mary Stuart, Le Comte Ory, Cenerentola, Ascanio, Cherubino, The Beggar's Opera, Alceste, Ariodante; Prof. of Singing, Royal Acad. of Music 2010–. *Honours:* Hon. DBE 2002; Bavarian Order of Merit 2005. *Address:* Department of Voice, Royal Academy of Music, London, NW1 5HT, England (office). *Telephone:* (20) 7873-7384 (office). *E-mail:* voice@ram.ac.uk (office); calasanctius@aol.com. *Website:* www.ram.ac.uk (office).

MURRAY, John Horton, BA, MM; American singer (tenor); b. 10 Oct. 1961, Brunswick, Germany; s. of William Murray and Nancy Adams; m. Louise Sweet; three c. *Education:* State Univ. of NY, Potsdam, Curtis Inst., Philadelphia, Lyric Opera, Chicago Center for Young Artists, Metropolitan Opera Lindemann Young Artist Devt Program. *Career:* debut as David in Meistersinger at Spoleto Festival 1992; performances of Stolzing, Don José, The Emperor in Frau Ohne Schatten and Aeneas in Les Troyens at the Metropolitan Opera 1995–2004; Don José, Verona Arena 1996; Stolzing and Bacchus, Lyric Opera of Chicago 1998; Menelaus in Strauss's Ägyptische Helena, Royal Opera, Festival Hall, London 1998; Bacchus in Santa Fe 1999 and Menelaus 2001; Apollo and Menelaus at Deutsche Oper Berlin, Parsifal in Edinburgh, Lohengrin at the Liceo, and La Scala debut as Bacchus 2000; Laca in Jenůfa for Geneva Opera, Paul in Tote Stadt for New York City Opera and Stolzing at RAI Orchestra Sinfonica Naz. 2001–02; Bacchus at Liceo and Rienzi at Antiken Festspiele, Trier 2002–03; Emperor for Metropolitan Opera, Bacchus at Seattle Opera 2003–04; Albrecht in Mathis der Maler for Radio Symphony Orchestra Vienna 2005, Otello, Lohengrin, Parsifal, Canio, Alvaro, Kaiser, Siegmund in Mannheim 2006–08, Bacchus at Washington Nat. Opera 2009, Stolzing at Cincinnati Opera 2010, Lohengrin at Buenos Aires 2011. *Recordings:* The Magician in Menotti's Medium, Wagner: Scenes from Lohengrin and Siegfried, Scenes from Tristan und Isolde. *Honours:* Nat. Inst. for Music Theater Prizes, George London Award 1988, Musician's Emergency Fund Winner 1990, Liederkranz Wagner Award 1991, Grammy Award for Secondary Soloist (Die Meistersinger von Nürnberg, conducted by Sir George Solti) 1997, New York City Opera Artist of the Year Contemporary Music 2001. *Current Management:* c/o Guy Barzilay Artists, 420 West 25th Street, Suite 4, New York, NY 10001, USA. *Telephone:* (212) 741-6118. *Fax:* (212) 741-2558. *E-mail:* guy@guybarzilayartists.com. *E-mail:* johnhortonmurray@aol.com (home). *Website:* www.johnhortonmurray.com.

MURRAY, Niall; singer (baritone); b. 22 April 1948, Dublin, Ireland; m. Barbara F. M. Murray; one d. *Education:* Royal Acad. of Music, Dublin. *Career:* debut as boy soprano in pantomime, Dublin; appearances as Curly in Oklahoma, Dublin 1970; opera debut as Bomarzo, Coliseum, London 1976; baritone lead in musicals, including at ENO, London; television and radio broadcasts; appeared in cabaret and musicals; opera appearances include Papageno, Schaunard, Figaro in Barber of Seville, and Lescaut in Manon; sang Iago at the Basle City Theatre 1988 (as Mario di Mario); sang Falstaff at Lübeck 1999. *Recordings:* Niall Murray Sings Irish Songs, Danilo, The Merry Widow, Robert in La Fille du Régiment.

MURRAY, William; singer (baritone); b. 13 March 1935, Schenectady, NY, USA. *Education:* Adelphi Univ., studied in Rome. *Career:* debut in Spoleto 1957, in Il segreto di Susanna by Wolf-Ferrari; appearances in Munich, Salzburg, Amsterdam and Frankfurt; mem., Deutsche Oper Berlin from 1969; sang Dallapiccola's Ulisse at La Scala 1970, and took part in the premiere of Nabokov's Love Labour's Lost, Brussels 1973; other roles include Don Giovanni, Verdi's Macbeth, Luna, Rigoletto and Germont, Puccini's Scarpia and Lescaut, Wagner's Wolfram and parts in We Come to the River by Henze, Orff's Antigonae and Paisiello's Re Theodoro in Venezia. *Honours:* Fulbright Scholarship 1956, Kammersänger of the Deutsche Oper Berlin.

MURTO, Matti Yrjö Juhani, Dip. of Music Theory, LicPhil; Finnish composer and academic; *Manager, Modus Musiikki Oy;* b. 12 July 1947, Tampere; m.; one s. one d. *Education:* Sibelius Acad., Univ. of Helsinki. *Career:* Headmaster, Music Conservatory Ostro Bothnia 1980–85; Gen. Man. Tampere Philharmonic Orchestra 1985–87; Headmaster, Savolinna Music School 1991–2000; Lecturer, Cen. Ostrobothnia Conservatory and Univ. of Cen. Ostrobothnia for Applied Sciences 2001–10; Man. Modus Musiikki Oy; freelance composer, arranger and musician. *Compositions include:* for orchestra: Polskafantasioita jousille (Reel Fantasies for Strings) 1980, Ultima Thule, suite for string orchestra 1982, Revontulet (Aurora Borealis), prelude for orchestra 1983, The Fiddlers for strings 1988, Soittoniekat, suite for string orchestra 1988–89; for soloist and orchestra: Concertino for violin and strings, Concerto for accordion and chamber orchestra 1999; chamber works: Quintet for accordion and string quartet 2007–08, String Quartet No. 1 2009, Sarja bandoneonille ja decacordelle (Suite for bandoneon and decacorde) 2011, Kaksi Kalevalaista näkyä (Two Visions from Kalevala) for clarinet and accordion 2012; for solo instrument: Partita for accordion 1998,Fennica, fantasia bandoneonille for bandoneon 2007, Partita per organo for organ 2013, Suomalainen sarja harmonikalle (Finnish suite for accordion) 2014; vocal and choral works: Joulukantaatti (Christmas Cantata) for mixed choir, soprano and baritone soloists, and orchestra 1996, Kaksi laulua V.A. koskenniemen runoihin 2007, Kolme laulua Kantelettaren runoihin for soprano, lapinrumpu (Sami drum) and accordion 2014–15; various orchestrations and arrangements. *Recordings include:* New Finnish Chamber Music 1997, A Flight Beyond Time 2001. *Publication:* Soivat soinnut, Introduction for Harmony 1994 (fifth edn 2013). *Address:* Modus Musiikki Oy, Puistokatu 6, 39500 Ikaalinen, Finland (office). *Telephone:* (40) 1698484 (office). *Fax:* (3) 4589021 (office). *E-mail:* info@modusmusiikki.fi (office); matti.murto@ippnet.fi (home). *Website:* www.modusmusiikki.fi (office).

MUSACCHIO, Martina; singer (soprano); b. 11 Feb. 1956, Aosta, Italy. *Education:* studied in Geneva with Ursula Buckel and in Florence, Munich and Zürich. *Career:* sang at Zürich Opera 1981–82, Lucerne 1982–85; guest appearances at Geneva, Düsseldorf, Venice, Mantua, Lausanne and Ravenna; roles have included Mozart's Susanna, Zerlina, Despina, Pamina and Papagena, Donizetti's Norina and Adina, Martha, Micaela, Euridice, Orff's Die Kluge and Ismene in Honegger's Antigone; sang Lisetta in La Rondine at Monte Carlo 1991; concert appearances throughout Switzerland and in Hamburg, Munich, Stuttgart, Paris, Venice and Madrid, notably in baroque repertoire.

MUSGRAVE, Thea, CBE, MusDoc; British composer; b. 27 May 1928, Edinburgh, Scotland; d. of James Musgrave and Joan Musgrave (née Hacking); m. Peter Mark 1971. *Education:* Univ. of Edinburgh and Paris Conservatoire, France (under Nadia Boulanger). *Career:* Lecturer, Extra-Mural Dept, Univ. of London 1958–65; Visiting Prof., Univ. of California, Santa Barbara, USA 1970; Guggenheim Fellow 1974–75, 1982–83; Distinguished Prof., Queen's Coll., CUNY 1987–2002. *Works include:* Chamber Concertos 1, 2 & 3 1966, Concerto for Orchestra 1967, Clarinet Concerto 1968, Beauty and the Beast (ballet) 1969, Night Music 1969, Horn Concerto 1971, The Voice of Ariadne (chamber opera) 1972–73, Viola Concerto 1973, Space Play 1974, Mary, Queen of Scots (opera) 1976–77, A Christmas Carol (opera) 1978–79, Harriet, A Woman Called Moses 1980–84, An Occurrence at Owl Creek Bridge (radio opera) 1981, Black Tambourine for women's chorus and piano 1985, Pierrot 1985, For the Time Being for chorus 1986, The Golden Echo 1987, Narcissus 1988, The Seasons (orchestral) 1988, Rainbow (orchestral) 1990, Simón Bolívar (opera) 1993, Autumn Sonata 1993, Journey through a Japanese Landscape (marimba concerto) 1993, On the Underground (vocal) 1994, Helios (oboe concerto) 1995, Phoenix Rising (orchestral) 1997, Canta, Canta for clarinet and ensemble 1997, Lamenting with Ariadne 1999, The Mocking Bird for baritone and ensemble 2000, Pontalba (opera) 2003, Turbulent Landscapes (orchestral) 2004, Wood, Metal, Skin (concerto for percussion and orchestra) 2004, Journey into Light for soprano and orchestra 2005, Two's Company (duet for oboe and percussion) 2005, Green for string ensemble 2008, Snapshots for piano 2009, Ithaca (SATB chorus) 2010, Towards the Blue (wind quartet and string quartet) 2010; chamber music, songs, choral music, orchestral music. *Honours:* Hon. DMus (CNAA, Smith Coll., Old Dominion Univ.); Koussevitzky Award 1972, 2000. *Current Management:* c/o Paula Mlyn, A440 Arts Group, 321 West 24th Street, Suite 19C, New York, NY 10011, USA. *Telephone:* (646) 498-0103. *E-mail:* paula.mlyn@gmail.com. *Website:* www.theamusgrave.com.

MUSOLENO, Rosemary; American singer (soprano); b. 1965. *Education:* Juilliard School, New York, studied with Renata Scotto. *Career:* debut at Opéra de Lyon, as Drusilla in Monteverdi's Poppea; sang at Lyon as Mozart's Susanna, Cherubino, Servilia and Zerlina; season 1991 as Poppea at St Etienne and Spoleto, USA; Colorado Opera and Los Angeles, 1994, as Liu in Turandot; Alice Ford in Falstaff for Long Beach Opera; frequent concert appearances. *Recordings include:* Applausus by Haydn. *Website:* www.onatech.com/GMMartynuk/rosemary.

MUSTONEN, Olli; Finnish pianist, composer and conductor; b. 7 June 1967, Helsinki; s. of Seppo Mustonen and Marja-Liisa Mustonen; m. Sole Mustonen. *Education:* began studies with harpsichord, studied piano with Ralf Gothóni and Eero Heinonen, composition with Einojuhani Rautavaara. *Career:* has played with many of the world's leading orchestras; has appeared at festivals including Berlin, Hollywood Bowl, BBC Proms and Salzburg; Artistic Dir Turku Music Festival 1990–92, Ludus Mustonalis concert series; Co-founder and Dir, Helsinki Festival Orchestra; Conductor, Tapiola Sinfonietta 2003–. *Major compositions:* Fantasia (for piano and strings) 1985, Toccata (for piano, string quartet and double bass) 1989, two Nonets (for two string quartets and double bass) 1995, 2000, Triple Concerto (for three violins and orchestra) 1998, Jehkin Iivana Sonata for piano 2006, Sinuhe Sonata for solo oboe 2005–06. *Honours:* Edison Award 1992, Gramophone Award for Best Instrumental Recording 1992. *Current Management:* Hazard Chase Limited, 48-49 Russell Square, London, WC1B 4JP, England. *E-mail:* info@hazardchase.co.uk.

MUTI, Riccardo; Italian conductor; *Music Director, Chicago Symphony Orchestra*; b. 28 July 1941, Naples; s. of Domenico Muti and Gilda Sellitto; m. Cristina Mazzavillani 1969; two s. one d. *Education:* San Pietro Conservatory, Majella, Naples and Milan Conservatory of Music. *Career:* Prin. Conductor, Maggio Musicale, Florence 1969–81; Prin. Conductor, Philharmonia Orchestra, London 1973–82, Music Dir 1979–82, Conductor Laureate 1982–; Prin. Guest Conductor, Philadelphia Orchestra 1977–80, Prin. Conductor and Music Dir 1980–92, Conductor Laureate 1992–; Music Dir, La Scala, Milan 1986–2005; Prin. Conductor, Filarmonica della Scala 1988–2005; Prin. Guest Conductor Designate, New York Philharmonic; Music Dir, Chicago Symphony Orchestra 2010–; Founder Orchestra Giovanile Luigi Cherubini; concert tours in USA with Boston, Chicago and Philadelphia Orchestras; concerts at Salzburg, Edinburgh, Lucerne, Flanders and Vienna festivals; also conducted Berlin Philharmonic, Bayerische Rundfunk Sinfonie Orchester, Vienna Philharmonic, New York Philharmonic and Concertgebouw Amsterdam; opera: Florence, Munich, Covent Garden, La Scala, Ravenna, Vienna, Accad. di Santa Cecilia (Rome), Accademico Dell'Accademia Cherubini (Florence). *Honours:* Hon. mem. American Acad. of Arts & Sciences, Hon. mem. Vienna Philharmonic 2011, Hon. Dir for Life, Rome Opera 2011; Grand Golden Medal of the City of Monaco, Grand Silver Ehrenkreuz Medal (Austria), Officer Order of Merit (Germany), Verdienstkreuz (First Class, Germany) 1976, Cavaliere Gran Croce (Italy) 1991, Légion d'honneur, Hon. KBE 2000, Russian Order of Friendship 2001, Silver Medal of the Salzburg Mozarteum 2001, Knight of the Grand Cross First Class of the Order of St Gregory the Great (Holy See) 2012; Hon. PhD (Weizmann Inst. of Science); Dr hc (Pennsylvania, Philadelphia, Bologna, Urbino, Milan, Cremona, Lecce); Guido Cantelli Award 1967, Diapason d'Or, Premio Critica Discografia Italiana, Prix Académie nat. du disque 1977, Deutschen Schallplatten Prize, Bellini d'Oro, Abbiati Prize, Grand Prix du disque for La Traviata (Verdi), Requiem in C minor (Cherubini) 1982, Disco d'Oro for Music for Films, Wolf Prize 2000, Musical America Award for Musician of the Year 2010, Grammy Award for Best Classical Album (for Verdi: Requiem) 2011, Birgit Nilsson Prize 2011, Prince of Asturias Prize for the Arts 2011. *Address:* Chicago Symphony Orchestra, Symphony Center, 220 South Michigan Avenue, Chicago, IL 60604, USA (office). *E-mail:* info@riccardomuti.com (office). *Website:* www.riccardomuti.com.

MUTTER, Anne-Sophie; German violinist; b. 29 June 1963, Rheinfelden/Baden; m. 1st Dithelf Wunderlich 1989 (deceased); m. 2nd André Previn 2002 (divorced). *Education:* studied with Prof. Aida Stucki, Winterthur, Switzerland. *Career:* began musical career playing piano and violin 1969; played in Int. Music Festival, Lucerne 1976; debut with Herbert von Karajan at Pfingstfestspiele, Salzburg 1977; soloist with numerous orchestras worldwide; has given world premieres of 24 works, including works by Sebastian Currier, Henri Dutilleux, Sofia Gubaidulina, Witold Lutoslawski, Norbert Moret, Krzysztof Penderecki, Sir André Previn and Wolfgang Rihm; also plays with string trio and quartet; Guest Teacher, RAM, London 1985; est. foundation promoting gifted young string players throughout the world 1997. *Recordings include:* Mozart: Five Violin Concertos 2005, Bach, Gubaidulina: Violin Concertos (with the Trondheim Soloists) 2008, Mendelssohn's Violin Concerto 2009, Brahms: The Violin Sonatas 2010, Rihm/Currier (ECHO Klassik Award for Concerto Recording of the Year/Violin – 20th/21st Century 2012) 2011. *Honours:* Hon. Pres. Mozart Soc., Univ. of Oxford 1983; Foreign Hon. mem. American Acad. of Arts and Sciences 2013; Hon. Fellow, Keble Coll., Oxford 2015; Order of Merit (Germany and Bavaria), Großes

Österreichisches Ehrenzeichen (Austria), Chevalier, Ordre national de la Légion d'honneur 2009; Dr hc (Norwegian Univ. of Science and Tech.) 2012; four Grammy Awards, Youth Music Prize (FRG) for violin 1970, for piano 1970, for violin 1974, Artist of the Year, Deutscher Schallplattenpreis, Grand Prix Int. du Disque, Record Acad. Prize, Tokyo 1982, Internationaler Schallplattenpreis 1993, Herbert von Karajan Award 2003, International Ernst von Siemens Music Prize 2008, Leipzig Mendelssohn Prize 2008, European St Ullrichs Prize 2009, Cristobal Gabarron Award 2009, Musical America Award for Instrumentalist of the Year 2011, Brahms Prize 2011, Erich Fromm Prize 2011, Gustav Adolf Prize 2011, Atlantic Council's Distinguished Artistic Leadership Award 2012, Lutoslawski Soc. Award 2015. *Address:* Sekretariat Anne-Sophie Mutter, Ismaninger Straße 75, 81675 Munich, Germany. *E-mail:* info@anne-sophie-mutter.de. *Website:* www.anne-sophie-mutter.de.

MYERS, Michael; American singer (tenor); b. 1955. *Education:* Curtis Institute, Philadelphia. *Career:* debut at Central City Opera 1977, in The Bartered Bride; US appearances in Minnesota, Tulsa, Cleveland, San Francisco, Los Angeles and Des Moines; season 1981–82 as Belmonte in Ottawa, Alfred in Die Fledermaus for Charlotte Opera, Faust for Providence and Virginia Operas and Jenik in Kentucky and Augusta; highlights of 1982–83 were debuts at the New York City Opera, as Rodolfo, Santa Fe Opera as Quint (Turn of the Screw), Monteverdi's Nerone with Canadian Opera and the Duke of Mantua for Hawaii Opera Theatre; sang Nick in the premiere of The Postman Always Rings Twice for St Louis Opera (1982) and repeated the role at the 1983 Edinburgh Festival; Scottish Opera debut 1984, as Idomeneo, returning as the Duke in Rigoletto and Cavalli's Orione; season 1984–85 included Percy to Joan Sutherland's Anna Bolena for Canadian Opera, Flotow's Lionel in Portland and Lord Puff in the US premiere of Henze's The English Cat, at Santa Fe; season 1985–86 featured debuts with Seattle Opera (Des Grieux in Manon), in Toulouse (Gounod's Roméo), Long Beach Grand Opera (Belmonte), Montpellier (Rimsky's Mozart) and with the Mostly Mozart Festival (Belfiore in La Finta Giardiniera); during 1986–87 at Philadelphia (Wagner's Steersman), Pittsburgh (Edgardo in Lucia di Lammermoor) with the Canadian Opera as Dimitri in Boris Godunov and the Mostly Mozart Festival as Agenore in Il Re Pastore; from 1987 sang Berg's Painter with the Chicago Opera, the Berlioz Faust with Lyon Opéra, Sergei in Lady Macbeth of Mtsensk with Canadian Opera, Boris in Katya Kabanova at Glyndebourne and Ismael in Nabucco in Philadelphia and New York; season 1992 as Tom Rakewell at Brussels and Percy in Anna Bolena at Santiago; Tom Rakewell at Madrid, 1996; Donizetti's Edgardo for New Israeli Opera, 1999; concert engagements include Rossini's Stabat Mater (Cincinnati May Festival) and Huon in Oberon for Radio France. *Honours:* First Prize 1979 Merola Program of the San Francisco Opera. *Current Management:* Columbia Artists Management, 1790 Broadway, New York, NY 10019-1412, USA. *Telephone:* (212) 841-9500. *Fax:* (212) 841 9744. *E-mail:* info@cami.com. *Website:* www.cami.com.

MYERS, Pamela; singer (soprano); b. 1952, Baltimore, MD, USA. *Career:* debut at San Francisco Western Opera 1977 as Mozart's Countess; sang the title role in Stephen Oliver's The Duchess of Malfi, Santa Fe 1978; appearances at New York City Opera from 1979, Scottish Opera 1980–81, as Lucia; Giessen 1981 in the title role of Menotti's La Loca, Amsterdam 1983 as Mozart's Constanze, Innsbruck Early Music Festival 1984 in Handel's Rodrigo; sang at Marseille 1988, 1991 as Desdemona and Ellen Orford; other roles have included Aennchen in Der Freischütz, Zerlina, Zerbinetta, Micaela, Luisa Miller, Violetta, Liu and Lady Macbeth; noted concert artist.

MYERS, Peter Joseph, BA, MA; composer; b. 3 Feb. 1962, Werribee, Vic., Australia. *Education:* La Trobe Univ. *Career:* faculty mem., La Trobe Univ. 1984–90, Pascoe Vale Girls' Secondary Coll. 1993–. *Compositions include:* Transformations for oboe 1983, Aftermath for concert band octet for winds 1984, Scintilla for orchestra 1986, Of Minds and Minds for ensemble 1987, Antipathy for mezzo and ensemble 1988, Towards the Equinox for chamber ensemble 1986, Vex for violin 1988, Homage to the Ancient for trombone, percussion and piano, Pasar for piano 1991, Bilanx for violin, cello, piccolo, clarinet and piano 1991, Demons Within for orchestra 1993, Paroxysms for string quartet 1993.

MYERSCOUGH, Nadia, LRAM, ARAM, Artist Dip. (IU), USA; British/Swiss violinist; b. 29 July 1967, London, England; d. of Clarence Myerscough. *Education:* Royal Acad. of Music, London, Indiana Univ., Bloomington, USA, studied with Clarence Myerscough, Franco Gulli, Rostislav Dubinsky, Luba Edlina, Shigeo Neriki. *Career:* soloist, recitalist and chamber music player; broadcasts on BBC Radio 3, Classic FM, France Music, Radio MEC Brazil, Polish Radio and TV; appearances at South Bank, Wigmore Hall, City of London Festival, Wexford Festival; soloist with the Lucerne Festival Strings, London Soloists, Kent Concert Orchestra, Bangkok Philharmonic; mem. New Helvetic Soc., Royal Soc. of Musicians, RAM Club. *Recordings:* Dvořák, Suk, Smetana, Vivaldi Concerto (Festival Strings, Lucerne), chamber music works by Alan Rawsthorne. *Radio:* broadcasts on BBC Radio 3, Classic FM, Radio MEC Brazil and Polish Radio. *Honours:* B.J. Dale Prize, Countess of Munster Award, Marianne and Kurt Dienemann Stiftung, English Speaking Union Fellowship and other study scholarships. *Current Management:* c/o M&M Management, 17 Salterton Road, London, N7 6BB, England. *Telephone:* (20) 7272-2547. *E-mail:* myerscough@waitrose.com (office).

N

NAAF, Dagmar; German singer (mezzo-soprano); b. 1934, Munich. *Education:* studied in Munich. *Career:* sang in Opera at Freiburg 1958–63, Munich 1963–66, Wiesbaden 1963–66 and Hanover 1966–70; engaged at Cologne 1967–69, Graz 1970–72, Staatsoper Munich 1974–76; guest appearances at Brussels, Berne, Marseilles, Rio de Janeiro, (Amsterdam, Octavian 1965), Barcelona and Vienna 1972; other roles have included Monteverdi's Ottavia, Handel's Cornelia, Gluck's Paride, Dorabella, Brangaene; Strauss's Composer and Clairon; Verdi's Preziosilla, Azucena, Amneris and Eboli; noted concert artist.

NADAREISHVILI, Zurab; Georgian composer; b. 4 Jan. 1957, Poti; m. Niho Shawdia 1985; one s. one d. *Education:* Music School, Poti and Tbilisi State Conservatoire. *Career:* debut in Tbilisi 1985; performed in St Petersburg 1987, Moscow 1988, Amsterdam 1992, USA 1993; teacher, Tbilisi State Conservatory; mem. Georgian Composers' Union. *Compositions:* two String Quartets, Brass Quintet, Orchestral Minatures, Symphonic Poem, Hymns for chamber orchestra, Variations for piano, Variations for piano and orchestra, instrumental pieces. *Recordings:* Hymns for chamber orchestra 1988. *Publications:* The Way to Music 1987, Musical Georgia 1997. *Honours:* Moscow Composers International Competition 1987, Georgian Composers' Union Award 1992, third place Moscow Prokofiev Competition 1997.

NADELMANN, Noëmi; singer (soprano); b. 1966, Zürich, Switzerland. *Education:* studied at Bloomington, Indiana. *Career:* sang at Lucerne Opera 1988–89, Zürich and Augsburg (as Norina in Don Pasquale); Theater am Gärtnerplatz, Munich from 1990, as Zerlina, Blondchen, Aennchen in Der Freischütz, Manon and Zerbinetta; Komische Oper Berlin 1994–95, as Traviata, Lucia di Lammermoor, Nedda and Musetta; Munich 1996, as Rosalinde in Die Fledermaus and the title role in Orff's Die Kluge; further appearances at Venice, Geneva and the Metropolitan, New York debut 2000, as Musetta; sang Rosalinde for Zürich Opera and Armida in Handel's Rinaldo at the Prinzregententheater, Munich 2000; Wiener Blut and Die lustige Witwe at Zürich 2002.

NADLER, Sheila; American singer (mezzo-soprano); b. 1945, New York, NY. *Education:* Manhattan School of Music, Opera Studio of the Metropolitan Opera, Juilliard School. *Career:* sang at San Francisco and New York City Opera 1970–72, Baltimore 1972–, notably in 1975 in the premiere of Inez de Castro by Pasatieri, Metropolitan Opera 1976–; sang Anna in Les Troyens at La Scala, 1982, and Clytemnestra in Elektra at Santiago, 1984; further appearances as Fricka and Waltraute in The Ring, at Marseilles, Lyon and Brussels and as Erda, Herodias, Jocasta in Oedipus Rex, Azucena, Ulrica, Mistress Quickly, Cornelia in Giulio Cesare and La Cieca in La Gioconda; sang Clytemnestra in Elektra at Seattle 1996; as Poulenc's Mme de Croissy, Santa Fe 1999.

NADOR, Magda; Hungarian singer (soprano); b. 16 Dec. 1955, Dorog. *Education:* Budapest Music Acad. *Career:* debut at Budapest National Opera 1979, as Mozart's Constanze; Komische Oper Berlin from 1982, as Mozart's Fiordiligi and Queen of Night, and Gilda in Rigoletto; guest appearances at Amsterdam (as Adele), Zürich, Düsseldorf and Munich; Vienna Staatsoper 1986, as Oscar in Un Ballo in Maschera; Queen of Night at Stuttgart and Graz 1987; Berlin and Wiesbaden 1991–91, as Isotta in Strauss's Die Schweigsame Frau; concerts include Salzburg Festival 1986.

NAEF, Yvonne; Swiss singer (mezzo-soprano); b. 1965. *Education:* studied in Zürich, Basle and Mannheim. *Career:* concert and recital appearances from 1987; Opera debut as Rossini's Cenerentola, followed by an engagement at St Gallen, as Ulrica, Ariodante, Gluck's Orfeo and Sara in Roberto Devereux, from 1992; Wiesbaden from 1993, as Preziosilla, Rosina, Suzuki, Fricka, Brangaene and Adalgisa; Monte Carlo 1994, as Giovanna Seymour in Anna Bolena, and La Scala Milan as Offenbach's Giulietta; Invalid Woman in Schoenberg's Moses and Aron at Amsterdam, Salzburg and the Festival Hall, London (1996); Appearances as Verdi's Amneris at St Gallen, Wiesbaden and the Deutsche Oper Berlin; Concert engagements in Prokofiev's Alexander Nevsky (at Naples), Mahler's Second Symphony (Venice), Bach's B Minor Mass (Lausanne) and Das Lied von der Erde (Toulouse); Bayreuth Festival 1997, as Waltraute and Second Norn, in The Ring; Season 2000–01 as Wagner's Venus at Hamburg, Stravinsky's Jocasta in Brussels, Anna in Les Troyens at Salzburg and Eboli at the Vienna Staatsoper (debut); Azucena at Covent Garden, and returned to Hamburg for Marina in Boris Godunov. *Honours:* Second Prize, Lieder and Oratorio section, 1987 Maria Callas Competition, at Athens. *Current Management:* c/o Künstleragentur Dr Raab & Dr Böhm, Plankengasse 7, 1010 Vienna, Austria; c/o Caecilia Lyric Department, Rennweg 15, 8001 Zürich, Switzerland. *Telephone:* 1-512 05 01 (Austria); 2213388 (Switzerland). *Fax:* 1-512 77 43 (Austria); 2117182 (Switzerland). *E-mail:* office@rbartists.at; caecilia@caecilia-lyric.ch. *Website:* www.rbartists.at; www.caecilia.ch.

NAFE, Alicia; singer (mezzo-soprano); b. 4 Aug. 1947, Buenos Aires, Argentina. *Education:* studied in Buenos Aires with Ferruccio Calusio and in Europe with Luigi Ricci and Teresa Berganza. *Career:* sang in Barcelona after winning competition there, debut in Verdi's Requiem; sang in Toledo and at the Bayreuth Festival 1975; mem., Hamburg Opera 1977–81; Geneva Opera 1981, in La Cenerentola; Lyon 1981, in Beatrice et Benedict by Berlioz;

sang Rosina with the Cologne Opera at the 1981 Edinburgh Festival; La Scala 1984, as Idamante in Idomeneo; Covent Garden 1985, as Rosina; guest engagements in Spain, South America, France, Germany and China; other roles include Carmen and Dorabella; sang Adalgisa at Covent Garden 1987; Metropolitan Opera debut 1988, as Sextus in La Clemenza di Tito and Ramiro in La Finta Giardiniera; sang Massenet's Charlotte at the Teatro Regio Parma 1990; Grandmother in La Vida Breve at Madrid 1998; also heard in oratorios and as song recitalist. *Recordings:* Mercedes in Carmen and La Vida Breve; Monteverdi Madrigals; Così fan tutte.

NAFORNITA, Valentina; Moldovan singer (soprano); b. 1987, Glodeni. *Education:* Nat. Univ. of Music, Bucharest, Romania. *Career:* mem. young artists programme, Wiener Staatsoper 2011–12, joined ensemble 2012–, debut as Musetta in La Bohème under Franz Welser-Möst and Najade in Ariadne auf Naxos; debut at Teatro alla Scala as Gilda in Rigoletto under Gustavo Dudamel 2012; appearances at Musikverein Vienna, with Netherlands Radio Philharmonic Orchestra at Concertgebouw Amsterdam, with Romanian Nat. Opera and George Enescu Philharmonic Orchestra. *Honours:* BBC Cardiff Singer of the World and Dame Joan Sutherland Audience Prize 2011. *Current Management:* c/o Intermusica Artists Management, 36 Graham Street, Crystal Wharf, London, N1 8GJ, England. *Telephone:* (20) 7608-9900. *Fax:* (20) 7490-3263. *E-mail:* info@intermusica.co.uk. *Website:* www.intermusica.co.uk.

NAGANO, Kent; American conductor; *General Music Director and Chief Conductor, Hamburg State Opera*; b. 22 Nov. 1951, Berkeley, Calif.; m. Mari Kodama; one d. *Education:* studied under Ozawa, Boulez and Bernstein. *Career:* first achieved int. recognition when he conducted Boston Symphony Orchestra in performance of Mahler's Symphony No. 9 1984; conducted US premiere of Messiaen's The Transfiguration; debut at Paris Opera conducting world premiere of Messiaen's St François d'Assise; debut, Metropolitan Opera, New York conducting Poulenc's Dialogues des Carmélites 1994; Music Dir, Berkeley Symphony Orchestra, Calif. 1978–2008, Opéra de Lyon 1988–98, Hallé Orchestra 1991–2000; Artistic Dir, Deutsches Symphonie-Orchester Berlin 2000–06; Prin. Conductor and Music Dir, Los Angeles Opera 2001–06; Music Dir, Montreal Symphony Orchestra 2006–, Bayerische Staatsoper 2006–13; Prin. Guest Conductor and Artistic Adviser, Gothenburg Symphony Orchestra 2013–; Gen. Music Dir and Chief Conductor, Hamburg State Opera and Philharmonic Orchestra 2015–. *Publication:* Erwarten Sie Wunder 2014. *Honours:* Officier, Ordre des Arts et des Lettres 1992, Order of the Rising Sun, Gold Rays 2009; Grammy Awards for Busoni's Dr Faust with Opéra Nat. de Lyon, Prokofiev's Peter and the Wolf with the Russian Nat. Orchestra, Saariaho's L'Amour de Loin with Deutsches Symphonie-Orchester Berlin (Best Opera Recording 2011), Bayerischer Verdienstorden 2013. *Current Management:* c/o Janet Marsden, International Classical Artists, Dunstan House, 14A St Cross Street, London, EC1N 8XA, England. *Telephone:* (20) 7902-0520. *Fax:* (20) 7902-0150. *E-mail:* info@icartists.co.uk. *Website:* www.osm.ca; www.kentnagano.com.

NÄGELE, Barbara; Austrian recorder player; b. 16 March 1973, Lustenau. *Education:* Hochschule für Musik und Theater, Zürich, Switzerland with Kees Boeke and Matthias Weilenmann. *Career:* mem., Trio O'Henry (with Claudia Gerauer and Martina Joos); appearances (among others) at Bludenzer Tage für Zeitgemässe Musik, Austria 1997; Festival of Ancient Music, Stary Sacz, Poland 2000; Festival Musica Nova, Sofia, Bulgaria 2001; Festival Bohemia-Saxony, Czech Republic 2001; cycle of premieres with works of Swiss composers, Zürich 2000–01; radio appearances (live recordings) include St Peter's Church, Zürich 1996; Great Hall of the HFMT, Zürich; radio features: Austrian Radio ORF 1 1998; Swiss Radio DRS 2 2000; Bulgarian radio and television, Sofia 2001; premieres Kees Boeke's The Unfolding 1997; Martin Derungs's A Set of Pieces 2000; Thomas Müller's Erste Etappe in Richtung farbiger Eindrücke 2000; Giorgio Tedde's Medio Aevo 2000; Andreas Nick's Trio pour flûtes à bec 2000; Annette Schmucki's tatsache. eisschollen; Der unzertrennliche anstoss abweichender labialität 2001; Gerald Bennett's Textures of Time 2001. *Honours:* Kiwanis Kammermusik-Wettbewerb, Zürich, 1995; International Recorder Competition, Calw, Germany, 1995; Orpheus Förderpreis, Zürich, 1997; Premio Bonporti, Rovereto, Italy, 1997; Migros Kammermusik-Wettbewerb, Zürich, 1999.

NAGELSTAD, Catherine; American singer (soprano); b. 1967, California. *Education:* San Francisco Conservatory, studied in Rome. *Career:* as Zdenka in Arabella and Magda in La Rondine, Southern California Festival; European debut as Mozart's Constanze, Hamburg 1993; concerts with Plácido Domingo in USA and Europe; Staatsoper Stuttgart as Musetta and Mozart's Vitellia; Venus in King Arthur; Tosca and Alcina 1998–99; season 1999–2000 with Constanze, Fiordiligi and Poppea, Elisabeth de Valois and Violetta at Stuttgart; Musetta at Covent Garden. *Honours:* winner Palm Springs, Pasalena Opera Guild Competitions 1991–92.

NAGY, Janos B.; Hungarian singer (tenor); b. 1943, Debrecen. *Education:* Bartók Conservatory, Budapest. *Career:* sang with Hungarian Territorial Army choir on tour, 1967–70; stage debut at Budapest, 1971, as Don José in Carmen; many performances in operas by Verdi and Puccini; Berlin 1978, in the Verdi Requiem; Warsaw National Opera 1979; mem., Deutsche Oper am

Rhein, Düsseldorf from 1981; other roles include Puccini's Des Grieux, Cavaradossi and Calaf, Verdi's Manrico, Duke of Mantua, and Macduff, Nemorino in L'Elisir d'amore and Pollione in Norma; guest appearances at opera houses in Germany and Switzerland; sang Radames with the Deutsche Oper am Rhein, Düsseldorf, 1989. *Recordings:* Boito's Nerone, Kodály's Te Deum, Psalmus Hungaricus and Missa Brevis, Christus by Liszt, Mosè in Egitto, Szokolay's Blood Wedding, Simon Boccanegra.

NAKAMURA, Hiroko; Japanese pianist; *Music Director, Hamamatsu International Piano Academy*; b. 25 July 1944, Tokyo; m. Shoji Fukuda 1974. *Education:* studied piano under Aiko Iguchi, Leonid Kochanski, Rosina Lhevinne, Zbigniev Dzriewiecki, Stefan Askenazy. *Career:* began playing piano aged three; debut with Tokyo Philharmonic Orchestra; Soloist NHK Symphony; performed with Moscow Philharmonic, State Acad. Symphony Orchestra of the USSR, Leningrad Philharmonic, USSR now Russian Fed.; has performed at over 3,700 concerts during her career, including tours of USA, Canada, UK, Europe, fmr USSR, People's Repub. of China and Repub. of China (Taiwan); first Japanese to win scholarships from Rockefeller Foundation and Juilliard School of Music, USA 1962; youngest winner of All-Japan Jr Student Piano Competition 1954, All-Japan Sr Student Piano Competition 1956, Japan Music Concours 1959; winner Juilliard Concours, Aspen Music Festival Prize, USA; youngest winner Int. Piano Competition, Warsaw; juror, Int. Tchaikovsky Piano Competition 1982–2007, Int. Chopin Piano Competition 1990–2005; Music Dir Hamamatsu Int. Piano Acad.; Chair. Hamamatsu Int. Piano Competition. *Recordings include:* Rachmaninov's Second and Third Piano Concertos, Tchaikovsky's First Piano Concerto, Chopin's First Piano Concerto; numerous other pieces with Sony. *Publications:* The Tchaikovsky Concours (Ohya Non-Fiction Prize), Savages Called Pianists. *Honours:* Medal for Merits to Culture Gloria Artis (Poland), Arthur Rubinstein Gold Medal (Poland), Medal with Purple Ribbon (Japan). *Current Management:* c/o Junichi Nihei, Japan Arts, 2-1-6 Shibuya, Shibuya-ku, Tokyo 150-8905, Japan. *Telephone:* (3) 3499-8097. *Fax:* (3) 3499-8092. *E-mail:* nihei@japanarts.co.jp. *Website:* www.japanarts.co.jp. *Address:* #1302, 2-3-34 Mita, Minato-ku, Tokyo 108-0073, Japan (home). *Telephone:* (3) 3454-6659 (home). *Fax:* (3) 3454-7547 (home).

NAKAMURA, Tomoko; singer (soprano); b. 1961, Japan; m. Uwe Heilmann. *Education:* studied at Detmold and with Elisabeth Schwarzkopf. *Career:* debut at Detmold Opera 1983, as Madama Butterfly; sang at the Stuttgart Staatsoper from 1986, notably as Mozart's Constanze (also at the Vienna Staatsoper 1992), Queen of Night and Donna Anna, Olympia in Les contes d'Hoffmann, and Gilda; numerous concert appearances. *Honours:* prizewinner Mozart Competition, Salzburg 1985.

NAKARIAKOV, Sergei; Russian musician (trumpet, flugelhorn); b. 10 May 1977, Gorky. *Career:* acclaimed performance at Korsholm Festival, Finland aged 12; debut at Salzburg Festival with Lithuanian Chamber Orchestra 1991; appeared at Schleswig-Holstein Musikfestival 1992; began recording career aged 15; numerous int. performances, including Royal Festival Hall and Royal Albert Hall, London, Hollywood Bowl in Los Angeles, Lincoln Center in New York; has performed with Tchaikovsky Orchestra, Munich Chamber Orchestra, Berliner Sinfonie Orchester, Bremen Philharmoniker, Toronto Symphony Orchestra, English Chamber Orchestra, Rotterdam Philharmonic; has collaborated with conductors, including Kent Nagano, Valery Gergiev, Vladimir Spivakov, Vladimir Ashkenazy, Emmanuel Krevine, Jesus Lopez-Cobos; festival appearances include Colmar, Menton, Salzburg, Montreux, Lucerne, Strasbourg, Cannes; frequent tours in Japan, USA, Canada, Germany. *Recordings:* Trumpet Works 1992, Trumpet Concertos 1993, Carmen Fantasy 1994, Baroque Trumpet Concertos 1996, Élégie 1997, Concertos for Trumpet 1999, No Limit 2000, From Moscow with Love 2001, Echoes from the Past 2002, Widmung 2012. *Honours:* Prix Davidoff, Schleswig-Holstein 1992, ECHO Klassik Award 2002. *Current Management:* c/o Alexandra Heinz Artists, Kleine Brunndnestraße 18, 22765 Hamburg, Germany. *Telephone:* (40) 39803790. *Fax:* (40) 39804903. *E-mail:* info@ah-artists.de. *Website:* www.ah-artists.de; www.nakariakov.com.

NALL, Cecily; American singer (soprano); b. 1960, Georgia. *Education:* studied in USA and Graz, Austria. *Career:* debut at Spoleto Festival 1985, as Zerbinetta in Ariadne and Naxos; season 1986 as Blondchen in Die Entführung at Santiago and Offenbach's Olympia for Miami Opera; Aachen Opera 1987–91, Darmstadt 1991–93; many guest appearances elsewhere in Europe; Cleveland 1988, as Mozart's Constanze; Cincinnati Opera from 1992, as Olympia, Sophie in Der Rosenkavalier, and Mozart's Susanna 1995.

NALLY, Donald, BMus, MM, DMusArts; American conductor; *Chorus Master, Lyric Opera of Chicago*; b. 27 Dec. 1960, Hilltown, Pa. *Education:* Univ. of Cincinnati Coll.-Conservatory of Music, Westminster Choir Coll., Princeton, NJ, Univ. of Illinois. *Career:* began career as Chair. Music Dept, Chicago Acad. for the Arts; Chorus Master, Opera Co. of Philadelphia (more than 50 operas produced) 1992–2003; Chorus Master, Spoleto Festival, Italy 1994–2001; Artistic Dir, Choral Arts Soc. of Philadelphia 1998–2002; Chorus Master, Welsh Nat. Opera 2003–06; Chorus Master, Lyric Opera of Chicago 2007–; Founder and Conductor, The Crossing (chamber ensemble) 2006–; Music Dir, Vocal Arts Ensemble of Cincinnati 2009–. *Address:* Lyric Opera of Chicago, 20 North Wacker Drive, Chicago, IL 60606, USA (office). *Telephone:* (312) 332-2244 (office). *E-mail:* dnally@lyricopera.org (office). *Website:* www.lyricopera .org (office).

NÁNÁSI, Henrik; Hungarian conductor; *General Music Director, Komische Oper Berlin*; b. 1975, Pécs. *Education:* Béla Bartók Conservatory, Univ. of Music and Performing Arts, Vienna. *Career:* solo-répétiteur, Stadttheater Klagenfurt 1999, First Kapellmeister 2002, conducted Mozart opera repertoire (The Magic Flute, Così fan tutte), the Italian mode (Don Carlos, Nabucco, Norma, La Cenerentola, Don Pasquale, Turandot, Madama Butterfly, Tosca), Tchaikovsky (Pique Dame), Stravinsky (The Rake's Progress), Offenbach (La Belle Helene), Lehar's Eva; First Kapellmeister, Theater Augsburg 2005–07, conducted Otello, Hansel and Gretel, Tosca and new productions of Berlioz's Beatrice et Benedict, Gounod's Romeo et Juliette, Donizetti's Maria Stuarda and Salieri's Axur, Re d'Ormus; fmr Musical Asst, Covent Garden Royal Opera House under Antonio Pappano, Opéra de Monte Carlo; apptd First Kappelmeister and temporary Head Conductor, Staatstheater am Gärtnerplatz, Munich 2007, conducted Le Nozze di Figaro, Fra Diavolo, L'Elisir d'amore, Il Barbiere di Siviglia, Boccaccio, Martha, and others), debut performances of Verdi's I Masnadieri and Giovanna d'Arco; guest conductor at Volksoper, Vienna (Carmen, La Traviata, La Bohème, Countess Mariza, The Bird Seller), Oper Frankfurt (La Bohème), Komische Oper Berlin (Fidelio), Staatstheater Braunschweig (Otello, The Riviera Girl), Nationaltheater Mannheim (The Magic Flute), Budapest Operetta Theatre (The Bat, The Land of Smiles) and Miskolc Int. Opera Festival (Duke Bluebeard's Castle, Gianni Schicchi); conducted inaugural Swiss performance of Verdi's early work of Alzira at Theater St Gallen; has conducted the Radio-Symphonieorchester Wien, Orchestre Symphonique de L'Opera de Toulon, Tiroler Symphonieorchester Innsbruck, Staatsorchester Braunschweig, Philharmonisches Orchester Augsburg, Sinfonieorchester St Gallen, Neue Philharmonie Westfalen; Gen. Music Dir Komische Oper Berlin 2012–13. *Current Management:* c/o IMG Artists, The Light Box, 111 Power Road, London, W4 5PY, England. *Telephone:* (20) 7957-5800. *Fax:* (20) 7957-5801. *E-mail:* kenticott@imgartists.com. *Website:* www.imgartists.com.

NAOURI, Laurent; French singer (baritone); b. 1964, Paris. *Education:* studied at Marseille, Guildhall School, London. *Career:* debut at Guglielmo in Così fan tutte; Lully's Phaeton and Roland at Lyon and Montpellier; Les Contes d'Hoffmann, Metz; Massenet's Des Grieux and Mozart's Figaro, Opéra Bastille, Paris; 1997–98 season: Jupiter in Orphée aux Enfers, Geneva; Antenor in Rameau's Dardanus; Bottom in A Midsummer Night's Dream, Lyon; Many appearances at Aix-en-Provence Festival; Season 1999–2000 as Melisso in Alcina at the Palais Garnier, Paris, and as Hucscar in Les Indes Galantes by Rameau; the Villains in Les Contes d'Hoffmann at Antwerp. *Recordings:* Hidraot in Gluck's Armide. *Current Management:* c/o Agence Artistique Thérèse Cédelle, Boulevard Malesherbes 78, 75008 Paris, France. *Telephone:* 1-49-53-00-02. *Fax:* 1-45-63-70-23. *E-mail:* Agence.Cedelle@wanadoo.fr.

NASH, Graham Thomas, LRAM; conductor; b. 21 June 1952, London, England; m. (divorced); one s. *Education:* Royal Acad. of Music. *Career:* debut conducting at Royal Albert Hall 1980, Kraków Radio Symphony Orchestra, Poland 1988 and London Philharmonic Orchestra 1985; conducting, Victor Hochhauser, Opera Gala Nights at Royal Albert Hall, Royal Festival Hall, Barbican 1980–89; guest conductor, London Festival Ballet; Music Dir, London City Ballet 1986–88; Kuopio Orchestra debut in Finland 1987; mem. Incorporated Soc. of Musicians. *Compositions include:* In Memoriam Lord Mountbatten for large orchestra 1979. *Honours:* North London Orchestral Soc. Prize for Conducting 1974, Blake Memorial Prize for Flute, Ensemble Prize 1974.

NASH, Peter Paul; composer; b. 1950, Leighton Buzzard, Bedfordshire, England. *Education:* Univ. of Cambridge with Robin Holloway. *Career:* Composition Fellow at Leeds Univ. 1976–78; Composer-in-Residence, Nat. Centre for Orchestral Studies 1983; Prod., BBC Radio 3 1985–87; critic and broadcaster, presenter of Music Week on Radio 3. *Compositions:* String Trio 1982, Wind Quintet, Insomnia for chamber ensemble, Etudes for orchestra (On the Beach, Percussion Study, Parting) 1983–84, Figures for harp, Earthquake scena for narrator, six players and quintet 1987, Symphony 1991.

NASH, Rebecca Errington, BA, GradDipEd, PGDip (opera); Australian singer (soprano); b. 1971, Melbourne, Vic. *Education:* studied with Dame Joan Hammond in Melbourne, Royal Coll. of Music, UK. *Career:* appearances throughout Australia as Pamina, Donna Elvira, Marguerite in Faust, Gilda, Micaela and Nedda; Mozart's Countess for Opera Australia at Sydney Opera House, 2000; other roles include Desdemona, Arabella, Jenůfa and Magda in La Rondine; concerts include Strauss Vier letzte Lieder under Daniel Harding; Beethoven 9 and Egmont under Frans Bruggen with Scottish Chamber Orchestra and The Orchestra of the 18th Century; Mendelssohn's Elijah under Kurt Masur as well as Verdi Requiem; Ein Deutsches Requiem; Mozart C Minor Mass; Mahler 4; The Creation; Messiah; Handel's Jephtha; Barena in Jenůfa; Fifth Maid in Elektra; First Maid in Daphne for Royal Opera Covent Garden; season 2003–04 included Marschallin in Der Rosenkavalier with ENO; Fifth Maid in Elektra under Donald Runnicles at BBC Proms; concerts with The Orchestra of the 18th Century, Mozart's Coronation Mass (RTVE Madrid), Dvořák Requiem (Danish Radio); season 2004–05 included Beethoven's 9th Symphony in Hong Kong with Frans Brüggen and the Orchestra of the 18th Century, Vier letze Lieder and Strauss Orchestral Songs with Sir Richard Armstrong and the Scottish Opera Orchestra; season 2006–07 included the Marschallin for Scottish Opera, Beethoven Mass in C with Olari Elts and Mozart Arias at the BBC Proms with Sir Roger Norrington, both with the Scottish Chamber Orchestra; season

2007–08 included Beethoven's 9th Symphony in Caracas with Gustavo Dudamel and the Simon Bolivar Youth Orchestra and with the Ulster Orchestra; Madama Butterfly for Scottish Opera and Kát'a Kabanová in Cologne under Markus Stenz; season 2009–10 included Miss Jessel in The Turn of the Screw with Boston Lyric Opera; season 2010–11 included production of Erwartung with New York City Opera; season 2012–13 brought debuts with Central City Opera (Miss Jessel), Teatro del Palacio de Bellas Artes, Mexico City (Kaiserin in Die Frau ohne Schatten), Virginia Symphony (Mahler 8: Una Poenitentiam and Les Noces both recorded), Chicago Lyric Opera (4th maid in Elektra); season 2014–15: role debuts as Judit in Duke Bluebeard's Castle conducted by JoAnn Falletta (Virginia Symphony) and title role in Ariadne auf Naxos (West Green Opera) as well as debut with Boston Symphony Orchestra and Andris Nelsons (5th Maid in Elektra) and Buffalo Philharmonic (Rachmaninoff's The Bells). *Honours:* Inaugural Dame Joan Sutherland Singing Award, Australian Nat. Acad. of Music 1996, The Herald-Sun Aria 1996, Marianne Mathy Award 1996. *Current Management:* c/o Kristin Cowdin, Guy Barzilay Artists, 420 West 25th Street, Suite 4F, New York, NY 10001, USA. *Telephone:* (212) 741-6118. *Fax:* (212) 741-2558. *E-mail:* kristin@guybarzilayartists.com. *Website:* www.guybarzilayartists.com.

NASRAWI, Douglas; American singer (tenor); b. 25 June 1960, Calif.; m. Marianne Kienbaum; three c. *Education:* vocal training in San Francisco and Paris. *Career:* appearances at numerous European opera houses, including José-Ramón Encinar's Figaro in Madrid and Lisbon, title role in Mozart's La Clemenza di Tito in Lille, Charles Chaynes' Jocasta in Rouen, Osman in Handel's Almira in Bremen, title role in Pennisis' Tristan at Biennale della Musica in Venice and Teatro Comunale di Bologna, Stravinsky Pulcinella in Metz, Avignon, Caen directed by Jean-Claude Malgoire; extensive repertoire includes both parts of the standard repertoire as Lenski, Italian singer, Des Grieux, Ismaele, Don José, Pollione, Erik, MacDuff and roles including Läerte (Hamlet), Gérald (Lakmé), Grimoaldo (Rodelinda), Prince Pao (The Chalk Circle); recent and upcoming projects include Edrisi (Krol Roger) in Amsterdam, Romeo in Karlsruhe, Narraboth in Frankfurt, Chlestakow (Der Revisor) in Augsburg, Tamino at the Vienna State Opera, Stravinsky's Persephone with Wiener Klangboden Festspielen and in Basel, Lancelot (Le roi Arthus) in Cologne, Panait (Greek Passion), Flaminio (L'amore dei tre re) and Lancelot at the Bregenz Festival, Don José, Peace, Wozzeck, Jimmy in Mahagonny and Die Liebe der Danae at Semperoper, Dresden, The Dwarf and Lancelot at the Théâtre de la Monnaie, Brussels, Peter Grimes, Don José, Lady Macbeth and The Dwarf in Berlin, Panait at Convent Garden, Beethoven's 9th Symphony in Tokyo, La Mort d'Orphée (Berlioz) in Bonn, Jacob's Ladder and The Dwarf at the Concertgebouw, Amsterdam, Rossini's Petite Messe Solennelle with the MDR, Leipzig, Captain Vere in Billy Budd at Cologne Opera, as well as the Captain in a new production of Wozzeck at Théâtre Royal de la Monnaie, Brussels, Don Juan in Erwin Schulhoff's Flammen and the title role in Zemlinsky's King Candaules at the Pfalztheater, Kaiserslautern, Shuiskij in Boris Gogunov in Klagenfurt and L'Hérisson in L'Étoile with the Berlin State Opera under Sir Simon Rattle. *Recordings:* Osman in Handel's Almira, Alecton and Apollon in Lully's Alceste, Schütz Symphoniae sacrae, Purcell Songs of Welcome and Farewell. *Current Management:* c/o Haydn Rawstron, 29A High Street, First Floor, West Wickham, Kent, BR4 0LP, England. *Telephone:* (20) 8777-6070. *Fax:* (20) 8777-4073. *E-mail:* enquiries@haydn-rawstron.com. *Website:* www.haydnrawstron.com; www.douglasnasrawi.com.

NASU, Teruhiko, BA, MA, MPhil; Japanese academic; b. 23 Dec. 1960, Tokyo; m. Machiko; one d. *Education:* Rikkyo Univ., Tokyo, Univ. of Cambridge, UK. *Career:* part-time Lecturer in Music, St Gregory's Institute for Religious Music 1991–, Toho Gakuen Junior Coll. 1993–97, Japan Lutheran Theological Coll. 1995–96, Rikkyo Univ. 1996–2000; Lecturer in Music, Senzoku Gakuen Coll. 1996–2000; Assoc. Prof. of Music, Aoyama Gakuin Univ.; mem. Musicological Soc. of Japan, Royal Musical Asscn, Plainsong and Mediaeval Music Soc., Japan Soc. of Liturgical Musicology. *Publications:* The Publication of Byrd's Gradualia Reconsidered, Brio xxxii 1995, On Versus and Versiclus, Grocheio's De Musica: A Japanese Translation 2001. *Honours:* Kan Memorial Scholarship 1984. *Address:* Aoyama Gakuin University 4-4-25 Shibuya, Shibuya-Ku, Tokyo, 150-8366 Japan (office). *Telephone:* (3) 3409-7921 (office). *Fax:* (3) 3409-5414 (office). *E-mail:* tnasu@cl.aoyama.ac.jp (office). *Website:* www.aoyama.ac.jp (office).

NATANEK, Adam Tadewsa; conductor; b. 23 July 1933, Kraków, Poland; m. Danuta Daniecka 1966. *Education:* Academy of Music, Kraków. *Career:* debut with Kraków Philharmonic Orchestra, 1960; Conductor, Lublin Philharmonic Orchestra, 1961–69; Head, Artistic Director, Chief Conductor, 1969–90; First Guest Conductor, Symphonic Orchestra, Valladolid, Spain, 1984–; Artistic Director, Chief Conductor 1990; Artistic Director Rzeszów Philharmonic and Music Festival in Iancur, Poland; Professor, Marie Curie-Skiodowska University, Lublin, –1992; Member of Jury, numerous music competitions; appearances throughout Europe, South Korea, Africa, Cuba and Latin America. *Recordings:* numerous radio and television recordings with orchestras including National Warsaw Philharmonic, Great Symphony Orchestra of Polish Radio and Television, Katowice, Polish Radio and Television Orchestra, Kraków; Ignacy Feliks Dobrzynski's Piano Concerto with the New Polish Symphony Orchestra. *Publications:* contrib. to Promoter and Reviewer, Maria Sklodowska-Curie University, Lublin and Academy of Music, Warsaw and

Poznań. *Honours:* Commander's Cross of the Order of Polish Revival. *Address:* ul Szczerbowskiego 13/10, 20-012 Lublin, Poland.

NATRA, Sergiu, MA; composer; b. 12 April 1924, Bucharest, Romania. *Education:* Nat. Music Acad., Bucharest, studied with Leo Klepper. *Career:* commissions of symphony works, chamber music, stage and film music in Romania; major commissions in Israel from the Israel Festival, Israel Philharmonic Orchestra, Israel Radio, Israel Composers' Fund; resident in Tel-Aviv from 1961; Prof. of Composition; examiner for higher musical education, Israel Ministry of Education and Culture 1964–71; Hon. Dir, World Harp Congress. *Compositions:* Three Corteges in the Street 1945, Suite for orchestra 1948, Sinfonia for strings, Music for violin and harp, Music for harpsichord and six instruments 1964, Music for oboe and strings 1965, Sonatina for harp 1965, Song of Deborah 1967, Variations for piano and orchestra 1966, Prayer for harp 1972, Sonatina for trumpet solo 1973, Sonatina for trombone solo 1973, Sacred Service 1976, From the Diary of a Composer 1978, Variations for harpsichord 1978, Hours for mezzo-soprano, violin, clarinet and piano 1981, Music for harp and three brass instruments 1982, Divertimento for harp and strings 1983, Ness Amim Cantata for solo voices, choir, chamber orchestra with harpsichord 1984, Music for violin and piano 1986, Sonatina for piano 1987, Music for NICANOR for harp solo and chamber ensemble 1988, Developments for viola solo and chamber orchestra 1988, Sonata for four harps 1993, Sonata for harp and string quartet 1997, Sound Picture for two pianos 1998.

NAUHAUS, Gerd Ernst Hermann, DipMus, DipMusEd, PhD; musicologist; b. 28 July 1942, Erfurt, Germany; m. Ursula Karsdorf 1965, two s. (one deceased) one d. *Education:* Martin Luther Univ., Halle-Wittenberg. *Career:* Dramaturg at Zwickau Opera House 1967; musicologist, Robert Schumann House, Zwickau 1970–, Vice-Dir 1980–93, Dir 1993; Vice-Chair. and Scientific Sec. Robert Schumann Soc., Zwickau; mem. German Musicological Soc., Saxon Cultural Council 1993–2002. *Publications:* Robert Schumann, Diaries and Household Books (complete scholarly edn) Vol. III 1982, Vol. II 1987, Clara Schumann Three-Part Songs After Poems by Geibel 1989, Piano Sonata in G minor 1991, March in E Flat Major 1997. *Honours:* Schumann Prize, Zwickau Town Council 1986.

NAYLOR, Peter Russell, MA, BMus, ARCM, FRCO; British composer; b. 5 Oct. 1933, London; s. of Alfred Douglas Naylor and Rebecca Kate Naylor. *Education:* Univ. of Cambridge, London Univ. *Career:* Lecturer, City Literary Inst., London 1963–65; Lecturer in Harmony and Counterpoint, and History, Royal Scottish Acad. of Music and Drama 1965–71; organist, Ashwell Festival, Herts. 1964–69; Assoc. Organist, Glasgow Cathedral 1972–85; Music Assoc., Scottish Opera for Youth 1975–80; Repetiteur, Shepway Youth Opera, Kent 1982–85; Organist, Lyminge Methodist Church, Kent 1986–; Organist, Postling Church, Kent 1988–; mem. British Acad. of Composers and Songwriters, Scottish Music Centre. *Compositions:* Symphony in One Movement: Tides and Islands, Organ Concerto, Beowulf for symphonic wind band, Odysseus Returning (three-act opera), Pied Piper (one-act opera), The Mountain People and Shipwreck (workshop operas), Earth was Waiting (cantata), Wassail Sing We for SA chorus, piano and percussion, A Hero Dies for 22 voices and clarsach, Movement for organ, Air and Variations for two pianos, Clarinet Quintet, Love and Life (five songs), Carols and Anthems, Daybreak to Starlight (16 pieces) for organ, The Oak Tree and the Cypress for speaker, mezzo-soprano, harp and organ 1998, Tides of Summer (five pieces) for organ 2001, Echoes and Reflections (four pieces) for organ 2002, Trumpet in three for organ 2004, Three Hymn Preludes for organ 2005, Four Miniatures for double bass and piano 2006, Trio for violin, clarinet and piano 2006, Variations for violin and organ 2006, Kilda Kaleidoscope for double bass and piano 2007, Dialogues and Explorations for cello and double bass 2008, Spring Fantasia for SATB choir, violin, clarinet and piano 2011, After Darkness 2011. *Recordings:* Eastern Monarchs, Elizabethan Singers, Louis Halsey and the Choir of St John's College, Cambridge, George Guest; Now the Green Blade Riseth, SATB Choir of Glasgow Cathedral, John R. Turner; Clarinet Quintet, Colin Bradbury and the Georgian Quartet; Movement and Stillness (four songs), Stephen Pusey (baritone), Peter Naylor (piano). *Publications:* The Oak Tree and the Cypress 1998, Movement and Stillness: Four Songs for Baritone and Piano 1998, Tides of Summer 2001, Five Bird Songs 2001, Echoes and Reflections 2002, Trumpet in 3 2004, Three Hymn Preludes 2005, Gabriel's Message, The Bell Carol, Three Wordless Songs for Organ 2006, Love Came Down at Christmas, Four Miniatures for Double bass and Piano 2006, Trio for Violin, Clarinet and Piano 2006, Variations for organ 2007, Trumpet in 3 (2) 2007, The Voice of My Beloved for High Voice and Piano 2009, After Darkness 2011. *Honours:* London Univ. Convocation Trust Prize 1959, Aschenberg Composition Prize 1959. *Address:* Over Nailbourne, North Lyminge, Folkestone, Kent, CT18 8EE, England (home). *Telephone:* (1303) 863284 (home).

NAYLOR, Steven, BMus, FRAM; British pianist, accompanist, vocal coach and opera administrator; *Director of Artistic Administration, Glyndebourne Festival*; b. 1956, Gwent, Wales. *Education:* Univ. Coll., Cardiff, at the Nat. Opera Studio and the Royal Acad., London; further piano studies with Geoffrey Parsons. *Career:* Accompanist and opera coach at many venues in the UK and abroad; Joined Glyndebourne, 1989, Head of Music, 1998–, Dir of Artistic Administration, 1999–; BBC Radio 3 broadcasts; further engagements at the Wexford and Buxton Festivals, the Munich Festival and the Hans Werner Henze Summer Acad., Germany; Canadian Opera, Singapore Arts Festival, Royal Opera House Covent Garden, English Nat. Opera and Paris

(Opéra and Châtelet); Netherlands Opera, Amsterdam. *Honours:* prizes for piano accompaniment at RAM, and Countess of Munster Musical Trust Scholarship; Jani Strasser Award, Glyndebourne 1993. *Address:* Glyndebourne Festival Opera, Glyndebourne, Lewes, East Sussex, BN8 5UU, England (office). *Telephone:* (1273) 812321 (office). *Fax:* (1273) 815016 (office). *E-mail:* steven.naylor@glyndebourne.com (office). *Website:* www .glyndebourne.com (office).

NAZERI, Hafez; Iranian composer and musician; s. of Shahram Nazeri. *Education:* Mannes Coll., New York. *Career:* performances with his father, Shahram Nazeri in Europe and Middle East; has performed as musician at Sfinks Festival, Belgium, Festa Del Popolo, Italy, Théâtre de la Ville, Paris, Beiteddine Festival, Lebanon, Walt Disney Concert Hall, Los Angeles, Carnegie Hall, New York; compositions performed by Armenian Philharmonic Orchestra at Royal Albert Hall, Sodra Theare, Stockholm, De Bijlike, Ghent, Fez Festival, Morocco; founder, the Rumi Ensemble 2000–, the Rumi Symphony Project (ensemble playing a mix of Eastern and Western classical string music); created a new musical instrument based on traditional four-string sitar, The Hafez. *Compositions include:* The Passion of Rumi, The Rumi Symphony 2007, Iranian Sounds of Peace 2009, Night Angel 2010. *Honours:* UCLA Creativity Award for Most Distinguished Young Composer, Irvine City Hall Award of Distinction in Kurdish Music. *Current Management:* International Music Network, 278 Main Street, Gloucester, MA 01930, USA. *Telephone:* (978) 283-2883. *Fax:* (978) 283-2330. *Website:* www.imnworld.com.

NEARY, Alice; British cellist; b. 15 Dec. 1972, London; d. of Martin Gerard James Neary and Penelope Neary (née Warren). *Education:* Chetham's School of Music, RNCM with Ralph Kirshbaum, SUNY, Stonybrook with Timothy Eddy. *Career:* debut playing Haydn's C major concerto with the London Symphony Orchestra, Barbican 1994; South Bank Show (ITV) appearance in programme on John Tavener 1995; Wigmore Hall, London, debut 1999; recitals for the Park Lane Group Series at the Purcell Room, for BBC Radio 3 and at Bridgewater Hall, Manchester; concertos with the English CO, in Canada with the Israel Symphony Orchestra (season 2000), Orchestra of St John's, London, and Royal Liverpool Philharmonic Orchestra; Bach's Solo Suites at St John's 2000; performances at the Int. Musicians Seminar, Prussia Cove, with National Tour 2000; festival engagements at Manchester Int. Cello Festival, Santa Fe Chamber Music Festival and Presteigne Festival (Artist-in-Residence 1999); recitals with pianist Gretel Dowdeswell and the Ovid Ensemble; Wigmore Hall recital April 2000. *Recordings include:* Innocence by John Tavener. *Honours:* Pierre Fournier Award, 1988; Silver Medal, 1994 Shell/London Symphony Orchestra Competition; Prize Winner, Adam Int. Cello Competition, New Zealand, 1997; Countess of Munster Musical Trust. *Address:* 7 Cornwall Avenue, Finchley, London, N3 1LH, England (home).

NEARY, Martin Gerard James, LVO, MA, DMus, FRCO; British conductor and organist; b. 28 March 1940, London, England; s. of the late Leonard W. Neary and of Jeanne M. Thébault; m. Penelope J. Warren 1967; one s. two d. *Education:* City of London School and Gonville & Caius Coll., Cambridge. *Career:* Asst Organist, St Margaret's Westminster 1963–65, Organist and Master of Music 1965–71; Prof. of Organ, Trinity Coll. London 1963–72; Organist and Master of Music, Winchester Cathedral 1972–87; Founder and Conductor Martin Neary Singers 1972–; Conductor Waynflete Singers 1972–87; Organist and Master of Choristers, Westminster Abbey 1988–98; has led Westminster Abbey Choir on tours to France, Germany, Switzerland, Hungary, USA, Russia, Ukraine; Guest Conductor Australian Youth Choir 1999–; Founder and Conductor Millennium Consort Singers 2007, including appearances at Disney Hall, Los Angeles; Pres. Cathedral Organists Asscn 1985–88, Organists' Charitable Trust 1988–, Royal Coll. of Organists 1988–90, 1996–98; Chair. Church Services Cttee, Musicians Benevolent Fund 1993–98, Herbert Howells Soc. 1993–; Artistic Dir Paulist Boy Choristers of California 1999–2003; many organ recitals and broadcasts in UK (including First Night of the Proms 2004), Europe, USA, Canada, the Far East and Australia; many choral premières; guest conductor English Chamber Orchestra, London Symphony Orchestra, Netherlands Chamber Choir, Netherlands Radio Choir, Nat. Lutheran Choir, University Voices Canada. *Compositions include:* Responses, carol arrangements, All Saints Mass, Mass of the Redeemer, O Worship the Lord, Joy and Woe, Christmas Recordings. *Recordings:* numerous recordings. *Publications:* edns of early organ music, contribs to organ journals. *Honours:* Hon. RAM; Hon. FTCL; Hon. Fellow, Royal School of Church Music. *Address:* 44 Radipole Road, Fulham, London, SW6 5DL, England. *Telephone:* (20) 7736-5268. *E-mail:* martin@mneary.co .uk.

NEBE, Michael, DipEd, MMus, LRAM; German cellist and conductor; b. 28 July 1947, Nordenbeck, Waldeck. *Education:* Dortmund Conservatorium, King's College, London, England, studied with Thurston Dart, Brian Trowell, Antony Milner, Geoffrey Bush, Royal Academy of Music with Florence Hooton and Colin Hampton, studied in Germany and Morley College, London with Lawrence Leonard, International Conductors' Seminar, Zlin, Czech Republic with Kirk Trevor, Jiri Belohlavek and Zdenek Bilek. *Career:* debut at Wigmore Hall, London, 1977; mem., London Piace Consort, London Piace Duo, both until 1987, Plaegan Piano Quartet; numerous performances as soloist and chamber music player throughout the UK; tours in Germany, Netherlands, USA, Canada, Australia; Conductor and Musical Director of Whitehall Orchestra (The Orchestra of the British Civil Service), 1990–; Assoc. Conductor, Surrey Sinfonietta until 1994; founder and Musical Director, Fine Arts Sinfonia of London, 1994–; appearances as conductor in

the UK, Germany Spain, Turkey; Teacher, conductor, freelance musician, soloist, translator, writer, lecturer and adjudicator; numerous live and recorded radio and television appearances, album recordings; conducted over 100 British and world premières; mem. Dvořák Society, Incorporated Society of Musicians, Musicians' Union. *Publications:* translation into German, Eta Cohen's Violin Tutor, 1979; Cello Tutor, 1984; articles for British newspapers and magazines. *Telephone:* (20) 8671-4408. *Fax:* (20) 8671-2848. *E-mail:* admin@fasinfonia.freeserve.co.uk. *Website:* www.fasinfonia .freeserve.co.uk.

NEBLETT, Carol; singer (soprano); b. 1 Feb. 1946, Modesto, CA, USA. *Education:* studied with Lotte Lehmann and Pierre Bernac. *Career:* sang with Roger Wagner Chorale from 1965; Stage debut as Musetta, New York City Opera 1969; Returned as Marietta in Die Tote Stadt, Poppea, and Margherita and Elena in Boito's Mefistofele; Chicago 1975, as Chrysothemis in Elektra; Veinna Staatsoper debut 1976 as Minnie in La Fanciulla del West, Covent Garden 1977; Metropolitan Opera debut 1979, as Senta in Der fliegende Holländer; Returned as Tosca, Amelia (Un Ballo in Maschera), Manon Lescaut and Alice Ford in Falstaff; Appearances in Dallas, Turin, Leningrad, Pittsburgh, Baltimore and San Francisco; Other roles include Violetta, Minnie in La Fanciulla del West, Mozart's Countess, Charpentier's Louise and Antonia in Les Contes d'Hoffmann; Salzburg Festival as Vitelia in La Clemenza di Tito (has also appeared as Vitelia in Jean-Pierre Ponnelle's film of the opera); Teatro Regio Turin 1987, in Respighi's Semirama; Sang Mme Lidoine in Les Dialogues des Carmélites at San Diego, 1990; Debut as Norma for Greater Miami Opera 1990; Aida for Cincinnati Opera; Season 1992 as Tosca for Opera Pacific at Costa Mesa, Queen Isabella in Franchetti's Cristoforo Colombo at Miami and as Amelia in Un Ballo in Maschera at Dublin; Sang the title role in Blitzstein's Regina at Costa Mesa, 1990. *Recordings include:* Die Tote Stadt (RCA); La Fanciulla del West (Deutsche Grammophon); La Bohème (HMV).

NEBOLSIN, Eldar; Russian pianist; *Professor of Piano, Hanns Eisler Musik Hochschule;* b. 24 Dec. 1974, Tashkent; m. Lidia Lorite; one d. *Education:* Tashkent Uspensky School of Music, Escuela Superior de Música Reina Sofia. *Career:* appearances include Ravinia Festival with Riccardo Chailly, with Chicago Symphony 1994, Berlin Philharmonie with V. L. Ashkenazy, Deutsche Symphony Orchestra 1995, Avery Fisher Hall with New York Philharmonic and Leonard Slatkin, Cleveland Orchestra 1996, with Paavo Berglung, Mstislav Rostropovich, Accad. Santa Cecilia; Prof., Int. Inst. for Chamber Music, Escuela Superior de Música Reina Sofía, Madrid 2001–; Prof., Conservatorio Profesional de Música Francisco Escudero, San Sebastián 2004–06; Prof. of Piano, Hanns Eisler Musik Hochschule 2013–. *Recordings:* Chopin and Liszt recital, Chopin Piano Concerto No. 1, Rachmaninov's Preludes for Piano 2007, Liszt's Piano Concerti, with Vasily Petrenko, Chopin Works for Piano and Orchestra, Philharmonic Orchestra of Warsaw, with Antoni Wit. *Honours:* Concertino Prague Radio Competition, Santander Piano Competition Paloma O'Shea, Sviatoslav Richter Prize 2005. *Current Management:* Musiespaña, Calle José Marañón nº 10, 4º izq., 28010 Madrid, Spain. *Telephone:* (91) 5913290. *E-mail:* humberto.oran@musiespana.com. *Website:* www.musiespana.com. *Address:* Avenida Escondite, nº 4 bis., Urb. Los Peñascales, Torrelodones, 28250 Madrid, Spain (office). *Telephone:* (60) 6349218 (office). *E-mail:* nebolsineldar@hotmail.com (home). *Website:* www .eldarnebolsin.com.

NEEF, Alexander, MA; German opera administrator; *General Director, Canadian Opera Company;* b. 22 Feb. 1974, Ebersbach an der Fils; m. Eloise Bellemont-Neef; one d. *Education:* Eberhard Karls Univ., Tübingen. *Career:* Intern, Salzburg Festival 2000, with Artistic Admin Dept 2001; joined RuhrTriennale 2001, Progamming Dir 2004; Casting Dir Opéra Nat. de Paris 2004–08 (worked on 80 operas); with New York City Opera 2007; Gen. Dir Canadian Opera Co. 2008–. *Address:* Office of the General Director, Canadian Opera Company, 227 Front Street E., Toronto, Ont. M5A 1E8, Canada (office). *Telephone:* (416) 363-6671 (office). *E-mail:* info@coc.ca (office). *Website:* www .coc.ca (office).

NEGRIN, Francisco Miguel; Mexican opera director; b. 5 June 1963, Mexico City. *Education:* studied in France. *Career:* staff producer at Théâtre Royal de la Monnaie, Brussels; assisted directors such as Patrice Chéreau, K. E. Herrmann and Graham Vick; associations with many opera houses, including Paris Châtelet, Salzburg Landestheater and Seattle Opera; directed premiere of his version of Debussy's The Fall of the House of Usher, Christ Church, Spitalfields 1986, London Int. Opera Festival and Lisbon Opera 1989; produced Werther at Opéra de Nice 1990, Orlando Paladino at Garsington Manor 1990, La Traviata and the Mozart pasticcio The Jewel Box at Opera North 1991, the first outside production to be invited by Glyndebourne to be performed there 1991, Così fan tutte at Seattle Opera, Don Carlos at Victoria State Opera, Melbourne, L'Heure Espagnole and La Colombe at the Guildhall School of Music 1993, Handel's Julius Caesar at Australian Opera, Sydney 1994, Melbourne 1995; world premieres of Tourist Variations and Visitatio Sepulchri by James Macmillan at Glasgow's Tramway and at Edinburgh Festival, Una Cosa Rara by Martin y Soler at Drottningholm Festival; Schoeck's Venus at Geneva 1997; Handel's Partenope for Glimmerglass Opera, New York 1998. *Recordings include:* Julius Caesar. *Current Management:* c/o Ian Stones, Harrison Parrott, 5–6 Albion Court, London, W6 0QT, England. *E-mail:* francisco@negrin.com. *Website:* www.negrin.com.

NEIKRUG, Marc Edward, MM; composer and pianist; b. 24 Sept. 1946, New York, NY, USA. *Education:* studied with Giselher Klebe in Detmold, Stony Brook State Univ. of New York. *Career:* commissions from the Houston Symphony and the St Paul Chamber Orchestra (Consultant on Contemporary Music 1978); Los Alamos premiere at the Deutsche Oper Berlin 1988; duo partnership with Pinchas Zukerman; visited London 1989; British premiere of Violin Concerto at South Bank and duo recital at the Barbican Hall. *Compositions:* Piano Concerto 1966, Solo Cello Sonata 1967, Clarinet Concerto 1967, two String Quartets 1969, 1972, Viola Concerto 1974, Suite for cello and piano 1974, Rituals for flute and harp 1976, Concertino for ensemble 1977, Fantasies for violin and piano 1977, Continuum for cello and piano 1978, Cycle for seven pianos 1978, Kaleidoscope for flute and piano 1979, Eternity's Sunrise for orchestra 1979–80, Through Roses (theatre piece) 1979–80, Mobile for orchestra 1981, Violin Concerto 1982, Duo for violin and piano 1983, Los Alamos (opera) 1988, Chettro Ketl for chamber orchestra 1994, Sonata Concertante for violin and piano 1994, String Quintet 1995, Pueblo Children's Songs for soprano and piano 1995, Piano Concerto 1996. *Honours:* NEA Awards 1972, 1974, Besançon Film Festival Prizes (for Through Roses) 1981, Int. Film and Television Festival, New York prize (for Through Roses) 1982.

NEILL, Stuart; American singer (tenor); b. 1965, Atlanta, GA; m. 4th Sandra Lopez 2008. *Career:* sang Rodolfo in La Bohème at San Francisco 1993 (also at Venice and the Deutsche Oper Berlin); season 1994–95 as Arturo in I Puritani at Santiago, Geneva, Venice and the Vienna Staatsoper; Dallas Opera 1996, as Don Ottavio; Metropolitan Opera debut in I Puritani 1997; other roles include Arnoldo in Guillaume Tell, Gualtiero in Bellini's Pirata, Fernando in La Favorita, Alfredo, Don Carlo, Tosca, Turandot; further appearances at the Lyric Opera Chicago, Naples and Nice, La Scala, Milan, Teatro La Fenice, Royal Opera, Teatro Colon, Alte Oper Frankfurt, Dallas Opera, Lyric Opera of Chicago, Atlanta Symphony Orchestra, New York Philharmonic, San Francisco Symphony, Boston Symphony, Staatskapelle Dresden. *Honours:* three Grammy Awards. *E-mail:* webmaster@stuartneill.com (office). *Website:* www.stuartneill.com.

NEL, Anton, BMus, DipMus, MMus, DMus; pianist and academic; b. 29 Dec. 1961, Johannesburg, South Africa. *Education:* Univ. of the Witwatersrand, South Africa, Univ. of Cincinnati, USA. *Career:* debut at Carnegie Recital Hall, New York 1986; performances with orchestras, including Chicago, Seattle, Cincinnati, Brooklyn; recitals and chamber music concerts throughout USA, Canada, Europe, parts of Africa; recitals in Alice Tully Hall, New York; Barbican Centre and QEH, London; many appearances at summer festivals, including Aspen, Ravinia; Prof. of Piano, Eastman School of Music, Rochester, NY. *Recordings:* Saint-Saëns: Carnival of the Animals, Haydn: Four Sonatas. *Honours:* first prize Walter W. Naumburg Int. Piano Competition, first prize Joanna Hodges Int. Piano Competition, prizes at Leeds and Pretoria Int. Piano Competitions.

NELSON, Esther; American/German arts administrator; *General and Artistic Director, Boston Lyric Opera*; m. Bernd Ulken; two c. *Education:* Kaiserslautern Univ., Germany. *Career:* fmrly head of press, marketing and devt depts, New Orleans Opera; fmr Gen. Dir, Nevada Opera; Gen. Dir and CEO, Glimmerglass Opera 1995–2002; man. consultant working with clients including European Int. Music and Arts Foundation, Cultural Diplomacy Inst., New York, Albany Symphony Orchestra, Virginia Opera, Nat. Endowment for the Arts 2002–08; Gen. and Artistic Dir, Boston Lyric Opera 2008–. *Address:* Boston Lyric Opera, 45 Franklin Street, Boston, MA 02110-1316, USA (office). *Telephone:* (617) 542-4912 (office). *Fax:* (617) 542-4913 (office). *Website:* www.blo.org (office).

NELSON, John; American conductor; *Honorary Music Director, Ensemble Orchestral de Paris*; b. 6 Dec. 1941, San José, Costa Rica; m. Anita Nelson. *Education:* Juilliard School, New York. *Career:* Conductor, Berlioz's Les Troyens, New York 1972, New York City Opera 1972–; from 1973 at Metropolitan Opera, conducting Cavalleria Rusticana, Pagliacci, Jenůfa, Il Barbiere di Siviglia, Carmen and L'Incoronazione di Poppea; conducted US premiere of Britten's Owen Wingrave, Santa Fe Opera; Music Dir, Indianapolis Symphony Orchestra 1977–88, St Louis Opera 1981–91 (thereafter Principal Guest Conductor), Caramoor Festival, New York; currently Music Dir, Ensemble Orchestral de Paris 1998–2008, Hon. Music Dir 2008–; tour of Europe 1987; guest engagements with leading orchestras in North America and Europe; debut with Lyon Opéra 1991 conducting Béatrice and Bénédict; conducted Benvenuto Cellini at Geneva Opera 1992; Offenbach's The Tales of Hoffmann at the Bastille; other productions include Handel's Xerxes, Massenet's Don Quichotte with Chicago Lyric Opera, Béatrice and Bénédict with WNO, Faust at Geneva Opera, Benvenuto Cellini with Rome Opera, Don Carlos at Lyon Opéra and a new opera at Lyon Opéra by Marcel Landowski, Verdi's Vespri Siciliani at Rome 1997 and Handel's Giulio Cesare 1998; has worked with many of the world's leading orchestras and opera houses, including the New York and Los Angeles Philharmonic Orchestras, the Symphony Orchestras of Boston, Chicago, Cleveland, Pittsburgh, San Francisco, the LSO, Philharmonia, RPO, Hallé, Bournemouth Symphony, Scottish Nat. Orchestra, the Radio Orchestras of Hamburg, Munich, Berlin, Saarbrucken, the Orchestras of Oslo, Rotterdam, the Hague, the New Japan, Hong Kong and Shanghai Philharmonics; conducted numerous works by Berlioz 2003, by Schumann 2007; Founder, Soli Deo Gloria org. to promote the performance of sacred works. *Recordings include:* Béatrice and Bénédict (Diapason d'Or Award 1992), Bach Arias with Kathleen Battle, Gorecki's Beatus Vir with Czech Philharmonic, Handel's Semele with English Chamber Orchestra and Kathleen Battle (Grammy Award for Best Operatic Recording 1993), Works of Paul Schönfield 1994, Gorecki's Miserere (with Chicago Symphony and Chicago Lyric Opera choruses). *Current Management:* c/o Peter Railton, International Classical Artists, The Tower Building, 11 York Road, London, SE1 7NX, England. *E-mail:* prailton@icartists.co.uk.

NELSON, Richard Lawrence, BA, MD; American epidemiologist, academic and musician; *Adjunct Professor, Epidemiology/Biometry, University of Illinois School of Public Health*; b. 11 Oct. 1946, Evanston, Ill.; s. of Richard Lawrence Nelson and Mary Jane Curtis; m. Susan Jane Berryman 1972; three s. two d. *Education:* Stanford Univ., Univ. of Chicago, studied French horn with Paul Navarro, Liss van Pechman, Arnold Jacobs and Flugel with Iwan Williams. *Career:* Prof. of Surgery, Univ. of Illinois at Chicago 1995–; mem. Illinois Brass Band 1993–2001, North American Brass Band Asscn, Int. Horn Soc., Historic Brass Soc., Chicago Brass Band 2002, Prairie Brass Band 2004–; Co-ordinating Ed., Colorectal Cancer Collaborative Group of the Cochrane Collaboration; mem. American Coll. of Surgeons. *Recordings:* Christmas Fantasy, Illinois Brass Band Live, Championship Brass, Shakin' not Stirred. *Publications:* contrib. to Wind and Song – Arnold Jacobs by Brian Frederickson 1996. *Honours:* North American Brass Band Champions 1996, 1997, 1998, 2000, 2001, Order of Brass Band World 2001, New Year's Honors List, Brass Band World. *Address:* 956 SPH, 1603 West Taylor, Chiacgo, IL 60612 (office); 2651 Hillside Lane, Evanston, IL 60201, USA (home). *Telephone:* (224) 410-5592 (office). *E-mail:* altohorn@uic.edu (office); shadow881@aol.com (home).

NELSON, Ron, BM, MM, DMA; American composer and academic; b. 14 Dec. 1929, Joliet, IL; m. Helen Mitchell (deceased); one s. one d. *Education:* Eastman School of Music, Rochester and Ecole Normale de Musique, Paris, France. *Career:* Prof. Emeritus 1993–. *Compositions:* The Birthday of the Infanta (opera) 1956, The Christmas Story 1958, Toccata for orchestra 1963, What is Man? 1964, Rocky Point Holiday 1969, This is the Orchestra 1969, Prayer for an Emperor of China 1973, Five Pieces for orchestra (after paintings of Frank Wyeth) 1975, Four Pieces (after the seasons) 1978, Three Autumnal Sketches 1979, Mass of LaSalle 1981, Nocturnal Pieces 1982, Three Settings of the Moon 1982, Medieval Suite 1983, Aspen Jubilee 1984, Te Deum Laudamus 1985, Danza Capriccio for saxophone 1988, Three Pieces (after Tennyson) 1989, Fanfare for the Hour of Sunlight 1989, Morning Alleluias 1989, The Deum Laudamus 1991, To the Airborne 1991, Passacaglin (Homage on B-A-C-H) 1992, Lauds (Praise High Day) 1992, Epiphanies, fanfares and chorales 1994, Chaconne (In memoriam. . .) 1994.

NELSONS, Andris; Latvian conductor; *Music Director, Boston Symphony Orchestra*; b. 18 Nov. 1978, Rīga; m. Kristine Opolais (q.v.); one d. *Education:* Emils Darzins Music School, Latvian Acad. of Music, St Petersburg Conservatory, Russia, pvt study with Mariss Jansons, master-classes with Neeme Järvi and Jorma Panula. *Career:* began career as trumpeter with Latvian Nat. Opera Orchestra; Asst Conductor Latvian Nat. Opera 2001–03, Prin. Conductor 2003–07; Prin. Conductor, Nordwestdeutsche Philharmonie, Herford 2003–; Music Dir City of Birmingham Symphony Orchestra 2008–15, Boston Symphony Orchestra 2014–; Chief Conductor, Gewandhausorchester Leipzig 2015–; regular guest appearances with Berliner Philharmoniker, Wiener Philharmoniker, Het Koninklijk Concertgebouworkest, Symphonieorchester des Bayerischen Rundfunks and Philharmonia Orchestra; regular guest at Royal Opera House Covent Garden, Wiener Staatsoper and the Metropolitan Opera New York. *Recordings include:* Strauss, Also sprach Zarathustra, Don Juan, Till Eulenspiegels lustige Streiche with City of Birmingham Symphony Orchestra, Wagner, Overture to Tannhäuser, Sibelius Symphony No. 2 with Boston Symphony Orchestra, Wagner, Der fliegende Holländer with Concertgebouw Orkest 2015, Shostakovich: Under Stalin's Shadow - Symphony No. 10 2015, Tchaikovsky: Slavonic March - Manfred Symphony 2015. *Honours:* Latvian Grand Music Award 2001, Preis der deutschen Schallplattenkritik, ECHO Klassik as Conductor of the Year. *Current Management:* c/o KDS UK, 40 St Martin's Lane, London, WC2N 4ER, England. *Telephone:* (20) 7395-0910. *Fax:* (20) 7395-0911. *E-mail:* karen.mcdonald@kdschmid.co.uk. *Website:* www.kdschmid.de; www.bso.org; www.gewandhausorchester.de.

NĚMCOVÁ, Miriam; Czech conductor; *Conducting Professor, Prague Conservatory*; b. 2 Aug. 1961, Prague; d. of Mudr Zvonimié Němec and Dagmar Němcová. *Education:* Prague Conservatory, Acad. of Music, Prague, Conservatoire Nat. Supérieur de Musique, Paris, France. *Career:* Choir Mistress, Rosa Chamber Chorus, Prague 1977–89, Charles Univ. 1980–85, Prague Radio 1987–88; Conductor Prague Madrigalists 1987–88, Asst Choir Mistress 1988–89; Conductor Liberec Opera Theatre 1989–90, Karlsbad Symphony Orchestra 1990, Prague Chamber Opera 1990–91, Karlovy Vary Symphony Orchestra 1991; Founder Praga Sinfonietta 1990; Artistic Dir and Conductor F. X. Šalda Theatre, Liberec 1991; Conducting Prof. Prague Conservatory 1995–, Dir Symphony Orchestra 1995–; Perm. Chief Conductor Hradec Králové Philharmonic 2001–. *Address:* Pražská Konzervatoř, Na Rejdisti 1, 110 00 Prague 1, Czech Republic (office). *Telephone:* (2) 22327206 (office). *Fax:* (2) 22326406 (office). *E-mail:* conserv@prgcons.cz (office). *Website:* www.prgcons.cz (office).

NEMETH, Géza; Hungarian violist; b. 1930. *Education:* Franz Liszt Acad., Budapest. *Career:* violist, Bartók Quartet 1957–; performances in nearly every European country and tours to Australia, Canada, Japan, New Zealand and the USA; festival appearances at Adelaide, Ascona, Aix, Venice, Dubrovnik,

Edinburgh, Helsinki, Lucerne, Menton, Prague, Vienna, Spoleto and Schwetzingen; tours of the UK, including concerts at Cheltenham, Dartington, Philharmonic Hall Liverpool, RNCM Manchester, the Wigmore Hall, the Sheldonian Theatre Oxford, Harewood House and Birmingham; repertoire includes standard classics and Hungarian works by Bartók, Durko, Bozay, Kadosa, Soproni, Farkas, Szabo and Lang. *Recordings include:* complete quartets of Mozart, Beethoven and Brahms, major works of Haydn and Schubert, complete quartets of Bartók. *Honours:* with mems of Bartók Quartet: Kossuth Prize, Outstanding Artist of the Hungarian People's Republic 1981, UNESCO/IMC Prize 1981. *Address:* Nippon Artists Management Inc., 5-4-10-3F Koishikawa Bunkyo, Tokyo 112-0002, Japan.

NENDICK, Josephine; British singer (soprano); b. 1940, Kent, England. *Education:* Royal Coll. of Music, Guildhall School of Music with Audrey Langford. *Career:* sang first at the Aldeburgh Festival, then premiered works by Boulez and Bo Nilsson at Darmstadt; has sung with such ensembles as Capricorn, Domaine Musical, Ensemble Musique Nouvelles, Music Group of London, Les Percussions de Strasbourg; festival engagements at Avignon, Berlin, Cheltenham, London (English Bach), Edinburgh, Prades, Royaun, Warsaw; repertoire includes Berg, Der Wein; Berio Magnificat, Chamber Music, Circles; Four Popular Songs, Sequenza; Boulez Improvisations sur Mallarmé, Le Marteau sans Maitre, Le Soleil des Eaux; Birtwistle Entractes and Sappho Fragments; Bussotti Le Passion selon Sade; Ravel Chansons Medécasses and three Poemes de Stephane Mallarmé; Schoenberg Pierrot Lunaire and Das Buch der Hängenden Gärten; Webern Songs Op 8 and Op 13; Bartók Village Scenes; works by Barraqué, Smith Brindle, Finnissy, Dillon, Cage, Crumb, Dallapiccola, Stravinsky, Babbitt, Ives and Satie; sang in Bach's Christmas Oratorio, Berlioz Les Troyens (Ascanius), Delius A Mass of Life; Mahler Das Lied von der Erde, Monteverdi L'Incoronazione di Poppea (Drusilla, at Bremen) and Mozart's Requiem and C minor Mass. *Recordings include:* Boulez Le Soleil des Eaux; Lutyens Quincunx, with the BBC Symphony Orchestra; Barraqué Sequence and Chant après Chant.

NERDRUM, Sonja; singer (mezzo-soprano); b. 1 Oct. 1953, Bern, Switzerland. *Education:* West London Inst. of Higher Education, studied with Eduardo Asquez, Jeffrey Talbot and Françoise Garner. *Career:* debut in Abbaye de Flaran, Gascogne, as Dorabella in Così fan tutte directed by Jean-Claude Auvray 1978; Dorabella in Angers, conductor Sylvain Cambreling; Apollo/Mirtillo in Handel's Il pastor fido at Den Norske Opera, in the Drottningholm production; Giacinta in Mozart's La finta semplice in Batignano, conductor David Parry; Zweite Dame in Die Zauberflöte at Opéra de Montpellier; Dorabella in Oslo Summer Opera, returning as Hermia in A Midsummer Night's Dream; La Baronne in La Vie parisienne for ENO; Donizetti's Maria Stuarda in Kristiansund; Marcellina in Le nozze di Figaro at Versailles and for Jean-Claude Malgoire at Tourcoing; Puccini's Tosca, touring Middle and Far East; concert repertoire includes Norwegian, French, Italian, German, English and Russian songs. *Honours:* Hon. RCM 1988.

NERSESSIAN, Pavel; pianist; b. 26 Aug. 1968, Ramenskoye, Moscow, Russia. *Education:* Central Music School, Moscow and Tchaikovsky Conservatory. *Career:* concert tours of Russia from 1972 and appearances in Spain, Hungary, Italy, France and Ireland; season 1992–93 in Cannes and Dublin, tour of Japan and appearances in Austria, England, Ireland, Canada, and the USA; Prof. of Piano, Moscow Conservatory. *Honours:* second prize Beethoven Competition, Vienna 1985.

NESCHLING, John; Brazilian conductor; b. 1947, Rio de Janeiro; m. Patrícia Melo; two s. *Education:* studied in Vienna with Hans Swarowsky, with Leonard Bernstein in the USA. *Career:* engagements with the London, Vienna and Berlin Radio Symphony Orchestras, New York and Israel Philharmonic, the Tonhalle, Zürich and the Italian Radio at Naples and Milan; opera appearances at Berlin (Deutsche Oper and Staatsoper), Stuttgart, Hamburg and Stockholm; Principal Conductor, San Carlo Lisbon 1981–88; Music Dir, Teatro de São Paulo, Teatro do Rio de Janeiro, St Gallen Theatre, Switzerland, Teatro Maasimo, Palermo, Opera de Bordeaux; Artistic Dir, Orquestra Sinfônica do Estado de São Paulo 1997–2009. *Compositions:* for film: Os Condenados 1973, Lúcio Flávio, o Passageiro da Agonia 1977, O Grande Desbum... 1978, O Cortiço 1978, Gaijin - Os Caminhos da Liberdade 1980, Bonitinha Mas Ordinária ou Otto Lara Rezende 1981, Álbum de Família 1981, Pixote: A Lei do Mais Fraco 1981, Kiss of the Spider Woman 1985, O Judeu 1996, Desmundo 2002. *Recordings include:* Il Guarany 1996. *Honours:* winner Int. Competition for Young Conductors, Florence, London Symphony Orchestra Int. Competition, Latin Grammy Award for Best Classical Album 2007. *Address:* c/o Orquestra Sinfônica do Estado de São Paulo, Praça Júlio Prestes S/N°, 01218-020, São Paulo, SP, Brazil (office). *E-mail:* orquestra@osesp.art.br (office). *Website:* www.osesp.art.br (office).

NESS, Arthur J., BMus, AM, PhD; American musicologist and academic (retd); b. 27 Jan. 1936, Chicago, Ill.; s. of Martin Ness and Rosetta Ness; m. Charlotte A. Kolczynski 1982. *Education:* Univ. of Southern California, Harvard Univ., New York Univ., Ludwig-Maxmillians-Universität, Munich, Germany (Fulbright Fellow). *Career:* Asst Prof., Univ. of Southern California 1964–76; Assoc. Prof. and Dept Chair., Daemen Coll. 1976–83; Visiting Prof., State Univ. of NY, Buffalo 1983–87; ed. and music engraver 1990–; Gen. Ed. Monuments of the Lutenist Art 1992–94; regular participant at int. confs on lute music in Tours, Freiburg, Milan, Aquila, Chicago, Amsterdam etc. *Compositions:* Three Poems by Kenneth Patchen for alto and piano. *Publications:* Lute Works of Francesco Canova da Milano (1497–1543) 1970, The Herwarth Lute Tablatures 1984, The Königsberg Manuscript (with John M. Ward) 1989, The Lute Works of Marco dall'Aguila (mysite.verizon.net/vzepq31c/marcodallaquila) 2010; major contrib. to New Grove Dictionary of Music 1980–2000, New Harvard Dictionary of Music 1986, Journal of American Musicological Society, Le Luth et sa Musique II 1985, Music in Context: Essays for John M. Ward 1985, New Grove Dictionary of American Music 1986; numerous reviews in Journal of the American Musicological Society, Journal of the Lute Society of America and in Notes: Quarterly of the Music Library Association. *Honours:* Merit Salary Award for excellence in teaching and scholarship, Daemen Coll. 1980, Cleary Award, New York Univ. for the outstanding dissertation in the humanities and social sciences for 1984, honoured with a three-vol. Festschrift published by the Lute Soc. of America 2011–12. *Address:* 2039 Commonwealth Avenue, Suite 10, Boston, MA 02135, USA. *Telephone:* (617) 254-6509. *E-mail:* arthurjness@verizon.net (office).

NESTERENKO, Evgeni, DipEng; Russian/Austrian singer (bass) and teacher; b. 8 Jan. 1938, Moscow, USSR; s. of Evgeni Nesterenko and Velta Baumann; m. Ekaterina Alexeyeva 1963; one s. *Education:* Leningrad Eng Inst. and Leningrad Conservatory with V. Lukanin. *Career:* debut as General Ermolov in War and Peace, Maly Theatre, Leningrad 1963; soloist with Leningrad Maly Opera and Ballet Theatre 1963–67; soloist with Kirov Opera 1967–71; teacher of solo singing, Leningrad Conservatory 1967–72, Moscow Conservatory 1975–93, Konservatorium Wien 1993–2003; soloist with the Bolshoi 1971–2003; mem. staff, Moscow Musical Pedagogical Inst. 1972–74; Chair. of Singing at Moscow Conservatoire 1975–93, Prof. 1981–93; USSR People's Deputy 1989–91; seasons at Budapest 1970, Vienna Staatsoper 1975, Metropolitan Opera 1975, Teatro Colón, Buenos Aires 1975, La Scala, Milan 1977, Covent Garden 1978, Verona Festival 1978, Munich 1978, Estonia 1980, Japan 1983, Barcelona 1984, Bregenz Festival 1986, Savonlinna Festival 1987, Hamburg 1986, Orange Festival 1990, Antwerp 1993, Hong Kong 2002, São Paulo 2006; mem. Int. Acad. of Creative Endeavours, Moscow 1991. *Roles include:* Boris Godunov, Ivan Khovansky and Dosifey (Khovanshchina), Igor and Khan Konchak (Prince Igor), Mephistopheles (Faust), Grigori (Quiet Flows the Don), General Ermolov and Kutuzov (War and Peace), Filippo II (Don Carlo), Attila, Zaccaria (Nabucco), Don Pasquale, Sarastro (Magic Flute), Bluebeard, Gremin (Eugene Onegin), Ivan Susanin, Old Convict (Lady Macbeth), Don Basilio, Enrico VIII, Moses, Water-Sprite (Rusalka), Don Bartolo. *Recordings:* Glinka's Ruslan and Lyudmila and Ivan Susanin, Tchaikovsky's Mazeppa, Iolanta and Eugene Onegin, Rachmaninov's Francesca da Rimini and Aleko, Songs by Shostakovich and Mussorgsky, Suite on Poems of Michelangelo and 14th Symphony by Shostakovich, Verdi Requiem, Nabucco, Attila and Trovatore, Gounod's Faust, Dvořák's Rusalka, Donizetti's Don Pasquale and L'Elisir d'amore, Bela Bartók's Bluebeard's Castle; videos: Verdi's Attila, Rachmaninov's Aleko, Mussorgsky's Boris Godunov and Khovanshchina, Glinka's A Life for the Tsar. *Publications:* Evgeni Nesterenko, Thoughts on My Profession 1985, Evgeni Nesterenko, Memoirs of a Russian Bass 2011. *Honours:* People's Artist of the USSR 1976, Viotti d'Oro Prize, City of Vercelli (Italy) 1981, Lenin Prize 1982, Melodia Golden Disc, USSR 1984, Giovanni Zenatello Prize, Verona (Italy) 1986, Hero of Labour 1988, Chaliapin Prize 1992, Wilhelm Furtwängler Prize (Germany) 1992, Austrian Kammersänger 1992, Casta Diva Prize 2001, Golden Pegasus Theatre Prize (Poland) 2004, Centaur with Gold Flower 2009.

NETHSINGHA, Andrew Mark, MA, FRCO, ARCM; British conductor and organist; *Director of Music, St John's College, Cambridge*; b. 16 May 1968, Worcs., England; s. of Lucian Nethsingha and Jane Nethsingha; m. Lucy; one s. two d. *Education:* Royal Coll. of Music, London, Univ. of Cambridge. *Career:* Asst Organist, Wells Cathedral 1990–94; Master of the Choristers and Organist, Truro Cathedral 1994–2002; Musical Dir Three Spires Singers and Orchestra 1994–2002; Dir of Music, Gloucester Cathedral 2002–07; Dir of Music, St John's Coll., Cambridge 2007–; Musical Dir Gloucester Choral Soc. 2002–07; Artistic Dir Three Choirs Festival 2002–07; Pres. Cathedral Organists' Asscn 2007–09; conducted Philharmonia, Royal Philharmonic Orchestra, City of Birmingham Symphony Orchestra, BBC Concert Orchestra, Aarhus Symphony Orchestra, Orchestra of St Luke's, Britten Sinfonia, London Mozart Players; conducted in China, South Africa, Singapore, Canada, Japan, Mexico, Hong Kong, USA and Europe; organ recitals include at Nôtre-Dame de Paris, Washington Nat. Cathedral; conducting venues have included BBC Proms, Royal Albert Hall, Amsterdam Concertgebouw, Tokyo Suntory Hall, Verbier Festival; mem. Inc. Soc. of Musicians, Royal Coll. of Organists. *Radio:* numerous broadcasts for BBC and in Japan, USA, The Netherlands, Switzerland, European radio, Canada, Hong Kong. *Television:* various BBC programmes, also stations in USA. *Recordings:* 11 CDs for Chandos with St John's College Choir; other discs for Abbey, Avie, Cantoris, Priory, St John's Coll.. *Honours:* Hon. Fellow, Royal School of Church Music, Guild of Church Musicians. *Address:* St John's College, K1 First Court, Cambridge, CB2 1TP, England (office). *Telephone:* (1223) 338683 (office). *E-mail:* an323@cam.ac.uk (office). *Website:* www.sjcchoir.co.uk (office).

NETREBKO, Anna; Austrian (b. Russian) singer (soprano); b. 18 Sept. 1971, Krasnodar, Russia; one s. with Erwin Schrott (q.v.). *Education:* Rimsky-Korsakov Conservatory. *Career:* debut at Mariinsky Opera Theatre, St Petersburg 1994, as Susanna; roles include Glinka's Ludmila with Kirov Opera, Gilda in Rigoletto and Kundry in Parsifal at St Petersburg; first appearance at Salzburg Festival 1998; tours with Kirov Opera as Pamina and Bizet's Micaela; sang Gilda at Washington 1999 and New York, Mimi at San Francisco 1999–2000 and New York; concerts with Rotterdam Philharmonic

Orchestra include London Proms and Teresa in Benvenuto Cellini, Royal Festival Hall 1999; sang Natasha in War and Peace at St Petersburg and London 2000; other roles include Zerlina and Louisa in Prokofiev's Betrothal in a Monastery at San Francisco, Rosina, Pamina and Xenia in Boris Godunov, Mozart's Servilia at Covent Garden 2002, Donna Anna in Don Giovanni at Salzburg 2003 and Covent Garden 2007, Violetta in La Traviata at Salzburg 2005, Norina in Don Pasquale in New York 2005, and Elvira in I Puritani 2006; role debuts as Leonora in Il trovatore at Berlin Staatsoper, in title role of Puccini's Manon Lescaut, Lady Macbeth in Bavarian State Opera's Macbeth, Marguerite in Gounod's Faust at Covent Garden, Vienna's Staatsoper and Festspielhaus, Baden-Baden 2013; title role in Giovanna d'Arco, La Scala 2015. *Recordings include:* Glinka's Ruslan and Ludmila, Mozart Album 2006, Souvenirs 2008, In the Still of Night 2010, Rossini's Stabat Mater (Gramophone Editor's Choice Award 2011), Anna Netrebko – Live at the Metropolitan Opera 2011, Anna Netrebko – Verdi 2013, Four Last Songs 2014. *Honours:* First Prize, All-Russian Glinka Vocal Competition, Moscow 1993, Third Prize, Rimsky-Korsakov Int. Competition for Young Opera Singers, St Petersburg 1996, Costa Diva Prize 1998, Golden Sophit Prize, St Petersburg 1999, Russian State Prize 2005, Bambi Award 2006, Classical BRIT Award for Singer of the Year 2007, Musician of the Year, Musical America Awards 2008, People's Artist of Russia 2008, ten ECHO Klassik Awards. *Current Management:* c/o Judith Neuhoff, Centre Stage Artist Management, Stralauer Allee 1, 10245 Berlin, Germany. *E-mail:* judith.neuhoff@centrestagemanagement.com. *Website:* www.annanetrebko.com.

NETTL, Bruno, BA, MA, PhD; American musicologist and writer; *Professor of Music and Anthropology Emeritus, University of Illinois;* b. 14 March 1930, Prague, Czechoslovakia; m. Wanda Maria White 1952; two d. *Education:* Indiana Univ., Univ. of Michigan Ann Arbor. *Career:* instructor in music 1953–54, Asst Prof. of Music 1954–56, 1959–64, Music Librarian 1958–64, Wayne State Univ., Detroit; Ed., Ethnomusicology 1961–65, 1988–2002, Yearbook of the Int. Folk Music Council 1975–77; Assoc. Prof. of Music 1965–67, Prof. of Music and Anthropology 1967–92, Prof. Emeritus 1992–, Chair Division of Musicology 1967–72, 1975–77, 1982–85, Univ. of Illinois, Urbana; numerous visiting lectureships and professorships, including Visiting Prof. of Music Harvard Univ. 1990, Distinguished Albert Seay Prof. of Music Colorado Coll. 1992, Visiting Hill Prof. of Music Univ. of Minnesota 1995, Benedict Distinguished Visiting Prof. of Music Carleton Coll. 1996; mem. American Acad. of Arts and Sciences, Coll. Music Soc., Int. Council for Traditional Music, Int. Musicological Soc., Soc. of Ethnomusicology (pres. 1969–71, hon. mem. 2001). *Publications:* North American Indian Musical Styles 1954, Music in Primitive Culture 1956, An Introduction to Folk Music in the United States (third edn, revised by H. Myers, as Folk Music in the United States: An Introduction 1976) 1960, Cheremis Musical Styles 1960, Reference Materials in Ethnomusicology 1961, Theory and Method in Ethnomusicology 1964, Folk and Traditional Music of the Western Continents 1965, Daramad of Chahargah: A Study in the Performance Practice of Persian Music (with B. Foltin Jr) 1972, Contemporary Music and Music Cultures (with C. Hamm and R. Byrnside) 1975, Eight Urban Musical Cultures: Tradition and Change (ed.) 1978, The Study of Ethnomusicology: 29 Issues and Concepts 1983, The Western Impact on World Music: Change, Adaptation, and Survival 1985, The Radif of Persian Music: Studies of Structure and Cultural Context 1987, Blackfoot Musical Thought: Comparative Perspectives 1989, Comparative Musicology and Anthropology in Music: Essays on the History of Ethnomusicology (ed. with P. Bohlman) 1991, Excursions in World Music (with others) 1992, Community of Music: An Ethnographical Seminar in Champaign-Urbana (ed. with others) 1993, Heartland Excursions: Ethnomusicological Reflections on Schools of Music 1995, In the Course of Performance: Studies in the World of Musical Improvisation (ed. with M. Russell) 1998, Encounters in Ethnomusicology 2002. *Honours:* Hon. LHD (Univ. of Chicago) 1993, (Univ. of Illinois) 1996, (Carleton Coll.) 2000, (Kenyon Coll.) 2002;hon. mem. American Musicological Soc. 1995; Koizumi Prize in Ethnomusicology, Tokyo 1994. *Address:* c/o University of Illinois, Department for Performing Arts, EPASW Bldg, 1040 W Harrison Street, MC-255, Chicago, IL 60607; 1423 Cambridge Drive, Champaign, IL 61821, USA.

NEUBAUER, Margit; singer (mezzo-soprano); b. 1950, Austria. *Education:* studied in Vienna. *Career:* sang at Linz Landestheater 1975–77, notably in 1976 premiere of Der Aufstand by Helmut Eder; engagements at Frankfurt Opera from 1977, Zürich 1978–79, Hamburg 1980–83, Deutsche Oper Berlin 1982–85; Bayreuth Festival 1981–86, as Sigrune in Die Walküre and a Flowermaiden in Parsifal; US tour with Deutsche Oper 1985; roles have included Cherubino, Flosshilde, Brigitte in Korngold's Tote Stadt, Annina, Rosenkavalier and the title role in Miss Jule by Bibalo; many concert appearances, notably in baroque music. *Recordings:* Parsifal at Bayreuth 1985, Bach B minor Mass and Handel Utrecht Te Deum.

NEUDAUER, Lena; German violinist; *Professor of Violin, Hochschule für Musik Saar;* b. 1984, Munich. *Education:* Mozarteum, Salzburg with Helmut Zehetmair, Thomas Zehetmair and Christoph Poppen. *Career:* played Vivaldi's Four Seasons with members of Munich Philharmonic in Japan and Munich aged 11; performances with orchestras including MDR Symphony Orchestra, Deutsche Radio Philharmonie Saarbrücken Kaiserslautern, Munich Chamber Orchestra, Nuremberg, Brandenburg and Munich Symphony Orchestra, Orchestra of the Staatstheater am Gärtnerplatz, German Chamber Acad. Neuss, Salzburg Chamber Soloists, Orchestre Nat. de Belgique, Orchestra di Padova e del Veneto, Polish Chamber Philharmonic; played under conductors including Christoph Poppen, Dennis Russell Davies, Mariss Jansons, David Stahl, Wojciech Rajski, Lavard Skou Larsen; contemporary music performances with Ensemble Intercontemporain and Pierre Boulez, Österreichische Ensemble für Neue Musik; festival appearances at Mozart Week, Salzburg, Mecklenburg-Vorpommern Festival, Schleswig-Holstein Music Festival, Braunschweig Classix, Chamber Music Festival Hohenstaufen, Gaia Chamber Music Festival Thun, Int. Pharos Chamber Music Festival, Music Festival Schloss Cappenberg, Festival of the Nations, Bad Wörishofen, Festival Musical Olympus, St Petersburg, Flandern Festival; Prof. of Violin, Hochschule für Musik Saar in Saarbrücken 2010–. *Recordings include:* Robert Schumann – Complete Works for Violin and Orchestra (Best Concert Recording, International Classical Music Awards 2011) 2010. *Honours:* First Prize, Mozart Prize, Richard Strauss Prize for best interpretation of Richard Strauss's Violin Concerto and Audience Prize, Leopold Mozart Int. Competition, Augsburg 1999. *Current Management:* c/o Daniela Wiehen Artists Management, Espellohweg 65, 22607 Hamburg, Germany. *Telephone:* (40) 3869-9927. *E-mail:* daniela@wiehen.de. *Website:* www.wiehen.de. *Address:* Hochschule für Musik Saar, Bismarckstraße 1, 66111 Saarbrücken, Germany (office). *Telephone:* (681) 967310 (office). *Fax:* (681) 9673130 (office). *Website:* www.hfm.saarland.de (office); www.lena-neudauer.de.

NEUENFELS, Hans; German stage director; b. 1941, Krefeld; m. Elisabeth Trissenaar; one s. *Career:* debut production, Il Trovatore at Nuremberg 1974; Frankfurt Opera 1976–80, with Macbeth, Aida, Die Gezeichneten by Schreker and Busoni's Doktor Faust; productions at Deutsche Oper Berlin 1982–86 have included La Forza del Destino, Rigoletto and Zimmermann's Die Soldaten; Paris Opéra 1989 with the premiere of York Höller's Der Meister und Margarita (the last production at the Palais Garnier before the opening of the Opéra Bastille); Il Trovatore at the Deutsche Oper 1996; Le Prophète by Meyerbeer at the Vienna State Opera 1998; Fledermaus, Salzburg Festival 2001; Idomeno, Deutsche Oper Berlin 2003; Zauberflote, Komiche Oper Berlin 2006.

NEUHOLD, Günter, MA; Austrian conductor; b. 2 Nov. 1947, Graz; m. Emma Schmidt; one s. *Education:* advanced courses with Franco Ferrara in Rome, Hans Swarowski in Vienna. *Career:* engaged at various German opera houses, 1972–80, ending as First Kapellmeister in Hanover and Dortmund; Music Dir, Teatro Regio di Parma, 1981–86, devoted mainly to Verdi operas and as Chief Conductor, Arturo Toscanini Symphonic Orchestra of Emilia Romagna; Chief Conductor, Musical Dir, Flanders Royal Philharmonic Orchestra, Antwerp, 1986–90, with tours, Germany, Italy, UK, France; Gen. Music Dir, Badisches Staatstheater Karlsruhe, 1989–95, conducting a Richard Strauss cycle and Ring des Nibelungen; Gen. Music Dir, Artistic Dir, Theater der Freien Hansestadt Bremen and Philharmonische Orchester Bremen, 1995–2002; Concerts with Wiener Philharmoniker, Staatskapelle Dresden, Philharmonic Orchestra Monte Carlo, Tokyo Philharmonic Orchestra, Tokyo Metropolitan Opera, radio orchestras of several German stations, also ORF, RAI, BBC, Radio-Television Moscow, CBC Canada, ABC Australia, Nat. Orchestra of Capitol Toulouse; Operas at Wiener Staatsoper, La Scala, Staatsoper Dresden, Nationaltheater München, Berliner Staatsoper, Deutsche Oper Berlin, Komische Oper Berlin, Oper Leipzig, Staatsoper Hamburg, Grand Théatre Genève, Opéra de Monte Carlo, Capitol Toulouse, Real Madrid, Philadelphia Opera, Teatro Colon, Buenos Aires, Teatro San Carlos, Naples; tours of USA, Japan, Russia; Appeared Salzburg Festival, 1978, 1980, 1983, 1986, Radio France Festival-Montpellier, Flanders Festival, Musikfestspiele Dresden. *Recordings:* Bach St Matthew Passion; Bartók's Bluebeard's Castle and Concerto for Orchestra; Brahms Symphony No. 1; Berlioz Damnation de Faust; Rolf Liebermann orchestral and vocal works; Mahler Symphonies Nos 1, 2, 3, 5; Puccini Madama Butterfly (vers 1904); Strauss's Dynastie; Wagner: Rheingold, Walküre, Siegfried, Götterdämmerung; and many more. *Honours:* Grand Decoration of Honour in Silver for Services to the Repub. of Austria 1999; First Prize, Contest in Florence, Marinuzzi Contest, San Remo 1976, Böhm Contest, Salzburg 1977, Second Prize, Swarowski Contest, Vienna, Third Prize, Cantelli Contest, Milan 1977. *Address:* Scheibengasse 14, 1190 Vienna, Austria (home). *Telephone:* (1) 369-57-49 (home). *E-mail:* neuhold@dirigent.at (office). *Website:* www.dirigent.at (home); www.neuhold.dirigent.at (home).

NEUMAN, Maxine Darcy, BMus, MMus; American/German concert cellist, academic and administrator; b. 1 July 1948, Philadelphia, Pa, USA; d. of Marvin Neuman and Helga Neuman (née Hennigson); m. Reinhard Humburg 1987; one d. one s. *Education:* Manhattan School of Music, New York. *Career:* cellist, New Jersey Symphony Orchestra 1969–71, Mostly Mozart Festival Orchestra, American Ballet Theatre, American Composers Orchestra 1971–80, Walden Trio 1972–, Contemporary Trio 1975–80, Crescent String Quartet 1979–, Berkshire Chamber Players 1980–85, St Luke's Chamber Ensemble 1980–, Breve, Ensemble for Early Music 1985–, Claremont Duo, Germany 1998–, Belmont Trio 2000–, Por el Tango 2006–; lead cello, Ron Carter Nonet 2014–; Prof. of Music, Bennington Coll., Vt 1981–95, Chair. Music Dept 1985–86, 1990; Prof. of Music, Williams Coll., Mass 1994–95, 1998; Prof. of Music, Hawthorne Valley School 1996–2000; mem. Faculty, School for Strings, New York 1996–, Hoff-Barthelson School, New York 2003–, Mannes Coll. 2008–; annual solo tours to Europe, S America, Japan, USA; festivals include Caramoor, Manchester Music Festival, Chamber Music Conference of the Northeast; Judge, Concert Artists Guild Competition 1986–; panelist, Mass Cultural Council 1996, 2001; mem. Bd of Dirs Bronx Opera Co. 1972–85, Chamber Music Conf. 1987–; Asst Music Dir, Chamber Music Conf.

2014–15, Assoc. Music Dir 2015–; mem. American Fed. of Musicians 1969–, Chamber Music America 1980–. *Recordings:* Nighthawks (film score); more than 98 CD releases on int. labels 1980–. *Honours:* Ford Foundation Grant 1971–72, Ford Foundation Award 1975, Winner, Nat. Arts Competition 1975, Double Award of Merit, Nat. Fed. of Music Clubs 1976, New York State Council on the Arts Grants 1979, 1981, 1995, 2001, Geraldine Rockefeller Dodge Grants 1982, 1992, 1994, Grammy Awards 1988, 1990, 2003, Int. Congress on Women in Music Award, UN 1990, Link Outreach Grant, Carnegie Hall 1994–2001, Carnegie Mellon Foundation Awards 2005, 2006, 2008. *Address:* 200 Claremont Avenue, New York, NY 10027 (home); 148 College Road, North Bennington, VT 05257, USA (office). *Telephone:* (212) 222-7896 (home); (802) 442-2349 (office). *E-mail:* cellomax@aol.com (office). *Website:* cellomax.com.

NEUMANN, Gunther; German singer (tenor); b. 22 Aug. 1938, Stablack. *Career:* debut in Potsdam 1965, as Belmonte; Komische Oper Berlin from 1969, notably as Idomeneo, Lohengrin, Verdi's Riccardo and Alvaro, Pinkerton and Rodolfo; modern repertory includes Alwa in Lulu, Sergei in Lady Macbeth and Schoenberg's Aron (Cologne 1995); guest engagements at the Vienna Staatsoper as Tannhäuser and Volksoper as Vitalino in Handel's Giustino 1995, Hamburg as Walther von Stolzing, Verona and Tel-Aviv (Handel's Belshazzar 1995); other roles include Offenbach's Bluebeard at Covent Garden 1989, Grischka in Rimsky's Kitezh at Komische Oper 1996; sang Calaf in Berlin 1998; season 2000–01 as Herod in Salome at Trier, Shuisky in Boris Godunov at the Komische Oper, Berlin, and Wagner's Loge at Meiningen.

NEUMANN, Wolfgang; singer (tenor); b. 20 June 1945, Waiern, Austria. *Education:* studied in Essen and Duisburg. *Career:* debut in Bielefeld 1973, as Max in Der Freischütz; sang at Augsburg from 1978, Mannheim from 1980; Maggio Musicale Florence 1983, as Tannhäuser; appearances in Zürich, Bologna, Munich and Hamburg; other roles include Wagner's Erik, Rienzi, Schoenberg's Aron (at Barcelona), Tristan, Lohengrin and Siegfried, Verdi's Otello, the Emperor in Die Frau ohne Schatten, Turiddu in Cavalleria Rusticana, Puccini's Calaf and Edgar in Reimann's Lear; concert repertoire includes Schoenberg's Gurrelieder and Das Lied von der Erde by Mahler; Metropolitan opera debut as Siegfried in the Met's new production of Siegfried by Otto Schenk/James Levine 1988; sang the Cardinal in Mathis der Maler at Munich 1989; Teatro Colón Buenos Aires 1990, as Rienzi in a concert performance of Wagner's opera; sang Wagner's Erik at the Deutsche Oper Berlin 2001; Siegfried in Götterdämmerung at Mannheim 2002.

NEUNECKER, Marie Luise; German horn player; *Professor of Horn, Hochschule für Musik Hanns Eisler, Berlin;* b. 17 July 1955, Erbes-Büdesheim. *Education:* studied with Erich Penzel in Cologne. *Career:* Second Horn, Frankfurt Opera 1978–79; Prin. Horn, Bamberg Symphony Orchestra 1979–89, Radio Symphony Orchestra Frankfurt 1981–89; solo performances with orchestras in Germany, Austria, France, Italy, Switzerland, USA and Japan; has appeared as soloist and chamber musician at Salzburg Festival, Marlboro Music Festival, Vienna Festive Weeks and Schleswig-Holstein Music Festival; chamber music with Frank Peter Zimmermann, Christian Tetzlaff, Lars Vogt and the Zehetmair/Petersen Quartet; Prof. of Horn, Hochschule für Musik und Darstellende Kunst, Frankfurt 1988–; Prof. of Horn, Hochschule für Musik Hanns Eisler, Berlin 2004–. *Recordings include:* Strauss Concertos, Britten's Horn Serenade, Mozart Masterpieces, Hindemith Horn Concerto, Horn Concertos by Russian Composers, works by Othmar Schoeck, Charles Koechlin and Ethel Smyth, Georg Lygeti Edition 7; also horn trios by Brahms, works of Hindemith, Kirchner, Brahms, Beethoven and Schumann. *Honours:* numerous awards, including German Music Competition, Bonn, First Prize ARD Competition, Munich, First Prize Concert Artists' Guild Competition, New York 1986. *Current Management:* c/o Künstlersekretariat Schoerke GmbH, Grazer Strasse 30, 30519 Hannover, Germany. *Telephone:* (511) 401048. *Fax:* (511) 407435. *E-mail:* info@ks-schoerke.de. *Website:* www.ks-schoerke.de. *Address:* Hochschule für Musik Hanns Eisler, Charlottenstrasse 55, 10117 Berlin, Germany (office). *Telephone:* (30) 90269700 (office). *Fax:* (30) 90269701 (office). *Website:* www.hfm-berlin.de (office).

NEUWIRTH, Olga, MA; Austrian composer; b. 4 Aug. 1968, Graz. *Education:* Conservatory of Music, San Francisco, USA, Vienna Acad. of Music and Performing Arts, Electroacoustic Inst., studied composition under Erich Urbanner, Elinor Armer, Adriana Hölszky, Tristan Murail and Luigi Nono; studied music technology at IRCAM, Paris. *Career:* jury mem. Munich Biennale 1994; mem. Composers' Forum, Darmstadt Summer School; Composer-in-Residence, Royal Philharmonic Orchestra of Flanders, Antwerp, Belgium 2000, Lucerne Festival 2002; mem. Acad. of the Arts, Berlin 2006. *Radio music:* Punch & Judy 1994. *Theatre music:* Ein Sportstück 1997, Abenteuer in Sachen Haut 2000, Virus 2000, Ein Sommernachtstraum 2000, Totenaupberg 2001, Philoktet 2002, Lost Highway 2003, Der jüngste Tag 2004. *Film score:* The Long Rain 1999, Das Vaterspiel 2009. *Compositions include:* Locus... doublure... solos 2001, Ecstaloop 2001, Torsion: transparent variation 2001, Verfremdung/Entfremdung 2002, Lost Highway 2003, ...ce qui arrive... 2004, ...miramondo multiplo... (trumpet concerto) 2006, Remnants of Songs... an Amphigory (viola concerto) 2009. *Recordings include:* Vexierbilder 1993, Loncera Caprifolium 1993, Sans Soleil 1994, Five Daily Miniatures 1994, Spleen 1994, Vampyrotheone 1995, Akroate Hadal 1995, Risonanze! 1996, Pallas/Construction 1996, Hooloomooloo 1996, Bählamms Fest 1997, Photophorus 1997, Todesraten 1997, Nova/Minraud 1998,

Hommage à Klaus Nomi 1998, Ad auras... in memoriam H 1999, Settori 1999, Morphologische Fragmente 1999, Clinamen/Nodus 1999, The Long Rain 2000, Construction in Space 2000, Inciendo/fluido 2000, Settori, Quasare/Pulsare, Neuwirth Music for Films 2009. *Honours:* Publicity Prize, austro mechana 1994, Ernst von Siemens Foundation Composers Prize, Munich, Hindemith Prize, Schleswig-Holstein Music Festival 1999, Ernst Krenek Prize 1999, Heidelberg Artist Prize 2008, Louis Spohr Music Prize, Braunschweig 2010, Österreichischer Staatspreis 2010. *Current Management:* c/o Frank Harders, Boosey & Hawkes, Bote & Bock GmbH, Lützowufer 26, 10787 Berlin, Germany. *Telephone:* (30) 25001300. *Fax:* (30) 25001399. *E-mail:* frank.harders@boosey.com. *Website:* www.boosey.com; www.olganeuwirth.com.

NEVILLE, Margaret; singer (soprano); b. 3 April 1939, Southampton, Hampshire, England. *Education:* studied with Ruth Packer and Olive Groves in London, Maria Carpi in Geneva. *Career:* debut at Covent Garden 1961 in Die Zauberflöte; appearances at Sadler's Wells, Scottish Opera, WNO, Barcelona, Aix, Berlin and Hamburg; Glyndebourne 1963–64 in Die Zauberflöte and L'Incoronazione di Poppea; roles included Mozart's Zerlina, Despina and Susanna, Verdi's Gilda, Donizetti's Norina and Humperdinck's Gretel; sang in the 1967 BBC production of Cavalli's L'Erismena. *Recordings include:* Hansel and Gretel. *Honours:* Mozart Memorial Prize 1962.

NEVSKAYA, Marina; Russian organist and composer; b. 1 Oct. 1965, Moscow. *Education:* Central Music School, Moscow Tchaikovsky State Conservatory, Royal Carillon School, Mechelen, Belgium. *Career:* debut in organ concert, Moscow, 1986; Festival of Young Composers, Moscow, 1985; recitals, Moscow Conservatory, 1987, 1988, Dnipropetrovsk and Yalta, Ukraine, 1989, Festival of Young Organists, Polotsk, Byelorussia, 1989; participation in Organ Forum, Kazan, 1990, international summer organ course, The Organ Art of Flor Peeters, Mechelen, 1990, 1991; International Organ Week, Vlaardingen, Netherlands, 1991, 1993; recitals, Vlaardingen, 1991, Belaya Tserkov, Ukraine, 1991, 1992, Dnepropetrovsk and Yalta, 1992, Krasnoyarsk, 1993; concert tours, Belgium and Netherlands, 1993, 1994, Italy, 1993, Siberia, 1994; recitals, St Petersburg, 1994, Yalta, 1995, 1996, 1999; organ soloist, Tver Philharmonic, 1992–; teacher of harmony, polyphony, analysis of musical form and piano, Academy of Fine Arts, Moscow, 1995–; participation in annual music festivals, Tver and Moscow; concert tour in Belgium with choir, 1998; recitals at the State Big Concert Hall of the Republic of Tatarstan in Kazan, 1998, 1999; recital at the Organ Festival in Brno, Czech Republic, 1999; participation in the Days of Russian Culture in Armenia in Yerevan, 1999. *Compositions:* Symphoniette; String Quartet; 2 Piano Sonatas; Sonata for Trumpet and Piano; Sonata for Violin and Organ; Suite for Organ; Poem for Viola and Piano; Vocal and Piano Cycles; Pieces for Wind Instruments; Pieces for Carillon and Other Chamber Works. *Recordings:* Italian, French and German Organ Music of the 17th–18th Centuries; Organ Recital, 5th International Bach Festival, Tver, 1997; Playing in the British Bach Film, 1993. *Address:* Tver Academic Philharmonic, Sovetskaya str 18/43, 170000 Tver, Russia.

NEWBOULD, Brian Raby, BA, BMus, MA; British writer, musicologist and fmr academic; *Professor Emeritus of Music, University of Hull;* b. 26 Feb. 1936, Kettering, Northants., England; m. 1st Anne Leicester 1960; one s. one d.; m. 2nd Ann Airton 1976; one d. *Education:* Univ. of Bristol. *Career:* Lecturer, Royal Scottish Acad. of Music, Glasgow 1960–65, Univ. of Leeds 1965–79; Prof. of Music, Univ. of Hull 1979–2001, Prof. Emer. 2001–; numerous talks/discussions on nat. radio, lectures with live illustrations by Allegri String Quartet, Chilingirian String Quartet, the Lindsays, London Mozart Trio, Jyväskylä Sinfonia. *Artistic achievements include:* realizations of Schubert's Symphonies No. 7 in E 1979, No. 10 in D 1981, completion of Symphony in D, D.708a commissioned by BBC Radio 3, completion of Schubert's Symphony No. 8 in B minor 1982, orchestration of Schubert's other symphonic fragments, completions of Schubert's String Trio in B flat 2000, Piano Sonata in C 2003; Patrick for narrator and small orchestra, completion of fragmentary Klavierstück 1995, transcription for clarinet and string quartet of Arpeggione Sonata 1996. *Publications include:* Musical Analysis in the Sixth Form, Music to an Unpurged Ear 1981, Schubert and the Symphony: A New Perspective 1992, Schubert: The Music and the Man 1997, Schubert Studies (ed.) 1998, Schubert the Progressive (ed.) 2003; contrib. to Musical Times, Music & Letters, 19th-Century Music, Current Musicology Music Review, Musiktheorie, Schubert-Jahrbuch, Schubert durch die Brille, The Schubertian, BBC Music Magazine, The Guardian, The Scotsman, Glasgow Herald, Daily Telegraph, Radio Times, Jewish Echo, Classic CD, Classical Music, Ovation, Journal of the Conductors' Guild, Beethoven Newsletter, Nieuwsbrief Franz-Schubert Stichting, Meddelelse Franz Schubert Selskabet Danmark, Music Teacher; chapters in edited vols. *Honours:* Hon. Vice-Pres. Schubert Inst. (UK), Scunthorpe and North Lincolnshire Concert Soc. *Address:* c/o Department of Music, University of Hull, Hull, HU6 7RX, England (office). *E-mail:* b.r.newbould@hull.ac.uk (office). *Website:* www.briannewbould.co.uk.

NEWLAND, Larry, BM, MM; American conductor; b. 24 Jan. 1935, Winfield, KS; m. Paula Kahn 1977, two d. *Education:* Oberlin Conservatory, Manhattan School of Music. *Career:* violist and keyboard player with New York Philharmonic 1960–74; Asst Conductor, New York Philharmonic 1974–85; Music Dir, Harrisburg, Pennsylvania Symphony 1978–94; Guest Conductor, New York City Ballet and orchestras worldwide 1974–; Chair Music Dept and Dir of Ensembles, Adelphi Univ., Garden City, NY 1990–; faculty mem., Int. Opera Workshop, Czech Republic 1997, Assoc. Artistic Dir 1998–; numerous broadcasts with New York Philharmonic and other orchestras. *Publications:* contrib. articles to Apprise. *Honours:* Harold Bauer Award 1957, Koussevitzky Conducting Prize 1961, Leonard Bernstein Conducting Fellowship 1962.

NEWMAN, Anthony, BS, MA, DMA, DipMus; American harpsichordist, organist, composer, fortepianist and conductor; b. 12 May 1941, Los Angeles, CA; m. Mary Jane Flagler 1968, three s. *Education:* Mannes Coll., Harvard Univ., Boston Univ., Ecole Normale de Musique, Paris. *Career:* debut, Carnegie Recital Hall; performing artist in USA and Europe from 1967 with Detroit Symphony, Boston Symphony, Los Angeles Symphony, New York Philharmonic and as conductor with Los Angeles Chamber, Y Chamber, New York, Scottish Chamber, and St Paul Chamber Orchestras; appearances with Israel Symphony, Calgary Symphony, Colorado Symphony, New Jersey Symphony, Youth Chamber Orchestra and Vienna Boys Choir, and St Stephens Cathedral, Vienna, Kraków Festival 1991, 1992. *Compositions include:* Concertino for piano and winds, Concerto for viola and strings, Symphony for string orchestra, Grand Hymns of Awakening for chorus, orchestra and bagpipes, works for organ solo, piano quintet, quartets for flutes and various smaller works, On Fallen Heroes sinfonia for orchestra 1988, Symphony for strings and percussion 1987, 12 Preludes and Fugues for piano, Symphony No. 1 and No. 2 for organ solo. *Recordings include:* Bach, baroque and classical repertoire, On Fallen Heroes, Brandenburg Concerti. *Publication:* Bach and the Baroque 1985. *Address:* State University of New York, Purchase, NY 10577, USA.

NEWMAN, Henry; British singer (baritone); b. 1950, England. *Career:* roles with Welsh National Opera include Zurga in Les Pêcheurs de Perles, Mozart's Count, Papageno, Don Alfonso and Don Giovanni, Marcello, Germont, Britten's Demetrius, Don Pasquale, Tomsky, Scarpia and Sharpless: further appearances with English National Opera, Opera North and Scottish Opera; season 1999–2000 as Foreman of the Mill in Jenůfa at Glyndebourne, Scarpia for Mid Wales Opera, the Forester in The Cunning Little Vixen for City of Birmingham Touring Opera and the Speaker in Die Zauberflöte for London City Opera; radio and television broadcasts.

NEWMAN, Leslie, BMus, MMus; Canadian flautist; b. 1969. *Education:* Univ. of Toronto, Yale Univ. with Thomas Nyfenger, Juilliard School of Music with Julius Baker, Mozarteum Salzburg, studied with András Adorján, Peter Lukas-Graf and Wolfgang Schulz. *Career:* debut performance with Carl Nielsen's Flute Concerto with the Toronto Symphony Orchestra aged 18; performances at Lincoln Center's Alice Tully Hall, New York; Salzburg Festival, Wigmore Hall, London; Taiwan's National Concert Hall; soloist, Toronto Symphony Orchestra tour to 1988 Winter Olympics Arts Festival at Calgary; performed major flute concerti with orchestras throughout Canada; recitalist on BBC Radio 3, UK, and CBC Radio, Canada; duo with pianist John Lenehan, debuted at Wigmore Hall, London, with live BBC broadcast; appearances at Canadian National Competitive Festival of Music; currently tutor at faculty of music, Univ. of Toronto. *Recordings include:* two solo albums, four concerti with CBC Vancouver Orchestra. *Honours:* winner Canadian National Competitive Festival of Music aged 17, Canada Council grants, Yale Univ. Outstanding Performance Major, prizewinner CBC National Young Performer's Competition, finalist New York Pro Musicis Int. Competition.

NEWMAN, Thomas Montgomery, MMus; American composer; b. 29 Oct. 1955, Los Angeles, Calif.; s. of Alfred Newman; m. Ann Marie Zirbes; three c. *Education:* Univ. of Southern California, Yale Univ. *Career:* mem. Broadcast Music, Inc. *Compositions for film:* Summer's End 1984, Reckless 1984, Revenge of the Nerds 1984, Grandview, USA 1984, Desperately Seeking Susan 1985, Girls Just Want to Have Fun 1985, The Man with One Red Shoe 1985, Real Genius 1985, Gung Ho 1986, Jumpin' Jack Flash 1986, Light of Day 1987, The Lost Boys 1987, Less Than Zero 1987, The Great Outdoors 1988, The Prince of Pennsylvania 1988, Cookie 1989, Men Don't Leave 1990, Welcome Home, Roxy Carmichael 1990, Career Opportunities 1991, Naked Tango 1991, The Rapture 1991, Deceived 1991, The Linguini Incident 1991, Fried Green Tomatoes 1991, The Player 1992, Whispers in the Dark 1992, Scent of a Woman 1992, Flesh and Bone 1993, Josh and S.A.M. 1993, Threesome 1994, The Favor 1994, Corrina, Corrina 1994, The Shawshank Redemption 1994, The War 1994, Little Women 1994, Unstrung Heroes 1995, How to Make an American Quilt 1995, Up Close & Personal 1996, Phenomenon 1996, American Buffalo 1996, The People vs Larry Flynt 1996, Mad City 1997, Red Corner 1997, Oscar and Lucinda 1997, The Horse Whisperer 1998, Meet Joe Black 1998, American Beauty (Grammy Award, BAFTA 2000) 1999, The Green Mile 1999, Erin Brockovich 2000, My Khmer Heart 2000, Pay It Forward 2000, In the Bedroom 2001, The Execution of Wanda Jean 2002, The Salton Sea 2002, Road to Perdition 2002, White Oleander 2002, Finding Nemo 2003, Lemony Snicket's A Series of Unfortunate Events 2004, Cinderella Man 2005, Jarhead 2005, Little Children 2006, The Good German 2006, Nothing is Private 2007, Wall-E 2008, Revolutionary Road 2009, Brothers 2009, The Debt 2010, Skyfall (BAFTA 2013, Grammy Award for Best Score Soundtrack for Visual Media 2014) 2012, Side Effects 2013, Saving Mr. Banks 2013. *Compositions for television:* The Paper Chase (series) 1978, The Seduction of Gina (film) 1984, Amazing Stories (episode 'Santa 85') 1985, Heat Wave (film) 1990, Against the Law (series) 1990, Those Secrets (film) 1992, Citizen Cohn (film) 1992, Arli$$ (series) 1996, Boston Public (series theme) 2000, Six Feet Under (series theme) 2001, Angels in America (mini-series) 2003, Katedralen 1.z 2004, The Newsroom (series) 2012, Lauren (series) 2013. *Current Management:* c/o Gorfaine/Schwartz Agency Inc., 4111 West Alameda

Avenue, Suite 509, Burbank, CA 91505, USA. *Telephone:* (818) 260-8500. *Website:* www.gsamusic.com.

NÉZET-SÉGUIN, Yannick; Canadian conductor; *Musical Director, Rotterdam Philharmonic Orchestra;* b. 1975, Montréal. *Education:* Conservatoire de Musique du Québec, Montréal, Westminster Choir Coll., Princeton, New Jersey. *Career:* f. vocal and instrumental ensemble La Chapelle de Montréal 1995; Musical Adviser L'Opéra de Montréal 2000–02; Artistic Dir and Prin. Conductor Orchestre Metropolitain du Grand Montréal 2000–08; Prin. Guest Conductor Victoria Symphony Orchestra 2003–06; Music Dir Rotterdam Philharmonic Orchestra 2008–; Prin. Guest Conductor London Philharmonic Orchestra 2008–; Music Dir Philadelphia Orchestra 2012–; has worked with orchestras in Canada and worldwide including Toronto Symphony, Staatskapelle Dresden, Rotterdam Philharmonic Orchestra, London Philharmonic Orchestra, Orchestre Nat. de France, Royal Stockholm Philharmonic, City of Birmingham Symphony Orchestra, Frankfurt Radio Symphony Orchestra, Orchestre Nat. du Capitole de Toulouse (European debut 2004), Scottish Chamber Orchestra, Swedish Radio Symphony Orchestra, Flemish Radio Orchestra, Orchestre Philharmonique de Monte-Carlo, Sydney Symphony Orchestra, New Zealand Symphony Orchestra; opera conducted includes Massenet's Portrait de Manon and Poulenc's La voix humaine for Barcelona Opera 2007; Met debut with Carmen 2009. *Recordings include:* Nino Rota's La Strada, Mahler's Symphony No.4, Saint-Saens' Organ Symphony (Felix Award), Bruckner's Symphony No.7, Stravinsky & Stokowski (Echo Klassik Conductor of the Year 2014) 2013, Mozart: Die Entführung Aus Dem Serail 2015. *Honours:* several Conseil Québécois de la Musique Prix Opus including Découverte de l'année 1999, Prix du public 1999, 2000, Canada Council for the Arts Virginia Parker Prize 2000, Royal Philharmonic Soc. Award for Best Young Artist 2009, Nat. Arts Centre Award 2010. *Address:* Rotterdam Philharmonic Orchestra, POB 962, 3000 AZ Rotterdam, Netherlands (office). *Telephone:* (10) 2177920 (office). *Fax:* (10) 4116215 (office). *E-mail:* info@rpho .nl (office); info@yannicknezetseguin.co.uk (office). *Website:* www.rpho.nl (office); www.yannicknezetseguin.com.

NG, Cheuk-yin, DMus; Chinese composer and sheng player; b. 1977, Hong Kong. *Education:* Chinese Univ. of Hong Kong, Int. Christian Univ., Tokyo, Japan. *Career:* composes for Western and Chinese instruments, particularly the sheng (ancient classical Chinese instrument); also arranges pop albums and concerts; f. experimental music group SIU2 (Sheng It Up2); Founding mem. The Gay Singers (a cappella group); fmr Artist Assoc. Hong Kong Sinfonietta; mem. Bd of Dirs Flower Music Co. Ltd; performed at Hong Kong Arts Festival 2008, New Vision Arts Festival 2008. *Compositions include:* Fly 2007, New Flowers Party, The Static Days, Rock Hard. *Recordings:* with SIU2: Open Door 2008. *Honours:* Hong Kong Theme Award, Hong Kong Chinese Orchestra Int. Competition for Chinese Orchestral Composition 2000, Konfusion 2010. *Address:* c/o Board of Directors, Flower Music Co. Ltd, 9/F Tack Building 48 Gilman Street Central, Hong Kong Special Administrative Region, People's Republic of China.

NICHITEANU, Liliana; Romanian singer (mezzo-soprano); b. 1962, Bucharest. *Education:* Bucharest Academy. *Career:* numerous engagements including Oslo as Rosina, 1989; Berliner Philharmonie, Fjodor in Boris Godunov, concerts and recordings (CD) with Claudio Abbado, 1993; Vienna, Rossini, Messa di Gloria, 1995; seasons 1995–97, sang Octavian at Frankfurt; Zerlina at the Mozart Festival, Madrid; Cherubino and Despina with Harnoncourt in Zürich; sang Te Deum, Bruckner, in Edinburgh Festival concert; Sang at Salzburg Festival with Valery Gergiev; Fatima in Oberon at Zürich, 1998; Der Rosenkavalier as Octavian in Opéra Bastille Paris and in Vienna, 1998, 2000, 2001; Così fan tutte as Dorabella, Munich, 2001 and 2002; concert repertory: Bach: Magnificat; St John Passion; Brahms Alto Rhapsody; Mahler; concert appearances worldwide in Bach B minor Mass; Mozart, Requiem and C minor Mass; Mahler, Des Knaben Wunderhorn; Mahler, 8th Symphony; Rossini, Stabat Mater and Messa di Gloria; Hindemith, Die junge Magd, Sieben Lieder for orchestra and alto. *Recordings:* Moussorgsky, Boris Godunov with Claudio Abbado; Mozart's Don Giovanni as Zerlina and in Così fan tutte as Dorabella, both with Alain Lombard. *Honours:* Belvedere Contest, two prizes and six special prizes, Vienna, 1989; Geneva CIEM contest, two prizes and Suisse Prize, 1991.

NICHOLAS, James, BM, MM, DMus; cellist; b. 25 Jan. 1957, Valley Stream, New York, USA. *Education:* Indiana Univ. *Career:* freelance cellist and baroque cellist; announcer and producer, Connecticut Public Radio WPKT Meriden, WNPR Norwich and WEDW Stamford and Greenwich. *Compositions:* Concerto for natural horn (Romantic) 1984, Panikhida (Mnemosynon) for unaccompanied natural horn 1987, three Sonatas for natural horn and piano 1985, 1993, 1995, Son of Horn Concerto 1988, Corni Duos 1991, Grande fantaisie en forme de potpourri pour cor à pistons en fa et pianoforte (ca 1838) 1991, Psalsima (Chants) for natural horn and small orchestra 1991, Return of the Shoe Quintet: The Sequel for horn and strings 1994, Mozart: Horn Concerto in Eb, K370b and 371 (reconstruction) 1994, Mozart: Horn Concerto in E, K494a (reconstruction) 1995. *Publications:* J. S. Bach–Six Sonatas and Partitas, An Urtext edition for viola 1986, J. S. Bach–Six suites for Cello, an attempt at an Urtext for viola 1986, J. S. Bach–Suite No. 6 S1012, a performing version for the four-stringed cello 1986, Edition of Horn Concerti from the Lund Manuscript 1989; contrib. to The Horn Call. *Honours:* performer's certificate Indiana Univ. 1978.

NICHOLLS, David Roy, MA, PhD, FRSA; British musicologist and composer; *Professor of Music, University of Southampton*; b. 19 Nov. 1955, Birmingham; m. Tamar Hodes 1984; one s. one d. *Education:* St John's Coll., Cambridge with Hugh Wood. *Career:* Keasbey Fellow in American Studies, Selwyn Coll., Cambridge 1984–87; Lecturer in Music, Keele Univ. 1987, Sr Lecturer in Music 1992, Prof. of Music 1995–2000; Prof. of Music, Univ. of Southampton 2000–. *Compositions include:* Pleiades for three groups of instruments 1979–80, The Giant's Heart for singers and instrumentalists 1983, two Japanese Miniatures for eight instruments 1988–89, Winter Landscape with skaters and birdtrap for string quartet 1989–90, Cantata: Jerusalem for soprano, double choir and double wind band 1990–91, String Quartet: NMC D006 1992, Bingham String Quartet. *Publications:* American Experimental Music 1890–1940 1990, new edn of Henry Cowell's New Musical Resources 1995, The Whole World of Music: A Henry Cowell Symposium (contrib. ed.) 1997, The Cambridge History of American Music (contrib. ed.) 1998, The Cambridge Companion to John Cage (contrib. ed.) 2002, John Cage 2007. *Address:* Department of Music, University of Southampton, Southampton, SO17 1BJ, England (office). *Telephone:* (23) 8059-3973 (office). *E-mail:* drn@soton.ac.uk (office).

NICHOLLS, Hyacinth; singer (mezzo-soprano); b. 10 Sept. 1956, Trinidad. *Education:* Guildhall School of Music and the National Opera Studio. *Career:* sang Cherubino, Octavian, Dorabella, Carmen and Dalilah while a student; Professional debut in 1985 at Wigmore Hall; sang in the European premiere of Virgil Thomson's Four Saints in Three Acts, Belgium, 1983; Glyndebourne Festival from 1986 in Porgy and Bess, Sang Purcell's Sorceress at Battersea Arts Centre, 1995; L'Enfant et les Sortilèges, Die Entführung, La Traviata, The Electrification of the Soviet Union as Natasha in the premiere, and as Varvara in Katya Kabanova; Tour of Italy in 1989 with Albert Herring; Other roles include Fenina in Nabucco and Humperdinck's Gretel; Sang in the Royal Opera's Garden Venture in 1989; Has performed the role of Carmen for several opera companies including English National Opera's Baylis Programme and the Royal Opera House's Education Programme; other roles include the title role in Gluck's Orfeo, Dalila, Third Lady (Magic Flute) and Suzuki (Madama Butterfly); Has recently returned from Syria where she sang the role of Dido in a production of Syria's first ever opera; Further roles include Carmen and Serena (Porgy and Bess); Concert repertoire includes Schumann Lieder with recital at St John's with Iain Burnside, Beethoven's Mass in C, the B minor Mass and the St Matthew Passion. *Honours:* Ricordi Opera Prize; Susan Longfield Award; winner, Maggie Teyte International Competition, 1985.

NICHOLLS, Rachel, BA Hons; British singer (soprano); b. 1965, Bedford, England; pnr Andrew Slater. *Education:* Trinity College of Music, Royal College of Music, London Royal Schools Opera. *Career:* concerts include Bach's B minor Mass in Tokyo, Handel's Messiah in Beijing and Royal Albert Hall, London, Rossini's Petite Messe solenelle in Rome, Brahms' Requiem at Royal Albert Hall, Mozart's Requiem with London Mozart Players, Nielsen's 3rd Symphony and Mendelssohn's Hymn of Praise with CBSO, Bach's St Matthew Passion and Handel's Apollo e Dafne, with the London Handel Orchestra, Choral Symphony, with the Hanover Band, Dixit Dominus Queen Elizabeth Hall, Mozart's Mass in C minor at St John Smith's Square, Bach's Magnificat and St John Passion, Fauré Requiem with Royal Scottish Nat. Orchestra, Elgar's Coronation Ode and Poulenc's Gloria in Westminster Abbey, Handel's L'Allegro for the London Handel Festival, Messiah in Halle, and the Vaughan Williams Sea Symphony at the Brighton Festival; recitals; specialist in French song, Lieder of Richard Strauss and Russian Song; opera with Royal Opera Covent Garden from 2001, as Flowermaiden in Parsifal and Echo in Ariadne auf Naxos, also Naxos Priliepa in The Queen of Spades, Pepik in The Cunning Little Vixen; with Scottish Opera from 2003, as Flora in the Knot Garden, Frasquita in Carmen, and with Scottish Opera on tour as Tatyana in Eugene Onegin; with English Touring Opera as Erismena, Dorabella in Cosí fan tutte, Elisa in Tolomeo; with Longborough Festival Opera as Fiordilligi in Cosí fan tutte; other roles include Donna Elvira, Puccini's Lauretta, Maria in Mazeppa, Micaela, Marenka and Mozart's Countess; has premiered contemporary song cycles by John McCabe, Cecilia Macdowall, David Matthews, Wendy Hiscocks. *Recordings include:* Bach B Minor Mass and Bach Cantatas, Hummel Mass in D Minor, Metella in Silla, David Matthews Movement of Autumn, Cecilia Mcdowall Magnificat. *Honours:* Queen Elizabeth Rose Bowl 2002, Lies Askonas Prize 2001, RCM Junior Fellowship 2001–02. *Current Management:* James Black Management, The Old Grammar School, High Street, Rye, East Sussex, TN31 7JF, England. *Telephone:* (1797) 224668 (office). *E-mail:* james@jamesblackmanagement.com. *Website:* www.jamesblackmanagement.com. *E-mail:* rachel@rachelnicholls.com. *Website:* www.rachelnicholls.com.

NICHOLLS, Simon, GRSM, ARCM, LRAM; British pianist; b. 8 Oct. 1951, London, England; m. Lorraine Wood 1976. *Education:* Royal College of Music. *Career:* performances in London, St John's Smith Square, Wigmore Hall, South Bank, Snape Maltings, Aldeburgh and at music clubs throughout the UK; broadcasts on BBC and ITV and radio; tours and broadcasts in France, Netherlands, Germany, Ireland, Greece and USA; piano teacher at Yehudi Menuhin School 1976–86; Prof., Royal College of Music 1985–; teacher, Birmingham Conservatoire 2000–; mem. ISM. *Recordings include:* Simon Nicholls Plays Scriabin. *Publications:* The Young Cellist's Repertoire, Recital Repertoire for Cellists with Julian Lloyd Webber; contrib. to Piano Journal; Music and Musicians; Tempo; Music Teacher, International Piano Quarterly.

NICHOLSON, George Thomas Frederick, BA, DPhil; British composer, pianist and conductor; *Reader in Composition, University of Sheffield*; b. 24 Sept. 1949, Great Lumley, Co. Durham, England; m. Jane Ginsborg 1984; one s. one d. *Education:* Univ. of York. *Career:* freelance teacher, Guildhall School of Music and Drama, London, Morley Coll., London 1978–88; recitals with Jane Ginsborg, soprano, and with Philip Edwards, clarinet, Triple Echo and with John Kenny, trombone; Lecturer, Keele Univ. 1988–96; Sr Lecturer in Music, Univ. of Sheffield 1996–2007, Head of Music 2003–05, Reader in Composition 2007–; mem. Classical Exec. Cttee, British Acad. of Songwriters, Composers and Authors. *Compositions:* Triple Echo (Trio Award, Gaudeamus Competition, Rotterdam) 1982; orchestral works: 1132, The Convergence of the Twain, Blisworth Tunnel Blues for soprano and orchestra, Chamber Concerto, Cello Concerto, Flute Concerto, Fenestrae, Concerto for orchestra, Short Stories for wind orchestra; chamber works: 4 string quartets, Winter Music, Ancient Lights, Movements, Stilleven, Three Nocturnes, Piano Sonata, Brass Quintet, The Arrival of the Poet in the City (melodrama) for actor and seven musicians, Muybridge Frames for trombone and piano 1992, Mots Justes for piano solo 1988–97, Catch, Shailing and Wambling 2001, Umbra/Penumbra for trombone and piano, Mister Biberian his Dompe for guitar solo 2002, Autumn Journey 2005, Sonant Formant morph 2006, Bagatelles for oboe and percussion 2007, Caesura for horn, violin and piano 2007, Tableaux vivants for ten instruments 2007, Recueillement for flute, horn, viola and harp 2007, Salve Regina for eight instruments 2008, The Darkening Green for oboe and piano 2008, Groundswell for 10 players 2009, Pas seul for piano solo, Harmonica for clarinet ensemble, Moonlight over Albion for clarinet, viola and piano 2011, Chiaroscuro for piano solo, Darkness Visible for bass clarinet and piano, Soundings for bass clarinet solo 2012, Tronie for piano solo 2013, Far Cry for alto sax and piano 2015, Shadow Play for flute and clarinet 2015; vocal: Aubade, Vignette, Peripheral Visions, Alla Luna for soprano, clarinet and piano, Letters to the World 1997–99, Idyll 2003, Embers 2004, For Tess 2009, Volte-face 2009, Along upon 2009, Further than Guess 2010, Toward the Rainbow 2014, (Fifty-second) Streets for vocal quartet 2015; electroacoustic: Dedans for trombone and live electronics 2010. *Recordings:* String Quartet No. 3, Peripheral Visions, Letters to the World, Spring Songs, Nodus, Mots Justes, Muybridge Frames, Umbra/Penumbra, The Arrival of the Poet in the City, Bagatelles. *Publications:* contrib. of articles to Composer Magazine 1983–87. *Honours:* Yorkshire Arts Composers' Award 1977, Greater London Arts Asscn Young Composer 1979–80. *Current Management:* c/o University of York Music Press, Department of Music, University of York, Heslington, York, YO10 5DD, England. *Telephone:* (1904) 432434. *Fax:* (1904) 432450. *E-mail:* info@uymp.co.uk. *Website:* www.uymp.co.uk. *Address:* Department of Music, University of Sheffield, Jessop Building, 34 Leavygreave Road, Sheffield, S3 7RD, England (office). *Telephone:* (114) 222-0479 (office). *E-mail:* g.nicholson@shef.ac.uk (office). *Website:* www.shef.ac.uk/music/staff/academic/gnicholson (office).

NICHOLSON, Linda; fortepianist; b. 1955, England. *Career:* mem., London Fortepiano Trio from 1978; duo with violinist, Hiro Kurosaki; solo recitals and concertos, performances of the Viennese classics on original instruments at major festivals and concert series throughout Europe, including Italy, Belgium, France, Germany, the UK and The Netherlands; 12 concert series of the complete piano trios of Haydn in London 1982, to mark the composer's 250th anniversary; complete piano trios of Beethoven at the Wigmore Hall 1987; season 1991 with Mozart Trios and quartets in London, tour on the early Music Network and lunchtime recitals at the QEH; played Mozart in Spain, Portugal and Germany; frequent radio broadcasts. *Recordings:* Complete Trios by Mozart; Trios by Haydn and Beethoven; Mozart Concertos; Complete Violin Sonatas by Mozart, with Hio Kuoselui.

NICKLIN, Celia Mhry, FRAM; musician and oboist; b. 28 Nov. 1941, Malmesbury, Wiltshire, England; m. Howard Gough 1964, three d. *Education:* Royal Acad. of Music, London and Hochschule für Musik Detmold, Germany. *Career:* Principal Oboe, City of Birmingham Symphony Orchestra 1962–63, London Mozart Players 1970, Acad. of St Martin-in-the-Fields 1970; Prof., Royal Acad. of Music, London. *Recordings include:* Vaughan Williams, Handel, Vivaldi Oboe Concertos with Academy of St Martin, Mozart with London Mozart Players.

NICOLAI, Claudio; singer (baritone); b. 7 March 1929, Kiel, Germany. *Education:* studied with Clemens Kaiser-Breme in Essen and Serge Radamsky in Vienna. *Career:* debut at Theater am Gärtnerplatz, Munich 1954; early engagements as a tenor then as baritone from 1956; appearances at Bregenz Festival, Vienna Volksoper and in Stuttgart, Hamburg, Brussels, Munich, Berlin, Paris, London, Stockholm, Oslo, Prague, Bucharest, Budapest, Zürich and Amsterdam; mem., Cologne Opera from 1964; sang in the 1965 premiere of Zimmermann's Die Soldaten and visited London 1969 for the British premiere of Henze's Der Junge Lord; sang with Oper der Stadt Köln from 1966; roles include Giovanni, Count, Papageno and Guglielmo; Tel-Aviv 1984 in Die Zauberflöte, Metropolitan Opera 1988, sang Don Alfonso at Brussels and Barcelona 1990 and Don Alfonso under John Eliot Gardiner at Amsterdam 1992; Prof., Musikhochschule Cologne; Salzburg Festival 1976–79; Nozze di Figaro, Giovanni, Vienna Staatsoper; 15 years guest at the Berlin Staatsoper and three times in Japan; Così fan tutte in Paris with J. E. Gardiner. *Recordings:* Der Freischütz; Die Fledermaus; Die Kluge; Highlights from Die Soldaten.

NICOLESCO, Mariana; singer (soprano); b. 28 Nov. 1948, Brasov, Romania. *Education:* studied in Romania, Conservatorio Santa Cecilia, Rome with

Jolanda Magnoni, studied with Elisabeth Schwarzkopf and Rodolfo Celletti. *Career:* debut in television concert, Voci Rossiniane International Award, Milan 1972; sang Violetta in La Traviata, Teatro Comunale, Florence 1976, Gran Teatro del Liceu, Barcelona 1976, 1978, 1981, also San Francisco Opera 1991; Violetta at Metropolitan Opera 1978, where she also appeared as Gilda in Rigoletto 1978, and Nedda in Pagliacci 1979, 1986, Donna Elvira in Don Giovanni, Teatro dell'Opera, Rome 1984, Munich Staatsoper and Munich Festival 1986–93, Tokyo 1988, La Scala, Milan 1987, 1988, 1993; also at La Scala, world premiere of Berio's La Vera Storia 1982, and Un Re in Ascolto 1986; Dargomishky's Stone Guest 1983, Mozart's Lucio Silla 1984, Luigi Rossi's L'Orfeo 1985, Jommelli's Fetonte 1988, three recitals 1988–93; Elettra in Idomeneo, Salzburg Festival 1990, 1991, Japan 1990, Dresden Semper Oper 1991; a true dramatic coloratura: Bellini's Beatrice di Tenda, La Fenice, Venice 1975, Donizetti's Maria di Rohan, Martina Franca Festival 1988, Elisabeth Queen of England in Roberto Devereux, Monte Carlo 1992, 1997; sang at first Christmas concert in the Vatican, televised worldwide 1993; Anna Bolena, Munich 1995; world premiere, Krzysztof Penderecki's Seven Gates of Jerusalem of the Holy City 1997; performed at leading opera houses worldwide; concerts at Royal Festival Hall London, Carnegie Hall New York, Musikverein Vienna, Boston Symphony Hall, Concertgebouw Amsterdam, Teatro Real Madrid, Cleveland Symphony Hall, Teatro alla Scala; Great Conservatory Hall, Moscow. *Recordings:* Bellini: Beatrice di Tenda; Donizetti: Maria di Rohan; Verdi: Simon Boccanegra; Puccini: La Rondine; Mozart: Le nozze di Figaro; World premiere: Meyerbeer cantata Gli Amori di Teolinda, Ravel cantatas Alcyone, Alyssa.

NICOLESCU, Antonius; singer (tenor); b. 17 Aug. 1946, Bucharest, Romania. *Career:* debut at Romanian Nat. Opera, Bucharest 1971, as Vladimir in Prince Igor; guest appearances at Athens, Berlin Staatsoper, and Heidelberg; Opéra Bastille, Paris 1992, as Hoffmann; Berne 1995, in Zandonai's I Cavalieri di Ekebu, Hamburg 1996, as Don José; other roles include Alfredo (Essen 1994), Pinkerton, Ernesto, Faust, Gerald in Lakmé, Lenky and Don Ottavio.

NICOLL, Harry; British singer (tenor); b. 1970, Coupar Angus, Perthshire, Scotland. *Education:* Royal Scottish Academy of Music and Drama. *Career:* sang with Scottish Opera Go Round from 1979 as Nemorino, Ferrando, Alfredo and Ramiro; appearances with Welsh National Opera as Valetto in L'Incoronazione di Poppea, Vasek, the Idiot in Wozzeck and Brighella and the Dancing Master in Ariadne; Sang with English National Opera in Pacific Overtures, Street Scene and The Mikado and with Scottish Opera in their Rossini double bill, as The Lover in the premiere of Judith Weir's The Vanishing Bridegroom in 1990, as Bardolph and as Almaviva; Other engagements with Opera North in Acis and Galatea and L'Heure Espagnole, Park Lane Group in La Finta Semplice, Glyndebourne Touring Opera as Pedrillo in Die Entführung, English Bach Festival in Versailles as Thespis in Rameau's Platée, Kammeroper Berlin in The Lighthouse, Il Re Pastore and Il Matrimonio Segreto; La Fenice Venice in Zaide, Frankfurt and Jerusalem as Roderigo in Otello, Cologne Opera as Vasek, The Bartered Bride, Opera Voor Vlaanderen, Pedrillo in Die Entführung, New Israeli Opera, Tel-Aviv, Idiot in Boris, Vasek in Bartered Bride, and as Almaviva, Barbiere; Théâtre des Champs Elysées as Medor in Roland by Lully; Has sung in several operas at the Batignano Festival; concert appearances in the UK and abroad. *Current Management:* Musicmakers International Artists Representation, Tailor House, 63–65 High Street, Whitwell, Hertfordshire SG4 8AH, England. *Telephone:* (1438) 871708. *Fax:* (1438) 871777. *E-mail:* musicmakers@ compuserve.com. *Website:* www.operauk.com.

NICOLLS, Sarah, LRAM, ARCM, LGSM, LTCL; British pianist; *Lecturer in Music, Brunel University*; b. 1 April 1974, Newcastle upon Tyne. *Education:* Chetham's School of Music, King's Coll., London, RAM, Guildhall School of Music and Drama. *Career:* debut recital Purcell Room, London (Park Lane Group Young Artists concert) 2001; recitals at Aldeburgh Festival, BBC Broadcasting House, London Sinfonietta State of the Nation weekend, Purcell Room 2002; multimedia concert 'Cinesthesia', Purcell Room, Bath Int. Festival Rising Stars recital, Wigmore Hall solo debut, festival performances in Austria, Holland and Aveiro Int. Piano Festival (Portugal), gave British premiere of Berio's Piano Sonata 2003; soloist with Britten-Pears Contemporary Ensemble, pianist in the Tate Ensemble; Lecturer in Music, Brunel Univ. 2005–; seminars given throughout UK; Berio recital in 'Ommaggio' Festival, Italian Cultural Inst., London, recitals at Bath and Cheltenham festivals, 'Cinesthesia II' 2004; performances in 2005 included concerto with BBC Nat. Orchestra of Wales, Queen Elizabeth Hall debut; festival performances in 2005 included Ravello and Reggello, Italy, Aldeburgh, Royal Castle, Warsaw, Warwick, Klara Festival in Belgium (broadcast on Klara Radio), Sligo, Ireland, Aldeburgh, Leeds FUSE; recitals at St George's Brandon Hill, Kettle's Yard, Cambridge, EPTA conference, Purcell Room and throughout UK 2005; Concerto commissioned by London Sinfonietta, performed at St Luke's LSO (with live BBC Radio 3 broadcast) 2005; performances with electronic trio, Alexander's Annexe at the IF Festival, London 2005; 'Les Nuits Sonores' Lyon 2005. *Recording:* the piano music of Niccolo Castiglioni. *Honours:* winner British Contemporary Piano Competition 2000. *Current Management:* c/o Margaret Murphy Management, 7 Grove Park, Wanstead, London E11 2DN, England. *Telephone:* (20) 8530-1305. *E-mail:* info@ margaretmurphy.com. *Website:* www.margaretmurphy.com. *E-mail:* info@ sarahnicolls.com. *Website:* www.sarahnicolls.com.

NIEHOFF, Beatrice; singer (soprano); b. 1952, Mannheim, Germany. *Career:* sang at Karlsruhe and Darmstadt 1977–82; later appearances in Hamburg, Zürich, Berlin and Vienna notably as Mozart's Constanze, Countess, Pamina and Fiordiligi, Dvořák's Rusalka, Weber's Agathe and Wagner's Elsa; modern repertory includes operatic roles in Fortner's Bluthochzeit, Zemlinsky's Der Kreidekreis, Hindemith's Mathis der Maler and Schoeck's Massimilia Doni; in 1988 sang Eva in a new production of Die Meistersinger at Essen and the Protagonist in the German premiere of Berio's Un Re in Ascolto at Düsseldorf; returned to Düsseldorf 1989 as Cleopatra in Giulio Cesare by Handel; sang Strauss's Chrysothemis at Aachen 1999.

NIELSEN, Svend; Danish composer; b. 20 April 1937, Copenhagen. *Education:* Univ. of Copenhagen, Royal Acad. of Music, Copenhagen. *Career:* debut in Copenhagen 1962; teacher, Royal Acad. of Music, Århus 1967–. *Compositions:* orchestral: Metamorphoses 1968, Nuages 1972, Symphony 1978–79, Nocturne 1981, Concerto for violin and orchestra 1985, Nightfall for chamber orchestra 1989, Symphony No. 2 1997; for voice and instruments: Three of Nineteen Poems 1962, Duets 1964, Romances 1970–74, Chamber Cantata 1975, Sonnets of Time 1978, Ascent Towards Akseki 1979; choral music: Motets 1982, Imperia 1982, Jorden 1983, Sommerfugledalen for 12 solo singers 1999; piano music: Romantic Piano Pieces 1974, five Inventions 1983; chamber: Rondo for flute quintet 1986, String Quartet 1987, Black Velvet for clarinet quintet 1988, Variations for double quintet 1989, Windscapes for brass quintet 1990, Aria for orchestra 1991, Aubade for orchestra 1994, Sinfonia Concertante for cello and chamber orchestra 1994, Shadowgraphs for ten instruments 1995, The Colour Blue for three ensembles 1998. *Recordings:* Carillons, Sinfonia Concertante, Nightfall. *Honours:* Carl Nielsen Prize 1981, Danish State lifelong grant 1982–, Schierbeck Prize 1995.

NIEMELA, Hannu; singer (baritone); b. 17 April 1954, Lohtaja, Finland. *Education:* Sibelius Acad., Helsinki, studied with Kim Borg and Hans Hotter. *Career:* debut at Zürich Opera 1985 as Marullo in Rigoletto; mem., Karlsruhe Opera 1985–89 and Staatstheater Mainz from 1989; guest engagements at Savonlinna and Schwetzingen Festivals and at Berne, Basle, Mannheim, Dresden, Prague, Leningrad and Strasbourg; Karlsruhe 1986 in the premiere of Der Meister und Margarita by Rainer Kunad; other roles have included Mozart's Count, Papageno and Don Giovanni, Gluck's Orestes, Escamillo, Wozzeck and Demetrius in A Midsummer Night's Dream, and Verdi's Macbeth and Falstaff; sang the title role in the German premiere of Le Roi Arthus by Chausson, Cologne 1996; Willy Brand in the premiere of Kniefall in Warschau by G. Rosenfeld, Dortmund 1998; season 2000–01 as Kurwenal and Count Luna at Dortmund and the title role in the premiere of Tüür's Wallenberg; Iago and title tole in The Death of Klinghoffer at Helsinki; noted concert artist.

NIES, Otfrid; violinist and writer on music; b. 5 May 1937, Giessen, Germany; m. Christel Nies-Fermor 1961, two s. two d. *Education:* studied with Max Rostal, Rudolf Kolisch. *Career:* mem., National Theatre Orchestra, Mannheim 1964–66; Leader, Stadttheaterorchester Hagen 1966–71, Staatstheaterorchester Kassel 1971–; presentation of music for player piano by Conlon Nancarrow at Documenta 7, Kassel 1982; founder of Archiv Charles Koechlin 1984; mem. Asscn Charles Koechlin, Paris, Internationale Schoenberg-Gesellschaft, Vienna. *Recordings:* Quintets, Op 80 for piano and strings, Op 156 for flute and harp, by Charles Koechlin; music for violin and player piano by Conlon Nancarrow. *Publications:* orchestration of Quartre Interludes, Op 214 for The Ballet Voyages, Op 222 1947, by Charles Koechlin 1986; contrib. many articles on Charles Koechlin in Das Orchester, Neue Zeitschrift fuer Musik, Fonoforum.

NIGOGHOSSIAN, Sonia; French singer; b. 3 April 1944, Arnouville-lès-Gonesse; d. of Nigoghos Nigoghossian and Hermine Keutahialian. *Education:* Conservatoire Nat. Supérieur de Musique et de Danse, France. *Career:* operatic debut Opéra de Nantes; numerous nat. and int. recitals; has taken part in Aix-en-Provence Festivals. *Operas include:* Les Indes Galantes, Alceste, The Marriage of Figaro, Così fan tutte, La Clemenza di Tito, The Barber of Seville, Tancrède, L'occasion fait le larron; many oratorios and Armenian music. *Recordings include:* Les Indes Galantes, Hyppolite et Aricie, Alceste, Les leçons de ténèbres, Auber: Le Cheval de Bronze 2003. *Film appearance:* La flûte enchantée de Mozart. *Honours:* First Prize for singing and lyric art, Conservatoire Nat. Supérieur de Musique et de Danse, Paris.

NIIMI, Tokuhide; Japanese composer; b. 5 Aug. 1947, Nagoya. *Education:* Univ. of Tokyo, Tokyo National Univ. of Fine Arts and Music. *Career:* faculty mem., Toho Gauden School of Music, Tokyo; mem. of bd of dirs, Japanese Composers' Soc.; mem. Japanese Federation of Composers. *Compositions include:* Percussion Concerto 1973, Enlacage I for chorus and orchestra 1977, Enlacage II for three percussionists 1978, Enlacage III for two marimbas and two percussionists 1980, two Symphonies 1981, 1986, Three Valses for piano duet 1986, two Piano Concertos (Eyes of the Creator) 1984, 1993, Under Blue Skies for children's chorus, mixed chorus and orchestra 1986, Ohju for cello 1987, Kazane for clarinet, violin and cello 1989, Au-Mi for soprano, violin, cello and piano 1989, Heteorhthmix for orchestra 1991, Chain of Life for chamber orchestra 1993, Planets Dance for six percussionists 1993, String Quartet 1994, Fusui for small orchestra 1994, The Cosmic Tree for koto and orchestra 1996, Soul Bird for flute and piano 1996, Spiral of the Fire for orchestra 1997, Fujin, Raijin for Japanese big drum, organ and orchestra 1997, Garden in the Light for piano quintet 1997, Towards the Silence for string orchestra 1998, Fairy Ring for clarinet and piano 1998. *Recordings:* Eye of the Creator,

Garden in the Light. *Honours:* Grand Prix of Composition Int. Competition of Ballet Music, Suisse Roman, Geneva. *Address:* 1-26-6-303, Chuo, Nakano-ku, Tokyo, Japan.

NIKITIN, Evgeny; Russian singer (bass-baritone); b. 1973, Murmansk. *Education:* St Petersburg Conservatoire. *Career:* appearances at Mariinsky Opera from 1996; Covent Garden debut 2000; Metropolitan debut 2002; Paris debut in Rubinstein's The Demon and title role of Boris Godunov at Théâtre du Châtelet; debut at Bayerische Staatsoper Munich as Jochanaan in Salome 2008; debut Vienna Staatsoper season 2014–15; current roles include Mozart's Figaro, Don Giovanni, Glinka's Ruslan, Mussorgsky's Boris Godunov, Wagner's Wotan, Der Wanderer, Der Fliegender Holländer, Friedrich von Telramund, Amfortas, Klingsor, Strauss's Jochanaan, Oreste; frequent performances as guest artist in major theatres through Europe, USA and Japan; orchestral concert soloist with Santa Cecilia, Rome, London Symphony Orchestra, Boston Symphony Orchestra, Berlin Radio Symphony, Bayerische Rundfunk, etc.; annual appearances at Stars of the White Nights Festival, St Petersburg. *Recordings include:* Boris Godunov. *Honours:* Honoured Artist of Russia, Prizewinner, Pechovsky, Rimsky-Korsakov and Tchaikovsky Competitions 1996–98. *Current Management:* c/o Claire Feazey, IMG Artists, 31–33 rue du Temple, 75004 Paris, France. *Telephone:* 1-44-31-44-38. *Fax:* 1-44-31-44-40. *E-mail:* cfeazey@imgartists.com. *Website:* www.imgartists.com.

NIKKANEN, Kurt; American violinist; b. Dec. 1965, Hartford, CT. *Education:* Boston Univ. with Roman Totenberg, Juilliard School, New York with Dorothy DeLay. *Career:* won first competition, 1976; Carnegie Hall debut, 1978, playing the Saint-Saëns Introduction and Rondo Capriccioso; 1980, played the Paganini 1st Concerto with the New York Philharmonic; Bruch 1st Concerto with the Boston Pops; appearances with the Hartford Symphony, Colorado Philharmonic, New Jersey Chamber Orchestra and Aspen Chamber Symphony; European debut, 1981, with recital tour of Finland; Cleveland Orchestra debut in the Glazunov Concerto, July 1988; British debut playing the Elgar Concerto with the Royal Liverpool Philharmonic conducted by Libor Pesek 1988; toured in Venezuela; debuted at the Kennedy Center in Washington, DC; further engagements with the Helsinki Philharmonic under James DePreist, and an orchestral/recital tour of Japan; season 1990–91, made debuts in London, Munich and Barcelona; season 1991–92, engagements with the San Francisco, New Orleans and Portland Symphonies; recital debuts in Vancouver, Berlin and Paris; played the Glazunov Concerto at the 1991 Promenade Concerts, London; 1995, BBC Scottish Symphony, Bergen Philharmonic, Seattle International Festival, Hallé Orchestra, Khumo Festival, Resedentie Orchestra of Holland; premiered John Adams's Concerto in Sweden with the Stockholm Philharmonic, John Adams conducting 1995; season 1996–97 included the Adams Concerto with the Hallé Orchestra, the New Zealand Symphony Orchestra and the Cincinnati Symphony, Dvořák and Brahms on Far East tour; performed Aaron Jay Kernis' Concerto for violin and guitar at the 1998 Aspen Festival, conducted by Hugh Wolff, and H.K. Gruber's Violin Concerto, Nebelsteinmusik performed with the Swedish Chamber Orchestra under the composer's direction 1999; gave a recital at Wigmore Hall, London performing Violin Dance, pieces inspired by dance forms; Meditations for flute and strings, 1997; Via Crucis for solo voices, chorus and orchestra, 1997; A Polish Folksong for soprano and orchestra, 1998; season 2001–02 with New York City Ballet, concerts with Auckland Philharmonic, Eugene Symphony Orchestra and return to Hong Kong Symphony Orchestra. *Recordings include:* Tchaikovsky and Glazunov Concertos. *Current Management:* c/o Nicholas Curry, Clarion/Seven Muses, 47 Whitehall Park, London, N19 3TW, England. *Telephone:* (20) 7272-4413. *Fax:* (20) 7281-9687. *E-mail:* admin@c7m.co.uk. *Website:* www.c7m.co.uk; www.kurtnikkanen.com.

NIKL, Pavel; Czech musician (viola); b. Moravia. *Career:* mem. Pavel Haas Quartet 2002–, performed in numerous concert halls including London's Wigmore Hall, Concertgebouw Amsterdam, Palais des Beaux-Arts Brussels, Auditorio Nacional Madrid, Zurich Tonhalle, Munich Herkulessaal, with Luxembourg Philharmonie and at Aldeburgh, Edinburgh, Verbier and Zeist festivals; BBC New Generation Artists scheme 2007–09; Artist-in-Residence, Cologne Philharmonie, Birmingham Town Hall, Prague Spring Festival 2014, Bodensee Festival 2015; tours to Australia, Japan and Korea 2015. *Recordings include:* with Pavel Haas Quartet: Janáček's Quartet No. 2 (Intimate Letters) and Haas' Quartet No. 2 (From the Monkey Mountains) (Gramophone Award for Best Chamber Recording 2007), Janacek's Quartet No. 1 (Kreutzer Sonata) and Haas' Quartets Nos. 1 and 3 2007, Prokofiev's String Quartets (Diapason d'or de l'année) 2010, Dvořák's String Quartets (Gramophone Award for Recording of the Year 2011), Franz Schubert works (Gramophone Award for Best Chamber Recording 2014) 2013, Smetana String Quartets (Gramophone Award for Best Chamber Recording 2015). *Honours:* with Pavel Haas Quartet: First Prize, Paolo Borciani competition 2005, ECHO Rising Stars Award 2007, Special Ensemble Scholarship, Borletti-Buitoni Trust 2010. *Current Management:* Intermusica Artists' Management, 36 Graham Street, Crystal Wharf, London, N1 8GJ, England. *Telephone:* (20) 7608-9918. *E-mail:* nfriemel@intermusica.co.uk. *Website:* www.intermusica.co.uk; www.pavelhaasquartet.com.

NIKODEMOWICZ, Andrzej; Polish composer and pianist; b. 2 Jan. 1925, Lvov; s. of Marian and Helena; m. Kazimiera Maria Grabowska 1952; one s. one d. *Education:* Conservatory of Lvov with Adam Soltys, studied with Tadeusz Majerski. *Career:* Prof. of Composition and Piano, Conservatory of Lvov 1951–73; Prof. of Faculty of Music, Univ. of Maria Curie-Sklodowska in Lublin 1980–; Prof., Faculty of Church Musicology, Catholic Univ., Lublin; mem. Polish Composers' Soc., Soc. of Authors ZAiKS. *Compositions include:* Ekspresje 66 miniatures for piano solo 1959–60, violin works, Songs for voice and piano, Chamber Concerto 1968, Composizione sonoristica for violin, violoncello and piano 1966–71, Musica concertante per tre for flute, viola and piano 1966–67, three nocturnes for trumpet and piano 1964, Symphonic music 1974–75, Concerto for violin and symphony orchestra 1973, choir music including 500 Polish Christmas carols, Glass Mountain (pantomime) 1969, 47 religious cantatas including Magnificat for choir of women and orchestra 1977–78, Evening Offering 1980, Hear My Cry, O God 1981, five lullabies for violin and piano 1991, four songs for soprano, trumpet and organ, George Herbert 1992, Variations, Ave maris Stella for organ 1993, Concerto for piano and symphony orchestra 1994; Laudate Dominum (cantata) 1985–87, Via Crucis (cantata) 1996, Concerto No. 2 for piano and symphony orchestra 2002, Concerto No. 3 for piano and symphony orchestra 2002, Concerto-meditazione for violoncello and symphony orchestra 2003, Concerto No. 4 for piano and symphony orchestra 2003, Concerto No. 5 for piano and symphony orchestra 2004, Concerto for violoncello and symphony orchestra No. 2 2005, Per Tromba ed archi 2005–06, Psalmus paenitentialis for voice and orchestra/organ 2006, Concerto No. 6 for piano and orchestra 2007, Concerto No. 7 for piano and symphony orchestra 2007, Little Concerto for horn and string orchestra 2007, Te, Matrem Dei, Laudamus 2007, Oratorio in honour of the Mother of the God of Marvellous Change 2008, Concerto in C for two pianos 2009, Three Lullabies for piano 2009, To Most Holy Virgin Merciful, cantata 2010, Two lullabies for voice and piano 2010, Six songs for voice and piano 2010, Impression for violoncello and piano 2010, Triptych – three songs for voice and organ 2010, Epitaph, cantata 2011, Triptych – three psalms in Jan Kochanowski's trans. (Psalm 105 for men's choir and baritone solo, Psalm 136 for mixed choir, Psalm 106 for mixed choir and baritone solo) 2011, Psalm 18 for men's choir and baritone solo 2011, Jubilate Deo for mixed choir 2011, Capriccio for violoncello solo 2011. *Recordings:* two cantatas, cycle of songs. *Publications:* contrib. several reviews in Ruch Muzyczny; subject of two books: Classic Romantic of the Present Time: Andrzej Nikodemowicz Early Works in Chamber Music by Agnieszka Schulz-Brzyska 2009, Sacred Music in Andrzej Nikodemowicz Musical Compositions by Ewa Nidecka 2010. *Honours:* Order Ĵ, Lvov 2005; Dr hc (Lwów Musical Acad.) 2003; Prize of Saint Friar Albert 1981, Mayor of Lublin City Award 1998, Asscn of Polish Composers Award 2000, Ministry of Culture Award 2000, Artistic Award of the City of Lublin 2002, Diploma and Medal of His Holiness Pope John II Pro Ecclesia et Pontifice 2003, Hon. Citizen of Lublin 2009. *Address:* ul Paryska 4/37, 20-854 Lublin, Poland (home). *Telephone:* (4881) 7415629 (home); (4881) 4438755 (home).

NIKODIJEVIĆ, Marko; Serbian/German composer and electronica artist; b. 4 Jan. 1980, Subotica, Serbia. *Education:* Univ. of the Arts, Belgrade with Srdjan Hofman and Zoran Erić, Hochschule für Musik Stuttgart with Marco Stroppa. *Career:* compositions influenced by techno and use digital technology; works featured at festivals including World New Music Days, Stuttgart 2006, UNESCO Rostrum of Composers, Paris 2009, and performed at festivals including Steirischen Herbst, Huddersfield Contemporary Music Festival, Warsaw Autumn, musica Strasbourg, MATA New York, Witten New Music Days and Donaueschingen Festival; works premiered by ensembles including Ives Ensemble, Nieuw Ensemble, Asko/Schönberg Ensemble, Nouvel Ensemble Moderne, Ensemble Insomnio, Ensemble ascolta, Brandenburger Symphoniker and Radio-Sinfonieorchester Stuttgart, and taken up by conductors such as Peter Eötvös (ORF Radio-Symphonieorchester Wien) and Ilan Volkov (BBC Scottish Symphony Orchestra). *Compositions include:* Sadness Untitled for 2 sopranos 2010, chambres de ténèbres, GHB/tanzaggregat for orchestra, grid/index for chamber ensemble, acid/glitch for ensemble, gesualdo abschrift/antiphon. *Recording:* Dark/Rooms 2013. *Honours:* grants and residencies in Weimar, Salzwedel, Baden-Baden and Paris, Brandenburg Biennale Composition Prize 2008, Gaudeamus Prize 2010, 2012, Siemens Foundation Composers' Prize 2013. *Address:* c/o Internationale Musikverlage Hans Sikorski, Johnsallee 23, 20148 Hamburg, Germany (office). *Telephone:* (40) 4141000 (office). *Fax:* (40) 41410040 (office). *E-mail:* contact@sikorski.de (office). *Website:* www.sikorski.de (office).

NIKOLOV, Nikola; singer (tenor); b. 1924, Sofia, Bulgaria. *Education:* studied in Sofia and Moscow, Russia. *Career:* debut in Varna 1947 as Pinkerton; sang at Varna until 1953, then at Sofia National Opera from 1955; appearances in Moscow and Leningrad 1950s, La Scala Milan 1958 as Jenik in The Bartered Bride; season 1958–60 at Wexford Festival, Vienna Staatsoper and Covent Garden as Radames; New York Metropolitan 1960 as Don José, State Operas of Berlin and Hamburg and Naples 1963 as Vasco da Gama in L'Africaine; sang further in Munich, Barcelona, Geneva, Belgrade, Budapest and Bucharest; other roles included Manrico, Turiddu, Cavaradossi, Calaf and Don Carlos. *Recordings:* Aida, Carmen, Boris Godunov, L'Africaine.

NIKOLOVA, Zistomira; singer (mezzo-soprano); b. 10 March 1949, Svilengrad, Bulgaria. *Career:* sang in opera houses throughout Yugoslavia, as Verdi's Azucena, Eboli and Amneris, Marina in Boris Godunov, Adalgisa in Norma, Carmen, Dalila, Marfa (Khovanshchina) and Clytemnestra; Staatstheater Karlsruhe, 1995–96, notably as Fricka and Waltraute in The Ring; Guest appearances in Moscow, St Petersburg, Mannheim, Leipzig and Marseilles; numerous concert appearances; sang Fortunata in Makernas's Satyricon at Zagreb, 1998. *Address:* Karlsruhe Opera, Baumeisterstrasse 11, 7500 Karlsruhe, Germany.

NIKOLSKY, Gleb; Russian singer (bass); b. 1959, Moscow. *Education:* Moscow Conservatory and La Scala, Milan. *Career:* soloist at the Bolshoi Theatre, Moscow, as Verdi's King Philip, Ramphis, Fiesco and Padre Guardiano, Boris, Dosifey, Ivan Susanin and Gounod's Mephistopheles; guest appearances in Italy, the USA and Zürich (Gremin in Eugene Onegin, 1990); Carnegie Hall 1990, as the Archbishop in Tchaikovsky's The Maid of Orleans; Metropolitan Opera from 1991.

NILON, Paul; British singer (tenor); b. 1961, Keighley, Yorkshire. *Education:* Royal Northern College of Music with Frederic Cox. *Career:* appearances with Opera 80 as Don Ottavio, the Duke of Mantua and Sellem in The Rake's Progress; La Fenice, Venice, as Sellem; Musica nel Chiostro in Batignano, Italy, as Jacquino in Beethoven's Leonora; Has sung Strauss's Scaramuccio and Mozart's Belmonte for Opera Northern Ireland, 1987–88; Mario and the Magician, Stephen Oliver, world premiere Batignano, 1988; with City of Birmingham Touring Opera sang Fenton in Falstaff and Mozart's Tamino; has sung with Opera North from 1988 as Hylas in The Trojans, Kudras in Katya Kabanova, Belfiore in La Finta Giardiniera, Leander in Nielsen's Maskarade (British premiere), Ferrando and Don Ottavio; engagements with New Israel Opera and English National Opera, 1990–92 as Ferrando, Narraboth in Salome and Telemachus in The Return of Ulysses; Tamino ENO, 1992–93, Duel of Tancredi and Clorinda; Tamino Scottish Opera, 1992, ENO, 1993; in Ariodante ENO, as Lurcanio, 1993; many concert appearances; Almaviva, Barbiere, ENO and New Israeli Opera; King Ouf in L'Etoile; Paolino in Secret Marriage; Benedict in Beatrice and Benedict, WNO; Pirro in Rossini's Ermione at Glyndebourne 1996; Alfredo for GTO and Grimoaldo in Rodelina (GTO, 1998); sang Monteverdi's Ulysses at Florence, 1999; season 2000–01 as Lurcanio in Ariodante at the Munich Staatsoper, with Opera North in Prague as Michel in Martinů's Julietta, Golo in Schumann's Genoveva at Edinburgh and Don Ottavio for ENO. *Recordings include:* L'Assedio di Calais by Donizetti and Vol. II and III in One Hundred Years of Italian Opera, Medea in Corinta by Mayr, Orazi e Curiazi, Mercadante.

NILSSON, Anders; Swedish composer; b. 6 July 1954, Stockholm; s. of the late Birger Nilsson and of Valborg Nilsson; m. Elzbieta Mysliwiec 1989; two d. *Education:* Music High School, Stockholm, Birkagården Folk High School, Stockholm, State Coll. of Music, Stockholm. *Career:* debut with first of Trois Pièces pour grand orchestre, with Danish Radio Symphony Orchestra, Copenhagen 1981; composer, conductor, Swedish Nat. Theatre Centre and Stockholm City Theatre 1975–78; full-time composer 1983–; represented at Int. Soc. for Contemporary Music World Music Days 1990, 1993, and elsewhere; mem. Swedish Composers' League, Int. Soc. for Contemporary Music. *Compositions:* selected works: Trois Pièces pour grand orchestre 1980–88, Reflections for soprano and chamber ensemble 1982, Resonance for piano 1985, Ariel for oboe, tape and string orchestra 1985, Cadenze for chamber orchestra 1987, Concerto for organ and orchestra 1987, Marimba Concerto 1988, Sinfonietta for orchestra 1992, Divertimento for chamber ensemble 1991, KRASCH for saxophone quartet and percussion ensemble 1993, Mountains for organ (First Prize, Grand Prix de Saint-Rèmy-de-Provence) 1994, Concerto Grosso I for saxophone quartet and orchestra (Christ Johnson Grand Prize 2000) 1995, Symphony No. I 1996, Mind the Gap for orchestra 1997, Piano Concerto for orchestra 1997, Concerto for marimba and orchestra 1998, Symphony No. II: Symphonic Dances 2001, Orbit: Concerto Grosso II for six percussionists and string orchestra 2001, Klassresan (one-act opera) 2002, Zarah (two-act opera) 2004–07, Jordens drömmer gröna, songcycle for baritone and orchestra 2007, Requiem for baritone, choir and orchestra (Music Soc. of Stockholm Award 2011, Swedish Music Publr Asscn Prize 'The Music of the Year' (music for large ensemble category) 2011) 2008–10, Violin Concerto 2011, Kira – in the house where I live (one-woman opera, for a tall woman and a half sinfonietta, libretto by Charlotte Engelkes and Sophie Holgersson) 2013. *Recordings:* Ariel, Cadenze, Concerto for organ and orchestra, Five Orchestral Pieces for piano, Reflections, KRASCH, Divertimento, Aria. *Publications:* contrib. to numerous articles to Nutida Musik, Swedish magazine for contemporary music. *Honours:* Gehrmans Music Publrs Rosenborg Prize 1988, Le Grand Prix de Saint-Rémy-de Provence 1992, Second Prize, Int. Contest of Composition inauguration of the Klais-organ in Hallgrim Cathedral, Reykjavik, Iceland 1993, Grand Prize of Christ Johnson's Prize Fund 2000, The Art Music Work of The Year Award, Swedish Asscn of Music Publrs 2011. *Address:* Fyrskeppsvägen 128, 121 54 Johanneshov, Sweden. *Telephone:* 70-6501854 (mobile). *E-mail:* anders@andersnilssoncomposer.com. *Website:* www .andersnilssoncomposer.com.

NILSSON, Bo; Swedish composer; b. 1 May 1937, Skelleftehamn; m. (divorced); two d. *Education:* studied with Micha Pedersen, K. G. St Clair Renard, Karl Birger Blomdahl. *Career:* debut as composer, Cologne 1956; freelance artist 1976–; compositions played worldwide. *Compositions include:* Brief an Gösta Oswald 1958–59, Drei Szenen 1960–61, Swedenborg Dreaming for electronic music 1969, Déjà Vu for woodwind quartet 1967, Déjà connu, Déjà entendu for wind quintet 1976, We'll Be Meeting Tomorrow for mixed choir, soprano, celesta and triangles 1970, Fatumeh for speaker, soloists, mixed choir, electronics and large orchestra 1973, La Bran for soprano, saxophone, mixed choir, orchestra and electronics 1975, Fragments for marimba, five Thai-gongs 1975, Floten aus der Einsamkelt for soprano and nine players 1976, Bass for bass tuba solo, six Javanian tuned gongs and Chinese gong 1977, Plexus for brass instruments, piano and percussion 1979, Wendepunkt-Infrastruktur-Endepunkt for brass quintet 1981, Autumn Song

for baritone and orchestra 1984, My Summerwind is Yours for baritone and orchestra 1984, Brief an Gösta Oswald, Arctic Romance 1995, A Spirit's Whisper in Swedenborg's Gazebo 1996, Arctic Air for orchestra 2001; film music, songs and jazz music. *Recordings include:* Introduction and Midsummer Tune; Quantitaten, Raga Rena Rama; Rendez-vous; You; Illness; Walz in Marjoram; Blue-Black Samba; The Last Lass; To Love; Lidingo Airport; Forward Waltz; The Swinging World of Bo Nilsson; The Missile; In the Loneliness of the Night; Ravaillac; A Spirit's Whisper, 1997. *Publications include:* Spaderboken 1962, Missilen eller Livet i en mossa 1994. *Honours:* Dr hc (Univ. of Lulea) 2000; State Artist grant 1974–, Christopher Johnson Grand Prize 1975, Hilding Rosenberg Prize 1993. *Address:* Sickla Allé 35 131 65 Nacka, Sweden. *Telephone:* (8) 716-96-96; (8) 782-89-23. *E-mail:* harpa@ bonilsson.se. *Website:* www.bonilsson.se.

NILSSON, Pia-Marie; Swedish singer (soprano); b. 1961. *Education:* Stockholm College of Music, State Opera School. *Career:* debut at Stockholm Folkoperan 1985 as the Queen of Night; sang at Royal Opera Stockholm and the Drottningholm Theatre, 1986–88 and Frankfurt Opera from 1989 as Sandrina in La Finta Giardiniera, Servilia in La Clemenza di Tito, Pamina, Oscar in Ballo in Maschera, Gilda and Sophie; French debut in 1991 as Donna Anna at Nancy; concert engagements in Scandinavia, Italy, Switzerland, Germany and Austria; engaged as Oscar for the Théâtre de la Monnaie, Brussels, 1995; season 1994–95, Ring Cycle, Frankfurt; season 1995–96 as Susanna at Frankfurt; broadcasting commitments in Scandinavia.

NIMSGERN, Siegmund; singer (baritone); b. 14 Jan. 1940, St Wendel, Germany. *Education:* studied with Paul Lohmann and Jakob Staempfli. *Career:* debut as Lionel in Tchaikovsky's Maid of Orleans, Saarbrucken 1967; sang in Saarbrucken until 1971, then Deutsche Oper am Rhein, Düsseldorf 1971–74; London Promenade Concerts 1972 as Mephistopheles in La Damnation de Faust; La Scala Milan and Paris Opéra 1973, Covent Garden 1973 as Amfortas in Parsifal; Paris 1977–82 as the Speaker in Die Zauberflöte, Creon in Oedipus Rex, Telramund in Lohengrin and Beethoven's Pizarro; Metropolitan Opera 1978 as Pizarro; Bayreuth Festival 1983–85 as Wotan in the Peter Hall production of Der Ring des Nibelungen; often heard as concert singer; Chicago Lyric Opera 1988 as Scarpia; sang Wotan in Das Rheingold at Bonn 1990, Don Pizarro in Fidelio at La Scala and Telramund at Frankfurt in 1991; sang Creon in Cherubini's Médée at Trier 1999. *Recordings:* St John Passion by Bach; Masses by Haydn and Hummel; Pergolesi's La Serva Padrona; Cantatas by Bach and Telemann; Bach's Magnificat; St Matthew Passion and Bach B minor Mass; Alberich in Das Rheingold; Mosè in Egitto; Die Schöpfung; Marschner's Der Vampyr.

NIQUET, Hervé; French conductor, harpsichordist and singer (tenor); *Music Director, Le Concert Spirituel;* b. 1957, Abbeville. *Career:* Choir Master, Opéra de Paris 1980–; mem. (tenor), Les Arts Florissants 1985–86; Founding Music Dir, baroque period instrument ensemble Le Concert Spirituel 1987–; BBC Proms debut, London 2012; Music Dir, Flemish Radio Choir and Principal Guest Conductor, Brussels Philharmonic 2011–; Guest Conductor, Akad. für Alte Music Berlin, Sinfonia Varsovia, Rias Kammerchor, Orchestre Philarmonique de Radio France, Orchestre de l'Opéra Nat. de Montpellier-Languedoc-Roussillon and others. *Recordings include:* over 20 CDs with Le Concert Spirituel. *Honours:* Chevalier, Ordre Nat. du Mérite, Officier, Ordre des Arts et Lettres. *Address:* Le Concert Spirituel, 42 rue du Louvre, 75001 Paris, France (office). *Telephone:* 1-40-26-11-31 (office). *Fax:* 1-40-13-91-35 (office). *E-mail:* info@concertspirituel.com (office). *Website:* www .concertspiritual.com (office).

NIRQUET, Jean; French singer (countertenor), conductor and musicologist; b. 15 Aug. 1958, Paris. *Education:* Sorbonne, Univ. of Paris, Strasbourg Music High School and Conservatory, Conservatory of Orléans with Jacqueline Bonnardot, Conservatory of Paris with Christiane Eda-Pierre, studied with Claude-Henry Joubert, Betsy Jolas. *Career:* engagements at opera houses of Paris, Lyon, Nice, Strasbourg, Karlsruhe and Helsinki; radio broadcasts in France, Germany and The Netherlands; at numerous festivals; film for Südwestfunk 2, Pasticcio of Handel-Martinoty 1985. *Recordings:* Handel's Alessandro, Cavalli's Serse, Charpentier's Vespers of the Annunciation, Te Deum and David et Jonathas, Gilles' Requiem, Prodomidès' H.H. Ulysse. *Publications:* Rose et Colas de Monsigny 1982, L'Irato de Méhul 1984, La Dramaturgie des Opéras de Lully dans l'etude des Tempi, Analyse d'Epiphanie d'André Caplet.

NISHIDA, Hiroko; Japanese singer (soprano); b. 17 Jan. 1952, Oita; m. Peter Bachmann; one d. *Education:* studied in Tokyo. *Career:* sang with the Bonn Opera 1979–81; appearances at Zürich Opera as Butterfly, Berne, Mimi, St Gallen, Micaela and the Forza Leonora at Berlin, Munich, Cologne, Frankfurt, Düsseldorf, Stuttgart and Mannheim; sang Butterfly with Opéra de Lyon 1990; further guest appearances at San Diego, Enschede and Amsterdam, Vienna Staatsoper, Hamburg, Prague, Sofia, Vancouver, Tokyo; other roles include Arminda in La Finta Giardiniera, Pamina, Manon Lescaut, Lauretta, Elisabeth de Valois and Kunigunde in Lortzing's Hans Sachs; concert repertoire includes works by Bach, Handel, Mozart, Schubert, Beethoven, Bruckner and Mahler; currently CEO Musikhaus Bachmann. *Address:* Metzgergasse 16, 9004 St Gallen, Switzerland (office). *Telephone:* (71) 2233931 (office). *Fax:* (71) 2233934 (office). *E-mail:* info@musikhaus -bachmann.ch (office). *Website:* www.musikhaus-bachmann.ch (office).

NISHIKAZE, Makiko, MA; Japanese composer and pianist; b. 22 April 1968, Wakayama. *Education:* Aichi Univ. of Fine Arts and Music, Mills Coll., CA,

USA, Hochschule der Künste, Berlin, Germany. *Career:* finalist, Forum '93 Int. Composition Competition, Montréal 1993; participant, Darmstadt Summer Course 1994; piano solo recitals, Berlin 1996, 1999; appeared at Chamber Music Festival in Kanagawa, Japan 1997; concerts in New York, Israel, Brazil, and Barcelona, Spain 1998. *Compositions:* Haiku for sextet 1994, Celestial Fruits for ensemble 1995, Shades I–V for piano 1995–96, Chant I–III for voice 1997–98, North Piano I–V for piano 1997, Lux for string quartet 1999, Oratorio for vocal ensemble 2000, Garden, Nocturnal for ensemble 2001. *Honours:* Berlin Senate grant 1994, Composition Prize, Stuttgart 1995, Akademie Schloss Solitude Fellowship 1999, State Schleswig-Holstein Prize 2000, State Niedersachsen Prize 2001. *Address:* Sophie-Charlotten Strasse 112, 14059 Berlin, Germany.

NISHIYAMA, Ikuko; Japanese pianist; b. 28 Dec. 1976, Tokyo. *Education:* Purcell School, London, UK, Hochschule für Musik und Darstellende Kunst, Vienna, Austria. *Career:* performed Shostakovich Piano Concerto No. 1 with London Gala Orchestra, Royal Festival Hall, London 1991; piano recital, Casals Hall, Tokyo, Japan 1998; Beethoven Piano Concerto No. 3 with Tokyo New City Orchestra 2003. *Recordings:* album of works by Mozart, Beethoven and Schumann. *Honours:* Third Prize Int. Beethoven Piano Competition 1997, First Prize Int. Chamber Music Competition, Greece 2000. *Address:* 3-30-18 Ozenji-nishi, Asao-ku, Kawasaki-shi, Kanagawa 215-0017, Japan (home).

NISHIZAKI, Takako; Japanese violinist; d. of Shiniji Nishizaki. *Education:* Toho School of Music, Juilliard School, New York. *Career:* studied with father, then became first student of Shinichi Suzuki, creator of Suzuki Method of violin teaching. *Recordings include:* complete Fritz Kreisler Edn. (ten vols.), many contemporary Chinese violin concertos, concertos by Spohr, Briot, Crui, Respighi, Rubinstein and Joachim; for Naxos: Vivaldi's Four Seasons, Mozart's Violin Concertos, sonatas by Mozart and Beethoven, also Bach, Mendelssohn, Tchaikovsky, Beethoven, Bruch and Brahms Concertos.

NISKA, Maralin; singer (soprano); b. 16 Nov. 1930, San Pedro, CA, USA. *Education:* studied with Lotte Lehmann. *Career:* sang widely in California from 1955; sang at San Diego Opera 1965 as Mimi in La Bohème, sang Floyd's Susannah with the Met National Company, at New York City Opera 1967 as Mozart's Countess returning as Turandot, Tosca, Salome and Janáček's Emilia Marty, and at Metropolitan Opera 1970–77 as Tosca, Musetta and Hélène in Les Vêpres Siciliennes; Italian debut as Marie in Wozzeck at Maggio Musicale Florence 1978; other roles have included Violetta, Madama Butterfly, Donna Elvira, Manon Lescaut and Marguerite in Faust.

NISKANEN, Jyrki; singer (tenor); b. 12 Feb. 1956, Finland. *Education:* Helsinki Sibelius Acad., studied with Vera Rozsa in London. *Career:* debut in Tampere 1986, as Tonio in La Fille du régiment; sang Alfredo at Helsinki 1989; Savonlinna Festival 1992–96, as Florestan and Verdi's Macduff; Théâtre du Châtelet, Paris 1994, as Siegmund; Florence 1995, in Zemlinsky's Eine Florentinische Tragödie; season 1996 as Siegmund at the Vienna Staatsoper, Tristan at Barcelona and Florestan in Rio de Janeiro; concerts in Europe and USA, include Requiems of Mozart and Verdi; season 1998 as Shostakovich's Sergei at Florence, Alvaro in La Forza del Destino at Savonlinna; sang Wagner's Lohengrin at Nice 1998 and Seville 1999; Tristan in Nice, Washington, Munich and Florence 2001; Loge and Siegmund at Catania; Beethoven's Ninth at la Scala 1999, and Gabriele Adorno at Catania. *E-mail:* sirkka.kuula-niskanen@pp.inet.fi.

NISSMAN, Barbara, BMus, MMus, DMus; American concert pianist, lecturer, recording artist, writer and clinician and producer; b. 31 Dec. 1944, Philadelphia, Pa. *Education:* Univ. of Michigan; studied with pianist, György Sandor. *Career:* American orchestral debut with Philadelphia Orchestra, Ormandy 1971; appearances with London Philharmonic, Royal Philharmonic, Rotterdam Philharmonic, L'Orchestre de la Suisse Romande, BBC Symphony, other BBC orchestras, Netherlands Chamber, Munich Philharmonic, Bavarian Radio Orchestras, etc.; USA: Philadelphia, Pittsburgh, Minnesota, Chicago, Cleveland, St Louis, National, New York Philharmonic Orchestras etc., with Ormandy, Muti, Mata, Skrowaczewski, Zinman, Slatkin, amongst others; concert tours of the Far East, Latin America, NZ and Soviet Union; presented Netherlands premiere of Ginastera Piano Concerto in Concertgebouw, Amsterdam 1978; UK premiere of Ginastera Piano Concerto No. 1 with BBC Symphony 1982; soloist at Gala 60th birthday concert for Ginastera with Suisse Romande 1976; Third Piano Sonata (1982) of Ginastera, dedicated to her; masterclasses given at Moscow and St Petersburg Conservatories, Fed. Univ. of Brazil, Royal Coll. of Music, UK, Canterbury Univ., NZ and throughout USA; first live performance of complete Prokofiev Piano Sonatas in three concerts, London and New York 1989; first performance of two-page fragment of Prokofiev's Sonata No. 3 1989; first performance of the three piano concertos by Ginastera at Univ. of Michigan, including official reintroduction of Concierto Argentino, unpublished concerto by Ginastera and world premiere of original version of Piano Concerto No. 2; first recording of all three Ginastera Piano Concertos 2011; first recording of unpublished Piano Sonata (1898) by Bartók discovered at Morgan Library; associated with 'A Concerted Effort' (Robert James Frascino AIDS Foundation benefit concert series) 2002–14. *Film:* Liszt – The 'Elvis' of the Keyboard, Part I in the Series 'Barbara & Friends', adapted for children (with actors from Greenbrier Valley Theater) (DVD) 2008. *Radio:* Co-host Composer of the Week – Alberto Ginastera (BBC Radio 3) 2006; numerous recitals recorded for BBC Radio 3, German Radio, Dutch Radio, Swedish Radio, Norwegian Radio, US Public Radio. *Television:* Barbara & Friends (BBC TV), Steinway Gala Concert at Carnegie Hall, Kennedy Center 25th Anniversary Gala. *Recordings:* Complete Solo and Chamber Music of Alberto Ginastera (two vols), Music of Franz Liszt, Complete piano sonatas of Prokofiev and other major works (three vols), Chopin by Nissman, Beethoven by Nissman, Bartók by Nissman (includes first performance of unpublished 1898 Sonata), Schumann by Nissman, Brahms by Nissman, Rachmaninoff by Nissman (two vols) 2007, Recital Favorites by Nissman, Vols 1–8, Complete Piano Concertos of Alberto Ginastera 2014, Fireworks! and Out of Doors, Three Oranges Recordings. *Publications:* Piano Sonata No. 3 by Alberto Ginastera (ed) 1982, Bartók and the Piano: A Performer's View 2002, Critical Edition of Ginastera's Second Piano Concerto (ed.) 2014; various articles and master classes written for music magazines; contrib. to The Pianist & His Craft. *Honours:* Martha Baird Rockefeller Grants, Nat. Endowment for the Arts Recital Grant, Stanley Medal, School of Music, Univ. of Michigan 1966, Athena Award, Univ. of Michigan 1983, Citation of Merit Award, School of Music, Univ. of Michigan 1996, Hall of Fame, Philadelphia High School for Girls 2006, West Virginia Governor's Arts Award 2008. *Address:* 892 Herns Mill Road, Lewisburg, WV 24901, USA (home). *Telephone:* (304) 645-6896 (home). *E-mail:* pianoconnect@barbaranissman.com (office); barbaranissman@frontier.com. *Website:* www.barbaranissman.com (office); www.threeorangesrecordings.com (office).

NITESCU, Adina; Romanian singer (soprano); b. 1965. *Education:* George Enescu Conservatoire, Bucharest, studied in Munich. *Career:* roles with the Opera Studio of the Bavarian State Opera included Mozart's Countess and Fiordiligi; Bucharest Opera debut as Mimi in La Bohème, 1993; further engagements as Donna Anna at Leipzig, Saarbrucken and Essen; Mimi at Cologne and Wiesbaden, Marzelline in Fidelio, Bregenz Festival and Gounod's Marguerite at the Deutsche Oper, Berlin, First Lady in Die Zauberflöte, and in Gluck's Armide to open the 1996 season at La Scala, Milan; other roles include Madama Butterfly and Cio-Cio-San in Madama Butterfly, Margherita in Mefistofele, Maddalena in Andrea Chenier, Nedda in I Pagliacci, Tosca, Manon Lescaut, Elisabetta in Maria Stuarda. *Honours:* stipendium from Georg Solti 1991–92. *Current Management:* c/o Angela Maria Blasi, Columbia Artists Management, 1790 Broadway, New York, NY 10019-1412, USA. *Telephone:* (212) 841-9500. *Fax:* (212) 841-9744. *E-mail:* info@cami.com. *Website:* www.cami.com.

NITSCHE, Horst; singer (tenor); b. 22 March 1939, Vienna, Austria. *Education:* Bruckner Conservatory, Linz. *Career:* sang at the Landestheater Salzburg from 1970, Vienna Staatsoper 1972; appearances in Vienna (also at Volksoper) as Monostatos, Don Curzio, Jacquino, Zorn in Meistersinger, Flavio in Norma and Missail in Boris Godunov; sang in the 1976 premiere of Kabale und Liebe by Einem; Salzburg Festival from 1977, in Salome, Don Carlos, Die Zauberflöte and Le nozze di Figaro. *Recordings:* Character roles in Il Trovatore, Der Rosenkavalier, Die Zauberflöte and Don Carlos.

NIXON, Marni; American singer (soprano), actress and teacher; b. 22 Feb. 1930, Altadena, CA; d. of Charles McEathron and Margaret (Wittke) McEathron; m. 1st Ernest Gold 1950 (divorced 1969, died 1992); m. 2nd Lajos Frederick Fenster 1971 (divorced 1975); m. 3rd Albert David Block 1983. *Education:* Los Angeles City Coll., UCLA, Univ. of S Calif., Tanglewood, MA. *Career:* actor Pasadena Playhouse, Calif. 1940–45; singer with Roger Wagner chorale (soloist) 1947–53, New England Opera Co., LA Opera Co., Ford Foundation TV Opera 1948–63, San Francisco Opera 1966, Seattle Opera 1971–73; classical recitals and appearances with symphony orchestras in USA, Canada, England, Israel, Ireland; private teacher, voice coach, conductor, masterclasses 1970–; head of apprentice div. Santa Barbara Music Acad. of West 1980; fmrly Dir opera workshop Cornish Coll. of the Arts, Seattle; judge Metropolitan Opera Int. American Music Awards, Nat. Inst. of Music Theatre 1984–87; mem. Nat. Assn of Teachers of Singing (pres. NY chapter 1994–). *Films:* Sound of Music 1964, I Think I Do 1996; voice dub: My Fair Lady (for Audrey Hepburn), The King and I (for Deborah Kerr), An Affair to Remember, West Side Story (for Natalie Wood), Disney's Mulan. *Plays:* My Fair Lady 1964, Taking My Turn 1983, Opal 1992–94, Cabaret 1998, Ballymore 1999, Follies 2001, 2005, James Joyce's The Dead 1999–2001, Nine 2002. *Television:* Boomerang (series) 1975. *Publications:* I Could Have Sung All Night (autobiog.), My Story (with Stephen Cole) 2006. *Honours:* four Emmy Awards for Best Actress, two Action for Children TV Awards, Chicago Film Festival Award 1977.

NIZIOŁ, Bartek; Polish musician (violin) and academic; b. 1974, Szczecin. *Education:* Acad. of Music Poznań, studied with Jadwiga Kaliszewska. *Career:* started playing violin aged five; as soloist has performed with Nat. Warsaw Philharmonic Orchestra, Sinfonia Varsovia, Polish Nat. Radio Symphony Orchestra, Berlin Symphony Orchestra, NDR Hannover, SWR Keiserslautern, Orchestre de Radio France, English Chamber Orchestra, London Symphony Orchestra, Tonhalle Zurich, Edmonton Symphony and others; concert tours to Asia, Africa, S. America and in Europe in halls including Salle Pleyel Paris, Barbican Centre London, Philharmonie Berlin, Santory Hall Tokyo, Vienna Konzerthaus, Music Conservatory Moscow; has lived in Switzerland since 1995; Prin. Violinist, Tonhalle Orchestra 1997–2003, Zurich Opera Orchestra 2003–12, Philharmonia Zurich 2012–; Prof. of Violin, Hochschule der Künste, Bern 2008–; Visiting Prof., Szymanowski Acad. of Music Katowice; Founder and Artistic Dir Piła Int. Masterclass Festival, Poland 2009–; jury mem. H. Wieniawski Int. Violin Competition, Poznań; Co-founder and leader, Berlinsky Quartet 2009–. *Recordings include:* Wieniawski - Violin Concerto No. 2 (Fryderyk Prize) 1996, Wieniawski - Pieces for Violin Solo, Two Violins and Violin with Piano

2001, Grażyna Bacewicz - Violin & Piano Works (Fryderyk Prize) 2004, Eugène Ysaÿe's Six Sonatas for Solo Violin (Fryderyk Prize) 2009, Luise Adolpha Le Beau: Chamber Music 2015. *Honours:* first prize, int. violin competitions in Lublin, Poznań, Adelaide, Pretoria, Brussels and Paris. *Address:* Hochschule der Künste, Papiermühlestrasse 13a, 3014 Bern, Switzerland (office). *Telephone:* (31) 8483999 (office). *E-mail:* bartek@barteknizioI.com (office). *Website:* www.hkb.bfh.ch (office); barteknizioI.com.

NKETIA, Joseph Hanson Kwabena; Ghanaian composer, academic and writer; *Director, International Centre for African Music and Dance, University of Ghana*; b. 22 June 1921, Mampong, Ashanti Region. *Education:* Presbyterian Training Coll. and Theological Seminary, Akropong, School of Oriental and African Studies, London, Trinity Coll. of Music, London, Birkbeck Coll., London, Columbia Univ. and Juilliard School of Music, New York, Northwestern Univ., Evnaston, IL. *Career:* composer from 1940; teacher, Presbyterian Training Coll. 1941–44, 1949–52, acting Principal 1954; Asst, SOAS, Univ. of London 1946–49; Research Fellow, Univ. Coll. of Ghana 1952–59, Sr Research Fellow 1959–61; Assoc. Prof., Univ. of Ghana, Legon 1962, Prof. 1963–65, Dir Inst. of African Studies 1965–79, Prof. Emeritus 1990–, Dir Int. Centre for African Music and Dance 1993–; Dir musical ensemble for Ghana Dance Troupe 1963–70; Prof., Univ. of Calif. at Los Angeles 1969–82, Prof. Emeritus 1982–; Horatio Appleton Lamb Visiting Prof. of Music, Harvard Univ. 1971; Visiting Prof. of Music, Univ. of Queensland, Brisbane, Australia 1979; Andrew Mellon Prof. of Music, Univ. of Pittsburgh, PA 1982–91, Chair. Dept of Music 1986–89, Andrew Mellon Prof. Emeritus 1992; Visiting Prof., China Conservatory of Music, Beijing; Langston Hughes Visiting Prof., Univ. of Kansas-Lawrence 1992; Cornell Visiting Prof. Dept of Music and Dance, Swarthmore Coll., PA 1995; Distinguished Hannah Prof. of Integrative Studies, Mich. State Univ., East Lansing 1997; Fellow, Ghana Acad. of Arts and Sciences 1959; mem. Exec Bd, Int. Folk Music Council 1959–70; mem. Int. Music Council 1962–66, 1978, exec. mem. 1971–77, mem. of honour 1980; mem. Scientific Bd, Int. Inst. for Comparative Music Studies and Documentation (Berlin) 1964; mem. Soc. for Ethnomusicology Council (dir at large 1968, vice-pres. 1972–73); mem. Int. Soc. for Music Educ. (bd dirs 1967–74, vice-pres. 1968–74); Chair. African Regional Secretariat, Int. Music Council (UNESCO) 1972; Regional Co-ordinator for Africa, Bd Dirs Universe of Music: A World History (UNESCO) 1980; mem. Int. Comm. for a Scientific and Cultural History of Mankind, UNESCO 1980–; mem. Scientific Cttee, Institut des Peuples Noir, Burkina Faso 1986; mem. Bd Dirs, African Studies Asscn 1986–90; mem. Int. Semiotic Inst. 1987; mem. African Music Soc., Historical Soc. of Ghana, Int. Council for Traditional Music, Nat. Music Asscn of Ghana (pres.). *Compositions include:* Adanse Kronkron (Divine Testimony) 1940, African Pianism: Twelve Pedagogical Pieces 1946–75, Suite for flute and piano 1959, Four Akan Solo Songs 1962, Canzona 1963, Antubam (Dirge for cello and piano) 1965, For Violin 1967, Four Flute Pieces 1969, Quartet No. 1 for Atenteben 1969, Quartet No. 2 for Ateneben 1969, Chamber Music in the African Idiom 1976. *Publications:* Akanfoo Anansesem 1949, Akanfoo Nnwom Bi 1949, Ananwoma 1951, Anwonsem 1952, Kwabena Amoa 1952, Akwansosem Bi 1952, Adae 1953, Semode 1954, Funeral Dirges of the Akan People 1955, The Writing of Twi: Asante Spelling 1955, Possession Dances in African Societies 1956, Kookoo ho Mpanisem 1959, African Music in Ghana: A Survey of Traditional Forms 1962, Drumming in Akan Communities of Ghana 1963, Folk Songs of Ghana 1963, Ghana: Music, Dance and Drama: A Review of the Performing Arts of Ghana 1965, Music in African Cultures: A Review of the Meaning and Significance of Traditional African Music 1966, Adowa Songs 1966, The Place of Authentic Folk Music in Music Education 1966, Our Drums and Drummers 1968, Creating a Wider Interest in Traditional Music: The Place of Traditional Music in the Musical Life of Ghana 1969, Ethnomusicology in Ghana 1970, Kokofu Ayan: Drum Language of Kokofu (Ashanti) 1973, The Music of Africa 1974, Ayan 1975, Collating and Disseminating Oral Sources of Musical Information 1977, Amoma 1978, Selected Reports in Ethnomusicology: Studies in African Music (ed., with Jacqueline C. DjeDje) 1984. *Honours:* elected to Ghana Acad. of Arts and Sciences 1959, hon. mem. Royal Anthropological Inst. of Great Britain and Ireland 1972; African Music Soc. Cowell Award 1958, Rockefeller Foundation Fellowship 1958–59; Ford Foundation Fellowship 1961, Grand Medal of Ghana 1968, Ghana Arts Award 1972, ASCAP Deems Taylor Award 1975, Int. Music Council-UNESCO Music Prize for Distinguished Service to Music 1981, Nat. Entertainment Critics and Reviewers Asscn of Ghana Flagstar Award 1993. *Address:* International Centre for African Music and Dance, University of Ghana, PO Box 25, Legon, Accra, Ghana (office). *Telephone:* (233) 21-500381 (office). *Website:* www.ug.edu.gh (office).

NOACK, Florian; Belgian pianist; b. 1990, Brussels. *Education:* Queen Elisabeth Musical Chapel in Exceptional Young Talent programme (aged 12), studied under Yuka Izutsu, Musikhochschule Köln, studied with Vassily Lobanov, Musikhochschule Basel and with Claudio Martinez-Mehner. *Career:* began playing piano aged four; has performed at festivals in China, S Korea, USA, France, Germany, Belgium; recitals in numerous halls, including Philharmonie Köln, Beijing Concert Hall, Palais des Beaux Arts Brussels, Oriental Art Centre Shanghai, Xinghai Concert Hall Guangzhou, Konzerthaus in Detmold, Comédie des Champs-Elysées, Paris; regular guest at festivals in France, including Chopin Festival, Annecy Festival, Piano en Valois, Esprit du Piano, Pianissimes; performs rare works from romantic and post-romantic repertoire; concert programmes include composers such as Lyapunov, Alkan, Medtner and Dohnanyi; has authored transcriptions of orchestral works by Tchaikovsky, Rachmaninov and Rimsky-Korsakov; as soloist, has performed with numerous orchestras including WDR Rundfunkorchester, Philharmonie Südwestfalen, Charlemagne Chamber Orchestra, Symphonic Orchestra of Aquitaine, Philharmonisches Orchester Zwickau. *Recordings include:* Sergei Lyapunov: Works for Piano Vol. 1 2013, Transcriptions and Paraphrases for Piano (Tchaikovsky, Rimsky-Korsakov and Rachmaninov) (Echo Klassik Award for Emerging Artist of the Year – piano 2015) 2014. *Honours:* grants and scholarships from Spes, Fondation Banque Populaire and Mozart Gesellschaft, prizewinner at Rachmaninov Int. Competition, Robert Schumann Int. Competition and the Piano Competition, Cologne. *Current Management:* Jeroen Tersteeg, Nymus Artists, Avenue du Beau Séjour 34, 1180 Brussels, Belgium. *Telephone:* (2) 3723005. *E-mail:* jt@nymusartists.com. *Website:* www.floriannoack.com.

NOBLE, Jeremy; musicologist, critic and broadcaster; b. 27 March 1930, London, England. *Education:* Worcester Coll., Oxford. *Career:* music critic for The Times 1960–63, The Sunday Telegraph 1972–76; Research Fellow, Barber Inst., Birmingham 1964–65; Assoc. Prof., State Univ. of New York, Buffalo 1966–70, 1976–; Fellow, Harvard Inst. for Renaissance Studies, Florence 1967–68; Leverhulme Research Fellow 1975–76; many broadcasts for BBC Radio 3. *Publications:* Purcell and the Chapel Royal, in Essays on Music 1959, Mozart: A Documentary Biography (co-trans.) 1965; contrib. entries on Josquin and Stravinsky (with E.W. White) for The New Grove Dictionary of Music and Musicians 1980; contrib. articles on Josquin, Debussy and Stravinsky for the Musical Times.

NOBLE, Timothy; American singer (baritone); b. 22 Feb. 1945, Indianapolis, IN. *Career:* sang supporting roles in Carmen, Turandot and Wozzeck with San Francisco Opera in 1981; Houston Opera from 1982 as Ping, Leporello and Falstaff; Colorado Springs Festival in 1982 as Rigoletto and Fort Worth and Opéra-Comique Paris in 1983 as Sharpless and Germont; Season 1985–86 at Santa Fe in the premiere of John Eaton's The Tempest, as Falstaff in Amsterdam and as Simon Boccanegra at Glyndebourne returning in 1988 as Germont; San Francisco in 1987 as Tomsky in The Queen of Spades, Venice in 1988 in Verdi's Stiffelio; Sang Shaklovity in Khovanshchina at the Metropolitan in 1988 and San Francisco in 1990, returning to New York in 1991 as Leporello; Opera Pacific at Costa Mesa and the Santa Fe Festival in 1991 as Renato and as Jack Rance in La Fanciulla del West; Other roles include William Tell, Amonasro, Macbeth, Iago, Tonio, Alfio, Di Luna and Scarpia; Sang Columbus in the premiere of The Voyage by Philip Glass at New York Metropolitan in 1992; Iago at the 1996 Holland Festival and Rigoletto for Flanders Opera, 1998; Sang Rigoletto, Antwerp and Gent, 1998, and Flying Dutchman at Indianapolis Opera; Iago at Amsterdam, 1999; Sang in Henze's Venus and Adonis at Toronto, 2001; Further engagements in musicals and as concert artist; Professor of Voice, Indiana University, 1999–. *Current Management:* c/o Janet Jarriel, JEJ Artists, 861 Fair Oaks Drive, Macon, GA 31204, USA. *Telephone:* (478) 742-1162. *Fax:* (646) 304-1188. *E-mail:* janet@jejartists.com. *Website:* www.jejartists.com.

NOCENTINI, Maria Costanza; Italian singer (soprano); *Teacher of Singing, Conservatory of Music G. Verdi, Como*; b. Florence, Tuscany. *Education:* G. B. Martini Conservatory of Bologna (studies with Suzanne Danco). *Career:* following her diploma, took part in a Mozart project managed by Claudio Desderi making her debuts in the roles of Despina in Così fan tutte, Susanna in Le nozze di Figaro and Zerlina in Don Giovanni; appearances in Italy at Teatro alla Scala, Teatro Regio di Torino, Teatro Valli di Reggio Emilia, Teatro di San Carlo di Napoli, Teatro Regio di Parma, Teatro dell'Opera di Roma, Teatro Comunale di Bologna, Teatro La Fenice di Venezia, Teatro Comunale di Firenze, Teatro Carlo Felice di Genova, Teatro Verdi di Trieste, Teatro Massimo di Palermo, Spoleto Festival, Festival of Martina Franca, Festival of Cremona, and abroad at Théâtre des Champs Elysées, New Israeli Opera, Salzburg Festival, Bayerischer Staatsoper, Teatro Municipal, Santiago, Chile, Wiener Staatsoper, Scottish Opera, Glasgow, Opéra de Nice, Teatro de La Maestranza, Seville, Glyndebourne Festival Opera, Tokyo Japan Opera Foundation, New Zealand Opera, and elsewhere; has appeared in the main soprano roles in such operas as Il Turco in Italia, La scala di seta, L'occasione fa il ladro, La Visita Meravigliosa by Nino Rota, Die Zauberflöte, L'Elisir d'amore, Werther, Le convenienze e inconvenienze teatrali, Aci e Galatea, Le due cinesi, La jaune princesse by Saint-Saëns, Rinaldo, Lucia di Lammermoor, Le nozze di Figaro, Semele, La Bohème, La gazza ladra, Orfeo ed Euridice, Falstaff, L'incoronazione di Poppea, Don Pasquale, Il matrimonio segreto, Rigoletto, Traviata; concert performances with several important orchestras and musical institutions, including Festival International, Beaune, Amici della Musica di Firenze, Accad. Nazionale di Santa Cecilia di Roma, Concertgebouw, Amsterdam, Wiener Konzerthaus, Festival Siglas de Oro, Madrid; has collaborated with conductors, including R. Alessandrini, M. Benini, F. Biondi, F. Brüggen, G. Carella, M. W. Chung, R. Clemencic, A. Davies, G. Gelmetti, M. Guidarini, C. Hogwood, L. Langrée, L. Maazel, R. Muti, D. Oren, D. Parry, E. Pidò, C. Rousset, C. Rovaris, J. Tate, as well as with stage directors, including P. Avati, F. Crivelli, A. Fassini, M. Hampe, N. Joël, P. L. Pizzi, L. Puggelli, J. Taymor, M. van Hoecke, G. Vick, H. Wernicke, F. Zeffirelli; appearances have included Donizetti's La figlia del reggimento (Maria) in Chieti and Bergamo, Oedipe in Cagliari, Incoronazione di Poppea in Sevilla and at Opernahus in Zurich, Falstaff in Verona La Scala di Seta in Palermo and La Bohème in Torre del Lago, Traviata with the Fondazione Toscanini in Zeffirelli's production, Don Giovanni (Donna Anna) in Glasgow, Stabat Mater by Pergolesi at Théâtre Royal de la Monnaie, Bruxelles, Turandot (Liù) in Wellington and Auckland, Beethoven's 9th Symphony conducted by Yutaka Sado on the occasion of the rebuilding of the Hyogo Performing Arts Center in Kobe, Japan, Traviata at Kungliga Operan Stockholm, Maria Stuarda at Teatro Bellini in Catania, Teatro La Fenice in Venice and Teatro Verdi in Trieste, Teatro Municipale in Piacenza, Teatro Pavarotti in Modena and Luisa Miller at Malmö Opera; teacher of singing, Conservatory of Music G. Verdi, Como 2012–14. *Recordings include:* Le convenienze ed inconvenienze teatrali, La princesse jaune by Saint-Saëns, Mercadante's Emma d'Antiochia, Donizetti's La figlia del reggimento, La Sonnambula, La Pietra del Paragone, Souvenir de Florence. *Honours:* Toti Dal Monte Prize 1992, Prize of Int. Viotti Competition 1992, Miguel Cervantes Prize and Best Rossini interpretation, Francesco Viñas Competition, Barcelona 1992. *Current Management:* c/o In Art Management, Via San Gregorio 53, 20124 Milan, Italy. *Telephone:* (02) 97374166; 335-8212239 (mobile). *Fax:* (02) 97374233. *E-mail:* info@inartmanagement.com. *Website:* www.inartmanagement.com; www.facebook.com/pages/Maria-Costanza-Nocentini/110607609082343?fref=ts.

NODA, Ken; pianist and arts administrator; b. 5 Oct. 1962, New York, USA. *Education:* studied with Daniel Barenboim. *Career:* London debut 1979 with the English Chamber Orchestra and Daniel Barenboim; later engagements with the Philharmonia, Berlin Philharmonic, Orchestre de Paris, Rotterdam Philharmonic, New York Philharmonic and Chicago Symphony; recitals in London, Toronto, Chicago, Lincoln Center New York, Hamburg and La Fenice, Venice; festival appearances at Mostly Mozart, New York, Ravinia and Tanglewood; 1986 debut with the Vienna Philharmonic in Salzburg; season 1986–87 in concerts with the Berlin Philharmonic, the Hallé and the Philharmonia; 1988 concerts with the Rotterdam Philharmonic playing Mozart under James Conlon, Beethoven's Triple Concerto with Pinchas Zukerman and Lynn Harrell at Ravinia; toured Japan with Ozawa and the New Japan Philharmonic; resumed concert career in New York with solo recitals at Metropolitan Museum of Art 1998, 92nd Street, New York 1999; lieder recitals with Jessye Norman 1998 and Hildegard Behrens 1999, both at Salzburg Festival; Musical Asst to the Artistic Dir, Artistic Administration, Metropolitan Opera.

NOEL, Rita; singer (mezzo-soprano); b. 21 Nov. 1943, Lancaster, SC, USA. *Education:* Eastman School, Queens Coll., studied in Charlotte, SC, in New York and in Vienna. *Career:* played violin and viola with the Vienna Chamber Orchestra and the Berlin Symphony; stage debut with the Metropolitan National Opera Company 1966, as Flora in Traviata; further appearances at the Theater am Gärtnerplatz Munich, Bielefeld, Amsterdam and Miami; other roles included Mozart's Cherubino and Sextus, Cornelia in Giulio Cesare, Carmen, Rosina, Octavian, Nickausse, Azucena and Santuzza; frequent concert engagements.

NOLAN, David, DipMus; violinist; b. 1949, Liverpool, England. *Education:* Royal Manchester Coll. of Music with Yossi Zivoni and Alexander Moskowski, studied in Russia. *Career:* debut with the Mendelssohn Concerto 1965; joined the London Philharmonic Orchestra 1972, Leader 1976–92; many appearances with the London Philharmonic Orchestra and other orchestras in concertos by Bach, Beethoven, Brahms, Bruch, Glazunov, Korngold, Mozart, Paganini, Saint-Saëns, Stravinsky, Tchaikovsky and Walton; Leader, Philharmonia Orchestra 1992–94, Bournemouth Symphony Orchestra 1997–2001; Solo Concertmaster, Yomiuri Nippon Symphony Orchestra, Tokyo 1999–. *Recordings:* The Lark Ascending by Vaughan Williams; The Four Seasons by Vivaldi; Mozart Rondo in C for violin and orchestra with the BBC Philharmonic. *Address:* 5-21-8-2F Nishi-Shinjuku, Shinjuku-ku, Tokyo 160-0023, Japan; Flat 1, 34 Craven Street, London, WC2N 5NP, England.

NOLEN, Timothy; American singer (baritone); b. 9 July 1941, Rotan, TX. *Education:* Manhattan School of Music, studied with Richard Fredericks and Walter Fredericks. *Career:* debut at New Jersey Opera Newark as Rossini's Figaro; sang Marcello in La Bohème with San Francisco Opera in 1968; Appearances in Chicago, Houston, Boston and Minneapolis; European debut at Rouen in 1974 as Pelléas; Sang at Amsterdam in 1974 in the premiere of The Picture of Dorian Gray by Kox, at Cologne, 1974–78 and Paris, Bordeaux, Aix and Nantes as Mozart's Count, Figaro and Guglielmo, Donizetti's Malatesta and Belcore, Monteverdi's Orpheus, and Dandini in La Cenerentola, Puccini's Gianni Schicchi, the Emperor in The Nightingale by Stravinsky and Ford in Falstaff; Sang in the premieres of Carlisle Floyd's Willie Stark and Bernstein's A Quiet Place, Houston in 1981 and 1983; Further engagements at Florence, Geneva, Miami, New York, City Opera and Philadelphia; Santa Fe Festival in 1992 as Mr Peachum in The Beggar's Opera and Frank in Die Fledermaus; Sang Malatesta at Chicago, 1995; Season 1998 as Somarone in Béatrice and Bénédict at Santa Fe and Don Pasquale at St Louis; Season 2001–02 as Rossini's Don Magnifico at Cincinnati and Trinity Moses in Mahagonny at Genoa. *Current Management:* c/o Thea Dispeker Inc, 59 East 54th Street, Suite 81, New York NY 10022, USA. *Telephone:* (212) 421-7676. *Fax:* (212) 935-3279. *E-mail:* info@dispeker.com. *Website:* www.dispeker.com.

NONOSHITA, Yukari; Japanese singer (soprano) and academic; *Associate Professor of Early Music, Tokyo Geijutsu Daigaku*; b. Ohita Pref. *Education:* Tokyo Nat. Univ. of Fine Arts and Music (now Tokyo Geijutsu Daigaku), Conservatoire Nat. de Saint-Maur, Ecole Normale de Musique de Paris, studies with Hiroko Nakamura, Mady-Mesplé, Camille Maurane and Gérard Souzay. *Career:* debut as Cherubino in Le Nozze di Figaro at Rennes; has appeared in operatic roles including Rosina in Il Barbiere di Siviglia at Rennes and Siébel in Faust at Rennes and Angers; has participated in Baroque Opera Project with Ryo Terakado; contemporary music performances of Toshiro Mayuzumi's Sphénogramme, Luciano Berio's Sequenza III under Hiroyuki Iwaki in Osaka and several premiere performances of new compositions; performed in various Japan premieres of operas, including Chabrier's Une éducation manquée and Fauré's Pénélope; Lecturer (part-time), Ueno-Gakuen Univ. 1994–2002, Tokyo Univ. of the Arts 2000–02; Assoc. Prof. of Early Music, Tokyo Geijutsu Daigaku 2002–. *Recordings include:* J.S. Bach's Complete Motets (BBC Music Magazine Award, Choral Category) 2011. *Honours:* First Prize, Concours d'interpretation de melodies francaises et japonaises 1986, First Prize, Concour Int. de l'UFAM en France 1988. *Address:* Tokyo Geijutsu Daigaku, 12-8 Ueno Kouen, Taito-ku, Tokyo 110-8714, Japan (office). *Website:* www.geidai.ac.jp (office).

NOONE, Michael, PhD; Australian conductor and academic; *Professor and Chair of Music Department, Boston University*; b. Sydney. *Education:* Univ. of Sydney, King's Coll., Cambridge, UK. *Career:* specialist in Renaissance music; Co-founder and Music Dir Ensemble Plus Ultra 2001–; fmrly Head of Musicology, Music Dept, ANU; held teaching positions at Cornell Univ., USA and Univ. of Hong Kong; currently Prof. and Chair Music Dept, Boston Coll., USA. *Recordings include:* with Ensemble Plus Ultra: Morales en Toledo (newly discovered liturgical pieces) 2005, Fernando de las Infantas Motetes 2005, several CDs of the music of Tomás Luis de Victoria including Hymns, Motets and Missa O Quam Gloriosum (Gramophone Award for Best Early Music Recording 2012) 2010, Guerrero: Missa Super Flumina Babylonis 2012, Zarlino's Canticum Canticorum 2012, also music of William Byrd and Atalanta Fuguiens; with Orchestra of the Renaissance: Morales Assumption Mass, Guerrero Requiem, Vivanco In Manus Tuas, Canticum Canticorum; with The Song Company: Spanish Battle Music in the Age of Discovery. *Publications include:* Music and Musicians in the Escorial Liturgy under the Habsburgs 1998, Códice 25 de la catedral de Toledo 2003. *Honours:* mem. Real Academia de Bellas Artes y Ciencias Históricas de Toledo; Premio Real Fundación for contrib. to Spanish music, from King Juan Carlos II 2007, Prelude Classical Award 2008, Boston Coll. Arts Council Faculty Award for his contribution to cultural life on campus and beyond 2012. *E-mail:* christoph.crepaz@crepazmusic.com. *Address:* Music Department, Boston College, Lyons Hall 408, 140 Commonwealth Avenue, Chestnut Hill, MA 02467, USA (office). *E-mail:* michael.noone@bc.edu (office); info@ensembleplusultra.com. *Website:* www.ensembleplusultra.com; www2.bc.edu/~noonemc (office).

NORBERG-SCHULZ, Elizabeth; Norwegian/Italian singer (soprano) and teacher; *Professor of Classical Voice, University of Stavanger*; b. 27 Jan. 1959, Norway; d. of Prof. Christian Norberg-Schulz and Anna Maria De Dominicis; m. Vittorio Bonolis; one s. *Education:* Accad. di Santa Cecilia, Rome with Rosina Laporta, Pears-Britten School, UK and studied with Elisabeth Schwarzkopf in Zurich. *Career:* principal roles include Pamina (Chicago, Madrid, Salzburg, Vienna, Bologna), Susanna (Milan, Vienna), Zerlina (Rome, Naples, Vienna), Asteria in Tamerlano (Florence, Halle, London, Paris), Adina (Milan, Rome, Naples, Vienna), Lucia (Vienna, Spoleto, Oslo), Norina (Munich, Hamburg, Macerata, Naples), Nannetta (Milan, Salzburg, Vienna, Madrid), Gilda (Vienna, Spoleto, Palermo, Treviso, Oslo), Oscar (Met, Chicago, Vienna, Oslo), Micaëla (Bastille, Rome, Oslo), Liù (Covent Garden, Athens, Bologna), Mimì (Glyndebourne, Oslo), Musetta (Florence, Vienna), Adele in Die Fledermaus (Met), Gretel (Chicago), Constance in Dialogues des Carmélites (Milan), Manon (Vienna); appearances at various int. opera houses, including Teatro alla Scala, Teatro dell'Opera di Roma, Teatro Carlo Felice de Bologna, Teatro Comunale di Firenze, Teatro Massimo di Palermo, Teatro Regio di Torino, Teatro San Carlo di Napoli, Teatro Carlo Felice di Genova, La Fenice, Metropolitan Opera, New York, The Lyric Opera of Chicago, Los Angeles Opera, Royal Opera, Covent Garden, Opéra Bastille, Théâtre des Champs Elysées, La Monnaie, Teatro Real di Madrid, Opéra de Genève, Bayerisches Staatsoper, Vienna Staatsoper and Norwegian Opera; performances with numerous int. orchestras, including Berlin Philharmonic (Schumann Requiem für Mignon and Brahms Requiem with Abbado), Vienna Philharmonic (Mozart Great Mass in C minor with Solti, Brahms Requiem with Abbado), I Filarmonici della Scala (Mozart Requiem with Muti, and with Gergiev), Orchestra Nazionale di RAI (Mahler 4° and Der Wein with Tate), Dresden Staatskapelle (Beethoven 9th, Strauss Lieder and Mozart Requiem, all with Sinopoli), Munich Philharmonic (Pergolesi Salve Regina with Abbado and Lily Boulanger Clairières dans le Ciel with Viotti), Bayerischer Rundfunk (Mahler 8° with Sir Colin Davies), Oslo Philharmonic (Mahler 4° with Sinopoli, opera recital with Jansons), Bergen Philharmonic (Mahler 4°, Berg Sieben Frühe Lieder, De Falla Atlantide, Brahms Requiem with Ceccato), New York Philharmonic (Debussy Le Martyr de Saint Sébastien with Masur), Chicago Symphony (Haydn Creation with Solti), San Francisco Symphony (Brahms Requiem with Blomstedt), Boston Symphony (L'Enfant et les Sortilèges with Osawa), Orchestre de Paris (Mahler 2° and Beethoven 9° with Bychkow, Brahms Requem with Masur); Artistic Dir Kirsten Flagstad Festival, Hamar 2005–10, Oslo Operafestival, Oslo 2005–; Prof. of Classical Voice and Interpretation, Univ. of Stavanger, Norway 2006–; Guest Prof., Nanjing Univ. of Arts, People's Repub. of China, The Barratt-Due Inst. of Music, Oslo, Norwegian Acad. of Music (NMH), Oslo, Norwegian Univ. of Science and Tech. (NTNU), Trondheim, Conservatorio Luisa D'Annunzio, Pescara, Italy, Accad. Filarmonica Romana, Rome, Accad. di Santa Cecilia, Rome. *Honours:* Kt, Order of Sankt Olav, Norway 2004, Commdr, Ordine al Merito della Repubblica Italiana 2007; Grieg Prize 1993, Grammy Award 1995, Baerenreiter Prize 1996, Sperimentale of Spoleto 1997, Minerva Prize

2004, Verdi Prize 2006. *Current Management:* c/o Owen/White Management, Flat 6, 22 Brunswick Terrace, Hove, East Sussex, BN3 1HJ, England. *Telephone:* (1273) 727127. *Fax:* (1273) 527038. *E-mail:* info@owenwhitemanagement.com. *Website:* www.owenwhitemanagement.com. *Address:* UiS, University of Stavanger, Det humanistiske fakultet, Bjergsted, 4036 Stavanger, Norway (office). *E-mail:* elizabeth.norberg-schulz@uis.no (office). *Website:* www.uis.no (office).

NORDAL, Jon; Icelandic composer; b. 1926. *Education:* Reykjavík Coll. of Music with Arni Kristjansson, Jon Thorarinsson and Dr V. Urbancic, studied with W. Frey and W. Burkhard in Zürich, Switzerland, in Paris and Rome, Darmstadt summer courses. *Career:* Pres., Reykjavík Coll. of Music. *Compositions:* orchestral: Concerto Lirico for harp and strings, Concerto for orchestra 1949, Concerto for piano and orchestra 1956, Sinfonietta Seriosa 1956, A Play of Fragments 1962, Adagio for flute, harp, piano and strings 1965, Stiklur 1970, Canto Elegiaco 1971, Leidsla 1973, Epitaphio 1974, The Winter Night 1975, Twin Song for violin, viola and orchestra 1979, Dedication 1981, Choralis 1982, Concerto for cello and orchestra 1983; chamber: Sonata for violin and piano, Fairy Tale Sisters for violin and piano, Chorale Prelude for organ 1980, Duo for violin and cello 1983, Requiem 1995, From Dream to Dream for string quartet 1997, Dreaming on a Dormant String for violin, cello and piano 1998, My Faith is but a Flicker for chorus 1999; choir music: Seven Songs for male chorus 1955. *Address:* c/o Reykjavík College of Music, Skipholti 33, 105 Reykjavík, Iceland.

NORDEN, Betsy; American singer (soprano); b. 17 Oct. 1945, Cincinnati, Ohio. *Education:* Boston Univ. *Career:* mem., Metropolitan Opera Chorus from 1969; solo appearances at the Metropolitan from 1972 in Le nozze di Figaro and as Papagena, Elvira in L'Italiana in Algeri, Constance in the Carmélites, Oscar and Despina in Così fan tutte 1990; sang in The Cunning Little Vixen at Philadelphia season 1980–81, Constance at San Francisco 1983 and Gretel at San Diego 1985; many concert appearances.

NORDIN, Birgit; Swedish singer (soprano); b. 22 Feb. 1934, Sangis, Norrbotten. *Education:* Stockholm Opera School, studied with Lina Pagliughi in Italy. *Career:* debut in Stockholm 1957 as Oscar in Un Ballo in Maschera; annual visits to the Drottningholm Opera from 1960, notably in operas by Mozart; sang at Wexford Festival 1963, 1965, and Glyndebourne Festival 1968 as Blondchen in Die Entführung; sang Jenny in Weill's Mahagonny at Copenhagen 1970, Berlin 1970 as soloist in Bach's St Matthew Passion and Christmas Oratorio; television appearance as Berg's Lulu and sang the Queen of Night in Bergman's film version of The Magic Flute 1974; oratorio engagements in Scandinavia, Germany, England and Austria; has sung with the Royal Opera Stockholm on tour to Covent Garden 1990 and the Edinburgh Festival; other roles include Mozart's Susanna and Pamina, Gilda, Rosina, Sophie in Der Rosenkavalier and Mélisande; sang Angelica in Handel's Orlando at Stockholm 2000. *Recordings:* Die Zauberflöte; Madrigals by Monteverdi; Video of Don Giovanni, as Donna Elvira. *Honours:* Swedish Court Singer 1973.

NORDIN, Lena; Swedish singer (soprano); b. 18 Feb. 1956, Visby. *Education:* Coll. of Music in Malmö and Stockholm, studied in Salzburg, Florence and Siena. *Career:* debut in Verdi's Luisa Miller; mem. of soloist ensemble of Royal Opera, Stockholm 1987; has performed numerous roles, including Cleopatra, Donna Anna, Antonia, Lauretta, Marguerite, Constanze, Violetta, Maria Stuarda, Contessa, Nedda, Norma and Sophie; has also sung at Drottningholm Court Theatre (Dido, and Regina in Soler's Cosa Rara); sang Strauss's Daphne in Salzburg and Marguerite at Savonlinna Festival; has guested at Wexford Opera Festival twice, including as Aspasia in Mozart's Mitridate; other roles include Adele, Contessa di Folleville in Rossini's Il viaggio a Reims and Donna Elvira; regular guest in Copenhagen, Dresden, London, Moscow and Seville; has sung Violetta at Nat. Opera of Helsinki, Elena in Vespri Siciliani, Amelia in Un Ballo in Maschera in Darmstadt; Odabella in Verdi's Attila and Die Prinzessin in Schreker's opera Das Spielwerk in Darmstadt, Elisabetta in Don Carlos, Madama Butterfly, Gutrune in Götterdämmerung, Lady Macbeth in Macbeth in Stockholm, Rosalinda in Die Fledermaus, Lina in Verdi's Stiffelio, Ortrud in Lohengrin, Mme Lidoine in Dialogues des Carmélites; concert engagements include performances in USA, France, Germany, Switzerland, Italy, UK and in Scandinavia. *Recordings:* title roles in Berwald's Estrella di Soria, Hallman's Solitär and in Naumann's Gustav Wasa; Carmina Burana; Arias by Mozart, Verdi and Gounod; Mary Stuart, Queen of Scots; Mozart Concert Arias 1996; Lehn Deine Wang: Swedish Songs by Stenhammer, Sjögren, Lindblad. *Honours:* Christina Nilsson Prize 1959, Birgit Nilsson Prize 1987, Svenska Dagblacket Prize 1987, Jussi Björling Prize 1997, Royal Court Singer, King Carl Gustaf, Litteris et Artibus, King Carl Gustaf 2003. *Address:* Östermalmsg 3, 11424 Stockholm, Sweden. *Website:* www.lenanordin.com.

NORDMANN, Marielle Isabelle; French harpist; b. 24 Jan. 1941, Montpellier; d. of Robert Nordmann and Josette Nordmann (née Trèves); m. Patrice Fontanarosa 1968; one s. two d. *Education:* with Lily Laskine and Conservatoire Nat. Supérieur de Musique, Paris. *Career:* Founder-mem. Trio Nordmann, Lily Laskine–Nordmann Duo; played with Bashmet, Duchable, Radulovic and others, under conductors Corboz, Menuhin, Janowski and others; teaching and concerts in Argentina 1989–99; set up masterclasses for children at Conservatoire Nat. Régional de Paris; Artistic Dir Les Musicales Festival, Bagatelle Orangery, Paris 2008–; cr. musical spectacle 'Voyage' with words by P. Coelho, photos by Clémence Bourgoin and lighting and staging by W. Schick 2008; gave world premiere of Concerto in C minor by romantic composer Elias Parish-Alvars (1808–49) in Israel 2008. *Recordings:* more than 20 recordings, including solo harp, concerts, chamber music and duos. *Honours:* Chevalier, Légion d'honneur, Officier, Ordre nat. du Mérite 1990, Chevalier, Ordre des Arts et des Lettres; Premier Prix Harpe, Premier Prix Musique de Chambre (Conservatoire Nat. Supérieur de Musique). *Address:* c/o Clémence Bourgoin, 3 Plumes Productions, 9 rue de l'abbé Rousselot, 75017 Paris, France. *Telephone:* (6) 17-35-11-54. *E-mail:* contact@marielle-nordmann.com (office). *Website:* www.marielle-nordmann.com.

NORDSTRØM, Hans-Henrik; Danish composer; b. 26 June 1947, Nakskov; m. Anne Kristine Smith; one s. *Education:* Royal Danish Acad. of Music, Copenhagen. *Career:* debut in Copenhagen 1990; Co-Artistic Dir Contemporary Music in Susaa Festivals held annually in Aug., 1993–; mem. Danish Composers' Soc. *Compositions:* Kybikos for wind band 1989–90, That Autumn for orchestra 1990–91, The Mountains in Monestiés for sinfonietta 1988, Tripthychos for three double basses and sinfonietta 1989–90, Dialogue for tuba and percussion 1991, Srebrenica for organ 1993, Tympanon for three percussion 1993, Reflections I for sextet 1992, Reflections II for violin and harp 1992, Reflections III for flugelhorn and piano 1993, Night for choir 1992, Clockwork and Raindrops for sextet 1991, Room/Space String Quartet I 1991–92, Seven Vignettes from Susaa for sinfonietta 1994, Andalusian Reflections for piano trio 1995, Sonata per l'Inverno for piano 1994–95, String Quartet II (Faroese) 1994, M 31 for clarinet trio 1995–96, Songlines for sinfonietta 1995, Carnac for sextet 1995, Images d'autumne for flute, clarinet and bassoon 1996, Icelandic Suite for reed quartet 1996, Fara fram vid for clarinet 1996, To Winter for saxophone quartet 1996–97, Sketches from Hirsholmene for sinfonietta 1997, La Primavera for flute, oboe, bassoon and harpsichord 1997, La rosa, la noche y el tiempo 1997, String Quartet III (Norwegian) 1998, Il Quadrato magico for reed quartet 1998–99, Abstractions for saxophone and percussion 1998, Entwicklungen for two accordions 1998, Flows for three flutes 1998, Fantasy for bass flute 1998, Tres Poemas de Federico García Lorca for mezzo, clarinet, cello, harp and percussion 1998, Birds of Susaa are Dreaming New Songs for saxophone quartet 1999, A Dream for flute and harpsichord 1998–99, Gravures en taille-douce for harpsichord 1998–99, String Quartet No. 4 (Hebredian) 1999, Asterion for violin 1999, Mykines for sinfonietta 2000, Limbo for violin, cello and piano 2000, Mouvements for piano trio 2000, Land of Shadows for bass clarinet and percussion 2000, Light for flute and guitar 2000, Fluctuations for four guitars 2000, Night Glow and Dawn Frosting for soprano and guitar 2000, Chac for organ 2001, Lost Traces for saxophone and percussion 2001, The Twelve Bens for string trio 2001, In the Woods for violin and sinfonietta 2001, Nada y todo for recorder quartet 2001, Imaginations for harpsichord 2002, '. . .if a Tone in the Night' for recorder and accordion 2002, Growth for brass quintet 2002, Fair Isle for cello, 12 woodwinds and four French horns 2002, Riverrun for sinfonietta 2002, Quarks for string trio 2002, Tingsomingenting for guitar 2003, A.L.P. for flute, clarinet, guitar, percussion and violin 2003, Following the Wake for piano trio 2003, Sketches from Iceland for piano quartet 2003, Morning Knight for mezzo, recorder, saxophone and percussion 2003, A.L.P. Too for viola and guitar 2003, Nuages d'automne for trombone and sinfonietta 2003–04, Nuvele Italiane for piano 2004, Nuages Élégiaques for trombone 2004, Triskele for wind quintet 2004, Roest for clarinet, bassoon and piano 2004, Ante Discum Solis for saxophone and harp 2004, Infinite Water for clarinet and electronics 2004, Dieciséis Fragmentos for mezzo, guitar and percussion 2004, Sjúrður for soprano and saxophone 2004, Anna Livia for mezzo and guitar 2004, Finnegan's for sinfonietta 2005, Stalingrad for four saxophones and two percussion 2005, The Place that is Not for saxophone and organ 2005, Endro Karnag for flute and violoncello 2005, Tres Retratos con sombra for mezzo, flute, violoncello and accordion 2006, Silent November for septet 2006, Días for accordion and harpsichord 2006, Another Kind of Stillness for bassoon and piano 2006, Rain for flute, percussion and electronics, Cantes de amor for mezzo and piano trio 2007, In the Wake of Ulysses for clarinet, violoncello and piano 2006–08, Nocturno del hueco for mezzo and guitar 2007, Klodens Vaerksted for mezzo, flute, cello and accordion 2007, Six Fragments from Macedonia (String Quartet No. 5) 2007, Snefnug for soprano, flute and piano 2008, In Front of the Sun for flute and piano 2008, Behind the Moon for flute and piano 2008, Mais les oiseaux chantent for bass flute and electronics 2008, Egyptian Nights for horn trio 2008, Between mountains for harp trio 2008, At the Nile for saxophone and percussion, De efterladte (Asger Jorn painting) for octet 2008, The New Fire for orchestra 2008–09, Nine Moments For Two Guitars 2010, Syv snefnug for mezzo, flute, cello and accordion 2010, The Surviving (Asger Jorn painting) for string quartet and 4-hand piano 2010, New work for orchestra 2010–11. *Recordings include:* Hans-Henrik Nordstrøm 1 1997, Hans-Henrik Nordstrøm 2 1999, Hans-Henrik Nordstrøm 3 2001, Hans-Henrik Nordstrøm 4: In the Woods 2003, Hans-Henrik Nordstrøm 5: North West 2005, Starting Points 2007, Finnegan's 2007, Hans-Henrik Nordstrøm LIVE 2010, Secrets (wind quintet) 2010, Lyric Sketches (fl, gt & acc.) 2011, Cycle II – The Year (Orchestra) 2010–11, Finn, again! (mezzo, fl & gt), String Quartet No 6 2012, Seven Soundscapes (sextet) 2012, Manos (fl, vla & acc) 2012, Impromptu pour piano 2012–13, Furari 2013, Four Poems (Tomas Tranströmer) 2013, Quatuor à l'aube de l'automne 2014, Ainola 2014, La cometa scomparsa (theorbo) 2014, Winter Dream (tenor sax) 2014, Orion 2015, Sphinx (sinfonietta) 2015, Out of the Darkness (eight double basses) 2015, Ikke en etude (bass trombone) 2015. *Honours:* Danish Art Foundation grants 1990–, Danish Composers' Soc. grant 2001, Wilhelm Hansen Foundation grants 2003, 2004, Composer of the Year, Bornholm

Music Festival 2003, Composer of the Year, Birkeroed 2004, Hakon Boerresen Hon. Prize 2007, Play-Danish-Day Composer's Portrait Copenhagen 2010. *Address:* Skovmarksvej 52, Vetterslev, 4100 Ringsted, Denmark (home). *E-mail:* hans-henrik@nordstroem.dk (office). *Website:* www.nordstroem.dk.

NOREJKA, Virgilius; Lithuanian singer (tenor) and administrator; b. 22 Sept. 1935, Siaulai. *Education:* studied in Vilnius. *Career:* debut at State Opera of Vilnius 1957 as Lensky in Eugene Onegin; sang in Lithuania as Alfredo, the Duke in Rigoletto, Werther, Don José, Almaviva and The Prince in The Love for Three Oranges; guest appearances in Moscow, Leningrad, Kiev and Kharkov; gave recitals and sang Russian folksongs, in addition to operatic repertoire; further engagements at the Berlin Staatsoper and in Poland, Bulgaria, Denmark, Finland, Italy, Austria, Hungary, USA and Canada; sang Radames at Hamburg Staatsoper and also appeared in operas by Lithuanian composers; Dir, Vilnius Opera 1975–.

NØRGÅRD, Per; Danish composer; b. 13 July 1932, Gentofte. *Education:* Royal Danish Acad. of Music, studied with Nadia Boulanger in Paris, France. *Career:* teacher, Odense Conservatoire 1958–61, Royal Acad. of Music 1960–65, Royal Acad. of Music, Århus 1965; Terrains Vagues premiered by the BBC Symphony Orchestra 2001. *Compositions include:* operas: Gilgamesh 1971–72, Siddharta 1974–79, The Divine Circus 1982, Nuit des Hommes 1995; orchestral: Symphony No. 1 1953–55, Voyage into the Golden Screen 1968–69, Twilight 1976–77, Symphony No. 3 in two movements 1972–75, Symphony No. 4 1981, Symphony No. 5 1990, Spaces of Time 1991, Symphony No. 6 1999; for string and wind orchestras: Metamorphosis 1953, Modlys 1970; chamber: eight String Quartets 1952–97, Fragment V 1961, Prelude and Ant Fugue (with a Crab Cannon) 1982, Lin for clarinet, cello and piano 1986; solo keyboard: Sonata in one movement 1953, Canon 1971; choral: Evening Land 1954, Frost Psalm 1975–76, Interrupted Hymn, Scream, Drinking Song, Piano Concerto 1995, Terrains Vagues for orchestra 2001; solo instruments and orchestra: Between in three movements for cello and orchestra 1985, Helle Nacht violin concerto 1987, King, Queen and Ace for harp and 13 instruments 1989; percussion: Iching solo 1982, nine Symphonies 1958–90, Violin Concerto No. 2 1993, Viola Concerto 1995, Organ Concerto No. 2 1996, Elf's Mirror for solo voices, chorus and orchestra 1996, nine String Quartets 1955–94. *Honours:* Nordic Council Prize for Music (for opera, Gilgamesh) 1974, Sonning Music Prize.

NORHOLM, Ib; Danish composer; b. 24 Jan. 1931, Copenhagen. *Education:* Royal Danish Acad. of Music, Copenhagen. *Career:* music critic with several major Copenhagen Newspapers; Prof. of Composition, Royal Danish Acad. of Music; organist in Copenhagen. *Compositions include:* Stanzas and Fields, Strofer Og Marker, Trio op 22, Fluctuations: The Unseen Pan, Exile for large orchestra, From My Green Herbarium, September-October-November, After Icarus, Tavole Per Orfeo, Invitation to a Beheading 1965, Isola Bella 1968–70, Den Unge Park 1969–70, Day's Nightmare 1973, Violin Concerto 1974, Heretic Hymn 1975, The Garden Wall 1976, The Funen Cataracts 1976, Essai Prismatique 1979, Lys 1979, Decreation 1979, The Elements, Moralities or There May be Several Miles to the Nearest Spider, Ecliptic Instincts, Apocalyptic Idylls 1980, Before Silence 1980, Haven Med Steir Der Deler Sig 1982. *Address:* Henningsens Allé 30B, 2900 Hellerup, Denmark.

NORMAN, Andrew; American composer; b. 1979. *Education:* Univ. of Southern California, Yale Univ. *Career:* works commissioned and premiered by Los Angeles Philharmonic, Royal Liverpool Philharmonic, Orpheus Chamber Orchestra, Minnesota Orchestra, Tonhalle Orchester Zurich, Grand Rapids Symphony; chamber music featured at venues including Le Poisson Rouge, MATA Festival, Tanglewood Festival, Los Angeles Philharmonic's Green Umbrella Series, Juilliard School Focus Festival, Aspen Music Festival; Composer-in-Residence, Los Angeles Chamber Orchestra 2012–; Berlin Philharmonic's Scharoun Ensemble portrait of the composer concert Melting Architecture 2010. *Compositions include:* chamber: Gran Turismo for violin octet 2004, Garden of Follies for alto saxophone and piano 2006, The Companion Guide to Rome for string trio 2010, Try for large chamber ensemble 2011; orchestral: Sacred Geometry 2003, Unstuck 2008, The Great Swiftness for chamber orchestra 2010, Apart 2011. *Honours:* ASCAP Nissim Prize 2005, Rome Prize 2006, Berlin Prize 2009, Aspen Music Festival Druckman Prize. *Current Management:* c/o Norman D. Ryan, Schott Music NY, 254 West 31st Street, 15th Floor, New York, NY 10001, USA. *Telephone:* (212) 461-6940. *E-mail:* ny@schott-music.com. *E-mail:* andrew@andrewnormanmusic.com (office). *Website:* www.andrewnormanmusic.com (office).

NORMAN, Daniel, BA, MEng(Oxon.), Dip RAM, ARAM; British singer (tenor); b. 2 July 1970, Ivinghoe, Bucks., England; m. Sarah Norman (née Moore); three s. *Education:* Lichfield Cathedral School, Shrewbury School, New Coll., Oxford, Banff Centre for the Arts, Britten Pears School, Aldeburgh, Tanglewood Music Center, Royal Acad. of Music, London. *Career:* concerts and song recitals in major venues in UK and Europe; prin. roles with Paris Opera, Bavarian State Opera, Glyndebourne, Royal Opera, ENO, Wexford Opera, Garsington, Opera North, New Israeli Opera, Opera Zuid, Nationale Reis Opera (Netherlands), New Kent Opera, Tête à Tête, Early Opera Co., Classical Opera Co., Opera Boston, Almeida Opera, Verona Opera. *Films:* Powder Her Face, Die Meistersinger. *Radio:* regular appearances on BBC Radio 3 and Classic FM, including Britten's St Nicolas and Les Illuminations, Mozart's Requiem, Maxwell Davies's Taverner, Britten War Requiem. *Television:* Birth of British Music. *Recordings include:* Billy Budd (Richard

Hickox), Hyperion Schubert Edition (Graham Johnson), Hugh Wood's Comus (Sir Andrew Davies), Brett Dean's Winter Songs (Berlin Phil. Wind Quintet), Britten Winter Words (Christopher Gould), Arne Artaxerxes (Ian Page), Schubert: Lieder Year by Year, Britten Canticles. *Current Management:* c/o Hazard Chase, 25 City Road, Cambridge, CB1 1DP, England. *Telephone:* (1223) 321400. *Fax:* (1223) 460827. *E-mail:* info@hazardchase.co.uk. *Website:* www.hazardchase.co.uk.

NORMAN, Jessye, MMus; American singer (soprano); b. 15 Sept. 1945, Augusta, Ga; d. of Silas Norman and Janie Norman (née King). *Education:* Howard Univ., Peabody Conservatory, Univ. of Michigan. *Career:* operatic debut, Deutsche Oper Berlin 1969; debut La Scala, Milan 1972, Royal Opera House, Covent Garden 1972; American operatic debut, Hollywood Bowl 1972; performer at Lincoln Center 1973–; tours in N and S America, Europe, Middle East, Australia; int. festivals including Aix-en-Provence, Aldeburgh, Berliner Festwochen, Edin., Flanders, Helsinki, Lucerne, Salzburg, Tanglewood, Spoleto, Hollywood Bowl, Ravinia; with leading orchestras from USA, UK, Israel, Australia; other performances include La Voix Humaine, Orchestre nat. de Lyon 2002; Founder and Pres. L'Orchidée Inc.; mem. Bd of Dirs Ms. Foundation, New York Botanical Garden, Nat. Music Foundation, City-Meals-on-Wheels (New York City); Trustee, Paine Coll., Augusta, Ga; spokesperson for Partnership for the Homeless; Fellow, American Acad. of Arts and Sciences. *Publication:* Stand Up Straight and Sing! 2014. *Honours:* Commdr des Arts et des Lettres 1984; more than 30 hon. degrees including Hon. MusDoc (Howard) 1982, (Univ. of the South, Sewance) 1984, (Univ. of Michigan) 1987, (Edinburgh) 1989; Hon. DMus (Cambridge) 1989; Vocal Winner, Int. Musikwettbewerb, Bayerischer Rundfunk (Germany) 1968, Grand Prix du Disque (Acad. du Disque Français) 1973, 1976, 1977, 1982; Deutsche Schallplatten Preis für Euryanthe 1975; Cigale d'Or (Aix-en-Provence Festival) 1977; Grammy Award 1980, 1982, 1985, Musician of the Year (Musical America) 1982, IRCAM Record Award 1982, Alumna Award (Univ. of Michigan) 1982, Edison Award for Lifetime Achievement, Amsterdam 2006, Grammy Lifetime Achievement Award 2006, Nat. Medal of Arts 2009, NAACP Spingarn Award 2013, Wolf Prize in Arts 2015. *Address:* 244 Mount Airy Road West, Croton On Hudson, NY 10520-3311, USA.

NORRINGTON, Sir Roger Arthur Carver, Kt, CBE, FRAM; British conductor; *Principal Conductor, Zurich Chamber Orchestra*; b. 16 March 1934, s. of Sir Arthur Norrington and Edith Joyce Carver; m. 1st Susan Elizabeth McLean May 1964 (divorced 1982); one s. one d.; m. 2nd Karalyn Mary Lawrence 1986; one s. *Education:* Dragon School, Oxford, Westminster School, Clare Coll. Cambridge, Royal Coll. of Music. *Career:* freelance singer 1962–72; Prin. Conductor, Kent Opera 1966–84; Guest Conductor with numerous British, American and European orchestras, appearances at BBC Proms and City of London, Bath, Aldeburgh, Edin. and Harrogate festivals; regular broadcasts UK, Europe, USA; Musical Dir London Classical Players 1978–97, London Baroque Players 1975–, Schütz Choir of London 1962, Orchestra of St Luke's, New York 1990–94; Prin. Conductor Bournemouth Sinfonietta 1985–89; Chief Conductor Camerata Salzburg 1997–2006; Prin. Conductor Radio Sinfonieorchester, Stuttgart 1998–2011, Zurich Chamber Orchestra 2011–; Co-Dir Early Opera Project 1984–90, Historic Arts 1986–90; numerous gramophone recordings. *Honours:* Cavaliere, Ordine al Merito della Repubblica Italiana, Ehrenkreuz Erster Klasse (Austria) 1999; Ehrenkreuz Erste Klasse (FRG) 2011; Hon. DMus (Kent) 1994, (York) 2013; ECHO Klassik Award for Symphonic Recording of the Year – 19th Century (for Elgar Enigma Variations) 2012. *Address:* Zürcher Kammerorchester, Seefeldstrasse 305, 8034 Zurich, Switzerland (office). *Telephone:* (44) 388-36-00 (office). *E-mail:* info@zko.ch (office). *Website:* www.zko.ch (office).

NORRIS, David Owen, MA, FSA, FRAM, FRCO; British pianist, broadcaster and academic; *Professor of Musical Performance, University of Southampton*; b. 16 June 1953, Northampton, England; s. of Albert Norris and Margaret Norris; two s. *Education:* Keble Coll. Oxford, Royal Acad. of Music, and privately in Paris. *Career:* Prof., RAM 1977–89; Dir Petworth Festival 1986–92; Artistic Dir Cardiff Festival 1992–95; Chair. Steans Inst. for Singers, Chicago 1992–98; Gresham Prof. of Music, London 1993–97; Prof., Royal Coll. of Music 2000–; Lecturer in Music and Head of Keyboard, Univ. of Southampton 2000–07, Prof. of Musical Performance 2007–; gave world premieres of Schubert's First Song Cycle and Elgar's Piano Concerto. *Compositions include:* oratorios: Prayerbook, Turning Points; other: Piano Concerto, Symphony, HengeMusic for saxophones, organ, film and poetry; song cycles, cantatas. *Recordings include:* complete piano music of Elgar, Dyson and Quilter, and the World's First Piano Concertos. *Radio:* Playlist (BBC Radio 4 series), regular contrib. to Building a Library (BBC Radio 3). *Television:* 'Chord of the Week' and 'Inside the Score' for BBC 2's Proms Extra; appearances in programmes on Elgar (including 'Imagine' on the Piano Concerto), Parry, Vaughan Williams, Music & Royalty, etc.. *Honours:* Hon. Fellow, Keble Coll., Oxford 2006; First Gilmore Artist Award 1991. *Address:* Music, Building 2, Highfield Campus, University of Southampton, Southampton, SO17 1BJ, England. *Telephone:* 7957-322091 (mobile) (office). *E-mail:* info@davidowennorris.com (home). *Website:* www.davidowennorris .com (home).

NORRIS, Geoffrey, BA, ARCM; British critic and musicologist; *Chief Music Critic, The Daily Telegraph;* b. 19 Sept. 1947, London. *Education:* Durham Univ., Univ. of Liverpool, Inst. of Theatre, Music and Cinematography, Russia. *Career:* music critic, The Daily Telegraph 1983, chief music critic 1995–, also for The Times; Lecturer in Music History, Royal Northern Coll. of

Music 1975–77; Commissioning Ed., New Oxford Companion to Music 1977–83; Prof., Rachmaninoff Music Inst., Tambov, Russia 2005–; mem Critics' Circle, The Arts Club. *Publications include:* Encyclopedia of Opera (co-author) 1976, Rachmaninoff 1976, 2nd edn 2001, Shostakovich: The Man and his Music (co-author) 1982, A Catalogue of the Compositions of S. Rachmaninov (co-author) 1982; contrib. to New Grove Dictionary of Music and Musicians 1980, 2001, Musical Times, Music Quarterly, Tempo, Music and Letters, BBC broadcasts. *Address:* The Daily Telegraph, 1 Canada Square, Canary Wharf, London, E14 5DT, England (office).

NORTH, Nigel; British lutenist, classical guitarist and academic; b. 5 June 1954, London, England. *Education:* Guildhall School of Music, Royal College of Music, studied with John Williams, Carlos Bonell, Francis Baines, Michael Schaffer in Germany. *Career:* performances from 1973 with the Early Music Consort of London, Academy of Ancient Music, Schütz Choir of London and Early Opera Project with Roger Norrington, Kent Opera, English Concert with Pinnock, Taverner Players, London Baroque, Trio Sonnerie, Raglan Baroque Players, and The Sixteen Choir and Orchestra; Professor of Lute at the Guildhall School from 1976; Solo debut at Wigmore Hall in 1977 with Bach recital on lute and played at Bach 300th anniversary concerts in London, 1985 with Maggie Cole; Solo recitals and tours from 1977 world-wide; Accompanist to such singers as Alfred Deller and Emma Kirkby; Summer Academies include The Lute Society of America, 1980–88 and Trio Sonnerie Summer School, 1989; Masterclasses, lectures and workshops in Sardinia, Rome, Venice, Vancouver, New York and San Francisco. *Recordings:* As soloist, music by Robert de Visée, Dowland, Bach and Vivaldi; Albums of Monteverdi, Handel, Purcell, Corelli and Vivaldi with London Baroque, Taverner Players, The English Concert, Academy of Ancient Music, Raglan Baroque Players, Trio Sonnerie and The Sixteen Choir and Orchestra (Monteverdi Vespers, 1988); Music by Bach, 1990s. *Publications:* Lute Music By William Byrd, 1976; Lute Music by Alfonso Ferrabosco, 1979; Continuo Playing on Lute, Archlute and Theorbo, 1987.

NORTH, Roger Dudley, LRAM; British composer and writer; b. 1 Aug. 1926, Warblington, Hants., England; m. Rosamund Shreeves 1965; two d. *Education:* Univ. of Oxford, Royal Acad. of Music, London. *Career:* various small choir and orchestra conductorship posts 1950–56; evening inst. teaching 1951–, including Morley Coll. 1963–91; numerous broadcasts for BBC 1960–70; mem. British Acad. of Songwriters, Composers and Authors. *Compositions:* Sonata for clarinet and piano 1956, Octet for clarinet, horn, bassoon, 2 violins, viola, cello and double bass 1960, Salle d'Attente (ballet suite) 1977, one-act opera, film music, music for dance and theatre, Many Light Orchestral and other pieces electronically realised on two CDs. *Publications:* The Musical Companion Book I 1977, ABC of Music (Musical Companion) 1979, Wagner's Most Subtle Art 1996; contribs: Thematic Unity in Parsifal (in Wagner Society Magazine), The Rhinegold – The Music (in English National Opera guide 1985). *Honours:* RAM William Wallace Exhbn 1949, RAM Battison Haynes Prize for Composition 1949, RAM Oliviera Prescott Gift for Composition 1950. *Address:* 24 Strand on the Green, London, W4 3PH, England (home). *Telephone:* (20) 8995-9174 (office). *E-mail:* rogernorth@talktalk.net (office).

NORTHCOTT, Bayan Peter, BA, BMus, DipEd; British music critic and composer; b. 24 April 1940, Harrow-on-the-Hill, Middlesex, England. *Education:* Univ. Coll., Oxford, Univ. of Southampton. *Career:* music critic for the New Statesman 1973–76, Sunday Telegraph 1976–86, The Independent 1986–; mem. music section Critics' Circle 1974–92. *Compositions include:* Hymn to Cybele 1983, Sextet 1985, Concerto for horn and ensemble 1996, instrumental music and songs. *Publications:* contrib. to New Grove Dictionary of Music and Musicians 1980, Music and Musicians, The Listener, Musical Times, Daily Telegraph, Guardian, Tempo, Dansk Musiktidsskrift, BBC Music Magazine (including articles on Goehr, Tippett, Maw, Davies, Carter, Jonathon Harvey and Poulenc).

NOSEDA, Gianandrea; Italian conductor; *Music Director, Teatro Regio Torino*; b. 23 April 1964, Milan; s. of Tarcisio Noseda and Angela Noseda; m. Lucia Belluso. *Education:* Milan Conservatoire, studied with Donato Renzetti at Accad. Musicale Pescarese, with Valery Gergiev and Myung-Wha Chung at Accad. Chigiana, Siena. *Career:* Prin. Guest Conductor, Mariinsky Theatre, St Petersburg 1997; Prin. Conductor Orquesta de Cadaqués 1998–; Prin. Guest Conductor, Rotterdam Philharmonic 1999–2003, Orchestra Sinfonica Nazionale della RAI 2003–06; Artistic Dir Stresa Festival 2000–; Prin. Conductor BBC Philharmonic Orchestra 2002–06, Chief Conductor 2006–11, Conductor Laureate 2011–12; Music Dir Teatro Regio, Turin 2007–; Prin. Guest Conductor, Israel Philharmonic Orchestra 2011–; Victor de Sabata Guest Chair, Pittsburgh Symphony Orchestra 2011–14; Music Dir, National Symphony Orchestra, Washington, DC 2016–; has also appeared with Cleveland Orchestra, Los Angeles Philharmonic, Chicago Symphony Orchestra, Philadelphia Orchestra, New York Philharmonic, Pittsburgh Symphony, Cincinnati Symphony, Boston Symphony, Toronto Symphony, Montreal Symphony, London Symphony Orchestra, London Philharmonic, City of Birmingham Symphony Orchestra, Chamber Orchestra of Europe, Swedish Radio Symphony Orchestra, Goeteborg Symphony Orchestra, Oslo Philharmonic, Finnish Radio Symphony Orchestra, Danish Nat. Symphony Orchestra, Tokyo Symphony, NHK Symphony Orchestra, Orchestre du Capitole de Toulouse, Orchestre Nat. de France, Orchestre de Paris, DSO Berlin, Frankfurt Radio Symphony Orchestra, Vienna Symphony Orchestra, Vienna Philharmonic Orchestra, Berlin Philharmonic Orchestra. *Publication:* Demo-

crazia della Musica (with Giorgio Soro) 2012. *Honours:* Cavaliere Ufficiale al Merito della Repubblica Italiana. *Current Management:* c/o Ettore F. Volontieri, Artists Management Company, Holbeinstrasse 31, 8008 Zurich, Switzerland. *Telephone:* (43) 2551447. *E-mail:* efv@artistsmanagement.com. *Website:* www.artistsmanagement.com. *Address:* c/o Florence Plouchart-Cohn, Teatro Regio di Torino, Piazza Castello 215, 10124 Turin, Italy (office). *Telephone:* (011) 8815381 (office). *Fax:* (011) 8815264 (office). *E-mail:* plouchart-cohn@teatroregio.torino.it (office). *Website:* www.teatroregio.torino.it (office); www.gianandreanoseda.com.

NOSSEK, Carola; singer (soprano); b. 10 Feb. 1949, Schwerin, Germany. *Education:* studied in Dresden and Schwerin. *Career:* debut at Dresden Staatsoper 1972, as Nanette in Lortzing's Der Wildschütz; Berlin Staatsoper from 1975, as Marenka in The Bartered Bride, Mozart's Servilia and Despino, Marzelline in Fidelio and Echo in Ariadne; Orff's Die Kluge 1990, Susanna 1991, and Nuri in Tiefland 1995; guest at Las Palmas Festival and elsewhere; concert repertory includes songs by Hanns Eisler and Schubert's Lazarus.

NOTARE, Karen; American singer (soprano); b. 1961. *Education:* Manhattan School of Music, New York. *Career:* debut in Madama Butterfly for New York City Opera, 1987; European debut as Leoncavallo's Zaza, at the 1990 Wexford Festival; Tosca with Greater Miami Opera and the Royal Danish Opera, Mimi at Nice, Desdemona in Hong Kong and Mariella in Mascagni's Piccola Marat at the 1992 Wexford Festival; Bonn Opera from 1994, as Manon Lescaut, Donna Elvira, and Lisa in The Queen of Spades; Concerts with the Pittsburgh and Cincinnati Symphonies, Verdi Requiem with the Eastern Connecticut Symphony Orchestra; Season 1996 with the Trovatore Leonora for Fort Worth Opera, and Tosca with Opera Zuid, Netherlands; Season 1999 as Salome in Dublin and as Santuzza in Auckland. *Current Management:* Pinnacle Arts Management, 889 Ninth Avenue, Second Floor, New York, NY 10019, USA. *Telephone:* 212-397-7915. *Fax:* 212-397-7920. *Website:* www.pinnaclearts.com.

NOTT, Jonathan; British conductor; b. 1962, Solihull, England. *Education:* choral scholar St John's Coll., Cambridge, Royal Northern Coll. of Music, Nat. Opera Studio. *Career:* Repetiteur then Conductor, Frankfurt Opera 1988–; First Kapellmeister, Wiesbaden Opera and Symphony Orchestra 1991–96, covering all main opera repertoire, including complete Ring Cycle of Wagner as part of Centenary Maifestspiele; Music Dir, Luzern Opera and Symphony Orchestra 1997–2003; Chief Conductor, Ensemble Intercontemporain 2000; Chief Conductor, Bamberger Symphoniker 2000–; Music Dir Designate, Tokyo Symphony Orchestra (2014–17); guest appearances with WDR Cologne, Leipzig Gewandhaus, Tonhalle, NDR Hamburg. NHK Symphony, Concertgebouw, and London, New York, Los Angeles, Munich and Berlin Philharmonics; world premieres of work by Ferneyhough, Rihm, Lachenmann. *Recordings:* with ASKO Ensemble, Moscow Philharmonic, orchestral works including the Requiem of Gyorgy Ligeti with Berlin Philharmonic, Complete Schubert Symphonies with Bamberger Symphoniker, Mahler Symphonies. *Current Management:* Askonas Holt, Lincoln House, 300 High Holborn, London, WC1V 7JH, England. *Telephone:* (20) 7400-1700. *Fax:* (20) 7400-1799. *E-mail:* info@askonasholt.co.uk. *Website:* www.askonasholt.com.

NOVIKOV, Leo, MMus; Australian (b. Russian) violinist and violin teacher; b. (Lev Novikov), 11 July 1964, Moscow, Russia; m. Tania Novikov 1989; three s. *Education:* Moscow State Acad. of Music Gnesins, Music Coll. of Moscow Conservatoire, Moscow Conservatoire Special Music School. *Career:* debut solo recital, Tbilisi Conservatoire, Georgia, with State Chamber Orchestra 1989; solo performances in Moscow, Georgia, Latvia 1989–92; solo performance in TV link-up broadcast from Moscow 1990; rank and file violinist, Moscow Philharmonic Orchestra, solo performer with Solo Performers Chamber Orchestra of Moscow Philharmonic 1990–93; Sr Teacher, Australian Inst. of Music 1993–2003; solo performances in Concert Hall of Sydney Opera House 1996, 1997, Melbourne Town Hall 2004, Sydney Town Hall 2005, and on nat. television; conducted first experimental master-classes on TV; currently teacher, Conservatorium of Music, Univ. of Sydney and Int. Grammar School, Sydney; mem. Musicians' Union of Australia, Australian String Teachers Asscn. *Recordings:* Golden Dreams 2000, Leo's Violin Magic 2004. *Honours:* Third Prize, First Int. Competition Golden Hanukiah, Germany 2003. *Address:* 915 Anzac Parade, Maroubra, Sydney, NSW 2035, Australia (home). *Telephone:* 402-870456 (mobile). *E-mail:* violin_magic@hotmail.com (office). *Website:* www.violinmagic.com.au (office).

NOVIKOVA, Julia; Russian singer (soprano); b. 1983, St Petersburg. *Education:* Rimsky-Korsakov Conservatory, St Petersburg. *Career:* made professional stage debut at Marinsky Theatre 2006; other stage appearances at Theater Dortmund, Oper Frankfurt, Vienna State Opera, Staatsoper Unter den Linden, Komische Oper Berlin, Carnegie Hall, New York, Budapest Nat. Opera. *Plays:* operatic appearances include: Britten, The Turn of the Screw, Offenbach, Les Contes d'Hoffmann, Rossini, Il Barbiere di Siviglia, Rimsky-Korsakov, The Golden Cockerel, Verdi, Rigoletto, Mozart, Die Zauberflöte, Verdi, Un Ballo in Maschera, Mozart, Die Entführung aus dem Serail, Richard Strauss, Ariadne auf Naxos, Donizetti, L'elisir d'amore, Humperdinck, Hansel and Gretel, Bellini, La Sonnambula, Donizetti, Don Pasquale. *Honours:* Concours de Genève Audience Prize 2007, Neue Stimmen Audience Prize, Germany 2007, Musik Debut First Prize, Germany 2008, Operalia Plácido Domingo World Opera Competition First Prize and Audience Prize, Budapest 2009. *Current Management:* TACT International Art Management, Tefelenstraat 120, 1107 Amsterdam, Netherlands. *Telephone:* (20) 69-77-091.

Fax: (20) 69-77-831. *E-mail:* info@tact4art.com. *Website:* www.tact4art.com; www.julianovikova.com.

NOVOA, Salvador; American singer (tenor) and voice teacher; *Voice Teacher, Boces Cultural Center;* b. 30 Oct. 1937, Mexico City, Mexico; m. Audrey; three s. one d. *Education:* Univ. of Mexico School of Music, studied with Felipe Aquilera Ruiz, Kurt Baum. *Career:* debut as Pinkerton in Madama Butterfly, Mexico Opera Co. 1960; Erik in Der fliegende Holländer with the Philadelphia Lyric Opera; several roles in various operas with the New York City Opera, including Don José and Cavaradossi, title roles in Bomarzo and Don Rodrigo, Faust in Mefistofele and Edgardo in Lucia di Lammermoor; has appeared with opera cos widely, including San Diego Opera, Houston Grand Opera, Boston Opera, Cincinnati Opera, Teatro Colón, Argentina, Opera Municipal de Marseille, Stuttgart Opera Company, Tehran; repertoire includes Radames, Andrea Chénier, Bomarzo (Pier Francesco), Carmen (Don José), Cavalleria Rusticana (Turiddu), Don Rodrigo, Faust, Macbeth, Macduff, Faust in Mefistofele, Pollione in Norma, Samson in Samson and Delilah; numerous other roles in various operas; symphonic repertoire includes Beethoven's 9th Symphony and Verdi's Messa da requiem. *Recordings include:* Bomarzo by Alberto Ginastera. *Honours:* Second Prize, Metropolitan Opera Regional Auditions, Mexico City 1959. *Address:* 4 Cedargate Lane, Westport, CT 06880-3759, USA (home). *E-mail:* snovoa@aol.com (home).

NOVOHRADSKY, Thomas; artistic director. *Education:* Univ. of Music and Dramatic Arts, Vienna. *Career:* Asst Stage Dir St Gallen Theatre, Switzerland 1980–82; apptd Asst Stage Dir Wiener Staatsoper 1982, Production Man. 1993–2001; has also worked for Teatro alla Scala, Salzburg Festival, Bregenz Festival; researcher New Nat. Theatre, Tokyo 1999–2001, Artistic Consultant (Opera) 2001–03; Artistic Dir (Opera) 2005–07. *Address:* c/o New National Theatre Tokyo, 1-1-1 Hon-machi, Shibuya-ku, Tokyo 151, Japan (office).

NOVOTNÁ, Květa; Czech pianist; b. 1 July 1950, Prague; d. of Josef Novotný and of the late Květa Novotná; two d. one s. *Education:* Acad. of Music, Prague. *Career:* Prof., Acad. of Music, Prague; Third Prize, Prague Spring Int. Competition 1972; Fourth Prize, Int. Competition Bolzano, Italy 1973, Int. Competition Naples, Italy 1973; finalist, Zwickau, GDR 1974. *Recordings include:* Schumann's Davidsbündlertänze, Papillons and Toccata 1989, Kinderszenen, Waldszenen and Faschingsschwank aus Wien 1991, Sonata and Novelleten 1992, Dvořák's Poetic Tone-Pictures 1992. *Address:* Kocanda 129, 252 42 Jesenice, Czech Republic. *Telephone:* (2) 6438343.

NOVOTNY, Jan, MgA; Czech pianist; *Professor of Piano, Prague Conservatory;* b. 15 Dec. 1935, Prague; m. 1985; two d. *Education:* Prague Conservatory, Acad. of Music Arts, Prague. *Career:* debut in Prague 1954; concert performances world-wide with frequent appearances at Prague Spring Festival, Smetana Int. Festival, Festival de Bonaguil, France and on Radio Prague, Bern, Gothenburg, Brussels, Paris and TV Prague; Prof. of Piano, Prague Conservatory 1961–, and Head of Piano Classes Dept 1988–95; Pres. Smetana Soc. 1991, Smetana Int. Piano Competition 1988–2003. *Recordings:* Beethoven's Sonatas Op. 10 No. 3, Op. 22, Op. 28, Op. 31 No. 1; Smetana's Complete Piano Works (seven CDs); Schumann's Phantasie C major Op. 17; F. X. Dussek's Piano Concertos; Bohuslav Martinů's 2nd Piano Concerto; Jaroslav Jezek's Complete Piano Works; J. L. Dussek's Last Piano Sonatas and Piano Concertos with Prague Chamber Philharmonic Orchestra, etc. *Publications:* Smetana: Piano Compositions (seven vols, complete edn); contrib. to Gramorevue (Prague). *Honours:* State Prize 1984, Annual Prize of Panton Ed., Prague 1987. *Address:* Prague Conservatory, Na Rejdisti 1, Prague 1, 110 00 (office); Achátová 18, Prague 5, 153 00, Czech Republic (home). *Telephone:* (2) 57911263 (home); 604-704743 (mobile). *E-mail:* novotny.piano@centrum.cz.

NOWACK, Hans; singer (bass); b. 1930, Waldenburg, Germany. *Education:* vocal studies. *Career:* sang at Heidelberg Opera from 1959, Bielefeld 1961 and Bremen Opera 1963–66; Essen Opera from 1967, with guest engagements at Vienna, Barcelona, Mexico, Venice, Lisbon and New Orleans; roles have included Osmin, Sarastro, Kaspar in Der Freischütz, Gurnemanz, Hunding, Rocco and Ochs; further visits to Hamburg, Munich, Berlin and Warsaw, as Jupiter in Rameau's Platée, Marke, the Commendatore, Daland, Boris Godunov and Hindemith's Cardillac.

NOWAK, Grzegorz; conductor; b. 1951, Poland. *Education:* Poznań Academy of Music, Eastman School of Music, Rochester, Tanglewood with Bernstein, Ozawa, Leinsdorf and Markevitch. *Career:* Music Director for Slupsk Symphony Orchestra, 1976–80; won first prize in 1984 at Ansermet Conducting Competition, Geneva; engagements followed with London Symphony, Montreal Symphony and Orchestre National de France; has also appeared with orchestras of Rome, Oslo, Stockholm, Copenhagen, Helsinki, Monte Carlo, Jerusalem, Madrid, Lisbon, Baltimore, Cincinnati, San Diego, Vancouver, Ottawa, Tokyo, Hong Kong, Geneva, Zürich, Baden-Baden, Milan, Saarbrücken, Rotterdam, Florence, Göteborg, Malmö, Birmingham, Liverpool, Bournemouth, Manchester, Belfast and Glasgow; Music Director of the Biel Symphony Orchestra, Switzerland; led the Polish premiere of Simon Boccanegra, Warsaw, 1997. *Recordings:* Ravel's Daphnis et Chloe and Bartók's Dance Suite with the London Symphony Orchestra. *Honours:* American Patronage Prize, 1984; Europaischen Förderpreis für Musik, 1985.

NUCCI, Leo; Italian singer (baritone); b. 16 April 1942, Castiglione dei Pepoli, Bologna; m. Adriana Anelli. *Education:* studied with Giuseppe

Marchesi and Ottaviano Bizzarri. *Career:* debut at Spoleto in 1967 as Rossini's Figaro; Sang Puccini's Schaunard at Venice in 1975, at La Scala Milan in 1976 as Figaro, at Covent Garden in 1978 as Miller in Luisa Miller and Metropolitan Opera from 1980 as Renato in Un Ballo in Maschera, Eugene Onegin, Germont, Amonasro and Posa in Don Carlos; Sang at Paris Opéra in 1981 as Renato and at Pesaro in 1984 in a revival of Rossini's Il Viaggio a Reims; Wiesbaden in 1985 as Rigoletto, at Salzburg Festival, 1989–90 as Renato, Turin in 1990 as Silvio in Pagliacci and Parma as Di Luna in Il Trovatore; Sang Iago in concert performances of Otello at Chicago and New York in 1991; Season 1992 as Luna at Turin, Tonio at Rome, Iago at Reggio Emilia, the Forza Don Carlo at Florence and Rossini's Figaro at the Festival of Caracalla; Sang Dulcamara at Turin, 1994; Sang Rossini's Figaro at the Verona Arena, 1996; Sang Macbeth at Buenos Aires, 1998; Season 2000–01 as Germont at Verona, Count Luna at La Scala, Verdi's Franesco Foscari for the San Carlo Opera, Naples, and Nabucco at the Vienna Staatsoper. *Recordings:* Donizetti's Maria di Rudenz; Ford in Falstaff; Il Viaggio a Reims; Aida; Simon Boccanegra; Otello; Rigoletto; Michonnet in Adriana Lecouvreur; Video of Il Barbiere di Siviglia, from the Metropolitan;. *Current Management:* c/o Opera Art, Via Isolalta Forette 11, 37068 Vigasio (VR), Italy; c/o International Creative Management, 4-6 Soho Square, London, W1D 3PZ, England. *Telephone:* (45) 6649911 (Italy); (20) 7432-0800 (England). *Fax:* (45) 6649912 (Italy). *E-mail:* info@operaart.it; classical@icmtalent.com. *Website:* www .operaart.it; www.icmtalent.com; www.leo-nucci.com.

NUNEMAKER, Richard E., BS, MM; American clarinettist and saxophonist; *Professor of Clarinet and Saxophone, University of St Thomas, Houston;* b. 30 Nov. 1942, Buffalo, NY; m. Lynda Perkins 1964; one s. one d. *Education:* State Univ. of New York Coll. at Fredonia, Univ. of Louisville, studied with Clark Brody, Jerome Stowell, James Livingston, Allen Sigel, William Willett. *Career:* bass clarinet, saxophone, Houston Symphony Orchestra 1967–2007; clarinet, saxophone, Houston Pops 1970–85; Cambiata Soloists 1970–84; Faculty, clarinet, saxophone, Asst Dir, Wind Ensemble, Univ. of St Thomas, Houston 1970–92; clarinet, saxophone, Music America Chamber Ensemble 1977–92; clarinet, saxophone, Pierrot Plus Ensemble, Rice Univ. 1987–92; clarinet and saxophone concertos with Lawrence Foster, Jorge Mester, Sergiu Comissiona, other conductors; frequent recitalist and soloist with chamber music ensembles on radio and TV, including new music; Prin. Clarinet, Orquesta Filarmonica de la Ciudad de México 1987; Clarinet and Saxophone Opus 90, New Directions in American Chamber Music 1990; Carnegie debut, New and Improvised Music Concert, music of Willian Thomas McKinley 1994; European debut, tour with Camerata Bregenz, conductor Christoph Eberle, Austria 1994; Prof. of Clarinet and Saxophone, Univ. of St Thomas, Houston 2007–; mem. Int. Conf. of Symphony and Opera Musicians, American Fed. of Musicians, Int. Clarinet Asscn, Houston Composers' Alliance. *Recordings:* From The Great Land, Logo I, America Swings, Stompin' At The Savoy; as exec. producer: Multiplicities, Golden Petals, Magical Place of My Dreams, Between Silence and Darkness, The Louisville Project (all contain music for clarinet and saxophone commissioned by Richard Nunemaker). *Publications:* If the Shoe Fits, Scales and Chords (A New Approach for all Instruments), The Effortless Clarinet. *Honours:* Distinguished Alumni Fellow, Univ. of Louisville 2002. *Current Management:* c/o Lyn-Rich Management, 4114 Leeshire Drive, Houston, TX 77025, USA. *Telephone:* (713) 665-8877. *Fax:* (713) 248-8894. *E-mail:* Lynrichmgt@aol.com. *Address:* 4114 Leeshire Drive, Houston, TX 77025, USA (home). *Telephone:* (713) 665-8877 (home); (713) 248-8894 (home). *Fax:* (713) 667-0283 (home). *E-mail:* rnunemaker@aol.com (home). *Website:* www.richardnunemaker.com.

NUSSBAUMER, Georg; composer; b. 24 Aug. 1964, Linz, Austria; m.; one d. *Education:* Bruckner Conservatory, Sweelinck Conservatory, Amsterdam, studied with W. v. Hauwe. *Career:* work performed at Konzerthaus, Vienna 1991, 1992, Ciurlionis Museum Kaunas 1992, Zur Kunst der Klangzucht, Linz 1993, Unerhörte musik, Berlin 1996, Ars electronica, Linz 1996, Atlas mapping, Bregenz 1997, Melos Ethos, Bratislava 1997, Insel Musik, Berlin 1997, Schaubühne Berlin 1999. *Compositions:* Für einen Klavierzyklus for piano 1994, Organ O Agie for organ 1991, Introibo ad altare dei (installation, action) for ensemble 1995, An Armorica for ensemble 1996, four String Quartets 1997, 1998, Icarusetude/Chopinyonnaise for piano 1999, Der Hebel des Lichts (installation) 1999. *Recordings include:* Lebenssee/3 Männer (with poet, Walter Pilar). *Honours:* prizes and scholarships from the Austrian Govt.

NUTTALL, Geoff, BA; American violinist; *Charles E. and Andrea L. Volpe Artistic Director for Chamber Music, Spoleto Festival USA;* b. College Station, Tex.; m. Livia Sohn; one s. *Education:* The Banff Centre, Univ. of Western Ontario, Univ. of Toronto. *Career:* Co-founder and first violinist, St Lawrence String Quartet (SLSQ); tours throughout North and South America, Europe, New Zealand, Australia and Asia; regular appearances at music festivals including Mostly Mozart, Ottawa Chamber Music Festival, Bay Chamber Concerts, Spoleto USA (quartet-in-residence 1999–); performed (with SLSQ) at Carnegie Hall, Lincoln Center, Metropolitan Museum, Kennedy Center, London's Wigmore Hall, Royal Concertgebouw Hall in Amsterdam, Theatre de Ville Paris, Tokyo's Suntory Hall, and the White House for President Clinton and guests; SLSQ was graduate ensemble-in-residence at Juilliard School, Yale Univ., Hartt School of Music, also Stanford Univ. 1999–; mem. faculty, Stanford Univ.; Assoc. Artistic Dir, Spoleto Festival USA 2008–09, Charles E. and Andrea L. Volpe Artistic Dir for Chamber Music 2010–. *Recordings:* with SLSQ: Robert Schumann Quartets (Juno Award for Best Classical Album, Canadian Acad. for Arts and Sciences, Preis der Deutschen Schallplattenkritik), Yiddishbbuk, Shostakovich Quartets Nos. 3, 7, and 8 2009. *Honours:* with SLSQ: First Prize, Banff Int. String Quartet Competition 1992. *Address:* Spoleto Festival USA, PO Box 157, 14 George Street, Charleston, SC 29402-0157, USA (office). *Telephone:* (843) 722-2764 (office). *Fax:* (843) 723-6383 (office). *E-mail:* info@spoletousa.org (office). *Website:* www.spoletousa.org (office).

NYIKOS, Markus Andreas, MMus; Swiss cellist; *Professor, University of the Arts, Berlin;* b. 9 Dec. 1948, Basel; m. Seraina Nyikos; one s. *Education:* Musik Akad., Basel with Paul Szabó, Konservatorium Luzern with Stanislav Apolín, masterclasses with Zara Nelsova, Pierre Fournier, Sándor Végh and Janáček Quartet. *Career:* cello solo at Festival of Strings Lucerne 1974–79 and with Philharmonische Virtuosen Berlin 1983–; Prof., Universität der Kunste, Berlin, 1979–; Guest Prof. at Shanghai Conservatory and other insts in Europe and Asia; mem. Gililov Quartet, Berlin; numerous concerts, radio appearances and masterclasses world-wide as soloist and chamber musician; duo with pianist Jaroslav Smýkal for more than 40 years. *Recordings:* Vivaldi, Cirri; Cello Concertos with Radio Sinfonie Orchestra Berlin; Brahms Sonatas in E minor and F major, with pianist, Gerard Wyss; Schubert's Arpeggione-Sonata in A minor and Brahms Sonata in D major with Gerard Wyss; With La Groupe Des Six, compositions by Auric, Poulenc, Honegger, and Milhaud, with pianist, Jaroslav Smýkal, Zoltan Kodály; works for cello and piano with Jaroslav Smýkal; Burkhard, Honegger, Martin, works for cello and piano, with Jaroslav Smýkal; seven CDs with Philharmonisches Klavierquartett Berlin: works by Brahms, Mozart, Schumann, Dvořák, Beethoven, Juon, Mahler, Schnittke, Suk, Strauss. *Honours:* Swiss Soloist Prize 1976, Gaspar Cassadò, Italy 1977. *Address:* Faculty of Music, Universität der Künste, Postfach 12 05 44, 10595 Berlin, Germany (office). *E-mail:* nyimark@web.de (office). *Website:* www.vdl.udk-berlin.de (office).

NYMAN, Michael, CBE; British composer; b. 23 March 1944, London. *Education:* Royal Acad. of Music, King's Coll. London. *Career:* composer, writer and music critic 1968–78; lecturer 1976–80; f. MN Records label 2005–. *Film and television soundtracks:* Peter Greenaway films: 5 Postcards from Capital Cities 1967, Vertical Features Remake 1976, Goole by Numbers 1976, A Walk Through H: The Reincarnation of an Ornithologist 1978, 1–100 1978, The Falls 1980, Act of God 1980, Terence Conran 1981, The Draughtsman's Contract 1982, The Coastline 1983, Making a Splash 1984, A Zed and Two Noughts 1985, Inside Rooms: 26 Bathrooms, London & Oxfordshire 1985, Drowning by Numbers 1988, Fear of Drowning 1988, Death in the Seine 1988, The Cook, The Thief, His Wife and Her Lover 1989, Hubert Bals Handshake 1989, Prospero's Books 1991; other films: Keep It Downstairs 1976, Tom Phillips 1977, Brimstone and Treacle 1982, Nelly's Version 1983, Frozen Music 1983, The Cold Room 1984, Fairly Secret Army 1984, The Kiss 1985, L'ange frénétique 1985, I'll Stake My Cremona to a Jew's Trump 1985, The Disputation 1986, Ballet méchanique 1986, Le miraculé 1987, The Man Who Mistook His Wife for a Hat 1987, Monsieur Hire 1989, Out of the Ruins 1989, Le mari de la coiffeuse 1990, Men of Steel 1990, Les enfants volants 1990, Not Mozart: Letters, Riddles and Writs 1991, The Final Score 1992, The Fall of Icarus 1992, The Piano 1993, Ryori no tetsujin 1993, Mesmer 1994, A la folie (Six Days, Six Nights) 1994, Carrington 1995, Anne no nikki (The Diary of Anne Frank) 1995, Der Unhold (The Ogre) 1996, Enemy Zero 1996, Gattaca 1997, Titch 1998, Ravenous 1999, How to Make Dhyrak: A Dramatic Work for Three Players and Camera, Truncated with Only Two Players 1999, Wonderland 1999, Nabbie no koi (Nabbie's Love) 1999, The End of the Affair 1999, The Claim 2000, Act Without Words I 2000, That Sinking Feeling 2000, La Stanza del figlio 2001, Subterrain 2001, 24 heures de la vie d'une femme 2002, The Man with a Movie Camera 2002, The Actors 2003, Nathalie... 2003, Charged 2003, Ident (Channel 5) 2004, Man on Wire 2007, The Eleventh Year 2009, The Trip 2010, 2 Graves 2010, Everyday 2012. *Other compositions:* orchestral: A Handsome, Smooth, Sweet, Smart, Clear Stroke: Or Else Play Not At All 1983, Taking a Line for a Second Walk 1986, L'Orgie Parisienne 1989, Six Celan Songs 1990, Where the Bee Dances 1991, Self Laudatory Hymn of Inanna and Her Omnipotence 1992, The Upside-Down Violin 1992, MGV (Musique à Grande Vitesse) 1993, On the Fiddle 1993, Concerto for Harpsichord and Strings 1995, Concerto for Trombone 1995, Double Concerto 1996, Strong on Oaks, Strong on the Causes of Oaks 1997, Cycle of Disquietude 1998, a dance he little thinks of 2001, The Draughtsman's

Contract for Orchestra 2001, Dance of the Engines 2002, Gattaca for Orchestra 2003, The Claim for Orchestra 2003, The Piano: Concert Suite 2003, Violin Concerto 2003; chamber music: First Waltz in D, Bell Set No. 1 1974, 1–100 1976, Waltz in F 1976, Think Slow, Act Fast 1981, 2 Violins 1981, Four Saxes (Real Slow Drag) 1982, I'll Stake My Cremona to a Jew's Crump 1983, Time's Up 1983, Child's Play 1985, String Quartet No. 1 1985, Taking a Line for a Second Walk 1986, String Quartet No. 2 1988, String Quartet No. 3 1990, In Re Don Giovanni 1991, Masque Arias 1991, Time Will Pronounce 1992, Songs for Tony 1993, Three Quartets 1994, H.R.T. 1995, String Quartet No. 4 1995, Free for All 2001, Five Who Figured Four Years Ago 2002, Mapping 2002, Yellow Beach 2002, 24 Hour Sax Quartet 2004, For John Peel 2004; instrumental: Shaping the Curve 1990, Six Celan Songs 1990, Flugelhorn and Piano 1991, For John Cage 1992, The Convertibility of Lute Strings 1992, Here to There 1993, Yamamoto Perpetuo 1993, On the Fiddle 1993, To Morrow 1994, Tango for Tim 1994, Elisabeth Gets Her Way 1995, Viola and Piano 1995, Titch 1997, Fourths, Mostly (for organ) 2001; dramatic works: Strange Attractors, The Princess of Milan, A Broken Set of Rules 1984, Basic Black 1984, Portraits in Reflection 1985, And Do They Do 1986, The Man Who Mistook His Wife for a Hat 1986, Miniatures/Configurations 1988, Letters, Riddles and Writs 1991, Noises, Sounds and Sweet Airs 1994, Facing Goya 2000, Man and Boy: Dada (opera) 2004; vocal: A Neat Slice of Time 1980, The Abbess of Andouillets 1984, Out of the Ruins 1989, Polish Love Song 1990, Shaping the Curve 1991, Anne de Lucy Songs 1992, Mozart on Mortality 1992, Grounded 1995, The Waltz Song 1995, The Ballad of Kastriot Rexhepi 2001, Mosè 2001, A Child's View of Colour 2003, Acts of Beauty 2004; with Michael Nyman Band: In Re Don Giovanni 1977, The Masterwork/Award-Winning Fishknife 1979, Bird List Song 1979, Five Orchestral Pieces Opus Tree 1981, Bird Anthem 1981, M-Work 1981, Love is Certainly, at Least Alphabetically Speaking 1983, Bird Work 1984, The Fall of Icarus 1989, La Traversée de Paris 1989, The Final Score 1992, AET (After Extra Time) 1996, De Granada a la Luna 1998, Orfeu 1998, The Commissar Vanishes 1999, Man with a Movie Camera 2001, Compiling the Colours (Samhitha) 2003, Three Ways of Describing Rain (Sawan; Rang; Dhyan) 2003, Zeit und Ziel 1814–2002, Manhatta 2003; dance: Flicker 2005. *Films:* Cine Opera 2009, Nyman with a Movie Camera 2010. *Recordings include:* film soundtracks, The Piano Sings 2005. *Publications:* Libretto for Birtwistle's Dramatic Pastoral, Down by the Greenwood Side 1968–69, Experimental Music: Cage and Beyond 1974; contribs: critical articles to journals, including The Spectator. *Honours:* Hon. DLitt. *E-mail:* myriam@michaelnyman.com. *E-mail:* office@michaelnyman.com. *Website:* www.michaelnyman.com.

NYQUIST, Kristian Benedikt, BA; American harpsichordist, fortepianist and teacher; *Teacher of Harpsichord, Fortepiano, Figured Bass-playing and Chamber Music, University of Music, Karlsruhe;* b. 16 Oct. 1964, Los Angeles, Calif.; m. Judith Nyquist 1991; two s. one d. *Education:* Staatliche Musikhochschule, Karlsruhe, Conservatoire Nat. de Région Rueil-Malmaison, Paris. *Career:* debut at Ernst Toch Saal, Mannheim, Germany 1986; concerts as recitalist, continuo player, duo partner and soloist in Germany, France, Belgium, Netherlands, Poland, Czech Repub., Switzerland, Russia, USA, Brazil; Lecturer, Univ. of Music, Mannheim 1989–2007; Lecturer, Univ. of Music, Karlsruhe 1995–2006, Prof. of Harpsichord, Fortepiano, Figured Bass-playing and Chamber Music 2006–; mem. Piano-Podium, Karlsruhe, Clavecin en France, pro cembalo (Italy), Händel-Gesellschaft, Karlsruhe. *Radio:* (for SWR Stuttgart): F. Devienne, 6 sonatas for oboe and continuo 2003, C.P.E. Bach Solo pieces for fortepiano 2004. *Recordings:* C.P.E. Bach, 5 Sonatas for harpsichord and flute 1996, J.S. Bach, 5 Flute Sonatas 1997, D'Anglebert Harpsichord Music 1998, Italian Serenade Works for Guitar and Fortepiano 2006, J.S. Bach Goldberg Variations 2007, Viennese Serenades for Guitar and Fortepiano 2010, Origins of the Romantic Piano – Works by Clementi, Field and Chopin 2011, Devienne Sonatas for Oboe resp. Bassoon and continuo 2012. *Publications:* Realisations of Figured-Bass Parts, Trio-Sonatas by Tartini, Sonata Pastorale by Campioni. *Honours:* Prix d'Excellence, Prix de Virtuosité, First Prize, Concours Musical de Region d'Ile de France 1991, Hon. Mention, Prague Spring Competition 1994. *Address:* Soonwaldstrasse 27, 55566 Bad Sobernheim, Germany (home). *Telephone:* (67) 516577 (home). *Fax:* (67) 516577 (home). *E-mail:* kristian.nyquist@arcor.de (home).

O

OAK, Kilsung, MA, DMA, PhD; South Korean composer; b. 7 May 1942, Tong Yung; m., one s. two d. *Education:* Long Island Univ., Columbia Univ. *Career:* mem., Group for Contemporary Music, 1972; Riverside Dance Festival, 1976; Seoul Symphony Orchestra, 1994; Prof. of Composition, Kyung Hee Univ.; mem. ASCAP, Korean Society of the I-Ching, Korean Composers' Association. *Compositions:* Duo for violin and piano 1992, Dahn for violin and piano 1992, GHI for violin and piano 1993, String Quartet 1995, Symphony 1997, Amorphosis for soprano and 12 percussionists 1997, Sonata for piano 1998, The Days of Indong for orchestra. *Honours:* Rappaport Prize 1971, Korean Arts and Culture Foundation Award 1995, 1998, Korean Film Critics' Soc. Best Film Award 1996. *Address:* Kyung Hee University, 1 Hoegi-dong, Dongdaemun-ku, Seoul 130-701, Republic of Korea (office). *E-mail:* ksohk@khu.ac.kr.

OAKLEY-TUCKER, John, AGSM; singer (baritone); b. 1959, Canada. *Education:* Guildhall School of Music, Britten-Pears School, Ravel Acad. with Peter Pears, Gerard Souzay, Elisabeth Schwarzkopf and Thomas Hampson, studied with David Pollard. *Career:* operatic debut in the title role of Britten's Owen Wingrave, conducted by Steuart Bedford, Aldeburgh, 1984; sang in Glyndebourne Opera Festival Chorus in Jenůfa, Arabella, Le nozze di Figaro and Falstaff, 1988–90; operatic roles include lead role, Tom in Hans Werner Henze's The English Cat, conducted by the composer, Berlin, 1989, Italy, 1990 and Barbican, London, 1991 as part of the Henze BBC Festival; title role in Eugene Onegin, Co-Opera, London, 1993; lead role of Pluto in the world premiere of Hilda Paredes' chamber opera, The Seventh Pip, Mexico City, 1993; Belcore with Island Opera, 1994; English tour with Camberwell Opera as Il Conte, 1994–95, both directed by Mark Tinkler; Pluto in The Seventh Pip, San Diego, 1995; further roles include Don Giovanni, Guglielmo, Papageno, Sid (Albert Herring) and Billy Budd; concert performances include Bach's St John's and St Matthew's Passion, Duruflé's Requiem, Dvořák's Requiem, Elgar's Apostles, Fauré's Requiem, Handel's Messiah, Mozart's Requiem, Orff's Carmina Burana, Rossini's Petite Messe Solennelle and Vaughan Williams Sea Symphony; toured UK, Spain, Portugal, singing Mahler's Kindertotenlieder for the Ballet Rambert, 1988–89; recital debut with Graham Johnson, Schumann's Dichterliebe and English Song, Purcell Room, 1987; performances with the Songmakers' Almanac; Schubert's Winterreise with Nicholas Bosworth, Purcell Room, 1992; recital tour of the Middle East with Iwan Llewelyn-Jones, 1993; Schubert's Die schöne Müllerin with Iwan Llewelyn-Jones, Purcell Room, 1994; other recitals in the UK and abroad; formed duo, Tucker and Rohr, 1996, with pianist Alard von Rohr, performances include Carnegie Hall in New York, 1998 and Konzerthaus, Berlin, 1999. *Recordings:* Tom in Hans Werner Henze's The English Cat (German television), 1991; Pluto in Hilda Paredes' The Seventh Pip (with Arditti String Quartet), 1995; Baritone Solo, Symphony No. 5, Alexander Lokshin conducted by Rudolf Barschai, 1997. *Honours:* Countess of Munster Musical Trust Scholarship. *Current Management:* Judith Newton, 75 Aberdare Gardens, London, NW6 3AN, England. *Address:* Sonnenallee 152, 12059 Berlin, Germany.

OBATA, Machiko; singer (soprano); b. 23 Feb. 1948, Sapporo, Japan. *Education:* studied in Tokyo and Cologne. *Career:* appearances with the Cologne Opera as Mozart's Pamina and Servila, Marzelline in Fidelio, Gretel, Liu and Flora in The Turn of The Screw; sang the Woodbird in Siegfried 1991; guest engagements at Strasbourg, Munich and the Opéra Comique in Paris; Salburg Easter and Summer Festivals 1991 as Barbarina in Le nozze di Figaro; sang the Princess in Les Brigands by Offenbach at Colgone 2001; frequent concert appearances.

OBERHOLTZER, William; American singer (baritone); b. 1947, Bloomington, IN. *Education:* Indiana State Univ. *Career:* debut in Indiana 1972 in Herakles by John Eaton; sang Marcello at St Gallen 1976, then at Saarbrucken 1978–81, Gelsenkirchen 1981–86 and Kassel from 1986; St John in Wolfgang von Schweinitz' Patmos 1990; engaged at Munster 1986–88 and made guest appearances at Düsseldorf as Marcello, Linz, Krefeld and Hannover; other roles include Mozart's Count and Don Giovanni, Valentin, Renato, Rigoletto, Ford, Paolo, Wagner's Wolfram and Amfortas, Strauss's Jochanaan and Mandryka, and Wozzeck; season 1998 as Matthes in Weill's Die Burgschaft, at Bielefeld; sang Dallapiccola's Prigioniero at Bielefeld 1999; concert engagements include Bach's St John Passion in Berlin and Carmina Burana.

OBERLIN, Russell; American academic and singer (countertenor); b. 11 Oct. 1928, Akron, OH. *Education:* Juilliard School. *Career:* founding mem., New York Pro Musica Antiqua and soloist with many orchestras, including New York Philharmonic, Chicago Symphony and Buffalo Philharmonic; Little Orchestra Soc., Clarion Concerts, Smithsonian Inst. Concert Series, CBS Radio Orchestra; masterclasses throughout USA; opera appearances in major roles at Covent Garden in Midsummer Night's Dream, San Francisco Opera, at Edinburgh and Vancouver Festivals and American Opera Soc.; solo recitalist throughout USA; radio and television broadcasts; Thomas Hunter Prof. of Music, Hunter Coll. and the Graduate Center of CUNY 1966–; founding bd mem., Waverly Consort, Berkshire (Mass) Concert Series, Soho Baroque Opera Co.; mem. Nat. Asscn of Teachers of Singing, Academia Monteverdiana, American Acad. of Teachers of Singing. *Recordings include:* A Russell Oberlin Recital; Russell Oberlin, Handel Arias; Russell Oberlin, Baroque Cantatas; Soloist with New York Philharmonic, Handel's Messiah; Bach's Magnificat in D; Soloist with New York Pro Musica, The Play of Daniel; Thomas Tallis's Sacred Music; Josquin des Pres' Missa Pange Lingua; Walton's Façade with Hermione Gingold; Numerous other recordings including recently reissued CDs including: Troubadour and Trouvére Songs. English Polyphony of the 13th and Early 14th Centuries, The French Ars Antiqua and William Byrd Music for Voice and Viols.

OBERLINGER, Dorothée; German musician (recorder), conductor and academic; *Professor and Director, Institute for Early Music, Salzburg Mozarteum;* b. 2 Sept. 1969, Aachen. *Education:* Hochschule für Musik und Tanz Köln, student of Günter Höller, also studied in Amsterdam with Walter van Hauwe and in Milan with Pedro Memelsdorff. *Career:* solo debut at Wigmore Hall, London 1998; recitals at festivals including Ludwigsburger Schlossfestspiele, Musikfestspiele Potsdam, Settimane Musicale Stresa, Nederlandse Oude-Musik-Network, Festival de Musica Antigua Sajazarra, Warsaw Beethoven Festival, Europäische Musikfestwoche Passau, Rheingau-Musikfestival, Tage der Alten Musik Regensburg, MDR-Musiksommer, Neue Bachgesellschaft: Bachfest: Salzburg, Thüringer Bachwochen, Bach Festival Arnstadt and Salzburger Bachgesellschaft: Bach-Zyklus; also played at Warsaw Philharmonie, Marianischer Saal Lucerne, Rosée Theatre in Fuji and Köln Philharmonie; guest soloist with ensembles including London Baroque and Musica Antiqua Köln; plays regularly with WDR Sinfonieorchester Köln and Detmolder Kammerorchester; Founder and Music Dir Ensemble 1700 (specialises in 17th/18th-century music) 2003–; has collaborated frequently with Italian ensemble Sonatori de la Gioiosa Marca; Univ. Prof. and Dir Inst. for Early Music, Salzburg Mozarteum 2004–; Dir Bad Arolsen Baroque Festival 2009–. *Recordings include:* with Ensemble 1700: Italian Sonatas (Echo Klassik Award for Best Instrumentalist of the Year) 2008, Telemann 12 Fantasias 2010, The Passion of Musick (with Vittorio Ghielmi) (Echo Klassik Award for Chamber Music Recording of the Year 2015) 2014; with Sonatori de la Gioiosa Marca: Flauto Veneziano (Diapason d'Or, Echo Klassik Award for Best Concerto Recording 2013) 2012. *Current Management:* c/o Nicola Oberlinger, Künstlerbüro Dorothee Oberlinger, Hochkreuzallee 171, 53175 Bonn, Germany. *Telephone:* (228) 97464412. *E-mail:* mail@dorotheeoberlinger.de. *Website:* www.dorotheeoberlinger.de. *Address:* Institute of Early Music, Mozarteum, Mirabellplatz 1, 5020 Salzburg, Austria (office). *Telephone:* (662) 61983135 (office). *Fax:* (676) 88122356 (office). *E-mail:* ruth.dyson@moz.ac.at (office). *Website:* www.moz.ac.at (office).

OBERMAYR, Christine; singer (mezzo-soprano); b. 30 May 1959, Wiesbaden, Germany. *Education:* studied in Mainz with Josef Metternich. *Career:* debut at Theater am Gärtnerplatz, Munich 1983 as Cherubino; sang a Flowermaiden at Bayreuth Festival 1984; roles in Munich have included Hansel, Flotow's Nancy, Nicklausse and Orlofsky; engagements at Wiesbaden 1984–89 as Carmen, Emilia, Otello, Olga, Janáček's Fox, the Composer in Ariadne and Ottavio in L'Incoronazione di Poppea; further appearances at the Theater an der Wien, the Paris Opéra and the Teatro Regio Turin; sang Lyubasha in Rimsky's Tsar's Bride 1985 and Mary in Der fliegende Holländer at Naples 1992; many concert and lieder performances. *Honours:* prizewinner in competitions at Vienna, Wiesbaden and Berlin.

OBERSON, René; composer, organist and academic; b. 27 June 1945, La Tour-de-Treme, Fribourg, Switzerland; m.; two s. one d. *Education:* teachers training coll., schools of music in Fribourg, Berne and Geneva. *Career:* organist at concerts in Switzerland and abroad, notably at Notre-Dame, Paris, France and Symphony Hall, Osaka, Japan; Prof., School of Music, Fribourg; reconstructed the Fourth Concerto for organ or harpsichord and string orchestra by the Swiss composer, Meyer von Schauensee (1720–98). *Compositions include:* L'Exilée 1983, Concerto for pan pipes 1984, Le Grand Cercle 1985, Homo Somniens 1988, Au Seuil de l'Ere du Verseau 1988, Jumière Divine, Omniprésente, Invulnerable for organ 1990, Espoirs for two trumpets, two trombones and organ 1990.

O'BRIEN, Eugene, MM, DMA; American composer and teacher; b. 24 April 1945, Paterson, NJ. *Education:* Univ. of Nebraska, studied with Bernd Alois Zimmermann at Cologne, Indiana Univ. with John Eaton and Iannis Xenakis, Cleveland Inst. of Music with Donald Erb. *Career:* teacher, Cleveland Inst. of Music 1973–81, Composer-in-Residence 1981–85; Assoc. Prof., Catholic Univ. of America, Washington, DC 1985–87; Indiana Univ. School of Music 1987–. *Compositions:* orchestral: Symphony 1969, Cello Concerto 1972, Dedales for soprano and orchestra 1973, Rites of Passage 1978, Dreams and Secrets of Origin for soprano and orchestra 1983, Alto Saxophone Concerto 1989; chamber: Intessitura for cello and piano 1975, Embarking for Cythera for eight instruments 1978, Tristan's Lament for cello 1979, Allures for percussion trio 1979, Psalms and Nocturnes for flute, viola da gamba and harpsichord 1985, Mysteries of the Horizon for 11 instruments 1987; vocal: Requiem Mass for soprano, chorus and wind ensemble 1966, Nocturne for soprano and ten instruments 1968, Elegy for Bernd Alois Zimmermann for soprano and ensemble 1970, Lingual for soprano, flute and cello 1972; other: Taking Measures (ballet) 1984. *Honours:* Guggenheim Fellowship 1984–85.

OCHANINE, Olivier, BMus, MMus; French conductor, flautist and bassist; *Music Director and Principal Conductor, Philippine Philharmonic Orchestra*; b. 7 Sept. 1979, Paris. *Education:* Univ. of Kentucky, Univ. of Southern California, Cincinnati Coll. Conservatory of Music, USA. *Career:* Auxiliary Contrabassist, Lexington Philharmonic Orchestra 1999–2001; Music Dir and Prin. Conductor, Philippine Philharmonic Orchestra 2010–; mem. Conductors Guild of America. *Honours:* Univ. of Southern California Thornton School Conducting Award 2003. *Address:* Philippine Philharmonic Orchestra, Cultural Center of the Philippines, CCP Complex, Roxas Boulevard, Pasay City, Manila, Philippines (office). *Telephone:* (2) 832-1126 (office). *Fax:* (2) 832-3683 (office). *E-mail:* ccp@culturalcenter.gov.ph (office). *Website:* www.philippinephil.org (office); www.olivierochanine.com.

OCHMAN, Wiesław; Polish tenor, producer and painter; b. 6 Feb. 1937, Warsaw; s. of Jan Ochman and Bronisława Ochman; m. Krystyna Ochman 1963; one s. one d. *Education:* Acad. of Mining and Metallurgy, Kraków 1960, studied with Prof. Gustaw Serafin, Kraków and with Prof. Maria Szłapak, Jerzy Gaczek and Sergiusz Nadgryzowski. *Career:* debut at Silesian Opera, Bytom 1960; soloist, Silesian Opera, Bytom 1960–63, Opera in Kraków 1963–64, Great Theatre, Warsaw 1964–75, Deutsche Staatsoper 1967, Hamburgische Staatsoper, Metropolitan Opera, New York, La Scala, Milan 1981; festivals at Glyndebourne, Salzburg, Orange; guest performances in operas in Paris, Munich, Frankfurt am Main, San Francisco, Miami, Chicago, Geneva, Budapest, Washington, Staatsoper in Vienna, Grand Theatre in Moscow, Staatsoper and Deutsche Oper in W Berlin, Teatro Colón in Buenos Aires, Gran Teatre del Liceu in Barcelona, Accademia Santa Cecila in Rome, Carnegie Hall in New York, Teatro de la Maestranza in Seville; participation in TV films including Eugene Onegin, Tcharevitch, Salome, Don Giovanni; numerous recordings; mem. Pres. Council for Culture 1992–95; Goodwill Amb. for UNICEF 1996. *Exhibitions:* 75 solo exhbns of paintings. *Operatic roles include:* Faust, Don Carlos, Cavaradossi in Tosca, Don José in Carmen, Dimitri in Boris Godunov, Edgardo in Lucia di Lammermoor, Arrigo in I vespri siciliani, Alfredo in La Traviata, Don Carlos in Don Carlos, Stefan in The Hunted Manor, Turiddu in Cavalleria Rusticana, Lensky in Eugene Onegin, Herman in Pique Dame, Tamino in Der Zauberflöte, Idomeneo in Idomeneo, Titus in La clemenza di Tito, Eric in Der Fliegende Holländer, Florestan in Fidelio, Shepherd in King Roger, Les pêcheurs de perles, Herod in Salome, Prince Golitsyn in Khovanshchina, Jontek in Halka, Laca in Jenůfa, Prince in Rigoletto, Don Ottavio in Don Giovanni. *Operas directed:* Mozart's Don Giovanni, Verdi's La Traviata 2000, Lehar's Tcharevitch 2001, Tchaikovsky's Eugene Onegin 2002. *Recordings include:* Jenůfa 1995, 2002, Halka 1995, Bruckner Masses 1996, Armida 1996, Stabat Mater/Legends 1997, Rusalka 1998, King Roger 1999, Great Operas of Richard Strauss 2001, Orchestral & Choral Works 2002, Te Deum/Lachrimosa 2003, Prokofiev: 50th Anniversary Edition – Limited Edition 2003, Cantatas 2004. *Honours:* Commdr's Cross with Star, Order of Polonia Restituta 2001; Minister of Culture and Art Prize 1973, The City of Warsaw Prize 1976, Pres. of Radio and TV Cttee Prize (1st Class) 1976, Prime Minister Prize (1st Class) 1979, Minister of Foreign Affairs Diploma 1977, 1986, Medal Maecenas of Art 1976, The City of Kraków Gold Award, Medal of Merit for Nat. Culture 1986.

OCHOTNIKOV, Nikolai; singer (bass); b. 1948, Russia. *Career:* Principal, Kirov Opera, St Petersburg; season 1990–91, with Kutuzov in War and Peace for the BBC and in Seattle; Edinburgh Festival 1991, as Dosifey in Khovanshchina; sang Boris Godunov at Helsinki and the New York Metropolitan Opera 1992; season 1995 as the King in Iolanta at Birmingham and the Prince in Rimsky's Invisible City of Kitezh with the Kirov at Edinburgh; other roles include Verdi's King Philip and Glinka's Ivan Susannin. *Recordings:* Khovanshchina, War and Peace.

O'CONNOR, Gerard; Irish singer (bass); b. Co. Galway. *Education:* University College, Cork and National Opera Studio, London. *Career:* appearances in Butterfly; Bohème; Figaro; Macbeth for Opera Ireland; Sparafucile in Rigoletto and Cieco in Mascagni's Iris at Holland Park; Il Barbiere di Siliglia by Paisiello, Wexford; Mamirov, Tchaikovsky Enchantress, Brighton; Chelsea Opera in Tannhäuser and Der Freischütz; Britten's Snug at Singapore; Season 1999: with Les Contes d'Hoffmann for Central Festival Opera; Rossini's Basilio for Castleward Opera; Varlaam in Boris Godunov for Opera Ireland; Company House Principal, English National Opera, 2001–; Boris in Lady Macbeth of Mtsensk, ENO and Dublin; Dikoy in Katya Kabanova for Opera Ireland; Croucher in the Silver Tassie, ENO and Dublin. *Honours:* National Opera Studio Guiness Bursary 1994–95. *Current Management:* Music International, 13 Ardilaun Road, London N5 2QR, England.

O'CONNOR, Mark; American musician (violin, guitar, bass, mandolin); b. 5 Aug. 1961, Seattle, Washington. *Career:* leader, own group, Nashville Strings; musician with artists including Paul Simon, James Taylor, Dolly Parton, Willie Nelson, Chet Atkins, Randy Travis, Michael Brecker; concerts include Barbican Hall (with Yo-Yo Ma), Montreux Jazz Festival, Carnegie Hall, New York; founder and Pres., Mark O'Connor Fiddle Camp and Strings Conference; Artist-in-Residence, UCLA 2008–09; mem, CMA. *Compositions include:* Fiddle Concerto 1995, The American Seasons: Seasons of an American Life 2000, Double Violin Concerto 2000, Double Concerto for Violin and Cello 2003, Violin Concerto No. 6: Old Brass 2005, Poets and Prophets. *Recordings include:* Pickin' in the Wind 1975, Markology 1978, On the Rampage 1979, Soppin' the Gravy 1979, False Dawn 1982, Meanings Of 1985, Stone from Which the Arch Was Made 1986, Elysian Forest 1988, Championship Years

1989, On the Mark 1989, Retrospective 1990, New Nashville Cats 1991, Johnny Appleseed (children's album with Garrison Keillor) 1992, Heroes 1993, The Night Before Christmas 1993, Fiddle Concerto for violin and orchestra 1994, Appalachia Waltz 1996, Liberty! 1997, Midnight on the Water 1998, Fanfare for the Volunteer 1999, Appalachian Journey (Grammy Award 2001) 2000, Hot Swing 2001, The American Seasons 2001, In Full Swing 2003, Crossing Bridges 2004, Double Violin Concerto 2005, Fiddle Camp, Vol. 1 2006, Folk Mass 2007. *Honours:* winner, classical guitar competition, aged 11, Country Music Asscn 's Musician of the Year, four times, Grammy Award, New Nashville Cats. *Current Management:* c/o Mark Alpert, Columbia Artists Management, 1790 Broadway, New York, NY 10019-1412, USA. *Telephone:* (212) 841-9500. *Fax:* (212) 841-9744. *E-mail:* info@cami.com. *Website:* www.cami.com. *E-mail:* mark@markoconnor.com (office). *Website:* www.markoconnor.com.

OCTORS, Georges; Belgian conductor; b. 1940, Zaire. *Education:* Brussels Conservatory with Francis de Bourguignon, studied with André Cluytens. *Career:* founded and conducted the Antwerp Bach Society Chamber Orchestra; Asst to Cluytens at the National Orchestra of Belgium, 1967; Music Dir, 1975–83, Resident Conductor, 1983–86, Conductor and Musical Adviser of Gelders Orchestra in Arnhem, 1986–; Musical Dir of the Chamber Orchestra of Wallonia, 1990; guest appearances in Amsterdam, Leningrad, London with London Symphony Orchestra at the Barbican Hall in 1990, and elsewhere. *Honours:* winner of various competitions as violinist.

ODINIUS, Lothar; German singer (tenor); b. Aachen; m. Hanna Dóra-Sturludóttir; two s. *Education:* Berlin Musikhochschule; master-classes with Bernd Weikl, Ingrid Bjoner, Alfredo Kraus and Dietrich Fischer-Dieskau. *Career:* debut in the oratorio Lazarus at Schubertiade, Feldkirch 1995; Mozart's Pedrillo, Bad Hersfeld Festival 1995; Braunschweig Staatstheater 1995–97; Salzburg Festival 1997; Mozarteum concerts; further appearances at Stuttgart, Bonn, Vienna Volksoper, Zürich 2001, Mannheim 2002, 2007, Copenhagen, Toronto 2009, Opéra National de Paris 2010, Bayreuth (debut) 2011, 2012, 2013, 2014; appeared at BBC Proms, Edinburgh Festival, Oregon Bach Festival; Glyndebourne tour as Tamino in Mozart's Magic Flute 2008; debut at Covent Garden 2010; lieder recitals in Paris, Basel, Bern, Cologne, Hamburg, Frankfurt and Berlin; close collaboration with Helmuth Rilling, Adam Fischer, András Schiff, Thomas Hengelbrock. *Recordings:* Bach's B-minor Mass and BWV 201 Geschwinde, Mozart's C-minor Mass (Levin), Davide penitente, Haydn's Schöpfungsmesse, Heiligmesse and Die Schöpfung, Schubert and Mozart Lieder, Lucio Vero in Jommelli's Il Vologeso, Lucio Silla, Il Re Pastore, Das Buch mit sieben Siegeln, Catulli Carmina, Der Sterngucker, Der Onkel aus Boston. *Current Management:* c/o Boris Orlob Management, Jägerstr. 70, 10117 Berlin, Germany. *Telephone:* (30) 204-50-839. *Fax:* (30) 204-50-849. *E-mail:* boris@orlob.net. *Website:* www.orlob.net; www.lotharodinius.com.

OEHRING, Helmut; German composer, guitarist and conductor; b. 16 July 1961, Berlin. *Education:* masterclasses at Berlin Akademie der Künste. *Career:* mem. Berliner Akademie der Künste 2005–. *Compositions include:* Coma 1 1991, Locked-In 1992, Wrong 1993–95, Documentation 1 1993–96, Dokumentaroper 1994–95, Das D'Amato System 1996, Sexton A 1996, Prae-Senz 1997, Live (with Iris ter Schiphorst) 1997, Philip 1997–2001, Requiem 1998, Marie B. 1998–99, Verlorenwasser 2000, BlauWaldDorf 2001, Berlin: Sinfonie einer Grossstadt 2001, Das Blaumeer 2003, wozzeck kehrt zurück 2003–04, Unsichtar Land 2004–05, Goya 1 2006, Goya 2 (Memoratorium) 2007. *Recordings include:* Dokumentaroper, Requiem. *Honours:* Deutschlandsender Kultur Hans Eisler prize 1990, WDR Cologne Young Composer's Award 1992, Orpheus Prize, Italy 1996, Hindemith Prize 1997, Schneider-Schott Music Prize 1998. *Address:* c/o Boosey & Hawkes, Komponisten Abteilung, Lützowufer 26, 10787 Berlin, Germany (office). *Website:* www.helmutoehring.de.

OELZE, Christiane; German singer (soprano); b. 9 Oct. 1963, Cologne; m. Bodo Primus; one d. *Education:* studied with Klesie Kelly-Moog and Erna Westenberger. *Career:* began singing in opera 1990; recital tours USA, S America, Japan; has worked with numerous major int. conductors and has appeared on all important European concert stages and at int. festivals, including Salzburg Festival; roles include Despina (Ottawa), Pamina (Leipzig, Lyon, Hamburg, Munich), Konstanze (Salzburg, Zurich), Anne Trulove (Glyndebourne), Regina (in Mathis der Maler, Covent Garden), Zdenka (Covent Garden), Zerlina (Covent Garden), Ännchen (in Der Freischütz, Covent Garden), Mélisande (Glyndebourne), Servilia (in La Clemenza di Tito, Covent Garden), Susanna (Salzburg), Ilia (in Idomeneo, Glyndebourne), Igluno (Palestina, Covent Garden), Sophie (in Rosenkavalier, Hamburg); Prof., Robert-Schumann-Hochschule, Dusseldorf, Germany 2003–08. *Recordings include:* several solo recitals, concert arias, Mass in C minor (Mozart), Christmas Oratorio, St John and St Matthew Passions, Webern songs and cantatas, Le nozze di Figaro and many others. *Television:* Pelléas et Mélisande, Glyndebourne 1999. *Honours:* winner, several lieder competitions, including Hugo-Wolf-Wettbewerb 1987, Hochschule Wettbewerb für Lied-Duo 1988. *Current Management:* c/o Künstleragentur, Augstein & Hahn, Sendlinger Str. 56, 80331 Munich, Germany. *E-mail:* kontakt@christianeoelze.de. *Website:* www.christianeoelze.com.

OERTEL, Christiane; singer (mezzo-soprano); b. 22 Dec. 1958, Potsdam, Germany. *Education:* Leipzig Hochschule. *Career:* mem., Komische Oper Berlin from 1988, as Cherubino, Olga, Dorabella and Carlotta in Die schweigsame Frau; debuts at Covent Garden, Hamburg and 1991 as Cherubino; Hamburg Cherubino; Japan visit with Covent Garden as Cherubino 1992; engaged at Theater Erfurt 1982–88; debut as La Cenerentola, G. Rossini, Komische Oper 1994; concert with Gewandhaus Leipzig under Kurt Masur; season 2000–01 at the Komische Oper as Mozart's Annio and Meg Page in Falstaff; Siebel in Faust at the Landestheater, Salzburg; many concert appearances.

OFENBAUER, Christian, MA; Austrian organist and composer; *Professor of Harmony and Counterpoint, Universität Mozarteum Salzburg*; b. 24 March 1961, Graz. *Education:* Klagenfurt Conservatory, Vienna Musikhochschule. *Career:* organist at Votivkirche, Vienna 1982–87; composer, TheaterAngelus-Novus 1982–87; mem. ensemble, Die Reihe 1983–92; freelance ed., Universal Edition 1985–1992; Visiting Prof. Vienna Musikhochschule 1991–92; Guest Prof. of Composition, Universität Mozarteum Salzburg 1994–97, Prof. of Harmony and Counterpoint 2001–. *Compositions include:* Tod des Hektor 1987, Medea 1990–94, unordentliche inseln/de la motte fouqué-vertonung 1995, Streichquartettsatz 1997, fancies/fancy papers (violin concerto) 1997. *Address:* Department for Composition and Music Theory, Universität Mozarteum, Mirabellplatz 1, 5020 Salzburg, Austria (office). *Telephone:* (662) 61-98-51-23 (office). *E-mail:* christian.ofenbauer@chello.at (office). *Website:* www.moz.ac.at (office).

OGAWA, Noriko; Japanese pianist; b. 28 Jan. 1962, Kawasaki. *Education:* Tokyo Coll. of Music High School, Juilliard School, New York, studied piano with Benjamin Kaplan. *Career:* concerto soloist from 1976 playing works by Mendelssohn, Tchaikovsky, Liszt, Schumann and Chopin; New York recital debut in 1982, London Wigmore Hall debut in 1988 playing Schumann's Fantasy and Liszt's Sonata; recitals throughout England and Ireland, Germany, Spain, France, Scandinavia, USA, Switzerland, Singapore; major appearances worldwide include the Harrogate Festival and the Tokyo and Yokohama Festivals; several recordings for the BBC, including Tchaikovsky B flat minor and Prokofiev No. 3 Concertos with Rozhdestvensky and the State Symphony Orchestra of the Russian Ministry of Culture; has appeared with Tokyo Symphony and Philharmonic, the Yomiuri Nippon Symphony Orchestra (with Jan Pascal Tortelier) and the Singapore Symphony; formed a duo with clarinettist, Michael Collins in 1988, performing at Wigmore Hall and various festivals; 1991 included performances with Philharmonia Orchestra at the Festival Hall, the Ulster Orchestra and Bournemouth Symphony; gave world premiere of a work by Lyn Davies at Lower Machen Festival and live BBC solo broadcast; duo with pianist Kathryn Stott 2001, gave premiere of double concerto Circuit by Fitkin with BBC Philharmonic, Piano 2003; performances include concertos with Minnesota Orchestra, Odense Symphony and ONL 2007; recitals in Kenya and Australia 2007; premieres include Dai Fujikura's Returning 2006, Earth Stream with Evelyn Glennie 2007, Yoshihiro Kanno recital at Suntory Hall 2008; adjudicated piano finals of BBC Young Musician 2000, 2002, 2004, Honens Int. Piano Competition 2006, Scottish Int. Competition 2007; appointed adviser for the new concert hall MUZA Kawasaki Symphony Hall 2004; performed premiere of Dai Fujikura's Ampere for piano and toy piano, with the Philharmonia Orchestra and Martyn Brabbins 2009; comm. of a ground-breaking series of four recital pieces from Kanno for piano and various traditional Japanese instruments or sounds 2009. *Recordings:* Czerny Etudes, Liszt, Prokofiev, Finzi Bagatelles, Rachmaninov Piano Concertos 2 and 3, Mussorgsky's Pictures at an Exhibition, Takemitsu complete solo piano works, Beethoven's Ninth (arranged by Wagner), Debussy complete solo piano works 2006, Tcherepnin Piano Concertos, Japanese piano pieces, Peterson-Berger piano pieces. *Honours:* Gina Bachauer Memorial Scholarship, Juilliard 1984, Japanese Ministry of Educ. Art Prize 1999, Cultural Prize from City of Kawasaki 2006. *Current Management:* c/o Libby Percival, Hazard Chase, 25 City Road, Cambridge, CB1 1DP, England. *Telephone:* (1223) 312400 (office). *Fax:* (1223) 460827 (office). *E-mail:* libby.percival@hazardchase.co.uk. *Website:* www.hazardchase.co.uk (office); www.norikoogawa.com.

OGDEN, Craig, BA(Mus), PGDipRNCM, PPRNCM, FRNCM; Australian classical guitarist; b. Perth; m. Claire Bradshaw; two c. *Education:* Univ. of Western Australia, Royal Northern Coll. of Music. *Career:* moved to UK 1990; recitals in UK, Europe, USA, SE Asia, S Africa and Australia; has performed concertos with London Symphony Orchestra, BBC Symphony, Royal Philharmonic, London Philharmonic, Philharmonia (with Vladimir Ashkenazy), Accad. di Santa Cecilia, Rome, Hallé, BBC Philharmonic, City of Birmingham Symphony, Royal Scottish Nat., Bournemouth Symphony, Royal Liverpool Philharmonic, BBC Nat. Orchestra of Wales, Northern Sinfonia, Britten Sinfonia, Riga Kammermusika, St Petersburg Festival Orchestra, English Chamber, English Symphony, English Sinfonia, Ulster Orchestra, London Concert Orchestra, Manchester Camerata, Nat. Orchestra of South Africa, Tasmania Symphony, West Australian Symphony and Melbourne Symphony Orchestras; festivals (with counter-tenor David Daniels) include Tanglewood, Ravinia and Mostly Mozart; has performed as chamber musician with Brodsky Quartet, Nash Ensemble and London Sinfonietta and in duos; featured in film Notting Hill; Prin. Lecturer in Guitar, Royal Northern Coll. of Music. *Recordings include:* 20th Century Classics by British Composers, A Quiet Thing (with counter-tenor David Daniels), all three solo Rodrigo guitar concertos, Music from the Novels of Louis de Bernières, Walton, Arnold and Berkeley concertos, The Complete Solo Guitar Music of Sir Lennox and Michael Berkeley, The Guitar Music of Paul Coles, Guitar Meditations, Tango Nuevo. *Current Management:* Patrick Garvey Management, 40 North Parade,

York, YO30 7AB, England. *Telephone:* (1904) 621222. *E-mail:* andrea@patrickgarvey.com. *Website:* www.patrickgarvey.com. *Address:* School of Strings, Royal Northern College of Music, 124 Oxford Road, Manchester, M13 9RD, England (office). *Telephone:* (161) 907-5254 (office). *E-mail:* margaret.kaye@rncm.ac.uk (office); craig@craigogden.com (office). *Website:* www.craigogden.com.

OGNOVENKO, Vladimir; Russian singer (bass); b. 1957. *Education:* Urals Conservatory. *Career:* sang at the Sverdlovsk Opera until 1984, then principal at the Kirov Opera, St Petersburg; Season 1991–92 as Bolkonsky in War and Peace at San Francisco, Boris Godunov at Helsinki and Varlaam in Boris Godunov at the New York Metropolitan (as guest with the Kirov); Palermo, 1993, in Rimsky's Sadko, San Francisco, 1995, as Farlaf in Ruslan and Lyudmila; Other roles in Lady Macbeth by Shostakovich, Ivan the Terrible by Rimsky, Prince Igor (as Galitsky) and Il Barbiere di Siviglia; Sang the Grand Inquisitor in Kirov Gala Concert, St Petersburg, 1998; Season 2000–01 in Shostakovich's Lady Macbeth at the Met, as Maljuta in The Tsar's Bride by Rimsky at San Francisco, Chub in Tchaikovsky's Cherevichii at Cagliari and Galitzky in Price Igor for Houston Opera; Mussorgsky's Boris Godunov at the London Proms, 2002. *Recordings include:* Videos of Prince Igor and Sadko.

OHLSSON, Garrick; American pianist; b. 3 April 1948, White Plains, NY. *Education:* Westchester Conservatory, Juilliard School with Sascha Gorodnitsky, studied with Olga Barabini, Rosina Lhevinne and Claudio Arrau. *Career:* appears regularly with major orchestras, including New York Philharmonic, Chicago Symphony, Boston Symphony, Philadelphia Orchestra, Los Angeles Philharmonic and with orchestras and in recital series throughout the world; complete cycle of Beethoven piano sonatas at Verbier, Tanglewood and Ravinia festivals. *Recordings include:* Complete Solo Works of Chopin and numerous other recordings. *Honours:* prizewinner at Busoni Piano Competition, Italy 1966, Gold Medal, Chopin Int. Piano Competition, Warsaw 1970, Montreal Int. Piano Competition 1970, Avery Fisher Prize 1994, Grammy Award for Best Instrumental Soloist Performance 2008, University Musical Society Distinguished Artist Award, Ann Arbor, Mich. 1998, Jean Gimbel Lane Prize in Piano Performance, Northwestern Univ. Bienen School of Music 2014. *Current Management:* Opus 3 Artists, 470 Park Avenue South, 9th Floor North, New York, NY 10016, USA. *Telephone:* (212) 584-7500. *Fax:* (646) 300-8200. *E-mail:* info@opus3artists.com. *Website:* www.opus3artists.com.

O'HORA, Ronan, FRNCM, FGSM; British pianist; *Head of Keyboard Studies, Guildhall School of Music and Drama*; b. 9 Jan. 1964, Manchester; m. Hannah Alice Bell 1991. *Education:* Royal Northern Coll. of Music. *Career:* recitals and concerts in the United Kingdom, USA, Australia, New Zealand, Germany, France, Italy, Austria, Switzerland, Spain, Denmark, Norway, Sweden, Belgium, Netherlands, Portugal, Ireland, Yugoslavia and Czechoslovakia; concerts with Philharmonia, Royal Philharmonic, BBC Symphony, Hallé, Bournemouth Symphony, Royal Liverpool Philharmonic, BBC Philharmonic, BBC Scottish, Zürich Tonhalle Orchestra, Netherlands Radio Symphony and Chamber Orchestras, Philharmonia Hungaria, Indianapolis Symphony, and Florida Philharmonic; Sr Tutor, Royal Northern Coll. of Music; Head of Keyboard Studies, Guildhall School of Music and Drama 1999–. *Recordings:* Concertos by Tchaikovsky, Grieg and Mozart with the Royal Philharmonic Orchestra; Britten complete music for two pianos with Stephen Hough; Numerous radio recordings in the United Kingdom, USA, France, Netherlands, Poland, Czechoslovakia, Portugal and Ireland. *Recordings:* more than 30 recordings including music of Chopin, Schubert, Brahms and Beethoven. *Honours:* Freeman of The City of London 2000; Silver Medal, Worshipful Company of Musicians 1984, Dayas Gold Medal 1985, Stefania Niedrasz Prize 1985. *Current Management:* Patrick Garvey Management, Cedar House, 40 North Parade, York YO30 7AB, England. *Telephone:* (1904) 621222 (office). *Fax:* (1723) 330050 (office). *E-mail:* patrick@patrickgarvey.com. *Website:* www.patrickgarvey.com. *Address:* 183 Honor Oak Road, Forest Hill, London, SE23 3RP, England (home). *E-mail:* ronanohora@tiscali.co.uk (home).

ÖHRN, Per-Erik, BA; Swedish artistic director, singer, translator and librettist; *Artistic Director, Drottningholms Slottsteater*; b. 18 Oct. 1946, Malmö. *Education:* Opera Acad. Göteborg, Univ. of Göteborg. *Career:* opera singer 1972–82; Stage Dir 1973–; Artistic Dir, Norrlands Operan, Umeå, Sweden 1988–96, Drottningholms Slottsteater 1996–; Sr Prof., Opera Acad., Göteborg, Univ. 2004–. *Address:* Drottningholms Slottsteater, Box 15417, Stockholm, 10765, Sweden (office). *Telephone:* (08) 55693100 (office). *Fax:* (08) 55693101 (office). *E-mail:* dst@dtm.se (office). *Website:* www.dtm.se (office).

OHYAMA, Heiichiro, AGSM; violinist, violist and conductor; b. 31 July 1947, Kyoto, Japan; m. Gail J. Ohyama, one s. *Education:* Toho Music High School, Toho Coll. of Music, Guildhall School of Music and Drama, UK and Indiana Univ., USA. *Career:* debut in New York; Prof. of Music, Univ. of California, Santa Barbara; Asst Conductor and Principal Violist, Los Angeles Philharmonic; Music Dir, Santa Barbara Chamber Orchestra and Crossroads Chamber Ensemble; Music Dir and Artistic Dir, La Jolla Chamber Music Festival; played at Marlboro Music Festival, Santa Fe Chamber Music Festival, Round Top Music Festival; mem. Musicians' Union (UK). *Honours:* Carl Flesch Int. Competition 1968, winner Young Concert Artist 1975.

OISTRAKH, Igor Davidovich, FRCM; Russian violinist and academic; *Professor, Conservatoire Royal de Musique, Brussels*; b. 27 April 1931, Odessa, Ukrainian SSR, USSR; s. of David Oistrakh; m. Natalia Zertsalova 1960; one

s. *Education:* Cen. Music School, Moscow, State Conservatory, Moscow. *Career:* concert debut 1948; many foreign tours, several concerts with father David Oistrakh; appears with major orchestras world-wide as soloist and conductor; joined Faculty of Moscow State Conservatory 1958, Lecturer 1965; Prof., Royal Conservatory of Music, Brussels, Belgium 1996–; teaches int. master-classes; Pres. Russian br. of ESTA, César Franck Foundation; Patron and fmr Jury mem. Benjamin Britten Int. Violin Competition, London. *Recordings include:* more than 100 recordings. *Honours:* Hon. mem. Beethoven Soc., Bonn, E. Ysaÿe Soc., Brussels, H. Wieniawski Soc., Poznań, J. Heifetz Soc., USA; winner of numerous competitions, asteroid 42516 Oistrach named in his (and his father's) honour, numerous awards. *Current Management:* c/o Master Recitals, Milestone, St Nicholas Avenue, Great Bookham, Surrey, KT23 4AY, England. *Telephone:* (1372) 457755. *E-mail:* info@masterrecitals.co.uk. *Address:* Conservatoire Royal de Musique, 30 rue de la Régence, Brussels, Belgium (office).

OKADA, Yoshiko; Japanese pianist; b. 5 Oct. 1961; m. Grzegorz Cimoszko, one s. *Education:* Ecole Normale de Musique, Paris, studied in Paris with Yvonne Loriod, in London with Maria Curcio and in Switzerland with Nikita Magaloff. *Career:* debut at Carnegie Hall, New York 1991; touring in recital and as soloist with orchestras throughout USA, Canada, Poland, Denmark, Belgium, Switzerland and France. *Recordings include:* albums of Mozart Sonatas and Concertos with Warsaw Chamber Orchestra.

OKE, Alan; British singer (tenor); b. 1954, London. *Education:* Scottish Acad. of Music and Drama, Glasgow, studied in Munich with Hans Hotter. *Career:* sang first in concerts, operas and oratorios as baritone; debut as tenor 1992; stage debut with Scottish Opera; roles include Papageno in Die Zauberflöte, Schaunard in La Bohème, Olivier in Capriccio; sang in Cavalli's L'Egisto in Frankfurt, Venice and Schwetzingen 1983; Covent Garden 1984 in Taverner by Maxwell Davies; took part in British premiere of Weill's Street Scene, Glasgow 1989; guest appearances with ENO and Opera North; sang Macheath in The Threepenny Opera, Leeds; Pluto in Orpheus in the Underworld, for Opera North; tenor roles include Rodolfo in La Bohème, Boris in Katya Kabanova, Alfredo in La Traviata for Opera North, Gaston and Alfredo in La Traviata for GTO; season 1998 as Ravel's Gonsalve and Puccini's Rinuccio at Auckland, Shuisky for New Sussex Opera, and in Caterina Cornaro at the QEH, London; Pinkerton in Madama Butterfly at Royal Albert Hall; the Armoured Man in The Magic Flute at Royal Opera House and Glyndebourne; Gherardo in Gianni Schicchi; Tanzmeister in Ariadne auf Naxos at Royal Opera House; Tchekalinsky in The Queen of Spades; Monostasos in The Magic Flute; Four Servants in Les Contes d'Hoffman at the Metropolitan Opera; Aschenbach in Death in Venice at Aldeburgh Festival, in Bregenz, Prague, Lyon; Gandhi in Satyagraha for ENO and Metropolitan Opera; Monostatos at the Met 2010–11; Gherardo in Gianni Schicci and Old Man Marshall in Turnage's new opera Anna Nicole, Royal Opera House 2011; concert performance of The Mask of Orpheus, Proms 2009. *Recordings include:* Mary's Music: Songs and Dances from the Time of Mary Queen of Scots 1992, Giuseppe in The Gondoliers 1993, Lehar, The Merry Widow 1997, Turnage, Anna Nicole 2011, Britten: Peter Grimes (BBC Music Magazine Opera Award 2014) 2013. *Honours:* Singer of the Year, Kultur magazine 2008, Best Performance Award, Prague Festival 2009.

OKERLUND, David; American singer (baritone); b. 1965, Kearney, NE. *Education:* Merola Opera Program, San Francisco. *Career:* appearances with San Francisco Opera as Don Giovanni, the Herald in Lohengrin, Eugene Onegin and Mozart's Count; Puccini's Sharpless in Tokyo and Guglielmo for Opera Carolina; Season 1998–99 as Stanley in the San Francisco premiere of A Streetcar Named Desire, and Gunther in Götterdämmerung; Germont in La Traviata for Vancouver Opera; Concerts include Carmina Burana, Die Schöpfung by Haydn and the Brahms Requiem. *Honours:* Adler Fellow, 1995. *Current Management:* c/o Harlequin Agency Ltd, 203 Fidlas Road, Llanishen, Cardiff CF14 5NA, Wales. *Telephone:* (29) 2075-0821. *Fax:* (29) 2075-5971. *E-mail:* peter@harlequin-agency.co.uk. *Website:* www.harlequin-agency.co.uk; www.DavidOkerlund.net.

OLAFIMIHAN, Tinuke; singer (soprano); b. 1961, London, England. *Education:* Colchester Institute, Morley College, National Opera Studio, London, studied with Elisabeth Schwarzkopf. *Career:* debut as Despina at the Queen Elizabeth Hall in 1989 with the National Opera Studio; Has sung Zerlina in Don Giovanni at the Snape Maltings, Messiah with The Sixteen under Harry Christophers and appearances with the Vivaldi Concertante at St John's Smith Square and in the St John Passion at Belfast; Sang Susanna in a production of Figaro by Colin Graham and Barbarina for Opera Northern Ireland and in Aix-en-Provence; Sang Carmina Burana at the Queen Elizabeth Hall in 1990 and Clara in the Covent Garden premiere of Porgy and Bess in 1992. *Honours:* Peter Stuyvesant Foundation Scholarship; Walter Legge/Elisabeth Schwarzkopf Society Award; Finalist, 1988 Richard Tauber Competition. *Current Management:* Stafford Law, Candleway, Broad Street, Sutton Valence, Kent ME17 3AT, England. *Website:* www.stafford-law.com.

OLAFSSON, Kjartan, BM, PhD; Icelandic composer; b. 18 Nov. 1958, Reykjavík; two d. *Education:* Reykjavík Coll. of Music, Inst. in Sonology, The Netherlands, Sibelius Acad. *Career:* debut in Reykjavík 1985; mem. Soc. of Composers in Iceland. *Compositions:* Reflex for orchestra 1988, Bribraut for clarinet trio 1993, Summary for tape 1994, Utstrok for orchestra 1995, Dimma for viola and piano, Dark Days for electronics and live performance. *Publications:* Calmus Theory Books 1–4; contrib. to CALMUS (Calculated Music). *Honours:* prize Competition for Young Composers, grants from Ministries of Iceland and Finland.

OLANO, Miguel; Spanish singer (tenor); b. 1962, Cenicero, La Rioja. *Education:* Madrid Conservatory, studied in Florence with Gino Bechi, in Siena with Carlo Bergonzi. *Career:* debut in Wels, Austria, 1991, as Rodolfo; appearances as Puccini's Edgar at Torre del Lago and as Cavaradossi at Vercelli, Bregenz and Salzburg; season 1995 with Don Carlos at the Paris Châtelet; further engagements as Puccini's Des Grieux at Livorno and Pisa, Manrico, Pollione (Norma) and Don Carlos at the Amsterdam Concertgebouw; other roles include Andrea Chénier, Turiddu and Calaf in Turandot; sang Don Juan in Margarita la Tornera by R. Chapi, opposite Placido Domingo, at Madrid 2000; US debut Washington Opera 2000, as Cavaradossi; season 2000–01 as Don Carlos and Calaf at Washington; Des Grieux at L'Opéra de Genève. *Current Management:* Musicaglotz, 11 rue le Verrier, 75006 Paris, France. *Telephone:* (1) 42-34-53-40. *Fax:* (1) 40-46-93-77. *E-mail:* general@musicaglotz.com. *Website:* www.musicaglotz.com; www.miguelolano.com.

OLCZAK, Krzysztof Robert; Polish composer and accordionist; b. 26 May 1956, Łódź; m. 1980; one s. one d. *Education:* Fr Chopin Academy of Music, Warsaw, Academy of Music, Gdansk. *Career:* solo and chamber concerts in Poland from 1978; Played with National Philharmonic, 1985, 1986 and Bialystok, Gdansk, Koszalin, Łódź, Opole, Poznań, Wroclaw, Austria, Finland, Germany, Italy, Norway, Sweden and Russian Philharmonic Orchestras; appearances at contemporary music festivals include Styrian Autumn, Austria, Warsaw Autumn, Poznań Spring, Gdansk Encounters of Young Composers; Conservatorium Legnica, 1987, 1991, Musik Biennale, Berlin in 1987, Musica Polonica Nova, Wroclaw in 1988, and Internationale Studienwoche, Bonn in 1991; Tour of Scandinavia with American Waterways Wind Orchestra in 1990; Lecturer at Gdansk Academy of Music. *Compositions include:* Accordion Solos: Manualiter, 1977, Phantasmagorien, 1978, Winter Suite, 1980, Fine Pluie, 1980, Berceuse, 1984, Rondino, 1985, Pozymk for 4 performers, 1982, Sea Spaces for Soprano and Prepared Piano, 1982, Cantata for Soprano, 2 Accordions, 1984, Sinfonietta Concertante for Percussion and Orchestra, 1985–86, Belt The Bellow for Tuba and Accordion, 1986, Trio, Homage to Karol Szymanowski, 1987, Intervals for Organ and 2 Accordions, 1987, Concerto for Accordion and Orchestra, 1989, Concerto Grosso for Wind Orchestra, 1990. *Address:* 11 Listopada 79, 80-180 Gdańsk, Poland.

OLDFIELD, Mark, BA (Hons), AGSM, Post Dip. (RCM); British singer (baritone); b. 1967, Sheffield, Yorks., England. *Education:* Colchester Inst. with Norman Tattersall and Rae Woodland, Guildhall School of Music and Drama with Ann Wood and Paul Hamburger, Royal Coll. of Music opera school with Kenneth Woollam and James Lockhart, Britten-Pears School, Snape, Suffolk with Hugues Cuenod, further studies with Michelle Wegwart and Jane Robinson. *Career:* operatic work has included Metcalf's Tornrak at Banff Centre, Canada, Papageno for London Opera Players, The Fisherman by Paul Max Edlin for London Int. Opera Festival 1989, Malatesta (Don Pasquale) for Opera Northern Ireland, Redburn (Billy Budd) and Onegin for Scottish Opera, Guglielmo (Così) and Marcello (La Bohème) in Malta, Poeta (Rossini's Il Turco in Italia) and John Sorel (Mennoti's The Consul) with Simon Callow, Mercurio (La Calisto) in Provence, Dancairo (Carmen) at Castleward, Tancredi (Missa e Combattimento) in Brussels/Antwerp, Romeo (Julia) for Opera Factory, Il Ragazzo (Knapik/Jan Fabre's Silent Screams) in Normandie/Antwerp/Kassel, Dunstan in Silas Marner, Birmingham with Graham Vick, I have seen someone (Eiriksdottir/Lontano) at the Riverside Studios, Don Giovanni, Bristol Old Vic/Martyn Brabbins; concerts include Brahms' Requiem, Snape Maltings, Bach's Magnificat, Las Palmas, Handel's Chandos Anthems with English Chamber Orchestra under Sir Charles Mackerras, Carmina Burana, Nigeria (British Council), Monteverdi Madrigals and Brahms' Liebeslieder (tour of northern Italy); teachers at Middlesex Univ.; facilitates projects for Streetwise Opera, London and Magdala, Nottingham; consultancy for coaching choirs (Vocalcraftwork.com). *Telephone:* 7932-075178 (mobile) (office). *E-mail:* contactme@markoldfield.net (office). *Website:* www.markoldfield.net.

OLDFIELD, Michael (Mike) Gordon; British musician (multi-instrumentalist) and composer; b. 15 May 1953, Reading, Berks., England; three s. two d. *Career:* solo artist; numerous tours, worldwide TV and radio broadcasts. *Recordings include:* albums: Tubular Bells (Grammy Award) 1973, Hergest Ridge 1974, Ommadawn 1975, Incantations 1978, Platinum 1979, QE2 1980, Five Miles Out 1982, Crises 1983, Discovery 1984, Islands 1987, Earthmoving 1989, Amarok 1990, Heaven's Open 1991, Tubular Bells II 1992, Elements 1994, The Songs of Distant Earth 1996, Voyager 1996, XXV The Essential 1997, Tubular Bells III 1998, Guitars 1999, Millennium Bell 1999, Tres Lunas 2002, Tubular Bells 2003 2003, Light + Shade 2005, Music of the Spheres 2008, Man on the Rocks 2014. *Website:* www.mikeoldfieldofficial.com.

O'LEARY, Timothy; American opera director; *General Director, Opera Theatre of Saint Louis*; b. 1975; m. Kara O'Leary. *Education:* Dartmouth Coll. *Career:* Grant Writer, New York City Opera 1997, Admin. Dir 2005–07; fmr Stage Dir, Glimmerglass Opera and Florida Grand Opera; fmr Man. Dir, Gotham Chamber Opera; Exec. Dir, Opera Theatre of Saint Louis Jan.–Oct. 2008, Gen. Dir Oct. 2008–. *Address:* Office of the General Director, Opera Theatre of Saint Louis, PO Box 191910, St Louis, MO 63119-7910, USA (office). *Telephone:* (314) 961-0171 (office). *Website:* www.opera-stl.org (office).

OLEDZKI, Bogdan; conductor; b. 25 June 1949, Stupsk, Poland; m. Ewa Gtowacka 1981. *Education:* Warsaw Music Acad. *Career:* debut with National Philharmonic Orchestra, Warsaw in 1974; Conductor in Warsaw, Radom and

Poznań, 1974–82; Principal Conductor for Rzeszow Philharmonic Orchestra, 1982–84; Conductor for Great Opera, Warsaw, 1984–; Guest Conductor with Philharmonic Orchestra, Poland and Salzburg-Aspecte, Edinburgh and Skopje Festivals. *Address:* Bandrowskiego 8 m 60, 01-496 Warsaw, Poland.

OLEG, Raphaël; French violinist; b. 8 Sept. 1959, Paris. *Education:* Paris Conservatoire. *Career:* international reputation as recitalist and with Europe's major symphony orchestras; Lucerne Festival in 1986 with the Czech Philharmonic and Vaclav Neumann; First Prize in Tchaikovsky International Competition in 1986; British debut in 1987 playing the Brahms Concerto with the London Symphony Orchestra under Jeffrey Tate; 1987 tour of European Festivals with the Orchestre National de France and Lorin Maazel; Engagements with the Concertgebouw under Chailly, Orchestre de Paris under Bychov, the Philadelphia Orchestra under Maazel and the Munich Staatsorchester under Sawallisch; British appearances with the Philharmonia, English Chamber Orchestra, Northern Sinfonia, Scottish Chamber Orchestra and City of London Sinfonia; Japanese debut in 1989 at Suntory Hall; Engagements in 1989–90 season included a tour of Italy with ECO and Tate, and a tour of France and Switzerland with the Academy of St Martin-in-the-Fields and Marriner; Gave recitals at Prague Spring Festival and Paris, concerts with the Orchestre National de France, and Polish Chamber Orchestra; 1990–91 toured Germany with Chamber Orchestra of Europe and Berglund, and Japan with the Nouvel Orchestre Philharmonique. *Address:* 4 bis rue Riquet, 31000 Toulouse, France (home).

OLESCH, Peter Otto; German singer (bass-baritone); b. 10 Sept. 1938, Andreashutte, Oberschlesien. *Education:* studied in Dresden with Rudolf Bockelmann. *Career:* debut at Berlin Staatsoper 1963 as a Flemish Deputy in Don Carlos; sang at the Berlin Staatsoper until 1982 in such roles as Masetto, Monterone, Bartolo, Pistol, Falstaff, Alberich, Alfio in Cavalleria Rusticana, Vaarlam and Rangier in Penderecki's The Devils of Loudun; sang at Leipzig Opera 1989 as Don Pasquale; many concert performances. *Recordings include:* Puntila by Dessau.

OLIVEIRA, Elmar; American violinist; b. 28 June 1950, Waterbury, CT. *Education:* Hart Coll. of Music, Hartford and Manhattan School of Music. *Career:* appearances with orchestras including New York Philharmonic, Cleveland, Baltimore, Chicago Symphony, Dallas, Montreal and Moscow Philharmonic. *Recordings include:* Sonata by Husa. *Honours:* first prize Naumberg Competition 1975, gold medal Tchaikovsky Int. Competition 1978.

OLIVER, Alexander; British singer (tenor); b. 27 June 1944, Scotland. *Education:* Royal Scottish Acad.; further studies in Vienna and with Rupert Bruce-Lockhart. *Career:* Netherlands Opera from 1971 in The Love For Three Oranges, Intermezzo, Peter Grimes, L'Ormindo and The Turn of the Screw; Scottish Opera in A Midsummer Night's Dream, Wozzeck, The Bartered Bride, Eugene Onegin and Mahagonny; Opera North as Nemorino in L'Elisir d'amore; Glyndebourne Opera in Il Ritorno d'Ulisse, Ariadne auf Naxos and Albert Herring in 1985; Covent Garden in Eugene Onegin, Le nozze di Figaro, Andrea Chénier, Manon and Albert Herring, 1989; Zürich Opera from 1978 in L'Incoronazione di Poppea and Les Contes d'Hoffmann; Brussels Opera in 1982 as Arbace in Idomeneo, returning for the world premiere of Le Passion de Gilles by Boesmans; Antwerp Opera and Canadian Opera debuts in 1983 in Death in Venice and Poppea; La Fenice Venice in Curlew River, La Scala Milan in the premiere of Riccardo III by Flavio Testi and sang Mime in a new production of Siegfried at Covent Garden in 1990; sang Shapkin in From the House of the Dead at Brussels in 1990, and at Salzburg in 1991 in Le nozze di Figaro; sang Schmidt in Werther for Netherlands Opera, 1996; concert engagements with the Concertgebouw Orchestra in the St John and St Matthew Passions of Bach and Stravinsky's Pulcinella; Houston Symphony and Chicago Symphony and frequent appearances with the Songmakers' Almanac; now retd. *Recordings include:* Videos of Gilbert and Sullivan's The Sorcerer and Pirates of Penzance.

OLIVER, John Edward, BMus, MMus, DMus; Canadian composer; b. 21 Sept. 1959, Vancouver. *Education:* McGill Univ., Montréal, Univ. of British Columbia, San Francisco Conservatory of Music. *Career:* works performed by New Music Concerto, Toronto 1982, 1987, Vancouver New Music 1982, 1990, Societé de Musique Contemporaine de Québec 1989, Canadian Opera Co. 1991; Composer-in-Residence, Banff Centre, Leighton Artist Colony 1989, 1990, and Music Dept 1990, 1991, Canadian Opera Co. 1989, 1991, Vancouver Opera 1992–; mem. Soc. of Composers, Authors and Music Publishers of Canada, American Federation of Musicians, Canadian Electro-acoustic Community. *Compositions:* Gugcamayo's Old Song and Dance 1991, El Reposo del Fuego 1987, Aller Retour 1988, Marimba Dismembered 1990, Before the Freeze 1984. *Publication:* contrib. 'New Music in British Columbia' (in Soundnotes, Fall edn) 1992. *Honours:* Canada Council Arts Awards 1984–87, 1991, prize CBC Nat. Radio Competition for Young Composers 1988, two prizes PROCAN Young Composers Competition 1989.

OLIVER, Lisi, BA, ALM, PhD; American stage director and translator; b. 13 Dec. 1951, Frankfurt am Main, Germany. *Education:* Smith College, Harvard University. *Career:* Stage Man., Bolshoi Opera US Tour, 1974; inaugural gala for President Carter, 1978; Production Stage Manager, Assistant Director, Opera Company of Boston, 1975–78; Asst Director, Komische Oper Berlin, 1979–80; Director, Opera Company of Boston, Opera New England, Skylight Comic Opera, Des Moines Metro Opera, Atlanta Opera, Baldwin-Wallace Conservatory, Opera Company of the Philippines, Massachusetts Institute of Technology, Wolftrap Farm Park, City of Boston First Night, 1980–90;

Director of Opera Studio, New England Conservatory, 1988–90; first projected titles at Bolshoi Opera, 1991; Director, Atlanta Opera Studio, 1989–95; Title Supervisor, Atlanta Opera, Director of Raymond Street Translations, Translation and Titles Rental Company; Prof. of Mediaeval Studies and Linguistics, Louisiana State University 1996–. *Publications:* translations of surtitles used by many American companies; The Beginnings of English Law 2002. *Honours:* Yvonne Burger Award, Smith College, 1973; Merit Award, Komische Oper, 1980; National Opera Institute Grant, 1978–80; Whiting Fellowship, Harvard University, 1994–95; Outstanding Graduate Faculty in English, LSU, 1997; Phi Beta Phi Award, LSU, 1998; BP Amoco Award for outstanding undergraduate teaching, 2001. *Address:* 2021 Cedardale Avenue, Baton Rouge, LA 70808 (home); Department of English/Interdepartmental Program in Linguistics, Louisiana State University, Baton Rouge, LA 70803, USA (office). *E-mail:* lolive1@lsu.edu (office).

OLIVEROS, Pauline, BA; American composer and musician; b. 30 May 1932, Houston, TX. *Education:* San Francisco State Coll. *Career:* Dir, San Francisco Tape Music Center 1966–67; Prof. of Music, Univ. of California, San Diego 1967–81, Dir Centre for Music Experiment 1976–79; Prof. of Music, Theater School for New Dance, Amsterdam 1985; Founder, Pres. and Co-Artistic Dir, Pauline Oliveros Foundation Inc. 1985–87, 1997–98; Prof. of Composition, Oberlin Conservatory of Music 1999; Visiting Prof., Stanford Univ. 1979, Mills Coll. 1985; Composer-in-Residence, Alfred Univ. 1996, 1998, Mills Coll. 1996, 1997, 1999, 2000, Northwestern Univ. 1996, Agnes Scott Coll. 2000, Univ. of Wisconsin, Madison Spring 2001; Summer Olympics, Los Angeles 1984; works performed and solo performances worldwide and with numerous orchestras. *Compositions include:* Roots for the Moment, Tara's Room, The Well and the Gentle, Tashi Gomang, Rose Moon, Sonic Meditations, Horse Sings from Cloud, Rattlesnake Mountain, Lullaby for Daisy Pauline, Spiral Madala, Bonn Feier, Double Basses at 20 Paces, Three Songs for soprano and piano, To Valerie Solanas and Marilyn Monroe, Jar Piece, Sound Patterns, Njinga the Queen King (music theatre) 1993, From Unknown Silences for ensemble 1996, Cicada Song for accordion 1996, Beyond the Mysterious Silence for low voice and ensemble 1996, Four Meditations 1997, Primordial/Lift 1998, Antigone's Dream 1999, The Heart of Tones 1999, Elan Trio The Space of Spirit 2000, Starkland Elemental Gallop 2000, Lunar Opera 2000, Sound Patterns and Tropes 2001. *Publication:* Software for People 1984. *Honours:* Hon. DMus (Univ. of Maryland) 1986; Gaudeamus Prize 1962, Guggenheim Fellowship 1973, Beethoven Prize, City of Bonn 1977, ASCAP Standard Award 1982–99, Nat. Endowment for the Arts Composer's Fellowship 1984, 1988. *E-mail:* ione .booking@gmail.com (office). *Website:* paulineoliveros.us.

OLLI, Kalevi; Finnish singer (bass-baritone); b. 1951. *Education:* Sibelius Acad., Helsinki with Eino-Johani Rautavaan. *Career:* sang Silvano in Un Ballo in Maschera at Helsinki 1977; sang at Frankfurt Opera 1978–84; appearances at the Savonlinna Festival as the Dutchman and concert engagements, including Lieder recitals, in Germany, Switzerland and elsewhere; sang in Boris Godunov at Royal Opera Stockholm Warlaan 1997, and at Deutsche Oper Berlin Alberich in Rheingold; sang whole Ring Cycle in Helsinki 1996–99; season 1998 as Alberich in Siegfried at Helsinki; sang in Sapporo, Japan with Tan Dum and Orchestra Theatre II 1999; mem. Finnish Composers, Finnish Drama Authors. *Recordings:* complete songs by Rachmaninov, Schumann's Dichterliebe with Toiva Kuula, Schwanengesang with Ulrich Koneftke. *Honours:* prizewinner in competitions at Savonlinna, Lappeenranta and Geneva 1977–81.

OLLMANN, Kurt; American singer (baritone); b. 19 Jan. 1957, Racine, WI. *Education:* studied with Gerard Souzay and others. *Career:* sang with the Milwaukee Skylight Opera, 1979–82; engagements in Santa Fe, Washington, DC, Milan and Brussels in operas by Debussy and Mozart; Pepsico Summerfare New York in 1987 as Don Giovanni, in the Peter Sellars version of Mozart's opera; sang under Bernstein in the Viennese premiere of A Quiet Place in 1986 and as Maximilian in a concert performance of Candide at the Barbican in London 1989; Seattle Opera in 1988 as Mercutio in Gounod's Roméo et Juliette; St Louis Opera 1989–90, as Purcell's King Arthur and Mozart's Count; many concert appearances; season 1992 in On The Town at the Barbican Hall and the title role in the US premiere of Bose's The Sorrows of Young Werther at Santa Fe; season 1999–2000 for Seattle Opera as the Speaker in Die Zauberflöte and Frédéric in Lakmé; currently lecturer in voice, Peck School of the Arts, Univ. of Wisconsin. *Recordings:* Count Paris in Roméo et Juliette, conducted by Michel Plasson; Candide and West Side Story conducted by the composer; Mercutio in Roméo et Juliette, under Leonard Slatkin 1996. *Telephone:* (414) 758-0293 (office). *E-mail:* tadmilo@aol.com (office). *Address:* Peck School of the Arts, 2400 E. Kenwood Blvd, Milwaukee, WI 53211, USA (office).

OLMI, Paolo; Italian conductor; *Music Director, Opéra National de Lorraine, Nancy*; b. 23 May 1954. *Education:* studied with Massimo Pradella and Franco Ferrara in Rome. *Career:* frequent appearances with major orchestras in Italy and abroad from 1979; opera debut at Teatro Communale di Bologna 1986; conducted Rossini's Mosè in Egitto at Rome 1988, later at the Bayerische Staatsoper, Munich; Deutsche Oper am Rhein, Düsseldorf, with Traviata, Théâtre des Champs Elysées with Rossini's Guillaume Tell; British debut 1991, with Royal Philharmonic in a concert performance of Nabucco; Bellini's Zaira at Catania 1990; concerts at the Schleswig-Holstein Festival, the Philharmonic Berlin, the Frankfurt Alte Oper and the Philharmonie in Munich; English Chamber Orchestra with Rostropovich as soloist; apptd Principal Conductor, RAI Rome 1991; Deutsche Oper Berlin 1992 with

La Forza del Destino; tour of Italy with the Royal Philharmonic 1993, Verdi Requiem at the Festival Hall 1994; conducted Mosè at Covent Garden 1994; Madama Butterfly at Copenhagen 1996; season 1998 with L''Elisir d'amore at Madrid; toured Italy with Royal Philharmonic Orchestra, London Philharmonic Orchestra and BBC Symphony Orchestra 1998–2001; Verdi Requiem with the London Philharmonic Orchestra at the Festival Hall 2001, Rigoletto in Rotterdam; Ballo in Maschera and Nabucco at Tokyo 2000–01; Music Dir, Opéra National de Lorraine, Nancy 2006–11; Music Dir, Orchestra Symphonique et Lyrique, Nancy 2006–. *Current Management:* c/o Brian Jauhiainen, Bel Canto Global Arts, 17 Auburn Avenue, Bay Shore, NY 11706, USA. *Telephone:* 718 772 024 (Mobile); (631) 206-0260. *Fax:* (866) 698-3059. *E-mail:* brian@belcantoglobal.com. *Website:* www.belcantoglobalarts.com. *E-mail:* info@paoloolmi.com. *Website:* www.paoloolmi.com/Paolo_Olmi___Conductor. *Current Management:* IMG Artists, The Light Box, 111 Power Road, London, W4 5PY, England. *Telephone:* (20) 7957-5800. *Fax:* (20) 7957-5801. *E-mail:* nmathias@imgartists.com. *Website:* www.imgartists.com.

OLMSTEAD, Andrea, BM, MA; American musicologist; *Faculty Member, New England Conservatory of Music*; b. 5 Sept. 1948, Dayton, Ohio; d. of Dr Edwin Guy Olmstead and Mary Alice Olmstead; m. Larry Thomas Bell 1982. *Education:* Hartt Coll. of Music, New York Univ., Juilliard School, New York. *Career:* mem. Faculty, The Juilliard School 1972–80, Boston Conservatory 1981–2004; Christopher Hogwood Research Fellow, Handel and Haydn Soc. 2005–07; mem. Faculty, New England Conservatory of Music 2007–, Boston Univ. (online faculty mem.) 2007–, Univ. of Massachusetts, Amherst 2009–10. *Libretto:* wrote opera libretto for Holy Ghosts by Larry Bell and based on the play by Romulus Linney. *Publications:* Roger Sessions and His Music 1985, Conversations with Roger Sessions 1987, The New Grove 20th Century American Masters 1987, The Correspondence of Roger Sessions 1992, Juilliard: A History 1999, Roger Sessions: A Biography 2008, Cultivating the Past: A Celebration of Hadley's 350th Anniversary 2009; contrib. to Journal of the Arnold Schoenberg Institute, American Music, Musical Quarterly, Tempo, Musical America, Perspectives of New Music, Music Library Association Notes, Journal of Musicology. *Honours:* three Nat. Endowment for the Humanities grants 1989, 1992, 2000, Outstanding Academic Book, Choice 1986, Outstanding Teacher of the Year Boston Conservatory 2000, 2004, six Visiting Scholar residencies, American Acad., Rome, four residencies at Virginia Center for the Creative Arts. *Address:* 73 Hemenway Street, Apt 501, Boston, MA 02115, USA. *Telephone:* (617) 262-1775. *E-mail:* andrea.olmstead@gmail.com. *Website:* www.holyghoststheopera.com.

OLSEN, Derrick; Swiss singer (bass-baritone) and administrator; b. 30 March 1923, Berne. *Education:* studied in Berne, Geneva and Lucerne. *Career:* sang at Grand Théâtre Geneva 1944–69, Basle 1950–55, with guest engagements at Holland and Schwetzingen Festivals, Buenos Aires, Milan, Berlin Staatsoper, Zürich, Lucerne and Marseilles; roles included Mozart's Count, Masetto and Alfonso, Pizarro, Rossini's Basilio and Bartolo, Iago, Germont and Melitone, Wagner's Dutchman, Telramund and Klingsor, Jochanaan, Malatesta and Achilles in Penthesilea by Schoeck; sang at Basle Opera 1952, 1958 in the premieres of Leonore by Liebermann and Titus Feuerfuchs by Sutermeister; concert premieres of oratorios by Honegger, Cantate de Noel 1953, Kelterborn and Frank Martin, Mystère de la Nativité 1958 and Martinů, Gilgamesh 1958; sang in the British premiere of Schoenberg's Von Heute auf Morgen, Royal Festival Hall 1963; mem., Quatuor Vocale de Genève; Artistic Dir, Radio Orchestra Beromunster, Zürich 1958–70. *Recordings:* Pelléas et Mélisande; Monteverdi's Combattimento; Sutermeister's Schwarze Spinne; Martin's Le Vin Herbé; Handel's Apollo e Dafne.

OLSEN, Frode; Norwegian singer (bass); b. 10 April 1952, Oslo; m. Yayoi Koizumi Olsen. *Education:* Opera State Conservatory in Oslo, studied in Düsseldorf. *Career:* joined Deutsche Oper am Rhein 1982–86, debut in Düsseldorf 1982; later mem. Badisches Staatstheater, Karlsruhe; repertoire includes Pimen in Boris Godunov, Gremin in Eugene Onegin, Zaccaria in Nabucco, Pogner in Die Meistersinger von Nürnberg, King Marke in Tristan und Isolde, Landgraf in Tannhäuser, Orest in Elektra, Timur in Turandot, Doktor in Wozzeck, Moses in Moses und Aron, Guenemanz in Parsifal, Vodnik in Rusalka, Astradamors in Le Grand Macabre, Rocco in Fidelio, Kottwitz in Der Prinz von Homburg, Wesener in Die Soldaten, Fasolt in Rheingold; title role in St François d'Assise; has also performed at Salzburg Festival, Wiener Volksoper, Den Norske Opera, Deutsche Oper Berlin, Leipzig Opera, Hamburgische Staatsoper, Glyndebourne Festival Opera, Netherlands Opera, Opéra de Marseille, Opéra de Monte-Carlo. *Recordings:* Astradamors in Le Grand Macabre with Salonen, Doktor in Wozzek with Metzmacher. *Current Management:* Athole Still Opera Ltd, Foresters Hall, 25–27 Westow Street, London, SE19 3RY, England. *Telephone:* (20) 8771-5271. *Fax:* (20) 8771-8172. *E-mail:* enquiries@atholestill.co.uk. *Website:* www.atholestill.com.

OLSEN, Keith, BM, MM; American/Italian singer (tenor); b. 13 June 1956, Denver, Colo. *Education:* San Francisco Conservatory, Franz Schubert Inst., Vienna, Univ. of Tennessee, Juilliard School of Music, New York. *Career:* US debut in Die Lustige Witwe with New York City Opera 1982; European debut as Rodolfo with Staatstheater Karlsruhe 1987; has sung 76 major tenor roles in 174 productions with 104 worldwide companies, including six consecutive years at Royal Opera House, Covent Garden, London, debut as Rodolfo, Boris in premiere of Katya Kabanova (Bernard Haitink, conductor), Cavaradossi in Tosca (Plácido Domingo, conductor), Radamès, Pinkerton; Opéra Bastille,

Paris debut as Adorno in Simon Boccanegra, opened 1998 season with Pinkerton, Cavaradossi (Seiji Osawa, conductor), Rodolfo; La Scala, Milan, debut as Loris in Fedora, Dick Johnson in Fanciulla del West; Arena di Verona, debut as Rodolfo, Pinkerton in the premiere of Madame Butterfly, Radamès, Don José; Staatsoper Berlin, debut as Vasco de Gama in L'Africaine, Il Trovatore, Radamès; Deutsche Oper Berlin premiere as Hoffmann; Opera of Rome as Eric in Der Fliegende Holländer and Radamès; Oper Wien as Cavaradossi; Andrea Chénier and Cavarodossi with Warsaw Naradowa; Opéra de Marseille as Werther; San Francisco Opera as Flamand in Capriccio; Barcelona, Helsinki, Los Angeles as Alfredo. *Films:* Verdi's Requiem from The Vatican (RAI1 and NTV Japan, Santi conducting), Puccini's Des Grieux, 100th anniversary performance (RAI1), Beethoven's Ninth (MDR, Masur conducting), Solo Orchestral Concert (Ceskà Televice), Turridu (SABC), Pinkerton (VCR, 41st Puccini Festival). *Recordings:* Verdi's Requiem (Plasson conducting), Radamès (DVD, Companions Opera), La Damnation du Faust, Handel's Rodrigo, The Three Sisters. *Current Management:* c/o Stage Door, Via San Giorgio 4, 40121 Bologna, Italy. *Telephone:* (051) 262126. *Fax:* (051) 271452. *E-mail:* info@stagedoor.it. *Website:* www.stagedoor.it. *E-mail:* kotenor@operamail.com (home). *Website:* www.keitholsen.com.

OLSEN, Stanford, BMus; American singer (tenor); *Professor of Voice, School of Music, Theatre & Dance, University of Michigan*; b. 1959, Salt Lake City, Utah. *Education:* Univ. of Utah, Metropolitan Opera Devt Programme. *Career:* for the Metropolitan Opera in New York has sung Arturo in Puritani, Don Ottavio, Ferrando, Belmonte, Idreno (Semiramide), Count Almaviva, Ernesto and Fenton; European career includes Don Ottavio at the Deutsche Oper Berlin, Rossini's Comte Ory for Netherlands Opera and Belmonte under John Eliot Gardiner; concert at the Mostly Mozart Festival New York, in Boston and elsewhere for the Handel and Haydn Society (Messiah and The Creation), for the Berlin Philharmonic (Berlioz Requiem, 1989) and at the Salzburg Festival with the International Bach Academy; New York recital debut at Alice Tully Hall 1990, with Die schöne Müllerin; season 1993–94 at the Ravinia Festival in Fidelio, with the Houston Symphony in Britten's War Requiem and a tour of Spain with Messiah, conducted by Helmuth Rilling; sang Iopas in Les Troyens at La Scala 1996; frequent judge for the Metropolitan Opera's Nat. Council Auditions; masterclasses at univs and conservatories, including CCM, Curtis, Eastman, Oberlin, Manhattan School of Music, Rice Univ., Univ. of Illinois, Univ. of Houston, Univ. of Southern California, and many others; has also worked with apprentices at the Tanglewood Festival, Opera Theater of St Louis, Santa Fe Opera, Ravinia Festival, Cleveland Art Song Inst., Aspen Music Festival, Utah Opera, Metropolitan's Lindemann Young Artist Program; fmr Artist-in-Residence and holder of the Shelfer Eminent Scholar in Music Chair, Florida State Univ.; currently Prof. of Voice, School of Music, Theatre & Dance, Univ. of Michigan. *Honours:* winner Metropolitan Opera Nat. Council Auditions 1986, winner Richard Tucker Foundation Career Grant 1989, awards from Opera America and Opera IndexWalter, W. Naumburg Award 1989, Emmy Award for PBS broadcast of Sondheim's Sweeney Todd with the New York Philharmonic, Coll.-Conservatory of Music's Alumnus of the Year Award, Univ. of Cincinnati 1989, Alumnus of the Year Award, Univ. of Utah Coll. of Fine Arts 2010. *Address:* University of Michigan School of Music, Theatre & Dance, Room 3061, E.V. Moore Building, 1100 Baits Drive, Ann Arbor, MI 48109-2085, USA (office). *Telephone:* (734) 764-8773 (office). *Website:* music.umich.edu (office).

OMACHI, Yoichiro; Japanese conductor; *Permanent Conductor, Tokyo Philharmonic Orchestra*; b. 22 Aug. 1931, Tokyo. *Education:* Tokyo Acad. of Music with Akeo Watanabe and Kurt Woss, Acad. of Music, Vienna with Karl Bohm, Franco Ferrara and Herbert von Karajan. *Career:* toured Japan 1957 with Karajan and the Berlin Philharmonic; guest conductor with the Berlin Philharmonic, Tonkunstler Orchestra, Vienna 1959; Chief Conductor, Tokyo Philharmonic Orchestra 1961; founder, Tokyo Metropolitan Symphony 1964; Guest Conductor, Vienna Symphony Orchestra 1964–67; Permanent Conductor, Dortmund Opera 1968–73; East Asian tour with the Tokyo Philharmonic 1973; season 1976–77 conducted Aida at Mannheim, Fidelio in Prague, Madama Butterfly at the Berlin Staatsoper and The Merry Widow in Tokyo; concerts in Japan, South America 1978–79; Madama Butterfly at the Vienna Staatsoper 1980, Permanent Conductor there 1982–84, including Attila on Austrian television and ballet performances; Prof. in Opera Faculty, Tokyo Acad. of Music; Permanent Conductor, Tokyo Philharmonic Orchestra 1999–. *Address:* Tokyo Philharmonic Orchestra, Tokyo Opera City Tower 8F, 3-20-2 Nishi Shinjuku, Shinjuku-ku Tokyo 163-1408, Japan (office).

O'MARA, Stephen; American singer (tenor); b. 1962, Brooklyn, New York. *Career:* sang widely in North America, including Turiddu and Radames at the New York City Opera; Vienna Staatsoper from 1991, as Don José and Pinkerton; Deutsche Oper Berlin, 1993, as José; season 1994–95 as Tom Rakewell at Glyndebourne and Luigi in Il Tabarro at Cologne; Royal Opera, Copenhagen, 1996, as Alvaro in La Forza del Destino; further appearances at Oslo, and the Bregenz Festival; season 1998 as Samson at Montpellier and Narr' Havas in the premiere of Fénélon's Salammbô, at the Paris Opéra Bastille; season 2000–01 as Verdi's Riccardo at Bregenz, Gabriele Adorno at Strasbourg, Radames for Houston Opera and Menelaus in Strauss's Die Aegyptische Helena at Cagliari. *Current Management:* Pinnacle Arts, 889 Ninth Avenue, Second Floor, New York, NY 10019, USA. *Telephone:* (212) 397-7911. *Fax:* (212) 397-7920. *E-mail:* jmiller@pinnaclearts.com. *Website:* www.pinnaclearts.com.

OMBUENA, Vicente; Spanish singer (tenor); b. 1949, Valencia. *Education:* studied in Valencia. *Career:* sang at first in concert, then with Mainz Opera 1989–91 as Don José, Erik, Cassio and Lysander in A Midsummer Night's Dream; sang at Hamburg Staatsoper from 1991, notably as Ernesto in Don Pasquale; season 2000–01 for New Israeli Opera at Savonlinna as Nemorino, in Tel-Aviv as Macduff; Verdi Requiem in Karlsruhe. *Recordings include:* Franchetti's Cristoforo Colombo.

OMILIAN, Jolanta; singer (soprano); b. 1956, Warsaw, Poland. *Education:* Chopin Acad., Warsaw. *Career:* debut in Venice 1979, as Violetta; sang widely in Germany, including Bonn and Dortmund and at the 1985 Macerata Festival as Elisabetta in Roberto Devereux; sang in Maria Stuarda at Palermo 1989, Donizetti's Parisina at Basle 1990 and Norma at Rio de Janeiro; other roles include Dorabella and Leonora in Trovatore, Amenaide in Tancredi, Fiorilla in Il Turco in Italia and Anaide in Mosè in Egitto. *Recordings include:* Adriano in Siria by Pergolesi, Il Bravo by Mercadante.

ONAY, Gülsin; Turkish pianist; b. 12 Sept. 1954, Istanbul; d. of Jochen and Gülen Reusch; m. 1st Ersin Onay 1975 (divorced 1986); one s.; m. 2nd Norbert Schappacher 1987 (divorced 1995); m. 3rd Anthony Scholl 2002. *Education:* Conservatoire Nat. Supérieure de Musique, Paris and under Nadia Boulanger, Monique Haas, Pierre Sancan and Bernhard Ebert. *Career:* first concert aged six; appearances with Warsaw Philharmonic, Staatskapelle Dresden and Berlin Radio Symphony Orchestra (Germany), Vienna Philharmonic Orchestra, Salzburg Mozarteum Orchestra (Austria), Tokyo Symphony, Japan Philharmonic (Japan), Royal Philharmonic Orchestra, English Chamber Orchestra (UK), and the Bavarian, Danish, Austrian and Finnish Radio Symphony Orchestras; prize-winner numerous int. competitions; Turkish State Artist 1986–. *Recordings include:* Debussy–Ravel 1989, Chopin–Debussy–Saygun 1990, Bartok–Saygun 1991, Saygun 1994, Piano Variations 1995, Rachmaninov 2001, Chopin 2004, Rachmaninov–Tchaikovsky 2007, Saygun 2008. *Honours:* Dr hc (Bosphorus) 1988, (Hacettepe, Ankara) 2005. *Current Management:* Konzertbüro Andreas Braun, Sülzgürtel 86, 50937 Cologne, Germany. *Telephone:* (221) 9420430. *Fax:* (221) 94204319. *E-mail:* braun@konzertbuero-braun.de. *Website:* www.konzertbuero-braun.de. *E-mail:* gulsin@gulsinonay.com (office). *Website:* www.gulsinonay.com.

O'NEIL, James; American singer (tenor); b. 1954, Shawnee, OK. *Career:* debut in Santa Fe 1978, in Salome; sang at St Gallen and Berne 1979–82; Bielefeld Opera from 1982, in Fennimore and Gerda by Delius, Schreker's Der singende Teufel and as Eleazar in La Juive; Staatsoper Berlin from 1985, as Arrigo in Les Vêpres Siciliennes, Turiddu and Lohengrin; Rome Opera 1991, as Leukippos in Daphne by Strauss; Parsifal at Chemnitz 1992, and Siegfried and Siegmund for Oslo Opera 1993–96; Los Angeles 1993, as Strauss's Emperor; season 1996 as Oedipus Rex, Théâtre du Châtelet, Paris, and the title role in the premiere of Zemlinsky's Der König Kandaules at Hamburg.

O'NEIL, Scott; American conductor; *Resident Conductor, Colorado Symphony Orchestra;* b. Salt Lake City, Utah. *Education:* Oberlin Coll. Conservatory, Eastman School of Music, Rice Univ. *Career:* Orchestral Dir High School for the Performing and Visual Arts, Houston 1999; fmr Music Dir Denver Young Artists Orchestra; Asst Conductor, Utah Symphony Orchestra 2000–02, Assoc. Conductor 2002–06; Assoc. Conductor, Colorado Symphony Orchestra 2006–11, Resident Conductor 2011–; Founder and Music Dir Rosetta Music Soc.; fmr Guest Conductor, Houston Symphony, Houston Youth Symphony, Phoenix Symphony, Annapolis Symphony, Florida Philharmonic, Tulsa Philharmonic, Portland Symphony (Maine), Lubbock Symphony, Boise Philharmonic, Salt Lake Symphony, Columbus Symphony, Ohio. *Address:* Colorado Symphony Orchestra, Boettcher Concert Hall, 1000 14th Street, #15, Denver, CO 80202, USA (office). *Telephone:* (303) 623-7876 (office). *Website:* www.coloradosymphony.org (office).

O'NEILL, Charles; American singer (tenor); b. 22 Sept. 1930, Ridgefield Park, NJ. *Education:* studied in New York. *Career:* debut at Fort Worth Opera 1958 as Radames; appearances at opera houses in Santa Fe, Cincinnati, Hamburg, Stuttgart, Berlin, Cologne, Frankfurt, Düsseldorf and Zürich; mem., Theater am Gärtnerplatz Munich, with guest engagements at Toronto, Vancouver, Belgrade and Basle; other roles have been Florestan, Don José, Don Carlos, Alvaro, Manrico, Otello, Turiddu, Samson, Cavaradossi, Rodolfo, Calaf, Andrea Chénier, Oedipus Rex by Stravinsky, Bacchus and Siegmund.

O'NEILL, Dennis, CBE, FTCL, ARCM; British singer (tenor) and teacher; *Director, Wales International Academy of Voice;* b. 25 Feb. 1948, Pontarddulais, Wales; s. of Dr William O'Neill and Eva Ann O'Neill (née Rees); m. Ellen O'Neill. *Education:* studied privately with Frederick Cox in London, and on scholarships to Italy with Campogalliani in Mantua and Ricci in Rome. *Career:* debut with State Opera of S Australia 1975–76; Prin. Tenor, Scottish Opera 1976–78; debuts at Covent Garden in Norma 1979, Glyndebourne as the Italian Singer in Der Rosenkavalier 1980, Vienna Staatsoper as Alfredo in La Traviata 1983, US debut at Dallas Opera in Lucia di Lammermoor 1983; has sung at leading opera houses world-wide and is noted for his performances of the operas of Verdi; long association with Royal Opera House, Covent Garden with over 200 performances, most recently in La Juive; for Metropolitan Opera has performed in La Traviata, La Bohème, Rigoletto, Aida, Pagliacci, Cavalleria Rusticana, Turandot; conceived and first Dir Int. Acad. of Voice at Cardiff Univ. 2007–10, Dir, Wales Int. Acad. of Voice, Univ. of Wales, Trinity St David, Cardiff 2011–; mem. jury, Cardiff Singer of the World 2015. *Honours:* Hon. RAM; Hon. Fellow, Cardiff Univ., Univ. of Wales, Trinity St David; Order of St John; Hon. DMus; Verdi Medal, Amici di Verdi 2005.

Current Management: c/o Jonathan Groves, Ingpen & Williams Ltd, 7 St George's Court, 131 Putney Bridge Road, London, SW15 2PA, England. *Telephone:* (20) 8874-3222. *Fax:* (20) 8877-3113. *E-mail:* jg@ingpen.co.uk. *Website:* www.ingpen.co.uk. *E-mail:* dennisoneill1@aol.com (office). *Website:* www.dennisoneilltenor.com.

O'NEILL, Fiona; British singer (soprano); b. 1958, England. *Education:* Royal Northern Coll. of Music, masterclasses at Aldeburgh. *Career:* solo roles have included Musetta, Norina and Donna Anna for Travelling Opera, Mabel in The Pirates of Penzance for New D'Oyly Carte, Serpetta in La Serva Padrona at the Northcutt Theatre in Exeter, and Salome for the Stockholm Folkopera at the Edinburgh Festival; ENO 1990–91 as Papagena and as Gerda in Fennimore and Gerda; sang the title role in Lakmé and Louise at the Bloomsbury Theatre and Pedrotti's Tutti in Maschera at the Britten Theatre; concert engagements include Kurt Weill songs at the Cheltenham and Edinburgh Festivals; premiere of Goehr's Sing Ariel at the 1990 Aldeburgh Festival and Handel's Solomon at Birmingham 1990; Royal Festival Hall debut with the Philharmonia Orchestra 1990 and debut at the Barbican with the RPO 1991; sang Mimi for Castleward Opera 1996.

O'NEILL, Robin; British bassoonist, conductor and teacher; *Professor of Conducting, Royal College of Music. Education:* Guildhall School of Music and Drama. *Career:* Founder mem. Chamber Orchestra of Europe; fmr Prin., English Chamber Orchestra and Endymion; Prin. Bassoonist, Philharmonia; Founder mem. Gaudier Ensemble and London Winds; conducted Philharmonia Orchestra and Chorus, London Philharmonic Orchestra, English Chamber Orchestra, BBC Scottish Symphony Orchestra, Belgrade Philharmonic Orchestra, Stavanger Symphony Orchestra, Johannesburg Philharmonic Orchestra, Trondheim Symphony Orchestra, Swedish Chamber Orchestra, Nordic Chamber Orchestra, City of London Sinfonia, Orchestra Ensemble Kanazawa Japan and Orchestras of Guildhall School of Music, RAM and Royal Coll. of Music; as chamber musician, worked with musicians including Mikhail Pletnev, Boris Berezovsky, Mitsuko Uchida, Christoph Eschenbach, Pinchas Zuckerman, Salvatore Accardo, Isabelle Faust and Alina Ibragimova; broadcasts on BBC, Swedish and South African Radio and Japan Broadcasting Corpn; Prof. of Conducting, Royal Coll. of Music; Prof. of Conducting, Umbria Int. Summer Music Acad., Assisi, Italy; Visiting Prof. of Bassoon, RAM 2012–; Music Dir, music theatre ensemble The Motion Group. *Recordings include:* Spohr Clarinet Concertos Nos 1 & 2 2005, Nos 3 & 4 2008. *Address:* 3A The Chandlery, 50 Westminster Bridge Road, London, SE1 7QY (office); Royal College of Music, Prince Consort Road, London, SW7 2BS, England (office). *E-mail:* oneill@robinoneill.com (office). *Website:* robinoneill .com (office).

ONKEN, Jan Moritz; German conductor; *Principal Conductor, Kazakh National Youth Symphony Orchestra;* b. 20 Aug. 1977, Wuppertal. *Education:* St Petersburg Conservatory, Bard Coll., NY. *Career:* intern Symphony Orchestra of Bavarian Radio, Munich 2004; Conductor and Artistic Dir Tonika Ensemble, Berlin 2005–07; Prin. Conductor, Kazakh Nat. Youth Symphony Orchestra 2007–. *Address:* Kazakh National Youth Symphony Orchestra, 65 Pobeda Avenue, Astana 010000, Kazakhstan (office). *Telephone:* (777) 548-53-03 (office). *E-mail:* info@janmoritzonken.com (office). *Website:* janmoritzonken.com/index.php.

ONO, Kazushi; Japanese conductor; *Principal Conductor, Opéra National de Lyon;* b. 1960, Tokyo. *Education:* National Univ., Tokyo, studied in Munich with Wolfgang Sawallisch and Giuseppe Patanè. *Career:* Music Dir Zagreb Philharmonic Orchestra 1990–96; Hamburg Opera debut 1995 with Rigoletto; Music Dir Karlsruhe Opera 1996–2002; repertory includes La Traviata, La Bohème, Henze's Junge Lord and The Ring, Norma, Der fliegende Holländer and Schreker's Der Schatzgräber; further concerts with the BBC and Bournemouth Symphony Orchestra; Music Dir Théâtre Royal de la Monnaie, Brussels 2002–08, producing Elektra by Strauss, I Due Foscari by Verdi, Ballata by Francesconi and Khovanshchina by Mussorgsky; symphonic debut with a performance of Mahler 7; season 2005–06 CBSO, La Scala Symphonic concerts, Vienna Radio Symphony, Leipzig Gewandhaus and tour of Japan with La Monnaie; Principal Conductor, Opéra Nat. de Lyon 2008–. *Current Management:* c/o Claire Parker-Paphitis, International Classical Artists, The Tower Building, 11 York Road, London, SE1 7NX, England. *Address:* Opéra National de Lyon, 1 Place de la Comédie, 69001, Lyon, France. *Website:* www .opera-lyon.com.

OOI, Datuk Chean See; Malaysian conductor; *Resident Conductor, Malaysian Philharmonic Orchestra;* b. 1965. *Education:* studied with Volker Wangenheim in Cologne, and with W. F. Hausschild and Dennis Russell Davies. *Career:* Principal Conductor, Classic Philharmonic Orchestra, Bonn 1991–94; guest conductor with German orchestras; performances of Fidelio and Die Zauberflöte at Bahia, Brazil 1998, 2000; Resident Conductor, Malaysian Philharmonic Orchestra (Dewan Filharmonik PETRONAS) 1997–; conducting workshops in Malaysia, Germany and France, and with the Jeunesses Musicales World Orchestra; season 1999–2000 with the Czech Virtuosi and Czech Philharmonic Choir. *Honours:* first prize Conductors' Competition at Halle, Germany. *Address:* Dewan Filharmonik PETRONAS, Level Two, Tower Two, PETRONAS Twin Towers, Kuala Lumpur City Centre, 50088 Kuala Lumpur, Malaysia (office).

OOSTWOUD, Roelof; singer (tenor); b. 16 Jan. 1946, Leeuwarden, The Netherlands. *Education:* Univ. of Toronto, studied with Louis Quilico. *Career:* guest appearances in opera throughout North America and in London,

Vienna, Paris and Amsterdam; Theater am Gärtnerplatz, Munich from 1978; North American premiere of Verdi's Stiffelio (title role) with the Opera Company of Boston 1978; premiere of Berio's Vera Storia at La Scala, Milan 1982; Düsseldorf from 1982, notably in Schreker's Die Gezeichneten, Henze's Bassarids (as Dionysus) and as Strauss's Bacchus 1995; Berne 1992, as Sergei in Lady Macbeth; Coburg 1996, as Verdi's Otello; concert and oratorio performances; sang Oreste in Gluck's Iphigénie en Tauride, Rio de Janeiro 1997.

OPALACH, Jan; American singer (bass-baritone); b. 2 Sept. 1950, Hackensack, NJ. *Education:* Indiana State University. *Career:* sang at various regional US operatic centres, New York City Opera from 1980 as Bartolo, Papageno, Schaunard, Kingfisher (Midsummer Marriage) and Leporello; Caramoor Festival, 1980, as Viltotta in the USA premiere of Haydn's La Vera Costanza; St Louis 1986 in USA premiere of Rossini's Il Viaggio a Reims; Sang at Seattle Opera, 1991–92, as the Music Master in Ariadne auf Naxos and Guglielmo in Così fan tutte; New York City Opera, 1991 as the Forester in The Cunning Little Vixen, Mozart's Figaro at Toronto; sang in Rossini Gala Opera at New York's Fisher Hall, 29 February 1992; New York Premiere, B A Zimmerman's Die Soldaten, Wesener, NYCO, 1992; New York Premiere, Tippett's Midsummer Marriage, King Fisher, 1993; World Premiere, Glass's The Voyage, Metropolitan Opera, 1992; American Premiere, Schnittke's Faust Cantata, American Symphony Orchestra with Botstein; Rossini's Italiana in Algeri, Taddeo, Netherlands Opera; Season 1997–98 in Handel's Serse at the New York City Opera. *Recordings:* Solo Bach Cantatas and Bach Ensemble; 2 world premiere recordings R Beaser's Seven Deadly Sins, D Russell, American Composers' Orchestra (ARGO); Syringa, Elliott Carter; Speculum Musicae (Bridge). *Honours:* NEA Recital Grant, 1986; W M Naumburg Vocalist Award, 1989; Metropolitan Opera Nationals Award; Hertogenbosch Vocalisten Concours, 1981. *Current Management:* c/o Janice Mayer and Associates, 250 West 57th Street, Suite 2214, New York, NY 10107, USA. *Telephone:* (212) 541-5511. *Fax:* (212) 541-7303. *E-mail:* jmayer@janicemayer.com. *Website:* www.janicemayer.com; www.janopalach.com.

OPIE, Alan, OBE; British singer (baritone); b. 22 March 1945, Redruth, Cornwall; m. Kathleen Smales; one s. one d. *Education:* Guildhall School of Music, London and London Opera Centre with Vera Rosza. *Career:* debut with Sadler's Wells Opera as Papageno in Die Zauberflöte 1969; appearances with ENO, Welsh Nat. Opera, Aldeburgh Festival and Santa Fe Opera; other roles include Mozart's Guglielmo, Rossini's Figaro, Verdi's Germont, Britten's Demetrius and Charles Blount (Gloriana) and Massenet's Lescaut; sang Wagner's Beckmesser with ENO 1984 and at Bayreuth 1987, 1988, Berlin 1990, Munich 1994; sang Germont with ENO 1990 and title role in Busoni's Doctor Faust; Glyndebourne Festival as Sid in Albert Herring 1990; season 1992 as The Fiddler in Königskinder for ENO, Balstrode in Peter Grimes at Glyndebourne, Melitone in The Force of Destiny and Papageno at the Coliseum; Balstrode at New York Metropolitan 1994; Panza in Don Quichotte, Paolo in Munich 1995; title role in world premiere of Berio's Outis at Las Scala, Milan 1996, again 1999 and Châtelet, Paris 1999; sang Rossini's Taddeo for ENO 1997; Balstrode in Peter Grimes at the New York Met 1998; season 1998 as Don Alfonso at Glyndebourne, Janáček's Gamekeeper at Spoleto and Sharpless in Madama Butterfly at the New York Met; sang Beckmesser in Meistersinger at Munich 1994, 1996, 1997, 1998 and Vienna 1999; season 2000–01 as Britten's Balstrode at the Vienna Staatsoper, Don Carlo in Ernani for ENO, Don Alfonso at Glyndebourne, Strauss's Faninal at the Met and Germont in La Traviata for the Royal Opera, Covent Garden; appearances as Germont for San Diego Opera 2010, Sulpice in La Fille du régiment, Covent Garden 2012, Germont in La Traviata, Covent Garden 2014. *Recordings include:* Maria Stuarda by Donizetti, The Bear, Rape of Lucretia, Troilus and Cressida, Barber of Seville, Hugh the Drover, Balstrode in Peter Grimes (Grammy Award 1996), Tonio in Pagliacci, Marcello in La Bohème, Beckmesser in Meistersinger (Grammy Award 1997). *Current Management:* c/o Allied Artists, 42 Montpelier Square, London, SW7 1JZ, England. *Telephone:* (20) 7589-6243. *Fax:* (20) 7581-5269. *E-mail:* info@alliedartists.co.uk. *Website:* www.alliedartists.co.uk.

OPOLAIS, Kristīne; Latvian singer (soprano); b. 12 Nov. 1979, Rēzekne; m. Andris Nelsons 2011; one d. *Education:* Jāzeps Vītols Latvian Acad. of Music, studied with sopranos Regina Frinberga and Lilija Greidāne and vocal coach Margarita Gruzdeva, and with Margreet Honig at Sweelinck Conservatory, Amsterdam. *Career:* started career as mem. chorus with Latvian Nat. Opera 2001–03, soloist 2003–07, operatic stage debut as Musetta in La Bohème, Riga 2003; debut at Staatsoper Unter den Linden, Berlin, as title role in Tosca 2006; debut at Teatro alla Scala, Milan as Pauline in The Gambler 2008, at Wiener Staatsoper as Mimi in La Bohème 2008, at Bavarian State Opera as title role in Dvorak's Rusalka 2010, at Royal Opera, Covent Garden as Cio Cio San in Madama Butterfly 2011; debut at Metropolitan Opera, New York as Magda in La Rondine 2013; opera repertoire includes Puccini roles (Tosca, Musetta, Mimi, Butterfly, Magda), Tatyana in Eugene Onegin, Rusalka, Jenufa, Violetta in La traviata, Tamara in The Demon; has worked with leading conductors, including Daniel Barenboim, Riccardo Chailly, Antonio Pappano, Daniel Harding, Louis Langrée, Andris Nelsons, Gianandrea Noseda, Marco Armiliato, Marc Minkowski, Fabio Luisi, Kirill Petrenko, Alain Altinoglu and Kazushi Ono; concert repertoire includes Verdi's Requiem, Wagner's Wesendonck Lieder, Strauss' Vier letzte Lieder, and Mahler's 4th Symphony; concert performances have included appearances at Salzburg Festival, Tanglewood, BBC Proms, with orchestras including

Symphonieorchester des Bayerischen Rundfunks, WDR Sinfonieorchester Köln, Tonhalle Orchester Zürich, Stockholm Philharmonic and Filarmonica della Scala, Royal Danish Orchestra; regular guest with City of Birmingham Symphony Orchestra. *Recordings include:* Puccini: Suor Angelica 2012, Tchaikovsky: Eugene Onegin (with Orchestra and Chorus of the Comunitat Valenciana) 2013, Simon Boccanegro (recording from Vienna Konzerthaus conducted by Massimo Zanetti) 2013, Manon Lescaut (RoH recording with Jonas Kaufmann, conducted by Antonio Pappano) 2015. *Honours:* Paul Sakss Singers Award 2004, Latvian Annual Theatre Award for Best Opera Artist 2005, Latvian Cultural Foundation Award 2005, Latvian Great Music Award 2006, 2007. *Current Management:* c/o Alan Green, Zemsky Green Artists Management, 104 West 73rd Street, New York, NY 10023, USA. *Telephone:* (212) 579-6700. *E-mail:* agreen@zemskygreen.com. *Website:* www.zemskygreen.com; kristineopolais.com.

OPPENHEIM, Martha Kunkel, MusM; American pianist; b. 25 June 1935, Port Arthur, Tex.; d. of Samuel Adam Kunkel and Grace Kunkel (née Moncure); m. Russell Edward Oppenheim 1960; two d. *Education:* Univ. of Texas, Juilliard School of Music, New York and American Conservatory, Fontainebleau, France. *Career:* piano soloist, Amarillo Symphony, Austin Symphony, Univ. of Texas Orchestra, San Antonio Symphony and Dallas Symphony TX and Heilbronner Kammer Orchestra, Germany; recitals in Texas, New York and France; mem. Halcyon Trio 1974–77; Asst Teacher Univ. of Texas 1957–59, 1968–69; pvt. teacher 1962–; mem. Music Teachers Nat. Asscn, Texas Music Teachers Asscn, San Antonio Music Teachers Asscn; winner of numerous local, nat. and int. competitions. *Address:* 9118 East Valley View Lane, San Antonio, TX 78217, USA (home). *E-mail:* moppenheim@satx.rr.com (home).

OPPENS, Ursula, BA; American pianist; *Distinguished Professor, Brooklyn College Conservatory of Music and CUNY Graduate Center;* b. 2 Feb. 1944, New York. *Education:* Radcliffe Coll., Juilliard School with Rosina Lhevinne, Guido Agosti and Leonard Shure. *Career:* debut in New York 1969; performances with Boston Symphony, New York Philharmonic and other leading American orchestras; recitals at Tully Hall, Kennedy Center; appearances at Aspen, Berkshire and Marlboro Festivals; co-founder and soloist, Speculum Musicae 1971–; performances of contemporary music; engagements with the Chamber Music Soc. of Lincoln Center and the Group for Contemporary Music; composers who have written for her include Anthony Braxton, Anthony Davis, John Harbison, Julius Hemphill, Tania Leon, Gyorgy Ligeti, Witold Lutoslawski, Conlon Nancarrow, Tobias Picker, Frederic Rzeweski, Alvin Singleton, Joan Tower, Lois Vierk, Christian Wolff, Elliott Carter, Amnon Wolman and Charles Wuorinen; John Evans Distinguished Prof. of Music, Northwestern Univ. 1994–2008; Distinguished Prof., Brooklyn Coll. Conservatory of Music and CUNY Graduate Center 2008–. *Recordings include:* Busoni, Mozart and Rzewski, Carter, Pianos Works 2008, Rzewski: The People United Will Never Be Defeated! 2015. *Honours:* winner Busoni Int. Piano Competition 1969, Avery Fisher Prize 1976. *Current Management:* Colbert Artists Management, 111 West 57th Street, New York, NY 10019, USA. *Telephone:* (212) 757-0782. *Fax:* (212) 541-5179. *E-mail:* nycolbert@colbertartists.com. *Website:* www.colbertartists.com.

OPRISANU, Carmen; Romanian singer (mezzo-soprano); b. 1964, Brasov. *Education:* Cluj Music Academy. *Career:* sang with the Romanian Opera at Cluj, 1986–93, and gave concerts with the Bucharest Radio Symphony Orchestra and the Georges Enescu Philharmonic (tours of Italy and Spain); Bucharest State Opera 1993, as Carmen and Rosina; Lucerne Theatre 1993–96, as Carmen, Suzuki, Isabella in L'Italiana in Algeri, the Composer (Ariadne auf Naxos), Sesto in La Clemenza di Tito and Adalgisa; season 1995 as Isabella at the Deutsche Oper Berlin and Sigismondo in the German premiere of Rossini's opera, at Wildbad; Charlotte in Werther, Rosina and Maddalena with the Zürich Opera; Season 1997–98, Rosina in Covent Garden and Barcelona, Cenerentola at Hamburg, Pierotto in Linda di Chamonix with La Scala, in Zürich as Fenena in Nabucco and Hänsel; Season 1998–99, Carmen and Charlotte in Amsterdam and Charlotte in Madrid; Season 2000 as Orlofsky for Zürich Opera, Rossini's Isabella for New Israeli Opera and Dulcinée in Don Quichotte at the Opéra Bastille, Paris. *Recordings:* Title role in Sigismondo; Orlofsky in Fledermaus and Elisabetta in Maria Stuerda (Nightingale Classics). *Honours:* Prizewinner at the 1992 Vienna Belvedere Competition and the 1995 Placido Domingo Operalia Competition, in Madrid; Winner, Leonard Bernstein International Oratorio and Song Competition, Jerusalem, 1996. *Current Management:* Hilbert Artists Management, Maximilianstrasse 22, 80539 Munich, Germany. *Telephone:* (89) 2907470. *Fax:* (89) 29074790. *E-mail:* agentur@hilbert.de. *Website:* www.hilbert.de; www.carmenoprisanu.com.

ORAMO, Sakari Markus; Finnish conductor and violinist; *Chief Conductor, BBC Symphony Orchestra;* b. 26 Oct. 1965, Helsinki; m. Anu Komsi; two s. *Education:* Sibelius Acad., Utrecht Conservatoire. *Career:* Founder-mem. Avanti Chamber Orchestra 1982–89; violinist and concertmaster, Finnish Radio Symphony Orchestra 1991, Assoc. Prin. Conductor 1994–2003, Chief Conductor 2003–12; further engagements with major Scandinavian orchestras, City of Birmingham Symphony, BBC Symphony and Philharmonic, London Sinfonietta and Rotterdam Philharmonic; Danish Radio Symphony 1994–, tour of Australia; Music Dir City of Birmingham Symphony Orchestra (CBSO) 1997–2008, Prin. Guest Conductor 2008–, season 2003–04 included Artistic Directorship of CBSO's musical festival Floof; Chief Conductor and Artistic Advisor, Royal Stockholm Philharmonic Orchestra and West Coast

Kokkola Opera 2008–; Chief Conductor Designate, BBC Symphony Orchestra 2012–13, Chief Conductor 2013–; co-f., together with his wife, Annika Mylläri and Robert McLoud, West Coast Kokkola Opera 2004, currently Vice-Chair. and Prin. Conductor; guest conductor with NDR Hamburg, New York Philharmonic, Berlin Philharmonic, Orchestre de Paris, Chicago Symphony, Hessischer Rundfunk, Vienna Symphony. *Recordings include:* Foulds' Dynamic Triptych 2006, Nørgård Symphonies Nos 1 & 8 (Gramophone Award for Best Contemporary Recording 2015) 2014; numerous recordings with Royal Stockholm Philharmonic, City of Birmingham Symphony Orchestra and Finnish Radio Symphony Orchestra. *Honours:* Hon. DUniv (Univ. of Central England) 2004; Hon. OBE 2009; Elgar Medal 2008. *Current Management:* c/o Harrison Parrott Ltd, 5–6 Albion Court, London, W6 0QT, England. *Telephone:* (20) 7229-9166. *Fax:* (20) 7221-5042. *E-mail:* info@harrisonparrott.co.uk. *Website:* www.harrisonparrott.com.

ORBAN, György; Hungarian composer; b. 12 July 1947, Tirgu-Mures, Romania. *Education:* Cluj Conservatory. *Career:* teacher of theory, Cluj Conservatory –1979; moved to Hungary; Ed., Editio Musica Budapest; teacher of composition, Music Acad., Budapest. *Compositions:* orchestra: Five Canons to Poems by Attile Joszef for soprano and chamber ensemble 1977, Triple Sextet 1980, two Serenades 1984, 1985, four Duos with soprano and clarinet 1979, soprano and double bass 1987, soprano and violoncello 1989, soprano and violin 1992, Sonata Concertante for clarinet and piano 1987, Wind Quintet 1984, Brass Music for Quintet No. 1 1987, Sonata for bassoon and piano 1987, Sonata for violin 1970, three Sonatas for violin and piano 1989, 1991, three Suites for piano 1986, 1997, 1998, four Piano Sonatas 1987, 1988, 1989; chorus and orchestra: Rorarte Coeli (oratorio) 1992, Regina Martyrum (oratorio) 1993, Missa No. 2 1990, No. 4 1991, No. 10 1993, Requiem 2003; chorus and chamber ensemble: Missa No. 7 1993, Flower Songs for female choir 1978, Chorus Book in Memory of S. A. No. 1 1984, Chorus Book No. 2, Book of Medallions (cycle of nine choruses) 1987, Stabat Mater 1987, Passion (oratorio) 1997, Christmas Oratorio 1998, Sketches from Verona for orchestra 1998, three string quartets 1994, 1994, 1998, about 40 Latin motets for mixed and female chorus; operas: Pikkó hertzeg 2000, Büvölet 2004. *Address:* 1016 Budapest, Mészáros u. 15–17 (office); 1121 Budapest, Adorján út 4, Hungary (home). *Telephone:* (1) 246-3136 (home).

ORBE, Javier Logioia; Argentine conductor; *Artistic and Music Director, Orquesta Filarmónica de Montevideo (Montevideo Philharmonic Orchestra).* *Education:* Conservatorio Nacional de Música, Instituto Superior de Arte del Teatro Colón, Buenos Aires, Inter-American Music Council, Washington, Vienna School of Music. *Career:* Principal Guest Conductor, Opera de Rio de Janeiro 2002–; has been Chief Conductor of National University of Cuyo Orchestra, Teatro Colón Philharmonic Orchestra, Estable del Teatro Argentino de La Plata, Córdoba Symphony Orchestra, Rosario Symphony Orchestra, Universidad de Concepción Orchestra, Chile; currently Artistic and Music Director, Orquesta Filarmónica de Montevideo (Montevideo Philharmonic Orchestra); has directed Ballet Company of Teatro Colón, Teatro Argentino, Southern Ballet Theatre of Warsaw, Bolshoi, Kirov, Prague, Black Swan, American Ballet, Royal Ballet of London. *Address:* Orquesta Filarmónica de Montevideo, Montevideo, Uruguay (office). *Telephone:* 19508145 (office); 19508147 (office). *E-mail:* filarmonica@filarmonica .org.uy (office). *Website:* www.filarmonica.org.uy (office).

ORCIANI, Patrizia; Italian singer (soprano); b. 1959, Fano, Urbino. *Education:* Bologna Conservatory. *Career:* debut as Fano 1983 as Mimi in La Bohème; has sung widely in Italy notably as Liu at the 1991 Verona Festival and as Handel's Cleopatra at the Valle d'Istria Festival; sang at the Bonn Opera, 1991–92; other roles include Donizetti's Adina and Norina, Rossini's Elvira, Micaela and Giulietta in Les Contes d'Hoffmann; season 1998 as Lucieta in Wolf Ferrari's Il campiello at Bologna and Venus in Tannhäuser at Palermo. *Recordings include:* Cimarosa's L'Italiana in Londra; Nina by Paisiello; Il Signor Bruschino. *Current Management:* Atelier Musicale, Via Caselle 76, San Lazzaro di Savena 40068, Italy. *Telephone:* (51) 19984444. *Fax:* (51) 19984420. *E-mail:* info@ateliermusicale.com. *Website:* www .ateliermusicale.com.

ORDONEZ, Antonio; Spanish singer (tenor); b. 27 Oct. 1948, Madrid. *Education:* studied in Madrid with Miguel Garcia Barrosa. *Career:* concert appearances in Spain and USA from 1980; opera debut at Teatro Zarzuela, Madrid 1982, as Pinkerton; sang Don Carlos at Liège 1986 and at Deutsche Oper Berlin 1988; Teatro Liceo Barcelona 1986, in Pacini's Saffo; further guest appearances as Cavaradossi at Dallas 1987, Calaf at Ravenna Festival 1988 and as Alvaro in La Forza del Destino at Washington 1989; San Francisco Opera 1991 as Foresto in Attila; other roles include Rodolfo, Deutsche Oper 1989, Alfredo, Riccardo, Gabriele Adorno and Edgardo in Lucia di Lammermoor, Liège 1987; sang Don José in Carmen at Earl's Court, London 1991.

ORE, Cecilie; Norwegian composer; b. 19 July 1954, Oslo. *Education:* Norwegian State Acad. of Music, studied in Paris, with Ton de Leeuw at Sweelinck Conservatory, Amsterdam, Inst. of Sonology in Utrecht. *Career:* frequent performances at Nordic and int. festivals; commissioned by BBC Symphony Orchestra; mem. Soc. of Norwegian Composers. *Compositions include:* orchestral music: Porphyre 1986 (Composer of the Year, Norwegian Soc. of Composers 1988), Nunc et Nunc 1994; chamber music: Helices for wind quintet 1984, Preasems Subitus for string quartet 1989, Erat Erit Est for ensemble 1991, Futurum exactum for string ensemble 1992, Lex Temporis for string quartet 1992, Ictus for six percussionists 1997, Semper Semper for

saxophone quartet 1998, Nunquam Non for ensemble 1999, Non Nunquam for string trio 1999, Cirrus for string quartet 2002, Cumulus for wind trio 2002, Schwirren for vocal ensemble 2003, Music drama: A – A Shadow Opera 2001, Dead Beat Escapement 2008, Adam & Eve – A Divine Comedy 2012, Come to the Edge! 2013, Dead Pope on Trial 2016. *Honours:* First and Second Prizes, Int. Rostrum for Electro-acoustic Music 1988, Arne Nordheim Prize 2004, Lindeman Prize 2015. *Address:* Ullevålsvn 61 B, 0171 Oslo, Norway. *Website:* www.cecilieore.no.

O'REGAN, Tarik, BA, MPhil, MA; British composer and broadcaster; b. 1 Jan. 1978, London, England. *Education:* Univs of Oxford and Cambridge. *Career:* fmr Composer-in-Residence, Corpus Christi Coll., Cambridge; Fellow Commoner in Creative Arts, Trinity Coll. 2007–12, Cambridge; compositions have been performed by BBC Symphony Orchestra, London Sinfonietta, BBC Singers, Los Angeles Master Chorale; based in New York and UK. *Compositions:* for chorus a cappella or chorus and one instrument: Agnus Dei 2001, Magnificat & Nunc Dimittis 2001, Cantate Domino, Corpus Christi Service 2001, Sequence for St Wulfstan 2003, Alleliua, laus et gloria 2004, Bring Rest, Sweet Dreaming Child 2004, De Sancto Ioanne Baptista 2004, Dorchester Canticles 2004, Gloria 2004, I Sleep, but My Heart Waketh, Lamentation 2005, Scattered Rhymes, We Remember Them 2005, The Windows 2005; for chorus and orchestra/ensemble: The Ecstasies Above, Threnody 2004, And There Was A Great Calm 2005, Triptych 2005; for solo voice and up to six players: The Tongue of Epigrams 1998, The Appointment 1999, Sainte 2002, Three Andrew Motion Settings 2005; for solo keyboards: Colimaçon for organ 1999, Three Piano Miniatures for piano 1999, Textures for organ 2004, Lines of Desire for piano 2005; for two to six players: Clichés 2000, Lexington 767 2002, Fragment for string quartet 2005, Fragments from a Gradual Process; for orchestra: Hudson Lullaby 2004, The Pure Good of Theory 2004. *Honours:* Columbia Univ. Fulbright Chester Schirmer Fellowship in Music Composition, Harvard Univ. Radcliffe Inst. Fellowship, Vocal Award, British Composer Awards 2005, Liturgical Award 2007. *Current Management:* c/o Jenny Wegg, Chester Novello & Co., 14–15 Berners Street, London, W1T 3LJ, England. *Telephone:* (20) 7612-7400. *Fax:* (20) 7612-7545 (office). *E-mail:* jenny.wegg@musicsales.co.uk. *Website:* www.musicsalesclassical.com; www .tarikoregan.com.

O'REILLY, Brendan; Irish violinist; b. 1935, Dublin. *Education:* Belvedere Coll., Dublin, Royal Acad. of Music with David Martin, studied with Andre Gertler in Brussels. *Career:* played with the Radio Eireann String Quartet in Cork, then freelancer with the Royal Philharmonic and the English Chamber Orchestra; co-founder, Gabrieli Quartet 1967, touring Europe, North America, the Far East and Australia; festival engagements in the UK, including Aldeburgh, City of London and Cheltenham; concerts every season in London, participation in the Barbican Centre's Mostly Mozart Festival; Artist-in-Residence, Univ. of Essex from 1971; has co-premiered works by William Alwyn, Britten, Alan Bush, Daniel Jones and Gordon Crosse, 3rd Quartet of John McCabe 1979, 2nd Quartets of Nicholas Maw and Panufnik 1983–80; British premiere of the Piano Quintet by Sibelius 1990. *Recordings include:* early pieces by Britten, Dohnányi's Piano Quintet with Wolfgang Manz, Walton's Quartets and the Sibelius Quartet and Quintet, with Anthony Goldstone.

O'REILLY, Graham Henry Meredith, BA, DipEd, LTCL, AMusA; Australian singer, conductor and musicologist; *Director, Ensemble William Byrd;* b. 4 Sept. 1947, Parkes, NSW; s. of Oscar Meredith O'Reilly and Winifred Lillian Jean Macfadyen; m. 1st Jill Barralet 1972 (divorced); one s. one d.; m. 2nd Brigitte Vinson 1986; two d. *Education:* Univ. of Sydney, Sydney Conservatorium of Music, Trinity Coll. of Music, London, UK. *Career:* debut with Messiah at Sydney Town Hall 1971; music teacher in Sydney 1970–73; concert and session singer, London 1973–82; dir for early music ensembles 1976–; Dir The Restoration Musick 1980–81, Psallite 1981–86, Ensemble William Byrd 1983–, Ensemble Vocal de Pontoise 1999–; singing teacher 1980–93; mem. Groupe Vocal de France 1982–86; solo oratorio and ensemble singer, specializing in early music; dir of workshops and masterclasses in early vocal music in UK, France, Portugal, Sweden and elsewhere; researcher of late Restoration stage music 1973–, pitch, voicing and tuning in Renaissance vocal music 1979–, Allegri Miserere and vocal practice in Sistine Chapel 2001–. *Recordings:* with Psallite: Music by Tallis, Byrd and Gibbons and Collected Works of Jon Dixon; with Groupe Vocal de France: Sacred Music of Giacinto Scelsi; with Ensemble William Byrd: English Music of the Seventeenth Century, Vol. 1: Orlando Gibbons, Vol. 2: Welcome Vicegerent, music of Henry Purcell; Palestrina: Canticum Canticorum; Handel: Music for Cannons, Vol. 1; three Chandos anthems; Handel: Dixit Dominus, Nisi Dominus; Music for San Marco (Monteverdi, Gabrieli), Domenico Scarlatti: Musica Sacra (Stabat Mater a 10, Missa Brevis etc.); Miserere (Allegri/Bai, F. Scarlatti, Leo); The Last Judgement, Marc-Antoine Charpentier; sacred music by João Rodrigues Esteves; Polish Baroque Music; Carissimi and Music in Rome in 1640; The Secret Garden – Music by Thomas Tallis. *Publications:* Music to Macbeth 1978, Allegri's Miserere in the Sistine Chapel 2016; article on the Allegri Miserere in journal Early Music 2016. *Honours:* Frank Busby Musical Scholarship, Univ. of Sydney 1967; three Chocs du Monde de la Musique, two Orphées d'Or de l' Acad. du disque lyrique, two Diapasons d'Or, Premio Internazionale del Disco Antonio Vivaldi (Italy), one Disc of the Month, one "definitive version" from the BBC etc. *Address:* 10 rue Massenet, 93600 Aulnay-Sous-Bois, France. *E-mail:* grabyrdy@gmail.com. *Website:* www .ensemblewilliambyrd.com.

ORGONASOVA, Luba; Slovak singer (soprano); b. 22 Jan. 1961, Bratislava. *Education:* Bratislava Conservatory. *Career:* concert and operatic engagements in Czechoslovakia 1979–83; Hagen Opera, West Germany, 1983–88 as Mozart's Ilia and Pamina, Gilda and Violetta, Lauretta and Sophie in Der Rosenkavalier; guest appearances in Nuremberg, Essen, Hamburg and Zürich; Vienna Volksoper 1988–89; Sang Pamina and Donna Anna at Aix-en-Provence Festival, 1988–89; Opéra de Lyon 1988 as Madame Silberklang in Der Schauspieldirektor; sang Constanze at Deutsche Oper Berlin and in Lisbon 1991, with concert performances of Die Entführung under John Eliot Gardiner in London and Amsterdam; other roles include Susanna, Atalanta in Handel's Serse, Marzelline, Cendrillon and Antonia, Les Contes d'Hoffmann; Sang Donna Anna at Chicago, 1995; season 1999–2000 as Donna Anna at the Opéra Bastille, Gluck's Euridice at Zürich and Elettra in Idomeneo at Salzburg; concert repertoire includes Janáček's Glagoltic Mass, Bruckner's Te Deum and the Missa Solemnis, all at Zürich, Haydn's Harmonie Mass at Bremen and Oratorios by Bach, Handel and Dvořák. *Recordings:* Die Zauberflöte. *Current Management:* Hilbert Artists Management, Maximilianstrasse 22, 80539 Munich, Germany; Opéra et Concert, 37 rue de la Chausée d'Antin, 75009 Paris, France. *Telephone:* (89) 2907470 (Germany); (1) 42-96-18-18 (France). *Fax:* (89) 29074790 (Germany); (1) 42-96-18-00 (France). *E-mail:* agentur@hilbert.de; agence@opera-concert.com. *Website:* www.hilbert.de; www.opera-concert.com.

ORKIS, Lambert Thomas, BM, MM; American pianist and educator; b. 20 April 1946, Philadelphia, PA; m. Janice Barbara Kretschmann 1972. *Education:* Curtis Institute of Music, Temple Univ. *Career:* world-wide performances; premiered solo works of George Crumb, Richard Wernick, Maurice Wright and James Primosch, including Wernick's Piano Concerto, Washington, DC and Carnegie Hall, New York, with National Symphony Orchestra, conducted by Mstislav Rostropovich 1991; recitals with cellist Mstislav Rostropovich 1981–, with violinist Anne-Sophie Mutter 1988–, with soprano Arleen Augér 1987–90, with soprano Lucy Shelton 1981–, with cellist Han-Na Chang 2001, with violinist Julian Rachlin 2000; founding mem., fortepianist, Castle Trio 1988–; pianist, Smithsonian Chamber Music Soc. 1983–; Honoured Artist, New Aspect International Arts Festival, Taipei, Taiwan 1996; pianist, Library of Congress Summer Chamber Festival 1986–89, American Chamber Players 1986–89, 20th Century Consort 1976–87; soloist with National Symphony Orchestra, Great Performances (PBS) 1983; soloist-in-residence 1983; principal keyboard, National Symphony Orchestra, Washington, DC 1982–; Faculty mem., Temple Univ., Philadelphia; Prof. of Piano, Co-ordinator of Master of Music programme in piano accompanying and Chamber Music 1968–; soloist, National Symphony Orchestra Piano 2000 Festival; trios with Anne-Sophie Mutter and Lynn Harrell 2001–2002; pianist, Bay Chamber Concerts Summer Music Festival 2002–, Kennedy Center Chamber Players 2003–; judge at Carnegie Hall Int. American Music Competition for Pianists 1985, Kennedy Center Friedheim Awards 1991, Trondheim Int. Chamber Music Competition 2003. *Recordings:* solo: Music of Louis Moreau Gottschalk, 1988; Schubert Impromptus, 1990; Schubert Moment Musicaux and 3 Klavierstücke, 1993; George Crumb, A Little Suite for Christmas, Richard Wernick, Sonata for Piano, 1986; Richard Wernick, Piano Concerto, with Symphony II, composer conducting, 1998; with Anne-Sophie Mutter: Berlin Recital, 1996, Beethoven Cycle of 10 Sonatas for Piano and Violin, 1998; Bartók Sonata No. 2, 1998; with Anner Bylsma: Works by Franchomme and Chopin, 1994, works by Brahms and Schumann, 1995; with Arleen Augér: Schubert Lieder, 1991; with Castle Trio: Beethoven Cycle of Piano Trios, 1989–92; Recital 2000, 2000; A Life With Beethoven (DVD), 2000; The Complete Violin Sonatas (DVD), 2001; Tango, Song and Dance, 2003; Keys to the Future, works of Richard Wernick and James Primosch, 2003. *Publications:* A Journey Back to Beethoven (article) 1998. *Honours:* Grammy Award, Best Chamber Music Performance 1999, Best Classical Album 1999, National Public Radio Critic's Choice Award 1999, Temple University Faculty Award for Creative Achievement 1982. *Address:* PO Box 6023, Arlington, VA 22206-0023, USA. *Telephone:* (703) 998-0791. *Fax:* (703) 998-6531. *E-mail:* orkispiano@lambertorkis.com. *Website:* www.lambertorkis.com.

ORLANDI MALASPINA, Rita; Italian singer (soprano); b. 28 Dec. 1937, Bologna; m. Massimiliano Malaspina. *Education:* studied with Carmen Melis in Milan. *Career:* debut at Teatro Nuovo Milan 1963 as Verdi's Giovanna d'Arco; sang widely in Italy, and at Covent Garden, London, Munich, Hamburg, Paris, Nice, Barcelona, Vienna and Buenos Aires; Metropolitan Opera debut 1968; other roles include Puccini's Tosca and Suor Angelica, Wagner's Elsa, Giordano's Maddalena and Verdi's Aida, Odabella, Leonora, Amelia, Abigaille, Desdemona, Luisa Miller, Elisabeth and Lucrezia (I Due Foscari); also heard in concert.

ORLOFF, Claudine, DipMus; Belgian pianist; b. 6 Jan. 1961, Brussels; m. Burkard Spinnier 1983, two s. *Education:* Conservatoire Royal de Musique, Brussels with J. C. Vanden Eunden and A. Siwy, studied with B. Lemmens. *Career:* recording for RTB 1978; regular appearances as soloist and in chamber music; often includes contemporary works in recital programmes, including Van Rossum's 12 preludes 1986; many concerts on two pianos (with Bukard Spinnier), Belgium, France, Germany, including Musique en Sorbonne, Paris 1991; radio engagement, Hommage a Milhaud (live, RTB Brussels) 1992. *Honours:* Ella Olin Prize, Brussels 1985. *Address:* c/o Conservatoire Royale de Musique, 30 rue de la Régence, 1000 Brussels, Belgium.

ORLOWSKY, David; German musician (clarinet); b. 1981, Tübingen. *Education:* Folkwang Hochschule Essen, studied with Manfred Lindner, Manhattan School of Music, with Charles Neidich and Ayako Oshima. *Career:* has appeared as soloist and with his trio (f. aged 16) at numerous festivals and venues, including Schleswig-Holstein Music Festival, Rheingau Music Festival, Beethovenfest, Lucerne Festival, Gidon Kremer's Lockenhaus Chamber Music Festival, Moritzburg Festival, also at Concertgebouw Amsterdam, Stiftung Mozarteum Salzburg, Berlin Konzerthaus, Leipzig Gewandhaus; collaborations with Danish String Quartet, pianist Igor Levit, mandolinist Avi Avital; as chamber musician has collaborated regularly with performers such as Daniel Hope, Andreas Haefliger, Vilde Frang, Fauré Quartet, Nils Moenkemeyer, vocal sextet Singur Pur, Vogler Quartet. *Recordings include:* with David Orlowsky Trio: Noema (ECHO Klassik Award ohne Grenzen 2008) 2007, Nessiah 2008, Klezmer Kings – A Tribute (ECHO Klassik Award 2015) 2014, Chronos 2015; other: with Singur Pur sextet: Jeremiah (ECHO Klassik Award ohne Grenzen 2011) 2010; with Vogler Quartet: Mozart and Golijov 2011. *Current Management:* Opus 3 Artists, Pariser Strasse 62, 10719 Berlin, Germany. *Telephone:* (30) 88910151. *Fax:* (30) 88910152. *E-mail:* sgrevesmuhl@opus3artists.com. *Website:* www.opus3artists.com; www.davidorlowskytrio.com.

ORMAI, Gábor; Hungarian violist; b. 1950. *Education:* Franz Liszt Acad., Budapest with Andras Mihaly, studied with the Amadeus Quartet and Zoltán Szekely. *Career:* founder mem., Takacs Quartet 1975; many concert appearances in Europe and the USA; tours of Australia, New Zealand, Japan, South America, England, Norway, Sweden, Greece, Belgium and Ireland; Bartók Cycle for the Bartók-Solti Festival at South Bank, London 1990; Great Performers series at Lincoln Center and Mostly Mozart Festival at Alice Tully Hall, New York; visits to Japan 1989, 1992; Mozart Festivals at South Bank, Wigmore Hall and Barbican Centre 1991; Bartók Cycle at the Théâtre des Champs Elysées 1991; Beethoven Cycles at the Zürich Tonhalle in Dublin, at the Wigmore Hall and in Paris 1991–92; Resident, Univ. of Colorado, London Barbican 1988–91; masterclasses at the Guildhall School of Music; plays Amati instrument made for the French royal family and loaned by the Corcoran Gallery, Gallery of Art, Washington, DC. *Recordings:* Schumann Quartets Op 41, Mozart String Quintets (with Denes Koromzay), Bartók 6 Quartets, Schubert Trout Quintet (with Zoltán Kocsis) Hungaroton; Haydn Op 76, Brahms Op 51, Nos 1 and 2, Chausson Concerto (with Joshua Bell and Jean-Yves Thibaudet); works by Schubert, Mozart, Dvořák and Bartók. *Honours:* winner Int. Quartet Competition, Evian 1977, winner Portsmouth Int. Quartet Competition 1979.

OROZCO-ESTRADA, Andrés; Colombian conductor; *Principal Conductor, Tonkünstler Orchestra of Lower Austria*; b. Dec. 1977, Medellín. *Education:* Vienna Music Acad. *Career:* Prin. Conductor Tonkünstler Orchestra of Lower Austria 2009–; Prin. Conductor Orquesta Sinfónica de Euskadi (Basque Nat. Orchestra) 2009–13; Music Dir designate, Houston Symphony Orchestra 2013–14, Music Dir 2014–(19); numerous other engagements as conductor, including Vienna Philharmonic, Munich Philharmonic, Leipzig Gewandhaus Orchestra, City of Birmingham Symphony Orchestra, Orchestre Nat. de France, Vienna Symphony Orchestra, Bamberg Symphony Orchestra, Deutsches Symphonie Orchester Berlin, Swedish Radio Symphony Orchestra, Frankfurt Radio Symphony Orchestra. *Recordings include:* albums: with Tonkünstler Orchestra: Mahler, Symphony No. 1 2009, Mendelssohn Bartholdy, Symphony No. 2 'Lobgesang' 2010, works by Muthspiel, Resch and Eröd 2011, Berlioz, Symphonie fantastique 2013. *Current Management:* c/o Nicholas Mathias, IMG Artists, The Light Box, 111 Power Road, London, W4 5PY, England. *Telephone:* (20) 7957-5800. *Fax:* (20) 7957-5801. *E-mail:* nmathias@imgartists.com; napollonov@imgartists.com. *Website:* www.imgartists.com. *Current Management:* Anna Studer, Künstleragentur Dr Raab & Dr Böhm GmbH, Plankengasse 7, 1010 Vienna, Austria. *Telephone:* (1) 512-05-0126. *Fax:* (1) 512-77-43. *E-mail:* studer@rbartists.at. *Website:* www.rbartists.at; orozcoestrada.com.

ORREGO-SALAS, Juan A., BA, MA; Chilean composer, academic and architect; *Professor Emeritus, Indiana University*; b. 18 Jan. 1919, Santiago; m. Carmen Benavente 1943; four s. one d. *Education:* State Univ. of Chile, Catholic Univ. of Chile, Univ. of Columbia, Princeton Univ., USA. *Career:* Conductor, Catholic Univ. Choir 1938–44; Prof. of Musicology, Faculty of Music, State Univ. of Chile 1942–61; Ed., Revista Musical Chilena 1949–53; Music Critic, El Mercurio 1950–61; Dir, Instituto de Extension Musical, Chile 1957–59; Chair. Music Dept, Catholic Univ., Chile 1951–61; Prof. of Music and Dir of Latin American Music Centre, Indiana Univ., USA 1961–87, Prof. Emer. 1987–; mem. Chilean Acad. of Fine Arts 1977–. *Compositions include:* orchestral: Variaciones serenas for strings 1971, Volte for chamber orchestra 1971, Symphony No. 4 1966, Violin Concerto 1983, Second Piano Concerto 1985, Cello Concerto 1992, Symphony No. 5 1995, Sinfonia in One Movement 1997, Fantasias for cello and orchestra 2000, Concerto Grosso 2002; chamber music: Trio No. 2 1977, Presencias 1972, Tangos 1982, Balada for cello and piano 1983, Partita 1988, two string quartets 1957, 1996, Piano Quintet 1997, Introduction and Allegro Concertante for one piano, four hands and chamber orchestra 1999, Secuencias for saxophone and percussion 2001, String Quartets Nos 3 and 4 2003; vocal music: Missa in tempore discordae 1969, The Days of God 1974–76, Bolivar for narrator, chorus and orchestra 1982, The Celestial City 1992; stage music: The Tumbler's Prayer (ballet) 1960, Widows (opera) 1989. *Publications include:* Music of the Americas (co-ed.) 1967, Encyclopedia Americana 1970, Latin American Literary Review 1975,

Encuentros, visiones y repasos 2005, Testimonios y Fantasias 2012; contrib. to Musical Quarterly, Tempo, Revista Musical. *Honours:* Dr hc (Catholic Univ., Chile) 1998; Nat. Prize for the Arts, Chile 1992. *Address:* 490 S Serena Lane, Bloomington, IN 47401, USA (home). *Telephone:* (812) 336-6005 (home). *E-mail:* jucar@ciswired.com (home).

ORSANIC, Vlatka; Croatian singer (soprano); *Professor of Singing, Academy of Music, Zagreb*; b. 29 Jan. 1958, Zabok; m. Igor Antic. *Education:* Acad. of Music, Ljubljana, Slovenia, advanced study at Kms Olivera Miljakovic, Vienna, Austria. *Career:* sang at Ljubljana Opera from 1979, as Lucia, Gilda, Elvira in I Puritani, Adina, Violetta, Queen of the night and Rossini's Rosina; at Belgrade as Lucia 1981, and guest appearances in all opera theatres in Yugoslavia; Salzbur Opera 1990–92, as Despina, Tamiri (Il re pastore), Euridice, Bastienne (Tokyo, Osaka); Semperoper Dresden as Mila (Osud) 1991; Darmstadt Opera from 1992, as Jenůfa, Rosalinde, Mimi, Mozart's Vitellia and Donna Anna, Tatiana and Traviata; Maggio Musicale Fiorentino Music Festival, Florence (Jenůfa, conducted by Semyon Bychkov, directed by Liliana Cavani) 1993; Essen 1995, as Shostakovich's Lady Macbeth 1996, Rusalka 2000, Jenůfa and Tosca; Katya Kabanova at Darmstadt 1996; Vienna Konzerthaus in War and Peace, Janáček's Mr Brouček and Schumann's Genoveva; concerts under conductor Michael Gielen at Berlin (Philharmonie, Konzerthaus), at Summer Festival in Salzburg, at Edinburgh Festival, in Frankfurt (Alte Oper), Köln (Philharmonie), Paris (Radio France, Théâtre du Châtelet); Wiener Festwochen, Konzerthaus: S. Prokofiev: War and Peace (Natasha), conductor Pinchas Steinberg; Verdi's Lady Macbeth, Komische Oper, Berlin 1997, as Ariadne 1998; as Mozart's Elettra at Salzburg Festspielhaus and as Verdi's Leonora (Trovatore) in Bonn; sang Shostakovich's Lady Macbeth at Meiningen 1999 and Verdi's at Leipzig, Verdis's Lady at Innsbruck 2001, Shostakovich's Lady Macbeth at Bremen 2002 and Zagreb 2004; Verdi's Abigaile 2000, Gounod's Marguerite 2003, Puccini's Tosca and Madama Butterfly 2004, Giodano's Andrea Chénier at Ljubljana 2005, Purcell's Dido in Zagreb 2008 and Ljubljana 2012, Princess in Rusalka 2011, Maddalena in Rigoletto 2013, Menotti's Miss Todd 2014, Herodias (Salome) in Ljubljana 2015; worked with directors including Joachim Herz, John Cox, Thomas Schulte-Michels, Liliana Cavani, Pet Halmen, Christine Mielitz, Andreas Homoki and Harry Kupfer and conductors Michael Gielen, Semyon Bychkov, Pinchas Steinberg, Heinz Holliger, Michael Schönwandt, Daniel Harding, Kiril Petrenko, Diter Rossberg, Tomaš Hanus, Rafael Frübeck de Burgos and Wladimir Jurowski; Several recitals with slovenian and croatian pianists; mem. Slovenian Nat. Opera, Ljubljana; Prof. of Singing, Acad. of Music, Zagreb 2003–, Head of Dept 2007–; Prof. of Singing, Acad. of Music, Ljubljana 2006–10. *Recordings:* A. Zemlinsky: Lyrische Symphonie, A. Berg: Altenberglieder 1994, Ludwig van Beethoven: Symphonie Nr 9 1994, B. A. Zimmermann: Requiem für einen jungen Dichter 1995, G. F. Händel: Neun deutsche Arien 2000, Vječni Orfej Varazdina 2012. *Honours:* Student's Highest Slovenian Cultural Award F. Prešeren 1977, First Prize, Int. Mario del Monaco Competition, Udine (Italy) 1979, Second Prize, Int. Competition, Ostend 1980, Croatian Award 'Marijana Radev' for Best Opera Role (Katerina Izmajlova), Zagreb 2004, Highest Croatian Cultural Award 'Milka Trnina' 2007, Annual Award for Best Pedagogic Achievement in Croatia 2011, Slovenian Award for Achievements in Opera-Theatre 'Samo Smerkolj' 2012, Slovenian Award for Cultural Achievements 'Julij Betetto' 2012, Sergije Rainis for the Contribution to the Vocal Art. *Address:* Muzička akademija, Gundulićeva 6, 10000 Zagreb, Croatia (office); Upančičeva 1, 1000 Ljubljana, Slovenia (home). *Telephone:* (1) 4810200 (office). *Fax:* (1) 8343759 (home). *E-mail:* vlatka.orsanic@gmail.com (home). *Website:* www.muza.hr (office).

ORTH, Norbert; German singer (tenor); b. 1939, Dortmund. *Education:* studied in Hamburg and Cologne, Dortmund Opera House School. *Career:* sang in Enschede, The Netherlands, then at opera houses in Düsseldorf, Nuremburg, Munich, Paris, Berlin and Stuttgart; Metropolitan Opera 1979, as Pedrillo in Die Entführung; Augsburg 1981, as Max in Der Freischütz; appearances at the Salzburg and Bayreuth Festivals; Loge in Das Rheingold 1984; sang Walther in Die Meistersinger at Hanover 1986; sang Tannhaüser at Kassel 1988, Lohengrin at Hanover and Wiesbaden; Walther in Die Meistersinger at the rebuilt Essen Opera 1988; Théâtre du Châtelet, Paris 1990, as Walther; season 1992 as Berg's Alwa at Dresden and Parsifal at Turin; also heard in the concert hall as lieder and oratorio singer. *Recordings:* Die Entführung; Schubert's Die Freunde von Salamanka; Augustin Moser in Die Meistersinger, Bayreuth 1974.

ORTIZ, Cristina; Brazilian pianist; b. 17 April 1950, Bahia; d. of Silverio M. Ortiz and Moema F. Ortiz; m. Jasper W. Parrott 1974; two d. *Education:* Conservatório Brasileiro de Música, Rio de Janeiro, Académie Internationale de Piano (with Magda Tagliaferro), France, Curtis Inst. of Music, (with Rudolf Serkin), USA. *Career:* New York recital debut 1971; London debut with LSO and André Previn 1973; has appeared in concerts with the Vienna Philharmonic, Berlin Philharmonic, the Concertgebouw, Chicago Symphony, New York Philharmonic, Israel Philharmonic, Los Angeles Philharmonic, leading British orchestras and has undertaken many tours of North and South America, the Far East, New Zealand and Japan; appeared with NHK Symphony, the Bergen Philharmonic and Philharmonia under Janowski 1997; played with conductors including Previn, Mehta, Kondrashin, Ashkenazy, Leinsdorf, Chailly, Masur, Salonen, Colin Davis, Janssons, Fedoseyev, Zinman, Rattle, Järvi and Fürst. *Honours:* First Prize, Van Cliburn Int. Competition, Texas 1969. *E-mail:* cristina.ortiz.name@gmail.com. *Website:* www.cristina.ortiz.name.

ORTIZ, Francisco; Spanish singer (tenor); b. 1948. *Education:* studied in Barcelona and Madrid. *Career:* debut in Barcelona 1973, as Foresto in Attila; further appearances as Foresto in London, Paris 1974, Madrid and Venice 1976, Toulouse 1979; New York City Opera 1973, as Turiddu, Nice 1974, as Radames, Geneva 1975, as Puccini's Des Grieux; sang Pollione in Norma at Amsterdam, Barcelona and Vienna 1978–80; Théâtre de la Monnaie Brussels 1981 as Cavaradossi, Sydney Opera 1982 as Manrico; further engagements at Hamburg, Santiago, Ernani 1979, Paris, Rio de Janeiro and the Vienna Staatsoper, Alvaro in La Forza del Destino; appeared with Canadian Opera Co. at Toronto as Pollione 1991; performances in Zarzuela and as concert artist.

ORTIZ, William, BM MA, PhD; Puerto Rican composer and academic; *Professor of Music and Humanities, University of Puerto Rico at Bayamón*; b. 30 March 1947, Salinas, Puerto Rico; s. of William Ortiz and Guillermina Alvarado Ortiz; m. Candida Rodríguez 1968; three d. *Education:* Puerto Rico Conservatory of Music, State Univ. of New York at Stony Brook, State Univ. of New York at Buffalo. *Career:* Guest Composer, Latin American Music Festival, Caracas, Venezuela 1991–2008; Premiered Composer, Casals Festival 1995; Composer-in-Residence, Atlantic Center for the Arts; Prof. of Music and Humanities, Univ. of Puerto Rico at Bayamón, also Dir Univ. Concert Band; Prof. of Music and Humanities, Conservatory of Music of Puerto Rico; Music Dir Ateneo Puertorriqueño 2005–; music critic, San Juan Star; mem. American Music Center, Coll. Music Soc.; contrib. to Musical Culture of Puerto Rico, Univ. of Puerto Rico at Bayamón 2012–13. *Compositions:* more than 140 compositions for various instruments, including Garabato, A Sensitive Mambo in Transformation, Trio Concertante en Tres Realidades, Loaisai, Nueva York Tropical, String Quartets No. 1 1976, String Quartet No. 2 1987, Graffiti Nuvorican 1988, Suspensión de Soledad en tres tiempos 1990, Caribe Urbano 1990, Rican (street opera) 1991, Unknown Poets from the Full-Time Jungle for soprano and piano 1992, Cantilena for guitar 1996, Fotografia de Héctor for guitar 1997, Tropicalización 1999, Montage para un Sueño en Mi for orchestra 2001, Esta es la tierra de los que aguantan callados y pacientes por un nuevo despertar (guitar concerto) 2001, Elogio a la Plena for band 2002, Cantos de la Calle 2003, Rito Ceremonial of the Church of the Spanglish Nación 2004, Ciudad en tropical jubilation (piano concerto) 2004, Música con Calle (percussion concerto) 2006, Songs of Coconut 2009, Araguaco Coabey 2009, Tránsito 2010, Mamerto (Zarzuela) 2010, Contrabando 2012, 2nd Avenue Jangueo 2013, Cartas por Deseno 2014, Trilogía Jabao 2014. *Publications include:* contrib. to Resonancias 2006, Perspectives on New Music, World Music Magazine, Musiké (Conservatory of Music Puerto Rico). *Honours:* Felipe Gutiérrez Espinosa Int. Composition Award 1980, Ateneo Puertorriqueño Music Composition Prize 1989, CAP Grant Award, American Music Center 2007, UNESCO Cultural Recognition, Puerto Rico 2015. *Address:* University of Puerto Rico at Bayamón, Bayamón, 00958 Puerto Rico (office). *Telephone:* (787) 779-2610 (home); (787) 993-0000 (office). *Fax:* (787) 993-8868 (office). *E-mail:* williamortizupr@yahoo.com (office). *Website:* www.williamortiz.com.

ORVAL, Francis, DipMus; American (b. Belgian) horn player and professor of music; *President, Concerts de Midi de la Ville de Liège*; b. 8 Sept. 1944, Liège, Belgium. *Education:* Conservatoire Royal de Musique de Liège, Belgium. *Career:* debut as First Solo Horn with Nat. Orchestra of Belgium under André Clutyens aged 16; 20 years' experience as Prin. Horn with major orchestras in Belgium and Luxembourg; has performed as soloist and recitalist world-wide; adjudicator for several competitions; Prof., Music Conservatories, Liège and Luxembourg; Co-Dir Grétry Music Acad., Liège; Artistic Music Dir, Acad. Internationale d'Eté de Wallonie; founder and organiser of two int. horn competitions 1977, 1981; Univ. Prof., USA 1983–91; Prof. of Horn, Musikhochschule, Trossingen, Germany 1991–2007; mem. Int. Horn Soc. (fmr officer). *Compositions:* Libre/Free/Frei for horn solo, Champaign for horn and piano, Method for natural horn, Triptych for horn alone, Transcription for horn of Bach's six suites for cello, Treatise: method and exercises and 21 études, Ensembles for horns. *Recordings include:* Haydn's Concerto for two horns, Belgian Contemporary Music, Schumann's Konzertstück, Weber's Concertino, The Berwald and Beethoven Septets with the Uppsala Chamber Soloists, Brahms Horn Trio, with A. Grumiaux and G. Sebok, Bach, Six Suites for Cello, arrangement for horn, Masterpieces for Horn and Piano with Jean-Claude Vanden Eynden, French Music for Brass and Piano, French Music for Trumpet, Horn, Trombone and Piano. *Publications:* Treatise: method and exercises and 21 études 2006; contrib. of articles to Brass Bulletin, Horn Call, Historic Brass Society Journal, Méthode for Natural Horn, Horn (transcription for Horn of J.S. Bach Suites for Violoncello). *Honours:* First Prize, Int. Music Competition, Louise MacMahon, Lawton, Okla, USA 1987. *Address:* Boulevard Piercot 14/052, 4000 Liège, Belgium (home). *Telephone:* (4) 223-71-77 (home); 473-867506 (mobile). *E-mail:* francis_orval@yahoo.com (home).

OSBORNE, Charles Thomas, FRSL; Australian/British writer, critic and poet; *Opera Critic, Jewish Chronicle*; b. 24 Nov. 1927, Brisbane, Qld; partner, Kenneth Thomson 2006. *Education:* Griffith Univ., studied with Archie Day, Irene Fletcher, Vido Luppi and Browning Mummery. *Career:* Asst Ed., London Magazine 1957–66; Asst Literary Dir, Arts Council of Great Britain 1966–71, Literary Dir 1971–86; Opera Critic, Jewish Chronicle 1985–; Chief Theatre Critic, Daily Telegraph 1986–92; mem. Editorial Bd, Opera magazine; mem. Critics' Circle, PEN. *Publications include:* The Gentle Planet 1957, Opera 66 1966, Swansong 1968, The Complete Operas of Verdi 1969, Letters of Giuseppe Verdi (ed.) 1971, The Concert Song Companion 1974, Wagner and his World 1977, The Complete Operas of Mozart 1978, W. H. Auden: The Life of a Poet 1980, The Dictionary of Opera 1983, Letter to W. H. Auden and Other Poems 1984, Giving It Way 1986, The Operas of Richard Strauss 1988, The Complete Operas of Richard Wagner 1990, The Bel Canto Operas of Rossini, Donizetti and Verdi 1994, The Pink Danube 1998, The Life and Crimes of Agatha Christie 2000, The Opera Lover's Companion 2004, Murder in Three Stages 2007, The Unexpected Guest 2008; contribs to anthologies, newspapers and journals including Opera, London Magazine, Spectator, Times Literary Supplement, Encounter, New Statesman, Observer, Sunday Times. *Honours:* Order of the Star of Italian Solidarity 2009; Dr hc (Griffith Univ.); Gold Medal 1993. *Address:* 125 St George's Road, London, SE1 6HY, England (home). *Telephone:* (20) 7928-1534 (home). *Fax:* (20) 7401-9099.

OSBORNE, Nigel, BA, BMus; British composer; *Reid Professor of Music, University of Edinburgh;* b. 23 June 1948, Manchester, England. *Education:* Univ. of Oxford with Kenneth Leighton and Egon Wellesz, and at Polish Radio Experimental Studio, Warsaw. *Career:* fmr Lecturer Univ. of Nottingham 1978; conducted the premiere of The Sun of Venice, Royal Festival Hall, London 1992; reworking of the Electrification of the Soviet Union on tour with Music Theatre Wales, including Linbury Theatre, Covent Garden, 2002; The Piano Tuner (Linbury Studio, Royal Opera House, London) 2004; currently Reid Prof. of Music, Univ. of Edinburgh; extensive composition for theatre, including Glyndebourne, ENO, Opera Factory, Wuppertal, Hebbel Theatre (Berlin), Shakespeare's Globe (London), the Ulysses Theatre (Istria), BBC Radio 3 and BBC2. *Compositions include:* Seven Last Words cantata (Radio Suisse Romande and Ville de Geneve Opera Prize) 1971, Heaventree for chorus 1973, Remembering Esenin for cello and piano 1974, The Sickle for soprano and orchestra 1975, Chansonier for chorus and ensemble 1975, Prelude and Fugue for ensemble 1975, Passers By for trio and synthesizer 1978, Cello Concerto 1977, I Am Goya for baritone and quartet 1977, Vienna, Zürich, Constance for soprano and quintet 1977, Figure/Ground for piano 1978, Kerenza at the Dawn for oboe and tape 1978, Orlando Furioso for chorus and ensemble 1978, Songs from a Bare Mountain for women's chorus 1979, In Camera for ensemble 1979, Under the Eyes for voice and quartet 1979, Quasi una fantasia for cello 1979, Flute Concerto 1980, Gnostic Passion for chorus 1980, Poem without a Hero for four voices and electronics 1980, Mythologies for sextet 1980, The Cage for tenor and ensemble 1981, Piano Sonata 1981, Choralis I–III for six voices 1981, Sinfonia I 1982, Sinfonia II 1983, Cantata piccola for soprano and string quartet, Fantasia for ensemble 1983, Wildlife for ensemble 1984, Alba for mezzo-soprano, ensemble and tape 1984, Zansa for ensemble 1985, Hell's Angles chamber opera 1985, Pornography for mezzo-soprano and ensemble, The Electrification of the Soviet Union opera after Pasternak 1986, Lumiere for string quartet and four groups of children 1986, The Black Leg Miner for ensemble 1987, Esquisse I and II for strings 1987, Stone Garden for Chamber Orchestra 1988, Zone for oboe, clarinet and string trio 1989, Tracks for two choirs, orchestra and wind band 1990, Eulogy (for Michael Vyner) 1990, Canzona for brass 1990, Violin Concerto 1990, The Sun of Venice (after Turner's visions of Venice) 1991, Terrible Mouth opera 1992, Sarajevo opera 1994, Forest-River-Ocean for carnyx, string quartet and electronics 2002, East 2006, Roma Diary 2007, The Piano Tuner 2007, Differences in Demolition 2007, Music for Children in Zones of Conflict and Post Conflict 2007, Concertino for Violin and Orchestra 2007. *Honours:* Netherlands Gaudeamus Prize, Radcliffe Award, Koussevitzky Award of the Library of Congress, Washington. *Address:* Department of Music, School of Arts, Culture and Environment, Edinburgh University, Room 211, Alison House, 12 Nicolson Square, Edinburgh, EH8 9DF, Scotland (office). *Telephone:* (131) 650-2424 (office). *Fax:* (131) 650-2425 (office). *E-mail:* n.osborne@ ed.ac.uk (office). *Website:* www.music.ed.ac.uk (office).

OSBORNE, Steven; British pianist; b. 1971, Scotland. *Education:* St Mary's Music School, Edinburgh with Richard Beauchamp, Royal Northern Coll. of Music, studied with Renna Kellaway. *Career:* concerto performances worldwide, has worked with conductors including Christoph von Dohnányi, Alan Gilbert, Vladimir Ashkenazy, Sir Charles Mackerras, Ludovic Morlot, Leif Segerstam, Andrew Litton, Ingo Metzmacher, Vladimir Jurowski, Kazuki Yamada and Jukka-Pekka Saraste; has worked regularly with UK orchestras including Philharmonia, City of Birmingham Symphony and BBC Philharmonic; has appeared regularly at BBC Proms and Wigmore Hall, London; recitals at halls including Konzerthaus Vienna, Amsterdam Concertgebouw, de Doelen Rotterdam, Philharmonie Berlin, Musikhalle Hamburg, Palais des Beaux Arts, Brussels, Suntory Hall, Tokyo, Kennedy Center, Washington DC and Carnegie Hall, New York; regular chamber music partners include Alban Gerhardt, Paul Lewis, Dietrich Henschel and Lisa Batiashvili; currently Int. Fellow in Piano, Royal Conservatoire of Scotland. *Recordings include:* solo: Mackenzie and Tovey Piano Concertos 2000, Nikolai Kapustin Piano Music 2000, Liszt: Harmonies poétiques et religieuses 2003, Alkan: Esquisses 2003, Debussy: The Complete Preludes 2006, Tippett: Complete Music for Piano 2007, Britten: Complete Works for Piano and Orchestra (Gramophone Award for Best Concerto Recording, Preis der Deutschen Schallplattenkritik) 2008, Rachmaninov Preludes 2009, Beethoven Piano Sonatas 2010, Ravel: The Complete Solo Piano Music 2011, Beethoven Bagatelles 2012, Mussorgski: Pictures at an Exhibition/Prokofiev (Gramophone Award for Best Instrumental Recording) 2013, Stravinsky Complete Works for Piano and Orchestra 2013; other: Shostakovich & Schnittke Cello Sonatas 2006, Messiaen: Vingt Regards sur l'Enfant Jésus 2002, Messiaen: Visions de l'Amen 2004, Alkan & Chopin Cello Sonatas 2008, Schubert Piano Duets 2010, Turangalîla Symphonie 2012, Britten: Complete works for solo cello 2013. *Honours:* First

Prize, Clara Haskil Int. Piano Competition 1991, Naumberg Foundation Int. Competition 1997. *Current Management:* Sulivan Sweetland, 1a Hillgate Place, Balham Hill, London, SW12 9ER, England. *Telephone:* (20) 8772-3470. *Fax:* (20) 8673-8959. *E-mail:* info@sulivansweetland.co.uk. *Website:* www .sulivansweetland.co.uk. *E-mail:* sgmo@stevenosborne.co.uk (office). *Website:* www.stevenosborne.co.uk (office).

OSKARSSON, Gudjon; Icelandic singer (bass); b. 1965, Reykjavík. *Education:* studied in Iceland and Italy (Osimo and Milan). *Career:* mem., Norwegian Opera from 1990, as Colline, Zuniga, Sparafucile and Raimondo (Lucia di Lammermoor); Fafner, Hunding and Hagen in The Ring, 1993–96 (also at Norwich, 1997); Further appearances at Mozart's Commendatore at Glyndebourne and Covent Garden (1996–97), as Raimondo at Munich and Fafner in Das Rheingold at La Scala (1996); Season 1998 with Titurel in Parsifal at Brussels, the Commendatore at Aix and King Mark for Scottish Opera; Concerts include: Tosca and Otello with the Israel Philharmonic Orchestra (1995–97), Act I of Die Walküre with the London Symphony Orchestra, Rocco in Fidelio under Carlo Rizzi and the Berlioz Messe Solennelle with the Gothenburg Symphony Orchestra; Further concerts with the Oslo and Bergen Philharmonics and the Trondheim Symphony Orchestra; Season 2000–01 as Priam in Les Troyens at Salzburg and Fafner in Das Rheingold at Toulouse. *Current Management:* c/o Anne-Kathrin Seibel, Allegro Artist Management, Yorckstrasse 81, 10965 Berlin, Germany. *Telephone:* (30) 78896635. *Fax:* (30) 78896711. *E-mail:* allegro@allegroartist.com. *Website:* www.allegroartist.com.

OSKOLKOV, Sergei Alexandrovich; composer and pianist; b. 9 March 1952, Donetsk, Ukraine; m. Natalia Semionovna Oskolkova 1986, two s. *Education:* Donetsk Music College with Galina Sladkovskaya, Leningrad Conservatory with Pavel Serebryakov, Vjacheslav Nagovitsin and Yuri Falik. *Career:* debut as pianist with Donetsk Philharmonic Orchestra 1972; performance of vocal compositions, Leningrad, 1975; publishing poetry and selling paintings and graphics, 1972–; participant as composer and pianist at international festivals in Berlin, Kazan, St Petersburg and Kalingrad, 1985; concert tours, Germany, France, Belgium, Ukraine, Kazakhstan, Latvia; mem. Union of Composers of Russia. *Compositions:* two String Quartets 1976, 1979; Sinfonietta for string orchestra 1979; 2 Concertos for piano and orchestra 1981, 1988; Count Nulin, opera, 1983; Set of Pieces and 2 Sonatas for piano 1994; music for Russian folk instruments; music for theatre and film. *Recordings:* Offenbach, Liszt, as pianist with St Petersburg Quartet, 1994; 2nd Piano Sonata and cycle of songs by Oskolkov, 1996; Mussorgsky and Tchaikovsky, as pianist, Radio St Petersburg, 1996. *Address:* St Petersburgsky Prosp 51, ap 5, Petrodvorets, St Petersburg 198903, Russia.

OSOSTOWICZ, Krysia; British violinist; b. 1960, England. *Education:* studied with Yehudi Menuhin and Sándor Végh. *Career:* founder mem., Chamber Ensemble Domus; leader, Endymion Ensemble; founder and leader, Dante String Quartet; many performances as soloist and chamber musician, with repertoire from baroque to Bartók. *Recordings include:* Les Vendredis (with Dante Quartet). *Current Management:* Connaught Artists Management Ltd, 2 Molasses Row, Plantation Wharf, London, SW11 3UX, England. *Telephone:* (20) 7738 0017. *Fax:* (20) 7738 0909. *E-mail:* classicalmusic@ connaughtartists.com. *Website:* www.connaughtartists.com. *E-mail:* krysia@ stradella.freeserve.co.uk.

OSTENDORF, John; American singer (bass-baritone); b. 1 Nov. 1945, New York. *Education:* Oberlin Coll. with Margaret Harshaw. *Career:* debut at Chautauqua Opera 1969, as the Commendatore in Don Giovanni; appearances at San Francisco, Houston, Baltimore, Toronto and Philadelphia; Amsterdam 1979 in the premiere of Winter Cruise by Henkeman; repertoire includes Don Alfonso, Basilio, Escamillo, Ramphis in Aida and Handel's Julius Caesar; many concert performances, notably in the baroque repertoire. *Recordings:* Bach's St John Passion and Handel's Imeneo, Joshua and Acis and Galatea.

ÖSTMAN, Arnold; Swedish conductor; b. 1939, Malmö; m. Kristina Modig. *Education:* Univ. of Paris, France, Univ. of Stockholm. *Career:* fmr Lecturer, State Acad. of Music and Drama, Stockholm; Chief Conductor and Dir Vadstena Acad. 1970–84; f. Norrlands Operan 1974, Gen. Admin. and Artistic Dir Drottningholm Court Theatre 1979–92; has conducted at opera houses including Covent Garden, Parma, Paris Bastille, Paris Garnier, Trieste, Cologne, Bonn, Toulouse, Nice, Vienna Staatsoper, Vienna Volksoper, Wexford, Washington, Lausanne, Gothenburg Opera, Graz Opera; symphonic conductor with orchestras including German radio orchestras of Hamburg, Cologne, Stuttgart and Baden-Baden, Stuttgart Philharmonic, Orchestre nat. de France, de Lille, orchestra of La Fenice, Venice, Adelaide Symphony Orchestra, Orchestra Sinfonia Siciliana, Scottish Chamber Orchestra, Acad. of Ancient Music, London, Royal Concertgebouw Orchestra, Amsterdam, Oslo Philharmonic Orchestra, Minneapolis Symphony Orchestra, Sydney Symphony Orchestra, Melbourne Symphony Orchestra, Rotterdam Philharmonic, Gothenburg Symphony Orchestra, Swedish Radio Orchestra; works regularly with Netherlands Radio Chamber Orchestra (symphonic and operatic); mem. Royal Swedish Acad. of Music. *Recordings include:* Così fan tutte, Le Nozze di Figaro, Don Giovanni, Die Zauberflöte (Diapason d'Or and Deutsche Schallplattenpreis), Gluck's Alceste for Naxos; co-producer two TV films: Christina the Winter Queen, Gustav III (both winners of Prix d'Italia). *Honours:* Chevalier, Légion d'honneur; Dr hc (Umeå) 1979; Hans Majestät Konungens Medal 2010. *Current Management:* c/o Haydn Rawstron Ltd, 29a

High Street, First Floor, West Wickham, Kent, BR4 0LP, England. *E-mail:* enquiries@haydn-rawstron.com. *Website:* www.haydnrawstron.com.

O'SULLIVAN, Cara; Irish singer (soprano); b. 1970, Cork. *Career:* engagements with WNO as Donna Anna and Violetta; at Garsington for Mozart's Fiordiligi and Constanze; the Queen of Night for Opéra de Nantes, 1999–2000; Helmwige in Die Walküre for the Royal Opera, 1998–99; concerts include the Verdi Requiem at the Albert Hall; Beethoven's Ninth; Elijah; Messiah in Barcelona with Paul McCreesh; Brahms Requiem; Poulenc's Gloria. *Honours:* winner Stanislav Moniuszko Vocal Competition, Warsaw 1996. *Current Management:* Harlequin Agency Ltd, 203 Fidlas Road, Llanishen, Cardiff, CF14 5NA, Wales. *Telephone:* (29) 2075-0821. *Fax:* (29) 2075-5971. *E-mail:* peter@harlequin-agency.co.uk. *Website:* www.harlequin-agency.co.uk.

OTAKA, Tadaaki; Japanese conductor; *Permanent Conductor, NHK Symphony;* b. 8 Nov. 1947, Kamakura; s. of Hisatada Otaka and Misaoko Otaka; m. Yukiko Otaka 1978. *Education:* Toho Gakuen Music School, Toho Gakuen Music Acad., Vienna Acad., Austria. *Career:* began studying violin 1951; Chief Conductor, Tokyo Philharmonic Orchestra 1971–, Conductor Laureate 1991–; Chief Conductor, Sapporo Symphony 1981–86, Prin. Conductor 1998–; Prin. Conductor, BBC Welsh Symphony Orchestra (now BBC Nat. Orchestra of Wales) 1987–95, Conductor Laureate 1996–; Chief Conductor, Yomiuri Nippon Symphony Orchestra 1992–98; apptd Music Adviser and Prin. Conductor, Kioi Sinfonietta, Tokyo 1995, Hon. Conductor Laureate 2003–; Dir Britten Pears Orchestra 1998–2001; Music Dir, Sapporo Symphony Orchestra 2004–; Perm. Conductor, NHK Symphony, Tokyo 2010–; Prin. Guest Conductor, Melbourne Symphony 2009–12; Artistic Dir New Nat. Theatre, Tokyo 2010–14; has conducted BBC Proms, and orchestras including City of Birmingham Symphony, Royal Liverpool Philharmonic, Royal Scottish Nat., Bournemouth Symphony, BBC Symphony, London Symphony, London Philharmonic, Rotterdam Philharmonic, Bamberg Symphony, Strasbourg Philharmonic, Bergen Philharmonic and Singapore Symphony. *Recordings include:* numerous recordings with BBC Nat. Orchestra of Wales including works by Takemitsu and Franck, and Britten's Peter Grimes with Yomiuri Nippon. *Honours:* Hon. Fellow, Welsh Coll. of Music and Drama 1993; Hon. CBE 1997; Dr hc (Univ. of Wales) 1993; Second Prize, Min-On Conductors Competition 1969, Suntory Music Award 1992, Elgar Medal 2000. *Website:* www.askonasholt.co.uk/artists/conductors/tadaaki-otaka. *Address:* NHK Symphony Orchestra 2-16-49 Takanawa, Minato-ku, Tokyo, 108-0074, Japan (office). *Telephone:* (3) 5793-8111 (office). *Fax:* (3) 3443-0278 (office). *Website:* www.nhkso.or.jp/en (office).

OTELLI, Claudio; Austrian singer (bass-baritone); b. 20 June 1960, Vienna. *Education:* Vienna Musikhochschule. *Career:* Bregenz Festival 1986, Vienna Staatsoper 1989–94; Salzburg Festival 1986, in Elektra; Rome Opera 1994, as Alfio and Tonio in Cav and Pag; since 1994, has performed with artists including Nicolas Brieger, Adolf Dresen, Johannes Schaaf, Chrisoph Nel, David Pountney, Calixto Bieito, Christoph Marthaler, Martin Kusej, Moshe Leiser, Patrice Caurier, Andrea Moses, Riccardo Muti, Claudio Abbado, Pinchas Steinberg, Stefan Soltesz, Lothar Zagrosek, Sylvain Cambreling, Michael Gielen, Manfred Honeck, Jeffrey Tate, Peter Schneider, Gabriel Feltz, Peter Eötvös and Michael Schönwandt at venues and festivals in Europe, USA and Japan, including Aalto Theater Essen (Il Conte in Le nozze di Figaro, Marcello in La Bohème, Mandyka in Arabella, Telramund in Lohengrin, Gregor Mittenhofer in Elegie für junge Liebende), Santa Fe Festival as Jochanaan in Salome, in Los Angeles as Il Conte in Figaro, Staatsoper unter den Linden as Graff in Der ferne Klang, Mailänder Scala and Théâtre du Capitole Toulouse as Gunther in Götterdämmerung, Teatro Regio Torino as Olivier in Capriccio, Opéra du Rhin Strasbourg as Amfortas in Parsifal, Opéra de Lyon as Don Pizarro in Fidelio, Grand Théâtre Geneva as Galilee, at the Ruhr triennale 2006, Lincoln Center Festival as Stolzius in Die Soldaten, Stadttheater Bern as De Flores in Die Vipern, Frankfurt Opera (Schischkow in In einem Totenhaus, Don Giovanni, Tonio in I Pagliacci, Jochanaan in Salome, Cardillac, Scarpia in Tosca, Ryuji in Das verratene Meer), Oper Leipzig as Telramund, New Nat. Theatre Tokyo as Dr Schön in Lulu and Sharpless in Butterfly, in Antwerp as Dreieinigkeitsmoses in Mahagonny, at Bregenz Festival as Scarpia in Tosca, Stadttheater Basel as Dr Schön in Lulu and Schischkow in Aus einem Totenhaus, Opéra Angers Nantes as Scarpia in Tosca, and Beaupertuis in Le Chapeau de paille d'Italie, KOB as Marquis de la Force in Dialogues des Carmélites, Dr Bloom in American Lulu, Nekrozar in Le Grand Macabre, Staatstheater Stuttgart as Graf Vitelozzo Tamare in Die Gezeichneten, Wozzeck, and Scarpia in Tosca; concerts. *Current Management:* c/o Artists Management Zürich, Rütistrasse 52, 8044 Zürich-Gockhausen, Switzerland. *Telephone:* (44) 8218957. *Fax:* (44) 8210127. *E-mail:* schuetz@artistsman.com. *Website:* www.artistsman.com.

OTEY, Louis; American singer (baritone); b. 1957. *Career:* repertoire includes Mr Astley in The Gambler, Scarpa in Tosca, Escamillo in Carmen, Figaro in Il Barbiere di Siviglia, the Count in Le Nozze di Figaro, Germont in La Traviata, Sam in A Quiet Place, Count di Luna in Il Trovatore, Nekrotzar in La Grand Macabre, Le Pere in Louise, Pascoe in The Wreckers, Eisenstein in Die Fledermaus, Emile du Becque in South Pacific, Danilo in The Merry Widow, Sharpless in Madama Butterfly, Dulcamara in L'Elisir d'Amore, Jokanaan in Salome, Antony in Antony and Cleopatra, the Four Villains in Les Contes d'Hoffman, Fieramosca in Benvenuto Cellini, Nazarie in La Senorita Cristina, Ezio in Attila, Iago in Otello, Arthur in Le Roi Arthus, Musiklehrer in Ariadne auf Naxos, Philosopher in Cherubin, The Consul in Chandos, in Adriana Lecouvreur, Doctor Atomic, Thais, title roles in Eugene

Onegin, Don Giovanni, Rigoletto, Macbeth, The Flying Dutchman; regularly performs at Metropolitan Opera, New York City Opera and across the USA and Europe. *E-mail:* louisotey@hotmail.com (office). *Current Management:* c/o Bernard Uzen, Pinnacle Arts Management, 889 Ninth Avenue, 2nd Floor, New York, NY 10019, France. *Telephone:* (212) 397-7915. *Fax:* (212) 397-7920. *Website:* www.pinnaclearts.com. *E-mail:* louisotey@hotmail.com (office). *Website:* www.louisotey.net.

OTT, Karin; Swiss singer (soprano); b. 13 Dec. 1945, Wädenswil, Zürich. *Education:* studied in Zürich and Germany. *Career:* sang first with the opera house of Biel-Solothurn; appeared in Mussorgsky's Sorochintsy Fair at Brunswick 1970; Zürich 1970, as Tove in Schoenberg's Gurrelieder; Paris Opéra as the Queen of Night in Die Zauberflöte; Salzburg Festival 1979–81; Venice 1981, in the premiere of Sinopoli's Lou Salomé; engagements at Stuttgart, Berlin, Zürich, Amsterdam and Vienna; sang Scoltarella in the premiere of the original version of Henze's König Hirsch 1985, as Kassel. *Recordings include:* Die Zauberflöte (conducted by Karajan).

OTTENSAMER, Andreas; Austrian musician (clarinet); *Principal Clarinettist, Berlin Philharmonic;* b. 1989. *Education:* Univ. of Music and Performing Arts, Vienna, studied with Johann Hindler, Orchestra Acad. of the Berliner Philharmoniker. *Career:* fmr mem. Gustav Mahler Jugendorchester; soloist and chamber musician in numerous venues including Musikverein Wien, Konzerthaus Wien, Brucknerhaus Linz, Musikverein Graz, Philharmonie Berlin, Tempodrom Berlin, De Doelen Rotterdam and Seoul Arts Center; worked with musicians including Murray Perahia, Leif Ove Andsnes, Leonidas Kavakos, Janine Jansen, Clemens Hagen and Yo-Yo Ma; Prin. Clarinettist, Deutsches Symphonie-Orchester Berlin, July 2010–February 2011, Berlin Philharmonic 2011–; f. The Clarinotts clarinet trio with father Ernst and brother Daniel 2005. *Recordings include:* Portraits: The Clarinet Album 2013, Brahms: The Hungarian Connection (Echo Klassik Award for Instrumentalist of the Year – Clarinet) 2015. *Website:* www .askonasholt.co.uk; andreasottensamer.com.

OTTENTHAL, Gertrud; German singer (soprano); b. 1957, Bad Oldesloe, Schleswig-Holstein. *Education:* studied in Lubeck. *Career:* sang at Wiesbaden Opera 1980, Hamburg 1981–82; engagements at Vienna Volksoper 1982, Salzburg Festival 1984, Vienna Festival 1986–88; sang Mozart's Countess at Klagenfurt 1984, Komische Oper Berlin 1986, returned to Berlin 1990 as Mimi; further appearances at Theater am Gärtnerplatz Munich, Barcelona and the Schwetzingen Festival; other roles include Agathe, Fiordiligi, Sandrina in La Finta Giardiniera, Rosalinde, Antonio and Arianna in Giustino by Handel; concert repertoire includes works by Bach, Handel, Mozart, Bruckner and Schubert; sang Elisabeth de Valois in the Komische Oper, Berlin 1999; season 2000 as the Queen in Zemlinsky's Der König Kandaules, at the Vienna Volksoper, and Wagner's Gutrune at the Erl Festival, Tyrol. *Recordings:* Werther, Der Rosenkavalier and Der Wildschütz; Mrs Ma in Der Kreidekreis by Zemlinsky; Donna Elvira in Don Giovanni, conducted by Neeme Järvi.

ÖTVÖS, Csilla; Hungarian singer (soprano); b. 23 June 1947, Budapest; m. Antal Szabados 1975. *Education:* Liszt Ferenc Acad. of Music. *Career:* debut in Ariadne auf Naxos, Zerbinetta 1974; numerous roles in the Hungarian State Opera, including Despina in Mozart's Così fan tutte, Rosina in Rossini's Il Barbiere di Sivigla, Norina in Don Pasquale, Adina in Elisir d'amore; appearances on Hungarian television, including Lehár's Die Lustige Witwe. *Recordings:* Szép Alom: Hungarian operettas and folk music, Operettcsillogás, operettas. *Honours:* Pro Kultúra Hungarica 1985, Bartók-Pásztory Prize 1992.

OUE, Eiji; Japanese conductor; *Conductor Laureate, Osaka Philharmonic;* b. 1957, Hiroshima. *Education:* studied at Toho School of Music and with Bernstein and Ozawa at Tanglewood from 1978. *Career:* asst to Bernstein at concerts in Paris, Vienna and Milan; Music Dir Erie Philharmonic, Pa 1991–95; Assoc. Conductor, Buffalo Philharmonic Orchestra 1987–91; Music Dir Minnesota Orchestra 1995; tours through USA and Europe 1997–98; Dir Grand Teton Music Festival, Wyo. 1997; further engagements with New York Philharmonic Orchestra, Philadelphia Orchestra, Oslo Philharmonic Orchestra, Santa Cecilia, Rome, Los Angeles Philharmonic Orchestra; Prin. Conductor NDR Symphony Orchestra, Hanover 1998–2009; Music Dir Osaka Philharmonic 2003–12, Conductor Laureate 2012–; Music Dir Barcelona Symphony Orchestra 2006–09; conducted Tokyo Philharmonic Orchestra 100th Anniversary World Tour 2014. *Recordings:* The Rite of Spring and The Firebird by Stravinsky, Strauss Ein Heldenleben and Mussorgsky, Antheil Piano Concertos 2006. *Honours:* Koussevitzky Prize 1980, Hans Haring Gold Medal, Salzburg Mozarteum 1981. *Current Management:* c/o IMG Artists, The Light Box, 111 Power Road, London, W4 5PY, England. *Telephone:* (20) 7957-5800. *Fax:* (20) 7957-5801. *E-mail:* dchandruang@imgartists.com. *Website:* www.imgartists.com.

OUNDJIAN, Peter; Canadian violinist and conductor; *Music Director, Toronto Symphony Orchestra;* b. 21 Dec. 1955, Toronto; m. Nadine Oundjian; one s. one d. *Education:* Royal Coll. of Music, London, Juilliard School with Ivan Galamian and Dorothy DeLay. *Career:* leader, Tokyo Quartet 1981–95; regular concerts in the USA and abroad; first cycle of the complete quartets of Beethoven at the Yale at Norfolk Chamber Music Festival 1986; repeated cycles at the 92nd Street Y (New York), Ravinia and Israel Festivals and Yale and Princeton Univs; Visiting Prof., Yale Univ. 1982–; Music Dir, Nieuw Sinfonietta, Amsterdam 1998–2003; Prin. Conductor and Artistic Advisor,

Caramoor Int. Music Festival; Prin. Guest Conductor and Artistic Advisor, Detroit Symphony Orchestra; Prin. Guest Conductor, Colorado Symphony Orchestra; Music Dir, Toronto Symphony Orchestra 2004–; Music Dir, Royal Scottish Nat. Orchestra 2012–. *Recordings:* Schubert's major Quartets; Mozart Flute Quartets with James Galway and Clarinet Quintet with Richard Stolzman; Quartets by Bartók, Brahms, Debussy, Haydn, Mozart and Ravel; Beethoven Middle Period Quartets. *Honours:* Stoutzker Prize, Royal Coll. of Music, Grand Prix du Disque du Montreux. *Current Management:* Harrison Parrott, 5–6 Albion Court, Albion Place, London W6 0QT, England. *Telephone:* (20) 7229-9166. *E-mail:* info@harrisonparrott.co.uk. *Website:* www .harrisonparrott.com.

OUSSET, Cécile; French pianist; b. 23 Jan. 1936, Tarbes. *Education:* Paris Conservatoire. *Career:* French début with Orchestre de Paris; British début, Edin. Festival 1980; U.S. début with LA Philharmonic 1984; first recital at Théâtre des Champs-Elysées 1987–88; played Debussy's Preludes on BBC TV 1988; retd from public performances 2006. *Recordings include:* concertos by Rachmaninov, Liszt, Saint-Saëns, Ravel, Grieg and Mendelssohn and recitals of Chopin, Debussy and Liszt. *Honours:* winner Van Cliburn, Queen Elisabeth of Belgium, Busoni and Marguerite Long-Jacques Thibaud competitions, Grand Prix du Disque for recording of Brahms 2nd Piano Concerto.

OUZIEL, Dalia; pianist; b. 28 Sept. 1947, Tel-Aviv, Israel; m. Jerrold Rubenstein 1969, one s. one d. *Education:* Rubin Acad., Tel-Aviv, Royal Conservatories at Mons and Brussels, Belgium. *Career:* soloist and chamber artist; performs at festivals. *Recordings include:* Beethoven Variations, Piano Solo; Mozart Concerti, Double Piano Concerto, Sonatas for Violin and Piano, complete Piano Duos; Violin-Piano Sonatas of Mozart, Brahms, Fauré, Copland, Ives, Mendelssohn, Ravel, Grieg, Villa-Lobos, others; Piano Trios of Fauré, Schubert, Brahms, Mendelssohn, others; Fauré Piano Quartets; Chausson Concerto; Schubert Trout; Mendelssohn Sextet; Beethoven Lieder.

OVCHINNIKOV, Vladimir Pavlovich; Russian pianist; *Professor of Piano and Director, Central Music School, Moscow Conservatory;* b. 1 Jan. 1958, Beleby, Urals. *Education:* studied with Anna Artobolevskaya and at Moscow Conservatory with Alexey Nasedkin. *Career:* London debut, Barbican Hall 1987; has since given recitals in UK, Europe, USA, Canada and Japan and appeared with BBC Symphony, BBC Philharmonic, Royal Philharmonic, Royal Scottish Nat., Royal Liverpool Philharmonic, Ulster Orchestra, Netherlands Philharmonic, Netherlands Radio Symphony Orchestra, Bournemouth Symphony, Chicago Symphony, Danish Radio Symphony, Hague Residentie, Hallé, Leipzig Gewandhaus, Montreal Symphony, Nat. Symphony of Wales, Philharmonia, Polish Nat. Radio Orchestra, Slovak Philharmonic, Zurich Tonhalle, Russian State Symphony Orchestra, Moscow Philharmonic, Moscow Radio Symphony, St Petersburg Philharmonic and other major orchestras; Lecturer in Keyboard Studies, Royal Northern Coll. of Music, UK from 1994; Prof. of Piano, Moscow Conservatory, Dir Cen. Music School 2011–; Guest Prof. of Piano, Sakuyo Univ., Japan; Chair. Jury, Int. Russian Rotary Children's Music Competition 2011. *Recordings include:* Shostakovich's Piano Concerto No. 1 coupled with Mussorgsky's Pictures at an Exhibition; Rachmaninoff's Études-Tableaux; Liszt's Transcendental Études; Prokofiev's Piano Sonatas; Sonatas for Violin and Piano by Grieg (with violinist Vinnitsky); Liszt, Tchaikovsky, Taneyev, Rubinstein for Gold Club. *Honours:* People's Artist of Russia 2005; Second Place, Montreal Int. Music Competition 1980, Jt Second Prize (no first prize awarded) (with Peter Donohoe), Moscow Tchaikovsky Competition 1982, First Prize, Leeds Int. Piano Competition 1987. *Current Management:* c/o Schmidt Artists International, Inc., 59 East 54th Street, Suite 83, New York, NY 10022, USA. *Telephone:* (212) 421-8500. *Fax:* (212) 421-8583. *E-mail:* info@schmidtart .com. *Website:* www.schmidtart.com/artists/vladimir_ovchinnikov. *Address:* Moscow Conservatory, Bolshaya Nikitskaya str. 13/6, 125009 Moscow, Russian Federation (office). *E-mail:* spravka@mosconsv.ru (office). *Website:* www.mosconsv.ru (office).

OVENS, Raymond, ARAM, FRAM; British violinist; b. 14 Oct. 1932, Bristol, England; m. Sheila Margharet Vaughan Williams; one s. one d. *Education:* Royal Acad. of Music. *Career:* debut at Wigmore Hall, London 1950; Leader, London Symphony Orchestra 1951; Principal Second Violin, Royal Philharmonic Orchestra 1956; Asst Leader, BBC Scottish Symphony Orchestra 1972, Leader –1980; Leader, Philharmonia Orchestra 1980–85, Orchestra of the ENO from 1985; has played concertos with the BBC Scottish Symphony, the Vancouver Symphony and the Philharmonia Orchestra; concerts and recitals for BBC; Leader, Lyra String Quartet, Ceol Rosh Chamber Group.

OVERMAN, Robert; American singer (baritone); b. 1957, North Carolina. *Career:* sang at the Landestheater, Salzburg, from 1984; Karlsruhe Opera, 1986–91; Guest appearances at Mannheim, Stuttgart and Zürich; Salzburg Festival, 1987; Leipzig Opera, 1990, as Count Luna; Bonn Opera from 1992, in Le Villi and La Rondine by Puccini, and as Iago; Sang Carlo in La Forza del Destino at Karlsruhe, 1993, and Jack Rance in La Fanciulla del West at Catania, 1995; Other roles include Germont, and Alfio in Cavalleria Rusticana. *Current Management:* c/o Sardos Artists Management, 180 West End Avenue, Suite 22B, New York, NY 10023, USA. *Telephone:* (212) 874-2559. *Fax:* (212) 721-7815. *E-mail:* info@ritasardos.com. *Website:* www .ritasardos.com.

OWEN, Barbara Jean, BMus, MMus, ChM Cert.; American organist and musicologist; b. 25 Jan. 1933, Utica, New York; d. of David Owen and Vera Owen. *Education:* Westminster Choir Coll., Boston Univ., North German Organ Acad., Acad. of Italian Organ Music. *Career:* Music Dir First Religious Soc., Newburyport Mass 1963–2002; Curator, American Guild of Organists Organ Library, Boston Univ. 1985–2012; Organist, St Anne's Episcopal Church, Lowell, Mass 2002–07; Ed. of Publs, Westfield Center for Early Keyboard Studies 2001–04; freelance researcher, lecturer, recitalist, teacher and organ consultant; mem. American Guild of Organists, Organ Historical Soc. (Pres. 1956–61, 1997–99), American Musical Instrument Soc., British Inst. of Organ Studies, Reed Organ Soc., Organ Historical Trust of Australia, Instituto de Organos Historicos de Oaxaca (Advisory Bd); Trustee, Methuen Memorial Music Hall. *Publications include:* editions of music: A Century of American Organ Music (four vols) 1975, 1976, 1983, 1991, Four Centuries of English Organ Music 1979, A Handel Album 1981, The Candlelight Carol Book 1981, 4 Centuries of Italian Organ Music 1994, A Pachelbel Album 1994, A Romantic Christmas 1995; books written: The Organs and Music of King's Chapel 1965, 1993, The Organ in New England 1979, E. Power Biggs, Concert Organist 1987; co-ed.: Charles Brenton Fisk, Organ Builder 1986, The New Grove Organ 1988, The Mormon Tabernacle Organ 1990, The Registration of Baroque Organ Music 1997, The Organ Music of Johannes Brahms 2007, Music on the Green 2009, The Great Organ 2011; contrib. to Grove's Dictionary (seventh edn), Grove's Dictionary of Musical Instruments, New Grove Dictionary of American Music, Harvard Dictionary of Music, various anthologies and periodicals, including The Diapason, The American Organist, The Tracker, BIOS Journal, Organ Yearbook, The Hymn, Bach Perspectives, Choir & Organ, 19th Century Music. *Honours:* Alumni Merit Award, Westminster Choir Coll. 1988, OHS Distinguished Service Award 1988, AMIS Curt Sachs Award 1994, Max Miller Book Award 2008, UU Partner Church Council Steward of Partnership Award 2011, AGO Hansen Award 2014. *Address:* 28 Jefferson Street, Newburyport, MA 01950, USA (home). *Fax:* (978) 465-2068 (home). *E-mail:* owenbar@juno.com (office).

OWEN, Lynn, BS, MS; American singer (soprano) and voice teacher; *Voice Teacher, Manhattan School of Music;* b. Kenosha, WI; m. Richard Owen 1960; three s. *Education:* Northwestern University, Juilliard School of Music, Vienna Academy of Music, Austria. *Career:* debut Constanze in Abduction from the Seraglio, New Orleans Opera, USA; La Fanciulla del West (Minnie), Fliegende Holländer (Senta), Metropolitan Opera, New York; Don Carlos (Elisabetta), Forza del Destino (Leonora), Il Trovatore (Leonore), Prince Igor (Jaroslavna), Zürich, Switzerland; Il Trovatore, Turandot, Fidelio (Leonora), Krefeld Opera, Hamburg and Frankfurt, Germany; Fanciulla del West, Central City, Fliegende Holländer, Aspen, USA; Ballo in Maschera, Othello, Calgary, Canada; Il Trovatore, Caracas, Venezuela; Siegfried (Brünnhilde), Art Park, New York; Isolde, Mexico City Opera; Concerts and recitals throughout USA and Europe; US premiere, Strauss, Aegyptische Helene, NY (title role); Frau Ohne Shatten (Dyer's wife; Die Walkuere (Sieglinde) NY; world premieres, US (Owen) Mary Dyer, The Death of the Virgin, Abigail Adams, Rain (Alice Tully, New York); Voice Teacher, Columbia Univ./Barnard Coll., New York 1983–, Manhattan School of Music 1993–; mem. Nat. Assn of Teachers of Singing, New York Singing Teachers' Assn. *Recordings:* Serenus Records, Vanguard Records, Vienna to Broadway, Aurora, Rain, Albany Records. *Publications:* contribs to music journals. *Honours:* Fulbright Scholar. *Address:* 21 Claremont Avenue, New York, NY 10027, USA (office). *Telephone:* (212) 864-4968 (office). *E-mail:* operaowen@aol.com (office). *Website:* www .lynnandrichardowen.com.

OWEN, Stephen; American singer (bass-baritone); b. 2 March 1949, Kunming, China. *Education:* Wheaton Coll., Princeton Theological Seminary. *Career:* began int. career as Gunther in Götterdämmerung, Salzburg 1990; ensemble singer, Staatstheater Kassel 2005–08, Theater Augsburg 2009–; repertoire includes Don Pizarro and Don Fernando in Fidelio, Jochanaan in Salome, Kurwenal in Tristan und Isolde, Orest in Elektra, Peter in Hänsel und Gretel, Alberich in Das Rheingold, the Herald in Lohengrin, Dr Schön in Lulu, Bluebeard in Bluebeard's Castle, Kissinger in Nixon in China, Grandpa Moss in The Tender Land, Creon in Oedipus Rex, Teufel in Tod und Teufel, Conductor in Prova d'Orchestra, Schaunard and Colline in La Bohème, Scarpia in Tosca, Amonasro in Aida, Sharpless in Madama Butterfly, Alfio in Cavalleria Rusticana, Leporello in Don Giovanni, Sparafucile in Rigoletto, Raimondo in Lucia di Lammermoor, Escamillo in Carmen, Paolo in Simon Boccanegra, Musiklehrer in Ariadne auf Naxos, Tod in Kaiser von Atlantis, Balstrode in Peter Grimes, Grand Inquisitor in Don Carlo, Dr Vigelius in Der Ferne Klang, Officer in In the Penal Colony, title role in Der Fliegende Holländer. *Current Management:* c/o Brian Jauhlainen, Bel Canto Global Arts, 17 Auburn Avenue, Bay Shore, NY 11706, USA. *Telephone:* (631) 206-0260. *Fax:* (866) 698-3059. *E-mail:* brian@ belcantoglobal.com. *Website:* www.belcantoglobalarts.com. *Telephone:* (172) 561-1580 (office). *E-mail:* showen@t-online.de (office). *Website:* www .stephenowenheldenbari.com.

OWENS, Anne-Marie; British singer (mezzo-soprano); b. 15 Aug. 1955, Jarrow, Tyne and Wear, England. *Education:* Newcastle School of Music, Guildhall School, National Opera Studio. *Career:* sang Gluck's Orpheus, Dido, Dalila and Angelina in La Cenerentola while student; professional debut as Mistress Quickly on the Glyndebourne Tour; for ENO has sung Charlotte, Rosina, Maddalena, Suzuki in Madama Butterfly, Bianca in The Rape of Lucretia, Solokha in the British premiere of Rimsky-Korsakov's Christmas Eve 1988, and Magdalene; Covent Garden 1989, as Third Lady in Die

Zauberflöte and Rossweise in a new production of Die Walküre; visit to the Vienna Staatsoper with the company of the Royal Opera 1992; sang Jocasta in Oedipus Rex for Opera North, followed by the title role in Ariane and Bluebeard by Dukas 1990; season 1992 in Les Contes d'Hoffmann at Covent Garden, as Baba the Turk in The Rake's Progress at Brussels and Preziosilla in The Force of Destiny for ENO; other roles include Arnalta in Monteverdi's Poppea (Glyndebourne Festival); Clotilde in Norma and the Hostess in Boris Godunov (Royal Opera); Baba the Turk (Brussels); Fidalma in Il Matrimonio Segreto (Lausanne); sang Venus in a new production of Tannhäuser for Opera North; T. Picker's Emmeline at the New York City Opera 1998; Kundry in Parsifal for Scottish Opera 2000; concert appearances with the City of Birmingham Symphony, BBC Symphony, London Mozart Players, Royal Liverpool Philharmonic; has sung at the London Proms, Aix-en-Provence, San Sebastien, Rouen and Detroit (US debut with Messiah); season 2000–01 as Kundry for Scottish Opera, Laura in La Gioconda (concert) and Arnalta in Poppea for ENO; Brangaene for Opera North and Azucena in Glasgow. *Current Management:* Hazard Chase, 25 City Road, Cambridge CB1 1DP, England. *Telephone:* (1223) 312400. *Fax:* (1223) 460827. *E-mail:* info@hazardchase.co.uk. *Website:* www.hazardchase.co.uk.

OWENS, David Bruce; American composer; b. 16 Oct. 1950; m. 1974; one s. two d. *Education:* Eastman School, Rochester, NY, Manhattan School, New York. *Career:* mem. American Soc. of Composers, Authors and Publrs (ASCAP). *Compositions include:* Sonatina for percussion solo 1969, Quartet for strings 1969, Encounter for orchestra 1970, Gentle Horizon for chamber ensemble 1972, Ricercar for band 1978, Concerto for viola and orchestra 1982, The Shores of Peace for chorus and chamber orchestra 1984, Fantasy on a Celtic Carol for viola and piano 1985, Jonah, opera in three acts 1986–89, One in Heart, processional for organ or orchestra or band 1988, My Frozen Well for SATB chorus 1991, Echoes of Edo for piano solo 1993, Trio for violin, horn and piano 1995, Double Concerto for euphonium, tuba and orchestra 1997, Sonata Organottone for organ and brass quintet 2007, Raking the Snow: Six Poems of Elisavietta Ritchie for voice and piano 2008, Concertino for cello and orchestra 2010, Sonata for two pianos 2010, Goldonda Songs, based on Harry Martinson's 'Aniara' for voices and chamber ensemble 2012, At the Landing – Verses from a Poet's Life, for voice, flute, viola and harp 2013, Trio Opalesco, for clarinet, viola and piano 2014, Sonata for cello and piano 2015, Sky Legends – Twelve Miniatures on the Signs of the Zodiac, for piano four-hands 2015; choral, piano and organ pieces. *Publications:* contribs: columns and articles on 20th-century music, also reviews of many books in Music, The Christian Science Monitor, Ovation, Musical America. *Honours:* ASCAP/Deems Taylor Award for Distinguished Criticism, for Christian Science Monitor column, Inside 20th Century Music 1983. *Address:* 75 Travis Road, Holliston, MA 01746, USA (home). *E-mail:* andreapressmusic@aol.com (office).

OWENS, Eric, BMus; American singer (bass baritone); b. 1970, Philadelphia. *Education:* Temple Univ., Curtis Inst. of Music. *Career:* debuts: Lodovico in Otello at San Francisco Opera 2002, Oroveso in Norma at Royal Opera House, Covent Garden and The Speaker in Die Zauberflöte at Paris Opera; debut at Metropolitan Opera as General Leslie Groves in Doctor Atomic and Sarrastro in Die Zauberflöte 2008; world premieres include title role in Elliot Goldenthal's Grendel with Los Angeles Opera and two roles created for him by John Adams, General Leslie Groves in Doctor Atomic at San Francisco Opera and Storyteller in A Flowering Tree at New Crowned Hope Festival in Vienna; sang Alberich in Das Rheingold, Siegfried and Götterdämmerung for Metropolitan Opera, Rigoletto, Il Trovatore and La Bohème for Los Angeles Opera, Hercules for Lyric Opera of Chicago, Ramfis in Aida for Houston Grand Opera and San Francisco Opera, Ariodante and L'Incoronazione di Poppea for ENO, Porgy for Washington Nat. Opera; concert performances include Lodovico in Otello with Chicago Symphony Orchestra in Chicago and Carnegie Hall, Beethoven's Missa Solemnis with Atlanta Symphony, and with Boston Symphony at Carnegie Hall, The Dream of Gerontius with Netherlands Radio Philharmonic, Mozart's Requiem with Handel and Haydn Soc., Brahms' Ein Deutsches Requiem at Carnegie Hall with Collegiate Chorale, Berlioz' Roméo et Juliette with Utah Symphony, Bach Cantatas with Chamber Music Soc. of Lincoln Center, Storyteller in Adams's A Flowering Tree with Atlanta Symphony Orchestra and Los Angeles Philharmonic and Jochanaan in Strauss's Salome with Cleveland Orchestra; has worked with conductors including James Levine, Riccardo Muti, Donald Runnicles, Jaap van Zweden, Giuseppe Finzi and Bernard Haitink; Carnegie Hall recital debut 2008, US recital tour with pianists Roberto Spano and Craig Rutenberg 2011–12; Artist-in-Residence, Glimmerglass Festival, New York (Aida, Kurt Weill's Lost in the Stars and a cabaret concert) 2012; mem. Bd of Trustees Nat. Foundation for Advancement in the Arts and Astral Artistic Services. *Recordings include:* Jackie O 1997, Mozart Requiem 2005, Adams: A Flowering Tree 2008, Glass Box 2008, John Adams Doctor Atomic (Grammy Award for Best Opera Recording 2012) 2008, Great Strauss Scenes 2010. *Honours:* ARIA Award 1999, Marian Anderson Award 2003, Opera News Award for invaluable contrib. to opera 2012. *Current Management:* c/o Stefania Almansi, IMG Artists, 111 Power Road, London, W4 5PY, England. *Telephone:* (20) 7957-5811. *E-mail:* salmansi@imgartists.com. *Website:* www.imgartists.com/artist/eric_owens; www.eric-owens.com.

OXENBOULD, Moffatt, AM; Australian artistic director and broadcaster; b. 18 Nov. 1943, Sydney. *Education:* National Institute for Dramatic Art. *Career:* Stage Man., Elizabethan Trust Opera 1963–65, Sutherland Williamson Opera, Sadler's Wells, London 1966–67; Planning Co-ordinator, Elizabethan Trust Opera—Australian Opera 1967–73; Artistic Administrator, Australian Opera 1974–84, Artistic Dir 1984–99 (retd); productions include The Rape of Lucretia 1971, Il Trittico 1978, La Clemenza di Tito 1991, Idomeneo 1994, Madama Butterfly 1997, La Bohème 1999; guest dir with Opera Australia, Houston Grand Opera since retirement; Presenter, ABC Classic FM 2000–; Chair. NIDA Bd of Studies. *Publications:* Joan Sutherland: A Tribute 1989; contrib. to various Australian publications. *Honours:* Dame Joan Hammond Award 1986, Green Room Award for contribution to opera 1999, Opera Australia Trophy 2000. *Address:* ABC Classic FM, GPO Box 9994, Sydney, NSW 2001, Australia (office).

OXLEY, James; singer (tenor); b. 1964, England. *Education:* Royal Coll. of Music, Univ. of Oxford, studied with Rudolf Piernay. *Career:* debut at the Royal Albert Hall 1991, under David Willcocks; concerts include Les Illuminations, and the Brahms Experience on South Bank 1992 and Edinburgh Festival 1993; season 1995–96 with Messiah (CBSO and Ulster Orchestras), and Alexander's Feast by Handel with the Brandenburg Consort; A Child of our Time in Oxford and Sweden, L'Enfance du Christ in Spain, and Britten's War Requiem; Bach's B Minor Mass on tour to France with Le Concert Sprituel; opera roles include Tamino (at Durham), Ottavio, Rodolfo and Alfredo; title roles in Britten's Prodigal Son, with Kent Opera; season 1996–97 with Purcell's King Arthur in France and The Fairy Queen at Schlossbruhl; Werther at Wexford, the Christmas Oratorio under Marc Minkowski, the Missa solemnis at the Festival Hall, London, and Messiah with the CBSO. *Honours:* first prize International Vocalisten Councours/Hertogenbosch 1994.

OZAWA, Seiji; Japanese conductor; b. 1 Sept. 1935, Shenyang, China; m. 1st Kyoko Edo; m. 2nd Vera Ilyan; one s. one d. *Education:* Toho School of Music, Japan with Prof. Hideo Saito, Tanglewood, USA and in Berlin under Herbert von Karajan. *Career:* Asst Conductor (under Leonard Bernstein), New York Philharmonic 1961–62 (including tour of Japan 1961); Guest Conductor, San Francisco Symphony, Detroit Symphony, Montréal, Minneapolis, Toronto and London Symphony Orchestras 1961–65; Music Dir Ravinia Festival, Chicago 1964–68; Music Dir Toronto Symphony Orchestra 1965–69, San Francisco Symphony Orchestra 1970–76, Boston Symphony Orchestra 1973–2002 (now Music Dir Laureate), Vienna State Opera 2002–10; Co-founder, Saito Kinen Orchestra 1987, Saito Kinen Festival Matsumoto 1992, Tokyo Opera Nomori 2005; toured Europe conducting many of the major orchestras 1966–67; Salzburg Festival 1969; toured USA, France, FRG, China 1979, Austria, UK 1981, Japan 1981, 1986, toured England, Netherlands, France, Germany, Austria and Belgium 1988; est. International Music Acad., Geneva 2005; makes frequent guest appearances with leading orchestras of America, Europe and Japan; has conducted opera at Salzburg, Covent Garden, La Scala, Vienna Staatsoper and Paris Opera; conducted world premiere, Messiaen's St Francis of Assisi, Paris 1983. *Honours:* Hon. mem. Vienna Staatsoper 2007; Chevalier, Légion d'Honneur 1999, Order of Friendship (Russia) 2011; Hon. DMus (Univ. of Mass., New England Conservatory, Wheaton Coll., Norton, Mass.); Dr hc (Univ. of Paris—Sorbonne) 2004; First Prize, Int. Competition of Orchestra Conductors, France 1959, Koussevitzky Prize for outstanding student conductor 1960, Laureate, Fondation du Japon 1988, Inouye Award 1994, Japan Art Asscn Praemium Imperiale 2011, Tanglewood Medal 2012, Kennedy Center Honoree 2015. *Current Management:* c/o Ronald A. Wilford, Columbia Artists Management Inc., 5 Columbus Circle at 1790 Broadway, New York NY 10019-1412, USA. *Website:* www.saito-kinen.com.

OZIM, Igor; Slovenian/German violinist and academic; *Professor of Violin, Universität Mozarteum, Salzburg;* b. 9 May 1931, Ljubljana, fmr Yugoslavia (now Slovenia); s. of Rudolf Ozim and Marija Kodric; m. Wonji Kim-Ozim. *Education:* Akad. za glasbo Ljubljana, Royal Coll. of Music, UK, studied with Prof. Max Rostal. *Career:* Prof. of Violin, Akad. za glasbo Ljubljana 1960–63, Staatliche Hochschule für Musik, Cologne 1963–96, Berne Conservatoire 1985–96, Hochschule für Musik, Vienna 1996–, currently Universität Mozarteum, Salzburg; mem. trio with Walter Grimmer and Ilse Dorati-von Alpenheim which performed and recorded all of Mozart's and Schubert's works –1995; concerts throughout Europe; Pres. Cen. Cttee European String Teachers' Asscn. *Honours:* Dr hc; First Prize, Int. Carl-Flesch Competition, London 1951, Munich 1953. *Address:* Department of Strings, Universität Mozarteum, Mirabellplatz 1, 5020 Salzburg, Austria (office). *Telephone:* (662) 61-98-0 (office). *E-mail:* igor.ozim@moz.ac.at (office). *Website:* www.moz.ac.at (office).

OZOLINS, Arthur Marcelo, BSc; Canadian concert pianist; b. 7 Feb. 1946, Lübeck, Germany. *Education:* University of Toronto, Canada, Mannes College of Music, New York, USA; studies with Pablo Casals, Jacques Abram, Nadia Boulanger, Nadia Reisenberg, Vlado Perlemuter. *Career:* debut, Toronto Symphony Orchestra, Toronto, 1961; Soloist with Royal Philharmonic, Hallé Orchestra, Stockholm and Oslo Philharmonic, Leningrad Philharmonic, Montreal Symphony, Toronto Symphony; Recitals, New York, London, Paris, Moscow, Leningrad, Buenos Aires, Sydney, San Paulo; 7 Tours, USSR; Television and radio performances, CBC, BBC, Swedish Radio; Concerto repertoire included works by Bach, Brahms, Beethoven, Mozart (K414, K466 and K503), Rachmaninov, Prokofiev, Tchaikovsky and Tippett (Handel Fantasy); mem, AFM; English Speaking Union. *Recordings:* The Complete Piano Concerti and Paganini Rhapsody of Rachmaninov with Mario Bernardi and the Toronto Symphony plus Dohnányi's Variations on a Nursery Song,

Healey Willan's Piano Concerto and Strauss Burleske; Numerous Solo recordings. *Honours:* 1st Prizes, Edmonton Competition, 1968, CBC Talent Festival, 1968; Juno Award, Best Classical Record, 1981; 7 Canada Council Awards. *Current Management:* Robert Gilder and Co., 91 Great Russell Street, London, WC1B 3PS, England. *Telephone:* (20) 7580-7758. *Fax:* (20) 7580-7739. *E-mail:* rgilder@robert-gilder.com. *Website:* www.robert-gilder .com.

OZOLINS, Janis Alfreds, DipMus; Latvian violoncellist, singer and conductor; b. 29 Sept. 1919, Riga; m. Adine Uggla 1951, two s. one d. *Education:* Conservatory of Latvia, studied with Prof. E. Mainardi in Rome, Royal Acad. of Music, Stockholm, Univ. of Uppsala. *Career:* debut on violoncello in Riga 1933; concert radio recitals, solo performances with orchestras in Latvia, Sweden, Denmark, the UK, Italy, Switzerland; Music Master 1956–; Conductor, Landskrona Symphony Orchestra, Sweden 1957; bass soloist, Beethoven's 9th Symphony with H. Blomstedt, Norrköping, Sweden 1961; Dir, Växjö Municipal School of Music and Municipal Music Dir, Växjö, Sweden 1964–84; conductor of operas and ballets, Växjö. *Honours:* Nat. Prize of Latvia 1944, Växjö Lions Club Culture Prize 1976, Swedish Orchestra Nat. Federation Royal Gold Medal 1977, 1984.

P

PAASIKIVI, Lilli; Finnish singer (mezzo-soprano); b. 1970. *Education:* Royal Academy, Stockholm, Royal College of Music, London with Neil Mackie, studied with Janet Baker. *Career:* debut with Noorland Opera 1993, as Ottone in Poppea; appearances at Paris Châtelet (Pilgrim in Saariaho's L'amour de loin 2001); Finnish National Opera from 1998 as Cenerentola, Suzuki, Dorabella, Marguerite (Berlioz Faust) and Rosina; Cordelia in the premiere of Sallinen's King Lear; Jitsuko Honda in premiere of Hosokawa's Hanjo at Aix Festival 2004. *Recordings:* Kullervo Symphony, The Tempest, The Maiden in the Tower, by Sibelius, Complete Alma Mahler Songs. *Current Management:* Harrison Parrott, 5–6 Albion Court, London, W6 0QT, England. *Telephone:* (20) 7229-9166. *Fax:* (20) 7221-5042. *E-mail:* info@harrisonparrott.co.uk. *Website:* www.harrisonparrott.com.

PABST, Michael; Austrian singer (tenor); b. 1955, Graz. *Education:* studied in Graz and Vienna. *Career:* Principal Tenor at Vienna Volksoper singing operetta and lyric opera roles 1978–84; dramatic repertoire from 1985, including Max in Der Freichütz, Munich; Bacchus, at Philadelphia, Stuttgart, Frankfurt and Houston; Lohengrin, at Hamburg and Zurich; Walther, at Cape Town and Trieste; Erik, at La Scala and Buenos Aires; Huon in Oberon, at La Scala; Florestan at the Savonlinna Festival and Siegmund at Liège; guest appearances at Vienna Staatsoper from 1991, with Florestan, The Drum Major in Wozzeck, Max, Jenik in The Bartered Bride, Erik; other roles include Hoffmann, Pedro in Tiefland, Luigi in Il Tabarro, Schubert's Fierrabras, Sergei, in Lady Macbeth, Strauss's Matteo, Aegisthus, Burgomaster in Friedenstag and Apollo. *Recordings include:* Heinrich in Schreker's Irrelohe 1995; season 1998 in Henze's Venus and Adonis at Genoa and as Bacchus in Ariadne at Toulouse.

PACE, Patrizia; Italian singer (soprano); b. 1963, Turin. *Education:* Turin Conservatory. *Career:* debut at La Scala 1984, as Celia in Mozart's Lucio Silla; has appeared in Milan as Micaela, Mozart's Despina, Susanna and Zerlina, Oscar, Lisa in La Sonnambula and in premiere Il Principe Felice by Mannino 1987; guest appearances at Deutsche Oper Berlin, Spoleto Festival and the Vienna Staatsoper as Oscar and Rossini's Elvira 1986, 1988, Gilda, Nannetta in Falstaff and Yniold; further engagements at Hamburg Staatsoper as Liu, Florence, Genoa, Palermo and Covent Garden 1991, 1993 as Gilda, and Yniold in Pelléas et Mélisande; other roles include Rosina, and Sofia in Il Signor Bruschino; season 1998 at Catania as Gilda and Marzelline; engaged as Nannetta in Falstaff for the Royal Opera 1999; sang Zobeida in Donizetti's Alahor in Granata at Palermo 1999, Zerlina at La Coruña 2000. *Recordings:* Barbarina in Le nozze di Figaro and Mozart's Requiem; Mozart's C minor Mass.

PACIOREK, Grażyna, BMus; Polish composer; b. 11 Dec. 1967, Zyrardow. *Education:* State School of Music, Warsaw, Acad. of Music, Warsaw with Prof. M. Borkowski, Polish Section ISCM, Kazimierz Dolny, Studio of Electro-acoustic Music, Acad. of Music, Kraków. *Career:* many performances at the composers concerts in Warsaw (Acad. of Music, Royal Castle) and in Kraków 1987–91; composed music for film aired on Polish television 1991; works presented in radio programme at Gdansk Meeting of Young Composers 1991 and fifth Laboratory of Contemporary Chamber Music 1991; mem. Polish Soc. for Contemporary Music, Polish Composers' Union Youth Circle. *Compositions include:* Monologue for oboe solo, Te-qui-la for six percussion group, Toccata for violin, cello and piano, string quartet, Muzyka Mapothana for oboe and accordiov, Concerto for viola and orchestra, also electronic music, film music.

PADMORE, Elaine Marguirite, OBE, BMus, MA, LTCL; British artistic director, broadcaster, singer, lecturer and writer; b. 3 Feb. 1947, Haworth, Yorks., England; d. of Alfred Padmore and Florence Padmore. *Education:* Newland High School, Hull, Arnold School, Blackpool, Univ. of Birmingham and Guildhall School of Music, London. *Career:* Lecturer in Liberal Studies, Coll. of Art, Croydon and Kingston 1968–70; Books Ed., Music Dept, Oxford University Press 1970–71; Producer, Music Div., BBC 1971–76, Chief Producer, Opera, BBC Radio 1976–83, Announcer, BBC Radio 3 1982–90, programmes include Parade, Music of Tchaikovsky's Russia, Festival Comment, England's Pleasant Land; opera singer; Lecturer in Opera, RAM 1979–86; Artistic Dir Wexford Festival Opera 1982–94, Opera Ireland 1989–91, Royal Danish Opera 1993–2000; Dir of Opera, Covent Garden 2000–11; currently freelance opera consultant and lecturer. *Publication:* Wagner (Great Composers series); contrib. to New Grove Dictionary of Music and Musicians. *Honours:* Hon. ARAM, Hon. FTCL, Hon. FBC; Kt, Order of the Dannebrog (Denmark) 1994; Hon. DMus (Birmingham); Hungarian Pro Musica Award for BBC Radio programme In Summertime on Bredon 1973, Prix Musical de Radio Brno for The English Renaissance 1974, Sunday Independent Award for Services to Music in Ireland 1985. *E-mail:* elainepadmore@gmail.com (home).

PADMORE, Mark Joseph; British singer (tenor); b. 8 March 1961, London; m. Victoria Mortimer 2009. *Education:* Kings Coll., Cambridge, studied with Erich Vietheer, Gita Denise, Janice Chapman and Diane Forlano. *Career:* singer at major festivals including Aix-en-Provence, Edinburgh, BBC Proms, Salzburg, Spoleto, Tanglewood, New York; opera house debuts include Teatro Comunale, Florence 1992, Opéra Comique, Paris 1993, Théâtre du Châtelet

1995, Royal Opera House, Covent Garden 1995, Scottish Opera 1996, Opéra de Paris 1996; sang Captain Vere in Britten's Billy Budd at Glyndebourne 2013; regular singer, Hilliard Ensemble 1986–90; singer with Les Arts Florissants 1991–2001; has performed in Charpentier's Médée, Rameau's Hippolyte, Purcell's King Arthur, Rameau's Zoroastre and Platée, Britten's Paul Bunyan, Mozart's Don Giovanni, Handel's Jephtha; recitals include St John Passion, St Matthew Passion, Bach's Weihnachtsoratorium, Schubert's Die Schöne Müllerin, John Eliot Gardiner's Bach Cantata Pilgrimage 2000. *Recordings:* over 50 recordings including Britten: Before life and after 2009, Schubert: Winterreise 2009, Schubert: Die schone Mullerin 2010, Schubert: Schwanengesang 2011, Beethoven: An die ferne Geliebte 2015. *Honours:* Gramophone Award for Best Solo Vocal Recording (for Schubert's Winterreise) 2010. *Current Management:* Maxine Robertson Management, 14 Forge Drive, Claygate, KT10 0HR, England. *Telephone:* (20) 7993-2917. *E-mail:* mr@maxinerobertson.com. *Website:* www.maxinerobertson.com; www.markpadmore.com (home).

PAĎOUROVÁ, Lýdie, (Lýdie Havláková); Czech singer (mezzo-soprano) and teacher; b. 30 Aug. 1957, Prague; m. Jan Padour 1979; one d. *Education:* Conservatoire of Prague, Univ. of Music, Prague. *Career:* debut at Nat. Theatre, Prague in Janáček's Katya Kabanova (Varvara) 1986, and Prokofiev's Betrothal in a Monastery (Klara), Tchaikovsky's Queen of Spades (Pavlina and Dafnis) 1987, Mozart's Le nozze di Figaro (Cherubino) 1988, Purcell's Dido and Aeneas (Dido), Tchaikovsky's Eugen Onegin (Olga), B. Martinů's Julietta (Pán), Trojí přání (Adelaida), Britten's The Beggar's Opera (Mrs Coaxer). *Films:* Poslední ples na ronovské plovárně 1974, Odysseus a hvězdy 1976, Marečku, podejte mi pero 1976, Podivný výlet 1978, Hildegarda von Bingen 2010. *Recordings:* Arias by Mascagni (Santuzza), Bizet's Carmen, Mozart's Dorabella, Thomas' Mignon, Purcell's Dido, Donizetti's Orsini (Lucrezia Borgia); complete opera: Prokofiev's Betrothal in a Monastery. *Address:* Na Lysinach 461/30, 14700 Prague, Czech Republic. *Telephone:* (2) 22988340. *E-mail:* lydieh@volny.cz. *Website:* www.agency-lydie.com.

PADRÓS, David; Spanish composer and pianist; b. 22 March 1942, Igualada, Barcelona. *Education:* Municipal Music School, Barcelona, Musikhochschule Trossingen, Germany, Konservatorium, Basel and in Zürich, Switzerland and Freiburg, Germany. *Career:* commissions and performances in European music festivals; mem. Associacio Catalana de Compositors. *Compositions include:* Styx for chamber ensemble, Heptagonal for piano, Crna Gora for chamber ensemble, Khorva for orchestra, Cal Ligrama (F1 in G) for piano, Dos Legendes for organ, Batalla for piano, harpsichord and strings, Musik im Raum for chamber ensemble, Jo-Ha-Kyu for orchestra, Arachne for chamber ensemble, Maqam for piano, Trajectories for violin, Confluences for brass ensemble, percussion and tape, Chaconne for string quartet and harpsichord, El Sermo de R. Muntaner for four mixed voices, four old wind instruments and organ, Ketjak for piano quartet, Recordant W. A. M. for clarinet and organ, La Sala de la Suprema Harmonia for chamber ensemble 1991, Jdeb for recorder quartet 1992, Seis Diferencias for organ 1992, Ghiza-i-ruh for flute, clarinet and piano 1993, Nocturne for flute, viola and clarinet 1992, Gjatams for piano quartet 1993, Xucla el silenci nocturn for flute, clarinet, violin and cello 1994, Qawwali for recorder quartet 1994, Klagelied for piano 1994, Manas for piano, percussion and wind quintet 1996, Cinco Tankas for mezzo, flute, clarinet and guitar 1996, Cheops for chamber orchestra 1997, Sunyata for flute and guitar 1997, 17 Cançons populars catalanes for piano 1998, Verwandlung for flute quartet 1999, Tres Poemas sonores for mixed chorus 1999, El temps segons Rama for orchestra 1999, Piano Concerto 2000–01, Acciones y reacciones for flute and piano 2000, Degung for recorder and vibraphone 2000, Projeccions for chamber orchestra 2001, Diario de noche for piano 2003, Lignes dans l'espace for flute in G 2004, Amalgames for clarinet and piano 2004, Instants for piano 2004, Metamorfosis Mozartiana for chamber orchestra 2005, Linies i Plans for orchestra 2006, Daha for bass clarinet 2006. *Recordings:* Musik in Raum, Arachne, Confluencies, Chamber Music, La Sala de la Suprema Harmonia, Materials, Klagelied, Verwandlung, Complete Piano Works, Cinco Tankas. *Publications:* contrib. to Revista Musical Catalana, Revista Quodlibet. *Honours:* Hans-Lenz-Preis, Germany 1969, Komposition-Preis der Stiftung Landis and Gyr, Switzerland 1976. *Address:* Rossello 213, 1-1, 08008 Barcelona, Spain (home). *Telephone:* (93) 2170943 (home).

PAGE, Anne, BMus, DipEd; Australian organist; b. 2 Dec. 1955, Perth, Western Australia. *Education:* Univ. of Western Australia, with Maire-Claire Alain at Conservatoire Nationale de Musique, Rueil-Malmaison, France, with Peter Hurford in Cambridge, and with Jacques van Oortmerssen at the Sweelinck Conservatory, Amsterdam. *Career:* organ recitalist in UK, Europe, USA and Australia; teacher and course dir; debut at Royal Festival Hall, London 1988; directed Cambridge Summer Recitals 1987–94; pioneered revival of serious interest in the harmonium; Prof. of Harmonium, RAM, London 2003; Music Co-ordinator and Curator, Historic Organ Sound Project, British Inst. of Organ Studies 2004–07; mem. Incorporated Soc. of Musicians, British Inst. of Organ Studies. *Recordings:* French Music for Harmonium (two vols) 1988, 1990, Sigfrid Karg-Elert: Music for Harmonium 1990, Two Mander Organs 1990, Veni Creator Spiritus: choral and organ music of Carl Rütti (with Cambridge Voices) 1998, J. S. Bach's Orgelbüchlein 1999, The Willis Organ of Emmanuel United Reform Church 2001, Olivier Messiaen: Livre du

Saint Sacrement 2002, César Franck: L'Organiste (two vols) 2008, The Historic Organ of Adlington Hall 2008; recordings on 23 organs of historic interest as part of Historic Organ Sound Project. *Honours:* Prix d'excellence à l'unanimité, Conservatoire Nationale de Musique 1981. *Website:* www.anne-page.co.uk.

PAGE, Charlotte; British singer (soprano); b. 1972, England. *Education:* Royal Coll. of Music, London. *Career:* first niece in Peter Grimes for Covent Garden, WNO 1999; Gretel for Opera Northern Ireland; Frasquita for Central Festival Opera; Zerlina for Pimlico Opera and Offenbach's Hélène, Holland Park; other roles include Mozart's Despina; Pamina, Second Lady and Cherubino; Clinene in Cavalli's L'Egisto; Mélisande for Atelier Lyrique, Orleans; on tour to France; further concerts in Tokyo and throughout the UK.

PAGE, Christopher Howard, BA, DPhl; British medievalist; b. 8 April 1952, London; m. 1st Régine Fourcade 1975 (divorced 2002); m. 2nd Anne Dunan 2004. *Education:* Univ. of Oxford, York Univ. *Career:* Prof. of Medieval Music and Literature, Univ. of Cambridge; frequent broadcaster on BBC Radio 3, both as lecturer and as dir of his ensemble, Gothic Voices; presenter of Radio 4 arts programme, Kaleidoscope; presenter Radio 3 series Spirit of the Age. *Recordings include:* directed Gothic Voices in Sequences and Hymns by Abbess Hildegard of Bingen (several awards) and many other recordings. *Publications:* Voices and Instruments of the Middle Ages, Sequences and Hymns by Abbess Hildegard of Bingen, The Owl and the Nightingale: Musical Life and Ideas in France, 1100–1300 1989, Latin Poetry and Conductus Rhythm in Medieval France 1997, Music and Instruments of the Middle Ages: Studies in Text and Performance 1997; The Christian West and Its Singers: The First Thousand Years 2010; many academic and scholarly contributions to Early Music, Galpin Society Journal, Proceedings of the Royal Musical Association, New Oxford History of Music, Cambridge Guide to the Arts in Britain, Early Music History, The Historical Harpsichord, Journal of the American Musicological Society. *Honours:* Fellow Fellowship of Makers and Restorers of Historical Instruments, Soc. of Antiquaries; prizewinner Innsbruck Int. Radio Prize 1981, Gramophone Awards, Royal Musical Asscn Dent Medal. *Address:* c/o Sidney Sussex College, Cambridge University, Cambridge, CB2 3HU, England (home). *Telephone:* (1223) 338800 (home).

PAGE, Steven; singer (baritone); b. 1950, England. *Education:* Opera Studio, London with Margaret Hyde. *Career:* sang Don Alfonso and Nick Shadow with Opera 80, (now English Touring Opera); For English National Opera he has sung the title role in Mozart's Don Giovanni, Tarquinius in The Rape of Lucretia, Albert in Werther, Paolo in Simone Boccanegra, Valentine in Faust and the Count in Marriage of Figaro and most recently the role of Figaro; For Scottish Opera he has appeared as Guglielmo in Così fan tutte, Marcello in La Bohème, Chorèbe in Les Troyens, Ford in Falstaff and the title role of Don Giovanni and the Count in Marriage of Figaro; He has also taken part in four seasons at the Buxton Festival in leading roles and has appeared with Opera Factory as Don Giovanni at the Queen Elizabeth Hall; For Glyndebourne Touring Opera has sung Nick Shadow in The Rake's Progress, Leporello in Don Giovanni, Anubis in Harrison Birtwistle's The Second Mrs Kong and Coyle in a new production by Robin Philips of Britten's Owen Wingrave; Made his debut Glyndebourne Festival as Nick Shadow in 1994 and returned as Leporello in Don Giovanni and Anubis; Sang Geronio in Rossini's Il Turco in Italia, Garsington, 1996; Season 1999 in Tippett's The Mask of Time at the London Prom concerts.

PAGLIARANI, Mario; Swiss composer; b. 27 June 1963, Mendriosa, Ticino canton. *Education:* Conservatorio di Milano, studied with Salvatore Sciarrino. *Compositions include:* Alcuni particolari oscuri 1983, Vie d'uscita 1986, Lucciole o imperi? 1989–90, Paesaggio-Madrigale 1991, Pierrot lunatique 1993, Cappuccetto rosso 1994, Bergweg 1995, Canzone fantasma 1996, Apparizione di Franz Schubert fra le onde 1997, Trio pozzanghera 1998, Rarefatto cantabile 1999. *Recordings:* Alcuni particolari oscuri, Paesaggio-Madrigale, Pierrot lunatique. *Honours:* Musica Ticinensis prize 1987, VI Concurso de obras musicales para Radio prize, Madrid 1995, Premio Meret Oppenheim 2008. *Address:* Vicolo dei Lironi 3, 6833 Vacallo 7, Switzerland (home).

PAGLIARI, Matteo; Italian conductor; *Principal Conductor, Orquesta Sinfónica Nacional (National Symphonic Orchestra), Peru;* b. 20 June 1974, Parma. *Education:* Conservatorio di Musica Arrigo Boito, Parma, Conservatorio Giuseppe Verdi, Como, Accademia Musicale Pescarese. *Career:* Musical Dir Città di Parma Youth Choir 1997; Artistic Dir and Principal Conductor, Città di Parma Mixed Choir 1998–2001; fmrly Asst Conductor to Riccardo Frizza 2002–03, Roberto Abbado 2004; Principal Conductor, Nat. Symphonic Orchestra, Lima, Peru 2009–; currently Prof. of Conducting Technique, School of Opera-Teatro Comunale, Bologna; other engagements with orchestras include: Symphonic Orchestra of Rome, Orchestra Sinfonica Nazionale della RAI. *Current Management:* Alessandro Panetto, Alessandro Panetto Management, Via Aeroporti 119–121, 36030 Caldogno, Italy. *Telephone:* (04) 441455748. *Fax:* (04) 441455747. *E-mail:* alessandro@apmanagement.eu. *Website:* www.apmanagement.eu. *Address:* Via N. Venturini 5, 43035 Parma, Felino, Italy (office); Teatro Comunale di Bologna Fondazione, Largo Respighi 1, 40126 Bologna, Italy (office). *Telephone:* 3406992049 (mobile); (51) 529958 (office). *E-mail:* matteopagliari@matteopagliari.com. *Website:* www.comunalebologna.it (office); www.matteopagliari.com.

PAGLIAZZI, Franco; Italian singer (baritone, dramatic tenor); b. 8 April 1937, Florence; m. Denise Serghieva 1965; one s. *Education:* Centro Lirico del Teatro Comunale, Florence, studied with Ettore Campogalliani. *Career:* debut as Cherubini's Elisa, Maggio Musicale Fiorentino 1960; as baritone, sang numerous Verdi roles, including Rigoletto, Conte di Luna, Amonasro, Iago, Posa, Carlo V; sang in theatres including Firenze Teatro Comunale, Naples San Carlo, Milan La Scala, Wiener Staatsoper, Dublin, Orange Festival, Sofia, Lugano, Brussels, Bielefeld, Amsterdam, Ostrava, Catania, and other venues until 1974; from 1976, singing as dramatic tenor under name Marc Alexander; sang roles including Enzo, Gabriele, Macduff, Manrico, Don Alvaro, Calaf; appearances include Gran Teatre del Liceu, Valencia, Rouen, Bordeaux, Braunschweig, Como, Mantova; recitals in Italy, Switzerland, Japan, until 1998; sang with conductors including Muti, Gavazzeni, Bartoletti, G. Patanè, Savini, Rivoli, Morelli, Wung Chung. *Recordings:* Un Converso in Cherubini's Elisa 1960, Arias from Il Trovatore, Ernani, Ballo in Maschera 1963, Conte di Luna in Il Trovatore 1968, Nello in Donizetti's Pia de Tolomei 1968. *Honours:* competitions, Milan, Associazione Lirico Concertistica Italiana 1960, Busseto Voci Verdiane 1962, Sofia Competition 1963, Vercelli Viotti First Prize 1964. *Address:* Via del Ghirlandaio 24, 50121 Florence, Italy (home). *E-mail:* pagliazziopera@yahoo.it (home).

PAHUD, Emmanuel; French flautist; b. 27 Jan. 1970, Geneva, Switzerland. *Education:* Paris Conservatoire, studied with Aurèle Nicolet. *Career:* Principal Flute of the Berlin Philharmonic 1992–, and many concerts as solo artist appearances at leading international festivals and chamber music societies throughout Europe and Japan; appeared with Zürich Tonhalle, Philharmonia, Danish National Radio, Auvergne, Vienna Chamber, Zürich Chamber, The Baltimore Symphony, the London Philharmonic, Bayerischer Rundfunk, Mariinski, Minnesota Symphony, Camerata Salzburg, Deutsche Kammerphilharmonie, Washington National Symphony, NHK Symphony, and Scottish Chamber Orchestras; festivals include New York Mostly Mozart, Salzburg, Budapest, Artist-in-Residence, Lucerne Festival 2006; collaborations with Matthias Pintscher, Michael Jarrell, Marc-André Dalbavie, Eric Le Sage, Yefim Bronfman, Hélène Grimaud, Jacky Terrasson. *Recordings include:* Mozart Concertos with the Berlin Philharmonic and Abbado 1997, French repertory with pianist Eric Le Sage 1998, Dalbavie Flute Concertos 2008, Bach Harpsichord and Flute Concertos 2009, Opium Mélodies françaises 2009, Fantasy: A Night at the Opera 2010, French Music for Winds (Echo Klassik Award for Instrumentalist of the Year – Flute) 2014. *Honours:* winner, Duino Int. Music Competition 1988, Kobe Int. Music Competition 1989, eight prizes, Concours de Genève 1992, Instrumentalist of the Year, Victoires de la Musique Awards 1997. *Current Management:* c/o Cæcilia, 29 rue de la Coulouvrenière, 1204 Geneva, Switzerland. *Telephone:* 8091520. *Fax:* 8091528. *E-mail:* caecilia@caecilia.ch; jmpeysson@caecilia.ch. *Website:* www.caecilia.ch. *Current Management:* Opus 3 Artists, 470 Park Avenue South, 9th Floor North, New York, NY 10016, USA. *Telephone:* (212) 584-7500. *Fax:* (646) 300-8200. *E-mail:* info@opus3artists.com. *Website:* www.opus3artists.com; www.emmanuelpahud.net.

PAÏDASSI, Solenne; French violinist. *Education:* Conservatoire de Musique, Geneva, Royal Acad. of Music, London, Curtis Inst. of Music, Philadelphia, Hochschule für Musik und Theater, Hannover. *Career:* performed as soloist with Orchestre de Radio-France, Sinfonia Varsovia Orchestra, NDR Philharmonic Orchestra, Orchestre Philharmonique de Nice, Korean Nat. Univ. of Arts Chamber Orchestra; worked with conductors including Shlomo Mintz, Jacek Kaspszyk and Jaime Martin; recitals and concerts in France, Switzerland, Korea, Japan, Germany, Poland, Mexico, Italy, Ukraine, USA, including at Tonhalle Zürich and Carnegie Hall, New York; festival appearances at La Folle Journée, Kanazawa, Japan, Festival Int. du Jeune Soliste, Antibes, Festival Int. de Sion Valais, Festival de Musique Sacrée, Nice, Int. Holland Music Sessions, Tongyeong Int. Music Festival; concerts with Sinfonia Varsovia Orchestra, Orchestra de Radio-France, Orchestre de Cannes 2011; took part as a 'New Masters on Tour' from The Int. Holland Music Sessions in an int. concert tour to Concertgebouw, Amsterdam and elsewhere 2011; mem. Il Gioco col Suono. *Honours:* Yehudi Menuhin: Live Music Now Scholarship, Winner, Baltic Int. Violin Competition 2008, Winner, Hanover Competition 2009, First Prize, Jacques Thibaud Int. Violin Competition 2010, Mozarteum Prize 2011. *E-mail:* info@solenne-paidassi.com. *Website:* www.solenne-paidassi.com.

PAIK, Byung-dong; South Korean academic; b. 26 Jan. 1936, Seoul; m. Woo Wha-ja 1969. *Education:* Shin-Heung High School, Jeon-joo; Coll. of Music, Seoul National Univ.; Stadtliche Hochschule für Musik, Hanover, Germany. *Career:* debut, Annual Korean New Composers Prize with Three Symphonic Chapters 1962; six composition recitals since first recital 1960–; has presented his works several times with National Symphony Orchestra, Seoul Philharmonic Orchestra and other ensembles; Prof., Personnel Management mem., Coll. of Music, Seoul National Univ.; Pres., Perspective Composers Group. *Compositions:* Major works, Symphonic Three Chapters, 1962; Un I, II, III, IV, V, VI for Instrumental Ensemble; Drei Bagetellen für Klavier, 1973; Concerto for Piano and Orchestra, 1974; Veranderte Ehepaar, 1986; In September for Orchestra, 1987; Contra, 1988. *Recordings:* Ein kleine Nachtleid für Violine und Klavier, SEM, Seoul, 1978; Guitariana for two Guitars, SEM, 1984; Byul-Gok 87, Jigu Record Corporation, Seoul, 1987. *Publications:* Musical Theory, 1977; Essays: Seven Fermatas 1979; Essays: Sound or Whispering, 1981; Harmony, 1984; Music for Culture, 1985; College Musical Theory, 1989; The Streams of Modern Music, 1990. *Address:* 214-1 Sangdo 1 dong, Dongjakgu, A-202 Sangdo Villa, Seoul, Republic of Korea.

PAIK, Kun-woo; South Korean pianist; b. 10 March 1946, Seoul. *Education:* Juilliard School, USA, studied with Rosina Levine, studied in London with Ilona Kabos and in Italy with Guido Agosti and Wilhelm Kempf. *Career:* interpreter of piano works of Ravel, Liszt, Scriabin and Prokofiev; has played with orchestras throughout N America and Europe, including Indianapolis Symphony, Rotterdam Philharmonic, Royal Philharmonic, London Symphony, BBC Symphony (soloist, Last Night of the Proms 1987), Orchestre Nat. de France, Polish Radio Nat. Symphony; Music Dir Festival International de Musique de Dinard-Emerald Coast; mem. jury, Tchaikovskyi Competition, Moscow 2007; recitals at maj. European music festivals; numerous recordings. *Honours:* winner, Naumburg Competition, Gold Medal, Busoni Int. Piano Competition, three Diapason d'Or awards. *Current Management:* . *E-mail:* prailton@vanwalsum.com. *Website:* www.vanwalsum.com. *E-mail:* kw@kunwoopaik.com (office). *Website:* www.kunwoopaik.com.

PAINTAL, Priti, BSc, MSc, MMus, PGCE; British composer; *Artistic Director, ShivaNova / Equator*; b. Delhi, India; partner Robert Maycock (deceased); one s. one d. *Education:* studied piano and composition in India and moved on to Univ. of York, Royal Northern Coll. of Music, Manchester and Inst. of Educ., London. *Career:* joined a family that included musicians trained in both Indian and Western traditions alongside eminent scientists and doctors; established herself writing for leading British performers; now based in UK and well known as a composer, performer, music producer and promoter; f. ensemble ShivaNova, brings together traditional, classical and jazz performers; has written group pieces and a mini-opera, Survival Song, for the Royal Opera's Garden Venture contemporary opera programme, led to full-length Biko, Royal Opera's first commission from an Asian and a woman composer, staged in London and Birmingham; other performers have included the Philharmonia Orchestra in premiere of Secret Chants, City of London Sinfonia, Bournemouth Sinfonietta, East of England Orchestra, Balanescu and Bingham string quartets, Park Lane Sextet, and numerous singers and instrumentalists; contrib. to radio and TV; has written for The Guardian; featured in The Independent and The Daily Telegraph, on Songlines, and BBC Radio 3 and on Womans' Hour (BBC Radio 4); mem. Bd Kent Music; fmr mem. Arts Council Music panel, Bd of South-East Arts, Bd of Overtones; Artistic Dir Women of the World, Equator World music and dance (promotions of ShivaNova). *Works include:* Survival Song 1988, Biko 1992, Gulliver 1995, Polygamy, Improvisations and other chamber works. *Recordings include:* Polygamy, Urban Mantras, Flying to the Sun, Moonlighting, Seventh Heaven, Secret Chants 2009. *Address:* Peregrine, Grange Road, St Michaels, Tenterden, Kent, TN30 6TJ, England (office). *E-mail:* PPaintal@aol.com (office); shivanova@aol.com (office); admin@shivanova.co.uk (office). *Website:* www.shivanova.com (office); www.myspace.com/shivanovacom; www.equatorfestival.com.

PAL, Támás; Hungarian conductor; b. 16 Sept. 1937, Gyula. *Education:* Franz Liszt Acad., Budapest with Janos Viski and Andréas Korody. *Career:* Conductor, Budapest State Opera 1960–75, notably at the Edinburgh Festival 1973 and the Wiesbaden May Festival 1974; Principal Conductor, Szeged Symphony Orchestra and Opera 1975–83; Permanent Conductor, Budapest Opera 1983–85; Artistic Dir of the open air summer music festival at Budapest 1987; has conducted operatic rarities such as Salieri's Falstaff, Liszt's Don Sanche and Il Pittor Parigino by Cimarosa; directed Aida at Szeged 1997. *Recordings include:* Liszt Piano Concerto No. 2 with the Hungarian State Orchestra; Brahms Symphony No. 3 and Academic Festival Overture with the Budapest Symphony Orchestra; Il Pittor Parigino (premiere recording).

PALACIO, Ernesto; Peruvian singer (tenor); b. 19 Oct. 1946, Lima. *Education:* studied in Peru and Milan, Italy. *Career:* debut as Almaviva in San Remo, Italy 1972; sang lyric roles in Milan, Rome, Venice, Trieste, Bologne, Turin, Genoa, Palermo, Naples, Parma, Catania; guest appearances in London (Covent Garden), New York (Metropolitan and Carnegie Hall), Buenos Aires (Colón), Berlin (Philharmonic), Edinburgh, Marseilles, Bordeaux, Lille, Nancy, Lyon, Strasbourg, Houston, Dallas, Zürich, Düsseldorf, Munich, Caracas, Chile; other roles include 18 operas of Rossini, Don Giovanni, Così fan tutte, Re Pastore, Die Zauberflöte, Finta giardiniera, Finta Semplice (Mozart); Elisir d'amore, Don Pasquale, La fille du Régiment, Esule di Roma, Torquato Tasso (Donizetti); sang in a revival of Ciro in Babilonia by Rossini at Savona 1988; appeared as Argirio in Tancredi opposite Marilyn Horne at Barcelona 1989, Bilbao 1991; Bonn Opera 1990, as Almaviva. *Recordings:* Mosè in Egitto; Il Turco in Italia; Miserere by Donizetti; Adelaide di Borgogna by Rossini; Vivaldi's Serenata a Tre; Torquato Tasso; Catone in Utica by Vivaldi; Unpublished arias by Rossini, conducted by Carlo Rizzi; Prince Giovanni in Una Cosa Rara.

PALACIO, Pedro Antonio, DipMus, MMus; Argentine composer; b. 15 April 1961, La Rioja; one s. one d. *Education:* studied in Córdoba, Argentina and in France. *Career:* debut with Variations for piano performed at National Festival for Contemporary Music, Argentina 1984; performance of works at Teatro Colón, Argentina, Festival Antidogma Musica, Italy, Mengano Quartett and WNC Ensemble, Cologne, and Turmheim Ensemble, Germany; Ensemble Stringendo, Ensemble Aleph at Festival of Evreux, BMA Ensemble at Nantes, Wozzeck Trio, ENMD-Montreuil Ensemble, France, World Music Days Festival, Zürich, Switzerland, Poland Broadcasting Symphony Orchestra, Symphony Orchestra of Cordoba, SACEM, France. *Compositions:* Axis, Triolaid, Quintolaid, Latidos, Yugoslavia Burning, Omphalo, Dämmerung, Laughs of Tokyo, Histoire d'Oiseaux Mathématiques, Quateur à Cordes No. 1 1998, Cuerdas Vocales 1998, El tiempo suspendido resonante II 2000. *Recordings:* albums: Dämmerung, Laughs of Tokyo, Histoire d'oiseaux mathématiques, Ensemble Aleph, El tiempo suspendido resonante II. *Publications include:* Roman-B for guitar 1987, Herejía for solo violin 1998. *Honours:* Essec-Invention Prize, France 1986, Icon Award, Italy 1988, Trinac Award, Argentina 1989, Prix André Jolivet, France 1991, Kazimierz Serocki Competiton, Poland 1996, Premio Alberto Ginastera, Argentina 1996. *Address:* 15 rue Surmelin, 75020 Paris, France (home).

PALAY, Elliot; American singer (tenor); b. 18 Dec. 1948, Milwaukee, Wis. *Education:* Indiana Univ., Bloomington with Charles Kullmann, studied with Clemens Kaiser-Breme in Essen. *Career:* debut at Lubeck 1972, as Matteo in Arabella; sang in Freiburg, Düsseldorf, Munich and Stuttgart; Komische Oper Berlin 1977, in Aufstieg und Fall der Stadt Mahagonny; returned to USA and sang at the New York City Opera; Santa Fe and Seattle 1983, as Siegfried in Der Ring des Nibelungen; Antwerp and Ghent 1983, as Siegmund in Die Walküre; Dresden 1984, in Wozzeck; other roles include Wagner's Tristan and Walther, Verdi's Radames and Ismaele, the Emperor in Die Frau ohne Schatten and Boris in Katya Kabanova; sang Siegfried with the Jutland Opera at Århus 1987; opera roles in Munich from 2000; fmr mem. Vocal Faculty, United States Int. Univ., San Diego, Calif.; fmr Resident mem. Los Angeles Music Center Opera; now retd.

PALECZNY, Piotr; Polish pianist and academic; *Artistic Director, International Chopin Festival*; b. 10 May 1946, Rybnik; m.; one s. *Education:* State Higher School of Music, Warsaw, studied under Prof. Jan Ekier. *Career:* soloist with orchestras including Warsaw Nat. Philharmonic Orchestra, Polish Radio Nat. Symphony Orchestra, Chicago Symphony, American Symphony, Royal Philharmonic, Concertgebouw, BBC London Orchestra, Yomiuri Nippon, Tonhalle Zürich, RAI Roma, Santa Cecilia, Mexico Nat., Buenos Aires Nat., Gewandhaus, Nat. Orchestra Madrid; has performed in major concert halls, including Carnegie Hall, Avery Fisher Hall and Alice Tully Hall, New York, Orchestra Hall, Chicago, Suntory Hall, Tokyo, Teatro Colon, Buenos Aires, Gewandhaus, Leipzig, Concertgebouw, Amsterdam, Royal Festival Hall, London; Artistic Dir Int. Chopin Festival, Duszniki Zdrój 1993–; Prof. of Piano Performance, Frederick Chopin Acad. of Music, Warsaw; judge, int. music competitions in Warsaw, Paris, Santander, Tokyo, Hamamatsu, Prague, Taipei, Cleveland, London; judge, Sendai Int. Music Competition, Japan 2010, Prix Amadèo de Piano 2011; f. master courses in music, Bordeaux, Amsterdam, Paris, Buenos Aires, Tokyo, Lugano, Warsaw. *Recordings include:* K. Szymanowski Concert Symphony No. 4, complete Ballads, Sonatas, and Concertos by Chopin, The Best of Fryderyk Chopin ('Fryderyk 1999' Award, Polish Phonographic Acad.), works by Paderewski, Szymanowski, Lutosławski. *Honours:* Kt's Cross, Order of Polonia Restituta, Gold Cross of Merit, Order of the Aguila Azteca (Mexico); winner, competitions in Sofia 1968, Munich 1969, Warsaw 1970, Pleven 1971, Bordeaux 1972, Grand Prix VIII Chopin Competition 1970, granted title of Prof. by Pres. of Poland 1998, Gloria Artis Gold Medal 2005. *Address:* International Chopin Festival, 57-340 Duszniki-Zdrój, Rynek 10, Poland (office). *Telephone:* (74) 8669280 (office). *E-mail:* chopin@festival.pl (office). *Website:* www.chopin.festival.pl (office).

PALEY, Alexander, MA, PhD; pianist; b. 9 Jan. 1956, Kishinev, USSR; m. 1978, one d. *Education:* Moscow Conservatory. *Career:* debut in Kishinev 1969; performed with Moscow Virtuosi (V. Spivakov) 1985–90, Bolshoi Theatre Orchestra 1986, Monte Carlo Philharmonic 1989, Colorado Symphony 1991; recitals, Châtelet, Paris 1990, Auditorium de Halles 1991, Strasbourg, Moscow, Prague, Berlin, Sofia; appeared with Nat. Symphony Orchestra, Wolf Trap Festival 1991 and Boston Pops 1991; chamber music with Fine Arts Quartet, New York Chamber Soloists, with V. Spivakov, Bella Davidovich, Oleg Krysa, D. Sitkovetsky and B. Pergamentshikov; Musical Dir, Cannes-sur-Mer Festival, France.

PALM, Mati-Johannes, MMus; Estonian singer (bass); *Professor of Singing, Estonian Academy of Music and Theatre*; b. 13 Jan. 1942, Tallinn; two c. *Education:* Tallinn Conservatoire, studied in Moscow and at La Scala. *Career:* sang with Estonian State Opera from 1967, notably as Boris, Basilio, King Philip, Ivan Khovansky, the Dutchman, Silva, Zaccaria, Raimondo, Colline and Gremin; guest appearances from 1980 in Helsinki as Attila, Savonlinna Festival as the Dutchman, Paris Opéra in 1988 as Pimen, at Karlsruhe in 1992 in Khovanshchina as Dosifei, Buenos Aires from 1991 in Iolanta and Lohengrin; sang King Philip in Don Carlos at Tallinn 1971, 2000; sang Mephistopheles in Boito's Mefistofele and Banquo in Verdi's Macbeth; further appearances in Moscow, St Petersburg, Prague and Berlin, with numerous concerts, including 55 cantatas and oratorios, including Bach's St John Passion, Handel's Messiah, Mozart's Requiem, Beethoven's Missa Solemnis, Rossini's Stabat Mater, Verdi's Requiem; judge at int. singing competitions; currently Prof. of Singing, Estonian Acad. of Music and Theatre. *Recordings:* M. Palm 1972, Arias of Verdi, Romances of A. Kapp and G. Sviridov, Mussorgsky's Boris Godunov (Pimen), Two Cantatas of J. S. Bach BWV 78 140, Estonian opera singer Mati Palm, Mati Palm sings Estonian and Italian Songs, A. Kapp's Oratorio Hiob, R. Tobias Oratorio Des Jona Sendung, Verdi's Nabucco (Zaccaria), E. Tubin Barbara von Tiesenhusen (Konguta). *Film recording:* Mati Palm is Singing 1972. *Honours:* State Order of the White Star; Gold Medal, Classical Singing Competition, Sofia, First Prize, Baltic States Young Singers Competition 1971, Silver Medal, F. Viñas Int. Competition, Barcelona 1972, Soviet Union State Prize 1983, G. Ots Prize, Gold Medal, I. Arhipova Foundation, Moscow 2012. *Address:* Estonian Academy of Music and Theatre, Rävala pst 16, 10143 Tallinn, Estonia (office). *Telephone:*

667-57-00 (office); 5-113703 (mobile). *Fax:* 667-58-00 (office). *E-mail:* mati .palm.001@mail.ee (home). *Website:* matipalm.blogspot.com.

PALMER, Dame Felicity Joan, DBE, FGSM; British singer (mezzo-soprano); b. 6 April 1944, Cheltenham, Glos.; d. of Sylvia and Marshall Palmer. *Education:* Erith Grammar School and Guildhall School of Music and Drama. *Career:* soprano, then mezzo-soprano; has performed at all major int. opera houses, including La Scala, Milan, Royal Opera House, Covent Garden, Opéra de Paris, Netherlands Opera and Glyndebourne, Metropolitan Opera, New York, Lyric Opera, Chicago. *Operas include:* Elektra, Semele, Mahagonny, Pelléas et Mélisande, The Ring Cycle, Falstaff, Un Ballo in Maschera, Katya Kabanova, Sweeney Todd, Dialogues des Carmélites, Peter Grimes. *Recordings include:* Poèmes pour Mi, Holst Choral Symphony, The Music Makers, Sea Pictures, Phaedra, songs by Poulenc, Ravel and Fauré, Victorian ballads. *Honours:* Kathleen Ferrier Memorial Prize 1970. *Current Management:* c/o Intermusica Artists' Management, 36 Graham Street, Crystal Wharf, London, N1 8GJ, England. *Telephone:* (20) 7608-9900. *Fax:* (20) 7490-3263. *E-mail:* mail@intermusica.co.uk. *Website:* www.intermusica.co.uk.

PALMER, Larry, DMA; American harpsichordist and organist; b. 13 Nov. 1938, Warren, OH. *Education:* Oberlin Coll. Conservatory and Eastman School at Rochester, Salzburg Mozarteum with Isolde Ahlgrimm and studied with Gustav Leonhardt at Haarlem. *Career:* recitalist on harpsichord and organ throughout the USA and Europe, with premieres of works by such composers as Vincent Persichetti and Ross Lee Finney; Harpsichord Ed., The Diapason from 1969; Prof. of Harpsichord and Organ, Southern Methodist Univ., Dallas 1970. *Recordings:* organ works of Distler and harpsichord pieces from the 17th–20th centuries. *Publications:* Hugo Distler and his Church Music 1967, Harpsichord in America: A 20th-Century Revival 1989.

PALMER, Peter Rodney, MA; British writer on music and translator; b. 7 March 1945, West Bridgford, Notts., England. *Education:* Gonville and Caius Coll., Cambridge. *Career:* apprentice stage Dir, Int. Opera Studio, Zürich 1967–69; Founder and Artistic Dir East Midlands Music Theatre; first British stage productions of works by Janáček, Krenek, John Ogdon, Schoeck; Founding Ed. Bruckner Journal 1997; Visiting Lecturer, Romantic and Modern Swiss Music, Pro Helvetia Foundation 1998–99; Symposium Speaker, Lucerne Festival 1999, Ivor Gurney Conf., Cambridge 2007. *Publications:* trans include: From the Mattress Grave, song cycle by David Blake 1980, Essays on the Philosophy of Music by Ernst Bloch 1985, Wagner and Beethoven by Klaus Kropfinger 1991, Late Idyll: The Second Symphony of Johannes Brahms by Reinhold Brinkmann 1995, Johann Faustus, libretto by Hanns Eisler in: Hanns Eisler: A Miscellany 1995; contrib. to Die Tat, Zürich, Music and Letters, Organists' Review, German Life and Letters, Tempo, The Musical Times, New Grove Dictionary of Music and Musicians, Musik in Geschichte und Gegenwart, Perspectives on Anton Bruckner 2001, Ivor Gurney Society Journal 2003, 2007, Reger-Studien 7 2004. *Address:* 2 Rivergreen Close, Bramcote, Nottingham, NG9 3ES, England (home). *E-mail:* peter@peterpalmer.wanadoo.co.uk (office).

PALMER, Rudolph Alexis, BA, BS, MM, DMA; American conductor, composer, pianist and educator; *Member, Conducting and Composition Faculty, Mannes College of Music, New School University;* b. 5 Aug. 1952, New York, NY; m. Madeline Rogers 1981. *Education:* Bucknell Univ., Mannes Coll. of Music, Juilliard School. *Career:* mem. Conducting and Composition Faculty, Mannes Coll. of Music 1982–; Dir Great Neck Choral Soc. 1983–84; Orchestra Dir, Horace Mann School 1988–93; Assoc. Conductor, Amor Artis Chamber Choir, Fairfield County Chorale; Conductor North Jersey Music Educators' Orchestra, Brewer Chamber Orchestra, Palmer Chamber Orchestra, Palmer Singers, Queen's Chamber Band. *Compositions:* Contrasts for four bassoons, O Magnum Mysterium, Songs of Reflection, The Vision of Herod, The Immortal Shield, orchestration of Leonard Bernstein's Touches, works for chamber groups, chorus and orchestra, including two string quartets, a symphony, Dance-Music (ballet), orchestral overtures and several dramatic cantatas. *Recordings:* as accompanist: Lieder (by women composers), The Unknown Dvořák; as conductor: Baroque Cantatas of Versailles, The Romantic Handel, Handel's Imeneo, Telemann's Pimpinone, Handel's Berenice, Handel's Siroe, Pergolesi's La Serva Padrona, Handel's Joshua, Handel's Muzio, A Scarlatti's Ishmael, Haydn's La Canterina, Handel Arias, with various artists, Handel's Muzio Scevola, Handel's Alexander Balus, Handel's Deidamia, Handel's Faramondo, Gluck's Il Parnaso Confuso, Gluck's La Corona; as chorusmaster: Bach, St John Passion. *Address:* 215 West 88th Street, Apt 7E, New York, NY 10024, USA (home). *Telephone:* (212) 787-6341 (office). *E-mail:* rudy.palmer@gmail.com (home).

PALMER, Ruth; British violinist; b. 1979. *Education:* Royal Acad. of Music, Royal Coll. of Music. *Career:* debut, Wigmore Hall, London 2004; has given recitals at Ravinia Festival, Chicago, Royal Opera House, Edinburgh Festival, Cheltenham Int. Festival of Music, Queen Elizabeth Hall, Purcell Room, Teatro Albeniz Madrid, Munich Opera House Gala, Snape Maltings; has performed with English Chamber Orchestra, London Chamber Orchestra, Ulster Orchestra, Royal Liverpool Philharmonic Orchestra; performed at World Economic Forum Annual Meeting, Davos, Switzerland 2008. *Recordings:* Shostakovich Violin Concerto No 1 & Violin Sonata 2006, Bartok Solo Sonata and Bach Partita No.2 2009. *Honours:* Countess of Munster Musical Trust Star Award, Classical BRIT Award for Young British Classical Performer 2007. *Current Management:* Bedlam Artists Agency, PO Box 34449, London, W6 0RT, England. *Telephone:* (7957) 982308. *E-mail:* hannah

.hawes@bedlammanagement.com. *Website:* www.bedlamartistsagency.com. *E-mail:* info@ruthpalmer.com (office). *Website:* www.ruthpalmer.com.

PALOLA, Juhani; Finnish violinist; *Teacher, Lahti Conservatory;* b. 25 Nov. 1952, Helsinki; m. Liisa-Maria Lampela 1977; two d. *Education:* Oulu Music Inst., Sibelius Acad., studied in Munich with Takaya Urakawa and in London with Eli Goren. *Career:* debut as soloist, Oulu Symphony Orchestra 1968; concerts as soloist and chamber musician 1968–, Finland, Sweden, Norway, Ukraine, Romania, Albania, Germany, Switzerland, USA, Austria; Prof. of Violin, Teachers' Training Coll., Rorschach, Switzerland; First Violin in Arioso Quartet, St Gallen 1986–97, Weimar Trio 1998–2004; teacher, Lahti Conservatory 2003–. *Recording:* Classic 2000. *Address:* Lummekatu 12, 15240 Lahti, Finland (home). *Telephone:* (40) 5955607 (home). *E-mail:* juhani .palola@phnet.fi (home). *Website:* www.phnet.fi.koti/paloj (home).

PALOMBI, Antonello; Italian singer (tenor); b. 1965, Umbria. *Education:* studied in Italy. *Career:* debut as Pinkerton in Germany 1990; appearances as Dourmont in La Scala di Seta at Pistoia and as the Duke of Mantua in Austria; Edoardo in La Cambiale di Matrimonio by Rossini at Macerata, Ferrando at Ravenna, Macduff at Livorno and Attalo in Rossini's Ermione in Berlin; Teatro Comunale, Pisa, as Alfredo, Ramiro (La Cenerentola), Don José and Monteverdi's Telemaco (Ritorno d'Ulisse); Nemorino at San San Gimignano, the Duke of Mantua in Tokyo and Sou Chong in Das Land des Lächelns at Florence; sang Edmondo in a new production of Manon Lescaut at Glyndebourne 1997; other appearances include Canio in Pagliacci, La Scala 2011 and Detroit 2012, Vasco de Gama in L'Africaine, La Fenice, Venice 2013, Radamès in Aida and Manrico in Il Trovatore at New York Met 2014–15; concerts include Pulcinella, at Pisa and Modena; Fenton in Falstaff at the 1999 London Proms. *Current Management:* Ouverture, Via Braccianese Claudia 44, 00062 Bracciano (Roma), Italy. *Telephone:* (6) 9986602. *Fax:* (6) 9986603. *E-mail:* info@ouverture.net. *Website:* www.ouverture.net.

PÅLSSON, Hans; Swedish pianist and professor of music; b. 1 Oct. 1949, Helsingborg; m. Eva Pålsson 1980; three s. one d. *Education:* Staatliche Hochschule für Musik und Theater, Hannover, Germany. *Career:* debut in Stockholm 1972; concerts in some 30 countries; performed in 30-part TV series, Dead Masters, Live Music 1994–99; dedicatee of 60 solo pieces and piano concertos; Prof., Lund Univ. 1987; juror at int. piano competitions, master-classes; mem. Royal Swedish Acad. of Music. *Recordings:* some 30 albums. *Honours:* Swedish First Prize, Nordic Music Prizes Competition 1972, Swedish Phonogram Award 1987, Royal Medal Litteris et Artibus 1997, Royal Medal, Royal Swedish Acad. of Music 2012. *Address:* Gotlandsvägen 4, 222 25 Lund, Sweden. *E-mail:* hanspalsson@telia.com. *Website:* www.hanspalsson .se.

PALUMBO, Donald; American chorus director; *Chorus Master, Metropolitan Opera;* b. Rochester, New York. *Career:* fmr Chorus Master Opera Theatre of St Louis, Dallas Opera; Music Dir Chorus pro Musica, Boston 1980–90; Chorus Dir Salzburg Festival 1999–2001; Chorus Master Lyric Opera of Chicago 1991–2007; Chorus Consultant Canadian Opera Co.; Chorus Master Metropolitan Opera, New York 2007–; has worked extensively in France with Opéra de Lyon, Théâtre du Châtelet and Aix-en-Provence Festival; collab. with conductors including Valery Gergiev, Lorin Maazel, Sylvain Cambreling, Christoph von Dohnányi and Ken Nagano. *Address:* The Metropolitan Opera, Lincoln Center, New York, NY 10023, USA (office). *Telephone:* (212) 799-3100 (office). *Website:* www.metoperafamily.org (office).

PALUMBO, Renato; Italian conductor, artistic director and teacher; b. 27 July 1963, Montebelluna, Treviso. *Career:* int. career began early with invitation to Istanbul State Opera for a production of Il Trovatore, followed by a six-year contract as music director; Music Dir Festival of Macao 1990–99; performed in South Africa, Germany, France, Japan and Spain, repertoire ranging from Rossini's Guillaume Tell to Wagner's Der Fliegende Holländer, from Mozart to Verdi and Puccini; invited to return to Italy for Il re and Mese Mariano by Umberto Giordano at Festival della Valle d'Itria in Martina Franca 1998; conducted Verdi's Simon Boccanegra in 1857 first version and Robert le Diable and Les Huguenots by Meyerbeer; conducted Carmen with José Carreras at Arena di Verona 1999, then I Due Foscari with Renato Bruson; debut at La Scala in Milan with revival of Donizetti's Lucrezia Borgia featuring Mariella Devia, Michele Pertusi, Marcelo Alvarez and Daniela Barcellona 2002; debut with I lombardi alla prima crociata at Teatro Regio in Parma 2003, returned for La traviata, Il trovatore and Il Corsaro; debut at Rossini Opera Festival in Pesaro with Adina, followed by Elisabetta regina d'Inghilterra, Bianca e Falliero and Otello; also conducted Sly by Wolf Ferrari in Turin and Rome, Les contes d'Hoffmann in Rome, Il trovatore, Rigoletto and Adriana Lecouvreur in Turin, Beatrice di Tenda at La Scala in Milan, Andrea Chénier and Elisabetta regina d'Inghilterra in Bologna, La cenerentola and I vespri siciliani in Genoa, Don Carlo in Palermo, Aida and Rigoletto in Verona, Nabucco in Venice, Un ballo in maschera in Paris, Rigoletto in London, Attila and Macbeth in Washington, Ernani, Cavalleria Rusticana and Pagliacci in Chicago, La Traviata and Don Carlo at Vienna State Opera, Manon Lescaut in Barcelona, I due Foscari, La battaglia di Legnano and Un Ballo in Maschera in Bilbao; repertoire also includes less popular titles, including Il re and Mese mariano by Giordano, Germania by Franchetti, Hans Heiling by Marschner and Meyerbeer's Robert le Diable and Les Huguenots; guest conductor at major int. theatres, including La Scala in Milan, Opéra de Paris, Covent Garden in London, Pesaro and Martina Franca Festivals, Washington, Chicago, Berlin, Tokyo, Bilbao and Barcelona, Genoa,

Turin, Parma, Verona, Florence, Naples, Palermo and Cagliari; apptd first Italian after Giuseppe Sinopoli, as Gen. Music Dir Deutsche Oper Berlin 2006; first conductor to conduct in rebuilt Teatro Petruzzelli in Bari with a rehearsal of Tosca 2009, official opening of theatre with Turandot 2009; opened 2010 Fenice season in Venice with Manon Lescaut, then conducted Un ballo in maschera in Bilbao and returned to Opera of Rome with Boito's Mefistofele; season 2010–11 began with opening of Chicago Lyric Opera with Verdi's Macbeth, followed by Il corsaro in Bilbao, I due Foscari in Trieste, Les Huguenots in Madrid, Paris and Madrid, Tosca and La traviata in Venice and Ernani in Tokyo; Il trovatore and Carmen in Palermo, Aïda in Chicago and Barcelona, La forza del destino in Barcelona, Un ballo in maschera in Turin, Il trovatore in Bologna, concerts in Venice and Cagliari. *Recordings:* Verdi: Simon Boccanegra, Il corsaro, Opera gala; Rossini: La cenerentola, Bianca e Falliero; Cilea: Adriana Lecouvreur; Meyerbeer: Robert le Diable, Les Huguenots; Giordano: Il re, Mese Mariano; Marschner: Hans Heiling; Franchetti: Germania. *Honours:* Cavaliere dell'Ordine al Merito; Bianca e Falliero Best Opera CD (M&D Musica e Dischi magazine) 2006, Germania (German Critics' Awards). *Current Management:* Punto Opera srl, piazza IV Novembre 16/b, 37064 Povegliano (VR), Italy. *E-mail:* gall@puntoopera.net. *Website:* www.puntoopera.net. *E-mail:* info@renatopalumbo.it. *Website:* www .renatopalumbo.it.

PAN, Yiming; Chinese pianist and educator; b. 9 July 1937, Shanghai; m. Ying Shi-Zhen 1960, two s. *Education:* Central Conservatory of Music, Beijing, studied with Li Chang-Sun, C. Stevenska in Poland, D. Klavchenko in teh fmr USSR. *Career:* teaching piano, 1959–91, Associate Professor, 1983–90, Deputy Director Piano Department, 1983–91, Professor of Piano, 1990–91, Central Conservatory of Music; moved to Singapore, 1991; Piano Professor, LaSalle-SIA, College of Arts; recitals and concerto concerts, main Chinese cities such as Beijing, Tianjin, Chengdu, Xian; recital on radio, Central People's Broadcasting, 1984; joint recitals, Beijing, with Professor Jacob Latiener of Juilliard School of Music and with Professor Razits of Indiana University; jury member, National Piano Competitions, China, formerly, and National Music Competitions, Singapore, 1991, 1993, 1995; mem. Resources Panel, National Arts Council of Singapore; Chinese Musicians Association. *Compositions include:* The Youth Piano Concerto, co-composer. *Recordings:* works of Beethoven, Chopin, Granados, and many Chinese composers. *Publications:* articles about piano performing and teaching; editor: The Album of 45 Piano Sonatas by Scarlatti, first Chinese edition; Foreign Piano Pieces for the Young, vols 1–6. *Honours:* 1st Prize, Piano Competition, Central Conservatory of Music, 1957. *Address:* Blk 38, #14-2406, Upper Boon Keng Road, Singapore 380038, Singapore.

PANAGULIAS, Ann; American singer (soprano); b. 1963. *Career:* sang Berg's Lulu at San Francisco, 1989, returned as Natasha in War and Peace; Marzelline in Fidelio and Musetta; Wexford Festival, 1991 as Eleanora in Donizetti's Assedio di Calais; Vancouver, 1992 as Norina, Los Angeles, 1992 as Pamina and Dallas, 1994 as Poppea; Washington Opera, 1995 as Marenka in The Bartered Bride; guest appearances at Geneva and Bordeaux, as Fiordiligi, and Paris, in Lully's Roland; Santa Fe Opera from 1992, notably in the US premiere of Bose's Werther and the world premiere of D. Lang's Modern Painters; sang Poulenc's Blanche for Portland Opera, 2000. *Current Management:* c/o Pinnacle Arts: Miller Division, 889 Ninth Avenue, 2nd Floor, New York, NY 10019, USA. *Telephone:* (212) 397-7911. *Fax:* (212) 397-7920. *E-mail:* jmiller@pinnaclearts.com. *Website:* www.pinnaclearts.com.

PANERAI, Rolando; Italian singer (baritone); b. 17 Oct. 1924, Campi Bisenzio, Florence. *Education:* studied in Florence with Raoul Frazzi and in Milan with Armani and Giulia Tess. *Career:* debut in Naples 1947 as Faraone in Rossini's Moses; sang at La Scala from 1951, debut in Samson et Dalila; Venice 1955 in the stage premiere of Prokofiev's The Fiery Angel; Aix in 1955 as Mozart's Figaro; Salzburg from 1957 as Ford in Falstaff, Masetto in Don Giovanni, Guglielmo in Così fan tutte and Paolo in Simon Boccanegra; sang in the Italian premiere of Hindemith's Mathis der Maler, Milan 1957; Covent Garden debut 1960 as Figaro; other roles include Verdi's Luna and Giorgio Germont, Henry Ashton in Lucia di Lammermoor and Marcello in La Bohème; appearances in Verona, Florence, Rome, San Francisco 1958, Moscow, Rio de Janeiro, Athens, Berlin, Munich and Johannesburg; returned to Covent Garden in 1985 as Dulcamara in L'Elisir d'amore; Maggio Musicale Florence 1988 as Puccini's Gianni Schicchi; sang Michonnet in Adriana Lecouvreur at the 1989 Munich Festival; Douglas in Mascagni's Guglielmo Ratcliff at Catania, 1990; returned to Covent Garden 1990, and to Barcelona 1998, as Dulcamara; season 2000–01 with Don Alfonso at the Opéra Bastille and Dulcamara at Frankfurt. *Recordings:* I Puritani; Così fan tutte; Il Trovatore; Falstaff; Il Barbiere di Siviglia; La Bohème; Aida; Verdi's Oberto; Parsifal with Maria Callas.

PANHOFER, Wolfgang; Austrian cellist; b. 6 June 1965, Vienna. *Education:* Hochschule Vienna with Benesch and Herzer, Royal Northern Coll. of Music with Ralph Kirschbaum, studied with B. Pergamenshikov, W. Pleeth, A. Schiff, Paul Tortelier. *Career:* debut with Dvořák Concerto, Grosser Wiener Musik-Vereinssaal; freelance mem., Vienna Philharmonic; soloist, most European countries, Japan, USA, Egypt, Korea, Turkey, India, Iran; concertos with Vienna Symphony Orchestra, Vienna Chamber Orchestra, almost all the Polish orchestras, Bombay Chamber Orchestra, Hamburg Symphony Orchestra, ABC Chamber Ensemble, Cairo Symphony Orchestra; appearances on BBC television with Paul Tortelier, Polish television with Philharmony Katowice, Austrian television with Franz Welser-Möst; played

with Josef Suk at the 150th Birthday Concert of Dvořák, Wiener Konzerthaus; Schleswig-Holstein Music Festival with Pergamenshikov; held masterclasses in Europe, USA, Japan, Republic of Korea, Egypt, Turkey and Iran; debut at Carnegie Hall, New York 2000; mem. ESTA, WUT (fmr pres.), Soc. for Modern Music and Literature. *Recordings:* Contemporary Austrian music, with Vienna J. S. Chamber Orchestra. *Honours:* Sir John Barbirolli Prize 1984, Anerkennungspreis der Alban Berg Stiftung.

PANKRATOV, Vladimir; Russian singer (bass); b. 1958, St Petersburg. *Education:* St Petersburg Conservatoire. *Career:* sang with the Kirov Opera in St Petersburg and on tour to Edinburgh, Italy, Sweden, France and Japan in Prince Igor, War and Peace and Khovanshchina; Italian roles include Sparafucile, Philip II, Fiesco, Dulcamara and Basilio; Sarastro, Leporello and Mozart's Commendatore; Guest engagements with Heidelberg Opera until 1995; Debut with Théâtre du Capitole Toulouse, 1996; Concert repertoire includes songs by Borodin, Glinka and Tchaikovsky, and the Requiems of Fauré, Mozart and Verdi; frequent concerts in Israel; teacher, Rubin Academy.

PANNELL, Raymond; Canadian composer and pianist; b. 25 Jan. 1935, London, ON. *Education:* Juilliard School with Steuermann, Wagenaar and Giannini. *Career:* taught at Toronto Royal Conservatory from 1959, directed opera workshops at Stratford Festival, Ontario 1966; Asst Dir and Resident Conductor, Atlanta Municipal Theater 1960; Dir of Youth Experimental Opera Workshop 1969; co-founder and Gen. Dir, Co-Opera Theatre, Toronto 1975. *Compositions:* stage works: Aria da Capo (one-act opera) 1963, The Luck of Giner Coffey (three-act opera), Go (children's opera) 1975, Midway 1975, Push (one-act developmental opera) 1976, Circe (masque) 1977, Aberfan (video opera) 1977, N-E-U-S (radio opera) 1977, Souvenirs (one-act opera) 1979, Refugees (vaudeville) 1986, The Downsview Anniversary Song-Spectacle Celebration Pageant 1979, Harvest (TV opera) 1980, The Forbidden Christmas (musical) 1990. *Honours:* Salzburg Television Opera Prize for Aberfan 1977.

PANNI, Marcello; Italian conductor and composer; b. 24 Jan. 1940, Rome; s. of Arnaldo Panni and Adriana Cortini; m. Jeanne Colombier 1970; one d. *Education:* Accad. di Santa Cecilia, Rome under Goffredo Petrassi and Conservatoire Nat. Supérieur, Paris under Manuel Rosenthal. *Career:* conducting debut, Festival of Contemporary Music, Venice 1969; has since achieved renown in field of avant-garde music conducting first performances of works by Berio, Bussotti, Cage, Feldman, Donatoni, Clementi, Sciarrino, Glass and others at all major European festivals and for Italian Radio; regular guest conductor for Accad. di Santa Cecilia, the Italian radio orchestras and other European orchestras performing full range of baroque, classical and modern works; opera debut with The Barber of Seville, Hamburg 1977 and has since conducted opera in all the principal opera houses in Europe; American debut with Elisir d'amore, Metropolitan Opera, New York 1988; conducted world premiere of Bussotti's Cristallo di Rocca (opera) at La Scala 1983; Bolshoi debut with Macbeth, Moscow 2003; Musical Dir Bonn Opera House 1994–97, Nice Opera House 1997–2001; Artistic Dir San Carlo Opera House, Naples 2001–02; Artistic Dir Accad. Filarmonica Romana 2001–04, 2007–09; Musical Dir Orchestra Sinfonica Tito Schipa, Lecce 2008–11; Milhaud Prof. of Composition and Conducting, Mills Coll., Oakland, Calif. 1980–84; mem. Accad. di Santa Cecilia 2003–. *Works include* symphonic and chamber music and music for experimental theatrical works; operas and sacred music: Hanjo (one act) 1994, Il giudizio di Paride (one act) 1996, The Banquet (one act) 1998, Missa brevis 2002, Garibaldi en Sicile (two acts) 2005, Apokàlypsis (oratorio) 2009. *Address:* 3 Piazza Borghese, 00186 Rome, Italy (home). *Telephone:* (06) 6873617 (home). *Fax:* (06) 6873617 (office). *E-mail:* marcellopanni@yahoo.it (office).

PANOCHA, Jiri; violinist; b. 1940, Czechoslovakia. *Education:* Prague Acad. of Arts. *Career:* Leader, Int. Student Orchestra in Berlin, under Karajan; co-founder, Panocha Quartet 1968; many concert appearances in Europe, the USA, Canada, Iraq, Mexico, Cuba and other countries; repertoire includes works by Smetana, Janáček, Dvořák, Martinů, Haydn, Mozart, Beethoven, Schubert, Bartók and Ravel. *Recordings include:* Dvořák late quartets and Terzetto; Haydn Op 33, Nos 1–6, D Major Op 64; Martinů Complete Quartets; Mendelssohn Octet (with Smetana Quartet); Mozart Oboe Quartet, Clarinet Quintet and Horn Quintet; Schubert Quartettsatz D703 (Supraphon). *Honours:* prizewinner (with Panocha Quartet) at Kromeriž 1971, Weimar 1974, Prague 1975, Bordeaux 1976, Grand Prix du Disque, Paris (for Martinů recordings) 1983.

PANTILLON, Christopher David, DipMus; Swiss cellist; b. 26 Jan. 1965, Neuchatel. *Education:* studied in Neuchatel, Basle Conservatory with Heinrich Schiff, Hochschule für Musik, Vienna with Valentin Erben. *Career:* numerous appearances as soloist or chamber player; mem., Trio Pantillon (with two brothers); concerts in Geneva, Zürich, Bern, Vienna, Paris, Rome, England, France, Germany, The Netherlands; appeared on Swiss television and radio; mem. ESTA. *Recordings include:* Kabalevsky: Cello-Concerto No. 1 in G Minor. *Honours:* second prize Swiss Youth Competition, Lucerne 1983.

PANUFNIK, Roxanna, ARAM, FRSA; British composer; b. 1968, London, England; d. of Andrzej Panufnik. *Education:* Royal Academy with Paul Patterson and Henze. *Career:* BBC researcher and presenter; visiting teacher of composition at various schools in England and Barbados; Composer-in-Residence, Royal County of Berkshire; performances of her music at all London's main concert venues and throughout the UK, Europe, Asia,

Antipodes and USA; mem. BAC&S, PRS, MCPS. *Compositions include:* Westminster Mass for Westminster Cathedral Choir; Olivia, string quartet; The Music Programme, chamber opera; Leda, ballet; Beastly Tales (words Vikram Seth) for voices and orchestra; Powers & Dominions, harp concertino; Orchestrated Samuel Arnold's opera Inkle and Yarico (1787) for its first modern performance, Barbados, 1997; The Upside Down Sailor, commissioned by Collegiate Wind Ensemble, for narrator and wind nonet, words by Richard Stilgoe. *Recordings:* Angels Sing (all Roxanna Panufnik's religious choral works), The Joyful Company of Singers, Westminster Cathedral Choir; The Upside Down Sailor (for narrator and wind nonet) with Richard Stilgoe & David Campbell's Soundwood Ensemble. *Current Management:* Universal Edition, 48 Great Marlborough Street, London, W1F 7BB, England. *E-mail:* uel.promotion@universaledition.com. *Website:* www.roxannapanufnik.com.

PANULA, Jorma; Finnish conductor, composer and academic; b. 10 Aug. 1930, Kauhajoki. *Education:* Sibelius Acad. *Career:* Artistic Dir and Chief Conductor, Turku Philharmonic Orchestra 1963–65, Helsinki Philharmonic 1965–72, Aarhus Symphony, Denmark 1970–73; Prof. of Orchestral Conducting, Sibelius Acad., Helsinki 1973–94; trains conductors in USA, France, Netherlands, Russia, Sweden, Italy, Australia and UK; fmr Visiting Prof. Music, Stockholm Royal Acad. of Music and Copenhagen Royal Acad. of Music, Yale Univ., Bartók Seminar, Hungary; f. Jorma Panula Foundation. *Music:* (operas) Jaakko Ilkka, The River Opera; musicals, church music, a violin concerto, a jazz capriccio and vocal music. *Honours:* Music Prize, Royal Swedish Acad. of Science 1997. *Address:* Jorma Panula Foundation, c/o Taco Kooistra, Sloterweg 1188, 1066 Amsterdam, Netherlands (office). *E-mail:* tckooistra@zonnet.nl (office). *Website:* www.jormapanula.com.

PANZARELLA, Anna Maria; French singer (soprano); b. 1970. *Education:* studied in Grenoble and Geneva, Royal College of Music and at the National Opera Studio. *Career:* debut as Fransquita in Carmen with Geneva Opera; appeared in La Rondine for Opera North, as Frasquita in Lisbon, and Stephano in Roméo et Juliette at Covent Garden; season 1995–96 as Puccini's Lauretta in Brussels, First Lady (Die Zauberflöte) at Aix and Amore in the world premiere of Goehr's Arianna at Covent Garden; season 1996–97 as Donna Elvira for Opera Zürich, Balkis in Haydn's L'Incontro Improvviso at Lausanne and Rameau's Aricie in Paris and New York; season 1997 as Adèle in Le Comte Ory for GTO and Despina at the Bastille, Paris; sang Erinice in Rameau's Zoroastre at the Brooklyn Academy of Music and Lyon Opéra, 1998. *Recordings include:* Mozart's Requiem with Les Arts Florissants and William Christie.

PAPANDREOU, Elena; Greek musician (classical guitar); *Assistant Professor, University of Macedonia, Thessaloniki;* b. 7 March 1966, Athens; d. of Andreas Papandreou and Ioanna Papandreou; m. Oscar Ghiglia. *Education:* Nat. Conservatory of Athens, Royal Northern Coll. of Music, UK, studied with E. Boudounis and O. Ghiglia, classes with G. Crosskey, A. Diaz, J. Bream, L. Brouwer and R. Chiesa. *Career:* has played in more than 30 countries and in concert halls including Carnegie Hall, New York, Tchaikovsky Concert Hall, Moscow, Queen Elizabeth Hall, London, Vienna Musikverein, Kölner Philharmonie, Birmingham Symphony Hall, Athens Concert Hall; has performed as soloist with ten orchestras in Greece, Italy, Turkey, Romania, Mexico, Singapore; currently Asst Prof., Univ. of Macedonia, Thessaloniki. *Recordings include:* albums: Love Music for Solo Guitar 1983, 22 Pieces for Solo Guitar 1984, The New Excursion 1986, Elena Papandreou 1990, Elena Papandreou Live 1992, Elena Papandreou, Guitar Recital 1998, Leo Brouwer, Guitar Music Vol. 2 2001, works by Nikita Koshkin 2003, works by Roland Dyens 2005, works by Nikita Koshkin 2012. *Honours:* First Prize, Maria Callas Competition, Greece, First Prize, Gargnano Competition, Italy, First Prize, Alessandria Competition, Italy, NAXOS Prize, Guitar Foundation of America Competition, Spyros Motsenigos Prize, Acad. of Athens 1992. *Address:* Nafpaktou 3-G, Pylaia, Thessaloniki 55535, Greece (home). *Telephone:* (2310) 916453 (home). *E-mail:* elpa@elenapapandreou.gr. *Website:* www.elenapapandreou.gr.

PAPAVRAMI, Tedi; Albanian/French/Swiss violinist, translator, writer, actor and violin teacher; b. 13 May 1971, Tirana, Albania. *Education:* Paris Conservatoire, with Pierre Amoyal. *Career:* numerous appearances in Europe and South Africa from 1988; festival engagements at Montreux, Newport and Schleswig-Holstein; season 1998–99 in Paris, Monaco, Germany, Italy and Spain; season 2000–01 with Stuttgart Chamber Orchestra; chamber music partners include François-Frédéric Guy (piano), Nelson Goerner (piano), Lawrence Power (viola); mem. Schumann piano quartet; debut tour of Japan with Paganini's 24 Caprices 2001; transposed harpsichord and organ music for performance on the violin (works by Scarlatti and Bach); trans. of works of Ismail Kadare (into French) 2000–. *Film:* played lead role in Josée Dayan's film adaptation of Dangerous Liaisons 2003. *Publications:* Fugue pour Violon Seul 2013; as trans. (into French) for Ismail Kadare: L'Envoi du Migrateur; Vie, Jeu et Mort de Lul Mazrek; Le Successeur; La Fille d'Agamemnon; Un Climat de Folie; Dante l'incontournable; Le dîner de trop; L'accident; L'entravée; as transcriber for violin: 12 Scarlatti harpsichord sonatas; Bach Fantasie und fuge for organ BWV 542; Bach harpsichord suite BWV 822. *Honours:* Rodolfo Lipizer Prize, Gorizzia 1985, First Prize, Paris Conservatoire 1986, Winner, Sarasate Competition, Pamplona 1993. *Address:* Haute école de musique de Genève, Case postale 5155, 1211 Geneva, Switzerland (home). *Website:* www.papavrami-tedi.com.

PAPE, Gerard Joseph, BA, MA, PhD; American composer; b. 22 April 1955, Brooklyn, NY; m. Janet Smarr Pape 1981, two s. *Education:* Columbia Univ., Univ. of Michigan, studied with George Cacioppo and William Albright. *Career:* Dir, Composer-in-Residence, Sinewave Studios 1980–91; music presented in over 25 Sinewave Studios concerts in Ann Arbor, MI; produced the annual Festival of Contemporary Orchestral, Ensemble and Electronic Music, Ann Arbor 1986–91; Dir, Les Ateliers, UPIC Paris, France (Electronic Music Studio) 1991–; mem. ASCAP. *Compositions include:* Ivan and Rena for four vocal soloists and orchestra 1984, Cosmos for large orchestra 1985, The Sorrows of the Moon for baritone and tape 1986, Folie à Deux for violin and piano 1986, Exorcism for baritone and orchestra 1986, Catechresis for soprano and orchestra 1987, Cerberus for organ and tape 1987, Vortex (String Quartet No. 2) 1988, Three Faces of Death for orchestra 1988, Piano Concerto 1988, Xstasis for ensemble and tape 1992, Two Electro-Accoustic Songs for voice, flute and tape 1993, Le Fleuve du Désir (String Quartet No. 3) 1994, Monologue for bass voice and tape 1995, Battle for four solo voices and tape 1996, Makbenach for saxophone, ensemble and tape 1996, Feu Toujours Vivant for large orchestra and live electronics 1997, Funeral Sentence for two sopranos and percussion 1998, Makbenach IV for trombone and tape 1998, Fabula for soprano and tape 1999, Aquarelles for clarinet and tape 1999, Mon Autre Peau for tape 1999, Les Cenci (opera) 2000. *Publications:* contrib. 'Complexity, Composition, Perception' (in Currents in Musical Thought) 1994, 'Luigi Nono and his Fellow Travellers' (in Contemporary Music Review). *Honours:* Michigan Council for the Arts grants to produce the Sinewave series of concerts, Meet the Composer 1989, eight ASCAP Standard Awards 1992–99.

PAPE, René; German singer (bass-baritone); b. 4 Sept. 1964, Dresden. *Education:* Dresden Musikhochschule. *Career:* mem., Dresden Kreuzchor 1974–81, tours to Japan and Europe; mem. Berlin Staatsoper 1988–, debut as the Speaker in Die Zauberflöte; sang in 1989 premiere of Siegfried Matthus's Graf Mirabeau at Berlin Staatsoper and has appeared there and elsewhere in Germany as Mozart's Figaro and Alfonso, Verdi's Banquo, Procida and King in Aida, Gremin in Eugene Onegin and Galitzky in Prince Igor; guest engagements at Frankfurt and Vienna Staatsoper; Salzburg Festival 1991, as Sarastro in Die Zauberflöte; many concert appearances, notably in Mozart's Requiem for the bi-centenary performances 1991; sang the Speaker in Die Zauberflöte at the Met 1995; appeared as King Henry in Lohengrin at Covent Garden 1997; season 1998 with Pogner in Die Meistersinger at the Berlin Staatsoper and Verdi's Philip II at Salzburg; season 2000–01 as King Mark at the Met, Pogner at the Berlin Staatsoper, Leporello for the Salzburg Festival and King Philip in Don Carlos at the Vienna Staatsoper; season 2002–03 as Massimiliano in I Masnadieri and Heinrich in Lohengrin at Covent Garden; season 2010–11 included Wotan in Die Walküre at La Scala, Filippo in Don Carlos, Tokyo and Nagoya; 2011–12 included Méphistophélès in Faust, Covent Garden and the Met, Filippo in Don Carlos, Bayerische Staatsoper and Staatsoper Wien, Tristan and Isolde, Rheingold and Die Walküre at Staatsoper Unter den Linden, Berlin; 2015 roles included Filippo in Don Carlos, Munich Opera, title role in Méphistophélès, Bayerische Staatsoper and Sarastro in Die Zauberflöte, Unter den Linden, Berlin. *Recordings:* Mozart's Requiem 1992, Bastien und Bastienne 2003, Die Zauberflöte 2006, Korngold's Das Wunder der Heliane 1993, Mendelssohn's Die Erste Walpurgisnacht 1993, Antigone 1995, Oedipus 1996, Busoni's Turandot 1993, Arlecchino 1995, Wagner's Die Meistersinger von Nürnberg 1994, Lohengrin 1998, Tannhäuser 2002, Tristan und Isolde 2005, Haydn's The Creation 1995, Beethoven's Missa Solemnis 1995, Triple Concerto 1995, Fidelio 2000, Symphony No. 9 2000, Mahler's Symphony No. 8 1997, Schmidt's Book of the Seven Seals 1998, Torsten Rasch's Mein Herz Brennt 2004, Gods, Kings and Demons 2008, Wagner 2011. *Honours:* Metropolitan Opera Guild Opera News Award 2006. *Current Management:* c/o Marianne Boettger, Artists Managenent, Dahlmannstrasse 9, 10629 Berlin, Germany. *Telephone:* (30) 3248527. *E-mail:* agency@boettger-berlin.de. *Website:* www.renepape .com.

PAPERNO, Dmitry; Ukranian pianist and academic; b. 18 Feb. 1929, Kiev, USSR; m. Ludmila Gritsay 1966, two d. *Education:* Moscow Tchaikovsky Conservatory. *Career:* debut recital, Moscow, 1955; pianist-soloist, Mosconcert; some 1,500 solo recitals and performances in the former Soviet Union, Eastern and Western Europe and Cuba including USSR State Orchestra, (Moscow, Leningrad and Brussels, Belgium EXPO 1958), Gewandhaus Orchestra, (Leipzig, 1960), Hallé Orchestra, (Manchester, 1967), and many others 1955–76; numerous concerts in USA, 1977–2001, also Netherlands, France, Belgium, Majorca and Portugal, 1985–2001; sonata recital with Mstislav Rostropovich, Pasadena, California, 1989; taught at Moscow State Gnesin Institute 1967–73; Full Prof. of Piano 1985, later Prof. Emer., DePaul University, Chicago 1977–2001; numerous masterclasses in the USA and Europe, including Tchaikovsky Conservatory, Moscow. *Recordings include:* Melodia, USSR; Works by Chopin, Liszt, Grieg, Schumann, Bach-Busoni, Debussy, Medtner; 2 videotapes for Moscow television: piano recital and Chopin F minor concerto with Moscow Radio and Television Orchestra under Gennady Rozhdestvenski; Selected Works of Scriabin, 1978, and Tchaikovsky's The Seasons, 1982; 7 CDs, USA; Russian Piano Music, 1989; Works of Bach-Busoni, Beethoven, Schubert, Brahms, 1990; Uncommon Encores, 1992; Chopin Live, including the 5th Chopin Competition, Warsaw, 1995, 1997; Paperno Live: Selected works from the 1960s and 1970s 1998, Through the Years: Recordings of a Moscow Pianist 2004. *Publications include:* Notes of a

Moscow Pianist 1983, Post Scriptum 1987, contrib. articles and reviews to magazines.

PAPIAN, Vag; Russian conductor and pianist; b. 1960. *Education:* Moscow and St Petersburg Conservatories. *Career:* performances as piano soloist throughout Russia from 1979; conducting studies, with Ilia Musin, led to Associate status with the Armenian SO, from 1987 (chief conductor, 1990); Associate Conductor, Been Sheva SO, Israel, from 1990; Music Director; Israel Camerata; soloist and Conductor with the Jerusalem Symphony; season 2000–01 with English Chamber Orchestra and a tour to Far East; further conducting engagements with New Japan Philharmonic and Malmö, Trondheim, Lucerne and Valencia Symphonies; Armenian PO, Israel CO, Belgrade SO and Bucharest Virtuosi; Productions of Don Giovanni, Carmen and Nielsen's Saul and David in Israel; Norma for Armenian Opera, 2001; concerts as pianist in Europe, North and South America and Far East; accompanist for Maxim Vengerov, violin. *Recordings include:* recitals.

PAPIS, Christian; French singer (tenor); b. 1960, Algrange. *Education:* Paris Conservatoire. *Career:* Glyndebourne Festival Opera from 1992 as Boris in Katya Kababova 1998, Lensky in Eugene Onegin and Gregor in The Makropulos Case 1997; further engagements as Don Ottavio in Dublin, Massenet's Des Grieux at Lausanne, Tamino throughout France and Berlioz's Bénédict in Toulouse; Werther in France and Netherlands, Alfredo for Opera Zuid, Don José in Bordeaux, Rodolfo in Amsterdam and Vincent in Gounod's Mireille at the Opéra Comique; the Berlioz Faust in Madrid, Matteo in Arabella and Gounod's Roméo at Geneva Opera; Idomeneo in Nantes, Števa in Jenůfa and Berg's Alva in Liège; Wagner's Froh in Geneva and Alim in Massenet's Le Roi de Lahore at St Etienne and Bordeaux.

PAPOULIAS, Althea-Maria; Canadian singer (soprano); b. 1968, Montréal. *Education:* Metill Univ., Montréal. *Career:* sang at Cologne Opera from 1993, as Pamina, Gretel and Elvira in L'Italiana in Algeri; Vienna Staatsoper, 1996 as Liu in Turandot; guest appearances as Agathe in Der Freischütz, Musetta, Puccini's Suor Angelica, Drusilla in Monteverdi's Poppea and Purcell's Dido; sang Mozart's Fiordiligi for Glyndebourne Touring Opera, 1998; sang Verdi's Alice Ford at the Vienna Volksoper, 2000; concerts include songs by Debussy, Ravel and Duparc. *Honours:* prizewinner Belvedere Competition, Vienna 1993.

PAPP, Christine; German singer (mezzo-soprano); b. 1959, Sonneberg. *Education:* studied in Weimar, Berlin and Milan, Italy. *Career:* sang at Meiningen Opera 1983–86; further appearances at Magdeburg, Potsdam and the Berlin Staatsoper; Frankfurt Opera from 1991 as Verdi's Azucena and Ulrica, Fidalma in Il Matrimonio Segreto, Mozart's Marcellina, Annina in Der Rosenkavalier and Santuzza; concert repertory includes Beethoven's Ninth; lieder recital in New York.

PAPPANO, Sir Antonio (Tony), Kt; British conductor and pianist; *Music Director, The Royal Opera, Covent Garden*; b. 30 Dec. 1959, Epping, London; m. Pam Bullock 1995. *Education:* studied in USA with Norma Verrilli, Arnold Franchetti and Gustav Meier. *Career:* Répétiteur and Asst Conductor New York City Opera, Gran Teatro del Liceo, Barcelona, Frankfurt Opera, Lyric Opera of Chicago early to mid-1980s; asst to Daniel Barenboim for Tristan und Isolde, Parsifal and the Ring cycle at Bayreuth Festival 1986; opera conducting debut with Norwegian Opera, Oslo 1987; Music Dir, Norwegian Opera 1990–92; Covent Garden debut conducting La Bohème 1990; Vienna Staatsoper debut conducting new production of Wagner's Siegfried 1993; season 1996 included the original Don Carlos in Brussels and at the Paris Théâtre du Châtelet; season 1997 Salome at Chicago and Eugene Onegin at the Metropolitan; Prin. Guest Conductor Israel Philharmonic Orchestra 1997–2000; seasons 1999–2001 Lohengrin at Bayreuth; Music Dir, Théâtre Royal de la Monnaie, Brussels 1992–2002, conducting a wide variety of titles; Music Dir, Royal Opera, Covent Garden 2002–; new productions of Ariadne auf Naxos, Wozzeck, Madama Butterfly and Pagliacci, revival of Falstaff 2002–03; Don Giovanni, Aida, Lady Macbeth of Mtsensk, Faust and Peter Grimes in 2003–04; Das Rheingold and Die Walküre 2005; Music Dir Orchestra dell'Accad. Nazionale di Santa Cecilia, Rome 2005–; 2008 performances at ROH included Don Giovanni, La fanciulla del West, Les contes d'Hoffmann; 2009 included Lulu, La Traviata, Il barbiere di Siviglia, Tristan und Isolde; 2010 Simon Boccanegra, Les Pêcheurs de perles; 2011 Turnage's new opera Anna Nicole, Werther, Macbeth and Tosca, among others; 2012 Die Meistersinger von Nürnberg, Le nozze di Figaro, Les Troyens, Otello; has conducted major orchestras, including Berlin Philharmonic Orchestra, Boston Symphony Orchestra, Chicago Symphony Orchestra, Cleveland Orchestra, London Symphony Orchestra, Los Angeles Philharmonic Orchestra, Orchestre de Paris, Oslo Philharmonic Orchestra, Munich Philharmonic Orchestra. *Recordings include:* many recordings as conductor including Puccini's La Rondine (Gramophone Award for Best Opera Recording and Record of the Year 1997), Il Trittico 1999, Britten's The Turn of the Screw (Choc du Monde de la Musique, Prix de l'Acad. du Disque Lyrique, Grand Prix Int., Orphées d'Or) 1999, Werther 1999, Manon (Gramophone Award for Best Opera Recording) 2001, Rachmaninov's Piano Concertos 1 & 2 2005, Madame Butterfly 2009, Verdi's Messa da Requiem 2009, Wagner: Tristan and Isolde 2011, Rossini: William Tell 2011, Tosca (Puccini) (BBC Music Magazine DVD Performance Award 2014), Nessun Dorma: The Puccini Album (with Jonas Kaufmann) 2015, Schumann (with Orchestra dell'Accademia Nazionale di Santa Cecilia) 2016, Brahms: Violin Concerto, Bartok: Violin Concerto (with Janine Jansen and London Symphony Orchestra) 2016; recordings as pianist: recordings with Rockwell Blake, Barbara Bonney and Han-Na Chang; Joyce & Tony - Live From Wigmore Hall (with Joyce DiDonato) 2015. *Television includes:* Pappano's Classical Voices (BBC series) 2015. *Honours:* Commendatore of Italian Repub. 2008, Cavaliere di Gran Croce, Order of Merit of Italian Repub. 2012; Olivier Award for Outstanding Achievement in Opera 2003, Royal Philharmonic Soc. Award for best conductor 2005, Assoc. Naz. Critici Musicali Premio Abbiati Prize for Conductor 2006, Inc. Soc. of Musicians Distinguished Musician Award 2012, Int. Opera Awards Best Conductor 2013, Bruno Walter Prize, Royal Philharmonic Soc. Gold Medal 2015. *Current Management:* c/o Peter Wiggins, IMG Artists, 31–33 rue du Temple, 75004 Paris, France. *Telephone:* 1-44-31-00-10. *E-mail:* pwiggins@imgartists.com. *Website:* imgartists.com/artist/antonio_pappano. *Address:* Royal Opera House, Bow Street, Covent Garden, London, WC2E 9DD, England (office). *Telephone:* (20) 7240-1200 (office). *E-mail:* info@roh.org.uk (office). *Website:* www.roh.org.uk (office).

PAQUETTE, Daniel; French composer and academic; *Professor Emeritus of History of Music, Université Lumière – Lyon II*; b. 1930, Morteau, Doubs; m. Madeleine Mougel 1957, one s. one d. *Education:* Nat. Conservatoire de Dijon, Nat. Conservatoire of Saint Etienne, Univ. of Paris, Sorbonne. *Career:* teacher of musical education, Lycées in Angiers 1952, Dijon 1953–64; Asst, Inst. of Musicology, Univ. of Strasbourg 1964–69; Lecturer, Univ. of Dijon 1970–72; Prof., Univ. of Lyon 1972–; Head Musicology Section, Univ. of Besançon, Univ. of Dijon (audio-visual education), Univ. of St Etienne; Leader, Philharmonic Choirs of Dijon and Voix Amies Dijon 1953–64, Univ. Orchestra, Strasbourg 1964–69; Prof. Emer. of History of Music, Université Lumière – Lyon II 1990–; mem. Academie de Dijon, Academie de Besancon, Academie de Mácon. *Compositions:* Les Dames des Entreportes (symphonic poem), operetta for children, Les Fantomes du Val au Faon, a cappella choral music based on ancient music of 16th–18th century, chamber music; music for films, J. J. Rousseau et la musique, J. Ph. Rameau musicien sensible et savant rigoureux; Oratorio for two choruses, four singers, string orchestra, piano and trumpet (based on verses by Lamartine, A Hymn of Peace), Grand Cantate for voice, orchestra, piano and organ 2005, Verses of Lamartine, Hymn à la concorde, Invention du piano à couleurs. *Publications:* L'Instrument de musique dans la Grece Antique 1984, Jean Philippe Rameau musicien bourguignon 1983, Musique baroque: aspects de la musique en France et à Lyon au XVIII 1990; contrib. articles in Dictionnaire de la Musique 1976–86, Die Musik in Geschichte und Gegenwart 1999, Dictionnaire de Jean Jacques Rousseau 1990, Dictionnaire de l'Ancien Regime 1996. *Honours:* Chevalier, Ordre des Palmes Académiques 1986; Prix de l'Academie de Dijon 1983. *Address:* Les Furtins, 71960 Berzé-la-Ville, France (home). *Telephone:* 3-85-37-76-40 (home). *Fax:* 3-85-37-76-46 (home).

PARATORE, Anthony, BM, MS; American concert pianist; b. 17 June 1946, Boston, MA. *Education:* Boston Univ., Juilliard School, New York. *Career:* debut at the Metropolitan Museum 1973; guest appearances with New York Philharmonic, Chicago, San Francisco, Detroit, Washington National, Denver, Boston, Indianapolis, Atlanta, San Diego, BBC London, Vienna Philharmonic, Berlin Philharmonic, Vienna Symphony, RAI Orchestra, Nouvel Philharmonique, Warsaw Philharmonic, Amsterdam Philharmonic, Rotterdam Philharmonic, Norwegian Chamber Orchestra, English Chamber Orchestra, Prague Chamber Orchestra, Bavarian Radio Orchestra, London Symphony Orchestra, Munich Chamber Orchestra; festival appearances, mostly Mozart, Salzburg, Berlin, Strauss Tage, Lucerne, Istanbul, Adelaide Festival in Australia, and Spoleto; PBS television special, The Paratores, Two Brothers, Four Hands; NPR radio, All Things Considered and A Note To You; mem., Boston Musicians' Asscn, Dante Alighieri Society. *Compositions:* premieres of new compositions; Wolfgang Rihm, Maskes; Manfred Trojan, Folia; William Bolcom, Sonata for two pianos in one movement. *Recordings:* Pictures at an Exhibition, Mussorgsky; Opera Festival for Four Hands; Mendelssohn Concerti for two pianos and orchestra; Variations for Four Hands; Schoenberg Chamber Symphony op 9; Stravinsky, Sacre du Printemps; Ravel; Bolero, Ma Mère L'Oye, Rapsodie Espagnole; Gershwin; Rhapsody in Blue, Concerto in F; Brahms Liebeslieder Waltzes, opus 52 and 65, Waltzes opus 39; Saint-Saëns, Carnival of the Animals; Variations on a Theme by Haydn Sonata in F minor, opus 34; Points on Jazz, by Dave Brubeck. *Publications:* contrib. to Keyboard Classics, Clavier magazine. *Honours:* First Prize, Munich International Music Competition, Duo-Piano Category 1974; George Washington Honor Medal 1998. *Current Management:* Konzert-Direktion Hans Adler, Auguste-Viktoria-Strasse 64, 14199 Berlin, Germany. *Telephone:* (30) 825-6333. *Fax:* (30) 826-3520. *Website:* www .musikadler.de.

PARATORE, Joseph D., BM, MS; American concert pianist; b. 19 March 1948, Boston, MA. *Education:* Boston Univ., Juilliard School. *Career:* debut at Metropolitan Museum of Art 1973; guest appearances with New York Philharmonic, Chicago Symphony, San Francisco, Detroit, Indianapolis, Atlanta, Washington National, Boston, Denver, San Diego, BBC London, Vienna Philharmonic, Berlin Philharmonic, Vienna Symphony, RAI, Nouvel Philharmonique, Warsaw Philharmonic, Amsterdam Philharmonic, Rotterdam Philharmonic, Norwegian Chamber Orchestra, English Chamber Orchestra, Prague Chamber Orchestra, Bavarian Radio Orchestra, London Symphony, Munich Chamber Orchestra; festival appearances, Lucerne, Istanbul, Adelaide Festival in Australia, Salzburg, Berlin, Strauss Tage, Spoleto, mostly Mozart; television appearances include: WGBH-PBS television special The Paratores, Two Brothers/Four Hands; radio: NPR All Things

Considered and A Note to You; mem., Boston Musicians' Asscn, Dante Alighieri Society. *Compositions:* Wolfgang Rihm, Maskes; Manfred Trojan, Folia; William Bolcom, Sonata for two pianos in one movement. *Recordings:* Mussorgsky–Pictures at an Exhibition and Opera Festival for Four Hands; Mendelssohn Concerti for Two Pianos and Orchestra; Variations for Four Hands; Schoenberg, Chamber Symphony op 9; Stravinsky, Sacre du Printemps; Ravel: Bolero, Ma Mère L'Oye, Rapsodie Espagnole; Gershwin: Rhapsody in Blue, Concerto in F; Brahms: Variations on a Theme by Haydn and Sonata in F minor, Liebeslieder Waltzes Op 52 and 65, Waltzes Op 39; Saint-Saëns, Carnival of the Animals; Points on Jazz, by Dave Brubeck. *Publications:* contrib. to Keyboard Classics – The Art of Transcribing Mussorgsky, Clavier magazine, Master Class, Ravel Ma Mère L'Oye. *Honours:* First Prize, Munich International Music Competition, Duo-Piano Category 1974, George Washington Honor Medal 1998. *Current Management:* Konzert-Direktion Hans Adler, Auguste-Viktoria-Strasse 64, 14199 Berlin, Germany. *Telephone:* (30) 825-6333. *Fax:* (30) 826-3520. *Website:* www .musikadler.de.

PARIK, Ivan; Czech conductor; *Chief Conductor, Josef Kajetan Tyl Theatre, Plzeň;* b. 1955. *Education:* State Conservatory, Prague, Universität für Musik und Darstellende Kunst, Vienna. *Career:* began career on internships in Munich and Bayreuth; has appeared with leading orchestras in Czechoslovakia and elsewhere in Eastern Europe; made debut, Prague 1972; Chief Conductor, Pilsen 1975, Ostrava Opera 1980; Conductor, Vienna Volksoper 1984–88; Dir of Opera, Plzeň 1988–91; Music Dir, Gars Festival 1990–; Guest Conductor, Prague Staatsoper 1991–; Gen. Music Dir, State Theatre, Ostrava 1991–92, City Theatre, Klagenfurt 1992–95; Prof., Universität für Musik und Darstellende Kunst, Vienna 2001–; Chief Conductor, Josef Kajetan Tyl Theatre, Plzeň 2006–; guest appearances in Dresden, Bilbao, Prague, Ulm, Brno, Nice; concert engagements in works by Mozart, Schubert, Berlioz, Brahms, Dvořák, Janáček, Debussy, Stravinsky and Strauss; mem. Slovak Music Union, ISCM. *Address:* Josef Kajetan Tyl Theatre, Prokopova 14, 301 00 Plzeň, Czech Republic (office). *E-mail:* operaschool@gmx.at (office). *Website:* ivanparik.com.

PÂRIS, Alain, LèsJ; French conductor; b. 22 Nov. 1947, Paris; m. Marie-Stella Abdul Ahad 1973. *Education:* Ecole Normale de Musique, Paris, studied with Bernadette Alexandre-Georges, Georges Dandelot, Pierre Dervaux, Louis Fourestier, Paul Paray. *Career:* debut in 1969; guest conductor with major French orchestras, including Orchestre de Paris, Orchestre National, Orchestre de Lyon, Toulouse, Strasbourg; performed with various orchestras abroad, including, Dresdner Philharmonic, Slovak Philharmonic, Orchestre de la Suisse Romande, Philharmonia Hungarica, Philharmonie George Enesco (Bucharest), Orchestra de la BRT (Brussels), and in Italy, Russia, Germany, Luxembourg, Greece, Iraq, Hong Kong, Spain and Turkey; Asst Conductor, Orchestre du Capitole de Toulouse 1976–77; Assoc. Conductor 1983–84, Permanent Conductor 1984–87, Opéra du Rhin, Strasbourg; producer of musical broadcasts for Radio France 1971–; Prof. of Conducting, Strasbourg Conservatory 1986–89; regular conductor of French Season Concerts, Capella Symphony Orchestra and Chorus, St Petersburg 1996–; mem. Société française de musicologie. *Publications:* Dictionnaire des interprètes et de l'interprétation musicale 1982, Dictionnaire Encyclopédique de la Musique (ed. French edn) 1988, Les Livrets d'opéra 1991, Dictionnaire Biographique des Musiciens (ed. French edn) 1995, various translations; contrib. to Encyclopaedia Universalis, Retz, Quid, Scherzo, Courrier Musical de France, Diapason, La Lettre du Musicien. *Honours:* first prize Concours International de Besançon 1968.

PARISOT, Aldo Simoes; Brazilian cellist and teacher; *Samuel Sanford Professor of Music, Yale University;* b. 30 Sept. 1920; m. Elizabeth Sawyer-Parisot; three s. *Education:* Yale Univ. and private studies with Thomazzo Babini and Ibere Gomes Grosso. *Career:* debut with the Boston Symphony, Berkshire Music Center 1947; principal cellist Pittsburgh Symphony 1949–50; tours of Europe, Asia, Africa, South America and throughout the USA from 1948; plays solo works by Bach and the sonatas of Brahms and Beethoven in recital; joined faculty of Peabody Conservatory 1956–58, Mannes Coll. 1962–66, New England Conservatory 1966–70; Prof. in School of Music, Yale Univ. 1958–, currently Samuel Sanford Prof. of Music; Music Dir Aldo Parisot Int. Cello Course and Competition, Brazil 1977; artist-in-residence, Banff Center for the Arts, Canada 1981–83; has given the premieres of works by Quincy Porter, Villa-Lobos (concerto No. 2 1955), Claudio Santoro (concerto 1963), Leon Kirchner (concerto for violin, cello and orchestra 1960), Alvin Etler (concerto 1971), Yehudi Wyner (De novo 1971) and Donald Martino; formed students at Yale Univ. into the 'Yale Cellos' ensemble. *Recordings include:* numerous recordings by the Yale Cellos. *Honours:* Dr hc (Shenandoah) 1999, Hon. DFA (Penn State) 2002; Ind. Univ. Eva Janzer Chevalier du Violincello 1980, UN Peace Medal 1982, American String Teachers' Asscn Award 1983, Gov.'s Arts Award, CT 1997, RNCM Award of Distinction 2001, Gustave Stoeckel Award 2002. *Address:* The School of Music, Yale University, PO Box 208246, New Haven, CT 06520-8246, USA (office).

PARK, Jong-min; South Korean singer (bass); b. 1986, Seoul. *Education:* Korea Nat. Univ. of Arts, Accademia Teatro alla Scala, Milan with Mirella Freni, Luciana Serra, Luigi Alva and Renato Bruson. *Career:* soloist at Christmas concert, Teatro alla Scala, Milan 2008; has given recitals at several int. concert halls including Bolshoi Theatre, Moscow, Philharmonia, St Petersburg, Teatro Pergolesi, Jesi, Italy, Auditorium Sony, Madrid; took part in Ravello Festival and Naples Theatre Festival, Italy; mem. Hamburgisch

Staatsoper ensemble 2010–; first solo lieder recital, Munich 2010. *Operatic repertoire includes:* Sarastro in Die Zauberflöte, Sparafucile in Rigoletto, Bartolo in Le nozze di Figaro, the King in Aida. *Honours:* numerous awards including Prix de la Chambre Professionnelle des Directeurs d'Opéra, XXVI Int. Hans Gabor Belvedere Competition 2007, First Prize for male voice and Critics' Prize, XII Int. Singing Competition, Bilbao, Spain 2008, First Prize and Audience Prize, First Stella Maris Int. Vocal Competition 2009, First Prize for male vocals, Int. Tchaikovsky Competition 2011, Birgit Nilsson Prize, Placido Domingo Operalia World Opera Competition, Moscow 2011. *Address:* Staatsoper Hamburg, Dammtorstrasse 28, 20354 Hamburg, Germany (office). *Website:* www.hamburgische-staatsoper.de (office).

PARKER, James (Jamie), MusD; Canadian pianist. *Education:* Vancouver Acad. of Music, Univ. of British Columbia, Juilliard School, studied with Kum Sing Lee and Adele Marcus. *Career:* Founder-mem. Gryphon Trio; regular tours across Canada and USA, and in Europe; education and outreach initiatives including multi-media project Constantinople and Listen Up! workshop for schools; Artist-in-residence (with Gryphon Trio), Assoc. Prof. and Rupert E. Edwards Chair in Piano Performance, Univ. of Toronto Faculty of Music; Artistic Advisor, Ottawa Chamber Music Soc.; as soloist, has performed with symphonies of Toronto, Vancouver, Nat. Arts Centre, Nova Scotia. *Recordings include:* Jamie Parker: Beethoven/Brahms/Chopin/Stravinsky 1988, Harry Somers: Celebration 2000, Azulão (with Isabel Bayrakdarian) (Juno Award for Classical Album of the Year 2004) 2003; with Gryphon Trio: Haydn: Four Piano Trios 1996, Dvořák/Mendelssohn: Piano Trios 1998, Mendelssohn/Lalo: Piano Trios 2002, Beethoven: Piano Trios Op. 1 Nos 1 & 3 2003, Canadian Premieres (Juno Award for Classical Album of the Year 2004) 2003, Mozart: Complete Piano Trios 2006, Shostakovich: Complete Works for Piano 2006, Christos Hatzis: Constantinople 2007, Schubert: Complete Piano Trios 2007, Tango Nuevo 2008, Beethoven: Piano Trios Op. 1 No. 2 and Op. 97 Archduke 2009, Beethoven: Piano Trios Op. 70 Nos 1 & 2 and Op. 11 (Juno Award for Classical Album of the Year 2011) 2010, Jeffrey Ryan: Fugitive Colours 2011, Broken Hearts & Madmen 2011, Great Piano Trios 2011, For the End of Time 2012. *Honours:* First Prize, Eckhardt-Gramatte Competition 1984, CBC Nat. Competition for Young Performers and Virginia P. Moore Award; (with Gryphon Trio) Walter Carsen Prize for Excellence in the Arts, Canada Council 2013. *Current Management:* Melvin Kaplan, Inc., 115 College Street, Burlington, VT 05401, USA. *Telephone:* (802) 658-2592. *E-mail:* music@melkap.com. *Website:* www.melkap.com. *E-mail:* jamie .parker@utoronto.ca (office). *Website:* www.gryphontrio.com (office).

PARKER, Jon Kimura, OC, MMus, DMA; Canadian pianist; b. 25 Dec. 1959, Vancouver. *Education:* Juilliard School and studied with Adele Marcus, Lee Kum-Sing, Edward Parker and Marek Jablonski. *Career:* debut in New York 1984, London 1984; performed with London Symphony, London Philharmonic, Toronto Symphony, Cleveland Orchestra, Minnesota Orchestra, Los Angeles Philharmonic, Philadelphia Orchestra, Scottish Nat. Orchestra, Berlin Radio Symphony, NHK Orchestra, Japan, and all Canadian orchestras; recital tours in Europe, Canada, North and South America, Far East and Australia; command performance for Queen Elizabeth II and the Prime Minster of Canada 1984; benefit performance of Beethoven's Emperor Concerto at Sarajevo, New Year's Eve 1995. *Television:* host of series, Whole Notes 1999–. *Recordings:* Tchaikovsky Piano Concerto No. 1; Prokofiev Piano Concerto No. 3 with André Previn and Royal Philharmonic Orchestra, 1986; Solo Piano Music of Chopin, 1987; Two Pianists are Better Than One, with Peter Schickele, 1994; Barber Piano Concerto with Yoel Levi and Atlanta Symphony, 1997. *Honours:* first prize and Princess Mary Gold Medal Leeds Int. Piano Competition 1984, Canadian Governor-General's Performing Arts Award 1996. *Current Management:* Opus 3 Artists, 470 Park Avenue South, 9th Floor North, New York, NY 10016, USA. *Telephone:* (212) 584-7500. *Fax:* (646) 300-8200. *E-mail:* info@opus3artists.com. *Website:* www.opus3artists .com; www.kimura.com.

PARKER, Moises; singer (tenor); b. 1945, Las Villas, Cuba. *Education:* studied in Munich, Juilliard School and Verdi Conservatory, Milan, studied with Tito Gobbi, Richard Holm and Hermann Reutter. *Career:* debut at New York City Opera 1976, as Don José; sang at Strasbourg Opera 1978–80 as Tamino, Hoffmann and Ratansen in Roussel's Padmâvatî; season 1981–82 with WNO and Scottish Opera as Rodolfo and Alvaro; Brunswick and Augsburg 1982–83 as Don José and Alvaro; Deutsche Oper Berlin as Pinkerton; sang Otello at Coburg 1984 and at Stuttgart and Klagenfurt 1989; Theater des Westens Berlin 1988–89, as Gershwin's Porgy, Würzburg 1990 as Bacchus; mem., Kiel Opera from 1988, notably as Turiddu in Cavalleria Rusticana and Win-San-Lui in Leoni's L'Oracolo 1990; sang Tannhäuser at Passau 2000; concert repertoire includes Messiah, Beethoven's Ninth and the Missa Solemnis, Elijah, Rossini's Stabat Mater and Messe Solennelle, Verdi's Requiem. *Honours:* prize winner Voci Verdiane Competition at Bussetto 1974, Francisco Vinas at Barcelona 1975.

PARKER, Roger; British writer on music; b. 2 Aug. 1951, London, England. *Education:* Univ. of London with Margaret Bent and Pierluigi Petrobelli. *Career:* Prof., Cornell University, USA 1982–94; Co-ordinating Ed., Donizetti Critical Edition 1988; founding Co-Ed., Cambridge Opera Journal 1989–98; University Lecturer in Music and Fellow, St Hugh's Coll., Oxford 1994–99; Prof. of Music and Fellow, St John's Coll., Cambridge 1999. *Publications:* Critical Edition of Verdi's Nabucco 1987, Giacomo Puccini (with A. Groos), La Bohème 1986, Reading Opera 1989, Studies in Early Verdi 1989, Analyzing Opera: Verdi and Wagner (with C. Abbate) 1989, Oxford Illustrated History of

Opera (ed.) 1994, Leonora's Last Act: Essays in Verdian Discourse 1997, The New Grove Guide to Wagner (with Barry Millington and Julian Rushton) 2006, The New Grove Guide to Verdi 2006, The New Grove Guide to Mozart and his Operas 2006; contrib. articles on Verdi and his operas in The New Grove Dictionary of Opera 1992. *Honours:* Dent Medal 1991.

PARKER-SMITH, Jane Caroline Rebecca, ARCM, LTCL; British concert organist; *Organist and Director of Music, German Christ Church, Knightsbridge, London;* b. 20 May 1950, Northampton, England; m. John Gadney 1996. *Education:* Barton Peveril Grammar School, Eastleigh, Hants, Royal Coll. of Music, postgraduate study with Nicolas Kynaston in London and Jean Langlais in Paris. *Career:* Westminster Cathedral, London 1970; Royal Festival Hall, London 1975; BBC Promenade Concert 1972; solo recitals at Jyvasklya Festival, Finland 1977, Stockholm Concert Hall, Sweden 1980, Hong Kong Arts Festival 1988, Roy Thomson Hall, Toronto, Canada 1989, City of London Festival 1992, Festival Paris Quartier d'Été 1995, American Guild of Organists Centennial Convention, New York, USA 1996, Festival Internazionale de Musica Organistica, Magadino, Switzerland 1999, Athens Concert Hall, Greece 1999, Cube Concert Hall, Shiroishi, Japan 2000, American Guild of Organists Nat. Convention, Philadelphia, USA 2002, Royal Festival Hall 2003, Severance Hall, Cleveland, USA 2003, Sejong Cultural Center, Seoul, S Korea 2004, Benaroya Concert Hall, Seattle, USA 2005, Esplanade Concert Hall, Singapore 2005, Walt Disney Concert Hall, Los Angeles, USA 2006, Verizon Hall, Philadelphia 2009, Lapua Organ Festival, Finland 2009, Monaco Cathedral 2009, Mariinsky Concert Hall, St Petersburg 2011, ZK Matthews Great Hall, UNISA, Pretoria, South Africa 2011, Davies Symphony Hall, San Francisco 2011; currently Organist and Dir of Music, German Christ Church, Knightsbridge, London; mem. Guild of Musicians and Singers, Incorporated Soc. of Musicians. *Recordings:* Widor Symphonies, Music for Trumpet and Organ with Maurice André; Liszt Organ Works, Saint-Saëns Organ Symphony No. 3, Janácek Glagolitic Mass with the City of Birmingham Symphony Orchestra, conductor Simon Rattle; Baroque Organ Concertos with Prague Chamber Orchestra, conductor Steuart Bedford; Popular French Romantics, Armagh Cathedral, Coventry Cathedral, Beauvais Cathedral; Lefébure-Wély Romantische Orgelmusik; Romantic and Virtuoso Organ Works, Vols 1–3. *Honours:* Hon. FGSM 1996, Hon. Fellow, North and Midlands School of Music 1997; Winner, Nat. Organ Competition 1970. *Address:* 174 The Quadrangle Tower, Cambridge Square, London, W2 2PL, England (home). *Telephone:* (20) 7262-9259 (home). *E-mail:* janeparkersmith@btconnect.com (home). *Website:* www.janeparkersmith.com.

PARKIN, Simon, BMus, ARCM; British composer, pianist and teacher; b. 3 Nov. 1956, Manchester, England. *Education:* Yehudi Menuhin School, Univ. of Manchester, Royal Northern Coll. of Music, Royal Coll. of Music. *Career:* performances in St John's, Smith Square, London, Wigmore Hall and QEH, London; performances as duo-partner in Budapest, Liszt Acad. and Berlin (Otto Braun Saal); resident pianist at ISM, LDSM and Lenk courses; compositions performed in London, New York, Frankfurt, Germany; broadcasts on German radio; teacher at Royal Northern Coll. of Music, Yehudi Menuhin School. *Compositions:* Ted Spiggot and the Killer Beans (opera), Le Chant des Oiseaux (choral work), Laughter and Tears (requiem for choir and orchestra), piano trio, string quartet, chamber concerto, several sonatas for solo instruments and piano. *Honours:* various univ. and coll. prizes, Morley Coll. Centenary Concerto Prize for chamber concerto.

PARKINSON, Del R., BM, MM, DM; American pianist and academic; *Professor, Boise State University;* b. 6 Aug. 1948, Blackfoot, Ida; s. of Douglas Parkinson and Jane Peck; m. Glenna M. Christensen 1986. *Education:* Indiana Univ., Juilliard School, New York, studied in London, UK. *Career:* debut at Wigmore Hall, London 1976; Carnegie Recital Hall, New York 1981; concerto appearances with Chicago Civic Orchestra, Utah Symphony, Boise Philharmonic, Guadalajara Symphony and Orquestra Sinfônica de Sorocaba; solo recitals in USA, England and Mexico; chamber music in USA and aboard Royal Viking Cruise Line; performer in American Piano Duo 1984–; performed with American Piano Quartet throughout USA, Asia and Europe 1989–95; Asst Prof., Furman Univ. 1975–76; Piano Co-ordinator, Ricks Coll. 1977–85; Prof., Boise State Univ. 1985–. *Recordings:* American Piano Quartet 1992, American Piano Duo: Celebrating Gershwin 1998, American Piano Duo: Mendelssohn Concerto 2004, American Piano Duo: Rachmaninoff: Duo Piano Works 2007. *Publications:* contrib. of record review for Journal of American Liszt Soc. of Charles Koechlin piano music 1984. *Honours:* Idaho Distinguished Teaching Award, Brigham Young Univ. 1984, Idaho Gov.'s Award for Excellence in the Arts 1988, Idaho Comm. on the Arts Career Fellowship 1997, Boise Mayor's Award for Artistic Excellence 2001, Foundation Scholar Award for Research and Creative Activity, Boise State Univ. 2003, Arts & Sciences Award for Research and Creative Activity, Boise State Univ. 2008, Int. Roster of Steinway Artists 2008, Idaho Award for Excellence in the Performing Arts, Brigham Young Univ. 2009, Arts & Sciences Award for Community Engagement, Boise State Univ. 2012. *Address:* Music Department, Boise State University, Boise, ID 83725, USA (office). *Telephone:* (208) 426-3300 (office). *E-mail:* dparkins@boisestate.edu (office). *Website:* www.boisestate.edu/music (office).

PARKMAN, Stefan; Swedish conductor and singer; *Professor of Choral Conducting, Uppsala University;* b. 22 June 1952, Uppsala; m. Anna Packalén Parkman; one d. one s. *Education:* Uppsala Univ., Royal Coll. of Music, Stockholm. *Career:* Conductor Boys' Choir, Uppsala Cathedral 1974–89, Royal

Philharmonic Chorus, Stockholm 1985–93, Acad. Chamber Choir of Uppsala 1983–; Chief Conductor Danish Nat. Radio Choir 1989–2002, Swedish Radio Choir 2002–05; Prof. of Choral Conducting, Uppsala Univ. 2000–; freelance appearances with numerous symphony orchestras and ensembles throughout Scandinavia, including the Royal Philharmonic Orchestra and Royal Opera, Stockholm; regular guest conductor of the BBC Singers (London), Nederlands Kamerkoor, Rundfunkchor (Berlin), RIAS Kammerchor Berlin, MDR Rundfunkchor Leipzig, Chor des Bayerischen Rundfunks München, NDR Chor Hamburg, Choeur de Radio France Paris, Trinity Church Choir, New York; regular teacher of master-classes and seminars in Sweden and overseas; appearances as a tenor soloist (mainly Evangelist parts) in baroque oratorios and passions; mem. Royal Swedish Acad. of Music 1998. *Recordings include:* UAK: Swedish a cappella I, Swedish a cappella II, Swedish a cappella III, En stjärna gick på himlen fram, Stemning, Kraus: Sorgemusik över Gustav III, Schnittke: Requiem, Gosskören, KFUM:s K-kör: Gloria Sanctorum, Frögdesång och lustig Dantz, Dygd och Ära, Runkfunkchor Berlin Hindemith: Körverk a cappella, Shchedrin: The sealed Angel, Pepping: Passionsbericht des Matthäus, BBC Singers Brahms. Zigeunerlieder, Op. 103, Radiokoret, Copenhagen Brahms, a cappella, I, Brahms, a cappella, II, Gade: Fünf Gesänge, Gubaidulina: Sonnengesang, Kodaly: Missa brevis och a cappella, Nielsen: Three Motets, Nörgård: Frostsalme, Pepping: Matteuspassion, Pizzetti: A cappella, Reger: A cappella, Schnittke: Minnesang/Körkonsert, Schnittke: 12 Penitential Psalms, S.S. Schultz: Yndigt dufter Danmark, R Strauss: A cappella, Masters of the Chandos label 20th Century a cappella, Royal Music from the Court of King Chr. IV, Scandinavian Contemporary a cappella , Nordic Light (Grieg, Alfvén, P-B, Stenh. mfl.) , Radiokören, Stockholm Hambraeus: Apocalipsis cum figuris), Övrigt Larsson: Orkestermusik). *Honours:* Kt of the Dannebrog 1997. *Address:* Uppsala University Choral Centre, PO Box 638, 75126 Uppsala, Sweden (office). *Telephone:* (18) 4717915 (office). *E-mail:* stefan.parkman@musik.uu.se (office). *Website:* www.korcentrum.uu.se (office).

PARMERUD, Åke; Swedish composer; b. 24 July 1953, Lidköping; s. of Harald Parmerud and Ing-Brit Parmerud; m. Mireille Leblanc; two s. *Education:* Gothenburg Conservatory, from 1978. *Career:* Lecturer in Computer Music and Composition Gothenburg Conservatory 1987; Lindblad-Studio of University of Gothenburg; mem. RAM 1998. *Compositions:* Time's Imaginary Eye, for soprano, tape and slides, 1980; Floden av glas, multimedia, 1978–82; Remaim, orchestra and tape, 1982; Yttringer, soprano and ensemble, 1983; Kren, 1984; Maze, 1985; Yàn, percussion, ensemble and tape, 1985; Isola for chamber orchestra and tape, 1986; Inori, harpsichord and synthesizer, 1987; Les objects obscurs, 1991; Inside Looking Out, computer and ensemble, 1992; Jeux imaginaires, 1993; Stings and Shadows, harp and computer, 1993; Renaissance, 1994; Grains of Voices, 1995; Mirage 1996; Efterbild, computer and orchestra, 1998; The Heart of Silence, multimedia, 1998, Les Flûtes en feu 2000, The Fire Inside, sound/video installation 2000, Substring Bridge for guitar and computer 2002, Bows, Arcs and the Arrow of Time for string orchestra, computer and video 2004, La Vie Mécanique tape 2004. *Honours:* 1st Prize Festival de Bourges 1978, 1980, 1984, 1986, 1991, Prix Ars Electronica 1990, 1994, 1st Prize Stockholm Electronic Arts Awards 1993, The Rosenberg Prize 1997, 1st Prize Metamorphosis Festival 1999. *Address:* Klostergången 3, 41318, Göteborg, Sweden. *Telephone:* (31) 494942 (office). *E-mail:* ake.parmerud@musik.gu.se (office).

PARNAS, Leslie; American cellist and academic; b. 22 Nov. 1932, St Louis, MO; m. Ingeburge Parnas; two s. *Education:* Curtis Inst. of Music, Philadelphia with Piatigorsky. *Career:* debut at New York Town Hall 1959; solo cellist in annual worldwide concert tours with leading orchestras; Dir, Kneisel Hall Summer Music School, Blue Hill, ME; teacher, St Louis Conservatory of Music 1982–; mem. Chamber Music Soc. of Lincoln Center, New York. *Honours:* Pablo Casals Prize, Paris 1957, Primavera Trophy, Rome 1959, prizewinner Int. Tchaikovsky Competition, Moscow 1962. *Address:* 6 Brentwood Avenue, Newton Center, MA 02459, USA (home). *E-mail:* ingelababy@aol.com (home). *Website:* leslieparnas.parnasmusic.com.

PARR, Patricia Ann, CM, DipMus; Canadian pianist and educator; b. 10 June 1937, Toronto, Ont.; two s. *Education:* Curtis Inst. of Music, Philadelphia, Pa, studied with Isabelle Vengerova, Gian-Carlo Menotti and Rudolf Serkin. *Career:* debut with Toronto Symphony aged nine; soloist with Philadelphia, Cleveland, Pittsburgh, Toronto Orchestras and others; New York Town Hall debut; soloist and chamber musician, appearing extensively in Canada and USA; in Trio Concertante toured Australia 1975, 1978; festival appearances include Marlboro, Stratford, Fontana, Marin County, Festival of the Sound; Founding mem. Amici Chamber Ensemble 1985, 20th season in Toronto, tours of Mexico, Jamaica, Eastern Europe, Eastern Canada; Faculty mem. Duquesne Univ. 1967–74, Univ. of Toronto 1974–2009 (Prof., Faculty of Music, retd), Royal Conservatory of Music 1982–90. *Recordings:* Musica Viva Series with clarinettist Joaquin Valdepeñas; with Violinist Lorand Fenyves; with hornist Eugene Rittich; with tenor Marc Dubois; ten albums as mem. Amici Chamber Ensemble. *Honours:* mem. Order of Canada 2009. *Address:* 1702–71 Charles Street East, Toronto, ON M4Y 2T3, Canada (office). *E-mail:* patricia@amiciensemble.com (home). *Website:* www.amiciensemble.com.

PARRA, Hèctor, MA; Spanish composer and academic; *Composition Teacher, IRCAM-Centre Pompidou;* b. 17 April 1976, Barcelona; m. Imma Santacreu. *Education:* Conservatorium of Music, Barcelona, studied composition under David Padros, Brian Ferneyhough and Jonathan Harvey, Conservatorium of Barcelona, IRCAM, Haute École de Musique de Genève, Univ. of Paris VIII;

composition workshops at Centre Acanthes and Royaumont, France and Takefu, Japan. *Career:* works performed by the Ensemble Intercontemporain, Klangforum Wien, Ensembe Recherche, Arditti Quartet, Tokyo Philharmonic Orchestra, Brussels Philharmonic, Barcelona Nat. Orchestra, etc.; comms from the French Govt, IRCAM-Centre Pompidou, Berlin Acad. of Arts, Münchener Biennale, Strasbourg Festival, Musée du Louvre, Selmer Soc., amongst others; works performed at int. festivals of Lucerne, Avignon, Warsaw Autumn, Wien Modern, Donaueschingen, Agora-IRCAM, Witten, Stuttgart Opera House, Bacelona Opera Liceu, Guggenheim New York, San Francisco Arts Festival, Vienna Konzerthaus, etc.; Prof. of Electroacoustic Composition, Conservatorium of Aragon 2005–11, currently at IRCAM-Centre Pompidou. *Compositions include:* Three pieces for piano 1999, Pulsions 2000, Antigone cycle 2002, Strette 2003, Andante sospeso 2003, Time Fields cycle 2002–04, Piano Trio No. 1 – Wortschatten 2004, L'aube assaillie 2005, Chamber Symphony – Quasikristall 2005, Ciel Rouillé 2005, Impromptu 2005, Vestigios 2005, Lumières Abyssales – Chroma I 2006, Arena 2006, String Trio 2006, Karst – Chroma II 2006, Zangezi (music theatre) 2007, Quatre miniatures 2007, String Quartet No. 1 – Leaves of Reality 2007, Piano Trio No. 2 – Knotted Fields 2007, Stimmen 2008, An Exploration of Light 2008, Sirrt die Sekunde 2008, Fibrillian 2008, Fragments on Fragility (string quartet) 2009, Stress Sensor 2009, Hypermusic Prologue (opera) 2009, La dona d'aigua 2009, 'I have come like a butterfly into the hall of human life' 2009, Stress Tensor 2009–11, Mineral Life 2010, Early Life 2010, Equinox 2010, Love to Recherche 2010, Piano Sonata 2010, Caressant l'Horizon 2011, InFALL 2011, Moins qu'un souffle 2012, Cos de matèria 2012, Te craindre en ton absence (opera) 2012–13, L'absència 2013, FREC 2012–13, Carícies cap al blanc 2013, Das geopferte Leben (opera) 2013. *Recordings include:* monographic CD of his trios and chamber music performed by the Ensemble Recherche 2008, Hypermusic Prologue (chamber opera, libretto by Lisa Randall), played by the Ensemble Intercontemporain and IRCAM 2010, Caressant l'Horizon 2012. *Honours:* Prize of the Nat. Inst. for Performing Arts and Music (Spain) 2002, Tremplin Prize, Ensemble Intercontemporain 2005, Donald Aird Memorial Int. Composition Prize of San Francisco 2007, Ernst von Siemens Composers Prize 2011. *Address:* c/o Durand-Salabert-Eschig (Universal Music Publishing Classical), 20 rue des Fossés Saint-Jacques, 75005 Paris, France. *Telephone:* 1-44-41-50-81. *Fax:* 1-44-41-50-77. *E-mail:* patricia.alia@umusic.com. *Website:* www.durand-salabert-eschig.com; hectorparra.net.

PARRISH, Cheryl; American singer (soprano); b. 6 Nov. 1954, Pasadena, TX. *Education:* Baylor Univ. and Vienna Musikhochschule. *Career:* sang at San Francisco Opera from 1983, as Sophie in Rosenkavalier and Werther and Mozart's Blondchen and Susanna (season 1990–91); Miami Opera 1987, 1991, as Ophelia in Hamlet and as Despina; sang Adele in Die Fledermaus at Toronto 1987 and San Diego 1991; Sophie in Der Rosenkavalier at Zürich Opera 1988 and has guested further at Florence and Santa Fe; Shepherd in Tannhäuser at Austin, Texas 1996; frequent concert appearances.

PARROTT, Andrew Haden, BA; British conductor and musicologist; b. 10 March 1947, Walsall, W Midlands, England; s. of R. C. Parrott and E. D. Parrott; m. 1st Emma Kirkby 1971; m. 2nd Emily Van Evera 1986; one d. *Education:* Queen Mary's Grammar School, Walsall, Merton Coll., Oxford. *Career:* Dir of Music, Merton Coll., Oxford 1969–71; Founder, Conductor and Dir Taverner Choir, Taverner Consort and Taverner Players 1973–; Music Dir and Prin. Conductor London Mozart Players 2000–06; Music Dir New York Collegium 2002–10; BBC Promenade Concerts debut 1977; fmr musical asst to Sir Michael Tippett; freelance orchestral and operatic conductor; occasional writer, lecturer and continuo player; Open Postmastership, Merton Coll. 1966–69; Leverhulme Fellowship 1984–85. *Recordings include:* more than 60 recordings of medieval and renaissance music and major works by Monteverdi, Purcell, Vivaldi, Bach, Handel, Mozart, Beethoven and 20th-century composers. *Publications include:* New Oxford Book of Carols (co-ed.) 1992, The Essential Bach Choir 2000 (German edn 2003); articles in Early Music and other journals. *Honours:* Hon. Research Fellow, Royal Holloway, Univ. of London 1995; Hon. Sr Research Fellow, Univ. of Birmingham 2000–. *Current Management:* Rayfield Allied, Southbank House, Black Prince Road, London, SE1 7SJ, England. *Telephone:* (20) 3176-5500. *E-mail:* info@rayfieldallied.com. *Website:* www.rayfieldallied.com/artists/andrew-parrott. *Address:* Mill Farm, Stanton St John, Oxford, OX33 1HN, England.

PARRY, Susan; British singer (mezzo-soprano); b. 13 Feb. 1963, Luton, Bedfordshire, England. *Education:* Birmingham University and the Royal Academy of Music. *Career:* Welsh National Opera from 1987, as the Witch in Hansel and Gretel, and Kate Pinkerton; English National Opera debut 1992, in the premiere of John Buller's The Bacchae; Company Principal with ENO from 1995, as the Kitchen Boy in Rusalka, Brangaene (first major role, 1996), Janáček's Fox, Strauss's Octavian and Composer, and Dorabella, (1997); Concerts include the Brahms Liebeslieder Waltzes under Antal Dorati, Messiah at the Albert Hall and Beethoven's Ninth at the Festival Hall; Season 1996 included concert of Gluck's Iphigénie en Tauride with the Orchestra of the Age of Enlightenment, Covent Garden debut in Alzira, and Tebaldo in Don Carlos at the London Proms; Falla's El Amor Brujo with the BBC Philharmonic Orchestra, Henze's La Cubana with the Ballet Rambert and an orchestration of Alma Mahler Lieder at Maastricht; Imelda in Verdi's Oberto at Covent Garden, 1997, Pierotto in Donizetti's Linda di Chamounix with the OAE and Hansel in concert with the CBSO under Mark Elder; Elizabeth I in new production of Mary Stuart, ENO 1998; Miss Jessel in The Turn of the Screw, Cincinnati (US debut); London Proms, 2002. *Current Management:* c/o Ingpen & Williams, 7 St George's Court, 131 Putney Bridge Road, London, SW15 2PA, England. *Telephone:* (20) 8874-3222. *Fax:* (20) 8877-3113. *E-mail:* info@ingpen.co.uk.

PARSONS, Brian Geoffrey, GRSM, ARCM; British singer (tenor); b. 6 Aug. 1952, Luton, England. *Education:* Boston County Music School, Lincolnshire, Royal Coll. of Music, Royal Coll. of Music Opera School. *Career:* Vicar choral, St Paul's Cathedral 1977–79; BBC Singers 1981–83; Groupe Vocal De France 1983–84; Opera 80 (now English Touring Opera) Count Almaviva, Il barbiere di Siviglia 1980; Lindoro, L'italiana in Algeri 1985; Prof. of Singing, Conservatoire National Supérieur de Musique, Lyon 1998–, Guildhall School of Music and Drama 2000–; mem. Incorporated Soc. of Musicians, Asscn of English Singers and Speakers. *Recordings:* Rameau: Castor et Pollux (English Bach Festival, conductor Charles Farncombe) 1983, Rameau: Naïs (English Bach Festival, conductor Nicolas McGegan) 1982. *Honours:* Finalist, National Federation of Music Societies Award 1977, Finalist, Richard Tauber Competition 1982. *Address:* 5 Montrose Avenue, London, NW6 6LE, England (home). *Telephone:* (20) 8969-4880 (home). *E-mail:* bgparsons@aol.com (home).

PÄRT, Arvo; Estonian composer; b. 11 Sept. 1935, Paide; m. Eleonora Pärt. *Education:* composition studies with Heino Eller at Tallinn Conservatory. *Career:* sound engineer, Estonian Radio 1958–67; freelance composer 1967–; first creative period starting with neoclassicist piano music 1958–68; experiments with serial techniques, aleatoricism ("incorporation of chance into the process of creation"), collage and sonic fields; his piece Credo from this period caused scandal in Soviet Estonia and was immediately banned 1968; new artistic re-orientation 1968–76; studied Gregorian chant, Notre Dame School and classic vocal polyphony; long silence broken by Symphony No. 3 1971 (sole work from this period); Für Alina 1976, first composition in tintinnabuli technique; emigrated to Vienna, Austria 1980; contract with Universal Edition; grant from German Academic Exchange Service (DAAD) 1981, moved to Berlin; began collaboration with ECM label and producer Manfred Eicher 1984; Int. Arvo Pärt Centre est. in Laulasmaa, Estonia 2010 (holds composer's personal archive); returned to Estonia where he resides 2010–; mem. Estonian Acad. of Sciences (Academician for Music), Tallinn 2011, Pontifical Council for Culture, Vatican City 2011; Academician for Music, Tallinn 2011. *Compositions include:* for chamber or symphony orchestra: Symphony No. 1 (Polyphonic) 1963, Symphony No. 2 1966, Symphony No. 3 1971, Symphony No. 4 (Classic Brit Award – Composer of the Year 2011) 2008, Nekrolog 1960, Perpetuum mobile 1963, Collage über B-A-C-H 1964, Pro et contra (concerto for violoncello and orchestra) 1966, Wenn Bach Bienen gezüchtet hätte … 1976–2001, Cantus in Memory of Benjamin Britten 1977–80, Fratres for different ensembles 1977, Tabula rasa for two violins or one violin and one viola, prepared piano and orchestra (Estonia SSR annual music award 1978) 1977, Festina lente 1986–90, Silouan's Song, 'My Soul Yearns after the Lord...' 1991, Trisagion 1992–94, Orient & Occident (Classical Brit Award – Contemporary Music Award 2003) 2000, Lamentate, Homage to Anish Kapoor and His Sculpture 'Marsyas' for piano and orchestra 2002, La Sindone 2005–13, Für Lennart in memoriam 2006, These Words … 2008, Silhouette, Hommage à Gustave Eiffel 2009–10, Swan-Song 2013, Sequentia 2014; for choir and orchestra: Our Garden (First Prize, Composers Forum, Moscow 1962) 1959, Credo 1968, Stabat Mater 1985–2008, Te Deum 1985–92, Miserere 1989–92, Berliner Messe for different instrumentation 1990–2002, Litany, Prayers of St John Chrysostom for each hour of the day and night 1994–96, Como cierva sedienta 1998–2002, Cantique des degrés 1999–2002, Cecilia, vergine romana 2000–02, Salve Regina 2011, In principio 2003, Adam's Lament (Tõnu Kaljuste, Sinfonietta Riga, Latvian Radio Choir, Vox Clamantis, Tallinn Chamber Orchestra, Estonian Philharmonic Chamber Choir, soloists Tui Hirv and Rainer Vilu, Grammy Award for Best Choral Performance 2014) 2010; chamber music: Quintettino 1964, Sarah Was Ninety Years Old 1976–89, In spe (later: An den Wassern zu Babel… for different ensembles) 1976, Pari intervallo (later for different ensembles) 1976, Arbos for different ensembles 1977, Spiegel im Spiegel for different ensembles 1978, De profundis 1980, Passio (Edison Classical Music Award 1989) 1982, Ein Wallfahrtslied/Pilgrims' Song 1984, Psalom for different ensembles 1985, Mozart-Adagio 1992–2005, My Heart's in the Highlands 2000, Salve Regina 2001, Estonian Lullaby for different ensembles 2002, Christmas Lullaby for different ensembles 2002, L'abbé Agathon for different ensembles 2004, Vater unser 2005–11, Sei gelobt, du Baum 2007, Alleluia-Tropus 2008, Missa brevis 2009; for choir a cappella: Solfeggio 1963, Missa syllabica for different ensembles 1977, Summa for different ensembles 1977, Sieben Magnificat-Antiphonen 1988–91, Magnificat 1989, Dopo la vittoria 1996–98, Kanon pokajanen 1997, Triodion 1998, Zwei Beter 1998, Which Was the Son of … 2000, Peace upon You, Jerusalem 2002, Most Holy Mother of God 2003, Da pacem Domine for different ensembles (Estonian Philharmonic Chamber Choir, conductor Paul Hillier, Grammy Award – Best Choral Performance 2007) 2004, Habitare fratres in unum 2012, Virgencita 2012–13, Kleine Litanei 2015; for piano: Partita 1958, Two Sonatinas 1958–59, Diagramme 1964, Für Alina 1976, Variations for the Healing of Arinushka 1977; for organ: Trivium 1976, Pari intervallo 1976–80, Annum per annum 1980, Mein Weg hat Gipfel und Wellentäler 1989. *Honours:* Hon. Citizen of Rakvere 1995, Paide 2009; Hon. mem. Royal Swedish Acad. of Music 1991, American Acad. of Arts and Letters 1996, Royal Acad. of Sciences, Letters and Fine Arts (Belgium) 2001, Royal School of Church Music (UK) 2003, Accad. Nazionale di Santa Cecilia (Italy) 2004; Hon. title 'Borderlander' from Borderland Foundation, Sejny, Poland 2003, Archon of Ecumenical Patriarchate 2013; Second

Class Order, Nat. Coat of Arms (Estonia) 1998, Commdr, Ordre des Arts et des Lettres 2001, Estonian Nat. Honour First Class 2006, Cross of Honour for Science and Art First Class (Austrian) 2008, Coat of Arms of Tallinn 2011, Chevalier, Légion d'honneur 2011, Estonian Evangelical Lutheran Church Cross of Merit First Class 2015, Austrian Decoration for Science and Art 2015; Dr hc (Estonian Acad. of Music) 1989, (Sydney) 1996, (Tartu) 1998, (Durham) 2002, (Nat. Univ. of Gen. San Martín, Argentina) 2003, (Freiburg) 2007, (Liège) 2009, (St Andrews) 2009, (Pontifical Inst. for Sacred Music) 2011, (Lugano) 2012, (St Vladimir's Orthodox Theological Seminary) 2014; DAAD Fellowship (German Academic Exchange Service), Berlin 1981, Ind. Russian Arts Award 'Triumph', Moscow 1997, Culture Award (Estonia) 1998, Herder Prize (Germany) 2000, Composition Award for choral work, C.A. Seghizzi, Gorizia, Italy 2003, Composer of the Year, Musical America 2005, European Church Music Prize (Germany) 2005, Int. Prize 'Baltic Star', St Petersburg 2007, Int. Brückepreis Award, European City of Görlitz/Zgorzelec 2007, Léonie Sonning Music Prize (Denmark) 2008, Lifelong Achievement Award (Estonia) 2009, Lifelong Achievement Award, Int. Istanbul Music Festival 2010, Baltic Image Enhancement Award (USA) 2010, Homage to Arvo Pärt by Konrad Adenauer Fund (Germany) 2011, Prize of Int. Festival Cervantino (Mexico) 2012, Estonian Music Council Composition Award 2012, Orlando-di-Lasso-Medaille (Germany) 2013, Praemium Imperiale (Japan) 2014, Tallinn Black Nights Film Festival (PÖFF) Lifetime Achievement Award 2015, Estonian Culture Endowment Annual Award 2016. *Current Management:* c/o Universal Edition AG, Boesendorferstrasse 12, 1010 Vienna, Austria. *Telephone:* (1) 337-23-0. *Fax:* (1) 337-23-400. *E-mail:* office@universaledition.com. *Website:* www.universaledition.com/paert. *E-mail:* info@arvopart.ee (office). *Website:* www.arvopart.ee.

PARTRIDGE, Ian H., CBE; British singer (tenor) and teacher; b. 12 June 1938, London, England; m. Ann Glover 1967; two s. *Education:* Clifton College, Royal College of Music, Guildhall School of Music. *Career:* debut at Bexhill, 1958; concerts and recitals worldwide; Covent Garden debut 1969; numerous broadcasts for BBC and worldwide TV; mem. Garrick Club, RSM (governor), PAMRA (dir). *Recordings:* Schöne Müllerin, Schubert; Dichterliebe and Liederkreis op 39-Schumann; On Wenlock Edge and Other Songs, V Williams; The Curlew, Peter Warlock; Songs by Fauré, Duparc, Delius, Gurney. *Honours:* Harriet Cohen Award, 1967; Prix Italia, 1977; Hon. RAM, 1996.

PASATIERI, Thomas; American composer; b. 20 Oct. 1945, New York. *Education:* Juilliard with Giannini and Persichetti, Aspen Music School with Darius Milhaud. *Career:* freelance composer 1965–; commissions from Nat. Educational Television, Houston Grand Opera, Baltimore Opera, Michigan Opera Theater, Univ. of Arizona, Evelyn Lear and Thomas Stewart; has taught at Juilliard School, Manhattan School of Music, Cincinnati Conservatory of Music; Artistic Dir, Atlanta Opera 1980–84; f. Topaz Productions (film music production co.) 1984. *Compositions include:* operas: The Trysting Place 1964, Flowers of Ice 1964, The Women 1965, La Divina 1965, Padrevia 1966, The Penitentes 1967, Calvary 1971, Black Widow 1972, The Seagull 1972, The Trial of Mary Lincoln 1972, Signor Deluso 1974, Inés de Castro 1976, Washington Square 1976, Three Sisters 1979, Before Breakfast 1980, The Goose Girl 1981, Maria Elena 1983, Three Sisters 1986, Frau Margot 2007, The Hotel Casablanca 2007; vocal: Selected Songs 1971, Heloïse and Abelard for soprano, baritone and piano 1973, Rites of Passage for voice and chamber orchestra or string quartet 1974, Three Poems of James Agee 1974, Permit Me Voyage for soprano, mixed chorus and orchestra 1976, Far from Love for soprano, clarinet, violin, cello and piano 1976, Songs Vol. One 1977, Songs Vol. Two 1980, Day of Love 1983, Mass for soprano, alto, tenor and bass soloists, mixed chorus and orchestra 1983, Canciones del Barrio 1983, Three Sonnets from the Portuguese 1984, A Joyful Noise for mixed chorus, brass sextet, organ, percussion 1985, Sieben Lehmannlieder for voice and orchestra 1988, Windsongs 1989, Alleluia for voice and orchestra 1991, Three Mysteries for mixed chorus 1991, The Harvest Frost for mixed chorus and chamber ensemble 1993, Bang the Drum Loudly for mixed chorus and piano or two-part treble chorus and piano 1994, Canticle of Praise for mixed chorus and organ 1995, Mornings Innocent for men's chorus, oboe, cello, harp and piano 1995, Three Poems of Oscar Wilde 1998, Windsong 2001, A Rustling of Angels 2003, Letter to Warsaw for voice and chamber orchestra 2003; instrumental: Piano Sonata No. 1 1966, Invocation 1968, Piano Sonata No. 2 1969, Cameos for solo piano 1969, Theatrepieces for clarinet, violin and piano 1987, Serenade for violin and chamber orchestra 1992, Concerto for piano and orchestra 1993, Concerto for two pianos and strings 1994, Quartet for flute and strings 1995, Sonata for viola and piano 1995, Sonata for flute and piano 1997, Piano Sonata No. 3 1999. *Address:* c/o Theodore Presser Company, 588 N Gulph Road, King of Prussia, PA 19406, USA (office). *E-mail:* thomas@thomaspasatieri.org (office). *Website:* www.thomaspasatieri.org.

PASCAL, Michel; French electro-acoustic composer and academic; *Professor of Electro-acoustic Composition, Conservatoire de Nice;* b. 12 Oct. 1958, Avignon; m. Maxime Pascal; two d. *Education:* CNSM Paris, CNR Marseille, INA-GRM and IRCAM, Paris with I. Xenakis, H. Dutilleux, W. Lutosławski and L. Berio. *Career:* debut as asst of Jean Etienne Marie, CIRM, Nice 1985–87, for studio and Festival of Contemporary Music; composer in many fields, including acoustic, choir, instrumental, dance music, music for theatre, film, video and television production; as synthesist, performer and creator of the Studio Instrumental, works played on hyperinstruments with live electronics; Prof. of Electro-acoustic Composition, Conservatoire de Nice

1986–; Artistic Dir acousmatic festival Microfolies, Aix en Provence – Acousmonium Rime Monaco 2005–10; mem., SACEM, SACD, Rainbow Across Europe. *Compositions include:* Falaises et Emergences, for tape 1981, Voiles, for choir and synthesizers 1987, Protos, for symphonic orchestra 1989, Sonic Waters No. 2 1989, Nausicaä 1991, Berceuses 1992, Puzzle 1995–99, Puissance 3, for string trio 1997, V° Concours Noroit 1997, Répertoires Polychromes 2 1998, Répliques 2007, Beyond 2009. *Recordings:* albums: Contribution to Nausicaa, Centre de la Mer, Boulogne 1990, Sonic Waters, with Michel Redolfi-Berceuse/Albin Michel 1990, Répertoires Polychromes 1999, Puzzle 1999; videos: Mille Mètres sous la Jungle 1995, Les Grottes ornées de Borneo 1996; other: music for Luc Henri Fage's film, French national television. *Publications:* Les Nouveaux Gestes de la Musique 1999, La composition est-elle transmissible? 2010. *Address:* Conservatoire à Rayonnement Régional, 127 Avenue de Brancolar, 06364 Nice, France (office). *Telephone:* 4-97-13-50-00 (office). *Fax:* 4-97-13-50-25 (office). *E-mail:* info@crr-nice.org (office); michel.pascal@freesbcc.fr (home). *Website:* www.crr-nice.org (office); studio-instrumental.org (home).

PASCHER, Hartmut; Austrian violinist and violist; b. 1956, Vienna, Austria. *Education:* Vienna Acad. of Music. *Career:* member of the Franz Schubert Quartet, Paracelsus String Quartet 1985–; many concert appearances in Europe, the USA and Australia, including the Amsterdam Concertgebouw, the Vienna Musikverein and Konzerthaus, the Salle Gaveau Paris and the Sydney Opera House; visits to Zürich, Geneva, Basle, Berlin, Hamburg, London, Rome, Rotterdam, Madrid and Copenhagen; festival engagements include Salzburg, Wiener Festwochen, Prague Spring, Schubertiade at Hohenems, the Schubert Festival at Washington DC and the Belfast and Istanbul Festivals; Tours of Australasia, USA; frequent concert tours of UK including appearances at the Wigmore Hall and Cheltenham Festival; teacher of the Graz Musikhochschule; masterclasses at the Royal Northern College of Music at Lake District Summer Music. *Address:* Paracelsusquartett, c/o Erich Petuelli, Kurrentgasse 12/26, 1010 Vienna, Austria (office). *E-mail:* pascherhartmut@hotmail.com (office). *Website:* www .paracelsusquartett.at.

PASCOE, John; British artistic director; b. 1949, Bath. *Career:* debut designed Julius Caesar for English National Opera, also seen in San Francisco, Geneva, the Metropolitan and on TV 1979; designed Lucrezia Borgia at Covent Garden and Alcina at Sydney, both with Joan Sutherland, Tosca for Welsh National Opera 1980; Producer and Designer: La Bohème in Belfast, Solomon at the Göttingen Festival 1984; Producer and Designer: Rameau's Platée in Spoleto Festival, also seen in BAM, New York; Designer: Orlando at San Francisco and Chicago; Così fan tutte in Dallas; Anna Bolena, with Joan Sutherland, in Toronto, Chicago, Detroit, Houston and San Francisco 1985–86; Designer: Amahl and the Night Visitors; Norma, in Santiago, 1987; Producer and Designer: Anna Bolena at Covent Garden; Norma in Los Angeles and Detroit, both with Joan Sutherland 1988; Producer and Designer: La Bohème in Bath; Designed: Tosca in Nice; Apollo and Hyacinthus at Cannes Festival, Madrid, Paris 1991, 1992; Producer and Designer: La Traviata in Bath; Designer: Anna Bolena in Washington, DC 1993; Founder, Bath and Wessex Opera. *Honours:* Evening Standard Award for Julius Caesar 1979. *Current Management:* c/o Robert Lombardo, Lombardo Associates, 61 West 62nd Street, Suite 6F, New York, NY 10023, USA. *Telephone:* (212) 586-4453. *E-mail:* robert@robertlombardo.com. *E-mail:* segretaria.jpascoe@live.co.uk. *Website:* www.johnpascoe.com.

PASCOE, Keith; violinist; b. 1959, England. *Career:* founder mem., Britten Quartet, debut concert at the Wigmore Hall 1987; quartet-in-residence, Dartington Summer School 1987, with quartets by Schnittke; season 1988–89 in the Genius of Prokofiev series at Blackheath and BBC Lunchtime Series at St John's Smith Square; South Bank appearances with the Schoenberg/ Handel Quartet Concerto conducted by Neville Marriner, concerts with the Hermann Prey Schubertiade and collaborations with the Alban Berg Quartet in the Beethoven Plus series; tour of South America 1988, followed by Scandinavian debut; season 1989–90 with debut tours of The Netherlands, Germany, Spain, Austria, Finland; tours from 1990 to the Far East, Malta, Sweden, Norway; Schoenberg/Handel Concerto with the Gothenburg Symphony; festival appearances at Brighton, the City of London, Greenwich, Canterbury, Harrogate, Chester, Spitalfields and Aldeburgh; collaborations with John Ogdon, Imogen Cooper, Thea King and Lynn Harrell; formerly resident quartet at Liverpool Univ.; teaching role at Lake District Summer Music 1989, and at Univs of Bristol, Hong Kong 1990. *Recordings:* Beethoven Op 130 and Schnittke Quartet No. 3, Vaughan Williams On Wenlock Edge and Ravel Quartet, Britten, Prokofiev, Tippett, Elgar and Walton Quartets.

PASHLEY, Anne; British singer (soprano); b. 5 June 1937, Skegness, England; m. Jack Irons; one s. one d. *Education:* Guildhall School of Music, London. *Career:* took part in sprinter 1956 Olympic Games, Melbourne; stage debut in Semele, with Handel Opera Soc. 1959; Glyndebourne debut 1962, in Die Zauberflöte; Covent Garden debut 1965, as Barbarina in Le nozze di Figaro; guest appearances with ENO, Scottish Opera, WNO, and at Edinburgh and Aldeburg Festivals; foreign engagements in France, Germany, Portugal, Spain, Belgium, Italy, Israel; leading roles in BBC television operas and numerous radio braodcasts; New Opera Co., London, in the British premiere of Hindemith's Cardillac 1970; mem. Equity. *Recordings include:* La Morte de Cléopâtre, Berlioz; Magnificat, Bach; Albert Herring and Peter Grimes, Britten.

PASINO, Gisella; Italian singer (mezzo-soprano); b. 1965, Genoa. *Education:* studied at Genoa with Maggia Olivero. *Career:* debut in Padua 1987 as the Princess in Suor Angelica; Rome 1987 as Amneris in Aida; sang Verdi's Preziosilla at Piacenza 1989; Anacoana in Franchetti's Cristoforo Colombo at Frankfurt 1991; season 1995–96 as Carmen at Rotterdam and the Princess in Adriana Lecouvreur at Livorno. *Recordings include:* Cristoforo Colombo. *Honours:* prizewinner at competitions in Genoa and Milan.

PASQUETTO, Giancarlo; Italian singer (baritone); b. 1959, Verona. *Career:* sang widely in Italy from 1984 as Alfio in Cavalleria Rusticana, Count Luna, Marcello, Verdi's Miller and Carlo in La Forza del Destino; Metropolitan Opera, New Yok 1989 as Miller; season 1993 as Nabucco at Bregenz, Germont at Verona and for New Israeli Opera 1998; Rigoletto at the Berlin Staatsoper and Tonio in Pagliacci at La Scala, Milan; further appearances as Guzman in Verdi's Alzira at Parma and at Covent Garden as Rigoletto 1994; other roles include Amonasro, Simon Boccanegra, Riccardo in I Puritani. *Recordings include:* Simon Boccanegra, from Glyndebourne 1998.

PASQUIER, Bruno; French violist; b. 10 Dec. 1943, Neuilly-sur-Seine. *Education:* Paris Conservatoire with Etienne Ginot and Pierre Pasquier. *Career:* Mix à Munich 1965; Queteur à cadas, string quartet 1972–83; leader viola section, Orchestre de Paris Opéra 1972; soloist, Orchestre National de France 1984–89; founder (with Regis Pasquier and Roland Pidoux), New Pasquier Trio 1970; solo performances with leading orchestras in France and abroad; Prof. of Viola and of Chamber Music, Paris Conservatoire 1983; plays a Maggilli viola c. 1620. *Honours:* Chevalier, Ordre des Arts et des Lettres 1991.

PASQUIER, Régis; French violinist; *Professor of Violin, Paris Conservatoire;* b. 10 Oct. 1945, Fontainebleau. *Education:* Paris Conservatoire, studied with Isaac Stern. *Career:* recitals, and concerts with leading orchestras, in Japan, Europe, Canada, USA and S America; soloist with Orchestre Nat. de France 1977–86; formed (with Bruno Pasquier and Roland Pidoux) the New Pasquier Trio 1970; sonata recitals with pianist Jean-Claude Pennetier; concerto repertoire ranges from standard classics to works by Xenakis and Gilbert Amy (Trajectoires); Prof. of Violin and of Chamber Music, Paris Conservatoire 1985; in demand for coaching, master-classes and on juries; plays a violin by Guarnerius (Del Gesù), Cremona 1734. *Recordings:* recordings include concertos by Mozart, Prokofiev, Berg and Bartók and violin sonatas by Prokofiev and Beethoven. *Honours:* Chevalier, Légion d'honneur 2005, des Arts et des Lettres; First Prize for Violin and Chamber Music, Conservatoire Nat. Supérieur de Musique de Paris. *Current Management:* c/o Christine Talbot-Cooper, International Artists, Stoneville Cottage, Gretton Fields, Chelthenham, Glos., GL54 5HH, England. *Telephone:* (1242) 620736. *Fax:* (1242) 620736. *E-mail:* talbotcooper@onetel.com. *Website:* www .ctcinternationalartists.com.

PASSOW, Sabine; German singer (soprano); b. 1960, Essen. *Education:* studied in Essen and Hannover. *Career:* sang in opera at Oldenburg from 1987; Komische Oper Berlin from 1991, as Mozart's Countess, Handel's Cleopatra, Marenka in The Bartered Bride, Micaela and Agathe; Arianna in Handel's Giustino, 1995; Alice Ford in Falstaff, 1996; guest at the Munich Staatsoper from 1986, notably in Strauss's Daphne and as Ismene in Mozart's Mitridate, 1990; guest with Komische Oper at Covent Garden, 1989; Tours of Japan, 1991 and 1994; Cleopatra at the Schwetzingen Festival, 1993; sang Elisabeth in Tannhäuser at Darmstadt, 1994 and at Cottbus in 1999; sang Anna in Seven Deadly Sins by Brecht/Weill; concerts of music by Bach; season 2000–01 as Butterfly at Cottbus, Elisabeth at Saarbrücken, Alice Ford for the Komische Oper and Agathe at the Eutin Festival. *Current Management:* c/o Neil Dalrymple, Music International, 13 Ardilaun Road, London, N5 2QR, England. *Telephone:* (20) 7359-5183. *Fax:* (20) 7226-9792. *E-mail:* music@ musicint.co.uk.

PATAKI, Eva, DipMus; Hungarian pianist; b. 19 Oct. 1941, Budapest; m. T. Bantay 1971. *Education:* Franz Liszt Music Academy, Budapest, studied with Carlo Zecchi in Salzburg. *Career:* debut recital, Budapest 1965; Asst, Mozarteum, Salzburg for five years; coach, Royal Opera, Stockholm 1967–; concerts, radio and television, with Helena Doese, Catarina Ligendza, C.-H. Ahnsjö, Nicolai Gedda, Gösta Winbergh and others, across Europe and in Moscow, St Petersburg and other venues 1967–; teacher of masterclasses; producer of concerts at Royal Opera, Stockholm 1985–. *Address:* Brahegatan 29, 114 37 Stockholm, Sweden (home). *Telephone:* (8) 662-11-34 (home).

PATCHELL, Sue; American singer (soprano); b. 1948, Montana. *Education:* studied in Montana and at Univ. of California, Los Angeles. *Career:* frequently performs role of Isolde, including at Théâtre Royal de la Monnaie Brussels, Danish Royal Opera, Copenhagen, in Trieste, Dortmund, Wiesbaden, Weimar, Mannheim, at Gran Teatre del Liceu, Barcelona and with Valery Gergiev at the Rotterdam Festival 2004; performed Chrysosthemis at Vienna State Opera, Hamburg State Opera, in Antwerp, at Festival in Tel-Aviv and in various gala concerts; sang Senta at Opera di Roma (Jeffrey Tate conducting), Houston Grand Opera, in Torino and at Hamburg State Opera; also sang Jenůfa in Hamburg; highlights at Vienna State Opera include Elisabeth (Tannhäuser), Eva (Die Meistersinger), the Marschallin (Der Rosenkavalier), Elsa (Lohengrin) and Salome; sang Chrysosthemis at Gran Teatre del Liceu, Barcelona (together with Eva Marton as Elektra), Eva in Meistersinger (with Bernd Weikl as Sachs) and Elsa in production of Lohengrin by Götz Friedrich; sang Eva in Paris, Budapest and at Opera House in Bonn, also performed Fidelio-Leonore; sang Brünnhilde in Siegfried at Opera House in Nuremberg

and at Wagner Festival in Wels; sang Freihild in Italian premiere of Guntram by Richard Strauss at Teatro Massimo Bellini in Catania, Cassandra in Les Troyens at Leipzig Opera House and Mannheim Nat. Theatre; has performed with numerous conductors, including James Levine, Gerd Albrecht, Sir Colin Davis, Jeffrey Tate, Ivan Anguélov, Heinz Fricke, Valery Gergiev, Fabio Luisi, Antonio Pappano, Donald Runnicles, Peter Schneider, Ulf Schirmer, Stefan Soltesz and others; has worked with stage dirs including Ruth Berghaus, Dieter Dorn, Götz Friedrich, Achim Freyer, Dietrich Hilsdorf, David Pountney, etc.; recitals of Wagner and Strauss songs, repertoire includes The Four Last Songs, the Wesendonk songs and Isoldes Liebestod amongst others. *Recordings include:* Das Dunkle Reich by Pfitzner. *Current Management:* c/o Mennicken PR Management, Heinrich-Zille-Street 19, Zeesen, 15711 Berlin, Germany. *E-mail:* info@mennicken-pr.com. *Website:* www .mennicken-pr.com.

PATERNOSTRO, Roberto; Austrian conductor; *Music Director, Israel Chamber Orchestra;* b. 1957, Vienna. *Education:* Music Univ. of Vienna with Hans Swarowsky, Music Univ. of Hamburg with György Ligeti and Christoph von Dohnanyi. *Career:* Asst to Herbert von Karajan, Berlin 1978–84; Conductor, Opera for Africa gala, Arena di Verona, Italy 1985; Gen. Music Dir Württembergische Philharmonie 1991–2000; Gen. Music Dir Staatstheater Kassel, Germany 1997–2007; debut with Munich Philharmonic orchestra for New Year's Concert 1999; debut with Vienna Symphoniker 2002; Artistic Dir and Conductor, Gustav-Mahler-Festival, Kassel 2005–; Music Adviser to Israel Chamber Orchestra 2009–, Artistic Dir 2010–; 2010–11 debuts: State Opera Prague, Cincinnati, Teatro Massimo Bellini Catania, first performance of an Israeli orchestra in Bayreuth (Wagner's Siegfried Idyll). *Recordings:* albums including: as conductor: Verdi, La Traviata 1990, Gala Opera Concert (with RSO Berlin) 1991, Great Overtures (with Tokyo Philharmonic Orchestra and Deutsches Symphonieorchester Berlin), Bizet, Carmen 1998, Puccini, Opera Arias and Duets 1998, Renato Bruson, Arie Antiche 2000, Poulenc/Mendelssohn, Concertos for Pianos, Die Grosse Wagner Operngala 2003, Wagner, Arien, Bruckner, The Symphonies 2009, Richard Strauss, Orchesterwerke, Mozart, Fremuarermusik 2009, Elisabeth-Maria Wachutka, Strauss/Beethoven/Wagner 2009, Historical Moment in Bayreuth – Israel Chamber Orchestra playing Mahler and Wagner in Bayreuth 2011. *Current Management:* c/o Iván Paley, VMC – Vienna Music Connection, Rodrigo Mora Wiedner Hauptstrasse 90–92/2/12, 1050 Vienna, Austria. *Telephone:* 676-757-3098 (mobile). *E-mail:* vmc@viemuc.com. *Website:* www.viemuc.com. *Address:* Yuval Shamir, General Manager, Israel Chamber Orchestra, 10 She'erit Israel Street, Tel-Aviv-Jaffa 68184, Israel (office). *Telephone:* (3) 5188845 (office). *E-mail:* ico2000@netvision.net.il (office); office@robertopaternostro.com. *Website:* www.ico.co.il (office); www .robertopaternostro.com.

PATIPATANAKOON, Annalee; Canadian musician (violin). *Education:* Indiana Univ., Curtis Inst. of Music, studied with Aaron Rosand, Franco Gulli and Miriam Fried. *Career:* Founder-mem. Gryphon Trio; regular tours across Canada and USA, and in Europe; education and outreach initiatives including multi-media project Constantinople and Listen Up! workshop for schools; Artist-in-Residence (with Gryphon Trio) and Asst Prof., Univ. of Toronto Faculty of Music; has taught and conducted masterclasses at Rice Univ., Stanford Univ., Royal Conservatory of Music, Hochschule für Musik Mainz, Domaine Forget, Orford Acad., Tuckamore Festival and School and Mount Royal Univ.; Artistic Advisor, Ottawa Chamber Music Soc. *Recordings include:* with Gryphon Trio: Haydn: Four Piano Trios 1996, Dvorak/ Mendelssohn: Piano Trios 1998, Mendelssohn/Lalo: Piano Trios 2002, Beethoven: Piano Trios Op. 1 Nos 1 & 3 2003, Canadian Premieres (Juno Award for Classical Album of the Year 2004) 2003, Mozart: Complete Piano Trios 2006, Shostakovich: Complete Works for Piano 2006, Christos Hatzis: Constantinople 2007, Schubert: Complete Piano Trios 2007, Tango Nuevo 2008, Beethoven: Piano Trios Op. 1 No. 2 and Op. 97 Archduke 2009, Beethoven: Piano Trios Op. 70 Nos 1 & 2 and Op. 11 (Juno Award for Classical Album of the Year 2011) 2010, Jeffrey Ryan: Fugitive Colours 2011, Broken Hearts & Madmen 2011, Great Piano Trios 2011, For the End of Time 2012. *Honours:* with Gryphon Trio: Walter Carsen Prize for Excellence in the Arts, Canada Council 2013. *Current Management:* Melvin Kaplan, Inc., 115 College Street, Burlington, VT 05401, USA. *Telephone:* (802) 658-2592. *E-mail:* music@melkap.com. *Website:* www.melkap.com; www.gryphontrio.com (office).

PATON, Iain; singer (tenor); b. 1960, Scotland. *Education:* Royal Scottish Acad., studied with David Keren in London. *Career:* appearances with Glyndebourne Festival and touring Opera in Capriccio, Death in Venice and Le nozze di Figaro, Don Curzio; sang in Judith Weir's The Vanishing Bridegroom for Scottish Opera at Glasgow and Covent Garden; season 1992–93, as Pedrillo in Die Entführung and in The Makropulos Case; season 1993–94, as Vanya in Katya Kabanova, Tamino and the Shepherd in Tristan und Isolde; sang Leicester in Maria Stuarda for Scottish Opera-Go-Round 1992; City of Birmingham Touring Opera in Mozart's Zaide; concert repertoire includes Liszt's Faust Symphony and appearances with Scottish Early Music Consort in Northern Ireland, Germany and Poland; sang Eurimachos in Dallapiccola's Ulisse for BBC 1993; season 1995–96 in Purcell's King Arthur and as Mozart's Pedrillo with Les Arts Florissants and Boris in Katya Kabanova at Dublin; season 1997 with Ferrando for Flanders Opera and Scottish Opera; sang Vasek in The Bartered Bride for Opera North 1998; sang Don Carlos in Les Indes Galantes by Rameau at the Palais Garnier, Paris

1999; season 2000–01 as Grimoaldo in Rodelinda at Göttingen and Lensky for Opera North; Almaviva in Il Barbiere di Siviglia, Vlaamse Opera, Ghent 2005. *Honours:* Glyndebourne Eric Vertier Award.

PATRIARCO, Earle; American singer (baritone); b. 1965. *Career:* many concert and recital engagements in Europe and the USA, with songs by Poulenc and Strauss; opera repertory includes Così fan tutte and The Queen of Spades; contestant at the 1994 Cardiff Singer of the World Competition; appearances with LA Opera, Metropolitan Opera, Seattle Opera. *Recordings:* Massenet, Manon 2000, Orff, Carmina Burana 2002.

PATTERSON, Paul Leslie, FRAM, FRNCM, FRSA; British composer and educator; *Manson Chair of Composition, Royal Academy of Music*; b. 15 June 1947, Chesterfield; m. Hazel Wilson 1981; one s. one d. *Education:* Royal Acad. of Music. *Career:* freelance composer 1968–; Art Council Composer-in-Asscn, English Sinfonia 1969–70; Dir Contemporary Music, Univ. of Warwick 1974–80; Composer-in-Residence, SE Arts Asscn 1980–82, Bedford School 1984–85; Prof. of Composition, RAM 1970–, Head of Composition/20th Century Music 1985–97, Manson Chair of Composition 1997–; Artistic Dir Exeter Festival 1991–97; Composer-in-Residence, Nat. Youth Orchestra 1997–; Visiting Prof. of Composition, Christchurch Univ., Canterbury. *Compositions:* Te Deum 1988, Symphony 1990, The Mighty Voice 1991, Songs of the West 1995, Rustic Sketches 1996, Hell's Angels 1998, Gloria 1999, Millennium Mass 2000, Orchestra on Parade 2006; performances world-wide by leading orchestras, soloists, ensembles, also film and TV music, including music for films from Hammer House of Horror. *Recordings:* Concerto for Orchestra, Little Red Riding Hood, Mass of Sea, Magnificat, with Bach Choir. *Publications:* Rebecca 1968, Trumpet Concerto 1969, Time Piece 1972, Kyrie 1972, Requiem 1973, Comedy for 5 Winds 1973, Requiem 1974, Fluorescences 1974, Clarinet Concerto 1976, Cracowian Counterpoints 1977, Voices of Sleep 1979, Concerto for Orchestra 1981, Canterbury Psalms 1981, Sinfonia 1982, Mass of the Sea 1983, Deception Pass 1983, Duologue 1984, Mean Time 1984, Europhony 1985, Missa Brevis 1985, Stabat Mater 1986, String Quartet, Harmonica Concerto, Magnificat and Nunc Dimitus 1986, Te Deum 1988, Tunnell of Time 1988, The End 1989, Violin Concerto 1992, Little Red Riding Hood 1993, Magnificat 1994, Royal Eurostar for the opening Channel Tunnel 1994, Songs of the West (overture) 1995, Deviations for String Octet 2001, City Within 2000, Cello Concerto 2002, Jubilee Dances 2002, Bug for solo harp 2003, Three Little Pigs 2004, Orchestra on Parade 2006, Allusions for two violins & strings, Brumba for organ 2007. *Honours:* Hon. FLCM 1997; Medal of Honour, Polish Ministry of Culture 1986; Leslie Boosey Award 1996. *Current Management:* Rosemary Dunn. *Telephone:* (1304) 831616. *E-mail:* ro .dunn@virgin.net. *Address:* 31 Cromwell Avenue, Highgate, London, N6 5HN, England (home). *Telephone:* (20) 8348-3711 (home). *E-mail:* paulpatterson@ hotmail.co.uk (home). *Website:* www.paulpatterson.co.uk.

PATTERSON, Susan; American singer (soprano); b. 1962. *Career:* sang widely in USA and made European debut in 1988 with the Welsh National Opera as Violetta; sang at San Francisco in 1988 and 1991 as Anne Trulove and Constanze; sang Gilda at Vancouver in 1989 and in Cherubini's Lodoiska at La Scala, 1990–91; sang at Rome Opera in 1991 as Adèle in Le Comte Ory, Fiordiligi at Cologne and Berenice in Rossini's L'Occasione fa il Ladro at Schwetzingen and Paris; sang Aspasia in Mozart's Mitridate at Amsterdam in 1992; Magda in La Rondine at St Louis, 1996; Rusalka for ENO, 1998; frequent concert appearances.

PATTON, Chester; American singer (bass); b. 1965, Columbia, MS. *Education:* San Francisco Conservatory of Music. *Career:* appearances with San Francisco Opera from 1993, as Don Basilio, the King of Egypt in Aida, First Nazarene in Salome, Colline, Raimondo and Lord Walton in I Puriatni; Bay Area credits include further appearances with West Bay Opera, Opera San José, Pocket Opera and Berkeley Contemporary Opera; Title role in the US premiere of Tippett's King Priam, San Francisco Opera Center; Debut with Opera Pacific as Basilio, Beethoven's Pizarro at Lyon, High Priest in Nabucco at the Opéra Bastille and Timur in Turandot (1997); Hawaii Opera Theater as Ferrando in Trovatore, Sparafucile and Colline. *Recordings include:* Mandarin in San Francisco Opera production of Turandot. *Current Management:* Matthew Laifer Artists Management, 410 West 24th Street, Suite 2i, New York, NY 10011, USA. *Telephone:* (212) 929-7429. *Fax:* (212) 633-2628. *E-mail:* laiferart@aol.com. *Website:* www.laiferart.com.

PAUK, György; British (b. Hungarian) violinist; *Professor of Violin, Royal Academy of Music*; b. 26 Oct. 1936, Budapest, Hungary; s. of Imre Pauk and Magdolna Pauk; m. Susan Mautner 1959; one s. one d. *Education:* Franz Liszt Acad. of Music, Budapest under Ede Zathureczky, Leo Weiner and Zoltán Kodály. *Career:* concerts all over Eastern Europe 1952–58 and rest of world; settled in Western Europe 1958, The Netherlands 1958–61, England 1961–; Prof. of Violin, RAM 1987–; Artistic Dir Mozart Bicentenary Festival, London 1991; Prof. of Violin, Winterthur-Zürich Konservatorium of Music 1994–2000; Prof. Emer., Franz Liszt Acad. of Music, Budapest; jury mem. at int. violin competitions; master-classes world-wide. *Recordings include:* numerous concertos, the complete violin/piano music of Mozart and Schubert, Handel and Brahms sonatas, Mozart string quintets, all Bartók's music for solo, duo and sonatas; first performances of Penderecki's violin concerto, UK, Japan, Sir Michael Tippett's Triple Concerto, London 1980, Lutosławski's Chain 2, UK, Netherlands, Hungary, with composer conducting, Sir Peter Maxwell Davies' violin concerto, Switzerland, Germany, William Mathias violin concerto, England. *Honours:* Hon. mem. and Prof., Guildhall School of Music and

Drama, London 1987; Hon. RAM 1990; highest civilian award, Hungarian Govt 1998; Paganini Prize 1956, Sonata Competition Prize, Munich 1957, Jacques Thibaud Prize 1959, Grand Prix for Bartók (Ovation Magazine, USA) 1982, Best Record of 1983 (Gramophone Magazine), Bartók-Pasztory Prize (Hungary). *Address:* Royal Academy of Music, Marylebone Road, London, NW1 5HT, England (office). *Telephone:* (20) 7873-7395 (office). *E-mail:* strings@ram.ac.uk (office). *Website:* www.ram.ac .uk (office).

PAUL, Thomas; American singer (bass); b. 22 Feb. 1934, Chicago, IL. *Education:* Juilliard School with Beverly Johnson and Cornelius Reid. *Career:* debut at New York City Opera 1962, as Sparafucile in Rigoletto; sang in New York, Pittsburgh, Washington, Vancouver, San Francisco and Montréal as Mozart's Figaro and Sarastro, Pogner in Die Meistersinger, Bartók's Duke Bluebeard, Padre Guardiano, La Forza del Destino; Ptolemy in Giulio Cesare by Handel; sang at Central City Colorado in the premiere of Robert Ward's Lady from Colorado 1964; many concert performances; Teacher, Eastman School, Rochester, Aspen School, Colorado. *Recordings include:* Brander in La Damnation de Faust.

PAULSEN, Melinda; singer (mezzo-soprano); b. 1970, USA. *Education:* Swarthmore Coll., Munich Hochschule, studied with Helmut Deutsche. *Career:* Opera Studio of the Bavarian State Theatre, Munich; appearances at Bregenz Festival, Wratislava Cantans, Poland; Ramiro in Mozart's La Finta Giardiniera at Klagenfurt 1998; many recital and concert engagements. *Recordings include:* Puck in Oberon. *Honours:* winner Int. ARD Competition, Munich 1992.

PAUSTIAN, Inger; Danish singer (mezzo-soprano); b. 1937. *Education:* studied in Copenhagen. *Career:* engaged at Kiel Opera 1965–67, Hanover 1967–69, Frankfurt 1969–78; guest appearances at Hamburg 1970, Munich 1971, Valencia 1976, as Ortrud in Lohengrin; Bayreuth Festival 1968–71, as Siegrune, Wellgunde and a Flowermaiden; sang at Zürich Opera 1976–77; other roles include Monteverdi's Penelope, Mozart's Marcellina, Magdalene, Brangaene, Herodias and the Nurse in Die Frau ohne Schatten; Verdi's Azucena, Amneris and Eboli, Guilietta in Les Contes d'Hoffmann, Larina in Eugene Onegin and Agave (The Bassarids by Henze); frequent concert performances.

PAUTZA, Sabin; composer and conductor; b. 8 Feb. 1943, Calnic, Romania; m. Corina Popa 1974, two d. *Education:* Bucharest Acad. of Music, Accademia Musicale Chigiana, Siena, Italy. *Career:* debut in Romanian Athenee, Romania 1964; Prof. of Harmony and Conducting, Iassy Acad. of Music 1965–84; Conductor, Iassy Acad. of Music Orchestra 1969–84; appearances, Bayreuth Wagner Youth Festival 1974, 1977, 1978, Carnegie Hall, New York 1984; extensively performed as a conductor in Europe, Australia and North America; Music Dir and Conductor, Plainfield Symphony Orchestra, NJ, USA 1987–. *Compositions:* Symphony No. 1 In Memoriam, Symphony No. 2 Sinfonia Sacra, Offering to the Children of the World for double choir, Games I, II, III, IV, V and VI for orchestra, three String Quartets 1976, 1977, 1979, Double Concerto for viola, piano and orchestra, Ebony Mass for choir, organ and orchestra, Another Love Story (opera for children), Laudae for chamber orchestra, five pieces for large orchestra, Nocturnes for soprano and orchestra, Haiku for soprano and chamber orchestra, Sinfonietta 1994, Rita Dove Triptych 1994, Chimes for percussion instruments 1995, String Quartet No. 4: Ludus Modalis 1998, Mood Swings microcantata for mezzo-soprano and piano on verses by Tristan Tzara, Ode to Hope cantata for soprano solo, choir and orchestra (dedicated to the new millennium), Antiphonon Melos–Dramatic oratorio 1969, revised 1999, Saxophone Concerto 1996, revised 2001, Sonata a Quatro for strings 1969, revised 2000. *Honours:* Dr hc (London Inst. for Applied Research); Romanian Acad. George Enesco Prize for Composition 1974, Romanian Union of Composers Prize 1977, Martin Luther King Jr Prize (for Chimes) 1995.

PAVIOUR, Sir Paul, JP, AM, FRCO, FRSA; British/Australian composer and musician (organ); *Consultant, Goulburn Regional Conservatorium;* b. 14 April 1931, Birmingham, England; s. of Hereward Paviour; m. Janet Margaret Paviour. *Education:* Univ. of London. *Career:* Faculty mem. All Saints Coll., Bathurst 1969–75; Conductor Goulburn Consort of Voices 1975–; comms from Goulburn Festival of the Arts, Australian Govt and others; Goulburn Coll. of Advanced Educ. 1975–84; Organist and Conductor with Argyle Operatic Soc. 1977–; Dir of Music for Opening of New Parl. House by HM the Queen 1988; Dir of Music, Goulburn Cathedral; currently Consultant, Goulburn Regional Conservatorium. *Compositions include:* Horn Concerto 1970, Missa Australis 1971, Take Kissing as a Natural Law for female voices and flute 1971, Four Carols 1972, A New Australian Mass 1973, All Systems Go for chorus and orchestra 1980, An Urban Symphony (No. 2) 1982, This Endris Nyghte, Christmas Cantata 1982, Concerto for oboe, strings and percussion 1983, Symphony No. 5 1985, Overture: Streetscape at Noon 1997, Per Ardua, Ad Astra 2001, Symphony No. 6 2001. *Honours:* Medal of the Order of Australia, Centenary Medal 2000; Harding Prize, Royal Coll. of Organists. *Address:* 4 Beppo Street, Goulburn, NSW 2580, Australia (home). *Telephone:* (2) 4821-2450 (home). *E-mail:* paulpav@exemail.com.au.

PAVLOVSKAYA, Tatiana; Russian singer (soprano); b. 1970, Murmansk. *Education:* St Petersburg Conservatoire. *Career:* engaged with the Kirov Opera, from 1995; currently Prin. Artist, Mariinsky Theatre, St Petersburg; roles have included Madama Butterfly, Tatiana in Eugene Onegin, Yaroslavna (Prince Igor); Mozart's Countess and Clara in Prokofiev's

Betrothal in a Monastery; further apearances as Paulina in The Gambler by Prokofiev, Natasha in War and Peace, Wagner's Elsa and Maria in Mazeppa; San Francisco Opera debut in Betrothal in a Monastery, under Gergiev; British debut as Maria at Glasgow, with the Kirov 1999; sang Sofya in the British premiere of Prokofiev's Semyon Kotko, with the Kirov Opera at Covent Garden 2000. *Honours:* winner Int. Pechkovsky Vocal Competition, Int. Competition for Young Singers, Wrocław, Poland. *Address:* c/o Mariinsky Theatre, 1 Theatre Square, St Petersburg, 190000 Russia (office). *Telephone:* (812) 3264141 (office). *Website:* www.mariinsky.ru/en (office).

PAY, Antony, MA; British clarinettist; b. 21 Feb. 1945, London. *Education:* Cambridge Univ., studied with John Davies and Wilfred Kealey. *Career:* debut with Mozart's Concerto with National Youth Orchestra on tour to Europe 1961; Principal Clarinet of the Royal Philharmonic 1968–78; London Sinfonietta 1968–83, including the premiere of Henze's The Miracle of the Rose, 1982; Principal with the Academy of St Martin-in-the-Fields 1976–86, Academy of Ancient Music 1983–94, Orchestra of the Age of Enlightenment 1986–; mem., Nash Ensemble 1986–93; teacher, Guildhall School, London 1982–90; frequent concerts as conductor and clarinettist. *Recordings include:* Berio Concertino, Concertos by Weber, Crusell and Mozart, Chamber works by Beethoven (Septet), Schubert (Octet), Mozart and Brahms (Quintets) and others. *Current Management:* Allied Artists, 42 Montpelier Square, London, SW7 1JZ, England. *Telephone:* (20) 7589-6243. *Fax:* (20) 7581-5269. *E-mail:* info@alliedartists.co.uk. *Website:* www.alliedartists.co.uk.

PAYER-TUCCI, Elisabeth; singer (soprano); b. 1944, Germany. *Career:* sang at the Berne Opera 1968–70 and at the Cologne Opera until 1976; New York 1980 as Irene in a concert rendition of Rienzi; sang the Siegfried Brünnhilde at the Metropolitan, Isolde at Rome and Ariadne at Lisbon; sang at Verona Festival as Turandot, Brünnhilde at Barcelona and Senta at Rio de Janeiro 1987; other roles have included Verdi's Amelia in Un Ballo in Maschera, the Forza Leonora, and Santuzza in Cavalleria Rusticana.

PAYNE, Anthony Edward, BA, FRCM; British composer; b. 2 Aug. 1936, London, England; s. of the late Edward Alexander Payne and (Muriel) Margaret Payne; m. Jane Manning (q.v.) 1966. *Education:* Dulwich Coll., London and Durham Univ. *Career:* freelance musical journalist, musicologist, lecturer, etc. with various publs and BBC Radio, active in promoting new music, serving on Cttee of Macnaghten Concerts (Chair. 1967) and Soc. for the Promotion of New Music (Chair. 1969–71), composed part-time 1962–73; full-time composer 1973–; Composition Tutor, London Coll. of Music 1983–85, Sydney Conservatorium 1986, Univ. of Western Australia 1996; Milhaud Prof., Mills Coll., Oakland, Calif., USA 1983; Artistic Dir Spitalfields Festival; Creative Arts Fellow, Royal Coll. of Music 2007–08; Professorial Fellow, Univ. of East Anglia; mem. Cttee Asscn Frank Bridge Trust; Vice-Pres. Delius Trust. *Compositions:* Paraphrases and Cadenzas 1969, Paean for solo piano 1971, Phoenix Mass 1972, The Spirits Harvest for full orchestra 1972, Concerto for Orchestra (Int. Jury Choice for Int. Soc. for Contemporary Music Festival 1976) 1974, The World's Winter for soprano and ensemble 1976, String Quartet 1978, The Stones and Lonely Places Sing (septet) 1979, Song of the Clouds for oboe and orchestra 1980, A Day in the Life of a Mayfly (sextet) 1981, Evening Land for soprano and piano 1981, Spring's Shining Wake for orchestra 1981, Songs and Seascapes for strings 1984, The Song Streams in the Firmament (sextet) 1986, Fanfares and Processional 1986, Half Heard in the Stillness for orchestra 1987, Consort Music for string quintet 1987, Sea Change (septet) 1988, Time's Arrow for orchestra 1990, The Enchantress Plays bassoon and piano 1990, Symphonies of Wind and Rain for chamber ensemble 1991, A Hidden Music 1992, Orchestral Variations: The Seeds Long Hidden 1993, Empty Landscape–Heart's Ease (sextet) 1995, Break, Break, Break for unaccompanied chorus 1996, Elgar's Third Symphony (commissioned by Elgar Trust to complete Elgar's sketches) 1997, Piano Trio 1998, Scenes from The Woodlanders for soprano and ensemble 1999, Of Knots and Skeins for violin and piano 2000, Betwixt Heaven and Charing Cross for unaccompanied chorus 2001, Visions and Journeys for orchestra (British Composers Award 2003) 2001, Poems of Edward Thomas for soprano and piano quartet 2003, Horn Trio 2005, Elgar's Sixth Pomp & Circumstance March (commissioned by Elgar Trust to complete Elgar's sketches) 2006, Windows on Eternity 2007, Piano Quintet 2007, Out of the Depths Comes Song for cello and piano 2008, From a Mouthful of Air for quintet 2009, The Period of Cosmographie for orchestra 2009, Second String Quartet (British Composer Award Chamber category 2011) 2010, Arrangement of Bruckner's Second Symphony for Chamber Ensemble 2012, The Undiscovered Country (octet) 2012. *Recordings include:* The Music of Anthony Payne (Gramophone Critics' Choice) 1977, Time's Arrow 1996, A Day in the Life of a Mayfly 1998, The Stones and Lonely Places Sing 2007, My Own Country (Warlock arrangements) 2008, Elgar/Payne Symphony No. 3 (six recordings), Elgar/Payne Pomp & Circumstance March No. 6 (three recordings), Elgar (orchestrated Payne) Crown of India. *Radio:* frequent talks for BBC Radio 3 (music matters, Proms, etc.). *Television:* appearances, BBC documentaries by John Bridcut on Elgar, Vaughan Williams, Parry and Delius. *Publications:* Schoenberg 1968, The Music of Frank Bridge 1984, Elgar's Third Symphony: The Story of the Reconstruction 1998; contrib. to Musical Times, Tempo, Music and Musicians, The Listener, Daily Telegraph, The Times, The Independent, Country Life. *Honours:* Hon. mem. Royal Philharmonic Soc. 1999; Hon. DMus (Birmingham) 2000, (Kingston) 2002, (Durham) 2007; Radcliffe Award 1975, South Bank Show Award 1998, Evening Standard Classical Music Award 1998, New York Critics' Circle Nat. Public Radio Award 1999, Classical CD Award 1999, Elgar Medal 2011. *Address:* 2 Wilton Square, London, N1 3DL, England (home). *Telephone:* (20) 7359-1593 (home). *E-mail:* paynecomp@gmail.com (office).

PAYNE, Nicholas; British opera company director; *Director, Opera Europa*; b. (Geoffrey John Nicholas Payne), 4 Jan. 1945, Bromley, Kent, England; s. of the late John Laurence Payne and of Dorothy Gwendoline Payne (née Attenborough); m. Linda Jane Adamson 1986; two s. *Education:* Eton Coll. and Trinity Coll., Cambridge. *Career:* worked for Paterson Concert Management 1967; Arts Council administration course 1967–68; joined finance dept Royal Opera House, Covent Garden 1968–70; Subsidy Officer, Arts Council 1970–76; Financial Controller, Welsh Nat. Opera 1976–82; Gen. Admin. Opera North 1982–93; Dir of Opera, Royal Opera House 1993–98; Gen. Dir ENO 1998–2002; Dir Opera Europa 2003–. *Honours:* Hon. mem. Guildhall School of Music and Drama, Royal Northern Coll. of Music; Dr hc (Leeds Metropolitan Univ.). *Address:* Opera Europa, 23 rue Léopold, 1000 Brussels, Belgium (office). *Telephone:* (2) 217-67-05 (office). *E-mail:* nicholas.payne@opera-europa.org (office). *Website:* www.opera-europa.org (office).

PAYNE, Patricia; New Zealand singer (mezzo-soprano); b. 1942, Dunedin; d. of Henry Payne and Margaret Payne; m. David Galloway 1974. *Education:* Otago Girls' High School, Dunedin Training Coll. *Career:* debut at Covent Garden 1974, as Schwertleite in Die Walküre: returned as Ulrica in Un Ballo in Maschera, Azucena, Erda in Das Rheingold, First Norn in Götterdämmerug and Filippyevna in Eugene Onegin 1989; as La Cieca in La Gioconda and as Erda, Barcelona 1974–75; Bayreuth Festival and San Francisco Opera 1977; played Ulrica at La Scala, Milan 1978; Verona Festival 1980; guest appearances at Frankfurt Opera and the Metropolitan, New York (debut 1980 as Ulrica, sang in La Gioconda 1983); has sung Gaea in the British premiere of Strauss's Daphne, Opera North 1987; appearances with English National Opera in The Love for Three Oranges, Salome and The Magic Flute; sang Prokofiev's Princess Clarissa with Opera North, Edinburgh Festival 1989; as Herodias in Salome at Wellington 1992; sang the Witch in Hansel and Gretel and Auntie in Peter Grimes at Wellington 1996; concert repertoire includes the Wesendonck Lieder, Bach's St John Passion (in Paris), the Alto Rhapsody and Beethoven's 9th (Spain), Alexander Nevsky and the Mozart Requiem (London, Festival Hall). *Recordings include:* Un Ballo in Maschera and Peter Grimes, Beethoven's Missa Solemnis. *Honours:* New Zealand Order of Merit 2001; Hon. DMus (Univ. of Otago) 2007; winner, Sidney Sun Aria Competition 1966, Queen Elizabeth II Arts Council Scholarship, Kathleen Ferrier Competition 1972. *Address:* 16 Farquharson Street, North East Valley, Dunedin, New Zealand (home). *Telephone:* (3) 473-1625 (home).

PAZDERA, Jindrich; Czech violinist, conductor and teacher; b. 25 July 1954, Zilina; m. 1982, one s. *Education:* Moscow State Conservatory, studied with Leonid Kogan. *Career:* debut in Bratislava, Violin Concerto No. 2, by Karol Szymanowski, with the Slovak Philharmonic Orchestra, 1974; concerts in Europe, America and Asia, as soloist with orchestras and as a chamber musician (violin and piano, Bohemia Piano Trio); teacher: Bratislava Secondary Music School, 1983–94; Prague Academy of Arts, 1991–; Reader of Violin, 1995–; repertoire: 25 violin concertos and many recital programmes; numerous first performances of contemporary Slovak and Czech works; mem. Slovak Music Asscn, Czech Asscn of Music Artists and Scientists, Stamic Quartet (string) 1st Violin 2001–. *Broadcast:* Schubert Complete Works for Violin and Piano 2000–03. *Recordings:* albums: Violin Concertos, Vivaldi 1990, Le Quattro Stagioni, Vivaldi 1992, Chamber Orchestra works by Suk, Barber, Bruckner and Shostakovich 1993, Piano Trio works by Beethoven, Dvořák 1995, Violin works by W. A. Mozart 1997, Dvořák, Serenade and Sextet in A major, live recording violin/piano recital in Kioi Hall Tokyo, Beethoven, Janáček, Martinů, Smetana 2003, Stamic Quartet, Smetena, Dvořák, Mozart, Schubert, Janáček 2002–03, Phantasies for violin/piano b Schubert, Suk, Milhaud 2004, Stamic Quartet: works by composers imprisoned in Terezin during World War II 2005, Violin/piano works by Hikaru Hayashi 2006, Quartet works by A. and P. Vranitzky 2009, Violin/piano works by Moyzes, Suchoň, Kardoš, Očenáš, Salva 2010. *Publications:* A Reconstruction of a W. A. Mozart's Sinfonia Concertante in A, for Violin, Viola and Cello (K104-320e), A World Premiere 1991, CD Recording 1997; Translations of Methodical and Muspsychological Works of Russian Authors (V. P. Bronin, G. Kogan); Selected Chapters from the Method of Violin Playing 1999 (2nd edn 2008). *Honours:* A Frico Kafenda Slovak National Music Award 1985. *Address:* Luzická 8, 120 00 Prague, Czech Republic. *E-mail:* jindrich@pazdera.biz. *Website:* www.pazdera.biz.

PEACOCK, Lucy; singer (soprano); b. 21 June 1947, Jacksonville, FL, USA. *Education:* North West Univ., Opera Studio of the Deutsche Oper Berlin. *Career:* debut in Berlin 1969, as the Milliner in Der Rosenkavalier; sang in Berlin as Flotow's Martha, Mozart's Pamina, Countess and Servilia, Cavalli's Calisto, Micaela in Carmen and Rosina in Il Barbiere di Siviglia; guest appearances in Düsseldorf, Vienna, Munich, Hamburg, Turin, Geneva, Paris and London; Bayreuth 1985, as Freia in Das Rheingold and in Die Walküre and Götterdämmerung; sang Eva in Die Meistersinger at the 1988 festival; sang Mathilde in Guillaume Tell at Catania 1987; Deutsche Oper Berlin as Marenka in The Bartered Bride and as Myrtocle in Die Toten Augen by d'Albert; created the title role in Desdemona und ihre Schwestern by Siegfried Matthus, Schwetzingen 1992; Princesse de Bouillon in Adriana Lecouvreur at Adelaide 1994; Gertrud in Hansel and Gretel at the Berlin Deutsche Oper 1998; season 2000 at the Deutsche Oper in Die Frau ohne Schatten and Der Rosenkavalier; television appearances include Martha, in Flotow's opera.

PEARCE, Alison Margaret, AGSM; British singer (soprano); b. 5 Aug. 1953, Bath, England. *Education:* Dartington College of Arts, Guildhall School of Music and Drama, studied with Pierre Bernac in Paris, Gerhard Husch in Munich. *Career:* debut, Wigmore Hall, London; international soloist, oratorio, concert, opera, recital; regular performances with choirs, orchestras and conductors, including Colin Davis, Charles Groves, David Willcocks, James Lockhart, Steuart Bedford, Sylvain Cambreling, Libor Pesek; festivals include Three Choirs, Cheltenham, Llandaff, St David's, Brighton, Flanders, France, Netherlands, Germany, Spain, Norway, Philippines, Poland, Israel; soloist at world premieres of Sinfonia Fidei (A. Hoddinott), Six Psalms (D. Muldowney), Music's Empire (J. McCabe), Hell's Angels (P. Patterson), Requiem (J. Bartley); regular int. television and radio broadcasts; opera debut, title role in Lucia di Lammermoor 1982; other roles include Violetta in La Traviata, Abigaille in Nabucco, Manon in Manon Lescaut, Elisabeth in Tannhäuser, Tosca, Fidelio; season 2003–04 in numerous recitals and opera galas, Mahler 8th, Verdi Requiem, Vaughan-Williams Sea Symphony, Tosca, R. Strauss Four Last Songs, Finzi Dies Natalis, Handel Messiah, Gounod Faust in UK, Italy, Belgium, Netherlands, Germany, Poland, China. *E-mail:* divapearce@ hotmail.com.

PEARCE, Michael, BA, BMus; Australian composer; b. 25 March 1954, Windsor, NSW. *Education:* University of Sydney, Sussex University with Jonathan Harvey, studied with Peter Sculthorpe. *Career:* faculty mem., New South Wales Conservatory 1981–, University of Sydney 1990; interest in urban aboriginal music; commissions from Synergy and Seymour Group. *Compositions include:* Kynesis for string quartet, flute, guitar and harpsichord 1978, Eulogy for flute, percussion and piano 1979, Interiors for violin, cello, flute, clarinet and percussion 1981, Deserts I for four percussion 1982, Deserts II and III for ensemble 1982–83, Chamber Symphony 1987, Canciones for soprano and seven instruments 1990, Oh Tierra, Espérame for soprano and piano 1991, Chamber Symphony No. 2 1991. *Honours:* Sarah Makinson Prize for Composition 1979.

PEARCE, Michael, MA (Cantab.); British singer (baritone); *Performance Tutor, University College, Chichester*; b. 1945, Chelmsford, Essex. *Education:* Choral Scholar at St John's College, Cambridge; Study with Otakar Kraus and Elizabeth Fleming. *Career:* concert appearances in China, Canada, Brazil and throughout Europe; Repertory includes Mozart Requiem (at Bruges), Monteverdi Vespers (Maastricht), Bach B Minor Mass (Turin and Edinburgh), Messiah (London and Brighton) and Brahms Requiem (Royal Festival Hall); Haydn's Theresienmesse at Windsor, The Creation at the London Barbican and Schöpfungsmesse at the Queen Elizabeth Hall; Opera roles include Ortel in Meistersinger and 5th Jew in Salome, both at the Royal Opera House, Claudius in Handel's Agrippina with Midsummer Opera, Lysiart in Weber's Euryanthe with New Sussex Opera and Beethoven's Rocco; Season 1996–97 with A Child of our Time by Tippett, the Berlioz Messe Solennelle and Elijah in Norway; Mozart's Requiem and Carmina Burana in Spain; Verdi Requiem at Canterbury Cathedral and Messiah with David Willcocks; Christus in Bach's St John Passion in London, St Matthew Passion at Salisbury and the B Minor Mass at Beverley Minster; Season 1998–99 with Germont for Opera Brava, Mozart's Count for Kentish Opera, Dundas in the premiere of David Horne's Friend of the People; Concerts include Missa Solemnis, B minor Mass, the Dream of Gerontius and A Child of Our Time. *Recordings include:* Handel Coronation Anthems under Simon Preston; Bach B Minor Mass, Edinburgh 1990. *Honours:* Winner, first English Song Award at the Brighton Festival. *Address:* 1 Homelands Copse, Fernhurst, Haslemere, Surrey GU27 3JQ, England.

PEARCE, Richard; British conductor, organist and pianist; b. 1965, England. *Education:* Trinity Coll., Cambridge and Guildhall School, London. *Career:* tours with Trinity Coll. Choir to North America and Far East; conductor, accompanist and organist throughout UK, including Purcell Room, Wigmore Hall, BBC and commercial broadcasts; accompanist at 1997 Cardiff Singer of the World Competition; Conductor, Whitehall Choir at St John's Smith Square (Handel's Israel in Egypt 2000), engagements with BBC Singers; season 1999–2000 with recitals at the Louvre, Paris and in Tokyo; performances at the London Prom Concerts and in France. *Recordings include:* Stanford, Fauré and Christmas Music, with BBC Singers; Mahler 4th Symphony, with Northern Sinfonia.

PEARLMAN, Martin, BA, MM; American conductor, harpsichordist and composer; b. 21 May 1945, Chicago, IL. *Education:* Cornell Univ. with Karel Husa, studied in The Netherlands with Gustav Leonhardt, Yale Univ. with Yehudi Wyner, studied with Ralph Kirkpatrick. *Career:* founder and Dir early music group, Banchetto Musicale 1973, renamed Boston Baroque 1992; faculty mem., Univ. of Massachusetts at Boston 1976–81; Prof. of Music and Historical Performance, Boston University Coll. of Fine Arts 2002–; many tours as harpsichordist in repertory which includes D. Scarlatti and Couperin family; US premieres of works by Handel, Rameau and other Baroque composers, as conductor; Handel's Semele at the Kennedy Center, Washington, DC 1995. *Recordings include:* Mozart Requiem 2006, Haydn: The Creation 2012, Monteverdi: Il Ritorno D'Ulisse In Patria 2015. *Publications include:* Performing editions of Monteverdi's L'Incoronazione di Poppea, Purcell's Comical History of Don Quixote, and Mozart's fragment, Lo Sposo Deluso; Complete edition of the harpsichord music of Armand-Louis Couperin. *Honours:* Erwin Bodky Award 1972, prizewinner Bruges Competition 1974.

PEARSON, Gail, BMus (Hons); British singer (soprano); b. 1970, Neath, Wales; m.; one s. *Education:* Royal Northern Coll. of Music. *Career:* has sung Pamina in production of The Magic Flute and Asteria/Tamerlano for Scottish Opera, Frasquita/Carmen for ENO, Naiad for Welsh Nat. Opera, Papagena/ Die Zauberflöte and Pernille/Maskarade at Royal Opera House, Covent Garden, Jano at Opéra Nat. de Lyon, Anne Page/The Merry Wives of Windsor at the Buxton Festival 2005, followed later by Lisette/La Rondine for Opera North and Gilda for Opera Holland Park; sang Musetta for ENO 2008, also Iris/Semele in concert at Grange Park (with recording), Bellezza in Handel's Il Trionfo del Tempo e del Disinganno for Transition Opera, 1st Priestess/ Iphigénie en Tauride at Royal Opera House, Agilea/Teseo for English Touring Opera, and Anne Truelove/The Rake's Progress for Opéra Angers Nantes; other appearances have included Nora/Riders to the Sea and Alison/The Wandering Scholar at Buxton Festival; other engagements included Oscar in Un Ballo in Maschera for Opera Holland Park 2009 and role of Antonia in Michael Berkeley's For You for Music Theatre Wales 2009, Woglinde and Waldvogel in Longborough Festival Opera's Ring Cycle 2013. *Honours:* Sir Geraint Evans Award, Welsh Music Guild. *Current Management:* c/o Athole Still Opera Ltd, Forresters Hall, 25–27 Westow Street, London, SE19 3RY, England. *Telephone:* (20) 8771-5271. *Fax:* (20) 8771-8172. *E-mail:* enquiries@ atholestill.co.uk. *Website:* www.atholestill.co.uk. *Address:* 12 Insole Place, Llandaff, Cardiff, CF5 2BW, Wales. *Telephone:* (29) 2057-5831. *E-mail:* gailpearson31@aol.com. *Website:* gail-pearson.weebly.com.

PECCHIOLI, Benedetta; Italian singer (mezzo-soprano); b. 1949. *Career:* debut Piccola Scala, as Clarina in La Cambiale di Matrimonio 1973; appearances at Monte Carlo from 1974, Rouen 1974–75, Maggio Musicale, Florence 1976–77, in Henze's Il Re Cervo and as Fenena in Nabucco; Spoleto Festival 1976, as Cenerentola, Geneva 1980, 1986, Brussels 1982, 1987; Metropolitan Opera debut 1983, as Rosina; further engagements at Teatro Regio Turin, Bilbao Festival, Teatro Massimo Palermo and Aix-en-Provence Festival (Meg Page 1971); concert appearances in the Ring at Paris and at Carnegie Hall, New York; La Scala, Milan 1989, in Rossi's Orfeo; other roles include Fidalma in Il Matrimonio Segreto, Liseta in Il Mondo della Luna, Erilda in Le Pescatrici by Haydn, Maddalena, Federica in Luisa Miller, Donizetti's Smeton in Anna Bolena and Orsini in Lucrezia Borgia, and Geneviève in Pelléas et Mélisande. *Recordings include:* Il Guiramento by Mercadante, Demetrio e Polibio by Rossini, Donizetti's Pia de Tolomei.

PECI, Aleksandër; composer; b. 24 April 1951, Tirana, Albania. *Education:* Jordan Misja Art Lyceum, Tirana and Tirana Conservatory. *Career:* Musical Dir, Përmeti 1974–77; Composer-in-Residence, Tirana Reuve Theatre 1977–99; Amsterdam Int. Composers' Workshop 1992. *Compositions:* Sonata for violin and piano 1972, Suite for flute and strings 1974, Two cello concertos 1974, 1982, Variations for horn and orchestra 1975, The Kids and the Wolf (ballet) 1979, Symphony No. 1 for vocal soloists and orchestra 1984, Piano Concerto 1980, Symphony No. 2 1985–88, Four Rhapsodies for orchestra 1977–87, Land of the Sun for low voice and orchestra 1989, Suite for string quartet 1990, Dialogue Liturgique 1993, Epic of Gilgamesh for narrator, solo female voices and tape 1997, Raindrops on Glass for soprano and tape 1997, Broken Dream for bassoon 1998, Remodelage for piano 1998, Le Paradis des enfants for children's chorus, piano, percussion and ensemble 1998, Polycentrum for strings 1999.

PECKOVÁ, Dagmar; Czech singer (mezzo-soprano); b. 4 April 1961, Chrudim; m. 1st J. Vejvoda; m. 2nd Aleš Kasprík 1997; one s.; m. 3rd Klaus Schiesser; one d. *Education:* Prague Conservatory. *Career:* soloist at Karlín Musical Theatre, Prague 1982–85; soloist with numerous cos including Czech Philharmonic 1985–, with Semper Opera, Dresden 1985–88, with State Opera Berlin 1989–92; guest appearances in Tokyo, Paris 1992, Bregenz Festival, Austria 1992, 1993, Hamburg 1993, Salzburg Festival 1993, 1995, 1996, Basel 1994, Zürich 1994, London 1995, Tel-Aviv 1996, La Corona Festival, Spain 1996, San Sebastien Festival, Spain 1996, Prague Spring Festival 1996, Frankfurt 1996; concert tours Austria, Switzerland, Germany, UK 1993, France, Japan 1990, 1994, USA 1997–99; charity concerts after floods in Czech Repub. 2002; roles include Leonora (Basel), Cherubino in The Marriage of Figaro (London), Rosina in The Barber of Seville (Berlin, Dresden), Carmen (Prague), Varvara in Katya Kabanova (Salzburg, Barcelona). *Recordings include:* Martinů—Nipponari 1991, Mozart—Che Bella 1994, Janáček— Moravian Folk Poetry in Song 1994, Mahler—Adagietto, Kindertotenlieder 1996, Songs of Mahler and Berio 1997, Janáček—Kátá Kabanová 1997, Janáček—Diary of One Who Disappeared 1999, recital of music by Wagner, Schoenberg, Zemlinsky and Brahms 2000, Lieder by Strauss, Schoeck, Berg 2001, Lieder by Dvořák 2001, Arias (live) 2002. *Honours:* First Prize, Antonin Dvořák Competition 1982, Second Prize, Brno Vocal Competition 1985, Czech Music Fund Award (for role of Eliza Doolittle in My Fair Lady) 1985, First Prize, Prague Spring Vocal Competition 1986, Berlin Critics' Prize (for role of Dorabella in Così fan tutte) 1989, European Foundation for Music Prize 1993, Thalia Prize (for Carmen) 2000.

PEČMAN, Rudolf; Czech academic; *Professor, Institute of Musicology, Masaryk University, Brno;* b. 12 April 1931, Staré Město u Frýdku (Frýdek-Místek); s. of the late Vladimír Pečman and Otilie Pečmanova (née Jarošová). *Education:* Masaryk University, Brno. *Career:* Asst 1955, Docent 1984, Prof. of Musicology 1990–, Philosophy Faculty, Masaryk Univ., Nummo Memoriali Ateneo Rector 1995–; Czech Music Counsel UNESCO 1997; mem. Czech Music Soc., G-F-Händel-Gesellschaft, Halle (Saale). *Publications:* Josef Mysliveček und sein Opernepilog 1970, Beethoven dramatik (Beethoven the

Dramatic Composer) 1978, Beethovens Opernpläne 1981, Josef Mysliveček 1981, Georg Friedrich Händel 1985, Eseje o Martinů (Essays about Martinů) 1989, F X Richter und seine 'Harmonischen Belehrungen' 1991, Style and Music 1600–1900 (in Czech) 2nd Ed 1996, The Attack on Antonín Dvořák (in Czech) 1992, The Stage Works of Ludwig van Beethoven (in Czech) 1999, Vladimír Helfert (in Czech) 2003, F.X. Šalda and Music (in Czech) 2004, Old Italian Music Contexts (in Czech) 2006. *Honours:* Smetana Prize 1974, Janáček Prize 1984, Mozart Prize 1987, Prize of Rector of Masaryk Univ., Brno. *Address:* Loosova 12, 638 00 Brno, Czech Republic (home). *Address:* Arna Nováka 1, 66088 Brno (office); Loosova 12, 63800 Brno, Czech Republic (home). *Telephone:* 549 494 623 (office); 548 520 261 (home). *Fax:* 549 497 478 (office). *E-mail:* music@phil.muni.cz (office).

PECORARO, Herwig; singer (tenor); b. 1959, Bludenz, Switzerland. *Education:* Bregenz Conservatory. *Career:* sang at the Graz Opera 1985–90 and Bregenz Festival from 1985 as a Priest in Die Zauberflöte and the Steuermann in Fliegende Holländer; sang at Vienna Staatsoper from 1991, notably as Pedrillo and Steuermann; other engagements at Nice and the Smetana Theatre in Prague; appeared at the Vienna Volksoper 1992 in Dantons Tod; season 2000–01 as Mozart's Pedrillo at the Vienna Staatsoper and Rosillon in Die Lustige Witwe at Leipzig.

PEDANI, Paolo; singer (bass); b. 1930, Italy. *Education:* studied in Milan. *Career:* sang in Cherubini's L'Osteria Portoghese and Falla's Vida Breve at La Scala 1950–51; appearances at Bologna, Genoa, Trieste and Venice from 1954, Wexford Festival 1956–59, Spoleto 1961; Aix-en-Provence Festival from 1959, in Haydn's Mondo della Luna and as Masetto; Venice 1966, in premiere of La Metamorfosi di Bonaventura by Malipiero; Florence 1976, in the Italian premiere of Henze's Il Re Cervo; guest appearances at Barcelona, Catania, Mexico City and Antwerp; other roles include Rossini's Alidoro, Don Magnifico, Taddeo and Basilio, Don Pasquale, Don Alfonso, Melitone in La Forza del Destino and Paisiello's Basilio; character roles from 1970.

PEDERSEN, Laura; American singer (soprano); b. 1969, Sioux City, IA. *Career:* debut as Donna Elvira in Don Giovanni for Tirana Opera, Albania 1996; theatre engagements at Lyric Opera, Cleveland 1991–94, educational outreach programmes, apprenticeships and main stage and leading roles; Cleveland Opera 1990–97, educational outreach programmes, mini-residencies, leading roles; Tirana Opera 1996, main stage leading role; Tulsa Opera, main stage role; Bremen Theater, Bremen, Germany, leading roles; performances as Norina in Don Pasquale, Maria in West Side Story, Oscar in The Masked Ball, Amour in Orphée, Susanna in Marriage of Figaro, Adele in Die Fledermaus. *Address:* c/o Encompass Arts, 119 West 72nd Street No. 371, New York, NY 10023, USA (office). *E-mail:* contact@encompassarts.com (office). *Website:* www.laurapedersen.com.

PEDERSON, Monte; American singer (bass-baritone); b. 1960, Sunnyside, WA. *Education:* studied in USA and with Hans Hotter in Munich. *Career:* debut at San Francisco Opera, as M Gobineau in Menotti's The Medium, 1986; Engaged at various opera houses in USA and at Bremen, 1987–88, notably as Szymanowski's King Roger; Montpellier and Bregenz, 1988–89, as Wagner's Dutchman; Minister in Fidelio at Orange, Deutsche Oper Berlin and Stuttgart, 1989–90; Sang Pizarro in a new production of Fidelio at Covent Garden, 1990, followed by concert performance at the Festival Hall, conducted by Lorin Maazel; Season 1990–91 as Shishkov in From the House of the Dead at Cologne, Orestes in Elektra at San Francisco and Amfortas at La Scala; Salzburg Festival, 1992, as Shishkov, Houston Opera, 1992, as Amfortas in a production of Parsifal by Robert Wilson; Other roles include Jochanaan in Salome, Basle, 1989, and Angelotti; Sang Nick Shadow at the 1996 Salzburg Festival; Golaud in Pelléas at Brussels, Scarpia at Stuttgart, 1998; Sang Kurwenal at the New York Met, 1999; season 2000 as Debussy's Golo at Toronto, Orestes in Elektra at the Munich Staatsoper and Britten's Claggart at Cagliari. *Recordings include:* Fidelio (video, Covent Garden). *Website:* www.operastars.com/monte_pederson.

PEDICONI, Fiorella; Italian singer (soprano); b. 1950. *Education:* Conservatorio Giuseppe Verdi, Milan. *Career:* appeared at first in Il Barbiere di Siviglia and I Puritani at opera houses in Italy; sang Violetta at Glyndebourne 1988, Gilda at Covent Garden 1989; appeared in Bussotti's L'Ispirazione at Turin 1991, as Sandrina in La Finta Giardiniera at Alessandria; has also sung in operas by Haydn, Pergolesi, Rossini, Respighi, Cimarosa and Donizetti at such opera centres as La Scala, Milan, San Carlo, Naples, La Fenice, Venice, Teatro dell'Opera, Rome, Grand Théâtre, Geneva, Théâtre des Champs Elysées, Paris and the Gran Liceo, Barcelona.

PEDUZZI, Richard; French stage designer and costume designer; b. 28 Jan. 1943, Argentan. *Education:* Academie de Dessin, Paris. *Career:* collaborations with producer Patrice Chéreau have included L'Italiana at Spoleto 1969, Les Contes d'Hoffman and Lulu at the Paris Opéra 1974, 1979, Der Ring des Nibelungen at Bayreuth 1976, Lucio Silla for La Scala, Théâtre des Amandiers in Nanterre and Théâtre de la Monnaie, Brussels 1984–85; Co-Artistic Director with Chéreau of Théâtre des Amandiers 1982–89; stage designs include Tony Palmer's production of Les Troyens, Zürich, Don Giovanni, Rome, Tristan and Isolde, La Scala; costume designs for War and Peace at San Francisco, Le nozze di Figaro, Salzburg.

PEEBLES, Antony Gavin Ian, BMus; British pianist; b. 26 Feb. 1946, Southborough, England; m. Frances Clark 1982 (divorced 1999); two s. two d. *Education:* Trinity Coll., Cambridge and studied with Peter Katin. *Career:*

debut, Wigmore Hall, London 1969; has given concerts worldwide; soloist with London Symphony, Royal Philharmonic, Philharmonia, Hallé, Royal Liverpool Philharmonic, City of Birmingham Symphony, BBC Philharmonic Orchestras and BBC Nat. Orchestra of Wales. *Recordings:* Copland Fantasy; Bartók Studies; Dallapiccola Quaderno Musicale di Anna Libera; Ravel Gaspard de la Nuit, Miroirs, Sonatine, Pavane; Recital of Liszt operatic transcriptions; Schubert Lieder transcribed by Liszt. *Honours:* first prize BBC Piano Competition 1971, first Prize, Debussy Competition, 1972. *Current Management:* Allegro Artists, Conifers, Roselands Avenue, Mayfield, East Sussex TN 20 6EB, England. *Address:* 130 Roehampton Vale, London SW15 3RX, England. *Telephone:* (20) 8788-0488. *E-mail:* antonypeebles@btopenworld.com.

PEEBLES, Charles Ross, MA, ARCM; British conductor; b. 31 Aug. 1959, Hereford, England. *Education:* Trinity Coll., Cambridge, Guildhall School of Music and Drama, Tanglewood. *Career:* orchestras worked with include City of London Sinfonia, City of Birmingham Symphony, Bournemouth Sinfonietta, European Community Chamber Orchestra, London Mozart Players, English Chamber Orchestra, BBC Symphony Orchestra, Scottish Chamber Orchestra, Nash Ensemble, Composers Ensemble, London Sinfonietta, Vienna Chamber Orchestra; from 1992 all major orchestras of Spain, including Orquesta Nacional de España; opera work includes Opera 80/English Touring Opera, Garsington Opera, Glyndebourne, Broomhill Opera. *Recordings:* Orchestral Works by M. Berkeley and Leighton, also Honegger's Amphion, Andrew Toovey's The Juniper Tree (opera). *Honours:* first prize Cadaques Int. Conducting Competition, Spain 1992.

PEEL, Ruth; British singer (mezzo-soprano). *Education:* Royal Northern Coll. of Music (RNCM). *Career:* opera roles have included Third Lady in Die Zauberflöte at Geneva and the 1994 Aix Festival, Kate Pinkerton at Antwerp and the Page in Salome at Covent Garden; Kate in Britten's Owen Wingrave for Glyndebourne Touring Opera, the title role in The Rape of Lucretia, under Stuart Bedford, and the Countess of Essex in Gloriana for Opera North; Concerts include recitals in the Covent Garden Festival, Wigmore Hall, Glasgow, Manchester and St John's Smith Square, London (Young Songmakers' Almanac, with Graham Johnson); concerts include Pergolesi's Stabat Mater at the Barbican Hall, Mahler's Second Symphony in Lithuania, Beethoven's Ninth in Japan under Ozawa and Holst Songs for the BBC; Beethoven's Ninth under Osawa for opening of Winter Olympics 1998; Mahler's Second Symphony in Brisbane, Holst and Brahms recitals for BBC Radio 3. *Recordings include:* Brahms recital. *Honours:* Claire Croiza French Song Prize, RNCM, Kathleen Ferrier Decca Prize 1993 Lieder Prize, RNCM.

PEETERS, Harry; Dutch opera singer (baritone-bass); b. (Henricus Hubertus Christina Peeters), 7 Aug. 1959, Roermond. *Education:* studied in Maastricht and Vienna. *Career:* debut at Vienna Volksoper as Rossini's Basilio 1984; Paris Opéra, in Rossini's Le Siège de Corinthe 1985; with Deutsche Oper am Rhein, Düsseldorf 1987–; Geneva as Bluebeard, by Dukas 1987–; Seneca in Poppea and the villains in Les Contes d'Hoffmann; San Francisco and Houston, Gurnemanz in Parsifal 1992; season 1994 as Sarastro at Los Angeles and in the premiere of P. Schat's Symposium at Amsterdam; Cologne Opera as Escamillo; Orestes in Elektra 1995; Ariodate in Handel's Xerxes; season 1998 as Kaspar in Der Freischütz at Cologne; Wagner's Amfortas for Netherlands Opera and Orestes at Catania; Sang Wotan at Münster, 1999; season 2000–01 at Cologne as Prus in The Makropoulos Case and Alberich in Das Rheingold; season 2003 in Götterdämmerung in Perth; season 2003–04 as Don Pizarro in Fidelio, Cologne; season 2004–05 as Graf Walter in Luisa Miller at Nationale Reisopera, Geisterbote in Frau Ohne Schatten at La Monnaie, Brussels; season 2005–06 as Mephisto in Faust at Opéra Royal de Wallonie; season 2006–07 as Monsieur de Pourceaugnac, Frank Martin in Geneva, Marke in Tristan und Isolde in Perth, Osmin in Die Entführung at La Monnaie, Brussels; season 2008–09 as Zacharias in Verdi's Nabucco at Nationale Reisopera; other repertory includes Idomeneo, Oedipus Rex, Poliuto by Donizetti and Monteverdi's Orfeo. *Recordings include:* Oedipus Rex (with Seiji Ozawa), Szenen aus Goethes Faust (with Claudio Abbado), Salome (with Seiji Ozawa), Idomeneo (with Sir Colin Davis), L'Orfeo (with René Jacobs), Nerone (with Kees Bakels), Fauré's Requiem (with Ed Spanjaard), Poliuto (with Oleg Caetani), Tancredi (with Roberto Abbado), The Magic Flute (with Sir Neville Marriner), The Magic Flute (with John Eliot Gardiner), Nabucco (with Walter Attanasi); DVDs include: L'incoronazione di Poppea (with René Jacobs), Kurt Weill's Aufstieg und Fall der Stadt Mahagonny (with Dennis Russell Davies). *Honours:* Verdi Prize, Int. Belvedere Singing Competition 1983. *Current Management:* c/o Alferink Artists Management, Herengracht 340, 1016 CG Amsterdam, The Netherlands; c/o Atelier Musicale S.r.l., Via Caselle 76, 40068 San Lazzaro di Savena, Italy. *Telephone:* (20) 664-31-51 (Netherlands); (051) 455706 (Italy). *Fax:* (20) 675-24-26 (Netherlands); (051) 463331 (Italy). *E-mail:* info@alferink.org; info@ateliermusicale.it. *Website:* www.alferink.org; www.ateliermusicale.it. *Address:* Rue d'Aubel 48, 4852 Hombourg, Belgium. *Telephone:* (87) 310137. *E-mail:* PeetersH@cs.com. *Website:* www.harrypeeters.com.

PEHRSON, Joseph Ralph, BA, MM, DMA; American composer and pianist; *Founding Director, Composers Concordance, New York City;* b. 14 Aug. 1950, Detroit, Mich.; m. Linda Past 1985. *Education:* Eastman School of Music, Univ. of Michigan, studied with Leslie Bassett, Joseph Schwantner and, informally, Otto Luening and Elie Siegmeister in New York. *Career:* has written works for a wide variety of media, including orchestra and chamber works, performed at numerous venues, including Merkin Hall, Weill Recital

Hall, Symphony Space in New York and throughout the US, Eastern Europe and Russia; Founder and Co-Dir Composers Concordance, New York 1983–; Goliard Concerts performed several pieces in Metropolitan New York area, in Warwick, NY and on a tour of southern states 1992, 1993; Residency, Univ. of Cincinnati Coll.-Conservatory of Music 1997; travelled to Russia for series of concerts arranged by composer Anton Rovner 2001, 2003; Organum for solo organ premiered by organist Carson Cooman and performed in Russia at Glinka Museum by Kirill Umansky as part of Moscow Autumn Festival 2005; Inner Voices II for percussion and near-just-intonation electronics premiered by DoubleStop Percussion Duo at William Paterson Coll. 2006, later at Connecticut Coll. 2006; Three Pianopieces performed by Juny Jung in Weill Recital Hall of Carnegie Hall 2006; Flautando for flute and guitar presented by New York Composers' Circle 2006; Levitations for viola and piano performed by American Modern Ensemble 2006; concert series in St Petersburg and Moscow, Russia 2008; participated in Festival 'From the Avant Garde to the Present Day', House of Composers, St Petersburg 2008; five pieces presented at Jurgenson Salon, Moscow 2008. *Compositions include:* for orchestra: Regions 1973, Sinfonia Concertante 1980, Manhattan Plaza Orchestral Painting 1988, Chromakkordion 1995; for chorus: Choral Confessions for SATB, flute, violin, cello, tambourine, based on chamber piece Confessions of the Goliards 1997; for chamber ensemble: De Rerum Natura for flute, oboe, clarinet, mandolin, tenor voice, percussion, two cellos 1974, Entropic Latitudes for flute, oboe, clarinet, trumpet, trombone, piano, two percussion, two violas, two cellos and contrabass 1974, New York Suite for flute, oboe, clarinet, trumpet, piano, viola and cello 1983, Hornucopia for ten horns 1988, Etheroscape for eight flutes 1989, Confessions of the Goliards for tenor voice, flute, violin and cello 1992, Lustspiel clarinet, violin, cello, piano 1993, Trumpet in a New Surrounding for trumpet and string quintet 1996, Wild, Wild West for oboe, clarinet, bassoon, piano, percussion, violin and cello 1997, Twang for rock band 1998, Blackjinn for woodwind quintet in the near just intonation 'Blackjack' scale 2003, Mandolini Majestici for mandolin ensemble plus recorder and concertina 2003, Windjammer for woodwind quintet 2006, Cracker for flute, alto sax, percussion, piano, electric guitar, bass guitar, violin and cello 2006, Slacker Cracker for string quartet 2006, Fire in the Evening for oboe, bassoon, guitar and viola 2008, Night Crawler for horn, bass trombone, electric guitar, bass guitar, violin and cello 2009; duos and trios: Arecibo for piano and percussion 1976, 12 Entelechies for clarinet and two violas 1977, Rites of Passage for bassoon and piano 1981, Changing Fantasy for flute, viola and piano 1983, Thanatopsis for baritone voice, violin and piano 1985, Romance for horn and piano 1985, Nature's Harmony for two horns in just intonation 1987, Chromotions for two pianos 1988, Violarimba for viola and marimba 1988, Tonreiter for clarinet and piano 1989, Lewis Carroll Songs for soprano and piano 1986–90, Exhilarations for clarinet, cello and piano 1993, Transcendence for violin and harp 1994, Spectral Harmony for alto sax and horn 1997, Doodle Doo for clarinet and piano 1999, Three Musicians for guitar, violin and viola 2002, Levitations for viola and piano 2003, Trump-it! for trumpet and piano 2004, Bass Desires for bass clarinet and piano 2005, Aura for bassoon and percussion 2005, Inner Voices II for electronics and two percussionists non-pitched 2005, Quixoddities for piccolo and bassoon 2007, B's Company for trumpet, horn and trombone 2007, Slick Clicks for violin and cello 2008, Lunar Tunes for flute, clarinet and piano 2009; for solo instruments: Approaches for solo trombone 197, Harmonic Etude for solo horn in just intonation 1987, The Nature of the Universe II for baroque flute 1998, One Small Step for Man for microtonal bassoon 1998, Profondo for bass flute 1998, Just in Time for guitar in just intonation 1999, Violahexy for viola and electronics 2000, Blackjack for trombone and electronics in near just intonation 'Blackjack' scale 2001, Blacklight for cello and electronics in near just intonation 'Blackjack' scale 2002, Organum for organ 2002, BlackandJill for soprano and electronics in near just intonation 'Blackjack' scale 2003, Transpian for piano and electronics in near just intonation 'Blackjack' scale 2006, Toast for Contrabass 2007, Prudendurance (solo piano version) 2008, I Won't Get Any Higher for bass trombone 2008, Phone for alto voice 2009, Motorfogger for electric cello 2009; electronic: Alignments for Univ. of Michigan electronic studio 1974, T and Serial for MIDI 1990, Wuuuu for solo theremin 1997, Unheard for MIDI in 1/8 tones 2000, Verklarte Neunzehn for MIDI in 19 tones per octave 2000, Hexy for MIDI using a 1.3.5.11 hexany six-note tuning on 1.11 2000, Beepy for MIDI using the Bohlen-Pierce scale 2001, The Tempest, Music for Shakespeare's play for MIDI in meantone tuning produced by Pulse Ensemble Theatre 2001, Blect for MIDI in the near just intonation 'Blackjack' scale 2002, Inner Voices for 'z3ta+' softsynth in the near just intonation 'Blackjack' scale 2005, microproj for 'z3ta+' softsynth in the near just intonation 'Blackjack' scale 2007. *Commissions include:* ensemble pieces from Belgian horn player Francis Orval, including Hornucopia, a piece for 10 horns, and a piece for solo horn in just intonation, Harmonic Etude 1987–91, premiered at Merkin Hall; Confessions of the Goliards for tenor and chamber ensemble from Goliard Concerts; ensemble piece Forest of Winds and two new solo pieces from flautist Gerardo Levy of New York Univ.; Trumpet in a New Surrounding from St Luke's Chamber Ensemble, performed at Dia Arts Center 1997; Wild, Wild West requested and performed by Liviu Danceanu's Archaeus Ensemble in Romania and Moldova 1997, 1999, 2004; several works in unusual tunings have been featured on Johnny Reinhard's American Festival of Microtonal Music continuously since 1980s. *Address:* c/o Composers Concordance, PO Box 3620548, New York, NY 10129-0548, USA (office). *Telephone:* (212) 564-4899 (office). *E-mail:* joseph@composersconcordance.org (office). *Website:* www.composersconcordance.org (office).

PEI, Yanling; Chinese actress; b. Aug. 1947, Shuning Co., Hebei Prov.; m. 1st Ding Bao Jin 1971 (divorced 1990); two d.; m. 2nd Guo Jing Chun. *Career:* Vice-Chair. Hebei Fed. of Literary and Art Circles 1993–, China Fed. of Literary and Art Circles 2001–; Chair. Hebei Professional Dramatists' Asscn; currently Dir Pei Yanling Co. of Hebei Prov. Peking Opera Theatre; mem. 7th CPPCC 1987–92, 8th CPPCC 1992–97. *Performances include:* The Man and the Ghost, Lotus Lantern, Ren gui qing (Woman-Demon-Human) 1987 and numerous others. *Honours:* Excellent Performing Artist Award, Ministry of Culture 1992, Plum Blossom Award 1986, 1995, Grand Plum Blossom Award 2009, White Magnolia Award for Special Achievement in the Performing Arts 2009.

PEINEMANN, Edith; German concert violinist; b. 3 March 1939, Mainz; d. of Robert Peinemann and Hildegard Peinemann (née Rohde). *Education:* studied under her father and later with Heinz Stauske and Max Rostal. *Career:* has performed with leading orchestras and conductors worldwide; orchestral debut, Carnegie Hall 1965; performed at Salzburg, Lucerne, Ravinia, Mozart, Marlboro Chamber Music Festivals; Prof. of Violin, Hochschule für Musik, Frankfurt 1976–; Int. Pres., European String Teachers' Asscn 2005–. *Honours:* First Prize, ARD competition, Munich 1956, Plaquette Eugène Ysaye 1858–1958. *Address:* Oberlindau 15, 60323 Frankfurt, Germany (office). *E-mail:* info@esta-int.com (office). *Website:* www.esta-int.com (office).

PELINKA, Werner, MA, DPhil; Austrian composer and pianist; b. 21 Jan. 1952, Vienna; m. Liliane Flühler 1976; two d. *Education:* Hochschule für Welthandel, Vienna, Univ. of Michigan, USA, Konservatorium der Stadt Wien, Hochschule für Musik und darstellende Kunst, Vienna, Univ. of Vienna. *Career:* concerts with horn player Roland Horvath (mem. of Vienna Philharmonic) as Ensemble Wiener Horn; teacher, Konservatorium Wien Privatuniversität, Toho-Vienna Music Acad. 1991–2000; Man. Viennese Children's Music Festival, Kinderklang 1992–2003; formation of a Tomatis Inst. in Vienna (training in Paris) 1994–95; concerts with Ensemble Imago (founder mem.) 2004–. *Compositions:* op. 1–47, including op. 1: Pater Noster, op. 5: Sinfonietta con Corale, op. 9: Trio Reflexionen, op. 14: Passio Silvae, op. 24: Concerto for Jon, op. 28: Die Erbsenprinzessin, Opera after Hans Christian Andersen (libretto by Martin Auer) 1995, op. 33: In adventu, op. 39: Cantata brevis. *Recordings:* Horn und Klavier 4 (op. 2, op. 5 and op. 8, with Werner Pelinka, piano and Roland Horvath, horn), Österreichische Komponisten der Gegenwart (op. 12, with Brigitte Hübner, contralto and Werner Pelinka, piano), Passio Silvae (op. 14, with Johannes Jokel, bass voice, Roland Horvath, horn and Werner Pelinka, piano), Horn und Klavier 5 (op. 24), New Music for Orchestra VMM (op. 5, with ORF Symphonic Orchestra conducted by Christo Stanischeff, soloist Erwin Sükar, horn), Trio Arabesque (op. 26, oboe, bassoon, piano with Tonkünstler Ensemble), Diagonal (concert pieces for strings, op. 27, with Ruse Philharmonic conducted by Tsanko Delibozov), Musik-Sprache-Dichtung-Musik (op. 9), J'aime le son du cor (op. 14, with Walter Fink, bass voice). *Publications:* Die Vertonungen des lateinischen Paternoster der nachklassischen Zeit (Diss 1985, Vienna). *Honours:* Karl Medaille des Ordens der Ritter des Heiligen Lazarus zu Jerusalem 2007. *Address:* Gusenleithnergasse 30, 1140 Vienna (office); Langwiesgasse 38, 1140 Vienna, Austria (home). *Telephone:* (1) 9148674 (home); (1) 9124290 (office). *Fax:* (1) 9124290 (office). *Website:* www.tomatis-institut.at.

PELLEGRINI, Maria; Italian singer (soprano); b. 15 July 1943, Pescara. *Education:* Opera School of the Royal Conservatory in Toronto. *Career:* debut with the Canadian Opera Company as the Priestess in Aida, 1963; sang Gilda 1965; appearances in Montréal, Toronto and Vancouver; Sadler's Wells Opera from 1967, Covent Garden from 1968, notably as Violetta, Micaela in Carmen and Madama Butterfly; guest appearances in Genoa, Bologna, Parma and Trieste and with the Welsh National Opera; US debut Pittsburgh, 1975; sang Musetta in Ottawa, 1980. *Recordings include:* Carmen. *Website:* maria_pellegrini.tripod.com/home.html.

PELLEGRINO, Ronald (Ron) Anthony, BM, PhD; American composer and musician; b. 11 May 1940, Kenosha, WI. *Education:* Lawrence Univ., Univ. of Wisconsin with Rene Leibowitz and Rudolph Kolisch. *Career:* electronic music studio at Univ. of Wisconsin from 1967; Dir of the electronic music studios, Ohio State Univ. 1968–70, Oberlin Conservatory 1970–73; Assoc. Prof., Texas Tech Univ., Lubbock 1978–81; founded electronic music performance ensembles Real Electric Symphony and Sonoma Electro-Acoustic Music Soc. *Compositions include:* electronic and mixed media: S&H Explorations 1972, Metabiosis 1972, Figured 1972, Cries 1973, Kaleidoscope, Electric Rags 1976, Setting Suns and Spinning Daughters 1978, Words and Phrases 1980, Siberian News Release 1981, Spring Suite 1982, Laser Seraphim and Cymatic Music 1982; tape and instruments: The End of the Affair 1967, Dance Drama 1967, Passage 1968, Markings 1969, Leda and the Swan 1970, Phil's Float 1974, Wavesong 1975, Issue of the Silver Hatch 1979. *Publications include:* An Electronic Music Studios Manual 1969. *Honours:* National Endowment for the Arts and National Endowment for the Humanities grants for founding the Leading Edge contemporary music series. *E-mail:* ronpell_1@earthlink.net (office).

PELLEKOORNE, Anne; singer (contralto); b. 1957, Amsterdam, The Netherlands. *Education:* Hamburg Musikhochschule. *Career:* concerts for German television and at Rome under Gerd Albrecht, Hindemith programme; appearances at Wiesbaden and Zürich in Die Zauberflöte and Die Walküre; Wagner's Ring at Rome; Bavarian State Opera from 1989 in Salome and Der

Rosenkavalier and the premiere of Bose's Schlachthof 5 1996; concert tour of Brazil 1996; sang Angustias in the premiere of Reimann's Bernarda Albas Haus, Munich 2000.

PELLETIER, Louis-Philippe; Canadian pianist and academic; b. 1945, Montréal. *Education:* studied with Lubka Kolessa, Claude Helffer, Harald Boje, Aloys Kontarsky. *Career:* Prof. of Piano and Chair Dept of Piano, McGill Univ. *Recordings:* Piano Works, Bach, Beethoven, Schumann, Brahms, Debussy, Boulez, Messiaen, Stockhausen, Xenakis, Schoenberg, Berg, Webern, Vivier, Papineau-Couture, Garant. *Honours:* first prize Arnold Schoenberg Piano Competition, Rotterdam 1979, Canadian Music Council Artist of the Year 1980.

PELLY, Laurent; French stage director and costume/set designer; Co-Director, *Théâtre National de Toulouse*; b. 1962, Paris. *Career:* staged his first play aged 16 and at 18 f. theatre company Le Pélican, Co-Dir 1989–; Dir Centre Dramatique Nat. des Alpes in Grenoble 1997–2007; Co-Dir Théâtre Nat. de Toulouse 2008–; operas directed include I Puritani, Giulio Cesare and Ariadne auf Naxos (Paris Opéra), L'heure espagnole/L'enfant et les sortilèges and Hänsel und Gretel (Glyndebourne Festival), La Traviata (Santa Fe and Teatro Regio, Turin), L'amour des trois oranges (Netherlands Opera), Pelléas et Mélisande (Theater an der Wien), The Cunning Little Vixen (Saito Kinen Festival and Maggio Musicale, Florence) and Platée (Paris Opera and Santa Fe); has directed numerous works by Offenbach, including Les Contes d'Hoffmann (Liceu, Barcelona, San Francisco and Opéra de Lyon), La Belle Hélène (Théâtre du Châtelet Paris, Santa Fe and English Nat. Opera), La vie parisienne (Lyon and Toulouse) and La Grande-Duchesse de Gérolstein (Châtelet Paris); Royal Opera House, Covent Garden debut 2007 as stage director and costume designer of La fille du régiment; L'heure espagnole and L'enfant et les sortilèges (Glyndebourne) 2012, Weill's Grandeur et décadence de la ville de Mahagonny (Théâtre du Capitole), Jules César (Opéra Garnier), Les Puritains (Opéra Bastille), Cendrillon (Liceu Barcelona), Le Comte Ory (Opéra de Lyon, La Scala Milan), Don Pasquale (Santa Fe). *Recordings include:* Ravel: L'heure espagnole/L'enfant et les sortilèges (DVD) (Gramophone Award for Best Opera Recording of the Year 2014) 2013. *Honours:* Prix de la Soc. des Auteurs et Compositeurs Dramatiques 2009, Prix Georges Lherminier (for Mille francs de récompense) 2010, whatsonstage.com award for Best New Opera Production (for L'enfant et les sortilèges at Glyndebourne) 2012. *Address:* Théâtre National de Toulouse, 1 Rue Pierre Baudis, 31000 Toulouse, France (office). *Telephone:* 5-34-45-05-16 (office). *E-mail:* l.khaidouri@tnt-cite.com (office). *Website:* www.tnt-cite.com (office).

PEÑA, Paco; Spanish flamenco guitarist, musical director and professor of flamenco guitar; *Director, Paco Peña Flamenco Company*; b. (Francisco Peña Perez), 1 June 1942, Córdoba; s. of Antonio Peña and Rosario Pérez; m. Karin Vaessen 1982; two d. *Career:* int. concert artist since 1968; f. Paco Peña Flamenco Co. 1970, Centro Flamenco Paco Peña, Córdoba 1981; Prof. of Flamenco, Rotterdam Conservatory, Netherlands 1985; composed Misa Flamenca 1991; produced Musa Gitana 1999, Voces y Ecos 2002; composed Flamenco Requiem 2004; produced flamenco dance show A Compas! 2006; devised dance productions Flamenco sin Fronteras 2009, Quimeras 2010, Flamenco Vivo 2011, Quimeras 2012. *Publication:* Toques Flamencos. *Honours:* Oficial de la Cruz de la Orden del Mérito Civil; Ramón Montoya Prize 1983, Arts Gold Medal in the Arts, John F. Kennedy Centre for the Performing Arts, Washington, DC 2012. *Current Management:* c/o MPM London, Suite 20, 1 Prince of Wales Road, London, NW5 3LW, England. *Telephone:* (20) 7681-7475. *Fax:* (20) 7681-7476. *E-mail:* MPM@pacopena.com. *Website:* www.pacopena.com.

PENCARREG, Wyn; British singer (baritone); b. (Wyn Griffiths), 22 May 1968, Wales; s. of Dilwyn Barrie Griffiths and Janet Griffiths. *Education:* Royal Northern Coll. of Music (RNCM), masterclasses with Geraint Evans, Brigitte Fassbaender and Sherrill Milnes. *Career:* Glyndebourne Chorus 1992–94; then Masetto (Don Giovanni) and Kuligin (Katya Kabanova); for Opera North: sang De Brétigny (Manon), Masetto and Leporello (Don Giovanni), Figaro (Le Nozze di Figaro) and Father (Hansel and Gretel); for English Touring Opera: sang Figaro, Lescaut (Manon), Papageno (The Magic Flute) and Helson (Paul Bunyan); for Mid Wales Opera: sang Count Almaviva (Le Nozze di Figaro), The Villains (The Tales of Hoffman), Ford (Falstaff), Sharpless (Madam Butterfly) and Leporello; for ENO: sang Surin (The Queen of Spades); for Royal Opera House: sang Papin (Babette's Feast), Fiorello (Il Barbiere di Siviglia) and Lalchand (The Firework Maker's Daughter); for Raymond Gubbay Ltd: performed Morales (Carmen), Schaunard (La Bohème) and Sharpless; for Lyric Opera, Dublin: sang Belcore (L'Elisir d'amore), Marcello (La Bohème) and Sharpless; sang the role of Luca (The Bear) for L'Opéra de Monte Carlo. *Radio:* numerous broadcasts on BBC Radio. *Honours:* Erich Viether Memorial Award 1995. *Current Management:* c/o Owen White Management. *Telephone:* (20) 8480-1152. *E-mail:* john@owenwhitemanagement.com. *Website:* www.owenwhitemanagement.com.

PENDACHANSKA, Alexandrina; singer (soprano); b. 1970, Bulgaria. *Education:* studied with her mother, Valeri Popova. *Career:* debut in concert at Sofia 1987, with Violetta's Act 1 aria; concert tour of Germany 1989; performances of Traviata in Sofia and Bilbao; performances of Lucia in Cairo and Sofia; performances of Gilda in a new production of Rigoletto for WNO 1991; concert engagements with the Sofia Philharmonic and other orchestras in Bulgaria, Moscow and Kiev; Lucia di Lammermoor (title role) in Dublin, Ophelia in Hamlet with Monte Carlo Opera 1991–92; sang Marie in La Fille

du Régiment at Monte Carlo 1996; Elisabetta in Donizetti's Roberto Devereux, Naples 1998; season 2000 as Donna Anna at Houston, Rossini's Ermione for Santa Fe Opera, Adalgisa in Florence and Lucrezia in Verdi's I Due Foscari at Naples. *Recordings include:* Antonida in A Life for the Tsar by Glinka. *Honours:* second prize Int. Competition, Bilbao 1988, winner Int. Dvořák Competition, Prague 1988, first prize Pretoria Music Competition 1990.

PENDERECKI, Krzysztof; Polish composer and conductor; b. 23 Nov. 1933, Dębica, Kraków Prov.; s. of Tadeusz Penderecki and Zofia Penderecka; m. Elżbieta Solecka 1965; one s. two d. *Education:* Jagiellonian Univ., and State Higher Music School (now Music Acad.), Kraków, studied composition first with Skołyszewski, later with Malawski and Wiechowicz, Kraków. *Career:* Lecturer in Composition, State Higher Music School, Kraków 1958–66, Prof. Extraordinary 1972–75, Prof. 1975–; Rector Kraków Conservatory 1972–87; Prof. of Composition, Folkwang Hochschule für Musik, Essen 1966–68; Musical Adviser, Vienna Radio 1970–71; Prof. of Composition, Yale Univ., USA 1973–78; Music Dir, Casals Festival, Puerto Rico 1992–2002; Music Man. Sinfonia Varsovia Orchestra 1997–; Guest Conductor China Philharmonic Orchestra 2000–; mem. Presidential Council of Culture 1992–; Corresp. mem. Arts Acad. of GDR, Berlin 1975, Academia Nacional de Bellas Artes, Buenos Aires 1982; Extraordinary mem. Arts Acad. of W Berlin 1975; mem. Royal Acad. of Music, Stockholm 1976, Acad. Nat. de Sciences, Belles-Lettres et Arts, Bordeaux, American Acad. of Arts and Letters 1999, Hong Kong Acad. for the Performing Arts 2001 etc.; Fellow, Royal Irish Acad. of Music. *Works include:* Psalms of David (for choir and percussion) 1958, Emanations (for two string orchestras) 1958, Strophes (for soprano, speaker and ten instruments) 1959, Anaklasis (for strings and percussion) 1959–60, Dimensions of Time and Silence (for 40-part mixed choir and chamber ensemble) 1959–60, String Quartet no. 1 1960, no. 2 1968, Threnody for the Victims of Hiroshima (for 52 strings) 1960, Polymorphia (for strings) 1961, Psalms (for tape) 1961, Fluorescences (for large orchestra) 1961, Sonata for Cello and Orchestra 1964, St Luke's Passion 1965–66, De natura sonoris (for large orchestra) 1966, Dies irae (for soprano, tenor, bass, chorus and large orchestra) 1967, Violin Concerto 1967–77, The Devils of Loudun (opera) 1968–69, Cosmogony 1970, De natura sonoris II (for wind instruments, percussion and strings) 1970, Canticum Canticorum Salomonis (for 16 voices and chamber orchestra) 1970–73, Partita (for harpsichord, guitars, harp, double bass and chamber orchestra) 1972, Symphony no. 1 1972–73, Magnificat (for bass solo, voice ensemble, double choir, boys' voices and orchestra) 1973–74, When Jacob Awoke (for orchestra) 1974, Paradise Lost (opera) 1976–78, Christmas Symphony No. 2 1979–80, Te Deum 1979–80, Lacrimosa 1980, Cello Concerto No. 2 1982, Viola Concerto 1983, Black Mask (opera) 1984–86, Der unterbrochene Gedanke (for string quartet) 1988, Adagio (for orchestra) 1989, Symphony No. 4 (Adagio for orchestra) 1989, Sinfonietta (for orchestra) 1990–91, Symphony No. 5 (for orchestra) 1991–92, Partita (for orchestra, rev. ed.) 1991, Ubu Rex (opera) 1991, Benedicamus Domine 1992, Benedictus 1992, Flute Concerto 1992–93, Quartet for Clarinet and String Trio 1993, Violin Concerto No. 2 1992–95, Symphony No. 3 1995, Agnus Dei from Versöhnung Messe (a cappella choir) 1995, Seven Gates of Jerusalem (oratorio) 1995–96, Passacaglia (chamber music) 1995–96, Larghetto (chamber music) 1997, Credo 1997–98, Sonata for Violin and Piano 2000, Sextet for Violin, Viola, Cello, Piano, Clarinet and French Horn 2000, Benedictus 2002, Resurrection Piano Concerto 2002, Largo for violoncello and orchestra 2003, Symphony No. 8 2005–07, Concerto per corno 'Winterreise' 2007–08, Quartetto per archi No. 3 2008, Drei chinesische Lieder 2008, Kaddisz 2009, Prelude for Peace 2009. *Honours:* Hon. RAM, London 1974; Hon. mem. Accad. Nazionale di Santa Cecilia, Rome 1976, Acad. Int. de Philosophie et de l'Art, Berne 1987, Musikkreis der Stadt, Duisburg 1999, Gesellschaft der Musikfreunds, Vienna 2000; Hon. Prof., Moscow Conservatory 1997, Cen. Beijing Conservatory 1998, St Petersburg Conservatory 2003, Komitas State Conservatory, Yerevan 2008; Officier, Ordre de Saint-Georges de Bourgogne (Belgium) 1990, Grand Cross Order of Merit (FRG) 1990, Commdr, Ordre des Arts et des Lettres 1996, Ordine al Merito della Repub. Italiana 2000, Commdr of the Three Star Order, Riga (Latvia) 2006, Order of the White Eagle (Poland) 2006; Dr hc (Univ. of Rochester, NY) 1972, (St Olaf Coll., Northfield, Minn.) 1977, (Katholieke Univ., Leuven) 1979, (Univ. of Bordeaux) 1979, (Georgetown Univ., Washington, DC) 1984, (Univ. of Belgrade) 1985, (Univ. Autónoma, Madrid) 1987; Hon. DMus (Glasgow) 1995, (Jagiellonian Univ., Krakow) 1998, (Ukrainian Nat. Tchaikovsky Acad. of Music) 1999, (Pittsburgh) 1999, (Lucerne) 2000, Univ. of St Petersburg, Yale Univ., Univ. of Leipzig 2003, and many others; Fitelberg Prize for Threnody for the Victims of Hiroshima 1960, also UNESCO award 1959, Polish Minister of Culture and Art Prize 1961, (First Class) 1981, Krakow Composition Prize for Canon 1962, North Rhine-Westphalia Grand Prize for St Luke's Passion 1966, also Pax Prize (Poland) 1966, Alfred Jurzykowski Foundation Award, Polish Inst. of Arts and Sciences in America 1966, Prix Italia 1967/68, State Prize (1st Class) 1968, Gustav Charpentier Prize 1971, Gottfried von Herder Prize 1977, Prix Arthur Honegger for Magnificat 1978, Grand Medal of Paris 1981, Sibelius Prize (Wihouri Foundation, Finland) 1983, Order of Banner of Labour (1st Class) 1983, Premio Lorenzo il Magnifico (Italy) 1985, Wolf Foundation Award 1987, Grammy Award Nat. Acad. of Recording Arts and Sciences (for Best Contemporary Composition) 1988, (for Best Instrumental Soloist Performance with Orchestra) 1999, (for Best Choral Composition) 2001, Grawemeyer Award for Music Composition 1992, City of Strasbourg Medal 1995, Crystal Award, World Econ. Forum, Davos 1997, Business Center Club Special Award, Warsaw 1998, AFIM Indie Award 1999, Köhler-Osbahr-Stiftung

Music Award 1999, Best Living Composer Award, Midem Classic Award, Cannes 2000, Príncipe de Asturias Award 2001, Roman Guardini Prize, Catholic Acad. of Music 2002, North Rhine-Westphalia Award 2003, Praemium Imperiale 2004, Gold Medal, Ministry of Culture (Armenia) 2009, Lifetime Achievement Award, Int. Classical Music Awards 2012. *Website:* www.penderecki.de.

PENDLEBURY, Sally; British cellist; b. 1960, England. *Education:* Chetham's School of Music, New England Conservatory and studied in Düsseldorf. *Career:* led cello section of the European Community Youth Orchestra 1982–85; mem., Chamber Orchestra of Europe; recitals with Natalia Gutman and Yuri Bashmet; co-founder, Vellinger String Quartet 1990; participated in masterclasses with Borodin Quartet at Pears-Britten School 1991; concerts at Ferrara Musica Festival, Italy and debut on South Bank with London premiere of Robert Simpson's 13th Quartet; BBC Radio 3 debut 1991; season 1992–93 with concerts in London, Glasgow, Cambridge, at Davos Festival, Switzerland and Crickdale Festival, Wiltshire; Wigmore Hall with Haydn (Op 54, No. 2), Gubaidulina and Beethoven (Op 59, No. 2), Purcell Room with Haydn's Seven Last Words.

PENHERSKI, Zbigniew, DipMus; Polish composer; b. 26 Jan. 1935, Warsaw; m. Malgorzata Penherska; one s. *Education:* Warsaw Conservatory of Music. *Compositions include:* Musica Humana for baritone, choir and symphony orchestra 1963, Missa Abstracta for tenor, reciting voice, choir and symphony orchestra 1966, Street Music, chamber ensemble 1966, Samson Put on Trial, radio opera 1968, 3 Recitativi for soprano, piano and percussion 1968, 3M-H1, electronic piece 1969, Instrumental Quartet 1970, Incantationi 1 Sextet for Percussion Instruments 1972, The Twilight of Peryn, opera in 3 parts 1972, Masurian Chronicles 2 for symphony orchestra and magnetic tape 1973, Radio Symphony for 2 1975, Anamnesis for symphony orchestra 1975, String Play for string orchestra 1980, Edgar: The Son of Walpor, opera in three parts 1982, Jeux Partis for saxophone and percussion 1984, 3 impressions for soprano, piano and four percussions 1985, Scottish Chronicles for symphony orchestra 1987, The Island of the Roses, chamber opera 1989, Signals for Symphony orchestra 1992, Cantus for mixed choir 1992, Signals No. 2 1995, Genesis for bass solo, vocal ensembles, reciting voices, selected instruments and electronic sounds 1995, Introduction and Toccata for clarinet, trombone, cello and piano 1998, Little Music for the End of Century for recorder, two percussions, organ and tape 1999, Cantus II for mixed choir 2000, Little String Litany for string orchestra 2002, Lamentations for baritone and string quartet 2003. *Honours:* Hon. Citizen of Kragujevac (Yugoslavia), Russe (Bulgaria), Ho-Chi-Minh (Viet Nam); Hon. mem. Scottish Soc. of Composers 1987; Silver Cross of Merit 1975, Prime Minister's Award for works for children and youth 1982. *Address:* ul. Krucza 24A, 05-120 Legionowo by Warsaw, Poland. *Telephone:* (22) 7844163. *E-mail:* zpenherski@neostrada.pl (home). *Website:* www.zaiks.org.pl; www.polmic.pl.

PENICKA, Miloslav, BMus, MMus; Australian (b. Czech) composer; b. 16 April 1935, Ostrava, Czechoslovakia; s. of Judr Soběslav and Jarmila Rybáková; m. Sandra Parton; two d. one s. *Education:* Prague Conservatorium and Prague Acad. of Music and Arts, Charles Univ., studied with František Pícha and Emil Hlobil. *Career:* Percussionist, Sydney Symphony Orchestra 1965–69; Abbotsleigh School, Wahroonga 1969–75; full mem. Australian Music Centre; mem. Australian Performing Rights Asscn. *Compositions include:* two Symphonies 1964, 2005, four Overtures 1972, 1975, 1989, 2003, two Orchestral Suites 1994, 1995, two Serenades for small orchestra 1958, 1961, two Piano Concertos 1963, 1996, Clarinet Concerto 1977, Cello Concerto 2007, Divertimento for violin, wind, timpani and bass 1963, four String Quartets 1962, 1969, 2002, 2007, Clarinet Quintet 1967, Piano Quartet 1973, two Piano Sonatas 1958, 1979, Sonatinas for violin and piano 1978, for cello and piano 1991, for piano 1978, for bassoon and piano 2007, four Pieces for flute and piano 1977, for oboe and piano 1995, Partita for cello 1991, Music for string orchestra: Divertimento 1972, Sonatina 1980, Partita 1987, Dance Suite 1991, three Piano Cycles: Kookaburra's Friends 1990, Musings 1996, Waratah and Others 2000, Mosaics for cor anglais quartet 2003, Pargamyshky for brass quintet 2005, Piano Trio 2005, Piano Quintet 2008, Oboe Quintet 2009, Quintet for piano, clarinet, horn and bassoon 2009, Gargoyles for wind quintet 2009, String Trio 2010, 10 songs for SATB on English Poetry 2012, piano pieces, vocal and theatre music. *Address:* 9 Warraroon Road, Riverview 2066 (home); Australian Music Centre, POB N690, Grosvenor Place 1220, Australia (office). *Telephone:* (2) 9428-5889 (home). *Website:* www.amcoz.com.au.

PENKOVA, Reni; Bulgarian teacher of singing and fmr singer (mezzo-soprano); b. 28 Oct. 1935, Tarnovo. *Education:* studied with Nadia Aladjem and Elena Doskova-Ricardi in Sofia, and Dimitar Kozhuharov, State Music Acad., Sofia. *Career:* debut in Burgas 1960, as Olga in Eugene Onegin; mem. Nat. Opera Sofia from 1964; guest appearances in The Netherlands and UK; Glyndebourne Festival as Olga, Pauline in The Queen of Spades, Dorabella in Così fan tutte and Meg Page in Falstaff 1971–77; Wexford Festival as Vanya in Glinka's Ivan Sussanin 1973; other roles include Gluck's Orpheus, Cherubino, Octavian in Der Rosenkavalier, Amneris, and Angelina in La Cenerentola; also heard in concert and oratorio; mem. Bulgarian Nat. Opera, Sofia –1991; Vocal Prof., State Music Acad., Sofia; further roles include Bartók (Bluebeard's Castle), as Judith 1975; Britten (Midsummer Night's Dream), as Oberon 1982; Verdi (Nabucco), as Fenena 1976; Bellini (Norma), as Adalgisa 1984; Donizetti (La Favorita), as Leonora 1985; Cilea (Adriana Lecouvreur), as La Princesse de Bouillon 1987; last roles included Bernstein's Candide (Old

Lady) 1995, Humperdinck's Hänsel und Gretel (Gertrude) 1998, Britten's Let's Make an Opera 2002. *Recordings include:* Prince Igor by Borodin, Francesca da Rimini Zandonai, Bulgarian operas Tsar Kaloyan by P. Vladigerov, Zografat Zahari by M. Goleminov and Yoan Kukuzel by Parashkev Hadzhiev. *Television:* Verdi's Falstaff. *Publications:* Galia Youncheva Operni pateki 2003, Nevena Koralova Razgovori v kadar í sad kadar 2004. *Honours:* Order of the Red Flag of Labour 1985; Silver Harp Union of Bulgarian Musicians and Dancers 1978, Golden Harp 1995. *Address:* ul Keshan 9, 1527 Sofia, Bulgaria (home). *Telephone:* (2) 8435831 (home). *E-mail:* maro_s@abv.bg (office).

PENN, William Albert, MA, PhD; American composer; b. 11 Jan. 1943, Long Branch, NJ. *Education:* State Univ. of New York at Buffalo with Henri Pousseur and Maurico Kagel, Michigan State Univ., Eastman School with Wayne Barlow. *Career:* faculty mem., Eastman School 1971–78; staff composer, New York Shakespeare Festival 1974–76; Folger Shakespeare Theatre and Sounds Reasonable Records in Washington from 1975. *Compositions include:* String Quartet 1968, At Last Olympus (musical) 1969, Spectrums, Confusions and Sometime for orchestra 1969, The Pied Piper of Hamelin (musical) 1969, Chamber Music No. 1 for violin and piano 1971, for cello and piano 1972, Symphony 1971, The Boy Who Cried Wolf is Dead (musical) 1971, Ultra Mensuram: Three Brass Quintets 1971, The Canticle (musical) 1972, Inner Loop for band 1973, Niagura 1678 for band 1973, Night Music for flute and chorus 1973, Miriors sur le Rubaiyat for piano and narrator 1974, Mr Toad's Wild Adventure for orchestra 1993, Saxophone Concerto 1995, The Revelations of St John the Divine for wind ensemble 1995, incidental music and songs. *Honours:* ASCAP Awards, NEA Fellowship.

PENNETIER, Jean-Claude; French pianist and conductor; b. 16 May 1942, Chatellerault. *Education:* Paris Conservatoire. *Career:* numerous solo appearances in Europe and elsewhere 1968–; chamber musician with Regis Pasquier (violin) and trio with E. Krivine and F. Lodeon; recitals with piano four hands; duo with clarinettist Michel Portal 1979–80; mem. of ensembles, including Domaine Musical, Musique Vivante, Ars Nova, Itineraire and Musique Plus; performer of contemporary music at the Roayn and La Rochelle festivals; has conducted the Ensemble Intercontemporain and the orchestras of French Radio; performed premieres of Maurice Ohana's 24 Preludes 1973 and Piano Concerto 1981, Nikiprovetski's Piano Concerto 1979; Prof. of Chamber Music, Paris Conservatoire 1985–. *Honours:* Chevalier, Légion d'Honneur 2002; winner Prix Gabriel Fauré, winner International Competition Montréal, second prize Long-Triubaud Competition, winner Geneva International Competition 1968. *Current Management:* Melvin Kaplan Inc., 115 College Street, Burlington, VT 05401, USA. *Telephone:* (802) 658-2592. *Fax:* (802) 658-6089. *E-mail:* music@melkap.com. *Website:* www.melkap.com.

PENNISI, Francesco; Italian composer; b. 11 Feb. 1934, Acireale. *Education:* Univ. Faculty of Arts, Rome, studied with Robert W. Mann. *Career:* co-founder of new music soc. in Rome, Nuova Consonanza 1960; participation in Palermo Int. New Music Week 1960–. *Compositions:* A Cantata on Melancholy 1967, Sylvia Simplex (music theatre) 1972, Fantasia for cello and orchestra 1997, La vigne di Samaria for chorus and orchestra 1974, Gläserner Tag for orchestra 1978, La partenza di Tisies for viola and orchestra 1979, Descrizione dell Isola Ferdinandea (chamber opera) 1983, Per Agamemnone for orchestra 1983, I mandolini e le chitarre for soprano and ensemble 1986, Aci il fume (radio opera) 1986, Tre Pezzi for clarinet, viola and piano 1987–90, Purpureass rosas for two sopranos, baritone and clarinet quartet 1990, Lesequie della luna (music theatre) 1991, Una cartolina da selim (omaggio a Mozart) 1991, The Wild Swans for soprano and ensemble 1992, Medea dixit for soprano and ensemble 1992–93, Tristan (music theatre after Ezra Pound) 1995, Altro efetto di luna for soprano and ensemble 1996, Scena for flute and orchestra 1997, chamber and solo instrumental music.

PENNY, Andrew Jonathan, ARNCM, GRNCM; British conductor; b. 4 Dec. 1952, Hull, Yorks., England; m. Helga Robinson 1988; one s. one d. *Education:* Royal Northern Coll. of Music, Manchester, studied clarinet with Sidney Fell and conducting with Charles Groves, Timothy Reynish and Edward Downes. *Career:* Musical Dir, Hull Philharmonic Orchestra 1982–. *Recordings include:* premiere recordings of Sullivan's ballet and theatre music, symphonies by Armstrong Gibbs, Edward German and Hubert Parry, film music by Vaughan Williams and William Walton, complete cycle of Malcolm Arnold Symphonies, Shakespearean Overtures of Castelnuovo-Tedesco. *Honours:* Ricordi Prize, Royal Northern Coll. of Music 1976. *Address:* 14 South Lane, Hessle, East Yorks., HU13 0RR, England.

PENRI-EVANS, David, BMus, MMus, DMA, PGCE, FTCL; British composer; b. 18 Jan. 1956, Wrexham, Wales. *Education:* Centenary Coll. of Louisiana, Univ. of Wales, Louisiana State Univ., USA, Trinity Coll., London; studied composition with Dinos Constantinides. *Career:* Teacher, Victoria Coll., Jersey 1979–81; Portsmouth Grammar School 1987–92; Dir of Music, Elmhurst Ballet School 1992–94, John Lyon School 1995–96, Brooklands Coll., Weybridge 1996–; Asst Prof., American Univ. in London 1987–; Founder-Dir Tempo New Music Festival 1987–94; Guest Composer, Louisiana Festival of Contemporary Music 1990, 1995, Conservatoire Nat. de Région de Rouen 2000; Chair. Portsmouth District Composers' Alliance; mem. BMI, Exec. Cttee British Acad. of Songwriters, Composers and Authors. *Compositions include:* many comms in UK and USA; Violin Prologue 1982, Brown Studies 1983, Symphony 1983, String Quartet, Dinas Brân 1984, Night Music 1985, Study in Grey, Opera 1985, Death in the Surf 1987, Textures 1990,

Sunrise with Sea Monsters 1990, Aurelia 1993, Sift 1994, Five Haiku for Peace 1995, Four Ways of Having Sex in Zero Gravity 2000, Rain Journal 2001, L'Indifferent 2006. *Address:* Brooklands College, Weybridge, Surrey, KT13 8TT, England (home). *E-mail:* david.penrievans@brooklands.ac.uk (office). *Website:* www.penrievans.free-online.co.uk/DPE_Web_01.

PEPER, Uwe; German singer (tenor); b. 20 May 1939, Hamburg. *Career:* debut as Mozart's Pedrillo in Halberstadt 1966; Komische Oper Berlin as Monostatos and Jacquino in Fidelio, Zürich, Frankfurt and Paris as Jacquino from 1969; Pedrillo at the Salzburg Festival 1990–91; Mime in The Ring at the Salle Pleyel, Paris 1992; in Boris Godunov and Andrea Chénier, Deutsche Oper Berlin 1995–96; sang Guillot in Massenet's Manon 1998; sang Jacquino in Fidelio, Strauss's Valzacchi and the Emperor in Turandot at the Deutsche Oper 1999–2001. *Recordings:* Salome, Die Entführung, Die Zauberflöte.

PEPI ALÓS, Jorge; Argentine pianist and composer; b. 28 March 1962, Córdoba. *Education:* Acad. Menuhin, Gstaad and studied with Edith Fischer, studied with Eric Gaudibert, Geneva. *Career:* concerto soloist and chamber musician (notably in two-piano duo with Edith Fischer) in Europe, USA and S America; long-term composing collaboration with Théâtre de l'Ephémère, Lausanne 1985–; organizer, Festival Int. de Piano de Blonay; teacher, Conservatoire Neuchatelois 1992–. *Compositions include:* Trio for piano, violin and cello 1982, Enouma Elish for orchestra 1982–83, Micro-Suite for piano 1983, Septet 1983, Three Moments for piano duo 1984, Block for piano 1986, Bagatelles for harp, clarinet and cello 1987, Metamorfosis I for piano 1989, La Caccia al tesoro (chamber opera) 1990–92, Metamorfosis II 1991, Extravagario 1992–93, Amalgama 1995, Metamorfosis III, Metamorfosis IV 1995, Puna for flute 1996, Cadenza 1997, Nachtstücke 1998–99, Vida Maravillosa y Buslesca del Cafe 1999–2000, Metamorfosis VI 2001, Quatre Études 2002–03. *Honours:* Orpheus Prize 1987, Association des Musiciens Suisses Prix d'étude 1988, Edition Musicale Suisse composition prize 1991, Soc. Suisse des Auteurs composition prize 1993, first prize Gerona Int. Competition 1995, Grand Prix Gilson 1995. *E-mail:* info@jorgepepialos.com (office). *Website:* www.jorgepepialos.com.

PERAHIA, Murray; American pianist and conductor; b. 19 April 1947, New York, NY; s. of David Perahia and Flora Perahia; m. Naomi (Ninette) Shohet 1980; two s. *Education:* High School of Performing Arts, Mannes Coll. of Music, studied with Jeanette Haien, Arthur Balsam, Mieczyslaw Horszowski. *Career:* debut, Carnegie Hall 1968; has appeared with many of world's leading orchestras and with Amadeus, Budapest, Guarneri and Galimir string quartets; regular recital tours N America, Europe, Japan; Co-Artistic Dir Aldeburgh Festival 1983–89; numerous recordings including complete Mozart Piano Concertos; Prin. Guest Conductor, Acad. of St Martin-in-the-Fields. *Recordings include:* Bach Partitas Nos 2, 3, 4 (Midem Classical Award for Solo Instrument Recording 2009) 2008, Bach Partitas Nos 1, 5, 6 2009, Brahms: Händel Variations 2010, Beethoven: Piano Sonatas Nos. 4,11,7 2013, Murray Perahia Plays Chopin 2014, The Art of Murray Perahia 2016. *Honours:* Dr hc (Univ. of Leeds), (Duke Univ.); Hon., FRCM, FRAM; Hon. KBE 2004; won Leeds Int. Piano Competition 1972, Kosciusko Chopin Prize 1965, Avery Fisher Award 1975, eight Gramophone Record Awards, three Grammy Awards, Royal Acad. of Music Bach Prize 2013, Wolf Prize in Arts 2015. *Current Management:* c/o Linda Petrikova, IMG Artists, Carnegie Hall Tower, 152 West 57th Street, 5th Floor, New York, NY 10019, USA. *Telephone:* (212) 994-3500. *Fax:* (212) 994-3550. *E-mail:* lpetrikova@imgartists.com. *Website:* www.imgartists.com; www.murrayperahia.com.

PEREIRA, Alexander; Austrian opera house director; *Artistic Director*, *Zurich Opera House*; b. 11 Oct. 1947, Vienna. *Career:* formerly Sec.-Gen., Vienna Concert House; Dir, Zurich Opera House 1991–2012, Artistic Dir 1996–2012; mem. Artistic Cttee, Zurich Festival 1996–; Artistic Dir, Salzburg Festival 2011–; Superintendent-designate, Teatro alla Scala, Milan 2013–. *Address:* Zurich Opera House, Falkenstrasse 1, CH– 8008 Zurich, Switzerland (office). *Telephone:* (44) 2686400 (office). *Fax:* (44) 2686401 (office). *E-mail:* info@opernhaus.ch (office). *Website:* www.opernhaus.ch (office).

PEREIRA, Clóvis; Brazilian composer; b. 14 May 1932, Caruaru; m. Rizomar Pereira 1955, two s. two d. *Education:* School of Arts, Boston Univ. and studied with Guerra Peixe. *Career:* debut as conductor with Lamento e Dansa Brasileira 1968; arranger, Radio Jornal do Commercio 1950; Head Music Dept, Television 1960; Chair., Conservatorio Pernambucano de Musica 1983; tour of USA as Brazilian representative and Conductor, Univ. of Paraiba Chorus, Int. Choir Festival 1974; Teacher, Univ. da Paraiba, Rio Grande do Norte e Pernambuco 1994. *Compositions:* Grande Missa Nordestina para coro, solistas e orquestra, three Peças Nordestinas, Terno de Pifes, Cantiga, Velame, Cantata de Natal, Poetas Nordestinos songs for voice and piano, Concertino para violino e orquestra de camara 1994. *Honours:* first prize Primeiro Concurso Nacional de e Orq de Camara 1964, Trofeu Cultural Cidade do Recife 1997.

PERÉNYI, Miklós; Hungarian cellist and composer; b. 5 Jan. 1948, Budapest. *Education:* Ferenc Liszt Music Acad. of Budapest, Accademia Santa Cecilia, studied with Enrico Meinardi in Rome, Ede Bande in Budapest, Pablo Casals in Zermatt. *Career:* started playing cello aged five, first public recital aged nine, Budapest; Violoncello Teacher and Lecturer, Ferenc Liszt Acad. of Music, Budapest 1974–, Prof. 1980–; numerous appearances at int. music festivals including Edinburgh, Lucerne, Prague, Salzburg, Vienna, Hohenems, Warsaw, Berlin, also cello festivals in Kronberg, Winterthur and Manchester, Festival Pablo Casals, Prades, France, as well as in Japan, China

and USA; collaborates with pianist András Schiff, including concerts at Schubertiade Festival, Austria, Wigmore Hall, London, Edinburgh and Ruhr Festivals; performed Lutoslawski's Cello Concerto with Berlin Philharmonic Orchestra and Sir Simon Rattle, Berlin, Essen and Paris 2013; tour with Israel Philharmonic and András Schiff 2013–14. *Recordings include:* works of Ernö Dohnányi, Ferenc Farkas, Zoltán Kodály, György Ligeti, András Mihály and Sándor Veress (with Dénes Várjon), Hungarian Cello Music, Haydn Cello Concertos 1991, Zoltán Kodály, Sonatas for Cello and Piano 1994, Complete Beethoven Sonatas (with András Schiff) 2004, Beethoven: Complete Music for Piano and Violoncello (with András Schiff) (Cannes Classical Award 2005) 2004, Bach, Brahms, Britten (with Dénes Várjon) 2010, Britten, Bach, Ligeti 2012, Schubert: String Quartet 2013. *Honours:* Prizewinner, Int. Pablo Casals Cello Competition, Budapest 1963, Liszt Prize 1970, Kossuth Prize 1980, Bartók-Pasztory Prize 1987. *Current Management:* c/o Impresariat Simmenauer GmbH, Kurfürstendamm 211, 10719 Berlin, Germany. *Telephone:* (30) 414-781-714. *Fax:* (30) 414-781-713. *E-mail:* oda.caspar@impresariat -simmenauer.de. *Website:* www.impresariat-simmenauer.de.

PERERA, Ronald Christopher; American composer and professor of music; *Elsie Irwin Sweeney Professor Emeritus of Music, Smith College*; b. 25 Dec. 1941, Boston, Mass. *Education:* Harvard Univ. with Leon Kirchner, Utrecht Univ. studios, the Netherlands. *Career:* Instructor, Syracuse Univ. 1968–70; Visiting Asst Prof., Dartmouth Coll. 1970; Prof., Smith Coll. 1971–2002, Elsie Irwin Sweeney Prof. Emer. of Music 2002–; mem. The American Soc. of Composers, Authors and Publrs (ASCAP). *Compositions include:* Piano Suite 1966, Mass 1967, Dove sta amore for soprano and tape 1969, Reverberations for organ and tape 1970, Alternate Routes for electronics 1971, Apollo Circling 1972, Five Summer Songs on poems of Emily Dickinson for mezzo and piano or orchestra 1972, Apollo Circling for soprano and piano 1972, Three Night Pieces for choir 1974, Three Poems of Günther Grass for mezzo, chamber ensemble and tape 1974, Fantasy Variations for piano and electronics 1976, Children of the Sun for soprano, horn and piano 1978, Tolling for two pianos and tape 1979, The White Whale for baritone and orchestra 1981, Crossing the Meridian for tenor and chamber ensemble 1982, Chamber Concerto for brass quintet, winds and percussion 1983, Earthsongs for choir 1983, The Canticle of the Sun for chorus 1984, Sleep Now for high voice and piano 1985, Shakespeare Songs for high voice and piano 1985, Out of Shadow for piano 1987, The Yellow Wallpaper (chamber opera) 1989, Music for flute and orchestra 1990, The Saints for orchestra 1990, The Outermost House cantata for mixed chorus, narrator, solo soprano and chamber orchestra 1991, Visions for two sopranos voice and chamber orchestra 1993, S (opera, based on novel by John Updike) 1995, The Golden Door cantata for speaker, mixed chorus and ensemble 1998, The Araboolies of Liberty Street (one-act opera) 2001, Piano Trio 2002, String Quartet 2003, The Star in the Pail for men's chorus and piano 2004, Why I Wake Early, eight poems by Mary Oliver for mixed chorus, string quartet and piano 2006, A Dickinson Set for mixed voices a cappella 2009, Hildegard Magnificat for men's or women's choir and organ 2009, Full Sun for organ 2011, North Country for mixed chorus and piano 2011, Waypoints for piano 2011, Hymnos for organ 2013, A Soldier's Carol for mixed voices a cappella 2014. *Publication:* Development and Practice of Electronic Music (co-ed.) 1975. *Honours:* ASCAP Awards for Composition 1972–2013, Artists Foundation of Massachusetts Fellowship 1978, four MacDowell Colony Fellowships 1974–88, Nat. Endowment for the Arts grants 1976, 1988. *Address:* 703 Fairway Village, Leeds, MA 01053, USA (home). *E-mail:* rperera@ronaldperera.com (office). *Website:* www.ronaldperera.com.

PERESS, Maurice; American conductor and musician (trumpet); b. 18 March 1930, New York. *Education:* New York Univ., Mannes Coll., studied conducting with Philip James and Carl Bamberger. *Career:* played trumpet before appointed by Bernstein as Asst Conductor of the New York Philharmonic 1961; conducted revivals of Candide, Los Angeles 1966, West Side Story, New York 1968; Music Dir, Corpus Christi Symphony Orchestra 1962–75, Austin Symphony 1970–73, Kansas City Philharmonic 1974–80; guest conductor in Brussels, Hong Kong, Vienna, Jerusalem and Mexico City; conducted the premiere of Bernstein's Mass at the opening of the Kennedy Center, Washington, DC 1971, and at the Vienna Staatsoper 1981; led the US premiere of Einem's Der Besuch der alten Dame at the San Francisco Opera 1972; has orchestrated, edited and conducted jazz music by Duke Ellington, Eubie Blake and Gershwin (60th anniversary concert of the Rhapsody in Blue, New York 1984); has taught at New York Univ., Univ. of Texas at Austin, Queens Coll., New York; Pres. Conductors' Guild of the American Symphony Orchestra League. *Recordings include:* Bernstein's Mass (musical dir), Organ Concertos 1 and 2 by Rheinberger (with E. Power Biggs and the Columbia Symphony Orchestra). *Publication:* Dvořák to Duke Ellington: A Conductor Explores America's Music and its African-American Roots 2005. *Current Management:* Gershunoff Artists LLC, 2731 NE 14 Street, Suite 3, Fort Lauderdale, FL 33304-1650, USA. *Telephone:* (954) 769-9105. *Fax:* (954) 769-9107.

PÉREZ, Alejo; Argentine conductor; b. Buenos Aires. *Education:* Univ. of Buenos Aires, Hochschule für Musik, Karlsruhe. *Career:* works with orchestras including Royal Stockholm Philharmonic Orchestra, Gewandhausorchester Leipzig, Orchestre Philharmonique de Radio France and Deutsches Symphonie-Orchester Berlin; noted for his large repertoire of interpretations of contemporary music; opera productions at Opéra Bastille, Opéra de Lyon, Opéra Comique, Théâtre des Champs-Élysées, Frankfurt Opera and Leipzig Opera; Guest Conductor and Musical Advisor, Teatro Real Madrid, invited to conduct the Orquesta Sinfónica de Madrid by Gerard Mortier in Wagner's Rienzi, Golijov's opera Ainadamar, Mozart's Don Giovanni and Rihm's La Conquista de Mexico; Music Dir Teatro Argentino de La Plata 2009–12. *Current Management:* c/o Karsten Witt Musik Management, Leuschnerdamm 13, 10999 Berlin, Germany. *Telephone:* (30) 214594220. *Fax:* (30) 214594101. *E-mail:* info@karstenwitt.com. *Website:* www.karstenwitt.com.

PÉREZ, José-María; Spanish singer (tenor); b. 1934. *Education:* studied in Spain and Switzerland. *Career:* sang at the Lucerne Opera, 1959–60, then at Innsbruck and Basle; sang at Graz Opera, 1963–84 in such roles as the Duke of Mantua, Don Carlos, Rodolfo, Calaf, Radames, Cavaradossi, Andrea Chénier, Alfredo and Turiddu; guest appearances in Switzerland and elsewhere as Vasco da Gamain L'Africaine, by Meyerbeer, Faust, Pelléas, Sergei in Lady Macbeth of Mtensk and Albert Gregor in The Makropulos Case; also active in operetta at Berlin, Barcelona and Vienna.

PÉRISSON, Jean-Marie; French conductor; b. 6 Sept. 1924, Arcachon. *Education:* studied with Jean Fournet in Paris, Igor Markevitch in Salzburg. *Career:* conducted the orchestra of the Salzburg Mozarteum in Austria and Germany, then led the French Radio Orchestra at Strasbourg 1955–56; Permanent Conductor, Orchestre Philharmonique of Nice; Musical Dir of the Nice Opera; conducted cycles of The Ring and the French premieres of Katerina Izmailova by Shostakovich 1964, Elegy for Young Lovers by Henze 1965 and Prokofiev's The Gambler 1966; gave Janáček's Katya Kabanova at the Salle Favart, Paris, and conducted the Monte Carlo Opera 1969–71; directed the Presidential Symphony Orchestra 1972–76, and worked in the French repertory at the San Francisco Opera; conducted Carmen at Peking 1982.

PERL, Alfredo; Chilean/German pianist, conductor and teacher; *Artistic Director, Detmold Chamber Orchestra;* b. 1965, Santiago, Chile. *Education:* Universidad de Chile with Carlos Botto, Cologne Musikhochschule with Günter Ludwig, studied with Maria Curcio in London, UK. *Career:* concerts throughout S America and Europe; debut in Int. Piano Series, Queen Elizabeth Hall, London 1992; performed complete Beethoven Sonata Cycle at London's Wigmore Hall, Santiago and Moscow 1996–97; BBC Proms debut, Royal Albert Hall 1997; has performed world-wide at major venues including Vienna Musikverein and Konzerthaus, London Barbican, Rudolfinum Prague, Munich Herkulessaal, Cologne Philharmonie, Hamburg Musikhalle, Leipzig Gewandhaus, Izumi Hall Osaka, Hamarikyu Asahi Hall in Tokyo, Teatro Colón in Buenos Aires, Sydney Town Hall and Sydney Opera House, Nat. Arts Centre in Ottawa, Great Hall of the Moscow Conservatoire, Vilnius Grand Philharmonic Hall; has performed at festivals including Schwetzingen, Bad Kissingen, Rheingau, Schleswig-Holstein, Beethovenfest Bonn, Bath Int. Music Festival, Harrogate Festival, al-Bustan Festival Beirut, Haydn Festival in Eisenstadt; played with orchestras including the London Symphony, BBC Symphony, Philharmonic, Welsh and Ulster Orchestras, Royal Philharmonic, Hallé Orchestra, Netherlands Philharmonic, Hague Residentie, Florida Philharmonic, Tokyo Symphony, Adelaide Symphony, Melbourne Symphony, Sydney Symphony, Mozarteum Orchestra, Orchestre de la Suisse Romande, Mitteldeutscher Rundfunk Leipzig, Gewandhaus Orchestra, Vienna Symphony and Orquestra Sinfônica do Estado de São Paulo; Prof., Detmold Musikhochschule 2007–; Artistic Dir Detmold Chamber Orchestra 2009–. *Television includes:* Chopin Preludes for Opus Arte (BBC). *Recordings include:* Complete Beethoven Sonatas and Diabelli Variations, Fantasias by Schumann, Liszt and Busoni, Liszt piano works and concertos, Grieg Concerto and Szymanowski Symphonie Concertante, Schubert Sonatas D. 958, 959, 960, Ravel complete piano works, Brahms Sonatas for clarinet and piano with Ralph Manno, Beethoven Cello Sonatas with Guido Schiefen, Das Lied von der Erde (version for chamber orchestra). *Honours:* prizewinner at numerous competitions, including Viña del Mar, Tokyo, Ferruccio Busoni, Bolzano, Beethoven Competition, Vienna, First Prize, Int. Piano Competition, Montevideo. *Current Management:* c/o EAS Musikmanagement GmbH, Kastanienallee 34, 14050 Berlin, Germany. *Telephone:* (30) 20076409. *Fax:* (30) 20076410. *E-mail:* andreea.butucariu@eas-musikmanagement.com. *Website:* www.eas-musikmanagement.com.

PERLMAN, Itzhak; Israeli violinist and conductor; b. 31 Aug. 1945, Tel-Aviv; s. of Chaim Perlman and Shoshana Perlman; m. Toby Lynn Friedlander 1967; two s. three d. *Education:* Shulamit High School, Tel-Aviv, Tel-Aviv Acad. of Music and Juilliard School, USA, studied with Ivan Galamian and Dorothy De Lay. *Career:* gave recitals on radio at the age of 10; went to USA 1958; first recital at Carnegie Hall 1963; has played with maj. American orchestras 1964–; has toured Europe regularly and played with maj. European orchestras, including Berlin Philharmonic, Concertgebouw Orchestra, London Philharmonic, English Chamber Orchestra; debut in UK with London Symphony Orchestra 1968; toured Poland, Hungary, Far East; played with Israel Philharmonic Orchestra in fmr Soviet Union; appearances at Israel Festival and most European Festivals; Music Advisor, St Louis Symphony 2002–04; Prin. Guest Conductor Detroit Symphony Orchestra 2001–05; Dorothy Richard Starling Foundation Chair, Juilliard School; numerous recordings. *Honours:* Hon. DMus (Univ. of S Carolina) 1982; Dr hc (Yale, Harvard and Yeshivah Univs); several Grammy awards, four Emmy Awards, Medal of Liberty (USA) 1986, EMI Artist of the Year 1995, Royal Philharmonic Soc. Gold Medal 1996, Nat. Medal of Arts (USA) 2000, Kennedy Center Honor, John F. Kennedy Center for the Performing Arts 2003, Grammy Lifetime Achievement Award 2008, Presidential Medal of Freedom 2015. *Current Management:* IMG Artists, Carnegie Hall Tower, 152 West 57th Street, 5th Floor, New York, NY 10019, USA. *Telephone:* (212) 994-3547. *E-mail:* dlai@imgartists.com. *Website:* www.itzhakperlman.com.

PERLMAN, Navah, BA; American pianist; b. 1970. *Education:* studied with Ronit Lowenthal, with Dorothy DeLay at Juilliard, Brown University. *Career:* season 1999–2000 with St Paul Chamber Orchestra, Nashville SO, Philadelphia Orchestra, Pittsburgh SO and Fort Worth Chamber Orchestras; European debut at Ruhr Festival, Bochum, 1999; further engagements with the Barcelona Symphony, Israel Philharmonic, New Japan PO, and National Orchestra of Mexico; recital and concert appearances with Kurt Nikkainen (violin) and Zuill Bailey (cello), including Kennedy Center, Metropolitan Museum, and Ravinia Festival; Beethoven's Triple Concerto throughout USA. *Current Management:* Martha Bonta, IMG Artists, Carnegie Hall Tower, 152 West 57th Street, Fifth Floor, New York, NY 10019, USA. *Telephone:* (212) 994-3500. *Fax:* (212) 994-3550.

PERLONGO, Daniel, MM; American composer; b. 23 Sept. 1942, Gaastra, MI. *Education:* Univ. of Michigan with Leslie Bassett and Ross Lee Finney, Academia di Santa Cecilia, Rome with Goffredo Petrassi. *Career:* Resident, American Acad. in Rome 1970–72; Prof. of Composition and Theory, Indiana Univ. of Pennsylvania 1980–. *Compositions include:* Piano Sonata 1966, Myriad for orchestra 1968, Intervals for string trio 1968, Missa Brevis 1968, Movement in Brass for 12 instruments 1969, Changes for wind ensemble 1970, Ephemeron for orchestra 1972, Variations for chamber orchestra 1973, Voyage for chamber orchestra 1975, two String Quartets 1973, 1983, Ricercar for oboe, clarinet and bassoon 1978, A Day at Xochimiloo for wind quintet and piano 1987, Lake Breezes for chamber orchestra 1990, Piano Concerto 1992, Arcadian Suite for horn and harp 1993, Three Songs for chorus 1994, Shortcut from Bratislava for orchestra 1994, Two Movements for orchestra 1995, Sunburst for clarinet and orchestra 1995. *Honours:* NEA Fellowships 1980, 1995.

PERRAGUIN, Hélène; French singer (mezzo-soprano); b. 7 Sept. 1963, Tours. *Career:* Paris Opéra-Comique from 1986 in Die Zauberflöte and Suor Angelica; Season 1988–89 in Massenet's Amadis at St Etienne; Wagner's Ring at the Théâtre du Châtelet, Paris and The Love for Three Oranges at Aix-en-Provence; Opéra Bastille, Paris, 1991 as Pauline in The Queen of Spades; Sang Carmen for Opéra de Lyon, 1996; Leonore in La Favorite at Metz, 1993; Other roles include Mozart's Cherubino and Dorabella; Siebel in Faust and Ursula in Béatrice et Bénédict by Berlioz. *Current Management:* c/o Agence Artistique Thérèse Cédelle, Boulevard Malesherbes 78, 75008 Paris, France. *Telephone:* 1-49-53-00-02. *Fax:* 1-45-63-70-23. *E-mail:* Agence.Cedelle@ wanadoo.fr.

PERRETT, Danielle Gillian, MMus, ILTM; British musician and teacher; b. 2 July 1958, London, England; m. *Education:* RCM Junior Department, Exeter Univ., London Univ. *Career:* musicianship and harp teacher, RCM Junior Department 1980–; debut, Purcell Room 1983; asst examiner, Trinity Coll. London 1988–; harp coach, Kent County Youth Orchestra 1985–; head of harp studies, London Coll. of Music 1996–; Mozart flute and harp concerto with Halstead, Brown, Hanover Band, Wigmore Hall 2001; performances at World Harp Congress, Prague 1999, Geneva 2002; broadcast for BBC World Service 2003; mem. Musicians' Union, Incorporated Soc. of Musicians, FITPRO, United Kingdom Harp Asscn, Clarsach Soc. *Compositions:* After Debussy, House Music, Lever Harp 2000, A Patchwork Suite, Technical Development for Harpists, Lift off for Harp (with David Gough). *Recordings:* Dussek and the Harp 1993, The Complete Chamber Music and Songs 1996, The Alabaster Box, Elis Pehkonen 2001, Tranquil Haven 2003. *Publications:* harp articles in UK Harp Association Magazine, reviews for BBC Music Magazine, features for World Harp Congress Review, magazines of Victorian Harp Society, South Australian Harp Society, Trinity College, London, Harp Syllabuses; contrib. to Incorporated Society of Musicians Music Journal, Clarsach Society London Branch Publications. *Honours:* Associated Board Sheila Mossman Prize 1974, Clothworkers Company Thomas Aitchison Trust Fund Award 1975, Henry and Lily Davis Trust, Arts Council Award 1982, Royal Overseas Harp Prize 1983, Music for small groups, Arts Council Award 1991, Freedom of Worshipful Company of Musicians 2003. *Current Management:* c/o J. Audrey Ellison International Artists' Management, 135 Stevenage Road, Fulham, London, SW6 6PB, England. *Telephone:* (20) 7381-9751. *Fax:* (20) 7381-2406. *E-mail:* audrey@ellison-intl.freeserve.co.uk. *Website:* www.ellison-intl .freeserve.co.uk; www.danielleperrett.co.uk.

PERRIERS, Danièle; French singer (soprano); b. 24 June 1945, Beaumont-le-Roger, Eure. *Education:* studied in Paris with Janine Micheau, Roger Bourdin and Fanelu Revoil. *Career:* debut in Marseille, 1968, as Sophie in Werther; has appeared in France at the Paris Opéra and the Opéra-Comique, and in Nice, Bordeaux, Lyon, Rouen, Toulouse and Strasbourg; also engaged at the Grand Théâtre de la Monnaie, Brussels, and in Liège and Monte Carlo; Glyndebourne Festival 1972–73 and 1976, as Despina and Blondchen; widely known in the Coloratura and light lyrical repertory and in operettas; sang also in works by Bizet, Boieldieu, Lecocq, Offenbach, Rossini and Richard Strauss. *Recordings:* Les Brigands by Offenbach; Die Entführung, Glyndebourne 1972; L'Amant jaloux by Grétry.

PERRY, Douglas R.; American singer (tenor); b. 19 Jan. 1945, Buffalo, NY. *Career:* sang at the New York City Opera from 1970 with his debut as Mozart's Basilio, and at Santa Fe Festival from 1971, notably in the US premieres of Reimann's Melusine in 1972 and Weir's A Night at the Chinese Opera in 1989; sang in the premieres of Glass's Satyagraha at Stuttgart in 1980 and The

Voyage at the Metropolitan in 1992; other modern repertory has included Menotti's Tamu Tamu at Chicago in 1973 and Bernstein's A Quiet Place at Houston in 1983; has also sung Rameau's Platée, M. Triquet in Eugene Onegin and Scaramuccio in Ariadne auf Naxos; sang Quint in The Turn of the Screw at Montreal, 1996; Orlofsky in Die Fledermaus at Miami, 1998. *Recordings:* Satyagraha, A Quiet Place.

PERRY, Elisabeth; British violinist; b. 1955, England. *Education:* Menuhin School, studied with Dorothy DeLay and Oscar Shumsky at Juilliard. *Career:* debut at South Bank, London, 1978; concerts in Cincinnati, Florida, Chicago, Colorado and San Francisco and showings at Carnegie Hall with Alexander Schneider; Bartók's Second Concerto in Chicago; further engagements in France, Switzerland, Italy and Germany; Leader of Deutsche Kammerakademie, 1987; concerts in Sviatoslav Richter's Festival of British Music at Moscow and Leningrad, 1987; US premiere of Schnittke's Quasi una Fantasia at Alice Tully Hall and the Berg Chamber Concerto at QEH under Lionel Friend; recital tour of New Zealand, 1990, and the Berg Violin Concerto in London; plays a Giovanni Grancini Violin on loan from Yehudi Menuhin. *Recordings include:* Bach's Double Concerto, with Menuhin; Kirschner's Duo for Violin and Piano. *Honours:* winner Concert Artists' Guild Competition, New York.

PERRY, Eugene; American singer (baritone); b. 20 Dec. 1955, Nashville, TN; m. Jessica Smith Perry; one s. *Education:* studied in New York. *Career:* debut as St Ignatius in Four Saints in Three Acts by Virgil Thomson, with the Opera Ensemble of New York 1986; sang Tarj in premiere of Under the Double Moon, by Anthony Davis, St Louis 1989; Don Giovanni in Peter Sellars' production of Mozart's opera at Purchase and elsewhere; European debut as Alidoro in La Cenerentola, Nice 1989; has sung Shiskov in US stage premiere of From the House of the Dead and as Stolzius in Die Soldaten by Zimmermann, New York City Opera; appeared as the Devil in Dvořák's Devil and Kate at St Louis, Théâtre de la Monnaie, Brussels, as Mamoud in premiere of The Death of Klinghoffer by John Adams, Mercutio in Cavalli's Calisto, in Glass' Sound of a Voice, Hotel of Dreams, Waiting for the Barbarians. *Recordings include:* Video of Don Giovanni; The Death of Klinghoffer. *Honours:* George London Award from National Institute of Music Theater 1986. *Current Management:* c/o Organisation Internationale Artistique, 16 avenue Franklin D. Roosevelt, 75008 Paris, France. *Telephone:* 1-42-25-58-34. *Fax:* 1-42-25-64-97. *E-mail:* oia@oia-poilve.com. *Website:* www.oia-poilve.com.

PERRY, Herbert; American singer (baritone); b. 1955, Nashville, TN. *Education:* studied in Texas and Arizona. *Career:* sang at the Houston and St Louis Operas from 1984; Sang at the Spoleto Festival at Charleston in 1987 as Citheron in Rameau's Platée, at Pepsico Summerfare in 1989 as Leporello in Don Giovanni, at Chicago Opera, Nice and Santa Fe in 1991 in I Puritani, as Mozart's Figaro and as Masetto, and sang Leporello at Toronto in 1992; Sang Mozart's Don Alfonso at Toronto, 1995; Season 1999–2000 in Weill's Die Burgschaft, at Charleston, and the premiere of In the Penal Colony by Philip Glass, for Seattle Opera. *Recordings include:* Video of Don Giovanni, in the production by Peter Sellars. *Current Management:* Pinnacle Arts: Miller Division, 889 Ninth Avenue, 2nd Floor, New York, NY 10019, USA. *Telephone:* (212) 397-7911. *Fax:* (212) 397-7920. *E-mail:* jmiller@pinnaclearts.com. *Website:* www.pinnaclearts.com.

PERRY, Janet, BMus; American singer (soprano); b. 27 Dec. 1947, Minneapolis, Minnesota; m. Alexander Malta. *Education:* Curtis Institute, Philadelphia, with Euphemia Gregory. *Career:* debut Linz 1969, as Zerlina in Don Giovanni; appearances in Munich and Cologne as Norina (Don Pasquale), Adina (L'Elisir d'amore), Blondchen (Die Entführung), Zerbinetta (Ariadne auf Naxos) and Olympia (Les Contes d'Hoffmann); guest engagements in Vienna, Frankfurt, Stuttgart and at the Aix-en-Provence Festival; Glyndebourne 1977, as Aminta in Die schweigsame Frau; numerous opera and operetta films for German television; Salzburg Festival; Sang Zerbinetta in Ariadne auf Naxos, RAI Turin, 1989; Violetta at the 1990 Martina Franca Festival; Season 1992 as Gluck's Eurydice at Bonn and Cleopatra in Giulio Cesare at the Halle Handel Festival. *Recordings:* Papagena in Die Zauberflöte, conducted by Karajan; Falstaff, Der Rosenkavalier, Beethoven's Ninth, Bruckner Te Deum; Nannetta in Falstaff; Egk's Peer Gynt. *E-mail:* janetperry@libero.it (office). *Website:* www.janetperry.com.

PERRY, Jennifer; singer (soprano); b. 1969, Rotterdam, The Netherlands. *Education:* Royal Acad. and the Guildhall School of Music, London. *Career:* concerts include Handel's Dixit Dominus on tour with the Tallis Scholars and regular appearances with other leading choral societies; other repertoire includes Mozart's C minor Mass and songs by Schubert and Duparc; operatic roles include Despina, Susanna and First Lady.

PERSSON, Miah; Swedish singer (soprano); b. Örnsköldsvik. *Education:* Conservatoire Kulturama, Opera Studio 67, Univ. Coll. of Opera, Stockholm. *Career:* appearances include Aix-en-Provence Festival, Berlin State Opera, Théâtre de la Monnaie, Brussels, Frankfurt Opera, New Zealand Festival, National Opera, Paris, Théâtre des Champs-Elysées, Paris, Opéra du Rhin, Strasbourg, Vienna Staatsoper, Stockholm Opera, San Francisco Opera, Los Angeles Opera; has performed under Vladimir Ashkenazy, Daniel Barenboim, Ivor Bolton, Pierre Boulez, Sir John Eliot Gardiner, Nikolaus Harnoncourt, Philippe Herreweghe, René Jacobs and Marc Minkowski; concert debut Salzburg Festival 2003 with the Vienna Philharmonic, opera debut in Salzburg as Sophie/Rosenkavalier under Semyon Bychkov 2004; debut Royal Opera House Covent Garden as Susanna in La Nozze di Figaro

and Glyndebourne Festival as Fiordiligi in Così fan tutte 2006; Fiodiligi in Cosi fan tutte, Met, New York 2010, Bayerische Staatsoper 2011–12; concerts and recitals include London (BBC Proms, Gabrieli Consort and London Players, Royal Festival Hall, Wigmore Hall), Amsterdam, Brussels, Dijon, Lille, Lucerne, New York (Carnegie Hall), Paris, Salzburg, Stockholm, Strasbourg, and Verbier Festival. *Recordings include:* Soul & Landscape 2003, Handel's Rinaldo (as Almirena), Haydn's Die Jahreszeiten, Bach: Magnificat, John Fernström's Songs of the Sea, Mozart: Un moto di gioia: Opera and Concert Arias 2006, Schumann Portraits 2011, Songs by Schubert, Grieg and Sibelius 2012. *Current Management:* Opern-Agentur, Tal 15, 80331 Munich, Germany. *Telephone:* (89) 29161661. *Fax:* (89) 29161667. *E-mail:* kursidem@opern-agentur.com. *Website:* www.opern-agentur.com.

PERTIS, Attila; Hungarian pianist; b. 5 March 1966, Budapest; m. Monika Egri 1991. *Education:* Bartók Conservatory, Budapest, Liszt Music Acad., Budapest and Music Acad., Vienna. *Career:* performances at Hungarian Days, London 1989, and Musikverein, Vienna 1991; appeared at Budapest Spring Festival and Carinthian Summer Festival, Austria; with Monika Egri founded Egri and Pertis Piano Duo 1980s; television and radio recordings, Hungary, Austria, Italy. *Recordings include:* albums: Journey Around the World 1995, Liszt: Opera Fantasies and Transcriptions for two pianos 1997–98. *Publications:* contrib. to Die Presse, Kronen Zeitung, Piano Journal. *Current Management:* Annart Artists Management, Barkács utca 7, 1221 Budapest, Hungary; J. A. Ellison, International Artists Management, 135 Stevenage Road, Fulham, London, SW6 6PB, England; Künstlermanagement Till Dönch, Weimarer Strasse 48, 1180 Vienna, Austria.

PERTUSI, Michele; Italian singer (bass); b. 1965, Parma. *Education:* studied in Parma with Carlo Bergonzi. *Career:* debut in Modena, as Silva in Ernani, 1984; appearances at Teatro Donizetti, Bergamo, Ravenna Festival and Teatro Comunale, Bologna; Teatro Regio, Parma, 1987–, notably as Dulcamara, 1992; Season 1992 as Mozart's Count at Orchestra Hall, Chicago, and Figaro at Florence; Sang Talbot in Maria Stuarda at Barcelona, Assur in Semiramide at Pesaro; other roles include Raimondo in Lucia di Lammermoor, Pagano in I Lombardi, and Rossini's Maometto; Sang Don Giovanni at Lausanne, 1996; Sang in Lucrezia Borgia at La Scala, 1998; Season 2000–01 as Rossini's Selim and Alidoro at Monte Carlo, Mahomet in Le Siège de Corinthe at Pesaro and Don Giovanni at Coruña; the Villiains in Hoffmann, and Alidoro, at Covent Garden, and the Berlioz Mephisto on London's South Bank; Don Alfonso at the Met and Guillaune Tell for the Vienna Staatsoper; London Proms, 2002. *Recordings include:* Mozart's Figaro, Assur, Alidoro, Silva, Lodovico in Otello; La Wally by Catalani. *Current Management:* c/o Atelier Musicale, Via Caselle 76, San Lazzaro di Savena 40068, Italy. *Telephone:* (51) 19984444. *Fax:* (51) 19984420. *E-mail:* info@ateliermusicale .com. *Website:* www.ateliermusicale.com.

PERUSKA, Jan; Czech violist; b. 1954. *Education:* studied in Prague with members of the Smetana Quartet. *Career:* violist with Stamic Quartet, Prague 1985–; performances at the Prague Young Artists and the Bratislava Music Festivals; tours to Spain, Austria, France, Switzerland, Germany and Eastern Europe; tour of the USA 1980, debut concerts in the UK at London and Birmingham, 1983; further British tours, 1985, 1987, 1988 (Warwick Arts Festival) and 1989 (20 concerts); gave the premiere of Helmut Eder's 3rd Quartet, 1986; season 1991–92 with visit to the Channel Islands (Festival of Czech Music), Netherlands, Finland, Austria and France, Edinburgh Festival and debut tours of Canada, Japan and Indonesia. *Recordings:* Shostakovich No. 13, Schnittke No. 4; Mozart K589 and K370; Dvořák, Martinů and Janáček complete quartets. *Honours:* (with members of Stamic Quartet): prizewinner, International Festival of Young Soloists, Bordeaux, 1977; winner, 1986 ORF (Austrian Radio) International String Quartet Competition (followed by live broadcast from the Salzburg Mozarteum); Academie Charles Cros Grand Prix du Disque, 1991, for Dvořák Quartets. *Current Management:* c/o Stamic Quartet, Henrik F. Lodding Svensk Konsertdirektion, Danska vägen 25 B, 41274, Gothenburg, Sweden. *Telephone:* (31) 83-00-95. *Fax:* (31) 40-80-11. *E-mail:* info@loddingkonsert.se. *Website:* www.loddingkonsert.se.

PERUSSO, Mario; Argentine conductor and composer; b. 16 Sept. 1936, Buenos Aires. *Career:* Deputy Conductor, Teatro Colón, Buenos Aires, giving his own opera Escorial 1989 and Puccini's La Rondine 1990; conducted Otello and Turandot at La Plata 1990–91; conducted Tosca at La Plata 1995. *Compositions include:* La Voz del Silencio (one-act opera) 1969, Escorial (one-act opera) 1989, Sor Juana Ines de la Cruz 1991–92, Guayaquil (lyric drama) 1993.

PERUZZI, Elio; Italian clarinettist and teacher; b. 14 Oct. 1927, Malcesine, Verona. *Education:* Canetti Inst., Vicenza and B. Marcello Conservatory, Venice. *Career:* debut at Olympic Theatre, Vicenza; soloist with Virtuosi di Roma, Solisti Veneti, Solisti di Milano 1950–; string quartets of Milan, Ostrava, Brno, Prague and Zagreb, and with Brno Philharmonic Orchestra, Bozen Orchestra, Padua Chamber Orchestra, Filarmonico di Bologna 1960–; Founder Bartók Trio (clarinet, violin, piano) 1958, Piccola Camerata Italian (mediaeval, Renaissance and Baroque instruments) 1967; performances in Europe, USA, South America, fmr USSR, Canada 1960–; Vice-Pres. Fondazione Musicale Omizzolo-Peruzzi, Centro Culturale Musicale Silvio Omizzolo; mem. Accad. Tiberina, Rome. *Recordings:* Mozart Clarinet Quintet with Moravian Quartet, 18th and 19th century music with Virtuosi di Roma. *Publications:* Esercizi e Studi Method for Recorder 1972, Sonatas by Robert Valentine for two recorders (ed.) 1973, G. Rossini Variations for clarinet and orchestra (ed.) 1978, A. Ponchielli's Il Convegno for two clarinets and piano (ed.) 1988. *Honours:* Il sigillo della Città di Padova. *Address:* Fondazione Musicale Omizzolo-Peruzzi, Via Dosso Faiti 4, 35141 Padua, Italy. *E-mail:* info@fondazioneomizzoloperuzzi.it.

PEŠEK, Libor; Czech conductor; *Chief Conductor, Czech National Symphony Orchestra;* b. 22 June 1933, Prague. *Education:* Prague Acad. of Musical Arts, studied conducting with Karel Ancerl, Vaclav Neumann and Václav Smetáček. *Career:* f. Prague Chamber Harmony 1958; Chief Conductor, Slovak Philharmonic 1980–81; Conductor-in-Residence, Czech Philharmonic Orchestra 1982–90, Germany tour 1998; Prin. Conductor and Artistic Adviser, Royal Liverpool Philharmonic Orchestra 1982–97, Conductor Laureate 1997–; Visiting Conductor, Prague Symphony Orchestra 1989–; Pres. Prague Spring Festival 1994–; Chief Conductor, Czech Nat. Symphony Orchestra 2007–; mem. Bd of Supervisors OPS Prague European City of Culture 1999–; has conducted Royal Liverpool Philharmonic Orchestra, Prague Spring Festival 2000; has conducted Philharmonia, London Symphony, Royal Philharmonic, BBC Philharmonic, Hallé, Oslo Philharmonic, Danish Radio, Los Angeles Philharmonic and Cincinnati, Dallas, Minnesota, Pittsburgh, Cleveland, Montreal, Indianapolis and Philadelphia orchestras, Orchestra of La Scala, Milan and Orchestre de Paris; charity concerts after floods in Czech Repub. 2002. *Recordings include:* works by Dvořák, Suk, Janáček, Martinů and Britten. *Honours:* Hon. mem. Preston Univ. 1997; Hon. Fellow, Univ. of Cen. Lancashire 1997; Hon. KBE; Classic Prize for Extraordinary Merit in Musical Culture (Czech Repub.) 1997, Journal Harmonie Lifelong Contrib. to Czech Culture 2002. *Current Management:* IMG Artists, The Light Box, 111 Power Road, London, W4 5PY, England. *Telephone:* (20) 7957-5800. *Fax:* (20) 7957-5801. *E-mail:* ajamieson@imgartists.com. *Website:* imgartists.com/artist/libor_peek.

PESKO, Zoltan, DipMus; composer and conductor; b. 15 Feb. 1937, Budapest, Hungary. *Education:* Liszt Ferenc Music Acad., Budapest, Accademia di S Cecilia, Rome, Italy with Goffredo Petrassi, studied with Pierre Boulez in Basel, Switzerland and Franco Ferrara in Rome, Italy. *Career:* debut as composer and conductor on Hungarian TV 1960; work with Hungarian television 1960–63; Asst Conductor to Lorin Maazel, West Berlin Opera and Radio Orchestra, Berlin 1969–73; performances at Teatro alla Scala 1970; Prof., Hochschule, Berlin 1971–74; Chief Conductor, Teatro Communale, Bologna, Italy 1974–; conducted Wagner's Ring at Turin 1988; concert performance of Mussorgsky's Salammbô at the 1989 Holland Festival; Teatro Lirico Milan 1990, premiere of Blimunda by Azio Corghi; has also led the premieres of Bussotti's Il Catalogo è questo 1960, Donatoni's Voci 1974, In Cauda 1982, Tema 1982, Atem 1985, Jolivet's Bogomile suite 1982, Dies by Wolfgang Rihm 1985, Fünf Geistliche Lieder von Bach by Dieter Schnebel 1985; season 1992 with Der fliegende Holländer at Naples and Le Grand Macabre at Zürich; conducted Fidelio at Rome 1996. *Compositions:* Tension for string quartet 1967, Trasformazioni 1968, Bildinis einer Heligen for soprano, children's choir and chamber ensemble 1969, Jelek 1974. *Honours:* Academia di S Cecilia, Rome Prize for Composition 1966, Italian Critics Premio Discografico for recording debut as conductor 1973. *Address:* 40125 Bologna, Teatro Communale, Largo Respighi, Italy.

PESKOVA, Inna; Russian violist; b. 1960, Moscow. *Education:* Moscow Conservatoire with Alexei Shislov. *Career:* co-founder, Glazunov Quartet 1985; many concerts in Russia and appearances in Greece, Poland, Belgium, Germany, Italy; works by Beethoven and Schumann at Beethoven Haus in Bonn; further engagements in Canada and The Netherlands; Teacher, Moscow State Conservatoire; Resident, Tchaikovsky Conservatoire; repertoire includes works by Borodin, Shostakovich, Tchaikovsky, in addition to standard works. *Recordings include:* albums of the six quartets of Glazunov. *Honours:* prizewinner Borodin Quartet and Shostakovich Chamber Music Competitions (with Glazunov Quartet).

PETCHERSKY, Alma; pianist; b. 1950, Argentina. *Education:* studied with Roberto Caamano in Buenos Aires, Maria Curcio in London and with Magda Tagliaferro and Bruno Seidlhofer of the Vienna Acad. *Career:* debut at Teatro Colón Buenos Aires with Bartók's 3rd Concerto; concert and broadcasting engagements in Russia, USA, Canada, Spain, Germany, Brazil, Czechoslovakia, Mexico and the Far East; London appearances at the Wigmore Hall. *Recordings:* works of the German, French and Russian schools, Latin-American and Spanish Romantic Composers; complete piano music by Ginastera.

PETERS, Roberta, DLitt, DMus; American singer (soprano); b. 4 May 1930, New York; d. of Sol Peterman and Ruth Peterman (née Hirsch); m. 1st Robert Merrill; m. 2nd Bertram Fields 1955; two s. *Education:* Elmira Coll., Ithaca Coll. *Career:* debut in Don Giovanni, Metropolitan Opera, New York 1950; has performed at numerous opera houses and festivals including Royal Opera House, Covent Garden, London, Vienna State Opera, Munich Opera and West Berlin Opera, Germany, Vienna and Salzburg, Austria, and Munich festivals, Bolshoi Theatre and Kirov Opera, USSR, now Russian Fed.; tours include USA, Russian Fed., Israel, People's Repub. of China, Japan, Taiwan, S Korea and Scandinavia; Chair. Nat. Inst. Music Theater 1991–; mem. Nat. Council of Arts 1992. *Publication:* A Début at the Met (co-author) 1967. *Honours:* Hon. LHD (Westminster) 1974, (Leligh) 1977; Hon. DMus (Colby) 1980; Hon. DFA (St John's) 1982; Hon. DLitt (New Rochelle) 1989; first American recipient of Bolshoi Medal; named Woman of the Year by Fed. of Women's Clubs 1964, Nat. Medal for Arts 1998. *Current Management:* c/o ICM, 825 Eighth Avenue,

New York, NY 10019, USA. *Telephone:* (212) 556-5600. *Fax:* (212) 556-5677. *Website:* www.icmtalent.com.

PETERSEN, Dennis; American singer (tenor); b. 11 May 1954, Iowa. *Education:* University of Iowa, San Francisco Opera's Merola Programme. *Career:* concert appearances in Mozart's Requiem, Messiah and Bach's Magnificat with St Paul Chamber Orchestra; Haydn's Theresienmesse at Spoleto Festival in Charleston; sang in Tippett's A Child of Our Time at Carnegie Hall and concerts with New Jersey and Baltimore Symphonies under David Zinman and Calgary Philharmonic under Mario Bernadi; engagements with San Francisco Opera from 1985, including: Don Quichotte, Captain in Wozzeck, Mime in Der Ring des Nibelungen, Die Meistersinger, and Tybald in Roméo et Juliette; Lyric Opera of Chicago debut in season 1992–93 as Mime in Das Rheingold under Zubin Mehta; sang Carlo in Donizetti's Il Duca d'Alba at Spoleto Festival; season 1994–95 at Chicago Lyric Opera in Boris Godunov, and Mime in Siegfried; Metropolitan Opera in Lady Macbeth of Mtsensk (debut) and as Bob Boles in Peter Grimes; season 1995–96 at San Francisco Opera in Anna Bolena and Madama Butterfly, Chicago Lyric Opera, Andrea Chénier – The Ring Cycle and Miami Opera in Ariadne auf Naxos; Leo in Antheil's Transatlantic for Minnesota Opera, 1998; sang Monostatos at the Met, 2000.

PETERSEN, Marlis; German singer (soprano); b. 1968, Sindelfingen, nr Stuttgart. *Education:* studied with Sylvia Geszty and at Hochschule für Musik, Stuttgart. *Career:* appearances at Nuremberg Opera from 1993, as Aennchen in Der Freischütz, Mozart's Blondchen, Oscar, Adele (Die Fledermaus), Rosina and The Queen of Night; concert engagements in Rome, Sydney, Athens, Porto, Madrid, Milan, Brussels, Amsterdam, Minneapolis and Boston; Deutsche Oper am Rhein from 1998, as Mozart's Serpetta and Susanna and Konstanze, Marie in La Fille du Régiment, Norina (Don Pasquale) and Ophelie (Hamlet); Season 2000–01 as Lulu at Kassel, Oscar at Bregenz, and Adele at the Opéra Bastille; Covent Garden debut as Zerbinetta in Ariadne auf Naxos 2002; sang Lulu at the Vienna Staatsoper 2002, Lulu at Hamburgische Staatsoper 2003, Braunfels' Die Vögel at Grand Théâtre de Genève; debut at the Met, New York as Adele in Fledermaus 2005, Lulu at Athens Megaron, Mozart's Il Re Pastore at Salzburg Festival and Adele and Lulu at Lyric Opera, Chicago, Kostanze Aix en Provence Festival; radio broadcasts on BR, SWR, HR, NDR, WDR, Rai. *Recordings:* Bach Cantatas (with Helmut Rilling), The Seasons (with René Jacobs). *Honours:* Prizewinner at Berlin and J. Offenbach Competitions 1990–91, Singer of the Year, Opernwelt 2004. *Current Management:* c/o Artists Management, 8044 Zürich, Switzerland. *Telephone:* (1) 8218957 (office). *Website:* www.marlis-petersen.de.

PETERSEN, Nils Holger, PhD; Danish composer; b. 27 April 1946, Copenhagen; m. Frances Ellen Hopenwasser 1971 (divorced 1989); one s. one d. *Education:* Univ. of Copenhagen, Univ. of Oslo, studied with Elisabeth Klein, Ib Norholm. *Career:* Minister of the Danish Church 1974–; Research Fellow, Univ. of Copenhagen 1990–, Research Lecturer 1995; External Prof. of Gregorian Studies, Univ. of Trondheim, Norway 1997–; freelance composer with compositions performed on radio and television, at Nordic Music Days and various concerts in many countries; mem. Danish Composers' Soc. , Nordic Soc. for Interart Studies (bd mem.). *Compositions:* piano and guitar solo works, Fool's Play (opera) 1970, Vigil for Thomas Beckett (liturgical opera) 1989, Church Cantatas 1971, 1974, 1976, Antiphony for Good Friday for nine instruments and voice, two wind quintets, solo works for violin, piano and organ, The Lauds of Queen Ingeborg (liturgical opera) 1991, Fragments of a Distant Voice electrophonic work (for the Danish State Radio) 1992, Concerto for clarinet in B and octet 1994, A Plain Song for piano. *Publications:* Kristendom i Musikken 1987, Liturgy and the Arts in the Middle Ages 1996; contrib. articles on theologico-musical aspects of the western culture in musical and theological papers. *Honours:* Hakon Borresen Memorial Prize 1993.

PETERSON, Claudette; American singer (soprano); b. 15 July 1953, Lakewood, OH. *Education:* San Francisco Conservatory. *Career:* sang at San Francisco Opera from 1975; Washington Opera 1979, as Blondchen in Die Entführung; Boston 1980, as Dunyasha in War and Peace; Chicago 1982, as Adele in Fledermaus; New York City Opera 1985–86, as Manon and Lisette in La Rondine; Sang Yum-Yum in The Mikado for Canadian Opera at Toronto 1986; other roles have included Lucia (Arizona Opera) and Gilda (Shreveport); further engagements at Buffalo, Houston, Geneva and Honolulu; frequent concert appearances. *Recordings include:* Musgrave's A Christmas Carol.

PETERSON, John Murray, BMus, MMus, PhD; Australian composer, university lecturer and author; *Lecturer, University of New South Wales;* b. 14 Jan. 1957, Wollongong, NSW. *Education:* Sydney Univ. *Career:* orchestral works performed by Queensland Philharmonic Orchestra, Sydney Youth Orchestra, Tasmanian Symphony Orchestra, West Australian Symphony Orchestra, New Zealand Symphony Orchestra and BBC Nat. Orchestra of Wales; choral works performed by Sydney Philharmonia and Royal Melbourne Philharmonic; broadcasts on ABC Classic FM and BBC Radio 3; participant, Australian Composers' Orchestral Forum 1998, 2001; currently Sr Lecturer, Univ. of New South Wales; mem. Australian Music Centre, Musicological Soc. of Australia. *Compositions:* Ex Tenebris Lux for orchestra 1989, At the Hawk's Well (music theatre piece) 1990, Walking On Glass for piano solo 1992, A Voice from the City for voice and small ensemble 1994, Eternity's Sun Rise for voice and piano 1995, Cyberia for orchestra 1996, The Still Point for cello and piano

1997, Diabolic Dance for violin and cello 1997, Rituals in Transfigured Time for orchestra 1997, Of Quiet Places for voice and guitar 1998, Port Kembla for orchestra 1998, Staring at the Sun for large mixed ensemble 1998, Drive for alto saxophone and piano 1998, Wired Life for mandolin duo 1999, Spike for cello duo 1999, At the Still Point for viola and piano 1999, Landmarks for brass quartet 1999, From Mountains to Sea for mixed sextet 1999, Moving Fast Through Autumn Light for solo mandolin 2000, Tallawarra for string quartet 2000, Encomium for clarinet and cello 2000, Illawarra Music for orchestra 2000, The Earth That Fire Touches for orchestra, soprano soloist and SATB chorus 2000, Five Islands for solo piano 2001, Nocturnalia for orchestra 2001, New England Dances for orchestra 2002, Liquid Steel for string quartet 2002, Woollungah Dances for three solo clarinets and orchestra 2002, The Velocity of Celebration for mixed ensemble 2003, Shadows and Light for soprano and tenor solo, SATB chorus, string orchestra and percussion 2004, Slowburn for mixed ensemble 2005, Mourning and the Light Within for SATB chorus and orchestra 2006, Songs from a Sunrise Land for female vocal quartet and string quartet 2006, Guilty Pleasures for mixed instrumental ensemble 2007, Under Sydney Skies for mandolin orchestra 2008, Sailing for the Sun for SATB Chorus 2008, Taking Flight for mixed ensemble 2009, Illawarra Dances for mandolin orchestra 2009, Waves for handbells and percussion ensemble 2009, Anniversary Music for orchestra 2009, These Guilty Pleasures for string quartet 2009, Race Against Time for cello and piano 2010, Impressions of Shanghai for solo piano 2010, Veni Creator Spiritus for unaccompanied SATB chorus 2010, Five Bagatelles for solo clarinet 2010, Ariadne's Thread for flute, clarinet and piano 2010, Dreams and Visions for mezzo-soprano, baritone, SATB chorus, string quartet and piano 2011, Anniversary Fanfare for brass and percussion 2012, Fabulous Beasts for clarinet, cello and piano 2012, Flames of Ancient Fires for wind band and taiko drums 2012, Double Entendre for string quartet and piano 2013, The Immortal Spark for double SATB chorus, string quintet, piano and percussion 2013, See, the Prismatic Colors Glisten for soprano, mezzo-soprano, clarinet, cello and vibraphone 2013, Shadow Dances for tenor saxophone and gamelan ensemble 2015, Emergence for mixed flute sextet 2015, String Quartet No. 3 2015, String Quartet No. 4 2015. *Publication:* The Music of Peter Sculthorpe 2014. *Honours:* semi-finalist, Masterprize, London 1997, 2001, Winner, Albert H. Maggs Composition Award 2005, winner, Australian Flute Festival Composition Competition 2015. *Address:* Music, School of the Arts and Media, University of New South Wales, Sydney, NSW 2052, Australia (office). *Telephone:* (2) 9385-4870 (office). *E-mail:* j.peterson@unsw.edu.au (office). *Website:* www.research.unsw.edu.au/people/dr-john-peterson (office).

PETERSONS, Ingus; Latvian singer (tenor); b. 12 Feb. 1959, Gulbene. *Education:* Rīga Acad. *Career:* debut in Rīga 1985 as Lensky in Eugene Onegin; sang at the Rīga Opera as the Duke of Mantua, Alfredo, Don Carlo and Nemorino; sang at Wexford Festival as Arturo in La Straniera by Bellini 1987, Opera North, Leeds as Edgardo in Lucia di Lammermoor 1988; sang Hoffmann at the Folksoperan Stockholm 1991; other roles have included Des Grieux in Massenet's Manon and the Italian Singer in Der Rosenkavalier; sang Rodolfo in La Bohème and Riccardo in Un ballo in maschera at Rīga Opera 2004. *Address:* c/o Latvian National Opera, Aspazijas Blvd 3, 1050 Rīga, Latvia. *Telephone:* 6707-3715. *Fax:* 6722-8930. *E-mail:* info@opera.lv. *Website:* www.opera.lv.

PETIBON, Patricia; French singer (soprano); b. 27 Feb. 1970, Montargis (Loiret). *Education:* Conservatoire Nat. Supérieur de Musique, Paris. *Career:* debut at Opéra Nat. de Paris In Rameau's Hippolyte et Aricie 1996; subsequently appeared in a variety of roles, including Blondchen in Mozart's Die Entführung aus dem Serail, Zerbinetta in Richard Strauss's Ariadne auf Naxos and Sophie in Der Rosenkavalier, Norina in Donizetti's Don Pasquale, Ophélie/Hamlet and Olympia in Offenbach's Les Contes d'Hoffmann, Serpetta/La Finta Giardiniera and the title role of Lakmé; has performed at Deutsche Oper am Rhein, the opera houses in Lyon and Nancy, the Théâtre du Capitôle de Toulouse and in Strasbourg, followed by debuts at Opéra Bastille in Paris in Massenet's Manon, Zürich Opera as Blondchen, and at Vienna State Opera as Olympia and Sophie; role debut as Susanna in Mozart's Le Nozze di FIgaro in Nancy 2006; appearances together with William Christie; has performed numerous Baroque opera roles, including Phani and Zima in Rameau's Les Indes Galantes at Opéra Bastille, Paris, Dalinda in Ariodante conducted by Marc Minkowski, at re-opening of Théâtre du Châtelet in Gluck's Orphée et Eurydice under Sir John Eliot Gardiner, Ariodante/Ginevra at Grand Théâtre de Genève; Giunia in Mozart's Lucio Silla at Theater an der Wien under Nikolaus Harnoncourt, with whom she first sang the role of Zelmira in Haydn's Armida at the Musikverein in Vienna and for a recording; has appeared under his baton as Mademoiselle Silberklang in Mozart's Der Schauspieldirektor in Salzburg and in Vienna's Musikverein, as Angelica in Haydn's Orlando Paladino at the Styriarte in Graz, and in Mozart's Schuldigkeit des Ersten Gebots at Theater an der Wien and at the Salzburg Mozartwoche; highlights of 2008/09 season have included a new production of Les Contes d'Hoffmann in Geneva, Alcina/Morgana at La Scala in Milano, Mitridate/Aspasia at Theater an der Wien and Così fan tutte/Despina at Salzburg Festival; sang Cunégonde/Candide at Wiener Konzerthaus and at Bremen Glocke; programme of arias by Mozart and Haydn at Vienna Musikverein and in Luxembourg, and in Versailles with Concerto Köln; sang Mozart's C-Minor Mass with Ivor Bolton as well as in a scenic recital with Susan Manoff and Olivier Py, both at the Salzburg Festvial 2009; frequent guest of conductors including Charles Dutoit for Carmina Burana at Théâtre des Champs-Elysées and Fabio Biondi for Caldara's La Passione di Gesù at Accad. di Santa Cecilia in Rome; appeared also in concert of Mozart arias together with Freiburg Baroque Orchestra at Wiener Musikverein; frequent recitals; appeared at Salzburg Festival together with Michael Schade and actor Tobias Moretti in a special Mozart programme of arias and selected texts for 250th anniversary year of Mozart 2006; solo recital Salzburg 2009; season 2009/10 was heard at Vienna's Musikverein as well as in Tokyo, Aix-en-Provence and Geneva; other highlights included a tour to Japan, debut as Lulu in Geneva, Carl Orff's Carmina Burana with Bavarian Symphony Orchestra under Daniel Harding in Munich, concerts with Venice Baroque Orchestra in Schwetzingen and Paris, and Mozart's Il Sogno di Scipione under Nikolaus Harnoncourt at Musikverein, Vienna; season ended with performance of the title role in new production of Lulu with Marc Albrecht and Vera Nemirova at the Salzburg Festival. *Recordings include:* Stratonice by Méhul, Sant'Alessio by Landi, Die Entführung, Acis and Galatea, Werther, Haydn's Armida, Les Fantaisies de Patricia Petibon, French Touch with French arias, solo recording with French baroque arias, Orlando Paladino with Nikolaus Harnoncourt, La Passione di Gesù with Fabio Biondi, album of arias by Gluck, Haydn and Mozart with Concerto Köln, album of Italian Baroque arias with Venice Baroque Orchestra. *Current Management:* c/o Künstleragentur Dr Raab & Dr Böhm, Plankengasse 7, 1010 Vienna, Austria. *Telephone:* (1) 512-05-01. *Fax:* (1) 512-77-43. *E-mail:* office@rbartists.at. *Website:* www.rbartists.at.

PETIT, Jean-Louis; French conductor, harpsichordist and composer; b. 20 Aug. 1937, Favrolles. *Education:* studied in Paris with Igor Markevitch, Pierre Boulez and Olivier Messiaen. *Career:* organized and conducted various ensembles in the regions of Champagne, 1958–63 and Picardy, 1964–70; performances on Radio and Television, tours of Europe and the USA; co-directed the Paris Summer Festival, 1972–77; founder mem. of contemporary music group, Musique Plus; Director of the Association musicale international d'echange (AMIE); Director of the Ecole Nationale de Musique of Ville d'Avray. *Compositions include:* Au-delà du signe for Orchestra; De Quelque Part Effondrée de l'homme for Quartet; Continuelles discontinués for Percussion; (82 Opus) transcriptions of early music. *Recordings include:* Works by Boismortier, Leclair, Marais, Rameau, Lully, Mouret, Devienne, Campra, Francoeur, Couperin and Mondonville; Roussel's Sinfonietta; Les Troqueurs by d'Auvergne; 2nd Symphonie of Gounod; Chamber Music by Saint-Saëns.

PETKOV, Dimiter; singer (bass); b. 5 March 1939, Sofia, Bulgaria; m. Anne-Lise Petkov. *Education:* Sofia Music Acad. with Christo Brambarov. *Career:* debut in Sofia as Ramfis and Zaccaria 1964; guest appearances, Glyndebourne Festival 1968, 1970, as Osmin and Gremin; Rostropovich Festival, Aldeburgh 1983; Earl's Court, London 1988; Birmingham Arena 1991; Daytona Festival with London Symphony Orchestra 1993; Arena di Verona as Philipp II 1969, as Zaccaria 1981, as Ramfis 1986, 1987; appearances at Vienna State Opera 1972–86, 1990, as Philip II, Ramfis, Boris, Khovansky, Mephisto; Madrid, Barcelona 1978–86, 1990; Chicago 1980; Bologna 1980–83, 1988; Catania, Palermo, Lecce 1981, 1984, 1986; La Scala, Milan 1981, 1984, 1989; Washington, DC 1982, 1984; Carnegie Hall, New York 1982, 1984, 1989; Zürich, Hamburg, Bonn 1984–85, 1990; Naples 1984, 1991; Rome 1987, 1992; Florence 1986–89, 1991; Monte Carlo 1986, 1989; Paris 1986, 1988; Deutsche Oper Berlin 1988–93; Dallas 1989, 1993; Opéra Bastille, Paris 1990–93; appeared with Berlin Philharmonic, London Symphony Orchestra, Nat. Symphony Washington, DC, Boston Symphony Orchestra at Tanglewood, Israel Philharmonic (Zubin Mehta) at Tel-Aviv, Montréal Symphony Orchestra, RAI Orchestras in Milan, Rome, Naples, Orchestre de Paris, Orchestre Nat. de France, Concertgebouw Amsterdam, St Petersburg Philharmonic Jerusalem Symphony, San Francisco Symphony; repertoire includes the Verdi bass roles, Philipp, Zaccaria, Fiesco, Bellini, Rossini, Donizetti, Mephisto by Gounod in French repertoire, all main roles in Russian repertoire, including Boris Godunov, Ivan Khovansky, Ivan Susanin; sang Shishkov in From the House of the Dead, Opéra du Rhin 1996; Old Prisoner in Lady Macbeth at Florence 1998; sang Ernani at Manaus. *Film appearance:* Werner Herzog's film, Fitzcarraldo. *Recordings:* Lady Macbeth of Mtsensk, Shostkovich 13th Symphony with London Symphony Orchestra, Aleko by Rachmaninov, Khovanshchina by Mussorgsky, Yolanta by Tchaikovsky, Mussorgsky cycles and Boris arias 1989, Boris Godunov 1992, Shostakovich Cycles 1993, Verdi Requiem 1994.

PETRE, Leonardus Josephus, BM; Belgian trumpet teacher; b. 27 Jan. 1943, Saint Triniden; m. Maes Arlette 1965, two s. *Education:* Univ. of Leuven, St Trinden en Hasselt, Conservatoire Royal, Brussels. *Career:* teacher of trumpet and several other brass instruments in several music schools; Prof. of Trumpet, Lemmens Inst., Leuven; many broadcasts as mem. of orchestra or soloist on Belgian and German radio and television; soloist at many classical concerts in Belgium, France, The Netherlands and Germany; trumpet soloist with The New Music Group and Collegium Instrumentale Brugense; mem., Xenakis Ensemble, The Netherlands; creator and leader of The Belgian Brass Quintet 2 1973–79; conductor of brass band and fanfare; specialist in playing Bach-trumpet (piccolo) and copies of very old trumpets; mem. Int. Trumpet Guild. *Recordings:* several cantatas of J. S. Bach with La Chapelle des Minimes, Brussels.

PETRENKO, Kirill; Russian conductor; *General Music Director, Bayerische Staatsoper*; b. 1972, Omsk. *Career:* debut as opera conductor 1995; Kapellmeister, Vienna Volksoper, Austria 1997–98; Gen. Music Dir Theater Meiningen, Germany 1999–2002; Gen. Music Dir Komische Oper Berlin

2002–07; Music Dir Bayerische Staatsoper (Bavarian State Opera), Munich 2013–; guest conductor of many opera companies and orchestras including: Maggio Musicale, Florence, State Opera Dresden, Vienna State Opera, Gran Teatre del Liceu, Barcelona, Opéra de la Bastille, Paris, Opéra de Lyon, Munich State Opera, Opera Frankfurt, Royal Opera House, Covent Garden, London, Berlin Philharmonic Orchestra, Duisburger Philharmonic Orchestra, Hamburg Philharmonic Orchestra, London Philharmonic Orchestra, Symphonieorchester des Bayerischen Rundfunks. *Recordings:* albums: Suk, Asrael Symphony 2004, Suk, A Summer's Tale 2006, Rachmaninov, Piano Concerto No. 2 2008, Suk, Tale of a Winter's Evening/The Ripening 2009. *Honours:* Int. Opera Awards Best Conductor 2014. *Current Management:* Michael Lewin Artists' Management International, Euroartists Künstlermanagement GmbH, Bastiengasse 27/1, 1180 Vienna, Austria. *Telephone:* (676) 375-19-63. *E-mail:* mertova@lewin-management.com. *Website:* www.lewin-management.com.

PETRENKO, Mikhail; Russian singer (bass); b. 1976, St Petersburg. *Education:* St Petersburg Conservatoire. *Career:* debut at Kirov Opera 1998, as Ivasenko in Prokofiev's Semyon Kotko; Young Singers' Acad. and Opera Co., Mariinsky Theatre, St Petersburg, 1998–; other roles have included Svetozar in Ruslan and Lyudmila, Mozart's Masetto, Fafner in Das Rheingold and the King of Egypt in Aida; sang Bermyata in Rimsky-Korsakov's The Snow Maiden, Amsterdam and London (concert performances) 1999–2000; Ivasenko in the British premiere of Semyon Kotko, with the Kirov Opera at Covent Garden 2000, Hunding in Die Walkure at Berliner Staatsoper 2004; appearances at Opéra Nat. de Paris, Metropolitan Opera (New York), La Scala (Milan), Bayerische Staatsoper, Royal Opera House, Covent Garden (London), Salzburg Festival, Aix en Provence Festival, BBC Proms, Royal Albert Hall, London. *Films:* Juan 2010. *Address:* c/o Mariinsky Theatre, 1 Theatre Square, St Petersburg, 190000, Russia (office). *E-mail:* post@mariinsky.ru (office). *Website:* www.mariinsky.ru/en (office).

PETRENKO, Vasily; Russian conductor; *Chief Conductor, Royal Liverpool Philharmonic Orchestra;* b. 7 July 1976, St Petersburg. *Education:* St Petersburg Capella Boys Music School, St Petersburg Conservatory, masterclasses with Ilya Musin, Mariss Jansons, Yuri Temirkanov, Esa-Pekka Salonen. *Career:* Resident Conductor St Petersburg State Opera and Ballet Theatre 1994–97; Prin. Guest Conductor St Petersburg State Orchestra of Classical and Contemporary Music 1998–; Chief Conductor State Acad. Orchestra of St Petersburg 2004–07; Chief Conductor Royal Liverpool Philharmonic Orchestra 2006–(18) (also Oslo Philharmonic); Prin. Conductor, Nat. Youth Orchestra of Great Britain 2009–13, European Union Youth Orchestra 2015–; Music Dir, Oslo Philharmonic 2013–; has also conducted St Petersburg Symphony and Chamber Orchestras, Royal Flemish Philharmonic Orchestra, Barcelona Symphony, Norrköping Symphony, BBC Nat. Orchestra of Wales, BBC Philharmonic, Swedish Radio Symphony, Netherlands Symphony, Spanish Nat. Orchestra, City of Birmingham Symphony, Moscow Philharmonic, Rotterdam Philharmonic, Orchestre National deu Capitole de Toulouse, London Symphony Orchestra, Netherlands Radio Philharmonic, Budapest Festival Orchestra, European Union Youth Orchestra, Russian Nat. Orchestra, Dallas Symphony, Cincinnati Symphony, Boston Symphony, St Louis Symphony, Los Angeles Philharmonic, San Francisco Symphony, Rundfunk-Sinfonieorchester Berlin, Oslo Philharmonic, Finnish Radio Symphony, Accad. Nazionale di Santa Cecilia, Roma, Czech Philharmonic, Chicago Symphony, NHK Symphony Tokyo, Sydney Symphony. *Recordings include:* symphonic works and concertos of Rachmaninov, Tchaikovsky, Liszt, Prokofiev, Elgar, Scriabin, Szymanowski, Higdon and Shostakovich Symphony cycle, including No. 10 (Gramophone Award for Best Orchestral Recording) 2011, Rachmaninov cycle, including Symphony No. 3 (ECHO Klassik Award for Newcomer of the Year/Conductor) 2012. *Honours:* Dr hc (Liverpool) 2009, (Liverpool Hope) 2009; First Prize, Shostakovich Choral Conducting Competition, St Petersburg 1997, Second Prize, Prokofiev Conducting Competition, St Petersburg 2003, First Prize, Cadaques Int. Conducting Competition, Spain 2004, Gramophone Awards for Best Young Artist 2007, for Best Orchestral Recording (for Tchaikovsky's Manfred Symphony) 2009, Classic BRIT Award for Best Male Artist 2012. *Current Management:* c/o Thomas Walton, IMG Artists, The Light Box, 111 Power Road, London, W4 5PY, England. *Telephone:* (20) 7957-5800. *Fax:* (20) 7957-5801. *E-mail:* aclarke@imgartists.com. *Website:* www.imgartists.com. *Address:* Royal Liverpool Philharmonic Orchestra, Philharmonic Hall, Hope Street, Liverpool, L1 9BP, England (office). *Telephone:* (151) 210-2895 (office). *Fax:* (151) 210-2902 (office). *Website:* www.liverpoolphil.com (office).

PETRI, Michala; Danish musician (recorder player); b. 7 July 1958, Copenhagen; d. of Kanny Sambleben and Hanne Petri; m. Lars Hannibal 1992 (divorced 2010); two d. *Education:* Staatliche Hochschule für Musik und Theater, Hannover. *Career:* debut aged five, Danish Radio 1964; soloist with Orchestra Tivoli, Copenhagen 1969; over 4,000 concerts in Europe, USA, Japan, China, Korea, Mexico, Canada and Australia; numerous appearances at festivals, performances on TV and radio; performs frequently with orchestras worldwide, also as duo with lutenist and guitarist, Lars Hannibal; has inspired and initiated various contemporary compositions by Malcolm Arnold, Vagn Holmboe, Per Nørgård, Thomas Koppel, Daniel Boertz, Gary Kulesha, Stephen Stucky, Joan Albert Amargos, Chen Yi and others; mem. Presidium, UNICEF Denmark; Vice-Pres. Cancer Asscn (Denmark). *Recordings include:* more than 60 albums, including 12 with Academy of St Martin-in-the-Fields, Bach Sonatas and Handel Sonatas with Keith Jarrett, Vivaldi Concertos with Heinz Holliger, Henryk Szeryng, contemporary concerts with English Chamber Orchestra and Danish Nat. Symphony Orchestra, six albums with Lars Hannibal, albums with Chen Yue, Kremerata Baltica, Chinese Recorder Concertos, English Recorder Concertos, Uğis Praulinš: The Nightingale (ECHO Klassik Award for World Premiere Recording of the Year 2012) 2011, two albums with Danish Nat. Vocal Ensemble. *Publications:* ed. of several works for Wilhelm Hansen and Moeck; Sheet Music Now. *Honours:* Hon. Prof., Royal Danish Acad. of Music; Kt of the Dannebrog 1995, Order Kt of First Grade 2010; Jacob Gade Prize 1969, 1975, Critics' Prize of Honour 1976, Nording Radio Prize 1977, Niels Prize 1980, Tagea Brandts Prize 1980, Maarum Prize 1981, Schroder Prize 1982, Deutscher Schallplattenpreis 1997, 2002, Sonning Music Prize 2000, H. C. Lumbye Prize 2000, European Soloist Prize 'Pro Europa' 2005, Danish Music Award 2006, three ECHO Klassik Awards. *Current Management:* c/o Lars Hannibal, Borgergade 142, 3rd, 1300 Copenhagen K, Denmark. *Telephone:* 40-15-05-77. *E-mail:* hannibal@michalapetri.com. *Website:* www.ourrecordings.com. *Address:* Nordskraenten 3, 2980 Kokkedal, Denmark (office). *Telephone:* 26-13-58-77 (office). *E-mail:* mail@michalapetri.com (office). *Website:* www.michalapetri.com.

PETRIC, Ivo; Slovenian musician, composer and conductor; b. 16 June 1931, Ljubljana; two d. *Education:* Music Acad., Ljubljana. *Career:* debut, Piano Trio 1952; Conductor, Slavko Osterc Ensemble (for contemporary music) 1962–82; Ed.-in-Chief, Composers Editions 1970–2002; Artistic Dir Slovenian Philharmonic 1979–95. *Compositions:* orchestral music; concertos for various instruments; chamber music; sonatas for various instruments with piano, three symphonies 1954, 1957, 1960, six string quartets 1956–2004, Trumpet Concerto 1986, Dresden Concerto for Strings 1987, Trois Images 1973, Dialogues Entre Deux Violons 1975, Sonata for violin solo 1976, Jeux Concertants for Flute and Orchestra 1978, Toccata Concertante for Four Percussionists and Orchestra 1979, Gallus Metamorphoses 1992, Scottish Impressions 1994, The Song of Life 1995, The Four Seasons 1995, The Autumn Symphony 1996, MacPhadraig's Scottish Diaries (three) for piano 1996, 2002, 2010, Grohar's Impressions II 1998, Three Places in Scotland 2002, Autumn Concerto for violin and orchestra 2003, Integrals for Mirjam after Kosovel's Poetry 2004, Concertino doppio for flute, horn and strings 2007, Duo concertante for viola and accordion 2007, Sinfonietta giocosa for strings 2007, Fantasiana: sonata for solo viola 2008, The Picture of Dorian Gray 2008, Toccata 2008, Concerto No. 2 for orchestra 2009, Fantasia Concertante for viola and orchestra 2009, Tha Landscapes of Memories for orchestra 2010, The Games for voice and orchestra (poems by Vasko Popa) 2011, Harpsody for two harps 2012. *Recordings:* 12 albums of orchestral, chamber and solo music. *Honours:* Hon. mem. Slovenian Philharmonic 2008, Asscn of Slovenian Composers 2012; Slovene State Preseren Foundation Prize 1971, First Prize, Wieniawski International Composition Competition for Violin 1975, Ljubljana Prize for Artists 1977, Oscar Espla International Competition, First Prize 1984, Kozina Award for six string quartets 2001, Preseren Foundation Prize 2016. *Address:* Bilecanska 4, 1000 Ljubljana, Slovenia (home). *E-mail:* ivo_petric@t-2.net (home). *Website:* www.ivopetric.com.

PETRINI, Anna; Swedish musician (recorder); b. Stockholm. *Education:* Royal Music Univ., Amsterdam Conservatory, The Netherlands. *Career:* soloist and chamber musician; has performed at home and abroad at festivals and halls including Warsaw Autumn, ISCM World New Music Days, Other Minds Festival, Musica Electronic Nova, Bath Int. Music Festival, Östersjöfestivalen, Stockholm Early Music Festival, Nordic Music Days, Huddersfield Contemporary Music Festival and Tokyo Opera City Recital Hall; performances broadcast on nat. radio in the Netherlands, Italy, Poland, Australia and Sweden; mem. early music ensembles Trio Stravaganti and El Escorial and duets with singer Susanne Rydén and lutenist Karl Nyhlin. *Recordings include:* solo: Crepusculo: Works for the Paetzold Contrabass Recorder (Nutida Sound Prize for Best New Music Recording) 2012. *Address:* c/o dB Productions, PO Box 60 252, 21609 Malmö, Sweden (office). *Telephone:* 739904875. *E-mail:* annapetrini@tele2.se. *Website:* www.annapetrini.com.

PETRINSKY, Natascha; Austrian singer (mezzo-soprano); b. 1966, Vienna. *Education:* studied in Israel. *Career:* began 2007/08 season creating title role of Phaedra (Henze) at German State Opera, Berlin and La Monnaie, Brussels, followed, at same theatre, by world premiere of role of Hannah in Pierre Bartolomé's La Lumière Antigone; sang role of Varvara in Kát'á Kabanová at De Nederlandse Opera (Jacob Kreizberg/Willy Decker); performed title role of Phaedra at Maggio Musicale (with Roberto Abbado) 2008 and at Alte Oper, Frankfurt (with Michael Boder); future engagements include Venus in Tannhäuser at Teatro dell'Opera di Roma, Das Liede von der Erde with Jeffrey Tate at Auditorio RAI, Naples, Klytämnestra in Elektra at La Monnaie, Brussels, Gräfin Geschwitz in Lulu at La Scala and Theater an der Wien, and Amneris in Aida at Oper Leipzig. *Recordings:* Wagner and Strauss Scenes with Deborah Voigt (Bavarian Radio Orchestra with Richard Armstrong), Carmen, role of Mercedes (Bavarian State Opera Orchestra with Giuseppe Sinopoli), Ariadne auf Naxos, role of Dryade (Teatro San Carlos Orchestra under Gustav Kuhn), Der Ring, Das Rheingold and Götterdämmerung, role of Wellgunde and Walküre, role of Waltraute (Netherlands Philharmonic Orchestra under Hartmut Haenchen). *Current Management:* c/o Andrea De Amici, Agenzia De Amici, Via Lazzaro Palazzi 19, 20124 Milan, Italy. *Telephone:* (02) 29536569. *Fax:* (02) 29532914. *E-mail:* info@agamici.it. *Website:* www.agamici.it; www.nataschapetrinsky.com.

PETRO, Janos; conductor, music director and composer; b. 5 March 1937, Repceszemere, Hungary; m. 1959, one s. one d. *Education:* Acad. of Music,

Budapest. *Career:* debut as composer, Vienna 1959; opera and concerts in Budapest, Vienna, Berlin, Dublin, Bratislava, Frankfurt, Hamburg, Graz; broadcasts on Radio Budapest, Vienna Symphonic Record Register, Television Budapest and Vienna; mem. Musicians' Alliance, Budapest (pres.). *Recordings include:* Goldmark: Concerto for Violin and Orchestra; Mendelssohn: Concerto for Violin and Orchestra; Haydn: Scena di Berenice and Concert Arias; P. Karolyi; Epilogus; P. Karolyi: Consolatio; Bizet: Symphony C-major; Bizet: Suite L'Arlesienne; Beethoven: Egmont Overture; Liszt: Les Préludes; Haydn: Symphony No. 104. *Honours:* F. Liszt Prize for Conductor, Budapest 1983, World Young Composer Prize, Vienna 1959, State Prize, Budapest 1982. *Address:* c/o Austroconcert International, Gluckgasse 1, 1010 Vienna, Austria.

PETROFF-BEVIE, Barbara, DipMus; German singer (soprano) and academic; b. 2 June 1934, Hamburg; m. Joseph Petroff 1973, one s. one d. *Education:* Hochschule für Musik, Hamburg, Bern and Geneva Conservatories. *Career:* debut as Constanze in Entführung aus dem Serail, Stadttheater Luneberg 1959, and as Clarice in Haydn's Il mondo della luna, Stadttheater Bern 1960; main appearances include Árhus (Denmark), Bern and Geneva (Switzerland), The Hague (Netherlands), Royal Opera Ghent (Belgium), Linz (Austria), Kiel (Germany), Grand Theatre, Geneva; sang as Carolina in Il matrimonio segreto, Gilda in Rigoletto, Blondchen and Constanze in Entführung, Musetta, Sophie in Der Rosenkavalier, Ännchen in Freischütz, Susanna in Figaro, Despina in Così fan tutte, Adele in Die Fledermaus, Rosina in Barbiere di Siviglia and Adina in L'Elisir d'amore; operettas: Maritza in Gräfin Maritza and Evelyne in Graf von Luxemburg.

PETRONI, Luigi; Italian singer (tenor); b. 1970. *Career:* debut in Cimarosa's Il Matrimonio Segreto at Teatro Regio, Turin; appearances in Philip Glass' The Civil Wars, Don Giovanni, Demophoon, Manon Lescaut, Semiramide, L'heure espagnole, Salome, Guillaume Tell, I Quatro Rusteghi, Il Barbiere di Siviglia, La Gazza Ladra, L'Inganno Felice, Una Cosa Rara, Le nozze di Figaro, Boris Godunov, L'Amor Rende Sagace, Anna Bolena, Il Turco in Italia, L'Elisir d'Amore, Fra Diavolo, Mavra, Turandot, Carmina Burana, L'Avaro, L'Intrigo della Lettera, Il Tabarro, I Pagliacci, Il Signor Bruschino, La Cambiale di Matrimonio, Don Pasquale, as Egoldo in Matilde di Shabran, Ernesto in Ricciardo e Zoraide, Eliezer in Moise et Pharaon, Neaco in Les Martyrs, Ippia in Saffo, Clistene in Olimpiade, Lindoro in L'Italiana in Algheri; regular performances at Teatro dell'Opera, Rome, Rossini Opera Festival, Pesaro, Teatro Massimo Bellini, Catania, Teatro La Fenice, Venice, Teatro Comunale di Bologna and across Italy, also with New Israeli Opera, in Monte Carlo, Montpelier, Angèrs, Zurich, Toulouse, Tokyo, Amsterdam. *Recording:* Elena da Feltre. *Honours:* winner International Enrico Caruso Competition, International Voice Contest, Turin.

PETROV, Petar Konstantinov; Bulgarian composer and pianist; b. 23 June 1961, Stara Zagora. *Education:* Musical School, St Zagora, State Musical Academy, Sofia. *Career:* debut in New Bulgarian Music 1984; Manager and Pianist in Chilorch-choire, Sofia 1988–91; Honorary Professor of Counterpoint, Bulgarian State Academy 1990–93; Professor of Counterpoint and Composition in Music School, St Zagora; Composition Masterclass of Profesor Anatol Vieru-Rumenia 1993–95; many appearances as Chamber Pianist with Rosed Idealov–Clarinet 1990–97. *Compositions:* Sonata, partita for violin solo 1986, Concerto Piccolo for flute, violin and piano 1987, The Christian Convert, for organ 1989, Studies Nos 1–19, for various solo instruments 1989–99, Ricercare, for three instruments 1990, Dialogues with Mr Galiley, for chamber ensemble 1997, In Memorium, for piano 1997, Dewy concerto for clarinet and 3 key instruments 1997, 6 Mediations for chamber ensemble 1997, Symphony No. 5, alla bulgarese, for electronic instruments 1998, Symphony No. 6 'Because these we are' 1998, Second concerto for Violin (Viola) and Orchestra 1998, Phantoms in Viennese Forest, six commentaries for piano 1998, Concerto for Piano and Orchestra, 'In memory of Erik Satie' 1999. *Recordings:* Concerto for Violin and Orchestra No. 1 1987, Symphony No. 1, Lamento 1987, Symphony No. 2, Katarsis 1990, Concerto Piccolo IV 1994, Dialogues with the Silence 1994, Estampie 1994, Symphony No. 3, Momento 1994, Symphony No. 4, Dona nobis pacem 1995, Bach Studies for Clarinet, Viola and Piano 1995, Messages I 1997, Toccata for Piano 1997, Messages II 1999.

PETROV-STOYKOVICH, Marina, MA; pianist and academic; b. 27 Dec. 1960, Kiev, Ukraine. *Education:* Central Music School for Gifted Children, Belgrade, Central Music School for Gifted Children, Kiev, College of Music, Belgrade, Moscow Conservatoire, Belgrade Academy of Music. *Career:* debut in Belgrade 1969; recital pianist 1969–; first appearance on television and radio in Belgrade 1969; subsequently played in Kiev and Moscow; tours in Yugoslavia; has also played in Norway and in the UK at venues including London, Dartington Hall and Bristol 1990–; piano teacher in the UK. *Address:* 28B Caedmon Road, London, N7 6DH, England.

PETROVA, Petia; singer (mezzo-soprano); b. 1970, Sofia, Bulgaria. *Career:* many appearances in Bulgaria and Germany; in operas by Rossini, Il Barbiere di Siviglia, La Donna del lago and L'Italiana in Algeri; engagements with the Hamburg State Opera include Rossini's Rosina, Suzuki in Madama Butterfly and Mercédès in Carmen. *Honours:* winner competitions in Sofia and Barcelona, finalist Cardiff Singer of the World Competition 1999.

PETRUSHANSKY, Boris; pianist; b. 3 June 1949, Moscow, Russia. *Education:* Central School of Music, Moscow Conservatoire. *Career:* many concert tours of Russia and appearances in Italy, Hungary, the UK, Germany, France, Japan and Australasia; repertoire includes works by Beethoven, Brahms, Liszt, Prokofiev, Shostakovich, Schnittke, Gubaidulina; Prof., Academica

Pianistica, Italy. *Recordings include:* works by Schnittke, Gubaidulina. *Honours:* prizewinner in competitions at Leeds 1969, Moscow 1970, Munich 1971, Casagrande 1975.

PETRUTSHENKO, Natalia, PhD; pianist; b. 21 Aug. 1963, Ulan-Ude, Russia. *Education:* studied in Kemerovo, Music High School, Nikolayev, Ukraine, Tchaikovsky Moscow Conservatoire with Prof. Dorenski. *Career:* comprehensive repertoire with orchestra and solo; participant in Rachmaninov Int. Competition for Pianists, Moscow and Int. Competition for Young Performers, Japan 1993; guest performance tour to Japanese towns; numerous concerts in major cities in Russia, Ukraine, Belarus, the Baltic states, Bulgaria and Romania; Prof., Music High School, Kurgan, Russia 1994; soloist, District Philharmonic Soc., Nikolayev, Ukraine 1995; moved to Varna, Bulgaria 1996; European tour.

PETUKHOV, Mikhail; pianist; b. 24 April 1954, Varna, Bulgaria. *Education:* studied in Kiev and at Moscow Conservatoire with Tatiania Nikolayeva. *Career:* many concerts in Russia, Italy, Belgium, The Netherlands, Czechoslovakia and Germany; played with Royal Scottish Orchestra 1992, followed by Tchaikovsky First Concerto with City of Birmingham Symphony under Yuri Simonov; repertoire has also included works by Purcell, Ravel, Handel, Stravinsky, Mendelssohn, Schumann, Schoenberg and Ives; Prof. in Piano, Moscow Conservatoire. *Honours:* third prize J. S. Bach Competition, Leipzig 1972, Queen Elizabeth Competition, Brussels 1975.

PFAFF, Luca; Swiss conductor; b. 25 Aug. 1948, Olivone; m. Dominique Chanet 1986; two s. *Education:* Univ. of Basel, Conservatorio G. Verdi, Milan, Musikakademie, Austria, Accademia Santa Cecilia, Italy. *Career:* Perm. Conductor of chamber orchestra Santa Cecilia, Rome 1980–84; Musical Dir Orchestre Symphonique du Rhin 1986–96; Founder, Ensemble Alternance, Paris; regular guest conductor of various orchestras including Bayerischer Rundfunk, Bamberg, BBC, Philharmonique de Radio France, National or Broadcasting Orchestras of France, Spain, Belgium, Greece, Mexico, Argentina, Sweden, Switzerland and Finland, Philharmonics of Oslo, Bergen, Helsinki, Monte-Carlo, Tonhalle-Zürich, Gulbenkian-Lisbon, Maggio Fiorentino, RAI Orchestra, Turin; teaching positions at Univs of Vienna and Graz, Conservatoire National Superieur, Paris, also in Madrid and Lisbon. *Recordings:* numerous recordings including works of Mozart, Dusapin, Johann Strauss, Bartok, Sibelius. *Address:* 5, Quai du Maire Dietrich, 67000 Strasbourg, France. *E-mail:* lucapfaff@hotmail.com.

PFISTER, Daniel, DipMus; Swiss composer; b. 6 Nov. 1952, St Gallen. *Education:* teachers training coll., Konservatorium Winterthur, Musikhochschule Zürich, studied with Hans Ulrich Lehmann, Hochschule für Musik und darstellende Kunst in Wien with Prof. Alfred Uhl, Otmar Suitner. *Career:* freelance composer; private teacher for music theory composition and piano 1982–; mem. SMPV Schweizerischer Musikpaedagogischer Verband. *Compositions:* Saitenspiel for two guitars 1982, Concerto for string orchestra 1982–87, Aeon for soprano and piano 1983, Aeon for soprano and orchestra 1983–84, Canto for soprano or flute or saxophone 1985–88, Canto for soprano (flute), clarinet and vibraphone 1986, Neun und Zehne auf einen Streich for guitar 1988, Touches for flute, oboe, clarinet, bassoon, horn, trumpet, snare drum, gong, xilorimba, vibraphone, guitar, piano, violin, viola and cello 1988–89, Bruchstuecke aus Touches 1988, 880 un satiesme for any instrument 1988, 12 kleine Odien for flute and guitar 1987–89, Max and Moritz for reciter and guitar 1990–91.

PHARR, Rachel Elizabeth Caroline, BMus, MMus; American harpsichordist; b. 15 April 1957, Picayune, MS; m. Bernard Gerard Kolle 1989. *Education:* Univ. of Southwestern Louisiana, Lafayette, Aspen Music School, Aspen Festival, Arizona State Univ., Tempe, Banff Centre School of Fine Arts, Canada. *Career:* harpsichordist with Houston Baroque Ensemble 1983–87, with Texas Chamber Orchestra in Houston, TX 1985–87; numerous concerts, Banff Centre, Banff, Alberta, Canada 1987–89; performed at Aspen Music Festival 1981, Breckenridge Music Inst. 1982, 1983; featured soloist in Houston Harpsichord Soc. presentation of the entire J. S. Bach Well-Tempered Klavier for Bach Tercentenary 1985; New Music America concerts 1986; tours as solo harpsichordist 1986; with Liedermusik Ensemble 1987; harpsichord accompanist, Banff Centre 1988–89; radio performances, KLEF, Houston and WWNO, New Orleans; television performance, NBC-Channel 4, Denver.

PHIBBS, Joseph, MMus, DMA; British composer; b. 1974, London, England. *Education:* The Purcell School, Harrow, King's Coll., London, Cornell Univ., USA. *Career:* Asst Lecturer in Composition, King's Coll. London 1995–96, Teaching Asst 2010, Lecturer in Composition 2013–14; Teaching Asst, Cornell Univ., USA; Composition Teacher, Wells Cathedral School 2008–09; Composition Tutor, The Purcell School 2009–; Composer-in-Residence, Exon Singers Festival 2010; Composer-in-Residence, Presteigne Festival 2011; Tutor in Composition, Univ. of Cambridge 2014–15. *Compositions include:* orchestral works: Soiree (Winner, BBC Young Composer's Forum) 1996, Dreams of a Summer Night 2000, In Camera 2001, Lumina (for BBC's Last Night of the Proms) 2003, Shruti 2008, Towards Purcell 2012, Rivers to the Sea (British Composer Award (Orchestral Category) 2013) 2012, Partita 2016; choral works: Ave verum corpus (SATB) 2002, Rainland (SATB and wind orchestra) 2003, St Margaret's Carol (SATB) 2004, Tenebrae (SATB and orchestra) 2004, Gaudeamus (SSA/SATB) 2008, Salve Regina (SATB), Shadows of Sleep (SATB and piano) 2010, Carol: Lullay lullay thou lytil child (SATB) 2014, Choral Songs of Hommage (SATB and piano) 2016, Missa Brevis (SSA) 2016), Carol:

Modyr whyt as lily flowr (SATB) 2016; chamber orchestra works: Cayuga (for Faber Millennium Series) 2000; chamber works: Broken Sequence 1996, Char Fragments 1999, Trio Semplice 2000, Ritual Songs and Blessings (for London Spitalfields Festival) 2002, La noche arrolladora (for BBC Proms) 2002, The Canticle of the Rose 2005 (for Belcea Quartet/Lisa Milne), Personnages 2005, Flex (for City of London Festival) 2007, Agea (for Presteigne Festival) 2008, The Silence at the Song's End 2008, The Palace of the Winds 2009, From Shore to Shore 2010, On a Deserted Shore 2012, Moon Songs 2013, Night and Silence: scena from Shakespeare (for Uzerche Festival) 2014; String Quartet No. 1 (for Rye Festival) 2014, L'ombra e la luce (for Alwyn Festival) 2015, String Quartet No. 2 (for Presteigne Festival) 2015, Letters from Warsaw (for Hampstead Festival) 2015. *Honours:* Purcell Prize, King's Coll., London 1995, British Academy Award, King's Coll., London 1995, Sage Fellowship, Cornell Univ. 1997, Robbins Composition Prize, Cornell Univ. 1998, Blackmore Prize in Composition, Cornell Univ. 2001, Koussevitzky Foundation Award 2014. *E-mail:* infojosephphibbs@yahoo.co.uk (office). *Website:* www.josephphibbs .com.

PHILIP, Robert Marshall, MA, PhD, ARCM; British writer, broadcaster and academic (retd); b. 22 July 1945, Witney, Oxon., England; m. Susan Tomes 2004; two d. from previous m. *Education:* Royal Coll. of Music, London, Peterhouse, Cambridge, Univ. (now Wolfson) Coll., Cambridge. *Career:* Jr Research Fellow, Univ. Coll. Cambridge 1972–74; Producer, BBC TV, Open Univ. Dept 1976–99; Lecturer in Music, Open Univ. 2000–10; freelance music critic and broadcast talks. *Radio:* contrib. to BBC Radio 3 series: The Long Playing Era, The Developing Musician, Vintage Years, Wartime at the National Gallery, Record Review, CD Review; to BBC World Service series: Composer and Interpreter, Musical Yearbook. *Publications:* Early Recordings and Musical Style 1992, Performing Music in the Age of Recording 2004. *Honours:* Organ Scholarship, Peterhouse, Cambridge 1964, Visiting Research Fellowship, Open Univ. 1995–98; Deems Taylor Award, American Soc. of Composers, Authors and Publrs (ASCAP) 1992. *Address:* 180 South Park Road, London, SW19 8TA, England. *E-mail:* robert.philip@lineone.net.

PHILIPPE, Michel; French singer (bass-baritone); b. 1943, Pau. *Education:* Paris Conservatoire. *Career:* sang at the Paris Opéra from 1971; appearances at the Orange and Aix-en-Provence Festivals, Hamburg Staatsoper, Royal Opera Stockholm, Geneva, Madrid and Rio de Janeiro; Chorèbe and Panthée in Les Troyens at Montréal 1993; other roles have included Rossini's Figaro, Marcello, Scarpia, Mozart's Count, Don Giovanni, Valentin in Faust and Iago. *Honours:* winner Voix et Musique Concours, Paris 1971.

PHILIPS, Daniel; violinist; b. 1960, USA. *Career:* recitalist at Lincoln Center's Alice Tully Hall, 92nd Street 'Y' and appearances with major orchestras; chamber musician at Santa Fe Festival, Spoleto Festival, Lockenhaus Kammermusikfest and the International Musicians' Seminar in Prussia Cove; co-founder, Orion Quartet; has given concerts at Kennedy Center, Washington, DC, at Gardner Museum, Boston and throughout USA; Carnegie Hall recital 1991 as part of the Centennial Celebration tribute to next 100 years of music making; concerts at Turku Festival in Finland; Prof. of Violin, State Univ. of New York; faculty mem., Aaron Copland School of Music. *Honours:* winner Young Concert Artists Int. Auditions.

PHILIPS, Leo; British violinist; b. 1960, England. *Education:* Yehudi Menuhin School, studied with Sándor Végh, Dorothy DeLay and Shmuel Ashkenasi. *Career:* concerts as chamber musician and soloist; fmr mem., Chamber Orchestra of Europe; Leader and Principal Dir, East of England Orchestra; co-founder, Vellinger String Quartet 1990; participated in masterclasses with Borodin Quartet at Pears-Britten School 1991; concerts at Ferrara Musica Festival, Italy; debut on South Bank with London premiere of Robert Simpson's 13th Quartet; BBC Radio 3 debut 1991; season 1992–93 with concerts in London, Glasgow, Cambridge, at Davos Festival, Switzerland and Crickdale Festival, Wiltshire; Wigmore Hall with Haydn (Op 54, No. 2), Gubaidulina and Beethoven (Op 59, No. 2), Purcell Room with Haydn's Seven Last Words. *Recordings include:* Elgar's Quartet and Quintet (with Piers Lane).

PHILLIPS, Margaret Corinna, GRSM, ARCM, FRCO; British organist and harpsichordist; *Professor of Organ, Royal College of Music;* b. 16 Nov. 1950, Exeter, Devon, England; d. of John George Phillips and Cora Frances Phillips (née Hurford); m. Dr David Richard Hunt. *Education:* Royal Coll. of Music, London, studied with Marie-Claire Alain in Paris, France. *Career:* debut at Royal Festival Hall 1972; Dir of Music, St Lawrence Jewry next Guildhall, London 1976–85; Prof. of Organ and Harpsichord, London Coll. of Music 1985–91; Tutor in Organ Studies, Royal Northern Coll. of Music 1993–97; Visiting Tutor 1997–2005; Co-founder with D. R. Hunt, English Organ School and Museum, Milborne Port 1996; Prof. of Organ, Royal Coll. of Music 1996–, Prof. in Charge of Organ 1998–2003; Pres. Inc. Asscn of Organists 1997–99; recitals throughout Europe, USA, Canada, Mexico, Australia; radio broadcasts in UK, Sweden, Denmark, The Netherlands, Australia; performances with London Choral Soc., BBC Singers, The Sixteen and London Mozart Players; Lecturer in English Church and Organ Music; mem. Inc. Soc. of Musicians, Royal Coll. of Organists (Council mem. 1982–2003). *Recordings include:* Festliche Orgelmusik, English Organ Music from Queen Elizabeth I to Queen Elizabeth II, D. Buxtehude, Orgelmusik i Karlskoga kyrka, Klosters Orgel, Organ Music of Saint-Saëns, 18th-Century English Organ Music, 19th-Century English Organ Music, Wesley, Music for Organ, Dances for Organ, Voluntaries and Variations, The Young Bach, John Stanley – the Complete

Voluntaries for Organ, Mendelssohn The Essential Organ Works, Springs of Genius, J.S. Bach – The Complete Organ Works, Capriccio – Contemporary Music for Organ. *Address:* The Manse, Chapel Lane, Milborne Port, Sherborne, Dorset, DT9 5DL, England. *Telephone:* (1963) 250022. *E-mail:* mp@margaretphillips.org.uk. *Website:* www.margaretphillips.org.uk.

PHILLIPS, Paul Schuyler, BA, MA, MM; American conductor, composer and author; *Senior Lecturer in Music and Director of Orchestras and Chamber Music, Brown University;* b. 28 April 1956, NJ; m. Kathryne Jennings 1986; two d. *Education:* Eastman School of Music, Rochester, NY, Columbia Univ., New York, Univ. of Cincinnati, Goethe Univ., Frankfurt, Germany, Mozarteum, Aspen Music Festival, Colo, Los Angeles Philharmonic Inst., Tanglewood, Mass, Music Acad. of the West, Santa Barbara, Calif. *Career:* conducting positions at Frankfurt Opera, Stadttheater Lüneburg, Greensboro Symphony, Greensboro Opera, Savannah Symphony, Savannah Symphony Chorale, Maryland Symphony, Rhode Island Philharmonic 1982–92; Music Dir, Brown Univ. Orchestra 1989–, currently Sr Lecturer in Music and Dir of Orchestras and Chamber Music; Music Dir, Pioneer Valley Symphony and Chorus 1994–; Guest Conductor San Francisco Symphony, Dallas Symphony, Detroit Symphony, Rochester Philharmonic, Louisville Orchestra, Charlotte Symphony, Columbus Symphony, Netherlands Radio Chamber Orchestra, Boston Acad. of Music, Commonwealth Opera, Opera Providence, Savannah Ballet, Festival Ballet of RI, Wisconsin Dance Ensemble, Amherst Ballet, Hampshire Choral Soc., Masterworks Chorale; mem. Bd of Dirs American Music Center. *Compositions include:* War Music, Brownian Motion, Celestial Harmonies, Miracle Songs. *Recordings:* with Iceland Symphony Orchestra, RTÉ Nat. Symphony of Ireland, Pioneer Valley Symphony. *Television:* documentary: The Burgess Variations (BBC). *Publications:* A Clockwork Counterpoint: The Music and Literature of Anthony Burgess 2010; contrib. to The New Grove Dictionary of Music and Musicians 2000, Portraits of the Artist in 'A Clockwork Orange' 2003, Anthony Burgess and Modernity 2008, Anthony Burgess: Music in Literature and Literature in Music 2009; articles in The Journal of Music, Music Analysis, Symphony Magazine, Anthony Burgess Newsletter. *Honours:* awards from: American Music Center, Univ. of Texas Harry Ransom Humanities Research Center, Rhode Island State Council on the Arts, New England String Ensemble, St Botolph Club Foundation, Awards for Adventurous Programming of Contemporary Music, The American Soc. of Composers, Authors and Publrs (ASCAP). *Address:* Brown University, Box 1924, Providence, RI 02912, USA (office). *Telephone:* (401) 863-1472 (office). *Fax:* (401) 863-1256 (office). *E-mail:* Paul_Phillips@ brown.edu (office). *Website:* www.brown.edu/Departments/Music (office); www.paulsphillips.com.

PHILLIPS, Peter; British choral director; *Director, The Tallis Scholars;* b. 15 Oct. 1953, Southampton, England; s. of Edmund Phillips and Caroline Trevor. *Education:* Winchester Coll., organ scholar St John's Coll., Oxford. *Career:* taught at Univ. of Oxford, Trinity Coll. of Music, Royal Coll. of Music; Founder-Dir The Tallis Scholars 1973–; founded Gimell Records 1980; regular concerts in UK and abroad, including Australia 1985–, USA 1988–, Far East 1989–; Promenade Concert debut with Victoria's Requiem 1988; UK concerts include Bath Festival 1979, BBC Proms 1988, 2001, 2003, 2007, 2008, 2011, Three Choirs Festival 2002; also conducted BBC Singers 2003–, Intrada of Moscow 2009–; Dir of Music, Merton Coll., Oxford 2008–, Bodley Fellow 2010–; mem. Chelsea Arts Club, MCC. *Recordings:* over 70 recordings including Lassus Music for Double Choir, John Sheppard Media Vita, Gesualdo Tenebrae Responsories, Cornysh Stabat Mater, Clemens non Papa Missa Pastores Quidnam vidistis, Victoria Requiem and Tenebrae Responsories, Cardoso Requiem, Josquin L'homme armé Masses (Diapason d'Or de l'année 1989), Byrd The Great Service and Three Masses, Medieval Christmas Carols and Motets, Palestrina Masses (4 CDs), Tallis Complete English Anthems and Spem in Alium, Taverner Missa Gloria Tibi Trinitas, Isaac Missa de Apostolis, Tomkins The Great Service, Tallis Lamentations of Jeremiah 2011, Tallis Missa Puer Natus, Obrecht Missa Maria Zart, Live in Rome, Live in Oxford, Music from the Sistine Chapel, Guerrero Missa Surge propera, Josquin Missa Sine nomine & Missa Ad fugam, Josquin Missa Malheur me bat & Missa Fortuna desperata, Flemish Masters, Victoria Lamentations of Jeremiah 2010, Josquin Missa De beata virgine and Missa Ave maris stella (Diapason d'Or de l'année 2012) 2011, Jean Mouton: Missa Dictes moy toutes voz pensées 2012. *Publications include:* contribs to The New Republic, Music and Letters, The Listener, The Spectator, The Guardian, The TLS, Proprietor, The Musical Times 1995–. *Honours:* Chevalier, Ordre des Arts et des Lettres 2005; with Tallis Scholars: Gramophone Magazine Record of the Year 1987, Gramophone Award for Early Music Record of the Year 1987, 1991, 1994, 2005. *Address:* The Tallis Scholars, c/o Hazard Chase Ltd, 25 City Road, Cambridge, CB1 1DP, England (office). *Telephone:* (1223) 312400 (office). *Fax:* (1223) 460827 (office). *Website:* www.thetallisscholars.co.uk (office).

PHILLIPS, Richard, MBE, BA; British festival director; *Festival Director, Leamington Music;* b. 15 Sept. 1940, Warwick; m. Veronica Phillips; two d. *Education:* Oundle School, Univ. of Oxford. *Career:* Sadler's Wells Opera 1966–70; York Arts Asscn 1970–80; Festival Dir, Warwick Arts Soc. 1982–2005, Charlecote Park Festival 1983–98, Norfolk and Norwich Festival 1986–91, Solihull Arts Festival 1990–92, King's Lynn Festival 1997, Stratford on Avon Music Festival 2000–07, Leamington Music 2006–. *Honours:* Hon. Fellow, Birmingham Conservatoire 2002; British Arts Festivals Asscn Award for Outstanding Contrib. to British Arts Festivals 2010. *Address:* Northgate,

Warwick, CV34 4JL, England (home). *Telephone:* (1926) 492468 (home); (1926) 497000 (office). *E-mail:* richard@leamingtonmusic.org (office). *Website:* www.leamingtonmusic.org (office).

PHILLIPS, Susanna; American singer (soprano); b. 1981, Birmingham, Ala. *Education:* Randolph School, Huntsville, Juilliard School, New York. *Career:* appeared with Santa Fe Opera 2009, Metropolitan Opera 2009; undertook Tully Recital Tour with Craig Terry 2009; toured with Metropolitan Opera 2010; featured artist, Metropolitan Opera Summer Recital Series, Central Park and Brooklyn Bridge Park; festival appearances at Fort Worth Opera Festival, Santa Fe Chamber Music Festival, Marlboro Music Festival, Greenwood Music Festival, Oklahoma Mozart Festival, Twickenham Fest, Alabama; has also appeared at Dallas Opera, Madison Opera, Metropolitan Opera, Minnesota Opera, Mississippi Opera, Opera Birmingham, Boston Lyric Opera, Carnegie Hall, Chamber Music Milwaukee; other appearances include: Baltimore Symphony Orchestra, Santa Barbara Symphony Orchestra. *Appearances include:* Donizetti, The Elixir of Love 2010, Mozart, Le Nozze di Figaro 2010, Gluck, Orfeo ed Euridice 2010, Mozart, The Magic Flute 2010. *Recordings:* albums: appears on Scott Wheeler, Wasting the Night: Songs (with William Sharp, Joseph Kaiser, Krista River and Donald Berman) 2009. *Honours:* Operalia First Prize and Audience Prize 2005, Metropolitan Opera National Council Auditions Winner 2005, MacAllister Award Winner 2005, George London Foundation Award 2005, Alice Tully Vocal Arts Debut Recital Award 2009, Metropolitan Opera Beverly Sills Artist Award 2010. *Current Management:* Matthew Horner, IMG Artists, Carnegie Hall Tower, 152 West 57th Street, 5th Floor, New York, NY 10019, USA. *Telephone:* (212) 994-3500. *Fax:* (212) 994-3550. *E-mail:* mhorner@imgartsts.com. *Website:* www .imgartists.com; susannaphillips.com.

PHILLIPS, Todd; American violinist; b. 1968. *Education:* Juilliard School with Sally Thomas, Salzburg Mozarteum with Sándor Végh. *Career:* mem. Orion String Quartet; performed as guest soloist with numerous orchestras including Pittsburgh Symphony, New York String Orchestra, Orpheus Chamber Orchestra; has appeared at Mostly Mozart, Ravinia, Santa Fe, Marlboro and Spoleto festivals, also with Chamber Music Society, Lincoln Center; faculty mem., Mannes Coll. of Music, Rutgers Univ. *Recordings include:* with Orion String Quartet: Mendelssohn's Quartet and Octet for Strings, Wynton Marsalis' At the Octoroon Balls and A Fiddler's Tale, Dvorak's String Quartet, The Chamber Music of Claude Debussy, Koch's The Adevntures of Hippocrates, Beethoven's String Quartets, Kirchner's Complete String Quartets. *Current Management:* Kirshbaum Demler and Associates, 711 West End Avenue, Suite 5KN, New York, NY 10025, USA. *Telephone:* (212) 222-4843. *Fax:* (212) 222-7321. *E-mail:* info@kirshdem.com. *Website:* www.kirshdem.com. *E-mail:* todd@orionquartet.com (office). *Website:* www.orionquartet.com.

PHILOGENE, Ruby Catherine, MBE; British singer (mezzo-soprano); b. 14 July 1965, London, England. *Education:* Curtis Inst., Philadelphia, Guildhall School of Music and Drama. *Career:* concert engagements with the San Francisco Symphony Orchestra, London Philharmonic and City of London Sinfonia; season 1994–95 included Mahler 2 with the Liverpool Philharmonic, Messiah under Yehudi Menuhin, Bach B Minor Mass and Schumann's Scenes from Faust with the London Philharmonic Orchestra, Janáček's Glagolitic Mass and Les Nuits d'Eté by Berlioz; opera appearances as Britten's Hermia (with the London Symphony Orchestra under Colin Davis), in Biber's Arminio at Innsbruck, the Page in Salome (Covent Garden 1997), in Handel's Orlando with the Gabrieli Consort and as Goehr's Arianna; season 1997–98 as Dorabella in Così fan tutte for Opera North and a new production of Parsifal in Brussels; other repertory includes the Sorceress in Dido and Aeneas (Staatsoper Berlin) and Smeraldine in The Love for Three Oranges, at Lyon and San Francisco; Carmen for Opera North 1998; Tokyo debut with Bach Collegium 2003; world premiere of Pierre Bartholomé's Oedipe sur la Route, La Monnaie, Paris 2003; Britten's Midsummer Night's Dream, La Monnaie 2004; regular concerts and opera with Rotterdam Philharmonic. *Recordings include:* A Midsummer Night's Dream, Arianna. *Honours:* Anna Instone Memorial Award 1990, Kathleen Ferrier Memorial Prize 1993. *Address:* Impulse Art Management, O. Z. Voorburgwal 72–74, 1012 GE, Amsterdam (office); Jacob Marisstraat 97-1, HX 1058 Amsterdam, The Netherlands (home); 22 Pine House, Avenue Gardens, Droop Street, London, W10 4EJ, England (home). *Telephone:* (20) 8400-1721 (England) (home). *Website:* www .philogene.net.

PHOENIX, Paul; British singer (tenor); m. Helena Phoenix; two s. *Education:* Royal Northern Coll. of Music. *Career:* chorister, St Paul's Cathedral; freelance singer and singing tutor 1991–97; mem., The King's Singers 1997–2014; has performed at venues including Concertgebouw, Amsterdam, Carnegie Hall, New York, Royal Albert Hall, London, Kennedy Center, Washington, DC, and Suntory Hall, Tokyo. *Recordings include:* with The King's Singers: 1605: Treason and Dischord 2005, Sacred Bridges 2005, Six 2005, Thomas Tallis Spem in Alium 2006, Landscape & Time 2006, The Quiet Heart 2007, Live at the Proms 2008, The Golden Age 2008, Simple Gifts (Grammy Award) 2008, Reflections 2008, Romance du Soir 2009, Swimming over London 2010; with Eric Whitacre, the Eric Whitacre Singers, Christopher Glynn, Laudibus and the Pavão Quartet: Light and Gold (Grammy Award for Best Choral Performance 2012) 2010.

PHOTINOS, Nicholas Constantine; American musician (cello). *Education:* Oberlin Conservatory, Cincinnati Coll.-Conservatory and Northwestern Univ.

Career: Co-founder and mem. contemporary music ensemble eighth blackbird 1996–, ensemble has commissioned and performed new works by composers such as Steve Reich, Frederic Rzewski, Jennifer Higdon, Stephen Hartke and Steven Mackey, and performed with orchestras including Cleveland Orchestra, Toronto Symphony and Atlanta Symphony at venues such as Carnegie Hall, Barbican, Sydney Opera House and Kennedy Center; residencies at univs and conservatories, including Univs of Richmond and Chicago, Oberlin Conservatory, Queensland Conservatorium, Southern Methodist Univ., Colburn School and Curtis Inst. of Music; teacher at Bang on a Can Summer Festival 2007–; has performed as mem., Cabrillo Festival Orchestra and Canton and Columbus Symphony Orchestras; performed and recorded with artists including Björk, Willco, Autumn Defense and violinist Zach Brock; also soloist and chamber musician. *Composition:* Mirage. *Recordings:* thirteen ways 2003, beginnings 2004, fred 2005, strange imaginary animals (Grammy Award for Best Chamber Music Performance 2007) 2006, Paul Moravec: The Time Gallery 2006, Steve Reich: Double Sextet 2010, Jennifer Higdon: On a Wire 2011, Steven Mackey: Lonely Motel: Music from Slide (Grammy Award for Best Small Ensemble Performance) 2011, meanwhile (Grammy Award for Best Chamber Music/Small Ensemble Performance) 2012. *Honours:* winner (with eighth blackbird) Fischoff Chamber Music Competition 1996 and numerous awards including Naumburg Chamber Music Award 2000, ASCAP Award for Adventurous Programming 1998, 2000, American Music Center Trailblazer Award 2007, Meet the Composer Award 2007. *Current Management:* David Lieberman Artists, PO Box 10368, Newport Beach, CA 92658, USA. *Address:* c/o eighth blackbird, 5315 North Clark Street, #104, Chicago, IL 60640-2113, USA (office). *Telephone:* (773) 484-8811 (office). *Fax:* (773) 961-7328 (office). *E-mail:* phot@eighthblackbird.org (office). *Website:* www .eighthblackbird.org (office).

PIA, Claude; Swiss singer (tenor); b. 1968, Berne. *Education:* studied with Gina Cigna in Milan, Nicola Gedda in Switzerland and Edita Gruberova. *Career:* appearances in Berne, Lucerne and Basle, 1993–96, as Belfiore in Il Viaggio a Reims, the Painter in Lulu, Rossini's Almaviva, Tamino, and Dinna in La Vestale; season 1996–97 as Ramiro in La Cenerentola at Lille and Mozart's Belmonte at Biel; season 1997–98 as Rodolfo at Biel, Nikolai's Fenton at Visp, Painter and Negro in Lulu at the Opéra Bastille, Hoffmann at Klagenfurt and Narraboth in Salome at Barcelona; season 1999–2000 at Lensky in St Etienne, Don Ottavio in Frankfurt, Arbace in Idomeneo at Toulouse and Belmonte for Nice Opéra; further engagements as Verdi's Fenton in Frankfurt, Belfiore in La Finta giardiniera, and in concerts throughout Europe.

PIANA, Dominique, MA; American harpist, teacher, performer and music editor, composer, arranger, publisher and writer and curator; *Professor of Harp, Holy Names University;* b. 5 July 1956, Eupen, Belgium; m. Will Joel Friedman 1985 (died 2013); one s. *Education:* Royal Conservatory of Music, Brussels, Claremont Grad. Univ., Calif. *Career:* Prof. of Harp, La Sierra Univ., Riverside, Calif. 1982–2001, Univ. of Redlands, Calif. 1985–2001, Holy Names Univ., Oakland, Calif. 2001–; master classes and lectures, solo, duo and lecture recitals, chamber music, concerti; duo recitals with tenor Greg Allen Friedman; Founder and Artistic Dir Pleasanton Chamber Players; Owner Harpiana Publs; Curator, Classical Concert Series, Firehouse Arts Center, Calif.; mem. touring roster California Arts Council 2000–02; mem. American Harp Soc. (Programme Chair. 1992 Nat. Conf., Pres. Bay Area Chapter 2011–13), Historical Harp Soc., American String Teachers Asscn, World Harp Congress, American Liszt Soc., OPERA America, Musical America, WAA. *Composition:* Mélodies imaginaires for solo harp 1995, La Chrysalide for solo harp 2009. *Recordings include:* Harpiana Productions: Fancy, entertaining music for harp 1984, Lulling the Soul, Carols of Love and Wonder 1992, The Harp of King David, Songs of Longing and Hope 1994, Beyond Dreams, The Spirit of Romanticism 1996. *Publications include:* contrib. to Revue Musicale Belge (Belgium), American Harp Journal, American String Teacher, Bulletin of Int. Asscn of Harpists (France), Music for Harp: Harpiana Publs (more than 250 titles), including Contemplation, The Franz Liszt Anthology for Harp (nine vols), The Music of Félix Godefroid (more than 30 titles), Tendresses (book and CD), Pastels, La Lyre d'Orphée (two baroque collections) and single works by Alberstoetter, Auber, Bach-Busoni, C.P.E. Bach, Beethoven, Blangini, Bochsa, Boussagol, Bruch, Burgmüller, Chopin, Creston, Debussy, Deleplanque, Dizi, Duparc, Dvořák, Finko, Fuchs, Galeotti, Godard, Godefroid, Gombau, Grétry, Hahn, Haydn, Hasselmans, Holý, Hummel, Kastner, Kienzl, Krumpholtz, Labarre, Larivière, Leoncavallo, Lorenzi, MacDowell, Méhul, Mendelssohn, Moór, Moszkowski, Mozart, Oberthür, Parish Alvars, Poenitz, Ponce, Posse, Reichardt, Rohozinski, Rossini, Schubert, Schuëcker, Schumann, Servais, Snoer, Steibelt, Stix, Strauss, Suppé, Thomas, Trneček, Vernier, Vierne, Wagner, Zabel, Zingel, Zlatkovsky. *Address:* 5662 Carnegie Way, Livermore, CA 94550, USA (home). *Telephone:* (925) 455-5333 (home). *E-mail:* dominiquepiana@gmail.com (home). *Website:* www.harpiana.com; www.dominiquepiana.com.

PIAU, Sandrine; French singer (soprano); b. 1969; m.; two c. *Education:* studied with Julius Rudel in Paris, with Rachel Yakar and René Jacobs at Versailles. *Career:* noted Handelian and Mozartian singer; trained as a harpist, began vocal studies while attending Nat. Conservatoire in Paris; performs regularly with conductors including William Christie, Philippe Herreweghe, Christophe Rousset, Gustav Leonhardt, Emmanuelle Haïm, Ton Koopman, René Jacobs, Marc Minkowski, Ivor Bolton, Fabio Biondi, Michel Corboz, Josep Pons and Louis Langrée; roles include Pamina/Die Zauberflöte,

Donna Anna/Don Giovanni, Cleopatra/Giulio Cesare, Titania/A Midsummer Night's Dream, Servilia/La Clemenza di Tito, Ismène/Mitridate Re di Ponto, Aennchen/Der Freischütz, Wanda/La Grande Duchesse de Gerolstein, Atalanta/Xerxes, Asteria/Tamerlano, Konstanze/Die Entführung aus dem Serail, Nanetta/Falstaff, Sophie/Werther, Mélisande/Pelléas et Mélisande; performs at Grand Théâtre de Genève, Théâtre des Champs Elysées, Théâtre du Châtelet, Opéra National de Bordeaux, Teatro Lirico di Cagliari, Opéra de Montpellier, Bayersiche Staatsoper, Le Capitole de Toulouse, Concertgebouw, Amsterdam, Teatro Communale di Firenze, Teatro Communale di Bologna, The Barbican, London, Berlin Philharmonic and Salle Pleyel; recitals at Wigmore Hall, London, Carnegie Hall, New York, Le Théâtre des Bouffes du Nord, Paris; festival appearances include Salzburg, Covent Garden, Aix-en-Provence, Montreux, Dresden, Verbier, Drottningholm, Festival du Printemps des Arts, Monte-Carlo, Mostly Mozart, New York. *Recordings include:* substantial operatic and recital discography, including Mozart Arias (Prix Charles Cros), Debussy Mélodies (Prix Ravel, Orphée Awards), Handel's Arias (Stanley Sadie Handel Recording Prize) 2005, Vivaldi 2006, Evocations 2007, Between Heaven and Earth 2009. *Honours:* Chevalier, Ordre des Arts et des Lettres. *Current Management:* c/o IMG Artists, 31 rue du Temple, 75004 Paris, France. *Telephone:* 1-44-31-44-38. *Fax:* 1-44-31-44-01. *E-mail:* cfeazey@imgartists.com. *Website:* www.imgartists.com.

PICCONI, Maurizio; Italian singer (bass-baritone); b. 1957. *Education:* studied at Osimo. *Career:* after winning competitions such as the Concours Bellini in 1983 and the Philadelphia International in 1985, sang widely in Italy; roles have included Rossini's Taddeo, Gianni Schicchi, Bartolo, Dulcamara, Belcore and Malatesta; sang at Zürich in 1988 as Sulpice in La Fille du Régiment, at Bonn in 1992 as Leporello and further appearances at Dublin, Bilbao, Amsterdam, Strasbourg and Philadelphia; sang Rossini's Bartolo at Pavia, 1995; sang Sulpice in La Fille du régiment at St Gallen, 2000. *Recordings include:* Il Furioso all'Isola di San Domingo by Donizetti. *Address:* Via Amedeo VIII N7, 00185, Rome, Italy. *E-mail:* mp@mauriziopicconi.it. *Website:* www.mauriziopicconi.it.

PICHLER, Günter; Austrian violinist and conductor; *Head of Strings Department, International Chamber Music Institute, Escuela Superior de Música Reina Sofía*; b. 9 Sept. 1940, Kufstein, Tirol. *Education:* studied in Vienna. *Career:* Leader, Vienna Symphony Orchestra 1958, Vienna Philharmonic 1961; Prof., Univ. of Music and Performing Arts, Vienna 1963–; Founder and Leader, Alban Berg Quartet 1971–2008; Guest Prof., Univ. for Music, Cologne 1993–2012; Head of Strings Dept, Int. Chamber Music Inst., Escuela Superior de Música Reina Sofia 2007–; annual concert series at Vienna Konzerthaus, Queen Elizabeth Hall, London, Théâtre des Champs Elysées, Paris, Opera Zürich, Philharmonie Cologne, Alte Oper Frankfurt, Madrid, and festival and concert engagements world-wide; Assoc. Artist at South Bank Centre, London; conducting engagements include Vienna, Israel, Irish and Norwegian Chamber Orchestras, London Mozart Players, Ensemble Orchestral de Paris, Orchestre della Toscana, Hallé Orchestra, Deutsche Kammerphilharmonie, Orchestre Nat. de Lille, Südwestdeutsche Philharmonie, Tokyo, Osaka and Sendai Philharmonic Orchestras and NHK Orchestra; Prin. Guest Conductor, Orchestra Kanazawa 2001–06, Artistic Advisor 2006–; US appearances include Washington, DC, Chicago, Boston, Philadelphia, Los Angeles, San Francisco and New York. *Recordings include:* Complete quartets of Beethoven, Brahms, Berg, Webern and Bartók; Late quartets of Mozart, Schubert, Haydn and Dvořák; Ravel, Debussy and Schumann Quartets; live recordings from Carnegie Hall (Mozart, Schumann); Konzerthaus in Vienna, Mozart; Complete Beethoven; Brahms, Dvořák, Smetana, Rihm, Schnittke, Berio, Janáček; Opéra-Comique Paris, (Brahms); as conductor: Haydn, Mozart, Beethoven symphonies, Piano and Violin Concertos, Brahms, Schoenberg, Webern; Berio, Ligeti, Strauss (Horn Concertos, Metamorphoses, Burleske, Capriccio) etc., Wagner, Verdi. *Honours:* Hon. mem. Vienna Konzerthaus; more than 30 prizes, including Grand Prix du Disque, Deutscher Schallplatenpreis, Edison Prize, Japan Grand Prix, Gramophone Magazine Award, Int. Classical Music Award 1992. *Current Management:* c/o Henrik F. Lodding, Svensk Konsertdirektion, Danska vägen 25B, 412 74 Göteborg, Sweden. *Telephone:* (31) 83-00-95. *Fax:* (31) 40-80-11. *E-mail:* info@loddingkonsert.se. *Website:* www.loddingkonsert.se; www.guenterpichler.com.

PICK-HIERONIMI, Monica Maria Anna; German singer (soprano); *Professor, Staatliche Hochschule für Musik, Cologne*; b. 14 Dec. 1943, Olpe; d. of Jacob Pick and Helene Schäfer; m. Otto Hieronimi 1968; one s. *Education:* Rheinische Musikschule, Cologne. *Career:* numerous nat. and int. opera and concert appearances including performances in Munich, Mannheim, Frankfurt, Stuttgart, Vienna Staatsoper, Hamburg, Barcelona Theatre del Liceu, Spain, Rome, Deutsche Staatsoper Berlin, Paris, Milan, Italy, Zurich, Switzerland, Brussels, Prague, Verona (first German Aida), Italy 1992, Carnegie Hall, New York 1992; has performed at many festivals, including Buxton, UK, Würzburg Mozartfest, Schleswig-Holstein, Karlsruhe Händelsfestspiele, Prague Spring Festival, Arena di Verona Int. Festival, Vienna Festival Weeks, Festival di Caracalla, Rome 1991, Oslo, Helsinki, Luxor; Prof., Staatliche Hochschule für Musik, Cologne 1992–. *Operas include:* Idomeneo, Don Giovanni, La Clemenza di Tito, I Puritani, Norma, La Forza del Destino, Otello, Il Trovatore, Nabucco, Un Ballo in Maschera, Aida, Der Rosenkavalier, Die Frau ohne Schatten, Ariadne auf Naxos. *Recordings:* Christ on the Mount of Olives 1987, Verdi's Requiem 1989, Don Giovanni 1991, Nabucco, under Guadagno with Arena di Verona 1996. *Honours:* Carpine d'Oro, Brescia 1990. *E-mail:* pickhieronimi@aol.com (home). *Website:* www.monica-pick-hieronimi.de (office).

PICKENS, Jo Ann; American singer (soprano); b. 4 Aug. 1950, Robstown, Tex.; d. of Anne Belle Sanders. *Education:* North Texas Univ. *Career:* started singing career in Chicago Lyric Opera; has perfomed in recital and concerts around the world and appeared with conductors including Solti, Dorati, Rattle, Norrington, Pesek and Sanderling; also appears in opera, notably Berlioz's The Trojans 1987 and Armide 1988. *Honours:* award, Int. Competition for Singers, Paris 1980, Metropolitan Opera Regional Auditions 1981, Benson & Hedges Gold Award 1981. *Current Management:* c/o Hispania Clásica SL, Calle Los Madrazo 16 bajo, 28014 Madrid, Spain. *Telephone:* (91) 4292625. *Fax:* (91) 4293530. *E-mail:* ediisprod@gmail.com. *Website:* www.joannpickens.com.

PICKER, Tobias, BM, MM; American composer; b. 18 July 1954, New York. *Education:* Manhattan School of Music with Charles Wuorinen, Juilliard School with Elliott Carter, Princeton Univ. *Career:* composer-in-residence, Houston Symphony Orchestra 1985–90; composer-in-residence, Santa Fe Chamber Music Festival, Pacific Music Festival; commissions from the American Composers Orchestra, San Francisco Symphony Orchestra, St Paul Chamber Orchestra, and Ursula Oppens; operas Emmeline, premiered at the Santa Fe Festival 1996, Fantastic Mr Fox, Los Angeles 1998; Cello Concerto premiered at the London Proms 2001; Artistic Adviser, Dicapo Opera Theatre, New York 2007–; apptd artistic dir, new opera co. based in San Antonio, Texas 2010–; mem. BMI; mem. American Acad. of Arts and Letters 2012. *Compositions include:* four sextets for various instruments 1973, 1973, 1977, 1981, Rhapsody for violin and piano 1979, three Piano Concertos 1980, 1983, 1986, Violin Concerto 1981, three Symphonies 1982, 1986, 1989, Serenade for piano and wind quintet 1983, Piano-o-rama for two pianos 1984, Encantadas for narrator and orchestra 1984, Dedication Anthem for band 1984, Old and Lost Rivers for orchestra 1986, String Quartet New Memories 1987, Piano Quintet 1988, Romances and Interludes (after Schumann) for oboe and orchestra 1990, Two Fantasies for orchestra 1991, Bang for piano and orchestra 1992, Violin Sonata Invisible Lilacs 1992, And Suddenly it's Evening for orchestra 1994, Suite for cello and piano 1998, Cello Concerto 2001, Tres sonetos de amor, Neruda Love Poems for baritone, orchestra, voice and piano, The Blue Hula for chamber ensemble; opera: Emmeline 1996, Fantastic Mr Fox 1998, Thérèse Raquin 2000, An American Tragedy 2006, Dolores Claiborne 2013. *Honours:* Bearns Prize, Columbia Univ. Charles Ives Scholarship 1978, Guggenheim Foundation Fellowship 1981, American Acad. of Arts and Letters Award in Music. *Current Management:* c/o Norman D. Ryan, Head of Contemporary Music, Schott Music Corporation, 35 E 21st Street, Eighth Floor, New York, NY 10010, USA. *Telephone:* (212) 368-0119 (office); (212) 358-4999 (office). *Fax:* (212) 871-0237 (office). *E-mail:* ny@schott-music.com (office). *E-mail:* mikael@tobiaspicker.com (office). *Website:* www.tobiaspicker.com.

PIDOUX, Roland; French cellist; b. 29 Oct. 1946, Paris. *Education:* Paris Conservatoire with André Navarra, Jean Hubeau and Joseph Calvet. *Career:* co-founder, Ensemble Instrumental de France; played with the orchestra of the Paris Opéra from 1968; mem., Via Nova Quartet 1970–78; joined Regis and Bruno Pasquier 1972, to form the Pasquier Trio; directed the record collection, Les Musiciens 1979; soloist, Orchestra National de France 1979–87; Prof. of Cello, Paris Conservatoire 1987; plays a Stradivarius of 1692.

PIECZONKA, Adrianne, OC, MusBac (Hons); Canadian singer (soprano); b. 2 March 1963, Poughkeepsie, NY, USA; m. Laura Tucker; one d. *Education:* Univ. of Western Ontario, Univ. of Toronto (Diploma in Operatic Performance). *Career:* began European career 1989 at Vienna Volksoper; mem. Vienna State Opera 1991–95, sang Countess in Marriage of Figaro; Donna Elvira and Donna Anna in Don Giovanni; Desdemona in Otello; Agathe in Der Freischütz; Eva in Die Meistersinger von Nürnberg; Tatyana in Eugene Onegin; Antonia in Les Contes d'Hoffmann; Die Tochter in Cardillac; Micaela in Carmen; UK operatic debut, Glyndebourne Festival 1995, Arabella 1996; sang Elsa in Lohengrin at Munich State Opera and in Los Angeles, Houston and Vienna; debut at La Scala as Donna Anna 1999, later as Marschallin in Der Rosenkavalier, Desdemona in Otello and Elisabeth in Tannhäuser; debut at Covent Garden as Donna Anna 2002; debut at Metropolitan Opera as Lisa in Pique Dame 2004, later sang Sieglinde in Die Walküre and Amelia in Simon Boccanegra; sang Elisabetta in Don Carlo at Salzburg Festival 2003, sang Marschallin in Der Rosenkavalier 2004; Bayreuth debut as Sieglinde 2006; sang Tosca at Los Angeles Opera 2008, at San Francisco Opera 2009, Berlin and Hamburg Operas 2009/10; debut singing Kaiserin in Die Frau ohne Schatten in Florence 2010; sings regularly with Canadian Opera Co. in Toronto; debut as Leonora in Fidelio in Toronto 2009; Paris Opera debut as Senta in Der Fliegender Holländer 2010; worked with James Levine, Riccardo Muti, Claudio Abbado, Sir Colin Davis, Christian Thielemann, Sir Georg Solti, Lorin Maazel, Zubin Mehta; appears frequently on BBC Radio, CBC and Austrian Radio ORF. *Recordings include:* First Lady in Die Zauberflöte conducted by Solti 1989, Die Fledermaus (Rosalinde) 1997, Complete Richard Strauss Orchestral Songs 1998, Don Giovanni (Donna Anna) 1999, Millennium Opera Gala 2000, Aids Gala Berlin 2003, Collection of Arias and Songs by Strauss and Wagner 2006, Beethoven: Ideals of the French Revolution 2008, Lohengrin 2009, Adrianne Pieczonka sings Puccini (Juno Award for Classical Album of the Year 2010) 2009. *Television:* Don Giovanni (Donna Elvira) (also video and DVD) 1995, Simon Boccanegra (Amelia) (DVD). *Honours:* Kammersängerin, Vienna State Opera 2007; Hon. PhD (McMaster);

Winner, s'Hertogenbosch Singing Competition, Netherlands 1988, Pleine-sur-Mer Singing Competition, France 1988, Dora Award for Best Operatic Performance (Canada) 2004, Premios Líricos Teatro Campoamor Award for Best Female Opera Singer 2008. *Website:* www.adriannepieczonka.com.

PIENAAR, Daniel-Ben; South African pianist and academic; *Curzon Lecturer in Performance Studies, Royal Academy of Music. Education:* Royal Acad. of Music, studied with Christopher Elton. *Career:* recitalist and chamber musician; debut in S Africa aged 14, playing Liszt's E-flat concerto; first played Bach six partitas in one concert 1999, Mozart piano sonata cycle 2000; other complete performances include Bach's Goldberg Variations and Well-Tempered Clavier, Beethoven's Diabelli Variations, Schubert's 12 major piano sonatas, Chopin ballades and waltzes; toured Japan with violinist Narimichi Kawabata, duo repertoire and solo recitals 1999–2005; other chamber music collaborations with Jonathan Freeman-Attwood, Martin Knizia, Giovanni Guzzo and Peter Sheppard-Skaerved; mem. Faculty, RAM 2005–, currently Curzon Lecturer in Performance Studies. *Recordings include:* Bach: The Well-Tempered Clavier Book 1 2003, Book 2 2005, La Trompette Retrouvée 2007, Orlando Gibbons Complete Keyboard Works 2007, Trumpet Masque 2008, Mozart Complete Piano Sonatas 2010, Bach Goldberg Variations 2011, Romantic Trumpet Sonatas 2011, Beethoven Diabelli Variations 2012. *Honours:* winner, Nat. Youth Music Competition (S Africa). *Address:* c/o Royal Academy of Music, Marylebone Road, London, NW1 5HT, England (office). *E-mail:* info@danielbenpienaar.com (office). *Website:* www.danielbenpienaar.com (office).

PIERARD, Catherine; British singer (soprano); b. 1960, England. *Career:* many appearances in the UK and Europe, with the Jerusalem Symphony Orchestra, City of London Sinfonia, Scottish Chamber Orchestra and Concertgebouw; opera roles have included Tatiana in Eugene Onegin, Fiordiligi and Donna Elvira with English Touring Opera 1994, Papagena in Die Zauberflöte at the 1990 London Proms, Purcell's Dido (Spitalfields Festival 1993), Gluck's Alceste, Iphigénie and Euridice; engagements with Roger Norrington in Orfeo at the Bath Festival and Purcell's Fairy Queen in Florence; Drusilla and Fortune in Monteverdi's Poppea under Richard Hickox; season 1995–96 in Mozart's C Minor Mass, Messiah with the Ulster and London Bach Orchestras and Ravel's Shéhérazade with the Bournemouth Symphony Orchestra; Biber's Arminio at the Salzburg and Innsbruck Festivals, Bach's Magnificat at Ottawa and Handel's Belshazzar with Nicholas Kraemer. *Recordings include:* Monteverdi Arias, Dioclesian and The Fairy Queen, Britten's Rape of Lucretia. *Telephone:* (20) 8995-3226. *Fax:* (20) 8742-7476. *E-mail:* catherinepierard@aol.com.

PIERSON, Alan; American conductor; *Artistic Director, Brooklyn Philharmonic Orchestra;* b. 12 May 1974, Chicago. *Education:* Massachusetts Inst. of Tech., Eastman School of Music; studied with Robert Spano, Stefan Asbury, Bradley Lubman, Gunther Schuller and David Epstein. *Career:* studied physics at MIT before turning to music; Founder and Artistic Dir Alarm Will Sound (20-mem. chamber orchestra); Prin. Conductor, Crash Ensemble, Dublin; Artistic Dir Brooklyn Philharmonic Orchestra 2011–; has collaborated with major composers and performers including Yo-Yo Ma, Steve Reich, John Adams, Augusta Read Thomas, David Lang, Michael Gordon, La Monte Young, Osvaldo Golijov, Julia Wolfe and Wu Man, and choreographers Akram Khan and Elliot Feld; has appeared as Guest Conductor with the London Sinfonietta, the Steve Reich Ensemble, Carnegie Hall's Ensemble ACJW, the Tanglewood Music Center Orchestra, the New World Symphony and The Silk Road Project, among other ensembles; Visiting Faculty Conductor, Jacobs School of Music, Indiana Univ. *Recordings include:* Alarm Will Sound Plays the Music of Aphex Twin, Silk Road Journeys with Yo-Yo Ma, premiere recording of Steve Reich's Variations with the London Sinfonietta, a/rhythmia, Steve Reich Tehillim/The Desert Music 2002. *Honours:* ASCAP Concert Music Award. *Current Management:* William Reinert Associates, 163 Amsterdam Avenue, #334, New York, NY 10023, USA. *Telephone:* (212) 799-5365 (office). *Fax:* (775) 259-5585 (office). *E-mail:* info@williamreinert.com (office). *Website:* www.williamreinert.com; www.alarmwillsound.com (office).

PIJAROWSKI, Marek; Polish conductor and pianist; *Chief Conductor, Tadeusz Szeligowski Poznań Philharmonic Orchestra;* b. 25 April 1951, Wrocław. *Education:* Music Acad., Wrocław, Hochschule für Musik, Vienna, also studied with Arvid Jansons. *Career:* made professional debut with Wrocław Philharmonic Orchestra 1973; Asst Conductor, Wrocław Philharmonic Orchestra 1974–75, Second Conductor 1975–80, Artistic Dir 1980–2001; Artistic Dir Musica Polonica Nova, Wrocław 1980–2000, Chopin Festival, Duszniki Zdroj 1986–87; Artistic Dir Łodz Philharmonic Orchestra 2002–05; Prof. of Conducting, Frederick Chopin Acad. of Music, Warsaw 2006–; Chief Conductor, Rzeszów Philharmonic Orchestra 2006–; Chief Conductor, Tadeusz Szeligowski Poznań Philharmonic Orchestra 2007–. *Honours:* winner, Int. Conducting Competition, Katowice 1974, Gloria Artis Medal 2004. *Address:* Tadeusz Szeligowski Poznań Philharmonic Orchestra, ul. Św. Marcin 81, 61-808 Poznań, Poland (office). *Telephone:* (61) 852-47-08 (office). *Fax:* (61) 852-34-51 (office). *E-mail:* sekretariat@filharmoniapoznanska.pl (office). *Website:* www.filharmoniapoznanska.pl (office).

PIKE, Jennifer; British violinist; b. 2000, d. of Jeremy Pike (q.v.) and Teresa Pike. *Education:* Guildhall School of Music and Drama, Univ. of Oxford. *Career:* debut aged 15 at BBC Proms and Wigmore Hall, London; mem. BBC Young Generation Artists programme; as soloist, has performed with

numerous orchestras, including BBC orchestras, London Philharmonic, London Symphony, Royal Liverpool Philharmonic, Orchestre Philharmonique de Strasbourg, City of Birmingham Symphony, Brussels and Bergen Philharmonics, Auckland Philharmonia, Tampere Philharmonic, Vienna Symphony, Nagoya Philharmonic, Adelaide Symphony and Malmö Symphony, Singapore Symphony, Philharmonia, Halle; performed Beethoven and Bruch concertos with Philharmonia and Hallé orchestras, Sibelius with Bergen Philharmonic and Bournemouth Symphony, Mozart with the Rheinische Philharmonie and Singapore Symphony Orchestra; world premiere with Scottish Chamber Orchestra 2011 of concerto composed for her by Haflidi Hallgrimsson; has worked with numerous conductors including Andris Nelsons, the late Richard Hickox, Sir Mark Elder, Christopher Hogwood, Sir Andrew Davis, Leif Segerstam, Tugan Sokhiev, Jiří Belohlávek, John Storgårds, James Gaffigan, Jukka-Pekka Saraste, Martyn Brabbins; performed Sibelius, Brahms and Tchaikovsky Concertos with the BBC Nat. Orchestra of Wales, BBC Scottish Symphony and BBC Philharmonic Orchestras for broadcast on BBC Radio 3; recital collaborators include harpsichordist Mahan Esfahani and pianists Martin Roscoe and Tom Poster; concerts at Mecklenburg-Vorpommern Festival (Germany), Musée d'Orsay in Paris, Musashino Foundation in Japan, and in New York; Artist-in-Residence, Univ. of Oxford; Amb., Prince's Trust; Patron, Lord Mayor of London's City Music Foundation. *Recordings include:* Schultz Violin Concerto (premiere) 2011, Schultz Sonatina for Solo Violin, Debussy, Ravel and Franck sonatas 2011, Rózsa's Violin Concerto and Variations on a Hungarian Peasant Song 2011, Chausson's Concert for Violin, Piano and String Quartet 2013, Brahms and Schumann sonatas 2013, Sibelius Violin Concerto 2014, Janacek's complete works for violin and piano 2014, Mendelssohn Violin Concerto 2015. *Honours:* BBC Young Musician of the Year 2002, London Music Masters Award, South Bank Show/Times Breakthrough Award. *Telephone:* (20) 8859-4846. *E-mail:* ian.roberts@astarpr.com. *E-mail:* jeremypike@lineone.net. *Website:* www.jenniferpike.com.

PIKE, Jeremy, MA, PhD, LRAM; British composer and pianist; *Head of Composition, Chetham's School of Music;* b. 20 Nov. 1955, London, England; m. Teresa Majcher 1981; two d. *Education:* King's Coll., Cambridge, Royal Acad. of Music, London. *Career:* British Council Scholarship to study composition with Henryk Gorecki in Poland, Katowice Acad. of Music 1978–79, and with Tadeusz Baird at Warsaw Acad. 1979; Dir of Contemporary Music, Univ. of Warwick 1981–87; Dir of Electroacoustic Music, RAM 1987–92; Head of Composition, Chetham's School of Music, Manchester 1989–. *Compositions include:* Bassoon Concerto, two Piano Concertos, A Street Under Siege for orchestra, The Crossing Point, Stamford Overture, six String Quartets, Oboe Quartet, Clarinet Quartet, Processions, Aphelion and Praesagium for violin and piano, eight Piano Sonatas, Missa Brevis for chorus and piano, Summer in Winter and other piano works; vocal works. *Honours:* Hon. ARAM; Churchill Fellowship in the Application of New Tech. to the Arts 1998. *Address:* Chetham's School of Music, Long Millgate, Manchester, M3 1SB, England (office). *E-mail:* jeremypike@chethams.com (office). *Website:* www.jeremypike.co.uk.

PIKE, Julian; British singer (tenor); b. 1948, England. *Education:* Royal Coll. of Music, studied with Pierre Bernac in France. *Career:* sang Don José in Peter Brook's version of Carmen in Paris, Zürich, Stockholm, Copenhagen and New York 1982–84; sang Michael in productions of Stockhausen's Donnerstag aus Licht in The Netherlands, Germany, Italy and London (Covent Garden 1985); tour with the European Community Youth Orchestra under Matthias Bamert 1985; Wexford Festival 1985, in Mahagonny; appearances with Kent Opera in Poppea and Rameau's Pygmalion; has sung in Henze's English Cat in Frankfurt, at the Edinburgh Festival and for the BBC; premiere productions of Montag aus Licht in Milan, Amsterdam, Frankfurt and Paris from 1988; sang Roderick in The Fall of the House of Usher by Glass with Music Theatre Wales 1989; Ligeti Festival at the South Bank 1989; other roles include the Dancing Master in Ariadne and Piet the Pot in Le Grand Macabre; season 1992 as Michael in the premiere of Stockhausen's Dienstag aus Licht at Lisbon and later at Amsterdam; recitals at the Bath, City of London, Camden and Aldeburgh Festivals; repertoire includes Bach, Monteverdi and contemporary music; tours of France, Germany, Belgium, The Netherlands, Poland, Finland and Austria (Salzburg); appearances with the Songmakers' Almanac and Fortune's Fire Lute Song Ensemble; Head of Vocal Studies, Birmingham Conservatoire 1999.

PIKE, Lionel John, BMus, MA, DPhil, FRCO, ARCM; British organist and academic; *Professor Emeritus of Music, Royal Holloway College;* b. 7 Nov. 1939, Bristol; m. Jennifer Parkes; two d. *Education:* Bristol Cathedral School, Pembroke Coll., Oxford. *Career:* Asst Organist, Bristol Cathedral 1957–59; Asst Organist, Royal Holloway Coll., London 1965, Organist and Dir of the Chapel Choir 1969–2005, Sr Lecturer in Music, later Prof. of Music –2005; Dean, Faculty of Music, Univ. of London; mem. Purcell Soc. (Cttee mem.), Vaughan Williams Soc., Robert Simpson Soc. (fmr Chair.), Havergal Brian Soc., Royal Musical Soc., Royal Coll. of Organists. *Compositions:* Monkey Music, The Pilgrim Way, Encircled by Sea, The Lyra Davidica Motets. *Recordings:* with the Chapel Choir of Royal Holloway Coll. 1993–2005. *Publications:* Beethoven, Sibelius and the Profound Logic, Hexachords in late Renaissance Music, Vaughan Williams and the Symphony, Pills to Purge Melancholy: the evolution of the English Ballett, Purcell: Symphony Anthems in The Works of Henry Purcell (ed.); contrib. to Tempo, Music and Letters. *Honours:* Limpus Prize, Royal Coll. of Organists. *Address:* 34 Alderside Walk,

Englefield Green, Egham, Surrey, TW20 0LY, England (home). *Telephone:* (1784) 435863 (home). *E-mail:* lionel.pike@gmail.com (home).

PILAND, Jeanne, BA; American singer (mezzo-soprano); b. 3 Dec. 1945, Raleigh, NC. *Education:* University of North Carolina, studied in New York with Gladys White and Prof. Carolyn Grant. *Career:* debut with New York City Opera 1972; performed with New York City Opera 1974–77; sang at the Deutsche Oper am Rhein 1977–; roles included Cherubino, Composer, Ariadne, Octavian in Der Rosenkavalier, Silla in Palestrina and the Child in L'Enfant et les Sortilèges; sang Hamburg 1981–, Munich 1985–, Ludwigsburg Festival 1984–, Vienna Staatsoper 1984, 1987, 1991, Paris, Dresden, Hamburg, Vienna, Nice, Monte Carlo, Amsterdam, 1987, Ariadne auf Naxos at Covent Garden and Aix-en-Province; has appeared as Octavian at Dresden 1986 for 75th Anniversary of World premiere, Cologne, Zürich, Nice 1986, and Monte Carlo 1987, Santa Fe 1988; Aix-en-Province, Munich, Hamburg 1988, as Idamante and Octavian; sang Octavia in L'Incoronazione di Poppea Annius, La Clemenza di Tito, at Geneva 1989; other roles include Rosina and Cenerentola, Preziosilla, Smeaton in Anna Bolena, Zerlina and Massenet's Charlotte, Concepcion in L'Heure Espagnole, Elena in La Donna del Lago, Marguerite in La Damnation de Faust, Clytemnestra, Iphigenia in Aulis, La Scala Milan, Cherubino, Dorabella, Adalgisa, Norma, Carmen, Charlotte in Werther, Olivia in the premiere of Trojahn's Was ihr wollt (Twelfth Night), Neris in Cherubini's Médée, Eboli in Don Carlos, Didon in Les Troyens, Gertrude in Hamlet, Fricka in Die Walküre, Maria Maria in Giorgio Battistellis' Fashion; concert repertoire includes, Berlioz, Les Nuits d'Eté, Shéhérazade, Mahler's Symphonies and Lied-Cycles; currently also teacher, Hochschule für Musik Robert Schumann, Düsseldorf. *Honours:* Ordre des Arts et des Lettres; Kammersängerin 2003. *Current Management:* c/o Dr. Werner Hellfritzsch, Paul Spiegel Internationale Künstler und Medienagentur, Postfach 11, 0938 Düsseldorf, Germany. *Telephone:* (211) 4983199. *Fax:* (211) 4983445. *E-mail:* info@paulspiegel.de. *Website:* www.paulspiegel.de. *E-mail:* info@jeanne-piland.de (office). *Website:* www.jeanne-piland.de.

PILAVACHI, Anthony; Irish stage director and lighting designer; b. 24 July 1962, Cyprus. *Education:* Guildhall School of Music and Drama. *Career:* debut with Pergolesi's La Serva Padrona at Monte Carlo 1983; Dir and Asst, Bonn Opera 1987–92, notably with Falstaff 1991; Dir and Asst, Cologne Opera 1992–95, notably with Peter Grimes 1994, Carmen at Bergen 1992, Il Barbiere di Siviglia and Traviata at Bogota 1994; season 1995–96 with Madame Butterfly at Halle/Saale, Un Ballo in Maschera at Freiburg, Carmina Burana at Dresden in the Zwinger Courtyard, Handel's Tolomeo at the Handel Festival Halle; season 1996–97 with Lulu at Lubeck, Orpheus in the Underworld at Freiburg; season 1997–98 with Tales of Hoffmann at Lübeck, The Love of Three Oranges, for the reopening of theatre at Freiburg, La Traviata at Gothenburg, Madama Butterfly at Lübeck; season 1998–99 with The Love of Three Oranges at Lübeck, Saul at Komische Oper Berlin, Daphne at Deutsche Oper Berlin, Faust at Freiburg; season 1999–2000 with Fliegende Holländer at Frankfurt, Dialogues of Carmelites and The Magic Flute at Freiburg; seasons 2000–02 with Cendrillon at Lübeck, Boris Godunov at Hannover Expo 2000, Così fan tutte at Bremen, Onegin at Freiburg, La Bohème at St Gallen, Fanciulla del West at Dessau and Figaro at Oldenburg; Season 2002–03 with world premiere of Verdi's Gustavo III at Gothenburg, Sweden, Il Tabarro and Gianni Schicchi at Lübeck, Lohengrin at Bremen, Cavalleria Rusticana and Pagliacci at Dessau; season 2003–04 with Rigoletto at Cottbus, German premiere of Verdi, Gustavo III at Darmstadt, Idomeneo at Oldenburg; season 2004–05 with Entführung aus dem Serail at Oldenburg, Eugene Onegin at St Gallen, and Don Giovanni at Cottbus; season 2005–06 with Freischütz at Krefeld, Clemenza di Tito and Nozze di Figaro at Oldenburg, Zar und Zimmermann at Bremen, La Finta Giardiniera at Nürnberg; season 2006–07 with Othello at Augsburg, La Belle Hélène at Dortmund; season 2007–08 with Rheingold at Lübeck, Barbiere di Siviglia at Schwerin, Freischütz at Sankt-Gallen, Switzerland and The Magic Flute at Lübeck; season 2008–09 with Walküre in Lübeck, Tosca at Bordeaux, Midsummer Night's Dream at Berne; season 2009–10 with Siegfried at Lübeck, Platée at Linz, Wildschütz at Weimar; season 2010–11 with Götterdämmerung and complete Ring Cycle at Lübeck, Falstaff at Lübeck, L'infedeltà delusa at Hamburg; season 2011–12 with Rosenkavalier at Lübeck and Linz; Season 2012–13 with Parsifal at Lübeck, Rigoletto; season 2013–14 with Tristan und Isolde and Der Wildschütz at Lübeck, Salome in Taiwan; season 2014–15 with La Damnation de Faust at Lübeck, The Canterville Ghost/ Getty (WP) and Pagliacci at Leipzig; Season 2015–16 with Capriccio at Meiningen, Werther at Chemnitz, My Fair Lady at Weimar; Season 2016–2017 with Cinq-Mars/ Gounod at Leipzig. *Recordings include:* R. Wagner's Ring des Nibelungen (DVD box set) (German Critic Award 2011, Echo Klassik Award for the Best Opera DVD 2012). *Honours:* Princess Grace of Monaco Scholarship 1983, German Critics' Prize for Wagner's Ring (DVD box set) 2011. *Address:* Siemensstrasse 2, 50825 Cologne, Germany. *Telephone:* (221) 5505936; (171) 9531791. *E-mail:* anthonypilavachi@gmx.de.

PILAVACHI, Costa, BA; Greek/Canadian music industry executive; *Senior Vice-President, Classical Artists and Repertoire, Universal Music Group International;* b. 8 May 1951, London, England; s. of Aristide Pilavachi and Frosso Pilavachi; m. Elisabeth Hajdu. *Education:* Carleton Univ., York Univ. *Career:* Dir of Music, St Lawrence Centre for Arts, Toronto 1979–81, Nat. Arts Centre, Ottawa 1981–85; Artistic Admin., Boston Symphony Orchestra 1985–89; Vice-Pres. of A&R, Philips Classics 1989–97, Pres. Philips Music Group 1997–99; Pres. Decca Music Group 1999–2006; Pres. EMI Classics

2006–08; Sr Vice-Pres. of Classical Artists and Repertoire, Universal Music Group Int. 2010–. *Address:* Universal Music Classical, 364–366 Kensington High Street, London, W14 8NS, England (office). *Telephone:* (20) 7471-5000 (office). *E-mail:* costa.pilavachi@umusic.com (office). *Website:* www .universalmusicclassical.com (office).

PILGRIM, Shirley, ARCM, Dip RAM; British singer (soprano) and teacher; *Singing Teacher, Queenswood School and Haileybury College;* b. 1957, London; m. 1979. *Education:* RAM with Ilse Wolf and Patricia Clark, Nat. Opera Studio. *Career:* sang with the Glyndebourne Festival and Touring Opera choruses; solo debut as Helena with the Touring Opera, in A Midsummer Night's Dream; appearances in Hong Kong, and at the Buxton and Wexford Festivals; with Opera East sang Mimi, and the Female Chorus in The Rape of Lucretia; Scottish Opera and ENO as Despina, and cover for various roles; New D'Oyly Carte Opera Co., Elsie in Yeomen of the Guard and Phyllis in Iolanthe; oratorio and concert engagements, notably at the Barbican Hall, London, and recitals including lighter American music; sang in Born Again directed by Sir Peter Hall at the Chichester Festival; other roles include the Countess in The Marriage of Figaro, Fiordiligi in Così fan tutte, Tosca, Mimi in La Bohème, Carmen, Santuzza in Cavalleria Rusticana; singing teacher, Queenswood School and Haileybury Coll. and privately. *Recordings include:* solo album: Shirley Pilgrim with Attitude, duet album (Lloyd Webber). *Address:* 85 Chichester Road, Edmonton Green, London, N9 9DH, England (office). *Telephone:* (20) 8803-9757 (office).

PILOU, Jeannette; singer (soprano); b. July 1931, Alexandria, Egypt. *Education:* studied with Carla Castellani in Milan. *Career:* debut in Milan 1958 as Violetta; sang widely in Italy as Mélisande, Mimi, Liu, Susanna, Manon, Nedda, Micaela, Marguerite and Nannetta; appearances in Barcelona, Buenos Aires, Hanover, Hamburg and Wexford; Vienna 1965 as Mimi; with Metropolitan Opera from 1967–86 with debut as Gounod's Juliette; Covent Garden 1971 as Madama Butterfly; sang at Monte Carlo 1973 in the premiere of Rossellini's La Reine Morte; other roles have included the female leads in Von Einem's Der Prozess, Gluck's Euridice, Marzelline in Fidelio and Magda in La Rondine; US appearances in Houston, Chicago, San Francisco, New Orleans and Philadelphia; sang Mélisande in Athens 1998. *Recordings include:* Micaela in Carmen.

PILZ, Gottfried; Austrian stage designer and costume designer; b. 1944, Salzburg; m. Isabel Ines Glathar; one s. *Education:* Academy of Arts, Vienna. *Career:* Asst, Vienna State Opera to Wieland Wagner, Luchino Visconti, Teo Otto, Luciano Damiani, Rudolf Heinrich and others 1965–69; Asst to Filippo Sanjust 1969–72; debut in Reimann's Melusine world premiere at Berlin, Edinburgh and Schwetzingen Festival, staged by Gustav Rudolf Sellner; operas, Dramatic Theatre and Ballets in Austria, Belgium, the United Kingdom, Netherlands, USA and Switzerland, principal in Germany; Exhibitions in Berlin, Kunsthalle Bielefeld, Düsseldorf, Kunsthalle Kiel and Wuppertal (Reflexe I–III, Aus-Grenzen I–III); debut as a producer with Rameau's Hippolyte et Aricie at Oper Leipzig 1993; collaborations with John Dew 1979–92 (Wagner's Ring, Krefeld 1981–85, The Unknown Repertory at Bielefeld 1983–91, Les Huguenots Deutsche Oper Berlin 1987 as well as Royal Opera House, Covent Garden 1991 and others); with Götz Friedrich (Der Rosenkavalier, Un Ballo in Maschera, Deutsche Oper Berlin 1993) with Gunther Krämer since 1990 at Kölner Schauspiel, with Nikolaus Lehnhoff at Oper Frankfurt and Leipzig; Munich and Zürich, Henze's new version of Der Prinz von Homburg 1992 and 1993; with Christine Mielitz, Rienzi at Komische Oper Berlin 1992, engaged for Henze's The Bassarids at Hamburg State Opera 1994 and also for 1994 at Oper Leipzig, Moses and Aron staged by George Tabori; Designs for the premiere production of Bose's Schlachthof 5, at the 1996 Munich Festival; Wagner's Ring at Helsinki 1996–99. *Current Management:* Artists Management Zurich, Rütistrasse 52, 8044 Zurich, Switzerland. *Telephone:* 448218957. *Fax:* 448210127. *Website:* www .artistsman.com.

PILZ, Janos; Hungarian violinist; b. 1960. *Education:* Franz Liszt Acad., Budapest, studied with Sándor Devich, György Kurtág and András Mihaly. *Career:* mem., Keller String Quartet from 1986, debut concert at Budapest 1987; played Beethoven's Grosse Fuge and Schubert's Death and the Maiden Quartet at Interforum 87; series of concerts in Budapest with Zoltan Kocsis, Deszö Ranki (piano) and Kalman Berkes (clarinet); further appearances in Nurembourg at the Chamber Music Festival La Baule and tours of Bulgaria, Austria, Switzerland, Italy (Ateforum 88 Ferrara), Belgium and Ireland; concerts for Hungarian radio and television. *Honours:* second prize Evian Int. String Quartet Competition 1988.

PINI, Carl; British violinist; b. 2 Jan. 1934, London, England. *Education:* studied with his father, Anthony Pini and in London. *Career:* fmr leader, Philomusica of London, English Chamber Orchestra and Philharmonia Orchestras 1974–; Leader, London String Quartet from 1968, Melbourne Symphony Orchestra from 1975; many chamber recitals in English works and the established repertory.

PINNOCK, Trevor David, CBE, ARCM, FRAM; British harpsichordist and conductor; b. 16 Dec. 1946, Canterbury, Kent; s. of Kenneth Pinnock and Joyce Pinnock. *Education:* Canterbury Cathedral School, Royal Coll. of Music, London. *Career:* Co-founder Galliard Harpsichord Trio, debut, London 1966, solo debut, London 1968, Dir The English Concert 1973–2003; Artistic Dir and Prin. Conductor Nat. Arts Centre Orchestra, Ottawa 1991–96, Artistic Adviser 1996–; f. European Brandenburg Ensemble 2006–, numerous tours and recordings; has toured Western Europe, USA, S America, Canada, Australia, Japan with The English Concert, as solo harpsichordist and as orchestral/opera conductor; debut at Metropolitan Opera, New York 1988; has worked with Opera Australia, Freiburg Baroque Orchestra, Salzburg Camerata, Salzburg Mozarteum Orchestra, Deutsche Kammerphilharmonie Bremen, Deutsches Symphonie-Orchester Berlin, Amsterdam Concertgebouw Orchestra. *Recordings include:* Rameau, Pièces de Clavecin (with Jonathan Manson, J. S. Bach, Sonatas for viola da gamba and obligato harpsichord, and works by Handel, C. P. E. Bach, Vivaldi, Scarlatti, 16th, 17th and 18th-century harpsichord music and most of the standard baroque orchestral/concerto/choral repertoire, Brandenburg Concertos (with European Brandenburg Ensemble) (Gramophone Award for Best Baroque Instrumental Recording 2008), Scarlatti: Sonatas 2015, The Harmonious Blacksmith 2015, Journey 2016. *Honours:* Gramophone Award for Bach Partitas BWV 825–30 2001. *Website:* www.askonasholt.co.uk; www.trevorpinnock.com.

PINSCHOF, Thomas, DipMus; flautist; b. 14 Feb. 1948, Vienna, Austria. *Education:* Conservatorium of Vienna with Camillo Wanausek, Indiana Univ., USA, studied with Aurèle Nicolet, masterclasses with Karl-Heinz Zöller, Jean-Pierre Rampal, Severino Gazzelloni. *Career:* debut, Wiener Musikverein, Brahms-Saal 1965; mem., Vienna Symphony Orchestra 1971–72; Berkshire Music Festival, Tanglewood, USA (with Scholarship Boston Symphony Orchestra) 1969; founder, ENSEMBLE I 1971–; Artist-in-Residence, ENSEMBLE I, Victorian Coll. of the Arts, Melbourne, Australia 1976; Acting Head Woodwind Dept, Lecturer in Flute and Chamber Music, Victorian Coll. of Arts, Melbourne –1988; Lecturer, Canberra School of Music, Melbourne Univ. *Publications:* music edns for various publishers, including own series, Pinschofon, with Zimmermann; contrib. to The Flautist, Flutenotes, Musikerzeihung, Österreichishce Musikzeitschrift, Kunst und Freie Berufe. *Honours:* second prize Int. Flute Competition, Severino Gazzelloni 1975, Alban Berg Foundation Award 1971, Australia Council Music Bd grant 1984–85, for project with Prof. Nikolaus Harnoncourt.

PINTSCHER, Matthias; German composer and conductor; b. 29 Jan. 1971, Marl. *Education:* Detmold Musikhochschule, Robert Schumann Hochschule, Düsseldorf. *Career:* commissions from Berlin Philharmonic, NDR Symphony Orchestra, Cleveland Orchestra, Chicago Symphony Orchestra, London Symphony Orchestra; Composer-in-Residence to the Nationaltheater, Mannheim 1999–2000, Cleveland Orchestra 2000–02; composer-in-residence, Konzerthaus Dortmund 2002–03, Lucerne Festival 2006, RSO Saarbrücken 2006–07, Kölner Philharmonie 2007–08; Prof. of Composition, Hochschule für Musik, Munich 2007–; has conducted numerous orchestras including Cleveland Orchestra, DSO Berlin, SWR Stuttgart, RSO Wien, Danish Radio Symphony, Orchestre National de Strasbourg, Orchestre Philarmonique de France; premiere of Thomas Chatterton, opera in two acts, Dresden Oper 1998. *Compositions include:* Invocazioni 1991, Partita 1991, Monumento I 1991, Omaggio a Giovanni Paisiello 1991, La Metamorfosi di Narciso 1992, Tableau/Miroir 1992, Dunkles Feld – Berückung 1993, Devant une Neige 1993, Départ (Monumento III) 1993, dernier espace avec introspecteur 1994, Nacht. Mondschein 1994, Choc (Monumento IV) 1996, Fünf Orchesterstücke 1997, a twilight's song 1997, Musik aus Thomas Chatterton 1998, Monumento V 1998, Hérodiade-Fragmente 1999, Sur depart 1999, in nomine 1999, Vers quelque part...– façons de partir 2000, Lieder und Schneebilder 2000, with lilies white 2000–01, 1 tenebrae 2000–01, Janusgeischt 2001, en sourdine 2002, L'Espace Dernier 2003, Gesprungene Glocken, Study I for Treatise on the Veil 2004, on a clear day 2004, Study II for Treatise on the Veil 2005, Reflections on Narcissus 2005, towards Osiris 2005, Verzeichnete Spur 2005, svelto 2006, Transir 2006, The Garden 2006, nementon 2007, Osiris 2007, Songs from Solomon's Garden 2009, Sonic Eclipse 2009–10, mar'eh 2011, Chute d'Etoile 2012. *Honours:* Fondation Prince Pierre de Monaco Prize1999, Kompositionspreis der Österfestspiele Salzburg 2000, Hindemith-Preis from the Schleswig-Holstein Music Festival 2000, Hans Werner Henze Prize (Westfälischer Musikpreis) 2002. *Current Management:* c/o Cathy Nelson Artists and Projects, The Court House, Dorstone, Herefordshire, HR3 6AW, England. *Telephone:* (1981) 551903. *E-mail:* cathy@cathynelson.co.uk. *Website:* www.cathynelson.co.uk; www.matthiaspintscher.com (home).

PIRES, Filipe; Portuguese composer; b. 26 June 1934, Lisbon; m. Ligia Falcao 1958. *Education:* Nat. Conservatory, Lisbon, Hannover Music High School. *Career:* Prof. of Composition, Porto Nat. Conservatory 1960–70; Prof. of Composition, Lisbon Nat. Conservatory 1972–75; Music Specialist, UNESCO, Paris 1975–79; concert tours in Europe (as pianist and composer); Prof. of Composition, Porto High School of Music 1993–2004; Artistic Dir, Nat. Orchestra, Porto 1997–99; mem. Portuguese Authors' Soc. (vice-pres. 1979–91, 1998–2001); retired 2004. *Compositions:* Figurations I for flute, Sonatine for violin and piano, Piano Trio, Figurations II for piano, Figurations III for two pianos, Three Poems by Fernando Pessoa for high voice and piano, String Quartet, Ostinati for six percussionists, Zoocratas (music theatre), Disimulation for guitar, Brass septet, Epos for orchestra, Ricercare for orchestra, Playing Ludwig for orchestra, Babel for speaker, tenor, baritone, bass, male choir and orchestra, Three Bagatelles for piano, Partita for piano, Varied Song for piano, Stretto for two pianos. *Recordings:* Piano Trio, Figurations I, Figurations IV, Ostinati, Figurations III, String Quartet, Canto Ecumenico (tape music), Litania (tape music), Homo Sapiens (tape music), 20 Choral Songs, Portugaliae Genesis for baritone, mixed choir and orchestra, Sintra, Akronos for orchestra, Sonata for piano, Sonorities Studies for piano, Figurations I for flute, Figurations II for piano, Figurations III for two pianos,

Figurations IV for harp, Sonatine for cello and piano. *Publications:* Theory of Counterpoint and Canon 1981, Oscar da Silva – Analytical and biographical study, Helena Costa – tradition and renewal 1996, Introduction to Claudio Carneyro's Work 2005. *Honours:* Concours Quatuor, Liège 1959, German Industry, Cologne 1959, Alfredo Casella, Naples 1960, Calouste Gulbenkian, Lisbon 1968. *Address:* R. Costa Cabral, 2219-4D, 4200 Porto, Portugal (home). *Telephone:* (22) 548-84-98 (home).

PIRES, Maria João; Portuguese pianist; b. 23 July 1944, Lisbon; m.; four c. *Education:* Lisbon Acad. of Music. *Career:* debut recital aged four; early concert tours of Portugal, Spain and Germany; int. career from 1970, with performances in Europe, Africa and Japan; British debut 1986; debut tour of N America 1988; appearances with numerous famous orchestras and conductors world-wide; repertoire includes Mozart, Schubert, Schumann, Beethoven and Chopin; f. Belgais Foundation for the Study of Arts 1999; moved to San Salvador, Brazil 2006. *Recordings include:* Complete Mozart Piano Sonatas (Edison Prize, Prix de l' Acad. du Disque Français, Prix de l' Acad. Charles Cros), Debussy Etudes (Grammy Award) 1990, Concertos by Mozart (Grammy Award) 1991, Beethoven Piano Concertos Nos 3 & 4 (Gramophone Award for Best Concerto Recording 2015) 2014. *Honours:* First Prize, Beethoven Int. Competition, Brussels 1970.

PISARENKO, Vitaly; Russian pianist; b. 24 July 1987, Kyiv. *Education:* Moscow State Conservatory, Codarts Conservatory, Rotterdam, the Netherlands. *Career:* has performed as soloist at festivals in Belgium, France, Germany, Netherlands, Italy, Hungary, Poland, USA and Lithuania, with orchestras including Netherlands Radio Philharmonic Orchestra, Franz Liszt Chamber Orchestra, North Netherlands Symphony Orchestra, Polish Nat. Philharmonic Orchestra, Moscow Symphony Orchestra; tours in S America, Indonesia and Europe; appearances across Europe and in Japan, Australia, S Korea, Turkey, Algeria and S Africa. *Recording:* Vitaly Pisarenko 2009. *Honours:* First Prize, Int. Franz Liszt Competition 2008. *Current Management:* c/o Liszt Competition Foundation, PO Box 550, 3500 AN Utrecht, The Netherlands. *Telephone:* (30) 286-22-58. *Fax:* (30) 231-65-22. *Website:* www .liszt.nl. *E-mail:* vitaly@vitalypisarenko.com. *Website:* www.vitalypisarenko .com.

PISARONI, Luca; Italian singer (bass-baritone); b. 1975, Busseto. *Education:* Verdi Conservatory, Milan. *Career:* professional debut as Figaro in Le Nozze di Figaro, Klagenfurt 2001; other operatic roles have included Masetto and Leporello in Don Giovanni, Publio in La Clemenza di Tito, Douglas D'Angus in La Donna del Lago, Hercules in Alceste, Colline in La Bohème, Melisso in Alcina, Guglielmo in Così fan tutte, Alidoro in La Cenerentola, Achilla in Giulio Cesare, Papageno in Die Zauberflöte; has performed at Metropolitan Opera, New York, Opéra Bastille and Théâtre des Champs-Elysées, Paris, Opéra National du Rhin, Nederlandse Opera, Amsterdam, Teatro Real, Madrid, Barbican Hall, London, and at the Salzburg, Whitsun, Aix-en-Provence, Glyndebourne and Tanglewood Festivals; has worked with conductors, including Nikolaus Harnoncourt, James Levine, Daniel Harding, René Jacobs, Ivor Bolton, Mark Minkowski; concert performances have included Zebul in Jephtha with the Berlin Philharmonic and Nikolaus Harnoncourt, Haydn's Requiem in C minor, Mozart's Mass in C Minor, Mozart's Coronation Mass, Vivaldi's Orlano Furioso in Toulouse and Brussels with Jean-Christophe Spinosi and Ensemble Matheus; sang the Count in Le Nozze di Figaro at Salzburger Festspiele, Lyric Opera of Chicago and Wiener Staatsoper 2015 and at the Metropolitan Opera 2016. *Recordings include:* Mozart, Mass in C minor 2006. *Honours:* special prize Darclée Competition, Romania 1997, Vienna State Opera Eberhard-Wächter-Medal 2001. *Website:* www.askonasholt.co.uk; www.lucapisaroni.com.

PISCHNER, Hans, PhD; German teacher, harpsichordist, musicologist and intendant; b. 20 Feb. 1914, Breslau. *Education:* Univ. of Breslau, studied with Bronislav von Pozniac and Getrud Wertheim. *Career:* Prof. 1949; Head of Radio Music Dept, Ministry of Culture 1950–54, Head of Music Dept 1954–56, representative 1956–62; Intendant, Deutsche Staatsoper, Berlin 1963–89; numerous appearances as soloist and accompanist in Europe, America and Japan; now retired; Chair. Neue Bach-Gesellschaft, Leipzig; Sr Pres. Int. Soc. for Young Artists, 'Bünneu Reif' 1995–. *Recordings:* numerous works by Bach, both as soloist and continuo player; Bach Sonatas with David Oistrakh. *Publications:* Music in China 1955, Die Harmonielehre Jean-Philippe Rameaus 1967, Premier en eines Lebens (autobiog.) 1986, Tasten, Taten, Träume 2006; contrib. several articles to professional journals. *Honours:* Handel Prize, Halle 1961, Nat. Prize (third class) 1961, Johannes R. Becher 1962, Nat. Prize (first class), Bundesverdienstkreuz der Bundesrepublik Deutschland 1999. *Address:* Friedrichstrasse 105C, 10117 Berlin, Germany.

PITTMAN, Richard Harding, BMus; American conductor; *Music Director, Boston Musica Viva, The Concord Orchestra and New England Philharmonic Orchestra;* b. 3 June 1935, Baltimore, Md; s. of Emory Harding Pittman and Lenetta Pittman; m. 1965; one s. *Education:* Peabody Conservatory, studied with Laszlo Halasz in New York, Sergiu Celibidache at Accad. Musicale Chigiana, Siena, Italy, with W. Brueckner Ruggeberg in Hamburg, with Pierre Boulez in Basel, Switzerland. *Career:* Instructor of Conducting and Opera, Eastman School of Music 1965–68; teacher of orchestral conducting and orchestra conductor, New England Conservatory 1968–85; Guest Conductor of Nat. Symphony, Washington, DC, BBC Orchestras, London Sinfonietta, Frankfurt Radio Symphony, Germany, Hamburg Symphony, BBC Concert Orchestra, City of London Sinfonia, Ulster Orchestra, Belfast,

Nebraska Chamber Orchestra, Lincoln, Dutch Ballet Orchestra, Amsterdam, and Kirov Opera Orchestra, St Petersburg, Russia; additional guest conductor, Banff Arts Festival, Canada, BBC Singers, American Repertory Theatre, Cambridge, Mass, Symphony Orchestra of Ireland, Dublin 1999, Seattle Symphony, Wash. 2000; Music Dir Boston Musica Viva 1969–, The Concord Orchestra 1969–, New England Philharmonic, Boston 1997–; Guest Conductor, Canadian Opera Co., Toronto 2000–02. *Recordings:* music by Ives, Berio, Davidovsky, Harris, Schwantner, Henry Brant, Wilson, Lieberson, Rands, Ellen Taaffe Zwilich, Shifrin, Musgrave, Crawford Seeger, William Kraft, John Harbison, Ezra Sims, Bernard Hoffer, Chou Wen-chung, Peter Child, Eitan Steinberg, Hale Smith, Ronald Perera. *Honours:* Fulbright Award, American Composers' Alliance Laurel Leaf Award, New York 1989, Peabody Conservatory Distinguished Alumni Award 1996, Award for Adventurous Programming (with New England Philharmonic), American Soc. of Composers, Authors and Publrs (ASCAP) 2003, Chamber Music America/ ASCAP Award for Adventurous Programming (with Boston Musica Viva) 2004, ASCAP Award for Adventurous Programming (with New England Philharmonic) 2011. *Address:* 41 Bothfeld Road, Newton Center, MA 02459, USA (home). *Telephone:* (617) 969-3629 (home); (617) 354-6910 (office). *E-mail:* richardpittman2001@yahoo.com (home). *Website:* richardpittmanconductor.com (office).

PITTMAN-JENNINGS, David; American singer (baritone); b. 1949, Oklahoma. *Education:* studied in America. *Career:* sang Lensky at Graz Opera 1977 and was engaged at Bremen 1981–85; sang at Paris Opéra 1982–83, as Don Fernando in Fidelio and Schaunard in La Bohème; sang Germont at Tel-Aviv 1988, and Wozzeck at Reggio Emilia 1989; mem., Karlsruhe Opera from 1990, singing Amfortas in Parsifal at Strasbourg 1991; season 1992 in Dallapiccola's Il Prigioniero, and as Mandryka in Arabella at the Vienna Staatsoper; other roles have included Guglielmo, the Count in Capriccio, Mozart's Count and Figaro, Lescaut, Chorèbe in Les Troyens, Marcello and Gluck's Orestes; sang in Schoeck's Venus at Geneva 1997; Genoa 1998 in Peter Grimes; season 2000–01 as Wozzeck at Santiago, Scarpia at Buenos Aires and Klingsor for the Edinburgh Festival; Cortez in Die Eroberung von Mexico, by Rihm, at Frankfurt, Orestes at Antwerp and Janáček's Forester in Ghent; concerts include Beethoven's Ninth, Elijah, Ein Deutsches Requiem and L'Enfance du Christ.

PITTSINGER, David; American singer (bass-baritone); b. 1962. *Career:* sang with San Francisco Opera from 1987; Brussels from 1988, as Verdi's Fiesco; Mephistopheles in Faust; Nick Shadow in Stravinsky's Rakes Progress; Shrecker's Der Ferne Klang; Mozart's Figaro and Don Giovanni at Nice, 1991, and Cologne, 1995; Salzburg, 1992, as Orbazzano in Rossini's Tancredi; Vienna Festival as Nick Shadow, 1993, and Lausanne, 1999; Season 1996–97, debuted as Olin Blitch in Carlisle Floyd's Susannah with Vancouver Opera; Performance of Bach's Christmas Oratorio with Amsterdamse Bach Solisten, Netherlands; Season 1997–98, debut at L'Opéra de Montréal, and also Macerata Festival as Mephistopheles in Gounod's Faust; Boito's Mefistofele for Pittsburgh Opera, 1997, and St Louis, 1998; Season 1998–99, duo-recital with soprano Patricia Schuman including works by Mozart, Verdi, Tchaikovsky, Dvořák, Bowles and Copland; Debut as Four Villains in Offenbach's Les Contes d'Hoffmann for Opera Company of Philadelphia; Sang Publio in La Clemenza di Tito in Paris; Metropolitan Opera in Don Carlo, Rake's Progress, 1998, and as Colline in La Bohème, 1999; season 2000–01 as Rossini's Alidoro in Brussels, Rossini's Selim in Buenos Aires and Tiresias in Oedipus Rex at Naples; Massenet's Don Quichotte, Buenos Aires 2005. *Recordings:* Simon Boccanegra by Verdi; La Calisto by Cavalli; Susannah by Floyd; Alfonso in Donizetti's Lucrezia Borgia. *Honours:* Grammy Award (for Susannah). *Address:* Columbia Artists Management Inc, 165 W 57th Street, New York, NY 10019, USA.

PIZARRO, Artur; Portuguese pianist; b. 1968, Lisbon. *Education:* studied with Sequeira Costa, with Jorge Moyano in Lisbon, and with Ado Ciccolini, Géry Moutier and Bruno Rigutto in Paris. *Career:* regular int. performances with leading conductors including Esa-Pekka Salonen, Sir Andrew Davis, Charles Dutoit, Franz Welser-Most, Ilan Volkov, Tugan Sokhiev, Yakov Kreizberg, Yannick Nezet-Seguin, Libor Pesek, Vladimir Jurowski, Sir Simon Rattle, Sir Charles Mackerras; as recitalist has performed at numerous venues and festivals including Kennedy Center, Washington, DC, Wigmore Hall, London, Aldeburgh Festival, Neues Gewandhaus, Leipzig, Frankfurt Alte Oper, Théâtre du Chatelet and Musee D'Orsay, Paris, Zürich Tonhalle, BBC Proms, London, NHK and Orchard Halls, Japan; chamber music appearances with Raphael Oleg, Christian Altenburger, Truls Mork, Toby Hoffmann, the St Lawrence, Muir and Petersen quartets; taught at GSMD 1998–2002; performed complete cycle of Beethoven Piano Sonatas, St John Smith's Square, London 2004–05; f. the Pizarro Trio with violinist Raphael Oleg and cellist Josephine Knight 2005. *Recordings include:* Milhaud, Music for Two Pianos (with Stephen Coombs) 1997, Vianna da Motta, The Romantic Piano Concerto 1999, Beethoven Piano Sonatas 2003, Beethoven, Last Three Piano Sonatas 2003, Chopin, Reminiscences 2005, Rodrigo, Complete Piano Works (Ed.'s Choice, Gramophone Magazine) 2005, Chopin, Second and Third Sonatas 2006, Lizst, Hungarian Rhapsodies 2006, Ravel, Complete Solo Works 2007, Piano Duo Music, with Vita Panomariovaite 2007, Ravel, Complete Piano Works, Vol. 2 2008. *Honours:* Medal of Cultural Merit, Portugal 2007; winner, Vianna da Motta Int. Piano Competition 1987, Greater Palm Beach Symphony Invitational Piano Competition 1989, Leeds Int. Pianoforte Competition 1990; Bordalo Prize 1998, Portuguese Press Award,

Portuguese Soc. of Authors Award, Medal of Culture of the City of Funchal, Medal of Cultural Merit from Portuguese Govt . *Current Management:* Komarova & Reinicke Artists Management, Ludwigkirchplatz 11, 10719 Berlin, Germany. *E-mail:* mail@komarova-reinicke.com. *Website:* www .arturpizarro.pt.

PIZER, Elizabeth; American composer and musician; b. 1 Sept. 1954, Watertown, NY; m. Charles Ronald Pizer 1974. *Education:* Watertown High School, Boston Conservatory of Music, Boston, MA. *Career:* numerous concert performances of her compositions internationally; many broadcasts of compositions throughout the USA 1979–86, and a live concert broadcast including pre-recorded material in Australia 1986. *Compositions:* Expressions Intimes for solo piano 1975, Quilisoly for flute and piano, or violin and piano 1976, Look Down, Fair Moon for voice and piano 1976, Elegy (fmrly known as Interfuguelude) for string orchestra, or string quartet, or wind quartet 1977, Fanfare Overture for symphonic band 1977–79, Five Haiku for soprano and chamber ensemble 1978, Five Haiku II for mezzo-soprano and piano 1979, Madrigals Anon for a capella choir 1979, Sunken Flutes for electronic tape 1979, String Quartet 1981, Lyric Fancies for solo piano 1983, Kyrie Eleison for a capella chorus 1983, Strains and Restraints for solo piano 1984, Nightsongs for voice and piano 1986, Arlington for electronic tape 1989, Embryonic Climactus for electronic tape 1989, Aquasphere for electronic tape 1990, Elegy in Amber (in memoriam Leonard Bernstein) for string orchestra 1993.

PIZZI, Pier Luigi; Italian stage director and set and costume designer; *Artistic Director, Sferisterio Opera Festival;* b. 15 June 1930, Milan. *Education:* Milan Polytechnic. *Career:* debut designing Don Giovanni at Genoa 1952; Artistic Dir, Sferisterio Opera Festival 2005–; designs and productions for operas including Handel's Ariodante and Rinaldo (seen at Reggio Emilia, Paris, Madrid and Lisbon), Rameau's Hippolyte et Aricie and Castor et Pollux, Gluck's Alceste; other work includes Les Troyens, to open the Opéra Bastille at Paris in 1990, followed by Samson et Dalila 1991, I Capuleti e i Montecchi at Covent Garden, Don Carlos at Vienna, La Traviata at Monte Carlo, Venice and Lausanne, Rossini productions at Pesaro include Otello and Tancredi; staged Gluck's Armide at La Scala to open the 1996–97 season; Rossini, Guillaume Tell, Rossini Opera Festival 1995; Verdi, Macbeth, Arena di Verona 1997, Britten's Death in Venice, Genoa 2001, La Traviata, Teatro Real, Madrid 2003, Massenet's Thaïs, Venice 2003, Salieri's Europa riconosciuta, La Scala Milan 2004, La Gioconda 2005, A Midsummer Night's Dream 2006, L'Orfeo 2008, Il Ritorno di Ulisse in Patria, Teatro Real, Madrid 2009, Die tote Stadt, Venice and Palermo 2009, Don Giovanni, Macerata 2009. *Honours:* Chevalier, Légion d'honneur, Officier, Ordre des Arts et des Lettres, Grand'Ufficiale al Merito (Italy), Commdr, Ordre du Mérite Culturel (Monaco); Dr hc (Macerata), (Accad. di Belle Arti, Verona); seven Abbiati Prizes, Premio Rubinstein. *Address:* Sferisterio Opera Festival, Piazza Mazzini 10, 62100 Macerata, Italy (office). *Telephone:* (0733) 261335 (office). *Fax:* (0733) 261499 (office). *E-mail:* info@sferisterio.it (office). *Website:* www .sferisterio.it (office).

PLA GARRIGOS, Adolf, DipMus; Spanish pianist; b. 4 Oct. 1960, Sabadell; m. Roser Farriol. *Education:* Public Conservatoire of Barcelona, Franz Liszt Acad., Budapest, Hungary, studied in Würzburg, Germany. *Career:* played at Int. Festivals of Barcelona, Madrid, Havana and St Petersburg, also at Pau Casals Festival in Spain, El Salvador and Prades, France; appeared in concerts in Italy, Germany and Hungary and on Spanish and Russian nat. radio, Catalan television; Dir, Professional Conservatoire of Sabadell 1989–93, 1996–97; council mem., Catalan Asscn of Performance 1994–. *Recording:* Ma De Guido (album of music by Schumann, Granados and Ravel as soloist) 1995.

PLACIDI, Tommaso; Italian conductor; b. 29 March 1964, Rome. *Education:* Geneva Conservatory, Switzerland, Vienna Acad. of Music, Austria and Accad. Musicale Chigiana, Siena. *Career:* Asst Conductor, London Symphony Orchestra; guest conductor in Europe, of the London Symphony Orchestra, Royal Philharmonic Orchestra, Vienna Symphony Orchestra, Spoleto Festival, Orchestre National du Capitole de Toulouse, Orchestre Philharmonique de Strasbourg, Orchestre Philharmonique des Pays de Loire, Orchestre de la Suisse Romande, Orchestre de Chambre de Lausanne, Wiener Kammerorchester, Orchestra Sinfonica RAI, Turin, Orchestra del Teatro Regio, Turin, Orchestra della Toscana, Florence, Orchestre Sinfonica Haydn Bolzano, Trento, Orchestra of Bratislava Opera House, Wrocław Philharmonic Orchestra, Philharmonisches Staatorchester Hallé, Radio Philharmonie Hannover des NDR, Orchestre Philharmonique de Liège, Orchestre Philharmonique du Luxembourg, Norddeutsche Philharmonie Rostock; also with Guangzhou Symphony Orchestra. *Recordings:* Tchaikovsky's Violin Concerto, Piano Concerto No. 1, Weber's Clarinet Concertos, Münchner Rundfunkorchester, Germany 1997, Bruch Concerto for Clarinet and Viola, Hannover Radio Philharmonic 2002. *Honours:* Dr hc (Accad. Musicale Chigiana) 1992; First Prize, Donatella Flick Conducting Competition, London 1986, First Prize, Besançon Conducting Competition 1992, Cesare Alfieri Prize awarded by Mrs Cristina Muti 1994. *Current Management:* c/o Xenia Evangelista, Merzbacherstraße 32, 80637 Munich, Germany. *Telephone:* (89) 12038285. *E-mail:* welcome@xeniaevangelista.com; x.e@xeniaevangelista.com; xenia .evangelista@me.com. *Website:* www.xeniaevangelista.com. *Address:* Chemin Taverney 5, 1218 Geneva, Switzerland (home). *Telephone:* (22) 3497938 (office). *Fax:* (22) 3497938 (office). *E-mail:* tommaso.placidi@bluewin.ch (office).

PLAGGE, Wolfgang Antoine Marie; Norwegian composer and pianist; b. 23 Aug. 1960, Oslo; m. Lena Rist-Larsen 1993. *Education:* studied with Robert Riefling and Jens Harald Bratlie in Norway, with Oistein Sommerfeldt, Johan Kvandal, Evgenij Koroliev, and Musikhochschule, Hamburg with Werner Krützfeld. *Career:* debut as pianist, Oslo 1972; first published work aged 12; numerous commissions. *Compositions include:* Music for two pianos 1982–89, Piano Sonata V 1985–86, Piano Sonata VI 1988–91, Vesaas-Sange: Baryton og Piano 1989–90, A Litany for the 21st Century: Sonata for horn and piano 1989, Festival Music for symphonic band 1989, for symphonic orchestra 1994, Concerto for horn and orchestra 1990, Canzona for brass quintet and pianoforte 1990, Concerto for violin and orchestra 1991, Concerto for two pianos and orchestra 1991, Solarljod: Solsanger fra Norron Middelalder 1992, Sonata II for bassoon and pianoforte 1993, Hogge i Stein: A Portrait of Trondenes Church and her People for narrator, choir, three soloists and orchestra 1994, Concerto for trumpet and orchestra 1994.

PLAISTOW, Stephen, MA, ARCM; British pianist, writer and broadcaster; b. 24 Jan. 1937, Welwyn Garden City, Herts., England; partner Sanchia Voilley (died 1989); one step-d. *Education:* Bedales School, Hants., Clare Coll., Cambridge. *Career:* freelance music journalist 1961–; BBC Music Producer 1962–74; Chair. British section of Int. Soc. for Contemporary Music (ISCM) and Music Section of Inst. of Contemporary Arts (ICA) 1967–71; Chair. British section of ISCM and Arts Council Contemporary Music Network 1976–79; mem. of Music Panel, Arts Council of GB 1972–79; Chief Asst to Controller of Music, BBC 1974–79, Ed. Contemporary Music, BBC 1979–92, Deputy Head, Radio 3 Music Dept 1989–92; freelance pianist and writer 1992–; mem. Royal Soc. of Musicians, Royal Musical Asscn, Samuel Blythe Soc., Haydn Soc. of GB, Royal Philharmonic Soc. *Radio includes:* regular contribs to BBC Radio 3, especially on musical performance and living composers. *Publications include:* contrib. to The Gramophone, The Guardian, Musical Times, Tempo, The Independent, Revista de libros. *Honours:* Hon. RAM 2003; Leslie Boosey Award 1994. *Address:* 5 Gloucester Court, 33 Gloucester Avenue, London, NW1 7TJ, England. *Telephone:* (20) 7485-2693. *E-mail:* stephen.plaistow@ ecosse.net. *Website:* sites.ecosse.net/stephen.plaistow.

PLANCHART, Alejandro Enrique, BMus, MMus, PhD; music historian and composer; b. 29 July 1935, Caracas, Venezuela; m. (divorced); one d. *Education:* Yale Univ. School of Music, Harvard Univ. *Career:* freelance arranger and composer, New York and New Haven 1960–64; Instructor/Asst Prof., Yale Univ. 1967–75; Assoc. Prof., Univ. of Victoria 1975–76, Univ. of California at Santa Barbara 1976–; Visiting Prof., Brandeis Univ. 1982–83. *Compositions:* Divertimento for percussion trio, Five Poems of James Joyce for soprano and piano. *Recordings:* 20 recordings of medieval and renaissance music with the Cappella Cordina, Lyrichord and Musical Heritage Society. *Publications:* The Repertory of Tropes at Winchester (two vols) 1977, Beneventanum Troporum Corpus (ed. with John Boe, 10 vols); contrib. to Guillaume Dufay's Masses: Notes and Revisions (in Musical Quarterly) 1972, Fifteenth Century Masses: Notes on Chronology and Performance (in Study Musicali 10) 1983, some 50 other titles. *Address:* 1070 Via Regina, Santa Barbara, CA 93111, USA.

PLANTINGA, Leon Brooks, BA, MMus, PhD; American musicologist, academic and writer; *Professor Emeritus of Music, Yale University;* b. 25 March 1935, Ann Arbor, Mich. *Education:* Calvin Coll., Michigan State Univ., Yale Univ. *Career:* mem. Faculty, Yale Univ. 1963–74, Prof. of Music 1974–2005, Prof. Emer. 2005–, Acting Chair Dept of Music 1978–79, Chair Dept of Music 1979–86, Dir Div. of Humanities 1991–97; mem. American Musicological Soc. *Publications include:* Schumann as Critic 1967, Muzio Clementi: His Life and Music 1977, Romantic Music: A History of Musical Style in Nineteenth-Century Europe 1984, Anthology of Romantic Music 1984, Beethoven's Concertos: History, Style, Performance 1999; contrib. to scholarly books and journals. *Honours:* Deems Taylor Award, American Soc. of Composers, Authors and Publrs 1985. *Address:* c/o Department of Music, Yale University, PO Box 208310, New Haven, CT 06520-8310, USA.

PLASSON, Michel; French conductor; *Music Director, Chinese National Symphony Orchestra;* b. 2 Oct. 1933, Paris. *Education:* Paris Conservatoire, studied in the USA with Leinsdorf, Monteux and Stokowski. *Career:* Musical Dir, Metz 1966–68; Dir of the Orchestra and of the Théâtre du Capitole de Toulouse 1968–83; operatic performances in Toulouse include Salome, Aida, Die Meistersinger, Faust, Parsifal, Carmen and Montségur by Landowski (world premiere 1985); Conductor, Orchestre National du Capitole de Toulouse 1983–2003, Conductor Emer. 2003–; Principal Conductor Dresden Philharmonic Orchestra 1994–2001; Music Dir Chinese Nat. Symphony Orchestra 2009–; at the Palais Omnisport de Paris-Bercy has conducted Aida, Turandot, the Verdi Requiem and Nabucco 1984–87; guest engagements with the Berlin Philharmonic Orchestra, London Philharmonic, Orchestre of the Suisse Romande, and the Gewandhaus Orchestra Leipzig; Paris Opéra, Geneva Opera, State Operas of Vienna, Hamburg and Munich, Zürich Opera, Covent Garden, Metropolitan Opera, Chicago and San Francisco; Principal Guest Conductor, Zürich Tonhalle Orchestra from 1987; conducted new production of Guillaume Tell at Covent Garden 1990; Il Trovatore at the Halle aux Grains, Toulouse 1990; Faust at the 1990 Orange Festival; returned to Covent Garden 1991, Tosca; season 1991–92 with Lucia di Lammermoor at Munich, Guillaume Tell at Covent Garden, Don Quichotte at Toulouse and Carmen at Orange; conducted La Forza del Destino at Orange 1996; original version of Boris Godunov at Toulouse 1998. *Recordings include:* La Vie Parisienne, La Grande Duchesse de Gérolstein, Chausson's Symphony, Saint-

Saëns Piano Concertos, premiere pressings of Roussel's Padmâvati, Magnard's Symphonies and Guercoeur, Symphonic poems by Chausson, Les Pêcheurs de Perles, Faust. *Honours:* Hon. Conductor for Life, Orchestre National du Capitole de Toulouse; Commdr, Légion d'Honneur. *E-mail:* cnso@ cnso.com.cn (office). *Website:* www.cnso.com.cn.

PLATILOVÁ, Dagmar, MusM; Czech harpist; b. 15 Aug. 1943, Slapy; d. of Josef Platilovi and Jarmila Platilovi; m. Myron Yadzyn 1971 (divorced 1985). *Education:* Acad. of Musical Arts, Prague, Hartt School of Music, Univ. of Hartford, USA and Juilliard School of Music, New York. *Career:* mem. Prague Duo (flute and harp) 1962–68, 1976–, New York Harp Ensemble 1972–75; Prin. Harpist Czech Radio Orchestra 1976–2002; freelance harpist 2002–; appearances include Cisac Int. Festival of Contemporary Music, Prague 1966, Int. Music Festival, Bergen, Norway 1967, 1974, Prague Spring Festival 1967, ICAM Festival, Hartford, CT 1969; Corresp. for World Harp Congress Review 1985–99; many TV appearances; numerous recordings. *Recordings:* albums: Compositions for Violin and Harp (with Josef Suk), Harp Concertos (Dussek and Krumpholtz), New York Harp Ensemble. *Address:* Tibetská 6/806, 160 00 Prague 6, Czech Republic (home). *Telephone:* (2) 35311932 (home).

PLATT, Ian; British singer (baritone); b. 1959, Fleetwood. *Education:* studied with John Cameron at Royal Northern College of Music. *Career:* sang Rossini's Figaro, Guglielmo, Papageno and Junius in The Rape of Lucretia for Royal Northern College of Music; Professional debut for Kent Opera, in La Traviata and Il Barbiere di Siviglia; Engagements with Opera 80 as Don Magnifico in La Cenerentola and Baron Zeta in The Merry Widow; New Sadler's Wells Opera as Agamemnon in La Belle Hélène; Sang Tom in Henze's The English Cat at Hebbel Theatre, Berlin and toured with Travelling Opera as Schaunard and Mozart's Figaro; Welsh National Opera and Scottish Opera, 1991, in La Traviata; Alcindoro in La Bohème for Glyndebourne Touring Opera, 1991; Pirate King, D'Oyly Carte, 1993; Don Magnifico, Welsh National Opera, 1993–94. *Recordings include:* Il Crociato in Egitto by Meyerbeer, Opera Rara.

PLATT, Richard Swaby, ARCA; British musicologist; b. 14 May 1928, London, England; m. 1st; two s. one d.; m. 2nd Diane Ibbotson 1977; one s. one d. *Education:* Royal Coll. of Art, studied with Walter Bergmann, Hugh Wood. *Career:* painter and printmaker, exhibiting at Royal Acad., London Group and others 1953–61; solo show of works, Leicester Galleries 1956; musicologist, specializing in 18th-century English music 1969; mem. Royal Musical Association. *Publications:* editions of William Boyce: 12 Overtures, Thomas Arne: four Symphonies, works by Croft, Roseingrave, Mudge, Fisher, Gli Equivoci by Stephen Storace, Peleus and Thetis by William Boyce; contrib. to New Grove 1980, 2001, Grove Opera 1992, Theatre Music 1700–1760 in Blackwell's History of Music in Britain vol. 4, The Symphony 1720–1840 1983, Semele by John Eccles: Judgement of Paris 1984, 2000, contrib. to BIOS 17 on Gerard Smith Organ Contract, Early Music on Richard Mudge 2000.

PLATT, Theodore, DMus; Russian conductor, composer, double bassist and harpsichordist; b. 8 Sept. 1937, Moscow. *Education:* Ippolitov-Ivanov Conservatory of Music, Moscow Conservatory of Music. *Career:* founder and Dir, four chamber ensembles, including first baroque and classical ensembles in USSR (Moscow) 1968–81, New York Concertino Ensemble 1981; live concerts on major classical music radio stations in USA; eight years as double bass soloist, Moscow Chamber Orchestra; discovered and premiered lost Baroque works; teacher of string instruments and voice; mem. Conductors Guild, Coll. Music Soc. *Compositions:* two symphony concertos, cycles of vocal compositions, one quartet.

PLATZ, Robert H. P.; German composer and conductor; b. 16 Aug. 1951, Baden-Baden. *Education:* studied with Wolfgang Fortner, Karlheinz Stockhausen, Francis Travis, IRCAM computer workshop for composers. *Career:* founded new music group Ensemble Köln, 1980; own concert series with Ensemble Köln, 1982; appeared at music festivals such as Musik der Zeit WDR and Musica Viva series of Munich, Donaueschingen and La Rochelle; performed at Salzburg Festival, Metz. *Compositions:* Schwelle, Full Orchestra and Tape; Chlebnicov, Ensemble and Tape; Maro and Stille, Soprano, Violin and Piano Solos, plus Ensembles and Choirs; Raumform, Clarinet Solo; Flotenstücke–Seven Pieces for Flute and Ensemble; Requiem for Tape; Pianoforte 2; Closed Loop, Guitar; Verkommenes ufer, opera (texts Heiner Müller); Quartett (Zeitstrahl) for String Quartet, 1986; Dunkles Haus, music theatre, 1991; Grenzgänge Steine, for soprano, 2 pianos and orchestra, 1993; Echo I–V, for ensemble 1994–98. *Publications:* Musikalische Prozesse, 1979; Uber Schwelle, 1980; Uber Schwelle II, 1981; Uber Tasten, 1983; Versuch einer Asthetik des Kleinen, 1984; Blumroder, Nicht Einfach, Aber Neu, 1980; Formpolyphone Musik, 1981; Stegen: Robert HP Platz, 1982; Van den Hoogen: Komplizierte Horbarkeit, 1982; Blumröder: Maro, 1984; Van den Hoogen: Raumform, 1984; Allendë-Blin: Uber Chielnicov, 1984; Record Maro, Irvine Arditi, Violin.

PLAVIN, Zecharia, BMus, MMus; pianist; b. 7 June 1956, Vilnius, Lithuania; m. 1984; one s. one d. *Education:* Ciurlionis School of Arts, S. Rubin Acad. of Music, Univ. of Tel-Aviv, Israel. *Career:* concerts with Israel Philharmonic Orchestra, Jerusalem Symphony Orchestra, Symphonietta of Beer-Sheva, Haifa Symphony Orchestra, and others; recitals on all major stages in Israel; concerts in Western Europe from 1988; numerous recordings for Israel Broadcasting Authorities; work for Israel Concert Bureau Omanuth Laam. *Honours:* first prize S. Rubin Acad. of Music Competition 1978, Nat. François Shapira Prize 1980, Israel Broadcasting Competition diploma 1985.

PLAZAS, Mary; British singer (soprano); b. 9 Sept. 1966, Wallingford. *Education:* Royal Northern Coll. of Music with Ava June, National Opera Studio. *Career:* solo recitals at Wigmore Hall, Purcell Room, Birmingham Town Hall and Royal Exchange Theatre, Manchester; concerts at Cheltenham and Aldeburgh Festivals; opera engagements include Poulenc's La Voix Humaine at Aix-en-Provence, Nannetta at Aldeburgh and Despina for Mid-Wales Opera; ENO debut 1992, as Heavenly Voice in Don Carlos; with Opera North 1992–, as the Gypsy in British premiere of Gerhard's The Duenna, Barbarina and Susanna in Figaro and Tebaldo in Don Carlos; sang in Opera Factory's Nozze di Figaro for Channel 4 television and appeared as Echo in Ariadne auf Naxos for Garsington Opera; joined ENO as Company Principal 1995 and sang Echo in Ariadne auf Naxos 1997; Tina in premiere of Dove's Flight for GTO at Glyndebourne 1998; season 2000–01 as Donna Elvira for GTO and Lauretta in Gianni Schicchi for ENO. *Honours:* Kathleen Ferrier Memorial Scholarship 1991.

PLECH, Linda; singer (soprano); b. 1951, Vienna, Austria. *Education:* studied in Vienna and at Salzburg Mozarteum. *Career:* sang as mezzo-soprano at Klagenfurt Opera 1976–77, Oldenburg 1980–84; soprano roles at Kaiserslautern 1985–86, Hamburg Staatsoper 1987–88 as Donna Anna and Elisabeth de Valois; Cologne 1989, as Jenůfa; Bregenz Festival 1988–89, as Senta in Der fliegende Holländer; sang the Trovatore Leonora at Deutsche Oper Berlin 1989, Ariadne auf Naxos at Antwerp; season 1991–92 as Senta at Geneva, Elisabeth in Tannhäuser at Barcelona; other roles include Marenka in The Bartered Bride and Giulietta in Les Contes d'Hoffmann.

PLESHAK, Victor Vasilievich; Russian composer; b. 13 Nov. 1946, Leningrad; two s. *Education:* Choral College of Chapel, St Petersburg Conservatoire with B. Tischenko. *Career:* debut with Many-coloured Balls, song cycle for children, verses by Akimya, Leningrad Radio. *Compositions include:* more than 17 musicals and operas, including The Red Imp, musical, 1980; The Knight's Passions, 1981; The Glass Menagerie, opera, 1987; A Tale of a Blot, New Year operetta, 1988; Caution Baba-Yaga, ecological opera; Inspector, an opera after Gogol, 1993; Choral Cycle, About Friendship, Love and Brotherhood, to verses by R Burns, 1983; Over 100 published songs including: V Pleshak, Songs for voice and piano (guitar, accordion), in Soviet Composer, 1988. *Recordings:* The Tale of a Dead Tsarevna and Seven Epic Heroes, opera in 2 acts; The Widow of Valencia, musical after the play by Lope de Vega; Oh These Pretty Sinners, musical farces after Lasage and Rabelais; Puss in Boots, musical after the play by Pierrot; Author of over 150 theatre performances including 30 musicals, and over 400 songs. *Compositions include:* The Turnip, opera after Russian folk tale, 1992; The Canterville Ghost, musical after story, 1994; Ruslan and Ludmila, after Russian fairy-tale, Pushkin, 1999. *Recordings:* Hymn of St Petersburg Region, 1997; Hymn of St Petersburg University, 1999. *Address:* Gorokhovaya Street 53 kv 29, 190031 St Petersburg, Russia.

PLETNEV, Mikhail Vasilievich; Russian pianist, conductor and composer; b. 14 April 1957, Arkhangelsk. *Education:* Moscow State Conservatory with Yakov Flier and Lev Vlasenko (piano), Albert Leman (composition). *Career:* gave recitals and played with orchestras in major cities of Russia, Europe, Japan and America; gained reputation as Russian music interpreter; Founder and Chief Conductor Russian Nat. Orchestra 1990–99, Hon. Conductor 1999–, head of Conductor Collegium 2006–; has performed with Haitink, Maazel, Chailly, Tennstedt, Sanderling, Blomstedt, Järvi, Thielemann; has conducted Philharmonia Orchestra, Deutsche Kammerphilharmonie, Norddeutsche Rundfunk Symphony Orchestra, London Symphony Orchestra, Berlin Philharmonic, Bayerische Rundfunk Symphony, Orchestre Nat. de France, Israel Philharmonic, San Francisco Symphony and Pittsburgh Symphony; teacher, Moscow Conservatory 1981–1992; f. Mikhail Pletnev Fund for the Support of National Culture 2006. *Honours:* First Prize, Int. Tchaikovsky competition, Moscow 1978, People's Artist of Russia 1990, State Prize of Russia 1982, 1993. *Current Management:* Opus 3 Artists, 470 Park Avenue South, 9th Floor North, New York, NY 10016, USA. *Telephone:* (212) 584-7500. *Fax:* (646) 300-8200. *E-mail:* info@opus3artists.com. *Website:* www.opus3artists.com. *Address:* Russian National Orchestra, Moscow 117335, Orchestrion, Garibaldi 19, Russia (office). *Website:* russiannationalorchestra.org (office).

PLISHKA, Paul; singer (bass); b. 28 Aug. 1941, Old Forge, PA, USA. *Education:* Montclair State Coll., studied with Armen Boyazjian. *Career:* debut with Paterson Lyric Opera 1961; Metropolitan Opera from 1967, as King Marke in Tristan, Procida in Les Vêpres Siciliennes, Varlaam and Pimen in Boris Godunov, Oroveso in Norman, Leporello and the Commendatore in Don Giovanni, Banquo in the Peter Hall production of Macbeth, and Philip II in Don Carlos; La Scala 1974, in La Damnation de Faust; San Francisco 1984, as Silva in Ernani; Teatro Liceo Barcelona 1985; Orange Festival 1987, as Phanüel in Massenet's Hérodiade; sang Daland in Der fliegende Holländer at the Metropolitan 1989; Procida at Carnegie Hall 1990; Opera Company of Philadelphia 1990, as the Mayor in La Gazza Ladra, Fiesco in Simon Boccanegra at the Metropolitan; Grand Park concerts Chicago, in Prince Igor; season 1991–92 as Giorgio in Puritani at Chicago, the Pope in Benvenuto Cellini at Geneva and Zaccaria at Montréal; sang Mozart's Bartolo at the Met 1997; Grand Inquisitor in Don Carlos at Salzburg 1998; sang Des Grieux in Manon at the Met 2001. *Recordings:* Crespel in Les Contes d'Hoffmann and Henry VIII in Anna Bolena; Norma; Le Cid and Donizetti's Gemma di Vergy; Faust; Wurm in Luisa Miller.

PLITMANN, Hila, MusM; Israeli singer (soprano); b. Jerusalem. *Education:* Juilliard School. *Career:* has worked with conductors including Kurt Masur, Robert Spano, Marin Alsop, Esa Pekka Salonen, Andrew Litton, Leonard Slatkin and Steven Sloane, with orchestras including New York Philharmonic, Los Angeles Philharmonic, Chicago Symphony, Atlanta Symphony Orchestra, Minnesota Orchestra, Nat. Symphony Orchestra, Pittsburgh Symphony Orchestra, Israel Philharmonic, Orpheus Chamber Orchestra, New Israeli Opera; soloist in world premieres of works by David Del Tredici, Esa Pekka Salonen, Oscar, John Corigliano, Aaron Jay Kernis and Eric Whitacre. *Film soundtrack:* The Da Vinci Code (soloist). *Recordings include:* John Corigliano's Mr Tambourine Man, David Del Tredici's Two Song Cycles for Voice & Piano, Paul Revere's Ride, The Da Vinci Code (soundtrack); with Eric Whitacre: Light and Gold (Grammy Award for Best Choral Performance 2012) 2010. *Honours:* Sony ES Prize for outstanding contribution to the vocal arts, Grammy Award for Best Classical Vocal Performance 2009. *Current Management:* c/o Mark Williams, IMG Artists, 152 W 57th Street #5, New York, NY 10019-3433, USA. *Telephone:* (212) 994-3500. *E-mail:* mwilliams@imgartists.com. *Website:* www.imgartists.com; www.hilaplitmann.com.

PLOEMACHER, Marije; Dutch violinist; b. 1983. *Education:* Utrecht Conservatory, Sweelinck Conservatory, Amsterdam, Royal Northern Coll. of Music, UK, pvt. tuition from Davina van Wely. *Career:* fmr leader and soloist, Youth String Orchestra of the Netherlands; fmr co-leader Nat. Youth Orchestra of the Netherlands (NJO); fmr mem. EU Youth Orchestra; plays with Navarra String Quartet 2002–. *Honours:* RNCM Professional Performance Diploma, RNCM Gold Medal 2005. *Current Management:* c/o Sue Hudson and Rosemary Pickering, Young Concert Artists Trust, 23 Garrick Street, London WC2E 9BN, England. *Telephone:* (20) 7379-8477. *Fax:* (20) 7379-8467. *E-mail:* info@ycat.co.uk. *Website:* www.ycat.co.uk. *E-mail:* mp@navarra.co.uk (office). *Website:* www.navarra.co.uk.

PLOSKINA, Victor; Ukrainian conductor; *Chief Conductor, Orchestra of the National Academic Opera and Ballet Theatre, Belarus*; b. Transcarpatian region. *Education:* M. Lysenko State Acad. of Music, Lviv. *Career:* Conductor, Orchestra of Dnipropetrovs'k Ballet and Opera House, Ukraine 1993–95, Chief Conductor 2002–03; Conductor, Nat. Symphony Orchestra of Ukraine 1995–; Chief Conductor, Nat. Theatre of Serbia, Novi Sad 2000–02; Chief Conductor, Crimean State Philharmonic Orchestra 2004–05; Chief Conductor, Orchestra of the Nat. Academic Opera and Ballet Theatre, Belarus 2007–. *Honours:* Honoured Artist of Ukraine 2000; winner, Stefan Turchak Conducting Competition 1998. *Address:* National Academic Opera and Ballet Theatre, 220029 Minsk, Parizhskaya Kommuna pl. 1, Belarus (office). *Telephone:* (17) 334-10-41 (office). *Fax:* (17) 334-07-72 (office). *E-mail:* belarus_opera@tut.by (office). *Website:* www.belarusopera.com (office).

PLOWRIGHT, Jonathan Daniel, Dip RAM, ARAM, FRAM; British pianist and academic; *Professor of Piano, Royal Conservatoire of Scotland*; b. 24 Sept. 1959, Doncaster, S Yorks., England; s. of Cyril James Plowright and Molly Plowright; m. Diane Rosemary Shaw 1990. *Education:* Stonyhurst Coll., Univ. of Birmingham, Royal Acad. of Music, Peabody Conservatory of Music, USA. *Career:* debut at Carnegie Recital Hall, New York 1984, Purcell Room, London 1985; has performed with all major UK orchestras and numerous int. orchestras; solo recitals throughout UK and many int. tours; regular BBC broadcasts and commercial recordings; performed world premiere of Constant Lambert's piano concerto, St John's Smith Square 1988; Head of Keyboard, Univ. of Chichester; currently Prof. of Piano, Royal Conservatoire of Scotland (fmrly Royal Scottish Acad. of Music and Drama). *Recordings include:* Capital Virtuosi, Brahms Solo Piano, Chopin Solo Piano, Vol. 1, Jonathan Plowright (recital), Paderewski (solo piano), Sigismund Stojowski Piano Concertos, Sigismund Stojowski (solo piano), Constant Lambert Piano Concerto, Rarities of Piano Music at Schloss vor Husum 2003, 2004, 2007, 2010, Paderewski (solo piano), Henryk Melcer Piano Concertos 2008, Hommage à Chopin 2010, Johann Sebastian Bach Piano Transcriptions 2010, Homage to Paderewski 2011, Zelenski & Zarebski Chamber Music 2012, Brahms Works for Solo Piano Vol. 1, 2, 3 2013–16, Zelenski Piano Concertos 2014, Rozycki Piano Concertos 2016. *Film:* pianist Ernest Ziegler in Florence Foster Jenkins 2016. *Honours:* RAM McFarren Gold Medal 1983, Fulbright Scholarship 1983, Countess of Munster Scholarship, Commonwealth Musician of the Year 1983, Gold Medal, Royal Overseas League 1983, winner, Baltimore Symphony Orchestra Awards 1984, winner, European Piano Competition 1989. *E-mail:* jonathan@jonathanplowright.com. *Website:* www.jonathanplowright.com.

PLOWRIGHT, Rosalind Anne, OBE, LRAM; British singer (mezzo-soprano); b. 21 May 1949, Worksop, Notts.; d. of Robert Arthur Plowright and Celia Adelaide Plowright; m. James Anthony Kaye 1984; one s. one d. *Education:* Notre Dame High School, Wigan, Royal Northern Coll. of Music. *Career:* began career at London Opera Centre 1973–75; Glyndebourne Chorus and Touring Co. 1974–77; debut with ENO as Page in Salome 1975, Miss Jessel in Turn of the Screw 1979 (Soc. of West End Theatre Laurence Olivier Award 1980), at Covent Garden as Ortlinde in Die Walküre 1980; Metropolitan Opera debut 2003; has also sung in Argentina, Austria, Chile, Denmark, France, Germany, Greece, Israel, Italy, Japan, Netherlands, Portugal, Spain, Switzerland, USA; wide repertoire as soprano, but has sung mezzo roles since 1999; principal roles (as soprano) include Ariadne, Alceste, Médée, Norma, Tosca, title role and Elizabeth I in Mary Stuart, Maddalena in Andrea Chénier, Antonia in The Tales of Hoffman, Donna Anna in Don Giovanni, Vitellia in La Clemenza di Tito, Madame Butterfly, Manon Lescaut, Suor Angelica, Giorgetta in Il Tabarro, Aida, Abigaille in Nabucco, Desdemona in Otello, Elena in I Vespri

Siciliani, Leonora in Il Trovatore, Amelia in Un Ballo in Maschera, Leonora in La Forza del Destino, Violetta in La Traviata; (as mezzo) Kostelnička in Jenufa, Amneris in Aida, Fricka in Das Rheingold and Die Walküre, Gertrude in Hansel & Gretel, Klytemnestra in Elektra, Madame de Croissy in Dialogues des Carmelites, Herodias in Salome. *Television:* House of Elliot 1992, The Man Who Made Husbands Jealous 1997. *Honours:* First Prize, 7th Int. Competition for Opera Singers, Sofia 1979, Prix Fondation Fanny Heldy, Acad. Nat. du Disque Lyrique 1985, Grammy 2009. *Current Management:* c/o Zemsky/Green Artists Management, 104 West 73rd Street, Suite 1, New York, NY 10023, USA. *Address:* 83 St Mark's Avenue, Salisbury, Wilts., SP1 3DW, England (home). *Website:* www.rosalindplowright.com (home); www.ros-sing.co.uk (home).

PLOYHAROVA-PREISLEROVA, Vlasta; Czech singer (soprano); b. 25 Jan. 1928, Zbynice, Klatovy; m. Frantisek Preisler Sr 1972; one s. one d. *Education:* Conservatory of Prague, Corso Academia Musicale Siena, Italy with Gina Cigna. *Career:* debut in Smetana's Bartered Bride at Janáček Theatre, Brno, 1958; appeared at Theatre Olomouc, 1956–84, Theatre Brno, 1960–64, Theatre Ostrava, 1967–77; operatic repertoire included: Puccini's Turandot and Madama Butterfly, Strauss's Rosenkavalier (as Sophie), Tchaikovsky's Eugene Onegin, Iolanta, Massenet's Manon, Verdi's Gilda, Bizet's Carmen, Gounod's Marguerite, Gluck's Orfeo and Euridice, Beethoven's Fidelio, Mozart's Don Giovanni, Così fan tutte, Offenbach's Les Contes d'Hoffmann and Janáček's Cunning Little Vixen and From the House of the Dead; also operas by Skroup, Dvořák, Fibich, V. Novak, V. Blodek, B. Martinů, Smetana, Pergolesi, Weber, Rossini, Flotow, J. F. Halévy, Lortzing, Rimsky-Korsakov, Leoncavallo, N. Zajc, A. Honegger; concert repertoire included: Bach's Magnificat, Beethoven's 9th Symphony, Mahler's 4th Symphony. *Honours:* International Competition, Toulouse, France, Silver Medal, 1957.

PLUDERMACHER, Georges; French concert pianist and academic; *Professor of Piano, Paris National Conservatoire*; b. 26 July 1944, Guéret. *Education:* studied with Geneviève Joy, Jacques Fevrier and Henriette Puig Roget at the Paris Conservatoire; further study with Geza Anda in Lucerne 1963–64. *Career:* numerous appearances throughout Europe, the Americas, Japan and China from 1965; contemporary repertory has included premieres of Archipel I and III by Boucourechliev 1967 and Synaphai by Xenakis 1971; engagements with the Domaine Musical, Musique Vivante and Orchestra of Paris Opéra, particularly for Ravel and Stravinsky Ballet evenings by Balanchine and J. Robbins; duos with Yvonne Loriod and chamber music with the Nouveau Trio Pasquier, Trio à cordes Français, Moraguès Wind Quintet, Michel Portal; classical and improvisation, lieder recitals with Ernst Häffliger; duo sonata recitals over 20 years with Nathan Milstein; numerous appearances with leading orchestras, such as the Chicago Symphony, London Symphony, London Sinfonietta, RAI Torino, UNAM Mexico, Orchestre de Paris, Orchestre Nat. de France and others, under prominent conductors, including Sir George Solti, Pierre Boulez, Ch.von Dohnanyi, Horst Stein, J. Cl. Casadesus, E. Krivine and many others; Prof. of Piano, Paris Nat. Conservatoire 1977–. *Radio:* numerous recordings and broadcasts in many countries. *Television:* Complete Beethoven Sonatas and Diabelli Variations recorded live at Paris Opera Bastille 1999; Ravel Concertos with J. Cl. Casadesus played before 16,000 people at the Lille stadium, and many others. *Recordings include:* Complete Sonatas by Mozart, Live recordings of Complete Beethoven and Schubert Sonatas; Estampes, Images, Children's Corner, Complete Etudes and Preludes by Debussy; Ravel Complete Piano Music (recorded live), Brahms Händel Variations and Fantasien Op. 116, Liszt B minor Sonata and Chopin 24 Preludes Op. 28, Two Pianos recordings with J. F. Heisser including Bartòk two pianos and Percussions Sonata, also La Mer, Images (for orchestra), Nocturnes by Debussy (A. Caplet and Ravel transcriptions), Sonata Recital with N. Milstein including Beethoven Kreutzer Sonata (his last recital in Stockholm). *Honours:* Third Prize, Viana da Motta Int. Competition, Second Prize, Leeds Int. Piano Competition 1969, First Prize, Geza Anda Competition 1979, Acad. Charles Cros Award for Beethoven Diabelli Variations recording; Acad. du Disque Français Award for Debussy Etudes recording. *Current Management:* Concerts de Valmalete, 7 rue Hoche, 92300 Levallois Perret, France. *Telephone:* 1-47-59-87-59. *Fax:* 1-47-59-87-50. *E-mail:* valmalete@valmalete.com; www.valmalete.com.

PLUJNIKOV, Konstantin; Russian singer (tenor); b. 1946. *Education:* St Petersburg Conservatory. *Career:* sang with the Kirov Opera, St Petersburg from 1971; roles have included Lensky, Vladimir in Prince Igor, Don Ottavio, the Duke of Mantua, Alfredo, Edgardo, Lucia di Lammermoor, Ernesto, Faust and Lohengrin; guest appearances with the Kirov Opera at San Francisco, 1993 and La Scala, Milan, as Agrippa in The Fiery Angel by Prokofiev, 1995; season 1998 as Shuisky in Boris Godunov with the Kirov Opera at Drury Lane, London and the New York Met. *Honours:* prizewinner at Glinka, Geneva and Bucharest Competitions.

PLUSH, Vincent, BM; Australian composer; b. 18 April 1950, Adelaide, SA. *Education:* Univ. of Adelaide, Univ. of California at San Diego, USA. *Career:* staff Music Dept, Australian Broadcasting Commission; teacher, New South Wales State Conservatorium of Music 1973–80; tutor Music Dept, Univ. of New South Wales 1979; founder The Seymour Group, Univ. of Sydney 1976; consultant for many arts bodies on federal, state and municipal levels; Composer-in-Residence, Musica Viva 1985; Artistic Dir, The Braidwood Festival 1989, 1991; Composer-in-Residence, ABC Radio 1987. *Compositions:* Chu no mai 1974–76, Encompassings 1975, Chrysalis 1977–78, Stevie Wonder's Music 1979, Aurores (from O Paraguay!) for solo instrument and ensemble 1979, The Maitland and Morpeth String Quartet for narrator and accompaniment 1979–85, Bakery Hill Rising for solo instrument and ensemble 1980, On Shooting Stars (homage to Victor Jara) for ensemble 1981, Facing the Danger for ensemble 1982, Gallipoli Sunrise for solo instrument and ensemble 1984, FireRaisers for solo instrument and ensemble 1984, The Wakefield Convocation for ensemble 1985, Helices (from The Wakefield Chronicles) for ensemble 1985, The Wakefield Chorales for brass band 1985–86, The Wakefield Chronicles for narrator and accompaniment 1985–86, Pacifica for orchestra 1986, The Wakefield Invocation 1986, The Wakefield Intrada 1986, The Muse of Fire for narrator and accompaniment 1986–87, The Love Songs of Herbert Hoover for ensemble 1987, March of the Dalmations for brass band 1987, also works for tape, vocal works, choral works, works for music theatre and arrangements.

PLUYGERS, Catherine, MMus, ARCM; British oboist and artistic director; b. 20 Nov. 1955, Colchester, Essex, England. *Education:* Univ. of London, Royal Coll. of Music, Banff Centre School of Fine Arts, Canada, Goldsmiths Coll. *Career:* freelance orchestral player with BBC, Royal Ballet Orchestra, Ulster Orchestra; founder mem., Thomas Arne Players, with Purcell Room debut 1985, Wigmore Hall debut 1986; recital tour, oboe and organ music, South Norway, sponsored by Norwegian Arts Council 1982; formed New Wind Orchestra (NEWO) 1985, New Wind Summer School 1988; premiered Sonata No. 2, opus 64, oboe and piano, dedicated to her by Dr Ruth Gipps 1986; BBC World Service broadcast 1986; NEWO South Bank Premiere, QEH 1986; formed London New Wind Music Festival, annual festival (Sept.–Nov.) of contemporary wind music 1998–; invited to Democratic People's Republic of Korea as part of promotion of music by women composers; also performed in USA and Far East. *Compositions:* Gloryland, Mixed Media one woman show on subject of War and The Square, A Mixed Media piece performed in Purcell Room 1990, by the Group Interartes and Hong Kong City Hall 1990. *Recordings:* English Music for oboe and piano, with accompanist Matthew Stanley 1984. *Current Management:* New Wind Management Ltd, 119 Woolstone Road, Forest Hill, London, SE23 2TQ, England.

PODGER, Rachel; British musician (violin); b. 1968. *Education:* Guildhall School of Music and Drama, studied with David Takeno and Micaela Comberti. *Career:* fmrly leader, Gabrieli Consort & Players; leader, The English Consort 1997–2002, touring extensively (often as soloist); Guest Conductor, Orchestra of the Age of Enlightenment 2004–, Arte dei Suonatori, Poland, Musica Angelica and Santa Fe Pro Musica, USA, European Union Baroque Orchestra, Holland Baroque Soc. and Handel and Haydn Soc.; soloist, Acad. of Ancient Music; tours with fortepianist Gary Cooper; Co-founder and Music Dir, Brecon Baroque Festival 2006–; f. Brecon Baroque ensemble 2007; Prof. of Baroque Violin, Guildhall School of Music and Royal Welsh Coll. of Music; teacher, Hochschule Bremen; Micaela Comberti Chair for Baroque Violin, Royal Acad. of Music, London 2008–; Visiting Prof., Royal Danish Acad. of Music. *Recordings include:* Bach Sonatas and Partitas for Solo Violin Vols 1 & 2 1998, 2000, Bach Sonatas for Violin and Harpsichord 2000, Telemann's Twelve Fantasies for Solo Violin 2002, Vivaldi/La Stravaganza: 12 violin concertos (Gramophone Award for Best Baroque Instrumental Recording 2003), complete Mozart Sonatas for violin and piano 2004–09, Mozart Violin Concerti 2009, Mozart/Haydn: Duo Sonatas 2011, Vivaldi/La Cetra: 12 Violin Concertos (Diapason d'Or de l'Année) 2012, Guardian Angel (BBC Music Magazine Instrumental Award 2014) 2013, Perla Barocca (Opus HD d'Or) 2014, Rosary Sonatas - Heinrich Ignaz Franz von Biber (1644-1704) 2015; with Brecon Baroque: Bach Violin Concertos 2010, Bach Double and Triple Concertos 2013, Vivaldi L'Estro Armonico (Diapason d'Or) 2015. *Honours:* Hon. mem. RAM, Royal Welsh Coll. of Music and Drama, Kohn Foundation Bach Prize. *Current Management:* c/o Percius, Advice Hub, 66 Devonshire Road, Cambridge, CB1 2BL, England. *Telephone:* (77) 1875-2481 (mobile). *E-mail:* info@percius.co.uk. *Website:* www.percius.co.uk; www.rachelpodger.com.

PODLEŚ, Ewa Maria; Polish singer (contralto); b. 26 April 1952, Warsaw; m. Jerzy Marchwinski; one d. *Education:* Chopin Music Acad., Warsaw, vocal study with Alina Bolechowska. *Career:* engagements include Metropolitan Opera (La Cieca in Ponchielli's La Gioconda), Seattle Opera (title role of Händel's Giulio Cesare, Adalgisa in Bellini's Norma and Erda in Wagner's Ring cycle), San Diego Opera (Cesare; Marquise in Donizetti's La fille du Régiment), San Francisco Opera (Principessa in Puccini's Suor Angelica), Canadian Opera Company (Cesare, Jocasta in Stravinsky's Oedipus Rex, Klytämnestra in Richard Strauss' Elektra and title role of Rossini's Tancredi), Houston Grand Opera (Ulrica in Verdi's Un Ballo in Maschera and the Marquise), Dallas Opera (Bertarido in Handel's Rodelinda and Erda), Milwaukee's Florentine Opera (Azucena in Verdi's Il Trovatore), Michigan Opera Theatre (Ulrica), Opéra de Monte Carlo (Countess in Tchaikovsky's Pique Dame), Madame de la Haltiere in Massenet's Cendrillon at Paris Opéra Comique and the Royal Opera, Covent Garden, Minnesota Opera (Malcolm in Rossini's La donna del lago) and Klytämnestra in Warsaw and Nice; appearances at New York's Carnegie Hall include Gluck's Orphée et Eurydice with the Oratorio Soc. of New York, Ulrica with Collegiate Chorale, baroque and Rossini programmes with Moscow Chamber Orchestra, Das Lied von der Erde with Philadelphia Orchestra and Szymanowski's Three Hymns with Sinfonia Varsovia; signature pieces include Rossini's cantata Giovanna d'Arco performed with Moscow Chamber Orchestra in Pittsburgh and at Lincoln Center's Avery Fisher Hall and with Toronto Symphony; presented in recital by Univ. Musical Soc., Ann Arbor, Mich., as Tancredi with Detroit Symphony and as Orfeo in a semi-staged version; has sung principal roles at Deutsche Staatsoper Berlin and Deutsche Oper Berlin, Frankfurt Alte Oper, Gran Teatre del Liceu, Teatro Bellini, La Scala Milan, La Fenice Venice, Teatro San Carlo, Warsaw's Nat. Theatre, Théâtre Châtelet and Opéra Bastille; mem. Warsaw's Teatr Wielki; has sung with the St Paul Chamber Orchestra, San Francisco, Detroit, Seattle, Montreal, American, Toronto, NHK, New World and Pittsburgh Symphonies, Maggio Musicale Fiorentino and Nat. Arts Centre Orchestras, Nat. Orchestra of Spain, Hong Kong and Dresden Philharmonics; has sung under conductors including David Atherton, Leon Botstein, Myung-Whun Chung, Gerard Schwarz, Neeme Jaervi, Lorin Maazel, Constantine Orbelian, Alberto Zedda and Pinchas Zukerman; recitalist on major art-song series of Cleveland, Atlanta, Vancouver, Philadelphia, St Paul, Chicago, Paris, Amsterdam, London, Toronto, Moscow, Warsaw, Montreal, San Juan, Québec and New York (Alice Tully Hall and the 92nd Street Y); festival invitations include New York's Bard Festival, Aix-en-Provence, Flanders, Montpellier and Lanaudière; sang both Azucena and Tancredi at Caramoor and in Rossini's Ciro in Babilonia 2012; numerous collaborations with Marc Minkowski and Les Musiciens du Louvre, including two recordings of Händel's Ariodante and Gluck's Armide. *Recordings include:* collaborations with Marc Minkowski and Les Musiciens du Louvre, including Handel's Ariodante and Gluck's Armide, Handel Arias, Russian Arias, three recital discs with pianist Garrick Ohlsson, including a release recorded live at Wigmore Hall. *Honours:* prizes at Athens and Geneva 1977, Moscow 1978, Toulouse 1979, Seattle Opera Artist of the Year 2003, major prizes at Tchaikovsky Competition, Moscow. *Current Management:* c/o Matthew Sprizzo, 18 Allison Avenue, Staten Island, NY 10306, USA. *Telephone:* (718) 987-2736 (home). *E-mail:* msprizzo@aol.com. *Website:* www.matthewsprizzo.com; www.podles.pl.

POGAČNIK, Miha; Slovenian violinist and music director; b. 31 May 1949, Kranj; m. Judith Csik 1974; one s. one d. *Education:* Musikhochschule Cologne, Indiana Univ. School of Music, USA, studied with Veronek, Ozim, Gingold, Rostal, Szeryng. *Career:* more than 100 concerts per season since 1977 in USA, Canada, Mexico, South America, Australia, NZ, China, Scandinavia, Western and Eastern Europe; Music Dir Chartres Festival d'Eté 1981–; Founder and Pres. IDRIART International, Geneva (Inst. for the Devt of Intercultural Relations through the Arts) now represented in 30 countries 1983–, Music Dir of some 20 IDRIART Festivals on five continents. *Address:* IDRIART, c/o Grad Borl, Ustanova Gandin Fundacija, Dolane 1, 2282 Cirkulane, Slovenia (office). *E-mail:* miha@mihavision.com (office). *Website:* www.mihavision.com.

POGORELICH, Ivo; Croatian concert pianist; b. 20 Oct. 1958, Belgrade; s. of I. Pogorelich and D. Pogorelich; m. Aliza Kezeradze 1980 (died 1996). *Education:* Tchaikovsky Conservatoire of Moscow, then studied with Aliza Kezeradze. *Career:* debut recital in Carnegie Hall, New York, USA 1981; has appeared in major concert halls throughout the world; f. Bad Wörishofen Festival (Germany) 1988; inaugurated Ivo Pogorelich Int. Solo Piano Competition, Pasadena, Calif. 1993; UNESCO Goodwill Amb. 1988; f. Sarajevo Charitable Foundation (to raise funds for people of Bosnia in fields of medicine and health) 1994; Fellow-Commoner, Balliol Coll., Oxford 1993. *Recordings include:* numerous recordings for Deutsche Grammophon, starting with a Chopin recital in 1981 and including works by Bach, Beethoven, Brahms, Chopin, Haydn, Liszt, Mozart, Mussorgsky, Prokofiev, Ravel, Scarlatti, Schumann and the Tchaikovsky Piano Concerto No. 1; Complete Recordings (box set) 2015. *Honours:* First Prize, Casagrande Competition, Terni, Italy 1978, First Prize, Montréal Int. Music Competition, Canada 1980, Special Prize, Int. Chopin Competition, Warsaw 1980. *Current Management:* August Faulend-Heferer, Eudora Kaciceva 5, 10000 Zagreb, Croatia. *Website:* www.ivopogorelich.com/en.

POGOSTKINA, Alina; German (b. Russian) violinist; b. 18 Nov. 1983, St Petersburg; d. of Alexander Pogostkin. *Education:* Hochschule für Musik Hanns Eisler, Berlin. *Career:* has appeared with conductors including Sir Mark Elder, Mikko Franck, Sakari Oramo, Jukka-Pekka Saraste, Mikhail Pletnev, Sir Roger Norrington, Gennadi Roshdestvensky, Christoph Eschenbach, Marek Janowski and Andrey Boreyko, and with orchestras including SWR-Sinfonieorchester, Stuttgart, hr-Sinfonieorchester Frankfurt, MDR Sinfonieorchester Leipzig, Czech Philharmonic Orchestra, Residentie Orkest, Kremerata Baltica, Finnish Radio Symphony Orchestra, BBC Scottish Symphony Orchestra and the Indianapolis Symphony Orchestra; tours to festivals and venues worldwide. *Honours:* first prize and Special Prize, Sibelius Int. Violin Competition 2005. *Current Management:* c/o Sabine Frank, Harrison Parrott Artist Management, Lucile-Grahn-Strasse 37, D-81675 Munich, Germany. *Telephone:* (89) 45726154. *E-mail:* sabine.frank@harrisonparrott.co.uk. *Website:* www.harrisonparrott.com; www.alinapogostkina.de.

POGSON, Geoffrey; British singer (tenor); b. 1966, England. *Education:* Univ. of Cambridge and Trinity Coll. of Music. *Career:* appearances with Glyndebourne Festival in The Queen of Spades 1995, ENO, Scottish Opera and Opera North; roles include Monostatos, Augustin Moser, Vere in Billy Budd, Quint in The Turn of the Screw and Cornwall in Lear. *Recordings include:* Remendado in Carmen conducted by Abbado.

POHJANNORO, Hannu, DMus; Finnish composer; *Senior Lecturer in Composition and Music Theory, School of Arts, Music and Media, Tampere University of Applied Sciences;* b. 4 July 1963, Savonlinna. *Education:*

Helsinki Conservatory, Sibelius Acad. *Career:* teacher, Sibelius Acad. 1992–93, 1998, 2005, Helsinki Conservatory 1992–95, Helsinki Univ. Dept of Musicology 1994–98, Espoo Music Inst. 1996–2000, Sibelius Acad. electronic music studio 1997–2000; Sr Lecturer in Composition and Music Theory, School of Arts, Music and Media, Tampere University of Applied Sciences 2005–; Vice-Pres. Finnish Composers' Asscn 2005–06; mem. of Bd Finnish Copyright Bureau (TEOSTO) 2005–06. *Compositions include:* Matkalla 1991, Kuvia, heijastuksia 1992, Eilisen linnut 1994, Saari, rannaton 1994, Korkeina aamujen kaaret 1996, Syksyn huoneet 1997, Kuun kiertoa kohti 1998, Paluu 2000, Carmen de Sole 2002, Ajan reuna 2003, XL 2003–04, Time Exposures 2004–05. *Compositions for stage:* incidental music for Juha 1998, Romu-Heikki 2004, Concerto for Four Horns and Orchestra 2011, images hommages 2011, sacred colours 2012. *Recordings:* Eilisen linnut, Kuun kiertoa kohti, Ajan reuna, Carmen de Sole. *Address:* c/o Fennica Gehrman Oy Ab, PO Box 158, 00121 Helsinki, Finland. *E-mail:* hannu.pohjannoro@tamk.fi (office). *Website:* www.fennicagehrman.fi/composers/pohjannoro-hannu.

POHJOLA, Seppo; Finnish composer; *Teacher of Composition, Eastern Helsinki College of Music;* b. 4 May 1965, Espoo; s. of Erkki and Aino Pohjola; m.; two c. *Education:* Espoo Coll. of Music (Composition), Sibelius Acad., Helsinki (Horn and Composition). *Compositions include:* chamber music: String Quartet No. 1 1989, Splendori 1991, Pixilated 1992, Gimla 1993, String Quartet No. 2 1995, Game Over 1996, String Quartet No. 3 2000, Liebelei 2001, New York New York 2001, Identifying the Beast 2001, Elämän Kevät 2002, Wedding March 2002, A Night at the Opera 2002, Express 2004, Virtaa! 2004, Dance in the Rain 2005, String Quartet No 4 2006, Quintet 2007; orchestral music: Symphony No. 1 2002, Tapiolandia 2003, Citius Altius Fortius 2004, Sisu for Yoko 2006, Symphony No. 2 2006; choral works: Oravan laulu 2000, Gloria 2001, Hommage a Schubert 2002, Ukri 2003, Terve kuu 2005, The Wicked Witch of the North 2007; operas: The Arabian Rabbit 2004, The Wardrobe 2004, My Dearest One 2005. *Honours:* winner Soc. of Finnish Composers New Tone Competition, Kuhmo Chamber Music Festival 2002. *Address:* Kirkkonummentie 29, 02140 Espoo, Finland (office). *Telephone:* (45) 6500633 (office). *E-mail:* sjpohjola@luukku.com (home).

POHL, Carla; singer (soprano); b. 1942, Johannesburg, South Africa. *Education:* studied in South Africa and at the Wiesbaden Conservatory. *Career:* sang at Pforzheim from 1970, Freiburg from 1979, notably as Tosca, Maddalena in Andrea Chénier, Marenka in The Bartered Bride and Strauss's Chrysothemis; Wiesbaden 1979–81; Deutsche Oper am Rhein, Düsseldorf from 1981, as Wagner's Elisabeth, Eva and Sieglinde, the Empress in Die Frau ohne Schatten, Strauss's Ariadne and Marschallin, and Leonore in Fidelio; guest appearances in Mannheim, Berlin, Nancy, Karlsruhe, Stuttgart, Vienna State Opera, Munich State Opera, Milan, Rome and Brunswick; tour of South Africa 1985; Deutsche Oper am Rhein 1987, as Rezia in Oberon; Deutsche Oper Berlin and Santiago Chile 1988, as Chrysothemis and Elsa; sang Wagner's Venus at Cape Town 2000.

POKA, Balazs; Hungarian singer (baritone); b. 1947, Eger. *Career:* soloist with the Hungarian Nat. Opera from 1976, as Rossini's Figaro and Dandini, Valentin, Eugene Onegin, and Carlo in La Forza del Destino; Bregenz Festival 1991 as Escamillo; season 1993 as Don Giovanni at Madrid and Lisbon, Busoni's Turandot at Opéra de Lyon; other roles include Germont, Marcello, Renato, Rodrigo and Puccini's Lescaut; sang Ping in Turandot; concert appearances at La Scala, Milan, Palermo, Bergamo, Hamburg, Amsterdam, Antwerp and Rome. *Recordings:* Kodály's Háry János; From Blues to Opera; La Bohème, Puccini; L'Arlesiana, Cilea; Judgement in Jerusalem, Szehely; Petroviks, Crime and Punishment.

POLA, Bruno; Italian singer (baritone); b. 1945, Rovereto, Trento. *Education:* Berlin Conservatory. *Career:* engaged at Kaiserslautern Opera 1968–71, Kiel 1972–73, Cologne 1974–77, Zürich Opera 1978–81; recitals and concerts throughout Germany, Netherlands, Switzerland and Austria; from 1982 engagements at such major opera centres as Milan, Rome, Lisbon, Vienna, Munich and Hamburg; Metropolitan Opera from 1988, in Cavalleria Rusticana, Il Barbiere di Siviglia, Gianni Schicci, Rigoletto, Don Giovanni, La Fanciulla del West, Falstaff, Simon Boccanegra, and L'Elisir d'amore; season 1995–97 in Cavalleria Rusticana and La Forza del Destino at the Met; Aida and Dulcamara at Vienna and Covent Garden; Amonasro in Aida at Santiago, Arena di Verona and Covent Garden; further opera appearances at Turin, Ascona, Montreal, Pittsburgh, Florence, Geneva and Houston; Melitone in La Forza del Destino at Savonlinna 1998; sang Falstaff at Deutsche Oper 2000–01.

POLASKI, Deborah, DPA; American singer (soprano) and teacher; b. 26 May 1949, Richland Center, Wis. *Education:* Marion College, Ind., Coll.-Conservatory of Music, Univ. of Cincinnati, Ohio, American Inst. of Int. Music, Graz, Austria. *Career:* professional debut singing role of Senta in Wagner's The Flying Dutchman 1976; performed in Milan, Munich, Berlin and on some smaller opera stages following studies in USA; est. int. reputation singing role of Brünnhilde in Harry Kupfer's production of The Ring in Bayreuth 1988; has since sung Brünnhilde more often than any other soprano since World War I; has sung at all major opera houses in Paris, London, Berlin (Staatsoper and Deutsche Oper), New York, Chicago, Sydney, Milan, Florence, Barcelona, Madrid, Dresden, Leipzig, Munich, Hamburg, Cologne, Vienna and Salzburg; repertoire includes other major Wagner roles: Senta, Venus in Tannhäuser, Ortrud in Lohengrin, Sieglinde and Kundry in Parsifal; won int. acclaim in role of Isolde, Freiburg 1984, in Stuttgart and Amsterdam late 1980s, at

Dresdner Semperoper 1995, followed by Salzburg (Abbado), Florence (Mehta), Tokyo (Abbado), Berlin (Barenboim), Barcelona (de Billy) and Hamburg (Young); equally well known as an interpreter of Richard Strauss; debut in Elektra 1984; performed role under many leading conductors and stage dirs; repertoire also includes roles of Marie in Wozzeck, Kostelnika in Jenůfa, Kassandra and Dido in Les Troyens and Leonore in Fidelio, as well as Ariane in Paul Dukas' Ariane et Barbe-Bleue 2006 and the Woman in Erwartung by Schönberg 2008; sang role of Kostelnika at Munich State Opera and Teatro Real, Madrid; concert performances with New York Philharmonic Orchestra (Maazel), Berliner Philharmoniker (Abbado), as well as with Zubin Mehta, James Levine, Semyon Bychkov, Bertrand de Billy, Vasily Petrenko, Fabio Luisi, Georges Prêtre and Simone Young; collaborations with Chicago Symphony Orchestra and the Orchestre de Paris, with Daniel Barenboim and the Staatskapelle; recitals with Barenboim in Berlin, Lieder recitals with Charles Spencer world-wide. *Recordings:* Wolf-Ferrari's Sly, Brünnhilde's Immolation with the Chicago Symphony, R. Strauss's Elektra (with Chorus and Symphony Orchestra of Westdeutscher Rundfunk, Cologne) 2005. *Honours:* Kammersänger (Austria) 2003. *Current Management:* c/o Michael Lewin Artists' Management International, Bastiengasse 27/1, 1180 Vienna, Austria. *Telephone:* (1) 310-60-96. *Fax:* (1) 310-60-94. *Website:* www.lewin -management.com. *E-mail:* sekretariat-polaski@web.de (office). *Website:* www .deborahpolaski.com.

POLAY, Bruce, BM, MA, DMA; American conductor, composer and educator; *Artistic Director and Conductor, Knox-Galesburg Symphony;* b. 22 March 1949, Brooklyn, NY; s. of Benjamin Polay and Joan Polay; m. Louise Phillips 1983; two s. three d. *Education:* Univ. of Southern California, California State Univ., Arizona State Univ., studied conducting with Herbert Blomstedt, Jon Robertson, Murray Sidlin, Alberto Bolet. *Career:* debut conducting in the USA, Lakewood (Calif.) Chamber Orchestra 1972, in Europe, Filarmonica de Stat Sibiu, Romania 1993; Artistic Dir and Conductor Knox-Galesburg (Ill.) Symphony 1983–; currently Prof. of Music, Knox Coll.; recent guest conducting in USA, Belarus, Mexico, Italy, Romania, Russia, Spain, UK and Ukraine; composer/scholar-in-residence, Lynn Univ. Conservatory of Music, Boca Raton, Florida 2008; mem. Bd of Advisors, Foundation for New Music 1997–, Music Panel, Ill. Arts Council 2005–; Composer-in-Residence, Lynn Univ. Conservatory of Music 2008; presented conducting masterclasses at Moscow Tchaikovsky Conservatory and Belorusian State Acad. of Music. *Compositions:* Encomium for three-part children's chorus, narrator and orchestra 1987, Concerto for tenor trombone 1991, Three Word Paintings for a cappella chorus 1991, Cathedral Images for orchestra 1993, Bondi's Journey: An Orchestral Rhapsody after Jewish Themes 1994, Sound Images: Pictures for an Exhibition for solo piano 1995, Anniversary Mourning for a cappella choir 1996, Concerto-Fantasie for piano and orchestra 1997, Sinfonia Concertante 1998, Y'Urning cycle for soprano, clarinet and piano 1998, Consolation for organ 1998, Amazing Grace for violin and piano 2001, Prelude for Kingsfold for organ 2001, Elegy for violin solo and small orchestra 2004, Suite of Preludes for organ 2005, Suite on Catalonian Folksongs for string orchestra 2005, 5 Novelettes for harps and string orchestra by Glazunov (arranged) 2006, Illumination for Orchestra 2007, String Quartet 2008, Four Score for Piano Solo 2009. *Recordings:* Cathedral Images 1996, Y'Urning 1999, Elegy for solo violin and small orchestra 2001, Suite of Preludes for organ 2002, Illumination for orchestra 2003, Suite on Catalonian Folksongs for string orchestra 2004, Three Duets for two violins on Catalonian Folksongs 2005, 5 Novelettes for String Orchestra by Glazunov, arranged by Polay 2006, Sparkle for Orchestra 2007 (revised 2012). *Publications:* Encomium 1987, Consolation for Organ 2001, Elegy for Solo Violin and Small Orchestra 2001, Semi-Suite for Violin, Cello and Piano 2002, Amazing Grace for Violin and Piano 2002, Solemnity for Brass Ensemble 2008, String Quartet 2008, Come, Thou Fount of Every Blessing for Violin and Piano 2009, Suite of Preludes for Organ 2013. *Honours:* Illinois Orchestra of the Year (with Knox-Galesburg Symphony) 1986, 1998, Illinois Conductor of the Year 1997, 2004, 2010, Knox Coll. Exceptional Achievement Award 1998, 2005, Programming of the Year Award 2006, Barlow Endowment for Music Composition 2007, Paul Harris Fellow, The Rotary Foundation of Rotary International 2010. *Address:* Knox College, Campus Box 5, Galesburg, IL 61401 (office). *Telephone:* (309) 341-7208 (office). *Fax:* (309) 341-7019 (office). *E-mail:* bpolay@knox.edu (office). *Website:* www.knox.edu/kgsymphony.xml (office).

POLEGATO, Brett; Canadian/Italian singer (baritone); b. 9 May 1968, Niagara Falls, Ont. *Career:* has appeared in 19 countries and participated as soloist in the Grammy Awards' Best Classical Recording of 2003: a recording of Vaughan Williams' A Sea Symphony with the Atlanta Symphony Orchestra; Season 2005–06, performed with the Cleveland Orchestra, Toronto Symphony Orchestra, Les Violons du Roy and Milwaukee Symphony Orchestra; sang in Jake Heggie's The End of the Affair at Seattle Opera, Die Rheinnixen at Opera Nat. de Lyon, Così fan tutte at Opera Nat. de Toulouse and Die tote Stadt at Geneva Opera; also sang title role of Don Giovanni for the first time at Vancouver Opera; appeared at inaugural Gala Concert of Canadian Opera Co.'s new opera house; numerous recitals. *Recordings include:* Ulbalde in Gluck's Armide, Messiah, Kalman's Die Herzogin von Chicago, To a Poet, solo recital, Bach Coffee and Peasant Cantatas. *Current Management:* c/o Simon Goldstone, Intermusica Artists Management Ltd, 36 Graham Street, Crystal Wharf, London, N1 8GJ, England. *E-mail:* sgoldstone@intermusica.co.uk. *Website:* www.brettpolegato.com.

POLENZANI, Matthew; American singer (tenor); b. 1968, Evanston, Illinois; m. Rosa Maria Pascarella; three c. *Education:* Eastern Illinois Univ., Young Artist Program, Lyric Opera of Chicago. *Career:* Metropolitan Opera debut as Boyar Kruschov in Boris Godunov 1997; has also sung with Los Angeles Opera, Lyric Opera of Chicago, Oper Frankfurt, Vienna State Opera, Bayerische Staatsoper, New York City Opera, Opéra de Bordeaux, Opéra Bastille de Paris, Rome Opera, Rossini Festival of Pesaro, San Francisco Opera, Seattle Opera, Teatro del Maggio Musicale Fiorentino, Théatre Royal de la Monnaie, Royal Opera House, Covent Garden; recital performances with leading orchestras including Chicago Symphony Orchestra, Cleveland Orchestra, Minnesota Orchestra, Munich Philharmonic, New York Philharmonic, Orchestra di Santa Cecilia, San Francisco Symphony; roles include: Boyar Kruschov in Boris Godunov, Alfredo in La Traviata, Roméo in Roméo et Juliette, Belmonte in Die Entführung aus dem Serail, Tebaldo in I Capuleti e i Montecchi, Edgardo in Lucia di Lammermoor, the Duke in Rigoletto, Don Ottavio in Don Giovanni, Tamino in Die Zauberflöte, David in Die Meistersinger von Nürnberg, Count Almaviva in Il Barbiere di Siviglia, Iopas in Les Troyens, Chevalier de la Force in Dialogues des Carmélites, Lindoro in L'Italiana in Algeri, Ferrando in Così fan tutte, Achille in Iphigénie en Aulide, Nemorino in L'Elisir d'Amore, title role in Werther. *Recordings include:* Live at the Verbier Festival 2007, Liszt: The Complete Songs 2010, Songs by Schubert, Beethoven, Britten and Hahn 2011. *Honours:* Richard Tucker Award 2004, Metropolitan Opera Beverly Sills Artist Award 2008. *Current Management:* IMG Artists, Carnegie Hall Tower, 152 West 57th Street, 5th Floor, New York, NY 10019, USA. *Telephone:* (212) 994-3500. *Fax:* (212) 994-3550. *E-mail:* bpalant@imgartists.com. *Website:* www.imgartists .com.

POLETAEV, Ilya, DMus; Russian pianist and harpsichordist. *Education:* Univ. of Toronto, Canada, Yale Univ., USA. *Career:* began studying piano in Moscow at age of six; moved to Israel aged 14; studied piano with Marietta Orlov and harpsichord with Colin Tilney; faculty mem., Yale Inst. of Sacred Music, Yale Dept of Music, Lecturer, Yale School of Music 2005–10; appearances with Toronto Symphony Orchestra, Hartford Symphony Orchestra, Filarmonica Mihail Jora di Bacau, Romania, Orchestra J-Futura, Trento, Italy; festival appearances at Caramoor Festival, Festival Lago Maggiore, Italy, Liszt Festival, Grottamare. *Recordings:* albums: Enescu, Complete Works for Violin and Piano 2011. *Honours:* Prize Winner, Southeastern Historical Keyboard Soc. Harpsichord Competition 2007, Concorso Sala Gallo Piano Competition First Prize, Audience Prize, Bach Prize, Orchestra Prize, Monza, Italy 2008, Grieg Int. Competition First Prize 2008, Nat. Stepping Stone Competition Laureate 2008, Int. Johann Sebastian Bach Piano Competition Winner, Leipzig 2010. *Current Management:* Astral Artists, 230 South Broad Street, Suite 300, Philadelphia, PA 19102, USA. *Telephone:* (215) 735-6999. *Fax:* (215) 735-6856. *E-mail:* astral@astralartists.org. *Website:* astralartists.org.

POLI, (Angelo) Antonio; Italian singer (tenor); b. 22 March 1986, Viterbo. *Education:* Accademia Santa Cecilia Opera Studio, Rome. *Career:* participant, Young Singer's Project of Salzburg Festival 2010; debut at Royal Opera House, London as Cassio (Otello) 2012; debut as recitalist at Wigmore Hall, London 2014; has performed with Roma Sinfonietta, Orchestra Nazionale di Santa Cecilia, London Symphony Chorus, Orchestra Sinfonica Siciliana, Orchestra di Roma e del Lazio; performances of numerous works including Mozart, Requiem, Mozart, Don Giovanni, Beethoven, Fidelio, Wagner, Tristan und Isolde, J.S. Bach, Magnificat, Donizetti, Lucia de Lammermoor, Penderecki, Polish Requiem. *Honours:* Int. Hans Gabor Belvedere Singing Competition First Prize and Audience Prize, Vienna 2010. *Current Management:* Mariano Horak or Stephanie Ammann, Cæcilia Lyric Department, Rennweg 15, 8001 Zürich, Switzerland. *Telephone:* (44) 221-33-88. *Fax:* (44) 211-71-82. *E-mail:* horak@caecilia-lyric.ch; ammann@caecilia-lyric.ch. *Website:* www.caecilia.ch/zurich.html.

POLIANSKY, Valerig K.; Russian conductor; *Chief Conductor and Artistic Director, State Academic Symphony Capella;* b. 19 April 1949, Moscow; m. Olga P. Lapuso, one s. one d. *Education:* State Conservatoire Tchaikovsky, Moscow. *Career:* debut at Moscow Operetta; conducted Shostakovich's Katerina Izmailova at Bolshoi Theatre; Conductor Chamber Choir of the Ministry of Culture 1980; Conductor State Chamber Choir 1990; Chief Conductor and Artistic Dir State Acad. Symphony Capella of Russia (Russian State Philharmonic Orchestra) 1992–. *Recordings:* Rachmaninov Vespers, Liturgia of St John Chrysostom, A Schnittke, Choir Concert; A Bruckner, Geistliche motetten, L Cherubini, Requiem in C minor, P Tchaikovsky, Liturgia of St John Chrysostom, various choruses; Orchestral Serenade. *Publications:* contrib. to Soviet Music, Music Life, Music in the USSR. *Honours:* Arezzo Prize for best conductor, 1975; Honoured Artist of the People of Russia 1996. *Address:* Pyatnitskaya str. 2, Moscow 115035 (home); Begovay 4 alleya 3-40, 125040 Moscow, Russia (home). *Telephone:* (495) 953-51-94. *Fax:* (495) 953-89-96. *E-mail:* gaskros@rambler.ru.

POLISI, Joseph W.; MA, MMus, DMA; American bassoon player and college president; *President, The Juilliard School;* b. 1947. *Education:* Univ. of Connecticut, Tufts Univ., Yale Univ., Conservatoire Nat. de Paris with Maurice Allard. *Career:* extensive solo and chamber bassoon performances throughout USA; fmr Dean, Coll.-Conservatory of Music, Univ. of Cincinnati, OH; fmr Dean of Faculty, Manhattan School of Music, New York; fmr Exec. Officer Yale Univ. School of Music, New Haven, CT; currently Pres., The Juilliard School, New York; Fellow, American Acad. of Arts and Sciences

2009–. *Recordings:* A Harvest of 20th Century Bassoon Music 1979. *Publication:* The Artist as Citizen 2005. *Honours:* hon. mem. RAM, England 1992; Hon. DHumLitt (Ursinius Coll.) 1986, (Juilliard School) 2005, Hon. DMus (Curtis Inst. of Music, Philadelphia) 1990, Dr hc (New England Conservatory) 2001; Musical America Educator of the Year 2005. *Address:* The Juilliard School, 60 Lincoln Center Plaza, New York, NY 10023, USA. *Telephone:* (212) 799-5000 (ext. 201) (office). *Website:* www.juilliard.edu (office).

POLIVNICK, Paul, BM; American conductor; b. 7 July 1947, Atlantic City, New Jersey; m. Marsha Hooks 1980. *Education:* Juilliard School of Music, New York, Aspen Music School, Colorado (summers), Berkshire Music Center, Tanglewood, Accademia Musicale Chigiana, Siena, Italy (summer). *Career:* Conductor, Debut Orchestra, Los Angeles 1969–73; Assoc. Conductor, Indianapolis Symphony Orchestra 1977–80; Assoc. Principal Conductor, Milwaukee Symphony Orchestra 1981–85; Music Dir, Alabama Symphony Orchestra, Birmingham 1985–93; Principal Conductor, Harmonia Classica of Vienna, Austria 1988–2003; Music Dir Oberlin Conservatory Orchestras 1997–2002; Music Dir, New Hampshire Music Festival 1993–2009, currently Conductor Laureate; mem. American Symphony Orchestra League; has also guest conducted over 40 orchestras. *Honours:* Dr hc (Montevallo Univ.) 1986. *Telephone:* (727) 298-8182. *Fax:* (727) 298-8182. *E-mail:* maestrop@tampabay.rr.com. *Website:* www.paulpolivnick.com.

POLLARD, Mark, BA, MA; Australian composer and music director; b. 14 Feb. 1957, Melbourne, Vic. *Education:* La Trobe Univ. *Career:* Sr Tutor, La Trobe Univ. 1983–85; Lecturer, Victoria Coll. of the Arts 1986–; music dir of various contemporary ensembles; commissions from Seymour Group, Australian Chamber Soloists, New Audience and others. *Compositions include:* Quinque II for tape 1979, Krebs for piano 1983, A Sympathetic Resonance for guitar 1989, Bass Lines for amplified double bass 1990, Carillon for Sacha for piano 1991, Two Drummings for Joe for choir 1991, The Quick or the Dead for string quartet 1992, A View from the Beach for orchestra 1994, The Art of Flirting for clarinet 1994, Inherit the Wind for English horn 1994. *Honours:* Spivakovsky Award 1993.

POLLASTRI, Paolo, DipSc, DipMus; Italian oboist; b. 12 July 1960, Bologna; m. Christine Dechaux 1988, two d. *Education:* studied in Bologna, Brussels, Accademia Chigiana, Siena. *Career:* First Oboe, Orchestra Giovanile Italiana, 1977; Genova, 1979; Rai Roma, 1981; Orchestra Regionale Toscana-Firenze, 1982–89; Accademia di S Cecilia, Roma, 1989; Solisti Veneti, 1984–89; television and radio broadcasts with RAI 1, 2, 3 (Solisti Veneti); Television Australiana (Solisti Veneti); Radio Israeliana (Accademia Bizantina); BBC (Solisti Veneti); played at Festivals in Montreux, Salzburg, Zagreb and Belgrade, Martigny and Vevey, Toulouse, Paris, Stuttgart, Edinburgh, Sydney, Melbourne and Canberra; winner of Italian competition to teach in conservatories, 1993; teacher, Studea di Musica, Fiesole, 1993–. *Recordings include:* Respighi, Solisti Veneti, Vivaldi oboe concertos, Malipiero, Respighi, Ghedini, Rota, Woodwind Quintet. *Publications:* IDRS 1998, I Fiati 1999; contrib. to Il Dopo Concerto, 1980–81; The Italian Academy of Woodwinds, 1988–89. *Address:* Via di Mugnana 3, 50027 Strada in Chianti, Florence, Italy.

POLLEI, Paul, BM, MM, PhD; American pianist and administrator; b. 9 May 1936, Salt Lake City, UT; m., two c. *Education:* Univ. of Utah, Eastman School of Music, Florida State Univ. *Career:* Prof. of Piano, Brigham Young Univ. 1963–2001; founder of Gina Bachauer International Piano Competition 1976–; creator of American Piano Quartet (2pianos/8hands) 1984–; teacher, lecturer, speaker; mem. Music Teachers' Nat. Asscn, European Piano Teachers' Asscn, World Federation of Int. Music Competitions. *Recordings:* American Piano Quartet. *Publications:* Essential Technique for the Pianist. *Honours:* The Madeleine Award 2002. *Address:* 138 W Broadway, Salt Lake City, UT, 84101, USA (office). *Telephone:* (801) 2974250 (office). *Fax:* (801) 5219202 (office). *E-mail:* paul@bachauer.com (office). *Website:* www.bachauer.com (office).

POLLET, Françoise; French singer (soprano); *Professor of Singing, Conservatoire National Supérieur de Musique et de Danse de Lyon*; b. 10 Sept. 1949, Boulogne Billancourt; one d. *Education:* Versailles Conservatory, Hochschule für Musik, Munich, studied with Ernst Haefliger, Erik Werba, Hermann Reutter, private studies later with Hanna Scholl, Helen Donath and Judith Beckmann. *Career:* debut as the Marschallin, Lubeck, 1983; sang at Lubeck –1986, performed as Santuzza, Fiordiligi, Donna Anna, Elisabeth in Tannhäuser, Amelia in Ballo in Maschera, Alice Ford, Giulietta, Ariadne, Arabella and la Voix Humaine, Agathe, Marseille and Metz, Vitellia in La Clemenza di Tito, Opéra-Comique, Paris, Elettra and Idomeneo, London, Dukas' Ariadne, Théâtre du Châtelet 1991; has sung Reizia in Oberon, Meyerbeer's Valentine, Catherine of Aragon in Saint-Saëns's Henry VIII, Elisabeth, Tannhaüser and Don Carlos, Magnard's Berenice, Cimarosa's Armida immaginaria, Gazaniga's Don Giovanni, Oskar Strauss's Lustigen Nibelungen, Montpellier; has sung Marschallin and Ariadne, Frankfurt, Cassandra and Philippe Boesman's world premiere of Reigen la cantatrice, Brussels and in Paris; in premiere of Liebermann's Freispruch für Medea, Hamburg 1995; has sung Leonore in Il Trovatore 1990, Madame Lidoine, 1995, Marschallin 1998, Toulouse; other operatic roles include Cassandra in Les Troyens, Mozart's Countess, Donna Anna, Valentine de St Bris, Meyerbeer, Mathilde in Guillaume Tell, Grete in Ferne Klang, Anita in Jonny spielt auf, Didon in Les Troyens, Alceste, Brünnhilde, Amelia; concert repertoire includes Schumann's Liederkreis, Berlioz's Les Nuits d'été, songs from Duparc, Schubert, Wolf, Poulenc, Fauré, Debussy, Ravel, Chausson, Strauss, Wagner, Schoenberg, Webern, and numerous contemporary creations (Florentz, Liebermann, Boesmanns, Cohen, Durrieux, etc.); fmr Prof. of Singing, Conservatoire Nat. Supérieur de Musique et de Danse de Lyon (now retd); private teaching sessions, master-classes. *Recordings include:* 4th Symphony by Guy Ropartz, La Vièrge in Jeanne d'Arc au Bûcher by Honegger, conducted by Ozawa, Les Troyens and La Damnation de Faust/Berlioz, conducted by Charles Dutoit, Gloria and Stabat Mater/Poulenc, conducted by Charles Dutoit, Poèmes pour Mi/Messiaen, conducted by Pierre Boulez, Integrale Webern, conducted by Pierre Boulez, Integrale Berlioz Melodies with Cord Garben, Vier letzte Lieder, Sieben frühe Lieder and Wesendonck Lieder, conducted by Klaus Weise, Airs d'Opéras Français and Les Huguenots/Meyerbeer conducted by Cyril Diederich, Les Nuits d'été Herminie/Berlioz, conducted by Stefan Sanderling, Les Nuits d'été and Poème de l'amour et de la Mer/Berlioz/Chausson, conducted by Armin Jordan, Mélodies avec Orchestre d'Henri Duparc, conducted by Jerome Kaltenbach, Live Recital from Berlioz up to Brel, conducted by Yutaka Sado, Italian Recital 'Vissi d'arte' conducted by Friedeman Layer, Recital Airs sacrés français, conducted by Jacques Mercier, La Petite Messe solennelle/Rossini, Requiem Lazare/Bruneau, Requiem le Déluge/Saint Saëns, La lyre et la harpe/Gounod, La Mort du nombre/Messiaen, all conducted by Jacques Mercier, Brahms Lieder with Roger Vignolles, piano. *Honours:* Chevalier des Arts et Lettres, Chevalier, Ordre nat. du Mérite; Show Original Victoires de la Musique, France, two Grammy Awards. *Website:* www.francoisepollet.com (office).

POLLETT, Patricia Engeline Maria, BMus, ARCM; violist and academic; b. 13 Oct. 1958, Utrecht, The Netherlands; m. Dr Philip Keith Pollett 1978, one s. *Education:* Univ. of Adelaide, Royal Coll. of Music, Hochschule der Kunst, Berlin, studied with Beryl Kimber, Peter Schidlof, Margaret Major, Bruno Giuranna. *Career:* mem., I Solisti Veneti 1983–84; founder mem., Perihelion contemporary ensemble; resident, Univ. of Queensland 1988–, later Assoc. Prof.; concerto soloist with Gulbenkian Orchestra, Lisbon 1984, Queensland Philharmonic Orchestra 1989, 1995, Queensland Symphony Orchestra 1990, 1991, 1994, Sydney Symphony Orchestra 1991, Mozart Symposium at Univ. of Otago, New Zealand 1991; commissioned new works for viola by Colin Spiers, Andrew Schultz, Nigel Sabin, Philip Bracanin, Ross Edwards, Colin Brumby (world premiere performances of these works), Robert Davidson, Stephen Cronin, Mary Mageau, Andrew Ford and Elena Kats-Chernin. *Recordings:* Tapestry; Points of Departure; Chamber Music of Andrew Schultz; Anthology of Australian Music; Evocations; Patricia Pollett: Viola Concerti; Solo: Viola Power, Australian works for viola.

POLLINI, Maurizio; Italian pianist; b. 5 Jan. 1942, Milan; s. of Gino Pollini and Renata Melotti; m. Maria Elisabetta Marzotto 1968; one s. *Career:* has played with Berlin and Vienna Philharmonic Orchestras, Bayerischer Rundfunk Orchestra, London Symphony Orchestra, Boston, New York, Philadelphia, LA and San Francisco Orchestras; has played at Salzburg, Vienna, Berlin, Prague Festivals; recordings for Polydor Int. *Recordings include:* Chopin's Nocturnes (Prix Victoire for Best Classical Recording) 2007, Bach's The Well-Tempered Clavier, Book 1 2010, Chopin Etudes Opp.10 & 25 (Gramophone Award for Best Historic Recording 2012) 2011, Brahms Piano Concerto No. 1 op.15 (ECHO Klassik Award for Concerto Recording of the Year/Piano – 19th Century 2012). *Honours:* First Prize Int. Chopin Competition, Warsaw 1960, Ernst von Siemens Music Prize, Munich 1996, Edison Classical Music Award for Best Instrumental Solo Recital 2007, Grammy Award for Best Instrumental Soloist Performance 2007, Disco d'Oro 2007, Praemium Imperiale 2010, RPS Instrumentalist Award 2012. *Current Management:* Harrison Parrott, 5–6 Albion Court, London, W6 0QT, England. *Telephone:* (20) 7229-9166. *Fax:* (20) 7221-5042. *E-mail:* info@harrisonparrott.co.uk. *Website:* www.harrisonparrott.com.

POLOLANIK, Zdenek, MgA; Czech (Moravian) composer; b. 25 Oct. 1935, Brno; m. Jarmila Linka; one d. one s. *Education:* Brno Conservatoire, Janáček Acad. of Performing Arts, Brno. *Career:* freelance composer from 1961–; composed 600 works including concert music and ballet, spiritual music for liturgical purposes and musical scores for film, radio, incidental music, etc; mem. Prítomnost composers' consortium, Prague. *Compositions include:* Variations for organ and piano 1956, Sinfonietta 1958, String Quartet 1958, Divertimento for 4 horns and strings 1960, 5 Symphonies 1961, 1962, 1963, 1969, Concentus resonabilis for 19 soloists and tape 1963, Musica Spingenta I–III 1961–63, Mechanism, ballet 1964, Horn sonata 1965, Popelka (Cinderella), puppet ballet 1966, Piano Concerto 1966, Concerto Grosso I and II 1966, 1988, Missa Brevis 1969, Song of Songs, oratorio 1970, Snow Queen, ballet 1978, Lady Among Shadows, ballet 1984, Summer Festivities for chorus and 2 pianos 1985, Christmas Message 1987, March for wind orchestra 1990, Easter Way, 14 songs for soprano and ensemble 1990, Small Mythological Exercises, melodrama 1991, Ballad for cello and piano 1992, Christmas Triptych for bugle and 4 trombones 1993, First One Must Carry the Cross, chamber oratorio for medium voice and synthesizer 1993, Eulogies, Psalms for chorus 1993, Psalms for women's chorus 1993, Cisařuv mim (Emperor's Mime) 1993, Chválozpevy 1994, Spor duše s tělem (Dispute of Soul with Body) 1994, Two Ballads for lower voice 1995, Prazská legenda (Prague Legend) 1995, Winterballad 1996, Sexton 1996, Horka blahoslavenství (Bitter Hallow) 1996, Citadella 1997, Cycles of Noels for organ, piano, large symphony orchestra 1997, Dulces cantilenae 1997, Cantus laetitiae 1997, Setkání (Ordinario and Proprio) 1997, Musica sacra 1999, Slavnostní konická mše (Solemn Konical mass) 2000, Baletní epizody (Ballettic episodes) 2001, Interludium 2001, Missa solemnis 2001, Capriccio for cello and orchestra

2002, Noc plná světla (Night of Full Light), opera 2009. *Recordings:* Missa Brevis 1994, Pastorale for Organ, Liturgical mass, Te Deum, Ave Maria 1996, Time and Joy of Merrymaking 1997, Ballad 1997, What's New 1997, Snow Queen 1998, Pierot 1999, Noel's Adventní (Advent) 1999, The Angel's Message to the World, Capriccio for cello and orchestra. *Publications:* contrib. to journals and books. *Honours:* Hon. Freeman Ostrovacice; Holyś Cyril and Method Decoration; Josef Blaha Prize for Music Composition, Cena Jihomoravského kraje 2005, Sv. Petra a Pavla Medal 2007, Svatovojtěšská stříbrná Medal 2010. *Address:* Osvobození 67, 66481 Ostrovačice, Czech Republic (home). *Telephone:* (546) 427417 (home). *E-mail:* zdenek.pololanik@capellen.cz (home). *Website:* www.volny.cz/pololanik.

POLOZOV, Vyacheslav M.; Ukrainian singer (tenor); b. 1950, Mariupol. *Education:* Kiev Conservatory. *Career:* debut at Kiev Opera 1977, as Alfredo in La Traviata; leading tenor at the Saratov Opera 1978; Leading tenor at Minsk Opera 1980; Bolshoi Opera Moscow, 1982, Alfredo and Turiddu; Sang Pinkerton at La Scala 1986; US debut with Pittsburgh Symphony Orchestra 1986, as Cavaradossi; US stage debut the Chicago Lyric Opera 1986, as Rodolfo in La Bohème; Further appearances at Washington, DC (1986, as Lykov, in The Tsar's Bride), New York (Met 1987, as Pinkerton); Palm Springs, as Cavaradossi; San Antonio (as Cavaradossi); Met (as Rodolfo, 1987, summer park concerts); Washington, DC, as Dimitri in Boris Godunov; Season 1987–88 with Calaf in New City Opera, repeated at the Bayerische Staatsoper Munich; Rome Opera as Lykov and the Metropolitan as Verdi's Macduff; Michigan Opera Theatre as Rodolfo in La Bohème, (1988 debut); Further debuts at the San Francisco Opera (1988 as Enzo, in La Gioconda), Carnegie Hall (1988, as Andrea Chénier), Canadian Opera Company (1989 as Cavaradossi), Greater Miami Opera (1989, as Alvaro in La Forza); Sang Pinkerton in San Francisco, 1989, Lyon Opéra (debut 1990), as Pinkerton, repeated in the Greater Miami Opera; appearance, at the 1990 Caracalla Festival, Rome, and Turiddu and Lensky with the Chicago Lyric Opera, 1990; Calaf with the Greater Miami Opera; Cavaradossi in the Houston Grand Opera, 1991; as Lensky in Hamburg; as Don Carlo in Denver at the Opera Colorado. *Recordings include:* Aleko by Rachmaninov, Boris Godunov. *Honours:* winner All-Russia Glinka Competition 1981; Sofia Competition, Bulgaria, 1984 (for the Duke of Mantua); Madama Butterfly Competition, Tokyo, 1987.

POLSTER, Hermann Christian; German singer; b. 8 April 1937, Leipzig. *Education:* Univ. of Leipzig. *Career:* sang with the Dresden Kreuzchor while a boy; many engagements with the Leipzig Bach Soloists, the chorus of St Thomas's Leipzig and the Leipzig Gewandhaus Orchestra; guest appearances Berlin; Munich, Frankfurt, Hamburg, Roma, Milano, Torino, Amsterdam (St Matthew Passion); Halle (Shostakovich 14th Symphony); Tokyo, Osaka (Bach: St Matthew and St John Passion, Beethoven's Ninth); Paris (Fidelio), Moscow, Buenos Aires, Rio de Janerio, Aix-en-Provence, Venice, Dubrovnik, Prague (Beethoven's Ninth); other repertoire includes Monteverdi's Vespers; Buxtehude Cantatas, Telemann Cantatas, Psalms, Serenades; Handel Saul, Acis and Galatea, Samson, Belshazzar, Judas Maccabaeus, Solomon, Jephtha, Hercules and Messiah; Bach Cantatas and Oratorios; Haydn Oratorios; Mozart Masses, Requiem, Solemn Vespers and Die Zauberflöte (Sarastro); Beethoven Missa Solomnis, Mass in C and Christus am Olberg; Mendelssohn Elijah, St Paul, Erste Walpurgisnacht; Schumann Paradies und die Peri; Verdi Requiem; Brahms Ein Deutsches Requiem; Mahler 8th Symphony; Janáček Glagolitic Mass; Stravinsky Oedipus Rex; Wagner Die Meistersinger (Pogner); Tchaikovsky Eugene Onegin (Gremin); Blacher The Grand Inquisitor; Shostakovich 13th Symphony, Songs of Michelangelo; Professur für Gesang Musikhochschule Leipzig, International Masterclasses, Juror in international competitions (Brussels, Moscow, Berlin, Leipzig); mem, Deutscher Musikrat, Bundesverband Deutscher Gesangspädagogen, Neue Detusche Bachesellschaft. *Recordings:* St Matthew Passion and Bach Cantatas; Elijah and Orff's Die Kluge; Beethoven: Fidelio (1804 version), Missa solemnis; Shostakovich Michelangelo Songs; Mozart Litaneien; Concert works conducted by Karl Böhm, Karajan, Herbert Kegel, Neville Marriner, Wolfgang Sawallisch and Kurt Masur. *Honours:* Kammersänger, Kunstpreisträger. *Address:* c/o Gewandhausorchester, Augustusplatz 8, 4109 Leipzig (office); Weissackerweg 7, 4827 Machern, Germany (home). *Telephone:* 34292-73798 (home). *Fax:* 34292-73798 (home). *E-mail:* Prof_Polster@web.de (home).

POLTÉRA, Christian; Swiss cellist; b. 9 Aug. 1977, Zurich. *Education:* studied with Nancy Chumachenco and Boris Pergamenschikow, and with Heinrich Schiff in Salzburg and Vienna. *Career:* BBC New Generation Artist Award 2004; performs as soloist with conductors including Bernard Haitink, Riccardo Chailly, Christoph von Dohnányi and John Eliot Gardiner and orchestras including Gewandhausorchester Leipzig, Munich Philharmonic, Oslo Philharmonic, Chamber Orchestra of Europe, Orchestre de Paris, BBC Symphony; US debut with American Symphony Orchestra 2006, also at Carnegie Hall 2006; chamber music with Leonidas Kavakos, Gidon Kremer, Kathryn Stott, Lars Vogt, Christian Tetzlaff, Leif Ove Andsnes, Mitsuko Uchida and Auryn, Guarneri and Zehetmair String Quartets and as mem. string trio with Frank Peter Zimmermann and Antoine Tamestit; festivals in Austria, Germany, Switzerland, UK. *Recordings include:* cello concertos of Toch, Dvořák, Schoeck, Dutilleux, Lutosławski; chamber music by Prokofiev, Fauré and Schubert, Dvorak: Silent Woods (Works for Cello and Piano) 2012, Poltera Cello Concertos 2012, Walton/Hindemith: Cello Concertos 2014. *Honours:* Borletti-Buitoni Award, BBC New Generation Artist 2004, European Concert Halls Org. Rising Star 2006. *E-mail:* christianpoltera@yahoo.de (office). *Website:* www.christianpoltera.com.

POLVERELLI, Laura; Italian singer (mezzo-soprano); b. 24 Aug. 1967, Siena. *Education:* Florence and Verona Conservatories, Accademia Chigiana, Siena, Munich Musikhochschule. *Career:* has sung several of the most important roles in opera houses in Italy and abroad, including venues such as Teatro alla Scala in Milan, Teatro del Maggio Musicale Fiorentino, Accad. Nazionale di Santa Cecilia in Rome, Teatro La Fenice in Venice, Bayerische Staatsoper in Munich, Hamburgische Staatsoper, Teatro Real in Madrid, Opéra de Lyon, Opéra de Montecarlo, Théâtre des Champs Elysées in Paris, Vlaamse Opera in Antwerp, Théâtre Royal de la Monnaie in Bruxelles, Opéra de Lausanne, Rossini Opera Festival in Pesaro, Glyndebourne Int. Festival, working with famous conductors including Claudio Abbado, Riccardo Muti, Zubin Mehta, Riccardo Chailly, Jeffrey Tate, Colin Davis, René Jacobs, amongs others; repertoire includes roles of Rosina in The Barber of Seville, Angelina in La Cenerentola, Isabella in L'Italiana in Algeri, Isolier in Le Comte Ory, Dorabella in Così Fan Tutte, Idamante in Idomeneo, Zerlina in Don Giovanni, Cherubino in Le Nozze di Figaro, Cornelia and Sesto in Handel's Julius Caesar, Goffredo in Rinaldo, Proserpina and Musica in Monteverdi's Orfeo, Poppea in L'inconorazione di Poppea, Irene in Handel's Tamburlaine, Licida in Pergolesi's L'Olimpiade, Meg in Verdi's Falstaff, Felicia in Il Crociato in Egitto, Jane Seymour in Donizetti's Anna Bolena, Elizabeth I in Donizetti's Maria Stuarda, Sesto in La Clemenza di Tito, Arsace in Vivaldi's Ercole sul Termodonte, Edwige in Guglielmo Tell; performances at La Scala Milan have included Puck in Weber's Oberon, Fenena in Nabucco with Riccardo Muti, Ascanio in Berlioz's Les Troyens with Colin Davis, Zaida in Il Turco in Italia with Riccardo Chailly; regular guest appearances at the Rossini Opera Festival where she has sung Corghi's Isabella, Isaura in Tancredo, Madame La Rose in La Gazzetta and Isolier in Le Comte Ory. *Recordings include:* Le nozze di Figaro and Così fan tutte; Zaida in Il Turco in Italia and Hemon in Traetta's Antigone. *Honours:* winner of several int. competitions. *Current Management:* c/o Raffaella Coletti Artists Management, via Maggio 35, 50125 Florence, Italy. *Telephone:* (055) 213705. *Fax:* (055) 282631. *E-mail:* info@raffaellacolettiam.com. *Website:* www.raffaellacolettiam.com (office); www.laurapolverelli.com (office).

POLYANICHKO, Alexander; Russian violinist and conductor; *House Conductor, Mariinsky Theatre*; b. 26 March 1953. *Education:* Rostov-on-Don Conservatoire with Prof. Matvey Dreier, St Petersburg Conservatoire with Prof. Ilya Musin. *Career:* fmr violinist with Leningrad Philharmonic Orchestra, under Evgeny Mravinsky; apptd Conductor Mariinsky (Kirov) Theatre 1989–; fmr Artistic Dir St Petersburg Orchestra; Dir of the Opera Dept, Mariinsky Theatre 1995–96; Artistic Dir State Chamber Orchestra of Belorussia, Minsk 1986–89; Prin. Conductor Bournemouth Sinfonietta 1997–2000; conducted the Mariinsky (Kirov) Opera and Ballet Theatre at the Edinburgh Festival (The Marriage) 1991, Los Angeles (The Nutcracker) 1993, Tel-Aviv (Khovanshchina) 1996; London debut conducting ENO's production of Eugene Onegin 1994, returning to ENO to conduct Eugene Onegin and Carmen 1997, 1998; season 1994–95 conducted La Bohème with Norwegian Opera in Oslo, The Fiery Angel with San Francisco Opera, and toured Australia for ABC and NZ with New Zealand Symphony Orchestra; season 1995–96 with La Bayadère at the Opéra Nat. de Paris, later touring with this production to the New York Met; debut at La Scala conducting the Mariinsky Opera's production of Mussorgsky's Khovanshchina 1998; conducted Lady Macbeth of Mtsensk for Stuttgart Opera 1998, returning in subsequent years to conduct The Queen of Spades, Tosca, Boris Godunov, Turandot, and La Traviata; Covent Garden debut 1999, conducting for the Royal Ballet, returning in 2000–01; seasons 1999–2000, 2000–01 and 2001–02 conducting La Traviata at Deutsche Oper Berlin; conducted Paris Opera in Stravinsky's Mavra, Prokofiev's The Prodigal Son and Weill's Seven Deadly Sins 2001; appearances at San Francisco Opera, conducting Turandot, La Bohème and The Cunning Little Vixen; at the Bolshoi Theatre, Moscow, conducting La Bohème, Tosca, The Queen of Spades Eugene Onegin, Boris Godunov; at the Royal Danish Opera, conducting The Queen of Spades, The Love of Three Oranges; at the Royal Opera House, Covent Garden, conducting The Queen of Spades and Cherevichki; conducted The Queen of Spades at Gothenburg Opera 2003, returning to conduct a new production of Boris Godunov 2005 and Eugene Onegin 2010; at the Opéra de Monte Carlo, conducted Boris Godunov 2006; conducted La Traviata, Hansel and Gretel, The Queen of Spades, Eugene Onegin, Mazeppa, The Barber of Seville for Welsh Nat. Opera; conducted Roméo et Juliette and Nutcracker for Opéra de Lyon, Carmen 2005 and Manon Lescaut 2009 for Australian Opera, Eugene Onegin for New Zealand Opera 2009, Rusalka 2010 and Il Trovatore 2012 for Opera Colorado; numerous guest appearances with leading European and US orchestras, including Chicago Symphony Orchestra 2009, 2010, and with leading Russian orchestras; Artistic Dir and Prin. Conductor Rostov Academic Symphony Orchestra 2012–; Prof., St Petersburg Conservatoire 1986–89, Minsk State Conservatoire 1986–89, Rostov-on-Don Conservatoire 2012; has taken part in numerous int. festivals, including Aldeburgh, Bergen, Edinburgh, Mikkele and Savonlinna, Golden Mask Festival (Moscow), The Avantgarde to the Contemporary Festival, St Petersburg, Shaliapin Festival, Kazan, Russia, Bulat Mizhilkiev Festival, Bishkek, Kyrgystan; mem. Jury, Rimsky-Korsakov Opera Singers' Competition 1996, Bulat Mizhilkiev Festival, BBC Cardiff Singer of the World Competition 2011; regular masterclasses for conductors in Bishkek and in St Petersburg organised by Royal Baltic Festival and Hermitage Music Acad. 2001–. *Honours:* Honoured Artist of

Russia; First Prize, All-Union Conductors' Competition 1988. *Current Management:* c/o Ingpen & Williams, 7 St George's Court, 131 Putney Bridge Road, London, SW15 2PA, England. *Telephone:* (20) 8874-3222. *Fax:* (20) 8877-3113. *E-mail:* info@ingpen.co.uk. *Website:* www.ingpen.co.uk. *Address:* Mariinsky Theatre, 19000 St Petersburg, Teatralnaya pl. 1, Russia (office). *Website:* www.polyanichko.ru (home).

POMERANTS-MAZURKEVICH, Dana, MMus, DipMus; violinist and academic; b. 11 Oct. 1944, Kaunas, USSR; m. Yuri Mazurekvich 1963, one d. *Education:* Moscow State Conservatory. *Career:* performed as mem. of Mazurkevich Violin Duo and also as a soloist in USSR, Poland, USA, Canada, Australia, England, France, Belgium, Germany, Hong Kong, Taiwan, Switzerland, Italy, Romania, Mexico and other countries; recorded for radio worldwide. *Recordings:* Works by Telemann, Prokofiev, Honegger, Sarasate, Spohr, Rawsthorne, Wieniawski, Shostakovich, Leclair, Handel and others; Masters of the Bow, Toronto, Canada; SNE, Montréal, Canada.

POMMIER, Jean-Bernard; French pianist and conductor; b. 17 Aug. 1944, Béziers; two d. by Irena Podleska. *Education:* Conservatoire de Paris, studied with Yves Nat and Pierre Sancan and conducting with Eugene Bigot, also worked with Eugène Istomin. *Career:* as pianist has appeared with conductors including: Herbert von Karajan, Bernard Haitink, Pierre Boulez, Riccardo Muti, Gennadi Rozhdestvensky, Leonard Slatkin, Zubin Mehta and Daniel Barenboim; has conducted numerous orchestras including Chamber Orchestra of Europe, Orchestre de Paris; debut with Royal Liverpool Philharmonic Orchestra 1991; Artistic Dir Northern Sinfonia, Newcastle-upon-Tyne 1996–99; Prin. Conductor Orchestra Filarmonica di Torino 1997; Founder and Artistic Dir Musikè International Acad.; fmr Artistic Dir Festival de Menton; mem. Faculty, Piano Dept, Rotterdam Classical Music Acad. 2011–; Visiting Fellow, St Chad's Coll., Durham; masterclasses in Chicago, London, Lausanne and Melbourne. *Recordings include:* Mozart Piano Concerti (with Sinfonia Varsovia), Poulenc Piano Concerti (with City of London Sinfonia), Brahms Cello Sonatas and Violin Sonatas, Complete Beethoven Piano Sonatas, complete Mozart Sonatas. *Honours:* Officier, Ordre nat. du mérite, Chevalier, Légion d'Honneur; Int. Competition for Young Musicians, Berlin, Prix de la Guilde des artistes solistes français, Diapason d'Or, Tchaikovsky Prize, Moscow. *Current Management:* Künstlersekretariat Barbara Golan, Barbara Golan-Oehninger, Stettbachstrasse 131h, 8051 Zürich, Switzerland. *E-mail:* infoatgolanartists.ch. *Website:* www.golanartists.ch/English/Pommier.html.

POMPILI, Claudio, BMus; Italian composer; b. 12 May 1949, Gorizia. *Education:* Univ. of Adelaide, studied with Richard Meale and Tristram Cary in Australia, with Franco Donatoni and Salvatore Sciarrino in Italy, IRCAM Studios, Paris. *Career:* faculty mem., Univ. of Adelaide 1983–84, Univ. of New England 1987–97; Assoc. Prof. and Dir, Conservatorium of Music, Univ. of Wollongong 1998–; commissions from Duo Contemporain, Perihelion and others. *Compositions include:* Medieval Purity in a Bed of Thorns for tape 1981–84, The Star Shoots a Dart for flute, clarinet, violin and cello 1985, Polymnia Triptych for soprano and large ensemble 1986, Songs for Ophelia for soprano 1989, Scherzo alla Francescana for double bass 1990, Trio for violin, guitar and double bass 1990, Zeitfluss: Teuflicher kontrapunkt for wind quintet 1990, Lo spazio stellato si riflette in suoni for baroque flute 1990, Ah, amore che se n'ando nell'aria for clarinet, viola and cello 1991, String Quartet 1992, El viento lucha a obscura con tu sueno 1993, Fra l'urlo e il tacere for bass clarinet 1993. *Honours:* Adolf Spivakovsky scholarship 1990.

POND, Celia Frances Sophia, BA, MA, LRAM; British cellist; b. 5 Jan. 1956, London; m. Ambrose Miller 1981. *Education:* Girton Coll., Cambridge, Royal Acad. of Music, London, Staatliche Hochschule für Musik, Rheinland. *Career:* cellist and coordinator, European Union Chamber Orchestra 1981–2012, performances in 73 countries; cellist with Trio Gardellino, recitals throughout Europe; cello and piano duo, Celia and Mary Pond 1983–89. *Recording:* Antonio Duni, Cantate da Camera Dedicate Alla Maesta di Giovanni V. *Publications:* contrib. to Early Music 1978, Solo Bass Viol Music in France. *Honours:* Edith Helen Major Prize, Cambridge 1976, German Govt Scholarship 1978. *Current Management:* c/o 5 Churchside, Fowey, Cornwall, PL23 1BX, England. *Telephone:* (1726) 832171. *E-mail:* classicconcert@aol.com (office). *Website:* foweyvalleymusic.org.uk. *Address:* Hollick, Yarnscombe, North Devon, EX33 3LQ, England (home). *Telephone:* (1271) 858249 (home). *Fax:* (1271) 858375 (home). *E-mail:* eucorch2@aol.com (office). *Website:* www.euco.org.uk (office); www.brandenburgbachsolisten.org.

PONDJICLIS, Sophie; French singer (mezzo-soprano); b. 1968. *Career:* appearances at Florence, the Paris Opéra Bastille, La Scala Milan, Palais Garnier, Hamburg Opera and Marseille; Paris Châtelet in Stravinsky's Les Noces, repeated in Rome; sang title role in Esther de Carpentras by Milhaud, 1992; Recitals at the Châtelet, Studio Bastille, Mannheim and Villa Medici in Rome; Further enagements as Carmen, Ruggiero in Alcina and Rossini's Rosina; season 2000–01 at the Berlin Konzerthaus as Ravel's Enfant, Mozart's Marcellina in Paris, Madrid and Barcelona, Isaura in Rossini's Tancredi at Marseille and Olga in Eugene Onegin at Geneva. *Recordings include:* Stabat Mater by Gouvy. *Honours:* winner Toti dal Monte Competition, Treviso. *Current Management:* c/o Musicaglotz, 11 rue le Verrier, 75006 Paris; c/o Organisation Internationale Artistique, 16 Avenue Franklin D. Roosevelt, 75008 Paris, France. *Telephone:* (1) 42-34-53-40 (Musicaglotz); 1-42-25-58-34 (OIA). *Fax:* (1) 40-46-93-77 (Musicaglotz); 1-42-25-64-97 (OIA). *E-mail:* general@musicaglotz.com; oia@oia-poilve.com. *Website:* www.musicaglotz.com; www.oia-poilve.com; www.sophie-pondjiclis.com.

PONIATOWSKA, Irena, PhD; Polish musicologist; b. 5 July 1933, Góra Kalwaria; m. Andrzej Poniatowski 1953 (died 1994); one d. *Education:* Warsaw Univ. *Career:* tutor, Inst. of Musicology, Warsaw Univ. 1970, Vice-Dir 1974–79, Asst Prof. 1984, Extraordinary Prof. 1991, Ordinary Prof. 1996–2003, Vice-Dean Faculty of History 1988–90, 1993–99; Pres. Council, Chopin Soc. 1975–85, Vice-Pres. 1985–90; Pres. Congress, Musica Antique Europae Orientalis, Poland 1988, 1991, 1994, 1997, 2000, 2003, 2006, Polish Chopin Acad. 1994, Congress Chopin, Warsaw, 1999, Council of Inst. of Fryderyk Chopin, 2001–; ed. of many encyclopaedias, including Polish Encyclopaedia of Music, Vols 1–5 1979–97. *Publications:* Beethoven Piano Texture 1972, The Chronicle of the Important Musical Events in Poland 1945–72 1974, Piano Music and Playing in XIX Century Artistic and Social Aspects 1991, Dictionary of Music for Schools 1991, 1997, History and Interpretation of Music 1993, 1995, Musical Work: Theory History, Interpretation (ed.) 1984, Maria Szymanowska 25 Mazurkas 1993, Chopin in the Circle of his Friends, Vols I–V (ed.) 1995–99, J. A. Hasse und Polen (co-ed.) 1995, 24 Préludes by Fryderyk Chopin (ed., facsimile edn with commentary) 1999, Henryk Wieniawski Polonaise Brillante pour le violon avec accompagnement de piano op. 4, urtext and critical edn 2000, Musica antique Europae Orientalis X Acta Musicologica (co-ed.) 1994, Bydgoszcz 1997, Bydgoszcz XI 1999, Bydgoszcz XII 2003, Bydgoszcz XIII 2004, Chopin and his Works in the Context of Culture, Vols 1–2 (ed.) 2003, Sonate Si-mineur of F. Chopin (co-ed.) 2005, Fryderyk Chopin (co-author) 2006; numerous articles in collective works; contrib. to Muzyka, Ruch Muzyczny, Rocznik Chopinowski, Chopin Studies, Hudobny Život, Quadrivium. *Honours:* hon. mem. Accad. Filarmonica di Bologna 1998; Officer's Cross, Order of Polonia Restituta 2000; Medal of Nat. Educ. Cttee 2004, Medal of Merits for Polish Culture 2004, Prize of Polish Composers' Union 2004, Argent Medal, Gloria Arfis 2006. *Address:* Filtrowa 63-38, 02-056 Warsaw, Poland (home). *Telephone:* (22) 8252850 (home); (22) 8279599 (office). *E-mail:* nifc@nifc.pl (office).

PONKIN, Vladimir; Russian conductor; b. 1951, Irkutsk, Siberia. *Education:* Gorky Conservatoire, studied with Rozhdestvensky in Moscow. *Career:* Asst Conductor, Bolshoi Theatre and Moscow Chamber Theatre; Conductor, Yaroslavl Philharmonic Orchestra, later with Russian State Cinema Orchestra; guest engagements with St Petersburg Philharmonic and Russian State Academic Symphony Orchestra; Chief Conductor and Music Dir, Russian State Maly Symphony from 1991; Music Dir, New Moscow State Symphony Orchestra; has toured to Italy, Hungary, Germany, Austria, Spain and Denmark; repertoire has included much contemporary music as well as standard works. *Honours:* winner Rupert Foundation Conducting Competition, London 1990.

PONOMARENKO, Ivan; Ukrainian singer (baritone); b. 1955. *Education:* Odessa Conservatory, studied with Irina Arkhipova. *Career:* sang first with Odessa State Opera Theatre as Escamillo, Don Giovanni, Renato in Un Ballo in Maschera, Germont and Amonasro; mem., Kiev Opera from 1981, touring with co. to Germany, Spain, The Netherlands, Hungary and France; sang at Strasbourg Festival 1993 as Nabucco; British debut on tour 1995; recitalist with a wide repertoire.

PONS, Josep; Spanish conductor; *Music Director, Orquesta Nacional de España;* b. 1957, Barcelona. *Education:* Escolania de Montserrat. *Career:* f. Orquestra de Cambra Teatre Lliure, Barcelona 1985; Music Dir Orquesta Ciudad de Granada 1994–2004; Artistic Dir Orquesta Nacional de España 2003–; Assoc. Principal Conductor, Gran Teatro del Liceo, Barcelona; guest conductor, many Spanish and European orchestras, orchestras in Israel and Australia. *Recordings:* albums: as conductor: Falla, Siete canciones populares españolas (with Victoria de los Angeles and Orquesta de Cambra Teatre Lliure) 1993, Gerhard, Cancionero de Pedrell (with Orquesta de Cambra Teatre Lliure) 1994, Albéniz, Pepita Jiménez (with Susan Chilcott, Francesc Garrigosa and Orquesta de Cambra Teatre Lliure) 1995, Falla, El corregidor y la molinera (with Ginesa Ortega and Orquesta de Cambra Teatre Lliure) 1995, Piazzolla, Concerto for bandoneon (with Pablo Mainetti) 1996, Falla, El Sombrero/Noches (with Josep Colom and Orquesta Ciudad de Granada) 1997, Stravinsky, Pulcinella (with Orquesta de Cambra Teatre Lliure) 1997, Falla, La Vida breve (with Mabel Perelstein, Antonio Ordoñez, Cor de Valencia and Orquesta Ciudad de Granada) 1998, Bizet, L'Arlésienne (with Orquesta Ciudad de Granada) 2000, Stravinsky, The Firebird (with Orquesta Ciudad de Granada) 2001, Rodrigo, Concerto de Aranjuez/Fantasia para un gentilhombre (with Orquesta Ciudad de Granada) 2002, Ginastera, Estancias/Concerto for Harp (with Magdalena Barrera and Orquesta Ciudad de Granada) 2003, Rota, La Strada/Il Gattopardo (with Benedetto Lupo and Orquesta Ciudad de Granada) 2005, Mompou, Suburbis/Les Impròperes (with Virginia Parramon, Jerzy Artysz and Cor de Valencia) 2007. *Honours:* Premio Nacional de la Música, Spanish Ministry of Culture 1999. *Address:* Orquesta y Coro Nacionales de España, Principe de Vergara 146, 28002 Madrid, Spain (office); Harmonia Mundi SA, Mas de Vert, BP 20150, 13631 Arles, France (office). *Telephone:* (91) 337-01-40 (office); (4) 90-49-90-49 (office). *Fax:* (91) 563-29-07 (office). *E-mail:* infosite@harmoniamundi.com (office). *Website:* ocne.mcu.es (office); www.harmoniamundi.com (office).

PONS, Juan; Spanish singer (baritone); b. 8 Aug. 1946, Ciutadella, Menorca. *Education:* studied in Barcelona. *Career:* sang at the Teatro Liceo Barcelona, at first as a tenor; Covent Garden 1979, as Alfio in Cavalleria Rusticana;

Barcelona 1983, Herod in Massenet's Hérodiade; Paris Opéra 1983, as Tonio in Pagliacci; Guest appearances in Munich, Madrid and at the Orange Festival; Verona Arena 1984–85, Amonasro; La Scala Milan 1985, as Rigoletto and as Sharpless in Madama Butterfly; Metropolitan Opera 1986, as Scarpia in Tosca; Well known as Verdi's Falstaff; (Munich Staatsoper 1987), San Francisco and Rome 1989; Also sings Renato in Un Ballo in Maschera and roles in operas by Donizetti; sang Verdi's Germont at Chicago 1988; Sharpless in Madama Butterfly at La Scala, 1990; Barcelona 1989, as Basilio in Respighi's La Fiamma (also at Madrid); Season 1992 as Tonio in Pagliacci at Philadelphia, Scarpia at San Francisco and Luna at Madrid; Sang Amonasro at the Verona Arena, 1994; Tonio at Los Angeles, 1996; Season 1998 as Count of Westmorland in Wolf-Ferrari's Sly at Zürich, and Renato at Milan; Season 2000–01 as Germont in Florence, Amonasro at the Verona Arena, Rigoletto for the Opéra Bastille and Nabucco at the Met. *Recordings:* Aroldo by Verdi; Pagliacci. *Current Management:* c/o 2wise artist management, Ronda Sant Pere 29 2°- 3ª, 08010 Barcelona, Spain; c/o Opera Art, Via Isolalta Forette 11, 37068 Vigasio (VR), Italy. *Telephone:* 93 304 11 68 (Spain); (45) 6649911 (Italy). *Fax:* (45) 6649912 (Italy). *E-mail:* miguelpons@2wiseartist.com; info@operaart.it. *Website:* www.2wiseartist.com; www.operaart.it.

PONSFORD, David Stewart, MA, PhD, FRCO, ARCM; British organist, harpsichordist, conductor and musicologist; *Conductor and Associate Lecturer, Cardiff University School of Music*; b. 18 Jan. 1948, Cardiff, Wales; s. of Howard William Ponsford and Olive Jeanie Ponsford; m. Vicki Frances Ponsford; one s. *Education:* Queen's Coll., Taunton, Royal Manchester Coll. of Music, Emmanuel Coll., Cambridge, Univ. of Cardiff. *Career:* Asst Organist, Wells Cathedral 1971–76; Organist, St Matthew's, Northampton; Conductor, Northampton Bach Choir 1977–79, Cheltenham Bach Choir 1981–88; organ, harpsichord and academic tutor, Birmingham Conservatoire 1982–91; harpsichord and organ tutor, Wells Cathedral School 1986–; Assoc. Lecturer in Performance Practice, Univ. of Cardiff 2000–, also Conductor, Univ. of Cardiff Choir and Univ. Chamber Orchestra; Ed. and contrib., Bios Journal 2003; Publs Officer, British Inst. of Organ Studies 2005–11. *Recordings:* Annus Mirabilis 1685, Harpsichord music by Bach, Handel, Scarlatti and Sandoni 1999, Vive Le Roy, organ music by Bach, Couperin, Gringy from Greyfriars Kirk, Edinburgh 1999, Complete J. S. Bach Violin Sonatas (with Jacqueline Ross) 2002, J. S. Bach Clavierübung Part 3 2003, Parthenia 2005, Handel Recorder Sonatas (with Alan Davis) 2005. *Publications:* The Organ of Gottfried Silbermann, in Choir and Organ 1997, Inégalité and Récits: Genre Studies in 17th century French Organ Music, in The Organ Yearbook 1998–99, J. S. Bach and the Nature of French Influence, in The Organ Yearbook 2000, edn of Biber: Mystery (Rosary) Sonatas 2007, Organ Music in the Reign of Louis XIV 2011; contrib. to The Musical Times, Choir and Organ, Organist's Review, The Organ Yearbook. *Honours:* Leverhulme Research Fellowship 2004. *Address:* School of Music, Cardiff University, 31 Corbett Road, Cardiff, CF10 3EB, Wales (office); Ford Cottage, Middle Duntisbourne, Cirencester, Glos., GL7 7AR, England (home). *Telephone:* (29) 2087-4381 (office); (1285) 651995 (home); 7932-140823 (mobile). *Fax:* (1285) 651995 (home). *E-mail:* Ponsfordd@Cardiff.ac.uk (office); dsponsford@aol.com (home). *Website:* www.davidponsford.org.

PONSONBY, Robert Noel, CBE, MA; British arts administrator; b. 19 Dec. 1926, Oxford, England; m. Lesley Black 1977. *Education:* Trinity Coll., Oxford. *Career:* staff mem., Glyndebourne Opera 1951–55; Artistic Dir Edinburgh Festival 1956–60; Gen. Admin. Scottish Nat. Orchestra 1964–72; Controller of Music, BBC 1972–85; Artistic Dir Canterbury Festival 1986–88; Admin. Friends of Musicians Benevolent Fund 1987–93. *Publication:* Short History of Oxford University Opera Club 1950, Musical Heroes 2009; conceived Choirbook for the Queen, a book of 44 anthems by living British composers for the Queen's Diamond Jubilee 2011; contribs to numerous magazines and journals; obituaries for The Times, The Independent and The Guardian. *Honours:* Hon. RAM 1975; Janáček Medal, Czech Govt 1980. *Address:* 11 St Cuthbert's Road, London, NW2 3QJ, England (home). *Telephone:* (20) 8452-1715 (home).

PONTES-LEÇA, Carlos de; Portuguese musicologist and music programmer; b. 26 Nov. 1938, Coimbra. *Education:* Coimbra Univ., Univ. of Navarra, Spain, Music Conservatories of Lisbon and Coimbra. *Career:* Asst Dir Music Dept, Calouste Gulbenkian Foundation, Lisbon 1978–2004, Artistic Adviser 2004–10; Assoc. Ed. (for music and dance) of the cultural magazine, Coloquio-Artes, Lisbon 1971–96; Artistic Dir Leiria Music Festival 1993–2001; writer of music programmes on Portuguese TV and radio, essays and lectures on history of music, opera and musical film, programme notes for Gulbenkian Foundation, San Carlos Theatre (Lisbon Nat. Opera) and recordings; commentator of opera performances on radio and TV; courses convenor at Portuguese Film Archive, Coimbra Univ. and Gulbenkian Foundation; collaborator, Int. Symposia on Music and Cinema, Salamanca Univ. 2006–; Founder-mem. Portuguese Music Council. *Publications:* contrib. to The New Grove Dictionary of Music and Musicians, Verbo Encyclopedia. *Address:* Campo Grande 300, 1700-097 Lisbon, Portugal. *E-mail:* cpontesleca@gmail.pt.

PÖNTINEN, Roland; Swedish pianist and composer; b. 4 May 1963, Stockholm; s. of Rikhard Pöntinen and Gunnel Pöntinen; m. Camilla Wiklund; one s. one d. *Education:* Stockholm Royal Music Acad. with Gunnar Hallhagen, further studies at School of Fine Arts, Banff, Canada. *Career:* debut, Royal Stockholm Philharmonic Orchestra, playing Franck's Symphonic Variations 1981; many appearances with leading orchestras, including all major Swedish ensembles, Oslo Philharmonic, Los Angeles Philharmonic, Hollywood Bowl, Jerusalem Symphony, BBC Symphony, Tonhalle Orchestra, Zurich, Accad. Santa Cecilia, Rome, Philharmonia Orchestra, Scottish Chamber Orchestra, Orchestre de la Suisse Romande; festival engagements include Bergen, Schleswig-Holstein, Ludwigsburg, Edinburgh, La Roque d'Anthéron Piano Festival, BBC Promenade Concerts, London (playing Grieg Piano Concerto, Ligeti Piano Concerto), Aldeburgh Festival, Berliner Festwochen, Maggio Musicale Fiorentino, Verbier Festival, Klavier Festival Ruhr, Piano Rarities Festival at Schloss vor Husum, Kuhmo Chamber Music Festival; recitals throughout Europe and USA (including Wigmore Hall, London and The Frick Collection, New York), Japan, Korea, Australia and NZ; premiere of composition Blue Winter played by Philadelphia Orchestra and Wolfgang Sawallisch, Carnegie Hall 1998; mem. Royal Swedish Acad. of Music. *Composition:* Blue Winter 1998. *Recordings include:* more than 90 albums of solo and chamber music, playing works by Busoni, Chopin, Janáček, Scriabin Piano Concerto (with Royal Stockholm Philharmonic Orchestra), Rachmaninov's Etudes-Tableaux, Selected works by Szymanowski, Debussy's Etudes, Pianorama: Piano music from films by Bergman, Kubrick, Fellini, Beineix etc., For Agnès – Music by Debussy, Schumann, Villa Lobos, Chick Corea etc. *Honours:* Litteris et Artibus (Royal Medal) for skills in the arts 2001. *Current Management:* c/o Robert Gilder & Co., 91 Great Russell Street, London, WC1B 3PS, England. *Telephone:* (20) 7580-7758. *Fax:* (20) 7580-7739. *E-mail:* rgilder@robert-gilder.com; ny_office@robert-gilder.com. *Website:* www.robert-gilder.com; www.rolandpontinen.com.

PONTVIK, Peter; Swedish composer, ensemble leader, musicologist and music producer; *Artistic Director, Stockholm Early Music Festival*; b. 29 April 1963, Copenhagen, Denmark; m. Daniela Valero; two s. *Education:* studied composition with Marino Rivero, Nat. Conservatory, Montevideo with Sara Herrera, Royal Acad. of Music, Stockholm with Sven-David Sandström, Acad. of Music, Karlsruhe, Germany with Wolfgang Rihm, Ferienkurse für Neue Musik, Darmstadt, and studied early music with Hans-Georg Renner. *Career:* grew up in Uruguay; debut in first performance of Reencuentro con Misiones for bandoneon at Taller de Música Contemporánea, Montevideo 1985; Founder and Artistic Leader of Ensemble Villancico, Stockholm 1995–, more than 300 concerts in 30 countries; radio broadcasts of several works, Swedish and German Broadcasting 1994–; Founder and Artistic Dir Stockholm Early Music Festival 2002–; mem. FST (Soc. of Swedish Composers), Int. Soc. for Contemporary Music; Founder NORDEM (Nordic Early Music Fed.) 2006–; Pres. REMA (European Early Music Network) 2011–; Promoter of European Day of Early Music 21 March 2013. *Compositions:* Amen for mixed choir 1989, Three Images for three recorders 1990, Candombe for wind orchestra 1990–91, Yeikó for bandoneon, percussion and dancer 1992–93, Allelu for mixed choir 1993, En kort mässa/Missa brevis for choir and brass quintet 1994, Sagitra for choir and percussion 1996–2002, Norr om himlen (song cycle) 2002, arrangements of Latin American Baroque music. *Television:* Ensemble Villancico (SVT) 2002, Stockholm Ealry Music Festival (SVT) 2008 and others. *Recordings:* with Ensemble Villancico: Cancionero de Upsala 1556, Music from a Pack of Cards, ¡A la xácara! – The Jungle Book of the Baroque (Latin American Baroque music), Hyhyhyhyhyhyhyhy – The New Jungle Book of the Baroque (Latin American Baroque music), The Källunge Codex 1622, ¡Una tonadilla nueva! – Ecuador Baroque, Tambalagumbá - Early World Music in Latin America. *Publications:* contrib. of articles to Codex kellungensis gåtfullt gotländskt musikfynd 2003. *Honours:* First Prize, Int. Competition for Choir Composition, Tolosa, Spain 1989, Ivan Lukacic Prize, Varazdin, Croatia (with Ensemble Villancico) 2001, Swedish Music Festivals Promoter of the Year 2004, Swedish Early Music Award 2010. *Current Management:* c/o Götgatan 62, 6 tr, 118 26, Stockholm, Sweden. *Telephone:* (8) 304329. *E-mail:* info@semf.se. *Website:* www.semf.se. *Address:* Tångvägen 9, 1 tr, 126 38 Hägersten, Sweden (home). *E-mail:* peter.pontvik@semf.se (home). *Website:* www.villancico.se (office); www.rema-eemn.net.

POOK, Jocelyn; British composer and violist; b. 14 Feb. 1960, Birmingham, England; d. of Wilfred Pook and Mary Cecil Williams. *Education:* King Edward VI School, Bury St Edmunds and Guildhall School of Music and Drama. *Career:* composes music for film, TV, theatre, dance and the concert platform; has toured and recorded with many leading names in pop, rock and classical music including The Communards (three-year tour), Laurie Anderson, Massive Attack, Ryuichi Sakamoto and Peter Gabriel; Assoc. Guildhall School of Music and Drama; mem. Jocelyn Pook Ensemble. *Musical scores include:* films: Strange Fish (Prix Italia 1994) 1994, Mothers and Daughters (Mention Speciale at Grand Prix Int. Video-Danse 1994) 1994, Blight (Golden Plaque Award, Chicago Int. Film Festival 1997) 1996, Eyes Wide Shut (Chicago Film Critics' Award 2000, ASCAP Award 2000) 1999, Comment j'ai tué mon père 2000, Time Out/L'emploi du Temps (Golden Lion Award) 2001, La Repentie 2002, Gangs of New York (featuring her track Dionysus from Untold Things album) 2003, Wild Side 2004, The Merchant of Venice 2004, Heidi 2005, Brick Lane (ASCAP Award) 2007, Caótica Ana 2007, The People v. Leo Frank 2009, Habitación en Roma 2010, Room 304 2011; TV: People's Century/Half the People (BBC) 1996, Saints and Sinners (S4C documentary series) 1997, The Lost Supper (Channel 4) 1998, Just Enough Distance (BBC 2) 1998, Trouble at the House (BBC 2) 1998, The Establishment (Channel 4 documentary series) 1999, Dancing Inside (BBC 2) 1999, Butterfly Collectors (Granada) (Best Title Music, Royal TV Soc.) 1999, In a Land of Plenty (BBC 2, co-written with Harvey Brough) 2001, Death on the Staircase 2004, The Government Inspector 2005, Storm Over Everest 2008, Going South 2009, DESH (British Composer Award 2012); opera: Ingerland

2010. *Dance includes:* Phantasmaton (Shobana Jeyasingh Dance Co.), Requiem (Darshan Singh Bhuller, performed by the Phoenix Dance Co. *Television commercials include:* Blow the Wind/Pie Jesu (Orange Mobile Phone TV advert) (Designers and Art Dirs Asscn Silver Award 1997) 1997, Ode to Why (Enron advertising campaign) 2000–01. *Recordings include:* Deluge 1997, Flood 1999, Untold Things 2001, Wild Side 2004, The Merchant of Venice 2004, Saint Joan 2008 (Olivier Award). *Honours:* American Soc. of Authors Composers and Publrs' Prize 1999, Multi-Media Award, British Composer Awards 2003. *Address:* c/o Laurence Aston, First Name, Suite 302, 43 Lancaster Gate, London, W2 3NA, England (office). *Telephone:* (20) 7706-8484 (office). *Fax:* (20) 7706-3434 (office). *E-mail:* info@firstname.org.uk (office). *Website:* www.jocelynpook.com (office).

POOLE, John, FRCO; British choral director; b. 1934, Birmingham, England; m. Laura McKirahan 1987, three s. *Education:* Univ. of Oxford. *Career:* fmr organist of London Univ. Church and Music Dir at Univ. Coll., London; founder, Bloomsbury Singers and Players; Dir of the BBC Singers 1972–90 and has directed the BBC Symphony Chorus and Singers in many concerts throughout the UK and abroad; Music Dir, Groupe Vocal de France 1990–95; Chief Guest Conductor, BBC Singers, with frequent performances of modern repertory; guest director worldwide. *Recordings:* Giles Swayne, Cry, with BBC Singers; Martin Mass, Britten, A Boy Was Born, BBC Singers, Westminster Cathedral Choristers; Chants d'Eglise with Groupe Vocal de France.

POOT, Sonja; singer (soprano); b. 3 Dec. 1936, Gravenzande, The Netherlands. *Education:* studied in Harare (Zimbabwe), Amsterdam and Vienna. *Career:* sang at Bonn Opera 1964–71, notably as Constanze in Entführung, and Donizetti's Lucia and Maria di Rohan; Nuremberg 1971–73, Stuttgart Staatsoper 1973–78; guest engagements at Basle, Amsterdam (Elsa 1978), Vienna Volksoper, Rome, Geneva (Elettra in Idomeneo 1973), Barcelona and Ottawa; other roles have included Mozart's Donna Anna, Queen of Night and Pamina, Anna Bolena, Lucrezia Borgia, Violetta, Amelia in Ballo in Maschera and Norina in Don Pasquale; many concert performances.

POP, Stefan; Romanian singer (tenor); b. 1987, Bistrita. *Career:* has performed at many opera houses in Vienna, Rome, Athens, Trieste, Hamburg: debuted at Israeli Opera 2010; roles include: Paolino in Cimarosa, Il matrimonio segreto, Normano in Donizetti, Lucia de Lammermoor, Nemorino in Donizetti, L'elisir d'amore, Rodolfo in Puccini, La Bohème, Alfredo in Verdi, La Traviata. *Honours:* Winner, Operalia Plácido Domingo World Opera Competition 2010. *Address:* Israel Opera Tel-Aviv-Yaffo, 19 Shaul Hamelech Boulevard, Tel-Aviv, Israel (office); Operalia, 230 rue du Faubourg Saint-Honoré, 75008 Paris, France (office). *Telephone:* (3) 6927777 (office); (1) 53-75-00-82 (office). *Fax:* (1) 75-43-92-15 (office). *E-mail:* operalia.paris@wanadoo.fr (office). *Website:* www.israel-opera.co.il (office); www.operalia.org (office).

POPE, Cathryn; British singer (soprano); b. 1960. *Education:* Royal Coll. of Music with Ruth Packer, National Opera Studio. *Career:* with ENO sang Papagena and Pamina in The Magic Flute, Anna in Moses, Susanna, Zerlina, Sophie in Werther, Leila in The Pearl Fishers, Gretel and Werther; sang Oksana in first British production of Christmas Eve by Rimsky-Korsakov, 1988; sang Amor in Orpheus and Euridice for Opera North; Royal Opera Covent Garden as Gianetta in L'Elisir d'Amor, Frasquita in Carmen and a Naiad in Ariadne auf Naxos; sang Gretel with Netherlands Opera 1990, Pamina at London Coliseum; sang in new productions of The Marriage of Figaro and Königskinder at Coliseum 1991–92; Gilda in a revival of Rigoletto 1992–93. *Recordings include:* Anne Trulove in The Rake's Progress, Barbarina in Le nozze di Figaro. *Address:* 31 Kenwood Drive, Hersham, Walton-on-Thames, KT12 5AX, England (home). *Telephone:* (19) 3224-8518 (home). *E-mail:* cathy@cathypope.com. *Website:* www.cathypope.com.

POPE, Michael Douglas, FRSA; British musician, radio producer, choral conductor and writer; b. 25 Feb. 1927, London; s. of Lt-Gen. Vyvyan Pope and Sybil Pope; m. 1st Margaret Jean Blakeney 1954, one s.; m. 2nd Gillian Victoria Peck 1967, one s. one d. *Education:* Wellington Coll., Guildhall School of Music and Drama. *Career:* served in Army 1945–48; mem. British Olympic team (athletics) 1948; joined BBC 1954, Asst, Music Div. 1960, Producer, music programmes and music talks 1966–80; planned and produced many programmes and series with BBC Chorus, subsequently BBC Singers; productions include revivals of works by Elgar, Stanford, Bantock (Omar Khayyám trilogy 1979), Pearsall, Bennett, Rootham, Hurlstone, Boyce (Solomon 1979), Parry (Prometheus Unbound 1980) and other composers; Royal Musical Asscn Centenary Concert 1974; premiere of Everyman, music drama by Kennedy Scott 1977; Missing Music 1972; The Direction of Modern Music 1980; Musical Dir, London Motet and Madrigal Club 1954–93; Guest Conductor, RTE; Hon. Sec., Royal Philharmonic Soc. 1983–85; mem. RMA, Incorporated Soc. of Musicians (Chair. Wiltshire Centre 2005–08), Elgar Soc. (Chair. 1978–88, Vice-Pres. 1988); Pres. London Athletic Club 1971–73. *Publications include:* King Olaf and the English Choral Tradition in Elgar Studies 1990; contrib. to DNB, Royal Coll. of Music Magazine. *Address:* Quarry Farm House, Chicksgrove, Salisbury, Wiltshire, SP3 6LY, England (home).

POPKEN, Ralph; German singer (countertenor); b. 1962, Wilhelmshaven. *Education:* studied in Hanover with Emma Kirkby. *Career:* sang in concerts and oratorios from 1984, in Europe and the USA; Opera debut, Hanover 1989 in Enrico Leone by Steffani; Handel Festival at Göttingen from 1992 in Agrippina, Ottone and Radamisto; Deutsche Staatsoper Berlin, 1992–95 in Graun's Cesare e Cleopatra, Gassmann's L'opera seria; Theater an der Wien 1998 and 1999–2000; Theater des Westens, Berlin in Chicago (musical); sang Narciso in Handel's Agrippina at Halle 1999–2000. *Recordings:* Radamisto, Cesare e Cleopatra; Bach-Cantatas.

POPLAVSKAYA, Marina; Russian singer (soprano); b. 1977, Moscow; m. Robert Hale 2006 (separated). *Education:* Bolshoi Theatre children's chorus, Ippolitov-Ivanov Music Acad., Moscow, Royal Opera House Jette Parker Young Artist's Programme, London. *Career:* began career as soloist, New Opera Theatre, Moscow 1996–98; soloist, K.S. Stanislavsky and V.I. Nemirovich-Dantchenko Opera and Ballet Theatre, Moscow 2002; Bolshoi Theatre debut as Ann in The Rake's Progress 2003, soloist Bolshoi Theatre 2004; Royal Opera house debut as Elisabetta in Don Carlo 2007; roles include: Ann Truelove in The Rake's Progress, Maria in Mazepa, Donna Anna in Don Giovanni, Tatiana in Eugene Onegin, Elisabetta in Don Carlo, Violetta in La Traviata, Desdemona in Otello, Prilepa in The Queen of Spades, Belinda in Dido and Aeneas, Rachel in La Juive, Ludmila in Ruslan and Ludmila, Marfa in The Czar's Bride, Oksana in Christmas Eve, Xenia in Boris Godunov, Luisa in The Duenna, Adina in L'Elisir d'Amore, Rosina in Il Barbiere di Siviglia, Pamina in The Magic Flute, Fiordiligi in Cosi fan tutte, Micaëla in Carmen, Marguerite in Faust, Rosalinda in Die Fledermaus, Senta in Der Fliegende Holländer, title roles in Aida, Iolanta, Snegourochka. *Honours:* winner, Panrussian Bella Voce Competition 1997, Elena Obraztsova Int. Competition, St .Petersburg 1999, Queen Elizabeth Int. Competition, Belgium 2000, Grand Prix, Int. Romanciada Competition 2004, Grand Prix, Maria Callas Int. Competition, Athens 2005. *Current Management:* Zemsky/Green Artists Management, 104 W73 Street Suite 1, New York, NY 10023, USA. *Telephone:* (212) 579-6700. *Fax:* (212) 579-4723. *E-mail:* bzemsky@zemskygreen.com. *Website:* www.zemskygreen.com.

POPLE, Ross; conductor and cellist; b. 11 May 1945, Auckland, New Zealand; m. 1st Anne Storrs 1965 (divorced); three s. one d.; m. 2nd Charlotte Fairbairn 1992; one s. *Education:* Royal Acad. of Music, London and Paris Conservatoire. *Career:* debut in London 1965; Principal Cello, Menuhin Festival Orchestra, BBC Symphony Orchestra 1976–86; Dir, London Festival Orchestra 1980–; founder Cathedral Classics, Festival of Music in Cathedrals, UK 1986–; London South Bank series, Birthday Honours 1988–; founder and developer, The Warehouse, Waterloo (home to London Festival Orchestra and recording studio) 1993. *Recordings:* Haydn, Boccherini, Mozart, Mendelssohn, Schoenberg, Vaughan Williams, Holst, Strauss, Arnold, Franck, Bach and others. *Honours:* Hon. RAM.

POPOV, Stefan; Bulgarian cellist; b. 1940. *Education:* studied in Sofia, Moscow Conservatory with Sviatoslav Knushevitsky and Mstislav Rostropovich. *Career:* debut in Sofia 1955; many concert appearances in Europe, North America and Asia, notably in London, Moscow, Boston, Florence, Geneva, Dublin, Genoa, Milan and Budapest; concerto repertoire includes works by Vivaldi, Haydn, Boccherini, Beethoven, Schumann, Dvořák, Brahms, Elgar, Hindemith, Milhaud, Honegger, Kabalevsky and Shostakovich; Don Quixote by Strauss; Respighi Adagio with Variations; Prokofiev Symphonie Concertante; Bloch Schelomo; sonata collaborations with the pianist Allan Schiller; taught at Boston Univ., New England Conservatory of Music. *Honours:* winner of competitions in Moscow 1957, Geneva 1964, Vienna 1967, Florence 1969, Techaikovsky Int. Competition, Moscow 1966.

POPOV, Valery; Ukrainian singer (tenor); b. 1965, Kharkiv. *Education:* Kharkov Inst. of Arts. *Career:* has sung at the Kiev and Kharkov Opera Houses; Principal, Brno Opera Theatre, Czech Republic from 1994; roles include Cavaradossi, Don Alvaro, Don Ottavio, Don Carlos, Turriddu, Samson and Alfredo; sang Don José on tour to France 1992; further appearances throughout Europe and North America; Jenik in The Bartered Bride at Ostrava 1998; sang Meyerbeer's Robert le Diable at Prague 1999; Robert in Tchaikovsky's Iolanta at Monte Carlo 2001. *Honours:* prizewinner Belvedere Int. Competition, Vienna.

POPOV, Vladimir; Russian singer (tenor); b. 29 April 1947, Moscow. *Education:* Tchaikovsky Conservatory, Moscow. *Career:* sang at Bolshoi Opera, Moscow 1977–81; studied further in Milan and moved to USA 1982, singing Ramirez in La Fanciulla del West at Portland; Metropolitan Opera debut 1984, as Lensky in Eugene Onegin; further engagements as Calaf at Houston 1986, as Cavaradossi at Philadelphia 1987, as Dimitri in Boris Godunov at Covent Garden 1988, and Hermann in The Queen of Spades at Washington 1989; sang Calaf with Covent Garden Co. at Wembley Arena 1991, Samson at Detroit and Canio in Pagliacci at Buenos Aires 1992; other roles include Ernani, Gabriele Adorno, Don José and Radames (San Francisco 1989).

POPOVA, Valeria; Bulgarian singer (soprano); b. 1945. *Education:* studied with father, Sacha Popov in Sofia and with Gina Cigna. *Career:* debut as Lauretta in Gianni Schicchi at Nat. Theatre, Belgrade; sang at Plovdiv Opera 1971–76, Sofia from 1976; guest engagements in former Soviet Union, Germany, Romania and Cuba; other roles include Violetta, Manon, Mozart's Countess, Jenůfa, Fiordiligi, Marguerite, Donna Anna, Pamina and Leonora in La Forza del Destino; sang Amelia in Ballo in Maschera at Milwaukee 1990; teacher, with pupils including Alexandrina Pendachanska. *Recordings include:* Arias by Puccini, Verdi, Massenet and Bellini.

POPOVICI, Doru; Romanian composer; b. 17 Feb. 1932, Resita. *Education:* Bucharest Conservatory, studied in Timosoara and Darmstadt. *Career:* Ed., Romanian radio and television 1968. *Compositions:* operas: Promethu 1964,

Mariana Pineda 1969, Interrogation at Daybreak 1979, The Longest Night 1983, Firmness 1989; orchestral: Triptyque 1955, Two Symphonic Sketches 1955, Concertino for strings 1956, Concerto for orchestra 1960, four Symphonies 1962, 1966, 1968, 1973, Poem Bizantin 1968, Pastorale Suite 1982; chamber: Cello sSonata 1952, Violin Sonata 1953, String Quartet 1954, Fantasy for string trio 1955, Sonata for two cellos 1960, Sonata for two violas 1965, Quintet for piano, violin, viola, cello and clarinet 1967, Piano Trio 1970, Madrigal for flute, clarinet, string trio and trombone, also cantatas, piano music, choruses, songs. *Publications include:* Elizabethan Music 1978, Italian Renaissance Music 1978.

PORTELLA, Nelson; Brazilian singer (baritone); b. 1945. *Education:* studied in Rio de Janeiro. *Career:* sang widely in South American opera houses from 1970, Teatro Liceo Barcelona from 1980, Naples from 1983 and Venice from 1985; Caracalla Festival 1986, Ravenna 1988; roles have included Don Giovanni, Leporello, Masetto, Germont, Iago, Sharpless, the Count in Capriccio and Wozzeck; currently singing tutor, Rio de Janeiro. *Recordings include:* Scarpia in Tosca, Mascagni's Le Maschere.

PORTER, David Hugh, BA, PhD; American classicist, pianist, harpsichordist and educator; *President and Professor Emeritus, Skidmore College;* b. 29 Oct. 1935, New York, NY; s. of Hugh Porter and Ethel Porter; m. 1st Laudie E. Dimmette 1958 (deceased); three s. one d.; m. 2nd Helen L. Nelson 1987. *Education:* Swarthmore Coll., Princeton Univ., Philadelphia Conservatory of Music, studied piano with Edward Steuermann, harpsichord with Gustav Leonhardt. *Career:* debut in Philadelphia 1955; piano and harpsichord recitals and lecture recitals throughout USA 1966–, in London and Edinburgh, UK 1977; performances on radio and TV 1967–; Prof. of Classics and Music, Carleton Coll. 1962–, W.H. Laird Prof. of Liberal Arts 1974–87, Pres. 1986–87; Pres. Skidmore Coll. 1987–98, Pres. Emer. 1999–, Tisch Family Distinguished Prof. of Liberal Arts 2008–14, Prof. Emer. 2014–; Harry C. Payne Visiting Prof. of Liberal Arts, Williams Coll. 2000–08; Case Distinguished Visiting Prof., Indiana Univ. 2008; Phi Beta Kappa Visiting Scholar 1994–95. *Publications:* Only Connect: Three Studies in Greek Tragedy, Horace's Poetic Journey, The Not Quite Innocent Bystander: Writings of Eduard Steuermann, Virginia Woolf and Logan Pearsall Smith: An Exquisitely Flattering Duet, Virginia Woolf and the Hogarth Press: Riding a Great Horse, The Omega Workshop and the Hogarth Press: An Artful Fugue, On the Divide: The Many Lives of Willa Cather, Seeking Life Whole: Willa Cather and the Brewsters; contrib. to Music Review and Perspectives of New Music; numerous articles in classical journals. *Honours:* Hon. DHumLitt (Skidmore Coll.) 1998; Hon. DLitt (Carleton Coll.) 2011; Philadelphia Conservatory of Music Steuermann Scholarship 1955, Academic Laureate Award, State Univ. of NY Foundation 1999, Denis Kemball-Cook Award 2005, Distinguished Service Award, American Philological Assscn 2012. *Address:* 5 Birch Run Drive, Saratoga Springs, NY 12866, USA (home). *Telephone:* (518) 587-0388 (home). *E-mail:* ddodger@skidmore.edu (office).

PORTMAN, Rachel Mary Berkeley, OBE; British composer; b. 11 Dec. 1960, Haslemere, Surrey, England; m. Uberto Pasolini; three d. *Education:* Worcester Coll., Oxford. *Career:* composer of film and TV scores, for US productions 1992–. *Compositions for film and television:* Experience Preferred... But Not Essential 1982, The Storyteller (TV series) 1986–88, 1990, Life is Sweet 1990, Oranges Are Not the Only Fruit (TV drama) 1990, Antonia and Jane 1991, Where Angels Fear to Tread 1991, Used People 1992, The Joy Luck Club 1993, Benny and Joon 1993, Friends 1993, Sirens 1994, Only You 1994, War of the Buttons 1994, To Wong Foo – Thanks for Everything! 1995, A Pyromaniac's Love Story 1995, Smoke 1995, The Adventures of Pinocchio 1996, Marvin's Room 1996, Emma (Academy Award for Best Music, Original Music or Comedy Score 1997) 1996, Addicted to Love 1997, The Cider House Rules 1999, Ratcatcher (Georges Delerue Prize, Ghent Int. Film Festival) 1999, Chocolat 2000, The Legend of Bagger Vance (Phoenix Film Critics Soc. Award for Best Original Score) 2000, The Emperor's New Clothes 2001, Hart's War 2002, The Truth About Charlie 2002, Nicholas Nickleby 2002, The Human Stain 2003, Mona Lisa Smile 2003, The Little Prince 2003, Lard 2004, The Manchurian Candidate 2004, Because of Winn-Dixie 2005, Oliver Twist 2006, The Lake House 2006, Miss Potter 2006, Infamous 2006, H2hOpe: The Water Diviner's Tale (BBC Proms) 2007, Little House on the Prairie Musical (theatre) 2008, The Duchess 2008, Grey Gardens (TV) 2009, London Assurance (Royal Nat. Theatre) 2010, Never Let Me Go (San Diego Film Critics Soc. Award for Best Score) 2010, Snowflower and the Secret Fan 2011, One Day 2011, The Vow 2012, Bel Ami 2012, Private Peaceful 2012, The Right Kind of Wrong 2013, Paradise 2013, Still Life 2013, Belle 2013, Dolphin Tale 2 2014, Bessie (Primetime Emmy Award for Outstanding Music Composition for a Limited Series, Movie or a Special (Original Dramatic Score) 2015) 2015. *Recordings include:* Rachel Portman Soundtracks (compilation album), numerous soundtrack recordings. *Honours:* British Film Inst. Young Composer of the Year Award 1988, Carlton TV/Rank Films Laboratories Award for Creative Originality 1996, Muse Award from New York Women in Film and Television 2000, BMI Richard Kirk Award 2010. *Current Management:* c/o Robert Messinger, First Artists Management, 4764 Park Granada, Suite 210, Calabasa, CA 91302, USA; Simon Platz, Bucks Music, Onward House, 11 Uxbridge Street, London, W8 7TQ, England. *Website:* www.rachelportman.co.uk.

POSADA (GOMÉS), Alejandro; Colombian conductor; *Chief Conductor, Orquesta Sinfónica de Castilla y León.* *Education:* Conservatorio de Bellas Artes, Medellín, Hochschule für Musik und Darstellende Kunst, Vienna.

Career: fmrly Chief Conductor, Sarajevo Philharmonic and Chamber Orchestra, Asst Conductor, Vienna Mozart Orchestra, Artistic Dir, Musikverein Pressbaum Orchestra, Chief Conductor, Baden City Orchestra, Assoc. Conductor, Orquesta Filarmónica de Medellín; Asst Conductor, Orquesta Sinfónica de Colombia 1996–; Chief Conductor, Orquesta Sinfónica de Castilla y León 2002–09; regular guest conductor in Spain and Colombia, also elsewhere in Europe and South America. *Honours:* Special Prize, Nicolai Malko Int. Conducting Competition, Copenhagen (Denmark). *Address:* Orquesta Sinfónica de Castilla y León, Avda Monasterio Nuestra Señora de Prado 2, 47014 Valladolid, Spain (office). *Telephone:* (983) 385604 (office). *Fax:* (983) 343577 (office). *E-mail:* fsiglo.orquesta@jcyl.es (office). *Website:* www.orquestacastillayleon.com (office).

POSADAS, Alberto; Spanish composer; b. 1967, Valladolid. *Education:* Madrid Royal Conservatory. *Career:* studied composition with Francisco Guerrero Marin; Professor and teacher of music 1991–, currently teaches at Music Conservatory of Majadahonda, Madrid; international recognition as composer 1993–; many commissions from festivals including Agora, Paris, Donaueschinger Musiktage, Musica Festival, Strasbourg, Ars Musica, Brussels; commissions from musicians including Esteban Algora, Andrés Gomis, Alexis Descharmes, Oiasso Novis; works performed by Ensemble intercontemporain, Ensemble L'itineraire, Ensemble Court-Circuit, Nouvel Ensemble Moderne, Quatuor Diotima, Arditti String Quartet, Orchestre National de France, Orchestre Philharmonique du Luxembourg. *Compositions include:* Apeiron, for orchestra 1993, Pri em hru, for ensemble 1994, A silentii sonitu, for string quartet (Audience Prize, Ars Musica Festival) 2002, Snefru, for accordion and electronics 2002, Liturgia Fractal, for string quartet 2003–07, Nebmaat, for ensemble 2004, Anamorfosis, for ensemble 2006 and numerous others. *Recordings:* albums: as composer: Quatuor Diotima, Liturgia Fractal 2009. *Address:* Kairos Music, Feldgasse 21, 1080 Vienna, Austria (office). *Telephone:* (1) 409-58-95 (office). *Fax:* (1) 408-35-06 (office). *E-mail:* kairos@kairos-music.com (office). *Website:* www.kairos-music.com (office).

POSCHNER-KLEBEL, Brigitte; Austrian singer (soprano); b. 1957, Vienna. *Education:* studied in Vienna with Gerda Scheyrer and Gottfried Hornik. *Career:* sang with Vienna Staatsoper 1982–, guest appearances at Aix-en-Provence Festival 1988–89, Fiordiligi, La Scala, Milan as Pamina 1986, Venice, Amsterdam and Tokyo; sang Susanna in Khovanshchina at Vienna Staatsoper 1989; other roles include Hansel, Rosalinde, Esmerelda, Sophie in Der Rosenkavalier, Xenia in Boris Godunov and Lucy in The Beggar's Opera; frequent concert appearances. *Recordings include:* Khovanshchina, Maidservant in Elektra (video).

POSSEMEYER, Berthold; German singer (baritone); b. 1950, Gladbeck, Westfalen. *Education:* studied in Cologne with Josef Metternich. *Career:* sang at first in concert and gave lieder recitals, notably in Paris, New York, Jerusalem, Hamburg, Turin and Venice; stage career from 1978, at first at Oldenburg, then from 1979 at Essen, as Rossini's Figaro, Papageno, Guglielmo, Eugene Onegin and Silvio in Pagliacci; sang at Gelsenkirchen Opera 1984–86, then returned to concerts; repertoire includes works by Bach, Mozart, Mendelssohn and Distler.

POSTNIKOVA, Viktoria; Russian pianist; b. 12 Jan. 1944, Moscow; m. Gennadi Rozhdestvensky 1969. *Education:* Moscow Central School of Music with E. B. Musaelian, Moscow Conservatoire with Yakov Flier. *Career:* many concert appearances in Europe, Russia and the USA from 1966; Repertoire includes music by Bach, Handel, Scarlatti, Haydn, Mozart, Liszt, Chopin, Mendelssohn, Schumann, Brahms and Rachmaninov; modern repertoire includes music by Busoni, Ives, Britten and Shostakovich; played in the British premiere of Schnittke's Concerto for piano duet and orchestra in London 1991. *Recordings:* Tchaikovsky Concertos, Busoni Concerto and complete piano works by Janáček, Tchaikovsky and Mussorgsky, Violin sonatas by Busoni and Strauss, Complete piano concertos of Brahms, Chopin and Prokofiev. *Honours:* Prizewinner at competitions in Warsaw 1965, Leeds 1966, Lisbon 1968 and Moscow 1970. *Current Management:* c/o Allied Artists, 42 Montpelier Square, London SW7 1JZ, England. *Telephone:* (20) 7589-6243. *Fax:* (20) 7581-5269. *E-mail:* info@alliedartists.co.uk. *Website:* www.alliedartists.co.uk.

POTOCNIK, Tone, (Gaudenzio); Slovenian pianist and organist; *Professor of Gregorian Chant, Piano and Polyphonic Music, Academy of Music, Ljubljana;* b. 13 Jan. 1951, Bukovica, Skofja Loka. *Education:* Acad. of Music, Ljubljana, Acad. of Music, Zagreb, Croatia, Acad. of Santa Cecilia, Rome, Conservatoire of Santa Cecilia, Rome, Rome Papal Inst. for Church Music, Licenza in Canto Gregoriano, Licenza in Musica Sacra. *Career:* Prof. of Gregorian Chant, Piano and Polyphonic Music, Acad. of Music, Ljubljana; f. first School of Gregorian Chant in Slovenia and Schola Cantorum – Cantate Domino; Koralni zbor (Coral Choir), Acad. of Music, Schola cantorum Labacensis, Schola Sitiensis; recording for RTV Slovenia–Cerkveno leto v Gregorijanskem koralu (Church year in Gregorian Chant); Tonus psalmorum; performs at ind. recitals as an organist; premiere performances of contemporary Slovene composers (L. Lebic, P. Ramovs, L. Vrhunc, M. Gabrijelcic); soloist and with RTV and Philharmonic Orchestra of Ljubljana; organ and piano accompaniment of instrumental and vocal soloists and chorus; specialises in the piano music of G. Gurdieff and T. de Hartmann, Inst. for the Harmonious Devt of Man; performances in Italy and other countries in Europe. *Recordings:* Eno je dete rojeno, with Komorni zbor Ave (The Child Was Born, with The Chamber Choir Ave); Ave Maria, with Branko Robinsak, tenor; Music Highlights of Baroque, with Norina Radovan, soprano and Tibor Kerekes, trumpet; Hugolin Sattner with Komorni Zbor Ave; Ch. Gounold – J.G. Rheinberger with Ljubljanski oktet; Ego sum Sesurrectio et Vita, Gregorian Coral songs with Schola Cantorum Labacensis; In Onore di Sua Eminenza Rev. Ma. Mons. Dr Franc Rode in Occasione della Nomina a Cardinale della Sacra Chiesa Romana with Andreja Zakonjšek and Marcos Fink; Kristus je vstal (Christ was Raised) with Komorni zbor Ave; Lojze Lebič, Symphony with Organ, with RTV orchestra of Ljubljana; author of vocal music for Processio Locopolitana (Passion of Škofja Loka) edited on CD, titled Glasba, Škofjeloški pasijon (Music, Passion of Škofja Loka); Boič (Christmas) with Slovenski Oktet. *Address:* Zabrdo 1, 4229 Sorica, Slovenia (home). *Telephone:* (41) 977282 (home). *E-mail:* potocniktol@gmail.com (office).

POTOURLIAN, Artin Bedros; Bulgarian composer and academic; b. 4 May 1943, Kharmanli; s. of Bedros Michael Potourlian and Siranoush Artin Papazian; m. Akopian Anahid Aram 1950; two s. *Education:* State Acad. of Music, Sofia, Yerevan State Conservatoire Komitas. *Career:* of Armenian descent; first public performances of compositions in Yerevan, Moscow and Tbilisi 1970–74; performances of Symphonies Nos 1 and 2 in Sofia 1976 and 1978; regular appearances in New Bulgarian Music Festival 1980–2013; authorial recitals of chamber compositions at Yerevan, Armenia 1987 and Sofia 1991, 2003, 2013; performances of Four Spiritual Songs (on themes by Nerses Shnorhali) for organ in Austria at Vienna, Klagenfurt, Anif 1991, at Friedrichshafen am Bodensee, Germany 1997, Grossräschen 2010 and elsewhere; participation in Holland-Bulgarian Music Festival, Sofia 1992, Musica Nova, AmBul, Sofia, Festival Neue Musik XVII, Randspiele Zepernick 2009, Europe through the Eyes of Russians/Russia through the Eyes of Europeans, Moscow 2011, St Petersburg Musical Spring 2011 and elsewhere; teacher of polyphony, State Musical Acad., Sofia 1990–2000, Assoc. Prof. 2000–05, Prof. of Polyphony 2005–13; performances at Salzburg of Arabesques, Confessions and Fantasia Worlds for two pianos, and participant in symposium West ruft Ost 1995; performances of Improvisations for clarinet and piano, Bratislava, Slovakia 1998, Triennale di Milano 2007; performances of Anagram-Labyrinth for piano, Berlin 2005, Melomonologos for solo viola, Vienna 2007, Fantasia Worlds, Kostroma, Moscow, Russia 2009 and elsewhere; mem. Soc. for Contemporary Music in Bulgaria, Bulgarian Composers' Union 1978–2013. *Compositions:* Sonata for violin and piano 1972, Music for three flutes, two pianos, tam-tam and strings 1977–78, Women's Cry (one-act opera) 1979, Poem for organ and symphony orchestra 1980, Chamber Concerto for piano and strings 1981, Concerto for violin and symphony orchestra 1983, Music in memory of Evariste Galois for symphony orchestra 1984, Confessions for piano 1985, Fantasia Worlds for 2 pianos 1985, Four Spiritual Songs on themes by Nerses Shnorhali 1988, Klavier Quintet 1989, Fantasia for piano and symphony orchestra 1990, Mosaici for symphony orchestra 1993, Divertimento for wind quintet, harp, harpsichord and percussion 1994, Piano Trio 1995, L'Infinito for mezzo soprano solo, baritone solo, chorus and symphony orchestra (poetry by Giacomo Leopardi) 1998, Kaissa's Temple for piano I, II 1998, 2000, Songs, Concerto for cello and chamber orchestra 1999, Concerto Grosso '87 2000, Klavier Quartet 2001, Elegia for symphony orchestra 2002, Melomonologue for viola solo 2003, Epigraph, Epistrophes, Epilogue for violin and viola 2004, Monumentum for string orchestra 2005, Sphynx for string trio 2005, Bagatelles for symphony orchestra 2006, Sonata for violin and piano No. 2 2006, Epitaphios for piano trio 2007, Sonata for cello and piano 2007, Avec Debussy à travers le labyrinthe du temps for flute and piano 2008, Ich habe eine gute Tat getan for tenor solo, chorus and symphony orchestra (poetry by Franz Werfel) 2009, Five Pieces in memory of Friedrich Goldmann for organ 2009, Petroglyphes for symphony orchestra 2012, and others. *Recordings:* Arabesques for piano, The Confession for piano, Kaissa's Temple for piano, Fantasia, Worlds for two pianos, Symphony No. 2 (documentary), Mosaici 1994, Fantasia for piano and symphony orchestra 2007, Avec Debussy à travers le labyrinthe du temps 2010, Expatriated Songs for mixed chorus 2013, Trio for trombone, tuba and double bass 2014 and others. *Publications include:* Metrorythmic tempo modulation 1992, Geometric Transformations of the Plane and the Space and Invention Polyphony 1999, Reflexive Counterpoint 2004. *Honours:* First Prize, Composition Competition, Pazardjik 1985, Prizes of Bulgarian Composers' Union (for Arabesques) 1983, (for Violin Concerto) 1989. *Address:* 1113 Sofia, Tsarigradsko shosse 8, Bl 4, Vch B, Bulgaria (home). *Telephone:* (2) 4809801 (home). *E-mail:* art_b_pot@hotmail.com (home).

POTT, Francis John Dolben, MA (Cantab.), MusB, PhD, FLCM; British composer, pianist and academic; *Chair and Head of Composition, London College of Music, University of West London*; b. 25 Aug. 1957, Oxon.; s. of the late John Antony Pott and Cynthia Margaret Pott (née Guillaume); m. Virginia Straker 1992; one s. one d. *Education:* New Coll., Oxford, Winchester Coll. and Magdalene Coll., Cambridge, studied with Robin Holloway, Hugh Wood, Hamish Milne. *Career:* freelance composition/performance; Tutor in Compositional Techniques, Univ. of Oxford 1987–89; Lecturer in Music, St Hugh's Coll. 1988; Lecturer in Music, Dir of Foundation Studies, West London Inst. 1989–91; John Bennett Lecturer in Music, St Hilda's Coll., Oxford 1992–2001; Visiting Tutor in Composition, Winchester Coll. 1991–96; piano recitalist and accompanist; Admin. Head of Music, London Coll. of Music, Univ. of West London 2001–02, Prof. of Composition 2007–, Head of Research Devt, London Coll. of Music 2002–08, currently Chair and Head of Composition; numerous TV and radio broadcasts; works performed and broadcast world-wide in approx. 40 countries. *Compositions:* organ: Mosaici di Ravenna 1981, Empyrean 1982, Fenix, Music for Lincoln Minster, organ, brass, percussion, timpani 1985, Passion Symphony Christus 1986–90 (premiered Westminster Cathedral 1991), Toccata for Organ 1991, Introduction, Toccata and Fugue 2001, Sonata Breve 2011; choral (church) and other works: Piano Quintet (premiered by The Twentieth Century Consort, Smithsonian Inst., USA 1993), solo piano works, Sonata for cello and piano (premiered at Wigmore Hall, London 1996), A Song on the End of the World 1999, Elgar Commission (oratorio), Three Choirs Festival, chorus, orchestra, soloists, organ, texts by Czeslaw Milosz and others (premiere Worcester Cathedral 1999), Cello Sonata revised 2000, The Cloud of Unknowing 2005, Performing Right Soc. commission (oratorio), premiered at London Festival of Contemporary Church Music 2006, Mass for eight parts 2011; numerous sacred choral works and compositions for piano solo. *Recordings:* Christus, organ symphony, 1992, Cello Sonata, David Watkin 1997, Sacred Choral: My Song is Love Unkown, The Souls of the Righteous, Tenebrae (conductor Nigel Short) 2003, Oratorio: The Cloud of Unknowing 2006, Word (cantata, texts by R. S. Thomas and from St John's Prologue) 2012, Einzige Tage (song cycle) 2011, Sonata for viola and piano 2013. *Honours:* Gerald Finzi Trust Memorial Award for Composition 1981, Lloyd's Bank Nat. Composing Competition 1982, Barclaycard Nat. Composing Competition 1983, First Prize, Second S.S. Prokofiev Int. Composing Competition, Moscow 1997, Hon. Mention (second from a field of 362 composers world-wide), Barlow Int. Composition Award (USA) 2004, Winner, Cheltenham Festival Int. Composition Award 2012. *Address:* London College of Music, University of West London, St Mary's Road, Ealing, London, W5 5RF (office); Choral Connections, 14 Stevens Close, Prestwood, Bucks., HP16 0SQ, England. *Telephone:* (20) 8231-2569 (office); (1494) 866389. *E-mail:* francis.pott@uwl.ac.uk (office); val@choralconnections.com. *Website:* www.uwl.ac.uk/music/London_College_of_Music.jsp (office); www.choralconnections.com; www.francispott.com.

POULENARD, Isabelle; French singer (soprano); b. 5 July 1961, Paris. *Education:* Ecole de l'Opéra de Paris, Certificat d'Aptitude. *Career:* spent seven years singing with Maîtrise de Radio-France followed by three years with Ecole Nationale d'Art Lyrique at Opéra de Paris; specializes in performing 17th and 18th century music; has taken part in numerous productions with Tourcoing Atelier Lyrique under the direction of Jean-Claude Malgoire; repertoire ranges from Baroque opera to contemporary works, including pieces by Mozart, Rossini, Weber, Poulenc and others; has worked with conductors including Charles Dutoit, Mstislav Rostropovich, William Christie, Marc Minkowski, Theodor Guschlbauer, René Jacobs, Richard Hickox, Mark Foster, Joël Suhubiette, Jérôme Corréas; performs regularly at recitals, notably at series of concert recitals organized for the inauguration of Opéra Bastille July 1989; interpreted role of Pamina in Mozart's Die Zauberflöte, directed by O. Desbordes and S. Ottin and filmed by France 3 TV channel and broadcast by both France 3 and Mezzo 2000; recent performances have included the roles of Norine (Don Pasquale/Donizetti), Zerline (Don Juan/Mozart), Madeleine (Le Postillon de Longjumeau/Adam), Vespetta (Pimpinone/Telemann) and more recently as Soeur Constance (Dialogues des Carmélites/Poulenc) as well as Suzanne in Mozart's Les Noces de Figaro in theatrical opera version featuring Beaumarchais' words and Mozart's music; interpreted role of Verdi's La Traviata in concert version under direction of Philippe Le Fèvre; involved in creation of Vespetta and Pimpinone inspired by works of Albinoni, Telemann, Pergolesi and Abattini 2006, performance staged by G.-P. Couleau, directed by J. Maillet and accompanied by Mensa Sonora ensemble, rerun in Paris region and around France 2007; has taught in conservatoires and regularly leads courses and master-classes both in France and abroad; participated in rerun in France and abroad of the show 'Je suis ton labyrinthe' (I am your labyrinth) staged by puppeteer, D. Lippe, accompanied by Fuoco e Cenere ensemble and directed by J. Bernfeld 2009; played role of Genio in l'Anima del Filosofo (opera by Haydn) in Tourcoing under direction of J.-C. Malgoire and staged by A. Baldi; sang title role in concert version of Manon (Massenet), Brest 2009. *Recordings:* more than 50 recordings, including role of Teutile in Montezuma (pasticcio opera by Vivaldi) (Victoire de la Musique 1993), Stabat Mater by Pergolesi (directed by J.-C. Malgoire), Bach's Mass in B Minor, directed by G. Leonhardt, role of Bellezza in Handel's Il trionfo del tempo e del disinganno, directed by M. Minkowski, recital recording Strozzi – Stradella, Office of Darkness (Leçons de Ténèbres) by Porpora with Les Paladins, directed by J. Corréas, Lieder & Sonaten by Johann-Friedrich Reichardt (received a «Choc» in Le Monde de la Musique) 1998; also other recordings of music by Cesti, Rameau, Couperin, Schütz, Strozzi, Stradella, Cavalli, Bach, Vivaldi, Albinoni, Scarlatti, Hasse, Porpora, Richter, Reichardt, Rigel, Fauré; Il Combattimento di Tancredi e Clorinda and Selva Morale e spirituale by Monteverdi; Armide and Comédies-Ballets by Lully; Le Malade imaginaire by Charpentier; Alessandro by Handel; La serva padrona by Pergolesi; Le Cinesi by Gluck; Le Temple de la Gloire, Platée and Les Indes Galantes by Rameau; La caravane du Caire by Grétry; L'incoronazione di Dario. *Honours:* Chevalier, Ordre des Arts et des Lettres 2003. *Telephone:* (6) 80-33-23-60 (office). *E-mail:* isabelle.poulenard@wanadoo.fr (home). *Current Management:* c/o Bureau de Concerts de Valmalète, 7 rue Hoche, 92300 Levallois Perret, France. *Telephone:* 1-47-59-87-59. *Fax:* 1-47-59-87-50. *Website:* www.valmalete.com. *E-mail:* contact@isabellepoulenard.com. *Website:* www.isabellepoulenard.com.

POULET, Michel; French cellist; b. 1960. *Education:* Paris Conservatoire with Jean-Claude Pennetier, studied with the Amadeua and Alban Berg Quartets. *Career:* mem., Ysaÿe String Quartet from 1986; many concert performances in France, Europe, America and the Far East; festival engagements at Salzburg, Tivoli (Copenhagen), Bergen, Lockenhaus, Barcelona and Stresa; many appearances in Italy, notably with the Haydn Quartets of Mozart; tours of Japan and the USA 1990, 1992. *Recordings:* Mozart Quartet K421 and Quintet K516, Ravel, Debussy and Mendelssohn Quartets. *Honours:* Grand Prix Evian Int. String Quartet Competition 1988, prizes for best performances of a Mozart quartet, Debussy quartet and a contemporary work, second prize Portsmouth Int. String Quartet Competition 1988.

POULSON, Lani; American singer (mezzo-soprano); b. 7 March 1953, Tremonton, UT. *Career:* freelance singer throughout Europe from 1984; sang as Charlotte, Ramiro, Carmen, Octavian and The Composer, Countess Geschwitz in Lulu at Théâtre Royal de la Monnaie, Brussels, Cherubino at Hamburg Staatsoper, Sextus in La Clemenza di Tito at Court Theatre, Drottningholm, as Dorabella at Montpellier 1988, as Andromeda in world premiere of Perseo ed Andromeda by Sciarrino in Stuttgart 1991, in world premiere of Das Schweigen der Sirenen by Riehm also in Stuttgart; appearances at Amsterdam, Antwerp, Berlin (Staatsoper), Budapest, Drottningholm, Düsseldorf, Frankfurt, Graz, Hamburg, Lisbon, Madrid, Mannheim, Montpellier, Munich, Strasbourg, Tel-Aviv, Trieste, Verona; concert repertory includes: St Matthew Passion, Mozart's Requiem and Beethoven's Mass in C; season 1993–94, sang performances of Sesto in Dresden, also as part of the Dresden Musikfestspiele; season 1994–95 included world premiere of Rihm's Das Schweigen der Sirenen at Staatstheater, Stuttgart returning to Dresden for further performances of La Clemenza di Tito; world premiere concert performance of L'Icone Paradoxale by Gerard Grisey 1996, and also in Strasbourg, Frankfurt and Reggio Emilia; season 1997–98, Ottavia in L'Incoronazione di Poppea, Utah Opera, and debut as Magdalene in Meistersinger in Lisbon; season 1998–99, new production of Al gran sole carico d'amore by Luigi Nono at Stuttgart, Mahagonny and Mamma Lucia in Cavalleria Rusticana in Stuttgart, Third Lady in Zauberflöte in Trieste, La Clemenza di Tito and Le Nozze di Figaro in Dresden, debut as Magdalene in Meistersinger in Lisbon, Der Rosenkavalier in Frankfurt and Ottavia L'Incoronazione di Poppea for Utah Opera; season 1999–2000 included Poppea for Columbus Opera and Al gran sole carico d'amore at Staatstheater in Stuttgart; roles include Charlotte in a production of Zimmermann's Die Soldaten, Brigitta in Die tote Stadt, lead role in Vivier's Kopemikus in Amsterdam, world premiere of Breitscheid's Im Spiegel Wohnen in Stuttgart, Jakobsleiter and Der feme Klang at Concertgebouw, Amsterdam, Beethoven's Ninth Symphony in Berlin, 2nd Norn in Madrid, Grisey's L'icone paradoxale in Vienna, Freiburg, Amsterdam, Berlin, Düsseldorf and Brussels, Dvořák's Requiem in Leipzig and Beethoven's Missa Solemnis in Maastricht. *Honours:* prizewinner, Concours the de Chant de la Ville de Toulouse, 1984; Grand Prizewinner, First Prize Mezzo and winner of Elly Ameling Prize for Lieder at the 's-Hertogenbosch the Vocal Competition. *Current Management:* c/o Haydn Rawstron Ltd, 29a High Street, First Floor, West Wickham, Kent BR4 0LP, England. *Telephone:* (20) 8777-6070. *Fax:* (20) 8777-4073. *E-mail:* enquiries@haydn-rawstron.com. *Website:* www.haydnrawstron.com.

POUNTNEY, David Willoughby, CBE, MA; British opera director; *Artistic Director, Welsh National Opera*; b. 10 Sept. 1947, Oxford, England; s. of E. W. Pountney and D. L. Byrt; m. 1st Jane R. Henderson 1980; one s. one d.; m. 2nd Nicola Raab 2007. *Education:* St John's Coll. Choir School, Cambridge, Radley Coll. and St John's Coll., Cambridge. *Career:* first opera production, Scarlatti's Trionfo dell'Onore, Cambridge 1967; Katya Kabanova at Wexford Festival 1972; Dir of Productions, Scottish Opera 1975–80, notably with Die Meistersinger, Eugene Onegin, Jenůfa, The Cunning Little Vixen, Die Entführung and Don Giovanni; Australian debut in Die Meistersinger 1978; world premiere of Philip Glass's Satyagraha, Netherlands Opera 1980; Prin. Prod. and Dir of Productions, ENO 1982–93, notably with The Flying Dutchman, The Queen of Spades, Rusalka, The Valkyrie and Lady Macbeth of Mtsensk; US debut with Houston Opera, Verdi's Macbeth, returning for world premiere of Bilby's Doll by Carlisle Floyd, Katya Kabanova and Jenůfa; produced Weill's Street Scene for Scottish Opera 1989; other productions include From the House of the Dead in Vancouver, Dr Faust in Berlin and Paris, The Fiery Angel at State Opera of South Australia, Adelaide, The Flying Dutchman, Nabucco and Fidelio for Bregenz Festival, The Excursions of Mr Brouček for Munich State Opera, world premiere of Philip Glass's The Voyage at the Met, The Fairy Queen for ENO, Der Kaukasianische Kreidekreis in Zurich, A Midsummer Night's Dream in Venice, Jenůfa, Rienzi and La Forza del Destino for the Vienna Staatsoper 2002, Turandot at Salzburg 2002, Lulu at Welsh Nat. Opera (WNO), world premiere of Philip Glass's Spuren der Verirrten in Linz, Die Zauberflöte in Bregenz; future plans include The Fall of the House of Usher and Guillaume Tell for WNO and The Passenger at Lincoln Center Arts Festival; Intendant and Artistic Dir, Bregenzer Festspiele 2003–13; Chief Exec. and Artistic Dir, Welsh Nat. Opera 2011–15, Artistic Dir 2015–. *Publications:* Powerhouse; The Doctor of Mydffai (libretto for Peter Maxwell Davies), Mr Emmett Takes a Walk (libretto for Peter Maxwell Davies), Kommilitonen (libretto for Peter Maxwell Davies); several trans. from German, Italian, Russian and Czech. *Honours:* Janáček Medal, SWET Award, Martinu Medal, Olivier Award; Chevalier des Arts et des Lettres, Knight's Cross, Order of Merit of the Repub. of Poland, Ehrenkreuz des Bundes Osterreich 2014. *Current Management:* IMG Artists, The Light Box, 111 Power Road, London, W4 5PY, England. *Telephone:* (20) 7957-5800. *Fax:* (20) 7957-5801. *E-mail:* bsegal@imgartists.com. *Website:* imgartists.com/artist/david_pountney. *Address:* Welsh National Opera, Wales Millennium Centre, Bute Place, Cardiff CF10 5AL, Wales (office). *Telephone:* (29) 2063- 5000 (office). *Website:* www.wno.org.uk (office).

POWELL, Christopher (Kit) Bolland, BMus, MSc; New Zealand/Swiss composer and academic (retd); b. 2 Dec. 1937, Wellington, NZ; m. Brigitte Bänninger 1966; one s. one d. *Education:* studied in NZ and Europe. *Career:* teacher of Maths and Music, New Zealand High School 1962–75; Lecturer, Christchurch Teachers' Colls 1975–84; has written experimental music for choruses and percussion, 15 song cycle settings of poems by Michael Harlow and three major works of experimental music theatre; computer music, Swiss Computer Music Centre 1985; Atelier UPIC, Paris 1987; mem. Composers' Asscn of NZ, Swiss Tonkünstlerverein. *Compositions include:* The Evercircling Light for choir, SATB and percussion 1980, Galgenlieder 1980, Christophorus for children's choir and orchestra 1981, Les Episodes for soprano, bass soloists and orchestra 1987, Chinese Songs for soprano and tape 1988, Concerto for two violins, strings and percussion 1989, Hauptsache man geht Zusammen hin (chamber opera) for SATB, speaker and instrumental ensemble 1989–93, Gargantua for wind orchestra 1990, Whale for solo trombone and tape 1993, Piano Poems 1994, Dies irae for men's choir, soprano and instrumental ensemble 1995, Clara Schumann for soprano, piano and tape 1996, Concerto for five percussionists and orchestra 1997, Koauau for eight flautists with 16 flutes (contrabass flute to piccolo) 1998, Salmagundi – Entertainment for brass ensemble 1998, Home Thoughts from Abroad for symphony orchestra 1999, Concerto for trombone, tuba and orchestra 2001, Rothko Variations for orchestra 2004, 4 Maui Legends: Clarinet Concerto 2007–10, Alles unter einem Hut for soprano and string orchestra, Francesca e Paolo for a cappella choir (SATB), Missa Profana for soloists (SATB), choir (SATB) and orchestra, Was Liebe ist for soprano and piano 2012, Microzoic Piano Suite for baritone and ensemble 2012. *Radio:* 75th birthday concert (Swiss and NZ radio) 2012. *Recordings:* Devotion to the Small 1980, The Evercircling Light 1982, Hubert the Clockmaker 1982, Whale 1994, Chinese Songs 1995. *Publications:* Workbook for University Entrance Prescription 1973, Musical Design 1975, Musik mit gefundenen Gegenständen 1982, Quite by Chance/Wie durch Zufall (dual language book about his life as a composer) 2014. *Address:* Promenadenstrasse 24, 8193 Eglisau, Switzerland (home). *Telephone:* (44) 8671348 (office). *E-mail:* powell.kit@gmail.com (home). *Website:* www.sounz.org.nz/composer; www.musicedition.ch/sme; www .kitpowell.ch; music.kitpowell.ch.

POWELL, Claire, FRAM, ARAM, LRAM; British opera singer (mezzo-soprano) and stage director; *Artistic Director, Absolute Opera*; b. 7 April 1954. *Education:* Royal Acad. of Music and London Opera Centre with Joy Mammen and Peter Harrison. *Career:* joined Glyndebourne Festival Opera and Royal Opera House, Covent Garden on completion of her studies; London debut recital Wigmore Hall 1979; numerous roles at Royal Opera have included Eboli in Don Carlos, Dalila in Samson et Dalila, Orolvsky in Die Fledermaus, Neris in Medea, Hermia in A Midsummer Night's Dream, Auntie in Peter Grimes, Maddalena in Rigoletto, Nicklaus in Tales of Hoffmann, Emilia in Otello; other roles include Carmen, Preziosilla in La Forza del Destino, Azucena in Il Trovatore, Quickly in Falstaff, Beatrice in Beatrice et Benedict, Baba the Turk in The Rakes Progress, La Duenna, Clairon in Capriccio, Annina in Der Rosenkavalier, Pauline in Pique Dame, La Mère, La tasse chinoise, La libellule in L'enfant et Les Sortilèges, Clarissa in Love of Three Oranges, Aunty and Sedley in Peter Grimes, Larina in Eugene Onegin, Miss Jessel in Turn of the Screw, Juno in Semele, Principessa di Bouillon in Adriana Lecouvreur, Zia Principessa in Suor Angelica, Margaret in Wozzeck, Genevieve in Pelléas et Melisande, La Cieca in La Gioconda, Mamma Lucia in Cavalleria Rusticana, Mary in Fliegende Holländer, Waltraute, which she has sung in all the major British opera cos and in Munich, Berlin, Hamburg, Frankfurt, Köln, Graz, Paris, Toulouse, Nantes, Brussels, Netherlands, Lausanne, Barcelona, Madrid, Rome, Trieste, San Francisco, New York City Opera, Toronto, Tokyo; has sung with many of the world's leading conductors, including Carlos Kleiber, Georg Solti, Bernard Haitink, Colin Davis, Georges Prêtre, Lorin Maazel, James Conlon, Philippe Jordan, Antonio Pappano; voice teacher in her native Cornwall; also teaches at Univ. of Exeter; Co-founder, Artistic Dir and Stage Dir Absolute Opera (AbOp) 2007–. *Recordings include:* Der Rosenkavalier (Strauss), La Duenna (Roberto Gerhard), El Amor Brujo (de Falla), Il Ritorno d'Ulisse in Patria (Monteverdi), Iernin (George Lloyd) and videos of Les Contes d'Hoffmann, Royal Opera House, Covent Garden, A Midsummer Night's Dream, Glyndebourne Festival Opera, Otello, Royal Opera House, Covent Garden. *Honours:* Richard Tauber Memorial Scholarship. *Current Management:* c/o Penelope Marland & Patricia Greenan Associates, 10 Roseneath Road, London, SW11 6AH, England. *Telephone:* (20) 7223-7319. *E-mail:* penelope@marlandartists.co.uk. *E-mail:* klaraki@btinternet.com (office).

POWER, Clement; British conductor; b. 1980, London. *Education:* Gonville & Caius Coll., Cambridge, Royal Coll. of Music, London. *Career:* Asst Conductor, London Philharmonic Orchestra 2005–06, Ensemble Intercontemporain 2006–08; worked with Pierre Boulez, Susanna Mälkki and Peter Eötvös; engagements included London Philharmonic Orchestra, Birmingham Contemporary Music Group, Philharmonia, Ensemble Intercontemporain, Nat. Youth Orchestra of Catalonia and Klangforum Wien and opening concert of Wien Modern Festival 2012; also conducted BBC Scottish Symphony Orchestra, Orchestre Philharmonique de Luxembourg, Orchestre de Bretagne, NHK Symphony Orchestra in Suntory Hall, Tokyo and Gran Teatre del Liceu, Barcelona; festivals include IRCAM Agora, Paris, Suntory Summer Music Festival, Tokyo, Ars Musica, Brussels, Huddersfield Contemporary Music Festival, Contempuls, Prague, Sacrum-Profanum Festival, Krakow and Rainy Days, Luxembourg; broadcasts on BBC Radio 3, ORF 1, France

Musique and NHK; Conductor, New London Chamber Choir. *Website:* www .nlcc.org.uk.

POWER, Lawrence; British violist; b. 1977, London. *Education:* Juilliard School of Music, New York, studied with Mark Knight in London and Karen Tuttle in New York. *Career:* debut as soloist with The Philharmonia, London; has worked with orchestras, including the Center Symphony of New York, New Zealand Symphony, Berlin Philharmonic Orchestra, LSO, BBC Nat. Orchestra of Wales, BBC Scottish, BBC Symphony, Nat. Youth Orchestra of Great Britain, CBSO, Musica Vitae Chamber Orchestra, ECO, Symphony Orchestra of The Curtis Inst. of Music; has performed at BBC Proms, Bath and Cheltenham Festivals, Verbier Festival, Wigmore Hall, South Bank Centre, Concertgebouw, Amsterdam, Alte Oper, Frankfurt; performs recitals with chamber musicians, including Mikhail Pletnev, Steven Isserlis, Vadim Repin, Truls Mork, Lisa Batiashvili; mem., Nash Ensemble of London, Leopold String Trio; has given world premieres of many pieces written for him, including John Kaefer's Viola Concerto (New York and Paris), Colin Matthews's Calmo (Purcell Room), Mark-Anthony Turnage's Eulogy (Cheltenham Festival) 2003, and On Open Ground viola concerto (Barbican Hall) 2004, Andrew Toovey's Viola Concerto (BBC Scottish) 2005. *Recordings include:* Bowen/Forsyth, Viola Concertos 2005, Hindemith: Sonatas for Viola and Piano 2009, Hindemith: Sonatas for Solo Viola 2010. *Honours:* third prize Maurice Vieux Int. Viola Competition, Paris 2000, winner William Primrose Int. Viola Competition. *Current Management:* c/o Thomas Hull, Ingpen and Williams, 7 St George's Court, 131 Putney Bridge Road, London, SW15 2PA, England. *Telephone:* (20) 8874-3222. *Fax:* (20) 8877-3113. *E-mail:* th@ingpen .co.uk. *Website:* www.ingpen.co.uk.

POWER, Patrick; New Zealand singer (tenor); b. 6 June 1947, Wellington. *Education:* Univs of Otago and Auckland, New Zealand, Univ. of Perugia, Italy. *Career:* principal lyric tenor with The Norwegian Opera in Oslo, Gärtnerplatz, Munich and Krefeld; Covent Garden debut 1983, as the Simpleton in Boris Godunov, followed by Britten's Serenade for the Royal Ballet; has sung Alfredo for Kent Opera, Rodolfo and Almaviva for Scottish Opera; Glyndebourne Festival as Flute and Des Grieux in Manon for Opera North; Wexford Festival in title role of Massenet's Le Jongleur de Notre Dame; overseas engagements as The Italian Tenor in Rosenkavalier and Fenton for Royal Danish Opera; Don Ottavio, Tamino and Rodolfo in Cologne; Belmonte in New Zealand and at Drottningholm; Le Comte Ory and Huon in Oberon at Lyon and Alceste in Paris; Alfredo, Tamino and Don Ottavio in Canada; Almaviva in San Francisco; season 1988–89, as Nadir in Les Pêcheurs de Perles in Pisa; Faust with Victorian State Opera; returned to Australia as Pinkerton, Hoffmann, Rodolfo and the Duke of Mantua; sang Nadir at Adelaide 1996; Don José for WNO; Principal Vocal Tutor, Eastern Inst. of Technology. *Recordings include:* Beethoven's 9th Symphony conducted by Roger Norrington, Balfe's Bohemian Girl conducted by Richard Bonynge, Nadir for Tulsa Opera 1997, Canio in Pagliacci for Opera Ireland 1998, Radames in Aida at Nantes, Angers and Rennes, France, Cavalleria Rusticana and Pagliacci for Opera New Zealand, Pinkerton in Madama Butterfly for Wellington Opera 1999. *Address:* c/o Wellington Orchestra, PO Box 11-977, Manners Street, Wellington, New Zealand. *E-mail:* admin@ wellingtonorchestra.co.nz.

POWERS, Anthony; British composer; b. 13 March 1953, London, England. *Education:* studied with Nadia Boulanger in Paris and with David Blake and Bernard Rands at York. *Career:* Composer-in-Residence, Southern Arts; Composer-in-Residence, Univ. of Wales, Cardiff Coll. *Compositions include:* Piano Sonata No. 2 1985–86, Stone, Water, Stars 1987, Horn Concerto 1989, Cello Concerto 1990, String Quartet No. 2 1991, Terrain for orchestra 1992, In Sunlight for violin and piano 1993, Symphony 1994–96, Fast Colours for ensemble 1997, Memorials of Sleep for tenor and chamber orchestra 1998.

POWTER, Adrian, BA; British singer (baritone); b. 5 Nov. 1970, Cambridge, England; s. of Michael Powter and Anne Powter. *Education:* Royal Northern Coll. of Music with Paddy McGuigan and Neil Howlett. *Career:* created Philip in Harrison Birtwistle's The Last Supper at Deutsche Staatsoper, Berlin 2000 (later at Glyndebourne Festival and Touring Operas, also in Milan, Turin); other roles have included The Abbot in Curlew River for Opéra de Rouen, Masetto in Don Giovanni for English Touring Opera, Jupiter in Peleus and Thetis and The Lion in Pyramus and Thisbe for Opera Restor'd, The Forester in The Cunning Little Vixen for Surrey Opera, Guglielmo in Così fan tutte, Figaro in Figaro's Wedding, Baron Douphol in La Traviata for Opera Project, Dr Falke in Die Fledermaus, Giuseppe in The Gondoliers, Pish-Tush in The Mikado for Carl Rosa Opera, Marullo in Rigoletto for Mid-Wales Opera, Zurga in Les Pêcheurs de Perles for Swansea City Opera, Schaunard in La Bohème for Castleward Opera, Bonario in La Capricciosa Corretta, Capulet in Romeo and Juliet, Rocco in Leonora for Bampton Classical Opera, Dandini in La Cenerentola, Marcello in La Bohème, Dr Bartolo in The Barber of Seville for The Garden Opera Company, Frank in Die Fledermaus for Scottish Opera on Tour; concerts throughout UK as well as in Germany, Ireland, Italy, Netherlands, Portugal, Singapore and China singing with orchestras including Acad. of Ancient Music, Darmstadt Hofkapelle, Orchestra of the Age of Enlightenment, Royal Liverpool Philharmonic Orchestra; sang Mahler's Lieder eines fahrenden Gesellen and world premiere of Howard Goodall's Eternal Light: A Requiem, the Rambert Dance Company; future engagements include Brétigny in Manon, Alcindoro/Benoit in La Bohème, Scottish Opera. *Radio:* Friday Night is Music Night with Catherine Bott and the BBC Concert Orchestra (BBC Radio 2). *Television:* Opera Works (series of opera master-classes with Jonathan Miller for BBC 2) 1998. *Current Management:* James Black Management, 9 Burnhams, Rye, East Sussex, TN31 7LW, England. *Telephone:* (1797) 224668. *E-mail:* james@jamesblackmanagement.com. *Website:* www.jamesblackmanagement.com. *Telephone:* (7971) 004898 (office). *E-mail:* adrianpowter@yahoo.co.uk (office).

PRAESENT, Gerhard; Austrian composer and conductor; *Professor, University of Music, Graz;* b. 21 June 1957, Graz; m. Sigrid Praesent-Koenig; two s. *Education:* Univ. of Music, Graz. *Career:* debut as composer, Weiz 1978; Asst, Univ. of Music and Dramatic Arts, Graz 1986–92, Prof. 1992–; more than 900 performances of works in 20 countries; several commissioned compositions for the Vienna Concert Hall, The Gesellschaft der Musikfreunde Vienna, Austrian Cultural Forums in New York and London, and Univ. of Graz, amongst others; numerous concerts, including festivals in Graz, Hong Kong, New York, Rome, Munich, Vienna; fmr Vice-Pres., Styrian Tone Arts Asscn, Pres. 2005–; mem. ISCM, OEKB, OEGZM. *Compositions include:* symphonic music: Symphonic Fragment, Hermitage, Configurations, Chaconne, Partita sagrada; works for strings: La Tâche, Sonata Regina per SF, Sounds of Wood, Missa for string quartet, Big Apple, Canzona, A. Rayas; chamber music: Trio intricato, Sonata del Gesù, Sonata al dente, Marcia funebre, Encore Piece, Rhapsodie; vocal music: Song, Fantasy on a Bach-Choral, Missa minima, Half-dark Songs, Pater Noster, Psalm. *Recordings:* radio recordings in Austria; ten albums, including La Tâche 1997, Sounds of Wood 1999, Music for Strings 2011. *Publications:* Information of the Styrian Tone Arts Asscn (ed.) 2003–; several articles on music theory in different print media. *Honours:* Hon. Assoc., Nat. Acad. of Music 2011; Austrian State Scholarship, CA Prize, Composition Prize, Berlin, Federal Music Award for Symphonic Fragment 1992, Reinl Prize (for La Tâche), Prize of the City of Vienna 1996, Theodor Koerner Prize 1997, 2010. *Address:* Badstrasse 58, 8063 Eggersdorf, Graz, Austria (home). *Telephone:* (311) 72025 (home). *E-mail:* praesent@telering.at (home). *Website:* www.alea.at.

PRANTL, Pavel, MA; Czech concertmaster and academic; b. 21 April 1945, Susice; m. Martina Maixnerova 1972; two s. *Education:* Conservatory of Music, Kromeriz, Acad. of Musical Arts, Prague, masterclasses with David Oistrakh. *Career:* debut with Czechoslovak Broadcasting Corpn 1956; mem. first violin group, Czech Philharmonic Orchestra 1967–76, Asst Concertmaster 1976–78; Concertmaster and Artistic Dir Prague Chamber Orchestra Without a Conductor 1978–80; Founder and Artistic Leader Prague Baroque Ensemble 1973–80; Concertmaster, Singapore Symphony Orchestra 1980–93; guest soloist with Prague Symphony Orchestra 1968, Moravian Philharmonic Orchestra 1975, Radio Plzeň Symphony Orchestra 1977, Singapore Symphony Orchestra 1981–87; numerous tours abroad, including festivals in Salzburg, Montreux, Edinburgh, Würzburg, Japan (Tokyo, Hokkaido) 1996, 1998, 2000, 2002, 2004, 2007, S Korea (Seoul), USA (Cornell Univ., Univ. of California at Los Angeles and at San Diego) 1997, 1999, 2001–03, 2007, Germany 1996, 1998, 2000–07, Spain 2000, 2002, 2005; Head of String Dept, Hong Kong Acad. for Performing Arts 1993–95; Dir Singapore Professional String Centre 1995; Concertmaster, Prague Radio Symphony Orchestra 1996, Prague Radio Chamber Orchestra 1996–2000; Founder, Artistic Dir and Concertmaster, Czech Philharmonic Chamber Orchestra 1996–; Artistic Leader Trio d'Archi di Praga, 1996–; Founder and Dir PPProduction Co.; Founder and Exec. Dir Int. Music Acad. Pilsen, Czech Repub.; violin masterclasses: Seoul Nat. Univ. 1993, Arai School of Music, Tokyo 1994, Meadowmount Summer School of Music 2004; mem. Jury, Kocian Int. Violin Competition 1991, 1993, 1996, 2000, 2002, Czech Nat. Violin Competition 1998, 2001; Head, Post-Educ. of Public Music School Teachers in the Czech Repub., Ministry of Educ. 2003–. *Recordings:* Ivo Blaha's Violin Concerto (world premiere) 1970, Czech Chamber Music, Czech Classical Violin Concertos 1991, Vivaldi Four Seasons 2000, Czech String Serenades 2004. *Honours:* Hon. Prof., Univ. of Brussels, Haute Ecole de Recherche, Paris; Hon. DFA (London Inst. of Applied Research). *Current Management:* c/o Stanton Management, 45-05 Newtown Road, Astoria, NY 11103, USA. *Telephone:* (718) 956-6092. *Fax:* (718) 956-5385. *E-mail:* TDStanton@StantonMgt.com. *Website:* www.ppproduction.cz; www.ima-pilsen.com.

PRATICO, Bruno; Swiss singer (bass-baritone); b. 1962, Aosta. *Education:* opera school of La Scala. *Career:* sang Rossini's Mustafà and Bartolo under Abbado at La Scala; Bologna in 1987 as Belcore, Reggio Emilia in 1988 as Gaudenzio in Il Signor Bruschino; has sung widely in Italy and guest appearances elsewhere include Opéra de Lyon in 1989, in Salieri's Prima La Musica poi le Parole, and Marseille in 1990 as Leporello; other repertory includes The Mikado (Macerata Festival), Zurga in Les Pêcheurs de Perles and Geronimo in Cimarosa's Il Matrimonio Segreto; Season 1998 in Don Pasquale at Genoa, La Rocca in Un Giorno di Regno at Parma and Don Magnifico in La Cenerentola at Pesaro. *Recordings include:* Leoncavallo's La Bohème; Lakmé and Paisiello's Don Chisciotte; Cimarosa's I Due Baroni di Rocca Azzurra. *Current Management:* c/o Atelier Musicale, Via Caselle 76, San Lazzaro di Savena 40068, Italy. *Telephone:* (51) 19984444. *Fax:* (51) 19984420. *E-mail:* info@ateliermusicale.com. *Website:* www.ateliermusicale .com.

PRATLEY, Geoffrey Charles, BMus, FRAM, ARCM, GRSM; British accompanist and duo pianist; *Professor, Trinity College of Music;* b. 23 March 1940, Woodford, Essex, England; s. of Reginald Charles Pratley and Edith Gwendoline Clarke; m. 1st Wendy Eathorne 1965; one d.; m. 2nd Vija Rapa 1987; one d. *Education:* Buckhurst Hill Co. High School and Royal Acad. of Music. *Career:* numerous concerts throughout the world with many int.

artists, including Baker, Domingo, Tortelier, Goossens, Brymer, Holmes, Streich and Milanova; Prof., RAM 1965–2005, Pres. RAM Club 2004–05; Prof., Trinity Coll. of Music 1990–2009; mem. Inc. Soc. of Musicians, Royal Soc. of Musicians. *Compositions:* Dorothy Parker Poems for female voice and piano 2000, Six Irish Folk-Songs and Six English Folk-Songs, arranged for voice and piano. *Radio:* numerous broadcast recitals with various singers and instrumentalists. *Television:* accompanist for Paul Tortelier's Cello Masterclasses and Jack Brymer's Clarinet Masterclass on BBC 2 TV. *Recordings:* Ivor Gurney Songs with C. Keyte. *Publications:* Handel Operatic Repertory Book 2: Arias for tenor and piano; Concert Master Series: Book 1 – Tchaikovsky Violin Solos with Piano; William Walton's Viola Concerto, new viola/piano score; Great Orchestral Cello Solos, for cello and piano (two books); Great Orchestral Violin Solos, for violin and piano; Great Operatic Melodies, arranged for piano duet. *Address:* Wryneck Mill, Hundred Foot Bank, Welney, Wisbech, Cambs., PE14 9TW, England (home). *Telephone:* (1366) 377484 (home); (7974) 654558 (mobile). *Fax:* (1366) 377484 (home). *E-mail:* gpratley@postmaster.co.uk (home). *Website:* www.piano-duet.co.uk.

PRATSCHKE, Sinead, MMus; Canadian singer (soprano); b. 1971. *Education:* Royal Coll. of Music, National Opera Studio. *Career:* operatic roles as Susanna, Poulenc's Thérèse, Handel's Dorinda, Tytania, Euridice, Cunegonde, Valencienne, Barbarina, Despina, Gretel, Musetta; recital appearances at Jubilee Hall, Aldeburgh Festival 1997, Songmakers' Almanac; oratorio performances include Apollo e Daphne, The English Concert at Queen Elizabeth Hall, Mozart's C Minor Mass, Switzerland, Magnificat, National Concert Hall in Dublin, Ireland, St Matthew Passion, National Orchestra of Wales at Brangwyn Hall, Aldeburgh Early Music Festival. *Recordings include:* Handel's Samson and Judas Maccabaeus (Maulbronn Handel Festival, Germany), Rodrigo Centenary Recording, Royal Philharmonic Orchestra, Zélide (Musikfestspiele Sanssouci, Berlin). *Honours:* Canada Council, Countess of Munster, Madeleine Finden, Ian Fleming Trust. *Address:* 70A Stondon Park, Forest Hill, London, SE23 1JZ, England. *Telephone:* (20) 8699-8060. *E-mail:* spratschke@hotmail.com.

PRATT, Stephen Philip, CertEd, BA, BMus; British composer, academic, broadcaster and conductor; *Professor of Music, Liverpool Hope University;* b. 15 June 1947, Liverpool, England; m. Monica Mullins 1972; one s. three d.; partner Patricia Turton 1997–. *Education:* Christ's Coll., Liverpool, Royal Manchester Coll. of Music, Univs of Reading and Liverpool. *Career:* broadcaster, BBC Radio Merseyside 1971–, BBC Radio 3, 1994–; Sr Lecturer in Music, Liverpool Hope Univ. 1972–2003, Head of Music 1991–, Prof. of Music 2003–; freelance conductor 1975–; part-time Lecturer, Open Univ. 1976–78, Lancashire Polytechnic 1983–, Univ. of Liverpool 1984–86 (Fellow 1993–); Prof. of Music, Gresham Coll., London 1997–2000, Prof. Emer. 2000–, Fellow 2000–06. *Compositions include:* Uneasy Vespers (Part I) for mixed choir, soloists and orchestra 1991, At The Turn of The Year for piano 1993, About Time for small ensemble with tape 1995, The Song Within 1997, Violin Concerto 1997 (revised 2003), Undulations and Other Movements 1998, Three Studies after John Cage 1998, Aphrodite's Rock 2001, Lovebytes for soprano and ensemble 2003, Double Act for ensemble 2006, Short Score for clarinet and piano 2006, Uneasy Vespers (Part II) for choir, orchestra and eight soloists 2008, Canto di Primavera 2010, On Reflection 2011, Entre Nous for solo cello 2012. *Publications:* Violin Concerto, Aphrodite's Rock, Lovebytes 2005, Double Act 2007, Short Score 2007, Uneasy Vespers (Part II) 2008, Strong Winds, Gentle Airs 2009, On Reflection 2011, Entre Nous 2012; contrib. to Arts Alive 1972–, Reviewer 1976–78, The Guardian, Classical Music 1975–78. *Honours:* Chandos Composition Prize, Musica Nova, Glasgow 1981. *Current Management:* c/o Edition HH, 68 West End, Launton, Bicester, Oxon., OX26 5DG, England. *Address:* 9 Wellington Avenue, Liverpool, L15 0EH, England (home). *Website:* www.hope.ac.uk (office).

PRAULIŅŠ, Uģis; Latvian composer; b. 17 June 1957, Riga. *Education:* Latvian Acad. of Music, studied with Jānis Ivanovs and Ģederts Ramans. *Career:* sound engineer, Latvian Radio 1981–86; fmrly producer, AMI Int. (Red Bus Recording Studios), London and Cinevilla film studio, Jumala; Composer-in-Residence, Latvian Ind. TV 1996–97; works recorded on disc or radio broadcast by Choir of Trinity Coll., Cambridge, Riga Cathedral Boys' Choir, Sonux Ensemble, Pro Coro, Michala Petri and Danish Nat. Vocal Ensemble, and performed in Canada, France, England and elsewhere; fmrly rock musician in bands Salve and Vecās Mājas 1986–93. *Compositions include:* orchestral and choral works including To the Light, Missa Rigensis, Laudibus in Sanctis, The Nightingale concerto for recorder and 20 solo voices, Overture-Fantasia for symphonic winds 2013, Old Stained Glasses of Riga, symphony, Rhapsody for Piano and Orchestra, Latvian Solstice in the New World. *E-mail:* praulins@hotmail.com.

PRECHT, Ulrika; Swedish singer (mezzo-soprano); b. 1959. *Education:* Opera Studio 67 and Stockholm State Opera, Stockholm. *Career:* debut at Royal Opera, Stockholm, as Cherubino, 1990; sang Dalila with Folkoperan Stockholm, 1991, and Nancy in Martha for Dublin Opera, 1992; season 1992–93 in Rossini's Il Signor Bruschino at Frankfurt, Eboli in Don Carlos at Stockholm and title role of Carmen at Sodertaleoperan; concert engagements throughout Scandinavia. *E-mail:* ulrika@ulrikaprecht.se. *Website:* www .ulrikaprecht.se.

PREECE, Dane Richard, BA, ARCM, LGSM, LTCL; British pianist, music director and repetiteur; *Head of Music, Arts Educational Schools, London;* b. 12 Feb. 1960, Hereford, England; s. of Ronald Preece and Maureen Preece.

Education: Univ. of Nottingham, Birmingham Conservatoire with Frank Wibaut. *Career:* concerto and recital appearances in major British venues and Huddersfield, Buxton and Warwick Festivals; pianist with Melachrino Strings and Orchestra 1987–93; accompanist, BBC radio and TV; repetiteur with D'Oyly Carte Opera Co., CBTO, Birmingham Music Theatre, Mid Wales Opera and Opera International; Guest Music Dir for RSC, Nat. Theatre, Chichester Festival Theatre, Theatre Royal Plymouth, West Yorkshire Playhouse, Crucible Theatre, Sheffield, Birmingham Repertory Theatre, Salisbury Playhouse, Royal Exchange Theatre, Manchester, New Wolsey Theatre, Ipswich, RAM and West End theatres; piano tutor and vocal coach, Birmingham Conservatoire 1988–2007; repertoire coach, RAM 2000–07; vocal master-classes/workshops in China, Switzerland, Italy, UK; currently Head of Music, Arts Educational Schools, London. *Recordings:* Spend Spend Spend (conductor), Bad Girls the musical (conductor), The Snowman (pianist). *Honours:* Hon. BC; Univ. of Nottingham Barber Organ Scholarship 1978, First Prize, Robert William and Florence Amy Brant Pianoforte Competition 1982. *E-mail:* danepreece@aol.com (home).

PREECE, Margaret; British singer (soprano); b. 1965, England. *Career:* appearances with ENO as Zerlina, Janáček's Vixen, Ninetta (Love for Three Oranges) and Nymph in Monteverdi's Orfeo; Elisabeth de Valois for Opera-Go-Round, in The Ring Saga for City of Birmingham Touring Opera and Oriana in Handel's Amadigi with Opera Theatre Dublin (also on tour to France); Alice Ford, Fiordiligi and Adina for English Touring Opera; Donizetti's L'Ajo nell Imbarazzo and Provenzale's Lo Schiavo di sua Moglie at Musica nel Chiostro, Batignano; season 1997 with the Queen of Night for Opera Theatre Dublin and Despina and Papagena for Opera North; British premieres of Kurt Weill's Love Life and Gershwin's Of These I Sing, both recorded for BBC Radio 3; concerts include Mozart's Davidde Penitente (at Seville), Beethoven's Missa solemnis, Dvořák Requiem and Paul Patterson's Mass of the Sea; further opera roles include Oscar (Ballo in Maschera), Cordelia in Reimann's Lear, Susanna, Mozart's Countess, Anne Trulove, and Gilda; regular performances as Mother Abbess, The Sound of Music, London 2007–.

PRÉGARDIEN, Christoph; German singer (tenor) and vocal teacher; *Professor, Hochschule für Musik und Tanz, Cologne;* b. 18 Jan. 1956, Limburg. *Education:* Frankfurt Hochschule für Musik, also studied in Milan and Stuttgart. *Career:* lyric tenor, noted as a Lieder singer; regular guest at festivals including Schubertiade Schwarzenberg, Rheingau Musik Festivals and Menuhin Festival, Gstaad; conducted Bach's St John Passion on a European tour with the ensemble Le Concert Lorrain and the Nederlands Kamerkoor 2012, second tour and also singing role of the Evangelist in a new recording of the work; appears regularly with orchestras world-wide, including Berlin and Vienna Philharmonics, Bavarian Radio Symphony, Amsterdam Concertgebouw Orchestra, Staatskapelle Dresden, Gewandhausorchester Leipzig, Nat. Orchestra of Spain, Philharmonia Orchestra, London, Philharmonie de Radio France, Boston Symphony, St Louis Symphony, Montreal Symphony and San Francisco Symphony; orchestral repertoire includes baroque, classical and romantic oratorios and passions, as well as works from the 17th century (Monteverdi, Purcell, Schütz) and 20th century (Britten, Killmayer, Rihm, Stravinsky); has collaborated with conductors including Barenboim, Chailly, Gardiner, Harnoncourt, Herreweghe, Luisi, Metzmacher, Nagano, Sawallisch and Thielemann; opera roles have included Tamino (Mozart's Die Zauberflöte), Almaviva (Rossini's Il Barbiere di Siviglia), Fenton (Verdi's Falstaff), Don Ottavio (Mozart's Don Giovanni) and the title roles in Mozart's La Clemenza di Tito and Monteverdi's Il Ritorno d'Ulisse in Patria; season 2012–13 at Wigmore Hall London, Musikverein Vienna, Berlin Philharmonie, La Monnaie de Munt Brussels, Malmö Konserthus and Cité de la Musique, Paris; taught at Hochschule für Musik and Theater, Zurich 2000–04; Prof., Hochschule für Musik und Tanz, Cologne 2004–. *Recordings:* more than 150 recordings with repertoire from the 16th to the 21st century, including Schubert's Die schöne Müllerin (accompanied by Michael Gees) (Gramophone Best Recording of the Year 2008, honoured at MIDEM as both Record and Vocal Recital of the Year 2009) 2008, Between Life and Death (songs by Schubert, Mahler, Wolf, Loewe, and others) (accompanied by Michael Gees) 2010, Hugo Wolf's Italienisches Liederbuch with soprano Julia Kleiter and pianist Hilko Dumno 2010, Wanderer (chamber ensemble versions of song cycles by Schumann, Killmayer and Mahler) with the Ensemble Kontraste 2011. *Publication:* multimedia book/DVD on vocal technique and musical interpretation (Schott's Master Class series). *Honours:* Preis der Deutschen Schallplattenkritik, Edison Awards 1995, 1998, Cannes Classical Award 1995, Diapason d'Or de l'Année 1996, 1997, Choc de la Musique 1997, Caecilia-Preis (Belgium) 1998, Orphée d'Or, Acad. du Disque Lyrique, Prix Georg Solti 1998, Preis der Deutschen Schallplattenkritik, Vierteljahresliste 1999. *Current Management:* c/o Karsten Witt Musikmanagement, Leuschnerdamm 13, 10999 Berlin, Germany. *Telephone:* (30) 214594235. *Fax:* (30) 214594101. *E-mail:* dh@karstenwitt.com. *Website:* www.karstenwitt.com. *E-mail:* info@pregardien.com (office). *Website:* www.pregardien.com.

PREIN, Johann Werner; Austrian singer (bass-baritone); b. 3 Jan. 1954, Trofaiach, Leoben. *Education:* studied with Herma Handl-Wiedenhofer in Graz. *Career:* sang in concerts and recitals from 1979; stage career from 1984, notably at Graz and Vienna; Bayreuth Festival, 1984–85, as Donner in Das Rheingold; Engaged at Gelsenkirchen from 1986; Guest appearances at the Vienna Staatsoper, Düsseldorf and Barcelona; Wiesbaden 1988, as King

Henry in Lohengrin; At Gelsenkirchen in 1989 sang Wagner in the first German production of Busoni's Doktor Faust, in the completion by Antony Beaumont; Other roles include: Mephistopheles (Faust); 4 villains in Les Contes d'Hoffmann; The Speaker in Die Zauberflöte; Biterolf and the Landgrave in Tannhäuser; Wotan in Der Ring des Nibelungen; Achilles in Penthesilea by Schoeck; Season 1998 with the Doctor in Wozzeck at Trieste and Weber's Kuno in Rome; Season 1999 as Strauss's Jochanaan and Faninal at Wiesbaden, followed by Talbot in Maria Stuarda. *Recordings include:* Lieder by Joseph Mathias Hauer (Preiser); Der Konthur in Schulhoff's Flammen, 1995. *Current Management:* c/o Theateragentur Kühnly, Wörth-strasse 31, 70563 Stuttgart, Germany. *Telephone:* (711) 7802764. *Fax:* (711) 7804403. *E-mail:* Kuehnly@aol.com. *Website:* Agentur-Kuehnly.de.

PREISLER, Frantisek, Sr; Czech opera stage manager and producer; b. 29 April 1948, Opava; m. Vlastimila Plosharova Preislerova 1972; one s. *Education:* Janáček Acad., Brno. *Career:* debut, Smetana's Two Widows at the Theatre Olomouc 1973; Producer, Theatre Olomouc 1973–80, Theatre Maribor, Ljubljana 1980–83; Coll. Lecturer, Janáček Acad., Brno 1982–92; Producer, Janáček Theatre, Brno 1983–92; Dir, Janáček Opera, Brno 1985–92; productions of over 60 operas from the Slav repertoire (Smetana's Bartered Bride, Two Widows and The Secret, Dvořák's Rusalka, Janáček's Jenůfa, Cunning Little Vixen and Kata Kabanova, Mussorgsky's Boris Gudunov and Khovanshchina, Tchaikovsky's Eugene Onegin, Borodin's Prince Igor) and also Bizet's Carmen, Puccini's Madama Butterfly, La Bohème, Gershwin's Porgy and Bess, Strauss's Rosenkavalier, Mozart's Le nozze di Figaro and Don Giovanni, Gounod's Faust, Rossini's Il Barbiere di Siviglia, Donizetti's L'Elisir d'amore, Verdi's La Traviata, Massenet's Werther and numerous others; mem. Free Artist.

PREMRU, Raymond Eugene, BMus; American composer and trombonist; b. 6 June 1934, Elmira, NY; m. (divorced); two d. *Education:* Eastman School of Music, Univ. of Rochester, New York. *Career:* mem., Phillip Jones Brass Ensemble 1960–; commissions from Cleveland Orchestra (Lorin Maazel), Pittsburgh Symphony (André Previn), Philadelphia Orchestra (Riccardo Muti), Philharmonia Orchestra (Lorin Maazel), London Symphony Orchestra (Previn), Royal Choral Soc. (Meredith Davies); Int. Trumpet Guild, York Festival, Cheltenham Festival, Camden Festival, Philip Jones Brass Ensemble; Visiting Prof. of Trombone, Guildhall School of Music, Eastman School of Music, Rochester 1987. *Compositions:* Music from Harter Fell, Quartet for two trumpets, horn and trombone, Divertimento for ten brass, Concertino for trombone, flute, oboe, clarinet and bassoon, Tissington Variations. *Publications:* contrib. to International Trombone Association Journal, Instrumentalist Magazine.

PRESCOTT, Duncan; British clarinettist; b. 1964, England. *Education:* Royal Academy of Music with Anthony Pay, studied with Karl Leister. *Career:* recitals at the Wigmore Hall and on the South Bank; mem., Nash Ensemble, with whom he has broadcast the Brahms, Reger and Weber Clarinet Quintets; Mozart Clarinet Concerto with the London Sinfonietta and the English String Orchestra; performances at many jazz venues, including Ronnie Scott's; Member of the Boronte Ensemble and duo partnership with pianist Scott Mitchell; further engagements in Germany, America, Israel, Russia, Japan, Hong Kong and Italy. *Recordings include:* virtuoso pieces with Scott Mitchell. *Honours:* Capitol Radio Music Prize; Lambeth Music Award; Frank Britton Award; Malcolm Sargent Music Award; Scholarships from the Myra Hess Trust, Countess of Munster Trust and the English Speaking Union.

PRESSLER, Menahem; pianist and academic; b. 16 Dec. 1923, Magdeburg, Germany; m. Sara Szerzen; one s. one d. *Education:* educated in Israel, studied with Petri and Steuermann. *Career:* Distinguished Prof. of Music, Indiana Univ., USA 1955–; soloist under Stokowski, Dorati, Ormandy, Mitropoulos; co-founder, Beaux Arts Trio 1955–2008, performed annually in the capitals of Europe and Americas, in residence at the Library of Congress, Washington, DC 1984–; appearances at festivals in Edinburgh, Salzburg, Paris; subscription concerts in New York, Metropolitan Museum and at Harvard Univ. *Recordings:* most of the trio repertoire, more than 50 records. *Honours:* Hon. Fellow, Jerusalem Acad. of Music and Dance 2007; Deutsche Bundesverdienstkreuz First Class 2005, Commdr, Ordre des Arts et des Lettres 2005; Dr hc (Univ. of Nebraska), (North Carolina School of the Arts); winner Debussy Prize, San Francisco, three Grand Prix du Disque, Gramophone Record of the Year Award, Prix d'honneur Montreux Prix Mondial du Disque, Musical America Ensemble of the Year (with Beaux Arts Trio) 1997, Gold Medal, Nat. Soc. of Arts and Letters, Lifetime Achievement Award, Int. Classical Music Awards 2011. *Telephone:* (812) 320-4389. *E-mail:* info@encoreartsmanagement.com. *Website:* www.encoreartsmanagement.com. *E-mail:* info@menahempressler.org (office). *Website:* www.menahempressler.org; www.beauxartstrio.org.

PRESTON, Katherine Keenan, BA, MA, PhD; American music historian; *Associate Professor of Music, College of William and Mary;* b. 7 Dec. 1950, Hamilton, OH; m. Daniel F. Preston 1971; one s. *Education:* University of Cincinnati, Evergreen State College, Olympia, WA, University of Maryland, Graduate Center of CUNY. *Career:* taught at University of Maryland, Catholic University, and Smithsonian Institution; Associate Professor, College of William and Mary, Williamsburg, Virginia, 1989–; mem. American Musicological Society; Sonneck Society for American Music. *Publications:* Books: Scott Joplin, Juvenile Biography, 1987; Music for Hire: The Work of Journeymen Musicians in Washington DC 1875–1900, 1992; Opera on the

Road: Traveling Opera Troupes in the USA, 1820–1860, 1993; The Music of Toga Plays (Introduction) in Playing Out The Empire: Ben Hur and other Toga Plays and Films, 1883–1908, edited by David Mayer, 1994; Editor of Irish American Theater, Vol. 10 in Series Nineteenth-Century American Musical Theater, 1994; contrib. various articles, including The 1838–40 American Concert Tour of Jane Shirreff and John Wilson, British Vocal Stars in Studies in American Music, 1994; Popular Music in the Gilded Age: Musicians' Gigs in Late Nineteenth-Century Washington DC, in Popular Music, 1985; Music and Musicians at the Mountain Resorts of Western Virginia, 1820–1900, in A Celebration of American Music, 1989; Numerous articles in The New Grove Dictionary of American Music, 1986 and The New Grove Dictionary of Opera, 1992. *Address:* 137 Pintail Trace, Williamsburg, VA 23188, USA.

PRESTON, Simon John, CBE, MusB, MA, FRAM, FRCM, FRCO, FRCCO, FRSA; British organist and conductor; b. 4 Aug. 1938, Bournemouth, Dorset, England; m. Elizabeth Hays. *Education:* Canford School, King's Coll., Cambridge. *Career:* Sub-Organist, Westminster Abbey 1962–67; Acting Organist, St Albans Abbey 1967–68; Organist and Lecturer in Music, Christ Church, Oxford 1970–81; Organist and Master of the Choristers, Westminster Abbey 1981–87; Conductor, Oxford Bach Choir 1971–74; Artistic Dir, Calgary Int. Organ Festival; Patron, Univ. of Buckingham; mem. Royal Soc. of Musicians, Council of Friends of St John's Smith Square; over 30 recordings. *Honours:* Edison Award 1971, Grand Prix du Disque 1979, Performer of the Year Award, American Guild of Organists 1987, Medal of the Royal Coll. of Organists 2014. *Address:* 15 St Margaret's Road, Oxford, OX2 6RU, England. *Telephone:* (1865) 512276.

PRESTON, Stephen; British flautist and choreographer; b. 24 May 1945, Skipton, Yorkshire, England. *Education:* Guildhall School of Music, London, studied with Geoffrey Gilbert and with Wieland Kuijken in Amsterdam. *Career:* flautist, Acad. of Ancient Music, English Baroque Soloists and London Classical Players; founder mem., English Concert (under Trevor Pinnock); Artistic Dir, MZT Dance Co.; choreographer for many early operas, including works by Gluck and Purcell. *Recordings include:* Concertos by Vivaldi, Trio Sonatas by J. S. Bach.

PRÊTRE, Georges; French conductor; b. 14 Aug. 1924, Waziers; s. of Emile Prêtre and Jeanne Prêtre (née Dérin); m. Gina Marny 1950; one s. one d. *Education:* Lycée and Conservatoire de Douai, Conservatoire national supérieur de musique de Paris and Ecole des chefs d'orchestre. *Career:* Dir of Music, Opera Houses of Marseilles, Lille and Toulouse 1946–55; Dir of Music, Opéra Comique, Paris 1955–59; Dir of Music, l'Opéra de Paris 1959, Artistic Dir 1966, Dir-Gen. of Music 1970–71; conductor of symphonic asscns of Paris and of festivals worldwide; also conducted at La Scala, Milan and major American orchestras; Conductor, Metropolitan Opera House, New York 1964–65, La Scala, Milan 1965–66, Salzburg 1966; First Visiting Conductor, Vienna Symphony Orchestra 1986–91, Opéra Bastille (Turandot) 1997, Opéra-Comique (Pelléas et Mélisande) 1998; Turandot at La Scala 2001; concert to celebrate 80th birthday, l'Opéra-Bastille 2004; conducted New Year concert, Vienna 2008, 2010. *Honours:* Hon. mem. Gesellschaft der Musikfreunde, Vienna, Hon. Conductor Wiener Symphoniker; Officier, Légion d'honneur 1971, Commdr 2003, Grand Officier 2009; Chevalier des Palmes Academiques, Haute Distinction République Italienne 1975, Commdr République Italienne 1980, Cross for Services Rendered to Science and the Arts, 1st Class (Austria), Cross of Honour of the City of Salzburg; Europa Prize 1982, Victoire de la musique Award for Best Conductor 1997. *Current Management:* Künstleragentur Dr. Raab & Dr. Böhm Gesellschaft m.b.H., Paniglgasse 18-20 / 14, 1040 Vienna, Austria. *E-mail:* zeugswetter@rbartists.at. *Website:* www.rbartists.at.

PREVIN, André George; American conductor, pianist and composer; b. (Andreas Ludwig Priwin), 6 April 1929, Berlin, Germany; s. of Jack Previn and Charlotte Previn (née Epstein); m. 1st Betty Bennett (divorced); two d.; m. 2nd Dory Langan 1959 (divorced 1970); m. 3rd Mia Farrow 1970 (divorced 1979); three s. three d.; m. 4th Heather Hales 1982 (divorced); one s.; m. 5th Anne-Sophie Mutter 2002 (divorced 2006). *Education:* Berlin and Paris Conservatories. *Career:* began career as film score composer, MGM studios, Los Angeles; Music Dir, Houston Symphony, US 1967–69; Music Dir and Prin. Conductor, London Symphony Orchestra 1968–79, Conductor Laureate 1979–; composed and conducted approx. 50 film scores 1950–65; guest conductor of most major world orchestras, also Royal Opera House, Covent Garden, Salzburg, Edinburgh, Osaka, Flanders Festivals; Music Dir, London South Bank Summer Music Festival 1972–74, Pittsburgh Symphony Orchestra 1976–84, LA Philharmonic Orchestra 1984–89; Music Dir, Royal Philharmonic Orchestra 1985–86, Prin. Conductor 1987–92; Chief Conductor and Music Dir, Oslo Philharmonic Orchestra 2004–06, Conductor Laureate 2006–. *Television:* series of television specials for BBC and for American Public Broadcasting Service. *Major works include:* Symphony for Strings 1965, Overture to a Comedy 1966, Suite for Piano 1967, Cello Concerto 1968, Four Songs (for soprano and orchestra) 1968, Two Serenades for Violin 1969, Guitar Concerto 1970, Piano Preludes 1972, Good Companions (musical) 1974, Song Cycle on Poems by Philip Larkin 1977, Every Good Boy Deserves Favour (music, drama, text by Tom Stoppard) 1977, Pages from the Calendar for solo piano 1977, Peaches for flute and strings 1978, Principals 1980, Outings for brass quintet 1980, Reflections 1981, Piano Concerto 1984, Triolet for Brass 1987, Variations for Solo Piano 1991, Six Songs for Soprano and Orchestra on texts by Toni Morrison 1991, Sonata for Cello and Piano 1992, The Magic

Number for soprano and orchestra 1995, Trio for Bassoon, Oboe and Piano 1995, Sonata for Violin 1996, Sonata for Bassoon and Piano 1997, Streetcar Named Desire (opera) 1998, The Giraffes Go to Hamburg for soprano, alto, flute and piano, Three Dickinson Songs for soprano and piano, Diversions for orchestra, Violin Concerto Anne-Sophie 2001, Double Concerto for Violin, Double Bass and Orchestra 2004, Double Concerto for Violin, Viola and Orchestra 2009, Brief Encounter (opera) 2009, Music for Boston 2012, Music for Wind Orchestra (No Strings Attached) 2014, Nonet (chamber music, premiered 2015). *Publications:* Music Face to Face 1971, Orchestra (ed.) 1977, Guide to Music 1983, No Minor Chords: My Days in Hollywood 1992. *Honours:* Hon. KBE 1996; Television Critics Award 1972, Acad. Award for Best Film Score 1959, 1960, 1964, 1965, Kennedy Center Honor 1998, Glenn Gould Prize 2005, London Symphony Orchestra Lifetime Achievement Award 2008, Gramophone Award for Lifetime Achievement 2008, 11 Grammy Awards, Recording Acad. Lifetime Achievement Award 2010. *Current Management:* c/o Tanja Dorn, IMG Artists, Carnegie Hall Tower, 152 West 57th Street, 5th Floor, New York, NY 10019, USA. *Telephone:* (212) 994-3540. *Fax:* (212) 994-3550. *E-mail:* tdorn@imgartists.com. *Website:* www.imgartists.com; www.andre-previn.com.

PREVITALI, Fabio; Italian singer (baritone); b. 1961, Venice. *Education:* Venice Conservatory. *Career:* debut as Luca in Salieri's Falstaff 1987; sang at Treviso 1987 as Albert in Werther, Frank in Die Fledermaus and in Linda di Chamounix; season 1988 at opera houses in Paris, Verona and Reggio Emilia; other roles in Don Giovanni, Maria Stuarda, La Bohème, Eugene Onegin and Semele. *Recordings include:* Franchetti's Cristoforo Colombo 1991.

PREVOST, André; Canadian composer; b. 30 July 1934, Hawkesbury, ON. *Education:* Conservatoire de Musique de Montréal, Paris Conservatoire with Olivier Messiaen, Ecole Normale, Paris with Henri Dutilleux, studied with Michel Philippot at ORTF, with Aaron Copland, Zoltán Kodály, Gunther Schuller and Elliott Carter at Berkshire Music Center, Tanglewood, MA. *Career:* Prof. of Composition and Analysis, Faculty of Music, University of Montréal; composed music played throughout Canada and also France, USA, England, Yugoslavia, India and New Zealand; commissions have been received from Jeunesse Musicales du Canada, Quintette de Cuivres de Montreal, Charlottetown Festival, Ten Centuries Concerts, Canadian Broadcasting, McGill Chamber Orchestra, l'Orchestre symphonique de Quebec, Communaute Radiophonique des Pays de Langue Francaise, London (Ontario) Symphony Orchestra, Société de Musique Contemporaine du Québec, Canadian Music Centre among others. *Compositions include:* orchestral: Célébration 1966; Chorégraphie I, 1972, II 1976, III 1976, IV 1978; Cosmophonie 1985; Diallele 1968; Evanescence 1970; Fantasmes 1963; Hommage 1970–71; Ouverture 1975; Scherzo 1960; Soloists with Orchestra: Concerto pour Violoncelle et Orchestre 1976; Le Conte de l'Oiseau 1979; Hiver dans l'Ame 1978; Paraphase 1980; Oboe Concerto, 1993; Chamber Music: Improvisation Pour Violon Seul 1976; Improvisation pour Violoncelle Seul 1976; Improvisation pour Alto Seul 1976; Mobiles 1959–60; Mouvement pour Quintette de Cuivres 1963; Musique pour l'Ode au St Laurent 1965; Mutations 1981; Quatuor 1958, No. 2 1972; Sonate pour Alto et Piano 1978; Sonate No. 1 pour Violoncelle et Piano 1962; No. 2 Pour Violoncelle et Piano 1985; Suite pour Quotuor a Cordes 1968; Triptyque 1962; Trois Pieces Irlandaises 1961; Solo Voice: Geoles 1963; Improvisation pour Voix et Piano 1976; Musique Peintes 1955; Chorus: Ahimsa 1984; Missa de Profundis 1973; Psalm 148 1971; Images d'un Festival for baritone, chorus and orchestra, 1993; Keyboard: Cinq Variations sur un Thème Grégorien 1956; Improvisation pour piano 1976; Variations en passacaille 1984.

PREY, Florian; German singer (baritone); *Festival Manager, Herbstliche Musiktage Bad Urach* and *Kleines Sommerfestival Remise Gauting;* b. 1959, Hamburg; s. of Hermann Prey and Barbara Prey; m.; two c. *Education:* Munich Musikhochschule. *Career:* gave lieder recitals and appeared in concert from 1982; Opera debut as the Count in Schreker's Der ferne Klang, Venice, 1984; sang in a staged version of St Matthew Passion at Teatro La Fenice, 1984; Silvio for Vienna Kammeroper, 1986; Stadttheater Aachen 1988–93, as Harlekin in Ariadne auf Naxos (Strauss), Falke (Strauss) and Papageno, Count, Figaro and Gulielmo (Mozart); Nationaltheater Mannheim as Papageno, Staatstheater am Gärtnerplatz, Munich, Musikverein, Vienna, Konzerthaus, Vienna, Philharmonie, Cologne and Munich; Festival Man., Herbstliche Musiktage Bad Urach 2006–, Kleines Sommerfestival Remise Gauting 2009–; writer of stage pieces and film scripts (Montag eine Parodie 1985). *Recordings:* Winterreise, Die schöne Müllerin, Abendlieder, Lieder von Franz Schubert und Y. Kilpinen, Telemann: Moralische Kantaten, Baroque cantatas by Bach, Händel, Telemann, Christmas songs, A.K. Böhm Lieder (three CDs), Opera: Die drei Wünsche, Postillion von Lonjumeau. *Honours:* Günther Klinge Preisträger. *Current Management:* c/o Künstlersekretariat Andreas Liebrandt, Ambach/Starnberger See, Holzbergstrasse 11, 82541 Münsing, Germany. *Telephone:* (8177) 1069. *Fax:* (8177) 26169. *E-mail:* info@liebrandt.com. *Website:* www.randt.com. *E-mail:* post@florianprey.de. *Website:* www.florianprey.de; www.kleines-sommerfestival.de.

PRIBYL, Luboš; Czech pianist; b. 29 Oct. 1975, Prague. *Education:* Prague Conservatoire with Prof. Radomír Melmuka, Academy of Music, Prague with Prof. Emil Leichner. *Career:* debut in Zlín, performance in the concert of the Zlín Symphony orchestra, 1989–; recital in the Beethoven festival in Teplice, 1992–; concerts in Bolzano, Brixen, Italy, 1994; concert tour in Japan (Tokyo, Sapporo, Obihiro, Asahikava), 1996; played Tchaikovsky's Concert No. 1, with orchestra of the Prague Conservatoire, 1997; short portrait on Czech television, 1997. *Recordings:* recordings on Czech Radio (Chopin, Tchaikovsky, Rachmaninov, Martinů, Jezek); album of piano recital (Haydn, Liszt, Semtana, Rachmaninov, Martinů, Jezek). *Honours:* Competition, Virtuosi per musica di pianoforte, Czech Republic, 1st Prize, 1988; Competition 'Citta di Senigallia', Italy, 5th prize, 1991; Beethoven Competition in Hradec nad Moravicí, Czech Republic, 1st Prize, 1992; F P Neglia Competition in Enna, Italy, 2nd Prize, 1993; Dr Václav Holzknecht Competition in Prague, 1st Prize, 1995; Mavi Marcoz Competition in Aosta, Italy, 5th Prize, 1995. *Address:* Smeralova 34, 170 00 Prague 7, Czech Republic.

PRICE, Curtis Alexander, AM, PhD, FRCM, FRNCM; American musicologist, academic and university administrator; *Warden, New College, Oxford;* b. 7 Sept. 1945, Springfield, Mo.; m. Rhian Samuel. *Education:* Southern Illinois Univ., Harvard Univ. with John Ward and Nino Pirotta. *Career:* teacher, Washington Univ., St Louis 1974–81; teacher, King's Coll. London 1981, Reader 1985, King Edward Prof. of Music 1988–95; Prin. RAM, London 1995–2008, also Prof., Univ. of London; Prof. of Music, Univ. of Oxford 2009–, also Warden, New Coll., Oxford; mem. Royal Musical Asscn (Pres. 1999–2002); Trustee Musica Britannica, Wigmore Hall; Gov. Purcell School, Winchester Coll., Lord Williams's School. *Publications include:* The Critical Decade for English Music Drama 1700–1710 1978, Music in the Restoration Theater: with a Catalogue of Instrumental Music in the Plays 1665–1713 1979, Henry Purcell and the London Stage 1984, H. Purcell: Dido and Aeneas (ed.) 1986, Italian Opera and Arson in Late Eighteenth-Century London 1989, The Impresario's Ten Commandments: Continental Recruitment for Italian Opera in London 1763–4 (with J. Milhous and R.D. Hume) 1992, Man and Music: The Early Baroque Era (ed.) 1993, Purcell Studies (ed.) 1995. *Honours:* Hon. RAM; Hon. KBE 2005. *Address:* New College, Oxford, OX1 3BN, England (office). *E-mail:* warden@new.ox.ac.uk (office). *Website:* www.new.ox.ac.uk/warden (office).

PRICE, Eileen, BEd, ARCM; British fmr singer (mezzo-soprano); b. Cardigan, Wales; m. Iain McWilliam (deceased); two s. (deceased). *Education:* Homerton Coll., Cambridge and Royal Coll. of Music, London. *Career:* has performed with all major British orchestras, and conductors, including Sir Malcolm Sergeant, Sir Adrian Boult, Swarowsky, Bryden Thomson and Sir John Barbirolli; own radio and TV series; appeared at Citizens Theatre, Glasgow and Royal Court Theatre, London; Head of Vocal Studies, Welsh Coll. of Music and Drama (retd); Teacher of Voice, Royal Holloway, Univ. of London 1991–, Jr Guildhall School of Music and Drama, London 1996–; Dir and Creator, Teachers of Singing Training Course for AOTOS; mem. and past chair. Asscn of Teachers of Singing (hon. life mem.), Asscn of Teachers of Singing (USA). *Honours:* RCM Jenny Lind Prize, Henry Leslie Prize, Clara Butt Prize, Tagore Medal for Most Distinguished Student of the Year. *Address:* Flat 2A 15 Marine Parade, Penarth, Cardiff, HA2 0HY, Wales (home). *E-mail:* eileenmcwilliam@icloud.com.

PRICE, Gwynneth Patricia; British fmr singer (soprano); b. 1935, Bath, England. *Education:* studied in London with E. Herbert-Caesari, and with Parry Jones at Trinity Coll. of Music. *Career:* has sung at opera houses throughout the world, including the Royal Opera House, Covent Garden, as the Priestess in Aida, Fortune Teller in Arabella, Milliner and Duenna in Rosenkavalier, Villager in Jenůfa 1993; sang title role in Menotti's The Old Maid and The Thief at Norfolk Festival 1992, Alice in Verdi's Falstaff; concert repertoire includes Verdi's Requiem, conducted by Colin Davis, Tosca, Santuzza in Cavalleria Rusticana; fmr mem. Council of the Friends of Covent Garden; Founder and Dir Floriale Singers and Covent Garden Singers; now one of Britain's English Language pronunciation specialists; has made guest appearances on BBC radio. *Honours:* Long Service Silver Medallist, 35 Years with Royal Opera. *Address:* 65 Lancaster Grove, Hampstead, London, NW3 4HD, England (home). *Telephone:* (20) 7794-6455 (home).

PRICE, Henry; American singer (tenor); b. 18 Oct. 1945, Oakland, CA. *Career:* many seasons at the New York City Opera, where he sang Telemaco in Monteverdi's Ulisse, Tamino, Almaviva, Narciso in Il Turco in Italia, Gennaro in Lucrezia Borgia and operetta roles; other appearances in Philadelphia and Miami, at the US Spoleto Festival and from 1983 in Europe, notably at the Mainz and Linz Operas.

PRICE, Janet, BMus, MMus, LRAM, ARCM; British singer (soprano); *Emeritus Teaching Fellow, Royal Welsh College of Music and Drama;* b. 5 Feb. 1938, Abersychan, Pontypool, Gwent, S Wales; m. Adrian Beaumont 1963. *Education:* Univ. of Wales Cardiff, studied with Nadia Boulanger in Paris, Olive Groves, Isobel Baillie and Hervey Alan. *Career:* singer in concerts with leading orchestras and conductors throughout UK and Western Europe; numerous premieres, including Belgian premiere of Tippett's Third Symphony, Festival of Flanders 1975; has sung opera with Glyndebourne Festival Opera, Welsh Nat. Opera Co., Kent Opera Co., Opera Rara, Handel Opera Soc., Northern Ireland Opera Trust, San Antonio Grand Opera, Tex., USA, BBC TV; has made a speciality of resurrecting neglected heroines of the Bel Canto period, the first person to sing a number of these roles in the modern era; highlights include: live commercial recording of Beethoven's 9th Symphony with Bernard Haitink and Concertgebouw Orchestra and Chorus, Tippett's 3rd Symphony with Haitink and London Philharmonic Orchestra, Stravinsky's Les Noces with Rozhdestvensky and BBC Symphony Orchestra and Chorus; sang role of Hecuba in Kent Opera's production of Tippett's King Priam (video); Prof. of Singing, RAM 1997–2007; Prof. of Singing, Royal Welsh Coll. of Music and Drama (RWCMD) 1984–2004, Emer. Teaching Fellow 2006–.

Publication: Haydn's Songs from a Singer's Viewpoint (article in The Haydn Yearbook) 1983. *Honours:* Hon. ARAM 2000; Hon. FRWCMD 2004; Winner British Art Council First Young Welsh Singers' Award 1964. *Address:* 73 Kings Drive, Bishopston, Bristol, BS7 8JQ, England (home). *Telephone:* (117) 924-8456 (home).

PRICE, Leontyne; American singer (soprano); b. (Mary Violet Leontine Price), 10 Feb. 1927, Laurel, Miss.; d. of James A. Price and Kate Price (née Baker); m. William Warfield 1952 (divorced 1973). *Education:* Central State Coll., Wilberforce, Ohio, Juilliard School of Music. *Career:* appeared as Bess (Porgy and Bess), Vienna, Berlin, Paris, London, New York 1952–54; recitalist, soloist 1954–; soloist, Hollywood Bowl 1955–59, 1966; opera singer, NBC-TV 1955–58, San Francisco Opera Co. 1957–59, 1960–61, Vienna Staatsoper 1958, 1959–60, 1961; recording artist RCA-Victor 1958–; appeared at Covent Garden 1958–59, 1970, Chicago 1959, 1960, 1965, Milan 1960–61, 1963, 1967, Metropolitan Opera, New York 1961–62, 1963–70, 1972, Paris Opéra as Aida 1968, Metropolitan Opera as Aida 1985 (retd); Fellow, American Acad. of Arts and Sciences; Trustee, International House. *Honours:* Hon. Vice-Chair. US Cttee of UNESCO; Order of Merit (Italy); Hon. DMus (Howard Univ., Cen. State Coll., Ohio); Hon. DHL (Dartmouth); Hon. DH (Rust Coll., Miss.); Hon. DHumLitt (Fordham); Presidential Medal of Freedom 1964, Kennedy Center Honor 1980, Nat. Medal of Arts 1985, Essence Award 1991, 20 Grammy Awards including for Lifetime Achievement 1989, Nat. Endowment for the Arts Opera Award 2008.

PRICE, Luke; singer (tenor); b. 1968, Germany. *Education:* chorister Westminster Cathedral, Trinity Coll., London. *Career:* appearances at Batignano Festival as Eufemio in Storace's Gli Equivoci; Apprentice in Die Meistersinger for Netherlands Opera and at Covent Garden; engagements in Opéra de Lyon, Paris Châtelet, Salzburg and Glyndebourne (festival and touring); other roles include Tchaikovsky's Lensky, Arturo in I Puritani and Camille in Die Lustige Witwe; mem., Covent Garden chorus from season 2000–2001; sang Janissary in revival of Mozart's Die Entführung 2000.

PRICE, Perry; American singer (tenor); b. 13 Oct. 1942, New York, PA; m. Heather Thomson. *Education:* Univ. of Houston, studied in London with Otakar Kraus and in New York. *Career:* debut in San Francisco as Des Grieux in Manon 1964; New York City Opera, Houston, Philadelphia, San Diego and Portland; sang further at Montréal, Vancouver, Toronto, Lisbon and Stadttheater Augsburg; other roles include Mozart's Ferrando, Don Ottavio and Tamino, Rossini's Almaviva and Lindoro, the Duke of Mantua, Edgardo, Nemorino, Faust and Hoffmann; active in concert and as teacher.

PRICK, Christoph; German conductor; b. 23 Oct. 1946, Hamburg. *Education:* studied in Hamburg with Wilhelm Bruckner-Ruggebourg. *Career:* Asst, Hamburg Staatsoper; Permanent Conductor, Trier Opera 1970–72, Darmstadt 1972–74; Musical Dir, Saarbrucken 1974–77, Karlsruhe 1977–84; Staatskapellmeister, Deutsche Oper Berlin 1977–84 (returned to conduct the premiere of Wolfgang Rihm's Oedipus 1987); conducted Così fan tutte at Los Angeles 1988, Arabella at Barcelona 1989; Music Dir, Los Angeles Chamber Orchestra 1992–95; conducted Fidelio and Tannhäuser at the Metropolitan 1992; Music Dir, City of Hannover, Germany from 1993; led Die Schweigsame Frau at Dresden 1998.

PRIDAY, Elisabeth; British singer (soprano); b. 1955, Buckingham, England. *Education:* Royal Academy of Music. *Career:* joined the Monteverdi Choir 1975: concerts at the Aix Festival, and BBC Promenade; sang in Handel Opera's Giustino 1983 and Hasse's L'Eroe Cinese at the 1985 Holland Festival; appearances with Roger Norrington for the Maggio Musicale Florence (Speranza in Orfeo) and Amor in Gluck's Orfeo with the Scottish Chamber Orchestra; Dido and Aeneas with the English Concert in Germany, London and the Brighton Festival Concert performances of Bach's B minor Mass in King's College, Cambridge, Handel's Carmelite Vespers with the European Baroque Orchestra, Alexander's Feast for RAI in Italy and Messiah at the Festival de Beaune in France and also QEH; Monteverdi Vespers in St John's Smith Square, Bristol, St Albans; concerts in France and England with Chiaroscuro and Climene in Gluck's La Corona at the City of London Festival; Paris 1991 with the Deller Consort. *Recordings:* Bach Motets with the Monteverdi Choir; Purcell's King Arthur, Music for the Chapels Royal and the Fairy Queen; Handel's Israel in Egypt, Semele and Dixit Dominus with the Winchester Cathedral Choir; Motets by Schütz and Monteverdi; Rameau's Les Boréades; Vivaldi Glorias (Nimbus); Dido and Aeneas with Trevor Pinnock and also with John Eliot Gardiner.

PRIETO, Carlos; cellist; b. 1 Jan. 1937, Mexico City, Mexico; m. Maria Isabel 1964; two s. one d. *Education:* Mexico City Conservatory of Music with Imre Hartman, studied with Pierre Fournier in Geneva, Leonard Rose in New York, USA. *Career:* mem., Trio Mexico 1978–81; int. career as concert cellist; many world tours from 1981; performances in Carnegie Hall and Lincoln Center, New York, Kennedy Center, Washington, DC, Salle Pleyel and Salle Gaveau, Paris, Philharmonic Hall, Leningrad, Concertgebouw, Amsterdam; has performed at int. music festivals; played at world premieres of many cello concerti, including those of Carlos Chavez, Joaquin Rodrigo. *Recordings include:* Complete Bach Suites for cello solo 1985, works by Paganini, Ponce, Rachmaninov, Fauré, Mendelssohn, Tchaikovsky. *Publications:* Alrededor del Mundo con el Violonchelo (autobiog.) 1987, Russian Letters 1965. *Address:* Gurtman and Murtha Associates Inc., 450 Seventh Avenue #603, New York, NY 10123-0101, USA.

PRIETO, Carlos Miguel, MBA; Mexican conductor and violinist; *Music Director, Orquesta Sinfónica Nacional de Mexico*; b. 1965, Mexico City; s. of Carlos and Maria Isabel Prieto; m. Isabel Mariscal; two d. *Education:* Princeton Univ., Harvard Univ., USA. *Career:* fmrly violinist with Cuarteto Prieto; Music Dir Mexico City Philharmonic Orchestra 1998–2002; Founder and Music Dir, Mozart-Haydn Festival 2000; Conductor, Youth Orchestra of the Americas 2002–; Music Dir Orquesta Sinfónica Nacional de Mexico 2007–; currently Music Dir and Principal Conductor, Louisiana Philharmonic Orchestra and Music Dir Huntsville Symphony Orchestra and Orquesta Sinfónica de Minería; guest appearances with numerous orchestras in North America, and in Mexico, Europe, Russia, Israel; notable appearances with Netherlands Radio Orchestra in Utrecht, Chicago Symphony Orchestra, Boston Symphony Orchestra at Tanglewood Festival, with soloist Yo-Yo Ma. *Recordings:* albums: as conductor: Guarnieri/Ibarra/Chávez, Conciertos y Chôro (with Carlos Prieto, Edison Quintana and Orquesta de las Américas) 2000, Revueltas (with Orquesta Sinfónica de Xalapa) 2004, Mozart, Piano Concertos Nos. 14, 23 and 25 (with Jorge Federico Osorio and Mozart-Haydn Festival Orchestra) 2006, Revueltas 2 (with Orquesta Sinfónica de Xalapa) 2007, Korngold, Violin Concerto/Schauspiel Overture/Much Ado About Nothing Suite (with Philippe Quint and Mineria Symphony Orchestra) 2009. *Honours:* Mozart Medal of Honor, Govt of Mexico and Embassy of Austria 1998, Mexican Union of Music and Theater Critics Conductor of the Year 2002. *Current Management:* Thea Dispeker Inc. Artists Management, 59 East 54th Street, Suite 81, New York, NY 10022, USA. *Telephone:* (212) 421-7676. *Fax:* (212) 935-3279. *E-mail:* info@dispeker.com. *Website:* www.dispeker.com. *Address:* Louisiana Philharmonic Orchestra, 1010 Common Street, Suite 2120, New Orleans, LA 70112, USA (office). *Telephone:* (504) 523-6530 (office). *Fax:* (504) 595-8468 (office). *E-mail:* info@lpomusic.com (office). *Website:* www .osn.bellasartes.gob.mx (office); www.lpomusic.com (office).

PRIETO, Joel; Spanish/Puerto Rican singer (tenor); b. Spain. *Education:* Manhattan School of Music. *Career:* debut as Tamino in Die Zauberflöte at Deutsche Oper, Berlin 2006; has performed at Palau de las Arts, Valencia, Scottish Opera, Salzburg Festival, Royal Opera House, Covent Garden, Gran Teatre del Liceu, Barcelona, Théâtre du Capitole, Toulouse, Bayerische Staatsoper, Munich, Grand Théâtre de Luxembourg, Teatro Municipal Santiago, Chile; has sung Ferrando in Così fan tutte, Fenton in Falstaff, Arlecchino in Pagliacci; concert performances include Haydn's Creation in Seville, Arturo in Lucia di Lammermoor in Dresden, Tybalt in Roméo et Juliette in Amsterdam; mem., Deutsche Oper, Berlin 2006–08; mem., Atelier Lyrique, Opéra Nat. de Paris 2006. *Honours:* first prize, Placido Domingo's Operalia Competition 2008. *Current Management:* c/o Elisabetta Hartl, Italartist Austroconcert Kulturmanagement, Gluckgasse 1, A- 1010 Vienna, Austria. *Telephone:* (1) 5132657. *Fax:* (1) 5126154. *E-mail:* austroconcert@ia -ac.com. *Website:* joelprieto.ia-ac.com.

PRIEW, Uta; singer (mezzo-soprano); b. 3 Aug. 1944, Karlovy, Varg, Czechoslovakia. *Education:* studied in Halle and Leipzig. *Career:* sang in opera at Weimar from 1970; Staatsoper Berlin from 1975 as Cenerentola; Selika in L'Africane, 1992; Clytemnestra, 1994; Fricka in Wagner's Ring, 1996; Bayreuth Festival, 1988–96 in The Ring and as Ortrud, Venus and Brangaene; Dresden Staatsoper, 1988 as Kundry; Deutsche Oper Berlin, 1990 as Amneris; Sang Clytemnestra at the Théâtre du Châtelet, Paris, 1996; Brangaene at Monte Carlo, 1998; Berlin Staatsoper 2000–01, as the Kostelnička in Jenůfa, Wagner's Mary and Herodias in Salome. *Recordings include:* video of Götterdämmerung. *Address:* Staatsoper Berlin, Unter den Linden 7, 1060 Berlin, Germany.

PRIMAKOV, Vassily; Russian pianist; b. 1979, Moscow. *Education:* Central Special Music School, Moscow with Vera Gornostaeva, Juilliard School (USA) with Jerome Lowenthal. *Recordings include:* Beethoven Sonatas, Chopin Concertos, Tchaikovsky: The Seasons and Grand Sonata, Chopin: 21 Mazurkas (NPR Recording of the Year 2009), Schumann: Carnaval, Kreisleriana, Arabeske, Dvorak: Piano Concerto, Op. 33, Poetic Tone-Pictures, Op. 85, Schubert: Dances and Impromptus, Mozart Concertos, Vol. 1, Vassily Primakov plays Brahms, Chopin & Scriabin. *Honours:* Winner, Cleveland Int. Piano Competition 1999, Silver Medal and Audience Prize, Gina Bachauer Int. Artists Piano Competition 2002, First Prize, Young Concert Artists Int. Auditions 2002, Classical Recording Foundation Young Artist of the Year 2007. *Address:* c/o Bridge Records, 200 Clinton Avenue, New Rochelle, NY 10801, USA (office). *Telephone:* (914) 654-9270 (office). *Fax:* (914) 636-1383 (office). *E-mail:* bridgerec@aol.com (office). *Website:* www .bridgerecords.com (office).

PRIMROSE, Claire; singer (mezzo-soprano); b. 2 Oct. 1957, Melbourne, Victoria, Australia. *Education:* Victorian Coll. of Arts, studied with Joan Hammond in Melbourne, with Gerard Souzay in Paris. *Career:* debut as mezzo-soprano in Australia, as soprano from 1990 as the sister in Holloway's Clarissa with ENO; mezzo-soprano roles include Krista in The Makropolous Case, Meg Page in Falstaff, Mercédès in Carmen, Cornelia in Giulio Cesare, title role in Cendrillon at Wexford Festival, Charlotte in Werther at Montpellier, Giulietta in Les Contes d'Hoffmann at Lille, Salud in La Vida Breve at Liège, Suzuki in Madama Butterfly for Opera North, Orlofsky in Die Fledermaus at the Hong Kong Festival, Dorabella in Così fan tutte, Sesto in La Clemenza di Tito for Opera Forum Holland; soprano roles include Leonore in Fidelio, Medea in Teseo, Athens Festival and Sadler's Wells, Dido in Dido and Aeneas at Bologna, title role in Alceste, Monte Carlo Festival and Covent Garden, Elettra in Idomeneo, Valencia Festival 1991, Chrysothemis for State

Opera of South Australia and Festival of Melbourne, Leonore in Fidelio with Australian Opera 1992–93; Paris debut as Alceste at Châtelet; Scandinavian debut as Elettra in Idomeneo, Helsinki, and with the New Israeli Opera in Tel-Aviv 1992; Fiordiligi, Lyric Opera of Queensland; Santuzza, Australian Opera 1994, 1996; numerous concert appearances include a Wigmore Hall recital with Roger Vignoles in Berlioz's Roméo et Juliette, Salle Pleyel, Paris, and Leonara in La Forza del Destino, Scottish Opera; sang Verdi's Lady Macbeth at Sydney 1998; season 2000–01 as Sieglinde at Brunswick and Senta in Dublin. *Honours:* winner Metropolitan Opera Competition, winner Pavarotti Int. Competition, Philadelphia. *Current Management:* Robert Lombardo & Associates, 61 W 62nd Street, Suite 6F, New York, NY 10023, USA. *Telephone:* (212) 586-4453. *Fax:* (212) 581-5771. *E-mail:* Robert@RobertLombardo.com.

PRING, Katherine; British singer (mezzo-soprano); b. 4 June 1940, Brighton, England. *Education:* Royal Coll. of Music with Ruth Packer, studied with Maria Carpi in Geneva and Luigi Ricci in Rome. *Career:* debut in Geneva 1966, as Flora in La Traviata; sang at Sadler's Wells from 1968, notably as Carmen, Dorabella, Poppea, Eboli, Azucena and Waltraute; sang in the 1974 British stage premiere of Henze's The Bassarids; Covent Garden debut 1972, as Thea in The Knot Garden; Bayreuth 1972–73, as Schwertleite in Die Walküre; Glyndebourne 1978, as Baba the Turk in The Rake's Progress; other modern roles included Kate in Owen Wingrave and Jocasta in Oedipus Rex; retired 1982. *Recordings:* Fricka and Waltraute in The Ring conducted by Reginald Goodall, The Magic Fountain by Delius.

PRING, Sarah; British singer (soprano); b. 1962, England. *Education:* Guildhall School, studied in Florence with Suzanne Danco and with Johanna Peters. *Career:* sang Norina, Susanna, Concepcion and Martinů's Julietta while a student in London, the Trovatore Leonora in Belgium; professional debut at Glyndebourne, 1988, as Alice in Falstaff, returning as Barena in Jenůfa; Glyndebourne Touring Opera as Glasha in Katya Kabanova, First Lady in Die Zauberflöte and Dorabella; Opera North debut, 1989, as Concepcion, Scottish Opera, 1991, as Mimi; concert appearances at Festival Hall (Jenůfa), Greenwich Festival (Judas Maccabaeus), Belfast (Beethoven's Ninth) and Purcell Room; sang Gluck's Euridice for Opera West, 1991; ENO debut, 1993, Princess Ida, Don Pasquale; ENO, 1993, Norina, Don Pasquale; ENO, 1994, Nannetta, Falstaff, also Glyndebourne Touring Opera, Second Niece, Peter Grimes. 1995, Second Niece, Paris Châtelet; Covent Garden debut 1996 as a Rhinemaiden in Götterdämmerung; Berta in Il Barbiere di Siviglia, 1997–98. *Honours:* jt winner John Christie Award 1990. *Current Management:* Musicmakers International Artists Representation, Tailor House, 63–65 High Street, Whitwell, Hertfordshire SG4 8AH, England. *Telephone:* (1438) 871708. *Fax:* (1438) 871777. *E-mail:* musicmakers@compuserve.com. *Website:* www.operauk.com.

PRINGLE, John, AM; Australian singer (baritone); b. 17 Oct. 1938, Melbourne, Vic. *Education:* studied in Melbourne and with Luigi Ricci in Rome. *Career:* debut with Australian Opera, as Frank in Die Fledermaus, 1967; many appearances with Australian Opera as Mozart's Don Giovanni and Leporello, Count and Papageno, Verdi's Posa, Ford, the Lescauts of Puccini and Massenet, Rossini's Barber, Britten's Death in Venice, Mozart's Figaro, Don Alfonso, Debussy's Golaud; Nick Shadow in The Rake's Progress, Andrei in War and Peace, Janáček's Forester and Robert Storch in Intermezzo (Glyndebourne, 1983); Also sings Olivier in Capriccio and appeared at Paris, Brussels and Cologne, 1980–85; Sang Beckmesser in Meistersinger for Australian Opera, 1988–89, Comte de Nevers in Les Huguenots, 1990; Appeared in Los Angeles and San Diego, 1992; Gianni Schicchi at Sydney, 1995 and sang Prus in The Makropulos Case at Sydney, 1996; Don Alfonso at Sydney, 1997–98; Teatro Regio, Turin, as Musiklehrer, 1998; Conjoint Professor of Vocal Studies, Newcastle University Conservatorium, 1998–; Sang Don Alfonso at Sydney, 2001. *Recordings include:* Video of Les Huguenots; Videos of Intermezzo and Love for Three Oranges (both Glyndebourne); Die Meistersinger (Australian Opera).

PRIOR, Benjamin; singer (tenor); b. 1943, Venice, Italy. *Career:* sang widely in Italy from 1967, with Edgardo at La Fenice Venice 1969; Wexford Festival 1971, in La Rondine and Vienna Staatsoper 1972, as Verdi's Riccardo; Barcelona 1971, as Percy in Anna Bolena, San Francisco 1980 (Alfredo), Buenos Aires 1981 (Pinkerton) and New Orleans Opera 1981–88; sang Pinkerton at Verona 1983, and has also sung Verdi's Rodolfo (Luisa Miller) and Foresto, Nemorino, Faust, Macduff, the Duke of Mantua and Des Grieux.

PRITCHARD, Edith; singer (soprano); b. 1962, Edmonton, Canada. *Education:* Univ. of Toronto and Royal Northern Coll. of Music, UK. *Career:* represented Canada at the 1991 Cardiff Singer of the World Competition; sang Fiordiligi at the 1991 Glyndebourne Festival and the Countess in Cornet Rilke by Siegfried Matthus with the 1993 Glyndebourne Tour; other roles include First Lady in Die Zauberflöte at Covent Garden 1992–93, Licenza in Mozart's Sogno di Scipione at Buxton Festival and the Heavenly Voice in Don Carlos for Opera North. *Honours:* Royal Northern Coll. of Music Brigitte Fassbaender Prize for Lieder, Glyndebourne John Christie Award 1992.

PRITCHARD, Gwyn Charles, DRSAMD; British composer and conductor; *Professor of Composition, Trinity Laban Conservatoire of Music and Dance;* b. 29 Jan. 1948, Richmond, Yorks., England; s. of William Hugh Pritchard and Kathleen Mary Haworth; m. Claudia Klasicka 1967; two d. *Education:* Royal Scottish Acad. of Music and Drama, studied cello with Joan Dickson, composition with Dr Frank Spedding. *Career:* Dir of Music, Salisbury Cathedral School 1969–70; BBC contract for documentary Young Composer

1972–73; freelance cellist and mem. of various chamber ensembles 1973–78; Artistic Dir and Conductor, Uroboros Ensemble 1981–; Founder Reggello Int. Festival of Music, Italy 2003, London Ear Festival 2013; currently Prof. of Composition, Trinity Laban Conservatoire of Music and Dance, London; compositions performed world-wide, including Warsaw Autumn Festival, Wien Modern, Huddersfield Contemporary Music Festival, ISCM World Music Days, Int. Composers' Forum, Mexico Festival, Weimar Spring Music Days, Zepernicker Randspiele, Klangwerkstatt Berlin, throughout Europe, in USA, China, Hong Kong, S Korea, Australia and NZ. *Compositions:* Concerto for viola and orchestra 1967, Tangents 1969, Music for double bass and harp 1969, Five Miniatures 1969, Spring Music 1972, Enitharmon 1973, Becoming 1974, Five Short Pieces for piano 1975, Ensemble Music for six 1976, Tetrad 1976, Nephalauxis 1977, Strata 1977, Jardenna 1978, Objects in Space 1978, Mercurius 1979, Duo with a Young Girl 1980, 1980, Earthcrust 1980, Visions of Zosimos 1981, Sonata for guitar 1982, Moondance 1982, Nocturne 1982, Lollay, Lollay 1983, Dramalogue 1984, Chamber Concerto 1985, Madrigal 1987, La Settima Bolgia 1989, Mercurius 1989, Eidos 1990, Janus 1991, Intermezzo 1992, Wayang 1993, Demise 1994, Das Mysterium der heiligen Dreifaltigkeit 1995, Break Apart 1995, Canzonetta Elusiva 1995, Raum Greift Aus 1996, Forse Mi Stai Chiamando 1997, From Time to Time 1999, Micropus 1 and 2 2002, Features and Formations 2003, The Fruit of Chance and Necessity 2004, Nebulae and Episodes 2005, In Passing 2005, Song for Icarus 2006, Capriccio Inquieto 2006, Two Movements for Solo Viola 2007, Luchnos 2007, Game 2007, Conflux 2007, The Firmament of Time 2008, Micropus 3 & 4 2008, Harmoniemusik 2009, Micropus 5 2009, Ariel Dreaming 2010, In the Silence of Turned Earth 2010, Capriccio Fluido 2010, Mercurius 6 2010, Novelette 2011, Kommos 2011, Pour le Musicien de Saint-Merry 2011, Nightfall 2011, Epyllion 2011, Res 2011, Prince Achmed in China 2012. *Address:* 40 Woolstone Road, London, SE23 2SG, England. *Telephone:* (20) 8699-8883. *E-mail:* mail@gwynpritchard.com. *Website:* www.gwynpritchard.com. *Current Management:* c/o Verlag Neue Musik, Grabbeallee 15, 13156 Berlin, Germany. *Telephone:* (30) 616981-0. *Fax:* (30) 616981-21. *E-mail:* vnm@verlag-neue-musik.de. *Website:* www.verlag-neue-musik.de.

PROBST, Dominique Henri; French percussionist, composer and conductor; b. 19 Feb. 1954, Paris. *Education:* La Sorbonne, Paris, Paris Conservatoire Nat. Superieur de Musique. *Career:* as musician at La Comédie Francaise and many other Paris theatres 1974–; titulary mem., Concert Colonne and Ensemble Percussion Four; Asst, CNSM, Paris 1978–; Prof., Levallois Conservatory of Music 1984–. *Compositions:* for theatre: King Lear 1978, Dom Juan 1979, Macbeth, Les Caprices de Marianne 1980, Les Plaisirs de L'Ile Enchantée 1980, Les Cenci 1981, Marie Tudor 1982, L'Esprit des Bois, Dialogues des Carmélites 1984, La Mouette 1985, L'Arbre des Tropiques 1985, Le Cid 1985, L'Hote et le Renegat, Thomas More Richard de Gloucester Bacchus 1987, Ascese-a-Seize for six percussion players, Les Plaisirs de l'Ile Enchantee for recorder, violin, guitar and percussion, Coda and Variation IV for guitar. *Publications:* contrib. to professional journals, including La Revue Musicale. *Honours:* Lili and Naida Boulanger Foundation Prize for Composition 1979, Académie des Beaux-Arts Marcel Samuel Rousseau Prize, Paris (for opera, Maximilien Kolbe) 1986.

PROBST, Wolfgang; German singer (bass-baritone); b. 16 Nov. 1945, Neuhausen. *Education:* studied in Munich with Marianne Scheck. *Career:* Staatsoper Stuttgart from 1971 as King Philip in Don Carlos, Wotan in The Ring, in the premiere of Glass's Akhnaten (1984), and as Bartók's Bluebeard (1996); Guest at Munich as Wotan, Jochanaan and Wagner's Dutchman; Orange Festival, 1979, as Klingsor, Dallas, 1980, as Wotan (US debut); Sang Orestes in Elektra at Buenos Aires, 1987, and Boris Godunov at Basle, 1990; Trieste, 1992–94, as Hans Sachs and Kaspar in Der Freischütz; Sang Pizarro in Fidelio at Stuttgart, 1998; Season 2000–01 at Stuttgart in the premiere of Adriana Hölszky's Giuseppe e Sylvia, and in Donizetti's La Convenienze Teatrali and I Pazzi per progetto. *Recordings include:* Der Freischütz (video from Stuttgart).

PROCHAZKOVA, Jarmila; Czech musicologist; b. 27 Feb. 1961, Trebic. *Education:* Brno Conservatoire, Mašaryk Univ., Brno. *Career:* scholarship-holder of the Leoš Janáček Fund, practice at Janáček Archives; custodian, Janáček Archive of the Music, History Dept of Moravian Museum in Brno; mem. of commission to edit Janáček's musical works. *Publications:* Leoš Janáček: Album for Kamila Stösslova 1994, Jarmil Prochazkova, Bohumir Volny, Leoš Janáček 1995; contrib. on Janáček's composition method, folk inspirations, sociological aspects to On the Genesis of Janáček Symphony Dunaj 1993, Leoš Janáček and the Czech National Band 1995.

PROCTER, (Mary) Norma; British singer (contralto) (retd); b. 15 Feb. 1928, Cleethorpes, Lincs.; d. of John Procter and Clarice Procter. *Education:* Wintringham Secondary School, Grimsby, vocal and music studies in London with Roy Henderson, Alec Redshaw, Hans Oppenheim and Paul Hamburger. *Career:* London debut at Southwark Cathedral 1948; operatic debut at Aldeburgh Festival in Britten's Rape of Lucretia 1959, 1960; first appearance at Royal Opera House, Covent Garden in Gluck's Orpheus 1961; specialist in concert works, oratorios and recitals; has performed at festivals and with major orchestras in Germany, France, Netherlands, Belgium, Spain, Italy, Portugal, Norway, Denmark, Sweden, Finland, Austria, Luxembourg, Israel and S America and with conductors including Bruno Walter, Leonard Bernstein, Jascha Horenstein, Bernard Haitink, Rafael Kubelik, Karl Richter, Pablo Casals, Malcolm Sargent, Charles Groves, David Willcocks, Alexander

Gibson, Charles Mackerras and Norman del Mar; Pres. Grimsby Philharmonic Soc. *Recordings include:* The Messiah, Elijah, Samson, Second, Third and Eighth Symphonies and Das Klagende Lied (Mahler), First Symphony (Hartmann), Scenes and Arias (Nicholas Maw), Le Laudi (Hermann Suter), Brahms and Mahler Ballads (with Paul Hamburger), Songs of England with Jennifer Vyvyan 1999, The Rarities (Britten) including world premiere release of 1957 recording of Canticle II – Abraham and Isaac (with Peter Pears and Benjamin Britten) 2001. *Honours:* Hon. RAM 1974. *Address:* 194 Clee Road, Grimsby, Lincs., DN32 8NG, England (home). *Telephone:* (1472) 691210 (home).

PROKINA, Elena; Russian singer (soprano); b. 16 Jan. 1964, Odessa, Ukrainian SSR, USSR. *Education:* studied in Odessa and at Leningrad Theatre Inst. and Leningrad Conservatory, USSR. *Career:* Kirov Theatre, Leningrad 1988–, as Emma in Khovanshchina, Violetta, Marguerite, Natasha in War and Peace (seen on BBC TV), Tatyana, Desdemona, Pauline in The Gambler, Jaroslavna in Prince Igor, Iolanta and Maria in Mazeppa; tours with the Kirov Co. in Europe and Kirov Gala at Covent Garden 1992–; appearances in Los Angeles as Donna Anna, and Lina in Stiffelio; Lisbon and Sydney as Tatiana; Shostakovich No. 14 with the London Symphony Orchestra under Rostropovich 1993; Covent Garden debut in 1994 as Katya Kabanova in a production by Trevor Nunn, returning 1995 as Desdemona; Katya at Covent Garden in 1997; Verdi's Amelia Grimaldi at Glyndebourne 1998; Sang in Rachmaninov's Aleko at BBC London Prom Concerts 1999; season 1999–2000 for Zürich Opera as Tatiana in Eugene Onegin, Giselda in I Lombardi, Lucrezia (I Due Foscari) and Tosca; Elisabeth de Valois 2001; Amelia Grimaldi at Sydney and Marie in Wozzeck for Dallas Opera 2000; recent appearances include Desdemona in Otello, Euryanthe, Amelia in Un Ballo in Maschera, Elsa in Lohengrin, Tatiana in Eugene Onegin and performances of Britten's War Requiem. *Current Management:* c/o Pro Artist, 54 Beaconsfield Road, London, SE3 7LG, England. *Telephone:* (20) 8858-0785. *Fax:* (20) 8269-1722. *E-mail:* aminah@proartist.co.uk. *Website:* www.proartist.co.uk.

PROMONTI, Elisabeth, DipMus; singer (soprano); b. 9 July 1942, Budapest, Hungary; one s. *Education:* Franz Liszt Music Acad., Budapest, Akad. Mozarteum, Salzburg, studied with Zoltan Zavodsky, Viorica Ursuleac, Friederike Baumgartner, Elisabeth Grümmer Int. Opera Studio, Opera Zürich. *Career:* debut as Aida, Bielefeld Municipal Theatre 1967; sang such roles as Aida, Amelia, Desdemona, Elisabeth, Donna Anna, Pamina, Countess, Elsa and Marie at opera houses of Bielefeld, Oberhausen, Kiel, Bremen, Heidelberg, Bordeaux, Vienna, Zürich 1967–75; concert singer 1975–; appearances on radio and tv; tours to Europe, USA and Canada; Dir Swiss Kodály Inst. 1983–95; Pres., Swiss Kodály Soc. 1991–96; Dir, Concorde Opera Management Ltd, Vienna 1998–. *Recordings include:* Zoltán Kodály, Epigrammes 1991, Folk Songs arranged by Great Composers 1993.

PROSTITOV, Oleg; Russian composer; b. 7 Sept. 1955, Stavropol; m. Grishina Lyudmila 1976; one s. one d. *Education:* Rimsky-Korsakov State Conservatoire, St Petersburg and St Petersburg Conservatoire with Prof. Mnatsakanyan. *Career:* debut in Stavropol 1972; participant in three int. music festivals, Baku 1987, Sofia 1990, St Petersburg 1991; Sonata-fantasy, Amadeus; mem. Union of the Composers of Russia. *Compositions:* five symphonies, two piano concertos, violin concerto, five children's musicals, chamber and vocal instrumental works (sonatas, suites, string quartets, cantatas, romances), about 100 songs. *Honours:* first prize for vocal cycle on the poems by S. Esenin for baritone and piano Young Musicians' Competition, St Petersburg 1978. *Address:* Krasnoyarsky Rabochy, 124-A Apt 25, 660095 Krasnoyarsk, Russia.

PROTSCHKA, Josef; German singer (tenor) and professor of singing; b. 5 Feb. 1944, Prague, Czechoslovakia; s. of Josef Protschka and Franziska Protschka; m. Christa Protschka; one s. two d. *Education:* Univs of Tubingen and Bonn (Staatsexamen 'mit Auszeichnung' in Philology and Philosophy), Hochschule für Musik und Tanz Köln with Erika Köth and Peter Witsch. *Career:* Giessen 1977–78, Saarbrücken 1978–80; leading tenor at Köln Opera from 1980, singing all main tenor parts in Ponnelle's Mozart cycle, Lionel, Tom Rakewell, Faust, Max, Lensky, Jenik in The Bartered Bride, José, Hermann (Queen of Spades), Loge, Erik, Eisenstein; freelance from 1985; debuts at Salzburg Festival and Vienna State Opera (Hans) 1985, La Scala and Semperoper Dresden (José) 1986, Bregenz Festival (Hoffmann) 1986, Maggio Musicale, Florence (Flamand/Capriccio) and Zurich Opera 1987, Wiener Festwochen (Fierrabras-Schubert) 1988, Hamburg State Opera as Florestan and Elis in Schreker's Schatzgräber 1989, Idomeneo 1990, Royal Opera, Brussels 1989, as Florestan and Lohengrin 1990, Florestan at Covent Garden and Tokyo NHK 1990; Oper Leipzig as Herodes 1996; US debut in Houston (Song of the Earth) 1991; appears regularly on stage at festivals and opera houses with leading conductors and producers; also lieder recitals, concerts, radio and TV productions; Prof., Hochschule für Musik und Tanz Köln 1995–2009, Rector 2002–09; Prof., Det Kongelige Danske Musikkonservatoriet, Copenhagen 1993–; master-classes throughout Europe, South Africa and China; contract teacher for classical singing; private teaching in studio for vocal interpretation (SVI), Pulheim, nr Köln 2012–; jury mem. for numerous int. singing competitions. *Recordings include:* more than 60 CD/DVD productions (numerous int. awards), including Haydn Die Schöpfung/Jahreszeiten (Harnoncourt), Schubert Lazarus/Stabat Mater (Sawallisch), W. A. Mozart Opernarien, Schubert Schöne Müllerin, Mendelssohn Lieder (complete), Mozart Lieder (complete), Schumann Dichterliebe, Op. 39/ Spanisches Liederspiel, Schoeck Massimila Doni, Zemlinski Traumgörge,

Schreker Der Schatzgräber, Hindemith Cardillac/Mathis der Maler, Schubert Fierrabras (Abbado), Fidelio (Florestan) and Flying Dutchman (Erik) (with Vienna Philharmonic and Dohnányi); videos: Fidelio (Covent Garden), Tales of Hoffmann (Bregenz Festival), Fierrabras (Theater an der Wien), Schatzgräber (Hamburg Opera), Missa solemnis (Uracher Musiktage), Ritorno di Ulisee (Salzburg Festival), Lieder recital (Urach), Soloportrait (NDR). *Address:* SVI, Malvenweg 6, 50259 Köln (office); Ringstrasse 17B, 50765 Köln, Germany (home). *Telephone:* 172-5203910 (mobile) (office). *E-mail:* josef .protschka@gmx.de (office).

PROUVOST, Gaetane; French violinist; b. Lille; m. Charles de Couessin 1985; four c. *Education:* Conservatoire Nat. Supérieur, Paris, Juilliard School of Music, New York with Ivan Galamian, studied with Chigiana in Siena, Italy, with D. Markevitch at the Institut des Hautes Etudes Musicales, Montreux, and with Zino Francescatti. *Career:* debut at Carnegie Hall 1974; soloist, Radio-France Orchestra, Orchestre Lamoureux, Bucharest Philharmonic, Gdansk Philharmonic, Ensemble Intercontemporain, Ensemble Forum; premiered Olivier Greif's Sonate, M. Rateau's Offrande lyrique, Paris 1984; participated in Etienne Perrier's film, Rouge Venitien; Prof., Conservatoire Nat. Supérieur de Musique, Paris; mem. Alumni Asscn of Conservatoire Nat. Supérieur de Musique, Paris. *Recordings:* Prokofiev's Sonatas op 80 and 94 for violin and piano, with A.L. el Bacha, Pierné's Work for violin and piano, with Laurent Cabasso, Farrenc's Work for violin and piano, with Laurent Cabasso, Zino Francescatti works. *Publications:* biography of Zino Francescati. *Honours:* prizewinner, Carl Flesch Int. Competition, London. *Address:* 7 rue des Volontaires, 75015 Paris, France (home). *Telephone:* 6-79-74-44-84 (mobile) (office). *E-mail:* gaetane.prouvost@free.fr (home).

PROUZA, Zdenek; cellist; b. 3 Aug. 1955, Prague, Czechoslovakia; m. Katherine H. Allen 1987. *Education:* Conservatory of Music, Prague, Acad. of Performing Arts, Prague, Hochschule für Musik, Vienna, Mozarteum, Salzburg and Accademia Musicale Chigiana, Siena. *Career:* debut recital in Prague 1973; Principal Cellist, Czech Chamber Orchestra and Nurnberg Symphony Orchestra; Co-Principal, Vienna Chamber Orchestra and Munich Chamber Orchestra; solo appearances in Czechoslovakia, Germany, Belgium, France, Italy, Austria, USA and Canada; mem. American Cello Soc. *Recordings:* Pauer, Radio Prague; Suk, Czech television; Suk, ORTF; Vivaldi, RAI; Saint-Saëns, Colosseum; Musical Heritage Society. *Honours:* Concertino Praga 1970, Beethoven Cello Competition 1972, Czech Cello Competition 1976, Czech Music Foundation Contemporary Performance Award 1977, 1978. *Address:* 820 West End Avenue, Suite 3C, New York, NY 10025, USA.

PROVOST, Serge; Canadian composer and academic; b. 1952, Saint-Timothée de Beauharnois, QC. *Education:* Conservatoire de Musique, Montréal, studied with Gilles Tremblay, Bernard Lagacé, Claude Ballif in Paris. *Career:* Prof. of Analysis, Trois-Rivières and Hull Conservatories; took part in Banff Centre Composers' Workshop 1979, Rencontres Internationales de la Jeunesse at Bayreuth Festival; has given organ recitals in France, Germany and Canada. *Compositions include:* Les Isles du Songe for choir, orchestra and percussion (first prize in composition for choir, orchestra and percussion) 1979, Cretes for two harpsichords 1980, Tetrarys for saxophone, harp, flute and piano 1988, Les Jardins Suspendus for four ondes martenots and piano 1984. *Honours:* first prize in analysis at Conservatoire de Paris 1981.

PROWSE, Philip; British stage director and stage designer; b. 29 Dec. 1937, Worcestershire, England. *Education:* Slade School of Fine Art, London. *Career:* teacher at Birmingham Coll. of Art; teacher Slade School of Fine Art 1995–99, Prof. 1999–03, now Emer.; designed ballets for Covent Garden, followed by Orfeo ed Euridice 1969, and Ariadne auf Naxos 1976; Dir Citizens Theatre, Glasgow 1970–; produced and designed Handel's Tamerlano for WNO 1982, and Les Pêcheurs de Perles for ENO 1987; designs for Jonathan Miller's production of Don Giovanni at ENO 1985 and The Magic Flute for Scottish Opera; work as producer and designer for Opera North includes Orfeo ed Euridice, Die Dreigroschenoper and Aida 1986, British premiere of Strauss's Daphne 1987, and La Gioconda 1993; staged the house premiere of Verdi's Giovanna d'Arco, Covent Garden 1996 (also at Opera North 1998); Prof., Slade School, Univ. Coll. London 1999–; Dir Citizens 1970–2004. *Current Management:* c/o Cruickshank Cazenove, 97 Old South Lambeth Road, London, SW8 1XU, England. *Telephone:* (20) 7735-2933.

PRUETT, Jerome; American singer (tenor); *Associate Professor of Vocal Studies, The Hartt School, University of Hartford*; b. 22 Nov. 1941, Poplar Bluff, Missouri. *Education:* studied with Thorwald Olsen in St Louis and with Boris Goldovsky in West Virginia. *Career:* debut, Carnegie Hall New York 1974, in a concert performance of Donizetti's Parisina d'Este; sang with New York City Opera; performances in Europe include Vienna Volksoper, in the premiere of Wolpert's Le Malade Imaginaire 1975, Théâtre de la Monnaie Brussels 1983, as Julien in Louise and as Boris in Katya Kabanova, Geneva Opera, as Debussy's Pelléas 1984; sang at Nancy, in Henze's Boulevard Solitude 1984; other roles include Mozart's Belmonte and Tamino, Nicolai's Fenton, Tonio in La Fille du Régiment and Ernesto in Don Pasquale, Boris in Katya Kabanova, Ferrando in Così fan tutte, Alfredo and Gounod's Faust; currently Associate Prof. of Vocal Studies, The Hartt School, Univ. of Hartford. *Recordings:* Louise (Erato). *Address:* The Hartt School, University of Hartford, 200 Bloomfield Avenue, West Hartford, CT 06117-1599, USA (office). *Telephone:* (860) 768-4454 (office). *E-mail:* jerpruett@aol.com (office). *Website:* harttweb.hartford.edu (office).

PRUNELL-FRIEND, Agustin, BMus, BA; Spanish singer (tenor); b. 1969, Tenerife, Canary Islands. *Education:* Guildhall School of Music and Drama, London, UK, Universidad La Laguna. *Career:* debut as Ramiro in Cenerentola at Madrid 1996; appearances at Teatro La Fenice (Nettuno in world premiere of Cavalli's Orione with Venice Baroque Orchestra, Maderna's Venetian Journal), Teatro Real, Madrid (Cefalo in new Pizzi production of Hidalgo's Celos Aun del Ayre Matan, conducted by Malgoire), Royal Opera House, Covent Garden (Acis in Acis and Galatea and M. de la Grille in EBF's production of Lully's Le Bourgeois Gentilhomme with Malgoire); sings regularly with Rafael Fruhbeck de Burgos and orchestras including Akademie Alte Musick Berlin, Rundfunk Berlin, Dresdner Philarmonie, Nacional de Espana, Sinfonica de Mexico, RAI Torino, Barroca di Venezia, Bergen Philharmonie; future engagements include the Evangelist in Matthaus-Passion with Fruhbeck de Burgos, Jephtha for Collegium Gent, Berlioz Requiem in Dresden, Los Angeles Philharmonic Opening Gala at Walt Disney Concert Hall and Esa-Pekka Salonen, Britten's War Requiem with Lorin Maazel, Sartorio's Orfeo with Alberto Zedda; lieder recitals with Graham Johnson and Orfeo with William Christie and Les Arts Florissants. *Recordings:* Rossini's Turco in Italia (Kicco Classics), Handel's Ode to St Cecilia and Carmina Burana (Sello RTVE), Beethoven's Fidelio and Cavalli's Orione, Cavalli's Apollo e Dafne. *Address:* Musiespaña, Humberto Orán. C/José Marañón 10, 4 Izda., 28010 Madrid, Spain (home). *Telephone:* (91) 591-3290 (home). *Fax:* (91) 591-3291 (home). *E-mail:* horan@musiespana.com (home). *Website:* www.agustinprunell.com (home).

PRUSLIN, Stephen Lawrence, BA, MFA; pianist and writer on music; b. 16 April 1940, Brooklyn, NY, USA. *Education:* Brandeis Univ., Princeton Univ., studied piano with Eduard Steuermann. *Career:* Taught at Princeton until 1964, then moved to London; Recital debut as pianist at Purcell Room, South Bank, 1970; Concert appearances with BBC Symphony and Royal Philharmonic; Recital accompanist to Bethany Beardslee, Elisabeth Söderström and Jan DeGaetani; Appearances with London Sinfonietta and the Fires of London (Co-founder), 1970–87; Repertoire has included works by Elliott Carter, Maxwell Davies (premiere of Piano Sonata), late Beethoven, Bach and John Bull; Collaborated with Davies on music for Ken Russell's film The Devils and has written other film and theatre music, including Derek Jarman's The Tempest; Articles on contemporary music, translation of Schoenberg's Pierrot Lunaire and librettos for Birtwistle's Monodrama, 1967, and Punch and Judy, 1968; Libretto for Craig's Progress by Martin Butler. *Recordings include:* albums as solo and ensemble pianist. *Publications include:* Peter Maxwell Davies: Studies from Two Decades (editor), London, 1979. *Telephone:* (20) 8948-7404. *E-mail:* stephanos@waitrose.com.

PRYCE-JONES, John, ARCO; British conductor; b. 1946, Wales. *Education:* studied in Penarth and Worcester, Corpus Christi College, Cambridge. *Career:* Asst Chorus Master and Conductor at Welsh National Opera, 1970–; freelance conductor in the UK and abroad until 1978; Chorus Master and Conductor with Opera North, 1978–; Head of Music, Scottish Opera, 1987; debut with ENO in The Mikado; Music Director of the New D'Oyly Carte Opera, 1990–92; first US visit of the company with The Mikado and The Pirates of Penzance; Artistic Director of the Halifax Choral Society; has conducted the Oslo Philharmonic, the Bergen Symphony and the Norwegian Broadcasting Orchestra; debut with Icelandic Opera, 1991, with Rigoletto; Principal Conductor and Musical Director, with Northern Ballet Theatre, 1992; Rigoletto, with Opera North, 1992; La Bohème with WNO 1993; conducted CBSO, BBC National Orchestra of Wales. *Recordings:* Pirates of Penzance; Mikado; Iolanthe; Gondoliers. *Honours:* Hon. MA. *Telephone:* (1422) 825594; (7768) 352399 (mobile). *E-mail:* jpj1@uwclub.net.

PRYOR, Gwenneth, DipMus, ARCM; Australian pianist; b. 7 April 1941, Sydney, NSW; m. Roger Stone 1972, one s. one d. *Education:* New South Wales Conservatorium of Music, Royal College of Music. *Career:* debut at Wigmore Hall, London; recitals and concerts in major cities in UK, Europe, North and South America and Australia; many records and radio broadcasts, both solo and chamber music; teacher, Morley College; mem. Incorporated Society of Musicians, Royal Society of Musicians. *Recordings:* Moussorgsky's Pictures at an Exhibition; Schumann's Carnaval and Papillons; Gershwin's Rhapsody in Blue and Concerto; with clarinettist Gervase de Peyer; Malcolm Williamson Concertos. *Honours:* Prize for Most Outstanding Student, New South Wales Conservatorium, 1960; 1st Prize, Australia House, 1963; Gold Medal, Royal College of Music, 1963. *E-mail:* gwenneth@gwennethpryor.co.uk. *Website:* www.gwennethpryor.co.uk.

PRZYTOCKI, Paweł; Polish conductor; *General Manager and Artistic Director, Karol Szymanowski Philharmonic Orchestra, Krakow*; b. 13 Sept. 1958, Krośnie. *Education:* Acad. of Music, Krakow under Jerzy Katlewicz, Bachakademie Stuttgart (Germany) with Helmuth Rilling. *Career:* worked with Krakow Philharmonic 1983–87, and with Grand Opera Theatre, Łódź 1987–; Conductor and Artistic Man., Baltic Philharmonic Orchestra, Gdańsk 1988–91; Music Dir Artur Rubinstein Philharmonic Orchestra, Łódź 1995–97; Conductor, Polish Nat. Opera, Warsaw 2005–; Gen. Man. and Artistic Dir Karol Szymanowski Philharmonic Orchestra, Krakow 2009–; regular Guest Conductor with most symphonic orchestras in Poland and with symphonic and chamber orchestras abroad, including Budapest Concert Orchestra, Orquesta Sinfónica de Xalapa, Real Filharmonia de Galicia, Capella Istropolitana in Bratislava, Neue Philharmonie Westfalen, Philharmonisches Staatsorchester Halle, Bilkent Symphony Orchestra in Ankara, Janáček Philharmonic Orchestra in Ostrava; tours and festivals including Athens Festival 1987, Musikfest Stuttgart 1988, Flanders Festival 1989, La Chaise-Dieu Festival 1996, Kissinger Sommer 1998, Bratislava Music Festival 1999, Augsburger Mozartsommer 2000, Prague Spring 2001, Vratislavia Cantans 2005; has performed at venues including Musikverein Vienna, Berlin Konzerthaus, Brussels Palais des Beaux Arts, Hamburg Musikhalle and Bonn Beethovenhalle. *Address:* Karol Szymanowski Philharmonic, ul. Zwierzyniecka 1, 31–103 Krakow, Poland (office). *Telephone:* (12) 6198726 (office). *Fax:* (12) 4224312 (office). *E-mail:* fk@filharmonia.krakow.pl (office). *Website:* www.filharmonia.krakow.pl (office).

PTASZYŃSKA, Marta, MA; Polish composer, percussionist and academic; *Professor of Composition, University of Chicago*; b. 29 July 1943, Warsaw; m. Andrew Rafalski 1974; one d. *Education:* Acad. of Music, Warsaw, Acad. of Music, Poznań, Centre Bourdan, ORTF, Cleveland Inst. of Music, studied with Nadia Boulanger and Olivier Messiaen in Paris, Tadeusz Paciorkiewicz and Witold Lutoslawski in Warsaw. *Career:* performances at int. festivals, including ISCM World Music Days, and int. conventions; radio and TV broadcasts in Poland and USA; teacher of composition and percussion, Warsaw Higher School of Music; Prof. of Composition at various univs in USA including Indiana Univ., Bloomington, Northwestern Univ., Cincinnati Coll. Conservatory, Univ. of California, Berkeley and Santa Barbara; Prof. of Composition, Univ. of Chicago 1998–, Helen and Frank Sulzberger Professorship in Composition 2005; comms from American and European orchestras, chamber groups and major insts including Chicago Symphony Orchestra, Cincinnati Symphony Orchestra, Polish Chamber Orchestra, Sinfonia Varsovia, Polish TV, BBC, Nat. Opera in Warsaw, and comms for musicians including Yehudi Menuhin, Ewa Podles, Keiko Abe, Evelyn Glennie. *Compositions:* Spectri Sonori for orchestra 1973, Siderals for 10 percussionists 1974, Un Grand Sommeil Noir 1977, Dream Lands, Magic Spaces 1978, Die Sonette an Orpheus 1981, Winter's Tale (Int. Rostrum of Composers at UNESCO Award 1985) 1984, Marimba Concerto 1985, Moon Flowers 1986, Oscar of Alva (opera on G. G. Byron's poem) (Polish Radio and TV Award) 1972, revised 1986, Songs of Despair and Loneliness 1988–89, Saxophone Concerto 1988, Poetic Impressions 1991, Holocaust Memorial Cantata 1992, Spider Walk 1993, Mister Marimba (opera for children) 1993–96, Liquid Light for mezzo-soprano, piano and percussion 1995, Concerto Grosso 1996, Letter to the Sun 1998, Inverted Mountain for orchestra 2001, Mosaics for string quartet 2002, The Drum of Orfeo for percussion and orchestra 2003, Pianophonia 2004, Elegia in Memoriam John Paul II for viola solo 2005, Magic Doremic (children's opera) 2006–07, The Lovers of the Valldemosa Monastery (opera on Chopin in Majorca commissioned for Chopin Bicentennial) 2008–10, Of Time and Space, concerto for percussion solo, electronics and orchestra 2009, Red Rays for flute and piano 2011, Blue Line for marimba solo 2011. *Radio:* many archive recordings on Polish Radio. *Recordings:* Space Model 1975, Epigrams 1977, Un Grand Sommeil Noir 1979, La Novella D'Inverno 1985, Concerto for Marimba 1985, Moon Flowers (recorded at BBC) 1986, Graffito 1988, Songs of Despair and Loneliness 1989, Poetic Impressions 1991, Holocaust Memorial Cantata 1992, Mister Marimba (opera) 1996, Mancala 1996, Touracou 1996, Spider Walk 1993, Ajikan, Variations for flute, Candenza, Concerto for flute, harp orchestra 2008. *Publications:* contrib. to Cum Notis Variorum, Polish music magazine Ruch Muzyczny, Polish Daily News in New York. *Honours:* Officer's Cross of Repub. of Poland 1995; Alfred Jurzykowski Music Award, New York 1997, Polish Govt Award 2000, ASCAP Awards, Benjamin Danks Award, American Acad. of Arts and Letters 2006, Fromm Music Foundation Award 2006, John Simon Guggenheim Award 2009, Special Award, Union of Polish Composers 2011. *Current Management:* c/o Union of Polish Composers, Rynek Starego Misat 27, 00-272 Warsaw, Poland. *Address:* University of Chicago, Department of Music, 1010 E 59th Street, Chicago, IL 60637 (office); Polish Music Publications, PWM, AL. Krasinskiego 11A, 31-111 Kraków, Poland. *Telephone:* (773) 702-8663 (office). *Fax:* (773) 753-0558 (office). *E-mail:* mptaszyn@uchicago.edu (office). *Website:* www.music.uchicago.edu (office); www.pwm.com.pl/ptaszynska (office); www .martaptaszynska.com.

PUDDY, Keith, FRAM; British academic, clarinettist and researcher; b. 27 Feb. 1935, Wedmore, England; m. Marilyn Johnston 1970; one s. *Education:* Royal Acad. of Music, London. *Career:* Principal Clarinet, Hallé Orchestra under Barbirolli aged 23; returned to London for solo and chamber music; fmr mem., The Gabrieli Ensemble, The Music Group of London, The New London Wind Ensemble; mem., The London Wind Trio and London Music Phoenix; Principal Clarinet and wind adviser on period instruments, New Queen's Hall Orchestra, London; performs and records on both modern and period instruments; Prof., Royal Acad. of Music and Trinity Coll. of Music, London; mem., London Wind Trio and New South Wales Queen's Hall Orchestra; freelance clarinettist, playing solo and chamber and also performing on early period instruments. *Recordings:* Brahms Sonatas, Brahms Quintet, Mozart Concerto, Mozart Quintet, Beethoven Septet, numerous solo period recordings. *Honours:* Hon. FTCL 1970, Leverhulme Trust Fellowships to study and research clarinets 1983, 1988.

PUGH, William; singer (tenor); b. 1 July 1949, Scotland. *Education:* Univ. of Oxford, Univ. of St Andrews, London Opera Centre, studied with Eduardo Asquez. *Career:* appearances in opera throughout Germany from 1981; Hildesheim 1981–84, Oberhausen 1984–86, Oldenburg 1986–91, Saarbrücken 1991–94 (as Werther, Mozart's Titus, Eisenstein, Danilo and Libenskof in the German premiere of Il Viaggio a Reims by Rossini); subsequently as guest artist in Mannheim 1994, Schaum der Tage (Denisov); 1995, Il Viaggio a

Reims; 1998–2000, the Painter in Lulu (Berg); Essen 2000, Faust (Gounod); Bielefeld 1993–94, Faust (Spohr) and the German premiere of The Duenna by Gerhard; other roles have included Belmonte, Ferrando, Don Ottavio, Almaviva, Hoffmann, Don José, Alfredo, the Duke of Mantua, Edgardo and Rodolfo.

PUHLMANN, Albrecht; German opera house director; *Director, Staatsoper Stuttgart;* b. 1955, Bad Segeberg; m.; two c. *Career:* Dir Basel Opera 1996–2001; Intendant, Staatsoper Hannover 2001–06, producing controversial avant-garde productions; Dir Staatsoper Stuttgart 2006–. *Address:* Staatstheater Stuttgart, Oberer Schlossgarten 6, 70173 Stuttgart, Germany (office). *Telephone:* (711) 20320 (office). *Website:* www.staatstheater.stuttgart.de (office).

PULEIO, Jacqueline; Panamanian pianist; b. 31 March 1961, Panamá; d. of Luis Puleio and Griselda Cervera; m. Pierre Deschamps 1980; three d. *Education:* Coll. Privado de Maria Inmaculada and Conservatoire Européen de Musique, Paris. *Career:* first piano recital aged ten; debut as soloist with Nat. Symphonic Orchestra at Nat. Theatre, Panamá 1975; Paris debut as Soloist with UNESCO Philharmonic Orchestra 1977; has given recitals at the Festival de Musique de Sceaux, Paris, with the Paillard Chamber Orchestra; other concerts and recitals (with Pierre Deschamps) include appearances in Paris, Santiago, Viña del Mar, Chile, Panama, Quito, Lima, London. *Recordings:* four CDs with Pierre Deschamps. *Honours:* Hon. Cultural Attaché, Embassy in Paris 1990; Diploma of Excellence, Conservatoire Européen de Musique, Paris 1979. *Address:* 35 rue Prosper Dufour, 78370 Plaisir les Gâtines, France. *Telephone:* 1-30-54-06-97. *Fax:* 1-34-81-23-57.

PULIEV, Michael; Bulgarian singer (bass-baritone); b. 27 March 1958, Sofia. *Education:* studied in Sofia with Boris Christoff. *Career:* sang at the Nat. Opera, Sofia 1984–86, then gave concerts in Bulgaria, People's Republic of China, Republic of Korea, Germany and Switzerland; sang at Stadttheater Bern 1986–87, Liège, as Mars in Orphée aux Enfers, Frère Laurent in Roméo et Juliette and roles in Mascagni's Nerone, Die Zauberflöte, Le nozze di Figaro, La Traviata and Andrea Chénier. *Honours:* winner Bulgarian Young Singers Competitions, prizewinner Maria Callas Competition, Athens 1984, Geneva Int. 1987.

PURCELL, Kevin John, BA, MMus, PhD, GradDipMus, GradDipEd; Australian conductor and composer; *Head, Conservatorium of Music, University of Tasmania;* b. 9 Sept. 1959, Melbourne, Vic.; s. of Lt Col Kevin Thomas Purcell and Marie Berchmans Purcell; m. Janine Hanrahan; one s. one d. *Education:* Latrobe Univ., Univ. of Melbourne, Univ. of Sydney, Moscow Conservatory, Russia, Janáček Acad., Brno, Czech Repub. *Career:* moved to UK 1994; worked for Cameron Mackintosh in London, roles including Musical Dir of Cats and Andrew Lloyd Webber's 50th Birthday concert 1996–98; moved to USA 1998; Prin. Conductor Cen. Ohio Symphony Orchestra 1999–2000; returned to Australia 2001; Dir of Music and Performing Arts, Central Queensland Univ. 2007–08; Head, Conservatorium of Music, Univ. of Tasmania 2008–; Composer-in-Residence Banff Centre for the Arts, Canada 1994, 1996; Composer, Nat. Orchestral Composers' School, Australian Broadcasting Corporation 1992, 1995; orchestras conducted include Dinu Lippati Philharmonic, Silesian State Orchestra, Hradec Krlov Filharmonie, Beethoven Chamber Orchestra, Georgian State Television and Radio Orchestra, L'Ensemble Intercontemporain Paris, Melbourne Symphony Orchestra, Queensland Orchestra, Tasmanian Symphony Orchestra, New Sydney Sinfonia; Artistic Dir Broadway to Australia 2009–; Exec. Producer Australian Shakespeare Festival 2010–; mem. Int. Jury, Prague Quadrennial of Performance Design and Space, Czech Repub. 2011. *Compositions include:* for orchestra: The Enchanter of Cyrmddin 1992, Murder in the Staromestsky Orloj 1995, Danger under the Moon 2001, The Witchlight 2003, Symphony No. 1 2007, La cathédrale dans le brouillard 2007, Valentine Lover's Concerto for alto saxophone 2009; for chamber orchestra: Three Brass Monkeys 1989, An Umbrella for Inclement Weather 1990, Kite Songs for a Crescent Moon 1991, Violin Sonata The Silent Well 2007, Night Piece (Alternative Version) 2008; solo works: The Breath of Angels for guitar 1994, Spells for flute 2007; musicals: Atlantis 2000, Rebecca – The Musical 2004; opera: The Mapmaker's Opera 2009. *Publications:* Reading and Writing Rock (co-author) 1992, Rock Essentials (co-author) 1995. *Honours:* Bellhouse Conducting Prize 1991, Willen van Otterloo Conducting Scholarship 1991, Sir Charles Mackerras Conductor's Award 1995, Tait Memorial Trust Conductor's Award 1996. *Address:* University of Tasmania Conservatorium of Music, 5–7 Sandy Bay Road, Hobart, Tasmania 7000, Australia (office). *Telephone:* (3) 6226-7373 (office). *Fax:* (3) 6226-7333 (office). *E-mail:* kevin.purcell@utas.edu.au (office); info@kevinpurcell.com.au (office). *Website:* fcms.its.utas.edu.au/arts/music (office); www.kevinpurcell.com.au.

PURKISS, Anthony John, GGSM (Lond.), FLCM, ARCM, ATCL, Dip. Adv. Studies (GSM); British pianist, composer and teacher; b. 13 Nov. 1943, Brighton, Sussex, England; s. of Sidney Charles Purkiss and Phyllis Ellen Purkiss (née Carter). *Education:* Brighton, Hove & Sussex Grammar School, Guildhall School of Music and Drama, London, studied piano with James Gibb (also Geraldine Peppin and Mary Peppin) and composition with Edmund Rubbra. *Career:* fmrly taught at Haywards Heath Grammar School, East Sussex Music Centre, Lewes, Trinity School of John Whitgift, Croydon, Steyning Grammar School, The Angmering School, Chichester Coll. of Arts, Science and Tech., Guildhall School of Music and Drama; fmr Artistic Dir, Brighton Coll. Concerts, Programme Advisor, Brighton and Hove Philharmonic Soc.;

currently teaches privately (piano and composition) and represents several concert artists. *Honours:* Wainwright Composition Scholarship, Composition Prize, Guildhall School of Music and Drama, Composers' Prize, Royal Amateur Orchestral Soc. *Address:* 35 Fonthill Road, Hove, East Sussex, BN3 6HB, England. *Telephone:* (1273) 774730. *E-mail:* tonypurkiss@talktalk.net.

PURVES, Christopher; British singer (baritone); b. 1960, England. *Education:* choral scholar King's Coll., Cambridge. *Career:* appearances with ENO, WNO and Opera Northern Ireland as Mozart's Figaro, Leporello, Masetto, the Speaker and Papageno; other roles include Don Pasquale, the Sacristan in Tosca, Dandini in La Cenerentola, Janáček's Forester and Melibeo in La Fedeltà Premiata (Garsington 1995); Melot in Tristan and Isolde for Scottish Opera 1998; concerts with such conductors as Colin Davis, Pesek, Rattle, Hickox, Christophers and Herreweghe. *Recordings include:* Israel in Egypt (with Gardiner), Purcell and Charpentier albums, Written on Skin (Gramophone Award for Best Contemporary Recording 2014) 2013. *Honours:* BBC Music Magazine Premiere Award 2014 (for George Benjamin: Written on Skin 2012). *Current Management:* c/o Sue Nicholls, Hazard Chase, 25 City Road, Cambridge, CB1 1DP, England. *Telephone:* (1223) 312400. *Fax:* (1223) 460827. *E-mail:* sue.nicholls@hazardchase.co.uk. *Website:* www.hazardchase.co.uk.

PURVS, Arvids; Latvian conductor, composer and music critic; b. 22 March 1926, Mengele; m Marija Falkenburgs 1952; one d. *Education:* violin, conducting and composition in private lessons; attended music seminars at Univs of Waterloo and Halifax, Canada. *Career:* Music Dir, St Andrew's Latvian Lutheran Church Choir, Toronto, Canada 1958–2009; Conductor, Women's Choir, Zile, Toronto 1974–2007; conductor at over 50 Latvian song festivals in the USA, Canada, Australia and Europe, leading orchestras and massed choirs of up to 4,000 voices, as in the Festival at the Royal Albert Hall, London 1977 and in the XXth National Song Festival, Riga, Latvia 1990; mem. Toronto Latvian Concert Assocn (pres. 1967–), Latvian Song Festival Assocn in Canada (chair. 1977–). *Compositions include:* Cantata of Psalms for soloists, chorus, orchestra and organ 1956, Calling of the Bells for chorus and orchestra 1972, Toward the Light for chorus, speaker, orchestra and organ 1975, Time cantata for chorus, string orchestra, timpani and organ 1980, Thus Said the Lord for chorus, orchestra and organ 1990. *Publications:* Pa skanosu vasaru (My Musical Summers) 2000. *Honours:* Arts Foundation of the Asscn of Latvians in the Free World Music Award 1977, 2001, Order of Three Stars, Latvian Republic 1997. *Address:* 65 Rivercove Drive, Etobicoke, ON M9B 4Y8, Canada (home). *Telephone:* (416) 621-1751 (home). *Fax:* (416) 621-8385 (home).

PUSAR, Ana; singer (soprano); b. 1954, Celje, Yugoslavia. *Education:* studied in Celje, School of Music, Ljubljana. *Career:* sang in Ljubljana from 1975 as Rosina, Manon, Tatiana, Dido, Nedda, Micaela, Desdemona and Poppea; Berlin Komische Oper 1979–85; appearances at the State Operas of Berlin and Dresden; guest appearances in Japan, Prague, Moscow, Leningrad, Edinburgh, Venice and Madrid; roles have included Mozart's Fiordiligi and Countess, Agathe, Ariadne, Elsa, Madama Butterfly and Ellen Orford; sang the Marschallin at reopening of Dresden Semper Oper 1985, Vienna Staatsoper from 1986 as Donna Anna, Arabella, Agathe and the Marschallin, Munich Staatsoper in Daphne, as the Countess in Figaro and Capriccio and Donna Anna; has also sung in Barcelona, Venice, Hamburg, Montréal, Geneva, Stuttgart, Lisbon, Toulouse, Graz and Cologne; season 1992 with Sieglinde in Die Walküre at Bonn; concert appearances in most major European centres; has worked with such conductors as Peter Schneider, Gerd Albrecht, John Pritchard, Nikolaus Harnoncourt and Lorin Maazel; from 1992 sang Tatiana at Venice 1993, Katya Kabanova at Zürich 1994 and Graz 1994 in Stiffelio, as Lina; Gertrud at Palermo 1995; sang Mozart's Countess at Ljubljana 2000. *Recordings include:* Der Rosenkavalier, Semper Opera; Bontempi Requiem; Dvořák Stabat Mater; Così fan tutte; Hugo Wolf, Lieder, 1990; Rachmaninov Lieder and Romances; Orfeo, 1994. *Honours:* winner Toti dal Monte Competition and Mario del Monaco Competition 1978, National Award of Slovenia 1979. *Current Management:* Music International, 13 Ardilaun Road, London, N5 2QR, England.

PUSHEE, Graham; Australian singer (countertenor); b. 1954, Sydney. *Education:* studied in London with Paul Esswood, Schola Cantorum Basiliensis, Basel, Switzerland. *Career:* debut, as Oberon in A Midsummer Night's Dream, Sydney 1973; concerts in Australia 1973–77; has sung Orlando, Poro, Scipione, Belshazzar and Admeto at Handel Festivals, as Giulio Cesare, Paris Opéra 1987, as Ruggiero in Alcina, Australian Opera, Sydney Opera North, as Andronico in Handel's Tamerlano, as Oberon, Staatsoper Berlin, as Endimione in Cavalli's La Calisto; further operatic roles include Orindo in L'Orontea, Monteverdi and Stradella, Handel's Giulio Cesare, Rinaldo, Semele, in La Calisto, in Tatiana by Azio Corghi, Handel's Tamerlano, in Dido and Aeneas, in Orpheus, Der Geduldige Sokrates, L'Orontea,. *Recordings include:* La Calisto, Handel Arias, Vivaldi's Solo Sacred Works. *Honours:* Churchill Fellowship Award 1977.

PUSZ, Ryszard; percussionist and teacher; b. 5 Feb. 1948, Frille, Germany; m.; one s. three d. *Education:* Elder Conservatorium with Richard Smith, Indiana Univ. with George Gaber. *Career:* music teacher 1970–73; worked in Education Dept of South Australia Music Branch 1974–86; Head of Percussion School of Music, ACTAFE 1986–; commissioned and premiered over 50 works for percussion, and performed Australian premieres of numerous works of prominent overseas composers; arranged many pieces for percussion solo and ensemble; orchestral percussionist, Australian Youth Orchestra 1964–70, Adelaide Symphony Orchestra, Adelaide Chamber Orchestra 1964–90; performed as soloist with many orchestras and ensembles, including Hungarian Youth Orchestra, Adelaide Symphony Orchestra, Prague Conservatory Percussion Ensemble, Stuttgart Musikhochschule Percussion Ensemble, Corpus Christi Percussion Ensemble (USA), and at numerous festivals, including Int. Percussion Festival, Bydgoszcz (Poland), Adelaide Festival of Arts, Banff Festival (Canada), Int. Barossa Music Festival, Perkusja 2001, Warsaw (Poland), as well as at music academies and concert halls throughout Europe, USA, the Far East and Australia; has conducted various percussion ensembles and other performing groups; discovered and developed a new, one-handed tremolo technique, applied in existing and new commissioned pieces; has worked with filmmakers, theatre directors and visual artists to produce performance projects for educational purposes and other productions; Music Dir, COME OUT '93 Festival; pioneered the teaching of instrumental music by distance mode in Australia; founder, The Percussion Soc. of Australia, Adelaide Percussions, Sonitus, Drumworks and Percusson (a double father-son percussion quartet). *Compositions include:* Baltika for steel band, Drumworks Quintet for 75 players, Keep on Drummin!, Three Camps Thrice, ForE (multiple perscussion solo), Tsunami (Taiko ensemble). *Publications:* Percussion: A Comprehensive Approach, Time and Again: Essentials of Percussion Practice. *Honours:* Sounds Australian Award for Most Significant Contribution by a South Australian to the Presentation of Australian Music, Australia Council Fellowship to present Australian compositions overseas. *Address:* School of Music, Adelaide Institute of TAFE, 279 Flinders Street, Adelaide, SA 5000, Australia. *E-mail:* rpusz@camtech.net.au.

PUTILIN, Nikolai Georgiyevich; Russian singer (baritone); b. 1954, Saratov region. *Education:* Krasnoyarsk Inst. of Arts, lessons with Nikola Nikolov in Bulgaria. *Career:* started career as singer of Variety Theatre; soloist, Syktyvkar Musical Theatre, Komi Repub. 1983–85; soloist, Musa Dzhalil Academic Theatre of Opera and Ballet (Kazan) 1985–92; soloist, Kirov (Mariinsky) Theatre, St Petersburg 1992–; has toured with Mariinsky Opera Company and independently to Germany, France, Spain, Italy, the Netherlands, Belgium, Finland, Great Britain, Japan, USA, Hungary, Czech Republic, Bulgaria, Korea, Israel and Luxemburg; has performed at Metropolitan Opera, New York, Chicago Lyric Opera, Royal Opera House and Covent Garden, London, La Scala, Milan, Accademia Santa Cecilia, Rome; has performed at Salzburg Festival. *Repertoire includes:* over 40 leading roles toured Metropolitan Opera, La Scala, Teatro Comunale di Firenze, Covent Garden, Bolshoi Theatre and others. *Honours:* winner, International Vocalists' Competition, Sofia 1988, Int. Chaliapin Competition 1989, State Prize of Russia, People's Artist of Tatarstan, People's Artist of Russia. *Address:* Mariinsky Theatre, 190000 St Petersburg, 1 Theatre Square, Russia (office). *Telephone:* (812) 326-41-41 (office). *Website:* www.mariinsky.ru/en (office).

PUTKONEN, Marko; Finnish singer (bass); b. 1947. *Education:* Sibelius Academy, Helsinki. *Career:* at the Finnish National Opera has sung Mozart's Bartolo, Nicolai's Falstaff, in Katerina Izmailova, Sallinen's Red Line and the 1990 premiere of Rautavaara's Vincent (as Gauguin); Guested at Los Angeles, 1992, in the premiere of Kullervo by Sallinen; further guest appearances at the Savonlinna Festival (Rocco, 1992), Zürich and Geneva.

PUTNAM, Ashley; American singer (soprano); b. 10 Aug. 1952, New York. *Education:* Univ. of Michigan with Elizabeth Mosher and Willis Patterson. *Career:* Norfolk Opera, Virginia from 1976 as Donizetti's Lucia and the title role in the US premiere of Musgrave's Mary Queen of Scots; NYC Opera debut 1978, as Violetta; later sang Bellini's Elvira, Verdi's Giselda, Thomas' Ophelia and Donizetti's Maria Stuarda; European debut 1978 as Musetta at Glyndebourne; returned for Arabella 1984; Lucia with Scottish Opera; Mozart's Fiordiligi at Venice and for BBC television, Sifare in Mitridate at Aix, Donna Anna in Brussels and Countess Almaviva in Cologne; Covent Garden debut 1986, as Janáček's Jenůfa; appearances at Santa Fe in Thomson's The Mother of Us All and in the title role of Die Liebe der Danaë 1985; Metropolitan Opera debut 1990, as Donna Elvira; Florence 1990, as Katya Kabanova; sang Ellen Orford in Peter Grimes at the Geneva Opera and Vitellia in La Clemenza di Tito at the 1991 Glyndebourne Festival; season 1991–92 as Fusako in the US premiere of Henze's Das Verratere Meer, at San Francisco, and the Marshallin at Santa Fe; Eva in Die Meistersinger at Cleveland 1995; sang St Teresa I in Thomson's Four Saints in Three Acts, Houston and Edinburgh 1996; concert engagements with the Los Angeles Philharmonic, New York Philharmonic and Concertgebouw Orchestras; regular concerts at Carnegie Hall. *Recordings:* The Mother of Us All, Mary Queen of Scots, Musetta in La Bohème.

PUTS, Kevin, MMus; American composer, pianist and academic; b. 1972, St Louis, Mo. *Education:* Eastman School of Music, Yale Univ. *Career:* works commissioned and performed throughout North America, Europe and the Far East; commissions from New York Philharmonic, Nat. Symphony Orchestra, Tonhalle Orchester Zurich, symphony orchestras of Baltimore, Cincinnati, Detroit, Atlanta, Colorado, Houston, Forth Worth, Utah, St Louis, Boston Pops, Minnesota Orchestra and chamber ensembles including Mirò Quartet, Eroica Trio, eighth blackbird, Pittsburgh New Music Ensemble and Chamber Music Soc. of Lincoln Center; Concerto for Everyone premiered at Carnegie Hall 1999; premieres performed by artists including Evelyn Glennie, Yo-Yo Ma, Bill Jackson and Makoto Nakura; Composer-in-Residence, Young Concert

Artists and California Symphony 1996, Forth Worth Symphony and Bravo! Vail Valley Music Festival 2007; Assoc. Prof. of Composition, Univ. of Texas at Austin 1999–2005; mem. Composition Faculty, Peabody Inst., Johns Hopkins Univ., Baltimore 2006–. *Compositions:* numerous orchestral, chamber and ensemble works including four symphonies and several concertos; works for solo instruments with and without orchestra; other: Silent Night (opera) (Pulitzer Prize for Music 2012). *Recordings:* works included on CDs including Violinguistics: American Voices, Alternating Current 2010, Playing the Edge: Music for Violin and Percussion 2010, River of Light 2011, Sound the Bells! 2011, American Portraits 2011. *Honours:* grants and awards from ASCAP, BMI, Charles Ives Scholarship, Barlow Int. Prize for Orchestral Music 1999, Guggenheim Fellowship, Rome Prize 2001–02, American Acad. of Arts and Letters Benjamin H. Danks Award for Excellence in Orchestral Composition 2003. *Address:* Peabody Conservatory, 1 East Mount Vernon Place, Baltimore, MD 21202, USA (office). *Website:* www.peabody.jhu.edu/conservatory (office); www.kevinputs.com.

PÜTZ, Ruth-Margret; German singer (soprano); b. 26 Feb. 1932, Krefeld; m. 1966; two d. *Education:* singing studies in Cologne and Hanover. *Career:* mem. Württemberg State Opera, Stuttgart 1959–, Vienna State Opera 1960–64, Hamburg Opera 1963–; guest appearances in Milan and Rome, Italy, London, Paris, Madrid, Lisbon, Moscow and Leningrad (now St Petersburg), USSR (now Russian Fed.), Stockholm, Helsinki and Buenos Aires; has performed at many festivals including Bayreuth, Salzburg, Austria and Edinburgh, UK; numerous recordings for Columbus, Electrola, CBS and Decca. *Honours:* Kammersängerin 1962; Soviet Culture Prize. *Address:* Herderstr. 5, 71229 Leonberg, Germany.

PUUMALA, Veli-Matti, MMus; Finnish composer; b. 18 July 1965, Kaustinen; m. Tiina Käkelä-Puumala; two c. *Education:* Sibelius Acad., Helsinki, Accad. Musicale Chigiana summer course with Franco Donatoni, Siena, Italy. *Career:* currently Prof. of Composition, Sibelius Acad. *Compositions include:* Scroscio 1989, Verso 1991, Ghirlande 1992, Tutta via 1993, String Quartet 1994, Chant Chains 1995, Chains of Camenae 1996, Soira 1996, Chainsprings 1997, Umstrichen vom Schreienden 1997–98, Taon concerto for double bass 1998–2000, Hommages Fugitives 2000–01, Seeds of Time piano concerto 2004, Anna Liisa, opera in three acts 2008, Mure 2008, Memorial Fragment 2008, Mure 2008, Rope 2012, Tear 2013, Rime 2013. *Honours:* Prix Italia 2001, Teosto Prize 2005, Erik Bergman Prize 2011. *Current Management:* c/o Fennica Gehrman, PO Box 158, 00121 Helsinki, Finland. *E-mail:* info@fennicagehrman.fi. *Website:* www.fennicagehrman.fi. *Address:* Sibelius Academy, PO Box 30, 00097, Uniarts, Helsinki, Finland (office). *Telephone:* (294) 47-2000 (office). *E-mail:* veli-matti.puumala@uniarts.fi (office). *Website:* www.musicfinland.fi (office); www.fennicagehrman.fi/composers/puumala-veli-matti.

PY, Gilbert; French singer (tenor); b. 9 Dec. 1933, Sete. *Career:* debut in Verviers, Belgium, 1964 as Pinkerton in Madama Butterfly; Paris Opéra from 1969, notably as Manrico, Don José, Samson, Florestan, Tannhäuser, Lohengrin and in La Damnation de Faust; Paris Opéra-Comique 1969, in the title role of Les Contes d'Hoffmann; Nice Opéra in the local premiere of Sutermeister's Raskolnikov; Toulouse 1970, in Gounod's La Reine de Saba; guest appearances in Vienna, Munich, Verona, Florence, Barcelona, New Orleans and Budapest; Turin 1973, as Lohengrin; sang at the 1987 Orange Festival as Jean in Massenet's Hérodiade; Aeneas in Les Troyens at Marseilles 1989. *Recordings include:* Carmen, La Vestale by Spontini.

PYATT, David; British horn player; *Principal Horn, London Philharmonic Orchestra*; b. 26 Sept. 1973, St Albans, Herts., England; m.; two c. *Education:* Selwyn Coll., Cambridge. *Career:* fmr Prin. Horn, Nat. Youth Orchestra and Nat. Youth Chamber Orchestra of GB; performed with London Symphony and Hallé Orchestras, English Chamber Orchestra and London Mozart Players from 1988; tours of Germany and Japan with BBC Nat. Orchestra of Wales; played Richard Strauss's Second Concerto at the BBC Proms, London 1993; repertoire ranges from Telemann, Haydn and Mozart to contemporary composers; broadcast on BBC and ind. radio and TV; season 1998–99 included debut at Salzburg Festival, concert with Deutsches Symphonie-Orchester, Berlin, and Promenade Concerts with BBC Symphony Orchestra; season 2001–02 with concerts in London and Europe, as soloist in Britten's Serenade; has performed with Columbus Symphony Orchestra, Salzburg Mozarteum Orchestra, Norrköping Symphony Orchestra, Istanbul State Symphony Orchestra, Gulbenkian Orchestra, Lisbon, Orquestra Sinfonica do Estado de São Paulo, Netherlands Radio Chamber Orchestra, BBC Nat. Orchestra of Wales, Orchestre Philharmonique de Radio France; soloist, Last Night of the Proms, Strauss No. 1 with BBC Symphony Orchestra under Leonard Slatkin 2004, Edinburgh Int. Festival Weber Concertino with Northern Sinfonia under Thomas Zehetmair 2004; Prin. Horn, London Symphony Orchestra 1998–2012; Prin. Horn, London Philharmonic Orchestra 2013–. *Recordings include:* Strauss Concerti, Britten Serenade, Mozart Concerti, Horn and Piano Works with Martin Jones, English Music with Anthony Rolfe Johnson, Peter Donohoe and Levon Chilingirian, Schubert's Auf der Strom with Michael Schade and Graham Johnson. *Honours:* BBC Young Musician of the Year Award 1987, Gramophone Magazine Young Artist of the Year 1996. *Address:* London Philharmonic Orchestra, 89 Albert Embankment, London, SE1 7TP, England (office). *Website:* www.lpo.org.uk.

PYAVKO, Vladislav Ivanovich; Russian singer (tenor); b. 4 Feb. 1941, Krasnoyarsk; s. of Nina Piavko and step-s. of Nikolai Bakhin; m. Irina

Arkhipova (died 2010); four s. two d. *Education:* State Inst. of Theatrical Art, Moscow. *Career:* studied under S. Rebrikov, Moscow, R. Pastorino, La Scala, Milan; mem. CPSU 1978–89; soloist with Bolshoi Opera 1965–89, Berliner Staatsoper 1989–96; teacher of singing and dramatic art, State Inst. of Theatrical Art 1980–89, Dean of School 1983–89; producer at Mosfilm 1980–83; Prof., Moscow State Conservatory 2000–; Pres. Int. Union of Musicians 2010–, The Arkhipova Foundation 2010–; has also sung at Teatro Colón, Buenos Aires, Teatro Comunale, Florence, Opéra Bastille, Paris, Nat. and Smetana Operas, Prague, Metropolitan, New York, Kirov, St Petersburg and in many other houses; also at many int. festivals; mem. Acad. of the Arts 1992. *Major roles include:* Hermann in Queen of Spades, Andrei in Mazeppa, Dmitry and Shuisky in Boris Godunov, Andrei and Golitsin in Khovanshchina, Radames, Otello, Manrico in Il Trovatore, Cavaradossi in Tosca, Pinkerton in Madam Butterfly, Don José in Carmen, Turiddu in Cavalleria Rusticana, Guglielmo Ratcliff, Sergei in Katerina Izmailova, Canio in Pagliacci and many other roles. *Film:* You're My Delight My Suffering… (Mosfilm) 1983. *Recordings include:* numerous recordings for leading int. labels including EMI, HMV, Philips, Chant du Monde, Columbia. *Publication:* Tenor, Vladislav Pyavko. *Honours:* Hon. Prof., Lomonosov Moscow State Univ. 2004–; Gold Medal in tenor section, Vervier Int. Competition 1969, Silver Medal, Tchaikovsky Int. Competition 1970, Gold Medal and Pietro Mascagni Silver Medal, Livorno 1984, Gold Plank of Cisternino, Italy 1993; People's Artist of USSR 1983, of Kyrgyzstan 1993, Prize of Moscow 2004 and other awards. *Address:* Bryusov, per. 2/14, stroenie 2, Apt 26, 125009 Moscow, Russia. *Telephone:* (495) 629-43-07 (home); (495) 629-60-29 (office). *Fax:* (495) 629-60-29 (office). *E-mail:* amguem@gmail.com (home).

Q

QUARRINGTON, Joel; Canadian musician (double bass); *Principal Double Bassist, London Symphony Orchestra*; b. Toronto. *Education:* Univ. of Toronto, studied with Thomas Monohan and Peter Madgett, also with Franco Petracchi and Ludwig Streicher in Italy and Austria. *Career:* Prin. Double Bassist of many ensembles, including Canadian Opera Company, Toronto Symphony Orchestra and Nat. Arts Centre Orchestra, Ottawa; Prin. Bassist, London Symphony Orchestra 2013–; solo appearances across Canada, USA, Europe and China; world premiere of John Harbison's Concerto for Bass with Toronto Symphony and conductor Hugh Wolf 2005; Visiting Artist, RAM 2014–; master-classes at Orford Arts Centre, Quebec; guest teacher, Danish and Polish Bass Socs, Beijing's China Conservatory, Australian String Acad., RAM, Double Bass Kaleidoscope, Michaelstein (Germany) and Fed. Univ. Rio Grande do Sul, Porto Alegre (Brazil); has performed with string quartets including Orford, Vermeer, Cleveland, Colorado, St Lawrence, Allegri, Artis, Leipzig and Tokyo Quartets and Pinchas Zukerman Chamber Players; three-times featured performer at biennial conventions of Int. Soc. of Bassists. *Recordings include:* solo recordings: Garden Scene: music of Korngold, Gliere, M. Weinberg, J.C. Bach and Bottesini (Juno Award for Best Classical Recording) 2010, Brothers in Brahms: music of Robert Fuchs, Schumann and Brahms 2013; Timothy Findley's The Wars (soundtrack, with Glenn Gould) 1982; Schubert's Trout Quintet with Yefim Bronfman 2008. *Honours:* Hon. RAM; Eaton Scholarship, Univ. of Toronto, winner, Geneva Int. Competition and CBC Talent Competition, Special Recognition Award for Outstanding Solo Performance, Int. Soc. of Bassists 2011. *Website:* joelquarrington.com.

QUASTHOFF, Thomas, BL; German singer (bass-baritone); *Professor, Hanns Eisler Music University*; b. 9 Nov. 1959, Hildesheim; m. Claudia Quasthoff. *Education:* Univ. of Hanover, studied with Charlotte Lehmann. *Career:* appeared regularly with world's leading orchestras under conductors including Abbado, Barenboim, Haitink, Jansons, Masur, Ozawa, Rattle, Rilling, Thielemann and Welser-Möst; debut at Oregon Bach Festival 1995; regularly appeared at New York's Carnegie Hall following recital debut in Schubert's Winterreise 1999; opera debut in role of Don Fernando (Fidelio) with Berlin Philharmonic under Sir Simon Rattle at Salzburg Easter Festival March 2003; debut at Vienna Staatsoper in role of Amfortas (Parsifal) under Donald Runnicles 2004, revived under Sir Simon Rattle 2005; fmr Artist-in-Residence, Vienna's Musikverein, Amsterdam Concertgebouw, Carnegie Hall and Lucerne Festival, and in Baden-Baden, Hamburg and at the Barbican Centre, London 2009–10; concert engagements included Haydn's Jahreszeiten and Bach's St Matthew Passion with the Berlin Philharmonic under Sir Simon Rattle, Elgar's Dream Of Gerontius with the Vienna Philharmonic, Mahler's Kindertotenlieder with Zubin Mehta, Brahms's Vier Ernste Gesäng under Simone Young as well as Mozart Arias under Lothar Zagrosek in Berlin; toured with Kammerorchester Wien-Berlin and a programme with Folksongs together with Max Raabe, Angela Winkler and Udo Samel; appeared in recital in Baden-Baden, London, Schwarzenberg, USA and on tour with lieder, duets and quartets by Schumann; concerts at Oregon Bach Festival (30th anniversary) as well as a jazz gala for opening of Salzburg Festival; Prof., Hanns Eisler Music Univ., Berlin 2004–; f. Lied competition, Berlin 2009–; retired from public performance 2012. *Recordings include:* Bach Cantatas (BBC Music Magazine Award 2006), St John Passion and Schumann Lieder (Grand Prix Gabriel Fauré, Paris), Schubert Goethe-Lieder, Fidelio under Colin Davis and Mozart Arias, Des Knaben Wunderhorn by Mahler, with Anne Sofie von Otter 2001, The Jazz Album 2007. *Publication:* The Voice: A Memoir 2008. *Honours:* Kammersänger 2009; Bundesverdienstkreutz 2004; Herbert von Karajan Music Prize 2009, Royal Philharmonic Soc. Gold Medal 2009; three Grammy Awards. *Current Management:* c/o Künstleragentur Dr Raab & Dr Böhm Gesellschaft, Plankengasse 7, 1010 Vienna, Austria. *Telephone:* (1) 512-05-01. *Fax:* (1) 512-77-43. *E-mail:* machreich@rbartists.at. *Website:* www.rbartists.at; www.thomas-quasthoff.com.

QUEFFÉLEC, Anne; French concert pianist; b. 17 Jan. 1948, Paris; d. of Henri Queffélec and Yvonne Pénau; m. Luc Dehaene 1983. *Education:* Conservatoire Nat., Paris. *Career:* since 1968 has played in tours of Europe, Japan, Israel, Africa, Canada and USA; has played with BBC Symphony, London Symphony, Royal Philharmonic, Bournemouth Symphony, Hallé, Scottish Chamber, City of Birmingham Symphony, Miami Symphony, NHK Tokyo, Tokyo Symphony orchestras, Nouvel orchestre philharmonique de Radio-France, Orchestre nat. de Radio-France, Orchestre de Strasbourg, Ensemble Intercontemporain, etc., under conductors including Zinman, Groves, Leppard, Marriner, Boulez, Semkow, Skrowaczewski, Eschenbach, Gardiner, Pritchard, Atherton, etc.; has played at numerous festivals including Strasbourg, Dijon, Besançon, La Roque d'Anthéron, La Grange de Meslay, Bordeaux, Paris, King's Lynn, Bath, Cheltenham, London Proms; judge in several int. piano competitions; master-classes in France (including Ecole normale de musique, Paris), England and Japan; Pres. Asscn des amis d'Henri Queffélec, Asscn musicale 'Ballades'. *Recordings include:* more than 30 records of music by Scarlatti, Handel, Chopin, Schubert, Fauré, Ravel (complete piano works), Debussy, Liszt, Hummel, Beethoven, Mendelssohn, Bach, Satie, complete piano works of Henri Dutilleux 1996 and Mozart and Haydn recitals. *Radio includes:* numerous appearances on BBC Radio 3, France Musique and Japanese radio. *Television includes:* numerous appearances on musical, but also literary and religious, programmes. *Honours:*

Chevalier, Légion d'honneur 1998, Officier, Ordre nat. du Mérite 2001; First Prize for Piano 1965, for Chamber Music 1966, Conservatoire Nat., Paris; First Prize, Munich Int. Piano Competition 1968, Prizewinner, Leeds Int. Piano Competition 1969, Best Classical Artist of the Year, Victoires de la Musique 1990. *Current Management:* c/o Christine Talbot-Cooper, International Artists, Stoneville Cottage, Gretton Fields, Cheltenham, Glos., GL54 5HH, England. *Telephone:* (1242) 620736 (home). *Fax:* (1242) 620736 (home). *E-mail:* talbotcooper@onetel.com. *Website:* www.ctcinternationalartists.com. *Address:* 15 avenue Corneille, 78600 Maisons-Laffitte, France (home). *Telephone:* 1-39-62-25-64 (home). *Fax:* 1-39-62-25-64 (home).

QUELER, Eve; American conductor; b. 1 Jan. 1936, New York. *Education:* Mannes Coll. of Music, New York, City Coll. of New York, piano with Isabella Vengerov, conducting with Carl Bamberger, Joseph Rosenstock, Walter Susskind and Igor Markevich. *Career:* began as pianist, asst conductor New York City Opera 1958 and 1965–70; later became a conductor; guest-conducted Philadelphia, Cleveland, Montréal Symphony, New Philharmonia, Australian Opera, Opéra de Nice, Opera de Barcelona, San Diego Opera, Edmonton Symphony, Nat. Opera of Czechoslovakia, Hungarian State, Hungarian Operahaz, Hamburg Opera, Pretoria, Hamilton, Ont., Opei Bonn and various other orchestras; Music Dir, Opera Orchestra of New York 1968–2011. *Recordings:* Puccini's Edgar, Verdi's Aroldo, Massenet's Le Cid, Boito's Nerone, Strauss' Guntram, Wagner's Tristan und Isolde, Janacek's Jenufa. *Publications:* articles in Musical America and Orpheus magazines. *Honours:* Chevalier, Ordre des Arts et des Lettres; Dr hc (Russell Sage Coll., Colby Coll.); Musician of the Month, Musical American Magazine, Martha Baird Rockefeller Fund for Music Award, Sanford Medal, Yale Univ., Nat. Endowment for the Arts Opera Honor 2010. *Current Management:* Robert Lombardo and Assoicates, 61 West 62nd Street, Suite 6F, New York, NY 10023, USA. *Telephone:* (212) 586-4453. *Fax:* (212) 581-5771. *E-mail:* robert@robertlombardo.com. *Website:* www.robertlombardo.com. *Address:* Opera Orchestra of New York, 239 West 72nd Street, Suite 2R, New York, NY 10023, USA (office). *Telephone:* (212) 799-1982 (office). *E-mail:* oony@tiac .net (office). *Website:* www.operaorchestrany.org (office); www.evequeler.com.

QUEYRAS, Jean-Guihen; Canadian/French musician (cello); b. 11 March 1967, Montréal; m.; three c. *Education:* Conservatoire de Lyon, Hochschule Freiburg, then studied with Timothy Eddy at Mannes Coll., USA. *Career:* moved to Algeria as a child then to Provence, France where he lived until he was aged 17; fmr protégé of Pierre Boulez, soloist with Boulez' Ensemble Intercontemporain 1990–2000; Co-founder and cellist, Arcanto Quartet with Tabea Zimmermann 2002–; gave world premieres of Ivan Fedele's cello concerto (Orchestre National de France, Leonard Slatkin) and Gilbert Amy's concerto (Tokyo Symphony Orchestra at Suntory Hall in Tokyo); has performed with numerous orchestras including Philharmonia, Orchestre de Paris, NHK Symphony, Tokyo Symphony, Philadelphia, Tonhalle Zürich, Leipzig Gewandhaus, Budapest Festival Orchestra, Orchestre de la Suisse-Romande and Netherlands Philharmonique, under conductors such as Franz Brüggen, Günther Herbig, Ivan Fisher, Philippe Herreweghe, Jiří Bělohlávek, Olivier Knussen and Sir Roger Norrington; regular soloist with early music ensembles such as Freiburg Baroque and Akadamie für Alte Musik Berlin; debut Carnegie Hall, New York with Concerto Köln 2004; debut BBC Proms 2008; regular appearances at Aldeburgh Festival, UK; regular chamber music partners include pianists Alexander Melnikov and Alexandre Tharaud and violinist Isabelle Faust; Co-Artistic Dir, Rencontres Musicales de Haute-Provence; Prof., Hochschule Freiburg 2002–. *Recordings include:* solo: Britten Suites for Solo Cello 1998, Schubert Arpeggione Sonata 2006, Bach Complete Cello Suites 2007, Debussy/Poulenc Sonates 2008; with Ensemble Intercontemporain: Ligeti Cello Concerto 1995, Boulez Sur Incises 2007; with Arcanto Quartet: Bartók String Quartets 2007, Brahms String Quartet 2008, Debussy/Dutilleux/Ravel String Quartets 2010, Schubert String Quintet op. 163 2012, Mozart String Quartet K421 2013; other: Beethoven/Hummel Piano Trios 2004, Dutilleux Symphonie No. 1 2004, Haydn Cellos Concertos 2004, Dvořák Cello Concerto 2005, 21st Century Cello Concertos 2009, Kodály/Kurtág/Veress Sonatas for cello and piano 2010, Vivaldi Cello Concerto 2011, Elgar Cello Concerto 2013, Berg/Schoenberg 2014, Beethoven trios 2014, Beethoven complete works for cello and piano 2014. *Honours:* Glenn Gould Protégé Prize 2002, Victoire Award for best solo instrumentalist 2008. *Website:* www.askonasholt.co.uk; www .jeanguihenqueyras.com.

QUILICO, Gino, OC; singer (baritone); b. 29 April 1955, New York, USA. *Education:* Univ. of Toronto, studied with Lina Pizzolongo and his father. *Career:* Canadian debut 1978, in a television performance of The Medium; mem., Paris Opéra from 1980, in operas by Rossini, Britten, Poulenc, Puccini, Gounod, Massenet and Gluck; British debut with Scottish Opera at the 1982 Edinburgh Festival, as Puccini's Lescaut; Covent Garden debut 1983, as Valentin in Faust; later London appearances as Puccini's Marcello, Donizetti's Belcore, Rossini's Figaro, Escamillo and Posa in Don Carlos 1989; Aix-en-Provence Festival 1985, 1986, as Monteverdi's Orfeo and Mozart's Don Giovanni; Metropolitan Opera debut 1987, as Massenet's Lescaut; Malatesta in Don Pasquale at Lyon; sang Dandini in La Cenerentola at the 1988 and 1989 Salzburg Festivals; Rome Opera 1990, as Riccardo in I Puritani; sang

Gluck's Oreste at the 1994 Vienna Festival; sang Iago at Cologne 1996; sang Escamillo at Metropolitan Opera and Munich Festival 1997; Zurga in Les Pêcheurs de Perles at Chicago and Barber of Seville in Seville 1998; season 1999–2000 as Donizetti's Enrico at Los Angeles, Massenet's Lescaut for La Scala, Iago in Montreal and Escamillo at the Munich Staatsoper. *Recordings include:* Lescaut in Manon, Dancairo in Carmen, Mercutio in Roméo et Juliette, Marcello in La Bohème, Malatesta in Don Pasquale, Salzburg Cenerentola (video) 1988. *Honours:* Grammy Award, Artist of the Year, Canadian Music Council 1988. *Telephone:* (514) 814-7789 (office). *E-mail:* s.decayette@mvconcerts.com (office). *Website:* www.ginoquilico.com.

QUILLA CROFT, Howard; British singer (baritone); b. 1966, Huddersfield. *Education:* Royal Coll. of Music, London and Nat. Opera Studio. *Career:* debut, Mozart's Count for the Opera Company 1993; appearances with Glyndebourne Touring Opera 1993–94, as Don Giovanni, A Captain in Eugene Onegin and Fiorello in Il Barbiere di Siviglia; Glyndebourne Festival 1994, in Eugene Onegin; further engagements as Escamillo in Carmen for British Youth Opera, and Fiorello for Opera Northern Ireland. *Honours:* Cuthbert Smith and Agnes Nicholls Trophy, Kirkless Young Musician of the Year. *Current Management:* Robert Gilder & Company, 91 Great Russell Street, London, WC1B 3PS, England. *Telephone:* (20) 7580-7758. *Fax:* (20) 7580-7739. *E-mail:* rgilder@robert-gilder.com. *Website:* www.robert-gilder.com.

QUING, Miao; Chinese singer (mezzo-soprano); b. 1955. *Education:* Peking Conservatory. *Career:* sang Carmen under the direction of Jacqueline Brumaire at Peking 1982; studied further at the Nancy Conservatoire and sang Butterfly from 1986 at Basle, Berlin, Lausanne, Toulon and Covent Garden; guested with the Peking Opera at Savonlinna as Carmen, sang Donna Elvira at Brunswick 1991, in Ariadne and Zauberflöte at the Bonn Opera; many concert engagements.

QUINN, Andrea, BA, ARAM; British conductor and music director; b. 22 Dec. 1964; m. Roderick Champ 1991; one s. two d. *Education:* Royal Acad. of Music, London, Nottingham Univ.; Bartók Int. Seminar, Hungary. *Career:* Music Dir London Philharmonic Youth Orchestra 1994–97, Royal Ballet 1998–2001; Music Dir New York City Ballet 2001–06; Music Dir Norrlands Opera and Symphony Orchestra, Umea, Sweden 2005–09; has conducted London Symphony Orchestra, London Philharmonic, Philharmonia, Royal Philharmonic, Hallé, Scottish Chamber, Northern Sinfonia, London Mozart Players and other leading orchestras in UK, Australia, Hong Kong, Sweden, Norway, Italy, Singapore; operas and music theatre pieces conducted include Misper (Glyndebourne), Four Saints in Three Acts (ENO), Harrison Birtwistle's Pulse Shadows (UK tour), Royal Opera House debut conducting Royal Ballet's Anastasia and on tour Cinderella in Turin and Frankfurt and Swan Lake in Japan, China and N America; Fellow, Trinity Coll. of Music 2000. *Dance:* conducted world premiere of Saint-Saens's Carnival of the Animals (choreography Christopher Wheeldon) 2003, Double Feature (Susan Stroman) 2004. *Address:* Urishay Barn, Michaelschurch Escley, Herefordshire, HR2 0LU, England (home). *E-mail:* quinnchamp@gmail.com. *Website:* www .andreaquinn.com.

QUINN, Gerard; British singer (baritone); b. 1962, Irvine, Scotland; m. Heather Lorimer, one d. *Education:* Napier Coll., Edinburgh, Royal Northern Coll. of Music, Manchester with Patrick McGuigan, Nat. Opera Studio, London, studied in Vienna with Otto Edelmann, and with Iris Dell'Acqua. *Career:* early appearances as Golaud in Pelléas et Mélisande, Escamillo, Mozart's Count and Junius in The Rape of Lucretia; Buxton Festival Opera 1985; Glyndebourne Festival debut 1987, in Capriccio; Glyndebourne Tour 1988, in La Traviata; Scottish Opera debut 1989, Donner in Das Rheingold; ENO debut 1990, as Pantaloon in The Love for Three Oranges, also for New

Israeli Opera; Royal Opera, Covent Garden debut as Flemish Deputy in Don Carlo 1989; Meru in Les Huguenots 1991, in 1994 Le Comte in the British premiere of Massenet's Chérubin; WNO debut 1993, Enrico in Lucia di Lammermoor 1995, Father, Hansel and Gretel, Germont in La Traviata; Bath and Wessex Opera, title role Rigoletto 1994; English Touring Opera 1994, Marcello, La Bohème; European Chamber Opera 1993, Count di Luna, Il Trovatore (also recorded) 1994, Count Alamaviva, Le nozze di Figaro and Rigoletto; Crystal Clear Opera, Sharpless, Madama Butterfly 1995; other roles performed include Nabucco, Germont, Ford, Michele in Il Tabarro, Tonio, Pagliacci, Zurga in The Pearl Fishers, Malatesta, Don Pasquale, Danilo in The Merry Widow, Don Giovanni and Eugene Onegin; sang Rolla in I Masnadieri for the Royal Opera in Savonlinna 1997; concert repertoire includes Elijah, Carmina Burana, Sea Symphony, Dream of Gerontius, Brahms Requiem and Britten's War Requiem.

QUITTMEYER, Susan; American singer (mezzo-soprano); b. 1955; m. James Morris; one s. one d. *Education:* Wesleyan Univ., IL and Manhattan School of Music. *Career:* sang with the America Opera Project, notably in the premiere of John Harbison's A Winter's Tale, at San Francisco 1979; guested at St Louis (debut in a revival of Martin y Soler's L'Arbore di Diana 1978), and sang further at San Francisco from 1981; sang in Montréal from 1983, Los Angeles 1984; Santa Fe 1984–88, notably in the US premiere of Henze's We Come to the River; further US appearances in Philadelphia, Cincinnati and San Diego; sang the Messenger in Monteverdi's Orfeo at Geneva 1986 and Sesto in Giulio Cesare at the Paris Opéra 1987; further engagements as Octavian for Netherlands Opera, Cherubino and Annius at Munich and Zerlina at the Vienna Staatsoper; Salzburg Festival debut 1991, as Idamantes in Idomeneo; concerts with the Los Angeles Philharmonic and the Symphony Orchestras of Oakland, Sacramento and San Francisco; Metropolitan Opera from 1987 as Nicklausse in Les Contes d'Hoffmann and Dorabella; sang Varvara in Katya Kabanova and Siebel with James Morris 1991; other roles include Meg Page, Cherubino, the Composer in Ariadne, Carmen, Pauline (The Queen of Spades) and Zerlina (Miami 1988); engaged as Siebel at San Francisco 1995; many concert appearances. *Telephone:* 1 877 9328 (Austria). *Fax:* 1 879 5396 (Austria). *E-mail:* akkcolbert@netway.at. *Website:* www.colbertartists.com.

QUIVAR, Florence; American singer (mezzo-soprano); b. 3 March 1944, Philadelphia. *Education:* Philadelphia Acad. of Music, Juilliard School New York. *Career:* concert appearances with the New York, Los Angeles and Israel Philharmonics, the Cleveland, Philadelphia and Mostly Mozart Festival Orchestras and the Boston Symphony; Metropolitan Opera debut 1977, roles include Marina in Boris Godunov, Jocasta in Oedipus Rex, Isabella in L'Italiana in Algeri, Fides in Le Prophète, Serena in Porgy and Bess, Ulrica in Un ballo in Maschera, Federica in Luisa Miller, Goddess in the premiere of La Amistad by A. Davis; guest appearances in Berlin, Florence, Geneva, Montréal and San Francisco; engagements include La Damnation de Faust in Geneva, the Wesendonk Lieder in Madrid and London, the Verdi Requiem with the Philharmonia Orchestra, Mahler's 3rd Symphony with the New York Philharmonic and performances with the Berlin Philharmonic under Giulini; festival appearances with the Israel Philharmonic in Salzburg, London, Lucerne, Florence and Edinburgh. *Recordings:* Rossini's Stabat Mater, Mahler's 8th Symphony under Seiji Ozawa, Mendelssohn's Midsummer Night's Dream, Berlioz's Romeo and Juliet, Virgil Thomson's Four Saints in Three Acts, Verdi Requiem, Un ballo in maschera, Luisa Miller, Schoenberg's Gurrelieder. *Current Management:* c/o Columbia Artists Management, 1790 Broadway, New York, NY 10019-1412, USA. *Telephone:* (212) 841-9500. *Fax:* (212) 841 9744 (USA). *E-mail:* info@cami.com. *Website:* www.cami.com.

R

RÄÄTS, Jaan; Estonian composer and teacher; *Professor Emeritus of Composition, Estonian Academy of Music*; b. 15 Oct. 1932, Tartu; s. of Peeter Rääts and Linda Rääts; m. 1st Marianne Rääts 1958; m. 2nd Ebba Rääts 1983; three c. *Education:* Tartu Music School with Aleksandra Sarv, Tallinn Conservatory with Mart Saar, Heino Eller. *Career:* mem. CPSU 1964–90; recording engineer, Estonian Radio 1955–66, Chief Dir Music Programmes, Estonian TV 1966–74; teacher of composition, Tallinn Conservatory (later Estonian Acad. of Music) 1968–70, 1974, Prof. 1990–2003, Prof. Emer. 2003–; initiated Estonian Music Days 1979; Vice-Chair. Estonian Composers' Union 1964–74, Chair. 1974–93. *Compositions include:* Symphony No. 1 1957, Symphony No. 2 1958, Symphony No. 3 1959, Symphony No. 4 Cosmic 1959, Concerto for chamber orchestra No. 1 1961, Violin Concerto No. 1 1963, Symphony No. 5 1966, Symphony No. 6 1967, Piano Concerto No. 1 1968, 24 Preludes 1968, Toccata 1970, Symphony No. 7 1973, 24 Estonian Preludes 1977, Violin Concerto No. 2 1979, 24 Marginalia 1979, 24 Marginalia for two pianos 1982, Piano Concerto No. 2 1983, Symphony No. 8 1985, Concerto for two pianos and symphony orchestra 1986, Concerto for chamber orchestra No. 2 1987, Piano Concerto No. 3 1990, Concerto for guitar and orchestra 1992, Concerto for trumpet and piano 1994, Concerto for violin and chamber orchestra 1995, Violin Concerto No. 3 1995, Five Sketches for Requiem for symphony orchestra 1999, Concerto for flute, guitar and symphony orchestra 2001, Symphony No. 9, Symphony No. 10, 10 piano sonatas, seven piano trios –2004, six string quartets. *Film scores:* Roosa kübar 1963, Null kolm 1965, Tütarlaps mustas 1966, Supernova 1966, Viini postmark 1967, Gladiaator 1969, Tuulevaikus 1971, Väike reekviem suupillile 1972, Ohtlikud mängud 1974, Aeg elada, aeg armastada 1976, Pihlakaväravad 1982. *Honours:* Order of the White Star (3rd Class) 2002; People's Artist of the Estonian SSR 1977. *Address:* c/o Estonian Composers' Union, A. Lauteri Street 7c, 10145 Tallinn, Estonia. *Telephone:* 646-6536 (office); 648-5744 (home). *E-mail:* heliloojate .liit@gmail.com (office); emie@emie.ee; ebba@hot.ee. *Website:* www.zzz.ee/ edition49 (office).

RABIN, Shira; Israeli violinist; b. 1 April 1970, Tel-Aviv. *Education:* Juilliard School and studied with Dorothy DeLay. *Career:* debut with the Israel Philharmonic 1979; appeared in the International Huberman Week with Isaac Stern and the Israel Philharmonic 1983; toured Europe 1983, Canada coast-to-coast tour 1985; played with Henryk Szeryng during Israel Philharmonic Jubilee Season 1987; soloist in the Stradivarius Year in Cremona; Israel representative in Italian Nights of Music with Zubin Mehta; gala concert at Carnegie Hall with Isaac Stern; Musical Discovery of 1989 in Italy, after recital debut in Milan; German debut 1991, with the Bavarian Radio Symphony Orchestra; US debut 1992 with the Philadelphia Orchestra under Riccardo Muti; further concerts with the Pittsburgh Orchestra under Lorin Maazel.

RACETTE, Patricia; American singer (soprano); b. 1967, San Francisco. *Education:* Merola Opera Program, San Francisco. *Career:* has sung with the San Francisco Opera from 1990, as Alice Ford, Rosalinde, Freia, Micaela, Mimi, Antonia and Mathilde in Guillaume Tell; other roles include Musetta for Netherlands Opera and at the Metropolitan 1994, Ellen Orford for Vancouver Opera and Gluck's Iphigénie en Tauride at St Louis; further appearances with the New York City and Vienna State Operas; concerts include the Messa per Rossini and Stephen Albert's Flower in the Mountain, at San Francisco; sang Emmeline Mostover in the premiere of Tobias Picker's Emmeline, Santa Fe 1996, Mathilde at Washington 1998; sang Violetta and Offenbach's Antonia at the Met 1999; season 2000–01 as Ellen Orford at La Scala, Luisa Miller for San Francisco Opera and Jenůfa in Washington; Poulenc's Blanche, Met 2003. *Current Management:* Opus 3 Artists, 470 Park Avenue South, 9th Floor North, New York, NY 10016, USA. *Telephone:* (212) 584-7500. *E-mail:* info@opus3artists.com. *Website:* www.opus3artists.com; www.patriciaracette.com.

RACHLIN, Julian; Lithuanian musician (violin, viola) and conductor; *Principal Guest Conductor, Royal Northern Sinfonia*; b. 8 Dec. 1974, Vilnius. *Education:* Konservatorium Wien, studied with Boris Kuschnir, private lessons with Pinchas Zukerman. *Career:* emigrated to Vienna 1978; youngest soloist ever to play with Vienna Philharmonic, making his debut under Riccardo Muti 1988; as violinist, has performed with leading conductors and orchestras including Munich Philharmonic/Lorin Maazel, Mariinsky Orchestra/Valery Gergiev, London Philharmonic/Andrey Boreyko, Bavarian State Orchestra/Zubin Mehta/Kirill Petrenko, also with Boston Symphony Orchestra/Asher Fisch, St Petersburg Philharmonic/Yuri Temirkanov and Orchestre Nat. de France/Daniele Gatti; gave world premiere of Krzysztof Penderecki's Concerto Doppio (dedicated to him) at Vienna Musikverein with Bavarian Radio Symphony Orchestra under Mariss Jansons 2012; performed concerts in Warsaw and the Asian premiere of the Concerto Doppio at Beijing Music Festival, in honour of Penderecki's 80th birthday; residency at Vienna Musikverein in 2014–15 includes opening the season with the Munich Philharmonic/Semyon Bychkov, conducting English Chamber Orchestra and playing in trio with Mischa Maisky and Daniil Trifonov; tour of Europe with Leipzig Gewandhaus Orchestra/Riccardo Chailly, and performances in China with China Philharmonic, Shanghai Symphony and Guangzhou Symphony/ Long Yu; as conductor, has led orchestras including Czech Philharmonic,

Israel Philharmonic, Acad. of St Martin in the Fields, Royal Northern Sinfonia, Orchestre Philharmonique de Nice, Moscow Virtuosi, Zurich Chamber Orchestra and Orchestra della Svizzera Italiana; Prin. Guest Conductor, Royal Northern Sinfonia 2014–; Dir Julian Rachlin & Friends Festival, Dubrovnik, Croatia 2012–; mem. Faculty, Konservatorium Wien Univ. 1999–; UNICEF Goodwill Amb. *Recordings include:* Bach: Goldberg Variations 2007, Shostakovich Piano Quintet 2007, violin concertos of Sibelius, Vivaldi, Brahms/Mozart, Saint-Saëns/Wieniawski, Prokofiev/Tchaikovsky. *Honours:* Eurovision Young Musician of the Year 1988. *Current Management:* c/o Alexia Blumenthal, Avenue Molière 355, 1180 Brussels, Belgium. *Telephone:* 479725078. *E-mail:* alexiablumenthal@gmail.com. *Address:* c/o Dmitri Kuschnir, Frankenberggasse 8/9, 1040 Vienna, Austria (office). *Telephone:* 6763149796 (office). *E-mail:* office@julianrachlin.com. *Website:* www.julianrachlin.com.

RADDATZ, Peter F.; German arts administrator; *Director-General, Stiftung Oper in Berlin (Berlin Opera Foundation);* b. Dec. 1953. *Career:* began career with Ministry of Finance 1981–84; Exec. Dir, Landesbühne Niedersachsen (State Theatre of Lower Saxony) 1984–88; Commercial Man., Schauspielhaus Theatre, Hamburg 1988–2001; Exec. Dir, Bühnen Köln (Cologne theatre, opera and dance org.) 2002–09; Dir-Gen., Stiftung Oper in Berlin (Berlin Opera Foundation) 2009–. *Address:* Stiftung Oper in Berlin, Am Wriezener Bahnhof 1, 10243 Berlin, Germany (office). *Telephone:* (30) 246477100 (office). *Fax:* (30) 246477102 (office). *E-mail:* y.heider@oper-in-berlin.de (office). *Website:* www.oper-in-berlin.de (office).

RADEMANN, Hans-Christoph; German choral conductor; *Principal Conductor, RIAS Kammerchor*; b. 1965, Dresden. *Education:* Musikhochschule Dresden. *Career:* Founder and Artistic Dir Dresdner Kammerchor 1985–; Dir Norddeutscher Rundfunk Chorus 1999–2004; Prin. Conductor RIAS Kammerchor 2007–; Founder and Artistic Dir Musikfest Erzgebirge 2010–; guest conducter with Bavarian, Central German and West Rundfunk orchestras, Radio Choir Berlin, Collegium Vocale Gent, Staatskapelle Dresden, Dresden Philharmonic Orchestra, Radio Philharmonic Hannover, Rotterdam Philharmonic Orchestra, Concerto Köln, Freiburg Baroque Orchestra and Akademie für Alte Musik Berlin; Prof. of Choral Conducting, Hochschule für Musik Carl Maria von Weber, Dresden 2000–. *Recordings include:* with Dresdner Kammerchor: Sacred Music of the Saxon-Polish Court 1997, Heinichen Missa No. 12/J.S. Bach Magnificat 2001, Johann Adolf Hasse: Requiem/Miserere 2006, Max Reger: Es waren zwei Königskinder 2007, Johann Adolf Hasse: Requiem in C 2011, Heinrich Schütz: Italienische Madrigale 2011, Heinrich Schütz: Psalmen Davids 2013, Heinrich Schütz: The Resurrection 2014; with RIAS Kammerchor: Mendelssohn: Lieder/Choral Works 2008, Ernst Krenek: Sechs Motetten nach Worten von Franz Kafka 2010, Wolfgang Rihm: Astralis & Other Choral Works 2012, C. P. E. Bach Magnificat (Gramophone Award for Best Baroque Vocal Recording 2014). *Honours:* Förderpreis der Landeshauptstadt Dresden 1994. *Address:* RIAS Kammerchor, Charlottenstrasse 56, 10117 Berlin (office); Chorbüro Dresdner Kammerchor, c/o MusikForum Dresden, Buchenstrasse 6, 01097 Dresden, Germany (office). *E-mail:* rademann@rias-kammerchor.de (office); office@dresdner-kammerchor.de (office). *Website:* www.rias-kammerchor.de (office); www.dresdner -kammerchor.de (office).

RADETA, Zdenko; Serbian composer and conductor; b. 16 Sept. 1955, Kragujevac; m. Miroslava Jankovic 1980, two s. one d. *Education:* Belgrade Univ., Tchaikovsky Conservatoire, Moscow. *Career:* debut with Four Sketches for chamber ensemble, 1974; singer in choir, Radio Television Belgrade; Producer, Radio Belgrade; Professor of Harmony and Counterpoint, Mokranjac Intermediate School, Belgrade; mem. Association of Composers of Serbia, SOKOJ. *Compositions:* 9 Piano pieces, 1972–90; Solo songs, 1974–84; 12 works for choirs, 1974–87; 1st String Quartet, 1980; Caleidoscope for 15 strings, 1985; Caleidoscope 2 for symphony orchestra, 1988; Gloomy Songs, Cyclus songs for voice, cor anglais and piano, 1998. *Recordings include:* Caleidoscope 2, 1st String Quartet, Remembrance for flute and piano, Wedding for mixed choir, and ballet Verities; Gloomy Songs, 1999. *Honours:* October Prize, City of Belgrade, 1974; SOKOJ Awards, 1983, 1984; 6 Awards from Association of Composers of Serbia. *Address:* Jurija Gagarina 186/4, 11070 Belgrade, Serbia.

RADIGUE, Eliane; French composer; b. 24 Jan. 1932, Paris; m. Arman 1953 (divorced 1971); one s. two d. *Education:* New York Univ., Univ. of Iowa, California Inst. of the Arts, USA, studied with Pierre Schaeffer and Pierre Henry. *Career:* work with electronic sounds on tape; performances include Salon des Artistes Décorateurs, Paris; Foundation Maeght, St Paul de Vence; Albany Museum of the Arts, New York; Gallery Rive Droite, Paris; Gallery Sonnabend, New York; Gallery Yvon Lambert, Paris; festivals include Como, Italy; Paris Autumn; Festival Estival, Paris; International Festival of Music, Bourges, France; New York Cultural Center; Experimental Intermedia Foundation, New York; Vanguard Theater, Los Angeles; Mills Coll., Oakland, California; Univ. of Iowa; Wesleyan Univ.; San Francisco Art Inst. *Compositions include:* Environmental Music 1969, OHMNT-Record Object 1971, Labyrinthe Sonore (tape music) 1971, Chry-ptus 1971, Geelriandre 1972, Biogenesis 1974, Adnos 1975, Adnos II 1980, Adnos III 1982, Prelude a Milarepa 1982, five songs of Milarepa 1984, Jetsun Mila 1986.

RADNOFSKY, Kenneth Alan, BM, MM; American saxophonist; b. 31 July 1953, Bryn Mawr, PA; m. Nancy Abramchuk 1977, two d. *Education:* Univ. of Houston, TX, New England Conservatory of Music, Boston. *Career:* Carnegie Hall debut 1985, performing Gunther Schuller Saxophone Concerto written for him; European debut 1987 with Leipzig Gewandhaus Orchestra under direction of Kurt Masur; saxophone soloist, Dresden Staatskapelle Orchestra, Pittsburgh Symphony Orchestra; solo works premiered or dedicated to him by Milton Babbitt, Donald Martino, Gunther Schuller, Morton Subotnick, Lee Hoiby, David Amram, Alan Hovhaness and John Harbison; saxophonist, Boston Symphony 1977–; soloist with BBC, Boston Pops and numerous US orchestras; mem. of faculty, New England Conservatory 1976. *Recordings:* soloist with New York Philharmonic in Debussy Rhapsody with Masur 1996, bass clarinet in Schoenberg Kammersymphonie with Felix Galimir.

RADULOVIĆ, Nemanja; Serbian musician (violin); b. 1985. *Education:* Conservatoire Nat. Supérieur Paris, with Patrice Fontanarosa, also studied with Joshua Epstein at Saarlandes Hochschule für Musik und Theater Saarbrücken and with Dejan Mihailović in Belgrade, master-classes with Yehudi Menuhin and Salvatore Accardo. *Career:* moved to Paris aged 14; int. career began when he stood in for Maxim Vengerov at Salle Pléyel, Paris 2006, playing Beethoven concerto with Orchestre Philharmonique de Radio France under Myung-Whun Chung; Carnegie Hall debut 2007; has appeared with leading orchestras in Europe, Asia and N America; tour of Japan; performs with own ensembles Les Trilles du Diable and Double Sens; recitals in Carnegie Hall, New York, Concertgebouw Amsterdam, Philharmonie Berlin, Salle Pléyel and Théâtre des Champs-Élysées, Paris, Megaron, Athens, Suntory Hall, Tokyo, Teatro Colón, Buenos Aires and Melbourne Recital Hall; partners include Marielle Nordmann, Laure Favre-Kahn and Susan Manof. *Recordings include:* Mendelssohn 2008, Les Trilles du Diable (Devil's Trills) 2009, Beethoven 2010, The 5 Seasons 2011, Après un Rêve 2013, Paganini Fantasy 2013, Carnets de Voyage (also known as Journey East) 2014. *Honours:* Dr hc (Niš); Victoires de la Musique Classique Award for Best Int. Newcomer 2005, Rising Star 2006 and Solo Instrumentalist of the Year 2014. *Current Management:* c/o Edward Pascall, IMG Artists,111 Power Road, London, W4 5P, England. *Telephone:* (20) 7957-5806. *E-mail:* epascall@imgartists.com. *Website:* www.imgartists.com; www.nemanjaviolin.com.

RAE, Caroline Anne Bodman, MA, DPhil (Oxon.), DipMus, ARCM; British pianist and musicologist; *Lecturer, School of Music, Cardiff University*; b. Leeds, Yorks.; sister of Charles Bodman Rae (composer); m. Peter Whittaker 1993; two s. *Education:* Somerville Coll., Oxford, Hochschule für Musik und Theater, Hannover, Germany, piano studies with Dame Fanny Waterman, Yvonne Loriod-Messiaen, David Wilde, Karl-Heinz Kämmerling. *Career:* debut as pianist in 1982; recitals in UK, Germany and France; two-piano duo with Robert Sherlaw Johnson; broadcasts for BBC, Channel 4, Radio 3, Radio France; research specialist in French music since Debussy and 20th-century music in Cuba; musical writings of Alejo Carpentier; lecture recitals in UK and Australia; guest lecturer at numerous univs and conservatories throughout the UK; Visiting Lecturer, Univs of Rouen, Paris 8, Paris-Sorbonne, Cologne; Visiting Scholar, St John's Coll. Oxford; programming consultant, BBC Nat. Orchestra of Wales, Philharmonia Orchestra of London; Tutor, Univ. of Oxford 1984–88; Lecturer in Piano, Oxford Polytechnic 1984, 1988; Lecturer, School of Music, Cardiff Univ. 1989–; UK univ. external examiner; mem. Royal Musical Asscn. *Publications include:* The Music of Maurice Ohana 2000; Music and Magic Realism, book chapters and numerous articles on 20th-century French and Latin American music including on Dutilleux, Messiaen, Jolivet, M.-F. Gaillard, Alejo Carpentier, Ohana; papers at numerous int. confs; contrib. to Music and Letters, Musical Times, Contemporary Music Review, Bulletin of Spanish Studies, Tempo, Cahiers Debussy, Les Cahiers du CIREM, NZM, Revista Música, Ethnomusicology, Notes, Monde de la Musique, Cahiers rémois de musicologie, New Grove Dictionary of Music and Musicians, New Grove Dictionary of Opera, Contemporary Composers Dictionary; CD booklet notes for Warners, Chandos. *Honours:* French Govt Scholarship, British Acad. research grant, AHRC research grant. *Address:* School of Music, Cardiff University, Corbett Road, Cardiff, CF10 3EB, Wales (office). *Telephone:* (29) 2087-4391 (office). *Fax:* (29) 2087-4379 (office). *E-mail:* rae@cardiff.ac.uk (office). *Website:* www.cf.ac.uk/music (office).

RAE, (John) Charles Bodman, MA, PhD, DMus, ARCM, FCLCM, FRSA; British/Australian composer, pianist, author and broadcaster; *Seventh Elder Professor of Music, University of Adelaide*; b. 10 Aug. 1955, Catterick, England; s. of Maj. John Rae and Mary Elizabeth Bodman Rae; brother of Caroline Rae; m. Dorota Kwiatkowska 1984. *Education:* Sidney Sussex Coll., Cambridge, Chopin Acad. of Music, Warsaw; piano with Dame Fanny Waterman; composition with Edward Cowie, Robert Sherlaw Johnson and Robin Holloway. *Career:* contribs as writer, presenter for BBC Radio 3 include Glocken, Cloches, Kolokola (six-hour series on European Bells); An Affair with Romanticism, features on Penderecki and Lutoslawski; Lecturer, Composition and Analysis 1979–81, 1983–92, Head of School of Creative Studies, City of Leeds Coll. of Music 1992–97; Visiting Composer, Univ. of Cincinnati Coll.-Conservatory of Music, OH, USA 1993; Director of Studies, Royal Northern Coll. of Music, Manchester 1997–2001; Seventh Elder Prof. of Music, and Dir/Dean, Elder Conservatorium of Music, Univ. of Adelaide 2001–, Chair. Academic Senate 2004–07; mem. Royal Musical Asscn; Fellow, British Acad. of Songwriters, Composers and Authors. *Radio:* Glocken, Cloches, Kolokola (BBC) 1990. *Compositions include:* Six Verses of Vision 1976, String Quartet 1981, Jede Irdische Venus 1982, Fulgura Frango 1986, Donaxis Quartet 1987, String Quartet No. 2 2004, Viola Concerto 2007, Toccata Agogica 2009, Partita Dalriada 2010. *Publications:* The Music of Lutoslawski 1994 (revised 1999), Muzyka Lutoslawskiego 1996, Lutoslawski Studies 2001. *Honours:* Fellowship, Leeds Coll. of Music 1999, Classical Music Award (Australia) 2005, inaugural Lutoslawski Medal 2005. *Current Management:* c/o Australian Music Centre, PO Box N690, Grosvenor Place, NSW 1220, Australia. *Telephone:* (2) 9247-4677. *Fax:* (2) 9241-2873. *E-mail:* info@australianmusiccentre.com.au. *Website:* www.australianmusiccentre.com.au/artist/bodman-rae-charles. *Address:* c/o Elder Conservatorium of Music, Elder Hall, University of Adelaide, SA 5005, Australia (office). *Telephone:* (8) 8303-3680 (office). *Fax:* (8) 8303-3665 (office). *E-mail:* charles.bodmanrae@adelaide.edu.au (office). *Website:* www.adelaide.edu.au/directory/charles.bodmanrae (office).

RAEKALLIO, Matti Juhani, DMus; Finnish pianist and academic; *Professor, Juilliard School*; b. 14 Oct. 1954, Helsinki; s. of Prof. Jyrki Arno Johannes Raekallio and Dr Eeva Liisa Laetitia Raekallio (née Mustakallio); m. 1st Sinikka Alstela 1977 (divorced 1996); m. 2nd Lara Lev 1998 (divorced 2013); one s. one d.; m. 3rd Sinikka Alstela 2013. *Education:* Juilliard School, USA, Turku Inst. of Music, pvt. lessons with Maria Diamond Curcio, London, at Vienna Music Acad., Austria, Leningrad Conservatory, Sibelius Acad., Finland, master-classes with Dmitry Bashkirov and Gyorgy Sebok. *Career:* debut as orchestra soloist, Turku 1971; solo, Helsinki 1975; extensive tours with all professional Finnish symphony orchestras 1971–; recitals in Nordic countries 1971–, in Finland 1975–, in Cen. Europe 1979–, in USA 1981–, in Japan 1990–; first US tour as orchestra soloist with Helsinki Philharmonic Orchestra 1983; recitals in Helsinki Festival 1981–97, Savonlinna Opera Festival 1988–2000, various other Finnish and Cen. European festivals; Beethoven Complete Sonatas in eight Finnish cities 1989–91; concerto repertoire includes over 60 works for piano and orchestra; Visiting Prof., Western Michigan Univ. 1984–85; Prof., Royal Swedish Coll. of Music, Stockholm 1994–1995; Assoc. Prof., Sibelius Acad., Helsinki 1994–2001, Prof. 2001–08; Prof., Hochschule für Musik und Theatre, Hanover, Germany 2005–10; Prof., Juilliard School, New York, USA 2007–14, 2015–; mem. Faculty, Bard Coll. Conservatory, NY, USA 2012–15; mem. Comm. for Research of Culture and Society, Acad. of Finland 1998–2000; mem. Bd of Dirs Soc. for Finnish Concert Soloists. *Radio:* several programmes for Finnish Nat. Public Radio (YLE). *Recordings include:* Complete Prokofiev Sonatas, about 20 other albums. *Publications:* Sormituksen strategiat (monograph study on piano fingerings) 1996; contrib. to several Finnish journals of music; articles in peer-reviewed journals of cognitive psychology, including Musicae Scientiae, Journal of Experimental Psychology, Music Perception. *Honours:* Dr hc (Estonian Acad. of Music) 2009. *Address:* Juilliard School, 60 Lincoln Center Plaza, New York, NY 10069, USA (office). *Telephone:* (212) 799-5000 (office). *E-mail:* mraekallio@juilliard.edu (office). *Website:* www.juilliard.edu (office).

RAFFAELLI, Piero; Italian violinist and violin teacher; b. 8 April 1949, Cesena; m. Santarelli Mariangela 1975; two d. *Education:* G. B. Martini Conservatory of Music, Bologna, masterclasses with various teachers. *Career:* debut, Italy 1968; radio appearances in Italy and Norway; Italian and European Concerts with Ensemble I Cameristi di Venezia; solo Concerts with Capella Academica of Vienna, Italy; Chamber Music Group Layer and Soloist, Italy; Europe, North America with Italian Ensembles 1971–73; Leader, Guitar Trio Paganini (also a viola player); duo recitals in Barcelona, Vienna, Berlin, Olso, Trondheim, Greece, Italy; Violin Teacher, Conservatory of Music, Bologna 1978–. *Recordings:* with Ensemble E Melkus, Solo Violin Works by M Kich (Yugoton) dedicated to him 1981, Contemporary Violin Chamber Music 1982. *Publications:* Revisions of Violin Works in First Printing for Zanibon and Violoncello 1979, A Vivaldi Concerto F 1 n 237 in D for violin, strings, cembalo 1980, N Paganini 3 Duetti Concertanti for Violin and Violoncello 1982. *Address:* Via Filli Latini 112, 47023 San Giorgio, Italy (home). *Telephone:* (0547) 324140 (home).

RAFFALLI, Tibère; French singer (tenor); b. 1954, Corsica. *Career:* sang Gabriele Adorno in Simon Boccanegra at Glyndebourne 1986 (Gonzalve in L'Heure Espagnole 1987); Bologna 1987, as the Berlioz Faust, Montpellier 1989, as Floresky in Cherubini's Lodoiska; season 1990–91 as Laërte in Hamlet by A Thomas at Turin, Julien in Louise at Liège and Berlioz's Bénédict for Opéra de Lyon; Strasbourg 1991, as Manalois in Martinů's Greek Passion; other roles include Edgardo in Lucia di Lammermoor and Massenet's Werther. *Recordings include:* L'Heure Espagnole.

RAFFANTI, Dano; Italian singer (tenor); b. 5 April 1948, Lucca. *Education:* La Scala School. *Career:* debut at La Scala School 1976, in Bussotti's Nottetempo; Verona 1978, in Orlando Furioso: Dallas 1980, in the US premiere of Vivaldi's opera; San Francisco 1980, as Almaviva in Il Barbiere di Siviglia; Houston 1981–82, as Giacomo in La Donna del Lago by Rossini; Metropolitan Opera from 1981, as Alfredo, Rodolfo, the Duke of Mantua, Edgardo, Goffredo in Handel's Rinaldo and the Italian Singer in Der Rosenkavalier; Teatro San Carlos Naples and Covent Garden, 1983 and 1984, as Tebaldo in I Capuleti e i Montecchi by Bellini; Guest appearances in Hamburg, Berlin, Santiago, Bilbao and at the Landestheater Salzburg; Maggio Musicale Florence 1989, as Idomeneo; Sang the Duke of Mantua at Turin, Dec 1989; Florence 1990, as Ugo in Donizetti's Parisina; Season 1992 as Cléomène in Le Siège de Corinthe by Rossini at Genoa. *Recordings include:* Fra Diavolo (Cetra); I Capuleti e i Montecchi; La Donna del Lago.

RAFFELL, Anthony; British singer (baritone); b. 1940, London, England. *Career:* sang first with a touring company with the works of Gilbert and Sullivan; Opera debut at Glyndebourne 1966, in Werther by Massenet; Sang at Gelsenkirchen, Karlsruhe and Bremen; debut, Covent Garden as Pantheus in The Trojans, 1969; mem. Stuttgart Opera 1985–; Metropolitan Opera debut 1983, as Kurwenal, in Tristan und Isolde, returning as Hans Sachs, 1985; appearances in Ring Cycles with ENO and in Seattle; further appearances as Klingsor in Turin, Wotan in Genoa, Jochanaan in Rio de Janeiro, Falstaff in Lisbon and at Parma, Trieste and Nancy; Metropolitan Opera 1989, as Gunther, in Götterdämmerung; Sang Telramund at Buenos Aires, 1991; regularly at Vienna State Opera, Hamburg, Berlin and Stuttgart; more recently in Buenos Aires in Tales of Hoffmann, as a guest, 1993; Sang Wotan/ Wanderer at Wiesbaden, 1994, Jochanaan in Switzerland, 1996 and Telramund and Wotan in Prague, 1997. *Recordings:* Video of Der Ring des Nibelungen, conducted by James Levine.

RAFTERY, J. Patrick; American singer (baritone); b. 4 April 1951, Washington, DC. *Education:* studied with Armen Boyajian. *Career:* debut at Chicago Lyric Opera 1980, as Shchelkalov in Boris Godunov; European debut 1982, at the Théâtre du Châtelet, Paris, as Zurga in Les Pêcheurs de Perles; Glyndebourne 1984, as Guglielmo; Santa Fe, New Mexico, 1984 in Verdi's Il Corsaro and Gwendoline by Chabrier; Covent Garden debut 1985, as Mozart's Count; Further appearances with the New York City Opera and in Hamburg, Brussels, and Cologne; Santiago 1988, as Luna in Il Trovatore; Rome Opera 1988, as Puccini's Lescaut; Sang Belcore in L'Elisir d'amore at Genoa in 1989; Other roles include Escamillo, Mercutio (Roméo et Juliette), Eugene Onegin, Valentin (Faust), Yeletsky in The Queen of Spades and Rossini's Figaro; Sang Rossini's Figaro at Vancouver, 1991; Matho in the premiere of Fénélon's Salammbô, Paris Opéra Bastille, 1998; Sang Mozart's Lucio Silla at Lausanne, 2001.

RAGACCI, Susanna; singer (soprano); b. 1959, Stockholm, Sweden. *Education:* studied in Florence, Italy. *Career:* sang first at Rome as Rossini's Rosina, then appeared at Florence, Venice, Palermo, Turin and La Scala Milan; sang Gilda in Dublin and at the Wexford Festival in Cimarosa's Astuzie Femminili; Opera de Wallonie at Liège 1987–88 as Rosina and as Egloge in Mascagni's Nerone; sang at Bologna in the 1987 Italian premiere of Henze's English Cat and at Florence as the Italian Singer in Capriccio; Théâtre du Châtelet, Paris 1992 as Sofia in Il Signor Bruschino. *Recordings:* Vivaldi's Catone in Utica and La Caduta di Adamo by Galuppi; I Pazzi per Progresso by Donizetti; L'Elisir d'amore.

RAGATZU, Rosella; Italian singer (soprano); b. 1964, Cagliari, Sardinia. *Education:* Cagliari Conservatory, studied with Magda Olivero and Claudio Desderi. *Career:* sang Fiordiligi at Spoleto 1987, Donna Anna at Treviso 1989; toured Italy, 1990, as Mozart's Countess and sang this role with Donna Anna at the 1991 Macerata Festival; further guest appearances at the Leipzig Opera, Teatro Regio Turin (in Don Carlos) and at Frankfurt in a concert of Franchetti's Cristoforo Colombo 1991, as Queen Isabella; Mozart's Countess at Turin, 1998; season 2000 as Mme Cortese in Il Viaggio a Reims at Liège and Rossini's Mathilde at the Vienna Staatsoper. *Honours:* winner Concorso Sperimento di Spoleto 1987, Concorso Toti dal Monte, Treviso 1989.

RAGIN, Derek Lee, BMus, MMT; American singer (countertenor); b. 17 June 1958, West Point, NY; s. of Ethel Yvonne Delaney; Alastair J. H. Boag, pnr. *Education:* Arts High School, Newark, NJ, Newark Boys' Chorus School, Newark Community Center of Arts, Oberlin Conservatory of Music. *Career:* debut with Opera-Festwoche der Alten Musik, Innsbruck, Austria 1983; recital debut, Wigmore Hall, London 1984; recital Aldeburgh Festival 1984; sang title role in Handel's Tamerlano at Lyon Opéra, France, at Göttingen Handel Festival; BBC debut recital 1984; debut at the Metropolitan Opera in Handel's Giulio Cesare 1988; recitals and oratorio in Frankfurt, Munich, Stuttgart, Cologne, Venice, Milan, Bologna, New York, Amsterdam, Maryland Handel Festival, London, Washington, Atlanta, Boston, San Francisco; made Salzburg debut in Gluck's Orfeo 1990; Gluck's Orfeo in Budapest 1991; season 1992 in Conti's Don Chisciotte at Innsbruck and as Britten's Oberon at Saint Louis; sang in Ligeti's Le Grand Macabre at the Paris Châtelet and the Salzburg Festival 1997; Hasse's Attilio regolo at Dresden 1997; sang in Legrenzi's La divisione del mondo at Innsbruck 2000; has worked with conductors including John Eliot Gardiner, Christoph Eschenbach, Kurt Masur, Alan Curtis, Ivan Fischer, Dennis Ressell Davies, Peter Eotvos, Jean Claude Malgoire, Frans Bruggen, Seiji Ozawa, Esa-Pekka Salonen, Reinhard Goebel, Paul Dyer, Robert Spano. *Recordings:* Purcell's Dido and Aeneas (role of Spirit) 1985, Handel's Tamerlano (title role) 1985, Handel's Giulio Cesare (roles of Flavio and Tolomeo), Handel's Saul, Vivaldi Cantatas, two recordings of Negro Spirituals with Moses Hogan, Ligeti's Le Grand Macabre 1998. *Honours:* First Prize in Purcell-Britten for Concert Singers 1983, First Prize, 35th Int. Music Competition, Munich 1986. *Current Management:* Colbert Artists Management Inc, 111 W 57th Street, New York, NY 10019, USA. *Telephone:* (212) 757-0782. *Fax:* (212) 541-5179. *E-mail:* nycolbert@colbertartists.com. *Website:* www.colbertartists.com. *Address:* Flat 8, The Old San, Glapthorn Road, Oundle, PE8 4JA, England (office). *Telephone:* (1832) 275717 (office). *E-mail:* Dragin1980@hotmail.com (office). *Website:* www.derekleeragin.net.

RAGNARSSON, Hjálmar Helgi, BA, MFA; Icelandic composer; b. 23 Sept. 1952, Isafjordur; m. Sigridur Asa Richardsdottir; two s. one d. *Education:* Isafjordur School of Music, Reykjavík Coll. of Music, Brandeis Univ., USA,

Rijksuniversiteit Utrecht-Instituut voor Sonologie, The Netherlands, Cornell Univ., USA. *Career:* Rector, Iceland Acad. of the Arts 1999–; mem. Composers' Soc. of Iceland (pres. 1988–92), Federation of Icelandic Artists (pres. 1991–98). *Music for theatre:* for Icelandic National Theatre and Reykjavík Municipal Theatre. *Music for film:* Tears of Stone 1995, No Trace 1998, for television films on Iceland State Television Service and Swedish State Television. *Compositions include:* Six songs to Icelandic Poems for voice and chamber ensemble 1978–79, Romanza for flute, clarinet and piano 1981, Canto for mixed choirs and synthesizer 1982, Mass for mixed choir 1982–89, Trio for clarinet, cello and piano 1983–84, Five Preludes for piano 1983–85, Tengsl for voice and string quartet 1988, Spjotalög for orchestra 1989, Raudur Thradur ballet music for orchestra 1989, Rhodymenia Palmata (chamber opera) 1992, Concerto for organ and orchestra 1997. *Publications:* A Short History of Icelandic Music to the Beginning of the Twentieth Century 1985, Tears of Stone (film script, co-author) 1995.

RAGUNATHAN, Sudha, MA; Indian classical Karnatic musician; *Founder and Managing Trustee, Samudhaaya Foundation*; b. (Geeta Sudha), 30 April 1968, Chennai; d. of Smt. Choodamani and Sri Venkatraman; m. M. C. Ragunathan; two c. *Education:* Ethiraj Coll. *Career:* vocalist specializing in Karnatic music; studied under Padmavibushan Sangeetha Kalanidhi, Dr M. L. Vasanthakumari; has travelled world-wide and participated in global music festivals; host of lecture demonstrations and conductor of workshops incorporating her diverse repertoire; participated in celebration of 50th Anniversary of Repub. of India with Vande Mataram by A. R. Rahman; has performed at Alice Tully Hall, Lincoln Centre and Broadway, New York to commemorate 50 years of the Bharatiya Vidya Bhavan; performed with Théâtre de la Ville, Paris; only Indian vocalist to have participated in Global Vocal Meeting organized by the Burghof Acad. of Music and Arts, Lorrach, Germany and produced by Stimmen Voices Int. Vocal Festival; performances in Norway, Switzerland, Tunisia and Israel 2011; teamed up with Amit Heri to present concerts in Karnatic fusion at The Hindu and The Times of India music festivals; forays into film music has had her singing for Ivan, Morning Raagas, Vaaranam Aayiram, Aadhavan, Mandhirappunnagai and Narthaki; has also composed pieces; Founder and Man. Trustee, Samudhaaya Foundation (charity) 1999–; took Karnatic music to the Corporation Schools 2010, 2011; lecture demonstrations and performances at select schools in Chennai. *Films:* has sung many film songs across all genres in Tamil, Telugu and Malayalam. *Radio:* 'A' Grade Artist, All India Radio. *Television:* numerous music programmes during key festivals; chief guest and judge for several reality shows. *Recordings include:* more than 200 albums, including San Marga 1994, Kaleeya Krishna 1994, Classical Vocal 1994, Padmashri 2004, Om Meditation 2004, Shakti 2005, Raagamala, 7th Sense. *Honours:* Amutha Isai Vani by Ikankai Thamil Sangam, USA 1988, Kalaimamani Award, Tamil Nadu Govt 1993, Sangeetha Choodamani, Sri Krishna Gana Sabha, Chennai 1997, Sangeetha Kala Sarathy, Sri Parthasarathy Swami Sabha, Chennai, Sangeetha Ratna 2003, Sangeetha Kalasagaram 2003, Padma Shri 2004, Award of Excellence, Rotary Club of Madras 2004, Virtuoso Award 2005, Gowri Manohari Award 2007, Gaana Padmam Award 2007, Rajiv Gandhi-Moopanar Award 2007, Best Performing Artist of the Season, Music Acad., Chennai 2008, Acharya Award 2008, Sangeetha Kala Saagara, Visakha Music Acad. of Visakhapatnam 2009, Pannisai Arasi, Thamizh Isai Manram, Thiruvaiyaru 2009, Sangeetha Rathnakara, Bhairavi Fine Arts Soc. 2010, Sangeetha Sampoorna, Poornathrayeesa Sangeetha Sabha, Tripunithura 2010, Sangeetha Kala Vishaaradh, Dombivili Fine Arts Soc., Mumbai 2010, Padmabhushan 2015; numerous other awards and titles. *Address:* 'Vasantham', 18/3 Cenotaph First Street, Alwarpet, Chennai 600 018, India (office). *Telephone:* (44) 24345001 (office). *E-mail:* sudha.sudharagunathan@gmail .com (office). *Website:* www.sudharagunathan.com.

RAIMONDI, Ildiko; Austrian singer (soprano); b. 11 Nov. 1962, Arad, Romania; m. Prof. Dr Herbert Zeman; two s. *Education:* Arad Conservatory. *Career:* sang at Chemnitz from 1983 and at the Vienna Kammeroper in Dresden and at the Landestheater Linz from 1988; Bregenz Festival 1991 (as Micaela) and further appearances at the Vienna Volksoper; mem. Vienna State Opera (Staatsoper); Lieder specialist; other roles have included Mozart's Zerlina, Susanna, Despina and Pamina, Sophie in Der Rosenkavalier, Rosalinde in Die Fledermaus, Gutrune in Götterdammerung; concerts include Masses by Mozart and Rossini, Die Schöpfung, the Verdi Requiem and Ein Deutsches Requiem; Marzelline in Fidelio at the 1996 Edinburgh Festival; Eurydice in Leopold I's Il figliol prodigo, Vienna 1997. *Publication:* Wenzel Johann Tomaschek: Gedicht von Goethe für den Gesang (ed.) 2003. *Honours:* Österreische Kammersängerin. *Address:* c/o Staatsoper Vienna, Opernring 2, 1010 Vienna (office); Kahlenbergerstr. 81, 1190 Vienna, Austria (home).

RAIMONDI, Ruggero; Monegasque singer (bass) and director; b. 3 Oct. 1941, Bologna, Italy; m. Isabel Maier 1987. *Career:* operatic debut in La Bohème, Spoleto Festival 1964; debut at Metropolitan Opera, New York in Ernani 1970; engagements include Don Giovanni, Le Nozze di Figaro, Faust, Attila, Nabucco, Don Carlos, Boris Godunov, Don Quichotte, Don Pasquale, Otello, Contes d'Hoffmann, Carmen, Il Viaggio a Rheims, Falstaff, I Vespri Siciliani, I Lombardi, L'Italiana in Algieri, Il Turco in Italia, Tosca, Assassinio nella Cattedrale, Così fan tutte and others; played role of Pagano in Verdi's I Lombardi alla prima crociata, anniversary concert on roof of Milan cathedral 2011. *Opera productions include:* Don Giovanni, The Barber of Seville, Don Carlos. *Films include:* Don Giovanni 1979, Six Characters in Search of a Singer 1981, La Truite 1982, Life is a Bed of Roses 1983, Carmen 1984, Boris

722 www.worldwhoswho.com

Godunov 1989, Tosca 2001, Assassinio nella cattedrale (opera) 2007, Rigoletto a Mantova 2010. *Television includes:* Boris Godunov staged by Joseph Losey at Opéra Nat. de Paris 1980, Six personnages en quête d'un chanteur by Maurice Béjart 1981, Verdi's Requiem 1982, Ernani directed by Kirk Browning (with Milnes and Pavarotti) 1983, Le nozze di Figaro directed by Jonathan Miller 1992, Tosca: In the Settings and at the Times of Tosca, directed by Brian Large (with Malfitano and Domingo) 1992, Il Turco in Italia with Cecilia Bartoli at Zurich Opera House 2001, Così fan tutte staged by Patrice Chéreau 2005. *Recordings include:* Verdi: Aida 1983, 2005, Rossini: L'Italiana in Algeri 1989, Puccini: Turandot 1990, Rossini: Il Viaggio a Reims 1990, Verdi: Don Carlos 1990, Rossini: Il barbiere di Siviglia 1993, Verdi: Un Ballo in Maschera 1998, Mozart: Le Nozze di Figaro 2003, Rossini: La Cenerentola 2003, Rossini: Il Barbiere di Siviglia (DVD) 2005, Verdi: Attila 2005. *Honours:* Commdr des Arts et des Lettres, Officier, Légion d'honneur, Kt, Order of Malta, Grand Ufficiale della Repubblica Italiana 1996, Citizen of Honour, Athens, Commdr du Mérite Culturel (Monaco) 1999. *Address:* 140 bis rue Lecourbe, 75015 Paris, France (office).

RAJNA, Thomas, DMus, ARCM; British composer, pianist and teacher (retd); b. 21 Dec. 1928, Budapest, Hungary; s. of Dr Nandor Rajna and Hella Eisen; m. Anthea Valentine Campion 1967; one s. two d. *Education:* Nat. Musical School, Budapest, Franz Liszt Acad. of Music, Budapest and Royal Coll. of Music, London. *Career:* freelance composer, pianist and teacher, London 1951–63; Prof. of Piano, Guildhall School of Music 1963–70; Lecturer, Univ. of Surrey 1967–70; Sr Lecturer in Piano, Faculty of Music, Univ. of Cape Town 1970–89, Assoc. Prof. 1989–93; launched own record label Amarantha Records 2001; Fellow, Univ. of Cape Town 1981. *Compositions include:* film and ballet music, orchestral and chamber music, two piano concertos, Harp Concerto 1990, Amarantha (opera in 11 scenes) 1991–94, Video Games (for orchestra) 1994, Rhapsody for clarinet and orchestra 1995, Fantasy for violin and orchestra 1996, Suite for violin and harp 1997, Stop All the Clocks (four songs on poems by W. H. Auden) 1998, The Creation – A Negro Sermon for unaccompanied choir 2000, Valley Song (opera) 2002–04, Tarantulla for violin and piano 2001, Violin Concerto 2007. *Recordings include:* works by Stravinsky (complete piano works), Messiaen: Vingt regards sur l'Enfant-Jesus; Scriabin, Granados (complete piano works), Liszt (Transcendental Studies), Schumann (A minor Piano Concerto and Piano Quintet and Quartet), Dohnanyi (Nursery Variations), The Hungarian Connection: Instrumental Works by Dohnányi and Rajna, Bach Harpsichord Concertos, Bartok 2nd and 3rd Piano Concertos, Stravinsky Capriccio, Prokofiev 3rd Piano Concerto, Barber Piano Concerto, A Garland of Spanish Songs; own compositions: Amarantha (opera), Valley Song (opera), Suite for violin and harp, Rhapsody for clarinet and orchestra, 1st Piano Concerto, Piano Preludes and Capriccio, 2nd Piano Concerto and Harp Concerto, Video Games and other orchestral works, The Creation – A Negro Sermon for chorus and orchestra, Violin Concerto. *Publications:* Dialogues for Clarinet and Piano 1970, Piano Preludes 1988, Music for Violin and Piano 1990, Concerto for Harp and Orchestra 1990; publs by Amarantha Music: Video Games for Orchestra 1994, Rhapsody for Clarinet and Orchestra 1995, Amarantha (opera) 1995, Fantasy for Violin and Orchestra 1996, Suite for Violin and Harp 1998, Stop All the Clocks – Four Songs on Poems by W. H. Auden 1998, Tarantulla for Violin and Piano 2001, Valley Song (opera) 2004, The Creation – A Negro Sermon for Chorus and Orchestra 2006, Violin Concerto 2007. *Honours:* DMus (Cape Town) 1985; Liszt Prize, Budapest 1947, Artes Award (SABC) 1981, UCT Book Award 1996, Cape Tercentenary Foundation Merit Award 1997. *Address:* 10 Wyndover Road, Claremont, Cape Town, West Cape 7708, South Africa (home). *Telephone:* (21) 6713937 (home). *Fax:* (21) 6713937 (home). *E-mail:* trajna@telkomsa.net (home).

RAKOWSKI, Andrzej, MA, MSc, PhD, DSc; Polish musicologist and acoustician; *Professor Emeritus, Fryderyk Chopin Academy of Music;* b. 16 June 1931, Warsaw; m. Magdalena Jakobczyk 1972; one s. two d. *Education:* Durham Univ., UK, Warsaw Univ. of Tech., Warsaw Univ., State Coll. of Music in Warsaw. *Career:* Prof. of Musical Acoustics, Fryderyk Chopin Acad. of Music, Warsaw 1963–2001, Prof. Emer. 2001–; Pres. 1981–87; part-time Prof., Inst. of Musicology, Warsaw Univ. 1987–2003; Chair. of Musicology, A. Mickiewicz Univ. 1997–2009; Visiting Prof., Central Inst. for the Deaf, St Louis, Mo., USA 1977–78, McGill Univ., Montreal, Canada 1985, Hebrew Univ., Jerusalem, Israel 1991, Univ. Nova de Lisboa, Portugal 2004; mem. Polish Music Council (Vice-Pres. 1984–89), Union of Polish Composers, Polish Acad. of Sciences (Pres. Acoustical Cttee 1996–2007), European Soc. for Cognitive Sciences of Music (Pres. 2000–03); Fellow, Acoustical Soc. of America 2001–. *Publications include:* Categorical Perception of Pitch in Music 1978, The Access of Children and Youth to Musical Culture 1984, Studies on Pitch and Timbre of Sound in Music (ed.) 1999, Creation and Perception of Sound Sequences in Music (ed.) 2002; contrib. over 100 articles on music perception and music acoustics to int. journals. *Honours:* Golden Cross of Merit 1973, Bachelor's Cross, Order of Polonia Restituta 1983, Officer's Cross 2002, Order of Polish Rebirth 2011. *Address:* Fryderyk Chopin Academy of Music, Okolnik 2, 00-368 Warsaw (office); Pogonowskiego 20, 01-564 Warsaw, Poland (home). *Telephone:* (22) 827-8303 (office); (22) 839-9456 (home). *Fax:* (22) 827-8310 (office). *E-mail:* rakowski@chopin.edu.pl. *Website:* www.chopin.edu.pl/angielskie/osobowe/rakowski.html (office).

RAMEY, Phillip, BA, MA; American composer, pianist and writer; b. 12 Sept. 1939, Elmhurst, Ill. *Education:* Int. Acad. of Music, Nice with A. Tcherepnin, De Paul Univ., Chicago with A. Tcherepnin, Columbia Univ., New York with

Jack Beeson. *Career:* Programme Ed., New York Philharmonic 1977–93; freelance composer, with premieres in New York, Boston, Sacramento, Chicago, London, Aldeburgh Festival, Tangier, Vilnius, Montreux; Vice-Pres. USA, The Tcherepnin Soc. 2002–. *Compositions include:* Meditation for piano 1959, Three Early Preludes for piano 1959, Suite for piano 1960–63, Incantations for piano 1960, Three Preludes for solo horn 1960, seven piano sonatas 1961, 1966, 1968, 1988, (for left hand) 1989, 2008, 2010, Sonata for three unaccompanied timpani 1961, Concert Suite for piano and small orchestra 1962 (revised, reorchestrated and expanded 1984 as Concert Suite for piano and orchestra), Cat Songs for soprano, flute and piano (text by T. S. Eliot) 1962, Music for brass and percussion 1964, Seven, They Are Seven: Incantation for bass-baritone and orchestra (text by Konstantin Balmont) 1965, Diversions for piano 1966, Two Short Pieces for piano 1967, Epigrams for piano (Book 1) 1967, Pen Sketches for piano 1967, Harvard Bells, Soundpiece for piano 1968, Toccata Breva for percussion 1968, Piano Fantasy 1969–72, three piano concertos 1971, 1976, 1994, Leningrad Rag (Mutations on Scott Joplin) for piano 1972, Memorial (In Memoriam Alexander Tcherepnin) for piano 1977, La Citadelle, Rhapsody for oboe and piano 1979, A William Blake Trilogy for soprano and piano 1980, Fanfare-Sonata for solo trumpet 1981, Canzona for piano 1982, Moroccan Songs to Words of Paul Bowles for high voice and piano 1982–86, Phantasm for flute and violin (or two violins) 1984, Proclamation for orchestra (orchestration of Aaron Copland's Proclamation for piano) 1985, Capriccio (Improvisation on a Theme from Youth) for piano 1985, Toccata No. 1 for piano 1986, Concerto for horn and strings 1987, Tangier Nocturne for piano 1989, Cantus Arcanus for piano 1990, Toccata No. 2 for piano 1990, Mirage for piano 1990, Burlesque-Paraphrase on a Theme of Stephen Foster for piano 1990, Rhapsody for cello 1992, Café of the Ghosts: Fantasy-Trio on a Moroccan Beggar's Song for violin, cello and piano 1992, Chromatic Waltz for piano 1993, Tangier Portraits for piano 1991–99, Praeludium for five horns 1994, Gargoyles for horn 1995, Elegy for horn and piano 1995, Nightfall: Aria for flute and piano 1996, Concertino for four horns, timpani and percussion 1996, Sonata-Ballade for two horns and piano 1997, Phantoms (Ostinato Etude) for piano 1997, Effigies for viola and piano 1998, Lyric Fragment for flute and harpsichord (or piano) 1998, Lament for Richard III for piano 2001, Color Etudes for piano and orchestra (arranged from Color Etudes for piano) 2002, Winter Nocturne for piano 2003, Ode for F.D.R. for piano 2004, Primitivo for Piano 2007, J.F.K.: Oration for Speaker and Orchestra 2007, Ballade for clarinet and horn 2008, Blue Phantom 2008, Djebel Bani (A Saharan Meditation) for piano 2009, Simon Songs: Six Poems for Baritone and Piano (text: John Simon) 2009, Simon Songs: Suite for Baritone and Orchestra (text: John Simon) 2009, Slavic Rhapsody (The Novgorod Kremlin at Night) for piano 2009–10, Bagatelle on 'Dies Irae' for piano 2010, Piano Sonata No. 7 2010, Bagatelle on 'Panis Angelicus' for piano 2010, Piano Sonata No. 8 2011–12, Concerto for Trombone and String Orchestra, Harp and Percussion 2012, Bagatelle on Twelve Tones for piano 2012, Bagatelle Romantique (on Themes of Alexander Tcherepnin) for piano 2013, Night of the Djinns for piccolo, contrabassoon and percussion 2013, Piano Sonata No. 9 (Ballade) 2013, Second Rhapsody for oboe and piano 2014. *Recordings include:* Piano Fantasy (with Bennet Lerner) 1984, Canzona for Piano (with Bennet Lerner) 1986, Color Etudes, Memorial, Chromatic Waltz, Piano Sonata No. 1, Piano Sonata No. 2, Piano Sonata No. 5 (for left hand), Piano Fantasy, Four Tangier Portaits, Toccata No. 2 (with Stephen Gosling) 2006, Diversions, Epigrams (Book 1), Leningrad Rag, Winter Nocturne, Toccata No. 1, Toccata No. 2, Ode for F.D.R., Piano Sonata No. 4, Primitivo (with Mirian Conti) 2008, Suite, Two Short Pieces, Toccata Giocosa, Slavic Rhapsody, Burlesque-Paraphrase on a Theme of Stephen Foster, Bagatelle on 'Dies Irae', Djebel Bani, Blue Phantom, Piano Sonata No. 6 (Sonata-Fantasia) (with Stephen Gosling) 2011, Incantations, Three Early Preludes, Cossack Variations, Epigrams (Book 2), Lament for Richard III, Piano Sonata No. 3, Piano Sonata No. 7 (with Stephen Gosling) 2013. *Publications:* Irving Fine: An American Composer in His Time (ASCAP Deems-Taylor/Nicolas Slonimsky Award for Outstanding Musical Biog. 2006) 2005. *Honours:* ASCAP Deems-Taylor/Nicolas Slonimsky Award for Outstanding Musical Biography 2006. *Address:* 825 West End Avenue, Penthouse F, New York, NY 10025, USA. *Telephone:* (212) 866-1063. *Fax:* (212) 866-2550. *E-mail:* bklisenbee@aol.com.

RAMEY, Samuel; American singer (bass-baritone); b. 28 March 1942, Kolby, Kan. *Education:* Wichita State Univ. with Arthur Newman, studied in New York with Armen Boyajian. *Career:* debut, New York City Opera as Zuniga in Carmen 1973, returned as Mephistopheles (Gounod and Boito), Attila, Don Giovanni, Henry VIII (Anna Bolena) and Massenet's Don Quichotte; Glyndebourne debut as Mozart's Figaro 1976; Nick Shadow in The Rake's Progress 1977; guest appearances in Hamburg, San Francisco, Chicago and Vienna, as Colline in La Bohème, Figaro, and Arkel in Pelléas et Mélisande; Covent Garden debut 1982, returned to London for a concert performance of Semiramide 1986 and as Philip II in Don Carlos 1989; Metropolitan Opera debut 1984, as Argante in Rinaldo 1986–87 as Walton in I Puritani and Escamillo; Pesaro 1984, in a revival of Rossini's Il Viaggio a Reims; Bartók's Bluebeard at the Met 1989; Pesaro Festival 1986 (Maometto II) and 1989 (La Gazza Ladra); Munich as Mephistopheles 1988; Don Giovanni at Salzburg from 1987, Metropolitan and Maggio Musicale, Florence 1990; season 1992–93 as Attila at San Francisco and Geneva, Rossini's Basilio at the Met, Philip II in Venice and New York, the Hoffmann Villains and Berlioz Mephistopheles at Covent Garden, and Nick Shadow at Aix-en-Provence; sang Mephistopheles in a new production of Faust at the Vienna Staatsoper 1997; other roles include the villains in Les Contes d'Hoffmann, Verdi's Renato and Banquo, and Mozart's Leporello; Covent Garden 1997, as Verdi's Fiesco and Oberto; Philippe in Don Carlo at the Paris Opéra Bastille 1998; season 2000–01 as Verdi's Zaccaria at Houston; Attila for the Chicago Lyric Opera and Rossini's Mustafà at the Met; Don Quichotte 2001. *Recordings:* Bach B Minor Mass, I Due Foscari, Un Ballo in Maschera, Ariodante, Lucia di Lammermoor, Maometto II, Petite Messe solenelle, Haydn's Armida, Le nozze di Figaro, The Rake's Progress, Il Turco in Italia, La Donna del Lago, Il Viaggio a Reims, Don Giovanni. *Honours:* inaugural mem. Wichita State Univ. Coll. of Fine Arts Hall of Fame 2015. *Current Management:* c/o Jeffrey Vanderveen, Opus 3 Artists, 470 Park Avenue South, Ninth Floor North, New York, NY 10016, USA. *Telephone:* (212) 584-7532. *E-mail:* jvanderveen@opus3artists.com. *Website:* www.opus3artists.com.

RAMICOVA, Dunya, MFA; American costume designer; b. 1950, Czechoslovakia. *Education:* Yale School of Drama Bachelor of Fine Arts, Goodman School of Drama. *Career:* collaborated with dir, Stephen Wadsworth on Jenůfa and Fliegende Holländer for Seattle Opera, Fidelio for Scottish Opera and La Clemenza di Tito for Houston Grand Opera; costume designs for Peter Sellars' production of Die Zauberflöte and The Electrification of the Soviet Union at Glyndebourne, Tannhäuser at Chicago, Nixon in China for Houston and St François d'Assise at Salzburg 1992; premiere of The Voyage by Philip Glass at the Metropolitan 1992, production by David Pountney; Covent Garden 1992, costumes for Alcina; costumes for the house premiere of Mathis der Maler, Covent Garden 1995, Tan Dun/Peter Sellars Peony Pavilion, Vienna 1998; Prof., Univ. of California at Merced 2004–. *Address:* c/o University of California at Merced, PO Box 2039, Merced, CA 95344, USA (office).

RAMIREZ, Alejandro; Colombian singer (tenor); b. 2 Sept. 1946, Bogota. *Education:* Conservatory of Bogotá, Musikhochschule Freiburg, studied with Annelies Kupper in Munich and Gunther Reich in Stuttgart. *Career:* sang in Pforzheim 1975–77, Kaiserslautern 1977–80; mem., Mannheim Opera 1980–82, Frankfurt from 1982; Covent Garden, London 1984 as Nemorino in L'Elisir d'amore; Vienna Staatsoper 1985 as Alfredo; Salzburg Festival 1985 in the Henze/Monteverdi Il Ritorno d'Ulisse; other roles include Belmonte, Don Ottavio, Tamino, Ferrando, Jacquino in Berlin 1984, Elvino in La Sonnambula, Rossini's Almaviva and Lindoro, Strauss's Narraboth and Flamand, Rodolfo and Edgardo; concert repertoire includes the Evangelist in the Bach Passions, and works by Handel, Bruckner, Schumann, Dvořák, Beethoven and Verdi; Bavarian State Opera as Don Ottavio, Frankfurt 1980–85; La Scala Milan 1988 as Henry Morosus in R. Strauss's Schweigsame Frau 1990; season 1992 as Rodolfo at Bonn and Tamino at Düsseldorf; Prof. of Singing, Musikhochschule of Mannheim, Germany; sang Pollione in Norma at Karlsruhe 2000. *Recordings include:* Schumann's Manfred, St John Passion and Christmas Oratorio by Bach, Sacred Music by Schubert, Mendelssohn and Charpentier, The Seven Last Words by Schütz, Mozart's Nozze di Figaro under Riccardo Muti.

RAMIRO, Yordi; singer (tenor); b. 1948, Acapulco, Mexico. *Career:* debut in Mexico City 1977, as Pinkerton; sang at the Vienna Staatsoper from 1978 and guested at the San Francisco Opera 1979, as Rinuccio in Gianni Schicchi; further appearances at Seattle as Alfredo, Barcelona as Rodolfo 1980, and Mexico City as Edgardo; Strasbourg 1983, as Gounod's Roméo; Covent Garden 1984, in Der Rosenkavalier and Arturo in I Puritani at the 1985 Bregenz Festival; Metropolitan Opera debut 1985, as Paco in La Vida Breve; other roles include Ernesto in Don Pasquale, Nemorino, the Duke of Mantua and Tebaldo in I Capuleti by Bellini. *Recordings include:* Rigoletto and La Traviata.

RAMNATH, Kala, BMus, MMus; Indian violinist; *Principal, Pandit Jasraj School of Music Foundation;* b. 29 May 1967, d. of Malathy Ramnath and T. N. Mani. *Career:* musician of N Indian classical genre; has performed at all major festivals throughout India and at World Music Festival in Montreal, Rhythms of India in Ottawa and S Asian Heritage Festival in Toronto, Canada, North Sea Jazz Festival in Cape Town, SA, Bath Festival, England; tours include USA, Canada, UK, Germany, Switzerland, Italy, France, Russia, SA, Middle East, Kenya, Tanzania, Australia; concerts at Queen Elizabeth Hall, London and Sydney Opera House, Carnegie Hall; leads first-ever African-Indian fusion band, Raga Afrika, also trans-genre band Four Elements, and Global Conversation, a band that plays raga-influenced jazz and jazz-inflected raga; Prin. Pandit Jasraj School of Music Foundation; mem. Advisory Bd Chinmaya Nada Bindu music school. *Recordings include:* Touching Air 2001, Samvad, Kala, Yashila, Twilight Strings, Nectar, Divine Wheel, Samaya, Nishigandha, Young Masters, Kala Ramnath, Passage Through Dawn, and numerous others. *Honours:* Pres.'s Award, AIR Music Competition 1984, Pandit Jasraj Gaurav Puraskar Award 1999, Sur Ratna, Sur Mani, Kumar Gandharva Nat. Award 2008. *Address:* 122, Bldg 3, Raheja Crest, Adarsh Nagar, Lokhandwala, Andheri (W), Mumbai 400 053, India. *Telephone:* (22) 42649439. *Fax:* (22) 26324897. *E-mail:* kala@kalaramnath.com. *Website:* www.kalaramnath .com.

RAMSAY, Dervla; Northern Irish singer (mezzo-soprano); b. 25 Aug. 1970, Derry, N Ireland. *Education:* Guildhall School of Music and Drama, London; Studies with Renata Scotto and Margarita Rinaldi. *Career:* debut, sang Volpino in Haydn's Lo Speziale, Bagno di Lucca 1994; Janissary in Mozart's Die Entführung at Covent Garden 2000; other roles include Countess Ceprano in Rigoletto, Page in Wagner's Lohengrin, Train bearer in Strauss' Elektra; mem. Royal Opera Chorus 1999–. *Honours:* winner, Ulster Bank's Music

Foundation Award for Young Musicians 1993, Concorso Intermazionale di Bagna di Lucca 1994.

RAN, Shulamit, PhD; American/Israeli composer; b. 21 Oct. 1949, Tel-Aviv, Israel; d. of Zvi Ran and Berta Ran; m. Abraham H. Lotan 1986; one s. *Education:* Mannes Coll. of Music, New York. *Career:* moved to USA 1963; William H. Colvin Prof. of Composition, Univ. of Chicago, Ill. 1973–2002; Andrew MacLeish Distinguished Service Prof., Dept of Music and Artistic Dir of Contempo (fmrly Contemporary Chamber Players), Univ. of Chicago 2002–; Visiting Prof., Princeton Univ., NJ 1987; Composer-in-Residence, Chicago Symphony Orchestra 1990–; Brena and Lee Freeman, Sr Composer-in-Residence, Lyric Opera of Chicago 1994; works performed by New York Philharmonic Orchestra 1963, Israel Philharmonic Orchestra 1971, Chamber Music Soc. (Lincoln Center, New York) 1987, Chicago Symphony Orchestra 1988, 1991, 1993, 1995, Philadelphia Orchestra 1990, Cleveland Orchestra 1991, 1993, Orchestre de la Suisse Romande, Amsterdam Philharmonic; piano performances in the USA, Europe and Israel; numerous comms; Fellow, American Acad. of Arts and Sciences. *Compositions include:* O the Chimneys 1969, Concert Piece for piano and orchestra 1970, Hyperbolae 1977, Verticals 1983, Sonata-Waltzer 1983, String Quartet No. 1 1984, Concerto da Camera I 1985, Concerto for orchestra 1986, Concerto for orchestra 1986, East Wind for solo flute 1987, Concerto da Camera II 1987, String Quartet No. 2: Vistas 1988–89, Mirage for five players 1990, Symphony (Pulitzer Prize in Music) 1991, Legends for orchestra 1993, Between two Worlds: The Dybbuk (opera) 1994–95, Soliloquy for Piano Trio 1997, Vessels of Courage and Hope for Orchestra 1998, Voices, Concerto for a Flautist with Orchestra 2000, Supplications for Chorus and Orchestra 2002, Violin Concerto 2003, Under the Sun's Gaze (Concerto da Camera III) 2003–04, Fault Line for Large Ensemble 2005–06, Credo/Ani Ma'amin, for Twelve Voices 2006, Song and Dance, Duo for Saxophones and Percussion 2007, The Show Goes On, Concerto for Clarinet and Orchestra 2008, Lyre of Orpheus for string sextet 2009, Silent Voices for reader and 14 players 2010, Perfect Storm for viola solo 2010. *Honours:* Dr hc (Mount Holyoke Coll.) 1988, (Spertus Inst.) 1994, (Beloit Coll.) 1996; Guggenheim Foundation Awards 1977, 1990, American Acad. and Inst. of Arts and Letters Award 1989. *Address:* University of Chicago, Department of Music, 1010 East 59th Street, Chicago, IL 60637, USA. *Telephone:* (773) 702-8484. *Fax:* (773) 753-0558.

RANACHER, Christa; singer (soprano); b. 12 Dec. 1953, Dollach in Kärnten, Austria. *Education:* studied in Vienna, masterclasses with Mario del Monaco and Elisabeth Schwarzkopf. *Career:* sang at Regensburg 1984–85, Monchengladbach from 1985, Leonore in Fidelio 1989; further appearances at Gelsenkirchen, Mannheim, Munster, Hannover, the Deutsche Oper Berlin, Staatsoper Munich and Zürich; season 1992 as Salome at Dusseldorf and Shostakovich's Katerina Izmailova at Berne; other roles include Mozart's Countess and Donna Anna, Agathe, Marenka in The Bartered Bride, Senta, and Ada in Wagner's Die Feen, Tosca, Santuzza, Zdenka, Arabella, Judith in the opera by Siegfried Matthus, Sophie in Cerha's Baal and Andromache in Troades by Reimann; sang Stella in Goldschmidt's Der Gewaltige Hahnrei, Bonn 1995; noted concert performer; season 2000 as Andromache in Troades, at Berlin, and Amélia in Clara by Hans Gefors, for Berne Opera.

RANCATORE, Desirée; Italian singer (soprano); b. 1972, Sicily. *Education:* studied with Margaret Baker-Genovesi. *Career:* debut in Mozart's Barbarina at the 1996 Salzburg Festival; appearances at Bologna in Figaro, at Parma in L'Arlesiana and as Frasquita in Carmen at Genoa; Flowermaiden in Parsifal at Florence and the Opéra Bastille, Paris; Sophie in Der Rosenkavalier at Palermo and Gilda at the San Francisco Opera, 2000–01; Covent Garden debut as Nannetta in Falstaff, repeated at the Vienna Staatsoper; further engagements in Don Carlos at Salzburg and Die Zauberflöte at the Bastille; Blonde in Die Entführung at Salzburg and in film conducted by Charles Mackerras. *Recordings include:* Nannetta in Falstaff, at Covent Garden (DVD). *Honours:* winner Maria Caniglia Competition 1996. *Current Management:* Atelier Musicale, Via Caselle 76, San Lazzaro di Savena 40068, Italy. *Telephone:* (51) 19984444. *Fax:* (51) 19984420. *E-mail:* info@ateliermusicale .com. *Website:* www.ateliermusicale.com.

RANDLE, Thomas (Tom); American singer (tenor); b. 21 Dec. 1958, Hollywood, Calif. *Education:* Univ. of Southern California. *Career:* concert appearances in the USA and Europe with the London Philharmonic Orchestra, Boston Symphony Orchestra and the Leipzig Radio Symphony Orchestra; has sung Berg and Stravinsky, and the US and world premieres of works by Tippett, Heinz Holliger and William Kraft, with the Los Angeles Philharmonic; often heard in works of Bach, Handel and Mozart; Bach's Christmas Oratorio in Leipzig; operatic repertoire includes all the major tenor roles of Mozart, Rossini and Donizetti, and French roles of Massenet and Thomas; British debut as Tamino in Nicholas Hytner's production of The Magic Flute (ENO 1988, returned 1989); European opera debut at the Aix-en-Provence Festival, France, in Purcell's The Fairy Queen; sang Monteverdi's Orfeo at Valencia 1989; Ferrando in Brussels and with Scottish Opera; sang Tamino at Glyndebourne 1991; sang Dionysius in the premiere of John Buller's The Bacchae and as Pelléas, ENO 1992; sang title role in reduced version of Pelléas et Mélisande with Peter Brook in Paris and on European tour, Netherlands Opera in world premiere of Peter Schaat's opera Symposion, based on Life of Tchaikovsky 1994; season 1994 returned to ENO to sing Tippett's King Priam and appeared in Britten's Gloriana at Covent Garden; Fairy Queen at ENO 1995; sang Idomeneo for Scottish Opera 1996, Mozart's Lucio Silla at Garsington 1998; engagements include Tom Rakewell in The Rake's Progress with Netherlands Opera; title role in Hasse's Solimano at the Staatsoper Berlin, Alfredo in La Traviata for Opera North; sang in the premiere of The Last Supper by Birtwistle, Berlin Staatsoper 2000; season 2000–01 as Schubert's Fierrabras at Buxton, Loge in The Rheingold for ENO, Berlioz's Bénédict for WNO and in Handel's Tamerlano at Halle; Handel's Samson at the London Proms 2002; Ulisse with ENO 2011; appearances with Teatro Real de Madrid in St François d'Assise 2011, Jack in Brokeback Mountain 2014, Admète in Alceste 2014; Aegisth in Elektra, La Scala 2014; Snaut in Solaris for Opéra de Lille, Théatre des Champs-Elyséees and Opéra de Lausanne 2015. *Recordings include:* Purcell's Fairy Queen with Les Arts Florissants, Tippett's The Ice Break with London Sinfonietta, Britten's War Requiem with BBC Scottish Symphony Orchestra, Luigi Nono, Canti di Vita e d'Amore with Bamberg Symphony Orchestra, Mozart's Requiem with German Nat. Youth Orchestra, Handel's Esther with Harry Christophers and The Sixteen, Requiem of Reconciliation with Helmuth Rilling and the Israel Philharmonic Orchestra, Handel's Messiah with the Royal Philharmonic Orchestra, Handel's Samson with Harry Christophers and the Symphony of Harmony and Invention, Terradellas, Sesostri 2011.

RANDOVÁ, Eva; Czech singer (mezzo-soprano); b. 31 Dec. 1936, Kolin. *Education:* studied with J. Svanova at Usti nad Labem, and Prague Conservatory. *Career:* sang first at Ostrava, as Eboli, Carmen, Amneris, the Princess in Rusalka, and Ortrud; Prague National Opera from 1969; Nuremberg and Stuttgart from 1971; Bayreuth Festival from 1973, as Gutrune, Fricka and Kundry; Salzburg Festival, 1975, Eboli in Don Carlos, conducted by Karajan; Covent Garden debut, 1977, as Ortrud; Returned to London as Marina, Venus, the Kostelnicka in Jenůfa, 1986, and Azucena in a new production of Il Trovatore, 1989; Metropolitan Opera, 1981, 1987, as Fricka and Venus; Orange Festival, 1985, as Marina in Boris Godunov; Vienna, 1987, in Rusalka; Sang Ortrud at San Francisco, 1989, Stuttgart, 1990; Sang Marina in Boris Godunov at Barcelona, 1990; Season 1992 as Clytemnestra at Athens; Covent Garden, 1994, as Kabanicha in Katya Kabanova (returned 1997); Sang Erda in Siegfried at Stuttgart, 1999; Grandmother in Jenůfa at Covent Garden, 2001; Frequent concert engagements; Jury Member, 1999 Cardiff Singer of the World Competition. *Recordings:* Bach cantatas; Santuzza in Cavalleria Rusticana; Mahler's Resurrection Symphony; Glagolitic Mass by Janáček; Šarka by Fibich; The Cunning Little Vixen and Jenůfa, conducted by Charles Mackerras.

RANDS, Bernard, MMus; American composer and conductor; b. 2 March 1934, Sheffield, Yorkshire, England. *Education:* Univ. of Wales, Bangor; studied in Italy with Dallapiccola, Boulez, Maderna and Berio. *Career:* instructor in the music dept, York Univ. 1968–74; Fellowship in Creative Arts, Brasenose Coll., Oxford 1972–73; Prof. of Music, Univ. of California, San Diego 1976; Visiting Prof., California Inst. of the Arts, Valencia 1984–85; worked at electronic music studios in Milan, Berlin, Albany (New York), Urbana; appearances as conductor of new music, notably with the London Sonor ensemble; founder mem., music theatre ensemble CLAP; mem. American Acad. of Arts and Letters 2004–. *Compositions include:* Serena, music theatre 1972–78; orchestral: Per Esempio 1968, Wildtrack I–III 1969–75, Agenda 1970, Mesalliance 1972, Ology for jazz group 1973, Aum 1974, Serenata 75b for flute, chamber orchestra 1976, Hirath for cello, orchestra 1987,... Body and Shadow... 1988; instrumental: Espressioni, series of piano pieces 1960–70, Actions for Six 1962, Formants I, II 1965–70, Tableau 1970, Memo 1–5, solo pieces 1971–75, Dejà I 1972, As all get out 1972, Etendre 1972, Response for double bass, tape 1973, Scherzi 1974, Cuaderna for string quartet 1975, Madrigali 1977, Obbligato for string quartet, trombone 1980,... In the Receding Mist... for flute, harp, string trio 1988, two string quartets 1974, 1994; vocal: Ballad 103 1970–73, Metalepsis for two mezzo-soprano 1971, Lunatici for soprano, ensemble 1980, Deja for two soprano, ensemble 1980, Sound Patterns for various combinations with voices, Canti del Sole for tenor, orchestra 1983, London Serenade 1984, Le Tambourin, suite 1, 2 1984, Ceremonial, 1, 2 1985–86, Serenata 85 1985, Requiescat for soprano, chorus, ensemble 1985–86,... Among the Voices... for chorus, harp 1988, Canzoni per Orchestra 1995, Symphony 1995, Cello Concerto 1996, Triple Concerto 1997, Requiescant for soprano, chorus and orchestra 1997, Opera commission for the Aspen Festival 1999. *Honours:* Hon. Fellow, Univ. of Wales, Bangor 2003; Pulitzer Prize for Canti del Sole 1984. *Address:* c/o Schott Music, 254 West 31st Street, Floor 15, New York, NY 10001, USA (office). *E-mail:* ny@schott-music.com (office). *Website:* www .schott-music.com (office); www.bernardrands.com.

RANGEL(-LATOUCHE), César, BMus, MMus, DMus, DipMus; Venezuelan pianist and educator; b. 3 April 1950, Caracas; m. María Cristina Graterol 1995; one s. *Education:* Juilliard School of Music, New York, Indiana Univ., Conservatory Juan Manuel Olivares. *Career:* debut at Carnegie Recital Hall, New York; extensive performances throughout USA; invited by Pres. of Venezuela to recital tour throughout the country; repertoire includes Bach's Goldberg Variations, complete cycle Beethoven Sonatas, Chopin 24 Preludes and Etudes, Ravel's Gaspard de la Nuit, Stravinsky's Petrouchka; performed Bartók's Second Piano Concerto, Int. Festival, Caracas; various television and radio broadcasts; performed Beethoven's Fifth Concerto with the Venezuelan Symphony Orchestra under Irwin Hoffmann; concert at Konzerthaus in Berlin of Beethoven's Fifth Piano Concerto, with Berliner Symphoniker under Eduardo Marturet; Teacher of Piano Performance, Master's Programme, Simón Bolívar Univ., Caracas. *Recordings:* Chopin Etudes op 10, 25, Schubert

Sonatas in G major and B Flat major, Beethoven Sonatas op 109, 110, 111, Beethoven's Emperor Concerto.

RANGELOV, Svetozar; Bulgarian singer (bass); b. 1967. *Education:* State Musical Acad., Sofia. *Career:* many concert and opera engagements in Bularia and elsewhere in Europe; opera debut as Ferrando in Il Trovatore with the Bulgarian Nat. Opera 1995; repertory also includes Le nozze di Figaro, Verdi's Vespri Siciliani and songs by Glière, Cui and Borodin; contestant at Cardiff Singer of the World Competition 1995.

RÁNKI, Dezsö; Hungarian pianist; b. 8 Sept. 1951, Budapest; s. of József Ránki and Edith Jecsmen; m. Edit Klukon 1979; two c. *Education:* Ferenc Liszt Music Acad. under Pál Kadosa. *Career:* has given recitals and appeared with several leading orchestras throughout Europe, including Berlin Philharmonic, Concertgebouw and London Philharmonic, and festivals such as Lucerne, Roque d'Anthéron, La Folle Journée in Nantes, Tokyo, Bilbao; regular concert tours of N America and Japan; four-hands piano recitals with Edit Klukon in European cities 1985–; has taught piano at Budapest Music Acad. since 1973. *Recordings include:* works by Bartók, Brahms, Haydn, Kadosa, Mozart, Ravel and Schumann. *Honours:* First Prize, Int. Schumann Competition, Zwickau, GDR 1969, Grand Prix Int. du Disque (Paris) 1972, Liszt Prize 2nd Degree 1973, Kossuth Prize 1978. *Current Management:* Interartists Amsterdam, Laing's Nekstraat 31, 1092 GT, Amsterdam, Netherlands. *Address:* Ördögorom Lejtő 11/B, 1112 Budapest, Hungary (home). *Telephone:* (1) 246-4403 (home).

RANKINE, Peter John, BMus, GradDipMus, MMus; Australian composer and conductor; b. 11 March 1960, Qld. *Education:* Queensland Conservatory and Univ. of Queensland. *Career:* faculty mem., Univ. of Queensland 1987, Queenland Univ. of Technology 1988–94; commissions from Queensland Wind Soloists, Australian Broadcasting Commission, Dance North, Opera Queensland, Canticum and others. *Compositions include:* Bunyip! (chamber opera) 1985, Three Movements for orchestra 1986, Eulogy for wind quintet 1987, Symphonia Dialectica 1988, From Fire by Fire for wind octet 1989, Celtic Cross for violin and chamber orchestra 1990, Time and the Bell clarinet concerto 1990, John Brown, Rose and the Midnight Cat for ensemble 1992, Surya Namaskar, Chaand Namaskar for horn and percussion 1993, Please No More Psalms (ballet score) for oboe, clarinet, percussion, violin and cello 1994, Media Vita for choir, clarinet, trombone and percussion 1997. *Honours:* Sounds Australian Awards 1990–91.

RAPER, Marion Eileen, BA, MA, LRAM; British pianist, vocal coach, teacher and accompanist; *Lecturer in Accompaniment, Italian for Singers and Piano, Leeds College of Music;* b. 18 Feb. 1938, Birmingham, England; m. 1st 1962 (divorced 1979); m. 2nd 2006. *Education:* Royal Acad. of Music, Univ. of London, Goldsmiths' Coll., London, Open Univ., Univ. of Manchester, Leeds Metropolitan Univ. *Career:* recitals throughout England with singers and instrumentalists; broadcasts for BBC and Capital Radio; Lecturer in Accompaniment, Italian for Singers and Piano, Leeds Coll. of Music 1985–; masterclasses; piano duo tours of Canada with Jennifer Hillman 1987, 1989; TV appearances (ITV and Channel 4); vocal coach, accompanist and teacher; examiner, Associated Bd of the Royal Schools of Music; Fellow, Incorporated Soc. of Musicians; mem. Royal Soc. of Musicians. *Address:* 3 Cavendish Drive, Guiseley, Leeds, LS20 8DR, England. *Telephone:* (1943) 873060; 7989-087507 (mobile). *E-mail:* marion.raper@mac.com.

RAPHANEL, Ghilaine; French singer (soprano); b. 19 April 1952, Rouen. *Education:* Rouen Conservatory, Paris Conservatoire with Janine Micheau. *Career:* sang Rosina in Il Barbiere di Siviglia at the Opera Studio of the Paris Opéra; Stadttheater Basle from 1980 as Gilda, Constanze, Juliette, Manon, and Titania in A Midsummer Night's Dream; guest appearances in Lyon and Nantes; Hamburg Staatsoper, 1985, as the Queen of Night and Zerbinetta; Aix-en-Provence Festival, 1985, Zerbinetta; sang at Mézières, 1988, as Amor in Orfeo ed Euridice; at Nancy, 1989, as Susanna; sang Nicolai's Frau Fluth at the Paris Opéra-Comique, 1995–96. *Recordings include:* Pousette in Manon, L'Etoile by Chabrier; Fiorella in Les Brigands by Offenbach; Marguérite de Valois in Les Huguenots. *Current Management:* Mondial Musique, 17 rue Brey, 75017 Paris, France. *Telephone:* (1) 55-37-93-50. *Fax:* (1) 55-37-93-51. *E-mail:* alfonsir@wanadoo.fr.

RAPPÉ, Jadwiga; Polish singer (contralto); b. 1957. *Education:* Univ. of Warsaw, Karol Lipinsky Acad. of Music, Wroclaw. *Career:* sang at first in concert and made stage debut at Warsaw in 1983; has sung throughout Europe in concert, notably with masses by Mozart, Bach and Beethoven and Szymanowski's Stabat Mater; performances of Erda in Wagner's Ring at the Deutsche Oper Berlin, Warsaw and Covent Garden from 1988; other operatic roles include Ulrica, Orpheus, Juno in Semele, Countess in The Queen of Spades, Gaea in Daphne, Erda in Siegfried; Lecturer, Vocal Dept, Frederic Chopin Collective State Music Schools 2005–; Artistic Dir, Chain VI Festival 2009; Chair. Anna and Jaroslaw Iwaszkiewicz Museum, Stawisko 2005–; Pres. Witold Lutoslawski Soc. 2006–09; mem. Polish Assicn of Music Artists 1977–. *Honours:* Gold Cross for Merit; First Prize and Gold Medal, Int. Johann Sebastian Bach Competition 1980, Gold Medal, Festival of Young Soloists, Bordeaux 1981. *Current Management:* Szwed Artists Management, 05-807 Podkowa Lesna, ul. Borsucza 64, Poland. *Telephone:* (22) 7589649. *Fax:* (22) 7589649. *E-mail:* office@szwedart.info. *Website:* www.szwedart.info. *E-mail:* office@rappe.pl (office). *Website:* www.rappe.pl.

RASILAINEN, Jukka; Finnish singer (bass-baritone); b. 1959, Helsinki. *Education:* studied in Rome and Helsinki. *Career:* debut at Savonlinna Festival, 1983, as Leporello; Lahti, 1984, as Rossini's Basilio; Dortmund Opera from 1986, as Verdi's Zaccaria and Ferrando, Galitzky in Prince Igor and Wozzeck; Karlsruhe, 1990, as Masetto and the Commendatore, in Don Giovanni; Vienna Staatsoper, 1991, as Wagner's Dutchman, Dresden, 1992–95, as Kaspar in Der Freischütz, Pizarro and Kurwenal; Finnish National Opera, 1996, as Wotan in Das Rheingold; Other roles include the Villains in Les contes d'Hoffmann, Scarpia, Amonasro and Jochanaan; Sang Strauss's Mandryka and Orestes at the Dresden Staatsoper, 1999; Season 2000–01 as Wagner's Wanderer at Mannheim, Wotan for the Zürich Opera and Jochanaan in Salome at Dresden. *Current Management:* c/o Opera Vladarski, Döblinger Hauptstraße 57/18, 1190 Vienna, Austria. *Telephone:* (1) 368-6960/6961. *Fax:* (1) 368-6962. *E-mail:* opera.vladarski@utanet.at.

RASKATOV, Alexander; Russian composer; b. 1953, Moscow. *Education:* Moscow Conservatory. *Career:* has received commissions from Gidon Kremer, Sabine Meyer Wind Ensemble, Netherlands Wind Ensemble, Hilliard Ensemble, Schoenberg Ensemble; composer-in-residence Stetson Univ., USA 1990; mem. Asscn for Contemporary Music. *Compositions:* 66 for soprano and 12 instruments 1990, Dolce far niente for cello and piano 1991, Xenia for chamber orchestra 1991, Commentary on a Vision for solo percussion and orchestra 1991, Kyrie eleison for solo cello 1992, Miserere for viola, violin, cello and orchestra 1992, Misteria brevis for piano and percussion 1992, Concerto for oboe and 15 strings 1993, Madrigal in Metal for five percussionists 1993, Eco perpetuo for solo bassoon, bass clarinet, trombone, percussion, harp, piano, cello and double bass 1993, Seven Stages of Hallelujah for soprano (with the use of percussion) and piano 1993, I will see a rose at the end of the path... for string quartet 1994, Litany for 15 musicians 1994, Xcos for cello and accordion 1994, Pas de deux for soprano (with tubular bells), soprano and tenor saxophones 1994, Farewell from the Birds of Passage for alto saxophone, percussion and strings 1994, Primal Song for viola and 15 string instruments 1995, Credo in Byzantinum for harpsichord or piano 1995, Songs of Sunset for mezzo-soprano, viola and piano 1995, Gebet for soprano and string quartet 1996, Resurrexit for soprano, mezzo-soprano and chamber orchestra 1996–97, Blissful Music for cello and chamber orchestra 1997, Quasi Hamlet for soprano and chamber ensemble 1997, Swinging the Dream Pendulum for violin and instrumental ensemble 1998, Ritual for voice and percussion 1997, Ritual II for four saxophones, percussion, piano and strings 1998–99, Paradise Lost? for wind ensemble 1999, Pro-Kofiev et Contra-Kofiev for wind instruments and percussion 1999, Before Thy Throne... for violin and percussion 1999, Circle of Singing-2 for baritone and piano 2000, Praise for four male voices and church bells 2000, In nomine for eight voices, wind instruments and percussion 2001, Voices of Frozen Land for seven voices, wind instruments and percussion 2001, Put-Path-Chemin-Weg for viola and orchestra 2003, Five Minutes from the life of W. A. Mozart. *Honours:* Salzburg Easter Festival composition prize 1998.

RASMUSSEN, Karl Aage; Danish composer, conductor and academic; b. 14 Dec. 1947, Kolding; m. Charlotte Schiotz 1975. *Education:* Acad. of Music, Århus and studied with Per Norgaard. *Career:* teacher, Acad. of Music, Århus 1970–, Royal Acad., Copenhagen 1980–; Dir, Conductor of chamber ensemble, The Elsinore Players 1975–; numerous duties at the New Music Dept, Danish Radio, co-editing The Danish Music Magazine; lectures in many European countries, USA; Artistic Dir, NUMUS Festival, Århus, and Esbjerg Ensemble 1991–; mem. Danish Music Council, Danish Arts Foundation. *Compositions include:* stage: Jephta (two-act opera) 1976–77, Majakovskij (two-act scenic concert piece) 1977–78, Jonas (musical play for radio) 1978–80, Our Hoffmann (opera) 1986, The Sinking of the Titanic (opera) 1994; orchestral: Symphony Anfang und Ende 1973, Contrafactum concerto for cello and orchestra 1980, A Symphony in Time 1982, Movements on a Moving Line 1985, Phantom Movements 1989, Litania 1994, Cosmology According to Chagall for piano and chamber orchestra 1996, Blissful Music for violin and orchestra 1997; chamber: Protocol and Myth 1971, Genklang 1972, A Ballad of Game and Dream 1974, Lullaby 1976, Berio Mask 1977, Le Tombeau de Père Igor 1977, Parts Apart 1978, Capricci e Dance 1979, Italiensk Koncert 1981, Ballo in Maschera 1981, Pianissimo Furioso 1982, A Quartet of Five 1982, Solos and Shadows 1983, Fugue/Fuga (Encore VIII) 1984, Surrounded by Sales 1985, Still string quartet 1988; solo instrument: Invention 1972, Antifoni 1973, Paganini Variations 1976, Fugue/Fuga 1984, Triple Tango 1984, Etudes and Postludes for piano 1990, I Will See a Rose at the End of the Path for string quartet 1994; vocal: Love is in the World 1974–75, One and All 1976, Encore Series I–XI 1977–85, Gebet for soprano and string quartet 1996, Resurrexi... for soprano, mezzo and chamber orchestra 1997, Praise for four voices 1998. *Honours:* Carl Nielsen Prize 1991.

RASMUSSEN, Paula; American singer (mezzo-soprano); b. 1965, California. *Career:* concert appearances with San Francisco Symphony under Nicholas McGegan in Bach Cantatas, the Los Angeles Master Chorale in Messiah, Bruckner's Te Deum and Pergolesi's Magnifict and with José Carreras in Dublin 1992; opera engagements as Nancy T'ang in the Peter Sellars production of Nixon in China at Los Angeles, Paris and Frankfurt; Lola in Cavalleria Rusticana with Long Beach Opera; Nancy in Albert Herring, Hansel, Anna in Les Troyens, Hippolyta in Midsummer Night's Dream and the Composer in Ariadne auf Naxos with the Los Angeles Music Center Opera; sang Handel's Serse at Cologne 1996 and Geneva 1998; season 2000 as Carmen at Cologne, Handel's Serse in Dresden and Cherubino for the New York City Opera. *Honours:* regional winner Metropolitan Opera Competition 1992.

RASMUSSEN, Sunleif; Faroese composer; b. 19 March 1961, Sandur. *Education:* Norges Musikkhøgskole, studied in Denmark with Bent Sørensen, Royal Danish Acad. of Music. *Compositions include:* Sig mær hví er foldin føgur (Tell Me Why the World is Pretty) 1982, Kvøldvísa um summarmála (Evening Tune in April) for choir 1983, Vár (Spring) for choir 1983, Sóljurnar og náttin (Marsh Marigolds and the Night) 1984, Blátt (Blue) for choir 1985, Skærur vindur (Pure Winds) for choir 1988, String Quartet No. 1 1989–90, Vetrarmyndir (Winter Pictures) for wind quintet and piano 1991, Tid, Ild, Baglæns (Time, Fire, Backwards) for choir and pre-recorded tape 1991–92, Syngjandi grót (Singing Rocks) 1992, Landid (The Land) 1992–93, Sum hin gylta sól (Like the Golden Sun) for piano and electronics 1993, Til Syvstjernen (To the Pleiades) for violin, flute, clarinet and piano 1993, Eitt ljós er kveikt (A Light has been Lit) for organ and tape 1993, The Song of the Sea for orchestra and tape 1994–95, Tilegnelse (Dedication) for mezzo-soprano and ensemble 1995, Symphony No. 1 (Oceanic Days) (Nordic Council Music Award 2002) 1995–97, Cantus Borealis for wind quintet 1996, Vox humana (electronic score) 1997, Pictures from the Sea's Garden for saxophone and percussion 1998, Arktis for mezzo-soprano and ensemble 1998, Trauer und Freude for 10 instruments 1999, Surrounded for chamber orchestra 2000, Sunshine and Shadows for string quartet 2000, Dem Livht entgegen for saxophone 2001, Nordisk Fanfare 2002, Enführung for chamber choir 2002, Four Gardens 2003, De graedendes nat for choir 2003, Songs of Seasons 2004, Movings and Melodies 2004, Suite for guitar solo 2007, Prelude to an Orchestra 2008. *Recordings include:* Symphony No. 1 Oceanic Days, Dem Licht Entgegen, Surrounded, Arktis, Mozaik / Miniature, Tilegnelse, Trauer und Freude. *Honours:* Hon. Pres. Faroese Arts Festival 2003. *Address:* c/o Edition Wilhelm Hansen, Bornholmsgade 1, 1266 Copenhagen, Denmark (office). *Website:* www.musicsalesclassical.com (office).

RATH, John Frédéric, BA; British singer (bass-baritone); b. 10 June 1956, Manchester, England. *Education:* Manchester University, Royal Northern Coll. of Music, Opera School at Basle; studied with Elsa Cavelti and Max Lorenz in Salzburg. *Career:* debut as Ramphis in Aida, RNCM; appearances with English Music Theatre Company, Glyndebourne Festival and Touring Company, Royal Opera House, Covent Garden, La Fenice, Venice, Maggio Musicale in Florence; roles include: Masetto in Don Giovanni, Argante in Handel's Rinaldo, Sparafucile in Rigoletto, Escamillo and Zuniga in Carmen; recently in Peter Brook's La Tragédie de Carmen in Paris, its European tour and New York as Escamillo; Kent Opera: Rocco in Fidelio; Nexus Opera: The Traveller in Britten's Curlew River at Wells Cathedral and filmed by BBC 2; Edinburgh Festival: Jochanaan in Salome; English Bach Festival: Charon in Handel's Alceste; appearances at various festivals; Prin. Bass with D'Oyly Carte Opera; concert and oratorio work throughout Europe including notable performances of Handel's Theodora in London, Spain and Italy, Bach Cantatas in New York and concert performances including Wotan in Das Rheingold and Die Walküre; Opera North: The Doctor in Berg's Wozzeck, 1993; Sarastro in Mozart's The Magic Flute, 1994; Nourabad in Bizet's Les Pêcheurs de Perles, 1995; cr. a new English version of Schubert's Winter Journey with the poet Miriam Scott and performed it; sang Herod in Stradella's San Giovanni Batista, Batignano, 1996; Satyr and Cythéron in Rameau's Platée in Berkeley, California, and Ferrando in Il Trovatore for Opera South in Cork, Ireland, 1998; sang Second Soldier in Salome and the Poet in Salieri's Prima la musica poi le parole for Oper Frankfurt, 1999; Ashby in La Fanciulla del West for Opera Zuid, Maastricht; King Philip, Don Carlos; Pizarro, Fidelio; Golaud, Pelléas et Mélisande for Stadtsoper Bremerhaven, 2002–03; Sebastian in d'Alberts' Tiefland; Wicks Booth, Sondheim Assassins; Iago, Otello and bass-baritone roles in Contes d'Hoffmann, also for Bremerhaven, 2003–04; Kaspar in Der Freischütz at Stadttheater, Bremerhaven, Schaunard in La Bohème, Der Sprecher in Die Zauberflöte, Dikoy in Katya Kabanova 2004–05, Mephisto in Faust, title role in Rigoletto, ein Musiklehrer in Ariadne auf Naxos 2005–06, Dr Schön in Lulu 2007, Jochanaan in Salome, Bremerhaven and Pforzheim 2008. *Film:* as Escamillo in film of Peter Brook's La Tragédie de Carmen. *Recordings:* The Gondoliers and Iolanthe with the D'Oyly Carte. *Publication:* The Song Cycles Winterreise and Die Schöne Müllerin (new English versions by Miriam Scott alongside the original German, illustrated by Esther Gruber). *Address:* Cwmllechwedd Fawr, Llanbister, Powys, LD1 6UH, Wales (home). *Telephone:* (1597) 840267 (home). *E-mail:* j.rath@hotmail.co.uk (home).

RATNER, Sabina Teller; Canadian musicologist; m. Jack Ratner; one s. one d. *Career:* fmr teacher, Vanier Coll.; currently Assoc. Prof. of Music, Univ. de Montréal; leading expert on French music of the 19th and 20th centuries, esp. the music of Saint-Saëns. *Music:* arrangements: Saint-Saëns' Henry VIII. Le Théâtre français de la musique 1992, Quatuor 1992, The Shorter Cello Works 1997, Sonate de Liszt 2002, Saint-Saëns: An Annotated Thematic Catalogue of his Complete Works 2002, Saint-Saens Oeuvres pour piano I, Saint-Saens Oeuvres pour piano II. *Publications:* contribs to Pipers Enzyklopädie des Musiktheaters 1994, Échos de France et d'Italie 1997, Regarding Fauré 1999, New Grove Dictionary of Music 2000. *Honours:* Univ. Scholar, McGill Univ.; Gov.-Gen.'s Medal for Academic Proficiency, MLA Best Article of a Music-Bibliographic Nature 1986, Best Music Research Book 2004. *Address:* 4595 Circle Road, Montréal, PQ H3W 1Y9, Canada (office). *Telephone:* (514) 489-4128 (office). *E-mail:* sabina.ratner@sympatico.ca (office). *Website:* www.musique.umontreal.ca (office).

RATTI, Eugenia; singer (soprano); b. 5 April 1933, Genoa, Italy. *Education:* studied with her mother. *Career:* concert tour with Tito Schipa, 1952; stage debut, 1954, in Sestri Levante; La Scala Milan from 1955, as Lisa in La Sonnambula, and in the premiere of Milhaud's David, 1955, and Dialogues des Carmélites, 1957; Holland Festival, 1955, 1961, as Nannetta and Adina; Edinburgh Festival, 1957, Il Matrimonio Segreto; Holland Festival, 1970, in Haydn's La Fedeltà Premiata; returned to Glyndebourne, 1973 and 1976, as the Italian Singer in Capriccio; Other roles include Zerlina in Don Giovanni, Susanna, Rosina, Musetta and Oscar. *Recordings:* Un Ballo in Maschera; Il Matrimonio Segreto; Aida; La Sonnambula; Don Giovanni, conducted by Leinsdorf.

RATTLE, Sir Simon Dennis, Kt, OM, CBE; British conductor; *Artistic Director and Chief Conductor, Berlin Philharmonic Orchestra;* b. 19 Jan. 1955, Liverpool; s. of Denis Guttridge Rattle and Pauline Lila Violet Rattle (née Greening); m. 1st Elise Ross 1980 (divorced 1995); two s.; m. 2nd Candace Allen 1996 (divorced 2004); m. 3rd Magdalena Kožená 2008; two s. one d. *Education:* Royal Acad. of Music. *Career:* has conducted Bournemouth Symphony, Northern Sinfonia, London Philharmonic, London Sinfonietta, Berlin Philharmonic, LA Philharmonic, Stockholm Philharmonic, Vienna Philharmonic, Philadelphia Orchestra, Boston Symphony orchestras, etc.; debut at Queen Elizabeth Hall, London 1974, Royal Festival Hall, London 1976, Royal Albert Hall, London 1976; Asst Conductor, BBC Symphony Orchestra 1977–80; Assoc. Conductor, Royal Liverpool Philharmonic Soc. 1977–80; Glyndebourne debut 1977, Royal Opera, Covent Garden debut 1990; Artistic Dir, London Choral Soc. 1979–84; Prin. Conductor and Artistic Adviser, City of Birmingham Symphony Orchestra (CBSO) 1980–90, Music Dir 1990–98; Artistic Dir South Bank Summer Music 1981–83; Jt Artistic Dir Aldeburgh Festival 1982–93; Prin. Guest Conductor, LA Philharmonic 1981–94, Rotterdam Philharmonic 1981–84; Prin. Guest Conductor Orchestra of the Age of Enlightenment 1992–; Artistic Dir and Chief Conductor Berlin Philharmonic Orchestra 2002– (announced in 2013 that he would step down in 2018); announced in March 2015 that he would become Music Dir of the London Symphony Orchestra (LSO) from Sept. 2017; conducted LSO at Opening Ceremony of London Olympics 2012; UNICEF Goodwill Amb. 2007–; Patron Elton John AIDS Foundation. *Honours:* Hon. Fellow, St Anne's Coll. Oxford 1991; Hon. Fellow, Soc. of Arts 2006; Officier, Ordre des Arts et des Lettres 1995; Order of Merit of the FRG; Chevalier, Légion d'honneur 2010; Hon. DMus (Liverpool) 1991, (Leeds) 1993, (RAM) 2011; won John Player Int. Conducting Competition 1973, Edison Award (for recording of Shostakovich's Symphony No. 10) 1987, Grand Prix du Disque (Turangalîla Symphony) 1988, Grand Prix Caecilia (Turangalîla Symphony, Jazz Album) 1988, Gramophone Record of the Year Award (Mahler's Symphony No. 2) 1988, Gramophone Opera Award (Porgy and Bess) 1989, Int. Record Critics' Award (Porgy and Bess) 1990, Grand Prix de l' Acad. Charles Cros 1990, Gramophone Artist of the Year 1993, Montblanc de la Culture Award 1993, Shakespeare Prize, Toepfer Foundation, Hamburg 1996, Gramophone Award for Best Concerto recording (Szymanowski Violin Concertos Nos 1 and 2), RSA Albert Medal 1997, Choc de l'Année Award (for recording of Brahms Piano Concerto Op. 15) 1998, Outstanding Achievement Award, South Bank Show 1999, Diapason Recording of the Year Award (complete Beethoven Piano Concertos) 1999, Gramophone Award for Best Opera Recording (Szymanowski's King Roger) 2000, Gramophone Awards for Best Orchestral Recording and Record of the Year (Mahler's Symphony No. 10) 2000, Comenius Prize (Germany) 2004, Classical BRIT Award (for Beethoven Symphonies) 2004, Schiller Special Prize, City of Mannheim 2005, Classical BRIT Award for Classical Recording of the Year (Holst's The Planets) 2007, Gramophone Award for Best Choral Recording (Brahms' Ein deutsches Requiem) 2007, Gold Medal 'Gloria Artis', Premio Don Juan de Borbón de la Música 2009, Wolf Prize in Music (shared with Plácido Domingo) 2012, ECHO Klassik Award for Symphonic Recording of the Year – 20th/21st Century (for Schönberg CD) 2012, voted into the inaugural Gramophone Hall of Fame 2012, Léonie Sonning Music Prize 2013. *Address:* Berlin Philharmonic Orchestra, Herbert-von-Karajan-Str. 1, 10785 Berlin, Germany (office). *Telephone:* (30) 25488999 (office). *Website:* www .berliner-philharmoniker.de (office); www.askonasholt.co.uk/artists/ conductors/simon-rattle.

RAUCH, Wolfgang; German singer (baritone); b. 27 Jan. 1957, Cologne. *Education:* studied in Cologne with Josef Metternich and in Italy with Mario del Monaco. *Career:* sang with the Deutsche Oper am Rhein Düsseldorf from 1984, member of the Bayerische Staatsoper Munich from 1987; Guest appearances at La Scala Milan, the State Operas of Vienna and Hamburg and the Deutsche Oper Berlin; Sang Papageno in Mozart bicentenary performances of Die Zauberflöte at Barcelona and Bonn, 1991; Other roles include Lortzing's Tsar, Marcello, Mozart's Guglielmo and Figaro, Count Perruchetto in Haydn's La Fedeltà Premiata, Silvio, Lionel in Tchaikovsky's The Maid of Orleans, Strauss's Count in Capriccio and Harlekin and the Herald in Lohengrin (Hamburg, 1998); Season 2000–01 as Puccini's Marcello at Hamburg, Strauss's Spirit Messenger at Barcelona and Lescaut in Henze's Boulevard Solitude for Covent Garden; Frequent concert and broadcasting engagements.

RAUNIG, Arno; German singer (countertenor); b. 1956, Klagenfurt. *Education:* Vienna Boys' Choir, Linz Conservatoire, studied with Kurt Equiluz in Vienna. *Career:* operatic debut, Stadttheater Klagenfurt 1990; many appearances in Baroque music throughout Europe, notably in works by Bach, Handel and Mozart in Vienna, Berlin and Hamburg; repertoire includes Mozart's

Ascanio in Alba and Idomeneo, Handel's Radamisto and Xerxes, Cesti's Pomo d'Oro and The Fairy Queen; Wiesbaden Festival, 1992, in the premiere of Der Park by Hans Gefors; sang Creon in the premiere of Medea by Osca Strasnoy, Spoleto 2000; appearances at Berlin Philharmonie, the Gewandhaus Leipzig, the Hamburg Concerthall, El Auditorio Nacional, Madrid, Paula de la Musica Catalana, Barcelona, in Bremen, the Tonhalle Zürich, the Herkulessaal, Munich, Wiener Musikverein, Wiener Konzerthaus. *Current Management:* Kultur-Management Wien, Hainburgerstrasse 26/26, 1030 Vienna, Austria. *Telephone:* (1) 890-54-04. *Fax:* (1) 890-54-04-4. *E-mail:* info@kultur -management.at. *Website:* www.kultur-management.at. *E-mail:* arno .raunig@gmx.at (office). *Website:* www.arno-raunig.at.

RAUTAVAARA, Einojuhani, MA; Finnish composer; b. 9 Oct. 1928, Helsinki; m. Sini Koivisto 1984. *Education:* Univ. of Helsinki, Sibelius Acad., Juilliard School of Music with Vincent Persichetti, New York, USA, Tanglewood Music Center with Aaron Copland and Roger Sessions, studied with Vladimir Vogel in Ascona, Switzerland, Kölner Musikhochschule with Rudolf Petzold, Germany. *Career:* Lecturer in Music Theory, Sibelius Acad. 1966–76, Prof. of Composition 1976–90; Art Prof., Finland 1971–76. *Compositions include:* operas: Kaivos 1957, Thomas 1983, Vincent 1986, House of the Sun 1990, Gift of the Magi 1993, Aleksis Kivi 1995, Rasputin 2003; other: Cantus Arcticus concerto for birds and orchestra, Angel of Dusk concerto for double bass and orchestra, concertos for cello and flute, three concertos for piano, concertos for violin, organ, double bass, clarinet, harp and percussion, Vigilia (Orthodox Mass), Missa a Cappella, two choir-operas, eight symphonies, cantatas (True & False Unicorn, In the Last Frontier, Independence Cantata 1967, Balada), four string quartets, two string quintets, Rubaiyat for baritone and orchestra; works for string orchestra: Autumn Gardens, The Fiddlers, Cantos I–V, A Finnish Myth, Bird Gardens, Adagio Celeste; works for orchestra: Angels and Visitations, Apotheosis, Before the Icons, Book of Visions, Isle of Bliss, Manhattan Trilogy, Modificata, A Requiem in Our Time, A Soldier's Mass, Tapestry of Life. *Recordings include:* Concertos (Colin Currie, Truls Mørk with Helsinki Philharmonic and John Storgårds) (Gramophone Award for Best Contemporary Recording 2012), Towards the Horizon (Gramophone Award 2012, Int. Classical Music Award) 2013. *Publications:* Omakuva (memoirs) 1989, Mieltymyksestä äärettömään (essays) 1998, Säveltäjä ja Muusa (with Sini Rautavaara) 2001. *Honours:* Kt's Cross of Merit (Hungary) 2012; Pro Finlandia, Commdr of the Finnish Lion; Golden Helsinki Medal; Hon. PhD (Oulu) 1983; MIDEM Classical Award 1997, 1998, ABC 1998, Supersonic 2010, Sibelius Prize; Composition contests: Cincinnati 1954, London 1966, Suomi Award 1997. *Current Management:* c/o Boosey & Hawkes, Aldwych House, 71–91 Aldwych, London, WC2B 4HN, England. *Website:* www.boosey.com.

RAUTIO, Nina; Russian singer (soprano); b. 21 Sept. 1957, Bryansk. *Education:* Leningrad Conservatoire. *Career:* sang first at the Leningrad State Theatre 1981–87; Bolshoi Opera from 1987; Western debut with Bolshoi Company at Metropolitan and Edinburgh Festival 1991, as Tatiana and as Oksana in Rimsky's Christmas Eve; season 1992, as Manon Lescaut at La Scala, conducted by Lorin Maazel, Verdi Requiem at Rome, Aida at Savonlinna Festival and in concert performances conducted by Zubin Mehta; sang with Pittsburgh Symphony on tour to Seville Expo 92 and as Elisabetta in Don Carlo to open the season at La Scala; season 1993–94, as Lisa in The Queen of Spades at Opéra Bastille Paris, Ballo in Maschera and Aida at Covent Garden, Verdi Requiem at Florence and the Festival Hall, Beethoven and Mahler in Pittsburgh, Desdemona at Orange Festival, Glagolitic Mass at La Scala and Amelia Boccanegra at Florence; season 1994–95, as Aida at Staatsoper Berlin and Amelia Boccanegra at Florence and Turin; season 1995–96, Metropolitan Opera debut as Aida; sang Aida at Verona Arena 1996 and Trovatore Leonora at Geneva 1998; sang Tosca at Glasgow 2000. *Recordings:* Manon Lescaut, Verdi Requiem, Guillaume Tell, Norma. *Current Management:* c/o Athole Still Opera Ltd, Foresters Hall, 25–27 Westow Street, London, SE19 3RY, England. *Telephone:* (20) 8771-5271. *Fax:* (20) 8771-8172. *E-mail:* enquiries@atholestill.co.uk. *Website:* www.atholestill.co.uk.

RAWLINS, Emily, BMus; American singer; b. 25 Sept. 1950, Lancaster, OH; m. 1982. *Education:* Indiana University, Curtis Institute of Music, Hochschule für Musik, Vienna. *Career:* debut in Basel, Switzerland; Basel Stadttheater, 1973–77; Deutsche Oper am Rhein, 1977–82; Debuts, Theater der Stadt Bonn, 1975, National Theater, Mannheim, 1976, Theater der Stadt Köln, 1977, Städtische Bühnen, Dortmund, 1979, Städtische Bühnen, Augsburg; San Francisco Opera, 1980; American premiere, Lear, Salzburg Festival, world premiere of Baal, 1981; Vienna Staatsoper, 1981; Teatro Nacional de São Carlos, Lisbon, 1982; Grand Théâtre de Genève, 1982; Houston Grand Opera, 1983; American premiere of Anna Karenina, Los Angeles Opera Theater, 1983; Appeared on television, ZDF Germany, 1981, 1982, ORF, Austria, 1981; Film appearances in Bartered Bride and Fra Diavolo, 1983, and Baal, 1984; Vienna State Opera, 1985; ORF with Wiener Symphoniker; Concert Opera Association, 1986; World premiere of Das Schloss, Opera National, Brussels, 1986; Sang Third Norn in Götterdämmerung at Cologne, 2000. *Recordings:* Baal (singing part of Sophie) 1985. *Address:* c/o Alferink, Appolaan 181, 1077 AT Amsterdam, The Netherlands.

RAWNSLEY, John, FRNCM; British singer (baritone); b. 14 Dec. 1950, England. *Education:* Royal Northern Coll. of Music. *Career:* debut with Glyndebourne Touring Opera 1975; later sang Verdi's Ford and Stravinsky's Nick Shadow on tour, Mozart's Masetto, Rossini's Figaro and Puccini's Marcello at Glyndebourne; Covent Garden debut as Schaunard in La Bohème

1979; French debut at Nancy as Tonio in Pagliacci 1980; ENO from 1982, as Amonasro and as Rigoletto in Jonathan Miller's production of Verdi's opera; tour to USA 1984; Italian debut as Verdi's Renato in Trieste 1985; La Scala Milan as Tonio 1987; guest engagements at Vienna Staatsoper, San Diego, Barcelona, Bilbao, Brussels and Geneva: roles include Paolo Albiani (Simon Boccanegra), Macbeth, Papageno, Don Alfonso and Taddeo in L'Italiana in Algeri; sang Rigoletto at Turin 1989, Simon Boccanegra in a concert performance at Royal Festival Hall 1990; Season 1992 as Rigoletto at Oslo and the Coliseum, and in The Beggar's Opera at Aldeburgh Festival; sang Falstaff for Opera Zuid, Netherlands 1994; sang Old Deuteronomy in Andrew Lloyd Weber's Cats at New London Theatre 1995–97; sang Albert Blossom in Doctor Dolittle at Apollo Theatre, Hammersmith, London 1998–99, then sang same role on nat. tour 2000–01; now singing mainly in musical theatre. *Recordings:* Rigoletto, Masetto in Don Giovanni, videos of Così fan tutte, Il Barbiere di Siviglia, La Bohème and Rigoletto. *Current Management:* c/o Irene Fawkes, Irene Fawkes Management, 91A Rivington Street, London, EC2A 3AY, England. *Telephone:* (20) 7729-8559. *Fax:* (20) 7613-0769. *E-mail:* irenefawkes@btconnect.com. *E-mail:* johnrawnsley@stageleft.demon.co.uk (home). *Website:* www.johnrawnsley.com.

RAXACH, Enrique; Dutch composer; b. 15 Jan. 1932, Barcelona, Spain. *Education:* studied in Darmstadt with Messiaen, Boulez, Stockhausen and Maderna. *Compositions include:* Estudis for strings, 1952; Six Movements for orchestra, 1955; Polifonias, for strings, 1956; Metamorphose I–II for orchestra, 1956–58; Metamorphose III for 15 solo instruments, 1959; Columna de fuego for orchestra 1958; Fluxion, for 17 players, 1963; Syntagma, for orchestra, 1965; Fragmento II for soprano, flute and 2 percussionists, 1966; Textures for orchestra, 1966; Inside Outside for orchestra and tape, 1969; Paraphrase for mezzo-soprano and 11 players, 1969; 2 String Quartets, 1961, 1971; Rite of Perception, electronic tape music, 1971; Interface for chorus and orchestra, 1972; Scattertime for 6 players, 1972; Sine Nomine for soprano and orchestra, 1973; Figuren in einer Landschaft for orchestra, 1974; Chimaera for bass clarinet and tape, 1974; Erdenlicht for orchestra, 1975; Aubade for percussion quartet, 1979; The Hunting in Winter for horn and piano, 1979; Am Ende des Regenbogens, for orchestra, 1980; Careful with that... for clarinet and percussionist, 1982; Chalumeau for clarinet quartet, 1982; Ode for flute and string trio, 1982; Vortice for 9 clarinets, 1983;... hub of ambiguity, for soprano and 8 players, 1984; Opus Incertum for chamber orchestra, 1985; Calles y sueños, for chamber orchestra, 1986; Obsessum for bassoon and 9 accordions, 1988; Nocturno del hueco for chorus, large ensemble and tape, 1990; Danses Pythiques for harp, 1992; Decade for bass clarinet and accordion, 1992; 12 Preludes for piano, 1993; Reflections inside, electronic tape music, 1994; Piano Concertino, 1995; Neumes for percussion sextet, 1996; Nocturnal Stroll for flute orchestra, 1996; Chapter Three for orchestra, 1997. *Address:* c/o Vereniging BUMA, PO Box 725, 1180 AS Amstelveen, The Netherlands.

RAYAM, Curtis; American singer (tenor); b. 4 Feb. 1951, Belleville, FL. *Education:* Univ. of Miami and studied with Mary Henderson Buckeley. *Career:* debut in Miami 1971, in Manon Lescaut; appearances in Dallas, Houston and Jackson Opera South; European debut at the Wexford Festival 1976, in Giovanni d'Arco by Verdi, returning as the Sultan in Mozart's Zaide and as Wilhelm Meister in Thomas' Mignon; Boston 1979, as Olympion in the US premiere of Tippett's The Ice Break, conducted by Sarah Caldwell; Amsterdam 1981, as Massenet's Werther; further engagements at Salzburg, Paris, Frankfurt and Venice; La Scala 1985, in Handel's Alcina, returning 1988 as Orcane in Fetonte by Jommelli; Spoleto 1988, as Creon in Traetta's Antigone; other roles include Rossini's Otello and Cleomene (L'Assedio di Corinto), Mozart's Idomeneo, Belmonte and Mitridate, Irus in Il Ritorno d'Ulisse, Nemorino and Puccini's Pinkerton and Rodolfo; sang Titus April in the premiere of Buchuland by Roelof Temmingh, Pretoria 1998. *Recordings include:* Treemonisha by Scott Joplin, Da-ud in Die Aegyptische Helena by Strauss. *Honours:* winner Dallas Competition 1974.

RAYMOND, Deborah, BMus; American singer (soprano); b. 26 Nov. 1951, Chicago, Ill.; m. Nando Schellen 1991. *Education:* School of Music, Univ. of Iowa and studied with Jean Kraft, Bill and Dixie Neill, Pauline Tinsley, Virginia Zeani. *Career:* debut with Netherlands Opera, Amsterdam 1983; leading roles include Salome at Staatsoper Dresden 1988, at Aachen 1989, at Salt Lake City, Utah 1993, at Charlotte, NC 1994, with Arizona Opera at Tucson and Phoenix 1995; Marie in Wozzeck, at Coburg 1989, at Spoleto Festival 1997; Woman in Erwartung, with Netherlands Radio Symphony Orchestra 1988, in Indianapolis 1994; Zoë in Stephen Climax (Hans Zender), La Monnaie Opera, Brussels 1990; Eine Diene in Reigen (Ph Boesmans/Luc Bondy), La Monnaie, Brussels 1991–93 (Strasbourg and Paris); Tatiana in Eugene Onegin, with the Bolshoi Opera of Belarus at Minsk 1993; Mimi in La Bohéme, USA 1994, 1996, 1997; title role in Tosca, USA 1996, 1998, 2000; Nedda in Pagliacci, USA 1997–98; Cio-Cio San in Madama Butterfly, USA 1997–99; appears often in concerts and recitals, in USA 1996, 1997, 1999, 2000, 2001; voice teacher at Northern Arizona Univ., Flagstaff, Ariz. from 2001. *Recordings include:* Reigen (Philippe Boesmans-Bondy). *Address:* c/o Sara Tornay, 155 West 72nd Street, New York, NY 10023, USA.

REA, John; Canadian composer; b. 14 Jan. 1944, Toronto, ON. *Education:* Univ. of Toronto with John Weinzweg, Princeton Univ. with Milton Babbitt. *Career:* teacher, McGill Univ. 1973, Dean of the Faculty of Music 1986–91; Composer-in-Residence, Mannheim 1984; founder mem. of Montréal music soc., Les Evénements du Neuf. *Compositions:* music theatre: Les Jours (ballet)

1969, The Prisoner's Play (opera) 1973, Hommage à Richard Wagner 1988, Com-possession 1980, Le Petit Livre des Ravalet (opera) 1983, Offenes Lied (operatic scenes) 1986, operatic scenes based on Dante's Inferno and Poe's Morella 1990–93: orchestral: Hommage à Vasarely 1977, Vanishing Points 1983, Over Time 1987, Time and Again 1987; chamber: Clarinet Sonatina 1965, Sestina 1968, Prologue, Scene and Movement for soprano, viola and two pianos 1968, Tempest 1969, What You Will for piano 1969, La Dernière Sirène for ondes martenot, piano and percussion 1981, Les Raison des Forces Mouvantes for flute and string quartet 1984, Some Time Later for amplified string quartet 1986; vocal: Litaneia for chorus and orchestra 1984.

REARICK, Barbara; American singer (mezzo-soprano); b. 1960. *Education:* Manhattan School of Music, Britten-Pears School with Nancy Evans and Anthony Rolfe Johnson. *Career:* concert and opera performances in the United Kingdom and USA; British debut, 1987, at Aldeburgh Festival as Britten's Lucretia; sang Copland's Old American Songs with Lukas Foss, piano, at the Snape Concert Hall; Other repertoire includes Messiah, Lieder eines fahrenden Gesellen, L'Enfance du Christ and Britten's Charm of Lullabies orchestrated by Colin Matthews, all at Snape; Ravel's Chansons Madécasses, Haydn Masses with the Orchestra of St John's Smith Square and Handel's Dixit Dominus at the Norfolk and Norwich Festival, American popular songs there, 1992, with Richard Rodney Bennett; Operatic repertoire includes Meg Page, Chautauqua Opera, Suzuki in Opera Delaware and Annina in Rosenkavalier in New York City Opera; Member of the Britten-Pears Ensemble, with performances throughout the United Kingdom and USA. *Current Management:* c/o Thea Dispeker Inc., 59 East 54th Street, Suite 81, New York NY 10022, USA. *Telephone:* (212) 421-7676. *Fax:* (212) 935-3279. *E-mail:* info@dispeker.com. *Website:* www.dispeker.com.

REAUX, Angelina; American singer (soprano); b. 1959, Houston, TX. *Career:* fmrly sang in various New York night clubs; sang Mimi in La Bohème at Rome 1987, and recorded the role with Leonard Bernstein; New York Acad. of Music 1989, as Dido by Purcell, Musetta at Boston and Despina at the Kentucky Opera 1993; other roles include Pamina, Nedda and the Woman in La Voix Humaine; sang The Queen of Sparta in La Belle Hélène for L'Opéra Français de New York 1996. *Recordings include:* La Bohème, Street Scene by Weill and Blitzstein's Regina.

REAVILLE, Richard; British singer (tenor); b. 1954, Nottingham, England; m. Cecilia Burel; two d. *Career:* appearances with ENO, WNO, Scottish Opera and Mid Wales Opera; Glyndebourne Festival and Tour, London Opera Players and festivals in the UK, Finland, France and Germany; Ernesto, Don Pasquale on tour to the Far East 1990; concerts throughout Europe, including engagements with the BBC Philharmonic Orchestra, Danish Radio Symphony Orchestra, Scottish Opera, Belgian Nat. Orchestra, Odense Philharmonic, Weimar Staatskapelle and various chamber ensembles; Mahler's Das Lied von der Erde with the Rander Orchestra (Denmark), Puccini's Messa di Gloria with the Ostrava Philharmonic Orchestra and Ligeti's Le Grand Macabre with the Odense Symphony Orchestra 1996–97; sang Second Judge in Param Vir's Broken Strings, Glasgow 1998. *Television:* Britten's Billy Budd (BBC 2), opera arias and duets programme (Finnish TV). *Radio:* Rossini's Petite Messe Solennelle (Danish Radio), Britten's Serenade for tenor, horn and strings (with Norwegian Radio Symphony Orchestra). *Recordings:* Puccini's Messe de Gloria (with Jihlava Choir and Ostrava Orchestra of Czech Repub.), Stuart Ward's A Celebration of Gods (with Divertimenti of London). *Address:* c/o Tivoli Artists, 3 Vesterbrogade, 1630 Copenhagen, Denmark. *Telephone:* (2) 5342093.

RECHBERGER, Herman, DipMus; Finnish composer and performer; b. 14 Feb. 1947, Linz, Austria; m. 1st Ilse Maier 1966, one s. one d.; m. 2nd Soile Jaatinen 1972, one s. two d. *Education:* studied in Linz, Sibelius Academy, Helsinki. *Career:* music teacher, choir conductor, 1975–79; Producer of Contemporary Music, Artistic Director of Experimental Studio, Finnish Broadcasting, 1979–84; state grant, 1985–; recitals of new recorder music, most European countries, Russia, Cuba, USA; performed own works, ISCM Music Days, Helsinki and Stockholm, 1978, Athens, 1979, Warsaw, 1992, and Helsinki Biennale, 1981, 1983; frequent performances and tours with ensembles Poor Knights; guest composer for Hungarofilm at Hungarian Broadcasting Company's Electronic Music Studio, 1985, and Slovak Radio (Rustle of Spring), 1986; Composer-in-Residence. *Compositions include:* orchestral: Consort Music 1, 2, 4, 5; The Garden of Delights; Venezia; 3 guitar concertos; Goya; Cello Concerto, 1999; operas: The Nuns; Laurentius nunc ad semper, 1998; The Night of Wishes, 2000; Ballet, The Changeling Princess, 1997; Radiophonic works: The Rise of Mr Jonathan Smith; Magnus Cordius, entries in a diary; vocal music: Vanha Linna; Hades; Dunk; Notturno inamorata; Seis Canciones de anochecer; Musica Picta for small children; Tape music: Cordamix; Narod; KV-622bis; Moldavia; Rustle of Spring; Multimedia: Zin Kibaru; Firenze 1582; Survol; La Folia; Chamber music: Consort Music 3 for brass nonet; El Palacio del Sonido for 3 guitars; Consort Music 6 for 12 recorders; Musical graphics and pictographic scores for educational purposes; many arrangements and reconstructions of early music and Ancient Greek music, e.g. the world's first opera, Jacopo Peri's Euridice. *Recordings include:* The King's Hunt, Esa-Pekka Salonen, French horn; Cordamix; Rasenie järi, Rustle of Spring; The Garden of Delights, Austrian RSO, conductor Leif Segerstam; Consort Music I, Clas Pehrson, recorders, Swedish RSO, conductor Leif Segerstam. *Address:* Laajavuorenkuja 5 B 11, 01620 Vantaa, Finland.

RECHNAGEL, Axel; Danish organist and cantor; b. 27 March 1936, Århus; m.; two d. *Education:* Århus Cathedral School, Univ. of Århus, State Acad. of Music, Århus, studied in Vienna, Austria and in the USA. *Career:* Organist, Ringkobing, 1961; Organist and Kantor, Nyborg, 1965; retd 1999; mem. Dansk Organist og Kantor Samfund; Det danske Orgelselskab. *Compositions:* Concerto for organ 1968, Toccata for organ 1996. *Publication:* Nyborg Vor Frue Kirke 1388–1988 (co-author). *Address:* Grejsdalen 5, 5800, Nyborg, Denmark.

RECTANUS, L. Hans, PhD; German academic; b. 18 Feb. 1935, Worms; m. Elisabeth Zilbauer; one s. one d. *Education:* Civic Music Academy and University, Frankfurt/Main, Academy of Music and Interpretive Art, University of Vienna, School for Protestant Church Music, Schlüchtern/Hesse, University of Frankfurt. *Career:* teacher of music, German literature for Gymnasium, 1960–63; Lecturer and Asst, University of Frankfurt/Main, 1963–66; Lecturer 1966–71, Prof. 1971–, Teachers' College, Heidelberg; mem. Präsidium, Hans Pfitzner Society, Munich; Society for Music Research, Cassel; Society of Professional Choirmasters. *Compositions:* edited Hans Pfitzner String Quartet in D minor, Trio for violin, violoncello and piano. *Publications:* Leitmotiv und Form in den Musikdramatischen Werken Hans Pfitzners, 1967; Neue Ansätze im Musikunterricht, 1972; Hans Pfitzner, Sämtliche Lieder mit Klavierbegleitung, vol. I, 1980, vol. II, 1983; contrib. to Die Musikforschung; Riemannmusiklexikon; Studien zur Musikgeschichte des 19 Jahrhundert; Mitteilungen der Hans Pfitzner-Gesellschaft; Festchrift H. Osthoff; Renaissance-Studien; Zeitschrift für Musik-Pädagogik; Lexikon der Musikpädagogik; Pfitzner-Studien. *Honours:* Kritiker-Preis 1956, Music Director Prize, Organist Prize. *Address:* Schlittweg 31, 6905 Schriesheim/Bergstr, Germany.

REDEL, Martin Christoph; German composer; b. 30 Jan. 1947, Detmold. *Education:* studied with Kelterborn and Gishele Klebe at Detmold, and with Isang Yun in Hanover. *Career:* Faculty, Detmold Hochschule from 1971, Professor of Composition 1979, Rector 1993; President of Jeunesses Musicales 1992. *Compositions include:* String Quartet, 1967; Strophen, for orchestra, 1970; Epilog for baritone, flute and guitar, 1971; Dispersion, for ensemble, 1972; Kammersinfonie II, 1972; Konfrontationen, for orchestra, 1974; Correspondences, for 2 percussion, 1975; Interplay for ensemble, 1975; Mobile, for oboe, clarinet and bassoon, 1976; Concerto for Orchestra, 1978; Espressioni, for woodwind quintet, 1980; Traumtanz for percussion and strings, 1981; Bruckner Essay for orchestra, 1982; Clarinet Quintet, 1988; Visions Fugitives for accordion and percussion, 1993; Teamwork, for 17 instruments, 1997; Vivo, for 4 percussion, 1997. *Publications:* Grundlagen des Kadenzspiels im Tonsatzunterricht 1975. *Honours:* Arthur Honegger Prize. *Website:* www.martin-redel.info.

REDGATE, Christopher Frederick; British oboist and academic; b. 17 Sept. 1956, Bolton, Lancashire; m. Celia Jane Pilstow 1981, two s. *Education:* Chetham's School of Music, Manchester and Royal Acad. of Music, London. *Career:* solo and chamber performances in England, Europe, USA; many performer-in-residence courses for composers; Artist-in-Residence, Victorian Coll. of the Arts, Melbourne, Australia, including recitals, lectures, recordings 1983; toured Canada 1985; American debut, Pittsburgh Int. Festival of New Music 1986–92; Prof. of Oboe, Darmstadt Int. School for Contemporary Music 1986–92; Evelyn Barbirolli Research Fellow, Royal Acad. of Music; performed regularly with the Phoenix Wind Quintet, Krosta Trio, Exposé, Lontano; TV and radio broadcasts in the UK and The Netherlands; many works written or commissioned for him by Michael Finnissy, James Clarke, Roger Redgate and others. *Recordings:* Pascilli for oboe; Platinum Fiction by Luca Francescin; Lost Lard, oboe music of Michael Finnissy; Quintets by Redgate, Fox and Clarke; Ferneyhough's Allegebrah and Coloratura, Electrifying Oboe 2014.

REDGATE, Roger; British composer; b. 3 June 1958, Bolton, Lancashire. *Education:* Chetham's School of Music, Manchester, RCM, London with Edwin Roxburgh, Freiburg Hochschule with Brian Ferneyhough. *Career:* co-founder, Ensemble Exposé 1984; Northern Arts Fellow in Composition; taught at Univs of Durham and Newcastle 1989–92; Professor in Composition, Goldsmiths Coll., London 1997–. *Compositions include:* two string quartets 1983, 1985, Eidos for piano 1985, Eperons for oboe and percussion 1988, Vers-Glas for 14 amplified voices 1990, Inventio for ensemble 1990, Celan Songs for soprano and ensemble 1991–94, Beuys for piano 1992, Feu la Cendre for cello 1992, Scribble for ensemble 1992, Eurydice (multimedia piece) 1993, Iro/ku for prepared piano 1994, ...still... for bass flute, violin, viola and cello 1995, arc 2000, rains true refuge 2004, Mirlitonnades 2005, Ausgangspunkte 2006, Residua 2009, Eperons 2009. *Honours:* Darmstadt Kranich-Steiner Prize for Composition 1988. *E-mail:* r.regate (@gold.ac.uk (office).

REEDER, Haydn Brett, BMus, MA; Australian composer, pianist and conductor; b. 27 Feb. 1944, Melbourne, Vic. *Education:* Univ. of Melbourne, La Trobe Univ. *Career:* Ed. of universal edn, Schott and Chester music publishers 1970–82; Lecturer, La Trobe Univ. 1984–88; commissions from Elision and Melbourne Windpower 1987–88. *Compositions include:* Mandala Rite for clarinet and guitar 1982, Strad Evarie for cello and piano 1984, Temi Distratti for trombone, cello and percussion 1985, Sirens' Hotel (chamber opera) 1986, Masks for piano 1986, Clashing Auras for wind octet 1989, Dance in a Mirror of Time for seven instruments 1989, Chants at Play with Solid Background 1990, Glances Repose for violin 1990, Draw Neat to the Bell for guitar 1990, Piano Pieces 1–3. *Honours:* prize Citta di Trieste Orchestral Competition.

REEDIJK, Alex; New Zealand arts administrator; *General Director, Scottish Opera. Career:* worked in the UK for Scottish Opera, Wexford Festival Opera, Opera Ireland, Garsington Opera –1998; Deputy Exec. Dir, later Exec. Dir, New Zealand Int. Festival of the Arts 1998–2002; Gen. Dir, NBR New Zealand Opera 2002–06; Gen. Dir, Scottish Opera 2006–. *Address:* Scottish Opera, 39 Elmbank Crescent, Glasgow, G2 4PT, Scotland (office). *Telephone:* (141) 248-4567 (office). *Fax:* (141) 242-0509 (office). *Website:* www.scottishopera.org.uk (office).

REEKIE, Jonathan, CBE; British music administrator; *Director, Somerset House Trust;* b. 2 Sept. 1964, s. of Dr Andrew Reekie and Virginia Reekie; divorced; two c. *Career:* began career, whilst still a student, working for Musica Nel Chiostro, Batignano, still mem. Bd of Dirs; Co. Co-ordinator, Glyndebourne Opera 1988–91; Founder and Dir Almeida Opera 1992–2002; Chief Exec. Aldeburgh Music 1997–2014; Trustee, Arts Foundation; Advisor, Paul Hamlyn Foundation Arts Programme Cttee 2007–; Dir, Somerset House Trust 2014–. *Productions:* nearly 30 new operatic works for Almeida Opera. *Honours:* Hon. FRAM 2010; Dr hc (Univ. of East Anglia) 2010. *Address:* Somerset House, Strand, London, WC2R 1LA, England (office). *Telephone:* (20) 7845-4600 (office). *E-mail:* info@somersethouse.org.uk. *Website:* www.somersethouse.org.uk (office).

REES, Jonathan; British violinist and director; b. 1963, England. *Education:* Yehudi Menuhin School, studied with Dorothy DeLay at Juilliard. *Career:* student engagements at the Windsor, Gstaad and Llandaff Festivals and three tours of The Netherlands; later recitals at the Bath, City of London, Brighton, Henley and Salisbury Festivals; concerto soloist with the Bournemouth Sinfonietta, Philharmonia, London Soloists Chamber Orchestra and the Royal Philharmonic; concerts with the Academy of St Martin in the Fields at Carnegie Hall, the Festival Hall and at St Martin's Church; Beethoven's Concerto with the Bournemouth Sinfonietta, 1990; director of the Scottish Ensemble: concerts in Edinburgh, elsewhere in Scotland and in Austria, Belgium, France, Germany, the Netherlands, Norway and North and Central America; festivals include Berlin, Guelph, Prague, Sofia, Cheltenham and Edinburgh; Royal Command Performances at the Palace of Holyrood House and at Balmoral. *Honours:* Prizewinner, 1978, BBC Young Musician of the Year Competition; first prize Royal Overseas League Competition, 1979. *Current Management:* J. Audrey Ellison International Artists' Management, 135 Stevenage Road, Fulham, London, SW6 6PB, England. *Telephone:* (20) 7381-9751. *Fax:* (20) 7381-2406. *E-mail:* audrey@ellison-intl.freeserve.co.uk. *Website:* www.ellison-intl.freeserve.co.uk.

REEVE, Stephen; British composer; b. 15 March 1948, London, England. *Education:* Liège Conservatoire with Henri Pousseur. *Career:* major comms for BBC South 1975, Inst. for Research and Co-ordination in Acoustics and Music 1980, Inst. of Contemporary Arts, London 1985; mem. PRS. *Compositions:* Narcisse et Échos for string quartet and high soprano 1967–68, 2013–14, The Kite's Feathers 1969–70, Japanese Haikai for mezzo and ensemble, Colour Music for woodwind quartet 1970, Poème: Couleurs du Spectre for orchestra with optional light projection 1972–73, Summer Morning by a lake full of colors, an expansion of Schoenberg's Farben for large orchestra 1974, ...aux régions éthérées... for three chamber groups 1975–76, 2013–14, Grande thèse de la petite-fille de Téthys, an ethnic encyclopaedia for solo cello 1980–87, L'Oracle de Delphes, music-theatre for brass quintet 1985, Strophe for solo rock and four classical guitars 1985–86, Les Fées dansent selon la mode, double scene for three to five dancer-percussionists and six to 10 or more actor extras 1988–89, O que Zeus apparaisse à l'horizon for gamelan ensemble and tape 1989–90, Volontaires d'Icare for harpsichord trio 1995, L'Alpha noir et l'Oméga violet, mélodies en drame for soprano and piano 2013–14. *Address:* 73 Knightsfield, Welwyn Garden City, Herts., AL8 7JE, England (home).

REEVES, Paul Edward; British opera singer (bass); b. 31 May 1974, England; s. of Antony William Edward Reeves and Jill Felicity Reeves; partner Ross Anthony Catterall. *Education:* Guildhall School of Music and Drama (GSMD), London with Rudolf Piernay, Nat. Opera Studio. *Career:* roles at GSMD included Budd in Albert Herring, Pasquale in The Aspern Papers by Argento and Rossini's Basilio; appearances as Mozart's Publio for the Glyndebourne Tour, Colline in La Bohème and Speaker in The Magic Flute for British Youth Opera; Ramphis in Aida for Ashleyan Opera, Mozart's Bartolo for Opera Box and Sarastro in Die Zauberflöte for Kentish Opera; season 2001 with the King in Raymond Gubbay's Aida at the Albert Hall, and Matthew in Birtwistle's The Last Supper at Glyndebourne; recitals at the Wigmore, Fairfield and Blackheath Halls; prin. roles with ENO, Royal Opera London, Scottish Opera, Welsh Nat. Opera, Glyndebourne Festival Opera, Opera North, Tenerife Opera, Toulon Opera, Staatsoper Berlin, Bregenz Opera Festival. *Honours:* Richard Lewis-Jean Shanks Award, Tillett Trust Award. *Current Management:* c/o Romy Günther, Bigger Fish Management & PR, Gothaerstr. 4, 10823 Berlin, Germany. *Telephone:* (30) 469959-20. *Fax:* (30) 469959-18. *E-mail:* opera@biggerfish.de. *Website:* www.biggerfish.de; www.paulreeves.biz (home).

REGAZZO, Lorenzo; Italian singer (bass); b. 1968, Venice. *Education:* studied with Regina Resnik and Sesto Bruscantini. *Career:* many appearances at the Rossini Festival, Pesaro, in La Scala di Seta, La Cenerentola and L'Ingano felice; Salzburg Festival as Publio in La Clemenza di Tito and in Les Boréades by Rameau, conducted by Simon Rattle; Further engagements in L'Italiana in Algeri at Munich and Venice, La Gazza Ladra, Rossini's Zelmira

(Lyon) and Il Viaggio a Reims (Bologna); Royal Opera House 2000–01, as Publio, Alidoro in La Cenerentola and Lorenzo in I Capuleti e i Montecchi; Performances in Don Giovanni at Vienna, Milan and Brussels, Handel's Agrippina in Paris and as Mozart's Figaro at the 2001 Salzburg Festival; concerts with the Berlin Philharmonic, under Claudio Abbado.

ŘEHÁNEK, František, PhDr; Czech philologist, musicologist and teacher; b. 13 Sept. 1921, Místek; m. Marie Řehánková-Motáčková 1954 (died 2006); one s. *Education:* Music School, Místek, Charles Univ., Prague, Univ. of Brno, studied violin with Gabriel Štefánek and Josef Muzika. *Career:* mem. Czech Soc. of Musicology. *Publications include:* Janáček's Teaching of Harmony (dissertation) 1965, Harmonic Thinking of Leoš Janáček 1993; contrib. Modality in Janáček's Music Theory (in Colloquium Probleme der Modalität, Leoš Janáček heute und morgen) 1988, Modality in the Works of Vítězslav Novák (in Zprávy Společnosti Vítězslava Nováka 17) 1990, To the Problem of Modality with Bohuslav Martinů (in Colloquium Bohuslav Martinů, his Pupils, Friends and Contemporaries) 1990, Alois Hába's Wallachian Suite (in Zpávy Společnosti Vitězslava Nováka 25, 26) 1995, Leoš Janáček and the Whole-Tone System 1998, On Harmonic Thinking of Leoš Janáček (in Hudebni věda) 2001, Fourth Chords of Leoš Janáček (in Miscellanea, Czech Soc. of Musicology) 2001, The Diatonic Modes with Leoš Janáček (in Hudebni věda) 2003, Leoš Janáček: Sonata for Violin and Piano (in Miscellanea, Czech Soc. of Musicology) 2006, Modulations of Leoš Janáček (in Miscellanea, Czech Soc. of Musicology) 2006, Bitonality in the Compositions of Leoš Janáček 2008. *Address:* Vlnařská 692, 460 01 Liberec VI, Czech Republic (home). *Telephone:* (720) 531925 (mobile) (home).

REHNQVIST, Karin; Swedish composer and academic; *Professor in Composition, Royal College of Music, Stockholm;* b. 21 Aug. 1957, Stockholm; m. Hans Persson 1982, one d. two s. *Education:* Royal Coll. of Music, Stockholm with Gunnar Bucht, Pär Lindgren and Brian Ferneyhough. *Career:* Conductor and Artistic Dir Stans Kör choir 1976–91; Composer-in-Residence, Svenska Kammarorkestern 1999–2003; Scottish Chamber Orchestra 1999–2003; currently Prof. in Composition, Royal Coll. of Music, Stockholm; mem. Soc. of Swedish Composers, Royal Sweden Acad. of Music 1997. *Compositions include:* Stråk for strings 1982, Dance for piano 1984, Davids nimm for three female voices 1984, Kast for strings 1986, Songs from the Saga of Fatumeh for male chours 1988, Here I am, Where are you? for girls' voices 1989, Skrin Violin Concerto 1990, The Triumph of Being for girls' voices 1990, Lamento for orchestra 1993, Sun Song for female voice, speakers and chamber orchestra 1994, Visletens lov for mixed chorus 1996, Arktis Arktis! for orchestra 2000–01, On a Distant Shore, concerto for clarinet and orchestra 2002, Teile dich Nacht for mixed choir and solo female voice 2002, Ljus av ljus (Lumière source de lumière) for children's choir and symphony orchestra 2003, Preludes for Large Orchestra 2006; opera, commissioned by The Stockholm Royal Opera. *Recordings:* Solsången, Dans, Davids nimm (solo version), Kast, Lamento – rytmen av en röst, Taromirs tid, Puksånger – Lockrop, Bara du går över markerna, Rädda mig ur dyn, Strömmar, Andrum, Lod, Wings, Sånger ur jorden, Triumf att finnas till, I Himmelen. *Publication:* Young People – New Music: An Introduction to Composition. *Honours:* Läkerol Arts Award 1996, Expressen's Spelmannen Prize 1996, Christ Johnsson Prize 1997, City of Stockholm Honour Prize 1999, Kurt Atterberg Prize 2001, Litteris et Artibus Medal from King of Sweden 2003, Rosenberg Award 2005/06, honoured with a major retrospective by Royal Stockholm Philharmonic Orchestra 2006, Hugo Alfvén Prize 2007. *Address:* Royal College of Music, Valhallavägen 105, Box 27711, 115 91 Stockholm, Sweden (office). *Telephone:* (8) 161800 (office). *Website:* www.kmh.se (office); www.editionreimers.se/tt/kr; www.mic.stim.se; www.karin-rehnqvist.se.

REIBEL, Guy; French composer; b. 19 July 1936, Strasbourg. *Education:* studied with Messiaen and Serge Wigg. *Career:* groupe de recherches musicales 1963–; Lecturer in Electro-acoustic Music, Paris Conservatoire; founder, Atelier des Choeurs, Radio France 1976; Dir, Groupe Vocal de France 1986–90, with many premieres; adviser to Cité De la Musique, La Villette 1983–89; Prof. of Composition, Paris Conservatoire 1976; collaborations with Pierre Schaeffer. *Compositions include:* Musaiques for two voices, percussion and orchestra 1987, Fugitivement à la surface de l'eau for ensemble 1989, Variations cinétiques for ensemble 1989, Etudes de flux for orchestra 1990, Métaphores for soprano and two guitars 1991, Le Coq et le renard for flute and chorus 1991, La Marseillaise des Mille for 500 voices and orchestra 1992, Calliphores for 12 voices 1995, Musique en Liesse for 12 brass and two percussion 1995, Trois Epigrammes de Clément Marot for chorus 1996, Surface Légèrement Spérique for tape 1996, Mamemimomusiques for orchestra 1997. *Publications include:* Essais sur l'idée musicale 1997.

REICH, Steve, MA; American composer; b. 3 Oct. 1936, New York; s. of Leonard Reich and June Carroll; m. Beryl Korot 1976; two s. *Education:* Cornell Univ., Juilliard School of Music, Mills Coll., studied composition with Berio and Milhaud, also studied at American Soc. for Eastern Arts and in Accra and Jerusalem. *Career:* f. own ensemble 1966; Steve Reich and Musicians have completed numerous tours world-wide 1971–; his music performed by maj. orchestras and ensembles in United States and Europe; Montgomery Fellowship, Dartmouth Coll.; Chubb Fellowship, Yale Univ. 2007; mem. American Acad. of Arts and Letters 1994–, Bavarian Acad. of Fine Arts 1995–, Royal Swedish Acad. of Music 2008–. *Works include:* Electric Guitar Phase for electric guitar and pre-recorded tape (arrangement of Violin Phase 1967) 2000, Tokyo/Vermont Counterpoint for KAT MIDI mallet and pre-recorded tape (arrangement of Vermont Counterpoint 1981) 2000, Three Tales (video opera, video by Beryl Korot) 2002, Dance Patterns for 2 xylophones, 2 vibraphones, 2 pianofortes 2002, Cello Counterpoint for amplified cello and multi-channel tape 2003, You Are (Variations) (text by Rabbi Nachman of Breslov (English), Psalms (Hebrew), Wittgenstein (English) and Pirke Avot (Hebrew) for amplified ensemble and voices, no brass, 2 marimbas, 2 vibraphones, 4 pianofortes, strings, and voices 2004, The Daniel Variations 2006, Double Sextet (Pulitzer Prize in Music 2009) 2008. *Recordings include:* Come Out, Violin Phase, It's Gonna Rain, Four Organs, Drumming, Six Pianos, Music for Mallet Instruments, Voices and Organ, Music for a Large Ensemble, Octet and Variations for Winds, Strings and Keyboards, Music for 18 Musicians, The Desert Music, Electric Counterpoint, Different Trains, The Four Sections, Nagoya Marimbas, City Life, Proverb, Hindenburg (in collaboration with Beryl Korot), Double Sextet. *Honours:* Commdr des Arts et Lettres 1999; Dr hc (Calif. Inst. of the Arts) 2000; recipient of three Rockefeller Foundation Grants 1975–81 and a Guggenheim Fellowship, Koussevitzky Foundation Award 1981, Schumann Prize, Columbia Univ. 2000, Regent Lectureship, Univ. of Calif., Berkeley 2000, Praemium Imperiale Music Laureate, Japan 2006, Polar Prize, Royal Swedish Acad. of Music 2007, awarded membership in Franz Liszt Acad., Budapest 2006. *Current Management:* Howard Stokar Management, 870 West End Avenue, New York, NY 10025-4918, USA. *Telephone:* (212) 866-5798. *Website:* www.stevereich.com.

REICHERT, Manfred; conductor; b. 5 May 1942, Karlsruhe, Germany. *Education:* Karlsruhe Hochschule, Univ. of Fribourg/Breisgau. *Career:* producer at South-West German Radio, Baden-Baden 1967–83; founded the chamber group, Ensemble 13 1973; directed the festivals Wintermusik and Musik auf den 49ten at Karlsruhe 1980, 1983; Artistic Dir, Festival of European Culture at Karlsruhe 1983–87; teacher, Hochschule für Musik at Karlsruhe from 1984; conducted the premieres of Hans-Jürgen von Bose's Variations for strings 1981, Wolfgang Rihm's Chiffre-Zyklus 1988, Gejagte Form 1989.

REID-SMITH, Randall; singer (tenor); b. 1959, Barboursville, WV, USA. *Education:* studied in Cincinnati and New York. *Career:* sang in concert and opera at Santa Fe, Dayton and Michigan; roles have included Don José, Rodolfo and Pinkerton; Brunswick Opera from 1990, as Don Ottavio, Rossini's Almaviva, Fenton in Falstaff and Nemorino; Dortmund Opera from 1993, as Tamino, Ferrando and the Duke of Mantua; sang Don Ottavio at Aachen 1995; guest appearances at Leipzig, Madrid, Vienna and Bregenz.

REIMANN, Aribert; German composer and pianist; b. 4 March 1936, Berlin. *Education:* Berlin Hochschule für Musik with Boris Blacher, Ernst Pepping and Rausch, Univ. of Vienna. *Career:* Prof. of the Contemporary Lied, Hamburg Musikhochschule 1974–83, Berlin Hochschule der Künste 1983; freelance composer, notably of operas; accompanist to Dietrich Fischer-Dieskau in lieder recitals; London premieres, Lear and The Ghost Sonata 1989; Opera Das Schloss premiered at the Deutsche Oper Berlin 1992, Bernarda Albas Haus premiered at the Bavarian State Opera, Munich 2000; mem., Berlin Akademie der Künste 1971, Bayerische Akademie der Schönen Künste 1976, Freie Akademie der Künste, Hamburg 1985. *Compositions:* operas: Ein Traumspiel (Strindberg) 1964, Melusine 1970, Lear (Shakespeare) 1978, Die Gespenstersonate (Strindberg) 1983, Troades (Euripides) 1985, Das Schloss (Kafka) 1992, Bernarda Albas Haus (García Lorca) 2000, Medea (Stillparzer) 2008–09; ballet: Stoffreste 1958 (revised as Die Vogelscheuchen) 1970; orchestral: Elegie for orchestra 1957, Cello Concerto 1959, Monumenta for wind and percussion 1960, Piano Concerto No. 1 1961, No. 2 1972, Sinfonie (from the opera Ein Traumspiel) 1964, Rondes for string orchestra 1967, Loqui for orchestra 1969, Music from the ballet Die Vogelscheuchen 1970, Variations for orchestra 1975, Sieben Fragmente 1988, Concerto for violin, cello and orchestra 1988–89, Neun Stücke 1993, Violin Concerto 1995–96, Concerto for Violin, Violoncello and Orchestra 1997, Cantus for clarinet and orchestra 2005; vocal: Ein Totentanz for baritone and chamber orchestra 1960, Hölderlin-Fragments for soprano and orchestra 1963, three Shakespeare Sonnets for baritone and piano 1964, Epitaph for tenor and seven instruments 1965, Verra la Morte cantata 1966, Inane for soprano and orchestra 1968, Zyklus for baritone and orchestra 1971, Lines for soprano and strings 1973, Wolkenloses Christmas Requiem for baritone, cello and orchestra 1974, Lear Symphony for baritone and orchestra 1980, Neun Sonette der Louize Labé, Chacun sa Chimère for tenor and orchestra 1981, Three Songs (poems by Edgar Allan Poe) 1982, Requiem for soprano, mezzo, baritone and orchestra 1982, Unrevealed for baritone and string quartet, Tre Poemi di Michelangelo 1985, Ein Apokalyptisches Fragment for mezzo, piano and orchestra 1987, Orchestration of Schumann's Gedichte der Maria Stuart 1988, Lady Lazarus for soprano solo 1992, Eingedunkelt for alto solo 1992, Nightpiece (James Joyce) for soprano and piano 1992, Findik Infinity for Soprano and Orchestra (Emily Dickinson) 1994–95, Schubert's Mignon Lieder for soprano and string quartet 1995, Kumi Ori for baritone and orchestra 1999, Drei Gedichte der Sappho for soprano and nine instruments 2000, Tarde for Soprano and Orchestra 2003; chamber: Piano Sonata 1958, Canzoni e Ricercare for flute, viola and cello 1961, Cello Sonata 1963, Nocturnos for cello and harp 1965, Reflexionen for seven instruments 1966, Spektren for piano 1967, Variationen for piano 1979, Invenzioni for 12 players 1979, Solo for cello 1981, String Trio 1987, Auf dem Weg for piano 1989–93, Solo for viola 1996, Metamorphosen for ten instruments 1997, Solo for clarinet 2000, ... ni una sombra for soprano, clarinet and piano 2006. *Honours:* Grand Cross for Distinguished Service of the Order of Merit 1985, Order of Merit of the State of

Berlin 1988, Ordre pour le Mérite for science and art 1993, Grand Cross with Star for Distinguished Service of the Order of Merit 1995, Commdr, Ordre du Mérite Culturel, Monaco 1999; Berlin Arts Award for Music (Young Generation) 1962, Rome Prize 1963, Schumann Prize, Düsseldorf 1964, Stuttgart Award for Young Composers 1966, Critics Award for Music, Berlin 1970, Ludwig Spohr Prize, Braunschweig 1985, Fondation Prince Pierre de Monaco Prix de composition musicale 1986, Bach Prize of the Free Hanseatic City of Hamburg 1987, Frankfurt Music Award 1991, German Asscn of Playwrights Goldene Nadel 1999, Arnold Schönberg Prize, Berlin 2006, Ernst von Siemens Music Prize 2011. *Current Management:* c/o Yvonne Stern-Campo, Schott Music GmbH & Co. KG, Weihergarten 5, 55116 Mainz, Germany.

REINEKE, Steven, BMus; American conductor and composer; *Principal Pops Conductor, National Symphony Orchestra;* b. 14 Sept. 1970, Tipp City, Ohio. *Education:* Miami Univ. *Career:* learned trumpet at an early age; 15 years as Assoc. Conductor, Cincinnati Pops Orchestra; Prin. Pops Conductor, Modesto Symphony Orchestra 2008–11; Music Dir New York Pops 2009–; Prin. Pops Conductor, Long Beach Symphony Orchestra 2009–11; Prin. Pops Conductor, Nat. Symphony Orchestra, Washington, DC 2011–; fmr Guest Conductor with the orchestras of Baltimore, Detroit, Edmonton, Houston, Indianapolis, Los Angeles, Toronto and Vancouver; Hollywood Bowl debut 2007; Carnegie Hall debut conducting New York Pops 25th Birthday Gala 2008; debuts with Boston Pops and Philadelphia Orchestra 2009; also composer of several symphonies and shorter pieces. *Compositions include:* Swan's Island Sojourn 1996, Into the Raging River 1999, Sedona 2000, Heaven's Light 2004, Festival Te Deum 2005, Goddess of Fire 2006, Symphony No. 1: New Day Rising 2007, Towards a New Horizon 2007, Celebration Fanfare 2008, Legend of Sleepy Hollow, Casey at the Bat, Sun Valley Festival Fanfare 2008. *Current Management:* c/o Peter Throm Management LLC, 2040 Tibbitts Court, Ann Arbor, MI 48105, USA. *Telephone:* (734) 222-8030. *Fax:* (734) 222-8031. *Website:* www.peterthrom.com; www.stevenreineke.com.

REINER, Thomas, BA, MMus, PhD; composer; b. 12 Aug. 1959, Bad Homburg, Germany. *Education:* La Trobe Univ., studied with Hans Werner Henze, Barry Conyngham and Peter Tahourdin, Univ. of Melbourne. *Career:* staff mem., Univ. of Melbourne 1990–91, Monash Univ. 1993–98. *Compositions include:* Journey and Contemplation for guitar and ensemble 1987, Moth and Spider for alto saxophone and percussion 1988, Paraphrase, Surge and Response for orchestra 1988, Bali Suite for ensemble 1989, Fantasy and Fugue for trombone 1989, Kalorama Prelude for piano 1989, Schumannianna: An Orchestration of Robert Schumann's Mondnacht 1991, Baby Orangutan for piano 1991, Words for six solo voices 1992, Three Sketches for cello 1993, Construction in Time for guitar and piano 1993, Oblique for flute 1994, Flexious for flute and guitar 1995–96, Septet for chamber ensemble 1996, Grace Notes for B flat clarinet 1997. *Publications:* articles on musical time and electronic dance music. *Honours:* prize International Witold Lutoslawski Composers Competition 1992, Dorian Le Gallienne Composition Award 1994, Albert H. Maggs Composition Award 1995, International Borwil Composer's Competition 1997.

REINHARDT-KISS, Ursula; singer (soprano); b. 3 Nov. 1938, Letmathe, Sauerland, Germany. *Education:* studied with Ellen Bosenius in Cologne and Irma Beilke in Berlin. *Career:* debut at Saarbrücken 1967 as Marie in Der Waffenschmied; sang in Saarbrücken until 1969 then Aachen 1969–71; guest appearances in Lubeck, Cologne, Zürich, Antwerp, Milan, Copenhagen and Rome; Drottningholm 1983 in Il Fanatico Burlato by Cimarosa; Komische Oper Berlin as Susanna and Lulu, and Dresden Staatsoper as Aminta in Die schweigsame Frau; sang at Graz 1985, in Angelica Vincitrice di Alcina by Fux, returning 1987 in the premiere of Der Rattenfänger by Cerha; also sings Salomé in Hérodiade by Massenet. *Recordings:* Sacred Music by Mozart; Lazarus by Schubert; Epitaph for Garcia Lorca, by Nono.

REINHART, Gregory; American singer (bass); b. 1955. *Career:* sang at Tourcoing, 1981, in Paisiello's Il Re Teodoro, Innsbruck, 1982 and 1987, in Cesti's Oronte and Semiramide; King of Scotland in Ariodante at Nancy (1983) and in Henze's English Cat at the Paris Opéra-Comique, 1984; Nice, 1986, as Henry VIII in Anna Bolena and at Aix-en-Provence as Ismenor in Campra's Tancrède; London concert performances of Poppea and Moses und Aron, 1988; Opéra-Bastille Paris, 1990, as Panthé in Les Troyens and Santa Fe, 1992, as Mozart's Commendatore; Sang Basil Hallward in the premiere of Lowell Liebermann's The Picture of Dorian Gray, Monte Carlo, 1996; Other roles include Lord Robinson in Il Matrimonio Segreto, Monteverdi's Seneca, Huascar in Les Indes Galantes and Douglas in Rossini's Donna del Lago; sang Claudio in Handel's Agrippina at Halle, 1999; Premiere of K... by Philippe Manouri at the Opéra Bastille, Paris, 2001; Metropolitan Opera debut in Die Zauberflöte 2006. *Recordings:* Handel's Tamerlano; Tancrède by Campra; Rameau's Zoroastre; Messiah. *Current Management:* Robert Gilder & Co., c/o Chase Thompson, Pinnacle Arts Management, 889 Ninth Avenue, 2nd Floor, New York, NY 10019, USA. *Telephone:* (212) 397-5299. *Fax:* (212) 397-7920. *E-mail:* cthompson@pinnaclearts.com.

REISSIG, Heiko Christian, (Jasper van Leeven); German singer (tenor), actor and stage director; b. 19 Feb. 1966, Wittenberge. *Education:* Univ. of Music and Theatre, Leipzig, Berlin and Munich. *Career:* opera singer and actor, Komische Oper, Berlin; Oper Leipzig; Theater Hof, Görlitz and other venues in Germany; actor, film and TV; singer, numerous festivals and concert tours abroad including Japan, Mexico and Austria; mem. Int. Yehudi Menuhin Soc., London, Int. Soc. Supporting Young Stage Artists (pres.),

BühnenReif. *Honours:* Music Prize 2002. *Address:* c/o BR - Künstlerskretariat, Postfach 67 02 34, 10207 Berlin, Germany. *Telephone:* 4 22 74 87. *E-mail:* heikoreissig@gmx.de. *Website:* www.heikoreissig.de.

REITER, Alfred; German singer (bass); b. Dec. 1965, Augsburg. *Education:* Munich Music Academy, studied with Astrid Varnay and Hans Hotter. *Career:* debut at Wiesbaden State Theatre, 1995 as Lefort in Lortzing's Zar und Zimmermann; Performances of Mozart's Sarastro at the Deutsche Oper Berlin, Ludwigsburg Festival, Vienna and Lisbon; Monteverdi's Seneca at Nuremberg and Stuttgart; Hans Schwarz and Titurel in Parsifal at the Bayreuth Festival, Pogner in Meistersinger at Nuremberg, Fafner in Siegfried at Geneva and in Das Rheingold at the Vienna Staatsoper; Royal Opera Covent Garden 2001–02 as Titurel and as Peneios in Strauss's Daphne (concert); Season 2002–03 as Sarastro in Salzburg, Paris and London, Timur in Turandot at San Francisco and Gurnemanz in Cardiff, Geneva and Bologna; Concerts include Haydn's Die Schöpfung (Ludwigsburg 2000) and Beethoven's Missa Solemnis (Philadelphia, 2001). *Current Management:* Balmer & Dixon Management AG, Kreuzstrasse 82, 8032 Zürich, Switzerland. *Telephone:* (43) 244-8644. *Fax:* (43) 244-8649. *Website:* www.badix.ch.

RELYEA, John; singer (bass); b. 1970, Canada. *Education:* studied with Jerome Hines. *Career:* appearances from 1995 with San Francisco Opera as Colline, and Mozart's Figaro; Metropolitan Opera as Alidoro in La Cenerentola and in Die Meistersinger and Lucia di Lammermoor; Escamillo at the Paris, Hamburg and Munich Operas; concerts include Elijah in San Francisco, Bach's B minor Mass with the Cleveland Orchestra and Magnificat in Philadelphia; Beethoven's 9th and Messiah with the Pittsburgh SO; Verdi Requiem under Antonio Pappano in Brussels and Frankfurt; Mozart's C minor Mass with the Boston SO, and Requiem in Pittsburgh 2001–02; further engagements at Covent Garden in La Bohème, Semele and Lucia di Lammermoor. *Honours:* winner Merola Grand Finals, San Francisco 1995, Richard Tucker Award 2004, Beverly Sills Artist Award 2009. *Current Management:* c/o Caroline Woodfield, Opus 3 Artists, 470 Park Avenue South, 9th Floor North, New York, NY 10016, USA. *Telephone:* (212) 584-7500. *Fax:* (212) 300-8200. *E-mail:* info@opus3artists.com. *Website:* www.opus3artists.com; www.johnrelyea.com.

REMEDIOS, Alberto Telisforo, CBE; British singer (tenor); b. 27 Feb. 1935, Liverpool; s. of Albert Remedios and Ida Remedios; brother of Ramon Remedios; m. 1st Shirley Swindells 1958; one s.; m. 2nd Judith Hosken 1965; one s. one d. *Career:* studied with Edwin Francis, Liverpool; joined Sadler's Wells Opera Co. 1955; sings regularly with ENO and Royal Opera House, Covent Garden; has made numerous appearances in USA, Canada, Argentina, Germany, France and Spain and appeared in concert with major British orchestras. *Recordings include:* Wagner's Der Ring des Nibelungen and Tippett's A Midsummer Marriage. *Honours:* Queen's Prize, Royal Coll. of Music; First Prize, Int. Singing Competition, Sofia, Bulgaria; Sir Reginald Goodall Award Wagner Soc. 1995.

REMEDIOS, Ramon; singer (tenor); b. 9 May 1940, Liverpool; s. of Albert Remedios and Ida Remedios; brother of Alberto Remedios. *Education:* Guildhall School of Music, Nat. School of Opera and London Opera Centre. *Career:* has sung with Opera For All, Scottish Opera, WNO and European companies; notably as Alfredo, Macduff, Ismaele in Nabucco, Grigory/Dimitri, Don Ottavio, the Duke of Mantua, the Painter in Lulu, Skuratov (From the House of the Dead), Tamino and Almaviva; ENO as Alfredo, Rodolfo, Don José, Pinkerton, Paris in La Belle Hélène, Smith in the British premiere production of Christmas Eve 1988 and Lensky in Eugene Onegin; Covent Garden 1990, as Uldino in a new production of Attila; television appearances in Top C's and Tiaras, and The Word by Rick Wakeman; season 1992 as Sir Bruno Robertson in I Puritani at Covent Garden; concert engagements include operatic arias in Glasgow, a Viennese Evening at the Festival Hall and Verdi's Requiem (Royal Festival Hall 1991). *Recordings include:* The Word, with the Eton College Choir; Kalman's Countess Maritza with New Sadler's Wells Opera; A Suite of Gods, songs by Rick Wakeman. *Honours:* Guildhall School of Music School Tenor Prize, Ricordi Prize and Countess of Munster Trust, finalist Kathleen Ferrier Competition.

REMENIKOVA, Tanya; American (b. Russian) cellist, cello teacher and academic; *Professor of Cello, University of Minnesota;* b. 31 Jan. 1946, Moscow, Russia; m. Alexander Braginsky. *Education:* Moscow Conservatoire, studied with Mstislav Rostropovich. *Career:* regular appearances in recitals and with various orchestras, including Israel Philharmonic, Orchestra Nat. de Belgique; tours to Europe, Taiwan, People's Repub. of China; New York debut 1979; North American tours to Chicago, New York, Washington, DC, Minneapolis, Los Angeles and elsewhere; currently Prof. of Cello, School of Music, Univ. of Minnesota; Fellow and Artist-in-Residence, Churchill Coll., Cambridge, UK 1981, 1986; premieres of Stephen Paulus' American Vignettes 1988, Judith Zaimont's Tanya Poems for cello solo, dedicated to Tanya Remenikova; mem. Coll. Music Soc., American String Teachers Asscn. *Radio:* broadcast performances on NPR, MPR, Radio Jerusalem, BBC, Flemish Radio (Belgium). *Recordings include:* Stravinsky: Suite Italienne, Shostakovich: Sonata Op. 40, Britten: Sonata in C, Rachmaninov: Sonata Op. 19, Grieg: Sonata Op. 36, Tanya: Poems for Cello Solo by Judith Zaimont. *Honours:* Laureate, Gaspar Cassado Cello Competition 1969, Eugene Ysaye Award for Musical Contrib., Brussels 1979, Schubert Club Teachers Award 1994, Master Teacher Studio Award, Minnesota Chapter, American String Teachers Asscn. *Address:* 4141 Dupont Avenue South, Minneapolis, MN 55409, USA (home).

Telephone: (612) 825-9537 (home); (612) 624-0809 (office). *E-mail:* remen001@umn.edu (office). *Website:* www.music.umn.edu (office).

REMEŠ, Vaclav; Czech violinist; b. 1950, Usti. *Education:* Prague Conservatory, studied with Marie Voldanova. *Career:* founder mem., Prazak String Quartet 1972–; tour of Finland 1973, followed by appearances at competitions in Prague and Evian; concerts in Salzburg, Munich, Paris, Rome, Berlin, Cologne and Amsterdam; tour of the UK 1985, including Wigmore Hall debut; tours of Japan, the USA, Australia and New Zealand; tour of the UK 1988, and concert at the Huddersfield Contemporary Music Festival 1989; recitals for the BBC, Radio France, Dutch Radio, the WDR in Cologne and Radio Prague; appearances with the Smetana and LaSalle Quartets in Mendelssohn's Octet. *Honours:* winner, Nat. Violin Competiton, Pisek 1973, Chamber Music Competition of the Prague Conservatory 1974, Grand Prix, International String Quartet Competition, Evian Music Festival 1978, National Competition of String Quartets in Czechoslovakia 1978, Best String Quartet of the Prague Spring Festival 1978. *Current Management:* c/o Světlana Jahodová, Jahoda Artists Management. *Telephone:* 603293985. *E-mail:* info@jahoda-arts.cz. *Website:* www.jahoda-arts.cz; www.prazakquartet.com.

REMMEREIT, Arild; Norwegian conductor and pianist. *Education:* Norwegian Conservatory of Music, Hochschule für Musik, Vienna, Accad. di Santa Cecilia, Rome. *Career:* Conductor, Wiener Residenz Orchester 1989–92; Artistic Dir State Opera of Ukraine 1992–95; Music Dir Rochester Philharmonic Orchestra 2011–; guest conductor, Baltimore Symphony, Bamberger Symponiker, BBC Scottish Symphony, BBC Symphony, Bergen Philharmonic, Bern Philharmonic, Cincinnati Symphony, Copenhagen Philharmonic, Dallas Symphony, Detroit Symphony Orchestra, Deutsches Symphonie Berlin, Filarmonica della Scala, Milan, Gelders Orchestra Arnhem, Graz Symphoniker, Gulbenkian Orchestra, Hallé Orchestra, Houston Symphony, Iceland Symphony, KBS Symphony, Limburg Symphony, Madison Symphony, Malaysian Philharmonic, Milwaukee Symphony, Montpellier Philharmonic, Mozarteum Salzburg, Munich Philharmonic, Nashville Symphony, National Arts Centre Orchestra, Ottawa, NDR Radio Philharmonic Hanover, Norwegian State Opera, Orchestra de Càmara Andrès Segovia, Orchestra del Maggio Musicale Fiorentino, Orchestre National du Capitole de Toulouse, Oslo Philharmonic, Pacific Symphony, Pittsburgh Symphony, Rheinland-Pfalz Philharmonic, Royal Scottish National Orchestra, RTÉ National Symphony, Seattle Symphony, Seoul Philharmonic, Stockholm Philharmonic, Tokyo Philharmonic, Utah Symphony, Vienna Symphony. *Current Management:* Opus 3 Artists, 470 Park Avenue South, 9th Floor North, New York, NY 10016, USA. *Telephone:* (212) 584-7500. *E-mail:* info@opus3artists.com. *Website:* www.opus3artists.com; www.remmereit.com.

REMMERT, Birgit; German singer (alto); b. 1966. *Education:* Detmold Musikhochschule with Helmut Kretschmar. *Career:* sang in Beethoven's Ninth under Nikolaus Harnoncourt in London 1991, and again under Giulini in Stockholm 1994; further concerts include Mendelssohn's Walpurgisnacht in Graz, Biber's Requiem and Vespers under Harnoncourt in Vienna, the song cycle Sunless by Mussorgsky, in Amsterdam, and Das Lied von der Erde under Philippe Herreweghe at the Théâtre des Champs-Elysées, Paris; as Martha in Tchaikovsky's Iolantha, Hamburg, as Erda in the Ring and Ulrica at Dresden; Zürich Opera, as Dalila, Suzuki and Third Lady in Die Zauberflöte; other repertory includes Mahler's Eighth and Das klagende Lied (with Chailly at the Concertgebouw), Mahler 3rd Symphony with Simon Rattle in Birmingham and the Nurse in Monteverdi's Poppea at Salzburg Festival; Mahler's Second with the CBSO under Rattle at the London Proms; sang Fricka in Das Rheingold and Die Walküre at the Bayreuth Festival; Mahler's Symphony of a Thousand at the London Proms. *Recordings include:* Beethoven's Ninth; Lieder by Brahms, Clara Schumann and Tchaikovsky; Bach Cantatas with Peter Schreier; Bruckner, Te Deum and F Minor Mass with Welser-Möst. *Honours:* Lieder Prize at the Palma d'oro Competition, Ligure. *Current Management:* c/o Opéra et Concert, 37 rue de la Chausée d'Antin, 75009 Paris, France. *Telephone:* 1-42-96-18-18. *Fax:* 1-42-96-18-00. *E-mail:* agence@opera-concert.com. *Website:* www.opera-concert.com.

RENDALL, David; British singer (tenor); b. 11 Oct. 1948, London, England; m. Diana Montague; four c. *Education:* Royal Academy of Music, Salzburg Mozarteum. *Career:* debut as Ferrando in Così fan tutte with Glyndebourne Touring Co. 1975; performances at Covent Garden 1975–2005, as the Italian Tenor in Der Rosenkavalier, Almaviva, Matteo, Rodolfo, Des Grieux in Manon and Rodrigo in a new production of La Donna del Lago by Rossini 1985; as Ferrando with Glyndebourne Festival 1976, returned as Belmonte and Tom Rakewell 1989; with ENO 1976–2005, as Leicester in Maria Stuarda, Rodolfo, Alfredo, Tamino and Pinkerton; European debut at Angers 1975, as the High Priest in Idomeneo; North American debut as Tamino, Ottawa 1977; New York City Opera debut as Rodolfo 1978; San Francisco debut as Don Ottavio 1978; regular performances with Metropolitan Opera 1980–2005, as Ottavio, Ernesto, Belmonte, Idomeneo, Lenski, Ferrando, Alfred in Die Fledermaus and Mozart's Titus; performed title role in La Damnation de Faust, Lyon Opéra 1983; further engagements in Amsterdam, Berlin, Paris, Milan, Hamburg, Tel-Aviv, Turin, Washington, Vienna, Dresden, Chicago, Santa Fe and Munich; other operatic roles include Gounod's Faust and the Duke of Mantua, Matteo, Cavaradossi, Don Antonio, stage premiere of Gerhard's The Duenna, Pinkerton in Madama Butterfly, Les Contes d'Hoffmann, Don José, Otello; many concert appearances in Europe and the USA; retd from the stage after an accident during a performance left him seriously injured 2005. *Recordings include:* Maria Stuarda, Così fan tutte, Ariodante, Mozart's Requiem, Beethoven's Missa solemnis, Madama Butterfly, Bruckner's Te Deum. *Honours:* Young Musician of the Year Award 1973, Gulbenkian Fellowship 1975.

RENICK, Therese; American singer (mezzo-soprano); b. 1963, St Louis, MO. *Education:* studied in Vienna with Hilde Zadek. *Career:* debut at Würzburg, 1985, in Der Barbier von Bagdad by Cornelius; Krefeld Opera, 1985–88, as Carmen and Azucena; Essen from 1989, as Verdi's Eboli, and Amneris, and Mozart's Dorabella; Salzburg, 1987–88, in Schoenberg's Moses und Aron; season 1995–96 as Ortrud in Lohengrin at Dessau and in the premiere of Bose's Schlachthof 5 at Munich; other roles include Santuzza, Venus in Tannhäuser and Fenena in Nabucco (Munich, 1996); concerts include the Requiems of Mozart and Verdi, and Beethoven's Ninth. *Current Management:* c/o Opernagentur Inge Tennigkeit, Kempener Strasse 4, 40474 Düsseldorf, Germany. *Telephone:* (211) 5160060. *Fax:* (211) 51600616. *E-mail:* opera@tennigkeit-ag.de. *Website:* www.tennigkeit-ag.de.

RENICKE, Volker; German conductor and academic; b. 3 July 1929, Bremen; m. Rey Nishiuchi 1975. *Education:* Nordwestdeutsche Musikakademie, Detmold, Accademia Chigiana, Siena with Paul van Kempen. *Career:* in Republic of Korea 1991, with Korean Symphony Orchestra in the Korean Orchestral Festival; Tokyo Mozart 200 Anniversary of Death, Idomeneo, 1991; in Seoul Opera Favorita and Fidelio at National Theatre, 1992; International Festival in Tsuyama, Japan, Mozart Tito, 1993; Salzburg Mozart Requiem, 1993; guest conducting and concerts in England, France, Germany, Netherlands, Luxembourg, Switzerland, Italy, Yugoslavia and Korea; concerts with all major Japanese orchestras; in Republic of Korea with Seoul Philharmonic Orchestra and Korean Symphony Orchestra; Zauberflöte and Traviata in Opernhaus Köln, 1995; mem. Kojimachi Rotary Club, Tokyo. *Recordings:* with Jörg Demus and NHK Orchestra members; Piano concertos of Bach, Haydn, Mozart, Debussy, Franck, Fauré; with Karl Suske, violin, and NHK Orchestra members; recordings of Vivaldi and Bach; Humperdinck's Hansel and Gretel, in Japanese, with Yomiuri Orchestra. *Address:* 5-26-15 Okuzawa, Setagaya-ku, 158 Tokyo, Japan.

RENNER, Jack L., BSc; American record company executive, recording engineer and academic; *Chairman, CEO and Chief Recording Engineer, Telarc International Corporation*; b. 13 April 1935. *Education:* Ohio State Univ. *Career:* fmr music teacher and professional trumpeter; co-founder, Telarc Int. Corpn (with Robert Woods) 1977, pioneered use of digital recording in classical and jazz music, made first digital recordings of an orchestra in the USA, currently Chair., CEO and Chief Recording Engineer; faculty mem., Cleveland Inst. of Music 1986–, currently Adjunct Prof. *Honours:* Dr hc of Musical Arts (Cleveland Inst. of Music) 1997; winner of nine Grammy Awards. *Address:* Telarc International Corporation, 23307 Commerce Park Road, Cleveland, OH 44122, USA (office). *Website:* www.telarc.com (office).

RENNERT, Jonathan, MA (Cantab.), FRCO, FRCCO, ARCM, LRAM; British organist, conductor and writer; *Director of Music, St Michael's, Cornhill*; b. 17 March 1952, London, England; s. of Sidney Rennert and Patricia Rennert; m. Sheralyn Ivil 1992; one d. *Education:* St Paul's School, London, Royal Coll. of Music (Foundation Scholar), St John's Coll., Cambridge (Organ Scholar), Univ. of Cambridge (Stuart of Rannoch Scholar in Sacred Music). *Career:* numerous recitals, concerts, recordings, radio and TV appearances worldwide as conductor, solo organist, accompanist or continuo player; Dir of Music, Holy Trinity Church, Barnes, London 1969–71; Musical Dir Cambridge Opera 1972–74; Dir of Music, St Jude's, Courtfield Gardens, London SW5; conductor American community choirs in London 1975–76; Acting Dir of Music, St Matthew's, Ottawa, Canada 1976–78; Dir of Music, St Michael's, Cornhill, London, Musical Dir St Michael's Singers 1979–; Musician-in-Residence, Grace Cathedral, San Francisco, USA 1982; Conductor Elizabethan Singers 1983–88; Festival Dir Cornhill Festival of British Music 1982–88; Admin. Int. Congress of Organists 1987; Course Dir and Chair. Cen. London Dist, Royal School of Church Music 1995–2007; Musical Dir London Motet and Madrigal Club 1994–; Dir of Music, St Mary-at-Hill, London, and Dir St Mary-at-Hill Baroque Chamber Orchestra and Bach Cantata Series 1996–2008; Master of the Reigate Choristers (from St Mary's Choir School) 1997–2000; Music Dir, St Cecilia Chorus 2009–; moderating and training examiner, Associated Bd of the Royal Schools of Music; Examiner and fmr Council mem. Royal Coll. of Organists; Warden, Performers' and Composers' Section, Incorporated Soc. of Musicians 2002–03; mem. Worshipful Co. of Musicians (Master 2003–04). *Publications:* William Crotch (1775–1847): Composer, Teacher, Artist 1975, George Thalben-Ball (biog.) 1979, Music, Musicians and Organs of St Michael's, Cornhill 2010; contrib. of articles to New Grove Dictionary of Music and Musicians, Die Musik in Geschichte und Gegenwart (DGG) and numerous other musical publs. *Honours:* Hon. Fellow, Royal Canadian Coll. of Organists. *Address:* 46 Doods Road, Reigate, Surrey, RH2 0NL, England (home). *Telephone:* (1737) 244604 (home). *E-mail:* jonathanrennert@hotmail.com (home).

RENSHAW, Kenneth; American musician (violin); b. 9 Oct. 1993. *Education:* San Francisco Conservatory, studied with Li Lin, Ruth Asawa San Francisco School of the Arts, New England Conservatory, studied with Donald Weilerstein, summer studies with Itzhak Perlman Music Program. *Career:* has appeared as soloist with orchestras in Europe, N America and Asia, including Lithuanian Nat. Orchestra, China Philharmonic, China NCPA Orchestra, Staatskapelle Weimar, San Francisco Symphony Youth Orchestra (SFSYO) and American Philharmonic, and played with conductors including

732 www.worldwhoswho.com

Michael Tilson Thomas, Sir Simon Rattle, Itzhak Perlman and Yan-Pascal Tortelier; S American debut as concerto soloist at Festival de Ushuaia, Argentina 2013; festivals in Europe in 2013 included Menuhin Festival in Gstaad, Mecklenburg-Vorpommern Festspiele and Fränkische Musiktage Festspiele; concertmaster, SFSYO 2008–10; chamber musician. *Honours:* First Prize, Los Angeles Philharmonic Competition 2009, SFSYO Concerto Competition 2009 and Louis Spohr Violin Competition (also Mozart Concerto Prize and Sonata Prize) 2010, American Philharmonic Young Artist Award 2011, First Prize, YES Foundation for the Arts Competition 2011 and Menuhin Int. Violin Competition 2012, Avanti Award 2012.

RENTOWSKI, Wieslaw Stanislaw Vivian; MA, MMus; composer and organist; b. 23 Nov. 1953, Bydgoszcz, Poland; m. Magdalena Kubiak 1985; one s. *Education:* Univ. of Łódź, Acad. of Music, Łódź, F. Chopin Acad. of Music, Warsaw and Louisiana State Univ. School of Music. *Career:* debut at Carnegie Hall, Lagniappe for eight instruments 1991; compositions performed at: International Festival of Contemporary Music, Warsaw Autumn 1984, 1986, 1987, 1989; Internationale Sinziger Orgelwoche, Bonn 1989, 1990; Festival International de Lanaudière, Canada 1989; International Festival of Contemporary Music, Baton Rouge, USA 1990, 1991; organist, many performances and recordings including solo recitals and chamber concerts in Warsaw, Banff, Toronto, Bayreuth, Baton Rouge and New Orleans. *Compositions:* Anagram 1986, Por día de años 1987, Chorea Minor 1989, Wayang 1989. *Publication:* contrib. article 'Intellectual Music Harmony', to Ruch Muzyczny music magazine, Poland 1989.

RENZETTI, Donato; Italian conductor; b. 30 Jan. 1950, Milan. *Education:* Conservatorio Giuseppe Verdi, Milan. *Career:* assisted Claudio Abbado in Milan; conducted the Verdi Requiem in Salzburg; gave Rigoletto at Verona 1981 and has since worked at most Italian opera houses; conducted the premiere of Corghi's Gargantua at Turin 1984; Paris Théâtre Musical, Macbeth; conducted La Sonnambula at the Chicago Lyric Opera 1988, and Le nozze di Figaro at Rome 1989; Bonn Opera and Teatro Fenice, Venice 1990, with Il Barbiere di Siviglia and Ernani; has given orchestral concerts in Italy and elsewhere; conducted Turandot at the 1996 Macerata Festival and at Dallas 1998. *Honours:* prizewinner Gino Marinuzzi International Competition 1976, bronze medal Ernest Ansermet Competition at Geneva 1978, Guido Cantelli Prize, Milan 1980.

RENZI, Emma; South African singer (soprano); b. (Emmerentia Scheepers), 8 April 1926, Heidelberg, Transvaal. *Education:* Coll. of Music, Kapstad, London Opera Centre, studied with Santo Santonocito in Catania, with Virginia Borroni in Milan. *Career:* debut in Karlsruhe as Sieglinde 1961; has sung in major cities world-wide, including Milan, Genoa, Lisbon, Buenos Aires, Barcelona, Edinburgh, Mexico City, Johannesburg, Naples, Rome and Munich; Italian Radio in Parisina by Mascagni 1977; Verona Arena 1989; other roles include Norma, Aida, Amelia in Un Ballo in Maschera, Tosca, Leonora in Il Trovatore, Turandot, the Duchess of Parma in Doktor Faust, Abigail, Lady Macbeth, Elisabeth, and Countess Almaviva; Head, Pretoria Technikon Opera School 1981–91; Sr Lecturer in Singing, Univ. of the Witwatersrand 1992–2003; runs pvt singing studio. *Recording:* Emma Renzi: A Tribute. *Honours:* Order for Meritorious Service 1987; Grande Ufficiale dell'Ordine Della Stella Della Solidarieta Italiana 2010; Hon. DMus (Potchefstroom) 2000; Vita Award 1986, Nederburg Special Award 1993, ATKV Award 1995, Adelaide Ristori (Italy). *Address:* 39 Auckland Avenue, Auckland Park, Johannesburg 2092, Gauteng, South Africa (home). *Telephone:* (11) 726-3974 (home). *Fax:* (11) 726-3974 (home). *E-mail:* emma.renzi@iburst.co.za (home).

REPIN, Vadim Viktorovich; Russian violinist; *Artistic Director, Trans-Siberian Arts Festival;* b. 31 Aug. 1971, Novosibirsk, Siberia; s. of Viktor Antonovich Repin and Galina Georgievna Repina. *Education:* Novosibirsk Music School, Hochschule für Musik, Lübeck with Zakhar Bron. *Career:* began playing violin aged five; first stage performance six months later; won gold medal in all age categories in Wienawski Competition, Poznań aged 11; debut recitals in Moscow and St Petersburg; debuts in Tokyo, Munich, Berlin, Helsinki 1985; Carnegie Hall 1986; has performed with all major orchestras and greatest conductors; regularly collaborates with Nikolai Lugansky and Itamar Golan in recital; other chamber music partners include Martha Argerich, Evgeny Kissin and Mischa Maisky; Season 2009–10: concerts with Muti in New York, with Thielemann in Tokyo, with Chailly in Leipzig, tour of Australia with London Philharmonic Orchestra and Vladimir Jurowski, and première of a violin concerto written for him by James MacMillan, performed with London Symphony Orchestra and Valery Gergiev; Artistic Dir Trans-Siberian Arts Festival 2013–. *Television:* Vadim Repin: A Magician of Sound (film documentary by Claudia Willke) 2010. *Recordings include:* Shostakovich No. 1 and Prokofiev No. 2 with the Hallé Orchestra under Nagano 1995, Prokofiev Violin Sonatas and Five Melodies with Berezovsky 1995, Tchaikovsky and Sibelius Concertos with the London Symphony under Krivine 1996, Tchaikovsky and Shostakovich piano trios with Berezovsky and Yablonsky 1997, Lalo Symphonie Espagnole with the London Symphony Orchestra under Nagano 1998, Tutta Bravura (with Markovich) 1999, Vadim Repin au Louvre (with Berezovsky, Barachovsky, Lakatos, Gothoni) 1999, Tchaikovsky and Myaskovsky violin concertos with the Kirov Orchestra under Gergiev 2002, A Night of Encores (recorded live with the Berlin Philharmonic under Jansons) 2004, Taneyev Piano Quintet and Trio (Gramophone Award for Best Chamber Recording 2006), Beethoven Violin Concerto (with Vienna Philharmonic and Riccardo Muti, coupled with

Beethoven's Kreutzer Sonata with Martha Argerich) 2008, Brahms Violin Concerto and Brahms Double Concerto (Truls Mørk, cello, with Gewandhaus Orchester Leipzig and Riccardo Chailly) 2009, Tchaikovsky and Rachmaninov trios with Mischa Maisky and Lang Lang (Echo Award) 2009, recital recording with Nikolai Lugansky 2010. *Honours:* Chevalier des Arts et des Lettres 2010; Tibor Varga competition winner, Sion 1985, winner, Reine Elisabeth Concours, Brussels (youngest ever winner) 1990, Victoire d'honneur (France) 2010. *Current Management:* c/o Interclassica Music Management, Schönburgstrasse 4, 1040 Vienna, Austria. *Telephone:* (1) 585-3980. *E-mail:* eleanorhope@interclassica.com. *Website:* www.interclassica.com; www.vadimrepin.com.

REPPEL, Carmen; singer (soprano); b. 27 April 1941, Gummersbach, Germany. *Education:* Hamburg Musikhochschule with Erna Berger. *Career:* debut in Flensburg 1968, as Elisabeth de Valois; has sung in Hanover, Hamburg, Frankfurt, Cologne, Mannheim, Wiesbaden and Kassel; Bayreuth Festival 1977–80, as Freia and Gutrune, and in Die Walküre and Parsifal; Wuppertal 1983, in a concert performance of Schwarzschwanenreich by Siegfried Wagner; San Francisco 1983, as Ariadne auf Naxos; sang Mozart's Electra at Stuttgart 1985; Hamburg and Vienna 1985, as Leonore and Chrysothemis; Munich Opera 1986, as Andromache in the premiere of Troades by Reimann; Zürich Opera 1986, Salome; further appearances in Berlin, Zürich, Barcelona, Milan and Tokyo; other roles include Fiordiligi, Donna Anna, Mélisande, Mimi, Liu, Marenka in The Bartered Bride, Violetta, Desdemona, Leonora in Il Trovatore, Ariadne, Salome, Elsa and Sieglinde; sang in Flavio Testi's Ricardo III at La Scala 1987; Sieglinde in Die Walküre at Bologna 1988; Strauss's Ariadne and Salome, Turin 1989; Salome at the Torre del Lago festival 1989. *Recordings include:* Freia and Gerhilde in Der Ring des Nibelungen, from Bayreuth; Les Troyens by Berlioz; Chrysothemis in Götz Friedrich's film version of Elektra.

RESA, Neithard; German violist; b. 1950, Berlin. *Education:* studied in Berlin with Michel Schwalbe, Cologne with Max Rostal, USA with Michael Tree. *Career:* Principal Viola, Berlin Philharmonic 1978; co-founder, Philharmonia Quartet, Berlin, giving concerts throughout Europe, USA and Japan; British debut 1987, playing Haydn, Szymanowski and Beethoven at Wigmore Hall; Bath Festival 1987, playing Mozart, Schumann and Beethoven; other repertoire includes quartets by Bartók, Mendelssohn, Nicolai, Ravel and Schubert; quintets by Brahms, Weber, Reger and Schumann. *Honours:* prizewinner German Music Foundation 1978.

RESCALA, Tim; Brazilian composer, arranger and musician (piano); b. (Luiz Augusto), 21 Nov. 1961, Rio de Janeiro; m. Claudia Mele 1995; one d. *Education:* Universidade Federal do Rio de Janeiro, studies piano with Maria Yêda Cadah, composition with Hans-Joachim Koellreutter. *Career:* works with both classical and popular music; founding mem. Estúdio da Glória (composers' cooperative) 1981; Musical Producer, TV Globo 1988–; Dir, Sala Baden Powell, Rio de Janeiro 2005–. *Compositions:* opera: O Homem que Sabia Português 1998, A Redenção pelo Sonho 1998, 22 Antes Depois 2002, À Sombra do Sucesso 2002; children's musical: Pianíssimo 1993, A Orquestra das Sonhos 1996, Papagueno 1997, O Cavalinho Azul 2001, A Turma do Pererê 2004; over 50 instrumental pieces. *Recordings:* Cliché Music, Estudio da Glória, Romance Policial, Desritmificações, Dolores, Giramundo. *Honours:* first prize, Villa-Lobos competition, Mambembe Prize 1993, Prize of Rio de Janeiro Municipality to write an opera, Shell Prize for Music 2001. *Website:* www.timrescala.com.br.

RESICK, Georgine; American singer (soprano); b. 1953. *Education:* studied with George London. *Career:* sang Sophie in Werther at Washington; Cologne Opera from 1981 as Marzelline in Fidelio, Oscar, Adina (L'Elisir d'amore) and Anne Trulove; Chicago Opera 1984, as Blondchen in Die Entführung; Drottningholm Festival 1985, as Mozart's Susanna and Constanze; Carolina in Il Matrimonio Segreto at Paris and Edinburgh; US appearances from 1986, including Hilde Mack in Henze's Elegy for Young Lovers at Long Beach Opera 1996. *Recordings include:* Così fan tutte, Le nozze di Figaro (video).

RESS, Ulrich; German singer (tenor); b. 29 Oct. 1958, Augsburg. *Education:* Augsburg Conservatory, studied with Leonore Kirchstein. *Career:* sang at Stadttheater Augsburg 1979–84, notably as Idamante and Rossini's Almaviva; engaged at Bayerische Staatsoper from 1984, as Mozart's Pedrillo and Monostatos, Verdi's Bardolph and Macduff, Beppe in Pagliacci and Pong in Turandot; sang the Steersman and Strauss's Truffaldino at Munich 1991; guest appearances at Bayreuth and Barcelona 1988–89, as David in Meistersinger, Strasbourg and Nice, Jacquino 1989; Munich Staatsoper 2000–01 in Carmen, Tannhäuser, Katya Kabanova, Falstaff and Arabella. *Recordings:* Young Servant in video of Elektra conducted by Abbado; Bardolph in Falstaff conducted by Colin Davis; Massimila Doni by Schoeck.

REVERDY, Michèle; composer; b. 12 Dec. 1943, Alexandria, Egypt; one d. *Education:* Sorbonne Univ. of Paris, Paris Conservatory with Alain Weber, Claude Ballif, Olivier Messiaen, Casa de Velazquez, Madrid. *Career:* teacher at lycées 1965–74; Prof. of Analysis, regional and municipal conservatories 1974–83; Prod., Radio-France 1978–80; Prof. of Analysis, Paris Conservatory 1983–. *Compositions include:* Kaleidoscope for harpsichord and flute 1975, Number One for guitar 1977, Météores for 17 instruments 1978, L'Ile aux Lumières for solo violin and string orchestra 1983, Scenic Railway for 16 instruments 1983, La Nuit Qui Suivit Notre Dernier Dîner for chamber opera 1984, Triade for guitar 1986, Trois Fantaisies de Gaspard de la Nuit for choir or 12-voice ensemble 1987, Sept Enluminures for soprano, clarinet, piano and percussion 1987, Propos Félins for string orchestra and children's choir 1988, Le Cercle du Vent for orchestra 1988, Vincent (opera based on the life of Vincent Van Gogh) 1984–89, Le Précepteur (opera, after Jakob Lenz) for coloratura soprano, soprano, mezzo-soprano, contralto, three tenors, two baritones, three basses and 20 instruments. *Recordings:* Michèle Reverdy (Scenic Railway, Sept Enluminures, Météores, Fugure, Kaleidoscope); Triade, Rafael Andia, guitar; Le Château, 1980–86, Opera for nine soloists, two choirs (men and children), orchestra, text from Franz Kafka. *Publications:* L'oeuvre pour piano d'Olivier Messiaen, 1978; Histoire de la Musique Occidentale, 1985; L'oeuvre pour orchestra d'Olivier Messiaen, 1988.

REVZEN, Joel, BMus, MMus; American conductor and pianist; *Artistic Director, Arizona Opera. Education:* The Juilliard School, New York. *Career:* Asst Conductor, St Paul Chamber Orchestra 1986–90; Founding Dean, St Louis Conservatory 12 years; Artistic Dir Berkshire Opera, Mass 1991–; Music Dir Fargo-Moorhead Symphony –2000; Artistic Dir and Prin. Conductor Western New York Chamber Orchestra 2000–03; Artistic Dir Arizona Opera 2003–, also Gen. Dir 2004–; on conducting roster Metropolitan Opera 1999–; guest conductor with Kirov Opera, Prague Symphony Orchestra, Prague Chamber Orchestra, Janáček Philharmonic, Sinfonia of Antwerp, Orchestre Nat. de Lyon, Norwegian Opera, Nat. Theatre Mannheim, Augsburg Symphony, Washington Opera, Minnesota Opera, Tucson Symphony, Dallas Symphony, Florida Philharmonic, Kennedy Center Chamber Players, Minnesota Orchestra, Nat. Symphony, Orchestra of St Luke's, Kansas City Symphony, Utah Symphony, San Antonio Symphony, Symphony of Southwest Florida, Seattle Symphony; as chamber musician has performed with Jaime Laredo, Sharon Robinson, Michael Tree, Arleen Auger. *Recordings include:* The Art of Arleen Auger 1994, Haydn, The Seasons 1995, Haydn, Die Schöpfung 1995, Larsen, Water Music 1997, Larsen, Symphony No. 4 2000, Mendelssohn, Concerto for piano and violin 2000, Feminine Escapes 2002, Music by Russell Peterson (composer and conductor) 2002. *Honours:* Dr hc (St Louis Conservatory of Music); Frank Damrosch Prize in Conducting, Berkshire Opera Silver Rose Award, Florida Grand Opera Henry C. Clark Conductor Award 2008. *Current Management:* c/o Karen Kriendler Nelson, KKN Enterprises, 277 West End Avenue, Suite 11A, New York, NY 10023-2681, USA. *Telephone:* (212) 496-5154. *Fax:* (212) 721-9566. *E-mail:* kknenterp@gmail.com. *Address:* Arizona Opera, 4600 N 12th Street, Phoenix, AZ 85014, USA (office). *Telephone:* (602) 266-7464 (office). *Fax:* (602) 266-5806 (office). *E-mail:* info@azopera.com (office). *Website:* www.azopera.com (office); joelrevzen.com.

REX, Christopher, BMus; American cellist; b. 2 Jan. 1951, Orlando, FL; m. Martha Anne Wilkins 1985; one s. one d. *Education:* Curtis Inst. of Music, Philadelphia, PA and Juilliard School, New York with Leonard Rose. *Career:* premiered Stephen Paul's Double Concerto with brother Charles, Lincoln Center, New York; seven years with Philadelphia Orchestra 1972–79; Principal Cello, Atlanta Symphony 1979–; Principal Cello, New York Philharmonic 1988 European tour; founder mem., Georgian Chamber Players; mem. NARAS, AFM. *Recordings:* Saint-Saëns, Muse and Poet with Martium Philharmonic. *Publications:* Mussorgsky's Pictures at an Exhibition (ed.), contrib. art work to Choral Journal. *Honours:* American Federation of Music Clubs Young Artist Competition 1979.

REY, Isabel; Spanish singer (soprano); b. 1966, Valencia. *Education:* Valencia Conservatory studied singing with Ana Luisa Chova, and in Barcelona with Juan Oncina and Tatiana Menotti. *Career:* debut in Bilbao 1987, as Amina in La Sonnambula; worked at Vienna's Konzerthaus, Musikverein and Staatsoper, Zürich Opera, Amsterdam Opera, Teatro Real, Madrid, Liceo de Barcelona, Fenice di Venezia, Nice, Salzburg Festival, Edinburgh Festival; over 55 operas in repertoire from Monteverdi to Stravinsky: Rigoletto, Elisir d'Amore, Don Pasquale, Dialogues des Carmélites (Blanche), Pelléas et Mélisande (Melisande), Rake's Progress (Ann); Mozart roles, including Donna Anna, Susanna, Fiordiligi, Pamina, Sandrina; concerts worldwide with José Carreras, Aragall, Pons 1993–. *Recordings:* albums: Nozze di Figaro, The Passion of Spain (with José Carreras), Damas del Canto (with Caballé, De los Angeles), Canciones para la Navidad (with A. Zabala), Natsu no Omoide (with I. Suzuki); DVDs of Nozze di Figaro, Don Giovanni, Il Ritorno d'Ulisse in Patria, King Arthur, Pelléas et Mélisande, La Finta Giardiniera, Don Pasquale, Semele. *Honours:* second prize, Toulouse contest 1987, first prize, Verviers contest, Bilbao contest. *Telephone:* (63) 9149393 (office). *E-mail:* manager@isabelrey.com (office). *Website:* www.isabelrey.com (office).

REYMOND, Valentin; Swiss conductor; b. 1954, Neuchâtel. *Education:* Conservatories of Bienne and Zürich. *Career:* asst at the Grand Théâtre Geneva; has assisted such conductors as Jean-Marie Auberson, Horst Stein, Armin Jordan and Roderick Brydon; Music Director of Opéra Décentralisé; concert and broadcast appearances with Orchestre de la Suisse Romande and Orchestre de la Radio Suisse Italienne, Orchestre de Chambre de Toulouse, Krasnoyarsk Symphony Orchestra (Siberia), Russian State Symphony Orchestra; operatic appearances: Traviata (Opéra de Lucerne); Rape of Lucretia (Opéra Décentralisé and Opéra de Lausanne); Albert Herring (Bern Opera, Opéra de Lausanne and Opéra de Nantes); Les Pêcheurs de Perles (Dublin Opera); Les Mamelles de Tirésias, Das Rheingold, Die Walküre, Le Roi Malgré Lui (Opéra de Nantes); L'Etoile (Opera North); Iphigénie en Aulide for Opera North, 1996. *Current Management:* c/o Neil Dalrymple, Music International, 13 Ardilaun Road, London, N5 2QR, England. *Telephone:* (20) 7359-5183. *Fax:* (20) 7226-9792. *E-mail:* music@musicint.co.uk.

REYNOLDS, Julian; British conductor and pianist; b. 1962, London, England. *Education:* Vienna Hochschule für Musik, studied with Albert Ferber. *Career:* debut recital at Wigmore Hall 1981; pianist with European Community Youth Orchestra 1980–85; Asst Musical Dir, Netherlands Opera 1986–94, conducting Bluebeard's Castle by Bartók, Luisa Miller and Mozart's Mitridate; A Midsummer Night's Dream 1993; Kirov Opera, St Petersburg, with La Traviata and Le nozze di Figaro; Otello at Stuttgart and The Cunning Little Vixen at Maastricht; concerts throughout the UK and The Netherlands; season 1998–99 with Haydn's Seasons at Melbourne and Luisa Miller at Mainz; Assoc. Conductor, Netherlands Opera from 1999, with L'italiana in Algeri, Figaro and L'Elisir d'amore; recital appearances with Barbara Bonney and Kiri Te Kanawa; Ravel's Ma Mère l'Oye, and own orchestrations of Alma Mahler songs.

REYNOLDS, Roger Lee, BSE, BM, MM; American composer; *Distinguished Professor, University of California at San Diego*; b. 18 July 1934, Detroit, MI; m. Karen Jeanne Hill 1964; two d. *Education:* Univ. of Michigan. *Career:* faculty mem., Univ. of California at San Diego 1969–, currently Distinguished Prof.; George Miller Visiting Prof., Univ. of Illinois 1971; founding Dir, Center for Music Experiment, Univ. of California at San Diego 1972–77; Visiting Prof., Yale Univ. 1981; Sr Research Fellow, ISAM, Brooklyn Coll. 1985; Valentine Prof. of Music, Amherst Coll. 1988; Rothschild Composer-in-Residence, Peabody Conservatory of Music, Baltimore 1992–93. *Compositions include:* The Emperor of Ice Cream 1961–62, A Portrait of Vanzetti 1962–63, Voicespace I-V 1975–86, Archipelago 1982–83, Odyssey 1989–93, Transfigured Wind I-IV 1984–85, Symphony [Vertigo] 1987, Symphony [Myths] 1990, Symphony [The Stages of Life] 1991–92, Ariadne's Thread 1994, last things, I think, to think about 1994, The Angel of Death 1994, The Red Act Arias 1997, Justice 1999–2001, Process and Passion 2002, Sanctuary 2004–08, Illusion 2006, Submerged Memories 2006, Elliott 2007–08. *Publications:* Mind Models: New Forms of Musical Experience 1975, A Searcher's Path: A Composer's Ways 1987, A Jostled Silence: Contemporary Japanese Musical Thought 1992–93, Form and Method: Composing Music 2002. *Honours:* Pulitzer Prize in Music 1989, National Institute of Arts and Letters Award 1971. *Address:* 624 Serpentine Drive, Del Mar, CA 92014, USA. *Website:* www.rogerreynolds.com.

RHODES, Cherry, BMus; American organist and academic; b. 28 June 1943, Brooklyn, NY; m. Ladd Thomas. *Education:* Curtis Inst. of Music, Philadelphia, PA, studied in Munich with Karl Richter, with Marie-Claire Alain and Jean Guillou in Paris, summer schools at Harvard and Univ. of Pennsylvania. *Career:* soloist, Philadelphia Orchestra, South German Radio Orchestra, Chamber Orchestra of French National Radio, Pasadena Chamber Orchestra, Phoenix Symphony Orchestra, Los Angeles Philharmonic; recitals, Lincoln Center, New York, Notre Dame, Paris, Royal Festival Hall, London, Los Angeles Music Center, Milwaukee Performing Arts Center, Orchestra Hall, Chicago, Meyerson Symphony Center, Dallas; numerous appearances at national and regional conventions of AGO; performances at several Bach festivals; international festivals Bratislava, Nuremberg, Paris, St Albans, Luxembourg, Vienna and throughout Poland; gave opening recital on new organ at John F. Kennedy Center in Washington, DC; broadcast performances in USA, Canada and Europe; adjudicator for national and international organ-playing competitions. *Publications:* Ascent for organ by Joan Tower (ed.), Prelude and Variations on Old Hundredth by Calvin Hampton (co-ed.).

RHODES, Phillip Carl, BA, MM; American composer; *Andrew W. Mellon Professor Emeritus of the Humanities, Carleton College*; b. 6 June 1940, Forest City, NC; s. of June H. Rhodes; m. Jane Carol Bowness Rhodes; one s. one d. *Education:* Duke Univ. with Iain Hamilton, Yale Univ. with Donald Martino, Mel Powell, Gunther Schuller and George Perle. *Career:* Composer-in-Residence, Ford Foundation and MENC Composers in Public Schools Program 1967–68; Asst Prof. of Music, Amherst Coll. 1968–69; Composer-in-Residence, City of Louisville and Faculty mem. Univ. of Lousiville 1969–72; Composer-in-Residence, Carleton Coll., Northfield, Minn. 1974–2006, Andrew W. Mellon Prof. of the Humanities 1985–2006, Prof. Emer. 2006–, Pres., Coll. Music Soc. 1985–87. *Compositions include:* Four Movements for chamber orchestra 1962, Three Pieces for solo violoncello 1965, Three Pieces for band 1967, Remembrance for symphonic wind ensemble 1967, Duo for violin and cello 1969, Autumn Setting for soprano and string quartet 1969, About Faces, ballet 1970, The Lament of Michal for soprano and orchestra 1970, Divertimento for small orchestra 1971, Oratorio from Paradise Lost 1972, Prayers from the Psalms 1972, String Trio 1973, Museum Pieces, for clarinet and string quartet 1973, Concerto for Bluegrass band and orchestra 1974, Quartet, for flute harp, violin and cello 1975, On the Morning of Christ's Nativity, cantata 1976, Mountain Songs for soprano and piano 1976, Reflections Eight Fantasies for piano 1976, Ceremonial Fanfare and Chorale, for 2 brass choirs 1977, Partita for solo viola 1978, Wind Songs for children's chorus and Orff instruments 1979, Visions of Remembrance for two sopranos and 12 instruments 1979, Ad Honorem Stravinsky 1981, In Praise of Wisdom, for chorus and brass choir 1982, Dancing Songs for treble choir 1985, Nets to Catch the Wind, for chorus and percussion 1986, The Gentle Boy, opera, premiered 1987, The Magic Pipe, opera 1989, Reels and Reveries, variations for orchestra 1991, Mary's Lullaby, for soprano, violin and organ 1993, Chorale and Mediatation (O Sacred Head Now Wounded) for women's voices and organ 1995, Fiddle Tunes, for violin and synthesized strings 1995, Cosmic Fantasies for band 1999, Three Appalachian Settings for SATB and Violin 2000, Two Appalachian Settings for String Quartet 2001, Shakespeare in

Song for High Voice, Clarinet in B flat and Piano 2001, March Parody (With Variations) for Concert Band 2002, Meditation Upon Lactantius' De Ave Phoenice for Bassoon and Harp 2002, Three Gershwin Settings for violin and piano 2004, Phoenix Resurgens for bassoon and piano 2009; solo instrumental pieces. *Honours:* Tanglewood Orchestra prizes 1962, 1965, BMI Student Composer Awards 1964, 1965, Margaret Lee Crofts Fellow 1965, John Day Jackson Prize 1966, Nat. Endowment for the Arts Grants 1974, 1975, 1976, Martha B. Rockefeller Grant 1976, Guggenheim Foundation Fellowship 1980, Nat. Endowment for the Humanities Grant 1984, McKnight Foundation Fellowship 1983, 1987, Bush Foundation Fellowship 1985, Nat. Opera Assn First Prize in New Opera Competition 1986, Jerome Foundation Grant 1994. *Address:* c/o BMI, 320 West 57th Street, New York, NY 10019, USA (office). *E-mail:* prhodes@carleton.edu (office). *Website:* www.prhodescomposer.com.

RHODES, Samuel, BA, MFA; American violist; b. 13 Feb. 1941, Long Beach, NY; m. 1968; two d. *Education:* Queens Coll., New York, Princeton Univ. *Career:* debut at Carnegie Recital Hall 1966; Faculty of Tanglewood and participant at Marlboro Festival 1960–; mem. Juilliard String Quartet 1969–2013; Faculty mem. Juilliard School 1969–, Co-Chair. Viola Dept 1992–2001, Chair. 2002–; fmr Artist-in-Residence, Michigan State Univ.; appearances include Great Performances (PBS TV) 1977, Hindemith: The Viola Legacy 3 Concert Series (Carnegie Recital Hall) 1985, CBS Sunday Morning 1986; recitals at Library of Congress, Washington, DC, Juilliard School; participant at Int. Hindemith Viola Festival, New York Chapter 1996–; has played recitals in Hamburg, Germany and Viola Congress in Cincinnati and Würzburg; jury mem. and recital giver at Tertis Competition 2013. *Composition:* Quintet for string quartet and viola. *Recordings include:* Schoenberg Quartets, Complete Beethoven Quartets, Mozart-Haydn Quartets, Complete Bartók Quartets, Schubert and Dvořák Quartets, Guest Artist with Beaux Arts Trio, Four Carter Quartets, Berg Lyric Suite, Complete Hindemith Quartets, Mendelssohn Op. 12, Op. 13, Hindemith Four Viola Solo Sonatas. *Honours:* Dr hc (Michigan State Univ.), (Univ. of Jacksonville), (San Francisco Conservatory); Grammy Awards 1971, 1976, 1985. *Address:* c/o Music Division, The Juilliard School, 60 Lincoln Center Plaza, New York, NY 10023-6588, USA (office). *Website:* www.juilliard.edu (office); www.juilliardstringquartet.org.

RHODES, Teddy Tahu; New Zealand singer (bass baritone); b. 1965. *Education:* Guildhall School, London with Ruldoph Piernay and David Harper, also studied with Maud Adams Taylor. *Career:* debut as Dandini in La Cenerentola with Opera Australia 1998; represented New Zealand at Cardiff Singer of the World Competition 1999; Sharpless in Madama Butterfly for Canterbury Opera 1999, Marcello and Silvio in Pagliacci for Opera New Zealand 1999; sang Mozart's Count and Britten's Demetrius for Opera Australia 2000–01; US debut as Joe in premiere of Jake Heggie's Dead Man Walking, San Francisco; sang Guglielmo, Belcore and the Herald in Lohengrin for Opera Australia 2001–02, Escamillo and Marcello for Dallas Opera 2001–02, Stanley in Previn's A Streetcar Named Desire for Washington Nat. Opera 2004, Don Giovanni for Cincinnati Opera 2004, Escamillo in Carmen for Dallas Opera 2004, Leander in The Love for Three Oranges and title role in Don Giovanni at Sydney Opera House 2005, Papageno in Die Zauberflöte for Welsh Nat. Opera, Il Conte Almaviva in Le nozze di Figaro for Houston Grand Opera 2005, Escamillo for Hamburg State Opera and Scottish Opera 2006, Il Conte Almaviva in Le nozze di Figaro for Opera Australia 2006; season 2007: Stanley for Staatsoper Vienna and Opera Australia, Escamillo for Théâtre du Châtelet, Guglielmo for Cincinnati Opera, title role in Don Giovanni for Opera Australia; season 2008: sang Ned Keene in Peter Grimes for The Metropolitan Opera, title role in Billy Budd for Santa Fe Opera and Opera Australia, Lescaut in Manon Lescaut for Leipzig Opera; season 2009: sang Escamillo for Bilbao Opera, Conte Almaviva in Le nozze di Figaro for Cincinnati Opera, Lescaut for Opera Australia, Stanley for Opera Australia; season 2010: sang Escamillo for The Metropolitan Opera, Conte Almaviva in Le nozze di Figaro for Washington Nat. Opera, Figaro in Le nozze di Figaro for Opera Australia; season 2011 sang Escamillo for Opera Australia, role debut as Scarpia in Tosca for West Australian Opera, Don Giovanni for Opera Australia; season 2012: sang Guglielmo for Washington Nat. Opera, Don Giovanni for Nat. Theatre, Bordeaux, role debut as Emile de Beque in South Pacific for Opera Australia. *Recordings include:* Fauré's Requiem and La naissance de Vénus, Handel's Messiah, Musical Renegades (CD/DVD), solo discs including Mozart Arias, The Voice (ARIA Best Classical Record Award), Vagabond, The Bach Arias, Mozart Requiem, Serious Songs as well as You'll Never Walk Alone (with David Hobson), appears on CD/DVD recording of The Little Prince directed by Francesca Zambello, Haley Westenra Live (CD/DVD), broadcast on PBS Great Performers series in USA 2005, Peter Grimes at the Metropolitan Opera (DVD), Metropolitan Opera's Carmen (DVD and shown in cinemas world-wide), Love for Three Oranges. *Honours:* awards include two Helpmann Awards/Best Male Operatic Performer for Dead Man Walking for State Opera of South Australia and in Sydney performances presented by Andrew McManus/Alexander Productions), Limelight Award for Best Performance by a Soloist with an Orchestra for his performances with the ACO 2006, Green Room Award for Best Male Artist in a Leading Role for his performance of Don Giovanni for Opera Australia, MO Award for Operatic Performer of the Year, Arts Foundation of New Zealand Laureate 2008. *Address:* c/o Jonathan Turnbull, Artist Manager, Askonas Holt Ltd, Lincoln House, 300 High Holborn, London, WC1V 7JH, England. *Telephone:* (20) 7400-1722. *Fax:* (20) 7400-1723. *E-mail:* jonathan.turnbull@askonasholt.co.uk. *Website:* www.askonasholt.co.uk. *Address:* c/o Kathryn Morrison Management, 1 Mimosa Court, Buxton, Vic. 3711, Australia. *Telephone:* (4) 0987-8016. *E-mail:* kmorrison.work@gmail.com.

RHYS-DAVIES, Jennifer, LTCL, GTCL, FTCL; Welsh/British singer (soprano); b. 8 May 1953, Panteg, Gwent; d. of Trevor Adams and Emily Adams. *Education:* Trinity College of Music, London. *Career:* opera debut with WNO as First Lady in Die Zauberflöte then Donna Elvira, Miss Jessel in Turn of the Screw, also in Dresden and Leipzig, and Lady Macbeth; further appearances as Constanze for Opera 80 and Donna Anna for ENO and Kent Opera on tour to Valencia; Opera North as Sandrina in La Finta Giardiniera, Aloysia in the Mozart-Griffiths pastiche The Jewel Box; sang Semiramide and Sieglinde at Nuremberg and Covent Garden Festival, Queen of Night for Dublin Grand Opera and Scottish Opera, 1993; Covent Garden and ENO debut 1993 as Berta in Barbiere di Siviglia and Mrs Fiorentino in Street Scene; concert engagements in Beethoven's Mount of Olives and Haydn's Seasons at Dublin, Handel's Dixit Dominus and Poulenc's Gloria for Stuttgart Radio, Angelica in Haydn's Orlando Paladino at Garsington; sang Clorinda in Cenerentola, The Duenna in Der Rosenkavalier, Amaltea in Moses, Widow in Babette's Feast at Royal Opera House, London, Lady Macbeth for WNO and Nuremberg, Italian Singer in Capriccio at Glyndebourne 1998, Hilda Mack in Switzerland, Olympia, Antonia, Giulietta, Les Contes d'Hoffman in France and Germany 2000, as Mozart's Marcellina at Garsington Elisabetta, Arminda and Elettra in Basel, The Queen of Night in Basel, Hanover, Garsington, Scotland and Stuttgart; Mrs Julian in Owen Wingrave for ROH and Lady Billows in Salzburg 2007–08. *Recordings include:* as Berta in Barber of Seville, various recordings for Opera Rara. *Honours:* Trinity College Kennedy Scott Prize, Rowland Jones Memorial Award. *Address:* 58 Park Place, Risca, New Port, Gewnt, NP11 6AS, Wales.

RHYS-EVANS, Huw; British singer (tenor); b. 1959, Tregaron, Ceredigion, Wales. *Education:* Royal Acad. of Music with Kenneth Bowen, Nat. Opera Centre. *Career:* debut at Carnegie Hall 2001; concert engagements worldwide; engagements include Ernesto in Don Pasquale, Ismaele Nabucco for WNO, Carlo/Goffredo in Armida, the title role in Le Comte Ory and Torvaldo from Torvaldo e Dorliska at the Rossini in Wildbad Festival, Count Almaviva from The Barber of Seville for Opera North and Spier Opera, South Africa, Pilade from Ermione and Idreno from Semiramide for Chelsea Opera Group, Belfiore from Il Viaggio a Reims at the Palace of Verseille and the Strasbourg Music Festival, Harris from Uncle Remus for Pegasus Opera, Flute from A Midsummer Night's Dream and Brighella from Ariadne auf Naxos for English Touring Opera, Vivaldo from Die Hochzeit des Camacho at the Flanders Int. Festival, Errico from La Vera Costanza for Bampton Classical Opera, Ferrando in Così fan tutte for Madrid Comic Opera, Opera d'Automne and Tours Opera, Don Ottavio from Don Giovanni for Bampton Classical Opera and for Perth Festival Opera, Belmonte from Die Entfuhrung aus dem Serail and Belmonte in Seraglio for The Opera Project, Nadir from The Philosopher's Stone for Collegium Musicum 90, Pang from Turandot for Lyric Opera Dublin and for Mid-Wales Opera, Brighella from Ariadne auf Naxos for the Norwegian State Opera, Young Servand from Electra at the BBC Proms, First Jew from Salome for the Bastille Opera, Third Jew from Salome for Marseille Opera, Hyllus for Handel Hercules at the Varazdin Baroque Festival, Croatia (with the Welsh Baroque Orchestra), roles in Cavalli's Erismena and Monteverdi's Orfeo with English Touring Opera. *Recordings include:* Judge in Le Calife de Bagdad, Gouvy Cantata Egill, Stabat Mater, Vivaldo in Die Hochzeit des Camacho, All Through the Night (Welsh songs with harp), Rossini's Torvaldo e Dorliska. *Honours:* Royal Nat. Eisteddfod of Wales Blue Riband Prize for Singer of the Year, Tenor Solo Award (three times), Great Grimsby Int. Competition for Singers Tenor Prize 1990. *Current Management:* c/o Musicaglotz, 11 rue le Verrier, 75006 Paris, France. *Telephone:* (1) 42-34-53-40. *Fax:* (1) 40-46-93-77. *E-mail:* general@musicaglotz.com. *Website:* www.musicaglotz.com; www.huwrhysevans.com.

RICCIARDI, Franco; singer (tenor); b. 1921, Italy. *Career:* debut in Naples, 1947, as Pinkerton; has sung widely in Italy, and notably at La Scala Milan from 1954, as Monostatos, Missail, Goro, Pang and Bardolph; Rome Opera 1963, as David in Die Meistersinger; Caracalla Festival and Verona Arena 1968–69; sang at Dallas Opera 1970, Martina Franca Festival 1982; other roles have included Borsa in Rigoletto, Arturo in Lucia di Lammermoor, Cassio and Shuisky.

RICCIARELLI, Katia; Italian singer; b. 18 Jan. 1946, Rovigo; m. Pippo Baudo 1986. *Education:* Benedetto Marcello Conservatory, Venice. *Career:* debut at Mantua 1969; appearances include Lyric Opera, Chicago, USA 1972, Royal Opera House, Covent Garden, London 1974, La Scala, Milan 1976, Metropolitan Opera Co., New York, USA 1975, San Francisco Opera, USA, Paris Opera, Verona Festival, Palermo 1997, Lecce 1998; f. Accademia Lirica di Katia Ricciarelli 1991; Artistic Dir Macerata Opera Festival 2003–05. *Operas include:* La Bohème 1969, 1974, I Due Foscari 1972, Suor Angelica 1976, Anna Bolena, Lucrezia Borgia, Imogene, Don Carlos 1989. *Recordings include:* I Due Foscari, Turandot, Carmen, Aida, Un Ballo in Maschera, Falstaff, Il Trovatore, La Bohème, Tosca. *Address:* C.D.A. Studio Di Nardo S.r.l., Via Cavour, 171, 00184 Rome, Italy. *Website:* www.katiaricciarelli.it.

RICE, Christine; British singer (mezzo-soprano); b. Manchester; m. Crispin Woodhead; two d. *Education:* Balliol Coll., Oxford, Royal Northern Coll. of Music. *Career:* operatic roles at Royal Opera House, Covent Garden have included Emilia in Otello, Suzuki in Madama Butterfly, Miranda in Ades' The Tempest, title role in The Rape of Lucretia, Sonyetka in Lady Macbeth of

Mtsensk; has also appeared at Bayerische Staatsoper, Munich as Ariodante, Teatro Real Madrid as Hermia in A Midsummer Night's Dream, and Seattle Opera as Dorabella in Cosi Fan Tutte; concerts throughout UK (including BBC Proms, Edinburgh Festival), Europe, North America; mem. BBC Radio 3's New Generation Artists scheme. *Recordings include:* De Falla's El Amor Brujo, Elgar's Sea Pictures, Berlioz Les Nuits D'Eté, Vincent d'Indy's Fervaal (Guilhen), Wolf's Spanisches Liederbuch, Lucia di Lammermoor (Alisa) 2002, Christine Rice 2005, Mozart, La Clemenza di Tito 2006, Respighi: Il Tramonto/ Pappano 2007. *Website:* www.christinerice.com.

RICH, Elizabeth; American pianist; b. 8 Feb. 1931, New York, NY; m. Dr Joel Markowitz 1952; two s. one d. *Education:* Juilliard School of Music, studied with Ernst Oster. *Career:* debut at New York Philharmonic Auditions, Young People's Concert, Carnegie Hall 1949; English premiere of Clara Schumann Piano Concerto, Beethoven Choral Fantasy, QEH, London 1985; complete cycle Mozart Piano Sonatas, New York 1984–85; guest artist at Mt Desert Festival of Chamber Music 1987–91, 1993–95; fourth recital, Alice Tully Hall, Lincoln Center 1993; Mozart Concerto and Bach Concerto, St Martin's-in-the-Field, London Chamber Soloists Orchestra 1993; opened Mozart Days at the Prague Festival in the Dvořák Hall, Prague 1997; Schumann Concerto, Bridgeport Symphony 1997; Mozart recital at Weill Hall, Carnegie Hall 2000; Weill Hall recital 2004; 'In Their Own Words', Bach, Schumann, Weber, Beethoven; Mozart Piano Concerto, K271, Purcell Room, London Chamber Soloists Orchestra 2001; Clara Schumann Concerto, Kalamazoo Symphony 2001; Appasionata with Eva Hoffman, Jewish Museum, New York 2009. *Publications:* contrib. articles 'Playing Late Mozart', in Piano Today, Winter 2001, 'On Late Style', in Pequod 2006. *Recordings:* Schumann's Novelettes and Carnaval 1991, Piano Concerti of Carl Maria von Weber and Clara Schumann 1995, Haydn and C.P.E. Bach Piano Works 1997, Complete Mozart Piano Sonatas 1998–2002, Mozart Piano Concerti K. 482 and 281 2008. *Current Management:* Liegner Management, PO Box 230884, New York, NY 10023, USA. *Telephone:* (212) 496-1515. *Fax:* (212) 787-9449. *E-mail:* liegnermgt@aol.com. *Website:* www .liegnermanagement.com. *Address:* 285 Central Park West, New York, NY 10024, USA (home). *Telephone:* (212) 787-9034 (home). *Fax:* (212) 579-6298 (home).

RICHARD, André; Swiss composer and conductor; b. 18 April 1944, Berne. *Education:* studied in Geneva, in Freiburg with Klaus Huber and Brian Ferneyhough. *Career:* Dir, Freiburg Inst. for New Music 1980–; Horizonte Concert Series, Freiburg until 1989; co-founder, Freiburger Solistenchor 1983, with concerts of works by Luigi Nono and others; Dir of experimental studio at Heinrich Strobel Foundation from 1989. *Compositions include:* Ritornelle for three percussion instruments 1976, Cinque for piano 1979, Trilogie for flute, oboe and harpsichord 1981, String Quartet 1982, Etude sur la carré rouge for chamber ensemble 1984–86, Echanges for orchestra and live electronics 1986, Musique de rue for six instruments and tape 1987, Glidif for bassoon, clarinet, two double basses and live electronics 1990. *Publications include:* articles on the music of Luigi Nono 1991, 1993.

RICHARDS, Timothy; British singer (tenor); b. 1970, Wales. *Education:* Royal Northern College of Music, studied with Dennis O'Neill. *Career:* concerts throughout the UK and Europe including Messiah, the Mozart and Verdi Requiems, The Creation and Rossini's Stabat Mater; opera roles include Alfredo for WNO, The Duke of Mantua at Innsbruck and Cassio in Otello at Basle; season 1999–2000 with Macduff in Leipzig and Rodolfo, Nemorino and Fenton for Dresden Opera; other roles include Tamino, British Youth Opera, Belmonte and Verdi's Ismaele. *Current Management:* Boris Orlob Management, Jägerstrasse 70, 10117 Berlin, Germany; Organisation Internationale Artistique, 16 avenue Franklin D. Roosevelt, 75008 Paris, France. *Telephone:* (30) 20450839 (Germany); 1-42-25-58-34 (France). *Fax:* (30) 20450849 (Germany); 1-42-25-64-97 (France). *E-mail:* info@orlob.net; oia@oia-poilve .com. *Website:* www.orlob.net; www.oia-poilve.com.

RICHARDSON, Carol; singer (mezzo-soprano); b. 1948, California, USA. *Education:* Occidental Coll., Los Angeles and studied with Martial Singher in Philadelphia, and in New York. *Career:* debut at Klagenfurt 1973, as Nicklause in Hoffmann; sang at Kiel from 1975, Bayreuth Festival 1976–81, in Parsifal; engagements at Bern Stadttheater until 1984, Cenerentola at Bielefeld 1988; other roles have included Dorabella and Cherubino, Rosina, Orlofsky, Nancy in Martha, Lola and Zerlina; further guest appearances at Hamburg, Gelsenkirchen, Karlsruhe and Hanover; noted concert performer; season 1998 at ENO in Purcell's Fairy Queen and the premiere of Dr Ox's Experiment by Gavin Bryars.

RICHARDSON, Marilyn, DipMus; Australian singer (soprano) and stage director; b. 1936, Sydney, NSW; m. 1st Peter Richardson 1954; three c.; m. 2nd James Christiansen 1974; three step-c. *Education:* New South Wales Conservatorium of Music. *Career:* Australian premiere of Schoenberg's Pierrot Lunaire, ISCM concert, Sydney 1958; debut with Basler Theater, Switzerland 1972, Lulu; Salome, debut with Australian Opera 1975, Aida; roles and operas include Four Sopranos in Tales of Hoffmann, Marschallin, Countess, Donna Anna, Katya Kabanova, Queen of Spades, Otello, Eva, Sieglinde, Elsa, Mimi, Rosalinda, Merry Widow, Laura in Voss, Leonore (Fidelio), Isolde 1990, and Tosca 1992; Emilia Marty in The Makropulos Case 1996; has appeared with all state companies; The Excursions of Mr Brouček, Fiordiligi, La Traviata, Madama Butterfly, Midsummer Marriage; Desdemona, Marguerite, Mistress Ford, Senta, Alcina, Cleopatra; soloist in a huge range of concert music, including Australian premieres of about 400 songs and vocal works; directed Les Pêcheurs de Perles at Adelaide 1996. *Honours:* Hon. DMus (Univ. of Queensland) 1993; Churchill Fellowship 1969, Australian Council Creative Fellowship 1991, Joan Hammond Award 1993.

RICHARDSON, Mark; British singer (bass-baritone); b. 1966, England. *Education:* Royal Manchester College of Music. *Career:* English National Opera Company Principal as Lamoral in Arabella, Masetto, Colline in La Bohème and France in Reimann's Lear, Varlaam in Boris Godunov, Leporello; Other roles in War and Peace, Der Rosenkavalier, Rimsky's Christmas Eve and The Pearl Fishers, Ariodate in Xerxes, Donald in Billy Budd, Hobson in Peter Grimes, Parson in The Cunning Little Vixen; Niklausse in Dr Ox's Experiment; Season 1995–96 as Bizet's Zuniga and Nourabad; Guest appearances at Buxton, as Mustafâ in L'Italiana in Algeri, Welsh National Opera (Angelotti and Rossini's Basilio) and the Bergen Festival (Sparafucile in Rigoletto); Sang Frank Maurrant in the Italian premiere of Street Scene, in Turin. *Current Management:* Robert Gilder & Co., 91 Great Russell Street, London, WC1B 3PS, England. *Telephone:* (20) 7580-7758. *Fax:* (20) 7580-7739. *E-mail:* rgilder@robert-gilder.com. *Website:* www.robert-gilder.com.

RICHARDSON, Meryl; British singer (soprano); b. 1965, England. *Education:* Royal Northern Coll. of Music with Neil Howlett, studied with Philip Thomas and Jeffrey Talbot. *Career:* appearances with ENO as Musetta in La Bohème, as Helmwige in Die Walküre, as Marianne Leitmetzer in Rosenkavalier, and as Aksinya in Lady Macbeth of Mdsensk; title role in British premiere of Barber's Vanessa and Brünnhilde in Die Walküre (chamber version) for the Covent Garden Festival; German debut in L'harmonia Drammatica by Vinko Globakar, with Bielefeld and Münster opera cos; other roles include Lady Macbeth (Buxton Festival), Leonora in La Forza del Destino, Anna Bolena and Elvira in Ernani, the title role in Vanessa; performances include The Ring, with South Australian Opera, Adelaide, American debut as Brünnhilde in Die Walküre, at the Met; concerts include Mozart's C minor Mass, Tippett's A Child of Our Time, Verdi Requiem, Bruckner's Mass in F minor, Stauss's Four Last Songs, Rossini's Messe Solennelle, Elgar's Spirit of England. *Film:* Ich Kann Nicht Bleiben (dir and prod.). *Address:* c/o ENO, London Coliseum, St Martin's Lane, Trafalgar Square, London, WC2, England (office).

RICHARDSON, Stephen; singer (bass); b. 1965, Liverpool, England. *Education:* Royal Northern Coll. of Music. *Career:* has sung at Glyndebourne and with GTO, ENO and WNO, Scottish Opera and Kent Opera; roles have included Mozart's Osmin, Sarastro and Commendatore, Colline, Sparafucile, Silva in Ernani and Rossini's Basilio; US debut with Messiah at Carnegie Hall and other concerts with leading British orchestras Montréal Philharmonic Orchestra and Prague Symphony Orchestra; premieres of Tavener's Eis Thanaton, Resurrection and Apocalypse, with other works by Gerald Barry, Birtwistle (Punch and Judy), Knussen, Mason and Casken; festival appearances at Aldeburgh, BBC Proms, Vienna, Hong Kong, Boston and Brussels; season 1996–97 with Colline and Sparafucile for WNO, Daland with Chelsea Opera Group and Tiresias in Oedipus Rex for the BBC; Baron Ochs for ENO 1999; season 2000–01 as Casken's The Golem at the Aspen Festival, Mr Flint in Billy Budd at Covent Garden and Fafner in The Rhinegold for ENO; Oliver Knussen's Where the Wild Things Are and Higglety, Pigglety, Pop! at the London Proms 2002. *Current Management:* Harrison Parrott, 5–6 Albion Court, London, W6 0QT, England. *Telephone:* (20) 7229-9166. *Fax:* (20) 7221-5042. *E-mail:* info@harrisonparrott.co.uk. *Website:* www.harrisonparrott .com.

RICHTER, Marga, MS; American composer; b. 21 Oct. 1926, Reedsburg, WI. *Education:* Juilliard School, New York with Rosalyn Tureck, William Bergsma and Vincent Persichetti. *Career:* freelance composer, with premieres at Salzburg, Chicago, Cannes, Cologne, Tucson, Atlanta, Brookville and New York. *Compositions include:* Clarinet Sonata 1948, Piano Sonata 1954, two Piano Concertos 1955, 1974, Aria and Toccata for viola and strings 1957, String Quartet 1958, Abyss (ballet) 1964, Bird of Yearning (ballet) 1967, Blackberry Vines and Winter Fruit for orchestra 1976, Requiem for piano 1978, Spectral Chimes/Enshrouded Hills for three orchestral quintets and orchestra 1980, Düsseldorf Concerto for flute, viola, harp, percussion and strings 1982, Seacliff Variations for piano, violin, viola and cello 1984, Lament for Art O'Leary for soprano voice 1984, Out of Shadows and Solitude for orchestra 1985, Qhanri-Tibetan Variations for cello and piano 1988, Quantum Quirks of a Quick Quaint Quark I–III for orchestra, organ and piano 1992–93, Variations and Interludes on Themes from Monteverdi and Bach concerto for piano, violin, cello and orchestra 1993, Riders to the Sea (one-act opera) 1996, choruses and songs. *Honours:* ASCAP Awards 1966–2002, NEA Fellowships 1978, 1980.

RICHTER, Max; British composer. *Education:* Royal Acad. of Music, studied with Luciano Berio in Florence. *Career:* co-f. contemporary classical ensemble Piano Circus; composer of music for concerts, installations, theatre, opera, film, ballet and dance; has collaborated with Tilda Swinton, Robert Wyatt, The Future Sound of London, Darren Almond, Vashti Bunyan, Random International, Hilary Hahn and Roni Size and worked with Wayne McGregor and the Royal Ballet, Lucinda Childs, NDT, Ballet du Rhin, American Ballet Theatre, Dresden Semper Oper, Dutch Nat. Ballet, Norwegian Ballet. *Music for installations:* The Anthropocene (White Cube), Rain Room (MoMA, New York). *Music for plays:* Macbeth (Nat. Theatre of Scotland on Broadway) 2013. *Film scores:* Spanien, Citizen Gangster, Waltz with Bashir (Best European

Composer, European Film Awards 2008), Coral: Rekindling Venus, Lore and Disconnect 2012; featured music on Shutter Island 2010. *Ballet scores:* Infra 2012 (premiered at Royal Opera House, London). *Chamber opera:* SUM 2012. *Compositions:* On the Nature of Daylight for strings, Autumn Music 2 for strings, The Four Seasons Recomposed for harp, harpsichord/strings 2012, Sum: Forty Tales from the Afterlives 2012. *Recordings include:* Memoryhouse 2002, The Blue Notebooks 2004, Songs From Before 2006, 24 Postcards in Full Colour 2008, Infra, Recomposed: Vivaldi Four Seasons (Klassik Ohne Grenzen Prize, ECHO Klassik Awards 2013) 2012. *Telephone:* 7740 900635 (mobile). *E-mail:* jane@janecarterproductions.com. *Website:* www.maxrichtermusic .com (office).

RICHTER DE VROE, Nicolaus; German composer and violinist; b. 1 Feb. 1955, Halle. *Education:* Moscow Conservatory, Berlin Akademie der Künste with Goldmann. *Career:* violinist with the Bavarian Radio Symphony 1988–; co-founder of XSEMBLE, Munich 1990. *Compositions include:* Tetra, series I–III, for differentiated quartets, 1984–91; Durchlässige Zonen I, for 13 instruments, 1985; String Quartet, 1986. Zu Fuss nach Island, graphic music, 1986; Isole de Rumore, for orchestra, 1988; Frag In Memorian Luigi Nono, for ensemble, 1990; Decemberhelft, for alto flute, guitar, cello and percussion, 1990; Naiss' orchestr' ance, 1992; Engfernt: Tänze, for ensemble, 1993; Shibuya movements for orchestra, 1993; Air't'rance, for ensemble, 1997; Éraflures, violin concerto, 1997. *E-mail:* n.devroe@web.de. *Website:* www .nicolaus-richter-de-vroe.kulturserver.de.

RICKARDS, Steven, BMusEd, MM, DM; American singer (countertenor), composer and music educator; b. 1955. *Education:* Florida State Univ., Tallahassee, Indiana Univ., Bloomington, Oberlin Coll. Baroque Performance Inst., Guildhall School of Music and Drama, London. *Career:* concert engagements with the Waverly Consort (New York), Chicago's Music of the Baroque, Concert Royal, New York, Ars Musica and Chanticleer; British appearances with the Ipswich Bach Choir and at the East Cornwall Bach Festival; tour of Ireland with the Gabrieli Consort and worldwide recitals with lutenist Dorothy Linell; has toured France and Michigan, USA with Messiah 1981–82; Carnegie Hall debut 1987, with the Oratorio Soc. of New York; Boston Early Music Festival in Handel's Teseo and Santa Fe Opera as Ariel in the premiere of John Eaton's The Tempest 1985; sang with the Opera Company of Philadelphia as Apollo in Death in Venice; revivals of Handel's Siroe in New York, Locke's Psyche in London, Hasse's L'Olimpiade in Dresden and Mondonville's De Profundis at Harvard; sang in John Adams's El Niño at the Châtelet Theatre in Paris 2000; teacher of singing, Univ. of Indianapolis and Butler Univ.; founder Echoing Air ensemble. *Compositions:* A Christmas Vision, All Good Gifts, Calm on the List'ning Ear of Night, Come Let Us Sing To The Lord, Come Thou Long Expected Jesus, Little Lamb, As the Lyre to the Singer, Behold the Tabernacle of God, Breathe on Me, Breath of God, Angels Did Sing, All of a Quiet Night He Did Come, The Power of Song. *Recordings include:* Bach cantatas 106 and 131 with Joshua Rifkin; St John Passion by Bach; Gradualia by Byrd with Chanticleer; Medarse in Siroe by Handel; Mass in B Minor by Bach; Buxtehude Project Vol. I Sacred Cantatas; T Campion Songs; J Dowland Songs. *Publication:* Twentieth Century Countertenor Repertoire 2008. *Current Management:* John Gingrich Management, PO Box 1515, New York, NY 10023, USA. *Address:* 123 East Westfield Boulevard, Indianapolis, IN 46220, USA (home). *Telephone:* (317) 252-4311 (home). *Website:* echoingair.com; www.stevenrickards.com.

RIDDELL, Alistair Matthew, BA, MA, PhD; Australian composer and computer technologist; b. 22 June 1955, Melbourne. *Education:* La Trobe Univ., Princeton Univ. *Career:* fellowships at Princeton and La Trobe Univs 1989–95; co-f. HyperSense Complex ensemble (with Somaya Langley and Simon Burton) 2003; collaborated on FyberMotion, a kinetic textile art project inspired by sound (with Belinda Jessup and Lucie Verhelst) 2005–09; Lecturer in Sound Art and Physical Computing, Centre for New Media Arts at Australian Nat. Univ. 2008–13; numerous stage performances. *Compositions include:* (most with computer-processed sound) Ligeti-Continuum 1982, Studies in Perception, Context and Paradox: Three-1 Existential Constellations, canon in six voices 1982, Bach-Inventio No. 4 1982, Atlantic Fears 1983, Core Image 1983, Atmisfearia 1989, Entering 2–12 1990, Third Hand 1991, Idyll Moment 1991, Heavy Mouse 1992, Z Says 1993, Triptychos 1995, autonomousAudio 2000. *Honours:* AC Artists and New Technology Program grant 1987. *E-mail:* alistair@alistairriddell.com. *Website:* www.alistairriddell .com.

RIDDELL, David; conductor; b. 1960, Elgin, Scotland. *Education:* St Andrew's Univ. and Guildhall School, London. *Career:* engagements for Den Jyske Opera, Denmark, in La Périchole, Butterfly, Cenerentola, The Pirates of Penzance, Paganini and Reesen's Farinelli 1992; Don Giovanni for Århus Summer Opera 1989–90, followed by Il Barbiere di Siviglia 1991; Die Fledermaus for Odense Symphony Orchestra 1992; British appearances with La Forza del Destino for Scottish Opera, Eugene Onegin for Opera 80 and Rimsky's Mozart and Salieri at the Royal Scottish Acad. of Music; regular concerts at the Guildhall School; season 1996 with Bach's Christmas Oratorio for the Randers Chamber Orchestra, and Burns International Festival Concert with the Northern Sinfonia in Scotland.

RIEBL, Thomas; violist; b. 1956, Vienna, Austria. *Education:* Vienna Acad. of Music, studied with Peter Schidlof and Sándor Végh. *Career:* led the violas of the World Youth Orchestra 1972; solo debut at the Vienna Konzerthaus 1972 and has since appeared with leading orchestras in Europe and North America, including the Chicago Symphony, Helsinki Radio, Bournemouth Symphony, Los Angeles and Vienna Chamber Orchestras; festival appearances at Salzburg, Vienna, Aspen, Ravinia, New York, Munich, Lockenhaus and Carinthian Summer Festival; concerts with the Juilliard Quartet, Gidon Kremer and Jessye Norman (Brahms Lieder Op 91); founder mem., Vienna Sextet; Prof. of Viola, Musikhochschule, Mozarteum, Salzburg from 1983. *Recordings include:* Brahms Lieder Op 91 with Brigitte Fassbaender and Irwin Gage. *Honours:* prizewinner Budapest international competition 1975, Munich international competition 1976, International Naumberg Viola Competition Ernst Wallfisch Memorial Award, New York 1982.

RIEDER, Jochen; German conductor; b. 12 Aug. 1970, Rheinland Pfalz. *Career:* Asst Conductor, Badische Staatstheater Karlsruhe 1992–95; Kapellmeister, Bremer Theater 1996–2001; Conductor, Zurich Opera 2001–14; Asst to Christian Thielemann for Bayreuth Festival production of The Mastersingers of Nuremberg 2001, 2002; freelance conductor 2014–; has worked with numerous singers including Peter Seiffert, Waltraud Meier, Nina Stemme, Thomas Hampson, José van Dam, Matthias Goerne, Renée Fleming, Matti Salminen and Michael Volle; regular collaborations with tenor Jonas Kaufmann; debut at Teatro alla Scala in Milan with Jonas Kaufmann and Orchestra Filarmonica della Scala 2015; guest conductor with numerous renowned orchestras including Royal Philharmonic Orchestra, Philharmonia Orchestra, Rundfunk-Sinfonieorchester Berlin, Tonhalle-Orchestra Zurich, Philharmonia Zurich, Orchestre Nat. de France, Tivoli Symphony Orchestra Copenhagen, Prague Symphony Orchestra, Athens State Orchestra, Norrköping Symphony Orchestra, Orchestre Métropolitain Montreal, Qatar Philharmonic, Orchestre Nat. de Belgique, Bochum Symphony Orchestra, Tirol Symphony Orchestra Innsbruck, Orquesta de Cadaqués, Symphony Orchestra of the Vienna Volksoper, Bruckner Orchestra Linz, Münchner Rundfunkorchester, Irish Chamber Orchestra, State Academic Symphony Orchestra of Russia (Svetlanov Orchestra), Symphony Orchestra of Hof (Germany), Zurich Chamber Orchestra, Basel Symphony Orchestra, Symphony Orchestra St. Gallen, Prague Radio Symphony Orchestra, Australian Opera and Ballet Orchestra, Sydney, Orchestra Victoria, Melbourne, Württembergische Philharmonie (Germany), Jyväskylä Sinfonia (Finland), Euro Asian Philharmonic Orchestra Seoul (South Korea), Orchestra Filarmonica della Scala Milano (Italy), Czech Nat. Symphony Orchestra, Staatskapelle Weimar, London Philharmonic Orchestra. *Recordings include:* as conductor: Schacher/Bardill: Die Rose von Jericho 2009, Schacher/Meyer: Die wilden Schwäne 2011, Du bist die Welt für mich/You Mean The World To Me (with Jonas Kaufmann) (Diapason d'or 2014, Classica – Choc de l'année 2014, Sony Gold Disc, BBC Music Magazine Opera Choice, Orphée d'Or) 2014. *Honours:* scholarship from Richard Wagner Soc. 1997. *E-mail:* mail@jochenrieder.com. *Website:* jochenrieder.com.

RIEDLBAUCH, Václav; Czech composer, academic and fmr government official; *Director, Bohuslav Martinu Foundation;* b. 1 April 1947, Dýšina; m.; two s. *Education:* Prague Conservatoire. *Career:* Lecturer, Prague Conservatory 1970–78; Lecturer, Prague Acad. of Performing Arts 1971, later Sr Lecturer, Head Dept of Composition 1990–2004; Artistic Dir Nat. Theatre Opera 1987–89; Programme Dir, Prague Congress Centre 1990–93; Ed.-in-Chief, Panton Publishers 1993–95, Dir 1996; Dir Gen., Czech Philharmonic Orchestra 2001–09; Minister of Culture 2009–10; currently Dir Bohuslav Martinu Foundation; Chair. Young Composers Section, Czech Composers' and Performing Artists' Union 1982. *Compositions include:* musical dramatic works: Macbeth (ballet for soloist and group dancers and large orchestra) 1979–82; symphonic works: The Rozmberk Sonata for Winds and Percussion Instruments 1971, Symphony 1972, Symphony with Refrain 1973, Concerto-Battle for Organ and Orchestra 1973, Deadly Rondo for Orchestra 1975, The Story – Symhonic narration 1983, Snake's Skin Shedding for trombone 1986, Preludes to the Exhibition's Openings for flute 1990; chamber instrumental music: Sonatina for James for Violin and Piano 1971, Cathedrals – Organ toccata 1972, The Picture (Still Life with a Dead Nightingale) for flute and piano 1974, Tale for Flute, Violin, Violoncello and Piano 1974, Lamento for Clarinet and Piano 1975, Ballads for Violin and Piano 1975, Stories for Bass-clarinet and Piano 1975, Allegri e Pastorali for wind quintet 1976, Luring for Flute and Piano 1977, Canons for Piano 1977, Parade for Organ 1978, Pastorali e Concerti for brass quintet 1978, Concertie Trenodi for wind octet 1979, The Curtain – Movement for organ 1982, Conjunction – Game for two organs or other keyboard instruments 1983, Epilogue: A Movement for bassoon and piano 1986, String Quartet No. 1 1986, A New Year Meditation for trumpet and organ 1989, Trio for violin, cello and piano 1981, A Small Stone Dance 1993, Wind Quintet No. 2 1999; vocal works: Touzenec pisni – Songs for Tenor and Piano After Verses by R. Tagore 1975, Songs from Rejdova for Soprano, Contralto, Violin and Piano 1976, Tesknice (nostalgic songs) – Three folk songs for two flutes-a-bec and three-part children's choir 1976, Wedding Singing for girls, female or male choirs after Sappho 1978, Rather-Or Cycle for Children – Seven children's choirs to words by R. Steindl 1978, Songs and Games to Excerpts from Shakespeare for six singers, two violins, oboe and violoncello 1979, Teachers Song (celebration of Bohemian baroque) for organ and children's choir to words by V. Fischer 1980, The Primer – Excerpts from beginnings at school – Four polyphonic pieces for children's choir 1980, Daidalos the Creator, for male choir with barytone solo after Ovid 1982; instructive works: Special Book of Prague – A book of polyphonic compositions for accordion 1972, Pastorale for Three Flutes-a-bec 1973, The Wizard – Accordion school for children 1973–76, SU South Bohemian Nocturnes, for two violins, violoncello, accordion and trumpet

1979, Reversals for children's accordion 1980, SU 2' Povidacky (talks) – Eight polyphonic pieces for two violins 1982. *Honours:* Artist of Merit 1987. *Address:* Bohuslav Martinu Foundation, Bořanovická 14, 18200 Prague 8 (office); Revoluční 6, 110 00 Prague 1, Czech Republic (home). *Telephone:* (2) 22310710 (home). *E-mail:* nadace@martinu.cz (office). *Website:* www.martinu.cz (office).

RIEGEL, Kenneth; American singer (tenor); b. 19 April 1938, Womelsdorf, Pa. *Education:* Manhattan School of Music, Berkshire Music Center, Metropolitan Opera Studio. *Career:* debut at Santa Fe Festival 1965 as the Alchemist in the US premier of Henze's König Hirsch, San Francisco Opera 1971, Metropolitan Opera, New York 1973, Vienna State Opera 1977, Paris Opéra 1979 as the Painter in the premiere of the three-act version of Lulu, La Scala 1979, Hamburg State Opera 1981, Geneva Opera 1981, Deutsche Oper, West Berlin 1983, and Bonn Opera 1983; sang the Leper in the premiere of Messiaen's St François d'Assise, Paris, 1983, at Brussels Opera 1984, and at Royal Opera Covent Garden 1985 in Der Zwerg by Zemlinsky; appeared in film, Don Giovanni 1988; at Stuttgart in 1989 as Dionysos in The Bassarids by Henze; season 1992 as Herod in Salome at Covent Garden and Salzburg; season 1996 with Aegisthus at Salzburg and the Inquisitor in Dallapiccola's Prigioniero at Florence; Herod in Salome at Santa Fe, 1998; title role in the premiere of K... by Philippe Manouri at the Opéra Bastille, Paris 2001. *Recordings include:* Der Zwerg, Damnation of Faust, Florentinische Tragoedie, Don Giovanni, Lulu, Mahler Symphony No. 8, Berlioz's Requiem. *Honours:* Hon. DHumLitt (St Bonaventure Univ.). *Current Management:* c/o Daniel Lombard, Musicaglotz, 29 rue Violet, 75015 Paris, France. *Telephone:* 1-42-34-53-47. *Fax:* 1-40-46-93-77. *E-mail:* contact@musicaglotz.com. *Website:* www.musicaglotz.com.

RIEU, André; Dutch violinist; *Leader, Johann Strauss Orchestra;* b. 1949, Maastricht; m. Marjorie Rieu 1975. *Education:* Conservatoires de Liège and Maastricht with Jo Juda and Herman Krebbers, Conservatoire de Bruxelles with André Gertier. *Career:* f. Maastricht Salon Orchestra 1978; violinist, Limburg Symphony Orchestra 1978–89; f. Johann Strauss Orchestra (JSO) 1987; f. André Rieu Productions 1987; tours with JSO in Europe, USA, Canada, Japan, Australia, NZ, South Africa. *Recordings include:* From Holland With Love 1994, The Vienna I Love 1996, The Christmas I Love 1997, Romantic Moments 1998, Celebration 1999, Walzertraum 2002, Romantic Paradise 2003, Forever Vienna 2009, Moonlight Serenade 2010, Dreaming 2010, Best of André Rieu 2010, And the Waltz Goes On (Classic BRIT Award – Classic FM Album of the Year 2012) 2011, 100 Years of Strauss 2011, Live in Brazil 2012, Home for Christmas 2012, Nuits magiques 2013, Music of the Night 2013, Love Letters 2014, Les mélodies du bonheur 2014, Un amour à Venise 2014, Arrivederci Roma 2015. *Honours:* Order of the Netherlands Lion 2002, Chevalier, Ordre des Arts et des Lettres 2009; World Music Award, Monte Carlo 1996, Médaille Charlemagne 2010, Gramophone Specialist Classical Chart Award 2010. *Address:* André Rieu Productions, Ursulinenweg 1A, 6212 NC Maastricht, Netherlands (office). *Telephone:* (43) 3516852 (office). *Website:* www.andrerieu.com (office).

RIFKIN, Joshua, BS, MFA; American conductor, musicologist and composer; *Professor of Music (Musicology and Ethnomusicology), Boston University;* b. 22 April 1944, New York; s. of Harry H. Rifkin and Dorothy Helsh; m. Helen Palmer 1995; one d. *Education:* Juilliard School, New York Univ., Göttingen Univ., Germany, Princeton Univs. *Career:* Musical Adviser and Assoc. Dir Nonesuch Records 1963–75; Asst. Assoc. Prof. of Music, Brandeis Univ. 1970–82; Dir The Bach Ensemble 1978–; Visiting Prof., New York Univ. 1978, 1983, 2000, Yale Univ. 1982–83, Princeton Univ. 1988, Stanford Univ. 1989, King's Coll. London 1991, Univ. of Basel 1993, 1997, Ohio State Univ. 1994, Univ. of Dortmund 1996, Schola Cantorum Basiliensis 1997, 2001, Univ. of Munich 2000; currently Professor of Music (Musicology and Ethnomusicology), Boston Univ.; Fellow, Inst. for Advanced Study, Berlin 1984–86; Guest Conductor English Chamber Orchestra, Los Angeles Chamber Orchestra, St Louis Symphony Orchestra, St Paul Chamber Orchestra, Scottish Chamber Orchestra, BBC Symphony Orchestra, Bayerische Staatsoper, San Francisco Symphony Orchestra, City of Glasgow Symphony Orchestra, Jerusalem Symphony Orchestra, Prague Chamber Orchestra. *Achievements include:* recreated J. S. Bach's Wedding Cantata BWV 216 (fragment, originally 1728) 2005. *Recordings:* Bach Mass in B minor 1982, Bach Magnificat 1983, numerous Bach cantatas 1986–2001, Rags and Tangos 1990, Haydn Symphonies 1994, Silvestre Revueltas 1999, rags by Scott Joplin, Mozart Posthorn Serenade, fanfares and sonatas by Pezel and Hammerschmidt, sonatas by Biber, vocal music by Busnois, Josquin. *Publications:* articles on Haydn, Schütz, Bach and Josquin in The Musical Times, Musical Quarterly and other journals, and in the New Grove Dictionary of Music and Musicians. *Honours:* Dr hc (Dortmund) 1999; Gramophone Award 1983. *Address:* Musicology and Ethnomusicology, School of Music, Boston University, 855 Commonwealth Avenue, Boston, MA 02215, USA (office). *E-mail:* jrifkin@bu.edu (office). *Website:* www.bu.edu/musicology (office).

RIGACCI, Susanna; singer (soprano); b. 1959, Stockholm, Sweden. *Education:* studied in Florence, Italy. *Career:* debut with Rome Opera, as Rossini's Rosina; appearances in opera throughout Italy, and guest at Dublin as Gilda in Rigoletto; Wexford Festival in Cimarosa's Astuzie Femminili; season 1987 in the Italian premiere of Henze's English Cat, at Bologna, and in Capriccio at Florence; season 1991–92 as Weber's Aennchen at Liège and Sofia in Rossini's Il Signo Bruschino at the Paris Théâtre du Châtelet. *Recordings include:* Vivaldi's Catone in Utica; L'Elisir d'amore.

RIGAL, Joel, MMus; French pianist; b. 17 Aug. 1950, Castres. *Education:* Univ. of Paris-Sorbonne, Aix en Provence and Marseilles Conservatories, studied with Pierre Barbizet and Paul Badura-Skoda, Vienna. *Career:* made debut: Vienna Theatre 1979; performances include Théâtre du Châtelet, Salle Gaveau, Musée de la Villette, Purcell Room, London, Opera, Cairo, Bibliotek Theatre, Rotterdam, Budapest Strings Orchestra; several television and radio appearances. *Recordings:* with Nadine Palmier: Mozart, Complete Works for Piano Duet and 2 Keyboards, French Music, The Golden Age; Schubert, The Final Masterpieces. *Publications:* Le clavier bien partagé (teaching manual) 1993; contrib. to Marsyas.

RIGBY, Jean Prescott, ARAM, ARCM, ABSM; British singer (mezzo-soprano); b. Fleetwood, Lancs.; d. of Thomas Boulton Rigby and Margaret Annie Rigby; m. James Hayes 1987; three s. *Education:* Elmslie Girls' School, Blackpool, Birmingham School of Music, RAM and Opera Studio. *Career:* studied piano and viola at Birmingham then singing at RAM with Patricia Clark, with whom she continues to study; Prin. Mezzo-Soprano, ENO 1982–90, roles include Mercedes, Marina, Lucretia, Dorabella, Octavian, Penelope, Jocasta, Helen (King Priam), Rosina; debut Covent Garden 1983, roles have included Tebaldo, Mercedes, Hippolyta, second Lady, Magic Flute and Olga, Eugene Onegin, Nicklausse (Hoffman), Irene in Theodora, Emelia in Otello, Geneviève in Pelléas and Mélisande, Edwige in Rodelinda; Glyndebourne debut 1984, sang Nancy in Albert Herring and Mercedes in Carmen 1985; American debut 1993; TV appearances in Così fan tutte and film on Handel; also sings concert repertoire and has made recordings with Giuseppe Sinopoli. *Recordings:* more than 50 recordings, ranging from Bach, Handel, Vivaldi and Debussy to Birtwistle and McMillan. *Honours:* Hon. FRAM 1989; Hon. Assoc., Birmingham Conservatoire 1996, Hon. Fellow 2007; numerous prizes and scholarships at RAM including Countess of Munster, Leverhulme, Peter Stuyvesant, RSA scholarships and the Prin.'s Prize; Royal Overseas League and Young Artists' Competition 1981. *Address:* c/o Hyperion Records, PO Box 25, London, SE9 1AX, England (office). *Telephone:* (20) 8318-1234 (office). *Fax:* (20) 8463-1230 (office). *E-mail:* info@hyperion-records.co.uk (office). *Website:* www.hyperion-records.co.uk (office).

RIHM, Wolfgang; German composer; b. 13 March 1952, Karlsruhe. *Education:* Hochschule für Musik Karlsruhe, with Eugen W Velte, studied with Stockhausen in Cologne and Klaus Huber in Freiburg. *Career:* teacher, Hochschule für Musik, Karlsruhe 1973–78, Prof. of Composition 1985–; freelance composer. *Compositions include:* operas: Deploration 1974, Jakob Lenz 1978, Oedipus 1987, Die Eroberung von Mexico 1992; orchestral: Three Symphonies 1969–76, Sub-Kontar 1975–76, La Musique Creuse Le Ciel for two pianos and orchestra 1979, Monodram for cello and orchestra 1983, Medea-Spiel 1988, Passion 1989, Schwebende Begegnung 1989, Dunkles Spiel 1990, La lugubre gondola for orchestra 1992, Vers une symphonie fleuve, I–IV 1994–98, Musik für oboe und orchester 1994, Styx und Lethe for cello and orchestra 1998, Marsyas for trumpet and orchestra 1998, Musick für Klarinette und orchester 1999; vocal: Hervorgedunkelt for mezzo and ensemble 1974, Umhergetrieben Aufgewirbelt, Nietzsche Fragments for baritone and mezzo, chorus and flute 1981, Lowry-Lieder (Wondratschek) 1987, Song Cycles for soprano and orchestra, Frau, Stimme for soprano and orchestra 1989, Mein Tod, Requiem In Memoriam Jane S 1990, Abschiedsstücke for female voice and 15 instruments 1993, Raumauge for chorus and five percussion 1994, Deutsches Stück mit Hamlet, for mezzo, baritone and orchestra 1997, In doppelter Tiefe for mezzo, alto and orchestra 1999; chamber music: Paraphrase for cello, percussion and piano 1972, Ländler for 13 strings 1979, 10 string quartets 1970–97, Gebild for trumpet, strings and percussion 1983, Duomonolog for violin and cello 1989; music for voice and piano, organ and piano. *Address:* Hochschule für Musik, Am Schloss Gottsaue 7, 76131 Karlsruhe, Germany (office). *Telephone:* (721) 66290 (office). *Fax:* (721) 6629266 (office). *Website:* www.hfm-karlsruhe.de (office).

RILEY, Howard, BA, MA, MMus, MPh; British musician (piano) and composer; b. 16 Feb. 1943, Huddersfield, Yorks., England. *Education:* Univ. of Wales, Indiana Univ., USA, York Univ. *Career:* festival, club, TV and radio appearances as solo and group pianist, throughout Europe and N America 1967–; Creative Assoc., Centre of the Creative and Performing Arts, Buffalo, NY, USA 1976–77. *Recordings include:* albums: Facets 1983, For Four On Two Two 1984, In Focus 1985, Live At The Royal Festival Hall 1985, Feathers 1988, Procession 1990, The Heat Of Moments 1991, Beyond Category 1993, The Bern Concert 1993, Inner Mirror 1996, Making Moves 1997, Short Stories 1998, One to One 1999, Synopsis 2000, Overground 2001, Airplay 2001, Consequences 2005, Two Is One 2006, Short Stories (Volume Two) 2007, Three is One 2008, The Monk and Ellington Sessions 2009, Solo in Vilnius 2010, The Complete Short Stories 1998–2010 2010, Live with Repertoire 2011, To Be Continued 2013. *Publications:* The Contemporary Piano Folio 1982. *Honours:* Bicentennial Arts Fellowship 1976. *Address:* Flat 2, 53 Tweedy Road, Bromley, Kent, BR1 3NH, England (home). *Telephone:* (20) 8290-5917 (home).

RILEY, Terry Mitchell, MA; American composer, pianist and raga singer; b. 24 June 1935, Colfax, Calif.; s. of Charles Riley and Wilma Ridlofi; m. Ann Yvonne Smith 1958; three c. *Education:* San Francisco State Univ., Univ. of California, studied with Duane Hampton, Adolf Baller and Pandit Pran Nath. *Career:* joined La Monte Young's Theater of Eternal Music 1965; Creative Assoc., Center for Creative and Performing Arts, Buffalo 1967; taught music composition and N Indian raga at Mills Coll. 1971–83; freelance composer and performer 1961–; launched Minimal Music Movt with composition and first performance of In C 1964; Founder-mem., Khaval ensemble 1989–93; f. The Travelling-Avantt-Gaard (theatre co.) 1992. *Compositions include:* The Harp of New Albion for solo piano in just intonation, Sunrise of the Planetary Dream Collector, Sri Camel, The Ten Voices of the Two Prophets, Chorale of the Blessed Day, Eastern Man, Embroidery, Song from the Old Country, G-Song, Remember This Oh Mind, The Ethereal Time Shadow, Offering to Chief Crazy Horse, Rites of the Imitators, The Medicine Wheel, Song of the Emerald Runner, Cycle of five string quartets, Trio for violin, clarinet and cello 1957, Concert for two pianos and tape 1960, String Trio 1961, Keyboard Studies 1963, Dorian Reeds for ensemble 1964, In C 1964, A Rainbow in the Curved Air 1968, Persian Surgery Dervishes for electronic keyboard 1971, Descending Moonshine Dervishes 1975, Do You Know How it Sounds? for low voice, piano and tabla 1983, Cadenza on the Night Plain for string quartet 1984, Salome Dances for Peace string quartet 1988, Jade Palace for orchestra and synthesiser 1989, Cactus Rosary for synthesiser and ensemble 1990, June Buddhas for chorus and orchestra 1991, The Sands for string quartet and orchestra 1991, Four Woelfi Portraits for ensemble 1992, The Saint Adolf Ring chamber opera 1993, Ritmos and Melos 1993, El Hombre string quartet 1993, Ascension for solo guitar 1993, The Heaven Ladder for piano four hands 1996, Three Requiem Quartets 1997, Autodreamographical Tales for narrator and instruments 1997, Uncle Jard for saxophone quartet and piano 1998, MissiGono 1998, DeepChandi for string orchestra, dancer and tape 1998, Banana Humberto 2000, Assassin Reverie for saxophone quartet 2001, Sun Rings for string quartet, choir and backing track 2002, ArchAngels for eight cellos 2003, Quando Cosas Malas Caen del Cielo 2003, Crazy World 2003, Worksong 2003, Baghdad Highway 2003, The Cusp of Magic 2004, Melodious Junkyard for piano 2004, Bruce's Travelling Machine for solo cello 2005, The Heaven Ladder, Book 6 2006, Giant-Hairy Nude-Warriors Racing down the Slopes of Battle 2006, SolTierraLuna 2007, The Universal Bridge 2008, The Transylvanian Horn Courtship 2009. *Honours:* Guggenheim Fellowship 1980. *Current Management:* c/o Tom Walsh, Associate Director of Music, The Cleveland Museum of Art, 11150 East Boulevard, Cleveland, OH 44106, USA. *Telephone:* (216) 707-2281. *E-mail:* tom@elisionfields.com. *Address:* Sri Moonshine Music, 13699 Moonshine Road, Camptonville, CA 95922, USA (office). *E-mail:* srimoonshinemusic@gmail.com (office). *Website:* www .terryriley.com.

RILLING, Helmuth; German conductor, chorus master, organist and academic; b. 29 May 1933, Stuttgart; m. Martina Greiner 1967; two d. *Education:* Staatliche Hochschule für Musik, Stuttgart with Johann Nepomuk David, Conservatorio di Santa Cecilia, Rome with Fernando Germani, studied conducting with Leonard Bernstein in New York. *Career:* founder and Dir, Gächinger Kantorei, Stuttgart 1954–; organist and choirmaster, Gedächtniskirche, Stuttgart 1957–98; London debut as organist 1963, as conductor 1972; taught organ and conducting, Berliner Kirchenmusikschule, Berlin-Spandau; Dir, Spandauer Kantorei 1963–66; founder, Bach-Collegium Stuttgart 1965–; Prof. of Conducting, Staatliche Hochschule für Musik, Frankfurt 1966–85; Dir, Frankfurter Kantorei 1969–81; co-founder and Artistic Dir, Summer Festival (now Oregon Bach Festival), Eugene, USA 1970–; teacher, Indiana Univ., Bloomington, USA 1976–77; founder and Dir, Sommer Acad. Johann Sebastian Bach Stuttgart 1979–99, Internationale Bachakademie Stuttgart 1981–, Bach Acads in Tokyo, Buenos Aires 1983, Santiago de Compostela, Spain, Prague, Kraków, Moscow, Budapest, Caracas; Chief Conductor, Real Filarmonía de Galicia, Santiago de Compostela, Spain 1996–2000; founder, Stuttgart Festival Choir and Orchestra 2001–; world wide int. appearances with own ensembles and as guest conductor and guest prof.; regular co-operation with Israel Philharmonic Orchestra, Cleveland Orchestra, Boston Symphony Orchestra, Minnesota Orchestra, LA Philharmonic, Toronto Symphony Orchestra, New York Philharmonic, Vienna Philharmonic Orchestra, Münchner Philharmoniker, Radio-Sinfonieorchester Munich; mem. Kungl. Musikaliska Akad., Stockholm 1993. *Recordings:* Cycle of Bach Cantatas with the Frankfurter Kantorei, the Gächinger Kantorei and the Figuralchor of Stuttgart 1970–84, Motets, Lutheran Masses, Choral Preludes and Orgelbüchlein by Bach, Magnificats by Schütz, Bach, Monteverdi and Buxtehude, Carissimi's Jephte and Judicum Salomonis, Handel's Belshazzar, Telemann's Ino and Pimpinone, Mozart's Concertos K364 and K190, Mass K317 and Vesperae Solennes de Confessore, Geistliche Chormusik, St Matthew Passion, Symphoniae Sacrae and Cantiones Sacrae by Schütz, Messiaen's Cinq Rechants, Edition Bachakademie: The Complete Works of Bach (172 albums) 1998–2000, Credo by Penderecki and Wolfgang Rihm's Deus Passus 2001–02. *Publications:* Johann Sebastian Bach, Matthäus-Passion, Einführung und Studienanleitung 1975, Johann Sebastian Bachs h-moll-Messe 1975. *Honours:* Hon. DFA (Concordia Coll., USA) 1990, Dr hc (Univ. of Oregon) 1999; Grand Prix du Disque 1985, UNESCO/IMC Music Prize 1994, Theodor Heuss Prize 1995, Int. Prize Compostela 1999, Cannes Classic Award 1999, Grammy Award for Best Choral Performance 2000, Hanns Martin Schleyer Prize 2001. *Current Management:* c/o Kristina Pauli, Internationale Bachakademie Stuttgart, Presse- und Öffentlichkeitsarbeit, Johann-Sebastian-Bach-Platz (Hasenbergsteige 3), 70178 Stuttgart, Germany. *Telephone:* (711) 6192117 (office). *Fax:* (711) 6192151 (office). *E-mail:* pr@bachakademie.de (office). *Website:* www .bachakademie.de (office).

RIMMER, John Francis; New Zealand composer; b. 5 Feb. 1939, Auckland. *Education:* University of Auckland, studied with John Weinzweig in Toronto. *Career:* Lecturer, University of Auckland 1974–99, Chair. in Music 1995; founder of electro-acoustic music studio. *Compositions include:* Symphony, 1968; Electro-acoustic: Composition nos 1–10, 1968–77; Seaswell, 1978; Projections at Dawn, 1985; Fleeting images, 1985; Beyond the Saying, 1990; A Vocalise for Einstein, 1991; La Voci di Galilea, 1995; Pacific Soundscapes with Dancing, 1995; Viola Concerto, 1980; Meeting Place for orchestra, 1984; Gossamer for 12 strings, 1984; With the Current, for ensemble, 1986; Symphony, the Feeling of Sound, 1989; Cloud Fanfares for orchestra, 1990; Millennia for brass ensemble, 1991; Bowed Insights, string quartet, 1993; The Ripple Effect, for ensemble, 1995; Flashes of Iridescence for piano, 1995; A Dialogue of Opposites, for cello, 1997; Memories, for youth orchestra, 1998; Galileo, chamber opera, 1998; Europa, Concerto for Brass Band and Orchestra 2002, Transcend, Concerto for Orchestra 2003, Thermal Labyrinths for Brass Band 2004. *Address:* 67 Marlborough Avenue, Glenfield, Auckland 1310, New Zealand (home). *Telephone:* (9) 444-8419 (home).

RINALDI, Alberto; Italian singer (baritone); b. 6 June 1939, Rome,. *Education:* Accademia di Santa Cecilia, Rome. *Career:* debut at Spoleto in 1963 as Simon Boccanegra; Teatro Fenice Venice in 1970 as Rossini's Figaro; Appearances in Milan, Rome, Naples, Paris, Rio de Janeiro, Ghent, Florence and Aix-en-Provence; Edinburgh Festival in 1973; Glyndebourne Festival in 1980 as Ford in Falstaff; Sang Mozart's Count on tour to Japan with the company of the Vienna Staatsoper, 1986; Sang at the Berlin Staatsoper in 1987 as Dandini in La Cenerentola; Pesaro and Cologne, 1988–89 in Il Signor Bruschino and Il Cambiale di Matrimonio; Bonn Opera in 1990 as Rossini's Figaro; Sang Blansac in La Scala di Seta at the 1990 Schwetzingen Festival; Season 1992 as Blansac at Cologne and Paris; Sang Geronio in Rossini's Il Turco in Italia, Brussels, 1996; Don Pasquale at Brussels, 1998; Season 2000–01 as Belcore at the Vienna Staatsoper and Rambaldo in Puccini's La Rondine at Rome. *Recordings:* Masetto in Don Giovanni; Il Matrimonio Segreto; Il Campanello; Pagliacci; Video of La Scala di Seta. *Current Management:* c/o Opera Vladarski, Döblinger Hauptstrasse 57/18, 1190 Vienna, Austria. *Telephone:* (1) 368-6960/6961. *Fax:* (1) 368-6962. *E-mail:* opera.vladarski@utanet.at.

RINALDI, Margarita; singer (soprano); b. 12 Jan. 1933, Turin, Italy. *Education:* studied in Rovigo. *Career:* debut in Spoleto 1958 as Lucia di Lammermoor; La Scala Milan 1959 as Sinaide in Mosè by Rossini; Dublin 1961 as Carolina in Il Matrimonio Segreto and Gilda; Verona Arena 1962, 1969; US debut at Dallas 1966 as Gilda; Glyndebourne Festival 1966 as Carolina; Bregenz Festival 1974, 1980 in Un Girono di Regno and as Alice Ford; further appearances in Barcelona, Chicago, San Francisco, Wexford, Rome, Naples and Turin; other roles include Amina, Norina, Linda di Chamounix, Marie in La Fille du Régiment, Bertha in La Prophète, Sophie, Ilia, Fiordiligi, Violetta, Oscar and the Marschallin; Maggio Musicale Florence 1977–78 as Amenaide in Tancredi and Helena in A Midsummer Night's Dream; retired from the stage 1981; many concert engagements. *Recordings include:* Lucia di Lammermoor, Rigoletto, Le Prophète, La Scala di Seta, L'Africaine, Ilia in Idomeneo.

RINGART, Anna; French singer (mezzo-soprano); b. 15 Jan. 1937, Paris. *Education:* studied with Irene Joachim and Marguerite Liszt in Paris, Hamburg Musikhochschule with Frau Anders-Mysz-Gmeiner. *Career:* sang at German opera centres, including Lubeck, Koblenz, Düsseldorf and Hamburg; sang at the Paris Opéra from 1973 under Karl Böhm, Pierre Boulez, Seiji Ozawa and Georg Solti, in a repertoire extending from Mozart to Schoenberg's Moses und Aron; appeared in the 1985 premiere of Docteur Faustus by Konrad Boehmer; Opéra-Comique 1988 as the Nurse in Boris Godunov; has sung at many festivals of contemporary music, notably with the group Contrasts.

RINGBORG, (Hans) Patrik Erland; Swedish conductor; b. 1 Nov. 1965, Stockholm. *Education:* Stockholm Inst. of Music, Royal Coll. of Music, Stockholm, further studies in Vienna and London. *Career:* debut Ystad Summer Opera, Akhnaten by Glass 1989; Städtische Bühnen, Freiburg, Bizet's Carmen 1992; Royal Opera, Stockholm, triple bill with Scheherazade 1993; conductor and coach since 1987, with Swedish Radio Choir 1988, Sächsische Staatsoper, Dresden 1988, Royal Opera, Stockholm 1989–93 (including TV), Canadian Opera Company 1992; 2nd Kapellmeister and Studienleiter, Städtische Bühnen Freiburg 1993–95, Co 1st Kapellmeister 1995–; Fellow, British Council. *Honours:* major scholarship, RAM, Stockholm 1987, 1st runner-up, First Competition for Opera Conductors, Royal Opera, Stockholm 1997, Opera Prize 2014. *Address:* Staatstheater Kassel, GMD-Sekretariat, Friedrichsplatz 15, D-34117, Kassel, Germany (office). *Telephone:* (561) 1094119 (office). *Fax:* (561) 1094212 (office). *Website:* www .staatstheater-kassel.de (office); www.ringb.org/en/.

RINGBORG, Tobias; Swedish violinist and conductor; b. 2 Nov. 1973, Stockholm. *Education:* Royal Univ. Coll. of Music, Stockholm with Harald Thedéen, Juilliard School, New York, USA. *Career:* debut playing Tchaikovsky Violin Concerto with Royal Stockholm Philharmonic Orchestra 1994; appearances with most Swedish and Danish orchestras; recitals throughout Europe and USA, including Concertgebouw, Amsterdam, Nat. Gallery of Art, Washington DC; conducting debut 2000; closely associated with Stockholm Royal Opera 2001–; Resident Conductor, Malmö Opera 2002–04; operatic engagements at Opera North, Scottish Opera, Oper Leipzig, Norwegian Opera, Danish Nat. Opera. *Recordings:* more than 20 recordings, including Joseph Marx's Sonata in A Major, Romantic Swedish Violin Concertos, Foroni: Cristina di Svezia. *Honours:* Soloist Prize, Royal Swedish Acad. of Music 1994, First Prize, Concours Int. de Musique de Chimay, Belgium 1995, Blomstedt Award 2010. *Current Management:* c/o Malin Gjörup, Svenska Konsertbyrån

AB, Karlbergsvägen 52, 113 37 Stockholm, Sweden. *Telephone:* (8) 665-88-88. *Fax:* (8) 665-80-66. *E-mail:* malin@svenskakonsertbyran.se. *Website:* www .svenskakonsertbyran.se. *E-mail:* info@tobiasringborg.com (office). *Website:* www.tobiasringborg.com.

RINGHOLZ, Teresa; American singer (soprano); b. 30 Dec. 1958, Rochester, NY. *Education:* Eastman School, Rochester, studied in San Francisco. *Career:* debut at Western Opera Theatre, San Francisco 1982 as Gilda; toured in the USA then sang in Europe from 1985 with debut at Strasbourg as Zerbinetta; Cologne Opera from 1985 as Liu, Sophie, Susanna, Despina, Pamina and Sandrina in La Finta Giardiniera; sang at the Salzburg Festival, 1987–88 and at Tel Aviv with the Cologne Opera Company; further appearances in opera and concert throughout Germany, France and Switzerland; other roles include Gretel, Oscar, Lauretta, Micaela, Marzelline and Adele in Die Fledermaus; season 1992 as the Wife in the premiere of Schnittke's Life With an Idiot, Amsterdam, and as Fanny in Rossini's La Cambiale di Matrimonio, Paris; sang at the Kennedy Center with the Washington Opera in 1994 as Susanna in Le nozze di Figaro; Violetta in Bogota and Fiordiligi in Barcelona, Seville and the Hamburg Staatsoper; sang Gluck's Alceste at Drottningholm, 1998; Tatiana in Eugene Onegin at Osnabrück, 2000. *Current Management:* MusiKado, Franz-Marc-Strasse 4, 50999 Cologne, Germany. *Telephone:* (221) 3579467. *Fax:* (221) 3579468. *E-mail:* musikado@musikado .com. *Website:* www.musikado.com.

RINGO, Jennifer; American singer (soprano); b. 1965. *Education:* University of Iowa, Juilliard School, New York, Merola Opera Program, Houston Grand Opera Studio. *Career:* appearances with San Francisco Opera, Houston Opera, Maggio Musicale (Florence) Grand Théâtre de Genève and Canadian Opera Co.; Poulenc's La Voix Humaine in New York and Cologne; other repertory includes Der Zwerg by Zemlinsky, Wozzeck and Enescu's Oedipe; concerts in Vienna, Berlin, Nice, Barcelona and Rotterdam; festival engagements at Aspen, Caramoor, Ravina, Tanglewood and Hollywood Bowl; season 2000–01 with Britten's Ellen Orford at Tours, Berg's Lulu Symphonie at Aspen, Donna Elvira and Mozart's Countess at Lisbon and Ullmann's Kaiser von Atlantis at Cincinnati. *Current Management:* Musicaglotz, 11 rue le Verrier, 75006 Paris, France. *Telephone:* (1) 42-34-53-40. *Fax:* (1) 40-46-93-77. *E-mail:* general@musicaglotz.com. *Website:* www.musicaglotz.com.

RINKEVICIUS, Gintaras; Lithuanian conductor; *Artistic Director and Chief Conductor, Lithuanian State Symphony Orchestra*; b. 20 Jan. 1960, Vilnius. *Education:* St Petersburg and Moscow Conservatoires. *Career:* Asst Conductor, Lithuanian Philharmonic Orchestra 1979; founder, Artistic Dir and Chief Conductor, Lithuanian State Symphony Orchestra 1988–; Artistic Dir and Chief Conductor, Latvian Nat. Opera 1996–2003, Chief Guest Conductor 2007–09; worked with soloists such as Natalia Gutman, Peter Donohoe, Oleg Kagan and Vladimir Ovchinikov; repertoire includes music by Dvořák, Mahler, Poulenc, Orff, Honegger, Prokoviev, Elgar and John Adams, in addition to standard works; guest engagements with Russian State Symphony, Moscow Philharmonic, St Petersburg Philharmonic, Berlin Symphoniker, Staatskapelle Weimar, at Frankfurt, Tampere, Tivoli in Copenhagen, Odense Symphony. *Honours:* Order of Grand Duke Gediminas, Fourth Class, Lithuania 1997, Order of Merit, Norway, Ordem do Merito Comemdador, Portugal, Order of Three Stars, Latvia, Grand Cross, Order of Merit, Lithuania 2009; winner, All-Union Conducting Competition at St Petersburg Conservatoire, first prize, Herbert von Karajan Conducting Competition 1985, second prize, Janos Ferencsik Competition, Budapest 1986, Lithuanian Nat. Prize 1994, Latvian Grand Music Prize 1997, 2000, Luminaries Prize, Konstantinas Čiurlionis Foundation 2010. *Current Management:* ZavArté Classic Artist Agency, Furutorpsgatan 43, 25227 Helsingborg, Sweden. *Fax:* (207) 100-82-07. *E-mail:* agency@zavarteclassic.com. *Website:* www.zavarteclassic.com. *E-mail:* letters@gintarasrinkevicius.lt (office). *Website:* www.gintarasrinkevicius.lt.

RINTZLER, Marius Adrian; German singer; b. 14 March 1932, Bucharest, Romania; m. Sanda Dragomir 1964. *Education:* Acad. of Music, Bucharest. *Career:* soloist with Bucharest Philharmonic 1959; debut in opera in Bucharest as Don Basilio in Il Barbiere di Siviglia 1964; went to Germany 1966; leading bass at Düsseldorf's Deutsche Oper am Rhein 1968–; guest singer with numerous opera cos, including Metropolitan, San Francisco, Glyndebourne, Paris, Brussels, Munich; repertoire includes various roles in Richard Strauss' Rosenkavalier (Ochs), Capriccio (La Roche), Schweigsame Frau (Morosus), in Rossini's La Cenerentola (Don Magnifico), Il Barbiere (Bartolo), in Richard Wagner's Ring (Alberich), in Mozart's Don Giovanni (Leporello), Die Entführung (Osmin); appears with major symphony orchestras in Europe and USA, including Philharmonia (London), Berlin Philharmonic, Cleveland Symphony; also gives recitals, TV appearances in England, Germany and France. *Honours:* Kammersänger. *Address:* Friedingstrasse 18, 40625 Düsseldorf, Germany (home). *Telephone:* (211) 297083 (home).

RISHTON, Timothy John, BA, MMus, PhD, ARCO; organist and musicologist; b. 14 Aug. 1960, Lancashire, England; m. Tracy Jane Hogg 1987, two s. one d. *Education:* Univ. of Reading, Univ. of Manchester, Univ. of Wales. *Career:* numerous recitals worldwide, including complete Stanley series, London 1981 and complete Bach Trio Sonatas, London and Salford 1983; complete Bach organ works, Norway 1988–89; concert tours in central Europe, the Arctic, Scandinavia, the Far East and USA; first performance of Smethergell Harpsichord Concerto, Tadley 1983; dedicatee of new compositions by Henning Somevvo and Hans-Olav Lien; lectures at Boxhill Summer School

annually 1985–90, Univ. of Oxford 1986, 1987, Univ. of Reading 1988; Norwegian Music Conservatoire, Trondheim 1993–; many public lectures in English, Welsh and Norwegian (some broadcast); many radio and television broadcasts 1984–; Univ. of Wales, Bangor 1984–87, 1989–91; organist and master of choristers, Collegiate Church of St Cybi, Holyhead and Parish Churches of Holy Island, Anglesey 1984–87; Univ. of Tromso 1998–; Reader in Performance Practice, Tromso 2001. *Compositions:* organ works. *Recordings:* with Aled Jones, 1985; Organ Works of the Eighteenth-Century, 1986; From Many Lands, 1991; Walther and Bach arrangements of Albinoni and Vivaldi, 2001; Contemporary Norwegian Organ Music, 2001. *Publications:* Aspects of Keyboard Music, Essays in Honour of Susi Jeans 1986, Organist in Norway 1989, Liturgisk orgelspill 1995, Voll Kyryje 1996.

RISLEY, Patricia; American singer (mezzo-soprano); b. 12 Jan. 1968, South Carolina. *Education:* Indiana University and Chicago Lyric Opera Center for American Artists. *Career:* Chicago Lyric Opera from 1995, as Siebel in Faust and in Berio's Un re in ascolto, Die Walküre, Die Zauberflöte and Norma; Metropolitan Opera from 1998 as Tebaldo in Don Carlo, Thisbe in Cenerentola and Mercédès in Carmen; European debut 1997 in Die Sieben Todsünden by Weill at Florence; Further roles include Mozart's Dorabella at St Louis, Farnace in Mitridate for Wolf Trap Opera and Cherubino at the Deutsche Oper, Berlin; Diana in La Calisto and Cesti's Orontea for Music of the Baroque, Gounod's Stephano and Meg Page in Falstaff at Chicago and Munich. *Current Management:* Balmer & Dixon Management AG, Kreuzstrasse 82, 8032 Zürich, Switzerland. *Telephone:* (43) 244-8644. *Fax:* (43) 244-8649. *Website:* www.badix.ch.

RISSET, Jean-Claude, PhD; French composer and researcher; b. 13 March 1938, Le Puy; s. of Raoul Risset and Renée Aubry; m. Rozenn Cornic; two c. *Education:* Ecole Normale Supérieure, Univ. of Paris, studied piano and composition with André Jolivet. *Career:* Bell Labs, USA 1964–69; CNRS 1969–72, Dir of Research, Laboratoire de Mécanique et d'Acoustique, Marseille 1985–, now Emer.; Head of Computer Dept, IRCAM, Paris 1975–79, with Pierre Boulez. *Compositions include:* Little Boy for tape 1968, Mutations I for tape 1969, Dialogues for four instruments and tape 1975, Inharmonique for soprano and tape 1977, Moments Newtoniens for seven instruments and tape 1977, Mirages for 16 instruments and tape 1978, Filtres for two pianos 1984, Sud 1985, Dérives for chorus and tape 1985–87, Phases for orchestra 1988, Electron Positron 1989, Duet for one pianist 1989, Lurai for Celtic harp and computer 1991, Triptyque for clarinet and orchestra 1991, Une Aube sans soleil for soprano and percussion 1991, Invisibles/Invisible for soprano and computer 1994, Mokee for bass, piano and tape 1996, Contre Nature for percussion and tape 1996, Elementa for tape 1998, Escalas for orchestra 2001, Resonant Sound Spaces 2002, Echappées for harp and tape 2004, Octant for tape 2004, Oscura for soprano and computer 2005, Pentacle for harpsichord 2006, Concerto for violin 2007, Multiples for piano and tape 2009, Kaleidophone (16 tracks) 2010, Otro 2011. *Recordings:* works appear on 30 albums. *Publications:* Du Songe au Son: entretiens avec Matthieu Guillot 2008; contrib. to Science, Musique en jeu, Esprit, Critique, Contemporary Music Review, Perspectives of New Music, Pour la Science. *Honours:* Commdr des Arts et des Lettres; Chevalier, Légion d'honneur; Hon. DMus (Edinburgh) 1994, (Cordoba, Argentina) 2000; Grand Prix Nat. de la Musique 1991, Médaille d'Or du CNRS 1999, Prix Ars Electronica 2007, Giga-Hertz Haupt Preis 2009. *Address:* Laboratoire de Mécanique et d'Acoustique, CNRS, 31 chemin Joseph Aiguier, 13402 Marseille Cedex 20, France (office). *Telephone:* (4) 91-16-42-10 (office). *Fax:* (4) 91-16-43-71 (office). *E-mail:* jcrisset@lma.cnrs -mrs.fr (office). *Website:* www.lma.cnrs-mrs.fr (office).

RITCHIE, Anthony Damian, PhD; New Zealand composer and academic; *Associate Professor of Music, University of Otago*; b. 18 Sept. 1960, Christchurch; s. of John and Anita Ritchie; pnr Sandy Garner; two c. *Education:* Canterbury Univ., Liszt Acad., Budapest, studied with Attila Bozay. *Career:* Lecturer, Canterbury Univ. 1985–87; Composer-in-Schools, Christchurch 1987; Mozart Fellowship at Otago Univ. 1988–89; Composer-in-Residence, Southern Sinfonia 1993–94; Lecturer in Composition, Otago Univ. 2001–06, Sr Lecturer in Music 2006–11, Assoc. Prof. of Music 2012–; Pres. Composers Asscn of NZ 2004–07; apptd arranger of nat. anthems for Rugby World Cup 2011. *Music for film and orchestra:* Southern Journeys 2000, Timeless Land 2004. *Compositions include:* Concertino for piano and strings 1981, Beginnings for orchestra 1987, Music for Tristan for piano 1988, The Hanging Bulb for orchestra 1989, To Face the Night Alone for baritone, chorus and orchestra 1990, As Long as Time for unaccompanied choir 1991, Berlin Fragments for soprano and piano 1992, Flute Concerto 1993, Symphony No.1 'Boum' 1993, Viola Concerto 1994, A Bugle Will Do for orchestra 1995, Then I Understood for choir and orchestra 1996, Guitar Concerto 1996, From the Southern Marches for choir and orchestra 1997, Revelations for orchestra 1998, Symphony No. 2 'The Widening Gyre' 1999, Ahua for choir and orchestra 2000, Piano Trio 2001, 24 Preludes for piano 2002, String Quartet No. 2 2002, 'Quartet' (chamber opera) 2003, Timeless Land for orchestra and film 2003, The God Boy (two-act opera) 2004, Clouds for trombone and brass band 2005, Clarinet Quintet 2006, Whalesong for bass and orchestra 2007, French Overture 2008, Wind Quintet 2009, Symphony No. 3 2010, Violin Concerto 2012, Symphony No. 4 2013; arrangements of the 20 nat. anthems for the Rugby World Cup, NZ 2011, This Other Eden (opera) 2014, Salaam for choir 2014, Lullabies for choir 2014. *Radio:* Composer of the Week, Radio New Zealand Concert 2011, A Bugle Will Do (recorded by BBC Symphony Orchestra, broadcast on BBC 3) 2014. *Recordings include:* Piano Preludes

2005, Anthony Ritchie: Symphonies Nos. 1 and 2 2007, New Zealand Poets in Song 2008, Remember Parihaka: Orchestral Music of Anthony Ritchie 2009, Expressions: Piano Music by Anthony Ritchie 2010, A Bugle Will Do: Symphonic Works by Anthony Ritchie 2011, Octopus: Chamber Music by Anthony Ritchie 2011, Concertino: Dance Music by Anthony Ritchie 2012, Stations Symphony No. 4 2014, Father & Son: Music of John and Anthony Ritchie 2015. *Publications:* musical scores: The Hanging 1999, Piano Trio 2004, Flute Concerto 2009, Symphony No. 3 2012, Meditation for violin and piano 2013, Revelations for orchestra 2014. *Honours:* Composers Asscn of NZ Trust Fund Award 1998. *Address:* Music Department, University of Otago, Box 56, Dunedin, New Zealand (office). *Telephone:* (3) 479-8881 (office). *E-mail:* anthony.ritchie@otago.ac.nz (office). *Website:* www.anthonyritchie.co.nz.

RITTERMAN, Dame Janet Elizabeth, DBE, MMus, PhD; British/Australian music college director (retd); b. (Janet Elizabeth Palmer), 1 Dec. 1941, Sydney, NSW, Australia; d. of Charles Eric Palmer and Laurie Helen Palmer; m. Gerrard Peter Ritterman 1970. *Education:* North Sydney Girls' High School and New South Wales State Conservatorium of Music, Australia, Univ. of Durham and King's Coll. London, UK. *Career:* pianist, accompanist, chamber music player, music educator; Sr Lecturer in Music, Middx Polytechnic 1975–79, Goldsmiths, Univ. of London 1980–87; Head of Music, Dartington Coll. of Arts 1987–90, Dean Academic Affairs 1988–90, Acting Prin. 1990–91, Prin. 1991–93; Visiting Prof. of Music Educ., Univ. of Plymouth 1993–2005; Dir Royal Coll. of Music 1993–2005; Chair. Assoc. Bd Royal Schools of Music (Publishing) Ltd 1993–2005, The Mendelssohn and Boise Foundations 1996–98, 2002–04, Advisory Council, Arts Research Ltd 1997–2005, Fed. of British Conservatoires 1998–2003; Vice-Pres. Nat. Asscn of Youth Orchestras 1993–, Royal Coll. of Music 2005–; mem. Music Panel, Arts Council of England 1992–98, Council Royal Musical Asscn 1994–2004 (Vice-Pres. 1998–2004), Bd ENO 1996–2004, Exec. Cttee Inc. Soc. of Musicians 1996–99, Arts and Humanities Research Bd 1998–2004 (Postgraduate Panel 1998–2002, Chair. Postgraduate Cttee 2002–04), Nominating Cttee Arts and Humanities Research Council 2005–07, Bd Nat. Youth Orchestra 1999–2007, Steering Cttee, London Higher Educ. Consortium 1999–2005, Arts Council of England 2000–02, Dept for Educ. and Skills Advisory Group, Music and Dance Scheme 2000–05, Council of Goldsmiths, Univ. of London 2002–07, Bd Anglo-Austrian Soc. 2005–11, Bd The Voices Foundation 2005–11, Advisory Bd Inst. for Advanced Studies in the Humanities, Univ. of Edinburgh 2005–, Advisory Council Inst. of Germanic and Romance Studies 2005–10 and Inst. of Musical Research, Univ. of London 2006–12, Educ. Advisory Group Nuffield Foundation 2007–09; Trustee, Countess of Munster Musical Trust 1993–, Prince Consort Foundation 1993–2005, Plymouth Chamber Music Trust 2006–10; Gov. Associated Bd Royal Schools of Music 1993–2005, Purcell School 1996–2000, Heythrop Coll., Univ. of London 1996–2006, Dartington Coll. of Arts 2005–08, Middlesex Univ. 2005–, Univ. Coll. Falmouth 2008–, Royal Welsh Coll. of Music and Drama 2010–; mem. Österreichischer Wissenschaftsrat 2002–12; mem. Court, Worshipful Co. of Musicians 2005–11; Fellow, Royal Northern Coll. of Music 1996, Dartington Coll. of Arts 1997, Univ. Coll., Northampton 1997, Guildhall School of Music and Drama 2000, Higher Educ. Acad. 2007, Heythrop Coll. 2008, Goldsmiths, Univ. of London 2009; Sr Fellow, RCA 2004; Assoc. Fellow, Inst. of Musical Research, Univ. of London 2006–; Chair. Int. Advisory Bd, Programme for Arts-based Research, Austrian Science Fund 2009–; mem. Conseil de fondation, Haute École de Musique de Genève, Switzerland 2009–. *Publications:* articles in learned journals in France, Germany, Australia and UK. *Honours:* Hon. RAM 1995; Hon. FGSM 2000; Hon. DUniv (Birmingham City) 1996, (Middlesex) 2005; Hon. DLitt (Ulster) 2004; Hon. DMus (Sydney) 2010.

RIVA, Ambroglio; Italian singer (bass); b. 1951, Ignazio, Milan. *Career:* debut, Teatro Nuovo Milan 1975, in Lucia di Lammermoor; has appeared widely in Italy, notably in La Bohème at Verona 1980 and at the Verona Arena in Aida and Carmen; sang in Donizetti's Martyrs at Bergamo, in Anna Bolena at Brescia and Sparafucile in Rigoletto at Ferrara; Valle d'Istria Festival 1985, as Polyphemus in Acis and Galatea; Maggio Musicale Florence 1990, as Angelotti in Tosca; further appearances at Salzburg, Würzburg and Berlin.

RIVENQ, Nicolas, LèsL; British singer (baritone); *Singing Teacher, Opera Junior Montpellier*; b. 18 April 1958, London; m. Séverine Rivenq; one s. three d. *Education:* Lycée Henri IV, Paris, studied with Madame Bonnardot in Paris, Conservatoire Nat. de Musique d'Orléans, with Michel Sénéchal at the School of the Paris Opéra, studied with Nicola Rossi-Lemeni at Indiana Univ., Univ. of Paris IV Sorbonne, Ecole Nationale Supérieure des Arts Décoratifs. *Career:* major operas and concerts 1986–95 include: Festival de Schwetzingen, Jacobs Gassman/Opera Seria; Teatro alla Scala di Milano, Montgomery Handel/La Resurrezione; Salzburg Festival, Jacobs Monteverdi/Orfeo; Festival d'Aix-en-Provence, Christie Rameau/Les Indes Galantes; Opéra de Paris, Christie Lully/Athys; Pesaro Festival, Simone Rossini/Le Comte Ory; Théâtres de Reggio Emilia/Modena, Marin Mozart/Così fan tutte; Piccolo Teatro di Milano, Marin Mozart/Così fan tutte; Opéra de Nice, Panni Rossini/La Cenerentola; Teatro di Bologna, Gatti Donizetti/Dom Sebastien; Martina Franca Festival, Palumbo Giordano/Il Re pastore; Teatro Regio di Torino, Pidò Mozart/Le nozze di Figaro; Opéra Nat. de Paris, Jordan Mozart/Le nozze di Figaro; Teatro alla Scala di Milano, Renzetti Donizetti/La Fille du Régiment; Teatro Massimo di Palermo, Malgoire Handel/Agrippina; Verona Festival, Salieri/Les Danaïdes; Opéra de Berlin, Jacobs Gassman/Opera Seria; 2000–05: Théâtre des Champs Elysées (TCE), Paris, Pidò Rossini/La Cenerentola; Opéra de Paris, Christie Rameau/Les Boréades; Teatro La Fenice, Minkovski Auber/Le Domino Noir; Opera di Roma, Gelmetti Gounod/Faust; Tokyo Opera City, Christie Purcell/The Fairy-Queen; Teatro La Fenice, Concerts inauguraux – Viotti Rossini/Petite Messe Solennelle – Muti Caldara/Te Deum; Tokyo Opera City, Mazzola Mozart/Così fan tutte; Opéra National de Paris, Christie Rameau/Les Indes Galantes Atelier Lyrique de Tourcoing/TCE, Malgoire Monteverdi/L'Orfeo/Il Ritorno D'Ulisse in Patria/L'Incoronazione di Poppea; 2005–10: Teatro delle Muse Ancona, Bartoletti Hindemith/Hin Und Zurück/Ravel/L'heure Espagnole; Teater an der Wien, Jacobs Handel/Giulio Cesare; Salle Pleyel, Kazushi Ono Ravel/l'Enfant et les Sortilèges; Macerata Festival, Tourniaire, F. Testi/Saül; Peking Opera, Bosman Mozart/Così fan tutte; Hong Kong Opera, Mozart/Le Nozze di Figaro; Glyndebourne Festival, Fischer Mozart/Così fan tutte; TCE, Paris, Malgoire Lully/Alceste; Innsbruck Festival, Jacobs Conti/Don Quixote; Théatre Anton Tchekov, Moscow, La Malfa Mozart/Così fan tutte; 2010–15: Théâtre du Bolshoi, Sinaisky Strauss/Der Rosenkavalier; Grand Théâtre de Genève, Guschlbauer Strauss/La Chauve-Souris; Festival Classica Montréal, Malgoire Dubois/Aben-Hamet; TCE, Paris, Malgoire Purcell/Dido and Aeneas/Christie Cavalli/La Didone; Opéra Comique Paris/BAM Brooklyn, Christie Lully/Atys; Théâtre du Bolshoi, Granovsky Strauss/Die Fledermaus; currently Singing Teacher, Opera Junior Montpellier. *Recordings include:* F. Alfano Cyrano de Bergerac M.Guidarini; H. Berlioz La Révolution Grecque M.Plasson; G. Bizet Carmen S. Ozawa; Carmen, M. Plasson; A. Campra Grands Motets W. Christie; Clérambault, Cantates W. Christie; A. Dauvergne, Les Troqueurs W. Christie; Donizetti, Lucie de Lammermoor, M. Benini; Il Fortunato, Inganno, A. Bosman; U. Giordano, Il Re R. Palumbo; G. F. Handel, Giulio Cesare, J. C. Malgoire; S. Landi, Il Sant' Alessio, W. Christie; J. Massenet, Roma, M. Guidarini; Don Quichotte M. Plasson; Manon, A. Pappano; S. Mercadante, Caritea Regina di Spagna, G. Carella; A. Messager, Fortunio, J. E. Gardiner; M. P. de Montéclair, Jephté, W. Christie; C. Monteverdi, L'Orfeo R. Jacobs; Il Combattimento, W. Christie; M. Ravel, Chansons, Madécasses; W. A. Mozart, Le nozze di Figaro/Don Giovanni/Così fan tutte, J. C. Malgoire; La finta giardiniera/Idomeneo, R. Jacobs; G. Pacini, L'Ultimo giorno di Pompei, G. Carella; L. Petitgirard, Elephant Man, L. Petitgirard; F. Poulenc, Le Bal Masqué; A. Plotino, Arts Mélodies et Chansons Ed. du centenaire; J. P. Rameau, Les Indes galantes, W. Christie; Les Grands Motets, P. Herreweghe; Les Grands Motets, W. Christie; Platée, J. C. Malgoire; Les Paladins, J. C. Malgoire; Varany Anacréon, W. Christie; G. Rossini, Robert Bruce; C. Saint-Saens, Requiem, J. Mercier; A. Vivaldi, Montezuma, J. C. Malgoire. *Recordings on film and DVD:* La Naissance d'un Chanteur, Nicolas Rivenq, Bruno Monsaingeon, Revcom Television; Bach Kaffee Cantata, Bauern Cantata, English Nat. Orchestra, Yehudi Menuhin, Revcom Television; Verdi, La Traviata, Zubin Mehta, Giuseppe Patroni, Griffi Andrea Andermann (RAI); Monteverdi La Guerra d'Amore, Ilinca Gheorghiu, William Christie (Arte); Une Leçon de William Christie (Arte); Alfano Cyrano de Bergerac, David and Frédérico Alagna, Lévon Sayan; Bernstein Mass Cochereau, Orchestre d'Orléans; Donizetti, La Fille du Régiment, Teatro alla Scala, Donato Renzetti; Gala Reopening of the Teatro La Fenice, Riccardo Muti; Lully Atys Les Arts Florissants, William Christie, Jean Marie Villégier; Mozart, Così fan tutte, Ivan Fischer, Nicholas Hytner, Glyndebourne; Petitgirard, The Elephant Man, Daniel Mesguich, Laurent Petitgirard, Marco Polo; Purcell Dido and Aeneas, Les Arts Florissants, William Christie; Rameau, Les Indes Galantes, Les Arts Florissants, William Christie; Les Boréades, Les Arts Florissants, William Christie; Salieri, Tarare Schwetzinger, Festspiele Jean Claude Malgoire. *Honours:* First Prize, G.B. Viotti Int. Vocal Competition 1990. *Current Management:* c/o Opéra et Concert, 37 rue de la Chausée d'Antin, 75009 Paris, France; c/o Atelier Musicale, Via Caselle 76, San Lazzaro di Savena 40068, Italy. *Telephone:* 1-42-96-18-18 (Paris); (051) 455706 (San Lazzaro di Savena). *Fax:* 1-42-96-18-00 (Paris); (051) 463331 (San Lazzaro di Savena). *E-mail:* agence@opera-concert.com; info@ateliermusicale.it. *Website:* www.opera-concert.com; www.ateliermusicale.com.

RIVERS, Malcolm; British singer (baritone); b. 19 April 1937, England. *Education:* Royal Coll. of Music, London. *Career:* has appeared in new productions at ENO of Tosca (Scarpia) and Die Soldaten (Eisenhardt), as Geistergebote in Marseille Opera's Die Frau ohne Schatten, in Arizona Opera's production of Rheingold (Alberich) and made his debut with Bordeaux Opera in Tosca (Sagrestano); other engagements include Commandant in From the House of the Dead at ENO, major role of The Judge in new production of Sweeney Todd for Opera North and Alberich for Arizona Opera; appeared in both La Traviata and Salome at Opera Ireland and recently in Marseille as Gunther in Götterdämmerung; most recent appearances include title role in The Mikado with D'Oyly Carte Opera Co. at the Savoy Theatre, London, Flint in Billy Budd at New Israeli Opera, Tel-Aviv and at Gran Teatre del Liceu, Barcelona, and role of Old Man in Ernest Bloch's Macbeth for KlangBogen Wien; also sang Gretch in Fedora for Opera Holland Park and has recently sung Quant in world premiere of John Wolf Brennan's Night.-Shift in St Gallen. *Current Management:* c/o Athole Still Opera Ltd, Foresters Hall, 25–27 Westow Street, London, SE19 3RY, England. *Telephone:* (20) 8771-5271. *Fax:* (20) 8771-8172. *E-mail:* enquiries@atholestill.co.uk. *Website:* www.atholestill.co.uk. *E-mail:* malcolmkingrivers@googlemail.com (home).

RIZZI, Carlo; Italian conductor; b. 19 July 1960, Milan. *Education:* Milan Conservatoire, studied with Vladimir Delman in Bologna, Accademia Chigiana with Franco Ferrara. *Career:* debut, Milan Angelicum in Donizetti's L'Aio nell'Imbarrazzo 1982; conducted Falstaff, Parma 1985 and widely in Italy with Rigoletto, La Traviata, Tancredi, Donizetti's Torquato Tasso,

Beatrice di Tenda, La Voix Humaine, Don Giovanni, L'Italiana in Algeri and Salieri's Falstaff; British debut at Buxton Festival with Torquato Tasso 1988; Netherlands Opera debut with Don Pasquale and productions of Fra Diavolo and Norma at Palermo 1989; Royal Philharmonic debut 1989, London Philharmonic debut 1990, Philharmonia debut 1991; Australian Opera with Il Barbiere di Siviglia and Lucrezia Borgia 1989–90; Tosca for Opera North and La Cenerentola at Covent Garden 1990; concert repertoire includes symphonies by Tchaikovsky and works by Haydn, Mozart, Beethoven and French composers; regular guest in Italy and Netherlands; US opera debut with Il Barbiere di Siviglia 1994; Don Giovanni and La Bohème for WNO 1996; Tristan and Isolde at Oxford and Bristol 1999; conducted Semiramide in Pesaro 2003; conducted Nabucco at the Met, I vespri siciliani in Zurich, Un ballo in maschera in Turin, Ariadne auf Naxos for WNO, Mefistofele in Amersterdam, Falstaff in Strasburg and Madama Butterfuly in Seville 2004; Music Dir, WNO 1992–2001, 2004–07, Guest Conductor 2007–. *Recordings:* L'Italiana in Algeri, Donizetti's Il Furioso sull'Isola di San Domingo, Rossini's Ciro in Babilonia, Paisiello's La Scuffiara, Piccinni's La Pescatrice, Arias for tenor and orchestra by Rossini (with Ernesto Palacio), Schubert, Liszt and Debussy with the London Philharmonic and Philharmonia. *Address:* c/o Welsh National Opera, Wales Millennium Centre, Bute Place, Cardiff, England (office). *Website:* www.wno.org.uk (office).

RIZZI, Lucia; singer (mezzo-soprano); b. 1965, Turin, Italy. *Education:* studied in Turin. *Career:* appearances throughout Italy, in Tokyo and at the Aldeburgh Festival, under such conductors as Myung Wha Chung, Gianandrea Gavazzeni and Semyon Bychkov; operas include Monteverdi's Poppea, Pergolesi's Frate ennamorato and Vivaldi's Farnace; roles include Mozart's Fiordiligi, Dorabella and Sesto, Clarice in La Pietra del Paragone and Rossini's Roggiero (Tancredi) and Cenerentola (both at Zürich 1996–97); further engagements in Luisa Miller, Falstaff, Boris Godunov, Lady Macbeth of the Mtsensk District (in Florence), Stravinsky's Rossignol and Les Noces (Monte Carlo) and the Italian premiere of Tchaikovsky's Cantata Moscow, at Genoa; other concerts in music by Vivaldi, Mahler and Schoenberg, at most Italian music centres; sang Rosmene in a revival of Pergolesi's Il prigionero superbo, Jesi 1998. *Recordings include:* Rossini Rarities.

RIZZO, Francis, BA; American stage director and administrator; b. 8 Nov. 1936, New York, NY. *Education:* Hamilton Coll. and Yale Univ. School of Drama. *Career:* American Dir, Spoleto Festival of Two Worlds 1968–71; Artistic Admin., Wolf Trap Farm Park for the Performing Arts 1972–78; Artistic Dir, Washington Opera 1977–87; as director staged productions for New York City Opera, Houston Grand Opera, Washington Opera, Wolf Trap, Opera Theater of St Louis, Santa Fe Opera, Baltimore Opera, Teatro Verdi, Trieste, Michigan Opera Theater, Théâtre Municipal, Marseilles; mem. American Guild of Musical Artists. *Publications:* contrib. to Opera News.

ROARK-STRUMMER, Linda; American singer (soprano); *Associate Professor of Voice, University of Tulsa;* b. 1952, Tulsa, OK; m. Peter Strummer. *Education:* Univ. of Tulsa. *Career:* sang Fiordilisi at St Louis 1977; engaged at Heidelberg 1979–80, Linz 1980–86 as Regina in the 1983 Austrian premiere of Lortzing's opera and in the premiere of In Seinem Garten Liebt Don Perlimpin Belinda by B. Sulzer; New York City Opera 1985 as Estabella in Attila; over 150 performances of Verdi's Abigaille, notably at the Deutsche Oper Berlin 1987, Ravenna 1988 and Montréal and Verona 1992; La Scala Milan 1988 as Lucrezia in I Due Foscari; sang Krasava in a concert performance of Smetana's Libuce at Carnegie Hall, New York; other roles include Lina in Stiffelio, the Forza and Trovatore Leonora, Arabella, Jenůfa and Antonia; guest engagements at Hamburg, Krefeld, Milwaukee and Venice; sang Norma for Opera Hamilton at Toronto 1991; Turandot at Portland 1996; Poulenc's Mère Marie at Portland 2001; Assoc. Prof. of Voice and Dir of Opera Workshop, Univ. of Tulsa. *Honours:* Zenatello d'Argento Award, Verona 1990. *Address:* School of Music, Tyrrell Hall 301, University of Tulsa, 600 South College, Tulsa, OK 74104, USA (office). *E-mail:* linda-strummer@utulsa.edu (office). *Website:* www.lindaroark-strummer.com.

ROBBIN, Catherine, OC, BA; Canadian singer (mezzo-soprano); *Assistant Professor and Director of Classical Vocal Studies, York University;* b. 28 Sept. 1950, Toronto, Ont. *Education:* Univ. of Toronto. *Career:* numerous appearances in Baroque music; sang in Handel's Messiah with English Baroque Soloists under Sir John Eliot Gardiner, Bach's B minor Mass with Monteverdi Choir and Handel's Orlando at BBC Proms 1989; opera performances include Olga in Eugene Onegin at Opéra de Lyon, Purcell's Dido and Handel's Orlando (role of Medoro) with Academy of Ancient Music, and Handel's Xerxes at Carmel Bach Festival; collaborations with Trevor Pinnock, Hogwood, Andrew Davis, John Nelson, Bernard Labadie and Charles Dutoit; repertoire includes Les Nuits d'Été by Berlioz, Mahler's Lieder eines Fahrenden Gesellen and Rückert Lieder, Elgar's Sea Pictures and the Brahms Alto Rhapsody; numerous recitals in Canada and USA and appearances at Aldeburgh Festival and with the Songmakers' Almanac; sang title role in North American premiere of Handel's Floridante in Toronto 1990; Annius in La Clemenza di Tito at Queen Elizabeth Hall, London 1990; sang in Handel's Rinaldo at Blackheath and Bromsgrove 1996; retd from public performance 2002; Asst Prof., Vocal Studies Program, Music Dept, York Univ., Toronto 2002–. *Recordings include:* Beethoven's Mass in C and Missa Solemnis; Messiah under Gardiner; Berlioz Songs, also Gardiner; Haydn's Stabat Mater with Trevor Pinnock and the English Concert; Orlando under Hogwood; Mahler Song Cycles. *Honours:* Gold Award, Int. Benson and Hedges Competition, Aldeburgh, UK. *Address:* Department of Music, Faculty of Fine Arts,

York University, 4700 Keele Street, Toronto, ON M3J 1P3, Canada (office). *Telephone:* (416) 736-5186 (office). *Fax:* (416) 736-5321 (office). *E-mail:* crobbin@yorku.ca (office). *Website:* www.yorku.ca/finearts/faculty/profs/robbin/robbin.htm (office).

ROBBINS, Julien; American singer (bass); b. 14 Nov. 1950, Harrisburg, PA. *Education:* Philadelphia Academy of Vocal Arts, studied with Nicola Moscona in New York. *Career:* debut in Philadelphia 1976, in Un Ballo in Maschera; Engagements at Santa Fe, Miami, Washington and Chicago; Metropolitan Opera from 1979, as Ramphis, Colline, Gremin and Don Fernando in Fidelio; Deutsche Oper Berlin 1990, as Abimelech in Samson et Dalila; Sang Masetto at the Metropolitan, 1990; World premiere, The Voyage, by Philip Glass, Metropolitan Opera (Second Mate and Space Twin), Nightwatchman in Meistersinger, 1993; Deutsche Oper, Berlin, Don Giovanni, 1992, 1993, Escamillo, 1993, Turandot, (Timur), 1992; Staatsoper Berlin, Barber of Seville, Basilio, 1992; 1993 Deutsche Oper, Berlin, Figaro in The Marriage of Figaro; Season 1994 at San Diego as Count Rodolfo in La Sonnambala at Lisbon as Escamillo in Carmen and the Dresdner Festival, Messiah; Le Comte Ory, Le Gouverneur, Glyndebourne, 1997–98; Alidoro in La Cenerentola, Achilles in Giulio Cesare for Metropolitan, 2000; Don Alfonso in Così fan tutte for Metropolitan Opera, 2001. *Recordings:* Salome, First Soldier, Berlin Philharmonic, 1991; Doctor, La Traviata, Metropolitan Opera, 1992. *Current Management:* c/o Martha Munro, Munro Artist Management, 786 Dartmouth Street, South Dartmouth, MA 02748, USA. *Telephone:* (508) 993-9011. *Fax:* (508) 993-9044. *E-mail:* operamom@aol.com. *Address:* 2805 Windy Hill Road, Allentown, PA 18103-4663, USA (home).

ROBERTI, Margherita; singer (soprano); b. 1930, Davenport, IA, USA. *Education:* Hunter Coll., Mannes School of Music, New York and studied in Italy. *Career:* debut at Teatro Alfieri Turin 1957, as Leonore in Il Trovatore; appeared at Covent Garden 1959 as Tosca; La Scala debut 1959 as Abigaille in Nabucco; engagements at the Verona Arena from 1959; Metropolitan Opera debut 1962 as Tosca; Edinburgh Festival 1963 as Luisa Miller and Glyndebourne Festival 1964 as Lady Macbeth; other roles include Elisabeth de Valois, Amelia in Un Ballo in Maschera, Hélène in Les Vêpres Siciliennes and Odabella in Atilla; guest appearances as concert artist in England and North America. *Recordings include:* Elena in Donizetti's Marino Faliero.

ROBERTS, Brenda; singer (soprano); b. 16 March 1945, Lowell, IN, USA. *Education:* Northwestern Univ., Evanstown with Hermann Baer, studied with Lotte Lehmann, Gerald Moore and Josef Metternich in Germany. *Career:* debut at Staatstheater Saarbrucken 1968 as Sieglinde in Die Walküre; German appearances at Düsseldorf, Essen, Frankfurt, Nuremberg, Wiesbaden and Wuppertal; mem., Hamburg Staatsoper; Bayreuth Festival 1974 as Brünnhilde in Siegfried; sang Isolde at Kassel 1983; American engagements in Baltimore, Chicago and San Francisco; Metropolitan Opera debut 1982 as the Dyer's Wife in Die Frau ohne Schatten; other roles include Salome at Vienna 1984 and Salome at Bremen 1986, Wagner's Senta and Elsa, Verdi's Elisabeth de Valois, Aida, Lady Macbeth, Leonora and Violetta, Mozart's Donna Elvira and Countess, Puccini's Tosca, Giorgetta and Turandot, Santuzza and Lulu; sang in a concert performance of Die Bakchantinnen by Egon Wellesz at Vienna 1985; Kiel Opera 1990 as Elektra and the title role in the premiere of Medea by Friedhelm Dohl; sang Schoenberg's Erwartung at Palermo 2000.

ROBERTS, Chris; record company executive. *Career:* fmr Pres., PolyGram Classics; Pres. of Classics & Jazz, Universal Music Group Int., Chair. Universal Classics Group, USA 1993–2010. *Address:* c/o Universal Music Group, 1755 Broadway, New York, NY 10019, USA (office). *Website:* www .universalmusicgroup.com (office).

ROBERTS, Deborah; British singer (soprano); b. 1952, England. *Education:* Nottingham Univ. and studied with Andrea von Ramm in Basle. *Career:* has sung with the Tallis Scholars on tours to Europe, Australia and the USA, appearing at most major festivals; guest concerts with the Deller Consort and the Consort of Musicke; frequent engagements with Musica Secreta, notably in the Early Music Centre Festival, the Lufthansa Festival of Baroque Music and at the National Gallery; Early Music Network tour of Britain with programme Filiae Jerusalem, sacred music for women's voices by Monteverdi, Carissimi, Cavalli, Viadana, Grandi and Marco da Gagliano; other repertoire includes works by Marenzio, Wert, Luzzaschi, Luigi Rossi and the composers Francesca Cacini and Barbara Strozzi; participation in lecture-recitals and workshops on performance practice and ornamentation. *Recordings:* with Musica Secreta, as musical director, Luzzaschi Madrigals for 1–3 Sopranos; Ensemble Music of Barbara Strozzi, 1994; over 30 recordings with Tallis Scholars. *Honours:* prizewinner Bruges Early Music Competition 1981.

ROBERTS, Eric; British singer (baritone); b. 16 Oct. 1944, Conway, North Wales. *Career:* opera debut as Papageno with WNO; has sung with various British cos, in roles including Guglielmo, Falke, Mozart's Figaro, Count and Trinity Moses in Mahagonny for Scottish Opera; ENO in Pacific Overtures and the British premiere of Rimsky's Christmas Eve 1988; mem. D'Oyly Carte Opera Co. 1988–90; further appearances as Don Alfonso for Opera North, Bartolo and Britten's Redburn for Scottish Opera, Don Isaac in the British premiere of Gerhard's The Duenna, Haly in L'Italiana in Algeri at Dublin, Eugene Onegin for Opera Omaha, Nebraska 1993; Australian debut as Bartolo, Lyric Opera of Queensland 1992; sang Don Isaac in Gerhard's The Duenna, Leeds 1996; concert engagements in Britten's War Requiem at Belgrade and L'Enfant et les Sortilèges at Rotterdam; season 2005–06 as

Bartolo in Il barbiere di Siviglia with WNO, Taxi Black/Dr Rook in One Touch of Venus, in Leeds, Ko-Ko in The Mikado with ENO, Dulcamara in L'elisir d'amore in Northington. *Current Management:* Musichall Ltd, Oast House, Crouch's Farm, Hollow Lane, East Hoathly, BN8 6QX, England. *E-mail:* info@musichall.uk.com. *Website:* www.musichall.uk.com.

ROBERTS, Kathleen; singer (soprano); b. 9 Oct. 1941, Hattiesburg, MS, USA. *Education:* Mississippi Coll., Texas Christian Univ., studied in Zürich and Darmstadt. *Career:* debut in St Gallen 1967 as Violetta; appearances at opera houses in Zürich, Geneva, Cologne and Frankfurt; mem., Darmstadt Opera as Marzelline in Fidelio, Micaela, Aennchen in Der Freischütz, Mozart's Pamina, Susanna and Constanze, Gretel, Martha and Mimi; modern repertoire has included Luise in Henze's Der Junge Lord and Laetita in The Old Maid and The Thief by Menotti; many concert appearances; teacher of singing in Darmstadt and elsewhere.

ROBERTS, Paul Anthony, BA; British pianist; b. 2 June 1949, Beaconsfield; two s. *Education:* Univ. of York, Royal Acad. of Music, , London. *Career:* juror, Int. Debussy Piano Competition, France 1982, 1984; cycle of Complete Debussy Piano Music at Purcell Room, London 1984; world premiere of Maurice Ohana's piano etudes in a live broadcast for Radio France 1986; premieres of Ohana work for BBC 1984, 1986, 1988; world premiere of original piano score of an unpublished opera by Debussy, Rodrigue et Chimène, BBC Radio 3 1988; Lecturer, then Prof. of Piano, Guildhall School of Music 1985–; Dir, International Piano Summer School, SW France; music at Ladevie. *Publications include:* contribs. to book reviews for Times Educational Supplement, Composer and Revue Musicale, Paris. *Website:* www.paulrobertspiano.com.

ROBERTS, Stephen Pritchard, ARCM, GRSM; British singer (baritone); *Professor, Vocal Faculty, Royal College of Music;* b. 8 Feb. 1949, Denbigh, Wales; s. of Edward Henry Roberts and Violet Pritchard. *Education:* Royal Coll. of Music, London. *Career:* professional lay cleric, Westminster Cathedral Choir 1972–76; sings regularly in London, the UK and throughout Europe with major orchestras and choral socs; has sung in USA, Canada, Israel, Hong Kong, Singapore, S Africa and S America; opera roles include Count in Marriage of Figaro, Falke in Die Fledermaus, Ubalde in Armide, Ramiro in Ravel's L'Heure Espagnole, Aeneas in Dido and Aeneas, Don Quixote in Master Peter's Puppet Show, Mittenhofer in Elegy for Young Lovers by Henze and Punch in Punch and Judy by Birtwistle; TV appearances include Britten's War Requiem, Weill's Seven Deadly Sins, Delius's Sea Drift, Handel's Jephtha and Judas Maccabaeus; has also taken part in numerous BBC Proms, including Penderecki's St Luke Passion 1983, Walton's Belshazzar's Feast 1984; has worked with numerous orchestras, vocal ensembles and conductors specialising in early and Baroque repertoire; concert and oratorio performer singing all major baritone roles by J. S. Bach, Mozart, Handel, Elgar and Britten, also choral symphonies by Mahler and Beethoven; sang in The Bach Choir's Easter performances of St Matthew Passion at Royal Festival Hall for 22 years; numerous recordings of the British baritone repertoire; Prof., Vocal Faculty, Royal Coll. of Music 1993–; visiting examiner and adjudicator for several music colls and orgs. *Recordings include:* numerous, many with King's Coll. and St John's Coll., Cambridge, and Bach Choir of London including: St Matthew Passion, Punch and Judy with London Sinfonietta, The Apostles with London Symphony Orchestra, Caractacus with London Symphony Orchestra, Fauré Requiem with Royal Philharmonic Orchestra, Messiah, Alexander's Feast, Carmina Burana with Berlin Radio Symphony Orchestra, St Luke Passion, King Priam with London Sinfonietta, and A Sea Symphony; Dyson Canterbury Pilgrims; three CDs of English Songs. *Address:* 144 Gleneagle Road, London, SW16 6BA, England (home). *E-mail:* srobertsbaritone@aol.com. *Website:* www.stephenroberts.uk.com.

ROBERTS, Susan; American singer (lyric-coloratura soprano); b. 1960; m. Dimitry Sitkovetsky 1983. *Career:* sang at first at the Bielefeld Opera then in Wiesbaden and Frankfurt; has sung Blonchen in productions of Die Entführung by Ruth Berghaus in Frankfurt, Giorgio Strehler in Bologna, Jean-Pierre Ponnelle in Cologne and Giancarlo del Monaco in Bonn; sang Minette in the premiere of Henze's English Cat at Frankfurt and again in Edinburgh and for the BBC; further appearances at the Bayreuth and Orange Festivals and other German theatres; Paris Opéra 1988 in the premiere of La Celestina by Maurice Ohana; season 1990–91 as Blondchen for Netherlands Opera and Zan in Blitzstein's Regina for Scottish Opera; concert engagements with radio orchestras in Vienna, Turin and Berlin, the National Orchestra of Spain, Orchestre Philharmonique Paris, Orchestre de Lyon and the Düsseldorf Symphonic; recitals at the Vassa, Lockenhaus and Schleswig-Holstein Festivals; season 1992 as Handel's Agrippina at the Buxton Festival; sang in Param Vir's Snatched by the Gods at the Almeida Theatre 1996; sang Poulenc's Thérèse for Grange Park Opera 1999. *Honours:* Martha Baird Rockefeller Foundation grant, Concours International Musicale Laureate, Geneva.

ROBERTSON, Christopher; American singer (baritone); b. 1964. *Education:* studied in San Francisco (Merola opera programme). *Career:* many appearances at Leading Opera Houses in North America and Europe; Metropolitan Opera, season 1992–93, as Marcello and Sharpless in Butterfly; Don Giovanni, 1995–96; European debut as Guglielmo at Frankfurt Opera, followed by Mozart's Count at Munich, Egberto in Verdi's Aroldo at Covent Garden, and Oreste in Gluck's Iphigénie en Tauride at the Berlin Staatsoper; Prus in The Makropulos Case at Vancouver, Germont for English National

Opera (1996) and Amonasro for San Francisco Opera (1997); Further engagements as Donner in Das Rheingold at Valencia, Count Luna with Florida Grand Opera, 1997 and Rigoletto with San Francisco Opera, also in 1997, Renato in Un Ballo in Maschera at Seattle and for Flanders Opera, and in Belgium, New Orleans, Montreal, Rio de Janeiro, Madrid and Santiago. *Honours:* Robert Jackson Memorial Grant, Richard Tucker Music Foundation. *Current Management:* c/o Columbia Artists Management, 1790 Broadway, New York, NY 10019-1412, USA. *Telephone:* (212) 841-9500. *Fax:* (212) 841 9744. *E-mail:* info@cami.com. *Website:* www.cami.com.

ROBERTSON, David; American conductor; *Music Director, St Louis Symphony Orchestra;* b. Santa Monica, California; m. Orli Shaham. *Education:* Royal Acad. of Music, London. *Career:* Conductor Jerusalem Symphony Orchestra 1985–87; Music Dir Ensemble Intercontemporain, Paris 1992–2000; Music Dir Orchestre Nat. de Lyon and Artistic Dir Lyon Auditorium 2000–04; Prin. Guest Conductor, BBC Symphony Orchestra 2005–12; Music Dir St Louis Symphony Orchestra 2005–(16); Chief Conductor and Artistic Dir, The Sydney Symphony 2014–; has conducted orchestras including Royal Concertgebouw, Orchestre de Paris, Berlin Philharmonic, Hamburg NDR Symphony, Bayerischer Rundfunk Symphonieorchester, Staatskapelle Dresden, Swedish Radio Orchestra, Filarmonica della Scala, Milan, Tonhalle Zürich, the Berlin, New York and Los Angeles Philharmonics and the symphony orchestras of Atlanta, Boston, Chicago, Cleveland, Dallas, Detroit and San Francisco; conducted US premieres of Berio's Stanze 2005, Saariaho's Adriana Songs 2006, Adams' Doctor Atomic Symphony 2008, Saariaho's Mirage 2009, Turnage's A Prayer Out of Stillness 2009, Mackey's Violin Concerto and Time Release 2009; world premiere of Danielpour's Songs of Solitude, with Philadelphia Orchestra and Thomas Hampson 2005, Fedele's Les 33 Noms 2009, Hayden's Substratum 2009, Meredith Monk's Weave with St Louis Symphony Orchestra 2010, Stephen McNeff's Concerto-Duo with BBC Symphony Orchestra 2010; French premiere of Birtwistle's Theseus Games, with Ensemble Intercontemporain 2005; opera engagements have included Metropolitan Opera, Opéra de Lyon, La Scala, Bayerische Staatsoper, Paris Châtelet, Hamburg State Opera, San Francisco Opera; has given master classes at Paris Conservatory, Juilliard School, Tanglewood, Aspen Music Festival; Fellow, American Acad. of Arts and Sciences 2010. *Recordings:* Milhaud, Works for Piano and Orchestra 1993, Edouard Lalo, Namoura, Musique de Ballet 1995, Silvestrov, Symphony No. 5 1996, Jessye Norman, In the Spirit 1996, Manoury, 60th Parallel 1999, Dusapin, Extenso 2000, Ginastera, Estacia 2001, Bartók, The Miraculous Mandarin 2002, Boulez, Rituel in memoriam Bruno Maderna 2003, Steve Reich, Different Trains 2004, Dvořák, Secrets of Dvořák's Cello Concerto 2005, Bolcom, Satie and Schoenberg "Surprise" 2007, Adams, Doctor Atomic Symphony 2009. *Honours:* Dr hc (Maryville Univ.) 2007, (Webster Univ.) 2009, (Westminster Choir Coll.) 2010; Musical America Conductor of the Year 2000, Ditson Conductor's Award 2006, ASCAP Morton Gould Award for Innovative Programming 2006, ASCAP Award for Programming of Contemporary Music 2009, 2010, Excellence in the Arts Award, St Louis Arts and Educ. Council 2010. *Current Management:* c/o Opus 3 Artists, 470 Park Avenue South, 9th Floor North, New York, NY 10016, USA. *Telephone:* (212) 584-7520. *Fax:* (646) 500-8220. *E-mail:* info@opus3artists.com. *Website:* www.opus3artists.com. *Address:* St Louis Symphony Orchestra, 718 North Grand Boulevard, St Louis, MO 63103, USA (office). *Telephone:* (314) 533-2500 (office). *E-mail:* artistic@stlsymphony.org (office). *Website:* www.stlsymphony.org (office).

ROBERTSON, John; Scottish singer (tenor); b. 20 Sept. 1938, Galashiels. *Education:* Sedburgh and Edinburgh Univs. *Career:* regular appearances with Scottish Opera; 850 performances in 50 roles, including Ferrando, Tamino, Ottavio, Albert Herring and Almaviva; has toured with the co. to Austria, Germany, Switzerland, Yugoslavia, Poland, Portugal and Iceland in The Turn of the Screw, The Rape of Lucretia and A Midsummer Night's Dream; appearances at Edinburgh as Tannhäuser and in Le nozze di Figaro; has directed the Edinburgh Opera in La Traviata, L'Elisir d'amore and La Sonnambula; oratorio and concert work throughout Scotland and on BBC and Scottish television; teaches voice in Glasgow and Edinburgh and at the School of Vocal Studies at the Royal Northern Coll. of Music, Manchester. *Recordings include:* Le nozze di Figaro.

ROBERTSON, Stewart John; British conductor, pianist and music director; *Artistic Director and Principal Conductor, Atlantic Classical Orchestra;* b. 22 May 1948, Glasgow, Scotland; m. Meryl Robertson; one s. one d. *Education:* Royal Scottish Acad. of Music, Bristol Univ., Vienna Acad., Salzburg Mozarteum, studied with Otmar Suitner, Hans Swarowsky and Denis Matthews. *Career:* Asst Chorus Master, Scottish Opera, Edinburgh Festival Chorus 1968–69; Chorus Master, London City Singers 1970–72; Conductor, Cologne Opera 1972–75; Music Dir, Tanz Forum, Zürich Opera 1975–76, Scottish Opera Touring Co. 1976–79; Asst Conductor, Oakland Symphony Orchestra 1985–86; Music Dir and Prin. Conductor, Glimmerglass Opera, New York 1987–2006, Dir Emer. 2006–; Music Dir and Prin. Conductor, Florida Grand Opera, Miami 1997–2009; Artistic Dir and Prin. Conductor, Opera Omaha 2005–08; Music Dir and Prin. Conductor, Atlantic Classical Orchestra 2005–; Guest Conductor for Netherlands Symphony Orchestra, North German Philharmonic, Louisville Orchestra, Ukraine State Philharmonic Orchestra, Sicily Symphony Orchestra, New York City Opera, Lyric Opera of Chicago, Deutsche Oper am Rhein, Royal Scottish Nat. Orchestra, BBC Scottish Symphony Orchestra, City of Birmingham Symphony Orchestra, Swiss-Italian Radio Symphony Orchestra, Buenos Aires

Philharmonic, Utah Symphony Orchestra, Montréal Opera, the Puccini Festival, Torre del Lago, Italy, Wexford Festival, Ireland; special interest in contemporary music having performed over 100 world premieres; especially noted for performances of British repertoire, in particular Benjamin Britten; radio broadcasts on BBC, NPR; TV appearances on PBS, Great Performances Series, Live From Lincoln Centre, Swiss Italian Television; numerous recordings on various labels. *Current Management:* c/o Dean Artists Management, 204 St George Street, Toronto, ON M5R 2W5, Canada. *Telephone:* (416) 969-7300. *E-mail:* admin@deanarts.com. *Website:* www.deanartists.com. *Address:* 81 Poppy Road, Carmel Valley, CA 93924, USA (home); Dunmore House, by Tarbert, Argyll, PA29 6XZ, Scotland (home). *Telephone:* (831) 659-4375 (Carmel Valley) (home); (1880) 821123 (Tarbert) (home). *Fax:* (831) 659-7959 (Carmel Valley) (home). *E-mail:* poppyroad@aol.com (home).

ROBINS, Brian Martin; British writer, lecturer, broadcaster and music historian; b. 2 Jan. 1940, Cheltenham, Glos., England; partner Anne Young; one s. one d. *Education:* Univ. of London. *Career:* classical record retailer 1957–90; adult educ. lecturer 1984–87; freelance writer and lecturer 2001–; Visiting Fellow, Univ. of Southampton; BBC Radio 3 broadcasts and script writing; mem. Royal Musical Asscn. *Publications include:* The John Marsh Journals (vol. 1) 1998 (revised edn 2011), The Catch and Glee in 18th Century Provincial England (in Concert Life in Eighteenth-Century Britain) 2004, Catch and Glee Culture in Eighteenth-Century England 2006, The John Marsh Journals (vol. 2) 2013; contrib. to New Grove Dictionary of Music and Musicians 2000, New Dictionary of National Biography 2004, Early Music, The Journal of the Royal Musical Association, Fanfare (USA), Goldberg Early Music Magazine (Spain), Gramophone, Early Music Today, Early Music Review, Opera Magazine (UK). *Honours:* Andrew W. Mellon Fellowship 1994, British Acad. Exchange Fellowship to Huntington Library, San Marino, USA 2000, Leverhulme Trust Fellowship 2001. *Address:* Lazerton Farm Cottage, Stourpaine, Blandford Forum, Dorset, DT11 8PW, England (home). *Telephone:* (1258) 489882 (home); 7866-641938 (mobile) (home). *E-mail:* brianrobins731@btinternet.com; brianrobins@earlymusicworld.com. *Website:* www.earlymusicworld.com.

ROBINSON, Christopher John, CVO, CBE, BMus, MA, FRCO; British organist and fmr conductor; b. 20 April 1936, Peterborough, Cambs., England; s. of the late John Robinson; m. Shirley Ann Churchman 1962; one s. one d. *Education:* St Michael's Coll., Tenbury, Rugby and Christ Church, Oxford. *Career:* Asst Organist, Christ Church, Oxford 1955–58, New Coll., Oxford 1957–58; Music Master, Oundle School 1959–62; Asst Organist, Worcester Cathedral 1962–63, Organist and Master of Choristers 1963–74; Organist and Choirmaster, St George's Chapel, Windsor Castle 1975–91; Conductor City of Birmingham Choir 1964–2002, Oxford Bach Choir 1977–97, Leith Hill Musical Festival 1977–80; Organist and Dir of Music, St John's Coll., Cambridge 1991–2003 (fmr Conductor Choir of St John's Coll.); Fellow, St John's Coll., Cambridge 1991–; Acting Dir, Clare Coll., Cambridge 2005–06; Pres. Royal Coll. of Organists 1982–84. *Recordings:* Parry, Cathedral Music 1994, Tavener, Sacred Works 1994, Mendelssohn, Church Music 1998, Howells, Requiem 1999, Tavener, Christmas Proclamation 2000, Britten, Rejoice in the Lamb 2000, Rubbra, Magnificat and Nunc Dimittis in A-flat 2001, Walton, English Choral Music 2002, Finzi, Lo, the full, final sacrifice Op. 26 2002, Leighton, Sacred Choral Music 2004, Elgar, Sacred Choral Music 2004, Duruflé, Requiem, Berkeley, Crux fidelis Op. 43 No. 1, Stanford, Anthems and Services. *Honours:* Hon. MMus (Birmingham) 1987; Hon. MusD (Lambeth) 2002; Hon. Fellow, Univ. of Central England 1990; Hon. RAM; Hon. FGCM 2002. *Current Management:* c/o Martin Denny Management Ltd, 11 High Street, Windsor, Berks. SL4 1LD, England. *Telephone:* (1753) 831353. *E-mail:* martin@martindenny.co.uk. *Address:* St John's College, Cambridge, CB2 1TP, England (office).

ROBINSON, Dean; Australian opera singer (bass); b. 20 Aug. 1968, Bathurst, NSW. *Education:* studied in Australia and at Royal Northern Coll. of Music, Manchester, UK. *Career:* opera engagements at Covent Garden in Don Carlos, Die Meistersinger, Lohengrin, Palestrina (also at Metropolitan Opera) and Ariadne auf Naxos; for ENO Colline in La Bohème, 2nd Soldier in Salome, Pluto in Orfeo and created role of Passauf in Gavin Bryars' Dr Ox's Experiment; Colline, Mr Ratcliffe in Billy Budd and Angelotti for Welsh Nat. Opera; Sparafucile and Sarastro for Scottish Opera; Colline, Sparafucile and Don Giovanni with Mid Wales Opera; Claudio in Agrippina, Polyphemus in Acis and Galataea, and King of Scotland in Ariodante, for The Early Opera Co.; Death in The Emperor of Atlantis for Mecklenburgh Opera; with English Touring Opera Sarastro, and Comte de Grieux in Manon; concerts include St John Passion at Westminster Abbey, Mozart Requiem with Eric Ericsson, Messiah with Sir John Eliot Gardiner and the English Baroque Soloists, L'enfance du Christ with Kent Nagano, Verdi's Requiem with Sir David Willcocks. *Recordings:* Don Pedro in Beatrice et Benedict with Sir Colin Davis and the London Symphony Orchestra; Masetto in Don Giovanni; Duca d'Argile in La Prigione di Edimburgo for Opera Rara and appearances on several Opera Rara recital discs. *Films:* First Officer in The Death of Klinghoffer for Channel 4 TV, Goffredo in Armida (Judith Weir) for Channel 4 TV. *E-mail:* deanrobinson@orange.net (home). *Current Management:* c/o Harlequin Agency Limited, 203 Fidlas Road, Cardiff, CF14 5NA, Wales. *Telephone:* (29) 2075-0821. *Fax:* (29) 2075-5971. *E-mail:* doreen@harlequin-agency.co.uk. *Website:* www.harlequin-agency.co.uk. *E-mail:* deanrobinson@orange.net (home).

ROBINSON, Ethna; Irish singer (mezzo-soprano); b. 20 June 1956, Dublin. *Education:* studied in Birmingham and at the Guildhall School, London. *Career:* ENO from 1984, as Rosette in Manon and in the British premiere of Akhnaten by Glass; Premieres of Birtwistle's The Mask of Orpheus, 1986, and Harvey's Inquest of Love, 1993; other roles have included Mozart's Dorabella and Cherubino, Hansel, Olga in Eugene Onegin, Berlioz's Béatrice, Margret in Wozzeck, and Pauline in The Queen of Spades; Tour of Russia with ENO, 1990; season 1998 as The Prioress in Suor Angelica for ENO, and Third Lady in The Magic Flute; Season 2000–01 as St Theresa III in Thomson's Four Saints in Three Acts, for ENO, and Larina in Eugene Onegin for Opera North. *Recordings include:* Video of ENO Mikado. *Current Management:* c/o Owen/White Management, Flat 6, 22 Brunswick Terrace, Hove, East Sussex BN3 1HJ, England. *Telephone:* (1273) 727127. *Fax:* (1273) 527038. *E-mail:* info@owenwhitemanagement.com. *Website:* www.owenwhitemanagement.com.

ROBINSON, Faye; American singer (soprano); b. 2 Nov. 1943, Houston, TX. *Education:* Texas Southern Univ. with Ruth Stewart, studied with Ellen Faull in New York. *Career:* debut at New York City Opera 1972, as Micaela; has sung Violetta, the Queen of Shemakha and Liu in New York; Washington Civic Opera 1973 as Violetta and Juliette; Jackson, FL 1974–75 as Desdemona and Adina; Aix-en-Provence 1975 in Der Schauspieldirektor and La Serva Padrona; engagements in Houston, Barcelona and Frankfurt; Buenos Aires 1980 in Les Contes d'Hoffmann; Schwetzingen Festival 1981 as Elektra in Idomeneo; Paris Opéra and Bordeaux 1982 as Juliette and Luisa Miller; other roles include Constanze, Norina and Oscar; sang in the premiere of The Mask of Time in Boston 1984 and in the first British performance of Tippett's oratorio; Cologne 1988 as Constanze. *Recordings:* Mahler's 8th Symphony, The Mask of Time.

ROBINSON, James; American opera producer; *Artistic Director, Opera Theater of Saint Louis*; b. Claremore, Okla. *Education:* studied composition with Dominick Argento. *Career:* began career as Asst, Santa Fe Opera; fmr Dir with New England Conservatory opera programme; Artistic Dir, Opera Colorado 2000–08; Artistic Dir, Opera Theater of Saint Louis 2009–; considered to be most widely performed opera dir in N America; has produced operas for New York City Opera, Canadian Opera Co., Santa Fe Opera, San Francisco Opera, Seattle Opera, Minnesota Opera, Boston Lyric Opera, Houston Grand Opera, Boston Lyric Opera, Opera Colorado, Royal Swedish Opera, Opera Ireland, Opera Australia, Welsh Nat. Opera. *Productions include:* Il Trittico, Nabucco, Norma, Abduction from the Seraglio, Nixon in China, La Bohème, Turandot, L'Elisir d'Amore, Hansel and Gretel, Giulio Cesare, Elektra, The Rake's Progress, Eugene Onegin, Katya Kabanova, Rinaldo, Radimisto, The Ghosts of Versailles. *Address:* Opera Theater of Saint Louis, PO Box 191910, St Louis, MO 63119-7910, USA (office). *Telephone:* (314) 961-0171 (office). *Website:* www.opera-stl.org (office).

ROBINSON, Michael Finlay, BA, BMus, MA, DPhil, DMus; British academic (retd); *Professor Emeritus of Music, Cardiff University*; b. 3 March 1933, Gloucester, England; m. Ann James 1961; two s. *Education:* Univ. of Oxford. *Career:* teacher, Royal Scottish Acad. of Music 1960–61; Music Lecturer, Univ. of Durham 1961–65; Asst Prof., McGill Univ., Montreal, Canada 1965–67, Assoc. Prof. 1967–70; Music Lecturer, Cardiff Univ. 1970–75, Sr Lecturer in Music 1975–91, Head of Music Dept 1987–94, Prof. of Music 1991–94, Prof. Emer. of Music 1995–. *Compositions:* String Quartet 1972, A Pretty How Town for baritone and eight instrumentalists 1983, Fantasy for unaccompanied cello 1997, The House of Bernarda Alba, opera 2005, A Welsh Garland for wind band 2007, A Gloucester Lad for tenor and orchestra 2014, other chamber music, songs. *Publications:* Opera Before Mozart 1966, Naples and Neapolitan Opera 1972, Giovanni Paisiello: A Thematic Catalogue of His Works Vol. 1 1991, Vol. 2 1993; contrib. to Proceedings of the Royal Musical Association, New Grove, Chigiana, Studi Musicali, Soundings, Early Music, Music and Letters, The Alternative Endings of Mozart's Don Giovanni (in Opera Buffa in Mozart's Vienna) 1997, Time in Western Music 2013. *Address:* Northridge House, Usk Road, Shirenewton, Mon., NP16 6RZ, Wales (home). *Telephone:* (1292) 641538 (home). *E-mail:* northridge33@icloud.com. *Website:* michaelfrobinson.org.uk.

ROBINSON, Paul; British singer (baritone); b. 1970, England. *Education:* chorister and choral scholar King's Coll., Cambridge, Royal Coll. of Music. *Career:* concerts include St John Passion at the London Bach Festival, Bach's Magnificat at Bristol Cathedral, Monteverdi Vespers in Vancouver, St Matthew Passion for Italian radio and Schubertiade recital at the Wigmore Hall; Mozart's Coronation Mass with the Royal Flanders Philharmonic Orchestra, Purcell's Indian Queen with the Acad. of Ancient Music, Messiah with the CBSO and Haydn's Mariazeller Mass at Canterbury Cathedral; opera roles include The Speaker in The Magic Flute for Opera West, Mangus in Tippett's Knot Garden and Janáček's Poacher and Britten's Demetrius for the RAM; season 1997–98 with the Brahms Requiem in London, Bach's Christmas Oratorio in Oxford, St John Passion with the Royal Liverpool Philharmonic Orchestra, Carmina Burana at Bristol and Handel's Joshua with the Acad. of Ancient Music. *Recordings:* albums with King's Coll. Choir, Robert in Hugh the Drover by Vaughan Williams.

ROBINSON, Peter, MA, FRCO; British conductor and vocal coach; *Artistic Director, British Youth Opera*; b. 24 June 1949, Hartlepool, England; s. of Eric Leslie Robinson and Winifred Robinson; m. Sally-Ann Shepherdson 2004. *Education:* West Hartlepool Grammar School, St John's Coll., Univ. of Oxford. *Career:* Asst Organist, Durham Cathedral 1970–71; associated with Glyndebourne Festival Opera music staff 1971–73; Head of Music Staff and Resident Conductor, Australian Opera 1973–80; Asst Music Dir, ENO 1981–89, conducting Le nozze di Figaro, Don Giovanni, Die Zauberflöte, Così fan tutte, Otello, Rigoletto, The Mastersingers, Madama Butterfly, Orfeo, Maria Stuarda, The Mikado, Carmen, Werther, Hansel and Gretel, Simon Boccanegra and The Turn of the Screw; conducted Così fan tutte in a production for BBC TV; has conducted in Australia for Victoria State Opera (Le Nozze di Figaro, Die Entführung, La Bohème), Opera Australia (Così fan tutte, Orfée), State Opera of South Australia (Don Giovanni, Otello, La Bohème, Così fan tutte), West Australian Opera, (Carmen, Roméo et Juliette, Lucia di Lammermoor), Opera Queensland (La Bohème, Madama Butterfly, Andrea Chénier, Turandot); in UK for Kent Opera (The Beggar's Opera and Don Giovanni), Opera Factory London (Marriage of Figaro, also for TV, The Coronation of Poppea), for Raymond Gubbay Ltd, Royal Albert Hall (Madama Butterfly, Tosca, Aïda, Carmen) 1998–2009, Opera Holland Park (Fidelio, Luisa Miller, Andrea Chénier, Rigoletto, L'amore dei tre re, La Gioconda, Un Ballo in Maschera) 2003–09, Scottish Opera (Falstaff) 2008, British Youth Opera (The Magic Flute, The Rape of Lucretia, Roméo et Juliette, Eugene Onegin, Albert Herring, La Rondine) 1996–2009; concerts with the LSO, LPO, RPO, BBCCO, etc; Prof., Guildhall School of Music & Drama; Visiting Coach, Nat. Opera Studio and Royal Acad. of Music; Artistic Dir British Youth Opera 2006–. *Current Management:* c/o Musichall Ltd, Oast House, Crouch's Farm, Hollow Lane, East Hoathly, BN8 6QX; 9 Westbury Road, Bounds Green, London, N11 2DB, England. *E-mail:* info@musichall.uk.com. *Website:* www .musichall.uk.com.

ROBINSON, Sharon, BM; American cellist; *Professor of Cello, Indiana University*; b. 2 Dec. 1949, Houston, TX; m. Jaime Laredo 1976. *Education:* North Carolina School of the Arts, Univ. of Southern California, Peabody Conservatory of Music. *Career:* debut in New York 1974; mem., Kalichstein-Laredo-Robinson Trio from 1976; soloist at Marlboro Music Festival, Mostly Mozart Festival and South Bank Festival in London, Edinburgh Festival, Madeira Bach Festival, Helsinki Festival and Tivoli Gardens; commissioned and premiered Ned Rorem's After Reading Shakespeare for solo cello and premiered Alan Shulman's Kol Nidrei for cello and piano, William Bland's Rhapsody for cello and piano, and Robert Blake's Cello Sonata; recent commissions and premieres include Double Concertos by Ned Rorem, Ellen Zwilich, Richard Danielpour, Daron Aric Hagen, triple concertos by Ellen Zwilich and David Ott; trios by Leon Kirchner, Arvo Pärt, Stanley Silverman, Hallgrimsson, Richard Danielpour, Ellen Zwilich, duos (violin and cello) by Robert Staren, David Ott, Maurice Gardner, Andrew Stein; Ensemble-in-Residence, Kennedy Center, Washington, DC 2002–; Tenured Prof. of Cello, Indiana Univ. 2005–; mem. Violoncello Soc. of America. *Recordings:* Vivaldi Sonatas, Fauré's Elegy, Debussy Sonata, Rorem's After Reading Shakespeare, Beethoven's Triple Concerto, Mendelssohn and Brahms Trios (with Kalich-stein-Laredo-Robinson Trio), Duos for Violin and Cello (with Jaime Laredo), Double and Triple Concertos by Ellen Zwilich, Double Concertos by Ned Rorem and Richard Danielpour, all works for strings and piano by Shostakovich and Ravel, complete Beethoven Trios Cycle. *Honours:* Pro Musicis Foundation Award 1974, Levintritt Award 1975, Avery Fisher Award 1979, Ensemble of the Year (Musical America) 2001, Samuel Sanders Collaborative Award 2002. *Address:* University of Indiana Bloomington, Merrill Hall MU114, 107 South Indiana Avenue, Bloomington, IN 47405-7000, USA (office). *Telephone:* (812) 856-7036 (office). *E-mail:* shhrobin@ indiana.edu (office). *Website:* www.indiana.edu (office).

ROBINSON, Timothy; British singer (tenor); b. 1968. *Education:* New Coll., Oxford and Guildhall School with William McAlpine. *Career:* began career giving recitals with orchestras including BBC Symphony Orchestra, Royal Philharmonic, Scottish Chamber Orchestra and Orchestra of the Age of Enlightenment; further concerts include Mozart's Davidde Penitente at Seville, Messiah in Singapore, Weber's Euryanthe at the Queen Elizabeth Hall, South Bank, London and Proms debut as Jupiter in Semele, under William Christie 1996; opera roles include Kudrjash in Katya Kabanova for Glyndebourne Touring Opera, Fenton and Scaramuccio (Ariadne auf Naxos) for English Nat. Opera and Jupiter at the Aix-en-Provence Festival (French premiere, 1996); mem. Royal Opera, appearing in such operas as Nabucco, La Traviata and Fedora; sang in British premiere of Pfitzner's Palestrina 1997; season 1997–98 in Katya Kabanova at Glyndebourne and in Turandot at the Paris Opéra; other roles include Don Ottavio, Tamino and Alfredo, with Travelling Opera; Arminio in Verdi's Masnadieri for the Royal Opera 1998; sang St John in The Kingdom by Elgar, London Proms 1999; London Proms, 2002; Third Jew in Salome for Salzburg Easter Festival 2011, Baden Baden Festival 2011, Royal Opera Covent Garden 2012; Don Basilio in Le nozze di Figaro, ENO 2011. *Recordings include:* Bach's Magnificat; Vaughan Williams Serenade to Music; Beethoven Cantatas, Purcell, Sacred Music 2000, Schumann, Liederkreis: Romanzen and Balladen 2000, Verdi, Opera Arias 2001, Fauré, Requiem 2003, Mozart, Great Mass in C Minor 2005, Smetana, The Bartered Bride 2005, Szymanowski, Harnasie, Orchestral Songs 2006, Schubert, Messe in Es/Mozart, Vesparae Solennes de Confessore 2009. *Current Management:* Askonas Holt, Lincoln House, 300 High Holborn, London WC1V 7JH, England. *Telephone:* (20) 7400-1700. *Website:* www .askonasholt.co.uk.

ROBISON, Paula; flautist; b. 8 June 1941, Nashville, TN, USA; m. Scott Nickrenz; one d. *Career:* founding mem., Chamber Music Soc. of Lincoln Center; jt recitalist with pianist Ruth Laredo and guitarist Eliot Fisk; soloist,

New York Philharmonic, Atlanta, American and San Francisco Symphony Orchestra; recitalist at numerous venues including Carnegie Hall and Kennedy Center and Wigmore Hall 1990; commissioned and premiered Kirchner's music for flute and orchestra with the Indianapolis Symphony, Toru Takemitsu's I Hear the Water Dreaming, Robert Beaser's Song of the Bells; numerous television appearances, including Live from Lincoln Center 1984–85, Christmas at the Kennedy Center, Sunday Morning (CBS); Co-Dir of Chamber Music, Spoleto Festival at Charleston, SC, and Spoleto, Italy 1978–1988; Blue Ridge Airs II for flute and orchestra, Kenneth Frazelle 1991; soloist, London Symphony Orchestra, Michael Tilson Thomas 1995; I Solisti Veneti, Claudio Scimone 1995. *Recordings include:* Flute Music of the Romantic Era, The Sonatas for Flute and Harpsichord by J. S. Bach (complete) and G. F. Handel (complete) with Kenneth Cooper, American Masterworks for flute and piano. *Address:* c/o London Symphony Orchestra, Barbican Centre, Silk Street, London, EC2, England.

ROBLES, Marisa, HRCM, FRCM; British concert harpist; b. 4 May 1937, Madrid, Spain; d. of Cristóbal Robles and María Bonilla; m. 3rd David Bean 1985; two s. one d. from previous marriages. *Education:* Madrid Royal Conservatoire of Music. *Career:* Prof. of Harp, Madrid Royal Conservatoire of Music 1958–63; Harp Tutor, Nat. Youth Orchestra of GB 1964–85; Prof. of Harp, Royal Coll. of Music, London 1969–94; Artistic Dir World Harp Festival, Cardiff, Wales 1991, World Harp Festival II 1994; appearances as soloist with all maj. orchestras in GB and throughout the world, including New York Philharmonic; chamber music performances with Marisa Robles and Friends, Marisa Robles Harp Ensemble, Marisa Robles Trio and other chamber groups; solo recitals in Australia, Canada, Europe, Japan, NZ, S America and the USA; many TV appearances and radio performances; masterclasses in GB and abroad; four recordings of Mozart's Flute and Harp Concerto with James Galway (q.v.) and more than 20 other recordings. *Publications:* several harp pieces and arrangements. *Address:* 38 Luttrell Avenue, London, SW15 6PE, England (home). *Telephone:* (20) 8785-2204 (home).

ROBLOU, David, ARAM, Dip RAM, LRAM, ARCM, ARCO; British conductor, harpsichordist, organist, pianist and vocal coach; b. 23 Dec. 1949, London, England. *Education:* Royal Acad. of Music, London, masterclasses with Nadia Boulanger (London) and Kenneth Gilbert (Antwerp). *Career:* Artistic and Musical Dir, Midsummer Opera; Prof., Guildhall School of Music and Drama 1974; mem. Musicians' Union, Incorporated Soc. of Musicians. *Recordings:* numerous chamber music recordings with New London Consort, including harpsichord solo, J. S. Bach: Brandenburg Concerto No. 5. *Current Management:* c/o Sounds Lyrical Artists Management, 109 Algernon Road, London, SE13 7AP, England. *Telephone:* (20) 7652-0070. *E-mail:* sounds.lyrical@ ntlworld.com. *Telephone:* (20) 8690-5652; 7973-758218 (mobile). *Fax:* (20) 7652-0070. *E-mail:* dj.roblou@ntlworld.com.

ROBSON, Christopher; Scottish opera and concert singer (countertenor), actor and singing teacher; b. 9 Dec. 1953, Falkirk, Scotland; s. of the late Salvation Army officers Brig. John Thomas Robson and Eva Elizabeth Robson (née Leathem); m. Laura Carin Snelling 1974 (divorced 1984); one s. (with Samantha Lambourne, separated) and one s. with current pnr Marie Reich. *Education:* Stockport Tech. High School, Portsmouth Tech. High School, Westcliff High School for Boys, Cambridge Coll. of Arts and Tech., Trinity Coll. of Music, London, singing studies with Nigel Wickens, James Gaddarn, pvt. singing studies with Paul Esswood and Helga Mott; master classes with Geoffrey Parsons; Britten-Pears School, studies with Peter Pears, John Shirley Quirk, Laura Sarti, Rae Woodland and Thomas Helmsley. *Career:* concert debut in Handel's Samson, Queen Elizabeth Hall, London 1975; opera debut, Handel's Sosarme, Barber Inst., Birmingham 1979; Guest Prin. Artist, ENO, London 1981–2012, Bavarian State Opera, Munich 1994–2006; prin. roles world-wide, including Kent Opera, Handel Opera Soc., Opera Factory, London, Royal Opera, Covent Garden, Glyndebourne, Frankfurt Opera, Sächsische Staatsoper, Dresden, Badische Staatstheater, Karlsruhe, Berliner Kammeroper, Houston Grand Opera, New York City Opera, Chicago Lyric Opera, Opera Factory Zürich, Nancy Opera, Innsbruck Tirolertheater, São Paulo Opera, Vlaamse Opera, Opera de Liège, Royal Opera Copenhagen; concerts and major festivals world-wide; radio and TV broadcasts world-wide; mem. Monteverdi Choir 1974–86, London Oratory Choir 1974–80, The Spieglers 1975–82, St George's Elizabethan Theatre, London 1975–76, Hilliard Ensemble 1979–81, Westminster Cathedral Choir 1980–85, King's Consort 1981–86, New London Consort 1982–2013; first countertenor to sing on Kiev Opera and Bolshoi Opera stages (Xerxes) on ENO Soviet Union tour 1990; UK premieres include Bruno Maderna's Satyricon (Habinnas), Aribert Reimann's Lear (Edgar/Mad Tom), Philip Glass's Akhnaten (title role), Olga Neuwirth's Lost Highway (Mystery Man); several roles created for world premieres, including Damon Albarn's Dr Dee (Kelley), John Lunn's The Maids (Claire), Jonathan Dove's Flight (Refugee), Alexander Strauch's Utoper (Thomas More/Seeker), Christoph Reiserer's President Jekyll (Prof. Weiss). *Plays:* Faust I & II (Goethe), Badische Staatschauspiel Karlsruhe. *Films:* Hell for Leather, A Night with Handel, Giulio Cesare, Xerxes, Rodelinda, Ariodante, Summertime Blues. *Television includes:* A Night with Handel (Channel 4/NVC/Warner Music), Xerxes (Thames TV/Channel 4/RM Arts/ Arthaus), Ariodante (BBC/RM Arts/Arthaus), Hail Bright Cecilia (Channel 4/ EMI), The Rake's Progress, Rodelinda (Bayerische Rundfunk), Flight (Chan-nel 4), Canticle IV (IdTv Holland/Arte), Giulio Cesare (Danish TV/Harmonia Mundi), Singing Voice Froschkoenig (Bavaria). *Recordings include:* Golem, John Casken; Flight, Jonathan Dove; Total Eclipse, Tavener; Resurrection,

Maxwell Davies; The Ice Break, Tippett; Kabbala, Clemencic; Venus & Adonis, Blow; Psyche, Locke; Artaxerxes, Arne; Magnificat, Cantatas 35/78/ 137, Johannes Passion, Bach; Xerxes, Ariodante, Giulio Cesare, Ezio, Belshazzar, Saul, Messiah, Handel; Gloria, Nisi Dominus, Vivaldi; St Cecilia Odes, Queen Mary Birthday Odes, Purcell; Requiem, Marienvespers, Biber; L'Orfeo, 1610 Marienvespers, Monteverdi; Missa Scala Aretina, Valls; Cadfael, Towns; Nine Lives of Thomas Katz, Scherrer, Doctor Dee (an English Opera), Damon Albarn. *Honours:* Bayerischer Kammersänger 2003; Young Musician Award, Greater London Arts Asscn 1979, first recipient of Wrocławskiego Szermierza Prize, Wrocław Int. Music Festival (Poland) 1991, Opernfestspiel Prize, Munich 1997, 2002. *Current Management:* c/o Neil Dalrymple, Music International, 13 Ardilaun Road, London, N5 2QR, England. *Telephone:* (20) 7359-5183 (office). *E-mail:* neil@musicint.co.uk. *Website:* www.musicint.co.uk. *E-mail:* contact@christopher-robson.com. *Website:* www.christopher-robson.com.

ROBSON, Elizabeth; singer (soprano); b. 1938, Dundee, Scotland; m. Neil Howlett. *Education:* Royal Scottish Acad. of Music and studied in Florence. *Career:* debut at Sadler's Wells 1961 as Micaela; appearances at Covent Garden throughout the 1960s as Musetta, Zdenka, Sophie, Susanna, Pamina, Marzelline and Nannetta in Falstaff; guest appearances with Scottish Opera as Zerlina and at the 1967 Edinburgh Festival as Anne Trulove in The Rake's Progress; sang also at Aix-en-Provence and La Scala Milan; noted concert artist. *Recordings:* Marzelline in Fidelio.

ROBSON, Nigel; singer (tenor); b. 1955, Argyllshire, Scotland. *Education:* Royal Northern Coll. of Music with Alexander Young. *Career:* sang with the Glyndebourne Festival Chorus and ENO from 1981 as Monteverdi's Orfeo and in the premiere of Birtwistle's The Mask of Orpheus 1986; British stage premiere of Weill's Der Protagonist; sang Ferrando in Così fan tutte and in David Freeman's production of Falstaff, in the premiere of Michael Finnissy's The Undivine Comedy and in Tippett's Songs for Dov conducted by Tippett; La Finta Giardiniera for Opera North and Don Ottavio in Don Giovanni for Opera Factory; Idomeneo at Munich 1996 and sang in new production of Monteverdi's Ulysses for Opera North 1997; appearances with the Monteverdi Choir and Orchestra including tours of Italy, Germany and France; performances of Monteverdi's Vespers in Venice and Orfeo in Spain as well as Idomeneo in Lisbon, Paris, Amsterdam and London; sang Handel's Jephtha at the Handel Festival in Göttingen and the Holland Festival; sang the Anonymous Voice in the British premiere of Tippett's New Year at Glyndebourne 1990; concerts at the Festival Hall with Janáček's Glagolitic Mass, with the Ensemble Intercontemporain in Paris and with the London Sinfonietta in Henze's Voices 1991; season 1992 as Claggart in Billy Budd for Scottish Opera and Nero in The Coronation of Poppea for Opera Factory; other roles include the title role in Idomeneo at the Bayerische Staatsoper; Ulisse in Il Ritorno d'Ulisse in Patria and Pandarus in Walton's Troilus and Cressida for Opera North; Laca in Jenůfa for WNO 1998; season 2000–01 as Peter Grimes at Maastricht, Golo in Schumann's Genoveva at Garsington and Britten's Captian Vere for Canadian Opera at Toronto. *Recordings include:* Handel's Tamerlano, Alexander's Feast and Jephtha, Tippett's Songs for Dov, Stravinsky's Renard, Arbace in Idomeneo, Britten's The Rape of Lucretia, Walton's Troilus and Cressida.

ROBSON, Richard; British singer (bass); b. 1964, County Durham, England. *Education:* Guildhall School with Otakar Kraus, studied with Arlene Randazzo. *Career:* debut as Badger in The Cunning Little Vixen and Antonio in Figaro, at Glyndebourne; Speaker in The Magic Flute and Gremin in Eugene Onegin, for Kent Opera; debut with Wiener Kammeroper as Rossini's Basilio 1990; festival engagements at Vienna Schonbrunn, Barcelona, Brighton, Hong Kong and Edinburgh; Colline and Sparafucile in Rigoletto for Bath and Essex Opera; Wexford Festival 1994–95, in Rubinstein's The Demon and as Il Cieco in Mascagni's Iris; further appearances in Iris at Rome and Munich and with the Chelsea Opera Group; season 1996–97 with Ramfis in Aida for Norwegian Opera and return to Wexford; concerts include Elgar's Apostles at Canterbury Cathedral, Rossini's Petite Messe in Strasbourg, Verdi Requiem in Croydon and Mozart's Requiem on tour to Germany; Creon in Cherubini's Médée and Frederico in Verdi's Battaglia di Legnano (St John's Smith Square and Chelsea Opera Group). *Current Management:* c/o Alexander European Management, 38 Lytton Grove, Putney, London, SW15 2HB, England. *Telephone:* (20) 8780-9377. *E-mail:* alexeuropra@aol.com.

ROCHAIX, François; Swiss stage director; b. 2 Aug. 1942, Geneva. *Education:* University of Geneva, Berliner Ensemble, East Berlin. *Career:* founder and Dir, the Atelier de Genève 1963–75, actor and director; Dir, Théâtre de Carouge 1975–81, 2002–08; freelance dir 1981–; Artistic Dir, La Fête des Vignerons 1999; has produced The Turn of The Screw and Death in Venice in Geneva, La Traviata for Opera North, Cardillac and Parsifal in Berne, Der Ring des Nibelungen, Die Meistersinger in Seattle, Tristan und Isolde for Opéra Lyon, Dialogues des Carmélites in Geneva; plays include A Doll's House, Henry IV, The Oresteia. *Address:* 7 Vy aux Vergnes, 1295 Mies, Switzerland (home).

ROCHAT, Michel, MMus; Swiss musician (clarinet), conductor and composer; b. 29 Jan. 1931, La Chaux de Fonds; m. Josette-Marie Rochat 1959; two d. *Education:* Conservatoires of Lausanne, Geneva and Paris with Louis Cahuzac, Basel Musikakademie with Erich Schmid, Klaus Huber, Jürg Wittenbach, Hans Ulrich Lehman, Jacques Wildberger. *Career:* clarinet teacher, Switzerland 1952, conducting in Switzerland 1960–; clarinet player,

Basel Contemporary Music Group 1968–72; Prof. and Dir Conservatoire Supérieur, Lausanne 1963–83; Guest Conductor in Belgium, Bulgaria, Italy, Greece, Romania, Russia, Switzerland, Venezuela 1976–85; Gen. Music Dir and Conductor, Izmir Nat. Symphony Orchestra 1982–85; Guest Conductor, Nat. Symphony Orchestra, Istanbul 1982–85; Prof., Nat. Inst. of Arts and Nat. Acad. of Arts, Taiwan 1985–; conductor in Taiwan, in Taipei City and Kaohsiung Symphony Orchestras, Taipei Bach Orchestra, Artist's Ensemble 1985–, Hwa Shing Children's Chorus 1989–90, Rong Shing Chorus 1993–96, Asia Int. Festival for Contemporary Music 1994, Dan Tie Orchestra 1995–, Music Camp for Chinese Music, Ilan 1996, Lan Yang Chinese Ensemble, performing at Int. Children's Festival and Taipei Chinese Music Festival 1996, Lan Yan Chinese Ensemble, Taiwanese Opera Ilan 1996–; Guest Conductor, Taipei Municipal Chinese Orchestra 1993–, Experimental Chinese Orchestra, Taipei, Taichung and Kaohsiung tours 1997, Festival I-Lan Taiwan 2003–04; mem. Swiss Musicians' Asscn. *Compositions include:* Taiwanese operas: Seven Words 1996, Kamalan Story 1997, Kavalan Princess 1998, Attaya Song 1999, The Mouse Bride Children 2000; arranged Taiwanese songs; hymns for Taoist Association 2000, Music, Dance and Theater (opera ballet), Flowers Listen (opera ballet) 2001, Improvisation and Dance for flute and piano, Christmas Songs for choir, brass and organ 2002, Avis for soprano and piano 2003, Alleluia for choir and brass ensemble 2003, Amen for choir and brass ensemble 2003, Treasures of I-Lan concerto for two violins and Chinese orchestra 2004, The Mouse's Wedding (ballet music) 2007, for symphony orchestra 2009, Alice in Wonderland (ballet music) 2007, Concerto for two flutes and orchestra 2007, Three Pieces for String Quartet 2008, Two Little Pieces for violin and piano 2008, Breath of Life (dance poem in three parts for principal clarinet and orchestra) 2013, Concert for violin, viola, percussion and string orchestra 2014), Concertante for piano, clarinet and string orchestra with percussion 2014, Escalade for piano solo 2014. *Recordings include:* Masterpieces of Chinese Music 1995, Chinese Contemporary Music 1995, Chinese Music for the Young 1996, Dan Tie Chinese Ensemble 1996, Concert for Dragon Boat Festival 1996, Religious Music, Christmas Songs, Chinese and Taiwanese Pieces 1999, Commemoration of Centenary 1999, Kamalan Princess 1999, Dao Anthems 2000, Flowers Listen 2000, Taipei Chinese Orchestra: Works from Lu Liang Whei 2002, Works of Wang, Chen, Guh and Rochat 2004. *Publications include:* To Know the Tonality 1995, Clarinet for Beginners 1996, Preparatory Exercises to the Conducting Technique 1996, Rudiments of Intervals and Notation 1996, Saxophone for Beginners 1997. *Honours:* First Prize, Rio de Janeiro Int. Conducting Competition, Gold Medal and Villa-Lobos Prize 1975, Medal of St-Laurent du Var (France) 1980, Award of Kaohsiung's School 1993, Lion's Club Best Music Teacher in Taiwan 1993, Award of Kaohsiung's mayor (Mr Wu Den Yi) 1994, Award of I-Lan County's President 1996. *Address:* Ch. des Ecoliers 7, 1305 Orbe, Switzerland (home). *Telephone:* (21) 861-29-30 (home). *Fax:* (21) 861-29-30 (home). *E-mail:* rochat@michelrochat.ch. *Website:* www .michelrochat.ch.

ROCHE, Elizabeth Barbara Winifred, BA; British musicologist and music critic; b. 12 March 1948, Southport, England; m. Jerome Roche (deceased), one d. *Education:* Univ. of Durham. *Career:* research on 18th-century German Catholic Church Music with Denis Arnold; research on rise of interest in early music in Britain from 1870 onwards; assisted Jerome Roche's work on 17th-century north Italian church music; mem. Royal Musical Asscn. *Publications:* A Dictionary of Early Music (with Jerome Roche); contrib. to New Grove Dictionary of Music and Musicians, New Oxford Companion to Music, The Musical Times, Early Music. *Address:* 31 Sideling Fields, Tiverton, EX16 4AG, England (home). *Telephone:* (1884) 254051 (home).

ROCHESTER, Marc, BMus, MA, PhD, ARCM, LRAM, FTCL; British music journalist, organist, conductor and adjudicator; b. 28 April 1954, London, England; m Magdelene Teresa de Rozario 1998. *Education:* University of Wales. *Career:* music critic, Western Mail 1975–80; correspondent for Organists' Review, Musical Times 1980–89, Independent 1987–, Gramophone 1989; sub-organist, Bangor Cathedral, 1978–80; Organist and Master of Choristers, Londonderry Cathedral, 1980–82; Music Tutor, New University of Ulster, Northern Ireland, 1980–84; solo recitalist; Choral Conductor; Examiner, Associated Board, Royal Schools of Music, Trinity College London, Northern Ireland Schools Examinations Council; University of London; Lecturer, Putra University, Malaysia, 1997–99; Programme Co-ordinator and Organist, Dewan Filharmonik Petronas, Kuala Lumpur. *Compositions:* hymn tunes, church music. *Recordings:* soloist, 20th-Century British Organ Music, 1983; Conductor, Hymns of C. F. Alexander, Derry Cathedral Choir, 1981; accompanist, Beaufort Male Voice Choir, 1977, 1978, Leila Carewe (soprano), 1980; A European Organ Tour. *Publications:* Frank Martin at Golgotha 1977, Traditional Welsh Musical Instruments (catalogue ed.); contrib. articles on 20th-century music. *Telephone:* (7950) 634870 (mobile). *Fax:* (1252) 783172. *E-mail:* marcroc@pc.jaring.my.

ROCKWELL, John Sargent, PhD; American journalist and author; b. 16 Sept. 1940, Washington, DC; s. of Alvin John and Anne Hayward; m. Linda Mevorach; one d. *Education:* Harvard Univ., Univ. of Munich, Germany, and Univ. of California, Berkeley. *Career:* music and dance critic, Oakland (Calif.) Tribune 1969; Asst Music and Dance Critic, Los Angeles Times 1970–72; freelance music critic, New York Times 1972–74, staff music critic 1974–91, Ed. Arts and Leisure section 1998, European Cultural Corresp. and Prin. Classical Recordings Critic, New York Times, Paris 1992–94, Sr Cultural Corresp. and Columnist 2002–04, Dance Critic 2005–06; Dir Lincoln Center

Festival, Lincoln Center for the Performing Arts, New York 1994–98; Distinguished Visitor, American Academy in Berlin 2008. *Publications include:* All American Music: Composition in the Late 20th Century 1983, Sinatra: An American Classic 1984, The Idiots 2003, Outsider: John Rockwell on the Arts 1967–2006 2006. *Honours:* Chevalier, Ordre des Arts et Lettres.

RODDE, Anne-Marie; French singer (soprano); b. 21 Nov. 1946, Clermont-Ferrand. *Education:* Conservatory of Clermont-Ferrand, Paris Conservatoire with Irene Joachim and Louis Nougera. *Career:* sang at Aix-en-Provence 1971 as Amor in Orfeo ed Euridice, Yniold in Pelléas et Mélisande at Paris 1972, in Cantate Nuptial by Milhaud and The Nightingale by Stravinsky; sang in Hyppolite et Aricie at Covent Garden, Falstaff, Cherubini's Médée, and Rosenkavalier at Paris Opéra House, Pelléas et Mélisande at Rome Opera House, Pearl Fishers at Stockholm Opera, Magic Flute debut 1991 at La Bastille Opéra, Magic Flute at Montréal and Bonn Opera; appearances in Amsterdam in Le nozze di Figaro and at Zürich and Barcelona; many appearances in the Baroque repertory including London Bach Festival in Les Boréades by Rameau; other roles include Zerbinetta, Oscar, Nannetta, Ravel's Child and Dirce in Médée, Paris Opéra in 1986; sang Frasquita in Carmen at Florence, 1993. *Recordings:* Les Indes Galantes by Rameau; Handel's Xerxes; Lully's Le Triomphe d'Alcide; Les Boréades; Honegger's Jeanne d'Arc au Bûcher; Messiah; Songs by Debussy; Avietta di Camera by Rossini; Songs by Widor; Works by Bellini, Donizetti and Gluck.

RODEN, Anthony; Australian singer (tenor); b. 19 March 1937, Adelaide; m. Doreen Roden. *Education:* Associated Australian Insurance Inst., Adelaide Conservatory. *Career:* debut at Glyndebourne, England; has sung with all major British opera companies, also in Prague, Hamburg, Barcelona, Madrid, Freiburg and Australia; numerous concerts for BBC with Geoffrey Parsons and British, Italian, French and Dutch orchestras; sang Peter Grimes, London, Samson and Tannhäuser, Melbourne 1992, Mahler's 8th Symphony, Royal Liverpool Philharmonic Orchestra, Florestan for Glyndebourne; Mahler, Das Lied von der Erde, Taiwan; Prin. Tutor, Royal Northern Coll. of Music; currently teaches in a pvt. studio. *Recordings include:* Britten War Requiem, Dresden Philharmonic Orchestra under Herbert Kegel, Le Cheval de Bronze, The Wreckers. *Honours:* John Christie Award 1971, Adelaide Conservatoire Opera Prize. *Address:* 33 Castlebar Road, Ealing, London, W5 2DJ, England (home). *E-mail:* anthonyroden@gmail.com (home).

RODERICK JONES, Richard Trevor, MMus, GRSM, ARCM, FRSA; British composer, conductor, pianist and musicologist; b. 14 Nov. 1947, Newport, Gwent, Wales; m. Susan Ann Thomason 1992. *Education:* Royal Coll. of Music and Univ. of Bristol. *Career:* Head of Music, South Warwickshire Coll., Stratford-upon-Avon 1970–79; Extramural Tutor, Univ. of Birmingham 1971–79; Musical Dir Nat. Youth Theatre of Wales 1978–87; Tutor, Welsh Coll. of Music and Drama 1979–93; Extramural Tutor, Univ. Coll. Cardiff 1980–93, 1997–; External Tutor, Univ. of Oxford 1993–95; Visiting Lecturer, Birmingham Conservatoire 2001–02; Composer-in-Residence, Alcester Grammar School 2002–12. *Compositions include:* piano concerto, three symphonies, three chamber concertos, three sinfoniettas, numerous choral works, including oratorio Altus Prosator, Missa Sarum, numerous chamber works, including two piano trios, piano quartet, stage works, including Me and My Bike (opera, BBC comm.), Chanticleer (church opera), Altar Fire (scenic celebration), Game Circle (scenic cantata), Sun Kingdom (opera), more than 30 scores for TV and stage. *Honours:* Cobbett Prize, Royal Coll. of Music 1970. *Address:* The Limes, 7 Manor Barns, Middle Street, Ilmington, Shipston-on-Stour, Warwicks., CV36 4LS, England (home). *Telephone:* (1608) 682209 (home). *E-mail:* rroderickjones@aol.com. *Website:* www.richardroderickjones .com.

RODESCU, Julian, BMus, MMus; Romanian singer (bass); b. 1 May 1953, Bucharest, Romania; m. Barbara Govatos 1983. *Education:* Juilliard School and studied with Giorgio Tozzi, William Glazier, Jerome Hines, Hans Hotter and Daniel Ferro. *Career:* debut as Plutone in Monteverdi's Il Ballo delle Ingrate with Brooklyn Opera 1980; Carnegie Hall debut 1989 with Rostropovich in world premiere of Shostakovich's Rayok; Teatro alla Scala with Riccardo Muti 1991, Boston Symphony with Seiji Ozawa in Boston Symphony Hall, Carnegie Hall and Tanglewood; appearances with Miami Opera, New York City Opera, Knoxville Opera, Aachen Stadttheater, Kennedy Center in Washington, DC, Alice Tully Hall, WHYY-TV Philadelphia, WQXR, WNCN New York, Central City Opera and Opera Delaware. *Recordings:* Shostakovich's Rayok, Tchaikovsky's Queen of Spades, Bortniansky's Complete Vocal Concerti. *Honours:* winner Luciano Pavarotti Competition 1988. *Current Management:* Robert Gilder & Co., c/o Chase Thompson, Pinnacle Arts Management, 889 Ninth Avenue, 2nd Floor, New York, NY 10019, USA. *Telephone:* (212) 397-5299. *Fax:* (212) 397-7920. *E-mail:* cthompson@pinnaclearts.com.

RODGERS, Joan, CBE, BA, FRNCM; British singer (soprano); b. 4 Nov. 1956, Whitehaven, Cumbria; d. of the late Thomas Rodgers and of Julia Rodgers; m. Paul Daniel 1988 (divorced); two d. *Education:* Whitehaven Grammar School, Univ. of Liverpool and Royal Northern Coll. of Music. *Career:* first maj. professional engagement as Pamina in The Magic Flute, Aix-en-Provence Festival 1982; début at Metropolitan Opera House, New York, in same role 1995; other appearances include title role of Theodora at Glyndebourne, The Governess in Turn of the Screw for Royal Opera House, Blanche in Dialogues des Carmélites for ENO and in Amsterdam, Marschallin in Der Rosenkavalier for Scottish Opera and title role of Alcina for English Nat. Opera; regular

appearances at Royal Opera House, English Nat. Opera, Glyndebourne, Promenade Concerts and with leading British and European cos; concert engagements in London, Europe and USA with conductors including Solti, Barenboim, Mehta, Rattle, Harnoncourt and Salonen; numerous recordings; Kathleen Ferrier Memorial Scholarship 1981. *Honours:* Dr hc (Liverpool) 2005; Royal Philharmonic Soc. Award as Singer of the Year 1997, Evening Standard Award for Outstanding Individual Performance in Opera 1997. *Current Management:* c/o Ingpen and Williams Ltd, 7 St George's Court, 131 Putney Bridge Road, London, SW15 2PA, England. *Telephone:* (20) 8874-3222. *Fax:* (20) 8877-3113. *Website:* www.ingpen.co.uk/artist/joan-rodgers.

RODGERS, Sarah Louise, BA (Hons), FRSA; British composer and conductor; *Partner, Impulse Music Consultants LLP;* b. 15 April 1953, Aylesbury, Bucks.; direct descendant of English composer Henry Purcell; m. Geraldine Allen. *Education:* Walthamstow Hall, Sevenoaks, Univ. of Nottingham. *Career:* composer 1982–; Chair. Composers' Guild of GB 1992–95; Dir Mechanical-Copyright Protection Soc. (joined with Performing Right Soc. to become MCPS-PRS Alliance 1997, rebranded PRS for Music 1999) 1999–; Founding Dir British Acad. of Songwriters, Composers and Authors (BASCA) 1999–, Chair. 2009–12, Concert Chair. BASCA 1999–2008, Chair. British Composer Awards 2003–12; Dir tutti.co.uk Ltd 2000–; Partner, Impulse Music Consultants LLP 2011–; Trustee, British Music Information Centre 1997–2008, PRS for Music Members' Benevolent Fund 2006–, The BASCA Trust 2010–; Conductor, New English Orchestra, Coventry and Leamington Spa Operatic Socs, Harlow Chorus, St John's Festival Orchestra and Chorus, City of London Sinfonia, Whiteacre Winds. *Compositions:* Spanish Sonata 1990, The Roaring Whirl 1992, Saigyo 1995, The King of the Golden River 2000, The Fire will Blaze Again 2003, In Your Shadow 2007, Dover Beach 2008. *Film:* Housekeeper of the Nation (Nat. Trust) 1985. *Recordings:* The Roaring Whirl 1995, The King of the Golden River 2000. *Publications:* contrib. to Music Journal (Incorporated Soc. of Musicians), The Works (British Acad. of Composers and Songwriters), scripts for BBC Radio 3. *Current Management:* c/o Impulse Music Consultants LLP, Pipers Mede, 8 Church Lane, Holme Hale, Norfolk, IP25 7DS, England. *Telephone:* (1760) 441441. *Fax:* (1760) 441448. *E-mail:* impulse@impulse-music.co.uk. *Website:* www.impulse-music .co.uk (office); www.tutti.co.uk.

RODRIGUEZ, Robert Xavier, MM, DMA; American composer, conductor and academic; *Endowed Chair, University Professor of Music, University of Texas at Dallas;* b. 28 June 1946, San Antonio, Tex.; m. Darlene Rodriguez. *Education:* Univ. of Texas, Austin, Univ. of California, Los Angeles, studied with Jakob Druckman at Tanglewood and Nadia Boulanger in Fontainebleau/Paris, masterclasses with Elliott Carter and Bruno Maderna at Tanglewood. *Career:* mem. Faculty, Univ. of Southern California 1973–75; mem. Faculty, Univ. of Texas, Dallas 1975–, currently Univ. Prof. of Music (Endowed Chair); Composer-in-Residence, Dallas Symphony Orchestra 1982–85, San Antonio Symphony Orchestra 1996–98; mem. Bd of Dirs American Music Center 2008–12, Artist Council of New Music USA, Advisory Bd Opera Hispanica. *Compositions include:* two Piano Trios 1970, 1971, Canto for soprano, tenor and chamber orchestra 1973, Favola Concertante for violin, cello and strings 1975, revised 1977, Variations for violin and piano 1975, Transfigurationis Mysteria for soloists, narrator, chorus and orchestra 1978, Favola Boccaccesca 1979, Estampie (ballet) for orchestra 1981, Semi-Suite for violin and orchestra 1981, Suor Isabella (opera) 1982, Trunks for narrator and orchestra 1983, Oktoechos (Concerto Grosso for orchestra) 1983, Seven Deadly Sins for wind ensemble 1984, Tango (chamber opera) 1985, Varmi'ts! for narrator, chorus and orchestra 1985, Monkey See, Monkey Do (children's opera) 1986, The Ransom of Red Chief (children's opera) 1986, A Colorful Symphony for narrator and orchestra 1987, We the People for narrator, chorus and orchestra 1987, The Old Majestic (opera) 1988, Invocations of Orpheus (trumpet concerto) 1989, A Gathering of Angels for orchestra 1989, Les Niais Amoureux for chamber ensemble 1989, Fantasia Lussuriosa for piano 1989, Ursa: Four Seasons for double bass and orchestra 1990, Frida (opera) 1991, Pinata for orchestra 1991, Tango di Tango for orchestra 1992, The Song of Songs for actor, soprano and chamber ensemble 1992, Meta IV for string quartet 1994, Hot Buttered Rumba for orchestra 1993, Mascaras for cello and orchestra 1994, Adoracion Ambulante (Con Flor y Canto) folk celebration for soloists, mariachis, percussion ensemble, chorus and orchestra 1994, Scrooge for bass-baritone, chorus and orchestra 1994, Forbidden Fire for bass-baritone, chorus and orchestra 1998, Sinfonia à la Mariachi for double orchestra 1998, Bachanale (Concertino for orchestra) 1999, The Last Night of Don Juan for actors, singers, dancers, puppeteers and orchestra 2000, Tequila Sunrise (Fanfare for brass, harp and percussion) 2000, The Tempest for actors and orchestra 2000, Gambits: Six Chess Pieces for horn and piano 2001, A Midsummer Night's Dream (incidental music) 2001, Smash the Windows for young concert band 2001, Flight: The Story of Wilbur and Orville Wright for narrator and orchestra 2002, Decem Perfectum (Concerto for woodwind quintet, brass quintet and wind ensemble) 2003, Food of Love for narrator/violin and piano 2004, Musical Dice Game for two string quartets and two string quartets 2005, The Dot and the Line: A Romance in Lower Mathematics for narrator and chamber ensemble 2005, The Versatility Rag for solo piano 2006, Agnus Dei (completion of Mozart's Great Mass in C minor) 2006, El Día de los Muertos for percussion sextet 2006, La Curandera (opera) 2006, Sor(tri)lege: Trio III for violin, cello and piano 2007, Tentado por la samba for cello and piano 2007, Musica, por un tempo for violin, clarinet, cello and piano 2008, Six Songs of E.E. Cummings for soprano and marimba or soprano and piano 2008, The Dot and the Line for narrator and orchestra 2011, Caprichos for piano solo 2012, De Rerum Natura for orchestra 2013, Xochiquetzal for violin and percussion sextet 2014, Fanfarria Son-Risa for orchestra 2015. *Recordings:* 20 CDs featuring his music. *Honours:* Guggenheim Fellowship 1976, Prix de Composition Prince Pierre de Monaco 1971, Prix Lili Boulanger 1973, American Acad. and Inst. of Arts and Letters Goddard Lieberson Award 1980, Distinguished Alumnus Award, School of Music, USC 1995, Aaron Copland Award 2001, 2011. *Current Management:* c/o Tammy Moore, G. Schirmer Inc., 180 Madison Avenue, 24th Floor, New York, NY 10016, USA. *Telephone:* (212) 254-2100. *Website:* www.musicsalesclassical.com/composer/long-bio/Robert-Xavier-Rodriguez. *Telephone:* (972) 883-2766 (office). *E-mail:* RobertXavierRodriguez@tx.rr.com (office). *Website:* www.robertxavierrodriguez.com.

ROE, Betty, MBE, LRAM, ARCM, ARAM, FRSA; British composer and fmr singer (soprano) and pianist; b. 30 July 1930, London, England; m. John Bishop (deceased); one s. two d. *Education:* Royal Acad. of Music. *Career:* organist and choirmaster, including Kensington 1958–68, 1978–88; Music Dir, London Acad. of Music and Dramatic Art 1968–78; professional soprano 1962–; John Aldiss Singers, St Clement Dane Chorale; founded NorthKen Chorale; Musical Dir NorthKen Concerts 1980–; f. Thames Publishing, specializing in English vocal music and books about British composers; festival adjudicator 1960–; Associated Bd examiner; Founder, Robish Music 2003; mem. Equity, Incorporated Soc. of Musicians, Asscn of Teachers of Singing, Performing Artists' Media Rights Asscn, Asscn of English Singers and Speakers, Royal Soc. of Musicians. *Compositions:* four chamber operas, musicals, cantatas, organ music, music theatre entertainments, choral music, piano, flute and other instrumental music, much of it for schools and young people. *Recordings:* Music's Empire, The Music Tree, The Family Tree. *Publications include:* Songs from the Betty Roe Shows (five vols), Pubs are People Places, Serious: Noble Numbers, Music's Empire, Conversation Piece for Horn and Piano, Soliloquy and Dialogue for Horn and Piano, Two Garden Songs for Soprano, Violin and Piano 2004. *Address:* 14 Barlby Road, Kensington, London, W10 6AR, England (home). *Telephone:* (20) 8969-3579 (home). *E-mail:* br@bettyroe.co.uk. *Website:* www.bettyroe.com.

ROEBUCK, Janine Lorraine Spence; British singer (mezzo-soprano); b. 5 Jan. 1954, Barnsley, South Yorks., England; d. of Kenneth Roebuck and Edna Roebuck. *Education:* Univ. of Manchester, Royal Northern Coll. of Music with Freddie Cox, Paris Conservatoire with Régine Crespin, Nat. Opera School, London, studied with Arwel Treharne Morgan. *Career:* appearances in La Buona Figliola, Buxton; as Rossini's Isabella for Opera 80; Lucille in The Silken Ladder and Clarina in The Marriage Contract for Scottish Opera; Mozart's Dorabella and Maddalena in Rigoletto for Pavilion Opera; Eduige in Handel's Rodelinda at Batignano; English Bach Festival in Dido and Aeneas and Gluck's Alceste, Monte Carlo and Covent Garden; operetta with D'Oyly Carte –1982, New Sadler's Wells Opera; shows with Richard Baker and Marilyn Hill Smith and BBC broadcasts; Mahler's Rückertlieder with Scottish Ballet; concerts in Coventry and Peterborough Cathedrals; Carmen in Middle East and Far East; opera recital at the Opera House in Manaus, Brazil; Thiske in Rossini's Cenerentola at the Linbury Theatre, Royal Opera House, Covent Garden; devised a tribute to Joyce Grenfell, Stately as a Galleon; Trustee, Action on Hearing Loss; Patron Auditory Verbal UK; after-dinner speaker. *Recordings:* Scrooge, with Tommy Steele, The Mikado – New D'Oyly Carte (video), Yeoman of the Guard, The Merry Widow 1986, HMS Pinafore 1987, The Songs of Rogers & Hammerstein 1995, Kiss Me Kate, with Edmund Hockeridge 1996, The King & I, with Keith Michell & Julia McKenzie 1997, Getting to Know You, Climb Every Mountain, People Will Say We're in Love, with Peter Skellern, When You Walk through a Storm – The Best of Andrew Lloyd Webber, Take That Look off Your Face, Taking It Easy 1996, People Will Say We're in Love – The Andrew Lloyd Webber Musical Box, Take That Look off Your Face, Romantic Favourites, Falling in Love with Love – Classical Tranquillity, O mio babbino caro, I Know That My Redeemer Liveth, The Word in Your Ear – Readings from the New Testament, Vols 6–10 and 11–15, Salvation Army, In trutina, I Know That My Redeemer Liveth, O mio babbino caro – Friday Night is Music Night Vol. 1 (BBC), Wanting You – Friday Night is Music Night Vol. (BBC), When I Marry Mr Snow, With One Look – Gilbert and Sullivan solo album 2012. *Honours:* AMI Champion Award for outstanding musical achievement despite being severely deaf 2009, listed in The Independent on Sunday 'Happy List' as one of 100 people who make Britain a better and a happier place to live 2010. *Address:* 55A Thorparch Road, London, SW8 4SX, England (office). *Telephone:* (20) 7978-1397 (office). *E-mail:* janine.roebuck@hotmail.com (office).

ROGÉ, Pascal; French pianist; b. 6 April 1951, Paris; m. Ami Rogé; two s. *Education:* Paris Conservatoire, private studies with Lucette Descaves, Pierre Pasquier and Julius Katchen. *Career:* debut in Paris 1969, London 1969; specialist in Ravel, Poulenc, Debussy, Satie; soloist with leading orchestras; Artistic Dir Incontri in Terra di Siena, Italy. *Honours:* Premiers Prix for Piano and Chamber Music at the Paris Conservatoire 1966, First Prize Marguerite Long-Jacques Thibaud Int. Competition 1971, Grand Prix du Disque and Edison Award 1984, Gramophone Award for Best Instrumental Recording 1988, Best Chamber Music Recording 1997. *Current Management:* Clarion/Seven Muses, 47 Whitehall Park, London, N19 3TW, England. *E-mail:* nick@c7m.co.uk. *Address:* 17 avenue des Cavaliers, 1224 Geneva, Switzerland. *Website:* www.pascalroge.net.

ROGER, David; stage designer; b. 1950, England. *Career:* for Opera Factory in London designed La Calisto, The Knot Garden, Osborne premiere of Hell's

Angels, Birtwistle premiere of Yan Tan Tethera 1986, a conflation of Gluck's Iphigenia operas, Ligeti's Adventures and Nouvelles Adventures, Mahagonny Songspiel, Così fan tutte, Don Giovanni, Reimann's The Ghost Sonata and The Marriage of Figaro 1991; other work has included Le Grand Macabre by Ligeti at Freiburg, Akhnaten by Philip Glass and The Return of Ulysses at ENO, La Bohème for Opera North and Manon Lescaut for Opéra-Comique in Paris; Madama Butterfly at the Albert Hall 1998.

ROGERS, Lesley-Jane, ARAM, GRSM, LRAM; British singer (soprano); b. 25 April 1962, Bristol, England; m. Robin Daniel 1988; one step-s. one step-d. *Education:* Royal Acad. of Music. *Career:* concert soloist specialising in contemporary music, oratorio, 'vocal concertos', solo cantatas and recitals; wide oratorio repertoire incorporating standard repertoire and unusual works; hundreds of solo cantatas, especially Bach and Telemann; more than 80 world premieres in recent years; dedicatee of various songs and song cycles; English Song devotee; Life mem. Nat. Early Music Asscn; mem. British Actors' Equity Asscn. *Radio includes:* broadcasts for BBC Radio 3, BBC Radio nan Gaidheal, TeleDiffusion de France, CKWR Canada. *Recordings include:* has appeared as soloist on numerous recordings, including Handel Tamerlano 1990, Caldara Madrigals and Cantatas 1992, Caldara Motets 1994, Peter Maxwell Davies Resurrection 1994, Peerson Private Musicke 1994, Carl Rütti Choral Music 1995, Percy Grainger Jungle Book: The Love Song of Har Dyal 1996, Sadie Harrison Taking Flight 2000, The Soprano Sings Schubert Lieder 2002, Julia Usher Sacred Physic 2002, Celtic Magic 2003, Stephen Dodgson High Barbaree 2004, The Soprano Sings English Song 2004, Seiber To Poetry 2005, Elizabeth Maconchy and Nicola Lefanu Reflections 2005, Grains of Sand: Music for and by Wilfrid Mellers 2006, Elis Pehkonen Turning World 2007, Christopher Wright A Vision of Heaven 2007, Brian Ferneyhough Choral Music 2007, John Joubert Song Cycles and Chamber Music 2007, Pied Piper: A Celebration of David Munrow 2009, Birdsongs in Silence: A Musical Portrait of Beth Wiseman and Geoff Poole 2010, David Lumsdaine White Dawn 2010, The Rose Tree Music for and by Basil Deane 2010, Orbits and Tangents: A Celebration for Sir John Manduell, Antony Hopkins: A Portrait 2012, Sounds of the Chionistra 2013, Of Times and Seasons: Songs and Anthems by Peter Lea-Cox 2013, Sonnets, Airs and Dances by Philip Wood 2015. *Honours:* Harry Farjeon Prize in Harmony 1982, Ella Mary Jacob Prize for Singing 1983, Greta G. M. Parkinson Prize in Piano 1984. *Address:* Hope Cottage, Meadow Court, High Street, Northleach, GL54 3EP, England (home). *Telephone:* (1451) 861492 (home). *E-mail:* info@lesleyjanerogers.co.uk. *Website:* www.lesleyjanerogers.co.uk.

ROGERS, Nigel David, BA, MA; British singer (tenor), conductor and teacher; b. 21 March 1935, Wellington, Shropshire, England; s. of Thomas Rogers and Winifred Rogers; m. Lina Rogers (née Zilinskyte); two d. *Education:* King's Coll., Cambridge, pvt. musical tuition in Rome and Milan, Hochschule für Musik, Munich. *Career:* began professional career with Early Music Group, Studio der Frühen Musik 1961; operatic debut at Amsterdam 1969; sang in Monteverdi's Ulisse and Orfeo under Harnoncourt at Vienna and Amsterdam 1971, 1976, L'Incoronazione di Poppea at Amsterdam under Leonhardt 1972, Il Combattimento at La Scala, Milan under Berio 1973; sang in British premiere of Arden Must Die by Goehr at Sadler's Wells 1974; sang title role in Handel's Teseo at Warsaw 1977; Prof. of Singing, Royal Coll. of Music 1978–2000; now freelance singer and teacher; conductor 1985–; directed and sang in the Serenata, La Gloria di Primavera by Alessandro Scarlatti (BBC invitation concert) 1996. *Recordings include:* Thomas Morley First Book of Ayres 1974, Monteverdi's 1610 Vespers and Orfeo (several prizes) 1975, Schubert's Die Schöne Müllerin 1975, John Dowland Lute Songs 1988, Sigismondo d'India 1991, Florentine Intermedi of 1589, Dido and Aeneas, Songs of Henry Lawes 1994, Symphonie Sacrae of Schütz 1995, Monteverdi's Vespers 1996. *Publications:* contrib. to various magazines and academic publs, including a chapter on voice, in Companion to Baroque Music (ed. by Julie Ann Sadie) 1991. *Honours:* Hon. mem. Royal Coll. of Music 1980. *Address:* Wellington House, 13 Victoria Road, Deal, Kent, CT14 7AS, England (home). *Telephone:* (1304) 379249 (home). *E-mail:* music@nigelrogers.org.uk (home).

ROGG, Lionel; Swiss organist and composer; b. 21 April 1936, Geneva; m. Claudine Effront 1957, three s. *Education:* Geneva Conservatory, studied with Nikita Magaloff, Pierre Segond. *Career:* Complete Bach organ works in ten recitals, Victoria Hall, Geneva, 1961; concerts (organ, harpsichord) worldwide; interpretative courses, USA, UK, Switzerland, Austria, Japan, Italy. *Compositions include:* organ: 12 chorales; Variations, Psalm 91, 1983; Introduction, ricercare, toccata; Cantata, Geburt der Venus; Also: Face à face, 2 pianos; Missa Brevis, chorus and orchestra; Concerto for organ and orchestra, 1992. *Recordings include:* Complete Bach organ works; Art of Fugue; Complete Buxtehude organ works; Rogg Plays Reger; Rogg Plays Rogg (organ compositions); Du Mage, Clérambault. *Publication includes:* Improvisation Course for Organists. *Honours:* Grand Prix du Disque 1970, Deutscher Schallplatten Preis 1980; Dr hc (Univ. of Geneva). *Website:* www.lionelrogg.ch.

ROGLIANO, Marco; Italian violinist; b. 26 Nov. 1967, Rome; m. Ciccozzi Antonella; one s. *Education:* Conservatory Santa Cecilia, Rome, Mozarteum of Salzburg and Acad. W. Stauffer. *Career:* debut at Helsingborg Concert Hall playing Sibelius Violin Concerto fo 47 with the Helsingborg Symphony Orchestra 1989; Casals Hall, Tokyo 1991; Paris 1993; Moscow 1993; with the Radio Symphonic Orchestra of Moscow 1994; Milan 1995; Rome 1996; Munich 1997; numerous radio and television broadcasts in France, Bulgaria, Sweden.

Recordings: Salvatore Sciarrino 1947, six Caprieei for solo violin 1976, Angelo Ragazzi, three Violin Concertos, Franz Adolf Berwald, The Violin Concerto.

ROGOFF, Ilan; Israeli concert pianist and conductor; b. 26 July 1943, Tel-Aviv; s. of Boris Rogoff and Sofija Rogoff; m. Vesna Zorka Mimiça 1985; two d. *Education:* Tel-Aviv Acad. of Music, Royal Conservatoire, Belgium, Mannes Coll. and Juilliard School, USA. *Career:* has performed all over Israel, Europe, N America, Latin America, S Africa, Japan and Far East with Israel Philharmonic Orchestra and many other orchestras; recognized for his interpretation of the Romantic composers, including Beethoven, Schumann, Brahms, Chopin, Liszt, César Franck, Rachmaninov, Tchaikovsky, Piazzolla; has performed twentieth-century and contemporary works including world premiere of concerti by John McCabe and by Ivan Erod; performs with various chamber music groups, including Enesco Quartet, Orpheus Quartet, Amati Trio, Festival Ensemble, Matrix Quintet, Sharon Trio and Quartet, soloists of Vienna Chamber Orchestra and Vienna Philharmonic Orchestra; conducting debut 1985, with Israel Philharmonic 1988; radio performances and TV appearances in UK, Spain, Austria, Germany, Israel, Canada, USA, SA, Colombia, Ecuador, Venezuela and Argentina; lectures and recital/lectures, master classes; juror at various int. music competitions. *Recordings include:* Chopin Concerti (version for piano and string quintet edited by him), transcriptions for piano solo of 12 works by Astor Piazzolla; 'Portraits' by Schumann; complete works by Chopin while in Mallorca; numerous works by Bach-Busoni, Beethoven, Schumann, Schubert, Beethoven, Liszt, Schubert/ Liszt and César Franck. *Publications:* Transcriptions for Piano Solo of Works by Astor Piazzolla, edited both Chopin Concerti for Piano and String Quintet; articles on music published in Scherzo magazine, Madrid, Piano magazine, London. *Honours:* various int. awards. *Address:* Estudio/Taller, Calle Bartomeu Fons 13, 07015 Palma de Mallorca, Spain (office). *Telephone:* (971) 707016 (home); 6-10980906 (mobile). *E-mail:* ilanrogoff@gmail.com (home). *Website:* www.ilanrogoff.com.

ROGOSIC, Marko, BA, MA; Serbian composer and academic; *President, Association of Composers of Montenegro;* b. 6 April 1941, Podgorica, Montenegro; s. of Vasilije Rogosic and Jana Rogosic; m. Gorica Rogosic; one s. one d. *Education:* Musical Acad., Belgrade; study tours throughout Europe, including London, Paris and Moscow. *Career:* Prof. of Music; Chief Ed. first Montenegrin Musical Herald; Pres. Asscn of Composers of Montenegro, Musicology and Ethnomusicology Inst. of Montenegro; mem. League of Composers' Asscn of Yugoslavia. *Compositions:* Seashore Water-Colour for clarinet and piano, Sonata in C-minor for piano, Sonata Fantasy for violin and piano, Concerto for contrabass and orchestra, Shepperds' Game for oboe or violin and piano, Suite for flute and fiddlers, Music for ballet Vladimir and Kosara, Simphony 'Cernogoria', Montenegrin Suite for string orchestra, The Dialogues for chamber orchestra, Variations for violin duo, Children Music, Nocturno for contrabass and string orchestra. *Publications:* Methodics of Music Education (reader for students) 1981, Monograph of Association of Composers 1996, Anthology of Soloist and Chamber Music of Montenegrin Composers 1998; numerous contribs to professional journals. *Honours:* New Composition Award 1987, 1994, 1995, Award for Life Deed. *Address:* Mitra Bakica 106, 81000 Podgorica, Montenegro (office). *Telephone:* (81) 248948 (office). *E-mail:* rogosic@yahoo.com.

ROHAN, Jiri; Czech double bass player; b. 11 Jan. 1965, Prague; m. Dana Skrovankova 1992; one d. *Education:* Prague Conservatory, Acad. of Music, Prague, Art Acad., Prague. *Career:* debut solo concert with Symphony Orchestra, Prague 1985; Czech Philharmonic Orchestra 1983–85; Suk Chamber Orchestra 1988–91; Munich Philharmonic Orchestra 1990; Czech String Ensemble 1992; Prague String Quintet 1993–97; Osaka Symphonic 1994. *Recordings include:* over 40 albums with several symphonic orchestras, over 10 albums with Suk Chamber Orchestra, two albums with Czech String Ensemble, three albums with Prague String Quintet, album with Czech Chamber Orchestra. *Publication:* Psychological Aspects of Music Listening 1993.

ROHNER, Ruth; singer (soprano); b. 18 Sept. 1935, Zürich, Switzerland. *Education:* studied in Winterhur and Amsterdam. *Career:* sang at the Opera of Biel-Solothurn 1960–61, Vienna Kammeroper 1960–62 and engaged at Zürich opera from 1962, notably in the premieres of Sutermeister's Madame Bovary 1967 and Kelterborn's Ein Engel Kommt Nach Babylon 1977; many performances in the lyric and coloratura repertory and in the first local performances of Burkhard's Ein Stern Geht auf Jakob and Krenek's Karl V; guest engagements at Berne, Basle, the State Operas of Hamburg and Munich, Düsseldorf, Strasbourg, Helsinki and Châtelet Paris; festival appearances at Lausanne, Wiesbaden and Athens; noted concert artist in oratorio and lieder.

ROHRL, Manfred; singer (bass); b. 12 Sept. 1935, Augsburg, Germany. *Education:* Augsburg Conservatory, studied with Franz Kelch and Margarethe von Winterfeld. *Career:* debut in Augsburg 1958 as Masetto; mem., Deutsche Oper Berlin, notably in the 1965 premiere of Der Junge Lord by Henze; guest appearances in Brussels, Nancy, Düsseldorf, Geneva, Zürich, Zagreb and Edinburgh; Netherlands Opera 1984 as Leporello; sang Waldner in Arabella at the Deutsche Oper Berlin 1988, and Dr Kolenaty in The Makropulos Case 1989; many performances in the buffo repertory; sang Taddeo in L'Italiana in Algeri with the Deutsche Oper 1992; Mozart's Bartolo at Glyndebourne 1994; sang Bartolo at the Deutsche Oper 2000.

ROJAS, Rafael; Mexican singer (tenor); b. 15 Sept. 1962, Guadalajara. *Education:* Univ. of Guadalajara, Royal Scottish Academy and Northern Coll. of Music, UK. *Career:* US debut as Alfredo in Traviata, Seattle, followed by Rafael Ruiz in El Gato Montes for Washington Opera; concerts include the Verdi Requiem with the Jerusalem Symphony Orchestra and the Hallé Orchestra; Lambeth Palace, London, Monmouth Cathedral, and the Glasgow Mayfest; season 1997–98 as Paco in La Vida Breve at Nice, Pinkerton for Glimmerglass Opera, USA, Werther at Boston, Rodolfo and Nemorino at Seattle and Verdi's Macduff for Houston Opera; season 2002–03 as Alfredo at Boston, Riccardo at Bregenz, Dick Johnson for Opera Zuid and Rodolfo at Melbourne; Don Carlos in Leipzig and Cavaradossi for Opera North. *Honours:* Domingo Prize, Placido Domingo Competition 1995. *Current Management:* c/o Cademi Artists Managment, C/ Esteban Garcia Chico 1-4c, 47003 Valladolid, Spain. *E-mail:* demiguel@cademi.eu. *Website:* www.cademi.eu.

ROLAND, Claude-Robert; Belgian conductor, organist and composer; b. 19 Dec. 1935, Pont-de-Loup; m. Anne-Marie Girardot 1963, one s. *Education:* Athénée Royal, Academy of Music, Châtelet, Conservatories in Liège, Paris, studied in Brussels with Messiaen and Defossez. *Career:* Organist, Notre Dame Church, Wasmes 1955–63, Basilica Charleroi 1963–67; Prof., Brussels Conservatory 1972–; performed works of Hoyoul, Lohet, Dumont, Buston, Schlick, Froidebise, Guillaume, Quatrefages; conducted works by Satie, Prokofiev, Guillaume, RTBF. *Compositions include:* Demain seulement (on poems by Alain Grandbois), Preludes for piano 1962, Rossignolet du bois for orchestra 1971, Rondeau for organ 1979, Thriller for trumpet and piano 1984, Datura 281 for piano 1987, Ricordanza for bass clarinet and piano 1989, music for Molière, Labiche, Turgenev and Ghelderode. *Recordings:* Compositeurs Liegeois, organ; Alpha; Musique au Chateau, organ and brass; Musica Magna. *Publications:* Orgues en Hainaut 1966; contrib. to Musique Vivante, Feuillets du Spantole, Hainaut-Tourisme, UWO.

ROLANDI, Gianna; American singer (soprano) and arts executive; *Vocal Consultant, The Patrick G. and Shirley W. Ryan Opera Center;* b. 16 Aug. 1952, New York; m. Andrew Davis. *Education:* studied with her mother and with Ellen Faull and Max Rudolf. *Career:* debut singing Offenbach's Olympia in Les Contes d'Hoffmann at New York City Opera 1975; Metropolitan Opera in 1979 as Sophie, later singing Olympia, Stravinsky's Nightingale and Zerbinetta; Glyndebourne debut in 1981 as Zerbinetta, returning in 1984 as Zdenka in Arabella and Susanna; ENO 1983 as Cleopatra in Giulio Cesare; San Diego in 1984 as Ophelia in Hamlet by Thomas; sang Lucia di Lammermoor at San Francisco in 1986, and Curiazio in a performance of Cimarosa's Gli Orazi e i Curizai, to mark the 200th anniversary of the French Revolution, at Rome Opera 1989; other roles include Gilda, the Queen of Night and parts in operas by Donizetti at the New York City Opera; sang Despina at Chicago 1993; concert tour of USA with BBC Symphony Orchestra 1996; Dir The Patrick G. and Shirley W. Ryan Opera Center (fmrly the Lyric Opera Center for American Artists), Chicago 2006–13, Vocal Consultant 2013–. *Address:* The Patrick G. and Shirley W. Ryan Opera Center, 20 North Wacker Drive, Chicago, IL 60606, USA (office). *E-mail:* giannarolandi@gmail.com.

ROLL, Michael; British pianist; b. 17 July 1946, Leeds, Yorks.; m. Juliana Markova; one s. *Education:* studied piano with Fanny Waterman. *Career:* debut, Royal Festival Hall playing Schumann Concerto with Malcolm Sargent 1958; regular appearances with major UK orchestras; played at Hong Kong Festival with London Philharmonic and toured Japan with BBC Symphony; also toured Netherlands, Germany, Switzerland, Spain and Eastern Europe; tours of Russia and Scandinavia in recital and with orchestra; conductors include Boulez, Giulini, Leinsdorf and Previn; visits to Aldeburgh, Bath, Edinburgh, Granada and Vienna Festivals; US debut with Boston Symphony Orchestra conducted by Colin Davis 1974; season 1987–88 with recitals in Milan, East Berlin, Dresden, Leipzig and London; season 1988–89 with London Symphony, Scottish Nat. Orchestra, Hallé, Bournemouth Symphony, Helsinki Philharmonic and Hong Kong Philharmonic Orchestras; recitals in London, Milan, Leipzig, Berlin and Dresden; played concertos at Promenade Concerts 1990, with Kurt Masur in Leipzig and London and Valery Gergiev in fmr Leningrad and UK; season 1991–92 played concertos with Skrowaczewski and the Hallé, BBC Philharmonic, BBC Scottish Orchestras and Leipzig Gewandhaus, recitals in the Int. Piano Series at Queen Elizabeth Hall and Klavierfestival Ruhr (Germany) with Helsinki Philharmonic under Comissiona, for the English Chamber Orchestra at the Barbican and New York debut recital 1992; performed complete cycle of Beethoven piano concertos with London Mozart Players, Barbican 1995; debut, Cologne Philharmonic Orchestra 2002; major Australian tour 2002; debuts with Orchestre de la Suisse Romande 2004, Dallas Symphony 2006, George Enescu Festival 2011, Budapest Philharmonic 2013; Prof., Folkwang Hochschule, Essen, Germany 1987–2009. *Recordings include:* Beethoven Piano Concertos (complete cycle). *Honours:* First Prize, Leeds Int. Piano Competition 1963. *Current Management:* c/o Martin Muller, Konzertdirektion, Uhrs Knappken 8, 59320 Ennigerloh-Ostenfelde, Germany. *Telephone:* (25) 24263480 (home). *Fax:* (25) 24263481 (home). *E-mail:* info@kdmueller.de. *Website:* www.kdmueller .de.

ROLLAND, Sophie; Canadian cellist; b. 18 July 1963, Montréal; d. of Pierre Rolland; m.; three c. *Education:* studied with Walter Joachim at Conservatoire de Musique du Quebéc, Montréal, at Coll.-Conservatory of Music, Cincinnati, studied with Nathaniel Rosen in New York, Pierre Fournier in Geneva and William Pleeth in London. *Career:* debut with Montréal Symphony Orchestra under Charles Dutoit 1982; regular appearances throughout Canada with all major orchestras, including the Montréal, Toronto and Vancouver Symphony Orchestras; toured in USA, France, Spain, UK, Germany, Switzerland, Bulgaria, Hungary, Yugoslavia, Finland and People's Republic of China; frequent guest at int. chamber music festivals, including Kuhmo, Dubrovnik and Parry Sound; duo partnership with pianist, Marc-André Hamelin since 1988; plays a 1674 cello by Petrus Ranta of Brescia. *Honours:* premier prix, L'Unanimité Montréal, study awards and scholarships from the Canadian and Québec Govts including Prix d'Europe, Canada, first prize Du Maurier Competition, Canada Arts Council Virginia P. Moore Prize. *Address:* 3 Sharon Road, Chiswick, London, W4 4PD, England (home). *E-mail:* sophier@onetel .com (office).

ROLOFF, Roger Raymond, BA, MA; singer (baritone); b. 22 Feb. 1947, Peoria, IL, USA; m. Barbara A. Petersen 1982. *Education:* Wesleyan Univ., Illinois State Univ., SUNY, Stony Brook. studied with Sam Sakarian in New York and with Hans Hotter. *Career:* debut at Deertrees Opera Theatre, Maine 1975; operatic roles include Wotan and Wanderer in The Ring, Jochanaan in Salome, and Ruprecht in Prokofiev's Fiery Angel; appearances with ENO, Deutsche Oper Berlin, Seattle, Kentucky, Dallas, San Diego and New York City Operas, Niedershsische Staatsoper Hannover, Hawaii Opera Theater, Houston Grand Opera and major orchestras in USA and Canada; concert appearances in Milwaukee, Boston, Los Angeles, Germany and Switzerland; sang the Dutchman in a concert performance of Der fliegende Holländer at Boston 1990, and Telramund in Lohengrin at Nice 1990.

ROLTON, Julian; pianist; b. 1965, England. *Career:* co-founder, Chagall Piano Trio at the Banff Centre for The Arts in Canada, resident artist; debut concert at the Blackheath Concert Halls in London 1991; further appearances at Barbican's Prokofiev Centenary Festival, Warwick Festival and the South Place Sunday Concerts at Conway Hall in London; Purcell Room recitals 1993 with the London premiere of Piano Trios by Tristan Keuris, Nicholas Maw and Dame Ethel Smyth composed 1880; premiere of Piano Trio No. 2 by David Matthews at Norfolk and Norwich Festival 1993; engaged at Malvern Festival 1994.

ROMANENKO, Yelena; singer (mezzo-soprano); b. 1951, Kharkov, Russia. *Education:* Inst. of Arts at Kharkov. *Career:* participated in the foundation of an opera programme with the State Opera Company of Kharkov; many performances in Russia and on tour in Europe and America, as Santuzza, Azucena, Eboli, Carmen, Dalila and Marfa in Khovanshchina; British debut on tour with the National Opera of the Ukraine 1995, as Marina in Boris Godunov and Fenena in Nabucco; concert recitalist in German, Czech and Russian works.

ROMANOVA, Nina; Russian singer (mezzo-soprano); b. 1946, Leningrad (later St. Petersburg). *Education:* Leningrad Academy of Music with Vera Sopina. *Career:* performed at Pushkin Theatre in Kishinov then from 1976 member of the Maly Theatre Leningrad, now St Petersburg; Roles have included Rosina in Barber of Seville, Azucena in Il Trovatore, Eboli in Don Carlo, Lady Macbeth, Carmen, Olga in Eugene Onegin, The Countess and Polina in The Queen of Spades, Marina in Boris Godunov and Marfa in Mussorgsky's Khovanshchina; Concerts include Alexander Nevsky by Prokofiev in Verona, St Matthew Passion, St John Passion, Mass in B minor by Bach, Mozart's Requiem, Verdi's Requiem, and Mahler's 2nd and 8th Symphonies; Guest performances with St Petersburg Mussorgsky State Academic Opera and Ballet Theatre, formerly Leningrad Maly Theatre, as member of the Opera Company; Sang in Italy at Palermo, Modena, Reggio Emilia, Parma, Ferrara, Ravenna and Catania, in France at Paris, Cannes and Nantes, New York and in Japan at Tokyo, Osaka, Hiroshima and Iokogama, Greece, Portugal and Netherlands; Sang in Rimsky's Invisible City of Kitezh at Bregenz, 1995. *Current Management:* Robert Gilder and Co., 91 Great Russell Street, London, WC1B 3PS, England. *Telephone:* (20) 7580-7758. *Fax:* (20) 7580-7739. *E-mail:* rgilder@robert-gilder.com. *Website:* www .robert-gilder.com.

ROMANOVSKY, Alexander; Italian (b. Ukrainian) pianist; b. 1984. *Education:* Kharkov Special Music School, Imola Piano Acad., Italy with Leonid Margarius, Royal Coll. of Music, London with Dmitry Alexeev. *Career:* gives recitals in Turin, Naples, Teatro della Pergola in Florence, Palermo, Auditorio Verdi and Teatro dal Verme in Milan, Accad. di Santa Cecilia, Rome; appeared as soloist with Mariinsky Orchestra under Valery Gergiev in St Petersburg, with Russian Nat. Orchestra under Michael Pletnev in Moscow, also with Royal Philharmonic Orchestra at the Barbican, London; has performed at festivals including La Roque d'Anthéron and Colmar, France, Klavier-Festival Ruhr, Germany, Chopin Piano Festival, Poland, Brescia and Bergamo, Italy, White Nights Festival, St Petersburg, East Neuk, Scotland, also at Ravinia Festival with Chicago Symphony and James Conlon and Vail Valley Music Festival, USA with the New York Philharmonic and Alan Gilbert. *Recordings:* Schumann Symphonic Etudes/Brahms Paganini Variations 2009, Rachmaninov Etudes-Tableaux Op. 39/Corelli Variations 2009, Beethoven Diabelli Variations 2011, Glazunov Concerti Nos. 1 and 2 2011. *Honours:* First Prize, Busoni Competition, Italy, Fourth Prize, Tchaikovsky Competition, Moscow. *Current Management:* c/o Mir Artists, Via Marsiglie 9D, 40020 Casalfiumanese (BO), Italy. *Telephone:* 393-1736701 (mobile). *E-mail:* tr@mirartists.com; www.mirartists.com; www.romanovsky.it.

ROMBOUT, Ernest; Dutch oboist; *Professor of Oboe, Conservatory of Music, Utrecht;* b. 30 Aug. 1959; m. Anne-Lou Langendyk 1995; one s. one d. *Education:* Staatliche Hochschule für Musik, Freiburg, Germany and studied with Heinz Holliger. *Career:* debut at Concertgebouw, Amsterdam 1983; soloist in major halls in Amsterdam, Berlin, Moscow, Munich, Lisbon, Paris, Zürich; festivals include Biennale of Venice, Donaueschinger Musiktage, Ludwigsburger Festspiele, Festival of New Music Middelburg, Takefu Festival, Japan, Summer Festival, Avignon, Summer Festival, Los Angeles; Prof. of Oboe, Conservatory of Music, Utrecht 1985–; masterclasses and workshops in The Netherlands, Russia, Austria and Liechtenstein 1993–; mem. of jury, Int. Oboe Competition (CIEM), Geneva 1998. *Recordings:* solo: Oboe Concertos, Haydn, Mozart, Theme and Variations by J. N. Hummel with the Concertgebouw Chamber Orchestra; Oboe Concertos by L. Francesconi, D. del Puerto; Omaggio all'Opera Lirica, arrangements of works by Rossini, Bellini, Donizetti, Verdi and others for oboe and harp with harpist Erika Waardenburg. *Honours:* prizewinner Ancona Competition of Winds, Italy 1979. *Address:* Oude Eemnesserstraat 34, 1221 HL Hilversum, The Netherlands (home). *E-mail:* erombout@tiscali.nl (home).

ROMERO, Angel; Spanish classical guitarist and conductor; b. 17 Aug. 1946, Malaga; one s. two d. *Education:* studied guitar with Celedonio Romero, conducting with Soltan Rushnia, Eugene Ormandy, Morton Gould, Ather Fiedler. *Career:* debut, Lobero Theatre, Santa Barbara, California 1958; first classical guitarist to perform at the Hollywood Bowl at West Coast premiere of Joaquin Rodrigo's Concerto de Aranjuez with the Los Angeles Philharmonic; performances with the Boston Symphony, Chicago Symphony, Philadelphia Orchestra, New York Philharmonic, Cleveland Orchestra, Orquesta National de Espana, Berlin Philharmonic, Concertgebouw-Amsterdam; Halls include Carnegie Hall, Musikverein-Vienna, Orchestra Hall, Chicago; performed for both Presidents Jimmy Carter and Richard Nixon, also the Pope at the Vatican; television appearances include the celebration of the 500th anniversary of Columbus' discovery at the United Nations with the Orquesta National de Espana, 1992; also with Arther Fiedler and the Boston Pops; performed with conductors including Eugene Ormandy, Raymond Leppard, Neville Mariner, Jesús López Cobos, Rafael Frühbeck de Burgos, Eduardo Mata, Giuseppe Patanè, Morton Gould, André Previn; conducted the Academy of St Martin-in-the-Fields, Pittsburgh Symphony Orchestra, San Diego Symphony Orchestra. *Compositions:* movie score for Bienvenido-Welcome. *Recordings:* Bella, Romero/Rodrigo, Remembering the Future, Vivaldi Concertos, Granados: Twelve Spanish Dances, Bach: The Music of Bach transcribed for the guitar, A Touch of Romance, A Touch of Class, Concierto de Aranjuez and Fantasia para un Gentilhombre, Spanish Guitar Virtuoso, Classic Guitar Virtuoso, Music of Rodrigo and Moreno Torroba, Guiliani: Guitar Concertos, Schifrin and Villa Lobos: Guitar Concertos, Rodrigo: Elogio de la Guitarra and Moreno Torroba, Music of Celedonio Romero, Moreno Torroba and Castelnuovo-Tedesco: Guitar Concertos, Claude Bolling: Concerto for Classic Guitar and Jazz Piano, Villa Lobos: Bachianas brasileiras. *Honours:* Gran Cruz, Orden de Isabel la Católica 2000; Mexican Academy Award (Ariel) for best original score, Recording Acad. President's Merit Award 2007. *Current Management:* c/o Jason Mainland, Vantage Artists, 45 Main Street, Suite 614, Brroklyn, NY 11201, USA. *Telephone:* (212) 229-2260. *Fax:* (212) 229-1133. *E-mail:* jmainland@vantageartists.com. *Website:* www.vantageartists .com. *Address:* Angel Romero Music, Inc., PO Box 906, San Marcos, CA 92069, USA (office). *Website:* www.angelromero.com.

ROMERO, Angelo; Italian singer (bass-baritone); b. 30 May 1940, Cagliari, Sardinia. *Education:* studied in Rome. *Career:* debut at Opera di Camera, Rome, as Monteverdi's Orfeo, 1966; Appearances throughout Italy, including Rome, Milan and Verona Arena (1982); Raimbaud in Le Comte Ory at Venice, 1988, Dandini in Cenerentola at Parma, 1990, and Geronimo in Il Matrimonio Segreto at Lausanne, 1993; Further guest appearances at Buenos Aires, Cincinnati, Geneva and Aix-en-Provence; Sang Cimarosa's Maestro di Capella for Rome Opera, 2001. *Recordings include:* Le Maschere by Mascagni; Donizetti's Gianni di Parigi. *Current Management:* c/o Giuseppe Oldani, Music Center, Viale Legioni Romane 26, 20147 Milan, Italy. *Telephone:* (2) 48702828. *Fax:* (2) 48700692. *E-mail:* info@musicenteronline.com. *Website:* www.musicenteronline.com.

ROMERO, Patricia, DipCNM, LCNM, LTCL; British/Mexican concert pianist, lecturer and María Fausta Patricia Romero Ponce; b. 20 Sept. 1953, Mexico City, Mexico; m. David Hanesworth; one s. *Education:* Conservatorio Nacional de Música, Mexico City, Trinity Coll., London, studied privately with Louis Kentner, master classes with Jorg Demus, Bernard Flavigny. Angélica Morales and John Lill and at Prussia Cove, Cornwall. *Career:* debut, Wigmore Hall, London 1976; performed widely in the UK, Spain, Switzerland, Italy, France, Greece and the Middle East; London appearances include Purcell Room, Wigmore Hall, Fairfield Halls, St John's Smith Square, Leighton House, St Martin in the Fields; performances with Orquesta Sinfónica del Bajio, Orquesta de la Universidad de Guadalajara, Orquesta Sinfónica de Coyoacan; radio broadcasts in Mexico City, Guadalajara and for the BBC; performed complete piano works of Maurice Ravel at the Purcell Room, London 1994; tours of Australia, NZ, Scandinavia and Russia 1998, of Argentina and Brazil 1999; concert with the Philharmonic of the Univ. of Hertfordshire 1999; tour of Turkey, Greece, Italy, France and Spain 2000, Spain and the Canary Islands 2001; concerts aboard the Arcadia and Oriana cruise ships 2002; tours of Spain, Switzerland and Mexico 2004, concerts in the UK 2004; formed a flute and piano duo (Cantilena) with Odinn Baldvinsson that has performed in several music clubs and halls in London; piano teacher, Trinity School, Croydon 2005–, Whitgift School 2008–; Piano Organizer for the Coulsdon and Purley Festival, Croydon 2011–; mem.

European Piano Teachers Asscn (UK), Incorporated Soc. of Musicians (Performers Section). *Recording:* Cantilena, with Odinn Baldvinsson 2009. *Honours:* First Prize, Yamaha Piano Competition 1971, Maud Seton Pianist Prize, London 1975, Herbert Shead Piano Competition, Trinity Coll. 1975. *Current Management:* c/o Hanesworth Concert Management, 114 Woodcote Grove Road, Coulsdon, Surrey, CR5 2AF, England. *Telephone:* (20) 8660-4096. *Fax:* (20) 8660-4096. *E-mail:* david.hanesworth@btopenworld.com (office). *Telephone:* (20) 8660-4096. *E-mail:* patricia.romero@btopenworld.com. *Website:* www.patriciaromeroconcertpianist.co.uk.

ROMERO, Pepe; American classical guitarist; b. 3 Aug. 1944, Málaga, Spain; s. of Celedonio Romero and Angelita Romero (née Gallego); m. 1st Kristine Eddy 1965; m. 2nd Carissa Sugg 1987; one s. three d. *Education:* various music acads in USA, including Music Acad. of the West. *Career:* began career in Seville, Spain, as part of Romero Quartet 1951, reformed in USA 1960; solo recordings plus others with Romero Quartet and various orchestras; Artist-in-Residence, Univ. of Southern California 1972, Distinguished Artist-in-Residence, Thornton School of Music, Univ. of Southern California 2004; taught at Univ. of California, San Diego 1984, Southern Methodist Univ. and Univ. of San Diego. *Publications include:* Guitar Method, Guitar Transcriptions for 1, 2 and 4 guitars. *Honours:* Order of Isabel la Católica (Spain); Dr hc (San Francisco Conservatory of Music), (Univ. of Victoria); Premio Andalucía de la Música 1996, President's Merit Award, Recording Acad. 2007. *Current Management:* Columbia Artists Management, Inc., 1790 Broadway, New York, NY 10019, USA. *E-mail:* tfox@cami.com. *Website:* www.peperomero.com.

ROMIG, James, BM, MM, PhD; American composer and academic; *Associate Professor of Theory and Composition, Western Illinois University;* b. 5 Aug. 1971, Long Beach, Calif.; m. Ashlee Mack. *Education:* Univ. of Iowa, Rutgers Univ., compositional studies with Charles Wuorinen, theoretical studies with Milton Babbitt. *Career:* fmr teacher, Univ. of Iowa, Rutgers Univ.; Asst Prof., Bucknell Univ. 2001–02; Assoc. Prof. of Theory and Composition, Western Illinios Univ. 2002–; Conductor and Music Dir Soc. of Chromatic Art; Asst Music Dir and Conductor of Helix, Rutgers Univ. new-music ensemble; played percussion with Joffrey Ballet, Handel and Haydn Soc. of Boston and the Symphony Orchestra, Percussion Ensemble and Center for New Music, Univ. of Iowa; comms/works performed by many US ensembles and orchestras; Guest Composer visits include Northwestern Univ., Columbia Univ., Cincinnati Conservatory, Juilliard School, American Acad. in Rome, Petrified Forest Nat. Park; numerous festival performances, including 50th Annual Fulbright Convention Music Gala, Berlin, Germany 1997, New Music Festival, William Paterson Univ. 2003, Total Music Festival, Tel-Aviv, Israel 2003, City Stages Music Festival (Birmingham, Alabama) 2004, Soc. for American Music Annual Conf. 2006, Third Int. Percussion Festival, Escuela Superior de Musica, Monterrey, Mexico 2006, Integrales New Music Festival, Univ. of Southern Mississippi 2008, SCI Region V Conf., Clarke Coll. 2009, PAS Day of Percussion, Purchase Coll., State Univ. of NY 2009, Festival of New Music, Florida State Univ. 2009, New Music Festival, Western Illinois Univ. 2010, Iowa Composers Forum Festival, Cedar Rapids, Ia 2010, New Music Festival/SCI Region VI Conf., Univ. of Central Missouri 2011, New Music Festival, Western Illinois Univ. 2011, Iowa Composers Forum Festival, Coe Coll. 2011; Petrified Forest Nat. Park Artist-in-Residence 2009; Grand Canyon Nat. Park Artist-in-Residence 2012; numerous lectures, masterclasses and paper presentations throughout US and abroad; numerous appointments as guest composer; mem. American Soc. of Composers, Authors and Publrs (ASCAP), American Music Center, Soc. for Music Theory, Pi Kappa Lambda Nat. Music Honor Soc. *Compositions:* solo works: Block for multi-percussion 1996, Vibraphone Sonata 1997, Gedanke for piano 1998, Vibraphone Sonata No. 2 1999, Sonnet 1 for violin 1999, Sonnet 2 for flute 1999, Sonnet 3 for clarinet 2001, Sonnet 4 for marimba 2002, Sonnet 5 for cello 2003, Sonnet 6 for bassoon 2003, Sonnet 7 for steel drums 2005, Oiseau Miró for flute 2001, Thread Sketches for piano 2001, Islands That Never Were for piano 2003, Piano Sonata 2004, Transparencies for piano 2004, A Slightly Evil Machine for multi-percussion 2005, Second Piano Sonata 2007, Disposition/Reflection for piano 2011; chamber works: Three Percussion Quartets 1991–92, Piano Trio for violin, cello and piano 1997, Double 1 for flute and marimba 1998, Double 2 for violin and marimba 1998, Spin for flute, violin, cello and keyboard percussion 1999, Variations for string quartet 1999, Shifting Brilliancies for oboe, vibraphone, contrabass and piano 2000, Negative Mirrors for flute, clarinet, violin, cello, vibraphone and piano 2001, Double 3 for trumpet and vibraphone 2003, The Frame Problem for percussion trio 2003, Islands That Never Were for vibraphone and piano 2003, Double 4 for flute and piano 2004, Ferocious Alphabets for clarinet and violin 2005, Small Worlds for flute, clarinet, violin, cello and piano 2006, Three Miniatures for flute, violin and glockenspiel 2006, Double 5 for trombone and piano 2007, Chronophonetic Alphabets for flute, clarinet, violin, cello, marimba and piano 2007, Recall Coordinator for flute and vibraphone 2008, Leaves from Modern Trees for flute and piano 2011, Walls Like These for cello and piano 2011; large ensemble works: Circulus and Invisible Cities for orchestra 1992–93, Six Pieces for string orchestra 1996, Trio for Orchestra for orchestra 1998, Negative Mirrors for orchestra 2002, Islands That Never Were for piano and string orchestra 2006, Glaciers for orchestra 2009, Percussion Concerto for percussion soloist and orchestra 2010. *Publications:* How to Listen to a New Piece of Music, A Conversation with Milton Babbitt, Parametric Counterpoint: Babbittonian Ideals in Composition and Performance. *Honours:* Rutgers Univ. Grad. Fellowship 1998, ASCAP Standard Award 1998–, Meet

the Composer grant 2003, Western Illinois Univ. Alumni Foundation Summer Stipend Grant 2004, 2006, Fellowship, Composers Conf., Wellesley Coll. 2008, American Acad. of Arts and Letters Awards in Music 2009, Hon. Mention, American Composers Orchestra Underwood New Music Readings 2011, Aaron Copland Award and Copland House Residency 2011. *Address:* School of Music, Western Illinois University, Macomb, IL 61455, USA (office). *E-mail:* jromig@jamesromig.com (home). *Website:* www.jamesromig.

RONCO, Claudio, MA; Italian cellist and composer; b. 16 Sept. 1955, Turin; m. Lone K. Loëll 1983; two s. *Education:* Conservatory of Music, Turin with Anner Bylsma and Christophe Coin. *Career:* debut at Como with the Clemencic Consort of Vienna 1982; soloist with the Clemencic Consort, Vienna 1982–; Hesperion XX, Ensemble 14, for ZDF 1991; television programme on Jewish music and solo recital for Radio Canada, Montréal. *Compositions:* Tombeau de Mr Farinelli for violin, violoncello and harpsichord 1994, Serenata Pastorale for three voices, violin, violoncello and harpsichord. *Recordings:* several recordings with Hesperion XX, Clemencic Consort, first recording of Veracini, Bonporti, Lanzetti, Paganini, Gade Heise trios.

RONGE, Gabriela Marie; German singer (soprano); b. 3 July 1957, Hanover. *Career:* sang in opera at Heidelberg from 1982, and Osnabruck from 1983 notably as Fiordiligi and Hanna Glawari; Further engagements at Hanover, 1985–87, Cologne, 1989, Frankfurt, Bonn, the Deutsche Oper Berlin and Brunswick; Bayerische Staatsoper Munich from 1987 as the Marschallin, Elsa, Eva and Agathe; Frankfurt in 1987 as Gluck's Iphigénie en Tauride, Paris Opéra in 1989 as Eva, and Isabella in Wagner's Das Liebesverbot at Palermo in 1991; Sang Aida at Schwerin, 1999; Brünnhilde in the Ring at Graz and Senta at the Deutsche Oper Berlin; Noted interpreter of Lieder.

RONI, Luigi; Italian singer (bass); b. 22 Feb. 1942, Vergemoli, Lucca. *Education:* studied with Sara Sforni Corti in Milan. *Career:* debut at Spoleto 1965 as Mephistopheles in Faust; sang in Milan, Rome, Turin, Venice, Palermo, Florence and Naples; Moscow in 1973 with La Scala Company; Guest appearances in Vienna, Munich, Berlin, London, Paris, New York, Chicago, Dallas and Houston; Orange Festival in 1984 as the Grand Inquisitor in Don Carlos; other roles include Mozart's Commendatore and Mussorgsky's Dosifey; La Scala in 1987 as Lodovico in Otello; Sang MacGregor in Mascagni's Guglielmo Ratcliff at Catania, 1990, Rossini's Basilio at Bonn, and Festival d'Orange in 1990 as the Grand Inquisitor in Don Carlos. *Recordings include:* Aida; Don Giovanni; Fernand Cortez by Spontini; Zaira by Bellini; Otello. *Current Management:* c/o Atelier Musicale, Via Caselle 76, San Lazzaro di Savena 40068, Italy. *Telephone:* (51) 19984444. *Fax:* (51) 19984420. *E-mail:* info@ateliermusicale.com. *Website:* www.ateliermusicale.com.

ROOCROFT, Amanda, FRNCM; British singer (soprano); b. 9 Feb. 1966, Coppull, Lancs.; d. of Roger Roocroft and Valerie Roocroft (née Metcalfe); m. 2nd David Gowland 1999; two s. *Education:* Royal Northern Coll. of Music. *Career:* appearances include Sophie in Der Rosenkavalier, Welsh Nat. Opera 1990, Pamina in The Magic Flute, Covent Garden 1991, 1993, Fiordiligi in Così fan tutte, Glyndebourne 1991, European tour with John Eliot Gardiner 1992, Bavarian State Opera 1993, 1994, Covent Garden 1995, Giulietta in I Capuleti e I Montecchi, Covent Garden 1993, Ginevra in Ariodante, ENO 1993, Donna Elvira in Don Giovanni, Glyndebourne 1994, New York Metropolitan Opera 1997, Amelia in Simon Boccanegra, Bavarian State Opera 1995, Mimi in La Bohème, Covent Garden 1996, Countess in Marriage of Figaro, Bavarian State Opera 1997, New York Metropolitan Opera 1999, Cleopatra in Giulio Cesare, Covent Garden 1997, Desdemona in Otello, Bavarian State Opera 1999, Covent Garden 2001, Jenůfa, Glyndebourne 2000, Berlin 2002, Katya Kabanova, Glyndebourne 1998, Covent Garden 2000, Meistersinger, Royal Opera House 2002; Jenůfa for ENO 2009, for Teatro Real Madrid 2009; title role in Katya Kabanova for WNO 2011; Feldmarschallin in Rosenkavalier for ENO 2012; Duchess in Powder Her Face, ENO 2014; debut at BBC Promenade Concert and Edin. Festival 1993; regular concert engagements and recitals; Fellow, Univ. of Cen. Lancs. 1992. *Recordings include:* Vaughan Williams Serenade to Music (with Matthew Best) 1990, Così fan tutte (with John Eliot Gardiner) 1993, Amanda Roocroft (solo album) 1994, Mozart and his Contemporaries 1996, Schoenberg String Quartet No. 2 (with Britten Quartet) 1994, Vaughan Williams Sea Symphony (with Andrew Davies), Mahler Symphony No. 4 (with Simon Rattle) 1998, Vaughan Williams Pastoral Symphony (with Bernard Haitink) 1998, Elgar, Complete Songs for Voice and Piano Vol 1 2007, Steve Nieve, Welcome to the Voice 2007, Vaughan Williams, Choral Works 2008, Beethoven: Symphony No. 9 2011, Hubert Parry: Works for Chorus and Orchestra 2013. *Television documentaries include:* The Girl from Coppull, The Debut (Granada TV), Hard Pressed for Signals (Channel 4), Jenufa (BBC Wales). *Honours:* Hon. DMus (Manchester) 2003, Kathleen Ferrier Prize 1988, Silver Medal, Worshipful Co. of Musicians 1988, Royal Philharmonic Soc./Charles Heidsieck Award 1990, Barclay Opera Award 2000, Outstanding Achievement In Opera (for Jenůfa, ENO 2006), Laurence Olivier Awards 2007. *Website:* www.askonasholt.co.uk/artists/singers/soprano/amanda-roocroft.

ROOLEY, Anthony, LRAM, FRAM; British lutenist, director, lecturer and researcher; b. 10 June 1944, Leeds, Yorks., England; three d. with Carla Rooley; one s. with Emma Kirkby. *Education:* Royal Acad. of Music. *Career:* teacher of guitar, lute, RAM 1968–71; Co-founder (with James Tyler) Consort of Musicke 1969–; dir and lutenist, many early music concerts, Europe, Middle East, USA; dir 1971–, often giving concerts of Renaissance theme; appearances on BBC, French and German TV and radio; int. festivals in Europe,

Scandinavia, USA; concerts with sopranos Emma Kirkby, Evelyn Tubb, alto Mary Nichols, tenor Andrew King, Simon Grant, Joseph Cornwell (Consort of Musicke mems), bass David Thomas, tenor Paul Agnew, other early music specialists; music-theatre includes staging of Le Veglie di Siena (music by Orazio Vecchi), Copenhagen, London 1988; collaboration with Italian commedia dell'arte actors La Famiglia Carrara in Marriage of Pantelone; Promenade Concert 1988, based on settings of poet Torquato Tasso; concerts in Tel-Aviv, New York 1988; Co-Dir (with Arjen Terpstra) record label, Musica Oscura; teacher in Japan, Padova, Basle, Dartington, promoting Renaissance attitudes to performance; Co-Dir (with Don Taylor), video Banquet of the Senses: Monteverdi's Madrigali Erotici; directed Semele, opera by Congreve and Eccles at Florida State Univ. 2003; first modern performance of William Hayes's The Passions: An Ode to Musick 2003, 2005, 2006; mem Viola da Gamba Soc., Galpin Soc., Wine Soc., Royal Soc. of Arts. *Recordings include:* Madrigals by Monteverdi, de Rore, Marini, Porter, Pallavicino, Marenzio, d'India; L'anime del Purgatorio (Stradella); Madrigals and Fantasias, Psalms and Anthems (John Ward); Arie Antiche, The Mad Lover (The Orpheus Circle); The Dark is my Delight (Women in Song); Maurice Greene: Songs and Keyboard works (The Handel Circle); The Mistress, The Mantle, Orpheus, Sound the Trumpets from Shore to Shore (Purcell), Madrigals and Part-songs (R.L. Pearsall), Semele (Eccles), The Passions (W. Hayes). *Publications include:* A New Varietie of Lute Lessons (album and book) 1975, The Penguin Book of Early Music (album and book) 1979, Performance: Revealing the Orpheus Within 1990, 2005; contrib. to Lute Society Journal, Early Music, Guitar. *Address:* c/o Consort of Musicke, 13 Pages Lane, London, N10 1PU, England. *Telephone:* (20) 8444-6565. *Fax:* (20) 8444-1008. *E-mail:* consort@easynet.co.uk.

ROOSENSCHOON, Hans, MMus, DMus; South African/Dutch composer; *Professor of Composition, Stellenbosch University*; b. 17 Dec. 1952, The Hague, The Netherlands; s. of Maarten Roosenschoon and Wilhelmina Christina van der Meer; m. Linda-Louise Badenhorst; two s. *Education:* Pretoria Conservatory, Royal Acad. of Music, London with Paul Patterson, Stellenbosch Univ., Univ. of Cape Town. *Career:* Production Man., South African Broadcasting Corpn (SABC), Cape Town 1980–95; Chair. Dept of Music and Dir of Conservatory, Stellenbosch Univ. 1998–2006, Prof. of Composition 2007–. *Compositions include:* Palette for strings 1977, Makietie for brass quintet 1978, Ars Poetica for baritone, double chorus and orchestra 1979, Ghomma for orchestra 1980, Firebowl for chorus 1980, Ikonografie for orchestra 1983, If Music Be 1984, Timbila for chopi xylophone ensemble and orchestra 1985, Horizon, Night Sky and Landscape for strings 1987, Does the Noise in my Head Bother You? for chorus and orchestra 1988, Mantis for chamber orchestra 1988, Fingerprints for piano 1989, Circle of Light, The Magic Marimba for orchestra 1991, Do-Re-Mi-Fabriek for orchestra 1992, Kô, Lat Ons Sing for double chorus 1993, Clouds Clearing for Strings 1994, To Open a Window for string quartet 1995, Ubuntu for chorus and orchestra 1996, A New Costume for the Emperor for piano trio 2000, Speculum Musicae for orchestra 2002, Klavierkant for piano 2004, Sky for double chorus 2004, Landskap for piano duo 2005, Menorah for orchestra 2005, Earth, Water, Air and Fire for orchestra 2006, To the Tune Of for flute, strings, piano and percussion 2007, Labyrinth (electronic) 2007, Curved Surface and Symmetry for organ 2013, ...or to err... for orchestra 2013, Die melkweg en die gebreekte snaar for mezzo, marimba and string quartet 2015. *Honours:* UNISA Composition Prize 1975, Dept of Nat. Educ. Composition Prize 1975, 1988, SAMRO Overseas Scholarship 1976, Arthur Lohr Scholarship 1978, Standard Bank Young Artist Award for Music 1987, Cape Tercentenary Foundation Award of Merit 1998. *Address:* Department of Music, Stellenbosch University, Private Bag X1, Matieland 7602, South Africa (office). *Telephone:* (21) 8083410 (office). *E-mail:* hroosen@sun.ac.za (office). *Website:* www.roosenschoon.co.za.

ROOT, Deane Leslie, BA, MMus, PhD; American musicologist, museum curator, teacher, librarian and editor; *Editor in Chief, Grove Music, Oxford University Press*; b. 9 Aug. 1947, Wausau, Wis.; s. of Forrest K. Root and Marguerite Root; m. Doris J. Dyen 1972; two d. *Education:* New Coll., Sarasota, Fla, Univ. of Illinois. *Career:* Faculty, Univ. of Wisconsin 1973; editorial staff, New Grove Dictionary of Music and Musicians, Macmillan 1974–76, Ed.-in-Chief Grove Music, Oxford University Press 2009–; Research Assoc., Univ. of Illinois 1976–80; Visiting Research Assoc., Florida State Univ. 1981–82; Curator, Stephen Foster Memorial and Adjunct Asst Prof. in Music, Univ. of Pittsburgh 1982–96, Chair. Music Dept 2002–07, Heinz Chapel Admin. 1983–95, Dir of Cultural Resources 1990–94, Adjunct Assoc. Prof. 1992–96, Prof. of Music, Dir and Fletcher Hodges Jr Curator, Center for American Music 1998–; Pres. Sonneck Soc. for American Music 1989–93; Del., American Council of Learned Socs 1996–99; mem. American Antiquarian Soc. Fellowship panels 2005, 2008, Nat. Endowment for the Humanities Review panels 1990–. *Recordings:* Proud Traditions, Musical Tribute to Pitt 1987. *Art exhibitions:* Pittsburgh Rhythms, Historical Soc. of Western Pa (consultant) 1990–96, perm. exhbn on Stephen Foster, Center for American Music, Univ. of Pittsburgh. *Television:* consultant, I Hear America Singing (PBS) 1996, Stephen Foster (PBS) 2001, Broadway: The American Musical (PBS) 2004. *Films:* music consultant, Gangs of New York (dir, Martin Scorsese) 2002. *Publications:* American Popular Stage Music 1860–1880, Music of Florida Historic Sites, Resources of American Music History (co-author), Music of Stephen C. Foster (co-ed.), Nineteenth Century American Musical Theater (series ed., 16 vols) 1994, Voices Across Time: American History Through Song (co-author) 2004, Emily's Songbook: Music in 1850s Albany (co-ed.) 2011; contrib. to New Grove Dictionary of Music and New Grove Dictionary of

American Music, American National Biography, various journals, yearbooks, conf. proceedings, articles in journals, multi-author books. *Honours:* Woodrow Wilson Fellow 1968, Music Library Asscn Book of the Year 1981, American Library Asscn Choice Award 1992, Soc. for American Music Distinguished Service 2000. *Address:* Department of Music, 205 Music Building, University of Pittsburgh, Pittsburgh, PA 15260, USA (office). *Telephone:* (412) 624-4126 (office); (412) 624-7775 (office). *Fax:* (412) 624-4186 (office). *E-mail:* dlr@pitt.edu (office). *Website:* www.music.pitt.edu (office).

ROOTERING, Jan-Hendrik; German singer (bass-baritone) and voice teacher; b. 18 March 1950, Wedingfeld, nr Flensburg; s. of Hendrikus Rootering; m. Marie-Pierre Rootering; one s. *Education:* studied voice with his father, and at Musikhochschule Hamburg. *Career:* debut at Metropolitan Opera, New York in role of Landgraf in Tannhäuser under James Levine 1986–87; sang in roles like Gurnemanz, Fasolt, Daland, Pogner, Gremin, Rocco, Sarastro, Alaska Wolf Joe, Count Walter, John Claggart, Il Commendatore, Don Basilio, Colline, Sparafucile, Baron Ochs, Inquisitore and Philipp at the Met –2006; first engagement at Bavarian State Opera as Geisterbote in Die Frau ohne Schatten 1982; Prof., Hochschule für Musik, Munich 1994; Prof., Folkwang Universität der Künste, Essen 2008–; regular guest appearances at major opera houses world-wide, including La Scala, Milan, Royal Opera House, Covent Garden, Opéra Basille, Paris, Chicago Lyric Opera, Vienna State Opera, Semperoper, Dresden and opera houses in San Francisco, Washington, New York, Berlin and Sydney; guest appearances at int. festivals including Munich Opera Festival, Salzburg Festival, Berlin Schubertiade, Beethoven Festival and Vienna Festivals, Opera Festival, Oslo and Ravinia; has sung almost all major bass roles of Mozart (Sarastro, Commendatore) and Wagner repertoire (Pogner, Fasolt, Fafner, Hunding, King Marke, König Heinrich, Gurnemanz, Daland, Landgraf, Hans Sachs, Wotan) as well as some roles of the Italian repertoire (Fiesco (Simon Boccanegra), Banquo (Macbeth); appeared as Hans Sachs in new production of Die Meistersinger at Bavarian State Opera under Zubin Mehta, at Opéra de Bastille, Paris, Vienna State Opera, Nederlandse Opera, Amsterdam, Royal Opera House, Covent Garden, Semperoper Dresden and Maggio Musicale Fiorentino; sang his first Wotan in Die Walküre in Stuttgart and at Vienna State opera 2004; sang Gurnemanz in Parsifal at Nederlandse Opera, Amsterdam, Oper Leipzig, Bavarian State Opera, Munich, Deutsche Oper, Berlin and at Semperoper, Dresden and Théâtre de la Monnaie, Brussels. *Honours:* Bavarian Kammersänger 1989, Hon. Prof., Hochschule für Musik, Munich 1994; Grammy Award for Best Opera Recording. *E-mail:* jhrootering@me.com.

ROREM, Ned, MA; American composer; b. 23 Oct. 1923, Richmond, IN. *Education:* American Conservatory, Chicago with Leo Sowerby, Northwestern Univ., Curtis Inst., Philadelphia, Juilliard School, New York, studied with Thomson and Copland. *Career:* lived in Morocco 1949–51, in France 1951–57; composer-in-residence Univ. of Buffalo 1959–61, Univ. of Utah 1966–67, Curtis Inst. 1980–, Manhattan School of Music 1985–, Yale Univ. 1998–; Pres., American Acad. of Arts and Letters 2000–03. *Compositions:* three symphonies 1951, 1956, 1959, four string quartets 1948, 1950, 1990, 1994, Design for orchestra 1953, A Childhood Miracle (opera) 1955, The Poets' Requiem 1955, The Robbers (opera) 1958, Eleven Studies for Eleven Players 1960, Ideas for orchestra 1961, Lift up your Heads for chorus and wind 1963, Lions (A Dream) for orchestra 1963, Miss Julie (opera) 1965, Letters from Paris for chorus and orchestra 1966, Sun eight poems for high voice and orchestra 1966, Water Music for clarinet, violin and orchestra 1966, Bertha (one-act opera) 1968, War Scenes for voice and piano 1969, three piano concertos 1950, 1951, 1969, Little Prayers for soprano, baritone and orchestra 1973, Air Music variations for orchestra (Pulitzer Prize 1976) 1974, Serenade on Five English Poems 1975, Hearing five scenes for singers and seven instruments 1976, Sunday Morning for orchestra 1977, The Nantucket Songs 1979, Remembering Tommy concerto for piano, cello and orchestra 1979, After Reading Shakespeare for solo cello 1980, The Santa Fe Songs for voice and piano quartet 1980, After Long Silence for soprano, oboe and strings 1982, An American Oratorio 1983, Winter Pages for five instruments 1982, Whitman Cantata 1983, Violin Concerto 1984, Septet, Scenes from Childhood 1985, Organ Concerto 1985, End of Summer for violin, clarinet and piano 1985, String Symphony 1985, Homer (Three Scenes from the Iliad) for chorus and eight instruments 1986, Goodbye My Fancy for chorus, soloists, orchestra 1988–89, The Auden Poems for tenor and piano trio 1989, Swords and Plowshares for four vocal soloists and orchestra 1991, Piano Concerto for left hand and orchestra 1992, Cor anglais concerto 1995, String Quartet No. 4 1995, Evidence of Things not Seen (365 songs to texts by 24 authors) 1997, Double Concerto for violin, cello and orchestra 1998, Evidence of Things Not Seen (36 songs for four voices and piano) 1999, Aftermath for voice and trio 2002, Cello Concerto 2002, Flute Concerto 2002, Mallet Concerto 2003, Our Town (opera) 2004–05; 100s of songs and 12 song cycles. *Publications:* Paris Diary 1966, Music from Inside Out 1966, New York Diary 1967, Music and People 1968, Critical Affairs 1970, The Later Diaries 1974, Pure Contraption 1974, Setting the Tone 1980, The Nantucket Diary 1985, Settling the Score 1988, Knowing When to Stop 1994, Other Entertainment (essays) 1995, Dear Paul, Dear Ned, Lies, A Diary (1986–99) 2001, A Ned Rorem Reader 2002, Wings of Friendship 2005. *Honours:* ASCAP Foundation Lifetime Achievement Award. *Address:* c/o ASCAP, ASCAP Building, 1 Lincoln Plaza, New York, NY 10023, USA.

RORHOLM, Marianne; Danish singer (mezzo-soprano); b. 1960. *Education:* Opera Academy at Copenhagen. *Career:* debut at Royal Opera, Copenhagen as

Cherubino; season 1984–85 sang Olga, Lola and Rosina at Copenhagen and as the Sorceress in Dido and Aeneas at Paris Opéra; Frankfurt Opera, 1985–88 as Rosina, Dorabella, Sextus in La Clemenza di Tito, Nicklausse and Octavian; sang Cherubino with the Israel Philharmonic under Daniel Barenboim and at the 1987 Ludwigsburg Festival; Bayreuth Festival in 1988 as a Flowermaiden in Parsifal; season 1988–89 included US debut with the Indianapolis Symphony under Raymond Leppard, a concert at Carnegie Hall, Cherubino at Glyndebourne and Isolier in Le Comte Ory for Netherlands Opera; regular appearances with the Deutsche Oper am Rhein, Düsseldorf, and Basle Operas; season 1992 as Annius in La Clemenza di Tito at Toulouse, Varvara in Katya Kabanova at Bonn, Purcell's Dido at Brussels and the Berlioz Marguerite at Amsterdam; season 2000 as Offred in the premiere of The Handmaid's Tale by Paul Ruders, at Copenhagen, and Carlotta in Die schweigsame Frau, at Århus; concert repertory includes Mahler's Das Lied von der Erde; sang Verdi's Preziosilla at Copenhagen, 1996 and Nicklausse in Les Contes d'Hoffmann at Dublin, 1998. *Recordings include:* Kate Pinkerton in Madama Butterfly; Salome under Giuseppe Sinopoli; Dryad in Ariadne auf Naxos. *Honours:* Carl Nielsen Scholarship, 1984; Elisabeth Dons Memorial Prize, 1985. *Current Management:* Ingpen & Williams Ltd, 7 St George's Court, 131 Putney Bridge Road, London, SW15 2PA, England.

ROS MARBA, Antoni; Spanish conductor; b. 2 April 1937, Barcelona. *Education:* Barcelona Conservatory, studied with Eduard Toldra, Celibidache at Accademia Chigiana and Jean Martinon at Düsseldorf. *Career:* debut in Barcelona 1962; Principal Conductor 1965–68, later Principal Guest Conductor and Artistic Consultant for Spanish Radio and Television Orchestras, for City of Barcelona Orchestra 1967–77, Spanish Nat. Orchestra 1978–81, and Netherlands Chamber Orchestra 1979–86; Principal Guest Conductor, Netherlands Chamber Orchestra (from unification with Netherlands Philharmonic Orchestra) 1986–; further appearances and tours worldwide, including Europe, North and South America, Japan and People's Republic of China, and with orchestras such as Berlin Philharmonic Orchestra; developed international career as an opera conductor with success at Teatro de la Zarzuela, Madrid and Gran Teatro del Liceu, Barcelona; Musical Dir, National Opera Theatre Real, Madrid 1989; season 1992 with the stage premiere of Gerhard's The Duenna at Madrid, repeated for Opera North; Idomeneo for Scottish Opera 1996. *Recordings include:* Haydn's Seven Last Words on the Cross, others with Victoria de Los Angeles, Teresa Berganza, English Chamber Orchestra and Netherlands Chamber Orchestra. *Honours:* National Music Prize of Spain, Ministry of Culture 1989, Arthur Honegger International Recording Prize (for Seven Last Words on the Cross), Cross of St Jordi Generalitat de Cataluna.

ROSAND, Aaron; violinist and teacher; b. 15 March 1927, Hammond, IN, USA. *Education:* studied with Marinus Paulsen, Leon Samenti and Efrem Zimbalist. *Career:* debut with the Chicago Symphony under Frederick Stock playing the Mendelssohn Concerto 1937; played at New York Town Hall 1948; European debut at Copenhagen 1955; tours of Europe, the Far East and Russia; appearances with leading orchestras in the USA; repertoire includes concertos by Lalo, Ries, Vieuxtemps, Joachim, Hubay and Wieniawski; taught at the Academie Internationale d'Eté in Nice from 1971, Peabody Conservatory, Baltimore and Mannes Coll., NY, and Curtis Inst., Philadelphia 1981–; plays a Guarneri del Gesu of 1741. *Recordings:* 15 albums. *Honours:* Chevalier Pour Mérite Cultural et Artistique 1965, Gold Medal of the Foundation Ysaÿe, Belgium 1967. *Current Management:* Jacques Leiser Artist Management, The Del Prado, 666 L/Pas Street, Suite 602, San Diego, CA 92103, USA.

ROSCA, Andreaiana; Romanian pianist and academic; b. 19 Nov. 1961, Bucharest; m. Alexandru-Ioan Geamana 1984. *Education:* Music High School Dinu Lipatti, Bucharest Univ. of Music, masterclasses with Bernard Ringeissen and Roger Vignoles. *Career:* debut aged 16 with Philharmonic Orchestra Ploiesti, Romania, playing Mozart's C minor concerto; concerts in Romania with major orchestras, including the Radio and Television Orchestra; numerous recordings for radio and television; recitals in Romania, Belgium; played at Verbier Festival, in Poland and Japan; repertoire includes Beethoven Piano Concertos; Liszt; Mozart; Schumann; Brahms; cycles of lieder and Romanian music, such as Enesun; accompanist for international singing competition for Radio Cologne, Germany; EPTA, Romania; Dinu Lipatti Foundation. *Recordings:* for Radio Cologne, lieder and Romanian piano repertoire. *Honours:* National Prizes 1979, 1980, 1982, 1986, Accompaniment Prize, Bianca 1993.

ROSCA, Marcel; Romanian singer (bass); b. 18 Oct. 1948, Bucharest; s. of Iov Rosca and Maria Rosca; three s. *Education:* Bucharest Univ. of Music. *Career:* fmr professional shooter; sang at Nat. Opera, Bucharest 1980–86; guest appearances at the Bolshoi Theatre, Moscow and in Poland, China, Vienna, Paris, Barcelona, Turin, Buenos Aires, São Paulo, Hamburg, Munich, Berlin, Stuttgart, Düsseldorf, Dresden, Bonn, Essen, Zurich, Basel, Budapest, Cuba and Korea; sang at Aalto Theater, Essen 1985–; roles include King Philip and Grand Inquisitor in Don Carlos, Zaccharias-Nabucco, Boris Godunov, Gremin in Eugene Onegin, Wagner's Hagen, Fafner, Hunding in Die Walküre, King Heinrich in Lohengrin, Kg. Marke, Figaro, Comendatore and Masetto, Osmin, Arkel in Pelléas et Mélisande, Sparafucile in Rigoletto, Sarastro, Mephisto-Faust, Mephistophele, Rocco, Pagno in I Lombardi, Peneios in Daphne, Waldner in Arabella, Don Pasquale, Walter in Luisa Miller; concerts throughout Europe and S America of the Verdi Requiem, Beethoven's Ninth and works by Dvořák; numerous TV appearances and recordings. *Films:* Pruncul, Petrolul si Ardelenii. *Honours:* Order of Sports, Romania,

Kammersänger, Germany; numerous Olympics, World and Europa Masters medals. *Address:* c/o Essen Aalto Theater, Rolandstrasse 10, 45128 Essen (office); Hagenaustrasse 13B, 45138 Essen, Germany (home). *Telephone:* (201) 798-8760 (office). *Fax:* (201) 798-8761 (office). *E-mail:* acsorm@googlemail.com (home).

RÖSCHMANN, Dorothea; German singer (soprano); b. 1969, Flensburg. *Education:* studied in Germany and with Vera Rozsa in London. *Career:* mem. Deutsche Staatsoper Berlin, appearing as Papagena, Iris (Semele) and Sophie in Der Rosenkavalier 1997; Salzburg Festival from 1995, as Susanna and in concert; further engagements as Zerlina at Tel-Aviv, Handel's Dorinda (Orlando) at Halle, Monteverdi's Drusilla at Munich and Dorina in Caldara's I Disingannati at the Early Music Festival Innsbruck; other roles include Weber's Ännchen at Berlin and Munich, Handel's Arianna (Giustino) at Göttingen and Servilia in La Clemenza di Tito, at the 1997 Salzburg Festival; season 1998 with Susanna at Salzburg and Donizetti's Norina at Brussels; sang Nannetta in Falstaff at Salzburg, 2001; season 2001–02 as Anne Trulove at the Munich Festival, Elmire in Keiser's Croesus, Staatsoper Berlin, Griselda (Scarlatti), Nannetta, Pamina, Zerlina and Fiordiligi; Covent Garden debut as Pamina 2003; concerts at Carnegie Hall, Vienna Musikverein, Leipzig Gewandhaus, Hamburg Musikhalle and Semperoper, Dresden. *Recordings include:* Pergolesi's Stabat Mater and Keiser's Masaniello Furioso; Messiah with Paul McCreesh and Bach's Secular Cantatas with Reinhard Goebbel; Bach's Weihnachtsoratorium and Telemann's Orpheus with René Jacobs, Bach, Dialogue Cantatas 2007, Mozart, Le Nozze di Figaro 2007, Songs My Mother Taught Me 2008, Handel, Famous Arias 2008.

ROSCOE, Martin; British pianist; b. 3 Aug. 1952, Halton, Cheshire, England. *Education:* Royal Manchester College of Music with Marjorie Clementi and Gordon Green. *Career:* appearances at Cheltenham, Bath, Leeds, and South Bank Music Festivals; performances at Royal Festival Hall, QEH, Royal Albert Hall, and Wigmore Hall in London with Hallé, City of Birmingham, Royal Philharmonic, Royal Liverpool Philharmonic, Northern Sinfonia, London Mozart Players, and BBC Philharmonic Orchestras; tours of Australia, Middle East and South America; further appearances at Harrogate Festival with Scottish National Orchestra, BBC, and Welsh Symphony Orchestras; played at the Promenade Concerts with BBC Symphony Orchestra 1987, and with French Philharmonic Orchestra 1989; recitals with violinist Tasmin Little, notably in the Kreutzer Sonata; mem. Incorporated Society of Musicians, Musicians' Union. *Recordings:* many for BBC Radio 3 including Piano Concertos of Berwald, Liszt, Beethoven, Stravinsky, Fauré, Vaughan Williams, and Shostakovich, solo works by Beethoven, complete Sonatas of Schubert, Debussy, Liszt and Bartók, concertos by Strauss and Szymanowski, solo commercial recordings with music by Liszt. *Honours:* Davas Gold Medal 1973, Silver Medal, Worshipful Company of Musicians 1974, British Liszt Piano Competition 1976, Sydney International Piano Competition 1981. *Current Management:* Hazard Chase Ltd, 25 City Road, Cambridge, CB1 1DP, England. *Telephone:* (1223) 312400. *Fax:* (1223) 460827. *E-mail:* info@hazardchase.co.uk. *Website:* www.hazardchase.co.uk.

ROSE, Gil, BMus, MFA; American conductor; *Founder and Music Director, Boston Modern Orchestra Project;* b. Pittsburgh, Pa. *Education:* Univ. of Cincinnati Coll. Conservatory of Music, Carnegie Mellon Univ. *Career:* Founder and Music Dir Boston Modern Orchestra Project 1996–; Music Dir Opera Boston 2003–; Artistic Dir Opera Unlimited Festival 2003–06; Guest Conductor Tanglewood Music Festival 2002, Netherlands Radio Symphony 2003; Artistic Dir Ditson Festival of Contemporary Music, Boston Inst. of Contemporary Art 2008; regular appearances with Boston Symphony Chamber Players; fmr Guest Conductor, American Composers Orchestra, Warsaw Philharmonic, Nat. Symphony Orchestra of the Ukraine, Cleveland Chamber Symphony, Orchestra della Svizzera Italiana, Nat. Orchestra of Porto. *Recordings:* numerous recordings with Boston Modern Orchestra Project including Samuel Barber: Vanessa 2003, Stephen Paulus: The Five Senses 2005, John Harbison: Ulysses 2008, John Cage: Sixteen Dances 2009, Louis Andriessen: La Passione 2009, Eric Moe: Kick & Ride 2011. *Honours:* Columbia Univ. Ditson Award 2007. *Address:* Boston Modern Orchestra Project, 376 Washington Street, # 101, Malden, MA 02148-1371, USA (office). *Telephone:* (781) 321-6868 (office). *E-mail:* gil@gilrose.info (office). *Website:* www.gilrose.info (office).

ROSE, Gregory, BA (Hons); British conductor, composer and academic; *Professor of Conducting, Trinity Laban Conservatoire of Music and Dance;* b. 18 April 1948, Beaconsfield, Bucks., England; s. of Bernard Rose, OBE and Molly Rose, OBE; m. Helen Ireland; one s. *Education:* Magdalen Coll., Oxford. *Career:* conductor, composer, founder of Singcircle, Circle 1977–; Music Dir London Jupiter Orchestra 1986–; Conductor, Reading Festival Chorus 1984–88; Conductor, London Concert Choir 1988–96; Conductor, Reading Symphony Orchestra 1986–91; Conductor Nat. Youth Choir of Wales 1986–89; has conducted Polish Nat. Radio Symphony Orchestra, St Petersburg Symphony Orchestra, Finnish Radio Symphony Orchestra, Odense Symphony Orchestra, London Philharmonic Orchestra, BBC Concert Orchestra, Ulster Orchestra, Nat. Symphony Orchestras of Estonia, Latvia, Lithuania, Eire, Netherlands Radio Chamber Orchestra London Philharmonia, Royal Scottish Nat. Orchestra, Estonian Philharmonic Chamber Choir, BBC Singers, Nederlands Kamerkoor, Groupe Vocal de France, WDR Choir, Steve Reich and Musicians; Series Dir, Cage at 70, Almeida Festival 1982 and Reich at 50, Almeida Festival 1986; has conducted operas by Bizet, Poulenc, Stravinsky, Scott Joplin, Virgil Thomson, Berthold Goldschmidt, Samuel

Barber, Nino Rota, Gian Carlo Menotti, Malcolm Williamson and Toshio Hosokawa; Prof. of Conducting, Trinity Laban Conservatoire of Music and Dance; has performed Stockhausen's Stimmung more than 50 times, including with composer at sound desk. *Music:* arranger/conductor for Diana Ross, Linda Ronstadt, Madness, Sasha & Shawna. *Compositions include:* Tapiola Sunrise, Birthday Ode for Aaron Copland, Cristalflood, Thambapani; works for chorus and many arrangements; completion of Hummel's Violin Concerto, Missa Sancta Pauli Apostoli (British Composer Award (Liturgical Section) 2006), Sha'alu Shlom Yerushalayim, Missa Sancti Dunstani, five sets of Evening Canticles, 12 masses; Danse macabre 2011, Avebury Stone Circles, etc. *Recordings:* Hyperion, Mouth Music, Stockhausen's Stimmung; Wergo, Son Entero by Alejandro Viñao; Continuum, music by Simon Emmerson; October Music, music by Trevor Wishart; Chandos, music by Janáček; numerous recordings for BBC radio and television, Channel 4, ITV and European radio stations. *Publications:* Violin Concerto by Johann Nepomuk Hummel completed and edited by Gregory Rose, Missa Sancta Pauli Apostoli, Four Spanish Carols, English carol arrangements, It's Snowing, A Song of Judith. *Address:* 57 White Horse Road, London, E1 0ND, England (home). *Telephone:* (20) 7790-5883 (home). *E-mail:* gr@gregoryrose.org. *Website:* www.gregoryrose.org.

ROSE, John Luke, BMus, LMusTCL, PhD; British composer, pianist, lecturer, writer and conductor; b. 19 July 1933, Northwood Hills, Middx. *Education:* Univ. of London, Trinity Coll. of Music. *Career:* debut, Univ. of Oxford 1958; Extension Lecturer in Music, Univ. of Oxford 1958–66; has taught in UK, USA, Canada, Fiji, New Zealand, Australia, India; lecturer, teacher and examiner, Trinity Coll. of Music 1960–; part-time teacher, St Marylebone Grammar School 1963–66; staff tutor, Dept of Extra-Mural Studies, Univ. of London 1966–84; mem. Assen of Univ. Teachers, British Acad. of Composers. *Compositions:* Symphony No. 1 The Mystic (Royal Philharmonic Soc. Prize) 1982, Piano Concerto 1977, Overture Macbeth 1977, Symphony No. 2 (Royal Philharmonic Soc. Prize) 1985, Symphonic Dances, String Quartet, Partsongs, two piano sonatas, various piano works, Blake's Songs of Innocence, The Pleasures of Youth (cantata), Hymns and Anthems, Apocalyptic Visions for piano, St Francis (musical play) 1985, Violin Concerto 1987, Odysseus (opera) 1987. *Publications:* Wagner's Tristan and Isolde: A Landmark in Musical History (introductory essay to libretto book) 1981, Ludwig, Wagner and the Romantic View (essay and lecture, V&A Museum exhibition). *Honours:* Hon. Fellow, Trinity Coll. London 1961.

ROSE, Jürgen; German stage designer; b. 25 Aug. 1937, Bernburg. *Education:* studied in Berlin. *Career:* ballet designs for the Stuttgart Ballet 1962–73; collaborations with director, Otto Schenk for Don Carlos and Die Meistersinger in Vienna, Simon Boccanegra and Der Rosenkavalier at Munich and Così fan tutte in Berlin; Bayreuth Festival 1972, 1990 with Tannhäuser and Der fliegende Holländer, in productions by Götz Friedrich and Dieter Dorn; Salome and Die Entführung in Vienna, Lucia di Lammermoor and Lohengrin in Hamburg; premiere of Isang Yun's Sim Tjong at Munich 1972; designed Die Zauberflöte for the Munich Opera and the 1981 Ludwigsburg Festival; Le nozze di Figaro for the 1997 Munich Festival; Bayreuth Festival, Tristan und Isolde 1999, Met New York, Premiere of H.W. Henze's L'Upupa, Salzburg Festival 2003; own direction in own stage and costume designs, including La Traviata 1994, Die Zauberflöte 1996, Bonn Opera/Don Carlo 2000 and The Cunning Little Vixen, Munich Opera 2002. *Recordings include:* video of Munich production of Die Zauberflöte.

ROSE, Matthew; British singer (bass); b. 1978, Brighton; s. of Robert and Dorothy Rose. *Education:* Curtis Inst. of Music, Philadelphia, USA. *Career:* mem. Britten-Pears Young Artist Programme, Aldeburgh; as mem. Young Artists Programme, Royal Opera House, Covent Garden 2003–05, sang Sciarrone in Tosca, Wagner in Faust, Collatinus in The Rape of Lucretia, Steward/Sentry in Lady Macbeth of Mtsensk, Jonas Fogg in Sweeney Todd, Schlemil in Les Contes d'Hoffmann, Judge in Philip Glass's Orphée and Montano in Otello; has since sung Tom in Un Ballo in Maschera, Zuniga in Carmen, Masetto in Don Giovanni, Bottom in A Midsummer Night's Dream, Colline in La Bohème, Crespel in Tales of Hoffmann and Polyphemus in Acis and Galatea at Royal Opera House, and performed at Welsh Nat. Opera (Figaro) and Glyndebourne Festival (Bottom, 2006 John Christie Award winner), Teatro Real Madrid (Collatinus), Opera de Lyon and Houston Grand Opera (Bottom), ENO (Colline and Der Sprecher); concert appearances include Edinburgh Int. Festival, BBC Proms with BBCSO, BBCPO, SCO, BBCNOW, Philharmonia, CBSO, LSO, RPO, OAE, Le Concert D'Astrée, Dresden Staatskappelle and Tonhalle Orchestra Zurich with conductors includling Sir Colin Davis, Mackerras, Dutoit, Harding, Gardner, Haim, Slatkin, Oramo, Tilson Thomas, Volkov, Norrington and Richard Hickox; future engagements planned at La Scala, Milan, Santa Fe Opera, Royal Opera House, Glyndebourne, Houston Grand Opera, Metropolitan Opera, New York and concerts in Los Angeles with Dudamel, New York, Paris and Vienna with Eliot Gardiner, Bergen with Lobos Cobez and Edinburgh with Ticciati. *Recordings include:* L'enfance du Christ and A Child of Our Time with Sir Colin Davis and LSO, Billy Budd with Harding and LSO, Schubert Mass in Eflat with Hickox and Mackerras and Tristan und Isolde with Pappano, Rossini's William Tell 2011. *Honours:* John Christie Award 2006, Independent Opera/Wigmore Hall Fellowship. *Address:* c/o EMI Classics, 27 Wrights Lane, London, W8 5SW, England (office). *Telephone:* (20) 7795-7000 (office). *Website:* www.emiclassics.com (office).

ROSE, Peter; British singer (bass); b. 1961, Canterbury. *Education:* Univ. of East Anglia; Guildhall School of Music with Ellis Keeler; Nat. Opera Studio. *Career:* debut as Commendatore in Don Giovanni with Glyndebourne Opera in Hong Kong, 1986 and on tour; Welsh Nat. Opera 1986–89 as Bartolo, Basilio, Prince Gremin in Eugene Onegin, Angelotti in Tosca, Osmin, Tutor in Count Ory and Marke in Tristan; Glyndebourne Touring Opera as Don Inigo in L'Heure Espagnole, Osmin and Basilio; Maggio Musicale Florence as Commendatore; Scottish Opera as Narbal in Les Troyens; sang in La Damnation de Faust in Chicago, BBC Proms and Salzburg Festival with Chicago Symphony under Solti; English Nat. Opera as Angelotti and Bottom; Covent Garden debut 1988 as Lord Rochefort in Anna Bolena then Cadmus in Semele, Bonze in Madama Butterfly, Lodovico in Otello, Nightwatchman in Meistersinger; Kecal in The Bartered Bride, Chicago Lyric Opera, Commendatore, Gessler in Guillaume Tell and Basilio at San Francisco 1991–92; also sang Walther in Luisa Miller, Amsterdam, 1st Nazarene in Salome, Salzburg, Bottom at Aix-en-Provence, Commendatore at Covent Garden in 1993, Mustafà (Italiana), Amsterdam, Pimen in Boris Godunov at New Israeli Opera, Ramfis in Aida, Hunding in Walküre, Berlin Staatsoper 1994 and Dosifei in Khovanshchina, Hamburg; other roles include Fasolt in Rheingold, Bottom at the Met; sang in Pfitzner's Palestrina at Covent Garden, 1997; Rachmaninov's Aleko, London Proms 1999; season 2000 as Silva in Ernani for ENO and King Mark in Tristan at Covent Garden; Britten's Claggart at Cologne, 2001; Ravel's L'Heure espagnole, London Proms 2002. *Recordings include:* Nozze di Figaro with Barenboim and the Berlin Philharmonic; Video of Clemenza di Tito for Glyndebourne; Salome with Dohnányi; Seven Deadly Sins (also on video); Barber of Seville (with Peter Moores); Beatrice Cenci, Goldschmidt; Ballo in Maschera, Teldec.

RÖSEL, Peter; German pianist; *Professor Emeritus, Hochschule für Musik, Dresden;* b. 2 Feb. 1945, Dresden; m. Heidrun Bergmann; one s. one d. *Education:* Tchaikovsky Conservatory, Moscow with Dmitri Bashkirov and Lev Oborin. *Career:* debut with Berlin Symphony 1964; performances at int. festivals, including Dresden, Salzburg, La Roque d'Anthéron, Edinburgh, BBC London Proms, Perth, Hollywood Bowl, Hong Kong; frequent guest with New York Symphony, Los Angeles Symphony, Montreal Symphony, Toronto Symphony and Detroit Symphony Orchestras, Philharmonia, Royal Philharmonic, Berlin Philharmonic, Deutsches Symphonie-Orchester Berlin, Radio Symphony Orchestra Berlin, Staatskapelle Dresden and Dresdner Philharmonie, Gewandhausorchester Leipzig, MDR-Sinfonieorchester, Mozarteum Orchester Salzburg and Netherlands Philharmonic; has played with conductors including Blomstedt, Boreyko, Dutoit, Fedossejew, Haenchen, Haitink, Harding, Herbig, Janowski, Kempe, Kitajenko, Kondrashin, Masur, Kurt Sanderling, Stefan Sanderling, van Steen, Stein, Temirkanov and Tennstedt; performed all Beethoven piano sonatas and concertos, Tokyo 2008–11; Prof. Emer., Hochschule für Musik, Dresden. *Recordings include:* complete concerti of Weber, Beethoven, Schumann and Rachmaninov, late concerti of Mozart, complete piano works of Brahms, complete sonatas of Beethoven, major piano sonatas of Mozart, Schubert and Schumann, various chamber music works. *Honours:* prizewinner, Moscow Tchaikovsky Competition and Montreal Piano Competition. *Current Management:* c/o Berliner Konzertagentur Monika Ott, Dramburgerstrasse 46, 12683 Berlin, Germany. *Telephone:* (30) 5144858. *Fax:* (30) 5142659. *E-mail:* berlinkonzert.ott@t-online.de. *Website:* www.berlinkonzert-ott.de; www.peter-roesel.de.

ROSELL, Lars-Erik; Swedish composer and organist; b. 9 Aug. 1944, Nybro. *Education:* Stockholm Royal Coll. of Music with Ingvar Lidholm. *Career:* teacher of counterpoint and composition, Stockholm Royal Coll. of Music 1972–, Prof. 2001–; freelance organist, with performances of contemporary music. *Compositions include:* Terry Riley for three pianos 1970, Poem in the Dark for mezzo and ensemble 1972, After the Fall (dramatic scene based on Arthur Miller) for vocal soloists and ensemble 1973, Visiones Prophetae (Biblical scene) 1974, Musik for cello and string orchestra 1975, Ordens källa scenic cantata 1980, Tillfälligt avbrott (chamber opera) 1981, Organ Concerto 1982, Amédée (chamber opera) 1987, Five Aphorisms for cello solo 1990, Fantasia Concertante for cello and orchestra 1992, The Illusionist (chamber opera) 1996, three Orchestral Songs for soprano and baritone 1999, Out of the Shadows (chamber opera) 2001, choir music, chamber music and other stage music. *Recordings include:* album: In Between. *Address:* Gnejsstigen 2, 19633 Kungsängen, Sweden. *E-mail:* lars-erik.rosell@kmh.se.

ROSEN, Nathaniel Kent; American cellist; b. 9 June 1948, Altadena, CA; m. Margo Shohl. *Education:* studied with Eleonore Schoenfeld in Pasadena, with Piatigorsky at the Univ. of Southern California, Los Angeles. *Career:* Asst to Piatigorsky 1966–76; solo debut with the Los Angeles Philharmonic 1969; New York debut 1970, Carnegie Hall; Principal Cellist, Los Angeles Chamber Orchestra 1972–76, Pittsburgh Symphony Orchestra 1977–79; Prof., Univ. of Illinois at Champaign-Urbana 1988–94; Prof., Manhattan School of Music 1981–88, 1994–; appearances with leading American and European orchestras and as recitalist and in chamber music. *Recordings:* complete music for cello and piano by Chopin, Shostakovich Cello Concerto No. 1, Brahms Sonatas, Bach Suites.

ROSEN, Robert Joseph, BMus; Canadian composer and performer; b. 20 May 1956, Melfort, SK; m. Deborah Alpaugh 1979; two s. one d. *Education:* Univ. of Alberta, Banff Centre, Darmstadt summer course, National Choreographic Workshop, Vancouver, studied with Violet Archer, Bruce Mather. *Career:* worked for short periods with John Cage, R. Murray Schafer, Witold Lutoslawski, Iannis Xenakis and Morton Feldman; broadcasts as performer on CBC national radio; compositions performed in Canada, Sweden, Germany, The Netherlands, France, Spain, USA, Italy and Australia by such notable performers as Robert Aitken, Jean-Pierre Drouet and Alan Hacker; founder mem. performing ensemble, Fusion 5; created film scores for documentaries produced by Helios Pictures for the National Film Board of Canada; Asst Dir of Music Programs, Banff Centre for the Arts from 1991; Musical Dir, Kokoro Dance. *Compositions:* From Silence for piano and orchestra, String Quartet 1979, Krikos I 1980, II 1982, Enigmas from the Muse, Meditation No. 1 for flute, violin and cello, No. 2 for small orchestra, No. 4 for two pianos, No. 5 Mosaic for flute and piano, No. 6 for piano, No. 7 Coro for 24 voices, In Anticipation of Beautiful Shadows for seven cellos, Mi Istakistsi for flute, percussion and string quartet, Zero to the Power for violin, cello, taiko percussion and electronics, Stones for two sopranos, tuba and percussion, Canyon Shadows: Stones, Animals for two sopranos, alpenhorn and tuba 1993. *Publications:* Canadian Composers at Banff, Celebration, Canadian Music Centre.

ROSEN, Rudolf; Swiss singer (baritone); b. 1960. *Education:* Berne Academy of Music with Jakob Stämpfli. *Career:* many concert engagements in Oslo, Stuttgart, Leipzig, Munich, Zürich and Geneva; conductors have included Neeme Järvi, John Nelson, Helmuth Rilling and Michel Corboz; Further engagements at Tel-Aviv and Mexico City; Heilbronn and Salzburg Festivals, 1996–97; concert repertoire from Lieder to Oratorios; Stuttgart State Opera from 2001, including engagement in Don Giovanni, La Finta Giardiniera; roles also include Bluebeard's Castle, Count in Le Nozze di Figaro, Papageno in Die Zauberflote, Posa in Don Carlo. *Honours:* prizewinner, Internaional Music Competition, Geneva 1997, ARD Music Competition Munich 1998, Belvedere Song Competition, Vienna. *Current Management:* Sabine von Imhoff Promotion, Holunderweg 71, 50858 Cologne, Germany. *Telephone:* (221) 481474. *Fax:* (221) 2831976. *E-mail:* info@svimhoff.de. *Website:* www.svimhoff.de.

ROSENBAUM, Victor, BA, MFA; American pianist, conductor and administrator; b. 19 Dec. 1941, Philadelphia, Pa; two d. *Education:* Brandeis and Princeton Univs, Aspen Music School; studied piano with Leonard Shure and Rosina Lhevinne, composition with Roger Sessions, Earl Kim and Edward T. Cone. *Career:* solo performances in USA, Japan, Brazil, Israel and Russia; chamber performances with Leonard Rose, Roman Totenberg, Arnold Steinhardt, Cleveland Quartet, Vermeer Quartet, Brentano Quartet, New World Quartet, at Tully Hall, Town Hall, New York, Jordan Hall, Boston; Conductor, Concerto Company chamber orchestra; fmr Faculty mem. Eastman School of Music, Brandeis Univ.; Faculty mem. New England Conservatory, Mannes Coll. of Music, Longy School of Music, Cambridge, MA (Dir and Pres. 1985–2001); masterclasses at Moscow Conservatory, St Petersburg Conservatory, Toho School, Tokyo, Jerusalem Music Center, RAM, London, Royal Coll. of Music, London, Guildhall School of Music, London; summer masterclasses in Vienna, Int. Keyboard Inst. and Festival, New York, Juilliard School, Yale Univ. etc. *Compositions:* for voice, piano, chorus, chamber ensemble and theatre pieces. *Recordings:* Beethoven: The Last Three Sonatas (Bridge), Schubert: Sonata, D959, Moments Musicaux (Bridge), John Harbison Trio. *Address:* 160 Lake Street, Brighton, MA 02135, USA (home). *Telephone:* (617) 254-9956 (office); (617) 645-3034 (mobile). *E-mail:* vrosenbaum@aol.com (home).

ROSENBERG, Pamela, BA, MA; German (b. American) music administrator and academic; *Dean of Fellows and Programs, American Academy in Berlin;* b. (Pamela Lyn Henry), 24 April 1945, Los Angeles, Calif.; m. Wolf Rosenberg (deceased); two c. *Education:* Univ. of California, Berkeley, Ohio State Univ., Guildhall School of Music and London Opera Centre, UK. *Career:* previous positions at Netherlands Opera, Amsterdam, Deutschen Schauspielhaus, Hamburg; Scenic Supervisor, subsequently Artistic Admin. Frankfurt Opera; Co-Dir (Co-Intendant) Stuttgart Opera 1991–2000; Gen. Dir San Francisco Opera 2001–06; Intendant (Gen. Man.) Berlin Philharmonic Orchestra 2006–10; Dean of Fellows and Programs, American Acad. in Berlin 2010–; Chair. Man. Bd, Barenboim Musikkindergarten Berlin, Musiktheater im Revier Foundation; Vice-Chair. Senate of Berlin-Brandenburgische Akad. der Wissenschaften; mem. Univ. Council (Hochschulrat) of Hochschule für Musik, Freiburg; mem. Bd of Advisors, Cogut Center for the Humanities, Brown Univ., Man. Bd, Liz Mohn Foundation; Trustee, Univ. of California, Berkeley Foundation. *Address:* American Academy in Berlin, Am Sandwerder 17–19, 14109 Berlin, Germany (office). *Telephone:* (30) 80483103 (office). *Fax:* (30) 80483111 (office). *E-mail:* pr@americanacademy.de (office). *Website:* www.americanacademy.de (office).

ROSENBOOM, David; American composer, performer and academic; *Dean of the School of Music, California Institute of the Arts;* b. 9 Sept. 1947, Fairfield, IA. *Education:* studied with Salvatore Martirano, Lejaren Hiller, Kenneth Gaburo, Gordon Binkerd, Bernard Goodman, Paul Roland, Jack McKenzie, Soulima Stravinsky and John Garvey, Univ. of Illinois, Urbana. *Career:* worked in commercial broadcast media; independent performer, composer and producer; special studies in physics, computer science, experimental psychology, and multi-media, New York Univ., and independently; has composed extensively for both instrumental and technological media; organized numerous performing groups, including the performance art group, Maple Sugar, Toronto (with Jacqueline Humbert and George Manupelli) and the open instrumental ensemble, Challenge, Oakland (with Braxton and Winant); has collaborated with many leading composers and musicians; Creative Assoc., Center for Creative and Performing Arts, State Univ. of NY,

Buffalo 1960s; Artistic Co-ordinator New York's Electric Circus 1960s; co-founder and Pres. Neurona Co., New York 1969–71; Prof. and Founder Dept of Music and Interdisciplinary Grad. Studies Programme, York Univ., Toronto 1972–79, Coordinator of Interdisciplinary Studies, Faculty of Fine Arts, Founding Dir Electronic Media Studios and Lab. of Experimental Aesthetics; teacher, Mills Coll., Oakland 1979–88, Darius Milhaud Prof. of Music, Head of Music Dept and Dir Center for Contemporary Music 1988; Head, Music Dept, California Inst. of the Arts 1984–90, fmr Co-Dir Center for Experiments in Art, Information and Tech. and Conductor of the New Century Players, Dean of School of Music 1990–; taught interdisciplinary subjects at San Francisco Art Inst. and California Coll. of Arts and Crafts; guest faculty mem. at numerous insts, including George A. Miller Visiting Prof., Univ. of Illinois 1995, Banff Centre for the Arts, Simon Fraser Univ.; has served as adviser, bd mem. and professional affiliate with nat. arts orgs in USA and Canada; has developed computer software for music, was co-designer of a computerized keyboard instrument with Donald Buchia, the Touché, and is co-author (with L. Polansky and P. Burk) of HMSL (Hierarchical Music Specification Language), a widely used music programming language. *Compositions include:* The Brandy of the Damned, music theatre 1967, How Much Better if Plymouth Rock Had Landed on the Pilgrims 1972, On Being Invisible 1976, In the Beginning I–IV, for Various Instrumental Combinations 1978–80, Future Travel for Piano, Violin and Computer Music System 1982, Champ Vital 1987, Systems of Judgement 1987, Predictions, Confirmations and Disconfirmations 1991, Extended Trio 1992, It Is About To... Sound, Interactive Computer Music Installation 1993, It Is About To... Vexations 1993, On Being Invisible II: Hypatia Speaks to Jefferson in a Dream (self-organizing opera with brain-evoked responses and interactive media) 1995, Brave New World: Music for the Play 1995, Seeing the Small In the Large (Six Movements for Orchestra) 1998, Bell Solaris (Twelve Movements for Piano) 1998, Naked Curvature for six instruments, whispering voices, sound effects, and HMSL software 2000, Four Lines for two to four instruments and electronic tracks 2001. *Recordings include:* A Precipice In Time (quintet with computer processing) 1966, How Much Better If Plymouth Rock Had Landed On The Pilgrims for unspecified instruments 1969, The Seduction of Sapientia for viola da gamba and electronics 1974, Suitable for Framing for two pianos 1975, South Indian Mrdangam, Brainwave Music 1976, On Being Invisible for brainwaves and computer music system 1977, And Out Come the Night Ears for piano and electronics 1978, In The Beginning (series of nine works for soloists, chamber ensembles, orchestra and electronics) 1978–81, Future Travel for computer and acoustic instruments 1982, Zones of Influence for percussion soloist and computer instrument 1984–85, Roundup (anthology of live electro-acoustic works) 1987, Systems of Judgment for computer music systems and various instruments 1988, Extended Trio for instruments and HMSL 1992, Two Lines (duets in collaboration with Anthony Braxton) 1995, On Being Invisible II 2000. *Publications include:* Biofeedback and the Arts: Results of Early Experiments 1975, The J. Jasmine Songbook (jtly) 1978, Collected Articles (1968–1982) 1984, In the Beginning – A Collection of Works, 1978–1981 1987, Music for Keyboard Instruments and Improvisation Groups, 1964–1981 1987, Collected Scores 1965–1973 1987, Extended Musical Interface with the Human Nervous System: Assessment and Prospectus 1990; contribs to Perspectives of New Music, Leonardo, Musicworks, Computer Music Journal, Performing Arts Journal, and others. *Address:* CalArts-School of Music, 24700 McBean Parkway, Santa Clarita, CA 91355-2397, USA (office). *Telephone:* (661) 253-7816 (office). *Fax:* (661) 255-0938 (office). *E-mail:* david@music.calarts.edu (office). *Website:* music.calarts.edu/~david (office).

ROSENKRANZ, Helge; Austrian violinist; b. 1962. *Career:* mem., Franz Schubert Quartet, Vienna 1989–; many concert engagements in Europe, USA, and Australia including Amsterdam Concertgebouw, Vienna Musikverein and Kozerthaus, Salle Gaveau, Paris and Sydney Opera House; visits to Zürich, Geneva, Basle, Hamburg, Rome, Rotterdam, Madrid and Copenhagen; festival engagements include Salzburg, Wiener Festwochen, Prague Spring, Schubertiade at Hohenems, Schubert Festival in Washington, DC, Belfast and Istanbul; tours of Australasia, Russia and USA; frequent concert tours to the UK; featured in Concerto by Spohr with Royal Liverpool Philharmonic, Liverpool and Festival Hall, London; many appearances at Wigmore Hall and at Cheltenham Festival; masterclasses at Royal Northern College of Music and Lake District Summer Music. *Recordings include:* Schubert's Quartet in G, D877, Dittersdorf Complete Quartets, Bach Violin Concertos, Mozart The Ten Celebrated String Quartets.

ROSENSHEIN, Neil; American singer (tenor); b. 27 Nov. 1947, New York. *Education:* studied in New York. *Career:* debut at Florida Opera 1972 as Almaviva in Il Barbiere di Siviglia; sang in Washington, Dallas, Boston and Santa Fe; European debut at Vaison-la-Romaine 1980 as Almaviva; further appearances in Geneva, Zürich and Paris; Covent Garden debut 1986 as Lensky in Eugene Onegin; Chicago Lyric Opera 1988 as Alfredo in La Traviata; sang in the premiere of The Aspern Papers by Dominick Argento, Dallas 1988; Berlioz Festival at Lyon 1989 as Benvenuto Cellini; other roles include Mozart's Tamino and Belmonte, Verdi's Fenton and Don Carlos, Massenet's Des Grieux and Werther at Turin, Sydney and Metropolitan 1989, and Števa in Jenůfa; season 1992–93 at the Metropolitan as Faust, Werther, Alfredo in Traviata and Léon in the premiere of Corigliano's The Ghosts of Versailles; sang the Berlioz Faust at Turin in 1992 and Peter Grimes at Sydney; sang Cavaradossi at Santa Fe, 1994. *Recordings include:* Eugene Onegin.

ROSEWELL, Michael; conductor; *Music Director, English Touring Opera.* *Career:* began his career working at Staatstheater Kassel, Staatstheater Wiesbaden, Nationaltheater Mannheim in Germany; joined staff Vienna State Opera; Artistic Dir London Phoenix Ensemble; Dir of Opera, Benjamin Britten Int. Opera School, RCM; guest conductor English Touring Opera, then apptd Assoc. Conductor 2005–, Music Dir 2008–; works conducted with English Touring Opera include Così fan tutte, Mary, Queen of Scots, Marriage of Figaro, Janáček's Jenufa; has also conducted at Clonter Opera Theatre, Aldeburgh Festival, ENO, Kent Opera, London Handel Festival, Bath Festival; numerous performances of works by Benjamin Britten, including A Midsummer Night's Dream, The Rape of Lucretia, world premiere of Plymouth Town (with RCM Sinfonietta) 2004; has also conducted Die Zauberflöte, Barber of Seville, La Bohème, Handel's Alessandro Severo, Gazzaniga's Don Giovanni. *Address:* English Touring Opera, 52–54 Rosebery Avenue, London, EC1R 4RP, England (office). *E-mail:* admin@englishtouringopera.org.uk (office). *Website:* www.englishtouringopera.org.uk (office).

ROSINSKI, Stefan; German opera administrator; b. 1961, Flensburg. *Education:* Hamburg Hochschule für Musik und Theater, studied theatrical direction with Friedrich Götz. *Career:* Asst Dir Aaltotheater, Essen 1988–90; worked in advertising, Hamburg 1990–91; freelance theatre producer, Hamburg 1993–96; screenplay writer 1996–99; fmr Lecturer, Univ. Frankfurt, Univ. Hamburg; Dir of Finance and Control Dept, Lower Saxony State Theatre 2003, Man. Dir 2004–06; Dir Bühnenservice (commercial services dept), Stiftung Oper in Berlin (Berlin Opera Foundation) 2006–09, also interim Dir Gen. 2007–09; Dir of Drama, Volksbühne Theatre, Berlin 2009–. *Address:* Volksbühne am Rosa-Luxemburg-Platz, Linienstraße 227, 10178 Berlin, Germany. *Telephone:* (30) 24065-5. *Fax:* (30) 24065-642. *E-mail:* dramaturgie@volksbuehne-berlin.de. *Website:* www.volksbuehne-berlin.de.

ROSKELL, Penelope, GMus, PPRNCM; British pianist; b. 1960, Oxford, England; m. Richard Griffiths 1985. *Education:* Royal Northern College of Music, studied with Guido Agosti in Rome. *Career:* solo pianist with tours worldwide at invitation of the British Council; concerts regularly in Europe, Scandinavia, USA, Africa, Asia, Middle and Far East; Broadcasts on BBC Radio 3, WFMT Radio Chicago and British and Polish television; Prof. of Piano, Royal College of Music, London; recitals at Wigmore Hall and Purcell Room; concerto engagements include recording with Oxford Pro Musica; tours with Manchester Camerata and the Bournemouth Sinfonietta under Simon Rattle. *Honours:* winner British Contemporary Piano Competition. *Telephone:* (20) 8802-6258. *E-mail:* peneloperoskell@yahoo.co.uk.

ROSS, Alex; American journalist and writer; b. 1968, Washington, DC; spouse Jonathan Lisecki. *Education:* St Albans School, Harvard Univ. *Career:* music critic, New York Times 1992–96, The New Yorker 1996–; McGraw Prof. in Writing, Princeton Univ. 2008. *Publications:* The Rest Is Noise: Listening to the Twentieth Century (Nat. Book Critics Circle Award, Guardian First Book Award 2008, Royal Philharmonic Soc. Award for Best Creative Communication 2009, Premio Napoli 2010, Grand Prix des Muses 2011) 2007, Listen To This (ASCAP-Deems Taylor Award) 2010, Da Capo Best Music Writing (ed.) 2011; contrib. to Studio A: The Bob Dylan Reader, Best American Essays, Da Capo Best Music Writing. *Honours:* Dr hc (Manhattan School of Music, New England Conservatory, Curtis Inst.); four ASCAP-Deems Taylor Awards for music criticism, Fellowships from American Acad., Berlin, Banff Centre, Canada and American Acad., Rome, American Music Center Letter of Distinction for contribs to the field of contemporary music, MacArthur Fellowship 2008, Arts and Letters Award, American Acad. of Arts and Letters 2011, Belmont Prize 2012. *Address:* The New Yorker, 4 Times Square, New York, NY 10036, USA (office). *Telephone:* (212) 286-5984 (office). *Website:* www.therestisnoise.com.

ROSS, Christopher; British pianist and conductor; b. 1961, England. *Career:* has worked with such musicians as soprano Jennifer Smith, cellist Raphael Wallfisch, violinist Dona Lee Croft (tour of the USA) and José Carreras (on two albums); many performances in France, Germany, Switzerland, Portugal, Namibia, Japan, Korea, India, Malaysia and London's concert halls; conducted Le Nozze di Figaro in Switzerland and Mozart's Requiem Mass in London 2003. *Honours:* accompanist's prize Richard Tauber Competition, accompanist's prize NFMS competition (twice). *E-mail:* chris_ross@ntlworld.com.

ROSS, Elinor; American singer (soprano); b. 1 Aug. 1932, Tampa, FL. *Education:* studied with Zinka Milanov in New York. *Career:* debut at Cincinnati Opera 1958 as Leonora in Il Trovatore; guest appearances in Boston, Chicago, Baltimore and Philadelphia; sang at Carnegie Hall in the 1968 US premiere of Verdi's Alzira; Metropolitan Opera from 1970 with debut as Turandot; European engagements at La Scala, Bologna, Palermo, Vienna, Budapest, Zagreb, Verona and Florence; other roles include Bellini's Norma, Verdi's Aida, Elisabetta, Amelia, Lady Macbeth and Abigaille, Mozart's Donna Anna, Puccini's Tosca and Giordano's Maddalena; sang Tosca at the Metropolitan 1973, and the Trovatore, Leonora at Buenos Aires 1974; frequent concert appearances.

ROSS, Elise; American singer (soprano); b. 28 April 1947, New York; m. Simon Rattle (divorced). *Career:* sang with the Juilliard Ensemble, New York and the Los Angeles Philharmonic Orchestra from 1970; performances of music by Berio in USA and Europe (Passagio in Rome); tour of Europe with the London Sinfonietta and appearances at Royan and Bath Festivals and in Venice and Warsaw; sang in Bussotti's Passion Selon Sade and Le Racine at La Scala in 1991; concerts with the Ensemble Intercontemporain, Paris from 1976; repertoire includes Berlin Cabaret songs, lieder by composers of the Second Viennese School, Chansons by Ravel and Debussy and lieder by Mozart, Schumann and Strauss; Shostakovich Symphony 14 with the Los Angeles Philharmonic and Ensemble Intercontemporain; has sung Cherubino for Opera North and for Long Beach Opera; sang Marie in Wozzeck at Los Angeles 1989, Mélisande with Netherlands Opera and Berlioz's Romeo and Juliette, Rotterdam, 1993.

ROSS, Graham; British conductor, composer and academic; *Fellow and Director of Music, Clare College, Cambridge;* b. 1985, Farnham, Surrey. *Education:* Clare Coll., Cambridge, Royal Coll. of Music. *Career:* Asst Conductor for Vladimir Jurowski, Sir Roger Norrington and Nicholas Collon and Chorus Master for Sir Colin Davies, Sir Mark Elder, Ivor Bolton, Edward Gardner, Richard Tognetti and Lars Ulrik Mortenson; currently Fellow and Dir of Music, Clare Coll., Cambridge; Principal Conductor, Dmitri Ensemble; Guest Conductor with ensembles including Orchestra of the Age of Enlightenment, London Mozart Players, Aalborg Symfoniorkester, Denmark, and Aurora, Kensington, Hertfordshire, East Anglia, and Covent Garden Chamber Orchestras; debuts at BBC Proms and Glyndebourne aged 25; Artistic Dir, Fringe in the Fen festival, Cambridgeshire. *Compositions include:* for orchestra: Variations on a Theme by Arnold Schoenberg for large ensemble 2005, Crossing Brooklyn Ferry for mezzo soprano, harp, double string orchestra 2006, Superstitions for chamber orchestra 2007, Echo for solo clarinet and orchestra 2008, Piano Triggers for large ensemble 2008, The Saffron Hour for orchestra 2009; for chorus a cappella: Deign at my hands for double SATB chorus and organ 2005, Two Southwell Motets 2005, Secret Music for SATB and organ 2007, Lullay, My Liking for two-part choir and piano/organ 2008, Ut tecum lugeam 2010, L'Heure du Berger for SATB chorus and harp 2010, To Make Much of Time, 7 songs for unison voices and piano 2011; for solo voice and small ensemble: The Dalliance of the Eagles for solo voices and piano 2008, The Wiry Concord for baritone and piano 2009, Through Galleried Earth for high voice and piano 2012, Translating the English for high voice and piano 1989 /2012; solo works: Toccatina for organ 2008, Scherzetto for organ 2009, Chaconne and Aus tiefer Not, both for organ 2010. *Recordings include:* James MacMillan: Seven Last Words from the Cross 2009, Vaughan Williams: Folk Songs from the Four Seasons 2009, Giles Swayne: Stabat Mater 2010, Judith Bingham: Jacob's Ladder 2011, Imogen Holst: Choral Works 2012, Veni Emmanuel 2013. *Current Management:* Ikon Arts Management Ltd, 114 Business Design Centre, Islington, London, N1 0QH, England. *Telephone:* (20) 7354-9199. *E-mail:* nicola@ikonarts.com. *Website:* www.ikonarts.com. *E-mail:* graham@grahamross.com (office). *Website:* www.grahamross.com (office).

ROSS, Walter, MMus, DMA; American composer; b. 3 Oct. 1936, Lincoln, NE. *Education:* Univ. of Nebraska, Cornell Univ. with Robert Palmer. *Career:* mem. music faculty, Univ. of Virginia 1967–. *Compositions:* Concerto for brass quintet and orchestra 1966, Five Dream Sequences for percussion quartet and piano 1968, two Trombone Concertos 1970, 1982, Canzona I and II for brass instruments 1969, 1979, In the Penal Colony (opera) 1972, three Wind Quintets 1974, 1985, 1989, A Jefferson Symphony for tenor, chorus and orchestra 1976, Concerto for wind quintet and strings 1977, String Trio 1978, Nocturne for strings 1980, Violin Sonata 1981, Concerto for bassoon and strings 1983, Suite No. 1 for chamber ensemble 1983, Concerto for oboe, harp and strings 1984, three Brass Trios 1985, 1986, 1986, Concerto for flute, guitar and orchestra 1987, Sinfonia Concertante for strings 1987, Oil of Dog for brass quintet and actor 1988, Concerto for euphonium, brass and timpani 1988, Scherzo Festivo for orchestra 1992, Summer Dances for oboe and marimba 1992, Clarinet Concerto 1994, Harlequinade for five wind instruments and piano 1994, also vocal music, including songs and choruses.

ROSSBERG, Dieter; German conductor; b. 1952, Hamburg. *Education:* Hamburg Acad. with Horst Stein, György Ligeti, Götz Friedrich and August Everding. *Career:* Principal Conductor/Kapellmeister and Deputy Gen. Music Dir in various opera houses in Germany and Austria 1975–92; from 1973 appeared as a guest conductor for opera concert and radio productions (NHK-Tokyo, Bayerische Rundfunk-München, Radio Hilversum, NDR, Danish and Norwegian Broadcasting Corporation) and festivals in Germany (Berlin, Bonn, Cologne, Essen, Hamburg, Hannover, Frankfurt and Munich) and abroad (Austria, Canada, Denmark, Estonia, France, Finland, Hungary, Italy, Japan, Tokyo, Monaco, The Netherlands, Norway, Slovenia, Sweden, Switzerland and Turkey); has worked with many noted instrumentalists and singers, including René Kollo, Gegam Grigorian, Ingvar Wixell, Peter Mattei, and stage directors and choreographers such as John Neumier; freelance conductor 1992–; more than 90 different operas in 1,000 performances, with a wide concert repertoire; has conducted many world premieres.

ROST, Andrea; Hungarian singer (soprano); b. 15 June 1962, Budapest; d. of Ferenc Rost and Erzsébet Privoda. *Education:* Ferenc Liszt Acad. of Music, Budapest, studied with Zsolt Bende. *Career:* operatic debut as Juliette in Gounod's Romeo et Juliette, Budapest 1989; solo artist at Wiener Staatsoper 1991; La Scala debut as Gilda in Rigoletto 1994; debut, Metropolitan Opera, New York as Adina in L'Elisir d'amore 1996; took part in Superconcert with José Carreras and Plácido Domingo, Budapest 1996; appeared as Elisabeth in Donizetti's opera, London 1997; debut, Tokyo Opera, as Violetta 1998; took part in concert in memory of Lehár with José Carreras and Plácido Domingo, Bad Ischl, Austria 1998; has also appeared at Staatsoper, Vienna, Salzburg

Festival, Opéra Bastille, Paris, Royal Opera House, Covent Garden and Chicago Opera; Lammermoori Lucia debut , Munchen, Wigmore Hall recital, London, Valencia recital 2002; Traviata debut, Deutsche Oper, Berlin, Desdemona, Otello, Tokyo, Lammermoori Lucia premier, Covent Garden, London 2003, Gilda, Rigoletto, Metropolitan, New York 2004. *Recordings include:* Mozart – Le nozze di Figaro (Susanna) 1994, Mahler – Symphony No. 8 1995, Verdi – Rigoletto (Gilda) 1995, Mendelssohn – Elias (die Witwe/ein Engel) 1996, Andrea Rost – Le delizie dell'amor 1997, Gaetano Donizetti – Lucia Di Lammermoori (Lucia) 1998, A Tribute to Operetta 1999, Amore II 2000, Escape Through Opera 2001, Erkel: Bánk bán (Melinda) 2003, . . .che cosa è amor. . . [Mozart Arias] 2004, Hungarian Songs – Bartók, Kodály, Ligeti 2008, Colours 2013, Opera Tales 2014. *DVD videos include:* Johann Strauss Gala 2000, Wolfgang Amadeus Mozart: Don Giovanni (Zerlina) 2000, A Verdi Gala from Berlin 2002, Erkel: Bánk bán (Melinda) (opera film) 2003. *Honours:* First Prize, Helsinki Competition 1989, Bartók Béla – Pásztory Ditta Award, Ferenc Liszt Artistic Merit of Honour 1997, Nat. Artistic Merit of Honour 1999, Medal Obersovszky, Prima Primissima Award 2003, Kossuth Prize 2004, Béla Bartók Memorial Award 2006, Mihály Székely Plaque 2011. *Current Management:* c/o Vera Meczner, Gradus Artist Management, 1061 Budapest, Dalszínház utca 10, Hungary. *E-mail:* vera.meczner@gradusartist.com. *Website:* www.gradusartist.com. *Address:* Nefelejes u. 27, 2040 Budaörs, Hungary (home). *Fax:* (23) 416-583 (home). *E-mail:* info@andrearost.com (home). *Website:* www.andrearost.com (home).

ROSTAD, Masumi Per, BMus, MMus; American violist. *Education:* Juilliard School. *Career:* fmr mem., Int. Sejong Soloists; currently mem. Pacifica Quartet, Faculty Quartet-in-Residence, Univ. of Illinois at Champagn/Urbana 2003–, Quartet-in-Residence, Metropolitan Museum of Art 2009–; faculty mem., Univ. of Illinois at Champagn/Urbana 2003–, Univ. of Chicago; as soloist, performed world premiere of Michael White's Viola Concerto, New York 1999. *Recordings:* with The Pacifica Quartet: String Quartets by Easley Blackwood 1999, Dvorak: String Quartet No. 13 in G Major and String Quintet in E-flat Major 2001, Mendelssohn: The Complete String Quartets 2005, Declarations: Music Between the Wars 2006, Elliott Carter: String Quartets Nos 1 and 5 (Grammy Award for Best Chamber Music Performance 2009) 2008. *Honours:* winner, Bronx Arts Ensemble Young Artist Competition, Lillian Fuchs Award for Outstanding Graduate Violist, Juilliard School, Grand Prize, Coleman Chamber Music Competition 1996, Walter F. Naumburg Chamber Music Award 1998, Chamber Music America's Cleveland Quartet Award 2002, Avery Fisher Career Grant 2006, Musical America Award for Ensemble of the Year 2009. *Current Management:* Melvin Kaplan Inc., 115 College Street, Burlington, VT 05401, USA. *Telephone:* (802) 658-2592. *Fax:* (802) 658-6089. *E-mail:* music@melkap.com. *Website:* www.melkap.com. *E-mail:* pacificaquartet@yahoo.com (office); masumiviola@yahoo.com (home). *Website:* www.pacificaquartet.com.

ROTH, Daniel; French organist and composer; *Organist, Église Saint-Sulpice, Paris*; b. 31 Oct. 1942, Mulhouse; m. Odile Mangin 1968; four c. *Education:* Paris Conservatoire with Maurice Duruflé, Rolande Falcinelli, Henriette Puig-Roget and Marcel Bitsch, also studied with Marie-Claire Alain. *Career:* Organist, Sacré-Coeur, Paris 1963–85, Église Saint-Sulpice 1985–; Prof. of Organ, Marseille Conservatoire 1973–79, later at Strasbourg Conservatoire; Visiting Prof., Summer Acad. at Haarlem, Netherlands; Prof., Catholic Univ. 1974–76; Resident Artist, Nat. Shrine, Washington, DC, USA 1974–76; Prof., Saarbrücken Musikhochschule, Germany 1988; Prof. of Organ, Musikhochschule, Frankfurt am Main, Germany 1995–2007. *Compositions include:* several works for organ published by Leduc, Bärenreiter, Schott (Mainz), Novello, and for flute and organ, choir and organ (Missa Brevis), and orchestra, published by Schott. *Recordings include:* works by Bach, Liszt, Franck, Guilmant, Boëly, Saint-Saëns, Widor, Vierne, Dupré and Jolivet. *Honours:* Hon. FRCO; Officier des Arts et Lettres, Chevalier de la Légion d'honneur; Florent Schmitt Prize for Composition, Acad. des Beaux Arts, Institut de France 2000, European Prize of European Sacred Music, Schwäbisch Gmünd Festival 2006. *Address:* Église Saint Sulpice, 75006 Paris, France (office). *Website:* www.danielrothsaintsulpice.org (office).

ROTH, David Robert, MMus, DMus, LRAM, ARAM; British violinist; b. 9 March 1936, Stockton-on-Tees, Co. Durham, England; m. Ruth Elaine West 1963; two s. *Education:* Univ. of Edinburgh, Royal Acad. of Music, London. *Career:* debut at West Linton, Peebles, Scotland 1954; with Netherlands Chamber Orchestra, Amsterdam 1960–64; played Bloch Sonata No. 1, Kol Israel Radio, Tel-Aviv 1962; Deputy Leader Northern Sinfonia Orchestra, Newcastle upon Tyne 1966–68; Second Violin, Allegri String Quartet 1969–99; taught at Univ. of Southampton 2000–11; mem. Incorporated Soc. of Musicians, Musicians' Union. *Recordings:* with Allegri String Quartet for Open Univ. and various labels. *Honours:* Hon. MM (Hull); Hon. DMus (Nottingham, Southampton). *Address:* 16 Oman Avenue, London, NW2 6BG, England (home).

ROTH, François-Xavier; French conductor; b. 1971, s. of Daniel Roth. *Education:* Conservatoire Nat. Supérieur de Musique. *Career:* Asst Conductor, London Symphony Orchestra 2000–02; Asst to Sir John Eliot Gardiner on productions of Les Troyens, Benvenuto Cellini, Falstaff; Assoc. Guest Conductor, BBC Nat. Orchestra of Wales 2008–11; Assoc. Conductor, Orchestre Philharmonique de Radio France 2008–10; Principal Guest Conductor, Navarra Symphonic Orchestra 2008–10; Music Dir, Orchestre Philharmonique de Liège 2009–10; Chief Conductor SWR Sinfonieorchester Baden-Baden und Freiburg 2011–; debut in N America with London Symphony Orchestra 2007; regular Guest Conductor, London Symphony Orchestra and Ensemble InterContemporain; f. Les Siècles orchestra 2003; concerts with Les Siècles in France, England, Portugal, Japan, Germany, Netherlands and France, and weekly appearances on TV programme Presto (France 2) 2007–. *Recordings include:* with Les Siècles: Chopin (with Denis Pascal) 2006, Franz Schubert: Le Voyage d'Hiver, Bizet/Chabrier (Diapason Découverte) 2007. *Honours:* winner, Donatella Flick Conducting Competition 2000. *Current Management:* c/o Mark Newbanks, Van Walsum Management, The Tower Building, 11 York Road, London, SE1 7NX, England. *Telephone:* (20) 7902-0520. *Fax:* (20) 7902-0530. *E-mail:* info@vanwalsum.com. *Website:* www.vanwalsum.com. *E-mail:* secretariat.fxroth@gmail.com (office). *Website:* www.francoisxavierroth.fr.

ROUDINE, Fédor; Russian musician (violin); b. 1992, Moscow; grandson of Edison Denisov. *Education:* studied in Paris with Miroslav Roussine, Philippe Coutelen, Alexandre Brussilovsky and Svetlin Roussev, and at Musikhochschule Köln with Zakhar Bron. *Career:* first appearance as soloist aged nine, with Perpignan Orchestra; has performed with Bulgarian Nat. Orchestra, Basel Symphony Orchestra, Sofia Soloists Chamber Orchestra, Nat. Orchestra of Opéra Bastille, Erfurt Philharmonic Orchestra, Arpeggione Chamber Orchestra, Moscow Musica Viva Chamber Orchestra, Georgian State Symphony Orchestra and Montreal Symphony Orchestra under conductors including Shlomo Mintz, Maxim Vengerov, Emil Tabakov and Alexander Rudin; as soloist, performed in halls in Paris including Comédie des Champs-Elysées, Théâtre Mogador, Salle Cortot and Bastille Opera Amphitheatre, in Germany at Gürzenich and Philharmonie in Köln, Tonhalle Düsseldorf, Philharmonie in Erfurt, Theater Hagen and Laeiszhalle in Hamburg; mem. Fratres trio. *Honours:* First Prize at several int. competitions including Andrea Postacchini, Louis Spohr, Yankelevitch, Aram Khachaturian and Lipizer Violin Competition 2013. *E-mail:* office@fedorroudine.com (office). *Website:* www.fedorroudine.com (office).

ROUILLON, Philippe; French singer (baritone); b. 1955, Paris. *Education:* Conservatoire National Supérieur de Paris, Ecole d'Art Lyrique de l'Opéra de Paris. *Career:* performed Golaud in Pelléas et Mélisande and High Priest of Dagon in Samson et Dalila, Vienna; Chorèbe in Les Troyens, Ruprecht in The Fiery Angel, Orest in Elektra, Renato in Un Ballo in Maschera, the High Priest of Dagon, The High Priest in Alceste and Thoas in Iphigénie en Tauride in Paris; Ruprecht, High Priest of Dagon, Gellner in La Wally and Escamillo in Carmen at Amsterdam; Jochanaan in Salome, Lisbon and Strasbourg; Guillaume Tell in Liège; Samson et Dalila and Les Contes d'Hoffmann in Zürich; Frequent appearances in Germany in a variety of leading baritone roles; Close collaborations with Festival of Bregenz, Austria; Further engagements include: Rigoletto in Leipzig, Tel-Aviv and Hamburg, Pagliacci in Hamburg, Macbeth and Guillaume Tell in Liège, Tosca in Amsterdam and Ballo in Maschera in Bregenz; Season 2000–01 as Macbeth at the Munich Staatsoper, Thaos in Iphigénie en Tauride at Salzburg and Scarpia for Bonn Opera. *Recordings include:* Thaïs by Massenet; Saint François d'Assise by Messiaen with Kent Nagano; Chant de Paix by Landowski; Henry VIII by Saint-Saëns; Le Déluge by Saint-Saëns; Lélio and La Damnation de Faust by Berlioz. *Honours:* First Place, Prix Opéra and Prix de Public, international competition in Verviers, 1979; First Prize, Rio de Janeiro Competition, 1983. *Current Management:* c/o Organisation Internationale Artistique, 16 Avenue Franklin D. Roosevelt, 75008 Paris, France; c/o Hilbert Artists Management, Maximilianstrasse 22, 80539 Munich, Germany. *Telephone:* 1-42-25-58-34 (France); (89) 2907470 (Germany). *Fax:* 1-42-25-64-97 (France); (89) 29074790 (Germany). *E-mail:* oia@oia-poilve.com; agentur@hilbert.de. *Website:* www.oia-poilve.com; www.hilbert.de.

ROULEAU, Joseph-Alfred, CC; Canadian singer (bass); *Honorary President, Jeunesses Musicales du Canada*; b. 28 Feb. 1929, Matane, Québec; s. of Joseph-Alfred Rouleau and Florence Bouchard; m. 1st Barbara Whittaker 1952; one d.; m. 2nd Renée Morreau; one s. one d. *Education:* Coll. Jean de Brebeuf, Montréal, Univ. of Montréal, Conservatoire of Music, Province of Québec. *Career:* debut at Montréal Opera Guild in Un Ballo in Maschera 1951; Royal Opera House, Covent Garden 1957–87, singing 48 roles; guest artist at prin. opera houses all over the world; tours of Canada 1960, Australia (with Joan Sutherland) 1965, Russia 1966, 1969, Romania, S Africa 1974, 1975, 1976; Paris Opera 1975, Metropolitan Opera, New York 1984, 1985, 1986, San Francisco 1986, 1987; roles include title role in Boris Godunov, Philip II and Inquisitore in Don Carlos, Basilio in Barber of Seville, Mephistopheles in Faust, Dosifei in Khovanshchina, title role in Don Quixote, Ramfis in Aida, Prince Gremin in Onegin, Father Lawrence in Roméo et Juliette, Colline in La Bohème, Raimondo in Lucia di Lammermoor, Titurel in Parsifal, Abimelech in Samson et Dalila, Crespel in Contes d'Hoffmann, Arkel in Pelléas et Mélisande, Sarastro, Osmin in Die Entführung, Daland in Der fliegende Holländer, Oroveso in Norma, Don Marco in The Saint of Bleecker Street, Trulove in The Rake's Progress, The Prince in Adriana Lecouvreur, Bartolo; Prof. of Voice, Univ. of Québec 1980–98, mem. Admin. Bd, Prof. Emer. 2004–; mem. Bd Corpn, Montréal Opera Co. 1980–; Pres., Jeunesses Musicales du Canada 1989–2014 (Prix Joseph Rouleau for Vocal Art named after him 1995), Hon. Pres. 2014–; Co-Founder and mem. Bd Concours Musical Int. de Montréal 2002–. *Recordings include:* scenes from Anna Bolena, Ruddigore, Roméo et Juliette (Gounod), L'Enfance du Christ (Berlioz), Semiramide, Lucia di Lammermoor, Don Carlos, Aida, Il Trovatore, Renard (Stravinsky), F. Leclerc's Songs, Les abîmes du rêve de Jacques Hétu (song cycle), French operatic arias (with Royal Opera House Orchestra), Boris Godunov (Prix Félix 2000), Don Carlos/Lucia di Lammermoor, L'Africaine (Meyerbeer), with

Domingo & Verrett, San Francisco Opera; Don Carlo, Royal Opera House Covent Garden. *Honours:* Grand Officier, Ordre Nat. du Québec 2004; Dr hc (Université de Québec à Rimouski, McGill Univ.); Prix Archambault 1967, La Société St Jean Baptiste Prix Calixa-Lavallée, Montréal 1967, Royal Opera House, Covent Garden Silver Medal 1983, Felix Award for Best Classical Artist of the Year 1989, Prix du Québec pour les Arts d'interprétation 1990, Panthéon de l'art lyrique du Canada 1992, Jeunesses Musicales du Canada Médaille du mérite exceptionnel 1995, Conseil québecois de la musique Prix Opus Hommage 2003, Prix du Gov. Gen. de Canada (Performing Arts Award) 2004, Opéra Canada Prix Ruby 2004, Médaille de la Ville de Marseille 2007, Gov. Gen.'s Mentorship Prize 2014. *Address:* c/o Jeunesses Musicales, 305 avenue du Mont-Royal Est, Montréal, PQ H2T 1P8 (office); 7 Roosevelt, Suite 20, Ville Mont-Royal, PQ H3R 1Z3, Canada (home). *Telephone:* (514) 739-3238 (home); (819) 688-3676 (home); (514) 845-4108 (ext. 232) (office). *Fax:* (514) 739-9135 (home); (514) 845-8241 (office). *E-mail:* joseph.alfred.rouleau@gmail .com (office); renee_rouleau@hotmail.com (home). *Website:* www.jmcanada.ca (office).

ROUSE, Christopher Chapman, BMus, MFA, DMA; American composer; b. 15 Feb. 1949, Baltimore, Md; m. Ann Jensen 1983, one s. two d. *Education:* Oberlin Conservatory, Cornell Univ. and studied with George Crumb. *Career:* Asst Prof., Univ. of Michigan at Ann Arbor 1978–81; Asst Prof., Eastman School of Music 1981–85, Assoc. Prof. 1985–91, Prof. 1991–2002; Composer-in-Residence, Indianapolis Symphony Orchestra 1985–86; Composer-in-Residence, Baltimore Symphony Orchestra 1986–88, New Music Advisor 1989–2000; Marie-Josée Kravis Composer-in-Residence, New York Philharmonic 2012–13; Prof., Juilliard School 1997–; Pres., Aaron Copland Fund for Music 2010–; mem., American Acad. of Arts and Letters 2002–. *Compositions:* Ogoun Badagris 1976, Ku-Ka-Ilimoku 1978, Mitternachtslieder 1979, Liber Daemonum 1980, The Infernal Machine (League of Composers/ISCM Prize) 1981, String Quartet 1982, Rotae Passionis 1982, Lares Hercii 1983, The Surma Ritornelli 1983, Gorgon 1984, Contrabass Concerto 1985, Phantasmata 1986, Phaethon 1987, Jagannath 1987, String Quartet No. 2 1988, Symphony No. 1 (Kennedy Center Friedheim Award) 1988, Bonham 1988, Iscariot 1989, Concerto per corde 1990, Karolju 1991, Violin Concerto 1992, Trombone Concerto (Pulitzer Prize in Music) 1993, Violoncello Concerto 1994, Flute Concerto 1994, Symphony No. 2 1994, Envoi 1996, Compline 1996, Der Gerettete Alberich 1998, Kabir Padavali 1999, Guitar Concerto 1999, Concert de Gaudi (Grammy Award for Best Contemporary Composition 2002) 2000, Rapture 2000, Clarinet Concerto 2001, Rapturedux 2001, The Nevill Feast 2003, Friandises 2006, Wolf Rounds 2006, Requiem 2007. *Honours:* Hon. DMus (State Univ. of New York) 2000; Rockefeller Foundation Grant 1980, Nat. Endowment for the Arts Fellowship 1981, Guggenheim Fellowship 1990, American Acad. of Arts and Letters Award 1993, DuPont Award, Delaware Symphony Orchestra 2001, Musical America Award for Composer of the Year 2009. *Current Management:* Boosey and Hawkes Inc., 35 East 21st Street, New York, NY 10010, USA. *Telephone:* (212) 358-5300. *Fax:* (212) 358-5303. *E-mail:* bhpromo@boosey.com. *Website:* www.boosey.com; www .christopherrouse.com.

ROUSSET, Christophe; French harpsichordist and conductor; *Musical Director, Les Talens Lyriques;* b. 12 April 1961, Avignon. *Education:* studied with Huguette Dreyfus, Kenneth Gilbert, Bob van Asperen and Gustav Leonhardt, chamber music with the brothers Kuijken and Lucy van Dael. *Career:* frequent solo appearances in France and throughout Europe; concertos with La Petite Bande, Musica Antiqua Köln, Acad. of Ancient Music; Asst for Les Arts Florissants; collaborations with artists, including William Christie, Agnès Mellon, Wieland Kuijken and Christopher Hogwood; conducts Les Arts Florissants, Il Seminario Musicale and other ensembles; founded Les Talens Lyriques (title from Rameau's Les Fêtes d'Hébé) 1991–, giving many performances of Baroque Opera; Monteverdi's Poppea in Amsterdam 1993, 1994, 1996, 2001, 2007; revival of Handel's Riccardo Primo at Fontevraud, France 1995, Handel's Admeto at Beaune and Montpellier and in Australia 1998, Wigmore Hall concerts 1999, Mozart's Mitridate at Le Châtelet, Paris 2000, Cavalli's La Didone, Lausanne 2000, Monteverdi's l'Incoronazione di Poppea, New York 2002, Cimarosa's Il Matrimonio Segreto, Paris 2002, V. Martin y Soler's La Capricciosa Corretta, Lausanne 2003, Lulli's Roland, Lausanne 2004, Mozart's Entführung aus dem Serail 2005, Salieri's La Grotta di Trofonio 2005, Handel's Alcina and Tamerlano, Drottningholm 2000, 2002, 2005, Rameau's Zoroastre at Drottningholm 2005, 2006, Monteverdi's Poppea, Toulouse 2006, Desmarest's Vénus et Adonis, Nancy 2006, Handel's Giulio Cesare, Paris 2006, Handel's Ariodante, Paris 2007; solo recital, Wigmore Hall, London 2013; Rameau's Les Indes Galantes, Barbican, London 2014; Gluck's Alceste, Wiener Staatsoper 2015; Rameau's Pygmalion, Trondheim, Norway 2016; Musical Dir Orchestre Français des Jeunes Baroque 2006–. *Recordings include:* Harpsichord Music by Bach, Rameau and Gaspard le Roux, Handel's Scipione and Riccardo Primo, Jommelli's Armida Abbandonata, Les Fêtes de Paphos by Mondonville, Mozart's Mitridate, Antigona by Traetta, complete keyboard works of Couperin, Rameau Overtures, Lulli's Persée, Lulli's Roland complete keyboard works of D'Anglebert, Handel Arias, Baroque Zarzuelas, Miserere by Leo, complete keyboard works of Forqueray, Salieri's La Grotta di Trofonio. *Publication:* Critical edition of La Capriciossa Coretta. *Honours:* Officier, Ordre des Arts et des Lettres, Chevalier, Ordre Nat. du Mérite; first prize Bruges Competition 1983, Gramophone Award 1998, Académie Charles Cros Grand Prix du Disque 2004, Traetta Prize 2013. *Current Management:* c/o Lorraine Villermaux, Les Talens Lyriques, 49 rue de Maubeuge, 75009 Paris. *Telephone:* 1-53-46-64-64 (office). *Fax:* 1-53-46-64-69

(office). *E-mail:* lv@lestalenslyriques.com (office). *Website:* www .lestalenslyriques.com (office). *Address:* 30 rue du Dragon, 75006 Paris, France (home). *Website:* christophe-rousset.com.

ROUTH, Francis John, BA, MA, ARAM, FRCO; British composer, pianist and writer; b. 15 Jan. 1927, Kidderminster, Worcs., England; m. 1st Virginia Anne Raphael 1956; m. 2nd Diana Florence Elizabeth Cardell Oliver 1991; two s. two d. *Education:* King's Coll., Cambridge, Royal Acad. of Music, London, studied with Matyas Seiber. *Career:* appeared as pianist, occasionally conducted in London and elsewhere, South Bank, radio broadcasts; Founder and Dir Redcliffe Concerts 1963–64; Ed. Composer (magazine of the Composers' Guild of Great Britain) 1980–88; Dir British Musical Heritage 2000–. *Compositions include:* Balulalow 1955, Fantasia 1 for organ 1958, A Sacred Tetralogy 1959–74, A Woman Young and Old 1962, Four Shakespeare Songs 1963, Elegy for soprano, violin and piano 1964, Songs of Farewell 1965, Sonatina for organ 1965, Songs of Lawrence Durrell 1966, Ode to the Evening Star 1967, Fantasia 2 for organ 1967, Horn Trio (unfinished) 1968, Dialogue for violin and orchestra 1968, Circles for soprano, clarinet, viola and piano 1969, Double Concerto 1970, Piano Quartet 1971, Spring Night 1971, Serenade for string trio 1972, Symphony I 1972, The Death of Iphigenia for soprano and 13 instruments 1972, Little Suite for piano 1974, Suite Cupid and Death 1974, On a Deserted Shore for soprano, mezzo soprano, tenor, baritone, choir, two pianos and percussion 1975, Cello Sonata 1 1975, Piano Concerto 1 1976, Mosaics 1976, At the round earth's imagined corners 1976, Oboe Quartet 1977, Fantasy for violin and pianoforte 1978, Scenes for orchestra 1978, Scenes for piano 1 1979, Vocalise 1979, Songs of Sir Walter Scott 1980, Songs of Dachine Rainer 1980, Love's Fool for soprano, flute and piano 1980, Ballade for piano 1982, Concerto for ensemble I 1982, Concerto for ensemble II 1983, Tragic Interludes for oboe 1984, Celebration for piano 1984, Dance Interludes for flute and guitar 1985, Elegy for piano 1986, Oboe Concerto 1986, Poème Fantastique for piano and orchestra 1986–88, Four Marian Antiphons for organ 1988, Romance 1989, Woefully Arrayed for soloists, choir and orchestra 1990, Fantasy Duo for violin and piano 1990, Romanian Dance 1990, Ripeness is all 1990, Concerto for ensemble III 1991, Suite for string orchestra 1992, Touraine Scenes for piano 2 1992, Three Shakespeare Songs 1992, Sonata for solo violin 1993, Cantate Domino for soprano, clarinet and strings 1993, Clarinet Quintet 1994, Capriccio 1995, Exultet coelum laudibus for organ 1995, Scenes for orchestra II 1997, Triumphal March 1997, Suite for Tbilisi concerto for ensemble IV 1997, Divertimento for string quartet 1998, Angels of Albion scenes for piano III 1998, Bretagne scenes for piano IV 1998, Sonata Festiva scenes for piano V 1999, Cello Sonata 2 1999, Andante for piano 2001, Agnus Dei 2002, Symphonic Variations 2003, Rondo capriccioso for piano 2003, Symphony II 2004, Alma Redemptoris Mater 2006, An English Organ Book 2006, A Parish Songbook 2006, The Well-Tempered Pianist 2008, Elegy for orchestra 2009, Symphony III 2012. *Recordings include:* A Sacred Tetralogy (organ Christopher Bowers-Broadbent) 1984, Celebration, Elegy (piano Jeffrey Jacob) 1986, Oboe Quartet, Tragic Interlude (oboe Robin Canter with Redcliffe Ensemble) 1992, A Woman Young and Old (soprano Margaret Field) 1995, Clarinet Quintet (clarinet Nicholas Cox with Redcliffe Ensemble) 1995, On a Deserted Shore 1996, Four Marian Antiphons, Exultet Coelum Laudibus 1998, Divertimento for string quartet (Bochmann Quartet) 1998, Scenes for piano III and IV 1999, Symphonic Variations 2003. *Publications:* The Organ 1958, Contemporary Music 1968, The Patronage and Presentation of Contemporary Music 1970, Contemporary British Music 1972, Early English Organ Music 1973, Stravinsky 1974; contrib. to various journals and The Annual Register 1980–2011. *Address:* Redcliffe Edition, 68 Barrowgate Road, Chiswick, London, W4 4QU, England (office). *Telephone:* (20) 8747-4730 (office). *Fax:* (20) 8747-4730 (office). *E-mail:* redcliffeedition@yahoo.co.uk (office). *Website:* www.redcliffe-edition.com (office); www.francisrouth.net (home).

ROUTLEY, Nicholas; conductor, composer and academic; b. 26 June 1947, England; m. Margo Adelson 1982, one s. two d. *Education:* George Heriot's, Edinburgh, St John's Coll., Cambridge, studied with Peter Feuchtwanger, Hans Heimler and Franco Ferrara. *Career:* debut as pianist, Wigmore Hall 1979; Conductor, Taiwan Symphony Orchestra 1984; Univ. of Cambridge 1973–75; Univ. of Sydney 1975–; Univ. of Hong Kong 1982–85, 1990–93; mem. Musicological Soc. of Australia. *Compositions:* Sicut Lilium for choir and vibraphone 1996, Sanctus for choir and percussion 1996, Like Snow five songs for voice and piano 1997, Icarus for orchestra 1997, Mycenae Lookout for baritone solo, choir, two pianos and percussion 1998. *Recordings:* The Hermit of Green Light (Australian vocal music) 1983, Monteverdi Vespers of 1610 1989, Josquin 1994, Clare MacLean: The Complete Choral Music 1995, Josquin: Secular Music 1996. *Publications:* A Practical Guide to Musica Ficta 1985, Arianna Thrice Betrayed (Gordon Athol Anderson Memorial Lecture) 1998, Symphony 2000; contrib. two articles on Debussy's Preludes, in Musicology Australia 1992, 1993.

ROWLAND, Daniel; British violinist; *First Violinist, Brodsky Quartet;* b. 1972, London. *Education:* Amsterdam Conservatoire, Royal Conservatory, Brussels. *Career:* has performed as soloist at Concertgebouw Amsterdam, Carnegie Hall, New York, Royal Albert Hall, London, Glinka Hall, St Petersburg, Symphony Hall, Birmingham, Gulbenkian Lisbon, and others; worked with orchestras across Europe under conductors including Andrei Boreiko, Djanzug Khakidze, Viktor Liberman, Lawrence Foster, Diego Masson, Lev Markiz, James Laughran, Jaap van Zweden; chamber musician and recitalist; masterclasses in Holland, the UK, Italy, Portugal and South

Africa; fmr Leader Allegri String Quartet; Leader Breitner String Quartet, Ensemble Contrechamps and the Quatour Contrechamps in Geneva, Switzerland, and Radius group in London; Guest Leader Philharmonia, BBC Symphony Orchestra; First Violinist Brodsky Quartet 2007–. *Honours:* several int. prizes including Brahms Soc. Brahms Prize, Baden Baden, Germany, Winner Oskar Back competition, Amsterdam Concertgebouw. *Current Management:* c/o Brodsky Quartet, Hazard Chase, 25 City Road, Cambridge, CB1 1DP, USA. *Telephone:* (1223) 312400. *Fax:* (1223) 460827. *E-mail:* robert.rountree@hazardchase.co.uk. *Website:* www.hazardchase.co.uk. *E-mail:* daniel@danielrowland.com (office). *Website:* www.brodskyquartet.co.uk (office); www.danielrowland.com.

ROWLAND, Gilbert, ARCM, ARCO; British harpsichordist and organist; b. 8 Oct. 1946, Glasgow. *Education:* Royal Coll. of Music, masterclasses in Dartington. *Career:* debut at Wigmore Hall 1973; harpsichordist, Wigmore Hall 1973, 1975, Purcell Room 1979, 1982, 1983, 1985, Greenwich Festival 1975–84, Berlin 1985; many recitals in North England; radio performances at BBC Concert Halls 1977–78; broadcasts of French harpsichord music 1984, Scarlatti Sonatas 1986, Soler Sonatas 1983. *Recordings:* Scarlatti Sonatas, Rameau keyboard works, Soler Sonatas. *Publication:* contrib. article on Scarlatti (for NEMA) 1985. *Current Management:* c/o Sylvia Junge Management, 7 Elton Close, Kingston upon Thames, Surrey KT1 4EE, England. *Telephone:* (20) 8977-9613. *E-mail:* sylviajunge@hotmail.com. *Address:* 418 Brockley Road, Brockley, London, SE4 2DH, England (home). *Telephone:* (20) 8699-2549 (home).

ROWLAND, Joan Charlotte, BA; pianist and teacher; b. 7 May 1930, Toronto, Canada; m. John Michael Thornton 1956; three s. one d. *Education:* Columbia Univ., New York, Royal Conservatory of Music, studied with Mona Bates in Toronto, with Eduard Steuermann at Juilliard School, New York. *Career:* debut with the Toronto Symphony under Ernest MacMillan 1942; recital debut in New York 1948; solo recitals in Canada, USA and Europe and for Canadian Broadcasting Corporation since 1942; two tours of USA and in London with Columbia Canadian Trio, and toured with Reginald Kell Players; soloist for various orchestras, including Toronto Symphony, Wiesbaden Orchestra, Mozarteum Orchestra, Mozart Festival Orchestra, and San Francisco and Buffalo Symphonies; toured with Piano Duo Schnabel in USA and Europe 1981–95. *Recordings:* Schubert Grand Duo and B flat Variations, Mozart Sonata in F major, Schubert E minor Sonata, Schubert Fantasy in F minor and Variations in A flat, all with Piano Duo Schnabel; solo recordings of Schumann Fantasy and Carnaval, Chopin Twenty-Four Preludes, Debussy Twenty-Four Preludes. *Publication:* contrib. 'Playing Four-Hands: A Pilgrim's Progress', in The Piano Quarterly 1986–87. *Honours:* first prize Kranichsteiner Modern Music Competition, Darmstadt, Germany 1954, first prize Mozarteum Piano Competition, Salzburg 1955. *Address:* 285 Riverside Drive, No. 4A, New York, NY 10025, USA (home).

ROWLAND-JONES, Simon Christopher, ARCM; British violist, composer, editor and teacher; *Professor, Royal College of Music;* b. 8 Sept. 1950, Colchester, Essex, England; s. of Robert Rowland-Jones and Penny Rowland-Jones (née Bergson). *Education:* Royal Coll. of Music (RCM), London. *Career:* mem. Chilingirian String Quartet 1971–78; solo debut, Carnegie Hall 1979; has performed with The Nash Ensemble, Villiers Piano Quartet, Chameleon, Arenski Ensemble; Prof., RCM 1990–2002, 2011–; Sr Tutor, Royal Northern Coll. of Music, Manchester 2002–11; Ed. new Peters Edn of Haydn String Quartets. *Compositions:* four String Quartets, Piano Quartet, String Trio, Rivers Gods, seven pieces for solo viola, String Quintet (Painting by Numbers) 1998, A Turn Outside (for Dame Josephine Barstow), Dark Night, Whirling 2007, Wiegenlied Variations for viola and piano 2008, Octet 2009, Teach Me Through Your Trees for baritone, viola and piano 2011. *Recordings include:* Dale, Phantasy and Suite; Bloch, Suites; Schubert, Schumann and Beethoven; Bach Solo Cello Suites, Vol. 1, Suites 1–3, after own edn/transcription. *Publication:* transcription of Bach Cello Suites 1998. *Address:* Pipers Croft, Friars Lane, Burnham Norton, King's Lynn, PE31 8JA, England (home). *Telephone:* 7796-263544 (mobile) (home). *E-mail:* simonrowlandjones@gmail.com.

ROXBURGH, Edwin; British conductor, composer and oboist; b. 6 Oct. 1937, Liverpool, England. *Education:* RCM with Herbert Howells and Terence McDonagh, St John's College, Cambridge, studied with Nadia Boulanger and Luigi Dallapiccola. *Career:* principal oboe of Sadler's Wells Opera, 1964–67, and soloist in contemporary music (Berio's Sequenza VII); teacher of composition at RCM, 1968–; founded 20th-Century Ensemble of London 1969. *Compositions include:* Night Music for soprano and orchestra 1969, How Pleasant to Know Mr Lear for narrator and chamber orchestra 1971, A Mosaic for Cummings for two narrators and orchestra, Montage for orchestra 1977, At the Still Point of the Turning World for amplified oboe and electronics 1978, Voyager for wind instruments 1989. *Honours:* Cobbett Medal 1970. *Telephone:* (1483) 282995. *E-mail:* springside@connectfree.co.uk.

ROYAL, Kate; British singer (soprano); b. 1979, London. *Education:* Guildhall School of Music and Drama, Nat. Opera Studio. *Career:* concert performances include Wagner's Das Rheingold with Sir Simon Rattle at BBC Proms and Festspielhaus Baden-Baden, Mendelssohn's Der Onkel aus Boston with the Bach Akademie Stuttgart under Helmuth Rilling, Mozart's Zaide at the Edinburgh Festival under Sir Charles Mackerras; US debut (Bach's St Matthew Passion) with Nat. Symphony Orchestra in Washington, DC under Helmuth Rilling; recitals in London, Edinburgh, Amsterdam, Barcelona,

Brussels and Cologne and at BBC Proms; has sung Pamina in Die Zauberflöte and Micaëla in Carmen for Glyndebourne Festival, Countess in Le nozze di Figaro and Governess in The Turn of the Screw for Glyndebourne on Tour, and Helena in A Midsummer Night's Dream for Teatro Real, Madrid and Glyndebourne Festival; debut Royal Opera House, Covent Garden as Miranda in Thomas Adès's The Tempest 2007; debut ENO in Monteverdi's The Coronation of Poppea 2007. *Recordings include:* Mahler's Symphony No. 4, Schumann's Liederkreis, Mendelssohn's Der Onkel aus Boston, Recital 2007, Midsummer Night 2009. *Honours:* Kathleen Ferrier Award 2004, John Christie Award 2004, Royal Philharmonic Soc. Young Artist Award 2007. *Address:* EMI Classics, 27 Wrights Lane, London, W8 5SW, England (office). *Telephone:* (20) 7795-7000 (office). *Website:* www.emiclassics.com (office); www.royalmidsummer.com.

ROZARIO, Patricia, OBE, BA, FRCM; Indian singer (soprano) and academic; b. 1960, Bombay; m. Mark Troop; one d. *Education:* Bombay Univ., Guildhall School of Music, Nat. Opera Studio, London, studied with Jeffrey Talbot. *Career:* has performed with numerous conductors, including Sir John Pritchard, Solti, Ashkenazy, Jurowski, Belohlavek, Gardiner, Pinnock, Ivan Fischer, Hickox and Andrew Davis; sung opera at Aix-en-Provence, Amsterdam, Lyon, Lille, Bremen, Antwerp, Wexford, English National Opera, Glyndebourne and Opera North; performed regularly with Graham Johnson in The Songmakers' Almanac programmes; solo recitals, South Bank, London and elsewhere; frequent performances of Bach, Handel, Mozart; Vaughan Williams' Serenade to Music, BBC Proms 1988; Schumann's Paradies und der Peri, Madrid with Gerd Albrecht; appearances at Bath and Eden. Festivals; world premiere of Taverner's Apocalypse, BBC Proms, also premiered John Casken's Farness with Northern Sinfonia and Chansons de Verlaine at Wigmore Hall, Jonathan Dove's Minterne; collaboration with Sir John Tavener wrote over thirty works for her; Prof., Royal Coll. of Music; teaches singing course at British Isles Music Festival summer music festival, Ardingly. *Operatic roles include:* Giulietta (Jommelli's La schiava liberata) for Netherlands Opera, Gluck's Euridice for Opera North, Mozart's Bastienne and Pamina for Kent Opera, Ilia on Glyndebourne tour, Ismene in Lyon production of Mithridate and Zerlina at Aix, Statue in Rameau's Pygmalion and Purcell's Belinda for Kent Opera; Florinda in Handel's Rodrigo at Innsbruck, Nero in L'incoronazione di Poppea and Massenet's Sophie; concert performance of Il re pastore, Queen Elizabeth Hall, London, world premiere of John Casken's Golem, as Miriam, Almeida Festival, London, Ismene at Wexford Festival 1989, cr. title role in premiere of Taverner's Mary of Egypt, Aldeburgh Festival 1992, season 1992–93 in Monteverdi's Il combattimento, ENO and Haydn's L'infedeltà delusa, Garsington Opera, Romilda in Serse, Brussels 1996. *Recordings include:* Mahler Symphony No. 4, London Symphony Orchestra, Songs of the Auvergne with John Pritchard (conductor), Haydn Stabat Mater with Trevor Pinnock (conductor), Golem (Gramophone Award 1991), Taverner: We Shall See Him As He Is, Mary of Egypt, To a Child Dancing in the Wind; Spanish Songs, Britten's Rape of Lucretia. *Honours:* Assoc., Guildhall School of Music; British Song Prize, Barcelona, Maggie Teyte Prize, Sängerforderungspreis, Salzburg Mozarteum, Guildhall School of Music Gold Medal, Asian Women of Achievement Arts and Culture Award 2002, Global Goan Award 2007, Pravasi Bharatiya Samman Award 2013. *Address:* Vocal Faculty, Royal College of Music, Prince Consort Road, London, SW7 2BS, England (office). *Website:* www.rcm.ac.uk/vocal (office); www.patriciarozario.com.

ROZE, Jeanine Michèle; French music promoter; b. 19 Aug. 1943, Aurillac (Cantal); d. of Henri Roze and Chana Roze (née Bernholc). *Education:* Lycée Lamartine, Paris, Univ. of Paris-IV Sorbonne. *Career:* Publicity Ed. Maillard agency 1962–63, Artistic Sec. 1964–75; artistic agent 1975–88; promoter of concerts etc., creator and organizer Liederabend Sunday Morning Concerts and Piano on the Champs-Elysées, at Théâtre de Champs-Elysées, in La Comédie des Champs-Elysées; narrator and music, Notes de lecture. *Publications include:* Schubert, album de famille (co-ed.) 1992, Musique en têtes (series of 16 musical post cards, ed.) 1992. *Honours:* Officier, Ordre des Arts et des Lettres. *Address:* 17 rue du Colisée, 75008 Paris, France. *Telephone:* (1) 42-56-90-10. *Fax:* (1) 43-59-54-37. *E-mail:* info@jeanine-roze-production.com. *Website:* www.jeanine-roze-production.com.

ROZHDESTVENSKY, Gennady Nikolayevich; Russian conductor; b. 4 May 1931, Moscow; s. of Nikolai Anosov and Natalia Rozhdestvenskaya; m. Viktoria Postnikova; one s. *Education:* Moscow State Conservatoire. *Career:* Asst Conductor, Bolshoi Theatre 1951, Conductor 1956–60, Prin. Conductor 1965–70, Artistic Dir 2000–01; Chief Conductor of USSR Radio and TV Symphony Orchestra 1961–74; Chief Conductor Stockholm Philharmonia 1974–77, 1992–95, Moscow Chamber Opera 1974–83; Founder, Artistic Dir and Chief Conductor State Symphony Orchestra of Ministry of Culture 1983–92; Prin. Conductor BBC Symphony Orchestra 1978–82, Vienna Symphony Orchestra 1980–83; has been guest conductor of numerous orchestras throughout Europe, USA and Asia; Chair of Conducting, Moscow State Conservatoire 1965–; Prin. Guest Conductor, Iceland Symphony Orchestra 2011–. *Publications:* The Fingering of Conducting 1974, Thoughts about Music 1975; numerous articles. *Honours:* Hon. mem. Swedish Royal Acad. 1975, Royal Acad., London, Hon. CBE 2014; Chevalier, Légion d'honneur, Order of the Rising Sun (Japan); People's Artist of the RSFSR 1966, People's Artist of the USSR 1976, Hero of Socialist Labour 1991, Lenin Prize 1970 and other awards. *Current Management:* Rayfield Allied, Southbank House, Black Prince Road, London, SE1 7SJ, England. *Telephone:* (20) 3176-5500. *Website:* www.rayfieldallied.com/artists/gennady-rozhdestvensky.

ROZSA, Pál; Hungarian composer; b. 14 March 1946, Szombathely; m. Éva Molnár 1977; two d. *Education:* Moscow State Univ., studied with Sándor Szokolay and Zsolt Durkó. *Career:* works performed world-wide; numerous works commissioned by renowned musicians; mem. Hungarian Composers' Union 1984–, Hungarian Music Soc. 1990–. *Compositions:* more than 540 works, including symphonic works, concertos, six operas, eight string quartets, wind quintets, brass music, songs, oratorios and cantatas, church music, wind band, transcriptions of classical works. *Recordings:* four albums, numerous recordings for Hungarian radio, one opera recorded by Hungarian TV. *Honours:* 18 works awarded first, second or third prizes at nat. or int. composers' competitions. *Address:* Csurgó u. 24/B, Örbottyán 2162, Hungary (home). *Telephone:* 20-3444086 (mobile) (home). *Fax:* (28) 816510 (office). *E-mail:* prozsa46@freemail.hu.

RÜBENACKER, Jutta; German violinist; *Professor of Violin, Hochschule für Musik und Theater, Hannover;* b. 25 May 1955, Karlsruhe, Germany; one s. *Education:* violin lessons and masterclasses. *Career:* mem., Bartholdy Quartet, Ensemble Neublang, Art Ensemble, Das Neue Ensemble, Rubernadzer Quartet, Duo Parlando; solo violist of the Sudwestdeubahe Kammer Orchester, Chamber Orchestra of Southwest Germany; concerts as soloist and chamber music, played mainly in Europe; masterclasses in Norway; many performances with Tatjana Prelevic, Xaver Thoma, David Wilde, Johannes Schollhorn, Stefan Schleiermacher, Tatjana Kumarova, Yougi Pagh-Pan, Sofia Gubaiduluia, Wolfgang Rihm; Prof. of Violin, Hochschule für Musik und Theater, Hannover 1993–. *Honours:* Hessischer Rundjunk-Preis 1974, Art and Promotion for music, Nieder, Sadisen 1998. *Address:* Hochschule für Musik und Theater, Emmichplatz 1, 30175 Hannover, Germany (office). *E-mail:* rueb.j@gmx.de (office). *Website:* www.hmt-hannover.de (office).

RUBENS, Sibylla; German singer (soprano); b. 1970, Nürtingen. *Education:* studied singing (concert and opera) at Staatliche Musikhochschule, Trossingen and at Hochschule für Musik, Frankfurt/Main, numerous masterclasses, including those of Edith Mathis and Elsa Cavelti, student of Irwin Gage's class for lied interpretation, Zurich. *Career:* recent highlights have included performances with the Royal Concertgebouw Orchestra under Philippe Herreweghe (including the Fauré Requiem), with Hartmut Haenchen (Bach's Magnificat and Brahms' Deutsches Requiem), Heinrich Schiff (Mahler's 4th Symphony and Beethoven's 9th Symphony in Vienna), as well as performances of Bach's St Matthew's Passion at New York's Carnegie Hall, with the RTVE Orchestra in Madrid and with the RAI Turin, Schumann's Requiem with the Munich Philharmonic under Christian Thielemann, Bach's Christmas Oratorio and Mass in B-minor in Montreal conducted by Kent Nagano and most recently a tour with the Budapest Festival Orchestra under Ivan Fischer through Europe (Mozart Vesperae Solennes de Confessore); has worked with conductors including Jun Märkl, Roger Norrington, Herbert Blomstedt, Marek Janowski, Riccardo Chailly; invited by Michael Gielen to perform with SWR Symphony Orchestra at two concerts in Schubert Mass in A-flat major 2010, by Christian Thielemann to sing both Mahler's 8th Symphony with the Munich Philharmonic 2010 and Bach's Christmas Oratorio in Dresden 2011; sang Mahler's 2nd Symphony in Milan and Mulhouse, Haydn's Creation with the Radio Philharmonic Orchestra Saarbrücken-Kaiserslautern, Bach's St John's Passion with the Leipzig Gewandhaus Orchestra and Bach's Christmas Oratorio with the Neubeuern Choral Society under Enoch zu Guttenberg and on tour with the Windsbach Boys' Choir 2010–11; performed Bach Cantatas with the Windsbach Boys' Choir in Dresden and Ansbach 2011; has worked closely with the Stuttgart Bachakademie and Helmuth Rilling for many years, with whom she travelled to Nashville, USA, Toronto, Canada (Bach Mass in B-minor) and Korea (Bach Magnificat); invited by the Bachakademie to perform at concerts featuring Schnittke's Requiem and Bach's Actus tragicus 2010; numerous lieder recitals, including Wolf's Italienisches Liederbuch (Italian Songbook) with Thomas Quasthoff at Schubertiade Festival in Schwarzenberg; previously accompanied by Irwin Gage, and now by various pianists, including Justus Zeyen, Michael Gees, Ulrich Eisenlohr and Anthony Spiri; guest performer at Ludwigsburger Schlossfestspiele and Heidelberger Frühling (Heidelberg Spring Festival), and in Barcelona, Amsterdam, Nuremberg, Stuttgart and Cologne. *Recordings include:* Schubert's Lazarus, arranged by Denisov, Mozart's Requiem, Lied recordings of Mozart, Schubert and Anselm Hüttenbrenner compositions, Bach Passions, Schumann Lieder and Songs Op. 27, Schubert Romantic Poets with Ulrich Eisenlohr, Humperdinck Lieder 2007, Mendelssohn's Symphony Cantata 'Lobgesang' with the Bavarian Radio Choir and Deutsche Radio Philharmonie Saarbrücken. *Current Management:* c/o KünstlerSekretariat am Gasteig, Rosenheimer Strasse 52, 81669 Munich, Germany. *Telephone:* (89) 44488790. *Fax:* (89) 4489522. *E-mail:* team@ks-gasteig.de. *Website:* www.ks-gasteig.de; www.sibyllarubens.de.

RUBIĶIS, Ainārs; Latvian conductor; b. 1978, Rīga. *Education:* Rīga Dome Choir School, Jāzeps Vītols Latvian Acad. of Music, masterclasses with Colin Metter, Jorma Panula, Mariss Jansons, Jozuas Domarkas and Leif Segerstram. *Career:* Prin. Conductor, Kamēr Youth Choir 1997–2006; Prin. Conductor, De Coro (Choir of Univ. of Latvia) 2000–; Teacher of Conducting, Rīga Dome Choir School 2001–08; took part as conductor and singer with Flemish Radio Choir in concert tour of Belgium and France 2005–06; Asst Conductor and mem. Latvian Radio Choir 2006–10; Conductor, Latvian Nat. Opera 2008–; int. conducting debut with Hungarian Nat. Opera Orchestra,

Miskolc 2009; UK debut with Royal Liverpool Philharmonic 2010; conducted Gustav Mahler Jugendorchester, Salzburg Festival 2011; appearances as Guest Conductor with Latvian Nat. Symphony Orchestra, Sinfonietta Rīga, Liepaja Symphony Orchestra, Bamberg Symphony Orchestra, Hong Kong Philharmonic, Oslo Philharmonic, Brussels Philharmonic, Novosibirsk State Opera and Orchestra. *Honours:* winner, Int. Gustav Mahler Conducting Competition 2010. *Address:* Latvian National Opera, Aspazijas bulv. 3, Rīga 1050, Latvia (office). *Telephone:* 6707-3777 (office). *E-mail:* info@opera.lv (office). *Website:* www.opera.lv (office).

RUBIN, Cristina; singer (soprano); b. 1958, Milan, Italy. *Education:* Milan Conservatoire, opera school of La Scala. *Career:* debut at Bergamo in 1985 as Mimi; sang Anna in Puccini's Le Villi at Torre del Lago and Trieste; sang at Teatro Goldoni in Venice as Agata in Il Flamino by Pergolesi, Trieste in 1987 as Suzel in L'Amico Fritz, as Mimi at Zürich in 1986 and Mozart's Countess at Piacenza; concerts with Beethoven's Missa Solemnis, Schumann's Manfred and Mendelssohn's Lobesgesang Symphony.

RUBINSKY, Sonia, MA; Brazilian pianist; b. 10 June 1957, Campinas, São Paulo; d. of Samuel Rubinsky Netto and Zlata Kaplan Rubinsky; m. Stephane Mallat. *Education:* Conservatório Musical Campinas, Rubin Acad. of Music, Jerusalem, Juilliard School, New York; studied with Vlado Perlemuter, Beveridge Webster, Jacob Lateiner, Olga Normanha and William Daghlian, master classes with Edward Aldwell, Leon Fleisher, Gina Bachauer, Claude Frank, Irma Wolpe, Murray Perahia and Arthur Rubinstein. *Career:* has lived in Israel, USA, currently in Paris, France; has played with Orchestra of St Luke's, New York, Richmond Symphony Orchestra, Phoenix Symphony Orchestra, Orquestra Sinfônica do Estado de São Paulo, Orquestra Sinfônica da Universidade de São Paulo, New York Women's Ensemble; has performed concerts at Carnegie Hall, Alice Tully Hall, Bargemusic, Merkin Concert Hall, New York, Hertz Hall, Berkeley, Jordan Hall, Boston, Tel-Aviv Museum of Art, Recanati Hall, Israel, Teatro Municipal de São Paulo, Sala São Paulo, Brazil, Aga-Zaal, Holland, Maison de la Radio, Paris; recorded complete Piano Works by Heitor Villa-Lobos; recorded Scarlatti, Mendelssohn, Mozart, Gabriela Lena Frank, Jorge Liderman; Artist-in-Residence, Edward Aldwell International Center, Jerusalem 2010–. *Recordings:* Villa-Lobos Piano Music Vols 1–8 (Vol. 1: one of five Best CDs of 1999, Gramophone Magazine, Vol. 5: Ed.'s Choice, Gramophone Magazine Oct. 2006, Vol. 8: Latin Grammy Award for Best Classical Album 2009) 1999–2009; has also recorded works by Debussy, Villa-Lobos, Messiaen, Mozart, Scarlatti and Jorge Liderman, currently recording 48 Songs Without Words (Mendelssohn). *Honours:* winner, Artists Int. Competition 1984, William Petschek Award, Carlos Gomes Prize 2006, 2009, Gramophone Magazine Award, Recitalist of the Year Award, São Paulo Asscn of Music Critics, Latin Grammy 2009. *Telephone:* (6) 71-71-79-67 (mobile). *E-mail:* feliperenault@yahoo.com.br. *Website:* www .arsvivaonline.com. *Telephone:* (6) 78-96-89-87 (mobile). *E-mail:* soniarubinsky@gmail.com (office). *Website:* www.soniarubinsky.com.

RUCKER, Mark; American singer (baritone); b. 1957, Chicago. *Career:* debut at Cincinnati, 1985, as Amonasro, in Aida; Philadelphia, 1986, as Verdi's Renato, New York City Opera, 1988, as Rigoletto; European debut at Nice, 1989, as Tonio in Pagliacci; Vienna Staatsoper, 1993, as Alfio in Cavalleria Rusticana; Verdi's Macbeth at New Orleans and Enrico in Lucia di Lammermoor for Portland Opera, 1994; Rigoletto for Milwaukee Opera, 1996; Season 2000 as Rigoletto at Miami and Amonasro in Amsterdam; Concerts include Messiah, Elijah and Donna nobis pacem by Vaughan Williams. *Recordings include:* Amonasro in Aida. *Honours:* winner Pavarotti Competition at Philadelphia 1985. *Current Management:* Wolf Piper Artists International, 13 East 69th Street, Suite 3R, New York, NY 10021, USA. *Telephone:* (212) 531-1514. *Fax:* (212) 861-6949. *E-mail:* info@wolfartists.com. *Website:* www.wolfartists.com; www.markrucker.com.

RUDAKOVA, Larisa; singer (soprano); b. 1964, Russia. *Career:* many performances in Russia and Eastern Europe in operas by Rossini (Il Barbiere di Siviglia), Donizetti (Lucia di Lammermoor), Charpentier (Louise) and Glinka (Ruslan and Lyudmila); also sings Rossini's Bel raggio lusinghier (Semiramide); contestant at the 1995 Cardiff Singer of the World Competition; sang Antonida in Glinka's A Life for the Tsar, St Petersburg 1998.

RUDENKO, Bela Andreyevna; Ukrainian singer (soprano); b. 18 Aug. 1933, Bokovo-Antratsit. *Education:* Odessa Conservatory with Olga Blagovidova. *Career:* debut at Odessa in 1955 as Gilda in Rigoletto; sang at Kiev from 1965 notably as Glinka's Ludmila, Rosina in Il Barbiere di Siviglia, Lakmé and Natasha in War and Peace; Bolshoi Theatre Moscow from 1972; also successful in operas by Ukranian composers. *Recordings include:* Ruslan and Ludmila and A Life for The Tsar, by Glinka. *Honours:* State Prize of USSR.

RUDERS, Poul; Danish composer; b. 27 March 1949, Ringsted, Denmark; s. of the late Poul Ruders Sr and Inge Ruders; m. Annette Gerlach 1995. *Education:* Royal Danish Music Acad. *Career:* performances with all major Danish symphony orchestras; performances by London Sinfonietta, Ensemble Intercontemporain, Speculum Musicae, New York Philharmonic, Berlin Philharmonic, Royal Danish Opera, ENO, Minnesota Opera, Canadian Opera Co., Philharmonia, Capricorn, Lontano; Psalmodies for Guitar and Ensemble 1990, and frequent performances of works at several int. festivals; mem. Danish Composers' Guild, Soc. for the Promotion of New Music, UK. *Compositions:* major orchestral pieces: Capriccio Pian e Forte 1978, Manhattan Abstraction 1982, Thus Saw St John 1984, The Drama Trilogy: Dramaphonia, Monodrama, Polydrama 1987–88, Himmelhoch-Jauchzend zum Tode betrübt, symphony 1989, Violin Concerto No. 2 1991, Solar Trilogy 1992–95, Symphony Nos 2–5 1997–2015; chamber works: String Quartet No. 1 1971, No. 2 1979, Four Compositions 1980, Greeting Concertino 1982, 4 Dances in one movement 1983, Vox In Rama 1983, Concerto in Pieces (commissioned by the BBC Symphony Orchestra) 1995, The Handmaid's Tale (opera commissioned by the Royal Theatre Copenhagen) 2000, Kafkas's Trial (opera with libretto by Paul Bentley, commissioned by The Royal Opera Co., Copenhagen) 2001–03, Selma Jezková, commissioned by The Royal Danish Opera 2005, Listening Earth (commissioned by the Berlin Philharmonic) 2002, Final Nightshade (commissioned by the New York Philharmonic) 2003; numerous solo pieces for various instruments. *Recordings include:* Four Dances, with London Sinfonietta conducted by Oliver Knussen 1983–89, Corpus Cum Figuris, commissioned by Ensemble Intercontemporain 1984–90, Corpus Cum Figuris: Point PCD 5084, Violin Concerto No. 1 Unicorn-Kanchana, 9114, Psalmodies: Bridge 9037, Symphony: Chan 9179. *Honours:* Charles Heidsieck Prize, Royal Philharmonic Orchestra, London 1991. *Current Management:* c/o Chester Music and Novello & Co., 14–15 Berners Street, London, W1T 3LJ, England. *Telephone:* (20) 7612-7400. *Fax:* (20) 7612-7545. *E-mail:* promotion@musicsales.co.uk. *Website:* www.chesternovello .com. *E-mail:* poulmus.ruders@mail.tele.dk (home). *Website:* www .poulruders.net.

RUDIAKOV, Shoshana; German (b. Latvian) pianist and academic; *Professor of Music, Vice-Rector and International Coordinator, Staatliche Hochschule für Musik und Darstellende Kunst, Stuttgart;* b. Rīga, Latvia. *Education:* Music School, Rīga and Moscow P. I. Tchaikovsky State Conservatoire, USSR (now Russian Fed.). *Career:* soloist in concerts and recitals, and appearances on radio and TV in UK, Germany, Italy, USA, Israel, Puerto Rico, Switzerland, Belgium, Netherlands, Yugoslavia, Japan, Chile, China; Prof. of Music, Vice-Rector and Int. Coordinator, Staatliche Hochschule für Musik und Darstellende Kunst, Stuttgart 1981–; teaching and performances at Manchester Music Festival, Vt, USA. *Address:* Staatliche Hochschule für Musik und Darstellende Kunst, Urbansplatz 2, 70182 Stuttgart (office); Bergstr. 47, 70186 Stuttgart, Germany (home). *E-mail:* shoshana.rudiakov@ mh-stuttgart.de (office). *Website:* www.mh-stuttgart.de (office).

RUDY, Mikhail; Russian/French pianist; b. 3 April 1953, Tashkent; m. Marie-Agnes Bousquet; two c. *Education:* Moscow Conservatory with Jakov Flier. *Career:* after winning prizes at competitions in Leipzig and Paris, made western debut 1977, playing Beethoven's Triple Concerto in Paris with Rostropovich and Stern; guest appearances with the Berlin Philharmonic, Orchestre de Paris, Concertgebouw, Boston Symphony, Montréal Symphony Orchestra, London Philharmonic and Toronto Symphony; US debut 1981 with the Cleveland Orchestra conducted by Lorin Maazel; festivals include Schleswig-Holstein, Berlin, Tanglewood, Lockenhaus and Vienna; Salzburg Easter Festival, 1987 with Karajan; chamber music concerts with the Amadeus Quartet until 1987, Guarneri Quartet and Vienna Philharmonic Wind Ensemble; London debut with the London Symphony Orchestra under Michael Tilson Thomas, 1988; Promenade Concerts 1989, Prokofiev's 2nd Concerto; debut with Dresden Staatskapelle, 1991; season 1991–92 with concerts in Cleveland and Munich; returned to Russia 1990, concerts with St Petersburg Philharmonic; fmr Music Dir St Riquier Festival; Waldbühne Concert with Berlin Philharmonic and Mariss Jansons 1994; Janáček, Stravinsky and Schubert concert at Wigmore Hall, London 1997; produced play The Pianist at the Manchester Int. Festival and directed Pictures at an Exhibition animated film (after Kandinsky's original 1928 staging) at Cité de la Musique in Paris 2010. *Exhibition:* Danser sa vie, Centre Pompidou 2011–12. *Plays:* The Pianist, Letters to Milena. *Film:* Désir Noir, Pictures at an Exhibition, after Kandinsky (video). *Television:* Le Roman d'un pianiste. *Recordings include:* Brahms and Ravel recital, Concertos by Rachmaninov and Tchaikovsky with St Petersburg Philharmonic and Mariss Jansons, Shostakovich Piano Concerto No. 1 with Berlin Philharmonic, Stravinsky: integral of Petroushka ballet (transcriptions: Stravinsky/Rudy), Wagner: Siegfried Idyll, Double Dream – two piano improvisations with jazz pianist Micha Alperin, Chopin 24 preludes and 2nd sonata. *Publications:* Le Roman d'un pianiste, l'impatience de vivre (autobiog.). *Honours:* Chevalier, Ordre des Arts et des Lettres; Prizewinner Bach Competition, Leipzig 1971, First Prize, Marguerite Long Competition, Paris 1975, Grand Prix du Disque Liszt, Budapest, Grand Prix du Disque Acad. Charles Cros (Scriabine), Grand Prix, Acad. Française (Rachmaninov concerti with Mariss Jansons, Szymanowski recital), Deutsche Schalplatten Kritik Preis (Shostakovich). *Current Management:* c/o Sulivan Sweetland, 28 Albion Street, London, W2 2AX, England. *Telephone:* (20) 7262-0333. *Fax:* (20) 7402-5851. *E-mail:* info@ sulivansweetland.co.uk. *Website:* www.sulivansweetland.co.uk. *E-mail:* mabousq@club-internet.fr (office).

RUDZINSKI, Zbigniew, MA; Polish composer; b. 23 Oct. 1935, Czechowice; m. Ewa Debska 1965; one d. *Education:* State High School for Music, Warsaw and Warsaw Univ. *Career:* Prof. of Composition, Acad. of Music F. Chopin, Warsaw 1973–, Head of Composition Dept 1980–81, Rector (Dir) 1981–84, Head of Co-operation Project, Acad. of Music F. Chopin and Keimyung Univ., Seoul, S Korea 1996–2007; Pres. Warsaw Dist, Polish Composers' Union 1983–85, Sec.-Gen. 1985–. *Compositions include:* orchestral: Sonata for two string quartets, piano and kettle drums 1960, Contra Fidem 1964, Moments Musicaux I–III 1965–68, Music by Night 1970; vocal/instrumental works: Four Folk Songs for soprano and piano 1955, Epigrams for flute, choir and percussion 1962, Study for C for ensemble ad libitum 1964, Symphony for

men's choir and orchestra 1969, Requiem for the Victims of Wars for choir and orchestra 1971, Tutti e Solo for soprano, flute, french horn and piano 1973, Strings in the Earth for soprano and string orchestra 1983, The Book of Hours songs for mezzo-soprano and piano trio 1983, Das Sind Keine Träume songs for mezzo-soprano and piano 1986; chamber: Sonata for clarinet and piano 1958, Trio for two clarinets and bassoon 1958, String Trio 1964, Impromptu for two pianos, three cellos and three percussion 1968, Quartet for two pianos and percussion 1969, Sonata for piano 1975, Campanella for percussion ensemble 1977, Tritones for percussion ensemble 1979, Three Romantic Portraits for 12 saxophones 1983, Three Pictures at an Exhibition for flute, piano and vibraphone 1996, String Quartet 2011; opera: The Mannequins 1981, Antigone 2001. *Address:* ul Poznanska 23 m 26, 00-685 Warsaw, Poland (home). *Telephone:* (22) 6296311 (home). *Fax:* (22) 8278310 (office); (22) 7591054 (home). *E-mail:* kataranka5432@interia.pl (home).

RUFFINI, Alessandra; Italian singer (soprano); b. 1961. *Education:* Milan Conservatory. *Career:* sang Arianna in Vivaldi's Giustino in 1985 and appeared as Gilda at Treviso and Rovigo in 1987; sang at Vicenza in 1988 as Elena in Gluck's Paride e Helena, Palermo 1991 as Mariana in Wagner's Das Liebesverbot, and at Rome Opera in 1992 as Rossini's Adina and Leila in Les Pêcheurs de Perles; other roles include Amina in La Sonnambula (Cremona, 1988) and Adina in L'Elisir d'amore (Piacenza 1992); sang Pauline in Donizetti's Les Martyrs, Nancy, 1996. *Recordings include:* Rosina in Morlacchi's Il Barbiere di Siviglia; La Locandiera by Salieri; La Cecchina by Piccinni. *Current Management:* Atelier Musicale, Via Caselle 76, San Lazzaro di Savena 40068, Italy. *Telephone:* (51) 19984444. *Fax:* (51) 19984420. *E-mail:* info@ateliermusicale.com. *Website:* www.ateliermusicale.com.

RUFO, Bruno; singer (tenor); b. 1941, Italy. *Career:* debut at Spoleto 1965 as Pinkerton; many appearances at La Scala Milan, Rome, Naples and as Radames 1981 at Verona Arena; further engagements at Bologna, Parma, Hamburg, Munich, Vienna, the Deutsche Oper Berlin and Düsseldorf; sang Manrico at Liège, and Samson in season 1986–87; television appearances have included Verdi's Ernani.

RUGGEBERG, Claudia; German singer (contralto); b. 1955, Hamburg. *Education:* studied in Hamburg with Judith Beckmann. *Career:* many appearances throughout Germany in concerts and recitals; Guest engagements at the Hamburg and Oldenburg Operas, Bregenz Festival, 1985–86 in Die Zauberflöte, and Gelsenkirchen and Stuttgart in 1987 in La Gioconda and Die Soldaten; Sang in Eugene Onegin at Zürich in 1991 and has appeared elsewhere including Barcelona, Bologna, Cologne and Krefeld; Has sung mainly in opera houses of Hamburg, Bonn, Cologne, Stuttgart, Aalto-Theater Essen; Ring Production (Erda), Dessau, Die Verurteilung des Lukullus, Handel, Giulio Cesare, 1992–97; Teatro Liceo Barcelona: Schoenberg Moses und Aron, Götterdämmerung, Walküre, Eugene Onegin; Teatro Communale Bologna: Walküre (Riccardo Chailly); Teatro alla Scala Milano, Elektra (Giuseppe Sinopoli), 1994; Asia-Concert tour with the Staatskapelle Dresden, Giuseppe Sinopoli: Elektra in Japan and Taiwan, 1995; Sang at Marseille, 1997 and Toulouse, 1999; Professor at the Essen Musikhochschule, 1990–. *Recordings:* albums: Braunfels: Die Verkündigung, 1994; Schoeck, Rohm, Shostakovich Lieder, 1997. *Current Management:* c/o Walter Beloch Artists Management, Via Melzi d'Eril 26, 20154 Milan, Italy. *Telephone:* (2) 33101922. *Fax:* (2) 3313643. *E-mail:* lirica@walterbeloch.com. *Website:* www .walterbeloch.com.

RŮIČKOVÁ, Zuzana; Czech harpsichordist; b. 14 Jan. 1927, d. of Jaroslav Růička and Leopoldine Lederer; m. Viktor Kalabis 1952. *Education:* Pilsen School of Music and Acad. of Performing Arts, Prague. *Career:* interned in concentration camps including Auschwitz and Bergen-Belsen 1942–45; concert harpsichordist in Europe, Japan, Canada and the USA 1956–; music teacher Acad. of Performing Arts (AMU) 1951–, Acad. of Music and Dramatic Art, Bratislava 1978–82, Zürich Masterclass, Switzerland 1969–; Prof. of Music AMU 1990–; mem. permanent cttee Prague Spring Festival, Concertino Praga Competition. *Recordings include:* more than 90 recordings, including works by J.S. Bach, Purcell, Handel, Haydn, Scarlatti. *Publications:* Královna Cembala, Reminiscences (ed.) 2005. *Honours:* Hon. mem. Nat. Early Music Asscn, Oxford, UK 1988, Neue Bachgesellschaft, Leipzig 2005, Dvořák Soc.; Chevalier, Ordre des Arts et des Lettres, France 2004; Dr hc (AMU) 2011; winner Arbeitsgemeinschaft der öffentlich-rechtlichen Rundfunkanstalten der Bundesrepublik Deutschland (ARD) Competition, Munich (Germany) 1956, State Prize of Merit 1970, Nat. Artist of Czechoslovakia 1989, Medal of Arts and Sciences, Hamburg, Germany 1992, Czech Critics' Medal 2003, Grand Prix du Disque Charles Cros, Medal of Merit for Arts, Czech Republic 2004, UNESCO-Czech Council of Music Award 2007, Charles IV Cultural Prize, Aachen 2011. *Address:* Slezská 107, 130-00 Prague 3, Czech Republic (home). *Telephone:* (2) 67312104 (home); 420 206678885 (mobile) (home). *E-mail:* ales@martinu.cz (office).

RUMBOLD, Ian Francis, BMus; British editor; *Senior Research Fellow, Bangor University;* b. 29 March 1956, Grantham, Lincs., England; m. Valerie Proctor. *Education:* King's School, Grantham, Univ. of Birmingham, Jesus Coll., Cambridge. *Career:* Research Fellow, Clare Hall Cambridge 1981–83; Sir James Knott Research Fellow, Newcastle upon Tyne 1983–85; freelance ed. and teacher 1985–86; Lecturer in Music, Univ. of Exeter 1986–87; Research Assoc. (New Berlioz Edn), Univ. of Manchester 1987–99, Royal Coll. of Music, London 1999–2003; Sr Research Fellow, Dept of Music, Univ. of Nottingham 2004–07, Lecturer 2007–08; Sr Research Fellow, Bangor Univ.

2010–12; Sr Research Fellow, Univ. of Manchester 2012–; mem. Advisory Bd 'Polski Rocznik Muzykologiczny'; mem. Royal Musical Asscn, Plainsong and Medieval Music Soc. *Publications:* edns for New Berlioz Edn Vols 14, 15 and 22b; Commentary of facsimile edn of St Emmeram Codex; Hermann Pötzlinger's Music Book: The St Emmeram Codex and its Contexts (with Peter Wright) 2009; contrib. to The New Grove Dictionary of Music and Musicians, The New Oxford Companion to Music and many journals. *Address:* 33 Selly Wick Drive, Selly Park, Birmingham, B29 7JQ, England. *Telephone:* (121) 472-4994. *E-mail:* ianrumbold@aol.com.

RUNKEL, Reinhild; German singer (mezzo-soprano); b. 25 Dec. 1943, Volkach am Main. *Education:* studied in Wuppertal. *Career:* sang at the Nuremberg Opera, 1975–82; guest engagements at Lisbon, Reggio Emilia, Paris and San Francisco, 1985, and Florence as Magdalene in Meistersinger in 1986; Salzburg Festival in 1987 in Moses and Aron by Schoenberg; Sang Fricka in Ring performances at Bologna, Stuttgart and Cologne, 1987–88; appearances at the Zürich Opera from 1985 as Herodias, Fricka and Clytemnestra in a Ruth Berghaus production of Elektra in 1991; Stuttgart Staatsoper in 1992 as Begbick in Aufstieg und Fall der Stadt Mahagonny; other roles include Erda, Waltraute, Brangaene, Lyon 1990, Jocasta in Oedipus Rex and the Nurse in Die Frau ohne Schatten; Fricka in Die Walküre for Netherlands Opera, 1998; Sang the Nurse in Die Frau ohne Schatten at La Scala and Munich, 1999; Clytemnestra in Elektra in Sydney and at the Savonlinna Festival, 2000; Frequent concert appearances. *Recordings include:* Fortune Teller in Arabella and Nurse in Die Frau ohne Schatten conducted by Solti; Beethoven's 9th. *Current Management:* c/o Astrid Winkler, Theateragentur Winkler, Grillparzerstrasse 46, 81675 Munich, Germany. *Telephone:* (89) 4705857. *Fax:* (89) 4707123. *E-mail:* astrid.winkler@agentur-winkler.com. *Website:* agentur-winkler.com.

RUNNICLES, Donald; British conductor; *General Music Director, Deutsche Oper Berlin;* b. 16 Nov. 1954, Edinburgh, Scotland. *Education:* Univs of Edinburgh and Cambridge, London Opera Centre. *Career:* Repetiteur, Mannheim Nat. Theatre from 1980, debut with Les Contes d'Hoffmann; Kapellmeister from 1984, conducting Fidelio, Le nozze di Figaro, Un Ballo in Maschera, Die Walküre and Parsifal; Prin. Conductor, Hanover from 1987, leading Salome, Jenůfa, Tosca, Don Giovanni, Werther; regular engagements with the Hamburg Staatsoper, including Turandot, The Bartered Bride, Die Zauberflöte, Manon Lescaut, Carmen, Don Carlos, Zar und Zimmermann, Il Trovatore, Il Barbiere di Siviglia, L'Elisir d'amore, Lady Macbeth of Mtsensk; Gen. Music Dir, Freiburg from 1989, with Lady Macbeth, Billy Budd, Peter Grimes; assisted James Levine at Bayreuth, then conducted Lulu at the Metropolitan 1988, followed by Der fliegende Holländer 1990, and Die Zauberflöte; conducted The Ring at San Francisco 1990; Vienna Staatsoper from season 1990–91, with Il Barbiere di Siviglia, Don Giovanni, Madama Butterfly, La Traviata and Prince Igor; Glyndebourne debut 1991, with Don Giovanni; Music Dir and Chief Conductor, San Francisco Opera 1992–2009; season 1992–93 with Lady Macbeth of the Mtsensk District at Vienna Volksoper; The Fiery Angel, Guillaume Tell, Boris Godunov at San Francisco; Don Giovanni at Munich; Tannhäuser at Bayreuth; Der Ring des Nibelungen at Bayreuth; other repertory includes Idomeneo at Hanover; Der Freischütz; symphonic engagements in Darmstadt, Odensee, St Gallen, Copenhagen and with NDR Orchestra, Hamburg; season 1997–98 at San Francisco with Death in Venice, Le nozze di Figaro and Pelléas et Mélisande; Billy Budd and the Ring at the Vienna State Opera 2001; led new production of Katya Kabanova at San Francisco 2002; conducted Schoenberg's Gurrelieder at the London Proms 2002; Tristan und Isolde (over three concerts) for the BBC SO 2002–03; conducted world premiere of John Adams's opera Doctor Atomic 2005; Music Dir, Grand Teton Music Festival 2005–; Gen. Music Dir Deutsche Oper Berlin 2009–; Chief Conductor, BBC Scottish Symphony Orchestra 2009–16, Conductor Emer. 2016–; Prin. Guest Conductor, Atlanta Symphony Orchestra. *Recordings include:* Mozart Requiem 2005, Wagner: Tristan und Isolde 2006, Orff: Carmina Burana 2008, Henryk Gorecki: Symphony No. 3 Symphony of Sorrowful Songs 2009, Highlights From The Ring – Siegfried Idyll 2010, Wagner: Arias (BBC Music Magazine Vocal Award 2014), Janácek: Jenufa (live recording from Deutsche Oper Berlin) 2014. *Honours:* San Francisco Opera Medal 2008. *Current Management:* c/o Opus 3 Artists, 470 Park Avenue South, 9th Floor North, New York, NY 10016, USA. *Telephone:* (212) 584-7500. *E-mail:* info@opus3artists.com. *Website:* www.opus3artists.com. *Address:* Deutsche Oper Berlin, Bismarckstrasse 35, 10627 Berlin, Germany (office). *Telephone:* (30) 3438401 (office). *Fax:* (30) 343 84 232 (office). *Website:* www.deutscheoperberlin.de (office); www.donaldrunnicles.com.

RUNSWICK, Daryl, MA; British composer, musician and singer (tenor); b. 12 Oct. 1946, Leicester, England. *Education:* Corpus Christi Coll., Cambridge. *Career:* Musical Dir, Footlights Club 1966–67; jazz bass player, especially with C. Laine and J. Dankworth 1968–82; concert bass player, especially with London Sinfonietta 1970–82; session player on bass, bass guitar, keyboards 1970–81; arranger and record producer, especially for King's Singers 1971–; composer of film and television music 1976–; tenor singer, Electric Phoenix 1983–; Musical Dir, Green Light Music Theatre Co. 1990–; Prof. of Composition and Media Studies, Trinity Coll. of Music, London. *Compositions:* Scafra Preludes, six Episodes forming a Threnody, Moto interrotto/Ripresso, Mouth Symphony, Four by Five, I Am a Donut, Four Nocturnes, Main-Lineing, From Two Worlds, Cool>Warm>Hot. *Recordings include:* with Electric Pheonix: Berio, Cage, Nordheim, Wishart; with London Sinfonietta: Songs for Dov,

Agon, King Priam; with Nash Ensemble: The Soldier's Tale. *Address:* 34A Garthorne Road, London, SE23 1EW, England.

RUOFF, Axel D., DipMus; German composer; b. 24 March 1957, Stuttgart. *Education:* State University for Music, Stuttgart, Academy for Music, Kassel, National University for Fine Arts and Music, Tokyo, Japan. *Career:* Head of Department, Stuttgart Music School, 1981–88; Lecturer, State University for Music, Trossingen, 1985–87; concurrently Guest Professor in Composition at Morioka College in 1988, selected for the Forum for Young Composers, Berlin; Fellowship from the Art Foundation of Baden, Württemberg; Fellowship from the Japanese Ministry of Culture for study at the National University for Fine Arts and Music in Tokyo; Professor at State University for Music, Stuttgart, 1992; broadcasts for German, other European and Japanese stations. *Compositions:* Procession for Orchestra, 1983; Concerto for flute and orchestra, 1984; Correlations, cello solo, 1983; Jemand In Vorbeigehen for voice and piano, 1984; Via Dolorosa for organ, 1985; Fassaden for violin solo, 1985; String Quartet, 1986; Salomo-Variations for choir, 1986; Nacht Und Träume for orchestra, 1987–88; String Quartet No. 2, 1988; Piano Concerto, 1989. *Honours:* Valentino Bucchi, Rome, 1985, 1987; 1st Prize, ICONS, Torino, 1988; 2nd Prize, Ensemblia, Mönchengladbach, 1986; 1st Prize, Corciano, Perugia, 1991. *Address:* Möhringer Land Str 53, 7000 Stuttgart 80, Germany.

RUOHONEN, Seppo; singer (tenor); b. 25 April 1946, Turku, Finland. *Education:* studied in Helsinki, with Luigi Ricci in Rome and with Anton Dermota in Vienna. *Career:* debut in Helsinki 1973 as Alvaro in La Forza del Destino; appearances with Finnish Nat. Opera as Verdi's Duke and Manrico, Tchaikovsky's Lensky and Hermann, and Don Ottavio; Savonlinna 1977 in The Last Temptations by Kokonnen, with Sallinen's The Red Line, repeated at the Metropolitan, New York 1983; San Diego Opera as Riccardo in Un Ballo in Maschera; returned to Savonlinna 1983 as Don Carlos and as Erik in Der fliegende Holländer; has sung at Frankfurt from 1978 and made guest appearances in Berlin, Dresden, Leeds, Glasgow, Stuttgart and Wiesbaden as the Duke of Parma in Doktor Faust, Puccini's Cavaradossi, Luigi and Pinkerton, and Jenik in The Bartered Bride; sang Florestan at the 1992 Savonlinna Festival; Inquisitor in Dallapiccola's Il Prigioniero for Tampere Opera 1996. *Recordings include:* The Last Temptations.

RUPP, Andrew, MA (Cantab.); British singer (baritone); *Baritone, The BBC Singers;* b. 1966, England; s. of Martin Rupp and Jacqueline Rupp; m. Tamsin Rupp; two s. *Education:* Kingswood School, Bath and St John's Coll., Cambridge; vocal studies with Linda Esther Gray and Philip Doghan. *Career:* prin. operatic roles with Glyndebourne Festival Opera, Berlin Staatsoper, Opera North, Glyndebourne Touring Opera, ENO, NI Opera, English Touring Opera, Festival d'Aix-en-Provence, Opera de Lausanne, Theatre de Caen, OTC Dublin, Buxton Festival, Music Theatre Wales and The Opera Group; solo oratorio and concert work in the UK, Europe, USA and China; has also performed and recorded with vocal ensembles, including The English Concert, The Cardinall's Musick, Polyphony, Tenebrae, Gabrieli Consort and King's Consort; mem. The BBC Singers. *Current Management:* c/o Athole Still Opera Ltd, Foresters Hall, 25–27 Westow Street, London, SE19 3RY, England. *Telephone:* (20) 8771-5271. *Fax:* (20) 8771-8172. *E-mail:* enquiries@atholestill .co.uk. *Website:* www.atholestill.com.

RUSHTON, Edward, MMus; British composer and pianist; b. 1972. *Education:* Chetham's School of Music with Renna Kellaway, Colin Touchin and Michael Ball, King's Coll., Cambridge with Robin Holloway and John York, RSAMD with James McMillan, attended summer schools with Sir Peter Maxwell Davies, Judith Weir, Magnus Lindberg, Colin Matthews, masterclasses with Irwin Gage at the Zürich Conservatory. *Career:* composer-in-residence, Musikfesttage of the Orpheum Stiftung, Zürich 2002; freelance composer and pianist; works performed and commissioned by Endymion Ensemble, London Sinfonietta, Schubert Ensemble, Birmingham Contemporary Music Group, Faber Music, Camerata Zürich, Tonhalle Orchestra Zürich, Vokalensemble Cantapella, Orchestra of the Nat. Theatre Mannheim; performances as accompanist with Harry White (saxophone). *Compositions:* opera: Leinen aus Smyrna 2001, The Young Man with the Carnation 2002, Philoctetes, Birds. Bark. Bones. 2004, Harley 2005; chamber music: Rounds, L'An Mil, Combat in the Year Thousand. *Honours:* British Composer Award British Acad. of Composers and Songwriters 2005.

RUSHTON, Julian Gordon, BA, MusB, MA, DPhil; British professor of music and writer; *Professor Emeritus, School of Music, University of Leeds;* b. 22 May 1941, Cambridge, England; s. of William Rushton FRS and Marjorie Rushton; two s. *Education:* Trinity Coll., Cambridge, Magdalen Coll., Oxford. *Career:* Lecturer, Univ. of East Anglia 1968–74; Lecturer in Music and Fellow, King's Coll., Cambridge 1974–81; West Riding Prof. of Music, Univ. of Leeds 1982–2002, Prof. Emer. 2002–; Dir Int. Musicological Soc. 2007–; Chair. Editorial Cttee, Musica Britannica 1993–; mem. Royal Musical Asscn (Pres. 1994–99), American Musicological Soc. (Corresp. mem.), Royal Soc. of Musicians, Royal Philharmonic Soc. *Publications include:* Berlioz: Huit Scènes de Faust, La Damnation de Faust, Cipriani Potter: Symphony in G minor (ed.), Elgar: Music for String Orchestra (ed.), Songs with Orchestra (ed.), Vaughan Williams: Serenade (1898) for Small Orchestra (ed.), Bucolic Suite (ed.), Flos campi (ed.), W. A. Mozart: Don Giovanni 1981, The Musical Language of Berlioz 1983, Classical Music: A Concise History 1986, W. A. Mozart: Idomeneo 1993, Berlioz: Roméo et Juliette 1994, Elgar: Enigma Variations 1999, The Music of Berlioz 2001, The Cambridge Companion to Elgar (ed. with Daniel Grimley) 2004, Mozart, an Extraordinary Life 2005,

Mozart (The Master Musicians) 2006, The New Grove Guide to Mozart and his Operas 2006, Europe, Empire, and Spectacle in Nineteenth-Century British Music (ed. with Rachel Cowgill) 2006, Elgar Studies (ed. with J.P.E. Harper-Scott) 2007, Let Beauty Awake – Elgar, Vaughan Williams, and Literature (ed.) 2010; Gen. Ed.: Cambridge Music Handbooks, Music in Context (with J. P. E. Harper-Scott); contrib. to New Grove Dictionary of Music and Musicians, New Grove Dictionary of Opera, other books and professional journals. *Honours:* Hon. Corresp. mem. American Musicological Soc.; Berlioz Soc. Medal 2015. *Address:* School of Music, University of Leeds, Leeds, LS2 9JT (office); 362 Leymoor Road, Golcar, Huddersfield, West Yorks., HD7 4QF, England (home). *Telephone:* (1484) 649108 (home). *E-mail:* j.g.rushton@leeds.ac.uk (office); julianrushton@btinternet.com (home).

RUSSELL, David, FRAM; British classical guitarist; b. 1953, Glasgow. *Education:* Royal Acad. of Music. *Career:* has performed in major halls in cities including New York, London, Tokyo, Los Angeles, Madrid, Toronto, Amsterdam and Denver; festivals and masterclasses worldwide; Fellow, Royal Acad. of Music 1997. *Recordings include:* Double Bass and Guitar (with Dennis Milne) 1978, Something Unique 1979, David Russel plays Antonio Lauro 1980, Guitar Duets (with Raphaella Smits) 1983, D. Milne Guitar Concerto 1984, 19th Century Music 1987, Handel, Bach, Scarlatti 1989, Tárrega: Integral de Guitarra 1991, Music of Barrios 1995, Music of Federico Moreno Torroba 1996, Rodrigo Concertos 1997, Message of the Sea 1998, Music of Giuliani 1999, David Russell Plays Baroque Music 2001, Reflections of Spain 2002, David Russell Plays Bach 2003, Aire Latino (Grammy Award for Best Instrumental Soloist Performance 2005) 2004, Spanish Legends 2005, Renaissance Favorites for Guitar 2006, Art of the Guitar 2007, Air on a G String 2008, For David 2009, Sonidos Latinos 2010, Grandeur of the Baroque 2012. *Honours:* winner Andrés Segovia Competition, José Ramírez Competition, Francisco Tárrega Competition, Medal of Honour, Conservatory of the Balearics 2003. *Address:* c/o Telarc International Corporation, 23307 Commerce Park Road, Cleveland, OH 44122, USA (office). *E-mail:* maria@davidrussellguitar.com (office). *Website:* www.telarc.com (office); www.davidrussellguitar.com.

RUSSELL, Lynda; British singer (soprano); b. 1963, Birmingham, England. *Education:* studied in London with Meriel St Clair and in Vienna with Eugene Ludwig. *Career:* has sung with Glyndebourne Opera as the Queen of Night, Fortuna in Monteverdi's Ulisse and Marzelline in Fidelio; opera engagements at Barcelona, Madrid, Nice, Venice, Vicenza, Rome, Bologna and Strasbourg; British appearances as Handel's Partenope and with Opera North and ENO, Trieste 1990 as Donna Elvira; concerts at the festivals of Athens, Barcelona, Granada, San Sebastian, Cuence, Venice, Berne, Munich and Siena; Brahms Requiem under Jesus Lopez-Cobos and Beethoven's 9th with Walter Weller; has sung Mozart's oratorios Davidde Penitente and Betulia Liberata in Italy; further repertoire includes Wolf's Italienisches Liederbuch, Beethoven's Missa Solemnis under Weller, and Ah, Perfido, Mozart's Exultate and Coronation Mass; Mozart bicentenary concerts in London, Birmingham, Winchester and Lahti in Finland 1991; season 1996–97 with Bach's Jauchzet Gott in Vienna, Britten's Illuminations in Scotland, Mozart's Requiem with the Ulster Orchestra, and Dalila in Handel's Samson with The Sixteen; sang Xanthe in Die Liebe der Danaë by Strauss at Garsington, 1999. *Recordings include:* Handel Dixit Dominus with The Sixteen.

RUSTIONI, Daniele; Italian conductor; *Principal Conductor, Orchestra della Toscana;* b. 18 April 1983, Milan; m. Francesca Dego. *Education:* Milan Conservatoire, studied with Gilberto Serembe, Accad. Musicale Chigiana, Siena with Gianluigi Gelmetti, Royal Acad. of Music, London. *Career:* debut Royal Opera House, Covent Garden (Aida) 2011, Teatro all Scala, Milan (La Bohème) 2012; regularly conducted at Italian opera houses including Teatro Regio Torino, La Fenice in Venice, Teatro Petruzzelli, Bari and Maggio Musicale Fiorentino and at festivals such as Rossini Opera Festival (debut 2012); has conducted at Opera North and Welsh Nat. Opera in UK, Glimmerglass Festival and Washington Nat. Opera in USA, Opéra Nat. de Lyon, Bayerisches Staatsoper, Nederlandse Opera in Amsterdam and Opernhaus Zürich in Europe; orchestral conducting has included Accad. Nazionale di Santa Cecilia, Sinfonica Nazionale della RAI, BBC Philharmonic, Orchestra della Svizzera Italiana, Helsinki Philharmonic, London Philharmonic and Orchestre Philharmonique de Montecarlo; Principal Guest Conductor, Orchestra della Toscana 2011–13, Principal Conductor 2014–; Music Dir, Teatro Petruzzelli, Bari 2013–14. *Recording:* Erwin Schrott Arias 2012. *Honours:* Int. Opera Awards Best Newcomer 2013. *Current Management:* Artists Management Company, Holbeinstrasse 31, 8008 Zurich, Switzerland. *Telephone:* (43) 2551447. *E-mail:* efv@artistsmanagement.com. *Website:* www.artistsmanagement.com.

RUTH, Sebastian, BA; American violist and music educator; *Founder and Artistic Director, Community MusicWorks;* b. 1975. *Education:* Brown Univ. *Career:* Founder and Artistic Dir Community MusicWorks, Providence, RI 1997–; Founding mem. Providence String Quartet; fmr mem. Boston Philharmonic Orchestra, Ocean State Chamber Orchestra, Wild Ginger Philharmonic; participated in Audubon String Quartet Seminar, Yellow Barn and Apple Hill Chamber Music Festivals, and Int. Musical Arts Inst.; mem. Bd of Dirs Int. Music Arts Inst.; mem. Advisory Bd Sphinx Org.; mem. Bd of Visitors, Longy School of Music. *Honours:* MacArthur Fellowship 2010. *Address:* Community MusicWorks, 1392 Westminster Street, Providence, RI 02909, USA (office). *Telephone:* (401) 861-5650 (office). *Fax:* (401) 861-3700

(office). *E-mail:* info@communitymusicworks.org (office). *Website:* www.communitymusicworks.org (office).

RUTHERFORD, James; British singer (bass-baritone); b. 1972, Norwich, Norfolk. *Education:* Durham Univ., Royal Coll. of Music, London with Margaret Kingsley, Nat. Opera Studio, London. *Career:* appearances as Hans Sachs in Die Meistersinger at Bayreuth Festival and Graz Opera; Germont for Graz Opera; Jochanaan for Montpellier Opera and Berlin State Opera; Barak for Graz Opera; Wolfram for San Francisco Opera; Donner in Das Rheingold for Lyric Opera of Chicago, Royal Opera House, Covent Garden and at BBC Proms; Kothner in Die Meistersinger at Covent Garden and Edinburgh Festival; Mozart's Figaro for Paris Opera, Welsh Nat. Opera (WNO), Glyndebourne Touring and Opera North; Leporello for Scottish Opera; Speaker for ENO; Argante in Handel's Rinaldo for Berlin Staatsoper, Innsbruck and Montpellier; Forester in Cunning Little Vixen for WNO; Nick Shadow for English Touring Opera and City of Birmingham Symphony Orchestra (CBSO); concerts include Britten's War Requiem at the Three Choirs' Festival, with Stockholm Philharmonic and in Riga Cathedral, Latvia; Walton's Belshazzar's Feast with CBSO, Bournemouth Symphony Orchestra (BSO) and BBC Scottish Symphony Orchestra; Vaughan Williams' Sea Symphony with the Royal Philharmonic Orchestra and Sudwest Rundfunk, Stuttgart; Holst's Savitri with CBSO; Delius' Sea Drift with BBC Philharmonic; Elgar's Dream of Gerontius at the Three Choirs' Festival, CBSO and Concertgebouw, Amsterdam; Elgar's The Kingdom with CBSO and BSO; Elgar's Apostles with CBSO, London Symphony Orchestra (LSO) and at BBC Proms; Brahms' Requiem with CBSO; Beethoven's Ninth Symphony with BSO and at BBC Proms; Mendelssohn's Elijah for Orchestra of the Age of Enlightenment and Northern Sinfonia; Handel's Belshazzar with Berlin Philharmonic; Handel's Jephtha with Stuttgart Bach-Akademie; Handel's Joshua at Klosterkonzerte Maulbronn; Handel's Apollo e Dafne with Freiburg Baroque Orchestra; Handel's Flavio with Acad. of Ancient Music; Handel's Messiah with Maggio Musicale, Florence, Royal Scottish Nat. Orchestra, BSO, Ulster Symphony Orchestra, Acad. of Ancient Music, English Consort, Huddersfield Chorus and at Royal Albert Hall; recitals for BBC Radio 3, at Wigmore Hall, St John's Smith Square, Bridgewater Hall, Manchester; Schubert's Winterreise at St George's, Brandon Hill, Bristol, for WNO and Buxton Festival. *Recordings include:* Prokofiev's Ivan the Terrible with BBC Symphony Orchestra, Faure's Requiem with BBC Philharmonic, Peter Grimes with LSO, Handel's Rinaldo with Freiburg Baroque Orchestra, Sullivan's Ivanhoe with BBC Nat. Orchestra of Wales 2010. *Honours:* Seattle Opera Int. Wagner Competition 2006. *Address:* c/o Chandos Records, Chandos House, 1 Commerce Park, Commerce Way, Colchester, Essex CO2 8HX, England (office). *Telephone:* (1206) 225200 (office). *Fax:* (1206) 225201 (office). *E-mail:* enquiries@chandos.net (office). *Website:* www.chandos.net (office).

RUTMAN, Neil, BMus, MMus, DMA; American pianist; b. 12 July 1953, California. *Education:* San Jose State University with Aiko Onishi, Eastman School of Music, University of Rochester, studied with Cecile Genhart, Peabody Institute of Johns Hopkins University with Ellen Mack, studied with Leon Fleisher, Frank Mannheimmer and Gaby Casadesus. *Career:* US debut at Carnegie Hall 1985; London debut at Wigmore Hall 1985; Washington, DC debut at Phillips Gallery in 1985; Associate Professor of Piano at Goucher College, Baltimore, 1983–; masterclasses on interpretation of French piano music of Fauré, Debussy, and Ravel, at Chateau de la Gesse, Toulouse, France, University of Colorado, Denver, 1986, and Wright State University, Dayton, OH, 1986; recitalist at Chateau de la Gesse in 1985, at Cheltenham International Festival of Music in 1986 and soloist for Denver Symphony in 1986; US State Department recital tour of Yugoslavia and soloist for Metropolitan Orchestra at Carnegie Hall in 1986; recitalist at Merkin Hall, NYC with three recitals of the music of Ravel, Debussy, Fauré and Poulence with American premiere each evening, 1987. *Recordings:* 3 Movements of Petrouchka by Stravinsky; 2 Mozart Piano Concerti, K482 and K414; Préludes Book 1 and 2 by Debussy. *Address:* 20990 Valley Green Drive, Apt 700, Cupertino, CA 95014-1846, USA.

RUTTER, Claire; British singer (soprano); b. 1972, South Shields, County Durham; m. Stephen Gadd. *Education:* Guildhall School of Music, National Opera Studio. *Career:* made US debut as Fiodoligi in Cosi fan Tutte for Dallas Opera; fmr principal with Scottish Opera; other roles include Amelia in Un Ballo in Maschera, Aida, Tosca, Elvira in Ernani, Alice Ford in Falstaff, Abigaille in Nabucco, Violetta in La Traviata, Donna Anna in Don Giovanni, Giovanna d'Arco, Countess in Le Nozze di Figaro, Miss Jessel in Turn of the Screw, Lucia di Lammermoor, Maddalena in Andrea Chenier, Mimi in La Bohème, Gilda in Rigoletto, Elettra in Idomeneo, Rosalinde in Die Fledermaus, Lucrezia Borgia; guest appearances with Opera Australia, Finnish Nat. Opera, Florida Grand Opera, ENO, Den Norske Opera, Opéra National du Rhin, Opéra de Montpellier, Bordeaux Opera, De Vlaamse Opera, Opéra de Bordeaux, Royal Scottish Nat. Opera, Welsh Nat. Opera. *Recordings include:* Rutter & Gadd: Family Album (also co-composer), The Mystic Trumpeter. *Telephone:* (1962) 860001 (office). *E-mail:* manager@ruttergadd.co.uk (office). *Website:* www.ruttergadd.co.uk.

RUTTER, John Milford, CBE, MA, BMus; British composer and conductor; *Director, The Cambridge Singers;* b. 24 Sept. 1945, London; m. JoAnne Redden 1980; two s. (one deceased) one step-d. *Education:* Highgate School and Clare Coll., Cambridge. *Career:* Dir of Music, Clare Coll., Cambridge 1975–79; part-time Lecturer in Music, Open Univ. 1975–87; Founder and Dir The Cambridge Singers 1981–. *Compositions include:* The Falcon 1969,

Fancies, for choir & chamber orchestra 1971, Gloria 1974, Bang! (opera for young people) 1975, The Piper of Hamelin (opera for young people) 1980, Requiem 1985, Partita for orchestra 1985, There is a Flower 1986, Magnificat 1990, I Believe in Springtime for chorus & orchestra 1992, Blow the Wind Southerly, folk song setting for voice & orchestra 1995, A Choral Amen, for chorus & orchestra 1997, As the Bridegroom To His Chosen for chorus & strings 1999, I my best beloved's am (unaccompanied choral work for BBC Sounding the Millennium series) 1999, Wings of the morning, for choir & orchestra 2002, Mass of the Children 2003, A crown of glory 2004, This Is the Day (commissioned for wedding of Prince William and Catherine Middleton) 2011, All Bells in Paradise, carol for chorus and organ 2012, The Gift of Life: Six Canticles of Creation 2015; numerous carols, anthems and songs; orchestral works and music for TV. *Recordings include:* original version of Fauré Requiem 1984, The John Rutter Christmas Album 2002, The Choral Collection 2005, The Very Best of John Rutter 2011, The Colours of Christmas 2011, Blessing 2012, The John Rutter Songbook 2014, The Gift of Life 2015. *Publications:* Opera Choruses (ed.) 1995, European Sacred Music (ed.) 1996, Christmas Motets (ed.) 1999. *Honours:* Hon. FGCM 1988, Hon. Fellow, Westminster Choir Coll., Princeton, Clare Coll., Cambridge 2001, Hon. Freeman Worshipful Co. of Barbers 2008, Hon. Bencher Middle Temple 2008; Hon. DMus (Lambeth) 1996; Dr hc (Anglia Ruskin Univ.) 2004, (Leicester) 2005, (Hull) 2008; Ivor Novello Classical Music Award 2007. *Address:* Old Laceys, St John's Street, Duxford, Cambridge, CB22 4RA, England (home). *Website:* www.johnrutter.com.

RUUD, Ole Kristian; conductor; b. 2 Oct. 1958, Oslo, Norway; m. Karen Johnstad Ruud 1988; two s. *Education:* Norwegian Acad. of Music, Sibelius Acad. *Career:* debut in radio concert with Oslo Philharmonic Orchestra 1985; Chief Conductor, North Norwegian Chamber Orchestra 1986–89, Trondheim Symphony Orchestra 1987–95, Norrkoping Symphony Orchestra 1996–99; touring concerts with Trondheim Symphony Orchestra, Germany 1988, 1995, Bergen Philharmonic, Germany 1991, Jeunesse Musicale Orchestra, Europe 1993, Berlin 1996, Stockholm Chamber Orchestra, Japan 1995, 1999; Prof. of Conducting, Oslo Acad. 1999–. *Recordings:* Norwegian Composers: Oslo Philharmonic, Trondheim Symphony, Stavanger Symphony Orchestra; International Composers: Swedish Radio Symphony Orchestra, Norrkoping Symphony Orchestra, Bergen Philharmonic, Trondheim Symphony. *Honours:* E. Grieg Prize 1992, Norwegian Newspaper Best Review Prize 1993, Lindeman Prize 1994, Johan Halvorsen Prize 1996.

RUUTTUNEN, Esa; Finnish singer (baritone); b. 11 March 1950, Nivala. *Education:* Helsinki Univ., Sibelius Acad., Helsinki. *Career:* Vicar, Temppelaukio Church, Helsinki 1975–84; appearances in lieder recitals and concerts of sacred music throughout Scandinavia and northern Europe and in USA; opera engagements at Helsinki and Savonlinna as Monterone, Escamillo, Pizarro, Enrico in Lucia di Lammermoor, Klingsor and Valentin; appeared as guest at Essen in Merikanto's Juha and at Los Angeles in premiere of Sallinen's Kullervo 1992; sang Alberich in Das Rheingold, Helsinki 1996; King Fisher in The Midsummer Marriage, Munich 1998; season 1999–2000 as Grigoris in The Greek Passion by Martinů, at Bregenz and Covent Garden; Enescu's Oedipe at Deutsche Oper Berlin and the General in premiere of Maria's Love by Kortekangas, Savonlinna; seasons 2000–05 included Alberich in Deutsche Oper Berlin, Stuttgart, The Flying Dutchman, Savonlinna with Deutsche Oper Berlin, Reykjavík, Oedipe with Vienna State Opera, Liceu, Barcelona, Bucharest, Kurwenal, Leipzig, Wotan in Helsinki, Oedipe/Tiresias, Teatro Colón, Buenos Aires; fmr Artistic Dir Jokilaakso Music Foundation, Nivala. *Recordings:* on DVD: Das Rheingold, Stuttgart 2002, Luther by Kari Tikka 2004, Pula! by Ilkka Kuusisto 2005. *Honours:* Pro Finlandia Medal, Helsinki 2001, Cultural Merit Medal, Romania 2004. *Address:* Metsikkötie 21, 01620 Vantaa, Finland. *Telephone:* (400) 422140. *E-mail:* esa.ruuttunen@gmail.com.

RUZICKA, Peter, PhD; German composer and intendant; b. 3 July 1948, Düsseldorf. *Education:* Hamburg Conservatory, studied in Munich and Berlin. *Career:* Intendant, Berlin Radio Symphony Orchestra 1979–87; Fellow Bavarian Acad. of Fine Arts, Munich 1985, Free Acad. of Arts, Hamburg 1987; music premiered at Gottingen, Stuttgart, Berlin, Hilversum, Hamburg, Munich, Vienna and Savonlinna. *Compositions:* Esta Noche for the victims of the Vietnam War 1967, Antifone-Strofe for 25 strings and percussion 1970, Elis for mezzo, oboe and orchestra 1970, Sonata for solo cello 1970, three string quartets 1970, 1970, 1992, Metastrophe for 87 instrumentalists 1971, Sinfonia for 25 strings, 16 vocalists and percussions 1971, Outside-Inside (music theatre) 1972, In Processo di Tempo for 26 instrumentalists and cello 1972, Versuch seven pieces for strings 1974, Stress for eight percussion groups 1972, Einblendungen for orchestra 1973–77, Feed Back for four orchestral groups 1974, Torso for orchestra 1974, Emanazione Variations for flute and four orchestral groups 1975, Zeit for organ 1975, Stille for cello 1976, Abbruche for orchestra 1977, Gestalt and Abbruch for voices 1979, Impuls zum Weitersprechen for viola and orchestra 1981, Satyagraha for orchestra 1985, ...der die Gesange zerschlug for baritone and ensemble 1985, Metamorphosen uber ein Klangfeld von Joseph Haydn for orchestra 1990, Vier Gesänge nach Fragmenten von Nietzsche for mezzo and piano 1992, Klangschatten for string quartet 1992, Tallis for orchestra 1993, ...Inseln, randlos for violin, chamber orchestra and chorus 1994.

RŮŽIČKA, Rudolf, MgA; Czech composer and academic; *Professor, Faculty of Informatics, Masaryk University, Brno;* b. 25 April 1941, Brno; s. of Antonin Růžička and Helena Růžička; m. Bozena Růžičkova 1967; two s. *Education:*

Brno Conservatory, Janáček Acad. of Performing Arts. *Career:* Prof. of Composition and Music Theory, Brno State Univ., Masaryk Univ. and Janáček Acad. of Arts; Chair. Asscn for Electroacoustic Music in the Czech Repub.; Pres. of Jury, Musica Nova Competition. *Film:* Creation. *Compositions:* more than 100 instrumental, chamber, vocal, electroacoustic and computer compositions. *Recordings:* some 60 compositions recorded for albums, radio and TV. *Publications:* Use of Computers in Creating Works of Art; contrib. of numerous articles on music theory of computer composition and automatic notation, to various publs. *Honours:* Hon. mem. Confed. of Chivalry, Sydney; Hon. Diploma (Masaryk Acad. of Art, Prague); numerous honours, prizes and awards for electroacoustic and computer music, including Int. Musica Nova Competition, Marcel Josse Competition. *Address:* Serikova 32, 637 00 Brno, Czech Republic. *E-mail:* ruzicka@fi.muni.cz; ruzickar@chello.cz; ruzickarudolf@gmail.com. *Website:* www.musica.cz/skladatele/ruzicka-rudolf.html.

RYABCHIKOV, Victor; Russian concert pianist, concertmaster and academic; b. 13 Feb. 1954, Tashkent, Uzbekistan; one d. *Education:* State Music Conservatory, Tashkent, Moscow State Conservatory. *Career:* concerts as soloist and with orchestras in various cities across Russia from 1979, and in France, Switzerland, UK, Sweden, the Netherlands, Italy, South Africa and Germany from 1993; numerous appearances on TV and radio in Russia, South Africa, Sweden and Switzerland; Founding Vice-Pres. Glinka Soc., Moscow 1997, Artistic Dir Glinka Festival, Moscow 1997; Wigmore Hall debut 2000; concert tours in Zimbabwe 2006, India 2008; mem. jury, Int. Forum 'Art XXI'. *Radio:* writer/presenter of series on Russian 19th-century composers, Radio Orphei 2002–03. *Recordings include:* Russian Piano Music of XIX Century 1994, Mikhail Glinka – Complete Piano Music (three vols) 1998, Complete Piano Music by Borodin and Kalinnikov 1999, Chopin in Stockholm 1999, Piano Music by Anton and Nikolai Rubinstein 2000, Tchaikovsky – The Seasons and other piano pieces 2002, Moments musicaux by Schubert and Rachmaninov 2003, Mikhail Glinka, Piano Pieces 2006, Complete Piano Music by Bortnyansky, Gribordov, Kalinnikov and Borodin 2006, Piano music by Anton Rubinstein 2009, 'Musical Diary' by St Seraphim (Chicgagov) 2011, Piano music by V. Rebikov 2012, Piano music of Gourilev (father) and Gourilev (son) 2012, Piano music of pre-Glinka composers (Kashin, Aliabiev, Field, Kozlovski, Handoshkin) 2012, Piano music by Tchaikovsky and Taneev (teacher and pupil) 2012–13. *Honours:* Winner Repub. Competition of Piano and Special Prize, Union of Composers, Uzbekistan 1976, APN Pianist of the Year, Moscow 1992, Medal for the Promotion of Russian Culture 2004, Medal for the Grand Merit in Russian Art 2009. *Address:* 143005 Odintsovo, ul. Kutuzovskaya 3, App. 382, Russia. *Telephone:* (495) 567-28-11; 926-2455258 (mobile). *E-mail:* rvprom@email.ru. *Website:* www.victorryabchikov.com.

RYABETS, Oleg; singer (male soprano); b. 28 June 1967, Kiev, Ukraine. *Education:* Kiev State Conservatory and Moscow State Acad. of Music with Profs K. Radchenko and Z. Dolukhanova. *Career:* debut in soprano part in Schnittke's Symphony No. 2 with Great Symphony Orchestra conducted by G. Rozhdestvensky, Bolshoi Moscow State Conservatory Hall 1990; professional stage performer 1977–; soloist, State Boys Choir and State Chapel Choir of Kiev, performing in European countries 1977–90; sang with Vivaldi State Chamber Orchestra in 17–19th-century music programme, in Russian and Italian tours 1990–93; soprano role in Pergolesi's Stabat Mater, Moscow and Prague 1992–93; Amour in Gluck's Orpheus, Hermitage Theatre, St Petersburg 1993; concerts and recitals in Moscow and St Petersburg, including special recital dedicated to official visit to Russia by Queen Elizabeth II, Tchaikovsky Great Concert Hall, Moscow 1994; performed in Petersburg's Seasons Music Festival and Ludwigsburg Festival conducted by W. Gönnenwein, sang in recital at French Embassy, Vienna, and appeared as Count Myshkin in world premiere of V. Kobekin's NFB at Sacro Art Festival, Bochum and Ludwigsburg, Germany 1995; Lenin in world premiere of The Naked Revolution by D. Soldier, New York 1997; Aminta in Galuppi's Il Re Pastore, Italy 1998. *Recordings:* Solo Soprano, Stabat Mater by G. Pergolesi 1993, Italian music of 17–18th centuries, Mr Soprano sings Bel Canto 1996, King Solomon's Song cantata composed for O. Ryabets by V. Kobekin.

RYAN, Barry; Australian singer (baritone); *Senior Lecturer in Voice and Opera, Sydney Conservatorium of Music;* b. 5 Jan. 1956; m. Anke Höppner. *Education:* Sydney Conservatorium (Diploma in Operatic Art). *Career:* has performed with many of Europe's leading opera cos, including Royal Opera, Covent Garden, La Scala, Milan, Paris Opéra, Bastille, Opéra Comique, Paris, Basle Opera, Switzerland, Deutsche Oper am Rhein, Düsseldorf, Flemish Opera, Antwerp; Prin. Artist with Cologne Opera 1988–92; Australian Opera debut in Die Meistersinger von Nuernberg 1993, has subsequently performed more than 30 roles for that co.; most recently performed Sharpless, Amonasro, Count di Luna, Renato, Marcello and Alex in world premiere of Bliss, also featured at Edinburgh Festival 2010; has performed with other opera cos, including Canterbury Opera, Christchurch, West Australian Opera, Opera Queensland; concert performances throughout Europe, Australia and Asia; appeared in televised performances in Germany, Belgium, the Netherlands, France and Australia; Season 2011: performances include roles of Sharpless in Madama Butterfly and George Milton in Of Mice and Men, and Schubert's Die Winterreise at Sydney Conservatorium of Music; Sr Lecturer in Voice, Sydney Conservatorium of Music. *Honours:* numerous awards for singing include Vienna State Opera Award, Shell Aria, Marten Bequest for Singing, Green Room Award. *Current Management:* c/o Patrick Togher Artists' Management, Suite 25, 450 Elizabeth Street, Surry Hills, NSW 2010, Australia. *Telephone:*

(2) 9319-6255. *Fax:* (2) 9319-7611. *E-mail:* pjtogher@ozemail.com.au. *Website:* www.patricktogher.com.

RYAN, Gary, GRSM, LRAM, LGSM; British musician (guitar, piano) and composer. *Education:* RAM. *Career:* London recital debut, Wigmore Hall 1994, later performed at Southbank Centre; concerto soloist and chamber musician; Prof. of Guitar, Royal Coll. of Music 1996–, Asst Head of Strings 2009–; Dir, Guitar France int. summer school 2006–; regular appearances on BBC TV and radio; as composer, broadcasts on Classic FM; Adjudicator, BBC Young Musician of the Year and at festivals and conservatoires across the UK; Fellow, Royal Coll. of Music 2013; composer of pieces for Trinity Guildhall Guitar Syllabus; electronic scores for theatre. *Compositions:* for solo guitar: Scenes from the Wild West 2003, Scenes from Brazil 2004, City Scenes 2005, Songs from Erin 2007, Benga Beat 2011; for guitar duo: Generator 2005, Dreams, Rest and Motion 2006, Bazaar 2008; for guitar trio: Latin Cabaret (Showgirls) 2005. *Recordings include:* The Magic of The Guitar 1996, Latin Temperament 2000, Worlds Apart 2003, Visions and Vistas 2008. *Publications:* Play Piazzolla (arrangements), Easy Scenes for Guitar Books 1 and 2. *Honours:* Hon. Assoc. RAM . *Address:* Royal College of Music, Prince Consort Road, London, SW7 2BS, England (office). *Telephone:* (1689) 840076 (office); (7875) 814060 (mobile) (office). *E-mail:* gary@garyryan.co.uk; garyryan@klh-artists.co.uk (office). *Website:* www.garyryan.co.uk (office).

RYAN, Kwamé; Canadian conductor; *Music Director, Orchestre National Bordeaux Aquitaine*; b. 1976. *Education:* Oakham School, England, Gonville and Caius Coll., Cambridge, studied with Peter Eötvös. *Career:* Asst Conductor Staatsoper Stuttgart –2003, gave premiere of Gérard Pesson's Pastorale; Gen. Music Dir Theater Freiburg and Philharmonisches Orchester Freiburg 1999–2003; Music Dir Orchestre Nat. Bordeaux Aquitaine 2007–, tours throughout Europe and Asia, new production of Tosca at Opéra de Bordeaux, tours in 2009–10 included performances at Folles Journeés, Bilbao and at Chorégies d'Orange Festival, also participted in first EVENTO Biennale in Bordeaux 2009; conducted new production of Peter Eötvös's opera Le Balcon in Bordeaux; will conduct Strauss's Ariadne of Naxos 2011; Music Dir Orchestre Français des Jeunes 2009–, annual tours and two concerts in the new Grand Théâtre de Provence in Aix-en-Provence 2009; Guest Conductor, City of Birmingham Symphony Orchestra, Royal Scottish Nat. Orchestra, Ensemble intercontemporain, Klangforum Wien; has conducted Radio-Sinfonieorchester Stuttgart des SWR, SWR Sinfonieorchester Baden-Baden und Freiburg, Symphonieorchester des Bayerischen Rundfunks, Bamberger Symphoniker, Bayerische Staatsphilharmonie, Deutsche Kammerphilharmonie Bremen and Ensemble Modern; has worked in N America with symphony orchestras of Baltimore, Detroit, Dallas, Indianapolis and Cincinnati, as well as New Jersey, Houston, Atlanta and Toronto; works closely with Peter Eötvös and conducted first French revival of composer's Tri Sestri at Opéra de Lyon and German premiere of Le Balcon; has also conducted productions at ENO, Edinburgh Festival and at Opéra Nat. de Paris (Bastille), where he conducted the world premiere of Pintscher's L'espace dernier. *Recordings include:* with Orchestre Nat. Bordeaux Aquitaine: Schubert's Symphony No. 9, Rachmaninov's Symphony No. 2. *Current Management:* c/o Harrison Parrott, 5–6 Albion Court, London, W6 0QT, England. *Telephone:* (20) 7229-9166. *Fax:* (20) 7221-5042. *E-mail:* info@harrisonparrott.co.uk. *Website:* www.harrisonparrott.com.

RYBARSKA, Lydia; singer (soprano); b. 1958, Czechoslovakia. *Career:* sang Rusalka at the National Theatre, Prague; season 1988–89 as Luisa Miller at Philadelphia and Amelia in Un Ballo in Maschera at Zürich; guest with the Slovak National Opera at Edinburgh 1990, in Prince Igor (as Jaroslavna) and Suchon's The Whirlpool; Bregenz Festival 1993, as Abigaille in Nabucco; Bratislava 1996, as Margherita in Mefistofele; further appearances at the Paris Opéra Bastille (as Amelia) and Stuttgart; concerts include Beethoven's Ninth in London and the Missa Solemnis in Vienna.

RYBNIKOV, Alexei; Russian composer; b. 17 July 1945, Moscow. *Education:* Moscow State Conservatoire P. I. Tchaikovsky, studied with Aram Khachaturian. *Career:* Dir, Russian State Symphony 1986–87; founder, Ribnikov Theatre Studio, Moscow 1990; performances of works throughout Russia, in USA, France, UK and Germany; mem. Russian Composers' Union 1969–, Russian Union of Cinematographers 1979–. *Films:* written scores for over 100 films. *Compositions include:* for theatre: The Star and Death of Joachino Murieti 1975, Juno and Avos 1979, Liturgy of the Heathens 1983–89, A Night Song, ballet 1997, Little Red Riding Hood 2007; chamber music: Andante for violin and piano 1957, Invention for organ 1957, Invention for three voices 1957, The Last Lead 1957, Suite for violin and piano 1959, Preludes 1960, Piano Sonatina 12 1960, Sonatina for cello and piano 1960, Six Preludes 1960, Khorovody Piano Sonata 1961, Piano Toccata 1963, Piano Sonata No. 2 1966, Concerto for solo piano 1972, Three Pieces for piano, Fugue; orchestral: The Russian Overture 1967, Sympony No. 1 1967–69, Skomorokh 1968, Overture for folk orchestra 1971, Symphony No. 3 1972–73, Symphony No. 2 1973–74, Ode for the 850th anniversary of Moscow 1997, Symphony No. 4 1999, Symphony No. 5 2005, Puss in Boots 2005, Symphony No. 6 2008; instrumental: Concerto for violin and orchestra 1967, Concerto for string quartet and orchestra 1970–71, Concerto for bayan and orchestra 1972, The Norhern Sphinx 2006, L'Oiseau Bleu 2006. *Honours:* People's Artist of Russia, Order of Prince Daniel of Moscow, Order of Friendship, Order of Diaghilev. *Website:* www.alexeyrybnikov.ru.

RYDL, Kurt; Austrian singer (bass); b. 8 Oct. 1947, Vienna. *Education:* studied in Vienna and Moscow. *Career:* debut in Stuttgart in 1973 as Daland in Der fliegende Holländer; Guest appearances in Venice, Barcelona and Lisbon; Sang at Bayreuth Festival in 1975; Vienna Staatsoper from 1976 as Rocco in Fidelio, Zaccaria in Nabucco, Procida in Vêpres Siciliennes, Mephistopheles in Faust, King Philip in Don Carlos, Kecal in The Bartered Bride, the Landgrave in Tannhäuser and Marke in Tristan und Isolde; Salzburg Festival in 1985 in Il Ritorno d'Ulisse by Henze/Monteverdi; Tour of Japan with Vienna Staatsoper in 1986; Sang Baron Ochs in Turin and at Monte Carlo and Florence in 1987 and 1989; Salzburg Festival, 1987–89 as Mozart's Osmin, and La Scala Milan in 1990 as Rocco; sang Pimen at Barcelona and Rocco at the 1990 Salzburg Festival; Season 1991–92 as Titurel at La Scala, Verdi's Zaccaria at the Vienna Volksoper, Ramfis in Aida at Tel-Aviv, Padre Guardiano at Florence and the Grand Inquisitor at the Verona Arena; Sang Hagen in Götterdämmerung at Covent Garden, 1995; returned 1997, in Pfitzner's Palestrina; Grand Inquisitor at Edinburgh, 1998; Season 2000–01 as Baron Ochs at the Deutsche Oper Berlin, Mozart's Osmin in Geneva, Dodon in The Golden Cockerel at Bregenz and Wagner's Pogner at Covent Garden; Morosus in Die schweigsame Frau at the Vienna Staatsoper and Wagner's Hagen (concert) in Sydney. *Recordings include:* Salome; Opera scenes by Schubert; Alceste; Manon Lescaut. *Current Management:* Italartist Austroconcert Kulturmanagement GmbH, Lothringerstrasse 14, 3400 Klosterneuburg, Austria. *Telephone:* (22) 4332614. *Fax:* (22) 4325819. *E-mail:* italartist@ia-ac.com. *Website:* www.ia-ac.com; www.kurt-rydl.com.

RYHÄNEN, Jaakko Sakari; Finnish singer (bass); b. 2 Dec. 1946, Tampere. *Education:* studied in Helsinki. *Career:* mem. Finnish Nat. Opera, Helsinki 1974–; appearances at the Savonlinna Festival and in Moscow and New York with the Helsinki Co.; further engagements in Madrid, Hamburg, Berlin, Munich, Zürich and Stuttgart; Paris Opéra in 1987, as Daland, and at Monte Carlo in 1988; season 1991 as Daland at Munich, Titurel in Parsifal at Tampere and Mozart's Bartolo at Helsinki; sang Daland at Santiago in 1992, and Sarastro at the Savonlinna Festival; sang Fiesco in the original version of Simon Boccanegra at Covent Garden 1997; Wagner's Daland at Lille, 1998; season 2000–01 as Verdi's Banquo for Cologne Opera, Fiesco and Boris Godunov in Helsinki and Sarastro at Savonlinna; Boris for the Deutsche Oper am Rhein; Gremin in Eugene Onegin, Commendatore in Don Giovanni, Sarastro in Die Zauberflöte for Helsinki Opera 2010–11; roles in Die Zauberflöte, Lohengrin and Don Giovanni at Savonlinna 2011–12; concerts with the Israel Philharmonic and throughout Scandinavia. *Current Management:* c/o Opera-Connection Alste & Mödersheim, Leibnizstrasse 94, 10625 Berlin, Germany. *Telephone:* (30) 31996688. *Fax:* (30) 31809739. *E-mail:* info@opera-connection.com. *Website:* opera-connection.com.

RYSANEK, Lotte; Austrian singer (soprano); b. 18 March 1928, Vienna. *Education:* Vienna Conservatory with Richard Grossman. *Career:* debut at Klagenfurt 1950 as Massenet's Manon; mem., Vienna Staatsoper as Marzelline in Fidelio, Marguerite in Faust, Pamina, Fiordiligi, Marenka in The Bartered Bride and Donna Elvira, and parts in operas by Wagner and Verdi; guest appearances at the Vienna Volksoper in Graz, Berlin, Düsseldorf and Hamburg; sang at Bayreuth 1958; well-known in operetta and as a concert singer. *Recordings include:* roles in operetta.

RYSANOV, Maxim, BMus, MMus; Ukrainian viola player and conductor; b. 1978. *Education:* Cen. Special Music School, Moscow, Guildhall School of Music and Drama, London. *Career:* regularly invited to perform as a soloist and chamber musician in UK and abroad; has performed with EU Youth Orchestra, Residentie Orkest, Amsterdam Sinfonietta, Orchestre Royale de Chambre de Wallonie (in China), Nat. Philharmonic, Guangzhou Symphony, Bayerischer Rundfunk Kammerorchester, Deutsche Staatsphilharmonie, Geneva Chamber Orchestra, Basel Sinfonie Orchester, Mostly Mozart Festival Orchestra, Grand Teton Festival Orchestra, Sinfonia Varsovia, Lithuanian Nat. Symphony Orchestra; has given recitals at many prestigious festivals including annual chamber music festivals at Vozvrashcheniye (Homecoming), Moscow, Lockenhaus, Cheltenham, Spitalfields, Britten, Aldeburgh, and Crescendo (France). *Recordings include:* Schnittke Concerto for Three 2006, Kancheli Styx & Tavener 2007, Romantic Expression 2007, The Myrrh Bearer 2007, Bach Inventions 2007, Brahms Viola 2008. *Honours:* Winner Valentino Bucchi Competition 1995, Lionel Tertis Competition 2003, Geneva Competition 2005, BBC Radio Three New Generation Artist 2007–09, Classic FM Gramophone Young Artist of the Year 2008. *Current Management:* c/o Lorna Neill, Music Inter Alia, 12 Eastcourt Road, Worthing, BN14 7DA, England. *Telephone:* (1903) 531668. *E-mail:* lorna@musicinteralia.com. *Website:* www.musicinteralia.com.

RYSSOV, Michail; singer (bass); b. 25 Aug. 1955, Crimea, Russia. *Career:* principal bass at the Opera in Minsk 1983–87, in Don Giovanni, Don Carlos, Aida, La Forza del Destino, Macbeth, Nabucco, I Vespri Siciliani, Faust, Eugene Onegin, Boris Godunov, Mefistofele; Treviso 1989, as the Commendatore in Don Giovanni; sang Ramfis at the Deutsche Oper Berlin and at the Verona Arena, Philip II at Deutsche Oper am Rhein, Düsseldorf, Prince Gremin and The Inquisitor in Don Carlos, at La Fenice, Venice; sang Ramfis in Aida at the 1996 Verona Arena; season 2000 as Verdi's Padre Guardiano at Verona and Procida at St Gallen, Kutzman in the premiere of Tatiana by Azio Corghi at La Scala. *Honours:* winner Glinka Competition 1984, Int. Verviers Competition, Belgium 1987, Int. Ettore Bastianini Competition, Siena 1988, Int. New Voice Competition, Pavia, Toti dal Monte Competition, Treviso 1989.

Current Management: Musicaglotz, 11 rue le Verrier, 75006 Paris, France. *Telephone:* 1-42-34-53-40. *Fax:* 1-40-46-93-77. *E-mail:* general@musicaglotz .com. *Website:* www.musicaglotz.com.

RZEWSKI, Frederic Anthony, BA, MFA; American composer and pianist; *Professor of Composition, Royal Conservatory, Liège;* b. 13 April 1938, Westfield, MA; m. Nicole Abbeloss; three c. *Education:* Harvard Univ. with Thompson and Piston, Princeton Univ. with Sessions and Babbitt, studied in Italy with Dallapiccola. *Career:* pianist and teacher in Europe from 1962; played in the premieres of Stockhausen's Klavierstuck X and Plus Minus; co-founded electronic ensemble, Musica Electronica Viva, Rome 1966; returned to New York 1971; Prof. of Composition, Royal Conservatory, Liège 1977–; Visiting Prof. of Composition, Yale Univ. 1984; mem. American Acad. of Arts and Letters 2009–. *Compositions include:* For Violin 1962, Composition for two 1964, Nature Morte for instruments and percussion 1965, Zoologischer Garten 1965, Spacecraft 1967, Impersonation (audiodrama) 1967, Requiem 1968, Symphony 1968, Last Judgement for trombone 1969, Falling Music for piano and tape 1971, Coming Together for speaker and instruments 1972, Piano Variations on the Song 'No Place to go but Around' 1974, The People United Will Never be Defeated (36 variations for piano) 1975, four Piano Pieces 1977, Satyrica for jazz band 1983, Una Breve Storia d'Estate for three flutes and small orchestra, A Machine for two pianos 1984, The Invincible Persian Army for low voice and prepared piano 1984, The Persians for four voices, actors and ensemble 1985, The Triumph of Death (oratorio) 1988, Roses for eight instruments 1989, Piano Sonata 1991, The Road for piano 1995–98, Scratch Symphony 1997, Spiritus for recorder and percussion 1997. *Recordings:* as pianist, numerous albums of contemporary music. *Address:* rue Meyerbeer 142, 1180 Uccle, Belgium (home).

S

SAARI, Jouko Erik Sakari; Finnish conductor and music director; b. 23 Nov. 1944, Stockholm, Sweden; m. Raija Syvänen; one s. one d. *Education:* Sibelius Acad., Helsinki Univ., Indiana Univ., USA. *Career:* Musical Dir Helsinki Opera Soc. 1971; Conductor Tampere City Orchestra 1973–74; Chorus Master, Nat. Opera Finland 1974–75, Conductor and Coach 1976–78; Musical Dir Lahti Symphony Orchestra 1978–84; Conductor Gothenburg Opera House, Stora Teatern 1984–85, Guest Conductor 1985–88; broadcast recordings with Finnish Radio Symphony Orchestra 1971, 1973–75, with Swedish Radio Symphony Orchestra 1974, 1976–77; concerts in USA, Canada, Germany, Hungary, Denmark, Sweden and Finland; Guest Conductor, Hämeenlinna Symphony Orchestra 1989–93; appearances on Swedish radio and on Finnish radio and TV; freelance conductor and organist. *Compositions:* for brass band recorded with Töölö Brass Band; for voice, choir, organ, strings, oboe, trumpets and brass published by Sulasol and Edition Tilli, Finland. *Address:* Laaksokatu 5 B 23, 15140 Lahti, Finland (home).

SAARIAHO, Kaija; Finnish composer; b. 14 Oct. 1952; m. Jean-Baptiste Barrière; one s. one d. *Career:* freelance composer of orchestral and instrumental music with live electronics and computers; music performed by most major orchestras and in most major festivals, including Salzburg Festival. *Compositions include:* Verbledungen 1984, Lichtbogen 1986, Du Cristal... à la fumée 1988–90, Graalthéatre for violin and orchestra (performed at BBC Proms, London 1995) 1994, Château de l'âme 1995, Lonh (Nordic Council Music Prize 2000) 1996, Graal Théâtre 1997, Oltra mar 1998, Miranda's Lament for soprano and ensemble 1998, Neiges for eight cellos 1998, L'amour de loin (opera, British premiere, Barbican Hall, London 2002) (Grawemeyer Award for Music 2003) 2000, Nymphea Reflection for orchestra 2001, Orion for orchestra 2002, Aile du Songe for flute and ensemble 2001, Cinq Reflects for soprano, baritone and orchestra 2001, Terrestre for flute and ensemble 2002, Asteroid 4179: Toutatis 2005, Adriana Mater (opera, European premiere, Opéra Bastille, Paris) 2006, Notes on Light (Royal Philharmonic Soc. Award for Large-Scale Composition 2010) 2006, La Passion de Simone 2008, Laterna Magica 2009, Leino et Pesanteur 2009, Emilie (opera) 2010, D'Om le vrai sens, concerto for clarinet and orchestra 2011. *Recordings:* Maa, Verblendungen, Lichtbogen, Io, Stilleben, L'Amour de loin (DVD) (BBC Music Magazine Award) 2006, Monographies 2009. *Honours:* Composer of the Year, Musical America Awards 2008, Michael Ludwig Nemmers Prize in Music Composition 2008, Léonie Sonning Music Prize 2010, Grammy Award 2011, and others. *Address:* c/o Chester Music, 14–15 Berners Street, London, W1T 3LJ, England. *Telephone:* (20) 7612-7400. *E-mail:* promotion@musicsales.co.uk. *Website:* www.chesternovello.com.

SAARINEN, Eeva-Liisa; Finnish singer (mezzo-soprano); b. 1951. *Education:* Sibelius Academy, Helsinki. *Career:* sang throughout Northern Europe from 1981 in concerts and recitals; stage debut at Helsinki in 1983 as Cherubino; further roles with the Finnish National Opera have been Rosina, Cenerentola, the Composer in Ariadne auf Naxos, Marja in Merikanto's Juha, and Hansel; has sung in the premieres of Sallinen's The King Goes Forth to France at Savonlinna in 1984 and Kullervo at Los Angeles in 1992; Fricka in Das Rheingold at Helsinki, 1996; sang in the premiere of Luther by Kari Tikka, Helsinki 2000. *Recordings include:* Kullervo Symphony by Sibelius.

SAARMAN, Risto; Finnish singer (tenor); b. 25 Jan. 1956, Jyvaskyla. *Education:* Sibelius Acad., Helsinki. *Career:* Finnish National Opera from 1984, at first as M Triquet in Eugene Onegin; Beppe; Borsa in Rigoletto; Don Curzio; Later sang: Tamino, Don Ottavio, Ferrando, Belmonte, Almaviva, Lensky and Albert Herring; Savonlinna Festival and Opéra de Lyon, 1987, as Tamino and Belmonte; Aix-en-Provence, 1990, as Belmonte and Almaviva; Sang Jacquino at the 1992 Savonlinna Festival; Concert engagements in the St John and St Matthew Passions; Masses by Haydn, Handel, Mozart and Beethoven; L'Enfance du Christ by Berlioz and Mendelssohn's Second Symphony; Lieder repertoire includes: Dichterliebe; Die schöne Müllerin; Songs by Strauss.

SABBATINI, Giuseppe; Italian singer (tenor); b. 11 May 1957, Rome. *Education:* Santa Cecilia Conservatory, Rome. *Career:* debut as opera singer in Edgardo in Lucia di Lammermoor at Spoleto 1987; played double bass in various Italian orchestras; following opera debut, has sung in Faust, La Bohème, Werther, Massenet's Manon, Linda di Chamounix, La Traviata, Rigoletto, I Puritani, L'Elisir d'amore, Fra Diavolo, Les Pêcheurs de Perles, Eugene Onegin, Idomeneo, Maria Stuarda, Les Contes d'Hoffmann, La Favorita, Falstaff, Guillaume Tell, Dom Sébastien, by Donizetti, Roméo et Juliette; performances at main theatres such as Teatro alla Scala, Milan, Vienna Staatsoper, Opéra-Bastille, Paris, Covent Garden, London, Chicago Lyric Opera, Suntory Hall, Tokyo, Carnegie Hall, New York City, Hamburg Staatsoper, San Francisco Opera; Gran Teatre del Liceu, Barcelona; Japan Opera Foundation Tokyo; sang in Massenet's Thais at Nice 1997, Arnold in Guillaume Tell at the Vienna Staatsoper 1998, in Gounod's Roméo in Turin, Donizetti's Roberto Devereux at Naples; concert repertoire includes Rossini's Stabat Mater, Rome, La Damnation de Faust, Florence, La Damnation de Faust in London and New York, Stabat Mater in Amsterdam, Massenet's Werther at Parma and Des Grieux at La Scala, Mozart's Mitridate at the Paris Châtelet, Lensky at the Vienna Staatsoper, Alfredo at Covent Garden; Beethoven's Ninth at the Ravenna Festival, Nemorinio for La Scala and Des

Grieux at the New York Met. *Recordings include:* La maga Circe, Gala Opera Concert–l'arte del belcanto, Le Maschere, by Mascagni, Canzone Sacre; Mozart Gala–Suntory Hall, Tokyo, Simon Boccanegra, La Bohème, Don Giovanni, Messe Solennelle, Recital, Mitridate, re di Ponto.

SABIN, Nigel, BMus; composer and clarinettist; b. 25 Nov. 1959, England. *Education:* Univ. of Adelaide, Manhattan School of Music with David del Tredici, studied with Richard Meale in Australia. *Career:* musician-in-residence, Univ. of Queensland 1988–95. *Compositions:* Job's Lament for clarinet 1984, Inner-City Counter-Points for clarinet, viola, cello and piano 1989, Four Studies for flute, clarinet, violin and guitar 1990, Points of Departure for violin, viola, piano and clarinet 1991, Time and Motion Studies: Postcards from France for clarinet and viola 1991, Voyages to Arcadia for small orchestra 1992, Terra Australia for soprano and ensemble 1992, Another Look at Autumn for piano 1993, Faint Qualm for piano 1993, Love Songs for orchestra 1993, Angel's Flight for small orchestra 1994. *Honours:* ASME Young Composers Awards 1981, 1984.

SACCÀ, Roberto; German singer (tenor); b. 12 Sept. 1961, Sendehorst, Westfalen. *Education:* Musikhochschule of Stuttgart and Karlsruhe. *Career:* sang in Germany from 1985 and in Israel, Switzerland, France and England; concert tour of Brazil 1987, with appearances at Teatro Municipal Rio de Janeiro; Stadttheater Würzburg 1987–88, Wiesbaden from 1988; sang at the Fermo Festival as Leandro in a 1990 revival of Paisiello's Le Due Contese; debut at La Scala, Milan with Henze's Das Verratene Meer 1990; Brussels and Salzburg Festival in Ulisse by Dallapiccola 1993, and Vienna, Musikvereinsaal 1993; mem., Zürich Opera 1994–97; sang Le Pêcheur in Le Rossignol at Salzburg Festival, and in Mozart's Der Schauspieldirektor under Harnoncourt 1994; season 1994–95 as Rinuccio in Puccini's Gianni Schicchi Bruxelles under Pappano, Vienna, title role of Orfeo, Alessandro in Mozart's Il Re Pastore under Harnoncourt, Don Ramiro in a new production of La Cenerentola, Don Ottavio in Don Giovanni and Almaviva in Il Barbiere di Siviglia; Fidelio under Solti in the Salzburg Festival; sang in Handel's Alcina at the 1997 Vienna Festival; season 1998 as Mozart's Ferrando at Glyndebourne and Lindoro in Paisiello's Nina at Zürich, with Cecilia Bartoli; season 1999 in Zürich as Oberon under Gardiner, Don Ottavio and Ramiro in Cenerentola; Berlin with Leukippos in Daphne under Thielemann and Don Ottavio in Baltimore; sang Alfredo in Traviata in Cologne and Munich and Tamino in The Magic Flute under Runniclers at San Francisco 2000, and Nemorino in L'Elisir d'amore there 2001; sang Haydn's Orfeo at Covent Garden 2001; Traviata and Magic Flute in Vienna; Berbiere in Paris; sang Tamino in Seville 2002, 2003; Rinuccio, Opéra Bastille, and Tokyo under Ozawa, Entfuhrung Munich 2004; inauguration concert of Le Fenice, Venice under Muti 2004; Tokyo Bohème under Ozawa; Entfuhrung Berlin; Traviata under Mehta in Munich; Rigoletto in Chile; inauguration performance La Fenice with La Traviata under Maazel in Venice. *Recordings:* Handel's Messiah; Capriccio with Vienna Philharmonic; Meistersinger von Nürnberg; Il Re Pastore; Don Giovanni and Cosí fan tutte under Harnoncourt and several solo albums. *Honours:* winner Opera Prize in Geneva, Switzerland 1989. *Current Management:* Mag Kurt-Walther Schober, Opernring 8-13, 1010 Vienna, Austria. *Website:* www.roberto-sacca.com.

SACCOMANI, Lorenzo; Italian singer (baritone); b. 9 June 1938, Milan. *Education:* studied in Milan with Vladimiro Badiali and Alfonso Siliotti. *Career:* debut in Avignon 1964 as Silvio in Pagliacci; sang the Herald in Lohengrin at Venice then appeared in many Italian houses, notably La Scala, Milan, in operas by Puccini, Gounod, Massenet and Verdi; London 1972 in a concert performance of Caterina Cornaro by Donizetti; US debut at Dallas 1972 as Henry Ashton in Lucia di Lammermoor; sang at Verona Arena 1983, and Geneva 1985 as Guy de Montfort in Les Vêpres Siciliennes; further appearances in Frankfurt, New York, Chicago and Buenos Aires; other roles include Escamillo, Zurga in Les Pêcheurs de Perles and Verdi's Nabucco, Germont, Ezio in Attila, Amonasro, Rigoletto, Luna and Francesco in I Masnadieri; season 1998 as Gérard in Andrea Chénier at Monte Carlo. *Recordings include:* Caterina Cornaro, Pagliacci.

SACHS, (Stewart) Harvey; American/Canadian/Swiss writer, music historian, teacher and fmr conductor; *Professor, Curtis Institute of Music;* b. 8 June 1946, Cleveland, Ohio; s. of Milton Sachs and Bella Sachs (née Bloom); m. 1st Barbara Gogolick 1967 (divorced); one s.; m. 2nd Maria Cristina Reinhart 2001 (divorced); one d. *Education:* Cleveland Inst. of Music, Oberlin Coll. Conservatory, OH, Mannes Coll. of Music, New York, Conductors' Workshop, Univ. of Toronto. *Career:* worked as conductor 1970–85; first published book 1978; full-time writer 1985–; Artistic Dir Società del Quartetto di Milano 2004–06; Lecturer, Harvard Univ., Univ. of Chicago, New York Public Library, Juilliard School, New York, Curtis Inst. of Music, Philadelphia, Univ. of Toronto, McGill Univ., Univ. of British Columbia, Freie Univ., Berlin, CUNY, Cleveland Inst. of Music, Italian Cultural Inst. in New York, Chicago, London, Toronto, Vancouver, Budapest, Warsaw, Tel-Aviv etc; currently Prof., Curtis Inst. of Music, Philadelphia; ed. of online articles and essays, OREL Foundation; consultant to Plácido Domingo on all writing projects; Leonard Bernstein Scholar-in-Residence, New York Philharmonic 2011–13. *Radio:* numerous music series and individual programmes for CBC, RAI, BBC, RSI (Italian Swiss Radio), and various US FM stations. *Television:*

Toscanini – The Maestro (documentary) 1985, for Bravo, PBS and other networks world-wide, Toscanini in His Own Words (docu-drama) 2009, for BBC, Arte and other networks world-wide. *Publications include:* Toscanini (biog.) 1978, Virtuoso 1982, Plácido Domingo's My First 40 Years (co-author) 1983, Music in Fascist Italy 1987, Arturo Toscanini from 1915 to 1946: Art in the Shadow of Politics (exhbn catalogue) 1987, Reflections on Toscanini 1991, Rubinstein: A Life (biog.) 1995, Sir Georg Solti's Solti on Solti (memoirs) (co-author) 1997, The Letters of Arturo Toscanini (ed. and trans.) 2002, The Ninth: Beethoven and the World in 1824 2010; contrib. to The New Yorker, Times Literary Supplement, New York Times, Atlantic, Wall Street Journal, La Stampa, Il Sole-24 Ore, Yale Review, Partisan Review, numerous other newspapers and periodicals; hundreds of CD liner notes for RCA/Sony BMG, Deutsche Grammophon and others. *Honours:* Dr hc (Cleveland Inst. of Music) 1999; Fellow, John Simon Guggenheim Foundation 1981, Cullman Center for Scholars and Writers, The New York Public Library 1999–2000, Nat. Endowment for the Humanities 2010–11. *Current Management:* c/o Denise Shannon Agency, Suite 1603, 20 West 22nd Street, New York, NY 10012, USA. *Telephone:* (212) 414-2911. *Fax:* (212) 414-2930. *E-mail:* dshannon@ deniseshannonagency.com. *Website:* www.deniseshannonagency.com. *E-mail:* harvey.sachs@gmail.com. *Website:* www.harveysachs.com.

SACKMAN, Nicholas; British composer; b. 12 April 1950, London, England. *Education:* Dulwich College, Nottingham University and Leeds University with Alexander Goehr. *Career:* ensembles and cadenzas performed in 1973 at the International Gaudaemus Week and the BBC Young Composers' Forum; A Pair of Wings for three sopranos and ensemble premiered at the 1974 ISCM Festival and Ellipsis for piano and ensemble premiered at Leeds Festival in 1976; Doubles for two instrumental groups and Flute Concerto commissioned by the BBC and String Quartet by the Barber Institute of Fine Arts, Birmingham; Alap for orchestra premiered by the BBC Philharmonic Orchestra in 1983 and Hawthorn for Orchestra premiered at the 1993 London Proms; taught in London; currently Sr Lecturer Music Dept, Nottingham University. *Compositions include:* Simplicia, musical for schools, 1980; The World A Wonder Waking for mezzo-soprano and ensemble, 1981; The Empress of Shoreditch, musical for schools, 1981; Holism for viola and cello, 1982; Time-Piece for brass quintet, 1982–83; Piano sonata, 1983–84; Corronach for ensemble, 1985; Sonata for trombone and piano, 1986; Paraphrase for wind, 1987; Flute concerto, 1988–89; String Quartet No. 2, 1990–91; Hawthorn for orchestra, 1993, revised 1994; Scorpio for multi-percussion and piano, 1995; Caccia for piano and orchestra, 1998; Koi for four flutes, 1999; Meld for piano, brass and percussion, 1999; Sextet for wind, 2000; Way Back When, for orchestra, 2000; Ballo, for ensemble, 2002; Mosaic, for orchestra, 2002; Fling, for flute, cello and piano, 2002; Cross hands, for piano, 2002; Puppets, for four percussionists, 2003; Vivace, for small orchestra, 2004. *E-mail:* nicholas@ sackman.co.uk. *Website:* www.sackman.co.uk.

SADÉ, Gabriel; Romanian singer (tenor); b. 1959. *Education:* studied in Israel and at the Guildhall School, London. *Career:* New Israeli Opera at Tel-Aviv from 1986, as Nemorino, Alfredo, Rodolfo, Faust and Pedrillo; Seattle Opera, 1991, as Don Ottavio; Stuttgart Staatsoper from 1992, as Jim Mahonney, Rodolfo and the Duke of Mantua; Tel-Aviv, 1994–95, as Dmitri in Boris Godunov and in the premiere of Tal's Josef; Cologne Opera, 1995–96, as Lensky and Pinkerton; other roles include Cavaradossi at Dresden, 1994, and Stuttgart, 1998, and Don José at Bologna and Modena; season 2000–01 as Radames at Cincinnati and Alpha in the premiere of Alpha and Omega by Gil Shohat, in Tel-Aviv. *Recordings include:* Verdi's Requiem. *Current Management:* Zemsky/Green Artists Management, 104 West 73rd Street, Suite 1, New York, NY 10023, USA. *Telephone:* (212) 579-6700. *Fax:* (212) 579-4723. *E-mail:* agreen@zemskygreen.com. *Website:* www.zemskygreen.com.

SADIE, Julie Anne, BA, BMus, MA, PhD; American/British cellist, viola da gamba player, lecturer and writer on Baroque music; b. (Julie Anne McCornack), 26 Jan. 1948, Eugene, Oregon; d. of Walter Stewart McCornack and Joan Eudora McCornack; m. 1st Daniel Vertrees 1968; m. 2nd Stanley Sadie 1978; one s. one d.; m. 3rd David Goode 2005. *Education:* Univ. of Oregon, Cornell Univ., City Univ. *Career:* taught at Eastman School of Music, Rochester, New York 1974–76, Queen's Coll., Taunton, Somerset 2002–05; freelance musician, lecturer and writer on Baroque music; Guest Lecturer in Baroque Music, King's Coll., London 1982; Guest Lecturer in Early Music, Royal Coll. of Music, London 1986–88; Ed. The Consort: European Journal of Early Music 1993–95; Admin. The Handel House Trust 1994–98; mem. Royal Soc. of Musicians 1996–, Holst Birthplace Trust 1999–2003, Cossington Concert Trust 2001–12; Ford Foundation Fellowship 1970–74. *Recordings:* as mem. of orchestra, with Acad. of Ancient Music in Mozart's Paris Symphony and with the English Bach Festival in Rameau's Castor et Pollux. *Publications include:* The Bass Viol in French Baroque Chamber Music 1980, Companion to Baroque Music (Ed.) 1991, The New Grove Dictionary of Women Composers (co-ed.) 1994; with Stanley Sadie, Calling on the Composer: a Guide to European Composer Houses and Museums 2005; contrib. to Gramophone, The Musical Times, Early Music, Chelys, Proceedings of the Royal Musical Association. *Honours:* Univ. of Oregon Distinguished Alumna Award 2005. *Address:* The Manor, Cossington, Bridgwater, TA7 8JR, England (home).

SAFFER, Lisa; American singer (soprano); b. 1964. *Career:* Philadelphia Opera 1987–88, as Flora in The Turn of the Screw, Susanna, and Poppea in Handel's Agrippina; Los Angeles Opera 1990, as Mozart's Re Pastore; Handel Festival at Göttingen 1992–93, as Poppea, in Ottone as Teofana, and Polinessa

in Radamisto; ENO 1996, and Opéra Bastille, Paris 1994, as Marie in Zimmermann's Die Soldaten; season 1996 as Cavalli's Calisto for Glimmerglass Opera, USA, and Despina in Così fan tutte at Philadelphia; season 1998 as Handel's Partenope for Glimmerglass Opera; sang Xanthe in Die Liebe der Danaë by Strauss at Avery Fisher Hall, NY 2000; Almirena in Handel's Rinaldo for New York City Opera; Lulu in a new production of Berg's opera for ENO (Royal Philharmonic Soc. Award 2003) 2002. *Recordings include:* Handel's Agrippina, Judas Maccabaeus and Radamisto. *Current Management:* Janice Mayer & Associates LLC, 250 W 57th Street, Suite 2214, New York, NY 10107, USA. *Telephone:* (212) 541-5511. *Fax:* (212) 541-7303. *Website:* www.janicemayer.com.

SAGLIMBENI, Rodolfo, BA, ARAM; Venezuelan conductor; *Artistic Director, Orquesta Sinfónica Municipal de Caracas;* b. 1962. *Education:* Royal Acad. of Music, UK, Accad. di Santa Cecilia, Italy. *Career:* Assoc. Conductor, Orquesta Sinfónica de Venezuela 1987–93; Founder and Music Dir Orquesta Sinfónica Gran Mariscal Ayacucho 1993–; Assoc. Conductor, Caracas Sinfonietta; Music Dir Teatro Teresa Carreño, Caracas 1999–2003; Artistic Dir Orquesta Sinfónica Municipal de Caracas 2003–; Prin. Guest Conductor, Orquesta Sinfónica Nacional de Colombia 2009–; guest conductor of orchestras in Argentina, Brazil, Chile, Colombia, Ecuador, El Salvador, France, Luxembourg, Mexico, Peru, Portugal, Romania, Spain, UK, USA; Prof. of Conducting, Canford Summer School, UK 1990. *Honours:* Orden José Félix Ribas 1991, Orden Waraira Repano 1999; Fellowship for the Americas, Kennedy Center, USA 1997, Premio Director de la Américas, Chile 1999, Premio Nacional del Artista 1999. *Address:* Orquesta Sinfónica Municipal de Caracas, Avenida Guaicaipuro, Edificio YMCA, PB, San Bernardino, Caracas 0500, Venezuela (office). *Telephone:* (212) 550-0522 (office). *Fax:* (212) 550-0767 (office). *E-mail:* saglimbeni@gmail.com (home); sinfonicamunicipal@ sinfonicamunicipal.org.ve (office). *Website:* www.sinfonicamunicipal.org.ve (office); rodolfosaglimbeni.com.

SAHAB, Selim, BA, MA; Egyptian conductor; *Artistic Director, National Arab Music Ensemble;* b. 1941, Palestine. *Education:* Moscow State Conservatoire P. I. Tchaikovsky. *Career:* teacher, Moscow State Conservatoire P. I. Tchaikovsky 1976–77; f. Beirut Co. for Arab Music, Lebanon 1980, performances in Syria, Tunisia, Oman and Egypt; teacher, Université Libanaise 1986–87, American Univ. in Beirut 1987–88; Prof., Higher Inst. of Music, Cairo 1988–90; Co-founder and Artistic Dir Nat. Arab Music Ensemble 1989–. *Honours:* Ordre National du Cèdre, Lebanon; numerous awards from Egyptian govt . *Address:* National Arab Music Ensemble, Cairo Opera House, PO Box 11567, El Borg Gezira, Cairo, Egypt (office). *Telephone:* (2) 7370603 (office). *Fax:* (2) 7370599 (office). *E-mail:* basma@selimsahab.com (home); info@cairoopera.org (office). *Website:* www.cairoopera.org/ national_arab_music_ensemble.aspx (office); www.selimsahab.com.

SAHBAI, Manuchehr, PhD; Iranian conductor and oboist. *Education:* Tehran Conservatory of Music, studied with Anton Kadletz, Hossein Nassehi, Shafighe Sedghi, Université des Sciences Humaines, Strasbourg. *Career:* began career as oboist, Tehran Symphony Orchestra; Prof. of Composition, Tehran Conservatory of Music and Univ. of Fine Arts; moved to Europe 1975; teacher, Musikschule Offenburg, Germany 1975–79; oboist and conductor, Sinfonieorchester St. Gallen, Switzerland 1979–91; Prof. of Oboe and Conducting, Landeskonservatorium für Vorarlberg, Feldkirch, Austria 1979–93; Artistic Dir and Chief Conductor, Tehran Symphony Orchestra 2007–10; guest conductor with Pasadena Symphony, Teplice Philharmonic, Orchestra Sinfonica di Bologna, Archi di Praga, Bulgarian State Philharmonic. *Address:* Quellenstrasse 8a, 9016 St Gallen, Switzerland (home). *Telephone:* 712885725 (home). *E-mail:* jas.capi@bluewin.ch (office). *Website:* www.sahbai.com.

SAHL, Michael, BA, MFA; American composer; b. 2 Sept. 1934, Boston, MA. *Education:* Amherst Coll., Princeton Univ. with Sessions, Berkshire Music Center, studied with Israel Citkowitz, and in Florence (Fulbright Fellowship). *Career:* Buffalo/Lukas Foss Ensemble 1965–66; Lincoln Center Repertory Company 1966; organist, Spencer Memorial Church; pianist/arranger for Judy Collins 1968–69; String Quartet 1969; Music Dir, WBAI-FM 1972–73; music theatre works 1975; Tango Project with William Schimmel 1981; film work 1963–. *Compositions include:* String Quartet 1969, Doina for violin and jazz trio 1979, Boxes (opera) (Seagrams Award in Opera) 1980, Symphony for big band with electric violin 1983, Tango from Exiles Cafe for piano solo 1984, Dream Beach (opera) 1987, Jungles for electric violin, electric guitar, piano, bass and drums 1992, John Grace Ranter (opera) 1996, Trio for violin, cello and piano 1997, Tropes on the Salve Regina, A Mitzvah for the Dead, Symphony 1983, Prothalamium. *Recordings include:* album: White Rabbit 1997. *Publication:* Making Changes: A Practical Guide to Vernacular Harmony 1977. *Honours:* Prix Italia (for Civilizations and its Discontents) 1980.

SAINSBURY, Lionel; British composer; b. 2 June 1958, Wilts., England. *Career:* Adjudicator, European Piano Teachers' Asscn Composers Competition 2001; mem., British Acad. of Songwriters, Composers and Authors, Performing Right Soc., Mechanical Copyright Protection Soc. *Compositions:* Fiesta for two pianos performed by Jeremy Filsell and Francis Pott, Grocer's Hall, London 1995, Twelve Preludes for piano premiered by Jack Gibbons, St John's Smith Square and featured in composer's own performance on Classic FM 1993, Violin Concerto first broadcast by Lorraine McAslan with BBC Concert Orchestra, conducted by Barry Wordsworth, BBC Radio 3 1995, Two

Nocturnes for strings premiered by William Boughton and the English String Orchestra, Malvern 1994, Cuban Dance No. 2 for violin and piano premiered by Tasmin Little and Piers Lane, Wigmore Hall 1993, Cuban Fantasy for piano first broadcast in composer's own performance on BBC Radio 3 2002, South American Suite for piano premiered by Jack Gibbons, Holywell Music Room, Oxford 1996, Two Cuban Dances originally for solo piano, arranged for piano four hands, premiered by Black/Katayama duo, Nuits Musicales de Beynac-en-Périgord 1998, Soliloquy for solo violin premiered by Oliver Lewis, Dartington Int. Summer School 1998, Incantation for piano premiered by the composer, St John's Coll., Oxford 2000, Intrada (first movt of Five Fantasias for guitar) premiered by Craig Ogden, Gloucester Three Choirs Festival 2007. *Recordings include:* Cuban Dance No. 2 for violin and piano 2003, Two Nocturnes for strings 2006, Violin Concerto 2009. *Honours:* Mendelssohn Scholarship 1980. *Website:* www.lionelsainsbury.com.

ST CLAIR, Carl; American conductor; *Music Director, Pacific Symphony Orchestra. Education:* Texas Univ. *Career:* Conducting Fellow, Tanglewood Music Centre 1985; asst conductor, Boston Symphony Orchestra 1986–90; conductor and Music Dir, Arin Arbor Symphony Orchestra 1985–92, Cayuga Chamber Orchestra 1986–92, Pacific Symphony Orchestra 1996–; Principal Guest Conductor, Radio-Sinfonieorchester Stuttgart 1998–2004; Gen. Music Dir, Deutsches Nationaltheater und Staatskapelle Weimar 2005–08; Gen. Music Dir, Komische Oper, Berlin 2008–10; guest conductor New York Philharmonic, Los Angeles Philharmonic, Philadelphia Orchestra, Austin Lyric Opera, and orchestras of Baltimore, Colorado, Houston, Minnesota, Indianapolis, Nashville, New Jersey, New Mexico, Phoenix, Pittsburgh, Saint Paul, San Antonio, San Jose, Seattle, Toronto, Montréal and Vancouver; has conducted European orchestras, including the radio orchestras of Stuttgart, Frankfurt, Saarbrücken, Hannover and Vienna, and the Frankfurt Opera Orchestra, Bamberg Symphony, Stuttgart Philharmonic, Essen Philharmonic, Staatsphilharmonie; has appeared at festivals, including Schleswig-Holstein Festival, Pacific Music Festival, Japan, Cabrillo Festival, Grant Park Music Festival, Round Top Festival, Tanglewood Festival. *Recordings:* Corigliano, Concerto for Piano and Orchestra 1994, Elliot Goldenthal, Fire Water Paper (A Vietnam Oratorio) 1996, Takemitsu, From Me Flows What You Call Time 1998, Villa-Lobos, Symphonies No. 1 and 11 1999, Villa-Lobos, Symphonies No. 4 and 12 2001, Foss, Piano Concertos and Elegy for Anne Frank 2001, Music of Gabrieli 2002, Danielpour, An American Requiem 2002, Villa-Lobos, Symphonies No. 3 and 9 2002, Mozart, Sinfonia Concertante (with Karen Dreyfus, Glenn Dicterow) 2003, Villa-Lobos, Symphony No. 7 2004. *Honours:* NEA/Seaver Conductors Award 1990. *Address:* Pacific Symphony Orchestra, 3631 South Harbor Boulevard, Suite 100, Santa Ana, CA 92704-8908, USA (office). *Telephone:* (714) 755-5788 (office). *Fax:* (714) 755-5789 (office). *E-mail:* info@pacificsymphony.org (office). *Website:* www.pacificsymphony.org (office).

SAINT-CLAIR, Carol; American singer (soprano); b. 1951, Texas. *Education:* Texas State Univ. *Career:* sang at Gelsenkirchen Opera 1977–82, Klagenfurt 1982–87 and Osnabruck Opera 1987–96; guest appearances throughout Germany and South America in such roles as Mimi, Marzelline in Fidelio, Euridice, Blanche in The Carmelites, Donna Anna and Tatiana in Eugene Onegin; frequent concert appearances; f. Saint-Clair Trio 1990.

ST HILL, Krister; Swedish singer (baritone); b. 1957. *Career:* debut as Escamillo 1982; roles in Sweden have included Sancho Panza in Massenet's Don Quichotte, Belcore and Nick Shadow in The Rake's Progress at Malmö City Theatre, Lord Sidney in Rossini's Il Viaggio a Reims, Bohème, Ned Keene, Peter Grimes, Valentin, Faust and Wolfram in Tannhäuser; Sang at Garsington Opera, Oxford, as Ernesto in Haydn's Il Mondo della Luna, at Houston as Donny in the premiere of New Year by Tippett in 1989, Glyndebourne Opera in 1990 in the British premiere of New Year and lieder recitals in Scandinavia and abroad which included Wigmore Hall recitals with Elisabeth Söderström. *Recordings include:* three solo albums; Title role in Jonny Spielt Auf by Krenek; Hindemith's Requiem. *Current Management:* c/o Good Company AB, Karlbergsvägen 64, 113 35 Stockholm, Sweden. *Website:* www.kristersthill.nu.

SAKAMOTO, Ryûichi, MA; Japanese composer, musician and actor; b. 17 Jan. 1952, Tokyo; m. Akiko Yano 1979. *Education:* Shinjuku High School, Composition Dept, Tokyo Fine Arts Univ. *Career:* began composing at age of ten; mem. group Yellow Magic Orchestra 1978–83; worked with David Sylvian 1982–83; solo recording artist, composer 1982–; conductor, arranger, music for Olympic Games opening ceremony, Barcelona, Spain 1992. *Film appearances:* Merry Christmas Mr Lawrence 1982, The Last Emperor 1987, New Rose Hotel 1998. *Film soundtracks:* Merry Christmas Mr Lawrence (BAFTA Award 1983) 1982, Daijôbu, mai furendo 1983, Koneko monogatari 1986, The Last Emperor (with David Byrne and Cong Su, Academy Award, Golden Globe Award, Grammy Award) 1987, Ôritsu uchûgun Oneamisu no tsubasa 1987, The Laser Man (title song) 1988, The Handmaid's Tale 1990, The Sheltering Sky (Golden Globe Award) 1990, Tacones lejanos 1991, Topâzu 1992, Wuthering Heights 1992, Wild Palms (TV series) 1993, Little Buddha 1993, Rabbit Ears: Peachboy 1993, Wild Side 1995, Snake Eyes 1998, Love is the Devil 1998, Gohatto 1999, Poppoya (theme) 1999, Femme Fatale 2002, Alexei to izumi 2003, Derrida 2003, Los Rubios 2003, Life Is Journey 2003, Appurushîdo 2004, Original Child Bomb 2004, Hoshi ni natta shonen 2005, Zarin 2005, Tony Takitani 2007, Silk 2007. *Recordings include:* albums: Thousand Knives 1978, B-2 Unit 1980, Hidariudeno (A Dream Of The Left Arm) 1981, Coda 1983, Ongaku Zukan (A Picture Book Of Music) 1984, Illustrated Musical Encyclopedia 1984, Esperanto 1985, Miraiha Yarô (A Futurist Chap) 1986, Media Bahn Live 1986, Oneamisno Tsubasa (The Wings Of Oneamis) 1986, Neo Geo 1987, Playing The Orchestra 1988, Tokyo Joe 1988, Sakamoto Plays Sakamoto 1989, Grupo Musicale 1989, Beauty 1989, Heartbeat 1991, Neo Geo (with Iggy Pop) 1992, Sweet Revenge 1994, Soundbites 1994, Hard To Get 1995, 1996 1996, Music For Yohji Yamamoto 1997, Smoochy 1997, Discord 1998, Love Is The Devil 1998, Raw Life 1999, Intimate 1999, Space 1999, BTTB 1999, Gohatto 1999, Complete Index of Gut 1999, Cinemage 2000, Casa 2002; singles: Bamboo Houses (with David Sylvian) 1982, Forbidden Colours (with David Sylvian) 1983, Field Work (with Thomas Dolby) 1986, Risky 1988, We Love You 1991, Moving On 1994, Prayer/Salvation 1998, Anger 1998, O Grande Amor 2001, World Citizen 2003, Sala Santa Cecillia 2005, Revep 2006, Koko 2008, Nord 2009, Three 2013. *Honours:* Order of the Cavaleiro Admissão (Brazil), Ordre des Arts et des Lettres 2009; UN Environment Programme's Echo Award, Golden Pine Award for Lifetime Achievement, Int. Samobor Film Music Festival 2013. *Current Management:* David Rubinson Management, PO Box 411197, San Francisco, CA 94141, USA. *Website:* www.sitesakamoto.com.

SAKS, Gidon; singer (bass-baritone); b. 5 Jan. 1960, Rechovot, Israel. *Education:* Univ. of Capetown, Royal Northern College of Music with John Cameron, Univ. of Toronto with Patricia Kern, Int. Opera Studio, Zürich. *Career:* debut at Stratford Festival Canada as The Mikado; Sang with Canadian Opera Company in Magic Flute, Belle Helene, Fanciulla del West, Poppea, Barbiere di Siviglia, Carmen, Merry Widow, Tales of Hoffmann, La Bohème, Anna Bolena, Fliegende Hollander, Luisa Miller, Beatrice et Benedict and Boris Godunov; Gelsenkirchen Opera in Hero und Leander, Punch and Judy, Der Freischütz, Poppea, Gianni Schicchi, Die Zauberflöte, Im Weissen Rossl, Die Blinden (world premiere), L'Italiana in Algeri, Barbiere di Siviglia, Der Rosenkavalier; Bielefeld Opera in Der Zauberflöte, Das Wunder der Heliane, Der Singende Teufel, La Juive, Verlorene Ehe von Katharina Blum (world premiere), Die Bakchantinnen, Street Scene, Ariadne auf Naxos; New Israeli Opera in La Bohème and Bartered Bride; Ariadne auf Naxos in Madrid; L'Incoronazione di Poppea in Brussels; Billy Budd, Don Giovanni, Giulio Cesare and Magic Flute for Scottish Opera; Billy Budd and Don Carlo in Geneva; Billy Budd, Fanciulla del West, Rigoletto, Semele with Vlaamse Opera; Boris Godunov in Dublin and Das Liebesverbot in Wexford; Fidelio and Freischutz at Berlin Staatsoper; Fidelio and Nozze di Figaro with Welsh Nat. Opera; Borish Godunov, Freischutz, Rake's Progress and Twilight of the Gods with English Nat. Opera; Harvey Milk in Houston, New York and San Francisco; Luisa Miller USA; Fidelio in Florence and Helsinki; Don Carlo in Palermo; Billy Budd, Salammbo and L'Espace Dernier at Bastille Paris; Nozze di Figaro in Cincinnati; concerts include Berliner Festwochen with Fischer Dieskau and Ashkenazy in Franck's Beatitudes, Shostakovitch 13th Symphony in Liverpool, Execution of Styenka Razin in Florence with Bychkov and Verdi Requiem in Toronto; As Dir and Designer: Puny Little Life Show in Cape Town; Wozzeck, Cavalleria Rusticana, Happy End and Don Giovanni in Manchester; Paisiello Barbiere in Gattierres, Grande Macabre in Vienna; Cosí fan Tutte, Eugene Onegin, Don Giovanni and Carmen for Aberdeen Int. Youth Festival; currently teaches at Ghent Conservatory, Belgium, also privately and in masterclasses. *Recordings:* Hercules, Billy Budd, Pilgrim's Progress, Silbersee, Ferne Klang, Der Kreidekries, Opera Gala, Harvey Milk. *Address:* c/o Ghent Conservatory, Hoogpoort 64, 9000 Ghent, Belgium (office). *E-mail:* gideon.saks@hogent.be (office). *Website:* cons.hogent.be (office).

SALA, Ofelia; Spanish singer (soprano); b. 1970, Valencia. *Education:* Valencia Conservatoire, studied with Victoria de los Angeles, Elly Ameling and Renata Scotto, Hochschule für Musik, Munich. *Career:* appearances in opera and concert at Leipzig, Lyon, Munich (Prinzregententheater), Vienna, Barcelona and Prague; repertoire includes Sophie in Der Rosenkavalier, Pamina, Gretel, Oscar, and Henze's Elizabeth Zimmer; Angel in Messiaen's St François d'Assise, in Outis by Berio at La Scala, Gilda, and Mozart's Servilia, Netherlands Opera; engaged with the Deutsche Oper Berlin 2001–; concerts include the Requiems of Brahms and Mozart, Haydn's Creation, Vivaldi's Gloria and Mozart's C minor Mass. *Honours:* prizewinner Montserrat Caballé, Francisco Viñas and Vervier Competitions. *Current Management:* Opéra et Concert, 37 rue de la Chausée d'Antin, 75009 Paris, France. *Telephone:* 1-42-96-18-18. *Fax:* 1-42-96-18-00. *E-mail:* agence@opera-concert.com. *Website:* www.opera-concert.com; www.ofeliasala.com.

SALAFF, Peter; American violinist; b. 1942. *Career:* mem., Cleveland Quartet 1968–92, with regular tours of the USA, Canada, Europe, Japan, Russia, South America, Australia, New Zealand and the Middle East; faculty mem., Eastman School Rochester and in residence at the Aspen Music Festival, co-founding the Center for Advanced Quartet Studies; tour of Russia and five European countries 1988; season 1988–89 with appearances at the Metropolitan Museum and Alice Tully, New York; concerts in Paris, London, Bonn, Prague, Lisbon and Brussels; appearances at Salzburg, Edinburgh and Lucerne Festivals; many complete Beethoven Cycles and annual appearances at Lincoln Center's Mostly Mozart Festival; in addition to standard works, repertory has included performances of works by Ives, John Harbison, Sergei Slonimsky, Samuel Adler, George Perle, Christopher Rouse and Toru Takemitsu. *Recordings:* repertoire from Mozart to Ravel and collaborations with Alfred Brendel in Schubert's Trout Quintet, Pinchas Zukerman and Bernard Greenhouse with Brahms' Sextets, Emmanuel Ax, Yo-Yo Ma and Richard Stoltzman.

SALERNO-SONNENBERG, Nadja; Italian violinist; *Music Director and Concertmaster, New Century Chamber Orchestra*; b. 10 Jan. 1961, Rome.

Education: Curtis Inst. of Music and Juilliard School. *Career:* moved to the USA aged eight; f. record label, NSS Music 2005; Music Dir and Concertmaster, New Century Chamber Orchestra 2008–. *Recordings include:* Speaking in Strings, Humoresque, Night and Day, Bella Italia, It Ain't Necessarily So, Vivaldi: The Four Seasons, Nadja Salerno-Sonnenberg: Sergio and Odair Assad. *Publication:* Nadja: On My Way (autobiog.) 1989. *Honours:* Hon. MMus (New Mexico State Univ.) 1999; Walter W. Naumburg Int. Violin Competition 1981, Avery Fisher career grant 1983, Ovation Award for Mendelssohn/Massenet/Saint Saëns 1988, Avery Fisher Prize 1999. *Current Management:* Opus 3 Artists, 470 Park Avenue South, 9th Floor North, New York, NY 10016, USA. *Telephone:* (212) 584-7500. *Fax:* (646) 300-8200. *E-mail:* info@opus3artists.com. *Website:* www.opus3artists.com. *Address:* New Century Chamber Orchestra, 665 3rd Street, Suite 200, San Francisco, CA 94107, USA (office). *Telephone:* (415) 357-1111 (office). *Fax:* (415) 357-1101 (office). *E-mail:* info@ncco.org (office); comments@nadjasalernosonnenberg .com (office). *Website:* www.ncco.org (office); www.nadjasalernosonnenberg .com.

SALLINEN, Aulis Heikki; Finnish composer and academic; b. 9 April 1935, Salmi; s. of Armas Rudolf Sallinen and Anna Malanen; m. 1st Pirkko Holvisola 1955 (died 1997); four s.; m. 2nd Maija Lokka 1999. *Education:* Sibelius Acad. *Career:* primary school teacher 1958–60; Man. Finnish Radio Orchestra 1960–70; Prof. of Arts, Sibelius Acad. 1965–76; mem. Bd of Dirs TEOSTO (Finnish Composers' Copyright Soc.) 1970–84, Chair. 1988–90; mem. Swedish Royal Music Acad. 1979–; mem. Finnish Composers' Soc., Sec. 1958–73, Chair. 1971–73; fmr mem. Bd Finnish Nat. Opera. *Compositions include:* eight symphonies, violin concerto, cello concerto, flute concerto, horn concerto and other orchestral music, five string quartets and other chamber music; film score for The Iron Age 1983. *Operas include:* The Horseman 1975, The Red Line 1978, The King Goes Forth to France 1982, Kullervo 1988, The Palace 1993, King Lear 1999. *Honours:* apptd Prof. of Arts for Life (by the Finnish Govt) 1981; Hon. DPhil (Turku) 1991, (Helsinki) 1994; Nordic Council Music Prize 1978, Wihuri Int. Sibelius Prize 1983.

SALMENHAARA, Erkki, PhD; Finnish composer and musicologist; b. 12 March 1941, Helsinki. *Education:* Sibelius Acad., Helsinki with Joonas Kokkonen and Vienna with Ligeti, Univ. of Helsinki. *Career:* faculty mem., Univ. of Helsinki 1963–; mem. Soc. of Finnish Composers (chair. 1974–76). *Compositions:* four Symphonies 1962, 1963, 1963, 1972, two Cello Sonatas 1960–69, 1982, Elegy for two string quartets 1963, Wind Quintet 1964, Requiem Profanum 1969, Quartet for flute, violin, viola and cello 1971, Nel Mezzo del Cammin di Nostra Vita for orchestra 1972, The Woman of Portugal (opera) 1972, Suomi-Finland Unsymphonic Poem 1967, Canzonetta per archi 1972, Illuminations for orchestra 1972, Horn Concerto 1973, Sonatine for two violins 1973, Canzona per piccola for orchestra 1974, Poema for violin or viola and strings 1976, Introduction and Chorale for organ and orchestra 1978, String Quartet 1978, Lamento per orchestra d'archi 1979, Concerto for two violins and orchestra 1980, Sonatine for flute and guitar 1981, Violin Sonata 1982, Sonatella for piano four hands 1983, Adagietto for orchestra 1982, Sinfonietta per archi 1985, Introduction and Allegro for clarinet, cello and piano 1985, Cello Concerto 1987, Isle of Bliss for baritone, soprano and orchestra 1990. *Publications include:* The History of Finnish Music 1995.

SALMINEN, Matti; Finnish singer (bass); b. 7 July 1945, Turku. *Education:* Sibelius Acad., Helsinki, and studied in Rome. *Career:* debut, Helsinki Opera as King Philip in Don Carlos 1969; sang in Cologne, Zürich and Berlin 1972–76 in the principal bass parts; La Scala, Milan 1973 as Fafner and at Savonlinna Festival 1975 as the Horseman, Sarastro, Philip, Don Carlos, Daland and Ramphis; sang at Bayreuth from 1978 as Daland, the Landgrave, Titurel, King Mark and in The Ring operas; Metropolitan Opera from 1981 as King Mark, Rocco, Osmin, Fasolt, Fafner, Hunding and Hagen; sang in Berlin 1985 and Munich 1987 as Fasolt, Hunding and Hagen; Prince Khovansky at San Francisco 1984, in Barcelona 1988, and Boris Godunov 1984 at Zürich and 1985 in Barcelona; sang in Zürich in the Ponnelle productions of L'Incoronazione di Poppea, Die Zauberflöte and Die Entführung and several principal bass parts in Vienna, Hamburg, Paris, Chicago and Tokyo; sang Hunding in Die Walküre at the Metropolitan 1990, also televised, Rocco in Fidelio at the Los Angeles Music Center, Daland at the 1990 Savonlinna Festival; season 1992–93 as Daland at the Metropolitan, Rocco at Zürich and Savonlinna, King Philip at the Deutsche Oper Berlin and Sarastro at the Savonlinna Festival; sang the Landgrave in Tannhäuser at Savonlinna 1996; sang Padre Guardiano in La Forza del Destino at Savonlinna 1998; season 2000–01 as Wagner's Hagen at the Deutsche Oper Berlin, Daland at Liège, King Mark for the Salzburg Festival, Gurnemanz for Washington Opera and Hunding in Zürich; title role in the premiere of Sallinen's Lear, at Helsinki; premiere of Rautavaara's Rasputin (title role) at Helsinki 2003. *Recordings:* St Matthew Passion, The Landgrave in Tannhäuser, The Ring, Sallinen's The Horseman, Daland, Mozart's Requiem, Osmin, Sarastro. *Honours:* Opera Actual magazine Award for best bass 2005. *Current Management:* Theateragentur Dr Germinal Hilbert, Maximilianstrasse 22, 80539 Munich, Germany. *Telephone:* (89) 2807470. *Fax:* (89) 29074730. *E-mail:* agentur@hilbert.de. *Website:* www.hilbert.de.

SALMON, Philip; British singer (tenor); b. 1960, England. *Education:* Royal College of Music. *Career:* debut recital at the City of London Festival followed by the St Matthew Passion with the Rotterdam Philharmonic, Beethoven's 9th with the Ulster Orchestra and Netherlands Philharmonic, and Mozart's Requiem with the Florida Philharmonic; Sang in Massenet's La Vièrge at St

Etienne in 1991; Operatic repertoire includes Mozart's Tamino and Belmonte for Pavilion Opera and Debussy's Pelléas at Marseille and Strasbourg, 1990–91; Sang Belmonte in Die Entführung at the Buxton Festival in 1991 and Albert Herring at St Albans; Sang Tamino at the Gaiety Theatre, Dublin, 1996. *Honours:* Young Musicians Recordings Prize.

SALOMAA, Petteri; singer (baritone); b. 1961, Helsinki, Finland. *Education:* Sibelius Acad., studied with Hans Hotter and Kim Borg. *Career:* debut at Finnish National Opera, Helsinki 1983, as Mozart's Figaro; appeared at the Ludwigsburg and Schwetzingen Festivals 1984; Wexford Festival 1985, as the King in Ariodante; Drottningholm from 1986, as Leporello and Nardo in La Finta Giardiniera; Geneva Opera 1987, as Papageno and Amsterdam 1988, as Masetto, conducted by Nikolaus Harnoncourt; North American debut 1988, with Messiah in San Francisco, followed by Figaro with Michigan Opera; season 1989–90 at Freiburg Opera as Faninal, Ned Keene, the Father in Hansel and Gretel and in Purcell's King Arthur; 1989–91 at Freiburg Opera as Billy Budd, Posa, Ned Keene and Belcore 1991 at Frankfurt Opera as Papageno and Guglielmo 1993 as Conte Robinson in Il matrimonio Segreto; sang in Purcell's King Arthur at the Châtelet and Covent Garden 1995; other roles include Oreste in Iphigénie en Tauride, Posa, Billy Budd and Albert in Werther; sang Silvio in Pagliacci with Tampere Opera 1996; sang in premiere of Bergman's The Singing Tree, Helsinki 1995; season 2000–01 in Legrenzi's La Divisione del Mondo, Swetzingen and Innsbruck Festivals; Captain in Death of Klinghoffer, by John Adams, Helsinki 2001. *Recordings include:* Beethoven's Ninth Symphony, La Finta Giardiniera, The Fiery Angel by Prokofiev, Peer Gynt with the Berlin Philharmonic, Le nozze di Figaro, Mendelssohn Elijah. *Honours:* first prize Nat. Singing Competition at Lappeenranta 1981.

SALOMAN, Ora Frishberg, AB, MA, PhD; American musicologist and academic; *Professor of Music, Baruch College and Graduate Center, City University of New York;* b. 14 Nov. 1938, Brooklyn, NY; d. of Rabbi Naphtali Frishberg and Lena Nidel Frishberg; m. Edward Barry Saloman 1968. *Education:* Columbia Univ., New York, studied violin with Vladimir Graffman and Ivan Galamian, chamber music with Raphael Hillyer, Claus Adam and William Kroll. *Career:* Prof. of Music, Baruch Coll. and The Graduate Center, CUNY, Leader, Baruch Faculty String Quartet 1972–77, Concert Master, Baruch Chamber Orchestra 1972–87, Violinist, Baruch Faculty Trio 1976–83, Chair. Dept of Music, Baruch Coll. 1978–84; Visiting Scholar in Residence, Queen's Univ., Ont., Canada 1999; mem. Editorial Advisory Bd American Music 1995–97. *Publications:* Essay in Music and Civilisation: Essays in Honor of Paul Henry Lang 1984, Essay in Music and the French Revolution 1992, Beethoven's Symphonies and J. S. Dwight: The Birth of American Music Criticism 1995, Essay in Mainzer Studien zur Musikwissenschaft: Festschrift Walter Wiora 1997, Essay in European Music and Musicians in New York City, 1840–1900 2006, Listening Well: On Beethoven, Berlioz, and Other Music Criticism in Paris, Boston, and New York, 1764–1890 2009, Essay in Music, American Made: Essays in Honor of John Graziano 2010, Essay in Oxford Handbook of Transcendentalism 2010; contrib. to Acta Musicologica, Musical Quarterly 1974, 1992, 1996, Music and Man, American Music 1988, 1990, International Review of the Aesthetics and Sociology of Music 1989, The Journal of Musicology 1992, The New Grove Dictionary of Opera 1992, St James International Dictionary of Opera 1993, Journal of the Royal Musical Association 1994, American National Biography 1999, Reader's Guide to Music 1999, Revised New Grove Dictionary of Music and Musicians 2001, Dictionary of Literary Biography 2001, Die Musik in Geschichte und Gegenwart 2001, The Opera Quarterly 2003, Encyclopaedia of New England Culture 2005, Journal of Musicological Research 2005, Musicorum 2008. *Honours:* Nat. Endowment for the Humanities Fellowship 1989. *Address:* Baruch College, Department of Fine and Performing Arts, City University of New York, Box B7-235, 1 Bernard Baruch Way, New York, NY 10010, USA (office). *Telephone:* (646) 312-4055 (office). *E-mail:* ora.saloman@baruch.cuny .edu (office). *Website:* www.baruch.cuny.edu/wsas/departments/arts (office).

SALONEN, Esa-Pekka, FRCM; Finnish conductor and composer; *Principal Conductor and Artistic Adviser, Philharmonia Orchestra;* b. 30 June 1958, Helsinki. *Education:* Sibelius Acad., Helsinki, studied composition with Rautavaara and conducting with Panula, studied composition with Niccolò Castiglioni and Franco Donatoni in Italy. *Career:* conducting debut with Finnish Radio Symphony Orchestra 1979; London conducting debut with the Philharmonia Orchestra 1983, Prin. Guest Conductor 1984–94, Prin. Conductor and Artistic Adviser 2008–; Prin. Guest Conductor, Oslo Philharmonic Orchestra 1985–; Music Dir and The Walt and Lilly Disney Chair, Los Angeles Philharmonic Orchestra 1992–2009; Prin. Conductor, Swedish Radio Symphony Orchestra 1985–95; Artistic Adviser, New Stockholm Chamber Orchestra 1986; Artistic Dir, Helsinki Festival 1995–96; Co-founder and Artistic Dir Baltic Sea Festival 2003–; Creative Chair, Tonhalle Zurich Orchestra 2014–15; Marie-Josée Kravis Composer-in-Residence, New York Philharmonic 2015–. *Compositions include:* orchestral: Concerto for alto saxophone and orchestra 1980–81, Giro 1982–97; chamber music: YTA I for alto flute 1985, YTA II for piano 1985, YTA III for cello 1986, Floof for soprano and chamber ensemble (UNESCO Rostrum Prize) 1990, Mimo II 1992, LA Variations 1996, Gambit 1998, Five Images after Sappho 1999, Mania 2000, Foreign Bodies 2001, Insomnia for orchestra 2002, Wing on Wing for soprano and orchestra 2004, Helix for orchestra 2005, Piano Concerto 2007, Nyx Violin Concerto (Univ. of Louisville Grawemeyer Award for Musical Composition 2012) 2009, Nyx for orchestra 2011, Karawane for orchestra and choir 2014.

Recordings include: numerous recordings, including Rite of Spring 2007, Orango 2009, Passion De Simone 2012, R Strauss Elektra (Gramophone Award for Best Opera Recording 2015) 2014. *Film appearance:* Sketches of Frank Gehry 2006. *Honours:* Hon. mem. American Acad. of Arts and Sciences 2010; Dr hc (Sibelius Acad.) 2003, (Hong Kong Acad. of Performing Arts) 2009, (Univ. of Southern California) 2010, (Royal Coll. of Music, London) 2011; Officier, Ordre des Arts et des Lettres 1998, Pro Finlandia Medal of the Order of the Lion of Finland; Siena Prize, Accad. Chigiana 1993, Royal Philharmonic Soc. Opera Award 1995, Litteris et Artibus Medal (Sweden) 1996, Royal Philharmonic Soc. Conductor Award 1997, Helsinki Medal 2005, Musical America Musician of the Year 2006, Artist of the Year, Int. Classical Music Awards 2011, 2014 Nemmers Composition Prize 2014. *Current Management:* c/o Fidelio Arts Ltd, 103 Whitecross Street, No 5, London, EC1Y 8JD, England. *Telephone:* (07733) 011145. *E-mail:* jessica@fidelioarts.com; mark@fidelioarts.com. *Website:* www.fidelioarts.com. *Address:* Philharmonia Orchestra, 6th Floor, The Tower Building, 11 York Road, London, SE1 7NX, England (office). *Telephone:* (20) 7921-3900 (office). *Fax:* (20) 7921-3950 (office). *E-mail:* orchestra@philharmonia.co.uk (office). *Website:* www.philharmonia.co.uk (office); www.esapekkasalonen.com.

SALTA, Anita; singer (soprano); b. 1 Sept. 1937, New York, USA. *Education:* studied in New York. *Career:* debut in Jacksonville 1959, as Aida; appearances at such German opera house centres as Stuttgart, Wuppertal, Nuremberg, Dortmund, Kassel, Essen and Hanover; other roles have included Gluck's Alceste, Mozart's Countess, Donna Elvira and Fiordiligi, Marguerite, the Trovatore and Forza Leonoras, Traviata, Desdemona, Hélène and Elisabeth de Valois; Tatiana, Antonida in A Life for the Tsar, Marenka, Mimi, Butterfly, Santuzza, Elsa, Eva, Chrysothemis, the Marschallin and Katerina Izmailova; many concert appearances.

SALTER, Robert; British violinist; b. 1960, England. *Education:* Wells Cathedral School and Guildhall School, London with David Takeno. *Career:* founder mem., Guildhall String Ensemble, with concerts in Europe, the Far East and North America; solo engagements at the Barbican and Wigmore Halls, London and elsewhere in England and Europe; Leader of Glyndebourne Touring Opera, 1992–; guest leader with the English Chamber Orchestra, London Pro Arte and orchestra of the Royal Opera (debut with Giulio Cesare at the Barbican 1997). *Recordings:* many albums with the Guildhall String Ensemble. *Honours:* GSMO prizes for solo and chamber music performance.

SALTER, Timothy, MA, LRAM, ARCO, MTC, FRCM; British composer, conductor and pianist; *Professor of Composition, Royal College of Music;* b. 15 Dec. 1942, Mexborough, Yorks., England. *Education:* St John's Coll., Cambridge, Univ. of London. *Career:* Musical Dir The Ionian Singers; pianist (chamber music) on tours in the UK and internationally; conductor and pianist on recordings and broadcasts; Prof. of Composition, Royal Coll. of Music; f. Usk Recordings to promulgate new and neglected works 1995. *Compositions:* instrumental works, chamber music, songs, choral and orchestral works. *Recordings include:* many choral and piano works, two string quartets and other chamber music, including Fantasy on a Theme by J. S. Bach for Piano, String Quartets Nos 1 and 2, Abstractions for oboe trio, Lacrimae rerum for cello, organ and chorus; English folk song arrangements; Katharsios for chorus, piano and percussion; Perspectives, set two, for piano, After the Sun for baritone, oboe/cor anglais and piano, Chimera for violin and piano. *E-mail:* info@ullagraymanagement.com. *Address:* 26 Caterham Road, London, SE13 5AR, England. *Telephone:* (20) 8318-2031. *E-mail:* ts@timothysalter.com (office). *Website:* www.timothysalter.com.

SALVATORI, Roberto; singer (baritone); b. 1970, Trinidad. *Education:* Guildhall School, London, England and the Britten/Pears School at Aldeburgh, masterclasses with Sena Jurinac and Sherrill Milnes. *Career:* roles with Pavilion Opera included Mozart's Don Giovanni, Count and Guglielmo, Rossini's Figaro, Donizetti's Enrico in Lucia di Lammermoor, Dr Malatesta and Belcore; Germont and Scarpia with European Chamber Opera, Sid in Albert Herring at Aldeburgh and Berkely in Marschner's Vampyr for BBC television; Principal, ENO from 1995, with Ping, Escamillo and Marcello (La Bohème) in first season; Stolzius in the British company premiere of Zimmerman's Soldaten 1996; season 1998–99 as Marcello and Escamillo for ENO and in Massenet's Esclarmonde for Chelsea Opera Group; sang Iago in Verdi's Otello at ENO and Jochanaan in Salome at the Spier Festival in South Africa. *Honours:* scholarship from the Countess of Munster Trust.

SALWAROWSKI, Jerzy Hubert; Polish conductor, music director and academic; *Artistic Director, Czestochowa Philharmonic Orchestra;* b. 7 Sept. 1946, Kraków; m. Ewa Czarniecka 1976, two s. *Education:* Kraków Music High School, Warsaw Chopin Music Acad. *Career:* Asst Conductor, Kraków Philharmonic Choir 1970–71; Second Conductor, Opole Philharmonic Orchestra 1972–78, Katowice-Silesian Philharmonic 1978–81; Substitute Art Dir, Silesian Philharmonic 1982–84, Polish Radio Nat. Symphony Orchestra 1985–; Guest Conductor, Łódź Great Opera House, tours in Europe; Artistic Dir, Pomeranian Philharmonic Orchestra 1988–90, Lublin State Philharmonic Orchestra 1991–93, Szczecin Symphony Orchestra and Torun Chamber Orchestra; Principal Guest Conductor, Szczecin Philharmonic Orchestra, Torun Chamber Orchestra; Artistic Dir festival, Torun 1999–2003: Music and Architecture; tours of Europe (France, Portugal, Spain, Germany) with symphony and opera music; Prof., Paderewski Music Acad. Poznań 1999–; Artistic Dir, Torun Symphony Orchestra 1999–2005, 2005–07, Czestochowa Philharmonic Orchestra 2005–; Dir, Orchestra and Opera Conductorship Inst.

Compositions: transcriptions and theatre music. *Recordings:* All Gershwin's Pieces for piano and orchestra (with A. Ratusinski) (Gold Plate Award 1993), All Symphonic Poems by M. Karlowicz, J. Sibelius: En Saga and Violin Concerto (with V. Brodski, for Musical Heritage Soc.), H. Wieniawski: Violin Concerto (with V. Brodski), Mozart: All Church Sonatas (with Pomeranian Philharmonic Orchestra and Karol Golebiewski) 1988, Lessel: Grand Rondeau and Piano Concerto (with Silesian Philharmonic and Jerzy Sterczynski) 1992, Mendelssohn, Hebrides Overture, Violin Concerto and 4th Symphony (Italian) (with Krzysztof Jakowicz) 1997, Famous Caprices (with Szczecin Philharmonic Orchestra) 2001, Brahms, Prokofiev Piano Concertos (with H. Salwarowski and Nat. Radio Orchestra) 2003. *Publications:* New Elaborations of Karlowicz Scores in PWM Edition; contrib. to Permanent Reviews. *Honours:* Silver Medal of Merit for Culture 'Gloria Artis' 2008. *Address:* Czestochowa Philharmonic Orchestra, Wilsona 16, 42-200 Czestochowa (office); ul. Wietnamska 63B, 40-765 Katowice, Poland (home). *Telephone:* (34) 3243437 (office); (32) 2018193 (home). *E-mail:* filharmonia@filharmonia.com.pl (office); jerzy@salwarowski.art.pl (home). *Website:* www.salwarowski.art.pl; www.filharmonia.com.pl.

SALZMAN, Eric, BA, MFA; American composer and writer on music; b. 8 Sept. 1933, New York. *Education:* Columbia Coll., Columbia Univ., Princeton Univ., studied with Otto Luening, Ussachevsky, Jack Beeson, Roger Sessions and Milton Babbitt, with Petrassi in Rome and Darmstadt. *Career:* music critic, New York Times 1958–62, New York Herald Tribune 1963–66; teacher, Queens Coll., New York 1966–68; Dir, New Images of Sounds, series of concerts at Hunter Coll.; founder, Quog Music Theater 1970, to explore new ideas in the performing arts; co-founder and Artistic Dir, American Music Theater Festival, Philadelphia 1983–. *Compositions include:* String Quartet 1955, Flute Sonata 1956, Inventions for orchestra 1959, Verses and Cantos for four voices, instruments and electronics 1967, Larynx Music (dance piece with tape) 1968, The Conjurer (multimedia spectacle) 1975, Civilization and its Discontents (opera buffa for radio) 1977, Noah (spectacle) 1978, The Passion of Simple Simon (for the Electric Circus, Greenwich Village), Variations on a Sacred Harp Tune for harpsichord 1982, Boxes (radio opera with Michael Sahl) 1983, Big Jim and the Small-Time Investors (music theatre) 1985, The Last Words of Dutch Schulz (music theatre) 1996, Body Language for mixed media 1996, adaptation of Gershwin's Strike Up The Band 1984. *Publications include:* 20th Century Music: An Introduction 1967, Civilization and its Discontents (with Michael Sahl), Making Changes (a handbook of vernacular harmony, with Michael Sahl), The New Music Theater 1998.

SAMOSHKO, Vitaly; Ukrainian pianist; b. 1973, Kharkiv. *Education:* Kharkiv Conservatoire, Accad. Pianistica, Isola, studied with Leonid Margarius. *Career:* has performed in over 25 countries at halls including Tonhalle Zürich, Théâtre du Châtelet Paris, Metropolitan Museum of Art and Steinway Hall, New York, Amsterdam Concertgebouw, Beethovenhalle Bonn, Yokohama Minato Mirai Hall, Okayama Symphony Hall, Kyoto Concert Hall, Teatro Gran Rex Buenos Aires; festivals include Klavier Festival Ruhr, Montpellier Radio France, Besançon, Música Romantica (Switzerland), Yokohama Piano Festival, Savannah Onstage (USA), Lanaudière (Canada), Echternach and Bourlinster (Luxembourg), Chopin Piano Festival (Poland), Flanders, Aulne and Wallonie (Belgium); has performed with orchestras including Tokyo Philharmonic, New Japan Philharmonic, Orchestre Symphonique de Montréal, Orchestre Philharmonique du Luxembourg, Orchestre Nat. de Belgique, Orchestre Philharmonique de Liège, Symfonieorkest Vlaanderen, St Petersburg State Symphony and Orchestre Nat. de Lille, with conductors including Charles Dutoit, Edvard Tchivzhel, Marc Soustrot, Gilbert Varga, Kazufumi Yamashita, Otaka Tadaaki and Louis Langrée; radio broadcasts for Radio Suisse Romande, Geneva, Westdeutscher Rundfunk, Cologne, Klara and Musique 3, Brussels; teacher, Ghent Conservatoire. *Recordings:* Schubert/Schumann/Scriabin/Prokofiev, Piano Studies Scriabin, Rachmaninov: Les Etudes-Tableaux, Rachmaninov: Piano Concerto No. 3 in D Minor. *Honours:* several awards including First Prize, Queen Elisabeth Prize, Brussels 2009. *Address:* c/o Conservatorium Gent, Hoogpoort 64, 9000 Ghent, Belgium (office). *E-mail:* vitaly.samoshko@telenet.be (office). *Website:* vitalysamoshko.com (office).

SAMPSON, Carolyn, BA (Hons); British singer (soprano); b. 1974, England. *Education:* Univ. of Birmingham. *Career:* opera includes Pamina in The Magic Flute (ENO), title role in Semele (ENO), La Musica and Euridice in Orfeo (Barbican, London), Julietta in The Tales of Hoffmann at the St Endellion Festival, First Niece in Peter Grimes for Opéra Nat. de Paris, Susanna in Le Nozze di Figaro (Montpellier); concert engagements with City of Birmingham Symphony Orchestra (Mahler 8), City of London Sinfonia (Hickox), Hallé Orchestra (Elder), Il Giardino Armonico (Antonini), Music of the Baroque Chicago (Bickett), RIAS Kammerchor (Reuss), Sonnerie, The King's Consort (including US tour 2001), The Sixteen (Christophers), Ex Cathedra (Skidmore), Scottish Chamber Orchestra (Kraemer), Collegium Vocale, Gent (Herreweghe), The Royal Concertgebouw Orchestra, Freiburg Baroque Orchestra, The English Concert (Pinnock), Orchestra of the Age of Enlightenment, Le Concert d'Astrée (Haim), Orchestre des Champs Elysées (Herreweghe); festival appearances include BBC Proms, Mostly Mozart (New York), Beaune, Leipzig, Saintes, Halle, Salzburg, Istanbul; recitals in the Proms Chamber Music series, The Wigmore Hall, BBC Wales, BBC Scotland, and Concertgebouw, Amsterdam. *Recordings include:* Kuhnau, Knüpfer, Vivaldi, Monteverdi, Zelenka, Lalande, Rameau, Bach, Orfeo, Buxtehude, Carmina Burana, Handel: Great Oratorio Duets (with Robin

Blaze) 2006, Exsultate Jubilate: Mozart Arias 2006, Handel: Solomon 2006, Victorious Love: songs by Purcell 2007, A French Baroque Diva (Gramophone Award for Best Recital Recording 2015) 2014. *Honours:* Artist of the Year, Gramophone Awards 2015. *Current Management:* c/o Ingpen & Williams, 7 St George's Court, 131 Putney Bridge Road, London, SW15 2PA, England. *Telephone:* (20) 8874-3222. *Fax:* (20) 8877-3113. *E-mail:* nw@ingpen.co.uk. *Website:* www.ingpen.co.uk.

SAMSING, Boris Leon; Danish violinist; b. 31 Dec. 1943, Copenhagen; m.; one s. one d. *Education:* Funen Acad. of Music, studied in Bern and Prague. *Career:* debut at Funen Acad. 1963; mem., Sonderjylland Symphony Orchestra 1964–69; Principal, Sjaelland Symphony Orchestra 1969–75; mem., Kontra Quartet 1973–, with tours worldwide and workshops; Principal, Danish Radio Symphony Orchestra 1975–; representative ensemble of the Danish State 1989–92; teacher, Royal Danish Acad. of Music. *Recordings:* music by Carl Nielsen, Per Norgaard, Rued Langgaard, Vagn Holmboe, Niels W. Gade, Poul Ruders, Hans Abrahamsen, Mozart, Schubert, Tchaikovsky, 33 recordings with the Kontra Quartet. *Honours:* Peder Moller Award, Gramophone Recording of the Year, Danish Musicians' Union Award.

SAMSING, Freddy; Danish musician (cathedral organ) and composer; *Organist, St Canute Cathedral, Odense;* b. 20 June 1946, Copenhagen; m. Anita Hyldgård Samsing 1997; one s. two d. *Education:* Royal Danish Acad. of Music, Copenhagen, studied conducting. *Career:* int. concert player, Northern Europe; solo appearances on TV and radio; solo appearances with nearly all Danish symphony orchestras; organist, St Canute Cathedral, Odense; jury mem., Int. Organ Competition, Odense; mem. Danish Assen of Organists and Cantors (DOKS). *Recordings:* as soloist/accompanist: works by Albinoni, Bach, Vivaldi, Monteverdi; trio with two outstanding trumpet players, Hovaldt and Son; solo trumpet by the Royal Danish Orchestra. *Address:* Fangel Bygade 34, 5260 Odense S, Denmark (office). *E-mail:* samsing@pc.dk (home).

SAMSON, (Thomas) James, BMus, MMus, PhD, LRAM, FBA; British academic; b. 6 July 1946, Northern Ireland. *Education:* Queen's Univ., Belfast, Univ. Coll., Cardiff Univ. *Career:* Research Fellow in Humanities, Univ. of Leicester, England 1972–73; Lecturer in Music, Univ. of Exeter 1973–86, Reader in Musicology 1986–91, Prof. of Musicology 1991–94; Badock Prof. of Musicology, Univ. of Bristol 1994–2002; Prof. of Music, Royal Holloway, Univ. of London 2002–; council mem. Royal Musical Assen. *Publications include:* Music in Transition 1977, The Music of Szymanowski 1980, The Music of Chopin 1985, Chopin Studies 1988, Man and Music vol. 7: The Late Romantic Era 1991, The Cambridge Companion to Chopin 1992, Chopin: The Four Ballades 1992, Chopin Studies 2 (with John Rink) 1994, Chopin (Master Musicians series) 1996, The Cambridge History of 19th Century Music 2002, Virtuosity and the Musical Work: Transcendental Studies of Liszt 2003; contrib. to Rocznik Chopinowski, Journal of the American Musicological Soc., Nineteenth-Century Music, Tempo, Journal of Musicology, Music Analysis, Music and Letters, Musical Times. *Honours:* Fellow of the British Acad. 2000; Szymanowski Centennial Medal 1982, Order of Merit, Polish Ministry of Culture 1990.

SAMUEL, Rhian, BA, BMus, MA, PhD; British composer and academic; *Professor Emeritus, City University, London;* b. 3 Feb. 1944, Aberdare, Wales; d. of David Hopkin Samuel and Gwenllian Forey; m. Curtis A. Price; one s. *Education:* Aberdare Girls' Grammar School, Univ. of Reading, Washington Univ., St Louis, USA. *Career:* Teacher of Composition, St Louis Conservatory, USA 1970s, Univ. of Reading 1984–95, Head of Dept 1993–95; Prof. of Music, City Univ., London 1995–2010, Prof. Emer. 2010–; currently Tutor in Composition, Magdalen Coll., Oxford; Co-Ed. Grove Dictionary of Women Composers 1994; Composer-in-Residence, 31st Pontino Festival, Italy 1995, Presteigne Festival 1996; comms from the BBC, Sinfonia 21, St Louis Symphony Orchestra, etc.; Judge, London Sinfonietta/Women in Music Composers' Prize 1995, Nat. Eisteddfod of Wales 1996, Britten Award 1996, Mendelssohn Scholarship 2000, Royal Philharmonic Prize 2001; Trustee Britten-Pears Foundation 1997–2002, Nat. Assen of Youth Orchestras 2001–05. *Compositions include:* Elegy-Symphony 1981, La Belle Dame sans Merci for chorus and orchestra 1982, A Song for the Divine Mass C for soprano, tenor chorus and orchestra 1987, Lovesongs and Observations for SATB chorus 1989, Encounters concerto for piano and orchestra 1991, The White Amaryllis (song cycle) 1991, The Cool Heart (song cycle) 1992, Clytemnestra for female voice and orchestra 1994, Brass Express for trumpet and orchestra 1994, Fantasy for five flutes 1995, Weeping Trellises for solo piano 1995, Scenes from an Aria 1996, Daughters' Letters for solo soprano, string orchestra and percussion 1996, Blythswood for viola and piano 1996, Dream-Images for solo piano 1997, Fantasy Quintet for five flutes 1997, Ymddiddan for two pianos 1998, Dear Night for SATB chorus 1998, Through Windows and the Balustrades Beyond for flute, viola and harp 1998, Dances of the Stream for full orchestra 1999, Tirluniau (Landscapes for full orchestra 2000, Shaping the Air for oboe and piano 2000, Cerddi Hynafol (Ancient Songs) for mezzo-soprano 2001, The Therapy of Moonlight for solo piano 2002, Primavera for wind quintet 2002, Songs of Earth and Air for medium voice and piano 2002, Tin Soldier for cello and piano 2002, Songlines for alto saxophone and piano 2003, Nantcol Songs for soprano and piano 2003, Everyday Dancing for clarinet quartet 2003, Little Serenade for Skaila for harp 2004, Serenade Duo for two pianos 2004, Trinity: Three Songs for soprano, flute and piano 2005, Gaslight Square II 2005, Dovey Junction for brass quintet 2005, Pan draw ust y nos/When the Calm of Night for SATB chorus and organ 2005,

Shards of Light for solo violin 2005, Little Duos for two clarinets 2006, Copper Ribbons and Silver Threads for harpsichord 2006, The Flowing Sand for baritone and piano 2006, Colours for soprano, trumpet and organ 2006, Dance of the Curlews for two harps 2008, A River for soprano, baroque oboe viola and harpsichord 2008, Emerging (lightly) for chamber ensemble 2008, Yr Alarch/The Swan for solo baritone 2009, The Last Dance for string quartet 2009, Far Across the Sea/Ymhell dros y môr for solo harp 2009, Lights in the City for full orchestra 2010, Spring Diary for baritone and piano 2010, Phantasy Trio for violin, cello and piano 2010, Mist on the Hills for accordion and string quartet 2010, Opposites for SATB chorus 2010, Summer Songs for high voice and piano 2010, The Path through the Woods for recorder and string orchestra 2011, Moon and Birds for mezzo-soprano and piano 2011, Moon and Birds for mezzo soprano, flute, harp and string quartet 2011, What Cheer? for SATB chorus and organ 2011, Mechanical and Fantastical Studies for solo piano 2011, Quartet: Threaded Light for string quartet 2012, Haze and the Absence of Clouds for soprano, string quartet and piano 2012, Fragile Landscapes for solo piano 2013, In Situ for tenor saxophone and piano 2013, Ave Regina Caelorum for SATB choir 2013, Brass Tacks for brass quintet 2013, The Gaze for soprano and piano 2013, His Gaze upon Ophelia for soprano, viola and piano 2013, Little Duos for two bassoons 2013, The Path through the Woods 2013, Love bade me welcome 2014, A Swift Radiant Morning 2015. *Recordings include:* various recordings including Light and Water: Deux Elles. *Publications:* contrib. to numerous journals, including articles on Birtwistle's operas Gawain and The Minotaur for Cambridge Opera Journal. *Honours:* First Prize, Greenwich Festival 1979, ASCAP/Rudolph Nissim Award 1983, Glyndwr Award 2006. *Address:* New College, Oxford, OX1 3BN, England (office). *Telephone:* (1865) 279589 (office). *E-mail:* r.samuel@city.ac.uk (office). *Website:* www.stainer.co.uk/samuel.html; www.rhiansamuel.com.

SAMUELSON, Mikael; singer (baritone); b. 9 March 1951, Stockholm, Sweden. *Education:* studied with Birgit Stenberg and Erik Werba. *Career:* has sung in Sweden from 1968 in opera, oratorio, music theatre and films; Royal Opera Stockholm as Rossini's Figaro; Drottningholm Theatre 1987, 1989, as Mozart's Figaro and Papageno; sang in Die Schöpfung 1988; appearances with the Stockholm Music Drama Ensemble in Pagliacci, Mahagonny and Death in Venice; television engagements in Drömmen om Thérèse by Werle and Kronbruden by Rangström; has appeared as cabaret artist in Sweden and Finland.

SÁNCHEZ, Ana Maria; Spanish singer (soprano); b. 1966, Elda, Alicante. *Education:* Alicante Conservatory, studied in Madrid with Isabel Penagos and Miguel Zanetwi. *Career:* sang in concerts and recitals in Spain, France and Germany; stage debut as Abigaille in Nabucco at Palma (1994) followed by Donna Anna at Valencia and elsewhere; Mathilde in Guillaume Tell at Lisbon, Leonora in La Forza de destino at Barcelona and Chrysothemis in Elektra at Valencia; sang the Trovatore Leonora at Zürich, season 1996–97, and has appeared further in Roberto Devereux and Tannhäuser in Bibao, Salud in La Vida Breve at Malaga and in Don Giovanni at Hamburg; engaged to return to Valencia 1998, as Gutrune in Götterdämmerung; concerts include the Verdi Requiem and song recitals. *Honours:* prizewinner in competitions at Bilbao and Enna (Italy), 1992–93. *Current Management:* c/o Columbia Artists Management, 1790 Broadway, New York, NY 10019-1412, USA. *Telephone:* (212) 841-9500. *Fax:* (212) 841 9744. *E-mail:* info@cami.com. *Website:* www .cami.com.

SAND, Annemarie; singer (mezzo-soprano); b. 26 Nov. 1958, Copenhagen, Denmark. *Education:* Royal Acad. of Music, Nat. Opera Studio. *Career:* appeared with ENO from 1987 as the Page in Salome, Linetta in The Love of Three Oranges, and Dryad in Ariadne auf Naxos; WNO 1989 as the Composer in Ariadne, conducted by Charles Mackerras; other roles include Mother Goose in The Rake's Progress, Nancy in Albert Herring, Charlotte, Octavian, Hansel and the Mother in Amahl and the Night Visitors; many concert appearances, including Mozart's Requiem at the Teatro San Carlo, Naples, and 12 concerts in Denmark 1989; season 1992 as Kate Pinkerton for ENO and in Oliver's Mario and the Magician at the Almeida Theatre; season 1993 included BBC Proms debut in The Wreckers, Ethyl Smyth. *Honours:* Elena Gerhardt Lieder Prize, Minnie Hauk Prize, Clifton Prize for Best Recital.

SAND, Malmfrid; Norwegian singer (soprano); b. 1955, Oslo. *Education:* studied in Oslo and London. *Career:* debut as Pamina in Die Zauberflöte at Oslo; appearances as Fiordiligi in Brussels, London and at the Bath Festival; Irene in Tamerlano for Orpheus Opera and Isaura in Jérusalem by Verdi for BBC Radio 3; Wexford Festival 1983, as the Queen in Marschner's Hans Heiling, returning as Donna Anna in Gazzaniga's Don Giovanni and in Busoni's Turandot; engagements as Electra in Idomeneo for the English Bach Festival and Manon for Dorset Opera, 1991; concert repertoire includes Vivaldi Gloria, Messiah, Dvořák's Requiem; concerts and recitals in Scandinavia, the USA and Europe, notably with the Stavanger Symphony, the Oslo NRK Symphony and the Harmonien Symphony Orchestra of Bergen; sang Mrs Maurrant in Weill's Street Scene, Turin, 1995.

SANDEL, Marina, PhD; German singer (mezzo-soprano); b. 1959, Stuttgart. *Education:* studied in Frankfurt and Stuttgart, and with Brigitte Fassbaender. *Career:* concert appearances in Europe and Israel from 1984; Essen Opera 1989–98, with guest engagements in opera at Karlsruhe, Mannheim and Ludwigsburg, Beslin, Kiel, Hannover, Stuttgart, Toulouse, St. Gallen, Schwerin, Kassel 1997–2007; roles have included Dorabella, Hansel, Laura in La Gioconda (Bremen, 1996) and Octavian in Der Rosenkavalier; Essen,

1996, in the premiere of Bibalo's Miss Julie and as Nicklausse in Les contes d'Hoffmann; Prof. of Voice, Martin Luther-Universität Halle-Wittenberg 2007–, also at Hochschule für Musik und Theater Hannover 2007–. *Publications:* various articles in Vox Humana. *Honours:* Welt Bewerb, Beslin 1984, Kultursenatoriu des Landes Sachsen-Anhalt 2007. *Current Management:* c/o Konzertdirektion Fritz Dietrich, Sigmund-Freud-Strasse 1, 60435 Frankfurt am Main, Germany. *Telephone:* 69544504. *Fax:* 695484107. *E-mail:* info@ konzertdirektion-dietrich.de. *Website:* www.konzertdirektion-dietrich.de. *Address:* Im Iangen Han 5, 70565 Stuttgart, Germany (home). *E-mail:* marina.sandel@hmt-hannover.de (home).

SANDERLING, Michael; German conductor and cellist; b. 1967, Berlin; s. of Kurt Sanderling and Barbara Sanderling; m. Krisztina Sanderling. *Education:* Berlin Musikhochschule. *Career:* Principal, Leipzig Gewandhaus Orchestra 1987–92, later with Radio Sinfonieorchester Berlin; solo career as violiinst, notably with the Boston Symphony Orchestra, Los Angeles Philharmonic Orchestra, Berlin and Bamberg Symphonies, Philharmonia, Royal Philharmonic Orchestra and Tonhalle Zürich, chamber concerts with the Trio Ex Aequo at the Schleswig-Holstein, Lucerne and Salzburg festivals 1992–2000; Artistic Dir and Chief Conductor, Kammerakademie Potsdam 2006–10; Chief Conductor, Dresdner Philharmonic Orchestra 2011–; guest conductor with Taipei Philharmonic Orchestra, China Philharmonic Peking, Nederlands Philharmonisch Orkest, Tonhalle-Orchester Zürich, Symphonieorchester des Bayerischen Rundfunks, Dresdner Philharmonie, Sächsische Staatskapelle Dresden, Rundfunk-Sinfonieorchester Berlin, MDR-Sinfonieorchester Leipzig, NDR Radiophilharmonie Hanover, Deutsche Radio Philharmonie Saarbrücken. *Recordings include:* Shostakovich Chamber Symphonies, Daniel Schnyder SubZERO, Sibelius Violin Concertos, Brahms Violin Concertos. *Honours:* prizewinner Maria-Canals Competition, Barcelona, J.S. Bach Competition, Leipzig and ARD Competition, Munich. *Current Management:* Artesystem Berlin, Kurfürstendamm 157, 10709 Berlin, Germany. *Telephone:* (30) 34902199. *Fax:* (30) 34902145. *E-mail:* bernds@artesystem.com. *Website:* www.artesystem.com.

SANDERLING, Thomas; conductor; b. 2 Nov. 1942, Nowosibirsk, USSR. *Education:* School of the Leningrad Conservatory, German High School of Music, East Berlin, Germany. *Career:* debut conducting Berlin Symphony Orchestra 1962; Chief Conductor, Reichenbach 1964; Music Dir of Opera and Concerts, Halle, Germany 1966; Permanent Guest Conductor, German State Opera, Berlin 1978–; has conducted at most major centres in Germany and throughout Europe, including Stockholm, Oslo, Helsinki, Milan, Rome, London, Salzburg and Amsterdam; gave the German premiere of Shostakovich's Symphonies 13 and 14 with Berlin Radio Symphony Orchestra 1969, and A. Petterson's 8th Symphony 1979; success with productions of Magic Flute and Marriage of Figaro at Vienna State Opera 1979; has worked with Rotterdam Philharmonic, Bournemouth Symphony Orchestra, Philharmonia (London), Vienna Symphony Orchestra and in Nice, Vancouver, Rochester, New Zealand, Japan, Israel and Australia, with productions of Figaro (Nice) and Don Giovanni (Austria and Helsinki). *Recordings:* Shostakovich: Michelangelo cycle (recording premiere) and Symphonies 2 and 4, Handel: Alexander's Feast and Italian Cantatas, Wolfgang Strauss: Symphony No. 1, Udo Zimmermann: Ein Zeuge der liebe. *Honours:* Berlin Critics' Award 1970.

SANDERS, Ernest H., MA, PhD; American musicologist and fmr professor of music; b. 4 Dec. 1918, Hamburg, Germany; m. Marion Hollander 1954; one s. one d. *Education:* Columbia Univ. *Career:* Lecturer, Dept of Music, Columbia Univ. 1954–58, Instructor 1958–61, 1962–63, Asst Prof. 1963–65, 1966–67, Assoc. Prof. 1967–72, Prof. 1972–86, Chair. Dept of Music 1978–85. *Publications include:* Polyphonic Music of the Fourteenth Century Vol. XIV: English Polyphony of the Thirteenth and Early 14th Centuries 1979, Vols XVI and XVII (co-ed.); contrib. of numerous articles on mediaeval polyphony in Journal of the American Musicological Soc., The Musical Quarterly, Acta Musicologica, Archiv für Musikwissenschaft, Music and Letters, Musica Disciplina, The New Grove Dictionary, various Festschriften; most of these collected in French and English Polyphony of the 13th and 14th Centuries: The Notation of Notre-Dame Organa Tripla and Quadrupla (article on Beethoven's Opp 125 and 123). *Honours:* Fulbright Research Scholarship (UK) 1965–66, Guggenheim Fellowship (supplementary) 1965–66, ACLS Fellowship 1969–70, Nat. Endowment for the Humanities Sr Research Fellowship 1973–74. *Address:* 885 West End Avenue, 8B, New York, NY 10025-3524, USA (home). *Telephone:* (212) 865-0527 (home). *E-mail:* sanders885@juno.com.

SANDERS, Graham, FLCM; British singer (tenor); b. 1963, Chichester, Sussex, England; m. *Education:* London Coll. of Music, and studied in USA with William McGraw at the Univ. of Cincinnati, James King and William Johns at Indiana Univ. *Career:* appearances at Bonn Opera as Roderigo in Otello (debut role), Laca in Jenůfa and Florestan in Fidelio; Bremen Opera 1994–2000, as Wagner's Erik and Walther, Bacchus in Ariadne auf Naxos and Canio in Pagliacci; further engagements as Siegmund in Die Walküre at Graz, Kiel and Darmstadt, Laca at Dresden and Polixenes in Ein Wintermärchen by Boesmans at Braunschweig; season 2001–02 as Otello at Budapest and Siegfried for Scottish Opera; engaged for Götterdämmerung at Edinburgh 2003. *Honours:* Lauritz Melchior Heldentenor Soc. scholarship 1990. *Current Management:* c/o Herbert Eckhoff Artist Management, 8404 Hurstbourne Court, Knoxville, TN 37919, USA. *E-mail:* gsanders@me.com. *Website:* www .dramatictenor.com.

SANDISON, Gordon; singer (baritone); b. 1949, Aberdeen, Scotland. *Education:* Royal Scottish Acad. *Career:* has sung with Scottish Opera from 1973 as Papageno, the Figaros of Rossini and Mozart, Malatesta, Don Giovanni, Belcore, Don Alfonso, Falstaff, Marcello; Covent Garden debut 1984, as Fléville in Andrea Chénier, followed by Mandarin, Morales, Starveling, Montano, Masetto and the Doctor and Shepherd in Pelléas et Mélisande; further appearances with ENO, Théâtre du Châtelet Paris, Opera Northern Ireland and the Glyndebourne, Wexford and Edinburgh Festivals; sang in Carmen at Earls Court, London and on tour to Japan; Rossini's Bartolo for ENO 1995; sang Frank in Die Fledermaus for Opera Holland Park 1998; season 2000–01 as the Mayor in Jenůfa at Glyndebourne and Rossini's Bartolo for ENO.

SANDMEIER, Rebekka, BA, MA, PhD, LRSM, Habil.; German musicologist; *Director, South African College of Music, University of Cape Town*; b. (Rebekka Fritz), Berlin. *Education:* Trinity Coll., Dublin, Ireland, Westfälische Wilhelms Universität, Münster. *Career:* Lecturer in Musicology, Trinity Coll., Dublin 1994–97, Conservatory of Music, Dublin 1996–97; violin teacher, Lüchow-Dannenberg 1997–98; Lecturer in Musicology, Münster Univ. 1999–2008; Prof. of Musicology, Potsdam Univ. 2009–10; Assoc. Prof. of Musicology, South African Coll. of Music, Univ. of Cape Town 2011–, Dir 2014–; concerts (early music) with The Cape Consort; mem. Editorial Bd Die Musik in Geschichte und Gegenwart 2001–07, Journal of the Musical Arts in Africa 2011–; mem. Exco, South African Soc. for Research in Music 2012–. *Publications:* Text and Music in German Operas of the 1920s 1998, Denen Kennern... Winifried Schlepphorst zum 65. Geburtstag 2002, Die Sammlung Nordkirchen: Kammermusik 2004, Geistliche Vokalpolyphonie und Frühhumanismus in England 2012; contrib. to Musikkonzepte, Archiv für Musikwissenschaft, Händel Handbuch, Die Musik in Geschichte und Gegenwart. *Honours:* Trinity Postgraduate Award 1992–95. *Address:* South African College of Music, UCT, Private Bag, Rondebosch 7701, South Africa (office). *E-mail:* rebekka.sandmeier@uct.ac.za (office).

SANDON, Nicholas John, BMus, PhD; musicologist; b. 16 Feb. 1948, Faversham, Kent, England; m. Edith Virginia Edwards 1975, one step-s. two step-d. *Education:* Univ. of Birmingham, Univ. of Exeter. *Career:* Lecturer in Music, Univ. of Exeter 1971–86, Head Music Dept 1983–86, Prof. of Music 1993–; Prof. of Music and Head Music Dept, Univ. Coll., Cork, Ireland 1986–93; mem. Royal Musical Asscn, Plainsong and Medieval Soc. (council mem.), Henry Bradshaw Soc. *Publications:* John Sheppard's Masses 1976, Oxford Anthology of Medieval Music 1977, The Use of Salisbury 1986–99, edns of English church music, gen. ed. of Antico Edition; contrib. to Early Music, Music and Letters, Musica Disciplina, Proceedings of the Royal Musical Association, Royal Musical Association Research Chronicle, Musical Times, Music Review, The Consort, BBC Radio 3, Journal of Theological Studies. *Honours:* Univ. Scholar at Birmingham 1967–70.

SANDSTRÖM, Sven-David; Swedish composer; b. 30 Oct. 1942, Motala; m. Gudrun Sandström. *Education:* Stockholm University, State College of Music with Lidholm, studied with Ligeti and Norgard. *Career:* joined faculty, State College of Music Stockholm 1980. *Compositions:* stage: Strong Like Death, Church opera, 1978; Hasta O Beloved Bride, chamber opera, 1978; Emperor Jones, music drama, 1980; Incidental Music for Strindberg's Dream Play, 1980; Ballet Den elfte gryningen, 1988; Music, ballet, 1995; The City, opera, 1998; Vocal: Pictures, 1969; Intrada, 1969; In the Meantime, 1970; Around a Line, 1971; Through and Through, 1972; Con tutta Forza, 1976; Clumination, 1977; Agitato, 1978; The Rest is Dross, 1980; Guitar Concerto, 1983; Invignings fanfar, 1988; Cello Concerto, 1989; Piano Concerto, 1990; Percussion Concerto, 1994; Concerto for recorder, harpsichord and strings, 1996; Soft Music for clarinet strings and percussion, 1996. Chamber: String Quartet, 1969; Mosaic for string trio, 1970; 6 Character Pieces, 1973; Metal, Metal for 4 percussionists, 1974; Utmost, premiered by Pierre Boulez, London 1975; Within for 8 trombones and percussion, 1979; Drums for timpani and 4 percussionists, 1980; Spring Music for percussion, 1997; Vocal: Inventions for 16 voices, 1969; Lamento, 1971; Birgitta-Music I, 1973; Expression, 1976; A Cradle Song/The Tiger, after Blake, 1978; Requiem, for the child victims of war and racism, 1979; Agnus Dei, 1980; Piano and organ music; Moses, Oratorio, 1997.

SANDVE, Kjell Magnus; Norwegian singer (tenor); b. 1957, Karmoy. *Education:* Oslo State Opera School. *Career:* sang at the Nationaltheater Weimar 1982–84, Norwegian National Opera at Oslo from 1983, with guest appearances at Copenhagen, Opéra Bastille as Hylas in Les Troyens, the Staatsoper Berlin as Belmonte 1989, and at Munich as Sifare in Mitridate 1990; other roles include Don Ottavio, Ferrando, Nemorino, Alfredo, Lensky and Nielsen's David; sang Verdi's Macduff at Oslo 2000. *Recordings include:* songs by Grieg.

SANTI, Nello; Italian conductor; b. 22 Sept. 1931, Adria, Rovigo. *Education:* Liceo Musicale in Padua, studied with Coltro and Pedrollo. *Career:* debut at Teatro Verdi, Padua 1951, Rigoletto; Conductor, Zürich Opera from 1958; Covent Garden debut 1960, with La Traviata; Vienna Staatsoper and Salzburg Festival debuts 1960; Metropolitan Opera 1962, Un Ballo in Maschera; regular appearances from 1976; La Scala, Milan 1971; Paris Opéra 1974; guest engagements in Berlin, Munich, Florence, Geneva, Lisbon and Madrid, in the operas of Rossini, Bellini, Donizetti, Verdi, Puccini and Mascagni; orchestral concerts with Orchestre National, Paris; RIAS, Berlin, and the Munich Philharmonic; New Philharmonia Orchestra and the London

Symphony; returned to Covent Garden 1982, La Fanciulla del West; conducted Aida in a new production by Vittorio Rossi; conducts regularly at the Metropolitan Opera House, New York, Arena di Verona and throughout Italy and Germany; Rigoletto at Verona 1997 and Nabucco at Zürich 1998; season 2003–04 included Barbiere di Siviglio, Nabucco, Tosca and Rigoletto with the Opera House of Zurich, Donizetti's Don Pasquale in Montecarlo, new productions of Bellini's I Capuleti e Montecci at the Opera of Rome and Verdi's Nabucco at the Summer Festival of Caracalla in Rome and a new production of Puccini's La Bohème at the Teatro San Carlo di Napoli; concert engagements included a summer concert with the Philharmonic Orchestra of Montecarlo, symphonic concerts with the Oslo Philharmonic Orchestra and further concerts with the NHK Symphony Orchestra in Tokyo. *Recordings:* Pagliacci; L'Amore dei Tre Re; Complete Verdi tenor arias, with Carlo Bergonzi; Aria recitals with Placido Domingo; Videos of Otello, La Bohème, Nabucco, Rigoletto, Andrea Chénier, Falstaff and the Verdi Requiem. *Honours:* Medallion de la Cité de Zürich, Commendatore of the Republic of Italy. *Current Management:* Robert Lombardo & Associates, 61 W 62nd Street, Suite 6F, New York, NY 10023, USA. *E-mail:* Robert@RobertLombardo.com. *Address:* Wildbachstrasse 77, 8008 Zürich, Switzerland (home).

SANTUNIONE, Orianna; singer (soprano); b. 1 Sept. 1934, Sassolo, Modena, Italy. *Education:* studied in Milan with Carmen Melis and Renato Pastorino. *Career:* after debut as Giordano's Fedora sang in Rome, Genoa, Bologna, Trieste, Naples, Parma and Palermo; Covent Garden, London 1965, as Amelia in Un Ballo in Maschera and Elisabeth de Valois; further appearances in Nice, Rouen, Turin, Venice, Munich, Hamburg, Amsterdam, Dallas, Philadelphia and Cincinnati; Verona Arena 1967–77; other roles include Desdemona, Elsa, Medea, Santuzza, Nedda, both Leonoras of Verdi, Mathilde in Guillaume Tell, Francesca da Rimini, Tosca, Madama Butterfly and Aida. *Recordings include:* Madame Sans-Gêne by Giordano, Pimmalione by Donizetti, Otello and Lohengrin (for Italian TV).

SAPAROVA-FISCHEROVA, Jitka; singer (soprano); b. 7 April 1964, Brno, Czechoslovakia; m. Miroslav Fischer 1991, one d. *Education:* High School of Musical Art. *Career:* debut in Mozart's Zauberflöte; soloist of chamber orchestra, baroque and renaissance music, Musica Aeterna 1985–86; soloist of Slovak National Theatre Opera from 1986; operas include Faust, Le nozze di Figaro, Rigoletto, Suor Angelica, Carmen; mem. Asscn of Slovak Theatres. *Recordings:* Rigoletto, La Sonnambula. *Honours:* first prize M. Schneider Trnaussee Competition 1985, laureate Antonín Dvořák Singing Competition.

SARADJIAN, Vagram; Armenian cellist; *Professor of Cello, Moores School of Music, University of Houston;* b. 15 July 1948, Yerevan. *Career:* debut in Yerevan 1956; US debut, Carnegie Hall 1994; recitals performed around the world in halls including Gaveau in Paris, La Scala in Milan, Victoria Hall in Geneva, Musikverein in Vienna, Teatro Colón Buenos Aires, Carnegie Hall in New York, Great Hall of the Moscow Conservatory, Leningrad Philharmonic Hall; int. tours; premiered works by composers including Alexander Tchaikovsky, Gia Kancheli, Karen Khachaturian; appearances include Valery Gergiev's Stars of the White Nights Festival in St Petersburg; extensive tour of Argentina and Uruguay; extensive European tour with Maxim Vengerov and Vag Papian; performances in Chicago, Los Angeles, Philadelphia, tours of Russia, Switzerland, Poland and Germany; teacher, Connecticut Coll., New London, Conn. and Oberlin Conservatory, Oberlin, OH; Faculty mem., Aaron Copland School of Music, Queens Coll., CUNY and Purchase Conservatory, State Univ. of NY; currently Prof. of Cello, Moores School of Music, Univ. of Houston, Tex. *Recordings:* Karen Khachaturian Cello Concerto (USSR Symphony Orchestra), Saint-Saëns: Concerto No. 1, Tchaikovsky Rococo Variations, Dvořák's Concerto in B Minor, Op. 104 (Moscow Philharmonic), Karen Khachaturian: Sonata for cello and piano, Eduard Mirzoian: Sonata for cello and piano. *Honours:* Winner Russian Nat. Competition aged 18, Fourth Prize, Tchaikovsky Int. Competition, Moscow 1970, Gold Medal, Geneva Int. Cello Competition, Switzerland 1975, Int. Music Festivals in Sofia 1976, Prague 1980, First Prize, Aram Khachaturian Int. Music Awards, New York 1990. *Address:* 120 School of Music Bldg, University of Houston, Houston, TX 77204-4017, USA (office). *E-mail:* cello@uh.edu (office).

SARASTE, Jukka-Pekka; Finnish conductor; b. 22 April 1956, Heinola; m. Marja-Lisa Ollila; three s. one d. *Education:* Sibelius Acad. *Career:* debut with Helsinki Philharmonic 1980; Prin. Conductor Scottish Chamber Orchestra 1987–91; Prin. Conductor and Music Dir Finnish Radio Symphony Orchestra 1987–2001, now Conductor Laureate; Music Dir Toronto Symphony Orchestra 1994–2001; Prin. Guest Conductor BBC Symphony Orchestra 2002–05; Chief Conductor and Music Dir Oslo Philharmonic Orchestra 2006–13, Conductor Laureate 2013–; Artistic Adviser, Lahti Symphony Orchestra 2008–11, Artistic Dir Lahti Sibelius Festival 2008–11; Chief Conductor WDR Symphony Orchestra, Cologne 2010–; has been guest conductor with Boston Symphony Orchestra, Cleveland Orchestra, San Francisco Orchestra, Frankfurt Radio Orchestra, NY Philharmonic Orchestra, London Philharmonic Orchestra, Orchestre Philharmonique de Radio France, BBC Symphony Orchestra, Munich Philharmonic Orchestra; has toured Japan, Hong Kong, Taiwan, Germany, USA, Canary Islands Festival; Artistic Adviser, Finnish Chamber Orchestra. *Recordings include:* complete Sibelius symphonies 1995 (with Finnish Radio Symphony Orchestra), Mussorgsky (with Toronto Symphony Orchestra), Nielsen Symphonies 4&5 (with Finnish Radio Symphony Orchestra), Romeo and Juliet Suite (Prokofiev). *Honours:* Dr hc (Univ. of York); Pro Finlandia Prize, Sibelius Medal, Finnish State Prize for Music. *Current Management:* Lothar Schacke, KünstlerSekretariat am Gasteig, Montgelasstrasse 2, 81679 Munich, Germany. *Telephone:* (89) 4448879–0. *E-mail:* lothar.schacke@ks-gasteig.de. *Website:* jukkapekkasaraste.com.

SARBU, Eugene; Romanian violinist; b. 6 Sept. 1950, Pietrari, nr. Rimnicu Vilcea. *Education:* studied in Bucharest and Parism Curtis Institute, Philadelphia with Ivan Galamian, Juilliard, New York, studied with Nathan Milstein in Zürich. *Career:* debut solo appearance aged six; won National Festival of Music Award in Bucharest, 1958; regular solo recitals and concerts in England; Promenade Concert debut, 1982; performances in USA, Europe, Australia and South America; Far East tour 1987–88, with the New Japan Philharmonic in Tokyo; plays a Cremonese Violin by Tomasso Balestieri made in 1756. *Recordings:* Sibelius Concerto (with the Hallé Orchestra) 1980, Vivaldi's Four Seasons and Mozart Concertos (with European Master Orchestra) 1988. *Honours:* winner Paganini and Carl Flesch Competitions 1978, George Enescu Medal 1995. *Address:* c/o Hispania Clásica SL, Los Madrazo 16 bajo, 28014 Madrid, Spain.

SARDI, Ivan; singer (bass); b. 7 July 1930, Budapest, Hungary. *Education:* Martini Conservatory Bologna with Antonio Mekandri. *Career:* debut at Brescia 1951, as Padre Guardiano in La Forza del Destino; sang in Naples, Bologna, Genoa, Trieste and Catania, as Mozart's Masetto and Bartolo and in Operas by Verdi; Glyndebourne 1956, as Don Alfonso; further appearances in Florence, Milan and Lisbon; Staatsoper Munich 1956–61; mem., Deutsche Oper Berlin from 1961; concerts in Munich, Hamburg, Vienna and elsewhere in Europe; sang Schigolch in Lulu at Dresden 1992. *Recordings:* Don Giovanni, Le nozze di Figaro, Verdi Requiem, Der junge Lord by Henze, Sparafucile in Rigoletto, Guillaume Tell.

SARFATY, Regina; singer (mezzo-soprano); b. 1932, Rochester, NY, USA. *Education:* Juilliard School, New York. *Career:* sang with New Mexico Opera from 1948; Santa Fe Opera from 1957, notably in the 1968 US premiere of The Bassarids by Henze; New York City Opera from 1958, as Cenerentola, Maria Golovin in the opera by Menotti, Jocasta (Oedipus Rex) and Dorabella; Frankfurt Opera from 1963, as Carmen and Octavian; sang Octavian at Glyndebourne 1960, and returned in 1984, as Adelaide in Arabella; sang Mme de Croissy in Dialogues des Carmélites at Baltimore 1984; mem., Zürich Opera, notably as the Countess Geschwitz in Lulu and in the premiere of Die Erretung Thebens by Kelterborn 1963. *Recordings:* excerpts from Die Walküre, conducted by Stokowski, The Rake's Progress, conducted by Stravinsky, Choral Symphony, conducted by Bernstein.

SARGENT, (Donald) Anthony, MA (Oxon.), FRSA; British arts manager; *General Director, The Sage Gateshead and North Music Trust;* b. 18 Dec. 1949, s. of Sir Donald Sargent, KBE, CB and Mary Raven; m. 1st Sara Gilford 1978 (divorced); m. 2nd Caroline Gant 1986; one d. *Education:* King's School, Canterbury, Oriel Coll., Oxford, Magdalen Coll., Oxford, Christ Church, Oxford. *Career:* numerous posts with BBC TV and radio 1974–86, including Man. Concert Planning 1982–86, Partnerships and Programme Devt Man. BBC Music Live 1999–2000; Artistic Projects Dir, South Bank Centre, London 1986–89; Head of Arts, Birmingham City Council 1989–99; Gen. Dir The Sage Gateshead and North Music Trust 2000–. *Publications:* several articles. *Honours:* Hon. Fellow, Birmingham Conservatoire 1999, Univ. of Sunderland 2005. *Address:* The Sage Gateshead, St Mary's Square, Gateshead Quays, Gateshead, NE8 2JR, England (office). *Telephone:* (191) 443-4601 (office). *E-mail:* anthony.sargent@thesagegateshead.org (office). *Website:* www .thesagegateshead.org (office).

SARGON, Simon A., BA, MS; American composer and pianist; *Meadows Distinguished Professor of Composition, Southern Methodist University;* b. 6 April 1938, Mumbai, India; m. Bonnie Glasgow 1961; one d. *Education:* Brandeis Univ., Juilliard School. *Career:* debut at Carnegie Hall with Jennie Tourel 1963; musical staff, New York City Opera 1960; Assoc. Conductor, Concert Opera 1962–68; pianist for concerts of Jennie Tourel 1963–71; Faculty mem. Juilliard School 1967–69; Chair of Voice, Rubin Acad., Jerusalem, Israel 1971–74; Faculty, Hebrew Univ., Jerusalem 1973–74; Dir of Music, Temple Emanu-El 1974–2001; Faculty, Southern Methodist Univ. 1983–, Meadows Distinguished Prof. of Composition 2009–; Judge, Nat. Composition Competition, Guild of Temple Musicians 1993, 1995, 2001, 2004, 2007; Judge, Distinguished Composer of the Year Award, Music Teachers' Nat. Asscn 2007. *Compositions:* Elul Midnight 1975, Bitter for Sweet 1982, Milestones 1983, After the Vietnam War 1985, Symphony No. 1: Holocaust 1985, Psalms of Qumram 1986, Questings 1990, Deep Ellum Nights 1991, Reb Mendele 1992, Waves of the Sea 1992, Legacy Trio 1993, Divertimento 1994, Klezmuzik 1995, The Singing Violin 1995, Implosions 1996, Moodswings 1997, Tapestries 1997, The Story of Ruth 2000, The Search Unending 2000, Janus Quartet 2001, Letters from Amherst 2002, Rap Sessions 2002, Vermeer Portraits 2002, The Town Musicians of Bremen 2003, Chagall Windows 2004, Homage to Hafiz 2004, Haas Trio 2005, The World of Anatevka 2005, Toward the Light 2006, Rapunzel 2006, Lift Off 2007, Fantasy on 'The Miller's Tears' 2008, Out of the Depths 2009, Horn Sonata 2010. *Television:* The Night of the Headless Horseman 1999, The Prophecies of Israel 2003. *Recordings:* Music for French Horn and Piano, Huntsman, What Quarry, Deep Ellum Nights, Shema, A Clear Midnight, Flame of the Lord, Questings, Divertimento for Piano. *Publications:* A Clear Midnight, A Voice Called, Ash un Flamen, At Grandfather's Knee, At Grandmother's Knee, Before the Ark, Bitter for Sweet, Break Forth, Sing Praise, Christmas in Black, Dusting Around with Scott's Rag, Psalm 150, Psalm 8, Flame of the Lord, Haas Trio, Homage to

Hafiz, Huntsman, What Quarry?, Intimations of Mortality, Jump Back, KlezMuzik, Let It Be You, Lord Make Me to Know My End, The Lord is my Strength, Loveliest of Trees, Patterns in Blue, Praise Ye the Lord, Psalm 1, The Queen's Consort, Reb Mendele, Shemà, Sing God's Praise, Sunflowers, Take Five, Waves of the Sea, Witness for my Lord. *Honours:* Hon. mem. American Conf. of Cantors 2003; Meadows Foundation Distinguished Prof. Award 2008–09, Sam Taylor Fellowship Award 2008–09; comms: Voices of Change 2007, Dallas Symphony Orchestra 2004, 2005, Yale Univ. 1999, Finalist, Nat. Opera Asscn Competition 1997, First Prize, Nat. Asscn of Teachers of Singing Competition 1993. *Telephone:* (214) 768-2241 (office); (214) 526-8084 (home). *E-mail:* ssargon@aol.com (home); ssargon@smu.edu (office). *Website:* www.simonsargon.com.

SÁRI, József; Hungarian composer; b. 23 June 1935, Lenti; m.; two d. *Education:* Ferenc Liszt Acad. of Music, Budapest. *Career:* tutor, Music School, Budapest 1962–71; freelance composer, Germany 1971–84; Teacher of Music Theory, F. Liszt Acad. 1984, Dir of Dept 1992; adviser at Hungarian Radio 1997; Composer's Portrait broadcast by three major radio stations, Germany 1992. *Compositions:* Fossils 1974, String Quartet 1975, Alienated Quotations for two pianos 1982, Symbols 1978, Attributes 1990, Questions for Hillel 1996, Concertino 1992–95, Zenith 1995, Parallel Lines which Cross before the Infinite, for flute and strings 1997, Con Spirito for orchestra 1998; Sonnenfinsternis (opera) 2000, Der Hutmacher (opera) 2008. *Recordings:* Time Mill; Farewell to Glenn Gould; Four Inventions; Fossils; Legend; complete works for flute; works for dulcimer and brass instruments. *Honours:* Erkel Prize, 1991; Bartók Pásztory Prize, 1995; Artist of Merit, 1998, Kossuth Prize 2009. *Address:* 2011, Budakalasz, Szent Laszlo 41, Hungary. *Website:* www.bmc.hu/sari.

SARICH, Paul, BSc; composer and percussionist; b. 18 Sept. 1951, Wellington, New Zealand. *Education:* Victoria Univ. of Wellington, studied with Leonard Salzedo and James Blades. *Career:* percussionist with various Australian bands and orchestras 1973–93; Lecturer, Victoria Coll. of the Arts 1991–; New Notations, London 1994–95. *Compositions:* Fantasia in G Minor for violin 1981, Sonata for side drum and three percussion 1981, Fantasia on a Fragment of Martinů for orchestra 1982, Chaconne in B Flat for tuba 1986, Concerto for bass trombone and orchestra 1986, Antiphons for two percussion 1986, Divertimento for viola, cello, double bass and percussion 1986, Five in the Afternoon for trumpet, keyboards and percussion 1986, Dance Suite for three tubas 1987, Concerto da Camera for percussion and strings 1988, Music for tubes and sticks 1988, Songs of Light and Shade for soprano and ensemble 1989, Concerto Pieces for timpani and piano 1990, Percussion Mass 1991, The Illusionist for bass and piano 1992, Fiesta for soprano, timpani, four percussion and flamenco dancers 1993, Essay for brass quintet and eight tubas 1993, Austranimalia for chorus, bass, percussion and piano 1994, Invocation and Dance for saxophone and clarinet trio 1994, Three Neruda Love Songs for soprano and ensemble 1994.

SARROCA, Suzanne; singer (soprano); b. 21 April 1927, Carcassonne, France. *Education:* Toulouse Conservatoire. *Career:* debut at Carcassonne 1949, as Massenet's Charlotte; sang Carmen in Brussels 1951; Paris Opéra and Opéra-Comique from 1952, as Tosca, Rezia, Marina (Boris Godunov), Aida, Marguerite in La Damnation de Faust, Leonore and Octavian 1957, 1966; also sang in Les Indes Galantes by Rameau; guest appearances in Marseille 1961 (Donna Anna), Rome 1965 (Elisabeth de Valois), and in Buenos Aires, Geneva, New York, London, Lisbon, Strasbourg and Toulouse; Salzburg Festival 1968, in Cavalieri's La Rappresentazione di Anima e di Corpo; further engagements in Rio de Janeiro, Hamburg and Vienna; modern repertoire included La Voix Humaine by Poulenc and Schoenberg's Erwartung; Dir, Centre d'art Lyrique at Strasbourg 1983–85.

SASAKI, Ken; pianist; b. 14 Sept. 1943, Sendai, Miyagi, Japan. *Education:* Univ. of Arts, Tokyo, Warsaw Conservatoire, masterclasses of Vlado Perlemuter in Paris, Danuta Lewandowska in Warsaw. *Career:* has given many concerts in France, Poland, The Netherlands, Switzerland, Austria, Germany, Japan; British debut 1972, at the Wigmore Hall; coast-to-coast tour of the USA 1979; QEH, London 1986 playing Bach's 1st Partita, Gaspard de la Nuit and Chopin's 2nd Sonata; further appearances with the Warsaw Chamber Orchestra and the Berlin Octet; other repertory includes concertos by Bach (D minor) and Beethoven (C minor and G major); Mozart K449 and K466; Chopin No. 1 and Schumann; Ravel in G; Rachmaninov Nos 1 and 3; Mozart Sonatas K310, K311; Chopin Sonatas, Etudes Ballades, Nocturnes, Preludes and Polonaise; Schumann Fantasie Op 17, Fantasiestücke, Etudes Symphoniques and Kreisleriana; Ravel Miroirs and Le Tombeau de Couperin; Debussy Images and Suite Bergamasque; Prokofiev 3rd and 7th Sonatas and Scriabin Etudes; Scarlatti Sonatas. *Recordings include:* Chopin Etudes. *Honours:* Stefanie Niekrasz Prize 1984.

SASS, Sylvia; Hungarian singer (soprano); b. 21 July 1951, Budapest. *Education:* Liszt Academy, Budapest with Ferenc Revhegyi. *Career:* debut at Budapest State Opera 1971, as Frasquita in Carmen; first major role as Gutrune, 1972; sang Giselda in I Lombardi, 1973 and repeated the role at Covent Garden, 1976; Sofia 1972, Violetta (also at Aix-en-Provence 1976); Scottish Opera debut 1975, Desdemona; at the Budapest Opera 1977, sang in the premiere of Mózes by Zsolt Durkó; Metropolitan Opera 1977, Tosca; guest engagements at the State Operas of Hamburg and Munich and at the Paris Opéra and La Scala Milan; other roles include Norma, Penelope (Il Ritorno d'Ulisse), Tatiana, Elvira (Ernani), Alceste, Odabella (Attila), Medea,

Santuzza, Elisabeth de Valois, Lady Macbeth, Donna Elvira and Donna Anna, Countess Almaviva, Mimi, Manon Lescaut, Turandot, Adriana Lecouvreur, Nedda (Pagliacci), Juliette and Marguerite by Gounod, and Salome (Budapest 1989); has sung Bartók's Judith on BBC television and in Montpellier and Metz, 1989; many concert performances in music by Strauss and Wagner; modern repertoire includes Sogno di un Tramonto d'Autunno by Malipiero; Wigmore Hall debut 1979, in songs by Strauss and Liszt; invited to return for András Schiff's Beethoven-Bartók series 1990; season 1993, as Adriana Lecouvreur at Budapest. *Recordings include:* Don Giovanni, Arias by Puccini and Verdi, Liszt and Bartók songs, Verdi Stiffelio, Il Trittico, Duke Bluebeard's Castle by Bartók, Wagner Wesendonck Lieder, Vier Letzte Lieder by Strauss, Medea, Ernani, I Lombards, Macbeth, Attila, Faust, Mózes by Durkó, Erkel's Hunyadi László.

SASSON, Deborah; singer (soprano); b. 1955, Boston, MA, USA; m. Peter Hofmann 1983 (divorced 1990). *Education:* Oberlin Coll. with Ellen Repp and Helen Hodam, New England Conservatory, Boston with Gladys Miller. *Career:* debut at Hamburg Staatsoper 1979, as Maria in West Side Story; sang at the Stadttheater Aachen 1979–81; guest appearances in Hamburg, Berlin, Venice and San Francisco; sang at the Bayreuth Festival from 1982; other roles include Norina, Adina, Gilda, Rosina, Despina and Zerlina. *Recordings include:* arias and duets with Peter Hofmann, Mahler's 8th Symphony (from Tanglewood).

SATO, Shunske; Japanese violinist; b. 1984, Tokyo. *Education:* Juilliard School, New York, with Dorothy DeLay from 1995. *Career:* debut at Philadelphia Orchestra 1994; appearances with the St Petersburg Philharmonic under Yuri Temirkanov, Nat. Symphony Orchestra, and with Christopher Hogwood, Baltimore and Minnesota Orchestras, and elsewhere in USA; Season 2000–01 with the Mariinsky Orchestra under Gergiev, Beethoven Concerto at the Bonn Festival, European tour with the St Petersburg Symphony Orchestra, Munich Radio Orchestra under Zdenek Macal; Swiss debut recital in Basle, and Italian concert with Riccardo Muti. *Address:* c/o Musicaglotz, 11, rue Le Verrier, 75006 Paris, France.

SATOH, Somei; Japanese composer; b. 19 Jan. 1949, Sendai. *Education:* studied in Japan. *Career:* freelance composer in advanced idioms, including non-Western techniques and instruments. *Compositions include:* Hymn for the Sun for two pianos and tape delay 1975, Cosmic Womb 1975, Incarnation I and II 1977–78, The Heavenly Spheres are Illuminated by Light for soprano, piano and percussion 1979, Birds in Warped Time I and II 1980, Lyra for two harps, percussion and strings 1980, Sumeru I and II 1982, 1985, A Journey Through Sacred Time 1983, Naohi for piano 1983, Hikari for trumpet and piano 1986, Shirasagi for string quartet 1987, Stabat Mater for soprano and chorus 1987, A Gate into Infinity for violin, piano and percussion 1988, Homa for soprano and string quartet 1988, Towards the Night for strings 1991, Kami No Miuri for mezzo and seven instruments 1991, Burning Meditation for baritone, harp, tubular bells and string quartet 1993, Lanzarote for soprano saxophone and piano 1993.

SAUER, Martin; German sound engineer and producer; *Partner, Teldex Studio Berlin;* b. 1958, Berlin. *Education:* Berlin Univ. of the Arts. *Career:* sound engineer, Tonstudio van Geest, Heidelberg 1982–92; broadcast producer, Radio France; producer Erato label 1995–96, Artistic Dir 1996–98; Man. Dir Teldec record co., Hamburg 1998–2001; producer Harmonia Mundi France 2002–; f. partner and freelance producer Teldex Studio Berlin 2002–; works with conductors including Daniel Barenboim, Nikolaus Harnoncourt, Kent Nagano and Réné Jacobs. *Honours:* five Gramophone awards, numerous other prizes. *Address:* Teldex Studio Berlin, Finckensteinallee 36, 12205 Berlin, Germany (office). *Telephone:* (30) 8439010 (office). *Fax:* (30) 84390149 (office). *E-mail:* info@teldexstudio.de (office). *Website:* www.teldexstudio.de (office).

SAUER, Ralph; American trombonist; b. Philadelphia, Pa. *Education:* Eastman School of Music with Emory Remington. *Career:* Prin. Trombonist, Toronto Symphony Orchestra 1968–74, also Prin. Trombonist, Canadian Opera Co. and CBC; Prin. Trombonist, Los Angeles Philharmonic 1974–2006; Los Angeles Philharmonic concerto debut 1979; Faculty mem. Music Acad. of the West; Visiting Prof., Arizona State Univ.; fmr Faculty mem. Univ. of Toronto; fmr Visiting Prof., Eastman School of Music; fmr Instructor, New World Symphony, Miami and Int. Brass Festival, Melbourne, Australia; Founding-mem. Summit Brass (brass ensemble). *Recordings include:* Orchestral Excerpts for Trombone 1994, Ralph Sauer Plays Handel, Telemann, Haydn 1995, OrchestraPro II: Trombone 2008. *Honours:* Int. Trombone Asscn Award 2011. *Address:* Music Academy of the West, 1070 Fairway Road, Santa Barbara, CA 93108-2899, USA (office). *Telephone:* (805) 969-4726 (office). *Website:* www.musicacademy.org (office).

SAUNDERS, Christopher; singer (tenor); b. 1971, Qld, Australia. *Education:* Univ. of Queensland, Guildhall School, London, England. *Career:* appearances with Opera Queensland from 1993, including Ernesto in Don Pasquale and Aufidio in the local premiere of Mozart's Lucio Silla; other roles include Jacquino for English Touring Opera, Tobias in Sweeney Todd for Opera North, Ferrando in Così fan tutte, and Jupiter in Handel's Semele; concerts include Britten's Serenade at the Barbican Hall and Britten's St Nicolas. *Honours:* The Hammond Prize, Qld.

SAUNDERS, Jenny; singer (soprano); b. 1970, England. *Education:* Royal Acad. of Music with Marjorie Thomas, studied with Mary Thomas. *Career:*

concerts include Mozart's C Minor Mass in Canterbury Cathedral, Mendelssohn's Elijah in Scotland, the Christmas Oratorio in Oslo and the Brahms Requiem at the St Endellion Easter Festival; further engagements with Messiah and Carmina Burana at the Albert Hall, Gounod's St Cecilia Mass and the Fauré Requiem at the Festival Hall and Mendelssohn's Midsummer Night's Dream with the Acad. of St Martin-in-the-Fields; appearances with the Opera Company as Helen in Mefistofele and Mozart's Barabarina and Susanna; season 1996–97 as Zerlina for Opera East, in Dido and Aeneas at Covent Garden and The Fairy Queen on tour to Spain and Greece; Despina for Country Opera and Nannetta for Palace Opera; 1997 concerts at St John's Smith Square (Exsultate Jubilate and St Matthew Passion) St Paul's Cathedral (Vivaldi's Gloria) and Wells Cathedral (Haydn's Creation); Papagena with Opera Factory; season 1998 with the Sandman and Dew Fairy in Hansel and Gretel for Palace Opera. *Honours:* winner soprano section Great Grimsby International Singers Competition 1992.

SAUNDERS, Rebecca; British composer; b. 19 Dec. 1967, London. *Education:* studied with Wolfgang Rihm at Musikhochschule Karlsruhe, and Nigel Osborne at Univ. of Edinburgh. *Career:* freelance composer; Resident Artist, Dortmund Konzerthaus 2005–06; Composer-in-Residence, Staatskapelle Dresden 2009–10. *Compositions include:* Trio 1991, Behind the Velvet Curtain for trumpet, piano, harp and cello 1992, Mirror, mirror on the wall 1994, The Under-Side of Green 1994, Crimson – Molly's Song 1 1995, Into the Blue for clarinet, bassoon, percussion, piano, cello and double bass 1996, G and E on A 1997, Duo 1996, Two Pieces based on Molly Bloom's Monologue, from Ulysses 1996, String Quartet for double bass 1998, Quartet for Clarinet, Accordion, Double Bass and Piano 1998, Dichroic Seventeen 1998, Cinnabar for ensemble 1999, Duo for viola and percussion 1999, Duo Four: Two Exposures 2001, In Chroma 2003, Insideout 2003, Vermillion 2004, Stirrings Still I 2008, Stirrings Still II (Royal Philharmonic Soc. Award for Best Chamber-Scale Composition) 2008, Murmurs 2009, Stasis 2011, Still, concerto for violin 2011, Ire, concerto for cello, strings and percussion 2012, fletch for string quartet (Arditti Quartet commission) 2012. *Honours:* prizewinner Berlin Acad. of Art 1995, Siemens Foundation Composer Prize 1996, Busoni Förderpreis, Paul Hindemith Prize, GEMA Deutscher Musikautorenpreis 2010. *Address:* c/o Edition Peters, Hinrichsen House, 10–12 Baches Street, London, N1 6DN, England. *Website:* www.editionpeters.com (office).

SAUTER, Lily; singer; b. 16 Nov. 1934, Zürich, Switzerland. *Education:* studied in Milan and Zürich. *Career:* sang at the Deutsche Oper am Rhein Düsseldorf 1961–64; Zürich Opera 1965–66; Stuttgart Staatsoper 1964–83; guest appearances at the State Operas of Hamburg and Munich, Berlin, Frankfurt, Barcelona, Venice, Milan, Genoa and Edinburgh; roles have included Mozart's Susanna, Blondchen and Despina, Rosina, Martha, Norina, Adina, Marzelline, Lortzing's Gretchen and Marie, Musetta, Nannetta, Sophie in Der Rosenkavalier, Aennchen, and Regina in Mathis der Maler; television appearances in Germany and Switzerland.

SAVAGE, Stephen Leon; pianist, conductor and teacher; b. 26 April 1942, Hertford, England; two s. *Education:* Vienna Akademie with Bruno Seidlhofer, Royal Coll. of Music with Cyril Smith. *Career:* debut at Wigmore Hall, London 1966; concerts on radio, television in England, Canada, Australia, Japan; concertos with Boult, A. Davis, Zollman and others, including first Australasian performance, Lutoslawski Concerto 1989; Dir, Brisbane Tippett Festival 1990; dedicatee of major works by Justin Connolly and Roger Smalley; Prof. of Piano and Co-Dir, 20th-Century Ensemble, Royal Coll. of Music 1967–81; Artistic Dir and Conductor, Griffith Univ. Ensemble, Brisbane, Australia; Master Teacher to Australian Nat. Acad. of Music, Melbourne; frequent residencies include Univs of Adelaide, Toronto, Hong Kong, Guildhall School of Music, Royal Acad. of Music, Royal Coll. of Music (Hon. Assoc. Prof.); noted for performances of classical repertoire and 20th-century music, including important first performances. *Recordings:* Roger Smalley, Accord for two pianos (with the composer), Tippett Sonatas 1 and 3, Beethoven Sonatas op 109, 110, 111. *Honours:* Dannreuther Prize 1964, Hopkinson Medal Worshipful Co. of Musicians 1965.

SAVALL, Jordi; Spanish musician (viola da gamba) and conductor; b. 1 Aug. 1941, Igualada, Barcelona; m. Montserrat Figueras (died 2011). *Education:* Barcelona Conservatory of Music and Schola Cantorum Basiliensis, Switzerland. *Career:* early collaborations with Ars Musica mid-1960s; teacher at Schola Cantorum Basiliensis from 1973; formed Hespèrion XX 1974; returned to Barcelona 1988; formed La Capela Reial de Catalunya 1988; created Le Concert des Nations 1989; many collaborations, including John Williams, Rafael Puyana, Michel Piguet, Stephen Preston, Trevor Pinnock, Ton Koopman, Christophe Coin, Christopher Hogwood; f. own label Alia Vox 1998, more than 70 titles published; EU Amb. for Cultural Dialogue 2008; UNESCO Amb. – Artists of Peace 2009. *Recordings include:* solo: Del Romànic Al Renaixement 1968, Recercadas Del Tratado De Glosas 1970, Canti amorosi 1975, François Couperin: Pièces De Viole 1976, Marin Marais: Pièces De Viole 1976, Sainte-Colombe: Concerts A Deux Violes Esgales 1976, Marin Marais: Pièces De Viole Du Quatrième Livre 1977, De Mr Demachy: Pièces De Viole 1977, The Punckes Delight And Other 17th Century English Music For Viol and Keyboard 1978, Antoine Forqueray: Pièces De Viole 1978, J. S. Bach: 3 Sonaten Für Viola Da Gamba Und Cembalo 1978, Lessons For The Lyra Viol 1980, Tobias Hume: Musical Humors 1983; with Hespèrion XX: Weltiche Musik Im Christlichen Und Jüdischen Spanien 1976, Canciones Y Danzas De España: Songs And Dances From The Time Of Cervantes 1977, Musicque De

Loye 1978, Cansós De Trobairitz 1978, El Barroco Español 1978, Scheidt: Ludi Musici 1978, Music From The Armada Years 1978, Libre Vermell De Montserrat 1979, Battaglie E Lamenti Schlacht Und Klage 1982, Couperin: Les Nations 1983, Brade: Consort Music 1983, Viva Rey Ferrando 1984, Hume: Poeticall Musicke 1985, Couperin: Les Apothéoses 1985, J. S. Bach: Die Kunst Der Fuge 1985, A. de Cabezón 1985, Johann Hermann Schein: Banchetto Musicale 1985, Harmmerschmidt: Vier Suiten Aus Erster Fleiss 1987, Ensaladas 1987, Eustache Du Caurroy: XXIII Fantasies 1988, Dowland: Lachrimae Or Seven Teares 1988, Juan del Enzina: Romances And Villancicos 1988, Tye: Lawdes Deo, Complete Consort Musicke 1989, Rosenmüller: Sonata Da Camera And Sinfonie 1989, Jenkins: Consort Music In Six Parts 1991, J. S. Bach: The Four Overtures 1991, Lope de Vega: Intermedios Del Barroco Hispánico 1991, J. S. Bach: The Brandenburg Concertos 1991, El Cancionero De Palacio 1992, El Cancionero De La Colombina 1992, Guerrero: Sacrae Cantiones 1993, Victoria: Cantica Beatae Virginis 1992, Folias And Canarios 1994, Locke: Consort Of Four Parts 1994, Jeanne La Pucelle 1994, Purcell: Fantasias For The Viol 1995, Scheidt: Ludi Musici 1997, Cabanilles 1644–1712 1998, William Lawes 1602–1645: Consort Sets in Five And Six Parts 2002, Istanbul: Dimitrie Cantemir 2009; with Le Concert des Nations: Marc-Antoine Charpentier: Canticum Ad Beatam Virginem Mariam 1989, Haydn: Seven Last Words Of Our Savior On The Cross 1991, Mozart: Requiem 1992, Vicent Martin I Soler: Una Cosa Rara 1992, Handel: Water Music/Music For The Royal Fireworks 1993, Marais: Alcione: Suites Des Airs À Jouer 1994, Arriaga: Symphony In D 1995, Beethoven: Symphony No. 3 1997, Purcell: The Fairy Queen/Prophetess 1997, Dinastia Borja with Hespèrion XXI (Grammy Award for Best Small Ensemble Performance) 2011, Rameau: L'Orchestre de Louis XV (Int. Classical Music Award for Best Baroque Instrumental Recording 2012) 2011. *Honours:* Officer, Ordre des Arts et des Lettres 1988; Grand Prix de l' Acad. du Disque Lyrique 1990, Generalitat de Catalunya Creu de Sant Jordi Award 1990, Medalla d'Or Parlament de Catalunya 2003, Prix Nat. de la Culture 2009, Léonie Sonning Music Prize 2012, York Early Music Festival Lifetime Achievement Award 2012. *Current Management:* c/o Fundació CIMA, Camí de la Font, 08193 Bellaterra, Spain. *Telephone:* (93) 594-47-60. *Fax:* (93) 594-47-70. *E-mail:* info@fundaciocima.org. *Website:* www .fundaciocima.org. *Address:* Alia Vox, Avinguda Bartomeu 11, 08193 Bellaterra, Spain (office). *E-mail:* aliavox@alia-vox.com (office). *Website:* www.alia-vox.com (office).

SAVASKAN, Sinan Carter, BA, MMus, PhD; British composer, conductor and teacher; *Head of Department for Academic Music, Westminster School;* b. 11 Aug. 1954; m. Sarah Carter; two s. two d. *Education:* Univ. of York, Univ. of Surrey, Univ. of London, Keele Univ., Middlesex, Chiswick Music Centre. *Career:* composer of over 50 orchestral, chamber and performing arts-related pieces; conductor and music dir, London-based ensembles, including Contemporary Arts Ensemble, Battersea Orchestra; Head, Dept for Academic Music, Westminster School, London; works featured at the 2002 International Rostrum of Composers, Paris; mem. Exec. Cttee British Acad. of Composers and Songwriters, PRS, MCPS. *Compositions:* over 50 works including String Quartet No. 3: Panic 1990, Anthems for the Sun No. 2 for organ 1994, Three Dances for chamber orchestra (BBC Philharmonic Forum Award) 1997, Symphony No. 2 1997, Symphony No. 3 1998, Symphony No. 4 2005. *Recordings:* Intercontinental Communication Disaster 1877, String Study No. 3. *Honours:* Dio Award (ACGB) 1985, BBC Symphony Orchestra Commission 1997, winner Foundation for Contemporary Performance Arts, USA 1998. *Address:* 27 Dorchester Court, London, SE24 9QX, England (home). *Website:* www.savaskan.org.

SAVIDGE, Peter; British singer (baritone); b. 1952, Essex, England. *Education:* Univ. of Cambridge. *Career:* debut at English Music Theatre, 1976, as Papageno; appearances with Opera North as Mozart's Count, Storch in Intermezzo, Don Giovanni, Valentin, Nardo in La finta giardiniera, Sharpless (Butterfly), Eugene Onegin; Welsh National Opera as Papageno, Marcello, Danilo, and Rossini's Figaro; Lescaut in Massenet's Manon, Ned Keene in Peter Grimes and the Baron in Massenet's Chérubin at Covent Garden, 1994; Seven baritone roles in Death in Venice at Nancy and Liège; Belcore (L'Elisir d'amore) at Opéra Comique, Paris; Ned Keene at Genoa, Strasbourg and Cologne; Season 1999–2000 world premiere of A Friend of the People by Horne at Scottish Opera; Count at Garsington; L'Anima del Filosofo by Haydn at Lausanne; Season 2000–01, title role in world premiere of Abélard et Heloïse for Strasbourg and Paris; 2003: Chnegos in Punch and Judy; Birtwistle in Porto; Gunther in Götterdämmerung for Scottish Opera and at Edinburgh Festival; Sang Szymanowski's Stabat Mater with Rotterdam Philharmonic, under Valerie Gergier, 2003. *Recordings include:* Britten's Albert Herring and Handel's Hercules; Mr Coyle in Channel 4's television film of Britten's Owen Wingrave, 2001; Bantock songs with David Owen Norris. *Current Management:* Musicmakers International Artists Representation, Tailor House, 63–65 High Street, Whitwell, Hertfordshire SG4 8AH, England. *Telephone:* (1438) 871708. *Fax:* (1438) 871777. *E-mail:* musicmakers@compuserve.com. *Website:* www.operauk.com. *Address:* 1 The Bank, Little Compton, Moreton-in-Marsh, Gloucestershire GL56 0RX, England (home).

SAVOVA, Galina; singer (soprano); b. 1945, Sofia, Bulgaria. *Career:* sang first at the Sofia Opera before an international career at the opera houses of Rome, Naples, Karlsruhe and Bologna; Metropolitan Opera debut 1982, as Amelia in Un Ballo in Maschera; Other roles include Chrysothemis (Elektra), Puccini's Minnie, Turandot and Tosca, Amelia (Simon Boccanegra), Yaroslavna in Prince Igor and Leonore; In 1989 sang Aida at the Teatro São Carlos, Lisbon; Chicago Lyric Opera, 1992 as Turandot; Season 2000–01 as Frosja in Semyon Kotko by Prokofiev, with Kirov Opera at Covent Garden, and Mme Blanche in Prokofiev's The Gambler at the New York Met.

SAVOVA, Olga B.; Russian actress and singer (mezzo-soprano); b. 14 Nov. 1964, Leningrad; m. Yefimov Dmitri; two s. *Education:* Leningrad State Inst. of Music Theatre and Cinematography, Leningrad State Conservatory. *Career:* actress at Leningrad Tovstonogov Drama Theatre –1995; singer at Mariinsky Opera Theatre (Kirov Opera) 1996–; repertoire includes Verdi's Requiem, Emilia in Othello, Eboli in Don Carlos, Flora in La Traviata, Carmen, Amneris and Preziosilla, Olga in Eugene Onegin, Prokofiev's Semyon Kotko, Azucena in Il Trovatore, Marfa in Tsar's Bride, Bobilikha in Rimsky-Korsakov's The Snow Maiden, Blanche in The Gambler by Prokofiev, Lyubov in Mazeppa, Marina Mnishek in Boris Godunov, Hélène in War and Peace, Paulina in The Queen of Spades and Teresa in La Sonnambula, The Nurse in Die Frau ohne Schatten; performances in France, Belgium, Holland, Italy, Japan, China and Israel. *Honours:* winner, Voci Verdiani Int. Competition, Italy 1992, Honoured Artist of Russia. *Address:* Mariinsky Opera Theatre, St Petersburg 130000, Teatralnaya pl.1, Russia (office). *Website:* www.mariinsky.ru/en (office).

SAWER, David, DPhil; British composer; *Professor of Composition, Royal Academy of Music*; b. 14 Sept. 1961, Stockport, Greater Manchester, England. *Education:* Univ. of York, studied with Richard Orton, Staatliche Hochschule für Musik Rheinland, Cologne, studied with Mauricio Kagel. *Career:* commissions from MusICA, Kirklees Metropolitan Council, Almeida Festival, London Sinfonietta, Birmingham Contemporary Music Group, BBC Proms, BBC Singers, BBC Symphony Orchestra and BBC Nat. Orchestra of Wales, Bath Int. Festival 2002, musikFabrik, Cheltenham Int. Festival, ENO, Opera North, Bregenz Festival, Danish Opera; directed premiere productions of Kagel's Pas de Cinq and Kantrimusik (Huddersfield Festival 1983, 1984) and as soloist in Kagel's Phonophonie at 1987 Summerscope season on the South Bank; conducted first UK performances of Kagel's Mare Nostrum (MusICA) and Szenario (Almeida Festival); music for radio and theatre productions; composer in association with the Bournemouth Orchestras 1995–96; Prof. of Composition, RAM, London. *Compositions:* music theatre: Etudes for 2–6 actors/musicians, two trumpets, percussion 1984, Food of Love for actress and piano 1988, The Panic, chamber opera, for four voices and six instruments 1990–91, From Morning to Midnight, opera, seven scenes, Sawer, from G. Kaiser: Von morgens bis mitternachts 1998–2001, Skin Deep (operetta) 2005–08, Rumpelstiltskin (ballet) 2009; orchestral: Byrnan Wood for large orchestra 1992, The Memory of Water for two violins and strings 1993, Trumpet Concerto 1994, The Greatest Happiness Principle 1997, Musica Ficta for chamber orchestra 1998, Piano Concerto 2002, From Morning to Midnight Symphonic Suite 2004, Flesh and Blood 2011; vocal: Rhetoric for soprano, viola, cello and double bass 1989, Songs of Love and War for 24 voices, two harps and two percussion 1990, Sounds: Three Kandinsky poems for chorus 1996, 1999, Stramm Gedichte for chorus 2001, Mutability for SSA children's choir 2005; chamber: Solo Piano for piano 1983, Cat's-Eye for chamber ensemble 1986, Take Off for instrumental ensemble 1987, Good Night for flute, harp, violin, viola and cello 1989, The Melancholy of Departure for piano 1990, Tiroirs for large ensemble 1996, Hollywood Extra for chamber ensemble 1996, Between for harp 1998, Rebus for chamber ensemble 2004. *Recordings include:* Tiroirs; From Morning to Midnight Suite; The Memory of Water; The Greatest Happiness Principle; Byrnan Wood; The Melancholy of Departure; Songs of Love and War. *Radio:* Swansong (with Nick Dear) 1989, The Long Time Ago Story (with Rose English) 2003. *Publications:* contrib. of entry on Kagel to New Grove Dictionary of Opera. *Honours:* DAAD Scholarship 1984–85, Sony Radio Award 1990, Fulbright-Chester-Schirmer Fellowship in Composition 1992–93, Paul Hamlyn Foundation Award 1993, Arts Foundation's Composer Fellowship 1995, British Acad. of Composers and Songwriters Award 2002, Civitella Ranieri Foundation Fellowship 2006. *Address:* 10 Normandy Road, London, SW9 6JH, England.

SAWYER, Philip John, BA, MA, MMus, ARCM, ARCO; British organist, continuo player and academic; b. 3 Feb. 1948, Birmingham, England; m. 1st Judith Susan Timbury 1981; m. 2nd Patricia Anne McAlister 1996. *Education:* Royal Coll. of Music, Peterhouse, Cambridge, studied in Amsterdam with Piet Kee, Nice Conservatoire with René Saorin. *Career:* Asst Dir of Music, Trent Coll. 1971–73; Lecturer, Napier Univ. (fmrly Napier Coll./Polytechnic) 1975–, Head of the School of Music 1987–99; Organist and Choirmaster: St Cuthbert's Parish Church, Edinburgh 1975–78, Nicolson Square Methodist Church, Edinburgh 1978–83, Dir of Music, St Andrew's and St George's Church, Edinburgh 1983–86; Dir of Music, St Mary's Collegiate Church, Haddington 1999–; organ recitals include Westminster Abbey, Notre Dame, Paris, Nice Cathedral, Monaco Cathedral, St Laurens, Alkmaar, St Bavo's RC Cathedral, Haarlem, Hillsborough Parish Church, N Ireland; univs of St Andrews, Edinburgh, Glasgow, Aberdeen; cathedrals at Edinburgh, Glasgow, Dundee; founder and Dir, Edinburgh Organ Week; first performances of newly-commissioned organ works by Alan Ridout and others; first performance of The Seven Sacraments of Poussin by John Mcleod in Edinburgh, Glasgow and London 1992; appearances as continuo player with Scottish Chamber Orchestra, Scottish Baroque Ensemble; Conductor, Scottish Chamber Choir 1994–97. *Recordings:* solo organ recitals for BBC Radio 3 and Radio Scotland, Harpsichord Continuo with Scottish Chamber Orchestra, with music by Handel, BBC Radio Scotland recording of first performance of The Seven Sacraments of Poussin 1992. *Publications:* contrib. various articles to journal of British Institute of Organ Studies.

SAXTON, Robert, BMus (Oxon.), MA (Cantab.), DMus (Oxon.), FGSM; British composer and university lecturer; *University Lecturer and Tutorial Fellow in Music, Worcester College, Oxford*; b. 8 Oct. 1953, London; s. of Ian Saxton and Jean Saxton (née Infield); m. Teresa Cahill. *Education:* St Catharine's Coll., Cambridge, Worcester Coll., Oxford, studied privately with Elisabeth Lutyens, Dr Robert Sherlaw Johnson (Univ. of Oxford) and Luciano Berio. *Career:* Lecturer, Univ. of Bristol 1984–85; Fulbright Arts Award, Visiting Fellow Princeton Univ., USA 1985–86; Head of Composition, Guildhall School of Music and Drama 1990–98; Head of Composition, RAM, London 1998–99; Univ. Lecturer and Tutorial Fellow, Worcester Coll., Oxford; mem. Bd South Bank Centre, London 1997–; mem. Royal Soc. of Musicians; Patron Soc. of English Speakers and Singers. *Compositions include:* orchestral: Ring of Eternity 1982, Concerto for Orchestra 1984, Viola Concerto 1986, In The Beginning 1987, Elijah's Violin 1988, Music to Celebrate the Resurrection of Christ 1988, Violin Concerto 1989, Cello Concerto 1992, Ring, Time for wind orchestra 1994; ensemble: Piccola Musica per Luigi Dallapiccola 1981, Processions and Dances 1981; vocal: Cantata No. 3 1981, Éloge for soprano and ensemble 1981, Chaconne for double chorus 1981, Caritas (opera) 1991, Paraphrase on Mozart's Idomeneo 1991; chamber: Chiaroscuro for percussion 1981, Piano Sonata 1981, Fantasiestuck for accordion 1982, The Sentinel of the Rainbow for sextet 1984, A Yardstick to the Stars 1994; choral: I Will Awake the Dawn 1987, At the Round Earth's Imagined Corners 1992, Psalm, a song of ascents 1992, O Sing unto the Lord a New Song 1993, Canticum Luminis for choir and orchestra 1994, Fanfare for the Golden Wedding Anniversary of Queen Elizabeth II, Songs, Dances and Ellipses 1997, Prayer Before Sleep 1997, Music for St Catharine 1998, Sonata on a Theme of William Walton for cello 1999, A Yardstick to the Stars 2000, The Dialogue of God and Zion for chorus 2000, Invocation, Dance and Meditation 2001, The Child of Light (carol), ...From a Distant Shore... 2001, Alternative Canticles 2002, Five Motets for nine voices 2003, Song without Words 2004. *Recordings:* Concerto for Orchestra, Sentinel of the Rainbow, Circles of Light, Ring of Eternity, Violin Concerto, In the Beginning, I Will Awake the Dawn, Paraphrase on Mozart's Idomeneo, Caritas, opera, At the Round Earth's Imagined Comers, Night Dance, Music to Celebrate the Resurrection of Christ, Chacony, Piano Sonata, A Yardstick to the Stars 2000, Eloge, Processions and Dances, Invocation, Dance and Meditation 2001, Songs, Dances and Ellipses 2001. *Publications:* The Process of Composition from Detection to Confection 1998; chapters in Cambridge Companion to the Orchestra 2003, Composing Music for Worship 2003; contrib. Where Do I Begin? (article in Musical Times) 1994, reviews in TLS. *Address:* Worcester College, Oxford, OX1 2HB, England (office).

SAY, Fazil; Turkish composer and pianist; b. 1970, Ankara. *Education:* Ankara State Conservatory, Robert Schumann Inst., Düsseldorf and Berlin Conservatory, Germany. *Career:* performances as soloist with orchestras, including New York Philharmonic, Israel Philharmonic, Baltimore Symphony, St Petersburg Philharmonic, Tokyo Symphony, BBC Philharmonic, Orchestre Nat. de France, Munich Philharmonic, Vienna Kammerorchester; has appeared world-wide at concert halls, including Concertgebouw Amsterdam, Berlin Philharmonie, Vienna Musikverein, Suntory Hall in Tokyo, Carnegie Hall, Avery Fisher Hall; has performed at festivals, including Lucerne Festival, Ruhr Piano Festival, Rheingau Music Festival, Verbier Festival, Montpellier Festival, Beethoven Festival Bonn, Salzburg Festival, Lincoln Center Festival, Harrod's Piano Series, World Piano Series in Tokyo; collaborations with musicians, including Yuri Bashmet, Shlomo Mintz, Maxim Vengerov, Akiko Suwanai, Patricia Kopatchinskaja, Sabine Meyer, Borusan Quartet, Abdullah Ibrahim, Bobby McFerrin; formed quartet with Kudsi Ergüner, performances at Montreux Jazz Festival, Istanbul Jazz Festival, Juan-les-Pins Festival; works commissioned by Turkish Ministry of Culture, Radio France and Kurt Masur, ETH Zürich, City of Vienna Mozart Year; Artist-in-Residence, Radio France 2003, Bremen Festival 2005, Konzerthaus Dortmund 2006–10, Tokyo Sumida Triphony Hall 2008, Paris Théâtre des Champs-Élysées 2010, Elbphilharmonie Hamburg 2010, Merano Festival 2010, Schleswig-Holstein Musik Festival 2011, Konzerthaus Berlin 2010–11, Hessischer Rundfunk Frankfurt 2012–13, Bodenseefestival 2014, Alte Oper Frankfurt 2015–16; apptd Amb. of Intercultural Dialogue 2008. *Compositions include:* Four Dances for Nasreddin Hoca for piano 1990, Fantasiestücke for piano 1993; chamber compositions: Symphony for string orchestra 1996, Sinfonia Concertante for piano and large orchestra 1994, 25 Songs for voice and piano 1994, Piano Concerto No. 2 'Silk Road' for piano and chamber orchestra 1994, Two Romantic Ballads for piano and strings 1995, Guitar Concerto 1996, Three Ballads for piano 1997, Black Earth for piano 1997, Violin Sonata 1997, Nazim oratorio for piano, vocalists, narrator, orchestra and chorus 2001, Piano Concerto No. 3 2001, Paganini Jazz for piano and orchestra 2003, Alla Turca (Jazz Fantasy after Mozart) for piano and orchestra 2003, Requiem for Metin Altiok oratorio for piano, chamber orchestra and chorus 2003, Ten Pieces for jazz quartet (with Kudsi Ergüner), Four Pieces for DJ and piano (with Mercan Dede) 2003, Patara 2005, Thinking Einstein 2005, Inside Serail 2006, Nirvana Burning for piano and orchestra 2010, Istanbul Symphony 2010, String quartet Divorce 2010, Trumpet Concerto 2010, Alevi develer raki masasinda for woodwind quintet 2011, Clarinet Concerto 2011, Hezarfen Concerto for ney and orchestra 2012, Mesopotamia Symphony 2012, Cello Sonata 4 Cities 2012, Universe Symphony 2012, Nietzsche and Wagner for piano 2013, Space Jump 2013, Gezi

Park 1 Concerto for two pianos and orchestra 2013, Gezi Park 2 Sonata for piano 2014, The Bells cantata 2014, Hermiyas 2014, Sait Faik 2014, Gezi Park 3 Ballad for mezzo-soprano, piano and string orchestra 2014, 1914. Overture for Orchestra 2014, Chamber Symphony 2015, Preludes for saxophone quartet and string orchestra with percussion 2015, Symphonic Dances 2015, Grand Bazaar 2015–16. *Recordings include:* Mozart, Piano Sonatas 1998, Bach 1999, Gershwin, Rhapsody in Blue 2000, Stravinsky, Le Sacre du Printemps 2000, Tchaikovsky, Piano Concerto No. 1 2001, Liszt, Piano Sonata in B minor, Mozart, Piano Concertos Nos 12, 21 and 23 2004, Beethoven, Appassionata 2005, Mussorgsky, Pictures at an Exhibition, Janaček, Piano Sonata I.X. 1905, Prokofiev, Piano Sonata No. 7 2012, Beethoven, Ravel, Say 2010; own compositions: Piano Concerto No. 2 'Silk Road' 1998, Nazim, Requiem for Metin Altiok, Black Earth 2004, Violin Sonata 2008, Violin Concerto 1001 Nights in the Harem, Summertime Variations, Patara Ballett, Alla Turca Jazz 2009, Istanbul Symphony, Hezarfen ney concerto 2012. *Honours:* winner, Young Concert Artists Int. Auditions 1994, Diapason d'Or 2000, Bremer Musikfest-Preis 2008, Special Jury Award (with Istanbul Symphony) Album Rheingau Musikpreis 2013 Prix International de la Laïcité 2015, Comité Laïcité République, France. *Current Management:* c/o Marianne Käch, Käch Artists & Promotion, Steintorweg 8, Hamburg 20099, Germany. *Telephone:* (40) 25336795. *Fax:* (40) 25336796. *E-mail:* marianne.kaech@kaechartists.com. *Website:* www.kaechartists.com; www.fazilsay.com.

SAYER, Roger Martin, ARCM, LRAM, FTCL; British organist; *Director of Music, Rochester Cathedral*; b. 1 May 1961, Portsmouth, Hants.; m. Nancy Sayer 1986, one s. one d. *Education:* Royal College of Music, organ scholar St Paul's Cathedral, London. *Career:* Organist and Dir of Music, Rochester Cathedral 1994–; Prof. of Organ, Trinity College of Music; Dir of Music, Rochester Choral Soc.; organ concerts in many parts of the world; Examiner, Associated Board of the Royal Schools of Music; Adjudicator, National Federation of Music and Drama. *Recordings:* Great European Organs; Hallgrimskirja, Iceland; Rochester Cathedra, A Classic Selection, Magnificat and Nunc Dimitus; A Choral Portrait, Vaughan Williams; A Classic Selection 2. *Honours:* Hon. FNMSM; third prize Int. Organ Competition, St Albans 1989, RCM Organ Prize 1989. *Address:* 107 Cecil Road, Rochester, Kent, ME1 2HR, England. *Telephone:* (7720) 773163 (mobile). *E-mail:* rms2001@bigfoot.com.

SAYERS, Gavin; British singer (tenor); b. 7 Jan. 1962, England. *Education:* Guildhall School of Music with Johanna Peters and Maureen Morelle. *Career:* sang Arturo in a concert performance of Lucia di Lammermoor, British premiere of Nino Rota's La Notte di un nevrastenico at Morley College 1990; concert repertoire includes Puccini's Messa di Gloria, Hiawatha's Wedding Feast by Coleridge-Taylor, Haydn's Nelson Mass and Maria Theresa Mass, Messiah and Mozart Mass in C, Hymn of Praise by Mendelssohn (2nd Symphony), Elijah (Harrow Choral 1990), Britten's Serenade (East Surrey Orchestra 1991) performed in a variety of amateur operatic performances.

SAYLOR, Bruce, BMus, MS, PhD; American composer; *Professor, Queens College* and *City University of New York*; b. 24 April 1946, Philadelphia, PA. *Education:* Juilliard School of Music with Hugo Weisgall and Roger Sessions, Accad. di Santa Cecilia, Rome with Petrassi and Evangelisti, CUNY Graduate School with Weisgall and George Perle. *Career:* Instructor, Queens Coll. 1970–76, Prof. 1979–; Instructor, New York Univ. 1976–79; Composer-in-Residence, Lyric Opera of Chicago 1992–94. *Compositions include:* My Kinsman, Major Molineux (opera in one act), It Had Wings (monodrama for mezzo and orchestra), Orpheus Descending (opera in two acts), The Scrimshaw Violin (opera in one act), When Samson Met Delilah (theatre), The Image Maker (opera in one act), Five Songs from Whispers of Heavenly Death for soprano and string quartet, Three Collects for mezzo and organ, Duo for violin and viola, Love Play for mezzo and ensemble, Four Psalms for voice and flute, Lyrics for soprano and violin, See You in the Morning for mezzo and ensemble, Song from Water Street for mezzo, piano, Swimming with Yevgeny for mezzo and ensemble, St Elmo's Fire for flute and harp, Cantos from The Inferno for clarinet and piano, Dante Suite for violin, Songs for cello, Reliquary for ensemble, Visions of Dante for piano, Liberating Chemistry for piano, Quattro Passi for piano, Preludes on American Hymns for organ, Cantilena for orchestra, Symphony in Two Parts: Turns and Mordents for flute and orchestra, Archangel for orchestra, Supernova for band, The Star Song for mezzo, flute, chorus and orchestra, A Scattering of Salts: concerto for piano, orchestra and chorus, Magnificat for soprano and orchestra, Dreams for two choruses and orchestra, In Praise of Jerusalem for chorus and orchestra, With Anthems Sweet for chorus and orchestra, The Idea of Us for chorus and orchestra, The Book in Your Hearts for mezzo, baritone, chorus and orchestra, Proud Music of the Storm for mixed and children's choruses and orchestra, Good News! for soprano, chorus and orchestra, Welcome the Morning Star for soprano, mezzo and orchestra, Francesco e il lupo for mezzo and orchestra, Images for orchestra, much choral music. *Recordings:* Jessye Norman at Notre-Dame 1990, Jessye Norman, In the Spirit 1997, and four song cycles performed by Constance Beavon. *Publications include:* The Writings of Henry Cowell. *Honours:* Gretchaninoff Prize 1965, Rogers and Hammerstein Scholarship 1968, Fulbright Fellowship 1969, NEA 1973, 1976, Mellon Foundation 1979–82, Guggenheim Fellowship 1982, Ingram Merrill Award 1990, Charles E. Ives Scholarship and Music Award, American Acad. of Arts and Letters. *Address:* 318 West 85th Street, New York, NY 10024, USA (home). *Telephone:* (718) 997-3857 (office).

SCALCHI, Gloria; singer (mezzo-soprano); b. 23 July 1956, Trieste, Italy. *Education:* studied with Iris Adami Corradetti and with Joseph Metternich in Munich; seminars at the Rossini Acad., Pesaro. *Career:* sang Angelina in La Cenerentola at Catania, 1988; further appearances at the Rome Opera as Emma in Rossini's Zelmira, conducted by Philip Gossett, and as Andromaca in Rossini's Ermione; Concertgebouw Amsterdam as Maffio Orsini, in Lucrezia Borgia; Verona as Rosina and Angelina; Bologna as Sinaide in Mosè; Carnegie Hall, Ermione; San Francisco, Zelmira; Monte Carlo, Roberto Devereux; Paris, Rossini's Petite Messe Solennelle and Vivaldi's Juditha Triumphans; Musikverein Vienna, Cherubini's D Minor Requiem; Rossini Festival Pesaro, 1990, as Somira in Ricciardo e Zoraide; Season 1996 as Verdi's Preziosilla at the Met and Pippo in La Gazza Ladra at Palermo; season 1998 as Donizetti's Léonor at Rome and Rosina at Genoa; season 1999–2000 as Hassem in Donizetti's Alahor in Granata, at Palermo, Rossini's Isabella at the Deutsche Oper Berlin and Fenena in Nabucco at the Verona Arena. *Recordings include:* Semiramide, La Favorite, Maometto II, Lucrezia Borgia, Stabat Mater, Messa da Requiem, Juditha Triumphans. *Honours:* G.Verdi Prize for best emerging singer, Parma 1991, Best interpreter of the year, Mondov 1992, Ebe Stignani Prize, Lugo di Romagna 1996, Ester Mazzoleni Prize, Palermo 2000. *Current Management:* Hilbert Artists Management, Maximilianstrasse 22, Munich 80539, Germany. *Telephone:* (89) 290747-0. *Fax:* (89) 29074790. *E-mail:* agentur@hilbert.de. *Website:* www.hilbert.de.

SCALTRITI, Roberto; Italian singer (baritone); b. 1969, Modena. *Education:* G. B. Martini Conservatory, Bologna, School of Music of Fiesole, studied with Ryland Davies. *Career:* debut as Alcindoro in La Bohème, Philadelphia 1986; appearances as Schaunard in Hamburg, as Masetto at Glyndebourne and the Festival Hall, Mozart's Count in Amsterdam and at the Opéra of Nice; Figaro with the Welsh National Opera, Publio in La Clemenza di Tito at the Théâtre des Champs-Elysées; further roles in La Gazza Ladra, Cimarosa's Maestro di Cappella and Handel's Rinaldo, Belcore in L'Elisir d'Amore, Don Giovanni, Alidoro in La Cenerentola, Monteverdi's Orfeo. *Recordings include:* Rigoletto with Riccardo Chailly, La Traviata with Zubin Mehta, Handel's Riccardo I with Christophe Rousset, Masetto in Don Giovanni, under Solti, Belcore in L'Elisir d'amore, Amadeus and Vienna–Arias with Christophe Rousset. *Honours:* winner Opera Company of Philadelphia Luciano Pavarotti International Voice Competition 1985. *Address:* Via San Benedetto 1841/B, 40018 San Pietro in Casale, Italy (home). *Telephone:* (051) 810176 (home).

SCANDIUZZI, Roberto; Italian singer (bass); b. 14 July 1958, Treviso. *Career:* debut as Bartolo in Mozart's Figaro under Riccardo Muti at La Scala 1982; appearances in opera at Paris, Munich, Hamburg, Amsterdam, Venice, Rome, Zürich; US Debut in Verdi's Requiem 1991; sang Fiesco in a new production of Simon Boccanegra at Covent Garden 1991; other conductors have included Patanè, Giulini, Colin Davis; festival engagements at Florence as Padre Guardiano in La Forza del Destino, Ramfis at Caracalla and Philip II and Zaccaria at Verona; repertoire includes Zaccaria, Verdi's Banquo, King Philip and Fiesco, Boito's Mefistofele, Cherubini's Creon, Verdi's Attila, Don Giovanni; has sung Verdi's Requiem in Verona, Dresden and Florence. *Recordings include:* Aida conducted by Mehta, I Puritani, Turandot and Simon Boccanegra. *Publication:* Une Voce che Colora la Musica 2007. *Current Management:* Atelier Musicale, Via Caselle 76, 40068 San Lazzaro di Savena, Italy. *Telephone:* (051) 19984444. *Fax:* (051) 19984420. *E-mail:* info@ateliermusicale.it. *Website:* www.ateliermusicale.it. *E-mail:* robertoscandiuzzi@hotmail.it (office). *Website:* www.robertoscandiuzzi.com.

SCARABELLI, Adelina; singer (soprano); b. 1950, Milan, Italy. *Education:* studied in Brescia. *Career:* sang at the Piccola Scala, Milan from 1977; La Scala Milan from 1981, debut as Barbarina in Le nozze di Figaro; Salzburg Festival 1984–85, as Despina and the Italian Singer in Capriccio; Florence 1988, as Lauretta in Gianni Schicchi; Rome Opera 1989, as Aminta in Mozart's Il re Pastore and as Susanna; sang Zerlina in Don Giovanni at Parma 1989; other roles include Mozart's Servilia in La clemenza di Tito and Ismene in Mitridate, Verdi's Oscar and Nannetta, Puccini's Musetta and Liu, and Micaela in Carmen; season 1996 as Rachelina in Paisiello's La Molinara at Bologna, and Olga in Fedora at La Scala; Anaide in Rota's Italian Straw Hat at Milan.

SCAUNAS MARKOS, Simona; pianist; b. 12 Nov. 1965, Rimnicu Vilcea, Romania. *Education:* High School of Art George Enescu, Bucharest, Conservatory of Arts and Music George Enescu, Iasi. *Career:* recitals at Romanian Athene, Bucharest 1989 and in other cities of Romania; participant in Young Talents Piatra-Neamt; Museum of Republic 1987–88; concerts with Bacau Symphony Orchestra 1987, Craiova Oltenia Philharmonic Orchestra 1988; radio broadcasts in musical programmes and with recitals 1987–88, and television 1987; participant in Young Talents Festival 1984, 1986, 1987, 1988; piano recitals and chamber music collaboration in German cities of Darmstadt, Erfurt, Freiburg, Gotha, Heiligenstadt, Nordhausen, Osnabrück, Sonderhausen, also in Poland and Italy; int. masterclasses for pianists.

SCEBBA, Miguel Angel; Argentine pianist, composer and academic; b. 6 Nov. 1948, San Martin, Buenos Aires. *Education:* Nat. Conservatory of Music, Buenos Aires, Tchaikovsky Conservatory, Kiev, studied in Moscow. *Career:* debut as piano soloist with Orchestra of San Martin, Buenos Aires, Beethoven Concerto No. 3 1966; concerts in more than 15 countries worldwide, including two tours in USSR 1981, 1985; int. festival, Settembre Musicale Triestino 1983; numerous appearances in Germany 1986–90, on Radio RIAS-Berlin, Tübingen, Konstanz; Teatro Colón, Buenos Aires 1992; Artist-in-Residence,

Miami Univ., OH, USA 1994–97; Full Prof., Nat. Univ. of San Juan, Argentina; t tours of Europe 2000. *Compositions:* five Symphonies 1987, 1996, 1998, 1999, 2001, Organ Book 1975, ten String Quartets. *Recordings:* Piano solo, Schumann, sonata op 22, Debussy, l'Isle Joyeuse, Ginastera sonata No. 1, Con Anima, São Paulo, Brazil, 1989; Argentina Musical, 1997; Liszt B minor sonata. *E-mail:* miguel.scebba@interredes.com.ar.

SCHAAF, Johannes; German stage director; b. 7 April 1933, Bad Cannstatt; m. Stella Kleindienst. *Education:* studied medicine. *Career:* worked at the Stuttgart Schauspielhaus, then directed plays in Ulm and Bremen; further theatre work at Munich (Twelfth Night), Vienna and Salzburg (Beaumarchais, Buchner and Lessing); opera productions have included Les Contes d'Hoffmann at Vienna Volksoper, Idomeneo at Vienna Staatsoper, Eugene Onegin in Geneva and Bremen, Capriccio and Die Entführung in Salzburg, Le nozze di Figaro, Così fan tutte, Idomeneo and Don Giovanni at Covent Garden, Fidelio and Die Frau ohne Schatten at Geneva Opera, The Nose in Frankfurt, Schreker's Der Ferne Klang in Brussels, Boris Godunov, New Israel Opera House, Simon Boccanegra in Stuttgart, Le nozze di Figaro, Stockholm, Katya Kabanova for San Francisco Opera. *Films:* as dir: Trotta 1971, Traumstadt 1973, Momo 1986. *Publications:* contrib. to Geo, on subjects including Chinese Opera.

SCHADE, Michael; singer (tenor); b. 23 Jan. 1965, Geneva, Switzerland. *Education:* Curtis Institute. *Career:* early experience as Ernesto in Belgium and Rameau's Pygmalion with Opera Atelier in Toronto; professional debut in 1990 as Jacquino with the Pacific Opera of British Columbia; sang Tamino at Bologna, 1991; appeared as Iago in Rossini's Otello at Pesaro; Vienna Staatsoper debut 1991 as Almaviva; season 1991–92 as Alfred in Fledermaus at Geneva, Almaviva with Edmonton and Canadian Operas, Ernesto with Vancouver Opera and Elvino in La Sonnambula at Macerata; season 1992–93 as Jacquino in San Francisco and the Chevalier in Dialogues des Carmélites at Geneva; sang Roderigo in Otello, 1993; engaged by Vienna Staatsoper as Ferrando, Almaviva, Nemorino, Tamino and Nicolai's Fenton; Salzburg Festival 1994 in a staged version of Mozart Arias; Cologne Opera as Telemaco in Monteverdi's Ulisse and Elvino at Trieste; sang Tamino, 1995, Haydn's Creation, 1995 and Fidelio, 1995; Oedipus Rex at Toronto, 1997; sang Tamino at Salzburg, 1997, and La Scala, 1998; appeared in Merry Widow at Paris Opéra 1998 and as Alfred in Fledermaus at the Metropolitan Opera 1998–99; concert repertoire includes Beethoven's Missa Solemnis, The Creation, The Seasons and Bach's St Matthew Passion, Mozart's Requiem, Carmina Burana, Schumann's Paradies und die Peri under John Eliot Gardiner and Elijah with the Cleveland Orchestra; Wagner's David at Chicago, 1999, Ottavio at Los Angeles, Vienna and Ravenna, 1999; season 2000–01 at the Met as Rossini's Almaviva and Tamino, Henry in Die schweigsame Frau at the Vienna Staatsoper, Cherubini's Jason at Salzburg (concert) and Idomeneo at Dresden. *Recordings include:* Haydn's Maria Theresa Mass under Trevor Pinnock; The Creation and The Seasons; St Matthew Passion, Elijah, St Paul under Rilling; Die Zauberflöte under Gardiner; Mozart Requiem under Abbado. *Honours:* Kammersänger (Austria) 2007. *Current Management:* Künstleragentur Dr Raab & Dr Böhm, Plankengasse 7, 1010 Vienna, Austria. *Telephone:* 1-5120501. *Fax:* 1-5127743. *E-mail:* office@rbartists.at. *Website:* www.rbartists .at; www.mschade.com.

SCHADLER, Elisabeth; pianist; b. 10 Nov. 1963, Feldbach, Styria, Austria. *Education:* Hochschule für Musik, Graz and masterclasses. *Career:* concerts and recitals at Vienna Konzerthaus and Musikverein; many European countries with Vienna Chamber Orchestra, Graz Symphony Orchestra; festival appearances; teacher, Kunstuniversität, Graz 1987–; mem. EPTA, Austria; Prof., Conservatory Klagenfurt 1999–. *Recordings:* Double concertos for violin, piano and orchestra 1996. *Honours:* second prize Int. Vercelli Competition 1985, second prize Int. Schubert Competition, Dortmund 1987, winner Int. Schubert and Music of the 20th Century Competition, Graz 1989, third prize in Lied.

SCHAEFER, Peter, BA, BMus, DCA; composer and musician (sitar); b. 14 Sept. 1956, Sydney, NSW, Australia. *Education:* Univ. of Sydney, Univ. of Wollongong, studied with Peter Sculthorpe, Barry Conyngham, Ustad Ali Akbar Khan, Ashok Roy. *Career:* faculty mem., New South Wales Conservatory 1984–90, Univ. of Wollongong 1990–92; founder mem., Peter Schaefer Ensemble; performer of Indian and electro-acoustic music. *Compositions:* Toward for string quartet 1980, See for synthesizer and/or computer and digital delay 1983, Petal… Silence for two pianos and tape 1983, Chien… Still for orchestra 1984, Spans for ensemble and tape 1989, Time Breathing (dance theatre) for ensemble and ape 1990, Quartet Vibra for string quartet and tape 1991, Open/Secret (music theatre for children) 1994, Expans Series (I–VII) for ensemble and tape 1990–, Tao Streams (orchestra project) 1995–. *Honours:* 2MBS-FM Radiophonic Tape Composition Prize 1985.

SCHAEFFER, Bogusław, DPhil; Polish/Austrian composer, music critic, playwright and pianist; b. 6 June 1929, Lwów (now Lviv, Ukraine); s. of Władysław Schaeffer and Julia Schaeffer; m. Mieczysława Hanuszewska 1953; one s. *Education:* State Higher School of Music (student of A. Malawski), Jagiellonian Univ., Kraków (student of Zdzisław Jachimecki). *Career:* wrote first dodecaphonic music for orchestra in Eastern Europe, Music for Strings: Nocturne 1953; Assoc. Prof., State Higher School of Music, Kraków 1963–98, Ordinary Prof. of Composition, Higher School of Music, Mozarteum, Salzburg 1986–89, Prof. 1989–; Chief Ed. Forum Musicum 1967–; leads int. summer courses for new composition in Salzburg and Schwaz, Austria 1976–. *Main*

compositions: Extrema, Tertium datur, Scultura, S'alto for alto saxophone, Collage and Form, Electronic Music, Visual Music, Heraclitiana, Missa Electronica, Jangwa, Missa Sinfonica, eight Piano Concertos, Maah, Sinfonia, Hommage à Guillaume for two cellos and piano 1995, Sinfonietta for 16 instruments 1996, Symphony in One Movement 1997, Enigma for Orchestra 1997, Four Psalms for choir and orchestra 1999, Musica Omogènea for 32 violins 1999, Si Quaeris Miracula for soprano and orchestra 2000, Model XXI (Wendepunkt) for piano 2000, De Profundis for soprano and chamber orchestra 2000, Monophonie VIII for 24 violins 2000, Ave Maria for soprano and orchestra 2000, opera Liebesblicke 2000, five violin concertos, three cello concertos, Concerto for vibraphone and orchestra 2001, Concerto for harp, Celtic harp and orchestra 2002, Concerto for saxophone, piano and orchestra 2002, 9th Symphony 2003, Concert for piano and choir 2004, For violin and electronics 2004, Blues VII for piano and orchestra 2004, Quartet for four cellos 2005, Panorama for orchestra 2005, Fragment III for two actors, clarinet, cello, piano and electronic media 2005, Second Symphony in One Movement 2005, OCSENOT for soprano and ensemble of seven instruments, Impresiónes Liricas for piano and electro-acoustic medias 2005, Model XXXIII for piano 2005, Contemporaneamente o Alternatamente for violin and piano 2005, Model XXXIV for piano 2006, Concerto for viola and 12 various instruments 2007, Quartet for four violins and chamber orchestra 2009, 10th Symphony 2010, SaVi for saxophone and violin 2011, Mini opera, also film and theatre music, Miserere, Organ Concerto, 17 string quartets, Orchestral and Electronic Changes, Concerto for Violin, Piano and Orchestra, Symphony/ Concerto for 15 solo instrumentalists and orchestra, Heideggeriana, Winter Musik for horn and piano, Concerto for percussion, electronic media and orchestra. *Plays:* 46 stage plays including: Three Actors 1970, Darknesses 1980, Screenplay for Sins of Old Age 1985, The Actor 1990, Rehearsals 1990, Séance 1990, Tutam 1991, Rondo 1991, Together 1992, Toast 1991, Harvest 1993, Promotion 1993, Gloss 1993, Daybreak 1994, Multi 1994, Largo 1996, Blockheads 1997, Stage Demon 1998, Alles 1998, Advertisement 1998, Walks Through Parc 1998, InOut 1998, Farniente 1998, Chance 1999, Dwa Te (Two Te) 2000, Skala 2000, Scale 2008, Something Multimedial 2009, Case; plays trans. into 17 languages. *Publications:* Nowa Muzyka. Problemy współczesnej techniki kompozytorskiej (New music. Problems of Contemporary Technique in Composing) 1958, Klasycy dodekafonii (Classics of Dodecaphonic Music) 1964, Leksykon kompozytorów XX wieku (Lexicon of 20th Century Composers) 1965, W kręgu nowej muzyki (In the Sphere of New Music) 1967, Mały informator muzyki XX wieku 1975, Introduction to Composition (in English) 1975, Historia muzyki (Story of Music) 1980, Kompozytorzy XX wieku (20th Century Composers) 1990, Trzy rozmowy (kompozytor, dramaturg, filozof) (Three Conversations: Composer, Playwright and Philosopher) 1992. *Honours:* Hon. mem. Int. Soc. for Contemporary Music 1998, Pro Sinfonica 2003; Gold Cross of Merit 1969; Kt's Cross of Polonia Restituta Order 1972; numerous prizes include G. Fitelberg Prize 1959, 1960, 1964, A. Malawski Prize 1962, Minister of Culture and Arts Prize 1971, 1980, Union of Polish Composers Prize 1977, Alfred Jurzykowski Award 1999. *Address:* Osiedle Kolorowe 4, m.6, 31-938 Kraków, Poland; St. Julienstrasse 7A, Apartment 27, 5020 Salzburg, Austria. *Telephone:* (12) 6441960 (Poland) (home). *E-mail:* bsch@ceti.pl (office).

SCHÄFER, Christine; German singer (soprano); b. 3 March 1965, Frankfurt. *Education:* Berlin Musikhochschule, studied with Arleen Auger and Aribert Reimann. *Career:* career in opera, concert and recital since 1988; regular guest at the Metropolitan Opera, New York, San Francisco Opera, Covent Garden, London, Paris, Vienna, Amsterdam, Brussels and all major German houses as well as most int. festivals, including Salzburg and Glyndebourne; regular concert appearances with most leading orchestras in USA and Europe, including Los Angeles and New York Philharmonic, Boston Symphony, Vienna Philharmonic, Berlin Philharmonic; conductors include Abbado, Barenboim, Boulez, Eschenbach, Levine, Harnoncourt, Rattle, Thielemann; recitals world-wide; repertoire consists of Mozart, Verdi, Handel and Strauss, also Lulu, Lucia, Ange and others. *Films:* several DVDs in opera and concert. *Television:* ARTE Portrait. *Recordings:* numerous CD recordings. *Honours:* prizewinner, Mozart Competitions in Vienna and Rome 1991. *Current Management:* c/o Artist Management Augstein & Hahn, Sendlinger Strasse 56, 80331 Munich, Germany. *Website:* www.christine-schaefer.com.

SCHÄFER, Markus; German singer (tenor); b. 13 June 1961, Andernach am Rhein. *Education:* studied in Koblenz, Karlsruhe. *Career:* sang at the Zürich Opera from 1985; Hamburg, 1986; Deutsche Oper am Rhein, Düsseldorf, from 1987; sang Fenton in Die Lustige Weiber von Windsor at Duisburg, 1991; Damon in Acis and Galatea at the Queen Elizabeth Hall; other concerts include the Evangelist in Bach's Passions; Messiah, Elijah, St Paul, Die Schöpfung and Rossini's Stabat Mater; opera roles include Paisiello's Almaviva, Pedrillo, Ramiro and Caramelo in Eine Nacht in Venedig; Mozart's Ferrando at the Berlin Staatsoper, 1997; Tamino at the Berlin Komische Oper, 1999. *Recordings include:* St Paul, Mendelssohn's Christus, Beethoven's Mass in C, Haydn's L'Infedeltà Delusa; Mozart's Mass K139. *Current Management:* Ariën Arts & Music Management, De Boeystraat 6, 2018 Antwerp, Belgium. *Telephone:* (3) 285-96-80. *Fax:* (3) 230-35-23. *E-mail:* arien@pandora.be.

SCHAFER, Raymond Murray; composer, writer on music and teacher; b. 18 July 1933, Sarnia, ON, Canada. *Education:* Toronto Conservatory with Guerrero and Weinzweg. *Career:* worked freelance for the BBC in Europe 1956–61; founder, Ten Centuries Concerts, Toronto 1961; Artist-in-Residence,

779

Memorial Univ., Newfoundland 1963–65, Simon Fraser Univ., British Columbia 1965; research into acoustic ecology from 1971. *Compositions include:* Concerto for harpsichord and eight instruments 1954, Minnelieder for mezzo and wind quintet 1956, Sonatina for flute and keyboard 1958, In Memoriam: Iberto Guerrero for strings 1959, Protest and Incarceration for mezzo and orchestra 1960, Brebeuf for baritone and orchestra 1961, Canzoni for Prisoners for orchestra 1962, untitled composition for orchestra 1963, Loving/Toi (music theatre) 1963–66, Requiems for the Party Girl 1966, Threnody 1966, Kaleidoscope for multi-track tape 1967, Son of Heldenleben for orchestra and tape 1968, From the Tibetan Book of the Dead for soprano, chorus and ensemble 1968, Yeow and Pax for chorus, organ and tape 1969, No Longer Than Ten Minutes for orchestra 1970, Sappho for mezzo and ensemble 1970, String Quartet 1970, Okeanos for four-track tape 1971, In Search of Zoroaster for male voice, chorus, percussion and organ 1971, Music for the Morning for the World 1970, Beyond the Great Gate of Light 1972, Arcana for low voice and ensemble 1972, East for chamber orchestra 1972, Paria I–X (music theatre) 1969–97, North White for orchestra 1972, String Quartet No. 2: Waves 1976, Adieu Robert Schumann for alto and orchestra 1976, Hymn to the Night for soprano and orchestra 1976, Cortège for orchestra 1977, Apocolypsis (music theatre) 1980, RA (multimedia piece based on the Egyptian God) 1983, Flute Concerto 1985, String Quartet No. 4 1989, Tristan and Iseult for vocal soloists 1992, Accordion Concerto 1993, String Quartets Nos 5 and 6 1989, 1993, The Falcon's Trumpet 1995, Musique pour la parque Fontaine for four bands 1995, Viola Concerto 1997, Seventeen Haiku for chorus 1997. *Publications include:* edn of Ezra Pound's opera Le Testament de Francois Villon 1960, British Composers in Interview 1963, Ezra Pound and Music 1977, The Thinking Ear 1986. *Honours:* Canada Council grants 1961, 1963, Ford Foundation Award 1968, Canadian Music Council Medal 1972, Donner Foundation grant 1972, Guggenheim Fellowship 1974.

SCHAFF, Gabriel Jacob Gideon Polin, BMus; American violinist; b. 9 Nov. 1959, Philadelphia, PA; m. Nancy McDill 1988, one d. *Education:* Manhattan School of Music, New York, New School of Music, Temple Univ., Philadelphia, studied with Erick Friedman, Norman Carol. *Career:* extensive symphonic, opera, ballet and chamber music performances at Lincoln Center, Carnegie Hall and throughout New York; violin soloist in Soviet-American exchange concerts, with performances in Philadelphia, New York, Moscow, Leningrad and Helsinki 1979–88; several commissions and premieres of works by US and Russian composers.

SCHAGIDULLIN, Albert; singer (bass); b. 1 May 1966, Baschkizia; m.; one s. *Education:* Moscow Conservatory. *Career:* debut in Dublin, Enrico Grand Opera 1991; Hamburg State Opera 1993–97; Easter and Summer Festival, Salzburg 1993, 1994; visited Tokyo with Vienna State Opera 1994; Salzburg 1998; Opera di Roma 1994; Bregenz Summer Festival 1995–96; Messa di Gloria, Vienna Symphony 1996; Oslo Philharmonic 1996; Munich Staatsoper 1997; Lyon Opéra 1998. *Recordings:* Boris Godunov, Three Sisters by Peter Eötvös. *Publications:* contrib. to F Times 1991, Hamburger Abendblatt 1992, Corriere della Sera 1994, Salzburger Nachrichten 1995, Opera International 1998, Opern Glas 1998. *Honours:* special prize for best young singer, Francisco Viñas Competition, Barcelona 1990, third prize Maria Callas Competition, Athens 1991, second prize Belvedere Competition, Vienna 1991, second prize CIEM Competition, Geneva 1991, first prize Vervier Competition 1991, winner Pavarotti Competition, Philadelphia.

SCHARBERTH, Irmgard; German opera producer and concert producer; b. 28 Nov. 1919, Hamburg. *Education:* Univs of Hamburg and Kiel. *Career:* opera and concert producer with Hamburg Staatsoper 1957–76, Bayerische Staatsoper, Munich 1976–77, Oper Stadt Köln, Cologne 1977–85; producer Gürzenichkonzerte, Cologne –1991. *Publications include:* Die Hamburger Staatsoper in Amerika 1967, Rolf Liebermann zum sechzigsten Geburtstag 1970, Musiktheater mit Rolf Liebermann 1975, Oper in Köln 1975–85, Michael Hampe 1985, Die Gürzenichorchester Köln 1988. *Address:* c/o Am Kiekeberg 24, 22587 Hamburg, Germany.

SCHARFENBERGER, Tobias; singer (baritone); b. 1 Sept. 1964, Grafelfing, Munich, Germany. *Education:* studied in Hannover and Karlsruhe. *Career:* sang at Stuttgart 1991 in the premiere of Perseo e Andromeda by Sciarrone; Deutsche Oper am Rhein at Düsseldorf as Ottakar in Der Freischütz and in Krenek's Orpheus; German premiere of Schnittke's Life with an Idiot, Gelsenkirchen 1991; Bielefeld Opera from 1995 as Papageno, Siegfried in Schumann's Genoveva and in the local premiere of Weir's Blond Eckbert 1996; season 1999–2000 as Nicomedes in Zemlinsky's König Kandaules at Cologne and as Kilian in Der Freischütz at the Komische Oper Berlin; concert and oratorio appearances.

SCHARINGER, Anton; singer (baritone); b. 5 March 1959, Austria. *Education:* Vienna Conservatory. *Career:* sang with the Salzburg Landestheater 1981–83, Vienna Volksoper from 1987; sang Dr Falke in Fledermaus at Amsterdam 1987; Mozart's Figaro at Ludwigsburg 1989; Salzburg Festival 1991; guest appearances at Cologne, Zürich; other roles include, Masetto and Guglielmo; sang the Captain in Gurlitt's Wozzeck at Florence 1998; many concert engagements, notably in sacred works by Bach; television appearances include Bass Solos in the St Matthew Passion, with the Neubeuern Choral Soc. and the Munich Bach Collegium. *Recordings include:* Die Zauberflöte with Les Arts Florissants 1996, Masetto in Don Giovanni, Mozart's L'Oca del Cairo.

SCHASCHING, Rudolf; singer (tenor); b. 12 April 1957, Engelhartszell, Austria. *Education:* Vienna Musikhochschule. *Career:* sang at the Saarbrucken Opera from 1983 as Tamino, Don Ottavio, Pinkerton, Cassio, Max, Oedipus Rex and Idomeneo; sang Loge, Siegmund and Siegfried 1987–90; guest appearances at the Vienna Staatsoper as Aegisthus 1992, Zürich and elsewhere; concerts include Beethoven's Ninth, Bruckner's Te Deum and Haydn's Seasons.

SCHAUERTE-MAUBOUET, Helga Elisabeth, BA; German/French organist; *Organ Teacher, Paris Conservatory*; b. 8 March 1957, Lennestadt, North Rhine-Westphalia, Germany; m. Philippe Maubouet 1988; one d. *Education:* St Franziskusschule, Olpe, Univ. of Cologne, Musikhochschule, Cologne, Conservatory of Rueil-Malmaison, France. *Career:* debut public appearance as organist aged ten; chief organist at local parish church aged 13; organist, German Lutheran Church, Paris 1982–; organ teacher, Conservatory Paris, 9th arrondissement and in Andresy 1993–; recitals, lectures, masterclasses, Europe and USA, including RAM, London, Univ. of Michigan, USA; performances on radio and TV in Germany, France, Denmark and USA; concerts include performance of complete organ works of Jehan Alain and Buxtehude, Paris 1986; first performance of Jean Langlais' organ works, BACH, Miniature II and Mort et Resurrection. *Recordings:* Integral of Jehan Alain's Organ Works, Complete Organ Works of Buxtehude, Poulenc Organ Concerto, Works of Boëllmann, Dubois, Langlais, Vierne, Max Reger, Marcel Dupré, Michel Corrette, Beauvarlet-Charpentier, Homilius, Walther, Kittel, Kellner, Buttstett, Armsdorff, Müthel. *Film:* Jean-Sebastien Bach. *Publications:* Jehan Alain: Das Orgelwerk, Eine monographische Studie 1983, Jehan Alain: L'Homme et l'Oeuvre 1985, Deutsche und französische Weihnachtslieder 1997, Noël dans la tradition, Traditionelle Weihnacht 1997, Boëllmann: Complete Organ Works, Vols I and II 2002, 2003, Vol. III 2004, Vol. IV 2012, Handbuch Orgelmusik 2002, Marc-Antoine Charpentier: Te Deum (H. 146/148), Messe de Minuit 2004, Dubois: Complete Organ Works Vol. I 2005, Vol. II 2006, Vol. IV 2007, Vol. V 2013, Louis Vierne: Complete Organ Works Vol. III 2008, Vol. VII (1–4) 2008–09, Vol. VIII (1–2) 2009, Vol. VI 2010, Vol. IX 2010, Vols I and II 2012; Jehan Alain: Complete Organ Works (three vols) 2011. *Honours:* Cultural Prize of Olpe 1987. *Address:* 25 rue Blanche, 75009 Paris, France. *Website:* www.bach-cantatas.com/Bio/Schauerte-Helga.htm.

SCHAVERNOCH, Hans; stage designer; b. 1955, Australia. *Education:* Vienna Akademie. *Career:* designed productions of Erwartung, Iphigénie en Aulide, Elektra and La Clemenza di Tito in Vienna; Tannhäuser and Werther at Hamburg, Orfeo and Die Zauberflöte at the Komische Oper Berlin; collaborations with producer Harry Kupfer in Berlin, at Salzburg for the premiere of Penderecki's Die schwarze Maske and the 1988 Ring des Nibelungen at Bayreuth; Metropolitan Opera with Der fliegende Holländer, Erwartung and Bluebeard's Castle; Paris Opéra with Der Rosenkavalier, Il Trittico, and Katya Kabanova; Royal Opera Covent Garden designs include Ariadne auf Naxos, Così fan tutte, Idomeneo, Elektra and La Damnation de Faust; other designs include Alceste at Versailles, Pelléas et Mélisande at Cologne, Liszt St Elisabeth in Vienna, Parsifal and the Ring at the Berlin Staatsoper and Khovanshchina in Hamburg; Rimsky's Legend of the Invisible City of Kitezh at the Bregenz Festival and Komische Oper, Berlin 1995–96; Boris Godunov at the Vienna Volksoper.

SCHEIBNER, Andreas; German singer (baritone); b. 18 Jan. 1951, Dresden. *Education:* studied in Dresden with Gunther Leib. *Career:* debut at Gorlitz 1972, as Dr Caius in Die Lustige Weiber Von Windsor; Sang at Butzen, 1974, Stralsund 1976–79, Postdam 1979–83; engaged at the Dresden Staatsoper from 1983; Roles have included Mozart's Don Giovanni, Guglielmo, Papageno, Belcore, Eugene Onegin, Count Luna, Silvio, Marcello, Lortzing's Zar and Kilian in Der Freischütz; Concert appearances in Austria, Netherlands, Poland and throughout Germany; Season 1999–2000 as the Count in Capriccio at Dresden, Barbier in Die schweigsame Frau for the Vienna Staatsoper, and Jochanaan in Salome at Zagreb; Hans Sachs in Madrid, 2001. *Recordings include:* Der Freischütz, conducted by C Davis; Bach Cantatas. *Current Management:* c/o Italartist Austroconcert Kulturmanagement, Gluckgasse 1, 1010 Vienna, Austria. *Telephone:* 1-5132657. *Fax:* 1-5126154. *E-mail:* austroconcert@ia-ac.com. *Website:* www.ia-ac.com.

SCHEIDEGGER, Hans Peter; Swiss singer (bass); b. 23 Feb. 1953, La Bottiere, Jura. *Education:* Berne University, studied in Essen with Jakob Stämpfli and Paul Lohmann. *Career:* debut at Geneva Opera 1983, as Curio in Giulio Cesare, conducted by Charles Mackerras; Has appeared at Lucerne and elsewhere in Switzerland as Fiesco (Simon Boccanegra), Britten's Theseus and Collatinus, Bartók's Duke Bluebeard, Zuniga, Leporello, Walter (Luisa Miller), Trulove (The Rake's Progress) and Rocco; Has sung at Karlsruhe from 1986, as King Henry (Lohengrin), Gremin, the Commendatore, Sarastro, Pogner and the Doctor in Wozzeck; Other roles include Zoroastro in Handel's Orlando, Publio in La Clemenza di Tito, and Ferrando in Il Trovatore; Sang Rocco and King Marke at Basle, 1990; Concert repertoire includes Bach Cantatas, B minor Mass, St John Passion and Christmas Oratorio; Beethoven Missa Solemnis; Dvořák Requiem, Te Deum and Mass in D; Haydn Schöpfung, Jahreszeiten, Harmonie and Nicholas Masses; Salve Regina; Handel Messiah, Saul and Hercules; Mozart Requiem and other Masses; Schubert Mass in A flat and G; Graun Der Tod Jesu; Keiser Markus Passion; Telemann Matthew and Luke Passions; Conductors have included Armin Jordan, Horst Stein, Jeffrey Tate, Roderick Brydon, Kurt Sanderling, Charles Farncombe, Wolfgang Gönnenwein and David Lloyd-Jones; Sang Wotan and the Wanderer at Hannover, 1999; Season 2000–01 as Enkidu in the premiere of Gilgamesh by V.D Kirchner, Monteverdi's Seneca, Rangoni in Boris Godunov and Strauss's Orestes. *Current Management:* Aria's di Novella Partacini & Alexandra Plaickner, Rappresentanza Artisti, Via Josef Weingartner, 4, 39022 Lagundo, Italy. *Telephone:* (0473) 200200. *Fax:* (0473) 222424. *E-mail:* info@arias.it. *Website:* www.arias.it.

SCHEJA, Steffan; pianist; b. 1950, Sweden. *Education:* Stockholm Coll. of Music, Juilliard School, New York. *Career:* debut concert with Swedish Radio Symphony Orchestra 1962; New York debut 1972, followed by concerts with the French Radio Symphony Orchestra, Philharmonia Hungarica, Munich Philharmonic, English Chamber Orchestra, NHK Symphony Tokyo and the major Scandinavian Orchestras; solo recitals and lieder accompanist to Håkan Hagegard, Barbara Bonney and Barbara Hendricks; Dir of Chamber Music Festival at Gotland, Sweden from 1986; broadcasting engagements, tours of Europe, the USA and Asia; recital programmes with violinist, Young Uck Kim. *Recordings include:* albums as concert soloist and as recitalist.

SCHELLE, Michael, BA, BM, MM, PhD; American composer and music educator; b. 22 Jan. 1950, Philadelphia, PA; m. Joyce Tucciarone 1972, one s. one d. *Education:* Villanova Univ., Butler Univ., Hartt School of Music, Univ., Univ. of Minnesota, studied with Aaron Copland. *Career:* teaching asst, Hartt School of Music, Univ. of Hartford 1974–77; Instructor and Teaching Assoc., Univ. of Minnesota School of Music 1977–79; Instructor, Carleton Coll. 19679; Instructor of Music, Jordan Coll. of Fine Arts, Butler Univ. 1979–81, Asst Prof. 1981–87, Assoc. Prof. 1987–, Composer-in-Residence 1981–, Dir New Music Ensemble 1981–; guest composer and lecturer at various univs and colls, with orchestras and at festivals; commissions include Indianapolis Symphony Orchestra, Buffalo Philharmonic Orchestra, Kansas City Symphony. *Compositions include:* stage: The Great Soap Opera (chamber opera) 1988; orchestral: Lancaster Variations 1976, Masque – A Story of Puppets, Poets, Kings and Clowns 1977, El Médico 1977, Pygmies for youth orchestra and tape 1982, Pygmies II for youth orchestra and speaker 1983, Golden Bells for orchestra and chorus 1983, completion of an unfinished score by N. Dinerstein, Oboe Concerto 1983, Swashbuckler! 1984, Concerto for two pianos and orchestra 1986, Kidspeace for orchestra and voices 1987, (restless dreams before) The Big Night 1989; symphonic band: King Ubu 1980, Cliffhanger March 1984, Seven Steps from Hell 1985; chamber music; Piano Pieces; vocal music: Swanwhite – Letters to Strindberg from Harriet Bosse cycle for soprano and piano 1980.

SCHELLEN, Nando; artistic director and stage director; b. 11 Oct. 1934, The Hague, The Netherlands; m. Deborah Raymond 1991. *Career:* Dir Nederlandse Operastichting, Amsterdam 1969–87; Stage Dir from 1982, with debut at Holland Festival with The Magic Flute 1982, American continent debut 1983 with Lohengrin at Toronto and Edmonton for the centennial of Richard Wagner's death; directed productions of Eugene Onegin 1986, and The Merry Wives of Windsor 1987 in Germany, and Salto Mortale 1989, Our Town 1990 in The Netherlands; Nabucco 1999 Bulgaria/The Netherlands; background managerial, musical and theatrical work; produced 14 world premieres during his engagement at Netherlands Operastichting, initiating major policy changes there, including expansion of season from initially 90 to 165 performances; Gen. Artistic Dir Sweelinck Conservatory of Music, Amsterdam 1991–93; Gen. Artistic Dir, Indianapolis Opera, USA 1993–96; Dir of Opera Workshop, Oberlin Summer School, Casaimaggiore 1998–; Dir of Opera Theater, Northern Arizona Univ., Flagstaff, AZ, USA 2000–; directed in USA The Telephone 1993, 2001, Rigoletto 1994, Erwartung 1994, Salomé 1995, Ariadne auf Naxos 1996, Così fan tutte 1997, 1998, 2001, Samson and Dalila 1998, Don Giovanni 2000, Into the Woods 2000, La Voix Humaine 2001, The Magic Flute 2001, Little Night Music 2002.

SCHELLENBERGER, Dagmar; singer (soprano); b. 8 June 1958, Oschatz, Germany. *Education:* Musikhochschule Dresden with Prof. Ilse Hahn. *Career:* from 1984 with Komische Oper, Berlin, singing: Donna Anna, in Dargomyzhsky's The Stone Guest; Eurydice, in Orfeo ed Eurydice; Rosalind (1995); guest artist in many German theatres including Dresden, as Aennchen in Freischütz and Laura in Weber's Die drei Pintos; in Leipzig as Hanna in The Merry Widow; Berlin Staatsoper as Agathe in Der Freischütz; Susanna in Le nozze di Figaro, at Hamburgische Staatsoper; US debut as Eurydice with Komische Oper Berlin and as Elena, in Donna del Lago 1992; Opéra de Bordeaux debut as Woglinde, in Das Rheingold; Italian debut with RAI Roma; Beethoven's 9th in Bordeaux 1992; title role in L'incoronazione di Poppea, Opéra de Marseille 1993; other engagements include: Countess in Le nozze di Figaro for Opera Northern Ireland; Anne in Marschner's Hans Heiling, Netherlands Opera; all four sopranos, Contes d'Hoffmann, Komische Oper Berlin; Donna Anna in Don Giovanni 1993; Adina in L'Elisir d'amore; Norina in Don Pasquale; Webern Cantatas with Beethoven Acad., Antwerp and Brussels; Brahms, Ein Deutsches Requiem with Berlin Philharmonic; Messiah with Cleveland Orchestra; Donna Anna at Strasbourg Festival; sang Anna Maria Strada in the premiere of Farinelli by Matthus, Karlsruhe 1998; season 2000–01 as Volkhova in Rimsky's Sadko at Venice and as Lehar's Hanna Glawari at the Leipzig Gewandhaus; as Iduna in Paul Burkhard's operetta The Fireworks 2014. *Recordings include:* Mozart's Bastien und Bastienne, Hasse's Mass with Capriccio, Handel's L'Allegro, il penseroso ed il moderato, Mozart's Kleinere Kirchenwerke, Solo Recital of Mozart Arias, Marenka in The Bartered Bride. *Honours:* winner Dvořák Int. Voice Competition 1982, Kammersängerin, Germany 1988. *E-mail:* office@dagmar -schellenberger.de. *Website:* www.dagmar-schellenberger.de.

SCHELLENBERGER, Hansjörg; German oboist and conductor; *Professor of Oboe, Escuela Superior de Música Reina Sofía*; b. 13 Feb. 1948, Munich. *Education:* Musikhochschule Munich, Tech. Univ. of Munich, Musikhochschule Detmold (Konzertexamen mit Auszeichnung). *Career:* Deputy Solo Oboist, Cologne Radio Symphony Orchestra 1971–75, Solo Oboist 1975–80; worked with Berlin Philharmonic Orchestra under Herbert von Karajan 1977, Solo Oboist 1980–2001; teacher, Hochschule der Künste, Berlin 1981–91; mem. Wind Ensemble of Berlin Philharmonic, Ensemble Wien-Berlin 1983–2013; Founder and Dir Haydn Ensemble, Berlin 1991–2001; regular performances as duettist with Rolf Koenen (piano), Wolfgang Schulz (flute), Margit-Anna Süss (harp); has performed as soloist with conductors including Claudio Abbado, Carlo Maria Giulini, Riccardo Muti, James Levine; teacher, Hochschule für Musik, Berlin 1981–91; Prof. of Oboe, Escuela Superior de Música Reina Sofía 2000–; masterclasses at Accad. Chigiana, Siena, Scuola di Musica, Fiesole, at his home in Sachrang, Bavaria 2003–; now mainly conductor with many different orchestras world-wide, including NHK Orchestra, Tokyo, Camerata Salzburg, Deutsche Radiophilharmonie Saarbrücken, Rundfunkorchester München, Vienna Symphony, amongst others; Chief Conductor Okayama Philharmonic Orchestra, Japan 2013–. *Recordings include:* about 50 albums, including Poulenc, Chamber Music 1989, Nielsen, Quintet for winds 1991, Mozart, Sinfonia Concertante K197b 1992, Salon Music of the 19th Century 1992, Hansjörg Schellenberger and Margit-Anna Süss, Duo Recital 1992, Mozart, Posthorn Serenade 1993, Mozart, Divertimenti 1994, Mozart and Beethoven, Quintets (with Daniel Barenboim) 1994, Wilhelm Friedemann Bach, Six Duets 1994, Lachner, Nonet/Piano Quintet 1995, Martin/Ibert/Lutosławski, Concertante 1998, Britten, Musik mit Oboe 1998, Bach, Sonaten 1998, Brahms/Mozart, Violin Concertos 2000, Romantic Oboe Concerti, Weber Symphonies and Piano Concerti of Mozart with Camerata Salzburg and Yu Kosuge, Telemann Fantasies and Kleine Kammermusik, Haydn Seven Last Words of Jesus Christ as Oboe Quartet together with Mozart's Oboe Quartet K370. *Honours:* First Prize, 'Jugend musiziert' 1965, Competition of German Conservatories 1971, Second Prize, Int. ARD Competition, Munich 1972, Cultural Promotion Prize of Bavaria 1972, Grammy Award 1990. *Address:* Escuela Superior de Música Reina Sofía, Plaza de Oriente s/n, 28013 Madrid, Spain (office). *Telephone:* (91) 3511060 (office). *Fax:* (91) 3510788 (office). *E-mail:* esmrs@albeniz.com (office). *Website:* www.escuelasuperiordemusicareinasofia.es (office); www.hansjoerg -schellenberger.de.

SCHELLHORN, Matthew; British pianist; b. 1977, Yorkshire, England. *Education:* Chetham's School of Music, Manchester, Univ. of Cambridge with David Hartigan, Maria Curcio, Ryszard Bakst and Peter Hill, studied in Paris with Yvonne Loriod-Messiaen. *Career:* guest soloist at several int. festivals including Three Choirs Festival, Windsor Festival, Presteigne Festival of Music and Arts, Sounds New, Canterbury, Kew Music Festival, Britten Sinfonia/BBC Radio 3 Tippett festival, Cambridge 2005; concerto performances with various ensembles including London Mozart Players, sinfonia ViVA, Cambridge Univ. Chamber Orchestra, Notes Inégales; has worked with numerous conductors including Baldur Brönnimann, Stephen Cleobury, Andrew Fardell, Jane Glover, David Hill, Russell Keable and Peter Stark; particularly noted for his performances of the music of Olivier Messiaen. *Recordings include:* Messiaen: Chamber Works 2008, Aisha Orazbayeva Outside 2011, Stations 2011. *Honours:* Hon. Fellowship for contrib. to music, Acad. of St Cecilia 2012. *Address:* c/o Signum Records, Suite 14, 21 Wadsworth Road, Perivale, Greenford, UB6 7JD, Middlesex, England (office). *Website:* www.matthewschellhorn.com (office).

SCHEMTSCHUK, Ludmilla; singer (mezzo-soprano); b. 14 Sept. 1946, Donetsk, Ukraine. *Education:* Odessa Conservatory. *Career:* sang at the Minsk Opera from 1970; Bolshoi Theatre Moscow from 1978, as Pauline (The Queen of Spades), Azucena, Amneris, Eboli, Dorabella, Ortrud, Fricka, Carmen and Charlotte (Werther); has sung at the Vienna Staatsoper from 1985 as Laura in La Gioconda, Marina (Boris Godunov), Ulrica and Marfa in Khovanshchina; guest appearances at the Verona Arena (Azucena 1985), Munich, Hamburg, Caracalla Festival, Rome and Stuttgart (Santuzza 1987); Countess in The Queen of Spades at Buenos Aires 1995; sang with Kirov Opera in Tchaikovsy's Mazeppa, as Lyubov 1998; season 2000 as Solokha in Tchaikovsky's Cherevichki, at Cagliari, and Ulrica at Barcelona; concert tours of Finland, Bulgaria and Hungary. *Recordings include:* La Gioconda (video).

SCHENK, Otto; opera producer; b. 12 June 1930, Vienna, Austria. *Education:* studied with Max Reinhardt, Univ. of Vienna. *Career:* debut opera production Die Zauberflöte, Salzburg Landestheater 1957; Don Pasquale at the Vienna Volksoper 1961; Vienna Festival 1963, Dantons Tod and Lulu; Salzburg Festival 1963, Die Zauberflöte and Der Rosenkavalier; Jenůfa at the Vienna Staatsoper 1964; Chief Stage Dir from 1965; further productions include Macbeth and Der Freischütz; opera productions in Frankfurt, Berlin, Munich (Der Rosenkavalier 1975) and Stuttgart; Metropolitan Opera from 1970; Tosca, Fidelio, Tannhäuser, Les Contes d'Hoffmann, Arabella and Der Ring des Nibelungen 1986–88; La Scala Milan 1974, Le nozze di Figaro, Covent Garden 1975, Un Ballo in Maschera; Savonlinna Festival 1991, The Bartered Bride; Elektra and Die Meistersinger at the Metropolitan 1992–93. *Recordings include:* Der Ring des Nibelungen (video, from the Metropolitan).

SCHERBACHENKO, Ekaterina; Russian singer (soprano); b. 1977. *Education:* Moscow State Conservatory. *Career:* mem. Bolshoi Theatre 2005–, roles include Natasha Rostova in War and Peace, Mimi in La Bohème, Liù in Turandot), Tatiana in Eugene Onegin, Micäela in Carmen and title role in

Iolanta; has performed at Opéra de Lyon, Opéra de Paris, France, Teatro alla Scala, Milan, Teatro Lirico di Cagliari, and in concert with Danish Nat. Symphony Orchestra, Royal Scottish Nat. Orchestra, St Petersburg Philharmonic (Ravenna Festival). *Honours:* BBC Cardiff Singer of the World 2009. *Current Management:* c/o Peter Wiggins, IMG Artists, 31–33 rue du Temple, Paris 75004, France. *Telephone:* 1-44-31-00-10. *Fax:* 1-44-31-44-40. *E-mail:* pwiggins@imgartists.com. *Website:* www.imgartists.com.

SCHERLER, Barbara; singer (contralto); b. 10 Jan. 1938, Leipzig, Germany. *Education:* Berlin Musikhochschule, studied with Margarete Barwinkel. *Career:* sang at Frankfurt 1959–64, Cologne Opera 1964–68, Deutsche Oper Berlin from 1968, notably in the 1984 premiere of Gespenstersonate by Reimann; guest appearances in London, Brussels, Lisbon, Mexico City, Zürich and Venice; noted concert artist, particularly in works by Bach. *Recordings:* Bach Cantatas, Masses by Mozart, Penthesilea by Schoeck.

SCHEUERELL, Douglas Andrew, BMus with distinction; American musician (tabla, guitar, voice) and academic; *Tabla Specialist, School of Music and Dance, University of Oregon*; b. 31 May 1948, Madison, Wis.; m. Victoria Ann Scheuerell 1992; one s. *Education:* Univ. of Wisconsin, Madison, Ali Akbar Coll. of Music, San Rafael, Calif., studied with Ali Akbar Khan, Swapan Chaudhuri, Jnan Prakash Ghosh, Samir Chatterjee. *Career:* musician, Madison 1966–74; Intern Choral Dir Sun Prairie High School, Wis. 1970; recording artist, Stas WHA and WHA-TV, Madison 1973–74; musician, composer, Missing Link Theatre Co., Berkeley, Calif. 1977–78; Faculty mem. East Bay Center for the Performing Arts, Berkeley 1977–78; Family Light Music School, Sausalito, Calif. 1978; Elizabeth Waters Dance Ensemble, Albuquerque, New Mexico 1979–80; accompanist, Univ. of New Mexico School of Dance, Albuquerque 1979–80; tabla soloist and accompanist, North Indian classical music 1988–; tabla tutor, Eugene, Ore. 1988–93; Faculty mem. and tabla specialist, Univ. of Oregon School of Music and Dance, Eugene 1993–; residencies in California schools, Nat. Endowment for the Arts 1977–78; performance grantee, Lane Regional Arts Council, Eugene 1989, 2010; faculty devt grantee, Univ. of Oregon, Eugene 1996; performances for Percussive Arts Soc., Asia Soc. *Film:* Musical Dir Wisconsin We Care. *Radio:* composed music for educational programming, WHA. *Recordings:* Badger A Go-Go, Vanish Into Blue, Communion, Loss, Structures. *Address:* School of Music and Dance, 1225 University of Oregon, Eugene, OR 97403-1225 (office); 1557 D Street, Springfield, OR 97477, USA (home). *Telephone:* (541) 346-5642 (office); (541) 484-9305 (home). *Fax:* (541) 346-0723 (office). *E-mail:* dougsch@uoregon.edu (office). *Website:* music.uoregon.edu/people/faculty/scheuerell.htm (office); dougmusic.info.

SCHEVCHENKO, Larissa; Russian singer (soprano); b. 1952, Kiev. *Education:* St Petersburg Conservatoire. *Career:* appearances with the Kirov Opera, St Petersburg, from 1976 as Aida, Olga in The Maid of Pskov by Rimsky-Korsakov, Lisa in The Queen of Spades and Maria in War and Peace; other roles include Tatiana, Leonora (Il Trovatore), Mimi and Maria in Tchaikovsky's Mazeppa; sang with the Kirov Opera in London, 1999–2000, as Katerina in Lady Macbeth of Mtsensk (Barbican Hall) and Maria in War and Peace (Covent Garden). *Honours:* Grand Prix in Holland, 1978 and Gold Medal in Belgium, 1979; Glinka All-Union Competition; Honoured Artist of the Republic and People's Artist of Russia.

SCHEXNAYDER, Brian; singer (baritone); b. 18 Sept. 1953, Port Arthur, TX, USA. *Education:* Juilliard School, New York. *Career:* sang in operas by Verdi and Puccini while at Juilliard; Metropolitan Opera from 1980 as Ashton (Lucia di Lammermoor), Marcello (La Bohème), Guglielmo and Lescaut in Manon Lescaut; Paris Opéra 1982–83, as Marcello; sang Marcello at the Metropolitan 1989, Valentin in Faust 1990.

SCHIAVI, Felice; singer (baritone); b. 4 July 1931, Vimercate, Italy. *Education:* studied with Riccardo Malipiero in Monza, Carlo Tagliabue, Carlo Alfieri and Enrico Pessina in Milan. *Career:* has sung widely in Italy from 1955, notably at Rome, Parma, Bologna, Trieste, Naples, Milan and Venice; Verona Arena 1977; Vienna Staatsoper 1984, as Paolo in Simon Boccanegra; further appearances in Nice, Marseille, Edinburgh, Prague, Barcelona, Moscow, Munich, Glasgow, Cardiff and Warsaw; other roles include Amonasro, Renato, Luna, Iago, Posa, Don Carlos (La Forza del Destino), Simon Boccanegra, Scarpia, Gerard, Barnaba and Escamillo.

SCHICK, Steven, MMus; American musician (percussion), conductor, writer and academic; *Distinguished Professor of Music, University of California, San Diego*; b. 1954, Iowa. *Education:* Univ. of Iowa, Staatliche Hochschule für Musik Freiburg, Germany. *Career:* champion of contemporary percussion music as performer and teacher; has commissioned and premiered more than 150 new works for percussion and performed works on major concert series, including Lincoln Center's Great Performers and Los Angeles Philharmonic's Green Umbrella concerts, and at int. festivals including Warsaw Autumn, BBC Proms, Jerusalem Festival, Holland Festival, Stockholm Int. Percussion Event, Budapest Spring Festival; percussionist, Bang on a Can All-Stars, New York 1992–2002; Artistic Dir, Centre Int. de Percussion, Geneva, Switzerland 2002–04; Founder and Artistic Dir, red fish blue fish percussion group; Resident Guest Conductor, ICE (int. chamber ensemble); apptd mem. Music Faculty, California State Univ.-Fresno 1983; Distinguished Prof. of Music, Univ. of California, San Diego 1991–, also holds Reed Family Presidential Chair; Lecturer in Percussion, Manhattan School of Music 1985–; Music Dir La Jolla Symphony and Chorus 2007–; Artistic Dir San Francisco Contemporary Music Players 2011–; Music Dir Ojai Festival 2015; Guest Lecturer,

Rotterdam Conservatory, Royal Coll. of Music, London; guest conducting appearances have included BBC Scottish Symphony Orchestra, Saint Paul Chamber Orchestra, Ensemble Modern, Asko/Schönberg Ensemble. *Recordings include:* John Luther Adams' The Mathematics of Resonant Bodies 2006, percussion music of Karlheinz Stockhausen 2014; with red fish blue fish: Complete percussion music of Iannis Xenakis 2006. *Publication:* The Percussionist's Art: Same Bed, Different Dreams 2006. *Honours:* First Prize in competition sponsored by American Wind Symphony Orchestra 1980, Kranichstein Prize, Darmstadt Summer Course 1982, American Composers Forum Champion of New Music 2014, inducted into Percussive Arts Soc. *Address:* UCSD Department of Music, Conrad Prebys Music Center, 9500 Gilman Drive MC 0099, La Jolla, CA 92093-0099, USA (office). *Telephone:* (858) 534-3752 (office). *E-mail:* sschick@ucsd.edu (office). *Website:* musicweb.ucsd.edu (office).

SCHIDLOWSKY, Leon; composer; b. 21 July 1931, Santiago, Chile. *Education:* Nat. Conservatory, Santiago, studied in Germany. *Career:* founder of performance group, Agrupacion Tonus, for the promotion of new music; teacher, Santiago Music Inst. 1955–63; Prof. of Composition, Univ. of Chile 1962–68; emigrated to Israel 1969; faculty mem., Rubin Acad., Tel-Aviv. *Compositions:* Jeremias for eight mixed voices and strings 1966, String Quartet 1967, Wind Quintet 1968, Sextet 1970, Bai Yar for strings, piano and percussion 1970, Rabbi Akiba, Scenic Fantasy 1972, Images for strings 1976, Lux in Tenebris for orchestra 1977, Adieu for mezzo and chamber orchestra 1982, Missa in Nomine Bach for chorus and eight instruments 1984, Trilogy for orchestra 1986, Ballade for violin and orchestra 1986, Piano Quartet 1988, String Quartet No. 2 1988, Laudatio for orchestra 1988, Kaleidoscope for orchestra 1989, Trio In Memoriam Vruno Maderna 1990, Sealed Room for 12 instruments 1991, Silvestre Revueltas (oratorio) 1994, Am Grab Kafkas for woman singer playing crotales 1994, I Will Lay My Hand Upon My Mouth for orchestra 1994, Dybbuk (opera) 1994, Laudate for chorus 1995, Absalom for orchestra 1996, Before Breakfast (monodrama) 1997, Lamento for soprano, string quartet and percussion 1998.

SCHIEFERSTEIN, Eva; German pianist and harpsichordist; b. 17 March 1955, Büdesheim; d. of Gerhard Schieferstein and Gertraud Schieferstein (née Klingler). *Education:* Ludwig Maximilians Univ., Munich, Richard Strauss Konservatorium, Munich, Salzburg Mozarteum; master classes with Elisabeth Leonskaja, Peter Feuchtwanger, Eckart Sellheim, Marina Horak and others. *Career:* debut at Municipal Hall, Friedberg, Germany 1983; specialised in contemporary music, lied accompaniment and chamber music; chamber concerts in Meran 1984, Berlin 1986, Bayreuth 1989, Reims 1991, Dresden 1992, Wartburg 1997, Salzburg 2002, Prague 2003, Salamanca 2009 and elsewhere; performed at Festivals for Contemporary Music, Bacau, Romania 1994, Bucharest, Romania 1995, Belgrade, Yugoslavia 1998, Pilsen, Czech Repub. 2006; recorded for Bavarian Broadcasting Station, Deutschland Radio, SWF Radio, Radio Berlin Brandenburg, Czech Radio; mem. European Piano Teachers' Asscn, GEDOK, Cttee Münchner Tonkünstlerverband. *Recordings:* as pianist/harpsichordist of Munich Flute Trio: Musik in Sanssouci, Oper im Salon, Masterpieces of Baroque Chamber Music, Noble Tafelmusik, Musik am Hofe August des Starken (Music at the Court of August the Strong), Friedrich der Grosse (Flute Music from Sanssouci), Münchner Flötentrio – Kompositionen für das Münchner Flötentrio; Dorothee Eberhardt 2008, Wilhelmine von Bayreuth 2010, Amüsantes und Rasantes 2012; Duo Elisabeth Weinzierl (flute) and Eva Schieferstein (piano): Flötenmusik von Komponistinnen (Flute Music by Female Composers) 2011, Hauptweg und Nebenwege 2012; as soloist: Carl Maria von Weber: Tänzerische Klaviermusik; Piano Duo Angela-Charlott Bieber & Eva Schieferstein: Dorothee Eberhardt, Kammermusik von Roland Leistner-Mayer. *Publications:* Piano Reduction: Paul Hindemith, Pantomime from the Opera Cardillac for 2 Flutes and Piano 2010. *Honours:* Special Prize as Lied Accompanist, Brahms Competition, Hamburg 1985. *Address:* Baldurstr. 31, 80637 Munich, Germany. *Telephone:* (89) 1576614. *Fax:* (89) 1576614.

SCHIEMER, Gregory, BMus, PhD; Australian composer, electronic instrument designer and academic; *Associate Professor of Music Technology*; b. 16 Jan. 1949, Dunedoo, NSW. *Education:* Univ. of Sydney, Control Data Inst., Macquarie Univ. *Career:* computer technician, Digital Equipment Australia 1976–81; Lecturer in Composition, New South Wales Conservatorium 1986–2002; Sr Lecturer in Music Technology, Faculty of Creative Arts, Univ. of Wollongong 2003, Assoc. Prof. 2004–; mem., Int. Computer Music Asscn; Sec. Australasian Computer Music Asscn. *Compositions include:* (most with purpose-built electronics) Laotian Wood for piccolo, flute, alto flute, soprano saxophone, tenor saxophone and harp, 1970–72; Brolga for computer generated tape, 1973; Iconophony for piano, 1973; Body Sonata for theremin controlled analogue electronics, 1974; A Rain Poem for theremin controlled digital synthesiser, 1975; Ground-Harp for theremin controlled analogue electronics, 1977; Karamojan Wood for 2 marimbas, 1978; Mandala I and II for Tupperware Gamelan, 1981–82; Porcelain Dialogue for Tupperware Gamelan, 1982–83; Monophonic Variations for percussion and interactive MIDI system, 1986; Music for Shreelata for percussion, Tupperware Gamelan and computer generated tape, 1986; Polyphonic Variations for percussion and interactive MIDI system, 1988; Spectral Dance for MIDI Tool Box and Tupperware Gamelan, 1991; Talk-Back Piano for MIDI Tool Box and Disklavier, 1991; Voltage-Control Piano Studies for MIDI Tool Box and Disklavier, 1991; Token Objects for MIDI Tool Box and Tupperware Gamelan, 1993; Machine Dance for MIDI Tool Box and clarinet, 1994; Shantivanam for carnatic violin and MIDI Tool Box, 1995; Shantivanam II for veena and A4 MIDI Tool Box, 1996; Vedic Mass for 2 sopranos and 2 mezzo-sopranos, 19998; Transposed Hexanies for computer generated tape, 2000–01; Tempered Dekanies for computer generated tape, 2002; Tampatablatarangalila for tabla and MIDI Tool Box, 2002; A Dekany In Memorian for computer generated tape, 2003. *Honours:* various grants, Univ. of Sydney 1990–95, Australia Council Composer's Fellowship for musical instrument design at CSIRO Div. of Radiophysics 1994, Australian Research Council Collaborative Project for musical applications of 3D audio with Lake Technology 1997, Australian Research Council Discovery Project for mobile J2ME musical instrument devt 2003–05, Research Infrastructure Grant for 3D audio, Univ. of Wollongong 2003, Australian Research Council Linkage Project with Capital Authority and Olympic Carillon International 2005–07. *Address:* Faculty of Creative Arts, Building 25, University of Wollongong, 2522, Australia (office). *Telephone:* (2) 4221-3584 (office). *Fax:* (2) 4221-3301 (office). *E-mail:* schiemer@uow.edu.au (office).

SCHIFF, Sir András, Kt; British (b. Hungarian) pianist; b. 21 Dec. 1953, Budapest; s. of Odon Schiff and Klara Schiff (née Csengeri). *Education:* Franz Liszt Acad. of Music, Budapest with Pal Kadosa, Gyorgy Kurtag and Ferenc Rados, pvt lessons with George Malcolm, England. *Career:* recitals in London, New York, Paris, Vienna, Munich, Florence; concerts with New York Philharmonic, Chicago Symphony, Vienna Philharmonic, Concertgebouw, Orchestre de Paris, London Philharmonic, London Symphony, Philharmonia, Royal Philharmonic, Israel Philharmonic, Berlin Philharmonic, Cleveland, Philadelphia, Washington Nat. Symphony; played at Salzburg, Edinburgh, Aldeburgh, Feldkirch Schubertiade, Lucerne and Tanglewood Festivals; f. Musiktage Mondsee Festival 1989 (Artistic Dir 1989–98); f. orchestra Cappella Andrea Barca 1999; Special Supernumerary Fellow, Balliol Coll., Oxford, UK 2011–. *Recordings include:* Bach Goldberg Variations, Bach Partitas, Bach Piano Concertos, Mendelssohn Concertos 1 and 2, all the Schubert Sonatas, Schubert Trout Quintet, Schumann and Chopin 2, all the Mozart Concertos, Bach Two- and Three-part Inventions, Bach Well-Tempered Klavier, Beethoven Violin and Piano Sonatas with Sandor Vegh, Beethoven Piano Concertos, Bartók Piano Concertos, Tchaikovsky Piano Concerto, Bach English Suites (Grammy Award 1990), Bach French Suites, Lieder with Peter Schreier, Robert Holl and Cecilia Bartoli, etc., Beethoven Piano Sonatas Op. 2 Nos 1–3 and Op. 7 No. 4 2005, Beethoven Piano Sonatas Op. Nos 6–8 2008, Schumann Geistervariationen (Int. Classical Music Award for Recording of the Year and Best Solo Instrument Recording 2012) 2011, Franz Schubert (double CD) 2015. *Television:* The Wanderer – A Film About Schubert with András Schiff (BBC Omnibus, narrator), Chopin with András Schiff (BBC Omnibus, narrator). *Honours:* Hon. Prof., Music Schools in Budapest, Detmold and Munich 2011–; Mem. of Honour, Vienna Konzerthaus 2012; Ordre pour le Mérite for Sciences and Arts 2012; Prizewinner at Tchaikovsky Competition, Moscow 1974 and Leeds Piano Competition 1975, Liszt Prize 1977, Premio dell'Accad. Chigiana, Siena 1987, RPS/Charles Heidsieck Award for best concert series of 1988–89, Wiener Flötenuhr 1989, Bartók Prize 1991, Instrumentalist of the Year, Royal Philharmonic Soc. 1994, Claudio Arrau Memorial Medal 1994, Kossuth Prize 1996, Sonning Prize, Copenhagen 1997, Palladio d'Oro della Città di Vicenza 2003, Musikfest Prize, Bremen 2003, Abbiati Prize 2007, RAM Bach Prize 2007, Wigmore Medal 2008, Klavier-Festival Ruhr Prize for outstanding achievements and to honour a lifetime's work as a pianist 2009, Schumann Prize, City of Zwickau 2011, Gold Medal, Royal Philharmonic Soc. 2013. *E-mail:* info@askonasholt.co.uk. *Website:* www.askonasholt.co.uk.

SCHIFF, Heinrich; Austrian cellist and conductor; b. 18 Nov. 1951, Gruunden. *Career:* London and Vienna debuts 1973; subsequently undertook extensive concert tours in Europe, Japan and USA appearing with numerous orchestras; interpreter of contemporary music including work of Lutosławski, Henze, Krenek and Penderecki and has given first performances of many new works; Artistic Dir Northern Sinfonia 1990–96; Prin. Guest Conductor, Deutsche Kammerphilharmonie 1990–92; apptd Prin. Conductor, Musikkollegium, Winterthur and Copenhagen Philharmonic Orchestra 1995; Chief Conductor, Vienna Chamber Orchestra 2005–08. *Current Management:* Künstlersekretariat Schoerke GmbH, Grazer Str. 30, 30519 Hannover, Germany. *E-mail:* info@ks-schoerke.de. *Website:* www.heinrichschiff.com.

SCHIFRIN, Lalo; Argentine pianist, composer, conductor and educator; b. 21 June 1932, Buenos Aires; m. Donna; three c. *Education:* Paris Conservatoire with Olivier Messiaen. *Career:* professional jazz pianist, composer and arranger 1950s–; represented Argentina, Paris Int. Jazz Festival 1955; founder of big band late 1950s; moved to USA 1958; played with Dizzy Gillespie, including European tour with Jazz at the Philharmonic Ensemble 1960–62; also played with Quincy Jones, Jimmy Smith, Sarah Vaughan, Ella Fitzgerald, Stan Getz and Count Basie; Tutor of Composition, Univ. of California at Los Angeles 1968–71; Musical Dir, Paris Philharmonic Orchestra 1987–92; Music Dir, Glendale Symphony Orchestra 1989–95; guest conductor of orchestras, including Atlanta Symphony Orchestra, Georgian State Symphony Orchestra, Houston Symphony Orchestra, Israel Philharmonic, London Philharmonic Orchestra, London Symphony Orchestra, Los Angeles Chamber Orchestra, Los Angeles Philharmonic, Mexico City Philharmonic, Mexico Philharmonic, Moscow Symphony Orchestra, National Symphony Orchestra of Argentina, Orchestra of Saint Luke (New York), Orchestre de la Suisse Romande (Geneva, Switzerland), Vienna Symphony Orchestra; Adviser to the Pres. in Cultural Affairs (Sec. of the Cabinet),

Argentina 1998. *Compositions include:* Concerto for double bass, Concerto for guitar and orchestra, Down Here on the Ground, Gone with the Wave, Harp Aujourd'hui, La Clave, Music for harp, Invocations, La Nouvelle Orleans, New Continent Suite, Pulsations, Rain Dance, Resonances, Spectrum, Tristeza on Piano, Tropicos, Piano Concerto No. 1, Piano Concerto No. 2 1992, Cantares Argentinos 1992, Christmas in Vienna 1992, Lili'Uokalani Symphony 1995, Rhapsody for Bix 1996, Concerto Caribeño for flute and orchestra 1997, Gillespiana Suite 1998, Latin Jazz Suite 1999, Esperanto 2000, Fantasy for screenplay and orchestra 2002, Symphonic Impressions of Oman 2003, Letters from Argentina 2005, Double Concerto for Piano, Trumpet and Orchestra 2007, Tangos Concertantes 2008, Elegy and Meditation 2009, Pampas (Latin Grammy Award for Best Classical Contemporary Composition 2010) 2009. *Compositions for film include:* Venga a bailar el rock 1957, El Jefe 1958, Rhino! 1964, Les Félins 1964, See How They Run 1964, The Way Out Men 1965, Once a Thief 1965, Dark Intruder 1965, The Cincinnati Kid 1965, The Liquidator 1965, Blindfold 1965, Wall Street: Where the Money is 1966, Way... Way Out 1966, The Making of a President: 1966, The Doomsday Flight 1966, Murderers' Row 1966, I Deal in Danger 1966, How I Spent My Summer Vacation 1967, The Venetian Affair 1967, Sullivan's Empire 1967, Cool Hand Luke 1967, The Fox 1967, The President's Analyst 1967, Mission Impossible Versus the Mob 1968, Coogan's Bluff 1968, Bullitt 1968, Hell in the Pacific 1968, The Rise and Fall of the Third Reich 1968, The Brotherhood 1968, U.M.C. 1969, Che! 1969, Eye of the Cat 1969, The Young Lawyers 1969, Pussycat, Pussycat, I Love You 1970, Kelly's Heroes 1970, The Aquarians 1970, I Love My Wife 1970, The Beguiled 1971, Pretty Maids All in a Row 1971, The Hellstrom Chronicle 1971, Earth II 1971, The Christian Licorice Store 1971, Dirty Harry 1971, Prime Cut 1972, The Wrath of God 1972, The Neptune Factor 1973, Enter the Dragon 1973, Hit! 1973, Egan 1973, Magnum Force 1973, Up from the Ape 1974, Night Games 1974, The Four Musketeers 1974, The Master Gunfighter 1975, Sky Riders 1976, Special Delivery 1976, Voyage of the Damned 1976, The Eagle has Landed 1976, Day of the Animals 1977, Good Against Evil 1977, Rollercoaster 1977, Telefon 1977, The President's Mistress 1978, Return from Witch Mountain 1978, Nunzio 1978, Escape to Athena 1979, Boulevard Nights 1979, Love and Bullets 1979, The Amityville Horror 1979, The Concorde... Airport '79 1979, The Nude Bomb 1980, The Big Brawl 1980, The Competition 1980, Chicago Story 1981, Caveman 1981, Los Viernes de la eternidad 1981, La Pelle 1981, Wait Until Dark 1982, The Seduction 1982, A Stranger is Watching 1982, Class of 1984 1982, Amityville II: The Possession 1982, The Sting II 1983, The Osterman Weekend 1983, The New Kids 1985, Private Sessions 1985, Command 5 1985, Bad Medicine 1985, Bridge Across Time 1985, Black Moon Rising 1986, Kung Fu: The Movie 1986, Triplecross 1986, Beverly Hills Madam 1986, The Ladies' Club 1986, Out on a Limb 1987, The Fourth Protocol 1987, Earth Star Voyager 1988, The Dead Pool 1988, Berlin Blues 1988, The Neon Empire 1989, Original Sin 1989, Return from the River Kwai 1989, Face to Face 1990, F/X2 1991, The Beverly Hillbillies 1993, Scorpion Spring 1996, Money Talks 1997, Something to Believe In 1998, Tango, no me dejes nunca 1998, Rush Hour 1998, Longshot 2000, Rush Hour 2 2001, Tom the Cat 2002, Bringing Down the House 2003, Biyik 2004, After the Sunset 2004, The Bridge of San Luis Rey 2004, Abominable 2006, Rush Hour 3 2007, Love and Virtue 2008, Love Story 2011, Sweetwater 2013, Tales of Halloween 2015. *Compositions for television:* music for episodes of The Man from U.N.C.L.E. 1965, Shipwrecked 1966, T.H.E. Cat 1966, Jericho 1966, National Geographic documentaries 1966, Mannix 1967, The Big Valley 1968–69, Medical Center 1969, The Young Lawyers 1970, The Partners 1971, Night Gallery 1972, The Sixth Sense 1972, Mission Impossible (BMI Composer's Award 2001) 1966–73, Petrocelli 1974, Planet of the Apes 1974, Bronk 1975, Starsky and Hutch 1975, Hollywood Wives 1985, A.D. 1985, El Quijote de Miguel de Cervantes 1991, A Woman Named Jackie 1991, Danger Theatre 1993. *Honours:* four Grammy Awards, Cable ACE Award, BMI Lifetime Achievement Award 1988, MIDEM Classique Festival Award 1990, Los Angeles Music Center Distinguished Artist Award 1998, SACEM Award for contribution to music, film and culture 2004, American Soc. of Music Arrangers & Composers Golden Score Award 2004; Chevalier, Ordre des Arts et des Lettres; Dr hc (Rhode Island School of Design), (Univ. of La Plata, Argentina). *Current Management:* c/o Rich Jacobellis, First Artists Management, 4764 Park Granada, Suite 210, Calabasas, CA 91302, USA. *Telephone:* (818) 377-7750. *E-mail:* rjacobellis@firstartistsmgmt.com. *Website:* www.firstartistsmgmt.com. *E-mail:* l2schifrin@aol.com (office). *Website:* www.schifrin.com.

SCHILDKNECHT, Gregor; Swiss singer (baritone); b. 18 Oct. 1936, Biel. *Education:* Univ. of Music, Vienna with Adolf Vogel, studied in Nuremberg with Domgraf Fassbänder, in Düsseldorf with Carino. *Career:* sang at the Oldenburg Opera 1965–67, Coburg 1968–73, Detmold 1973–74, Krefeld 1974–77, and Bielefeld 1977–80; guest engagements from 1980 at the Berlin Staatsoper, Hamburg, Düsseldorf, Karlsruhe, Geneva, Amsterdam, Brussels and Prague; roles have included parts in operas by Mozart, Donizetti, Rossini; Verdi's Luna, Rigoletto, Germont, Macbeth, Posa, Amonasro and Carlo in La Forza del Destino; Wolfram, Scarpia, the villains in Hoffmann and Mandryka in Arabella; concert engagements in Germany, Netherlands, Switzerland and USA. *Address:* 2555 Brügg bei Biel, Switzerland.

SCHILLER, Allan, ARCM, DipMus; British pianist; b. 18 March 1943, Leeds, Yorks. *Education:* Royal College of Music, Moscow Conservatoire. *Career:* debut with Hallé Orchestra with John Barbiroli, Leeds Town Hall, 1954; Edinburgh Festival, Scotland, 1954; Promenade Concert, London, 1957; subject of Philpott File, television documentary; toured in Canada, Europe,

Russia; Prof., Guildhall School of Music; mem. Incorporated Society of Musicians, Bristol Savages. *Recordings:* Recital, 1958; Chopin and Mozart; Bridge and Elgar Quintets with Coull Quartet; Complete Chopin Waltzes. *Honours:* Harriet Cohen Medal 1966. *Current Management: c/o* Camerata Artists, 4 Margaret Road, Birmingham B17 0EU, England. *Telephone:* (121) 426-6208. *Fax:* (211) 608-0676. *E-mail:* jrhumphreys@yahoo.co.uk. *Address:* 14 Lilymead Avenue, Knowle, Bristol 4, Avon, England. *Telephone:* (117) 972-3423 (office). *E-mail:* allan.schiller@virgin.net (office). *Website:* www .allanschiller.com (home).

SCHILLER, Christoph; Swiss violist; b. 17 May 1951, Zürich; m. Louise Pelerin 1981, one s. *Education:* Realgymnasium Zürichberg, Matura, University of Zürich, North Carolina School of Arts, Accademia Chigiana, Siena, Italy and Nordwestdeutsche Musikakademie, Detmold, Germany. *Career:* Violist, New Zürich String Quartet 1973–88, with tours in Europe, Israel, Scandinavia and North and South America; viola soloist with orchestras throughout Europe; Prof., Zürich and Basle Conservatories; founder and Artistic Dir, Ensemble Mobile 1989–. *Recordings:* Charles Koechlin, Viola Sonata; Willy Burkhard, works for viola; Giacinto Scelsi, Solo and Chamber Music; String Quartets by Brahms, Mendelssohn, Debussy, Ravel, Dvořák, Grieg and Haydn; chamber works by various Swiss composers. *Honours:* Swiss Musicians' Asscn Soloist's Prize 1976. *Address:* Bombachstr 21, 8049 Zürich, Switzerland.

SCHIML, Marga; singer (mezzo-soprano); b. 29 Nov. 1945, Weiden, Germany; m. Horst Laubenthal. *Education:* studied with Hanno Blaschke in Munich and with Hartmann-Dressler in Berlin. *Career:* debut at Basle Opera 1967, in Tigrane by Hasse; has sung in Vienna, Munich, Graz, Basle and Zürich; appearances at the Orange and Salzburg Festivals; Bayreuth Festival 1981, 1986, as Magdalene in Die Meistersinger and in Parsifal and Der Ring des Nibelungen; sang at Turin 1986, as Fricka in Das Rheingold; Maggio Musicale Florence 1989, Annina in Der Rosenkavalier. *Recordings:* Puck in Oberon, La Clemenza di Tito, Mozart Masses, Der Ring des Nibelungen, Choral Symphony, Masses by Weber.

SCHIMPF, Alexander; German pianist; b. 1981, Göttingen. *Education:* Hochschule für Musik, Würzburg. *Honours:* first prize, Int. Beethoven Piano Competition 2009, Cleveland Int. Piano Competition 2011. *Current Management: c/o* Konzertdirektion Fritz Dietrich GmbH, Sigmund-Freud-Strasse 1, 60435 Frankfurt am Main, GermanyFax: 0 e-mail:. *Telephone:* (69) 545658. *Fax:* (69) 5484107. *E-mail:* fdietrich@konzertdirektion-dietrich.de. *Website:* www.konzertdirektion-dietrich.de. *Address:* Hofstraße 14 1/2, 97070 Würzburg, Germany (home). *E-mail:* mail@alexander-schimpf.de (office). *Website:* www.alexander-schimpf.de.

SCHINDHELM, Michael; German music administrator and novelist; *Culture Director, Sama Dubai;* b. 1960, Eisenach. *Education:* Internationalen Universität Woronesh, Voronezh State Univ. *Career:* Dir Theater Nordhausen 1990–92, Gera City Theatres 1992–96, Basel Theatre 1996–2005; Gen. Dir Stiftung Oper Berlin (Berlin Opera Foundation) 2005–07; Culture Dir, Sama Dubai 2007–. *Television:* Lied von der Steppe (documentary, co-dir). *Publications:* novels: Roberts Reise 2001, Zauber des Westens 2001, Das Kamel auf der Startbahn 2004, Die Herausforderung 2005; trans.: Anton Chekhov, Onkel Wanja, Maxim Gorki, Nachtasyl; libretto: Lied von der Steppe. *Address: c/o* Sama Dubai, Dubai Health Care City, Building 51–52, PO Box 72527, Dubai, United Arab Emirates (office). *Telephone:* (4) 4279100 (office). *Fax:* (4) 3635305 (office). *E-mail:* info@sama-dubai.com (office). *Website:* www .sama-dubai.com (office).

SCHIPIZKY, Frederick Alexander, BMus, MMus, DMus; Canadian composer, conductor, bassist and teacher; b. 20 Dec. 1952, Calgary, Alberta; m. Ruth Fagerburg 1984. *Education:* Univ. of British Columbia, studied with Elliot Weisgarber, Jean Coulthard, Harry Freedman, Sophie Eckhardt-Gramatte Courtenay, Victoria Conservatory with Murray Adaskin, Juilliard School, New York with Roger Sessions, David Diamond and David Walter, Univ. of Toronto with John Beckwith and John Hawkins. *Career:* broadcasts on CBC radio and television with Vancouver Symphony Orchestra, and as composer, conductor and bassist; Bassist, Vancouver Symphony Orchestra; teacher of theory and composition, Vancouver Acad. of Music; faculty mem., Courtenay Youth Music Centre 1986; performed with Montréal Symphony Orchestra; faculty mem., Douglas Coll. from 1989; performed with Esprit Orchestra and Arraymusic; Assoc. Composer, Canadian Music Centre; mem. Canadian League of Composers. *Compositions:* Symphonic Sketches 1977, Fanfare for the Royal Visit 1983, Divertimento for string orchestra 1983, Symphony No. 1 1985, Symphony No. 2 1988, From Under the Overture 1990, Aurora Borealis 1992, Concerto for contrabass and orchestra 1994.

SCHIRMER, Astrid; singer (soprano); b. 8 Nov. 1942, Berlin, Germany. *Education:* Berlin Musikhochschule with Johanna Rakow and Elisabeth Grümmer. *Career:* debut in Coburg 1967, as Senta in Der fliegende Holländer; has sung at the Hanover Opera and widely in Germany, notably in Cologne, Mannheim, Berlin, Stuttgart and Nuremberg; guest appearances in Barcelona and Zürich; other roles include Santuzza, Leonore, Brünnhilde, Aida, Amelia (Un Ballo in Maschera), Sieglinde, Ariadne, Arabella, Tosca, Turandot and Lady Billows in Albert Herring; many concert appearances.

SCHIRMER, Ulf; German conductor; *Artistic Director, Symphonieorchester des Bayerischen Rundfunks;* b. 1959, Eschenhausen. *Education:* studied in Bremen and Hamburg with Horst Stein and Christoph von Dohnányi. *Career:*

began professional career at Mannheimer Nationaltheater 1980; Asst to Lorin Maazel at the Vienna Staatsoper; Gen. Music Dir and Artistic Dir, Hessisches Staatstheater Wiesbaden 1988–91; Resident Conductor and consultant, Vienna State Opera 1991–95; Chief Conductor, Danish Radio Symphony Orchestra 1995–98; Prof. Hochschule für Musik, Hamburg 2000–; Artistic Dir, Symphonieorchester des Bayerischen Rundfunks 2006–; Music Dir Opera Leipzig 2009–; has made regular guest appearances with Bregenzer Festspiele, Salzburger Festspiele, Grazer Oper, the Pariser Bastille, Teatro alla Scala, Deutsche Oper Berlin, Berliner Philharmoniker, Bamberger Symphoniker, Staatskapelle Dresden, Orchestre de la Suisse Romande, at Teatro alla Scala, Opera Bastille, Nat. Theatre, Tokyo. *Recordings include:* Capriccio, Lulu, Maskarade. *Current Management: c/o* Rudolf Berger, Overtones, Prinz Eugenstrasse 58/9–10, 1040 Vienna, Austria. *Telephone:* (1) 815-15-35-0. *Fax:* (1) 815-15-35-20-0. *E-mail:* schirmer@overtones.eu. *Website:* www.overtones.eu; www.ulfschirmer.com (home).

SCHIRRER, René; French singer (bass-baritone); b. 1957. *Education:* studied in Strasbourg, Basle and Salzburg. *Career:* sang with Groupe Vocal de France and with Lyon Opéra from 1983; Edinburgh Festival 1985; in Pelléas et Mélisande and Chabrier's Etoile; Aix-en-Provence in Lully's Psyché 1987; Karlsruhe as Rangoni in Boris Godunov and Montreal 1990; Les Troyens 1993; Herald in Lohengrin at Lyon 1995; appearances with Opéra du Rhin, Strasbourg, including title role in Honegger's Les Aventures du Roi Pausole 1998; other roles include Peter Quince, Zaccaria in Nabucco and Rossini's Basilio; sang Gounod's Frère Laurent at Strasbourg and Indra in Le Roi de Lahore by Massenet at St Etienne 1999–2000. *Recordings:* Le Roi Arthus by Chausson, Iphigénie in Aulide, Handel's Tamerlano and Leclair's Scylla et Glaucus.

SCHLAEPFER, Jean-Claude, DipMus; Swiss composer and teacher; *Professor, Haute Ecole de Musique, Geneva;* b. 11 Jan. 1961, Geneva. *Education:* Haute Ecole de Musique, Geneva, Acad. of Music, Paris with Betsy Jolas. *Career:* Prof., Dept of Harmony and Analysis, Haute Ecole de Musique, Geneva; Prof., Dept of Musical Languages, Univ. of Geneva. *Compositions include:* Esquisses en trois tableaux for violin and piano 1987, Instances I for piano or harpsichord 1987, Les Mots (3 melodies) for mezzo soprano and piano 1987–88, 3 Caprices, for violin in memory of N. Paganini, 1988, Impressions for 15 strings solo 1988; 5 Pieces for orchestra, in homage to Anton Webern, 1988, Dialogues, for solo violoncello 1989; Stabat Mater for soprano, mixed choir and orchestra 1990, 7 Preludes for two pianos 1991; Motets for soprano voice, viola da gamba and harp 1992, Trois rêves (Three Dreams) on poems by Georg Trakl for narrator, soprano, alto, wind quintet, string quartet and piano 1992, Concerto Solitude for violin and chamber orchestra 1993; Instances II for solo horn (commissioned by Geneva International Music competition) 1993, Visibili et Invisibili, for men's and children's choir a capella, 1994, Exil for symphony orchestra (commissioned by Orchestre de la Suisse Romande) 1994–95, Instances III for marimba alone 1994, Psaume for flute (C and G), oboe (and English horn), violoncello and organ 1994, Ascensus for trumpet and string orchestra 1995, L'impossible absence for symphony orchestra 1995, La Rose de Jéricho for soprano voice and piano 1995, Chant de lune for flute, oboe, clarinet, percussion, violin, viola and violoncello 1996, Missa Brevis for soprano and string quartet 1996, He de Re for violoncello and piano 1996, Instances IV for violin solo 1997–98, Trio à Karin for violin, violoncello and piano 1999, Lamentations de Jérémie for string orchestra 2000. *Recordings:* Impressions; Stabat Mater and 7 Preludes for two pianos, Radio Suisse Romande, Jean-Claude Schlaepfer, Portrait (including Exil, Motets, Ascensus, Missa brevis, Chant de lune, Trio à Karin, Visibili et invisibili). *Honours:* Composition Award, Geneva Conservatory 1988. *Address: c/o* Editions Bim, PO Box 300, 1674, Vuarmarens, Switzerland. *Telephone:* (21) 909-1000. *Fax:* (21) 909-1009. *E-mail:* admin@editions-bim.com. *Website:* www.editions-bim .com.

SCHLEE, Thomas Daniel, DrPhil; Austrian composer, organist, festival director and editor; *Director, Carinthian Summer Festival;* b. 26 Oct. 1957, Vienna; m. Claire Aniotz 1986; one s. one d. *Education:* Theresianische Akad. and Hochschule für Musik, Vienna, Conservatoire Nat. Supérieur de Musique, Paris, France, Univ. of Vienna. *Career:* numerous organ concerts, Europe, USA and fmr USSR; participant, various int. festivals; Music Dramaturg, Salzburger Landestheater 1986–89; teacher, Wiener Musikhochschule and Univ. of Salzburg 1988–90; Artistic Dir Bruckner Hall Linz and Int. Bruckner Festival 1990–98; Project Dir, La Cité Céleste by the Guardini Foundation, Berlin, Pres. 1998–2001, mem. Bd of Dirs; Music Dir, Brucknerhaus Linz, Upper Austria 1990; Vice-Dir Int. Beethoven Festival, Bonn 1999; Dir Carinthian Summer Festival, Austria 2004–. *Compositions include:* organ, vocal, instrumental and orchestral music; Ich, Hiob (church opera). *Recordings include:* Messiaen at La Trinité, E. Reuchsel, music for violin and organ. *Publications include:* contrib. to Ecrivains Français et l'Opéra (Légende de Tristan, Tournemire) 1986, Studien zur Wertungsforschung 20 (Cinq Rechants by Messiaen) 1988, Meilensteine der Musik 1991, Olivier Messiaen, La Cité céleste 1998, Georges Auric 2000, Les solitudes de Jean Françaix 2001, Abkehr und Einkehr (Musik & Kirche) 2005, Der Aspekt der Materialsammlung bei Olivier Messiaen 2006; contrib. to numerous music journals; ed. Universal Organ series; Almanach zum Internationalen Beethovenfest Bonn 1999–2000. *Honours:* Officier, Ordre des Arts et des Lettres 2005, Ehrenkreuz für Wissenschaft und Kunst 2012; Joaquín Rodrigo Medal 1997, Landeskulturpreis für Musik Oberösterreich 1998, Kirchenmusikpreis der Stadt Neuss 2002, Förderungspreis des Österr.

Bundeskanzleramtes 2003, Kulturmedaille des Landes Oberösterreich 2007, Österreichischer Kunstpreis für Musik 2010. *Address:* Hofmühlgasse 7A /7, 1060 Vienna, Austria. *E-mail:* schlee@carinthischersommer.at (office). *Website:* www.carinthischersommer.at (office).

SCHLEIERMACHER, Steffen; German pianist, composer and concert promoter; b. 1960, Halle. *Education:* Mendelssohn Bartholdy Acad. of Music Leipzig, student of Gerhard Erber (piano), Siegfried Thiele and Friedrich Schenker (composition) and Günter Blumhagen (conducting), Acad. of Arts Berlin, student of Friedrich Goldmann (composition), Cologne Acad. of Music, student of Aloys Kontarsky (piano). *Career:* has performed as soloist with Gewandhausorchester Leipzig, Deutsche Sinfonieorchester Berlin, Münchner Philharmoniker, Orchestre de la Suisse Romande and others, under conductors including Vladimir Ashkenazy, Friedrich Goldmann, Ingo Metzmacher, Vladimir Jurowski and Fabio Luisi; concert tours through several European, South American and Far Eastern countries; directed Musica Nova series at Gewandhaus Leipzig 1988–; f. Ensemble Avantgarde 1989; directed January Festival at Museum of Fine Arts in Leipzig 1993–2000 and annual KlangRausch festival at Mitteldeutsche Rundfunk 2000–10; commissions from numerous orgs including Oper Bonn, Gewandhausorchester Leipzig, Kirchenmusikfestival Oslo, WDR Sinfonieorchester, musikFabrik, RIAS Kammerchor, Gewandhausorchester Leipzig, Akademie für Alte Musik Berlin, Orchestre Français des Jeunes, Konzerthausorchester Berlin and Festival Pélerinages Weimar. *Commissions include:* Kokain 2004, Gegen Bild for orchestra 2006, Das Leuchten der singenden Kristalle for orchestra 2009, Die Beschwörung der trunkenen Oase 2009, Das Tosen des staunenden Echos 2009, Ataraxia 2009, Four Pieces to interpolate the Bach Mass 2008. *Recordings include:* more than 60 CDs including: first ever artist to record complete piano works by John Cage; teachers, friends, colleagues (Echo Klassik Award for Solo Recording of the Year (20th/21st century/piano) 2015). *Honours:* Chevalier des arts et des lettres 2010; Gaudeamus Competition Prize 1985, Eisler Prize 1986, Kranichstein Music Prize 1986, Christoph and Stephan Kaske Foundation Prize, Munich 1991, Fellowship of the German Acad. at Villa Massimo, Rome 1992, Japan Foundation Fellowship 1997, Fellowship of Cité des Arts, Paris 1999. *Address:* Gewandhaus Leipzig, Augustusplatz 8, 04109 Leipzig, Germany (office). *Website:* www .schleiermacher-leipzig.de (office).

SCHLEMM, Anny; singer (mezzo-soprano); b. 22 Feb. 1929, Neu-Isenburg, Frankfurt, Germany. *Education:* studied with Erna Westenberger in Berlin. *Career:* sang at the Berlin Staatsoper and the Berlin Komische Oper from 1949; Cologne Opera 1950–51; has sung at Frankfurt Opera from 1951; guest appearances in Hamburg, Munich and Berlin; Glyndebourne 1954, as Zerlina; Bayreuth Festival 1978–86, as Mary in Der fliegende Holländer; Netherlands Opera Amsterdam 1978, Herodias and Clytemnestra; Cologne 1981, as the Kostelnicka in Jenůfa; Covent Garden debut 1984, Madelon in a new production of Andrea Chénier; other roles include Susanna, Desdemona, the Marschallin, Octavian and Marenka in The Bartered Bride; sang Clytemnestra in Elektra at Stuttgart 1989; modern repertoire has included Miranda in Martin's The Tempest, Europera I and II by Cage (premiere at Frankfurt 1987), Mumie in Reimann's Gespenstersonate and Mother in Cerha's Baal (Vienna 1992); sang the Countess in The Queen of Spades for Opera Flanders 1999 and Mamma Lucia in Cavalleria Rusticana at Frankfurt 2001. *Recordings:* Madama Butterfly, Pagliacci, Hansel und Gretel, Der fliegende Holländer from Bayreuth, Andrea Chénier (video).

SCHLICK, Barbara; singer (soprano); b. 21 July 1943, Würzburg, Germany. *Education:* Musikhochschule Würzburg, studied with Paul Lohmann in Wiesbaden, and in Essen. *Career:* engaged by Adolf Scherbaum for his Baroque Ensemble 1966; concert engagements in Munich, Hamburg, Rome, Geneva, Paris, Prague, Leningrad and New York; Russian tour 1971 and tour of the USA and Canada with the Chamber Orchestra of Paul Kuentz 1972; tour of Israel and USA 1975–76 with the Monteverdi Choir under Jürgen Jürgens; festival appearances in Aix, Paris, Berlin, Kassel and Herrenhausen; sang at the Göttingen Handel Festival 1980, York Early Music Festival 1988, C.P.E. Bach's Die Letzten Leiden; further appearances at the Haydn series on South Bank with the Orchestra of the Age of Enlightenment and in Mozart's Requiem with the Amsterdam Baroque Orchestra; repertoire includes Carissimi's Jephte, Vivaldi's Gloria, Passions and Cantatas by Bach, Handel's Messiah, Acis and Galatea and Caecilia Ode, Haydn's Creation and Seven Last Words, Mozart's Requiem and Stravinsky's Cantata, and songs by Dowland, Purcell, Handel, Scarlatti and Haydn. *Recordings include:* Gagliano's La Dafne, Bach's St Matthew Passion, Jephtha by Reinthaler, Hasse's Piramo e Tisbe, Handel's Giulio Cesare and Rosalinda.

SCHMECKENBECHER, Jochen; German singer (baritone); b. 1967, Heidelberg. *Education:* studied in Cologne with Kurt Moll. *Career:* sang at Hagen Opera 1990–93, as Mozart's Count and Dandini in Cenerentola; The Count in Lortzing's Wildschültz; Komische Oper Berlin from 1993 as Papegano, Silvio and Schaunard, and in Rimsky's The Tale of Tsar Saltan; Further engagements at Hamburg, Bonn, the Châtelet, Paris and Geneva Opera; season 1997–98 with Papageno at Dallas Opera; Frequent concert appearances. *Current Management:* c/o Opern-Agentur und Artists' Mgt Lewin, Tal 28, 80331 Munich, Germany. *Telephone:* (89) 29161661. *Fax:* (89) 29161667. *E-mail:* kursidem@opern-agentur.com. *Website:* www.opern-agentur.de.

SCHMID, Benjamin, DipMus; Austrian violinist; b. 13 Sept. 1968, Vienna, Austria. *Education:* Music Univs of Salzburg, Vienna, Philadelphia, Curtis Inst., Magister Artium, Salzburg. *Career:* debut at Salzburg Festival 1986; over 500 concertos and recitals, St Petersburg Orchestra, Paris, London, Berlin, Vienna, in Europe, USA, Canada and Japan; chamber music and violin solo recitals, radio and television broadcasts in Europe, USA and Canada; professional jazz player; repertory includes more than 50 concertos from baroque to contemporary music; the three great cycles for violin solo; most of the important duo sonatas from 18th-century and contemporary music; Guest Prof., Hochschule Mozarteum, Salzburg 1996–98. *Recordings:* concertos: all of Bach, three Mozart, Haydn C major, Brahms D major, violin concerto, violin solo, Bach: six sonatas and partitas, Paganini, Ysaÿe: six sonatas, recitals, Brahms, Ravel, Kreisler solo recital. *Honours:* first prize Concours-Menuhin, Paris 1985, Leopold Mozart, Augsburg 1991, Carl-Flesch-Int. 1992.

SCHMIDT, Andreas; German singer (baritone); *Kammersänger Professor*, *Hochschule für Musik und Theater, Munich*; b. 30 June 1960, Düsseldorf; m. Jeanne Pascale 2003; two s. three d. *Education:* studied piano, organ, conducting in Düsseldorf, singing in Düsseldorf and Berlin. *Career:* youngest mem. Deutsche Oper Berlin 1983; debut Hamburg State Opera 1985, Munich State Opera 1985, Covent Garden London 1986, Vienna State Opera 1988, Geneva Opera 1989, Salzburg Festival 1989, Aix-en-Provence Festival 1991, Metropolitan New York 1991, Edin. Festival 1991, Paris Bastille 1992, Paris Garnier 1993, Glyndebourne Festival 1994, State Opera Berlin 1995, Amsterdam Opera 1995, Bayreuth Festival 1996; has sung with major orchestras, including Berlin, Geneva, Vienna, Munich, Hamburg, London, Paris, Rome, Amsterdam, Copenhagen, Stockholm, Helsinki, New York, Israel Philharmonic orchestras, Cincinnati, Cleveland, Chicago, San Franciso and Philadelphia Symphony orchestras, La Scala, Milan, and with conductors including Bernstein, Solti, Levine, Barenboim, Sinopoli, Thielemann, Conlon, Eschenbach, Masur, Nagano and others; Prof., Hochschule für Musik und Theater, Munich 2010–. *Recordings include:* more than 130 CDs. *Honours:* Hon. mem. Richard-Wagner-Verband; First Prize, Deutscher Musikwettbewerb, several German and int. awards and prizes. *Current Management:* c/o Hartmut Haase, Artists Management, Aalgrund 8, 31275 Lehrte, Germany. *Telephone:* (5175) 953232. *Fax:* (5175) 953233. *E-mail:* artists@t-online.de. *Website:* www.artists-haase.de.

SCHMIDT, Anne-Sophie; French singer (soprano); b. 1968. *Education:* Strasbourg Conservatoire. *Career:* debut with Aminta in Mozart's Il Re Pastore and Fiordiligi at Marseille, 1990; appearances in Figaro and Boris Godunov, and as Italian Singer in Capriccio at the Salzburg Festival; Berlin Staatsoper in Honegger's Jeann d'Arc au Bûcher, in Haydn's I Pescatrici at Toulouse, as Donna Elvira at Nancy and Poulenc's Blanche de la Force at Toronto; also seen at Savonlinna and the London Proms; season 1995 as Mélisande at Marseilles, followed by performances at the Paris Châtelet, Turin, Bucharest and Bologna; further engagements in Werther, opposite Alfredo Kraus, at Seville, and concerts with leading European orchestras; sang Susanna at Compiègne (1997) and Poulenc's La Voix Humaine, 2000. *Recordings include:* Arias from operas by Gounod and Massenet and Mélodies by Satie. *Current Management:* Musicglotz, 11 rue le Verrier, 75006 Paris, France.

SCHMIDT, Annerose; German pianist and academic; b. 5 Oct. 1936, Wittenberg. *Education:* Hochschule für Musik, Leipzig with Hugo Steurer. *Career:* debut in Wittenberg 1945; numerous engagements as soloist with orchestras, including Gewandhaus Orchestra, Leipzig, Dresden State Orchestra, Royal Philharmonic Orchestra, London, New Philharmonic Orchestra, London, Cleveland Orchestra, Chicago Symphony Orchestra, Tonhalle Orchestra, Zürich, Danish Radio Symphony Orchestra, Copenhagen, Concertgebouw Orchestra, Amsterdam, Residentie Orchestra, The Hague, NHK (Japan Broadcasting Orchestra) Symphony Orchestra, Tokyo; many festival appearances, including Salzburg, Holland, Prague Spring, Berlin, Dresden, Warsaw Autumn; Prof., Hochschule für Musik Berlin 1986–; television appearances include Beethoven's 5th Piano Concerto; Rector, Hanns Eisler Hochschule für Musik, Berlin 1990–. *Honours:* diploma Int. Chopin Competition, Warsaw 1954, first prize Int. Robert Schumann Competition, Zwickau 1956, Artist's Prize 1961, Nat. Prize 1965, Gold Bartók Medal 1974.

SCHMIDT, Carl Brandon, AB, AM, PhD, DipMus; academic and writer; b. 20 Oct. 1941, Nashville, TN, USA; m. Elizabeth Jane Kady 1967; two s. one d. *Education:* Stanford Univ., Harvard Univ., Fontainebleau School of Music, studied with Boulanger at Solfège-Dieudonné. *Career:* conducting debut at Stanford, California 1963, London 1971; Asst Prof., Wabash Coll. 1970–73, Bryn Mawr Coll. 1973–79; Prof., Univ. of the Arts 1978–. *Publications:* Antonio Cesti: Il Pomo d'oro (Music for Acts III and V from Modena, Biblioteca Estense, Ms Mus E 120), Recent Researches in the Music of the Baroque Era, Vol. 42 1982, A Catalogue Raisonné of the Literary Sources for the Tragédies Lyriques of Jean-Baptiste Lully, Jean-Baptiste Lully: The Collected Works (gen. ed.), The Music of Francis Poulenc (1899–1963): A Catalogue, Jean-Baptiste Lully: Actes du colloque/Kongressbericht; contrib. to The New Grove Dictionary of Opera 1992, Journal of Musicology.

SCHMIDT, Emma; Austrian pianist; b. 8 Feb. 1944, Vienna; m.; one s. *Education:* Hochschule für Musik, Graz, masterclasses in Salzburg and Siena. *Career:* teacher, Coll. of Music, Graz and Hanover; soloist in Vienna, Salzburg, London, Berlin, Hamburg, Düsseldorf, Hanover, Brussels, Warsaw, Belgrade, Budapest, Bilbao, La Coruna, Segovia, Zagreb, Moscow, Rome, Milan, Turin,

Florence, Palermo, New York, Chicago, Buenos Aires, São Paulo; several tours in Korea and China; radio productions across the world; TV concerts. *Recordings include:* La Ricordanza by Carl Czerny; George Gershwin's Rhapsody in Blue and 3 Preludes; Leoš Janáček, Piano Sonata and On the Overgrown Path I; Scott Joplin, Ragtimes; Alfred Schnittke, Concerto for Piano; Erwin Schulhoff's Concerto for piano; Franz Schubert, Winterreise; Smetana, Bohemian Dances; Alexandre Tansman, Sonatine Transatlantique; P.I. Tchaikovsky, Piano Trio; Alban Berg, Op. 1 Piano Sonata; Arnold Schönberg, 3 Klavierstücke Op. 11; J.S. Bach-Ferruccio Busoni, Chaconne; F. Schreker-I. Strasfogel, Kammersymphonie. *Honours:* Austrian Cross of Honour for Science and Arts 2002; Bösendorfer Prize, Vienna 1969, First Prize, Vittorio Gui Chamber Music Competition, Florence 1979. *Address:* Scheibengasse 14, 1190 Vienna, Austria (home). *Telephone:* (676) 5199630 (mobile) (office). *E-mail:* pianist@emma-schmidt.at (office). *Website:* www .emma-schmidt.at (home).

SCHMIDT, Hansjürgen, DipMus, MMus; German composer; b. 26 Aug. 1935, Jena-Burgau; m. Annemarie Illig 1959; two s. *Education:* Friedrich-Schiller Univ., Jena, Franz Liszt Hochschule Weimar, Akademie der Künste Berlin. *Career:* freelance composer in Jena from 1970; Lecturer in Theory of Music, Weimar 1986–87, Volkshochschule in Erlangen 1990–; mem. Union of Composers, Thüringen. *Compositions:* Winterpastorale 1976, Streichquartett II 1979, Schwanengesang 1983, Nachtstück and Toccata 1987, Sinfonie III 1989, Chthulu Suite, Schütz-Fantasie. *Honours:* Kunstpreis of the District of Gera 1980.

SCHMIDT, Manfred; singer (tenor); b. 27 June 1928, Berlin, Germany. *Education:* studied with Jean Nadolovitch and with Herbert Brauer in Berlin. *Career:* concert singer from 1956; many radio concerts; from the Bielefeld Opera moved to Cologne 1965, singing Ernesto, Ottavio, Tamino, Almaviva and other lyric roles; sang at the festivals of Salzburg, Holland, Perugia, Flanders and Prague; guest appearances in London, Paris and Milan. *Recordings include:* opera excerpts.

SCHMIDT, Maria (Mia) Margarete Gertrud, MA; German composer; b. 5 Jan. 1952, Dresden; m. Wolfgang Motz; one d. *Education:* Univs of Munich and Tübingen, Fachhochschule, Munich and Musikhochschule, Freiburg. *Career:* composition studies with Milko Kelemen, Brian Ferneyhough, Klaus Huber and Messias Maiguashca; currently freelance composer, Freiburg; performances in Amsterdam, Berlin, Paris, Rome, Tokyo, Vienna, Zürich and festivals of contemporary music in Darmstadt, Erice, Frankfurt, Graz, Krefeld and Witten; scholarships from Rosenberg-Stiftung 1985, Heinrich-Strobel-Stiftung des Südwestfunks 1995, 1999, 2001, Johann-Joseph-Fux Kompositionstipendium 1997, 1999, 2002, 2003. *Compositions include:* Ihre Geschichte 1985, Mondwein 1985, Vollmond 1986, A Rose is a Rose 1988, Für Fanny 1990, 5 Stücke für Bläserquintett und Kontrabaß 1992, Aïda domí 1996, Requiem für Fanny Goldmann 1998, Der Fall Franza 2000, Hades House for cello and tape 2002, Streichtrio 2003, Fantasie I and II for harp 2003, Malina 2005, Vom Lichte her kommend 2006. *Honours:* Forum junger Komponisten competition award, Cologne 1985, 1992, Special Prize Eighth Int. Composition Competition, GEDOK, Mannheim 1985, First Prize (Chamber Music), Premio Europa competition, Rome 1985, Förderpreis für das Musikprotokoll des Steirischen Herbstes, Graz 1986, Chamber Music Prize, IRINO, Tokyo 1987, prize from first Int. Kompositionswettbewerb. des Schweizer Frauenmusik-Forums, Berne 1992, Johann Joseph Fux Musikpreis des Landes Steiermark 1998, Johann Joseph Fux Opernkompositionswettbewerb des Landes Steiermark 2000. *Address:* Sickingenstr 31, 79112, Freiburg, Germany (home). *Telephone:* (761) 33479 (home). *E-mail:* mia.schmidt@gmx.de. *Website:* www.miaschmidt .de.

SCHMIDT, Peter-Jurgen; German singer (tenor); b. 25 Jan. 1941, Meiningen. *Education:* studied in Weimar. *Career:* debut at Weimar 1968, as Oberto in Alcina; sang at Weimar until 1980, Staatsoper Berlin from 1981, notably in 1989 premiere of Graf Mirabeau by Siegfried Matthus; guest appearances in concert and opera at London, Oslo, Linz, Salzburg, Graz and Germany, Japan and Republic of Korea; Schwetzinger Festival 1989, as Bacchus in Ariadne auf Naxos; other roles include Don José, Hoffmann, Radames, Walther Von Stolzing, Lohengrin and Laca in Jenůfa; season 1999–2000 at Chemnitz and the Brooklyn Acad. of Music in the premiere production of Weill's The Eternal Road. *Recordings include:* Levins Muhle by Udo Zimmermann and Graf Mirabeau.

SCHMIDT, Wolfgang; German singer (tenor); b. 1955, Kassel. *Education:* Frankfurt Musikhochschule. *Career:* sang first with the Pocket Oper Nuremburg, then at the Court Theatre Bayreuth 1982–84; Kiel 1984–86; Dortmund from 1986, notably as Otello and as Siegfried in Wagner's Opera; appearances at the Eutin Festival 1983–87, as Tamino, Max and Huon in Oberon; Bregenz Festival 1989, as Erik in Fliegende Holländer; Bayreuth 1992, as Tannhäuser; further engagements in Essen, Karlsruhe, Hanover, Stuttgart; sang First Armed Man in Die Zauberflöte at the 1991 Salzburg Festival; Tristan at the Opéra Bastille, Paris 1998; season 1999 as Siegfried at San Francisco, Loge, Siegmund and Siegfried in Hannover; Walther and Florestan for Deutsche Oper am Rhein; Siegfried and Siegmund at the Berlin Staatsoper and Cologne 2000; sang Siegfried at the 2002 Bayreuth Festival; season 2009 at Düsseldorf included Rheingold, Walküre, Siegfried and Salome; appearances as Mime in Rheingold and Siegfried in Bayreuth 2010 and Vienna 2011; Hauptmann in Wozzeck, Bayerische Staatsoper 2012, Tokyo 2014; concert repertoire includes the Missa Solemnis with appearances in

Mexico City, Parma, Prague. *Recordings include:* Die Zauberflöte, Weill's Lindberghflug. *Current Management:* Theateragentur Marx, Abensbergstr. 49a, 80993 Munich, Germany. *E-mail:* ks@wolfgangschmidt.com (office). *Website:* www.wolfgangschmidt.com.

SCHMIDT-MADSEN, Philip; Danish organist and conductor; *Artistic Director, Pro Musica Copenhagen*; b. 29 Nov. 1982, Copenhagen. *Education:* Royal Danish Acad. of Music with Bine Bryndorf and Hans Fagius, Hochschule für Künste, Bremen, Germany with Hans Davidsson, Rudolf Kelber and Martin Böcker. *Career:* mem. Copenhagen Boys' Choir 1993–96; Organist, St Paul's Roman Catholic Church, Taastrup 1999–2002; Artistic Dir, Pro Musica Copenhagen 2004–; Conductor, Almshouse Choir 2006–07; Choir Man., Sankt Annae Girls' Choir 2008–; Lecturer in Choral Singing, also Choir Man. and Organist, Copenhagen Girls' Choir 2009–11; Asst Organist, Grundtvig Church, Copenhagen 2011; solo recitals and concert appearances across Denmark and in Europe including Westminster Cathedral, London. *Honours:* First Prize and Commotio Prize, Carl Nielsen Int. Organ Competition 2011, Léonie Sonning Music Scholarship 2012. *Address:* Tagensvej 37, 2.tv, 2200 Copenhagen N, Denmark (office). *Telephone:* 26-74-70-40 (office). *E-mail:* philip@schmidt-madsen.dk (office). *Website:* www.schmidt-madsen .dk (office).

SCHMIEGE, Marilyn, BMus, MMus; singer (mezzo-soprano); b. 1955, Milwaukee, Wisconsin, USA. *Education:* Valparaiso Univ., Boston Univ., Zürich Opera Studio. *Career:* debut at Wuppertal as Dorabella 1978; Theater am Gärtnerplatz, Munich as Cherubino, Rosina, Hänsel, Orlovsky 1978–82; Teatro La Fenice, Venice 1981; Aix-en Provence as Zaide in Il Turco in Italia 1982; Munich Radio 1982 as Dido by Jan Novák conducted by Kubelik 1982; Düsseldorf as Cherubino 1983; La Scala title role in Orfeo by Rossi 1983; Vienna Staatsoper debut as Rosina, later as Octavian, the Composer 1985; Stuttgart as Charlotte in Werther, later as Lady Macbeth of Mtensk, Marguerite in Berlioz's Damnation de Faust 1985; Aldeburgh Festival in Das Lied von der Erde 1985; Hamburg Staatsoper as the Composer and Rosina 1985, later as Venus in Tannhäuser; Dresden Staatsoper as the Composer, Octavian 1986, later as Kundry; New York Philharmonic with Novák's Dido, 1986; Cologne as Lady Macbeth 1988; Munich Staatsoper Octavian 1988 later as Cherubino, Jeanne d'Arc, Silla in Palestrina, Dorabella, Venus 1991; Carmen at Berlin Komische Oper 1991; Judith in Berlin Schauspielhaus 1993; Amsterdam as Marie in Wozzeck and at the Paris Châtelet as Waltraute in Götterdämmerung 1994; sang Marie in Wozzeck at Catania 1996; Kundry in Parsifal for Nationale Reisopera, Netherlands 1998; season 1999–2000 as Countess Geschwitz in Lulu at Liège and Sieglinde for the Vienna Staatsoper. *Recordings include:* Vivaldi's Catone in Utica, Galuppi's La Caduta d'Adamo, Haydn Cantatas and Orfeo ed Euridice, Cherubino in Mozart's Figaro, Dido by Novák, Schreker Die Gezeichneten, Mélodies of Gabriel Fauré 1994.

SCHMÖHE, Georg; German conductor; *Chief Conductor, Münchner Symphoniker*. *Career:* f. his own orchestra, aged 15; Chief Conductor, Orquesta Sinfónica de Venezuela 1980–83; Chief Conductor, Nürnberger Symphoniker 1989–92; Music Dir Staatsheater Kassel 1992–97; Chief Conductor, Tiroler Symphonieorchester 1997–2004; Chief Conductor, Tiroler Landestheater 2004–; Chief Conductor, Münchner Symphoniker 2006–; guest conductor, Deutsche Oper Berlin, Hamburgische Staatsoper, Münchner Philharmoniker, Symphonieorchester des Bayerischen Rundfunks, Opéra National de Paris. *Address:* Münchner Symphoniker, Drachslstrasse 14, 81541 Munich, Germany (office). *Telephone:* (89) 4411960 (office). *Fax:* (89) 44119615 (office). *Website:* www.muenchner-symphoniker.de (office).

SCHNAPKA, Georg; singer (bass); b. 27 May 1932, Schlesisch Ostrau, Czechoslovakia; m. Elisabeth Schwarzenberg. *Education:* Bruckner Conservatory, Linz with Andreas Sotzkov. *Career:* debut at Heidelberg 1954, as Repela in Wolf's Der Corregidor; sang 1964–85 at the Vienna Volksoper in the buffo repertory, also appeared with the Vienna Staatsoper; guest appearances in Hamburg, Munich, Stuttgart, Saarbrucken, Düsseldorf, Wuppertal, Cologne and Frankfurt; further engagements in Florence (Maggio Musicale), Venice, Amsterdam, Strasbourg, Lisbon, Bucharest and Zürich; American centres include New York City Opera, Baltimore and Washington, DC; main roles have included Philip II in Don Carlos, Daland, Fafner, Hunding, Sarastro, Pimen, Osmin, Leporello, Nicolai's Falstaff, Baron Ochs and Rossini's Bartolo; many concert engagements.

SCHNAUT, Gabriele; singer (mezzo-soprano, soprano); b. 24 Feb. 1951, Mannheim, Germany. *Education:* studied in Frankfurt with Elsa Cavelti, in Darmstadt with Aga Zah-Landzettel and in Berlin with Hannelore Kuhse. *Career:* sang in Stuttgart from 1976; Darmstadt 1978–80; mem., Mannheim Opera from 1980; Bayreuth Festival from 1977, as Waltraute, Venus and Sieglinde; Chicago 1983, as Fricka in a concert performance of Die Walküre; Dortmund 1985, as Isolde; has sung at Stuttgart, Frankfurt, Hamburg, Barcelona, Rome and Warsaw; Covent Garden debut 1989, as Sieglinde in a new production of Die Walküre conducted by Bernard Haitink; sang in Düsseldorf and Hamburg 1989, as Lady Macbeth and Els in Schreker's Der Schatzgräber; Brünnhilde in Die Walküre at Cologne 1990; Bayreuth 1987–89, as Ortrud in Lohengrin; sang Isolde at San Francisco 1991, Elektra at the Opéra Bastille, Paris 1992; sang the Walküre Brünnhilde at the 1997 Munich Festival, Isolde at Catania 1996; other roles include Octavian, Sextus (La Clemenza di Tito), Dorabella, Carmen, Brangaene, Kundry and Marie in Wozzeck; season 1998 as Isolde at Cologne and 1999 as Elsa at Bayreuth; sang

Isolde at Covent Garden 2000; season 2001–02 as Isolde at Amsterdam, Turandot at the Vienna Staatsoper and Brünnhilde in new productions of Die Walküre and Siegfried at the Munich Staatsoper. *Recordings include:* St Matthew Passion by Bach, Sancta Susanna and Lieder by Hindemith.

SCHNEBEL, Dieter; German composer; b. 14 March 1930, Lahr. *Education:* Freiburg Hochschule für Musik, Darmstadt, Univ. of Thubingen. *Career:* active in the Lutheran Church from 1976; Prof. of Experimental Music and Musicology, Berlin Hochschule für Musik; work with the experimental theatre group, Die Maulwerker from 1978; collaborations with Achim Freyer on Maulwerke and Cage-up. *Compositions include:* Maulwerke (music theatre) 1968–74, Laut-Gesten-Laute, Zeichen-Sprache and St Jago (music and pictures on Kleist 1989–91); orchestral: Compositio 1956, Webern Variations 1972, Canones 1975, In motu proprio 1975, Diapason 1977, Orchestra 1977, Schubert-Phantasie 1978, Wagner-Idyll 1980, Thanatos-Eros 1982, Sinfonie-Stucke 1985, Beethoven-Sinfonie 1985, Mahler Moment for strings 1985, Raumklang X 1988; chamber: Reactions 1961, Visable Music I 1961, Nostalgie for conductor 1962, Espressivo (music drama) for pianist 1963, Concert sans orchestre for piano and audience 1964, Ansclage-auschlage 1966, Quintet 1977, Pan for flute 1978, Monotonien for piano and electronics 1989; vocal: Fur Stimmen (… missa est) for chorus 1961, Glossolalie 61 1961, Bach-Contrapuncti for chorus 1976, Jowaegerli for two speakers, voices and chamber ensemble 1983, Lieder ohne Worte 1980–86, Missa Dahlemer Messe 1984–87, Sinfonie X for orchestra 1992, Majakowskis Tod (chamber opera) 1987, Totentantz (ballet-oratorio) 1989–94, Motetus II for two choruses 1997, Ekstasis for soprano, chorus and orchestra 1997, Museumstücke I/II for mobile voices and instruments, Produktionprozesse series 1968–75; graphic works including mo-no: Musik Zum Lesen 1969. *Publications include:* Study of Stockhausen's early works: Mauricio Kagel 1970, Denkbare Musik: Schriften 1952–72, Anschläge-Ausschläge (essays) 1993.

SCHNEEBERGER, Hansheins; violinist; b. 16 Oct. 1926, Berne, Switzerland. *Education:* Berne Conservatory, studied with Carl Flesch in Lucerne and with Boris Kamensky. *Career:* debut in the Swiss premiere of Bartók's Second Violin Concerto 1946; teacher, Biel Conservatory 1948–58, Basle Musikakademie 1961–91; Leader,String Quartet 1952–59, North German Symphony Orchestra, Hamburg; premieres of Martin's Violin Concerto and Bartók's First Concerto 1952, 1958 with Paul Sacher; further performances of music by Klaus Huber, Heinz Holliger and Elliott Carter. *Recordings include:* Schumann sonatas and concerto, Bach sonatas and partitas for solo violin, Bartók sonata for solo violin.

SCHNEIDER, Bernhard; Austrian chorus master; *Chorus Master, Opera North;* b. Vienna. *Education:* Hochschule für Musik und Darstellende Kunst, Vienna. *Career:* Asst Chorus Master Vienna State Opera 1998–2001; Chorus Dir Nationaltheater Mannheim and Seefestspiele Moerbisch 2002–06; Chorus Master Opera North 2007–. *Address:* Opera North, Grand Theatre, 46 New Briggate, Leeds, LS1 6NU, England (office). *Telephone:* (113) 243-9999 (office). *Fax:* (113) 244-0418 (office). *E-mail:* info@operanorth.co.uk (office). *Website:* www.operanorth.co.uk (office).

SCHNEIDER, David E., AB, MA, PhD; American musicologist and clarinetist; b. 14 June 1963, Berkeley, CA; m. Klára Móricz 1994. *Education:* Harvard Univ., Univ. of California at Berkeley, studied with Donald Carrol, Leon Russianoff, Pasquale Cardillo, Greg Smith, Robert Marcellus, Nancy Garniez, Leon Kirchner and György Kurtag. *Career:* mem., Alaria Chamber Ensemble, New York 1986–88; Valentine Prof. of Music, Amherst Coll., Amherst, MA 1997–; mem. American Musicological Soc. *Recordings:* Copland Clarinet Concerto 1988. *Publications:* Bartók and Stravinsky 1995, The Culmination Point as a Fulcrum Between Analysis and Interpretation 1996, A Context for Béla Bartók on the Eve of World War II 1991. *Honours:* American Musicological Soc. 50 Fellowship 1996. *Address:* Amherst College, Box 2258 Music, Amherst, MA 01002-5000, USA. *E-mail:* deschneider@amherst.edu.

SCHNEIDER, Gary M.; American conductor and composer; b. 1950. *Career:* founder, Music Dir and Principal Conductor, Hoboken Chamber Orchestra; debut in Europe at the International Zelt Musik Festival in Freiburg; New York debut with the American Composers' Orchestra performing his Concerto for jazz clarinet and orchestra; has also conducted the Chamber Symphony of Princeton, and the New York Festival Orchestra; Artist-in-Residence at Denison University, Ohio and Composer-in-Residence at the Rockport (Massachusetts) Chamber Music Festival. *Compositions include:* Sonata for solo cello, 1976; String Quartet, 1977; Study for a Ballet, for piano, 1981; Piano Sonata, 1989; Nocturne for bassoon and strings, 1988; The Bremen Town Musicians, 1989; The Tell-Tale Heart and The Voice of Eternity for soloists and ensemble. *Address:* c/o ASCAP, ASCAP Building, 1 Lincoln Plaza, New York, NY 10023, USA.

SCHNEIDER, Gundula; singer (mezzo-soprano); b. 1965, Dresden, Germany. *Education:* studied in Karlsrule and at Dresden Music Academy; masterclasses with Brigitte Fassbaender and Sena Jurinac. *Career:* appearances from 1997 with Dortmund Opera as Carmen, the Composer in Ariadne auf Naxos, Hansel, and Orlovsky in Die Fledermaus; guest engagements in Dresden, Strasbourg and the Komische Oper Berlin as Annio in La Clemenza di Tito; Cherubino at Dusseldorf and Bellini's Adalgisa at Kassel; festival engagements at the Dresdner Musikfestspiele and Rossini Festspiele Bad Wildbad; recitals in the Paris Opéra-Comique, Liederhalle Stuttgart and Carnegie Hall, New York. *Honours:* special prize 27th Antonin Dvorak International Singing Competition 1992, laureate Brahms Internationaler

Wettbewerb, Hamburg 1994, Pro Musicis Int. Award 1995. *Current Management:* Pro Musicis, 140 W 79th Street, Suite 9F, New York, NY 10024, USA. *Telephone:* (212) 787-0993. *Fax:* (212) 362-0352. *Website:* www.promusicis.org.

SCHNEIDER, Peter; conductor; b. 26 March 1939, Vienna, Austria. *Education:* Acad. for Music and Dramatic Art, Vienna, studied with Hans Swarowsky. *Career:* sang with the Wiener Sängerknaben as a boy; Head of Studies at the Landestheater Salzburg from 1959 (conducting debut with Handel's Giulio Cesare); Principal Conductor in Heidleberg 1961, Deutsche Oper am Rhein, Düsseldorf from 1968; performances of operas by Janáček, Berg, Wagner, Mozart, Verdi and Dallapiccola; guest conductor in Warsaw, Florence and Edinburgh; Music Dir, Bremen 1978–85, Mannheim 1985–87, Bayreuth Festival from 1981; Der fliegende Holländer, Der Ring des Nibelungen and Lohengrin; conducted the Vienna Opera in Der Rosenkavalier on 1986 tour of Japan, and the Vienna Philharmonic at the Salzburg Festival; further appearances as a conductor of opera in Vienna, Berlin, London, Bologna, Barcelona, Madrid, San Francisco; Die Soldaten by Zimmermann at the Vienna Staatsoper 1990; conducted Tristan und Isolde in Japan 1990 and San Francisco 1991; Music Dir, Bavarian State Opera, Munich 1993; led Walküre and Meistersinger at the 1997 Munich Festival; Lohengrin at Barcelona 2000.

SCHNEIDER, Urs; Swiss conductor and music director; b. 16 May 1939, St Gallen. *Education:* Zürich Conservatory, studied conducting with Rafael Kubelik, Igor Markevitch, Otto Klemperer. *Career:* debut with own orchestras at age 15; founder, Conductor, Artistic Dir, Ostschweizer Kammerorchester, Camerata Helvetica; guest conductor, USA; Music Dir, Camerata Stuttgart; Music Dir, Camerata Academica Salzburg; Chief Conductor, Music Dir, Haifa Symphony Orchestra; concerts, operas, radio and television; guest conductor, numerous major orchestras and opera houses worldwide; over 4,000 performances in 70 countries; competition adjudicator, Concours des Jeunes Chefs d'Orchestre, Festival Int. de Besançon; jury mem., Conductors' Competition, Silvestri, Bucharest and competitions in Israel, Taiwan and USA; Principal Conductor, Artistic Dir, Nat. Taiwan Philharmonic Orchestra; First Guest Conductor of Prague Chamber Soloists; mem. Swiss Musicians' Asscn, Schweiz Berufsdirigenten Verband. *Recordings:* 60 records. *Honours:* Hon. MFA Int. (New York) 1969; Cultural Prize, City of St Gallen. *Address:* Gattestrasse 1B, 9010 St Gallen, Switzerland. *Telephone:* (71) 2223980 (office). *E-mail:* urs.schneider.conductor@sunrise.ch (office). *Website:* www .ursschneider.com (office).

SCHNEIDER-MALIPIERO, Victoria, BM, MM; American singer (soprano); b. 28 Oct. 1952, Reading, Pa; m. Riccardo Malipiero 1988 (died 2003). *Education:* Eastman School of Music, Rochester, NY, Staatliche Hochschule für Musik, Stuttgart (Performer's Certificate, Bühnenreife). *Career:* debut Staatsoper Stuttgart, Germany 1981; regular collaboration with Staatsoper Stuttgart and numerous concert appearances throughout Germany 1981–85; increased activity, Italy 1984–; appearances at Teatro alla Scala, Milan, Teatro Comunale di Bologna, Teatro dell'Opera di Roma, Teatro dell'Opera di Genova; numerous concerts with major Italian orchestras, Santa Cecilia, Rome, with Radio Orchestras (RAI) of Milan, Turin, Naples; Festival Wien Modern 1992; Paris debut at Théâtre du Châtelet 1993; Berg's Altenberg-Lieder and Der Wein with Staatsorchester Saarbrücken 1995; Frankfurt Opera 2000, Rome Opera 2001; concert repertoire ranges from baroque to contemporary, including Handel's Messiah, Beethoven's Mass in C Major and Missa Solemnis, Mozart's Mass in C Minor, Mahler's Kindertotenlieder, numerous Strauss Orchesterlieder, Wagner's Wesendoncklieder, Berg's Sieben Frühe Lieder, Shostakovich's Seven Lyrics of Alexander Blok, Dallapiccola's An Mathilde and Commiato, R. Malipiero's Loneliness, Ennio Morricone's Frammenti di Eros; numerous world premieres with works by R. Malipiero, S. Sciarrino, Donatoni, Gentilucci, Guarnieri and others; numerous concerts, including Schoenberg's Op. 10, with Arditti String Quartet 1989–93, Elliott Carter with the Ensemble Contrechamps and the Nieuw Ensemble 1998, 1999, Shostakovich and Beethoven with the Ensemble Recherche 1999–2000, Bach with the Orchestra Sinfonica Abruzzese 2000, Verdi and Schoenberg with the Quartetto di Fiesole 2001, Schoenberg Festival, Bari 2003, R. Malipiero's Voicequintet with the Quartetto di Torino 2004, Festival Musica in Alto Lario 2005, FIU Music Festival, Miami 2007, 2009, 2011, Villa Vigoni Convention and concerts 2008, 2010; master classes, Lake Como 2007, 2008, 2009, 2010; Founder and Pres. Centro Internazionale di Studi 'Riccardo Malipiero'. *Radio recordings include:* Vara Radio (Netherlands), Suddeutscher Rundfunk (Stuttgart), Bayerischer Rundfunk (Munich), Radio Bremen, RSI (Lugano), Italian National Radio RAI. *Honours:* Kirsten Flagstad Grant. *Address:* Via Bellera 22, 22010 Pianello Lario, Como, Italy. *Telephone:* (0344) 82790; 348-4043651 (mobile). *E-mail:* vsmalipiero@aol.com. *Website:* www.victoriamalipiero.com.

SCHNEIDERMAN, Helene, BMus, MMus; American singer (mezzo-soprano); b. 15 Nov. 1956, Flemington, NJ; d. of Paul Schneiderman and Judy Schneiderman; m. Michael Flamme; two c. *Education:* Westminster Choir Coll., Princeton, Univ. of Cincinnati Conservatory of Music. *Career:* sang at Heidelberg Opera 1982–, Stuttgart 1984–, with guest appearances at Düsseldorf, Munich, Orlando and New York City Opera; season 1990 with the Rossini Festival at Pesaro and Smeaton in Anna Bolena at the Concertgebouw; other roles have included (more than 60 roles) Monteverdi's Penelope Isabella, Carmen, Cesare and Rosina at Stuttgart; Covent Garden season 1995–96, as Cherubino and Dorabella; appearances with conductors, including Bernard Haitink, Salzburg 1993, Bernstein, Arias and Barcarolles,

Bonn, Gabriele Ferro, Sir Colin Davis, London, and Alberto Zedda, Pesaro; San Francisco Opera: Alcina (Bradamante) Rosina; Seattle Opera: Tales of Hoffmann (Niklaus, Muse), Olga in Onegin, Isabella in Italian Girl in Algiers; Cornelia in Haendel's Julius Caesar 2007; guestings in USA and Europe; mem. Stuttgart Opera Soloist Ensemble. *Recordings include:* Copland's Eight Poems of Emily Dickinson, Anna Bolena CD with Gruberova, various CD and DVD productions, including most recently Salzburger Festspiele Traviata with Anna Netrebko and Rolando Villazon. *Honours:* Kammersängering 1998. *Current Management:* Robert Gilder & Co., 91 Great Russell Street, London, WC1B 3PS, England. *Telephone:* (20) 7580-7758. *Fax:* (20) 7580-7739. *E-mail:* rgilder@robert-gilder.com. *Website:* www.robert-gilder.com. *E-mail:* schneidermansing@aol.com.

SCHNELLER, Oliver, MA, DMA; German composer and saxophonist; b. 26 March 1966, Cologne. *Education:* Univ. of Bonn, New England Conservatory, Columbia Univ., New York, with Tristan Murail, IRCAM. *Career:* compositions performed at festivals including Festival Agora Paris, Musica Strasbourg, Maerzmusik Berlin, Witten Tage für Neue Kammermusik, Ultraschall, Tremplins Paris, Int. Chamber Music Confs in Singapore and Göteborg, Musicacoustica Beijing, Aspen and Tanglewood and by ensembles including Ensemble Modern, musikFabrik, Ensemble Intercontemporain and Ensemble Cairn; as saxophonist, performed with ensembles including George Russell Big Band, Gustav Mahler Youth Symphony under Seiji Ozawa and as soloist with Tanglewood Music Center Orchestra; Dir, Electronic Music Studio, CUNY 1996–98; Artistic Dir, Tracing Migrations Festival featuring contemporary works of composers from Arab countries 2004; curated House of World Cultures, Berlin 2005; Prof. of Composition, Stuttgart Conservatory of Music 2009–10. *Commissions include:* for orchestra: Gammes 1995, Tightrope Dance 1996, Metall 2006–08; for ensemble: Quaestio for chamber orchestra 1994, Aquavit for 8 instruments 1999, Clair/Obscur for 7 instruments and live electronics, Musica ficta for flute, oboe, clarinet, piano, percussion and electronics; for solo/small group: Kumoijoshi for koto and soprano saxophone 1995, Reed-Weed for saxophone 1996, Marsyas for amplified flute and cello 1996, Aurora for piano 1997, Five Miniatures After Maurice Sendak for brass trio 1998, Topoi for clarinet, violin, cello and piano 2000, String Space for violin, viola, cello and live electronics 2005, Engine for accordion and 5 loudspeakers 2006, Resonant Space for 2 pianos and 2 percussions 2007; vocal: Three Songs After Hopkins, Shelley and Meredith for soprano and piano 1994, Candidum lilium for 2 sopranos, 2 tenors, bass voices and live electronics 1997; also electroacoustic works. *Honours:* grants and fellowships from Tanglewood Music Festival, IRCAM, Meet the Composer and German Acad. Villa Massimo in Rome, Ernst von Siemens Music Foundation Composers Prize 2010. *E-mail:* osmusik@yahoo.com (office). *Website:* www.oliverschneller.net (office).

SCHNITZLER, Michael; violinist; b. 1940, California, USA. *Education:* Vienna Music Acad. *Career:* mem. and soloist, Wiener Solisten chamber orchestra 1963–67; first Concertmaster, Vienna Symphony, with over 1,000 concerts, touring USA, Japan and Europe; performances of Haydn and other composers in Vienna and elsewhere from 1968; co-founder, The Haydn Trio of Vienna 1968, performing in Brussels, Munich, Berlin, Zürich, London, Rome, Paris; New York debut 1979 and frequent North American appearances with concerts in 25 states; Prof. of Violin, Vienna Music Univ. 1983–; debut tour of Japan 1984, with further travels to the Near East, Russia, Africa, Central and South America; series at the Vienna Konzerthaus Soc. from 1976, with performances of more than 100 works; summer festivals at Vienna, Salzburg, Aix-en-Provence, Flanders and Montreux; masterclasses at the Royal Coll. and Royal Acad. of London, Stockholm, Bloomington, Tokyo and the Salzburg Mozarteum; Leader, Vienna Johann Strauss Orchestra 2000–; masterclasses, Univ. of Indiana, Bloomington, Eastman School, Rochester, Mozarteum, Salzburg, RAM, RCM, London, Sweden, The Netherlands and Japan; juror at int. competitions in Vienna, Salzburg and Osaka. *Recordings:* Complete Piano Trios of Beethoven and Schubert, Mendelssohn D Minor, Brahams B Major, Tchaikovsky A Minor, Schubert Trout Quintet; albums of works by Haydn, Schumann, Dvořák and Smetana. *Address:* Sternwartestrasse 58, 1180 Vienna, Austria.

SCHOLL, Andreas; German singer (countertenor); b. 10 Nov. 1967, Eltville. *Education:* Schola Cantorum Basiliensis, Switzerland. *Career:* mem. Kiedricher Chorbuben choir as child; soloist, Pueri Cantors Gathering, St Peter's Basilica, Rome 1981; debut int. recital at Théâtre de Grévin, Paris 1993; opera debut in Handel's Rodelinda, Glyndebourne Festival Opera, England 1998; title roles in Handel's Giulio Cesare in Egitto 2002 and Partenope 2008, Royal Danish Opera; debut at Metropolitan Opera, New York in Rodelinda 2006; performed at Belgian Royal Wedding Dec. 1999; teacher, Schola Cantorum Basiliensis, Basel 2000–; numerous int. tours and recitals, working with the world's leading Baroque conductors and ensembles, including London Proms 2005, Liceu Barcelona 2011, Adelaide Opera 2011; title role in Giulio Cesare in Egitto at Salle Pleyel, Paris 2010, Salzburg Festival 2012; Bertarido in Rodelinda, Met Opera 2011; Athamas in Semele, Salzburger Pfingstfestspiele 2015. *Recordings include:* Handel's Messiah, Solomon, Italian Cantatas and Opera Arias, Bach's Christmas Oratorio, St Matthew Passion, St John Passion, Solo Cantatas for Alto and B Minor Mass, Vivaldi's Stabat Mater (Gramophone Award) 1996, Nisi Dominus (Edison Award) 2001, Monteverdi's L'Orfeo and 1610 Vespers, works by Pergolesi and Caldara; Heroes (Echo Classic Award) 1999, Wayfaring Stranger 2001, Arcadia 2003, Arias for Senesino (Classical BRIT Award for Singer of the Year 2006) 2005, Crystal

Tears (with Julian Behr) 2008, Bach Cantatas 2011, O Solitude, Songs & Arias by Purcell (BBC Music Magazine Vocal Award 2012) 2011, Wanderer 2012, Quarter to Six (with Idan Raichel) 2013, Bach: Cantatas for Solo Alto 2014, Monteverdi: Vespro della Beata Vergine 2015. *Honours:* Conseil de l'Europe Award 1992, Fondation Claude Nicolas Ledoux Award 1992, Cannes Classical Award 1998, Artist of the Year, German Kultur Radio 1998, Belgian Musical Press Union Prize 1999, European Culture Prize 2009, Rheingau Musikpreis 2015. *Current Management:* Harrison Parrott Ltd, 5–6 Albion Court, London, W6 0QT, England. *Telephone:* (20) 7229-9166. *E-mail:* info@harrisonparrott.co.uk. *Website:* www.harrisonparrott.com.

SCHOLLUM, Benno, MA; Austrian singer (baritone); b. 1953, Klagenfurt; s. of Robert Schollum. *Education:* Vienna Musikhochschule with Josef Greindl and Robert Schollum, masterclasses in New York and Vienna with Sena Jurinac and others. *Career:* performed in Austria and elsewhere in operettas by Lehar, Johann Strauss, Milloecker and Offenbach; operas by Mozart, Britten, Lortzing, Mascagni; lieder by Loewe, Schubert, Wolf, Strauss, Grieg, Brahms and others; oratorios include Schmidt's Das Buch mit Sieben Siegeln, the Brahms Requiem and Cantatas and Masses by Bach and Mozart; festival appearances at Vienna, Antibes, Carinthian Summer and Gstaad; guest engagements in France, Yugoslavia, Italy, USA, South America, South Africa, Germany, The Netherlands and Luxembourg; Berlin Philharmonic debut in Herbst by Antal Dorati; British debut 1991 with the English Symphony Orchestra in Arias by Mozart; stage roles include Papageno; teacher, Vienna Musikhochschule from 1983. *Recordings include:* Schubert's Winterreise with Graham Johnson; Beethoven's Symphony No. 9 with Yehudi Menuhin. *Publications include:* Sprecherziehung in der Praxis der Gesangsausbildung 1993.

SCHOLZ, Andreas; singer (baritone); b. 14 Dec. 1964, Leipzig. *Education:* Felix Mendelssohn Musikhochschule, Leipzig. *Career:* sang at Leipzig Opera from 1991, as Zuniga in Carmen, Schaunard, Guglielmo, Lortzing's Tsar Peter, Rossini's Figaro and Sander in Grétry's Zémire et Azore; further appearances in Schoenberg's Moses and Aron and Hiller's Der Jagd; Dresden Opera as the Constable in Strauss's Friedenstag; soloist with the Leipzig Gewandhaus Orchestra; further concerts in Munich and Berlin. *Honours:* prizewinner at Competitions in Karlovy Vary and Berlin 1990.

SCHOLZE, Rainer; singer (bass); b. 13 May 1940, Sudetenland Germany. *Education:* Cologne Musikhochschule. *Career:* sang in the Chorus of the Lübeck Stadt Theatre 1962–66; discovered by Gerd Albrecht and sang small roles; studied further and sang solo at Lübeck from 1966–70; engaged at Brunswick 1970–71, Kassel 1971–81; appeared at Kiel 1981–83 and made guest outings to Munich, Dresden, Hamburg; often appeared in operas by Mozart, Rossini, Lortzing and notably as Baron Ochs. *Recordings include:* Masetto in Don Giovanni, Reinmar in Tannhäuser, Larkens in Fanciulla del West.

SCHOMBERG, Martin; singer (tenor); b. 7 Nov. 1944, Hoxter, Westfalen, Germany. *Education:* Hamburg Musikhochschule with Jakob Stämpfli. *Career:* debut at Mainz 1972, as Lenski in Eugene Onegin; many appearances at the opera houses of Cologne, Hamburg, Düsseldorf; Zürich Opera in lyric roles and in the 1974 premiere of Ein Wahrer Held by Klebe; concert engagements at the Salzburg Festival and elsewhere; roles have included Mozart's Belmonte, Ottavio and Tamino, Nencio in Haydn's L'Infedeltà Delusa, Florindo in Le Donne Curiose by Wolf-Ferrari, the Italian Tenor in Rosenkavalier and Alfred in Fledermaus.

SCHONBECK, Uwe; singer (tenor); b. 1961, Essen, Germany. *Education:* Essen Musikhochschule. *Career:* appearances at Krefeld Opera from 1985; Frankfurt 1990 and at the Deutsche Oper am Rhein at Düsseldorf; Geneva 1991 as Mime in The Ring, also at Frankfurt 1995; Vienna Staatsoper 1993 as Herod in Salome; Salzburg 1994 as Sellem in The Rake's Progress; Munich 1996 as Billy II in the premiere of Bose's Slaughterhouse Five; other roles include Arnalta in Monteverdi's Poppea; Rameau's Platée and Nemorino; modern repertory includes Troades by Reimann, Judith by Matthus, Macbeth by Bibalo. *Recordings include:* Stephen Climax by Hans Zender.

SCHÖNBERG, Stig Gustav; Swedish composer and organist; b. 13 May 1933, Vastra Husby. *Education:* Stockholm Musikhogskolan, studied composition with Lars-Eric Larsson, Karl-Birger Blomdahl, organ with Flor Peeters in Belgium. *Career:* freelance composer with performances throughout Sweden; many concert tours and church performances throughout Scandinavia, Europe, USA and Japan as organist. *Compositions include:* Introduction and Allegro for strings 1959, Concerto for organ and strings 1962, Sinfonia Aperta 1965, three Concertinos for strings 1966, Madeleine and Conrad (ballet) 1967, Fantasia for strings 1967, numerous String Quartets 1961–84, Impromptu Visionario for orchestra 1972, Flute Sonata 1974, Concerto for two flutes and strings 1976, Symphony No. 2 1977, Pastoral for horn and organ 1979, Concerto for organ and orchestra 1982, Missa Coralis 1983, Missa da Pacem 1985, Concerto for organ and brass orchestra 1987, Sonata alla ricercata for organ and violin 1989, Bassoon Concerto 1992, Te Deum for choir and strings 1993, Gloria 1994, Symphony No. 3 1996, Variations on a Swedish Folktune for string orchestra 1999, Prince Hat Under the Earth (children's opera) 1999, Concerto for piano and orchestra 2001, Dance of the Crocodile for soprano and string quartet 2002, Concerto for violin and orchestra 2002, Messa Misura for two voices and organ or wind orchestra 2003, Missa for two voices and organ 2003, Capriccio elegante for two violins 2004, Sonata for violin and organ 2004, Symphony No. 4 2004; also choruses and songs. *Honours:* Royal Swedish Acad. of Music Award for Organ 2003. *Current Management:* c/o STIM, Sandhamnsgatan 79, PO Box 27327, 102 54 Stockholm, Sweden. *Telephone:* (411) 533730 (home). *E-mail:* sgschoenberg@ home.se (home).

SCHÖNE, Wolfgang, DipMus; singer (bass-baritone); b. 9 Feb. 1941, Bad Gandersheim, Germany. *Education:* studied with Naan Pold in Hanover and Hamburg. *Career:* Winner of awards from 1966 at Bordeaux, Berlin, Stuttgart and 's-Hertogenbosch; Concert tours and lieder recitals in Belgium, Netherlands, France, Denmark, USA, Mexico, Argentina and England; Appeared in film, The Chronicle of Anna Magdalena Bach; Opera career from 1970 at the State Operas of Stuttgart, Vienna and Hamburg, notably as Guglielmo, Wolfram and Count Eberbach in Der Wildschütz by Lortzing; Schwetzingen Festival 1983 as Tom, in the premiere of The English Cat by Henze; Komische Oper Berlin in 1984 as Golaud in Pelléas et Mélisande; Sang in the 1984 reopening of the Stuttgart Opera, as Don Giovanni; Season 1988–89 sang Gunther at Turin, Alidoro in Cenerentola at Salzburg and Barak at Cologne; Hamburg in 1990 as Wolfram; Sang Orestes and Pentheus in The Bassarids at Stuttgart in 1989; Sang Wolfram in Hamburg in 1990, the Count in Capriccio at 1990 Salzburg Festival, Dr Schön in Lulu at the Paris Châtelet, 1992; Amfortas in Parsifal at the Opéra Bastille, Paris, 1997; Gunther in Götterdämmerung for Netherlands Opera, 1998; Season 2000–01 as the Wanderer in Siegfried at Stuttgart, Prus in The Makropulos Case at Hamburg, Amfortas in the Albert Hall, London, Strauss's Barak in Barcelona and Marschner's Hans Heiling for the Deutsche Oper, Berlin; Hans Sachs in Hamburg, 2002. *Recordings:* Bach Cantatas; St Matthew Passion by Schütz; Theresienmesse by Haydn; Bach B minor Mass; Doktor und Apotheker by Dittersdorf; Giulio Cesare by Handel; Lulu; Video of Der Freischütz.

SCHØNWANDT, Michael, BMus; Danish conductor; *Music Director, Royal Danish Opera and Orchestra*; b. 10 Sept. 1953, Copenhagen; m. Amalie Malling 1991. *Education:* Copenhagen Univ., Royal Acad. of Music, London, England. *Career:* debut in Copenhagen 1977; concerts throughout Europe, Debut Royal Danish Opera 1979; Guest Conductor: Covent Garden, London, Paris Opéra, Wiener Staatsoper, Bayreuth Festival; Principal Guest Conductor, Théâtre Royal de la Monnaie, Brussels 1984–87; Principal Conductor, Collegium Musicum, Copenhagen 1981–; Principal Guest Conductor Nice Opera, 1987–91; Danish Radio Symphony Orchestra 1989–2000; Principal Conductor, Berliner Sinfonie Orchestra 1992–98; Permanent Conductor, Vienna State Opera 1990; conducts regularly in London (Philharmonia, BBC), Paris, (Orchestre Philharmonique), Vienna, Berlin, Hamburg; Music Dir, Royal Danish Opera and Orchestra 2000–(11); Chief Conductor, Netherlands Radio Chamber Philharmonic 2010–. *Recordings include:* Mozart Piano Concertos and Violin Concertos; Beethoven Piano Concertos; Niels W Gade Complete Symphonies; Kuhlau's Lulu, Complete Opera; Schoenberg and Sibelius Pelléas and Mélisande, Berlioz Requiem; Richard Strauss: Salome, complete opera; Weyse: Complete Symphonies; Nielsen: Complete Symphonies; DVD: Wagner's Ring cycle, Nielsen's Maskarade. *Honours:* numerous musical prizes, Denmark; Carl Nielsen Prize 1997. *Current Management:* Ingpen & Williams, 7 St George's Court, 131 Putney Bridge Road, London, SW15 2PA, England. *Telephone:* (20) 8874-3222. *Fax:* (20) 8877-3113. *E-mail:* info@ingpen.co.uk. *Address:* Soendermarksvej 10, 2500 Valby, Denmark (home).

SCHOPPER, Michael; singer (bass-baritone); b. 1942, Passau, Germany. *Education:* Munich Musikhockschule. *Career:* debut with Bach's Christmas Oratorio under Karl Richter 1968; many appearances in concerts and opera in the baroque and classical repertory; in Europe, N and S America; founded ensemble Musica Poetica, for performance of renaissance and baroque music 1974; sang Monteverdi's Seneca at Montpellier 1989; and in Cavalli's Giasone at the Châtelet, Paris; Innsbruck Festival 1990–93 in Cesti's L'Orontea, as Sancho Panza in Conti's Don Chisciotte and Monteverdi's Seneca and Nettuno; Frankfurt 1994 as Pfalzgrafen in Holzbauer's Gunther von Schwarzburg and Polyphemus in Handel's Acis and Galatea at Göttingen; Magdeburg 1996 in the title role of Telemann's Der neumodische Liebhaber Damon. *Recordings:* Giulio Cesare and Bach cantatas, Bach Matthew Passion, Telemann's Pimpinone, Winterreise, Poppea and Stradella's San Giovanni Batista, Keiser's Masaniello Furioso, Gunther von Schwarzburg.

SCHRANZ, Karoly; violinist; b. 1950, Hungary. *Education:* Franz Liszt Acad., Budapest with András Mihaly, studied with the Amadeus Quartet and Zoltán Szekely. *Career:* founder mem., Takacs Quartet 1975; many concert appearances in Europe and USA; tours of Australia, New Zealand, Japan, South America, UK, Norway, Sweden, Greece, Belgium and Ireland; resident at the London Barbican 1988–91, with masterclasses at the Guildhall School of Music; visits to Japan 1989, 1992; Bartók Cycle for the Bartók-Solti Festival on the South Bank, London 1990; Great Performers Series at Lincoln Center and Mostly Mozart Festival at Alice Tully Hall, New York; appeared at Mozart Festivals at South Bank, Wigmore Hall and Barbican Centre 1991; Bartók Cycle at the Théâtre des Champs Elysées 1991, and Beethoven Cycles at the Zürich Tonhalle, in Dublin, at the Wigmore Hall and in Paris 1991–92; plays Amati instrument made for the French royal family and loaned by the Corcoran Gallery, Gallery of Art, Washington, DC. *Recordings:* Schumann Quartets, Op 41; Mozart String Quintets, with Denes Koromzay; Bartók 6 Quartets; Schubert Trout Quintet, with Zoltán Kocsis; Haydn Op 76; Brahms Op 51, Nos 1 and 2; Chausson Concerto, with Joshua Bell and Jean-Yves Thibaudet; Works by Schubert, Mozart, Dvořák and Bartók. *Honours:* winner

Int. Quartet Competition, Evian 1977, winner Portsmouth Int. Quartet Competition 1979.

SCHREIBMAYER, Kurt; singer (tenor); b. 1953, Klagenfurt, Germany. *Education:* Graz Musikhochschule. *Career:* sang at Graz 1976–78, then at the Vienna Volksoper; further appearances at the Theater am Gartnerplatz Munich 1987–88, Deutsche Oper am Rhein Düsseldorf from 1987, Hamburg Staatsoper and the Zürich Opera; Théâtre Royal de la Monnaie, Brussels from 1987 as Steva in Jenůfa and Luka in From The House of the Dead 1990; Bayreuth Festival engagements 1986–90, as Froh, Walter von der Vogelweide and Parsifal; returned to Vienna Volksoper 1988 as Max in Der Freischütz; has sung at Liège as Lohengrin 1988–89; other roles include Fra Diavolo, Babinsky in Shvanda the Bagpiper, Pedro in Tiefland, Gomez in Die drei Pintos, Wenzel in Zemlinsky's Kleider Machen Leute, and parts in operettas; sang in Mona Lisa by Max von Schillings at the Vienna Volksoper 1996 and Dimitri in Boris Godunov 1998; season 2000 as Shuisky in Boris Godunov and Zemlinsky's König Kandaules at the Vienna Volksoper, Siegmund in Graz.

SCHREIER, Peter; German singer (tenor) and conductor; b. 29 July 1935, Meissen. *Education:* Dresden Hochschule für Musik. *Career:* joined school of Dresden Staatsoper 1959, stage debut as First Prisoner (Fidelio) 1961; mem. Berlin State Opera Company 1959–63; joined Berlin Staatsoper 1963; has appeared at Vienna State Opera, Salzburg Festival, La Scala, Milan, Sadler's Wells, London, Metropolitan Opera, New York and Teatro Colón, Buenos Aires; recital debut London 1978; debut as conductor with Berlin Staatskapelle 1970; has conducted recordings of several choral works by J. S. Bach, Mozart and Schubert; retd as opera singer 1999, continues to conduct; mem. Musical Academies of Munich and Berlin 1989–, Royal Swedish Arts Acad. 1989–. *Honours:* Hon. mem. Musical Soc. of Vienna 1986–; Bundesverdienstkreuz; Sonning Award 1988, Ernst von Siemens Music Prize 1988, Georg Philipp Telemann Prize 1994, Wartburg Prize 1994, European Church Music Prize, Royal Acad. of Music/Kohn Foundation Bach Prize 2009, Hugo Wolf Medal, Internationale Hugo-Wolf-Akademie, Stuttgart 2011, International Mendelssohn Prize 2011. *Current Management:* California Artists Management, 449 Springs Road, Vallejo, CA 94590-5359, USA. *E-mail:* don@calartists .com.

SCHRÖDER, Jaap, DipMus; Dutch violinist; b. 31 Dec. 1925, Amsterdam; m. Agnès Jeanne Françoise Lefèvre; three d. *Education:* Amsterdam Conservatory, Ecole Jacques Thibaud, Paris, France. *Career:* debut in The Netherlands 1949; Leader, Radio Chamber Orchestra 1950–63; Founder chamber music ensembles, Quadro Amsterdam, Concerto Amsterdam 1962–69, Quartetto Esterhazy 1973–81, Smithson String Quartet 1983–94, Skalholt String Quarter 1996; Prof. of Violin, Amsterdam Conservatory, Yale School of Music, Basel Schola Cantorum; mem. Netherlands String Quartet 1952–69. *Music includes:* recordings of 170 titles. *Publications:* Bach's Solo Violin Works: A Performer's Guide 2007. *Address:* Gerard Brandtstraat 18, 1054 JK Amsterdam, The Netherlands (home). *E-mail:* jaapschroder@wanadoo.nl.

SCHROTT, Erwin, Uruguayan singer (bass-baritone); b. 21 Dec. 1972, Montevideo; one s. with Anna Netrebko. *Education:* studied singing with Franca Mattiucci. *Career:* operatic debut as Roucher in Andrea Chénier, Montevideo aged 22; with Teatro Municipal, Santiago, Chile –1996, sang Timur in Turandot, Colline in La Bohème, Sparafucile in Rigoletto and Ramfis in Aida; Italian stage debut at Teatro Regio di Torino in Boris Godunov 1996; debut at Vienna State Opera as Banquo in Verdi's Macbeth 1999; debut at New York Metropolitan Opera as Colline in La Bohème 2000; debut at Royal Opera House as Leporello in Don Giovanni 2003; debut at Salzburg Festival as Leporello 2008; has sung his interpretation of title role in Mozart's Don Giovanni at Royal Opera, Covent Garden, Teatro alla Scala, Maggio Musicale Fiorentino, Washington Opera, Los Angeles Opera, as well as in Seville and Turin and with Metropolitan Opera on tour to Japan; has sung in numerous operatic theatres including Teatro alla Scala, Metropolitan Opera, Opera Nat. de Paris, Washington Opera, Vienna State Opera, Teatro Colon of Buenos Aires, Royal Opera, Covent Garden, Maggio Musicale Fiorentino, Hamburg State Opera, Theatre Royale de la Monnaie, Teatro Comunale, Firenze, Teatro Carlo Felice, Genoa, Los Angeles Opera, amongst others; numerous concert appearances including jt concert with Anna Netrebko conducted by Plácido Domingo in Centro de Bellas Artes, San Juan, Puerto Rico 2007, gala concert for 5th Abu Dhabi Music and Arts Festival, with Anna Netrebko and Elīna Garanča 2008, solo concert at Münchner Residenz 2008, jt concerts with Anna Netrebko and Jonas Kaufmann at Waldbühne, Berlin, Stadthalle, Wien and Königsplatz, Munich 2011, with Anna Netrebko and Ramon Vargas, Albert Hall, London 2012, solo concerts at Salzburger Festspiele 2014 and Los Angeles Opera 2015. *Opera repertoire includes:* major Mozart roles of Don Giovanni, Leporello and Figaro, Pagano in Verdi's I Lombardi, title role in Verdi's Attila, Banquo in Macbeth, Escamillo in Carmen, Méphistophélès in Gounod's Faust and title role in Boito's Mefistofele. *Honours:* scholarship for studies in Italy 1996; first prize in Plácido Domingo Operalia Singing Competition 1998; named Distinguished Citizen of Montevideo 2015. *Current Management:* c/o Alan Green, Zemsky Green Artists Management, 104 West 73rd Street, New York, NY 10023, USA. *Telephone:* (212) 579-6700 (office). *E-mail:* agreen@zemskygreen.com (office). *Website:* www.zemskygreen.com (office). www.erwinschrott.com (office).

SCHROTT, Thomas; Italian violinist; *Violinist, Festival Strings Lucerne*; b. 24 Nov. 1966, Milan. *Education:* Milan Conservatory, Parma Conservatory A. Boito, Mannes Coll. of Music, New York; studied violin with Aaron Rosand and

Lewis Kaplan; master-classes, Mozarteum, Salzburg, Centre Int. de Formation Musicale, Nice, Accad. Musicale Chigiana, Siena, Scuola di Musica di Fiesole. *Career:* played extensively in Italy for most concert socs, including Teatro alla Scala di Milano, Pomeriggi Musicali di Milano, Ravello Festival, Sagra Musicale Umbra, Bologna, Teatro Comunale, Mantua, Teatro Bibiena, Piccolo Teatro di Milano, Accad. Musicale Pescarese, Accad. Filarmonica Romana (Teatro Olimpico), Turin, Lingotto (Auditorium G-Agnelli), Piccolo Teatro Regio, Genoa, Teatro Modena, Cantiere d'Arte Contemporanea di Montepulciano; many concerts in USA, Japan, Switzerland, Germany, Austria, France, Finland, Romania, South Africa, India, Bahrain, Mauritius, Turkey; soloist, various orchestras including: Moldova Symphony Orchestra, Orchestra della Sagra Musicale Umbra, Festival Strings Lucerne, Bombay Chamber Orchestra, M. Jora Philharmonic Orchestra, Bacau; violinist, Festival Strings Lucerne 1995–, performs regularly at European festivals including Lucerne Festival, Musikverein in Vienna, Alte Oper Frankfurt, Köln Philharmonie, Rencontres Musicales d'Evian, Naantali Festival, Ossiach Festival, Festival G. Enescu, Bucharest, Engadiner Konzertwochen, Festival di Stresa, 21st Musicbiennale, Zagreb, Biennale di Venezia 2001, SKIP Festival, St Petersburg, DOM Cultural Centre, Moscow, Quirinale, Rome 2003; other appearances include Barbican Centre, Royal Albert Hall, London; Prin. Violin, Sentieri Selvaggi, Milan; performer (with Daniel Bosshard) complete cycle of J. S. Bach's sonatas for violin and harpsichord; Guest Concertmaster, Stresa Festival Orchestra (G. Noseda conductor), Orchestra Internazionale d'Italia, Milano Classica, Orchestra da Camera della Lombardia, Orchestre de Pays de Savoy; collaborations with pianist Paul Gulda, Alessandro Baricco, Michael Nyman, James MacMillan, Gavin Bryars, Ludovico Einaudi, and actors Claudio Bisio, Moni Ovadia, Lella Costa. *Radio:* Radio Popolare Milano, RAI Euroradio, New York Public Radio, Swiss Radio DRS2. *Recordings:* F. Chopin – Complete Chamber Music; with Sentieri Selvaggi: La Formula del Fiore, Musica Coelestis, Bad Blood, Child, La Buona Novella; other: Audible Noise, Milioni di Minuti, Ludovico Einaudi. *Address:* Via Treviglio 17, 20128 Milan, Italy (home). *Telephone:* (02) 2592609 (home). *E-mail:* thschrott@libero.it (home).

SCHUBACK, Thomas; Swedish conductor and pianist; b. 1943. *Education:* Stockholm Coll. of Music. *Career:* Conductor, Royal Opera Stockholm from 1971–91; Artistic Dir Nationalmusei Kammarorkester (National Museum Chamber Orchestra), Stockholm 1993–; productions at the Drottningholm Theatre include L'Incoronazione di Poppea, L'Arbore di Diana by Martin y Soler, Mozart's Così fan tutte and Gluck's Paride ed Elena; Musical Dir, Lyric Opera of Queensland from 1982; guest appearances with San Diego Opera and at Sydney and Copenhagen; season 1992–93 included performances with the Drottningholm Theatre at the Barbican Centre, London; concerts with major Swedish orchestras and elsewhere in Scandinavia, USA and Australia; lieder accompanist to Gösta Winbergh, Barbara Bonney and others; Prof. of Vocal Coaching, State Oper School, Stockholm; mem. Royal Acad. of Music 1995–. *Recordings include:* Electra by Haeffner. *Honours:* Litteris et Artibus 2007. *Address:* Nationalmusei Kammarorkester, PO Box 16176, 103 24 Stockholm, Sweden.

SCHUCH, Herbert; Romanian pianist; b. 1979, Temesvar. *Education:* Mozarteum, Salzburg with Karl-Heinz Kämmerling. *Career:* debut Gasteig, Munich 1996; debut London Philharmonic Orchestra at the Royal Festival Hall, London 2005, also 2007; solo performances with orchestras including Georgian Chamber Orchestra, Lithuanian Chamber Orchestra, Mozarteum Orchestra, Salzburg, Nuremburger Sinfoniker and Chamber Orchestra of Lausanne; in 2006 with Orchestre Nat. de Lyon, Munich Chamber Orchestra, London Mozart Players, Munich Symphony; appearances in 2007 include Tonhalle, Zürich and Musikverein, Vienna; recitals in Rome, Int. Beethoven Festival, Bonn, Int. Keyboard Festival, New York, Konzerthaus in Vienna; also chamber music with violinists Julia Fischer, Mirijam Contzen and Alina Pogostkin, cellists Julius Berger and Sebastian Klinger, and Szymanowski, Henschel and Ysaye quartets; teacher Inst. for Highly Talented Music Students. *Recordings include:* works of Schumann and Ravel, Mozart/Beethoven Quintets for Piano & Winds (ECHO Klassik Award for Chamber Music Recording of the Year/Wind – 17th/18th Century) 2012. *Honours:* First Prize Int. Piano Competition Usti nad Labem (Czech Repub.) 1993, First Prize and Special Prizee European Music Competition for Youth, Dublin (Ireland) 1996, First Prize and Critics' Prize Alessandro Casagrande Competition (Italy) 2004, First Prize London Int. Piano Competition 2005, Int. Beethoven Competition in Vienna. *Current Management:* Italartist Austroconcert Kulturmanagement GmbH, Lothringerstrasse 14, 3400 Klosterneuburg, Austria. *Telephone:* (22) 4332614. *Fax:* (22) 4325819. *E-mail:* italartist@ia-ac .com. *Website:* www.ia-ac.com. *E-mail:* herbert.schuch@gmx.de (office). *Website:* www.herbertschuch.com.

SCHUDEL, Regina; singer (soprano); b. 1964, Zürich, Switzerland. *Education:* Berlin Hochschule and Opera Studio of the Vienna Staatsoper. *Career:* debut in Vienna 1988 as Quiteria in Die Hochzeit des Camacho by Mendelssohn; Berlin Kammeroper from 1988, as Leda in Europa und der Stier by Helge Jorus and in Henze's Elegy for Young Lovers; sang Rosina in Paisiello's Il Barbiere di Siviglia; guest appearances at Krefeld, the Bregenz Festival and throughout Germany and Switzerland; many concert and recital engagements; Leipzig Opera from 1991. *Recordings:* Die Hochzeit des Comacho, Das Wunder der Heliane by Korngold, Wozzeck by Manfred Gurlitt.

SCHUDEL, Thomas, BSc, MA, DMA; Canadian composer; b. 8 Sept. 1937, Defiance, OH, USA. *Education:* Ohio University, studied with Leslie Bassett

and Ross Lee Finney, University of Michigan. *Career:* faculty mem., University of Regina, Canada, 1964–; bassoonist, Regina Symphony Orchestra, 1964–70. *Compositions:* Set No. 2, for brass and wind quintets, 1963; Violin Sonata, 1966; String Quartet, 1967; 2 Symphonies, 1971, 1983; Variations, for orchestra, 1977; Winterpiece, for chamber orchestra and dancers, 1979; Triptych, for wind ensemble, 1979; A Dream Within a Dream, for chorus, 1985; A.C.T.S, for narrator and ensemble, 1986; Dialogues, for trombone and percussion, 1987; Concerto, for piccolo, strings and percussion, 1988; Concerto, for alto trombone and chamber orchestra, 1990; An Emily Dickinson Folio, for soprano and ensemble, 1991; Trigon, for 2 saxophones and percussion, 1992; A Tangled Web, for chamber orchestra, 1993; The Enchanted Cat, children's operetta, 1993; Pick Up The Earth, Gold and Rose, and Another Love Poem, all for chorus, 1994; Sinfonia Concertante, for saxophone quartet and band, 1994. *Honours:* first prize, 1972 City of Trieste International Competition. *Address:* 149 Shannon Road, Regina, SK S4S 5H6, Canada.

SCHULDT, Clemens; German conductor and violinist; b. 1983, Bremen. *Education:* studied violin at Robert Schumann Hochschule, Düsseldorf with Markus Stenz and Paavo Järvi; conducting studies in Düsseldorf with Rüdiger Bohn, in Vienna with Mark Stringer and in Weimar with Nicolas Pasquet. *Career:* Asst Conductor, London Symphony Orchestra 2010–11; has also conducted numerous int. orchestras including BBC Nat. Orchestra of Wales, Deutsches Symphonie-Orchester, WDR Rundfunkorchester Cologne, Hamburger Symphoniker, Orquesta Sinfonica y Coro de RTVE Madrid, Osaka Symphony, Ho Chi Minh City Ballet Symphony Orchestra Vietnam, Slovak Sinfonietta, Beethoven Acad. Orchestra, MDR Sinfonieorchester Leipzig, Bremer Philharmoniker, Mariinsky Theatre Orchestra; Dir Schumann Camerata, Orchestra of the Konrad-Adenauer-Foundation; has played as violinist with Deutsche Kammerphilharmonie Bremen and Gürzenich Orchestra Cologne. *Honours:* winner, Donatella Flick Conducting Competition 2010. *Current Management:* Konzertdirektion Schmid, Postfach 34 09, 30034 Hanover, Germany. *Telephone:* (366) 07-60/-27 (office). *Website:* www .kdschmid.de (office).

SCHULTE, Eike Wilm; German singer (baritone); b. Plettenberg. *Education:* Cologne Musikhochschule with Joseph Metternich, Salzburg Mozarteum. *Career:* mem., Deutsche Oper am Rhein Düsseldorf 1956–69, Bielefeld Opera 1969–73 and Hessisches Staatstheater Wiesbaden 1973–88; sang the Herald in Lohengrin at Bayreuth 1988 and toured Japan with the Bayreuth Festival Company 1989; Munich Staatsoper from 1989 as Faraone in Mosè by Rossini, the Father in Hansel and Gretel and Schtschelkalov in Boris Godunov; baritone role in staged performances of Carmina Burana 1990; sang Beckmesser in Die Meistersinger at the Paris Opéra and in Munich; guest engagements in Vienna, Hamburg, Cologne, Bonn, Trieste, Rome and Brussels, notably as Figaro and Rigoletto; sang Kurwenal in Japan in 1990 conducted by Peter Schneider, Mahler's 8th Symphony with the London Philharmonic under Klaus Tennstedt in 1991; season 1991–92 included: Lohengrin at Vienna State Opera, Zemlinsky, VARA Holland and Brahms Requiem with Hamburg Philharmonic; season 1993–94 included: Hansel and Gretel, Rosenkavalier and Meistersinger in Munich, Ariadne auf Naxos in Cologne and Rigoletto in Tel-Aviv; season 1994–95 included: Gunther in a new Ring production at Paris, Tannhäuser at Bayreuth Festival and debut with the Philadelphia Orchestra in Ariadne auf Naxos in Philadelphia and Carnegie Hall, New York; sang the Herald in Lohengrin at the Accademia di Santa Cecilia, Rome 1996 and at New York Met 1998; also in 1998–99 sang Meistersinger at the Deutsche Oper Berlin; Alidoro in Cenerentola in Dresden, Rosenkavalier at the Munich Opera Festival and Parsifal in Chile; season 1999–2000 debuts with Gunther at La Scala, Herald in Lohengrin at Florence Opera and Beckmesser at the Lyric Opera, Chicago; season 2002–03 with Meistersinger at the Royal Opera House in London and the Vienna State Opera, Die Zauberflöte and Der Rosenkavalier in Munich, Götterdämmerung at the Tenerife Festival, Fidelio in Milan and Monte Carlo, Lohengrin in Berlin and La Cenerentola in San Fransisco. *Recordings include:* Berlioz's L'enfance du Christ, Wagner's Lohengrin, Beethoven's 9th, Haydn's Creation and Wagner's Das Rheingold. *Current Management:* c/o Haydn Rawstron Ltd, 29a High Street, First Floor, West Wickham, Kent BR4 0LP, England. *Telephone:* (20) 8777-6070. *Fax:* (20) 8777-4073. *E-mail:* enquiries@haydn -rawstron.com. *Website:* www.haydnrawstron.com; www.eike-wilm-schulte .de.

SCHULTZ, Andrew, BMus, PhD; Australian composer and professor of music; *Professor of Music, University of New South Wales, Sydney;* b. 18 Aug. 1960, Adelaide, SA. *Education:* Queensland Univ., studied with Colin Brumby, Univ. of Pennsylvania, USA with Richard Wernick and George Crumb, King's Coll. London, UK with David Lumsdaine. *Career:* Head of Composition and Music Studies, Guildhall School of Music and Drama, London, UK 1997–2002; Prof. of Composition and Dean of Faculty of Creative Arts, Univ. of Wollongong, NSW 2002–08; Prof. of Music, Univ. of New South Wales, Sydney 2008–; compositions performed and broadcast widely in Australia, USA, Europe; comms from Univ. of Melbourne, Perihelion, Seymour Group, Elision, Flederman, Queensland Philharmonic Orchestra, Hunter Orchestra, Sydney Symphony Orchestra, Guildhall School, 4MBS-FM, Duo Contemporain, Musica Nova, Melbourne, Adelaide, Tasmanian and Queensland Symphony Orchestras. *Compositions include:* Spherics for flute, trombone, one percussion, piano, synthesizer and cello 1985, Stick Dance for clarinet, marimba and piano 1987, Sea-Change for piano 1987, Black River (opera)

1988, Barren Grounds for clarinet, viola, cello and piano 1990, Ekstasis for six solo voices 1990, Calling Music for chamber orchestra 1991, The Devil's Music for large orchestra 1992, Diver's Lament for large orchestra 1995, Violin Concerto 1996, In Tempore Stellae: Symphony No. 1 for choir and orchestra 1998, Going into Shadows (three-act opera) 2000, Journey to Horseshoe Bend (orchestral cantata) 2003, Song of Songs for 18 voices 2004, Falling Man/ Dancing Man for organ and orchestra 2005, The Children's Bach (two-act opera) 2007, Symphony No. 2 for orchestra 2008, Beach Burial (choir and orchestra) 2009, To the Evening Star (song cycle) 2009, Clarinet Quintet 2010, Violin Sonata 2010, Wind Quintet 2011. *Recordings:* approx. 60 works recorded commercially. *Honours:* Australia Council Music Bd Composer Fellowship 1982, Queensland Univ. Medal 1982, Fulbright Award 1983, Commonwealth Postgraduate Research Award 1983, Commonwealth Scholarship and Fellowship Plan Award 1985, Albert H. Maggs Composition Award 1985, King's Coll. London Hilda Margaret Watts Prize 1986, Australian Nat. Composers' Opera Award 1988, Australia Council Composer Fellowship 1990, APRA Classical Composition of the Year 1994, Australia Council Project Fellowship 2004, Schueler Orchestral Award 2007, Australia Council Fellowship 2008–09, Paul Lowin Composition Prize 2009. *Address:* School of the Arts and Media, University of New South Wales, Sydney, NSW 2052, Australia (office). *Telephone:* (2) 9385-3871 (office). *Fax:* (2) 9385-6812 (office). *E-mail:* a.schultz@unsw.edu.au (office). *Website:* www.andrewschultz.net.

SCHULZ, Gerhard; Austrian violinist; b. 23 Sept. 1951. *Education:* studied in Vienna, Düsseldorf and USA. *Career:* Second Violin, Alban Berg Quartet from 1978; many concert engagements, including complete cycles of the Beethoven Quartets in 15 European cities 1987–88, 1988–89 seasons; Bartók-Mozart cycle in London, Vienna, Paris, Frankfurt, Munich, Geneva and Turin 1990–91; annual concert series at the Vienna Konzerthaus and festival engagements worldwide; Assoc. Artist at the South Bank Centre, London; US appearances in Washington, DC, San Francisco, and New York's Carnegie Hall. *Recordings:* complete quartets of Beethoven, Brahms, Berg, Webern and Bartók, quartets of Mozart, Schubert, Haydn, Dvořák, Ravel and Debussy, works of Mozart, Schumann, Brahms. *Honours:* Grand Prix du Disque, Deutsche Schallplatenpreis, Edison Prize, Japan Grand Prix, Gramophone Magazine Award.

SCHULZ, Walther; Austrian cellist; b. 1940, Vienna. *Education:* studied in Vienna. *Career:* debut in New York 1979; debut tour of Japan 1984; performances of Haydn and other composers in Vienna and elsewhere from 1968; co-founder of the Haydn Trio of Vienna 1968 and has performed in Brussels, Munich, Berlin, Zürich, London, Paris and Rome; frequent North American appearances with concerts in 25 states; further travels to the Near East, Russia, Africa, Central and South America; series at the Vienna Konzerthaus Soc. from 1976, with performances of more than 100 works; summer festivals at Vienna, Salzburg, Aix en Provence, Flanders and Montreux; masterclasses at the Royal Coll. and Royal Acad. in London, Stockholm, Bloomington, Tokyo and the Salzburg Mozarteum. *Recordings:* Complete Piano Trios of Beethoven and Schubert, Mendelssohn D Minor, Brahms B major, Tchaikovsky A Minor, Schubert Trout Quintet; albums of works by Haydn, Schumann, Dvořák, Smetana. *Address:* c/o Haydn Trio, Sternwartest. 58, 1180 Vienna, Austria (office).

SCHUMAN, Patricia; American singer (soprano); b. 4 Feb. 1954, Los Angeles. *Education:* Santa Cruz University. *Career:* sang minor roles with San Francisco Opera then appeared with the Houston Opera and in a touring company; engagements at the NYC Opera, the Paris Opéra, Teatro La Fenice Venice and in Washington DC; sang on tour with Peter Brook's version of Carmen; Théâtre de la Monnaie Brussels from 1983 as Dorabella, Zerlina, and as Angelina in La Cenerentola; St Louis 1986 and in US premiere of Il Viaggio a Reims by Rossini; Théâtre du Châtelet, Paris 1989, in the title role of L'Incoronazione di Poppea; Miami Opera and Long Beach Opera 1989, as Antonia in Les Contes d'Hoffmann and as Mozart's Countess; Seattle Opera 1990, as Blanche in Les Dialogues des Carmélites; has also sung at the Vienna Staatsoper and in the concert hall; Metropolitan Opera debut, Donna Elvira, 1990; The Voyage, by Glass 1996; Covent Garden debut 1992, as Donna Elvira; Salzburg Festival 1997, in La Clemenza di Tito, also at Covent Garden 2000; sang Schumann's Genoveva in Leeds and London 2000, Alice Ford in Falstaff at Cologne and Covent Garden 2001. *Recordings:* Roggiero in Rossini's Tancredi, Messiah, Handel, Video of Monteverdi's Poppea, Schwetzingen 1993.

SCHUNK, Robert; singer (tenor); b. 5 Jan. 1948, Neu-Isenburg, Frankfurt, Germany. *Education:* Frankfurt Musikhochschule with Martin Grundler. *Career:* sang at Karlsruhe 1973–75; Bonn Opera 1975–77; Dortmund 1977–79; Bayreuth Festival from 1977, as Siegmund, Erik and Melot; Hamburg Staatsoper 1981, as the Emperor in Die Frau ohne Schatten; Bregenz Festival 1983, Max in Der Freischutz; engagements in Munich, Vienna, Frankfurt, London, Cologne and Berlin; tour of Japan with the Hamburg Staatsoper 1984; sang Florestan at the Met and Naples 1986–87; Siegmund in New York and Munich 1987, 1989; Emperor in Die Frau ohne Schatten and Vladimir in Prince Igor at Munich 1989; sang Wagner's Erik at Naples 1992; Florestan in Fidelio at Catania 1998. *Recordings include:* Erik in Der fliegende Holländer (from Bayreuth).

SCHURMANN, Gerard; Dutch/British/American composer and conductor; b. (Eduard Gerhard Schurmann), 19 Jan. 1924, Kertosono, Java; s. of Johan Gerhard Schurmann and Elvire Stephanie Adeline Dom; m. 1st Vivien Hind;

one d.; m. 2nd Carolyn Nott 1973. *Education:* studied with Alan Rawsthorne, Kathleen Long, Franco Ferrara. *Career:* Aircrew, 320 Squadron, RAF 1941–45; acting Netherlands Cultural Attaché, London 1945–48; resident orchestral conductor, Radio Hilversum 1948–51; freelance composer and conductor 1950–; guest conductor in France, Italy, Spain, Switzerland, Czechoslovakia, Germany, Netherlands, Scandinavia, Ireland, USA; mem. Performing Right Soc., American Soc. of Composers, Authors and Publrs, Mechanical-Copyright Protection Soc., APC, Acad. of Motion Picture Arts and Sciences, BAFTA, Composers' Guild of Great Britain, Phyllis Court Club. *Compositions include:* orchestral: six Studies of Francis Bacon 1969, Variants 1970, Attack and Celebration 1971, Piano Concerto 1972–73, Violin Concerto 1975–78, The Gardens of Exile concerto for cello and orchestra 1989–90, Overture Man in the Sky 1994, Concerto for orchestra 1994–95; chamber, instrumental: Serenade 1971, Contrasts 1973, Leotaurus 1975, Wind Quintet for flute, oboe, clarinet, horn and bassoon 1976, two Ballades for piano: Hukvaldy and Brno 1981, Duo for violin and piano 1984, Quartet for piano and strings (violin, viola, cello, piano) 1986, Ariel for oboe 1987, Quartet No. 2 for piano and strings 1997, String Quartet 2003; vocal, choral: Song Cycle Chuenchi 1966, Summer is Coming madrigal for SATB unaccompanied 1970, The Double Heart cantata for SATB unaccompanied 1976, Piers Plowman (opera cantata in two acts) 1979–80, Nine Slovak folk songs for high voice and piano or orchestra 1988, Six Songs of William Blake 1997, Gaudiana Symphonic Studies for orchestra 1999–2002, Trio for clarinet, cello and piano 2001, String Quartet 2003, Sonata for strings 2004, Partita for clarinet, violin and piano 2005, Autumn Leaves for violin and piano 2007, Canzonetta for viola and piano 2009, String Quartet No. 2 2011–12, Four Pastoral Preludes for piano 2012, Romancing the Strings for string orchestra 2013. *Recordings:* Six Studies of Francis Bacon, Variants, Chuench'i, The Double Heart, Claretta, Piers Plowman, The Gardens of Exile, Piano Concerto, Violin Concerto, Concerto for Orchesta, Duo for violin and piano, Attack and Celebration, The Film Music of Gerard Schurmann, The Gambler, Man in the Sky. *Publications:* contrib. of introductory essay to three vols on Alan Rawsthorne 1984, two further essays on a long friendship with Alan Rawsthorne in The Creel, essay about working on the music for the film Lawrence of Arabia 1990. *Honours:* Bursary Award from British Arts Council 1973, British Council Int. Music Award 1980, US State Dept Visiting Fellowship Award 1980, Fellowship Grant, Nat. Endowment for the Arts 1985–86, etc.. *Address:* 3700 Multiview Drive, Hollywood Hills, Los Angeles, CA 90068, USA (home). *E-mail:* gerardschurmann@aol.com (office). *Website:* www.gerard-schurmann.com.

SCHÜTZ, Siiri, Artist Dipl.; German concert pianist; b. 26 July 1974, Berlin. *Education:* Carl Phil E. Bach Gymnasium, Berlin, studied with Annerose Schmidt at the Hochschule für Musik, Berlin, with Leon Fleisher at the Peabody Conservatory, Baltimore, Md, USA, with Pavel Gililov at Musikhochschule, Cologne, masterclasses with Alfred Brendel, Murray Perahia, Louis Lortie and Yoheved Kaplinsky. *Career:* performed in place of Claudio Arrau in Cologne Philharmonic and Murray Perahia in Düsseldorf; debut with Berlin Philharmonic Orchestra, conducted by Claudio Abbado (concert recorded and used in film, The First Year) 1991; further concerts include Schleswig Holstein Festival, Lucerne Piano Festival, Bayreuther Festspiel, Schwetzinger Mozart Festival and the Ruhrfestspiele; as soloist, played with Tonhalle Orchestra, Zürich, Bern Symphony Orchestra, Berlin Rundfunk Symphony Orchestra, MDR Symphony, Shenzen Symphony, amongst others; played chamber music during the Berliner Festwochen and in Faust Cycle of Philharmonic Orchestra in Berlin with mems of the Munich and Berlin Philharmonic Orchestra and soloists including David Garrett, Alina Pogostkin, the Jacques Thibaud Trio, Georg Faust, Emilia Baranowska and Christoph Poppen. *Film:* The First Year (Columbia Artists Management Inc.) (producer Peter Gelb) 1992. *Recordings include:* Fascination of Variation 2006. *Honours:* Gold Medal, Int. Piano Competition, Ust nad Labem 1989, Jütting Award, Stendal 1996, fellowship support from Jürgen Ponto Stiftung Dresdner Bank, German Exchange Service, Deutsche Grammophon Gesellschaft, Yehudi Menuhin Foundation and the Keyboard Trust, London. *Current Management:* Konzert-Direktion Hans Adler, Auguste-Viktoria-Str. 64, 14199 Berlin, Germany. *Telephone:* (30) 825-6333. *Fax:* (30) 826-3520. *Website:* www.musikadler.de. *Address:* Wilhelmplatz 3, 14109 Berlin, Germany. *Telephone:* (30) 8049-7015. *E-mail:* info@siiri-schuetz.de. *Website:* www.siiri-schuetz.de.

SCHWAGER, Myron August, BMus, MMus, MA, PhD; American academic; b. 16 March 1937, Pittsfield, MA; m. 1st Katharine Lake 1961; one s. one d.; m. 2nd Laurie Beth Lewis 1982; m. 3rd Susan Welch 1999. *Education:* Massachusetts Inst. of Tech., Boston Univ., New England Conservatory of Music, Harvard Univ. *Career:* Worcester Community School of the Performing Arts; Jesuit Artists Inst., Italy; Chair. Dept of Music History, Hartt School of Music, Univ. of Hartford, Conn. 1974–92, Prof. Emer. 1993–; fmr Prin. Cellist, Springfield Symphony Orchestra; appearances with Cambridge Soc. for Early Music, Boston Chamber Players, Consortium Musicale, Hawthorne Trio, Hartford Chamber Orchestra, and Karas String Quartet; revived and reconstructed Francesco Cavalli's La Virtu de'strali d'Amore, Venice, 1642 at Wadsworth Atheneum, Hartford 1987. *Publications:* contrib. to The Creative World of Beethoven 1971, Current Musicology, Music and Letters, Early Music, Musical Quarterly, Studi musicali, American Music Teacher, The Beethoven Journal, Clavier. *Address:* 64 Avonwood Road, B16, Avon, CT 06001, USA (home).

SCHWANBECK, Bodo; singer (bass-baritone); b. 20 July 1935, Scherwin, Germany. *Education:* studied with Franz-Theo Reuter in Munich, K.H. Jarius in Stuttgart. *Career:* debut in Detmold 1959, as Varlaam in Boris Godunov; has sung in Frankfurt, Hamburg, Munich, Manheim, Düsseldorf, and Lisbon and at the NYC Opera, Zürich Opera 1967, in the premiere of Madame Bovary by Sutermeister; French television as Mustafà in L'Italiana in Algeri; Théâtre de la Monnaie, Brussels 1986; sang at Madrid 1988, in Lulu; Brussels 1990, in From the House of the Dead; Covent Garden 1990, as Waldner in Arabella; sang Antonio in Figaro with the Royal Opera on tour to Japan 1992; other roles include Baron Ochs, Osmin, Alfonso, Pizarro, Leporello, Mephistopheles, Nicolai's Falstaff, Don Pasquale, Dulcamara, Golaud, Don Magnifico and Wozzeck; sang in Lulu at Palermo 2001; frequent concert appearances.

SCHWANEWILMS, Anne; German singer (soprano). *Education:* Cologne Musikhochschule with Hans Sotin. *Career:* mem., Cologne Opera Studio 1990–92, Cologne Opera 1993–95; freelance 1995–; engagements have included Die Walküre in Essen and Klagenfurt, Sieglinde/Walküre in Freiburg, Die Zauberflöte in Trieste (with Arnold Östman) and Salome with the Cologne Radio Symphony Orchestra; debut at the Bayreuth Festival in 1996 in roles of Gerhilde in Die Walküre and Gutrune in Götterdämmerung whilst covering the role of Kundry and has been reinvited to Bayreuth each year since; returned to Turin in 1998 to perform Gutrune and 3rd Norn in concert performances of Götterdämmerung; season 1999–2000 with Sieglinde at Bonn and Berlin, Senta at Lübeck, Adriano and Gutrune at Berlin; a new production of Götterdämmerung at Stuttgart and her first performance of Senta at the Hamburg State Opera 2000; concerts have included Zemlinsky's Der Zwerg with the Gürzenich Orchestra in Cologne, Mahler's Symphony No. 8 in Udine and a concert at the Kongresshalle in Lübeck (Weber/Schubert/Rubinstein) with Erich Wächter; further engagements with return visits to Bayreuth and concerts in Japan, Die Walküre (Gerhilde) in Hamburg, Hänsel und Gretel (Hexe) in Stuttgart, Wagner's Rienzi (Adriano) at the Komische Oper in Berlin, Die Walküure (Sieglinde) in Bonn, role of Judith in Barbe Bleue at the Brussels Opera and at the Schouwbund in Rotterdam, Beethoven's Symphony No. 9 in Leipzig for MDR and Wesendoncklieder (in the Mottl edition) in Freiburg; sang Beethoven's Leonore at the Châtelet 2002; Weber's Euryanthe at the London Proms 2002; engaged at Glyndebourne 2002–03, as Weber's Euryanthe and Mozart's Electra; Covent Garden debut as Chrysothemis in Elektra 2003; Ariadne in Ariadne auf Naxos, Covent Garden 2004. *Recordings:* Beethoven's Ninth (with Seiji Ozawa), Mahler's Eighth (with Riccardo Chailly), a Strauss recital (with the Hallé Orchestra), Mendelssohn's Lobgesang (with the Gewandhaus Orchester), Strauss Lieder recital for the BBC (with Roger Vignoles). *Honours:* Opernwelt magazine Singer of the Year 2002. *Current Management:* Haydn Rawstron Ltd, 29a High Street, First Floor, West Wickham, Kent Br4 0LP, England. *Telephone:* (20) 8777-6070. *Fax:* (20) 8777-4073. *E-mail:* enquiries@haydn-rawstron.com. *Website:* www.haydnrawstron.com.

SCHWANTNER, Joseph, BM, MM, DM; American composer; b. 22 March 1943, Chicago. *Education:* American Conservatory of Music, Chicago, Northwestern University. *Career:* fmr faculty mem., Juilliard School, Eastman School of Music, Yale School of Music; composer-in-residence, St Louis Symphony 1982–85, Cabrillo Music Festival 1992; mem. American Acad. of Arts and Letters. *Compositions include:* Chronicon for bassoon and piano 1968, Consortium I and II for flute and ensemble 1970–71, Modus Caeliestis for orchestra 1973, Elixir for flute and 5 players 1975, And the Mountains Rising Nowhere for orchestra 1977, Canticle of the Evening Bells for flute and 12 players 1977, Wild Angels of the Open Hills, Song Cycle for soprano and ensemble 1977, Aftertones of Infinity for orchestra (Pulitzer Prize 1979) 1978, Sparrows for soprano and chamber ensemble 1979, Wind Willow, Whisper for chamber ensemble 1980, Dark Millennium for orchestra 1981, Through Interior Worlds for ensemble 1981, Distant Runes and Incantations for piano and orchestra 1984, Someday Memories for orchestra 1984, Witchnomad, Song Cycle for soprano and orchestra 1984, Dreamcaller, Song Cycle for soprano, violin and chamber orchestra 1984, A Sudden Rainbow for orchestra 1984, Toward Light for orchestra 1986, Piano Concerto 1988, Freeflight for orchestra 1989, A Play of Shadows, Fantasy for flute and orchestra 1990, Velocities for marimba 1990, Percussion Concerto 1991 (premiered 1995), Through Interior Worlds (ballet) 1992 (concert version 1994), Symphony 'Evening Land' for soprano and orchestra 1995, In Memories Embrace… for strings 1996, Beyond Autumn for horn and orchestra 1999, Angelfire for violin and orchestra 2002, September Canticle for organ, brass, percussion, piano and strings 2002, New Morning for the World for narrator and orchestra 2004, Recoil for orchestra 2004, Morning's Embrace for orchestra 2006, Chasing Light for orchestra 2008. *E-mail:* schwantner@schwantner.net (office). *Website:* www.schwantner.net.

SCHWARTNER, Dieter; singer (tenor); b. 6 Feb. 1938, Plauen, Germany. *Education:* studied in Dresden. *Career:* debut in Plauen 1969 as the Baron in Der Wildschütz; sang at Plauen until 1972, then at Dresden 1972–78, and Dessau 1978–79; mem., Leipzig Opera from 1979 singing Ligeti's Le Grand Macabre and the Duke of Parma in Busoni's Doktor Faust in 1991; guest appearances in Dresden and at the Berlin Staatsoper; other roles have included Tamino, Faust, Max, Lionel in Martha, Florestan, Don José, Alvaro in La Forza del Destino and Walther von Stolzing; many concert engagements.

SCHWARTZ, Elliott Shelling, AB, MA, EdD; American composer, writer and academic; *Professor Emeritus of Music, Bowdoin College;* b. 19 Jan. 1936, Brooklyn, NY; m. Dorothy Rose Feldman 1960; one s. one d. *Education:* Columbia Univ. *Career:* Instructor, Univ. of Massachusetts 1960–64; Asst Prof., Bowdoin Coll., Brunswick, Me 1964–70, Assoc. Prof. 1970–75, Prof. of Music and Chair. of Dept from 1975, now Prof. Emer. of Music; Prof. of Composition, Ohio State Univ. 1985–86, 1988–91; visiting appointments, Trinity Coll. of Music, London, UK 1967–, Univ. of California, San Diego 1978–79, Robinson Coll., Cambridge, UK 1993–94, 1998–99, 2007, 2010–12; mem. American Soc. of Univ. Composers, Coll. Music Soc. (Past Pres.), American Composers' Alliance. *Compositions:* Timepiece 1794 for chamber orchestra 1994, Rainbow for orchestra 1996, Alto Prisms for eight violas 1997, Mehitadel's Serenade for saxophone and orchestra 2001, Rainforest with Birds 2001, Voyager for orchestra 2002, Riverscape 2003, Summer's Journey for concert bands 2005. *Recordings:* Grand Concerto, Extended Piano, Mirrors, Texture for Chamber Orchestras, Concert Piece for Ten Players, Chamber Concertos I–VI, Cycles and Gongs, Extended Clarinet, Dream Music with Variations, Celebrations/Reflections for Orchestra, Memorial in Two Parts, Chiaroscuro, Elan, Aerie for six flutes, Equinox for orchestra, Voyager for orchestra, Timepiece 1794 for chamber orchestra. *Publications:* The Symphonies of Ralph Vaughan Williams 1964, Contemporary Composers on Contemporary Music (co-ed.) 1967, Electronic Music: A Listener's Guide 1973, Music: Ways of Listening 1982, Music Since 1945: Issues, Materials and Literature (with Daniel Godfrey) 1993; contrib. to professional journals. *Honours:* Gaudeamus Prize (Netherlands) 1970, Maine State Award in the Arts and Humanities 1970, Nat. Endowment for the Arts grants 1978–83, Rockefeller Foundation residencies, Bellagio, Italy 1980, 1989. *Address:* PO Box 451, South Freeport, ME 04078, USA. *Telephone:* (207) 865-3722. *Fax:* (207) 865-6652. *E-mail:* eschwart@bowdoin.edu. *Website:* www.schwartzmusic.com.

SCHWARTZ, Sergiu; American concert violinist, academic and conductor; b. Romania. *Education:* Juilliard School, New York with Dorothy DeLay, Guildhall School, London with Yfrah Neaman, Rubin Acad., Tel-Aviv with Rami Shevelov, also studied with Stefan Gheorghiu in Romania and with Sándor Végh, Felix Galimir, Leon Fleisher, Isaac Stern and Sergiu Celibidache. *Career:* New York debut at Carnegie Recital Hall; London debut at Wigmore Hall in the Outstanding Israeli Artists series; N American debut at Museum of Fine Arts, Montreal; soloist with leading orchestras in Europe, Israel and throughout USA, including Dresden Staatskapelle, Jerusalem Symphony, London Symphony, Sarajevo, Dresden and Slovak Philharmonics, European Community Chamber Orchestra, Nat. Orchestra of Mexico, Chicago's Grant Park Festival Orchestra and numerous other distinguished ensembles in USA and world-wide; collaborations in performances with conductors including Sergiu Commissiona, James Judd, Peter Maag, Giuseppe Sinopoli and Bruno Weil; performances in major concert halls, including Lincoln Center, Carnegie Recital Hall and 92nd Street Y, New York, Kennedy Center, Washington, DC, Barbican Hall, Queen Elizabeth Hall and Wigmore Hall, London, Jerusalem Theatre, Accad. Santa Cecilia, Rome; Artist Faculty at Bowdoin, Summit and Killington (USA) int. music festivals and frequent guest at int. music festivals, including Newport, Interlochen (USA), Keshet Eilon (Israel), Kuhmo (Finland), Interlaken (Switzerland), Qingdao (China), and in Switzerland, Finland, UK, France, Romania and Bulgaria; conductor with European Community Chamber Orchestra, Concentus Hungaricus, Sarajevo Philharmonic, Israel Camerata Orchestra, Lynn Univ. Philharmonia and Chamber Orchestra, CSU String Orchestra; broadcasts for major radio and TV stations, including BBC, NPR and CNN; has given master classes at music schools, colls and univs throughout USA, including Interlochen Arts Acad., UCLA, Univ. of Southern California, Colburn School, Oberlin Conservatory, Eastman School, San Francisco Conservatory, Idyllwild Arts Acad., Boston Univ., DePaul Univ., Cleveland Inst. of Music, Carnegie Mellon, LaGuardia School for the Performing Arts, New York, RAM, London, Reina Sofia Acad. of Music, Madrid, Jerusalem Acad. of Music, Mount Royal Conservatory (Canada), Korea Nat. Univ. of Arts, Seoul, Busan Univ. (S Korea), Shanghai and Beijing Central Conservatories (China), Univ. of Music & Performance Arts, Graz (Austria), Haute Ecole de Musique de Lausanne (Switzerland), Novosibirsk State Conservatory (Russia); master courses in Romania, Bulgaria, Switzerland, Netherlands, Germany, Israel; judge at int. violin competitions, including Tchaikovsky (Russia), Pablo Sarasate (Spain), Henryk Szeryng (Mexico), Michael Hill (New Zealand), Mozart (Salzburg, Austria), Wieniawski (Poland), David Oistrakh (Russia), Novosibirsk (Russia), Postacchini (Italy), Sphinx (USA) and other competitions in France, Italy, Canada and USA; fmr Prof., The William B. and Sue Marie Turner Distinguished Faculty Chair in Violin, Schwob School of Music, Columbus State Univ.; Prof., Haute Ecole Musique de Lausanne-Sion, Switzerland. *Radio:* live broadcast recitals for the BBC, Kol Hamusica classical music station (Israel) and on NPR's Performance Today; broadcasts on major classical radio stations across USA. *Recordings:* extensive violin and chamber music repertoire. *Honours:* America-Israel Cultural Foundation Award, NEA Solo Recitalist Fellowship, Nat. Foundation for the Advancement of the Arts, prizewinner int. violin competitions in USA, UK, Switzerland and Chile, Regents' Teaching Excellence Award, Columbus State University/University System of Georgia Regents. *Current Management:* c/o Joanne Rile Artists Management, 93 Old York Road, Suite 212, Jenkintown Commons, PA 19046, USA. *Telephone:* (215) 885-6400. *Fax:* (215) 885-9929. *E-mail:* joanner@rilearts.com. *Website:* www.rilearts.com.

SCHWARZ, Dietmar; German arts organisation executive; *Director of Opera, Theater Basel;* b. 1957, Biberach an der Riss. *Education:* Ludwig Maximilian Univ., Munich, Univ. Paris-Sorbonne (Paris IV). *Career:* Artistic

Dir Ruhr Festival Break America 1990–93; worked at Theater Freiburg, Bremen Theatre and Frankfurt Opera; Opera Dir Nationaltheater Mannheim 1998–2006; Dir of Opera, Theater Basel 2006–; apptd Dir Deutsche Oper (2012–17). *Address:* Theater Basel, Elisabethenstrasse 16, 4051 Basel, Switzerland (office). *E-mail:* info@theater-basel.ch (office). *Website:* www.theater-basel.ch (office).

SCHWARZ, Gerard; American conductor; b. 19 Aug. 1947, Weehawken, NJ; m. Jody Greitzer 1984; two s. two d. *Education:* Professional Children's School, Juilliard School. *Career:* joined American Brass Quintet 1965; Music Dir Erick Hawkins Dance Co. 1966, Eliot Feld Dance Co. 1972; Co-Prin. Trumpet, New York Philharmonic 1973–74; Founding Music Dir Waterloo Festival 1975; Music Dir New York Chamber Symphony 1977–2002, LA Chamber Orchestra 1978–86; est. Music Today series, Merkin Concert Hall, New York 1981 (Music Dir 1988–89); Music Advisor, Mostly Mozart Festival, Lincoln Center, New York 1982–84, apptd Music Dir 1984; Music Advisor, Seattle Symphony 1983–84, Prin. Conductor 1984–85, Music Dir 1985–2011, now Jack Benaroya Conductor Laureate; Music Dir Royal Liverpool Philharmonic Orchestra 2001–06; currently Music Dir All-Star Orchestra, Music Dir Eastern Music Festival, North Carolina; Guest Conductor, Cosmopolitan Symphony, Aspen Festival Chamber, Tokyo Philharmonic, Residentie, The Hague, St Louis Symphony, Kirov, St Petersburg, Royal Liverpool Philharmonic and Vancouver Symphony Orchestras, City of London Symphonia and London Mozart Players; has conducted numerous orchestras, including Hong Kong Philharmonic, Jerusalem Symphony, Israeli Chamber and English Chamber Orchestras, London Symphony, Helsinki Philharmonic and Monte Carlo Philharmonic Orchestras, Ensemble Contemporain, Paris and Nat. Orchestra of Spain; operatic conducting debut, Washington Opera 1982; has also conducted Seattle Opera 1986, San Francisco Opera 1991 and New Japan Philharmonic 1998; fmr Artistic Advisor, Tokyo Philharmonic, Tokyu Bunkamura's Orchard Hall; Chair. Young Musicians Excelling. *Recordings include:* nearly 350 recordings on such labels as Naxos, Delos, EMI, Koch, New World, Nonesuch, Reference Recording, RLPO Classics, Columbia/Sony, RCA. *Honours:* Hon. Fellow, John Moores Univ., Liverpool 2001, given hon. title of Gen. by State of Wash. for contributions as an artist and citizen; Hon. DFA (Fairleigh Dickinson Univ., Seattle Univ.); Hon. DMus (Univ. of Puget Sound); Conductor of the Year, Musical America Int. Directory of the Performing Arts 1994, Ditson Conductor's Award, Columbia Univ. 1989, Concert Music Award, American Soc. of Composers, Authors and Publishers 2002, Impact Lifetime Achievement Award, Nat. Acad. of Recording Arts and Sciences 2003, four Emmy Awards. *Current Management:* AOR Management, Inc., 6910 Roosevelt Way NE, PMB221, Seattle, WA 98115, USA. *E-mail:* aormanagement@gmail.com (home). *Website:* www.aormanagement.com/artists/gerard-schwarz; www.gerardschwarz.com; www.allstarorchestra.org; easternmusicfestival.org.

SCHWARZ, Hanna; singer (mezzo-soprano); b. 15 Aug. 1943, Hamburg, Germany. *Education:* studied in Hamburg, Hanover and Essen. *Career:* debut at Hanover 1970, as Maddalena in Rigoletto; Eutin 1972, as Carmen; mem., Hamburg Staatsoper from 1973; guest appearances in Zürich 1975–, San Francisco 1977–, Vienna, Paris (Preziosilla 1977), Deutsche Oper Berlin (Cherubino 1978); Munich Staatsoper 1974, 1980, 1984; Bayreuth Festival 1976–85, as Fricka and Erda; sang in the first complete performance of Berg's Lulu, Paris Opéra 1979; Holland Festival 1985, as Brangaene in Tristan und Isolde; Paris 1987, as Cornelia in Giulio Cesare; sang Fricka in Das Rheingold at Bonn and Cologne 1990; season 1992 as Orpheus and Fricka at Bonn; sang Fricka at the New York Met 1996–97; Mephistophila and Helen in the premiere of Schnittke's Historia von D. Johann Fausten, Hamburg 1995; sang Brangaene at Cologne 1998; season 2000–01 as Fricka in the Ring and Berg's Countess Geschwitz at the Met; Waltraute at Cologne, the Nurse in Die Frau ohne Schatten at Dresden and Herodias for the Hamburg Staatsoper. *Recordings include:* Die Zauberflöte, The Queen of Spades, Lulu, Mahler's Rückert Lieder, Apollo et Hyacinthus by Mozart, Die Lustige Witwe; Les Contes d'Hoffmann, Humperdinck's Königskinder, Die Heimkehr aus der Fremde by Mendelssohn; Rhinedaughter in The Ring; Fricka in the Bayreuth Ring; Martha in Schubert's oratorio Lazarus; Mother in Hänsel und Gretel.

SCHWEEN, Astrid; cellist; b. 1960, New York, USA. *Education:* Juilliard School. *Career:* soloist with the New York Philharmonic; co-founder, Lark String Quartet; concert tours to Australia, Taiwan, Hong Kong, People's Republic of China, Germany, The Netherlands; US appearances at The Lincoln Center, New York, Kennedy Center, Washington, DC, in Boston, Los Angeles, Philadelphia, St Louis and San Francisco; repertoire includes quartets by Haydn, Mozart, Beethoven, Schubert, Dvořák, Brahms, Borodin, Bartók, Debussy and Shostakovich. *Honours:* gold medals at the Naumberg Competition 1990, Shostakovich Competition 1991, prizewinner Premio Paulio Borciani 1990, Karl Klinger Competition 1990, London Int. String Quartet Competition 1991, Melbourne Chamber Music Competition 1991.

SCHWEIGER, Stephanie Kreszenz Berta; German composer; b. 19 Dec. 1964, Regensburg. *Education:* studied in Regensburg, Munich and Berlin, Hochschule der Künste Berlin with Gösta Neuwirth, Walter Zimmermann and Dieter Schnebel. *Career:* first compositions 1980; composer and pianist in experimental ensemble 1983–88; radio broadcast at Westdeutscher Rundfunk, Sender Freies Berlin and other stations; performances include Darmstadt summer courses and festivals in Rome, Paris, Berlin, Leipzig and elsewhere; collaborations with Anna Clementi, Barre Bouman, ConGioco Ensemble, Accroche Note, Barbara Thun, Ariane Jessulat and others;

commissions from Berlin Senate 1993, from G-Lock, Passau 1994–98; mem. Freunde Guter Musik, Berlin. *Compositions:* 1au9tu9mn3 for four instruments and dancer 1993, ekloge for mezzo-soprano, viola, guitar and percussion 1996–97, frango phragmón for accordion 1996–97, Skira for flute, violoncello and accordion 1997, exilata for soprano and clarinet or bassoon 1998; film music: nine pieces of music (One more time before I die) 1990, Die Vergessenen 1997.

SCHWEIKART, Dieter; singer (bass); b. 9 Jan. 1942, Iserlohn, Germany. *Education:* studied in Wuppertal with Becker-Brill and with Thomas Lo Monaco in Rome. *Career:* sang in Saarbrucken from 1964; appearances at Düsseldorf, Krefeld and Bonn; Hanover from 1976; has sung in Dortmund, Hamburg, Frankfurt, Helsinki, Florence, Copenhagen and Cologne; Bayreuth Festival 1983–86, as Hans Foltz in Die Meistersinger and as Fafner in Der Ring des Nibelungen; sang Daland in Der fliegende Holländer at Naples 1992; Crespel in Les Contes d'Hoffmann at Cologne 1998; season 2000–01 at Cologne as Fafner and Sarastro.

SCHWEIZER, Alfred; Swiss composer; b. 4 Nov. 1941, Sevelen. *Education:* Univ. of Berne, Berne Conservatory, Music Acad. of Basle, Swiss Centre for Computer Music. *Career:* Prof., Winterthur Conservatory 1970–71; Prof., Biel Conservatory 1971–2003, Acting Dir 1979–80; Man. Classic 2000 1982–; mem. Schweizerischer Tonkünstlerverein, Schweizerischer Musikpädagogischer Verband. *Compositions include:* seven pieces for orchestra, Summer-Symphony for small orchestra, Concerto for piano; Music for piano 4-hd and strings, two Concertinos for violin and strings, Woodwind Quintet, Music for piano #1–10, two Miniatures for piano, Music for guitar #1–6, Metamusic for percussion and strings, Concerto for Swiss folk instruments and small orchestra, Canon for open orchestra, The Year in Naïve Music, Christmas Music, Quartet ATON open music, Glendaloug open music for flute, clarinet, violin, cello, piano and percussion, Music for viola, Music for viola d'amore, Music for harp and guitar, Music for accordion, Septet for flute, clarinet, bassoon, piano, violin, viola, cello, Etincelles for piano and percussion, Lichtes Wasser for flute, violin, viola and two guitars, Burleske for four bassoons, Pulsations for soprano saxophone, trumpet and marimba, COSMOS-5 for string quintet and sound track; ...ins Unendliche for violin, clarinet, double bass and didgeridoo, Music for brass numbers 1 and 2, Hip Hop for wind ensemble, Music for Christian for brass and two keyboards. *Recordings include:* Orchestral Pieces numbers 1, 2, 3, Piano Concerto, Concertinos for Violin and Strings, Quartet ATON open music, Music for Piano numbers 1–10, Metamusic, Music for Guitars numbers 1, 2, 3, 4. *Honours:* Second Prize, Int. Composers Competition, San Remo, Recognition Prize, Pro Arte Foundation, Berne, Recognition Prize, Canton Berne, Culture-Prize, City of Biel 2001. *Current Management:* c/o Müller & Schade AG, Moserstrasse 16, 3014 Bern, Switzerland. *Telephone:* (31) 3202626. *E-mail:* musik@mueller-schade.com. *Website:* www.mueller-schade.com. *Address:* Oberi Chros 22, 2513 Twann, Switzerland. *E-mail:* classic2000@bluewin.ch. *Website:* www.classic2000.ch.

SCHWEIZER, Daniel; Swiss conductor; b. 6 Nov. 1953, Herisau; m. Michiko Tsuda 1980, two s. *Education:* Zürich Konservatorium, Musikhochschule Essen, Musikhochschule Freiburg. *Career:* debut with Zürich Symphony Orchestra 1981; founder, Zürich Symphony Orchestra 1981; concerts at festivals in Spain and Estoril, Portugal; guest conductor in Germany, Czechoslovakia, Italy, France, Austria, Singapore, Republic of Korea, USA, Mexico, Estonia; mem. Schweizerischer Tonkünstlerverein. *Recordings:* Jecklin: Paul Muller, orchestral works; Motette: Marcel Dupré, Symphony G minor op 25, Dupré Concerto op 31 Demessieux op 9, Jongen Symphonie Concertante op 81, Classic 2000; Alfred Schweizer, orchestral works.

SCHWEIZER, Verena; singer (soprano); b. 9 May 1944, Solothurn, Switzerland. *Education:* Zürich Conservatory, studied in Frankfurt, in Basle with Elsa Cavelti, in Aachen and Freiburg, and in Mannheim with Anna Reynolds. *Career:* sang at Aargau 1971–72, Mainz 1973–75, Dortmund 1975–83; sang at Freiburg from 1985 and guested at Stuttgart (1986 as Jenůfa, 1990 as Marenka in The Bartered Bride); Ludwigsburg 1984–89, as Fiodriligi and Mozart's Countess; further appearances in Leeds (with the Dortmund Opera), Geneva, Cologne, Düsseldorf and Wiesbaden; other roles include Susanna, Zerlina, Marcellina, Adina, Gilda, Micaela, Nannetta, Mimi, Sophie in Der Rosenkavalier, Anne Trulove and Desdemona; concert engagements in Paris, Rome, Buenos Aires and Copenhagen; St Gallen 1983, in the premiere of P. Huber's Te Deum. *Recordings include:* Christmas Oratorio by Saint-Saëns, Magnificat and other sacred music by Vivaldi, Così fan tutte, Hindemith's Cardillac.

SCHWENNIGER, Aurelia; singer (mezzo-soprano); b. 1938, Austria. *Career:* sang at the Landestheater Linz 1962–64, Augsburg 1964–66, and at the Nationaltheater Mannheim 1968–78; roles have included Zenobia in Handel's Radamisto, Rosina, Fenena in Nabucco, Eboli, Amneris, Magdalene, the Composer in Ariadne auf Naxos, Silla in Palestrina, Janáček's Fox and Tchaikovsky's Maid of Orleans; guest appearances at the Vienna Staatsoper, Rome and Cologne Operas and the Teatro San Carlos at Lisbon.

SCHWETS, Stanislav; Russian singer (bass); b. 28 Jan. 1974, Ekaterinburg. *Education:* Moscow State Conservatory with Prof. P. Gluboky and Prof. V. Chachava. *Career:* debut as Banquo in Verdi's Macbeth, Dublin Opera 1996; filmed in masterclass by Galina Vishnevskaya, Moscow 1993; frequent broadcasts on Russian television; sang Rogozhin and David in world premieres of N.F.B. and Young David by V. Kobekin, at Sacro Art Festival, Germany 1995, 1997; sang in Te Deum by Handel and in Mass in B flat by

Mozart, conducted by W. Gönnenwein at Lüdwigsburger Festival 1996; sang Daland in Der fliegende Holländer for Metz Opera, France 1997, and with Mariinsky company, conducted by Valery Gergiev in Toulouse and Madrid 1997; 1998 engagements with Basilio in Rossini's Il Barbiere di Siviglia and Leporello in Don Giovanni at Frankfurt Opera, Daland with Mariinsky Theatre conducted by Gergiev in Lisbon, and Pimen in Boris Godunov at Dublin; sang in concerts with V. Chachava in Moscow, St Petersburg and other Russian cities; performed in Ekaterinburg in recital with Elena Obraztsova and Vazha Chachava; soloist with Helikon Opera 2006–. *Honours:* Grand Prix and Special Prize, Belvedere Int. Singers Competition, Vienna 1994; Prizewinner, Rimsky-Korsakov Int. Singers Competition, St Petersburg 1996. *Address:* Helikon-Opera, 19 Bolshaja Nikitskaja Street, 125009 Moscow, Russia (office). *Telephone:* (495) 6900971 (office). *Fax:* (495) 6911323 (office). *Website:* www.helikon.ru (office).

SCIAMA, Pierre; singer (countertenor); b. 1960, England. *Education:* Guildhall School with David Pollard and David Roblou, GSM Early Music Course. *Career:* sang Reason in Cavalieri's La Rappresentazione di Anima e di Corpo, Morley Coll. 1987; Purcell's Fairy Queen at the GSM conducted by William Christie; sang in Rameau's Pygmalion at the QEH and in Gluck's Alceste at Covent Garden and in Monte Carlo; Acis and Galatea with Midsummer Opera in Tours and St John's Smith Square, London 1989; appeared in Dido and Aeneas with the Early English Opera Soc. and as Apollo in Grabu's Albion and Albanus; Armindo in Handel's Partenope with Midsummer Opera.

SCIARRINO, Salvatore; Italian composer; b. 4 April 1947, Palermo. *Education:* Accademia di Santa Cecilia in Rome, studied with Tulio Belfiore. *Career:* Artistic Dir, Teatro Comunale in Bologna; teacher in Milan, Florence and Citta del Castello; Milan Conservatory from 1974. *Compositions:* instrumental pieces: Berceuse for orchestra 1967, Quartetto 1967, Da un divertimento 1970, Sonata du camera 1971, Arabesque for two organs 1971, Rondo for flute and orchestra 1972, Romanza for viola d'amore and orchestra 1973, Variazioni for cello and orchestra 1974, two Piano Trios 1974, 1986, two Quintets 1976, 1977, Clair de Lune for piano and orchestra 1976, Kindertotenlied for soprano, tenor and chamber orchestra 1978, Flos Forum for chorus and orchestra 1981, Nox apud Orpheum for two organs and instruments 1982, String Trio 1983, three Piano Sonatas 1976, 1983, 1986, Violin Concerto: Allegoria nella notte 1985, Morte di Borromini for narrator and orchestra 1989, Lohengrin 'azione invisible' 1983, Perseo e Andromeda 1991, Luci Miei Traditrici (opera) 1998, Infinito nero (theatrical piece) 1998, Notturni for piano 1999, Cantare con silenzio for chorus, flute and percussion 1999, Settimo quartetto for string quartet 1999.

SCIMONE, Claudio; Italian conductor and musicologist; b. 23 Dec. 1934, Padua. *Education:* studied with Franco Ferrara, Dmitri Mitropoulos and Carlo Zecchi. *Career:* founder and Principal Conductor of chamber ensemble, I Solisti Veneti 1959; performances of 18th- and 19th-century Italian music, Mozart, Schoenberg and modern works (Donatoni, Bussotti, Malipiero and others); tours of USA, Europe and Japan; wrote for La gazzetta del Veneto 1952–57; teacher, Venice Conservatory 1961–67; teacher of chamber music, Verona Conservatory 1967–74; Dir, Padua State Conservatory of Music from 1974; conducted Il Barbiere di Siviglia at Caracalla 1992 and at the Verona Arena 1996. *Recordings include:* more than 200 recordings with I Solisti Veneti and other orchestras (London Philaromia, Royal Philharmonic, English Chamber Orchestra, Bamberger Symphoniker, others), including L'Elisir d'amore (Ricciarelli, Carreras); Vivaldi flute concertos and Orlando Furioso; Concerti Grossi by Albinoni, Corelli and Geminiani; Marcello La Cetra; Italian flute and oboe concertos; Rossini string sonatas and Mozart's Salzburg Divertimenti; Operas by Rossini, including Zelmira 1990. *Publications:* edns of concertos by Tartini, complete edn of Rossini, Segno, Significato, Interpretazione 1974; contrib. numerous articles to music journals. *Honours:* Elizabeth Sprague Coolidge Memorial Medal 1969, Grammy Award, Grand Prix du Disque de l'Academie Charles Cros, Academie du Disque Lyrique. *Address:* I Solisti Veneti, Piazzale Pontecorvo 4A, 35121 Padua, Italy (office). *Telephone:* (049) 666128 (office). *Fax:* (049) 8752598 (office). *E-mail:* info@solistiveneti.it (office). *Website:* www.solistiveneti.it (office).

SCOGNA, Flavio Emilio; Italian composer and conductor; *Principal Conductor, Ensemble Contemporaneo Accademia Nazionale di S. Cecilia;* b. 16 Aug. 1956, Savona; m. Fiorenza Iademarco 1993; two s. *Education:* N. Paganini Conservatory, Genoa, Univ. of Bologna, studied conducting with Franco Ferrara in Rome. *Career:* works performed in major int. venues, including Italian Radio, Rome, Naples, Centre Pompidou, Paris, Vienna Konzerthaus, and broadcast, RAI, BBC, Radio France, ORF, BRT; many comms, Italian Radio, Vienna Konzerthaus, Pomeriggi Musicali of Milan; Prin. Conductor Ensemble Contemporaneo Accad. Nazionale di S. Cecilia; conductor, musical groups, nat. and int. orchestras such as RAI, Israel Symphony Orchestra, Radio Broadcasting of Spain, Hungarian State Symphony Orchestra; appearances on Italian Radio, Teatro Massimo, Palermo, Teatro Opera Roma, Teatro Comunale, Firenze; teacher in several Italian conservatories such as S. Pietro a Maiella, Naples, and G. Rossini, Pesaro. *Compositions include:* Arioso per Guillermo 1984, Serenata for ensemble 1984, Anton (one-act opera) 1984, Incanto for string trio 1985, Come un'onda di luce for oboe, clarinet, violin, viola, cello 1985, Canto del mare for flute, violin, cello 1985, Cadenza seconda for piano 1986, Sinfonia concertante for orchestra 1986–87, Frammento (after Mario Luz's poem) for soprano, piano 1987, La mar for marimba 1987, Concertino for 10 instruments 1987, Tre

invenzioni for piano 1988, Risonanze for string quartet 1988, Fluxus for orchestra 1988, Verso for three winds and three strings 1988, Rifrazioni for soprano and orchestra 1989, Alternanze for piano and strings 1989, Musica reservata for strings and orchestra 1990, Salmo XII for mezzo-soprano, baritone, orchestra 1990, Relazioni for ensemble 1991, La memoria perduta (two-act opera) 1991–93, Diaphonia for viola, orchestra 1992, Trame for trumpet 1993, Aulos for oboe 1993, Concentus for orchestra 1994–95, Amadeus Mio Caro for chamber orchestra 1998. *Recordings:* as conductor: Planc, chamber ensemble, Serenata, Incanto, Anton, Alternanze, and many others for leading recording cos. *Current Management:* Mrs. Philharmonica, Piazza del Colosseo 9, 00184 Rome. *Telephone:* (06) 77203017. *Fax:* (06) 70495523. *E-mail:* md9081@mclink.it. *Website:* mrsphilharmonica.it. *Address:* Via Gradoli 56, 00189 Rome, Italy (home). *Telephone:* (06) 33266646 (home). *Fax:* (06) 33266646 (home). *E-mail:* flavioscogna@libero.it (home); info@flavioemilioscogna.it. *Website:* www.flavioemilioscogna.it.

SCORSIN, Giuseppe; singer (bass); b. 6 July 1961, Treviso, Italy. *Education:* Cremona Univ. and Verdi Conservatory, Milan. *Career:* debut at Treviso 1990, as Bartolo in Le nozze di Figaro; appearances at Monte Carlo in Gianni Schicchi, at Rovigo in La Bohème and La Scala in Franchetti's Cristoforo Colombo; Zürich Opera from 1992, in Semiramide, Butterfly, Lohengrin, The Rape of Lucretia, Macbeth, Salome, Otello, Roméo et Juliette and Die Zauberflöte; Lucerne Opera as Philip II in Don Carlo and at Lugano in Mendelssohn's Die Erste Walpurgisnacht; further roles include Bellini's Oroveso, Rossini's Don Basilio and Ferrando in Il Trovatore, Pistola in Falstaff; season 1996 in The Gambler at La Scala, as Orbazzano in Tancredi at Winterthur, and Don Basilio throughout Italy; Zürich Opera 1997–98, as Sparafucile in Rigoletto; Il Prefetto in Linda di Chamounix (also at Bologna), Raimondo in Lucia di Lammermoor; Ashby in La fanciulla del West; Fabrizio in Wolf-Ferrari's Il Campiello at Bologna 1998. *Honours:* winner Toti dal Monte Competition, Treviso 1990.

SCOTTO, Renata; Italian singer (soprano); b. 24 Feb. 1935, Savona; m. Lorenzo Anselmi; one s. one d. *Education:* Giuseppe Verdi Conservatory with Emilio Ghiriardini. *Career:* debut as Violetta, Teatro Nuovo, Milan 1953; joined La Scala opera co. from 1954; London debut at the Stoll Theatre 1957; US debut in Chicago 1960; Covent Garden debut 1962, as Madama Butterfly; roles at the Metropolitan Opera from 1965, directed Butterfly at the Metropolitan 1986 and sang there for the last time in 1987; numerous festival appearances; sang roles in Adriana Lecouvreur, Andrea Chénier, Anna Bolena, Cavalleria Rusticana, Der Rosenkavalier (Marschallin), Elektra (Klytämnestra), Edgar, Falstaff, Gilda, I Capuleti e i Montecchi, I Lombardi, I Puritani, I Vespri Siciliani (Helena), L'Elisir d'amore, La Bohème, La Sonnambula (Amina), La Straniera, La Traviata, La Voix Humaine, Lucia di Lammermoor, Madama Butterfly, Manon Lescaut, Otello, Pagliacci, Pirata, Robert le Diable, The Medium, Tosca, Trittico, Turandot; as stage dir: Il Pirata, Bellini Festival, Catania, Madama Butterfly, Arena di Verona, Genoa, Thessaloniki, Ancona, Dallas Opera, Lucia di Lammermoor, Thessaloniki, Tosca, Traviata, Sonnambula, Florida Grand Opera, Sonnambula, Detroit. *Publication:* More Than a Diva (autobiog.) 1984. *Honours:* Commendatore della Reppublica; Dr hc (Saint John's Univ.); Metropolitan Opera Guild Opera News Award 2006. *Current Management:* c/o Robert Lombardo Associates, 61 West 62nd Street, Suite 6F, New York, NY 10023, USA. *Telephone:* (212) 586-4453. *Fax:* (212) 581-5771. *E-mail:* lewis@rlombardo.com. *Website:* www.rlombardo.com.

SCUDERI, Vincenzo; American singer (tenor); b. 1961, New York. *Education:* studied in New York and with Franco Corelli. *Career:* Long Island Opera, Pinkerton, Turiddu, Rodolfo; appearances at Plovdiv and Zürich as Ishmaele in Nabucco and as Radames, 1987–89; sang the Duke of Mantua on tour throughout France, 1989; sang arias from Chénier and Fanciulla del West in tribute concert to Franco Corelli, Purchase, New York, 1991; Radames at the Baths of Caracalla, 1991.

SEAMAN, Christopher, MA, ARCM; British conductor; b. 7 March 1942, Faversham, Kent, England; s. of Albert Edward Seaman and Ethel Margery Seaman (née Chambers). *Education:* Canterbury Cathedral Choir School, The King's School, Canterbury, King's Coll., Cambridge. *Career:* Prin. Timpanist, London Philharmonic Orchestra 1964–68; Asst Conductor BBC Scottish Symphony Orchestra 1968–70, Chief Conductor 1971–77; Chief Conductor Northern Sinfonia Orchestra 1973–79; Prin. Conductor BBC Robert Mayer Concerts 1978–87; Conductor-in-Residence, Baltimore Symphony Orchestra 1987–98; Chief Guest Conductor Utrecht Symphony Orchestra 1979–83; Music Dir Naples Philharmonic Orchestra, Fla 1993–, Rochester Philharmonic Orchestra, NY 1998–2011; Artistic Advisor, San Antonio Symphony; Dir Symphony Australia Conductor Programme; appears as guest conductor world-wide and has appeared in USA, Germany, France, the Netherlands, Belgium, Italy, Portugal, Spain, Australia and throughout UK. *Publication:* Inside Conducting 2013. *Honours:* Hon. FGSM 1972. *Current Management:* c/o Harrison Parrott, 5–6 Albion Court, Albion Place, London, W6 0QT, England. *Telephone:* (20) 7229-9166. *Fax:* (20) 7221-5042. *E-mail:* info@harrisonparrott.co.uk. *Website:* www.harrisonparrott.com/artist/profile/christopher-seaman.

SEARCY-HEITMAN, Imke Anne; German cellist; b. 5 March 1941, Lübeck; d. of Hans Heitmann and Annelise Heitmann (née Boysen); m. David Searcy 1966 (divorced 1968). *Education:* Staatliche Hochschule für Musik, Freiburg and New England Conservatory, USA. *Career:* solo cellist, Bergen, Norway

1966–67, Herford 1968–73; cellist, Radio Sinfonie Orchestra, Frankfurt 1973. *Recordings:* Offenbach: Quatre Pièces 1980, Strauss: Drei Romanzen 1980. *Honours:* First Prize New England Conservatory Competition, Boston, USA 1965. *Address:* Ringstr 19, 61389 Schmitten, Germany. *Telephone:* (6084) 3100.

SEARS, Nicholas; singer (tenor); *Head of Vocal Studies, Royal College of Music;* b. 1965, Australia. *Education:* Trinity College, Cambridge and Guildhall School of Music, London. *Career:* performed as a baritone singing major roles with the WNO, Opera North, ENO, Scottish Opera and La Monnaie, Brussels; concert appearances with the Songmakers' Almanac, the London Philharmonic Orchestra, the London Symphony Orchestra and the BBC Symphony and Philharmonic Orchestras; having changed to tenor, made debut as the Chevalier in Poulenc's Dialogues des Carmélites at Aldeburgh and has since sung Achilles in King Priam in Antwerp, Lysander in Midsummer Night's Dream, Essex and Spirit of the Mask in Gloriana, Telemachus in Ulisse and Agenore in Re Pastore for Opera North, Chevalier in Carmélites, Lucano in Poppea for WNO, Damon in Acis and Galatea in Frankfurt, Grimoaldo in Rodelinda for OTC in Ireland, High Priest in Idomeneo, Aufidio in Lucio Silla and Da-ud in Die Aegyptische Helena for Garsington, Sailor in Dido and Aeneas at Covent Garden, and Shepherd in Orfeo in Lugano; further engagements for Opera North, Pluto in Orfeus in the Underworld, Grimaldo in Rodelinda in New York, Gloriana in Barcelona, and Handel's Il Trionfo di Tempo e del Disinganno in Italy, Spain, Mexico, France and Belgium; sang in Rodelinda at the 2000 Buxton Festival; Head of Vocal Studies, Royal Coll. of Music, London 2006–. *Recordings:* On this Bleak Hut by Philip Grange with the Gemini Ensemble; Lysander (Dream); Spirit of the Mask in Gloriana for the BBC. *Address:* Royal College of Music, Prince Consort Road, London SW7 2BS, England (office). *Telephone:* (20) 7589-3643 (office). *E-mail:* info@rcm.ac.uk (office). *Website:* www.rcm.ac.uk (office).

SEBESTA, Ronald, DipMus; Slovak clarinettist; b. 22 July 1967, Senica. *Education:* Bratislava Conservatory, Acad. of Music, Bratislava, Boulogne Conservatory, France. *Career:* co-founder, VENI ensemble for contemporary music, with concerts in Bratislava (Evenings of New Music Festival), Prague, Berlin, Vienna, Perugia, Bucharest; projects (workshops and concerts) with Younghi Pagh Paan, Siegfried Palm, Hans Deinzer, Louis Andriessen, James Tenney, Hugh Davies; solo performance of Giacinto Scelsi's Kya 1990; VENI ensemble recording for Die Hessische Rundfunk in Frankfurt 1993; first clarinettist, Slovak Radio Symphony Orchestra, Bratislava; solo performance at Vienna Modern Festival 1994; co-founder, Vapori del Cuore improvising group 1994; solo performance of Mozart and Brahms Clarinet Quintets 1995; first clarinet, Cappela Istropolitana chamber orchestra, Bratislava 1995–; co-founder, Opera Aperta ensemble, for classical and contemporary chamber music 1997–; solo performances of Mozart Clarinet Concerto 1997–; mem. Int. Soc. for Contemporary Music (Slovak section). *Recordings:* albums with VENI ensemble 1990, 1992, 1995, album with Opera Aperta ensemble 2002, album of Vapori del Cuore: Alpine Songs 2003. *Address:* Fandlyho 1, 81103 Bratislava, Slovakia. *E-mail:* info@operaaperta.com. *Website:* www .operaaperta.com.

SECUNDE, Nadine; American singer (soprano); b. 21 Dec. 1953, Independence, OH. *Education:* Oberlin Conservatory, Indiana University School of Music with Margaret Harshaw, studied in Germany. *Career:* engaged first at the Hessisches Staatstheater Wiesbaden; Member of the Cologne Opera, where her roles have been Katya Kabanova, Elsa, Agathe, Elisabeth, Chrysothemis and Ariadne; Vienna Staatsoper debut as Sieglinde, Hamburg Staatsoper as Katya; Bayreuth Festival debut 1987, as Elsa in a Werner Herzog production of Lohengrin; returned 1988, as Sieglinde in the Harry Kupfer production of Der Ring des Nibelungen; Covent Garden and Chicago 1988, as Elsa and Elisabeth; returned to London 1990, as Chrysothemis; sang Elisabeth at Munich, 1994, (also televised); concert engagements include the Choral Symphony with the Los Angeles Philharmonic, conducted by Previn, and with the Orchestre de Paris under Barenboim; Penderecki's Dies Irae with the Warsaw Philharmonic; sang Chrysothemis at Covent Garden 1997, and in the 1997 Munich premiere of Henze's Venus and Adonis; Netherlands Opera 1998 as Brünnhilde in Götterdämmerung; sang Chrysothemis at Munich 2000 and Isolde at the Teatro Colón, Buenos Aires; Brünnhilde at Bilbao 2002. *Honours:* Fulbright Scholarship. *Current Management:* Ingpen & Williams Ltd, 7 St George's Court, 131 Putney Bridge Road, London, SW15 2PA, England.

SEERS, Mary; British singer (soprano); b. 1958, England. *Education:* Girton Coll., Cambridge, studied in Rome and London. *Career:* appearances with the Landini Consort, the Consort of Musique, The Scholars and the Hilliard Ensemble; festival engagements at Aix-en-Provence, Schleswig-Holstein and Greenwich; tour of the UK and Italy 1988 with Pärt's St John Passion; concerts in Sydney and Tokyo 1989 with John Eliot Gardiner and the Monteverdi Choir; concerts include Bach B minor Mass, Wrocław (Poland) with City of London Sinfonia; other repertoire includes Mozart's C minor Mass, the Monteverdi Vespers (Bruges Festival), Messiah (St Martin in the Fields) and music by Finzi and Purcell; further engagements at the Almeida, Cheltenham and Orkney Festivals and concerts with the Scottish Chamber Orchestra and the East of England Orchestra; US concerts in Chicago and New York, Pärt's St John Passion; opera with Music Theatre Wales, role of Madeleine in Philip Glass, The Fall of The House of Usher; festival appearances include Warsaw Contemporary Music Festival (Pärt Passio) 1992; Monteverdi Vespers with The Sixteen.

SEGAL, Uriel (Uri); Israeli orchestral conductor; *Adjunct Senior Lecturer in Music (Orchestral Conducting), Jacobs School of Music, Indiana University;* b. 7 March 1944, Jerusalem; s. of Alexander Segal and Nehama Segal; m. Ilana Finkelstein 1966; one s. three d. *Education:* Rubin Acad., Jerusalem and Guildhall School of Music, UK. *Career:* debut with Tivoli Orchestra, Copenhagen 1969; Prin. Conductor Bournemouth Symphony Orchestra 1980–82, Philharmonia Hungarica 1981–85; Music Dir Israeli Chamber Orchestra, Chautauqua Festival, NY 1990–2007, Louisville Orchestra, Ky 1998–2004; Founder/Chief Conductor, Century Orchestra, Osaka, Japan 1990–98, Laureate Conductor 1998–; currently Adjunct Senior Lecturer in Music (Orchestral Conducting), Jacobs School of Music, Ind. Univ.; fmr Prin. Guest Conductor Stuttgart Radio Symphony; orchestras conducted include Berlin Philharmonic, Stockholm Philharmonic, Concertgebouw, Orchestre de Paris, Vienna Symphony, Israel Philharmonic, London Symphony, London Philharmonic, Philharmonia, Orchestre de la Suisse Romande, Warsaw Philharmonic, Spanish Nat. Orchestra, Pittsburgh Symphony, Chicago Symphony, Detroit Symphony, Dallas Symphony, Houston Symphony, Montréal Symphony and Rochester Symphony; tours have included Austria, Switzerland, Spain, Italy, France, UK, Scandinavia and the Far East; operatic debut conducting The Flying Dutchman at Sante Fe Opera 1973, has since conducted opera in Italy, France, Germany, Japan, Israel and USA. *Recordings include:* Mahler Symphony No. 4 (with NZ Symphony Orchestra), music by Britten (Bournemouth Symphony), Stravinsky's Firebird Suite and Symphony in C with the Suisse Romande Orchestra), Mozart Piano Concertos with Radu Lupu and the English Chamber Orchestra, Schumann's Piano Concerto with Ashkenazy and the London Symphony, Beethoven Piano Concertos with Rudolf Firkusny and the Philharmonia, Mozart Piano Concertos with Alicia de Larocha and Wiener Symphoniker. *Honours:* First Prize, Int. Mitropoulos Conducting Competition, New York 1969. *Current Management:* c/o Michal Schmidt Artists Management, 59 East 54th Street, Suite 83, New York, NY 10022, USA. *Telephone:* (212) 421-8500. *E-mail:* mws@schmidtart.com. *Telephone:* (54) 801-9086 (Israel) (home). *Fax:* (77) 332-5508 (office). *E-mail:* uriel@urielsegal.com; usegal@indiana.edu. *Website:* www.urisegal.com; music.indiana.edu.

SEGERSTAM, Leif, DipMus; Finnish conductor and composer; *Chief Conductor Emeritus, Helsinki Philharmonic Orchestra;* b. 2 March 1944, Vasa. *Education:* Sibelius Academy, Helsinki, Juilliard School of Music, New York, USA. *Career:* debut as violin soloist Helsinki 1963; Conductor, Royal Opera Stockholm 1968–72, Musical Director 1971–72; First Conductor, Deutsche Oper Berlin 1972–73; General Manager Finnish National Opera 1973–74; Chief Conductor ORF (Austrian Radio) Vienna 1975–82; Musical Director, Finnish Radio Symphony Orchestra, Helsinki 1977–87: Principal Guest Conductor 1987–; General Music Director, Staatsphilharmonie Rhenland-Pfalz 1983–89; Honorary Conductor 1989; Conductor of the Danish Radio Symphony Orchestra 1988; Chief Conductor of the Helsinki Philharmonic Orchestra 1995–2007; Acting Prof. of Conducting, Sibelius Acad. 1997–; led Tannhäuser at the 1997 Savonlinna Festival and began a new Ring cycle at Stockholm with Das Rheingold; conducted Die Walküre and Siegfried at Helsinki, 1998; mem. Royal Academy of Music, Sweden. *Compositions include:* Divertimento for strings 1963, Six Cello Concertos, Three Piano Concertos, 234 Symphonies 1977– (nos. 20–25 to be given without conductor), 11 Violin Concertos, Six Double Concertos; many works for orchestra under title Composed orchestral works called Thought, the most famous being, Monumental Thoughts, Martti Tavela in memorium; Orchestral Diary Sheets, Five Songs of Experience after Blake and Auden for soprano and orchestra 1971, 30 String Quartets, Three Piano Trios, Four String Trios, Episodes for various instrumental combinations. *Recordings:* works by Mahler, Sibelius, Brahms, Scriabin, Petterson, Schnittke, Rott, Ruders, Koechlin, Schmitt, Roussel, Caplet, Roger-Ducasse and own compositions. *Honours:* Nordic Council Music Prize 1999, Midem Classical Award 2007, BBC Music Magazine Recording of the Year 2007, State Prize for Music 2004, Sibelius Medal 2005. *Current Management:* Patrick Garvey Management, 40 North Parade, York YO30 7AB, England. *Telephone:* (1904) 621222. *Fax:* (1723) 330050. *E-mail:* patrick@patrickgarvey.com. *Website:* www .patrickgarvey.com.

SEIFERT, Gerd-Heinrich; German horn player; b. 17 Oct. 1931, Hamburg; m. 1957, three s. one d. *Education:* Music High School, Hamburg, studied with Albert Doscher. *Career:* debut as soloist, Horn Concerto (Strauss) 1948; substitute, Hamburg Philharmonic Orchestra 1947–49; Solo Horn, Düsseldorfer Symphoniker 1949–64, Bayreuth Festival 1961, Berlin Philharmonic Orchestra 1964–; performed with Düsseldorfer Waldhorn Quartet, also 13 Bläser Philharmonic Orchestra and Philharmonic Octet, Berlin; teacher of horn, Music High School, Berlin 1970–. *Recordings:* with Berlin Philharmonic Orchestra/Octet (Hindemith), Octet, Nonet (Spohr), Serenade for 13 wind instruments by Mozart, and other chamber music, Concert Piece for four horns (Schumann). *Honours:* first prize ARD Competition, Munich 1956, Grand Prix du Disque.

SEIFERT, Ingrid; Austrian/British violinist; b. 27 Jan. 1952, Vöcklabruck; m. Charles Medlam. *Education:* studied violin at Salzburg Mozarteum, Vienna Akad., and in the Netherlands. *Career:* played with Concentus Musicus, Vienna; Co-founder (with Charles Medlam) London Baroque 1978; with London Baroque led first performance of Scarlatti's Una Villa di Tuscolo and a revival of Gli Equivoci Sembiante, for the BBC; season 1990–91 included Dido and Aeneas at Paris Opéra, music by Blow and Lully, Opéra Comique,

Aci, Galatea e Polifemo in Spain, Netherlands and England, cantatas by Handel and Rameau in Austria, Sweden and Germany, with Emma Kirkby; other recent repertoire includes Charpentier Messe de Minuit; 4 Violin music by Telemann, Vivaldi and Wassenaar; Bach Brandenburg Concertos; Monteverdi Tancredi and Clorinda; Salzburg Festival debut 1991, with music by Mozart; further festival engagements at Bath, Beaune, Versailles, Ansbach, Innsbruck, Edinburgh, Istanbul, Utrecht; numerous concerts in Japan and USA. *Recordings:* about 80 recordings, including Marais La Gamme; Theile Matthew Passion; Bach Trio Sonatas; Charpentier Theatre Music; Handel Aci, Galatea e Polifemo; Blow Venus and Adonis; Purcell Chamber Music; Purcell Fantasias; Bach Violin Sonatas; Monteverdi Orfeo; Handel German Arias; A Vauxhall Gardens Entertainment; English Music of the 18th Century; François Couperin Apothéose de Lulli, Corelli Chamber Music; Complete Trios of Handel, Purcell; Chamber Music by Lawes; Pachelbel, Complete Chamber Music; Vivaldi Sonatas op. 1; Handel Latin Motets, with Emma Kirkby; Bach Trio sonatas; Rameau Pièces de Clavecin en concert; 17th and 18th Century Trio Sonatas (English, French, German and Italian); Rameau Cantatas; CPE Bach Trio Sonatas; Stravaganze Napoletane. *Address:* Brick Kiln Cottage, Hollington, nr Newbury, Berks. RG20 9XX, England (home). *Telephone:* (1635) 254331 (home). *E-mail:* ingrid.seifert@btinternet.com (office).

SEIFFERT, Peter; German singer (tenor); b. 4 Jan. 1954, Düsseldorf; m. Lucia Popp 1986 (died 1993). *Education:* Robert Schumann Musikhochschule Düsseldorf. *Career:* sang first with the Deutsche Oper am Rhein Düsseldorf in Der Wildschütz and Fra Diavalo; mem., Deutsche Oper Berlin from 1982, notably as Lensky, Jenik in The Bartered Bride, Huon (Oberon) and Faust; Bayerische Staatsoper Munich 1983, as Fenton in Die Lustigen Weiber von Windsor; returned in Der Barber von Bagdad by Cornelius and as Narraboth and Lohengrin; Vienna Staatsoper and La Scala Milan debuts 1984; Covent Garden debut 1988, as Parsifal in a new production of Wagner's opera conducted by Bernard Haitink; season 1988–89 sang Faust at the Deutsche Oper Berlin and Lohengrin in Munich (repeated 1990); sang at Salzburg 1992, as Narraboth; concert engagements include Mozart's Requiem with Giulini in London, and the Choral Symphony with Muti in Philadelphia; sang Walther von Stolzing in Die Meistersinger at the 1996 Bayreuth Festival; season 1998 with Max in Der Freischütz at Rome; season 2000–01 as Lohengrin at the Deutsche Oper Berlin, Walther in Munich in, Rienzi in Dresden and Erik for Zürich Opera; Parsifal at Bayreuth, 2002. *Recordings:* Elijah; Zar und Zimmerman; Matteo in Arabella, conducted by Jeffrey Tate; Die Fledermaus, conducted by Domingo; Gianni Schicchi (Patanè); Erik in Der fliegende Holländer, conducted by Pinchas Steinberg; The Choral Symphony (Muti) and Mozart's Mass in C Minor with Levine; Mendelssohn's Lobgesang and Beethoven's Symphony No. 9 with Sawallisch; solo albums of operetta; Freischitz; Fidelio; Liszt, Faust Symphony, conducted by Simon Rattle. *Honours:* Kammersänger of the Bavarian State Opera. *Current Management:* Hilbert Artists Management, Maximilianstrasse 22, 80539 Munich, Germany. *Telephone:* (89) 2907470. *Fax:* (89) 29074790. *E-mail:* agentur@hilbert.de. *Website:* www.hilbert.de.

SEIFRIED, Reinhard; German conductor; b. 25 July 1945, Freising; m. Fenna Kügel 1991, two d. *Education:* Hochschule für Musik, Munich. *Career:* Asst Conductor with Rudolf Kempe, Rafael Kubelik, Karl Richter, Leonard Bernstein; debut as conductor in Staatstheater am Gärtnerplatz, Munich 1976; Conductor, Nürnberg 1986; Chief Conductor, Remscheider Symphoniker 1991; Music Dir and Chief Conductor, Oldenburgisches Staatsorchester 1993–; guest conductor in Europe, Japan and USA. *Recordings:* Mendelssohn-Bartholdy symphonies (with Irish National Symphony Orchestra, Dublin), Smetana, Ma Vlast (with Slovak State Philharmonic Košice). *Address:* c/o Oldenburgisches Staatstheater, Theaterwall 18, 26122 Oldenburg, Germany.

SEILER, Mayumi; German/Japanese violinist; b. 1963, Japan. *Education:* studied in Japan and at the Salzburg Mozarteum with Sándor Végh. *Career:* concerts with the Australian Chamber Orchestra, Hong Kong Philharmonic, Royal Philharmonic, the Acad. of St Martin in the Fields and the 1994 London Proms; Dir and soloist, City of London Sinfonia, featured soloist with Royal Philharmonic, the Berlin Symphony, the Moscow Symphony, the Hong Kong Philharmonic, the Australian Chamber Orchestra, Camerata Academica Salzburg and the Toronto Symphony Orchestra; Founder and Artistic Dir Via Salzburg Chamber Orchestra. *Honours:* Salzburg Mozarteum Christina Rechter Steiner Prize. *Current Management:* Via Salzburg Chamber Orchestra, PO Box 1116, T.D.C. Postal Station, 77 King Street West, Toronto, ON M5K 1P2, Canada. *Telephone:* (416) 972-9193. *E-mail:* info@viasalzburg.com. *Website:* www.viasalzburg.com. *Telephone:* (613) 882-6025. *E-mail:* mayumiseiler.hkim@gmail.com. *Website:* www.mayumiseiler.com.

SEILTGEN, Annette; German singer (mezzo-soprano); b. 26 June 1964, Wuppertal. *Education:* Leopold Mozart Conservatory, Augsburg and the Studio of the Bavarian State Opera. *Career:* Kassel Opera, 1990–92, as Rosina, Wellgunde in The Ring and Strauss's Composer; Theater am Gärtnerplatz, Munich, 1992–96; as Hansel, Cherubino, Rosina and Cornet in Matthus's Die Weise von Liebe und Tod; Guest appearances from 1989 at Mannheim, Heidelberg, Bielefeld, and Hannover notably as Octavian in Der Rosenkavalier; Deutsche Oper am Rhein at Düsseldorf from 1996, with Andronico in Handel's Tamerlano, 1998; Guest appearance in Madrid at the Theatro Real as Sextus in Mozart's La Clemenza di Tito, 1999; Season 1999–2000 as Dusseldorf as Olga in Three Sisters by Peter Eötvös, Ruggiero in Alcina and three roles in Lulu; Guest appearances in Nice and Santiago de Chile; Other roles include Don Ramiro in La finta giardiniera by Mozart. *Current Management:* c/o Organisation Internationale Artistique, 16 avenue Franklin D. Roosevelt, 75008 Paris, France. *Telephone:* 1-42-25-58-34. *Fax:* 1-42-25-64-97. *E-mail:* oia@oia-poilve.com. *Website:* www.oia-poilve.com.

SEIPP, Joachim; German singer (bass-baritone); b. 1956, Pohlheim; one d. *Education:* studied with Prof. Martin Gründler, Frankfurt Musikhochschule, Prof. Carla Castellani, Milan and with Milkana Nikolova, Vienna. *Career:* sang at Kiel Opera, 1982–86; Karlsruhe 1985–86; Hanover 1986–91; Landestheater Innsbruck from 1991; Repertoire; Marquese di Posa, Rigoletto, Iago, Scarpia, Wotan in Rheingold, Four Villains in Les Contes d'Hoffmann, Carmina Burana by Carl Orff, Germont, Ford in Falstaff and Mozart's Count; Title role in Dallapiccola's Il Prigioniero; Guest appearances at the Ludwigsburg Festival as the Count, 1987 and 1989; Sang at Wiesbaden in Henze's Das verratene Meer, 1990; Der Kaiser von Atlantis by Victor Ullmann, La Monnaie, Brussels; Sang at Innsbruck as Iago (1999) and Albert in Werther, 2001; Der Fliegende Holländer in Domstufen Festival in Erfurt under the direction of Werner Herzog; Further roles include Kurwenal in Tristan und Isolde and Pizarro in Fidelio under Brigitte Fassbaender and Conte Luna in Il Trovatore and Amonasro in Aida; Concert repertory includes Schubert's Schwanengesang, Wolf's Italian Song Book and all great oratorios and major concert pieces. *Recordings:* Carmina Burana with Orchestra Tenerife under Victor Pablo 1996, Die Frau Ohne Schatten under Fassbaender 2004. *Honours:* First Prize, VdmK Gesangswettbewerb, Berlin. *Current Management:* Robert Gilder and Co., 91 Great Russell Street, London, WC1B 3PS, England. *Telephone:* (20) 7580-7758. *Fax:* (20) 7580-7739. *E-mail:* rgilder@robert-gilder.com. *Website:* www.robertgilder.com. *Address:* Birchach 20, 6112 Wattenberg, Austria (home). *Telephone:* (5224) 52309 (home). *E-mail:* seipp.austria@web.de (home).

SEIVEWRIGHT, (Robert) Peter, BA, MA, FRCO; British concert pianist, jazz pianist and academic; *Professor in Residence, Afghanistan National Institute of Music*; b. 11 July 1954, Skipton, N Yorks., England. *Education:* Worcester Coll., Oxford; FRCO Diploma, three years' postgraduate piano study at Royal Northern Coll. of Music with Ryszard Bakst. *Career:* Tutor, Univ. of Keele 1979–83; Instructor in Music, Univ. of Leicester 1980–84; Lecturer in Music, Royal Scottish Acad. of Music and Drama 1984–2008; Prof. of Music, Acad. for the Performing Arts, Univ. of Trinidad and Tobago, Port of Spain, Trinidad 2008–11; Prof. in Residence, Afghanistan Nat. Inst. of Music, Kabul 2012; concerts throughout the UK, Ireland, Norway, Austria, Germany, Italy, Belgium, Denmark (eight recital tours), Latvia, Estonia, Kazakhstan, Viet Nam, Australia (five concert tours), Afghanistan, China, India, Kuwait, Trinidad and Tobago, USA and Russia, including Huddersfield Contemporary Music Festival 1983, 1984, Århus Festival, Denmark 1986, Munch-Museum, Oslo 1986, Heilbronn Int. Piano Forum, Germany 1993, Int. Masters of the Keyboard series, Bruges, Belgium 1994, Int. All-Stars Piano Festival, Liepaja, Latvia 1997, Wagner Hall, Riga, Nat. Concert Hall, Hanoi, Viet Nam, Melba Hall, Melbourne, Australia, Concert Hall of the Forbidden City, Beijing, China, Philharmonic Hall, Arkhangelsk, Russia, Philharmonic Hall, Almaty, Kazakhstan, Bosendorfer-Sal, Vienna, Opera House, Ho Chi Minh City, Moscow House of Music 2012; piano concerto performances with leading orchestras, including Hallé Orchestra, Milton Keynes City Orchestra, Scottish Sinfonietta, Orchestra of Scottish Opera, Strathclyde Sinfonia, Scottish Baroque Soloists, Paragon Ensemble, Bradford Chamber Orchestra, Liepaja Symphony Orchestra, Kazakhstan State Academic Symphony Orchestra, Beijing Symphony Orchestra, Calcutta Chamber Orchestra, Ho Chi Minh City Symphony Orchestra; radio recordings for BBC Scotland, BBC Radio 3, Radio Denmark, 3MBs and ABC (Australia). *Recordings include:* Contemporary Scottish Piano Music, Complete Piano Music of Carl Nielsen (two CDs) 1995, Piano Music by Victor Bendix 1998, Complete Piano Sonatas of Baldassare Galuppi 1706–1785, Variations and Fugue on a Theme of Telemann and Variations and Fugue on a Theme of Bach by Max Reger, Louis Glass Piano Music (double CD), J. S. Bach Piano Concertos with Scottish Baroque Soloists, American Piano Sonatas, J. S. Bach Goldberg Variations. *Address:* The Old Joinery, Lintfieldbank, by Coalburn, Lanarkshire, ML11 0NJ, Scotland. *Telephone:* (1555) 820840; 7747-023247 (mobile). *E-mail:* peterseivewright@hotmail.com. *Website:* www.divine-art.com/AS/seivewright.htm.

SELBIG, Ute; German singer (soprano); b. 18 Aug. 1960, Dresden. *Education:* Dresden Musikhochschule until 1985. *Career:* sang with Dresden Kreuzchor; tours of Japan, 1988 and Canada, 1991; mem., Dresden Opera from 1985, as Zerlina, Nannetta, Aennchen in Der Freischütz, Musetta, Susanna, Sophie in Der Rosenkavalier, Pamina and Fiordiligi; guest appearances throughout Europe and at Los Angeles and St Louis; Zdenka in Arabella at Geneva, 1994; Guardian of the Threshold in Die Frau ohne Schatten at Dresden, 1997; season 2000–01 at Dresden as Donna Elvira, Pamina, Marzelline in Fidelio and Ilia in Idomeneo (concert). *Recordings:* Mozart Arias; Sacred Music by Mozart; Das Lied von der Glocke by Bruch. *Honours:* prizewinner in competitions at Prague and Leipzig. *Current Management:* Hannagret Bueker Agentur für Musiktheater und Konzert, Fuhsestrasse 2, 30419 Hannover, Germany. *Telephone:* (511) 2716910. *Fax:* (511) 2717873. *E-mail:* mail@buekervoice.de. *Website:* www.buekervoice.de.

SELBY, Kathryn Shauna, BA, MM; Australian concert pianist; b. 20 Sept. 1962, Sydney. *Education:* Sydney Conservatorium of Music, Univ. of Washington, Seattle, Bryn Mawr College, PA, Curtis Inst. of Music, Juilliard School of Music. *Career:* debut, YMCA, 92nd Street, NY 1981; Wigmore Hall in London in 1987; appearances with Sydney Symphony Orchestra, Philadelphia

Orchestra, Pittsburgh, St Louis and Cincinnati Symphony Orchestras, Calgary and Erie Philharmonic, Indianapolis Symphony Orchestra, Shreveport Symphony Orchestra, among others; as Chamber Musician at Spoleto Festival, Australia in 1986, Marlboro Music Festival, Caramoor Festival, Concerto Soloists of Philadelphia, Hartford Chamber Orchestra, Kennedy Center Washington; Founding Member of Selby, Pini, Pereira Trio, Australia with appearances and tours, Musica Viva in Australia, 1985, 1987; ABC Film, Mozart in Delphi with Australian Chamber Orchestra for ABC Australia; recitals in New York, Washington DC, Seattle, Portland, Pittsburgh, Philadelphia, Sydney, London and Munich; began Selby and Friends performance series 1988–; founding mem., Macquarie Trio Australia 1993–2006. *Honours:* Rachmaninoff Prize, Curtis Inst. of Music, Australia Council Fellowship 2007–08. *Address:* PO Box 18, Northbridge, NSW 2063, Australia (office). *Telephone:* (2) 9969-7039 (office). *Fax:* (2) 9958-7111 (office). *E-mail:* info@selbyandfriends.com.au (office). *Website:* www.selbyandfriends .com.au.

SELBY, Philip; British composer; b. 6 Feb. 1948, s. of the late George Selby and Sarah Selby (née Knott); m. Rosanna Burrai 1974; one s. *Education:* Manor Park Grammar School, Nuneaton, Royal Northern Coll. of Music. *Career:* composition studies with G. Petrassi, C. Camilleri and Karlheinz Stockhausen; appeared as guitar soloist, Birmingham Town Hall 1966, Royal Albert Hall, London 1970, All-India Radio and TV, Pakistani TV, Youth Palace, Tehran, Istanbul Univ.; debut as composer with first performance of From the Fountain of Youth (for guitar and chamber orchestra), Leamington 1975; mem. British Acad. of Composers and Songwriters, Inc. Soc. of Musicians, Performing Right Soc. *Compositions include:* Suite for guitar 1965–67, Two Meditations for Piano 1972–74, Symphonic Dance for orchestra 1973, Ten Little Studies for Guitar Solo 1973–76, Fantasia for guitar 1974, Rhapsody for piano and orchestra 1975, Three Scottish Songs for voice and violin 1975, A Nature Meditation for violin and small orchestra, Guitar Concerto 1976–77, Suite for String Quartet 1977–78, Sonatina for piano 1978, Spirit of the Earth for flute 1978, Branch Touches Branch, pastorale 1979, Isa Upanishad (cantata sacra for double chorus and orchestra) 1979–87, Sonata for timpani 1980, Greek Suite for Oboe Solo 1981, Siddhartha (dance symphony) 1981–84, Logos for trumpet 1982, Ring Out Ye Bells (carol) 1988, Symphony of Sacred Images (for soprano and bass soli, double chorus and orchestra) 1986–92, Anthem for Gibraltar (unison voices and organ) 1994, Beatus Vir (motet) 1995, String Quartet No. 1 (Non Potho Reposare, Amore Coro) 1996–97, Autoritratto Vittorio Alfieri (for soprano, violin and guitar) 1998, Sonata Atma Brahma for Piano 1998–99, Fear No More the Heat of the Sun, madrigal 2001, Agape for solo violin 2001–02, Agape II for solo viola 2002, Eight Poems of J. G. Brown, song cycle 2005, Four American Portraits for speaking choir 2006, Ode to Earth and Sky (for double string orchestra) 2007–08. *Honours:* Chevalier, Ordre Souverain et Militaire de la Milice du Saint Sépulcre 1988. *Address:* Hill Cottage, Via 1 Maggio 93, 00068 Rignano Flaminio, Rome, Italy. *Telephone:* (0761) 507945.

SELDIS, Dominic; British musician (double bass); *Principal Double Bass, Concertgebouw Orchestra;* b. 22 June 1971, Bury St Edmunds. *Education:* Chetham's School of Music, RAM, studied under Robin McGee, Mozarteum Salzburg under Klaus Stoll. *Career:* Prin. Solo Double Bassist, Royal Concertgebouw Orchestra, Amsterdam 2008–; previously Prin. Bass, BBC Nat. Orchestra of Wales; Guest Prin. with Royal Philharmonic Orchestra, London Symphony Orchestra, Halle, London Sinfonietta, and Acad. of St Martin-in-the-Fields and freelance with many other symphony/chamber orchestras world-wide; mem. John Wilson Orchestra; recitals with pianist James Pearson at music festivals in UK and Europe and in concert halls including Wigmore Hall and Southbank Centre; concerto soloist with London Symphony Orchestra, Philharmonia Orchestra, BBC Nat. Orchestra of Wales, Concertgebouw Chamber Orchestra and others; as chamber musician, has played world-wide with numerous musicians; Prof., RAM, London; masterclasses in Amsterdam, London, Sydney, New York, Helsinki, Beijing, Düsseldorf and Zurich; tutor, Nat. Youth of Orchestra of Great Britain and Youth Orchestra of the Americas; appeared frequently at BBC Proms, BBC Young Musician of the Year and on radio and TV programmes in Holland and UK; performed/recorded with pop musicians including Tina Turner, Rod Stewart, Seal, Spice Girls, Tom Jones, Shirley Bassey, Wouter Hamel and Giovanca; f. pop orchestra The Love Philharmonic. *Television includes:* Het Orkest van Nederland (co-host, RTL 4), Maestro series (judge, BBC 2) 2008. *Honours:* Hon. Fellow, RAM. *Address:* The Royal Concertgebouw Orchestra, Postbus 78098, 1070 LP Amsterdam, The Netherlands. *E-mail:* info@ dominicseldis.com. *Website:* dominicseldis.com.

SELEZNEV, Georgi; Georgian singer (bass); b. 21 Oct. 1938, Tbilisi. *Education:* studied at Toilisi and the Leningrad Conservatory. *Career:* bass soloist at the Maly Opera Leningrad 1972–78; appearances with the Bolshoi Opera Russia 1978–, on tour to Western Europe and USA; solo debut in the West as Konchak and Galitzky in Prince Igor at Trieste, 1985; returned as Dosifei, in Khovanshchina; title role in Salammbô by Mussorgsky for RAI in Rome; appeared in numerous int. tours of Bolshoi Company; engagements include Verdi Requiem under Chailly, with Royal Concertgebouw Orchestra in Amsterdam; Oroveso, with Joan Sutherland as Norma, at Opera Pacific and with Michigan Opera; Boris at Wiesbaden Festival; Pimen in Opéra du Rhin, Strasbourg, repeated at Bordeaux, 1993; returned to Bordeaux as Timur, in production of Turandot, director Alain Lombard, 1994; Boris Godunov at St

Petersburg, 1997. *Recordings include:* Salammbô, Oroveso in Norma. *Honours:* Lenin Prize.

SELIG, Franz-Josef; German singer (bass); b. 11 July 1962. *Education:* Cologne Musikhochschule with Claudio Nicolai. *Career:* concert tours of Italy, Germany, France, Switzerland, Netherlands and Turkey; engaged at the Essen Opera from 1989, as the King in Aida, Herr Reich in Die Lustige Weiber von Windsor and Sarastro in Die Zauberflöte; Sang Mozart's Speaker at Frankfurt, 1991, and Fafner in Das Rheingold at Covent Garden; US debut in Fidelio at San Francisco, 1995; St John Passion with Solti, 1997–98; Season 1998 with Mozart's Sarastro, and Samiel and Hermit in Der Freischütz at La Scala; season 1999–2000 as Mozart's Commendatore at La Scala and the Vienna Staatsoper, Camillo in the premiere of Wintermärchen by Boesmans, at Brussels, and King Marke for the Deutsche Oper Berlin; other roles include Hermann in Tannhäuser. *Recordings include:* Die Zauberflöte; Sacred Music by Mozart. *Current Management:* c/o IMG Artists, 31–33 rue du Temple, 75004 Paris, France. *Telephone:* 1-44-31-00-10. *Fax:* 1-44-31-44-40. *E-mail:* pwiggins@imgartists.com. *Website:* www.imgartists.com.

SELLARS, Peter, BA; American theatre and opera director and professor of theatre and arts; *Professor, Department of World Arts and Cultures, University of California, Los Angeles;* b. 27 Sept. 1957, Pittsburgh. *Education:* Harvard Univ. *Career:* Dir, Boston Shakespeare Co. 1983–84; Dir and Man., American Nat. Theater at J.F. Kennedy Center, Washington, DC 1984–86; Artistic Advisor, Boston Opera Theatre 1990; currently Prof., Dept of World Arts and Culture, UCLA; Fellow, MacArthur Foundation, Chicago 1983; fmr Visiting Prof., Center for Theatre Arts, Univ. of California, Berkeley; Artistic Dir, New Crowned Hope Festival 2006–. *Libretto:* Doctor Atomic (Adams). *Productions include:* Ajax, Armida, Così fan tutte, The Death of Klinghoffer, Die Zauberflöte, Don Giovanni, The Electrification of the Soviet Union, Le Grand Macabre, Idomeneo, The Lighthouse, The Marriage of Figaro, Mathis der Maler, Merchant of Venice, The Mikado, El Niño, Nixon in China, Orlando, The Rake's Progress, Saul and Orlando, St François d'Assise, Tannhäuser, Theodora, Zangezi, Mozart's Zaide (Mostly Mozart Festival at Lincoln Center, New York 2006), Saariaho's La Passion de Simone 2006, Adams' A Flowering Tree 2006, Othello (New York City's Public Theater) 2009, Adams' Nixon in China (Metropolitan Opera) 2011, Vivaldi's Griselda (Santa Fe Opera) 2011, Tristan and Isolde (Helsinki Festival) 2012, (Toronto) 2013, (Real Opera Madrid) 2014, (Paris Opera) 2014, Johannes-Passion (Baden-Baden) 2014. *Honours:* Erasmus Prize 1998, The Dorothy and Lillian Gish Prize 2005, Opera News Award for invaluable contrib. to opera 2011, Polar Music Prize 2014, Musical America Award 2014. *Address:* Department of World Arts and Cultures, UCLA, Glorya Kaufman Hall 114, 120 Westwood Plaza, Suite 150, PO Box 951608, Los Angeles, CA 90095-1608, USA (office). *Telephone:* (310) 825-3951 (office). *E-mail:* djmalecki@aol.com. *Website:* www .wac.ucla.edu (office).

SELLHEIM, Eckart, DipMus; German pianist; b. 29 Oct. 1939, Danzig. *Education:* Hamburg Conservatory, Musikhochschule Cologne, Cologne Univ. *Career:* Lecturer, Rheinische Musikschule, Cologne 1963–69; Prof. of Piano, Musikhochschule Cologne 1969–83; teacher of piano and piano chamber music, Univ. of Michigan, Ann Arbor, USA 1983–89; teacher of piano accompanying, Dir of Accompanying, Arizona State Univ., Tempe 1989–; concert tours of Europe, USA, Latin America, Middle East; duo with Friedrich-Jürgen Sellheim (cello) 1965–. *Recordings include:* with Fr. J. Sellheim (cello): Mendelssohn, two Cello Sonatas; two Variations Concertantes; Lied Ohne Worte, 1976; Brahms, two Cello Sonatas, 1977; Schumann, Fantasiestücke, Adagio und Allegro, Stücke im Volkston, 1978; Schubert, Arpeggione-Sonata, Chopin, Cello Sonata, Polonaise Brillante, Grand Duo Concertant, 1980; Ravel, Violin Sonata, 1985. *Publications:* Spielbuch für Klavier (ed.); contrib. to Friedrich Gruetzmacher 1966, Oskar von Pander 1968, Instrumentale Ausbildung-Klavier 1980, Die Klavierwerke W. Fr. Bachs, Concerto 1984.

SELTZER, Dov, BS; Romanian composer, conductor and musician; b. 26 Jan. 1932, Iasi; m. Grazielle Fontana 1968, one step-s. *Education:* Haifa and Tel-Aviv Conservatory, Mannes Coll. of Music, State Univ. of New York, studied with Mordecai Setter, Herbert Bruen. *Career:* Music Dir and Composer, Israel Army Nachal Theatrical Group 1950–53; music teacher, Afek School, Haifa; Arranger and Music Dir, Oranim Zabar Folk Singers and Theodore Bikel for Elektra, Columbia Co., USA 1956–58; music teacher, Mannes Coll. of Music, New York 1958–60; freelance composer, conductor for theatre, musicals, films, records in Israel, USA, France, Italy, UK, Germany and elsewhere; conducted concert of his music, Israel Philharmonic and Jerusalem Symphony Orchestra 1987; Music Dir and Conductor, Three Penny Opera (film version) 1988. *Compositions include:* 15 musicals including: The Megillah 1966, Kazablan 1967, I Like Mike 1968, To Live Another Summer 1971, Comme la neige en été 1974, Stempeniu (symphonic poem) 1985, This Scroll (cantata for Ben Gurion centenary) 1986, Thieves in the Night (music for German TV series) 1988, The Assisi Underground, Hassidic Rhapsody for violin solo and symphonic orchestra 1989–90, The Gold of the Ashes (rhapsodic poem) 1991–92, Notre Dame de Paris (opera after novel by Victor Hugo) 1993–94, Lament to Yitzhak (requiem in memory of Yitzhak Rabin) 1998.

SELWAY, Emma; British singer (mezzo-soprano); b. 1970, England. *Education:* Royal Academy, London and National Opera Studio. *Career:* debut as Kate Pinkerton in Madama Butterfly for English National Opera, 1995; sang Cefisa in Rossini's Ermione at Glyndebourne, 1995 (Musician in Manon

Lescaut, 1999); Glyndebourne Tour 1996 and 1999, as Mozart's Dorabella and Sesto; Further engagements as Dorabella for Opera North, Idamante for Opera Northern Ireland and Cenerentola for Welsh National Opera; Sang Charlotte in Die Soldaten by Zimmermann, and Strauss's Octavian for English National Opera; Concerts include Debussy's Le Martyre de St Sebastian (Hallé Orchestra) and Mahler's 2nd symphony, with the Jersey Symphonic Orchestra; Anna in Weill's Seven Deadly Sins at Batignano. *Current Management:* c/o Owen/White Management, Flat 6, 22 Brunswick Terrace, Hove, East Sussex BN3 1HJ, England. *Telephone:* (1273) 727127. *Fax:* (1273) 527038. *E-mail:* info@owenwhitemanagement.com. *Website:* www.owenwhitemanagement.com.

SEMENCHUK, Ekaterina; Russian singer (mezzo-soprano); b. 1976, Minsk. *Education:* Minsk Music School; Byelorussian Music Acad., St Petersburg Conservatoire. *Career:* Young Singers' Acad. of the Mariinsky Theatre, St Petersburg, from 1999; roles have included the Nurse and Olga in Eugene Onegin, Marta in Iolanta, Puccini's Suzuki, Lyubasha in The Tsar's Bride by Rimsky-Korsakov and Pauline in The Queen of Spades; sang Lehl in Rimsky's The Snow Maiden and Sonya in War and Peace with the Kirov Opera at Covent Garden 2000. *Recordings include:* Stravinsky, Oedipus Rex 2010. *Honours:* Diplomas for opera and recital singing, Int. Dvórak Competition, Prague 1997; Winner, Int. Obraztsova competition 1999. *Current Management:* c/o Deborah Sanders, IMG Artists, The Light Box, 111 Power Road, London, W4 5PY, England. *Telephone:* (20) 7957-5842. *Fax:* (20) 7957-5801. *E-mail:* dsanders@imgartists.com. *Website:* www.imgartists.com.

SEMMINGSEN, Tuva; Norwegian singer (mezzo-soprano); b. 1975. *Education:* Royal Danish Opera with Prof. Kirsten Buhl-Moller, Ingrid Bjoner and Anthony Rolfe Johnson. *Career:* professional debut in role of Cherubino in Figaro at Theatre Royal, Copenhagen and Gran Teatro Fenice, Venice 2001; appeared as Angelina in La Cenerentola, Heksemutter Mortensen, Parsifal, Maskarade, Rosina in Il Barbiere di Siviglia and Sesto in Giulio Cesare for Royal Danish Opera; Feodor in Boris Godunov for Teatro Nacional de Sao Carlos; British operatic debut in La Gazzetta by Rossini, Garsington Opera; concerts: Mozart and Rossini arias with Gothenburg Symphony Orchestra under Mario Venzago, Schubert's Mass in E Flat with Danish Nat. Symphony and Choir under Andras Schiff, Mozart Requiem with Trondheim Symphony Orchestra, Juditha Triumphans with The King's Consort, Judas Maccabaeus with Danish Nat. Symphony Orchestra, Bach Cantatas with Danish Radio Symphony Orchestra and Haydn's Stabat Mater for Danish Radio Sinfonietta. *Recordings include:* Vivaldi's Sum in Medio and Gloria e Imeneo with The King's Consort (Hyperion). *Current Management:* Harrison Parrott Ltd, 5–6 Albion Court, Albion Place, London, W6 0QT, England. *Telephone:* (20) 7229-9166. *Fax:* (20) 7221-5042. *E-mail:* info@harrisonparrott.com. *Website:* www.harrisonparrott.com.

SEMPERE, José; Spanish singer (tenor); b. 9 Jan. 1955, Catalonia. *Education:* Barcelona Conservatory, La Scala Opera School, Milan. *Career:* debut as Ford in Salieri's Falstaff, Parma, 1987; appearances at Modena, Ferrara, Rome and Reggio Emilia; season 1991–92 as the Duke of Mantua at Covent Garden, London, in Auber's Masaniello at Ravenna and Ernesto in Don Pasquale at Naples; guest appearances at Oslo, 1989 as Rodolfo and at Bergamo, Donizetti's Poliuto, 1993; Madrid as Edgardo in Lucia di Lammermoor; sang at St Etienne, 1993 and as Duke of Mantua at Verona, 1994; Arturo i Puritani, Vienna Staatsoper and Lisbon, 1995–96; sang Don Pedro in Persiani's Ines de Castro at Jesi, 1999. *Recordings include:* Poliuto. *Current Management:* Iberkonzert, Calle Rodríguez Arias 23 - 6° - D 10, 48011 Bilbao, Spain. *Telephone:* (94) 4104746. *Fax:* (94) 4218582. *E-mail:* agencia@iberkonzert.com. *Website:* www.iberkonzert.com.

SENDEROVAS, Anatolijus; Lithuanian composer; b. 21 Aug. 1945, Uljanovsk, Russia; s. of Michailas Senderovas and Ila Senderova; one d. *Education:* Lithuanian Acad. of Music, Vilnius, Rubin Israel Acad. of Music at Tel-Aviv Univ., St Petersburg N. Rimski-Korsakoff Conservatory. *Career:* Composer-in-Residence, Osnabrück Music Festival, Germany 2004; invited as an hon. guest to Europäischer Musik Sommer, Berlin 2004; Guest Composer, 54th Festival Pablo Casals, Prades, France 2005, Int. Cello Congress, Kobe Japan 2005, Internationales Gitarren Festival, Münster, Germany 2006, Manchester Cello Festival 2007, 'Guitar Gems', Netanya (Israel) 2010, Radio Autumn 2010, Prague (Czech Repub.), Music of Our Age, Münster 2012, etc; currently freelance composer; Exec. Sec. Lithuanian Composers' Union; numerous broadcasts of compositions on radio and TV. *Film:* music for film Ghetto. *Dance:* ballet: Maria Stuart, Maiden and Death, Desdemona. *Compositions:* A Maiden and Death (ballet), staged at Lithuanian Opera and Ballet Theatre, Vilnius 1982, Mary Stewart (ballet), staged at Vanemuine Theatre, Tartu, Estonia 1986, 1988, Desdemona (ballet), staged at Lithuanian Nat. Opera and Ballet Theatre (Best Stage Work Award, Lithuanian Composers' Union) 2005, Symphony No. 2 (Music Festival, St Petersburg) 1984, Two Songs of Shulamith for voice and piano 1992, Der Tiefe Brunnen for voice and five instruments 1993, Paratum cor Meum: Concerto for cello, mixed choir, piano (clavinova) and symphony orchestra 1995, Simeni Kahotam al Libeha (Set Me As A Seal on Your Heart) for soprano, bass, percussion solo and symphony orchestra 1995, Shma Israel (Hear, O Israel) for cantor, male choir and symphony orchestra 1997, Cantus I, Cantus II for cello solo 1997, Concerto in Do for cello and symphony orchestra 2002, premiered at the Young Euro Classic, Berlin 2002 by D. Geringas and Lithuanian Symphony Orchestra, conducted by Robertas Servenikas, Guitar Concerto 2006, David's Song for Cello and String Quartet 2006, Violin Concerto 2007, Concerto for

Bayan and Symphony Orchestra 2007, Concerto for percussion solo and chamber orchestra 2011, Cello Concerto No. 3 2012. *Publications:* contrib. to Berliner Zeitung 1977, Ruch Muzyczny 1978, Frankfurter Allgemeine Zeitung 1982, Festival Zeitung 1992, The Independent 2003, International Arts Manager 2002, Die Welt 2002, Der Tagesspiegel 2002, International Art Manager, No. 14 2002 etc. *Honours:* Kt's Cross, Order of Lithuanian Grand Duke Gediminas 1996, Officer's Cross, Order of Merit of Lithuania 2006; Lithuanian Nat. Award 1997, European Composer's Prize 2002, Prize for the best Lithuanian stage work 2005, Second Prize, Int. Composers Competition, Prague 1993, Diploma, Int. W. Lutosławski Contest, Kil, Sweden 1994, WIPO Creativity Award and Gold Medal 2008, Latga-a Gold Stare 2010. *Address:* Lakstingalu 5, 15173 Nemencine, Vilnius raj, Lithuania (home). *Telephone:* (6) 999-9576 (home). *Fax:* (5) 237-0995 (home). *E-mail:* asenderovas@yahoo.com (home). *Website:* www.mxl.lt/senderovas.

SÉNÉCHAL, Michel; French singer (tenor); b. 11 Feb. 1927, Tavery. *Education:* Paris Conservatoire. *Career:* debut at Théâtre de la Monnaie, Brussels 1950; many appearances at the Paris Opéra and Opéra Comique and elsewhere in France; roles have included Ferrando, Don Ottavio, Tamino, Hylas in Les Troyens, Rossini's Almaviva and Comte Ory; successful in character roles, such as Rameau's Platée (Aix 1956, Brussels Opéra Comique 1977), Erice in Cavalli's L'Ormindo (Glyndebourne), M. Triquet in Eugene Onegin, Valzacchi and Scaramuccio in Ariadne auf Naxos; Glyndebourne debut 1966, as Gonzalve in L'Heure Espagnole; Salzburg Festival 1972–88, notably as Mozart's Basilio; Metropolitan Opera debut 1982, as the Villains in Les Contes d'Hoffmann, returned 1997 and 2002 as Basilio; season 1985 with the premieres of Landowski's Montségur at Toulouse and Boehmer's Docteur Faustus at the Paris Opéra; Dir, Opera School at the Opéra 1980–. *Honours:* Officier, Ordre National de la Légion d'Honneur, Officier, Ordre des Arts at des Lettres, Commandeur, Ordre du Mérite National.

SENN, Marta; Swiss singer (mezzo-soprano); b. 1958, Switzerland. *Education:* legal training in Columbia; musical study in USA. *Career:* Rosina and in title role of Rossi's Orfeo, at several American Opera Houses and La Scala, 1984; Charlotte in Stuttgart, Paris, Hamburg and Nantes; Giulietta in Les Contes d'Hoffmann in Madrid; Isabella in Rome; Massenet's Dulcinée at the Liceo, Barcelona; US tour with Placido Domingo; Annius in La Clemenza di Tito and Rossini's Angelina at the Salzburg Festival, 1988; Season 1988–89, as Sara in Roberto Devereux at Naples and Meg in new production of Falstaff at Bologna; Fenena in Nabucco and Verdi's Preziosilla at Verona Arena; Carmen at Munich State Theatre; Carmen at Stuttgart State Theatre; Liceo, Barcelona, Olympics Arts Festival; Charlotte in Werther; concerts and recording role of Salud, in La Vida Breve, Venezuela and Minnesota Orchestra, 1993; debut role of Carmen, Paris Opéra, 1994; Charlotte, in Lisbon and Rome; Dorabella in Toulon and Fidalma in Il Matrimonio Segreto at Bologna; Season 1996 as Charlotte at Naples. *Recordings include:* Maddalena in Rigoletto, from La Scala, conducted by Riccardo Muti; Musetta, in La Bohème, at Venice; Lola in Cavalleria Rusticana; Salud in La Vida Breve, Mata conducting, 1993; El Amor Brujo, original version. *Honours:* winner, Concours Int. de Paris 1982, First Prize, Baltimore Opera Nat. Auditions 1982. *Current Management:* c/o Fedeli Opera International, via Montegrappa 3, 40121 Bologna, Italy. *Address:* c/o Dorian Recordings, 8 Brunswick Road, Troy, NY 12180-3795, USA. *Telephone:* (518) 274-5475. *E-mail:* info@dorian.com.

SEO, Sun-young, MMus; South Korean singer (soprano); b. 1984. *Education:* studied at Korea Nat. Univ. of Arts, Seoul with Choi Hyun-soo, and at Robert Schumann Musikhochschule, Düsseldorf with Michaela Krämer, masterclasses in Salzburg with Grace Bumbry and in Seoul with Kwangchul Youn. *Operatic repertoire includes:* Fiordiligi in Così fan tutte, Donna Anna in Don Giovanni, Adina in L'elisir d'amore, Agathe in Der Freischütz, Marguerite in Faust, Micaëla in Carmen, Mimi in La Bohème, Liu in Turandot, Nedda in I Pagliacci, Wally in La Wally. *Honours:* First Prize, Francisco Viñas Int. Vocalists Competition, Barcelona 2010, Grand Prix, Maria Callas Grand Prix Competition, Athens 2011, winner, XVI Int. Tchaikovsky Competition, Moscow 2011. *Current Management:* c/o Mengino Artists Management, Masurenstrasse 1b, 81929 Munich, Germany. *Telephone:* (89) 99109932 (office). *E-mail:* mengino@hotmail.com. *Address:* c/o Robert Schumann Hochschule Düsseldorf, Fischerstrasse 110, 40476 Düsseldorf, Germany (office). *Website:* www.rsh-duesseldorf.de (office).

SEOW, Yitkin, LRSM; Singaporean pianist. *Education:* Yehudi Menuhin School and Royal Coll. of Music, London. *Career:* moved to UK 1967; toured USA 1972; toured Russia for BBC 1988. *Performances include:* Promenade Concerts, Royal Albert Hall and Royal Festival Hall (with Philharmonia Orchestra), London 1975; appeared at Beethovenfest, Bonn 1977, Hong Kong Arts Festival (with Berlin Radio Symphony Orchestra) 1977, Promenade Concerts (with Royal Philharmonic Orchestra) 1982, Poland 1984, Hong Kong Asian Arts Festival 1984, with St Petersburg Philharmonic 1988. *Recordings:* Satie, Schubert 1989. *Television:* appeared on French TV with Yehudi Menuhin, Mozart Concerto (BBC). *Honours:* First Prize, BBC Piano Competition 1974, winner, Rubinstein Competition 1977, Bronze Medal and Special Prize for Brahms Paganini Variations.

SEPEC, Daniel; German musician (violin); b. 1965, Frankfurt am Main. *Education:* studied with Dieter Vorholz at Musikhochschule Frankfurt and Gerhard Schulz at Hochschule für Musik, Vienna; master-classes with Sandor Végh and Alban Berg Quartet. *Career:* Leader, Deutsche Kammerphilharmonie Bremen 1993–, appears regularly as a soloist under such conductors as Daniel Harding, Thomas Hengelbrock, Frans Brüggen and Trevor Pinnock; frequently appears as leader of original instruments ensemble, Balthasar Neumann Ensemble; Guest Leader, Chamber Orchestra of Europe, Camerata Academica Salzburg and Camerata Bern, also as soloist with Acad. of Ancient Music and Wiener Akademie; performs as chamber musician with Schubertiade Hohenems 1995–; f. trio with flautist Eugen Bertel and guitarist Alexander Swete, also with pianist Andreas Staier and cellist Jean-Guihen Queyras (concert debut 2004); co-f. Arcanto Quartet 2004; Prof. of Violin, Hochschule für Musik Basel 2010–14; Prof., Musikhochschule Lübeck 2014–. *Recordings include:* Beethoven: Sonatas for Piano and Violin (using a violin that belonged to the composer, on loan from Beethoven House in Bonn) 2006, Beethoven/Hummel: Piano Trios 2008, Biber: Rosenkranzsonaten (Jahrespreis der Deutschen Schallplattenkritik 2011) 2010, Schumann: Sonatas for Piano & Violin 2010, Vivaldi: Le Quattro Stagioni/La Follia 2011, Beethoven: Violin Sonatas/Piano Trios 2014; with Arcanto Quartet: Mozart String Quartet K421, Schubert String Quintet op. 163, Ravel/Dutilleux/Debussy String Quartets, Bartók String Quartets. *Current Management:* c/o Karsten Witt Musik Management, Leuschnerdamm 13, 10999 Berlin, Germany. *Telephone:* (30) 214594. *Fax:* (30) 214594101. *E-mail:* info@karstenwitt.com. *Website:* www.karstenwitt.com. *Address:* Musikhochschule Lübeck, Grosse Petersgrube 21, 23552 Lübeck, Germany (office). *Telephone:* 45115050 (office). *Website:* www.mh-luebeck.de (office).

ŞERBAN, Andrei; Romanian theatre and opera director; *Director, Oscar Hammerstein II Center for Theatre Studies, Columbia University*; b. 21 June 1943, Bucharest; s. of Gheorghe Şerban and Elpis Şerban; m.; two c. *Education:* Bucharest Theatrical and Cinematographic Art Inst. *Career:* int. scholarships Ford 1970, Guggenheim 1976, Rockefeller 1980; associated with Robert Brustein's American Repertory Theatre Company for more than 20 years 1970–; worked also with LaMama Theatre, Public Theater, Lincoln Center, Circle in the Square, Yale Repertory Theatre, Guthrie Theatre, ACT, New York City, Seattle and Los Angeles Operas; in Europe: at Paris, Geneva, Vienna, and Bologna Opera Houses, Welsh Nat. Opera, Covent Garden, Théâtre de la Ville, Helsinki Lilla Teatern, Comédie Française, among others; worked with Shiki Co. of Tokyo, Japan; has delivered numerous lectures; Gen. Man. Nat. Theatre of Romania 1990–93; Dir, Oscar Hammerstein II Center for Theatre Studies, Columbia Univ., New York 1992–. *Productions include:* (in Romania) Ubu Roi 1966, Julius Caesar 1968, Jonah 1969, An Ancient Trilogy (Medea, The Trojan Women, Elektra) 1990; (in USA) Medea (Euripides) 1972, Fragments of a Trilogy (Medea, Elektra, The Trojan Women) 1974, As You Like It 1976, The Cherry Orchard 1977, Uncle Vanya 1979, The Umbrellas of Cherbourg 1980, The Seagull 1981, Three Sisters 1983, The King Stag 1985, The Miser 1988, Twelfth Night 1989, Sweet Table at the Richelieu 1989, Hamlet 1999 (in France, at the Comédie Française), L'Avare 2000, Le Marchand de Venise 2001, Lysystrata 2002 Pericles 2003, Cleansed 2006, Uncle Vanya 2005, King Lear 2006, Cries and Whispers (in Romania, three UNITER Awards including Best Dir 2011) 2011, Hedda Gabler 2012, Angels in America (in Hungary, Best Dir, Hungarian Theatre Critics Asscn 2013) 2013, Chung Young 2014. *Opera productions include:* Eugene Onegin 1980, Turandot 1984, Norma 1985, Fidelio (Covent Garden) 1986; Paris Opera: L'Ange de feu 1991, Lucia Di Lammermoor 1995, The Puritans 1997, L'Italienne à Alger 1998, Les Indes Galantes 1999, La Khovantchina 2001, Les Vêpres Siciliennes 2003, Otello 2004; Wiener Staatsoper: Les Contes d'Hoffman 1993, Die Lustige Witwe 1999, Werther 2005, Manon 2007, etc. *Honours:* Order of the Star of Romania (Steaua României); Prize for the Best Performance, World Students' Theatre Festival, Zagreb 1965, Obie Awards, Tony Award, George Abbott Award, Soc. of Stage Dirs and Choreographers, prizes at Avignon, Belgrade and Shiraz Festivals. *Address:* School of the Arts, Columbia University, 601 Dodge Hall, Mail Code 1807, 2960 Broadway, New York, NY 10027, USA (office). *Telephone:* (212) 854-3408 (office). *Fax:* (212) 854-3344 (office). *E-mail:* as160@columbia.edu (office).

SERBO, Rico; singer (tenor); b. 9 May 1940, Stockton, CA, USA. *Education:* studied in San Francisco. *Career:* debut in San Francisco 1965 as Ramiro in Cenerentola; sang in Opera at Seattle, Santa Fe and San Francisco, Europe from 1970, notably with Netherlands Opera and at Koblenz, Essen and the Theater am Gärtnerplatz Munich; further engagements at San Diego, New York City Opera, Houston, Toronto and Vancouver; sang at New Orleans, as Arvino in the US premiere of I Lombardi; Deutsche Oper and Theater des Westens Berlin, and at Belfast; other roles have included Mozart's Ferrando and Tamino, Almaviva, Ernesto, Fenton, Alfredo, Tom Rakewell, Rodolfo, Boito's Faust, Lord Barrat in Der Junge Lord and Tony in Elegy for Young Lovers. *Recordings include:* Donizetti's L'Assedio di Calais.

SERDIUK, Nadezhda; Russian singer (mezzo-soprano); b. 1975, Moscow. *Education:* Tchaikovsky Conservatoire, Moscow and Young Singers' Academy at the Mariinsky Theatre, St Petersburg, masterclasses with Christa Ludwig, Marilyn Horne and Renata Scotto at the Metropolitan Opera Young Singers' Programme. *Career:* roles with Kirov Opera have included Gluck's Orfeo, Olga in Eugene Onegin, Nadezhda in Vera Sheloga by Rimsky-Korsakov and Lyubava in Sadko; sang Beautiful Spring in Rimsky's Snow Maiden with the Kirov at Amsterdam and London (Covent Garden), 1999–2000; other roles include Lyubasha in Rimsky's The Tsar's Bride. *Honours:* prizewinner, International Glinka and Rimsky-Korsakov Vocal Competitions, 1998.

SEREBRIER, José, MA; American conductor and composer; b. 3 Dec. 1938, Montevideo, Uruguay; s. of David Serebrier and Frida Serebrier (née Wasser); m. Carole Farley 1969; one d. *Education:* Univ. of Minnesota, Curtis Inst. of Music, studied composition with Aaron Copland and Vittorio Giannini and conducting with Antal Dorati and Pierre Monteux. *Career:* started conducting at age of 12; moved to USA 1956; guest conductor in USA, S America, Australia and Europe; Assoc. Conductor, American Symphony Orchestra, with Leopold Stokowski 1962–68; conducted alongside Leopold Stokowski world première of Charles Ives' Fourth Symphony, Carnegie Hall, New York 1964; conducted first performance in Poland of Charles Ives' Fourth Symphony 1971 and premieres of over 500 works; Rockefeller Foundation Composer-in-Residence with Cleveland Orchestra 1968–70; Music Dir Cleveland Philharmonic Orchestra 1968–71; Artistic Dir Int. Festival of the Americas, Miami 1984–, Miami Festival 1985– (also Founder), Festival Miami; toured frequently with Russian Nat. Orchestra in S America and China. *Compositions include:* Solo Violin Sonata 1954, Quartet for Saxophones 1955, Pequeña música (wind quintet) 1955, Symphony No. 1 1956, Momento psicológico (string orchestra) 1957, Solo Piano Sonata 1957, Suite canina (wind trio) 1957, Symphony for Percussion 1960, The Star Wagon (chamber orchestra) 1967, Nueve (double bass and orchestra) 1970, Colores mágicos (variations for harp and chamber orchestra) 1971, At Dusk, in Shadows (solo flute), Andante Cantabile (strings), Night Cry (brass), Dorothy and Carmine (flute and strings), George and Muriel (contrabass), Winter (violin concerto) 1995, Winterreise (for orchestra) 1999; composed music for several films; all compositions published and recorded; over 350 recordings to date. *Television includes:* int. TV broadcast of Grammys Ceremony, LA 2002, conducting suite from Bernstein's West Side Story. *Recordings include:* more than 300 recordings with major orchestras. *Publications include:* orchestration of 14 songs by Edvard Grieg 2000, orchestration of Gershwin's works 2002, Suite from Janacek's Makropoulos Case 2004; more than 100 works published. *Honours:* two Guggenheim Fellowships, Ford Foundation Conducting Award, Nat. Endowment for the Arts Comm. Award 1969, Ditson Award for Promotion of New Music, Columbia Univ. 1980, Deutsche Schallplatten Critics' Award 1991, UK Music Retailers' Asscn Award for Best Symphony Recording (for Mendelssohn symphonies) 1991, Diapason d'Or Recording Award, France, Best Audiophile Recording (for Scheherazade), Soundstage 2000, BMI Award, Koussevitzky Foundation Award, Latin Grammy for Best Classical Album of 2004 (for Carmen Symphony with Barcelona Symphony Orchestra). *Address:* 20 Queensgate Gardens, London, SW7 5LZ, England (office). *Fax:* (212) 662-8073 (New York) (office). *E-mail:* caspi123@aol.com (office). *Website:* www.joseserebrier.com.

SEREMBE, Gilberto; Italian conductor and academic; *Professor of Conducting, Italian Conducting Academy, Milan*; b. 17 Dec. 1955, Milan; m. Elisabetta Brusa 1997. *Education:* Conservatory G. Verdi, Milan, Accad. Chigiana, Siena. *Career:* Prof. of Composition, Conservatorio 'Luca Marenzio', Brescia 1979–81; Asst, Teatro alla Scala, Milan 1980; Prof. of Orchestral Rehearsing, Mantova Conservatorio 1982–83, Conservatorio G. Verdi, Milan 1984–86, Brescia Conservatorio 1986–88, Genoa Conservatorio 1989–97; Prof. of Orchestral Conducting, Accad. Musicale Pescarese 1988–2010; Prof. of Conducting and Conductor, Orchestra of the Conservatorio of Brescia 1997–; Prof. of Conducting, Accad. Italiana per la Direzione d'Orchestra 2011–12, Italian Conducting Acad., Milan 2013–; Guest Conductor, Pomeriggi Musicali Orchestra, Milan 1976–77, 1980–83, 1987, 1990, 1992, 1994, 2009, 2010, AIDEM Orchestra, Florence 1979, Angelicum Chamber Orchestra, Milan 1980–83, San Remo Symphony Orchestra 1980–87, Teatro Massimo Symphony Orchestra, Palermo 1986–88, Orchestra Regionale della Toscana, Florence 1986–88, 1995, Stradivari Orchestra, Milan 1991–92, and Hungarian tour 1991, Teatro Regio Symphony Orchestra, Turin 1991, Toscanini Symphony Orchestra, Parma 1993, Brescia Symphony Orchestra 1996, 1998, 1999, Orchestra Sinfonica Triveneta 1997–98, Filarmonia Veneta of Teatro Comunale, Treviso 1997, Orchestra Sinfonica del Condervatorio di Brescia 1997–2009, Orchestra Stabile di Bergamo 1998, Orchestra Sinfonia di Pescara 1999, 2001, 2003, 2005, 2008; abroad at Gothenburg Symphonic Orchestra, Sweden 1989, BRT Radio Television Symphony Orchestra, Brussels 1991, Turku Philharmonic, Finland 1991, Tirana Radio and Television Symphony Orchestra, Albania 1994–95, Summer Stage in Conducting, Valencia, Spain 1999. *E-mail:* gilberto.serembe@italianconductingacademy.com (office). *Website:* www.italianconductingacademy.com (office); www.gilbertoserembe.it.

SERGEYEVA, Tatyana Pavlovna; Russian composer and musician (piano, organ, clavichord); *Executive Secretary, Russian Composers Union*; b. 28 Nov. 1951, Kalinin (now Tver); d. of Korovkin Pavel Petrovich and Vershinskaya Yevgenya Analolyevna; m. Vikharev Ivan Timofeyevich. *Education:* Moscow State Conservatory. *Career:* concertmaster for class of symphony conducting, Moscow State Conservatory 1975–88; music teacher Little Music Studios (pvt school) 1997–; works performed in festivals of contemporary music in USA, Scotland, France, Belgium, Germany, Finland, Italy, Poland; performs as pianist, organist, clavichordist; mem. Composers' Union 1982–; currently Exec. Sec., Russian Composers Union. *Works include:* three piano concertos 1975, 1985, 2000, concerto for bass and string orchestra 1980, for trombone and orchestra 1986, for violin and keyboard instruments, sonatas for trombone and cello 1986, for cello and organ 1988, for violin and organ 1994, variations on the theme of T. Tolstaya 1991, variations for violin, organ and winds, variations on the theme of Juan Idalgo for 4 cellos, vocal cycles on lyrics of Russian poets of the 18th century and Antiquity, instrumental ensembles. *Repertoire includes:* Bach, Beethoven, Liszt, Mendelssohn, Chopin, Busoni, Russian music by Bortnyansky, Tchaikovsky, Balakirev, N. Rubinstein, Arensky, N. Cherepnin, A. Rubinstein, contemporary music. *Recordings include:* Sergeyeva: The Musical World (conductor Dmitry Liss, Ural State Philharmonic Orchestra) 2000, Reverie 2004, Serenade 2004, In the Country Estate 2005, Toccata e fuga 2006, Alla maniera italiana 2007, Dreams of the Past 2010, Gagliarda 2011, The Extraordinary Concert 2011, At the Sea 2012, Etude 2013. *Honours:* D. Shostakovich Composer's Prize 1987, Honored Artist of the Russian Fed. 1995, Laureate, Sergei Prokofiev Int. Competition of Composers 2003. *Address:* Novopeschanaya str 19/10, apt 165, 125252 Moscow, Russia. *Telephone:* (095) 930-78-21.

SERKIN, Peter Adolf; American concert pianist; b. 24 July 1947, New York; s. of Rudolf Serkin and Irene Busch; m. Regina Serkin; five c. *Education:* Curtis Inst. of Music, studied with Lee Luvisi, Mieczyslaw Horszowski, and Rudolf Serkin, also studied with Ernst Oster, Marcel Moyse, and Karl Ulrich Schnabel. *Career:* debut, New York 1959; taught at Juilliard School, Curtis Inst. of Music; currently teaches at Bard Coll. Conservatory of Music, Longy School of Music; Founder mem. TASHI; concert appearances in recital and with orchestras worldwide including Philadelphia, Cleveland, New York, Chicago, Berlin, London, Zürich, Paris, Japan, Vienna; has premiered works composed for him by Knussen, Takemitsu, Lieberson, Berio; has given benefit performances to aid hunger and war victims. *Honours:* Dr hc (New England Conservatory) 2001; Grammy Award 1966, Premio Accademia Musicale Chigian Siena 1983. *Current Management:* CM Artists, 127 West, 96th Street, #13B, New York, NY 10025, USA. *Telephone:* (212) 864-1005. *Fax:* (212) 864-1066. *Website:* www.cmartists.com/artists/peter-serkin.htm; www.bard.edu/conservatory.

SERMILÄ, Jarmo Kalevi, MA; Finnish composer and musician (trumpet, flugelhorn); b. 16 Aug. 1939, Hämeenlinna; m. Ritva Vuorinen 1962. *Education:* Helsinki Univ., Sibelius Acad. *Career:* worked for Finnish broadcasting co. (YLE), Artistic Dir YLE Experimental Studio 1973–79; Pres. Finnish Section, Int. Soc. for Contemporary Music 1975–79; Composer-in-Residence, Hämeenlinna 1977–82; freelance composer 1982–; Artistic Dir Time of Music Contemporary Music Festival, Viitasaari 1987–99; state grant for composition 1990; mem. Soc. of Finnish Composers, Vice-Pres. 1981–2005. *Compositions include:* A Circle of the Moon, Allegria, At Bizarre Exits, La Place Revisitée, Labor, Manifesto, Merlin's Mascarade (ballet), Mimesis 2, Movimenti, On the Road, Pentagram, Quattro Rilievi, Random Infinities, Technogourmet, Train of Thoughts, Wolf Bride (ballet). *Recordings:* Quattro Rilievi, At Bizarre Exits, Random Infinities, Movimenti, Technogourmet, Citymusic. *Honours:* Hon. Prof. 2005; hon. mem. Finnish Composers' Soc. 2005; Hon. Reward, Sibelius Fund of the Finnish Composers' Soc. 2006; Janáček Medal 1978, Hämeenlinna City Music Prize 1981, Smetana Medal 1984, Häme Prov. Art Soc. Award 1988, State Grant for Composition 1990–2003. *Address:* Niittykatu 7 A 7, 13100 Hämeenlinna, Finland (home). *E-mail:* jarmo@sermila.net (home). *Website:* www.sermila.net.

SEROV, Edward; Russian conductor; b. 9 Sept. 1937, Moscow; Guenrietta Serova 1961, two s. *Education:* Gnessin Institute, Moscow, Tchaikovsky Conservatoire, Kiev, Rimsky-Korsakov Conservatoire, Leningrad. *Career:* debut at Kiev Opera, 1960; Conductor, Leningrad Philharmonic Orchestra, 1961–68, 1985–90; Founder, Chief Conductor, Uljanovsk Philharmonic, 1968–77; Chief Conductor, Leningrad Chamber Orchestra, 1974–85; Founder, Chief Conductor, Volgograd Philharmonic Orchestra, 1987–; Professor, Leningrad (now St Petersburg) Conservatoire, 1987–; Chief Conductor, Odense Symphony Orchestra, Denmark, 1991–96; Chief Conductor Saratov Philharmonic Orchestra, 1995–; Foreign Tours: Japan, USA, France, Germany, Austria, Spain, Sweden, Norway, Finland, Denmark, Czechoslovakia, Hungary, Yugoslavia, others. *Recordings include:* works of Webern, Tishchenko, Arensky, Mozart, Rubenstein, Tchaikovsky, Prokofiev, Sviridov, Purcell, Tartini, Bartók, Slonimski, Hindemith, Mendelssohn, Bach, Nielsen, Rossini, Ginastera, Shostakovich, Rodrigo, Elgar, Suk, Schumann, Spohr and Schubert. *Publications:* contrib. to The Exploit of Service to Music; The Soviet Music Magazine, 1980; About Conductor's Art, The Soviet Music, 1980; The original Symphonic Narration, The Music Life magazine, 1984; Meditation about G Sviridov to book on Sviridov; Others. *Honours:* People's Artist of Russia Honorary Title, President of Russia, 1990; Order of Honour, President of Russia, 1998.

SERRA, Enric; Spanish singer (baritone); b. 24 July 1940, Barcelona; one s. one d. *Education:* studied in Barcelona. *Career:* debut at Teatro del Liceo, Barcelona 1966, as Morales in Carmen; has sung in Spain (Madrid, Valencia, Bilbao, La Coruña, Oviedo, Valladolid, Zaragoza, Seville, Las Palmas and Barcelona) from 1969, notably as Falstaff, Scarpia, Escamillo, Enrico, Belcore and Alcandro in Pacini's Saffo 1987; guest engagements in Zürich, Cologne, Bonn, Cologne, Essen, Berlin, Frankfurt, Genoa, Turin, Lisbon, Bayreuth, Vienna, Nice, Tours, Naples, Venice, Bogotá and Caracas, as Don Pasquale, Rossini's Figaro, Alfonso (La Favorita) and Don Carlos in La Forza del Destino; at Schwetzingen as Italiana in Algeri and Lescaut in Manon Lescaut and at Barcelona 1990; Don Magnifico in La Cenerentola at Hamburg 1998; sang Belfiore in Haydn's Il mondo della luna at Maastricht 1999; other roles include Mozart's Leporello and Alfonso, Escamillo, Valentin in Faust, Scarpia, and Verdi's Count Luna; concert repertoire includes Falla's L'Atlantida (Madrid 1977); Rossini's Barbiere at München's Bayerische Staatsoper 1989, and also at the New York Metropolitan Opera 1997–98; further roles include Massenet's Mandy, Marcello, Albert, Michonet and Grand Prêtre from Saint-Saëns' Samson et Dalila; concerts in Madrid's Teatro Real, Barcelona's Palau Musica, Paris' Salle Pleyel and ORTF, London's Royal Festival Hall, Rome's RAI, Tokyo's Suntory Hall and Granada's Music Festival. *Recordings include:* Madama Butterfly, Tosca, Italiana in Algeri, Otello, Il barbiere di Siviglia, Romeo y Julieta, El Pessebre, Caterina Cornaro, Maria Stuarda, La Villana. *E-mail:* enricserrallobet@telefonica.net (office).

SERRA, Luciana; Italian singer (soprano); b. 4 Nov. 1946, Genoa. *Education:* Genoa Conservatoire and with Michele Casato. *Career:* debut at Budapest Opera 1966, in Cimarosa's Il Convito; mem. of Tehran Opera 1969–76; sang Gilda in Rigoletto at Genoa 1974; Bologna 1979, in La Sonnambula; Covent Garden 1980, as Olympia in Les Contes d'Hoffmann; Rossini's Aureliano in Palmira at Genoa 1980; Hamburg 1982 and La Scala Milan 1983, as Lucia; US debut at Charleston as Violetta; Chicago Lyric Opera 1983 as Lakmé; Parma 1986 as Lucia; Rossini Opera Festival Pesaro 1987 in L'Occasione fa il ladro (Rossini); Vienna 1988 as the Queen of Night; Maggio Musicale Florence 1989, as Elvira in I Puritani; sang Gilda at Turin 1989, Hanna Glawari at Trieste 1990; Santiago 1990, as Donizetti's Marie; Schwetzingen Festival 1990, in Fra Diavolo at La Scala and Pamira in Le Siège de Corinthe at Genoa; sang Olympia at Genoa 1996; other roles include Rosina, Fiorilla; Ophelia, Philine; Bellini's Giulietta; Norina; Adina; Linda di Chamounix and Marie in La Fille du Régiment; season 1998 with Gounod's Juliette at Palermo and Puccini's Lauretta at Torre del Lago; Rossini's Rosina at Santiago, 2000; concert appearances in pre-classical works and music by Vivaldi, Mozart, Rossini and Rimsky-Korsakov. *Recordings:* Zerline in Fra Diavolo (Cetra); Torquato Tasso by Donizetti; Die Zauberflöte; Les Contes d'Hoffmann; Don Pasquale, Barbiere di Siviglia, Gianni di Parigi; Fille du Régiment; La Scala di Seta and L'Occasione fa il Ladro. *Current Management:* Allied Artists Agency, 42 Montpelier Square, London, SW7 1JZ, England.

SERRAIOCCO, Danielo; singer (bass); b. 1960, San Giovanni Teatino, Italy. *Education:* Accademia di Santa Cecilia, Rome. *Career:* debut at Spoleto 1987 as Raimondo in Lucia di Lammermoor; sang at Spoleto in Così fan tutte, Don Carlos, Mahagonny and L'Italiana in Algeri; Savonna 1988 in a revival of Rossini's Ciro in Babilonia; season 1990 as Wurm in Luisa Miller at Rome, in La rosa bianca e la rose rossa by Simone Mayr and in Britten's The Rape of Lucretia at Naples; Santa Domingo 1992, as Columbus in the premiere of 1492 by A. Braga; concerts include Bach and Mozart at Florence; Puccini's Messa di Gloria and Mozart's Requiem in London; Schubert's Mass in G, Rome. *Recordings:* Angelotti in Tosca, La Fanciulla del West.

SERVADEI, Annette, BMus, BA, FTCL, LTCL(T), LRSM(P), UDLM, UTLM, HND; British pianist, piano teacher and painter; b. 16 Oct. 1945, Durban, Natal, S Africa; d. of Louis Kearney and Moira Birks Kearney; m. Achilles Servadei 1972 (divorced 1981); one s. one d. *Education:* studied with concert pianist mother, further studies in Milan, Detmold, Salzburg, London with Ilonka Deckers, Klaus Schilde, Carlo Zecchi, Wilhelm Kempff, studied Fine Art and Electronic Sound Production, Univ. of Kent. *Career:* first radio broadcast aged 10; concert debut with Durban Symphony Orchestra aged 12; debut, Wigmore Hall, London 1972; recitals and concertos in UK, Western Europe, USA, Africa; frequent radio and TV broadcasts; Sr Piano Tutor, UOFS Bloemfontein 1974; Wits Univ., Johannesburg 1977–81; festival adjudicator, lecture recitals, master-classes; played world premiere, Tavener's Palintropos, London 1980; Gordon Kerry: Perpetual Angelus, London 1991; championed music of Sibelius and Dohnányi; career interrupted 1997–2005; resumed public performances, specialising in Mozart 2005–; mem. Inc. Soc. of Musicians. *Recordings include:* Britten and Khachaturian Piano Concertos with London Philharmonic Orchestra 1987, Mendelssohn, Schumann and Brahms piano pieces, Sibelius complete piano music (five CDs) 1994–96, Dohnányi Piano Music, Vols 1 and 2, Sibelius: Piano Album (28 Miniatures For Piano) 2007, Khachaturian Concertos 2008, Sibelius Serenade - Piano Works 2015. *Honours:* UK Sibelius Soc. Artist of the Year 1993. *Telephone:* (1227) 369501. *E-mail:* annette.servadei@yahoo.co.uk. *Website:* annetteservadei.co.uk.

SERVILE, Roberto; Italian singer (baritone); b. 1959, Genoa. *Education:* studied with Paride Venturi. *Career:* sang Don Carlos in Ernani at Modena and Marcello with Bohème at Treviso 1984; Marcello with Pavarotti at Philadelphia 1986; Rome Opera 1989 in a revival of Rossini's Zelmira and 1994 as Enrico in Lucia di Lammermoor; Genoa 1990 as Luna in Il Trovatore, Macerata 1992 as Germont; further appearances at Naples from 1993, Santiago 1994 and Hamburg 1995; season 1996 as Osaka in Mascagni's Iris at Rome and Azo in Donizetti's Parisina at Wexford; season 1997–98 as Enrico at La Scala; High Priest in Samson and Delilah, Eugene Onegin at Turin and Nottingham in Roberto Devereux at Naples; other roles include Verdi's Posa, Macbeth and Ford, Oreste in Iphigénie en Tauride, Escamillo, Belcore and Zurga in Les Pêcheurs de Perles; season 2000–01 as Count Luna at Parma, Puccini's Lescaut at Catania and Belfiore in Verdi's Un giorno di regno at Bologna; performed in La Bohème at La Scala, Milan 2005, Un Ballo in Maschera, Zürich 2005. *Recordings:* Il Trovatore, Il Barbiere di Siviglia, Falstaff, Rigoletto (video), Marin Faliero (video), La Bohème (video). *Honours:* Bastianini Awards 1987, Ester Mazzoleni, Palermo 1992, Giacomo Lauri Volpi, Rome 1994, Golden Tiberini, S. Lorenzo in Campi 1995, Bellini Award, Como 1995, Carlo Alberto Capell, Carpi 1997, Opera Award, Milan 2001, Rosa D'Argento, Palermo 2002, Gianni Poggi Award, Piacenza 2005. *Current Management:* c/o Atelier Musicale, Via Caselle 76, San Lazzaro di Savena 40068, Italy. *Telephone:* (51) 19984444. *Fax:* (51) 19984420. *E-mail:* info@ateliermusicale.com. *Website:* www.ateliermusicale.com.

ŠESTÁK, Zdeněk, PhDr; Czech composer; b. 10 Dec. 1925, Citoliby; m. Marie Zatecka 1950; one s. one d. *Education:* Gymnasium, Louny, Conservatorium de la Musique, Prague, Charles Univ. *Career:* Prof. of Music 1952–57; freelance composer 1957–; Dramaturge, Centre for Symphonic Music, Radio Czechoslovakia, Prague 1968–70; mem. Asscn of Music Artists Tchèques. *Compositions include:* Symphonie II 1970, Symphonie III 1971, Cycle des Cantates Spirituels sur les Textes de psaume 1972–92, Homage à Apollinaire 1972, Portrait du poète Konstantin Biebl 1974, Concerto for string orchestra 1974, String Quartet V: Concentus musicus 1975, Manon Lescaut: Cantata de chambre d'aprés Vítěslav Nezval 1975, String Quartet: Labyrinth of the Soul 1976, Sonata Symphonica 1976, Sonata da Camera 1978, Symphonie IV 1978, Symphonie V Chronos 1978, Pushkin's Vigil 1978, Symphonie VI L'Inquietude Eternelle du Coeur 1979, Variations Symphoniques: Making the Moment Alive 1980, Sursum corda concerto for violin 1981, Meditations de Socrates concerto for viola 1982, Memoria: La Fresque Symphonique de Variation 1983, Fatum: Vocale-Symphonique Fragment d'Après Sophocles 1983, Jean le Violiniste concerto for violin 1985, Queen Dagmar (oratorium) 1989, Les Cycles des Chants sur Vers de Villon, Michelangelo Buonarotti, Hora, Macha, Jelen, Sefl, King Salamon, Le Testament Ancien (Book of Ecclesiasticas), Evocations Paschales for trumpet and organ 1992, Dies Laetitiae sonata for trumpet and organ 1993, String Quartet VI: Variations de Mácha 1993, String Quartet VII: Soliloquia 1994, Partita Capricciosa: Hommage à Jan Vent 1997, Symposium musicum, Suite pour les instruments à vent 1997, Herakleitos (Movimenti musicali per novem stromenti a fiato) 1998, String Quartet IX: Sisyfos 1999, String Quintet II: Conscientia temporis 2000, String Sextet: Laus Vitae 2001, Euripides. Bresque dramatique pour l'orchestre symphonique 2001, Concerto for Violoncello I: La lumière de l'espoir 2002, Concerto for Violoncello II: La voie de la connaissance 2005. *Publications:* La Musique de Maîtres de Citoliby de 18 Siècle 1968, Musica antiqua Citolibensis (musical/historical anthology) 2006. *Address:* Pracska 2594-87, 106 00 Prague 10, Czech Republic (home). *Telephone:* 222966714 (home).

SETZER, Philip; American violinist; b. Cleveland, OH. *Education:* The Juilliard School, New York, studied with Josef Gingold, Rafael Druian, Oscar Shumsky. *Career:* has performed with symphony orchestras, including Aspen Chamber, Memphis, New Mexico, Puerto Rico, Nat., Omaha, Anchorage, and the Cleveland Orchestra; festival appearances include Marlboro Music Festival; performed world premiere of Paul Epstein's Matinee Concerto 1989; founder mem. and co-leader Emerson String Quartet 1976–, performing at Alice Tully Hall, Lincoln Center and Carnegie Hall, New York, Wigmore Hall, South Bank Centre and Barbican Centre, London, Aspen Music Festival, Stony Brook Int. Chamber Music Festival; commissions and premieres with Emerson String Quartet include compositions by Mario Davidovsky 1979, Ronald Caltabiano 1981, Maurice Wright 1983, George Tsontakis 1984, Gunther Schuller 1986, John Harbison 1987, Richard Danielpour 1988, Richard Wernick 1991, Wolfgang Rihm 1993, Paul Epstein 1994, Ned Rorem 1995, Edgar Meyer 1995, Ellen Taaffe Zwillich 1998, Andre Prévin 2003, Joan Tower 2003, Nicholas Maw 2006; faculty mem. Isaac Stern Chamber Music Workshops, Carnegie Hall and Jerusalem Music Center; has given master-classes at RAM, Curtis Inst., San Francisco Conservatory, Cleveland Inst. of Music, The Mannes School; artist-in-residence and Visiting Prof. of Violin and Chamber Music, State Univ. of New York at Stony Brook. *Recordings:* with Emerson String Quartet: Schubert, Der Tod und das Mädchen/Beethoven, Quartetto Serioso 1990, Bartók, Complete String Quartets (Grammy Awards for Best Classical Recording, Best Chamber Performance) 1990, Prokofiev, String Quartets Nos 1 and 2 1992, Schubert, String Quintet in C 1992, Ives/Barber, String Quartets (Grammy Award for Best Chamber Performance) 1993, Dvořák, Piano Quartet/Piano Quintet 1994, Dvořák, American Quartet/Tchaikovsky, Quartet No. 1/Borodin, Quartet No. 2 1995, Mozart, String Quartets KV 387 and 421 1995, Debussy/Ravel, String Quartets 1995, Webern, Works for String Quartet/String Trio Op. 20 1995, Schumann, Piano Quintet Op. 44/ Piano Quartet Op. 47 1996, Beethoven, The String Quartets (Grammy Award for Best Chamber Performance) 1997, Beethoven, Key to the Quartets 1997, Meyer, String Quintet/Rorem String Quartet No. 4 1998, Curt Cacioppo, Monsterslayer 1998, Mozart, Flute Quartets 1999, Schubert, String Quintet/Late Quartets 1999, Mozart/Brahms, Clarinet Quintets 1999, Shostakovich, The String Quartets 2000, The Emerson Encores 2002, Bach, The Art of Fugue 2003, Haydn, The Seven Last Words 2004, Harbison/Wernick/Schuller, American Contemporaries 2005, Mendelssohn, The Complete String Quartets 2005, Intimate Voices 2006, The Little Match Girl 2006, Brahm's String Quartets 2007, Bach Fugues 2008, Intimate Letters 2009. *Honours:* Dr hc (Middlebury Coll., Vermont) 1995; Hartford Univ. Medal for Distinguished Service 1994, Avery Fisher Prize 2004, Grammy Awards for Best Chamber Music and Classical Record of the Year (for Shostakovich Quartets) 2001, for Best Chamber Music Performance (for Intimate Letters) 2010. *Current Management:* c/o Matthew Zelle, IMG Artists, 152 W 57th Street, Fifth Floor, New York, NY 10019, USA. *Telephone:* (212) 994-3500. *Fax:* (212) 994-3550. *E-mail:* mzelle@imgartists.com. *Website:* www.imgartists.com; www.emersonquartet.com.

SEVERIN, Denis; musician (cello) and academic; *Professor of Cello, University of Music, Geneva.* *Education:* Moscow Tchaikovsky Conservatory, studied with D. Miller, Geneva Univ. of Music with D. Grossgurin, Music Acad. Basel with Th. Demenga and Schola Cantorum Basiliensis with Christophe Coin; master-classes with J. Starker, N. Gutman, A. Meneses, A. Bylsma, T. Monk, and G. Hoffman. *Career:* currently Prof. of Cello, Univ. of Music, Geneva and Univ. of the Arts Bern; regular Guest Prof., Centro superior de musica

Katarina Gurska, Madrid, Spain, Nat. Univ. of the Arts Kharkov, Ukraine, Jāzeps Vītols Academy of Music Riga, Latvia, Beijing Central Conservatory of Music; also offers regular master-classes and oversees student music projects; mem. jury of music competitions in France and Switzerland; Pres. Art Without Borders; mem. Organizing Cttee, European String Teachers Asscn; has performed as soloist or chamber musician in numerous halls world-wide including Queen Elizabeth Hall, London, Concertgebouw Amsterdam, Musikverein Vienna, Philharmonic Soc. Concert Hall, Prague, Radio France Concert Hall, Paris, Tonhalle Zurich, Lutoslawski Concert Hall, Warsaw and at festivals in Germany, Austria, Spain, Belgium, Poland, Turkey, Singapore and Brazil. *Recordings include:* Bach: Brandenburg Concertos 2007, Rachmaninov: Works for cello and piano 2009, Vivaldi: Harmonie Universelle 2008, Works of G. M. Cambini 2010, Luise Adolpha Le Beau: Chamber Music (Echo Klassik Award for Best 19th Century Chamber Recording of the Year 2015) 2014. *Address:* Haute Ecole, 2000 Neuchâtel, Switzerland (office). *Telephone:* (32) 9302121 (office). *E-mail:* denis.severin@hesge.ch (office). *Website:* www.hesge.ch (office); www.denisseverin.com.

SEXTON, Timothy A. P., BMus (Hons), Grad. DipEd, GAICD; Australian composer, arranger, conductor, singer (bass) and adjudicator and radio broadcaster; *CEO and Artistic Director, State Opera of South Australia;* b. 1960, McLaren Vale, S Australia; m. Suzanne Walker 1984; one s. one d. *Education:* Elder Conservatorium of Music, Univ. of Adelaide, studied composition with Richard Meale and Bozidar Kos, conducting with Shalom Ronly-Riklis, Gianluigi Gelmetti and David Porcelijn. *Career:* debut conducting Tasmanian Symphony Orchestra 1994, Adelaide Symphony Orchestra 1994; bass soloist, world premiere of Propriocepts Symphony 1997; bass soloist, Australian premiere of Flamma Flamma 1998, conducted Don Pasquale, Riders to the Sea, Mavra, State Opera of South Australia (SOSA) 1998, The Mikado, SOSA, Mahogonny Songspiel, Treemonisha 1999, Bernstein Mass, AICSA 2001, The Turn of the Screw, SOSA 2001, Akhnaten, Sweeney Todd, SOSA 2002, Einstein on the Beach 2004, 2006, Little Women, Satyagraha 2007, Underneath 2008, Different Fields 2010, Maria de Buenos Aires 2010, 2011, Moby Dick 2011, Orpheus in the Underworld 2012, Ode to Nonsense (world premiere) 2013, Philip Glass Trilogy 2014; Founder and Chief Conductor, Adelaide Art Orchestra Inc. 2001; CEO and Artistic Dir State Opera of South Australia 2011–; mem. Music Arrangers' Guild of Australia, Australian Inst. of Co. Dirs; broadcaster on ABC Classic FM (Australia) and ABC 891 (Adelaide). *Compositions include:* Newcastle Coal Cantata, Escape of the Chrysalids (opera), Whispering Winds (choral song cycle), The Hole in the Sky (cantata), A Children's Century (choral song cycle), Pete McGynty and the Dreamtime (musical), Unity Blues (musical), A Coming of Age (choral cantata), Songs For A Distant Land (choral song cycle), The Rime of the Ancient Mariner (orchestral work) 2013. *Recordings:* Australia, Be Proud; Fanfare; A Universal Christmas. *Films:* as composer and conductor: The Marriage of Figaro 2008; conductor: The King is Dead 2011, The Old Man Who Read Love Stories 2001, When Human Voices Wake Us 2003; actor: Thunderstruck. *Publications:* contrib. to Sounds Australian; Sing Out; many opera programmes throughout Australia. *Honours:* Centenary of Fed. Medal (for services to music) 2003; Henry Krips Memorial Conducting Scholarship 1994, 1997, Ruby Award for Sustained Contrib. to the Arts by an Individual 2008, South Australian of the Year (Arts Category) 2009. *Address:* PO Box 211, Marleston BC, SA 5033, Australia (office). *Telephone:* (8) 8226-4790 (office). *Fax:* (8) 8226-4791 (office). *E-mail:* tsexton@saopera.sa.gov.au (office). *Website:* www.saopera.sa.gov.au (office); www.adelaideartorchestra.com.au (home).

SFIRIS, Konstantin; singer (bass); b. 1958, Waltessinikon, Arcadia, Greece. *Education:* Athens Nat. Conservatory, Cologne Musikhochschule. *Career:* sang at the Vienna Staatsoper 1981–87; Graz Opera from 1986, notably in the premieres of Der Rattenfänger by Cerha and Rashomon by Makayo Kuba; guest appearances in opera and concert at Bregenz, Barcelona, San Francisco and Geneva; sang Sparafucile in Rigoletto at Liège 1989; other roles include Philip II and the Grand Inquisitor in Don Carlos, Zaccaria in Nabucco, Procida (I Vespri Siciliani), Hunding in Die Walküre and Pimen in Boris Godunov; wide concert repertory. *Honours:* winner Treviso Int. Competition 1981.

SGOURDA, Antigone; singer (soprano); b. 6 June 1938, Saloniki, Greece. *Education:* Athens Conservatory, Vienna Music Acad. *Career:* sang at Bonn Opera 1960–62, Essen 1962–66; Glyndebourne Festival 1962–63, as Fiordiligi, and First Lady in Die Zauberflöte; festival appearances at Schwetzingen, Holland and Athens 1971–73; Zürich Opera 1968–82, notably in operas by Mozart, including Lucio Silla; Frankfurt Opera 1968–82; guest engagements at Dusseldorf, Vienna, Stuttgart and Munich (Israel tour 1974); sang Donna Anna in Don Giovanni at Edinburgh 1973 and Philadelphia 1977; other roles have included Tatiana, Verdi's Amelia (Ballo in Maschera), Alice Ford, Violetta, and Aida; Katya Kabanova, Elizabeth I in Donizetti's Roberto Devereux, Arabella and Ariadne. *Recordings include:* Don Giovanni, Beatrice di Tenda by Bellini.

SHABALTINA, Svitlana; Ukrainian pianist and harpsichordist; b. 3 Feb. 1948, Kiev. *Education:* Kiev Music School, Gnessin Acad. of Music, Moscow. *Career:* debut at Kiev Int. Festival of the Contemporary Music 1982; Early Music Festival, Kraków 1990; Kiev Int. Festival, Ukraine and the World of Baroque; Bach's Concertos for two harpsichords with Elizabieta Stefanska and the Kiev Chamber Orchestra, Kiev Organ Hall 1994; recital of Slav composers' music, Germany 1994; played music of Russian and Ukrainian composers for piano and flute, Tolouse, France 1996; baroque music for harpsichord and flute, Teatro Regio di Torino, Italy 1998; recital harpsichord music, Kiev Philharmonic Hall 1998; Prof. of Piano and Harpsichord in Ukraine. *Recordings:* Ukraine early and contemporary music for Kiev radio and television 1972–98, music for harpsichord 1997, Beethoven sonata op 111, Schumann Kreisleriana op.16, Luboš Fiser Sonata 4 for piano 1998. *Honours:* diplomas for accompanist Ukraine Cello Competition, Kcharkow 1984, Int. Cello Competition, Kyshynev 1985.

SHADE, Ellen; singer (soprano); b. 17 Feb. 1948, New York, USA. *Education:* Juilliard Opera Center, studied with Cornelius Reid and at Sanata Fe Opera. *Career:* debut in Frankfurt 1972, as Liu in Turandot; sang Micaela at Pittsburgh 1972 (US debut); further engagements in Cincinnati, Milwaukee, Dallas and New Orleans; Chicago 1976, as Emma in Khovanshchina, returning as Eve in the premiere of Penderecki's Paradise Lost 1978; Metropolitan Opera debut, as Eva in Die Meistersinger; New York City Opera 1981, Donna Elvira; sang in Paradise Lost at La Scala 1979 and has made further European appearances at Hamburg, Brussels, Vienna (Florinda in Schubert's Fierrabras, conducted by Abbado), and Geneva (Katya Kabanova 1988); returned to the Metropolitan as Sieglinde in Die Walküre, conducted by James Levine; season 1992 as the Empress in Die Frau ohne Schatten, at Amsterdam and Salzburg; other roles include Verdi's Alice Ford, Wagner's Elsa and Freia, Climene in Cavalli's Egisto and Agathe in Der Freischütz; as a concert singer has appeared with the New York Philharmonic, the Chicago Symphony and the Orchestras of Boston, Cleveland, Los Angeles, Minnesota, St Louis, Pittsburgh and the National Symphony and in Europe with the Radio Orchestras of Frankfurt, Berlin, Stuttgart, Baden-Baden, Rome and Turin; invited to teach French Art Song with the Ravinia Festival in Chicago; Revival of Die Frau ohne Schatten in Amsterdam; Aida with the Metropolitan Opera; sang Arabella at Covent Garden 1996. *Recordings include:* Hans Pfitzner Cantata Von Deutscher Seele with the Frankfurt Radio Orchestra conducted by Horst Stein; television recordings include Strauss's Empress and Saffi in Der Zigeunerbaron.

SHADE, Nancy Elizabeth; American singer (soprano); b. 31 May 1949, Rockford, Ill. *Education:* De Pauw Univ., Indiana Univ.; studied voice with Vera Scammon. *Career:* debut at Kentucky Opera Theatre, 1968, as Leonora in Il Trovatore; Lulu, Frankfurt Opera; Countess in Figaro, Hamburg State Opera; Manon Lescaut, Munich State Opera; Marguerite in Faust, San Francisco Opera; Madama Butterfly, New York City Opera; Marie in Die Soldaten, Lyon; Santa Fe 1984, in US premiere of Henze's We Come to the River; Stuttgart 1988, as Marie in Die Soldaten (repeated Vienna 1990); Sang Schoenberg's Erwartung at the Prague State Opera, 2000. *Honours:* First Prize, Nat. Metropolitan Auditions 1968. *Current Management:* Thea Dispeker, 59 East 54th Street, New York, NY 10022, USA.

SHAGUCH, Marina; Russian singer (soprano); b. 1964, Krasnodar. *Education:* Arts School in Maikop, St Petersburg State Conservatoire. *Career:* sang at the Kirov Opera Theatre season 1991–92, notably in Mussorgsky's Sorochinsky Fair and Il Trovatore; concert debuts at Grand Hall of the Moscow Conservatoire; Glinka Capella in St Petersburg; further appearances throughout Russia, USA, Germany, Wales; concert repertoire has included works by Handel, Mozart, Rimsky, Schumann, Schubert, Wolf, Dvořák and Brahms; performed in The Legend of the Invisible City of Kitezh with Kirov Opera at the Barbican, 1995. *Honours:* winner Mussorgsky All-Russia and Glinka National Singing Competitions, second prize Tchaikovsky International Competition. *Current Management:* c/o Musicaglotz, 11 rue le Verrier, 75006 Paris, France. *Telephone:* 1-42-34-53-40. *Fax:* 1-40-46-93-77. *E-mail:* general@musicaglotz.com. *Website:* www.musicaglotz.com.

SHAHAM, Gil; American violinist; b. 19 Feb. 1971, Champaign-Urbana, IL. *Education:* Rubin Academy, Jerusalem, studied in Aspen and at Juilliard with Dorothy DeLay. *Career:* debut concert with the Jerusalem Symphony conducted by Alexander Schneider; appeared with the Israel Philharmonic under Zubin Mehta, 1982; engagements with the New York Philharmonic; season 1987–88 with the London Symphony Orchestra at the Barbican, Bavarian Radio Orchestra in Munich, the RAI Turin and recitals at La Scala and in Munich; debut with the Philadelphia Orchestra and tour of South America 1988; season 1988–89 with the Berlin Philharmonic, Orchestre de Paris, Frankfurt Symphony and the Philharmonia under Sinopoli; Bruch and Sibelius Concertos with the London Symphony Orchestra, 1989; recital debut at the Wigmore Hall, London, 1990; season 1995–96 with the Israel Philharmonic, the London Symphony Orchestra, CBSO, Vienna Symphony Orchestra and the Philharmonia Orchestra; Recitals throughout Europe and the Far East. *Recordings include:* Bartók's Concerto No. 2 (Boulez/Chicago Symphony Orchestra); Messiaen's Quartet for the End of Time, Elgar's Violin Concerto. *Honours:* First Prize, Claremont Competition, Israel 1982, Avery Fisher Prize 2008. *Current Management:* Opus 3 Artists, 470 Park Avenue South, 9th Floor North, New York, NY 10016, USA. *Telephone:* (212) 584-7500. *Fax:* (646) 300-8200. *E-mail:* info@opus3artists.com. *Website:* www .opus3artists.com. *Current Management:* Harrison Parrott, 5–6 Albion Court, London, W6 0QT, England. *Telephone:* (20) 7229-9166. *Fax:* (20) 7221-5042. *E-mail:* info@harrisonparrott.co.uk. *Website:* www.harrisonparrott.com.

SHAMBADAL, Lior; Israeli conductor; *Music Director, Orquesta Filarmónica de Bogotá;* b. Tel-Aviv. *Education:* Universität Mozarteum, Salzburg, Austria, Johannes Gutenberg-Universität Mainz, Germany. *Career:* Chief Conductor, Haifa Symphony Orchestra 1980–86; Chief Conductor, Kibbutz Chamber Orchestra of Tel-Aviv 1986–93; Music Dir Pfalztheater, Kaiserslau-tern, Germany 1993–2000; Chief Conductor, Berliner Symphoniker 1997–; Chief Conductor, RTV Symphony Orchestra, Ljubljana 2000–03; Prin. Guest Conductor, Liepaja Symphony Orchestra 2008–; Prin. Guest Conductor, Chengdu Symphony Orchestra, Cen. Music Conservatory, Sichuan, China 2008–; Music Dir Orquesta Filarmónica de Bogotá 2009–; guest conductor with orchestras in Argentina, Austria, Brazil, Canada, China, Germany, Denmark, Finland, France, Hungary, Israel, Italy, Mexico, Netherlands, Poland, Romania, Russia, Serbia, South Korea, Switzerland, Turkey, USA. *Current Management:* Arbetter Artists, Neugasse 1, 8810 Horgen, Switzerland. *Telephone:* 432431825. *Fax:* 432431826. *E-mail:* jill@arbetter-artists .com. *Website:* www.arbetter-artists.com; www.shambadal.com.

SHAMEYEVA, Natalia; Russian harpist and teacher; *Professor, Russian Academy of Music;* b. 30 Dec. 1939, Moscow; m.; one s. *Education:* Moscow Middle Special Music School, Gnessin Musical Pedagogical Inst., postgraduate courses, Moscow Conservatory. *Career:* soloist, Moscow Concert Org. 1962–70; Solo Harpist, Bolshoi Theatre Orchestra 1970–85, Prin. Harpist 1985–2003; teacher, Moscow Conservatory 1967–70, Musical Pedogical Inst. 1977–79; teacher, Russian Acad. of Music 1985–96, Asst Prof. 1996–2004, Prof. 2004–; master classes in USA, the Netherlands, Switzerland, UK, Japan, Italy, Belgium, Canada, China and Hong Kong; performances on major stages and radio stations in Moscow and other Russian cities; performances abroad in Europe, USA, Canada, Japan, China, Hong Kong and Israel; world premieres of Schnittke's Concerto for oboe, harp and orchestra, Baltin's Bylina for harp and orchestra, Kikta's Scotland Suite for two harps and orchestra, Elegie of Morning and Night Mists for oboe, English horn, harp and orchestra, Ulyanich's Dreamings for harp, flute, saxophone and viola; first performances in Russia of Quintets by Villa-Lobos, V. d'Indy, A. Roussel, A. Caplet, Quartet by Haydn; mem. Russian Harp Soc., Corpn of World Harp Congress. *Recordings include:* solo and chamber compositions for harp. *Publications include:* The History & Development of Harp Music in Russia, Moscow 1994, The Development of Harp Music in Russia, Bloomington 1997, V. Dulova, Creative portrait, in Dulova's book, The Art of Harp Playing 1975. *Honours:* Master of Art Criticism 1992, Honoured Artist of Russia 1993, Second Prize, Laureate of the all Union Competition 1963, Third Prize, Int. Harp Contest, Israel 1965, First Prize, Int. Harp Contest, USA 1969, Gold Medal, Moscow Composers' Union 2009. *Address:* Moscow 125581, Liapidevskogo 14-68, Russia (home). *Telephone:* (495) 456-9196 (home). *E-mail:* natshameyeva@mail.ru.

SHAMIR, Michal; Israeli singer (soprano); b. 1960, Tel-Aviv. *Education:* Rubin Academy of Music, Tel-Aviv, studied in London. *Career:* operatic debut at Gluck's Euridice; followed by Cherubino and Elvira in L'Italiana in Algeri; European debut at Hamburg as Susanna, followed by Pamina, Gretel and Frasquita; Geneva Opera 1987, as Larissa in the premiere of La Forêt by Liebermann; appearances with Frankfurt Oper as Susanna, Despina, Gilda, Marzellina and Jenny in Mahagonny; has returned to Tel-Aviv for Violetta, Nedda and Marguerite; Basle Opera in Zemlinsky's Der Zwerg; mem., Deutsche Oper Berlin; concert repertoire includes Lutoslawski's Chantefleurs et Chantefables, performed with the composer in San Francisco and Helsinki; British debut as Violetta in La Traviata with Opera North; First Tatiana in Eugene Onegin at Lausanne, Switzerland; Violetta in Tel-Aviv; sang Jenůfa at Essen and Omega in the premiere of Alpha and Omega, by Gil Shohat for New Israeli Opera 2001. *Current Management:* Bureau de Concerts de Valmalete, 7 rue Hoche, 92300 Levallois Perret, France. *Telephone:* 1-47-59-87-59. *Fax:* 1-47-69-87-50. *Website:* www.valmalete.com.

SHANAHAN, Ian Leslie, BMus; Australian composer; b. 13 June 1962, Sydney, NSW. *Education:* Univ. of Sydney, studied with Eric Gross and Peter Sculthorpe. *Career:* faculty mem. Dept of Music, Univ. of Sydney 1994–, New South Wales Conservatory 1989–94; commissions from Roger Woodward 1993 and others. *Compositions:* Echoes/Fantasies for bass clarinet and percussion 1984, Arcturus Timespace for amplified mandolin and percussion 1987, Solar Dust for mandolin 1988, Cycles of Vega for clarinet and two percussion 1988–90, Lines of Light for amplified recorders and percussion 1991–93, Ritual Canons for four tubas 1982–93, Dimensions Paradisim for alto flute 1993, Arc of Light for piano 1993, Gate of Remembrance for amplified piano 1993. *Honours:* Adolf Spivakovsky Prize 1991.

SHANKAR, Anoushka; Indian sitar player, conductor and composer; b. 9 June 1981, London; d. of Ravi Shankar and Sukanya Shankar. *Education:* San Dieguito Acad., San Diego, Calif., USA. *Career:* professional debut in New Delhi 1995, aged 13; regular performances since 1997 at major concert halls in India, Europe, USA and Asia, including tours with Ravi Shankar ensemble; first solo tour 2000; fundraising concerts for the Tibet Foundation Peace Garden 2000, Ramakrishna Centre, Kolkata 2000, Siri Fort Auditorium, New Delhi (conducting debut) 2001, World Economic Forum, New York 2002, Rainforest Foundation Benefit Concert, Carnegie Hall 2002, Elizabeth Glazer Pediatric AIDS Foundation Concert 2002, A Concert for Peace and Reconciliation, Lincoln Center's Avery Fisher Hall, New York 2003, Adopt a Minefield, Germany 2005. *Film appearance:* Dance Like a Man 2003. *Recordings include:* solo: Anoushka 1998, Anourag 2000, Live at Carnegie Hall 2002, Rise 2006, Breathing Under Water (with Karsh Kale) 2007, Traveller (Best Artist, Songlines Music Awards) 2012, Traces of You 2013, Home 2015. *Publication:* Bapi, the Love of My Life (pictorial biog. of Ravi Shankar) 2002. *Honours:* House of Commons Shield 1998, Nat. Council on Youth Leadership Award 1998, San Dieguito Acad. Award 1999, Woman of the Year (India) Award 2003. *Current Management:* Sulivan Sweetland, 1 Hillgate Place, Balham Hill,

London, SW12 9ER, England. *Telephone:* (20) 8772-3470 (home). *Fax:* (20) 8673-8959 (home). *E-mail:* info@sulivansweetland.co.uk. *Website:* www .sulivansweetland.co.uk; www.anoushkashankar.com.

SHAO, En, FRNCM; Chinese/British conductor; *Music Director and Principal Conductor, Taipei Chinese Orchestra;* b. 1954, Tianjin. *Education:* Peking Centre Music Conservatory, Royal Northern College of Music, UK. *Career:* Deputy Principal Conductor of the Chinese Broadcasting Symphony Orchestra and Principal Guest Conductor of the Central Philharmonic Orchestra of Ogina and the National Youth Orchestra; engagements in Europe from 1988; Associate Conductor of the BBC Philharmonic Orchestra 1990; Principal Conductor and Artistic Adviser of the Ulster Orchestra 1993; guest appearances with the Bournemouth Symphony, Northern Sinfonia, Royal Liverpool Philharmonic and other BBC orchestras; London debut 1992 with the London Symphony Orchestra; European engagements with the Oslo Philharmonic, the Berlin Symphony and the Czech Philharmonic; Prague Autumn Festival 1993; concerts with the ABC Orchestras in Australia and the Hong Kong Philharmonic; North American showings with the Toronto Symphony and the Colorado and Vancouver Symphonies; Royal Philharmonic Orchestra debut 1994; Principal Conductor, Euskadi Orchestra, Spain; Principal Guest Conductor and Artistic Advisor, Ulster Orchestra 1992–95; Music Dir and Principal Conductor Macao Orchestra 2003–08; Chief Conductor RTV Slovenia Symphony Orchestra 2006–; Principal Guest Conductor China Nat. Symphony Orchestra 2006–; Music Dir and Principal Conductor Taipei Chinese Orchestra 2007–. *Honours:* Lord Rhodes Scholarship; First Edward Van Beinum Scholarship; winner Hungarian Television Conductors Competition. *Current Management:* IMG Artists, The Light Box, 111 Power Road, London, W4 5PY, England. *Telephone:* (20) 7957-5800. *Fax:* (20) 7957-5801. *E-mail:* epascall@imgartists.com. *Website:* www.imgartists.com. *Address:* 40 Ploughmans Way, Macclesfield, SK10 2UN, England (home). *Telephone:* (1625) 428069 (home). *E-mail:* shaoenyi@aol.com (home).

SHAPIRO, Joel, AB; American concert pianist and teacher; *Professor Emeritus of Piano and Director, Young Concert Artists' European Auditions, Hochschule für Musik und Theater, Leipzig;* b. 28 Nov. 1934, Cleveland, Ohio. *Education:* Columbia Coll., New York, Brussels Royal Conservatory, Belgium with Stefan Askenase. *Career:* debut in New York 1963; London debut as soloist with Royal Philharmonic Orchestra 1968; extensive annual concert tours including piano recitals, concertos and chamber music in the world's leading music centres; numerous radio and TV broadcasts; Prof. of Piano, Univ. of Illinois, 1970–93; Prof. of Piano and Prorektor, Hochschule für Musik und Theater, Leipzig 1994–2001, Prof. Emer. 2001–; Dir Young Concert Artists' European Auditions, Leipzig 1994–; Artistic Dir Int. Summer Music Acad., Leipzig 1999–2005. *Publication:* contrib. to Das Beethoven-Lexikon. *Honours:* Winner, Young Concert Artists Int. Auditions, New York City 1961, First Prize, Darche Competition, Brussels 1962, Harriet Cohen Int. Bach Award, London 1963, Awards from The Int. Inst. and Rockefeller Foundation. *Address:* KBB, Hochschule für Musik, Postfach 100809, 04107 Leipzig, Germany. *E-mail:* ycaleipzig@comcast.net (office); joelshapiro@comcast.net (office).

SHARAF, Hisham; Iraqi musician (clarinet). *Education:* Baghdad School of Folk Music and Ballet. *Career:* currently Dir Iraqi National Symphony Orchestra, Baghdad, also Dir School of Music and Ballet. *Address:* Iraqi National Symphony Orchestra, Baghdad Convention Center, Green Zone, Baghdad, Iraq.

SHARNINA, Ljubov; Russian singer (soprano); b. 1962, Moscow. *Education:* Gnessin Institute, Moscow. *Career:* sang at the Nemirovitsch-Danschenko Theatre Moscow from 1986, notably as Tatiana, Lisa, Iolanta, Nedda, Lisa in La Battaglia di Legnano, Zemfira in Rachmaninov's Aleko and Imogene in Bellini's Pirata; guest engagements as Aida at Birmingham and Manchester, Desdemona at Achen 1990, the Trovatore Leonora at Leipzig 1991 and Maria in Tchaikovsky's Mazeppa at Amsterdam 1991; many concert appearances in Cologne, Vienna, St Petersburg and North America.

SHARP, Norma; singer (soprano); b. 1945, Shawnee, OK, USA; m. Jens Niggemeyer; one s. *Education:* Kansas Univ., USA, Hochschule für Musik, Hamburg, Cologne. *Career:* mem. opera houses of Regensburg, Augsburg, Karlsruhe as lyric soprano 1970–77; freelance opera singer 1978–, regular guest at Berlin, Hamburg, Munich, Frankfurt, Cologne, Düsseldorf, Vienna; further guest appearances at Dresden, Hannover, Stuttgart, Amsterdam, Antwerp, Ghent, Zürich, Basel, Bern, Geneva, Milan, Rome, Naples, Madrid, London, Glasgow, Prague, Budapest; festival appearances at Bayreuth 1977–81, Glyndebourne, Vienna; concerts throughout Europe; Prof. of Voice, Hochschule für Musik, Hanns Eisler, Berlin 1992–. *Recordings:* Tales of Hoffmann, Peer Gynt, Ring of the Nibelung, Tannhäuser. *Address:* Seestr 119, 13353 Berlin, Germany.

SHAULIS, Jane; American singer (mezzo-soprano); b. 1950, New Jersey. *Education:* Philadelphia Academy and Curtis Institute. *Career:* appearances with New York City Opera 1977–90; Metropolitan Opera, 1990–, notably in the premieres of The Ghosts of Versailles by Corigliano and The Voyage by Glass; further New York appearances in Idomeneo, Elektra, Die Zauberflöte, The Ring, I Lombardi, Arabella and Peter Grimes; season 1996–97 as Mozart's Marcellina, Mdme. Larina in Eugene Onegin and Marthe in Faust; Glyndebourne, 1990–, as Nan in New Year by Tippett and Ragonde in Le Comte Ory, 1997; other roles include Amneris at Buffalo, Azucena and Herodias for Kentucky Opera and the Countess in Andrea Chénier at Chicago;

Fricka, Erda and Waltraute in The Ring at Artpark. *Current Management:* c/o Pinnacle Arts: Miller Division, 889 Ninth Avenue, Second Floor, New York, NY 10019, USA. *Telephone:* (212) 397-7911. *Fax:* (212) 397-7920. *E-mail:* jmiller@pinnaclearts.com. *Website:* www.pinnaclearts.com.

SHAVE, Jacqueline; British violinist; b. 1960, England. *Career:* co-founder, Brindisi String Quartet at Aldeburgh 1984; Wigmore Hall debut 1984, with Peter Pears; concerts in a wide repertory throughout the UK, in France, Germany, Spain, Italy and Switzerland; festival engagements at Aldeburgh, Arundel, Bath, Brighton, Huddersfield, Norwich and Warwick; first London performance of Colin Matthews 2nd Quartet 1990; quartet by Mark Anthony Turnage 1992; many BBC recitals; Resident Artist, Univ. of Ulster. *Recordings include:* quartets by Britten, Bridge and Imogen Holst, works by Pierné and Lekeu. *Honours:* prizewinner Banff Int. String Quartet Competition.

SHAVERZASHVILI, George; Georgian composer and classical and jazz pianist; *Head of Jazz Department, Georgian-Anglo International Association for Culture and the Arts;* b. 4 Aug. 1950, Tbilisi; s. of Alexander Shaverzashvili and Aza Kavtaradze; m. Nino Meskhi; one d. *Education:* State Conservatory, Tbilisi. *Career:* debut, piano 1970, composer 1980, Tbilisi; concerts in Tbilisi, Moscow, St Petersburg, Tallinn, Budapest, Bratislava; Prof. of Composition, Tbilisi State Conservatory; Head of Jazz Dept, Georgian-Anglo Int. Asscn for Culture and the Arts 2005–; mem. Georgian Composers' Union. *Compositions:* Quintet for piano and string quartet, three Sonatas for piano, two Concertos for piano and orchestra 1984, 1991, two Concertos for violin 1990, 1995, Sonata for violin, Trio for piano, flute and clarinet 1997, Alegg for string orchestra 1998, two Piano Fantasies 1998, 1999, Mass for chorus and orchestra 1999, Maestoso for piano 2000, Clouds for symphony orchestra 2003, Trio for piano, violin and cello 2004, Piano Suite from five pieces 2005, String Quartet No. 1 2006, No. 2 2010. *Honours:* Laureate of Transcaucasus Int. Piano Competition, Baku 1972, second prize Moscow Int. Competition of Composers 1985. *Address:* D. Agmashenebeli str. 123, 0164 Tbilisi (office); Mosashvili Street 8, Ap 6, 380062 Tbilisi, Georgia (home). *Telephone:* (32) 968678 (office); (32) 954861 (office); (32) 224157 (home). *Fax:* (32) 968678 (office). *E-mail:* geomic@mail.ru (office). *Website:* www.geomic.org.ge (office).

SHAW, Caroline Adelaide, BMus, MMus; American violinist, singer, composer and academic; *Doctoral Fellow in Composition, Princeton University;* b. 1973, North Carolina. *Education:* Rice Univ., Yale Univ. *Career:* musician since early childhood; fmr Thomas J. Watson Fellow; Doctoral Fellow in Composition, Princeton Univ. 2010–; mem. Roomful of Teeth (vocal quartet); also performs as violinist with American Contemporary Music Ensemble; has worked with Trinity Wall Street Choir, Alarm Will Sound, Wordless Music, Signal, The Yehudim, Victoire, Mark Morris Dance Group Ensemble, Opera Cabal, Yale Baroque Ensemble; work has been performed by So Percussion, Brentano String Quartet, Edward T. Cone Performers-in-Residence (Princeton); regular collaboration with artist Jane Philbrick as part of permanent landscape installation 'The Expanded Field' at Massachusetts Museum of Contemporary Art. *Recording:* Roomful of Teeth 2012. *Honours:* Pulitzer Prize for Music (for composition Partita for 8 Voices) 2013. *Address:* Department of Music, Princeton University, Princeton, NJ 08544, USA (office). *Telephone:* (609) 258-4241 (office). *E-mail:* hello@carolineshaw.com (office). *Website:* carolineshaw.com (office).

SHAW, Kenneth; American singer (bass-baritone); b. 1955, Georgia. *Career:* debut in New Orleans 1980, as Morales in Carmen; appearances at New Orleans and Kentucky Operas as Mozart's Count, Germont and Escamillo 1989; Scarpia and Nilakantha in Lakmé; season 1986–87 as Sharpless in Butterfly at New York City Opera; Mefistofele at Three Cities Opera; concert performance of Jenůfa at Carnegie Hall 1988; Saratoga Festival, New York as Marcello; other roles include Jochanaan in Salome; Sarastro, Kentucky Opera 1998. *Recordings include:* Jenůfa.

SHAW, Teresa; singer (mezzo-soprano); b. 1965, England. *Education:* Royal Acad. of Music. *Career:* concert appearances in Debussy's Le Martyre de Saint Sebastien with the London Philharmonic under Kurt Masur; Vivaldi's Gloria with Richard Hickox; Handel's Dixit Dominus and Haydn's Nelson Mass conducted by David Willcocks; The Dream of Gerontius at the York and Ripon Festival 1991; The Apostles and the Glagolitic Mass at Canterbury; operatic roles include Octavian, Third Lady in Die Zauberflöte, Dorabella (Opera Factory) and Female Chorus in Goehr's Triptych; season 1991 included Purcell Room, Conway Hall and Wigmore Hall recitals; premiere production of The Death of Klinghoffer by John Adams in Lyon and Vienna; season 1992 in title role of Oliver's Beauty and the Beast, at Portsmouth; season 1996 as the Composer in Ariadne auf Naxos for Castleward Opera. *Recordings include:* Sorceress in Dido and Aeneas and Brahms Liebesliederwalzer, conducted by John Eliot Gardiner. *Honours:* winner Great Grimsby Int. Singing Competition 1989.

SHCHEDRIN, Rodion Konstantinovich; Russian composer and pianist; b. 16 Dec. 1932, Moscow; s. of Konstantin Mikhailovich Shchedrin and Konkordia Ivanovna Shchedrin; m. Maya Plisetskaya 1958. *Education:* Moscow Conservatoire. *Career:* Chair. RSFSR (now Russian) Union of Composers 1973–90; USSR People's Deputy 1989–91; f. International Maya Plisetskaya and Rodion Shchedrin Foundation 2000; mem. Acad. of Fine Arts, Berlin 1989–, Bavarian Acad. of Fine Arts. *Compositions include:* operas: Not Only Love 1961, Lenin Oratory 1972, Dead Souls 1976, Lolita 1994, The Enchanted Wanderer 2002, Boyarinya Morozova 2006; ballets: Little Humpbacked Horse 1960, Carmen Suite 1967, Anna Karenina 1972, The

Seagull 1980, Lady with a Lapdog 1985; for orchestra: three symphonies 1958, 1965, 2000, 5 concertos for orchestra 1963, 1968, 1988, 1989, 1998; Self-Portrait 1984, Stykhira 1988, Old Russian Circus Music 1989; 6 concertos for piano and orchestra 1954, 1966, 1973, 1992, 1999, 2003, Concerto for cello and orchestra 1994, Concerto for trumpet and orchestra 1995, Two Tangos by Albéniz for orchestra 1996, Concerto dolce for viola and string orchestra 1997; other: Poetoria 1974, Musical Offering for organ and nine soloists 1983, The Sealed Angel (Russian Liturgy) 1988, Nina and the Twelve Months (musical) 1988, Piano Terzetto 1996, Concerto Cantabile (for violin and strings) 1997, Preludium for 9th Symphony by Beethoven 1999, Lolita-serenade 2001, Parabola concertante (for cello and strings) 2001, Dialogue with Shostakovich 2001, The Enchanted Wanderer (concert opera) 2002, Tanja-Katya 2002, My Age, My Wild Beast 2003; works for chamber orchestra, piano, violin, organ and cello and song cycles, music for theatre and cinema. *Honours:* Hon. mem. American Liszt Soc., Rachmaninov Soc., Int. Music Council, Hon. Prof., Moscow Conservatoire, St Petersburg Conservatoire; Lenin Prize, USSR and Russian State Prizes, Russian Union of Composers Prize, Shostakovich Prize, Beethoven Soc. Prize. *Address:* International Maya Plisetskaya and Rodion Shchedrin Foundation, Weihergarten 9, 55116 Mainz (office); Theresienstrasse 23, 80333 Munich, Germany (home); 25/9, Tverskaya St, apt. 31, 103050 Moscow, Russia (home). *Telephone:* (89) 285834 (home); (495) 299-72-39 (home). *Fax:* (89) 282057 (home). *E-mail:* infoplisetskaya.de (office); infoshchedrin.de (office); rshchedrin@yahoo.com. *Website:* www.shchedrin.de (office).

SHEBANOVA, Tatiana; Russian pianist; b. 12 Jan. 1953, Moscow; m. 1986, one s. *Education:* Moscow Conservatory. *Career:* represented Moscow Conservatory, various international competitions and meetings; live concert performances include appearances in Czechoslovakia, Belgium, France, Germany, Switzerland, Italy, Netherlands, Greece, Portugal, Austria and many tours: Japan, Philippines, Yugoslavia, Poland, Spain; repertoire includes some 30 recitals, 30 piano concertos; first interpretation of Bach's 12 choral preludes in Feinberg's transcription, Moscow Conservatory; teacher, Warsaw and Bygdoszoz Academies of Music, Poland. *Recordings:* works by Tchaikovsky, Chopin, Szymanowski, Rachmaninov, Bach, Debussy, Brahms.

SHEERIN, Mairead; singer (soprano); b. 1972, England. *Education:* Birmingham Conservatoire, Royal Coll. of Music with Margaret Kingsley. *Career:* concert engagements in Haydn's Paukenmesse and Harmoniemesse, Elijah, Mozart's Requiem and Coronation Mass, Messiah, the Fauré Requiem and Monteverdi's Vespers; European tour with the St Matthew Passion, as soloist with the English Concert under Trevor Pinnock 2001; London Handel Festival 2001, as Clelia in Muzio Scevola; other roles include Serpetto in La Finta Giardiniera, Ravel's Enfant, Purcell's Sorceress and Yum-Yum in The Mikado. *Honours:* D'Oyly Carte Scholar, London Royal Schools Opera.

SHEFFIELD, Graham, CBE, BMus; British arts administrator; *CEO, West Kowloon Cultural District Authority, Hong Kong. Education:* Univ. of Edin., City Univ., London. *Career:* joined BBC 1976, producer/sr producer for Radio 3, Radio 4, World Service; Music Dir, South Bank Centre, London 1990–95; Artistic Dir, Barbican Centre, London 1995–2010; CEO, West Kowloon Cultural District Authority, Hong Kong 2010–; mem. Royal Philharmonic Soc. (Chair. 2006–); Chair., Int. Soc. for the Performing Arts 2003–06; mem. ACE London Regional Council 2002–04, Int. Artistic Asscn Luminate Festival 2007–. *Honours:* Dr hc; Chevalier, Ordre des Arts et des Lettres 2006. *Address:* West Kowloon Cultural District Authority, 6/F, 98 Caroline Hill Road, Causeway Bay, Hong Kong (office). *Telephone:* 28950127 (office). *Fax:* 28950016 (office). *Website:* www.wkcda.hk (office).

SHEFFIELD, Philip; British singer (tenor); b. 1960, Kenya. *Education:* Univ. of Cambridge, Guildhall School and Royal College of Music, studied with Philip Langridge and Malcolm King. *Career:* season 1989–90 in L'Incoronazione di Popea at Brussels, Hans Jürgen von Bose's 63: Dream Palace at Munich and Capriccio at Glyndebourne; Cavalli's Egisto for the Berlin Kammeroper, Scaramuccio at Antwerp and the Count in Die Tote Stadt in Netherlands; Other Repertoire Encludes Mozart's Ferrando and Tamino, and Agenore in Il Re Pastore; Lensky, Tamino, and Belmonte for Lucerne Opera; Recent Concert performances include Britten's Nocturne with the Berlin Symphony Orchestra in the Philharmonie, and again in Montepulciano, Haydn's L'isola disabitata in the Vienna Konzerthaus with Heinz Holliger, Alexander Goehr's Eve Dreams in Paradise with the BBC Philharmonic, Henze's Kammermusik 1958 in Amsterdam, Schreker's Der Schatzgraeber for the Dutch Radio Philharmonic Orchestra in the Amsterdam Concertgebouw, Stravinsky's Renard with the Ensemble Modern in Frankfurt, Berlin and Vienna, Bach's St John Passion (Evangelist) with the North Netherlands Orchestra, Berio's Sinfonia in Leningrad and Messiah in Antwerp with the Royal Flanders Philharmonic; many appearances throughout the UK, including Monteverdi's Orfeo at the Proms, Poppea in the QEH and Bach's B Minor Mass in Canterbury, all with Roger Norrington; operatic performances include Ferrando in Così fan tutte; Shere Khan and Harry in Baa Baa Black Sheep; Chevalier in Der Ferne Klang; Belmonte in Die Entführung; Tamino in Die Zauberflöte; Lensky in Eugene Onegin; sang Theseus in Goehr's Arianna at Cambridge, 1996; Janáček's Schoolmaster (Vixen) at Birmingham, 1998. *Recordings include:* Berio's Sinfonia with Pierre Boulez; Baa Baa Black Sheep for BBC and Radio, Tippett's Midsummer Marriage for Thames television, 63 Dream Palace for Bayerischer Rundfunk. *Current Management:* Musicmakers International Artists Representation, Tailor House, 63–65 High Street, Whitwell, Hertfordshire SG4 8AH, England. *Telephone:* (1438) 871708. *Fax:* (1438) 871777. *E-mail:* musicmakers@compuserve.com. *Website:* www.operauk.com.

SHEFSIEK, David, MMus; American opera house director; *Managing Director, Vancouver Opera. Education:* Univ. of British Columbia, Carnegie Mellon Univ. *Career:* fmr singer with Des Moines Opera, Sarasota Opera, Ohio Light Opera; previous admin. positions include Dir of External Affairs Pittsburgh Opera; fmr Dir of Resource Development Vancouver Opera, currently Man. Dir; fmr teaching positions at Univ. of British Columbia, Carnegie Mellon Univ.; Exec. Dir Pacific Opera Victoria 2006–. *Address:* Vancouver Opera Offices, 835 Cambie Street, Vancouver, BC V6B 2P4, Canada (office). *Telephone:* (604) 682-2871 (office). *Fax:* (604) 682-3981 (office). *E-mail:* dshefsiek@vancouveropera.ca (office). *Website:* www.vancouveropera.ca (office).

SHELLEY, Howard Gordon, OBE; British concert pianist and conductor; b. 9 March 1950, London; s. of Frederick Gordon Shelley and Anne Taylor; m. Hilary MacNamara 1975; one s. one step-s. *Career:* professional debut at Wigmore Hall, London 1971; soloist with all London and prov. British orchestras; regular tours to USA and Canada, Australia, Hong Kong and Europe; three piano concertos written for him (Cowie, Chapple, Dickinson); conducting debut with London Symphony Orchestra 1985; Assoc. Conductor, London Mozart Players 1990–92, Prin. Guest Conductor 1992–98, Conductor Laureate 2013–; Music Dir and Prin. Conductor, Uppsala Chamber Orchestra, Sweden 2001–03; opera conducting debut 2002; current engagements as conductor or soloist or combined role of conductor/soloist. *Repertoire:* from Mozart through Liszt to Gershwin; first pianist to perform in concert complete solo piano works of Rachmaninov 1983. *Recordings include:* more than 150 recordings, including complete solo piano music of Rachmaninov (nine vols) and complete Rachmaninov song-cycle (three vols), vols of solo piano music by Chopin and Schumann, Hummel solo piano works, the complete Clementi sonatas (six double CDs) and a survey of Mendelssohn's music for piano solo, piano concertos of many British composers including Alwyn, Lennox Berkeley, Carwithen, Dickinson, Ferguson, Leighton, Rubbra, Tippett, Vaughan Williams and Britten, the symphonies of Alice Mary Smith, Gershwin's piano concerto and rhapsodies, piano concertos of Balakirev, Korngold (Left Hand), Liapounov, Hindemith's Four Temperaments, Szymanowski's Symphony No. 4 and Messiaen's Turangalila; conducting from the keyboard, has recorded Mendelssohn's piano concertos and Mozart piano concertos (six vols); Hummel piano concertos (eight vols), Cramer piano concertos with London Mozart Players; with Tasmanian Symphony Orchestra, piano concertos by Moscheles, Herz, Hiller, Kalkbrenner, Pixis, Döhler & Dreyschock, Rosenhain & Taubert, Godard; with Ulster Orchestra, first two vols of classical piano series: Dussek, Steibelt; with Orchestra of Opera North: Schumann, Grieg and Saint-Saëns piano concertos and the complete works for piano and orchestra of Beethoven (two-CD set); conducting the Royal Philharmonic Orchestra has recorded Mozart symphonies 35 and 38 and Schubert symphonies 3 and 5; with Tasmanian Symphony Orchestra: Reinecke symphonies 2 and 3; with Orchestra Svizzera Italiana in Lugano: Haydn's London symphonies and symphonies of Spohr; with Ulster Orchestra: Steibelt: Piano Concertos 2015. *Television includes:* documentary on Ravel with Tasmanian Symphony Orchestra (Australian Broadcasting Co.) featured as presenter, conductor and pianist (Gold Medal for Best Arts Biog., 40th New York Festival Awards); documentary on Rachmaninov by Hessische Rundfunk (Channel 4). *Honours:* Hon. FRCM 1993; Dannreuther Concerto Prize 1971. *Current Management:* Caroline Baird Artists, Stable Cottage, High Street, Culham Oxon., OX14 4NA, England. *Telephone:* (1235) 521771. *E-mail:* caroline@carolinebairdartists.co.uk. *Website:* www.carolinebairdartists.co.uk. *Address:* 38 Cholmeley Park, London, N6 5ER, England.

SHELTON, Lucy, BA, MusM; American singer (soprano). *Education:* Pomona Coll., New England Conservatory of Music. *Career:* Asst Prof. of Voice, Eastman School of Music, Univ. of Rochester 1979; Visiting Prof., Cleveland Inst. of Music 1986; appearances at Chamber Music NW, Bethlehem, Bach, Casals, Tanglewood and Aspen Music Festivals, with all major US orchestras, at BBC Promenade Concerts (London); numerous recitals and guest appearances; premières of Carter, Knussen, Ruders, Grisey, Albert, Schwantner, Smirnov, others; teacher, New England Conservatory, Tanglewood Music Center. *Honours:* Walter W. Naumburg Prize (jtly) 1977.

SHENG, Bright, BMus, MA, DMA; American (b. Chinese) composer, conductor and pianist; *Leonard Bernstein Distinguished Professor of Composition, University of Michigan*; b. 6 Dec. 1955, Shanghai. *Education:* Shanghai Conservatory of Music, Queens Coll., City Univ. of New York, Columbia Univ., studied with Chou-Wen Chung, Mario Davidovsky, George Perle, Hugo Weisgall, Leonard Bernstein. *Career:* Composer-in-Residence, Lyric Opera of Chicago 1989–92, Seattle Symphony Orchestra 1992–95, 2000–01; Assoc. Prof., Univ. of Michigan 1995–97, Prof. of Music 1997–2003, Leonard Bernstein Distinguished Prof. of Composition 2003–; Artistic Advisor, Yo-Yo Ma's Silk Road Project 1998–2003; Composer-in-Residence, New York City Ballet 2006–08; Y.K. Pao Distinguished Visiting Prof., Hong Kong Univ. of Science and Tech.; Artist-in-Residence, Queens Coll., CUNY; comms include Three Songs for Pipa and Cello from Pres. Clinton, honouring Premier Zhu Rongji's visit to USA 1999, Beijing Olympic Games 2008. *Compositions include:* Three Pieces for orchestra 1982, Trio for flute, harp and cello 1982, Five Pieces for oboe and cello 1983, Two String Quartets 1984, Suite for piano 1984, Four Poems From the Tang Dynasty for mezzo and piano 1984, Adagio for chamber orchestra 1987, Three Poems From the Sung Dynasty for soprano and chamber orchestra 1987, H'un (Lacerations): In Memoriam 1966–76 for orchestra 1988, Three Pieces for viola and piano 1987, My Song for piano 1988, Three Chinese Love Songs for soprano, viola and piano 1988, Three Chinhai Folk Songs for chorus 1989, Four Movements for piano trio 1990, The Song of Majnun (opera) 1992, Prelude for orchestra 1994, China Dreams 1995, Postcards 1997, The Silver River (musical, libretto by David Henry Hwang) 1997, Spring Dreams 1998, Flute Moon 1999, Nanking! Nanking!, a threnody for pipa and orchestra 2000, Red Silk Dance, a capriccio for piano and orchestra 2001, Tibetan Swing 2002, Madame Mao (opera) 2003, Phoenix 2004, Shanghai Overture 2007, The Nightingale and the Rose (ballet) 2008. *Honours:* Hon. Prof., Shanghai Conservatory of Music, Wuhan Conservatory of Music, Yunnan Arts Acad.; three Nat. Endowment for the Arts Fellowships, Charles Ives Scholarship Award, American Acad. of Arts and Letters, Michigan Arts Award 2000, MacArthur Foundation Fellowship 2001, American Award in Music, American Acad. of Arts and Letters 2001, ASCAP Achievement Award 2002. *Current Management:* c/o G. Schirmer Inc., 257 Park Avenue South, New York, NY 10010, USA. *Telephone:* (212) 254-2100. *Fax:* (212) 254-2013. *E-mail:* amelia.lukas@schirmer.com. *Website:* www .schirmer.com. *Address:* School of Music, University of Michigan, 1100 Baits Drive, Ann Arbor, MI 48109-2085, USA (office). *Telephone:* (734) 647-9413 (office). *Fax:* (734) 763-5097 (office). *E-mail:* bsheng@umich.edu (office). *Website:* www.brightsheng.com.

SHENG, Zhongguo; Chinese violinist; b. 1941, Chongqing, Sichuan Prov.; s. of Sheng Xue and Zhu Bing; m. Seta Hiroko. *Education:* Moscow Acad. of Music, USSR, studied with Leonid Kogan. *Career:* fmr Instructor, Cen. Acad. of Music; solo performer (First Class), Nat. Symphony Orchestra; performed Bach's concerto for two violins with Yehudi Menuhin 1979; performed 15 concerts in five Australian cities 1980; mem. 7th, 8th, 9th, 10th sessions CPPCC; Founder Sheng Zhongguo Foundation; Chair. Chinese Violin Soc. *Recordings:* numerous albums, including Butterfly Lovers Violin Concerto, Tchaikovsky Concerto, with Louis Frémaux. *Honours:* Hon. Prof., Central Conservatory of Music and over 20 other music colls; prize at Int. Tchaikovsky Violin Competition 1962, 1st Prize for Musical Instruments at Competitive Performance by Troupes and Insts (Ministry of Culture) 1981. *Telephone:* (10) 64917519 (home). *Fax:* (10) 64917519 (home). *E-mail:* ich23248@nifty.com (home).

SHENYANG; Chinese bass baritone; b. 1984, Tianjin. *Education:* Shanghai Conservatory of Music, Zhou Xiaoyan Opera Centre with Prof. Ping Gu, Juilliard School, USA. *Career:* operatic roles include Masetto in Don Giovanni at Verona Philharmonic Theatre and Zhou Xiaoyan International Opera Center 2005, Don Alfonso in Così fan tutte in France and Germany with Berliner Sibelius Orchestra 2006, Colline in La Bohème; concert performances include Eastern-Asia Music Festival in Korea and Beijing Music Festival; fmr mem. Metropolitan Opera's Lindemann Young Artist Development Program; debut with Metropolitan Opera 2009; has appeared with Daniel Barenboim, Antonio Pappano, James Levine and James Conlon. *Recordings include:* Super Bass, Winterreise. *Honours:* First Prize, Don Giovanni Singing Competition, Verona 2005, Orfeo Singing Competition, Verona 2007, Int. Opera Competition, Verona, Cardiff Singer of the World Competition 2007, Alice Tully Vocal Arts Debut Recital Award 2008, Borletti-Buitoni Trust Award 2008. *Current Management:* IMG Artists, 31-33 rue du Temple, Paris 75004, France. *Telephone:* 1-4431-0010 (office). *Fax:* 1-4431-4440 (office). *E-mail:* pwiggins@imgartists.com (office). *Website:* www.imgartists.com (office).

SHEPPARD, Craig; pianist; b. 26 Nov. 1947, Philadelphia, USA. *Education:* Curtis Inst. of Music, Juilliard School of Music. *Career:* Sr Artist-in-Residence, Univ. of Washington, Seattle; teacher, Yehudi Menuhin School, Surrey 1978–88; teacher, Univ. of Lancaster 1979–81; teacher, Guildhall School of Music and Drama 1981–86; concert experience as soloist in most American and all the major British, German and Italian orchestras; television appearances on PBS (USA) and BBC (UK). *Recordings:* Liszt, Rachmaninov, Rossini, Jolivet. *Honours:* Arthur Rubinstein Prize, silver medal Leeds Int. Pianoforte Competition, Dealey Award, Young Musicians' Foundation of Los Angeles first prize.

SHEPPARD, Honor, FRMCM; British singer (soprano); b. 1931, Leeds, Yorks.; d. of George Sheppard and Winifred Sheppard (née Tonkin); m. Robert Elliott; one s. one d. *Education:* Leeds Girls' High School, Royal Manchester Coll. of Music. *Career:* recitalist and oratorio singer; appearances at major British and European festivals; First Soprano with the Deller Consort, specialising in 17th and 18th century music; extensive tours of N and S America, Canada and Europe 1961–; numerous broadcasts; Tutor in Vocal Studies, Royal Northern Coll. of Music 1987–. *Recordings include:* Belinda in Dido and Aeneas, conducted by Alfred Deller; The Fairy Queen, The Indian Queen and King Arthur; Handel's Acis and Galatea. *Honours:* Curtis Gold Medal, Royal Manchester Coll. of Music. *Address:* The Firs, 27 The Firs, Bowdon, Cheshire WA14 2TF, England (home).

SHEPPARD, Kerrie; singer (soprano); b. 1970, Mansfield, England. *Education:* Studied at the Guildhall School and the National Opera Studio. *Career:* appearances as Mimi in La Bohème at the Mananan Festival; premiere production of Birtwistle's The Second Mrs Kong at Glyndebourne; other roles include Micaela, Donna Elvira, Fiordiligi in Così fan tutte; concerts include engagements with the Bangkok Symphony, Exultate Jubilate by Mozart at Chichester, Beethoven's Mass in C at the Fishguard Festival, Carmina

Burana; concerts with the Liverpool Philharmonic and Bournemouth Symphony Orchestras. *Honours:* Kathleen Ferrier Competition Decca Prize 1995.

SHEPPARD SKAERVED, Peter; violinist; *Research Fellow, Royal Academy of Music;* b. 1966, England. *Education:* Royal Acad. with Ralph Holmes, Sidney Griller and Erich Gruenberg, and studied in Boston with Louis Krasner. *Career:* dedicatee of over 200 works for solo violin, including Henze, Matthews and Rochberg; regular appearances in over 30 countries; recordings on Naxos, Metier, Chandos; duo partnership with pianist Aaron Shorr; leader of the Kreutzer Quartet; Principal Lecturer at the Royal Acad. of Music from 1993, currently Research Fellow; Visiting Prof. Blair School of Music, Carl Nielsen Conservatory. *Address:* c/o Royal Academy of Music Strings Faculty, Marylebone Road, London, NW1 5HT, England (office). *Telephone:* (20) 7480-5145 (home). *E-mail:* sheppardskaerved@aol.com (home).

SHERBA, John; American violinist; b. 10 Dec. 1954, Milwaukee, Wis. *Career:* mem. (second violin) Kronos Quartet 1978–; many performances of contemporary music, including premieres of the works of John Cage (30 pieces for string quartet), Pauline Oliveros (The Wheel of Time) and Terry Riley (G-Song, Sunrise of the Planetary Dream Collector and Cadenzas on the Night Plain); formerly quartet-in-residence at Mills Coll, Oakland; from 1982 resident quartet at the Univ. of Southern California; appearances at the Monterey Jazz Festival, Carnegie Recital Hall, San Quentin Prison and London's South Bank; New York debut 1984; noted for cross-over performances of jazz and popular music in arrangement. *Recordings include:* with Kronos: Schnittke: Complete String Quartets 1998, Philip Glass: Dracula (soundtrack) 1999, Caravan 2000, Terry Riley: Requiem for Adam 2001, Steve Reich: Triple Quartet 2001, Nuevo 2002, Mugam Sayagi: Music of Franghiz Ali-Zadeh 2005, You've Stolen My Heart (with Asha Bhosle) 2005, Górecki: String Quartet No.3 (songs are sung) 2007, The Fountain (soundtrack) 2008, Jerry Riley: The Cusp of Magic 2008, Floodplain 2009. *Honours:* with Kronos: Musical America Musicians of the Year 2003, Nat. Acad. of Recording Arts and Sciences President's Merit Award 2005. *Address:* c/o Kronos Quartet, 1242 Ninth Avenue, San Francisco, CA 94122, USA (office). *Telephone:* (415) 731-3533 (office). *Fax:* (415) 664-7590 (office). *E-mail:* janet@kronosarts.com (office). *Website:* kronosquartet.org (office).

SHERE, Charles; American composer and writer on music; b. 20 Aug. 1935, Berkeley, CA; m. Lindsay Remolif Shere. *Education:* Univ. of California at Berkeley, San Francisco Conservatory. *Career:* Music Dir at California radio stations 1964–73; Instructor, Mills Coll., Oakland 1973–84; critic, Oakland Tribune 1972–88; co-founder and publisher, EAR (monthly new-music magazine). *Compositions include:* Fratture for seven instruments 1962, Small Concerto for piano and orchestra 1964, Ces desirs du vent des Gregoriens for tape 1967, Nightmusic for diminished orchestra 1967, Handler of Gravity for organ and optional chimes 1971, Symphony for orchestra 1976, Tongues for poet, chamber orchestra and tape 1978, String Quartet No. 1 1980, The Bride Stripped Bare by Her Bachelors, Even (opera) 1981, 1984, Certain Phenomena of Sound for soprano and violin 1983, Concerto for violin with harp, percussion and small orchestra 1985, Requiem with oboe 1985, Ladies' Voices (chamber opera) 1987, Symphony in three movements 1988, I Like it to be a Play for tenor baritone, bass and string quartet 1989, Sonata: Bachelor Machine for piano 1989, What Happened? (chamber opera, after Gertrude Stein), three Stein Songs for soprano, violin, piano and bass clarinet 1997, Trio for violin, piano and percussion 1997.

SHERIFF, Noam; Israeli composer and conductor; *Music Director and Principal Conductor, New Haifa Symphony Orchestra;* b. 7 Jan. 1935, Tel-Aviv; m.; four c. *Education:* Hebrew Univ., Jerusalem, Berlin-Hochschule für Musik, Salzburg Mozarteum. *Career:* first premiere of work, Festival Prelude, by Israel Philharmonic Orchestra 1957; teacher of composition and conducting, Hebrew Univ. Jerusalem, Tel-Aviv Univ., Hochschule für Musik, Cologne, Universität Mozarteum Salzburg 1963–; Music Dir Israel Symphony Orchestra Rishon Le-Zion 1989–95; Prof. of Composition and Conducting, Rubin Acad. of Music, Tel-Aviv Univ. 1990–; Music Dir Israel Chamber Orchestra 2002–; Music Dir and Prin. Conductor, New Haifa Symphony Orchestra 2004–; Dean of Music Faculty, ONO Academic Coll., Israel. *Compositions:* for orchestra: Festival Prelude 1957, Song of Degrees 1959, Heptraprism 1965, Israel Suite 1967, Chaconne 1968, May Ko Mashma Lan 1976, Essay 1977, Prayers 1983, La Follia Variations 1984, A Vision of David 1986, Akeda 1997; for chamber orchestra: Debka Rafiah 1960, Destination 5 1961, Metamorphoses on a Galliard 1967, Two Epigrams 1968, Sonata 1973, Before the Gate of Gloom 1974, May Ko Mashma Lan 1976, String Quartet 1982, String Quartet No. 2 1996, Gomel Le'ish Hassid 1997; concertos: Song of Songs 1981, Concerto for Violin and Orchestra 1986, Concerto for Cello and Orchestra 1987, Scarlattiana 1994; instrumental: Klavier Sonate 1961, Confession 1966, Arabesque 1966, Piece for Ray 1966, Invention 1967, Butterflies 1973, Simple Tune 1973, Chant 1973, Mirkam for Chen 1982, Partita 1984, Dodecalogue 1984, For Ella 1991, Sonate à trois 1998; vocal music: Ashrei 1961, Little Ayelet 1975, Nocturnes 1982, Mechaye Hamethim 1987, Songs of Degrees 1987, A Sephardic Passion 1992, Psalms of Jerusalem 1995, Genesis 1998, Lullabies and Madrigals 1998. *Honours:* Acum Prize, Emet Prize 2005, Israel Prize 2011. *Address:* PO Box 1678, 40500 Even Yehuda, Israel (home). *E-mail:* info@noamsheriff.com (office). *Website:* www.noamsheriff.com.

SHERMAN, Alexandra; singer (mezzo-soprano); b. 1970, St Petersburg, Russia. *Education:* Victorian College of the Arts, Melbourne, Royal College of Music with Margaret Kingsley and studied in Jerusalem. *Career:* concert engagements include Bach's Passions, Elijah, Messiah, Mozart's Requiem and Vivaldi's Gloria; Lieder eines fahrenden Gesellen in Melbourne and Sydney, Les Nuits d'été and Elgar's Sea Pictures; season 1999 included Prokofiev's Alexander Nevsky with the Queensland Symphony Orchestra, Pergolesi's Stabat Mater, and Russian Songs at St John's Smith Square; season 2000–01, with Messiah in Manchester, B minor Mass in York, Schubert's A flat Mass with the London Mozart Players and Mahler's 2nd Symphony in Melbourne; London Handel Festival 2001, as Guido in Flavio and Irene in Muzio Scevola; European tour with the Academy of Ancient Music in Bach's Magnificat, 2001. *Honours:* Queen's Trust for Young Australians Award, Joan Sutherland Award. *Current Management:* Musicmakers International Artists Representation, Tailor House, 63–65 High Street, Whitwell, Hertfordshire SG4 8AH, England. *Telephone:* (1438) 871708. *Fax:* (1438) 871777. *E-mail:* musicmakers@compuserve.com. *Website:* www.operauk.com.

SHERRATT, Brindley, ARAM, DipRAM; British singer (bass); b. 1965, England; m.; two c. *Education:* RAM. *Career:* debut with WNO, as Leporello; appearances as Wurm in Luisa Miller at Lausanne, Commendatore in Don Giovanni and Basilio in Barbiere for Garsington Opera and the King in Ariodante for Reisopera, The Netherlands; concerts include St Matthew Passion (London Proms 2002), Les Noces by Stravinsky under Boulez in Paris, The Creation with Trevor Pinnock at the Lucerne Festival and Messiah with Robert King in the USA; Bach Cantatas and Haydn Masses with John Eliot Gardiner; season 2002–03 as Melisso in Alcina at the New York Met, Verdi's Ferrando and Gremin in Eugene Onegin for WNO and Britten's Theseus at La Monnaie, Brussels; concerts with Gardiner and Christophe Rousset; Sarasto for ENO, Commendatore and Claudio in Agrippina for Santa Fe Opera; Hobson in Peter Grimes in Salzburg with the Berlin Philharmonic and Sir Simon Rattle; season 2005–06 as Jeronimus in Maskerade at ROH, Rocco in Fidelis at Glyndebourne, Sparafucile at ENO, Commendatore (Don Giovanni) and Claudio (Agrippina) at Santa Fe Opera; Balducci in Benvenuto Cellini at the Salzburg Festival 2007; season 2008–09 included Don Basilio, Pimen and Sparafucile for ENO; Ramfis and Il Re in Aida, Royal Opera 2011; Banco in Macbeth, Bordeaux 2011–12; Narbal in Les troyens and Lodovico in Otello for Royal Opera 2012. *Recordings:* Haydn, 6 Great Masses 2006.

SHERRY, Fred; American cellist and chamber musician; b. 1948, Peekskill, NY; m. Carol Archer. *Education:* Juilliard School. *Career:* worked closely with composers Milton Babbitt, Luciano Berio, Elliott Carter, Aaron Copland, Lukas Foss and Toru Takemitsu and jazz pianist and composer Chick Corea; premiered Mario Davidowsky's Divertimento for Cello and Orchestra with American Composers Orchestra, later performed with Municipal Orchestra of Buenos Aires and San Francisco Symphony; Concerto Five written for him by Charles Wuorinen 1988, premiered at New York City Ballet, and performed again at Carnegie Hall 1989–90; cr. Bach Cantata Sundays series, St. Ann's Church, Brooklyn; Founding mem. Tashi ensemble; performed with Los Angeles Philharmonic, New Japan Philharmonic, Boston Symphony Orchestra, L'Orchestre de la Suisse Romande; festivals include Tanglewood, Chamber Music Northwest, Bridgehampton, Angel Fire, Casals, Spoleto; mem. Chamber Music Soc. of Lincoln Center 1984–, Artistic Dir 1989–92; mem. of faculty, Juilliard School 1992–. *Address:* The Juilliard School, 60 Lincoln Center Plaza, New York, NY 10023-6588, USA (office). *Telephone:* (212) 799-5000 (office). *Website:* www.juilliard.edu (office).

SHEVCHENKO, Oxana; Kazakhstani pianist; b. 1987, Almaty. *Education:* Moscow State Tchaikovsky Conservatory, Royal Coll. of Music, London. *Career:* has performed as soloist and with orchestras in Russia, Ukraine, Italy, Hungary, Germany, Portugal, Lithuania, Latvia, Japan, Panama, Columbia and Syria. *Recording:* Oxana Shevchenko 2010. *Honours:* First Prize, B. Dvarionas Int. Piano Competition and Special Prize for best interpretation of a 20th century concerto, Vilnius, Lithuania 2004, Third Prize and Public Prize, Sendai Int. Music Competition, Japan 2007, Third Prize, Shanghai China Int. Piano Competition, China 2009, Fourth prize, Int. Music Critics Prize, Special Prize for best interpretation of F. Busoni's work, Ferruccio Busoni Int. Piano Competition, Italy 2009, First Prize, Scottish Int. Piano Competition 2010. *Address:* c/o Delphian Records, 34 Wallace Avenue, The Meadows, Wallyford, East Lothian, EH21 8BZ, Scotland (office). *Telephone:* (845) 644-9308 (office). *Fax:* (7092) 165783 (office). *E-mail:* psb@ delphianrecords.co.uk (office). *Website:* www.delphianrecords.co.uk (office).

SHI, Fu; Chinese composer; b. (Guo Shifu), Sept. 1929, Xiangtan, Hu'nan Prov. *Education:* Cen. China Advanced Arts Teachers Training Coll. *Career:* joined PLA 1950; joined CCP 1983. *Publications:* Uygur Folk Songs, Kazakh Folk Songs.

SHICOFF, Neil; American singer (tenor); b. 2 June 1949, Brooklyn, New York; s. of Sidney Shicoff; m. Judith Haddon. *Education:* Juilliard School, studied with Jennie Tourel. *Career:* debut, Kennedy Center Washington in Verdi's Ernani 1975; as Rinuccio in Gianni Schicchi with Metropolitan Opera 1976–; European career 1976–; repertory includes Don José in Carmen, Peter Grimes, Maurizio in Adriana Lecouvreur, Paco in La Vida Breve, Nemorino in L'Elisir d'Amore, Edgardo in Lucia di Lammermoor, Poliuto, Andrea Chenier, Faust, Romeo in Romeo et Juliette, Eléazar in La Juive, Don Ottavio in Don Giovanni, Des Grieux in Manon, Werther, Raoul in Les Huguenots, Hoffmann in Les Contes d'Hoffmann, Rodolfo in La Bohème, Pinkerton in Madama Butterfly, Luigi in Il Tabarro, Cavaradossi in Tosca, Alfred in Die Fledermaus, Sänger in Der Rosenkavalier, Narraboth in Salome, Lenski in Eugene Onegin, Aroldo, Foresto in Attila, Riccardo in Un Ballo in Maschera, Don Carlo,

Ernani, Rodolfo in Luisa Miller, Macduff in Macbeth, Tenore in Messa da Requiem, Duca in Rigoletto, Alfredo in La Traviata, Manrico in Il Trovatore. *Recordings:* Macduff and the Duke of Mantua for Philips; Foresto in Attila, conducted by Muti. *Honours:* Chevalier, Ordre des Arts et des Lettres, Ehrenkreuz fuer Wissenschaft und Kunst 1 Klasse, Austria, Kammersänger and Ehrenmitglied, Vienna State Opera. *Current Management:* Theateragentur Dr Germinal Hilbert, Maximilianstrasse 22, 80539 Munich, Germany. *Telephone:* (89) 29074730. *Fax:* (89) 29074790. *E-mail:* agentur@hilbert.de. *Website:* www.hilbert.de; www.shicoff.com.

SHIFRIN, Kenneth (Ken) Allen, BA, PhD, JP; American lecturer, tenor trombonist, alto trombonist, tenor tubist and bass trumpeter and music publisher; *Artistic Director, Posaune Voce Trio;* b. 25 Aug. 1952, Washington, DC; s. of Joseph Shifrin and Rosalind Shifrin. *Education:* Duke Univ., Univ. of Oxford, UK. *Career:* debuts: US/British premiere of Leopold Mozart Konzert für Posaune 1974, 1996; world premiere of D to A for Ken Shifrin and Digital Analogue by David Maves; Assoc. Prin. Trombone, Israel Philharmonic 1976–77; Co-Solo Trombone, Radio Sinfonie Stuttgart 1977–78; Prin. Trombone, Israel Radio Symphony 1978–92; Prin. Trombone, City of Birmingham Symphony Orchestra 1982–94; Artistic Dir Posaune Voce Trio 1994–; Publr and Dir Virgo Music 1987–; Leopold Mozart, Concerto for Alto Trombone, British premiere 1996, Czech premiere 1997; Leopold Mozart, Agnus Dei, British premiere 1996; Wolfgang Amadeus Mozart, Jener Donnerworte Kraft 1996; Elizabeth Raum, Three Jazz Moods, British and USA premieres 1997; Word, St Thomas Sonata, premiere 1999; Guest Artist, Int. Janacek Music Festival, Dvořák Int. Music Festival, Int. Smetana Music Festival, Malta Int. Arts Festival; masterclasses presented including Prague, Vienna, Manchester, Kiev, Bratislava, Univ. of Texas, Univ. of Illinois, Duke Univ. and Washington, DC; British Acad. Research Board Fellowship 1998–2004; Univ. of Sciences of the Czech Repub. Scholar Exchange Fellowship 1998–2004. *Honours:* James Ingham Halstead Scholar, Univ. of Oxford, Oxford Univ. Press Music and Letters Award. *Address:* 47 Colebank Road, Hall Green, Birmingham, B28 8EZ, England (home). *Telephone:* (121) 778-5569 (office). *Fax:* (121) 778-5569 (office). *E-mail:* kvalita@aol.com (home). *Website:* www .posaunevocetrio.com.

SHIH, Patricia; violinist; b. 1971, Canada. *Education:* studied in Vancouver, Indiana Univ. with Josef Gingold. *Career:* season 1987 with recitals in Warsaw and at the Carnegie Hall, New York; many appearances with leading orchestras in the USA and Europe; Prokofiev's 2nd Concerto with the Toronto Symphony Orchestra 1994. *Honours:* prizewinner Seattle Young Artists Festival 1985, Wieniawski Competition, Warsaw 1986.

SHILAKADZE, Shavleg; Georgian composer and conductor; *Professor, Tbilisi State Conservatoire;* b. 21 Feb. 1940, Tbilisi; m. Liana Shilakadze 1964; two s. one d. *Education:* Z. Paliashvili Special Music School, V. Saradjishvili Conservatoire, Tbilisi, Rimsky-Korsakov State Conservatoire, Leningrad. *Career:* debut in composition, Tbilisi 1959, in conducting, Tbilisi 1967; Founder Ensemble Camerata Tbilisi; concerts at Tbilisi, Moscow, Leningrad, Kiev, Minsk, Tallinn, Vilnius and elsewhere 1976–85; Founder and Artistic Dir Concertino Tbilisi chamber orchestra 1988–; concerts at Tbilisi, Germany 1990, 1991, 1993, 1995, 1996, 1997, Spain 1993, Switzerland 1996, 1997, London and Edinburgh, UK 1998; Prof., Tbilisi State Conservatoire; mem. Union of Georgian Composers. *Compositions include:* Sonata for piano, Sonata for viola and piano, Sonata-Ballade for violin solo, Sonata for cello solo, Epitaph chamber symphony, From Ancient Georgian Poetry cantata, To David Agmashenebeli cantata, To Saint Nina cantata, Vocal Cycle for soprano and piano, Vocal Cycle for bass and piano, Concerto for oboe and strings, Concerto brevis for seven percussionists, Concerto for viola and orchestra, Concerto for orchestra, five symphonies, Psalms Symphony for baritone, mixed chorus and symphony orchestra, Concerto for oboe and chamber orchestra, Pages of Love (cantata), Concerto stretta for bassoon and chamber orchestra, Concerto giocoso for three trumpets and two percussionists, Concerto for violin, Double concerto for violin and viola, Canticle (string quartet), Capriccio (string quartet), Lamentatione (string quartet), Prayer (cantata), Penitential Psalms (oratorio). *Recordings:* R. Gabitchvadze's Chamber Symphony No. 4 1980, G. Japaridze's Metamorphoses chamber symphony 1983, Sh Shilakadze's Epitaph (Camerata Tbilisi, conductor Sh Shilakadze) 1983. *Publications:* contrib. of articles about Tbilisi's musical life 1982, the unity of creative forces 1984. *Honours:* Georgian Order of Honour 2000; Nat. Prize 2012. *E-mail:* concertino@mail.com (home). *Website:* www .shavleg-shilakadze.ge.

SHILLITO, Helen Claire, BMus; British horn player; b. 18 Oct. 1975, Newcastle-upon-Tyne. *Education:* Royal College of Music, London, with Julian Baker, Tim Brown and Susan Dent; Franz Liszt Acad., Budapest, with Adam Friedrich; CESMD, Saintes, France, with Claude Maury and Martin Murner (natural horn). *Career:* co-founder of Aurora Ensemble (wind quintet) 1995, giving wind quintet performances at ORF studios, Vienna, Purcell Room (London), English Music and Cheltenham International Festivals, South Bank Rimsky-Korsakov Festival and International Akademie Prag-Wien-Budapest; co-founded Ensemble Piros (wind and strings) 2002, Alla Caccia (horn, violin and piano trio) 2003; joined Broadwood Ensemble (wind and piano) 2002; launched outreach education scheme Sounds Exciting 2000; has played with The Acad. of St Martin-in-the-Fields, BBC Symphony Orchestra, Northern Sinfonia, City of London Sinfonia, Scottish Symphony Orchestra, Scottish Ballet, Welsh Nat. Opera and (on the natural horn) with Europa Galante and Orchestre Champs-Elysées; mem. (with Aurora Ensemble) Live

Music Now!. *Radio:* with Aurora Ensemble: BBC Radio 3 Young Artists' Forum Broadcasts 1999. *Honours:* Prague-Vienna-Budapest Internationale Sommerakademie scholarship winner (with Aurora Ensemble) 1997, winner, Outstanding Musicians Series (with Aurora Ensemble) at St Martin-in-the-Fields 1998 and 1999, winners, Manchester Mid-day Concert Series 2003, winners, Park Lane Group Series 2004. *Address:* 40 Westgate Road, Faversham, Kent ME13 8HF, England (office); 47 Salisbury Gardens, Jesmond, Newcastle-upon-Tyne NE2 1HP, England (home). *Telephone:* (7887) 835827 (office); (1795) 532432 (home). *E-mail:* helen@auroraensemble .com (office). *Website:* www.auroraensemble.com (office).

SHIMADA, Toshiyuki, MusB; Japanese/American conductor; *Music Director, Yale Symphony Orchestra;* b. 23 Dec. 1951, Tokyo; s. of Ron Shimada and Matsue Shimada; m. Eva Virsik; one s. *Education:* Univ. of Southern California, California State Univ., Northridge, Univ. of Vienna for Music and Performing Art. *Career:* moved to USA aged 15; Assoc. Conductor, Houston Symphony Orchestra 1981–85; Music Dir Portland Symphony Orchestra, Portland, Maine 1986–2006; Music Dir Yale Symphony Orchestra, Yale Univ. 2005–, Assoc. Prof. of Conducting, Yale School of Music and Yale Univ. Dept of Music; Music Dir E Connecticut Symphony Orchestra, New London and Orchestra of the S Finger Lakes, Corning, NY; fmr Music Dir Nassau Symphony Orchestra, New York, Cambiata Soloists, Houston, Shepherd School Symphony Orchestra, Rice Univ., Young Musicians' Foundation Debut Orchestra, Los Angeles; fmr Artistic Adviser Tulare Country Symphony Orchestra; frequent Guest Conductor with int. orchestras including Lithuanian State Symphony Orchestra, Moravian Philharmonic Orchestra, Karlovy Vary Symphony Orchestra, Prague Chamber Orchestra, Slovak Philharmonic, Tonkünstler Orchestra Nieder-Österreich, Vienna, Orchestre Nat. de Lille, France, Royal Scottish Nat. Orchestra, Orquesta Filhamonico de Jalisco, Guadalajara, Mexico; has also guest conducted the Houston Symphony, Honolulu Symphony Orchestra, Chautauqua Symphony Orchestra, San Jose Symphony Orchestra, Boston Pops Orchestra, Pacific Symphony, Edmonton Symphony Orchestra and many other US and Canadian orchestras. *Recordings include:* 15 CDs including Toshiyuki Shimada Conducts 2007. *Honours:* Hon. DFA (Maine Coll. of Arts) 2006. *Current Management:* William Reinert Associates, Inc., 163 Amsterdam Avenue, #334, New York, NY 10023, USA. *Telephone:* (212) 799-5365 (office). *E-mail:* tshimada@toshiyukishimada.com (office). *Website:* www.toshiyukishimada.com (office).

SHIMELL, William; British singer (baritone) and actor; b. 23 Sept. 1952, Ilford, Essex, England; s. of W. Shimell and F.E. Shimell; m. Olga Slavka 1996. *Education:* Westminster Abbey Choir School, St Edward's School, Oxford, Guildhall School of Music and Drama, Nat. Opera Studio. *Career:* debut with Kent Opera in Rigoletto 1980; known for interpretations of Don Giovanni, Count Almaviva (Marriage of Figaro) and Don Alfonso (Così fan Tutte), has sung in opera houses world-wide including La Scala, Milan, Metropolitan Opera House, New York, Paris Opéra, Rome Opera, Vienna Staatsoper, Covent Garden, London; Assoc. Guildhall School of Music and Drama. *Films:* Certified Copy 2010, Amour 2012. *Television:* as himself: Mozart – His Life with Music (series) 1985, The Fabulous Picture Show (series) 2010, Cinema 3 (series) 2010; actor: L'enfance du Christ (film) 1986, Hercules (film) 2005, The Rake's Progress (film) 2008.

SHIMIZU, Takashi; Japanese violinist; b. 13 Jan. 1953, Yokosuka; m. Harue Shimizu 1973; one s. *Education:* Yokosuka High School, Univ. of Southern California, USA and Guildhall School of Music, London, England. *Career:* debut in Tokyo; performed with the Royal Philharmonic Orchestra, BBC Philharmonic Orchestra, London Mozart Players, City of Birmingham Symphony Orchestra, The Hague Philharmonic; many television appearances in France, Belgium, Spain, USSR and Japan. *Honours:* bronze medal Queen Elisabeth Competition, second prize and Beethoven Sonata Prize Carl Flesch Competition, first prize Granada Int. Competition. *Address:* 18 Alyth Garden, London, NW11, England.

SHIN, Youngok; singer (soprano); b. 1961, Republic of Korea. *Education:* Juilliard School, New York. *Career:* debut at Spoleto Festival, USA, 1989 as Mozart's Susanna; Metropolitan Opera, New York, from 1990 as Gilda in Rigoletto and roles in Rossini's Semiramide and Bellini's Bianca e Fernando at Catania, 1991; Oscar in Ballo in Maschera at Paris Opéra Bastille, 1993; Gilda at Covent Garden, 1994; season 1995–96, as Lucia di Lammermoor at Toronto and Elvira in I Puritani at Turin; other roles include Leila in Les Pêcheurs de Perles. *Recordings:* Bianca e Fernando, Semiramide, Ave Maria.

SHINALL, Vern; American singer (baritone); b. 22 June 1936, St Louis. *Education:* Indiana University, Bloomington with Charles Kullman. *Career:* debut with Kansas City Opera, as Scarpia in Tosca, 1964; Appearances at opera houses in Philadelphia, Boston, Houston, New Orleans and St Paul; Main career at New York City Opera; Roles have included Escamillo, Pizarro in Fidelio, Rigoletto, Amonasro, Count Luna, Mephistopheles in Faust and Barnaba in La Gioconda; Wagner's Dutchman, Telramund and Wotan, Don Giovanni and the baritone roles in Les Contes d'Hoffmann; Modern repertory includes John Proctor in The Crucible by Robert Ward and Olin Blitch in Susannah by Carlisle Floyd; Many concert engagements.

SHINOZAKI, Yasuo; Japanese conductor; *Artistic Director and Chief Conductor, Kymi Sinfonietta;* b. 19 Feb. 1968, Kyoto; m. Asuka Shinozaki 1998; one s. one d. *Education:* Toho-Gakuen Music Univ. and Music Grad. School, Vienna Nat. Music Univ., Austria, Accad. Musicale Chigiana, Italy, Tanglewood, USA. *Career:* debut with Bolzano and Trento Orchestra, in Trento, Italy 1993; opera debut, Tokyo 1993; conducted Bolzano and Trento Orchestra 1993, Szeged Symphony Orchestra 1996, Tokyo City Philharmonic Orchestra 1998, Shinsei (Japan) Symphony Orchestra 1999, Hong Kong Philharmonic Orchestra 2008, Helsinki Philharmonic 2008, Johannesburg Philharmonic 2008, KwaZulu-Natal Philharmonic 2008, London Philharmonic 2009; Artistic Dir and Chief Conductor Kymi Sinfonietta 2007–. *Honours:* Second Prize, Antonio Pedrotti Int. Conducting Competition 1993, Jt Second Prize, Second Int. Sibelius Conducting Competition 2000. *Current Management:* c/o Hazard Chase, 25 City Road, Cambridge, Cambs., CB1 1DP, England. *Telephone:* (1223) 312400. *Fax:* (1223) 460827. *E-mail:* info@ hazardchase.co.uk. *Website:* www.hazardchase.co.uk. *E-mail:* yasuo@ yasuoshinozaki.com. *Website:* www.yasuoshinozaki.com.

SHIRAI, Mitsuko; singer (contralto); b. 1952, Japan. *Education:* studied in Stuttgart. *Career:* appearances in Europe, Israel, Japan and USA; recitals with piano accompanist Hartmut Holl and concerts with the Berlin Philharmonic, New Japan Philharmonic, Atlanta Symphony, Nouvel Orchestre Philharmonique de Paris and the Vienna Symphony; Conductors include Chailly, Inbal, Ahronovitch, Ferencic and Sawallisch; Repertoire includes Mahler Symphony No. 8, Berlioz Les Nuits d'Été, Berg 7 Early Songs, Hindemith Das Marienleben, Complete vocal works of Webern, Schubert Winterreise and Lieder by Brahms, Wolf and Schumann; Concert performances of Mozart's Lucio Silla, Wagner's Das Liebesverbot and Ariane et Barbe-Bleue; Opened Suntory Hall Tokyo with Alexander Nevsky by Prokofiev; Stage debut Frankfurt 1987, as Despina in Così fan tutte; Masterclasses with Hartmut Holl at the Savonlinna Festival, Schleswig-Holstein Festival, Aldeburgh Festival, in Switzerland and USA and at Isaac Stern's Music Centre in Jerusalem. *Recordings:* Mozart, Schumann and Brahms Lieder (Capriccio); Bach, Mozart and Spohr Lieder; Sacred music by Mozart (Philips); Frauenliebe und-leben by Schumann; Lieder by Mendelssohn and Schumann. *Honours:* winner of competitions in Vienna, 's-Hertogenbosch, Athens and Munich; winner Robert Schumann Prize, Zwickau, 1982. *Current Management:* c/o Janice Mayer and Associates, 250 West 57th Street, Suite 2214, New York, NY 10107, USA. *Telephone:* (212) 541-5511. *Fax:* (212) 541-7303. *E-mail:* jmayer@janicemayer.com. *Website:* www.janicemayer.com.

SHIRASAKA-TERATINI, Chieko; singer (mezzo-soprano); b. 1956, Tokyo, Japan. *Education:* studied in Tokyo, Hamburg Musikhochschule. *Career:* many opera appearances from 1981, notably at Bremerhaven and Bonn; guest engagements at Hamburg, Innsbruck, Bremen and Montpellier; roles have included Octavian, Hansel, Siebel in Faust, Mozart's Annio, Suzuki in Madama Butterfly, Verdi's Eboli, Preziosilla and Fenena in Nabucco; Ottavia in L'Incoronazione di Poppea, and Rossini's Rosina and Isabella; many concert and rectial appearances, notably in USA, Japan, Poland and The Netherlands. *Honours:* prizewinner 's-Hertogenbosch Competition 1980.

SHIRLEY, George Irving, BEd; American singer (tenor) and academic; *Joseph Edgar Maddy Distinguished University Professor Emeritus of Music (Voice), School of Music, Theatre and Dance, University of Michigan;* b. 18 April 1934, Indianapolis, Ind.; s. of Irving E. Shirley and Daisy Shirley (née Bell); m. Gladys Lee Ishop 1956; one s. one d. *Education:* Wayne State Univ. *Career:* New York premiere with Amato Opera in Verdi's Aroldo 1961; debuts with Metropolitan Opera, New York Opera, Festival of Two Worlds (Spoleto, Italy), Santa Fé Opera 1961, Teatro Colón, Buenos Aires 1965, La Scala, Milan 1965, Glyndebourne Festival 1966, Royal Opera, Covent Garden, Scottish Opera 1967, Vienna Festival 1972, San Francisco Opera 1977, Chicago Lyric Opera 1977, Théâtre Municipal d'Angers 1979, Edin. Festival 1979, Nat. Opera Ebony, Philadelphia 1980, Spoleto Festival, Charleston, SC 1980, Tulsa Opera, Okla 1980, Ottawa Festival 1981, Deutsche Oper 1983, Guelph Spring Festival 1983, Bregenz Festival, Austria 1998; Glimmerglass Opera, Cooperstown, NY 1999, Eugene Opera, Ore. 2009; Prof. of Voice, Univ. of Maryland 1980–87; Prof. of Music, Univ. of Michigan School of Music, Theatre & Dance 1987–2007, Joseph Edgar Maddy Distinguished Univ. Prof. of Music (Voice) 1992–2007, Prof. Emer. 2007–, also Dir Emer., Vocal Arts Div.; mem. Bd Santa Fe Opera, Sullivan Foundation, Voice Foundation; mem. Univ. of Michigan Soc. of Fellows 1989, American Acad. of Teachers of Singing 1990. *Honours:* Hon. HDH (Wilberforce Univ.) 1967, Hon. LLD (Montclair State Coll.) 1984, Hon. DFA (Lake Forest Coll.) 1988, Hon. DHumLitt (Northern Iowa) 1997, (Wayne State Univ.) 2013; numerous awards including Nat. Arts Club Award 1960, Concorso di Musica e Danza (Vercelli, Italy) 1960, Grammy Award (for recording of Mozart's Così fan tutte) 1968, Distinguished Scholar-Teacher Award, Univ. of Md 1985–86, Univ. of Mich. School of Music Alumni Asscn Distinguished Achievement Award 2005, Opera Noire Grazioso Award, New York 2005, Dr. Charles H. Wright Legacy Award for Excellence in Fine Arts, Detroit 2006, Nat. Asscn for Study and Performance of African American Music Trail Blazer Award 2007, Lifetime Achievement Award, Nat. Asscn of Teachers of Singing 2014. *Address:* University of Michigan School of Music, Ann Arbor, MI 48109-2085, USA (office). *E-mail:* gis@umich.edu (office). *Website:* www.music.umich.edu (office).

SHKOSA, Enkelejda; Albanian singer (mezzo-soprano); b. 29 Sept. 1969, Tirana. *Education:* State Conservatory, Acad. of Fine Arts, Tirana and Conservatorio di Music Giuseppe Verdi, Milan, Italy. *Career:* made int. debut in Moise et Pharaon at Rossini Opera Festival, Pesaro; other roles in L'occasione fa il ladro, Otello, Roberto Devereux, Maria Stuarda, Dom Sébastien, Carmen, Madama Butterfly, Il Barbiere di Siviglia, Rigoletto, Così fan Tutte, La Damnation de Faust, La Cenenterola, Suor Angelica, L'Italiana in Algheri, I Capuleti e I Montecchi, Werther, La Favorita, Les

Contes d'Hoffman; many appearances at La Scala, Milan, Naples, Turin, Barbican Centre London, Strasbourg Cathedral, Opéra Bastille, Paris, Stockholm, Amsterdam, Bologna, Naples, Monte Carlo and Brussels. *Honours:* winner Leyla Gencer Competition, Istanbul 1995. *Current Management:* c/o Opera Rara 134-146 Curtain Road, EC2A 3AR London, England. *Telephone:* (20) 7613-2858. *Fax:* (20) 7613-2858. *E-mail:* info@opera-rara .com. *Website:* www.opera-rara.com.

SHMITOV, Alexei; Russian organist and pianist; b. 1957, Moscow. *Education:* Moscow Conservatoire with Roisman and Nikolayeva. *Career:* many concerts in Russia as organist and pianist; piano concertos by Bach in Vilnius, Lithuania, and the Sonatas for violin and harpsichord and violin with Viktor Pikaisen; organ recitals in Lithuania, Estonia, Latvia; Bach Festival in Berlin; recitals with the tenor Alexei Martynov, in music by Bach, Handel, Scheidt, Schütz, Mendelssohn, Schumann and Verdi; recitals at the Prokofiev Centenary Festival in Scotland 1991; organ repertoire includes works by Bach, Widor, Taneyev, Liszt and Shostakovich. *Honours:* second prize Dom Zu Speyer Organ Competition, Germany.

SHOKOV, Vladimir; cellist; b. 1950, Crimea, Russia. *Career:* co-founder, Rachmaninov Quartet 1974, under auspices of the Sochi State Philharmonic Soc., Crimea; many concerts in Russia, from season 1975–76 tours to Switzerland, Austria, Bulgaria, Norway, Germany; participation in the 1976 Shostakovich Chamber Music Festival at Vilnius, and in festivals in Moscow and St Petersburg; repertoire has included works by Haydn, Mozart, Beethoven, Bartók, Brahms, Schnittke, Shostakovich, Tchaikovsky and Meyerovich. *Honours:* prizewinner All-Union Borodin String Quartet Competition.

SHORE, Andrew, BA; British singer (baritone); b. 30 Sept. 1952, Oldham, England; m. Fiona Macdonald 1976; three d. *Education:* University of Bristol, Royal Northern College of Music, London Opera Centre. *Career:* as stage manager and singer, Opera For All, 1977–79; debut as Antonio in Marriage of Figaro, Kent Opera, 1981; English National Opera debut, 1988, as Don Alfonso in Così fan tutte; Covent Garden debut, 1992, as Trombonok in Rossini's Il viaggio a Reims; Paris Opéra debut, 1995, as Sacristan in Tosca; US debut, 1996, as Dulcamara in L'Elisir d'amore, at San Diego; Principal roles with all British opera companies and in Paris, Lyon, Hamburg, Barcelona, Amsterdam, Copenhagen, Brussels, Vancouver, Ottawa, Tel-Aviv; Particularly known for Falstaff, Don Pasquale, Dulcamara, Don Alfonso, Papageno, Bartolo, Gianni Schicchi, and in the serious repertoire for Wozzeck, King Priam and Šiškov in Janáček's House of the Dead; Gianni Schicchi for ENO, 1998; Season 2000–01 as Janáček's Kolenaty at Hamburg, Mozart's Bartolo at Glyndebourne and Tippett's King Priam for ENO; Engaged as Hans Sachs for Opéra de Nantes, 2003. *Recordings:* Bartolo in Barber of Seville; Sacristan in Tosca; Benoit and Alcindoro in La Bohème; Dulcamara in L'Elisir d'amore; Title role in Don Pasquale; Video recording of Kolenaty in Janáček's Makropulos Case. *Current Management:* Ingpen & Williams Ltd, 7 St George's Court, 131 Putney Bridge Road, London, SW15 2PA, England.

SHORE, Clare, BA, MMus, DMA; American composer; b. 18 Dec. 1954, Winston-Salem, NC. *Education:* Wake Forest Univ. with Annette LeSiege, Univ. of Colorado with Charles Eakin and Cecil Effinger, Juilliard School of Music with David Diamond, Vincent Persichetti and Roger Sessions. *Career:* teacher, Fordham Univ., Manhattan School of Music, Univ. of Virginia, George Mason Univ. 1981–; numerous commissions; works performed in Carnegie Recital Hall, Alice Tully Hall, Lincoln Center, Merkin Concert Hall, Spoleto Festival, Charleston, The Barns of Wolf Trap, Nat. Gallery of Art, throughout USA and abroad. *Recordings include:* July Remembrances, Nightwatch, Oatlands Sketches. *Honours:* Contemporary Records Soc. grant 1988. *Address:* 12329 Cliveden Street, Herndon, VA 22070, USA.

SHORE, Howard; Canadian film score composer; b. 18 Oct. 1946, Toronto, Ont. *Education:* Berklee Coll. of Music, Boston. *Career:* f. rock band Lighthouse; Musical Dir Saturday Night Live TV comedy show 1970s; began composing film music 1978; has collaborated on films by David Cronenberg, Peter Jackson; mem. ASCAP. *Film scores include:* I Miss You, Hugs and Kisses 1978, The Brood 1979, Scanners 1980, Videodrome 1983, Nothing Lasts Forever 1984, After Hours 1985, Fire with Fire 1986, The Fly 1986, Heaven 1987, Nadine 1987, Dead Ringers 1988, Big 1988, Signs of Life 1989, She-Devil 1989, The Local Stigmatic 1989, An Innocent Man 1989, Made in Milan 1990, The Lemon Sisters 1990, Naked Lunch 1991, The Silence of the Lambs 1991, A Kiss Before Dying 1991, Prelude to a Kiss 1992, Single White Female 1992, Philadelphia 1993, Mrs Doubtfire 1993, Guilty As Sin 1993, Sliver 1993, M. Butterfly 1993, Nobody's Fool 1994, The Client 1994, Ed Wood (Los Angeles Film Critics' Asscn Award) 1994, Se7en 1995, Moonlight and Valentino 1995, White Man's Burden 1995, Before and After 1996, The Truth About Cats and Dogs 1996, Striptease 1996, Looking For Richard 1996, Crash 1996, That Thing You Do! 1996, The Game 1997, Cop Land 1997, Gloria 1999, Existenz 1999, Dogma 1999, Analyze This 1999, The Yards 2000, High Fidelity 2000, Esther Kahn 2000, The Cell 2000, Camera 2000, The Score 2001, The Lord of the Rings: The Fellowship of the Ring (Acad. Award for Best Original Score 2002, Grammy Award for Best Soundtrack) 2001, Spider 2002, Panic Room 2002, The Lord of the Rings: The Two Towers 2002, Gangs of New York 2002, The Lord of the Rings: The Return of the King (Golden Globe Award for Best Original Score 2004, Acad. Award for Best Song, for 'Into the West' 2004) 2003, The Aviator (Golden Globe Award for Best Original Score 2005) 2004, The Departed 2006, The Last Mimzy 2007, Eastern Promises 2007, Doubt 2008,

The Betrayal 2008, The Twilight Saga: Eclipse 2010, Edge of Darkness 2010, A Dangerous Method 2011, Hugo (Frederick Loewe Award) 2011, The Spider 2011, The Rise of Theodore Roosevelt 2011, The Hobbit: An Unexpected Journey 2012, Cosmopolis 2012. *Opera:* The Fly. *Honours:* Officier, Ordre des Arts et des Lettres; Dr hc (Berklee Coll. of Music), Hon. DLitt (York Univ., Toronto) 2007; Career Achievement for Music Composition Award, Nat. Bd of Review of Motion Pictures, ASCAP Lifetime Achievement Award 2004, Max Steiner Film Music Achievement Award, City of Vienna 2010. *Current Management:* Gorfaine/Schwartz Agency Inc, 4111 West Alameda Avenue, Suite 509, Burbank, CA 91505-4161, USA. *Telephone:* (818) 260-8500 (office). *Website:* www.gsamusic.com (office); www.howardshore.com.

SHOSTAKOVICH, Maksim Dmitriyevich; American (b. Russian) conductor and pianist; b. 10 May 1938, Leningrad (now St Petersburg); s. of the late Dmitriy Shostakovich and of Nina Varzar; m. 1st; one s.; m. 2nd Marina Tisie 1989; one s. one d. *Education:* Cen. Music School, Moscow Conservatory, studied conducting under Rabinovich, Gauk, Rozhdestvensky. *Career:* Asst Conductor, Moscow Symphony Orchestra; Conductor, State Academic Symphony Orchestra; piano debut age 19 in father's Second Piano Concerto; Prin. Conductor and Artistic Dir USSR Radio and TV Symphony Orchestra; requested and granted political asylum in USA while on tour with USSR Radio and TV Symphony Orchestra, Nuremberg 1981; conducted Nat. Symphony Orchestra, on Capitol steps, Washington, DC, USA 1981; Prin. Guest Conductor Hong Kong Philharmonic 1982; Music Dir New Orleans Symphony Orchestra 1986–91; toured Western Europe with USSR Radio and TV Symphony Orchestra, Japan, USA 1971–81; has conducted all maj. N American orchestras and many in Europe, Asia, S America; conducted premiere of father's 15th Symphony and recorded virtually all father's symphonies in USSR; has performed with leading soloists, including Emil Gilels, Oistrakh, Rostropovich. *Honours:* Hon. Music Dir Louisiana Philharmonic Orchestra 1993–94. *Current Management:* Judie Janowski, Columbia Artists Management LLC, 5 Columbus Circle at 1790 Broadway, New York, NY 10019-1412, USA. *E-mail:* info@cami.com. *Address:* PO Box 273, Jordanville, NY 13361, USA.

SHRAPNEL, Hugh Michael, BMus; British composer; b. 18 Feb. 1947, Birmingham, England; m. Ruth Shrapnel; one d. *Education:* Eltham Coll., Royal Acad. of Music and Goldsmiths Coll. *Career:* Scratch Orchestra 1969–72; Promenade Theatre Orchestra 1970–72; People's Liberation Music 1975–79; Co-founder Redlands Consort 1992, Vermilion 2002; compositions widely performed in London, provinces and abroad, including Wigmore Hall, Purcell Room, San Diego, Conway Hall, Univ. of Redlands, Texas, Leighton House, London, Slaughterhouse Gallery; Composer-in-Residence, Music Works, London 1993–96; mem. British Acad. of Songwriters, Composers and Authors, Performing Right Soc. *Compositions include:* Cantation I and II 1970, Four Toy Pianos 1971, Variation for Viola 1984, The Window of Today 1987–2008, Autumn Pieces 1989, South of the River 1993–95, Cat Preludes 1994, West Pier 1997, Woodlands Collection 2000, Not in Our Name 2003, Beelzebub's Barrel Organ 2003–05, Coronal 2004, Winter Songs 2010, String Trio 2011, Tomorrow's Seed 2011, Hilly Fields 2013. *Honours:* Lady Holland Prize for composition 1969. *Address:* 91A Ermine Road, Lewisham, London, SE13 7JJ, England (home). *Telephone:* (20) 8690-2994 (home); 7968-327413 (mobile) (home). *E-mail:* hugh@shrapnel39.freeserve.co.uk (home). *Website:* hughshrapnel.com.

SHTODA, Daniil; Russian singer (tenor); b. 1977, St Petersburg. *Education:* Glinka Capella, St Petersburg Conservatoire. *Career:* debut, sang Fyodor in Boris Godunov at the Mariinksy Theatre while a child; Young Artists' Acad. of the Mariinsky Theatre from 1998, soloist with Mariinsky Opera Co. 2007–; repertoire includes Lensky in Eugene Onegin, Elvino in La Sonnambula, The Indian Guest in Sadko by Rimsky-Korsakov, and Tsar Berendai in The Snow Maiden (concert) with the Kirov Opera at Covent Garden 2000; Wigmore Hall recital 2002; London Proms 2002. *Honours:* winner Mario Lanza Vocal Competition, third Rimsky-Korsakov and 11th Tchaikovsky Competitions. *Address:* Mariinsky Opera Company, Mariinsky Theatre, 1 Theatre Square, St Petersburg, 190000, Russia (office). *Telephone:* (812) 3264141 (office). *Website:* www.mariinsky.ru/en (office).

SHUI, Lan; Chinese conductor; *Music Director, Singapore Symphony Orchestra;* b. Hangzhou. *Education:* Shanghai Conservatory, Beijing Cen. Conservatory, Boston Univ., USA. *Career:* made professional debut with Beijing Central Philharmonic Orchestra 1986; Conducting Affiliate, Baltimore Symphony Orchestra 1992–94; Assoc. Conductor, Detroit Symphony Orchestra 1994–97; Music Dir Singapore Symphony Orchestra 1997–; Chief Conductor, Copenhagen Philharmonic Orchestra; guest conductor with Los Angeles Philharmonic, New York Philharmonic, Cleveland Orchestra, Bamberg Symphony, Deutsche Radio Philharmonie, Frankfurt Radio Symphony, Stuttgart Radio Symphony, Calgary Philharmonic, Detroit Symphony Orchestra, Houston Symphony, Danish Radio Symphony, Orchestra National des Pays de la Loire, Bern Symphony, Tampere Philharmonic. *Recordings:* over 16 recordings including Seascapes 2007, Movement 2008. *Honours:* Distinguished Alumni Award, Boston Univ., Cultural Medallion, Singapore. *Current Management:* Harrison Parrott, 5–6 Albion Court, Albion Place, London, W6 0QT, England. *Telephone:* (20) 7229-9166. *E-mail:* info@ harrisonparrott.co.uk. *Website:* www.harrisonparrott.com. *Address:* Singapore Symphony Orchestra, 4 Battery Road, #20-01, Bank of China Building, Singapore 049908, Singapore (office). *E-mail:* ssonet@singnet.com.sg (office). *Website:* www.sso.org.sg (office).

SHULMAN, Andrew; cellist and conductor; b. 1960, London, England. *Education:* RAM, RCM with Joan Dickson and William Pleeth. *Career:* Principal Cellist, Philharmonia for five years, followed by solo and conducting career; repertoire includes concertos by Dvořák, Elgar, Beethoven (Triple), Vivaldi and Haydn; Strauss's Don Quixote and Bloch's Schelomo; founder mem., Britten Quartet, debut concert at the Wigmore Hall 1987; Quartet-in-Residence, Dartington Summer School 1987, with quartets by Schnittke; season 1988–89 in the Genius of Prokofiev series at Blackheath and BBC Lunchtime Series at St John's Smith Square; South Bank appearances with the Schoenberg/Handel Quartet Concerto conducted by Neville Marriner, concerts with the Hermann Prey Schubertiade and collaborations with the Alban Berg Quartet in the Beethoven Plus series; tour of South America 1988, followed by Scandinavian debut; season 1989–90 with debut tours of The Netherlands, Germany, Spain, Austria, Finland; tours from 1990 to the Far East, Malta, Sweden, Norway: Schoenberg/Handel Concerto with the Gothenburg Symphony; festival appearances at Brighton, the City of London, Greenwich, Canterbury, Harrogate, Chester, Spitalfields and Aldeburgh; collaborations with John Ogdon, Imogen Cooper, Thea King and Lynn Harrell; fmr resident quartet, Liverpool Univ.; teacher, Lake District Summer Music 1989, Univ. of Bristol, Univ. of Hong Kong 1990; conductor of various orchestras, including RCM String Ensemble, Proteus Orchestra, Norfolk Youth Orchestra, Leicester Symphony Orchestra, Britten-Pears Orchestra, Ambache Chamber Orchestra, Salomon Orchestra. *Recordings:* Beethoven Op 130 and Schnittke Quartet No. 3, Vaughan Williams On Wenlock Edge and Ravel Quartet, Britten, Prokofiev, Tippett, Elgar and Walton Quartets, Vivaldi Concertos, Delius and Dyson. *Honours:* Piatigorsky Artist Award in Boston, USA 1989–90.

SHUTOVA, Marina; singer (mezzo-soprano); b. 1961, Moscow, Russia. *Education:* Tchaikovsky Conservatory, Moscow, and studied with Judith Beckmann in Hamburg. *Career:* sang with the Bolshoi Opera at Moscow from 1981; La Scala Milan debut 1989, as Clara in Prokofiev's Duenna (repeated at Edinburgh and Glasgow with the Bolshoi in 1990); Metropolitan Opera debut 1991, as Olga in Eugene Onegin; season 1992/93 as Amneris at Düsseldorf, Azucena at Liège and concerts in Hamburg; season 1995/6 as Sonia in War and Peace in Vienna, Dalila at Toulon and Maddalena in Rigoletto at Orange; other roles include Solocha in Rimsky's Christmas Eve (Edinburgh 1992).

SHUTTLEWORTH, Anna Lee, ARCM, BA (Hons); British cellist and academic; *Cello Teacher, University of Leeds;* b. 2 May 1927, Bournemouth, Dorset, England; d. of Henry Lee Hadwen Shuttleworth and Inez E. D. Lee Shuttleworth; m. 1st Noel Taylor; m. 2nd David Sellen. *Education:* St Christopher's School, Hampstead, Talbot Heath School, Bournemouth, Royal Coll. of Music, Boise scholarship to study with Pablo Casals and Enrico Mainardi. *Career:* cellist in Vivien Hind Quartet 1947; fmr Prin. Cellist, Sadler's Wells and English Sinfonia, also played with Philomusica, Jacques, Boyd Neel and BBC Concert Orchestras; broadcasts as soloist; recitals in London with Bernard Roberts in Purcell Room; Prof., Royal Coll. of Music (RCM) 1967–96; examiner, Associated Bd of Royal Schools of Music 1969–96; cello teacher, Univ. of Leeds 1996–, also Univ. of Christchurch, Canterbury and privately; cellist in Georgian Quartet and Leonardo Piano Trio with David Roth, Maureen Smith and Ian Brown; cello and piano recitals with John Thwaites 2003; mem. European String Teachers Asscn, Inc. Soc. of Musicians, Musicians' Union, Royal Soc. of Musicians. *Recordings include:* cello continuo on recordings by Alfred Deller. *Publications include:* Playing the Cello 1971, Anna Shuttleworth (autobiog.) 2009; contrib. to The Strad 1997, ESTA and NEEMF Magazines 2001–08. *Honours:* Hon. FRCM; RCM Leslie Alexander Prize, Boise Scholarship for study abroad. *Address:* 1 Buckingham Road, Leeds, W Yorks. LS6 1BP, England (home). *Telephone:* (113) 275-8509 (home); (1227) 261975 (home). *E-mail:* selshut@btinternet.com (home). *Website:* annashuttleworth.com.

SICHKIN, Emilian Boris; composer; b. 14 Aug. 1954, Kiev, Ukraine. *Education:* Moscow Conservatory of Music, Gorky Conservatory of Music, Gnesins Coll. of Music, Audio Inst. of America, studied with Prof. Berlin. *Career:* debut at Carnegie Hall 1991; performances include Winds of Freedom at Carnegie Hall 1991; Concerto for Astronauts 1988, 1989; piano recital, Carnegie Hall 1988; television appearance and radio broadcasts; mem. ASCAP, American Composers' Forum. *Compositions:* Concerto for Astronauts, Winds of Freedom symphonic suite, The Demon (ballet), Romeo and Juliet symphonic tragedy, Little Mermaid symphonic overture.

ŠICHO, Robert; Czech singer (tenor); b. 1967, Prague. *Education:* State Conservatory, Prague, Music Acad., Prague, studied with Jana Jonasová. *Career:* soloist of the State Opera, Prague; appearances in many major theatres in the Czech Republic; frequent guest, Austria, Belgium, Norway, Netherlands, Germany, Greece, Switzerland, Japan; operatic roles include Ferrando in Così fan tutte, Tamino in Die Zauberflöte, Almaviva in Il Barbiere di Siviglia, Alfredo in La Traviata, Lensky in Eugene Onegin, Leandro in Busoni's Arlecchino, Prince in Rusalka, Hoffmann in Les contes d'Hoffmann, Turiddu in Cavalleria rusticana and Don José in Carmen; operetta roles include Rosillon in Die Lustige Witwe, title role in Paganini and Octavio in Giuditta (Lehar), Caramello in Eine Nacht in Venedig, Bárinkay in Der Zigeunerbaron (J. Strauss) and Paris in Offenbach's La Belle Hélène; extensive concert repertoire includes Mozart's Requiem, Verdi's Requiem, Orff's Carmina Burana, Beethoven's Ninth, Rossini's Messe Solennelle and Stabat Mater and Telemann's Die Tageszeiten; sentenced to 10 years imprisonment on murder charges 2009. *Recordings include:* Caramello in

Strauss's Ein Nacht in Venedig 1990, Telemann's Die Tageszeiten, for Czech radio and television 1995, Carmina Burana for radio and television 1998, Charpentier's Te Deum, for radio and television 1999.

SICILIANI, Alessandro; Italian conductor and composer; b. 5 June 1952, Florence. *Education:* Milan Conservatoire, Accademia Chigiana in Siena with Franco Ferrara. *Career:* many appearances at leading opera centres in Italy, notably Rome, Naples, Palermo and Florence; further engagements in Marseilles, Barcelona, Nice, Liège, New Orleans and Philadelphia; Metropolitan Opera debut 1988, with Pagliacci and Cavalleria Rusticana; symphonic engagements throughout the USA, Far East and Europe; Principal Guest Conductor, Teatro Colón, Buenos Aires from 1988, Teatro Municipal, São Paulo from 1988; Music Dir, Columbus (Ohio) Symphony Orchestra from 1992. *Compositions include:* Cantata, L'Amour peintre (ballet), Giona (oratorio).

SIDLIN, Murry, MM; American conductor and academic; b. 6 May 1940, Baltimore, Md. *Education:* Academia Chigiana, Siena, Cornell Univ., Peabody Conservatory of Music, Johns Hopkins Univ. *Career:* Asst Conductor, Baltimore Symphony Orchestra 1971–73; Dir Maryland Ballet Co. 1971–73; Prin. Conductor, Baltimore Chamber Players 1971–73; Resident Conductor, Nat. Symphony Orchestra under Dorati 1973–77, Wolf Trap American Univ. Music Acad. 1974; Host and Conductor, Children's TV series Music is... 1977; Music Dir Tulsa Philharmonic Orchestra 1978–80; Music Dir New Haven Symphony 1977–88, Long Beach Symphony 1980–88, Resident Conductor, Aspen Music Festival 1978–93; Resident Conductor, Oregon Symphony Orchestra 1994–2002; Dean, Benjamin T. Rome School of Music, Catholic Univ., Washington, DC 2002–10, currently Prof. of Conducting; currently Founder-Pres. Defiant Requiem Foundation; Co-founder, Assoc. Dir and Program Coordinator, American Acad. of Conducting, Aspen; Artistic Dir Cascade Festival of Music; guest conductor with St Louis Symphony, orchestras of San Francisco, Pittsburgh, Minnesota, Atlanta, Colorado, Utah, Florida, Jerusalem, orchestras of Madrid, I Solisti Veneti, Honolulu, Seattle, Monte Carlo, Vancouver, Victoria, and Edmonton and Quebec, George Enescu Philharmonic of Bucharest, Czech Nat. Symphony, MVD Orchestra of Budapest, Iceland Symphony, Boston Pops, San Antonio Symphony and Opera, Houston Symphony; regular performances with Lindberg Orchestra of Holland; mem. Int. Bd of Govs Jerusalem Acad. of Music and Dance 2013–. *Television:* Music Is.... *Honours:* winner, Baltimore Symphony Orchestra Young Conductor's Competition 1962, Educator of the Year, Nat. Asscn of Ind. Schools of Music in America 1997, Distinguished Alumnus Award, Peabody Conservatory of Music, Johns Hopkins Univ. 2011, Excellence in Arts Award, City Choir of Washington 2011, Medal of Valor, Simon Wiesenthal Center 2013. *Telephone:* (212) 977-6779. *E-mail:* hughkaylor@msn.com. *Address:* Defiant Requiem Foundation, PO Box 6242, Washington, DC 20015, USA (office). *Telephone:* (202) 244-0220 (office). *E-mail:* msidlin@defiantrequiem .org. *Website:* www.defiantrequiem.org; www.murrysidlin.com.

SIDOROVA, Svetlana; singer (mezzo-soprano); b. 1970, St Petersburg, Russia. *Education:* St Petersburg Conservatoire, studied in Italy with Alberto Zedda and Carlo Bergonzi, and with Christa Ludwig. *Career:* appearances from 1992 in Vienna, Paris, Berlin and Bologna (Janacek's Makropulos Case 1994); Italiana in Algeri at the Pesaro Festival and Jocasta in Oedipus Rex at St Petersburg; Verdi's Amneris at Cologne, Kundry in Parsifal for the Kirov Opera and Eboli in Don Carlos at Essen; sang in Pacini's L'Ultimo giorni di Pompeii at the Martina Franca Festival and Falla's Atlantida at Granada; concerts include the Brahms Alto Rhapsody, Bach's Magnificat, Rossini's Stabat Mater (at Pesaro), Beethoven's Ninth and Alexander Nevsky by Prokofiev (Bologna); other opera roles include Carmen, Ulrica, Maddalena and Olga in Eugene Onegin (Deutsche Oper, Berlin). *Honours:* prizewinner at competitions in Athens, Sienna, Brussels, Tokyo and Barcelona.

SIEBER, Gudrun; singer (soprano); b. 1953, Germany. *Education:* Düsseldorf Opera Studio. *Career:* mem., Deutsche Oper am Rhein Düsseldorf 1974–83; Deutsche Oper Berlin from 1977, notably in the 1984 premiere of Reimann's Gespenstersonate; sang at the Bayerische Staatsoper Munich 1978–84, in operas by Gluck, Mozart and Lortzing; Schwetzingen Festival 1980, 1982, Salzburg Festival 1981, 1984, 1986 as Papagena in Die Zauberflöte; also sang Papagena at the Théâtre des Champs-Elysées, Paris 1987; sang in a double bill of Il Maestro di Capella (Cimarosa) and La Serva Padrona at the Deutsche Oper foyer 1990; other roles include Marie in Zar und Zimmermann; Amour in Hippolyte et Aricie and Kristen in Miss Julie by Bibalo; sang Papagena and Marie in Lortzing's Zar und Zimmermann at the Deutsche Oper Berlin 1999; Shepherd in Tannhäuser 2001; many concert appearances. *Recordings include:* Schumann's Manfred.

SIEBERT, Isolde; German singer (soprano); b. 1960, Hunfield, Hesse. *Education:* studied in Fribourg. *Career:* mem. of the Basle Opera 1982–85; sang at Darmstadt 1985–87, debut as Zerbinetta; Hanover Opera from 1987, as Blondchen, Susanna, Gretel, Tytania in A Midsummer Night's Dream, and Papagena; Bregenz Festival and Liège 1986, 1988, as the Queen of Night in Die Zauberflöte; sang in the 300th anniversary performance of Steffani's Enrico Leone, Hanover 1989; many concerts and recital appearances; sang La Reine de la nuit in Die Zauberflöte, Beaune 2004, Europa in Europa riconosciuta, La Scala, Milan 2004. *Recordings include:* Dvořák's Biblical Songs Op99 2002, Von Winter's Clarinet Concerto and Aria 2004. *Current Management:* Hannagret Bueker Agentur für Musikthater und Konzert, Fuhsestrasse 2, 30419 Hannover, Germany. *Telephone:* (511) 2716910. *Fax:*

(511) 2717873. *E-mail:* mail@buekervoice.de. *Website:* www.buekervoice.de; isolde-siebert.com.

SIEDEN, Cyndia; American singer (soprano); b. 10 Sept. 1961, Glendale, Calif.; one s. *Education:* studied at Olympia, Washington, and with Elisabeth Schwarzkopf. *Career:* sang Cunegonde in Candide for New York City Opera 1989; sang Sifare in Mozart's Mitridate at Wexford Festival 1989, the Queen of Night in Toulon, Adele in Fledermaus for Scottish Opera and Offenbach's Olympia at Seattle; Salzburg Festival debut as Amor in Orfeo ed Euridice, conducted by John Eliot Gardiner; appearances with Bayerische Staatsoper Munich as Rosina, Helena in premiere of Reimann's Troades 1986, Zerbinetta and Fiakermilli in Arabella; further engagements at Nice as Blondchen and Aminta in Die schweigsame Frau at Palermo; sang Xenia in concert performance of Boris Godunov conducted by Abbado 1984, Verdi's Oscar for Washington Opera, Donizetti's Marie with Florida Opera West, Nannetta at Omaha and Fido in US professional premiere of Britten's Paul Bunyan, St Louis; season 1990–91 as Blondchen at Théâtre du Châtelet, Paris, and on tour to Amsterdam, London, Lisbon and Stuttgart; appearances as the Queen of Night at Opéra Bastille, Paris, and Lucia di Lammermoor at Seattle; Zerbinetta for ENO and at Vienna Staatsoper; season 1992–93 with Sophie in Der Rosenkavalier at the Châtelet; sang in Mozart's Mitridate at Salzburg 1997; Handel's Rodelinda at Halle 1996; sang Gilda in Rigoletto for Flanders Opera 1999; season 2000–01 as the Queen of Night for ENO and Gilda for Vlaamse Opera, Antwerp; Lulu at the Metropolitan Opera 2001; sang Morgana in Alcina at Göttingen 2002; Zerbinetta in Tokyo 2003; sang Ariel in world premiere of Thomas Adès's The Tempest at Covent Garden 2004, also in Frankfurt 2014; Queen of the Night at the Metropolitan Opera 2008; concert repertoire includes Mozart's C minor Mass (Cleveland Orchestra, Royal Concertgebouw Orchestra, St Louis Symphony, Atlanta Symphony), Carmina Burana (Los Angeles Philharmonic, Atlanta, Seattle, Portland, Nashville), Bach's St John Passion at the Concertgebouw under Frans Brüggen, and Candide at the Barbican Centre, London. *Recordings include:* Guardian of the Threshold in Die Frau ohne Schatten, conducted by Sawallisch; Orfeo ed Euridice; Die Entführung aus dem Serail, Gardiner; Die Zauberflöte, Gardiner; Arias for Aloysia Weber (Mozart), Orchestra of the 18th Century, Bruggen; Der Schauspieldirector; Die Schweigsame Frau, Bayerische Rundfunk. *Current Management:* c/o Caroline Phillips Management, 11 Pound Pill, Corsham, Wilts., SN13 9HZ, England. *Telephone:* (1249) 716716 (home). *Fax:* (1249) 404123 (home). *E-mail:* info@caroline-phillips.co.uk (home). *Website:* www.caroline-phillips.co.uk.

SIEGEL, Jeffrey, DMA; pianist; b. 18 Nov. 1942, Chicago, IL, USA; m. Laura Mizel 1973, one s. one d. *Education:* Juilliard School of Music, studied with Rudolph Ganz, Rosina Lhevinne, Franz Reizenstein, Ilona Kabos. *Career:* debut as soloist, Chicago Symphony 1958; soloist with orchestras of New York, Philadelphia, Boston, Cleveland, Los Angeles, London Symphony, London Philharmonic, Royal Philharmonic, Philharmonia, BBC Orchestras, NHK Orchestra of Japan, Orquesta Nacional de Buenos Aires, Teatro Colón, Berlin Philharmonic; recitals in Carnegie Hall, Royal Festival Hall, Concertgebouw, Brussels, Berlin, Munich, Zürich, Tokyo, Tel-Aviv, Oslo, Stockholm; television appearances and frequent radio broadcasts. *Compositions:* Cadenza for Mozart C Minor Concerto. *Recordings:* Dutilleux Sonata and Hindemith Third Sonata, Gershwin complete works for piano and orchestra (with St Louis Symphony) 1974, solo works of Rachmaninov. *Honours:* silver medal Queen Elisabeth Competition, Brussels 1968, Dr hc (Nat. Coll. of Education, Evanston, IL) 1976. *Address:* c/o Kansai Opera Group, 3–3–9 Bingo-Cho, Chyno-Ku, Osaka, Japan.

SIEGEL, Laurence Gordon, BA, MM; American conductor; b. 23 July 1931, New York, NY; m. 1959; one d. *Education:* City Coll. of New York, New England Conservatory, Boston, Berkshire Music Center, Tanglewood with Boris Goldovsky and Leonard Bernstein. *Career:* Conductor, NBC Symphony, Carnegie Hall concerts including tribute to Fritz Kreisler; appeared with Honolulu Orchestra, Shreveport Festival Orchestra, Alexandria Symphony, Jacksonville Symphony and Opera Co., Connecticut Grand Opera Co.; Dir, Miami Int. Music Competition, Theater of Performing Arts, Miami Beach for seven seasons; worldwide conducting includes Orquesta Sinfónica del Salvador, Orquesta Sinfónica de Las Palmas, Spain, Manila Metro Philharmonic Orchestra and Opera Asscn, Teatro Sperimentale di Spoleto Orchestra, Belgrade Symphony, Filharmonica de Stat Oradea-Romania and RAI Milan Orchestra; Music Dir and Conductor, Puccini Festival Orchestra, Italy 1984, Pan-American Sinfónica 1991–, also Festival of the Continents, Key West, Florida; Music Dir, North Miami Beach Orchestra; Guest Conductor, Kensington Symphony (California), São Paulo Symphony, Brazil, Orquesta Sinfónica Ciudad Asunción, Paraguay 1994; Chief Conductor, Sakai City, Osaka Opera, Japan; numerous operas conducted, including Così fan tutte, Faust, Madama Butterfly, Tosca, La Bohème, La Traviata, Otello, Rigoletto, Die Fledermaus, Ernani, Il Trovatore, Suor Angelica, Hansel and Gretel, Samson and Delilah, La Périchole, Elisir d'amore, Carmen 1991, 1992, Merry Widow 1992–. *Recordings:* works of Tchaikovsky (with New Philharmonia Orchestra, London), albums with London Symphony Orchestra, London Philharmonic Orchestra, Royal Philharmonic Orchestra and London Festival Orchestra. *Honours:* Hon. DMus 1993; numerous citations and medals of honour. *Address:* 5225 La Gorce Drive, Miami Beach, FL 33140, USA.

SIEGEL, Wayne, BA, DipMus; composer; b. 14 Feb. 1953, Los Angeles, USA; m. 1980, one s. one d. *Education:* Univ. of California at Santa Barbara, Royal Danish Acad. of Music, Århus. *Career:* composer and performer in Europe and

USA, including many radio and television broadcasts and numerous commissions; performances include Danish Radio Festival, Copenhagen 1980, Nordic Music Days, Helsinki 1980, 1984, German radio 1981, New Music America, Chicago 1982, Warsaw Autumn Festival 1984, Rostrum, Stockholm 1988, Wigmore Recital Hall 1997, Sydney Opera House 1998, 1999, Cunningham Dance Studio, New York 1999; Administrative Dir, West Jutland Symphony and Chamber Ensemble 1984–86; Dir, Danish Inst. of Electro-acoustic Music 1986–. *Compositions:* String Quartet 1975–79, East LA for four marimbas or two guitars 1975, Narcissus ad fontem 1976, Mosaic 1978, Autumn Resonance 1979, Domino Figures 1979, Music for 21 clarinets 1980, Watercolor, Acrylic, Watercolor 1981, Polyphonic Music 1983, 42nd Street Rondo 1984, Devil's Golf Course 1985, Last Request 1986, Cobra 1988, Tracking 1991, Livstegn (opera) 1994, Jackdaw 1995, Movement Study 1996, Savannah 1997. *Honours:* Danish Art Council three-year grant for composition 1978–81.

SIEGELE, Ulrich, DPhil; German musicologist and academic; b. 1 Nov. 1930, Stuttgart. *Education:* Univ. of Tübingen. *Career:* Lecturer in Musicology, Univ. of Tübingen 1965–71, Prof. of Musicology 1971–95. *Publications:* Die Musiksammlung der Stadt Heilbronn 1967, Kompositionsweise und Bearbeitungstechnik in der Instrumentalmusik Johann Sebastian Bachs 1975, Bachs theologischer Formbegriff und das Duett F-Dur 1978, Zwei Kommentare zum Marteau sans maître von Pierre Boulez 1979, Beethoven/Formale Strategien der späten Quartette 1990, Die Orgeln des Musikwissenschaftlichen Instituts im Pfleghof zu Tübingen 1992, Johann Ulrich Steigleder, Ricercar Tablatura (1624) 2008, Johann Ulrich Steigleder: Vierzig Variationen über "Vater unser im Himmelreich" (1626/27) 2012, Johann Sebastian Bach komponiert Zeit (vol. 1) 2014; contrib. of articles to periodicals, collections by several authors, and musical encyclopaedias, including Bach: Das Wohltemperierte Klavier I, Ulrich Siegele zum 70.Geburtstag (biog.) 2002. *Address:* Holunderweg 20, 24229 Schwedeneck, Germany (home). *Telephone:* (430) 8189476 (home). *E-mail:* ulrich.siegele@gmx.de (home).

SIERRA, Roberto; Puerto Rican/American composer and academic; *Professor, Cornell University;* b. 9 Oct. 1953, Vega Baja. *Education:* Puerto Rico Conservatory of Music, Univ. of Puerto Rico, Royal Coll. of Music, London, Univ. of London, Inst. of Sonology, Utrecht, Hamburg Hochschule für Musik with Gyorgy Ligeti. *Career:* Asst Dir, Cultural Activities Dept, Univ. of Puerto Rico 1983–85, Dir 1985–86; Dean of Studies, Puerto Rico Conservatory of Music 1986–87, Chancellor 1987–; Prof., Cornell Univ.; fmr Composer-in-Residence, Milwaukee Symphony Orchestra, Philadelphia Orchestra, Puerto Rico Symphony Orchestra, New Mexico Symphony; several comms; numerous works performed in USA and Europe. *Compositions include:* Salsa on the C String for cello and piano 1983, Salsa for wind quintet 1983, Cantos Populares for chorus 1983, Cinco Bocetos for clarinet 1984, El Mensajero de Plata (chamber opera) 1984, Concerto Nocturnal for harpsichord, flute, clarinet, oboe, violin and cello 1985, Jubilo for orchestra 1985, Memorias Tropicales for string quartet 1985, Dona Rosita for mezzo-soprano and wind quintet 1985, El Sueño de Antonia for clarinet and percussion 1985, Invocaciones for voice and percussion 1986, Cuatro ensayos orquestales for orchestra 1986, Glosa a la sombra for mezzo-soprano, viola, clarinet and piano 1987, Essays for wind quintet 1987, Mano a mano for two percussionists 1987, El Contemplado (ballet) 1987, Glosas for piano and orchestra 1987, Introduccion y descarga for piano, brass quintet and percussion 1988, Descarga for chamber ensemble or orchestra 1988, Entre terceras for two synthesizers and computer 1988, Tributo for harp, flute, clarinet and string quartet 1988, Bayoán (oratorio) 1991–93, Trio Tropical for violin, cello and piano 1991, Evocaciones for violin and orchestra 1994, Lux Aeterna for chorus 1996, Alegría for orchestra 1996, Cuentos for chamber orchestra 1997, Concerto for percussion and orchestra 1998, Fandangos, Missa Latina, Sinfonia No. 1 (Winner, Kenneth Davenport Competition 2004) 2003, Folias 2004, Concierto Barroco 2004, Variations on a Souvenir 2008, also piano pieces, harpsichord pieces. *Honours:* Acad. Award in Music, American Acad. of Arts and Letters 2003. *Current Management:* c/o Cynthia B. Herbst, American International Artists Inc., 356 Pine Valley Road, Hoosick Falls, NY 12090, USA. *Fax:* (518) 686-1960 (home). *E-mail:* cynthia@aiartists.com. *Website:* www.aiartists.com. *E-mail:* rs58@cornell.edu (office); info@robertosierra.com (office). *Website:* www.robertosierra.com.

SIGHELE, Mietta; singer (soprano); b. 1944, Rovereto, Italy; m. Veriano Luchetti. *Education:* studied in Milan and Rome. *Career:* debut as Butterfly at Spoleto; appearances at opera houses throughout Italy and in Vienna, Barcelona, Buenos Aires, Montréal, Chicago, Dallas and New Orleans; Verona Arena from 1979, as Micaela in Carmen; Ravenna Festival 1986 and Torre del Lago 1989 as Butterfly; Metropolitan Opera 1989 as Micaela; season 1991 as Liu in Turandot, at Verona and Prioress in The Carmelites at Rome; engagements in operas by Mozart, Janáček, Wagner and Tchaikovsky. *Recordings:* Priestess in Aida, Meyerbeer's L'Africaine (in Florence) 1971.

SIGMUNDSSON, Kristinn; Icelandic singer (bass-baritone); b. 1 May 1951, Reykjavík. *Education:* Academy of Music, Vienna, studied in Washington DC. *Career:* mem., Wiesbaden Opera from 1989 as Don Giovanni, the Speaker in Die Zauberflöte and Eugene Onegin; Royal Court Theatre Drottningholm, 1989–90 as Agamemnon and Thoas in Gluck's Iphigénie operas; Season 1990–91 includes: Geisterbote in Die Frau ohne Schatten at the Concertgebouw, Beethoven's 9th with the Essen Philharmonie and St John Passion in the Hague; Recital at the Stratford-upon-Avon Scandinavian Festival; Malcolm in La Donna del Lago for Vara Radio, Netherlands, 1992; Concert appearances with the Dutch Radio Orchestra, the Rotterdam Philharmonic and the NDR Symphony Orchestra, Hamburg; Season 1991–92 included: Don

Giovanni at Stuttgart Opera, Mozart's Requiem at Drottningholm and Barber of Seville at Geneva; Season 1993–94 included: Alidoro and Speaker in Geneva, Mathis der Maler in Barcelona and Lady Macbeth of Mtsensk at the Maggio Musicale in Florence; Sang in a new production of The Bartered Bride at the Grand Théâtre in Geneva, 1994; Sang Mephistofeles in La Damnation de Faust at the Opéra National in Paris; Colline in 1996; Sang Klingsor in Parsifal at the Opéra Bastille, Paris, 1997; Season 1997–98 as Rossini's Mustafà at Dresden, the Hermit in Der Freischütz for the Royal Opera at the Barbican and Grand Inquisitor in Don Carlos at the Opéra Bastille, Paris; Season 2000 as Banquo at Cologne, Cherubini's Creon at Salzburg (concert) and Rossini's Mustafà for the Vienna Staatsoper; Season 2001–02 engagements included Barbiere at the Paris Bastille, Don Giovanni in Munich and Berlin, Lucia di Lammermoor in Munich, Die Walküre and Parsifal in Cologne and Eugene Onign in Hamburg, Nabucco at the Arena di Nimes; Season 2002–03 with Der Rosenkavalier and a revival of Walküre in Cologne, Meistersinger at Covent Garden, Gounod's Faust, Parisfal, Der fliegende Holländer, Meistersinger and La Juive at the Opéra National de Paris, La Damnation de Faust in San Francisco, Don Giovanni in Munich, Don Carlos in Dallas, Der Rosenkavalier in Dresden and Die Walküre in Naples. *Recordings include:* Commendatore in Don Giovanni, conducted by Arnold Östman. *Honours:* prizewinner Belvedere Singing Competition, Vienna 1983, winner Philadelphia Opera Competition 1983. *Current Management:* c/o Guy Barzilay Artists, 360 West 28th Street #6B, New York, NY 10001, USA. *Telephone:* (212) 741-6118. *Fax:* (212) 741-2558. *E-mail:* guybar@aol.com. *Website:* guybarzilayartists.com.

SIGURBJORNSSON, Thorkell; Icelandic composer; b. 16 July 1938, Reykjavík. *Education:* Reykjavík Coll. of Music, studied in USA. *Career:* Creative Assoc., State Univ. of New York, USA 1973; research musician, Centre for Music Experiment, Univ. of California, San Diego 1975; Head of Theory and Composition, Reykjavík Coll. of Music, Iceland 1968–74; mem. Icelandic League of Composers (fmr pres.). *Compositions include* Bukolla 1974, Wiblo 1976, Cadensa and Dance, Seascape, Albumblatt 1975, The Bull Man (ballet), Caprice 1986; chamber music: Differing Opinions, Intrada 1971, For Renée 1973, A Short Passion Story, Hasselby Icelandic Folk Songs 1976, Ballade 1960, Happy Music 1971, Kissum 1970, Copenhagen Quartet, For Better or Worse 1975, Solstice 1976, Auf Meinen Lieben Gott 1981, Three Faces of Pantomine 1982; choir music: Ode 1975, Five Laudi 1973, Beginning 1978, Hosanna Son of David, Palm Sunday 1978, The Artificial Flower, Seven Christmas Songs, David 121 1984, Evening Prayers 1983; children's music: Seven Songs from Apaspil, Apaspil (opera) 1966, Velferd, Four Icelandic Folk Songs, Three Songs, Gigjuleikur, The Ugly Duckling 1981, The Last Flower 1983; electronic music: La Jolla Good Friday I 1975, La Jolla Good Friday II 1975, fipur 1971, Race Track 1975, Trifonia for orchestra 1990, Missa Brevis 1993, Visit for string quartet 1993, Life, Dreams and Reality for orchestra 1993, Runes for horn and orchestra 1994, The Girl in the Lighthouse (children's opera) 1997, Symphony 1998, Wheel of Fortune (chamber opera) 1998.

SIKI, Bela; Hungarian pianist; b. 21 Feb. 1923, Budapest; m. Yolande Oltramare 1952; one s. one d. *Education:* Univ. of Budapest, Acad. Franz Liszt, Budapest, Conservatoire de Genève, Switzerland. *Career:* numerous concert tours worldwide; appearances with major orchestras around the world; extensive concert tours and masterclasses in Japan, Australia, USA and Canada 1988. *Recordings:* works by Bach, Ravel, Liszt (B minor sonata), Beethoven (late sonatas) and Bartók. *Publication:* Piano Literature 1981. *Honours:* Liszt Competition, Budapest 1942, 1943, Concours International d'Executions Musicales, Geneva 1948.

SIKORA, Elizabeth; British singer (soprano); b. 1950, Edinburgh, Scotland. *Education:* Royal Scottish Academy, Elsa Mayer Lismanns Opera Workshop. *Career:* appearances with the Royal Opera Covent Garden in London and on tour to Los Angeles, La Scala Milan, Japan, Repub. of Korea and Greece; solo roles in Die Meistersinger, Butterfly, Die Frau ohne Schatten, Manon Lescaut, Parsifal, Rigoletto and Simon Boccanegra; sang in the British premieres of Henze's Pollicino and Menotti's The Boy Who Grew Too Fast; appearances as Carmen in Oundle and Germany with Royal Opera Education; Annina in La Traviata at the Albert Hall; appearances at Covent Garden in Rigoletto 2009, 2012, The Gambler 2010, Electra 2013. *Current Management:* Helen Sykes Artists' Management, 100 Felsham Road, Putney, London, SW15 1DQ, England. *Telephone:* (20) 8780-0060. *Fax:* (20) 8780-8772. *E-mail:* helen@helensykesartists.co.uk. *Website:* www.helensykesartists.co.uk.

SILJA, Anja; German singer (soprano) and producer; b. 17 April 1940, Berlin; m. Christoph von Dohnányi (divorced); one s. two d. *Education:* studied with Egon van Rijn. *Career:* began concert career aged ten at Berlin Titania Palace; stage debut Brunswick 1956, as Rosina; mem. Stuttgart and Frankfurt operas 1958–59; sang the Queen of Night at Aix 1959; sang at Bayreuth Festival 1960–67, as Senta, Elsa, Eva, Elisabeth and Venus; London debut at Sadler's Wells Theatre as Leonore/Fidelio 1963; Covent Garden debut as Leonore 1969, returned as Cassandre in Les Troyens, Senta, Marie in Wozzeck, Kostelnicka in Jenůfa; Metropolitan Opera debut 1972, returned as Salome, Marie and Kostelnicka; with Vienna Staatsoper 1959–, in roles including Queen of Night, Salome, Elektra, Lulu; Paris Opéra 1964–, as Salome and Brünnhilde; Glyndebourne Opera debut as Kostelnicka 1989; sang the Nurse in Die Frau ohne Schatten at San Francisco 1989; debut as opera producer at Brussels with Lohengrin 1990; sang Emilia Marty at Glyndebourne 1995; season 1997 in The Makropoulos Case at Glyndebourne and as Herodias at Covent Garden;

Geschwitz in Lulu at Düsseldorf 2000; Clytemnestra at Madrid, Geschwitz and Herodias at Amsterdam, The Makropoulos Case at Aix and The Bassarids in Amsterdam, Pierrot Lunaire by Schoenberg at Aix 2003; season 2004 as Madame de Croissy in Milan and Mère Marie in Hamburg and Paris (both in Dialogues des Carmélites), Emilia Marty in Berlin, Clytemnestra (Elektra) in Oviedo, Gräfin Geschwitz (Lulu) in Munich; season 2005 as Kostelnicka in Lyon and Barcelona, Emilia Marty in Lyon and Berlin, Janáček's Osud in Vienna, and Gräfin Geschwitz in Munich. *Recordings include:* Der fliegende Holländer, Tannhäuser, Lohengrin and Parsifal from Bayreuth, Lulu, Wozzeck, Jenůfa (Grammy Award) 2001, Pierrot Lunaire, Salome, Erwartung, The Makropoulos Case. *Publication:* Die Sehnsucht nach dem Unerreichbaren (autobiog.) 1999. *Honours:* Kammersängerin; Bundesverdienstkreuz 1988; Janacek Medal, Opera News Award for invaluable contrib. to opera 2012. *Current Management:* Artists Management Zürich, Rütistrasse 52, 8044 Zürich-Gockhausen, Switzerland. *Telephone:* (1) 8218957. *Fax:* (1) 8210127. *E-mail:* schuetz@artistsman.com. *Website:* www.artistsman.com.

SILLA, Frederick; singer (tenor) and composer; b. 1948, Vienna, Austria. *Education:* Vienna Musikhochschule with Friedrich Cerha and Anton Dermota. *Career:* sang first at the Stadttheater Krefeld, then appeared at opera houses in Ulm, Kiel, Munster and Gelsenkirchen; opera, Jagdszenen aus Niederbayern, premiered at Karlsruhe 1979; mem., Staatstheater am Gärtnerplatz Munich from 1985; roles have included Mozart's Ottavio, Tamino, Ferrando and Belmonte, Nemorino and Hoffmann; modern repertoire includes parts in The Lighthouse by Maxwell Davies, Jakob Lenz by Wolfgang Rihm and Die Veruteilung des Lukullus by Dessau; guest engagements in Pisa, Venice and Madrid; concert appearances in Germany and elsewhere.

SILVA, Stella; singer (mezzo-soprano); b. 6 Jan. 1948, Buenos Aires, Argentina. *Education:* studied in Buenos Aires and Vercelli, Italy. *Career:* debut in Bordeaux 1969, as Preziosilla in La Forza del Destino; many appearances in Opera Houses at Parma, Lyon, Nice, Strasbourg, Hamburg, Vienna, Berlin, Barcelona and Buenos Aires; Verona Arena 1973–74, as Amneris; other roles have included Carmen, Ulrica, Eboli, Azucena, Adalgisa, Charlotte, Dalila and Ortrud; Laura in La Gioconda, Leonora, Gluck's Orpheus and Holofernes in Vivaldi's Juditha Triumphans; frequent concert appearances.

SILVA-MARIN, Guillermo Osvaldo, BA, DipMus; singer (tenor) and artistic director; b. 11 April 1944, Ponce, Puerto Rico. *Education:* Univ. of Puerto Rico, Univ. of Toronto, Canada. *Career:* Artistic Dir, Metropolitan Music Theatre, Scarborough 1976–79; founder and Artistic Dir, Toronto Operetta Theatre 1985; founder, Summer Opera Lyric Theatre 1986; Gen. Man., Opera in Concert 1994; staged over 21 operas and operettas, including Donizetti's Elixir of Love, Rossini's Barber of Seville, Lehar's Land of Smiles, Offenbach's La Vie Parisienne and Strauss's Gypsy Baron with the Toronto Operetta Theatre, Summer Opera Lyric Theatre, Opera de San Juan and Sault Ste Marie Opera; 16 performances as tenor with the Canadian Opera Co., including Richard Strauss's Ariadne auf Naxos and Leoncavallo's Pagliacci; appearances with Opera Lyra, Cincinnati Opera Asscn, New York City Opera, Metropolitan Opera, Mexico State Symphony, Toronto Symphony, Edmonton Symphony, Puerto Rico Symphony, Carnegie Hall, Canadian Broadcasting Corporation, CFMX-FM, including Stravinsky's Oedipus Rex, Strauss's Die Fledermaus, Zeller's The Bird Seller and Puccini's La Bohème.

SILVASTI, Jorma; Finnish singer (tenor); b. 9 March 1959, Leppavirta. *Education:* studied in Savonlinna, Sibelius Academy Helsinki, and in Frankfurt. *Career:* appearances with the Finnish National Opera at Helsinki from 1980; Frankfurt 1981–82, Krefeld, 1982–85; Karlsruhe, 1985–88; Savonlinna Festival from 1983 as Jenik (Bartered Bride), the Steersman in Fliegende Holländer and Tamino; premiere of Veitsi by Paavo Heikinen 1989; sang Ottavio at the Vienna Volksoper, 1988, Henry Morosus in Schweigsame Frau at Dresden, 1989; further engagements at Essen, Karlsruhe and Bremen; Created Kimmo in Sallinen's Kullervo with the Company of Finnish National Opera at the Dorothy Chandler Pavilion, Los Angeles, 1992; other roles include Ferrando, Fenton, Gluck's Pylades, Almaviva, Števa in Jenůfa, Lensky, Belmonte (Vienna State Opera, 1993) Nemorino, Alfredo; noted concert and oratorio performer; Gregor in premiere of Sansibar by E. Meyer at Schwetzingen with Bavarian State Opera Munich, 1994; Faust at the Dorothy Chandler Pavilion, Los Angeles; further engagements: Stuttgart, Düsseldorf, Frankfurt, Hannover, Hamburg, Munich, Vienna State Opera; sang Petruccio in The Palace, by Sallinen, at the 1996 Savonlinna Festival; sang Parsifal at Brussels, 1998; season 2000–01 as Berg's Alwa at the Vienna Staatsoper, Manolios in Martinů's The Greek Passion at Covent Garden and Edmund in the premiere of Sallinen's Lear, for Finnish National Opera; Laca in Jenůfa at Covent Garden, 2001; Dvorák's Stabat mater at the London Proms, 2002. *Current Management:* Vilja Valkeinen, Allegro Artist Management, Lars Sonckin kaari 16, 02600 Espoo, Finland. *Telephone:* (9) 462-007. *Fax:* (9) 5259-4200. *E-mail:* allegro.artist@dlc.fi. *Website:* www.allegroartist.com.

SILVER, Sheila, BA, PhD; American composer; *Professor of Music, Stony Brook University;* b. 3 Oct. 1946, Seattle, Wash.; d. of Robert Silver and Fannie Silver; m. John Feldman; one s. *Education:* Univ. of Washington, Seattle, Inst. for European Studies, Paris, Univ. of California, Berkeley, Stuttgart Hochschule für Musik with György Ligeti, Brandeis Univ. with Arthur Berger and Harold Shapero, Tanglewood and further study in Paris and London. *Career:* freelance composer, with performances throughout USA; has worked with film, including scores Alligator Eyes and Dead Funny; teacher of composition, then Prof. of Music at State Univ. of New York, Stony Brook 1979–. *Compositions include:* String quartet 1977, Galixidi for orchestra 1977, Dynamis for horn 1979, Canto for baritone and chamber ensemble 1979, Chariessa for soprano and orchestra (after Sappho) 1980, Two Elizabethan Songs for chorus 1982, Ek Ong Kar for chorus 1983, Dance Converging for viola, horn, piano and percussion 1987, The Thief of Love (opera) 1987, Window Waltz for bass clarinet, horn, strings, harpsichord, piano and percussion 1988, Song of Sarah for string orchestra 1988, Cello Sonata 1988, Oh, Thou Beautiful One for piano 1989, Dance of Wild Angels for chamber orchestra 1990, Six Préludes for piano 1991, Three Preludes for orchestra 1992, To the Spirit Unconquered trio for violin, cello and piano 1992, Transcending (three songs for Michael Dash, in memoriam) 1995, From Darkness Emerging harp and string quartet 1995, Piano Concerto 1996, Four Etudes and a Fantasy string quartet No. 2 1997, Winter Tapestry for chamber ensemble 1998, Subway Sunset for oboe and piano 1999, As the Earth Turns for oboe, bassoon, tape and video 1999, Chant for bass and piano 2000–04, Fantasy on an Imaginary Folk Song for flute and harp/string orchestra 2001, Lullaby for bassoon and piano 2001, Moon Prayer for two violins, two viola, two celli 2002, Midnight Prayer for orchestra 2003. *Recordings include:* To the Spirit Unconquered, Fantasy Quasi Theme and Variation, Piano Concerto and Six Preludes for Piano, Shirat Sarah, The Thief of Love, Who the Hell is Bobby Roos? (film score), The Wooden Sword, chamber opera in one act (Beverly and Raymond Sackler Prize in Music Composition 2007), The White Rooster, Cantata for women's vocal quartet, 6 Tibetan singing bowls and percussion (composed for Tapestry). Twilight's Last Gleaming, for two pianos and percussion, film score for documentary, EVO: Ten Questions Everyone Should Ask About Evolution. *Honours:* Radcliffe Inst. Award 1978, Rome Prize 1979, American Acad. and Inst. of Arts and Letters Composer Award. *Address:* PO Box 292, Spencertown, NY 12165, USA (office). *Telephone:* (518) 392-3843 (office). *E-mail:* sheila@sheilasilver.com (office). *Website:* www.hummingbirdfilms.com (office).

SILVERMAN, Faye-Ellen, BA, AM, DMA; American composer and academic; b. 2 Oct. 1947, New York; d. of the late Harry Ezra Silverman and Paula Silverman (née Hauptman). *Education:* Mannes Coll. of Music, Barnard Coll., Harvard Univ., Columbia Univ. *Career:* Teaching Asst, Columbia Univ. 1972–74; Adjunct Asst Prof., CUNY 1972–77; Asst Prof., Goucher Coll. 1977–81; Grad. Faculty, Dept of Music History and Literature, Peabody Inst., Johns Hopkins Univ. 1977–85; Faculty, Center for Compositional Studies, Aspen Music Festival 1986; part-time Assoc. Prof. The New School for Music, Mannes Coll. 1991–, Eugene Lang Coll., The New School for Liberal Arts 2000–13; works performed live and/or on radio and TV in numerous countries, including performances by Baltimore Symphony, Brooklyn Philharmonic, Greater Bridgeport Symphony, New Orleans Philharmonic, International Experimental Music Festival, Bourges, France, ISCM (Korea section), Nieuwe Oogst (Belgium), Grupo Musica Hoje (Brazil), Corona Guitar Quartet (Denmark), Monday Evening Concert series (LA), Aspen Music Festival, Jauna Muzika (Lithuania); Virginia Center for the Creative Arts residency 2007, 2010, 2011, 2014. *Compositions include:* more than 90 published compositions, including Oboe-sthenics (chosen to represent USA at Int. Rostrum of Composers/UNESCO 1982) 1981, Winds and Sines for orchestra (Indiana State Univ. Orchestral Composition Contest 1982) 1981, Restless Winds for woodwind quintet 1986, Adhesions for orchestra 1987, A Free Pen, a cantata for narrator, soloists, chorus and chamber ensemble 1990, Journey Towards Oblivion for soprano, tenor and chamber ensemble 1991, Just For Fun for chamber orchestra 1994, At The Colour Cafe for brass choir 1997, Dialogue Continued for horn, trombone and tuba 2000, Wilde's World for tenor, viola and guitar 2000, Reconstructed Music for piano trio 2002, The Wings of Night for mezzo and baritone soloists, SATB chorus and guitar 2008, Conversations Continued for alto flute and clarinet 2011, Shifting Colors for guitar, percussion, double bass, and piano 2012. *Recordings include:* Oboe-sthenics by James Ostryniec, Zigzags by Velvet Brown, 2nd recording by Joanna Ross Hersey, Passing Fancies, Restless Winds and Speaking Alone by Aspen Music Festival Contemporary Ensemble under Stephen Mosko, Taming the Furies performed by Bryan Guarnuccio on Points of Entry: The Laurels Project, Vol. 2, Manhattan Stories: The Music of Faye-Ellen Silverman, Dialogue, Dialogue Continued, Left Behind, Love Songs, Protected Sleep, Taming the Furies, Translations, Transatlantic Tales: Danish Delights, In Shadow, Pregnant Pauses, Processional, 3 Guitars, Wilde's World. *Television:* Adhesions, WKAR TV. *Publications include:* 20th Century Section of the Schirmer History of Music; journal articles. *Honours:* winner, Parents' League Competition (aged 13) 1961, Macdowell Fellowship 1981, Gov.'s Citation 1982, 30 Sept. 1982 Faye-Ellen Silverman Day declared in Baltimore, Md by Mayor Donald Schaeffer, Yaddo Fellow 1984, Composers' Conf. Fellow 1985, Rockefeller Foundation residency, Bellagio 1987, Virginia Liebeler Biennial Grant for Mature Women, Nat. League of American Pen Women 2002. *Telephone:* (212) 627-5162 (home). *E-mail:* fayenote@post.harvard.edu (home); silvermf@newschool.edu (office). *Website:* www.fayeellensilverman.com.

SILVERMAN, Stanley Joel; American composer; b. 5 July 1938, New York, NY; s. of Meyer Silverman and Eva Kass Silverman; one s. one d. *Education:* Boston Univ., Mills Coll., Columbia Univ., Berkshire Music Centre. *Career:* writer of incidental music for plays; composer of operas, chamber music and film music; two comms from Chamber Music Soc. of Lincoln Center; his music has been performed at int. festivals including Autumn Festivals of Paris and Madrid, European Cultural Centre of Delphi, Greece, Stratford Festival of Canada, Royal Exchange Theatre, Manchester, UK, RSC, Stratford-upon-Avon and London, UK, Shakespeare's Globe Theatre, London, UK; Advisor/Consultant, Rockefeller Foundation 1980; Advisor, Nat. Opera Inst., Washington, DC 1982; mem. Bd American Music Center, New York 1981–84, Theatre Communications Group 1986, Bd Dirs Lincoln Center Inst. 1970–2005. *Compositions include:* operas and musical plays: Elephant Steps, Tanglewood 1968, Dr Selavy's Magic Theatre, Stockbridge and Off Broadway 1972, Hotel for Criminals, Stockbridge and Off Broadway 1974, The American Imagination 1978, Up From Paradise (with Arthur Miller) 1980, Madame Adare, New York City Opera 1981, The Columbine String Quartet Tonight, Stockbridge 1981, Up from Paradise, New York 1983, The Golem 1984, Africanus Instructus, New York 1986, A Good Life, Kennedy Center 1986, Black Sea Follies, Stockbridge and Off Broadway 1986, Love and Science 1990, In Celebration 1990, Eridos 1999, Shakespeare and Our Planet 2001, Reveille (Trio No. 2) 2010, 2011; film scores: Nanook of the North 1975, Simon 1979, Eyewitness 1981, I'm Dancing As Fast As I Can 1982; theatre music: Bent 1979, Othello 1982, The Little Foxes 1982, Private Lives 1983, The Bluebird of Happiness 1987, Caucasian Chalk Circle 1987, The Merchant of Venice 1989, Timon of Athens 1991, Measure for Measure 1992, St Joan 1993, Timon of Athens 1993, The Government Inspector 1994, The Molières Comedies 1994, Twelfth Night 1994, Uncle Vanya 1995, The Capeman (musical by Paul Simon) 1998, Ah, Wilderness! Lincoln Center Theater; TV music: Behind the Scenes with David Hockney. *Honours:* Obie Award 1968, Drama Desk Award 1973, Naumburg Foundation Comm. Award 1977, Koussevitzky Foundation Comm. Award 1974, Grammy Award (as arranger) 1997, Guggenheim Fellowships, grants from Nat. Endowment for the Arts, Rockefeller Foundation, Ford Foundation. *Current Management:* c/o Kathy Lombard, 31 Rockinghorse Road, Rancho Palo Verde, CA 90275, USA. *Telephone:* (212) 221-0200. *Fax:* (212) 221-0253. *E-mail:* kl@kmlfirm.com. *Website:* www.kathylombard.com. *Address:* c/o Primary Wave Music Publishing, 116 East 16th Street, 9th Floor, New York, NY 10003 (office); 2600 Netherland Avenue, Apt 2406, Riverdale, NY 10463, USA (home). *E-mail:* BenRenaMus@aol.com (office). *Website:* www.stanleysilverman.com.

SILVERTHORNE, Paul; British violist. *Career:* Principal Violist, London Sinfonietta 1988–, London Symphony Orchestra 1991–; solo performances worldwide, recitals, masterclasses and summer schools; Prof., Royal Acad. of Music. *Recordings include:* Brahms Sonatas Op 120 and Songs with Viola 1989, Britten, Hindemith, Shostakovich 1993, Rózsa Viola Concerto 1994, John Biggs Concerto for Viola Winds and Percussion 1999, David Baker Concert Piece for Viola and Orchestra 2000, Invocations 2001, Michael Berkeley Viola Concerto 2003, Vaughan Williams Flos Campi 2004. *Current Management:* Robert Gilder & Company, 91 Great Russell Street, London, WC1B 3PS, England. *Telephone:* (20) 7580-7758. *Fax:* (20) 7580-7739. *E-mail:* cathy@robert-gilder.com; www.robert-gilder.com. *E-mail:* mail@paulsilverthorne.com (office). *Website:* www.paulsilverthorne.com.

SILVESTRELLI, Andrea; Italian singer (bass); b. 1966, Ancona. *Education:* Rossini Conservatory, Pesaro. *Career:* debut as Rodolfo in La Sonnambula at Spoleto, 1989; sang Fiesco in Simon Boccanegra 1989, Banquo in Macbeth at Jesi and the Commendatore at Bologna and Rome; season 1992–93 as Colline at Naples, the Monk in Don Carlos at La Scala and Baldassare in La Favorita at Philadelphia; Macerata Festival as Monterone in Rigoletto, Sarastro in Die Zauberflöte; Commendatore in Don Giovanni for the Holland and Ludwigsburg Festivals, Scottish Opera and in Toulouse 1995–96; Florence 1996 in Il Prigioniero by Dallapiccola and Capello in Bellini's I Capuleti at the Opéra Bastille; season 1999–200 as Verdi's Lodovico at Munich, Oroveso in Norma at Geneva and Sparafucile (Rigoletto) at the Chicago Lyric Opera; Concerts in Italy and elsewhere. *Recordings include:* Don Giovanni, Don Carlos, Mahler's 8th Symphony.

SILVESTRINI, Roberta; academic and composer; b. 3 Jan. 1964, Milan, Italy; m. Lorenzo Brunelli 1996. *Education:* G. Rossini Conservatory, Pesaro, G. B. Martini Conservatory, Bologna, studied with Franco Donatoni at Chigiana and S Cecilia Acads, and with Ennio Morricone. *Career:* debut at Institut Français, Naples 1987; collaborated with int. solists, theatrical companies, national and foreign ensembles; works performed at major venues and festivals including La Fenice Venice, Carnegie Hall New York, Harvard Univ., Gaudeamus Amsterdam, Acads S Cecilia and Chigiana; broadcasts for RAI radio and television, Bayerische Rundfunk and others; Dir, San Giovanni Choir; Prof., Fermo State Conservatory of Music; Artistic Dir, Asscn for Ancient and Contemporary Music. *Compositions include:* La Toile d'araignée for flute quartet 1989, Charmant for double bass 1990, Agité for double bass 1991, Crescendo intenso for violin, viola, cello, vibraphone, marimba 1992, Energique for piano 1993, Nuances éclatantes for saxophone quartet 1993, Animé for viola 1993, Pour Toi for guitar 1994, Epaisseurs No. 2 for four flutes and two pianos 1995, Sursauts for two percussionists 1995, L'Acquata for narrator and piano 1998, Spruzzi d'onde for string quartet 1998, Monsiue Oz Nerol le Fou for bass clarinet 1999. *Honours:* finalist Premio 900 Musicale Europeo 1987, SIAE Scholarship 1991.

SILVESTROV, Valentin Vasilyevich; Ukrainian composer; b. 30 Sept. 1937, Kiev. *Education:* Kiev State Conservatory, studied with Boris Lyatoshinsky and Lev Revutsky. *Career:* took courses at an evening music school while training to become a civil engineer 1955–58; compositions performed in USSR and numerous countries in Europe and in USA; Visiting Composer, Almeida Music Festival, London 1989, Gidon Kremer's Lockenhaus Festival, Austria 1990, and at other festivals in Denmark, Finland, and the Netherlands; Visiting Fellow, German Academic Exchange Service, Berlin 1998–99. *Compositions include:* five symphonies for large symphony orchestra 1963–82, Symphony for baritone with orchestra Echo Momentum on verses of A. Pushkin 1987, string quartets 1978, 1988, Dedication – symphony for violin and orchestra 1991, Mertamusica for piano and orchestra 1992, numerous chamber ensembles, piano pieces, vocal cycles, choruses, Metamusic 1993, Dedication for violin and orchestra 1993, Sixth Symphony 2002. *Honours:* S. Koussevitsky Prize (USA) 1967, Prize of Gaudeamus Soc. (Netherlands) 1970. *Address:* Entuziastov str. 35/1, Apt. 49, 252147 Kiev, Ukraine (home). *Telephone:* (44) 517-04-47 (home).

SIMA, Gabriele; singer (mezzo-soprano); b. 1955, Salzburg, Austria. *Education:* Salzburg Mozarteum and Vienna Musikhochschule. *Career:* sang in the baroque repertoire with the Viennese ensemble, Spectaculum and studied with Nikolaus Harnoncourt from 1979; Opera Studio of the Vienna Opera 1979–82; sang at the Vienna Staatsoper from 1982, Tebaldo in Don Carlos 1989; Salzburg Festival from 1980, notably as Johanna in the premiere of Cerha's Baal 1981 and in the 1984 premiere of Berio's Un Re in Ascolto; guest appearances at the Hamburg Staatsoper and at Zürich, Berlin from 1988; opera and concert tour of Japan 1989; other roles include Rosina, Cherubino, Octavian, Siebel, Annio (Titus), Idamante in Idomeneo, Feodor (Boris), Dorabella (Così), Zerlina; season 2000–01 as Giunone in Legrenzi's La divisone del mondo, at Innsbruck and Schwetzingen; Handel's Agrippina at Graz and Carlotta in Die schweigsame Frau for the Opéra Bastille. *Recordings:* Handel's Jephtha, Tannhäuser (as Shepherd), Barbiere di Siviglia (as Berta).

SIMCOCK, Iain Hamilton, FRCO; British organist and choirmaster; *Music Director, Académie Vocale de Paris;* b. 13 March 1965, Hemel Hempstead, Herts., England. *Education:* Solihull School, Christ Church Coll., Oxford, St Georges Chapel, Windsor Castle. *Career:* recitals for major venues all over UK and Europe; Sub-organist of Westminster Abbey and Asst Master of Music, Westminster Cathedral 1988–95; Founder Int. Bach Ensemble; currently Music Dir Académie Vocale de Paris; frequent broadcaster for BBC Radio 3; recitals at Nôtre Dame de Paris, Strasbourg Cathedral, BBC Proms, Royal Albert Hall; frequent tours of Scandinavia, Germany and France. *Recordings:* first performance of 'Christus' (passion symphony for organ) – Francis Pott; Vierne Symphonies. *Publications:* contrib. of articles on Music of Louis Vierne to the Musical Times. *Honours:* Hon. ARAM for services to sacred music; Second Grand Prix, Chartres Int. Organ Competition. *Address:* Académie Vocale de Paris, 76 rue de la Verrerie, 75004 Paris, France (office). *Telephone:* 6-77-52-35-70 (mobile) (office). *E-mail:* direction@academievocale-paris.org (office). *Website:* www.academievocale-paris.org (office).

SIMENSEN, Bjorn; Norwegian opera company director; *General Director, Norwegian National Opera;* b. 28 June 1947, Lillehammer. *Career:* Dir, Göteborg Symphony Orchestra 1980–84; Gen. Dir, Norwegian Nat. Opera 1985–. *Honours:* Commdr of St Olav 2008. *Address:* Den Norske Opera, Postboks 8800, Youngstorget, 0028 Oslo, Norway (office). *Telephone:* 23315000 (office). *Fax:* 23315030 (office). *E-mail:* bjorn.simensen@operaen.no (office). *Website:* www.operaen.no (office).

SIMMONDS, Victoria; British singer (mezzo-soprano); b. Lancashire. *Education:* Guildhall School of Music and Drama. *Career:* debut with ENO 2000, Co. Prin. 2000-05; sang in Les Troyens with London Symphony Orchestra under Sir Colin Davis at the BBC Proms 2003; title role of Carmen at Royal Albert Hall 2005; has also sung in UK for Grange Park Opera, Garsington Opera, Opera Holland Park and Buxton Festival and performed with Netherlands Opera, Stuttgart and Hallé Opera, and with Berlin Philharmonic (Wellgunde in Das Rheingold) under Sir Simon Rattle at Aix-en-Provence Festival 2006 and at Salzburg 2007; cr. title role in Jonathan Dove's The Adventures of Pinocchio at Opera North 2010; in concert, has sung in Le Comte Ory and title role in L'Enfant et les Sortilèges at Concertgebouw Amsterdam 2007, and worked with the Philharmonia and Hallé orchestras, and at Salzburg and Edinburgh Festivals; sang Marie in world premiere of George Benjamin's Written on Skin at Aix 2012, also at Covent Garden, Amsterdam, Capitole de Toulouse, Maggio Musicale Florence, Opéra Comique Paris and at festivals in Tanglewood, Munich and Vienna; world premiere of Joanne Lee's The Way Back Home for ENO at Young Vic 2014. *Recordings include:* Bellini: Il pirata, Janáček: Katya Kabanova (Varvara), Rossini: Ermione (Cefisa), Benjamin: Written on Skin (Marie) (Gramophone Award for Best Contemporary Recording 2014) 2013. *Current Management:* c/o Ingpen & Williams, 7 St George's Court, 131 Putney Bridge Road, London, SW15 2PA, England. *Telephone:* (20) 8874-3222. *Fax:* (20) 8877-3113. *E-mail:* jg@ingpen .co.uk. *Website:* www.ingpen.co.uk.

SIMON, Abbey; American pianist; b. 8 Jan. 1920, New York, NY; m. Dina Levinson Simon 1942; one s. *Education:* Curtis Inst. of Music, Philadelphia. *Career:* debut at Town Hall, New York, as winner of Walter W. Naumberg Award 1940; concert tours in recital and with orchestra on six continents 1940–; fmr Prof. of Piano, Juilliard School of Music, New York; Cullen Chair for Distinguished Prof., Univ. of Houston, Texas. *Recordings:* Complete Chopin repertoire for solo piano and orchestra, Complete Ravel repertoire for solo piano and orchestra, all Rachmaninov's works for piano and orchestra plus transcriptions, Beethoven and Mozart Woodwind quintets Mendelssohn Variations and Songs Without Words; many other recordings include the Piano Virtuoso and works by Schumann, Saint-Saens, Brahms and Liszt.

Honours: Hon. Dr of Arts (Chapman Univ.); First Prize, Walter W. Naumburg Piano Competition, Best Recital of the Year, Fed. of Music Clubs, New York, Nat. Orchestral Award, Elizabeth Sprague Coolidge Medal, London, Harriet Cohen Foundation, London. *Address:* 45 Chemin Moise Deboule, 1209 Geneva, Switzerland (home). *E-mail:* info@abbeysimon.com (office). *Website:* www.abbeysimon.com.

SIMON, Geoffrey; Australian conductor; b. 3 July 1946, Adelaide, SA. *Education:* Melbourne University, Juilliard School and Indiana University, USA. *Career:* guest appearances with leading orchestras, 1974–; Music Dir, Australian Sinfonia London, Albany Symphony Orchestra, New York 1987–89, Cala Records, London 1991–; Artistic Adviser, Sacramento Symphony, California 1993–94, Music Dir 1994–; regular concerts with The London Philharmonic, London Symphony and English Chamber Orchestras; other engagements with the Munich, Israel and New Japan Philharmonic Orchestras, the American, City of Birmingham, Sapporo and Tokyo Metropolitan Symphonies, the Orchestras of the Australian Broadcasting Corporation and the Australian Opera; conducted the Royal Philharmonic Orchestra in the premiere of Paul Patterson's 1st Symphony at the Cheltenham Festival; mem. Stokowski Soc. (vice-pres. 1993–). *Recordings:* music by French composers of the 1920s and rare music by Respighi and Tchaikovsky; Patterson's Mass of the Sea; The Warriors and other works by Percy Grainger; Music by Debussy, Ravel, Respighi, Brahms, Borodin, Mussorgsky, Saint-Saëns and Barry Conyngham; The London Cello Sound–the 40 cellos of the London Philharmonic, Royal Philharmonic Orchestra, BBC Symphony Orchestra and the Philharmonia Orchestra, similarly, the London Violin Sound, the London Viola Sound and the London Trombone Sound. *Honours:* prizewinner, John Player International Conductor's Award, 1974; Prix de la Ville de Paris, Académie du Disque Français, 1985; Gramophone Award (for Respighi recordings). *Telephone:* (20) 8883-7306. *Fax:* (20) 8365-3388. *E-mail:* geoffreysimon@aol.com. *Website:* www.geoffreysimon.com.

SIMON, Laszlo; pianist and academic; b. 16 July 1948, Miskolc, Hungary; m. Sabine Simon 1978; two d. *Education:* studied in Stockholm, Hannover, New York with Hans Leygraf, Ilona Kabos, Claudio Arrau. *Career:* debut 1966; appearances in Hamburg, Rome, Stockholm, Helsinki, Oslo, Berlin, Tokyo, Seoul, London, Porto; Prof., Karlsruhe State Acad. 1977–, Hochschule der Kunste, Berlin 1981–, in Stockholm 1988–; masterclasses at Murashino Acad., Tokyo 1988–. *Recordings:* Liszt, Clementi, Kodály, Schubert, de Frumerie, Velte. *Honours:* third prize Busoni Competition, first prize Casagrande Competition.

SIMONELLA, Liborio; singer (tenor); b. 10 Jan. 1933, Cordoba, Argentina. *Education:* studied in Buenos Aires with Mario Melani and Angel Celega. *Career:* debut at Teatro Colón, Buenos Aires, as Roberto in Le Villi by Puccini 1967; sang Jason in the premiere of Medea by Guidi-Drei 1973; Teatro Colón, Rio de Janeiro and Santiago as Verdi's Alfredo and Duke of Mantua, Don José, Andrea Chenier, Hoffmann, Rodolfo and Cavaradossi; season 1984 as Saint-Saëns's Samson at Santiago and Pierre in War and Peace at the Teatro Colón; other roles have included Canio in Pagliacci and Aegisthus in Elektra; many concert engagements.

SIMONETTI, Riccardo; British singer (baritone); b. 10 Jan. 1970, Leigh, Lancashire, England. *Education:* Royal Northern College of Music with Robert Alderson. *Career:* sang Rodimarte in Scarlatti's Il Trionfo d'Onore at Liège, Trento, Caen and Brussels; English National Opera from 1996, notably as Bill in Mahagonny (debut role) and Papageno; Ping in Turandot at Nice, Albert in Werther for English Touring Opera, Britten's Demetrius for the Broomhill Trust and Belcore for Clonter Farm Opera; Season 1997 with Mozart's Count for English Touring Opera and a principal contract with ENO; Season 1998 with ENO in The Tales of Hoffmann and the premiere of Dr Ox's Experiment by Gavin Bryars; Concerts include the St Matthew Passion with the Liverpool Philharmonic Orchestra, Messiah under David Willcocks and concerts with the Liverpool Philharmonic Choir. *Honours:* Winner, Anne Ziegler/Esso Award, 1993. *Current Management:* c/o James Black Management, The Old Grammar School, High Street, Rye, East Sussex, TN31 7JF, England. *Telephone:* (1797) 224668; 7810 436773 (mobile). *Fax:* (1797) 224668. *E-mail:* james@jamesblackmanagement.com. *Website:* www .jamesblackmanagement.com.

SIMONOV, Yuri Ivanovich; Russian conductor; *Music Director, Moscow Philharmonic Orchestra;* b. 4 March 1941, Saratov; s. of opera singers at Saratov Opera; m. Olga Mouzyka; one s. *Education:* Leningrad Conservatory (now St Petersburg State Conservatory) with Kramarov (viola) and Rabinovich (conducting). *Career:* debut 1953, conducting school orchestra; led several opera productions while a student; Prin. Conductor Kislovodsk Philharmonic 1968–69; Asst Conductor Leningrad Philharmonic 1968–69; Prin. Conductor Bolshoi Theatre, Moscow from 1970, toured with Prince Igor to the Metropolitan Opera 1975; premieres include Shchedrin's ballet Anna Karenina 1972, Das Rheingold at Bolshoi Theatre 1979; teacher, Moscow Conservatory from 1978; Music Dir and Chief Conductor Belgian Nat. Orchestra, Brussels 1994–2002; Music Dir Moscow Philharmonic Orchestra 1998–, Liszt-Wagner Orchestra, Budapest; frequent guest conductor with British orchestras; performances include Eugene Onegin by Tchaikovsky 1982 and La Traviata 1986 at Covent Garden, Mahler Festival in Paris with London Philharmonic Orchestra 1989, The Queen of Spades at Bastille Opéra, Paris 1993, concert tours of Japan with NHK Orchestra 1993–95, Der Ring des Nibelungen at Budapest Opera House 1995–98, Shostakovich Symphony No. 4 with Belgian

Nat. Orchestra 1996; debut with Orchestre de la Suisse Romande 2003, Warsaw Nat. Philharmonic 2004; toured Japan with Moscow Philharmonic 2004–12; debut with Beethovenhalle Orchestra, Bonn 2004, Budapest Festival Orchestra 2005; led Moscow Philharmonic Orchestra on tours to USA, Japan and Czech Repub. 2005; toured Spain, UK and Korea and conducted a new production of Die Meistersinger von Nürnberg at Hungarian Opera House, Budapest 2005–06; frequent guest conductor with Het Brabants Orkest 2008–12; debut with Strasbourg Philharmonic Orchestra 2010; world tour in connection with 70th anniversary (China, Spain, Germany, Ukraine, Romania, South Korea, UK, Russia); debut with Polska Filharmonia Baltycka in Gdansk 2012; Chair. of Jury, All-Russia Conductors Competition 2011, 2015; Prof. of Conducting, St Petersburg Rimsky-Korsakov Conservatoire 2006–. *Recordings include:* Glinka, Ruslan and Lyudmila (opera with the Bolshoi), Anna Karenina (ballet with the Bolshoi), Wagner: excerpts and overtures, Mahler: Symphony No. 1 (with RPO), Tchaikovsky: Romeo and Juliet and 1812 Overture, Prokofiev: Romeo and Juliet and Lieutenent Kijé. *Honours:* Order of Merits in Culture (Poland) 1988, Order of Honour 2001, Officer Cross Order of Merit (Hungary) 2001, Commdr Order of the Star (Romania) 2003, Order of Achievements before the Fatherland, IV Grade 2011; Laureate, All-USSR Conductors Competition 1966, winner, Accad. di Santa Cecilia Competition, Rome 1968, Artist of Merit of the USSR 1981. *Current Management:* c/o Robert Slotover, Rayfield Allied, Southbank House, Black Prince Road, London, SE1 7SJ, England. *E-mail:* robert.slotover@rayfieldallied.com (home). *Website:* www.yurisimonov.com.

SIMONYAN, Mikhail; Russian violinist; b. 1986, Novosibirsk. *Education:* Curtis Inst. of Music. *Career:* recitals in USA and Russia; toured with Nat. Philharmonic of Russia; concerts/solo performances with major Russian orchestras, New World Symphony, Vienna Tonkünstler Orchestra, Cincinnati Symphony Orchestra, New Jersey Symphony, Pittsburgh Symphony Orchestra; worked with conductors including Valery Gergiev, Mikhail Pletnev, Constantine Orbelian, Vladimir Spivakov, Arnold Katz, Kristjan Järvi, Leon Botstein and Yehudi Menuhin. *Recording:* Prokofiev Sonatas for Violin and Piano 2009. *Honours:* Yehudi Menuhin Foundation Award, Virtuoso of the Year, St Petersburg 2000, Nat. Acad. of Achievement Award in the Performing Arts 2003, Classical Recording Foundation Young Artist Award 2008. *Current Management:* c/o Tanja Dorn, IMG Artists, Carnegie Hall Tower, 152 West 57th Street, 5th Floor, New York, NY 10019, USA. *Telephone:* (212) 994-3540. *Fax:* (212) 994-3550. *E-mail:* tdorn@imgartists.com. *Website:* www.imgartists.com; www.mikhailsimonyanviolin.com.

SIMPSON, Dudley George, DipMus (Hons); Australian composer, conductor and pianist; b. 4 Oct. 1922, Melbourne, Vic.; m. Jill Yvonne Bathurst 1960; one s. two d. *Education:* Melbourne Univ. with Vera Porter and Victor Stephenson, studied orchestration with Elford Mack in Melbourne, Dr Gordon Jacob in England, composition with John Ingram in Australia. *Career:* debut conducting 1st and 2nd M.D. Borovansky Ballet, Royal Ballet, Covent Garden; Guest Conductor, Royal Ballet, Covent Garden 1960–62; prin. conductor at British and European festivals, including Monte Carlo, Nice, Athens and Middle East 1961–63; two world tours with Dame Margot Fonteyn and Rudolph Nureyev 1962–64; Conductor, Tokyo Philharmonic Orchestra ballet festival 1985; conducted premiere of own ballet work, Class at Covent Garden 1986; Paul Harris Fellow 2004. *Compositions:* The Winter Play (ballet, Sadler's Wells Royal Ballet), Here We Come (ballet, transcription for orchestra, Canadian Nat. Ballet), Class (ballet, Royal Ballet School), Marguerite and Armand (for Fonteyn and Nureyev, transcription for orchestra), The Pastoral Symphony; numerous TV themes and incidental music, including Shakespeare Canon (for BBC), A Trilogy of Psalms for choir, numerous Doctor Who scores. *E-mail:* dudd007@bigpond.com.

SIMPSON, Marietta, BME, MM; American singer (mezzo-soprano) and academic; *Professor of Music (Voice), Jacobs School of Music, Indiana University*; b. 1954, Philadelphia. *Education:* Temple Univ., State Univ. of New York at Binghamton. *Career:* sang in concert with the Atlanta Symphony Orchestra and in Dallas, Los Angeles, Cincinnati and Detroit; Virginia Opera, 1985 as Pat in the premiere of Harriet, A Woman Called Moses by Thea Musgrave; Glyndebourne Festival, 1986–87; As Maria in Porgy and Bess, also at Covent Garden in 1992; sang Alto Rhapsody by Brahms at Carnegie Hall, 1988; Virgil Thomson's Four Saints in Three Acts at Houston, Edinburgh and San Diego 1996; currently Prof. of Music (Voice), Jacobs School of Music, Indiana Univ. *Recordings include:* Porgy and Bess, Mendelssohn's Elijah. *Address:* Music Addition, MU003, Jacobs School of Music, Indiana University, 1201 East Third Street, Bloomington, IN 47405, USA (office). *Telephone:* (812) 855-2721 (office). *E-mail:* simpsonm@indiana.edu (office). *Website:* www.music.indiana.edu (office).

SIMS, Ezra, BA, BMus, MA; American composer and academic; b. 16 Jan. 1928, Birmingham, Ala. *Education:* Birmingham Southern Coll., Yale Univ. School of Music, US Army Language School, Mills Coll. *Career:* Music Dir, New England Dinosaur Dance Theatre 1968–74; mem. Theory Faculty, New England Conservatory 1976–78; Pres. Dinosaur Annex Music Ensemble 1977–81; Lecturer, Mozarteum 1992–93; Guggenheim Foundation Fellowship 1962; Fellow, Nat. Educ. Asscn 1976, 1978; Massachusetts Artists Foundation Fellowship 1979. *Compositions include:* Twenty Years After 1978, All Done from Memory 1980, Ruminations 1980, Phenomena 1981, Sextet 1981, Solo After Sextet 1981, Quartet 1982, Pictures for an Institution 1983, String Quartet No. 4 1984, Night Unto Night 1984, The Conversions 1985, Solo in Four Movements 1987, Quintet 1987, Flight 1989, Night Piece 1989, Concert Piece 1990, Duo 1992, Invocation 1992, Stanzas 1995, Duo 1996, If I Told Him 1996, Kumo Sudare 1999, String Quartet No. 5 2001, Musing and Reminiscence 2003. *Publications include:* contrib. to Apologia pro Musica Sua, Jaarboch 1992, Stichting Huyghens-Fokker, Reflections on This and That, in Perspectives of New Music Vol. 29 No. 1, Yet Another 72-Noter, in Computer Music Journal Vol. 12, No. 4. *Honours:* American Acad. of Arts and Letters Award 1985, Distinguished Achievement Award 2009. *Current Management:* c/o Rosalie Calabrese Management, Bos 20580 Park West Station, New York, NY 10025-1521, USA. *E-mail:* rcmgt@yahoo.com. *Address:* 229 Hurley Street #2, Cambridge, MA 02141, USA (home). *Telephone:* (617) 895-9579 (office); (617) 864-8781 (office). *E-mail:* ezrsims@aol.com (home). *Website:* www.ezrasims.com.

SIMSON, Julie, BMusEd, MMus; American singer (mezzo-soprano) and academic; b. 13 Feb. 1956, Milwaukee, WI. *Education:* Western Michigan University, University of Illinois. *Career:* New York recital debut, Weill Recital Hall, Carnegie Hall 1989; radio appearance, The Listening Room, New York Times Radio 1989; Lyric Opera Cleveland debut as Minerva in The Return of Ulysses 1991; Opera Colorado debut as Emilia in Otello 1991; other opera appearances with Santa Fe Opera, Dallas Civic Opera, Opera Colorado, Houston Opera Association; appeared as soloist with Milwaukee, Des Moines, Missoula, Denver, Cheyenne symphonies; George Crumb Festival featuring Ancient Voices of Children, Prague, Czech Republic; solo recital at Prague Spring Festival 1994; sang Suzuki in Madama Butterfly at Colorado Opera Festival 1999; La Dama in Macbeth for Opera Colorado 1999; soloist in Mahler's 2nd Symphony with the Omaha Symphony Orchestra 1999; Assoc. Prof. of Voice, University of Colorado. *Recordings:* Horatio Parker's Hora Norissima; Mahler's 8th Symphony. *Honours:* Mozart Prize, International Belvedere Competition, Vienna, 1985; Winner, East and West Artists International Competition for Carnegie Hall Debut; National 2nd Place Winner, NATS Artist Award. *Address:* University of Colorado-Boulder, College of Music, Campus Box 301, Boulder, CO 80309-0301, USA.

SINGER, Malcolm John; British composer and conductor; *Director of Music, The Yehudi Menuhin School*; b. 13 July 1953, London, England; m. Sara Catherine Nathan 1984. *Education:* Magdalene Coll., Cambridge, studied with Nadia Boulanger in Paris and Gyorgy Ligeti in Hamburg. *Career:* teacher, Yehudi Menuhin School; Dept of PCS, Guildhall School of Music and Drama; teacher of composition, Guildhall School of Music and Drama and the Yehudi Menuhin School; Dir of Music, Yehudi Menuhin School 1998–; mem. APC, British Acad. of Songwriters, Composers and Authors. *Compositions include:* Time Must Have a Stop for orchestra and piano solo 1976, The Icarus Toccata for piano duet 1979, A Singer's Complaint 1979, Making Music for narrator and orchestra 1983, Nonet for strings 1984, Sonata for piano 1986, Yetziah, Music for Dance 1987, Piano Quartet 1989, York, a cantata 1990, Kaddish for a cappella choir 1991, Honk for Ugly Culture 1992, A Hopeful Place, for Yehudi Menuhin's 80th Birthday 1996, Dragons 1998, The Jailer's Tale 2010. *Honours:* Cobbett Medal, The Worshipful Co. of Musicians 2012. *Address:* 29 Goldsmith Avenue, London, W3 6HR, England (home). *Telephone:* (20) 8992-2318 (home). *E-mail:* malcolmsinger@yehudimenuhinschool.co.uk (office). *Website:* www.malcolmsinger.co.uk.

SINGLETON, Alvin; American composer; b. 28 Dec. 1940, Brooklyn, NY; m. Lisa D. Cooper. *Education:* New York Univ., Columbia Univ., Juilliard School, Berkshire Music Center, Tanglewood, Mass, Yale Univ., Accad. Naz. di Santa Cecilia, Rome, Italy, Ferienkurse für Neue Musik, Darmstadt, Germany and Instituto Musicale, Vicenza, Italy. *Career:* mem. Woodwind Quintet, Berkshire Music Festvial 1969; freelance composer, Graz, Austria 1973; Composer-in-Rresidence, Atlanta Symphony Orchestra 1985–88, Spelman Coll. 1988–91; Master Artist, Atlantic Center for the Arts 1992; Composer-in-Residence, Calif. State Univ., Los Angeles 1996; UNISYS Composer-in-Residence, Detroit Symphony Orchestra 1996–97, Ritz Chamber Players, Jacksonville, Fla 2002–03, Visiting Composer-in-Residence, Tirana, Albania 2008. *Compositions include:* Epitaph (choral) 1966, String Quartet No. 1 1967, Woodwind Quintet 1968–69, Cinque for piano 1969, Argoru I for piano 1970, Argoru II for cello 1970, A Seasoning 1971, Argoru III for flute 1971, Be Natural for strings 1974, Kwitana for chamber orchestra 1974, Messa (soprano, chorus and chamber ensemble) 1975, Dream Sequence (opera) 1976, Extension of a Dream (percussion) 1977, Le Tombeau du Petit Prince for harpsichord 1978, Argoru IV for viola 1978, Again for chamber orchestra 1979, Et nunc (alto flute, bass clarinet and double bass) 1980, Necessity is a Mother (drama) 1981, A Yellow Rose Petal for orchestra 1982, Inside-Out for piano four hands 1983–84, La flora (chamber ensemble) 1983, Argoru Va for bass clarinet 1984, Argoru Vb for alto flute 1984, Apple for clarinet quartet 1984, Akwaaba (chamber orchestra) 1985, Changing Faces for piano 1986, Shadows for orchestra 1987, After Fallen Crumbs for orchestra 1987, Fallen Crumbs (choral) 1987, Alleluia (choral) 1987, Gospel (choral) 1988, Argoru VI for marimba 1988, Bernsteinlied (soprano, flute and piano)1988, Eine Idee ist ein Stück Stoff (An Idea is a Piece of Cloth, for string orchestra) 1988, Secret Desire to be Black for string quartet 1988, Between Sisters (soprano, flute, vibraphone and piano)1990, Sinfonia Diaspora (orchestra) 1991, Even Tomorrow for orchestra 1991, Durch Alles for orchestra 1992, 56 Blows for orchestra 1993, Intezar for string trio 1993, Cara Mia Gwen for orchestra 1993, Fifty Times Around the Sun (for clarinet and piano) 1994, Argoru VII for vibraphone 1994, Somehow We Can for string quartet 1994, Sing to the Sun (for narrator, children's chorus, chamber ensemble) 1995, Blues Konzert (piano concerto) 1995, Umoja: Each One of us Counts for narrator and orchestra 1996, Ein kleines Volkslied (chamber ensemble) 1997, In Our Own House (for chamber ensemble) 1998, Praisemaker (for chorus and orchestra) 1998, Mookestueck for electric viola 1999, Jasper Drag (for clarinet, violin and piano) 2000, When Given a Choice (for orchestra) 2004, Truth (for chamber orchestra) 2006, Through It All (for wind quintet) 2008, Brooklyn Bones (for tenor, chorus and orchestra) 2008, After Choice (for string orchestra) 2009. *Recordings including:* albums: Shadows 1992, Extension of a Dream 2002, Somehow We Can 2002, Sing to the Sun 2007, Sweet Chariot 2014. *Honours:* New York Univ. Marion Bauer Memorial Award 1967, Yale Univ. Rena Greenwald Memorial Prize 1969–70, Yale Univ. Woods Chandler Memorial Prize 1970–71, Kranischsteiner Musikpreis, Darmstadt 1974, Austrian Radio Musik-protokoll Kompositionpreis, Graz 1979, 1981, NEA grants 1980, 1990, MacDowell Colony fellowships 1987, 1989, 1991, 1994, 1995, 1997, City of Atlanta Mayor's Fellowship in the Arts 1989, ASCAP Standard Award 1997–98, Guggenheim Fellowship 2003. *Current Management:* c/o Norman D. Ryan, Schott Music Corporation, 254 West 31st Street, 15th Floor, New York, NY 10001, USA. *Telephone:* (212) 461-6940. *E-mail:* norman.ryan@schott-music.com. *Website:* www.schott-music.com; www.alvinsingleton.com.

SINYAVSKAYA, Tamara Ilyinichna; Russian singer (mezzo-soprano); b. 6 July 1943, Moscow; m. Muslim Magovaev 1974. *Education:* Moscow Music Coll. and State Theatre Art Inst. *Career:* soloist with Bolshoi Theatre 1964–; studied at La Scala, Milan 1973–74; currently Head, Dept of Vocal Training, Russian Acad. of Theatre Arts (GITIS). *Opera roles include:* Olga in Tchaikovsky's Eugene Onegin, Carmen, Blanche and Frosya in Prokofiev's Gambler and Semyon Kotko, Vanya in Glinka's A Life for the Tsar, Ratmir in Glinka's Ruslan and Lyudmila, Lyubasha in Rimsky-Korsakov's The Tsar's Bride, Varvara in Not Love Alone. *Honours:* Order of Merit 2001, Order of Lomonosov First Degree 2004; First Prize, Int. Singing Competition, Sofia 1968, Grand Prix Int. Singing Competition, Belgium 1969, First Prize, Int. Tchaikovsky Competition, Moscow 1970, People's Artist of RSFSR 1976, People's Artist of USSR 1982, Irina Arkhipova Prize 2004. *Address:* Department of Vocal Training, Russian Academy of Theatre Arts (GITIS), Moscow, 125009, Malyy Kislovskiy pereulok, 6, Russia. *Website:* gitis.net.

SIPPOLA, Una; singer (mezzo-soprano); b. 1959, Janakkala, Finland. *Education:* Sibelius Acad., Helsinki. *Career:* debut in Helsinki 1985 as Amneris in Aida; Savonlinna Festival from 1986; Freiburg Opera from 1989, notably as Jane Seymour in Anna Bolena 1991–92; season 1992 at Hagen as Lizzie Borden in Jack Beeson's opera; Deutsche Oper am Rhein from 1993, as Eboli in Don Carlos, Venus in Tannhäuser; Laura in La Gioconda and Brangaene and Kundry; Bayreuth Festival 1995 as Venus; Dresden Staatsoper 1996, 1998 as Brangaene and Amneris; Deutsche Oper Berlin from 2000, as Ortrud and other dramatic repertory; many concert appearances. *Recordings include:* Rossini's Petite Messe.

SIRKIA, Raimo; Finnish singer (tenor); *CEO, Sir-Production Oy*; b. 7 Feb. 1951, Helsinki; s. of Raimo A. Sirkia and Lidia Sirkia; m. Cynthia Makris; one s. one d. *Education:* Sibelius Academy in Helsinki, studied in Rome and London. *Career:* sang at Savonlinna Festival 1982–2007, Kiel Opera 1983–85, as Tamino, Lionel in Martha, Pollione and Cavaradossi; sang dramatic roles at Dortmund Opera from 1985 as Riccardo, Manrico, Otello, Alvaro, Walther, Parsifal, Don José, Bacchus, Huon in Oberon, Narraboth and Vladimir in Prince Igor; guest appearances at the Deutsche Oper am Rhein and mem. 1991–2000, Dresden, Stuttgart, Brunswick, Karlsruhe, Basle, Stockholm, Copenhagen, Bordeaux and the Deutsche Oper Berlin (as Manrico 1989), Hanover, Essen, Hamburg (Calaf 1992); mem. Finnish Nat. Opera at Helsinki 1989–2006, singing Edgardo and Alfredo there and at Tallinn 1990; sang at Savonlinna as Radames and as Erik in Der fliegende Holländer 1990; sang Idomeneo at the Finlandia Hall, Helsinki 1991; has appeared as a guest soloist at many important opera houses throughout Europe; role of Canio at the Royal Opera House in Stockholm followed by new production of Pagliacci in Tampere, Finland 1996; debut as Tannhäuser in the Savonlinna Opera Festival's new production 1996, as Siegmund 1996; Siegfried in new production of Wagner's Ring at the Finnish National Opera 1997; sang Siegmund at Helsinki 1998, Lohengrin, Athens 1999, Bayreuth 2000, Turin 2001, Macduff, Deutsche Oper, Berlin 2000, Tristan, Darmstadt 2000, Manrico and Otello, Finnish Nat. Opera 2000, Tristan, Venice 2002, Calaf, Savonlinna 2003, 2004, Singapore 2003; Artistic Dir Savonlinna Opera Festival 2002–07; frequent concert appearances; currently CEO Sir-Production Oy. *Recordings include:* Jää mun lähellein 1984, Der fliegender Holländer (video) 1989, Opera Arias 1992, Amado mio 1994, Symphony No. 8 Mahler 1994, Juha 1995, Lemmen Virtaa 1996, Valkea Joulu – White Christmas 1996, Pohjalaisia (opera) 1997, Die Feen (opera) 1998, Die Loreley (opera) 2003, Mare and Her Son (opera) 2005. *Honours:* Order of the Lion of Finland; Pro Finlandia Medal 2003. *Current Management:* Sir-Production Oy, Hietalahdenkatu 4 A 8a, 00180 Helsinki, Finland. *Telephone:* (40) 5001313. *E-mail:* sirproduction@raimosirkia.com. *Website:* www.sirproductions.com. *Address:* Hietalahdenkatu 4 A 8a, 00180 Helsinki, Finland (office). *E-mail:* mail@raimosirkia.com (office). *Website:* www.raimosirkia.com.

SISA, Hans; singer (bass); b. 1947, Linz, Austria; m. Sophia Larson. *Education:* Salzburg Mozarteum. *Career:* appearances at the Theater am Gärtnerplatz, Munich, Bregenz Festival, Essen, Kiel and Lucca; roles have included Verdi's Padre Guardiano, Fiesco, Ferrando and Sparafucile; Rossini's Basilio, Donizetti's Raimondo, Mozart's Count and King Henry in Lohengrin; sang Nicolai's Falstaff at Basle 1989, and Sarastro at Graz 1995; season 1999–2000 included Salome at Graz, Beethoven's 9th Symphony at Aachen, Freischütz at Savonlinna and the Landgraf in Tannhäuser at Baltimore, USA; further engagements in Rheingold and Götterdämmerung at Graz 2001; other roles include Bellini's Oroveso, Berkley in Der Vampyr by Marschner and the Hermit in Der Freischütz; many concert appearances, including Mahler's Das Klagende Lied, for Italian Radio.

SISMAN, Elaine Rochelle, AB, MFA, PhD; American musicologist; *Anne Parsons Bender Professor, Columbia University*; b. 20 Jan. 1952, New York, NY; m. Martin Fridson 1981, one s. one d. *Education:* Cornell Univ., Princeton Univ. *Career:* Instructor, Univ. of Michigan 1976–79, Asst Prof. 1979–81; Asst Prof., Columbia Univ., New York 1982–90, Assoc. Prof. 1990–94, Prof. 1995–2004, Dept Chair. 1999–2005, Anne Parsons Bender Prof. 2004–; mem., American Musicological Soc. (pres. 2004–06). *Publications:* Haydn and the Classical Variation 1993, Mozart's Jupiter Symphony 1993, Haydn and his World 1997; contrib. to Haydn Studies 1981, Small and Expanded Forms: Koch's Model and Haydn's Music, in Musical Quarterly 1982, Haydn Kongress, Vienna 1982, 1986, The Orchestra: Origins and Transformations 1986, The New Harvard Dictionary of Music 1986, Haydn's Theater Symphonies, in Journal of the American Musicological Society 1990, Brahms and the Variation Canon, in 19th-Century Music 1990, Pathos and the Pathétique, in Beethoven Forum 1994, Genre, Gesture and Meaning in Mozart's Prague Symphony 1997, After the Heroic Style, in Beethoven Forum 1997. *Honours:* Nat. Endowment for the Humanities Fellowship 1981–82. *Address:* Department of Music, Columbia University, 604 Dodge Hall, MC 1811, New York, NY 10027, USA (office). *Telephone:* (212) 854-7728 (office). *Fax:* (212) 854-8191 (office). *E-mail:* es53@columbia.edu (office).

SITKOVETSKY, Dmitry; American/British violinist, conductor, arranger and television presenter; *Music Director, Greensboro Symphony Orchestra*; b. 27 Sept. 1954, Baku, USSR (now Azerbaijan); s. of Julian Sitkovetsky and Bella Davidovich; m. Susan Roberts; one d. *Education:* Moscow Conservatory, Juilliard School of Music, New York (Artistic Diploma). *Career:* debut with Berlin Philharmonic 1980; appearances with Vienna Symphony Orchestra, Orchestre de Paris and the Amsterdam, Rotterdam, Munich and Royal Philharmonic Orchestras in Europe and the Chicago, Cincinnati, Detroit, Montréal and Toronto Symphony Orchestras in N America, Carnegie Hall debut 1986; Artistic Dir Korsholm Festival, Finland 1983–93, Seattle Int. Music Festival 1992–97; Music Dir and Prin. Conductor Ulster Orchestra, NI 1996–2001; Music Dir Tuscan Sun Festival, Cortona, Italy 2003–06; Artist-in-Residence, Orchestra de Castilla & Leon, Valladolid, Spain 2006–09; currently Music Dir Greensboro Symphony Orchestra, Greensboro, N Carolina. *Television:* role of Arkady Greenberg in film Heavy Sand (Russian Moscow TV) 2007, presenter of series Visiting with Dmitry Sitkovetsky for the Kultura channel (Russia). *Recordings include:* Stravinsky: A Soldier's Tale 2012, Chopin: 12 Preludes 2013; more than 50 transcriptions. *Publications:* transcriptions: Bach – Goldberg Variations for String Trio 1985, 2012, Dohnányi – Serenade for string orchestra 1990, Shostakovich – String Symphony Op. 73 1991, Bach Sinfonias for string trio, Bach Dance Suite Nos 1 and 2 for string orchestra 2014. *Honours:* First Prize, Fritz Kreisler Competition, Vienna 1979, Avery Fisher Career grant 1983. *Current Management:* c/o Tanja Dorn, IMG Artists GmbH, Theaterstrasse 2, 30159 Hannover, Germany. *Telephone:* (511) 4378134. *E-mail:* tdorn@imgartists.com. *Website:* www.imgartists.com; www.greensborosymphony.org.

SITSKY, Larry, AM, DFA, FAHA; Australian composer, pianist, musicologist, teacher and broadcaster; *Professor Emeritus, Australian National University*; b. 10 Sept. 1934, Tientsin (now Tianjin), China; m. 1961; one s. one d. *Education:* New South Wales State Conservatorium, Sydney, San Francisco Conservatory of Music, USA with Egon Petri, Australian Nat. Univ. *Career:* first recital aged 11; moved to Australia 1951; many recitals, including contemporary Australian music, USA 1959–61; numerous comms; piano teacher, Queensland State Conservatorium of Music; Guest Lecturer, Queensland Univ. 1961–65; Head of Keyboard Studies, Canberra School of Music, ACT 1966–78, Head, Dept of Composition and Electronic Music 1978–81, Head, Dept of Composition and Musicology 1981–; external examiner in composition, piano performance, Australian univs and colls of advanced educ.; Artistic Dir Bi-Centennial Recording Project; Dir Australian Contemporary Music Ensemble; Composer-in-Residence, Univ. of Cincinnati, USA 1989–90; Dir Conf. on Music and Musicians in Australian Culture 1930–60, 1993; promotion to Reader, ANU 1993, granted Personal Chair 1994, Distinguished Visiting Fellow 2005, now Prof. Emer.; Adjunct Prof., Monash Univ. 2004–10. *Compositions include:* opera: The Fall of the House of Usher 1965, Lenz 1970, De Profundis 1982, Fiery Tales 1975, The Golem 1980, De Profundis 1982, Three Scenes from Aboriginal Life 1988, Incidental Music to Faust 1996, completion of Ferruccio Busoni's opera Dr Faust 2007; major works for piano solo: The Way of the Seeker 2004, Dimensions of Night 2008, Retirer d'en Bas de l'Eau: Sonata #1 (for piano in 4 movements) 2009, The Golden Dawn 2009, Sonata #2 2011, Birth-Ceuse 2011, Sonatina Seconda in Extremis 2012, Sonata #3 for piano (comprising the "Sonatina Seconda" and the "Birth-ceuse"), Sonata #4 (for piano The Sufi Path) 2013, A Small Wedding Gift for Adam and Chanel 2013; orchestral: Symphonic Elegy 1962, Apparitions 1966, Prelude for Orchestra 1968, A Song of Love 1974, Six Orchestral Songs for Low Voice 1980, Suite for concert band 1987, At the Gate 1992, Symphony in Four Movements 2000, Symphony No. 2 for piano and orchestra 2003, Symphony No.3, on the notes E, G and C 2008, Pamiatuyi Jana Sedivku for string orchestra 2009, Concerto for Young Pianist with Second Piano 2012; song cycles: A Festival of Lanterns I & II and Letter from the Trenches

2014–15, Trio No.10 for flute, percussion, piano: Sandakan 2015, melodrama on Yeats' Purgatory, for computer screen; numerous other works including concerti, vocal music, keyboard music, chamber music, film scores. *Recordings include:* The Golem, Piano concerto, chamber instrumental music, solo piano music. *Publications include:* Music of the 20th Century Avant Garde, Australian Piano Music of the 20th Century, The Repressed Russian Avant Garde 1900–1929, Busoni and the Piano, Complete Piano Music of Roy Agnew (ed.), Anton Rubinstein 1998, Australian Piano Music of the 20th Century, Australian Chamber Music with Piano. *Honours:* Dr hc (ANU) 1997; Advance Australia Award 1989, Critics Circle Award 1994, Artist of the Year 2001, Centenary Medal 2003, Portia Geech Award 2010. *Address:* 29 Threlfall Street, Chifley, ACT 2606, Australia (home). *Telephone:* (2) 6125-5765 (office); (2) 6281-1008 (home). *E-mail:* Larry.Sitsky@anu.edu.au (office).

SITU, Gang, MMus; Chinese composer; b. 6 Dec. 1954, Shanghai. *Education:* Shanghai Teachers' University, Music and Arts Institute of San Francisco, USA. *Career:* Instructor in Music Theory, Music Department, Shanghai Teachers' University, 1979–85; Music Director, Chinese Cultural Productions, 1990–; Composer-in-Residence, Alexander String Quartet, 1998–2000; Composer-in-Residence, Meet the Composer 1998; mem. BMI, American Composers' Forum, National Association of Composers, Society of Composers Inc. *Compositions:* Symphonic Suite, 1988; Circle Series for Dance, 1992–94; Double Concerto for Violin and Erhu, 1994; Common Ground, 1994; Songs From the Land, San Francisco Suite, 1997; String Quartet No. 1, 1998; Rondo–String Quartet No. 2, 2000; Strings Calligraphy, 2000; String Symphony, 2000. *Recordings:* Sunlight, 1994; Dynaities, 1996; Concerto for Violin, Erhu and Strings, 1998; Songs from the Land, 1998. *Honours:* commissioning awards, Ross McKee Foundation, 1994; SF California Art Commission, 1996; Composers Fellowship, Californian Arts Council, 1995. *E-mail:* gangsitu@aol.com.

SIUKOLA, Heikki; Finnish singer (tenor); b. 20 March 1943. *Education:* Sibelius Academy, Helsinki. *Career:* sang in opera at Tempere and Helsinki; engaged at Wuppertal 1972–79, Krefeld 1980–83; season 1989 as Erik at Oslo, Siegmund in Naples and Tristan at Basle and Nancy; sang Tristan at Lyon 1990; Tannhäuser at Montpellier 1991; other roles include, Andrea Chénier, Alfredo, Cavaradossi, Don Carlos, Pinkerton, Dick Johnson, and Hoffmann; Florestan in Fidelio, Lohengrin, Parsifal and Bacchus; sang Samson for Palm Beach Opera, 1998; sang Tristan at Strasbourg and Buenos Aires, 2000; Siegmund at the Vienna Staatsoper. *Current Management:* c/o Theateragentur Heidi Steinhaus, Auerfeldstrasse 26, 81541 Munich, Germany; c/o Walter Beloch Artists Management, Via Melzi d'Eril 26, 20154 Milan, Italy. *Telephone:* (89) 93930110 (Munich); (2) 33101922 (Milan). *Fax:* (89) 93930111 (Munich); (2) 3313643 (Milan). *E-mail:* Steinhaus@heidi-steinhaus.de; lirica@walterbeloch.com. *Website:* www.heidi-steinhaus.de; www.walterbeloch.com; www.sfo.com/~mvogt/bio/HeikkiS.html.

SIURINA, Ekaterina; Russian singer (soprano); b. Ekaterinburg; m. Charles Castronovo; one s. *Education:* Russian Acad. of Theatrical Arts, Moscow. *Career:* began career as soloist, Moscow Municipal Theatre Novaya Opera; debut at Royal Opera House, Covent Garden as Olympia in Les Contes d'Hoffmann 2004; Metropolitan Opera New York debut as Gilda in Rigoletto 2008; has also appeared with Opera Nat. de Paris, Salzburg Festival, Deutsche Staatsoper, Wiener Staatsoper, Opéra Royal de Wallonie, Santa Fe Opera, Houston Grand Opera, Glyndebourne Festival Opera, Teatro Municipale, Salerno, Montpellier Opera, La Scala, Milan, Deutsche Oper Berlin, Salzburg Festival, San Diego Opera; roles include: Olympia in Les Contes d'Hoffmann, Adina in L'Elisir d'Amore, Giulietta in i Capuleti e i Montecchi, Servilia in La Clemenza di Tito, Ilia in Idomeneo, Zerlina in Don Giovanni, Leila in The Pearl Fishers, Lauretta in Gianni Schicchi, Susanna in Le nozze di Figaro, Pamina in Die Zauberflöte, Gilda in Rigoletto, Najade in Ariadne auf Naxos, Amina in La Sonnambula. *Honours:* winner Rimsky Korsakov Competition, St Petersburg. *Current Management:* c/o Zemsky Green Artists Management, 104 West 73rd Street, Suite 1, New York, 10023, USA. *Telephone:* (212) 579-6700. *Fax:* (212) 579-4723. *E-mail:* bzemsky@zemskygreen.com. *Website:* www.zemskygreen.com; ekaterinasiurina.com (home).

SJÖBERG, Gitta-Maria; Swedish singer (soprano); b. 1957. *Education:* Århus Conservatory and Opera Studio. *Career:* debut as Mimi in La Bohème at Århus 1987; currently lead soprano, Royal Danish Opera; appearances with Jutland Opera, Århus and Royal Opera Stockholm as Desdemona, Madama Butterfly and Donna Elvira, Micaela in Carmen, Amelia in Simon Boccanegra, Desdemona in Otello, Amelai in Simon Boccanegra, Elisabetta in Don Carlo, Leonora in Il Trovatore, Eva in Die Meistersinger, lead roles in Aida, Madama Butterfly, Mimi, Manon Lescaut, Rusalka, Tosca; guest appearances at Umea as Amelia in Un Ballo in Maschera, Mimi in La Bohème at Bonn Opera, Emilia Marty in The Makropulos Case at Dusseldorf. *Current Management:* Tivoli and Crescendi Artists, Laederstraede 9, 4, 1202 Copenhagen, Denmark. *Website:* www.crescendi.org.

SJÖBERG, Johan-Magnus Göran; Swedish organist, cantor and composer; b. 7 June 1953, Östra Grevie; m. Cajsa Finnström 1983, one s. one d. *Education:* Coll. of Music, Malmö. *Career:* Music Dir, Sankt Hans Church, Lund 1974–2003, performed at Poznán Spring Festival, Warsaw Autumn Festival, Festival for Contemporary Church Music, Sweden; Organist, Lund Alhelgonaförsamling 2003–; leader Helgonakören, Motettkör vocal ensembles; teacher Malmö Conservatory 1995–2008; mem. Swedish Composers' Soc.

Compositions include: for organ: Eli, Eli sabaktani 1980, Et vidi caelum 1980, O magnum mysterium 1981, Missa Brevis 1981, Ur djupen ropar jag till dig 1981, Surrexit Dominus vere, Alleluia 1982, Improperierna 1982, O beata virgo 1983, Piece dÓrgue 1983, Stabat Mater 1983, "...eternety..." 1984, Agnus Dei 1984, Hoc Modo Credo II 1985, Hoc Modo Credo 1985, Mobil 1985, Alleluia 1985, Te Deum laudamus 1985, Sound pattern 1 1986, Mmusic 1986, Concerning 1986, Growing fragments 1987, Summermusic-86 1987, Canvas 1988, Bells 1990, Once again 1991, Chaconne-92 1992, Respons 1992, Four Minimal Dances for a Minimal Instrument 1993, Magnificat 1993, Once again, once more, but... 1983, Loops 1983, On a ground 1994, En kort fantasi 1994, Vuolle 1994, On another ground 1994, Drone 1995, Liturgi 1996, Hymn 1996, Triptyk 1997, ConFusion 1997, Alleluia on a Ground 1998, Kom i ditt rike ,Kantat 1998, Nio enkla imitationer 1999, Speccio per organo 2000, Cantilenor 2001, Passacaglia för en orgel och två organister 2001, Tre Intermezzi 2002, Tre Luther-koraler 2003, Rondo per Organo 2004, Missa per Organo 2005, Laetentur coeli 2006, Missa Passacaglia per organo 2007, Två Orgeltoccator 2008, Tre Invocationer för altsaxofon och orgel 2009; numerous other compositions for voice and other instruments. *Honours:* Culture Award, Lund 1988. *E-mail:* dirigent@helgonakoren.se (office). *Website:* user.tninet.se/~mvk425a/index.htm; www.helgonakoren.se; www.motetten.se.

SJÖHOLM, Monica; singer (soprano); b. 1945, Sweden. *Education:* Stockholm Music High School. *Career:* sang at Vastenda and with the Ensemble Sangens Makt from 1972; Norrlandsoperan, Umea, from its foundation 1974, notably in L'Italiana in Algeri, as Donna Elvira, Rosina and Amelia (Un Ballo in Maschera); other roles have included Alice Ford, Begbick in Weill's Mahagonny, Ragnhild in Den bergtagna by Ivan Hallström, Flora in The Medium, and in Fortunato by Ian MacQueen 1993; frequent concert appearances throughout Scandinavia.

SJÖSTEDT, Sten; singer (tenor); b. 1945, Malmö, Sweden. *Education:* studied in Malmö, Salzburg Mozarteum. *Career:* debut at Trier Opera 1969, as Rodolfo in La Bohème; Malmö Opera 1969–74, notably in a revival of Dal Male il bene, by Abbatini; Stora Theatre, Gothenburg from 1974; guest appearances at San Diego (Ferrando 1971), Oslo (as Massenet's des Grieux) and Århus (as Hoffmann); other roles have included Tamino, Manrico, Riccardo (Un Ballo in Maschera), Lensky and Faust; modern repertory has included the title role in The Voyage of Edgar Allan Poe, by Dominick Argento. *Recordings include:* Tintomara, by Werle.

SKALICKI, Wolfram; stage designer; b. 1938, Vienna, Austria; m. Amrei Skalicki. *Education:* studied in Austria. *Career:* stage designs for San Francisco Opera from 1962, The Rake's Progress, The Ring 1967–72, Aida, Lady Macbeth of Mtsensk, L'Africaine, Andrea Chénier and Salome; collaborations with costume designer Amrei Skalicki at the Vienna Burgtheater, Volksoper and Staatsoper; productions in Lyon, Munich, Toronto, Buenos Aires, Hamburg, Miami, Athens and Geneva; operas have included Lulu, Boris Godunov, Tristan und Isolde, Death in Venice, Hérodiade and Giovanna d'Arco; Andrea Chénier at the Metropolitan, Boris at Pittsburgh, Falstaff for Canadian Opera, Ariadne at Los Angeles; The Queen of Spades in Santiago and Elektra for Seattle Opera; exhibitions at Bayreuth, Vienna, Zürich, New York and San Francisco; Prof., Univ. for Music and the Performing Arts, Graz.

SKARECKY, Jana, BMus, MMus, ARCT; Canadian composer, teacher and artist; b. 11 Nov. 1957, Prague, Czechoslovakia; m. Paul Polly; two d. *Education:* Wilfrid Laurier Univ., Ont., Royal Conservatory of Music (RCT), Toronto, Univ. of Sydney, Australia. *Career:* teacher of piano and theory, Canada and USA 1977–; mem. Faculty of Piano Theory, Royal Conservatory of Music, Toronto; painter, working with acrylics; compositions performed in N America, Europe, Australia, NZ and Japan; mem. Canadian League of Composers, Asscn of Canadian Women Composers, Canadian Music Centre. *Exhibitions:* annual exhbns in Mississauga, Ont. 2003–11; has also exhibited in Toronto, in Brampton, Stratford and Odense, Denmark. *Compositions include:* Sea Window for brass quintet 1983, Three Movements on Bach Themes for trumpet and strings/trumpet and organ 1984, Oresteia for solo double bass 1986, Rose of Sharon for solo harp 1985, Night Songs for four percussionists 1986, The Sign of the Four for solo tenor recorder 1986, Aquamarine for orchestra 1986, Dayspring for mezzo-soprano and piano 1987, Lullabies for voice 1988, Flame of Roses for flute, cello and piano 1989, The Living Wind for mezzo, flute, cello and harp 1990, Consort Royal recorder quartet 1990, Sonata for viola and piano 1992, On Her Wings for solo organ 1993, La Corona three motets 1993, Sinfonia Lauretta for string orchestra 1994, Into the Centre of Our Heart for chamber ensemble 1994, The Eye of the Phoenix for cello 1995, Love is Come Again for SATB choir 1995, Water, Fire, Air and Earth for piano 1996, Streams for large orchestra 1997, Green and Gold for soprano and piano 2001, Song of Life for SATB choir 2001, Planet Earth for soprano and piano 2002, The Beginning of the Wind for baritone and piano 2004, One More Veil That Falls Away for cello and piano 2004, Dream for piano 2005, Back to Babylon for choir 2006, Emily the Way You Are (opera) 2008, What Draws Us Together for bass clarinet and cello 2010, Opera Scenes 2011, Water Colours for piano 2011, Birds in the Hickory Tree for piano 2012, Deep Peace for choir 2012, Will You Dance for two violins 2012. *Recordings:* Flame of Roses (on Spinners of Starlight album, produced by the Ardeleana Trio), Jesus Christ is King of Kings (on Christmas around the World album by The Renaissance Singers). *Publications:* Birds in the Hickory Tree (piano), Water Colours (piano). *Address:* 2466 Westbrook Road, RR#1, Binbrook, ON

L0R 1C0, Canada (home). *Telephone:* (905) 692-9696 (office). *E-mail:* skarecky@gmail.com (office). *Website:* www.janaskarecky.com.

SKARENG, Per; Swedish classical guitarist; b. 28 June 1959, Gavle; m.; two d. *Career:* debut concert playing Rodrigo's Concierto de Aranjuez with Swedish Radio Symphony Orchestra 1985; has also performed with Stockholm Royal Philharmonic Orchestra, Norrkoping Symphony Orchestra, Estonia Symphony Orchestra, Gavleborgs Symphony Orchestra, Pietersaari Symphony Orchestra; Macedonian Philharmonic Orchestra; tours of Argentina, Cuba, Estonia and Switzerland, Finland; Sr Lecturer, Music College, Pietarsaari, Finland, Mälardalens Univ., Sweden; Senior Master, Royal College of Music, Stockholm; guest lecturer, Music College in Stockholm, Oslo and Copenhagen; Artistic Director, International Guitar Festival, Galve. *Recordings:* El Colibri, Dag Wiren Little Serenade, recording with flautist Tobias Carron 1995, recording with Tobias Carron with South American and Spanish music 1998. *Address:* School of Education, Culture and Communication, Mälardalens University, Högskoleplan 1, Rosenhill, 721 23 Västerås, Sweden (office). *Telephone:* (21) 10-15-13 (office). *Fax:* (21) 10-15-60 (office). *E-mail:* per.skareng@mdh.se (office).

SKELTON, Stuart Lindsay, AMusA, MM; Australian singer (tenor); b. 12 Nov. 1968, s. of Ralph and Lesley Skelton; partner Sarah Noble. *Education:* St Andrew's Cathedral School, Sydney, Univ. of Cincinnati, USA. *Career:* roles include: Lohengrin (Berlin State Opera, Deutsche Oper Berlin, Baden-Baden Festival, Trieste, Bologna, Dresden Semperoper), Peter Grimes (Opera Frankfurt, ENO, Opera Australia, Opera de Oviedo), Samson (Perth Int. Festival), Dimitrij (BBC Proms), Siegmund (Metropolitan Opera, State Opera South Australia, Hamburg State Opera, Zurich Opera, Seattle Opera, Paris Opéra Bastille), Florestan (Vienna State Opera, Stuttgart Opera, Palm Beach Opera), Kaiser (Opera Frankfurt, Hamburg State Opera), Erik (Berlin State Opera, Deutsche Oper Berlin, Vienna State Opera, Hamburg State Opera, Opéra Nationale de Strasbourg, Opera Colorado, ENO), Laca (Opera Frankurt, ENO, Opéra Nationale de Bordeaux), Prince in Rusalka (Paris Opéra Bastille), Bacchus (New Israeli Opera), Don José (San Francisco Opera, Opera Australia), Max (Hamburg State Opera, Bavarian State Opera), King Arthur in Merlin (Teatro Real Madrid), Canio (West Australian Opera), Drum Major (Metropolitan Opera, Santa Fe Opera), Herman (Sydney Symphony), Parsifal (Opera Frankfurt, Zurich Opera, ENO); numerous other performances with: Deutsche Oper Berlin, ENO, Opera Australia, Metropolitan Opera, Zurich Opera, Hamburg State Opera, State Opera South Australia, Düsseldorf Opera, St Louis Symphony, Palm Beach Opera, Vienna State Opera, Opera Frankfurt, Opera Colorado, Melbourne Symphony Orchestra, Opera North, Bavarian State Opera, Bamberg Symphony, Boston Symphony Orchestra, Orchestre Symphonique de Montréal, Los Angeles Philharmonic Orchestra, Luxembourg Symphony Orchestra, Dallas Symphony Orchestra, NHK Symphony Orchestra, Tokyo, Sydney Symphony Orchestra, London Symphony Orchestra, BBC Symphony Orchestra, Bavarian Radio Symphony Orchestra, NDR Symphony Hamburg, San Francisco Symphony, Boston Symphony, Chicago Symphony. *Recordings include:* Elgar The Dream of Gerontius/Sea Pictures (Gramophone Award for Best Choral Recording 2015) 2014. *Honours:* Marianne Mathy Award, McDonald's Aria Award, Winner, Belvedere Competition, Vienna, Green Room Award 2009, Helpmann Award 2005, 2010, Int. Opera Awards Best Male Singer 2014. *Current Management:* c/o Bill Palant, IMG Artists, Carnegie Hall Tower, 152 West 57th Street, 5th Floor, New York, NY 10019, USA. *Telephone:* (212) 994-3527. *Fax:* (212) 994-3550. *E-mail:* bpalant@imgartists.com. *Website:* www.imgartists.com; www.stuartskelton.com.

SKEMPTON, Howard; British composer, accordionist and music publisher; b. 31 Oct. 1947, Chester; m. Sue Skempton (née Lordon) (died 2008); one s. *Education:* studied with Cornelius Cardew. *Career:* freelance composer; tutor in composition, Birmingham Conservatoire. *Compositions include:* Lento for orchestra 1990, Concerto for hurdy gurdy and percussion 1994, Gemini Dances for flute, clarinet, violin, cello, percussion and piano 1994, Shiftwork for percussion quartet 1994, Chamber Concerto 1995, We Who With Songs for chorus and organ 1995, Winter Sunrise (string trio) 1996, Delicate (ballet) 1996, The Flight of Song for chorus 1996, Two Poems of Edward Thomas for choir 1996, Into My Heart an Air that Kills for soprano, piano, 2 violins, viola and cello 1996, Concerto for oboe and accordion 1997, Clarinet Quintet 1997, Hot Noon in Malabar for soprano and piano trio 1997, Ballade for saxophone quartet and strings 1997, Concertante for violin and strings 1998, Prelude for orchestra 1999, The Voice of the Spirits for choir 1999, He Wishes for the Cloths of Heaven for choir 1999, Murallennium for choir and wind band 2000, The Bridge of Fire for choir 2001, Catch for string quartet 2001, Sarabande for string orchestra 2002, Rise up, my love, for choir 2002, Emerson Songs for soprano and baritone 2003, That Music Always Round Me for choir and orchestra 2003, Magnificat and Nunc Dimittis (The Edinburgh Service) for treble voices and organ 2003, Eternity's Sunrise for flute, clarinet, harp and string quartet 2003, Tendrils for string quartet 2004, Ben Somewhen for flute, clarinet, harp, violin, viola, two cellos and double bass 2005, Pavilion for clarinet, viola and piano 2006, The Moon is Flashing for tenor and orchestra 2007, Three Motets for choir 2007, Only the Sound Remains for viola and chamber ensemble 2009, Field Notes for oboe, violin, viola and cello 2014; numerous piano pieces, including Images 1989, Expectancy for string quartet and chamber choir 2008, Notti Stellate a Vagli for solo piano 2008, Five Rings Triples for 8 church bells 2011, The Rime of the Ancient Mariner 2015, Piano Concerto 2015. *Honours:* Hon. mem. RAM 2012; Royal Philharmonic Soc.

Award for Chamber-Scale Composition 2004, British Acad. of Composers and Songwriters British Composer Award (Chamber) 2005, British Composer Award (Vocal), British Acad. of Composers and Songwriters 2008. *Address:* c/o Repertoire Promotion Music Department, Oxford University Press, Great Clarendon Street, Oxford, OX2 6DP, England (office). *E-mail:* repertoire.promotion.uk@oup.com (office).

SKETRIS, Paul; Canadian singer (bass); b. 2 June 1960, Sarnia, Ont. *Education:* Univ. of Toronto, Univ. of Freiburg, Germany. *Career:* sang at Frankfurt Opera 1991–93, Magdeburg 1993–, in more than 100 roles, including Sarastro, Gremin, King Philip, Hunding, Rocco, Daland, Mephisto, Mozart's Bartolo and Alfonso, Fafner and Henry, in Lohengrin; premiere of Goldschmidt's Beatrice Cenci 1994; guest at Toronto, Vancouver, Hamilton and Japan (tour, Aida 2003) opera houses and Aldeburgh Festival; concerts include Beethoven's Ninth, Shostakovich's 14th Symphony, Bach's B minor Mass and Christmas Oratorio, Messiah, Mozart Requiem and Verdi Requiem; Canadian music features in his recital programmes; singing teacher, Univ. of Magdeburg 1997–2009. *Recordings:* Winterreise 2000, Christmas Music (Stille Nacht) 2003. *Address:* c/o Theater Magdeburg, Universitätsplatz 9, Pf 1240, 39104 Magdeburg, Germany. *Website:* www.paulsketris.de.

SKIDMORE, Jeffrey, OBE; British choral conductor and artistic director; *Music Director, Ex Cathedra. Education:* Magdalen Coll., Oxford. *Career:* Founder and Artistic Dir Ex Cathedra choral group, also associated Consort and Baroque Orchestra; has commissioned more than 10 new works and conducted world premieres by composers including Fyfe Hutchins, Gabriel Jackson, John Joubert, Daryl Runswick, Peter Sculthorpe and Peter Wiegold; research and performance of neglected choral works of 16th, 17th and 18th centuries; has prepared new performing editions of works by Araujo, Charpentier, Lalande, Monteverdi and Rameau; Artistic Dir Early Music programme, Birmingham Conservatoire; gives choral training workshops and teaches at summer schools in UK and abroad; regularly directs choral programme at Dartington Int. Summer School; Classical Music Programmer, Kilkenny Festival 2005; Research Fellow, Univ. of Birmingham. *Recordings include:* with Ex Cathedra: Shared Ground, Gabrieli Sacred Symphonies, Britten to America, A French Baroque Diva (with Carolyn Sampson) (Gramophone Award for Best Recital Recording 2015) 2014, Brazilian Adventures. *Honours:* Hon. Fellow, Birmingham Conservatoire. *Current Management:* Ikon Arts Management, 114 Business Design Centre, 52 Upper Street, London, N1 0QH, England. *Telephone:* (20) 7354-9199. *E-mail:* info@ikonarts.com. *Address:* Ex Cathedra, CBSO Centre, Berkley Street, Birmingham, B1 2LF, England (office). *Telephone:* (121) 616-3410 (office). *Website:* www.excathedra.co.uk.

SKINNER, David, MMus, DPhil; American choral director, musicologist, singer and record producer; *Fellow and Osborn Director of Music, Sidney Sussex College, Cambridge;* b. 1964, California. *Education:* Univ. of Edinburgh, Christ Church, Oxford, UK. *Career:* moved to UK in 1987; choral scholar, Christ Church, Oxford 1989–94, Postdoctoral Fellow of British Acad., Christ Church 1997–2001, Lecturer in Music, Magdalen Coll. 2001–06; Fellow, Dir of Studies and Osborn Director of Music, Sidney Sussex Coll., Cambridge, also Conductor, Choir of Sidney Sussex Coll.; co-f. The Cardinall's Musick 1989; worked with early music ensembles including The Tallis Scholars, The Sixteen, Hilliard Ensemble and King's Singers; f. Alamire choral ensemble 2005; Artistic Dir, Obsidian recording label; writer and broadcaster, music adviser for Music and Monarchy series, BBC 2; mem. Medieval Music Soc. *Recordings include:* with the Cardinall's Musick: complete works of Nicholas Ludford 1993–94, Robert Fayrfax 1995–99 and William Byrd 1997–, John Merbecke: Latin Church Music 1996, William Cornish: Latin Church Music 1997; with Alamire: Philippe Verdelot: Madrigals for a Tudor King 2007, Josquin Desprez: Missa d'ung aultre amer, Motets & Chansons 2007, Thomas Tomkins: These Distracted Times 2007, Henry's Music: Motets from a Royal Choirbook 2009, Henry: Mind of a Tyrant (Philip Sheppard) 2009, Thomas Tallis & William Byrd: Cantiones Sacrae 1575 2011, John Taverner: Imperatrix inferni 2011, Deo gracias Anglia! 2012; with Alamire Cornett & Sackbut ensemble: The Spy's Choirbook (Gramophone Award for Best Early Music Recording 2015) 2014; other: Byrd: Infelix ego (Gramophone Award for Recording of the Year 2010). *Publications:* The Arundel Choirbook 2003, Nicholas Ludford I: Mass Inclina cor meum and Antiphons 2003, Nicholas Ludford II: Six-part Masses and Magnificat 2004, The Tallis Psalter: Psalms and Anthems 2013. *Current Management:* Percius, Advice Hub, 66 Devonshire Road, Cambridge, CB1 2BL, England. *E-mail:* info@percius.co.uk. *Website:* www.percius.co.uk. *Telephone:* (1223) 761563 (Sidney Sussex) (office). *E-mail:* director.music@sid.cam.ac.uk (office).

SKINNER, John York, BMus, LRAM, ARAM; British singer (countertenor); b. 5 March 1949, York, England; m. 1st Juanesse Adele Reeve 1970 (divorced); m. 2nd Janet Lesley Budden 1976; two d. *Education:* York Minster Song School, Colchester Inst., Royal Acad. of Music, London. *Career:* debut, Kassel Opera, West Germany; broadcasts on BBC, WDR, NDR, ORTF and Italian radio; opera appearances at Royal Opera House, Covent Garden, La Scala, Milan, Scottish Opera, Festival Ottawa and English Music Theatre; fmr Dir of Music, Llandaff Cathedral School. *Recordings:* works of John Dowland with Consort of Musicke, Handel's Partenope, other Mediaeval, Renaissance and Baroque music. *Honours:* Hon. mem. Royal Coll. of Music, London 1982. *Address:* Ysgubor Garreg, Cefn Gorwydd, Llangammarch Wells, Powys, LD4 4DN, Wales (home).

SKOGLUND, Annika; Swedish singer (mezzo-soprano); b. 5 Nov. 1960, Vanersborg, Alvsborg. *Education:* Royal Acad. of Music, Gothenburg, studied in London. *Career:* sang Cherubino at Drottningholm 1988, followed by Suzuki at the Royal Opera in Stockholm; returned to Drottningholm as Ramiro in La Finta Giardiniera and made Italian debut at Venice as Isolier in Le Comte Ory; further engagements as Cherubino at Oslo, Suzuki in Stockholm and the Countess in Maw's The Rising of the Moon at the 1990 Wexford Festival; concert repertoire includes the lieder eines Fahrenden Gesellen with Oregon Symphony; songs of the Auvergne and Kindertotenlider and Das Lied von der Erde. *Recordings include:* La Finta Giardiniera (video). *Current Management:* c/o Helena Friberg Artists Management, Nibblevägen 25, 2 tr, 177 36 Järfälla, Sweden. *E-mail:* annika@annikaskoglund.com. *Website:* www.annikaskoglund.com.

SKOVHUS, Bo; Danish singer (baritone); b. 22 May 1962, Ikast; s. of Freddy Jorgensen and Birthe Skovhus; one d. *Education:* Music Acad., Århus, Royal Music Acad. and Opera School, Copenhagen, and in New York. *Career:* debut in Don Giovanni, Vienna Volksoper 1988, debut as Silvio, Pagliacci Vienna Staatsoper 1991; regular guest singer with all major orchestras and opera cos including Metropolitan, New York, San Francisco, Houston, Munich State Opera, Hamburg State Opera, Berlin, Cologne, Covent Garden, Dresden, etc.; many recitals in Europe, USA and Japan; numerous lieder recitals with Helmut Deutsch, Stefan Vladar, Yefim Bronfman, Lief Ove Andsnes, Christoph Eschenbach and Daniel Barenboim; repertoire includes Don Giovanni, Almaviva in Le Nozze di Figaro, Guglielmo in Così fan tutte, Wolfram in Tannhauser, Olivier in Capriccio, Barber in Schweigsame Frau, Wozzeck, Hamlet, Billy Budd, Eugene Onegin, Yeletsky in Pique Dame, Danilo in Lustige Witwe, Eisenstein in Die Fledermaus, Mandryka in Arabella, Beckmesser in Die Meistersinger von Nürnberg, Kurwenal in Tristan und Isolde, Storch in Intermezzo. *Recordings include:* Don Giovanni (twice), Le Nozze di Figaro (three times), The Merry Widow, Britten's War Requiem, Carmina Burana, Fidelio, Das Lied von der Erde, Wozzeck, Mirror of Perfection (Blackford), I Pagliacci, Der Waffenschmied (Lortzing), Maskarade (Nielsen), Venus (Schoek), Die Schöne Müllerin, Schwanengesang (Schubert), Dichterliebe (Schumann), Liederkreis Op. 24 (Schumann), Eichendorff Lieder (Wolf), Italienisches Liederbuch (Wolf), Faust (Spohr), Oberon (Weber), Die Orchesterlieder (Strauss), Lyrische Sinfonie (Zemlinsky) (twice), Lieder (Zemlinski), arias by Britten, Gounod, Korngold, Verdi, Wagner, Thomas, Massenet and Tchaikovsky, Don Carlos, Tote Stadt, Brahms Requiem and Triumphlied, Mahler Knaben Wunderhorn/Klenau, Rilke, Scandinavian Orchestra Songs, Orchestra Songs by Schubert, Frühe lieder, Rückert lieder, Abschied, aus lied von der Erde (Mahler). *Honours:* Kammersänger (Austria) 1997; Kt's Cross, Order of the Dannebrog. *Current Management:* c/o Balmer & Dixon Management AG, Kreuzstrasse 82, 8032 Zurich, Switzerland. *Telephone:* (43) 2448644. *Fax:* (43) 2448649. *E-mail:* balmer@badix.ch. *Website:* www.badix.ch.

SKRAM, Knut; Norwegian singer (baritone); b. 18 Dec. 1937, Saebo. *Education:* Montana University, studied with George Buckbee, Paul Lohmann in Wiesbaden, Luigi Ricci in Rome and Kristian Riis in Copenhagen. *Career:* Oslo Opera from 1964 with debut as Amonasro in Aida; In 1967 won first prize in Munich Radio International Competition; Sang at Glyndebourne Festival, 1969–76, as Mozart's Guglielmo, Papageno and Figaro; Così fan tutte for French television in 1977; Sang at Aix-en-Provence, 1977–, in operas by Mozart and at Spoleto Festival in Italy from 1978; Concert appearances in Europe and America with regular broadcasts on television and radio in Scandinavia; Sang at Lyon in 1984 as Tchaikovsky's Eugene Onegin; Sang Jochanaan in Salome with the Berlin Staatsoper on tour to Japan in 1987, Amfortas, Amonasro and Kurwenal in Berlin, 1988–89 and appeared as Pizarro in Tel-Aviv and Buenos Aires in 1988; Bolshoi Opera debut in 1988 as Scarpia; Season 1989–90 sang in The Makropulos Case at the Deutsche Oper Berlin, Amfortas at the Spoleto Festival, Charleston, and Don Giovanni at Trieste; Sang Hans Sachs at Nice in 1992; Sang the Wanderer in Mike Ashman's production of Siegfried, Oslo, 1996; Season 1999–2000 as Scarpia at the Opéra-Comique, Paris, Creon in Oedipus Rex at Brussels. *Recordings include:* Video from Glyndebourne Festival of Le nozze di Figaro in 1973; Many recitals of Norwegian Songs.

SKRIDE, Baiba; Latvian violinist; b. 1981, Riga. *Education:* studied in Riga and at Conservatory of Music and Theatre, Rostock. *Career:* has worked with numerous orchestras including Berlin Philharmonic, Boston Symphony Orchestra, Sinfonieorchester des Bayerischen Rundfunks, Orchestre de Paris, London Philharmonic, Royal Stockholm Philharmonic, Oslo and Helsinki Philharmonics, Iceland Symphony, Sydney Symphony and NHK Symphony, and collaborated with conductors such as Christoph Eschenbach, Paavo and Neeme Järvi, Andris Nelsons, Sakari Oramo, Vasily Petrenko, Yannick Nézet-Séguin, Jukka Pekka Saraste, John Storgårds; debut with Concertgebouw Orkest Amsterdam performing Britten's violin concerto 2015; Artist-in-Residence, City of Birmingham Symphony Orchestra 2015–16; regular appearances with to Stockholm, Oslo and Helsinki Philharmonic, Iceland Symphony, BBC Nat. Orchestra of Wales, Royal Scottish Nat. Orchestra, Zurich Opera Orchestra and Hamburger Philharmoniker; debuts in USA include New York Philharmonic, Nat. Symphony of Washington, Toronto Symphony 2015–16; debuts with Orquestra Sinfônica do Estado de Sao Paulo and Filharmonica de Minas Gerais; tour with New Zealand Symphony; chamber music includes performances at Concertgebouw Amsterdam and Wigmore Hall, London in duo recitals with her sister, pianist Lauma Skride,

also trio performances with Daniel Müller-Schott at Schleswig-Holstein Musikfestival and in Bonn; trio with Sol Gabetta and Bertrand Chamayou. *Recordings include:* Bach/Bartok/Ysaÿe 2005, Brahms Violin Concerto with Stockholm Philharmonic/Oramo 2011, Stravinsky/Martin concerto with BBC Nat. Orchestra of Wales/Fischer 2012, Schumann Violin Concertos with Danish Nat. Symphony/Storgårds 2013, Tchaikovsky with CBSO/Nelsons, Szymanowski concertos (German Critics Prize) 2014, Nielsen and Sibelius concertos and 2 Serenades 2015. *Honours:* 1st Prize, Queen Elisabeth Competition 2001. *Current Management:* c/o KD Schmid UK, 40 St Martin's Lane, London, WC2N 4ER, England. *Telephone:* (20) 7395-0916. *Fax:* (20) 7395-0911. *E-mail:* karen.mcdonald@kdschmid.co.uk. *Website:* www .kdschmid.co.uk; baiba-skride.com.

SKRIPKA, Sergei Ivanovich, MMus; Russian conductor; *Art Director and Principal Conductor, Russian State Symphony Orchestra of Cinematography*; b. 5 Oct. 1949, Kharkov; m. Skripka Evgenija 1975; two d. *Education:* Kharkov Inst. of Arts, Moscow State Conservatoire with Prof. Leo Ginzburg. *Career:* debut with Zhukovsky Symphony Orchestra 1975; first performance in USSR of R. Keiser's St Markus Passion with Moscow Chamber Orchestra 1982; tour with Zhukovsky Symphony Orchestra 1991; Britten's War Requiem in Berlin 1991; Mozart's Requiem and Beethoven's 9th Symphony, with Russian State Symphony Orchestra of Cinematography, Frankfurt am Main, Germany 1992; Prof., Russian Acad. of Music (Gnessin's Inst.) 1980–2007; Artistic Leader and Prin. Conductor Russian State Symphony Orchestra of Cinematography and Zhukovsky Symphony Orchestra; mem. Professional Soc. of Cinematography 1988. *Recordings:* Minin and Pozharsky, Liberation of Moscow (oratorio by Degtyarev) 1990, Cello Concertos by Glièr and Mosolov with S. Sudzilovsky (cello) 1996, Russian Overture and Symphonies Nos 2 and 4 by Shebalin, Carmen-Suite by Bizet-Shchedrin (Zhukovsky Symphony Orchestra) 2006. *Honours:* Hon. Person in Russian Arts 1993, People's Artist of the Russian Fed. 1998, Government Prize for Culture 2010. *Address:* 107045 Moscow, ul. Sretenka 4/1 (office); 123181 Moscow, ul. Isakovskogo 12-1-208, Russia (home). *Telephone:* (495) 624-51-71 (office). *Fax:* (495) 624-51-71 (office). *E-mail:* kinoorkestr@mail.ru (office); sergeiskripka@gmail.com (home). *Website:* www.rgsok.ru (office).

SKROWACZEWSKI, Stanisław; Polish/American conductor and composer; *Principal Guest Conductor, Deutsche Radio Philharmonie*; b. 3 Oct. 1923, Lwów (now in Ukraine); s. of Paweł Skrowaczewski and Zofia Skrowaczewska (née Karszniewicz); m. Krystyna Jarosz 1956 (died 2011); two s. one d. *Education:* Lwów Conservatoire and State Higher School of Music, Kraków, further composition studies with Nadia Boulanger and P. Klecki, Paris. *Career:* Conductor Wrocław Philharmonic Orchestra 1946–47; Artistic Dir and First Conductor, Silesian Philharmonic Orchestra, Katowice 1949–54; First Conductor, Kraków Philharmonic Orchestra 1955–56; Dir Nat. Philharmonic Orchestra, Warsaw 1957–59; Musical Dir Minnesota Orchestra 1960–79, now Conductor Laureate; Prin. Conductor and Musical Adviser, Hallé Orchestra 1984–91; Musical Advisor, St Paul Chamber Orchestra 1986–88; Milwaukee Symphony 1992–94; Prin. Conductor, Yomiuri Nippon Symphony Orchestra, Tokyo 2007–10, Hon. Conductor Laureate 2010–; Prin. Guest Conductor, Deutsche Radio Philharmonie; tours in Europe, N and S America, Israel, Japan, Australia. *Compositions include:* Symphony for String Orchestra, three other symphonies, Muzyka Nocą (Music by Night, suite of nocturnes), four string quartets, two overtures, Cantique des Cantiques (voice and orch.), Prelude, Fugue, Post-Ludium (orch.), English Horn Concerto 1969, Ricercari Notturni (orchestral), Clarinet Concerto, Violin Concerto 1985, Fanfare for Orchestra 1987, Sextet 1988, String Trio 1990, Triple Concerto 1992, Chamber Concerto 1993, Passacaglia Immaginaria 1995, Musica a quattro 1998, Concerto for Orchestra 1999, Trio for piano, clarinet and bassoon, six piano sonatas, Music for Winds 2009; also music for opera, ballet, film and theatre; recordings for Mercury, Philips, Angel, RCA Victor, IMP, Erato, Arte Nova, Vox, Albany. *Honours:* Commdr Cross of Polonia Restituta Order; Hon. DHL (Hamline Univ., St Paul, Minnesota) 1961; Hon. DMus (Macalester Coll., St Paul, Minn.) 1977; Dr hc (Univ. of Minnesota) 1979, (New England Conservatory of Music), (Univ. of Wrocław), (Karol Szymanowski Acad. of Music, Katowice); Second Prize for 'Overture' 1947, Szymanowski Competition, Warsaw 1947, Second Prize, Int. Competition for String Quartet, Liège, Belgium 1953, State Prize (3rd Class) 1956, First Prize, Int. Conductor's Competition, Rome 1956, Conductor's Award of Columbia Univ., New York 1973, Third Prize, Kennedy Center Friedheim Award Competition (for Ricercari Notturni) 1978; 5 ASCAP Awards for imaginative programming with Minneapolis Symphony 1961–79, Gold Medal, Bruckner-Mahler Soc. 1999, McKnight Distinguished Artist Award 2004, Kilenyi Medal of Honor, Bruckner Soc. of America 2011. *Current Management:* c/o Intermusica Artists' Management Ltd, 36 Graham Street, Crystal Wharf, London, N1 8GJ, England. *Telephone:* (20) 7608-9900. *Fax:* (20) 7490-3263. *E-mail:* mail@intermusica.co.uk. *Website:* www.intermusica.co.uk; www .seekingtheinfinite.com (office).

SKRZYPCZAK, Bettina, DMus; Polish composer, musicologist and music teacher; *Professor, Music Department, Lucerne University of Applied Sciences and Arts*; b. 25 Jan. 1962, Poznań. *Education:* Poznań and Music, Basel Musikakademie Studio for Electronic Music, Kraków Acad. of Music. *Career:* Lecturer in Music History, Theory and Aesthetics of Music, Univ. of Lucerne, Switzerland 1995–, Prof. 2002–; Lecturer, Internationale Ferienkurse für Neue Musik, Darmstadt, Germany 2004; Guest Prof., Bydgoszcz Music Acad., Poland. *Compositions include:* Sonata for two pianos 1985, ABC 1986, What is

Black, What is White 1987, Lob der Erde 1991, Caleidoscopio 1992, Landschaft des Augenblicks 1992, Notturno 1992, String Quartet 1993, Acaso 1994, Nonett für Bläser und Kontrabass 1994, 'SN 1993 J' 1995, Oboe Concerto 1996, Fantasie 1997, Piano Concerto 1998, Konzert für klavier und Orchester 1998, Mouvement 1999, Mazurka 2000, Miroirs 2000, Arcato 2000, Cercar 2001, Vier Figuren 2001, Scène 2001, Daphnes Lied 2002, String Quartet No. 4 2003, Amoureske 2003, In un soffio 2003, Phototaxis 2003, Weissagung 2003, Aria 2004, Lettres 2004, Initial 2005, anomalia Lunae media 2007, Flash 2007, Illuminationen 2008, Aus der Ferne 2011. *Recordings include:* Portrait Bettina Skrzypczak with String Quartet No. 3 (DVD), Portrait Bettina Skrzypczak (including Scène, Miroirs, Toccata sospesa, 'SN 1993 J', Fantasie, Piano Concerto). *Honours:* awards at Zagreb Music Biennale competition for young composers 1988, Tadeusz Baird competition, Warsaw 1990, Mannheim Int. Competition for Women Composers 1994, Basle Förderpreis 1996, Riehen Kulturpreis 2004. *Address:* Hochschule für Musik Lucerne, Zentralstrasse 18, 6003 Lucerne, Switzerland (office). *E-mail:* bettina.skrzypczak@hslu.ch (office). *Website:* www.bettina-skrzypczak.com.

SLABBERT, Wicus, BA; singer (baritone); b. 1941, Kroonstad, South Africa. *Education:* Univ. of Pretoria, studied with Josef Metternich in Germany. *Career:* sang in German repertory at Düsseldorf from 1968 and Italian from 1973; appearances at Essen 1974–79 as Germont, Don Carlo, Rigoletto, Don Giovanni, Count Almaviva in Figaro, Scarpia, Jochanaan, Mandryka and Beckmesser; Staatsoper Kassel from 1979 notably as Macbeth, Iago, the Villains in Hoffmann and Dr Schön; guest engagements at the Bregenz Festival from 1988 in Les Contes d'Hoffmann and Der fliegende Holländer, at Düsseldorf, Stuttgart, Theater am Gärtnerplatz Munich and Pretoria; mem., Vienna Staatsoper from 1991, with performances as Boris in Lady Macbeth of Mtsensk and as Nabucco 1992; festival engagements at Edinburgh, Florence, Stockholm and Warsaw; sang at Teatro Colón Buenos Aires 1992 as Wagner's Dutchman, Alberich in the Ring and Tosca; Vienna Volksoper 1996, in Mona Lisa by Max von Schillings; Shostakovich's Boris in Bonn 1998; season 2000 as Falstaff, Nick Shadow and Gyges in Zemlinsky's Der König Kandaules, at the Veinna Volskoper; Dutchman at Dusseldorf. *Recordings include:* Bohni in Zemlinsky's Kleider Machen Leute.

SLATFORD, Rodney Gerald Yorke, OBE, FRNCM; British double bassist, publisher and administrator; *Chairman, The Yorke Trust*; b. 18 July 1944, Cuffley, Herts., England. *Education:* Royal Coll. of Music (RCM), London with Adrian Beers. *Career:* Prin. Bass, Midland Sinfonia, Academy of St Martin-in-the-Fields and English Chamber Orchestra until 1981; edited and published works for his own Yorke Edition, devoted to double bass literature; Founder-mem. The Nash Ensemble 1965–94; guest appearances with leading string quartets; tours to Australia, NZ and the Far East; debut double bass recital at Sydney Opera House; lectures in USA; Prof. in Residence, Kusatsu Int. Summer Acad., Japan 1984; teacher, Toho Acad., Tokyo and Beijing Conservatoire; Prof., RCM, London 1974–84; Head of School of Strings, Royal Northern Coll. of Music, Manchester 1984–2001; est. teaching method for double bass 1978; Founder and Chair. The Yorke Trust 1985–; Founder and Dir RNCM Junior Strings project 1991–2001; Chair. European String Teachers Asscn 1992–96; regular presenter on BBC Radio 3 1993–2001; Pres. and Trustee, Northern Lights Symphony Orchestra 2009. *Recordings include:* Rossini's Duetto in solo recording with The Academy of St Martin-in-the-Fields, numerous recordings with The Nash Ensemble and English Chamber Orchestra. *Publications:* The Bottom Line 1985; contrib. to The Strad Magazine, New Grove Dictionary of Music and Musicians 1980; numerous works for double bass in Yorke Edition catalogue; ABRSM Time Pieces for double bass 2009. *Honours:* Hon. RCM. *Address:* The Yorke Trust, Grove Cottage, Southgate Road, South Creake, NR21 9PA, England (office). *Website:* www.yorketrust.org (office).

SLATINARU, Maria; singer (soprano); b. 25 May 1938, Jassy, Romania. *Education:* Bucharest Conservatory with Arta Florescu and Aurel Alexandrescu. *Career:* debut at Bucharest 1969 as Elisabeth de Valois; appearances as guest at Mannheim, Stuttgart, Zürich, Wiesbaden and Düsseldorf; sang at Basle and Florence 1983 as Giorgetta in Il Tabarro, Strasbourg 1984 as Elisabeth in Tannhäuser and has sung Tosca in San Francisco, Dallas 1988 and elsewhere; other roles include Verdi's Abigaille and Amelia in Simon Boccanegra, Leonore in Fidelio, Wagner's Sieglinde, Senta and Elsa, Santuzza and Puccini's Turandot, Minnie and Manon Lescaut.

SLATKIN, Leonard Edward; American conductor and pianist; *Music Director, Detroit Symphony Orchestra*; b. 1 Sept. 1944, Los Angeles, Calif.; s. of Felix Slatkin and Eleanor Aller; m. 4th Cindy McTee 2011; one s. from previous marriage. *Education:* Indiana Univ., Los Angeles City Coll., Juilliard School; studied violin, piano, viola, composition, conducting. *Career:* debut Carnegie Hall 1966; Founder, Music Dir and Conductor St Louis Symphony Youth Orchestra 1979–80, 1980–81; Asst Conductor Youth Symphony of New York, Carnegie Hall 1966, Juilliard Opera, Theater and Dance Dept 1967, St Louis Symphony Orchestra 1968–71, Assoc. Conductor 1971–74, Music Dir and Conductor 1979–96; Prin. Guest Conductor Minn. Orchestra 1974–, Summer Artistic Dir 1979–80; Music Dir New Orleans Philharmonic Symphony Orchestra 1977–78; Music Dir Nat. Symphony Orchestra, Washington, DC 1996–2008; Prin. Conductor BBC Symphony Orchestra 2000–04; Prin. Guest Conductor Royal Philharmonic Orchestra 2005–, Pittsburgh Symphony Orchestra 2008–; Music Dir Detroit Symphony Orchestra 2008–; Music Dir Orchestre National de Lyon 2011–; guest conductor with orchestras worldwide, including most major US orchestras, Montréal, Toronto, Vienna, Vienna State Opera, London Symphony, London Philharmonia, English Chamber, Concertgebouw, Royal Danish, Stockholm, Scottish Nat., NHK Tokyo, Israel, Berlin, Stuttgart Opera; festivals include Tanglewood, Blossom, Mann Music Center, Mostly Mozart and Saratoga; Founder and Dir Nat. Conducting Inst.; currently teaches at Indiana University Jacobs School of Music, Manhattan School of Music, Juilliard School. *Publication:* Conducting Business (ASCAP Deems Taylor Special Recognition Award 2013) 2012. *Honours:* Chevalier, Légion d'honneur, Declaration of Honour in Silver (Austria); Dr hc (Julliard School, Indiana Univ., Michigan State Univ., Washington Univ. in St Louis); seven Grammy Awards, Nat. Medal of Arts, Gold Baton Award, American Symphony Orchestra League. *Current Management:* R. Douglas Sheldon, Columbia Artists Management Inc., 1790 Broadway, New York, NY 10019-1412, USA. *E-mail:* rdsheldon@cami.com. *Address:* Office of Leonard Slatkin, Detroit Symphony Orchestra, 3711 Woodward Avenue, Detroit, MI 48201, USA (office). *Telephone:* (313) 576-511 (office). *Fax:* (313) 576-5109 (office). *Website:* www.detroitsymphony.com (office); www.auditorium-lyon.com/L-Orchestre/Orchestre-national-de-Lyon; www.leonardslatkin.com.

SLAVICKÝ, Milan; Czech composer, producer, writer on music and lecturer; b. 7 May 1947, Prague; s of the late Klement Slavický and of Vlasta Slavická; m. Eva Hachova 1972; two s. *Education:* Charles Univ., Prague, Janáček Acad. of Music Arts, Brno. *Career:* Sr Music Producer of Classics, Supraphon 1973–81; Producer of Electro-acoustic Music, Radio Prague 1981–82; free-lance composer and producer 1982–90; Lecturer, Film Faculty, Acad. of Music Arts, Prague 1990–94, Asst Prof. of Composition 1994–97, Assoc. Prof. 1997–2001, Prof. 2002–; Asst Prof. of Musicology, Charles Univ. 1990–97, Assoc. Prof. 1997–2001, Prof. 2002–, Vice-Dir Inst. of Musicology; lectures given throughout Europe and many papers presented at congresses; compositions performed widely at leading festivals and broadcast world-wide; numerous radio broadcasts. *Compositions:* orchestral: Hommage à Saint-Exupéry, Terre des hommes, Porta coeli, Two chapters from the Revelation, Ich dien, Synergy, Morning Thanksgiving, Requiem; Concerto: Way of the Heart for violin, wind and percussion; chamber: Musica lirica, Musica notturna, Brightening I–IV, two string quartets (Dialogues with the Silence, Advent Contemplations); organ music and compositions for solo instruments; vocal: Stay with Us, Sweet Loving for soprano and ensemble, Media Vita for soprano and viola, Veni Sancte Spiritus for soprano and ensemble, Electro-acoustic: In Praise of Harpsichord, Variations on a Laser Ray, Brightening V or Prague Autumn, Adventus. *Recordings:* more than 550 albums as producer for many labels. *Publications:* Interviews from the House of the Artists, Gideon Klein: A Fragment of Life and Work. *Honours:* Carl-Maria-von Weber Prize, Dresden 1976, 1979, Second Prize, Competition from Czech Ministry of Culture 1980, Prize of Town Brasilia 1985, Czech Music Critics' Award 1992. *Address:* Lukešova 39, 142 00 Prague 4, Czech Republic. *Telephone:* (2) 44471567 (office). *Fax:* (2) 44471870 (home). *E-mail:* milan.slavicky@iol.cz (office). *Website:* www.musica.cz/slavicky (office).

SLAVKOVA, Maria; singer (soprano); b. 1958, Tarnova, Bulgaria. *Career:* sang at the Nat. Opera, Sofia from 1987; Mainz Opera from 1984 and Mannheim from 1990, as La Gioconda, Tosca, Senta, Leonore in Fidelio, Aida, Butterfly, Odabella in Attila and Margherita in Mefistofele; guest appearances at Munich as Smetana's Marenka and Tokyo (Santuzza); Gelsenkirchen 1995, as Leonore (also at Leipzig 1996), Brunswick 1994, as Elisabeth in Tannhäuser; Wagner's Sieglinde at Hamburg and Abigaille in Nabucco at Vienna; Venus and Elisabeth in Tannhaüser at Limoges and Toulon.

SLAWSON, A. Wayne, BA, MA, PhD; American composer and academic; *Professor Emeritus of Music, University of California at Davis*; b. 29 Dec. 1932, Detroit, Mich.; partner Jannalee Smithey. *Education:* Univ. of Michigan, Harvard Univ. *Career:* Asst Prof. of Theory of Music, Yale School of Music, Conn. 1967–72; Assoc. Prof., Univ. of Pittsburgh, Pa 1972–84, Chair. Dept of Music 1972–78, Prof. of Music 1984–86; Prof. of Music, Univ. of California at Davis 1986–2001, Chair. Dept 1996–2001, Prof. Emer. 2001–; Fellow, American Council of Learned Socs 1978–79. *Compositions:* electronic music works: Wishful Thinking About Winter 1966, Variations for two violins 1977, Colors 1981, Greetings 1985, Sound Color 1985, Quatrains Miniature 1986, If These Two Tolled (computer music) 1990, Interpolations of Dance for string quartet 1992, Grave Trunks for computer music and video tape (with Harvey Himelfarb) 1992, Warm Shades octet for singers and woodwinds 1993, Match for orchestra 1994, Dual II for computer-synthesised, speech-derived sound and sound poet 1997, Autumn Rounds for computer-synthesised, speech-derived sound 1999, Rap Soft for computer-synthesized, speech-derived sound 2000, Snow for computer-synthesised, speech-derived sound 2001, Papa for computer-synthesised, speech-derived sound 2005, Prelude on Aus tiefer North for organ 2005, Canzona for Brass Quintet 2006, Winter Rounds for computer-synthezized, speech-derived sound, Here in Silence for computer-synthesized, speech-derived sound, Mixed Doubles for computer-synthesized, speech-derived sound 2012. *Publication:* Sound Color 1985, Color-Class and Pitch-Class Isomorphisms: Composition and Phenomenology, Perspectives of New Music; contrib. of book reviews to Journal of Music Theory 1986, Perspectives of New Music. *Honours:* Soc. for Music Theory Outstanding Publication Award. *Address:* 8555 Yank Gulch Road, Talent, OR 97540, USA (home). *E-mail:* awslawson@ucdavis.edu (office); ygm@yankgulchmusic.com (office). *Website:* www.yankgulchmusic.com (office).

SLEPKOVSKA, Denisa; Slovak singer (mezzo-soprano); b. 1965, Košice. *Education:* Košice Conservatory. *Career:* appearances with Slovak National

Opera at Bratislava, with guest appearances in Greece, Austria, Germany, Edinburgh, Spain and Jerusalem; Concerts at Munich, Passau and Baden-Baden, 1992–95; repertory includes Puccini's Suzuki, Mozart's Apollo and Cherubino, Verdi's Maddalena and Fenena; Nicklausse in Les Contes d'Hoffmann, Rossini's Rosina and Vlasta in Šárka by Fibich. *Recordings include:* Respighi's Bella dormente and Lucrezia. *Current Management:* c/o Neil Dalrymple, Music International, 13 Ardilaun Road, London, N5 2QR, England. *Telephone:* (20) 7359-5183. *Fax:* (20) 7226-9792. *E-mail:* music@musicint.co.uk.

SLIMÁČEK, Jan; Czech composer; b. 31 July 1939, Kelč; m. Marie Chvatíková 1964; two d. *Education:* Prague Conservatory. *Career:* debut with Symfonietta for strings, tape recording Czech Radio; Music Dir, Radio Plzeň 1967–93; Sonatina for strings, Northern Music Festival, Ontario 1988, Vassa 1992; Divertimento for flute and piano, Inter Music Festival, Brno 1983, Graz Wien 1993; Quattro Intermezzi per orchestra gera 1983, Musical Festival Rostow Don 1988; Concertino for accordion, electravox and orchestra gera 1976, Nuremberg 1982, Bern, 1983; Dramatic Picture Szczecin, Weimar 1979; Piano Quartet, Warsaw 1977; Three Etudes for piano, Bristol 1981; Prof. of Music, Gymnasium Plzeň 1993–2004; mem. Asscn of Musicians and Musicologists. *Compositions include:* Piano Quartet, Sonatina for strings, Three Etudes for piano, Dramatic Picture, songs for children's choir and piano, Variations for strings and harpsichord, Quattro Intermezzi per orchestra, The Victory Overture for orchestra, Musica per orchestra, Three Miniatures for chamber orchestra, Music per ottoni. *Address:* Mohylová 109, Plzeň 312 06, Czech Republic (home). *E-mail:* j.slimacek@seznam.cz (home).

SLOANE, Steven; American conductor; *Chief Conductor, Stavanger Symphony Orchestra*; b. 1958, Los Angeles. *Education:* Univ. of California, Los Angeles. *Career:* began career as Orchestral and Choral Dir, Israel Conservatory of Music and Music Dir, Tel-Aviv Philharmonic Orchestra; Prin. Resident Conductor, Frankfurt Opera 1985–92; Music Dir Long Beach Opera 1992–94; Music Dir Bochumer Symphoniker 1994–; Music Dir Spoleto Festival 1996–2000; Music Dir Opera North 1999–2003; Music Dir American Composers Orchestra 2002–06; Chief Conductor, Stavanger Symphony Orchestra 2007–; conducted world premieres of Stewart Wallace's The Bonesetter's Daughter, San Francisco Opera, Elliot Goldenthal's Grendel, Los Angeles Opera; guest conductor with Israel Philharmonic Orchestra, Jerusalem Symphony, Israel Chamber Orchestra, Haifa Symphony, Israel Sinfonietta, New Israeli Opera, New York City Opera, Seattle Opera, Wolf Trap Opera, Utah Symphony, New Mexico Symphony, San Francisco Symphony, Chicago Symphony, Edmonton Symphony, Welsh Nat. Opera, Opera North, Bournemouth Symphony Orchestra, City of Birmingham Symphony, Philharmonia Orchestra, Deutsche Oper am Rhein, Cologne Radio Symphony Orchestra, Beethovenhalle Orchestra Bonn, Komische Oper Berlin, Bavarian Radio Orchestra, Stuttgart Chamber Orchestra, Orchestre National de Lyon, Prague Chamber Orchestra, Orchestra del Teatro di San Carlo, Naples, Sydney Symphony, Tokyo Metropolitan Orchestra. *Current Management:* Opus 3 Artists, 470 Park Avenue South, 9th Floor North, New York, NY 10016, USA. *Telephone:* (212) 584-7500. *E-mail:* info@opus3artists.com. *Website:* www.opus3artists.com. *Address:* Stavanger Symphony Orchestra, Sandvigå 27, Bjergsted, 4007 Stavanger, Norway (office). *Telephone:* 51-50-88-30 (office). *E-mail:* post@sso.no (office). *Website:* www.sso.no (office).

SLOBODENIUK, Dima; Russian conductor; *Music Director, Orquesta Sinfónica de Galicia*; b. Moscow. *Education:* studied violin at Central Music School and Conservatory under Zinaida Gilels and J. Chugajev, also at Middle Finland Conservatory and Sibelius Acad. under Olga Parhomenko; conducting studies at Sibelius Acad. under Leif Segerstam, Jorma Panula and Atso Almila; also studied under Ilja Musinin and Esa-Pekka Salonen. *Career:* moved to Finland early 1990s; Prin. Conductor Oulu Symphony 2005-08; Music Dir Orquesta Sinfónica de Galicia 2013–, concerts with soloists including Vilde Frang, Helen Juntunen, Julian Steckel and Angela Denoke; has appeared as guest conductor with Baltimore and Cincinnati Symphonies and St Paul Chamber Orchestra, Oslo and Bergen Philharmonics, Orchestre Nat. de Belgique, London's Philharmonia, Orchestre National de Radio France, Residentie Orchestra, Trondheim Symphony, Lutoslawski Philharmonic Wroclaw, Netherlands Radio Philharmonic Orchestra in Amsterdam's Concertgebouw, RAI Turin, Netherlands Philharmonic, Lucerne Symphony, SWR Stuttgart, Ulster Orchestra, Orchestre Philharmonique de Monte Carlo; has conducted new music chamber ensemble Avanti!, featuring works of Helena Tulva, Thomas Larcher, Magnus Lindberg and Esa-Pekka Salonen, for concerts in Vienna Konzerthaus. *Current Management:* c/o Emma-Jane Wyatt, Konzertdirektion Schmid, 40 St Martin's Lane, London, WC2N 4ER, England. *Telephone:* (20) 7395-0910. *Fax:* (20) 7395-0911. *E-mail:* emma-jane.wyatt@kdschmid.co.uk. *Website:* www.kdschmid.co.uk. *Address:* Palacio de la Ópera, Glorieta de América 3, 15004 A Coruña, Spain (office). *Telephone:* (981) 252021 (office). *Fax:* (981) 277499 (office). *E-mail:* dima@dimaslobodeniouk.com. *Website:* www.sinfonicadegalicia.com (office); www.dimaslobodeniouk.com.

SLONIMSKY, Sergey Michailovich, PhD; Russian composer, teacher and pianist; *Professor, St Petersburg Conservatoire*; b. 12 Aug. 1932, Leningrad (now St Petersburg); s. of Michail Slonimsky and Ida Slonimskaya (née Kaplan); m. Raisa Slonimskaya (née Zankisova) 1973; one s. one d. *Education:* Leningrad Conservatoire. *Career:* mem. Teaching Faculty, Music Theory and Composition, Leningrad (now St Petersburg) Conservatoire 1958–, Prof. 1976–; mem. Bd CIS Composers' Union (also mem. St Petersburg Br.). *Works include:* 13 symphonies 1958–2004, orchestral and vocal works, chamber works, opera, ballet, songs and choral pieces, including Carnival Overture 1957, Concerto Buffa, chamber orchestra 1966, Antiphones (string quartet) 1969, Virinea opera 1969, Icarus (ballet in three acts) 1973, Master and Margarita (chamber opera in three acts) 1970–85, Merry Songs for piccolo, flute and tuba 1971, Sonata for violoncello and piano 1986, Mary Stuart (opera performed at 1986 Edinburgh Festival, USSR and abroad), Hamlet (opera) 1990–94, Cerch: dell'Inferno secondo Dante 1992, 24 Preludes and Fugues for piano 1994, Ivan the Terrible 1994 (opera premiered at Samara 1998), 24 Preludes and Fugues for piano 1995, King Lear (opera after Shakespeare) 2001, The Magic Nut (ballet) 2005. *Recordings include:* Requiem 2003, Magic Nut (ballet, libretto by Mihail Shemiakin) 2005. *Publications:* musicological study of Prokofiev's symphonies 1964, Burlesques, Elegies, Dithyrambs 2000, Free Dissonance 2005. *Honours:* Cavalier of Commdr's Cross of Poland; RSFSR Glinka State Prize 1983, RSFSR People's Artist 1987, State Prize of Russia 2002. *Address:* St Petersburg Conservatoire of Music, 190000 St Petersburg, 3, Teatralnaya Square (office); 191186 St Petersburg, Canal Griboedova 9-97, Russia (home). *Telephone:* (812) 571-85-85 (home). *Fax:* (812) 571-58-11 (office). *E-mail:* sloh@rambler.ru (home). *Website:* eng.conservatory.ru (office).

SLORACH, Marie; singer (soprano); b. 8 May 1951, Glasgow, Scotland. *Education:* Royal Scottish Acad. of Music and Drama. *Career:* mem., Scottish Opera 1974–81, with roles including Marzelline in Fidelio, Marenka in The Bartered Bride, Zerlina in Don Giovanni, Eva in Die Meistersinger, Tatiana in Eugene Onegin, Fiordiligi in Così fan tutte and Jenifer in The Midsummer Marriage; sang at Wexford Festival in Wolf-Ferrari's I Gioelli della Madonna and Smetana's The Kiss; sang with ENO as Lisa in The Queen of Spades and Donna Elvira in Don Giovanni, Glyndebourne Touring Opera as Mozart's Donna Anna and Electra and Amelia in Simon Boccanegra; Opera North in Carmen, Die Meistersinger, Katya Kabanova and Così fan tutte, Dorset Opera as Gabriella di Vergy and Giovanna d'Arco and Australian Opera in Sydney as Amelia; sang Ellen Orford in a new production of Peter Grimes for Opera North 1989; concert engagements with the Hallé, Liverpool Philharmonic and Scottish Nat. Orchestras, London Mozart Players and London Sinfonietta.

SLUYS, Jozef; Belgian organist; *Chief Organist, Cathedral of SS Michael and Gudule, Brussels*; b. 22 Oct. 1936, Gaasbeek; two s. one d. *Education:* Lemmens Inst., Malines, Royal Conservatoire of Music, Brussels. *Career:* Prof. of Organ, Lemmens Inst., Louvain –1987; Dir Acad. of Music, Schaerbeek, Brussels 1968–95; organist, Cathedral of SS Michael and Gudule, Brussels 1971–, currently Chief Organist; Artistic Dir Cathedral Concert series and Brussels Int. Organ Week; founder-Dir Historical Concerts, Church of Our Blessed Lady, Lombeek; recitalist; performed on radio and television, Belgium and abroad; appearances in many European countries; toured fmr Soviet Union 1987, USA, Zaïre, NZ, S Africa; represented Belgium at first World Organ Festival, Cambridge, UK; Cultural Amb. of Flanders 1996–97. *Recordings:* On the Walcker organ in Riga: works of F. Mendelssohn 1987, Organ works of Belgian composers A. De Boeck, E. Tinel, J. N. Lemmens, J. Jongen, Flor Peeters, Chamber music of Marcel Dupré, J. S. Bach works on organs of Gottfried Silbermann, Romantic Music of Belgian Composers: works for organ (Van Bever, Brussels) viola, violin, piano and cello 1999, Jacques Nicolaas Lemmens: works for organ (Cavaillé-Coll-orgel, St Etienne), Flor Peeters: works for organ (organ Cathedral, Bruges), Joseph Jongen: works for organ (Sauer-organ Erlöserkirche), Peeter Cornet: opere integrali per organo del Maestro Fiammingo, Abraham van den Kerckhoven (on Severyn-organ Sint-Martinuskerk, Cuyk, Netherlands), J. S. Bach, Lemmens, van den Kerckhoven, Langlais, Messiaen, Dupré: works for organ (on Grenzing-organ, Brussels Cathedral), Organ Music from Ecclesiastical Principality of Liège, Josef Gabriel Rheinberger: works for organ, violin and cello (Walhorn), Georg Böhm (on Trost-organ, Waltershausen), Georg Böhm (on Arp-Schnitger-organ, Uithuizen, Netherlands), Johann Sebastian Bach (on Silbermann-organ, Ponitz), Johann Sebastian Bach (on Volckland-Hesse-organ, Mülberg), Meisterwerke der deutschen Romantik (Grenzing organ, Brussels Cathedral). *Honours:* Commdr, Ordre des Arts et Lettres 1990; Fuga Trophy 2000. *Address:* Domstraat 8, 1602 Vlezenbeek, Belgium (home). *Telephone:* (2) 219-26-61 (office); (2) 532-50-80 (home). *Fax:* (2) 219-26-61 (office); (2) 532-50-80 (home). *E-mail:* semorgweek@yucom.be (office); jozef@sluys.org (home). *Website:* www.jozef.sluys.org (home).

SMALLEY, Denis Arthur, MusB, BMus, DipMus, DPhil; New Zealand composer; *Professor Emeritus of Music, City University, London*; b. 16 May 1946, Nelson. *Education:* Univ. of Canterbury, Victoria Univ. of Wellington, Paris Conservatoire, France, Univ. of York, UK. *Career:* Head of Music, Wellington Coll. 1969–71; Northern Music Critic, The Guardian 1972–75; Composition Fellow 1975–76, Sr Lecturer in Music, Univ. of East Anglia, Norwich 1976–94; Prof. of Music, City Univ., London 1994–2009, Prof. Emer. 2009–. *Compositions:* Gradual 1974, Pentes 1974, Ouroboros 1975, Pneuma 1976, Darkness After Time's Colours 1976, Chanson de Geste 1978, The Pulses of Time 1979, Word Within 1981, Vortex 1982, Tides 1984, Clarinet Threads 1985, O Vos Omnes 1986, Wind Chimes 1987, Piano Nets 1990, Valley Flow 1992, Névé 1994, Empty Vessels 1997, Base Metals 2000, Ringing Down the Sun 2002, Resounding 2004, Spectral Lands 2011. *Recordings:* Gradual, Pentes, Chanson de Geste, The Pulses of Time, Pneuma, Vortex, Tides, Clarinet Threads, Wind Chimes, Piano Nets, Valley Flow, Névé, Base Metals, Empty Vessels, Tides, Pentes. *Publications:* The Listening Imagination: Listening in the Electro-acoustic Era 1992; contrib. to The Language of Electro-Acoustic

Music, Musiques et Recherches, Interface, Contemporary Music Review, Organised Sound, Ouïr, Écouter, Comprendre Après Schaeffer 1999. *Honours:* Hon. DLitt (Huddersfield); Fylkingen Prize 1975, 1st Prize, Bourges Electroacoustic Awards 1983, Special Prize, Int. Confed. of Electroacoustic Music 1983, Prix Ars Electronica 1988. *E-mail:* d.smalley@city.ac.uk (office). *Website:* www.city.ac.uk/music (office).

SMALLWOOD, Robert, BMus; composer; b. 22 July 1958, Melbourne, Australia. *Education:* Univ. of Melbourne, Accademia Chigiana, Siena, studied with Barry Conyngham and Nigel Butterley. *Career:* Musician-in-Residence, Orange City 1987–90. *Compositions include:* Trio Sonatina for two clarinets and piano 1976, Discovery for orchestra 1979, Sunshine Disaster for choir and band 1981, Reminiscences for clarinet and percussion 1982, Kyrie 1984, Elements for speaker, children's chorus and band 1985, Wake Up My Soul for children's and adult choirs, and orchestra 1987, Living Land for chorus, children's choir and ensemble 1988, Three Little Poems for speaker, flute, clarinet and cello 1980, Psalm 150 for soprano, chorus, strings, piano and organ 1991, Three Greek Dances for flute/piccolo, clarinet and string quartet 1993. *Honours:* Twin Cities Church Musicians Competition 1992.

SMEDING, Marten; Dutch singer (tenor); b. 1960. *Education:* studied with Maria Pluister-Leentvaar, Ge Neutel, Bernhard Kruysen, Robert Holl, Henk Smit. *Career:* sang in choir of Nederlandse Opera 1991; appearances at Théâtre de la Monnaie, Brussels, in Salome, Khovanshchina, Parsifal and Otello season 1999–2000; Holland Festival 1996, in Enescu's Oedipe; Netherlands Opera from 1992, in Samson et Dalila, Parsifal and The Carmelites; Strauss's Bacchus at Frankfurt and Gounod's Faust in Romania; concerts include Evangelist in the Bach Passions, Lieder by Schubert and Schumann, and Janáček's Diary of One who Disappeared; Pompeo in Benvenuto Cellini with the Rotterdam Philharmonic Orchestra at the Festival Hall, London 1999. *Honours:* semi-finalist 's-Hertogenbosch Singers' Competition, The Netherlands. *Current Management:* Pollock Artists Management Amsterdam, PO Box 15069, 1001 MB, Amsterdam, Netherlands. *E-mail:* pollock@chello.nl. *Website:* www.pollock.nl/html/marten-smeding.html.

SMEETS, Roger; singer (baritone); b. 1959, Maastricht, The Netherlands. *Education:* Maastricht Conservatory. *Career:* sang with Netherlands Opera from 1984, including the 1985 premiere of Wintercruise by Henkemans; Komische Oper Berlin as Don Giovanni, Eugene Onegin and Wagner's Dutchman; Opera Zuid in Kerkrade from 1990, notably as Mozart's Figaro; major roles with Netherlands Opera; Steuermann in Tristan at Amsterdam 2001.

SMETANIN, Michael, BM; Australian composer; *Chair of Composition, Sydney Conservatorium, University of Sydney*; b. 1 Oct. 1958, Sydney. *Education:* New South Wales State Conservatorium of Music, Australian Broadcasting Corporation orchestral summer schools, studied with Louis Andriessen at Royal Conservatorium, The Hague. *Career:* Composer-in-Residence, Musica Viva, 1988; jury mem. Int. Gaudeamus Music Week 1999; Chair. of Composition Sydney Conservatorium Univ. of Sydney 2002–. *Compositions:* Ensemble: Per Canonem, 1982, revised 1984, Lichtpunt, 1983, The Speed Of Sound, 1983, Ladder Of Escape, 1984, Track, 1985, Vault, 1986, Bellvue ll, 1987, Fylgir, 1989, Spray, 1990, Strange Attractions, 1991; Orchestral: After The First Circle, 1982, Black Snow, 1987, Zyerkala, Blitz, 1989; Women and Birds in Front of the Moon, 1991; Vocal: 3 Songs, 1981, The Skinless Kiss Of Angels, for mezzo, baritone and ensemble, 1992; Tube-makers, 1995; Adjacent Rooms, 1992; Children's music: Music for Children and Dancers, 1988; Instrumental and keyboard: Afstand, 1983, Sting, 1987, Stroke, 1988. *Recordings include:* albums: Ladder Of Escape; Spray; Sting, Skinless Kiss of Angels. *Honours:* Paul Lowin Orchestral Award 1999. *Address:* c/o Australian Music Centre, PO Box N690, Grosvenor Street, Sydney 2000, Australia. *Telephone:* (2) 9634-1612 (home). *E-mail:* msmetanin@conmusic.usyd.edu.au (office).

SMIETANA, Krzysztof, FGSM; Polish violinist; b. 11 Oct. 1956, Kraków. *Education:* Secondary High School of Music, Kraków Acad. of Music, Guildhall School of Music and Drama, London. *Career:* debut 1974; appearances with major orchestras such as London Symphony Orchestra, Philharmonia, BBC Symphony Orchestra; performed at 1997 Proms Festival; numerous broadcasts for BBC Radio 3 and Polish National Radio; very active in chamber music; leader with orchestras such as Chamber Orchestra of Europe, London Symphonietta and London Symphony Orchestra; violinist in London Mozart Trio; Prof. of Violin at Guildhall School of Music and Drama. *Recordings:* Brahms – Sonatas for Violin and Piano, with Caroline Palmer; Panufnik – Violin Concerto, with London Musici; Fauré Violin Sonatas, with John Blakely, piano; Stravinsky – Violin Concerto, with Philharmonia, conducted by Robert Craft. *Honours:* Prizes at competitions: Thibaud, Paris; Kreisler, Vienna; Flesch, London; Brahms, Hamburg; Lipizer, Gorizia.

SMIRNOFF, Joel; American violinist and conductor; *President, Cleveland Institute of Music*; b. New York; s. of Zelly Smirnoff; m. Joan Kwoon. *Education:* Univ. of Chicago, Juilliard School. *Career:* fmr mem., Boston Symphony Orchestra; mem. chamber music faculty, Tanglewood Music Center 1983–, Head of String Studies 1995–2000; mem. Juilliard String Quartet 1986–2009, Leader 1997–2009; mem. chamber music faculty, Juilliard School 1986–2009, violin faculty 1989–2009, Co-Chair. 1992–97, Chair. 1997–2009; Pres., Cleveland Inst. of Music 2008–; has conducted San Francisco Symphony Orchestra, Saint Paul Chamber Orchestra, Louisiana Philharmonic, Phoenix Symphony, Chicago Philharmonic, Texas Music Festival Orchestra, Amarillo Symphony, Western New York Chamber Orchestra, New World Symphony, Juilliard Symphony, Tanglewood Music Center Orchestra. *Address:* Cleveland Institute of Music, 11021 East Boulevard, Cleveland, OH 44106, USA (office). *Telephone:* (216) 791-5000 (office). *E-mail:* info@cim.edu (office). *Website:* www.cim.edu (office).

SMIRNOV, Dmitri Nikolayevich; Russian composer; b. 2 Nov. 1948, Minsk; m. Elena Firsova 1972; two c. *Education:* Moscow Conservatoire with Nikolai Sidelnikov, Edison Denisov and Yuri Kholopov, studied with Philip Herschkowitz. *Career:* Ed., Sovetsky Kompositor publishing house 1973–80; freelance composer 1980–; operas Tiriel and The Lamentations of Thel (after William Blake) (chamber) performed in Freiburg and Almeida Theatre, London; Symphony No. 1 The Seasons in Tanglewood 1989; oratorio A Song of Liberty premiered in Leeds 1993; Prof. and composer-in-residence, Keele Univ. 1993–98; Oratorio Song of Songs premiered in Geneva 1998; Visiting Fellow, Goldsmiths Coll. of Music, London 2002–. *Compositions include:* five piano sonatas 1967, 1980, 1992, 2000, 2001, three violin sonatas 1969, 1979, 1997, two piano concerti 1971, 1978, six string quartets 1973, 1985, 1993 (two), 1994, 1998, two piano trios 1977, 1992, three symphonies 1980, 1982, 1995, three violin concerti 1990, 1995, 1996, two cello concerti 1992, 2001, Songs of Destiny for voice and organ 1980, Six Poems by William Blake for voice and organ, Dirge Canons for ensemble, Serenade for ensemble 1981, Farewell Song for viola and harp, Fantasia for saxophone quartet, The Night Rhymes for voice and orchestra 1982, Two Ricercares for strings 1993, Tiriel 1985, Partita for solo violin 1985, Thel 1986, Mozart Variations for orchestra, The Visions of Coleridge for voice and ensemble 1987, The Songs of Love and Madness for voice and ensemble 1988–92, Angels of William Blake for piano 1988, Blake's Pictures (visionary ballet) for ensemble 1988–92, From Evening to Morning for mixed chorus 1990, Trinity Music for clarinet, violin and piano 1990, A Song of Liberty 1991, Three Blake's Songs for voice and ensemble 1991, Job's Studies for solo clarinet 1991, Wonderful Stories for voice and ensemble 1991, The Angels of Albion for piano 1991, Diptich for organ 1992, Orcades for solo flute 1992, Piano Quintet 1992, Ariel's Songs for voice and ensemble, Magic Lamb for voice and ensemble, The Bride in her Grave (opera) 1995, Between Scylla and Charybdis for strings, Song of Songs for soprano, tenor, chorus and orchestra 1997, MMass, Opus 111 for clarinet, cello and piano, Twilight for voice and ensemble 1998, Three Quarks for Muster Msrk for percussion, Portrait for wind ensemble, Shadows in Light for viola and harp 1999, Well Tempered Piano 2000, Saga for solo cello, Innocence of Experience for tape 2001, Metaplasms I and II for piano, The Stony Path for voice, cello and piano 2002, Triple Concerto No. 2 for violin, harp and double-bass with orchestra, Dream Journey for voice, flute and piano 2003. *Publications:* Philip Herschkowitz: A Geometer of Sound Crystals (in English) 2003; contributed articles on Webern, Boulez, Ligeti, Ferneyhow, Birtwhistle, Shostakovich, Denisov, Schnittke, Gubaidulina, others. *Honours:* first prize for solo for harp, Maastricht 1976. *Current Management:* Boosey & Hawkes, First Floor, Aldwych House, 71–91 Aldwych, London, WC2B 4HN, England. *E-mail:* composers.uk@boosey.com (office). *Website:* www.boosey.com/smirnov. *E-mail:* dmitrismirnov@ntlworld.com (home).

SMIRNOV, Oleg; cellist; b. 1950, Moscow, Russia. *Education:* Moscow Conservatoire with Prof. Kosolapova. *Career:* co-founder, Amisted Quartet 1973 (later renamed Tchaikovsky Quartet); many concerts in Russia with a repertoire including works by Haydn, Mozart, Beethoven, Schubert, Brahms, Tchaikovsky, Borodin, Prokofiev, Shostakovich, Bartók, Barber, Bucchi, Golovin, Tikhomirov; concert tours to Mexico, Italy and Germany. *Recordings include:* recitals for the US Russian Company Arts and Electronics. *Honours:* prizewinner Béla Bartók Festival and the Bucchi Competition.

SMITH, Angus; British tenor and arts organisation executive; *Member, The Orlando Consort and Artistic Director, Music in the Round*; m. Jenny Smith; two d. *Education:* St John's Coll., Cambridge, Guildhall School of Music and Drama, London. *Career:* worked with Monteverdi Choir, Taverner Consort, Tallis Scholars, Gabrieli Consort; as mem. The Orlando Consort chamber music ensemble, performed over 31 world premieres 2000–; collaborated with instrumentalists, singers and composers including the Perfect Houseplants jazz quartet, Calefax Reed Quintet, British composer Tarik O'Regan, Estonian Philharmonic Chamber Choir, and tabla player Kuljit Bhamra; regular performers at London's Wigmore Hall and South Bank Centre; numerous festivals in Spain, Belgium, Germany, Austria, Greece, Estonia, France, Poland, Czech Republic, Russia, Italy, Portugal, Sweden and UK, including Spitalfields, Bury St Edmunds, Aldeburgh, St David's, Stour, Deal, Brinkburn, Hexham, Cheltenham and Chester Festivals, Manchester Early Music Series, City of London Festival, St Magnus Festival in Orkney, Huddersfield Contemporary Music Festival, Three Choirs Festival, Beverley and York Early Music Festivals; also featured at events in North America, including Boston Early Music Festival; tours to Japan, Peru, Bolivia and Colombia; debut at BBC Proms 1997, Edinburgh Int. Festival 1998; solo performances with English Chamber Orchestra, Scottish Chamber Orchestra, Sir Roger Norrington, Richard Hickox, Ivan Fischer and others; Creative Projects Assoc., Oundle Int. Festival 2009–; Artistic Dir Music in the Round 2010–. *Recordings include:* with The Orlando Consort: The Mystery of Notre Dame, Loyset Compère 1445-1518, Popes and Antipopes (Papal music from the 14th and 15th Centuries), Passiontide (15th Century Flemish Easter music), Missa De plus en plus by Ockeghem, The Saracen and the Dove (Music for the courts of Padua and Pavia), Motets by Josquin Desprez, The Works of John Dunstaple (Gramophone Early Music CD of the Year 1996), The Call of the

Phoenix (Gramophone Early Music CD of the Year 2003), Machaut's Messe de Notre Dame/O'Regan's Scattered Rhymes 2008, Extempore, Extempore II, Mantra: Musical conversations across the Indian Ocean 2010. *E-mail:* angus@orlandoconsort.com (office). *Website:* www.orlandoconsort.com (office).

SMITH, Carol; British singer (soprano); b. 1960, Huddersfield, England. *Education:* Guildhall School and National Opera Studio. *Career:* appearances at Glyndebourne in Albert Herring and L'Enfant et les Sortilèges; Melissa in Handel's Amadigi for Dublin Opera Theatre at Prague, Paris and Warsaw; Handel's Solomon at the Prague Spring Festival and Tamerlano at Melbourne and Lisbon; recitals include Carnegie Hall and the Aldeburgh Festival; concerts with the Philharmonia, London Mozart Players, Hallé Orchestra and Berlin Symphony Orchestra; Mozart's C minor Mass at Tenerife and Henze's Der Prinz von Homburg (as Natalie) for the BBC; season 1999 with Haydn's Seasons for City of London Sinfonia and Beethoven's 9th for Northern Sinfonia. *Recordings include:* Rossini's Ricciardo e Zoraide. *Honours:* Concert Artists Guild Award, New York.

SMITH, Catriona; British singer (soprano); b. 1963, Scotland. *Education:* Royal Scottish Academy, University of Toronto Opera Division. *Career:* sang Britten's Lucretia and Miss Wordsworth at the Banff Summer Arts Festival in 1988, Cathleen in Riders to the Sea by Vaughan Williams at Toronto and Pamina for British Youth Opera; Wigmore Hall recital debut 1988; sang at Kent Opera as Juno in The Return of Ulysses; festival engagements include Aldeburgh in Goehr's Triptych and English Bach Festival in Idomeneo; sang Clorinda in La Cenerentola at Covent Garden 1991 and engaged at the Stuttgart Staatsoper 1991–95; other roles include Mozart's Countess, Rossini's Berta, Dido, Frasquita, Susanna and Barbarina in Le nozze di Figaro; roles in Stuttgart include Pamina, Gilda, Nayad, Sophie in Der Rosenkavalier, Erénoira (world premiere) and Zerlina; Madeline in Debussy's Fall of the House of Usher, 1996; Morgana in Alcina at Stuttgart, 1998; season 2000–01 as Offenbach's Olympia, at Stuttgart, and Norina in Donizett's I Pazzi per progetto. *Honours:* winner Maggie Teyte Competition 1987. *Current Management:* Opernagentur Inge Tennigkeit, Kempener Strasse 4, 40474 Düsseldorf, Germany. *Telephone:* (211) 5160060. *Fax:* (211) 51600616. *E-mail:* opera@tennigkeit-ag.de. *Website:* www.tennigkeit-ag.de.

SMITH, Craig; British singer (baritone); b. 1960, England. *Education:* Royal Northern College of Music with Nicholas Powell. *Career:* roles at the RNCM included Sharpless, Pandolfe in Cendrillon, Zurga in Les Pêcheurs de Perles and Lionel in The Maid of Orleans by Tchaikovsky; Cecil in Jonathan Miller's production of Maria Stuarda at Buxton and Smirnov in Walton's The Bear, at Los Angeles; Zürich Opera from 1995, as Morales in Carmen, Paris in Roméo et Juliette and the Wig Maker in Ariadne auf Naxos; Other roles include Nabucco (Bad Hersfeld, 1996) and Sharpless, with the Royal Liverpool Philharmonic; Concert repertory includes CPE Bach's Magnificat, Rossini's Petite Messe Solennelle at Winchester Cathedral, L'Enfance du Christ at the Queen Elizabeth Hall, London, Carmina Burana at the Royal Concert Hall, Glasgow, and in Terra Pax by Frank Martin, at Schaffhausen and Ravensburg. *Honours:* Peter Moores Foundation and Robert Stanley Ford Scholarships. *Current Management:* c/o Foxroe Artist Management, 103 Nottingham Road, New Basford, Nottingham NG7 7AJ, England. *Telephone:* (115) 847-8719. *Fax:* (115) 847-8719. *E-mail:* info@foxroe.com. *Website:* www.foxroe.com.

SMITH, Jennifer; British singer (soprano) and academic; *Professor of French Mélodie and Voice, Royal College of Music, London*; b. 13 July 1945, Lisbon, Portugal; d. of Arthur William Smith and Olga Hoffer Smith; one s. one d. *Education:* Lisbon Conservatory and French Lycée, Lisbon, studied with Jorge Croner de Vasconcellos and Gertrud Mersiovsky in Lisbon, Winifred Radford in London, Pierre Bernac in London and Paris, Hans Keller in London. *Career:* debut, sang Jephtha, Carissimi, Lisbon 1966; sang in Europe before moving to England 1971; operatic roles have included Countess Almaviva for WNO, Scottish and Kent Operas; Gluck's Orfeo at the Wexford Festival; Rameau's Les Boréades and Hippolyte et Aricie at Aix-en-Provence; L'Incoronazione di Poppea conducted by Leonhardt; Aminta in Il Re Pastore, Lisbon; Cybelle in Lully's Atys at the Opéra-Comique Paris and in New York; Electra in Mozart's Idomeneo, Lisbon 1995; Praskovia Ossipovna in Shostakovich's The Nose, Lausanne; Foresta's Wife and Screech Owl in Janáček's The Cunning Little Vixan, ROH debut 2002; concert repertoire includes works by Bach, Handel, Poulenc, Purcell, Britten and Berlioz (Les Nuits d'Eté); appearances with the English Chamber Orchestra, London Bach Orchestra, the English Concert, Steinitz Bach Players and the Orchestra of the Age of Enlightenment; conductors include Rattle, Willcocks, Leppard, Pinnock, Gardiner, Boulez, Mackerras and Kempe; tour of Europe with the B Minor Mass, conducted by Frans Brueggen; song recitals in Portugal, France, Germany, Switzerland, Belgium and UK; TV appearances include Scarlatti's Salve Regina with George Malcolm, Handel's Judas Maccabaeus conducted by Norrington and Purcell's Come, Ye Sons of Art Away; sang the Queen of Night (Mozart Experience, London) conducted by Norrington, QEH 1989; Rameau at Versailles (Flore and Nais) with the English Bach Festival 1989; season 1992 as Music in Monteverdi's Orfeo at ENO, Iphigénie en Tauride with the English Bach Festival at Covent Garden and in Conti's Don Chisciotte at Innsbruck; sang the Queen of Night with Hamilton Opera 1996; title role in the first performance since 1744 of Artaserse by Terradellas, Barcelona 1998; sang The Cunning Little Vixen, Covent Garden 2002, La Nozze di Figaro, Aix-en-Provence, France, also in Japan and in Baden-Baden, Germany 2002, Shostakovitch's The Nose, Lausanne, Switzerland 2002, Nantes and Angers, France 2002; Castor et Pollux conducted by John Eliot Gardiner, Paris 2007; Prof. of French Mélodie and Voice, Royal Coll. of Music, London 1998–. *Recordings:* Bach Mass in B Minor, Magnificat/Corboz, Cantata 208; Carissimi Jephté; Falla Retablo de Maese Pedro and Psyche/Rattle; Gabrieli Sacrae Symphoniae; Handel Hercules and L'Allegro/Gardiner, Il Trionfo del Tempo, Silete Venti/Pinnock, Messiah, Amadigi; Haydn Mariazeller Mass and Little Organ Mass/Guest; Lully Dies Irae, Miserere and Te Deum/Paillard; Rameau's Nais/McGegan, Castor et Pollux/Farncombe and Les Boréades/Gardiner; Purcell King Arthur, Indian Queen and Fairy Queen/Gardiner, Come Ye Sons of Art/Pinnock; Vivaldi Gloria and Kyrie/Corboz, Beatus Vir and Dixit Dominus/Cleobury; Schubert Lieder; Platée (Rameau), Titon et l'Aurore (Mondonville) Alycone (Marais) Il Trionfo del Tempo (Handel), La Resurrezione (Handel), all with Marc Minkowski; Xerxes (Handel) with McGegan; Orphée aux enfers (Offenbach), with Minkowski; French Cantatas; Saudade, amor e morte, with Manuel Morais; Ottone (Handel) with Robert King; King Alfred (Arne); Chants de L'âme (Greif) with the composer at the piano; The Nose (Shostakovitch) 2004, Fauré Complete Mélodies 2004–05. *Films:* England my England 1995. *E-mail:* je.ma.smith@care4free.net (home).

SMITH, Malcolm; American singer (bass); b. 22 June 1933, Rockville Center, NY; m. Margaret Younger. *Education:* Oberlin Conservatory and Indiana University, Bloomington. *Career:* debut as Inquisitor in Prokofiev's The Fiery Angel, New York City Opera, 1965; sang at the City Opera until 1970, New York Metropolitan from 1975; guest appearances at Chicago, Seattle, Houston, Miami and San Francisco; Deutsche Oper am Rhein, Dusseldorf, from 1972, with further engagements in Milan, Vienna and throughout Germany; season 1985–86 as Ramphis in Aida at Cincinnati and Fafner in Das Rheingold at Turin; Paris Théâtre du Châtelet, as Mephisto in Schumann's Faust and Salzburg Festival 1986 in the premiere of Die schwarze Maske by Penderecki; Dusseldorf 1991, as Drago in Schumann's Genoveva; season 2000–01 as Debussy's Arkel at Cincinnati, the Grand Inquisitor (Don Carlos) and Mussorgsky's Pimen at Dusseldorf; further roles in operas by Beethoven, Rossini, Mussorgsky and Wagner (King Marke at Trieste 1969). *Recordings include:* Tristan und Isolde, Das Rheingold, War and Peace, Oedipus Rex, Mahler's 8th Symphony. *Current Management:* c/o Thea Dispeker Inc., 59 East 54th Street, Suite 81, New York NY 10022, USA. *Telephone:* (212) 421-7676. *Fax:* (212) 935-3279. *E-mail:* info@dispeker.com. *Website:* www.dispeker.com.

SMITH, Maureen Felicity; British violinist; b. Leeds, Yorks.; m. Geoffrey Rivlin 1974; two d. *Education:* Royal Manchester Coll. of Music, Indiana Univ., USA. *Career:* debut at Royal Festival Hall 1961; soloist with most leading British orchestras; debut at London Promenade Concerts 1965; regular broadcasts for BBC Radio 3 and numerous TV appearances; appearances at major festivals, including Aldeburgh and Leeds, Brighton, Cheltenham, English Bach and Three Choirs; Prof. of Violin, Royal Coll. of Music, London 1997–, Deputy Head of Strings 2002–; mem. European String Teachers Asscn. *Recordings:* Mendelssohn Violin Concerto, Milhaud Duos, Brahms and Mahler Piano Quartets, Mozart and Haydn violin and viola duos. *Honours:* Hon. ARAM 1996; BBC Violin Competition 1965, Gulbenkian Foundation Fellowship 1966, Leverhulme Fellowship 1966. *Address:* Royal College of Music, Prince Consort Road, London, SW7 2BS (office); 8 Heath Close, London, NW11 7DX, England (home). *Telephone:* (20) 7591-4863 (office). *E-mail:* mfsmith@rcm.ac.uk (office); maureensmithriv@btinternet.com (home).

SMITH, Philip, BM, MM; American musician (trumpet); *Principal Trumpet, New York Philharmonic Orchestra*; b. 1 April 1952, London, England; s. of Derek Smith; m.; two c. *Education:* Juilliard School. *Career:* mem., Chicago Symphony 1975; co-prin. trumpet, New York Philharmonic Orchestra 1978, prin. trumpet 1988–; worked with conductors, including Zubin Mehta, Kurt Masur, Erich Leinsdorf, Leonard Bernstein, Neeme Järvi, Bramwell Tovey; notable performances with New York Philharmonic include world premieres of Joseph Turrin's Trumpet Concerto, Lowell Liebermann's Concerto, Siegfried Matthus's Double Concerto for Trumpet, Trombone, and Orchestra, and the US premiere of Jacques Hetu's Trumpet Concerto; performed Turrin's Chronicles (world premiere) with Univ. of New Mexico Wind Ensemble; appeared as guest soloist with Edmonton Symphony, Newfoundland Symphony, Columbus Symphony, Leipzig Gewandhaus, South Dakota Symphony, Pensacola Symphony, Hartford Symphony, and Beaumont Symphony, also with US President's Own Marine Band, La Philharmonie des Vents des Québec, Hanover Wind Symphony, Ridgewood Concert Band, many major univ. wind ensembles, US Army Brass Band, Goteborg Brass (Sweden), Black Dyke Mills and Ridged Containers Bands (UK), Hannaford Street Silver Band and Intrada Brass (Canada), numerous US and Salvation Army brass bands; has contributed to festivals, including Caramoor Int. Music Festival, Grand Teton Music Festival, Swiss Brass Week, Bremen Trumpet Days, Oslo Trumpet Week, Harmony Ridge Festival, Scotia Festival of Music, numerous Int. Trumpet Guild conferences; guest teacher The Juilliard School; mem. Resounding Praise ensemble. *Recordings:* Orchestral Excerpts for Trumpet 1995, Philip Smith 1997, Fandango 2000, My Song of Songs 2002. *Address:* New York Philharmonic, Avery Fisher Hall, 10 Lincoln Center Plaza, New York, NY 10023-6990, USA (office). *Website:* www.newyorkphilharmonic.org; www.principaltrumpet.com.

SMITH, Richard Langham, BA, FRSA; British musicologist and academic; *Research Professor, Royal College of Music*; b. 10 Sept. 1947, London, England; m. Susan Rebecca Parsons; one d. *Education:* Univ. of York, further study with Edward Lockspeiser and at Amsterdam Conservatory. *Career:* harpsichordist and musicologist, specialising in French music; Lecturer, Univ. of Lancaster –1979, City Univ., London –1995, Univ. of Exeter 1995–2005; Visiting Prof. of Music, Gresham Coll. 2003–04; Arnold Kettle Distinguished Scholar, Open Univ. 2005–; Visiting Lecturer, Univ. of Cambridge 2005–; Head of Grad. School, Royal Coll. of Music, London 2008–, Research Prof. 2011–; frequent broadcaster on BBC Radio 2, 3 and 4, and France Musique; Lecturer, Martin Randall Travel 2008–. *Compositions:* reconstruction of Debussy's unpublished opera, Rodrigue et Chimène premiered at Opéra de Lyon 1993, his edn of Bizet's Carmen used by Paris (Chatelet) and Opéra-Comique 2010. *Publications:* Debussy on Music (trans. and ed.) 1977, Debussy, Pelléas et Mélisande, Cambridge Opera Handbook (with R. Nichols) 1989, Debussy Studies 1997, Debussy: Rodrigue et Chimène, Durand (ed.) 2003, Bizet: Carmen Vocal Score, orchestral material on hire 2013; contrib. of numerous articles and reviews on Debussy in journals, including Music and Letters, Times Literary Supplement, 19th Century Music, Cahiers Debussy, Musical Times, The Listener, Early Music, The Strad; chapters in numerous multi-author books. *Honours:* Chevalier des Arts et des Lettres. *Address:* Higher Summerlands, 4 Longlands, Dawlish, Devon, EX7 9NE, England (home). *Telephone:* (1626) 864105 (home). *E-mail:* langhamsmith@gmail.com (home); rlanghamsmith@rcm.ac.uk (office).

SMITH, Robert Dean, BME, BM, MM; American/Swiss singer (tenor); b. 1965, Kansas; m. Janice Harper-Smith. *Education:* Pittsburg State Univ., The Juilliard School, New York. *Career:* lyric-baritone roles in German opera houses early in career; tenor repertoire has included Wagner's Walther, Parsifal, Tristan and Lohengrin, Verdi's Don Carlo and Manrico, Enzo in La Gioconda and Beethoven's Florestan; Don José, Pinkerton, Cavaradossi, Des Grieux in Manon Lescaut, Giordano's Andrea Chenier; Bayreuth Festival 1997–2008, as Walther von Stolzing and Siegmund in Die Walküre, Lohengrin and Tristan; further engagements in Vienna, New York, Paris, Barcelona, Tokyo and Berlin; season 2007–08 with Ariadne auf Naxos at the Royal Opera, Wagner's Lohengrin at Vienna State Opera and Tannhäuser at the Berlin State Opera; engaged as Tristan in Madrid 2008, as Andrea Chenier, Toulouse 2009; other concerts include Das Lied von der Erde, Gurre-Lieder and Beethoven's 9th Symphony. *Current Management:* Opera & Concert, 37 rue de la Chaussée d'Antin, 75009 Paris, France. *Telephone:* 1-42-96-18-18. *Fax:* 1-42-96-18-00. *E-mail:* agence@opera-concert.com. *Website:* www.opera-concert .com; www.robertdeansmith.com.

SMITH, Roger; British cellist; b. 1949, England. *Career:* fmr mem. Acad. of St Martin in the Fields and mem. of the Acad. of St Martin's Octet; teacher, Menuhin School; currently living and playing in southern France. *Address:* c/o Academy of St Martin in the Fields Chamber Ensemble, Station House, Staverton, Totnes, Devon TQ9 6AG, England. *E-mail:* rogersmithcello@ googlemail.com (home).

SMITH, Trefor Leslie, BMus, MA, ARMCM; British pianist; b. 4 July 1948, Aberdeen, Scotland. *Education:* Aberdeen Univ., Liverpool Univ., Royal Manchester Coll. of Music, State Coll. of Music, Hamburg, studied with Wilhelm Kempff, Vlado Perlemuter, Paul Badura-Skoda and Hans Leygraf. *Career:* numerous appearances in Germany, the UK, France, Italy, Spain, Norway, Ireland, Austria, USA, India, Turkey, Poland and Russia; various radio recordings; staff mem., later Prof. of Piano, Musikhochschule, Hamburg. *Recordings:* Piano Music by Theodore Kirchner (1823–1903), Brahms Piano Sonatas and Beethoven Piano Sonatas.

SMITH, Wilma; New Zealand violinist; b. 1960. *Education:* New England Conservatory. *Career:* Leader of the Boston-based Lydia Quartet; co-founder, New Zealand String Quartet, under the auspices of the Music Federation of New Zealand; debut concert in Wellington 1988; concerts at the Tanglewood School in the USA, the Banff Int. Competition in Canada, and performances with the Lindsay Quartet at the 1990 Int. Festival of the Arts; soloist, New Zealand Symphony Orchestra; Artist-in-Residence, Victoria Univ.; tour to Australia 1990 for Music Viva Australia; tours of New Zealand 1992; concerts in New York 1993.

SMITH-LOMBARDINI, Maryelizabeth Anne, BMus, MMus; singer and artistic director; b. 1 Sept. 1957, Norfolk, VA, USA; m. Danilo Lombardini 1987. *Education:* Univ. of Michigan at Ann Arbor, G. Verdi Conservatory, Milan, Italy, La Scala Opera Studio, Vienna State Opera, Austria. *Career:* debut in Azio Corghi's Gargantua, Teatro Regio, Turin 1984; specialist in 20th-century music; Vienna State Opera and Genoa Opera debuts 1985; La Scala 1991, in leading role in Henze's Das Verratene Meer, returning 1992 as Andromeda in Sciarrino's Perseo e Andromeda 1993 for Donatoni's Il Velo Dissolto 1996 for Berio's Outis; Catania and Venice debuts 1997; concert activity includes regular appearances at La Fenice, Venice; Artistic Dir, Laboratorio Lirico, Sicilian Chamber Music Soc. 1994–96; Prof., A. Scontrino State Music Conservatory, Trapani 1995–96; Artistic Dir, Operalaboratorio, City of Palermo Foundation Teatro Massimo-Ars Nova 1997–; Dir, Palermo-Detroit Cultural Exchange for Opera (Young Artists) 1998–. *Recordings:* La Griselda (Vivaldi), Stabat Mater (Boccherini). *Address:* Via del Celso 95, 90134 Palermo, Italy.

SMITH-MAXER, Carolyn; singer (soprano); b. 1945, Oklahoma City, USA. *Education:* studied in Chicago. *Career:* debut with Basle Opera 1967, as Gilda in Rigoletto; sang as Komische Oper Berlin from 1969, notably as Gershwin's Bess; Staatsoper Berlin 1974, in the premiere of Kunad's Sabellicus; Dresden Staatsoper 1976, as Mozart's Constanze; appeared at the Frankfurt Opera

until 1984 and sang at Bremen 1989–90; frequent opera and concert engagements in Chicago; repertory has included soubrette and coloratura roles.

SMITHERS, Don Le Roy, BS, PhD; music historian; b. 17 Feb. 1933, New York, USA; m. 2nd 1967; one d.; one s. one d. (from previous marriage). *Education:* Hofstra Univ., New York Univ., Columbia Univ., New York, Univ. of Oxford, England, studied with Prof. Arthur Mendel at Princeton Univ. *Career:* Assoc. Prof., Dept of Fine Arts and School of Music, Syracuse Univ. 1966–75; lectures and papers on baroque ornament, Festival Books, the history of music and musical instruments and the history of musical performance for various groups, colls and univs; solo concert performances on baroque trumpet, cornetto, and various renaissance wind instruments; co-founder, Musical Dir and fmr Conductor, Oxford Pro Musica, Oxford 1965–. *Recordings:* some 50 solo and ensemble recordings with various European and American groups including New York Pro Musica, The Leonhardt Consort, Concentus Musicus Wien and Early Music Consort of London. *Publications include:* The Music and History of the Baroque Trumpet Before 1721 1973, A Catalogue of Telemann's Music with Brass 1995; contrib. many articles to professional journals and book chapters. *Honours:* Research Fellow Princeton Univ. 1978, Japan Foundation grantee, ASECS/Folger Inst. Fellowship 1984.

SMITKOVA, Jana; Czech singer (soprano); b. 26 Dec. 1942, Prague. *Education:* Prague Conservatory, Prague Music Acad. *Career:* debut in Liberec 1967, as Nancy in Martha by Flotow; sang with the Brno Opera 1968–70, Ceske Budejovice 1970–73; mem., Komische Oper Berlin from 1973, debut as Katya Kabanova; frequent guest appearances in Dresden, notably as Agathe in Der Freischütz at the 1985 reopening of the Semper Opera House; has also sung at the Nat. Theatre, Prague, and in other East European centres; sang Ludmila in Harry Kupfer's production of The Bartered Bride at Covent Garden 1989, on visit with the co. of the Komische Opera; other roles include Pamina, Puccini's Butterfly and the leading role in Die Kluge by Orff. *Recordings include:* Der Freischütz, Beethoven's Ninth. *Honours:* Prague Spring Festival Prize 1963.

SMITS, Stefanie, DipMus; German singer (soprano); b. 13 Sept. 1966, Speyer, Rhein. *Education:* Hochschule für Musik, Karlsruhe, Hochschule für Darstellende Kunst und Musik, Frankfurt am Main. *Career:* debut at Telemann Festival, Magdeburg, as Nigella in Der neumodische Liebhaber Damon 1996; Donna Anna in Don Giovanni in Berlin 1997; debut with Norske Opera Oslo as Tosca in Kristiansand 1998; Dame in George Taboris's production of Magic Flute in Berlin 1998; guest performance as Suor Angelica at Frankfurt 1999; engaged with Landestheater Coburg to sing Mimi in La Bohème, Arabella, Rosalinde in Fledermaus and Manon by Massenet. *Recordings:* Der neumodische Liebhaber Damon with La Stagione Frankfurt with DLF Köln. *Honours:* Stiftung Frederique Brion scholarship, Basel 1991, silver medal Maria Callas Competition, Athens 1997.

SMOLYANINOVA, Soya; singer (soprano); b. 1960, Russia. *Education:* Gnessin Inst., Moscow. *Career:* appearances at the Bolshoi Opera from 1986, as Tatiana, Lisa in The Queen of Spades, Emma (Khovanshchina), Yaroslavna (Prince Igor), the Trovatore Leonora, Tosca and Desdemona; guest appearances at Leipzig, Dresden and the Deutsche Oper Berlin, as Amelia, Tosca and Tatiana; soloist with the Gewandhaus Orchestra, Leipzig, and other leading orchestras; Semper Oper Dresden from 1995, as Abigaille in Nabucco, Madama Butterfly and the Forza Leonora; season 1996 as Leonora and Tosca at Antwerp; engaged as Turandot 1998.

SMYTHE, Russell; Irish singer (baritone); b. 19 Dec. 1949, Dublin. *Education:* Guildhall School of Music and London Opera Centre. *Career:* sang Pantalon in L'Amour des Trois Oranges (BBC TV); recent appearances include Monteverdi's Orfeo with Opéra de Lausanne, Sharpless at Deutsche Staatsoper, Berlin, Starek in Jenůfa, Aeneas in Dido and Aeneas, Arbace in Idomeneo and Hastings in Richard III for De Vlaamse Opera, Redburn in Billy Budd for New Israeli Opera, Der Barbier in Die Schweigsame Frau, Fernando in La Gazza Ladra and Musiklehrer in Ariadne auf Naxos for Garsington and the Mayor in Jenůfa and Page in Sir John in Love for ENO; most recent appearances include Niceno in Vivaldi's L'incoronazione di Dario at Garsington, Manoah in Samson at the Buxton Festival, Ping for De Vlaamse Opera and Hastings in Richard III for Opéra Nat. du Rhin 2010. *Recordings:* Nardo, Brussels Opera, Thésée in Hippolyte et Aricie, Rameau; Der Mann Die Glückliche Hand (WDR Cologne), Menotti's The Telephone, Billy Budd, Teucer in Rameau's Dardanus; extensive recording for BBC Radio 3, Opera Rara series of 19th Century works, King Edward III L'Assedio di Calais. *Current Management:* c/o Athole Still Opera Ltd, Foresters Hall, 25–27 Westow Street, London, SE19 3RY, England. *Telephone:* (20) 8771-5271. *Fax:* (20) 8771-8172. *E-mail:* enquiries@atholestill.co.uk. *Website:* www.atholestill .co.uk. *E-mail:* rss@easynet.co.uk (home).

SNIPP, Peter; British singer (baritone); b. 1964, London. *Education:* Guildhall School of Music and Drama. *Career:* appearances as Masetto with Opera North and in the title role of the premiere of Judith Weir's The Vanishing Bridegroom for Scottish Opera; Eugene Onegin for Kentish Opera and in Zaide and Les Boréades for City of Birmingham Touring Opera; Principal with English National Opera from 1994, singing Malatesta, Harlequin (Ariadne), Guglielmo and Patroclus in King Priam; Concerts include the War Requiem in Finland, Carmina Burana under Jane Glover and the Steersman in Tristan with the London Philharmonic Orchestra; Sang in

Henze's Prince of Homburg for ENO, 1996, as Papageno, 1998 and as Figaro in Le Nozze in 1999. *Recordings include:* Il Barbiere di Siviglia, with ENO.

SNOWMAN, (Michael) Nicholas, OBE, MA; British music administrator and business executive; *Chairman, Wartski;* b. 18 March 1944, London, England; s. of the late Kenneth Snowman and Sallie Snowman (née Moghilevkine); m. Margo Michelle Rouard 1983; one s. *Education:* Hall School and Highgate School, London, Magdalene Coll., Cambridge. *Career:* Asst to Head of Music Staff, Glyndebourne Festival 1967–69; Co-founder and Gen. Man. London Sinfonietta 1968–72; Admin. Music Theatre Ensemble 1968–71; Artistic Dir Institut de Recherche et de Coordination Acoustique/Musique (IRCAM), Centre d'Art et de la Culture Georges Pompidou 1972–86; Co-founder and Artistic Adviser, Ensemble Intercontemporain 1975–92, mem. Bd 1992–, Vice-Chair. 1998–; mem. Music Cttee, Venice Biennale 1979–86; Artistic Dir Projects in 1980, 1981, 1983, Festival d'Automne de Paris; Programme Consultant, Cité de la Musique, La Villette, Paris 1991–92; Gen. Dir (Arts), South Bank Centre, London 1986–92, Chief Exec. 1992–98; Gen. Dir Glyndebourne Opera 1998–2000, Opera Nat. du Rhin, Strasbourg 2002–09; Chair. Wartski (jewellers) 2002– (co. made wedding rings for Prince Charles and Camilla Parker-Bowles 2005 and for Prince William and Kate Middleton 2011); mem. British Section, Franco-British Council 1995–; Trustee, New Berlioz Edn 1996–; Gov. RAM, London 1998–. *Radio:* Desert Island Discs (BBC Radio 4) 1990. *Publications:* The Best of Granta (co-ed.) 1967, The Contemporary Composers (series ed.) 1982–; papers and articles on music, cultural policy and France. *Honours:* Chevalier, Ordre des Art et des Lettres (France) 1985, Officier 1990; Order of Cultural Merit (Poland) 1990; Chevalier, Ordre nat. du Mérite (France) 1995. *Address:* Wartski, 14 Grafton Street, London, W1S 4DE, England (office); 9 rue de Bain Finkwiller, 67000 Stasbourg, France (home). *Telephone:* (20) 7493-1141 (office); (6) 64-77-81-30 (home). *Fax:* (20) 7409-7448 (office). *E-mail:* wartski@wartski.com (office). *Website:* www.wartski.com (office).

SNYDER, Barry, BM, DipArt, MA; pianist and teacher; b. 6 March 1944, Allentown, PA, USA. *Education:* Eastman School of Music, Univ. of Rochester. *Career:* debut as soloist with Allentown Symphony Orchestra; has performed throughout the USA, Canada, Europe, Poland, S America and Asia; appearances with orchestras of Montréal, Atlanta, Houston, Baltimore, Detroit and Kraków in Poland; chamber music with Jan DeGaetani, Dong-Suk Kang, Zvi Zeitlin, Ani Kavafian, Bonita Boyd, Cleveland Quartet, Composers' Quartet, Eastman Brass Quintet, New York Brass Quintet; founder mem., Eastman Trio, with tours to Europe and S America; Prof. of Piano, Eastman School of Music 1970–; has given masterclasses with solo recitals. *Recordings include:* Dohnányi (solo recording), Dohnányi chamber works (with Cleveland Quartet), complete cello music of Fauré (with Steven Doone, cellist), Stephen Jaffe's Two Piano Sonata (with Anton Nel).

SOAR, David; British singer (bass); b. Notts. *Education:* Royal Acad. of Music, Nat. Opera Studio. *Career:* worked as freelance organist, singer and conductor; Dir of Music, All Saints Parish Church, Kingston; joined Welsh National Opera (WNO), later returned as Assoc. Artist; opera performances include Colline in La bohème and Masetto in Don Giovanni (Metropolitan Opera), Peter Quince in A Midsummer Night's Dream, Escamillo in Carmen, Mr Flint in Billy Budd and Collatinus in The Rape of Lucretia (Glyndebourne), Le Duc Roméo et Juliette (Salzburg Festival), Quinault in Adriana Lecouvreur (Royal Opera House Covent Garden), Nilakantha Lakmé (Opera Holland Park), Basilio in The Barber of Seville, Roy Disney in The Perfect American and Bernardino in Benvenuto Cellini (English National Opera) and Leporello in Don Giovanni, Figaro in Le nozze di Figaro, Escamillo and Sparafucile in Rigoletto (WNO); concert performances include Seneca in L'incoronazione di Poppea, First Nazarene in Salome (Bournemouth Symphony), Frère Laurent in Roméo et Juliette and The Dream of Gerontius, The Midsummer Marriage at BBC Proms (BBC Symphony), Haydn's Die sieben letzte Worte (Orchestre des Champs Elysées), Handel's Saul (BBC Singers), Messiah (The English Concert and Acad. of Ancient Music and Britten Sinfonia), Stravinsky (Collegium Vocale), Weill's The Seven Deadly Sins (Hallé), Belshazzar's Feast (BBC Philharmonic), Wozzeck (Philharmonia), Masetto in Don Giovanni (SCO) and Beethoven's Symphony no. 9; has worked with conductors including Sir Andrew Davis, Herreweghe, Bicket, Egarr, Elder, Storgårds, Salonen, Ticciati and Mackerras. *Recordings include:* Cilea: Adriana Lecouvreur, Elgar's The Dream of Gerontius (Gramophone Award for Best Choral Recording 2015). *Website:* www.askonasholt.co.uk.

SOBEHARTOVA, Jitka; Czech singer (soprano); b. 1950. *Education:* studied in Prague. *Career:* sang in operetta at the Karlin Music Theatre, Prague; opera roles at Usti nad Labern 1977–84, including Marenka in The Bartered Bride, Susanna, and Marguerite in Faust; Nat. Theatre, Prague from 1984, notably as Zerlina in Don Giovanni, Musetta (La Bohème), Aennchen (Der Freischütz) and roles in operas by Dvořák and Smetana; many concert appearances in Eastern Europe. *Recordings include:* The Cunning Peasant by Dvořák.

SOBOLEVA, Galina; Russian cellist; b. 1960, Moscow. *Education:* Moscow Conservatoire with Valentin Berlinsky. *Career:* mem., Prokofiev Quartet (founded at Moscow Festival of World Youth and the Int. Quartet Competition, Budapest); many concerts in former Soviet Union and on tour to Czechoslovakia, Germany, Austria, USA, Canada, Spain, Japan and Italy; repertoire includes works by Haydn, Mozart, Beethoven, Schubert, Debussy, Ravel, Tchaikovsky, Bartók and Shostakovich.

SOCCI, Gianni; singer (bass); b. 19 March 1939, Rome, Italy. *Education:* Accademia di Santa Cecilia, Rome, studied with Franco Cavara. *Career:* debut at Piccolo Teatro Comico, Rome 1965, as Achmed in Paisiello's Il Re Teodoro in Venezia; sang in the buffo repertory at opera houses in Milan, Rome, Naples, Florence, Turin, Venice, Genoa and Trieste; guest appearances in Brussels, Copenhagen, Toulouse, Strasbourg, Paris, Cologne, Frankfurt, Philadelphia, Montréal, Québec, Monte Carlo and Barcelona; many performances in operas by Mozart, Cimarosa, Rossini and Donizetti; sang at Teatro Lirico, Milan 1975 in the premiere of Al Gran Sole Carico d'Amore by Luigi Nono; concert engagements in Italy and elsewhere.

SOFFEL, Doris; German singer (mezzo-soprano); b. 12 May 1948, Hechingen; m. Karl-Erik Norrman; one d. *Education:* studied with Marianne Schech in Munich, Musikhochschule. *Career:* Bayreuth Youth Festival 1972, in Das Liebesverbot; Stuttgart State Opera 1973–80; sang Waltraute at Bayreuth Festival; noted in Bach and other baroque music; sang at Bregenz Festival 1977 as Puck in Oberon, Carmen in Stuttgart, Zürich, Oviedo 1978–97, Fricka in Basel Ring 1978; sang Monteverdi's Poppea in Toronto 1983 and took part in the Hamburg premiere of J.C. Bach's Amadis de Gaule; sang at Covent Garden 1983 as Sextus in La Clemenza di Tito and Orlovsky in Die Fledermaus; Fricka (Solti/Hall), Bayreuth Festival 1983; Mahler 3rd (Tennstedt), New York Carnegie Hall 1983; sang Donizetti's Lucretia Borgia and Bellini's Norma with Joan Sutherland 1983, 1985; sang in the world premiere of Reimann's Troades, Munich 1986; sang Octavian in a production of Der Rosenkavalier at the renovated Brussels Opera House, and Angelina in La Cenerentola at the Berlin Staatsoper 1987; L'Italiana in Algeri/Isabella, Schwetzingen, Zürich, Cologne 1987; television appearances include Das Lied von der Erde 1988; sang Mère Ubu in the premiere of Penderecki's Ubu Rex at Munich 1991; season 1992 as Cassandra in Reimann's Troades at Frankfurt and Elizabeth in Donizetti's Maria Stuarda at Amsterdam; Verdi's Preziosilla at Munich 1994; also appeared as Judith in Bartók's Bluebeard's Castle, Deutsche Oper Berlin (Kout/Friedrich) 1994, 1997, 2003, as Charlotte in Werther in Madrid and Parma with Alfredo Kraus, Damnation of Faust, Munich 1995, as Klytämnestra in Strauss' Elektra, Salzburg 1996, in Kundry at the Deutsche Oper Berlin 2000, 2004, Venice 2005, as Fricka and Waltraute for Cologne Opera, Countess Geschwitz in Palermo and Schoeck's Penthesilea for the Maggio Musicale, Florence, as Ortrud in Lohengrin at Bologna 2002, as Clairon in Strauss's Capriccio, Turin 2002, Cagliari 2003 and Paris 2007, Berlioz's Mort de Cléopatre, Berlin 2003, as Amme in Strauss's Frau ohne Schatten, Los Angeles 2004, Dresden and Toulouse 2006, Amsterdam 2008, Berlin 2009, as Fricka in Amsterdam Ring 2004–05, in Dresden and at La Scala, Milan 2010, as Herodias in Salome, Rome 2004, Seville 2005, Munich 2008, Dresden and Amsterdam 2009, Madrid and Washington 2010, in Verdi's Requiem, Vienna 2006, in Gurrelieder Montreal 2006, as Marfa in Mussorgsky's Khovanschina, Munich 2007, 2008, Frank Martin in Terra Pax, Dresden, Leipzig 2007, in Mahler's Lied von der Erde, Frankfurt 2007, as Kabanicha in Janáček's Katya Kabanova in Cologne 2008, as Jezibaba in Dvořák's Rusalka in Brussels 2008, as Klytämnestra in Strauss's Elektra in Munich 2009, Brussels 2010. *Recordings include:* Bach Cantatas and Magnificat, Flotow's Martha, Lortzing's Der Wildschütz, Haydn's St Cecilia Mass, Das Liebesverbot, Schumann's Requiem, Zemlinsky's Eine Florentinische Tragödie, Troades, Parsifal, Mahler No. 2, Beethoven's Missa Solemnis and 9th Symphony, Wolf's Der Corregidor, Mahler 3, Mahler 8, Kindertotenlieder, Lieder eines fahrenden Gesellen, Mahler's Rückertlieder, Virtuoso Arias, Anna Bolena, Soffel sings Belcanto, Werther, Soffel sings Lieder, Brahms's Lieder, Berg's Lulu, Reuther-Lieder, Das Rheingold, Die Walküre, Parsfial, Chovanschina. *Honours:* Kammersängerin (Germany), Royal Order of the Northern Star (Sweden). *Current Management:* Agency Boris Orlob Management, Jägerstrasse 70, 10117 Berlin, Germany. *Telephone:* (30) 20450839. *Fax:* (30) 20450849. *E-mail:* boris@orlob.net. *Website:* www.orlob.net.

SOGNY, Michel, MA, DPhil; artistic director, manager, composer and writer; b. 21 Nov. 1947, Pau, France. *Education:* Ecole Normale de Musique de Paris. *Career:* debut with piano recital of own compositions, Paris 1990; new piano method 1978; producer, int. recitals of gifted pupils; founder, Paris Piano School 1974; numerous radio and television programmes; television film on Liszt 1982; educational methods adopted by ILO, Geneva 1985; creation of Michel Sogny Foundation for young and talented under-privileged children 2000; treasurer, French Asscn Franz Liszt, Paris 1972. *Compositions:* numerous concert pieces for piano, numerous didactic compositions for piano. *Recordings:* Michel Sogny Live at Espace Cardin 1990, Prolegomenes to a Musical Eidetic, Michel Sogny Live at Villa Schindler. *Publications:* Admiration Créatrice Chez Liszt 1975, La Methode et Questions 1984, Le Methode et Action 1987; contrib. to Tribune de Genève 1993, record critic for classical review, Harmony, Paris 1980. *Honours:* Peace Medal of UN, New York 1986, Hon. Dip (UNESCO) 1995.

SOHAL, Naresh; British composer; b. 18 Sept. 1939, Harsipind, Punjab, India. *Education:* Univ. of Punjab, London Coll. of Music, Univ. of Leeds. *Career:* Asht Prahar performed by London Philharmonic Orchestra under Norman del Mar at the Royal Festival Hall 1970; BBC have commissioned seven major works, including The Wanderer (first performed during the 1982 Promenade Concerts under Andrew Davis), From Gitanjali (commissioned by Philharmonic Soc. of New York, first performed by New York Philharmonic Orchestra under Zubin Mehta 1985); represented the West in two East-West encounters in the Netherlands and Bombay 1983; mem. BBC Central Music Advisory Cttee and the equivalent cttee in Scotland; mem. Soc. for the

Promotion of New Music. *Compositions include:* orchestral: Indra-Dhanush 1973, Dhyan I 1974, The Wanderer 1982, Tandava Nritya 1984, Satyagraha 1997; chamber and instrumental: Shades I 1974, Shades II 1975, Shades III 1978, Chakra 1979, Shades IV 1983, Brass Quintet No. 2 1983, String Quartet No. 2 2004; vocal and choral: Inscape 1979, The Wanderer 1981, From Gitanjali 1985, Songs of the Five Rivers 2002, Three Songs from Gitanjali 2004; music theatre: Maya 1997. *Television music includes:* score for Sir William in Search of Xanadu (for Scottish TV), score for three episodes of End of Empire (Granada TV) 1985. *Publications:* contrib. to Tempo Magazine. *Honours:* Padmashri from Govt of India for Services to Western Music 1987. *Address:* c/o British Music Information Centre, 11 Stratford Place, London, W1; 55 Drakefell Road, London, SE14 5SH, England (home). *Telephone:* (20) 7635-5132 (home). *E-mail:* naresh.sohal@gmail.com (office). *Website:* www.nareshsohal.org.uk.

SOHN, Sung-rai, BM, MFA; South Korean/American violinist, conductor and teacher; *Director of Chamber Music and String Orchestra, Sarah Lawrence College;* b. 23 Sept. 1950, Seoul, S Korea; m. Patricia Esposito Gilleran 1980; one s. three step-d. *Education:* Peabody Conservatory of Music (full scholarship student of Berl Senofsky), Baltimore, Md, Sarah Lawrence Coll. (full scholarship student of Dorothy DeLay), Quartet Seminar, Juilliard School of Music, Music Acad. of the West. *Career:* grand prize winner in solo violin and chamber music in Korea 1967; debut as a winner of Artists Int. Competition and Jack Kahn Music Award, Carnegie Recital Hall, New York 1980; Founder, Music Dir/Conductor Sarah Lawrence Coll.-Nyack Coll. String Orchestra; Founder, First Violinist, Laurentian String Quartet; Chair Adjudicator of the New York Music Competition; appeared in Rising Star, Live, and the Bosendorfer Concert Series, WNYC, New York, The Listening Room, WQXR, New York, NPR, Kansas Television Network, Maine Television Network, Korean Nat. TV (KBS Radio), Sendai Television Network, Japan; toured Canada, USA, Europe, Africa and Asia. *Recordings:* Barber String Quartet Op. 11, Rochberg String Quartet No. 3, C.P.E. Bach Concerto in A major, Ginastera Piano Quintet, Dvorak Romance. *Publications:* Careers in Music, 1980. *Address:* 69 Mile Road, Suffern, NY 10901, USA.

SOJAT, Tiziana; singer (soprano); b. 28 April 1955, Rome, Italy; d. of Alda Noni. *Education:* studied with her mother and Elisabeth Schwarzkopf. *Career:* debut in Dublin 1984, as Elsa in Lohengrin; sang Mimi at Ljubljana 1984; concert performances of Dido and Aeneas and Gianni Schicchi at Lausanne 1985; sang with the company of San Carlo, Naples, in Pergolesi's Stabat Mater at New York; Croatian Nat. Opera at Zagreb 1988 as Sieglinde in Die Walküre; Marseilles 1989 as Elena in Mefistofele; engaged at Karlsruhe Opera from 1989, notably as Butterfly and Arabella; concert performances at Turin, Dubrovnik, Rome and Milan; freelance career, giving several concerts and lieder in Tokyo, one of which for the Richard Strauss Soc. of Japan 1995-. *Recordings include:* Lieder by Wolf, Schumann, Liszt and Mahler, War Songs by Franz Lehar and Kurt Weill 1996.

SOJER, Hans; singer (tenor); b. 20 March 1943, Innsbruck, Austria. *Education:* studied with Franziska Lohmann. *Career:* debut at Innsbruck 1967 as David in Meistersinger; sang at Innsbruck until 1971, Bonn 1971–73, Wiesbaden 1973–81, and Hanover 1981–; roles in operas by Rossini, Donizetti, Mozart, Wagner and Strauss, at Graz, Cologne, Mannheim, Düsseldorf, Frankfurt, Berlin, Lisbon and Karlsruhe; sang at Bregenz and Schwetzingen Festivals; sang the Steersman and Narraboth at Barcelona 1988, Ernesto at Kiel and Count Riccardo in Wolf-Ferrari's Quattro Rusteghi at Hanover 1991; concert repertoire includes Beethoven's 9th and cantatas and Passions by Bach. *Recordings include:* Brighella in Ariadne auf Naxos.

SOKHIEV, Tugan; Russian conductor; *Music Director, Orchestre National du Capitole de Toulouse;* b. 1977, Vladikavkaz. *Education:* St Petersburg State Rimsy-Korsakov Conservatoire. *Career:* Guest Conductor, Berlin Philharmonic, Vienna Philharmonic, Mahler Chamber, Philharmonia Orchestra, NHK Symphony, Rotterdam Philharmonic, Orchestra of Santa Cecilia, Orchestre Nat. de France, Orquesta Nacional de España, Finnish Radio Symphony, State Symphony Orchestra of Russia, Vienna State Opera (The Queen of Spades 2010), Welsh Nat. Opera, Iceland Nat. Opera, Bavarian Staatsoper, Aix-en Provence-Festival 2004, Houston Grand Opera, Nuremberg Opera; conducts regularly at Mariinsky Theatre, St Petersburg; Prin. Guest Conductor, Orchestre Nat. du Capitole de Toulouse, France 2005–08, Music Dir 2008–; Chief Conductor and Music Dir Deutsches Symphonie-Orchester Berlin 2012–. *Recordings:* Tchaikovsky Fourth Symphony, Mussorgsky Pictures at an Exhibition, Prokofiev Peter and the Wolf, Rachmaninov Symphonic Dances. *Honours:* prize-winner Prokoviev Int. Conducting Competition 1999, named 'Révélation musicale de l'année' by French Critics' Union 2005. *Address:* Orchestre National du Capitole de Toulouse, BP 41408, 31014 Toulouse Cedex 6, France (office). *Website:* www.onct.mairie-toulouse.fr (office).

SOKOLOV, Grigory Lipmanovich; Russian pianist; b. 18 April 1950, Leningrad (now St Petersburg). *Education:* Leningrad Conservatory (pupil of Moisey Halfin). *Career:* numerous guest appearances in London, Paris, Vienna, Berlin, Madrid, Salzburg, Munich, Rome and New York; has worked with leading conductors including Myung-Whun Chung, Neeme Järvi, Herbert Blomstedt, Valery Gergiev, Sakari Oramo, Trevor Pinnock, Andrew Litton, Vassilly Sinajskij, Jukka-Pekka Saraste, Alexander Lazarev, John Storgards, Moshe Atzmon, Walter Weller and Evgeny Svetlanov; has performed with orchestras including New York Philharmonic, Montreal

Symphony, Münchner Philharmoniker, Leipzig Gewandhaus, Philhannonia, Amsterdam Concertgebouw and Detroit Symphony; Prof., Leningrad (now St Petersburg) Conservatory 1975–. *Recordings include:* several live recordings including works by Bach, Beethoven, Brahms, Chopin, Rachmaninoff, Prokofiev, Schubert, Schumann, Scriabin and Tchaikovsky; DVD of 2002 Paris recital directed by Bruno Monsaingeon. *Honours:* Second Prize, All-Union Competition of Musicians 1965, First Prize, Int. Tchaikovsky Competition 1966, People's Artist of Russia 1988. *Current Management:* Artists Management Co., Piazza R. Simoni 1, 37122 Verona, Italy. *E-mail:* panozzo@amcmusic.com. *Website:* www.amcmusic.com/en/artists/biography/grigory-sokolov. *E-mail:* info@grigory-sokolov.com (office). *Website:* www.grigory-sokolov.com (office).

SOKOLOV, Ivan Glebovitch; Russian composer, pianist and educator; b. 29 Aug. 1960. *Education:* Gnesin Musical College, composition with Nik Sidelnikov, piano with Lev Maumov. *Career:* Assistant Probationer under Nik Sidelnikov, 1984–86, Moscow Conservatoire; Concerts, as soloist and others in Moscow, Leningrad, Sverdlovsk, Kharkov, Briansk, Tashkent, Alma-Ata, Lvov and Tallinn among others, 1985–; Repertoire includes Stockhausen, Cage, Crumb, Scriabin, Shostakovich, Prokofiev, Debussy and Brahms; Festival appearances include Moscow Autumn, 1987–90, Alternative, 1988–90, Festival of Music in Russia and Germany, 1990, and Schleswig-Holstein Music Festival, Hamburg, 1991; Solo concert, playing Chopin in 1991; Teacher of Composition at Musical College, 1986–; Leader of classes in Instrumentation and Musical Score Reading at Moscow Conservatoire, 1988–. *Compositions include:* 10 Pieces for flute and piano, 1983; The Night, cantata, 1983; Rus Pevutchaya, cantata, 1985; Blazhenstvo I Beznadezhnos, vocal cycle, 1986; Volokos for piano, 1988; Sonata for flute and piano, 1988; 13 Pieces for piano, 1988; Eshtche, 7 pieces for piano, 1988; Knigy Na Stole for piano, 1989; Zvezda for soprano and piano, 1990; O, flute solo, 1990; Korably V More for 2 pianos, 1990; Igra Bez Natchala I Konza for percussion, 1991; Mysli O Rachmaninove for piano, 1991; Summer for narrator, actress and strings, 1994; Opera-Cryptophonics, 1995; KA-24 Non-Preludes, for piano and percussion ensemble, 1995; Secret Letters for violin, viola, piano and synthesizer, 1995; I. Sokolov, for fortepiano, 1997. *Address:* uliza Staryi Gaiy, dom 1, korpus 1, Kvartira 116, 111539 Moscow, Russia.

SOLARE, Juan María; Argentine/Italian composer and pianist; *Teacher and Conductor, University of Bremen;* b. 11 Aug. 1966, Buenos Aires; s. of Juan Solare and Beatriz Entenza. *Education:* Conservatorio Nacional, Buenos Aires; Postgraduate studies, Musikhochschulen, Cologne and Stuttgart. *Career:* Prof., Conservatorio, Tandil, 1986–93; Teacher and Conductor, Univ. of Bremen, Germany 2002–; Piano Teacher, Musikschule of Bremen 2002–; piano recitals (tango music and contemporary music); composition comms from Centro para la Difusion de la Musica Contemporanea, Madrid 2002, 2004, Kunststiftung NRW, Düsseldorf 2003, Landesmusikrat Bremen, Germany 2004; compositions performed at Ferienkurse, Darmstadt 1992, 1994, 1998; columnist, Clasica 1990–, Doce Notas 1996–; interviews with diverse musicians including Kagel, Berio, Lachenmann, Stockhausen, Juan Carlos Zorzi, Rihm, Nuria Schönberg-Nono, Luis de Pablo, Pedro Sáenz. *Compositions:* more than 250 works including Venticinco de Agosto (chamber opera) 1983, Neverness (string quartet), Passacaglia uber Heidelberg (trio), Pope for voice, An Angel of Ice and Fire for orchestra, Subte (radio piece), El es (piano trio), Palmas for 8 percussionists, Faq (piano four hands), Anamnesis (septet), Sufi Motetten for choir, piano music (about 30 pieces); music for Internet animations (art movies) and short films. *Publications:* Musica y Ajedrez, Planteo de un método 1998, El encuentro de Mahler y Freud 1996, Una ventana a El Sur 2001, Dónde estás, hermano?: die ewige Utopie 2001, Mis Maestros de Composición 2001, Gequälte Satire 2002, La música de Al Capone 2003, Doce aspectos del Doce 2003, Interkultur in der Elektroakustischen Musik Iberoamerikas 2004, Cage ajedrecista 2005, Bauernstruktur und die Generalbasslehre 2007, Analizando el análisis 2008. *Honours:* First Composition Prize, Promociones Musicales de la Argentina 1990, Third Prize, Walter Witte Viola Foundation, Frankfurt 2001, prize winner, Brewer Komponistenwettbewerb, Bremen, Germany 2004, Second Prize (as pianist of ensemble Die Kugel) 6th Internationaler Wettbewerb für junge Kultur, Düsseldorf 2000; scholarships from Fundacion Antorchas, Argentina 1986, 1988, Internationales Musikinstitut, Darmstadt 1992, 1994, German Academic Exchange Service 1993–94, Instituto de la Juventud, Spain 1996, Ministerio de Educación y Cultura, Spain 1996, Heinrich-Strobel Foundation, Baden-Baden 1998–99, Künstlerhauser Worpswede, Germany 2001–02, Landesmusikrat Bremen, Germany 2004. *Address:* Adam-Stegerwaldstr. 15, 51063, Cologne, Germany (home). *Telephone:* (221) 881474 (home). *Fax:* (221) 881474 (home). *E-mail:* donsolare@gmail.com (home). *Website:* www.tango.uni-bremen.de (office); www.ciweb.com.ar/solare (home).

SOLBIATI, Alessandro, DipMus; Italian composer; b. 5 Sept. 1956, Busto Arsizio; m. Emuanuela Piemonti 1985, one s. one d. *Education:* Univ. of Milan, Conservatory G. Verdi, Milan. *Career:* debut at biennale, Venice 1981; numerous commissions from Teatro alla Scala, RAI, French Ministry of Culture, Radio France, Mozarteum, South Bank of London, Gulbenkian Foundation, Lisbon, Univ. of Paris; performances at numerous festivals including Lille, Avignon, Strasbourg, Radio France Presences 1992, 1994, 1997, Huddersfield, England, Wien Modern, Holland Festival, Zagreb, Musicale of Florence, Sydney, Maastricht, Moscow. *Compositions:* Trio d'archi 1981, Sonata 1986, Nel Deserts 1986, Canto per Ania for cello and instruments 1992, Quartetto con lied for string quartet and child's voice 1992, Inno (radiophonic production) 1997, Sinfonia for orchestra 1998, Sonata for piano 1998. *Publications:* 'Progettualita Pormale nell'Ultimo Moderna', in Studies in Bruno Maderna 1989; contrib. to journals and periodicals. *Honours:* first prize Int. Composition Award, Turin 1980, first prize RAI-Paganini Int. Composition Award, Rome 1983, Targa d'Argento, Prize Saint Vincent 1983.

SOLDH, Anita; Swedish singer (soprano); *Voice Teacher, Musikkonservatoriet, Falun;* b. 26 Sept. 1949, Stockholm. *Education:* Stockholm Univ., Stockholm and Vienna Music Acads, studied with Erik Saéden, and with Luigi Ricci in Rome. *Career:* sang with Norrlands Opera 1975–77, notably as Britten's Lucretia and Mozart's Countess, Royal Opera Stockholm from 1977 with debut as Eva in Die Meistersinger, returning as Senta, Elizabeth, Arabella, Octavian, Chrysothemis, Mozart's Countess, Elvira, Vitelia and Pamina, Tchaikovsky's Tatiana and Maid of Orleans, Brussels 1984, as Cherubino; Bayreuth Festival as Blumenmädchen in Parsifal 1982–84, Freia in Das Rheingold 1983–84, Gerhilde in Valkyrie 1983–84; sang Elsa in Lohengrin at Stockholm 1989 and First Lady in Die Zauberflöte at the Drottningholm Court Theatre, and the Queen in Vogler's Gustaf Adolf och Ebba Brahe 1990; season 1991–92 as Agave in the premiere of Backanterna by Daniel Börtz, production by Ingmar Bergman, and at Drottningholm in Haeffner's Electra and as Gluck's Eurydice; concert repertoire includes Schoenberg's Erwartung, Berg's Frühe Lieder and Haydn's Schöpfung; voice teacher responsible for vocal education, Musikkonservatoriet, Falun 2004–. *Video:* Idomeneo (as Elletra), Titus (as Vitelia), Zauberflöte (as 1st Lady), Don Giovanni (as Zerlina), all from Drottningholm. *Recordings:* albums: Daniel Körtz: Backanterna (Stockholm Royal Opera), Wagner: Die Walkyrie, Sjoslakovitj: Blok-songs (with Stockholm Arts Trio). *Honours:* Kammersängerin (Horsängare) 1992. *Current Management:* Svenska Konsertbyrån AB, Jungfrugatan 45, 114 44 Stockholm, Sweden. *Telephone:* (8) 665 80 88 (office). *Fax:* (8) 665 80 66 (office). *E-mail:* info@svenskakonsertbyran.se. *Website:* www.svenskakonsertbyran.se. *Address:* Granmorvägen 9, 795 70 Stockholm, Sweden (home). *Telephone:* (2) 482 08 86 (home). *E-mail:* anita.soldh@telia .com (home).

SOLÉN, Christer; Finnish singer (tenor); b. 1939, Gustavs. *Education:* Royal Music Academy, Stockholm, studied with Luigi Ricci in Rome. *Career:* sang at Herrenhausen 1969–70, as Sextus in Handel's Giulio Cesare; Norrlandsoperan at Umea from 1974, as Rossini's Lindoro, Don Ottavio, Male Chorus in The Rape of Lucretia; Folksoperan Stockholm from 1981, as Pinkerton, Radames and Tamino; Stora Theatre Gothenburg in The Lighthouse by Peter Maxwell Davies (1984) and title role in The Voyage of Edgar Allan Poe, by Argento; other roles have included Hoffmann, Fatty in Weill's Mahagonny, Oedipus Rex, and Eufemio in Gli Equivoci, by Storace; many concert appearances throughout Europe.

SOLLBERGER, Harvey, BA, MA; American composer, conductor and flautist; *Distinguished Professor of Music, University of California, San Diego;* b. 11 May 1938, Cedar Rapids, IA; s. of Jakob Sollberger and Marguerite Sollberger (née Dennler); m. Marla Sollberger; two d. *Education:* Univ. of Iowa, Columbia Univ., New York with Jack Beeson and Otto Luening. *Career:* co-founder, Group for Contemporary Music, New York 1962. co-dir 1962–89; regular tours as flautist and conductor; faculty mem., Columbia Univ. 1966–82; Dir Manhattan School of Music Contemporary Ensemble 1972–82; faculty mem., Indiana Univ. School of Music 1983–92, Dir School of Music's New Music Ensemble 1983–89; Distinguished Prof. of Music, Univ. of California at San Diego 1992–; Dir SONOR 1993–98; Music Dir, La Jolla Symphony and Chorus 1997–2005; Resident Composer, American Acad., Rome 1989; Composer-in-Residence, San Francisco Contemporary Music Players 1990; fmr visiting prof. Amherst College, SUNY Stony Brook, SUNY Purchase, Temple Univ., CUNY City Coll. of New York, William Paterson Coll., Philadelphia Coll. of the Performing Arts; works have been performed by Speculum Musicae, New York New Music Ensemble, Da Capo Chamber Players, New York Philharmonic, San Francisco Symphony, San Francisco Contemporary Music Players, Univ. of Chicago Contemporary Ensemble, Domaine Musical (Paris), Incontri di Musica Sacra e Contemporanea (Rome), SONOR, June in Buffalo, Tanglewood, Composer Inc. and others; comms from San Francisco Symphony, Fromm Foundation/Tanglewood, Koussevitzky Foundation (2), Walter W. Naumberg Foundation, Nat. Endowment for the Arts, New York State Council on the Arts, Music from Japan, San Francisco Contemporary Music Players, Guild Trio, Nat. Flute Asscn, and many individual artists; has conducted the San Francisco Symphony, Buffalo Philharmonic, San Diego Symphony, Slee Sinfonietta and new music ensembles in Baltimore, Boston, Buffalo, Chicago, Cleveland, Indianapolis, Los Angeles, New York, Philadelphia, San Diego and San Francisco; has given recitals and performances of contemporary flute music in New York, Rome, Tokyo, Athens, Hiroshima, Fukuoka, Albany, Ann Arbor, Bowling Green (OH), Los Angeles, San Francisco, Washington, Iowa City, Champaign, Bloomington (Ind.), Buffalo, San Diego, Boston, Provo (UT); US State Dept-sponsored tours to Greece, Cyprus and Japan. *Compositions include:* Chamber Variations for 12 players 1964, music for Sophocles's Antigone (electronic) 1966, Musica Transalpina: two motets for soprano, baritone and nine players 1970, Folio (11 pieces) for bassoon 1976, Sunflowers for flute and vibraphone 1976, Music for Prepared Dancers 1978, Interrupted Night for five instruments 1983, Double Triptych for flute and percussion 1984, Persian Golf for strings 1987, Aurelian Echoes for flute and alto flute 1989, Passages for soloists, chorus and orchestra 1990, The Advancing Moment for flute, clarinet, violin, cello, piano and percussion 1993, CIAO, Arcosanti for eight instru-

ments 1994, In Terra Aliena for five soloists and orchestra 1995, Grandis Templum Machinae for soprano, mezzo, baritone, chorus and 21 instruments 1996, To the Spirit Unappeased and Peregrine for flute and clarinet 1998, New Millennium Memo for solo flute 2000, Passacaglia on a Theme of Anton Webern for solo clarinet 2000, 70 @ 70 for solo flute 2004, Nemesis for clarinet and piano 2007. *Honours:* Guggenheim Fellowships 1969, 1973, Award for service to contemporary music, Fromm Foundation 1980. *Current Management:* 301 East Elm Street, Strawberry Point, IA 52076, USA. *Telephone:* (563) 933-4041 (office). *E-mail:* marlacarnicle@hotmail.com (office). *Address:* Department of Music 0326, University of California, San Diego, La Jolla, CA 92093, USA (office). *Telephone:* (858) 534-7291 (office). *E-mail:* hsollberger@ucsd.edu (office).

SÖLLSCHER, Göran; Swedish classical guitarist; b. 31 Dec. 1955, Växjö; m. Kerstin Söllscher; one s. one d. *Education:* Malmö Conservatory, Royal Conservatory of Copenhagen. *Career:* recitals and concerts worldwide with Scandinavian orchestras and others including Camerata Bern, Japan Philharmonic Orchestra, English Chamber Orchestra, Royal Philharmonic Orchestra, Chamber Orchestra of Europe; performed under conductors such as Claudio Abbado, Rafael Frühbeck de Burgos, Sir Alexander Gibson, Sixten Ehrling, Woldemar Nelsson and Esa-Pekka Salonen; tours of N America, Europe, Japan and China; Adjunct Prof., Malmö Acad. of Music 1994–2001, Prof. 2002–; mem. Royal Swedish Acad. of Music. *Recordings include:* albums: Bach Complete Lute Works 1983, 1984, Fernando Sor 1987, Rodrigo 1990, Here, There and Everywhere 1995, Preludes, Songs, Homages 1999, I Hear the Water Dreaming 2000, From Yesterday to Penny Lane 2000, Eleven-String Baroque 2004, The Renaissance Album 2005, Reverie 2007. *Honours:* Winner, Concours Int. de Guitare, Paris 1978. *Current Management:* Künstleragentur Dr Raab & Dr Böhm, Plankengasse 7, 1010 Vienna, Austria. *Telephone:* 1-5120501. *Fax:* 1-5127743. *E-mail:* office@rbartists.at. *Website:* www.rbartists.at; www.sollscher.nu.

SOLODCHIN, Galina; violinist; b. 29 April 1944, Tientsin, People's Republic of China. *Education:* New South Wales Conservatorium. *Career:* freelance musican, including mem., Delmé Quartet from 1967; many performances in Europe in the classical and modern repertory; concerts at the Salzburg Festival and the Brahms Saal of the Musikverein Vienna; season 1990 included Haydn's Seven Last Words in Italy and elsewhere, three Brahms programmes at St John's Smith Square on piano; concerts at St David's Hall, Cardiff with Quartets by Tchaikovsky and Robert Simpson including premiere of his 13th Quartet; appearances in Bremen, Hamburg and Trieste followed by festival engagements 1991; other repertory includes works by Paul Patterson, Daniel Jones, Wilfred Josephs, Iain Hamilton and Bernard Stevens. *Recordings include:* Haydn's Seven Last Words; Vaughan Williams's On Wenlock Edge; Gurney's Ludlow and Tame; Simpson Quartets 1–9 and String Trio; Daniel Jones 3 Quartets and Bridge No. 2; Bliss's No. 1 and 2; Josef Holbrooke Piano Quartet and Clarinet Quintet; Brahms Clarinet Quintet; Dvořák F major Quartet; Verdi Quartet; Strauss A major Op 2; Hummel No. 1, 2 and 3; Bernard Stevens Theme and Variations and Quartet No. 2 and Lyric Suite for String Trio; Beethoven Op 74 and Op 95; Favourite Encores.

SOLOMON, Maynard Elliott, BA; American music historian and writer; b. 5 Jan. 1930, New York; m. Eva Georgiana Tevan 1951; two s. one d. *Education:* Brooklyn Coll., City Univ. of New York, Columbia Univ., New England Conservatory of Music. *Career:* Co-founder and Co-owner, Vanguard Recording Soc. Inc. 1950–86; teacher, CUNY 1979–81; Visiting Prof., SUNY at Stony Brook 1988–89, Columbia Univ. 1989–90, Harvard Univ. 1991–92, Yale Univ. 1994–95; Scholarly Adviser, Beethoven Archive, Bonn 1995–; mem. Graduate Faculty, Juilliard School 1998–; Assoc. Ed., American Imago 1976; mem. PEN. *Publications include:* Marxism and Art 1973, Beethoven 1977, 1998, Myth, Creativity and Psychoanalysis 1978, Beethoven Essays 1988, Mozart: A Life 1995, Some Romantic Images in Beethoven 1998, Late Beethoven: Music, Thought, Imagination 2003; contrib. articles to Beethoven Jahrbuch: Music and Letters, Musical Quarterly: 19th Century Music, Journal of the American Musicological Soc. *Honours:* Hon. DMA; ASCAP–Deems Taylor Awards 1978, 1989, 1995, Kinkeldey Award American Musicological Soc. 1989. *Address:* 1 West 72nd Street, Apt 56, New York, NY 10023, USA.

SOLTESZ, Stefan; Austrian conductor; *Artistic Director, Aalto Musiktheater;* b. 6 Jan. 1949, Nyiregyhaza, Hungary. *Education:* Vienna Hochschule für Musik with Dieter Weber, Hans Swarowsky, Reinhold Schmidt and Friedrich Cerha. *Career:* Conductor, Theater an der Wien, Vienna 1971–73; Coach and Conductor, Vienna Staatsoper 1973–83; Salzburg Festivals 1978, 1979, 1983 as asst to Karl Böhm, Christoph von Dohnányi and Herbert von Karajan; Guest Conductor, Graz Opera 1979–81; Perm. Conductor, Hamburg Staatsoper 1983–85, Deutsche Oper, Berlin 1985–97; Gen. Music Dir, State Theatre, Brunswick 1988–93; Music Dir, Flanders Opera, Antwerp/Ghent 1992–2011; Guest Conductor, Opéra Royale de Wallonie, Liège, Bavarian State Opera, Munich, Bonn Opera, Leipzig Opera, Vlaamse Opera Antwerp, Stuttgart State Theater, Nederlandse Oper at Amsterdam, Festival de Radio France et Montpelleier, Aix-en-Provence, Paris Opéra, Vienna State Opera, Frankfurt Opera, Semper Opera, Dresden, Teatro Bellini, Catania, Hamburg Opera, Teatro Colón, Buenos Aires, Washington Opera, Kennedy Center and Royal Opera House, London, San Francisco Opera, Zürich Opera, Tokyo Nikikai Opera, Grand Théatre de Genève, Opera di Roma, Hungarian State Opera Budapest; festivals in Montpellier, Aix-en-Provence, Savonlinna, Finland; toured Japan with German State Opera Unter den Linden; concerts in Bologna, Hamburg, Mexico City, Naples, Paris, Salzburg, Turin, Vienna, Munich, Essen, Berlin, Karlsruhe, Hanover, Dresden, Genoa, Basel, Rome, Trieste, Bern, Catania, Budapest, Nagoya and Zagreb among others; Artistic Dir, Aalto Musiktheater, Essen, Germany 1997–2013; Music Dir, Essen Philharmonic Orchestra 1997–2013. *Recordings include:* Swan Lake Excerpts with Vienna Symphony; La Bohème with Lucia Popp and Francisco Araiza; Opera Arias with Lucia Popp; Opera Arias with Grace Bumbry; Don Giovanni, by Giuseppe Gazzaniga, with Munich Radio Orchestra; The Chalk Circle by Alexander Zemlinsky; Orchestral Songs by Hugo Wolf with Dietrich Fischer-Dieskau, Works by Berg and Henze. *Honours:* Hon. Citizen of the Ruhr Dist; Hon. Prof.; Hon. Conductor, Brunswick; Cultural Prize, Foundation of Savings Banks of the Rhineland (Germany) 2004, Aalto Musiktheater, Essen voted Opera House of the Year in Opernwelt magazine critics' survey 2008. *Current Management:* c/o Hilbert Artists Management, Maximilianstrasse 22, 80539 Munich, Germany. *Telephone:* (89) 290747-0. *Fax:* (89) 290747-90. *E-mail:* agentur@hilbert.de. *Website:* www.hilbert.de. *Address:* Aalto Musiktheater Essen, Opernplatz 10, 45128 Essen, Germany (office). *Telephone:* (201) 8122291 (office). *Fax:* (201) 8122280 (office).

SOLUM, John Henry, BA; American concert flautist, writer, educator and arts advocate; b. 11 May 1935, New Richmond, Wis.; m. Millicent Hunt 1960; two s. *Education:* Princeton Univ., studied with William Kincaid in Philadelphia. *Career:* solo debut 1953; soloist, Philadelphia Orchestra 1957; New York debut recital 1959; soloist chamber music player world-wide; guest appearances with orchestras in more than 50 cities, many radio broadcasts, festival appearances in Europe, N America; teacher, Vassar Coll. 1969–71, 1977–, Indiana Univ. 1973, Oberlin Conservatory 1976; Co-Dir Bath Summer School of Baroque Music, UK 1979–89, Connecticut Early Music Festival 1982–99; Chair. Hanoverian Foundation 2000–; arts advocate. *Recordings:* Ibert, Jolivet, Honegger Flute Concertos 1975, Two Malcolm Arnold Flute Concertos 1977, Romantic Music for Flute and Orchestra 1978, Mozart Flute Concertos 1980, Telemann Duets 1981, Bach Flute Sonatas 1988, Vivaldi Bullfinch Concerto 1992, Bach, Handel, Telemann Trio Sonatas 1992, Sonatas by Telemann, Handel, Vinci, Scarlatti, J. C. Bach, C. P. E. Bach, Mozart 1994, Works by Kupferman, Laderman, Beeson, Luening, Kraft and Nowak 1994, Handel Trio Sonata in C Minor 1995, Hummel's chamber arrangements of Mozart symphonies 35 and 36 1997, Shadow by David MacBride 1995, Works by J. S. Bach, C. P. E. Bach, W. F. Bach and J. C. Bach 2001, Trio Sonatas by de la Barre, Hotteterre, Couperin, Leclair 2003, Music composed for Lord Abingdon by Haydn, Abel, Gretry, J. C. Bach 2003, Six Concertos for Two Flutes by Telemann 2004, Ten Suites for Two Flutes by de la Barre 2007, Three Inventions for Two Alto Flutes by Leo Kraft 2008, Telemann Chamber Music in the French style 2008, German Baroque Music 2010. *Publication:* The Early Flute 1992. *Honours:* Winner Philadelphia Orchestra Youth Contest 1957, Distinguished Service Award, Nat. Flute Asscn 1998, Distinguished Advocate Award, Connecticut Comm. on Arts and Tourism 2008. *Address:* 10 Bobwhite Drive, Westport, CT 06880, USA. *E-mail:* jhsolum@optonline.net.

SOLYOM, Janos Paul; Swedish (b. Hungarian) concert pianist and conductor; b. 26 Oct. 1938, Budapest, Hungary; s. of Dr I. Solyom and M. Weill; m. Camilla Lundberg 1987. *Education:* Franz Liszt Acad. of Music, Budapest, private studies with Ilona Kabos in London and Nadia Boulanger in Paris. *Career:* int. concert career 1958–; mem. Royal Swedish Acad. of Music. *Honours:* Pro Patria Gold Medal; Royal Swedish Medal for Outstanding Artistic Merit 'Litteris et Artibus'. *Address:* Norr Mälarstrand 54, 112 20 Stockholm, Sweden. *Telephone:* (8) 652-42-72. *E-mail:* pianos@solyom.com. *Website:* www.solyom.com.

SOLYOM, Stefan; Swedish conductor; *General Music Director and Principal Conductor, Deutsches Nationaltheater and Staatskapelle Weimar*; b. 1979, Stockholm. *Education:* Royal Coll. of Music, Stockholm, Sibelius Acad., Helsinki. *Career:* regular collaborations with Royal Stockholm Philharmonic, Gothenburg Symphony Orchestra, Lahti Symphony Orchestra, Frankfurt Radio Symphony Orchestra, MDR Symphony Orchestra Leipzig, Royal Swedish Opera, NDR Symphony Orchestra Hamburg and Deutsche Kammerphilharmonie Bremen; debut with Royal Swedish Opera 1999, for whom he has conducted Ingvar Lidholm's A Dream Play, Mozart's The Magic Flute, Carl Unander-Scharin's Hummelhonung (world premiere), Offenbach's The Tales of Hoffmann, Gefors' Christina and Rossini's The Barber of Seville; other operatic engagements include The Barber of Seville (Komische Oper Berlin) 2002, Strauss's Die Fledermaus (Komische Oper and Royal Swedish Opera), Gounod's Roméo et Juliette (Frankfurt Opera, Munich Opera), Puccini's Tosca (Frankfurt Opera and Opéra Nat. de Paris), Leoni's L'Oracolo & Puccini's Le Villi (Frankfurt Opera), Verdi's Falstaff and Il Trovatore (Royal Swedish Opera); Assoc. Guest Conductor, BBC Scottish Symphony Orchestra 2006–09; Gen. Music Dir and Prin. Conductor, Deutsches Nationaltheater and Staatskapelle Weimar 2010–; Prin. Guest Conductor, Norrköpings Symfoniorkester. *Website:* www.stefansolyom.com.

SOLYOM-NAGY, Sandor; singer (baritone); b. 21 Dec. 1941, Siklos, Hungary. *Education:* Ferenc Liszt Acad. of Music, Budapest. *Career:* Budapest State Opera 1964–; numerous guest performances in Berlin, Brussels, Bratislava, Prague, Cologne, Barcelona, Moscow, Leningrad, Genoa, Rome, The Hague, Rotterdam, Paris, Rio de Janeiro, São Paulo, Sofia, Varna and Vienna; frequent guest appearances with Bavarian State Opera, Munich, Germany and Vienna State Opera, Austria, and in Japan; regular guest artist at Bayreuth Festival from 1981, including Grail Knight in Parsifal 1992; sang

Palatine Gara in Erkel's Hunyadi László at Budapest 1989; sang Amonasro at Budapest 2000. *Recordings include:* Liszt's Christus Oratorio, The Legend of Elisabeth, Via Crucis, Goldmark's The Queen of Sheba, Agamemnon in Gluck's Iphigénie en Aulide, the title role in Kodály's Háry János and in Strauss's Guntram and Respighi's La Fiamma. *Honours:* Liszt Prize 1972, Merited Artist of Hungary 1977, Hector Berlioz Prize, French Record Acad. Grand Prix, Prix Charles Cros, Golden Orpheus Prize, Excellent Artist of Hungary 1987, Kossuth Prize 1998.

SOMACH, Beverly, BS; American violinist; b. 17 Jan. 1935, New York, NY; m. S. George Silverstein 1959; two s. two d. *Education:* Columbia Univ., Univ. of California, Los Angeles with Jascha Heifetz. *Career:* recitals at Town Hall, Carnegie Hall, Lincoln Center, Alice Tully Hall, New York; recitals in London (Wigmore Hall, Purcell Room), Edinburgh, Glasgow, Stockholm, Copenhagen, Zürich, Paris, Tokyo, Hong Kong, Montréal; soloist with orchestras, including New York Philharmonic, Chicago Symphony, Los Angeles Symphony, American Symphony, Orchestra Luxembourg. *Publications:* contrib. to New York Times, Musical America.

SOMFAI, László, DipMus, DMus; Hungarian musicologist and academic; *Professor Emeritus, Ferenc Liszt Academy of Music*; b. 15 Aug. 1934, Jászladány; m. Dorrit Révész-Somfai; one s. one d. *Education:* Ferenc Liszt Acad. of Music, Budapest, Hungarian Acad. of Sciences, Budapest. *Career:* Music Librarian at Nat. Széchényi Library, Budapest –1962; Head of Budapest Bartók Archives, Inst. for Musicology, Hungarian Acad. of Sciences 1972–2004; Prof. of Musicology, Ferenc Liszt Acad. of Music 1980–2004, Prof. Emer. 2005–; mem. Zentralinstitut der Mozartforschung, Salzburg, Joseph Haydn Institute, Cologne, Hungarian Acad. of Sciences, American Musicological Soc., British Acad., Academia Europaea; fmr Pres. Int. Musicological Soc. *Publications include:* Haydn als Opernkapellmeister (co-author) 1960, Joseph Haydn: Sein Leben in Zeitgenössischen Bildern 1966, Anton Webern 1968, The Keyboard Sonatas of Joseph Haydn 1979, 18 Bartók Studies 1981, Béla Bartók: Composition, Concepts and Autograph Sources 1996; studies on Haydn, Liszt, Stravinsky, Webern and Bartók; critical editions in Mozart Neue Ausgabe, Gluck Neue Ausgabe, Musica Rinata; Ed.: Documenta Bartókiana. *Address:* Falk Miksa u 12, V4, 1055 Budapest, Hungary.

SOMMERHALDER, Giuliano; Swiss/German trumpeter and pedagogue; b. (Julian Sommerhalder), 16 July 1985, Zurich; son of Prof. Max Sommerhalder and Regina Maria Sommerhalder (née Reichel). *Education:* Conservatorio G. Verdi, Como, Italy with Pierluigi Salvi and Detmold Coll. of Music with Max Sommerhalder; master classes with Maurice André, Stephen Burns, Pierre Dutot, Bo Nilsson, Markus Stockhausen, Mark Gould, Pierre Thibaud and James Thompson. *Career:* grew up in Italy; played in Claudio Abbado's Orchestra Mozart, Bologna 2004, and was chosen by Lorin Maazel as solo trumpeter for his Orquestra de la Comunitat Valenciana; solo trumpeter, Leipzig Gewandhaus Orchestra under Riccardo Chailly 2006–11; mem. brass quintet Italian Wonderbrass 2006–; Prin. Trumpet, Royal Concertgebouw Orchestra Amsterdam under Mariss Jansons 2011–13; substitute Prin. Trumpet, La Scala, Milan 2013; freelance performing artist 2013–; mem. Radio 3 New Generation Artists scheme 2008–10; appeared as soloist on both modern and historic instruments throughout Europe, in USA, Latin America, Australia and Asia, at halls including Vienna Musikverein and Berlin Philharmonie and at festivals including Lucerne, City of London and Schleswig-Holstein; appeared as soloist with ensembles including BBC Symphony Orchestra, NDR Symphony Orchestra Hamburg, Indianapolis Symphony Orchestra, Deutsches Symphonie-Orchester Berlin, Zürich Tonhalle Orchestra, NDR Philharmonic Orchestra Hannover, Melbourne Symphony Orchestra, Zurich, Munich, Lithuanian and Basle Chamber Orchestras, Moscow Soloists and MDR Symphony Orchestra Leipzig. *Radio:* broadcasts on BBC Radio 3 2008–10, various radio broadcasts in Switzerland and Germany. *Recordings include:* solo: Romantic Virtuosity 2010, Amilcare Ponchielli Concertos (ECHO Klassik Awards Concerto Recording of the Year/Wind Player 2012) 2011; with others: Johann Friedrich Fasch Concerti & Ouvertures 2009, four Gewandhaus Orchestra albums; chamber music: Pines of Rome with Italian Wonderbrass brass quintet. *Honours:* First Prize, Int. Trumpet Competition, Moscow Tchaikovsky Conservatoire 1997, European Culture Prize, Munich 1999, Berlin 2002, First Prize, Prague Spring Competition 2003, Second Prize, Int. Music Competition of the ARD, Munich 2003, shared Second Prize (no first prize awarded), Int. Maurice André Trumpet Competition, Paris 2003, ECHO Klassik Awards, Berlin 2012. *Current Management:* c/o Konzertagentur Dagmar Körner, Bergstraße 15, 85120 Hepberg, Germany. *Telephone:* (8456) 9189290. *E-mail:* dkoerner@konzertagentur-koerner.de. *Website:* www.konzertagentur-koerner.de. *E-mail:* info@giulianosommerhalder.com (office). *Website:* www.giulianosommerhalder.com (office).

SOMMERVILLE, James; Canadian horn player and artistic director; *Artistic Director, Hamilton Philharmonic Orchestra*; b. Toronto. *Education:* Univ. of Western Ontario, Univ. of Toronto. *Career:* fmrly played for Toronto Symphony Orchestra, Montreal Symphony Orchestra, Canadian Opera Co. Orchestra, Symphony Nova Scotia, Chamber Orchestra of Europe; Principal Horn, Boston Symphony Orchestra 1998–; Artistic Dir, Hamilton Philharmonic Orchestra 2007–; festival appearances include Festival of the Sound, Vancouver Chamber Music Festival, Scotia Festival, Banff Int. Festival of the Arts; has performed premieres of Christos Hatzis' Winter Solstice, Ligeti's Hamburg Concerto, John Williams' Horn Concerto, Weber's Concertino, Elliot Carter's Horn Concerto; mem., music faculty, Tanglewood Music Center, the

Longy School, New England Conservatory of Music. *Recordings include:* Mozart Horn Concertos (Juno Award for Best Classical Recording) 1998, Britten's Serenade for Tenor, Horn, Stings and Canticle III. *Honours:* winner, Int. Music Competition, Munich, Int. Music Competition, Toulon, CBC Young Performers Competition. *Address:* Hamilton Philharmonic Orchestra, 1002-105 Main Street East, Hamilton, ON L8N 1G6, USA (office). *Telephone:* (905) 526-1677 (office). *Fax:* (905) 526-0616 (office). *E-mail:* jsommerville@hpo.org (office). *Website:* www.hpo.org (office).

SOMTOW, S.P.; Thai/American composer and author; *Artistic Director, Siam Philharmonic Orchestra and Opera Siam (formerly Bangkok Opera);* b. (Somtow Papinian Sucharitkul), 30 Dec. 1952, Bangkok. *Education:* Eton Coll. and St Catharine's Coll., Cambridge, UK. *Career:* Artistic Dir Asian Composers Expo 1978; fmr Perm. Rep. to the Int. Music Council of UNESCO; turned to novel writing 1980s; Artistic Dir Siam Philharmonic Orchestra and Bangkok Opera (f. by him in 2001); f. Thai Composers Asscn; fmr Pres. Horror Writers Asscn. *Compositions include:* Views from the Golden Mountain (first to combine Thai and Western instruments) 1975, Madana (opera) 1999, Requiem – In memoriam 9/11, Mae Naak (opera) 2002, Kaki (ballet) and Mahajanaka Symphony, composed for the King of Thailand's 72nd birthday, Ayodhya (opera), The Silent Prince (opera). *Publications include:* as S. P. Somtow: Vampire Junction, Jasmine Nights (semi-autobiog.), Tagging the Moon, Fairy Tales of Los Angeles, Dragon's Fin Soup, The Bird Catcher (World Fantasy Award for Best Novella 2010). *Honours:* numerous awards for his novels, Ministry of Culture Silpathorn Kittikhun Award 2008. *Address:* Opera Siam, 34 Soi Pipaht 2, Silom Road, Bangkok 10502, Thailand (office). *Telephone:* (2)231-5273 (office). *Fax:* (2) 231-5280 (office). *E-mail:* intendant@ bangkokopera.com (office). *Website:* www.bangkokopera.com (office); www .somtow.com.

SONDEREGGER, Peter; Swiss composer and musician; b. 2 Oct. 1960, St Gallen. *Education:* Konservatorium Basel with Jacques Wildberger, Musikhochschule Karlsruhe, Germany with Wolfgang Rihm. *Career:* performer of 16th- and 17th-century music. *Compositions:* Delirien I–III, chamber ensembles and live electronics, 1981–83; Piano Concerto No. 1, 1985; Tombeau per tre Clarinetti, 1985; Eclairs Errants, piano and orchestra, 1986–87; Webern-Variations to Symphony Op 21, for orchestra, 1987; Zeit, Verjüngendes Licht, clarinet, viola and guitar, 1987–88; 73 Pezzi Degli Scrovegni, piano, 1989–90; Missa Incontri, piano trio, 1990–91; Auslöschung, for panflute and double-string quartet, 1991; Conductus II, violin and organ, 1993–94; Various other compositions for chamber ensembles, piano solo, guitar Solo; Quaenam sit divina caligo, for female voices and violins, 1994; La Mallorquina, for violin and piano, 1995; Conductus IV for 2 saxophones. *Recordings:* Tombeau per tre Clarinetti; Zeit, Verjüngendes Licht. *Honours:* scholarships to Heinrich Strobel-Stiftung des Südwestfunks 1986, Schweizerischer Tonkünstlerverein 1987. *Address:* Unterdorf 10, 4203 Grellingen, Switzerland.

SØNDERGÅRD, Thomas; Danish conductor; *Principal Conductor and Musical Adviser, Norwegian Radio Orchestra;* b. 1969, Holstebro. *Education:* studied percussion at Royal Danish Acad. of Music with Gert Mortensen. *Career:* began career as timpanist with European Union Youth Orchestra 1989–92; solo timpanist, Royal Danish Orchestra 1992; Faculty mem. Royal Danish Acad. of Music 2001–02; debut as conductor with Royal Danish Opera, conducting world premiere of Ruders' Kafka's Trial 2005; Prin. Conductor and Musical Adviser, Norwegian Radio Orchestra 2009–; Prin. Conductor, BBC Nat. Orchestra of Wales 2012–; Prin. Guest Conductor, Royal Scottish Nat. Orchestra 2012–; has conducted several major productions at various European opera houses, including for Royal Danish Opera Il barbiere di Siviglia, Le Nozze di Figaro and La bohème and for Royal Danish Ballet Rite of Spring and Pulcinella; orchestras conducted include Royal Stockholm Philharmonic, Rotterdam Philharmonic, Deutsche Kammerphilharmonie, Nat. Arts Centre Orchestra Ottawa, Orkester Norden, Finnish Radio Symphony Orchestra, Orchestre Nat. du Capitole de Toulouse, Orchestre Nat. d'Ile de France. *Recordings include:* Ruders Kafka's Trial 2006, Nielsen Cantatas 2009, Prokofiev & Sibelius: Violin Concertos. *Address:* Norwegian Radio Orchestra, RA 14, 0340 Oslo, Norway (office). *Website:* www.nrk.no (office).

SONDHEIM, Stephen Joshua, BA; American composer and lyricist; b. 22 March 1930, New York, NY; s. of Herbert Sondheim and Janet Fox. *Education:* George School, Newtown, Pa, Williams Coll., private instruction. *Career:* Pres. Dramatists' Guild 1973–81, Council mem. 1981–; Visiting Prof. of Drama and Musical Theatre, Univ. of Oxford, UK Jan.–June 1990; mem. American Acad. and Inst. of Arts and Letters 1983–, American Theater Hall of Fame 2014–. *Compositions include:* television: Topper (co-author) 1953, Evening Primrose (music and lyrics) 1967; lyrics: West Side Story 1957, Gypsy 1959, Do I Hear a Waltz? 1965, Candide 1973; music and lyrics: A Funny Thing Happened on the Way to the Forum 1962, Anyone Can Whistle 1964, Evening Primrose 1966, Company 1970, Follies 1971, A Little Night Music 1973, The Frogs 1974, Pacific Overtures 1976, Sweeney Todd 1978, Merrily We Roll Along 1981, Sunday in the Park with George 1984, Into the Woods (Drama Critics' Circle Award 1988) 1986, Follies 1987, Assassins 1990, Passion 1994, Bounce 2003 (renamed Road Show 2008); anthologies: Side by Side by Sondheim 1976, Marry Me a Little 1980, You're Gonna Love Tomorrow 1983, Putting It Together 1993; screenplays: (with Anthony Perkins) The Last of Sheila 1973, Birdcage 1996, Getting Away with Murder 1996; film scores: Stavisky 1974, Reds 1981, Dick Tracy 1989; incidental music: The Girls of Summer 1956, Invitation to a March 1961, Twigs 1971, Company: A Musical 2007, Sweeney Todd 2007, Into the Woods 2014.

Publications: Finishing the Hat 2010, Look, I Made a Hat: Collected Lyrics (1981–2011) 2011. *Honours:* Antoinette Perry Awards for Company 1971, Follies 1972, A Little Night Music 1973, Sweeney Todd 1979; Drama Critics' Awards 1971, 1972, 1973, 1976, 1979; Evening Standard Drama Award 1996; Grammy Awards 1984, 1986; Nat. Medal of Arts 1997, Praemium Imperial 2000, Special Tony Award for Lifetime Achievement in the Theatre 2008, Presidential Medal of Freedom 2015. *Current Management:* c/o John Breglio, 1285 Avenue of the Americas, New York, NY 10019, USA.

SONEK, František, MgrA; Czech pianist and conductor; b. 12 April 1933, Opava; s. of František Sonek and Maria Melecká; m. Lubomíra Záskodná 1959 (deceased 2013); two d. *Education:* Ostrava Conservatory, Janáček Acad. of Music Arts, Brno. *Career:* debut with ballet Fairy Tale about John by Oskar Nedbal in Theatre Ostrava (as conductor), Czechoslovakia; teacher, Conservatories of Ostrava and Brno 1965–69, Janáček Acad. of Music Arts, Brno (mainly as pianist and choral répétiteur) 1969–2003; Pianist and Choral Répétiteur, Opera House of Opava 1960–64; Pianist, Choral Répétiteur and Conductor, State Ballet Theatre, Ostrava 1964–68; Asst Conductor, Janáček Opera in Brno (music of Smetana, Dvořák, Janáček, Bizet, Moniuszko, Rimsky-Korsakov, Tchaikovsky) 1968–2006; Chief Conductor, Amateur Symphony Orchestra of Railwaymen, Brno 1978–2004. *Recordings:* Janáček's operas Jenůfa and Excursions of Mr Brouček. *Address:* Milénova 12, Brno 38, 63800, Czech Republic (home). *Telephone:* (548) 522872 (home).

SONNTAG, Ulrike; German singer (soprano); *Professor of Singing, Hochschule für Musik, Stuttgart;* b. 1959, Esslingen. *Education:* studied with Eva Sava, Irmgard Hartmann-Dressler, Dietrich Fischer-Dieskau. *Career:* debut as Oriane in Amadis de Gaul by J.C. Bach as guest with the Hamburg Staatsoper 1983; sang at Stadttheater Heidelberg 1984–86; Nationaltheater Mannheim 1986–88; has appeared in concerts all over Europe, festivals of Salzburg, Vienna, Berlin, Frankfurt, Schwetzingen and in USA (Los Angeles), China, Brazil, Japan, Uruguay, Paraguay, Argentina; mem. Stuttgart Opera 1988–95, as Euridice, Susanna, Donna Elvira, Marcellina, Pamina, Marenka, Ännchen, Micaela, Nedda, Frau Fluth, Gretel, Sophie in Der Rosenkavalier; sang Ännchen in Der Freischütz at the 1988 Ludwigsburg Festival 1992; mem. Vienna State Opera 1991–94, repertoire including Susanna, Pamina, Micaela, Zdenka, Musetta, Sophie, Donna Elvira; Freischütz production, Trieste 1994; Wildschütz production, Cologne 1994; Lieder tour, Moscow and St Petersburg 1994; Orfeo 1995; guest appearances with Deutsche Oper, Berlin; Frankfurt, Belinda, Marcellina, Musetta; Monte Carlo, Ännchen 1990; Cairo, Rosina in Haydn's La Vera Costanza 1990; Tel-Aviv Opera with Der Freischütz 1996; appeared in Don Giovanni at Berlin in 1997; season 1998 in Cagliari with Wagner's Die Feen and with Carmen at St Margarethen in Austria; lieder recitals in Europe, South America, Russia; Prof. of Singing, Hochschule für Musik, Stuttgart 2005–; voice and interpretation master classes in Paris, Riga, Bucharest, Budapest, Bulgaria and elsewhere. *Recordings include:* Bach's Cantatas, B minor Mass, Amadis; Stravinsky's Les Noces; Bruch's Achilleus; Mahler's Das Klagende Lied; Mignon's Lieder; Schubert, Schumann, Wolf, Milhaud songs and chamber music; Hindemith's Das Unaufhörliche, Der Freischütz, Die Zauberflöte, Carmen (DVD), Herbsttag (Rilke Songs), Wiegenlieder. *Address:* In den Burggärten 3, 72622 Nürtingen, Germany (home). *E-mail:* ulrike.sonntag@ mh-stuttgart.de.

SOOTER, Edward; singer (tenor); b. 8 Dec. 1934, Salina, KS, USA. *Education:* Friends Univ. in Wichita with Elsa Haury, Kansas Univ. with Joseph Wilkins, Hamburg Musikhochschule with Helmut Melchert. *Career:* debut at Bremerhaven 1966, as Florestan; sang in Kiel, Karlsruhe, Wiesbaden, Munich, Frankfurt and Cologne; Metropolitan Opera from 1979, as Florestan, Tannhäuser, Otello, Aeneas in Les Troyens, Walther, Tristan and Lohengrin; sang Siegmund in Ring cycles at Seattle; New Orleans Opera 1992, as Florestan; other roles include Parsifal, Don José, Canio, Aegisthus, Manrico, Ernani, Samson, and Babinsky in Schvanda the Bagpiper; sang Siegmund at Flagstaff 1996.

SOPRONI, Jozsef; Hungarian composer; b. 4 Oct. 1930, Sopron. *Education:* Budapest Acad. of Music. *Career:* faculty mem., Bela Bartók School, Budapest from 1957–62; faculty mem., Budapest Acad. of Music 1962–77, Prof. 1977–88, Rector 1988–94. *Compositions include:* Concerto for strings 1953, ten String Quartets 1958–94, Carmina polinaesiana cantata for women's chorus and ensemble 1963, Ovidi metamorphoses for soprano, chorus and orchestra 1965, two Cello Concertos 1967, 1984, Symphony No. 1 1975, Horn sonata 1976, Symphony No. 2 The Seasons 1977, Six Bagatelles for wind quintet 1977, Late Summer Caprices for string trio and piano 1978, two Violin Sonatas 1979, 1980, Symphony No. 3 Sinfonia da Requiem for soloists, chorus and orchestra 1980, Violin Concerto 1983, Comments on a Theme by Handel for orchestra 1985, Antigone (opera) 1987, Three Pieces for orchestra 1988, Magnificat for soloists, chorus and orchestra 1989, Missa Scarbantiensis 1991, Missa Choralis 1992, Missa super B-A-C-H 1992, Litaniae Omnium Sanctorum 1993, Pslam XXIX for chorus, organ, trumpet and trombone 1993, Missa Gurcensis for chorus and ensemble 1994, Symphony No. 4 1994, Te Deum for soloists, chorus and orchestra, Livre d'orgue (nine pieces) 1994, Symphony No. 5 1995, Symphony No. 6 1995, 12 Piano Sonatas 1996–98, Piano Concerto 1997, Chamber Concerto No. 2 for 12 instruments 1998, Das Marienleben for soprano and piano 1998, piano music, songs and choruses.

SØRENSEN, Bent; Danish composer; b. 18 July 1958. *Education:* Royal Danish Acad. of Music, Jutland Music Acad., studied with Ib Nørholm and Per

Nørgård. *Career:* opera Under the Sky premiered at Royal Danish Theatre, Copenhagen 2004; commissions from Leif Ove Andsnes, Christian Lindberg, London Sinfonietta, Ensemble Intercontemporain; works performed by Danish Nat. Radio Orchestra Oslo Sinfonietta; regular cooperation with Bergen Int. Festival; Prof., Royal Danish Acad. of Music; Visiting Prof. of Composition, RAM 2008–; Composer-in-Residence Huddersfield Contemporary Music Festival, UK 2011. *Compositions include:* string quartets: Alman 1984, Adieu 1986, Angels' Music 1988, Schreie und Melancholie 1994; orchestral: The Echoing Garden for soloists, choir and orchestra 1992, Sterbende Gärten violin concerto 1993, Symphony 1996, La Notte piano concerto 1998, Birds and Bells for trombone and 14 instruments 1995, The Little Mermaid for soprano solo, tenor solo, girls' choir and orchestra, 2004–05, Exit Music 2007, Sounds Like You 2008, La Mattina piano concerto (British Composer Award, international category 2011) 2009, Tunnels de Lumière 2010; opera: Under the Sky 2003; sound installation: The White Forest 2011, Saudades Inocentes. *Recordings include:* Sterbende Gärten 1996, Birds and Bells 1999, Shadowland 1999, The Little Mermaid 2006, Ockeghem/Sorensen: Requiem 2012. *Honours:* Nordic Council Music Prize 1995, Wilhelm Hansen Composer Prize 1999. *Address:* c/o Royal Academy of Music, Marylebone Road, London, NW1 5HT, England (office). *Website:* www.ram.ac.uk.

SORENSON VON GERTTEN, Iwa Cecilia; Swedish singer (soprano); b. 5 Sept. 1946, Gothenburg; m. Gustf von Gertten 1980, two s. *Education:* Music Conservatory, Gothenburg, Staatliche Hochschule für Musik, Cologne, School of Theatre and Opera, Gothenburg. *Career:* debut in Malmö, as Norina in Donizetti's Don Pasquale 1978; opera soloist at Malmö Stadsteater 1978–79 and Royal Opera of Stockholm 1979–; roles include Rosina in The Barber of Seville, Musetta in La Bohème, Sophie in Der Rosenkavalier, Zdenka in Arabella, Fiordiligi in Così fan tutte, Susanna in The Marriage of Figaro, Blonde in The Abduction from the Seraglio, Aminta in Il Re Pastore, Violetta in La Traviata, Marguerite in Faust, and Olympia in Tales of Hoffmann; roles in operettas include Adele in Die Fledermaus, Laura in Der Bettelstudent by Millöcker, Josephine in HMS Pinafore, and Fiametta in Boccacio by Von Suppé; concert repertoire includes Handel's Messiah and Judas Maccabaeus, Haydn's Creation, Mendelssohn's Elijah, and Mozart's Requiem and Mass in C minor; recitals with piano of German lieder, French art songs, Swedish repertoire and contemporary music. *Recordings:* mostly 19th- and 20th-century Swedish music. *Honours:* Gramophone Awards 1983–85.

SORG-ROSE, Margarete; German composer and publisher; b. 11 April 1960, Remscheid; d. of Margarete Sorg. *Education:* piano and conducting studies in Mainz, composition in Cologne with Hans Werner Henze and Krzysztof Meyer, Univs of Mainz and Tübingen. *Career:* Bachchor (choir) coach, Mainz 1985–87; Production Asst Zweites Deutsches Fernsehen (ZDF), Mainz 1987; freelance composer 1992–; works performed at nat. and int. concerts and festivals, including Festival Cantiere Int. d'Arte Montepulciano (Italy) 1990; compositions include pieces for orchestra, choir, Lieder and chamber music. *Honours:* Johann-Wenzel-Stamitz-Förderpreis for Composition 1993, Kompositionsauftrag des Landes Rheinland-Pfalz 1994, Kompositionsaufträge der Villa-Musica-Stiftung 1995, 1997, Auftragskomposition der Mozart-Gesellschaft Kurpfalz e.V. 1996, Art-Gedok-Nadel 1996 and other prizes. *Address:* Henkellstr. 3, 65187 Wiesbaden, Germany. *Fax:* 1805060 34445898 (office). *E-mail:* margaretesorg-rose@t-online.de.

SOROKINA, Elena, MA, PhD; Russian pianist and music historian; b. 6 April 1940, Moscow; m. Alexander Bakhchiev 1962, one d. *Education:* Central School of Music, Moscow State Conservatory. *Career:* debut in duet concert (with husband), Mozart, Schubert, Central Arts House, Moscow; Prof., Moscow State Conservatory 1965–, Chief and Chair of Russian Music History 1992–; regular duet performances, Beethoven, Mozart, Weber, Schumann, Schubert, Brahms, Glinka, Borodin, Rachmaninov, other Russian composers, music genres, history of Moscow Conservatory, 1969–; series of television programmes, chamber music concerts, 1970s; tours lecturing on Russian music, France, Austria, Latin America; international/national festivals of music, Moscow, Leningrad (with husband); Mozart International Festival, Tokyo (1991); British tour (Cambridge, London), Soviet and British modern piano duets; concerts with husband, Israel, Italy, Germany, USA, 1992–93; eight programmes, all Schubert piano duets, with husband; piano duo festivals, Novosibirsk and Ekaterinburg, 1993–95; works dedicated to her and husband by Boyarsky, Lubovksy, Fried, Manukyan and Moore. *Recordings include:* piano duets with husband: Rachmaninov; Russian Salon Piano Music; Mozart; Schubert; Music of France; Weber, Schumann, Mendelssohn; V Persichetti; Bartók, Lutoslawski; Enescu; albums: Music of Old Vienna; J. S. Bach, his family and pupils; Music for six and eight hands (with G. Rozhdestvensky, V. Postnikova). *Publication:* Piano Duet 1988. *Address:* 4-32 Koshkin Str, Moscow 115409, Russia.

SOTIN, Hans; German singer (bass); b. 10 Sept. 1939, Dortmund; m. Regina Elsner 1964; three c. *Education:* Dortmund Musikhochschule. *Career:* with Opera House, Essen 1962–64; State Opera, Hamburg 1964–, State Opera, Vienna 1970–; perm. mem. Bayreuth Festival 1971–; pvt singing teacher. *Recordings include:* Tannhäuser, Aida, Fidelio, Salome, Così fan tutte, Die Walküre, Parisfal, Paukenmesse. *Honours:* Forderpreis des Landes, Friedrich Oberdörfer Preis, Kammersänger.

SOUDANT, Hubert; Dutch conductor; *Music Director, Tokyo Symphony Orchestra;* b. 16 March 1946, Maastricht. *Education:* Maastricht Conservatory, studied with Franco Ferrara in Italy and at Netherlands Radio Course in

Hilversum. *Career:* Asst Conductor with Hilversum Radio Orchestra 1967–70; has conducted Orchestra of Radio France and Nouvel Orchestre Philharmonique, with which he gave the French premiere of Mahler's 10th Symphony at Strasbourg in 1979; conducted premieres of Rene Koering's opera Elseneur and Nana Symphonie by Marius Constant 1980; Conductor Symphony Orchestra of Utrecht 1982; Musical Dir with Orchestra Sinfonica dell'Emilia Romagna Arturo Toscanini, Parma 1988; Music Dir Tokyo Symphony Orchestra 2004–; guest conductor in England, Germany, Belgium, Italy, Scandinavia, South Africa and Japan. *Recordings:* Tchaikovsky 4th and 6th Symphonies and Romeo and Juliet with London Philharmonic, Liszt Piano Concertos with London Philharmonic Orchestra. *Honours:* winner Int. Competition for Young Conductors at Besançon 1971, second prize Herbert von Karajan Int. Conducting Competition 1973, first prize Guido Cantelli Int. Conducting Competition, Milan 1975, City of Salzburg Medal 2004. *Address:* Tokyo Symphony Orchestra, Muza Kawasaki Central Tower, Fifth Floor, 1310 Omiya-cho, Saiwai-ku, Kawasaki, Kanagawa, 212-8554, Japan (office). *Telephone:* (4) 4520-1518 (office). *Fax:* (4) 4543-1488 (office). *E-mail:* tokyosymphony@musicinfo.com (office). *Website:* www.tokyosymphony.com (office).

SOUKUPOVA, Vera; Czech singer (contralto); b. 12 April 1932, Prague. *Education:* studied in Prague with L. Kaderabek and A. Mustanova-Linkova. *Career:* sang in concert from 1955; stage debut 1957 at Pilsen; mem., Prague Nat. Opera from 1960; tour of Russia 1961 and sang Dalila in Bordeaux; guest appearances in Vienna, France and Switzerland; sang at State Operas of Hamburg and Berlin 1969–71; Prague Nat. Opera 1983 as Radmila in Smetana's Libuše. *Recordings:* Erda in The Ring, Dvořák's Stabat Mater, Lieder by Mahler, Choral Symphony, Libuše, The Brandenburgers in Bohemia, The Bride of Messina by Fibich, Oedipus Rex, Janáček's Glagolitic Mass.

SOUNOVA, Daniela; singer (soprano); b. 17 May 1943, Prague, Czech Republic. *Education:* studied in Prague. *Career:* debut at the Nat. Theatre Prague from 1973, notably in the 1974 premiere of Coriolanus by Jan Cikker and lyric roles in operas by Mozart, Smetana, Bizet, Puccini and Prokofiev; guest appearances at Bologna and the Edinburgh Festival; sang Donna Elvira in the bicentenary performances of Don Giovanni, in Prague 1987; Savonlinna Festival 1991, in Dvořák's Rusalka; many concert and recital engagements. *Recordings include:* Rusalka, The Jacobin by Dvořák, The Bride of Messina by Fibich, Don Giovanni, Mahler's 8th Symphony.

SOUSTROT, Marc; French conductor; b. 15 April 1949, Lyon. *Education:* Lyon Conservatoire, Paris Conservatoire with Manuel Rosenthal. *Career:* Asst to André Previn with the London Symphony Orchestra 1974–76; Deputy Conductor, Orchestre Philharmonique of the Loire 1976, then Musical Dir; Artistic Dir, Nantes Opera 1986–90; conducted the premieres of Claude Baliff's Fantasio Grandioso 1977, 1st Piano Concerto by Maurice Ohana 1981, and Concerto for orchestra by Alain Louvier 1987; conducted Tristan and Isolde at Nantes 1989, Manon Lescaut 1990, Les Contes d'Hoffmann at Geneva 1990, and Carmen at the Bregenz Festival, Austria; conducted Rheingold at Bonn 1997. *Recordings:* Trumpet Concertos with Maurice André; music by Franceschini, Scarlatti, Vivaldi, Tartini and Telemann with the Monte Carlo National Opera Orchestra. *Honours:* winner Rupert Foundation Competition for Young Conductors, London 1974, Int. Competition at Besançon 1975.

SOUTHGATE, Sir William David, Kt, BMus, MA; New Zealand conductor and composer; *Conductor Laureate, Christchurch Symphony Orchestra;* b. 4 Aug. 1941, Waipukarau. *Education:* Otago Univ., Guildhall School of Music, UK. *Career:* freelance composer in London and guest musical director of the RSC; Conductor and arranger for the Phoenix Opera Company; Musical Director of the Wellington Youth Orchestra from 1977; Musical Director of the Christchurch Symphony Orchestra 1984–97, Conductor Laureate 1997–; has conducted operas by Rossini, Verdi and Johann Strauss for the Wellington and Canterbury Opera Companies; presenter of music programmes on New Zealand radio and television; toured Finland as conductor 1986, Sweden and Finland 1989; debut on Honolulu Symphony 1989; tour of New Zealand with the Royal New Zealand Ballet Co. 1989; premieres of children's opera Faery Tale and Cello Concerto in New Zealand 1990; also performed with Dunedin Sinfonia, St Matthews Chamber Orchestra, New Zealand, SWF Sinfonia Orchestra, Christchurch Symphony Orchestra, New Zealand Symphony Orchestra, Halle Orchestra, Sydney Symphony Orchestra, Royal Philharmonic Orchestra, Royal Scottish Nat. Orchestra, Helsinki Philharmonic, Berlin Radio Symphony Orchestra. *Recordings include:* Second Symphony. *Honours:* Hon. DMus (Otago); Ricardi Conductors' Prize, Guildhall School of Music and Drama, second prize, Besançon Conducting Competition, Composers' Asscn Kirk-Burnand Prize, Composers' Asscn Brown Citation, Wellington Music Award for Services to Music 2003. *Address:* Christchurch Symphony Orchestra, PO Box 3260, The Arts Centre, Level One, Cnr Hereford Street and Rolleston Avenue, Christchurch 8013, New Zealand (office). *Telephone:* (3) 379-3886 (office). *Fax:* (3) 379-3878 (office). *Website:* www.christchurchsymphony.co.nz (office).

SOVERAL, Isabel; Portuguese composer; b. 25 Dec. 1961, Oporto. *Education:* Lisbon Conservatory with Joly Braga Santos, New York State Univ. at Stony Brook. *Career:* Lecturer, Univ. of Aveiro. *Compositions:* Contornos I for two clarinets 1987, II for oboe and bassoon 1987, III for four clarinets 1990, Pensando, enredano sombras for low voice and orchestra 1991, Quadramorphosis 1993, Anamorphoses I for clarinet and tape 1993, II for marimba, vibraphone and tape 1994, III for violin and tape 1995, IV for cello and tape 1997, V for string quartet 1997, Le Navigateur du soleil incandescent for baritone, chorus, orchestra and tape 1998, Un Soir for baritone and ensemble 1998.

SOVIERO, Diana; American singer (soprano); b. 1952. *Career:* sang first at St Paul 1974, appearing as Lauretta in Gianni Schicchi and as Massenet's Manon; joined the New York City Opera 1976 and sang further at Miami, San Francisco and Chicago; Metropolitan Opera debut 1986 as Juliet in Roméo et Juliette; European engagements at Paris, Rome, Florence, Milan, Vienna and Hamburg; Geneva 1988 as Gretchen in Doktor Faust by Busoni, Philadelphia and San Diego 1988 as Margherita in Mefistofele and Marguerite in Faust; sang Juliet and Manon at Montréal 1989; Covent Garden debut 1989 as Nedda; season 1992 as Tosca with Opera Pacific at Costa Mesa, Puccini's Trittico heroines at Dallas, Manon Lescaut at Miami and Adriana Lecouvreur at Sydney; other roles include Puccini's Butterfly and Mimi, Leila in Les Pêcheurs de Perles and Norina in Don Pasquale; sang Maddalena in Andrea Chénier at Seattle, 1996 and Monte Carlo 1998; Tosca for Palm Beach Opera, 1998. *Current Management:* Pinnacle Arts Management, 889 Ninth Avenue, Second Floor, New York, NY 10019, USA. *Telephone:* (212) 397-7915. *Fax:* (212) 397-7920. *Website:* www.pinnaclearts.com.

SOYER, Roger; singer (bass); b. 1 Sept. 1939, Thiais, France. *Education:* Paris Conservatoire with Georges Daum and Georges Jouatte. *Career:* sang at the Paris Opéra from 1963; sang at La Scala Milan 1963 as Tirésias in Les Mamelles de Tirésias by Poulenc, Aix-en-Provence Festival from 1965 as Pluto in Monteverdi's Orfeo, Don Giovanni, Don Basilio and Arkel, Paris 1965 in Rameau's Hippolyte et Aricie, Wexford Festival 1968 in La Jolie Fille de Perth by Bizet and US debut at Miami 1973 as Frère Laurent in Roméo et Juliette by Gounod; sang at Paris Opéra from 1972 in the premiere of Sud by Stanton Coe, and as Don Giovanni, Procida in Les Vêpres Siciliennes, Ferrando in Il Trovatore, Colline and Mephistopheles, Metropolitan Opera 1972 and Edinburgh Festival 1973 as Don Giovanni in a new production of Mozart's opera under Daniel Barenboim; guest appearances in Cologne, Brussels, Geneva, Chicago, Lisbon, Prague, San Antonio and Salzburg; sang Rodolfo in La Sonnambula at Geneva 1982, Sulpice in La Fille du Régiment at Dallas 1983 and sang in L'Heure Espagnole at Turin 1992. *Recordings:* Les Troyens and Benvenuto Cellini conducted by Colin Davis, Les Pêcheurs de Perles, L'Enfance du Christ, Mozart's Requiem, Lakmé, Werther, Maria Stuarda by Donizetti, Pelléas et Mélisande, Dardanus by Rameau, David et Jonathas by Charpentier.

SPACAGNA, (Susan) Maria, BMus, MMus; American singer (soprano) and voice teacher; b. 8 Dec. 1946, Rhode Island; d. of Aquilino (William) Spacagna and Assunta (Sue) Vestri Spacagna; m. Roger Everett Fowler; one c. *Education:* New England Conservatory, Juilliard Opera School, New York. *Career:* sang with Dallas Opera from 1977, New York City Opera 1978, St Louis Opera 1982, and Detroit 1986; sang Puccini's Liu at Toronto 1983 and appeared at Santa Fe, New Orleans and Trieste 1987; debut at La Scala, Milan as Madama Butterfly 1988; sang as Ismene in Traetta's Antigone at Spoleto Festival 1988, Mimi for New Orleans Opera 1989, Liu and Madama Butterfly at Costa Mesa California and Greater Miami Opera 1990; debut at Metropolitan Opera as Luisa Miller 1991; appearances at Memphis, Cologne Opera, La Fenice, Venice, Arena di Verona, Festival Pucciniano in Torre del Lago, Deutsche Oper Berlin, Dallas Opera, San Francisco Opera, Opera Theater of Montreal, Canadian Opera in Toronto, Capetown Opera (South Africa), Nat. Opera of China (Shanghai), Mexico, Teatro Municipao (Rio de Janeiro); roles include Violetta, Gilda, Amelia in Simon Boccanegra, Lina in Stifelio, Desdemona, Luisa Miller, Leonora in Trovatore, Susanna, Zerlina, Norina, Adina Marguerite, Rusalka, Micaela, Lauretta and Mascagni's Lodoletta; currently Lecturer in Voice, Boston Univ. Coll. of Fine Arts. *Recordings:* has recorded Madama Butterfly, Lodoletta and L'Arlesiana by Cilea. *Honours:* awards from Metropolitan Opera Nat. Council, Paris Int. Competition, Verdi Competition, Busseto, Rockefeller Foundation, George London Nat. Assn Inst., Minna Kaufmann Rudd Distinguished Performance Award, Rhode Island Pell Award for Excellence in the Arts. *Address:* College of Fine Arts School of Music, Boston University, 855 Commonwealth Avenue, Boston, MA 02215, USA (office). *Telephone:* (617) 353-3341 (office). *E-mail:* laspacagna@cox.net (office). *Website:* www.bu.edu/cfa/music (office).

SPAGNOLI, Pietro, (Zorro); Italian singer (baritone); b. 22 Jan. 1964, Rome. *Education:* Cappella Musicale Pontificia, Conservatorio di Santa Cecilia. *Career:* mem., Cappella Musicale Pontificia (Sistine Chapel Choir) from age 8 to 13; stage debut as Gaffredo in Bellini's Il Pirata at the Festival della Valle d'Itria, during same year performed role of Tracollo in Pergolesi's Livietta e Tracollo, Teatro Comunale di Firenze; operatic roles have included Don Giovanni and Leporello in Don Giovanni, Figaro in Il Barbiere di Siviglia, Figaro and Conte d'Almaviva in Le nozze di Figaro, Dandini in La Cenerentola, Don Alfonso and Guglielmo in Così fan tutte, Belcore and Doctor Dulcamara in L'elisir d'amore, Malatesta in Don Pasquale, Lescaut in Manon Lescaut, Silvio in I Pagliacci, Conte Asdrubale and Macrobio in La pietra del paragone; other operas include L'Orfeo, La serva padrona, Il matrimonio segreto, La Vita Nova, Capriccio, Pulcinella; concert performances have included Bach's Messa in B minor, Haydn's Die Schöpfung, Schubert's Die Winterreise; performed roles of Marcello and Schaunard in La Bohème, 100th anniversary of Bohème, Teatro Regio, Turin 1996; Covent Garden debut as Figaro in Il barbiere di Siviglia 2009; Metropolitan Opera debut as Dandini in

Cenerentola 2014; has appeared at numerous prestigious opera houses worldwide and worked with conductors including Rinaldo Alessandrini, Maurizio Benini, Richard Bonynge, Bruno Campanella, Riccardo Chailly, M. W. Chung, Daniele Gatti, Gianluigi Gelmetti, Renè Jacobs, Julia Jones, Philippe Jordan, Alain Lombard, Jesus Lopez-Cobos, Fabio Luisi, Gerard Korsten, Gustav Kuhn, Lorin Maazel, Riccardo Muti, Marc Minkowski, Daniel Oren, Antonio Pappano, Evelino Pidò, Stefano Ranzani, Carlo Rizzi, Hubert Soudant, Jordi Savall, Christian Thielemann, Marcello Viotti, Alberto Zedda; has worked with stage directors including Irina Brook, Robert Carsen, Liliana Cavani, Pippo Crivelli, Paul Curran, Gilbert Deflò, Roberto De Simone, Dario Fo, Michael Hampe, Werner Herzog, Ulrike and Karl-Ernst Herrmann, Gino Landi, Giorgio Marini, J. L .Martinoty, J. M. Flotats, Jonathan Miller, Moni Ovadia, Giuseppe Patroni-Griffi, Pier'Alli, Pierluigi Pizzi, Thomas Richter, Luca Ronconi, Emilio Sagi, Jerome Savary, Fabio Sparvoli, Stefano Vizioli, Franco Zeffirelli. *Recordings include:* L'Elisir d'amore; Rossini's Tancredi; numerous recordings for Erato, Harmonia Mundi, Ricordi, Astrae, Opera Rara, Nuova Era, Tactus, Bongiovanni, Claves, Novalis, Naxos. *Honours:* Winner, Pergolesi Nat. Competition, Rome 1987. *Current Management:* Irene Gall Management, Via Don G.Durgante 12 A, 37068 Vigasio, Italy. *Telephone:* (342) 9151023 (mobile) (home). *E-mail:* gall@irenegall.net. *Website:* www.irenegall.com.

SPAHLINGER, Mathias; German composer; b. 15 Oct. 1944, Frankfurt. *Education:* studied with Erhard Karkoschka and Konrad Lechner. *Career:* Lecturer, Hochschule der Kunst, Berlin 1978–81; Prof., Karlsruhe Hochschule für Musik 1983–90; Prof. of Composition, Freiberg 1990–. *Compositions:* Morendi for orchestra 1974, Éphémène for percussion and piano 1977, Extension for violin and piano, String Quartet 1982, Intermezzo for piano and orchestra 1986, Passage/Paysage for orchestra 1990, Und als wir for 54 strings 1993, Gegen unendlich for ensemble 1995, Akt, eine Treppe Herabsteigend for trombone, bass, clarinet and orchestra 1998. *Honours:* Boswil Foundation Prizes.

SPANO, Robert; American conductor and pianist; b. 1970, Conneaut. *Education:* Oberlin Conservatory, Curtis Inst. . with Max Rudolf. *Career:* Music Dir and Robert Reid Topping Chair., Atlanta Symphony Orchestra 1997–; Music Dir, Brooklyn Philharmonic; Dir Festival of Contemporary Music, Tanglewood 2003–04; Music Dir, Aspen Music Festival 2011–; appearances with symphonies of Boston, Houston, San Francisco and Chicago; opera engagements at Santa Fe (US premiere of Saariaho's L'amour de loin 2002), New York (Saariaho's Château de l'âme) and Houston (Eugene Onegin); season 2002–03 with the Cleveland and St Louis Symphonies, L'Amour de loin with the BBC Symphony Orchestra and the City of Birmingham Symphony Orchestra; further modern repertory includes El Niño by Adams, Del Tredici's Child Alice and Billy Budd (Seattle Opera); chamber musician (piano) with mems. of American orchestras. *Recordings include:* Rimsky-Korsakov: Scheherazade and Vaughan Williams: A Sea Symphony, Del Tredici: Paul Revere's Ride and Theofanidis: The Here and Now. *Honours:* Dr hc (Bowling Green State Univ., Curtis Inst. of Music) 2004; Conductor of the Year, Musical America Awards 2008. *Address:* Atlanta Symphony Orchestra, 1280 Peachtree Street NE, Atlanta, GA 30309-3552 (office); c/o Jason Bagdade, Opus 3 Artists, 470 Park Avenue, 9th Floor North, New York, NY 10016, USA. *E-mail:* aso-info@woodruffcenter.org. *Website:* www.atlantasymphony.org; www.robertspanomusic.com.

SPARNAAY, Harry Willem; Dutch bass clarinettist; b. 14 April 1944, Amsterdam; m. Roswitha Sparnaay-Mol. *Education:* Amsterdam Conservatory. *Career:* debut in Amsterdam 1969; performances with many leading orchestras including the BBC Symphony, Rotterdam Philharmonic, ORTF, Concertgebouw and Radio Chamber Orchestra Hilversum; soloist at festivals of Warsaw, Zagreb, Graz, Madrid, Poitiers, Witten, Como, Paris, Naples and the ISCM World Music Days at Boston, Athens and Bonn; concerts in Europe and America; Prof. of Bass Clarinet and Contemporary Music, Sweelinck Conservatory, Amsterdam-Rotterdam Conservatory and Royal Conservatory, The Hague; composers who have written for him include Donatoni, Ferneyhough, Bussotti, Isang Yun and Barry Anderson (premiere of ARC) 1987; appeared at Hudderfield Festival 1987 with Time and Motion Studies by Ferneyhough; tour of the UK 1989 on the Contemporary Music Network, playing Echange by Xenakis. *Recordings:* Bass Clarinet Identity, Harry Sparnaay/Lucien Goethals, Composers' Voice, Music by Thon Tbuynel, Music by Earle Brown, Bass Clarinet Idenitity 2, The Garden of Delight. *Honours:* first prize for bass clarinet soloist Int. Gaudeamus Competition 1972.

SPASOV, Bozhidar; Bulgarian composer and musicologist; b. 13 Aug. 1949, Sofia. *Education:* Moscow Conservatory with Edison Denisov. *Career:* Lecturer, Sofia Acad. of Music from 1976, Folkwang Hochschule, Essen 1990–; music performed at festivals in Dresden, Essen, Darmstadt and Rome. *Compositions:* The Bewitched (chamber opera) 1975, Sinfonie 1978, Konzertmusik for wind, percussion and two pianos 1982, Dialog I for two ensembles 1983, Glagolitic Concerto for mezzo, harpsichord and 13 strings 1984, The Beginning for mezzo and ensemble 1987, De Profundis for ensemble 1988, Violin Concerto 1988, Prabel 12 for chamber ensemble 1992, Oboe Concerto 1995, Sandglass for trombone, keyboard and electonics 1996, The Flight of the Butterfly for mezzo, flute and harpsichord 1997.

SPEACH, Bernadette; American composer; b. 1 Jan. 1948, Syracuse. *Education:* Columbia Univ., New York, studied in Siena with Franco Donatoni, State Univ. of New York at Buffalo with Morton Feldman. *Career:*

administrator, Composers' Forum 1988–94, The Kitchen 1995–. *Compositions:* Shattered Glass for percussion 1986, Telepathy Suite for speaker and ensemble 1998, Inside Out for piano 1987, Les Ordes pour quatre for string quartet 1988, Resoundings for piano four hands 1990, It Came to me in a Dream for baritone and ensemble 1990, Trio des trois I–III 1991–92, Angels in the Snow for piano 1993, Woman Without Adornment for speaker and ensemble 1995, Parallel Windows: Unframed for piano and orchestra 1995. *E-mail:* BSpeach@aol.com. *Website:* www.kallistimusic.com/Speach.html.

SPEISER, Elisabeth; Swiss singer (soprano); b. 15 Oct. 1940, Zürich; m. Hans Jecklin; two c. *Education:* Acad. of Music, Winterthur. *Career:* debut in Zürich; concerts in all European countries and North and South America; guest at many festivals; many concerts with Karl Richter; opera debut as Pamina in Die Zauberflöte, Ludwigsburger Schloss Festspiele 1972–73, Glyndebourne Festival 1973, Mélisande, St Gallen 1974; Euridice, Ludwigsburger Schloss Festspiele 1975; many Lieder recitals with Irwin Gage; television and radio appearances in Germany, Italy, Switzerland; Glyndebourne Festival as Euridice 1982; mem, Swiss Tonkunstlerverband. *Recordings include:* Secular Cantatas and Geistliche Lieder by JS Bach, Caecilien Mass by Haydn, Carissimi Cantatas, Berg/Schoenberg Lieder, Gluck's Orfeo ed Euridice, Schubert, Lieder 1984 and 1989, Brahms, Lieder 1985, Haydn's Arianna a Naxos and English songs 1987. *Address:* Ruelle du Château 4, 1742 Autigny, Switzerland (home).

SPELINA, Karel; Czech violist; *Professor of Viola and Chamber Music, Prague Conservatory;* b. 2 Nov. 1936, Plzeň; m. Marie Husickova 1958; two d. *Education:* Tech. Coll., Conservatory of Music, Plzeň. *Career:* debut with Plzeň Radio Quartet 1963; Prin. Viola, Plzeň Radio Orchestra 1962–70, Czech Philharmonic Orchestra 1970–2002; mem. Ars Rediviva Ensemble 1970–2002, Martinů Piano Quartet 1979–2002; Prof. of Viola and Chamber Music, Prague Conservatory 1994–; has played concertos and orchestral works by Berlioz, J. Reicha, A. Vranitzky, J.V. Stamitz, J.K. Vanhal, J.S. Bach, Martinů, and other composers; sonatas and chamber music by Bach and sons, Telemann, Handel, Mendelssohn, Hindemith, Brahms, Shostakovich, Martinů, Honegger, Milhaud, and others; mem. AHUV, Prague; teacher, Sándor Végh Int. Chamber Music Acad., AMEROPA Int. Chamber Music Acad. *Recordings:* Sonatas of C.P.E. Bach and W.F. Bach, Sonatas of A. Honegger and D. Milhaud, Sonatas of Hindemith, Concertos of Josef Reicha, Complete Sonatas of J.K. Vanhal, first World Recording 1997, Concertos and Chamber Music of Zdenek Lukas, Sonatas of Mendelssohn, Shostakowich and Elegy of Glazunov. *Honours:* City of Plzeň Prize 1968. *Address:* Sturova 32/1153, 142 00 Prague 411, Czech Republic (home). *E-mail:* kspelina@volny.cz (home).

SPEMANN, Alexander; German singer (tenor) and composer; b. 1 June 1967, Wiesbaden. *Education:* Peter Cornelius Conservatory, Mainz with Gertie Charlent, Frankfurt Musikhochschule with Martin Grundler. *Career:* debut tenor solo in Beethoven's Ninth, Milan, 1989; stage debut as First Armed Man in Die Zauberflöte at Wiesbaden; many concert and opera appearances at Essen, Vienna, Stuttgart, Cologne, Frankfurt, Munich and Hamburg; Engaged with Bonn Opera from 1993–97, singing Kronthal in Lortzing's Wildschütz, and making debut in a Wagner role as Erik in Der Fliegende Holländer; freelance film and theatre music composer, including music for the Hessiche Staatstheater, Wiesbaden; engaged with Darmstadt since 1997 as young heroic tenor, singing Son-Chong in Land des Lächelns, Don José in Carmen and many other roles; sang Berg's Alwa at Mainz, 1999; season 2000–01 as Florestan in the 1805 version of Fidelio, Don José and Herod in Salome. *Recordings include:* Count Rudolf in Weber's Silvana (Marco Polo); Jenik in The Bartered Bride, with the orchestra of North German Radio. *Honours:* winner Robert Stolz Competition, Hamburg 1996. *Current Management:* c/o Esther Schollum Artists' Management, Guntramsdorfer Straße 12/2, 2340 Mödling bei Wien, Austria. *Telephone:* 223641004. *Fax:* 2236410044. *E-mail:* es@art-mgmt.com. *Website:* art-mgmt.com.

SPENCE, Patricia; singer (mezzo-soprano); b. 12 Jan. 1961, Salem, OR, USA. *Education:* studied in San Francisco. *Career:* debut at San Francisco Opera as Anna in L'Africaine; has performed the Princess in Suor Angelica, Mother Goose in The Rake's Progress and Meg Page in Falstaff at San Francisco; New York City debut 1988, as Rosina; Opera Colorado 1989 as Mistress Quickly; European debut as Edwige in Guillaume Tell at Verona followed by Mozart's Requiem at St Petersburg, Malcolm in La Donna del Lago at La Scala 1992, and Cenerentola with Phoenix Opera, Arizona; further engagements as Farnace in Mitridate at St Louis, Tsaura in Tancredi at La Scala, Lola at the Arena di Verona, Cenerentola at Covent Garden, (UK debut 1993), and Ramiro in La Finta Giardinera for WNO; recitals at Göttingen and Hesse Handel Festivals, further Handel performances with Nicholas McGegan and appearances with San Francisco, Detroit, St Louis and Sacramento Symphonies, and Fresno and Mexico City Philharmonics; sang Handel's Poro at the Halle Festival 1998. *Recordings include:* Flora in La Traviata, Handel's La Resurrezione, Messiah and Ottone (conducted by McGegan). *Honours:* Merola Opera Programme Il Cenacolo Award, San Francisco Opera Centre 1987.

SPENCE, Toby; British singer (tenor); b. (Edward Tobias Spence), 22 May 1969, Hertford, Herts.; s. of Dr Magnus Peter Spence and Gillian Sara Spence. *Education:* New Coll., Oxford and Opera School of the Guildhall School. *Career:* early career included operatic debut with Welsh Nat. Opera as Idamante in Idomeneo 1995; appearances include Tom Rakewell in Stravins-

ky's The Rake's Progress in Vienna 2008, Madrid 2009 and London 2010, Elgar's Dream of Gerontius with Vienna Philharmonic in Vienna and as Laertes in Thomas' Hamlet at The Metropolitan Opera, New York 2010, Ferdinand in Thomas Adès' The Tempest, St John in Handel's La Resurrezione in a recording with Le Concert d'Astrée under the direction of Emmanuelle Haïm, title role in Faust, ENO 2010, Don Ottavio in Don Giovanni at Glyndebourne 2011, David in Die Meistersinger von Nürnberg, Covent Garden 2011–12, title role in La Clemenza di Tito, Bayerische Staatsoper andd Wiener Staatsoper 2014, Eistenstein in Die Fledermaus, Met Opera 2015–16; broad repertoire spanning Monteverdi, Wagner and Adès; also concert performances; co-f. (with conductor Edward Gardner) song recital series Wardsbrook Concerts 2013. *Recordings:* numerous recordings with EMI, Virgin, BMG, Deutsche Grammophon, Chandos, Linn and Hyperion. *Honours:* RPS Singer Award 2012. *Address:* 18 Sudeley Street, London, N1 8HP, England (office). *E-mail:* tobyspence@mac.com (office).

SPERSKI, Krzysztof, MA; violoncellist and teacher; b. 11 June 1942, Kraków, Poland; m. Janina Duda 1967 (divorced 1986); one s. *Education:* Academy of Music, Gdansk with Prof. R. Suchecki, Academy of Music, Poznań, Academy of Music, Łódź. *Career:* debut recital by Association of Polish Artist Musicians, Gdansk, 1964; soloist of symphony concerts, recitals, chamber concerts in Poland and foreign concert tours, Finland, the United Kingdom, Sweden, Germany, Romania, Bulgaria, Iceland, Czechoslovakia, Austria, Greece, Italy, Denmark, Lithuania, Peru, Switzerland, Netherlands, Belgium, Russia, Chile; Professor of Cello, Academy of Music, Gdansk; Guest Professor, Music Masterclasses, Mynämäki, Finland, 1976, International Music Seminar, Kozani, Greece, 1990–99, Masterclasses Santiago, Chile, 1998–2000, Lima, Peru, 2000; mem, Association of Polish Artist Musicians. *Recordings:* albums: Slavic Music 1994, Music Treasures of Gdansk 1997. *Publications:* About faults of position, left and right hand of young cellists, 1979; Characteristics of Musical Utterance, 1981; Remarks of Performing Violoncello Baroque Music in the Light of Traditions and Contemporary Requirements, 1988; Polish Violoncello Pedagogic Literature, 1988. *Honours:* Award for Polish Culture, 1979; Distinction of Merit, Town of Gdansk, 1981; Gold Cross of Merit, 1985. *Address:* ul Goralska 55/A/9, 80-292 Gdańsk, Poland.

SPICER, Paul, BMus, ARCM, ARCO, FRSA; British choral conductor, composer, record producer and teacher; *Head of Choral Conducting, Birmingham Conservatoire;* b. 6 June 1952, Bowdon, Cheshire, England; s. of John Harold Vincent Spicer and Joan Sallie Spicer. *Education:* New Coll., Oxford, Oakham School, Royal Coll. of Music, London, Durham Univ. *Career:* taught music at Uppingham School and Ellesmere Coll. 1974–84; Producer, BBC Radio 3 1984–86; Sr Producer, BBC Midlands Region 1986–1990; Founder-Dir, Finzi Singers 1987–; Artistic Dir, Lichfield Int. Arts Festival 1990–2001; Dir, Abbotsholme Arts Soc. 1990–2001; Conductor, Birmingham Bach Choir 1992–, Royal Coll. of Music Chamber Choir 1995–2008, Whitehall Choir, London 2000–, Birmingham Conservatoire Chamber Choirs 2001–; Prof. of Choral Conducting, Royal Coll. of Music 2000–08; Head of Choral Conducting, Birmingham Conservatoire 2003–; teacher of choral conducting techniques, Oxford Univ. 2006–; freelance conductor, composer, writer, teacher and broadcaster 2001–; Chair. Finzi Friends; Vice-Pres. Herbert Howells Soc.; mem. Council of Lichfield Cathedral; Patron, The Howells Singers; Trustee, Finzi Trust, Schulze Trust; Adviser, Sir George Dyson Trust. *Compositions include:* The Darling of the World for choir and orchestra 1986, Piano Sonata 1988, A Song for Birds (song cycle) 1990, Prelude in homage to Maurice Duruflé for organ 1990, Kiwi Fireworks for organ 1994, Dies Natalis for choir 1995, Man, Wretched Man for choir and organ 1997, Easter Oratorio for choirs, orchestra, soloists 2000, The Deciduous Cross for choir and orchestra 2003, Suite for Organ 2001, How Love Bleeds for choir 2005, Advent Oratorio for choir, orchestra and soloists 2009, Unfinished Remembering for choir, orchestra and soloists 2014. *Recordings include:* God's Great New Day: Extracts from Easter Oratorio, fifteen CDs with Finzi Singers, three CDs with Birmingham Bach Choir, including J. S. Bach: The Seven Motets, four CDs with Birmingham Conservatoire Chamber Choir. *Radio:* many programmes devised and presented for BBC Radio 1984–90, contribs to many programmes on BBC Radio 3 and BBC Radio 4 1990–. *Television:* film for Open Univ. on Howells and Gurney. *Publications include:* Herbert Howells 1998, George Dyson 2014. *Honours:* Hon. Research Fellow, Univ. of Birmingham 2000–; Hon. Fellow, Birmingham Conservatoire 2001, Univ. Coll., Durham 2014; Walford Davies Organ Prize Royal Coll. of Music, British Acad. Major Award 2007. *Current Management:* c/o Valerie Withams, Choral Connections, 14 Stevens Close, Prestwood, Great Missenden, HP16 0SQ, England. *Telephone:* (1494) 866389. *Fax:* (1494) 866389. *E-mail:* val@choralconnections.com. *Website:* www.choralconnections.com. *Address:* 4 The Close, Lichfield, Staffs., WS13 7LD, England (home). *Telephone:* (1543) 305019 (home). *E-mail:* paul@paulspicer.com (home). *Website:* www.paulspicer.com.

ŠPIČKA, Daniel Hilarius; Czech architect, music festival director, early music instrument maker and collector; *Architect and Designer, Hulec & Špička Architekti;* b. 5 Feb. 1939, Prague; m. Victoria W. Reilly 1973; two d. *Education:* Czech Tech. Univ., Prague, evening courses at Prague Conservatoire. *Career:* debut with Vejvanovsky Consort, Prague 1959; with Camerata RSX 1977; Valtice Baroque Festival 1989; Founder, Camerata RSX, first authentic Renaissance Consort in Czech Repub.; Co-founder Valtice Baroque Opera Festival, South Moravia, Czech Repub.; performances on Czech and Austrian TV, BBC and Czech Radio; Dramaturg, Valtice Baroque Opera Festival 1989–; noted for introducing authentic early music performances to

Czech music scene; mem. Czech Music Soc. (Early Music Br.); Architect and Designer, Hulec & Špička Architekti, worked on project for Valtice Castle Theatre (1791) involving complete restoration (including Baroque machinery, original lighting)– June 2015. *Exhibitions include:* numerous exhbns in Czech Repub. and abroad; Restoration of Baroque Theatres in Bohemia and Moravia 2004, 2006. *Recordings:* Gagliano: La Dafne 1992, Monteverdi: Balli 1994. *Publications include:* contrib. to various Czech music magazines 1982–, articles on Valtice Festival in The Independent 1990, Die Presse 1990, 1992, on the Restoration of Chateau Valtice Baroque Theatre 1991, The Times 1992. *Honours:* Czech Design Award 2007. *Address:* Hulec & Špička Architekti, Na Bitevni plani 44, 140 00 Prague 4 (office); U. Mrázovky 7, 15000 Prague 5, Czech Republic. *Telephone:* 73-7325292 (mobile). *E-mail:* spickovi@volny.cz; coraarch@volny.cz (office). *Website:* www.hs-architekti.cz (office); festivalvaltice.com (office).

SPIERS, Colin James, BA; Australian composer and pianist; *Senior Lecturer in Composition, The Conservatorium, Newcastle University*; b. 24 July 1957, Brisbane, Qld. *Education:* Queensland Conservatorium. *Career:* Faculty mem. Univ. of Queensland 1980–90; Faculty mem. The Conservatorium, Newcastle Univ. 1990–, currently Sr Lecturer in Composition; Founding mem., Perihelion Ensemble; solo pianist, recital accompanist and composition teacher. *Compositions include:* Fantasy on Theme of Keith Jarrett for piano 1987, Divertimento for strings 1987, Tales from Nowhere for piano 1988, Sonata for solo viola 1988, Day of Death and Dreams for tenor and piano 1989, UWJ for viola and piano 1991, Flecks for piano 1991, Cadenzas and Interludes for string orchestra 1991, Deranged Confessions, Desperate Acts, Divine Symmetry, Delicate Games piano sonatas 1990–98, ZYJ for trumpet and piano 1993, Music, Like the Dark Husk of Earth, Abiding for string orchestra 1994, NSJ for clarinet, bassett-horn and piano 1995, Mutations for piano 1996, five Bagatelles for piano 1996–97, Sonata for cello and piano 1999, The Last Thoughts of Prokofiev for piano 2003, Blue into Blue for orchestra 2004, Collide for orchestra 2004, Arc of Infinity for strings 2006, Memory for soprano and orchestra 2007, A Slender Strand of Memories for four vocal soloists, SATB choir and orchestra 2009. *Honours:* Queensland Conservatorium Medal of Excellence 1979, Jean Bogan Composition Prize 1995. *Address:* 16 Kimian Avenue, Waratah West, NSW 2298, Australia (home). *Telephone:* (02) 4921-8925 (office). *E-mail:* Colin.Spiers@newcastle.edu.au (office).

SPIEWAK, Tomasz, BEd; Australian (b. Polish) pianist and composer; b. 12 Sept. 1936, Kraków; s. of Antoni Spiewak and Janina Mermon; one s. one d. *Education:* State Primary and Secondary Music School, Kraków, Jagiellonian Univ., Kraków and Univ. of Melbourne, Australia. *Career:* full-time teacher, Box Hill Coll. of Music, Melbourne, Australia 1982–2001; two years in Polish army ensemble, Desant as pianist, composer and arranger; five years in Polish comedy theatre, Wagabunda as musical dir, pianist, composer, arranger and bandleader; two years in Polish radio and TV orchestra as pianist, composer and arranger; pianist, organist and arranger in a quartet, toured through Scandinavia 1971–74; currently part-time teacher of aural training, Defence Force School of Music, Melbourne. *Compositions include:* Quartet for Saxophones in four movements 1988, 11 studies for marimba 1988–94, three marimba duets 1988–94, six preludes for vibraphone 1988–95, Sonatina for B flat saxophone and piano 1990, Duo Sonata for tenor and baritone saxophones 1990, Trio for alto and baritone saxophones and piano 1991, Sonata for trombone and piano 1992, Roller Coaster for violoncello 1996, pieces for bassoon and piano 1996, Floral Suite for alto saxophone and piano 2000, Scherzetto for baritone saxophone and piano 2000, Walking Dance for baritone saxophone and piano 2000, Second Quartet for saxophones, featuring baritone saxophone 2000, Kaleidoscope for alto saxophone and piano 2002, Blue Ride for alto saxophone and piano 2002, Palindrome for saxophone quartet 2003, Quartet for Saxophones No. 3 (from Rag to Funk) 2003, six pieces for saxophone solo 2004, six pieces for clarinet solo 2004, Sonata for tenor saxophone and pianoforte 2005, The Koonung Trail Suite (six movts) for three clarinets and bass clarinet 2006, Thea's Tunes (six short pieces for violoncello solo) 2007, Funky Bassoon (five short pieces for bassoon and piano) 2008, Dance Sketches for marimba solo 2010. *Publications:* Aural Training for Musicians and Music Students Vols I–IV 1991–96, The Performing Ear (with Jenni Hillman) 2001, Vocalises for Modern Singers Vols I–III 2002, Essential Instrumental Ensemble Kit: Exercises in sight reading and aural training 2005. *E-mail:* tspiewak@bigpond.net.au (home). *Website:* www.reedmusic.com (office).

SPIEWOK, Stephen; singer (tenor); b. 1 Dec. 1947, Berlin, Germany. *Education:* Musikhochschule, Weimar, studied with Johannes Kemter in Dresden. *Career:* debut at Weimar 1971, as Nicolai's Fenton; Dresden Staatsoper 1971–80, notably in the 1979 premiere of Vincent, by Kunad; Leipzig Opera and Berlin Staatsoper 1980–90, including the 1984 premiere if Kunad's Amphitryon; Ludwigsburg Festival 1989, as Ephrain in the premiere of Judith, by S. Matthus; sang Arbace in Idomeneo at the Komische Oper, Berlin, and Morosus at Wiesbaden (Die schweigsame Frau, by Strauss); guest appearances throughout Europe and in Japan as Tamino, the Duke of Mantua, Števa in Jenůfa, and Andres in Wozzeck; many concert engagements.

SPILLER, Andres; Argentine oboist and conductor; b. 24 Dec. 1946, Buenos Aires; m. Marcela Magin; two s. one d. *Education:* Conservatorio Nacional, studied in Hochschule für Musik, Cologne, Germany, summer courses with Heinz Holliger, Bruno Maderna, Franco Ferrara, Michael Gielen, Volker Wangenheim and Hans Swarowsky. *Career:* Asst Conductor, Nat. Symphony Orchestra 1994–2011; currently Oboe Soloist, Nat. Symphony Orchestra, Camerata Bariloche; Soloist of Bach Acad., Buenos Aires; Conductor, La Plata Chamber Orchestra 1978–2005; performed with Koeckert Quartet in Munich; other European appearances include Madrid, Rome and Radio Zürich; toured America and Europe with Camerata Bariloche; Prof. of Oboe and Chamber Music. *Recordings:* Death of an Angel, Tango, Recent Works for Oboe, with Marcela Magin, viola. *Honours:* DAAD Fellowship for study in Germany, Sociedad Hebraica Prize, 2nd Prize, Promociones Musicales, Premio Konex, 1989, 1999. *Address:* Medrano 47, 5°A, 1178 Buenos Aires, Argentina (home). *Telephone:* (11) 49811470 (home). *Fax:* (11) 49811470 (home). *E-mail:* spillermagin@fibertel.com.ar.

SPINNLER, Burkard; pianist; b. 17 July 1954, Goldbach, Germany; m. Claudine Orloff 1983, two s. one d. *Education:* Musikhochschule Würzburg with J. von Karolyi, Brussels Royal Conservatory with J. Cl. Vanden Eynden, Ecole de Maitrise Pianistique, studied with Eduardo del Pueyo in Brussels. *Career:* debut with Univ. Orchestra at Würzburg 1978; recording for Bavarian radio 1979, for Belgian Radio RTB 1984; appearances as soloist and in chamber music in Germany, Belgium and France; special L. Godowsky commemorative programme 1989; regular concerts on two pianos with Claudine Orloff, including Musique en Sorbonne, Paris 1991; live radio engagement, Hommage à Milhaud, RTB Brussels 1992, 1999; private research of Liszt unpublished works and 136 unedited letters of Francis Poulenc; teacher, Brussels Conservatory 1985–; further live recordings for Belgian and French radio 1995, 1998. *Publication:* Zur Angemessenheit Traditionelles Formbegriffe in der Analyse Mahlerscher Symphonik, in Form und Idée in G Mahlers Instrumentalmusik 1980. *Address:* 109 Avenue E. Van Becelaere, 1170 Brussels, Belgium.

SPINOSI, Jean-Christophe; French conductor and violinist; *Founder and Music Director, Ensemble Matheus*; b. 1964, Corsica; m.; five c. *Career:* originally a violinist, studied conducting at an early age; f. the quartet Matheus 1991, became the Ensemble Matheus at the Quartz in Brest, made a series of recordings with the ensemble of Vivaldi's previously unrecorded works 2005, released several albums and four opera recordings; musical collaborations with artists including Cecilia Bartoli, Marie-Nicole Lemieux, Natalie Dessay and Philippe Jaroussky; has conducted his ensemble in a new production each year at the Théâtre du Châtelet, Paris 2007–; has worked with leading directors, including Pierrick Sorin (Rossini's La pietra del Paragone 2007), Oleg Kulik (Monteverdi's Vespers of the Blessed Virgin Mary 2009) and Claus Guth (Handel's Messiah at the Theater an der Wien 2009); teamed up with Kamel Ouali for his production of Orlando Paladino; productions at Opéra de Paris and Théâtre des Champs-Elysées have included performances of Mozart's Die Zauberflöte; invited by mezzo-soprano Cecilia Bartoli to perform a series of concerts with her 2011, European tour in Munich, Prague, Baden-Baden and at the Château de Versailles; works regularly with numerous orchestras, including the Wiener Staatsoper, Deutsches Symphonie Orchester at the Berlin Philharmonie, Orchestre Philharmonique de Monte-Carlo, Frankfurt Radio Symphony Orchestra, Orchestre du Capitole de Toulouse, Scottish Chamber Orchestra, New Japan Philharmonic, Royal Stockholm Philharmonic Orchestra, Rundfunk Sinfonie Orchester Berlin, Orquesta de Castilla y Leon, Wiener Symphoniker or Spain's Orquesta Nacional, and collaborates with the City of Birmingham Symphony Orchestra, NDR Radiophilharmonie Hannover, Mozarteum Orchester Salzburg, Verbier Festival Chamber Orchestra and Orchestre de Paris; season 2013–14 saw continued association with Cecilia Bartoli in the Rossini cycle, with Otello at Théâtre des Champs-Elysées, Paris, La Cenerentola in Salzburg (Whitsun and summer) and Italiana in Algeri in Dortmund; gave a new performance of La Pietra del Paragone at Théâtre du Châtelet, Paris 2014, following 15 performances of Handel's Orlando in Lorient, Brest, Rennes, Toulouse and Versailles (France). *Recordings include:* albums: Vivaldi's La verità in cimento, Orlando Furioso, La Griselda (BBC Music Magazine Opera Award 2006), La Fida Ninfa, Stabat Mater, Heroes (with Philippe Jaroussky) (Double Gold Disc); DVDs: Vivaldi's Orlando Furioso (at Théâtre des Champs-Elysées), Handel's Messiah (at Theater an der Wien), Rossini's La Pietra del Paragone (at Théâtre du Châtelet). *Honours:* Chevalier des Arts et des Lettres 2006; Diapason d'Or, Choc de l'année du Monde de la Musique, Premio internazionale del disco Antonio Vivaldi, Venice, Grand Prix de l' Acad. Charles Cros, Prix Caecilia, Belgium, Victoire de la Musique Classique, Best Opera Conductor, Acad. du disque lyrique 2007. *Current Management:* Ensemble Matheus, Le Quartz, Square Beethoven, 60 rue du Château, 29210 Brest Cedex 1, France. *Telephone:* (2) 98-33-95-03. *Fax:* (2) 98-33-95-01. *E-mail:* info@ensemble-matheus.fr. *Website:* www.ensemble-matheus.fr.

ŠPITKOVA, Jela; Slovak violinist; *Professor of Violin, University of Music, Vienna*; b. 1 Jan. 1947, Novo Mesto; d. of Dr Pavel Spitka and Olga Spitkova; one s. *Education:* Bratislava Conservatory, studied in Vienna with Riccardo Odnoposoff, Prague Coll. of Music, Tchaikovsky Conservatory Moscow with David and Igor Oistrakh. *Career:* has performed with leading Czech Orchestras and in 60 other countries, including South and North America and Africa; recitals in Paris, Rome, Moscow, Berlin, Prague, Amsterdam, Tokyo, Rio de Janeiro and Vienna; television and radio recordings in Spain, Norway, Denmark, Austria, France, Finland and Russia; Leader of the Mozarteum Orchestra 1980; soloist with Slovak Philharmonic in Bratislava; repertoire includes concertos by Tchaikovsky, Brahms, Beethoven, Sibelius, Mendelssohn, Mozart, Bach and Haydn, Lalo Symphonie Espagnole, Sonatas by Brahms, Beethoven, Franck, Schumann, Prokofiev, Mozart, Handel, Debussy and Dvořák; Concertmaster, Mozarteum Orchestra in Salzburg 1980–94; teacher of violin, Vienna Music Acad. 1985–; Prof. of Violin, Banska Bystrica Music Acad., Slovakia; Prof., Prague Music Acad. 2002–; Prof., Bratislava Music Acad. 2004–; Prof. of Violin, Univ. of Music, Vienna 2006–. *Recordings:* albums and recordings for Slovak Radio: Mendelssohn Violin Concerto in E Minor; Bruch Violin Concerto; Chausson, Poème; Tchaikovsky Serenade Melancholique; Brahms Sonata Nos 1, 2 and 3; Ravel's Tzigane; Sibelius Violin Concerto; Suchon Sonatine op 11; Haydn Violin Concerto in C Major; Dittersdorf Violin Concerto in G Minor, Sibelius Violin Concerto in D Minor, Tchaikovsky Violin Concerto in D Major, Beethoven Violin Concerto in D Major, Suk Fantasy in G Minor, Lalo Symphonie Espagnole, Hummel Concerto for Violin, Piano and Orchestra, Schuman Sonatas Nos 1 and 2, Debussy Sonata, Enescu Sonata No. 2. *Honours:* third prize Nat. Youth Festival, Sofia 1968, three prizes in int. violin competition Tibor Varga, Switzerland 1969, third prize int. competition Emily Anderson, Royal Philharmonic Soc., London 1969. *Address:* Belopotockeho 2, 81105 Bratislava, Slovakia (home). *Telephone:* (2) 52492535 (home). *E-mail:* jela.spitkova@post.sk (home); jspitkova@yahoo.com (home). *Website:* www.jelaspitkova.com.

SPIVAKOV, Vladimir Teodorovich; Russian violinist and conductor; *Artistic Director and Principal Conductor, National Philharmonic of Russia;* b. 12 Sept. 1944, Ufa, Bashkortostan; m. Satinik Saakyants; three d. *Education:* Moscow State Conservatory, postgraduate with Yury Yankelevich. *Career:* studied violin since age of six with B. Kroger in Leningrad; prize winner in several int. competitions including Tchaikovsky, Moscow; Founder and Conductor Chamber Orchestra Virtuosi of Moscow 1979–; Founder and Artistic Dir Music Festival in Colmar, France 1989–; Artistic Dir and Chief Conductor, Russian Nat. Symphony Orchestra 1999–2003; Founder, Artistic Dir and Prin. Conductor Nat. Philharmonic of Russia 2003–; Artistic Dir and Prin. Conductor, Moscow Virtuosi Chamber Orchestra; guest conductor of several orchestras including Chicago Symphony Orchestra, LA Philharmonic, London Symphony Orchestra, English and Scottish Chamber Orchestras; Pres. Moscow Performing Arts Centre 2003–; f. Spivakov Foundation 1994. *Recordings include:* more than 20 CDs on Capriccio, RCA Victor Red Seal and BMG Classics including works by Brahms, Berg, Chausson, Franck, Prokoviev, Ravel, Tchaikovsky, Richard Strauss, Schubert, Sibelius, Shostakovich. *Honours:* Officier, Ordre des Arts et des Lettres 1999, Chevalier, Légion d'Honneur 2000; Dr hc (Moscow Lomonosov Univ.) 2002; USSR State Prize 1989, USSR People's Artist 1990, Triumph Prize, Nat. Cultural Heritage Award, Russia's Artist of the Year 2002, First Prize Montreal Competition, Marguerite Long St Jacques Thibaud Competition, Paris, Nicolo Paganini Int. Violin Competition, Genoa, Int. Tchaikovsky Competition, Moscow. *Address:* c/o Columbia Artists Management, 1790 Broadway, New York, NY 10019, USA; National Philharmonic of Russia, Moscow 115054, Office 208, 52/8 Kosmodamianskaya Embankment, Russia; Vspolny per. 17, Apt 14, Moscow, Russia. *Telephone:* (495) 290-23-24 (Moscow); (495) 730-1367 (Nat. Philharmonic). *Fax:* (495) 730-3778 (Nat.Philharmonic). *Website:* www.nfor.ru/eng; spivakov.ru; www.mvco.ru/en.

SPOTORNO, Marianangela; Italian singer (soprano); b. 1970, Rome. *Education:* studied with Magda Laszlo and Elio Battaglia. *Career:* debut as Elisabetta in Cimarosa's Il Matrimonio Segreto, for the Walton Trust at Ischia and in Scotland 1992; sang in Offenbach's Barbe-bleue at Bologna and Messina, Mozart's Fiordiligi and Susanna at Cagliari; sang the title role in Manon Lescaut at the Glyndebourne Festival 1997, and engaged 1997–98 as Antonia in L'Elisir d'amore; concerts include Beethoven's Christus am Olberge at Treviso, opera concert with Domingo in Finland; sang the voice of the soprano Guiditta Pasta for Italian television film of the life of Giulio Ricordi.

SPRATLAN, Lewis, BA, MM; American composer; b. 5 Sept. 1940, Miami, FL. *Education:* Yale Univ. with Yehudi Wyner, Gunther Schuller and Mel Powell, Tanglewood with George Rochberg and Roger Sessions. *Career:* faculty mem., Pennsylvania State Univ. 1967–70; faculty mem., Amherst Coll. from 1970, Chair. of Music Dept 1977–94, Prof. from 1980. *Compositions include:* Missa Brevis 1965, Cantate Domine for men's chorus, winds and tape 1968, Serenade for six instruments 1970, Moonsong for chorus and ensemble 1970, Two Pieces for orchestra 1971, Woodwind Quintet 1971, Fantasy for piano and chamber ensemble 1973, Ben Jonson for soprano, violin and cello 1974, Life is a Dream (opera) 1977, Coils for ensemble 1980, String Quartet 1982, When Crows Gather for three clarinets, violin, cello and piano 1986, Hung Monophonies for oboe and 11 instruments 1990, Night Music for violin, clarinet and percussion 1991, In Memoriam for soloists, chorus and orchestra 1993, A Barred Owl for baritone and five instruments 1994, Concertino for violin, cello, baritone and five instruments 1994, Concertino for violin, cello and double bass 1995, Psalm 42 for soprano, baritone and ensemble 1996.

SPRATT, Geoffrey Kenneth, BA, PhD; British musician; *Director, Cork School of Music;* b. 16 Sept. 1950, London, England; m. 1st Frances Vivien Squire; two s.; m. 2nd Elizabeth Searls. *Education:* Univ. of Bristol. *Career:* professional freelance flute and viola player with Cyprus Broadcasting Company Orchestras 1969–70, and various British orchestras 1970–76; part-time Tutor, Open Univ. 1973–76, Univ. of Bristol 1974–76; Lecturer in Music, University Coll. Cork (UCC), Ireland 1976–92; Founder-Conductor, UCC Choir and Orchestra 1976–92; Conductor, UCC Choral Soc. 1978–86, Galway Baroque Singers and Orchestra 1983–92, Madrigal '75 Chamber Choir 1985–97; Dir Cork School of Music 1992–; Founder and Conductor, Irish Youth Choir 1982–2007, Fleischmann Choir of the Cork School of Music

1992–2013, Canticum Novum Chamber Choir 1998–; Guest Conductor RTÉ Nat. Symphony Orchestra 1980–, RTÉ Concert Orchestra 1980–, RTÉ Chorus, RTÉ Chamber Choir, Irish Chamber Orchestra, Orchestra St Cecilia; Chairman, Asscn of Irish Choirs 1984–2006, Cork Orchestral Soc. 1992–2013; Founder and Artistic Dir Asscn of Irish Choirs' Annual Summer School of Choral Conductors 1980–2005. *Recordings:* Choral music of Séamas de Barra sung by the Irish Youth Choir and Madrigal '75, Sacred Choral Music of Angel Climent sung by the Irish Youth Choir. *Publications:* Catalogue des oeuvres de Arthur Honegger 1986; co-author with M. Delannoy, Honegger 1986. The Music of Arthur Honegger 1987. *Honours:* Napier Miles Prize, Univ. of Bristol 1972. *Address:* Cork School of Music, Union Quay, Cork, Ireland (office). *Telephone:* (21) 4807307 (office). *E-mail:* geoffrey.spratt@cit.ie (office). *Website:* www.cit.ie/csm.

SQUIRES, Shelagh; British singer (mezzo-soprano); b. 17 Aug. 1936, England. *Education:* Guildhall School, London. *Career:* debut at Glyndebourne 1968, in Die Zauberflöte; sang Cherubino for Phoenix Opera, 1969; Sadler's Wells/English National Opera from 1972, as Mozart's Marcellina, Tisbe in Cenerentola, Filippevna in Eugene Onegin, Emilia in Othello, and Mamma Lucia in Cavalleria Rusticana; Appearances in the first local stage performances of War and Peace; Penderecki's The Devils of Loudun, Janáček's Osud (1984), Christmas Eve by Rimsky-Korsakov, and the premiere of Robin Holloway's Clarissa (1990); other roles in The Ring of the Nibelung, as Rosette in Manon, Jezibaba in Rusalka and Mrs Sedley in Peter Grimes. *Recordings include:* Othello, The Ring, Gloriana (video).

SRABRAWA, Daniel; violinist; b. 1948, Kraków, Poland. *Education:* studied with Z. Slezer in Kraków. *Career:* Leader, Kraków Radio Symphony Orchestra 1979; mem., Berlin Philharmonic Orchestra 1983, Leader 1983; co-founder, Philharmonic Quartet Berlin, giving concerts throughout Europe, USA and Japan; British debut 1987, playing Haydn, Szymanowski and Beethoven at Wigmore Hall; played at Bath Festival 1987 with Mozart, Schumann and Beethoven op 127; other repertoire includes quartets by Bartók, Mendelssohn, Nicolai, Ravel and Schubert, and quintets by Brahms, Weber, Reger and Schumann.

SRAMEK, Alfred; singer (bass); b. 5 April 1951, Nichtelbach, Vienna, Austria. *Education:* studied with Ludwig Weber and Hilde Zadek. *Career:* sang with the Vienna Staatsoper from 1975 in Palestrina and as Don Pasquale, Dulcamara, Beckmesser, Masetto, Leporello and Figaro; sang at Salzburg Festival from 1976, and Bregenz Festival 1982; season 2000–01 at the Vienna State Opera in Lulu, Figaro (as Bartolo), Wozzeck and Billy Budd; Dulcamara in L'elisir d'amore; many concert appearances. *Recordings:* Lohengrin, Wozzeck, Don Giovanni, Ariadne auf Naxos, Die Lustigen Weiber von Windsor, Karl V by Krenek, Video of Wozzeck (as First Workman, conducted by Abbado).

STAAHLEN, Torhild; Norwegian singer (mezzo-soprano); b. 25 Sept. 1947, Skien; m. Neil Dodd 1975. *Education:* Music Conservatory, Oslo, Nat. Opera School. *Career:* debut in Oslo, as Suzuki in Madama Butterfly 1971; has sung 65 roles from the mezzo-alto repertoire, including the title role in Carmen, Octavian in Der Rosenkavalier, Azucena in Il Trovatore, Ulrica in Un Ballo in Maschera, Amneris in Aida, Erda in Das Rheingold, Waltraute in Götterdämmerung, La Principezza in Suor Angelica, Olga in Eugene Onegin, Prince Orlovsky in Die Fledermaus, and Valencienne in The Merry Widow; character roles include Heriodas in Salome, Marcellina in The Marriage of Figaro, La Vecchia Madelon in Andrea Chenier, and The Secretary in Jeppe by Geir Tveitt; frequent radio and television broadcasts; sings many oratorios, including the Bach Passions and Handel's Messiah; concert repertoire includes Brahms' Alto Rhapsody, Wagner's Wesendonck Lieder, Beethoven's Ninth Symphony, Mahler's Second and Fourth Symphonies, Elgar's Sea Pictures, Heise's Bergljot, Handel's Samson, and Pergolesi's Stabat Mater; guested in Sweden, Denmark, Finland, Germany, England, Scotland and the USA; has sung under conductors, including Heinrich Hollreiser, Paavo Berglund, Maurice Handford, Heinz Fricke, Antonio Pappano, Michael Schönwandt, Silvio Varviso, Erich Wächter and Berislav Klobuchar; inaugurated Torhild Staahlen Prize for Singers, Musicians and Composers 1991; mem. Norsk Musikerforbund, Norsk Operasangerforbund. *Recording:* Expression 1991. *Honours:* Fund for Performing Artists State Artist's Stipendium, Friends of Music in Telemark Prize of Honour 1981, City of Oslo Cultural Stipendium, Vel Medal. *Address:* Breidablikkveien 24, 1167 Oslo, Norway.

STAAR, René; Austrian composer and violinist; b. 30 May 1951, Graz. *Education:* Sibelius Acad., Helsinki, Vienna Hochschule für Musik with Hans Swarowsky and Roman Haubenstock-Ramati, studied with Nathan Milstein in Zürich. *Career:* co-founder, Ensemble Wiener Coll. 1986; mem., Vienna Philharmonic Orchestra from 1988; Dir, Graz-Petersburg Ensemble 1993; founder, Ensemble Wien-Paris 1996. *Compositions:* Structures I–VI for various ensembles 1981–82, Just an Accident (requiem) 1985, Das Wachsende Schloss for violin and orchestra 1986, Bagatellen auf den Namen György Ligeti for piano 1989–96, Metamorphosen eines labyrinths for violin and strings 1991, Versunkene Träume for string quartet 1993, Metropolitan Midnight Music 1993, Heine Fragments for soprano, baritone and ensemble 1997, Monumentum pro Thomas Alva Edison for violin, guitar and double bass 1998.

STABELL, Carsten; Norwegian singer (bass); b. 5 Sept. 1960, Trondheim. *Education:* Norwegian Opera School, Oslo. *Career:* debut in Oslo 1984 as the

King in Aida; sang at Stuttgart Opera from 1986 as Osmin, Sarastro, the Commendatore, Pietro in Simon Boccanegra and the Hermit in Der Freischütz; Sang Rustomji in Philip Glass's Satyagraha in 1990; Concert repertoire includes Bach's Magnificat and St John Passion, Messiah, Judas Maccabaeus, Acis and Galatea, Die Schöpfung, the Requiems of Mozart and Verdi and Liszt's Christus; Engaged as the Commendatore at Opera Geneva and Sarastro at the Opéra de Paris Bastille in 1991, and in Perseo e Andromeda by Sciarrino at La Scala Milan in 1992; Season 1998 with Oroveso in Norma at Philadelphia and Fafner in Siegfried for Netherlands Opera; Sang Fasolt at Edinburgh, Daland in Ghent, King Marke for Houston Opera and Banquo at the Vienna Staatsoper, 2000–01. *Current Management:* c/o Ann Braathen Artist Management, Folkskolegatan 5, 11735 Stockholm, Sweden. *Telephone:* (8) 55690850. *Fax:* (8) 55690851. *E-mail:* info@braathenmanagement.com. *Website:* www.braathenmanagement.com.

STABLER, Gerhard; German composer; b. 20 July 1949, Wilhelmsdorf. *Education:* Detmold Music Acad., Essen Hochschule with Nicolaus Huber and Gerd Zacher, studied with Stockhausen, Kagel and Ligeti at Cologne and Darmstadt. *Career:* Stanford Univ. computer music centre 1983, 1986; Fellowship in Composition, Heinrich-Strobel-Stiftung 1985–86; Niederdachsen Scholarship 1987–88; faculty mem., Essen Hochschule 1989–94; Japan Foundation Scholarship 1994; concerts, lecture tours and guest professorships in Europe, Asia and North and South America from 1985. *Compositions include:* Drüber for eight screamers, cello and tape 1972, Das Sichere ist nicht sicher (spiral rondo) for eight instruments and tape 1982, Schatten Wilder Schmerzen for orchestra 1985, Warnung mit Liebeslied for harp, accordion and percussion 1986, ...strike the ear... for string quartet 1988, October for flute, violin and double bass 1988, Den Müllfahren von San Francisco for 17 instruments 1990, Ungaretti Lieder for mezzo or baritone and percussion 1990, Sünde, Fall, Beil (opera after Catherine Howard by Dumas) 1992, Traum 1/9/92 for soprano saxophone, cello, piano and ensemble 1992, Cassandra Complex (music theatre) 1994, (Apparat) for chorus, clarinet, accordion, double bass and percussion 1994, Karas Krähen for tape 1994, Winter, Blumen for countertenor, or solo string instruments 1995, Internet (various works for solo instruments or chamber music ensembles) 1995–98, Spuren for saxophone quartet 1995, Dalí for piano solo 1996, Poetic Arcs for ensemble 1996, Cassandra (music for dance) 1996, Burning Minds for 12 voices 1997, Bridges for mezzo and accordion 1997, Ausnahme Zustand for orchestra 1998, Time for Tomorrow (music theatre) for voice, percussion and tape 1998, Metal Seasons for violin solo, brass ensemble, percussion and aeroplanes 1999. *Honours:* Cornelius Cardew Memorial Prize, London 1982.

STACY, Thomas; American oboist and English hornist; b. 15 Aug. 1938, Little Rock, AR. *Education:* Eastman School of Music, Univ. of Rochester, NY. *Career:* solo English horn, New Orleans Symphony Orchestra 1960–61, San Antonio Symphony Orchestra 1961–62, Minneapolis Symphony Orchestra 1962–72, New York Philharmonic Orchestra 1972–2010 (retd); guest engagements with leading orchestras throughout USA; commisioned and premiered works by Stanislav Skrowaczewski, Gunther Schuller, Ned Rorem and Vincent Persichetti; teacher, Juilliard School, NY 1973–, Mannes Coll. of Music 1998–, Manhattan School of Music 2008–; has given masterclasses at the Royal Acad., London and throughout Asia; Dir, Stacy English Horn Seminar. *Recordings include:* Copland: Symphony No. 3/ Quiet City 1990, Rorem, Persichetti, Hodkinson: Three Concerti 1995, New York Legends 1995, Skrowaczewski Concerto for English Horn and Orchestra 1997, Plaintive Melody 2003, Fuchs: An American Place, Eventide, Out of the Dark 2005, Oboe D'Amore Concertos 2008. *Address:* Manhattan School of Music, 120 Claremont Avenue, New York, NY 10027, USA (office). *E-mail:* tom@thomasstacy.com (office). *Website:* www.thomasstacy.com.

STADELMANN, Christian; German violinist; b. 1958, Berlin. *Education:* studied with Charlotte Hampe and Thomas Brandis in Berlin. *Career:* fmr mem., Junge Deutsche Philharmonie, co-founder of its chamber orchestra; mem., Berlin Philharmonic 1985, leader of the second violins 1987; second violinist, Philharmonia Quartet, Berlin 1986; many concerts with the quartet in Europe and regular tours to the USA, Japan and South America. *Recordings include:* quartets by Reger, Beethoven, Shostakovich, Szymanowski, Janáček. *E-mail:* chr.stadel@googlemail.com.

STADLER, Irmgard; Austrian singer (soprano); b. 28 March 1937, Michaelbeuern, Salzburg. *Education:* Salzburg Mozarteum, Vienna Acad. of Music. *Career:* debut in Stuttgart 1962, as Micaela; Salzburg Festival 1961–62, in Idomeneo, Mozart's Requiem 1962–63; Glyndebourne Festival 1967–72 as Sicle in L'Ormindo, Donna Elvira, Juno in La Calisto and the Composer in Ariadne auf Naxos; mem. Stuttgart Opera from 1963; guest appearances in Vienna, Munich, Berlin, Lisbon, Venice and Rome; most important roles include Elvira, Cherubino, Fiordiligi, Elektra (Idomeneo), Octavian and Marschallin, Eva, Gutrune, Alice, Agathe, Marenka (Bartered Bride), Rusalka, Jenůfa, Katya Kabanova, Lisa (Queen of Spades), Tatiana, Marina and Marie in Wozzeck; concert appearances in sacred music by Bach, Mozart, Bruckner and lieder recitals; sang Theresa in the premiere of Giuseppe & Sylvia by Adriana Hölszky, Stuttgart 2000. *Honours:* Kammersänger 1970; Hon. mem. State Opera of Stuttgart 2003–. *Address:* Payerstr. 10, 70184 Stuttgart, Germany (home).

STADLMAIR, Hans; Austrian conductor; b. 3 May 1929, Neuhofen. *Education:* Vienna Acad. of Music with Clemens Krauss and Alfred Uhl, studied with Johann Nepomuk David in Stuttgart. *Career:* Conductor, Stuttgart

Chorus; Conductor, Munich Chamber Orchestra 1956; tours of Europe, North and South America, Asia, Africa, Canada and India; conducted own realisation of the Adagio from Mahler's 10th Symphony. *Compositions:* Concerto Profano for violin, cello and orchestra, Concerto Capriccioso for two flutes and orchestra, Adagietto for strings, Ecce Homo, five Novelletten for strings, Sinfonia 'Da Pacem Domine' für alphorn, röhrenglocken and strings 1988, Lacrimae Metamorphosen for strings, Essay for clarinet and strings. *Recordings:* W. A. Mozart, Piano Concertos Nr 8 KV246, Lützow and Nr 9 KV271, Jeunehomme; F. Danzi: Phantasie on La ci darem la mano from Don Giovanni, K. Stamitz; Concerto for Clarinet Nr 3 B flat (E. Brunner–Clarinet); Haydn's Seven Last Words; Scarlatti Il Giardino di Amore; Mozart Bassoon Concerto, Clarinet Concerto and Violin Concerto K219; Vivaldi Four Seasons; Koch-Schwann: Hans Stadlmair. *Honours:* Medaille: München Leuchtet 1989, Bundesverdienstkreuz am Bande 1989, Musikpreis der Stadt München 1994.

STADLMAIR, Vincent; Austrian cellist; b. 1959, Vienna. *Education:* Vienna Acad. of Music. *Career:* mem. of the Franz Schubert Quartet, Vienna 1983–95; Prof. of Chamber Music, Hochschule für Musik, Graz 1985–92; teacher, Vienna Acad. of Music 1995–99; mem. Mozarteum Orchestra, Salzburg 1997–99; Principal Cellist, Ålborg Symfoniorkester 2000–; also mem. Mira-Quartet; many concert engagements in Europe, USA, and Australia including appearances at the Amsterdam Concertgebouw, the Vienna Musikverein and Konzerthaus, the Salle Gaveau Paris and the Sydney Opera House; visits to Zürich, Geneva, Basle, Berlin, Hamburg, Rome, Rotterdam, Madrid and Copenhagen; festival engagements include Salzburg, Wiener Festwochen, Prague, Spring Schubertiade at Hohenems, the Schubert Festival at Washington, DC and the Belfast and Istanbul Festivals; tours of Australasia, Russia and USA; frequent concert tours of the UK; featured in the Quartet Concerto by Spohr with the Liverpool Philharmonic in Liverpool at the Festival Hall; many appearances at the Wigmore Hall and Cheltenham Festival; teacher at the Vienna Conservatory and Graz Musikhochschule; masterclasses at the Royal Northern Coll. of Music, Lake District Summer Music. *Recordings include:* Schubert's Quartet in G, D887, Complete Quartets of Dittersdorf, Mozart's String Quartet in D, K575, and String Quartet in B flat, K589. *Address:* Ålborg Symphony Orchestra, Kjellerupsgade 14, 9000 Ålborg, Denmark (office). *Telephone:* 98-13-19-55 (office). *E-mail:* info@aalborgsymfoni.dk (office). *Website:* aalborgsymfoni.dk (office).

STAEHELIN, Martin, DipEd, DipMus, PhD; Swiss musicologist; b. 25 Sept. 1937, Basel; m. Elisabeth Schenker; three c. *Education:* Music Acad., Basel, Univ. of Basel. *Career:* teacher of Latin, Greek and music, Basel 1963; musicology teacher, Univ. of Zürich 1971–76; Head of Beethoven Archives, Bonn, Germany 1976–84; teacher, Univ. of Bonn 1976–77, Prof. 1977–83; Prof., Univ. of Göttingen 1983–2002, Emeritus Prof. 2002–; Hon. Dir of J. S. Bach Institut, Göttingen 1992–2006; mem. Akad. der Wissenschaften, Göttingen 1987–; Corresp. mem. American Musicological Soc. 2012. *Publications:* H. Isaac, Messen (ed.) 1970, 1973, Der Grüne Codex der Viadrina 1971, Die Messen Heinrich Isaacs (three vols) 1977, H.G. Nägeli u. L. van Beethoven 1982, Musikalischer Lustgarten (with U. Konrad and A. Roth) 1985, Allzeit ein buch. Die Bibliothek W.A. Mozarts (with U. Konrad) 1991, J. Obrecht Collected Works 1994, Die Mittelalterliche Musik-Handschrift W1 1995, Gestalt und Entstehung musikalischer Quellen im 15. u. 16. Jh 1998, Der Basler Schultheiss E. Wolleb und seine satirische Schrift "Die Reise nach dem Concerte" 1999, Neues zu Werk und Leben von P. Wilhelmi 2001, Kleinüberlieferung mehrstimmiger Musik vor 1550 in deutschem Sprachgebiet, Lieferung IX: Neue Quellen des Spätmittelalters aus Deutschland und der Schweiz 2012, Ist die sogenamte Mozartische Bläserkonzertante KV 297b echt? 2013; contrib. to Archiv für Musikwissenschaft; Die Musikforschung; Fontes Artis Musicae; Schweizer Beiträge zur Musikwissenschaft; Tijdschrift van de Vereniging voor Nederlandse Muziekgeschiedenis; Schweizerisches Archiv für Volkskunde, Acta Organologica, Augsburger Jahrbuch für Musikwissenschaft, Nachrichten/Abhandlungen der Akademie der Wissenschaften zu Göttingen, Hist-Phil. Kl, Neues Musikwissenschaftliches Jahrbuch. *Honours:* Dr hc (Münster) 2011; Dent Medal, Royal Musical Asscn 1975, Glarean-Preis, Swiss Musicological Soc. 2009. *Address:* c/o Musicology Seminar of Georg August University, Kurze Geismarstrasse 1, 37073 Göttingen, Germany (office).

STAFFORD, Ashley George, BA, MA; British singer (countertenor); b. 3 March 1954, Holland, near Oxted, Surrey, England; m. Shauni Lee McGregor 1977; two s. *Education:* Westminster Abbey Choir School, Trinity School Croydon, Christchurch Coll., Oxford with Simon Preston, studied with Douglas Guest, Hervey Alan, Paul Esswood, Helga Mott, Jessica Cash. *Career:* debut, Purcell Room 1975; sang in opera at Aix-en-Provence, Lyon, Oxford and London and in concert at major festivals throughout Europe, in Sydney and Melbourne, Japan, Taiwan, USA and Canada including Bath, Edinburgh, Three Choirs, Berlin, Rome, Venice, Madrid, Barcelona, Lisbon, New York, Boston and Ottawa; many appearances on radio and on television including Messiah in France; Visiting Professor of Voice at Royal College of Music, London 1989; mem, Incorporated Soc. of Musicians, Equity; cttee mem., Royal Soc. of Musicians. *Recordings include:* Purcell's Ode to St Cecilia, King Arthur, From the Nativity of Time (Songs sacred and secular), Handel's Israel in Egypt, Dettingen Te Deum, Valls's Mass Scala Aretina, Motets by Bach, Power, Dunstable and Josquin, Haydn's Nelson Mass, Scarlatti's Stabat Mater, Schütz's Muzikalisches Exequien, Handel's Alexander's Feast. *Honours:* Young Musician, Greater London Arts Asscn.

STAHLHAMMER, Semmy, DipMus, BMus; Swedish violinist; b. 5 March 1954, Eskilstuna. *Education:* Royal Music Coll., Stockholm, Juilliard School of Music, USA, Curtis Inst. of Music, studied with Jaime Laredo, Ivan Galamian, Felx Galimir, Isidore Cohen, Szymon Goldberg, Paul Makanowitsky, Josef Silverstein, Josef Gingold, Nathan Milstein, Isaac Stern and Henryk Szeryng. *Career:* debut with Stockholm Philharmonic Orchestra 1964; First Concertmaster, Stockholm Royal Opera 1979–83; Artistic Dir, Chamber Music in The Mirror Hall 1982–; Artistic Dir, Chamber Music in the Parks 1986–; teacher at Stockholm Royal Music Coll. 1987–. *Recordings:* Collections of Swedish 20th-century music, Alfred Schnittke's Labyrinths, J.S. Bach's Sonatas and Partitas for Solo Violin. *Honours:* winner J.S. Bach Int. Violin Competition, Washington, DC 1985.

STAHMER, Klaus Hinrich, PhD; German composer; b. 25 June 1941, Szczecin, Stettin, Poland. *Education:* Hamburg Musikhochschule, Kiel Univ. *Career:* Lecturer, Würzburg Hochschule für Musik 1969–79, Prof. 1979–2004; Dir Tage der Neuen Musik 1972–2000; Dir Würzburg New Music Studio 1989–2000. *Compositions include:* Threnos in memoriam Paul Hindemith 1963, Rotations 1963, Zwei kleine Spruchmotetten 1964, Sonatine 1964, Dedications 1964, Vier Transformationen 1972, Tiere wie du und ich 1973, 15 Duette 1973, Quasi un requiem for speaker and string quartet 1974, Patterns 1974, Mobile Aktionen 1975, I Can Fly 1975, Musik für Mallets 1976, Tre paesaggi 1976, Rapsodia piccola 1976, Espace de la solitude (ballet) 1977, Multiples 1977, Parole ultime 1978, Die Landschaft in meiner Stimme 1978, Marsiada 1978, Paysages visionaires 1979, Flutist's Landscape 1979, Vocal Landscape 1979, Pages for four 1979, Aristofaniada 1979, Parisiada 1979, La voce del fiume 1980, Lieblose Psalmen 1980, Canti della vita 1980, Now 1980, Flippermusic 1980, Wintermärchen 1981, Odysseia 1981, König Wiedehopf 1981, Davids Lobgesang 1982, Die Nashörner 1983, Soundscape (sound sculptures) 1985, Momentaufnahmen for speaker and ensemble 1986–89, Musik der Stille for piano 1994–98, Noa, Noa for ensemble 1996, Sacred Site for piano 1996, Em-bith-kâ for string quartet 1998, People Out of Nowhere 2000, Mazewot 2001, The Way Lost 2003, Silence is the Only Music 2003, Redland 2005, Épitaphe 2006, Zansetsu 2006, Jing Zhan I 2007, Feng Yu 2007, Jing Zhan III 2008, Flüchtige Augenblicke 2008, Zikkrayat 2009, Gesänge eines Holzsammlers I and II 2009, One Stops searching, one grows silent 2009. *Honours:* Würzburg Arts Prize 1995, Händel Prize 1999. *Address:* c/o GEMA, Rozenheimerstr 11, 8166 Munich, Germany (office). *E-mail:* kontakt@khstahmer.de (office). *Website:* www.khstahmer.de.

STAICU, Paul, DipMus; conductor, academic and horn player; b. 7 June 1937, Bucharest, Romania; m. Irina Botez 1963; one s. *Education:* Prague Acad. of Music, Vienna Acad. of Music with Hans Swarowsky. *Career:* debut as horn soloist 1954, as conductor 1963, Bucharest Radio and Philharmonic Orchestra; Horn Soloist 1954–79; Solo Horn, Bucharest Philharmonic 1961–69; Chief Conductor, Chamber Orchestra 1966; Prof. of Chamber Music 1966–; Camerata 1978; H. von Karajan Foundation, Medal with Camerata Orchestra 1974; Prof. of Horn, Bucharest Music Acad. 1969–89, Chief Conductor of Symphony Orchestra 1975–78; Chief Conductor, Symphony and Chamber Orchestra, Constanta Romania 1978–79; Prof., Conservatoire of Music, Montbeliard, France 1990; Dir, School of Music, Exincourt, France 1990; Chief Conductor, Ensemble Orchestral Montbeliard, France 1992; television and radio performances in Romania and abroad; summer classes at Bayreuth, Gourdon, Europe, USA and Canada tours; mem. Munich and Prague Int. Music Competitions. *Recordings:* No. 3, Beethoven Horn Sonata; Mozart and Beethoven Quintets; Mozart's Horn Concertos as Soloist and Conductor; Haydn Concertos as Conductor; Haydn Symphonies 100–103 as Conductor; radio: Beethoven Symphony No. 4, Schoenberg Verklärte Nacht and Shostakovich's Symphony No. 14. *Publication:* Studiu introductiv si exercitii zilnice pentru corn (Introductory studies and daily exercises for horn).

STAIER, Andreas; German harpsichordist and pianist. *Education:* studied in Göttingen, Hannover and Amsterdam. *Career:* harpsichordist, Musica Antiqua, Köln 1983–86; Prof., Schola Cantorum, Basel, Switzerland 1987–96; performances with Concerto Köln, Freiburger Barockorchester, Akademie für alte Musik, Berlin, Orchestre des Champs-Elysées, Paris; festival appearances include Festival de La Roque d'Anthéron, Festival de Saintes, Festival de Montreux, Edinburgh Int. Festival, Styriarte Graz, Schubertiade Schwarzenberg, Schleswig-Holstein Musik Festival, Bach-Fest Leipzig, Bachtage Berlin, Bachwoche Ansbach and Kissinger Sommer; performances at Konzerthaus Vienna, Philharmonie Berlin, Kölner Philharmonie, Gewandhaus Leipzig, Alte Oper Frankfurt, Tonhalle Düsseldorf, Wigmore Hall and Royal Festival Hall, London, De Singel, Antwerp, Concertgebouw Amsterdam, Palais des Beaux Arts, Brussels, Tonhalle Zürich, Théâtre des Bouffes du Nord, IRCAM, Théâtre des Champs Elysées, Paris, Teatro della Pergola, Florence, Sala Filarmonica Rome, Toppan Hall, Suntory Hall, Tokyo, Carnegie Hall, New York; collaborations with Anne Sophie von Otter, Pedro Memelsdorff and Alexej Lubimov, Christoph Prégardien, Daniel Sepec, Jean-Guihen Queyras. *Recordings:* Haydn Piano Sonatas, J. S. Bach Harpsichord Works, C.P.E. Bach Harpsichord Works, Chamber Music, Lieder, D. Scarlatti, L. Dussek, Schubert and Schumann, piano solo works, concertos and lieder; Mozart Piano Sonatas, Beethoven Piano Trios, Schumann piano works, violin and piano works, Bach Goldberg Variations, CPE Bach Harpsichord Concertos (Gramophone Award for Baroque Instrumental Recording 2011), ...pour passer la mélancolie (Gramophone Award for Baroque Instrumental Recording 2013). *Honours:* Int. Classical Music Awards Artist of the Year 2014. *Current Management:* c/o Andreca Butucariu, European Artistic Services,

Hessischestrasse 6, 10115 Berlin, Germany. *Address:* Franzstr 19, 50931 Cologne, Germany (home). *Website:* www.andreas-staier.de.

STALDER, Hans Rudolf; Swiss clarinettist and musician; b. 9 July 1930, Zürich; m. Ursula Burkhard 1957. *Education:* Konservatorium, Zürich, Bayerische Staatskonservatorium, Würzburg, Germany, and studied with Louis Cahuzac in Paris. *Career:* int. soloist on clarinet, Bassethorn and Chalumeau, also with chamber music groups, including Stalder Quintet, Zürich Chamber Ensemble, Zürich Clarinet Trio; teacher, Musik Akademie, Basle and Schola Cantorum Basiliensis; mem. Schweizerischer Tonkunstler-verein. *Recordings include:* first recording of Mozart Clarinet Concerto in original version with bassetclarinet 1968, Bassethorn Concerto from A. Rolla, Das Chalumeau ein Portrait. *Address:* Wengi 2, 8126 Zumikon, Switzerland (home).

STALLMAN, Robert, BMus, MMus; American flautist, editor, arranger and teacher; b. (Robert Wooster Stallman, Jr), 12 June 1946, Boston, Mass; s. of R. W. Stallman and Virginia Blume Stallman; m. Hannah Woods 1981. *Education:* New England Conservatory of Music and Paris Conservatoire, France; studied with Jean-Pierre Rampal, Alain Marion, G. Crunelle, J. Pappoutsakis. *Career:* notable solo appearances include Library of Congress, Washington, DC, Carnegie Hall, Weill Hall, Avery Fisher Hall, New York, Symphony Hall, Boston, Salle Pleyel, Paris, Suntory Hall, Tokyo, Wigmore Hall, London, Martinů Hall, Prague, Vienna Konzerthaus; radio and TV broadcasts nationwide and abroad; guest artist appearances include American Symphony, Mostly Mozart Festival, Netherlands Chamber Orchestra and Suk Chamber Orchestras, Royal Philharmonic Orchestra, No. Sinfonia, Czech Chamber Orchestra, Odessa Philharmonic, Lincoln Center Chamber Music Soc., Chamber Orchestra of Philadelphia, Speculum Musicae, Alexander, Artis, St Lawrence, Muir, Mendelssohn, Martinů, Orion and Vlach String Quartets; festivals in Brazil, Canada, Czech Repub., Finland, France, Greece, Netherlands, Spain, China, Japan, USA; Founder and Artistic Dir Cambridge Chamber Players and Marblehead Music Festival 1976–96; composers for whom he has premiered works include Elliott Carter, Richard Danielpour, Stephen Dodgson, Robert Helps, John Harbison, Lee Hoiby, Karel Hurnik, Karel Husa, Ondrej Kukal, William T. McKinley; faculty mem. Aaron Copland School of Music, Queen's Coll., New York 1980–, Acad. Internationale d'Eté, Nice, France 1985, Boston Conservatory 1986–90, Domaine Forget, Quebec, Canada, New England Conservatory 1978–82; masterclasses in USA, Canada, Brazil, Mexico, England, France, Germany, Czech Repub., Japan, Ukraine, China; ed. of flute repertoire, International Music Co., New York 1984–, G. Schirmer, New York 1996–, Kalmus, USA 2005–, Ludwig Masters, USA 2005–, Doblinger Verlag, Vienna 2006–; Co-founder, Artistic Dir and artist, Bogner's Café Recordings 2006–. *Radio:* NPR Performance Today and Weekend Edition 2007. *Recordings include:* Mozart, New Quintets for Flute and Strings, New Schubert Works for Flute and Strings, Incantations (20th century solo flute works), Blavet Sonatas, Handel Sonatas, Leclair Sonatas, Bach Sonatas, The American Flute, Mozart Sonatas, Schubert Sonatas, Telemann Concerti, Vivaldi Concerti, Dodgson Concerto with the Northern Sinfonia, McKinley Concerto with the Prism Orchestra, The Nightingale in Love (Flute Music of the French Baroque). *Publications include:* Flute Workout: 14 Melodic Exercises for Technical Mastery; 70 publs include growing list of Mozart-Stallman and Schubert-Stallman arrangements for flute and strings. *Honours:* Fulbright grant, Paris 1968–69; Chadwick Medal, New England Conservatory 1968, Koussevitsky Fellowship, Tanglewood 1971, C. D. Jackson Prize, Tanglewood 1971, Nat. Endowment Solo Recitalist Award 1983, Arcadia Foundation grant 1994. *Address:* Bogner's Café, 1530 Locust Street, Suite 11-A, Philadelphia, PA 19102-4426, USA (office). *Telephone:* (215) 893-9443 (office); (215) 893-9030 (home). *E-mail:* robert@bognerscafe.com (office); info@bognerscafe.com (office). *Website:* AboutRobertStallman.com (office).

STAMENOVA, Galina, violinist; b. 5 Oct. 1958, Sofia, Bulgaria. *Education:* studied with her mother and Juilliard School of Music, New York with Dorothy DeLay. *Career:* debut with André Previn and London Symphony Orchestra at Royal Festival Hall; American debut with Dallas Symphony 1984; performances with most leading British orchestras, Antwerp Philharmonic and orchestras in Bulgaria; radio and television broadcasts in Bulgaria, The Netherlands, the UK and Belgium; accomplished recitalist, having appeared at Harrogate and Aspen Music Festivals, live on BBC and Radio VARA in the Netherlands and several other European countries. *Recordings:* Saint-Saëns No. 3, Chausson-Poème, Sofia Radio Orchestra with Vassil Stefanov conducting. *Honours:* several first prizes for young violinists.

STAMM, Harald; German singer (bass); b. 29 April 1938, Frankfurt am Main. *Education:* studied with Franz Fehringer. *Career:* debut at Gelsen-kirchen 1968; sang at Cologne and Frankfurt, Hamburg Staatsoper 1975, in the premiere of Der Gestiefelte Kater by Bialas; many appearances in German opera houses and in Budapest Venice, Rome and Nice; Metropolitan Opera from 1979; Salzburg Festival 1985, in the Henze version of Monteverdi's Ulisse; Bregenz Festival 1986, as Sarastro in Die Zauberflöte; other roles include Mozart's Commendatore, Beethoven's Rocco, Verdi's Grand Inquisitor and Zaccaria, Wagner's Daland, Marke, Fasolt and Hunding and Massenet's Don Quixote; Covent Garden debut 1987 as Raimondo in Lucia di Lammermoor; sang the King in Schreker's Der Schatzgräber at Hamburg 1989, King Henry in Lohengrin at Brussels and Lisbon 1990; season 1992 as Gurnemanz at Eseen; King Henry in Lohengrin at Hamburg 1998; Hamburg State Opera 1999–2000, as Arkel in Pelléas and Wagner's Landgrave; also heard in recital and concert; Prof., Hochschule der Künste, Berlin 1993. *Recordings:* Lieder by Liszt and Franz, Vier Ernste Gesänge by Brahms, Dittersdorf's Doktor und Apotheker, Schumann's Manfred, Massimila Doni by Schoeck. *Honours:* Kammersänger, Hamburg Opera 1989.

STANDAGE, Simon Andrew Thomas, MA; British violinist and conductor; *Musical Director, Collegium Musicum 90*; b. 8 Nov. 1941, High Wycombe, Bucks., England; s. of Thomas Ralph Standage and Henrietta Florence Standage (née Sugg); m. Jennifer Ward 1964; three s. *Education:* studied in Cambridge and with Ivan Galamian in New York. *Career:* Assoc. mem. London Symphony Orchestra and sub-leader of the English Chamber Orchestra; Founder-mem. and soloist, English Concert 1973; Leader, Richard Hickox Orchestra and City of London Sinfonia; Founder Salomon String Quartet 1981, giving performances of Classical repertoire on period instruments; Prof. of Baroque Violin, RAM, London 1983–; Founder and Musical Dir Collegium Musicum 90 1990–; Assoc. Dir Academy of Ancient Music 1991–95; Prof. of Baroque Violin, Dresdner Akad. für Alte Musik 1993–2004, Franz Liszt Acad., Budapest 2011–. *Recordings:* Vivaldi Op. 8 (including Four Seasons), Op. 3 (L'Estro Armonico), Op. 4 (La Stravaganza), Op. 9 (La Cetra), J.S. Bach Violin Concertos, Leclair complete concertos, Mozart and Haydn complete violin concertos, Mozart mature string quartets and quintets, Haydn quartets Opp. 17, 20, 33, 42, 50, 54/55, 64, 71/74, 77 and 103. *Publication:* Historical Awareness in Quartet Performance (in Cambridge Companion to the String Quartet). *Honours:* Hon. mem. RAM; Medal for Services to Polish Culture, Georg-Philipp-Telemann Preis 2010. *Address:* 106 Hervey Road, London, SE3 8BX, England. *E-mail:* standages@pobox.com.

STANHOPE, David; composer, conductor and horn player; b. 19 Dec. 1952, Sutton Coldfield, England. *Education:* studied in Melbourne, Australia. *Career:* moved to Australia 1958; Second Horn, Australian Symphony Orchestra 1970; Conductor, Australian Opera 1986–, conducted Berg's Lulu 1994, The Turn of the Screw 2005. *Compositions include:* Quintet No. 3 for brass quintet 1983, The Australian Fanfare for nine trumpets in three choirs 1983, Four Concert Studies for four trombones 1985, Felix Randall for high voice and piano 1986, Concerto for band 1988, Droylsden Wakes for wind or brass band 1990, Folksongs for band 1990–91, Endpiece for orchestra 1991, Three Poems for soprano and string orchestra, String Songs, Three Folksongs for brass quintet. *Honours:* prizewinner Int. Horn Soc. Composition Contest 1979. *Address:* c/o APRA, 1A Eden Street, Crows Nest, NSW 2065, Australia.

STANHOPE, Paul Thomas, BA, MA; Australian composer; b. 25 Nov. 1969, Wollongong, NSW. *Education:* Univ. of Sydney, Univ. of Wollongong, studied with Peter Sculthorpe. *Career:* faculty mem., Univ. of Wollongong 1994–95, Univ. of Sydney 1995–. *Compositions include:* Liquid Marimba for tape 1991, Morning Star for string quartet 1992, Missa Brevis for chorus 1992, The Taste of Midnight for flute, piano and clarinet 1993, Morning Star II and III for ensemble 1993, Kandeyala for orchestra 1994, Satz for mandolin quartet 1994, Rin for tape 1994, Snap for clarinet 1994, Geography Songs for chorus 1994–95, No More than Movement... or Stillness for tape 1995, Kraftwerk Overture for string orchestra 1995, Rain Dance for violin, two violas and cello 1995, Stars Sounding for orchestra 1996. *Honours:* Australian Voices Festival Young Composers Award 1995.

STANKOV, Angel Mirchov, MBE; Bulgarian violinist, conductor, college principal and academic; *Professor of Violin and Chamber Music, Bulgarian State Academy of Music*; b. 28 April 1948, Sofia; m. Meglena Stankova; one d. *Education:* State High School, Bulgarian State Music Acad., Sofia, studied in London with Prof. Parikian of the Royal Acad. of Music. *Career:* debut with Pleven Philharmonic Orchestra, Beethoven Concerto 1970; regular appearances with Sofia Phiharmonic Orchestra and foreign orchestras; broadcasts on Bulgarian radio and TV; Concert Master, Sofia Philharmonic 1981–2000; live recital, Hague Radio 1991; North France and Soviet TV appearances 1991; foreign tours to almost all European countries and Cuba; int. music festivals, including Llandaff (UK) 1975, Brno (fmr Czechoslovakia) 1989, Warsaw, Bydgoscz and Crete (Greece) 1983; currently Prof. of Violin and Chamber Music, Bulgarian State Acad. of Music, Vice-Rector (Prin.) 1999; performer as soloist; mem. of violin duo with Josif Radionov); conducted entire Beethoven Symphonies Cycle 1999–2000; Conductor 10th Anniversary of British Council, Sofia Concert 2001; First Violin, Sofia Quartet 2002; teacher for one term, North Carolina School of the Arts 2003; recitals in the USA 2003; master classes at Franz Liszt Hochschule, Weimar Univ., Univ. of Las Vegas 2005, ISA Semmering and Nis Univ.; conducted concert dedicated to 125 years of diplomatic relations between Bulgaria and GB 2005; Pres. of jury, Nedyalka Simeonova and Vasko Abadjiev competitions, Bulgaria; mem. of jury, Int. Competition, Kloster Schoenthal, Germany 2005, Maria Judina, St Petersburg, Russia 2006, Carl Flesch, Hungary; conducted first Carl Nielsen concert in Bulgaria. *Honours:* Hon. MBE 2009; Crystal Lyra of Bulgarian Union of Musicians, First Prize and Gold Medal, First Int. Chamber Music Festa, Osaka 1993, Zolotaya Murza for performances of Russian music 2006, Hon. Medal, Bulgarian Acad. of Music 2008, Sladkopoina Chuchuliga Award, Pazardjik. *Address:* 58 William Gladstone Street, 1000 Sofia, Bulgaria (home). *Telephone:* 9812689 (home). *Fax:* 9812689 (home).

STANKOVYCH, Yevhen Fedorovych; Ukrainian composer; b. 19 Sept. 1942, Svaliava. *Education:* Kiev Conservatory. *Career:* works performed throughout Russia and in USA and Asia; composer-in-residence at Berne 1996. *Compositions:* Prometheus, ballet 1985, Five Symphonies 1973, 1975, 1976, 1977, 1980, String Quartet 1973, Dictum, for ensemble 1987, Black

Elegy for chorus and orchestra 1991, Kaddish-Requiem for tenor, bass, chorus and orchestra 1991, Music for Heavenly Musicians for woodwind quintet 1993, Requiem for Those Who Died of Famine 1993, Sonata for clarinet 1996, Elegy for string quartet 1997, Ave Maria for orchestra 1997, May Night, and The Night before Christmas, ballets after Gogol. *Address:* c/o RAO, 6a B. Bronnaya, Moscow 103670, Russia.

STANTCHEV, Ognian Nikolov; violist and academic; b. 1937, Sofia, Bulgaria. *Education:* State Acad. of Music, Sofia, Paris Conservatory with Joseph Calvet, Tchaikovsky Conservatory, Moscow, Russia. *Career:* Lecturer, State Acad. of Music, Sofia 1962–81, Asst Prof. 1981–88, Prof. 1988–; First Viola, Sofia Philharmonic Orchestra 1962–66; Violist, Orpheus Quartet 1966–72, Tilev Quartet, Bulgarian Nat. Radio 1972–78; First Viola, Sofia Philharmonic Orchestra 1979–88; Violist, Sofia Quartet, Bulgarian Nat. Radio 1988–93; numerous concerts and many broadcasts of chamber music, especially string quartets; numerous concert tours in Czech Republic, Hungary, Germany, Austria, Poland, France, Italy, England, USA and Greece; holds masterclasses, Summer Acad. Prague-Vienna-Budapest 1997–; jury mem. viola competition in Vienna 1998; mem. Union of Musicians, Bulgaria. *Recordings:* Shostakovich Sonata for viola and piano; Debussy string quartet op 10; Prokofiev string quartet op 50; Four quartets for flute and strings, Mozart; Mozart quartet K 458; Haydn op 76 No. 2; Borodin string quartet No. 1; Sofia String quartet; for Bulgarian radio: Britten, Lachrimae op 48; Hindemith, Meditation. *Honours:* prizewinner int. competitions in Helsinki for stringed instruments 1962, second prize Stringed Quartet Competition, Kolmar, France 1978.

STANZELEIT, Susanne, DipMus; German violinist; b. 1968. *Education:* Folkwang Hochschule in Essen with Leonid Kogan, Guildhall School of Music with Yfrah Neaman, masterclasses with Nathan Milstein, Sándor Végh and György Kurtag at Prussia Cove. *Career:* recitals throughout Germany, Italy, Hungary, Netherlands, Canada, USA and England; concerto appearances with leading orchestras, leader of Werethina Quartet (Haydn, Mendelssohn and Bartók at Purcell Room, 1993) and Prometheus and Ondine Ensembles; Purcell Room Recital, 1993 with Julian Jacobson, playing Strauss, Schubert's C Major Fantasy and Beethoven, op 96; broadcasts with BBC Radio 3, teaching and performing with the Paxos Festival in Greece, Dartington Summer School (1993) and international Bartók Festival in Hungary. *Recordings:* Bartók's music for violin and piano, Delius sonatas for violin and piano, Stanford, Bantock, Dunhill.

STAPP, Olivia; singer (mezzo-soprano); b. 30 May 1940, New York, USA. *Education:* studied with Oren Brown in New York, Ettore Campogalliani and Rodolfo Ricci in Italy. *Career:* debut at Spoleto Festival 1960 in L'Amico Fritz; sang in Vienna, Berlin, Wuppertal, Turin and Basle; sang at Indiana Univ. at Bloomington in the 1971 premiere of Eaton's Heracles; sang at New York City Opera from 1972, notably as Carmen and Norma, Metropolitan Opera from 1982 as Lady Macbeth and Tosca, Paris Opéra 1982, La Scala, Milan 1983–84 as Turandot and Electra in Idomeneo, and Geneva 1985 as Elena in Les Vêpres Siciliennes; other roles include Verdi's Ulrica and Mistress Quickly, Santuzza, Dorabella, Isabella, Rosina, Idalma in Il Matrimonio Segreto and Jocasta in Oedipus Rex; sang Lady Macbeth at Geneva and Venice 1986, Elektra and Abigaille at Frankfurt and Zürich 1988–89, at Paris 1989 in La Noche Triste by Prodomidès, and sang Shostakovich's Katherina at Hamburg 1990. *Recordings include:* Cyrano de Bergerac by Alfano.

STAROBIN, David Nathan, BM; American classical guitarist; b. 27 Sept. 1951, New York, NY; m. Rebecca Patience Askew 1975; one s. one d. *Education:* Peabody Conservatory, studied with Manuel Gayol, Abert Valdes Blain and Aaren Shearer. *Career:* debut at Carnegie Recital Hall, New York 1978; European debut, Wigmore Hall, London 1979; played the premiere performances of over 200 new compositions written for him including solo works, concerti and chamber music; composers who have written for him include Elliott Carter, Charles Wuorinen, Barbara Kolb, David Del Tredici, Tod Machover, Milton Babbitt, Roger Reynolds, Robert Saxton, Mel Powell, Elisabeth Lutyens, Lukas Foss, Poul Ruders, George Crumb and Mario Davidovsky; Member of Speculum Misicae; f. Bridge Records 1981–; mem. music faculty, Manhattan School of Music 1993–, Chair., Guitar Dept 1993–2004; has also taught at Brooklyn Coll., Bennington Coll., North Carolina School of the Arts, State Univ. of New York. *Recordings:* New Music with Guitar, vols 1, 2, 3 and 4, A Song From The East, music from Russia and Hungary, Twentieth Century Music for Voice and Guitar, Newdance. *Publications:* editor: Looking for Claudio 1978, Three Lullabies 1980, Changes 1984, Acrostic Song 1983. *Honours:* AFIM Award Best Solo Classical Album, Newdance 1999, Harvard Univ. Fromm Grant, Avery Fisher Grant, Distinguished Alumni Award, Peabody Conservatory. *Address:* Bridge Records Inc, 200 Clinton Avenue, New Rochelle, NY 10801, USA (office). *Telephone:* (914) 654-9270 (office). *Fax:* (914) 636-1383 (office). *E-mail:* dstarobin@msmnyc.edu (office). *Website:* www.bridgerecords.com (office).

STARYK, Steven S., OC, FRCM; Canadian violinist, concertmaster and academic; *Professor Emeritus, University of Washington, Seattle*; b. 28 April 1932, Toronto, Ont.; m. 1963; one d. *Education:* Royal Conservatory of Music, Toronto, private studies in New York. *Career:* debut in Toronto; Concert Master, Royal Philharmonic, London, Concertgebouw Amsterdam, Chicago Symphony and Toronto Symphony; Prof. of Violin, Amsterdam Conservatory, Oberlin Conservatory, Northwestern Univ., Univ. of Victoria and Acad. of Music, Vancouver; Visiting Prof., Univ. of Ottawa, Univ. of Western Ontario;

Prof., Royal Conservatory of Music, Toronto; Prof., Faculty of Music, Univ. of Toronto; Prof. and Head String Div., Univ. of Washington, Seattle, USA 1987–98, Prof. Emer. 1998–; organizer of Quartet Canada; Leader CBC String Quartet; extensive concert tours, radio and TV broadcasts in N America, Europe and the Far East. *Recordings:* 190 compositions on 45 albums, completed 30-CD anthology 2008. *Publication:* Fiddling with Life (biog., co-author) 2000. *Honours:* Hon. Fellow, Glenn Gould School, Royal Conservatory of Music 2008; Hon. DLitt (York Univ., Toronto) 1980; Canada Council Arts Awards 1967, 1975, Shevchenko Medal 1974, Queen Elizabeth Centennial Award 1978, Univ. of Washington, Seattle Distinguished Teaching Award 1995, Queen Elizabeth II Diamond Jubilee Award 2012. *Telephone:* (416) 932-0159 (office). *Website:* www.starykanthology.ca.

STAUD, Johannes Maria; Austrian composer; b. 1974, Innsbruck. *Education:* in Vienna and Berlin with Michael Jarrell and Hanspeter Kyburz, among others. *Career:* works commissioned, premiered and performed by orchestras including Berlin Philharmonic, Cleveland Orchestra, RSO Wien, Ensemble Modern, Vienna Philharmonic, Arditti Quartet, Bavarian Radio Symphony Orchestra, Scharoun Ensemble, Hugo Wolf Quartet, Tiroler Landestheater Innsbruck/Oper Köln, Lucerne Symphony Orchestra, RSO Wien; Capell-Compositeur, Staatskapelle Dresden 2010–11; Composer-in-Residence, Lucerne Festival 2013–14; works performed at festivals including Schleswig-Holstein 2009, Klangspuren Schwaz 2012, 2013, Salzburg 2013. *Compositions include:* Apeiron 2004–05, On Comparative Meteorology, Contrebande (On Comparative Meteorology II), Segue—Musik für Violoncello und Orchester, Über trügerische Stadtpläne und die Versuchungen der Winternächte (Dichotomie II), Tondo for orchestra, Celluloid for bassoon, Der Riss durch den Tag (monodrama for narrator and ensemble), Maniai for orchestra, Caldera for soprano, clarinet and piano, K'in, Die Antilope (opera). *Honours:* Int. Rostrum of Composers Prize 2003, Ernst von Siemens Composers Prize 2004, Paul Hindemith Prize, Schleswig-Holstein Festival 2009. *Current Management:* c/o Katrin Gann, Karsten Witt Music Management, Leuschnerdamm 13, 10999 Berlin, Germany. *Telephone:* (30) 214594239. *E-mail:* kg@karstenwitt.com. *Website:* en.karstenwitt.com/johannes-maria-staud.

STAUFFER, George Boyer, BA, PhD; American university administrator, musicologist and organist; *Dean, Mason Gross School of the Arts, Rutgers University*; b. 18 Feb. 1947, Hershey, Pa; partner Renee Anne Louprette; one s. *Education:* Dartmouth Coll., Columbia Univ. and studied with John Weaver and Vernon de Tar. *Career:* Dir of Chapel Music and organist, Columbia Univ. 1977–99; Adjunct Asst Prof. of Music, Yeshiva Univ. 1978–79; Asst Prof., later Assoc. Prof., later Prof. of Music, Hunter Coll. and Grad. Center, CUNY 1979–2000; Pres. American Bach Soc. 1996–2000; Dean, Mason Gross School of the Arts, Rutgers Univ., NJ 2000–. *Publications include:* Organ Preludes of J. S. Bach 1980, J. S. Bach as Organist (co-ed.) 1986, The Forkel—Hoffmeister and Kuhnel Correspondence (ed.) 1990, Bach Perspectives 2 (ed.) 1996, J. S. Bach: Mass in B minor 1997, Organ Technique: Modern and Early (co-author) 2002, The World of Baroque Music (ed.) 2006, Yale Music Masterworks series (Gen. Ed.); contrib. to Early Music, Musical Quarterly, Bach-Jahrbuch, New York Review of Books. *Honours:* IREX Fellowship 1980, Guggenheim Fellowship 1985, Fulbright Fellowship 2000, ACLS Fellowship 2000, Bogliasco Fellowship 2005. *Address:* 33 Livingston Avenue, New Brunswick, NJ 08901, USA (office). *Telephone:* (848) 932-9360 (office); (732) 246-2618 (home). *Fax:* (732) 932-8794 (office). *E-mail:* stauffer@masongross.rutgers.edu (office). *Website:* www.masongross.rutgers.edu (office).

STEBLIANKO, Alexei; singer (tenor); b. 1950, Russia. *Education:* Leningrad Conservatory. *Career:* debut at the Kirov Theatre Leningrad as Lensky, also sang there as Radames, Manrico, Don José, Des Grieux, Andrei in Mazeppa, Herman in The Queen of Spades, Andrei Khovansky, Dmitri in Boris Godunov, Cavaradossi, Lohengrin, Canio and Pierre Bezukhov in War and Peace; tours of Europe with the Kirov Company, including Covent Garden debut as Hermann 1987; sang at La Scala 1982 as Aeneas in Les Troyens, and Covent Garden 1989–90 as Jason in Médée, Vladimir in Prince Igor, both being new productions, and Manrico; season 1992 as Otello at Reggio Emilia; television appearances include Prince Igor, also on video; sang Herman in The Queen of Spades at Bonn 1996; season 2000 as Pierre in War and Peace, as guest with the Mariinsky Co. at Covent Garden; Mussorgsky's Boris Godunov at the London Proms 2002.

STECKEL, Julian; German cellist; b. 1982. *Education:* studied with Ulrich Voss, Gustav Rivinius, Boris Pergamenschikow, Heinrich Schiff and Antje Weithaas. *Career:* concerts as soloist with Bavarian Radio Symphony Orchestra, Royal Philharmonic Orchestra, Radio Symphony Orchestras of Berlin, Stuttgart, Saarbrucken, Copenhagen and Warsaw, Orchestre de Paris, Kremerata Baltica, St Petersburg Philharmonic Orchestra, Bavarian State Orchestra, Franz-Liszt Chamber Orchestra of Budapest, Zürich, Munich and Stuttgart Chamber Orchestras, Konzerthaus Orchestra Berlin and Symphonic Orchestra Düsseldorf; worked with conductors such as Sir Roger Norrington, Mario Venzago, Christopher Hogwood, Heinrich Schiff, Andrey Boreyko, Michael Sanderling, Daniel Raiskin, Andrew Litton, Lan Shui and John Storgårds; chamber music partners included Lars Vogt, Christian Tetzlaff, Antje Weithaas, Isabelle Faust, Baiba and Lauma Skride, Alexander Lonquich, Veronika Eberle, Antoine Tamestit and Paul Rivinius and Ebène, Vogler and Guarneri quartets; festivals included Spannungen Festival Heimbach, Schleswig-Holstein, Mecklenburg-Vorpommernm, Rheingau, Mosel, Lucerne, Ludwigsburg, Bonn, Schwetzingen, Zermatt, Mondsee, Cambrai and Menton; Prof. of Cello, Rostock Univ. of Music and Drama 2011–. *Recordings include:* Korngold-Goldschmidt-Bloch Cello Concertos (ECHO Klassik Awards Newcomer of the Year/Cello 2012) 2011; with Paul Rivinius: Mendelssohn Works for Cello & Piano 2009, French Cello Sonatas 2011. *Honours:* First Prize, Rostropovitch Competition, Paris, Int. Pablo Casals Competition, Kronberg, Int. Lutosławski Competition, Warsaw, Grand Prix Feuermann, Berlin, First Prize, Audience Prize, Chamber Orchestra Prize and Oehms Classics Prize, ARD Int. Music Competition, Munich 2010, Borletti-Buitoni Trust Fellowship, Verbier Festival Prize. *Current Management:* Künstlersekretariat Astrid Schoerke, Grazer Strasse 30, 30519 Hannover, Germany. *Telephone:* (511) 26090750. *E-mail:* a.schoerke@ks-schoerke.de. *Website:* www.ks-schoerke.de. *E-mail:* julia.kadar@premiertone.com (office).

STEDRON, Milos; Czech composer; b. 9 Feb. 1942, Brno. *Education:* Brno Acad. *Career:* researched Janáček's music; administrator, Moravian Museum in Brno 1963–72; teacher of theory, Univ. of Brno from 1972. *Compositions include:* operas: The Apparatus (after Kafka) 1967, Culinary Cares 1979, The Chameleon, or Josef Fouche 1984; ballets: Justina 1969, Ballet Macabre 1986; orchestral: Concerto for double bass and strings 1971, Diagram for piano and jazz orchestra 1971, Music for Ballet 1972, Wheel Symphony 1972, Cello Concerto 1975, Sette Villanelle for cello and strings 1981, Musica Concertante for bassoon and strings 1986, Lammento for viola and orchestra 1987; chamber: Musica Ficta for wind quintet 1968, String Quartet 1970, Trium Vocum for flute, cello and drums 1984, Danze, Canti and Lamenti for string quartet 1986, Qudra for ensemble 1992, Trio for violin, cello and piano 1993, String Quartet 1994, Dances of King Lear for cello, early music instruments and percussion 1996, Annals of the Predecessors of the Avant-garde for chamber orchestra 1997; vocal: Mourning Ceremony (cantata) 1969, Vocal Symphony for soprano, baritone and orchestra 1969, Attendite, Populi cantata for chorus and drums 1982, Dolorosa Gioia Ommaggio á Gesualdo (madrigal cantata) 1978, Death of Dobrovsky (cantata oratorio) 1988, Missa Sine ritu for mezzo and cello 1996, solo instrumental music and piano pieces.

STEEL, George R., BA; American theatre and opera director and conductor; *General Manager and Artistic Director, New York City Opera*. *Education:* St Albans School, Washington, DC, Yale Univ. *Career:* f. Vox Vocal Ensemble 1995; Man. Producer, Tisch Center for the Arts, New York 1995–97; Exec. Dir, Miller Theatre, Columbia Univ. 1997–2008, staged US premieres of Xenakis's Oresteia, Carter's What Next?, Neuwirth's Lost Highway; f. Gotham City Orchestra 1998; Gen. Dir, Dallas Opera Oct. 2008–Jan. 2009; Gen. Man. and Artistic Dir, New York City Opera 2009–. *Honours:* Chamber Music America Award for Adventurous Programming 2002, 2005, Trailblazer Award, American Music Center 2003, ASCAP Concert Music Award 2003. *Address:* New York City Opera, David H. Koch Theater, 20 Lincoln Center, New York, NY 10023, USA (office). *Telephone:* (212) 870-5632 (office). *Fax:* (212) 724-1120 (office). *E-mail:* artistic@nycopera.com (office). *Website:* www.nycopera.com (office).

STEELE-PERKINS, Crispian; British musician (trumpet); b. 18 Dec. 1944, Exeter, Devon, England; m. Jane Elisabeth Mary 1995. *Education:* Guildhall School of Music, London. *Career:* many appearances in the Baroque repertoire at the Barbican and Royal Festival Halls with the City of London Sinfonia and the English Chamber Orchestra; Sadler's Wells Opera 1966–73; Royal Philharmonic 1976–80; played Haydn's Trumpet Concerto at the 1982 Edinburgh Festival; performances on the Natural Trumpet with The King's Consort, The English Baroque Soloists, The Taverner Players and The Parley of Instruments; Prof. of Trumpet, Guildhall School of Music 1980; workshops and masterclasses as preludes to concert presentations; season 1989–90 in Boston, Tokyo, Lisbon, Stuttgart and Gstaad; British festival engagements at Edinburgh, the Proms, City of London, Cambridge, Chester, Dartington, Leeds and Glasgow; US tour in 1988 and tour of Japan in 1990; mem. The King's Consort 1985–2009; full-time trumpet soloist 1990–; Bach's Magnificat with The Sixteen at Queen Elizabeth Hall, London 2000; mem. Royal Soc. of Musicians. *Recordings include:* 16 solo albums, Mr Purcell's Trumpeter (with the City of London Sinfonia under Richard Hickox), Messiah (featuring English trumpet of Handel's time), Shore's Trumpet, Let the Trumpet Sound, Six Trumpet Concertos, some 80 film tracks. *Publications:* contrib. of articles to Historic Brass Journal. *Honours:* Christopher Monk Award, Historic Brass Soc. 2004. *Address:* 5 Westfield Gardens, Dorking, Surrey, RH4 3DX, England (home). *Telephone:* (1306) 885339 (office). *E-mail:* crispiansp@trumpet1.co.uk (office). *Website:* www.crispiansteeleperkins.com.

STEFANESCU, Ana Camelia; Romanian singer (soprano); b. 8 June 1974, Bucharest. *Education:* Dinu Lipatti High School of Music, Bucharest and Univ. of Music, Bucharest with Ionel Voineag and Prof. Andreiana Rosca. *Career:* Prin. Artist, Romanian Nat. Opera, sang numerous roles including Lucia/Lucia di Lammermoor, Rosina/The Barber of Seville, Zerbinetta/Ariadne auf Naxos, Queen of the Night/The Magic Flute and Zerlina/Don Giovanni; recent European engagements have included Queen of the Night/Die Zauberflote with Deutsche Staatsoper Berlin, Graz Opernhaus and Opera de Nice, Faure's Requiem with Orquesta Sinfonica de Bilbao, L'Enfant et les Sortilèges at Teatro Real in Madrid and with Orquesta de Valencia, and Ligeti's Requiem with Orquesta Nacional de Espana; future engagements include further Queen of the Night/Die Zauberflote performances with Deutsche Oper, Berlin; several concerts and recitals in Romania, Spain, Poland, Switzerland, France, Holland, Luxembourg and the UK, including a concert in her native Romania, where she was the soprano soloist with José

Carreras. *Honours:* prizewinner, Verviers Int. Competition, Queen Elisabeth Int. Music Competition, Belgium, Romanian Critics' Award 1997.

STEFANESCU-BARNEA, Georgeta; Romanian pianist and academic; *Professor of Music, Spiru Haret University*; b. 25 April 1934, Satu-Mare; m. Jean Barnea 1958; two s. *Education:* Lyceum, Campulung Muscel, Cluj, G. H. Dima Acad. of Music, Cluj, Ciprian Porumbescu Conservatory, Bucharest, studied in Weimar, Germany, Switzerland, France. *Career:* piano teacher, Music Lyceum 1957–60; Univ. Lecturer, Ciprian Porumbescu Conservatory, Bucharest 1960–91, Univ. Reader 1991–, Prof. 1995–2000; Prof. of Music, Spiru Haret Univ. 2000–; numerous concerts and piano recitals in Romania, Germany, Switzerland, Czechoslovakia, England; appearances on Romanian radio and television, Radio Weimar, Suisse Romande Radio, Geneva. *Publications include:* Mihai Burada–Homage Album (three vols) 1993, Martian Negrea–Piano Pieces 1994, Romanian Sonatines for Piano (ed., two vols) 1994, many other pedagogical albums by H. Herz, Schubert, Grieg, Chopin, Haydn, Mozart and Beethoven, Romanian Sonatines for Piano (ed.) 1985, Lieds of Romanian Contemporary Creation (ed., two vols) 1987, Little Pieces for Piano Four Hands (ed., three vols) 1989, Album of Little Romanican Pieces for Piano 1997, Romanian Pieces for Piano of the XIXth Century (ed., three vols) 2004, Piese Preclasice si Clasice for piano 2004, Studii si Piese for piano 2005, Spre ethosul romanesc prin creatiile pentru pian de ieri si de azi 2007. *Address:* Blv. 1 Mai (Compozitorilor) 32, Bl F8, Sc. B, Apt 24 Sect Vl, 061634 Bucharest 66, Romania (home). *Telephone:* (21) 7252429 (home). *E-mail:* georgetabarnea@yahoo.fr (home); ushm@spiruharet.ro (office).

STEFANOVIĆ, Ivana; Serbian composer; b. 14 Sept. 1948, Belgrade. *Education:* Belgrade Acad. of Music, studied with Gilbert Amy in Paris. *Career:* Radio Belgrade from 1976, founder of Sound Workshop 1985, and head of music production 1990. *Compositions:* Hommage à François Villon for voices and early instruments 1978, Fragment of a Possible Order for two pianos and ensemble 1979, Interpretation of a Dream for flute, two speakers and tape 1984, Lingua/Phonia/Patria 1989, Psalm for mezzo and choir 1990, Isadora (ballet) 1992, Tree of Life for strings 1997. *Address:* c/o SOKOJ, PO Box 213, Mišarska 12–14, 1100 Belgrade, Serbia.

STEFANOWICZ, Artur; Polish singer (countertenor); *Professor, Music University, Warsaw*; b. 5 Oct. 1967, Szczecin. *Education:* Chopin Music Univ. with Jerzy Artysz, studied with Paul Esswood and Jadwiga Rappe. *Career:* has appeared with numerous orchestras and ensembles since 1991, including Orchestra Teatro La Fenice, Lithuanian Nat. Symphony Orchestra, Dublin Symphony Orchestra, Prague Nat. Theatre Orchestra, Sinfonia Varsovia, Warsaw Soloists, Clemencic Consort, Capella Savaria, Musica Aeterna, Hedos Ensemble, Combattimento Consort Amsterdam, Il Fondamento, Collegium Instrumentale Brugense, Les Arts Florissants, The Netherlands Wind Ensemble, Orchestra of the Age of Enlightenment, Akad. für Alte Musik, Lautten Compagney, working with conductors including Karol Teutsch, William Christie, Leopold Hager, Philippe Entremont, Zdenek Kosler, Rudolf Bibl, Frieder Bernius, Christophe Coin, Willem de Friend, Paul Dombrecht, Patrick Peire, Roy Goodman, Noel Davis, Sir Charles Mackerras, Harry Bicket, Peter Eötvös, Gennadi Rozhdestvensky, René Jacobs, Philip Pickett, Rinaldo Alessandrini, Andrey Boreyko, Michael Hofstetter; engagements include, amongst others, Opéra Comique, Paris (Ascanio in Alba/Ascanio), Massachusetts Int. Festival of the Arts and Florida Grand Opera, Miami (L'Incoronazione di Poppea/Ottone), Queen Elizabeth Hall, London, Théâtre Royal de la Monnaie, Brussels, Nat. Concert Halls in Dublin, Taiwan, Tel-Aviv and Warsaw (recitals), Mörbisch Seefestspiele (Die Fledermaus/Orlofsky), Rotterdam Schouwburg and De Nederlandse Opera (The Rake's Progress/Baba the Turk), Warsaw Chamber Opera (Mozart roles: Farnace, Ascanio, Apollo), Aix-en-Provence, Beaune, London, Palermo (European tour with Les Arts Florissants, Vespro della Beata Vergine), Concertgebouw (New Year Concert, songs by Nyman and Bedford), ENO (Xerxes/Arsamenes, Orfeo et Euridice/Orfeo), Glyndebourne Festival Opera, Music Festival, Montreux, Théâtre du Châtelet, Opernhaus Halle and Handel Festspiele Halle (Rodelinda/Unulfo), New York City Opera (Orfeo et Euridice/Orfeo), Deutsche Staatsoper Berlin, Théâtre des Champs Elysées and Festwochen für Alte Musik, Innsbruck (Griselda by Scarlatti/Ottone), De Vlaamse Opera (Festival van Vlaanderen, Chichester Psalms by Bernstein), Budapest Chamber Opera (title parts in Orlando, Tigrane by Vivaldi), Opera Nat. du Rhin (Il Tito by Cesti/Domitiano), Teatro Liceo Salamanca, Teatro Arriaga Bilbao (Theodora/Didimus), Dublin Opera (Giulio Cesare/Tolomeo), Musik Biel/Bienne (Giulio Cesare), Nationale Reisopera Enschede (Ariodante/Polinesso), Komische Oper Berlin (Tamerlano), Halle Handel Festspiele, Bayreuth Barok Festspiele (Teseo/Arcane), Winnipeg Symphony Orchestra, Berliner Philharmonie, Warsaw Philharmonic (Seid Nuchtern und Wachet by Sznittke); Prof., Music Univ., Warsaw. *Recordings include:* Mozart – Rare Opera Arias 1991, Pergolesi, Vivaldi – Stabat Mater 1993, Die Fledermaus 1996, The Vision of Escaflowne 1997, Majewski, Skrzek – The Roe's Room 1997, Brain Powered 1998, Monteverdi – Vespro della Beata Vergine 1998, Handel, Vivaldi – Cantatas 2000, Vivaldi – Il Tigrane (world premiere, live) 2004. *Honours:* Venanzio Rauzzini Prize for Best Counter-tenor at Mozart Singing Competition, Vienna 1990. *Current Management:* c/o Szwed Artists' Management, 64 Borsucza Street, 05-807 Podkowa Lesna, Poland. *Telephone:* (22) 7589649. *E-mail:* office@szwedart.info. *Website:* www.szwedart.info.

STEFÁNSSON, Finnur Torfi, MA; Icelandic composer; b. 20 March 1947, Akranes; m. 1st; two s. one d.; m. 2nd; two d.; m. 3rd Steinunn Johannesdottir 2002. *Education:* Univ. of Iceland, Univ. of Manchester, UK, Reykjavík Coll. of Music, Univ. of California, USA. *Career:* elected mem. Parl. 1978; Ombudsman, Ministry of Justice 1980; Lecturer, Reykjavík Coll. of Music 1991–94; music critic 1991–94; composer 1994–; mem. Icelandic Soc. of Composers. *Compositions:* for orchestra: Piece I 1986, Piece II 1988, Piece III 1992, Piece IV 1995, Piece V 1997, Piece VI 2001, Piece VII 2003, Piece VIII 2005, Piece IX 2008, Piece X 2011, Piece XI 2013, Piece XII 2015; opera: The Shinbone and the Shell 1992, Hallgerdur Langbrok 2012; oratorios: The Seventh Word of Christ 2003, When Jesus was brought forth 2007; concertos: Concerto for violin and orchestra 1996, Concerto for clarinet, bassoon and orchestra 1991, Concerto Grosso 1992, Concerto for violin and orchestra 2004, Concerto for piano and orchestra 2010; chamber music: string quartets 1989, 1994, 1998, 2010, wind quintets 1993, 1996, violin and piano 1985, 1998, flute and piano 2001, clarinet and piano 1993, solo piano 1987, 1995, 1997, 2011; choral: My Mother Said 1999, Cradle Song 1996, Christmas Night 2001; song cycles: About Love 2006, Reykjavik Poems 2009, Lieder of Themes 2015; solo songs to Icelandic and English texts. *Recording:* Waves in the Field 2000. *Address:* Vesturfold 44, 112 Reykjavik, Iceland. *Telephone:* (354) 426-7303. *E-mail:* finnurtorfi@hive.is. *Website:* finnurtorfi.com.

STEFFENS, Walter; academic and composer; b. 31 Oct. 1934, Aachen, Germany. *Education:* studied with Toni and Max Spindler, Rolf Agap, Musikhochschule Hamburg with Klussmann, Maler and Philipp Jarnach, Univ. of Hamburg. *Career:* Docent (lecturer) in Composition and Music Theory, Hamburg Conservatorium 1962–69; Prof. of Composition and Music Theory, masterclasses, Hochschule für Musik, Detmold 1969–. *Compositions:* operas: Eli (libretto by composer, after Mystery of the Sorrow of Israel by Nelly Sachs) 1967, Under Milk Wood (libretto by composer, after Dylan Thomas) 1973, Grabbes Leben (libretto by Peter Schütze) 1986, Der Philosoph (libretto by Schütze) 1990, Die Judenbuche (libretto by Schütze, after Annette von Droste-Hülshoff) 1993, Bildvertonugen (over 50 individual musical settings after paintings by Bosch, Marc Chagall, Klee, Picasso, Soto and others) 1977, 1992; also chamber music, lieder, concertos, symphonies, ballet music and oratorio.

STEFIUK, Maria; singer (soprano); b. 1967, Kiev, Ukraine. *Education:* Kiev State Conservatoire. *Career:* debut at Kiev Opera 1982 as Violetta; many appearances in Kiev, Moscow and St Petersburg as Lucia, Zerlina, Marguerite de Valois, Mimi, Leila in Les Pêcheurs de Perles and Marfa in The Tsar's Bride; guest engagements in Dresden, Madrid, Wiesbaden, London, Paris, Washington, Tokyo and Sydney, including many concert appearances; sang at La Scala Milan in Sorochintsy Fair by Mussorgsky.

STEGER, Ingrid; singer (soprano, mezzo-soprano); b. 27 Feb. 1927, Roding, Germany. *Education:* Musikhochschule, Munich. *Career:* debut as Azucena in Passau 1951; sang in opera at Augsburg 1952–54, Kassel 1954–59, Trier 1958–60 and Oberhausen from 1960; further engagements at Berlin Staatsoper 1965–68, Parma and Venice 1965, 1968, Salzburg Easter Festival 1967, Graz 1974–75 and Karlsruhe 1975–77; sang Elektra at San Francisco 1973 and appeared further at the state operas of Vienna, Hamburg and Stuttgart; sang until 1986 in such roles as Rodelinda, Leonore, Senta, Elsa, Ortrud, Elisabeth, Isolde, Kundry, the Composer in Ariadne, Lady Macbeth, Amneris, Amelia in Un Ballo in Maschera, Santuzza, Turandot, Judith in Bluebeard's Castle and Schoeck's Penthesilea. *Recordings include:* Die Walküre (conducted by Karajan).

STEGER, Maurice; Swiss musician (recorder) and conductor; b. 15 May 1971. *Education:* Zurich Conservatory, Zurich Musikhochschule, studied recorder and ancient music with Pedro Memelsdorff and Kees Boeke and conducting with Marcus Cree. *Career:* has performed as soloist and/or conductor with numerous period instrument ensembles, including Akademie Alte Musik Berlin, The English Concert, Musica Antiqua Köln, Europa Galante and I Barocchisti, and also with Zurich Chamber Orchestra, Sinfonieorchester Frankfurt, Musikkollegium Winterthur, Berlin Baroque Soloists (Berlin Philharmonic), Les Violons du Roy, Canada, NDR Radiophilharmonie; first recorder player from the West to perform with the Traditional Taipei Chinese Orchestra. *Recordings include:* Telemann: Recorder Works 2005, Mr Corelli in London 2010, Una Follia di Napoli 2012, Vivaldi: Concerti per flauto (Echo Klassik Award for Instrumentalist of the Year/Flute 2015) 2014. *Honours:* Karajan Prize 2002, Diapason d'or. *Current Management:* Künstlersekretariat Schoerke, Grazer Str. 30, 30519 Hanover, Germany. *Telephone:* (511) 26090754. *E-mail:* a.schoerke@ks-schoerke.de. *Website:* www.ks-schoerke.de; mauricesteger.com.

STEIGER, Anna; American singer (soprano); b. 13 Feb. 1960, Los Angeles, CA. *Education:* Guildhall School of Music, London, studied with Vera Rozsa and Irmgard Seefried. *Career:* associated with Glyndebourne Opera from 1983 singing Micaela on tour 1985, Poppea at the 1986 festival and in the 1987 premiere production of Osborne's The Electrification of the Soviet Union; sang at Lausanne Opera in 1985 in La Cenerentola, Opera North in 1986 as Musetta, Covent Garden Opera from 1987 in Parsifal and Jenůfa, ENO in The Makropulos Case, and Geneva Opera as Concepcion in L'Heure Espagnole; sang Despina in Così fan tutte for Netherlands Opera 1990, and Eurydice in Milhaud's Les Malheurs d'Orphée at the Queen Elizabeth Hall 1990; season 1991–92 as Despina at Stuttgart, a Hooded Figure in the premiere of Osborne's Terrible Mouth at the Almeida Theatre, and Zerlina for Netherlands Opera; sang in Verdi's Un Giorno di Regno for Dorset Opera, 1994; sang the Marquise in La Fille du régiment at St Gallen, 2000; concert engagements include BBC recitals, Clarissa's Mad Scene by Holloway with the London

Symphony, Les Illuminations with Bournemouth Sinfonietta and Fauré's Requiem with Scottish National Orchestra. *Recordings include:* Poème de L'Amour et de La Mer by Chausson, with the BBC Scottish Symphony Orchestra. *Honours:* Peter Pears Award, 1982; Richard Tauber Award, 1984; John Christie Award, 1985. *Current Management:* c/o Musicaglotz, 11 rue le Verrier, 75006 Paris, France; c/o Atelier Musicale, Via Caselle 76, San Lazzaro di Savena 40068, Italy. *Telephone:* 1-42-34-53-40 (France); (51) 19984444 (Italy). *Fax:* 1-40-46-93-77 (France); (51) 19984420 (Italy). *E-mail:* general@musicaglotz.com; info@ateliermusicale.com. *Website:* www.musicaglotz.com; www.ateliermusicale.com.

STEIGER, Rand, BMus, MFA; American composer and conductor; b. 18 June 1957, New York. *Education:* New York High School of Music and Art, Manhattan School of Music, California Inst. of the Arts with Brown, Subotnick and Powell, Yale Univ. with Elliott Carter, Betsy Jolas and Jakob Druckman, IRCAM electronic music studios, Paris, France. *Career:* faculty mem., Univ. of Costa Rica 1984–85, California Inst. of the Arts 1982–87, Univ. of California at San Diego from 1987; conductor and dir of contemporary music performances with SONOR at San Diego and with the Los Angeles Philharmonic New Music Group; mem. new music ensemble, E.A.R., California Inst. of the Arts 1981–; Composer Fellow, Los Angeles Philharmonic 1987–88. *Compositions include:* Brave New World for voices and electronics 1980, Dialogues II for marimba and orchestra 1980, Quintessence for six instruments 1981, Currents Caprice (electronic) 1982, Kennedy Sketches for marimba and vibraphone 1982, In Nested Symmetry for 15 instruments and electronics 1982, Tributaries for chamber orchestra 1986, Tributaries for Nancarrow for six computer-controlled pianos 1987, ZLoops for clarinet, piano and percussion 1989, Mozart Tributary for clarinet quintet 1991, The Burgess Shale for orchestra 1994, Resonant Vertices for ensemble 1996, Frames for ensemble 1998, Diaspora for cello and percussion 1999, Lemma I and II for percussion and electronics 1997, 1999.

STEIN, Caroline; German singer (soprano); b. 1963. *Education:* Musikhochschule, Cologne. *Career:* debut at Würzburg Municipal Theatre; recent engagements include Erste Dame in productions of Die Zauberflöte conducted by Claudio Abbado and Sir Colin Davis, Venus/Gepopo in Le grand Macabre for San Francisco Opera, Hilda Mack in new productions of Elegie für Junge Liebende at Staatsoper Berlin and Staatstheater am Gärtnerplatz, Konstanze in Die Entführung aus dem Serail for Staatstheater Oldenburg, Violetta in La Traviata for Norwegian State Opera, the Angel in Faustus Nacht at Staatsoper Berlin, Opéra de Lyon and Theatre du Châtelet and Erste Dame for Teatro San Carlo, Naples; 2010 season: concert engagements at Alte Oper Frankfurt, Corum Montpellier and Salle Grimaldi Monte Carlo; debut with Sir Simon Rattle and Berliner Philharmonic at Salzburg and Lucerne Festivals in Ligeti's Mysteries of the Macabre 2010; repeats performance in Faustus for Staatsoper Berlin and will also appear as the solo figure in Dusapin's Medeamaterial 2010. *Current Management:* c/o Athole Still Opera Ltd, Foresters Hall, 25–27 Westow Street, London, SE19 3RY, England. *Telephone:* (20) 8771-5271. *Fax:* (20) 8771-8172. *E-mail:* chris@atholestill.co.uk. *Website:* www.atholestill.co.uk.

STEIN, Peter; German stage director; b. 1 Oct. 1937, Berlin; m. Maddalena Crippa 1999. *Education:* Munich Univ. *Career:* worked with Munich Kammerspiele from 1964, directing Saved by Edward Bond 1967; directed plays by Brecht in Munich, Goethe and Schiller in Bremen; co-founder, Berlin Schaubuhne Co. 1970 (Artistic Dir –1985), Vietnam-Discourse 1968, The Mother 1970, Peer Gynt 1971, Oresteia 1980, The Three Sisters 1984; debut as Opera Dir with Das Rheingold in Paris 1976, As You Like It 1977; for WNO directed Otello 1986, Falstaff 1988, Pelléas et Mélisande 1992, Peter Grimes 1999; Dir of Drama, Salzburg Festival 1992–97; staged Schoenberg's Moses und Aron at Salzburg 1996; Faust I & II 2000, Simon Boccanegra 2000, The Seagull 2003, Blackbird 2005, Troilus and Cressida 2006, Electra with Nat Theatre of Greece 2007. *Recordings include:* videos of WNO productions, as director for television.

STEINAUER, Mathias, DipMus; Swiss composer; b. 20 April 1959, Basel; m. Elena Gianini 1991. *Education:* Musik-Akademie, Basel, studied with P. Efler, R. Moser, R. Stuter, J. Wildberger, and G. Kurtág in Budapest. *Career:* various concerts of own music, radio productions, film music 1982–; founder, Komponisten Forum 1982; teacher of music theory and composition, Hochschule für Musik and Theater Winterthur, Zürich 1986. *Compositions include:* Music for xylophone, marimba and two musical boxes 1984, Musik in fünf Teilen for three cellists and two percussionists 1985, Andante for percussion trio 1985, Vier Klangbilder for baritone, large orchestra, female choir and 18 recorders (words by H. Erni) 1986, Visions for 12 wind instruments, two percussionists and piano 1987, Drei Skizzen for string quartet 1987, Duat, 14 Signs for chamber orchestra 1988, ...wir Risse im Schatten... Concerto for flute and orchestra 1988–89, Blutenlese for two choirs, soprano, children's voice and ensemble (words by 12 authors) 1990–91, Undici Duettini for violin and viola 1991, Speculum Sibyllinum 1992, Omaggio ad Italo Calvino for clarinet, horn, violin and piano 1993, Il rallentando della sarabanda for piano, percussion and orchestra 1993–95, Die Gehaubte Braut (wedding music) for mezzo-soprano and organ 1994, Jahreszeiten for percussion trio 1994, Alta fedeltà for two violins and tape 1996, Rumori cardiacl for flute, clarinet, violin, cello and piano 1996, Nacht: Pipe Dreams for chamber orchestra, Koren Fantasie 1997.

STEINBACH, Heribert; singer (tenor); b. 17 May 1937, Duisberg, Germany. *Education:* studied in Düsseldorf, Cologne with Clemens Glettenberg. *Career:* sang at the Cologne Opera 1964–66, and Staatstheater Karlsruhe 1966–68; mem., Deutsche Oper am Rhein Düsseldorf 1968–76, and Munich Staatsoper 1977–80; sang at Bayreuth Festival 1971–76 as Froh and Melot; guest engagements at the Paris Opéra 1976, 1978, and Lisbon and Barcelona 1978; sang Loge in Das Rheingold at the 1979 Maggio Musicale Florence and again at the Teatro Colón Buenos Aires 1982; sang Tristan at Lausanne 1983, Walther von Stolzing at the Metropolitan 1985, followed by Siegfried at Kassel; sang at Teatro Regio Turin 1987–88 as Siegmund in Die Walküre; at the first season of the new Musiektheater Rotterdam 1988 sang Siegfried in Der Ring des Nibelungen; sang Herod in Salome 1989 at Lyric Opera of Queensland. *Recordings:* Pfitzner's Palestrina, Tristan und Isolde conducted by Bernstein, Die Soldaten by Zimmermann.

STEINBERG, Pinchas; Israeli conductor; b. 12 Feb. 1945. *Education:* studied in New York and Tanglewood, and with Boris Blacher in Berlin. *Career:* took part in the 1964 Tanglewood Festival; Prof. and Asst, Univ. of Indiana; Assoc. Conductor, Lyric Opera Chicago from 1967, making debut with Don Giovanni; conducted leading orchestras in Europe from 1972; Conductor, Frankfurt Opera from 1979, and has led performances in Stuttgart, Hamburg and Berlin and at Covent Garden, Paris Opéra and the San Francisco Opera; Musical Dir at Bremen 1985–89; Chief Conductor, Verona Arena 1989; Conductor, Austrian Radio Symphony Orchestra, notably in Janáček's Everlasting Gospel and Dvořák's Te Deum 1990; appeared at Bregenz Festival 1990 with Catalani's La Wally and conducted Rossini's Tancredi at the 1992 Salzburg Festival; L'amore dei tre re at the 1994 Montpellier Festival; further opera includes Rienzi for Radio France, Rigoletto at Orange, Nabucco at the Opéra Bastille, Tosca at Houston and Trovatore in Geneva; Un Ballo in Maschera at Monte Carlo 1998; Die Walküre at Toulouse 1999; Principal Conductor, Vienna Radio Symphony Orchestra 1989–96, Orchestre de la Suisse Romande 2002–05. *Honours:* winner Florence Int. Conductors' Competition 1972. *Current Management:* Opus 3 Artists, 470 Park Avenue South, 9th Floor North, New York, NY 10016, USA. *Telephone:* (212) 584-7500. *Fax:* (646) 300-8200. *E-mail:* info@opus3artists.com. *Website:* www.opus3artists.com.

STEINBERGER, Birgid; German singer (soprano); *Professor of Song Interpretation, Vienna Conservatory*; b. 1966, Burghausen. *Education:* studied with Wilma Lipp in Salzburg, Charlotte Lehmann in Hanover and Kurt Widmer in Basel. *Career:* debut in Heidelberg 1991, as Serpetta in La Serva padrona by Pergolesi; sang at Basle Oper 1992–94, then at Vienna Volks and State Operas, as Susanna, Marzelline in Fidelio, Papagena, Pamina, Marie in Lortzing's Zar and Zimmermann, Nicolai's Anne, and Musetta in La Bohème; operetta roles include Franziska in Wiener Blut, Rosalinde and Adele in Die Fledermaus and Lehar's Valencienne, Titania in Britten's Sommernachtstraum; Prof. of Song Interpretation, Vienna Conservatory. *Recordings:* Così fan tutte 2001, Le Nozze di Figaro 2002, Don Giovanni 2003, Songs by Kraus 2005, Songs by Schubert 2006. *Honours:* prizewinner, Hugo Wolf Competition, Stuttgart 1990. *Address:* c/o Volksoper, Währingerstrasse 78, 1090 Vienna, Austria (office). *E-mail:* b.steinberger@inode.at (home).

STEINECKER, Anton; Slovak composer; b. 9 Dec. 1971, Bratislava. *Education:* Bratislava Conservatory, Kroměříž Conservatory, Czech Republic, Acad. of Music and Drama, Bratislava with Jozef Sixta and Dušan Martincek, Acad. of Music and Drama, Prague with Svatopluk Havelka and Juraj Filas, Jerusalem Rubin Acad. of Music and Dance with Mark Kopytman, Acad. of Music and Drama, Bratislava with Dušan Martincek and Vladimír Bokes, Hochschule für Musik Saar, Germany with Theo Brandmüller, also studied with Tadeáš Salva. *Career:* debut, Ground for oboe and viola, Mirbach Concert Hall, Bratislava 1993; works performed at festivals in Slovakia, Czech Repub., Germany, Russia, Israel, France, Austria, Poland and USA; Lecturer, Acad. of Arts, Banská Bystrica, Slovakia 2001–02; masterclasses Bohemia Festival, Czech Repub. with Dušan Martinček 1996, Eighth Int. Summer Programme in Composition, CASMI, Czech Repub. with Ladislav Kubík 2001, Ostrava New Music Days and Festival, Czech Repub. with Jean-Yves Bosseur, Alvin Lucier, Petr Kotik, Christian Wolff and Tristain Murail 2001, 2003, Int. Music Acad. Masters of Pontelevoy, France with Mark Kopytman 2002, New Music Acad. Masters of Pontelevoy, France with Mark Kopytman 2002, New Music Darmstadt, Germany with Brian Ferheyhough and Chaya Czerhovin 2003, Days for Interpretation and Performance Praxis, Hochschule für Musik Saar, Germany with Theo Brandmüller and Toshio Hosokawa 2003, 2004; mem. Slovakian Composers' League. *Compositions:* Piano Trio 1994, Jaj, Bože môj! for a capella SATB choir (third prize Year of Slovak Music Composition Competition 1995) 1993–94, Ground for oboe and viola 1993, Invention for violin, viola or cello 1994–95, Preludium e Quasi una passacaglia for string orchestra 1994, Impressions for piano 1995–96, Moments musicaux for string trio 1996, Notturno for horn 1996, String Quartet No. 1 1996–98, Variants for clarinet 1998, String Trio 1998–99, Memories for percussion 1998–99, Wind Quintet 2000, String Quartet No. 2 Choral Variations 2000, Es umfingen mich die Wogen des Todes Cantata for baritone, SATB choir and chamber orchestra 2000, Chamber Opera in Four Scenes (libretto by Daniila Charms) 2001, String Quartet No. 3 Preludium – Fragmente 2001–02, Preludium for violoncello, violin or viola 2001–02, Notturni for cimbalom 2001–04, Impressions for clarinet 2002, Quasi una sonata for cimbalom 2003–05, Quintet for cimbalom and string quartet 2003. *Recordings include:* with Slovak Radio: Ground for oboe and viola 1994, Notturno for horn 1997, String Trio 2001, Wind Quintet 2001, Preludium e Quasi una passacaglia for string orchestra

2002, Notturni for cimbalom 2004; with Saarlandischem Rundfunk Saarbrücken: Impressions for clarinet 2003, Notturni for cimbalom 2004; other: Kohelet for baritone and piano trio 2000, Miserere mei Domine for a capella, SAATB choir 2002, Preludium for violincello 2002. *Publication:* contrib. to Slovak Music 1998. *Honours:* most-played composition prize Slovak Protection League of Authors 2004. *Address:* Tolsteho 2, 81106 Bratislava, Slovakia (home). *E-mail:* anton_steinecker@hotmail.com (home).

STEINER, Elisabeth; singer (mezzo-soprano); b. 17 March 1935, Berlin, Germany. *Education:* studied in Berlin with Frida Leider. *Career:* sang at the Städtischen Oper Berlin from 1961 with debut in Blacher's Rosamunde Floris; sang at Salzburg Festival 1962 as Artemis in Gluck's Iphigenia in Aulis; discovered by Rolf Liebermann and engaged for the Staatsoper Hamburg; sang in many premieres there, including Von Einem's Der Zerrissene 1964, Penderecki's The Devils of Loudun 1969, Kelemen's Der Belagerungszustand 1970 and Stefen's Under Milk Wood 1973; appeared often at Bayreuth and in guest engagements at the Maggio Musicale Florence, Metropolitan Opera, New York and La Scala, Milan; sang at Vienna Staatsoper 1980 in the premiere of Jesu Hochzeit by Gottfried von Einem; sang the Countess in Lortzing's Wildschütz, Hamburg 1994. *Recordings:* roles in Tiefland, Die Fledermaus, The Devils of Loudun, Rienzi and Eine Nacht in Venedig.

STEINER, Paul; Swiss singer; b. 19 Aug. 1948, Horgen, nr Zürich. *Education:* studied with Elsa Cavelti in Basle, Adalbert Kraus in Stuttgart. *Career:* many appearances in opera houses in Switzerland, notably at Paolino in Il Matrimonio Segreto, Milford in Rossini's Cambiale di matrimonio, Marquis in Zar und Zimmermann by Lortzing; concert engagements throughout Germany and Switzerland in repertory from Baroque to contemporary music; many premiere performances, including Une songe d'une nuit d'été, by R. Gerber, Biel 1984. *Recordings include:* Cantatas by Mozart and Schubert; Markus Passion, attributed to Bach (Collegium Musicum); Lieder by Othmar Schoeck. *Address:* c/o Stadttheater Biel, Burggasse 19, 2502 Biel, Switzerland.

STEINHARDT, Arnold; American violinist; b. 1 April 1937, Los Angeles, CA. *Education:* Curtis Inst., Philadelphia with Ivan Galamian. *Career:* debut with Los Angeles Philharmonic 1951; Asst Concertmaster, Cleveland Orchestra under George Szell; performed in chamber music with Rudolf Serkin at the Marlboro Festival; co-founder, Guarneri String Quartet 1964–2009; many tours of America and Europe, notably in appearances at the Spoleto Festival 1965, to Paris with Arthur Rubinstein and London 1970, in the complete quartets of Beethoven; noted for performances of Viennese classics, works by Walton, Bartók and Stravinsky; season 1987–88 included opening concert in New Concert Hall at Shufmotomo Festival, Japan and British appearances at St John's Smith Square and QEH; faculty mem., Curtis Inst., Univ. of Maryland. *Recordings include:* Mozart's Quartets dedicated to Haydn; Complete Quartets of Beethoven; Piano Quintets of Schumann, Dvořák and Brahms (with Arthur Rubinstein); Piano Quartets by Fauré and Brahms. *Honours:* Edison Award (for Beethoven recordings) 1971. *Address:* School of Music, University of Maryland, 2110 Clarice Smith Performing Arts Center, College Park, MD 20742-1620, USA (office). *Telephone:* (301) 405-5549 (office). *Fax:* (301) 314-9504 (office). *E-mail:* asteinha@umd.edu (office). *Website:* www.music.umd.edu/faculty/music_directory/string/arnold_steinhardt (office); www.arnoldsteinhardt.com.

STEINSKY, Ulrike; singer (soprano); b. 21 Sept. 1960, Vienna, Austria. *Education:* studied with Margaret Zimmermann, Hilde Zadek and Waldemar Kmentt in Vienna. *Career:* many performances as Constanze in Die Entführung while a student; debut at the Vienna Staatsoper 1983 as the Queen of Night; has also sung in Die Zauberflöte with the Cologne Opera in Tel-Aviv, Covent Garden in Los Angeles 1984 and at the 1985 Bregenz Festival; appeared with the Bayerische Staatsoper Munich 1984–90 and at Zürich from 1985 as Zerline in Fra Diavolo season 1989–90; further guest engagements at Cologne, Dortmund, Barcelona as Fiakermilli in Arabella 1989 and at Hamburg 1990; season 1992 as Fiakermilli at La Scala; other roles include Adele in Die Fledermaus, Musetta, Zerlina, Pamina, Despina, Aennchen and Papagena; has also sung in operettas by Oscar Straus, Lehar and Millöcker; concert performances of Così fan tutte, Don Giovanni and Mozart's La Finta Giardiniera; sang Pamina at the Loreley Festival 2000. *Recordings include:* Die Fledermaus.

STEJSKAL, Margot; singer (soprano); b. 9 Feb. 1947, Engelsdorf, Leipzig, Germany. *Education:* studied in Weimar, Leipzig Musikhochschule with Hannelore Kuhse. *Career:* debut in Cottbus, as Musetta 1975; sang in opera at Cottbus until 1977, Staatsoper Dresden 1977–80, and Chemnitz 1980–84; sang Sophie in Der Rosenkavalier at the opening of Semper Oper Dresden 1985; guest appearances at Berlin Staatsoper and elsewhere in Germany; other roles have included Blondchen, Susanna, Nannetta and Adele in Die Fledermaus; many concert appearances. *Recordings include:* Der Rosenkavalier.

STELLA, Antonietta; singer (soprano); b. 15 March 1929, Perugia, Italy. *Education:* Accademia di Santa Cecilia, Rome. *Career:* debut as Leonora in Il Trovatore, Spoleto 1950; Rome debut 1951, as Leonora in La Forza del Destino; Germany from 1951, in Stuttgart, Wiesbaden and Munich; sang as guest all over Italy; Verona Arena and La Scala debuts 1953; at the New York Metropolitan (debut 1956) sang Aida, Butterfly, Tosca, Elisabeth de Valois (Don Carlos), Violetta and Amelia (Un Ballo in Maschera); at Naples 1974 sang in the premiere of Maria Stuarda by de Bellis. *Recordings:* roles in Verdi's Simon Boccanegra, Un Ballo in Maschera, Don Carlos, Il Trovatore,

Aida and Il Battaglia di Legnano, Donizetti's Linda di Chamounix, Puccini's La Bohème and Tosca, Giordano's Andrea Chénier.

STELLUTO, George Edward, MMus; American conductor; *Music Director, Peoria Symphony Orchestra;* b. Washington, DC. *Education:* Western Virginia Univ., Yale Univ. School of Music. *Career:* Music Dir, Las Vegas Music Festival 1998–2006; Asst Conductor, Chicago Symphony Orchestra at the Ravinia Festival; Resident Conductor, The Juilliard School; performed with Ukrainian Nat. Orchestra, New York City Ballet, Int. Contemporary Ensemble, Boston's Alea III and Central Conservatory Orchestra in Beijing as part of Juilliard's 2008 tour of China and for 100th anniversary tours of Europe and America; festivals include Aspen, Peter Britt, Focus!, Quartet Program, Kiev Int., and Ukrainian Summer; Advisor, Sinfonia por La Vida, Ecuador; Music Dir Peoria Symphony Orchestra 2010–. *Address:* Peoria Symphony Orchestra, Foster Arts Center, 203 Harrison Street, Peoria, IL 61602 (office); The Juilliard School, 60 Lincoln Center Plaza, New York, NY 10023-6588, USA (office). *Telephone:* (212) 799-5000 (Juilliard) (office); (309) 637-2787 (Peoria) (home). *Website:* www.peoriasymphony.org (office).

STEMME, Nina; Swedish singer (soprano); b. 1966, Stockholm. *Education:* studied in Stockholm. *Career:* Stockholm Royal Opera as Cherubino 1994; Stora Theatre Gothenburg as Donna Elvira and Butterfly; Bayreuth Festival as Freia in Das Rheingold 1994–95; Cologne Opera from 1995, as Pamina, Butterfly, Mozart's Countess, and Mimi 1998; sang Katerina in Martinů's Greek Passion at Bregenz 1999; Elsa at Basle and Tosca for Cologne Opera; season 2000–01 as Senta at Antwerp, Marguerite for the Savonlinna Festival and in Frankfurt, Manon Lescaut for ENO and Tatiana in Brussels, Senta at the New York Met; sang Elisabeth in Tannhäuser at the Deutsche Oper, Berlin 2003; Isolde in Tristan und Isolde at Glyndebourne 2003, 2007 and Bayreuth 2005; Elisabeth in Tannhauser at Geneva, and Amelia in Un Ballo in maschera at the Royal Opera House, London 2005; Arabella in Gothenburg and Aida in Zurich 2006; Ariadne in Geneva 2007; Amelia in Simon Boccanegra at the Royal Opera House 2008; Sieglinde and Brünnhilde in The Ring of the Nibelung, Leonora in La Forza del Destino, Vienna State Opera 2007–08; Isolde in Tristan and Isolde, Zurich Opera, Salome, Gran Teatro del Liceu, Barcelona 2008–09; title role Ariadne auf Naxos, Metropolitan Opera, New York 2010, Vienna Staatsoper 2011; Leonora in Fidelio, La Scala 2011, Royal Opera House, London 2011; title role in Tosca, Vienna Staatsoper 2012; Brünnhilde in San Francisco 2011, La Scala 2012, Vienna Staatsoper 2013, Munich 2013; title role in Turandot, Opernhaus Zürich 2015, Münchner Opernfestspiel 2016; title role in Elektra, Metropolitan Opera 2016; many concert appearances. *Recordings include:* Capriccio and the Vier Letze Lieder 2007, Fidelio 2011, Tristan and Isolde 2012, Greek Passion, Der König Kandaules, The Flying Dutchman, Highlights from Salome, In Flanders' Fields, Wesendonck Lieder 2013, Songs by the Sea. *Honours:* Dr hc (Lund) 2016; winner Placido Domingo's Operalia Competition 1993, finalist Cardiff Singer of the World Competition 1993, named Court Singer by King Carl XVI Gustaf of Sweden 2006, awarded Litteris et Artibus Medal, King Carl XVI Gustaf of Sweden 2008, Int. Opera Awards Best Female Singer 2013, City of Stockholm Honorary Prize 2014. *Current Management:* Artists Management Zürich, Rütistrasse 52, 8044 Zürich-Gockhausen, Switzerland. *Telephone:* (44) 821 89 57. *Fax:* (44) 821 01 27. *E-mail:* schuetz@artistsman .com. *Website:* www.artistsman.com.

STENE, Randi; Norwegian singer (mezzo-soprano); b. 1967. *Education:* Norwegian State Acad. of Music, Oslo, Opera Acad., Copenhagen. *Career:* Salzburg Festival from 1992, in Salome and Dallapiccola's Ulisse; premiere of Reigen by Boesmans at Brussels 1993; season 1993–94 as Octavian at the Théâtre du Châtelet, Paris, and Dorabella at the Royal Opera, Copenhagen; season 1995–96 with Cherubino at Covent Garden, Olga in Eugene Onegin at the Opèra Bastille, Paris, and Carmen in Brussels; returned to London 1997 as Silla in new production of Palestrina by Pfitzner; Hansel at the Théâtre du Châtelet, Paris 1997; concert repertory includes Szymanowski's Stabat Mater (London Proms 1996), Dvořák's Requiem (Edinburgh Festival 1996), Missa Brevis by Bach (Salzburg), the Christmas Oratorio, Zemlinsky's Maeterlinck Lieder and Falla's Three Cornered Hat (with the Berlin Symphony Orchestra); Schubert's A-flat Mass with the Oslo Philharmonic Orchestra and Sibelius's Kullervo Symphony with the Stockholm Philharmonic Orchestra. *Recordings include:* Vivaldi Cantatas; Opera Arias, with Kathleen Battle; Salome, under Christoph von Dohnányi; Kullervo Symphony. *Honours:* Finalist, Cardiff Singer of the World Competition 1991. *Address:* c/o Simax Classics, Akersgata 7, Oslo 0158, Norway (office). *E-mail:* simax@grappa.no (office). *Website:* www.simax.no (office).

STENZ, Markus; German conductor; *Chief Conductor and General Music Director, City of Cologne;* b. 28 Feb. 1965, Bad Neuenahr. *Education:* Cologne Musikhochschule, Salzburg with Gary Bertini and Noam Sheriff, Tanglewood with Leonard Bernstein and Seiji Ozawa. *Career:* with Ozawa and Bernstein at Tanglewood 1988; asscn with Hans Werner Henze includes Elegy for Young Lovers at Venice 1988, and The English Cat in Berlin 1989; premieres of Das Verratene Meer (Berlin 1990) and Venus und Adonis (Munich 1997), L'Upupa und der Triumph der Sohnesliebe (Salzburger Festspiele 2003); Musical Dir, Montepulciano Festival 1989–95; conducted Figaro at Los Angeles 1994 and Hamburg 1996; ENO debut 1995, Don Giovanni; Principal Conductor, London Sinfonietta 1994–98, leading it at the 1994 Proms in Music by Kurtag, Ives and Xenakis; season 1993–94 with the Berlin Symphony Orchestra, Scottish Chamber Orchestra and BBC Symphony Orchestra; season 1994–95 included debuts with the Hallé Orchestra, Royal Stockholm Philharmonic, and

Philharmonic of Rotterdam, Helsinki and Hamburg; debut appearances with the Sydney and Melbourne Symphony Orchestras in season 1995–96 and Prom concert with Weill's Der Silbersee; other operas include Henze's Bassarids in Hamburg 1994, Hans Zender's Stephen Climax in Brussels and Weill's Mahagonny in Stuttgart; season 1997–98 included debuts with the Minnesota Orchestra and the Chicago Symphony Orchestra; Chief Conductor and Artistic Dir, Melbourne Symphony Orchestra 1998–2004; Chief Conductor, Gürzenich-Orchester Köln 2003–; Gen. Music Dir, City of Cologne 2004–; Principal Guest Conductor, Hallé Orchestra 2009–. *Current Management:* Ingpen & Williams, 7 St George's Court, 131 Putney Bridge Road, London, SW15 2PA, England. *Telephone:* (20) 8874-3222. *Fax:* (20) 8877-3113. *E-mail:* info@ingpen.co.uk. *Website:* www.ingpen.co.uk.

STEPANOV, Oleg; Latvian pianist; b. 2 May 1956, Riga; m. Natasha Vlassenko 1981, one d. *Education:* Moscow Tchaikovsky Conservatory. *Career:* appeared as duo with cellist, Daniel Shafran; appeared solo and as chamber music musician in Germany, Italy, Hungary, Sweden, Poland, Cuba, Bulgaria, Russia, Hong Kong and Australia; Lecturer in Piano, Queensland Conservatorium, Griffith University, Brisbane, Australia; founder, Artistic Director, The Lev Vlasenko Piano Competition, Brisbane. *Honours:* First Prize, Grand Prize, Vittorio Gui Chamber Music Competition, Citta di Firenze, Italy, 1988. *Address:* 26 Ninth Avenue, St Lucia, Brisbane, Qld 4067, Australia.

STEPHAN, Erwin; singer (tenor); b. 23 June 1949, Worms, Germany. *Education:* studied in Frankfurt, Osnabruck and Karlsruhe, and with James King. *Career:* debut at Flensburg 1978; sang in opera at Luneburg, Coburg and Giessen; Saarbrucken 1984–86 in debut as Florestan and sang Tannhäuser from 1985, notably at Dortmund, Bremen, Geneva and the 1986 Orange Festival; Freiburg 1987 as Otello, Huon in Oberon at Catania and Max in Der Freischütz at Cologne; US debut 1989 as Walther von Stolzing at Seattle; other roles have included Don José and Ismaele in Nabucco; opera performances at Semper Oper Dresden and concert showings in France, Austria, Switzerland, Japan and South America.

STÉPHANY, Anna, BMus, MMus; British/French singer (mezzo-soprano); b. 14 Dec. 1977. *Education:* King's Coll., London, GSMD, Nat. Opera Studio. *Career:* operatic roles include Dorabella in Così fan tutte, Juno in Semele for British Youth Opera; Concepçion in L'Heure Espagnole, title role in Mignon, Marcellina in Le Nozze di Figaro for Guildhall School of Music and Drama(GSMD); sang with Glyndebourne Festival Chorus 2002, 2003; has appeared as soloist with The Bach Choir, Holst Singers, The Philharmonia Chorus, Highgate Choral Soc., Britten Symphonia, Orchestra of St John's, Flemish Radio Orchestra, Leith Hill Festival, The New London Orchestra; Handel's Messiah with Sir David Willcocks, Royal Albert Hall 2003, 2005; recitals with Simon Lepper, Roger Vignoles; performances at Wigmore Hall, Oxford Lieder Festival, Barber Inst. Birmingham. *Honours:* Samling Scholar; Clonter Opera Prize 2005, Joaninha Trust Award 2005, Kathleen Ferrier Award 2005, GSMD Gold Medal 2005. *Current Management:* c/o Sue Nicholls, Hazard Chase, 25 City Road, Cambridge, CB1 1DP, UK. *E-mail:* sue.nicholls@ hazardchase.co.uk. *Website:* www.annastephany.com.

STEPHEN, Pamela Helen; British singer (mezzo-soprano); b. 1965, England; m. Richard Hickox. *Career:* debut as Cathleen in The Rising of the Moon, Wexford, 1990; appearances with Opera North as the Composer in the Mozart/Griffiths Jewel Box, Cherubino, Donna Clara in Gerhard's Duenna and Cynthia in Benedict Mason's Playing Away (Munich and London); Prince in Massenet's Cenrillon for WNO, Dafne in Peri's Euridice at Batignano and Juno in Semele for the City of London Festival; Season 1999–2000 with Sonya in War and Peace at Spoleto, Verdi's Maddalena for Los Angeles Opera, and Nero in Agrippina by Handel; Concerts including Haydn's Nelson Mass at the London Proms, Britten's Phaedra with the Los Angeles CO and Dream of Gerontius for the Scottish National Orchestra; Elgar's Sea Pictures at Lisbon. *Current Management:* c/o Neil Dalrymple, Music International, 13 Ardilaun Road, London, N5 2QR, England. *Telephone:* (20) 7359-5183. *Fax:* (20) 7226-9792. *E-mail:* music@musicint.co.uk.

STEPHENSON, Donald James, ARCM; British singer (tenor); b. 15 Feb. 1947, Leeds; m. (divorced); one s. one d. *Education:* Royal Manchester Coll. of Music, Nat. Opera Studio, ITEC. *Career:* ENO 1972–75; English Opera Group 1975; English Music Theatre 1976–78; freelance opera singer 1978–; festival appearances in the UK and Europe; film Death in Venice (Benjamin Britten, English Music Theatre); regular television and radio broadcasts; principal tenor, WNO; roles include Radames in Aida, Don José in Carmen, title role in Parsifal, Siegmund in Die Walküre, Max in Der Freischütz; Glyndebourne and Aldeburgh Festivals; numerous British premieres; world premieres include No. 11 Bus (Peter Maxwell Davies, London, Rome and New York) 1985; other appearances include Freiburg Opera in roles, including Alwa in Lulu 1986, Erik in Fliegende Holländer 1988; Scottish Opera as Florestan in Fidelio 1984, Red Whiskers in Billy Budd 1987; Opera North as Mark, Midsummer Marriage, Tippett 1985, Wiesbaden 1986; Florestan, Fidelio at Regensburg and Kaiserslautern Operas 1987–88, Hoffmann in Tales of Hoffmann, Stockholm 1990, First Jew in Salome, ENO 1991, Bob Boles in Peter Grimes 1992; Missa Solemnis, RAH 1992; sang Filaura in Cesti's Il Pomo d'Oro at Batignano 1998; mem. Equity, Int. Therapy Education Council. *Honours:* Arts Council Scholarship to study with Otakar Kraus 1974.

STEPHENSON, Michael, BMus, MMus; American saxophonist; b. 16 Nov. 1963, Charlotte, NC; m. Cheryl Ann Swanson 1988. *Education:* North Carolina School of Arts, Ithaca Coll. *Career:* debut with New Century Saxophone Quartet, Carnegie Hall, New York 1993; performances at the White House, Ambassador Auditorium, Boston Symphony Hall, Concertgebouw (Amsterdam, The Netherlands), Kennedy Centre. *Recordings:* with New Century Saxophone Quartet: Drastic Measures, Main Street USA, Home Grown, New Century Christmas, standard repertoire. *Address:* 102 Prince Road, Greenville, NC 27858, USA.

STEPHINGER, Christoph; German singer (bass); b. 4 June 1954, Herrshing. *Education:* Munich Hochschule, the Opera Studio of Bayerische Staatsoper, studied with Kurt Moll. *Career:* sang at Bielefeld Staadtheater, 1982–86, Staatstheater Hannover from 1986; guest appearances at Düsseldorf, Dortmund, Karlsruhe, Hamburg, Berlin, Nice and Spleto; Roles have included Wagner's Guernemanz, King Henry, Pogner and Daland, Mozart's Commendatore, Osmin, Sarastro and Alfonso, Kecal in The Bartered Bride and Jim in Maschinist Hopkins by Max Brand (at Bielefeld); concert repertoire includes Herod in L'Enfance du Christ by Berlioz, with the Gächinger Kantorei under Helmuth Rilling in 1989; sang Fasolt and Hunding in new productions of Das Rheingold and Die Walküre at Hannover in 1992; Season 1999–2000 as Leporello at the Theater am Gärtnerplatz, Munich, and Lotharo in Mignon. *Current Management:* Opernagentur Inge Tennigkeit, Kempener Strasse 4, 40474 Düsseldorf, Germany. *Telephone:* (211) 5160060. *Fax:* (211) 51600616. *E-mail:* opera@tennigkeit-ag.de. *Website:* www .tennigkeit-ag.de.

STEPTOE, Roger Guy, BA, ARAM; British composer, pianist and teacher; *Professor of Harmony and Analysis, Conservatoire de Brive-la-Gaillarde;* b. 25 Jan. 1953, Winchester, Hants., England. *Education:* Univ. of Reading, Royal Acad. of Music. *Career:* debut as composer at Purcell Room 1977, as pianist at Wigmore Hall 1982; first Vaughan Williams Composer-in-Residence, Charterhouse 1976–79; Prof. of Composition, RAM, London 1980–91; US debut as composer and pianist at Federal Hall, NY 1991; Admin. of Contemporary Music Projects, RAM 1989–91, for Int. Composer Festivals 1991–93; Prof. of Harmony and Analysis, Conservatoire de Brive-la-Gaillarde, France 2001–; French debut as pianist and composer, Salle Cortot, Paris 2003; Artistic Dir Festival de Musique Classique d'Uzerche, France; mem. Inc. Soc. of Musicians. *Compositions include:* opera: King of Macedon (libretto by Ursula Vaughan Williams) 1979; orchestral: Dance Music for symphonic brass 1976, Two Miniatures for strings 1977, Oboe Concerto 1982, Tuba Concerto 1983, Clarinet Concerto 1989, Cello Concerto 1991, Cheers 1993, Impressions Corréziennes 1999, This Side of Winter 2002, Sinfonietta for organ and 15 solo strings 2005–06, Dance Music 2009, Concerto in one movement for horn and orchestra 2009–10; choral: Two Madrigals 1976, In Winter's Cold Embraces Dye (cantata for soprano, tenor, chorus and chamber orchestra) 1985, Life's Unquiet Dream (cantata for baritone, chorus and chamber orchestra) 1992, Motet: The Spirit of the Lord God is Upon Me 2009; chamber: String Quartet No. 1 1976, No. 2 1985, No. 3 2002, No. 4 2003, Clarinet Quintet 1981, Four Sonnets for brass quintet 1984, Oboe Quartet 1989, Piano Quartet 2001, De l'angélus du matin à l'angélus du soir for four Cristal Baschet 2004, Dourando as trevas for two tubas and vibraphone 2005, Seven miniatures for piano trio 2008, New York Fanfares for brass quintet 2011; vocal: Aspects for high voice and piano 1978, Chinese Lyrics for soprano and piano 1982, Chinese Lyrics for mezzo or counter-tenor and piano 1983, The Bond of the Sea for bass-baritone and piano 1983, Five Rondos for soprano, baritone and piano 1989, Sonnets to Delia for baritone and piano 1993, Three Paul Verlaine Songs for mezzo-soprano, viola and piano 2009, Five Shakespeare Songs for tenor and piano 2011; instrumental: Three Preludes for piano 1976, Piano Sonata No. 1 1980, No. 2 1988, No. 3 2003, Prelude for guitar 1981, Equinox for piano 1981, Violin Sonata No. 1 1983, No. 2 1986, In the White and the Walk of the Morning (five poems for two guitars) 1989, Prelude La Dame de Labenche 2001, Prelude for viola and piano 2002, Sonata for trumpet and organ 2008, Sonatine I for solo viola 2009, Sonatine II for cello and piano 2009, Sonatine III for organ 2009, Sonatine IV for oboe and piano 2010, Sonata for viola and piano 2010, Sonatine 5 for violin and piano 2011, Toccata for organ 2011. *Current Management:* c/o Editions BIM, PO Box 300, 1674 Vuarmarens, Switzerland. *Telephone:* (21) 9091000. *E-mail:* jm@editions-bim.com. *Website:* www .editions-bim.com. *Address:* c/o Stainer & Bell Ltd, Victoria House, 23 Gruneison Road, London, N3 1DZ, England; 7 rue Jean Gentet, 19140 Uzerche, France (home). *Telephone:* (5) 55-73-75-99 (home). *E-mail:* roger .steptoe@nordnet.fr. *Website:* www.rogersteptoe.com.

STERN, David; American conductor; *Chief Conductor, Palm Beach Opera;* b. 21 May 1963, New York; s. of Isaac Stern and Vera Stern; m. Katharina Wolff; two d. *Education:* Yale Univ., Juilliard School. *Career:* Music Dir, Philharmonisches Orchester, Westphalen 1995, Prin. Guest Conductor 1998–; Music Dir, European Acad. of Music, Aix-en-Provence 1997–2000; led the Philharmonia Orchestra, London at Albert Hall in Yehudi Menuhin Memorial Concert; collaborations with Peking Festival and several orchestras in China; Prin. Guest Conductor, Opéra de Rouen 2001; regular appearances with period instrument orchestra, Concerto Köln, including tours of Europe and USA 2002–03; Founder and Artistic Dir, Opera Fuoco, Paris 2003–; Music Dir, Opéra de St Gallen, Switzerland 2008–12; Music Dir, Israel Opera 2008–14; Dir Shanghai Baroque Festival 2014–; Dir of Opera, Crested Butte Music Festival, Colo 2015–; Chief Conductor, Palm Beach Opera 2015–. *Current Management:* c/o IMG Artists, The Light Box, 111 Power Road, London, W4 5PY, England. *Telephone:* (20) 7957-5800. *Fax:* (20) 7957-5801. *E-mail:* labrahams@imgartists.com. *Website:* www.imgartists.com. *Address:* Palm

Beach Opera, 415 South Olive Avenue, West Palm Beach, FL 33401, USA. *Website:* pbopera.org; davidstern.co.

STERN, Michael; American conductor; *Music Director and Principal Conductor, Kansas City Symphony*; b. 1959; m. Shelly Cryer; two d. *Education:* Harvard Univ., Curtis Inst. of Music, studied wth Max Rudolf. *Career:* apptd conducting asst to Christoph von Dohnányi, Cleveland Orchestra 1986, Asst Conductor 1987–91; debut New York Philharmonic at Avery Fisher Hall 1986; Perm. Guest Conductor, Orchestre Nat. de Lyon 1991–96; Chief Conductor, Saarbrücken Radio Symphony Orchestra 1996–2000, tours of Spain, Portugal, China and Switzerland; fmr Principal Guest Conductor, Orchestre Nat. de Lille; f. IRIS Orchestra, Germantown, Tenn., Music Dir 2000–; Music Dir and Principal Conductor, Kansas City Symphony 2005–; guest conductor with orchestras including New York Philharmonic, Philadelphia Orchestra, and Symphony Orchestras of Chicago, Pittsburgh, St Louis, Atlanta, Houston, Baltimore, Cincinnati, Seattle, Toronto, Montreal, Indianopolis and Washington, DC and in Europe with Royal Stockholm and Oslo Philharmonics, Bergen Symphony, Beethovenhalle Orchestra Bonn, Deutsche Symphoniker Berlin, Vienna and Budapest Radio Symphony Orchestras, Israel, Moscow and Helsinki Philharmonics, Santa Cecilia Orchestra Rome, Bavarian Radio Symphony Orchestra, Chamber Orchestra of Lausanne, Tonhalle Orchestra Zürich, London Symphony Orchestra, London Philharmonic, BBC Symphony Orchestra, English Chamber Orchestra, Nat. Symphony of Taiwan, Singapore Symphony and NHK Symphony Orchestra, Tokyo; regular performer at Aspen Festival. *Recordings include:* The Romantic Piano Concerto: Rubinstein/Scharwenka 2005, Shakespeare's The Tempest 2008, Britten's Orchestra (Grammy Award for Best Surround Sound Album 2011) 2010, and works of Chin, Hartke, Leshnoff, Rorem and Zwilich. *Publications:* as co-ed.: The Grammar of Conducting (3rd edn) 1995, Max Rudolf, A Musical Life (writings and letters) 2001. *Honours:* Hon. DMA (Univ. of Missouri, Kansas City Conservatory of Music and Dance) 2011. *Address:* Kansas City Symphony, 1703 Wyandotte, Suite 200, Kansas City, MO 64108, USA (office). *Telephone:* (816) 471-1100 (office). *Fax:* (816) 471-0976 (office). *E-mail:* kcsinfo@kcsymphony.org (office). *Website:* www.kcsymphony.org (office); irisorchestra.org (office).

STERNBERG, (E.) Jonathan, AB; American conductor; b. 27 July 1919, New York; m. Ursula Hertz 1957 (died 2000); one s. one d. *Education:* Washington Square Coll., New York Univ., Harvard Summer School, Juilliard School of Music, Manhattan School of Music, studied with Leon Barzin and Pierre Monteux. *Career:* initial engagements, Nat. Youth Administration Symphony Orchestra 1940–42; Shanghai Municipal Symphony 1945–46; professional debut, Vienna Symphony Orchestra 1947; guest conductor with major orchestras and opera cos worldwide 1950–; Conductor, Halifax Symphony Orchestra, NS, Canada 1957–58; Musical Dir Royal Flemish Opera 1962–66, Harkness Ballet, New York 1966–68, Atlanta Opera and Ballet 1968–69; Visiting Prof. of Conducting, Eastman School of Music, Univ. of Rochester 1969–71; Prof., Temple Univ. Coll. of Music 1971–89, Prof. Emer. 1989–; Lecturer, Chestnut Hill Coll., Phila 1989–92; Faculty, Int. Conductors' Workshops and Masterclasses, Zlin, Marienbad, Karlsbad (Czech Repub.), Kharkov, Ukraine, Philadelphia, New York 1989–2006; conducted premiere performances in Europe, S Africa, China and USA of music by Bloch, Ives, Rorem, Blackwood, Persichetti, Prokofiev, Messiaen, Lajtha, von Einem, Diamond, Skrowaczewski, Hindemith; Ed.-at-Large Podium Notes (Conductors' Guild newsletter) 1982–; Artistic Dir and Musical Dir, Philadelphia Bach Festival 2004–08; mem. Int. Arts Medicine Asscn (vice-pres. 1981–85), Bartok Soc. of America (Vice-Pres. 1972–78), Conductors' Guild (Vice-Pres. 1991–96, Hon. Life mem. 2003). *Recordings include:* several Haydn symphonies, Nelson Mass, Mozart Posthorn Serenade, several Bach cantatas, Rossini Stabat Mater, Prokoviev Piano Concerto No. 5 (Brendel), Mozart Piano Concerti (Badura-Skoda), Handel Organ Concerti (Leonhardt), Schubert Symphonies Nos 2, 4, 5, Bassett Variations for Orchestra, Ives Set of Pieces, Telemann Pimpinone. *Publications include:* contributed a series of articles 'Scores and Parts' (corrections from published edns of conductors' scores and previously unavailable orchestral parts used by players) to Journal of the Conductors' Guild 1983–2000. *Honours:* Citation Award for Outstanding Service to American Music 1972, Temple Univ. Faculty Research Award 1983, Distinguished Alumnus Award Third Street Music School Settlement 1988, Maestro Soc. Conducting Teacher of the Year 2001, Lifetime Achievement Award, Conductors' Guild 2009, Max Rudolf Award, Conductors' Guild 2010. *Address:* 5 West Chestnut Hill Avenue, Philadelphia, PA 19118, USA (home). *Telephone:* (215) 242-8444 (office). *Fax:* (215) 242-3772 (office). *E-mail:* maestro@temple.edu.

STERNDALE-BENNETT, Barry Monkhouse, BA, PGCHE, FIAM, FRSA, ALCM; British singer (tenor), music administrator, lecturer and writer; b. 9 March 1939, London, England. *Education:* Univs of Chicago and London, London Coll. of Music. *Career:* appearances as soloist at festivals in UK, Europe and Canada; mem. Philharmonia Chorus 1962–93, including recordings, radio and TV; mem. Waynflete Singers 1980–95, then several chamber choirs; Consultant to Bd of Trinity Coll. of Music 2000–05; Visiting Fellow, Univ. of Reading 1996–2005; Chair. Music Preserved 2004–07; Trustee and Dir, Nat. School for Young Chamber Music Players (ProCorda) 2004–08, Benslow Music Trust 2003–12; Deputy Chair. Regents Coll., London 2005–10, Asscn of British Choral Dirs 2009–12, Guildford Inst. 2011–14; mem. British Music Soc., Royal Philharmonic Soc., Int. Mendelssohn Foundation (UK); Custodian of Sir William Sterndale-Bennett collection of important 19th century British music in collaboration with Bodleian Library, Oxford. *Publications:* contributed several articles to Journals of the British Music Society, RAM. *Honours:* Hon. ARAM . *Telephone:* 7753-958726 (mobile).

STERNKLAR, Avraham; American pianist, composer and educator; b. (Alberto Sternklar), 21 Oct. 1930, Trieste, Italy; m. Evelyn Katz 1953; one s. *Education:* studied piano with L. Kestenberg and composition with M. Seter, O. Partos and P. Ben Haim in Israel, Juilliard School of Music, New York, USA, studied piano with J. Friskin and E. Steuermann and composition with V. Giannini; grad. work in chamber music. *Career:* debut in Tel-Aviv, Israel; recitals, broadcasts and performances with Israel Philharmonic, Jerusalem Symphony; music corresp., Israel Broadcasting Service 1949–52; numerous concerts throughout USA, Canada and Europe as soloist, chamber musician and as soloist with orchestras; guest performer at festivals; lecturer at seminars and workshops; specialist in contemporary music; premiered many works, several of which recorded; faculty mem. Chamber Music Workshop, sponsored by Training Orchestra, Long Island and New York Univ.; appeared in concerts with Mischa Elman, Ruggiero Ricci, Oscar Shumsky, Zvi Zeitlin, Tossy Spivakovsky, Jascha Horenstein, Ramy Shevelov, Anne Yarrow, the Hofstra String Quartet and the Bayview Chamber Players; Assoc. Prof. of Piano Performance, Aaron Copland School of Music, Queens Coll. 1992; mem. Bd of Dirs Long Island Composers Alliance. *Compositions:* for piano: Sonatinas, Sonata, Trapezium, Etudes, A Promise Fulfilled (set of ten piano pieces based on the paintings of Tea Sternklar), The General Schwarzkopf March (works for one piano four hands and for two pianos), Violin and Piano Sonata, Cello and Piano Sonata, Clarinet and Piano Sonata, Introduction and Dance for flute and piano, also songs, chamber music, choral works, recorder works, 12 Duets for two violins, educational music, Etudes for piano, Sonatina for flute, oboe and bassoon, Silhouettes for solo harp. *Honours:* Juilliard School Scholarships for five years, 17 Meet the Composer Awards, three Piano Quarterly Magazine Awards, ASCAP Plus Award. *Address:* 14 Jerold Street, Plainview, NY 11803, USA (home). *E-mail:* composers@verizon.net; composersmeister@gmail.com. *Website:* www.clearstarinternational.com/asbio.html.

STEUERMAN, Jean Louis; Brazilian pianist; b. 16 March 1949, Rio de Janeiro; m. Monica Laport 1981; two s. *Career:* debut in Rio de Janeiro 1963; appearances world-wide with major orchestras, British debut 1976; engagements with Royal Philharmonic under Menuhin, Britten's Concerto at Athens Festival, with London Symphony Orchestra under Abbado and Liverpool Philharmonic and Gewandhaus Orchestra under Masur; tour of Japan in 1989 with Stuttgart Chamber Orchestra, Schumann's Concerto with the Hallé Orchestra; further tours of Switzerland, with EC Youth Orchestra under James Judd, Italy and Japan, with the Gustav Mahler Youth Orchestra of Vienna, Czechoslovakia and Ireland; recitals in San Francisco and Scotland; chamber music concerts with leading instrumentalists notably at Menuhin Festival in Gstaad and Kuhmo Chamber Music Festival. *Recordings include:* Bach Partitas, Italian Concerto, French Overtures, Chromatic Fantasia and Fugue, Capriccio, Preludes and Fugues, Concerti, Scriabin Sonatas 3, 4 and 5, Girolamo Arrigo: Pièces pour piano, Mendelssohn: Piano Concertos Nos. 1 & 2, Bach: Variations Goldberg, Bernstein: Symphony No. 2 The Age of Anxiety; West Side Story Symphonic Dances; Candide, J.S. Bach: Klavierkonzerte BWV 1052, 1056 & 1058. *Honours:* winner, Leipzig Bach Competition 1972. *Current Management:* c/o Veronique Jourdain Artists Management, 29 rue Violet, 75015 Paris, France. *Telephone:* 1-83-62-18-64. *Fax:* 1-83-68-16-59. *E-mail:* office@veroniquejourdain.com. *Website:* www.veroniquejourdain.com.

STEWART, Donald George, MusB; American musician (clarinet), composer and music industry executive; *President, Trillenium Music Company*; b. 8 Jan. 1935, Sterling, Ill.; s. of Donald Balmer Stewart and Elinore Maud Denison; m. Susan Ann Trainer 1963 (divorced 1979); one d. *Education:* Indiana Univ., Manhattan School of Music, School of Jazz; studied with Ray Harris, Bernhard Heiden, Gunther Schuller, clarinet with Russianoff, Cioffi and Moyse. *Career:* second clarinet, Birmingham Symphony Orchestra, Ala 1954–56, Florida Symphony, Orlando 1963; played with numerous jazz ensembles, including Ornette Coleman, David Baker, Sammy Davis 1957–65; freelance copyist 1958–88; woodwind in Orchestra USA 1963–65, various orchestras, New York 1967–72; arranger and orchestrator, Harkness Ballet 1968–71; Founder Boehm Quintette, New York 1968–88, debut at Carnegie Recital Hall 1972; more than 1,000 chamber music concerts, festival appearances, with Boehm Quintette and other groups; Co-Prin. Clarinet, Sarasota Pops 2005–08; Lead Alto, Sarasota Jazz Ensemble and Good Time Groove 2005–10; Music Asst, New York State Council on Arts 1970–74; panellist, Vermont Council on the Arts 1976–78; Founder Chamber Music America 1978, Bd mem., Treas. 1982; Founder and Pres. Trillenium Music Co. 1986–; Pres. Opera North, Norwich, Vt 1987–89, Bd mem. 1985–95; mem. Bd Vermont Symphony Orchestra 1989–93; mem. ASCAP, American Fed. of Musicians, American Soc. of Music Copyists (mem. Bd Dirs 1970–87, Treas. 1984–87), American Music Centre, Music Publrs' Asscn, Retail Print Music Dealers' Asscn. *Compositions include:* Seven Little Etudes for orchestral woodwind section, Gesualdo Stanzas for large ensemble, 200-bar Passacaglia, two string quartets, Sonata No. 1 for horn and piano, No. 2 for wind quintet, String Quartet Nos 1 and 2, Saxophone Quartet, Brass Quintet, Duet for flute and bass clarinet, Violin Sonatina, Never Leave Me Blue for SSAATTBB, piano and string bass, Piccolo Concerto 1973, August Lions for youth orchestra 1978, Song of Arion 1985, First Blue Symphony for large orchestra 1988, A Book of Sliding Things for eight trombones, tuba and bass 1989, Green

Mountain Christmas Card (opera) 1993, Never Seek to Tell Thy Love for voice and ensemble 1998, Duo for violin and cello 1999, Sinfonia for strings and percussion 2000, A Quartet of Flutes 2003, Third Symphony (Op. 43) Continuo Canti, Period Pieces with NooGlu (Op. 47), Third Wind Quintet, Metric Measures (Op. 48) 2008, Fourth Symphony (Music for Clarinet and Orchestra Op. 49), The Good Time Groove Op. 50 2010; transcriber, composer, arranger. *Recordings include:* three records with Boehm Quintette, Marlboro Recordings, Music of Arthur Berger. *Publications:* more than 100 titles in print 1970–. *Address:* Trillenium Music Co., PO Box 51059, Sarasota, FL 34232-0329 (office); 1515 Firethorne Lakes Drive, Sarasota, FL 34240, USA (home). *Telephone:* (941) 377-7375 (office). *Fax:* (941) 377-9043 (office). *E-mail:* don@trillmusic.com (office). *Website:* www.trillmusic.com (office).

STEWART, Jeffrey; British singer (tenor); b. 1970, Surrey. *Education:* Guildhall School and National Opera Studio. *Career:* appearances with Opera North in The Thieving Magpie and The Magic Flute (Tamino); Nadir in The Pearl Fishers for ETO and Narraboth in Salome for ENO; Edgardo in Lucia di Lammermoor for European Chamber Opera and Ernesto at Düsseldorf; other roles include Don José at Dartington, Steva in Jenůfa, Maurizio in Adriana Lecouvreur, 1999, the Duke of Mantua in Rigoletto, Ferrando in Cosi fan Tutti; Season 1999–2000 as Count Ivrea in Un giorno di regno, and Italian Singer in Der Rosenkavalier, Ernesto in Don Pasquale, Nemorino in Elisir D'Amore, Pinkerton in Madama Butterfly; concerts include Bach's Mass in B minor, Beethoven's Ninth Symphony, Berlioz's Te Deum, Britten's St. Nicholas, Elgar's Dream of Gerontius and The Kingdom, Handel's Messiah, Israel in Egypt and Dettingen Te Deum, Haydn's Nelson Mass and Lobgesang, Monteverdi's Vespere della Beata Vergine, Mozart's Mass in C, Coronation Mass, Mass in C Minor and Missa Domenicus, Puccini's Messa do Gloria, Rachmaninov's The Bells, Rossini's Stabat Mater and Petite Messe Solenelle, Stainer's Crucifixion, Verdi's Requiem, Weil's Seven DEeadly Sins. *E-mail:* jeff@jeffstewart.co.uk (office). *Website:* www.jeffstewart.co.uk.

STEWART, Murray, MA, FRCO (CHM), ARCM, LRAM; British conductor; *Artistic Director and Principal Conductor, London Pro Arte Orchestra and London Pro Arte Baroque;* b. 20 Feb. 1954, Barnet, Herts., England. *Education:* Trinity Hall, Cambridge, studied organ with Peter Hurford, Daniel Roth in Paris, conducting with Harold Gray, Meredith Davies and Sir Charles Mackerras. *Career:* as organist recorded complete works of Franck and works by Vierne; currently Artistic Dir and Prin. Conductor, London Pro Arte Orchestra and London Pro Arte Baroque; conducted premieres by Ropartz, Langlais, Sallinen, Kokkonen, Szymanowski, Howells, Patterson, Chapple, Hellawell, Burgon, Blake, Hakim, Walker and Leighton; guest conducting engagements with the Philharmonia Orchestra, Royal Philharmonic Orchestra, Bournemouth Symphony Orchestra, Bournemouth Sinfonietta, Ulster Orchestra, City of London Sinfonia, and with the Prague Radio Symphony Orchestra, Sinfonia Viva, Orchestra da Camera, Musici de Praga and the Aarhus Symphony Orchestra; Guest Conductor, West German Radio Choir, Danish Nat. Opera Chorus, Pamplona Chamber Choir, Spain; former conductor, Collegium Musicum of London, Bristol Choral Soc., East London Chorus, London Forest Choir, Nottingham Harmonic Soc. and Finchley Children's Music Group. *Recordings include:* works by Jean Langlais, Mozart's Requiem, complete orchestral works of Maurice Duruflé (with BBC Concert Orchestra), Rodriguez de Ledesma's Requiem Mass (world premiere recording). *E-mail:* office@londonproarte.co.uk (office). *Website:* www.londonproarte.co.uk (office).

STEWEN, Henrico, DMus; Dutch/Finnish organist; *Freelance Organist, Henrico Stewen Music Production;* b. 1970. *Education:* Sibelius Acad., Helsinki, Amsterdam Conservatory with Jacques van Oortmerssen, Hans Davidsson and Hans van Nieuwkoop. *Career:* works as concert organist and church musician, gives lectures and masterclasses. *Recording:* Max Reger—Organ Works (Echo Klassik Award Solo Recording of the Year, 20th/21st century) 2011. *Publication:* The Straube Code: Deciphering the Metronome Marks in Max Reger's Organ Music 2008. *Address:* Ruusukuja 1K, 02270 Espoo, Finland. *Telephone:* (44) 0583358. *E-mail:* hmstewen@hotmail.com (office). *Website:* www.henricostewen.tk.

STIER, Eckehard; German conductor; *Music Director, Auckland Philharmonia Orchestra;* b. 1972, Dresden. *Education:* Carl Maria von Weber Conservatory, Dresden. *Career:* sang as boy soprano, Dresden Kreuzchor; Staff Conductor, Opera Theater of Chemnitz 1995–2003; Chief Conductor, Görlitz Theatre and New Lausitz Philharmonic Orchestra 2003; Australian debut with Melbourne Symphony Orchestra 2006; Music Dir, Auckland Philharmonia Orchestra 2009–; has appeared with numerous orchestras including Sächsischen Staatskapelle Dresden, Melbourne Symphony Orchestra, Auckland Philharmonia Orchestra, Staatskapelle Halle, Robert Schumann Philharmonie Chemnitz, MDR-Sinfonieorchester, Dresdner Sinfonikern, Münchner Symphonikern, NRT Radio Orchester Zagreb; also plays jazz piano. *Repertoire:* repertoire of 70 stage works and almost 150 symphonic works. *Current Management:* Generalmanagement Konzertdirektion Martin Müller, Uhrs Knäppken 8, 59320 Ennigerloh-Ostenfelde, Germany. *Telephone:* (25) 24-26-34-80. *Fax:* (25) 24-26-34-81. *E-mail:* info@kdmueller.de. *Website:* www.kdmueller.de. *E-mail:* eckehard.stier@t-online.de (office). *Website:* www.eckehardstier.com.

STILES, Frank, BSc, BMus, LGSM, AGSM; British composer, conductor and violist; b. 2 April 1924, Chiswick, London, England; m. 1st Estelle Lewis 1969; m. 2nd Elizabeth Horwood 1988. *Education:* Imperial Coll., Durham Univ.,

Paris Conservatoire. *Career:* served in RAF 1942–46; Prin. Conductor, Priory Concertante of London; Composer-in-Residence, Protoangel Visions, Normanby by Spital, Lincs. 2003–; mem. Composers' Guild of GB, Incorporated Soc. of Musicians, Royal Soc. of Musicians, Asscn for British Music (Chair.), British Acad. of Songwriters, Composers and Authors, Performing Right Soc., Mechanical-Copyright Protection Soc. *Compositions:* Dramatic Cantata, Masada, Man's Four Seasons song cycle, Triple Concerto, Mirage for solo piano, Concoid organ work, In Memoriam choral work, String Quartet No. 6, five symphonies, seven concertos, other orchestral works, works for string orchestra, five string quartets, trios, duos and solo works, various other chamber, choral and vocal works, Four Miniatures for solo clarinet, Fantasia for 12 violas, The Great Lakes symphonic suite, Three Songs for Mezzo-Soprano and Piano, Sonata No. 3 for viola and piano 2005, Sonata for solo viola 2006, String Quartet No. 7 2011, String Trio, String Quintet (two violas). *Recordings:* Guitar Sonata, String Quartet No. 3, Keyboard Sonata, Concerto For Five, First Piano Concerto, Equinox for Solo Piano, Sonata for Solo Violin No. 2 2000, Sonata for Violin and Piano No. 2 2000, String Quartet No. 6 2001. *Publications:* contrib. to Composer, Musician 1979–84, Classical Musicians Speak Out 2004. *Honours:* City of London Prize for Composition 1955, Gold Medal for Composition, Paris Conservatoire 1955. *Address:* 43 Beech Road, Branston, Lincoln, LN4 1PP, England. *Telephone:* (1522) 791662.

STILLER, Andrew Philip, BA, MA, PhD; American composer; b. 6 Dec. 1946, Washington, DC; Ernestine Steiner 1975. *Education:* Univ. of Wisconsin, State Univ. of New York. *Career:* Center of Creative and Performing Arts 1971–73; Decapod Wind Quintet 1975; Age of Reason Ensemble 1981; Buffalo New Music Ensemble 1984–85; Network for New Music 1986–89; solo shows, Buffalo 1979, 1972, 1973, 1976; works also heard at North American New Music Festivals 1984, 1985; consultant, New Grove Dictionary of Opera 1990; founder and Dir, Kallisti Music Press 1991–; mem. ASCAP. *Compositions:* orchestral: Periodic Table of Elements, Foster Song, Magnification: Procrustean Concerto 1994; numerous chamber music works, including sonata, chamber symphony, various pieces for keyboard and vocal. *Recordings:* A Descent into the Maelstrom, The Mouse Singer, A Periodic Table of the Elements, The Water is Wide (Daisy Bell), Sonata a3 pulsatoribus. *Publications:* Handbook of Instrumentation 1985, Buffalo Philharmonic Orchestra 1985; contrib. to Opus, Philadelphia Inquirer, Buffalo News, Revised New Grove Dictionary of Music and Musicians, New Grove Dictionary of Opera, Musical Quarterly, Musical America. *Address:* 810 South Saint Bernard Street, Philadelphia, PA 19143, USA.

STILWELL, Richard Dale, MusB; American singer (baritone) and academic; b. 6 May 1942, St Louis, Mo.; s. of Otho John Clifton and Tressie Stilwell (née Parrish); m. 1st Elizabeth Louise Jencks 1967 (divorced); m. 2nd Kerry M. McCarthy 1983; two s. *Education:* Anderson Coll., Univ. of Indiana. *Career:* with Metropolitan Opera Co., New York 1970–; appearances in major roles with Washington Opera Soc., Marseille Opera, Santa Fe Opera, San Francisco Opera, Paris Opera, La Scala, Covent Garden, Hamburg State Opera, Glyndebourne Opera Festival, Vancouver Opera, Chicago Opera, Israel Philharmonic, Boston Symphony, LA Philharmonic, among others, and at Tanglewood Festival; soloist with Nat. Symphony, Washington, Chicago Symphony, American Symphony, Carnegie Hall, Boston Symphony, LA Philharmonic, among others; currently Prof. of Voice, Music Conservatory, Chicago Coll. of Performing Arts, Roosevelt Univ.; mem. American Guild of Musical Artists. *Honours:* Nat. Soc. of Arts and Letters Award 1963, Fisher Foundation Award, Metropolitan Opera Auditions 1965. *Address:* AUD 926, Music Conservatory, Chicago College of Performing Arts, 430 South Michigan Avenue, Chicago, IL 60605, USA (office). *Telephone:* (312) 341-4337 (office). *E-mail:* rstilwell@roosevelt.edu (office). *Website:* www.roosevelt.edu/CCPA/MusicConservatory.aspx (office).

STOCKDALE, Jonty, BA, DPhil, FLCM; British composer; *Principal, Royal Northern College of Music;* b. 1963, Doncaster; m. Catherine Stockdale; one d. *Education:* Univ. of Huddersfield, York Univ. *Career:* fmr Sr Lecturer and Head of School (Popular Music and Recording), Univ. Coll., Salford; Dir of Studies, Leeds Coll. of Music 1995–2005; Head of Music and Assoc. Dean, Victoria Coll. of the Arts, Melbourne, Australia 2005–08; Prin., Royal Northern Coll. of Music 2008–; compositions have received over 40 public performances at UK and Scandinavian festivals and venues; as both performer/composer has performed or had work featured at ICA, London, Nettlefold Festival, Huddersfield Contemporary Music Festival, York Spring Festival of Contemporary Music, Oxford Univ. Concert Series, Bergen Int. Festival of Contemporary Music, Lowry Centenary Festival, Oslo Konserthus, Reykjavik Konserthus; fmr BAFTA jury mem.; mem. Cttee, Melbourne Prize for Music 2007; mem. Editorial Bd, Jazz Research Journal (Equinox). *Compositions:* several contemporary and electro-acoustic compositions. *Address:* Office of the Principal, Royal Northern College of Music, 124 Oxford Road, Manchester, M13 9RD, England (office). *Telephone:* (161) 907 5273 (office). *E-mail:* jonty.stockdale@rncm.ac.uk (office). *Website:* www.rncm.ac.uk (office).

STOCKER, Markus; violoncellist; b. 2 April 1945, Basel, Switzerland; m. Mei-Lee Ong 1975; two d. *Education:* Univ. of Basel, Acad. of Music, Basel with August Wenzinger. *Career:* performances in London, Paris, Vienna, Berlin, New York, Tokyo, Beijing; concerts throughout Europe, USA, Far East, Israel and Russia; performed at Lucerne, Salzburg and Menuhin Festivals, Marlboro and Lockenhaus; appearances with Rudolf Serkin, Martha Argerich, Sándor Végh, Gidon Kremer; Professor at Winterthur and

Zürich Conservatories; piano trio with violinist Wanda Wilkomirska and pianist Werner Genuit 1985; European premiere, Cello Concerto by Oscar Morawetz, Memorial of Martin Luther King, Zürich 1995; Prof. of Cello, Queensland Conservatorium, Brisbane 1995–; mem. Asscn of Swiss Musicians, Indooroopilly LC. *Recordings:* Bach Suites, Mendelssohn Complete Works for Cello and Piano, works by Martin, Honegger, Rachmaninov and Shostakovich with Victor Yampolsky 1994. *Honours:* first prize Bloomington, IN, USA 1972, Grand Prix Maurice Marechal Int. Cello Competition, Paris 1972, soloist's prize Asscn of Swiss Musicians 1973.

STOCKHAUSEN, Markus; German musician (trumpet) and composer; b. 2 May 1957, Cologne. *Education:* Cologne Hochschule für Musik. *Career:* debut with K-H Stockhausen's Sirius, Washington, DC, 1976; participation in the premieres of Aries 1977, and the Licht cycle of operas; Donnerstag (Michaels Reise um die Erde 1981), Samstag (oberlip-pentanz 1984) and Dienstag (Invasion and Pietà 1991); jazz collaborations including the group Possible Worlds,1995–; duo partners include the pianist Majella Stockhausen; film and theatre music composition with brother, Simon Stockhausen; Lecturer, Cologne Hochschule für musik from 1996. *Recordings include:* Michaels Reise um die Erde, New Colours of Piccolo Trumpet 1993, Clow and Jubilee 1996. *Address:* Hochschule für musik, Dagobertstrasse 38, 50668 Cologne, Germany.

STOCKIGT, Janice Beverley, BMus, PhD, FAHA; Australian musicologist and academic; *Honorary Principal Fellow, Melbourne Conservatorium of Music, University of Melbourne*; b. (Janice Bevereley Larsen), 14 July 1938, Melbourne; d. of Walter Harold Larsen and Thelma May Larsen; two d. *Education:* Univ. of Melbourne. *Career:* Hon. Prin. Fellow, Melbourne Conservatorium of Music, Univ. of Melbourne 2006–; mem. Australian Acad. of Humanities, Australian Musicological Soc. *Publications include:* Jan Dismas Zelenka (1679–1745): A Bohemian Musician at the Court of Dresden 2000, A Study of English Influence on Musical Taste and Programming: New Choral Works Introduced to Audiences by Melbourne Philharmonic Society 1876–1901, 19th Century Music Review 4: 29–53 2005, Two more Vivaldi Finds in Dresden, Eighteenth-Century Music 3/1: 35–61 2006, This Rare and Precious Music: Preliminary Findings on the Music Collection of the Catholic Court Church (1765), Musicology Australia 27: 1–18 (with Michael Talbot) 2006, Music senza nome dell'Authore: anonymous works in the music collection of the Dresden Hofkirche 1765, Studi vivaldiani 7: 3–52 2007; contrib. to The Oxford Companion to Australia, The New Grove Dictionary of Music and Musicians; co-edited and contributed to Music at German Courts, 1715–1760: Changing Artistic Priorities 2011, Bach's Missa BWV 232I in the context of Catholic Mass settings in Dresden, 1729–1733, in Jan Smaczny: Exploring Bach's B-minor Mass 2013 (pp. 39–53). *Honours:* Chancellor's Prize, Univ. of Melbourne 1994, Harbison-Higinbotham Research Scholarship 1994, Woodward Medal, Univ. of Melbourne 2001, Derek Allen Prize, British Acad. 2001. *Address:* Melbourne Conservatorium of Music, Conservatorium Building, University of Melbourne, Parkville, Vic. 3010, Australia (office). *E-mail:* j.stockigt@unimelb.edu.au (office).

STØDLE, Tori; Norwegian pianist; b. 1 July 1942, Oslo; m. Hakon Stodle 1975; one s. one d. *Education:* studied with Robert Riefling in Oslo, Jurgen Uhde in Stuttgart, and Adele Marcus in New York. *Career:* debut in Oslo 1970 and New York 1990; recitals in Norway, UK, Germany, Russia, Italy, Netherlands, Denmark and USA; several television and radio programmes for Norwegian broadcasting; guest artist at major music festivals, including Chamber Music Festival at Tromso, Bergen Festival and North Norwegian Festival; piano soloist for world premieres of Ketil Vea's Piano Concertos Nos 1 and 3; Music from the Top of the World, recital of music by 19th- and 20th-century Norwegian composers, sponsored by various Norwegian organizations, Weill Recital Hall, Carnegie Hall, New York 1990; The Dream of a Sound, television portrait 1991; promotes new music; works dedicated to her by several Norwegian composers; Assoc. Prof. of Piano, North Norwegian Music Conservatory, Tromso; mem. of two Norwegian music asscns, European Piano Teachers' Asscn. *Recordings:* Music From The North, Music From The Top Of The World, Berg, Bibalo and Brahms 1996, Landscapes in Music (works by Norwegian composer David Monrad Johansen) 2000. *Honours:* Northern Lights Prize 1991. *Address:* Fogd Dreyersgt 21, 9008 Tromso, Norway (office).

STOIANOV, Konstantin; violinist; b. 1950, Russia. *Education:* Antwerp Conservatory, studied in Berlin and Würzburg. *Career:* numerous solo appearances with leading orchestras; radio broadcasts in Belgium, France and Italy; Leader, Royal Philharmonic Orchestra of Flanders; Co-Leader, London Philharmonic 1990; Prof., Int. Menuhin Acad. at Gstaad.

STOICA, Adrian-Oliviu, MA; Romanian pianist; b. 27 Oct. 1955, Cluj-Napoca; m. Marcela-Iustina Stoica 1979. *Education:* George Dima Academy of Music, Cluj (scholarship), studied with Georg Sava, Harald Enghiurliu, Ferdinand Weiss, masterclasses in Weimar, Germany with Rudolf Kehrer. *Career:* debut with Mozart's Concerto in C major, K 415, with Oradea Symphony Orchestra, 1972; Permanent Piano Soloist, Sibiu State Philharmonic Orchestra, 1989–91; recitals; guest soloist, concerts with all philharmonic orchestras in Romania; tours abroad include Washington, DC, Midland-Odessa (TX), New York, 1979, Boston, MA, 1993, 1994, New Jersey, 1994, Galesburg and Monmouth, IL, 1996, USA; Thuringia, 1979, Hannover-Langenhagen, 1994, 1996, Germany; Czech Republic, 1984; Poland, 1985; Russia and Baltic Republics, 1986, 1989; Valencia, Spain, 1992, 1994; Lecturer, Univ. of Music, Bucharest. *Recordings:* Paul Richter: Op 58, Concerto in C minor for piano and orchestra, and op 121, Variations for piano and orchestra. *Honours:* Fellowship, Romanian Ministry of Culture.

STOJADINOVIĆ-MILIĆ, Milana, MA; Serbian composer; *Associate Professor of Harmony and Analysis, Department of Musical Theory, Belgrade University*; b. 13 July 1962, Belgrade; m.; two s. *Education:* Belgrade Univ. *Career:* debut, String Quartet Melodia, Radio Belgrade Programme for Classical Music 1985; Prof. of Harmony and Analysis, High School for Music, Belgrade; fmr Asst in Dept of Music Theory, Faculty of Music, Belgrade Univ., currently Assoc. Prof. of Harmony and Analysis; live performances at festivals in Yugoslavia, Slovenia, Croatia, Germany, Italy, Bulgaria, Greece, UK, France, Russia; mem. Asscn of Composers of Serbia. *Compositions:* Melody for string quartet 1985, Dream for flute and piano 1986, Mimicry for symphony orchestra 1987, Aurora Borealis for symphony orchestra 1989, Duo Symbolico for piano and symphony orchestra 1994, Kaleidoscope for wind quintet 2001, Tango Sentimental for violin, double bass, accordion and piano (in memory of Astor Piazzola) 2002, Haven't You Forgotten Something? for flute and bassoon 2002, Tears, a cycle of ten miniature songs for voice (soprano), alt-flute and piano (first live performance, Belgrade) 2003, Fragment of Interim for soprano, flute and piano 2005, Neoromantico, trio for flute, violin and piano 2008, EOL for cello trio 2008, The Sky above Studenica for piano 2009, Rock Jazz Roll Etude for piano 2010, Tell Me for harp duo 2010, Neoromantico 2 for clarinette, violin and piano 2012, Tango per tre for violin, cello and piano 2013, Tango per tre nuovi for flute, violin and piano 2013, Secret agent from Timpanius (mini rhapsody for piano) 2013, So shall be light! for piano 2013, Fragments of Interim 2 for soprano, flute, violin and piano 2013, Little Pieces for Young Pianists (Chopinessa, The first-called…) 2013. *Recordings:* albums: Aurora Borealis 1989, Duo Simbolico 1995, Contemporary Music from the Balkans 1999, Kaleidoscope 2002, Tango Sentimental, New Tango After Piazzola 2002, Fragment of Interim 2008; pieces on The International Review of Composers. *Publications:* Four Spiritual Verses by Marko Tajcević – the force of prism in interlacing of modal and tonal harmonic solutions 2004, Anthology of Theoretical Works, Harmony and Analysis as a Creative Process 2010, Anthology of Theoretical Works 2013. *Honours:* three Asscn of Composers of Serbia Awards 1985, 1986, 1988, two Int. Festival of Composers Awards 1992, 1994, Belgrade October Prize 1987, Vasilije Mokraniac Prize 1989, 1994, Josip Slavenski Prize 1987. *E-mail:* composas@gmail.com (office).

STOJANOVIĆ, Milka; Serbian singer (soprano); b. 13 Jan. 1937, Belgrade. *Education:* La Scala Opera School, studied with Zinka Milanov. *Career:* sang with Belgrade National Opera from 1960, notably at Edinburgh Festival in 1962 and at Oslo and Lausanne in 1968 and 1971; further appearances at Graz, 1962, Metropolitan Opera, 1967–68, Vienna, Bari, Munich, Cologne and Barcelona, 1970–71; Opera and concert engagements in Denmark, England, Hungary, Hamburg, Frankfurt, Dresden, Berlin, Zürich, Oslo, Copenhagen, Helsinki, Rome, Venice, Bologna, Palermo, Syracuse, Valencia, Athens, Ankara, Cairo, Caracas, Russia, Sofia, Budapest, Bucharest, and Czechoslovakia; Also festival appearances at Prague Spring and Salzburg; Roles have included Verdi's Aida, Desdemona and Amelia in Un Ballo in Maschera, Leonore, Mimi, Liu, Mozart's Countess, La Gioconda, Marenka, Santuzza and Tatiana; roles in Verdi's Simon Boccanegra, Traviata and Vespri Siciliani, Madama Butterfly, Fidelio, Lohengrin, Tchaikovsky's Queen of Spades, Borodin's Prince Igor.

STOJANOVIĆ-KUTLAČA, Svetlana, BA, MA, DA; Serbian harpsichordist; *Professor of Harpsichord, Josip Slavenski Music School, Belgrade*; b. 2 May 1957, Skopje, Macedonia; m. Djuro Kutlaca 1980, one d. *Education:* Univ. of Arts, Belgrade, one-year specialization with Genoveva Galves, Madrid, Spain, masterclasses with Huguette Dreyfus, Kristine Daxelhofer, Marc Kroll, Colin Tilney and Paul Simmonds. *Career:* 17 solo recitals in Spain, UK and Switzerland and over 100 in Serbia and Montenegro; as harpsichord duo mem., appeared with Stephane Becchy, Maria Luisa Baldasari, Hilary McQueen, Jacques Etienne Rouge, Steven Devine, Agnes Varollyay; as accompanist with David Dor, Stefan Milenković, Karolina Beter, Dragan Karolić, Predrag Gosta and Predrag Djoković; associated with Belgrade Philharmonic Orchestra and RTS Orchestra; Prof. of Harphichord, Josip Slavenski Music School, Belgrade. *Recordings:* seven CDs of harpsichord solo pieces by Balbastre, F. Couperin, Rameau, Dufly, Scarlatti, M. Kuzmanovic and pieces by W. Byrd and John Bull on clavichord; Ed. Studio for Early Music. *Publications:* several articles in music journals. *Address:* Branicevska 11, 11000 Belgrade, Serbia. *E-mail:* svetlanastojanovic.kutlaca@gmail.com.

STOKER, Richard, FRAM, ARAM, ARCM; British composer, actor, conductor, writer and poet and painter; b. 8 Nov. 1938, Castleford, Yorks.; s. of Bower Morrell Stoker and Winifred Stoker; m. Gillian Patricia Watson 1986. *Education:* Breadalbane House School, Castleford, Univ. of Huddersfield with Harold Truscott, Coll. of Art, Royal Acad. of Music and Drama, composition with Sir Lennox Berkeley, conducting with Maurice Miles, pvt. study with Nadia Boulanger in Paris (Mendelssohn Scholarship), Arthur Benjamin, Eric Fenby, Benjamin Britten. *Career:* performance debut with BBC Home Service 1953, Nat. and Int. Eisteddfods, Wales 1955–58; conducting debut 1956; Asst Librarian, London Symphony Orchestra 1962–63; Prof. of Composition, RAM 1963–87 (tutor 1970–80); composition teacher, St Paul's School 1972–74, Magdalene Coll., Cambridge 1974–76; Ed. The Composer magazine 1969–80; Magistrate, Inner London Comm. 1995–2003, Crown Court 1998–2003; Adjudicator, Royal Philharmonic Soc. Composer's Award, Cyprus Orchestral Composer's Award from Ministry of Culture 2001–, BBC

Composer's Awards; mem. Composers' Guild 1962– (mem. Exec. Cttee 1969–80); Founder-mem. RAM Guild Cttee 1994– (Hon. Treas. 1995–); Founder-mem. European-Atlantic Group 1993–; mem. Byron Soc. 1993–2000, Magistrates' Asscn 1995–2003, English and Int. PEN 1996–2005; mem. and Treas. Steering Cttee Lewisham Arts Festival 1990, 1992; Founder-mem. Atlantic Council 1993, RSL, Creative Rights Alliance 2001–; concert appearances as pianist including Queen Elizabeth Hall, Purcell Room, Leighton House, RAM, Pizza on the Park, Barnet Festival; mem. RAM Guild. *Art exhibitions:* various works in pvt. collections including Trinity Coll. of Music. *Compositions include:* four symphonies 1961, 1976, 1981, 1991; 12 nocturnes; two jazz preludes; overtures: Antic Hay, Feast of Fools, Heroic Overture; three string quartets, three violin sonatas, Partita for Violin and Harp or Piano, Sonatina for Guitar, two piano sonatas, three piano trios, A York Suite for piano, Piano Variations, Piano Concerto, Partita for Clarinet and Piano, Wind Quintet; organ works: Partita, Little Organ Book, Three Improvisations, Symphony; Monologue, Passacagalia, Serenade, Petite Suite, Nocturnal, Festival Suite; choral works and song cycles: Benedictus, Ecce Homo, Proverb, Psalms, Make Me a Willow Cabin, Canticle of the Rose, O Be Joyful, A Landscape of Truth; piano works: Zodiac Variations, Regency Suite, A Poet's Notebook; vocal works: Music That Brings Sweet Sleep, Aspects of Flight, Four Yeats Songs, Four Shakespeare Songs, Johnson Preserv'd (three-act opera), Thérèse Raquin, Chinese Canticle, Birthday of the Infanta; music for film and stage includes Troilus and Cressida, Portrait of a Town, Garden Party, My Friend – My Enemy. *Recordings:* appearances on numerous CDs and records. *Films:* appearances include Red Mercury Rising, Woken, Daddy's Girl, Portrait of a Town, Lear and Goneril, The Shrink, Bedtime Story, The Usual, The End of the Line, The Queen, The Da Vinci Code, Ancient Cataclysms, Vagabond Shoes, Encounter, Bouquet, Interval, Home Guard Ron, Pirates of the Caribbean IV. *Television:* Mary Tudor (four-part series), Comment (Channel 4), Europe, Dirty Weekend in Hospital, Happiness (BBC), Troilus and Cressida. *Radio:* interviews and discussions on BBC Radio 3, 4, World Service, Radio Leeds, New York Times Radio, Radio New York, Wall Street Radio, Radio Algonquin. *Publications include:* Portrait of a Town 1970, Words Without Music 1974, Strolling Players 1978, Open Window – Open Door (autobiog.) 1985, Tanglewood (novel) 1990, Between the Lines 1991, Diva (novel) 1992, Collected Short Stories 1993, Sir Thomas Armstrong: A Celebration 1998, Turn Back the Clock 1998, A Passage of Time 1999; contrib. to anthologies, including Triumph, Forward, Outposts, Spotlight, Strolling Players, American Poetry Soc. publs, reviews and articles for periodicals, including Records and Recording, Books and Bookmen, Guardian, Performance, The Magistrate, poems in numerous anthologies and internet publs; contrib. to Oxford Dictionary of Nat. Biography (nine entries) 2004, 2006 (adviser 2003–). *Honours:* BBC Music Award 1952, Eric Coates Award 1962, Dove Prize 1962, Nat. Library of Poetry (USA) Editors' Choice Award 1995, 1996, 1997. *Telephone:* 7906-843812 (mobile). *E-mail:* r_stoker@btinternet.com. *Website:* www.richardstoker.co.uk.

STOKES, Harvey J., BM, MM, PhD; American composer, oboist and academic; *Professor of Music, Hampton University*; b. 14 Sept. 1957, Norfolk, Va; m.; one s. two d. *Education:* East Carolina Univ., Univ. of Georgia, Michigan State Univ. *Career:* currently Prof. of Music, Hampton Univ., Va. *Compositions include:* Symphonies Nos 1–5, String Quartet Nos 1–4, Dominion Fragments, Ethnic Impressions for soprano saxophone, alto saxophone and piano, Chamber Concerto No. 1 for oboe and string quartet, Concerto No. 2 for oboe and strings, Oboe Concerto No. 3 for chamber orchestra, Clarinet Concerto for chamber orchestra, Flute Concerto for chamber orchestra, Piano Concerto for orchestra, Wedge Dream for strings, Piano Sonatas Nos 1–6, Values and Proposals Nos 2, 3 and 6, DIVA Suite for bassoon and piano, Suite for Five Winds, Music for 12 Trumpets, In Memoriam SCA, Sonata for violin and piano, Sonata for violoncello and piano, Second Sonata for oboe and piano, Sonata for viola and piano, Sonata for horn and piano, Sonata for flute and piano, Quintet No. 3 for winds, Quintet No. 4 for winds, Trio Expressivo for flute, clarinet and piano, Three Psalm Fragments, The Triumphant Men for wind ensemble. *Recording:* Harvey J. Stokes: String Quartets 1, 2, 3 1998, Harvey J. Stokes: The Complete Wind Quintets 1, 2, 3, 4 2011. *Publications:* A Selected Annotated Bibliography on Italian Serial Composers 1989, Compositional Language in the Oratorio The Second Act 1992. *Honours:* First Prize, New England Conservatory New Works Competition 1983, First Prize, Lancaster Summer Arts Festival Orchestral Composition Contest 1983. *Address:* 1412 Hastings Drive, Hampton, VA, 23663, USA (office). *Telephone:* (757) 727-5410 (office); (757) 768-6263 (home). *Fax:* (757) 727-5084 (office). *E-mail:* harvey.stokes@hamptonu.edu (office); hstok1412@msn.com (home).

STOLL, David Michael, MA (Oxon.), ARAM, FRSA; British composer; b. 29 Dec. 1948, London. *Education:* Worcester Coll., Oxford, Royal Acad. of Music. *Career:* Music Dir, Greenwich Young People's Theatre 1971–75; subsequently freelance composer; fmr mem. Bd of Dirs British Acad. of Songwriters, Composers and Authors (fmr Chair.); consultant on music and creativity in schools and colls; Seminar Dir In Tune in Europe (UK Dept for Culture, Media, Sport and EC) 1998; Project Leader, Building Music (Dept for Educ. and Skills) 2003–04; fmr mem. Bd European Composers' Forum; mem. Inc. Soc. of Musicians; masterclasses in composing, songwriting and creative thinking in further and higher educ. *Plays:* Little Fir Tree, The Drummer Boy of Waterloo, You, Me and a Piano. *Compositions:* concert music includes: Piano Quartet 1987, Sonata for two pianos 1990, Piano Sonata 1991, String Trio 1992, Fanfares and Reflections (wind sextet) 1992, String Quartet No. 1 1994, Monument 1995, The Bowl of Nous (cantata) 1996, False Relations (opera) 1997, Motet in Memoriam 1998, Midwinter Spring (symphonic poem) 1998, String Quartet No. 2 1999, Cello Concerto 2000, Octave Variations (tuba quartet) 2001, The Path to the River (octet) 2001, Cello Sonata 2001, Fools by Heavenly Compulsion (String Quartet No. 3) 2002, Sonnet for string orchestra 2002, Pot-Pourri for orchestra 2002, Theatre Dreams for brass quintet 2003, A Colchester Suite for pipes 2003, String Quartet No. 4 2005, Gallions Concerto 2006, The Song of Deborah for mezzo-soprano with string quartet 2007, Sinfonietta for 12 Clarinets 2008; media music: comms include several signature tunes and considerable media and library (production) music; theatre: several scores, including Teller of Tales (musical, co-composer), As You Like It (RSC production) 2003, Henry VIII (A&BC theatre co. for RSC) 2006, Gulliver (musical) 2007, Cuckoo Rock (musical) 2013; educational works for schools (including for ABRSM music medals series) and children's songs including Sealsongs 2008. *Recordings:* Chamber Music 1993, The Shakespeare Suite 2000, String Quartets 2001, The Fair Singer 2002, What Fools These Mortals Be 2009, String Quartet No. 3 2013, String Quartet No. 4 2013. *Publications:* Building Music: Teaching Composing at Key Stage 2 2005, Key Stage 2 Composing: The Complete Scheme of Work (First and Best in Education) 2006; various articles; contrib. to Music Futures series, several articles on music, philosophy and related subjects. *Honours:* Hadow Open Scholarship in Composition to Worcester Coll., Oxford 1967. *E-mail:* davidstoll@btconnect.com (office). *Website:* www.davidstoll.co.uk (office).

STOLL, Klaus; German double bassist; b. 24 May 1943, Rheydt. *Education:* Cologne Musikhochschule. *Career:* mem. Niederrheinische Sinfoniker 1959–65; Berlin Philharmonic from 1965, Prin. Bass 1992–; Prof., Salzburg Mozarteum 1990–; premieres include Skalkottas Concerto and concertos for cello and double bass by Harald Genzmer and Helmut Eder; numerous duo recitals with cellist Jörg Baumann, as Philharmonisches Duo Berlin 1981–94; further engagements with András Schiff, Heinz Holliger, Ruggiero Ricci and Viktoria Mullova; plays Maggini Bass of 1610. *Publications include:* Repertoire Philharmonisches Duo Berlin (ed.).

STOLLERY, Pete, BMus (Hons), MA, PhD, PGCE, FRSA; British composer, performer, academic and researcher; *Professor in Composition and Electroacoustic Music, University of Aberdeen*; b. 24 July 1960, Halifax, Yorks.; s. of Derek Stollery and Rena Stollery; m. Catherine Sutcliffe 1988; two s. one d. *Education:* Univ. of Birmingham. *Career:* fmr Ed. Journal of Electro-acoustic Music, Res Musica; fmr Programme Dir BMus Educ., Univ. of Aberdeen, Prof. in Composition and Electroacoustic Music, fmr Head of Music, fmr Head of School of Educ.; frequent radio broadcasts and performances around the world; fmr Chair. Sonic Arts Network; Chair. Sound Festival 2010. *Compositions include:* Shortstuff 1993, Shioum 1994, Altered Images 1995, Onset/Offset 1996, Peel 1997, ABZ/A 1998, Thickness 2000, Vox Magna 2003, Banchory Ears 2004, Serendipities and Synchronicities 2004, Still Voices 2005, Fields of Silence 2005, Resound 2005, Scènes, Rendez-Vous 2006, Planar 2006, Back to Square One 2007, b3:dz 2008, 74 Degrees North 2009–10, Three Cities 2011, Aurphones 2012, Diverse Tremblings 2013, Lost Princes 2013, Dulax 2014, of the swan 2014, From Aberdeen to the Hamlets of the Argentine 2014, Image 16 2015, Granite Sound 2015. *Publications:* Some Perspectives on Musical Gift and Musical Intelligence, British Journal of Music Education 2002, The Wow Factor? Development of Student Music Teachers' Talents in Scotland and Australia, Educational Philosophy and Theory 2005, Taking Part in Music: Case Studies in Ethnomusicology (vol. 9) 2013. *Honours:* Musica Nova 1994, 2003, 2007, 2013, 2015, CIMESP 1997, Pierre Schaeffer Award 1998, Bourges 2003, 2007, Sounds Electric 2007, Prix Destellos 2009. *Address:* Room 011, School of Education, University of Aberdeen, MacRobert Building, King's College, Aberdeen, AB24 5UA, Scotland (office). *Telephone:* (1224) 274601 (office). *Fax:* (1224) 274900 (office). *E-mail:* p.stollery@abdn.ac.uk (office). *Website:* www.abdn.ac.uk/education/staff/details.php?id=p.stollery (office).

STOLTZMAN, Richard Leslie, BA, MM; American clarinettist; b. 12 July 1942, Omaha, NE. *Education:* Ohio State Univ., Yale Univ. studied with Donald McGinnis, Kalmen Opperman and Keith Wilson. *Career:* debut at Metropolitan Museum, New York; teacher, California Inst. of the Arts, Valencia 1970–75; Program Dir, Western Region of Young Audiences 1971–74, also Bd mem.; co-founder (with Peter Serkin, Ida Kavafian and Fred Sherry) of chamber group, Tashi 1973; Mozart concert debut at Carnegie Hall 1976; performed with Amadeus Quartet at the Aldeburgh Festival 1978, and New York Philharmonic with James Levine 1979; performances with the Cleveland, Emerson, Guarneri, Tokyo and Vermeer Quartets; concert programmes with transcriptions and commissioned pieces; debut at the Promenade Concerts, London with Mozart's Concerto 1989; premiere of Rautavaara Concerto with BBC and Leonard Slatkin 2003. *Compositions:* edition of Schubert's Arpeggione Sonata, Sonatinas in A minor (D385), and in D minor (D384), Saint-Säens's Romanza for clarinet and harp, Corigliano and Copland Concerti with London Symphony Orchestra, Mozart Concerto with English Chamber Orchestra. *Recordings include:* World premiere Toru Takemitsu's Fantasma/Cantos with BBC Wales; Brahms and Weber Quintets with Tokyo Quartet; Mozart, Beethoven and Brahms Trios with Yo-Yo Ma and Emmanuel Ax; Schubert and Schumann with Richard Goode; Laser Disc, Vienna Konzerthaus, 1791, 1891, 1991–Mozart, Brahms, Takemitsu, with Rafael Frubeck de Burgos; Finzi Concerto and Bagatelles with Guildhall Concerti for Richard Stoltzman by Einar Englund, Lukas Foss, William T McKinley with Berlin Radio Orchestra under Lukas Foss; Steve Reich, New York Counterpoint. *Publications:* The Richard Stoltzman Song Book, Aria:

The Clarinet as Opera Diva. *Honours:* Avery Fisher Prize 1977, 1986, Yale Univ. Order of Merit, Grammy Award 1983, 1996, Emmy Award (for Copland Concerto Video).

STONE, Carl Joseph; American composer and radio producer; b. 10 Feb. 1953, Los Angeles, CA. *Education:* California Inst. of the Arts with Morton Subotnick. *Career:* Independent Composers' Asscn from 1974; Dir, KPFA Radio; performances and lectures throughout Japan 1989. *Compositions:* electro-acoustic: Thoughts in Stone 1980, Ho ban for piano 1984, Wave Heat 1984, Samanluang 1986, Shing Kee 1986, Jang toh 1988, Chao nue 1990, Noor mahal 1991, Kamiya bar 1992, Acid Karaoke 1994, Electric Flowers for pipa 1994, Mae ploy for string quartet 1994, The Wagon Wheel for pipa 1995, Sampling Neurosis 1996, Wei fun 1996. *Honours:* Asian Cultural Council grant 1989.

STONE, Elisabeth; British cellist; b. 1975, England. *Education:* Royal Coll. of Music with Simon Rowland-Jones, studied with Chillingirian Quartet. *Career:* co-founder, Tavec String Quartet at RCM 1999; frequent performances at music soc. venues throughout UK; London engagements at QEH, St Martin-in-the-Fields and Serpentine Gallery (BBC Proms); National Gallery 2001, performing Schubert's Octet as mem. Piros Ensemble (founded 2000); workshops and other educational projects, notably in the NE of the UK. *Honours:* prizewinner Music d'Ensemble Competition, Paris 2001, Rio Tinto Ensemble Prize, Helen Just String Quartet Prize.

STONE, Karen; British opera house director and fmr singer; b. Yorkshire. *Education:* RAM, Conservatorio di Musica Santa Cecilia, Rome. *Career:* fmr opera singer, gave numerous performances; prod. and dir at venues, including Glyndebourne Festival, Brighton Festival, ROH, Maggio Musicale Fiorentino, Teatro Lirico di Parma, Opéra de Monte Carlo, Teatro Communale di Bologna, Bavarian State Opera, Houston Grand Opera, Los Angeles Opera, Auckland Opera Co., Teatro Colón-Bogotá, Savonlinna Opera Festival; fmr Asst Dir Freiburg Opera; fmr Staff Producer and Dir ENO; Deputy Dir Cologne Opera, then Dir 1995–2000; Gen. Man. Theatres of Graz, Austria 2000–03; Gen. Dir Dallas Opera 2003–07. *Address:* c/o Dallas Opera, Campbell Center I, 8350 N Central Expressway, Suite 210, Dallas, TX 75206, USA (office). *Website:* www.dallasopera.org (office).

STONE, William; American singer (baritone); b. 1944, Goldsboro, NC. *Education:* Duke University and University of Illinois. *Career:* sang at first in concert and oratorios; Opera debut as Germont in La Traviata in 1975 at Youngstown, Ohio; European debut in 1977 at Spoleto Festival in Napoli Milionaria by Nino Rota, and New York City Opera debut in 1981; Sang at Lyric Opera Chicago in 1978 as Adam in the premiere of Penderecki's Paradise Lost and again at La Scala in 1979; Maggio Musicale Florence in 1979 as Wozzeck, as Orestes in 1981, at Opéra Comique in Paris in 1984 as Purcell's Aeneas, Aix-en-Provence in 1987 as Ford in Falstaff; Further guest engagements at Trieste, Rome, Naples and Brussels as Germont, Paolo and Simone in Simon Boccanegra; Many appearances at the New York City Opera including Mozart's Count in 1990 and sang at Santa Fe in 1980 in the US premiere of Schoenberg's Von Heute auf Morgen; Sang at Wexford Festival in 1989 as the Templar in Marschner's Der Templer und die Jüdin; Other roles include Rossini's Figaro, Enrico, Malatesta, Verdi's Ezio and Posa, Zurga, Albert in Werther, Golaud, Alfio and Eugene Onegin; Sang the title role in the US stage premiere of Busoni's Doktor Faust, New York City Opera, 1992; Sang Wozzeck at the 1994 Spoleto Festival; Sharpless in Butterfly at Chicago, 1998; Concert repertoire includes the St Matthew Passion, Messiah, Missa Solemnis, Beethoven's 9th and Ein Deutsches Requiem. *Recordings:* Mussorgsky's Salammbô; Hindemith's Requiem; Walton's Belshazzar's Feast; Robert Ward's Arias and Songs; Bach B minor Mass; Mahler's Symphony No. 8; Schubert's Mass in G; Bach's Magnificat; Mozart's C minor Mass; Video of Messiah with Robert Shaw. *Current Management:* c/o Janice Mayer and Associates, 250 West 57th Street, Suite 2214, New York, NY 10107, USA. *Telephone:* (212) 541-5511. *Fax:* (212) 541-7303. *E-mail:* jmayer@janicemayer .com. *Website:* www.janicemayer.com.

STORGÅRDS, John; Finnish conductor and violinist; *Chief Conductor, Helsinki Philharmonic Orchestra. Education:* Sibelius Acad., Helsinki. *Career:* made conducting debut 1996; Artistic Dir Chamber Orchestra of Lapland 1996–; Prin. Guest Conductor, Helsinki Philharmonic Orchestra 2003–08, Chief Conductor 2008–; Artistic Dir Korsholm Music Festival 2004–06, Avanti Summer Sounds Festival; Chief Conductor, Tampere Philharmonic Orchestra 2006–09; Prin. Guest Conductor, BBC Philharmonic 2011–; guest conductor with Oulu Symphony Orchestra, Tapiola Sinfonietta, Tampere Philharmonic Orchestra, BBC Symphony Orchestra, Royal Stockholm Philharmonic, Orchestre Nat. de Belgique, Gothenberg Symphony, Radio-Sinfonie-Orchester Frankfurt, Danish Nat. Symphony Orchestra, Stuttgart Philharmonic Orchestra, MDR Leipzig Orchestra, Ensemble Intercontemporain, Sydney Symphony, Melbourne Symphony, New Zealand Symphony, St Paul Chamber Orchestra, Scottish Chamber Orchestra. *Honours:* Finnish State Prize for Music 2002. *Current Management:* c/o Karen McDonald, Konzertdirektion Schmid UK Ltd., 40 St Martin's Lane, London, WC2N 4ER, England. *Telephone:* (20) 7395-0910. *Fax:* (20) 7395-0911. *E-mail:* mail@kdschmid.co .uk. *Website:* www.kdschmid.de. *Address:* Helsinki Philharmonic Orchestra, Finlandia Hall, Mannerheimintie 13, PO Box 4400, 00099 Helsinki, Finland (office). *Telephone:* (9) 40241 (office). *Fax:* (9) 406484 (office). *E-mail:* john .storgards@hel.fi (office). *Website:* www.hel.fi (office); www.johnstorgards .com.

STOROJEV, Nikita; Russian opera and concert singer (bass) and professor of voice/opera; *Associate Professor, Butler Music School, University of Texas, Austin;* b. 9 Nov. 1950, Harbin, China; s. of Leonid Storozhev and Valentina Storozheva; m. Tatiana Storozheva; one s. one d. *Education:* Tchaikovsky Conservatoire, Moscow. *Career:* Bolshoi Theatre, Moscow from 1976; Prin. Soloist, Moscow Philharmonic Soc. from 1975; appearances from 1983 at Vienna, Paris, Milan, Rome, Florence, Berlin, London, New York, San Francisco, Madrid, Tokyo, Amsterdam, Toronto etc.; sang Boris Godunov, Varlaam, Pimen, Ivan Khovansky, Kontchak, Igor, Gremin, King Rene, Zaccaria, Ramphis, Filippo, Grand Inquisitor, Ferrando, Fiesco, Basilio, Sarastro, Dalland, Fafner, Mephistopheles etc.; concerts with orchestra: Prokofiev's Ivan the Terrible, Rimsky-Korsakov, Mozart and Salieri, Verdi Requiem, Mozart Requiem, Mussorgsky's Songs and Dances of Death, Shostakovich Symphonies Nos 13 and 14, Auerbach Russian Requiem, Gorecki's Beatus Vir etc.; song recitals with David Ashkenazi and Tatiana Storozheva. *Recordings include:* 25 CDs and five DVDs, including Shostakovich – 13th and 14th Symphonies, Rimsky-Korsakov, Mozart and Salieri, Russian Songs, Prokofiev – Ivan the Terrible, Shostakovich – Songs of the Forest, Gorecki – Beatus Vir, Mozart – Idomeneo, Verdi – Don Carlos, Verdi & Puccini, Eötvös – Three Sisters, Shostakovich – Rayok, Mussorgsky – Boris Godunov, Russian Arias, Tchaikovsky and Rachmaninov Songs. *Honours:* Diapason d'or, Choc de la Musique, Winner, Int. Tchaikovsky Competition, Moscow. *Current Management:* c/o Sardos Artists Management, 180 West End Avenue, New York, NY 10023, USA. *Telephone:* (212) 874-2559. *E-mail:* info@ ritasardos.com. *Website:* www.ritasardos.com. *Address:* Butler Music School, University of Texas at Austin, 1 University Station E3100, Austin, TX 78712-0435, USA (office). *Telephone:* (512) 471-9440 (office). *E-mail:* siberianbass@ yahoo.com (office). *Website:* www.music.utexas.edu (office); www .nikitastorojev.com.

STOTT, Kathryn Linda, ARCM; British pianist; b. 10 Dec. 1958, Nelson, Lancs.; d. of Desmond Stott and Elsie Cheetham; m. 1st Michael Ardron 1979 (divorced 1983); m. 2nd John Elliot 1983 (divorced 1997); one d. *Education:* studied at Yehudi Menuhin School under Marcel Ciampi, Vlado Perlemuter and Louis Kentner and at Royal Coll. of Music, London under Kendall Taylor. *Career:* debut, Purcell Room, London 1978; has since performed extensively in recitals and concertos both in UK and in Europe, Far East, Australia, Canada and USA; frequent appearances at Henry Wood Promenade concerts; Dir Fauré and French Connection Festival, Manchester 1995, Piano 2000, Manchester 2000, Piano 2003, Manchester 2003, Chopin and His Legacy, Leeds 2005; Artistic Dir Manchester Chamber Concerts Soc. 2008–14; Visiting Prof., RAM, Norwegian Acad. of Music, Oslo; regular collaborations with cellist Yo-Yo Ma. *Recordings include:* 30 recordings, including premieres of concertos by George Lloyd and Michael Nyman. *Honours:* Martin Scholarship 1976, Churchill Scholarship 1979, Croydon Symphony Award, Chappell Medal, Royal Amateur Orchestral Soc. Silver Medal 1979; Chevalier, Ordre des Arts et des Lettres 1996. *Address:* c/o Jane Ward, 60 Shrewsbury Road, Oxton, Merseyside, CH43 2HY, England. *Telephone:* (151) 513-2716. *Fax:* (151) 513-2716. *E-mail:* jane@kathrynstott.com. *Website:* www.kathrynstott .com.

STOUT, Alan Burrage, MA; American composer; b. 26 Nov. 1932, Baltimore, MD. *Education:* John Hopkins Univ., Peabody Conservatory, Univs of Copenhagen and Washington, Seattle, with Vagn Holmboe, Wallingford Riegger and Henry Cowell. *Career:* Music Department at Northwestern University, 1962–; George Lieder, Second Symphony, Fourth Symphony and Passion premiered by the Chicago SO. *Compositions:* 10 String Quartets, 1953–62; 4 Symphonies, 1959–1970; George Lieder for baritone and orchestra, 1962; Cello Sonata 1965; Solo for soprano and orchestra, 1968; Nocturnes for mezzo, speaker and ensemble, 1970; Pulsar for brass and timpani, 1972; Passion, for orchestra, 1975; Five Visages de Laforgue for soprano and orchestra, 1997; Pilva for orchestra and organ, 1983; Tryptich for female voices, chorus and orchestra, 1983; Waves of Light and sound, for chamber orchestra, 1993; Brass Quintet, 1997; Stele, for organ, 1997.

STOYANOV, Boyko Stoykov; composer, conductor, pianist and music teacher; b. 4 May 1953, Sliven, Bulgaria; m. Rikako Akatsu (deceased); two d. *Education:* Bulgarian State Acad. of Music, Sofia, Frederick Chopin Acad. of Music, Warsaw, Poland, Toho Gakuen School of Music, Tokyo, Japan. *Career:* Conductor, Varna Philharmonic Orchestra 1983–; Iwaki Symphony Orchestra, Japan 1984–; private music school, Iwaki Musica 1984; Tokyo debut with Tokyo Symphony Orchestra 1986; Conductor, Tenerife Symphony Orchestra 1991–; Kaguyahime, opera for children, premiered in Vienna 1993; broadcasts on Bulgaria Radio Varna, Japan Fukushima Central Television, TV V and NHK, Radio RFC, Poland Radio, Austria Television; mem. Piano Teachers' Nat. Asscn, Japan, Japan Computer Music Asscn. *Honours:* first prize (Folk Song Section) Bulgarian Nat. Folk Music Competition 1959, Varna Prize for Popular Song 1965, second prize for conducting and arrangement Bulgarian Nat. Folk Music Competition 1972, distinction Wrocław Arrangement Competition 1979, Int. Composers' Competition 1985, Int. Electro-acoustic Music Competition 1990.

STOYANOVA, Krassimira; Bulgarian singer (soprano); b. 1969. *Education:* Ruse Conservatory, University of Plovdiv. *Career:* debut as Violetta in La Traviata at Opava, 1994; appearances at the National Theatre, Sofia, as Gilda in Rigoletto, Susanna in Le Nozze di Figaro, Cecilia in Il Guarany, Delia in Fosca, Rachel in La Juive, Vitellia in La Clemenza di Tito, Ilia in Idomeneo 1995–; with Vienna Staatsoper 1998–; further engagements as Mozart's

Countess, Nedda in Pagliacci, Donna Anna in Don Giovanni, Valentine in Les Huguenots, Lida in La Battaglia di Lignano, Anna in Anna Bolena, Micaela in Carmen, Antonia in Les Contes d'Hoffmann, Mimi in La Bohéme; concerts include Beethoven's Ninth Symphony, conducted by Philippe Herreweghe in Europe and Japan, and under Riccardo Muti at the Ravenna Festival. *Recordings include:* Slavic Opera Arias (Int. Classical Music Award for Best Vocal Recital Recording 2012) 2011. *Honours:* Kammersängerin 2009. *Current Management:* Hilbert Artists Management, Maximilianstrasse 22, 80539 Munich, Germany. *Telephone:* (89) 2907470. *Fax:* (89) 29074790. *E-mail:* agentur@hilbert.de. *Website:* www.hilbert.de; www.krassimira-stoyanova .com.

STRAHAN, Derek William, BA; Australian composer, actor, singer and writer; *Director, Revolve Pty Ltd*; b. 28 May 1935, Penang, Malaysia; m. (divorced); one s. one d. *Education:* Campbell Coll., Belfast, Univ. of Cambridge. *Career:* Dir, Revolve Pty Ltd; script assessor and mem., Australian Writers' Guild; mem. Australian Music Centre, APRA, Music Arrangers' Guild of Australia, Media Entertainment and Arts Alliance; represented artist with Australia Cultural Fund of Australian Business Arts Foundation. *Radio:* presenter Words and Music, Sweet and Hot (Eastside Radio FM) 1984–2010. *Television:* Number 96 (212 episodes), Chopper Squad, Glenview High, Carrots!, Flying Start. *Film and TV appearances:* Fantasy 1991, Inspector Shanahan Mysteries (episode, Cult of Diana) 1992. *Film and TV writing:* The Unisexers (TV series) 1975, Chopper Squad (TV series) 1978, Leonora (screenplay, also dir) 1984, Fantasy (screenplay, also dir) 1991. *Compositions for film:* 30 documentaries, including Shell's Australia 1969–73, Aliens Among Us 1974, Garden Jungle 1974, Artisans of Australia 1985; films, including Leonora 1984, Fantasy 1991. *Compositions include:* String Quartet No. 1: The Key 1980, Clarinet Quintet No. 1 in D: The Princess 1980, The Quay for orchestra 1986, Rose of the Bay song cycle for mezzo-soprano, clarinet and piano 1987, String Trio No. 1 in F 1987, Piano Trio in F 1987, Sydney 200 for orchestra 1988, China Spring for cello and piano 1989, Escorts Trio 1989, Atlantis for flute and piano 1990, Solo Cello Suite No. 1 1991, Solo Cello Suite No. 2 1992, Atlantis Variations for piano 1992, Voodoo Fire for clarinet, percussion and keyboards 1994, Eden in Atlantis for soprano, flute and piano 1994, Clarinet Concerto No. 1 2001, Eden in Atlantis (opera libretto) 2002, Calypso in Exile for soprano and wind quintet 2003, Space Trilogy for trumpet and piano 2009. *Publications:* contrib. numerous articles to music publs and websites. *Address:* POB 422, Cronulla, NSW 2230, Australia (office). *Telephone:* (2) 8544-0184 (office). *Fax:* (2) 8544-0184 (office). *E-mail:* dstrahan@ revolve.com.au (home). *Website:* www.revolve.com.au (home).

STRAKA, Peter; German singer (tenor); b. 22 Feb. 1950, Zlin, Czechoslovakia. *Education:* Düsseldorf Conservatory, Cologne Music High School, International Opera Studio, Zürich. *Career:* mem., Zürich Opera; Guest at many opera houses and in concert; Appearances include New York Metropolitan debut as Boris and Kudryasch in Katya Kabanova under Charles Mackerras, 1991, returning as Boris, 1999; Season 1991–92 as Alwa in Lulu at the Châtelet, Paris, Titus in La Clemenza di Tito in Nice; Florestan at Zürich Opera 1992, also Berlin State Opera, Covent Garden, Nice, Paris; returned to the Châtelet as Lenski in Eugene Onegin; Lurcano in Monteverdi's Poppea, Salzburg Festival 1993; opened Season 1993 as Erik in Der fliegende Holländer at Bastille Opéra, Paris, then Loge in Rheingold at the Châtelet, Boris at Zürich; Mazal and Petrik in Janáček's Excursions of Mr Brouček and Narraboth in Salome under Mackerras at Bavarian State Opera, Munich 1995; Erik at Munich State Opera and Zürich, Boris at the Bastille, Alwa in Copenhagen programme, Oedipus in Oedipus Rex at Zürich 1996; Prince in Rusalka at Zürich Opera, Laca in Jenůfa at Amsterdam Opera for Holland Festival's 50th anniversary, Mahoney in Mahagonny at the Bastille 1997; Laca in Zürich, Siegmund in Walküre at Caracas Opera 1998; season 2000–01 at Zürich Opera as Elemer in Arabella, Narraboth, and Berg's Alwa; Boris in Katya Kabanova at the Munich Staatsoper; concerts with London Philharmonia, Munich Philharmonic under Celibidache, Bavarian Radio Orchestra under Colin Davis, Concentus Musicus Wien under Harnoncourt, other leading orchestras and conductors; concert repertoire includes Mahler's 8th Symphony, Janáček's Glagolitic Mass and Our Father, Beethoven Ninth, Zivny in Janáček's Osud, Bruckner's Te Deum, Puccini's Messa di Gloria, Stravinsky's Oedipus, Bach B minor Mass, Richard Strauss lieder. *Recordings include:* several operatic and concert performances. *Current Management:* Aria's di Novella Partacini & Alexandra Plaickner, Rappresentanza Artisti, Via Josef Weingartner, 4, 39022 Lagundo, Italy. *Telephone:* (0473) 200200. *Fax:* (0473) 222424. *E-mail:* info@arias.it. *Website:* www.arias.it.

STRASHKO, Yevgeny; Russian singer (tenor); b. 1967, Crimea. *Education:* St Petersburg Conservatoire, Musikhochschule Graz and Salzburg. *Career:* appearances with the Kirov Opera, St Petersburg, from 1995 as Tamino, Alfredo, Steersman in Der fliegende Holländer and Young Gypsy in Rachmaninov's Aleko; further roles include Tchaikovsky's Lensky and Herman, Dimitri in Boris Godunov, Kuragin in War and Peace and Prokofiev's Semyon Kotko; sang in Rimsky-Korsakov's Snow Maiden (Concert) with the Kirov Opera at Covent Garden, 2000; also appeared as Genarro in Prokofiev's Maddalena and gives recitals of Russian German and Italian songs. *Honours:* prizewinner at competitions in Russia, Germany and Sweden.

STRASNOY, Oscar; French/Argentine composer, conductor and pianist; b. 12 Nov. 1970, Buenos Aires. *Education:* studied piano, conducting and composition at Conservatorio Nacional Superior de Música, Buenos Aires with Aldo Antognazzi and Guillermo Scarabino, Conservatoire Nat. Supérieur de

Musique, Paris with Guy Reibel, Michaël Levinas and Gérard Grisey, Hochschule für Musik, Frankfurt with Hans Zender. *Career:* Music Dir Orchestre du Crous de Paris 1996–98; Artist-in-Residence, Herrenhaus-Edenkoben, Germany 1999, Akad. Schloss Solitude Stuttgart, Germany 2003, Villa Kujoyama Kyoto (Institut Français), Japan, Civitella Ranieri Foundation, Umbria, Italy 2006; featured composer at Festival Présences (Radio France/Théâtre du Châtelet Paris) 2012; operas performed at Spoleto, Rome, Reims, Rennes, Paris Opéra Comique and Théâtre du Châtelet, Hamburg, Bordeaux, Aix-en-Provence Festival, Teatro Colón Buenos Aires; song cycle Six Songs for Unquiet Traveller premiered by Nash Ensemble and Ann Murray in a concert to inaugurate the newly refurbished Wigmore Hall, London 2004; stage work Midea (2) premiered at Teatro Caio Melisso in Spoleto 2000 and Rome Opera 2001; compositions recorded by ensembles including 2e2m, Musicatreize, Neue Vocalsolisten Stuttgart and Orchestre Philharmonique de Radio France. *Compositions include:* 12 stage works: Midea (2) (Orpheus Prize, Italy) 2000, Opérette 2003, Geschichte (operetta a cappella) 2004, Underground (live-accompanied score to Alan Asquith's 1928 silent film, played at the Louvre and Cine Doré Madrid, Mozarteum Argentino and in Kyoto and Tokyo) 2004, Fabula (musical) 2005, L'instant (opera) 2006, Le Bal (opera) 2008–09, Un Retour (chamber opera) 2009-10, Cachafaz (opera) 2010, Dido and Aeneas (opera for seven singers, two pianos, two brass instruments and two percussion players) 2011, Slutchai = Incidents (opera) 2012, Requiem (opera in two acts) 2013; others: Hochzeitsvorbereitungen (mit B und K) (secular cantata), several song cycles and numerous other vocal, chamber and orchestral works. *Honours:* Founding Recipient, Grüneisen Foundation (Mozarteum Argentino) conducting scholarship, Guggenheim Fellowship for Music Composition 2007. *Address:* c/o Editions Chant du Monde, 31-33 rue Vandrezanne, 75013 Paris (office), Editions Billaudot, 14 rue de l'Échiquier, 75010 Paris, France (office). *Telephone:* 1-53-80-12-30 (Chant) (office); 1-47-70-14-46 (Billaudot) (office). *Fax:* 1-53-80-12-18 (Chant) (office); 1-45-23-22-54 (Billaudot) (office). *E-mail:* pianco@chantdumonde.com (office); cdardenne@billaudot.com (office). *Website:* www.chantdumonde.com (office); www.billaudot.com (office); www.oscarstrasnoy.info (office).

STRATAS, Teresa Anastasia Strataki, OC; Canadian singer (soprano); b. (Anastasia Stratakis), 26 May 1938, Toronto, Ont.; d. of Emmanuel Stratas and Argero Stratakis; m. Tony Harrison. *Education:* Univ. of Toronto. *Career:* began singing career in nightclubs in Toronto; debut at Toronto Opera Festival 1958; won audition to Metropolitan Opera, New York 1959; performances there include Berg's Lulu, Jenny in Brecht and Weill's Mahagonny, Suor Angelica, Lauretta and Giorgetta in Il Trittico; major roles in opera houses worldwide include Paris (Lulu 1979), Brussels (Lulu 1988), Boston (Mimi 1989), Chicago (Mélisande 1992); appeared as Violetta in Zeffirelli's film of La Traviata 1983; appeared in Broadway musical Rags 1986; cr. role of Marie Antoinette in Ghosts of Versailles, premiered Metropolitan Opera, NY 1992; Il Tabarro and Pagliacci at the Met 1994. *Honours:* Hon. LLD (McMaster Univ.) 1986, (Toronto) 1994, (Rochester) 1998, (Juilliard School of Music), (Royal Conservatory of Music); Hon. DLitt (York Univ.) 2000; Canadian Music Council Performer of the Year 1979, Drama Desk Award for Leading Actress in a Musical on Broadway 1986–87, Gemini Award for Best Supporting Actress (for Under the Piano) 1997, three Grammy Awards, Opera Canada Award for Creative Artist 2003.

STRATE, Petra-Ines; German singer (soprano); b. 7 Sept. 1945, Jessen an der Alster. *Education:* Magdeburg Musikhochschule, studied with Gunther Leib, Dresden. *Career:* debut at Magdeburg 1971, as Pamina in Die Zauberflöte; sang at Magdeburg until 1973; Halle Opera from 1973, Leipzig Opera from 1984; guest appearances throughout Germany as Mozart's Countess, Donna Anna and Fiordiligi, Agathe in Der Freischütz, and Liu in Turandot; many appearances in operas by Handel at the Halle Festival; often heard in oratorios by Bach, Haydn and Handel.

STRAUCH, Jacek; British singer (baritone); b. 1953, London, England. *Education:* Cambridge Univ., Royal Coll. of Music and National Opera Studio, London. *Career:* debut at Kent Opera in 1978 as Rigoletto; sang in opera at Würzburg 1980–82, and Saarbrucken 1982–85; guest appearances in Modena and Pretoria, South Africa in 1985, Berne Opera in 1987 as Wozzeck, English National Opera in 1988 as Alfio and as Jaroslav Prus in The Makropulos Case; season 1988–90 as Amfortas, Iago and the Hoffmann Villains at Brunswick, Kurwenal at Saarbrücken and Gunther in Götterdämmerung; Other roles include Mozart's Count; broadcast engagements in Germany, England and Norway; sang Pacheco in the premiere of Macmillan's Ines de Castro, Edinburgh 1996; season 2000–01 as Wotan in The Ring at Graz, followed by Nicolai's Falstaff, Verdi's Renato at Barcelona and Tomsky in The Queen of Spades for the Munich Staatsoper. *Honours:* winner Kathleen Ferrier Competition 1978. *Current Management:* Künstleragentur Die Stimme, Karlstrasse 22A, 76571 Gaggenau-Bad Rotenfels, Germany. *Telephone:* (72) 25770995. *E-mail:* wolfganga.palm@web.de. *Website:* www .wapagenturdiestimme.de.

STRAUCH, Pierre; French cellist and composer; b. 1958, Alsace. *Education:* studied cello with Jean Deplace. *Career:* mem. Ensemble Intercontemporain 1978–; performed, premiered and recorded many 20th century works by composers such as Iannis Xenakis, Luciano Berio, Bernd Alois Zimmermann, Olivier Messiaen and Brian Ferneyhough; co-f. Festival A Tempo de Caracas 1994. *Compositions include:* works for cello, other solo instruments and ensemble: La Folie de Jocelin, Preludio imaginario, Faute d'un royaume for solo violin and seven instruments, Deux Portraits for five violas, Trois Odes

Funèbres for five instruments, Quatre miniatures for cello and piano, La Descalera del dragón (In memoriam Julio Cortázar) (commissioned by Ensemble Intercontemporain); voice: Impromptu acrostiche for mezzo soprano and three instruments, La Beauté for three female voices and eight instruments. *Recordings include:* Joel F. Durand Concerto pour piano et orchestra, trio à cordes; numerous recordings with Ensemble Intercontemporain. *Address:* Ensemble Intercontemporain, 223 Avenue Jean-Jaurès, 75019 Paris, France (office). *Telephone:* 1-44-84-44-75 (office). *Website:* www .ensembleinter.com (office).

STRAUSSOVA, Eva; singer (soprano); b. 7 June 1934, Cheb, Czechoslovakia. *Education:* studied with Elisa Stunzner and Dresden Opera Studio with Rudolf Dittrich. *Career:* debut at Landestheater Dessau 1959 as Helmwige in Die Walküre; sang at Dessau until 1963, notably as Eva in Die Meistersinger, then joined the Staatsoper Berlin in roles, including Wagner's Elisabeth and Gutrune, Amelia in Un Ballo in Maschera, Donna Anna, Turandot, Elektra, Fiordiligi, Leonore and Katerina Izmailova; guest engagements in Switzerland, Germany, Russia and Austria; sang Isolde at Aachen Opera.

STREATFEILD, Simon; British violist and conductor; b. 3 May 1929, Windsor, Berkshire, England; m. Elizabeth Winship; two d. *Education:* Eton Coll., Royal Coll. of Music. *Career:* Principal Viola, Sadler's Wells Opera 1953–55, London Symphony Orchestra 1956–65, Vancouver Symphony Orchestra, Canada 1965; Asst Conductor, Vancouver Bach Choir 1967, Assoc. Conductor 1972–77, Music Dir and Conductor 1969–81; season 1970–71 included concerts with City of Birmingham Symphony, Royal Choral Soc., BBC and Vancouver Bach Choir in The Netherlands; Visiting Prof., Faculty of Music, Univ. of Western Ontario 1977–81; Conductor, Regina Symphony Orchestra, Canada 1981–84, Manitoba Chamber Orchestra 1982–, Québec Symphony Orchestra 1984–; has also conducted National Arts Centre Orchestra in Ottawa, Danish Radio Symphony, Oslo Philharmonic, Belgian Radio Symphony. *Recordings include:* Telemann Viola Concerto, Berlioz Harold en Italie.

STREET, Tison, MA; American composer and violinist; b. 20 May 1943, Boston, MA. *Education:* Harvard Univ. with David Del Tredici and Leon Kirchner. *Career:* Lecturer, Berkeley 1971–72, Harvard Univ. 1979–83, Boston Univ. 1995–; Co-Leader, Boston Ballet Orchestra 1992–97; commissions from the New York Philharmonic Orchestra and Boston Ballet Orchestra. *Compositions:* String Quartet 1972, String Quintet 1974, Adagio for oboe and strings 1977, Montsalvat for orchestra 1980, Divertimento for piano 1983, Six Fantasies on a Hymm Tune for string quartet 1984, Violin Concerto 1986, Fantasia for six cellos 1988, Bright Sambas for orchestra 1993, Symphony No. 2 1993, Ave maris stella for chorus 1994, The Jewel Tree (ballet) 1998. *Honours:* Prix de Rome 1973, Guggenheim Fellowship 1981.

STREHLE, Wilfried; German violist; *Principal Violist, Berliner Philharmoniker*; b. 1947, Schorndorf. *Education:* studied at Stuttgart and Detmold Hochschulen. *Career:* violist with Sudfunk-Sinfonie-Orchester at Stuttgart; soloist with Chamber Orchestra Tibor Varga –1971, principal violist with Berliner Philharmoniker 1971–; co-founder, Brandis String Quartet 1976, Berliner Philharmonic Sinfonietta 2005–; has performed chamber concerts in Paris, Munich, Hamburg, Milan, Tokyo and London with Wiener Singverein, Berlin Philharmonic, Tibor Varga Chamber Orchestra, Consortium Classicum, Katsaris Quartet; festival engagements at Edinburgh, Tours, Bergen, Salzburg, Lucerne, Florence and Vienna; co-premiered the third Quartets of Gottfried von Einem and Giselher Klebe in 1981 and 1983, and the Clarinet Quintet of Helmut Eder 1984; tutor, Berliner Philharmoniker Orchestra Acad., Universität der Künste, Berlin. *Recordings include:* albums in the standard repertory from 1978, Quartets by Beethoven, Schulhoff, Weill and Hindemith, and the Schubert String Quintet. *Honours:* European Chamber Music Award 1997. *Address:* Berliner Philharmonie, Herbert-von-Karajan-Strasse 1, 10785 Berlin, Germany (office). *Telephone:* (30) 254880 (office). *E-mail:* akademie@berliner-philharmoniker.de (office). *Website:* www .berliner-philharmoniker.de (office).

STREIT, Kurt; singer (tenor); b. 14 Oct. 1959, Itazuke, Japan. *Education:* University of New Mexico with Marilyn Tyler. *Career:* mem. of apprentice programmes at San Francisco and Santa Fe, also at the Texas Opera Theater; appearances with the Milwaukee Skylight Comic Opera and in Dallas; European career with the Hamburg Staatsoper singing in operas by Mozart, Donizetti and Rossini; guest appearances at Schwetzingen 1987, Aix-en-Provence 1989, Salzburg 1989 and at Glyndebourne as Tamino in the 1990 production of Die Zauberflöte by Peter Sellars; also ssng at opera houses in Vienna, Munich, Brussels, Leipzig, Düsseldorf and San Francisco 1990; Covent Garden debut 1992 as Ferrando; concert engagements with the London Symphony, Orchestre National de France, St Petersburg Philharmonic, Hamburg Staatsorchester and the English Chamber Orchestra; Promenade Concerts in London in a 1990 concert performance of Die Zauberflöte; sang Orfeo in Haydn's Orfeo ed Euridice at South Bank, London, 1997; Belmonte at Covent Garden, 1996; Grimoaldo in Rodelinda at Glyndebourne, 1998; season 2000–01 as Mozart's Tito for the New York City Opera, Almaviva in Seattle, Rossini's Ramiro in Los Angeles and Cassio in Otello at Covent Garden. *Recordings include:* Gluck's Echo et Narcisse; Ferrando in Così fan tutte (also at Glyndebourne 1990), with Daniel Barenboim and the Berlin Philharmonic; Die Entführung aus dem Serail. *Current Management:* IMG Artists, The Light Box, 111 Power Road, London,

W4 5PY, England. *Telephone:* (20) 7957-5800. *Fax:* (20) 7957-5801. *E-mail:* salmansi@imgartists.com. *Website:* www.imgartists.com.

STRINDBERG, Henrik; composer; b. 28 March 1954, Kalmar, Sweden. *Education:* Stockholm Royal Coll. of Music with Gunnar Bucht, Brian Ferneyhough and Sven-David Sandström. *Career:* Asst to Sandström 1985–87; computer music programs, IRCAM, Paris 1987–89. *Compositions:* In Yellow and Red suite for orchestra 1979, String Quartet 1982, Hustle and Bustle for ensemble 1984, Scenario for wind band 1984, Petite Chronique Berlinoise for two pianos 1984, Bambu (electro-acoustic) 1984, Midsummer for soprano and ensemble 1986, The First Lay about Gudrun for mezzo and guitar 1987, Within Trees for orchestra 1988, Etymology for piano, string quartet, soprano, saxophone and double bass 1990, Two Pianos 1992, Nattlig Madonna for chamber orchestra 1994, Clarinet Concerto 1998.

STROHM, Reinhard, PhD, FBA; German musicologist; *Professor of Music, University of Oxford*; b. 4 Aug. 1942, Munich. *Education:* Univ. of Munich and Technical Univ., Berlin with Carl Dahlhaus. *Career:* Lecturer 1975–83, King's Coll. London, Prof. 1990–96; Prof., Yale Univ. 1983–90; Heather Prof. of Music, Univ. of Oxford 1996–2007, Prof. of Music 2007–; Visiting Prof., Institut für Musikwissenschaft, Univ. of Vienna 2009; Fellow, Wissenschaftskolleg zu Berlin 2010–11; corresponding mem. American Musicological Soc., Göttinger Akad. der Wissenschaften. *Publications include:* Hasse, Scarlatti, Rolli 1975, Wagner Collected Edition (co-ed) 1970–82, Zu Vivaldis Opern schaffen 1975, Italienische Opernarien des Frühen Settecento, 1720–1730 1976, Die Italienische Oper im 18 Jahrhundert 1979, Music in Late Medieval Bruges 1985, Essays on Handel and Italian Opera (contrib.) 1985, Music in Late Medieval Europe 1987, The Rise of European Music, 1380–1500 1993, On the Dignity and the Effects of Music: Two Fifteenth-Century Treatises (with J. D. Cullington) 1996, Dramma per musica: Italian Opera Seria in the Eighteenth Century 1997, Song Composition in the 14th and 15th Centuries: Old and New Questions 1997, The Eighteenth Century Diaspora of Italian Music and Musicians 2001, Music as Concept and Practice in the Late Middle Ages (The New Oxford History of Music, Vol. III, with B. Blackburn) 2001, The Operas of Antonio Vivaldi 2008; contrib. to learned books and journals. *Honours:* Hon. mem. Slovenian Acad. of Sciences 2009; Royal Musical Asscn Dent Medal 1977, Glarean Music Prize 2008, Leverhulme Emer. Fellowship 2008. *Address:* Faculty of Music, Oxford University, St Aldgate's, Oxford, OX1 1DB, England (office). *E-mail:* reinhard.strohm@music.ox.ac.uk (office). *Website:* www.music.ox.ac.uk (office).

STROPPA, Marco; Italian composer, researcher and educator; *Professor of Composition and Computer Music, University for Music and the Performing Arts, Stuttgart*; b. 8 Dec. 1959, Verona. *Education:* Verona, Milan and Venice Conservatories, Massachusetts Inst. of Tech., USA. *Career:* composer and researcher, Institut de Recherche et Coordination Acoustique/Musique (IRCAM), electronic music studios, Paris from 1982; Prof. of Composition and Computer Music, Univ. for Music and the Performing Arts, Stuttgart 1997–. *Compositions:* Traiettoria for piano 1984, Etude pour Pulsazioni for 18 instruments 1985–89, Spirali for string quartet 1988, élet...fogytiglan for 15 instruments 1989–98, Träumen vom Fliegen (ballet) 1990, Leggere il decamerone 1990, Miniature estrose for piano 1991–95, Danza per miniature estrose (ballet) 1995, Auras 1996, Upon a Blade of Grass for piano and orchestra 1996, From Needle's Eye for trombone and 11 instruments 1998, opus nainileven for woodwind quintet 2003, Ay, there's the rub for clarinet, viola and piano 2004, Ossia, Seven Strophes for a Literary Drone 2005, Let me sing into your ear for amplified bassett horn and chamber electronics 2010. *Publications:* several articles in int. magazines. *Honours:* Kompositionpreis, Salzburg Easter Festival 1996. *Current Management:* c/o Casa Ricordi – Universal Music Publishing Ricordi srl., Promotion Department, Via Benigno Crespi 19, Area MAC 4, 20159 Milan, Italy. *Telephone:* (02) 80282812. *Fax:* (02) 80282882. *E-mail:* Promozione.Ricordi.Italy@umusic.com. *Website:* www .ricordi.com. *Address:* Hochschule für Musik, Urbanstr. 25, 70182 Stuttgart, Germany (office). *Telephone:* (711) 2124655 (office). *Fax:* (711) 2124639 (office). *E-mail:* stroppa@mh-stuttgart.de (office). *Website:* www.marcostroppa.eu.

STROW-PICCOLO, Lynn; singer (soprano); b. 17 June 1947, Waterburg, CT, USA. *Education:* Hartford Univ., studied with Carlo Alfieri in Parma. *Career:* debut at Siena Opera, 1975; Season 1976-77 as Leoncavallo's Zaza for RAI, and guest appearances in San Diego, and Turin; Further engagments at New Orleans, Santiago, Miami, Oslo and Marseille; Norma in Bellini's opera at Covent Garden, 1987; La Scala, Vienna Staatsoper and elsewhere in Europe as Maria Stuarda, both Leonoras of Verdi, Elisabeth in Don Carlos, Desdemona, Odabella and Amelia (Un Ballo in Maschera); Manon Lesaut, Mascagni's Isabeau, and Sieglinde in Die Walküre. *Honours:* winner Giuseppe Verdi Competition, Bussetto 1974.

STRUCKMANN, Falk; German singer (baritone); b. 23 Jan. 1958, Heilbronn. *Education:* Stuttgart Musikhochschule. *Career:* debut in Kiel, 1985; Kiel Opera, 1985–89, Basle Opera, 1991; Vienna State Opera, 1990, as Scarpia and Escamillo; Berlin State Opera from 1992, as Amfortas, the Wanderer in Siegfried, the Dutchman, Pizarro and Jochanaan in Salome; Bayreuth Festival from 1993 as Kurwenal, Donner, Gunther and Amfortas; Kurwenal and Wotan at the Vienna State, US debut Chicago, 1995, as Orestes in Elektra (concert); New York Metropolitan debut, 1997, as Wozzeck; La Scala, 1997, as the Wanderer; Berlin Staatsoper, 1996 and 1998, as Telramund and Hans Sachs; Other roles include Barak in Busoni's Turandot, Rangoni in Boris Godunov and Bartók's Bluebeard; Sang Kurnwenal at

Florence, Wozzeck at the Berlin Staatsoper and Strauss's Barak in Vienna, 1999; Season 2000–01 as Gunther for Cologne Opera, Pizarro at the Met, Hans Sachs in Madrid, Wagner's Dutchman and Wotan in Berlin. *Recordings include:* Tristan und Isolde, and Lohengrin conducted by Barenboim; Video of Parsifal, Berlin 1992; Bluebeard's Castle, under Eliahu Inbal. *Honours:* Kammersänger 2007. *Current Management:* Michael Lewin International Artists' Management, c/o EUROARTISTS Künstlermanagement GmbH, (Geschäftsführerin: Elisabetta Hartl) Gluckgasse 1/1, 1010 Vienna, Austria. *E-mail:* office@lewin-management.com. *Website:* www.lewin-management.com.

STRUMMER, Peter, Baron von Freifeld; American (b. Austrian) singer (bass-baritone); *Adjunct Voice Teacher and Opera Director, University of Tulsa;* b. 8 Sept. 1948, Vienna, Austria; grand-s. of Max Scheindel; m. Linda Roark. *Education:* Cleveland Inst. of Music, Juilliard School of Music, studied with Yi-Kwei Sze, Oren Brown, Prof. Alexander Kolo and Dr Thomas Lomonaco. *Career:* debut as Antonio in Le Nozze di Figaro with the Atlanta Symphony Orchestra 1972; Metropolitan Opera debut as Beckmesser 1985; debut with New York City Opera as the Sacristan in Tosca 1998–99; season 1999–2000 engagements included San Francisco Opera as Benoit/Alcindoro in La Bohème and as Borov in Giordani's Fedora for the Domingo Gala, New York City Opera as Don Prudenzio in Il Viaggio a Reims and as the Sacristan in Tosca, De Brétigny in Manon with Milwaukee's Florentine Opera Company, the Sacristan in Tosca with Manitoba Opera, Geronte in Manon Lescaut with Opera Pacific, and a concert performance as Alberich in Das Rheingold with L'Opéra de Montréal; season 2001–02 included appearances at San Francisco Opera as the Sacristan in Tosca and as Bogdanovic in The Merry Widow, New York City Opera as the Sacristan in Tosca and as Colonel Vandeveer in John Philip Sousa's The Glass Blowers, Opera Colorado as the Sacristan in Tosca, and Florentine Opera as Faninal in Der Rosenkavalier; season 2002–03 engagements included New York City Opera as Talpa in Il Tabarro and as Simone in Gianni Schicchi, Dr Bartolo in Il Barbiere di Siviglia with New York City Opera, Mustafa in L'italiana in Algeri with L'opéra de Montréal, Sulpice in La Fille du Régiment with Opera Ontario, and Benoit/Alcindoro in La Bohème with Utah Opera; season 2003–04 engagements include San Francisco Opera as Benoit/Alcindoro in La Bohème and as the Badger in The Cunning Little Vixen, New York City Opera in the title role of Don Pasquale and as Candy in Of Mice and Men, Florentine Opera and Opera Lyra Ottawa in the title role of Don Pasquale, and New Orleans Opera as Alberich in Das Rheingold; other roles include Baron Zeta in The Merry Widow, Beckmesser in Die Meistersinger von Nürnberg, Bottom in A Midsummer Night's Dream, Dansker in Billy Budd, Dikoj in Katya Kabanova, Don Alfonso in Così fan Tutte, Don Magnifico in La Cenerentola, Dr Bartolo in Le Nozze di Figaro, Dulcamara in L'Elisir d'Amore, Fabrizio in La Gazza Ladra, Frank in Die Fledermaus, Kecal in The Bartered Bride, Leporello in Don Giovanni, Mamma Agatha and the Impresario in Viva la Mamma, Melitone in La Forza del Destino, Raimbaud and the Gouverneur in Le Comte Ory, Shishkov in From the House of the Dead, the Mayor in Jenůfa, the Music Master in Ariadne auf Naxos, the Parson in The Cunning Little Vixen, Varlaam in Boris Godunov; numerous radio and TV broadcasts, including Melitone in La Forza del Destino and the Sacristan in Tosca (CBC) and the Music Master in Ariadne auf Naxos (PBS). *Television:* Sacristan in Tosca, Canadian Opera, Fra Melitone in La Forza del Destino, Canadian Opera, Musik Lehrer in Ariadne auf Naxos, PBS, Benoit in La Bohème, Live from Lincoln Center, Merry Widow, San Francisco Opera. *Recordings include:* Devilshoof in The Bohemian Girl, with Central City Opera. *Current Management:* Pinnacle Arts Management/Uzan Division, 889 Ninth Avenue, Suite 1, New York, NY 10019, USA. *Telephone:* (212) 397-7926. *Fax:* (212) 397-7920. *E-mail:* Vuzan@pinnaclearts.com. *Website:* www.pinnaclearts.com; www.peterstrummer.com.

STRUSIŃSKA, Ewa, MA; Polish conductor; *Music Director and Principal Conductor, Szczecin Philharmonic Orchestra;* b. 19 July 1976, Stalowa Wola. *Education:* Fryderyk Chopin Univ. of Music, Warsaw, Royal Northern Coll. of Music, Manchester, UK. *Career:* following graduation spent a year as Asst Conductor, Częstochowa Philharmonic Orchestra; won position of Jr Fellow in Conducting at Royal Northern Coll. of Music and moved to UK; extensive operatic and ballet repertoire as an Asst Conductor at Polish Nat. Opera and Polish Nat. Ballet – Teatr Wielki, Warsaw, collaborating on pieces including Nabucco, The Flying Dutchman, Madame Butterfly, Cinderella, Sleeping Beauty, The Nutcracker, Halka; Polish Nat. Opera debut with Medeamaterial by Dusapin; other opera work includes appearances at Royal Northern Coll. of Music (Janáček's The Cunning Little Vixen and Mozart's The Marriage of Figaro) and Buxton Opera Festival (Bennet's All the King's Men and McNeff's Tarka the Otter); has worked with orchestras, including BBC Nat. Orchestra of Wales, Bamberg Symphony, Hallé Orchestra, Hofer Symphony, Sinfonietta Baden, Uppsala Chamber Orchestra, Warsaw Philharmonic, Nat. Polish Radio Orchestra, Częstochowa Philharmonic, Rzeszów Philharmonic, Koszalin Philharmonic, Szczecin Philharmonic, Opole Philharmonic, Warsaw Nat. Opera Philharmonic, Beethoven Acad. Orchestra, Sinfonia Iuventus, Johannesburg Philharmonic, Gävle Symphony, Norrlands Opera Symphony, Slovak Sinfonietta and the Northern Sinfonia; chosen by London Symphony Orchestra to be one of three participants in a master class by Valery Gergiev 2008; Asst Conductor with the Hallé Orchestra, Manchester (first female asst conductor of a British orchestra) 2008–10, numerous concerts across UK, simultaneously held position of Music Dir with Hallé Youth Orchestra; collaborated with Royal Ballet at Covent Garden 2010; Music Dir and Prin.

Conductor, Szczecin Philharmonic Orchestra 2013–. *Honours:* honoured with title of Amb. of Stalowa Wola by her home city in recognition of her achievements in Poland and abroad; Grand Prix, St Petersburg (with choir Tutti Cantamus) 2000, Laureate, Gustav Mahler Int. Conducting Competition, Bamberg, Germany. *Address:* Szczecin Philharmonic Orchestra, pl. Armii Krajowej 1, 70-455 Szczecin, Poland. *Telephone:* 7894-350307 (UK, mobile); (60) 9779234 (Poland). *E-mail:* info@ewastrusinska.com. *Website:* www.ewastrusinska.com.

STRYCZEK, Karl-Heinz; German singer (baritone); b. 5 May 1937, Nichelsdorf. *Education:* Leipzig Musikhochschule. *Career:* debut at Dresden-Radebeul 1964, as Germont; Dresden Staatsoper from 1966, Berlin Staatsoper, 1970; Premiere of Levins Muhle by U Zimmermann at Dresden, 1973; Guest appearances at Paris Opéra, Helsinki, Wiesbaden and Barcelona (Telramund in Lohengrin, 1992); Dresden, 1992 and 1994, in Hoffmann and as Oger in Reimann's Melusine; Other roles include Pizarro, Wozzeck, Scarpia, Mozart's Count, Amonasro, Iago and Carlos in La Forza del Destino; Dresden Staatsoper 2000–01 as the Speaker in Die Zauberflöte, and in the premiere of Celan, by Peter Ruzicka; Many concert and oratorio engagements. *Recordings include:* Donner in Das Rheingold; Die Kluge and Carmina Burana.

STUART, Debra; British singer (mezzo-soprano); b. 1969, Scotland. *Education:* Royal Scottish Academy and the Guildhall School of Music. *Career:* opera appearances at Covent Garden, English National Opera and with the English Touring Opera; roles include Mozart's Annius and Dorabella, Rosina, Meg Page and Britten's Hermia; concerts with Frans Brüggen and the Songmakers' Almanac; sang in A Midsummer Night's Dream at Aldeburgh in 1995 and festival engagements at Aix-en-Provence and Bordeaux; further repertoire includes Les Nuits d'Été (BBC); sang Luca in the premiere of Woolrich's In the House of Crossed Desires, Cheltenham, 1996.

STUBBS, Stephen; American chitarrone player, archlute player and ensemble director; b. 1951, Seattle; m. Maxine Eilander. *Career:* debut as lutenist, Wigmore Hall, London 1976; Prof. of Lute and Performance Practice, Hochschule für Kunste, Bremen 1980–2006; debut as opera dir with Stefano Landi's La Morte d'Orfeo, Flanders Festival 1987; Dir, Tragicomedia, ensemble performing in the Renaissance and Baroque repertory; Francesca Caccini's La Liberazione di Ruggiero dall'Isola d'Alcina at the 1989 Swedish Baroque Festival, Malmö; conducted Monteverdi's L'Incoronazione di Poppea for Norrlands Opera in Umeå, Sweden 1993; conducted Monteverdi's L'Orfeo at Netherlands Opera, Amsterdam 1995; f. Teatro Lirico ensemble 1996–; co-Artistic Dir, Boston Early Music Festival 2003–; co-f. Seattle Acad. of Baroque Opera 2006–; f. opera company, Pacific Operaworks 2009. *Compositions:* Pegasus and the Griffin, one-hour chamber opera for three singers and chamber ensemble, libretto by Peter Bockström, performed Malmö, 1994. *Recordings include:* solo lute recordings: David Kellner's XVI. Auserlesene Lauten-Stücke, J. S. Bach, S L Weiss, David Kellner, Jacques St Luc, Gaultier, Gallot and Logi Lute Suites; with Tragicomedia: Proensa, My Mind to Me a Kingdom, A Musicall Dreame, Orpheus I Am, Sprezzatura, Il Ballo dell'Ingrate (and other theatrical music by Monteverdi), The Notebook of Anna Magdalena Bach, Le Canterine Romane (music for 3 sopranos by Luigi Rossi), Monteverdi Vespers; with Teatro Lirico: Love and Death in Venice, Folia. *Publications:* contrib. L'Armnonia Sonora: continuo orchestration in Monteverdi's L'Orfeo, to Early Music 1994. *Address:* Seattle Academy of Baroque Opera, 1525 NE Elskin Place, Seattle, WA 98125, USA (office). *Telephone:* (206) 913-2073 (office). *E-mail:* info@seattleacademyofbaroqueopera.com (office); info@pacificoperaworks.org (office). *Website:* www.seattleacademyofbaroqueopera.com (office); www.pacificoperaworks.org (office).

STUDEBAKER, Thomas; American singer (tenor); b. 1970, Illinois. *Career:* debut at St Louis Opera 1995; appearances throughout USA, including engagements with the Metropolitan (Ruiz in Il Trovatore); sang Narraboth in Salome at Santa Fe, 1998; season 1999–2000 with appearances at Montréal and Seattle. *Honours:* finalist in Singer of the World Competition, Cardiff 1999. *Current Management:* Columbia Artists Management, 1790 Broadway, New York, NY 10019-1412, USA. *Telephone:* (212) 841-9500. *Fax:* (212) 841-9744. *E-mail:* info@cami.com. *Website:* www.cami.com.

STUDER, Cheryl; American singer (soprano); *Professor of Voice, Hochschule für Musik, Würzburg;* b. (Cheryl Lynn Studer), 24 Oct. 1955, Midland, Mich.; m. 3rd Michalis Doukakis; two d. (by previous m.). *Education:* Interlochen Arts Acad., Oberlin Coll., Univ. of Tennessee, Hochschule für Musik, Vienna. *Career:* studied singing with Gwendolyn Pike, at Berkshire Music Centre, at Tanglewood with Phyllis Curtin at Hochschule für Musik, Vienna with Hans Hotter; Fellow, Tanglewood Berkshire Music Center 1975–77; engaged for concert series with Boston Symphony Orchestra by Seiji Ozawa 1979; opera debut as First Lady in The Magic Flute, Munich 1980–82; with Darmstadt State Theatre, Germany 1982–84, Deutsche Oper, Berlin 1984–86; US debut as Micaela in Carmen, Lyric Opera of Chicago 1984; debut at Bayreuth 1985, Royal Opera House, Covent Garden 1987, Metropolitan Opera, New York 1988; debut as Adelaide in Arabella, Hamburg State Opera 2014, as Madame de Croissy in Dialogues des Carmelites, Stadttheater Klagenfurt 2015; sings wide variety of roles, especially Wagner, Verdi, Mozart and Strauss; professional stage directing debut with Bavarian Chamber Opera Company with Il barbiere di Siviglia from Rossini 2010; Prof. of Voice, Hochschule für Musik Würzburg 2003–; Chair., Maria Callas Grand Prix Int. Voice Competition. *Honours:* Hon. Prof., Beijing Central Conservatory; Int.

Music Award 1993, Vocalist of the Year (USA) 1994, Terras Sem Sombre 2011, Ovation Award 2012, Furtwängler Preis; numerous awards for recordings including Grand Prix du Disque - Prix Maria Callas, Orphée d'Or, Cannes Classical Award and two Grammys. *Address:* Hochschule für Musik, Hofstallstrasse 6-8, 97070 Würzburg, Germany (office). *E-mail:* studouk@aol .com (office). *Website:* www.hfm-wuerzburg.de (office); www.cherylstuder .com.

STUDER, Ulrich; singer (baritone); b. 27 Aug. 1945, Bern, Switzerland. *Education:* Bern Conservatory and Musikhochschule Munich. *Career:* many appearances at opera houses in Italy, The Netherlands (The Hague), Austria (Innsbruck), Australia and Czechoslavakia; concert and broadcast engagements in Switzerland, Germany and France, notably in Bach's Sacred Music and contemporary works by Burkhard, Milhaud and Huber; recitals featuring German lieder and French chansons; opera performances at Bern 1979–83, and at Basle, Lausanne and Munich; roles have included Morales in Carmen, Belcore, Malatesta, Valentin, Creonte in Haydn's Orfeo, Masetto, Suppé's Boccaccio and Monteverdi's Orfeo; season 2000–01 at Halle as Don Alfosno, Escamillo, and Elmiro in Rossini's Otello (concert). *Recordings include:* Cantatas by Bach and Charpentier, Messe des Morts by Gilles, Cantatas by Vivaldi, Elviro in Handel's Serse, Lully's Armide, Erode in Stradella's San Giovanni Battista.

STUDNICKA, Vladimir; composer and music director; b. 24 Aug. 1935, Czechoslovakia; two d. *Education:* Conservatory of Music. *Career:* debut with Suite for orchestra, performed by Janáček Philharmonic Orchestra 1957; teacher at music school 1961–75; Music Dir, Radio Ostrava 1975–; founder and Conductor, Beskydska Muzika Harmonic Folk Orchestra. *Compositions include:* Suite for orchestra 1957, The May Dance 1973, The Beskydy Nocturno1984, The Ondra's Dance 1985, The Round 1985, Salut JV Stich-Punto for 12 horns 1986; concert pieces for orchestra, adaptations of folk songs of the Janáček region, chamber and symphony works. *Publication:* Slazsky Dance Musikvarlag Rundal 1993.

STUMPF, Peter Daniel, BM, DipArt; American cellist; b. 16 Jan. 1963, Syracuse, NY. *Education:* Curtis Inst. of Music, New England Conservatory, studied with David Wells, Orlando Cole, Lawrence Lesser. *Career:* debut with Boston Symphony Orchestra, Symphony Hall, Boston 1979; participant at Marlboro Music Festival 1985–; tours with Music from Marlboro; mem., Philadelphia Chamber Music Soc. Players 1994–; piano trio with Mitsuko Uchida and Mark Steinberg 1995–; solo recitals at the Jordan Hall, Boston 1989–90, Phillips Collection, Washington, DC 1991, 1994, 1996, Corcoran Gallery, Washington, DC 1997; solo appearances at Aspen Festival, Colorado 1984, Boston Philharmonic 1989, Virginia Symphony 1992, National Repertory Orchestra 1992, Philadelphia Orchestra Chamber Music Series 1990–; chamber music with Wolfgang Sawallisch in Carnegie Hall and Concertgebouw; teacher of chamber music, Curtis Inst. of Music 1994–; mem. bd of trustees, Yellow Barn Festival, Putney, Vt 1995–. *Honours:* second prize Evian Int. String Quartet Competition 1983, first prize Aspen Concerto Competition for Cello 1984, first prize Washington Int. Competition 1991.

STUMPHIUS, Annegeer; Dutch singer (soprano); b. 1963. *Career:* Glyndebourne Touring Opera 1987, as Fiordiligi; Munich Festival 1988, as Europa in Strauss's Die Liebe der Danaë; sang Britten's Helena at Glyndebourne 1989; First Lady in Die Zauberflöte 1991; season 1991 as Vitellia in La Clemenza di Tito at Enschede and Zürich, Ilia in Idomeneo at Amsterdam; season 1993–94 as Ellen Orford at Munich and Vitellia at Dresden; Munich 1996, as Echo in Ariadne and Naxos; Jenůfa at Hildesheim 2001; further engagements as Donna Anna at Dresden, Jenůfa at Hildesheim, Mozart's Countess at Salzburg and Donna Elvira at Munich; Wellgunde and Helmwige in Munich Ring, under Zubin Mehta. *Recordings include:* Bach B minor Mass, Haydn's Seasons, Mendelssohn Lobgesang, Bach St John Passion, Gluck Pilgrims to Mecca.

STUPPNER, Hubert, PhD; Italian composer; b. 18 Jan. 1944, Trodena, nr Bolzano. *Education:* Bolzano Conservatory, Univ. of Padua, Darmstadt with Ligeti, Xenakis and Stockhausen. *Career:* founder, Int. Festival of Contemporary Music at Bolzano 1975; Dir, Bolzano Conservatory from 1981. *Compositions:* Historia Naturalis for soprano, mezzo, six voices, two flutes and two percussion 1976, Totentanz (chamber opera) 1978, Die Stimme der Sylphiden for orchestra 1979, Quasi una Sinfonia 1981, Chamber Concerto 1981–84, String Quartet No. 1 1984, No. 2 1987, No. 3 1990, Symphony No.1 1985, Piano Concerto 1984, Chamber Symphony 1986, Symphony No. 2 1986, Café Eros (for theatre) 1986, Salomes Tanz for soprano and orchestra 1988, Bergkristall for violin and piano 1989, Hiob (oratorio) 1991, Folk Songs for soprano and ensemble 1994, Corrida for orchestra 1996.

STUR, Svetozar; conductor and composer; b. 21 Feb. 1951, Bratislava, Czechoslovakia; m. Nadezda Sturova 1977. *Education:* Conservatoire in Bratislava, Acad. of Music and Performing Arts, Bratislava. *Career:* debut with Taras Bulba by Janáček with the Slovak Philharmonic Orchestra, Bratislava 1977; Artistic Head of Orchestra, Slovak Folklorist Ensemble, Lucnica 1972–77; Asst Conductor, Slovak Philharmonic Orchestra, Bratislava 1977–79; First Conductor, Cairo Conservatoire Orchestra 1979–80, Symphony Orchestra of Czech Radio, Bratislava 1980–81; recorded own compositions for film and television with Fisyo Orchestra, Prague 1980; Asst Conductor, Slovak Nat. Theatre, Bratislava 1980–87; Conductor, Slovak State Folk Ensemble, Bratislava 1988–90; freelance composer for film, television and theatre from 1991.

STURROCK, Kathron; British pianist; b. 17 July 1948, Bournemouth, England. *Education:* Royal College of Music, studied with Alfred Brendel in Vienna, Mstislav Rostropovich in Moscow. *Career:* concert and television appearances throughout Europe and in North America, India and Australia; regular performances for the BBC and concerts in the major London halls; Dir of chamber music ensemble, The Fibonacci Sequence; taught at Morley College, the Royal College of Music, Royal Academy of Music and the Birmingham School of Music; Artist-in-Residence, Brisbane Conservatoire 1987; British Council tour of Oman 1989; BBC recitals include Schubert's Wanderer Fantasy, Beethoven Op 109, and Rawsthorne Ballade; Prom debut 1994 in Rawsthorne Second Piano Concerto with Piers Lane. *Recordings include:* Bliss Viola Sonata with Emanuel Vardi; Beethoven Spring Sonata; Brahms Violin and Viola Sonatas; cello sonatas by Beethoven, Schnittke, Shostakovich and Kabalevsky; songs by Rebecca Clarke with Patricia Wright; chamber works of Alan Rawsthorne; songs by Sir Arthur Bliss. *Honours:* Sofia International Opera Competition, as accompanist; Martin Musical Scholarship Fund and The Countess of Munster Award, RCM. *Address:* 81 Lacy Road, London, SW15 1NR, England. *Telephone:* (20) 8780-3266. *E-mail:* fibsequence@btinternet .com. *Website:* www.fibonacci-sequence.co.uk/Kathron.htm.

STUTZMANN, Nathalie; French singer (contralto) and conductor; b. 6 May 1965, Suresnes; d. of Christian Dupuy and Christiane Stutzmann. *Education:* Lycée Henri Poincaré, School of Lyrical Art at Paris Opera, studied singing with Christiane Stutzmann, Michel Sénéchal, Hans Hotter and conducting with Jorma Panula. *Career:* numerous concerts under the direction of Herbert von Karajan, Seiji Ozawa, Sir Simon Rattle, Nikolaus Harnoncourt, Yannick Nézet-Séguin and others; has performed with Berlin Philharmonic, Vienna Philharmonic, Orchestre de Paris, London Symphony Orchestra, others; numerous lieder recitals with Swedish pianist Inger Södergren since 1990s; f. Orfeo 55 chamber orchestra (ensemble playing on both baroque and modern instruments) 2009; Guest Conductor, London Philharmonic Orchestra, Orquestra Sinfônica de São Paulo, Washington Nat. Symphony Orchestra, Rotterdam Philharmonic Orchestra, Spanish Nat. Orchestra, Bergen Philharmonic, Konzerthaus Orchestra Berlin, RTE Nat. Symphony of Ireland, Oslo Philharmonic, Royal Stockholm Philharmonic, Monte-Carlo Philharmonic Orchestra, New Japan Philharmonic, Baltimore Symphony, Detroit Symphony Orchestra, Orchestre Nat. de Bordeaux, Royal Liverpool Philharmonic 2015–16; Artist-in-Residence, Metz Arsenal; teacher, Geneva Haute école de musique, Switzerland; Associated Artist, Orquestra Sinfônica de São Paulo, Orchestre de chambre de Paris. *Film:* Portrait (DVD). *Recordings include:* numerous recordings including Handel Opera Arias 1994, Pergolesi Stabat Mater/Salve Regina 1993, Schumann Lieder 1994, Bach St Matthew Passion 1997, Chausson Mélodies 1997, Brahms Lieder 1998, Mahler Symphony No. 2 2000, Poulenc Mélodies 2000, Schubert Winterreise 2003, Vivaldi Prima Donna 2011, Une cantate imaginaire 2012, Handel Heroes from the Shadows 2014. *Honours:* Officier des Arts et des Lettres, Chevalier, Ordre nat. du mérite, Officier du mérite culturel Monte-Carlo; First Prize in Piano, Bassoon and Chamber Music, Nancy Conservatory, Winner, Neue Stimmen Int. Singing Competition 1987, Grammy Awards, Deutscher Schallplatten Prize, Diapason d'Or, Choc Monde de la Musique. . *E-mail:* stutzmannoffice@ gmail.com (office). *Website:* www.nathaliestutzmann.com; www.orfeo55.com.

STYLES, Luke Raymond, BMus, MMus; British/Australian composer; b. 17 Oct. 1982, Brisbane, Queensland, Australia. *Education:* Royal Acad. of Music, London, Universität für Musik und Darstellende Kunst, Vienna with Detlev Muller-Siemens, Hochschule für Musik, Karlsruhe with Wolfgang Rihm, King's Coll., London with George Benjamin. *Career:* works have been performed by the London Philharmonic Orchestra, BBC Singers, Kreutzer Quartet, members of Ensemble Modern, Lontano and London Sinfonietta; music has featured at festivals including the Wien Modern, Aldeburgh Music Festival, Glyndebourne Festival, Tête à Tête: The Opera Festival, Darmstadt Int. Festival for New Music, ISCM Festival, Vienna, Park Lane Group 50th Anniversary concert series; participated in Jerwood Opera Writing Programme at Aldeburgh Music 2010–11; Artistic Dir Ensemble Amorpha; Young Composer in Residence, Glyndebourne 2012–14. *Honours:* numerous awards, commissions and scholarships. *Address:* 108 Burnt Ash Road, London, SE12 8PU, England. *Telephone:* 7870-230794 (mobile). *E-mail:* lukestylescomposer@ gmail.com. *Website:* www.lukestyles.com.

SUART, Richard Martin, ARAM, FRAM; British singer (baritone); b. 5 Sept. 1951, Blackpool, England; s. of George Frederick Suart and Nora Martha Suart; m. Susan Cook 1981 (died 2011); two s. (one deceased) one d. *Education:* Chorister at King's Coll., Cambridge, Sedbergh School, Choral Scholar in choir of St John's Coll., Cambridge, Royal Acad. of Music, London. *Career:* roles in contemporary opera include The Black Minister in Le Grand Macabre, Der Gatte in Reigen for Reisopera, Dad/Café Manager in Greek for ENO, Old Musician in Broken Strings (Param Vir) for Netherlands Opera, Mr Walter in Michel van der Aa's After Life, Chaplinoperas (Mason) throughout Europe with Ensemble Modern, Eight Songs for a Mad King in London, Paris, Helsinki, Milan and Strasbourg, Stan Stock in Playing Away (Mason) also French Amb. in Of Thee I Sing (Gershwin), General Snookfield in Let 'Em Eat Cake (Gershwin), Barabashkin in Paradise Moscow (Shostakovich) for Opera North; other roles include Frank in Die Fledermaus, Benoit and Alcindoro in La Bohème for ENO, the Lord Chancellor in Iolanthe, Don Inigo Gomez in L'Heure Espagnole for Grange Park Opera, Jack Point in The Yeomen of the Guard, King Arthur in Gwyneth and the Green Knight for Music Theatre Wales, Garsington Opera performances include Don Magnifico in La

Cenerentola, Antonio in Le Nozze de Figaro; Savoy Opera performances include the patter roles in Gilbert and Sullivan, particularly Ko-Ko (The Mikado), in London, Venice, New York; presents show As a Matter of Patter; mem. D'Oyly Carte 1988–; frequent visits to N America for Gilbert and Sullivan galas; debut at The Hollywood Bowl singing Pangloss in Candide and narrating 2010; Vice-Pres. Gilbert and Sullivan Soc. *Television:* The Little Prince, Eight Songs for a Mad King, Suart Sings Sullivan. *Recordings include:* most of the Savoy operas, Candide, A Midsummer Night's Dream, The Rose of Persia, The Fairy Queen, Ligeti's Le Grand Macabre, The Geisha, The Maid of the Mountains, The Contrabandistas, The Little Prince, Tom Jones, Songs from the shows of Lionel Monckton, Give Me a Smile (songs and music of World War II). *Publication:* They'd None of 'Em be Missed 2008. *Current Management:* Musichall Ltd, Oast House, Hollow Lane, East Hoathly, East Sussex, BN8 6QX, England. *Telephone:* (1825) 840437. *E-mail:* info@musichall.uk.com. *Website:* www.musichall.uk.com. *Address:* Yardley Bank, 29 Yardley Park Road, Tonbridge, Kent, TN9 1NB, England (home). *E-mail:* richard@richardsuart.co.uk (home). *Website:* www.richardsuart.co.uk.

SUBEN, Joel Eric, BMus, MFA, PhD; American conductor, composer and academic; *Artistic Director, Save The Music, Inc.*; b. 16 May 1946, New York, NY; m. 1st Judith Ann Gundersheimer 1979 (divorced 1985); m. 2nd Linda Rodgers 1993. *Education:* Eastman School of Music, Brandeis Univ., Hochschule Mozarteum Salzburg (conducting with Otmar Suitner), Akademia Muzyczna im. Karola Szymanowskiego (composition with Henryk Mikołaj Górecki), Curtis Inst. master class in conducting (Sergiu Celibidache), pvt. conducting study with Jacques-Louis Monod. *Career:* Music Dir and Permanent Conductor, Peninsula Symphony of Virginia 1982–87; Music Dir and Conductor, Center Orchestra, NJ 1986–88; Guest Conductor for American Symphony Orchestra, New York, Silesian Philharmonic Orchestra, Warsaw Nat. Philharmonic Orchestra, Sudeten Philharmonie, Rzeszów Philharmonic Orchestra, Częstochowa Philharmonic Orchestra, Białystok Philharmonic, Polish Radio Nat. Symphony Orchestra, Slovak Radio Symphony Orchestra, Bratislava, North Bohemian Philharmonic Orchestra, Janáček Philharmonic Orchestra, Moravian Philharmonic Orchestra (Czech Repub.); Dir of Orchestras, Coll. of William and Mary, Virginia 1983–92; Guest Lecturer, NY Philharmonic Pre-Concert Lecture Series 1989; Co-founder, Vice-Pres. and Artistic Dir, Save the Music, Inc. (non-profit org.) 1991–; Music Dir, Composers Chorus 1992; Music Adviser, Wellesley Philharmonic, Mass 1993–96. *Compositions include:* Rondo 1966, Make a Joyful Noise 1967, Sonata da Camera 1966, Adagietto 1967, Face of an Addict 1967, Offertory 1967, Psalm 121 1967, Lovemusic 1968, Agréments for flute 1971, Serenade for 12 instruments 1979, Five Goethe Songs 1980, Sonatina for piano 1981, The Birth of Euphrosyne 1983, Gesualdo Triptych for string orchestra 1984, Idylls for two pianos 1986, Symphony in Old Style for orchestra 1987, Academic Overture 1987, Suite of Dances for 2 Guitars 1987, Winter Love 1988, Song Book for treble voices 1989, Concerto Classico for flute and small orchestra 1991, Breve Sogno for large orchestra 1994, Fantasy-Variations for violin and orchestra 1999, Seven for a cappella chorus 2004, Ciacconetta for viola and orchestra 2008, Three Images for cello and orchestra 2010, A Memory of Youth for piano trio 2012. *Honours:* Winner Nat. Composers Competition, American Guild of Organists 1967, Eastman Sacred Song Competition 1967, Virginia Music Teachers Asscn Comm. 1981, (American) Music Teachers Asscn Composer of the Year 1982, Washington Square Contemporary Music Series Composers Competition 1986, Bucks Co. (Pa) Symphony Composition Prize 1987. *Address:* Save the Music Inc., PO Box 6268, West Side Station, Hoboken, NJ 07030-6268, USA (office). *Telephone:* (201) 798-1099 (office). *E-mail:* mail@save-themusic.org (office). *Website:* www.save-themusic.org (office).

SUBLETT, Virginia, BMus, MMus, DMusArts; American singer (soprano) and academic; *Professor, Department of Music, North Dakota State University*; b. 29 July 1952, Kansas City, Kansas. *Education:* Louisiana State Univ., Univ. of California, San Diego, studied with Carol Webber, Isabel Penagos and Michael Jackson Parker. *Career:* sang Queen of the Night in The Magic Flute (Mozart), New York City Opera and San Diego Opera; La Princesse and Le Rossignol in L'Enfant et les Sortilèges (Ravel), New York City Opera; Nannetta in Falstaff (Verdi), Tytania in A Midsummer Night's Dream (Britten), and Oberto in Alcina (Handel), Los Angeles Opera; Ismene in Mitridate (Mozart) and Servilia in La Clemenza di Tito (Mozart), L'Opéra de Nice; numerous appearances as soprano soloist with Los Angeles Philharmonic Orchestra, San Diego Symphony Orchestra, Illinois Symphony Orchestra, New Jersey Symphony Orchestra, and Los Angeles Baroque Orchestra; founder and Co-Conductor, Cappella Gloriana vocal ensemble 1996; mem. adjunct faculties, Univ. of California, San Diego and Univ. of San Diego 1992; Dir of Choral Scholars and Univ. Community Choir, Univ. of California, San Diego 1997–99; Prof., Dept of Music, North Dakota State Univ. 2004–; mem. American Guild of Musical Artists, Nat. Asscn of Teachers of Singing, American Choral Directors' Asscn. *Address:* 218F Music Education Building, Department of Music, Division of Fine Arts, North Dakota State University, PO Box 6050, Fargo, ND 58108-6050, USA (office). *Telephone:* (701) 231-8258 (office). *E-mail:* virginia.sublett@ndsu.edu (office). *Website:* www.ndsu.edu/finearts/music (office).

SUBOTNICK, Morton Leon, MA; American composer and academic; b. 14 April 1933, Los Angeles, Calif.; s. of Jack Jacob Subotnick and Rose Luckerman; m. 1st Linn Pottle 1953 (divorced 1971); one s. one d.; m. 2nd Doreen Nelson 1976 (divorced 1977); m. 3rd Joan La Barbara 1979; one s. *Education:* Univ. of Denver, Mills Coll. *Career:* Co-founder San Francisco Tape Music Center 1961–65; fmr Music Dir Ann Halprin's Dance Co. and San Francisco Actors' Workshop, fmr Music Dir Lincoln Center Repertory Theatre; Dir of electronic music at original Electric Circus, St Mark's Place, New York 1967–68; Artist-in-Residence, New York Univ. School of the Arts 1966–69; apptd Co-Dir Center for Experiments in Art, Information and Tech., California Inst. of Arts, Valencia 1969, also Co-Chair. Composition Dept; Visiting Prof. in Composition, Univ. of Maryland 1968, Univ. of Pittsburgh 1969, Yale Univ. 1982, 1983; Composer-in-Residence DAAD, West Berlin 1981, MIT 1986. *Compositions include:* Silver Apples of the Moon, The Wild Bull, Trembling, The Double Life of Amphibians, The Key to Songs, Return: The Triumph of Reason (electronic composition in honour of the return of Halley's Comet) 1986, In Two Worlds 1987–88, And The Butterflies Begin to Sing 1988, A Desert Flowers 1989, All my Hummingbirds have Alibis, Jacob's Room (opera) 1993, Making Music 1996, Intimate Immensity 1997, Echoes from the Silent Call of Girona 1998. *Honours:* Brandeis Award for Music 1983, American Acad. of Arts and Letters Composer Award, SEAMUS Lifetime Achievement Award 1998, ASCAP John Cage Award, ACO Lifetime Achievement Award. *Address:* 25 Minetta Lane, Apt 4B, New York, NY 10012, USA. *E-mail:* morts@creatingmusic.com. *Website:* www.mortonsubotnick.com.

SUDBIN, Yevgeny; Russian pianist; b. 1980, St Petersburg. *Education:* St Petersburg Conservatory with Lyubov Pevsner, Hochschule Hanns Eisler, Berlin, Purcell School of Music, London with Christopher Elton, and RAM. *Career:* has performed concerts and recitals throughout Europe and N America, including Rudolfinum, Prague, Philharmonie, Cologne, Gewandhaus, Leipzig, Schauspielhaus, Berlin, Nat. Concert Hall, Dublin, Salle de l'UNESCO, Paris, Serate Musicali, Milan, British Embassy, Paris, Tonhalle, Zurich, Konzertreihe, Wolfsberg, Nuits Romantiques Festival, France, Sommets Musicaux and the Verbier Festival, Switzerland; chamber music concerts with the Chilingirian String Quartet and violinists Ilya Gringolts and Julia Fischer. *Recordings:* London Octave, Better Baroque, Scarlatti Piano Sonatas 2005, Sudbin plays Rachmaninov 2005, Tchaikovsky Piano Concerto No. 1 and Medtner Piano Concerto No. 1 2008, Rachmaninov Piano Concerto No. 4 and Medtner Piano Concerto No. 2 2009. *Honours:* first prize Steinway Piano Competition, Berlin 1992, 1993, 1995, winner Concertino Praga Int. Piano Competition 1994, second prize Vendome Prize 2000, prize winner Dublin Int. Piano Competition 2000, Alfred Brendel Prize, Philharmonia Orchestra Musical Prize, winner Jaques Samuels Piano Competition 2003, Orpheum Public Award for the best interpretation of a Mozart Concerto. *Current Management:* c/o Nigel Grant Rogers, Grant Rogers Musical Artists' Management, 8 Wren Crescent, Bushey Heath, Hertfordshire WD23 1AN, England. *Telephone:* (20) 8950-2220. *Fax:* (20) 8950-3570. *E-mail:* info@ngrartists.com. *Website:* www.ngrartists.com. *Address:* c/o BIS Records AB, Stationsvägen 20, Åkersberga 184 50, Sweden (office).

SUHONEN, Antti; singer (bass-baritone); b. 5 Nov. 1956, Nurmes, Finland. *Education:* Sibelius Acad., Nat. Opera Studio, Helsinki, Int. Opera Studio, Zürich, masterclasses with Charles Farncombe, Herbert Brauer and Victoria de los Angeles. *Career:* debut at Zürich 1986, engaged at Karlsruhe 1987–91, and at Helsinki from 1991–; made guest appearances at Dresden, Wiesbaden, Hanover and Mannheim and also at Munich State Opera, Berlin State Oera, Essen and Royal Opera in Copenhagen; Karlsruhe 1989, in shared premiere of Graf Mirabeau by Siegfried Matthus; appearances at Helsinki and elsewhere as Mozart's Leporello, Masetto, Figaro and Alfonso, Sparafucile, Dulcamara, Basilio, Varlaam and Rangoni in Boris Godunov, Melitone in La Forza del Destino, Méphistopélès in Gounod's Faust; sang Klaus in premiere of Linkola's Elina, Helsinki 1992 and Fruitseller in Bergman's The Singing Tree in Helsinki 1995; with Berlin State Opera, Wagner's Ring, Kupfer and Barenboim 1996; Savonlinna Festival 1992, as Don Fernando in Fidelio; Bluebeard in Bartók's Bluebeard's Castle 1994; sang Ossip in The Palace, by Sallinen at the 1996 Savonlinna Festival; season 1999 with the Israel Philharmonic Orchestra under Zubin Mehta in Ariadne auf Naxos, Chicago Symphony Orchestra under Pierre Boulez in Schoenberg's Moses und Aron and the Finnish Nat. Opera in Wagner's Ring; season 1999–2000 as Wagner's Gunther in Helsinki and the Forester in The Cunning Little Vixen, for the Deutsche Oper Berlin; guest appearances at Deutsche Oper, Berlin 2000–; frequently appears as soloist in numerous concerts. *Recordings:* Rautavaara: Thomas 1986, Sampo 1995, Mozart: Die Zauberflöte 1988, Pacius: Kung Karls Jagd 1991.

SUKIS, Lilian; singer (soprano); b. 29 June 1939, Kaunas, Lithuania. *Education:* Toronto Univ., Canada. *Career:* debut in Toronto 1964, as Lady Billows in Britten's Albert Herring; Metropolitan Opera from 1965, notably as Pamina in Die Zauberflöte; Bayerishe Staatsoper, Munich, and elsewhere in Germany from 1969, as Violetta, Mozart's Countess and Fiordiligi, Micaela in Carmen, Liu in Turandot, and Verdi's Luisa Miller; sang Strauss's Daphne at Munich, and in the 1972 premiere of Sim Tjong by Isang Yun. *Recordings include:* Ascanio in Alba, by Mozart, Die Lustige Weiber von Windsor, Mozart's La finta giardiniera.

SULEIMANOV, Stanislav; Russian singer (bass); b. 1945, Baku. *Education:* Baku Conservatory. *Career:* sang at the Bolshoi Theatre Moscow from 1977; since 1989 also the creator of the first Contract Musical Theatre 'Forum'; repertoire includes: Boris and Varlaam in Boris Godunov, Rimsky's Salieri, Scarpia in Tosca, Malatesta in Rachmaninov's Francesca da Rimini, Boris in Lady Macbeth, Pontius Pilate in Master and Margarita by S. Slonimsky; guest appearances throughout Russia, USA, Japan, Netherlands, Belgium, Luxembourg, Italy, Spain, Greece and Germany; concerts and Lieder recitals. *Address:* Halturinskaja str 4-1-58, 107392 Moscow, Russia.

SULLIVAN, Ghillian; Australian singer (soprano); b. (Gillian Trotter), 31 Dec. 1949, Adelaide, SA; d of Robin Trotter; m. John Miller; one s. one d. *Education:* studied in London with Audrey Langford. *Career:* debut with Opera 80 as Mozart's Countess 1980; season 1981–82 as Britten's Tytania for GTO and Donizetti's Adina for Opera North; Fiordiligi at Sydney 1983; Leeds in the premiere of Rebecca by W. Josephs and English premiere of Krenek's Jonny spielt auf 1983–84; Wiesbaden and Aachen as Constanze 1985–86; Cologne as Musetta 1987; Victoria State Opera debut as Donna Elvira 1986; ENO from 1989, including tour of Russia; Prin. Guest Artist, Opera Australia 1985–; many major roles, including Traviata, Lucia, Gilda, Donna Anna and Rosalinde; guest appearances at all state companies and with Sydney Symphony Orchestra; sang Bizet's Leila and Rosalinde in Die Fledermaus at Sydney 2000; concert and oratorio engagements. *Recordings include:* solo album: Vocal Gems. *Address:* 11 Hillview Street, Cooks Hill, NSW 2305, Australia (office). *Telephone:* 41-2681568 (mobile) (office).

SULZEN, Donald, MMus; American pianist and accompanist; b. 17 Feb. 1955, Kansas City, KS. *Education:* Ecole Normale de Musique de Paris, Univ. of North Texas. *Career:* performed at major festivals throughout the world; regular appearances with well-known singers, such as Julie Kaufmann, Michiè Nakamaru, Anna Caterina Antonacci, Daphne Evangelatos, Doris Soffel, Marilyn Schmiege, Ofelia Sala, James Taylor, Laura Aikin and Thomas Cooley; pianist Munich Piano Trio 2001–; television and radio performances for Bayerischer Rundfunk Munich, WDR Cologne, Radio France Paris, RAI 1 Rome, Nippon TV Tokyo, RAI 3 Naples; teacher, Richard Strauss Conservatory and Hochschule für Musik, Munich; Visiting Prof. Shenyang Conservatory of Music, China 2008–09. *Recordings include:* Gabriel Fauré Melodies with Marilyn Schmiege (Le Monde de la Musique Prix du Choc 1994), Johannes Brahms Lieder und Duette with Julie Kaufmann and Marilyn Schmiege, George Enescu Cello Sonatas with Gerhard Zank, Franz Liszt Songs–Schmiege, Hans Pfitzner Lieder with Julie Kaufmann, Songs of John Duke with James Taylor and works of Alberto Ginastera, including solo piano pieces, Songs and Cycles of Ned Rorem with Laura Aikin, Songs and Trios of Joseph Haydn with Julie Kaufmann and the Munich Piano Trio, Songs and Trios of Joseph Haydn with James Taylor and the Munich Piano Trio, Felix Mendelssohn Piano Trios, Astor Piazzolla Tangos and Canciones. *Address:* Baaderstr. 19, 80469 Munich, Germany (home). *E-mail:* djsulzen@aol.com (home).

SUMEGI, Daniel; singer (bass); b. 1965, Australia. *Education:* studied in Australia, Venice (Italy), Vienna (Austria), San Francisco and New York (USA). *Career:* appearances with San Francisco Opera from 1991 in La Traviata, Andrea Chénier, A Midsummer Night's Dream, Der Rosenkavalier, Capriccio, Il Trovatore, Fiery Angel, Die Meistersinger, Pique Dame, Tannhäuser, King Priam, Salome and Aida; La Bohème at the Golden Gate Theatre 1996; world premiere in Asdrubila, Barcelona Olympic Games 1992; season 1994–95 with Hermit in Freischutz at Trieste, Sarastro at Victoria State Opera; season 1995–96 with Ramfis and Rossini's Basilio for Australia Opera, Gounod's Mefisto and Verdi's Banquo for Holland's Reiseopera, Britten's Theseus at Turin, Gremin for Victorian State Opera; Seneca in Monteverdi's Poppea for Glimmerglass Opera at Brooklyn Acad., Ratcliffe in Billy Budd at the Opéra Bastille and Alonso in Il Guarany for Washington Opera; season 1996–97 Ramphis and the Commendatore for Victoria State Opera, Basilio for Opera Australia, Commendatore in Oviedo, and Sarastro in Die Zauberflöte for Bonn Opera; season 1997–98 Colline and Saint Saens Old Hebrew for Opera Australia, Banquo at Houston, Peter Grimes and Boris Godunov at Metropolitan Opera, Sant Saens High Priest at Palm Beach, Billy Budd at Opera Bastille, Lady Macbeth of Mtsensk at Opera Nantes; season 1998–99 with Faust at Opera Australia, Wagner's Hagen at State Opera of South Australia, The Crucible and Boris for Washington, Pizzaro at Utah, Mefisto in Minneapolis and Fafner in Sydney; season 1999–2000 with I Lombardi in Santiago de Chile, Ramphis and the Commendatore in Houston, I Puritani's Georgio, Tosca's Scarpia and Otello's Lodovico in Washington and Baron Ochs for WNO; season 2000–01 as Fiesco for Opera Australia and Mahler's 8th for Olympic Games, Scarpa in Adelaide, Mozart's Speaker in San Diego, Verdi's Grand Inquisitor in DC and Richard Tucker Gala at Covent Garden; season 2001–02 as Wagner's Klingsor in Adelaide, Hoffmann Villains and Kurwenal for Opera Australia, Opera de Montréal Gala Concert, Don Carlo at the Met, Wagner's Pogner in Antwerp and Daland in San Diego; Washington Opera Japan Tour of Tosca, Otello and Sly; season 2002–03 as Scarpia at WNP, Medea's Creonte in Montpellier, Puccini's Timur in Dallas, Daland in Minneapolis, Escamillo for Opera Australia, Elijah for Sydney Philharmonia and Stiffelio's Jorg for Minneapolis, Daland at Austin Lyric and Escamillo at WNO; season 2003–04 with Messiah in Minnesota, Dutchman in Sydney and Austin. *Honours:* winner Melbourne Sun Aria 1987, Sydney McDonald's Aria 1994, Met Opera National Council Auditions 1994, Sullivan Foundation grant 1994. *Current Management:* Vincent & Farrell Associates, 165 East 83 No. 5E, New York, NY 10028, USA; Ingpen & Williams Ltd, 7 St George's Court, 131 Putney Bridge Road, London, SW15 2PA, England.

SUMMERLY, Jeremy, BA, MMus; British conductor and musicologist; b. 28 Feb. 1961, Stoke-on-Trent. *Education:* Lichfield Cathedral School, Winchester Coll., Univ. of Oxford, London Univ. *Career:* Studio Man., BBC Radio 1982–89; Lecturer in Academic Studies, Royal Acad. of Music 1989–95, Head of Academic Studies 1996–2007, Sterndale Bennett Lecturer in Music 2007–; co-f. Oxford Camerata 1984; f. Oxford Camerata Instrumental Ensemble 1992, Royal Acad. Consort 2002; Conductor, Schola Cantorum of Oxford 1990–96,

conducted choir of Queen's Coll., Oxford 2013–14; debut as conductor at BBC Promenade Concerts, July 1999; Dir of Music, Christ Church, Chelsea 1999–2002, now Dir of Music St Luke's, Chelsea; Guest Conductor, New London Chamber Choir, Cardinall's Musick, Chalice Consort, San Francisco, Ensemble Gombert, Melbourne, Tallis Chamber Choir, Elysian Singers of London; freelance contrib. to BBC Radio, including Record Review and CD Review (BBC Radio 3) 1990–, The English Cadence (BBC Radio 3) 1995, Choir Works (BBC Radio 3) 1996–98, Front Row (BBC Radio 4) 2002–; mem. Royal Musical Asscn, American Musicological Soc. *Recordings include:* Schütz: Christmas Story 1995, J. S. Bach: Magnificat 1995, Fauré Requiem 1994, Handel: Coronation Anthems 2002, Nicolas Gombert: Magnificat I (Salve Regina, Credo, Tulerunt Dominum) 2006, Hildegard Von Bingen: Celestial Harmonies, Responsories and Antiphons 2008. *Publications:* Gaudete: Medieval Songs and Carols 1999, Passetime with Good Company: Medieval Songs 2002, Fair Oriana: Elizabethan Madrigals 2002, Thomas Tallis: English Sacred Music 2004; contrib. to Early Music, The Musical Times, Choir and Organ, Leading Notes, Classic CD. *Honours:* Hon. ARAM 1997, Hon. FASC 2002, Hon. mem. RAM 2006; European Cultural Prize, European Asscn for the Encouragement of the Arts 1995. *Address:* Oxford Camerata, 11 Hurst Street, Oxford, OX4 1EZ, England (office). *E-mail:* j.summerly@oxfordcamerata.com (office). *Website:* www.oxfordcamerata.com (office).

SUMMERS, Hilary, BA, DipRam, ARAM; British singer (contralto); b. 1965, Newport, Gwent, Wales; m. Benjamin Mazower. *Education:* Reading Univ., Royal Acad. of Music and Nat. Opera Studio. *Career:* appearances worldwide in primarily baroque and contemporary repertoire; created the role of Stella in Elliot Carter's opera What Next? at Berlin Staatsoper 1999, and Irma in Peter Eotvos' opera Le Balcon at Aix-en-Provence Festival 2002; premiere and world tour of George Benjamin's opera Into the little Hill 2006–08; has sung Pierre Boulez' Le marteau sans maitre with the ensemble intercontemporain conducted by the composer in Paris, Rome, Cologne, Lucerne and New York; other concerts with Boulez include Stravinsky's Les noces (BBC proms 2005 and Paris 2007) and Le Visage nuptial by Boulez (Chicago Symphony Orchestra) 2005; Messiah tour (The King's Consort) 2007; with the Early Opera Company (Rosmira in Partenope 2005, Juno/Ino in Handel's Semele 2007); with Les Talens Lyriques (Penelope in Monteverdi's Il ritorno d'Ulysse in patria 2007); with Les arts florissants (Medoro in Handel's Orlando 1995–96); also Sorceress in a production of Purcell's Dido and Aeneas by Deborah Warner 2007. *Recordings include:* Le Marteau sans Maitre with Pierre Boulez and the Ensemble intercontemporain, Messiah with the King's College Choir, Handel's Orlando with Les arts florissants, Handel's Lotario with il Complesso barocco, Handel's Partenope and Semele with the Early Opera Company, Vivaldi's la Senna festeggiante and Rossini's La petite messe solonelle with The King's Consort. *Honours:* Worshipful Co. of Musicians Silver Medal, Royal Acad. of Music Shinn Fellowship, Royal Acad. of Music Recital Diploma, Grammy Award for Best Chamber Ensemble disc 2006. *Current Management:* c/o Ingpen & Williams, 7 St George's Court, 131 Putney Bridge Road, London, SW15 2PA, England. *Telephone:* (20) 8874-3222. *Website:* www.ingpen.co.uk.

SUMMERS, Jonathan, OAM; Australian/British singer (baritone); b. 2 Oct. 1946, Melbourne, Vic., Australia. *Education:* studied with Bettine McCaughan in Melbourne and with Otakar Kraus in London. *Career:* debut with Kent Opera 1975 as Rigoletto; Royal Opera House Covent Garden company mem. 1976–86; roles include High Priest in Samson et Dalila, Figaro in Barber of Seville and Marriage of Figaro, Papageno, Balstrode, Marcello, Demetrius, Silvio, Sharpless, Paolo, Ford, Nabucco and Iago; other UK appearances include ENO as Rigoletto, Rodrigo, Renato, Macbeth, Boccanegra, Onegin, Kurwenal, Don Carlos, Marcello, Balstrode, Amfortas, Zurga; Scottish Opera as Count Almaviva, Don Giovanni, Germont, Traveller in Death in Venice; Opera North as the High Priest, Germont, Onegin, Amonasro, Rigoletto, Barnaba, Michele, Tonio, Malatesta and Geppetto; Glyndebourne as Ford in Falstaff; Welsh Nat. Opera as Germont, Nabucco, Rigoletto, Tonio, Alfio and Kurwenal; European engagements at Berlin, Cologne, Frankfurt, Hamburg, Munich, Brussels, Florence, Toulouse, Avignon, Paris Opéra and Geneva; US debut as Marcello, Metropolitan Opera 1988, then Enrico and Marcello, Chicago Lyric Opera 1990, Prus in Vec Makropoulos, Houston Grand Opera; Australian debut as Germont in La Traviata 1981; roles for Opera Australia include di Luna, Renato, The Four Villians, Iago, Michele, Scarpia, Falstaff, Nabucco, Rigoletto, Wozzeck, Boccanegra, Alfio, Tonio, Scarpia, Dutchman, Schicchi, Wolfram; roles for State Opera of South Australia include Amfortas in Parsifal, Gunter in Wagner's Ring Cycle; has also appeared in Montreal, San Diego, Santiago, Cape Town, Hong Kong, Seoul, Tokyo, Bergen, Savonlinna, also sings regularly for Israel Opera, Tel-Aviv; recent appearances include the Butler in Rufus Wainwright's Prima Donna, Sadler's Wells, London 2010, Paolo in Simon Boccanegra, Royal Opera House, London 2010, Geppetto in The Adventures of Pinocchio, Opera North 2010, Germont Père in La Traviata, Opera Australia, Sydney 2010, 2012, Scarpia in Tosca, Orchestra Sinfonica Siciliana, Palermo 2011, Balstrode in Peter Grimes, Royal Opera House, London 2011, Tomsky in The Queen of Spades, Opera North 2011, Mr Redburn in Billy Budd, ENO, London 2012, Balstrode in Peter Grimes, New Nat. Theatre, Tokyo 2012, Don Carlaos in La forza del Destino, Opera Australia 2014, Iago in Otello, ENO, London 2014, Germont in La Traviata, Opera Queensland 2015, Le Bailli in Werther, Royal Opera House, London 2016. *Recordings include:* Peter Grimes (Grammy Award for Best Opera Recording 1979), La Bohème, Samson et Dalila, The Bohemian Girl, Gloriana,

A Sea Symphony, Carmina Burana, videos of Samson et Dalila, Il Trovatore and Nabucco. *Honours:* Green Room Award for Best Male Artist 1988, 2000, Helpmann Award for Best Supporting Male Performer 2002, for Best Male Performer 2003, 2007. *Current Management:* c/o Patricia Greenan, 7 White Horse Close, 27 Canongate, Edinburgh, EH8 8BU, Scotland. *E-mail:* patricia@ greenanartists.fsnet.co.uk. *Website:* www.jonathansummers.co.uk.

SUMMERS, Patrick; American conductor; *Artistic and Music Director, Houston Grand Opera;* b. 14 Aug. 1963, Indiana. *Education:* Indiana Univ. School of Music. *Career:* conducted season preview concerts with San Francisco Opera from 1989; Opera Center Showcase productions include Handel's Ariodante, Reimann's Ghost Sonata and Shield's Rosina; projects for the Merola Opera Program include La Bohème, Butterfly, Pasquale and Falstaff; Lucia di Lammermoor for Western Opera Theater; Music Dir, San Francisco Opera Center, leading Carmen and La Bohème on tour to Japan 1991, 1993 and La Fille du Régiment for the Opera Guild 1994; performances with San Francisco Opera include Tosca, US premiere of Rossini's Ermione and local premiere of his Otello; La Traviata and Così fan tutte; associated with Shanghai Conservatory of Music in productions of Rigoletto and Don Pasquale; Asian premiere of Tosca at Shanghai Opera House; Italian debut in season 1993–94 with Manon Lescaut for Rome Opera; Canadian debut with Lucia di Lammermoor at Calgary; Australian debut with Cenerentola at Sydney and Melbourne 1994; L'Incoronazione di Poppea for Dallas Opera 1995, Tosca at Lisbon; Artistic and Music Dir, Houston Grand Opera 1998–2014; Nabucco at Opera Australia 2005; Prin. Guest Conductor, San Francisco Opera 2009–14. *Honours:* named Outstanding San Franciscan by the San Francisco Chamber of Commerce 1991. *Address:* c/o Houston Grand Opera, 510 Preston Street, Houston, TX 77002, USA. *Website:* www.houstongrandopera.org.

SUNDINE, Stephanie; American singer (soprano); b. 1954, Illinois. *Education:* studied in Illinois and New York. *Career:* sang with the New York City Opera, 1981–84 as Ariadne, Santuzza and Margherita in Boito's Mefistofele; sang the title roles in the US premieres of Prokofiev's Maddalena at St Louis 1982 and Judith by Siegfried Matthus at Santa Fe 1990; best known as Strauss's Salome at Covent Garden (debut) 1988, Metropolitan Opera (debut) 1990 and WNO 1991; sang Isolde at Nantes in 1989 and Fusako in the premiere production of Henze's Das Verratene Meer at the Deutsche Oper Berlin 1990; other roles include Janáček's Emilia Marty, Tosca, La Gioconda and Elsa; sang the Foreign Princess in Rusalka at San Francisco, 1995. *Current Management:* Hubbard Levine Management, 133 West 71st Street 8A, New York, NY 10023 USA. *Telephone:* (212) 787-2443. *Fax:* (212) 877-8213. *Website:* www.hubbardlevine.com.

SUNDMAN, Ulf Johan, DipMus; Swedish organist and music director; b. 27 Feb. 1929, Stockholm; m. Anna-Greta Persson 1954; one d. *Education:* Hogre Organistexamen, Hogre Kantorsexamen, Musiklararexamen, RAM, Stockholm, Int. Acad. for Organ, Haarlem, Netherlands. *Career:* organist, Skelleftea St Olovs Church 1954–81, Gavle Heliga Trefaldighets Church 1981–94; organ concerts in Sweden, Finland, Norway, Germany, Austria, Netherlands, Switzerland, France, Italy, Spain, Czechoslovakia, Poland, USSR 1974, 1976, 1979, Denmark and Belgium; organ music festivals, Gottingen 1972, 1987, Vilnius 1974, Madrid 1982, Naples, Toulon 1983, Ratzeburg 1985, Verona and Asola 1986, Buren 1987, Gottingen 1987, Zug 1988, Biella 1988; concerts on Radio Sweden and Radio Netherlands. *Recordings include:* Soviet (Melodia) Sweden (Proprius), (Opus 3). *Honours:* RAM P. A. Berg Medal, Stockholm, Culture Prize of the Town of Skelleftea 1972, Province of Vasterbotten 1973, Gavle 1994.

SUNG, Shi-yeon; South Korean conductor; b. 1975, Pusan. *Education:* Universität der Künste Berlin, Royal Coll. of Music, Stockholm, Hanns Eisler School of Music, Berlin. *Career:* debut in Berlin 2002; Chief Conductor, Capella Academica, Humboldt Univ., Berlin 2003–06; Asst Conductor, Boston Symphony Orchestra 2007–09; has conducted Seoul Philharmonic Orchestra, Bamberg Symphony Orchestra, Frankfurter Museumorchester, Nürnberg Symphony, Princeton Symphony Orchestra, Berliner Sinfonie-Orchester, Berliner Symphoniker, Arnhem Philharmonic, Helsingborg Symphony, Stockholm Opera Orchestra, Royal Stockholm Philharmonic Orchestra, Milwaukee Symphony, Los Angeles Philharmonic, Rotterdam Philharmonic Orchestra; festivals include Tanglewood and Kapfenburg. *Honours:* winner, Sir Georg Solti Int. Conductors Competition 2006, Bamberg Gustav Mahler Conducting Competition 2007. *Current Management:* c/o Libby Abrahams, IMG Artists, The Light Box, 111 Power Road, London, W4 5PY, England. *Telephone:* (20) 7957-5800. *Fax:* (20) 7957-5801. *E-mail:* labrahams@ imgartists.com. *Website:* www.imgartists.com.

SUNNEGARDH, Thomas; Swedish singer (tenor); b. 11 July 1949, Stockholm. *Education:* Royal School of Music, Stockholm. *Career:* sang at Vadstena Academy, 1978–79; appeared in Die Fledermaus and Der Vogelhändler with National Touring Company; Royal Opera Stockholm from 1982 as Albert Herring, Walther von der Vogelweide, Taverner, Ferrando, Fra Diavolo, Tamino and Steuermann in Der fliegende Holländer; has sung Lohengrin in Stockholm, Moscow with Bolshoi, Wiesbaden and Stuttgart conducted by Silvio Varviso, 1990; Macduff at the Bergen Festival, 1988; other roles include Florestan, Erik and Parsifal in Denmark and Antwerp, and parts in Iphigénie en Aulide and Genoveva at Deutsche Oper am Rhein, and Die Meistersinger at Nice, 1992; season 1991–92 sang Lohengrin at Barcelona, Parsifal at Århus, Die Meistersinger at Nice Opera, Der fliegende Holländer at Royal Opera Covent Garden, Das Lied von der Erde with London Philharmonic Orchestra;

season 1992–93 with Meistersinger at Brussels, Deutsche Oper Berlin, Munich, Tokyo, Stuttgart, Dutchman/Erik in Munich, Parsifal in Essen and Deutsche Oper Düsseldorf, Lohengrin in Frankfurt, Berlin, Tokyo and Toulouse; season 1993–94 in Lohengrin in Frankfurt, Der fliegende Holländer in Munich, and Walter in Stuttgart; season 1994–95 with Walter von Stolzing in Stuttgart, Fidelio and Lohengrin in Düsseldorf and Toulouse; sang Paul in Korngold's Die tote Stadt at Stockholm, 1996; engaged for Lohengrin in Seville and concert performances of Wozzeck with the Swedish Radio Symphony Orchestra and Rheingold at the Canary Islands Festival; season 2001–02 with Capriccio in Stockholm, Tannhäuser in Gothenburg; Berg's Alwa and Rhiengold/Loge in San Francisco, a Wagner Gala Concert in San Diego, concert performances of Fidelio in Lübeck, performances of Beethoven IX at the Gewandhaus in Leipzig, concerts for RAI Torino (Bach's Magnificat and Chapentier's Te deum) and a new production of Gefors' Clara at the Royal Opera Stockholm; season 2002–03 with The Bells by Rachmaninov at Malmö and Tristan in Gothenburg, and further performances of Tannhäuser at the Royal Opera Stockholm. *Recordings:* role of Froh with Cleveland Orchestra under Christoph von Dohnányi, 1993. *Current Management:* Artistsekretariat ulf Törnquist, Sankt Eriksgatan 100, 2 tr., 113 31 Stockholm Sweden.

SUNSHINE, Adrian, BA; American conductor, teacher and lecturer; b. 1940, New York City; m. Sheila Genden; one s. one d. *Education:* San Francisco State Univ., Univ. of California, Berkeley, pvt. instrumental studies with Gabriel Sunshine (father), Janet Hale, Georg Gruenberg, Herman Reinberg; conducting teachers: Pierre Monteux, Leonard Bernstein, Paul Klecki. *Career:* performances: Philharmonia Orchestra, London, BBC Orchestras, BBC Opera, São Carlos Opera, Lisbon; Berlin, Leningrad, Cleveland, Geneva, Paris, Vienna, Bournemouth, Philharmonia Hungarica, Athens, Thessaloniki, Budapest, Bucharest, Cluj, Lausanne, Lugano, Amsterdam, Denmark, Sweden, Poland, Miami, San Francisco, Buenos Aires, Rio de Janeiro, São Paulo, Caracas, Mexico City, Israel, Ankara, Madrid, Barcelona, Bilbao, Lisbon, Luxembourg, Bangkok, Kuala Lumpur, Taipei, Durban, Cape Town, Johannesburg, etc.; festivals include Blossom, Athens, São Paulo, Montreux-Vevey, Ascona, Beijing, London, Cheltenham, Gulbenkian, Reims, Lille, Sevilla, Romania, Chamonix, San Sebastian, Sion, Cadiz; Founder and fmr Conductor San Francisco Chamber Orchestra; Music Dir Gulbenkian Orchestra, Lisbon, London Chamber Players; Prin. Guest Conductor, Romania; Dir Crete Int. Festival; Co-conductor Camerata Budapest; Perm. Guest Conductor Bucharest Philharmonic Orchestra; Visiting Prof., Romanian Acad. of Music; fmr Visiting Prof., Bowling Green State Univ., Ohio; Visiting Lecturer, Smith Coll., Mass; Guest Lecturer, Univ. of London Inst. of Educ.; Dir Orchestra-in-Residence Music Programme, Middlesex Univ., London; mem. Conductors' Guild. *Recordings:* works by Schoenberg, Shostakovich, Perera, Wheelock and Ives. *Publications:* Various articles on music. *Honours:* Dr hc.

SURJAN, Giorgio; singer (bass); b. 21 Oct. 1954, Rijeca, Yugoslavia. *Education:* studied in Ljubljana and at the Opera School of La Scala. *Career:* sang in Yugoslavia from 1977; La Scala, 1980, in a concert version of Mussorgsky's Salammbô; Pesaro Festival, 1984 and 1987, in Il Viaggio a Reims and Ermione; Aix Festival, 1988, as Publio in La Clemenza di Tito and Astarotte in Rossini's Armida; season 1991–92 as Rossini's Alidoro at Covent Garden, Gluck's Thoas at La Scala and Frère Laurent in Gounod's Roméo et Juliette at Martina Franca; Season 1995–96 as Polidoro in Rossini's Zelmira at Pesaro, Fiesco in Simon Boccanegra at Turin, and the Villains in Hoffmann at Genoa; Season 1998 as Balthasar in La Favorita at Rome, Governor in Le Comte Ory at Florence, Banquo at Genoa and Escamillo at Macerata; season 2000–01 as Monteverdi's Seneca in Florence, Rossini's Mosè in Verona, Rodolfo in La Sonnambula at Palermo, Alfonso (Luzrezia Borgia) in Bologna and Walter in Luisa Miller for Opéra Lausanne. *Recordings include:* La Forza del Destino, Anna Bolena, Salammbô.

SUSHANSKAYA, Rimma, PhD; Russian violinist; b. 1950, Leningrad. *Education:* Leningrad and Moscow Conservatoires with David Oistrakh. *Career:* moved to America 1977; numerous concerts in the USA, S America, throughout Russia and in Europe; orchestras include Czech, Moscow, and St Petersburg Philharmonic Orchestras and Prague Radio Symphony Orchestra; orchestral and recital tours of Russia, Finland and Czechoslovakia; London recital debut 1987 at the Wigmore Hall, followed by Tchaikovsky's Concerto with the Royal Liverpool Philharmonic Orchestra and the City of Birmingham Symphony Orchestra. *Honours:* first prize Prague Int. Competition, Ysaye Medal. *Address:* c/o The Administrator, The Virtuoso Violin, 29 Johnson Road, Erdington, Birmingham, B23 6PU, England. *Website:* www.rimma -sushanskaya.com.

SUSTIKOVA, Vera, PhD; Czech musicologist; b. 9 Jan. 1956, Uh Hradiste; m. Sustik Jaroslav 1982, one d. *Education:* Charles Univ., Prague, Conservatory of Brno, masterclasses with Prof. Cotsiolis in Greece. *Career:* debut at Muzeum of Czech Music in Prague; 100 let spolecen pusobeni smetanova dila, Prague 1984; Bedrich Smetana 1824–1884, Prague 1994; opera and song without singing musical Melodram, Stanford, CA 1996; Fibich-Melodrama-Art nouveau, Prague 2000; author of exhibitions, History of Czech Musical Culture 1986; Smetana-Dvořák, Litomyšl 1988; B. Smetana's Memorial in Benatky nj 1991; Bedrich Smetana, Legend of my Country, Montréal, Ottawa, Toronto 1994; Zdeněk Fibich 1850–1900, Prague 2000–01; dramaturgist and dir of concert tour with melodramas of Zdeněk Fibich, Los Angeles, San Francisco, Stanford, Portland, Vancouver, Montréal, Toronto, New York 1996; founder and dramaturgist of international workshops of melodrama from 1997; International Festival of Concert Melodrama, Prague from 1998; International

Zdeněk Fibich Competition in the interpretation of melodrama, Prague from 1999. *Publications include:* Bedrich Smetana: Legend of My Country 1994, Zdeněk Fibich: Master of Scenic Melodrama 1996, Zdeněk Fibich 1850–1900 2000, Zdeněk Fibich: Concert Melodramas Christmas Eve and Water Sprite 2003. *Address:* Pstrossova 35, Prague 1 11008, Czech Republic.

SUTER, Jeremy Langton, MA, FRCO, ARCM, ARSCM; British organist; b. 3 March 1951, London, England; m. Susan; two d. *Education:* Royal Coll. of Music, Magdalen Coll., Oxford. *Career:* organist and Choirmaster, All Saints, Northampton 1975–81; Asst Organist, Chichester Cathedral 1981–91; Master of Music, Carlisle Cathedral 1991–, also Dir, The Abbey Singers; mem. Royal Coll. of Organists, Incorporated Soc. of Musicians. *Honours:* Hon. FGCM 2009 . *Address:* 6 The Abbey, Carlisle, CA3 8TZ, England (home). *Telephone:* (1228) 526646 (home). *Fax:* (1228) 547049 (office). *E-mail:* jeremysuter@hotmail.com (home).

SUTER, Louis-Marc, PhD; Swiss musicologist and academic; *Professor Emeritus, University of Berne;* b. 2 Feb. 1928, Fribourg; m. Monique Suter 1955; four s. *Education:* Univ. of Fribourg, Berne Conservatory, Geneva. *Career:* debut 1955; Int. Academic Orchestra, Salzburg; Lausanne Chamber Orchestra; Suisse Romande Orchestra; fmr Prof. of Musicology, Univ. of Berne, now Prof. Emer.; mem. Int. Soc. for Musicology, Soc. Suisse de Musicologie, Asscn Suisse des Musiciens. *Publications:* four concert works for Serbian composers 1989, Norbert Moret, compositeur 1993, Le langage musical de l'Europe occidentale 2005; contrib. to Claude Debussy: Pour les accords, Etude No. 12 pour piano (in Revue Musicale de Suisse Romande) 1983, Ronsard: Les Amours de 1552 mises en musique (in Actes du Colloque de Neuchâtel) 1985, Pelléas et Mélisande in Performance (in Debussy in Performance) 1999, Indice d'acuité et fréquence dans les graduels en La (in Etudes Grégoriennes XXVII) 1999, Des Graduels en La? (in Etudes Grégoriennes XXXIV) 2007. *Address:* route du Pré de l'Ile 1, 1752 Villars-sur-Glâne, Switzerland (office). *Telephone:* (264) 025 845 (home).

SUTHERLAND, Rosalind; British singer (soprano); b. 8 May 1963, Glasgow, Scotland. *Education:* qualified as a nurse, London Coll. of Music and Royal Northern Coll. of Music. *Career:* appearances include Madama Butterfly (WNO, San Francisco Opera, Opera North), Nedda in Pagliacci (Minneapolis Opera, WNO, New Israeli Opera), Liu in Turandot (WNO, Mannheim Opera), Mimi in La Bohème (San Francisco Opera, ENO, WNO, New Israeli Opera), Jenůfa (WNO), Micaela in Carmen (WNO), Governess in Turn of the Screw (Minneapolis Opera), Musetta in La Bohème (Toronto Opera Co.). *Honours:* Peter Moores Scholarship, winner Anne Ziegler Prize for a Singer Showing Outstanding Promise.

SUTTER, Ursula; singer (mezzo-soprano); b. 26 March 1938, Berne, Switzerland. *Education:* studied in Berne and Stuttgart. *Career:* sang at Biel-Solothurn 1961–63, Trier 1963–64, Essen 1964–66 and engaged at Stuttgart Staatsoper 1966–85, notably in the premiere of Orff's Prometheus 1968; guest appearances at State Operas of Vienna, Munich and Hamburg, Cologne, Nuremberg and Düsseldorf; further engagements at Bucharest, Lisbon, Monte Carlo, Essen and Schwetzingen Festival (premiere of Henze's The English Cat 1983); roles have included Dorabella, Cherubino, Rosina, Isabella, Maddalena, Preziosilla, Magdalene in Meistersinger, the Composer in Ariadne and Britten's Lucretia.

SUWANAI, Akiko; Japanese violinist; b. 1972, Tokyo. *Education:* Toho Gakuen School of Music with Toshiya Eto, Columbia Univ. and Juilliard School of Music with Dorothy DeLay and Cho-Liang Lin, Hochschule der Künste, Berlin with Uwe-Martin Haiberg. *Career:* solo performances and recitals world-wide since becoming the youngest ever winner of the Tchaikovsky Competition, Moscow; has performed with conductors including Bychkov, Rostropovich, Rozhdestvensky, Ozawa, Marriner, Conlon, Previn, Svetlanaov, Maazel, Mehta; concert engagements with orchestras including Berlin Philharmonic, London Symphony Orchestra, Philharmonia Orchestra, Orchestre de Paris, New York and Los Angeles Philharmonics, Boston Symphony, Nat. Symphony Orchestra of Washington, Philadelphia, Pittsburgh, Cincinnati and Minnesota; performances at Ravinia, Lockenhaus, Marlboro, Rheingau, Schleswig Holstein and Berlin Festivals. *Recordings include:* Bruch Concerto No. 1 (Acad. of St Martin-in-the-Fields under Neville Marriner) 1997, Slavonic Album (Budapest Festival Orchestra under Iván Fischer), Tchaikovsky and Mendelssohn Concertos (Czech Philharmonic under Vladimir Ashkenazy), Takemitsu's Far Calls, Coming Far (NHK Symphony Orchestra), Bach Concertos 2005. *Honours:* Winners Gala, Tchaikovsky Competition, Moscow, Prizewinner, 35th Int. Paganini Violin Competition, Fourth Int. Japan Competition, Queen Elizabeth Int. Competition, Belgium. *Current Management:* c/o Harrison Parrott, 5–6 Albion Court, London, W6 0QT, England. *Telephone:* (20) 7229-9166. *Fax:* (20) 7221-5042. *E-mail:* info@harrisonparrott.co.uk. *Website:* www.harrisonparrott.com.

SUZUKI, Hidetaro; Japanese violinist and conductor; b. 1 June 1937, Tokyo; m. Zeyda Ruga 1962; two s. one d. *Education:* Toho School of Music, Tokyo, Curtis Inst. of Music, Philadelphia, PA, USA, studied with Efrem Zimbalist. *Career:* debut in Tokyo 1951; Concertmaster, Québec Symphony, Canada 1963–78; Prof., Conservatory of Province of Québec 1963–79; Prof., Laval Univ. 1970–79; Concertmaster, Indianapolis Symphony, IN 1978–; concert appearances as soloist, recitalist, conductor, the UK, Western Europe, Soviet Union, Central America, USA, Canada, Japan, South East Asia; Dir of Chamber Music Series, Suzuki and Friends 1980; served as jury mem. Montréal Int. Competition 1979, Int. Violin Competition 1982, 1986, 1990,

1994. *Recordings:* albums: Beethoven Sonatas, Hidetaro Suzuki Encore, Franck, Ravel Sonatas, Beethoven Piano Trios (Marlboro Festival), violin/piano repertoires with pianist Zeyda Ruga Suzuki. *Honours:* Laureat of Tchaikovsky Int. Competition 1962, Queen Elizabeth Int. Competition 1963, 1967, Montréal Int. Competition 1966. *Address:* 430 W 93rd Street, Indianapolis, IN 46260, USA.

SVANIDZE, Natela; Georgian composer; b. 4 Sept. 1926, Akhaltsikhe; m. Peter Tomadze 1952; one d. *Education:* Tbilisi State Univ., Tbilisi State Conservatoire. *Career:* debut with symphonic poem, Samgori, conducted by Odyssey Dymitriady, Tbilisi 1951; apptd Prof., Georgian State Inst. of Theatre and Cinema, Tbilisi 1991; Bd mem. Georgian Composers' Union. *Compositions include:* Samgori (symphonic poem) 1951, Improvisation for violin and piano 1956, Fairytale for piano 1960, Kvarkvare (symphonic poem) 1963, Burlesque (symphonic poem) 1966, Symphony No. 1 for strings, piano and percussion instruments 1967, Pirosmani (oratorio) 1972, Lamentatia Georgica oratorio for speaker, female sextet, two choruses, instruments and tape 1974, Symphony No. 2 for large orchestra 1983, Gaul-Gavkhe cantata for mixed choruses and large orchestra 1995, Monodrama for voice, piano, cassa a pedal, piatto and tape 1999. *Honours:* Honoured Art Worker of the Georgian SSR 1981.

ŠVARC-GRENDA, Ivana; Croatian pianist; b. 17 Feb. 1970. *Education:* Music Academy, Zagreb, Peabody Conservatory of Music, Baltimore, Hochschule der Kunste, Berlin and Mozarteum, Salzburg. *Career:* solo appearances at Carnegie Recital Hall; Lincoln Center Library, New York; Kennedy Center, Washington, DC; Philharmonie Berlin; Alte Oper Frankfurt; chamber music appearances, Salle Cortot, Paris; Philharmonie Berlin; Schauspielhaus Berlin; Glinka Hall, St Petersburg; orchestra appearances with Zagreb Philharmonic, Solisti di Zagreb and Croatian Chamber Orchestra; Berlin Symphony Orchestra; gives masterclasses at International Summer school, Hvar, Croatia. *Recordings include:* cello-piano duo with Monika Leskovar. *Honours:* winner Kosciuszko Chopin Competition, New York, Croatian National Artists Competition, Milka Trnina Prize for the Best Croatian Musician 1996, Porin Award for the Best Croatian Recording 1996.

SVECENY, Jaroslav; violinist; b. 8 Dec. 1960, Hradec Kralove, Czechoslovakia; m. Monika Svecena. *Education:* Prague Conservatoire, Prague Acad. of Arts with Vaclav Snitil, masterclasses with Nathan Milstein in Zürich and Gidon Kremer in Kuhmo. *Career:* concert appearances across Europe, the USA, Russia; participated in several festivals in Berlin, Constance, Helsinki, Bilbao, Madrid, Granada, Havana, Prague, Leipzig and Palermo; repertoire includes concertos by Dvořák, Beethoven, Brahms, Mozart, Bach, Vivaldi, Haydn, Reicha and Martinů, Reicha complete works for violin and piano, Benda 24 Capriccios, and sonatas by Brahms, Beethoven, Dvořák, Benda, Handel and Ysaÿe. *Recordings include:* Reicha four Sonatas, Grand Duo Concertante and Rondo, Sonatas by Benda, Stamitz, Corelli, Handel and Tartini, Vivaldi Four Seasons. *Honours:* winner Pablo de Sarasate Int. Violin Competition.

SVEINSSON, Atli Heimir; Icelandic composer and conductor; b. 21 Sept. 1938, Reykjavík. *Education:* Reykjavík Coll. of Music, Cologne Hochschule für Musik with Petzold and B.A. Zommermann, studied with Pousseur and Stockhausen at Darmstadt and Cologne. *Career:* freelance composer and conductor throughout Iceland and Scandinavia; mem. Soc. of Icelandic Composers (chair. 1972–83). *Compositions include:* Tautophony for orchestra 1967, Flower Shower for orchestra 1973, Flute Concerto 1975, Septet 1976, Twenty-One Sounding Minutes for flute 1980, Bassoon Concerto: Trobar Clus 1980, The Silken Drum (opera) 1982, Trombone Concerto: Jubilus 1984, Recitation for piano and orchestra 1984, Bicentennial for string quartet 1984, Trio for violin, cello and piano 1985, The Night on our Shoulders for soprano, alto, women's chorus and orchestra 1986, Dreamboat Concerto for violin, harpsichord and orchestra 1987, Vikivaki (television opera) 1990, Opplaring for soprano and wind instruments 1991, Dernier Amour (chamber opera) 1992, Rockerauschen, Bruit des Robes for chamber orchestra 1993, Poem to the Virgin Mary for chorus 1995, The Isle of Moonlight 1995, Signs of Fire for piano and wind 1995, Discords for cello, strings and piano 1997, Independent People (incidental music) 1999, The Conversion of Iceland (opera) 2000. *Honours:* Nordic Council Prize 1976. *Address:* Holtsgata 22, Reykjavík 101, Iceland (home). *Telephone:* 5622337 (home). *E-mail:* ahs@centruno.is (home).

SVENDEN, Birgitta; Swedish singer (mezzo-soprano); *Managing and Artistic Director, Royal Swedish Opera;* b. 20 March 1952, Porjus. *Education:* Stockholm Opera School. *Career:* has sung at the Royal Opera in Stockholm as Cherubino, Olga and Erda; sang a Rhinemaiden in The Ring under Solti at Bayreuth 1983, at Nice Opéra from 1985 in Carmen and as Meg Page and Anna in Les Troyens; created Queen Christina in Hans Gefors' opera 1988; sang at Metropolitan Opera from 1988 as Erda in Das Rheingold and Siegfried and Maddalena in Rigoletto, Seattle Opera 1989 as Magdalena in Die Meistersinger, Ravinia Festival Chicago in Mahler's 3rd Symphony under James Levine, and at La Scala, Munich and San Francisco 1990 as Magdalena, Erda and First Norn; Covent Garden debut 1990 in a new production of Siegfried under Bernard Haitink; sang at Théâtre du Châtelet, Paris, as Margret in a production of Wozzeck by Patrice Chéreau under Daniel Barenboim; engaged for BBC Philharmonic in Verdi's Requiem 1991, Gürzenich Orchestra in Mahler's 3rd 1992, and Los Angeles Philharmonic in Mahler's 3rd; sang in Eugene Onegin and Die Meistersinger at Metropolitan Opera 1993; season 1993 with Mahler's 3rd at Boston and Carnegie Hall under Ozawa, Mahler's 3rd and 8th at Rome and Rotterdam under Conlon, Missa Solemnis at Paris under Solti, and Octavian in Der Rosenkavalier at Paris Châtelet; season 1994 with new Ring productions at Bayreuth, Covent Garden and Cologne; season 1996–97 as Wagner's Magdalena at Bayreuth, Erda at the Met; season 2000–01 as Erda in Das Rheingold at the Met and Brigitta in Die tote Stadt at Strasbourg; mem. Royal Swedish Acad. of Music; Artistic Dir Royal Swedish Opera 2009–, Man. Dir 2010–. *Recordings:* Das Rheingold, Mahler, Elgar, Siegfried, Zemlinsky. *Honours:* Royal Court Singer (Hovsångerska), by King of Sweden 1995. *Address:* Royal Swedish Opera, PO Box 16094, 103 22 Stockholm, Sweden (office). *Telephone:* (8) 791-43-00 (office). *Fax:* (8) 791-44-44 (office). *E-mail:* birgitta.svenden@operan.se (office). *Website:* www.operan.se (office).

SVENSSON, Peter; Austrian singer (tenor); b. 1963, Vienna. *Career:* sang in the 1988 Vienna Festival under Claudio Abbado; season 1991–92 at the Prague State Opera, as Wagner's Rienzi and Zemlensky's Der Zwerg and Eine Florentinische Tragödie; Lucerne, 1993, as Strauss's Bacchus (also at Cologne); sang Tannhäuser at Prague, 1994, and Claudio in Das Liebesverbot by Wagner at Wexford; season 1995–96 as Hermann in The Queen of Spades at Mainz, Tannhäuser at Meinigen and in the premiere of The Marx Sisters at Bielefeld; guest appearances as Siegmund at the Châtelet, Paris, and as Max in Der Freischütz, Florestan and Strauss's Herod; sang Oedipus Rex at Naples, 2001. *Current Management:* Opera Vladarski, Döblinger Hauptstrasse 57/18, 1190 Vienna, Austria. *Telephone:* (1) 368-6960. *Fax:* (1) 368-6962. *E-mail:* opera.vladarski@utanet.at. *Website:* www.petersvensson.de.

SVETE, Tomas, DipMus, MA; Austrian composer, conductor and academic; *Professor of Composition, University of Maribor*; b. 29 Jan. 1956, Ljubljana, Slovenia; m.; one d. *Education:* Acad. of Music, Ljubljana, Hochschule für Musik und Darstellende Kunst, Vienna with Prof. F. Cerha, studied with Otmar Suitner and Dieter Kaufmann in Vienna. *Career:* debut composition performance, Ljubljana 1978; works performed in Ljubljana, Skopje, Opatija, Zagreb-Music Biennial, Vienna, Salzburg, Prague, Brno-Moravian Autumn, Amsterdam, Rotterdam, Taipei, Tel Aviv, Darmstadt, Hartford, Graz, Middleburgh, Torino, Trieste, Klagenfurt, Spittal-Drau, Tirana, Leipzig, Melk and St Pölten-Niederösterreich; Conductor, Slovene Philharmonic and Pro Arte Orchestras, of Singkreis Währing, Vienna and Brno Radio Symphony Orchestra; Prof. of Composition, Karl Prayner Conservatory, Vienna; concert of own works in Brahmssaal, Musikverein, Vienna; freelance composer in Vienna; Prof. of Composition, Pedagogical Faculty, Univ. of Maribor, Slovenia; Guest Prof. of Composition, Univ. of Hartford, Conn., USA 1999–2000. *Compositions include:* Requiem 1991, The Rape from Laudach Sea (opera) 1993, Isomerisms for Chamber Ensemble, Rappresentazione Sacra for double bass solo and flute quartet 1994, Sonata Solaris for violoncello and piano 1994, Sacrum Delirium cantata for soloists, chorus, ensembles and orchestra (Italian Prize) 1994, Hommage à Slavko Osterc for piano 1995, Evocazione for soprano and chamber ensemble 1995, Poet and Rebellion (opera) 1996, Concert de la Nuit for double bass, violin, harp and orchestra 1997, Kriton (opera after Plato) 2000, Gothic Windows for Orchestra 2004, Pierrot et Pierrette (opera) 2007, Granatapfel (children's opera) 2009, Antigona (opera) 2009, Lilium pedibus detrue for chamber ensemble 2009, Apologie of Socrates (opera) 2010, First Symphony 2011, Deux aquarelles écméliques for flute, viola and harp 2010, Arc-en-ciel for quintet 2010, Exclamations for saxophone solo 2011, Second symphony 2010, Viola concerto 2012, Violin concerto 2013, Tristesses de la Lune for wind quintet. *Recordings include:* Jugoton 1986, Kriton 1991, De Profundis 2001, Portrait of Toma Svete 2004. *Honours:* Theodor Körner Prize, Vienna 1992, Prize of Slovene Radio and TV 1992, first prize Competition of Composers, Gorizia, first prize Johann-Joseph-Fux Opernkompositionswettbewerb, Graz 2000, Glazer Prize, City of Maribor 2002. *Address:* Koroska 160, 2001 Maribor (office); Prušnikovaz 2, 2000 Maribor, Slovenia (home); Hetzendorferstrasse 163/4/14, 1120 Vienna, Austria (home). *Telephone:* 40975224 (mobile). *E-mail:* tomaz.svete@chello .at; tomaz.svete@uni-mb.si (office).

SVETLEV, Michail; singer (tenor); b. 6 March 1943, Sofia, Bulgaria. *Education:* Sofia Conservatoire. *Career:* debut in Passau as Manrico 1971; appearances in Munich, Hamburg, Berlin and Vienna, and La Scala, Milan 1979; US debut as Riccardo in Un Ballo in Maschera at Washington, DC 1980; further US appearances at Houston 1980, San Francisco 1980, 1983, and Philadelphia 1982; sang Dmitri in Boris Godunov at Covent Garden 1983, and has appeared elsewhere as Verdi's Radames and Gabriele Adorno, Andrea Chénier and Cavaradossi; season 1985–86 as Hermann in The Queen of Spades at Marseilles and Lykov in Rimsky's The Tsar's Bride at Monte Carlo; other roles include the Duke of Mantua, Don Carlos, Bacchus, Lensky, Edgardo and the Prince in Rusalka.

SVIRIDOV, Evgeny; Russian violinist; b. 17 Feb. 1989, St Petersburg. *Education:* St Petersburg Conservatoire. *Career:* performed at festivals including Schleswig-Holstein, Graz Chamber Music, Early Music Festival in St Petersburg, Bach Chamber Music Festival Leipzig, Alter Musik Zeitfenster Berlin; has performed with orchestras in Russia including Mariinsky Theatre Orchestra, St Petersburg Philharmonic, Moscow Symphony Orchestra under Yury Bashmet; concerts as soloist and chamber musician in Russia, Europe, USA and South America. *Recording:* Bach/Biber Sonatas 2011. *Honours:* Bach Prize, Yehudi Menuhin Int. Competition for Young Violinists 2008, Winner (violin category), Int. Johann Sebastian Bach Competition 2010. *Address:* c/o European Union of Music Competitions for Youth, Trimburgstrasse 2/V, 81249 Munich, Germany (office). *Telephone:* (89) 87100242 (office). *Fax:* (89) 87100290 (office). *E-mail:* info@emcy.org (office).

SVOBODA, Tomas; American/Czech composer, pianist, conductor and academic; *Professor Emeritus of Music, Portland State University*; b. 6 Dec. 1939, Paris, France; s. of Antonin Svoboda and Milada Svoboda; m. Jana Demartini 1965; one s. one d. *Education:* Conservatory of Music, Acad. of Music, Prague, Czechoslovakia, Univ. of Southern California, USA. *Career:* debut with FOK Prague Symphony Orchestra, Symphony No. 1, Op. 20 1957; Prof. Emer. of Music, Portland State Univ.; 1,300 orchestral performances world-wide; numerous comms; 50 recordings. *Compositions include:* Symphonies 1–6, two concertos for piano and orchestra, 10 string quartets, Children's Treasure Box (Vols 1–4) for piano, Czernogorsk Fugue for choir (Op. 14), Troika in Taiga for piano (Op. 21), Classical Sonatine for oboe and piano (Op. 28), Ballade for bassoon and piano (Op. 35), Sonata for viola and piano (Op. 36), Baroque Quintet (Op. 37), Bagatelles 'in a Forest' for piano (Op. 42), Nine Etudes (in Fugue Style), vols 1 and 2 for piano (Op. 44 and 98), Concertino for oboe, brass choir and timpani (Op.46), Offertories for organ vol. I (Op. 52a), Chorales from 15th Century for English horn and strings (Op. 52f), Reflections for orchestra (Op. 53), Sonata for Two Pianos (Op. 55), Sinfonietta (à la Renaissance) (Op. 60), Duo for flute and oboe (Op. 65), Child's Dream for children's choir and orchestra (Op. 66), Prelude and Fugue for string orchestra (Op. 67), Four Waltzes for piano (Op. 68), Sonata for violin and piano (Op. 73), Discernment of Time for gong solo (Op. 74), Concerto for violin and orchestra (Op. 77), Pastorale for flute (Op. 78), Celebration of Life cantata on Aztec poetry (Op. 80), Suite for piano and five percussionists (Op. 83), Nocturne for piano (Op. 84), Passacaglia and Fugue for piano trio (Op. 87), Five Studies for two timpanists (Op. 88), Overture of the Season (Op. 89), Wedding March for organ (Op. 94), March of the Puppets for guitar, xylophone and four temple blocks (Op. 95), Trio for woodwind trio (Op. 97), Sonata for guitar (Op. 99), Nocturne for orchestra (Op. 100), Morning Prayer for four percussion (Op. 101), Suite for guitar (Op. 102), Festive Overture (Op. 103), Scherzo for bassoon (Op. 104), Baroque Trio for vibraphone, electric guitar and piano (Op. 109), Autumn for koto (Op. 110), Woodwind Quintet (Op. 111), Brass Quintet (Op. 112), Ex Libris (Op. 113), Toccatina for oboe (Op. 114), Serenade for orchestra (Op. 115), Trio for piano trio (Op. 116), Chorale in E flat for piano quintet (homage to Aaron Copland) (Op. 118), Phantasy for piano trio (Op. 120), Suite for piano four hands (Op. 124), Concerto for chamber orchestra (Op. 125), Storm Session for electric guitar and bass guitar (Op. 126), Journey cantata for mezzo-soprano, baritone, choir and orchestra (Op. 127), Intrata for brass quintet (Op. 127a), Dance Suite for orchestra (Op. 128), Veritas Veritatum for male choir (Op. 129a), Six Fragments for woodwind trio (Op. 131), Concerto No. 2 for piano and orchestra (Op. 134), Swing Dance for orchestra (Op. 135a), Oriental Echoes for string orchestra (Op. 140), Duo for xylophone and marimba (Op. 141), Meditation for oboe and strings (Op. 143), Quartet for four French horns (Op. 145), Suite for cello (Op. 147), Concerto for marimba and orchestra (Op. 148), Forest Rhythms for flute, viola and xylophone (Op. 150), Duo Concerto for trumpet and organ (Op. 152), Remembrance chorale for trumpet and orchestra (Op. 152a), Aria for soprano and four instruments (Op. 153), Sonatine for flute, clarinet and piano (Op. 154), Nocturne for organ four hands (Op. 155), Conversations for 2 clarinets (Op. 157), Four Visions for 3 pianos (Op. 158), Summer Trio for oboe, clarinet and bassoon (Op. 159), Farewell Matinée for brass quintet (Op. 160), Partita in D for viola da gamba and harpsichord (Op. 161), Benedictus for piano (Op. 162), Concealed Shapes for two pianos, xylophone and marimba (Op. 163), Dreams of a Dancer for flute, clarinet and piano (Op. 164), Chaconne for strings (Op. 166a), Sonata for clarinet and piano (Op. 167), Sonata No.1 for string orchestra (Op. 168), Spring Overture for orchestra (Op. 172), Sonata No. 2 for Orchestra (Op. 173), Trio Chorales for flute, clarinet and piano (Op. 177), Prayer for clarinet and string quartet (Op. 189), Vortex for orchestra (Op. 197). *Recordings include:* Piano Works, Piano Trios, String Quartets 1–4 Vol. 1, 5–8 Vol. 2, Four Visions, music for one, two and three pianos; Chamber Music with clarinet, Nine Etudes in Fugue Style for piano, Vols 1 and 2, Op. 44, 98, Dreams of the Dancer, Music from Bohemia; Children's Treasure Box for piano in four vols; Symphony No. 4 (Apocalyptic), Op. 69; Ex Libris, Op. 113 for orchestra; Passacaglia and Fugue for piano trio, Op. 87 (Mirecourt Trio); Concerto for chamber orchestra, Op. 125; Trio for flute, oboe and bassoon, Op. 97; Concerto for marimba and orchestra, Op. 148; Concerto Nos 1–2 for piano and orchestra; Overture of the Season for orchestra; Symphony No. 1 (Of Nature) for orchestra; Duo Concerto for trumpet and organ, Op. 152; Autumn for koto solo, Op. 110; String Quartets 9-12 Vol. 3 (Martinů Quartet – all quartets); Concerto for Clarinet and Orchestra, Op. 205. *Honours:* Portland State Univ. Branford Price Millar Award for Faculty Excellence 1983, ASCAP Foundation/Meet the Composer Award 1985, Oregon Governor's Arts Award 1992, American Record Guide Critics Choice Award (for Piano Trios) 2001, Regional Arts and Culture Council Award, Oregon 2002, BMI Award for Music Accomplishments 2009. *Address:* c/o Thomas C. Stangland Co., PO Box 19263, Portland, OR 97280, USA. *Website:* www.tomassvoboda.com.

SWAFFORD, Jan, BA, MMA, DMA; American writer, composer and academic; b. (Jan Lewis Johnson), 10 Sept. 1946, Chattanooga, Tenn.; s. of Charles Monroe Johnson and Lucille Swafford Johnson; m. Julie Pisano 1973 (divorced 1979). *Education:* Harvard Univ., Yale Univ. School of Music. *Career:* Asst Prof., Boston Univ. School for the Arts 1977–78; Visiting Asst Prof., Hampshire Coll., Amherst 1979–81, Amherst Coll. 1980–81; freelance composer and writer 1981–; Lecturer in English, Tufts Univ. 1988–2013; Prof., Theory, Musicology and Composition, Boston Conservatory 2004–14; guest lecturer, Boston

Symphony, Los Angeles Philharmonic, Rockport Music, others; Massachusetts Artists Foundation grant 1983, Harvard-Mellon Fellowship 1988, Nat. Endowment for the Arts Composers Fellow 1991, Nat. Endowment for the Arts Fellowship 1990, Fulbright Fellowship 1995. *Compositions include:* Passage for piccolo, strings and percussion 1975, Landscape with Traveller for orchestra 1981, Shore Lines for soprano and flute 1982, Labyrinths for violin and cello 1983, Midsummer Variations for piano quintet 1985, Chamber Sinfonietta for chamber orchestra 1988, They Who Hunger for piano quartet 1989, Requiem in Winter for string trio 1991, From the Shadow of the Mountain for string orchestra 2001, They That Mourn for piano trio 2002, In Time of War for cello and piano 2007, The Silence at Yuma Point for solo cello 2013. *Publications include:* The Vintage Guide to Classical Music 1992, The New Guide to Classical Music 1993, Charles Ives: A Life with Music 1996, Johannes Brahms: A Biography 1997, Beethoven: Anguish and Triumph 2014; contrib. articles and reviews to Symphony, New England Monthly, Musical America, Slate, Guardian Int.; programme/liner notes for Boston, Chicago and San Francisco Symphonies, and Sony, Naxos and RCA recordings. *Honours:* L.L. Winship-PEN New England Award 1997, Deems Taylor Award for music writing 2013. *E-mail:* JanSwaff@aol.com (home).

SWANSTON, Roderick Brian, BMus, MA, LRA, ARCM, FRCO FRCO; British academic; b. 28 Sept. 1948, Gosport, England. *Education:* Stowe School, Royal Coll. of Music, Pembroke Coll., Cambridge, Royal Schools of Music. *Career:* Organist at Christ Church, Lancaster Gate 1972–77 and St James, Sussex Gardens 1977–80; Conductor of Christ Church Choral Soc. 1972–80; part-time Tutor at Dept of Extra Mural Studies, Univ. of London 1972–; apptd Academic Adviser in Music to Birkbeck Coll., Univ. of London, Centre for Extra Mural Studies 1987; Visiting Prof., Darmouth Univ. 1995, 1999; Prof., Royal College of Music –2004; Visiting Lecturer for many orgs including ENO, Royal Opera House, Covent Garden, BBC, Univ. of Oxford and Goldsmiths Coll., London; mem. Incorporated Society of Musicians 1972–, Pres. 2008–09. *Compositions include:* A Time There Was for Tenor, Choir and Strings; Let Us Gather Hand In Hand for Choir and Brass à 5, recorded by BBC. *Recordings:* organ recital from Framlingham Parish Church. *Publication:* Concise History of Music. *Address:* 1, Berstede Road, London, W6 9NP, England (home).

SWAYNE, Giles, MA, ARAM; British composer; b. 30 June 1946, Hitchin, Herts.; s. of Sir Ronald Swayne and Charmian Cairnes. *Education:* Trinity Coll. Cambridge, RAM, London, Accad. Chigiana, Siena; studied with Nicholas Maw, Harrison Birtwistle, Alan Bush and Oliver Messiaen. *Career:* early work performed by Soc. for the Promotion of New Music and at Aldeburgh and Bromsgrove Festivals; Orlando's Music and Pentecost Music performed by several major orchestras; opera repetiteur at Wexford Festival 1972–73 and Glyndebourne 1973–74; mem. teaching staff, Bryanston School 1974–76; first major int. success with composition Cry for 28 voices for BBC premiered London 1980, later 1988, Proms 1983, 1994, also Amsterdam Concertgebouw 1982, Vienna Modern Festival and Stuttgart 1997; companion piece Havoc premiered Proms 1999; visited West Africa in 1980 to study the music of the Jola people of Senegal and The Gambia; lived in Ghana 1990–96; taught composition, Univ. of Cambridge 2001–14, Composer-in-Residence, Clare Coll. 2008–14; mem. Inc. Soc. of Musicians, Mechanical-Copyright Protection Soc., Performing Right Soc. *Compositions include:* Six Songs of Love and Lust 1966, La Rivière 1967, The Kiss 1967, Three Shakespeare Songs for soprano, alto, tenor, bass (SATB) choir 1969, Four Lyrical Pieces for cello and piano 1970, The Good Morrow for mezzo-soprano and piano 1971, Paraphrase for organ 1971, String Quartet No. 1 1971, Canto for guitar 1972, Canto for piano, Canto for violin 1973, Orlando's Music for orchestra, Synthesis for two pianos 1974, Pentecost-Music for orchestra, Alleluia! for SA choir, harp, percussion 1976, String Quartet No. 2 1977, A world within (ballet for tape) 1978, Phoenix Variations for piano, Cry for 28 amplified voices and electronic treatment 1979, The Three Rs for primary school orchestra, Freewheeling for violin, viola, bass 1980, Count-Down for SATB choir, Riff-Raff for organ, A Song for Haddi for ensemble 1983, Le Nozze di Cherubino (opera), Naaotwa Lalà for orchestra 1984, Missa Tiburtina for SATB choir 1985, Into the Light for ensemble, Nunc Dimittis for SATB choir and organ 1986, O Magnum Mysterium for treble voices and organ 1986, Tonos for ensemble 1987, Veni Creator 1 and 2 for SATB choir and organ, Songlines for Flute and Guitar, The Coming of Saskia Hawkins for organ 1987, Harmonies of Hell for large ensemble, The Song of Leviathan for large orchestra 1988, No Quiet Place for SA choir and ensemble, No Man's Land for solo bass voice, SATB choir, ensemble 1990, Circle of Silence for 6 male voices 1991, Zebra Music for piano, The Song of the Tortoise for narrator, SATB, small orchestra 1992, The Owl & the Pussycat I for narrator, ensemble, String Quartet No. 3 1993, Fiddlesticks for violin and bass, Goodnight, Sweet Ladies for soprano and piano, Squeezy for accordion 1994, Ophelia drowning for flute and SATB choir, Mr Leary's Mechanical Maggot for string orchestra, Chinese Whispers for organ and orchestra, Miss Brevissima for SATB choir, Petite Messe Solitaire for SATB choir and unison voices, Winter Solstice Carol for flute and SATB choir, Groundwork theorbo, Merlis Lied for voice and piano 1998, The Flight of the Swan for flute and SATB choir, Perturbèd Spirit for countertenor and organ, The Akond of Swat for two narrators and ensemble 2000, Mancanza for solo guitar and orchestra, The Murder of Gonzago for wind quintet 2001, The Owl & the Pussycat II for treble voices and piano, Sangre viva for trumpet and piano 2003, Swayne's Canon for three violins and continuo 2003, Stabat mater for SATB choir and soloists, Stations of the Cross Book I for organ, Mr Bach's Bottle-Bank for organ 2004, Magnificat II for SATB choir, organ, Lonely hearts for SATB choir 2004, Elegy for a wicked world for mixed ensemble, Epithalamium for mezzo-soprano and string quartet, Nunc dimittis II for SATB choir, organ, Sinfonietta concertante for small orchestra, Two little motets for SA choir, organ, A Clare Eucharist for SATB choir, organ, Ten Terrible Tunes for piano, Creepy-crawlies for viola and piano, Aspects of Paradise for flute and piano, Symphony No. 1: a small world for large orchestra, Agnes Wisley's Chillout Fantasy for large wind orchestra, Suite No. 1 for solo cello, Leonardo's dream for alto sax & piano, Threnody for string quartet 2007, Bagatelles 1–4 for piano, Magnificat III for ATTB soli, Two carols for SATB choir, organ, lute 2008; Toil and trouble for double bass and piano, The human heart for SATB choir, String quartet No. 4, The joys of Travel for tenor and piano, Adam lay ybounden for solo cello, SATB choir, O mysteria for solo flute, SATB choir 2009, Hubbub for solo flute 2010, God is Gone Up 2014. *Current Management:* c/o DeNovo Arts, London, England. *Telephone:* (20) 7372-5048. *E-mail:* info@denovoarts.com. *Website:* www.denovoarts.com. *Telephone:* (20) 8964-3384 (office). *E-mail:* gs@gonzagamusic.co.uk (office). *Website:* www.gonzagamusic.co.uk (office); www.gilesswayne.com.

SWEENEY, William; British composer; b. 5 Jan. 1950, Glasgow, Scotland. *Education:* Royal Scottish Acad., Royal Acad. of Music, London with Harrison Birtwistle and Alan Hacker. *Career:* Lecturer on Composition, Univ. of Glasgow. *Compositions:* Three Poems from Sangschaw for soprano, three clarinets and piano 1977, Maqam for orchestra 1984, Sunset Song for orchestra 1986, The Heights of Macchu Picchu for soprano, harp and percussion 1988, The New Road for tenor saxophone and orchestra 1989, El Pueblo for baritone and ensemble 1989, Concerto Grosso for nine clarinets, strings and timpani 1990, St Blane's Hill for orchestra 1991, A Set for the Kingdom for strings 1991, Two Lyrics for two sopranos and chorus 1992, A Drunk Man Looks at the Thistle for speaker, baritone and ensemble 1992, The Woods of Rassay for soprano, baritone and orchestra 1993, Seeking Wise Salmon for soprano, clarinet, trombone and two synthesizers 1994, October Landscapes for orchestra 1994, The Lost Mountain for wind band 1996, All that Came in the Coracle for mezzo and ensemble 1999, Sonata for Cello and Piano (British Composer Award Instrumental Solo/Duo category) 2011.

SWEET, Sharon; singer (soprano); b. 16 Aug. 1951, New York, USA. *Education:* Curtis Inst., Philadelphia with Margaret Harshaw, studied with Marinka Gurewich in New York. *Career:* sang in private recitals at Philadelphia then appeared in the title role in concert performance of Aida at Munich 1985; Dortmund Opera 1986–88, debut as Elisabeth in Tannhäuser; Deutsche Oper Berlin from 1987, notably as guest in Zürich and Japan as Elisabeth and in the Ring; Paris Opera and Hamburg 1987 as Elisabeth de Valois; season 1987–88 as Desdemona in Brunswick, Dvořák's Stabat Mater at the Salzburg Festival, Gurrelider in Munich under Zubin Mehta and Wagner's Elisabeth at the Vienna Staatsoper; Norma in a concert performance of Bellini's opera at Brussels 1988; US debut as Aida at San Francisco 1989; season 1992 as Aida in Dallas and the Trovatore Leonora at Orange; sang in the house premiere of Verdi's Stiffelio at the Metropolitan season 1993–94 returned 1997, as Aida; Aida at Covent Garden 1995, returned as Turandot 1997; Norma at Rome 1999; sang Turandot at the Dresden Staatsoper 2001. *Recordings include:* Verdi's Requiem.

SWENSEN, Joseph Anton; American conductor, composer and violinist; *Founder and Director, U-HAC International*; b. 4 Aug. 1960, New York, NY; m. 2nd Kristina Algot-Sörensen; three s. (one from previous m.). *Education:* Juilliard School. *Career:* Prin. Guest Conductor Stockholm Chamber Orchestra 1994–97, Lahti Symphony Orchestra 1995–2000; Prin. Conductor Scottish Chamber Orchestra (SCO) 1996–2005, Conductor Emer. 2005–; Prin. Guest Conductor BBC Nat. Orchestra of Wales 2000–03; Prin. Conductor Malmö Opera och Musiktheater 2006–11; Prin. Guest Conductor and Artistic Advisor Ensemble Orchestral de Paris 2009–12; Founder and Dir Habitat4Music 2012–; toured Japan with SCO 1995, USA 1999; debut at Edinburgh Int. Festival with SCO 1998; cycle of Beethoven performances to mark 25th anniversary of SCO 1999; conducted new production of The Marriage of Figaro at the Royal Danish Opera 1999; Guest Conductor with City of Birmingham Symphony, Finnish Radio Symphony, Hallé Orchestra, Orchestra Nat. du Capitole de Toulouse; Prof. of Music, Indiana Univ. Jacobs School of Music 2013–; own orchestral works have been performed by various orchestras. *Recordings include:* Mendelssohn, Sibelius, Brahms, Prokofiev, Dvořák. *Honours:* Dr hc (St Andrew's, Scotland) 2001; Leventritt Foundation Scholarship 1978, Avery Fisher Career Grant 1982. *Current Management:* c/o Victoria Rowsell Artist Management Ltd, 34 Addington Square, London, SE5 7LB, England. *Telephone:* (20) 7701-3219. *Fax:* (20) 7701-3219. *E-mail:* management@victoriarowsell.co.uk. *Website:* www.victoriarowsell.co.uk; www.josephswensen.com.

SWENSEN, Robert, BMus, MMus; American singer (tenor); *Associate Professor of Voice, Eastman School of Music*; b. 1961. *Education:* Univ. of Arizona, Juilliard School, Univ. of Southern California. *Career:* sang at the New Jersey Festival, 1987 and 1988, as Rossini's Count and Britten's Lysander; season 1990 with Tybalt in I Capuleti e i Montecchi at Geneva and Nadir in Les Pêcheurs des Perles at the Paris Opéra-Comique; Carnegie Hall, New York, 1992, as George Brown in La Dame Blanche by Boieldieu; Matsumato Festival, 1993, as Oedipus Rex and Amenofi in Nabucco at Venice; season 1995–96 in Mozart's Mitridate at Turin and Gianetto in La Gazza Ladra at Palermo; other roles include Ferrando in Cosi fan Tutte; concerts include Mozart's Requiem at Cologne; Asst Prof. of Voice, Madison School of Music, Univ. of Wisconsin 1996–97; Assoc. Prof. of Voice, Univ. of Arizona School of Music and Dance 1997–2001; Assoc. Prof. of Voice, Eastman School of Music 2001–. *Recordings include:* Bach's St John Passion, Haydn's Orfeo ed

Euridice, Bach's Christmas Oratorio, Oedipus Rex, Barber: Anthony and Cleopatra (Grammy Award for Best Classical Recording). *Honours:* winner, Concert Artists Guild Int. Competition, New York 1987, Premio Giuseppe Borgati Concorso, Italy 1987. *Address:* Department of Voice and Opera, Eastman School of Music, 26 Gibbs Street, Rochester, NY 14604, USA (office). *Telephone:* (585) 274-1492 (office). *E-mail:* rswensen@esm.rochester.edu (office). *Website:* www.esm.rochester.edu (office).

SWENSON, Ruth Ann; American singer (coloratura soprano). *Career:* debut in San Francisco, CA 1983, Royal Opera House, Covent Garden, London 1996; has sung in Berlin, Geneva, Paris, etc. *Operas include:* Orlando, Rigoletto, Elisir d'amore, Lucia di Lammermoor, Puritani, Semele. *Recordings include:* Coloratura Arias from the Golden Age 1996, Roméo et Juliette (with Placido Domingo) 1996. *Honours:* San Francisco Opera Medal 2008.

SWERTS, Piet, (Pierre Rochus), PhD; Belgian composer, conductor and pianist; *Professor of Composition, Lemmens Institute, Leuven*; b. (Piet Jozef Raymond Maria Swerts), 14 Nov. 1960, Tongeren; m. Patricia Vanheukelom; three c. *Education:* Leuven Univ. Coll. of Arts. *Career:* Prof. of Composition, Lemmens Inst., Leuven; mem. Royal Acad. of Belgium 2013. *Film:* film music for Atlantic. *Compositions:* String Quartet No. 1 1982, Piano Concerto No. 1 1984, Piano Concerto No. 2 1986, Ajas (opera) 1986, St Mark Passion for soloists, choirs and orchestra 1988, Rotations for piano and orchestra 1988, Magma for concerto for violin, cello and strings 1989, Symphony No. 1 1990, Les Liaisons dangereuses (opera) 1994, Symphony No. 2 Morgenrot 2000, Wings piano concerto 2002, Nursery Songs for soprano and orchestra 2003, Dance of Uzume for alto saxophone and concert band 2004, The Song of Songs 2007–08, 24 Emulations for piano solo 2011, Hat City Sonata for alto saxophone and piano 2011–12, Piano Concerto No. 6 2012, Les Roses 2012, The Sack of Louvain 2013. *Publication:* Moments musicaux 2014. *Honours:* Baron Flor Peeters Prize 1983, Prijs Lemmens Tinel for piano and composition 1985, BAP Prize 1985, SABAM Prize 1986, Camille Huysmans Composition Prize 1986, Prize for Composition of the Province of Limburg 1986, First Prize, Concours Musical Int. Reine Elisabeth de Belgique 1993. *Address:* Lemmensberg 3, 3000 Leuven, Belgium (home). *E-mail:* piet.swerts@skynet.be (home); piet.swerts@luca-arts.be (office). *Website:* www.zodiaceditions.eu; www.pietswerts.be.

SWIERCZEWSKI, Michel; French conductor; b. 1960. *Education:* studied with Jean-Claude Hartemann in Paris and Charles Mackerras at the Vienna Hochschule. *Career:* made debut 1976 and was then asst conductor to Pierre Boulez and Peter Eötvös at the Ensemble Intercontemporain, 1983–85 and for Claudio Abbado at La Scala, including the premiere of Nono's Prometeo, 1985–86; Paris Opéra in 1986 with Georges Prêtre; has conducted such contemporary music ensembles as Itineraire, Musique Oblique, Antidogma and New Music Ensemble, giving many premieres; guest engagements in France, Germany, Italy, Spain, Portugal and Australia; conducted Die Fledermaus at Lyon, 1996. *Recordings:* La Conférence des Oiseaux by Michael Levinas; Works by Roussel with the Gulbenkian Foundation Orchestra; Complete Symphonies of Méhul. *Honours:* Finalist, 1984 Tanglewood International Conducting Competition; Prize, Villa Medicis Hors Les Murs. *Current Management:* Agence Thelen, 15 avenue Montaigne, 75008 Paris, France.

SWINNEN, Peter; Belgian composer; *Founder and President International Society of Contemporary Music (ISCM)-Flanders*; b. 31 Jan. 1965, Lier. *Education:* Royal Conservatory, Brussels, Muziekkapel Konigin Elisabeth, Waterloo, masterclasses with Michael Finnissy and Brian Ferneyhough. *Career:* taught cello at music schools 1990–97; teacher of analysis, Royal Conservatory, Brussels 1992–, of music technology 2002–, of composition 2004–; software development for aural training at Leuven Univ. 1997–2004, for musical analysis at Brussels Univ. 2004–; Founder and Pres. ISCM–Flanders 2005–; freelance work for BRTN-television; frequent performances of live electronics with various ensembles. *Compositions include:* FugaEneas (symphonic poem) 1990, Riflessione (violoncello concerto) 1991, The Petrifying Blue (chamber opera) 1992, The Black Lark's Ballad (symphonic poem, tribute to Frank Zappa) 1995, IdoVisu (oboe concerto) 1995, Quar'l (clarinet quartet) 1996, Canzone (for violin and piano) 1996, Gogutos (string quartet) 1998, Toaminá'k (recorder quartet) 1998, Sinfonia I 1998, Point d'Appui (violin/alto, declamation and electronics) 1999, Rinducele (harp quintet) 1999, Dorce (violin/viola/violoncello) 1999, Ciaccona (violin and piano) 2000, Annotazione 2000, Pas-de-deux 2001, Maitre Tsa (mini opera for children) 2003, Sinfonia II: A Broken Consort 2004, Quantsi (string quartet) 2004, Samoki (string trio and computer game) 2005, Nevrištec (string quartet) 2006, Hodechtri (ensemble and electronics) 2006, Ottarctra (piano trio) 2007. *Compositions for films:* Andres 1992, Het Verhoor 1998, The Voice of the Violin 1998, La petite peau-blanche devait courber la tête devant l'Empéreur Hirohito 2003. *Dance:* Hombre alado 1995, Laborintus 1996, La Vieille dame et la fille nomade 1998. *Recordings include:* Ciaccona, The Black Lark's Ballad, Quar'l. *Honours:* Prijs CERA – Jeugd en Muziek Vlaanderen 1991, Prov. of Antwerp Prijs voor Muziekcompositie 1992, Prix de Musique Contemporaine, Québec 1997, winner Queen Elisabeth Int. Music Competition Nat. Composition Contest, Belgium 1997, 2001, Laureaat van de Koninklijke Vlaamse Academie van België voor Wetenschappen en Kunsten 2005. *E-mail:* info@lantromusic.be. *Website:* www.lantromusic.be. *Address:* Boerderijstraat 26/8, 1082 Brussels, Belgium (home). *Telephone:* (2) 425-24-18 (home). *E-mail:* info@peterswinnen.be (home). *Website:* www.peterswinnen.be (home).

SYDEMAN, William; American composer; b. 8 May 1928, New York. *Education:* Mannes Coll. with Roy Travis, Hartt Coll., studied with Goffredo Petrassi and Roger Sessions. *Career:* Lecturer, Mannes Coll. 1959–70, Rudolf Steiner Coll., Calif. 1980–88; commissions from Boston Symphony Orchestra and Chamber Music Soc. of the Lincoln Center. *Compositions include:* over 600 chamber, orchestral and choral works, including Three Concertos da Camera for violin and orchestra 1959, 1960, 1965, Piano Sonata 1961, Homage to L'Histoire du Soldât 1962, Three Studies for orchestra 1959, 1963, 1965, Music for viola, winds and percussion 1996, Concerto for piano four hands and orchestra 1967, Full Circle for three solo voices and ensemble 1971, 18 Duos for two violins 1976, Duo for violin and cello 1979, A Winter's Tale (incidental music) 1982, Sonata for violin and piano 1987, Duo for cello and double bass 1992, Duo for oboe and piano 1996, Jonathan's Trombone 1996, The Odyssey (opera). *Honours:* Boston Symphony Merit Award, Koussevitzky Foundation, Nat. Inst. of Arts and Letters.

SYLVAN, Sanford, BMus; American singer (baritone); *Professor, Schulich School of Music, McGill University*; b. 1953. *Education:* Manhattan School of Music. *Career:* debut concert with New York Philharmonic Orchestra, under Pierre Boulez, 1977; sang at Marlboro Festival from 1982 and collaborated with Peter Sellars as Handel's Orlando, as Mozart's Don Alfonso 1986, and Mozart's Figaro 1987; premieres of Nixon in China by John Adams at Houston 1987, and The Death of Klinghoffer at Brussels 1991; Albert Hall, London 1990, as Xun in Tippett's The Ice Break; Glyndebourne, as Leporello 1994; Houston, New York and Edinburgh, as St Agnatius in Virgil Thomson's Three Saints in Four Acts 1996; Klinghoffer at Barbican Hall, London 2002; BBC Proms, London 2002; currently Prof., Dept of Performance, Schulich School of Music, McGill Univ., Montreal, Canada. *Films:* The Death of Klinghoffer (dir Woolcock), Mozart: Così fan tutte, Le nozze di Figaro (dir Sellars). *Recordings include:* JS Bach: Cantatas, Fussell: Wilde, Fauré: L'Horizon Chimerique, Beloved that Pilgrimage, Martin: The Glass Hammer, Adams' Nixon in China (Grammy Award, Emmy Award), The Death of Klinghoffer, The Wound Dresser. *Current Management:* c/o Donald E. Osborne, California Artists Management, 564 Market Street, Suite 420, San Francisco, CA 94104-5412, USA. *Telephone:* (415) 362-2787. *Fax:* 415-362-2838. *E-mail:* camdon@aol.com; don@calartists.com. *Website:* www.calartists.com. *Address:* Department of Performance, Schulich School of Music, Strathcona Music Building, 555 Sherbrooke Street West, Montreal, QC H3A 1E3, Canada (office). *Telephone:* (514) 398-4535 (loc. 094732) (office). *Fax:* (514) 398-1540 (office). *Website:* www.mcgill.ca/music (office).

SYLVESTER, Michael; singer (tenor); b. 21 Aug. 1951, Noblesville, IN, USA. *Education:* studied with Margaret Harshaw at Bloomington. *Career:* sang Radames and Pinkerton at Stuttgart 1987, at Cincinnati Opera from 1987 as Pinkerton and Sam in Floyd's Susannah, New York City Opera debut 1987 as Rodolfo in La Bohème; further engagements at La Scala and Santiago as Pinkerton 1990, Paris Opéra as Pollione in Norma, Hamburg Staatsoper as Rodolfo and Don José, and Vienna Staatsoper as Cavaradossi; Covent Garden debut 1990 as Samson, followed by Gabriel Adorno in a new production of Simon Boccanegra 1991; sang at Bregenz Festival 1990 as Hagenbach in La Wally; Metropolitan Opera debut 1991, as Rodolfo in Luisa Miller, followed by Don Carlos 1992; appearances as Radames at Deutsche Oper Berlin, Chicago, Orange Festival and Seattle 1992; further engagements at Bonn as Bacchus 1990, San Francisco as Calaf, Venice as Don Carlos and Geneva as Foresto in Attila; sang Radames at the Met 1996–97; season 2000–01 as Eleazar in La Juive for New Israeli Opera, Giasone in Cherubini's Médée at Montpellier, Calaf at the Met, Gabriele Adorno for Australian Opera and Puccini's Dick Johnson in Toronto. *Recordings include:* title role in Oberon, Don Carlos (conducted by James Levine), Simon Boccanegra (video, from Covent Garden with Solti conducting).

SYNKOVÁ, Milada; Czech pianist, harpsichordist and opera repetiteur; b. 16 May 1933, Bratislava, Czechoslovakia. *Education:* Conservatoire of Music, Brno, Univ. of Bratislava. *Career:* debut at Slovak Nat. Theatre, Bratislava 1963; concerts worldwide; harpsichordist, pianist and Asst to Prof. Viktor Málek (Conductor), Chamber Orchestra Camerata Slovaca 1969–2013; singer, pianist and Asst to Prof. Ladislav Holásek (Conductor), Bratislava City Choir 1973–; performed in chamber orchestras in Edinburgh, Jerusalem, Budapest and Seoul; co-operates regularly (with Prof. Milau Sládek) with The Mime Theatre ARENA, Bratislava –2007; taught professional training courses in piano, singing and Czech music at Sungshin Women's Univ., Seoul, Republic of Korea 2000; opera teacher, Suncheon Summer Music Camp, Republic of Korea 2004, 2005, 2007, 2008; worked with Milan Sládek Pantomimentheater, Cologne, Germany 2005; currently Tutor, Acad. of Music Arts, and Opera Repetiteur, Opera of the Slovak Nat. Theatre; collaborations with Australian soprano, Louise Hudson 2004–. *Recordings include:* several recordings for Czechoslovak radio, television. *Address:* Salviova 52, 82101 Bratislava 2, Slovakia (home). *Telephone:* 43421130 (home). *E-mail:* milad@stonline.sk.

SYRUS, David; British conductor; *Head of Music, Royal Opera House*; b. 1945, England. *Education:* Univ. of Oxford and London Opera Centre. *Career:* repetiteur, Royal Opera, Covent Garden 1971–81, Head of Music Staff 1981–93, Head of Music and Asst Conductor 1993–; Prof., Royal Coll. of Music, London; has conducted, for Royal Opera, Mozart's Le nozze di Figaro, Don Giovanni, Così fan tutte, La clemenza di Tito and Die Zauberflote, Wagner's Der fliegende Hollander, Verdi's La Traviata and Falstaff, Janacek's Jenůfa and Katya Kabanova, Strauss's Salome, Elektra and Ariadne auf Naxos, Smetana's The Bartered Bride, Britten's The Turn of the Screw and Tippett's

The Midsummer Marriage; Asst Conductor at Bayreuth Festival for seven reasons, at Salzburg 1991–; Guest Conductor with Israeli Ballet, Garden Venture, at St John's Smith Square and Ludlow Festival; other operas conducted include Les Pecheurs de Perles, Die Walkure (with Manchester Camerata, Britten's Let's Make an Opera, Menotti's Amahl and the Night Visitors (also recorded with Opera House Orchestra), and many world premieres of smaller-scale music-theatre pieces, including British premieres of works by Menotti and Henze; orchestras conducted include BBC Symphony Orchestra, Bamberg Symphony Orchestra and London Sinfonietta; continuo player and accompanist in Lieder recitals and at Wigmore Hall, London, Musikverein, Vienna, Carnegie Hall, New York and many other venues in Europe; conducted Zemlinsky's Eine florentinische Tragodie, Spoleto Festival 2003; has conducted with Vesselina Kasarova a series of concerts including excerpts from operas by Handel, Mozart, Gluck and Rossini, in Barcelona, Prague, Brussels, Schwetzingen Festival and Japan. *Recordings:* first lieder record with Hildegard Behrens for EMI, has played harpsichord and fortepiano continuo in recordings of Mozart and Rossini for Decca and BMG. *Address:* Royal Opera House, Bow Street, Covent Garden, London, WC2E 9DD, England (office). *Telephone:* (20) 7240-1200) (office). *E-mail:* info@roh.org.uk (office). *Website:* www.royaloperahouse.org (office).

SZABADI, Vilmos; Hungarian violinist; b. 10 March 1959, Budapest. *Education:* Liszt Acad. of Music. *Career:* debut with 2nd violin concerto, Bartók Festival, Royal Festival Hall, London 1988; regular performer in Finland; masterclasses in Finland, Greece and Hungary; Royal Philharmonic Orchestra; BBC Philharmonic; RTE Concert Orchestra, Ireland; played at Wigmore and Barbican Halls, RFH, London; St David's, Cardiff; Ulster, Belfast; Nat. Concert Hall, Dublin; Concertbegouw, Amsterdam; RAI Auditorium, Torino; Auditorio Nacional, Madrid; Châtelet, Conservatoire, Paris; Konzerthaus, Vienna; Liederhalle, Stuttgart; Helsinki, Finlandia, New York, Washington, Toronto, Montréal, Israel, Turkey, Republic of Korea, Taiwan; performed at celebration in honour of Georg Solti's 80th birthday, Buckingham Palace, London 1992; Stradivarius serie for Spanish royalty, Madrid 1995; Artistic Dir, Castle Chamber Music Festival, Hungary. *Recordings:* 21 albums include Dohnányi violin concertos, recordings for many radio and television stations. *Honours:* Midem Festival World Best Performance Prize, Cannes 1999, Hungaroton Prize, first prize Hungarian Radio Competition, Jenö Hubay, third prize Jean Sibelius 1985, Franz Liszt Prize 1993. *Current Management:* c/o Michael Brewer, 8 Edward Court, 317 Hagley Road, Birmingham, B16 9LQ, England. *Telephone:* (121) 454-3160. *Fax:* (121) 454-0225. *E-mail:* mbam@dsl.pipex.com. *Website:* www.mbam.co.uk; www.szabadi.com.

SZABO, Peter; cellist; b. 1965, Romania. *Education:* Kolozsvar Acad., Budapest. *Career:* played the Dvořák Concerto at Weimar 1981, with the Jena Philharmonic and is soloist with the Concentus Hungaricus and Budapest Festival Orchestra; soloist and chamber musician in USA, Mexico, Republic of Korea and throughout Europe; recitals and recordings with pianist Denes Varjon.

SZARÁN, Luis; Paraguayan conductor, composer and musicologist; *Music Director, Orquesta Sinfónica de la Ciudad de Asunción;* b. 24 Sept. 1953, Encarnación. *Education:* Conservatório Santa Cecilia, Rome, Italy. *Career:* first compositions performed at Festival de Música Contemporánea de Ouro Preto, Brazil 1975, 1978, Encuentros de Compositores de Latinoamérica, Santiago, Chile 1988, 1989, in Belo Horizonte, Brazil 1989, Buenos Aires 1990, Young Artists Festival, Bayreuth, Germany; Conductor, Orquesta Sinfónica de la Ciudad de Asunción 1978–90, Music Dir 1990–; Artistic Dir Festival de Música de Cascavel, Brazil 1990–95; Founder and Music Dir Camerata Filarmônica de Cascavel, Domenico Zipoli Ensemble, Venice 1997–; Founder and Dir Sonidos de la Tierra project 2002–. *Compositions:* Preludio Sinfónico 1973, Trozos para cuerdas 1975, Añesú for voice and orchestra 1976, Tríptico Barrettiano 1983, Mbocapú for orchestra 1989, La Magdalena for trombone and orchestra 1992, Las Musarañas 1973, Sonata for violin and piano 1975, Pequeña Suite for violin and strings 1975, Sonata for piano 1978, El Río for voice and instruments 1979, Encarnaciones suite for piano 1985, Variaciones en puntas for wind quintet 1986, Mbokapu for orchestra 1990, Miniaturas for oboe and piano 1990, Meditación por la caída del Muro de Berlin 1992, Rastros for flute and piano 1997, Concertino Uche Nuni y el Tagua 1998, La Cruz del Sur for soprano, violin and strings 2001, Chaidi: los últimos sonidos 2007. *Publications include:* Música en las Reducciones Jesuíticas de América del Sur (co-author) 1992, Mangore: Vida y Obras de Agustín Barrios 1994, Diccionario de la Música en el Paraguay 1997, Misa a San Ignacio de Domenico Zipoli 1688 – 1726 1999, Domenico Zipoli: Una vida, Un enigma 2000. *Honours:* Comendador, Orden Nacional del Mérito 2002, Ordre des Arts et des Lettres 2002; Premio Nacional de Música 1997, Orbis Guaraniticus Medal 2001, Vivaldi Medal 2002, Skoll Foundation Prize 2005, Medalla José Asunción Flores 2005. *Address:* Orquesta Sinfónica de la Ciudad de Asunción, Estación Ferrocarril Pdte. Carlos A. López, Eligio Ayala 571 con Mexico, Asunción, Paraguay (office). *Telephone:* (21) 492-416 (office). *E-mail:* sfa@pol.com.py (office). *Website:* www.sfa.org.py (office); www.sonidosdelatierra.org.py (office); www.luisszaran.org.

SZE, Jean Yi-Ching, BA, BS, MA, MS; American (b. Chinese) composer, zheng player and music teacher; b. 14 May 1956, Shanghai, China. *Education:* Shanghai Conservatory of Music, Coll. of St Elizabeth and Virginia Tech Univ., USA. *Career:* mem. American Music Center, American Soc. of Composers, Authors and Publrs (ASCAP), New Jersey Music Teachers Asscn. *Compositions include:* Shi for string quartet, Mountain for electric violin, zheng, bamboo flute, Autumn for string orchestra with bamboo flute, Flute Solo, Eastern View and Tradition Suite for violin and zheng, A Spring Morning at Miao Mountain for bamboo flute and zheng, Three Poems of Tang Dynasty for soprano, bamboo flute, yang qing, zheng, ban hu and pipa, The Sword and the Silk for lute and pipa 2000, The Pearl and the Thread for viola and pipa 2001, Nature for violin and piano 2003, White, Peace, Snow Mountains V for flute, piano and narrator 2006, Jasmin Flower Capriccio for zheng 2008, The Only Time Left for chorus 2010, A Letter from Mountain Village for er hu and flute 2010, A Brook at My Backyard for piano. *Publication:* Twentieth Century Music for Flute and Piano or Flute Solo. *Honours:* Second Prize, Shanghai Nat. Music Competition 1983, Asia Artist Award, USA 2001. *Address:* 13 Joann Court, Monmouth Junction, NJ 08852, USA (home). *Telephone:* (732) 329-3245 (home). *E-mail:* jeansze@comcast.net (office).

SZEGEDI, Anikó; Hungarian pianist; b. 22 March 1938, Budapest; d. of Ernö Szegedi; m. J. Szavai 1966; one d. *Education:* F. Liszt Acad. of Music, Budapest. *Career:* debut with Chopin Piano Concerto, Budapest Acad. of Music 1961; concerts in Budapest, Vienna Brahms Saal, Leningrad, Kiev, Dresden, London, Berlin, and Paris Salle Gaveau. *Recordings:* Beethoven Eroica Variations, Haydn Sonatas, Beethoven Piano Concerto and Triple Concerto (with D. Koracs and M. Pereuy), Schumann Carnaval, Kreisleriana. *Honours:* third prize Int. Schumann Piano Concerts, Zwickau 1963, F. Liszt Prize, Budapest 1973. *Address:* Szt Istvan krt 16, 1137 Budapest, Hungary (home); 93 boulevard de Port-Royal, Paris 75013, France (home). *E-mail:* szentistvan16@netquick.hu (home). *Website:* szegedianiko.hu/.

SZEGHY, Iris, ArtD; Slovak composer; b. 5 March 1956, Presov, Czechoslovakia; d. of Imrich Szeghy and Sophia Szeghy-Izso; m. Pedro Zimmermann. *Education:* Kosice Conservatory, Acad. of Music, Bratislava. *Career:* Resident Composer, Akad. Schloss Solitude, Stuttgart 1992–93; Visiting Composer, Univ. of California, San Diego, USA 1994; Composer-in-Residence, Hamburg State Opera 1995, STEIM Studio Amsterdam 1995, Kunstlerhauser Worpswede 1999; several portrait concerts, Hamburg, San Diego, Stuttgart, Bremen; participation in many festivals of music; Composer-in-Residence, Künstlerhaus Boswil, Switzerland 2001, Künstler Wohnung Stein am Rhun, Switzerland 2002. *Compositions:* Concerto for violoncello and orchestra 1989, Homewards for symphony orchestra 1997, De Profundis for voice and two melodic instruments 1990, Midsummer Night's Mystery for two percussionists 1992, Musica folclorica for clarinet, percussion and piano 1996, Vielleicht, dass uns etwas aufginge for soprano and string orchestra 2003, Anrufung des Grossen Bären for soprano, flute and piano 2003, Ad Parnassum for strings upon pictures of Paul Klee 2005, Hesse-Fragments for voice and piano 2006, String Trio 'Goldberg' 2007; broadcasts on various radio stations, especially Swiss, German and Slovak. *Recordings include:* Portrait, Hastedt Verlag Bremen 2001. *Honours:* several composition scholarships and prizes. *Current Management:* c/o Pedro Zimmermann, Nürenbergstrasse 17, 8037 Zürich. *E-mail:* pedrozim@hispeed.ch. *Address:* Nürenbergstrasse 17, 8037 Zürich, Switzerland (home). *Telephone:* (44) 3632966 (home). *E-mail:* szeghy@hispeed.ch (home). *Website:* www.szeghy.ch.

SZEMZO, Tibor; Hungarian composer and performer; b. 7 Feb. 1955, Budapest. *Education:* Budapest Acad. *Career:* composer for diverse groups; mem. of quartet, Group 180; solo performances; mem. of ensemble, The Gordian Knot 1998; performed at Contemporary Music Week, Budapest 1981–, Autumn Festival, Paris 1982, Steyerischer Herbst, Austria, New Music America, Houston 1986, Donaufest, St Polten 1988, Dokumenta, Kassel, Wiener Festwochen 1988, Ars Electronica, Linz 1988–89, Urban Aboriginal Festival, Berlin 1992, NIPAF, Nagano 1993, Music Now from Hungary, Yoahama 1994, Warsaw Autumn Festival, Poland 1995, Unsung Music 1996, Izumiwaka '96, Tokyo, Zona Europa de Est 1996, Romania Literatur Im Marz, Vienna, and in other countries. *Recordings:* Water Wonder 1983, Snapshot from the Island 1987, Private Exits 1989, Meteo/The Dreams of Eckermann 1990, Sub-Carpathia 1981, Ain't Nothing but a Little Bit of Music for Moving Pictures 1992, The Conscience/Narrative Chamber Pieces 1993, Duo 1984, The Last Hungarian PVC 1994, The Sex Appeal of Death/Airy Wedding 1994, Tractatus 1995, Symultan 1997, Relative Things 1998.

SZETO, Caroline, BMus (Hons), MMus (Hons), PhD; Australian composer; b. 15 Sept. 1956. *Education:* Univ. of Sydney, studied with Peter Sculthorpe. *Career:* worked at Univ. of Sydney 1990–91; comms from ABC 1991, Sydney Metropolitan Opera 1993, Song Co. 1994, 1997, Sydney Mandolins 1995, 1997, Bernadette Balkus and Michael Kieran Harvey 1999, ENERGEX Brisbane Festival 2000, Nat. Festival of Women's Music 2001, ISCM-ACL World Music Days 2007, Fed. of Australasian Mandolin Ensembles Music Festival 2008. *Compositions include:* Three Pieces for guitar 1984, Catalogue for string quartet 1985, C.C. 33 for concert band 1985, Sheng for orchestra 1986, Images of Li Po for ensemble 1987, Missa Brevis 1987, Energy for orchestra 1990, Study No. 1 and 2 for tuba 1990, Moon on Night's Water for piano 1990, Lament of the Boobook for computer-based instruments 1991, Yunny's Treat for piano 1991, ABC Fanfare for orchestra 1992, In a Garden for computer-based instruments 1992, A Game for violin 1992, The Third Station of the Cross for clarinet, double bass and percussion 1993, The Sweet Apple for six vocal soloists 1994, Energy II for orchestra 1994, Mandolin Dance 1995, Prelude for mandolin ensemble 1997, Monkeys Cry for six vocal soloists and two percussionists 1997, Cycles for guitar 1997, Mandolin Concerto 1998–99, Buffo for bassoon and piano 1998, Toccata for two pianos 1999, Cello Dance for cello and piano 1999, Impulse for oboe, clarinet, French horn and bassoon 2000, Dawn Day Dusk for koto and guitar 2001, Stringing 2007, Carryin' On 2008, Mirror for ensemble 2009, Maai Maai for vocal and ensemble 2010, Moon Rhyme for piano 2010. *Recordings:* Yunny's Treat 1991, Mandolin Dance 1995, Energy for Orchestra 1997, ABC Fanfare for Orchestra 1997, Moon on Night's Water 1998, Prelude 1999, Cello Dance 2004, Stringing 2007. *Honours:* Ignaz Friedman Memorial Prize 1985, Donald Peart Memorial Prize 1986, two first prizes City of Sydney Eisteddfod 1991, Australia Council for the Arts Composer Fellowship 1994. *Address:* PO Box 163, Mosman, NSW 2088, Australia (office). *E-mail:* mail@carolineszeto.com (office). *Website:* www .carolineszeto.com.

SZEVERENYI, Ilona; Hungarian academic and dulcimer player; b. 12 Aug. 1946, Gyula; m. Ferenc Gerencser 1967. *Education:* Liszt Ferenc Acad. of Music, Budapest with Ferenc Gerencser. *Career:* regular concerts as soloist and with chamber orchestras, Hungary and throughout Europe 1968–; founder, dulcimer duo 1972; numerous recitals in France, Germany, Italy; premieres of more than 70 works, including three concertos by contemporary composers; with students, founded Pantaleon ensemble for four dulcimers 1996; teacher, Béla Bartók Music Secondary School 1986–, Liszt Ferenc Acad. of Music 1989–; Ddeveloped curriculum for low, medium and advanced levels of dulcimer instruction. *Compositions:* several published compositions for dulcimer. *Recordings include:* Pieces for two dulcimers 1980, Contemporary works for dulcimer solo 1986, selection from J. S. Bach's pieces arranged for dulcimer solo 1995, Lachrymae (featuring the music of J. Dowland, S.L. Weiss and J.S. Bach) 2003. *Publications:* Cimbalon Tutor (co-author) 1982, publications in field of music education; contrib. to Parlando music journal. *Address:* Krecsanyi utca 12, 1025 Budapest, Hungary.

SZIGETI, István; Hungarian composer; b. 16 Oct. 1952, Budapest; Orsolya Srankó; two d. *Education:* Béla Bartók Conservatory, Budapest with Miklós Kocsár and Sándor Szokolay, Ferenc Liszt Acad. of Music with Zoltán Pongrácz. *Career:* worked for Hungarian Radio 1975–; Musical Ed. 1982–; Artistic Dir, electro-acoustic music studio, Hungarian Radio HEAR Studio 1994–; Head of Young Composers' Group, Budapest 1986–89; Pres., Hungarian Composers' Union; Pres., László Lajtha Soc. *Compositions include:* various recordings of chamber, opera, electroacoustic music, symphonic and choral music. *Honours:* special prize Int. GMEB Electro-acoustic Music Centre Composers' Competition, Bourges 1981, 1984, Kodály Scholarship 1984, Lajtha Prize 1999, Erkel Prize 2000, Artisjus Pirze. *E-mail:* szigetiis@t -online.hu (home).

SZILAGYI, Karoly; singer (baritone); b. 1949, Oradea Mare, Romania. *Education:* Cluj Conservatory. *Career:* sang Morales and Rigoletto at the Cluj Opera, then engaged at the Gelsenkirchen Opera 1980–85, Essen 1985–89; guest appearances at the Vienna Staatsoper, Zürich Opera and St Gallen and throughout Germany, Hungary and Austria; Liège 1990, as Rigoletto; also sings in operas by Donizetti and Puccini; sang Coppelius in Les Contes d'Hoffmann at Essen 1996; sang Verdi's Miller at Essen 2001.

SZMYTKA, Elzbieta; Polish singer (soprano); b. 1956, Prochowice. *Education:* studied in Kraków with Helena Lazarska. *Career:* sang at the Kraków Opera from 1978 then at Bytom and Wroclaw; toured West Germany and Luxembourg as Blondchen in Die Entführung; sang widely in Western Europe from 1983 notably at Ghent, Antwerp and Brussels as Despina, Blondchen and Serpina, and as Nannetta, 1987–88; sang at Aix-en-Provence Festival, 1987–88 as Nannetta and as Servilia in La Clemenza di Tito, Holland Festival in 1987 as Serpina in La Finta Giardiniera, at the Vienna Staatsoper in 1988 as Papagena, and in Amsterdam and Antwerp in 1989 as Gilda and Zerbinetta; sang at Glyndebourne Festival in 1991 as Ilia in Idomeneo and Servilia in La Clemenza di Tito, Salzburg Summer Festival in 1992 as Alyeya in From the House of the Dead and Mozartwoche in 1993 as Cinna in Lucio Silla; sang Vitellia in Gluck's La Clemenza di Tito at the Théâtre des Champs-Elysées, Paris, 1996; other roles include Susanna, Norina and Aennchen in Der Freischütz; engaged for Mozart's Lucio Silla and Entführung at the 1997 Salzburg Festival; season 1999–2000 as Mozart's Elettra at Lyon, Mélisande in Toronto and Donna Anna for the Berlin Staatsoper. *Recordings include:* La Finta Giardiniera; Despina in Così fan tutte; Mozart Arias; Die Entführung; Il Matrimonio Segreto; music by Szymanowski conducted by Simon Rattle. *Current Management:* Ariën Arts & Music Management, De Boeystraat 6, 2018 Antwerp, Belgium. *Telephone:* (3) 285-96-80. *Fax:* (3) 230-35-23. *E-mail:* arien@pandora.be.

SZŐNYI, Erzsébet; Hungarian musician; b. 25 April 1924, d. of Jenő Szőnyi and Erzsébet Piszanoff; m. Dr Lajos Gémes 1948; two s. *Education:* Music Acad., Budapest and Paris Conservatoire, France. *Career:* teacher of music at a Budapest grammar school 1945–48, Music Acad., Budapest 1948–; leading Prof. of Music Acad. 1960–81; Vice-Pres. Int. Soc. for Music Educ. 1970–74; Co-Chair. Hungarian Kodály Soc. 1978–2003, Chair. 2007–, Co-Chair. Bárdos Soc. 1988–, Forum of Hungarian Musicians 1995–; Hon. Pres. Hungarian Choir Asscn 1990–; Gen. adviser on methodology; Int. Kodály Soc. 1979–; mem. Chopin Soc. of Warsaw, Liszt Soc. of Hungary; mem. Hungarian Acad. of Art 1992–, Hungarian Composers' Soc. 1999–. *Compositions include:* Concerto for Organ and Orchestra; symphonic works: Musica Festiva, Divertimento 1 and 2, Prelude and Fugue, Three Ideas in Four Movements; operas: Tragedy of Firenze, A Gay Lament, Break in Transmission, Elfrida (madrigal opera) 1987–, several children's operas; chamber music, oratorios, vocal compositions, etc. *Publications:* Methods of Musical Reading and Writing, Kodály's Principles in Practice, Travels in Five Continents, Twentieth-Century Musical Methods. *Honours:* Dr hc (Duquesne Univ., Pittsburgh) 2006; Erkel Prize 1959, Hungarian Repub. Medal 1993, Apácai Csere János Prize 1994, Bartók-Pásztory Prize 1995, 2004, Prize for Artistic Excellence 2000, Zoltán Kodály Prize 2001, Hungarian Heritage Prize 2004, Hungarian Choir Asscn Medal 2004, Kossuth Prize 2006, Prima Prize 2011. *Address:* Ormódi-utca 13, 1124 Budapest XII, Hungary (home). *Telephone:* (1) 356-7329 (home).

SZÖRENYI, Suzana, DipMus; Romanian pianist and academic; *Professor, Academy of Music, Bucharest*; b. 23 Oct. 1929, Bucharest; m. Corneliu Radulescu 1968 (divorced). *Education:* C. Porumbescu Bucharest National Univ. of Music, studied with Dusi Mura and Dagobert Buchholz. *Career:* debut recital, Romanian Atheneum, Bucharest 1946; Prof., Acad. of Music, Bucharest; soloist, with symphony concertos, piano solo recitals, piano duets, lieder, chamber music, tours abroad; recordings for Romanian broadcasting, from Romanian and int. repertoire; premieres of recorded and stage performances of Romanian music by George Enescu, Constantin Silvestri, Hilda Jerea, Dan Constantinescu and others; premieres of works by Beethoven, Brahms, Schumann and Mendelssohn in Romania; participated in George Enescu International Festival, Bucharest 1988; tour of Germany and Switzerland with Cornelia Binonzetti (violin) 1991, of Austria 1996; participated in the Gala, EPTA Congress in Romania, Constanto 1992; interpretation of Nietzsche's works; lieder, violin, piano and four-hands works; participated as accompanist at several int. contests with singers and instrumentalists in France, Switzerland, Poland, Hungry, Russia, Czech Republic and Romania; participated as soloist with the G. Enescue Philharmonie Orchestra in the opening concert of the International Piano Competition and Festival, Dinu Lipattis, Bucharest 1995. *Recordings:* Lieder by Brahms with Marta Kessler; Romanian Lieder with Emilia Petrecu; Romanian Dances for two Pianos by Dinu Lipatti with Hilda Jerea; Beethoven's complete works for piano–four hands; Symphony Concertante for Two Pianos and String Orchestra by Dinu Lipatti, and George Enescu's works for piano–four hands with Corneliu Radulescu; Original four-hands works by Brahms, Schumann, Mendelssohn-Bartholdy and Max Reger (with Corneliu Radulescu). *Honours:* Nat. Order for Faithful Service, Romania 2004; M. Jora Soc. of Music Critics Award for lifetime achievement 2000. *Address:* 021158 Bucharest, Colentina 37, VI/26, sect. 10 (home); 010102 Bucharest, str. Stirbey Vodă 33, sect. 1, Romania (office). *Telephone:* (21) 6883939 (home); (21) 3146341 (office). *E-mail:* unmbrectorat@xnet.po (office).

SZOSTTEK-RADKOVA, Krystina; singer (mezzo-soprano); b. 14 March 1933, Katowice, Poland. *Education:* Katowice Conservatory with Faryaszevska and Lenczevska. *Career:* debut in Katowice 1960 as Azucena in Il Trovatore; Nat. Opera Warsaw from 1962 as Eboli, Amneris, Ortrud, Kundry and other roles in the dramatic mezzo repertory; guest engagements in Vienna, Hamburg, Berlin, Prague, Sofia, Belgrade, Moscow and Leningrad; sang at Paris Opéra 1981 as Ulrica in Un Ballo in Maschera, Grand Théâtre, Geneva 1983 as Herodias in Salome and appeared at the Théâtre de la Monnaie, Brussels, and the Opéra de Lyon in operas by Verdi and Wagner; sang Fricka in The Ring at Warsaw 1988; concert tours of France and S America. *Recordings:* opera albums and works by Penderecki and Tadeusz Baird.

SZUCS, Marta; singer (soprano); b. 1964, Hungary. *Education:* studied violin, then singing in Budapest. *Career:* sang in concert in Hungary and abroad 1976–78; guest appearances at Hamburg Staatsoper and Frankfurt from 1979; mem., Hungarian Nat. Opera from 1981, with debut as Gilda; further engagements at Vienna Staatsoper, La Traviata's Violetta 1985–87, Scottish Opera as Gilda 1984 and Anna in Anna Bolena 1989, Liège 1986–87 as Lucia di Lammermoor, and Monte Carlo 1988 in Cimarosa's Il Pittore Parigino; sang Anaide in Moïse et Pharaon by Rossini at Budapest 1992.

SZYMAŃSKI, Paweł; Polish composer; b. 28 March 1954, Warsaw. *Education:* Warsaw Acad. of Music with Tadeusz Baird, studied in Vienna with Roman Haubenstock-Ramati. *Career:* lecturer, Faculty of Composition, Theory and Conducting, Music Acad. Warsaw 1982–87; compositions have been performed all over the world, including Austria, Britain, Canada, Denmark, Germany, France, Holland, Japan, Hungary, Mexico, Sweden, Italy, USA; many works commissioned by European institutions and festivals and performed by world-renowned musicians. *Compositions include:* String quartet 1975, Partitas I–IV for orchestra 1977–86, Gloria, for female chorus and orchestra 1979, 10 Pieces, for sting trio 1979, La folia, tape 1979, Appendix, for ensemble 1983, Lux Aeterna, for chorus and ensemble 1984, Trope, for piano 1986, Through the Looking Glass I and II for chamber orchestra 1987, 1994, III for harpsichord and string quartet 1995, A Study of Shade, for chamber orchestra 1989, Quasi una Sinfonietta 1990, Miserere, for male voices and ensemble 1993, Piano Concerto 1994, Sonata for piano 1995, Recalling a Serenade, for clarinet and string quartet 1996, Muzyka filmowa 1996, Viderunt omnes for choir and ensemble 1998, Prelude and Fugue for piano (2000), Qudsja Zaher (opera in two acts for solo voice) 2005 (premiered at Grand Theatre Warsaw 2010), Gigue for cello solo 2006, Chamber music/ Silesian Quartet 2006, A Photo from The Birthday Party, Eals (Oomsu) for symphony orchestra 2009, A piu corde for piano and harp 2011. *Address:* c/o ZAiKS, 2 Hipoteczna Street, 00 092 Warsaw, Poland. *Telephone:* (4822) 828 17 05. *Fax:* (4822) 828 13 47. *E-mail:* sekretariat@zaiks.org.pl. *Website:* www .zaiks.org.pl.

T

TABACHNIK, Michel; Swiss/French conductor and composer; *Chief Conductor, Vlaams Radio Orkest*; b. 10 Nov. 1942, Geneva, Switzerland; m. Sabine Tabachnik 1981; two s. one d. *Education:* studied piano, conducting, writing and composition. *Career:* asst to Markevitch and Boulez; debut with BBC, London; Nat. Orchestra, Paris; Berlin Philharmonic; has conducted all major orchestras, including NHK Tokyo, Orchestre de Paris, Israel Philharmonic, Berlin Philharmonic, London Philharmonic, St Cecilia, Rome, Suisse Romande, Geneva, Concertgebouw, Amsterdam; Chief Conductor Gulbenkian Foundation Orchestra Lisbon, Orchestre Philharmonique de Lorraine, Ensemble InterContemporain Paris; Prof. of Conducting, Faculty of Music, Univ. of Toronto 1984–91, Royal Acad. of Music, Copenhagen 1993–2001; Founder and Artistic Dir des Jeunes de la Méditerranée 1984–96; Artistic Dir Orchestre des Jeunes du Québec 1985–89; Chief Conductor Noord Nederlands Orkest 2005–11; Chief Conductor and Artistic Dir Vlaams Radio Orkest (Brussels Philharmonic) 2008–. *Compositions:* Supernovae for 16 instruments 1967, Frise pour Piano 1968, Fresque for 33 instruments 1969, Invention à 16 voix for 23 instruments 1972, Mondes for two orchestras 1972, Sillages for string orchestra 1972, D'autres Sillages for magnetic tape and 8 percussions ad libitum 1972, Movimenti for orchestra 1973, Éclipses for piano 1974, Argile for four percussions 1974, Trois Impressions for nine instruments 1975, Les Perséïdes for orchestra 1981, Cosmogonie for orchestra 1981, L'Arche for soprano and chamber orchestra 1982–2009, 7 Rituels Atlantes for a cappella 1984, Pacte des onzes for soloists, double choir, orchestra and tape 1985–2008, Élévation for choir and orchestra 1990, Cycle of Haïsha: Prélude à la Légende for choir and orchestra 1989, La Légende de Haïsha for six voices, double choir and orchestra 1989–2009, Le Cri de Mohim for six voices and orchestra 1991, Évocation for choir and orchestra 1994, Concerto pour piano et orchestre de chambre 2003, Nord for orchestra 2006, Dyptique/Echo for solo violin 2008. *Recordings:* Beethoven, Wagner, Brahms, Dvořák, Honegger, Liszt, Nielsen, Fauré, Tabachnik, Schumann, Grieg, Lalo, Saint-Saëns, Xenakis. *Publications:* Bouc émissaire 1997, Il était une fois un enfant, Novel 1999, De la musique avant toute chose 2008. *Honours:* Artist of the Year, Centro Internazionale di Arte e Cultura, Rome 1995. *Address:* 1985 Villaz-La Sage, Switzerland (office). *E-mail:* office@tabachnik.org (office). *Website:* www.tabachnik.org.

TABAKOV, Emil; Bulgarian conductor and composer; b. 21 Aug. 1947, Russe; m. Buryana Tabakova; two s. *Education:* Bulgarian State Music Acad. *Career:* Conductor Russe Philharmonic Orchestra 1976–79; Founder and Conductor Bulgarian State Conservatoire Chamber Orchestra of Sofia 1977; Music Dir and Conductor Sofia Soloists Chamber Orchestra 1979–88, touring worldwide; Conductor Sofia Philharmonic Orchestra 1985–87, Prin. Conductor 1987, Music Dir and Conductor 1988–2000, with tours world-wide; Music Dir and Conductor Belgrade Philharmonic Orchestra 1994–99; Minister of Culture of Bulgaria 1997; Artistic Dir New Year Musical Festival, Sofia 1999–2004; Music Dir and Conductor Bilkent Symphony Orchestra, Ankara 2002–08; Dir Music Dept, Bulgarian Nat. Radio 2008–13, Prin. Conductor, Bulgarian Nat. Radio Symphony Orchestra 2008; guest conductor in Denmark, Sweden, Germany, Poland, Brazil, Russia, Greece, France, Russia, Japan, S Korea, Italy, Portugal, Mexico, Taiwan, Slovenia, Macedonia, Finland, Canada, S Africa, UK and USA; numerous radio and TV broadcasts. *Compositions:* eight symphonies, Concerto for double bass and orchestra, Turnovgrad Velki 1393 (cantata), Concerto for percussion instruments, Concerto for two flutes and orchestra, Concerto for piano and orchestra, Concerto for violin, percussion instruments and mixed choir, Requiem for soloists, orchestra and mixed choir, Concerto for violoncello and orchestra, Concerto for viola and orchestra, Astral Music for orchestra, Ad infinitum for orchestra, Concert for 15 string instruments, Concert piece for trumpet and string orchestra, Lamento for 12 double basses, Concert piece for orchestra, Concerto for orchestra, Five Bulgarian Dances for orchestra, Concerto for four traditional Bulgarian drums and orchestra, chamber music. *Recordings include:* with Sofia Soloists Chamber Orchestra, Sofia Philharmonic Orchestra: Mozart: The Complete Church Sonatas, Mendelssohn: The Complete Youth Symphonies, Mahler's Complete Symphonies, Brahms' Complete Symphonies, Overtures, German Requiem, Piano Concertos, Bartók's Concerto for Orchestra, Stravinsky's Fire Bird, Beethoven's Symphonies, works by J.S. Bach, Handel, Haydn, Mendelssohn, Shostakovich, Britten and Schoenberg, Rachmaninov and Bruckner, Berlioz, R. Strauss, Scriabin, Tchaikovsky, Dvořák, Verdi. *Honours:* prizewinner, Nikolai Malko Int. Competition for Young Conductors, Copenhagen 1977. *Address:* Bulgarian National Radio, 4 Dragan Tzankov Blvd, 1040 Sofia, Bulgaria (office). *Telephone:* (2) 9336352 (office). *Fax:* (2) 9634295 (office). *E-mail:* emiltabakov@hotmail.com (home). *Website:* www.emiltabakov.dir.bg.

TABAKOVA, Dobrinka, BMus, MMus, PhD; Bulgarian composer; b. 1980, Plovdiv. *Education:* Alleyn's School, Royal Acad. of Music Junior Dept, Guildhall School of Music and King's Coll. London, UK, summer courses at Centre Acanthus, France and Prague and Milan Conservatoires, masterclasses with John Adams, Louis Andriessen, Alexander Goehr, Marek Kopelent, Philippe Manoury, Alessandro Solbiati, Olav Anton Thommessen and Iannis Xenakis. *Career:* moved to London 1991; fmr Composition Fellow, Guildhall School of Music and Pres. Contemporary Music Soc.; has been Composer-in-Residence, Oxford Chamber Music Festival, Leicester Inter-national Chamber Music Festival and Utrecht International Chamber Music Festival, Kremerata Baltica Festival in Sigulda, Latvia; guest composer at Lockenhaus Festival, Austria and Julian Rachlin & Friends Festival, Dubrovnik; Composer-in-Residence, Orchestra of the Swan 2014–16, culminating in a work for 400th anniversary of Shakespeare's death at Holy Trinity Church in Stratford-upon-Avon; commissions from Royal Philharmonic Soc., violinist Maxim Rysanov, cellist Kristina Blaumane and Amsterdam Sinfonietta, among others; collaborative projects with Janine Jansen, Gidon Kremer, Natalie Clein, Milos Karadaglic, Choir of Merton College, Oxford, Lithuanian Chamber Orchestra and Voices of Ascension, New York. *Compositions include:* works for chamber, ensemble, string orchestra, orchestra and soloist, solo/duo instrumental, vocal/choral and stage/multimedia. *Recordings include:* String Paths 2013. *Honours:* Jean-Frédéric Perrenoud Prize, Vienna Int. Music Competition, composition prizes from Amsterdam, London, New York, Neuchâtel, Vienna and Warsaw, Adam Prize, King's Coll. London 2007, First Prize and Sorel Medallion in Choral Composition, New York 2011, won award for her anthem for Queen's Golden Jubilee, performed at St Paul's Cathedral. *Address:* c/o ECM Records, Postfach 600 331, 81203 Munich, Germany. *Telephone:* (89) 851048. *Fax:* (89) 8545652. *E-mail:* ecmrecords@ecmrecords.com. *Website:* www.dobrinka.com.

TACHEZI, Herbert; Austrian organist, harpsichordist and composer; b. 12 Feb. 1930, Wiener Neustadt. *Education:* Vienna Music Acad. *Career:* teacher at Vienna secondary schools 1952–67; teacher Vienna Acad. 1958, Prof. from 1972; performances with the Vienna Soloists and Solisti di Zagreb from 1960; keyboard soloist, Concentus Musicus 1964–; organist, Vienna Hofmusikkapelle 1974; concert tours throughout Europe and in the USA. *Compositions:* sacred vocal music, keyboard works, chamber and orchestral music. *Recordings include:* Handel Organ Concertos, Organ works by J. S. and C. P. E. Bach. *Honours:* Theodor Körner Prize, Vienna 1965. *Current Management:* c/o AKM, Baumanstrasse 10, Postfach 259, 1031 Vienna, Austria.

TACUCHIAN, Ricardo, BMus, DMA; Brazilian composer and conductor; *Professor, Federal University of Rio de Janeiro*; b. 18 Nov. 1939, Rio de Janeiro; m. Maria de Fátima G. Tacuchian; two s. *Education:* Universidade do Brasil, Universidade Fed. do Rio de Janeiro, Univ. of Southern California, USA. *Career:* Prof., Universidade Fed. do Rio de Janeiro –1995; Prof., Universidade Fed. do Estado do Rio de Janeiro (UNIRIO) 1995–, Pro-Rector 1999–2000; Visiting Prof., State Univ. of NY at Albany 1998, Universidade Nova de Lisboa 2002–03; Prof., Centro de Estudios Brasileños, Universidad de Salamanca 2011; Conductor, UNIRIO Chamber Orchestra 2002–04; more than 1,500 public presentations of his music in Asia, Europe and the Americas; numerous music commissions, including from FUNARTE (Nat. Foundation of the Arts), Bank of Brazil Cultural Centre, Rio de Janeiro Town Hall, Rio de Janeiro State Govt, Amazonas State Govt, Appolon Art Foundation (Germany), North/South Consonance (New York); Life mem. Academia Brasileira de Música (Pres. 1993–97, 2006–09) 1981, Academia Brasileira de Arte 2013. *Compositions include:* symphonic pieces, cantatas, chamber music, instrumental soli and tape music. *Recordings:* 70 albums (seven albums exclusive to his music). *Publications:* O Requiem Mozartiano de José Maurício (in Revista Brasileira de Música 19) 1991, Estrutura e Estilo na Obra de Béla Bartók (in Revista Brasileira de Música, v. 21, 1–17) 1994–95, Música pós-moderna no final do século (in Pesquisa e Música No. 2, 25–40) 1995, Fundamentos Teóricos do Sistema-T, Debates: Cadernos do Programa de Pós-graduação (in Música 1, 45–68) 1997; contrib. of more than 100 papers to Brazilian music journals. *Honours:* Hon. Conductor, Santa Maria Symphony Orchestra 1996; ALMB Brasilia Carlos Gomes Laurel Prize Medal 1996; Univ. of Southern Calif. Academic Achievement Award 1990, grants and scholarships from Fulbright Comm., Rockefeller Foundation, Other Minds, Appolon Stiftung, Capes and CNPQ (both in Brazil). *E-mail:* abmusica@abmusica.org.br. *Website:* www.abmusica.org.br. *Address:* Rua Carlos Góis 327, Ap. 702, 22440-040 Rio de Janeiro, RJ, Brazil (home). *Fax:* (21) 25113350 (home). *E-mail:* rtacuchian@terra.com.br (home). *Website:* sites.google.com/site/tacuchianmusica.

TADDEI, Marc; New Zealand conductor and trombonist; *Music Director, Wellington Orchestra*; b. USA. *Education:* Juilliard School, USA. *Career:* Prin. Trombonist, New Zealand Symphony Orchestra 1987–2001; Assoc. Conductor, Auckland Philharmonia Orchestra 2001–05; Music Dir Christchurch Symphony 2001–05; Music Dir Wellington Orchestra 2007–; Producer, Rattle Records 2008–10; guest conductor with Queensland Symphony, Sydney Symphony, Melbourne Symphony, Tasmanian Symphony, Adelaide Symphony, Orchestra Victoria, New Zealand Symphony, the Auckland Philharmonia, Oregon Symphony, Richmond Symphony, Fort Worth Symphony, New Haven Symphony, Louisiana Philharmonic, Chamber Orchestra of Hong Kong, Silesian State Opera, Opera New Zealand. *Recordings:* conducted over 20 recordings. *Current Management:* Maxima Artist Management Ltd., PO Box 1072, Auckland 1140, New Zealand. *Telephone:* (9) 522-1620. *E-mail:* info@maximaltd.com. *Website:* www.maximaltd.com. *Address:* Wellington Orchestra, PO Box 11-977, Wellington 6142, New Zealand (office). *Telephone:* (4) 801-3882 (office). *Fax:* (4) 801-3888 (office). *E-mail:* marc.taddei@xtra.co.nz (home); admin@wellingtonorchestra.co.nz (office). *Website:* www.wellingtonorchestra.co.nz (office).

TAGLIASACCHI, Monica; Italian singer (mezzo-soprano); b. 1959, Turin. *Education:* studied in Venice. *Career:* sang in Rossini's Tancredi at Turin and at La Scala in Rossini's Il Viaggio a Reims, I Lombardi and Die Frau ohne Schatten; Suzuki in Madama Butterfly at Ravenna, Verona and Zürich; guest appearances at the Vienna Staatsoper in L'Italiana in Algeri, at Philadelphia as Dorabella and at Florence as Pantalis in Boito's Mefistofele; Bayerische Staatsoper at Munich 1991; sang Teresa in La Sonnambula at Rome 1996.

TAGLIAVINI, Luigi Ferdinando, PhD; Italian organist, harpsichordist and musicologist; b. 7 Oct. 1929, Bologna. *Education:* Conservatoires of Bologna and Paris with Marcel Dupré (organ) and Riccardo Nielsen (composition), Univ. of Padua. *Career:* teacher of organ 1952–54, librarian 1953–60, Martini Conservatory, Bologna; Organ Prof., Monteverdi Conservatory, Bolzano 1954–64; founder and co-editor, L'Organo 1960; many concert appearances in Europe and N America, playing the harpsichord and organ; Visiting Prof., Cornell Univ. 1963, SUNY, Buffalo 1969; Dir, Inst. of Musicology at Fribourg Univ. 1965, Prof. 1971–2000, Prof. Emer. 2000–; Ed., Monumenti di Musica Italiana. *Recordings include:* two-organ works (with Marie-Claire Alain). *Publications:* contrib. to Neue Mozart-Ausgabe, 3 vols: Ascanio in Alba, Betulia Liberata, Mitridate Re di Ponto; Articles in L'Organo, Musik in Gesicht und Gegenwart, Ricordi, La Musica, Larousse de la Musique. *Address:* c/o Department of Musicology, University of Fribourg, Miséricorde, Bureau 2020, Av. de l'Europe 20, 1700 Fribourg, Switzerland (office).

TAÏRA, Yoshihisa; Japanese composer; b. 3 March 1937, Tokyo. *Education:* studied in Tokyo and with Messiaen at the Paris Conservatoire. *Career:* Lecturer at Ecole Normale de Musique, Paris; music performed by the Ensemble Intercontemporain, in Tokyo and Tanglewood and throughout Europe. *Compositions include:* Hierophonie II for 15 instruments 1970, III for four flutes 1971, Stratus for flute and harpsichord and 22 strings 1971, Trans-Appearance for 29 instruments 1977, Delta for chamber orchestra 1981, Pénombres I-IV for various instruments 1981–91, Tourbillon for six percussions 1984, Monodrame I for percussion 1984, II for bassoon 1986, III for guitar 1988, Polydère for orchestra 1987, Hexaphonie, for string sextet 1992, Pentamorphe for wind quintet 1993, Filigrane for flute and piano 1994, Réminiscence flute concerto 1998. *Honours:* Lily Boulanger Prize, 1971; Prix Florent Schmitt, 1985; Officier, Ordre des Arts et des Lettres.

TAKÁCS, Klára; Hungarian singer (mezzo-soprano); b. 24 April 1945. *Education:* Ferenc Liszt Acad., Budapest. *Career:* has sung at the Hungarian State Opera from 1973, notably as Orpheus, Adalgisa, Goldmark's Königin von Saba, Cenerentola and Cherubino; guest appearances at Europe's leading opera houses and concert halls; sang with the Vienna Staatsoper on a tour to Japan 1986, Teatro Colón Buenos Aires in 1987 as Charlotte and as Eudossia in La Fiamma by Respighi and sang Mozart's Marcellina at the 1992 Salzburg Festival. *Recordings:* Médée by Cherubini with Sylvia Sass; Die Königin von Saba; Boito's Nerone; Hunyádi Lászlo by Erkel; Haydn's Apothecary; Mozart's Requiem; Liszt's Legend of Saint Elizabeth; Missa Solemnis by Beethoven; Mahler Lieder eines Fahrenden Gesellen; Kodály's Háry János; Sacred Music by Haydn. *Honours:* prizewinner Erkel Int. Singing Competition, Budapest 1975, Liszt Prize Laureate, Grand Prix de L'Academie du Disque, Paris three times, Kossuth Prize 2014, 2015. *Address:* c/o Hungarian State Opera, Nepoztarsasag utja 22, 1061 Budapest, Hungary.

TAKÁCS, Tamara; Hungarian singer (mezzo-soprano); b. 1950. *Education:* Ferenc Liszt Acad., Budapest with Joszef Reti. *Career:* has sung at Hungarian State Opera House from 1978 as Vivaldi's Griselda, Orpheus, Mozart's 2nd Lady and Dorabella, Verdi's Azucena, Maddalena, Ulrica, Emilia, Mrs Quickly and Eboli, Wagner's Waltraute and Magdalena, Charlotte and Carmen; sang Orzse in Kodály's Háry János 1988; appeared as Judit in Duke Bluebeard's Castle at Covent Garden 1989 on a visit with the Hungarian State Opera; season 1992 as Public Opinion in Orphée aux Enfers, at Budapest; concert repertoire includes Purcell's Ode for St Cecilia's Day, Vivaldi's Stabat Mater, Gloria, Juditha Triumphans and Nisi Dominus, Donizetti and Verdi Requiems, Messiah and Rossini's Stabat Mater. *Address:* c/o Hungarian State Opera, Nepoztarsasag utja 22, 1061 Budapest, Hungary.

TAKÁCS-NAGY, Gábor; Hungarian/Swiss violinist and conductor; *Music Director, Verbier Festival Chamber Orchestra* and *Manchester Camerata*; b. 17 April 1956, Budapest, Hungary; s. of László Takács-Nagy and Matild Pataki; m. Lesley de Senger (née Townson) 1991; two d. *Education:* Béla Bartók Conservatory, Franz Liszt Music Acad. of Budapest. *Career:* f. Takács String Quartet 1976, Takács Piano Trio 1996, Mikrokosmos String Quartet 1998, Camerata Bellerive 2005; concert tours from 1980 every year throughout Europe, every other year in Australia, USA, Japan, South America; Prof., Haute Ecole de Musique, Geneva 1997–; Music Dir Verbier Festival Chamber Orchestra 2007–, Weinberger Kammer Orchestra 2007–, MAV Symphony Orchestra, Budapest 2010–12, Manchester Camerata 2011–; Prin. Guest Conductor, Budapest Festival Orchestra 2012–; Prin. Artistic Partner, Irish Chamber Orchestra 2013–. *Honours:* Hon. RAM; First Prize Evian Competition 1977, Menuhin Competition (Portsmouth) 1981, Scholarship Award, Banff School of Fine Arts, Franz Liszt Prize 1983. *E-mail:* Lesley@bellerive-festival.ch (office). *Address:* Case postale 186, 1245 Collonge-Bellerive, Switzerland (home). *E-mail:* ldstn@hotmail.com (home). *Website:* www.bellerive-festival.ch; www.gabortakacsnagy.com.

TAKAHASHI, Takako; Japanese pianist; b. Sapporo. *Education:* Toho Gakuen School of Music, Tokyo and Polish Nat. Frederic Chopin Music Acad., studied with Nobuyoshi Kato, Jan Ekier, Koji Shimoda. *Career:* currently based in Poland; has performed at festivals, including Yokohama Int. Piano Concert, Marianske Lazne Int. Chopin Festival, Duszniki Int. Chopin Festival, Nohant Int. Chopin Festival, Rimini Int. Music Festival. *Recordings:* Russian Piano Masterpieces 1994, Voyage de Chopin Vols 1–6. *Honours:* second prize and best contemporary music performance Porto City Int. Music Competition 1989, first prize Radziwill Int. Piano Competition, Antonin, Poland, fifth prize Int. Frederic Chopin Piano Competition, Warsaw 1990, Chopin Soc. Prize for best recital 1996. *Address:* c/o Exton Records, 6-5-8 Akasaka, Minato-ku, Tokyo 107-0052, Japan (office). *E-mail:* takako@japoland.pl (office). *Website:* www.takako-takahashi.com.

TAKEZAWA, Kyoko; Japanese violinist; b. 30 Oct. 1966, Nagano. *Education:* Juilliard School with Dorothy DeLay, Toho Gakuen School of Music, Tokyo with Kenji Kobayashi. *Career:* concerts with Philadelphia Orchestra under Charles Dutoit, New York Philharmonic under Zubin Mehta, Chicago Symphony, Boston Symhony, BBC Symphony Orchestra under Andrew Davis, Leipzig Gewandhaus orchestra, and London Symphony Orchestra with Michael Tilson Thomas; numerous appearances with leading orchestras in Europe, North America and Japan; Mainly Mozart Festival, New York 1999; Co-Dir Suntory Festival Soloists of Suntory Hall, Tokyo, including collaborations with Isaac Stern (violin), Yo-Yo Ma (cello), Wolfgang Sawallisch (piano) and Josef Suk (violin); Royal Concertgebouw Orchestra, Amsterdam with the Elgar Violin Concerto, conducted by Leonard Slatkin 2001; Szymanowski's Violin Concerto No. 1 at BBC Proms, London 2002; chamber music performances in Europe and North America; Jury mem., Indianapolis Violin Competition 2002, 2014, Menuhin Violin Competition. *Recordings include:* Elgar Concerto, with Bavaria Radio Symphony Orchestra under Colin Davis; Bartók's Second Violin Concerto with London Symphony Orchestra under Tilson Thomas; both Mendelssohn Concertos, with Bamberg Symphony Orchestra under Klaus Peter Flor; Barber's Violin Concerto with the Saint Louis Symphony Orchestra under Leonard Slatkin, Tchaikovsky and Prokofiev's Second Violin Concerto with Moscow Radio Symphony Orchestra. *Honours:* Gold Medal Second Quadrennial Int. Violin Competition 1986, winner Indianapolis Violin Competition, Idemitsu Award for Outstanding Musicianship. *Current Management:* c/o Kajimoto Music Management Inc., Kahoku Building 3F, Chuou-ku Ginza 8-6-25, Tokyo, Japan. *Telephone:* (3) 3574-0969. *Fax:* (3) 3574-0980. *E-mail:* concert@kajimotomusic.com. *Website:* www.kajimotomusic.com. *Current Management:* c/o Opus 3 Artists, 470 Park Avenue South, 9th Floor North, New York, NY 10016, USA. *Telephone:* (212) 584-7500. *Fax:* (646) 300-8200. *E-mail:* info@opus3artists.com. *Website:* www.opus3artists.com; www.kyokotakezawa.com.

TAKOVA, Davina; Bulgarian singer (soprano); b. 1968, Sofia. *Career:* appearances with Sofia Opera from 1992, with guest appearances at La Scala, as the Queen of Night and Lucrezia Borgia, and the Royal Opera as Rimsky's Queen of Shemakha and Violetta 2001; Gilda at Geneva, Rome, Frankfurt and Detroit; Lucia di Lammermoor at Bergamo, Florence, Amsterdam Concertgebouw and Tel-Aviv; Teatro Real, Madrid, in revival of 1660 opera by Juan Hidalgo, Celos aun del aire matan; Violetta in Berlin, Munich, Hamburg and Verona (Arena); season 2001–02 as Pamyre in Rossini's Le Siège de Corinthe at Lyon, Bellini's Elvira at Trieste and Violetta at Geneva. *Honours:* winner, Francisco Vinas Computation 1993, Toti del Monte Competition 1994.

TALARICO, Rita; Italian singer (soprano); b. 30 May 1941, Rome. *Education:* studied in Rome with Gabriella Besanzoni, Accademia di Santa Cecilia with Maria Teresa Pediconi. *Career:* debut as Eleonora in Il Furioso all'Isola di San Domingo by Donizetti, at the Spoleto Festival 1967; has sung at leading Italian opera houses and in Lyon, Rouen, Montreal, New York and Philadelphia; other roles include Elvira in I Puritani, Amina in La Sonnambula, Leila in Les Pêcheurs de Perles, Mimi, Violetta, Medora in Il Corsaro, Elsa, Agathe, Donna Anna, Susanna, Countess Almaviva, Marguerite, Carolina in Il Matrimonio Segreto and Margherita in Mefistofele; sang at La Scala 1985, in Orfeo by Luigi Rossi. *Recordings include:* Il Furioso all'Isolo di San Domingo.

TALBOT, Michael Owen, BA, BMus, PhD, ARCM, FBA; British writer; *Professor Emeritus of Music, University of Liverpool*; b. 4 Jan. 1943, Luton, Beds., England; s. of Alan Talbot and Annelise Talbot; m. Shirley Mashiane 1970; one s. one d. *Education:* Royal Coll. of Music, London, Clare Coll., Cambridge. *Career:* Lecturer, Univ. of Liverpool 1968–79, Sr Lecturer 1979–83, Reader 1983–86, James and Constance Alsop Prof. of Music 1986–2003, Prof. Emer. of Music 2003–; mem. Royal Musical Asscn, Società Italiana di Musicologia; mem. int. advisory bd, Fondazione Giorgio Cini; Corresp. Fellow, Ateneo Veneto. *Publications include:* Vivaldi 1978, Albinoni: Leben und Werk 1980, Antonio Vivaldi: A Guide to Research 1988, Tomaso Albinoni: The Venetian Composer and his World 1990, Benedetto Vinaccesi: A Musician in Brescia and Venice in the Age of Corelli 1994, The Sacred Vocal Music of Antonio Vivaldi 1995, Venetian Music in the Age of Vivaldi 1999, The Musical Work: Reality or Invention (ed.) 2000, The Finale in Western Instrumental Music 2001, The Business of Music (ed.) 2002, The Chamber Cantatas of Antonio Vivaldi 2006, Vivaldi and Fugue 2009, The Vivaldi Compendium 2011; contrib. to professional journals, including Early Music, Music and Letters, Music Review, Musical Times, Journal of the Royal Musical Association, Soundings, The Consort, Note d'Archivio, Händel Jahrbuch, Informazioni e Studi Vivaldiani, Studi Vivaldiani, Journal of Eighteenth Century Music, Recercare, Royal Musical Association Research Chronicle. *Honours:* Cavaliere del Ordine al Merito (Italy) 1980; Oldman Prize 1990, Serena Medal 1999.

Address: School of Music, University of Liverpool, Liverpool, L69 7WW, England (office). *Fax:* (151) 794-3141 (office). *E-mail:* mtalbot@liv.ac.uk (office).

TALI, Anu; Estonian conductor; *Artistic Director, Nordic Symphony Orchestra;* b. 18 June 1972. *Education:* Tallinn Music High School, Estonian Acad. of Music, Sibelius Acad., Finland, St Petersburg Conservatory, Russia with Ilya Mussin and Leonid Kortshmar. *Career:* conducting debut with the Estonian Nat. Symphony Orchestra; guest conductor with Lahti SO, Oulu SO, Tampere PO and Jyväskylä Chamber Orchestra in Finland, Tonkünstler SO and I Frauen Kammerorchester in Austria, Norrlands Opera and Gävle SO in Sweden, Liepaja SO, Latvia, Bratislava Soloists, Slovakia, Vanemuine Opera, Estonia, Moscow SO, Tokyo PO, Japan Philharmonic, Frankfurt Radio SO, Strasbourg Philharmonic, Tyrol SO, New Jersey SO; co-f., Artistic Dir and Conductor Nordic Symphony Orchestra (fmrly Estonian-Finnish Symphony Orchestra) 1997–, with themed seasons, Musical Capitals of the World 1998–99, Life and Death 1999–2000, Symphony 2000–01, Musica Grande 2001–02, Passion or Passion 2002–03, A la Russe 2003–04. *Recordings:* with Nordic SO: Swan Flight 2001, Action Passion Illusion 2005. *Current Management:* c/o Stafford Law, Candleway, Broad Street, Sutton Valence, Kent ME17 3AT, England. *Telephone:* (1622) 840038. *Fax:* (1622) 840039. *E-mail:* staffordlaw@btinternet.com. *Website:* www.stafford-law.com. *Address:* Nordic Symphony Orchestra, c/o Estonia Concert Hall, Estonia Avenue 4, Tallinn 10148, Estonia (office).

TALICH, Jan; violist; b. 30 Oct. 1945, Pilzen, Czechoslovakia. *Education:* Prague Conservatory. *Career:* co-founder, Talich Quartet 1961; after success in competitions at Komeriz and Belgrade gained title of Laureate from the Asscn of Int. Music Festivals, Bayreuth; violist, Talich Quartet 1972; appearances in Europe and North America, Egypt, Iraq, Indonesia and Japan; annual visits to France from 1976, including the complete Beethoven quartets; engagements with festivals and music clubs in the UK; played at Wigmore Hall, London 1991, with the quartets of Smetana, Beethoven's Op 74, Brahms A minor and Mozart D minor, and at Bath and Bournemouth Festivals 1991; played at QEH 1991, and Janáček's 2nd Quartet for BBC 2 The Late Show. *E-mail:* talich.quartet@gmail.com.

TALLEY-SCHMIDT, Eugene; American singer (tenor) and academic; b. 10 Feb. 1932, Rome, GA; m. Jeanette Lombard Pecorello 1960, two s. *Education:* San Diego State Coll., Indiana Univ., Opera Arts, Atlanta, GA, Teatro dell'Opera, Rome, Italy, Teatro Lirico, Spoleto, Italy, studied with Ethel Wilkerson in Rome, GA, John Walsh and Raoul Couyas, San Diego, CA. *Career:* US debut as Jenik in The Bartered Bride at San Diego, CA; European debut as Fritz in L'Amico Fritz at Spoleto, Italy; leading tenor with Deutsche Oper am Rhein, Düsseldorf, Staatsoper Hamburg, Wuppertal and Munster Operas; sang over 50 leading tenor roles at opera houses in USA and Europe; television and radio performances in Europe and America; performed at int. festivals and appeared with Atlanta, Birmingham, Mobile, Miami, Palm Beach, Indianapolis, Rome, and San Diego Symphony Orchestras. *Recordings:* Robert Schumann, Complete Duets for tenor and soprano.

TALMI, Yoav, OQ, DipMus; Israeli conductor, composer and pianist; *Head of Conducting Program, Buchmann-Mehta School of Music, Tel-Aviv University;* b. 28 April 1943, Kibbutz Merhavia; s. of Avraham Talmi and Sarah Talmi; m. Er'ella Talmi 1964; one s. one d. *Education:* Rubin Acad. of Music, Tel-Aviv, Juilliard School of Music, USA, summer study courses with Walter Susskind in Aspen, Bruno Maderna in Salzburg, Jean Fournet in Hilversum, Erich Leinsdorf at Tanglewood. *Career:* Co-conductor, Israel Chamber Orchestra, Tel-Aviv 1970–72; Artistic Dir and Conductor, Arnhem Philharmonic Orchestra 1974–80; Prin. Guest Conductor, Munich Philharmonic Orchestra 1979–80; Music Dir and Prin. Conductor, Israel Chamber Orchestra 1984–88; Music Dir New Israeli Opera 1985–89; Music Dir San Diego Symphony, USA 1989–96; Artistic Dir and Conductor, Orchestre Symphonique de Québec, Canada 1998–2011, Conductor Emer. 2011–; Chief Conductor, Hamburg Symphony 2000–04; Prin. Guest Conductor, Israel Chamber Orchestra 2008–12, Music Dir and Conductor 2012–13; guest conductor with the Berlin and Munich Philharmonics, London Symphony and Philharmonia, London and Royal Philharmonics, Amsterdam's Concertgebouw, Israel and New Japan Philharmonics, NHK Symphony, Vienna Symphony, St Petersburg and Oslo Philharmonics, Tonhalle Orchestra, Zürich, Detroit, Pittsburgh, Houston, Dallas, St Louis and Montreal Symphonies, Los Angeles and New York Chamber Symphonies; currently Head of Conducting Program, Buchmann-Mehta School of Music, Tel-Aviv Univ. *Compositions include:* The Zahal March (official march of the Israeli army) 1963, Dreams for choir a capella, Music for Flute and Strings 1965, Overture on Mexican Themes 1969, Three Monologues for solo flute 1982, Fanfare for double-brass ensemble 1990, Elegy for Strings, Timpani and Accordion (Dachau Reflections) 1997, Israeli Suite for flute and chamber orchestra 2004, The Double Marriage of Figaro, paraphrase 2006, 'De Profundis' for choir and orchestra 2011, Animi Motus for orchestra and children's choir 2014. *Recordings include:* Bruckner's Symphony No. 9, Oslo Philharmonic; Tchaikovsky's Symphony No.1, Bach's Metamorphosis, Debussy's Children's Corner, Quebec Symphony Orchestra; Mendelssohn's Symphony No. 1, Piano Concertos; Glière's Symphony No. 3, Rachmaninov's Isle of the Dead, Brahms's Sextet – Four Serious Songs, Berlioz's Overtures, Symphonie Fantastique, Romeo and Juliet and Harold in Italy, San Diego Symphony; Tchaikovsky's Souvenir de Florence, Schoenberg's Verklärte Nacht, Bloch, Barber, Puccini and Grieg, Israel Chamber Orchestra. *Publication:* A

Conductor's Career: From the Kibbutz to Quebec (memoir). *Honours:* Québec-City Medal 2008; Dr hc (Laval Univ.) 2000; Boskovitch Prize for Composition, Israel 1965, Koussevitzky Memorial Conducting Prize, Tanglewood 1969, Rupert Foundation Conductors' Competition, London 1973, Ahad Ha'am Award, Los Angeles Centre for Jewish Culture and American-Israel Cultural Foundation 1997, Frank Peleg Prize, Ministry of Culture, Israel 2008, Opus Prize for Best Performance Concert in the province of Quebec, City of Montreal 2009, Israeli Prime-Minister Prize for Composer, Jerusalem 2013. *Current Management:* c/o Michal Schmidt Artists International, 59 East 54th Street, Suite 83, New York, NY 10022, USA. *Telephone:* (212) 421-8500. *Fax:* (212) 421-8583. *E-mail:* mws@schmidtart.com. *Website:* www.schmidtart.com. *Address:* 17 Amir Gilboa Street, Apt 18, Tel-Aviv 6967130, Israel (home). *Telephone:* 3-6097942 (office). *Fax:* 3-6415472 (home). *E-mail:* talmi@netvision.net.il (home). *Website:* www.yoavtalmi.com.

TALVI, Ilkka Ilari; Finnish violinist and concertmaster; b. 22 Oct. 1948, Kuusankoski; m. Marjorie Kransberg 1984; three d. *Education:* Sibelius Academy, Helsinki with Arno Granroth, Univ. of Southern California, USA with Jascha Heifetz, Curtis Institute of Music with Ivan Galamian, with Riccardo Odnoposoff in Vienna and Gabriel Bouillon in Paris. *Career:* debut with orchestra aged 10; recital debut aged 15, Helsinki; performances as soloist and recitalist in Europe and USA; lecturer at Sibelius Academy, Finland 1969–75 and at Pori School of Music 1970–76; Concertmaster with Malmö Symphony, Sweden 1976–77; working in motion picture business at Los Angeles, USA 1977–85; Principal with Los Angeles Chamber Orchestra 1979–85; Guest Concertmaster Seattle Opera 1983–85, Concertmaster 1985–2004; Concertmaster, Waterloo Festival, New Jersey 1988–, Rainier Symphony Orchestra. *Recordings include:* Klami Violin Concerto, Albert Im Concordiam. *Honours:* numerous honours and prizes in Finland. *Address:* Rainier Symphony Orchestra, PO Box 58182, Seattle, WA 98138, USA (office). *Telephone:* (206) 781-5618 (office). *E-mail:* questions@RainierSymphony.org (office); talvi.violinstudio@gmail.com (home). *Website:* www.rainiersymphony .org (office); schmaltzuberalles.blogspot.com.

TAMAR, Iano; Georgian singer (soprano); b. 15 Oct. 1963, Kashbergi. *Education:* Tbilisi Conservatory. *Career:* sang at the Tbilisi Opera from 1989; best known in the title role of Rossini's Semiramide, which she sang at the Pesaro Festival, under Alberto Zedda and at the Zürich Opera; has also sung the Rossini Stabat Mater at Dresden, Natasha in War and Peace, Mozart's Countess and Amelia in Un Ballo in Maschera; sang Ottavia in Pacini's L'Ultimo giorno di Pompei, Martina Franca Festival; Lady Macbeth at Naples and Fiordiligi at Miami; sang Fausta in Massenet's Roma at Martina Franca; sang Amelia in Un Ballo in Maschera at Bregenz, Lady Macbeth for the Deutsche Oper Berlin, Donna Anna at La Coruña and Elvira in Ernani at the Vienna Staatsoper. *Address:* Opéra et Concert, 37 rue de la Chausée d'Antin, 75009 Paris, France. *Telephone:* 1-42-96-18-18. *Fax:* 1-42-96-18-00. *E-mail:* agence@opera-concert.com. *Website:* www.opera-concert.com; www.iano -tamar.com.

TAMAYO, Arturo; Spanish conductor; b. 3 Aug. 1946, Madrid. *Education:* Royal Conservatoire, Madrid, studied with A. Barrera, Francisco Cales and Gerardo Gombau. *Career:* concerts in Spain from 1967; studied further with Pierre Boulez at Basle and at the Musikhochschule Fribourg-in-Brisgau; studied conducting with Franc Travis 1971–76, and composition with Wolfgang Fortner and Klaus Huber; assisted Huber at Fribourg from 1974 and directed concerts of contemporary music; frequent appearances at the Deutsche Oper Berlin from 1982, notably with the 1983 premiere of Wolfgang Rihm's ballet, Tutuguri; conducted the premiere of Kelterborn's Ophelia at the 1984 Schwetzingen Festival, and Maurice Ohana's La Celestine at the Paris Opéra 1988; Théâtre des Champs Elysées in Paris 1990 with the local premiere of La Noche Triste by Jean Prodomidès; Graz 1996, Busoni's Doktor Faust. *E-mail:* arturotamayo@arturotamayo.com. *Website:* www .arturotamayo.com.

TAMBOSI, Olivier; French opera director; b. 7 July 1963, Paris. *Education:* Vienna Univ., Acad. of Music and Performing Arts, Vienna. *Career:* formed Neue Oper Wien 1989, Artistic Dir –1993; productions included Idomeneo, Medea, Die Zauberflöte, Macbeth, Hartmann's Simplicius, Telemann's Pimpinone, Don Pasquale and Lulu; Artistic Dir Klagenfurt Opera 1993–96, with Elisir d'amore, Manon Lescaut, Death in Venice, Così fan tutte, Cav and Pag, Les Contes d'Hoffmann and Rigoletto; productions from 1996 include Der Rosenkavalier and Lulu at Mannheim; Macbeth at Strasbourg; Bohème and Jenůfa at Hamburg 1999–2000; Pelléas et Mélisande at Linz, Falstaff for the Lyric Opera of Chicago; Tristan at Berne; Mozart's Die Entführung in Klagenfurt; season 2000–01 with Jenůfa at Covent Garden and Saariaho's L'Amour de Loin at Berne; Lulu at Klagenfurt 2002; Un Ballo in Maschera at Chicago 2003, Jenůfa, Met Opera, New York 2003, Luisa Miller at Covent Garden 2003; Zauberflöte at Linz 2003; Traviata at Strasbourg 2003, Gluck's Orfeo at Nürnberg 2004; Schreker's Irrelohe at Vienna Volksoper 2004; Rigoletto at Dublin 2004; Wozzeck at Mannheim 2005; Falstaff at Houston 2005; Jenůfa at Barcelona 2005; Manon Lescaut at Chicago 2005; Lucia di Lammermoor at Linz 2005; Don Giovanni at Zagreb 2006; Manon Lescaut at San Francisco 2006; Jenůfa at Met Opera, New York 2007; Zemlinsky's Zwerg and Florentinische Tragödie at Bard Summerscape Festival 2007; Idomeneo at Lucerne Festival 2007; Traviata at Linz 2007; Falstaff at Chicago 2008; Künneke's 'Vetter aus Dingsda' at Vienna Volksoper 2008; Nozze di Figaro at Linz 2009; Butterfly at Guadalajara 2009; Fledermaus at Dortmund 2009; Lucia di Lammermoor at Bregenz 2010; Otello at Saarbrücken 2010;

Meistersinger at Linz 2010; Makropoulos Case at San Francisco 2010; Falstaff at Hanover 2011; Manon Lescaut at Florence 2011; Gräfin Mariza at Linz 2011; Maria Stuarda at Linz 2011; Makropoulos Case at Helsinki 2012; Entführung at Saarbrücken 2012. *Current Management:* c/o IMG Artists, 31-33 rue du Temple, 75004 Paris, France. *Telephone:* 1-44-31-00-10. *E-mail:* salmansi@imgartists.com. *Website:* www.imgartists.com.

TAMESTIT, Antoine; French viola player; b. 1979, Paris. *Education:* Conservatoire de Paris, studied with Jean Sulem, Yale Univ., studied with Jesse Levine, Hanns Eisler Hochschule, Berlin, studied with Tabea Zimmermann. *Career:* New York, Boston and Washington recital debuts 2003; selected to participate in BBC Radio 3's New Generation Artists Scheme 2004; repertoire ranges from the Baroque period to the contemporary; has performed and recorded many world premieres; played George Benjamin's Viola, Viola with Tabea Zimmermann at Feldkirch Festival before recording it in 2003; premiered the Concerto for two violas by Bruno Mantovani, written for Tabea Zimmermann and himself with Orchestre Philharmonique de Radio France, Liège Orchestra and WDR Cologne; concerto written for him by Austrian composer Olga Neuwirth 2009, premiered in Vienna, Berlin, Tokyo, and in Paris with Orchestra Philharmonique de Radio France 2011; as soloist, has worked with Bavarian Radio Symphony Orchestra, Leipzig Gewandhaus Orchestra, Deutsches Sinfonie-Orchester Berlin, Dresden Philharmonic Orchestra, RSO Stuttgart, with major French orchestras, including Orchestre Philharmonique de Radio France, Orchestre de la Suisse Romande under Marek Janowski and with several BBC symphony orchestras; played with Vienna Philharmonic Orchestra under Riccardo Muti at Lucerne Festival 2008, with Franz Welser-Möst 2011; played in opening concerts of the Mostly Mozart Festival in New York together with Louis Langrée and Christian Tetzlaff 2011; chamber music partners include Gidon Kremer, Leonidas Kavakos, Christian Tetzlaff, Emmanuel Pahud, Jean-Guihen Queyras, Renaud and Gautier Capuçon, Nicholas Angelich, Natalia Gutman, the Ebène and the Hagen quartets; invited to play at festivals including Lockenhaus, Rheingau, Schwarzenberg, Lucerne, Verbier, Salzburg and Newport; also regularly plays in string trio with Frank-Peter Zimmermann and Christian Poltera; in recital, works with German pianist Markus Hadulla playing in major halls world-wide, including Amsterdam Concertgebouw, Vienna Musikverein, Carnegie Hall, Wigmore Hall in London, Megaron in Athens, Palais des Beaux-Arts in Brussels, Konserthus in Stockholm and Cité de la Musique de Paris as part of ECHO's Rising Stars programme; performed at Lincoln Center, New York 2006; Prof., Cologne Musikhochschule; plays on a viola made by Stradivarius in 1672, loaned by the Habisreutinger Foundation. *Recordings:* solo recording of Bach and Ligeti 2007, Mozart's Sinfonia Concertante with Renaud Capuçon, Louis Langrée and Scottish Chamber Orchestra, Schnittke Concerto with Warsaw Philharmonic and D. Kitajenko, Schubert's Trout Quintet with Christian Tetzlaff, Marie-Elisabeth Hecker, Alois Posch and Martin Helmchen, an all-Schubert recording with soprano Sandrine Piau, complete Fauré Piano Quartets with Trio Wanderer, Berlioz Harold in Italy with Marc Minkowski, Solo Bach Suites, as well as Mozart and Beethoven String Trios with the Trio Zimmermann. *Honours:* First Prize, Maurice Vieux Competition, Paris 2000, William Primrose Competition, Chicago 2001, Young Concert Artists Int. Auditions 2003, First Prize, 53rd ARD Munich Int. Music Competition 2004, Borletti-Buitoni Trust Award (co-recipient) 2006, Victoires de la Musique Révélation de l'Année 2007, Förderpreis Deutschlandfunk 2008, Credit Suisse Young Artist Award 2009. *Current Management:* c/o Agence Artistique Jacques Thélen, 15 avenue Montaigne, 75008 Paris, France. *Telephone:* 1-56-89-32-00. *Fax:* 1-56-89-32-01. *E-mail:* jthelen@wanadoo.fr. *Website:* www.premiumwanadoo.com/jacquesthelen; www.tamestit.org.

TAMMEL, Leili; Estonian singer (mezzo-soprano); b. 29 July 1943, Saaremaa; d. of Karl Tammel and Liina Tammel (née Kärner); one s. *Education:* Leningrad (now St Petersburg) Conservatoire, Russia and with Vladimir Neroda. *Career:* soloist, Estonia Opera, Tallinn 1973–; Lecturer, Estonian Music Acad., Tallinn 1986–; soloist, Camerata Tallinn Ensemble 1986–; has toured Italy, Germany, Portugal, Hungary, Australia, etc 1989–; has played leading roles at Opéra Comique, Paris, Komische Oper Berlin, Halle Opera and Karlsruhe State Opera, Germany, Danish Royal Opera, Copenhagen, Swedish Royal Opera, Stockholm, Finnish Nat. Opera, Helsinki, Latvian Nat. Opera, Rīga, Maria Theatre, St Petersburg, Bosra Festival, Syria 1987, Savonlinna Opera Festival, Finland 1987; mem. jury various nat. and Int. singing contests 1990–; specializes in works of modern Estonian composers and has performed leading roles in operas and oratorios written for her. *Operas include:* Il Trovatore 1975, 1989, Don Carlos 1976, 1994–, Luisa Miller 1981, Carmen 1982, 1987–88, Alcina 1985, 1989, Un ballo in maschera 1985, Khovanshchina 1987, Cavalleria rusticana 1993. *Recordings include:* Recitals with Camerata Tallinn 1987, 1995, works of Kuldar Sink 1989, 1996, works of Veljo Tormis 1990; numerous film and video recordings. *Honours:* Georg Ots Vocal Prize 1987; named People's Artist of the Repub. of Estonia 1989. *Address:* Estonian Music Academy, Rävala pst 16, Tallinn 10143 (office); Estonia Theatre, Estonia pst 4, Tallinn 0105, Estonia (office). *Telephone:* (2) 6675768 (office). *Website:* www.ema.edu.ee (office).

TAMULENAS, Eva; singer (mezzo-soprano); b. 1943, Narva, Estonia. *Education:* studied in Milwaukee, USA and in Vienna. *Career:* sang first with the Royal Opera Copenhagen, at Gelsenkirchen from 1977; roles have included Hansel, Rosina, Orlofsky, Olga, Maddalena and the title role in Miss Julie by Antonio Bibalo; Einem's Der Besuch der alten Dame 1991; sang Third Lady in Die Zauberflöte at Gelsenkirchen 2000; many concert engagements.

TAMULIONIS, Jonas; Lithuanian composer; b. 10 Jan. 1949, Alytus; m. (divorced); two s. *Education:* Vilnius Pedagogical Inst., Lithuanian State Conservatoire with Prof. Eduardos Balsys. *Compositions include:* for string quartet: Two Quartets 1973, 1982, Diary 1978; for string orchestras: Concertino 1974, Toccata Diavolesca 1988, Pastoral Suite 1990, Three symphonies 1976, 1978, 1986; for wind orchestra: Festive Overture 1978, Spanish Rhapsody 1981; sonatas: for two guitars 1978, two pianos 1979, two birbynes (Lithuanian folk wind instrument) 1988; for chamber orchestra: Epitaph 1981; cantatas: I Sing of Lithuania 1981, Children's Earth (verse by J. Marcinkevicius) 1988, To My Motherland (verse by J. Mikstas) 1989, Sinfonia Rustica 1989; oratorio: Six Dedications to the Town (text by various Lithunanian poets) 1985, Reminiscence for two violins and two accordions 1989, Recollection for glass instruments 1992, Trio for flute, viola, guitar and piano 1993; vocal music: Seven Love Elegies for soprano and chamber ensemble 1982, Summer Psalms for soprano and piano (verse by J. Marcinkevicius) 1985, Three Prayers for baritone and piano (verse by B. Brazdzionis) 1989; for choir: Single Words 1980, The Tears of Ablinga 1984, Tres retratos con sombra (verse by F. García Lorca) 1992, Los Juegos 1997; for accordion: Sonatina 1978, Metamorphoses 1984, Polyphonic Pieces 1990, Ten Etudes 1995; for guitar: Eleven preludes 1982, Suite of Intervals 1987. *Recordings:* On The Coast 1990, Numerations, Patterers 1992, Ex Anima 1994, Home Psalames 1995, The Sea 1996. *Honours:* second prize Symphony No. 1, Moscow, Russia 1967, first prize Canciones de la Tierra, Spain 1995, first prize Oda al Atlántico, Spain 1997, first prize Los Juegos, Spain 1997.

TAN, Dun, MA; Chinese composer; b. 18 Aug. 1957, Si Mao, Hunan Province; s. of Tan Xiang Qiu and Fang Qun Ying; m. Jane Huang 1994. *Education:* Cen. Conservatory of Music, Beijing and Columbia Univ., USA. *Career:* violist, Beijing Opera Orchestra 1976–77; Vice-Pres. Cen. Conservatory of Music 1978–; works performed by major orchestras in China and at festivals world-wide; has conducted orchestras including Royal Concertgebouw, London Symphony, New York Philharmonic, Berlin Philharmonic, BBC Symphony and Filarmonica della Scala; four recordings of his major orchestral works, oriental instrumental music, chamber music and electronic music issued by China Nat. Recording Co.; orchestral piece commissioned by Inst. for Devt of Intercultural Relations Through the Arts, USA for Beijing Int. Music Festival 1988; Artistic Dir Fire Crossing Water Festival, Barbican Centre, London 2000; composed music for Olympic Games medal ceremonies, Beijing 2008; commissioned by Google/YouTube to compose internet Symphony Eroica; named UNESCO Goodwill Amb. 2013. *Film scores:* Aktion K 1994, Nanjing 1937 1995, Fallen 1997, In the Name of the Emperor 1998, Wo hu cang long (Crouching Tiger Hidden Dragon) (Grammy Award 2001, Acad. Award 2001, British Acad. Film Award 2001, Classical BRIT Contemporary Music Award 2001) 2000, Ying xiong (Hero) 2002. *Compositions:* orchestral works: Li Sao (symphony) 1979, Five Pieces in Human Accent for piano 1980, Feng Ya Song for string quartet 1982, Fu for two sopranos, bass and ensemble 1982, Piano Concerto 1983, Symphony in two movements 1985, On Taoism for orchestra 1985, Traces for piano 1989, Eight Colours for string quartet 1989, Silk Road for soprano and percussion 1989, Orchestral Theatre I: Xun 1990, Soundshape 1990, Silent Earth 1991, Elegy: Snow in June 1991, Jo-Ha-Kyu 1992, Death and Fire: Dialogue with Paul Klee 1992, Orchestral Theatre II: Re 1992, CAGE for piano 1993, Circle for four trios, conductor and audience 1993, The Pink 1993, Autumn Winds for instruments and conductor ad lib 1993, Memorial Nineteen for voice, piano and double paper 1993, Orchestral Theatre III: Red 1993, Yi concerto for cello 1994, Ghost Opera 1994, Marco Polo 1995, A Sinking Love 1995, Heaven, Earth, Mankind symphony for the 'Bian Zhong' bronze bells (composed in celebration of the Hong Kong handover) 1997, Concerto for Six 1997, Heaven Earth Mankind 1997, Peony Pavilion 1998, 2000 Today: A World Symphony for the Millennium: A Musical Odyssey for the Ages 1999, Water Passion after St Matthew 2000, Crouching Tiger Concerto 2000, The Map concerto for cello, video and orchestra 2003, Eight Memories in Watercolor 2003, Secret Land: for Orchestra and 12 Violoncelli 2004; opera: Out of Beijing 1987, Nine Songs 1989, Marco Polo 1994, Peony Pavilion 1998, Tea 2002, Eight Memories in Watercolor 2003, The First Emperor (opera score, libretto co-writer) 2006. *Honours:* second place, Weber Int. Chamber Music Composition Competition, Dresden 1983, Suntory Prize 1992, Grawemeyer Award 1998, Musical America Composer of the Year 2003. *Address:* 367 West 19th Street, Suite A, New York, NY 10011, USA (office). *Telephone:* (212) 627-0410 (office). *Fax:* (917) 606-0247 (office). *E-mail:* tan_dun@hotmail.com (office). *Website:* tandun.com (office).

TAN, Lihua; Chinese conductor; *Music Director and Principal Conductor, Beijing Symphony Orchestra;* b. 22 Oct. 1955, Jiangsu; m. Lumin Qiao 1980, one d. *Education:* Shanghai Conservatory of Music. *Career:* debut conducting Bruch's Violin Concerto and Dvořák Symphony No. 9, Wuhan Orchestra, Wuhan, China; Conductor, Chinese Ballet, 1990–96; Conductor, China Central Philharmonic Symphony Orchestra, 1993–; Music Dir and Principal Conductor, Beijing Symphony Orchestra; Chinese premieres include: Pines of Rome, Dvořák Symphony No. 7, Prokofiev Symphony No. 5; guest conductor of New York Youth Symphony, Seattle Federal Way Symphony, Russian National Symphony; venues include New York City's Avery Fisher Hall, Lincoln Center; Moscow's Tchaikovsky Conservatory of Music. *Recordings:* Beethoven Symphony No. 5; Brahms Symphony No. 4, with Beijing Symphony Orchestra; Dvořák Symphony Nos 8 and 9; Haydn Symphony No. 94;

Mendelssohn, Saint-Saëns and Tchaikovsky Violin Concertos, China Central Philharmonic Symphony Orchestra. *Address:* Beijing Symphony Orchestra, No. A-1 Eight Poplar, Shuang Jing, Chao-Yang District, Beijing 100022, People's Republic of China (office). *Website:* www.bjso.cn (office).

TAN, Melvyn, FRCM; British concert pianist; b. 13 Oct. 1956, Singapore; s. of the late Tan Keng Hian and Wong Sou Yuen. *Education:* Anglo-Chinese School, Yehudi Menuhin School, Royal Coll. of Music. *Career:* has been performing on concert stage since early 1980s; following graduation, performed on historical instruments, culminating in original recordings of Beethoven sonatas for EMI and a tour on Beethoven's own piano in Europe and UK; tours regularly and extensively in Europe, Australia, the Far East and USA; has performed in most major venues and music festivals worldwide; returned to Singapore after a self-imposed exile of nearly 32 years for a homecoming concert 2011, continues to visit Singapore regularly to perform and encourage young musical talent; Artist-in-Residence, Yong Siew Toh Conservatory of Music, Singapore 2012–15. *Recordings include:* Debussy Préludes 2005, Beethoven Complete Piano Concertos with London Classical Players under Sir Roger Norrington, Beethoven and Schubert piano works, Mozart Piano Concert K414, Beethoven Concerto No. 2 with London Chamber Orchestra directing from keyboard. *Television:* featured extensively on the BBC soundtrack of Pride and Prejudice with music by Carl Davis. *Current Management:* Mark Stephan Buhl Artists Management, Geylinggasse 1, 1130 Vienna, Austria. *E-mail:* dtoennesmann@gmail.com. *Website:* www.msbuhl.com; www.melvyntan.com.

TANAKA, Karen, BM; Japanese composer and academic; b. 7 April 1961, Tokyo. *Education:* Tōhō Gakuen School of Music, Tokyo, intern at IRCAM, Paris, pvt studies with Tristan Murail in Paris, Luciano Berio in Florence. *Career:* Visiting Assoc. Prof., Univ. of California, Santa Barbara; Visiting Assoc. Prof., Univ. of Mich. School of Music. *Compositions include:* Anamorphose (piano concerto) 1986, Crystalline I, II and III 1988, 1995, 2000, Initium 1993, Wave Mechanics 1994, Echo Canyon 1995, The Zoo in the Sky 1995, The Song of Songs 1996, Night Bird 1997, Frozen Horizon 1998, Children of Light 1999, Water and Stone 1999, Techno Etudes 2000, Guardian Angel 2000, Departure 2000, Lost Sanctuary 2002, Rose Absolute 2002, Urban Prayer 2004, Herb Garden 2005. *Honours:* Japan Symphony Foundation Award 1985, Gaudeamus Prize 1987, Bekku Prize 2005. *Current Management:* c/o Chester Music, 14-15 Berners Street, London, W1T 3LJ, England. *Website:* www.chesternovello.com. *Address:* Herb Alpert School of Music at CalArts, California Institute of the Arts, 24700 McBean Parkway, Valencia, CA 91355, USA (office). *Telephone:* (661) 253-7816 (office); (661) 222-2778 (office). *E-mail:* ktanaka@calarts.edu (office). *Website:* www.music.calarts.edu (office).

TANENBAUM, David; American musician (guitar) and academic; *Chair of Guitar Department, San Francisco Conservatory of Music;* b. 1956. *Education:* San Francisco Conservatory, Peabody Conservatory, studied with Rolando Valdez-Blain, Aaron Shearer and Michael Lorimer; master-class with Andres Segovia. *Career:* concert debut aged 16; has performed world-wide, first American guitarist to be invited to perform in China 1988; appeared as soloist with Los Angeles Philharmonic, San Francisco Symphony, Minnesota Orchestra, London Sinfonietta, Oakland Symphony and Vienna's ORF orchestra, with conductors including Esa-Pekka Salonen, Kent Nagano and John Adams; featured soloist at int. festivals, including Bath, Luzern, Frankfurt, Barcelona and Vienna as well as numerous guitar festivals; premiered Peter Maxwell Davies's Sonata 1984; many works written for him such as Hans Werner Henze's guitar concerto An Eine Aolsharfe, which he premiered throughout Europe and recorded with the composer conducting, four works by Aaron Jay Kernis, two pieces by Roberto Sierra and a suite by Lou Harrison; long association with Ensemble Modern; as chamber musician has collaborated with Kronos, Shanghai, Alexander and Chester String Quartets and guitarist Manuel Barrueco; mem. World Guitar Ensemble, currently Chair of Guitar Dept, San Francisco Conservatory of Music; fmrly Artist-In-Residence Manhattan School of Music. *Recordings include:* albums of music by John Adams, Ástor Piazzolla, Steve Reich, Michael Tippett and Hans Werner Henze, among others. *Publication:* The Essential Studies (three books). *Honours:* Musical America Young Artist of the Year 1983, 1989, Nat. Endowment for the Arts grant 1993, Outstanding Prof. Award, San Francisco Conservatory of Music 1995. *Current Management:* c/o Donald E. Osborne, California Artists' Management, 564 Market Street, Suite 420, San Francisco, CA 94104-5412, USA. *Telephone:* (415) 362-2787. *Fax:* (415) 362-2838. *E-mail:* don@calartists.com. *Website:* www.calartists.com. *E-mail:* scarlatti@davidtanenbaum.com. *Website:* www.davidtanenbaum.com.

TANG, Muhai, DipMus; Chinese conductor; *Chief Conductor, Belgrade Philharmonic and Artistic Director, Zhenjiang Symphony;* b. 10 July 1949, Shanghai; s. of Tang Xiaodan. *Education:* Music Conservatory at Shanghai, Music Hochschule, Munich, Germany. *Career:* conducted the Berlin Philharmonic, London Philharmonic, Orchestre de Paris, San Francisco Symphony, Montréal Symphony, Santa Cecilia Orchestra, Rome, Tonhalle Orchestra Zürich, Helsinki Philharmonic, Hallé Orchestra, Scottish Nat. Symphony Orchestra, Nat. Symphony Orchestra of Spain, Mozarteum Orchestra Salzburg, Polish Chamber Orchestra, Oper Orchestra Hamburg, Frankfurt, Munich, Bonn, Monte Carlo, Radio Symphony Orchestras of Munich, Berlin, Hamburg, and Cologne; Chief Conductor, Peking Central Philharmonic and Gulbenkian Orchestra of Lisbon 1987–2000; Chief Conductor, Finnish Nat. Opera 2003–06; Conductor Laureate and Artistic Adviser, Queensland

Orchestra 2005–; Artistic Dir and Chief Conductor, Zurich Chamber Orchestra 2006–11, Prin. Guest Conductor 2011–; Artistic Dir Shanghai Philharmonic Orchestra 2009–, Zhenjiang Symphony Orchestra 2009–; Prin. Guest Conductor Hamburg Symphony Orchestra 2009–; Chief Conductor Belgrade Philharmonic Orchestra 2010–. *Current Management:* IMG Artists, The Light Box, 111 Power Road, London, W4 5PY, England. *Telephone:* (20) 7957-5800. *Fax:* (20) 7957-5801. *E-mail:* bcanniere@imgartists.com. *Website:* www.imgartists.com.

TANGGAARD, Svend Erik; Danish composer and writer; b. 25 Jan. 1942, Copenhagen; m. Margit Bendtsen 1980; two d. *Education:* studied with Helge Bonnen in Copenhagen, studied in Munich. *Career:* debut at Royal Acad. of Fine Arts 1962; performances of own works by Danish Radio Symphony Orchestra, Ålborg Symphony Orchestra, Southern Jutland Symphony Orchestra, Odense Symphony Orchestra and Moritz Fromberg Quartet; several transmissions on Danish Radio, NDR and Swedish Radio; performances at the Art Asscn, Gronningen and other art galleries. *Compositions:* five symphonies, Concerto for orchestra, 12 String Quartets, three Fuga String Quartets op 150, Piano, Violin (two), Viola, Cello, Oboe, Flute, Trumpet and Clarinet Concertos, Overtures Nos 1 and 2 for chamber orchestra, Concertos Nos 1, 2 and 3 for 14 wind instruments, two double basses and percussion, Concerto for violin, viola and orchestra, Vox Humana for orchestra, soprano, bass and tape recorder, The Bells for orchestra and reader, Songs, three Wind Quintets, three Solo Cello Suites, two Solo Violin Sonatas, Piano Sonata, Day and Night, three Italian Prayers for mezzo-soprano and viola, three Cantatas for tenor and wind quintet, 25 Selected Songs from Omar Khayyam's Rubaiyat for basso and three instruments, songs for small ensembles, Memoria Futuris Nos II and III for string orchestra 1997, Nos IV and V for wind quintet 1998, Opus 200, String Quartet No. 16 1999.

TANGUY, Eric; French composer; b. 27 Jan. 1968, Caen. *Education:* Caen Conservatoire, Darmstadt Ferienkurse, Conservatoire Nat. Supérieur de Musique, Paris, studied with Horatiu Radulescu, Ivo Malec and Gérard Grisey. *Career:* composer-in-residence, French Acad. in Rome 1993–94, Champagne-Ardenne 1995, Lille 1996, Orchestre de Bretagne 2001–03. *Compositions include:* Avènement de la ligne 1988, Alloys 1988, Océan N.Y. Fantaisie 1989, Azur B 1990, Azur C 1990, Towards 1991, Wadi 1992, Solo 1993, Concerto pour violon 1990, Towards 1991, Concerto pour flûte et 16 instruments 1992, Célébration de Marie-Madeleine 1995, Le Jardin des délices 1996, Éclipse 1999, Concerto for cello and orchestra No. 2 2000, Chronos (opera) 2002, Ouverture 2002, Prière 2003, Sénèque, dernier jour 2004, Salve Regina 2005. *Honours:* Darmstadt Stipendienpreis 1988, Villa Medici extramural prize 1989, Paris Conservatoire first prize for composition 1991, Darmstadt Kranichstein Musikpreis 1992, Villa Medici Award 1992, Institut de France André Caplet Prize 1995, SACEM Hervé Dugardin Prize 1997, Composer of the Year, Victoires de la Musique Classique 2004, 2008. *Current Management:* Concerts de Valmalete, 7 rue Hoche, 92300 Levallois Perret, France. *Telephone:* 1-47-59-87-59. *Fax:* 1-47-59-87-50. *Website:* www.valmalete.com; www.eric-tanguy.com.

TANGUY, Jean-Michel; flautist; b. 15 Nov. 1944, France. *Education:* Lycee Français, Berlin, studied with Jean-Pierre Rampal in Nice and Paris, Aurèle Nicolet in Berlin and in Freiburg, Breisgau Staatliche Hochschule für Musik. *Career:* debut with Orchestra der Beethovenhalle, Bonn, Germany; performances with Bonn Orchestra, Rotterdam Philharmonic, Orchestre National Belgique, Brussels; Chargé de Cours Conservatoire Royal de Bruxelles; Prof. of Flute, Hochschule für Musik, Heidelberg-Mannheim 1992–; jury mem. Int. Jean-Pierre Rampal Flute Competition 1994, 1998; guest mem. Nat. Flute Convention, Chicago 1986, Atlanta 1999; masterclasses in Belgium, France, Italy, Germany, Austria, Republic of Korea. *Recordings:* Telemann Flute Concertos, Heidelberger Chamber Orchestra, J.S. Bach Trios, C.P.E. Bach–Sonatas, J.S. Bach–Flute Sonatas, Sommermusik with Belgian Windquintett. *Honours:* prizewinner Int. Music Competition, Geneva 1973, DAAD scholarship.

TANYEL, Seta; pianist; b. 1950, Istanbul, Turkey. *Education:* Vienna Hochschule for Musik with Dieter Weber, studied with Louis Kentner in London. *Career:* orchestral and recital debuts in New York, Philadelphia, Detroit and London 1978; extensive touring in Europe, the Middle East, Russia and the USA, performing with such orchestras as the Vienna Symphony, Israel Philharmonic, Stuttgart Philharmonic, the Philharmonia and London Symphony Orchestra; taught at Yehudi Menuhin School in London 1986–89; faculty mem., Adamant Music School 2004–; pianist of both standard and lesser-known Romantic piano repertoire; performances include the revival in the piano music of Xaver Scharwenka. *Recordings include:* Shostakovich, Khachaturian, Poulenc and Bax 2-piano works, Brahms and Beethoven solo recital, Grieg and Schumann Piano Concertos with London Symphony Orchestra, Brahms Piano Concerto No. 1 with the Philharmonia, Scharwenka Piano Concerto No. 1 and Chopin Piano Concerto No. 1, with the Philharmonia/Rizzi, Chopin, Sharwenka and Moszkowski solo recitals, Scharwenka chamber works with piano, Stenhammar Piano Concertos. *Honours:* prizewinner Int. Beethoven Competition, Vienna 1973, Arthur Rubinstein Piano Master Competition, Israel 1974, Queen Elisabeth of Belgium Competition 1975. *Address:* Adamant Music School, PO Box 22, Adamant, VT 05640, USA (office). *Telephone:* (802) 229-9297 (office). *E-mail:* queries@adamant.org (office). *Website:* www.adamant.org (office).

TAPPY, Eric; singer (tenor); b. 19 May 1931, Lausanne, Switzerland. *Education:* studied with Fernando Carpi in Geneva, Ernst Reichert in Salzburg and Eva Liebenberg in Hilversum. *Career:* debut in Strasbourg 1959, as the Evangelist in Bach's St Matthew Passion; concert performances of Milhaud's Les Malheurs d'Orphée and Martin's Le Mystère de la Nativité and Monsieur de Pourceaugnac; sang in the premiere of Klaus Huber's Soliloquia 1962; stage debut at Opéra-Comique Paris 1964, as Rameau's Zoroastre; sang at Herrenhausen 1966, as Monteverdi's Orfeo, Geneva Opera 1966, in the premiere of Milhaud's La Mère Coupable, and Hanover 1967, in L'Incoronazione di Poppea; Covent Garden debut 1974, in the title role of La Clemenza di Tito; US debut 1974, as Don Ottavio at San Francisco, returning in Poppea and as Idomeneo 1977–78; sang at Rome Opera 1980 as Titus; appearances in Chicago, Drottningholm, Aix-en-Provence, Salzburg as Tamino, Amsterdam, Lyon, Brussels and Lisbon; other roles include Schoenberg's Aron, Pelléas, Lysander in A Midsummer Night's Dream, Don Ramiro, Lensky and Stravinsky's Oedipus; concert repertoire includes music by Handel, Haydn, Campra, Carissimi, Vivaldi, Bach, Berlioz and Schütz; retired 1982. *Recordings include:* Monteverdi's Orfeo and Poppea; Zoroastre; Pelléas et Mélisande; Die Jahreszeiten by Haydn; Die Zauberflöte; La Clemenza di Tito.

ŢĂRANU, Cornel, DMus; Romanian composer and conductor; b. 20 June 1934, Cluj; s. of Francisc Ţăranu and Elisabeta Ţăranu; m. Daniela Mărgineanu 1960; one d. *Education:* Gheorghe Dima Acad. of Music, studied with Sigismund Toduta, Paris Conservatoire, studied with Nadia Boulanger and Olivier Messiaen, also studied with György Ligeti, Bruno Maderna and Christoph Caskel. *Career:* joined Faculty, Gheorghe Dima Acad. of Music, Cluj-Napoca 1957, Asst Prof. 1970–90, Prof. of Composition 1990–; Founder and Conductor of Ars Nova, contemporary music ensemble; Vice-Pres. Romanian Composers' Union 1990–; Artistic Dir Modern Festival Cluj 1995–; mem. Romanian Acad. 1993–. *Works include:* Sonatas for flute, oboe, clarinet and percussion, Sonata for double bass solo, viola sonata, one piano concerto, cantatas, four symphonies, Séquences, Incantations, Symmétries, Alternances, Raccords for orchestra, two Sinfoniettas for strings, Garlands for chamber orchestra, Don Giovanni's Secret for chamber opera, Chansons nomades (oratorio), Chansons sans amour (lieder), Sempre Ostinato for saxophone and ensemble, Chansons sans réponse, Hommage à Paul Célan, Memento and Dedications (cantatas), Miroirs for saxophone and orchestra, Prolégomènes for chamber orchestra, Orpheus (cantata), Tombeau de Verlaine for mixed choir, Mosaïques for saxophone and ensemble, Testament for choir 1988, Chansons interrompues for voice and ensemble 1993, Cadenze Concertante for cello and chamber orchestra 1993, Trajectoires for ensemble 1994, Crisalide for saxophone, tape and ensemble, Five Tzara Songs for voice and piano, Remembering Bartók for oboe and ensemble, Enescu's 'Caprice Roumain' for violin and orchestra (new arrangement) 1995, Responsorial for clarinet 1996, Antiphona for flute and orchestra 1996, Flaine Quintette for winds 1997, Laudatio per Clusium for voice and instruments 1997, Saturnalii for baritone and ensemble 1998, Three Labiş Poems for bass and piano 1998, Cadenze per Antiphona for flute and solo 1998, Siciliana Blues for piano and chamber orchestra 1998, Concerto for oboe and strings 1998, Oreste-Oedipe (chamber opera) 1999–2001, Concerto Breve for flute orchestra 2001, Modra Rijeka for choir 2002, Shakespeare Sonnets for voice and ensemble 2003, Baroccoco for baroque ensemble 2004, Rimembranza for orchestra 2004, Sinfonia da Requiem for choir and orchestra 2005, Sax-Sympho for saxophone and orchestra 2006, Madrigals (verse by Blaga, Vinea, Attila, Ady); also film and theatre music. *Publications include:* Enesco dans la conscience du présent 1981. *Honours:* Chevalier, Ordre des Arts et des Lettres 2002, Great Officer, Order of Cultural Merit 2004; Prize of the Romanian Composers' Union 1972, 1978, 1981, 1982, 2001, Grand Prize 2005, Prize of the Romanian Acad. 1973, Koussevitsky Prize 1982. *Address:* Str. Nicolae Iorga 7, 400063 Cluj-Napoca, Romania (home). *Telephone:* (264) 593879 (office); (264) 443283 (home). *Fax:* (264) 593879 (office). *E-mail:* corneltaranu@yahoo.com (office). *Website:* www.corneltaranu.com.

TARARA, Stefan; German violinist; b. 2 May 1986, Heidelberg; s. of Viorel Tarara and Lavinia Tarara. *Education:* studied at Univ. of Music and Performing Arts, Mannheim with Zakhar Bron. *Career:* stage debut aged four; has performed at numerous int. festivals, including Salzburg Festival 2005, Int. Next Generation II, Dilsberg Festival, Heidelberg Spring Music Festival, EXPO 2000, Hanover, European Youth Festival of the Arts, Paris. *Honours:* First Prize, Ètienne Vatelot Violin Competition, Paris 1997, Valsesia Musica Violin Competition 2006, H. Wieniawski and K. Lipiński Violin Competitions 2006, First Prize and Special Prize for best interpretation of a virtuoso work, Henri Marteau Int. Violin Competition 2005, First Prize, 30th Rodolfo Lipizer Int. Violin Competition 2011. *Address:* Bauamtsgasse 12, 69117 Heidelberg, Germany (office). *Telephone:* (6221) 162362 (office). *Fax:* (6221) 164508 (office). *E-mail:* info@stefan-tarara.com (office). *Website:* www.stefan-tarara.com (office).

TARASCHENKO, Vitalij; singer (tenor); b. 1953, Kyrgyzstan. *Career:* sang in opera at Moscow and Warsaw; Florence, 1990, as Prince Vsevolod in Rimsky's Kitezh; Dimitri in Boris Godunov at Bologna; Bregenz Festival, 1993, as Andrei in Mazeppa and Ismaele in Nabucco; season 1993–94 as Calaf at Hamburg and Amsterdam, Turiddu at the Vienna Staatsoper and Hermann in The Queen of Spades at the Paris Opéra Bastille; Venice and Zürich, 1995, as Andrei and Lensky in Eugene Onegin; mem., Bolshoi Opera, Moscow from 1992; other roles include Vladimir in Prince Igor, Gabriele Adorno in Simon Boccanegra, and Cavoradossi; season 1997–98 as Prince Guidon in Rimsky's Tsar Saltan, at Florence, and Paolo in Rachmaninov's Francesca da Rimini, at St Petersburg; sang Dimitri in Boris Godunov with the Bolshoi Company in London, 1999; season 1999–2000 as Ugo in Mascagni's Parisina, at Montpellier, and Tchaikovsky's Herman for WNO.

TARASSOVA, Marianna; singer (mezzo-soprano); b. 1962, St Petersburg, Russia. *Education:* St Petersburg Conservatoire, masterclasses at Aldeburgh. *Career:* appearances with the Kirov Opera from 1993, as Carmen, Amneris, Cherubino, Olga in Eugene Onegin, Purcell's Dido, Konchakovna in Prince Igor and Blanche in The Gambler by Prokofiev; other roles include Lyubava in Sadko and Young Boy in The Invisible City of Kitezh, both by Rimsky-Korsakov, Polina in The Queen of Spades, Marfa (Khovanshchina) and Clara in Prokofiev's Betrothal in a Monastery; concert repertory includes Mahler Symphony No. 3, the Verdi Requiem and songs by Shostakovich for mezzo and orchestra; recitals and concerts in the USA, and worldwide tours with the Kirov Opera, including summer season at the Royal Opera, Covent Garden 2000.

TARBUK, Mladen, DipMus; Croatian composer and conductor; *Principal Conductor, Symphonic Orchestra of Croatian Radio and Television*; b. 19 July 1962, Sarajevo; s. of Milan Vukomanović and Olga Vukomanović; m. Jasna Cizmek 1994; three s. *Education:* Music Acad., Zagreb, Hochschule für Musik und darstellende Kunst, Graz, Hochschule für Musik und darstellende Kunst, Vienna. *Career:* conductor, Das Rheingold, Tosca, Elektra, Così fan tutte, Zagreb 1991, Udo Zimmermann's White Rose, Maribor 1991; world premiere of Schwertsik's Café Museum, Deutschlandsberg, Tannhäuser, Così fan tutte, Prague 1993, Zrinski, Zagreb 1994–2000, Julius Caesar, Zagreb 1999, Carmen, Skopje 2003, Marriage of Figaro, Sarajevo 2003, Simone Boccanegra, Zagreb 2003, Lady Macbeth of Mtensk, Zagreb 2004, Andre Chenier, Jesi 2004, Madama Butterfly, Opera Lyra Ottawa 2004, Swan Lake, Lecce 2004, Macbeth, Cavalleria and Pagliacci, La Wally, Abduction from Serail, German Opera at Rhine, Düsseldorf 2004–06, Tristan und Isolde, Zagreb 2005; Lecturer, Zagreb Music Acad. 1989, Sr Lecturer 1997, Asst Prof. of Music Theory 1997, Assoc. Prof. 2005–; Chief Conductor Symphonic Wind Orchestra, Croatian Mil. Forces 1992–99; Prin. Conductor Symphonic Orchestra of Croatian Radio and TV 1999–; Gen. Dir Croatian Nat. Theatre Zagreb 2002–05; concerts with Orquesta Sinfonica del Estado Mexico, ICO Venezia-Giulia-Friuli, Zagreb Philharmonic Orchestra, ICO Tito Schipa 2003, Orquesta Sinfonica Extremadura, Orchestra da Camera Firenze, Belgrade Philharmonic Orchestra, Heidelberger Philharmoniker 2004, Hungarian Symphony Orchestra Budapest 2006; composer, selected performances and recorded works: world premiere of Martyre d'un jongleur, Gaudeamus Amsterdam 1990, world premiere of Medida del tiempo, Konzerthaus Vienna 1991; recording of A Tre for ORF, 1993, recording of Zildjian Concerto for HoneyRock 1994, selected for performance, World Music Days, Manchester 1998, Osor Suite at the concert of composers from Alpe-Adria region, Moscow Autumn festival 1996, Unserious Variations at Europamusicale Munich, 1998, authorial CD with Dreamers and Flute Concerto on it 2002, opening night of World Music Days, Zagreb 2005 with world premiere of ballet, A Streetcar Named Desire. *Compositions include:* 4 strophes for string quartet 1988, Transfigurations for wind quintet 1989, Medida del Tiempo for soprano, marimba and strings 1990, A tre for string trio 1990, Ancient Croatian Music for orchestra 1991, Discusiones amorosas for choir 1993, An die Gleichgeschaltenen for mezzosoprano and chamber ensemble 1994, Zildjian Concerto for percussion and winds 1995, Concertino for alto saxophone and winds, Concerto grosso for trumpet, french horn, trombone and strings 1997, Concerto for saxophone quartet, strings and percussion 2001, Dreamers song cycle for soprano and chamber ensemble 2002, Concerto for flute and orchestra 2002, L'irreparable for chamber ensemble 2004, A Streetcar Named Desire (ballet) 2005, Prelude, Aria And Fugue for 15 strings 2005, D for symphonic wind band 2006. *Radio:* recording of over 12 hours of symphonic music by Croatian composers, Haydn's Symphony No. 56, Schreker, Kammersinfonie. *Television:* numerous concerts with Orchestra of Croatian Radio and Television. *Recordings:* Zildjian Concerto, Sticks&Strings&Winds, recorded by Honey & Rock; Croatian Masses. *Film:* music for A Lottery Chase. *Publications:* articles in magazine WAM. *Honours:* Order of Croatian Morning Star with Shape of Marko Marulić; Special Award for Best Interpretation of Janaček's Sinfonietta, Smetana-Dvořak-Janaček Int. Conductors Competition, Olomouc 1992, Dr Ernst Vogel Prize, Stockerau 1993, First Prize, Int. Competition for Choral Competition, Tolosa 1993, Šulek Prize 1993, Porin Prize 1998, 2001, Slavenski Prize 2002, Lisinski Prize 2006, Papandopulo Prize 2006. *Telephone:* 26116545. *Fax:* 26116567. *E-mail:* luizclaudiodasilva@hotmail.com. *Address:* Bleiweisova 18, 10000 Zagreb (office); Katicev Prilaz 7, 10010 Zagreb, Croatia (home). *Telephone:* 16685863 (home). *Fax:* 16685863 (home). *E-mail:* mtarbuk@xnet.hr (home). *Website:* www.pricerubin.com/classical/conductors/index.php (office).

TARLING, Judith, BA (Hons), MA; British violinist and violist; b. 1947, Brighton, Sussex, England. *Education:* Royal Acad. of Music, Royal Coll. of Music and Birkbeck Coll., London. *Career:* mem. and leader of the Parley of Instruments 1981–; frequent tours of the UK and abroad, including the British Early Music Network; performances in Spain, France, Germany, Sweden, Netherlands, Poland, Czechoslovakia, USA and Colombia; US debut in New York 1988; many concerts with first modern performances of early music in new edns by Peter Holman; numerous broadcasts on BBC Radio 3 and elsewhere; English Eighteenth-Century Music, such as Dr Arne at

Vauxhall Gardens, William Boyce's Solomon, and John Stanley Six Concertos in seven parts, Op. 2, these works performed with Crispian Steele-Perkins on trumpet and Emma Kirkby as soprano, among others; Prin. Viola, Brandenburg Consort, with recordings including Bach Brandenburg Concertos and Suites; Handel arias, flute concertos by Quantz and C.P.E. Bach; Prin. Viola, Hanover Band 1981–2002, with numerous recordings including complete symphonies of Beethoven, Schubert and Haydn; also Leader, Essex Baroque Orchestra, Leeds Baroque Orchestra, The Consort of Twelve; repertoire includes Renaissance Violin Consort Music, such as Music by Michael Praetorius, Peter Philips, music for Charles I by Orlando Gibbons and Thomas Lupo, Baroque Consort Music by Monteverdi and Matthew Locke anthems, motets and ceremonial music, Purcell Ayres for Theatre, Georg Muffat's Armonico Tributo sonatas of 1682, Heinrich Biber's Sonate tam Aris, Quam Aulis Servientes of 1676, Vivaldi sonatas and concertos for lute and mandolin, concertos for recorders, and J.S. Bach's Hunt Cantata, No. 208, Italian and German sacred music with Robin Blaze; various public lectures on the subject of rhetorical performance of music 2008–; teaching and lecture tours of USA 2010, 2012, visiting Juilliard School, New York, Longy School of Music, Jacobs School of Music, Univ. of Indiana, Yale, Harvard, Boston Univs and Oberlin Coll., Cleveland, Ohio; visits to São Paulo, Brazil to speak at rhetoric conf. and give performances with students 2012–13; keynote speaker, Tel-Aviv Conservatory of Music at Int. Seminar and Conf. 'Training Early Musicians in the Age of Recordings' 2013. *Publications:* Baroque String Playing for ingenious learners 2000, The Weapons of Rhetoric: A Guide for Musicians and Audiences 2004, Speaking with Quintilian 2009, Handel's Messiah: A Rhetorical Guide 2013. *Honours:* Hon. ARAM . *Address:* 3 North Street, Punnetts Town, Heathfield, East Sussex, TN21 9DT, England. *E-mail:* judytarling@btinternet.com. *Website:* www.judytarling.com.

TARR, Edward Hankins, DPhil; American musician (trumpet) and musicologist; b. 15 June 1936, Norwich, Conn.; s. of Donald B. Tarr and Ruth Wilkinson Tarr; m. 2nd Irmtraud Tarr; two c. *Education:* Univ. of Hamburg, studied trumpet with Roger Voisin in Boston, Adolph Herseth in Chicago, musicology with Leo Schrade in Basle. *Career:* Founder, Edward Tarr Brass Ensemble 1969, numerous performances of Renaissance, Baroque and contemporary music in Europe and USA; early repertoire includes trumpet works of Torelli; modern repertoire includes works by Kagel, Stockhausen and Krol; has collaborated on reconstruction of early instruments with German firm Meinl and Lauber and Swiss firm Adolf Egger and Son; trumpet teacher, Rheinische Musikschule Cologne 1968–70; cornett and natural trumpet teacher, Schola Cantorum Basiliensis 1972–2001; trumpet teacher, Basle Conservatory 1974–2001; apptd Baroque trumpet teacher, Musikhochschule Karlsruhe 2001, Prof. 2003–13; Baroque trumpet teacher, Musikhochschule Lucerne 2002–05; brass ensemble teacher, Musikhochschule Frankfurt am Main 2003–07; Dir Trumpet Museum, Bad Säckingen, Germany 1985–2003. *Publications include:* Die Trompete 1977, East Meets West 2003, Articulation in Early Wind Music (co-author with Bruce Dickey) 2007; over 70 articles to The New Grove 1980 and 2001 edns, contribs to performing edns of Baroque, Classical and Romantic Music; numerous articles in professional journals. *Honours:* Hon. DrMus (Oberlin Coll.) 2003; European Soloist Prize, European Foundation for Culture 2013. *Website:* www.tarr-online.de.

TARRÉS, Enriqueta; singer (soprano); b. 18 March 1934, Barcelona, Spain. *Education:* Barcelona Conservatory with Concepción Callao de Sanchez Parra. *Career:* debut in Valencia 1956, as the Trovatore Leonora; sang in Spain, notably at the Teatro Liceo, Barcelona, Basle and Wuppertal Opera 1960–64, Glyndebourne 1962, 1964, as Ariadne and Elettra in Idomeneo, and Hamburg Staatsoper from 1964, visiting Sadler's Wells 1966 as the Empress in the first British performance of Die Frau ohne Schatten by Strauss; engaged with Düsseldorf, Cologne and Stuttgart Operas; sang at Metropolitan Opera 1973 as Mimi, Lausanne 1983 as the Marschallin, Verona 1984 as Carmen, and sang the Mother in Luis de Pablo's El Viajero Indiscreto at the Teatro de la Zarzuela, Madrid 1990; frequent concert appearances. *Recordings:* Falla's Atlantida, Orff's Trionfi, Les Huguenots, Idomeneo. *Address:* c/o Arena di Verona, Piazza Brà 28, 37121 Verona, Italy.

TARUSKIN, Richard Filler, PhD; American musicologist, critic and writer; *Professor of Musicology, University of California, Berkeley*; b. 2 April 1945, New York. *Education:* Columbia Univ. *Career:* Asst Prof., Columbia Univ. 1975–81, Assoc. Prof. of Music 1981–87; Visiting Prof., Univ. of Pennsylvania 1985; Assoc. Prof., Univ. of California, Berkeley 1986–89, Prof. 1989–; Hanes-Willis Visiting Prof., Univ. of North Carolina at Chapel Hill 1987; music critic for Opus, New York Times; Fulbright-Hays Traveling Fellowship 1971–72; Guggenheim Fellowship 1987; mem. American Musicological Soc. *Publications include:* Opera and Drama in Russia 1981, Antoine Busnois: The Latin-Texted Works (ed., two vols) 1990, Musorgsky: Eight Essays and an Epilogue 1993, Stravinsky and the Russian Traditions: A Biography of the Works Through Mavra (two vols) 1995, Text and Act: Essays on Music and Performance 1995, The Oxford History of Western Music (six vols) 2005, The Danger of Music and Other Anti-Utopian Essays 2009, On Russian Music 2009; contributed articles on Russian composers and operas in New Grove Dictionary of Opera (four vols) 1992; many articles and reviews in professional journals and general periodicals. *Honours:* Dent Medal, England 1987, ASCAP Deems Taylor Award 1989. *Address:* Department of Music, University of California, 216 Morrison Hall, Berkeley, CA 94720-1200, USA (office). *Telephone:* (510) 642-6185 (office). *Fax:* (510) 642-8480 (office). *E-mail:* taruskin@berkeley.edu (office). *Website:* ls.berkeley.edu/dept/music/Taruskin.html (office).

TARVER, Kenneth; singer (tenor); b. 1965, Detroit, USA. *Education:* Oberlin Coll. Conservatory and Yale Univ. School of Music. *Career:* Stuttgart Staatsoper 1994–97, as Tamino, Ferrando, Almaviva and Lindoro; Tamino in Don Giovanni at Aix-en-Provence, Milan, Stockholm and Tokyo 1998; season 2000–01 at Covent Garden, London, as Fenton in Falstaff and Roderigo in Otello by Rossini; further appearances at the Deutsche Oper and State Opera, Berlin, and the New York City Opera; concerts include Bach's St Matthew Passion, conducted by Chailly and Berlioz series in London, conducted by Colin Davis 2000; Roméo et Juliette, Béatrice et Bénédict and Les Troyens; London Proms 2002. *Recording:* Falstaff (DVD, at Covent Garden) 2000. *Honours:* winner Metropolitan Opera Nat. Competition. *Address:* Guy Barzilay Artists, 360 West 28th Street #6B, New York, NY 10001, USA (office). *Telephone:* (212) 741-6118 (office). *Fax:* (212) 741-2558 (office). *E-mail:* guybar@aol.com (office). *Website:* www.guybarzilayartists.com (office).

TASKOVA, Slavka; singer (soprano); b. 16 Nov. 1940, Sofia, Bulgaria. *Education:* Accademia di Santa Cecilia with Gina Cigne, studied in Milan with Lina Pagliughi. *Career:* debut, Milan 1966 as Rosina in Il Barbiere di Siviglia; has sung in Venice, Bologna, Berlin, Munich, Paris, Vienna, Sofia, Warsaw and Zagreb; sang at Schwetzingen Festival 1971, in the premiere of Reimann's Melusine, Teatro Lirico Milan 1975, in the premiere of Nono's Al Gran Sole Carico d'Amore, and Genoa 1983 as Violetta. *Recordings include:* Anacréon by Cherubini. *Address:* c/o Teatro Carlo Felice, 16100 Genoa, Italy.

TATE, Jeffrey Philip, CBE, MA, MB, BChir; British conductor and physician; b. 28 April 1943, Salisbury, Wilts.; s. of Cyril H. Tate and Ivy Ellen Naylor (née Evans). *Education:* Farnham Grammar School, Christ's Coll., Cambridge and St Thomas's Hosp. London. *Career:* trained as medical doctor 1961–67; joined London Opera Centre 1969; joined staff of Royal Opera House, Covent Garden 1970; made recordings as harpsichordist 1973–77; Asst to Pierre Boulez for The Ring, Bayreuth 1976–81; Asst to Sir John Pritchard, Cologne Opera 1977; conducted Gothenburg Opera, Sweden 1978–80; Metropolitan Opera début 1979; Covent Garden debut 1982; Chief Guest Conductor, Geneva Opera 1983–95; Prin. Conductor, English Chamber Orchestra 1985–, Royal Opera House, Covent Garden 1986–91; Prin. Guest Conductor, Royal Opera House, Covent Garden 1991–94, Orchestre Nat. de France 1989–98; Chief Conductor and Artistic Dir Rotterdam Philharmonic Orchestra 1991–94; Chief Conductor Minnesota Orchestra Summer Festival 1997–; Prin. Guest Conductor Teatro La Fenice 1999; Musical Dir Teatro di San Carlo, Naples 2005–12; Prin. Conductor, Hamburger Symphoniker 2008–; appears with maj. orchestras in Europe and America; numerous recordings with English Chamber orchestra; Pres. Asscn for Spina Bifida and Hydrocephalus 1989–, Music Space Trust 1991–. *Honours:* Hon. DMus (Leicester) 1993; Hon. Fellow, Christ's Coll., Cambridge, St Thomas's and Guy's Hosp. Medical School; Grand Prix du Disque (for complete recording of opera Lulu) 1995, Premio della Critica Musicale 'Franco Abbiati' Spettacolo prize (for Königskinder, with Paul Curran) 2003; Officier, Ordre des Arts et des Lettres 1995, Chevalier, Légion d'honneur 1999.

TATTERMUSCHOVA, Helena; singer (soprano); b. 28 Jan. 1933, Prague, Czechoslovakia. *Education:* Prague Conservatory with Vlasta Linhartova. *Career:* debut in Ostrava 1955 as Musetta; National Theatre Prague from 1959; visited Edinburgh with the company 1964, 1970 in the British premieres of Janáček's From The House Of The Dead and The Excursions of Mr Brouček; guest appearances at opera houses in Barcelona, Brussels, Amsterdam, Warsaw, Naples, Venice and Sofia; repertoire includes works by Janáček, Smetana, Mozart, Puccini and Strauss; also sang in concert. *Recordings:* Orfeo ed Euridice; Trionfi by Orff; The Makropulos Case; From the House of the Dead; Glagolitic Mass; The Cunning Little Vixen.

TATUM, Nancy; American singer (soprano); b. 25 Aug. 1934, Memphis, TN; m. Wiley Tatum. *Education:* studied with Zelma Lee Thomas in Memphis, Samuel Margolis and Wiley Tatum in New York. *Career:* debut, Saarbrucken 1962 as Santuzza; has sung in Paris, Geneva, Lyon, Minneapolis, Vancouver and Sofia; mem., Deutsche Oper am Rhein, Düsseldorf from 1964, and Metropolitan Opera from 1973; further appearances in Budapest, Bucharest, Zagreb, Brussels and Amsterdam; repertoire includes major roles in operas by Wagner and Verdi.

TAUB, Robert David, AB, MMus, DMA; American concert pianist; b. 25 Dec. 1955, New York, NY; m. Tracy Elizabeth Milner 1983. *Education:* Princeton Univ., Juilliard School. *Career:* concert pianist performing throughout the USA, Europe, Asia and Latin America with orchestras including the MET Opera Orchestra, Boston Symphony Orchestra, LA Philharmonic, BBC Philharmonic, Philadelphia Orchestra; Concerto and solo repertoire covering the Baroque to contemporary music; numerous works composed for him by Milton Babbitt, Mel Powell, Jonathan Dawe, David Bessell, Ludger Brummer and others; performances broadcast live on nat. radio including BBC, RTE, NPR. *Recordings:* Beethoven, Complete Piano Sonatas; Scriabin, Complete Piano Sonatas; Milton Babbitt, Piano Works, Three Compositions; Schumann, Davidsbündlertänze and two Lizst transcriptions; Mel Powell, Duplicates: Concerto for 2 Pianos, 1990; Persichetti, Piano Concerto; Sessions, Piano Concerto; Bartók, Sonata; Shifrin, Responses; Kirchner, Sonata. *Television:* featured in US nat. TV special The Big Idea. *Publications:* Playing the Beethoven Piano Sonatas; contrib. to many music journals. *Current Management:* California Artists Management, 41 Sutter Street, Suite 420, San

Francisco, CA 94104-4903, USA. *Telephone:* (415) 362-2787. *E-mail:* don@ calartists.com. *Website:* www.calartists.com.

TAUTU, Cornelia; Romanian composer; b. 10 March 1938, Odorhei; m. Valentin Curocichin 1976, one d. *Education:* Ciprian Porumbescu Conservatory, Bucharest, Long Island Univ., NY, USA. *Compositions:* symphonic: Counterpoint for string orchestra, Segments for string orchestra, Inventions for piano and orchestra, Dice symphonic sketch, Palingenesia–Poem for 1907 for orchestra, Engravings for orchestra, sinfonietta, Symphony No. 1 1907, 1987, Concerto for piano and orchestra 1989; chamber: Concerto for 12 instruments, Inventions for piano, Collage for string quartet, Carol Echoes quintet for flute, oboe, clarinet, bassoon and horn, Homage for Peace for string quintet, Sonata, Trio for flute, piano and harp, eight progressive pieces for piano 1988, Three Lieder (rhymes by M. Eminescu); choral: Triptych 1991, Dixatuor for ensemble and percussion 1993, Inventions No.2 for piano and orchestra 1996, Palingenesia septet 1996. *Composition for film:* Tragic Holiday. *Composition for stage:* Prometheus (Aeschylus), La Locandiera (Goldoni), Medees (Seneca), Cherry Orchard (Chekhov). *Address:* c/o UCMR-ADA, Cala Victoriei 141, 71102 Bucharest, Romania.

TAVENER, Alan, BA, MA, ARCO/ARCM; British conductor, organist and manager; b. 22 April 1957, Weston-Super-Mare, Avon, England; m. Rebecca Jane Gibson 1980. *Education:* organ scholar Brasenose Coll., Oxford. *Career:* Dir of Music, Univ. of Strathclyde 1980–; founder Dir, Cappella Nova 1982–; conducted several world premieres of new choral works, including John Tavener's Resurrection, Glasgow 1990 and James MacMillan's Seven Last Words, Glasgow 1994. *Recordings:* Robert Carver, the Complete Sacred Choral Music 1990, Scottish Medieval Plainchant, Columba, most Holy of Saints 1992, Twentieth Century Scottish Choral Music 1992, Sacred Music for Mary Queen of Scots 1993, Sacred Music of Robert Johnson 1996, Scottish Medieval Plainchant, The Ceremonies of St Kentigern 1997, Now Let Us Sing: A Scottish Christmas 1998, The Thistle and the Rose 2003, Tenebrae: Sacred Music of James MacMillan 2007. *Address:* Director of Music, University of Strathclyde, Livingstone Tower, Richmond Street, Glasgow, G1 1XH, Scotland (office). *Website:* www.strath.ac.uk/music (office); www.cappella-nova .com (office).

TAYLOR, Ann; British singer (mezzo-soprano); b. 1966, Wrexham, North Wales. *Education:* Royal Northern College of Music, Guildhall School and the National Opera Studio. *Career:* appearances with Opera North as Ramiro in La Finta Giardiniera, Feodor in Boris Godunov (also at the London Proms), Cherubino, and Donna Clara in the British premiere of Gerhard's The Duenna; Dorabella, Ramiro, Phoebe in Yeomen of the Guard and Handel's Ariodante for Welsh National Opera; Kristina in The Makropulos Case and Oreste in La Belle Hélène for Scottish Opera, Rosina and Mozart's Annius for Glyndebourne Touring Opera; Premiere of Berkeley's Baa Baa Black Sheep at the 1993 Cheltenham Festival; Schumann's Manfred at Monnaie, Brussels, and Cherubino for the Bavarian State Opera; Concerts include Chabrier's La Sulamite at the Queen Elizabeth Hall, Schumann's Scenes from Faust at the 1994 Edinburgh Festival, Les Nuits d'Eté, and Nancy in Albert Herring under Steuart Bedford; Season 1997 with Hänsel for Opera Zuid, and Glyndebourne Festival debut, as Kate in Owen Wingrave; Sang the Stewardess in the premiere of Jonathan Dove's Flight for GTO at Glyndebourne, and also GFO (television) 1998 and Rosina in the Barber of Seville for Opera North; Pippo in The Thieving Magpie and Varvara in Katya Kabanova with Opera North, 1999, and Sarah in Tobias and the Angel for Almeida Opera; Concert, Les Noces, Stravinsky Ensemble Modern, Barbican. *Recordings include:* The Duenna; Baa Baa Black Sheep; Albert Herring; Flight by Jonathan Dove; Messiah, with Hallé Orchestra. *Current Management:* Ingpen & Williams Ltd, 7 St George's Court, 131 Putney Bridge Road, London, SW15 2PA, England.

TAYLOR, Daniel; Canadian singer (countertenor); b. 1969. *Education:* McGill Univ., Univ. of Montréal. *Career:* concerts with Tafelmusik, Netherlands Radio Chamber Orchestra, Dallas Symphony Orchestra, Portland Baroque, Winnipeg and Quebec Symphonies, Kammerchor Stuttgart and American Bach Soloists; repertoire includes Messiah (at Göttingen), St Matthew Passion (Berkeley), King Arthur (with Les Violons du Roi), and Rodelinda; sang Bertarido in Rodelinda at Broomhill and Halle 1996, Tolomeo in Giulio Cesare at Rome 1998, Handel's Israel in Egypt at the London Proms 2002; founder and Artistic Dir, Theatre of Early Music. *Recordings include:* over 60 albums including Jommelli, La Didone Abandonata, and Zelenka Missa Omnium Sanctorum, The Voice of Bach.

TAYLOR, Hilary; singer (soprano); b. 1970, Melbourne, Australia. *Education:* Melbourne Conservatorium, Victorian Coll. of Arts, Nat. Opera Studio, London. *Career:* appearances with Victorian State Opera, Australian Opera, Glyndebourne and Salzburg Festivals, and Raymond Gubbay productions; concerts with Tasmanian and Melbourne Symphonies and BBI Classic Café recitals from the Floral Hall, Covent Garden; Royal Opera engagements in Der Rosenkavalier, The Greek Passion by Martinů, Turandot and Die Entführung. *Honours:* Opera Foundation Australia Shell Covent Garden Scholarship 1996. *Address:* Royal Opera House (chorus), Covent Garden, London, WC2, England.

TAYLOR, James; American singer (tenor); *Associate Professor of Voice, Institute of Sacred Music, Yale University;* b. 1966, Dallas, TX. *Education:* Texas Christian Univ., Munich Hochschule with Adalbert Kraus. *Career:* debut as Tony in West Side Story, with the Fort Worth Symphony Orchestra 1990; Prof. of Voice, Musikhochschule, Augsburg, Germany 2001–05; Assoc.

Prof. of Voice, Inst. of Sacred Music, School of Music, Yale Univ. 2005–; opera appearances include Monteverdi's Ulisse, Der Fliegende Holländer, the Grand Priest in Idomeneo; concerts include Bach's St Matthew Passion in Munich, the St John Passion, Cantatas, B Minor Mass, Christmas Oratorio; Beethoven's Missa Solemnis; Mendelssohn's Elijah; Mozart's Requiem, Mass in C Minor; Haydn's Stabat Mater, The Creation, Orlando Paladino; Berlioz's Requiem; Mendelssohn's Paulus; Britten's War Requiem, Serenade for Tenor and Horn; Handel's Messiah, Schmidt's The Book of the Seven Seals. *Recordings include:* Orff's Catulli Carmina, Bach's Magnificat and Mass in A (with Helmuth Rilling), Missa solemnis and Mendelssohn's St Paul (Herreweghe). *Address:* Institute of Sacred Music, Yale University, 409 Prospect Street, New Haven, CT 06511, USA (office). *Telephone:* (203) 432-5180 (office). *Fax:* (203) 432-5296 (office). *Website:* www.yale.edu/ism (office).

TAYLOR, Paul Wegman; American conductor; b. 30 Sept. 1954, Cleveland, Ohio. *Education:* studied with Willem Wegman, Juilliard School with John Chambers and John Cerminaro, San Francisco State Univ. with David Gilbert, Maurice Peress, Walter Hugler, Queens Coll., CUNY. *Career:* freelance in New York, including solo horn, Greenwich Symphony Orchestra; New York Philharmonic, Metropolitan Opera and numerous other engagements, including chamber music 1975–83; Kammerphilharmonie Budweis CR Wiener Oper Theater 1992–94; conductor, choirs and amateur orchestras in Zürich 1993–2000; Guest Conductor, Tonhalle Orchestra 1994; founder and Conductor, Mauritius Ensemble, Switzerland 1995–; guest engagement, Kammerphilharmonie, Budweis, CR 1995; Thuner Stadtsorchester, Switzerland 1998; Artistic Dir Switzerland; mem. Conductors' Guild, International Horn Soc. *Recordings include:* Hornist with the New York Philharmonic: Ein Heldenleber, Strauss; Ring Excerpts, Wagner. *Honours:* winner Conducting Competition, Biel, Bienne Summer Acad. 1994. *Current Management:* c/o Andi Howard Entertainment, 30765 Pacific Coast Highway, Malibu, CA 90265, USA. *Telephone:* (310) 589-8604. *E-mail:* fhansen@apany.com. *Website:* www.andihowardentertainment.com; www.paultaylorsax.com.

TAZZINI, Rinaldo, BA; American producer and artistic director; b. 15 Feb. 1942, New York, NY; m. Helen Neswald 1965; one s. two d. *Education:* High School of Music and Art, New York, Hunter Coll., Mannes School of Music with Paul Berl and Carl Bamberger, Conservatorio di Cherubini, Florence, Italy with Cecilia Castelana-Zotti, Accademia di Chigiana with Gino Bechi, Accademia di Santa Cecilia with Tito Gobbi. *Career:* sang at New York City Opera 1971–72, Teatro dell'Opera, Rome, Italy 1972–74, Teatro Massimo Bellini at Catania 1974, Teatro Lonigo 1974; Artistic Dir and Dir of Productions, Brooklyn Opera Soc., USA 1977–; Madama Butterfly at Japanese Garden in New York, being the first opera for television shot on location in USA 1980; Prod., Dir of the George Gershwin Festival Tour 1982; Creator, Dir, Hot Rags Musical at Lincoln Center 1983. *Address:* c/o Bernard Lewis, The Brooklyn Opera Society, Borough Hall, Brooklyn, NY 11201, USA.

TCHAIKOVSKY, Aleksandr Vladimirovich; Russian composer and pianist; b. 19 Feb. 1946, Moscow; m. 1st; one s. one d.; m. 3rd; one d. *Education:* Moscow State Conservatory. *Career:* pianist and chamber musician 1967–; joined Faculty, Moscow P. I. Tchaikovsky Conservatory 1976, fmr Prof. and Composition Chair, Composition Dept; Artistic Consultant, Mariinsky Theatre, St Petersburg 1996–; Artistic Dir Moscow State Philharmonia 2003–; mem. Bd of Dirs Pervyi Kanal. *Compositions include:* operas: Grandfather Is Laughing 1976, Three Sisters (after A. Chekhov) 1994; ballets: Inspector 1960, Battleship Potemkin 1988, Legend of the Ancient Town of Yelets, Tamerlane and the Virgin Mary and Violist Davydov; symphonies 1985, 1991 (Aquarius), two piano concertos, two viola concertos, Distant Dreams of Childhood for violin and viola 1990, Concerto-Buff for violin and marimba 1990, Triple Concerto for piano, violin and cello 1994, folk operas Tsar Nikita and Motya and Savely for two soloists and folk instruments, Quartet (after A. Pushkin) 1997–99; chamber music, incidental music to theatre and film productions. *Honours:* winner, Hollybush Festival Prize (USA) 1987, People's Artist of Russia 1998. *Address:* Mariinsky Theatre, 190000 St Petersburg, Theatre Square, 1; 125040 Moscow, Leningradsky prosp. 14, Apt. 4, Russia (home). *Telephone:* (495) 151-54-18 (home). *Website:* www.mariinsky.ru/en/company/orchestra/piano/alexander_tchaikovsky (office).

TCHERNIAKOV, Dmitri; Russian opera director, producer and set designer; b. 1970, Moscow. *Education:* Russian Acad. of Theatre Arts. *Career:* came to int. attention as producer, The Legend of the Invisible City of Kitezh for Mariinsky Theatre 2001, also staged at Lincoln Center Festival, New York 2003; London debut at ENO 2011; New York debut at Metropolitan Opera 2013; directed Lady Macbeth of the Mtsensk District for ENO 2015, also Parsifal in Berlin and Lulu at Bavarian State Opera 2015; has worked with European opera houses including La Scala, Milan, Liceu Barcelona, Bolshoi Theatre, Moscow, Madrid, Novosibirsk, Bavarian State Opera, Munich, Aix-en-Provence Festival, Tel-Aviv, Deutsche Oper Berlin, Opéra Bastille and Opéra de Paris. *Operas produced include:* The Legend of the Invisible City of Kitezh, The Rake's Progress, Aida, Eugene Onegin, Wozzeck, Don Giovanni, A Life for the Tsar, Macbeth, The Tsar's Bride, Simon Boccanegra, Jenůfa, La Traviata, Prince Igor, Il Trovatore. *Honours:* several Golden Mask awards, Int. K. S. Stanislavsky Prize, Franco Abbiati Italian Music Critics' Prize, Designer of the Year, Opernwelt magazine, winner, Best Dir and Best New Production, Int. Opera Awards 2013. *Current Management:* c/o JL Artist Management, Fredericiastrasse 10C, 14050 Berlin, Germany. *Telephone:* (30)

30830820. *Fax:* (30) 30830820. *E-mail:* lukjanova@jl-artistmanagement.com. *Website:* www.jl-artistmanagement.com.

TCHISTJAKOVA, Irina; Russian singer (mezzo-soprano); b. 1965, Moscow. *Education:* Gnessin Russian Acad. of Music, Moscow. *Career:* soloist with the Theatre Studio of the Gnessin Acad. from 1988; prin. with Moscow Municipal Theatre 1990–, tour of Italy 1991, as Ratmir in Glinka's Ruslan and Lyudmila; performances include Marina in Boris Godunov at Liège, the Verdi Requiem at Lincoln Center, New York and Orchestra Verdi, Milan, Ruslan and Lyudmila at Carnegie Hall, Marfa in Khovanshchina, the Bolshoi, Marina at Turin and Salzburg, Eugene Onegin and The Queen of Spades at Trieste and Teatro de la Maestranza, Seville, Cherubino at Kirov Opera, St Petersburg, Marguerite in La Damnation de Faust, Amneris and Eboli, Rusalka with the Bayerischer Rundfunk, War and Peace and The Queen of Spades at La Bastille, Jean d'Arc with Montpellier Opera, Boris Gudunov at Teatro Real, Madrid; concert repertory includes Skriabin's 1st Symphony in Sweden and Germany, Beethoven's Ninth and Prokofiev's Alexander Nevsky with the Philharmonia Orchestra, Tchaikovsky's Moscow Cantata with Bern Symphony Orchestra. *Recordings include:* Verdi Arias on Capriccio, Azucena in Il Trovatore, Prokofiev's On Guard for Peace 2009. *Honours:* winner Viñas Singing Competition, Barcelona 1993. *Address:* Chandos Records Ltd, Chandos House, 1 Commerce Park, Commerce Way, Colchester, Essex, CO2 8HX, England (office). *Telephone:* (1206) 225200 (office). *Fax:* (1206) 225201 (office). *E-mail:* enquiries@chandos.net (office). *Website:* www.chandos.net (office).

TE KANAWA, Dame Kiri Jeanette Claire, ONZ, DBE, AC; New Zealand singer (soprano); b. (Claire Mary Teresa Rawstron), 6 March 1944, Gisborne, North Island; adopted d. of Thomas Te Kanawa and Nell Te Kanawa; m. Desmond Park 1967 (divorced 1997); one s. one d. *Education:* St Mary's Coll., Auckland, London Opera Centre. *Career:* first appearance at Royal Opera, Covent Garden, London 1970, Santa Fe Opera, USA 1971, Lyon Opera, France 1972, Metropolitan Opera, New York, USA 1974; appeared at Australian Opera, Royal Opera House Covent Garden, Paris Opera during 1976–77 season; appeared at Houston Opera, USA and Munich Opera 1977; debut La Scala, Milan 1978; Salzburg Festival 1979; San Francisco Opera Co. 1980; Edinburgh Festival, Helsinki Festival 1980; sang at wedding of HRH the Prince of Wales 1981; sang the premiere of Paul McCartney's Liverpool Oratorio, written by Carl Davis, at Liverpool Cathedral and in London 1991; voice of the theme of the Rugby World Cup, performing first recorded version of World in Union 1991; appeared in 2000 Today on 1 January 2000; returned to the Cologne Opera House for two final performances of the Marschallin in Rosenkavalier 2010; final opera performance before retirement was cameo role in La fille du régiment at Royal Opera House, London 2014; appeared in ITV's Downton Abbey playing Dame Nellie Melba, an Australian operatic soprano 2013; Founding Trustee and Chair. Kiri Te Kanawa Foundation 2004–; Hans Christian Andersen Amb. 2005–; Patron Ringmer Community Coll. *Operas include:* Boris Godunov, Parsifal, The Marriage of Figaro (Countess)Otello, Simon Boccanegra, Carmen, Don Giovanni, Faust, The Magic Flute, La Bohème, Eugene Onegin, Così fan tutte, Arabella, Die Fledermaus, La Traviata, Der Rosenkavalier, Manon Lescaut, Samson, Don Carlos, Capriccio, Vanessa. *Recordings include:* Don Giovanni (as Elvira), Così fan tutti (as Fiordiligi), Carmen (as Michela), Mozart Vespers, Mozart C Minor Mass, The Magic Flute (Pamina), Siegfried (Woodbird), The Marriage of Figaro, Hansel and Gretel, La Bohème, Capriccio, Otello, Die Fledermaus, French and German arias and songs, Maori songs 1999, Strauss songs with orchestra, Songs of the Auvergne, West Side Story, The Very Best of ... 2003, Kiri Sings Karl 2006. *Publications:* Land of the Long White Cloud (children's book) 1989, Opera for Lovers (with Conrad Wilson) 1997. *Honours:* Hon. Fellow, Somerville Coll., Oxford 1983, Wolfson Coll., Cambridge 1997; Hon. Mem. RAM; Hon. LLD (Dundee) 1982; Hon. DMus (Durham) 1982, (Oxford) 1983, (Nottingham) 1992, (Waikato) 1995, (Cambridge) 1997; Hon. DLitt (Warwick) 1989, (Sunderland) 2003, (Auckland), (Chicago); Classical Brit Award for Lifetime Achievement 2010, Kiri Prize competition to find a gifted opera singer of the future est. in her honour 2010, Edison Classical Music Award 2012, World Class New Zealand Award 2012. *Current Management:* c/o Kiri Te Kanawa Foundation, PO Box 38387, Howick, Auckland 2045, New Zealand; c/o Kiri Te Kanawa Foundation (UK), 23B Prince of Wales Mansions, Prince of Wales Drive, London, SW11 4BQ, England. *Telephone:* (9) 5349398 (Auckland) (office); (20) 8332-9829 (London) (office). *Fax:* (9) 5340629 (Auckland) (office); (20) 8332-7049 (London) (office). *E-mail:* foundation@kiritekanawa.org (office); gillian.newson@btopenworld.com (office). *Website:* www.kiritekanawa.org (office).

TEARE, Christine; British singer (soprano); b. 1959, Isle of Man. *Education:* Royal Academy of Music with Marjorie Thomas, studied with Rudolf Piernay. *Career:* debut with Welsh National Opera, Cardiff, as Donna Anna 1983; Covent Garden 1983, as Helmwige, Ortlinde and Third Norn in The Ring; season 1985–86 as a Flower Maiden in Parsifal for English National Opera, and Donna Anna for Opera North; Welsh National Opera 1985–89 as Mozart's Countess, Amelia in Un Ballo in Maschera, Third Norn in Götterdämmerung, Berta in Barbiere di Siviglia and the Empress in Die Frau ohne Schatten; broadcasts with the BBC. *Recordings include:* Osud by Janáček, and Parsifal (ENO and WNO; EMI). *Current Management:* Robert Gilder and Co., 91 Great Russell Street, London, WC1B 3PS, England. *Telephone:* (20) 7580-7758. *Fax:* (20) 7580-7739. *E-mail:* rgilder@robert-gilder.com. *Website:* www.robert-gilder.com; www.christineteare soprano.co.uk.

TEDE, Margery; American singer (mezzo-soprano); b. 1940. *Education:* San Francisco State Coll., Madrid Conservatory, Spain and Hochschule für Musik, Berlin, Germany. *Career:* sang with the San Francisco Opera as Fricka, Amneris, Azucena, Judith in Bluebeard's Castle, Jocasta and Herodias in Salome; sang Countess Carolina in the local premiere of Henze's Elegy for Young Lovers, conducted by Christopher Keene; Lake Tahoe Summer Music Festival as Susan B. Anthony in Virgil Thomson's The Mother of Us All; concert appearances with the San Francisco Symphony under Seiji Ozawa and in Mozart's Coronation Mass in New York; sang in opera, concerts and recitals in Europe, Central America, Alaska and the South Pacific; sang the world premiere of Roger Nixon's Three Transcendental Songs in New York and songs by Charles Ives in Hamburg; retired as singer and active as teacher. *Honours:* Int. Scholarship from the Federation of Music Clubs. *Address:* Steorra Enterprises, 243 West End Avenue, Suite 907, New York, NY 10023, USA.

TEITELBAUM, Richard Lowe, BA, MMus; American composer and teacher; b. 19 May 1939, New York, NY. *Education:* Haverford Coll., Yale Univ. School of Music, Mannes School, Accademia di Santa Cecilia, Rome, studied with Luigi Nono in Venice, Wesleyan Univ. World Music Program. *Career:* founder mem., Musica Electronica Viva, Rome 1966; Instructor, California Inst. of the Arts 1971–72; founder and Dir, Electronic Music Studio, Art Inst. of Chicago 1972–73; Co-Dir and Visiting Prof., York Univ., Toronto 1973–76; soloist at Berlin Philharmonic Hall, Concertgebouw, Centre Pompidou, WDR Cologne among others 1984–86; Visiting Prof., Vassar Coll.; Prof., Bard Coll. 1988–89; mem. American Music Center, Composers' Forum, Coll. Music Soc., Int. Computer Music Soc. *Compositions include:* Intersections for piano 1964, In Tune for live electronics 1966, Time Zones 1977, Hi Uchi Ishi 1977, Digital Piano Music 1983, Concerto Grosso for robotic pianos, winds, trombone and synthesizers, Iro Wa Nioedo for 20 Buddhist monks, Golem (interactive opera) 1989–94, Dal Niente for midi piano, sampler and computer 1997. *Honours:* Fulbright Scholarships, Italy 1964–66, Japan 1976–77, Meet the Composer/NEA grant, Mary Flager Cary Trust 1976, 1979, 1988.

TELLEFSEN, Arve; Norwegian violinist; b. 13 Dec. 1936, Trondheim. *Education:* studied with Arne Stoltenberg, Henry Holst and Ivan Galamian in New York. *Career:* numerous recitals and concerts in Europe; Prof., Acad. of Music, Oslo from 1973; tour of Norway 1985, with the RPO under Ashkenazy; Oslo Philharmonai concerts 1987, with Mariss Jansons, Neeme Järvi and Esa-Pekka Salonen; British engagements with David Zinman, Jerzy Maksymiuk, Marek Janowski, Okko Kamu, Vernon Handley and Kurt Sanderling; festival concerts at Schleswig-Holstein, Lockenhaus and Montreux; founded Oslo Chamber Music Festival 1989; season 1997 premiered the Concerto by Nordheim, with the Oslo Philharmonic Orchestra. *Recordings include:* concertos by Nielsen, Shostakovich, Berwald, Aulin, Valen, Sinding, Svendsen and Sibelius; Beethoven and Grieg Sonatas; Bruch and Beethoven concertos with the London Philharmonic Orchestra; Shostakovich 1 and Sibelius with the Royal Philharmonic. *Honours:* first prize Princess Astrid Competition for Young Norwegian Artists 1956, Harriet Cohen Int. Award 1962, Bergen Festival Prize 1964, Grieg Prize 1973.

TEMBE, Bongani, BMus, MMus; South African arts administrator and singer (tenor); *CEO and Artistic Director, KwaZulu-Natal Philharmonic Orchestra*; b. Durban; m. Linda Bukhosini; one d. *Education:* Juilliard School, USA. *Career:* fmr resident singer, Playhouse Co., Durban; first black South African singer to appear in prin. role in nationally televised opera production, appearing in Der Fliegende Holländer 1987; other operatic roles include Faust and Tamiro in Die Zauberflöte; Deputy Dir Nat. Philharmonic Orchestra of South Africa 1994–96; CEO and Artistic Dir KwaZulu-Natal Philharmonic Orchestra 1996–; mem. Nat. Arts Council of South Africa 1995–2002; mem. Bd of Dirs State Theatre, Pretoria, Playhouse Co., Durban. *Address:* KwaZulu-Natal Philharmonic Orchestra, PO Box 5353, Durban 4000, South Africa (office). *Telephone:* (31) 369-9438 (office). *Fax:* (31) 369-9403 (office). *E-mail:* ceo@kznpo.co.za (office). *Website:* www.kznpo.co.za (office).

TEMESI, Mária, DipMus; Hungarian singer (soprano); b. (Maria Toth), 1957, Szeged. *Education:* Franz Liszt Academy, studied in Szeged, masterclasses at Weimar Music Academy and Mozarteum, Salzburg. *Career:* debut at Budapest State Opera as Elsa, in Wagner's Lohengrin, under G. Patanè, 1982; appearances include Staatsoper Hamburg, Oper der Stadt Köln, Semperoper Dresden, Staatsoper Berlin, Komische Oper Berlin, Opernhaus Zürich, Teatro Farnese Parma, Teatro de la Zarzuela Madrid, Opéra de Nice, Théâtre du Capitole Toulouse, Opera Company of Philadelphia, Smetana Theatre Prague, Herodes Atticus Ampthitheatre Athens, Opernhaus Graz, Montevideo Teatro Solis, Uruguay; Main Roles: Vitellia in La Clemenza di Tito, Adriana Lecouvrer, Tatiana, Lisa in The Queen of Spades, Amelia in Ballo in Maschera, Leonora in Trovatore, Elisabeth de Valois, Elena in Vespri Siciliani, Desdemona, Alice in Falstaff, Elsa in Lohengrin, Eva in Meistersinger, Elisabeth in Tannhäuser, Estrella in Schubert's Alfonso und Estrella, Sieglinde in Die Walküre, Mimi in La Bohème and Manon in Manon Lescaut; Brünnhilde in Götterdämmerung at Budapest, 1998; Concert performance of Guntram by Strauss, Manhattan Cable television, New York; Götterdämmerung (Gutrune); Mahler's 2nd Symphony under Dorati; Handel's Messiah under Gönnenwein; La Clemenza di Tito conducted by John Pritchard, Cologne; Liederabenden, Budapest Music Academy; Lisbon Fundacao Calouste Gulbenkian; Cairo Academy of Arts; Beethoven: Missa Solemnis (Milano, RAI); Verdi: Requiem; Dvořák, Requiem; Britten: War Requiem (Zagreb); Rossini: Stabat Mater; Pergolesi: Stabat Mater. *Recordings:* Liszt,

Missa Choralis; Mahler, 8th Symphony. *Honours:* prizewinner in competitions in Athens, 1979, Toulouse, 1980; 1st Prize, Rio de Janeiro, 1981; winner Pavarotti Competition, Philadelphia, 1985; Szekely Mihaly Plaquette, Budapest, 1995.

TEMIRKANOV, Yuri Khatuyevich; Russian conductor; *Music Director and Principal Conductor, St Petersburg Philharmonic Orchestra*; b. 10 Dec. 1938, Nalchik, Repub. of Kabardino-Balkaria; s. of Khatu Sagidovich Temirkanov and Polina Petrovna Temirkanova; m. Irina Guseva (deceased); one s. *Education:* Leningrad Conservatoire. *Career:* First Violinist with Leningrad Philharmonic Orchestra 1961–66; Conductor for Maly Theatre and Opera Studio, Leningrad 1965–68; Chief Conductor, Leningrad Philharmonic Orchestra 1968–76, Kirov Opera and Ballet Co. 1976–88; Prof., Leningrad Conservatoire 1979–88; Artistic Dir, State Philharmonia 1988–; Prin. Guest Conductor, Royal Philharmonic Orchestra and Philadelphia Orchestra; Chief Conductor, Royal Philharmonic Orchestra 1992–97; Prin. Guest Conductor, Danish Radio Orchestra 1997–2008; Music Dir, Baltimore Symphony Orchestra 1999–2007, Music Dir Emer. 2007–; Music Dir and Prin. Conductor, St Petersburg Philharmonic Orchestra 2007–; Prin. Guest Conductor, Bolshoi Theatre, Russia 2007–; Music Dir, Teatro Regio di Parma 2009–; guest conductor of major orchestras in Europe and Asia, including Berlin Philharmonic, Vienna Philharmonic, Dresden Staatskapelle, London Philharmonic, London Symphony, Royal Concertgebouw Orchestra, Santa Cecilia, Rome and La Scala and in USA the major orchestras in New York, Philadelphia, Boston, Chicago, Cleveland, San Francisco and Los Angeles. *Opera productions include:* Porgy and Bess (at Maly); Peter the Great (at Kirov), Shchedrin's Dead Souls (at Bolshoi and Kirov), Tchaikovsky's Queen of Spades and Eugene Onegin (Kirov) 1979. *Honours:* Hon. Academician, Santa Cecilia; Commdr, Order of the Star of Italy 2012; USSR People's Artist 1981, Glinka Prize, USSR State Prize 1976, 1985, 2002, Abbiati Prize for Best Conductor 2002, Pres.'s Medal 2003. *Current Management:* c/o Nicholas Mathias, IMG Artists, The Light Box, 111 Power Road, London, W4 5PY, England. *Telephone:* (20) 7957-5800. *Fax:* (20) 7957-5801. *E-mail:* nmathias@imgartists.com. *Website:* imgartists.com/artist/yuri_temirkanov.

TEMPERLEY, Nicholas, BA, BMus, MA, PhD, ARCM, ARCO; American musicologist and academic; *Professor Emeritus of Music, University of Illinois at Urbana-Champaign*; b. 7 Aug. 1932, Beaconsfield, Bucks., England; s. of Arthur Cecil Temperley and Joyce van Oss; m. Mary Dorothea Sleator 1960; one s. two d. *Education:* Royal Coll. of Music, London, King's Coll., Cambridge. *Career:* Asst Lecturer in Music, Univ. of Cambridge and Fellow, Clare Coll., Cambridge 1961–66; Asst Prof. in Musicology, Yale Univ., USA 1966–67; Assoc. Prof. of Music, Univ. of Illinois at Urbana-Champaign 1967–72, Prof. 1972–96, Prof. Emer. 1996–, Chair. Musicology Div. 1972–75, 1992–96; Ed.-in-Chief Journal of the American Musicological Soc. 1978–80; Gen. Ed. Oxford Studies in British Church Music 1986–95; Pres. North American British Music Studies Asscn 2003–06; Nat. Arts Assoc., Sigma Alpha Iota 2004–; Fellow, Nat. Endowment for the Humanities 1975–76. *Publications include:* editions: Raymond and Agnes, Edward J. Loder, performed Cambridge 1966, Symphonie Fantastique, Berlioz, New Berlioz Edition 1972, English Songs 1800–60, Musica Britannica (Vol. 43) 1979, London Pianoforte School 1766–1860, (20 vols) Garland 1984–87; Haydn's Creation, with authentic English text 1987; books: Music of English Parish Church (two vols) 1979, Athlone History of Music in Britain: Romantic Age (Vol. 5) 1981, Haydn: The Creation 1991, The Hymn Tune Index (four vols) 1998, Bound for America: Three British Composers 2003, William Sterndale Bennett: Lectures on Musical Life 2006, Studies in English Church Music 2009; contrib. to numerous musical journals, New Grove Dictionary. *Honours:* Hon. Fellow, Guild of Church Musicians 1990–; Otto Kinkeldey Award for Best Musicology Book 1979. *Address:* 805 West Indiana Street, Urbana, IL 61801, USA (home). *E-mail:* ntemp@illinois.edu (office). *Website:* hymntune.library.illinois.edu (office).

TENENBOM, Steven; American violist; b. 1965, USA. *Education:* Curtis Inst. of Music with Michael Tree and Karen Tuttle. *Career:* mem. Orion String Quartet, TASHI, Opus One Piano Quartet; fmr mem. Galimir Quartet; appeared as guest artist with Guarneri String Quartet, Emerson String Quartets, the Beaux Arts Trio, Kalichstein-Laredo-Robinson Trio, Chamber Music Society, Lincoln Center, Utah Symphony Orchesra, Rochester Philharmonic, Cincinnati Chamber Orchestra, Brandenburg Ensemble; has appeared at Mostly Mozart, Aspen, Ravinia, Marlboro, June Music, Chamber Music Northwest, music from Angel Fire, and Bravo! Colorado festivals; faculty mem., Mannes Coll. of Music, Curtis Inst. of Music, Bard Coll. Conservatory of Music. *Honours:* Coleman Chamber Music Award. *Current Management:* Kirshbaum Demler and Associates, 711 West End Avenue, Suite 5KN, New York, NY 10025, USA. *Telephone:* (212) 222-4843. *Fax:* (212) 222-7321. *E-mail:* info@kirshdem.com. *Website:* www.kirshdem.com. *E-mail:* steve@orionquartet.com (office). *Website:* www.orionquartet.com.

TENNFJORD, Oddbjorn; Norwegian singer (bass); b. 1941, Oslo. *Education:* Bergen and Oslo Conservatories, studied in Essen with Clemens Kaiser-Breme, in Rome with Luigi Ricci and in London with Roy Henderson. *Career:* has sung with the Norske Opera Oslo from 1971 as Osmin, Don Pasquale, Basilio, Falstaff, Pogner, Boris Godunov, Sarastro, Wotan, King Marke, Gremin and Fiesco; Concert and opera engagements for Norwegian radio and television, in Germany, Italy, Poland, Sweden, Denmark, Israel, Yugoslavia, France and USA; appearances with Scottish Opera as The Commendatore, Daland, Sarastro and Fafner; Bologna in 1988 and Ravenna Festival in 1989

as the Grand Inquisitor in Don Carlos; Sang with Scottish Opera as Fafner in Das Rheingold and the Commendatore and as Daland at Oslo in 1989; Numerous guest appearances world-wide include: Baron Ochs and Daland in Montpellier, Daland in Cologne, Tokyo, Barcelona and Las Palmas, Baron Ochs in Osaka, The Grand Inquisitor in Bologna and Ravenna, Sarastro, Fafner, The Commendatore and Frank (Die Fledermaus) with the Scottish Opera; Since 1994 freelance: Gurrelieder with Mariss Jansons and the Oslo Philharmonic Orchestra, King Marke in Brussels with Antonio Pappano, Duke Bluebeard with Neeme Järvi and Gothenburg Symphony Orchestra, Vespri Siciliani, Rheingold and Die Walküre at Den Norske Opera; Season 1996–97 included Baron Ochs at Deutsche Oper, Berlin, Boris Godunov at Kungliga Operan, Stockholm, Marke and Commendatore in Brussels and Der Friedenstag and Don Giovanni at Sächsische Staatsoper, Dresden; Season 1998–99, Sang Wagner's Klingsor at Brussels, Baron Ochs at Royal Opera, Stockholm, Daland at Hamburg Staatsoper and The National Opera, Oslo.

TENSTAM, Ulrika; Swedish singer (mezzo-soprano); b. 20 Feb. 1963, Stockholm. *Education:* studied in Gothenburg Univ. of Music, Opera School, Stockholm. *Career:* debut as Ramiro in Mozart's La finta Giardiniera, Oslo 1987; appearances at Drottningholm Festival as Klytemnestra in Gluck's Iphigénie en Aulide, and other roles 1988–; with Royal Opera Stockholm 1992–, roles include Rosina in Il Barbiere di Siviglia, Nicklausse in Les Contes d'Hoffmann, Dalila, the Mother in Szokolay's Blood Wedding, Hermia in A Midsummer Night's Dream, Gluck's Orpheus, Marcellina in Le Nozze di Figaro, Melibea in Il Viaggio a Reims, Hélène in La belle Hélène, Carmen, Die Amme in Die Frau ohne Schatten, Gräfin Geschwitz in Lulu, Herodias in Salome, Baba the Turk, Judith in Duke Bluebeard's Castle, Orfeo, Suzuki, Ulrica in Un Ballo in Maschera, Magdalen in Die Meistersinger von Nürnberg; frequent concerts throughout Scandinavia, Europe and Asia; sang in world premiere of Näsflöjten. *Honours:* Kasper Award 1991. *Current Management:* c/o Good Company AB, Upplandsgatan 62, 113 28 Stockholm, Sweden. *Telephone:* (8) 545-805-54. *Fax:* (8) 34-43-54. *E-mail:* maria@goodcompany.se. *Website:* www.goodcompany.se.

TENZI, Fausto; singer (tenor); b. 1 April 1939, Lugano, Switzerland. *Education:* studied in Milan. *Career:* sang at La Scala Milan, Théâtre des Champs Elysées, Paris, Teatro Comunale, Bologna and in Florence, Lucerne, Aachen and Perugia; engaged at Buxton Festival, England and made concert appearances in Rome, Paris, Berlin, Moscow, Leningrad and North America; other roles include Don José, Edgardo, Manrico, Don Carlos, Pinkerton, Rodolfo, Turiddu and Ivan Khovansky in Khovanshchina. *Recordings include:* The Queen of Spades, Scriabin's 1st Symphony.

TER LINDEN, Jaap; Dutch musician (cello, viol) and conductor; *Music Director, Mozart Akademie*; b. 10 April 1947, Rotterdam. *Career:* co-f. Musica da Camera; fmr Principal Cellist, Musica Antiqua Köln, The English Concert and Amsterdam Baroque Orchestra; Founding Music Dir, Mozart Akademie 2000–; regular Guest Dir and soloist, Arion Ensemble (Canada); led period instrument orchestras including Boston Handel and Haydn Soc., San Francisco Philharmonia Baroque, Portland Baroque, European Union Baroque, Concerto Köln and Amsterdam Bachsoloists; chamber music partners included pianist Ronald Brautigam, violinists Elizabeth Wallfisch, Andrew Manze and John Holloway and harpsichordists Richard Egarr and Lars Ulrik Mortensen. *Recordings include:* Buxtehude Complete Chamber Music 2002, Corelli Trio Sonatas 2006, Hellendaal Cello Sonatas 2006, Bach Cello Suites 2006; with Mozart Akademie: Complete Mozart Symphonies 2005. *Current Management:* Joh. Adriaan Moens Artist Management, Nassaukade 5, 1052 CE Amsterdam, Netherlands. *Telephone:* (20) 6844322. *Fax:* (84) 8676757. *E-mail:* hans@moens-artists.nl. *Website:* www.moens-artists.nl; www.jaapterlinden.com (office).

TERAMOTO, Mariko, BA, MA, PhD; Japanese musicologist and academic; *Professor, Musashino College of Music*; b. 6 June 1948, Tokyo. *Education:* Musashino Coll. of Music, Tokyo, Nat. Univ. of Fine Arts and Music, Tokyo, Univ. of Frankfurt am Main, Germany. *Career:* Lecturer, Nat. Univ. of Fine Arts and Music 1985–89, 1996–97, 2005, 2015; Asst Prof., Meisei Univ. 1984–87, Prof. 1988–97; Lecturer, Musashino Coll. of Music 1984–97, Asst Prof. 1998–2001, Prof. 2002–; mem. Int. American and Japanese Musicological Soc., Gesellschaft für Musikforschung, Internationale C.-M.-von-Weber-Gesellschaft, Internationale Heinrich Schütz Gesellschaft. *Publications include:* Die Psalmmotettendrucke des Johannes Petrejus in Nürnberg 1983, Katalog der Musikdrucke des Johannes Petrejus in Nürnberg 1993, Shihen-no-Ongaku (Music of the Psalms) 2004; contrib. to Journal of the Japanese Musicological Society, musicological reference books. *Address:* 2-10-16 Shimo-ochiai, Shinjuku-ku, Tokyo 161-0033, Japan (home).

TERENTYEVA, Nina Nikolayevna; Russian singer (mezzo-soprano); b. 9 Jan. 1946, Kusa, Chelyabinsk Region; d. of Nikolai Fedorovich Terentyev and Tatyana Vladimirovna Terentyev; one d. *Education:* Leningrad State Conservatory (class of Olga Mshanskaya). *Career:* soloist, Kirov (now Mariinsky) Theatre 1971–77, Bolshoi 1979. *Russian repertoire includes:* Marta in Khovanshchina, Lubasha in Tsar's Bride, Lubava in Sadko, Marina Mnishek in Boris Godunov, also Amneris in Aida, Azucena in Il Trovatore, Delila in Samson and Delila, Eboli in Don Carlos, Santuzza in Cavalleria Rusticana and others; participated in productions of maj. theatres of the world including Covent Garden (Amneris 1995), Metropolitan-Opera (Eboli 1993), La Scala (oratorio Ivan Grozny with R. Muti 1994), also in Deutsche Oper and Staatsoper Berlin, Munich, Hamburg, Bordeaux, Los Angeles opera houses;

participated in int. festivals; concert repertoire comprises Russian classics. *Honours:* People's Artist of Russia. *Address:* Bolshoi Theatre, 103009 Moscow, Teatralnaya pl. 1, Russia (office). *Telephone:* (495) 971-67-61 (home).

TEREY-SMITH, Mary, BMus, MA, PhD; British musicologist, conductor and vocal coach; *Professor Emerita, Western Washington University;* b. (Mary Terey), 4 Dec. 1933, Budapest, Hungary; m. C. A. C. Smith (deceased). *Education:* Liszt Acad. of Music, Univ. of Vermont, USA, Eastman School of Music, Univ. of Rochester. *Career:* debut as conductor, Tatabanya Symphony Orchestra, Budapest 1951; vocal coach, then asst conductor, Hungarian State Opera 1950–56; resident conductor, Tatabanya Symphony Orchestra 1951–56; vocal coach, Toronto Royal Conservatory Opera School, Canada 1957–58; Asst Prof., Western Washington Univ. 1967–72, Assoc. Prof. 1972–85, Prof. of Music History and Literature 1985–2001, Prof. Emer. 2001–; Dir Western Washington Univ. Opera Workshop 1967–75, Dir of the Collegium Musicum Ensemble 1969–2001 (five biannual European summer tours with the Collegium Musicum 1990–2000, performing in Hungary, Italy, Austria, Switzerland, Liechtenstein, Slovakia and Romania); musical adviser and frequent conductor of Capella Savaria 1999–, with tours in Baroque music; research project on the church music of Gregor J. Werner, editing J.F. Fasch: Passio Jesu Christi; editing J.P. Rameau's opera: Abaris ou Les Boréades. *Recordings:* as conductor: Four Orchestral Suites from Operas by J. P. Rameau (with Capella Savaria Baroque Orchestra) 1996, Syrens, Enchanters and Fairies—18th-Century Overtures from the London Stage (directed with Capella Savaria Baroque Orchestra), Thomas Arne The Complete Solo Cantatas, G. J. Werner Masses and Offertories composed for the Esterházy Family, J.F. Fasch Passio Jesu Christi, T.A. Arne Theatre Overtures and Cantatas, Great Britain Triumphant 2011. *Publications:* French Baroque Partbooks in the Uppsala University Library 1979, Joseph Kämpfer, a Contrabass Virtuoso from Pozsony (Bratislava) 1983, French Baroque Orchestral Dances (ed.) 1986, Prosperina Rapita: An Unknown Opera Fragment 1990, International Dictionary of Opera: Rameau: Les Boréades (essay) 1993; contrib. to Orchestral Practice in the Paris Opéra 1690–1764 (in Studia Musicologica xxxi) 1989, The Spread of the French Influence in Europe (in Studia Musicologica xxxi) 1989, Passio Jesu Christi by J. F. Fasch (in The Fasch Yearbook) 1997, articles in Revised New Grove Dictionary of Music 2000–01; articles published in Canada, Hungary and USA; reviews for Music and Letters. *Honours:* Canada Council grant 1966–67, ACLS grant 1975–76, Harvard Fellowship 1976, Deutscher Akademischer Austausch Dienst (DAAD) grant 1987. *Address:* Department of Music, Western Washington University, 516 High Street, Bellingham, WA 98225-9107, USA (office). *Telephone:* (360) 650-3130 (office). *Fax:* (360) 650-7538 (office). *E-mail:* tereysm@gmail.com (office).

TERFEL, Bryn, CBE; British singer (bass-baritone); b. (Bryn Terfel Jones), 9 Nov. 1965, Pantglas, Snowdonia, Wales; s. of Hefin Jones and Nesta Jones; m. Lesley Halliday 1987 (divorced); three s. *Education:* Ysgol Dyffryn Nantlle, Penygroes, Gwynedd and Guildhall School of Music and Drama. *Career:* debut, Welsh Nat. Opera (WNO) as Guglielmo 1990; sang Mozart's Figaro at Santa Fe Opera and ENO 1991; Royal Nat. Opera, Covent Garden debut as Masetto in Don Giovanni 1992, repeated on tour to Japan; sang at Salzburg Festival as the Spirit Messenger in Die Frau ohne Schatten, and as Jochanaan in Salome 1992; Leporello in Don Giovanni 1994; further appearances at Vienna Staatsoper as Mozart's Figaro 1993, at Chicago as Donner in Das Rheingold, debuts at New York Metropolitan Opera 1994, Sydney Opera House 1999; frequent guest soloist with Berlin Philharmonic Orchestra; sang in the Brahms Requiem under Colin Davis and at Salzburg Easter Festival under Abbado (Herbert von Karajan In Memoriam) 1993; sang Nick Shadow in The Rake's Progress for WNO 1996, Figaro at La Scala 1997, Scarpia for Netherlands Opera 1998, Falstaff at the reopening of the Royal Opera House, Covent Garden 1999; four male roles in Les Contes d'Hoffmann and Don Giovanni, both at Metropolitan Opera, New York, and Nick Shadow in The Rake's Progress for San Francisco Opera 1999–2000; baritone roles in Les Contes d'Hoffmann at the Opéra Bastille, Sweeney Todd in Chicago, and Falstaff and Don Giovanni at Covent Garden 2002–03; Mephistopheles in Faust, Wotan in Das Rheingold and Die Walküre at Covent Garden 2004; Scarpia and the Flying Dutchman for the Royal Opera House 2009; Die Meistersinger von Nürnberg, WNO 2010; Wotan in Das Rheingold, Metropolitan Opera, New York 2010, Die Walküre 2011; Scarpia in Tosca for WNO, Staatsoper Hannover, Opera Monte Carlo, Wiener Staatsoper and Opéra Nat. de Paris 2015–16; many concert appearances in Europe, USA, Canada, Japan and Australia; Pres. Nat. Youth Choir of Wales, Festival of Wales; Vice-Pres. Llangollen Int. Eisteddfod; Founder, Faenol Festival 2000–. *Recordings include:* Salome, Le nozze di Figaro, An Die Musik, Wagner Arias, Britten's Gloriana, Beethoven's Ninth Symphony, Brahms' Requiem, Schwanengesang, Cecilia and Bryn, If Ever I Would Leave You, Handel Arias, Vagabond (Caecilia Prize 1995, Gramophone People's Award 1996) 1995, Opera Arias (Grammy Award for best classical vocal performance) 1996, Something Wonderful (Britannia Record Club Members' Award) 1997, Don Giovanni 1997, Bryn (Classical BRIT Award for Best Album 2004) 2003, Simple Gifts (Grammy Award for Best Classical Crossover Album 2007) 2005, Tutto Mozart! 2006, First Love: Songs from the British Isles 2008, Elgar's The Dream of Gerontius (Gramophone Award for Best Choral Recording) 2009, Bad Boys 2009, At His Very Best 2010, Carols & Christmas Songs 2010, Tosca (Puccini) (BBC Music Magazine DVD Performance Award 2014), Wagner: Der Ring des Nibelungen (with Met Opera, Grammy Award for Best Opera Recording 2013) 2012, Don Giovanni 2015, Der Fliegende Holländer 2015.

Honours: Hon. Fellow, Univ. of Wales, Aberystwyth, Welsh Coll. of Music and Drama, Univ. of Wales, Bangor; Hon. DMus (Glamorgan) 1997; White Robe, Gorsedd, recipient Kathleen Ferrier Scholarship 1988, Gold Medal Award 1989, Lieder Prize Cardiff Singer of the World Competition 1989, Gramophone magazine Young Singer of the Year 1992, British Critics Circle Award 1992, Int. Classical Music Awards Newcomer of Year 1993, Classical BRIT Award for Male Artist of the Year 2004, 2005, Nordoff-Robbins Silver Clef Classical Award 2006, Queen's Medal for Music 2006. *Current Management:* c/o Doreen O'Neill, Harlequin Agency, 203 Fidlas Road, Cardiff, CF14 5NA, Wales. *Telephone:* (29) 2075-0821. *Fax:* (29) 2075-5971. *E-mail:* doreen@harlequin-agency.co.uk. *Website:* www.harlequin-agency.co.uk.

TERRACINI, Lyndon; Australian singer (baritone); *Artistic Director, Opera Australia;* b. 1950. *Education:* studied in Australia. *Career:* debut with Australian Opera at Sydney Opera House as Sid in Albert Herring 1976; has performed roles from the traditional repertoire including Renato in Un Ballo in Maschera, Escamillo in Carmen, Don Giovanni, Marcello in La Bohème, Figaro in The Marriage of Figaro; notable performances have included title role in Rosa: A Horse Drama by Louis Andriessen and Peter Greenaway for the Netherlands Opera, Amsterdam (world premiere) 1994, 1998, title role in Stephen Climax by Hans Zender for Frankfurt Opera, Elliott Carter's Syringa at the Tonhalle, Zürich, 8 Songs for a Mad King, Royal Theatre, Copenhagen, Podewil Theatre, Berlin, Barossa Music Festival, Brisbane Biennial, Huntington and Sydney Festivals, role of Byron in Mer de Glace by Meale/Malouf for The Australian Opera, Gregor in Metamorphosis by Brian Howard, Der Alte in Reimann's Die Gespenstersonate for Opera Factory Zürich in the Stadttheaters of Bern, Luzern and Zürich, title role in Sondheim's Sweeney Todd for the State Opera of South Australia (Australian premiere), El Cimarron at the Adelaide, Melbourne, Perth, Barossa and Darwin (Guitar) Festivals, Sancio Panza in Henze and Paisiello's Don Quichotte, Montepulciano Festival, (world premiere) Italy, title role in Alley: The Opera at the NZ Int. Festival, Experimentum Mundi at the Adelaide Festival, lead role in The Voluptuous Tango by Dominic Muldowney, Frankfurt, Macheath in The Threepenny Opera, Festival of Perth, Rzewski's Coming Together, The Orestia and Kassandra (Xenakis) for Contemporary Music Events, Melbourne, Dominic Muldowney's The Fall of Jerusalem (world premiere), title role in Gaugin, Melbourne Festival, Mr Barbecue for Northern Rivers Performing Arts and at Brisbane Powerhouse with the Queensland Orchestra, world premiere of Love in the Age of Therapy for the Melbourne and Sydney Festivals 2003; concert appearances have included Mozart's Requiem with the BBC Philharmonic Orchestra, a Charles Ives Recital with Ensemble Modern, Alte Oper, Frankfurt; Artistic Dir and CEO, Queensland Music Festival 2000–05, Brisbane Festival 2006–09; Adjunct Prof., Univ. of Queensland 2005–; Artistic Dir, Opera Australia 2009–; mem. Int. Jury, Venice Biennale for Music 2006. *Television:* The Marriage of Figaro (Channel 4, UK). *Recordings include:* The Voluptuous Tango. *Publication:* A Regional State of Mind 2007. *Honours:* Dr hc in Music Theatre (Central Queensland Univ.) 1999; Hon. DUniv (Southern Cross Univ.) 2001, (Queensland Univ. of Tech.) 2007; Fellowship, Music Fund of the Australia Council for the Arts 2000, Dame Elisabeth Murdoch Cultural Leadership Award, Australian Business ARTS Foundation 2005. *Current Management:* c/o Arts Management Pty Ltd, Level 1, 405 Elizabeth Street, Surry Hills, NSW 2010, Australia. *Telephone:* (2) 9211-9422. *Fax:* (2) 9211-9466. *E-mail:* enquiries@artsmanagement.com .au. *Website:* www.artsmanagement.com.au.

TERRANOVA, Vittorio; Italian singer (tenor); b. 18 June 1945, Licata, Sicily. *Education:* Liceo Musicale v. Bellini, Catania, Conservatorio di Musica Giuseppe Verdi, Milan, Univ. of Pavia. *Career:* debut as Arturo in I Puritani, Mantua 1970; many appearances at opera houses throughout Italy, and at the Spoleto and Florence (Maggio Musical) festivals; guest engagements at the Vienna Staatsoper, Bregenz festival, Teatro Colón Buenos Aires, New York City Opera and Chicago Lyric Opera; other roles have included Verdi's Fenton, Alfredo and the Duke of Mantua, Nadir in Les Pêcheurs de Perles, Don Ottavio, Ferrando, Faust, Lyonel in Martha, Alamiro in Belisario; many concert engagements; Prof. of Voice, Conservatorio di Musica Giuseppe Verdi 2001–. *Address:* Department of Singing and Musical Theatre, Conservatorio di Musica Giuseppe Verdi, Via Conservatorio 12, 20122 Milan, Italy (office). *E-mail:* info@consmilano.it (office). *Website:* www.consmilano.it (office).

TERVO, Markku; singer (bass); b. 1955, Helsinki, Finland. *Education:* Sibelius Acad., Helsinki, studied with Hendrik Rootering. *Career:* sang with Finnish Nat. Opera 1977–79, Karlsruhe Opera 1981–86, Krefeld 1986–89, Freiburg 1989–94; returned to Karlsruhe 1994; roles have included Mozart's Osmin and Sarastro, Rossini's Basilio, Verdi's Ferrando, Sparafucile and King Philip (Don Carlos); Wagner's Daland and Hagen, and Claggart in Billy Budd; guest engagements throughout Germany and in Luxembourg; concerts throughout Europe, notably with Bach's Christmas Oratorio, St John Passion and Magnificat, L'Enfance du Christ by Berlioz, the Verdi Requiem and Shostakovich 13th Symphony (Babi-yar). *Recordings include:* Götterdämmerung. *Address:* c/o Staatstheater Karlsrhe, Baumesterstrasse 11Pf 1449, 7550 Karlsruhe, Germany.

TERZAKIS, Dimitri; Greek composer; *Professor Emeritus, Felix Mendelssohn-Bartholdy Musikhochschule;* b. 12 March 1938, Athens; s. of Angelos Terzakis and Louisa Terzakis; m. Magdalena; one d. *Education:* Hellenic Conservatory, Athens, Cologne Musikhochschule with Bernd Alois Zimmermann. *Career:* Co-founder Greek Soc. for Contemporary Music 1966; Lecturer, Robert Schumann Inst., Düsseldorf, Germany 1974; teacher and Prof. of

Composition, Düsseldorf Hochschule 1987–93, Berner Hochschule 1990–94, Felix Mendelssohn-Bartholdy Musikhochschule, Leipzig 1994–2006, Prof. Emer. 2006–. *Compositions include:* Ikona for strings 1963, Oboe Concerto 1968, Okeaniden for chorus and orchestra 1968, Ichochronos (electronic) 1968, Torquemada (opera) 1976, Circus Universal (chamber opera) 1976, five string quartets 1969, 1976, 1982, 1990, 1998, Tropi for orchestra 1976, Passionen (oratorio) 1979, Erotikon for soprano and three instruments 1979, Lachesis for orchestra 1984, Hermes (opera) 1984, Brass Quintet 1984, Six Monologues for soprano and orchestra 1985, Violin Concerto 1986, Das sechste Siegel for chorus and ensemble 1987, Per aspera ad Astra for orchestra 1990, Ikaros-Daidolos for soprano quartet and brass orchestra 1990, Der Holle Nachklang II for soprano and organ 1993, Daphnis und Chloe for soprano and viola 1994, Lieder ohne Worte for soprano 1994, Alto saxophone concerto 1995, Pensées for piano 2002, Mythen (Rapsodia) 2002, Drei Götter für zwei Klaviere 2009, Das Spiegelbild einer Frau for soprano and violin, Musik für einen Aulosspieler for oboe 2012, Fantasien for cello 2012. *Honours:* Dr hc; Apollo Award, Acad. of Athens. *Address:* Pölitzstraße 26, 04155 Leipzig (home); c/o Edition Gravis, Grabbeallee 15, 13156 Berlin, Germany. *Telephone:* (341) 9614431 (home); (30) 6169810. *E-mail:* dimitriterzakis@gmx.de (home); info@editiongravis.de. *Website:* www.dimitriterzakis.com; www.editiongravis.de.

TERZAKIS, Zachos; Greek singer (tenor); b. 1945, Athens. *Education:* University of Athens, Apollonion Odeon, Athens. *Career:* engaged at National Lyric Theatre of Athens, roles included Alfredo in La Traviata, Pinkerton in Madama Butterfly and Elvino in Sonnambula; sang in Athens Festival; Greek radio and television broadcasts; German debut as Turiddu in Cavalleria rusticana, Kiel, 1978; engaged in Bielefeld, roles included Cassio in Otello, Singer in Rosenkavalier and Tamino in Magic Flute, 1979–82; mem., Nuremberg Opera, roles included Rodolfo in Bohème, Almaviva in Barbiere di Siviglia and Adorno in Simon Boccanegra, 1982–87; from 1987, freelance opera singer, appearances in many European venues including Opernhaus Zürich, Staatsoper Berlin, Volksoper Wien and National Opera Athens; sang Hoffman at Bregenz Festival, 1987; other festival appearances include Luzerner Festwochen and Casals Festival in Puerto Rico; Debut as Titus in Staatsoper Vienna, and Jason in Medea by Mikis Theodorakis in Bilbao, 1991; Teatro dell Opera, Rome, as Rudolf von Habsburg in Mayerling, 1993; numerous concert recitals, including Tivoli Copenhagen, Concert House Stockholm and Palais des Beaux Arts, Brussels; Stage Dir, Medea, at Meiningen 1995, and German translator. *Recordings:* Greek opera, Mother's Ring by Kalomiris, tenor solo, 1985; Penderecki's Polish Requiem, 1992; Missa Solemnis; Lehar's Operetta Highlights; Die lustige Witwe; Markopoulos's Orpheus Liturgy. *Honours:* Gold Medal of Excellence, Apollonion Odeon, Athens, 1976; First Prize, Maria Callas Scholarship Competition, 1976.

TERZIAN, Alicia; Argentine composer, conductor, musicologist, lecturer and academic; *Artistic Director/Conductor, Fundacion Encuentros Internacionales de Musica Contemporanea;* b. 1 July 1934, Córdoba; m. (divorced); one d. *Education:* Nat. Univ. of Argentina, studied with Alberto Ginastera, Gilardo Gilardi, Roberto García Morillo, Floro Ugarte, studied Armenian ancient religious music (microtones) in Venice with Dr Leoncio Dayan and in Vienna and Yerevan. *Career:* debut premiere of String Quartet, Wagneriana Asscn, Buenos Aires 1955; more than 2,000 lectures on 20th century music history world-wide; performances for radio and TV and more than 400 concerts world-wide; as composer, works performed world-wide by leading soloists, orchestras and chamber ensembles; has taught at numerous univs in Argentina; Founder and Artistic Dir/Conductor Encuentros Internacionales de Música Contemporánea (promotes music written by Argentine and S American composers) 1968–; Pres. Argentine Music Council, UNESCO 1985–2005; mem. Int. Council, UNESCO (Vice-Pres. 1990); mem. Nat. Acad. of Fine Arts (Chile); UN Amb. of Peace 2014. *Compositions include:* stage: Hacia la luz (ballet) 1965, Bestiela (theatre music) 1981, El enano (theatre music) 1964; orchestral works: Three Pieces for strings, orchestra or guitar quartet 1954, Concerto for violin 1955, Atmosferas for symphonic band 1969, Carmen Criaturalis for solo horn, string orchestra and percussion 1971, Off the Edge for baritone, string orchestra and percussion 1992; chamber music: Y cuya luy es como la profunda oscuridad, group and tape 1982, Les yeux fertiles for mezzo and group with percussion 1997, Au delà des rêves for piano, clarinet and violin 2001, Song to Vahan 2005; instrumental: Libro de canciones de Federico Garcia Lorca for voice and piano 1954, Atmosferas for duo piano 1969, Yagua ya yuca for solo percussion 1992, Canto a Vahan for piano and tape 1996, Offer to Bach for organ 2000, Le viol des anges for four to six percussionists 2000/01; multimedia: Sinfonia Visual en dos movimientos, tape and slides 1972, Canto a mí misma for string orchestra, tamtam and electronic sound transformation and loudspeakers in concert hall 1986, Buenos Aires me vas a matar 1990, Frémissement for organ and tape 2000, Canto a Vahan (mezzo and ensemble) 2004. *Recordings:* Violin Concerto, Voces and Canto a mi misma, 1997; Toccata for Piano; Juegos para Diana. *Honours:* Hon. mem. Int. Music Council 2003, Acad. of Music, Valencia 2013; First Prize of Municipality of Buenos Aires 1964, Francisco Solano Award 1968, Outstanding Young Musicians Prize, Argentina 1970, Nat. Fund for the Arts Prize 1970, First Nat. Prize for Music 1982, Gomidas Int. Prize 1983, Médaille des Palmes Académiques, France 1992, St Sahuk and St Mesrop Medals, Pope Vasken I of Armenian Church 1992, Alberto de Castilla Medal (Colombia) 1994, Mozart Medal, Int. Music Council 1995, Most Outstanding Musician in Argentina, Parl. of Argentina 2013. *Telephone:* (11) 4832-1436. *E-mail:* nidiamag@hotmail.com. *Address:* Santa Fe 3269-4B, Buenos Aires 1425, Argentina (home). *Telephone:* (11) 4822-1383 (office). *Fax:* (11) 4822-1383 (office). *E-mail:* aterzian@aliciaterzian.com.ar (office). *Website:* www.aliciaterzian.com.ar.

TERZIAN, Anita; French singer (mezzo-soprano); b. 12 Oct. 1947, Strasbourg. *Education:* Juilliard School, New York with Jennie Tourel. *Career:* debut in Brussels in 1973 as Rosina; has appeared at many operatic centres in Europe and the USA; Opéra du Rhin, Strasbourg, Brussels, Liège and San Francisco Opera; Best known in such coloratura mezzo repertoire as Rossini's Isabella and Sinaide in Mosè, Elisetta in Il Matrimonio Segreto and Sesto in La Clemenza di Tito; other roles include Carmen, Charlotte, Olga, Orlofsky and Konchakovna in Prince Igor; Many concert appearances. *Recordings include:* title role in Handel's Serse.

TETZLAFF, Christian; German violinist; b. 29 April 1966, Hamburg. *Education:* Lubeck Conservatory with Uwe-Martin Haiberg, studied in Cincinnati with Walter Levine. *Career:* debut at the Berlin Festival and with the Cleveland Orchestra, followed by regular appearances with the Berlin and Vienna Philharmonic, London Symphony Orchestra, City of Birmingham Symphony Orchestra, Orchestra Philharmonie de Paris, Gewandhausorchestra Leipzig, Munich Philharmonic, NHK Orchestra Tokyo, the New York Philharmonic, Boston and Chicago Symphonies and Academy of St Martin in the Fields; season 1996–97 with the Houston Symphony Orchestra under Eschenbach and the Boston Symphony Orchestra under Franz Welser-Möst; Brahms Double Concerto and Shostakovich No. 1 with the Bavarian Radio Symphony Orchestra; Bach Sonatas and Partitas in Brussels and Paris 1997; Vienna Philharmonic concert at the 1997 Salzburg Festival; chamber music series at the Vienna Konzerthaus; has collaborated with Leif Ove Andses, Yo-Yo Ma, Sabine Meyer and Heinrich Schiff; Beethoven's Concerto at the 1999 London Prom concerts; Berg's concerto at the London Proms 2002; has worked with many distinguished conductors, including Boulez, Dohnanyi, Eschenbach, Gatti, Harding, Herreweghe, Paavo Jarvi, Levine, Nagano, Salonen, Saraste, Slatkin, Tilson Thomas and Vanska. *Recordings include:* Bach Sonatas and Partitas, Mozart Violin Concertos (with the Deutsche Kammerphilharmonie), Complete works for violin and orchestra by Sibelius, Mendolssohn and Schumann concertos/Schumann's Fantasy for Violin and Orchestra, Szymanowski Concerto pour violon no. 1/Symphone no. 3 (Diapason d'Or de l'année 2011), Schumann Complete Works for Piano Trio (Gramophone Award for Best Chamber Recording 2012) 2011. *Current Management:* Harrison Parrott, 5–6 Albion Court, London, W6 0QT, England. *Telephone:* (20) 7229-9166. *Fax:* (20) 7221-5042. *E-mail:* info@harrisonparrott.co.uk. *Website:* www.harrisonparrott.com.

TEZIER, Ludovic; French singer (baritone); b. 1968, Marseille. *Education:* studied in Paris and Switzerland. *Career:* engagements with Lyon, Marseille, Tours and Bordeaux Operas; Opéra-Comique, Paris, as Don Giovanni, Marcello, Escamillo, Harlequin (Ariadne auf Naxos), Sharpless, and Britten's Demetrius; Season 1996–97 in Handel's Radamisto and as Frédéric in Lakmé at Marseilles, Guglielmo at Bordeaux; Mozart Count, Marcello and Belcore at Lyon; Season 1997–98 as Malatesta, and Mercutio in Roméo et Juliette, at Bordeaux, with Escamillo, Don Giovanni and Talbot in Donizetti's Maria Stuarda at the Opéra-Comique; Glyndebourne 1997–98, as Comte Ory in a new production of Rossini's opera. *Honours:* Opera Singer of the Year Award, Les Victoires 2013.

THALLAUG, Edith; Norwegian singer (mezzo-soprano); b. 16 June 1929, Oslo. *Education:* studied with Giurgia Leppee and Joel Berglund in Stockholm. *Career:* stage debut as actress 1952; song recital in Oslo 1959; stage debut as Dorabella at Gothenburg 1960; sang at Royal Opera Stockholm from 1964, notably as Carmen, Cherubino, Rosina, Bradamante in Alcina, Maddalena in Rigoletto, Eboli, Azucena, Amneris, Venus, Fricka, Waltraute, Octavian and The Composer in Ariadne, Judith in Bluebeard and Miss Julie; frequent appearances at the Drottningholm Court Theatre from 1964; sang at Glyndebourne Festival 1971 as Dorabella, Basle 1976 in Schoenberg's Gurrelieder and on Swedish television as Carmen; guest engagements in Oslo, Copenhagen, Moscow, USA, Japan, Korea, Germany, La Scala Milan, Italy, Paris, Prague and Vienna. *Recordings include:* Songs by De Falla, Montsalvatge, Ravel and many other recordings of Scandinavian Songs; Opera Arias, Songs by Grieg, and duets with Gösta Winbergh. *Honours:* Kt First Class, Royal Norwegian Order of St Olav 1983; Critic Prizes for La Cenerentola, Oslo 1972, Court Singer 1976, Grieg Prize 1978, Drottningholm Court Theater Gold Medal 1979, Litteris et Artibus 1982. *Address:* Porfyrvägen 10A, 141 43 Huddinge, Sweden (home).

THARAUD, Alexandre; French pianist; b. 9 Dec. 1968, Paris. *Career:* as soloist, has performed with numerous orchestras including Symphonieorchester des Bayerischen Rundfunks, Münchner Rundfunkorchester, Orchestre Philharmonique de Radio France, Orchestre Nat. de France, Orchestre du Capitole de Toulouse, Orchestre Nat. de Lyon, Orch Nat. de Lille, Orchestre Nat. de Bordeaux Aquitaine, Estonian Nat. Symphony Orchestra, Orquestra Sinfonica do Estado de São Paulo, Umeå Symphony Orchestra, Japan Philharmonic Orchestra, Singapore Symphony, Taiwan Nat. Symphony Orchestra, Malaysian Philharmonic, Les Violons du Roy and Bolshoi Theatre Orchestra and London Philharmonic Orchestra at venues including Köln Philharmonie, Bern Casino, Essen Philharmonie, Royal Festival Hall, London, Southbank Piano Series, Rudolfinum Prague, Krakow Philharmonic, Théâtre des Champs Elysées, Cité de la Musique, Concertgebouw Amsterdam, Teatro Colón Buenos Aires, John F. Kennedy Center and Seoul Arts Center; festivals have included Piano aux Jacobins, La Roque d'Anthéron, BBC Proms

Chamber Music, Lufthansa Festival of Baroque Music, Sacrum profanum in Krakow, Schleswig-Holstein and Rimini Festivals; Artistic Dir Amadeus Festival, Switzerland 2011; Resident Artist, MC2 Grenoble. *Recordings include:* solo: Bach: Concertos pour piano, Scarlatti: Sonates pour piano, Chopin: Journal intime, Le Boeuf sur le toit (Victoires de la musique classique Recording of the Year, ECHO Klassik Awards Klassik Ohne Grenzen Prize 2013) 2012, Autograph 2013; with Jean-Guihen Queyras: Hungarian Cello Music, Arpeggione, Debussy/Poulenc. *Honours:* Chevalier, Ordre des Arts et des Lettres 2009; Grand Prix du Disque Charles Cros 2003. *Current Management:* c/o Catherine Le Bris, CLB Management, 5 passage Piver, 75011 Paris, France. *E-mail:* catherine@clbmanagement.co.uk. *Website:* www.clbmanagement.co.uk; www.alexandretharaud.com (office).

THEISEN, Kristin; Norwegian singer (soprano); b. 13 Jan. 1955, Oslo; one d. one s. *Education:* Oslo Univ., Music Conservatorium, Oslo, Norwegian State Opera School, studied in Vienna, Salzburg and Bayreuth, studied with Erna Skaug, Ingrid Bjoner, Kim Borg, Anna Reynolds and Jean Cox. *Career:* debut recital, Oslo 1979; as opera singer, Leoncavallo's Nedda, Gelsenkirchen 1982; has appeared in Hamburg, Frankfurt, Nuremberg, Catania, Strasbourg, Eutin, Basel and Lubeck; television, radio and film in Norway, Austria and Poland; important opera roles include Agathe in Freischütz, Rezia in Oberon, Susanna in Figaro, Giulietta in Hoffmann, Ellen Orford in Peter Grimes, Euridice in Orpheus and Euridice, Sieglinde in Walküre, Senta in Holländer; Leader, Norwegian Opera Singer Soc. *Recordings:* Zigeunerlieder with Audin Kayser, piano; Irmgard in Franz Schreker's opera Flammen, conducted by Frank Strobl; Norwegian Children's Songs (with Audin Kayser, piano). *Honours:* hon. mem. Robert Stolz Soc. 2001, Norwegian Opera Singers' Asscn 2005. *Address:* Sarbuvollveien 8A, 1363 Høvik, Norway (home). *Telephone:* 67590546 (home); 93497417 (office). *E-mail:* ktheiser@sensewave.com (home).

THEODOLOZ, Annelise; Swiss singer (soprano); b. 1954. *Education:* studied with Carl Flesch and Tibor Varga, Lausanne Conservatory and Guildhall School of Music and Drama, London. *Career:* debut as Dorabella in Così fan tutte and Dalila in Samson et Dalila, National Hungarian Opera under conductor János Kovács; has performed as soloist in major concert halls and on radio, with Orchestre de la Suisse Romande, Israel Chamber Orchestra, Bach Solisten Amsterdam, Orchestre National de Lyon and many others all over Europe, in the Middle East, Japan and Canada; French debut as Bradamante in Handel's Alcina 1998; further roles include Berlioz's Béatrice et Bénédict in Nancy and Tours under M. Ossonce; debut as soprano lirico spinto with Leonora's aria from Verdi's La Forza del Destino at Geneva, 2000. *E-mail:* csch@iprolink.ch.

THEODORAKIS, Mikis; Greek composer and politician; b. 29 July 1925, island of Chios; s. of Georges Michel Theodorakis and Aspasia Poulaki; m. Myrto Altinoglou 1953; one s. one d. *Education:* Athens Conservatoire, Paris Conservatoire, France. *Career:* joined resistance against German occupation of Greece 1942; arrested and deported during civil war 1947–52; moved to Paris 1953 and studied under Olivier Messiaen; first public concert Sonatina (for pianoforte), Paris 1954; set to bouzouki music the poem Epitaphios by Iannis Ritsos 1958–59 and subsequently wrote numerous other successful songs; ballet music for Antigone (first performed in London by Dame Margot Fonteyn), Stuttgart Ballet, others; returned to Greece 1962; Leader, Lambrakis youth movt; MP 1963; imprisoned for political activities 1967, released April 1970; lived in Paris 1970–74; resgnd from CP March 1972; MP 1981–1986 (resgnd), 1989–93 (resgnd), Minister of State 1990–92 (resgnd); f. Cttee for Greek-Turkish Friendship 1986. *Works include:* Sinfonia (oratorio) 1944, Love and Death (voice, strings) 1945–48, Assi-Gonia (orchestra) 1945–50, Sextet for Flute 1946, Oedipus Tyrannus (strings) 1946, Greek Carnival (ballet suite) 1947, First Symphony (orchestra) 1948–50, Five Cretan Songs (chorus, orchestra) 1950, Orpheus and Eurydice (ballet) 1952, Barefoot Battalion (film) 1953, Suite No. 1 (four movements, piano and orchestra) 1954, Poèmes d'Eluard (Cycle 1 and Cycle 2) 1955, Suite No. 2 (chorus, orchestra) 1956, Suite No. 3 (five movements, soprano, chorus, orchestra) 1956, Ill Met by Moonlight (film) 1957, Sonatina No. 1 (violin, piano) 1957, Les amants de Teruel (ballet) 1958, Piano Concerto 1958, Sonatina No. 2 (violin, piano) 1958, Antigone (ballet) 1958, Epitaphios (song cycle) 1959, Deserters (song cycle) 1958, Epiphania (song cycle) 1959, Honeymoon (film) 1960, Phoenician Women – Euripides (theatre music) 1960, Axion Esti (pop oratorio) 1960, Electra-Euripides (film), Phaedra (film) 1962, The Hostage (song cycle) 1962, The Ballad of the Dead Brother (musical tragedy) 1962, Zorba the Greek (film), The Ballad of Mauthausen (song cycle) 1965, Romiossini (song cycle) 1965, Lisistrata – Aristophanes (theatre music) 1966, Romancero Gitano (Lorca) (song cycle) 1967, Sun and Time (song cycle) 1967, Arcadias Nos. 1–10 (song cycles) 1968–69, Canto General (Pablo Neruda) (pop oratorio) 1972, Z (film), Etat de Siège (film) 1973, Ballads (song cycle) 1975, Symphony No. 2 (orchestra and piano) 1981, Messe Byzantine (Liturgie) 1982, Symphony No. 3 (orchestra, chorus, soprano) 1982, Sadoukeon Passion (cantata for orchestra, chorus, soloists) 1983, Liturgie No. 2 1983, Symphony No. 7 (orchestra, chorus, soloists) 1983, Requiem 1985, Kostas Kariotakis (opera in two acts) 1985, Beatrice (song cycle) 1987, Faces of the Sun (song cycle) 1987, Symphony No. 4 1987, Memory of Stone (song cycle) 1987, Like an Ancient Wind (song cycle) 1987, Canto Olympico (symphony) 1991, Medea (opera) 1990, Electra (opera) 1993. *Publications include:* La Dette, Journals of Resistance 1972, Ballad of the Dead Brother, Culture et dimensions politiques 1973, Star System, Antimanifeste, Les chemins de l'Archange (autobiog.), 4 vols 1986–92. *Honours:* Hon. mem. Acad. of Athens 2013; Gold Medal, Moscow Shostakovich Festival 1957, Copley Prize, USA 1957, First Prize Athens Popular Song Festival 1961, Sibelius Award, London 1963, Gold Medal for Film Music, London 1970, Socrates Prize, Stockholm 1974, First Literary Prize, Athens 1987; Lenin Int. Peace Prize 1982. *Address:* Epifanous 1, Akropolis, 117 42 Athens, Greece. *Telephone:* (1) 9214863. *Fax:* (1) 9236325. *Website:* en.mikis-theodorakis.net.

THEURING, Günther; Austrian conductor and academic; *Professor, University of Music, Vienna*; b. 28 Nov. 1930, Paris, France. *Education:* choirboy in Vienna, univ. studies in law and musicology, Univ. of Music Vienna with Hans Swarowsky and Ferdinand Grossmann. *Career:* Regens Chori at St Rochus Church, Vienna 1950; Conductor, Vienna Acad. Chorus 1954; Founder and Conductor, Vienna Jeunesse-Chorus 1959; Conductor, Contraste Ensemble for Contemporary Music 1971; concerts with Munich, Leipzig and Berlin Radio Choirs, Rias Chamber Choir, Berlin, Danish Radio Choir, Copenhagen, ORF Choir, Vienna and others; conductor of orchestras, including Vienna Symphony Orchestra, ORF Symphony Orchestra, Tonkünstler Orchester Wien, Mozarteum Orchestra, Salzburg, Orchestra della Scala, Milan, Jerusalem Symphony Orchestra; Gewandhausorchester, Leipzig, Danish Radio Orchestra, Copenhagen, Leipzig Radio Orchestra, Prague Symphony, Slovakian Philharmonic, Bratislava, and Vienna Chamber Orchestra; Pres. and Artistic Dir, Vienna master courses 1971–; Prof. Ordinarius, Univ. of Music, Vienna 1973–; Music Dir, Alpbach European Forum –1982; Artistic Dir, First World Symposium for Choral Music, held in Vienna 1987. *Recordings include:* concert extracts. *Honours:* Gold Badge of Service 1970, Cross of Honour for Science and Arts 1984; first prize, Choir Competition, Arezzo 1956, Ferdinand Grossmann Prize 1999. *Address:* Landstrasser Hauptstrasse 67, Vienna 1030, Austria (office). *Telephone:* 6645027530 (office); 17146125 (home). *Fax:* 17146125 (home). *E-mail:* guenther.theuring@aon.at. *Website:* www.wiener-meisterkurse.at (office).

T'HEZAN, Helia; French singer (soprano); b. 23 Aug. 1934, Rieumes. *Education:* Toulouse Conservatoire, Musikhochschule, Berlin. *Career:* debut, Bordeaux 1958 in Armide by Lully; sang at the Paris Opéra and the Opéra-Comique from 1959, Covent Garden 1965 in the title role of Gluck's Iphigénie en Tauride, Glyndebourne 1966 as Charlotte in Werther, and Monte Carlo 1973 in the premiere of La Reine Morte by Rossellini; has sung at Lyon, Marseille, Geneva, Rome, Trieste, Turin, Lisbon and Philadelphia; sang at the Paris Opéra 1988 as Juno in Orphée aux Enfers. *Recordings include:* Manon by Massenet.

THIBAUDET, Jean-Yves; French pianist; b. 7 Sept. 1961, Lyon. *Education:* Paris Conservatoire, Lyon Conservatory of Music. *Career:* began piano studies at age five and made first public appearance at age seven; appears with major orchestras in USA and Europe including Royal Concertgebouw, London Philharmonic, Royal Philharmonic, Orchestre Nat. de France, etc.; regular visitor to major US and European music festivals; in recital has collaborated with mezzo-sopranos Brigitte Fassbaender and Cecilia Bartoli, Renee Fleming and cellist Truls Mørk; debut, BBC Promenade Concerts 1992. *Recordings include:* recorded more than 50 albums, including Piano Concerti Nos. 2&5 2007, Aria—Opera Without Words 2007, Gershwin 2010, Satie: The Complete Solo Piano Music, Ravel Piano Music 2011, Rachmaninov: Piano Concertos 2012; jazz albums include Reflections on Duke: Jean-Yves Thibaudet Plays the Music of Duke Ellington, Conversations With Bill Evans. *Films:* Portrait of a Lady 1997, Bride of the Wind 2001. *Television:* Piano Grand! (PBS/Smithsonian Special) 2000. *Honours:* Chevalier, Ordre des Arts et des Lettres 2001, Officier, Ordre des Arts et des Lettres 2012; Premier Prix du Conservatoire, Paris Conservatory 1976, winner, Young Concert Artists Auditions 1981, Echo Award 1990, 1998, Schallplattenpreis 1992, Gramophone Award 1998, Edison Prize 1998, Choc de la Musique 1999, 2003, Diapason d'Or for his recordings of works by Debussy 2000, Premio Pegasus, Spoleto Festival 2002, Echo Classical Music Awards 2002, Victoire d'Honneur, Victoires de la Musique 2007. *Current Management:* c/o Jack Mastroianni, IMG Artists, Carnegie Hall Tower, 152 West 57th Street, 5th Floor, New York, NY 10019; c/o M. L. Falcone Public Relations, 155 West 68th Street, Suite 1114, New York, NY 10023, USA. *E-mail:* jmastroianni@imgartists.com. *Website:* www.jeanyvesthibaudet.com.

THIEDE, Helga; German singer (soprano); b. 6 Feb. 1940, Berlin, Germany. *Education:* Berlin Musikhochschule. *Career:* debut, Schwerin 1967, as Marina in Wolf-Ferrari's Quattro Rusteghi; sang at Schwerin until 1971, Dessau 1972–84 and Dresden Staatsoper from 1984; roles have included Leonore in Fidelio 1989, Chrysothemis in Elektra (also at Berlin Staatsoper and Kiel), Ariadne, the Marschallin, Wagner's Eva and Elisabeth, Eglantine in Euryanthe, the Mother in Dallapiccola's Il Prigioniero, and the Kostelnička in Jenůfa 1996; many concert engagements throughout Germany. *Address:* c/o Semper Opera, Theaterplatz 2, 01607 Dresden, Germany.

THIELEMANN, Christian; German conductor; *Music Director, Münchner Philharmoniker*; b. 1 April 1959, Berlin. *Education:* Berlin Hochschule für Musik, Karajan Foundation Orchestra Acad., Berlin. *Career:* musical coach in Berlin, with Karajan from 1979, at Berlin, Salzburg and Munich; asst to Daniel Barenboim at Paris, Berlin and Bayreuth; Principal Conductor, Deutsche Oper am Rhein Düsseldorf 1985; Music Dir, Nuremberg Opera 1988–92; American debut season 1991–92, with Elektra at the San Francisco Opera; Der Rosenkavalier at the New York Met 1993, Arabella 1994; regular concerts with the New York Philharmonic Orchestra and Philadelphia and Minnesota Orchestras; British debut with Jenůfa at Covent Garden 1988, returning for Elektra 1994 and the British premiere of Pfitzner's Palestrina 1997; further opera includes Capriccio in Florence, The Makropulos Case in Bologna, Don Giovanni in Berlin and Lohengrin on tour to Japan with the Deutsche Oper Berlin; season 1996 with Otello in Bologna (Principal Guest Conductor), Tristan and Meistersinger with the Deutsche Opera; further concerts with the Chicago Symphony Orchestra, Philharmonia Orchestra and the Munich Philharmonic Orchestra; Strauss's Aegyptische Helena for the Royal Opera at the Festival Hall 1998; returned to Covent Garden with Palestrina 2001; Music Dir, Deutsche Oper Berlin 1997–2004, Guest Dir 2004–; Music Dir Münchner Philharmoniker 2004–11; Musical Advisor, Bayreuther Festspiele 2008–; Chief Conductor, Staatskapelle Dresden (2012–). *Recordings include:* Wagner and Strauss, with René Kollo; Beethoven Cantatas, orchestral music by Wagner, Strauss and Pfitzner, Schumann 2nd Symphony and Beethoven Nos 5 and 7, Wagner's Parsifal 2006; Video of Arabella, from the Met, with Kiri Te Kanawa, Brahms: Klavierkonzert Nr.1 (ECHO Klassik Award for Concerto Recording of the Year/Piano – 19th Century 2012) 2011. *Address:* Munich Philharmonic Orchestra, Kellerstrasse 4/111, 81667 Munich, Germany (office). *Telephone:* (49) 894809851 (office). *E-mail:* presse.philharmoniker@muenchen.de (office). *Website:* www.mphil.de (office).

THIEME, Helga; German singer (soprano); b. 27 Feb. 1937, Oberlengsfeld. *Education:* studied in Frankfurt. *Career:* sang in opera at Basle 1962–65, Bielefeld 1965–67, Wiesbaden 1967–68, Hamburg 1968–83, notably in the premieres of The Devils of Loudun by Penderecki 1969 and Josef Tal's Ashmedai 1971, Bremen 1974–76, St Gallen from 1980 and Zürich 1984–85; guest engagements at Berne, Deutsche Oper Berlin, state operas of Munich and Stuttgart, Düsseldorf, Vienna Volksoper, Barcelona and Cologne; roles have included Susanna, Zerlina, Despina and the Queen of Night, Norina and Adina, Lortzing's Gretchen and Marie, Gilda, Aennchen, Marenka, Sophie in Der Rosenkavalier, Isotta in Die schweigsame Frau and Ida in Henze's Junge Lord. *Recordings include:* The Devils of Loudun. *Address:* c/o Staat Hochschule für Musik, 30175 Hannover, Germany.

THIEME, Ulrich, DipMus, PhD; German recorder player, musicologist and teacher; b. 5 Aug. 1950, Hamm. *Career:* television appearances with broadcasts for several German stations, 1969–; recorder teacher, Acad. of Music, Cologne 1973–78, Acad. of Music, Hannover 1978–; concert tours throughout Europe, Eastern Asia and South America and numerous concerts with recorder and lute-guitar duo in Germany; mem. European Recorder Teachers Assen, German Section (fmr vice-pres.). *Recordings:* Jürg Baur's Tre Studi per Quattro; Bach's Brandenburg Concertos; Baroque Recorder Music by various composers including Delalande, Bonocini and Mancini. *Publications:* Studien zum Jugendwerk A Schoenbergs, 1979; Affektenlehre im Barocken Musikdenken, 1984. *Honours:* first prize German Young Musicians' Competition 1967. *Address:* c/o Staatliche Hochschule für Musik, D-3 Hannover, Germany.

THIOLLIER, François-Joël; French/American concert pianist; b. 12 Nov. 1943, Paris; m. Beatrice Fitch 1978; one s. *Education:* studied in Paris with Robert Casadesus, Juilliard School. *Career:* played first concert in New York, aged five; many concerts in over 30 countries including appearances with the Orchestre de Paris, Nouvel Orchestre Philharmonique, Moscow and Leningrad Philharmonic Orchestras, the Hague Residentie Orkest, Tokyo and Berlin Philharmonics and RAI in Italy; concert halls include Amsterdam Concertgebouw, Théâtre des Champs Elysées, Teatro Real of Madrid, Accademia di Santa Cecilia, Rome, and Victoria Hall Geneva; played the Busoni Concerto in Berlin. *Recordings:* over 40 albums including Complete works of Rachmaninov and Gershwin, Beethoven Sonatas Op 27 No. 2, Op 13 and Op 57, Liszt Sonata and Complete Songs for Tenor and Piano, Brahms Sonata Op 5, Paganini Variations, Mozart Sonata K330 and Quintet K452. *Honours:* Officier, Ordre des Arts et des Lettres 2004; prizewinner at tnt. piano competitions including Viotti, Casella, Busoni, Pozzoli, Montreal, Tchaikovsky Moscow, Marguérite Long, Paris, Queen Elisabeth, Brussels. *Website:* fjthiollier.com.

THOMALLA, Hans, DMA; German composer; b. 1975, Bonn. *Education:* Musikhochschule Frankfurt, Stanford Univ., USA. *Career:* apptd Asst Dramaturge, Stuttgart Opera 1999–, later Dramaturge and Artistic Advisor to the Dir; works commissioned by groups including Stuttgart Opera, Arditti Quartet and Ensemble Recherche and performed in Europe and USA including festivals at Tanglewood, Chicago, Milwaukee Unruly Music, Donaueschingen, Wien Modern, Witten, Ultraschall Berlin, Takefu, Steirischer Herbst, Festival d'Automne, Paris (composer portrait) and Zurich Contemporary Music Days 2008; Asst Prof. of Composition, Northwestern Univ., USA. *Compositions include:* chamber works: Bebungen string trio 2006, Momentsmusicaux for 5 instruments 2003–04, Lied for saxophone, vibraphone and piano 2008, Albumblatt for string quartet 2010, Capriccio for clarinet, violin, viola and cello 2012; other: Rauschen for two speakers and orchestra 1998, Fremd (opera for Stuttgart Opera main stage) 2005–11, Cello Counterpart for cello solo 2006, Ausruff for large ensemble 2007, 1 2 three 4 1 2 three 4 for large orchestra 2009, Percussion Counterpart, Rhapsody for 4 reverberating sound objects 2009. *Honours:* fellowships from DAAD, Studienstiftung des deutschen Volkes, Stanford Humanities Center, MacDowell Colony and SWR-Experimentalstudio; Kranichsteiner Musikpreis 2004, Christoph Delz Prize 2006, Ernst von Siemens Foundation Composers Prize 2011. *Address:* Northwestern University School of Music, 711 Elgin Road, Evanston, IL 60208-1200, USA (office). *E-mail:* h-thomalla@northwestern.edu (office). *Website:* www.hans-thomalla.com (office).

THOMAS, Augusta Read, MMus; American composer; b. 24 April 1964, Glen Cove, NY. *Education:* Northwestern Univ., Yale Univ. with Jacob Druckman, Harvard Univ. Soc. of Fellows, Royal Acad. of Music, London. *Career:* freelance composer; faculty mem., Eastman School of Music, Rochester, NY 1993–2001; Prof. of Music, Northwestern Univ., Chicago, IL 2001–07; Mead Composer-in-Residence, Chicago Symphony Orchestra 1997–2006; mem. bd of dirs American Music Center 2000–, Chair. 2005–08; mem. American Acad. of Arts and Letters 2009–. *Compositions include:* Vigil for cello and chamber orchestra 1992, Ligeia chamber opera (Int. Orpheus Prize) 1994, Words of the Sea for orchestra 1996, Orbital Beacons for orchestra 1997, Ritual Incantations cello concerto 1999, Ceremonial for orchestra 1999, Daylight Divine 2001, Prayer Bells for orchestra 2001, In My Sky at Twilight 2002, Silver Chants the Litanies (homage to Luciano Berio) for solo horn and ensemble, Tangle for orchestra, Galaxy Dances ballet for orchestra, Gathering Paradise for solo soprano and orchestra, Grace Notes for orchestra, Terpsichore's Dream for orchestra, Carillon Sky for violin and chamber orchestra. *Honours:* Int. Orpheus Prize for Opera, Spoleto Italy 1994, Charles Ives Fellowship 1994, Rockefeller Foundation grant 1997, New York State Artist Fellowship 1998, Koussevitzky Award 1999, Siemens Award 2000, American Acad. Award 2001. *Address:* c/o PO Box 769, Lee, MA 01238, USA. *Telephone:* (617) 306-8112 (office). *E-mail:* artz4gusty@aol.com (office). *Website:* www.augustareadthomas.com.

THOMAS, Caryl, MA, ARCM, FRWCMD; British harpist; *Head of Harp Department, Royal Welsh College of Music and Drama*; b. 23 Oct. 1958, Aberystwyth, Dyfed, Wales; m. Huw Williams 1985. *Education:* Welsh Coll. of Music and Drama, New York Univ., USA. *Career:* debut, Carnegie Hall, New York 1981; freelance harpist, concentrating on solo and concert work with emphasis on BBC Radio 3 and Channel 4 TV broadcasting; appearances include London debut at Wigmore Hall, New York debut at Carnegie Recital Hall, concerto soloist with BBC Nat. Orchestra of Wales 1982, Mozarteum Orchestra in Salzburg, Austria 1984; Chair. Artistic Cttee for 7th European Harp Symposium, Cardiff 2007, World Harp Congress, Cardiff 2020; Head of Harp Dept, Royal Welsh Coll. of Music and Drama, Fellow; mem. Bd of Dirs World Harp Congress. *Recordings:* Mozart Concerto for flute and harp (with London Philharmonic Orchestra, flautist Jonathan Snowden and conducted by Andrew Litton) 1987, French Impressions (with Prometheus Ensemble). *Address:* Hendre'r Wenallt, St Athan Road, Cowbridge, Vale of Glamorgan, CF71 7HY, Wales (home). *Fax:* (1446) 771931 (home). *E-mail:* caryl.thomas.ehs@btinternet.com.

THOMAS, David; British singer (bass); b. 26 Feb. 1943, Orpington, Kent, England; m. Veronica Joan Dean 1982; three d. *Education:* St Paul's Cathedral Choir School, London, King's School, Canterbury, Choral Scholar, King's Coll., Cambridge. *Career:* began singing as boy chorister in St Paul's Cathedral Choir, London; repertoire from Baroque and Classical, and includes works by Walton, Tippett, Britten, Stravinsky, Schoenberg and Schnittke; tours to Europe, USA and Japan; appearances at int. festivals, including Tanglewood, Salzburg, Edinburgh, Lucerne, Stuttgart, Aldeburgh and BBC Promenade Concerts; has appeared with many of the major symphony orchestras and ensembles in UK, including City of Birmingham Symphony, London Philharmonic, Royal Philharmonic, Philharmonia, Hallé, Royal Liverpool Philharmonic, Chamber Orchestra of Europe, London Classical Players, Scottish Chamber Orchestra, Manchester Camerata, Northern Sinfonia, Taverner Consort, Acad. of Ancient Music and London Baroque, and has worked regularly with conductors including Simon Rattle, John Eliot Gardiner, Nicholas McGegan and Christopher Hogwood; notable engagements in UK include TV recording of Beethoven's 9th Symphony with London Classical Players conducted by Roger Norrington, Handel's Orlando at BBC Proms conducted by Christopher Hogwood and Die Schöpfung with Chamber Orchestra of Europe and Frans Bruggen; regular concerts with soprano Emma Kirkby and lutenist Anthony Rooley; sang Sarasto in Covent Garden Festival's production of Die Zauberflöte and the Commendatore in Don Giovanni and General Spork in Cornet Cristoph Rilke's Song of Love and Death for Glyndebourne Touring Opera; other engagements have included performances of the Christmas Oratorio in Leipzig and Berlin, a series of Messiahs in Italy and concerts with the Orchestre de la Suisse Romande, Fundaçao de Sao Carlos in Lisbon, Wiener Akademie, with Kammerchor Stuttgart in concerts in Göttingen, and Handel's Serse and Resurrezione in Brighton and Göttingen; engagements in USA have included Messiah with Los Angeles Philharmonic in the Hollywood Bowl, Haydn's Creation with Boston Symphony Orchestra and Simon Rattle, Messiah at Lincoln Center with Acad. of Ancient Music, Schubert's Winterreise at Cornell University and Handel's Judas Maccabaeus, Susanna and Theodora with Philharmonia Baroque and Nicholas McGegan; currently mem. staff, Trinity Laban Conservatoire of Music and Dance, London. *Recordings include:* more than 100 records, including Handel's Serse (Hanover Band/Nicholas McGegan), Handel's Susanna, Apollo and Daphne and Judas Maccabeus (Philharmonia Baroque/Nicholas McGegan), Handel's Semele, Purcell's Fairy Queen and Bach's Magnificat (Monteverdi Choir/English Baroque Soloists/John Eliot Gardiner), Handel's Messiah, Orlando, Athalia, etc. (Acad. of Ancient Music/ Christopher Hogwood), Handel's Acis, Galatea e Polifemo (London Baroque/ Charles Medlam), Handel's Messiah and Israel in Egypt, Bach's B Minor Mass and St John Passion (Taverner Consort & Players/Andrew Parrot), Handel's Messiah (Bach Collegium, Japan/Masaaki Suzuki), Coffee Cantata with Emma Kirkby, Mozart's Requiem (Hanover Band/Roy Goodman), Stravinsky's Pulcinella (City of London Sinfonia/Richard Hickox) and The Creation

(City of Birmingham Orchestra/Simon Rattle), Beethoven Choral Symphony (American Bach Soloists/Jeffrey Thomas); solo record Arias for Montagnana, Handel. *Address:* Trinity Laban Conservatoire of Music and Dance, King Charles Court, Old Royal Naval College, London, SE10 9JF, England (office). *Telephone:* (20) 8305-4444 (office). *E-mail:* d.thomas@trinitylaban.ac.uk (office); davidthomas@london.com (home). *Website:* www.trinitylaban.ac.uk (office).

THOMAS, Gwion; British singer (baritone); b. 1954, Wales. *Education:* Royal Northern Coll. of Music. *Career:* appearances with WNO, Royal Opera Garden Venture, Kent Opera and the Aldeburgh Festival (in the title role in the premiere of Lefanu's Wildman 1995); other roles include Orestes, Mozart's Don Giovanni, Count and Papageno, and Britten's Tarquinius, Billy Budd and Ned Keene; TV appearances in Weir's Night at the Chinese Opera and Scipio's Dream; concerts with BBC Symphony Orchestra, London Philharmonic Orchestra; Visiting Tutor, Birmingham Conservatoire. *Address:* The Vicarage, Station Road, Brixworth, Northampton, NN6 9DF, England. *Telephone:* (1604) 882-014. *E-mail:* gwionthomas1@btinternet.com. *Website:* www.gwionthomas.com.

THOMAS, Matthew Elton; Canadian singer (baritone); b. 1963. *Career:* performances as Kuligin in Katya Kabanova for the Canadian Opera Co., and Marcello in La Bohème at Vancouver; Mozart's Count, Guglielmo and Don Giovanni at the Banff Centre of the Performing Arts; Ourrais in Gounod's Mireille and Le Conte in Massenet's Grisélidis for Opera in Concert, Toronto; British performances include Rigoletto for Clonter Opera Farm and English Touring Opera 1996; Rossini's Figaro for ETO, Belcore (L'Elisir d'amore) for Mid Wales Opera and Valentin in Faust for Dublin Grand Opera Society; further appearances as Hercules/The Herald in Gluck's Alceste for Scottish Opera and Don Giovanni for Opera on a Shoestring, Glasgow; concert repertoire includes Carmina Burana, Messiah, Elijah, and the Requiems of Brahms, Fauré and Duruflé.

THOMAS, Michael Tilson (see Tilson Thomas, Michael)

THOMAS, Nova; American singer (soprano); b. 1960, North Carolina. *Education:* Univ. of Bloomington with Eileen Farrell. *Career:* debut as Mimi in La Bohème at North Carolina; appearances at opera houses in Cologne, Hamburg, Belfast (Opera Northern Ireland), St Louis, Seattle, San Diego, Detroit and New York City Opera; season 1991–92 in Cologne and Paris as Giulia in La Scala di Seta; roles have included Violetta, the Four Heroines in Les Contes d'Hoffmann, the Trovatore Leonora and Anna Bolena; further engagements as Mozart's Constanze for Cologne Opera, Norma with Seattle Opera and Hoffmann under Richard Bonynge; sang Adalgisa in Norma at Philadelphia 1998. *Recordings include:* title role in The Bohemian Girl, under Bonynge. *Honours:* winner Metropolitan Opera Nat. Council Auditions 1984.

THOMAS, Peter; British violinist; b. 1944, South Wales. *Education:* studied in England. *Career:* Second Violinist, Allegri Quartet 1963–68; co-founder, Orion Piano Trio, becoming resident ensemble at Southampton Univ.; Leader, BBC Nat. Orchestra of Wales 1972, then Philharmonia; Leader, City of Birmingham Symphony Orchestra; Artistic Dir, Birmingham Ensemble; String Adviser to Gustav Mahler Youth Orchestra, Vienna; Purcell Room, London recital 1993, with works by Schubert, Berio (Sequenza VIII), Schoenberg and Busoni (2nd Sonata). *Honours:* Menuhin Prize at Bath Festival 1958, BBC Prize for British and Commonwealth Ensembles (with Orion Piano Trio). *Address:* Camerata Artists, 4 Margaret Road, Birmingham B17 0EU, England.

THOMASCHKE, Thomas Michael; German singer (bass); *Professor of Vocals, Hochschile für Musik, Dresden;* b. 2 Aug. 1943, Pirna; m. 1964; one s. one d. *Education:* Dresden Hochschule für Musik. *Career:* debut in Freiberg, Germany, in Tosca 1963; sang in Leipzig, Dresden, and at the Komische Oper Berlin in the 1960s; La Scala, Bavarian State Opera, Glyndebourne, Covent Garden, Paris, Lisbon, Buenos Aires, Vienna, Edinburgh, Cape Town, Rome, Florence and Amsterdam; has sung Figaro, Don Giovanni, Rocco in Fidelio, Sarastro in The Magic Flute, Gurnemanz in Parsifal, Ramphis in Aida; Artistic Director of Festival Mitte Europa 1992–; Prof. of Vocals, Hochschile für Musik, Dresden 2004–. *Recordings include:* Bach and Handel, conducted by Nikolaus Harnoncourt; Weber, Freischütz, Philips, Colin Davis; Beethoven 9th Symphony, Yehudi Menuhin. *Publications:* contrib. to Opernwelt. *Honours:* Federal Cross of Merit, Germany 2004; Schumanpreis 1966, Tschaikowskypreis 1970, 1st Prize, Preis Hertogenbosch 1971. *Address:* Hochschile für Musik Carl Maria von Weber, PF 120039, 01001 Dresden, Germany (office). *Telephone:* (351) 4923600 (office). *Fax:* (351) 4923657 (office). *E-mail:* rektorat@hfmdd.de (office). *Website:* www.hfmdd.de (office).

THOME, Diane, DMus; American composer, pianist and academic; b. 25 Jan. 1942, Pearl River, NY. *Education:* studied with Dorothy Taubman in New York, Robert Strassburg, Darius Milhaud at Aspen, Roy Harris at Inter-American Univ., PR, Princeton Univ. with Milton Babbitt, studied with Alexander Boscovich in Israel. *Career:* music teacher, Princeton Univ., NJ 1973–74; theory and 20th-century music teacher, SUNY, Binghamton 1974–77; Prof. of Theory and Composition, Univ. of Washington School of Music, Seattle; mem. SCI Inc., BMI, CMS. *Compositions include:* chamber: three pieces 1958, three movements 1958, Sonatine 1960, Suite 1961, Quartet 1961, Constellations 1966; electronic music: Le Berceau de Miel 1968, Spectrophonie 1969, Polyvalence 1972, January Variations 1973, Los Nombres 1974, Alexander Boscovich Remembered 1975, Anais 1976, Sun-

flower Space 1978, Winter Infinities 1980, To Search the Spacious World 1986, The Ruins of the Heart for soprano, orchestra and tape 1991, Angels for Virtual Reality Artwork 1992, The Palaces of Memory for large chamber ensemble or chamber orchestra and tape 1993, Masks of Eternity 1994, Unseen Buds for chorus and tape 1995, Unfold, Entwine 1998, Like a Seated Swan for viola and tape 2000; multimedia works: In My Garden 1956, Caprice 1957, Night Passage 1973, Bright Air/Brilliant Fire, Levadi (Alone), Unseen Buds; orchestral: three movements 1962, S'Embarquement 1971, The Golden Messengers 1984, Lucent Flowers 1988; piano works: Sonatine 1959, Pianismus; sacred works: Three Psalms 1979; vocal: Ash On An Old Man's Sleeve 1962, Spring and Fall: To a Young Child 1962, Cantata 1964, Songs on Chinese Verses 1964, The Yew Tree 1979, Three Sonnets by Sri Aurobindo (settings for soprano and orchestra) 1984, Celestial Canopy 1999.

THOMPSON, Adrian; British singer (tenor); b. 1954, London, England. *Education:* Guildhall School of Music and Drama, London. *Career:* opera engagements with the Glyndebourne Festival, Scottish Opera, Handel Opera Society and at the Buxton, Aldeburgh, Wexford, Lausanne and Göttingen Festivals; roles include Ariodante, Snout and Flute in A Midsummer Night's Dream, Albert Herring, Podesta, Pedrillo in Die Entführung, Le nozze di Figaro, Così fan tutte, Bardolph in Falstaff, Conti's Don Quixote in Sierra Morena, the Simpleton in Boris Godunov and Nurse in L'Incoronazione di Poppea; sang Alfred in Die Fledermaus at Belfast, 1990, the title role in Haydn's Orlando Paladino at Garsington Manor, Oxford, and Britten's Flute at Sadler's Wells, 1990 (Snout at Glyndebourne, 1989); concert performances throughout Europe and the UK in works by Purcell, Bach, Handel, Berlioz, Schoenberg and Tippett; Britten repertoire includes Les Illuminations, The Serenade, Nocturne, Canticles and Song Cycles; appearances with leading British orchestras, the Netherlands Chamber Orchestra, Nash Ensemble and Stockholm Bach Choir; frequent Promenade Concerts and recitals at the Aldeburgh, Bath, Lichfield and Buxton festivals; has sung Schubert's Die schöne Müllerin at the Wigmore Hall and songs by Schubert and Schoenberg at South Bank; recitals in Israel, Canada, Germany, France and Switzerland; recitals in USA, Salome in Netherlands, Handel's Tamerlano at Karlsruhe and Irus in Monteverdi's Ulisse at the Coliseum, London, 1992–93; sang Grimoaldo in Rodelinda with Broomhill Opera, 1996; Schoolmaster in Janáček's Vixen at Spoleto, 1998; Albert Gregor in The Makropulos Case at Cologne, 2000. *Recordings include:* Gurney's Ludlow and Teme; Beggar's Opera. *Current Management:* Hazard Chase, 25 City Road, Cambridge CB1 1DP, England. *Telephone:* (1223) 312400. *Fax:* (1223) 460827. *E-mail:* info@hazardchase.co.uk. *Website:* www.hazardchase.co.uk.

THOMPSON, Donald Prosser, AB, MA, PhD; American academic, conductor and writer; b. 28 Feb. 1928, Columbus, OH; m. Ana Christina Figueroa Laugier 1972; two s. one d. *Education:* Univ. of Missouri, Akademie für Musik, Vienna, Austria, Eastman School of Music, Univ. of Iowa. *Career:* Prof. and Chair Dept of Music, Univ. of Puerto Rico 1956–85 (retd); conductor of opera, music theatre, television, San Juan, Puerto Rico 1956–; music critic, San Juan Star 1957–60, 1975–94; consultant in arts management 1985–. *Publications:* contrib. to Manual para monografias musicales 1980, The New Grove Dictionary of Music 1980, The New Grove Dictionary of American Music 1986, Music Research in Puerto Rico 1982, The Puerto Rico Symphony Orchestra 1985, The New Grove Dictionary of Opera 1992, El joven Tavarez: nuevos documentos y nuevas perspectivas 1993, Diccionario de musica española e hispanoamericana 1994; contrib. to journals, including Revista musical chilena 1984, African Music 1975–76, Inter American Music review 1989, Revista musical de Venezuela 1989, Bibliografia musicologica latinoamericana 1992, 1993, Latin American Music Review 1983, 1985, 1990, 1993.

THOMPSON, Lesleigh Karen, BMus, MMus; Australian composer and pianist; b. 8 Nov. 1966, Bulawayo, Rhodesia (now Zimbabwe). *Education:* Univ. of Melbourne, studied with Brenton Broadstock, Stephen Ingham. *Career:* Lecturer in Music Techniques, Univ. of Melbourne 1993–96; examiner, Australian Music Examinations Bd 1997–. *Compositions include:* Toccata for piano 1989, Captive for ensemble 1991, Enost for string quartet 1992, Sonata for Piano: Mad Men, Mad Times 1992, Sphygmus for piano 1992, Exuviae for piano 1993, Facade for guitar 1994, Clandestine for orchestra 1994, Sweet Talk for guitar and cello 1995, Roulette for piano 1996. *Honours:* New Audience Award for Composition 1990, Albert H. Maggs Award 1993.

THOMPSON, Margaret (Meg), BMAS; American singer (mezzo-soprano); b. 26 Aug. 1962, Glen Cove, NY; d. of William James Thompson and Margaret Faris Thompson; one s. *Education:* New England Conservatory, Boston, Univ. of Delaware, Salzburg Mozarteum with Grace Bumbry. *Career:* more than 70 operatic roles in Germany, Austria, Spain and USA; roles have included Fricka, Eboli, Strauss's Octavian and Composer, Judith in Duke Bluebeard's Castle, Venus in Tannhäuser, Charlotte in Werther, Queen of the Spirits in Marschner's Hans Heiling, Britten's Oberon, Suzuki, and Margaretha in Schumann's Genoveva, Suzuki, Hänsel, Jo in Adamo's Little Women, The Witch in Rusalka; engagements include Teatro Real Madrid, Volksoper Wien, Leipzig, Wiesbaden, Avery Fisher Hall and New York City Opera, Lincoln Center, Carnegie Hall, Spoleto Festival USA, Washington Nat. Opera, Kennedy Center, Los Angeles Opera; performed opposite Placido Domingo, Anna Netrebko, Matti Salminen, Patricia Racette, Vladimir Chernov and Carol Vaness; worked with conductors including Placido Domingo, James Conlon, Peter Schneider, Asher Fisch, M. Rostropovich, Julius Rudel and Kent Nagano; numerous recital and concert works at major concert halls around the world from Mahler, Bach, Mozart, Beethoven, Handel, Bruckner,

Haydn, Mozart, Schumann, Verdi and Penderecki; Vice-Pres. American-Austrian Soc. *Honours:* Winner, Sylvia Geszty Competition, Luxembourg, Christa Ludwig Akad. Austria Prize, Best Young Singer, Opernwelt, Best Singer of the Year, German Opertaler. *Current Management:* c/o Randsman Artists Management, 250 West 57th Street, Suite 2401, New York, NY 10107. *Telephone:* (212) 290-2281. *E-mail:* randsman@aol.com. *Address:* 33 South Shore Drive, Dover, DE 19901, USA. *Telephone:* (302) 697-1248 (office). *E-mail:* margthom16@aol.com (office). *Website:* www.margaretthompson.com.

THOMPSON, Martin; American singer (tenor); b. 1956. *Career:* many appearances at leading European and American opera houses; roles have included Werther, Hoffmann, Gounod's Roméo, Edgardo, Pinkerton, Peter Grimes, Don José, Lensky, Rodolfo, and Orombello in Bellini's Beatrice di Tenda; concerts include Beethoven's Ninth Symphony at San Francisco, Cherubini's Mass in D Minor (Stuttgart) and Britten's War Requiem; season 1997–98 with Covent Garden and Metropolitan Opera debuts (as the Duke of Mantua, and Pinkerton), Hoffmann in Philadelphia and Pinkerton at Santa Fe; other repertory includes Tom Rakewell (Philadelphia, 1997), the title role in Mozart's Mitridate (Wexford Festival, 1988), Nadir in Les pêcheurs de Perles and the title role in Argento's Voyage of Edgar Allan Poe (Dallas Opera); Santa Fé Opera 1999–2000, as Don José, Pinkerton and the Duke of Mantua; Puccini's Des Grieux for ENO 2000, Foresto in Attila at Chicago and Rodolfo in Luisa Miller for the Deutsche Oper Berlin. *Website:* www.aracnet.com/~cornflak.

THOMPSON, Michael, FRAM; British horn player; *Professor of Horn, Royal Academy of Music;* b. 4 Jan. 1954, London. *Education:* RAM, London with Ifor James. *Career:* Principal Horn, BBC Scottish Symphony Orchestra 1972–75, Philharmonia Orchestra, London 1975–85, London Sinfonietta; Prof. of Horn (Aubrey Brain Chair), Royal Acad. of Music 1984–; concert repertory includes concertos of Haydn and Mozart, Sea Eagle by Maxwell Davies, and Des Canyons aux Etoiles, by Messiaen; premieres of works by Benedict Mason, Simon Bainbridge and Anthony Powers. *Recordings include:* Standard Concertos and the Quintets of Franz Danzi and Antoine Reicha. *Address:* Royal Academy of Music, Marylebone Road, London, NW1 5HT, England. *Website:* www.ram.ac.uk.

THOMPSON, (Robert) Ian, MA, ARCM, ARCO; British singer (tenor), harpsichordist, conductor and artistic director; b. 5 April 1943, Bradford, Yorks.; m. Judith Welch 1970. *Education:* Queens' Coll., Cambridge, Royal Coll. of Music, London; singing with Campogalliani, Italy. *Career:* BBC Chorus 1966–67; Vicar Choral, St Paul's Cathedral, London 1967–77; opera and concert singer with Kent Opera and Opera North; debut, Royal Opera House, Covent Garden 1993; since debut at Rossini Festival, Pesaro 1991; has appeared regularly at leading European theatres, including La Scala, Milan, San Carlo Naples, Regio, Turin, Bastille and Châtelet, Paris, Strasbourg, Bordeaux and Lyon; broadcasts in most European countries; Visiting Lecturer, Royal Scottish Acad. of Music and Drama, Glasgow 1996–; Artistic Dir Lonsdale Music; 60e Parallèle with Philippe Mancury; Ariadne auf Naxos, with Giuseppe Sinopoli; Musical Dir Cockermouth Harmonic Society; mem. Incorporated Soc. of Musicians, Royal Coll. of Organists, The Alpine Club, Amaryllis Consort. *Recordings:* with Pro Cantione Antiqua, Early Music Consort, Società Cameristica di Lugano and Capella Clementina; Dr Wittkop in 60 Parallèle, Scaramuccio in Ariadne auf Naxos. *Address:* Hill Top, Tearnside, Kirkby Lonsdale, Cumbria, LA6 2PU, England (home).

THOMSON, Brian Edward, AM; Australian theatre designer; b. 5 Jan. 1946, Sydney; s. of Austin Thomas Thomson and Adoree Gertrude Thomson. *Education:* Applecross Sr High School, Perth Tech. Coll., Univ. of New South Wales. *Career:* Supervising Designer, closing ceremony of Olympic Games, Sydney 2000; Production Designer, Centennial of Fed. Ceremony 2001; Designer, opening and closing ceremonies, Rugby World Cup 2003. *Musicals include:* Hair, Jesus Christ Superstar (London and Australia), The Rocky Horror Show (original London production and worldwide), Chicago, The Stripper, Company, Chess, The King and I (Broadway production 1996 (Tony Award), London Palladium), How to Succeed in Business Without Really Trying, South Pacific, Hello, Dolly!, Merrily We Roll Along, Grease, Happy Days. *Theatre includes:* Housewife Superstar!!! (London and New York); The Threepenny Opera (opening season, Drama Theatre, Sydney Opera House); Big Toys (the Old Tote); A Cheery Soul, Chinchilla, Macbeth, The Doll Trilogy, The Ham Funeral, A Midsummer Night's Dream, The Crucible, The Home-coming, Uncle Vanya, Death and the Maiden, Coriolanus, Falsettos, King Lear, Arcadia, Medea, Mongrels, Third World Blues, After the Ball, White Devil (also at Brooklyn Acad. of Music), Up for Grabs (all for Sydney Theatre Co.); Arturo Ui, Rock-Ola (Nimrod); Lulu, Shepherd on the Rocks Crow (State Theatre Co. of S Australia); Ghosts, The Tempest, The Master Builder, Buzz, Frogs, Aftershocks, Radiance, Up the Road, Burnt Piano, The Laramie Project (Company B Belvoir); Angels in America (Melbourne Theatre Co.); Soulmates, One Day of the Year (Sydney Theatre Co.), My Zinc Bed, Buried Child (Company B Belvoir), Dame Edna Back With A Vengeance, Broadway 2004, Three Furies, Sydney Festival 2005. *Film and television includes:* Barlow and Chambers, Shadow of the Cobra (both mini-series); Shirly Thompson vs. the Aliens, The Rocky Horror Picture Show, Starstruck, Rebel, Night of Shadows (also dir), Ground Zero, Turtle Beach, Frauds. *Dance includes:* Synergy, Fornicon (Sydney Dance Co.), Tivol (Sydney Dance Co. and Australian Ballet). *Opera includes:* Death in Venice, The Makropulos Affair (Adelaide Festival), Turandot, Aida, Summer of the Seventeenth Doll (Vic. State Opera), Voss, Death in Venice, Tristan und Isolde, Katya Kabanova, The Eighth Wonder

(The Australian Opera), Billy Budd (Welsh Nat. Opera, Opera Australia, Canadian Nat. Opera), Sweeney Todd (Lyric Opera of Chicago), La Traviata (Helpmann Award 2012). *Honours:* Australian Film Inst. Award for production design, Rebel 1985, Ground Zero 1987, Sydney Theatre Critics' Award for Best Designer 1989, 1992, 1993, 1994, Mo Award 1994, 1995. *Address:* The Opera Centre - Sydney, 480 Elizabeth Street, Surry Hills NSW 2010, Australia. *Website:* opera.org.au/aboutus/our_artists/creative_teams/brian_thomson.

THOMSON, Heather; Canadian singer (soprano); b. 7 Dec. 1940, Vancouver; m. Perry Price. *Education:* Toronto Conservatory with Herman Geiger-Torel and Irene Jessner. *Career:* debut, Toronto 1962 in Hansel and Gretel; debut with Sadler's Wells as Micaela followed by Mimi, Marguerite in Faust and Anne Trulove in The Rake's Progress; Canadian Opera Co. roles include Manon, Rosalinda in Die Fledermaus, Donna Anna and Donna Elvira in Don Giovanni, Ellen in Peter Grimes, Marguerite in Faust, Mother in Hansel and Gretel, Mimi in La Bohème, Tatyana in Eugene Onegin, Lady Billows in Albert Hessing, and world premieres of Heloise and Abelard by Wilson, and Mario and The Magician by Sommers and the title role in Beatrice Cenci, by Goldschmidt in Magdeburg, Germany; has sung with WNO as well as throughout the British Islies, Holland, Czech Republic, Germany, Chile, Monterideo, Poland, Norway, China, the Phillipines and in USA; roles with New York City Opera include Violetta, Nedda, Donna Anna and Donna Elvira, Marguerite, Rosalinda, and Agathe in Der Freischütz; 1993–94 season as Lady Macbeth in Chemnitz in Germany, Violetta in La Traviata in Toledo, Ohio, Hanna in The Merry Widow at Victoria, BC and concerts in Germany and Canada; sang Rosalinda in Die Fledermaus in Regina, Sash 2002; teacher, School of Music, Univ. of British Columbia, Vancouver, and at the New England Vocal Studios, which she established in Danbury, CT 1997–. *Recordings:* sang Manon for CBC television, Lady Billows in Albert Herring for CBC and BBC radio, Mother in Hansel and Gretel for CBC-Radio.

THOMSON, Neil; British conductor; b. 1966, London, England. *Education:* Royal Academy of Music with George Hurst, Royal College of Music with Norman del Mar and Christopher Adey. *Career:* Director, Manson Ensemble at RAM giving many performances during the Messiaen Festival in 1987 and the Henze Festival in 1988; conducted major orchestral and instrumental works of Paul Patterson at venues around the UK; founded the contemporary music group, Terre Nova 1986, with its debut at St John's Smith Square; concerts at the Purcell Room, South Bank and the Huddersfield Contemporary Music Festival; worked with such soloists as Christopher Bunting in Dvořák's Cello Concerto and the Brahms Double Concerto with Emanuel Hurwitz; And Suddenly It's Evening by Elisabeth Lutyens with Philip Langridge, and Philip Gammon with Saint-Saëns's 2nd Concerto; concerts with the Royal Tunbridge Wells Symphony Orchestra; Music Director, Sadler's Wells Youth Ballet Workshop; concerts with the Bombay Chamber Orchestra in India. *Honours:* National Association of Youth Orchestras bursary for conductors. *Current Management:* Tom Croxon Management Ltd, 22 Hurst Road, Buckhurst Hill, Essex IG9 6AB, England. *Telephone:* (20) 8279-2516. *Fax:* (20) 8504-2200. *E-mail:* tom@tomcroxonmanagement.co.uk. *Website:* www.tomcroxonmanagement.co.uk.

THORBURN, Melissa Rachel, BMus, MMus; American singer (mezzo-soprano); *Adjunct Professor, Canisius College;* b. 9 July 1956, Monmouth, Ill.; m. Timothy Richard Sobolewski 1985; one s. *Education:* Louisiana State Univ., New England Conservatory, studied with Yvonne Lefébure in Paris, private study with Phyllis Curtin. *Career:* Handel's Messiah with Philadelphia Orchestra annually 1987–91; Berlioz's L'Enfance du Christ with Seattle Symphony, Wash. 1987; Gounod's Faust as Siebel with Deutsche Oper, Berlin 1988; Pergolesi's Stabat Mater with Puerto Rico Symphony 1988; Mozart's Le nozze di Figaro as Cherubino with Sarasota Opera, Fla 1988; Mozart's Requiem with Los Angeles Philharmonic 1991; Handel's Messiah with Nat. Symphony 1992; Mozart's Requiem and Schubert's Mass in E flat with Indianapolis Symphony conducted by Richard Hickox 1994; Bach's B Minor Mass Minor with Winter Park Bach Festival, Fla 1994; Bach's Christmas Oratorio and Cantata No. 78 with Baldwin-Wallace Bach Festival, Ohio 1995; Mendelssohn's Lobgesang with Vancouver Symphony and recitals at the Bermuda Festival 1996; Mendelssohn's A Midsummer Night's Dream with Philadelphia Orchestra conducted by Charles Dutoit 1997, and with St Louis Symphony 1998; Vivaldi's L'Olympiade with Little Orchestra Soc. 1999; Beethoven's 9th Symphony with Buffalo Philharmonic Orchestra 2001; Humperdinck's Hansel & Gretel as the Witch with Berlin Philharmonic 2002, 2003; recitals in France 2003, 2006, 2008, 2010; Roland Martin's Riders to the Sea as Maurya with Opera Sacra, Buffalo, NY 2010; Vivaldi's Gloria with Berlin Philharmonic 2012; Adjunct Prof., Canisius Coll., Buffalo. *Recordings:* Vaughan Williams's Serenade to Music with the New York Virtuosi Chamber Symphony; Sousa's Désirée with Pocono Pops. *Honours:* First Prize Winner, Metropolitan Opera Auditions, New England Region 1982. *Address:* Fine Arts Department, Canisius College, 2001 Main Street, Buffalo, NY 14208, USA (office). *Telephone:* (716) 888-2542 (office).

THORN, Benjamin, BA, PhD, DipEd; Australian composer, editor and recorder player; b. 31 Jan. 1961, Canberra, ACT. *Education:* Univ. of Sydney. *Career:* freelance performer and composer; Nat. Printing Industry Training Council 1991–2000; currently Ed. and Producer, Orpheus Music; Curator Museum of Printing at New England Regional Arts Museum, Armidale; Lecturer in Creative Arts Educ., Univ. of New England. *Exhibitions:* solo exhbns of collages at New England Regional Art Museum 2001, 2005. *Play:* Apotheosis

(Armidale Playhouse) 2000. *Compositions include:* Visioni di Cavoli for ensemble 1985, Pipistrelli Gialli for bass recorder and live electronics 1985, Chasing for three recorders 1985, Croutons II for clarinet 1985, Magnificat for chorus 1985, The Voice of the Crocodile for bass recorder 1988, The Pobble for chorus 1988, Chick Peas for two mandolins 1990, Two Diagonals and a Squiggle for recorder and percussion 1991, Missa Sine Verbum 1991, Croutons III for baroque flute 1992, Croutons IV for harpsichord 1992, Songs for my father's wedding for bass recorder 1995, Chocolate Bulbul, Forestry in New England, Purple Pavans Perhaps, We Hate Brussel Sprouts, Locked in, Bell Play (included in World Music Days 2012), Any Blue Cat Dances. *Publications:* ed. two vols of recorder music, Recorders at Large, Works of Sitsky, Strozzi and Castello. *Honours:* Jt Winner, Fellowship of Australian Composers Competition 1991, Winner, New England Art Soc. Sculpture Prize 2010. *Address:* 21 North Street, Armidale, NSW 2350, Australia (home). *Telephone:* (2) 6772-5889 (home). *E-mail:* info@orpheusmusic.com.au (office). *Website:* www.orpheusmusic.com.au (office).

THORN, Penelope; British singer (soprano); b. 19 Sept. 1957, Kent, England. *Education:* Guildhall School of Music and studied with Tito Gobbi in Italy. *Career:* sang with Karlsruhe Opera from 1980 as Adriana Lecouvreur, Alice Ford, Amelia in Ballo in Maschera, Princess in Rusalka, Giorgetta in Il Tabarro, Freia, Giulietta and Armida in Handel's Rinaldo, also at Barcelona; sang at Düsseldorf and Mannheim, then appeared at Hannover from 1985 as Tosca, Abigaille and Jenůfa; Freia and Gutrune in Der Ring des Nibelungen for Deutsche Oper am Rhein; guest appearances at Giessen in Menotti's Mara Golovin 1986 and at Bielefeld as the Forza Leonora and Asteria in Boito's Nerone; Zürich as Freia and Gutrune and at Nice as Minnie in La Fanciulla del West; has sung Senta at Freiburg, Lyon and Mannheim, Strauss's Empress at Karlsruhe and Bremen and Third Norn in Götterdämmerung at Munich Staatsoper and in Berlin, under Christian Thielemann; appearances at Saarbrücken as Aida, Salome, Leonore, Butterfly and Elsa; engaged as Salome at Stuttgart 1996; sang Third Norn in Götterdämmerung at Deutsche Oper Berlin 2000. *Honours:* winner Voci Verdiane, Bussetto 1985. *Current Management:* Konzertdirektion Fritz Dietrich GmbH, Sigmund-Freud-Strasse 1, 60435 Frankfurt am Main, Germany. *Telephone:* (69) 544504. *Fax:* (69) 5484107. *E-mail:* info@konzertdirektion-dietrich.de. *Website:* www.konzertdirektion-dietrich.de.

THORNER-MENGEDOTH, Jane; singer (soprano); b. 1955, Seattle, USA. *Education:* studied at Seattle, Munich, Milan and Geneva. *Career:* sang in concert at Vienna, with Schreker's Das Spielwerk und die Prinzessin and Pfitzner's Von deutscher Seele; Geneva Opera 1984, as Alceste; season 1985 as Salome at Seattle, Leonore at Lucerne, Tippett's Andromache at Nancy and Schreker's Princess at Wuppertal; sang Abigaille in Nabucco at the Bregenz Festival 1993–94; other roles include Cherubini's Medea, Wagner's Senta, Sieglinde and Gutrune; festival engagements at Lucerne, Basle and Lausanne; concerts with the Berlin Philharmonic Orchestra, Metropolitan Orchestra Tokyo and Orchestra of the Santa Cecilia, Rome.

THORNTON-HOLMES, Christopher; British singer (baritone); b. 1959, England. *Education:* Royal Northern College of Music. *Career:* Glyndebourne Tour and Festival from 1985, as Morales in Carmen, Jankel in Arabella, Paolo in Simon Boccanegra, Narumov in The Queen of Spades and Zaretsky in Eugene Onegin (1994); Engagements with Scottish Opera Go Round as Puccini's Sharpless, and Don Giovanni, Amonasro for New Sussex Opera and Verdi's Renato and Rigoletto, Mozart's Count and Eugene Onegin; Further engagements at the Royal Opera, Covent Garden, and La Scala Milan. *Recordings:* Emilia di Liverpool by Donizetti (Opera Rava).

THORSEN, Marianne; Norwegian violinist; b. 1972, Trondheim. *Education:* studied in Norway, Suzuki Institute, London, the Purcell School, and the Royal Academy in London with György Pauk. *Career:* solo performances in Berlin, with the Slovak Chamber Orchestra, Philharmonia, BBC Symphony Orchestra and orchestras throughout Norway; recitals at the Bergen International Festival; Member of the Leopold String Trio. *Recordings:* Svendsen's Romance with the Stavanger Symphony Orchestra; Albums with the Trondheim Soloists. *Current Management:* c/o Ingpen & Williams, 7 St George's Court, 131 Putney Bridge Road, London, SW15 2PA, England. *Telephone:* (20) 8874-3222. *Fax:* (20) 8877-3113. *E-mail:* info@ingpen.co.uk.

THURLOW, Sarah, BMus, MMus, PGDipRCM, DipRCM, ARCM; British clarinettist; b. 1974, Bromley, Kent, England. *Education:* Royal Coll. of Music with Robert Hill, Stephen Trier and Michael Harris, Scuola Internazionale di Perfezionamento Musicale, Bobbio, Italy with Hans Deinzer, studied with Andrew Marriner and Nicholas Bucknall. *Career:* debut at St John's Smith Square 1996; Philharmonia/David Parry recital debut, accompanied by Nigel Clayton, Purcell Room 1999; solo recitals include Kirckman concerts, Park Lane Group broadcast, Fresh Young Musicians, Purcell Room; numerous appearances for music clubs and societies; concertos, including touring with European Union Chamber Orchestra; orchestral as freelance with London Symphony Orchestra, Acad. of St Martin in the Fields, Sinfonia 21, London Chamber Orchestra, Orchestra of the Age of Enlightenment, BBC Philharmonic, Manchester Camerata, Viva, Philharmonia, English Baroque Soloists, Glyndebourne Touring Opera; chamber, founded Contemporary Consort 1998–; performances at Cheltenham, Brighton, Kings Lynn and York Late Music Festivals. *Current Management:* c/o Morgensterns Diary Service, PO Box 3027, South Croydon, Surrey, CR2 6ZN, England. *Telephone:* (20) 8681-

0555. *E-mail:* teleteam@morgensterns.com. *Website:* www .morgensternsdiaryservice.com.

THURMER, Harvey; Austrian violinist; b. 1950, Vienna. *Education:* Vienna Acad. of Music. *Career:* mem. of the Franz Schubert Quartet, 1983–90; many concert engagements in Europe, USA, and Australia including showings in the Amsterdam Concertgebouw, the Vienna Musikverein and Konzerthaus, the Salle Gaveau Paris and the Sydney Opera House; visits to Zürich, Geneva, Basle, Berlin, Hamburg, Rome, Rotterdam, Madrid and Copenhagen; festival engagements include Salzburg, Wiener Festwochen, Prague Spring Schubertiade at Hohenems, the Schubert Festival at Washington DC and Belfast and Istanbul Festivals; tours of Russia, Australasia and USA, and frequent concert tours of the UK; featured in the Quartet Concerto by Spohr with the Liverpool Philharmonic at the Liverpool Festival Hall; Wigmore Hall series includes Master Concerts, Russian Series, Summer Nights, and Coffee Concerts; performance of Alun Hoddinott's Quartet at the 1989 Cheltenham Festival featured on BBC Welsh television; teacher at the Vienna Conservatory and Graz Musikhochschule; masterclasses at the Royal Northern Coll. of Music and at the Lake District Summer Music. *Recordings include:* Schubert's Quartet in G, D877; Complete Quartets of Dittersdorf.

THWAITES, Penelope Mary, AM, BMus; British pianist and composer; b. 18 April 1944, Chester, England; m. Edward Jackson 1981, one s. one d. *Education:* Melbourne University, Australia, studied with Albert Ferber, William Reed. *Career:* debut at Wigmore Hall, London, 1974; regular concerts and broadcasts in London; tours worldwide, concertos with leading orchestras, Australia, the UK, America; lectures, lecture recitals, radio, television and video appearances; Artistic Dir, First London International Grainger weekend 1998; founder and Chair., Performing Australian Music Competition, London, 2001. *Compositions include:* Ride! Ride!, 1976; Dancing Pieces, 1989; A Lambeth Garland, 1990; Instrumental and organ works. *Recordings:* Australian Piano Music, 1981; Percy Grainger: complete original music for 4 hands, with John Lavender, Vol. 1, 1989, Vol. II, 1991, Vol. III, 1993; Percy Grainger: Chosen Gems for Piano, solo, 1992; Her own songs recorded, 1985, 1991; Ten recordings in Chandos Grainger Edition; Musical, Ride, Ride, 1999. *Publications:* contrib. to The Singer 1996, BBC Music Magazine 1997. *Honours:* International Grainger Society Medallion 1991. *Telephone:* (20) 7794-5090. *E-mail:* thwaites.jackson@virgin.net.

THYM, Jürgen, DipMus, PhD; musicologist; b. 2 July 1943, Bremervörde, Germany; m. Peggy Dettwiler 1992. *Education:* Hochschule für Musik, Berlin, Case Western Reserve Univ., studied with Reinhard Schwarz Schilling, Ernst Pepping, Josef Rufer, Reinhold Brinkmann, Rudolph Stephen and Jon G. Suess. *Career:* Visiting Instructor, Oberlin Coll., USA 1973; Instructor, Asst Prof., Assoc. Prof., Prof. 1973–, Chair of Musicology 1982–, Eastman School of Music, Rochester, NY. *Publications:* The Solo Song Settings of Eichendorff's Poems by Schumann and Wolf 1974, trans. of Kirnberger's The Art of Strict Musical Composition 1982, trans. of Schenker's Counterpoint 1987, 100 Years of Eichendorff Songs 1983, Schoenberg Collected Works Edition Vol. XIV 1988, Vol. XIII 1993; contrib. articles to Journal of Music Theory, Notes, American Choral Review, Comparative Literature, Journal of Musicological Research, Fontes Artis Musicae, Musica Realtà and Aurora, Eichendorff year book, Essays on Mendelssohn and Schumann.

TIBBELS, Nicole; British singer (soprano); b. 1960, England. *Education:* Sheffield University and the Guildhall School, London. *Career:* sang with the Swingle Singers and has made many concert appearances in music by Berio; other repertory includes Dies by Wolfgang Rihm, Mason's Concerto for Viola Section, Nenia by Birtwistle, and songs by Stravinsky; opera engagements as the Queen of Night with Richard Hickox, and the European Chamber Opera, Alice Ford and Rossini's Clorinda for Pimlico Opera, Serpina in La Serva Padrona for Broomhill Opera and Mozart's Constanze for Perth Festival Opera; Royal Opera Covent Garden debut 1997, as La Comtesse in Massenet's Chérubin; 1997–98 appearances as La Folie in Platée by Rameau and Fido in Paul Bunyan; premieres of works by Maxwell Davies, Bainbridge, Berio, Michael Finnissy, Jonathan Lloyd and Nigel Osborne. *Recordings include:* Berio's Sinfonia, and works by Bryars, Smalley, Cage and Stockhausen. *Current Management:* Allied Artists, 42 Montpelier Square, London, SW7 1JZ, England. *Telephone:* (20) 7589-6243. *Fax:* (20) 7581-5269. *E-mail:* info@ alliedartists.co.uk. *Website:* www.alliedartists.co.uk.

TIBERGHIEN, Cédric; French musician (piano); b. 1975. *Education:* Conservatoire Nat. Supérieur de Musique et de Danse, Paris, studied with Frédéric Aguessy and Gérard Frémy. *Career:* numerous concerts and recitals world-wide including at Carnegie Hall and Kennedy Center in USA, Royal Albert Hall, Queen Elizabeth Hall, Wigmore Hall and Barbican in UK, Salle Pleyel and Théâtre des Champs Elysées in Paris, Berlin's Bechstein Hall, Salzburg's Mozarteum, Sydney Opera and Tokyo's Bunka Kaikan and Asahi Halls; residency with Strasbourg Philharmonic 2014–15; has appeared with orchestras including Boston Symphony, Cleveland Orchestra, Washington National Symphony, Seattle Symphony, Hamburger Philharmoniker, Dresden Philharmonic, Tonhalle Orchestra Zurich, Orchestre de la Suisse Romande, Budapest Festival Orchestra, Czech Philharmonic, BBC Symphony, Philharmonique de Radio France, Orchestre de Paris, Orchestre Nat. de France, Sydney Symphony, Tokyo Philharmonic and New Japan Philharmonic; has collaborated with conductors including Christoph Eschenbach, Jiri Belohlavek, Yannick Nézet-Séguin, Simone Young, Myung-Whun Chung, Kurt Masur, Ivan Fischer, Jeffrey Tate, Louis Langrée, Ludovic Morlot,

Stéphane Denève and Enrique Mazzola; regular chamber music partners include Alina Ibragimova, Antoine Tamestit and Pieter Wispelwey. *Recordings include:* six recital discs: Debussy, Beethoven Variations, Bach Partitas, Chopin and Brahms Ballades, Brahms Hungarian Dances, Chopin Mazurkas; with Alina Ibragimova: Schubert, Ravel and Lekeu, Szymanowski, complete Beethoven violin sonatas; others: French melodies with Sophie Karthäuser, César Franck's Symphonic Variations and Les Djinns, Brahms's Concerto No.1 with the BBC Symphony and Jiri Belohlavek, Szymanowski 2014. *Honours:* CNSMD Premier Prix 1992, prizewinner at major int. piano competitions including Bremen, Dublin, Tel–Aviv, Geneva, Milan, First Prize and five special awards, including Audience Award and Orchestra Award, Long-Thibaud Competition, Paris 1998. *Website:* www.askonasholt.co.uk/artists/instrumentalists/piano/cdric-tiberghien.

TICCIATI, Robin; British conductor; *Principal Conductor, Scottish Chamber Orchestra*; b. 1983, London, England. *Education:* St Paul's School, London, Univ. of Cambridge. *Career:* trained as violinist, pianist and percussionist; fmr mem. Nat. Youth Orchestra of GB; began conducting aged 15 under guidance of Sir Colin Davis and Sir Simon Rattle; has conducted London Symphony Orchestra, Los Angeles Philharmonic, Philadelphia Orchestra, Rotterdam Philharmonic, Gothenburg Symphony Orchestra, Orchestra of the Age of Enlightenment, Accad. Naz. di Santa Cecilia, Rome, Filarmonica della Scala, Milan, Leipzig Gewandhaus Orchestra, Swedish Radio, Cleveland Orchestra, Tonhalle Orchestra, Zurich; Prin. Conductor and Artistic Dir Gävle Symphony Orchestra, Sweden 2006–09; Music Dir, Glyndebourne on Tour 2007–09; Prin. Conductor, Scottish Chamber Orchestra 2009–; Prin. Guest Conductor, Bamberger Symphoniker 2010–13; Music Dir, Glyndebourne Festival Opera 2014–. *Honours:* Arthur Belgin Medal for Most Outstanding Musician of the Year 2002, Borletti-Buitoni Trust Fellowship 2005. *E-mail:* rachel.bertaut@askonasholt.co.uk. *Website:* www.askonasholt.co.uk.

TICHY, Georg; Austrian singer (baritone); b. 9 June 1944, Vienna. *Education:* studied with Hilde Zadek in Vienna. *Career:* debut at Vienna Staatsoper 1973 in Tristan und Isolde; sang in Vienna in operas by Verdi, Rossini, Mozart, Puccini, Britten and Wagner; Sang at Maggio Musicale Florence in 1984 as Rigoletto and at Bregenz Festival in 1986 as Papageno; Sang in Schubert's Fierrabras and Wagner's Lohengrin at Vienna in 1990; Sang Ned Keene in the house premiere of Peter Grimes, Vienna Staatsoper, 1996; Season 2000–01 at Covent Garden as Faninal in Der Rosenkavalier, Don Carlo in Ernani and Verdi's Renato for the Vienna Staatsoper; Frequent concert appearances. *Recordings:* Ariadne auf Naxos; Parsifal; Alfonso und Estrella by Schubert. *Current Management:* c/o Opera Vladarski, Döblinger Hauptstrasse 57/18, 1190 Vienna, Austria. *Telephone:* (1) 368-6960/6961. *Fax:* (1) 368-6962. *E-mail:* opera.vladarski@utanet.at.

TIEBOUT, Torsten; violist; b. 21 Sept. 1963, Kassel, Germany. *Education:* music studies in Hamburg, Hannover, Trossingnen and Helsinki with Prof. Stanley Weiner, Hatto Beyerle, Emile Cantor, Hermann Voss and Teemu Kupiainen; masterclasses with Csaba Erdlyi, Kim Kashkashian, Bruno Giuranna, Tabea Zimmermann, Rainer Moog and Wolfram Christ. *Career:* debut as soloist, with Helsinki University Orchestra in first performance in Finland of revised version of Bartók's Viola Concerto, conductor John Storgårds, 13 April 1996; mem., Finnish Radio Symphony Orchestra 1991–95; Principal, Tampere Philharmonic Orchestra 1995–96; Principal Violist, Helsinki Philharmonic Orchestra 1996–. *Recordings:* numerous radio recordings as chamber musician with Cable Quartet, especially contemporary music.

TIEPPO, Giorgio; singer (tenor); b. 1953, Varese, Italy. *Education:* Giuseppe Verdi Conservatory, Milan, studied with Pier Miranda Ferraro. *Career:* sang in concert from 1977 and made opera debut at Pavia 1983, as Don Ruiz in Donizetti's Maria Padilla; appeared as Don Ruiz in Parma and Ravenna and sang further in La Bohème and Lucia di Lammermoor at Bergamo; Pinkerton in Butterfly at Genoa, Bologna, Turin and New Orleans; Vienna, Mannheim and Dublin debuts as Cavaradossi; Verona Arena in Nabucco, Il Trovatore, Un Ballo in Maschera, Norma and Aida; appearances at the Zürich Opera as Rodolfo (season 1996–97), Cavaradossi, and Luigi in Il Tabarro; further engagements in New York, Dallas, Berlin, Rome and Helsinki. *Honours:* winner Voci Nuove Verdiane Competition, Bergamo, Voci Verdiane in Busseto.

TIERNEY, Vivian; British singer (soprano); b. 26 Nov. 1957, London, England; m. Alan Woodrow. *Career:* sang as Prin. Soprano with D'Oyly Carte Opera Co.; freelance 1982–, at first with Sadler's Wells Opera Co. in Kalman's The Gypsy Princess and Lehar's The Count of Luxembourg; Edwige in Offenbach's Robinson Crusoe for Kent Opera; Hanna Glawari in Die Lustige Witwe for Opera North; ENO from 1987 as Frasquita, Euridice in Orpheus in the Underworld and Regan in the British premiere of Reimann's Lear 1989; sang title role in world premiere of Robin Holloway's Clarissa 1990; has sung with Freiburg Opera as Lady Macbeth of Mtsensk, Ellen Orford and Giulietta (Les Contes d'Hoffmann); has appeared in Handel's Alceste at Versailles; Mimi in La Bohème at Montpellier Festival; Euridice in Milhaud's Les Malheurs d'Orphée at Frankfurt; Donna Anna for Flanders Opera; sang in Sullivan's cantata The Golden Legend for Colorado Springs Orchestra; appearance with Opera 80 as Donna Anna; Marie in Wozzeck (Almeida Festival 1988); other roles include the Marschallin in Der Rosenkavalier, Jenny (in Mahagonny), Rosalinde in Die Fledermaus, and Malinka in The

Excursions of Mr Brouček; Mimi in La Bohème for ENO 1992; Gypsy Princess (Los Angeles); sang Ellen Orford in a new production of Peter Grimes at Glyndebourne 1992; Renata in The Fiery Angel in Freiburg 1993; Berg's Marie for Opera North 1993; sang Gutrune in Götterdämmerung at Covent Garden 1996; season 1998 with Jitka in Smetana's Dalibor for Scottish Opera; season 2000 as Korngold's Marietta at Cologne, Ellen Orford at Glyndebourne and Mrs Foran in premiere of The Silver Tassie, by Turnage, for ENO; other engagements include Max von Schilling's Mona Lisa at Stadttheater St Gallen, The Death of Klinghoffer for Opera OT, London premiere of Michael Nyman's Man and Boy for Almeida Opera, Rosa in world premiere of Joan Guinjoan's opera Gaudi at the Teatre del Liceu, Barcelona, Ellen Orford in Peter Grimes for the Teatro Comunale di Modena, Teatro Comunale di Ferrara and Teatro Reggio Emilia, Marie in Wozzeck at Liceu Barcelona, Mrs Gobineau in The Medium at Opera de Monte Carlo, Miss Jessel for Teatro Municipal Santiago di Chile, Miss Wingrave in Owen Wingrave for Royal Opera House Covent Garden at the Linbury.

TIKKA, Kari Juhani, DipMus; Finnish conductor and composer; b. 13 April 1946, Siilinjärvi; m. Eeva Relander 1979, three s. one d. *Education:* Sibelius Acad., Helsinki, studied with Arvid Jansons and Luigi Ricci. *Career:* debut in Helsinki 1968; Conductor, Tampere Theatre 1969–70, Finnish Nat. Opera, Helsinki 1970–72, 1979–, Finnish Radio Symphony Orchestra 1972–76, Royal Swedish Opera, Stockholm 1975–77, Symphony Orchestra Vivo, Helsinki 1986–97; guest conductor in Scandinavia, Western and Eastern Europe, Israel and USA. *Compositions:* Frieda (opera), Luther (opera), Two Aphorisms, Due Pezzi, many songs, cantatas, The Prodigal Son (oratorio), Cello Concerto, music for choir and chamber music. *Recordings:* Vivo-Tikka; Triplet; Jumala on rakkaus; Armolaulu: Armolaulu, VIVO Finlandia. *Address:* Mannerheimintie 38 A 4, 00100 Helsinki, Finland. *E-mail:* kari.tikka@kolumbus.fi.

TILLEY, David; British singer (baritone); b. 1960, England. *Education:* studied with Mark Wildman and David Mason. *Career:* appearances in Das Liebesverbot by Wagner at Wexford and Howard Goodall's Silas Marner for CBTO; Lesbo in Handel's Agrippina at Cambridge, Frost King in Purcell's King Arthur at Croydon and Adonis in Blow's Venus and Adonis; other roles include Leporello and parts in Purcell's Fairy Queen (English Bach Festival 2001) and Jonathan Dove's Tobias and the Angel for the Almeida Festival; further roles in Rigoletto and Die Zauberflöte.

TILLI, Johann; Finnish singer (bass); b. 11 Nov. 1967, Kerimäki. *Education:* Sibelius Academy, Helsinki. *Career:* appearances at the Savonlinna Festival, Finland, as Sarastro, the King in Aida, Banquo and Landgraf and other roles; National Opera, Helsinki, as Lodovico and High Priest Baal (Nabucco); Commendatore and Rossini's Basilio at Oslo, with further engagements at Amsterdam, Brussels, Tel-Aviv and Hannover; Member of the Hamburg Opera from 1990; First Bass with Düsseldorf Oper, 1996–97; Has worked with many conductors including Abbado, Cillario, de Burgos, Fricke, Harnoncourt, Steinberg, Sawallisch and Wallberg; Three Bass Concert with Matti Salminen, Jaakko Ryhänen and conductor Leif Segerstam in Helsinki, 1995; Wotan in Die Walküre at Helsinki, 1998; Season 2000–01 as Fasolt at Bayreuth, Gremin for Cologne Opera and Colonna in Wagner's Rienzi at Dresden (concert). *Recordings include:* Gazzaniga's Don Giovanni (Sony Classics); Mahler's 8th Symphony; Schumann Genoveva; Dessau: Haggaddah; Highlights from Savonlinna; Lady Macbeth of the Mtsensk District (DGG). *Current Management:* Fazer Artists' Management, Nervanderinkatu 5 E 46, 00100 Helsinki, Finland. *Telephone:* (9) 4542470. *Fax:* (9) 446841. *E-mail:* info@fazerartists.fi. *Website:* www.fazerartists.fi.

TILLIKAINEN, Sauli; singer (baritone); b. 7 Dec. 1952, Finland. *Education:* Sibelius Acad., Helsinki, studied in Vienna with Anton Dermota and Hans Hotter. *Career:* debut concert 1981; sang with the Finnish Nat. Opera from 1984 and as guest at the Moscow Bolshoi, Stockholm, Dresden and Copenhagen; roles have included Guglielmo, Don Giovanni, Escamillo, Mozart's Count, Germont, Eugene Onegin, Ruprecht in The Fiery Angel and the title roles in Lionardo by Werle and Thomas by Rautavaara; Kennedy Center, Washington, in Ein Deutsches Requiem and the Kullervo Symphony by Sibelius; sang Valmonte in Sallinen's The Palace, Savonlinna Festival 1996; season 2000–01 as Helsinki as Edgar in the premiere of Sallinen's Lear, and Germont in Traviata; Lieder recitals in music by Schubert and Schumann.

TILLING, Camilla; Swedish singer (soprano); b. 1972, Linköping; two s. *Education:* Gothenburg Univ., Royal Coll. of Music with Margaret Kingsley. *Career:* debut as Camiletta and Mergelina, in intermezzi by Jommelli, Vadstena Summer Opera; appearances in Gothenburg as Offenbach's Olympia, Sophie in Der Rosenkavalier, and Rossini's Rosina 2000–01; Mozart's Blonde and Susanna in London and Aix; Corinna in Il Viaggio a Reims for New York City Opera, Purcell's Belinda in Geneva and Nannetta in Falstaff at the New York Met 2001; Fiordiligi in Così fan tutte at Théâtre des Champs-Elysées 2012; concerts include Handel's Saul in Brussels, and engagements with the London Mozart Players, King's Consort and Corydon Singers; Glyndebourne Festival debut 2000, as First Niece in Peter Grimes.

TILNEY, Colin; British harpsichordist; b. 31 Oct. 1933, London, England. *Education:* studied with Mary Potts at Cambridge, Gustav Leonhardt in Amsterdam. *Career:* soloist and ensemble player in the UK and Europe from the early 1960s; US debut in 1971; repertoire has included music by Renaissance and Baroque composers; has performed on various clavichords, harpsichords, virginals and early pianos, employing both historical instruments and modern copies. *Recordings include:* Parthenia, a collection of pieces by Byrd, Bull and Gibbons published in 1611; Complete Keyboard Works of Matthew Locke and the Suites of Purcell and Handel; Bach's Toccatas, 1990. *Publications include:* Edition of the harpsichord music of Antoine Forqueray.

TILSON THOMAS, Michael, (MTT); American conductor, pianist and composer; *Music Director, San Francisco Symphony Orchestra;* b. 21 Dec. 1944, Los Angeles, Calif.; s. of Theodor Thomas and Roberta Thomas; m. Joshua Robison 2014. *Education:* Univ. of Southern California. *Career:* conductor, Young Musicians' Foundation Orchestra, Los Angeles 1963–67; conductor and pianist, Monday Evening Concerts 1963–68; musical Asst Bayreuth 1966–67; Asst Conductor, Boston Symphony Orchestra 1969, Assoc. Conductor 1970–71, Prin. Guest Conductor 1972–74; New York debut 1969; London debut with London Symphony Orchestra (LSO) 1970; Dir Young People's Concerts, New York Philharmonic 1971–77; Music Dir Buffalo Philharmonic 1971–79; Prin. Guest Conductor, Los Angeles Philharmonic 1981–85; Music Dir Great Woods Inst. 1985, Music Dir Great Woods Festival 1987–88; Prin. Conductor, LSO 1988–95, Prin. Guest Conductor 1995–; Founder and Artistic Dir New World Symphony 1988–; Music Dir San Francisco Symphony Orchestra 1995–; Artistic Dir Pacific Music Festival; Dir YouTube Symphony Orchestra 2009–; guest conductor with orchestras and opera houses in USA and Europe. *Compositions include:* Poems of Emily Dickinson, premiered by Renée Fleming and San Francisco Symphony Orchestra. *Recordings include:* more than 120 recordings, including Mahler Symphonies 1, 3 and 6 (with San Francisco Symphony Orchestra), four-hand version of Stravinsky's Rite of Spring (with Ralph Grierson), Charles Ives' 2nd Symphony (with Concertgebouw Orchestra), complete works of Carl Ruggles (with Buffalo Philharmonic), various musicals by Weill and Gershwin, works of Bach, Beethoven, Prokofiev, Reich and Cage, Mahler's Seventh Symphony (with San Francisco Symphony Orchestra) 2007, Mahler's Eighth Symphony and Adagio from Symphony No. 10 2009, Adams' Harmonielehre & Short Ride In A Fast Machine (with San Francisco Symphony Orchestra) (Grammy Award for Best Orchestral Performance 2013) 2012, Beethoven: Piano Concerto No. 3, Mass in C Major 2015, Mason Bates: Works For Orchestra 2016. *Honours:* Chevalier, Ordre des Arts et des Lettres; Tanglewood Koussevitzky Prize 1968, Ditson Award for contrib. to American music 1994, Musical America Conductor of the Year 1994, American Music Center Award 2001, two Gramophone Awards, seven Grammy Awards including Best Classical Album 2004, 2007, 2010, Classic FM Gramophone Award for Artist of the Year 2005, Nat. Medal of Arts 2010. *Address:* MTT Inc., 1745 Broadway, 18th Floor, New York, NY 10019 (office); San Francisco Symphony, Davies Symphony Hall, 201 Van Ness Avenue, San Francisco, CA 94102, USA (office). *Telephone:* (212) 246-7726 (New York) (office). *Fax:* (212) 489-5217 (New York) (office). *E-mail:* skashiyama@sfsymphony.org (office). *Website:* www .sfsymphony.org (office); www.michaeltilsonthomas.com.

TIMARU, Valentin, BMus, DMus, PhD; Romanian composer; *University Professor of Musical Theory, Gheorghe Dima Music Academy;* b. 16 Oct. 1940, Sibiu; s. of Simion Timaru and Elena Timaru; m. Maria Chisbora 1976; one s. one d. *Education:* Gheorghe Dima Conservatory, Cluj, studied with Sigismund Toduta, Bucharest Conservatory of Music, studied with Anatol Vieru. *Career:* debut as author of musical portrait 1970; music teacher, Buftea, Bucharest 1964–68; music inspector for Cultural Dept of Cluj Dist 1968–70; Asst in Musical Theory, Gheorghe Dima Music Acad. 1970, Lecturer in Musical Forms 1977, Prof. of Musical Theory 1990–. *Compositions:* instrumental: two string quartets 1968, 1992, Symphony No. 1 1972, No. 2 1988, No. 3 1988, No. 4 1990, No. 5 1999, Violin Concerto 1976, Double Concerto for double bass and percussion 1980, Viola Concerto 2008; vocal: four cantatas for choir and orchestra 1971, 1976, 1980, 1992, three oratorios 1981, 1984, 1999, Lorelei (opera) 1989, Liturgy for mixed choir (Liturgy of Ioan Chrysostomos) 1994, The Ciuleandra Ballet (after the novel of Liviu Rebreanu) 1998; lieder, works for choirs, miscellaneous chamber music. *Publications:* Musical Form Theory Vol. I 1990, Vol. II 1994, Vol. III 1998, Enescian Symphonism (Analysis of Enescu's Symphonies) 1992, The Art of Musical Ensemble (Orchestral and Vocal) 1998, Our Holy Music 2001, Dictionary of Notions and Terminology 2003, Musical Analysis Between Genre Conscience and Form Conscience 2003. *Honours:* Romanian Composers' Union Prize 1986, 1992, 1995, 2003, 2010, Romanian Acad. Prize 1995; Kt Order of Cultural Merit 2004. *Address:* Gheorghe Dima Music Academy, 25 I.C. Bratianu Street, PO Box 195, 400750 Cluj-Napoca, Romania (office). *Telephone:* (264) 442809 (office). *Fax:* (264) 593879 (office). *E-mail:* v_timaru@ yahoo.fr.

TINNEY, Hugh; Irish pianist; *Lecturer in piano, Royal Irish Academy of Music;* b. 28 Nov. 1958, Dublin; s. of Sean Tinney and Sheila Tinney. *Education:* Trinity Coll., Dublin, private piano studies with Mabel Swainson, Louis Kentner, Bryce Morrison and Maria Curcio. *Career:* debut, Purcell Room, London 1983; performed concertos and recitals in over 30 countries; recitals at Queen Elizabeth Hall in London, Musikverein, Vienna, Kennedy Center, Washington; appearances at festivals include Newport, Rhode Island, Granada, and Prague Spring Festival; performances with Gulbenkian, Lisbon, Spanish National, Spanish Radio, and Brazil Symphony Orchestras; proms debut in 1989 with BBC Nat. Orchestra of Wales; other performances with British orchestras such as London Philharmonic, Philharmonia, Royal Philharmonic, Royal Liverpool Philharmonic, City of Birmingham and Royal Scottish Orchestras; Lecturer in piano, Royal Irish Acad. of Music; Artistic Dir, Music Festival in Great Irish Houses series 2000–06; tours of China with

Acad. Chamber Ensemble 2012–14. *Television:* Piano - King of Instruments (principal pianist in Sean O'Mordha documentary) (RTE television) 2003. *Recordings:* Liszt's Harmonies Poétiques et Religieuses, Liszt Recitals, Mendelssohn's Concertos for two pianos, Raymond Deane's After Pieces, A Sheaf of Songs (song recital with Bernadette Greevy), Ian Wilson's Violin/ Piano Duo Music, Raymond Deane's Noctuary, A Portrait. *Honours:* Hon. DMus (Nat. Univ. of Ireland) 2007; winner, Pozzoli Competition 1983, Paloma O'Shea Competition 1984. *E-mail:* info@hughtinney.com. *Website:* www .hughtinney.com.

TINSLEY, Pauline, LRAM; British singer (soprano); b. 27 March 1928, Wigan; m. G. M. Neighbour; one s. one d. *Education:* Northern School of Music, Manchester, Opera School, London, studied with Eva Turner and Eduardo Asquez. *Career:* professional engagements in the UK from 1961 include London debut as Desdemona, Rossini's Otello; leading roles in Verdi's I Masnadieri, Ernani, Il Corsaro and Bellini's Il Pirata; WNO from 1962 as Susanna, Elsa, Lady Macbeth, Sinaide in Rossini's Moses, Abigaille, Aida, Tosca, Turandot, Kostelnicka in Jenůfa, Elektra and Dyer's Wife in Frau Ohne Schatten 1981; Sadler's Wells/ENO from 1963 as Gilda, Elvira in Ernani, Fiordiligi, Queen of Night, Countess, Donna Elvira, Beethoven's Leonore and Fidelio, Leonora in Force of Destiny, Elizabeth in Mary Stuart 1973, Mother/Witch in Hansel and Gretel 1987, Kabanicha in Katya Kabanova 1989; Covent Garden from 1965 as Overseer in Elektra, Amelia in Un Ballo in Maschera 1971, Helmwige and 3rd Norn in The Ring, Santuzza 1976, Mère Marie in Carmélites 1983, Lady Billows in Albert Herring 1989; various roles with Scottish Opera including Kostelnicka and with Opera North (Fata Morgana in Love for Three Oranges) and with Handel Opera Soc.; from 1966 performed abroad in Germany, Netherlands, Italy, USA, Canada, Switzerland, Czechoslovakia, Spain and Belgium; concerts, recitals, broadcasts and television operas; Wexford Festival as Lady Jowler in The Rising of the Moon 1990; sang Lady Billows at Garsington 1996; sang Grandmother Burya in Jenůfa, for Opera North 1995 and 2002, and for Netherlands Opera 1997 and 2001. *Recordings include:* Electra in Idomeneo. *Current Management:* Music International, 13 Ardilaun Road, Highbury, London, N5 2QR, England. *Telephone:* (20) 7359-5183. *E-mail:* music@musicint.co.uk. *Website:* www.musicint.wd-uk.com.

TIPO, Maria; Italian pianist; b. 23 Dec. 1931, Naples. *Education:* studied with Ersilla Cavallo. *Career:* debut public piano performance aged four; many solo engagements from 1949 throughout Europe, USA, Central and South America, Africa, Russia, Japan and the Middle East, including many performances in the USA after discovery by Arthur Rubinstein 1952; teacher at the Bolzano, Florence and Geneva Conservatories; performances of works by Clementi, Scarlatti and other Italian composers, Beethoven, Mozart, Schumann, Ravel, Debussy, Chopin, Brahms; has performed with the Berlin Philharmonic, Vienna Philharmonic, Boston Symphony, London Philharmonic, Concertgebouw Orchestra in Amsterdam, Czech Philharmonic, Orchestre de Paris, Salzburg Mozarteum, La Scala in Milan, S Cecilia in Rome and many others; chamber music performances with the Amadeus Quartet, Salvatore Accardo and Uto Ughi; judge at many int. competitions; Pres., Centro Studi Musicali F. Busoni. *Recordings include:* Piano Sonatas by Clementi; Bach's Goldberg Variations; Eighteen Scarlatti Sonatas. *Honours:* prizewinner Geneva Competition 1949, Queen Elisabeth of the Belgians Competition 1952, Music Critics' Prize 1985, Gargano Award, Ernest Hemingway Award.

TIRIMO, Martino, FRAM, FRSAMD, Dip RAM, ARAM; British concert pianist and conductor; *Professor, Trinity Laban Conservatoire of Music and Dance;* b. 19 Dec. 1942, Larnaca, Cyprus; s. of Dimitri Tirimo and Marina Tirimo; m. Mione J. Teakle 1973; one s. one d. *Education:* Bedales School, England (Cyprus Govt Scholarship), Royal Acad. of Music, London, Vienna State Acad. *Career:* first public recital, Cyprus 1949; conducted seven performances of La Traviata with singers and musicians from La Scala, Milan, at Cyprus Opera Festival 1955; London debut, Wigmore Hall 1965; gave first public performance of complete Schubert sonatas (including unfinished ones with own completions), London 1975; first public performance of Beethoven piano concertos cycle directed from keyboard in two consecutive evenings, Dresden 1985, London 1986; first performance of Tippett piano concerto in several European countries 1986–2013; concerto performances with major orchestras world-wide as well as recitals, radio and TV appearances in Europe, USA, Canada, SA and the Far East 1965–; four series of performances of complete Beethoven piano sonatas 2000, two series devoted to the major piano works of Robert and Clara Schumann 2001; six-concert series devoted to the major piano works of Chopin 2002; Mozart piano concertos series, directing from keyboard 2001–; f. Rosamunde Trio with violinist Ben Sayevich and cellist Daniel Veis 2002; performed with Vienna Philharmonic during Olympics, Athens Festival 2004, Olympic Games torch bearer 2004; performed complete Mozart solo piano works in several series of eight concerts, including at Cadogan Hall, London 2006; performed Chopin entire works in ten concerts in various countries, including at King's Place, London 2010; Tchaikovsky series at King's Place, London 2012; Prof., Trinity Coll. of Music (now Trinity Laban Conservatoire of Music and Dance) 2003–; mem. jury in various int. piano competitions 1995–. *Film score:* The Odyssey 1998. *Recordings:* more than 50 albums, including complete piano works of Mozart, Beethoven, Debussy and Janáček; Brahms piano concertos, Chopin concertos, Tippett piano concerto, Rachmaninov concertos, complete Schubert piano sonatas, complete Mendelssohn works for piano and cello, Tchaikovsky, Shostakovich and Dvořák piano trios (Rosamunde Trio), several other recordings with mixed repertoire. *Television:* live performance of Tippett piano concerto from Coventry Cathedral for BBC TV in celebration of composer's 90th birthday and 50th birthday of UN. *Publications include:* urtext edn of complete Schubert piano sonatas in three vols 1997–99. *Honours:* Hon. Prof., Middlesex Univ. 2004–; prizewinner, Int. Beethoven Competition, Vienna 1965, Liszt Scholarship, Boise Foundation Scholarship, Gulbenkian Foundation Fellowship 1967–69, Jt Winner, Munich Int. Piano Competition 1971, Winner, Geneva Int. Piano Competition 1972, Gold Medal, Associated Bd of Royal Schools of Music 1959, Macfarren Medal, Royal Acad. of Music 1964, Silver Disc 1988 and Gold Disc 1994 for recording of Rachmaninov 2nd Concerto and Paganini Rhapsody, Nemitsas Foundation Prize 2011, and other prizes and awards. *Telephone:* (210) 6015224 (Athens). *Fax:* (210) 6994520 (Athens). *E-mail:* deskaps@otenet.gr. *Address:* 1 Romeyn Road, London, SW16 2NU, England. *Telephone:* (20) 8677-4847. *E-mail:* martino@tirimo.fslife.co.uk. *Website:* www.martinotirimo.com.

TISCHENKO, Leonid; Ukrainian singer (bass); b. 1969, Kiev. *Education:* Moscow and Kiev Conservatories. *Career:* has sung with the Nat. Opera of the Ukraine at Kiev, as Pimen (Boris Godunov), Verdi's King Phillip and Gremin in Eugene Onegin; concerts at Strasbourg 1999, in the Mozart Requiem, and at the Concertgebouw Amsterdam in Rossini's Stabat Mater; further engagements with the Verdi Requiem and other works in Germany, Italy, the USA, Austria, France and Hungary; has also conducted the Ukraine State Symphony Orchestra.

TISNE, Antoine; French composer; b. 29 Nov. 1932, Lourdes. *Education:* Paris Conservatoire with Riviere and Darius Milhaud. *Career:* Inspector of Music, Ministry of Culture 1967–92; Inspector for the municipal conservatories of Paris from 1992; Prof. of Composition and Orchestration, Paris Conservatoire. *Compositions include:* four piano concertos, 1959, 1961, 1962, 1992; four string quartets, 1956, 1979, 1979, 1989; Cantique de Printemps, 1960; Wind Quintet, 1961; Violin Sonata, 1963; Cosmogonies for three orchestras, 1967; Violin Concerto, 1969; Ondes Flamboyantes for strings, 1973; Impacts for ondes martenots and two string orchestras, 1973; Isle de Temps for ondes martenot sextet, 1980; La Ramasseuse de sarments, music theatre, 1982; Instant, ballet, 1985; L'Heure des Hommes, oratorio, 1985; Reliefs irradiants de New York, for orchestra, 1979; Le Chant des Yeux, oratorio, 1986; Les Voiles de la nuit, 1991; De la Nuit et L'Aurore, for oboe and strings, 1991; La Voix de l'Ombre, for flute and string trio, 1991; Dans la lumière d'Orcival, for chorus, 1992; Invocation, for baritone and orchestra, 1993; Pour l'amour d'Alban, opera. *Honours:* Grand Prix Musical, Paris 1979.

TITOV, Alexander; Russian conductor; b. 1950, St Petersburg. *Education:* St Petersburg Conservatoire. *Career:* assistant conductor to Gennadi Rozhdestvensky and Mstislav Rostropovich; Conductor at the Kirov Opera and Ballet, St Petersburg from 1991; Repertoire has included La Traviata, Prokofiev's The Gambler and Love for Three Oranges, Stravinsky's Rossignol, Katerina Izmailova and Ruslan and Lyudmila; Ballets include Chopiniana, The Sleeping Beauty, The Firebird and Schéhérazade; conducted the Kirov Ballet in summer season at Covent Garden, 2000; Professor at the St Petersburg Conservatoire. *Honours:* winner International Minon Competition, Tokyo 1988.

TITTERINGTON, David Michael, BA; British organist; b. 10 Jan. 1958, Oldham. *Education:* Pembroke Coll., Oxford, Conservatoire National de Rueil-Malmaison, Paris with Marie-Claire Alain. *Career:* debut at the Royal Festival Hall, 1986; recitals in cathedrals and halls throughout the UK; concert tours of Germany, Scandinavia, France, USA, Far East, New Zealand and Australia; appearances at major international festivals at Hong Kong, Harrogate, Istanbul, Adelaide, Sydney and Brighton; concert hall appearances include Wigmore Hall, Royal Festival Hall, Munich, Acad. for Performing Arts, Hong Kong; television appearances; Prof. of Organ, Royal Acad. of Music, London 1990–; concertos with Berlin Symphony, BBC Symphony Orchestra, City of London Sinfonia and English Sinfonia; recitals, concertos and masterclasses worldwide at major venues and festivals, including BBC Proms, Hong Kong, Sydney, New Zealand, Tokyo; Head of Organ Studies, Royal Acad. of Music 1996–. *Recordings include:* Messiaen; La Nativité du Seigneur; Eben; Job; Eberlin; Toccatas; over 30 recordings for BBC and networks worldwide. *Publications include:* edited works of Petr Eben; Organ Works (ed.). *Current Management:* c/o Owen White Management 22, Brunswick Terrace 6, Hove, East Sussex, BN3 1HJ, England. *Telephone:* (1273) 727-127. *Fax:* (5601) 527-038. *E-mail:* info@owenwhitemanagement .com. *Website:* www.owenwhitemanagement.com.

TITUS, Alan; American singer (baritone); b. 28 Oct. 1945, New York, NY. *Education:* studied with Askel Schiotz at the Colorado School of Music and with Hans Heinz at Juilliard. *Career:* debut in Washington, DC 1969 in La Bohème; sang the Celebrant in the premiere of Bernstein's Mass at Washington, DC 1971; sang at New York City Opera 1972 in Summer and Smoke; European debut at Amsterdam 1973 in Debussy's Pelléas; sang at Metropolitan Opera 1976 as Harlekin in Ariadne auf Naxos, Glyndebourne 1979 as Guglielmo, Deutsche Oper am Rhein Düsseldorf 1984 as Don Giovanni, and Santa Fe 1985 in Strauss's Intermezzo; engagements at Aix-en-Provence, Hamburg and Frankfurt; sang at Maggio Musicale Florence 1987 as Olivier in Capriccio; sang Dandini at San Francisco 1987, at Munich as Valentin and sang in Mathis der Maler 1989, Bologna 1990 as Storch in the Italian premiere of Intermezzo; sang Kovalyov in The Nose by Shostakovich at Frankfurt 1990; season 1992–93 in Arabella at La Scala, the title role in

Donizetti's Il Duca d'Alba at Spoleto, and Hans Sachs at Frankfurt; sang the title role in Hindemith's Mathis der Maler at Covent Garden 1995; sang Pizarro in Fidelio at Rome 1996; Altair in Strauss's Aegyptische Helena at the Festival Hall 1998; season 2000–01 as Kurwenal at Covent Garden and Strauss's Barak for the Dresden Staatsoper; sang Wotan in The Ring at Bayreuth 2001. *Recordings include:* Haydn's La Feldeltà Premiata; La Bohème; L'Elsir d'Amore; Don Giovanni; La Wally; Le nozze di Figaro; Falstaff; Paradies und die Peri; Genoveva; Carmen. *Current Management:* L. S. Artists, Lydia Störle, Orlando Strasse 8, 8000 Munich 2, Germany.

TITUS, Graham, MA, FRCO; British singer (baritone); b. 15 Dec. 1949, Newark, Nottinghamshire, England. *Education:* Clare Coll., Cambridge, Cologne Musikhochschule. *Career:* debut, Purcell Room, London 1974; appearances with New Opera Co., Handel Opera and ENO; radio recitals from 1974; concert tour of South America; recital and oratorio work throughout the UK, including the Aldeburgh Festival 1975, the Glyndebourne Festival 1979 as Guglielmo. *Honours:* winner Young Musician Competition 1974, 's-Hertogenbosch Competition 1977.

TJEKNAVORIAN, Loris; Iranian composer and conductor; b. 13 Oct. 1937, Iran; s. of Haikaz Tjeknavorian and Adriné Tjeknavorian; m. 1st Linda Pierce 1964 (divorced 1979); one s.; m. 2nd Julia Cory Harley-Green 1986; m. 3rd Naira 2004. *Education:* Tehran Conservatory of Music, Vienna Acad. of Music, Salzburg Mozarteum, Austria, Univ. of Michigan, USA. *Career:* several works published in Vienna following graduation 1961; given scholarship to study with the late Carl Orff 1963–64; lived in Salzburg and worked on opera Rostam and Sohrab; began studying conducting in USA 1965; Composer-in-Residence, Concordia Coll., Moorhead, Minn. 1966–67; Head of Instrumental and Opera Departments, Moorhead Univ., Minn. 1966–70; numerous recordings with leading orchestras, including London Symphony Orchestra, Royal Philharmonic Orchestra, London Philharmonic Orchestra; works have been performed by major orchestras, including Vienna Symphony, London Philharmonic, American Symphony; Prin. Conductor and Artistic Dir Armenian Philharmonic Orchestra 1989–2000. *Compositions include:* more than 80 works (five symphonies, five operas, a requiem, chamber music, concerto for piano, violin, guitar, cello and pipa (Chinese lute), ballet music, choral works and an oratorio, and more than 40 film scores), including Requiem for the Massacred 1975, Simorgh (ballet music), Lake Van Suite, Erebouni for 12 strings 1978, Credo Symphony Life of Christ (after medieval Armenian chants) 1976, Liturgical Mass, Violin Concerto, oratorios Lucifer's Fall and Book of Revelation, Mass in Memoriam 1985, Othello (ballet), ballet suites for orchestra, five symphonies. *Honours:* Order of Homayoun; Austrian Presidential Gold Medal for Artistic Merit 2010, Highest Medal of Repub. of Armenia, Highest Order of Arts of Iranian Islamic Repub. *Address:* Vogelsanggasse 39–41/30, 1050 Vienna, Austria. *E-mail:* ltjeknavorian@ yahoo.com. *Website:* www.loristjeknavorian.com.

TOCZYSKA, Stefania; Polish singer (mezzo-soprano); b. 19 Feb. 1943, Gdansk. *Education:* Gdansk Conservatory with Barbara Iglikovska. *Career:* debut, Danzig as Carmen 1973; sang in Poland as Azucena, Leonora in La Favorita and Dalila; Western debut in 1977 as Amneris at Basle Opera; sang at Vienna Staatsoper 1977 as Ulrica in Un Ballo in Maschera, returning as Carmen and as Verdi's Azucena, Eboli and Preziosilla; sang at Munich and Hamburg 1979 as Eboli in Don Carlos, San Francisco Opera as Laura in La Gioconda, Amneris and in Roberto Devereux, Royal Opera Covent Garden 1983–84 as Azucena and Amneris, Bregenz Festival and Chicago Lyric Opera 1986 as Giovanna Seymour in Anna Bolena, Houston Opera 1987 as Adalgisa and Amneris, and Barcelona 1987 and Hamburg 1990 as Venus in Tannhäuser; sang Laura in La Gioconda at the Metropolitan Opera 1989, at Washington and Houston 1990 as Amneris and Dalila, and appeared in Aida at the Caracalla Festival at Rome 1990; season 1992 as Azucena at Munich, Massenet's Dulcinée at Toulouse, Donizetti's Maria Stuarda at Barcelona and Carmen at the Munich Festival; sang Amneris at the Met 1997; season 2000–01 as Amneris at Maastricht, and in Moniuszko's The Haunted Castle at Warsaw.

TODD, Will, BA, MMus; British composer; b. 14 Jan. 1970, Durham, England; s. of Derek and Iris Todd; m. Bethany Halliday; one s. two d. *Education:* Bristol Univ. with Raymond Warren and Adrian Beaumont. *Compositions:* Isambard Kingdom Brunel (opera, premiered at Colston Hall, Bristol) 1993, Saxophone Concerto 1993, Midwinter for chorus 1994, St Cuthbert (oratorio, premiered at Durham Cathedral) 1996, Violin Concerto 1996, The Burning Road (commissioned for Crouch End Festival Chorus) 1996, The Screams of Kitty (musical, with librettist David Simpatico, performed at Boston Conservatory) 2001, The Blackened Man (opera, with librettist Ben Dunwell, Linbury Studio Theatre Covent Garden) (prizewinner Int. Giuseppe Verdi Competition) 2002, Mass in Blue (commissioned by Herts. Chorus) 2003, Sweetness and Badness (opera, with librettist Michael Wicherek, Welsh Nat. Opera) 2006, Requiem 2009, Te Deum 2009, Clarinet Concerto 2009. *Recordings:* The Burning Road, Saint Cuthbert (Northumbrian Anthology), Mass in Blue. *Telephone:* (7767) 623093 (office). *E-mail:* will@willtodd.com (office). *Website:* www.willtodd.com.

TODISCO, Nunzio; Italian singer (tenor); b. 1942. *Career:* has sung in Italy and at Orange, Lisbon, Rome and Zürich from 1970; US debut at San Francisco 1978 as Pollione in Norma; sang Loris in Fedora at the Metropolitan Opera and in Naples 1989; sang at Verona Arena 1989 as Ismaele in Nabucco; other roles include Verdi's Carlo in I Masnadieri, Foresto in Attila, Arrigo in

La Battaglia di Legnano, Manrico, Ernani and Radames, Puccini's Dick Johnson, Luigi and Cavaradossi and Licinius in La Vestale by Spontini; sang Ismaele at Verona 1992.

TODOROV, Nedyalcho Georgiev, MA; Bulgarian violinist and academic; b. 27 Oct. 1940, Plovdiv; m. Veneta Assenova Todorova 1967, one s. one d. *Education:* State Acad. of Music, Sofia, Gnessini State Music Pedagogy Inst., Moscow. *Career:* Violin Teacher, Secondary School of Music, Plovdiv 1964–67; Violin Prof., Deputy Rector 1974–79, Rector 1979–83, Acad. of Music and Dance Art, Plovdiv; Dir 1970–72, Concertmaster 1976–79, Plovdiv Philharmony; 1st Violinist, Plovdiv String Quartet 1978–; Dir Educational Dept, Ministry of Culture, Sofia 1983–91; recitals, soloist with orchestra, chamber music concerts; repertoire includes concertos of Bach, Mozart, Beethoven, Mendelssohn, Bruch, Hindemith, Shostakovich, V. Stoyanov, Ivan Spassov, sonatas, pieces, duos, trios, quartets. *Recordings:* Luigi Boccherini: String Quartet Op 33 No. 6, A major; Quintet for oboe, violins, viola and violoncello Op 45 No. 1, G major, Quintet Op 45 No. 2, F major, Quintet Op 45 No. 3, D major with Plovdiv String Quartet and Boryu Pamoukchiev, oboe, 1988; 4 concertos for violin, oboe and orchestra: Telemann, C minor, Fasch, D minor, Vivaldi, B flat major, Bach, D minor, soloists: self, violin, Pamoukchiev, oboe, with Jambol Chamber Orchestra, conductor N Sultanov, 1988. *Publications:* 1st performances, recordings, editions (pieces for violin and piano, duos for 2 violins and chamber ensembles by modern Bulgarian composers), 6 vols, 1977–88; Recordings, editions (collections of classical concertos for oboe and violin), 1990; Bulgarian Violin Literature (editor), catalogue, 1992; Avramov Catalogue, 1999. *E-mail:* todorov@inet.bg.

TODOROVIC, Nicholas; New Zealand singer (bass-baritone); b. 1965, Christchurch. *Education:* Univ. of Canterbury and Queen's Conservatorium of Music. *Career:* appearances with Mercury Opera, Auckland, as Hermann in The Queen of Spades and Morales in Carmen; Don Giovanni with the Lyric Opera of Queensland and Papageno with Victoria State Opera; British debut as the villains in Les Contes d'Hoffmann, for Stowe Opera; further roles as Masetto for Victoria State Opera and Johnny Dowd in the premiere of Summer of the Seventeenth Doll by Richard Mills, at the Melbourne Int. Arts Festival; Masetto in Don Giovanni for Auckland Opera (with Kiri Te Kanawa) and Schaunard in La Bohème at Melbourne, Rambaldo in La Rondine for Opera Holland Park, London, Jude in Salome for Adelaide Opera. *Current Management:* c/o Jamari Artist Management, 29/72 Sandford Street, St Lucia, Qld 4067, Australia. *Telephone:* (7) 3371-6137. *Fax:* (7) 3871-0635. *E-mail:* james@jamari.com.au.

TODOROVICH, Zoran; Bulgarian singer (tenor); b. 1962. *Education:* Belgrade Conservatoire, studied in Zagreb with Zinka Milanov. *Career:* National Theatre, Belgrade, from 1985 as Rossini's Almaviva, Shuisky in Boris Godunov and Donizetti's Tonio; State Opera Hanover 1994–99; Pinkerton at the Vienna and Berlin State Operas, 1997–98, Faust at the Deutsche Oper, Berlin; season 1999–2000 as Leopold in La Juive (Vienna), US debut as Rodolfo at San Francisco, Lensky for Nice Opera and Alfredo in La Traviata at Zürich; season 2000–01 as Lensky in Tokyo, Rodolfo at Hamburg and the Berlioz Faust in Zürich; further engagements in Roberto Devereux by Donizetti in Munich, Edgardo and the Duke of Mantua for Hamburg Opera and Alfredo at Frankfurt; concerts include the Verdi Requiem (Munich), Gounod's Mors et Vita and Rossini's Stabat Mater; other opera roles include Mozart's Titus (at Madrid). *Recordings include:* Mors et Vita. *Current Management:* c/o Opera-Connection Alste & Mödersheim, Leibnizstrasse 94, 10625 Berlin, Germany; c/o Teddy Gerstel, Gerstel International Opera Management, Stockerstrasse 10, 8002 Zürich, Switzerland. *Telephone:* (30) 31996688 (Germany); 76 391 88 01 (Switzerland). *Fax:* (30) 31809739 (Germany); 44 253 14 53 (Switzerland). *E-mail:* info@opera-connection.com; gerstel@swissonline.ch. *Website:* opera-connection.com.

TOFFOLUTTI, Ezio; stage designer; b. 1941, Venice, Italy. *Education:* Accademia delle Belle Arti, Venice. *Career:* designer, Volksbuhne, Berlin 1971–79; collaboration with such opera producers as Harry Kupfer, Johannes Schaaf and Jerome Savary (Rossini's Le Comte Ory at the 1997 Glyndebourne Festival, also televised); engagements also include Rigoletto in Berlin, Die Meistersinger at La Scala, and Idomeneo at the Salzburg Festival; Grand Theatre, Geneva, with Così fan tutte and at the Palais Garnier, Paris; season 1997–98 with Il Matrimonio Segreto in Vienna and Die Entführung aus dem Serail at Trieste.

TOGNETTI, Richard; Australian violinist, conductor and composer; *Artistic Director, Australian Chamber Orchestra;* b. Wollongong. *Education:* Sydney Conservatorium, Berne Conservatory, Switzerland. *Career:* Leader, Australian Chamber Orchestra 1989–, later apptd Artistic Dir; Artistic Dir, Maribor Festival, Slovenia 2007–; as violinist has performed with Sydney Symphony Orchestra; as conductor performances include Sydney Festival, with Handel and Haydn Soc., Hong Kong Philharmonic, Camerata Salzburg, Tapiola Sinfonietta, Irish Chamber Orchestra, Nordic Chamber Orchestra. *Compositions:* as co-composer: Master and Commander (film-score) 2003, Horror-scopes 2005, The Red Tree 2008. *Recordings include:* as soloist: Bach's Sonatas and Partitas for Solo Violin (ARIA Award for Best Classical Album) 2006, Bach Violin Concertos (ARIA Award for Best Classical Album) 2007, Bach Sonatas for Violin and Keyboard (ARIA Award for Best Classical Album) 2008. *Honours:* three hon. doctorates; Tschumi Prize 1989, Nat. Living Treasure of Australia 1999. *Address:* Australian Chamber Orchestra, PO Box R21, Royal Exchange, NSW 1225, Australia (office). *Telephone:* (2) 8274-3800

(office). *Fax:* (2) 8274-3801 (office). *E-mail:* headoffice@aco.com.au (office). *Website:* www.aco.com.au (office).

TOIVANEN, Heikki; singer (bass); b. 1947, Mikkeli, Finland; m. Ingrid Haubold. *Education:* Sibelius Acad., Helsinki, studied in Germany. *Career:* sang at the Finnish Nat. Opera 1973–74, Wuppertal 1974–76, Karlsruhe 1977–84, Bayreuth Festival 1977–78, as Fasolt and Titurel; guest appearances throughout Europe and in South America; many concert engagements.

TOKAREV, Nikolai; Russian pianist; b. 15 Sept. 1983, Moscow; s. of Alexander Tokarew and Lyubov Rosenova. *Education:* Gnessin Music School, Moscow, Royal Northern Coll. of Music, Manchester, Robert-Schumann Music School, Düsseldorf. *Career:* public debut at age six with solo recital, Moscow 1989; started touring Europe and Japan at age 14; has appeared with numerous orchestras, including Camerata Salzburg, Tonhalle Orchester Zurich, Nat. Philharmonic of Russia, BBC Philharmonic Orchestra; regular guest at int. festivals, including Ludwigsburger Schlossfestspiele, Schleswig-Holstein Musik Festival, Rheingau Musik Festival, Kissinger Sommer, Davos Musik Festival, Festspiele Mecklenburg-Vorpommern, Mosel Musikfestival 2008, Estonian Int. Pianists Festival 2008. *Recordings:* No 1 2007, French Album 2008. *Honours:* winner 10th Eurovision Grand Prix of Young Musicians, Bergen 2000, Orpheum Public Award at 8th Int. Orpheum Music Festival, Zurich 2006, Echo Klassik Award for Best New Male Artist 2008. *Current Management:* Sony BMG Music Entertainment, Schlegelstrasse 26b, 10115 Berlin, Germany. *Telephone:* (30) 13888-7364 (office). *Fax:* (30) 13888-7389 (office). *E-mail:* presse_classical@sonymusic.com (office). *Website:* www .nikolaitokarew.de.

TOKODY, Ilona; Hungarian soprano; b. 27 April 1953, Szeged; d. of András Tokody and Ilona Nagy. *Education:* Liszt Ferenc Music Acad. *Career:* joined State Opera, Budapest 1976; regular guest performer with Staatsoper Wien and Deutsche Oper West-Berlin; appearances in opera houses and concert halls worldwide, including Metropolitan Opera House, Royal Opera House Covent Garden, Vienna State Opera, San Francisco Opera, Teatro Colón, Buenos Aires, Liceo, Barcelona, Bavarian State Opera, San Carlo, Naples, Rome Opera, Bolshoi, Carnegie Hall, New York, Musikverein, Vienna, Royal Opera, Copenhagen; mem. Hungarian Acad. of Arts; Life Mem., Halhatatlanok Társulata. *Operatic roles include:* leading roles in La Forza del Destino, Don Carlos, Suor Angelica, Madama Butterfly, Il Trovatore, Aida, La Juive, La Bohème, Manon Lescaut, Nedda in I Pagliacci, Micaela in Carmen, Alice in Falstaff, Giselda in I Lombardi, Desdemona in Otello. *Recordings include:* Suor Angelica, Nerone, La Fiamma, Brahms Requiem, Il Tabarro, Guntram, Iris, Ilona Tokody – Portrait Of The Artist 1995, Beethoven – Symphony No. 9 2000. *Honours:* Cross of the Order of Merit 1994; won Kodály singing competition 1972, Erkel competition of Inter-konzert Agency 1973, Ostend competition operatic category 1976; Franz Liszt Prize 1980, Artist of Merit of Repub. of Hungary Award 1983, Kossuth Prize 1985, Repub. of Hungary Outstanding Artist Award 1990, Bartók-Pásztory Prize 2010, Székely Mihály Plaque 2010, Hazám-díj 2012, Master Artist, Hungarian State Opera House 2013.

TOLE, Vasil S., PhD; Albanian composer, musicologist and ethnomusicologist; *President, Albanian Music Council;* b. 22 Nov. 1963, Përmet; s. of Sofokli Tole and Janulla Tole; m. Enkeleida Tole; two d. *Education:* Tirana Conservatory, Folkwang Hochschule, Essen, Athens Univ. *Career:* Music Dir, Naïm Frashëri Palace of Culture 1988–91; Artistic Dir, Elrena Gjika Ensemble 1988–91; Lecturer, Tirana Conservatory 1991–; founder, New Albanian Music Asscn 1993; founder, Ton de Leeuw Int. Competition for New Music, Tirana 1997; Dir, Theatre of Opera and Ballet, Tirana 1997–99; Dir, State Ensemble of Folk Songs and Dances 1997–99; Dir of Dept for Cultural Heritage, Ministry of Tourism and Culture 2001–; Pres. Albanian Music Council; mem. Acad. of Sciences of Albania, Int. Music Council. *Compositions include:* Suite 1986, Symphonic Poem 1987, Kontrast 1989, Concerto for Orchestra 1990, Epitaf dhe britmë 1992–93, Pheromones 1993, Genotype 1996, Trias 1996, RIP 1997, Dikotomi 2000, Eumenides (opera) 2004. *Recordings:* Trias 1997, Epitaf dhe britmë 1998. *Publications:* Music and Literature 1997, SAZET 1998, Albanian folk polyphony 1999, Etnostructure and Etnosemantic 2000, Encyclopedia of Albanian Folk Music 2001, The Albanian National Anthem 2003, The Albanian Intangible Heritage 2004, Cluster, Musicology and Composition 2004, Odysseus and the Sirens: A Temptation Towards the Iso-Polyphonic Region of Epirus, A Homeric Theme with Variations 2005, The Encyplopedia of Albanian Folk Iso-Polyphony 2007, Usta Lave Bariu 2008, Pse qane kuajt e Akilit 2011, 100 kenge, himne dhe marshe patriotike shqiptare 2012. *Honours:* Asscn of Albanian Composers Prix des Jeunesses Musicales 1990, Ministry of Culture MUZA Prize 2001, prizewinner, Dimitri Mitropoulos Int. Competition for Composers, Athens, Greece 2001. *Address:* Rr. 'Sitki Çiço', Pallatet 9 kate, Shkalla 2, Ap. 4, Tirana (office); c/o Rr. Hodo BEG, P. 12 Kate, Ap. IV-D, Tirana, Albania. *Telephone:* (4) 2370414 (office); (69) 2055551. *Fax:* (4) 2370414 (office); (68) 3855455. *E-mail:* vasiltole@gmail.com (office); vasiltole@hotmail.com (home). *Website:* www.isopolifonia.com; www.vasiltole.com.

TOLIVER, Zelotes Edmund, BMus, MM, DMus; American singer (basso cantante) and academic; b. 8 Jan. 1948, Greenport; s. of Zelotes Toliver and Dorothy May Toliver (née Howard); m. Sabine E. Toliver (née Mählmann) 1957; two s. one d. *Education:* Illinois Wesleyan Univ.; studied with Prof. Willis Patterson, Vienna, Austria and Prof. Franz Schuch-Tovini, Univ. of Michigan. *Career:* Vienna Staatsoper as Pistol in Falstaff, Nightwatchman in

Die Meistersinger, Hector in Les Troyens, First Soldier in Salome, Capitan in Boris Goudonov, Lorenzo in I Capuleti e Montecchi, Balthazar in Amahl and the Night Visitors; Coburg Opera 1985–87; Graz Opera 1987–92, Dortmund 1992–95; sang Fasolt, Fafner, Hunding and Hagen in Ring cycles at Graz, Salzburg Landestheater and Dortmund 1988–95, as the King in Aida, Detroit 1985, as Boito's Mefistofele, Linz 1988, as Hunding and Fafner, Paris Châtelet 1994, and in The Rake's Progress 1996, Gurnemanz in Parsifal, King Marke in Tristan, Gremin in Eugene Onegin and Sarastro in the Magic Flute, Enschede 1998–2001; further appearances in Amsterdam, Berlin, Brussels, Munich, Tokyo, Zürich and New York; frequent solo and oratorio concert engagements. *Radio:* concerts broadcast in Austria (ORF), Bavarian Radio, Netherlands Classic Radio. *Television:* Andrea Chenier – The Vienna State Opera, Wagner – Ring des Nibelungen (complete), Graz Opera. *Recordings include:* Bonze in Madama Butterfly, Song of Old Souls (Spiritual CD). *Honours:* Mid-Atlantic Region Winner, Metropolitan Opera Auditions, Washington, DC, Prize Winner, VIth Tchaikovsky Music Competition, Moscow, Stipendium from Nat. Opera Inst., Faculty European Study Award. *Current Management:* c/o Alferink Artists Management, Herengracht 340, 1016 CG Amsterdam, Netherlands. *Telephone:* (20) 6643151. *Fax:* (20) 6752426. *E-mail:* info@alferink.org. *Website:* www.alferink.org; www.zedmundtoliver.com.

TOMASI, Loretta, OBE; Australian opera company director; b. Balingup, Western Australia. *Education:* St Thomas More Coll., Univ. of Western Australia. *Career:* fmr chartered accountant with Coopers & Lybrand, Perth, Melbourne and London 1979–87; Financial Controller, Tyndall Holdings PLC, London 1987–90; Finance Dir, Stoll Moss Theatres (became Andrew Lloyd Webber's Really Useful Theatres group) 1990–2000, Man. Dir Really Useful Theatres 2000–02; Exec. Dir and Finance Dir, ENO 2003–05, Chief Exec. 2005–13. *Address:* c/o English National Opera, London Coliseum, St Martin's Lane, London, WC2N 4ES, England.

TOMASONI, Omar; Italian musician (trumpet); b. 1984, Orzinuovi. *Education:* Conservatorio Luca Marenzio, Brescia, studied with Sergio Malacarne. *Career:* mem. EU Youth Orchestra 2001–03; fmr Prin. Trumpeter, Orchestra Filarmonica della Scala, Janáček Festival Orchestra; Prin. Trumpeter, Orchestra del Maggio Musicale Fiorentino under Zubin Mehta 2004–08; also worked as substitute with Royal Concertgebouw Orchestra, Mozart Orchestra and Mahler Chamber Orchestra; apptd Prin. Trumpeter, Orchestra dell'Accad. Naz. di Santa Cecilia, led by Sir Antonio Pappano 2008; Prin. Trumpeter, Royal Concertgebouw Orchestra 2013–; soloist and chamber musician; mem. and Co-founder Italian Wonderbrass wind quintet 2006–. *Recordings include:* Pines of Rome (with Italian Wonderbrass). *Honours:* Bronze Medal of the Italian Repub. 2003. *Address:* Stichting Koninklijk Concertgebouworkest, Postbus 78098, 1070 LP Amsterdam, Netherlands (office). *Telephone:* 203051010. *Fax:* 203051001. *E-mail:* info@concertgebouworkest.nl. *Website:* www.concertgebouworkest.nl.

TOMASSON, Tomas; Icelandic singer (baritone); b. 28 Dec. 1966, Reykjavík. *Education:* Reykjavík Coll. of Music, Royal Coll. of Music Opera School, London, UK. *Career:* sang at first with Icelandic Opera, as Sparafucile (Rigoletto), Mozart's Sarastro and Lodovico in Otello; made transition from bass to baritone 2005; other roles include Colline in La Bohème, Conte Rodolfo in La Sonnambula, Ferrando in Il trovatore, Frate and Grand Inquisitore in Don Carlo, Raimondo in Lucia di Lammermoor, Pimen in Boris Godunov, Gremin in Eugene Onegin, Escamillo in Carmen, Fasolt in Rheingold, Fafner in Rheingold and Siegfried, title roles in Der fliegende Holländer, Don Giovanni, Wozzeck, Lear and Rigoletto, Tomsky in Pikovaya Dama, Ruprecht in The Fiery Angel, Hans Sachs in Die Meistersinger von Nürnberg, Kurwenal in Tristan und Isolde and Klingsor in Parsifal. *Current Management:* c/o Atelier Musicale S.r.l, via Caselle 76, 40068 San Lazzaro di Savena, Italy. *Telephone:* (051) 455706. *Fax:* (051) 463331 (office). *E-mail:* info@ateliermusicale.it (office). *Website:* www.ateliermusicale.it (office).

TOMES, Susan, MA (Cantab.), ARCM; British pianist and writer; b. 26 May 1954, Edinburgh, Scotland; d. of the late Albert Henry Tomes and Catherine Mary Brodie; m. Dr Robert Philip; one d. *Education:* King's Coll., Cambridge. *Career:* Founder-mem. Domus 1980–95; Founder-mem. Florestan Trio 1995–2012; pianist, Gaudier Ensemble 1993–; solo pianist. *Recordings include:* more than 50 CDs of solo and chamber music, including numerous albums with Domus, the Florestan Trio and the Gaudier Ensemble; solo recording of Billy Mayerl's piano music; solo recording of Mozart's piano concertos K413–415 with the Gaudier Ensemble. *Publications:* Beyond the Notes 2004, A Musician's Alphabet 2006, Out of Silence 2010; contrib. to The Cambridge Companion to Recorded Music 2009, The Guardian, Financial Times, numerous music magazines. *Honours:* numerous awards, including three Gramophone Awards 1985, 1995, 1999, Classic CD Award 1999, Royal Philharmonic Soc. Award 2000, several Diapasons d'Or, several Deutsche Schallplattenpreise, Walter Wilson Cobbett Medal for distinguished services to chamber music 2013. *E-mail:* susan@susantomes.com (office). *Website:* www.susantomes.com.

TOMITA, Yo, BMus, MMus, PhD; Japanese musicologist and academic; *Professor, Queen's University, Belfast;* b. 17 Dec. 1961, Fukushima. *Education:* Musashino Academia Musicale, Tokyo and Univ. of Leeds, UK. *Career:* Postdoctoral Research Fellow, Queen's Univ., Belfast 1995–2000, Lecturer 2000–01, Reader 2001–06, Prof. 2006–; Sr Fellow, Bach-Archiv Leipzig 2011–; Gerhard Herz Visiting Bach Prof., Univ. of Louisville, USA 2012; mem. Royal Musical Asscn, Neue Bach-Gesellschaft, American Bach Soc., Soc. for Musicology in Ireland, Japan Musicological Soc., Advisory Council Bach Network UK, Editorial Bd Understanding Bach. *Publications include:* J.S. Bach's Das Wohltemperierte Clavier II 1993, edns of Fugal Composition: A Guide to the Study of Bach's 48 by Joseph Groocock 2003, Bach Studies from Dublin (with Anne Leahy) 2004; contrib. to Oxford Composer Companions: J.S. Bach 1999, Cambridge Mozart Encyclopedia 2006, Henle Urtext edn of Das Wohltemperierte Klavier II 2007, Ashgate Baroque Composers: Bach 2011; numerous journal articles. *Honours:* Martha Goldsworthy Arnold Fellowship, Riemenschneider Bach Inst., Berea, USA 2002. *Address:* School of Creative Arts, Queen's University, Belfast, BT7 1NN, Northern Ireland (office). *Telephone:* (28) 9097-5206 (office). *E-mail:* y.tomita@qub.ac.uk (office). *Website:* www.qub.ac.uk/schools/SchoolofCreativeArts/Staff/ProfessorYoTomita (office).

TOMLINSON, Sir John Rowland, CBE; British singer (bass); b. 22 Sept. 1946, Accrington, Lancs.; s. of Rowland Tomlinson and Ellen Greenwood; m. Moya Joel 1969; one s. two d. *Education:* Accrington Grammar School, Manchester Univ. and Royal Manchester Coll. of Music. *Career:* debut at Glyndebourne Festival 1972, ENO 1974, Royal Opera House, Covent Garden 1976; since then has appeared in many operas throughout Europe and N America, including Parsifal, Tristan und Isolde and Lohengrin; has sung role of Wotan/Wanderer in The Ring Cycle, Bayreuth Festival 1988–98; other significant roles include Boris in Boris Godunov, ENO (Manchester) 1982, Don Basilio in Il Barbiere di Siviglia, Covent Garden 1985, Moses, ENO 1980, Fiesco in Simon Boccanegra, ENO 1988, Mephistopheles in Damnation of Faust, Santiago, Chile 1990, Attila, Opera North 1990, Filippo II in Don Carlos, Opera North 1992, König Marke in Tristan and Isolde, Bayreuth Festival 1993, Mephistopheles in Damnation of Faust, La Fenice, Venice 1993, Claggart in Billy Budd, Covent Garden 1994, Hans Sachs in Die Meistersinger, Berlin Staatsoper 1995, Kingfisher in Midsummer Marriage, Covent Garden 1996, Bluebeard in Bluebeard's Castle, Berlin Philharmonic 1996, Four Villains in Tales of Hoffmann, ENO 1998, Moses in Moses and Aaron, New York Metropolitan Opera 1999, Golaud in Pelléas et Mélisande, Glyndebourne 1999, Mephistopheles in Damnation of Faust, Munich Staatsoper 2000, Hagen in Götterdämmerung, Bayreuth 2000, Baron Ochs in Rosenkavalier, Staatsoper Dresden 2000, Borromeo in Palestrina, Covent Garden 2001, Gurnemanz in Parsifal, New York Metropolitan 2001. *Honours:* Hon. FRNCM; Hon. DMus (Sussex) 1997, (Manchester) 1998; Singer of the Year, Royal Philharmonic Soc. 1991, 1998, 2008, Evening Standard Opera Award 1998, Soc. of London Theatre's Special Award, Olivier Awards 2007. *Current Management:* Music International, 13 Ardilaun Road, Highbury, London, N5 2QR, England. *E-mail:* dan@musicint.co.uk. *Website:* johntomlinson.org.

TOMMASI, Carlo; stage designer; b. 1950, Italy. *Education:* Brera Acad. *Career:* designs for Rigoletto at Munich, in production by Roman Polanski, Carmen in Tokyo, Otello at Bregenz and Tannhäuser in Frankfurt; premiere production of Berio's La Vera Storia, La Scala 1982, La Cenerentola in Brussels 1983 and L'Incoronazione di Poppea at Nancy; further designs at La Monnaie for The Cunning Little Vixen, Der Rosenkavalier, Der fliegende Holländer and Der Freischütz; collaborations with Nicholas Joël at Théâtre du Capitole, Toulouse, for Falstaff 1991 and Roméo et Juliette 1993, also at the Royal Opera, Covent Garden; further work includes Leonore at Genoa and Les Contes d'Hoffmann at Toulouse.

TOMOWA-SINTOW, Anna; Bulgarian singer (soprano); b. 22 Sept. 1943, Stara Zagora; m. Albert Sintow; one d. *Education:* Nat. Conservatory of Sofia with Zlatew Tscherkin and Katja Spiridonowa. *Career:* debut at Leipzig Opera 1967; joined Deutsche Staatsoper, Berlin 1973; guest engagements at all leading European and US opera houses, with conductors including Karajan, Böhm, Haitink, Kleiber, Solti, Abbado, Muti, Maazel, Mehta, Levine, Chailly, Davis, Barenboim, Thielemann; N America debut in San Francisco 1974, at Met, New York 1978, Chicago 1981; numerous tours in Japan, also with La Scala and Berlin Philharmonic under von Karajan; regular guest at Salzburg Festival 1973–91. *Recordings include:* Lohengrin, Le Nozze di Figaro, Don Giovanni, Die Zauberflöte, Der Rosenkavalier, Ariadne auf Naxos, Madame Butterfly, La Traviata, Tosca, Eugene Onegin, Aida, Otello, Capriccio, Andrea Chénier, Simon Boccanegra, Prince Igor, Mozart Coronation Mass, Mozart Requiem, Bach Magnificat, Brahms German Requiem, Verdi Requiem, Strauss Four Last Songs (Orphée d'Or) and Capriccio monologue, Beethoven Missa Solemnis and 9th Symphony, recitals of Verdi arias and of Italian and German arias. *Roles include:* Arabella, Ariadne, Marschallin, Salome, Madelaine in Capriccio, Ägyptische Helena, Countess Almaviva, Fiordiligi, Donna Anna, Elsa in Lohengrin, Elisabeth in Tannhäuser, Sieglinde, Aida, Traviata, Leonora in La Forza del Destino, Amelia in Ballo, Simone Boccanegra, Elisabetta in Don Carlo, Yaroslavna in Prince Igor, Tatjana in Onegin, Tosca, Madama Butterfly, Turandot, Manon Lescaut, Norma, Santuzza, Das Wunder der Heliane, etc. *Honours:* Dr hc; Kammersängerin, Vienna and Berlin, two Grammy Awards (for Ariadne and Don Giovanni/Donna Anna), three Orphée d'Or awards. *E-mail:* contact@tomowa-sintow.com. *Website:* www.tomowa-sintow.com.

TOMTER, Lars Anders; violist; b. 30 Nov. 1959; one d. *Education:* Max Rostal Bern Conservatory, Sándor Végh, Mozarteum, Salzburg. *Career:* solo performances, USA, Germany, Austria, Scandinavia, Spain, Hungary, France, UK; soloist with such orchestras as Acad. of St Martin-in-the-Fields, City of Birmingham and Frankfurt Radio Symphony Orchestra, Philharmonic Orchestra of Frankfurt, Hungarian National Philharmonic

Orchestra, Los Angeles Chamber Orchestra, Oslo and Bergen Philharmonics, Danish Radio Symphony Orchestra, Stockholm New Chamber Orchestra, Gavleborg, Norwegian Radio, Trondheim and Stavanger Symphony Orchestras; Proms debut with RPO 1998; Artistic Dir, Risar Chamber Music Festival; Walton's concerto at the London Proms 2002. *Recordings:* Walton Concertos; Franck and Vieuxtemps Sonatas; Mozart's Sinfonia Concertante with Norwegian Chamber Orchestra and Iona Brown; Schumann and Brahms Sonatas with Pianist Leif Ove Andsnes. *Current Management:* c/o Stephannie Williams Artists, 9 Central Chambers, Wood Street, Stratford-upon-Avon, Warwicks. CV37 6JQ, England. *Telephone:* (1789) 266272. *Fax:* (1789) 266467. *E-mail:* enquiries@swartists.co.uk.

TONE, Yasunao; American composer and multimedia artist; b. 31 March 1935, Tokyo, Japan. *Education:* Japanese National University, Chiba, Tokyo University of the Arts. *Career:* founded performance group Ongaku at Tokyo, 1960; wrote tape pieces Geography, and Music performed by Merle Cunningham Dance Company; moved to New York, USA 1972, participating in avant garde and computer music festivals in North America and Europe, FLUXUS festivals 1979–87 and Venice Biennale 1990. *Compositions include:* Intermedia Art Festival, 1969; Multi Performance, 1972; Voice and Phenomenon, 1976; The Wall and the Books, 1982; Word of Mouth, 1988. *Publications include:* Can Art be Thought 1970. *Honours:* New York Foundation for the Arts Fellowship 1987.

TOOLEY, Sir John, Kt, MA; British arts administrator and arts consultant; b. 1 June 1924, Rochester, Kent, England; s. of the late H. R. Tooley; m. 1st Judith Craig Morris 1951 (divorced 1965); three d.; m. 2nd Patricia J. N. Bagshawe 1968 (divorced 1990); one s.; m. 3rd Jennifer Anne Shannon 1995 (divorced 2003). *Education:* Repton School and Magdalene Coll., Cambridge. *Career:* Sec., Guildhall School of Music and Drama 1952–55; Asst to Gen. Admin., Royal Opera House, Covent Garden 1955–60, Asst Gen. Admin. 1960–70, Gen. Admin. 1970–80, Gen. Dir 1980–88; Dir London Philharmonic Orchestra 1998–2010, Britten Estate 1989–96, South Bank Bd 1991–97, Compton Verney Opera Project 1991–97, Welsh Nat. Opera 1992–2000, David Gyngell Holdings Ltd 1996–97; Pres. Salisbury Festival 1988–2005; Chair. Rudolf Nureyev Foundation 1995–2008, Almeida Theatre 1990–97, Salisbury Cathedral Girl Choristers Trust 1995–2006, , Monument Insurance Brokers Ltd 1997–2002; Gov. Royal Ballet 1994–97; consultant, Int. Man. Group 1988–97, Ballet Opera House, Toronto 1989–90, Istanbul Foundation for Culture and Arts 1993–2008, Antelope Films 1993–; adviser, Borusan Philharmonic Orchestra, Istanbul 2005–08; Trustee Britten Pears Foundation 1988–99, Walton Trust 1988–2000, Wigmore Hall 1989–2001, Almeida Theatre 1990–2002, Performing Arts Labs 1992–97, Cardiff Bay Opera House 1995–96, Sidney Nolan Trust 1995–, Mozartfest, Bath 2001–. *Publication:* In House 1999. *Honours:* Hon. FRAM; Hon. FGSM; Hon. FRNCM; Hon. mem. Incorporated Soc. of Musicians; Hon. Fellow, Magdalene Coll., Cambridge 2005; Commendatore of Italian Repub. 1976; Hon. DUniv (Univ. of Central England) 1996; Queen Elizabeth II Coronation Award 2005. *Address:* 18 Grange Court, Cambridge, CB3 9BD, England (home). *Telephone:* (1223) 358737 (office); (1223) 351995 (home). *Fax:* (1223) 358737 (office). *E-mail:* tooley@btinternet.com (home).

TOOVEY, Andrew; British composer; b. 21 Feb. 1962, London, England. *Education:* Univs of Surrey and Sussex with Jonathan Harvey, at Dartington with Morton Feldman. *Career:* music has been performed by Alan Hacker, Michael Finnissy, the Mistry Quartet and the Endimion Ensemble; Dir, Ixion 1987–, giving performances of works by Cage, Feldman, Ferneyhough, Finnissy, James Dillon and Xenakis; Young Concert Artists Trust Assoc. Composer 1993–; Composer-in-Residence, Banff Centre, Canada 1997. *Compositions:* chamber and ensemble: Winter Solstice 1984, String Quartet (Tippett Prize) 1985, Cantec for viola and piano (Bernard Shore Composition Award) 1986, Ate (Terra Nova Prize) 1986, Shining for violin and cello 1987, Shining Forth 1987, Shimmer Bright for string trio 1988, White Fire 1988, Snow Flowers 1988, Black Light 1989, An Die Musik 1989, Adam 1989; solo instruments: Veiled Wave 1 and 2 for flute and clarinet 1985, Artaud for piano 1986, Fragments after Artaud 1988, Lament, Strathspey, reel for violin 1988, Out Jumps Jack Death and Down There By the Sea for piano 1989, UBU (two-act opera) 1990–92, The Juniper Tree (one-act opera) 1993, The Moon Falls through the Autumn for piano 1995, Out! for two pianos and orchestra 1995, Red Icon for large symphony orchestra 1996, Oboe Concerto 1997, In the Shallow Grave (opera) 1999. *Address:* c/o Boosey & Hawkes, Aldwych House, 71–91 Aldwych, London, England.

TOPCHJAN, Eduard; Armenian conductor; *Artistic Director and Principal Conductor, Armenian Philharmonic Orchestra*; b. 1971, Yerevan. *Education:* Yerevan Conservatory. *Career:* co-f. Serenade Chamber Orchestra 1991; Artistic Dir and Principal Conductor, Armenian Philharmonic Orchestra 2000–; Principal Guest Conductor, Yerevan Int. Music Festival 2007–. *Recordings include:* Khachaturian/Shostakovich 2006. *Honours:* Meritorious Worker of Art Award, Ministry of Culture of Armenia 2007. *Address:* c/o Armenian Philharmonic Orchestra, Aram Khachaturian Concert Hall, 46 Mashtots Avenue, 0002 Yerevan, Armenia (office). *Telephone:* (1) 0560645 (office). *Fax:* (1) 0564965 (office). *E-mail:* philharmonic@apo.am (office). *Website:* www.apo.am (office).

TÖPPER, Hertha; singer (mezzo-soprano); b. 19 April 1924, Graz, Austria. *Education:* Graz Conservatory. *Career:* debut in Graz 1945 as Ulrica in Un Ballo in Maschera; sang in Graz 1945–52, at Munich Staatsoper from 1952

notably in the 1957 premiere of Hindemith's Die Harmonie der Welt, at Bayreuth Festival from 1951 as Brangaene and Fricka, and visited Covent Garden with the Munich Co. 1953 as Clairon in Capriccio; sang at San Francisco 1960 and Metropolitan Opera 1962 as Octavian in Der Rosenkavalier, and at Munich 1972 in the premiere of Isang Yun's Sim Tjong; other roles include Verdi's Eboli and Amneris, Mozart's Dorabella, Magdalena in Die Meistersinger and Nancy in Martha; sang Branhaene with Bayreuth Co. in Osaka; retired from stage 1981; often heard in sacred music by Bach; Prof., Munich Musikhochschule from 1971. *Recordings:* Die Meistersinger; Bluebeard's Castle; Oedipus Rex; Schoenberg's Gurrelieder; Bach's B minor Mass; Octavian in Der Rosenkavalier from London's Covent Garden. *Honours:* Bayer Kammersängerin 1955, Deutsches Bundes Verdienstkreuz 1 Klasse 1985, Bayer Maximiliansorden für Wissenschaft und Kunst 1995; Bayer Verdienstorden 1962. *Address:* Knöbelstrasse 2, 80538 München, Germany.

TORADZE, Alexander; pianist; b. 1955, Tbilisi, Georgia. *Education:* Tchaikovsky Conservatory, Moscow. *Career:* Resident in the USA from 1983, giving concerts in every major centre and appearing with such conductors as Ashkenazy, Dutoit, Eschenbach, Masur, Mehta, Ozawa and Rattle; European engagements with the Kirov Orchestra (under Valery Gergiev) Rotterdam Philharmonic Orchestra, London Symphony and Philharmonic, CBSO and Philharmonia Orchestra; Season 1997 with the Los Angeles Philharmonic Orchestra under Esa-Pekka Salonen, Toronto Symphony Orchestra under Jukka-Pekka Saraste, the Orchestra National de France and the Rotterdam Philharmonic Orchestra under Gergiev; Festival appearances at the London Proms, Hollywood Bowl, St Petersburg White Nights, Saratoga and Schleswig-Holstein; Martin Endowed Prof. in Piano, Indiana Univ. South Bend 1991–; Prokofiev's concerto No. 3 in C major at the London Proms, 2002. *Recordings include:* Prokofiev's 7th Sonata, Ravel's Miroirs, Three Movements from Petrushka, Pictures at an Exhibition, Gaspard de la Nuit (EMI/Angel); Prokofiev Concertos, with the Kirov Orchestra and Gergiev (Philips Classics). *Current Management:* c/o Ettore F. Volontieri, EFV Consultants, Via Antonio Allegri da Correggio 1, 00196 Rome, Italy. *Telephone:* (06) 45423164. *Fax:* (06) 45423174. *E-mail:* ettore.f.volontieri@efvconsultants.com. *Website:* www.efvconsultants.com. *Current Management:* c/o Douglas Sheldon, Columbia Artists Management Inc., 1790 Broadway, New York, NY 10019, USA. *Telephone:* (212) 841-9541. *Fax:* (212) 841-9517. *Website:* www.cami.com; www.toradzepianostudio.org.

TORCHINSKY, Yuri; Ukrainian violinist; b. 1949, Kharkiv; one s. *Education:* Tchaikovsky Conservatory, Moscow. *Career:* debut with Brahms Violin Concerto with the Kharkov Philharmonic Orchestra conducted by Vakhtang Gordania; Leader, Bolshoi Theatre, Moscow with numerous performances, concerts and tours, as soloist and orchestra leader, worldwide including the Metropolitan Opera in New York and at many opera theatres and concert halls in USA, Italy, Austria, France, Netherlands, Germany, Japan and elsewhere; radio broadcasts with recitals in Moscow and on television in Yugoslavia; several appearances at the Albert Hall in London, television and radio recordings of Promenade Concerts performance, at the Barbican Hall, Royal Festival Hall, New Symphony Hall and Town Hall in Birmingham; many concerts and recordings as guest leader of London Symphony Orchestra, as well as tours to France, Switzerland, Austria, Portugal and Italy; solo appearances at Royal Opera House 1995; guest leader with such orchestras as BBC Nat. Orchestra of Wales, Philharmonia, Royal Philharmonic, and BBC Manchester; Leader, Royal Ballet Symphonia Orchestra of the Birmingham Royal Ballet.

TORKE, Michael, BMus; American composer and pianist; b. 22 Sept. 1961, Milwaukee, Wis.; s. of Thomas Torke and Diane Torke. *Education:* Eastman School of Music, Rochester. *Career:* commissions from New York City Ballet, New York City Opera, New York Philharmonic, Metropolitan Opera, Nat. Ballet of Canada, San Francisco Symphony, London Sinfonietta and Walt Disney Co.; f. Ecstatic Records to re-release the complete Argo Decca catalogue as well as new releases; publishing entity Adjustable Music. *Compositions:* Laetus for piano solo 1982, Ceremony of Innocence for flute, clarinet, violin, cello and piano 1983, Ecstatic Orange for ensemble 1984, Vanada for keyboards, brass and percussion 1984, The Yellow Pages 1984, Bright Blue Music for ensemble 1985, Verdant Music for ensemble 1986, The Directions (one-act opera based on The Yellow Pages) 1986, Adjustable Wrench for ensemble 1987, Black and White for wind instruments, percussion and synthesizer 1988, Copper for brass quintet and orchestra 1988, Ash for orchestra or chamber orchestra 1989, Slate (ballet for Concertante Group and orchestra) 1989, Rust for piano and wind instruments 1989, Run for orchestra 1992, Four Proverbs for voice and ensemble 1993, King of Hearts (chamber opera) 1994, Book of Proverbs for soprano, baritone, chorus and orchestra 1996, Overnight Mail and Change of Address for ensemble 1997, Brick Symphony 1997, Pentecost for soprano, organ and strings 1997, Strawberry Fields (chamber opera) 1999, Four Seasons (oratorio) 1999, Rapture (concerto for percussion and orchestra) 2001, An American Abroad 2002, The Contract (ballet) 2002, An Italian Straw Hat (ballet) 2004, Two Girls on the Beach for woodwind quintet 2005, Bays of Huatulco for piano 2006, Central Park West (opera) 2007, Tropical for ensemble 2007, Plans for orchestra and chorus 2008, Song of Ecclesiastes for baritone and piano 2008. *Honours:* Prix de Rome, Koussevitsky Foundation Award. *Telephone:* (702) 837-3367 (office). *E-mail:* michael@michaeltorke.com (office). *Website:* www.michaeltorke.com.

TÖRNQUIST, Pirkko; Finnish singer (soprano); b. 1955. *Education:* Helsinki Conservatory and Sibelius Acad., studied with Vera Rozsa in

London, Nicolai Gedda in Stockholm and with Anitta Välkki. *Career:* many appearances as opera and concert singer throughout Finland and Europe; Finnish Nat. Opera, Helsinki from 1990, as Amelia in Ballo in Maschera, Tosca, Tatiana in Eugene Onegin, Mozart's Countess and Elsa in Lohengrin; Maija in Pohjan's Daughter, by Merikanto; Savonlinna Festival 1990–91, as Aida; sang Sieglinde in Die Walküre at Helsinki 1998. *Honours:* prizewinner Vienna Belvedere Competition 1993.

TORRES, Victor; singer (baritone); b. 1965, Buenos Aires, Argentina. *Education:* studied in Buenos Aires and with Gerard Souzay. *Career:* debut, Bilbao 1991, as Germont; sang in South Africa as Verdi's Posa and Luna; Teatro Colón, Buenos Aires, from 1993, as Masetto in Don Giovanni and Paolo Orsini in Rienzi; season 1993–94 at the Châtelet, Paris, and Lyon as Germont; further appearances as Donizetti's Enrico at the Paris Opéra and as Purcell's Aeneas and Bartók's Bluebeard at San Francisco; season 1997–98 as Don Alfonso in Così fan tutte at the Berlin Staatsoper and Germont at Opéra de Nancy; many concert engagements, notably in Bach's St John Passion, Messiah, Haydn's Creation and Schumann's Scenes from Faust; sang Yeletzky in The Queen of Spades at Florence 1999. *Recordings include:* Monteverdi Vespers.

TORRES-SANTOS, Raymond, BA, MA, PhD; American composer, arranger, keyboard player, conductor and music educator and music critic; *Dean, College of Arts, California State University, Long Beach;* b. 19 June 1958, Puerto Rico. *Education:* Puerto Rico Univ. and Conservatory of Music, Univ. of California, Los Angeles, Ferienkurse für Neue Musik, CCRMA, Stanford Univ., Centro di Sonologia Computazionale, Padua Univ., Italy. *Career:* arranger, Music Dir, for American singers and entertainers; composer of film music, studio musician in Hollywood; Prof., California State Univ., San Bernardino 1986–91; Chair of Music Dept, Univ. of Puerto Rico 1991–93; Chancellor, Puerto Rico Conservatory of Music 1994–98; Prof., CUNY 2000–08; Dean, Coll. of Arts and Communication, William Paterson Univ. 2008–11; Dean, Coll. of Arts, Calif. State Univ., Long Beach 2011–. *Compositions include:* Sinfonietta Concertante for orchestra 1980, Summertime for clarinet consort 1982, Exploraciones for string orchestra 1982, Areytos: a Symphonic Picture 1985, Enchanted Island for piano and tape 1986, Monchin del Alma (ballet) 1988, El País de los Cuatro Pisos: A Symphonic Overture 1988, Viaggio Senza Destinazione for tape 1988, Danza for orchestra 1991, La Cancion de las Antillas: A Symphonic Poem 1992, Fantasia Caribeña for orchestra 1992, Salsa y tres soneos for piano or harp solo, Requiem for mezzo-soprano, baritone, mixed chorus, children's choir and orchestra 1995, Odalisque (ballet) 1997, Concertino for clarinet, French horn, piano, percussion and strings 1998, Trio for clarinet, cello and piano 1998, Overture for orchestra 1998, Conversation with Silence for soprano and ensemble 1999, Millennium Symphony for orchestra 2000, Jersey Polyphony for chorus 2000, Juris Oratorio for chorus 2000, Predatory Gestures for flute and pre-recorded sounds 2001, Al Padre: A Prayer for tenor, chorus and orchestra 2003, Aves Eco, Aliento y Sonido for two sopranos and piano 2005, Musica Naturalis for chamber ensemble 2006, Recordar es vivir for orchestra 2010, Symphonia: Resonantia Luminosa Infinita for brass and orchestra 2014; performed and/or commissioned by the Casals Festival, Vienna Philharmonic, New Jersey Chamber Music Society, Continuum, Bronx Arts Ensemble, Quintet of the Americas, Paquito D'Rivera, Inter-American University, Youth Symphony of the Americas, San Juan Ballet and Pops Orchestra, American Composers Orchestra, and Symphony Orchestras from Puerto Rico, Queens, London, Pacific, Taiwan, Warsaw, Vancouver, Toronto, Washington, China, Northwestern Univ. and Univ. of California at Los Angeles. *Recordings:* 25 as arranger and/or conductor. *Address:* PO Box 361743, San Juan, PR 00936-1743, USA (office).

TORTELIER, Yan Pascal; French conductor and violinist; b. 19 April 1947, Paris; s. of the late Paul Tortelier and of Maud Tortelier; m. Sylvie Brunet-Moret 1970; two s. *Education:* Paris Conservatoire and Berkshire Music Centre, UK, music studies with Nadia Boulanger, studies in conducting with Franco Ferrara. *Career:* debut as concert violinist, Royal Albert Hall 1962; has since toured extensively world-wide; Konzertmeister, Assoc. Conductor of Orchestre du Capitole de Toulouse 1974–83; Prin. Conductor and Artistic Dir, Ulster Orchestra 1989–92; Prin. Conductor, BBC Philharmonic 1992–2003, Conductor Laureate 2003–10, Conductor Emer. 2010–; Prin. Guest Conductor, RAM, Pittsburgh Symphony Orchestra 2005–08; Prin. Conductor, Orquestra Sinfónica de São Paulo 2009–11, Hon. Guest Conductor 2012–; guest conducting with San Francisco Symphony, Dresden Philharmonic, London Philharmonic, Minnesota Orchestra, Baltimore Symphony, St Petersburg Philharmonic, Sydney Symphony, Melbourne Symphony etc. *Recordings include:* Ravel/Debussy/Massenet (BBC Music Magazine Orchestral Award 2012). *Publication:* première orchestration of Ravel's Piano Trio (world première concert 1992). *Honours:* Hon. DLitt (Ulster) 1992; Dr hc (Lancaster) 1999; First Prize for Violin, Paris Conservatoire 1961. *Current Management:* c/o Nicholas Mathias, IMG Artists, The Light Box, 111 Power Road, London, W4 5PY, England. *Telephone:* (20) 7957-5800. *Fax:* (20) 7957-5801. *E-mail:* nmathias@imgartists.com. *Website:* imgartists.com/artist/yan_pascal_tortelier.

TORZEWSKI, Marek; Polish singer (tenor); b. 1960. *Education:* Poznań Academy of Music. *Career:* debut, Łódź Opera 1984 as Edgardo in Lucia di Lammermoor; sang in Idomeneo at the Théâtre de la Monnaie Brussels, 1984; appearances in La Finta Giardiniera at Vienna, Salzburg, Amsterdam, Berlin and New York, 1985; further engagements at Brussels and in Hamburg,

Montpellier, Philadelphia and Lausanne; season 1989–90 in L'Incoronazione di Poppea in Paris, Rosenkavalier, Così fan tutte and Fierrabras by Schubert in Brussels, Don Ottavio at Toulouse and Glyndebourne Festival debut as Fenton in Falstaff; season 1991–92 as Tamino at Lausanne, Alfredo for Scottish Opera and the Mozart Requiem under Muti at La Scala, Milan; debut with the Berlin Philharmonic 1992, singing in Nono's Il Canto Sospeso, under Abbado; Opera National de Lisbon, Eugene Onegin – Lensky, Staatsoper Leipzig, Così fan tutte – Ferrando, 1993; Théâtre Municipal de Lausanne, Iphigénie en Tauride – Pylade, 1994. *Recordings include:* Il Canto Sospeso. *E-mail:* marektorzewski@hotmail.com (office). *Website:* www.marektorzewski.com.pl.

TOTH, Gwendolyn Joyce, DMus; American musician and conductor; *Artistic Director, Art of the Early Keyboard, Inc.;* b. 28 July 1955, Cleveland, Ohio; d. of Ernest J. Toth and Ruth M. Toth (née Office); m. 1st Philip M. Rosenberg 1981 (divorced 1988); m. 2nd Dongsok Shin 1989; one s. two d. *Education:* Middlebury Coll., Southern Methodist Univ., City Univ. of New York, Yale Univ., Amsterdam Conservatory. *Career:* Music Dir St Francis of Assisi Church, New York 1989–2007; Lecturer in Harpsichord, Mannes Coll. of Music, New School Univ.; collaboration with Mark Morris Dance Group 1997–2002; Lecturer in Harpsichord, Mason Gross School of the Arts, Rutgers Univ. 2001–04; mem. Harpsichord Faculty, Montclair State Univ. 2007–; Music Dir Immanuel Lutheran Church 2007–; Orchestra Dir, Manhattan Coll. 2008–; Harpsichord Adjunct Faculty, Hunter Coll., CUNY 2008–11; Choral Dir, Coll. of Mount Saint Vincent 2011–12; currently Artistic Dir, Art of the Early Keyboard, Inc. *Recordings include:* Orfeo, Love Letters From Italy, I Don't Want to Love, Organ Music of Heinrich Scheidemann, Bach: Goldberg Variations, Meantone Organs in Holland, Monteverdi Madrigals, Book 5, The Arp Schnitger Organ in Noordbroek, Soli Deo Gloria: Solo Cantatas of Johann Rosenmüller. *Plays include:* I'll Never See the Stars Again. *Publications include:* contrib. of articles to Early Music America Magazine 2005. *Honours:* First Prize, American Guild of Organists 1977, 1979, Opera News Top Ten Conductors 1989, Newell Jenkins Prize 2001. *Address:* Art of the Early Keyboard, Inc., 170 West 73rd Street, No. 3C, New York, NY 10023, USA (office). *Telephone:* (212) 967-9157 (office). *Fax:* (212) 799-0690 (office). *E-mail:* artekgwent@aol.com (office). *Website:* www.artekearlymusic.org (office).

TOVEY, Bramwell, FRAM; British conductor and composer; *Music Director, Vancouver Symphony Orchestra;* b. 1955, England. *Career:* many concerts in a broad repertoire throughout Europe and Canada, including numerous premieres; Artistic Dir, Winnipeg Symphony Orchestra 1989–2001, establishing the Winnipeg New Music Festival; Music Dir, Vancouver Symphony Orchestra 2000–; Chief Conductor and Music Dir, Orchestre Philharmonique du Luxembourg 2002–06; debut, Concertgebouw, Amsterdam 2004; Principal Guest Conductor, Los Angeles Philharmonic 2008–; guest conductor with orchestras, including NYPO, Toronto Symphony, National Arts Centre Orchestra, Trondheim Symphony in Norway, New York Philharmonic, Royal Scottish Nat. Orchestra, London Philharmonic; Fellow, Royal Acad. of Music, London, Royal Conservatory of Music, Toronto. *Compositions include:* Cello Concerto 2001, Requiem for a Charred Skull (Juno Award for Best Classical Composition 2003), Eighteen (film score) 2005. *Honours:* Member of the Order of Manitoba 2000; Hon. DJur (Manitoba), (Winnipeg), (Kwantien Univ. Coll.); Joan Chalmers Nat. Award for Artistic Direction 1999. *Current Management:* IMG Artists, Carnegie Hall Tower, 152 West 57th Street, 5th Floor, New York, NY 10019, USA. *Telephone:* (212) 994-3539. *Fax:* (212) 995-3550. *E-mail:* artists@imgartists.com. *Website:* www.imgartists.com. *Address:* Vancouver Symphony Orchestra, Orpheum Theatre, 601 Smithe Street, Vancouver, BC V6B 5G1, Canada (office). *Website:* www.vancouversymphony.ca (office).

TOWER, Joan Peabody, MA; American composer; b. 6 Sept. 1938, New Rochelle, NY. *Education:* Bennington Coll., Columbia Univ. *Career:* pianist, Da Capo Chamber Players 1969–84; apptd Assoc. Prof., Bard Coll., New York 1972; Composer-in-Residence, St Louis Symphony 1985–87; comms from Contemporary Music Soc., Jerome Foundation, Massachusetts State Arts Council, Schubert Club, Richard Stolzman, St Louis Symphony, Elmar Oliveira, NY Philharmonic, Chicago Symphony, Fromm Foundation, Nat. Endowment for the Arts; Guggenheim Fellow 1976; Nat. Endowment for the Arts Fellow 1974, 1975, 1980, 1984; New York State Council for Arts Award 1980; American Acad. and Inst. of Arts and Letters Award in Music 1983. *Compositions include:* Amazon, Amazon II, Sequoia, Silver Ladders (Grawemeyer Award, Univ. of Louisville 1990) 1985, Breakfast Rhythms, Black Topaz, Wings, Fantasy, Cello Concerto, Piano Concerto, Clarinet Concerto, Made in America (Grammy Award for Best Classical Composition 2008). *Address:* Bard College, Annandale-On-Hudson, NY 12504, USA.

TOWSE, David, ARCM, LRAM; British violinist; b. 1956, Bridlington, England. *Education:* Royal Coll. of Music with Leonard Hirsch, Peter Element and Herbert Howells. *Career:* leader of the East Riding County Youth Orchestra and British Youth Symphony Orchestra 1972; leader of the London Youth String Ensemble while at the Royal Coll. of Music; with Royal Philharmonic Orchestra 1978–98, Assoc. Leader 1982, (performances of piano quintets and quartets with the Forellen Ensemble (mems of the RPO) at music clubs and festivals throughout the UK; freelance in and around London, guest leading, directing and coaching ensembles, teaching and performing as a soloist, also chamber music both for concerts and private functions. *Address:* 47 Abbotswood Road, London, SW16 1AJ, England (home).

TRACK, Gerhard; Austrian conductor and composer; *Artistic Director, World Choral Festival*; b. 17 Sept. 1934, Vienna; m. Micaela Maihart 1958; two s. *Education:* Acad. of Music and Performing Arts, Vienna, Teacher Training Coll., Vienna. *Career:* mem. Vienna Boys' Choir 1942–48; debut as conductor with Vienna Boys' Choir 1953; Conductor, Vienna Boys' Choir 1953–58; Music Dir, St John's Symphony Orchestra; Assoc. Prof. of Music, St John's Univ. Men's Chorus, Minnesota, USA 1958–69; Music Dir, Metropolitan Youth Symphony Orchestra, Minneapolis, Minnesota 1965–69; Music Dir, Pueblo Symphony Orchestra, Chorale and Youth Symphony; founder annual Mozart Festival, Pueblo, CO, USA; Thatcher Prof. of Music, Univ. of Southern Colorado, Pueblo, CO 1969–86; Music Dir and Conductor, Choral Soc. of Young Vienna (Jung-Wien) 1986–96, Orchester Pro Musica Int. and Vienna Serenade Orchestra, Vienna 1986–; teacher, Conservatory of the City of Vienna and Hochschule for Music and Performing Arts, Vienna 1987–89; Dir, Conservatory of the City of Vienna 1989–99; Pres., Austrian Composers' Soc. 1988–92; Music Dir, Vienna Male Choral Soc. 1990–2003, Hon. Conductor 2005–; Conductor, Salute to Vienna Concerts, USA and Canada 2000–; Artistic Dir, World Choral Festival, Austria 2001–; guest conductor in Europe, USA, Asia and Australia; Pres. and founder, PMI Music Publication, CA. *Compositions include:* over 600 compositions, orchestral works, choral compositions and arrangements, one opera, chamber music, songs, three children's operas, 11 masses, oratorio Abraham and Isaac. *Publications:* contrib. to Sacred Music, Oesterreichische Musikzeitschrift, Wienerlied-Magazin. *Honours:* Golden Hon. Cross for Merit, Republic of Austria, Golden Hon. Cross of Vienna and Hon. Cross for Science and Art, First Class, Austria. *Current Management:* PMI, 10730 Riverside Drive, North Hollywood, CA 91602, USA. *Telephone:* (818) 769-3517 (office). *Address:* Praterstrasse 76/8, 1020 Vienna, Austria. *Telephone:* (1) 2167333. *E-mail:* gerhard.track@chello .at (home).

TRAMA, Ugo; Italian singer (bass); b. 4 Aug. 1932, Naples. *Education:* studied with Emilia Gubitosi in Naples, Accademia Chigiana, Siena and Accademia di Santa Cecilia, Rome. *Career:* debut at Spoleto Festival 1951, as Banquo in Macbeth; sang in Cairo and the Italian provinces; Holland Festival 1960, as Fiesco in Simon Bocanegra; Wexford festival 1961, as Silva in Ernani; Dallas Opera 1961; San Francisco Opera 1965; Appearances at the Maggio Musicale Florence, Teatro Liceo Barcelona and Strasbourg; Glyndebourne 1964–79, as Asdrubale in La Pietra del Paragone, Giove and Pane in Calisto, Atinoo and Tempo in Il Ritorno d'Ulisse, Bartolo in Le nozze di Figaro, Pistol in Falstaff and Farfallo in Die schweigsame Frau. *Recordings include:* Ramphis in Aida, La Cenerentola, Il Ritorno d'Ulisse.

TRAN, Quang Hai, MA, PhD, DipMus; French ethnomusicologist, educator, composer and musician; b. 13 May 1944, Linh Dong Xa, Vietnam; s. of Dr Tran Van Khe and Nguyen Thi Suong; m. Bach Yen 1978; one d. *Education:* Nat. Conservatory of Music, Saigon, Sorbonne Univ., Paris, Institut d'Ethnologie, Centre d'Etudes de Musique Orientale, Institut de Musicologie, Paris. *Career:* ethnomusicologist, Musée Nat. des Arts et Traditions Populaires 1968–87, Musée de l'Homme, Paris 1968–2009; Prof., Centre d'Etudes de Musique Orientale 1970–75; Lecturer of South East Asian music, Univ. of Paris X—Nanterre 1988–95; more than 3,500 concerts in 70 countries 1966–; played at many int. music festivals and in films, including Le chant des Harmoniques (co-author, actor, composer) 1989, The Song of Harmonics 2006, Hai, un musicien vietnamien à Paris 2014; mem. Soc. for Ethnomusicology, USA 1969–, Int. Council for Traditional Music, Slovenia 1976–, Int. Musicological Soc., Switzerland 1977–, Int. Asscn of Sound Archives, Australia 1978–, Soc. for Asian Music, USA 1978–, Société de Musicologie, France 1980–, European Seminar in Ethnomusicology, Switzerland 1983–, French Soc. for Ethnomusicology (Founding mem.) 1985–, Center for Vietnamese Studies, France 1987–, Int. Center of Khoomei, Russia 1995–, Int. Jew's Harp Soc. UK 2002 (founding mem.); Exec. Bd mem. Int. Council for Traditional Music 2005–09. *Films include:* Le Chant des Harmoniques (dir Hugo Zemp, co-authors: Tran Quang Hai and Hugo Zemp, produced by CNRS Audio-visuel) 1989, Hai: parcours d'un musicien vietnamien à Paris (dir Pierre Ravach) 2005. *Compositions include:* Ve Nguon (electro-acoustic) 1975, Shaman 1982, Nui Ngu Sông Huong (monochord) 1983, Voyage chamanique for voice 1986, Solo Thai for zither 1989, Tambours 89 for percussion and tape 1989, Vinh Ha Long 1993, Hôn Viêtnam 1993, Nostalgie au Pays Mông for Jew's harp 1997, Vietnam Mon Pays for Jew's harp 1997, Tuva Tuva for Jew's harp with overtone singing 1997, Ambiance des Hauts Plateaux du Vietnam for Jew's harp 1997, also some 300 pop songs. *Recordings include:* 23 recordings of Vietnamese music 1971–97, four DVDs on overtone singing 2004, 2005, 2006, two DVDs on traditional music of Viet Nam 2000, 2009. *Publications include:* Am Nhac Viet Nam 1989, Musique du Monde (with Michel Asselineau and Eugène Bérel) 1993, Musiques et Danses Traditionnelles d'Europe 1995, Tuyen tap 50 cakhuc (book of 50 Songs, with Vo My Ngoc) 1999; contrib. to New Grove Dictionary of Music and Musicians 1980, 2001 edns, New Grove Dictionary of Musical Instruments 1984, Encyclopedia Universalis, authored more than 500 articles for 30 Vietnamese magazines in America, Europe, Asia and Australia. *Honours:* Hon. mem. Scientific Soc. of Vietnamese Professionals, Canada 1992–, Inst. of Musicology, Hanoi 2004–, Centre de recherche d'ethnomusicologie (CREM); Chevalier, Légion d'honneur 2002; Dr hc (Int. Univ. Foundation, USA), (Albert Einstein Int. Acad., USA) 1989; Grand Prix, Acad. Charles Cros, Paris 1983, 1997, Gold Medal, Acad. of Asia 1986, Grand Prize, Int. Scientific Film, Parnu (Estonia) 1990, Prize for Best Ethnomusicological Film, Parnu 1990, Prize for Best Film on Scientific Research, Int. Film Festival, Palaiseau (France) 1990, Grand Prize, Int. Scientific Film Festival, Montreal 1991, Special Prize for Overtone Singing, Kyzyl, Tuva 1995, Medal of Cristal 1996, Medal of Honour, City of Limeil-Brévannes (France) 1998, Special Performer Prize, Jew's Harp Int. Festival, Molln, Austria 1998, Medal of Honour for his work, Grand Gold category (France) 2009, diplomas from Vietnam's Guinness Book of Records as the 'King of Spoons' 2010 and 'the person who has performed on the Vietnamese Jew's harp in greatest number of countries in the world' 2012. *Address:* 12 rue Gutenberg, 94450 Limeil-Brévannes, France (home). *Telephone:* 1-45-69-55-77; 6-50-25-73-67 (mobile). *E-mail:* tranquanghai@gmail.com. *Website:* www .tranquanghai.info; haidiphonie.wordpress.com; tranquanghai1944 .wordpress.com.

TRANTER, John; British singer (bass); b. 1946, Chesterfield, Derbyshire, England. *Education:* London Opera Centre, studied with John Dethick in Sheffield. *Career:* debut as Hobson in Peter Grimes, Châtelet Opera in Paris; Opera for All; Kent Opera as the Commendatore in Don Giovanni and Seneca in L'Incoronazione di Poppea; ENO from 1976 as Sarastro, Colline, Monterone in Rigoletto, Verdi's Grand Inquisitor Opera North as Zaccaria in Nabucco, Rossini's Don Basilio, Daland in Der fliegende Holländer, Gremin in Eugene Onegin, Pogner in Die Meistersinger and Trulove in The Rake's Progress; Welsh Nat. Opera as Wagner's Fasolt and Hagen, and Grigoris in The Greek Passion; other engagements in Nancy, Nîmes, Wellington and Lausanne; other roles include Oroveso in Norma, Ramphis in Aida, Nourabad in Les pêcheurs de Perles, Henry VIII in Anna Bolena and Tiresias in Oedipus Rex; Fafner at Covent Garden and Pope Leone in Attila at Covent Garden 1990; Banquo in Metz, France, and engagements in Marseille; debut in Pittsburgh as Varlaam in Boris 1991; season 1992 as Melchtal in Guillaume Tell at Covent Garden and Monterone for Opera North; has sung in concert at the Royal Albert Hall, Royal Festival Hall, Canterbury Cathedral, York Minister and Leeds Town Hall; also sang with the Scottish Opera as Gremin, King in Aida and in Billy Budd, Pearl Fishers; sang Fafner in Siegfried and the King in Aida at Santiago 1996–98; Hobson in Peter Grimes at La Scala 2000. *Current Management:* c/o Music International, 13 Ardilaun Road, Highbury, London, N5 2QR, England.

TRAUBOTH, Andrea; German singer (soprano); b. 2 April 1959, Seefeld, Munich, Germany. *Education:* studied in Munich. *Career:* sang with the Dortmund Opera 1983–86, Munich Staatsoper from 1986 and Cologne Opera from 1988; Dresden 1986–87, notably as Musetta and Donna Anna; further appearances at the Komische Oper, Berlin, La Scala, Milan, Madrid, Cologne, as Agathe in Der Freischutz, Laura in News of the Day, Freia in Das Rheingold, Eva in Die Meistersinger von Nürnberg, Elsa in Lohengrin, Chrysothemis in Elektra, Leonore in Fidelio, Arabella, Katja Kabanova, Rusalka and First Lady in Die Zauberflöte; concerts in Netherlands, Greece, France and England. *Current Management:* c/o Beate I. Mennicken, Heinrichzillestrasse 19, 15711 Zeesen, Germany. *Telephone:* (3375) 5249877. *Fax:* (3375) 5249878. *E-mail:* info@mennicken-pr.com. *Website:* www.mennicken-pr.com.

TREACHER, Graham; British conductor, composer and academic; b. 1932, England. *Career:* conducted the London New Music Singers 1958–63, with the first performances of works by Davies and Bennett, British premieres of works by Penderecki and Schoenberg; tours of Europe, Henry Wood Promenade Concerts; Conductor at Morley College, London, Holst Choir and Opera Group; Director of the Thaxted Festival, Essex until 1963; Asst Chorus Master Royal Opera House, Covent Garden 1962–64 for the British premiere of Schoenberg's Moses und Aron; Assoc. Conductor of the BBC Scottish Symphony Orchestra and Chorus, 1964–67; Dir of the Purcell School, London, 1968–70; Dir of Music at the University of Warwick, 1969–70; Lecturer in Style, Interpretation and Conducting, University of York, 1972–85; founder of the Amati Ensemble, baroque quartet, playing harpsichord and chamber organ, 1978–85; Dir and Conductor, Northern Music Theatre 1980–84, with first performances of works by Vic Hoyland, Philip Grange and British premieres of Kagel and Henze; Artistic Dir of the John Loosemore Early Music Centre, Devon, 1988–92. *Compositions include:* music for children, vocal and instrumental music including music for strings, percussion and celestine, for the 1990 Orkney Summer Festival; choral music with settings of Chaucer and Christmas music. *Publications include:* editions of Gesualdo (Cantiones Sacrae 1603) and Pallavicino's three act Carnival opera Messalina, for performance at the Vadstena International Opera Festival, Sweden; Dixit Dominus by Pallavicino. *Telephone:* (1297) 445193. *E-mail:* g.treacher@virgin .net.

TREE, Michael, DipMus; American violinist and violist; b. 19 Feb. 1934, Newark, NJ; m. Johanna Kreck; one s. one d. *Education:* Curtis Inst. of Music. *Career:* debut, Carnegie Hall 1954; soloist with major American orchestras; solo and chamber music appearances at festivals, including Israel, Athens, Spoleto, Casals, Marlboro; founder mem., Guarneri String Quartet 1964–2009; faculty mem., Curtis Inst. of Music, Univ. of Maryland, Rutgers Univ., Manhattan School of Music; pres., first American String Quartet Congress at Univ. of Maryland and Smithsonian Inst. 1989. *Recordings:* over 60 chamber music works, complete Beethoven quartets, 10 works for piano and strings with Artur Rubinstein; collaborations with Emanuel Ax, Jaimie Laredo, Leonard Rose, Alexander Schneider, Rudolf Serkin and Pinchas Zuckerman. *Honours:* Hon. DFA (Univ. of South Florida), (State Univ. of New York at Binghampton); New York City Seal of Recognition 1982. *Address:* School of Music, University of Maryland, 2110 Clarice Smith Performing Arts Center, College Park, MD 20742-1620, USA (office). *Telephone:* (301) 405-5549 (office). *Fax:* (301) 314-9504 (office). *E-mail:* mtree@umd.edu (office). *Website:* www.music.umd.edu/faculty/music_directory/string/michael_tree (office).

TREFAS, György; Hungarian singer (bass); b. 6 Oct. 1931, Budapest; m. Katalin Szabó 1972. *Education:* studied with Werner Alajos, Makai Mihály, Lendvay Andor, Hetényi Kálmán. *Career:* mem. Hungarian Army Musical Ensemble 1952–57; singer with Csokonai Theatre, Debrecen, Hungary 1957–2007; repertoire includes Verdi's King Philip in Don Carlos, Attila and De Silva in Ernani, Rocco in Fidelio, Duke in Bluebeard, Bartók's Duke Bluebeard's Castle, Zaccaria in Nabucco, Mephisto in Faust, Angelica, Sarastro in Die Zauberflöte, Osmin in Entführung, Gremin in Eugene Onegin. *Honours:* Order of Merit, Hungary 2006; Ferenc Liszt Prize 1968. *Address:* c/o Csokonai Theatre, 4024 Debrecen, Kossuth u. 10, Hungary (office).

TREKEL, Roman; German singer (baritone); b. 1962, Pirna, Saxony. *Education:* Berlin Musikhochschule, studied with Siegfried Lorenz and Hans Hotter. *Career:* sang with the Berlin Staatsoper from 1986, notably in Erwin and Elmire by Reichardt 1987 and Ullmann's Emperor of Atlantis 1989; many roles in operas by Mozart in Berlin and elsewhere; season 1992 as Ulysses in Erendira by Violet Dinescu and as Tarquinius in The Rape of Lucretia with the Berlin Kammeroper; concerts and lieder recitals in Europe; Berlin Staatsoper 1999–2001, as Leonhard in Die Brautwahl by Busoni, Ottokar in Der Freischütz and Don Alfonso. *Honours:* prizewinner Dvořák Competition 1985, Karlovy Vary 1987, DDR Competition Germany, Int. Lieder Competition Walter Gruner in London 1989.

TREKEL-BURCKHARDT, Ute; German singer (mezzo-soprano); b. 3 Nov. 1939, Pirna, Saxony. *Education:* studied in Berlin with Rita Meinl-Weise. *Career:* debut, Komische Oper Berlin 1963, as the Page in Salome; sang at the Komische Oper until 1978, then joined the Staatsoper Berlin; guest appearances in Vienna, Cologne, Brussels, Madrid and Dresden; Cologne 1984, as Renata in The Fiery Angel by Prokofiev; Nancy 1985, as The Woman in Schoenberg's Erwartung; created Queen Marguerite in Sutermeister's Le roi Bérenger at Munich 1985; other roles include the Countess Geschwitz in Lulu, Mozart's Sextus and Cherubino, Verdi's Eboli, Amneris and Ulrica, Strauss's Nurse (Die Frau ohne Schatten), Composer and Octavian, and Wagner's Fricka, Kundry and Ortrud (Wiesbaden 1988); sang Venus in Tannhäuser as guest with the Berlin Staatsoper at Las Palmas in 1986; sang Clytemnestra in Elektra at the Komische Oper Berlin, 2000; many concert appearances.

TRELEAVEN, John; British singer (tenor); b. 10 June 1950, Cornwall. *Education:* studied in London and Naples. *Career:* with Welsh Nat. Opera has sung Tamino, Alfredo in La Traviata, Pinkerton, Nadir in Les Pêcheurs de Perles and Mark in The Midsummer Marriage; at ENO his roles have included Don José, Cavaradossi, Faust (Berlioz), Erik in Der fliegende Holländer, the Prince in Rusalka, Hoffmann, Don Carlos and Wozzeck in a new production of Berg's Opera 1990; Royal Opera, Covent Garden, debut as Tamino, followed by Froh in Das Rheingold and Peter Grimes 1989; appearances with Scottish Opera have included Florestan, Jenik in The Bartered Bride, Werther and Radames; Opera North as Dick Johnson in La Fanciulla del West, Cavaradossi, Radames and Peter Grimes; Further engagements in The Damnation of Faust at the Adelaide Festival, Pylades in Iphigénie en Tauride at the Paris Opéra, Verdi's Attila at the Concertgebouw, Amsterdam and Prince Golitisin in Khovanshchina at the San Francisco Opera 1990; concert performances include a 1981 debut at Royal Festival Hall in Puccini's Messa di Gloria and Rossini's Stabat Mater; Verdi Requiem under Nello Santi at the 1984 Festival de la Mediterranée; Dream of Gerontius with Scottish Nat. Orchestra 1989; concert performance of Bernstein's Candide at Barbican, London 1989; Season 2000 sang Lohengrin at Barcelona 2000, at Karlsruhe, as Apollo in Daphne, Siegmund and Tristan, Siegfried at Mannheim and Chemnitz; sang Weill's Jim Mahonney at Genoa and Tristan in Amsterdam 2001; Tristan for BBC Symphony Orchestra at Barbican, London 2002–03; Season 2003–04 sang Lohengrin at Hamburgische Staatsoper, Siegfried at Lyric Opera, Chicago, Die Walküre with Bamberger Symphoniker, Götterdämmerung in Tokyo, Siegfried and Götterdämmerung at Gran Teatre del Liceu, Barcelona, Tristan at Opéra de Rouen; Season 2004–05 sang Tristan (konzertant) at Lucerne Festival, Siegfried and Götterdämmerung in Helsinki, Liederabend in Wiesbaden, Gurrelieder in Melbourne, Siegfried at Staatsoper, Vienna, Tristan in Mannheim Gala, Die Walküre for Semperoper Dresden, Meistersinger in Hamburg, Das Lied von der Erde in New Orleans, Gurrelieder in Los Angeles, Siegfried and Götterdämmerung for Lyric Opera, Chicago, Meistersinger and Lohengrin in Hamburg, Tristan in Frankfurt and Brisbane at Queensland Music Festival; Hon. Prof., Faculty of Arts, Thames Valley Univ. 2007–. *Recordings include:* solo parts: Le Prophète, Meyerbeer, conducted by Henry Lewis; L'Assedio di Calais, Donizetti; Il Trovatore, Colin Davis, with José Carreras; Il Tabarro, Maazel with Placido Domingo; Rachmaninov Vespers, Candide, Leonard Bernstein; Videos of Rusalka for English National Opera; Richard Dauntless in Ruddigore; Candide; John Treleaven as Siegfried in Siegfried and Götterdämmerung at the Gran Teatre del Liceu Barcelona on DVD 2006. *Current Management:* Theateragentur Dr Germinal Hilbert, Herr Rudolf Meindl, Maximilianstrasse 22, 80539 Munich, Germany. *Telephone:* (89) 290-747-0. *Fax:* (89) 290-747-90. *E-mail:* meindl@hilbert.de. *E-mail:* mennicken.beate@t-online.de. *Website:* www.johntreleaven.com.

TRELIŃSKI, Mariusz; Polish opera, film and theatre director; *Artistic Director, Polish National Opera.* *Education:* State School of Film, Television and Theatre, Łódź. *Career:* began career working for Television Theatre; Artistic Dir Karol Irzykowski Studio 1990–92; dir of plays, including Lautréamont-Dreams (Studio Theatre), Macbeth (Powszechny Theatre); opera directing debut with Madama Butterfly, Polish Nat. Opera, Warsaw 1999 (with subsequent productions in Washington 2001, Mariinsky Theatre, St Petersburg 2005); other operas directed in Warsaw include Szymanowski's King Roger (Karol Szymanowski Award 2001) 2000, Otello 2001, Eugene Onegin 2002, Don Giovanni 2002 (also for Los Angeles Opera 2003), The Queen of Spades 2004 (also for Staatsoper, Berlin 2003); has also directed Giordano's Andrea Chénier for Washington Nat. Opera 2004, Teatr Wileki, Poznań 2004, Polish Nat. Opera 2005; Artistic Dir Opera Narodowa (Polish Nat. Opera), Teatr Wielki, Warsaw 2005–. *Films as director:* Zad Wielkiego Wieloryba (Stern of the Giant Whale, TV) 1987, Pożegnanie jesieni (The Farewell to Autumn) 1990, Łagodna (The Gentle One) 1995, Egoiści (Egoist) 2000. *Honours:* Andrzej Munk Award 1990, Minister of Culture Award for Best Debut 1990. *Address:* Opera Narodowa, Teatr Wielki, Plac Teatralny 1, PO Box 59, Warsaw 00-950, Poland (office). *Telephone:* (22) 692-05-01 (office). *Fax:* (22) 826-04-22 (office). *E-mail:* office@teatrwielki.pl (office). *Website:* www.teatrwielki.pl (office).

TRETYAKOV, Viktor Viktorovich; Russian violinist; b. 17 Oct. 1946, Krasnoyarsk; m. Natalia Likhopoi; one d. *Education:* Moscow Conservatory, pupil of Yury Yankelevich. *Career:* concert career since mid-1960s, soloist of Moscow Philharmonic 1969; tours Europe, USA, Japan; participant in numerous European music festivals; Artistic Dir and Conductor, Moscow (now Russian) Chamber Orchestra 1983–90; Prof. and Head of Chair of Violin, Tchaikovsky Moscow State Conservatory 1979–; Prof., Hochschule für Musik, Cologne 1996–; Jury Pres. International Tchaikovsky Competition 1986–94. *Honours:* First Prize, All-Union Competition of Violinists 1965, First Prize, Int. Tchaikovsky Competition 1966, Lenin Komsomol Award 1967, People's Artist of the RSFSR 1979, Glinka State Award of the RSFSR 1981, USSR People's Artist 1987, Shostakovich Premium 1997, Triumph Prize 2003.

TREW, Graham Donald, MVO, MMus, AGSM, PGCE, FRSA; British singer (baritone), teacher and adjudicator; b. 18 July 1948, Epping, Essex. *Education:* Guildhall School of Music and Drama, Univ. of London, Bretton Hall. *Career:* performed with English Opera Group, Nottingham Music Theatre, Cockpit Opera Workshop (20 productions and title role in video of Marriage of Figaro); recitals, Wigmore Hall, Purcell Room, QEH, Barbican, Royal Nat. Theatre; oratorio and concerts throughout UK, Europe, USA, Caribbean and South Africa; English song recitals for BBC Radio 3, Friday Night is Music Night, Songs from the Shows, Melodies for You, for BBC Radio 2; Gentleman of Her Majesty's Chapel Royal, St James's Palace 1975–2002; Prof., RAM 2005–07; Assoc. Prof., Trinity Coll. of Music; teaches privately and at Tonbridge School; master-classes and prize adjudicator, RAM, Trinity Coll., Guildhall, Birmingham Conservatoire, Leeds Coll. of Music; adjudicator throughout England, including British Fed. of Music Festivals; Chair. Asscn of English Singers and Speakers 2005–15; Pres. Knighton and Dist Concert Soc. 2007–; mem. Equity, Royal Soc. of Musicians. *Recordings:* English song recordings with Roger Vignoles, recordings with John Alley, Marcello-Cantatas, Rodolphe, Florence, The Holy Boy with Simon Weale, James Bowman and Richard Lewis. *Honours:* Gold Medal, Guildhall School of Music and Drama 1973, Gramophone Magazine Award for Vocal Record of the Year (for A Shropshire Lad) 1980, Queen's Silver Jubilee Medal 1977, Queen's Golden Jubilee Medal 2002. *Address:* Melin-y-Grogue, Llanfair Waterdine, Knighton, Powys, LD7 1TU, Wales (home). *Telephone:* (1547) 510327 (home). *Fax:* (1547) 510327 (home). *E-mail:* graham.trew@virgin.net (home).

TRIFONOV, Daniil; Russian pianist; b. 5 March 1991, Nizhny Novgorod. *Education:* Gnessin State Musical Coll., Moscow with Tatiana Zelikman, composition classes with Vladimir B. Dovgan, Cleveland Inst. of Music with Sergei Babayan. *Career:* performed with Vienna Philharmonic Orchestra (tour and subscription concerts in Vienna), London Symphony Orchestra, Mariinsky Orchestra (with Gergiev), Israel Philharmonic (with Mehta), Russian Nat. Orchestra (with Pletnev), New York Philharmonic (with Gilbert), Chicago Symphony, Royal Philharmonic (with Dutoit), Boston Symphony (with Guerrero), Cleveland Orchestra (with Gaffigan), BBC Philharmonic (with Sinaisky), Philharmonia Orchestra (with Maazel), Orchestre Philharmonique de Radio France, Orchestra di Santa Cecilia, Warsaw Philharmonic; collaborations with Vladimir Fedoseyev, Pietari Inkinen, Sir Neville Marriner, Diego Matheuz, Gabor Takacs-Nagy, Antoni Wit, Nikolai Zneider; has given performances at Wigmore Hall, Queen Elizabeth Hall London, Musikverein Vienna, Salle Pleyel Paris, Parco della Musica Roma, Carnegie Hall New York, Suntory Hall Tokyo and venues across North and S America, Europe and Asia; major festivals include Verbier, Montreux, Tivoli, Edinburgh, Lucerne, Lockenhaus, Grafenegg, La Roque d'Anthéron, Klavier Festival Ruhr and Schloss Elmau, Blossom, Ravinia and Chautauqua Festival. *Recordings:* Trifonov Plays Chopin, Chopin Works for Piano, Concerto in E minor Op.11 2011, Chopin Piano Concerto No. 1 2011, Rachmaninov Variations 2015. *Honours:* several awards including Third Prize, Chopin Piano Competition, Warsaw 2010, First Prize, Gold Medal and Grand Prix, XIV Int. Tchaikovsky Competition, Moscow 2011, First Prize, Arthur Rubinstein Int. Piano Master Competition, Tel-Aviv 2011. *Current Management:* c/o Studiomusica, Via Farini 53, 41121 Modena, Italy. *Telephone:* (059) 245486. *Fax:* (059) 235875. *E-mail:* classical@studiomusica.net. *Website:* www.studiomusica.net; www.daniiltrifonov.com.

TRIFONOVA, Olga; Russian singer (soprano); b. 1969, St Petersburg. *Education:* St Petersburg Conservatoire. *Career:* appearances at the Mariinksy Theatre, St Petersburg, from 1994 as Mozart's Queen of Night and Barbarina, Rosina, Lucia di Lammermoor, Xenia in Boris Godunov, Frasquita in Carmen and Louisa in Prokofiev's Betrothal in a Monastery; Salzburg debut 1998, as Flowermaiden in Parsifal, New York Met 1999, in The Queen of Spades; Sang the title role in The Snow Maiden by Rimsky-Korsakov (Concert) with the Kirov Opera at Covent Garden, 2000; Other roles include Stravinsky's Nightingale, Amina in La Sonnambula, Gilda, Glinka's Lyudmila and Chloë/Prilepa in The Queen of Spades. *Recordings include:* Le Rossignol (London Philharmonic under Robert Craft).

TRIMARCHI, Domenico; Italian singer (bass-baritone); b. 21 Dec. 1940, Naples. *Education:* Naples Conservatory, Accad. di Belle Arti and with Gino Campese. *Career:* debut at Teatro La Fenice Venice as Belcore in L'Elisir d'amore 1964; has sung widely in Italy (Verona Arena 1975–78), Edinburgh, London, Stuttgart, Frankfurt, Chicago and Dubrovnik; Teatro Regio Parma as Falstff in the operas by Salieri and Verdi 1987; repertoire also includes Leporello, Alfonso, Papageno, Arbace and Count Almaviva (Mozart), Varlaam (Mussorgsky), Germont, Paolo and Fra Melitone (Verdi), Dulcamara, Belcore, Don Pasquale, Malatesta, Enrico and Alfonso (Donizetti), Dallapiccola's Job, Marcello, Sharpless and Gianni Schicchi (Puccini); sang Donizetti's Mamma Agata at Luga di Romagna 1988, Marchese in Linda di Chamounix at Trieste 1989, Leporello at Parma; sang in Wolf-Ferrari's Quattro Rusteghi at Geneva 1992. *Recordings:* Haydn's La Vera Costanza, L'Incontro Improvviso and Il Mondo della Luna, Il Barbiere di Siviglia, Vivaldi's Tito Manlio, Tosca (Philips), Elisa e Claudio by Mercadante, La Straniera by Bellini, La Cenerentola (CBS), Pimpinone by Albinoni. *Honours:* winner Venice Int. Competition 1970. *Address:* Studiomusica s.r.l., Via Farini 53, 41100 Modena, Italy. *Telephone:* (059) 245486. *E-mail:* gabriele.monici@studiomusica.net. *Website:* www.studiomusica.net.

TROJAHN, Manfred; composer; b. 22 Oct. 1949, Cremlingen, Brunswick, Germany. *Education:* Niedersächsische Musikschule, Brunswick, Hamburg Hochschule. *Career:* freelance composer, including Residency at the Villa Massimo in Rome 1979–80; teacher of composition, Robert Schumann Hochschule, Düsseldorf 1991. *Compositions include:* Opera Enrico 1991, four symphonies 1973, 1978, 1985, 1992. three string quartets 1976, 1980, 1983, Fünfsee-Bilder für messosopran und orchester 1979–83, Flute Concerto 1983, Requiem 1985, ...une campagne noire de soleil (seven ballet scenes) for chamber ensemble 1983–93, Sonatas for violin and cello 1983, Variations for orchestra 1987, Cinq Epigraphes for orchestra 1987, Fragmente für Antigone – six pieces for string quartet 1988, Transir for orchestra 1988, Aubade for two sopranos 1990, Ave Maria for chorus 1991, Grodek for baritone and eight instruments 1991, Quattro Pezzi for orchestra 1992, Divertissement for oboe and chamber orchestra 1993, Cornisches Nachtlied for orchestra 1994, Was ihr Wollt (As You Like It, opera) 1997–98, Liebeslieder for soprano and orchestra 1997, Palinsesto for soprano and string quartet 1997, Violin Concerto 1999, La Clemenza di Tito (by Mozart with newly composed recitatives by Trojahn) 2002, Limonen aus Sizilien: Drei italienische Geschichten (opera) 2003, Occhi mie for tenor 2002, Three Songs by John Keats for mezzo-soprano and six instruments 2002, Rhapsodie for clarinet and orchestra 2002.

TROPP, Vladimir; Russian pianist; b. 9 Nov. 1939, Moscow; m. Tatiana Zelikman 1961; one s. *Education:* Gnessin Children's Music School, Gnessin Specialized Music School, Gnessin Institute. *Career:* concert tours in Russia, Netherlands, USA, Italy, Japan, Finland, Germany, Ireland, Costa Rica, Republic of Korea, Czechoslovakia, Cuba; masterclasses and concerts in American univs, conservatories of Holland and Ireland, London Royal Acad. of Music, Italy, France, Japan; numerous chamber music festivals; performances on radio and television in Russia, Netherlands, Germany, USA, Finland, Costa Rica; performances with major orchestras; Prof. of Piano, Dept of Russian, Gnessin Acad. of Music, Chief of Piano Dept. *Recordings include:* works by Chopin, Brahms, Tchaikovsky, Rachmaninov, Scriabin, Medtner. *Publications:* contrib. articles to magazines and newspapers in Russia. *Address:* Dmitry Ulianov Str 4, Block 2, Apt 251, Moscow 117333, Russia.

TROST, Rainer; German singer (tenor); b. 1966, Stuttgart. *Education:* Munich Hochschule with Adalbert Kraus. *Career:* mem., Hanover Staatstheater 1991–95; sang Ferrando in Così fan tutte at the Hamburg Opera 1992 and toured in Mozart's opera with the Monteverdi Choir and Orchestra; sang Ferrando at Munich 1993, Don Ottavio at Dresden and Vienna, Tamino in Geneva and Berlin 1994, and Eginhard in Schubert's Fierrabras at Florence 1995; further engagements at the Cologne Opera, Opéra National de Paris, as Belmonte in Vienna and Hamburg and as Ferrando at Covent Garden, Glyndebourne, 1994 (debut role), returning 1997; season 1998–99 sang Orsino in the premiere of Manfred Trojahn's Was ihr Wollt, Munich, Entführung, Don Giovanni and Zauberflöte in Vienna, Don Giovanni in Hamburg and concerts of Tristan und Isolde with the Berlin Philharmonic under Abbado; season 1999–2000 included Zauberflöte and Fidelio in Munich, Cosí fan tutte at Salzburg Festival with Abbado, Katya Kabanova for Netherlands Opera and concerts for Gesellschaft der Musikfreunde in Vienna; season 2001 as Fenton and Ferrando in Munich, Belmonte at Hannover and Des Grieux in Henze's Boulevard Solitude at Covent Garden; further engagements include Don Giovanni, Zauberflöte, Così fan tutte, Fidelio and Falstaff in Munich, Zauberflöte at Vienna State Opera and Così fan tutte in Salzburg, with concert engagements of Fidelio in Munich and Katja Kabanowa in Brussels and Barcelona; concerts include Mozart's Mass in C Minor, with the Monteverdi Choir and Orchestra; Die Schöpfung, with the Hamburg Philharmonic Orchestra and the Cologne Radio Symphony Orchestra, Bach's Christmas Oratorio (NDR SO) and the St Matthew Passion, with the Concertgebouw Orchestra. *Recordings include:* Così fan tutte. *Current Management:* Haydn Rawstron Ltd, 29a High Street, First Floor, West Wickham, Kent BR4 0LP, England. *Telephone:* (20) 8777-6070. *Fax:* (20) 8777-4073. *E-mail:* enquiries@haydn-rawstron.com. *Website:* www.haydnrawstron.com.

TROTTER, Thomas Andrew, MA, ARCM, FRCO; British organist; *Organist, City of Birmingham*; b. 4 April 1957, Birkenhead, England. *Education:* Royal Coll. of Music, London, Univ. of Cambridge, Conservatoire Rueil-Malmaison, France. *Career:* debut at Royal Festival Hall 1980; regular broadcasts on BBC Radio 2 and 3; performances at festivals throughout Europe; Proms debut 1986; concert tours of USA, Australia and Japan; Organist, St Margaret's Church, Westminster, London 1982–, City of Birmingham 1983–; Resident Organist, City of Birmingham Symphony Hall 2001–; Messiaen recitals, Edinburgh Festival 1994. *Recordings:* The Grand Organ of Birmingham Town Hall, Liszt Organ Works and Reubke Sonata, Jehan Alain Organ Works, Charles-Marie Widor Organ Works, Antonio Soler Concertos for Two Organs, Olivier Messiaen Organ Works, The Ride of the Valkyries: Organ Transcriptions, Liszt Organ Works Vol. 2, Mozart Organ Works, Marcel Dupré Organ Works, Olivier Messiaen Organ Works Vol. II, Edward Elgar Organ Works, Restored to Glory, C.P.E. Bach Organ Works, R. Schumann Organ Works, Grand Organ Prom, The Town Hall Tradition (DVD), A Shropshire Idyll (DVD). *Honours:* Hon. DUniv (Univ. of Central England, now Birmingham City Univ.) 2004, Hon. DMus (Birmingham) 2006; RCM Walford Davies Prize 1976, Organ Scholar St George's Chapel, Windsor and King's Coll., Cambridge (John Stewart of Rannoch Scholarship in Sacred Music 1979), First Prize and Bach Prize, St Alban's Int. Organ Competition 1979, Prix de Virtuosité 1981, Royal Philharmonic Soc. Award for Best Instrumentalist 2001, Int. Performer of the Year, American Guild of Organists (New York Chapter) 2012, Royal Coll. of Organists Medal 2016. *Current Management:* c/o Patrick Garvey Management, 43 Greencroft Street, Salisbury, Wilts., SP1 1JF, England. *Telephone:* (1904) 621222. *E-mail:* patrick@patrickgarvey.com. *Website:* www.patrickgarvey.com.

TROUP, Malcolm, DPhil, DMus, LLD, FGSMD, ARCT, FRSA; British/Canadian concert pianist, academic, author, editor and lecturer; *Professor Emeritus of Music, City University*; b. 22 Feb. 1930, Toronto, Ont., Canada; s. of William John Troup and Wendela Mary Seymour-Conway; m. Carmen Lamarca Subercaseaux; one d. *Education:* Univ. of York, Royal Conservatory of Music, Toronto, Guildhall School of Music and Drama, London, Saarlandisches Konservatorium, Germany with Walter Gieseking. *Career:* debut with CBC Symphony Orchestra, Toronto aged 17; recitals and concertos with leading orchestras in Europe, N and S America, Australia, China and Hong Kong; premieres and dedicatee, important modern works; frequent broadcaster with the BBC, CBC, ABC; external examiner, Univs of Oxford, York, Keele, London; mem. int. juries, Chopin Competition of Australia, CBC Nat. Talent Competition, Young Musician of the Year; First Dvořák Int. Piano Competition 1997, Rome 1997, 2002, 2010, First Claudio Arrau Int. Piano Competition, Chillan, Chile 2003, Gina Bachauer Int. Piano Masters Competition, Salt Lake City, USA 2006, First European Union Piano Competition, Prague 2009; Vice-Pres. World Piano Competition, London; Pres. of Jury, First EPTA Int. Piano Competition, Zagreb 1999, Reykjavík 2000, Int. Ernest Bloch Music Competition 2009, 2010, 2011, 2012, Int. Israeli Music Competition, Royal Coll. of Music, London; invited as Guest Performer by Australian Broadcasting Corpn during Bicentenary to tour the country with Olivier Messiaen; Founder and Head of Music Dept, City Univ., London 1976–2003; Visiting Prof., Instituto de Musica, Catholic Univ. of Chile, Santiago 2010; Chair. European Piano Teachers' Asscn 1978–, Beethoven Piano Soc. of Europe 1992–, Int. Ernest Bloch Soc. 2009–; Pres. Oxford Int. Piano Festival 1999–, Vice-Pres. 2009–; Founder and Vice-Pres. Asociación Latinoamericana de Profesores de Piano (ALAPP/Chile); Gov., Music Therapy Charity 1978–2008; Trustee, Jewish Music Inst., Mendelssohn Scholarship & Boyce Foundation 1980–. *Recordings include:* Vingt Regards (Messiaen), Catalogue d'Oiseaux (Messiaen). *Publications:* The Piano Journal (ed. 1996–); contrib. to The Messiaen Companion 1995, The Science and Psychology of Music Performance 2002. *Honours:* Hon. Prof., Univ. of Chile 1966, Freeman of the City of London 1971, Liveryman of Worshipful Co. of Musicians 1973 (Court mem. 1991, Master 1999); Hon. DMus (City Univ.), Hon. LLD (Memorial Univ., Newfoundland); Commonwealth Medal, Harriet Cohen Int. Awards 1965, American Liszt Soc. Liszt Medal 1998. *Address:* Music Department, City University, Northampton Square, London, EC1V 0HB, England (office). *Telephone:* (20) 7040-8284 (office). *Fax:* (20) 7040-8561 (office). *E-mail:* malcolmtroup@yahoo.co.uk (home). *Website:* www.bpse.org (office).

TROWELL, Brian Lewis, MA, PhD; British academic; b. 21 Feb. 1931, Wokingham, Berkshire, England; m. Rhianon James 1958, two d. *Education:* Christ's Hospital, Gonville and Caius Coll., Cambridge. *Career:* Asst Lecturer, later Lecturer in Music, Birmingham Univ. 1957–62; freelance scholar, Conductor, Opera Prod., Lecturer and Ed. 1962–67; Head, BBC Radio Opera 1967–70; Regents' Prof., Univ. of California, Berkeley, USA 1970; Reader in Music, KCL 1970, Prof. of Music 1973; Visiting Gresham Prof. of Music, City Univ. 1971–74; King Edward Prof. of Music, Univ. of London, King's Coll. 1974–88; Chair. of Editorial Cttee, Musica Britannica 1983–93; Pres., Royal Musical Asscn; Chair., Handel Inst. Trust and Council 1987–98; Heather Prof. of Music, Univ. of Oxford 1988–96; Prof. Emeritus 1996–. *Publications:* Pelican History of Music: The Early Renaissance (vol. II) 1963, Four Motets by

John Plummer 1968, John Dunstable: Complete Works (co-ed., revised edn) 1970, Invitation to Medieval Music (vol. 3, ed.) 1976, (vol. 4) 1978, opera translations; contrib. to dictionaries of music and articles in books and learned journals, including: Libretto II, The New Grove Dictionary of Opera 1992, Acis, Galatea and Polyphemus: a serenata a tre voci?, Music and Theatre: Essays in Honour of Winton Dean 1987, Elgar's Use of Literature in Edward Elgar Music and Literature 1993.

TRPČESKI, Simon; Macedonian pianist; b. 18 Sept. 1979, Skopje. *Education:* Univ. of St Cyril and St Methodius, Skopje and studied with Boris Romanov. *Career:* concert appearances in Romania, Bulgaria, Italy, France, Portugal and Republic of Korea; played Prokofiev's Third Concerto at the World Piano Competition, London 2000; played at Jacobins Festival, Toulouse 2000; further concerts in Russia, Yugoslavia, Czech Republic, Turkey, Canada, Switzerland, Norway, UK, Australia and USA; repertoire centres on Russian music and Chopin; Wigmore Hall, London debut, concerts in Australia and Malaysia; Royal Festival debut with the Philharmonia Orchestra; engagements include collaborations with Sydney and Melbourne Symphony Orchestras, the Tonhalle Orchestra, the Bergen Philharmonic, Seattle Symphony, Royal Liverpool Philharmonic, Scottish Chamber Orchestra, Stockholm Philharmonic Orchestra and the Hallé Orchestra, New York Philharmonic, London Philharmonic; recitals at Queen Elizabeth Hall, London, BBC Proms, San Francisco Symphony with Ashkenazy. *Honours:* Winner, Yamaha Music Foundation of Europe, Skopje 1998, Second Prize, World Piano Competition, London 2000, Young Artist Award, Royal Philharmonic Soc. 2003, Gramophone Award 2003. *Current Management:* IMG Artists, The Light Box, 111 Power Road, London, W4 5PY, England. *Telephone:* (20) 7957-5800. *Fax:* (20) 7957-5801. *E-mail:* bcanniere@imgartists.com. *Website:* www.imgartists.com.

TRUAX, Barry, BS, MM; Canadian composer; b. 10 May 1947, Chatham, ON. *Education:* Queen's Univ. Kingston, Univ. of British Columbia, Inst. of Sonology, Univ. of Utrecht. *Career:* collaboration with Murray Schafer at World Soundscape Project in Vancouver; Dir of Sonic Research Studio and Prof. in Communication Dept, Simon Fraser Univ. 1976–, and School for the Contemporary Arts. *Compositions include:* Four Sonic Landscapes 1971–79, Gilgamesh for voices, chorus, ensemble and tape 1974, Nautilus for percussion and tape 1976, East Wind for amplified recorder and tape 1981, Nightwatch for marimba and tape 1982, Etude for cello and tape 1983, Divan and Wings of Nike for computer images and tape 1985–87, Tongues of Angels for English horn and oboe d'amore 1988, Dominion for chamber ensemble and tape 1991, Song of Songs for oboe d'amore, tape and computer images 1993, Bamboo, Silk and Stone for Asian instruments and tape 1994, Inside for bass oboe and tape 1995, Wings of Fire for cello and tape 1996, Androgyne, Mon Amour for double bass and tape 1997, Powers of Two for singers, dancers, video and tape 1995–99, Twin Souls, Islands. *Publications include:* Handbook for Acoustic Ecology 1978, (on CD-ROM) 1999, Acoustic Communication 1984. *Honours:* magisterium Int. Electro-acoustic Competition, Bourges 1991.

TRUBASHNIK, Simon, DipMus; oboist; b. 16 Sept. 1939, Odessa, Ukraine; m. (divorced); one d. *Education:* Central Music School for Gifted Children, Moscow Conservatoire. *Career:* solo debut, Youth Festival, Berlin 1955; Principal Oboe, Moscow Philharmonic Orchestra 1955–72, Principal Oboe, Moscow Chamber Orchestra 1958–72; Assoc. Principal Oboe, Israel Philharmonic Orchestra 1972–75; Principal Oboe, Belgium Nat. Opera 1976–85; Principal Oboe, Halifax Symphony, Canada 1986–87; Prof., Royal Conservatory of Music, Toronto 1987–; solos with Moscow Philharmonic and Moscow Chamber Orchestras (world tours), Radio Luxembourg Orchestra of Belgium, Mozart Chamber Orchestra, Brussels, Opera Orchestra of Ghent, Toronto Chamber Players, Kingston Philharmonic, McGill Chamber Orchestra; mem. American Federation of Musicians. *Recordings:* Bach Concerto (with David Oistrakh) and Concertos by Mozart and Strauss with Moscow Philharmonic Orchestra; Italian Baroque Concerts with Luxembourg Radio Orchestra; 100 Orchestral Records with Moscow Philharmonic Orchestra. *Honours:* gold medal Moscow Conservatoire 1958.

TRUDEL, Alain; Canadian trombonist and conductor; *Music Director, Orchestra London Canada;* b. 13 June 1966, Montréal. *Education:* Conservatoire de musique du Québec with Joseph Zuskin. *Career:* began musical career as trombone soloist, solo debut at age 18; Prin. trombone Barcelona Symphony Orchestra 1986–87; Founding-mem. and trombonist, Nouvel Ensemble Moderne, Montréal 1989–95; Leader and Music Tutor, Camp Musical des Laurentides, Québec 1988–2004; Tutor, Conservatoire de musique du Québec 1997–; Glenn Gould Professional Music School (Royal Conservatory of Music) 2005–; Conductor, Toronto Symphony Youth Orchestra 2004–; Music Dir Orchestre Symphonique de Laval 2006–; Artistic Dir and Prin. Conductor, Nat. Broadcast Orchestra, Vancouver 2008–11; Music Dir Orchestra London Canada 2011–; Prin. Guest Conductor, Victoria Symphony Orchestra; conducting debut with Opéra de Montréal 2009, Opéra de Quebec 2010; debut with Orchestre Symphonique de Montréal, Gävle Symphony Orchestra, Sweden and St Petersburg Cappella Symphony Orchestra 2010/11 season; has conducted orchestras in UK, USA, Sweden, Russia, Japan, Hong Kong, South America. *Honours:* Amb. of Canadian Music, Canadian Music Centre 2011; numerous awards including Canada Council for the Arts Virginia Parker Prize 1996, Le grand prix du disque Président de la République de l'Académie Charles Cros (France), Heinz Unger Prize for conducting 2007, Prix Opus, Prix Juno. *Address:* Orchestra London Canada, 609 Wellington Street,

London, ON N6A 3R6, Canada (office). *Telephone:* (519) 679-8778 (office). *Website:* alaintrudel.com; www.orchestralondon.ca (office).

TRUE, Stefanie, BFA, BMus; Canadian singer (soprano). *Education:* York Univ., Toronto with Catherine Robbin, Royal Conservatoire, The Hague with Michael Chance, Jill Feldman, Diane Forlano and Barbara Pearson. *Career:* performs regularly in Europe, North and Central America, appearing in operas, oratorios, and solo recitals; known particularly for concert performances of major works of Bach, Händel, Mozart, Vivaldi. *Operatic repertoire includes:* Euridice in Orfeo ed Euridice, Cephise in L'Europe Gallante, Poppea in Agrippina, Adelaide in Lotario, Serpina in La Serva Padrona, Belinda in Dido and Aeneas, Papagena in Die Zauberflöte, Susanna in Le Nozze di Figaro. *Recordings include:* Händel Complete Cantatas Vol. 1 2006, Vol. 2 2009, Händel Aminta e Fillide, Händel Aci, Galatea e Polifemo 2008, Händel La Resurrezione 2009, Lully Ballets et recits italiens 2009, Arne Overtures and Cantatas 2011. *Honours:* Adair Prize, London Handel Singing Competition 2011. *Address:* c/o Centaur Records Inc, 136 St Joseph Street, Baton Rouge, LA 70802, USA (office). *Telephone:* (316) 23850639 (mobile) (office). *E-mail:* stefanietrue@gmail.com (office). *Website:* stefanietrue.weebly.com (office).

TRUEFITT, Alison; British singer (soprano); b. 1958, England. *Education:* Univ. of London and Royal Acad. of Music. *Career:* debut, sang at the Purcell Room, London 1979; has appeared in recital with the Songmakers' Almanac and with the BBC in songs by Britten, Bartók, Fauré, Holst, Milhaud, Poulenc and Tippett; with orchestra or ensemble in works by Gerald Finzi, Stephen Dodgson and Frank Martin; Promenade Concerts debut in La Forza del Destino; sang Gluck's Iphigenia with Opera Factory 1985, created Kathe in John Metcalf's The Crossing (tours of the USA, the UK and Canada); sang in the British stage premiere of Schubert's Fierrabras, Univ. of Oxford 1986; ENO 1988, as Manassah in Salome; sang Donizetti's Rita, Madame Herz in Mozart's Impresario and Musetta with London Chamber Opera 1988; appearances with London Chamber Opera 1988; appearances as the Queen of Night with Birmingham Touring Opera 1988–89; other repertory includes Leila in Les Pêcheurs de Perles, the Governess in The Turn of the Screw, Britten's Phaedra and Major Stone in Weill's Happy End; translated Orfeo for Opera North 1990, and has provided several sets of surtitles for Covent Garden.

TRUSSEL, Jacques; American singer (tenor); b. 7 April 1943, San Francisco, CA. *Education:* Ball State Univ., Muncie, Indiana and studied in New York. *Career:* sang at first in concert then made opera debut at the Oberlin Festival 1970, as Pinkerton; has appeared in Boston, Dallas, Houston, Santa Fe, New Orleans, Chicago from 1976, Pittsburgh 1979, Washington 1981 and San Francisco as Loge in Das Rheingold 1990; sang Don José at Cincinnati 1988 and has appeared as Rodolfo, Cavaradossi, Berg's Alwa, Araquil in La Navarraise by Massenet, Števa in Jenůfa, Max (Der Freischütz) and Nero in L'Incoronazione di Poppea, at Geneva 1989; sang in Houston in the title role of Hugh the Drover by Vaughan Williams 1973 and in the 1974 word premiere of The Seagull by Pasatieri; European debut Spoleto Festival 1976, as Hermann in The Queen of Spades; sang Alwa at Florence 1985 and at Chicago 1987; Covent Garden and Nancy 1989, as Peter Grimes and as Sergei in the French premiere of Lady Macbeth of Mtsensk by Shostakovich; appeared with Greater Miami Opera 1990, as Pollione in Norma; London appearances 1991, as Don José; season 1991/92 as Alexey in the US premiere of The Gambler, at Chicago; Sergei at the Opéra Bastille, Monteverdi's Nero in Florence, Don José in Birmingham and Roderick in The Fall of the House of Usher by Philip Glass at the Maggio Musicale; sang Golitsin in Khovanschina at Brussels 1996; Herod in Salome at Vancouver 1998 and at Cincinnati 2000.

TRYON, Valerie Ann, LRAM, FRAM, ARCM; Canadian (b. British) concert pianist and academic; b. 5 Sept. 1934, Portsmouth, Hants., England; d. of Kenneth Montague Tryon and Winifred Tryon (née Lunan). *Education:* Royal Acad. of Music, London and with Jacques Fevrier, Paris. *Career:* performances in UK include Cheltenham Festival, Royal Festival Hall, Royal Albert Hall, Croydon; has performed throughout Canada and the USA, including Library of Congress, Washington, DC; fmrly pianist in Rembrandt Trio; Artist-in-Residence, McMaster Univ., Hamilton, Ont. 1978–86, Assoc. Prof. 1986–2009. *Recordings include:* Liszt's Sonata for Violin and Piano, Rachmaninov, Valerie Tryon plays Richard Baker's most requested pieces, These You Have Loved, Valerie Tryon Piano, The Joy of Piano, Debussy Songs (Juno Winner with Claudette Leblanc) 1994, Music by Busoni, Ravel Complete Piano Music, Scarlatti Sonatas, Mozart Sonatas, Schubert Sonatas, Schumann's Fantasie in C major, Piano Music by Liszt (2-CD set), Music by Chopin (3-CD set), Four Pieces by Alun Hoddinott, Mozart Piano Concerti and Rondo in A, Rachmaninov Piano Concerto No. 1, Franck Symphonic Variations, Ravel Piano Concerto in G. *Honours:* Hon. DLitt (McMaster Univ.); Dove Prize 1955, Harriet Cohen Int. Music Award 1967, Franz Liszt Medal of Honour, Hungarian Ministry of Culture 1986, Juno Award 1991. *Current Management:* c/o Howard Greenwood Concert Management, 64 Hazel Close, Whitton, Twickenham, TW2 7NR, England. *Telephone:* (20) 8894-0391. *Fax:* (20) 8287-9428. *E-mail:* howardmusic@virginmedia.com; howard@howardgreenwood.freeserve.co.uk. *Address:* 609 Tuscarora Drive, Ancaster, ON L9G 3N9, Canada (home). *Telephone:* (416) 648-5883 (home). *E-mail:* vtryon1@cogeco.ca (office). *Website:* www.artset.net/ValerieTryon.html.

TRYTHALL, (Harry) Gilbert (Gil), Jr, BA, MMus, DocMusArts; American composer and academic; *Adjunct Professor, Brookhaven College, Dallas*; b. 28 Oct. 1930, Knoxville, Tenn.; s. of Harry Gilbert Trythall and Clara Hannah Akre; m. Carol King; two d. *Education:* Univ. of Tennessee, Northwestern Univ., Cornell Univ., studied with David Van Vactor, Wallingford Riegger, Robert Palmer, Donald Grout, Julius Herford, Richard Lert, Thor Johnson. *Career:* Asst Prof. of Music, Knox Coll., Galesburg, Illinois 1960–64, Prof. of Music Theory and Composition 1964–75; Chair. School of Music, George Peabody Coll. for Teachers, Nashville, Tenn. 1973–75; Prof. of Music, Univ. of Virginia 1975–96, Dean, Creative Arts Center 1975–81; Visiting Prof., Universidade Federal do Espírito Santo in Vitória, Brazil 1999–2001; Adjunct Prof., Brookhaven Coll., Dallas, Tex. 2002–; guest lecturer at various colls and univs. *Compositions:* operas: The Music Lesson 1960, The Terminal Opera 1982, revised 1987, The Pastimes of Lord Caitanya, chamber opera 1992; orchestral: A Solemn Chant for strings 1955, Symphony No. 1 1958, revised 1963, Harp Concerto 1963, Dionysia 1964, Chroma I 1970, Cindy the Synthe (Minnie the Moog) for synthesizer and strings 1975; chamber: Flute Sonata 1964, A Vacuum Soprano for brass quintet and tape 1966, Entropy for brass, harp, celesta, piano and tape 1967, Echospace for brass and tape 1973; choral music; piano pieces; organ music; electronic scores; mixed media pieces; film music. *Publications include:* Principles and Practice of Electronic Music 1974, Eighteenth Century Counterpoint 1993, Sixteenth Century Counterpoint 1994; music educ. software at www.musicstudy.com. *Address:* KBA Software, 7740 Bantry Lane, Dallas, TX 75248, USA (office). *Telephone:* (972) 407-1081 (office). *E-mail:* htrythal@yahoo.com (office). *Website:* www.musicstudy.com (office).

TSCHAIKOV, Basil Nichols, FRCM, FRSA; British clarinettist; b. 30 May 1925, London, England; m. 1st; two d.; m. 2nd Dorothy Gallon 1966. *Education:* Royal Coll. of Music, London. *Career:* London Philharmonic Orchestra 1943–47; Royal Philharmonic Orchestra 1947–55; Philharmonia Orchestra 1958–79; Visiting Lecturer, Middlesex Polytechnic 1959–79; Prof., Royal Coll. of Music 1964–84; Dir, Nat. Centre for Orchestral Studies, Goldsmiths Coll., London 1979–89; Artistic and Exec. Dir, Nat. Orchestra of Europe 1989–90; Ed.-in-Chief Musical Performance, Harwood Academic Publrs 1993–2001; mem. Musicians' Union, Music Preserved (fmrly Music Performance Research Centre) (Chair. 1987–2003, Pres. Emer. 2003–). *Publications include:* Play the Clarinet Teacher's Handbook: How to Be a Musician. *Honours:* Hon. mem. Royal Coll. of Music 1966. *Address:* Apartment 31, Royal Arch Court, Earham Road, Norwich, NR2 3RU, England (home). *Telephone:* (1603) 766123 (home). *E-mail:* bnickt@homecall.co.uk.

TSCHAMMER, Hans; German singer (bass); b. 1945, Silesia. *Education:* Würzburg Musikhochschule and Salzburg Mozarteum. *Career:* sang at the Deutsche Oper am Rhein from 1975, notably as Pogner, Hagen, Daland, the Landgrave in Tannhäuser and Gurnemanz; guest appearances at Hamburg, Zürich and San Francisco (Hunding, 1983); Bayreuth Festival 1985–86; further appearances at the New York Metropolitan 1983, Bregenz Festival as Daland 1990, and Covent Garden as Rocco 1991; other roles include the Commendatore in Don Giovanni and Prince Gremin (Toulouse, 1990 and 1993); season 1994–95 as Sarastro at Turin and Gurnemanz at Montpellier; season 1998 as King Marke for Flanders Opera and at Monte Carlo; sang Rocco in Fidelio at Rome, Daland in Dresden and Pogner for the Deutsche Oper Berlin 2000; concerts include Mozart's C minor Mass. *Current Management:* c/o Peter Seyfferth Artists Management, Avenue de la Concorde 385, 06190 Roquebrune, Cap Martin, France. *Telephone:* 4-93-35-01-05 (France). *Fax:* 4-93-35-02-17 (France). *E-mail:* peter@seyfferth.de. *Website:* www.seyfferth.de. *Address:* Sonnenbichlweg 3, 82319 Stamberg, Germany.

TSCHERGOV, Michail; Bulgarian singer (tenor, baritone); b. 1 Oct. 1928, Novo Selo. *Education:* studied in Sofia. *Career:* sang with the Vraza Opera 1952–53 (debut as Nemorino), at Rostock 1966–68, as Max, Alvaro and Dimitri; sang widely in Eastern Europe as Otello, Canio, Des Grieux and Pedro in Tiefland; other roles have included Calaf, Don José, Florestan, Tannhäuser, Siegmund and Rodolfo; Sang Otello at Frankfurt, 1988, and from 1990 such baritone roles as Verdi's Rigoletto and Renato.

TSONEVA, Plamena, MA; Bulgarian musicologist and arts manager; *Production Manager, Varna Summer International Music Festival*; b. 19 Nov. 1954, Baltchik. *Education:* Dobri Hristov High School of Music, Varna, Pancho Vladigerov Music Acad., Sofia, Acad. for Music and Dance, Plovdiv, Int. Centre for Culture and Management, Salzburg and Linz Univ., Austria. *Career:* Dept of Culture, Dobrich Municipality 1978–85; Bulgarian Nat. Inst. of Culture, Dobrich Br. 1985–88; musicologist and Production Man., Varna Summer Int. Music Festival and Summer Int. Music Acad. 1988–; recent projects include Balkan Musicians in Varna Summer Festival 2002, Varna Summer Int. Music Acad., with assistance from the British Council, Folkwang Hochschule, Essen, Germany 2002, meeting point of Young Talents supported by EC Culture 2000 Programme; participation in, as rep. of the Varna Festival, projects initiated by European Festivals Asscn 1998–2003. *Publications include:* catalogues and brochures for Varna Summer Int. Music Festival, texts and articles about the festival image, programmes and performers 1989–2010; papers in annual Books of Salzburg Symposium 2003, 2004, 2005, 2006 edns; in Varna Summer Int. Festival and Creative Urban Policy summary; 'The Balkan City – Stage for the End of the XXth Century' in conf. book for Yugoslav Performing Arts Centre, Belgrade 2000; script for a documentary, 'Choir Singing in Dobrich' (Bulgarian Nat. TV/Varna Br.) 2002. *Address:* Varna Summer International Music Festival,

Varna Municipality, 43 Osmi Primorski Polk Blvd, 9000 Varna, Bulgaria (office). *E-mail:* tsoneva@varnasummerfest.org (office). *Website:* www.varnasummerfest.org (office).

TSONTAKIS, George; American composer; b. 24 Oct. 1951, New York. *Education:* Juilliard School, Karlheinz Stockhausen, Rome, studied with Roger Sessions. *Career:* freelance composer; faculty mem., Aspen Music School, Colorado 1976–, founding dir Aspen Contemporary Ensemble 1991–98; Asst in Electronic Music, Juilliard 1978; Asst Prof., Brooklyn Coll. Conservatory 1986–87; Distinguished Faculty Composer-in-Residence Bard Coll. *Compositions include:* Scenes from the Apocalypse for soloists, chorus and orchestra 1978, The Epistle of James, Chapter I for narrator, chorus and orchestra 1980, Erotkritos oratorio for chorus and orchestra 1982, Five Signs and a Fantasy for orchestra 1985, Fantasia Habanera for orchestra 1986, four string quartets 1980, 1984, 1986, 1989, Bird-wind Quintet 1983, Brass Quintet 1983, Brass Quintet 1984, Saviours for soprano, chorus and orchestra 1985, The Past, The Passion for 15 players 1987, Galway Kinnell Songs for mezzo, piano and string quartet, The Sowers of the Seed for orchestra 1989, Heartsounds quintet for piano and strings 1990, Stabat Mater for soprano, chorus and orchestra 1990, four symphonic quartets 1992–96, Gemini for horn, violin, cello and piano 1996, Dust for horn, violin and piano 1998, Violin Concerto 1998, Violin Concerto No. 2 (Grawemeyer Award for Music Composition 2005) 2003. *Honours:* Charles Ives Living, American Acad. of Arts and Letters 2006. *Address:* c/o Aspen Music School, 2 Music School Road, Aspen, CO 81611, USA.

TSOUPAKI, Calliope; composer and pianist; b. 27 May 1963, Piraeus, Greece. *Education:* Hellinicon Conservatory, Athens, Nikos Skalkottas Conservatory, Hague Royal Conservatory with Louis Andriessen, summer courses at Darmstadt with Iannis Xenakis, Olivier Messiaen and Pierre Boulez. *Career:* freelance composer and pianist; Gaudeamus Int. Music Week at Amsterdam 1991, 1993; Composer-in-Residence, Budapest Young Artists' Foundation 1993; featured composer at San Francisco Other Minds Festival 1995. *Compositions include:* Eclipse for orchestra 1986, Earinon for eight horns and percussion 1986, Revealing Moment for alto flute 1987, Moments I and II for piano 1988, For Always for female voice, tape and lights 1989, Your Thouht for voice, tape and lighting 1989, Silver Moments for two pianos and two percussion players 1989, Mania for amplified violin 1989, Visions of the Night for amplified chamber ensemble 1989, Sappho's Tears for violin, tenor recorder and female voice 1990, When I was 27 for amplified viola and double bass 1990, Song for Four for string quartet 1991, Echoing Purple for violin and ensemble 1992, Eros and Psyche for wind octet and double bass 1992, Orphic Fields for flute, two harps and two pianos 1993, Phantom for tuba 1994, Her Voice for harp 1994, Ethra for flute, string trip and harp 1995, Epigramma for chorus and orchestra 1995, Lineos for chorus and ensemble 1995, Hippolutos (music theatre after Euripides) 1996, Medea (for stage) 1996, Interface for ensemble 1996, Siren for narrator and chamber orchestra 1997, No Name I for oboe and violin 1997, E guerre morte (after Tasso) for chorus and ensemble 1997.

TSUDA, Yuya; Japanese pianist; b. 1982, Sendai. *Education:* Tokyo Nat. Univ. of Fine Arts and Music, Berlin Univ. of the Arts. *Honours:* first prize and Audience Prize, Sendai Int. Music Competition 2007. *Address:* c/o Paul Devoyon, Universität der Künste Berlin, Institut für Künstlerische Ausbildung/Klavier, Einsteinufer 43-53, D-10587 Berlin, Germany (office). *E-mail:* pdevoyon@aol.com (office). *Website:* www.pascaldevoyon.com/devoyonprof/ (office).

TSUJII, Nobuyuki; Japanese pianist; b. 1988, Tokyo. *Education:* Ueno Gakuen Coll. of Music. *Career:* first solo recital aged 12 Suntory Hall (Small Hall), Tokyo 2000; tours throughout Japan, and in Europe and USA; US debut, Carnegie Hall 2000, UK concerto debuts with Orchestra Europa at Queen Elizabeth Hall, London and Philharmonic Hall, Liverpool, German recital debut at the Klavier-Festival Ruhr at Harenberg City Centre, Dortmund; has also performed with NHK Symphony Orchestra, Japan Philharmonic Orchestra, Orchestre des Concerts Lamoureux, Slovak Philharmonic Orchestra, Tokyo Symphony Orchestra. *Recordings include:* Début 2007, Rachmaninov: Piano Concerto No.2 2008. *Honours:* first prize, All Japan Blind Students Music Competition 1995, Critics' Award, Int. Frederik Chopin Piano Competition 2005, Nancy Lee and Perry R. Bass Gold Medal, Van Cliburn Int. Piano Competition, USA 2009. *Current Management:* c/o Dorothy Currie, IMG Artists London, The Light Box, 111 Power Road, London, W4 5PY, England; c/o Concert Imagine, 35 Kaitai-cho, Shinjuku-ku, Tokyo 162-0802, Japan. *Telephone:* (20) 7957-5800 (London); (3) 3235-7772 (Tokyo). *Fax:* (20) 7957-5801 (London); (3) 3235-3855 (Tokyo). *E-mail:* dcurrie@imgartists.com; chirashi@concert.co.jp. *Website:* www.imgartists.com; www.concert.co.jp; www.nobupiano1988.com.

TSUTSUMI, Tsuyoshi; Japanese cellist and academic; *President, Toho Gakuen School of Music, Tokyo*; b. 28 July 1942, Tokyo; m. Harue Saji 1978; one s. one d. *Education:* Toho Gakuen High School of Music, Tokyo, Indiana Univ., USA. *Career:* debut in Tokyo, Japan 1955; soloist (Iwaki), European Tour, NHK Symphony Orchestra of Tokyo 1960; soloist (Ozawa), Chicago Symphony, Ravinia Festival, Ravinia Park, Chicago, Illinois, USA 1967; soloist (Ozawa), American and European Tour, New Japan Philharmonic 1974; soloist (Akiyama), American Symphony, New York City 1978; soloist (Ceccato), Czech Philharmonic, Prague, Czechoslovakia 1984; Prof. of Music, School of Music, Univ. of Illinois, Urbana, USA; Prof. of Music, School of

Music, Indiana Univ., Bloomington, USA 1988–; Pres. Toho Gakuen School of Music, Tokyo 2004–. *Recordings:* Bach, Unaccompanied Suites, complete; Beethoven, Sonatas and Variations (Turini, piano); Dvořák Concerto, Czech Philharmonic (Košler, conductor); Haydn, Concertos, English Chamber Orchestra; Yashiro Concerto, Tokyo Symphony Orchestra, conducted by Ohtomo. *Publications:* An Illinois Diary (The Cello and I), 1991, My Life with Cello 2003. *Honours:* First Prize, Int. Casals Competition, Budapest, Hungary 1963, Prize, Nat. Acad. of Arts (Japan) 1993. *Address:* 2715 Bluff Court, Bloomington, IN 47401 (home); School of Music, Indiana University, Bloomington, IN 47405, USA (office). *Telephone:* (812) 339-4629 (home); (812) 855-1552 (office). *Fax:* (812) 332-9523 (home); (812) 856-5006 (office).

TSYDYPOVA, Valentina; singer (soprano); b. 1955, Buritia, Russia. *Education:* Novosibirsk Conservatory. *Career:* sang at the Ulan-Ude Opera Theatre 1984–89; Novosibirsk Opera Theatre 1989–92; Kirov Opera St Petersburg from 1992, notably on tour to Italy, Israel, Spain, the Met Opera in New York, France, Finland and Germany; guest appearances as Butterfly at the Opéra Bastille, Paris 1993 and in Hamburg and Berlin, Tosca at the Savonlinna Festival and Gorislava in Ruslan and Lyudmila at San Francisco; other roles include Tchaikovsky's Tatiana, Maria (Mazeppa) and Lisa, Elisabeth de Valois, Desdemona, Aida, Santuzza and Yaroslavna; Concerts include Wigmore Hall recital 1995 and the Verdi Requiem at the Bastille Opéra. *Recordings include:* Rimsky's Sadko and Glinka's Ruslan and Lyudmila, with the Kirov Opera. *Honours:* People's Artist of the Buriatian Republic.

TSYPIN, George; set designer; b. 1954, Russia. *Education:* studied architecture in Moscow and set design in New York, USA. *Career:* collaborations with producer Peter Sellars include premiere of Osborne's The Electrification of the Soviet Union (1987) and Handel's Theodora (1996) at Glyndebourne; premiere production of The Death of Klinghoffer by John Adams seen at Brussels, San Francisco, Lyon and New York, 1991; Messiaen's St Francois d'Assise (1992) and Le Grand Macabre by Ligeti (1997) at the Salzburg Festival; first staging by British company of Hindemith's Mathis der Maler, Covent Garden 1995; further engagements with Salome and Katerina Izmailova at the Kirov, St Petersburg; The Gambler at La Scala, Die Zauberflöte in Florence and Orfeo and Euridice in Zürich; Oedipus Rex in Japan, Rigoletto for Canadian Opera with further work on Tannhäuser, Don Giovanni and Pelléas et Mélisande; engaged for The Ring at Netherlands Opera (concluding with Götterdämmerung, 1999).

TUCCI, Gabriella; Italian singer (soprano); b. 4 Aug. 1929, Rome. *Education:* Accademia di Santa Cecilia, studied with Leonardi Filoni. *Career:* debut at Teatro Giglio Lucca 1951, as Violetta; Spoleto Festival 1952, as Leonora in La Forza del Destino; Florence 1953, as Cherubini's Médée; tour of Australia 1955; La Scala, Milan from 1959, as Mimi and in the Italian premiere of A Midsummer Night's Dream; Verona Arena 1959–69; US debut San Francisco 1959, as Madeleine in Andrea Chénier; Metropolitan Opera 1960–73 as Butterfly, Aida, Euridice, Leonora in Trovatore and La Forza del Destino, Violetta and Marguerite; Covent Garden 1960, as Tosca; appearances at Buenos Aires, Sydney, Oslo, Johannesburg, Dallas, New Orleans and Philadelphia; other roles include Desdemona, Anaide in Mosé by Rossini, Luisa Miller, Micaela and Elvira in I Puritani; Teacher, Indiana Univ. from 1983. *Recordings:* Pagliacci, Il Trovatore, Requiems by Bellini and Donizetti.

TUCEK, Rene; Czech singer (baritone); b. 8 Jan. 1936, Plzeň. *Education:* studied in Plzeň with M. Gartnerova and in Vienna with F. Schuch-Tovini. *Career:* debut at Brno 1960, as Count Luna in Il Trovatore; sang first in Brno, Plzeň and Ceske Budejovice; Prague National Theatre from 1971, in the standard repertory and in operas Prokofiev, Martinů, Gershwin and Myslivicek; Guest appearances in Spain, Austria, Bulgaria, Luxembourg and Cuba; Has sung in concert and in song recitals; Teacher at the Prague Conservatory from 1973. *Recordings:* The Jacobin by Dvořák and operas by Smetana.

TUCKER, Mark; British singer (tenor); b. 10 Aug. 1958, England. *Education:* Univ. of Cambridge and Guildhall School of Music and Drama, London. *Career:* active as concert and opera singer with particular interest in Italian repertoire, has performed and recorded alongside many of its leading exponents, including Gardiner, Harnoncourt and Jacobs; career highlights include a performance at QEH as title-role of Monteverdi's L'Orfeo; appearances at Salzburg Festival in Monteverdi Vespers of 1610 under Harnoncourt, and again under John Eliot Gardiner at Basilica San Marco, Venice; world premiere of Shchedrin's Vek Moy with Ashkenazy (piano) and Koelner Philharmonie; operatic engagements include L'Orfeo with Pinchgut Opera in Sydney, Hyllos (Hercules) in Potsdam, Platee in Lisbon, Eurimaco (Il ritorno d'Ulisse in patria) with Boston Baroque, Danceny in world premiere of Swerts' Les liaisons dangereuses for Flanders Opera, Gomatz (Zaide) at La Monnaie and for Opera du Rhin, Lysander (A Midsummer Night's Dream) in Turin, The Novice (Billy Budd) for Royal Opera, Covent Garden and Marzio (Mitridate) under Christophe Rousset at Theatre du Chatelet, Paris; concerts have included Elgar's Dream of Gerontius with Orchestra dell'Accademia Nazionale di Santa Cecilia under Ashkenazy, Andromeda Liberata with Venice Baroque Orchestra under Marcon, Beethoven's Mass in C for La Fenice under Gardiner; appearances with London Symphony Orchestra in L'enfant et les sortileges under Previn, Handel's Messiah with New York Philharmonic conducted by Hickox. *Recordings include:* A Midsummer Night's Dream, L'incoronazione di Poppea, Bach B Minor Mass, Fennimore and Gerda by

Delius 1997, Percy Grainger Songs, Vivaldi's Andromeda Liberata. *Current Management:* Harrison Parrott, 5–6 Albion Court, London, W6 0QT, England. *Telephone:* (20) 7229-9166. *Fax:* (20) 7221-5042. *E-mail:* info@harrisonparrott .com. *Website:* www.harrisonparrott.com.

TUCKWELL, Barry Emmanuel, AC, OBE, FRCM, FRSA; Australian horn player, conductor and academic; b. 5 March 1931, Melbourne; s. of Charles Tuckwell and Elizabeth Hill; m. 1st Sally E. Newton 1958; one s. one d.; m. 2nd Hilary J. Warburton 1971; one s.; m. 3rd Susan T. Levitan 1992. *Education:* Sydney Conservatorium. *Career:* French horn player with Melbourne Symphony Orchestra 1947, Sydney Symphony Orchestra 1947–50, Hallé Orchestra 1951–53, Scottish Nat. Orchestra 1954–55, Bournemouth Symphony Orchestra, London Symphony Orchestra 1955–68; f. Tuckwell Wind Quintet 1968; Conductor Tasmanian Symphony Orchestra 1980–83; Music Dir and Conductor Maryland Symphony Orchestra 1982–98; Guest Conductor Northern Sinfonia 1993–; Prof. of Horn, RAM, London 1963–74; also taught in USA at Dartmouth Coll., Pomona Coll., Peabody Conservatory, Colorado Mesa Univ.; joined Faculty of Music, Univ. of Melbourne (now Melbourne Conservatorium of Music) as Prin. Fellow 2005, currently Prin. Fellow; Pres. Int. Horn Soc. 1969–76, 1993–95; mem. Bd of Dirs London Symphony Orchestra 1957–68, Chair. 1961–68; mem. Chamber Music Soc. of Lincoln Center 1974–81. *Publications:* Playing the Horn, 50 1st Exercises 1978, The Horn (Yehudi Menuhin Music Guides) 1981, entire horn repertoire of G. Schirmer Inc. (Ed). *Honours:* hon. degrees from RAM, Guildhall School of Music and Drama, Sydney Univ.; Harriet Cohen Int. Award for Solo Instruments 1968, George Peabody Medal for outstanding contribs to music in America, JC Williamson Award 2007. *Address:* University of Melbourne, The Conservatorium Building (Gate 12), Royal Pde, Parkville, Melbourne, Vic. 3010, Australia (office). *Website:* conservatorium.unimelb.edu.au/staff/ barrytuckwell (office).

TULACEK, Thomas; violinist; b. 26 April 1955, Prague, Czech Republic. *Education:* Prague Conservatory, Prague Acad. of Musical Arts, Guildhall School of Music, UK. *Career:* First Violin Section, BBC Scottish Symphony Orchestra 1985–89; Leader, New Chamber Orchestra, Oxford 1990–; Assoc. Prof., Trinity Coll. of Music, London 1991; recital work has taken him to countries such as Italy, Switzerland, France, Israel and the Czech Republic; recordings for Czech Radio and Radio Vatican; since 1990 has been performing regularly with the English pianist Steven Wray, forming piano trio with Jaroslav Ondracek; concerto performances include works by Prokofiev, Bruch, Haydn, Mozart, Nielsen, with the Teplice Symphony Orchestra, Czech Republic.

TUMA, Jaroslav; Czech organist; b. 1956. *Education:* Prague Acad. of Performing Arts with Milan Sleehta and Zuzana Ruzicková, summer school at Haarlem, Netherlands with Hans Haselböck, studied improvisation and Bach interpretation with Piet Kee. *Career:* laureate of organ competitions in Prague, Linz, Leipzig, Nuremberg and Haarlem; festival appearances by Nuremberg, Linz, Prague and Mechelen; engagements in Europe, Japan and the USA; concerts with Czech Philharmonic Orchestra, three-year cycle of complete organ works by J. S. Bach in Prague 1990–93; repertoire includes works by Bach, Franck, Liszt, Reger, Hoffhaimer, Sweelinck, Isaac and Husa; accompanies major soloists on the harpsichord; teacher, Prague Acad. of Arts. *Recordings:* L. and H. Hassler, Muffat; Handel; Series organs of Bohema I–IV, Czech compositions for harpsichord. *Address:* c/o Prague Academy of Performing Arts, Malostranské nám. 12, 118 00 Prague, Czech Republic (office). *E-mail:* jaroslav.tuma@volny.cz (office). *Website:* www.jaroslavtuma .cz.

TUMAGIAN, Eduard; singer (baritone); b. 1944, Bucharest, Romania. *Career:* sang at Bucharest from 1968 as Papageno, Alfonso, Mozart's Count, and Wolfram in Tannhäuser; Opéra du Rhin Strasbourg from 1974, as Germont, Iago, Enrico in Lucia di Lammermoor, Scarpia, Marcello, Belcore, Escamillo and Eugene Onegin; guest appearances at Lyon, Stuttgart, Karlsruhe and Orange; sang Rigoletto at Basle 1981 and appeared further with WNO and ENO, Frankfurt (Renato 1983), Nice (I Puritani and Vespri Sicilaini, Montfort), I Due Foscari and Riccardo III by Flavio Testi; Paris Opéra 1985, as Germont; US debut 1986 at Pittsburgh as Don Carlo in La Forza del Destino; Carnegie Hall New York in concert performances of Béatrice et Bénédict and Nabucco; other appearances at the Deutsche Oper Berlin, Staatsoper Hamburg, Vienna Staatsoper (Scarpia in season 1988–89), Toulouse (La Franciulla del West) and Oviedo Festival (Simon Boccanegra and La Favorita); season 1991 as Nabucco at Trieste and Buenos Aires, Rigoletto at Philadelphia; sang Vaudémont in Iolanta and Verdi's Germont at Orange and Baltimore 1999; concert repertoire includes music by Bach, Handel, Beethoven, Mussorgsky, Britten and Shostakovich (14th Symphony at the 1984 Salzburg Festival). *Recordings include:* Miller in video of Luisa Miller from Opéra de Lyon, Napoleon in War and Peace, Turandot.

TUMANYAN, Barseg; Armenian singer (bass-baritone); b. 1958, Yerevan. *Education:* Komitas Conservatoire, La Scala, Milan, studied with Evgeny Nesterenko at the Moscow Conservatoire. *Career:* sang with the Spenderian Opera (Armenia) from 1980; Performances of Basilio at the Teatro San Carlo Naples 1988; Appeared in Gala Concert for Armenia at Covent Garden 1989, and invited back to sing in La Bohème, Les Contes d'Hoffmann and Carmen; US debut with Boston Opera as Ramfis in Aida, 1989; Appearances in USA, 1989 with the Armenian State Opera; Sang Colline in La Bohème at Covent Garden and Monte Carlo, 1990; King Philip in Don Carlos at Los Angeles;

Wigmore Hall recital, June 1990; Sang Moser in I. Masnadieri with the Royal Opera, 1998; Sang Ramphis in Aida at Dublin, and Gounod's Mephisto at Lyon, 2000. *Honours:* Prizewinner, Bussetto Competition, 1983; 2nd Prize, Tchaikovsky Competition, Moscow 1986; Joint First Prize, Rio de Janeiro Competition, 1987.

TUNLEY, David Evatt, AM, MMus, DLitt, FAHA; Australian musicologist and academic; *Professor Emeritus and Honorary Senior Research Fellow, Department of Music, University of Western Australia;* b. 3 May 1930, Sydney; s. of Leslie Tunley and Marjorie Tunley; m. Paula Patricia Laurantus 1959; one s. two d. *Education:* The Scots Coll., State Conservatorium of Music. *Career:* Music Master, Fort Street Boys' High School, Sydney 1952–57; joined staff of Dept of Music, Univ. of Western Australia 1958, apptd Personal Chair. of Music 1980, now Emer., Head Dept of Music 1985–90, Hon. Sr Research Fellow in Music 1994–; studied under Nadia Boulanger with French Govt Scholarship 1964–65; Scholar-in-Residence, Rockefeller Foundation, Bellagio, Italy 1987; Fowler Hamilton Visiting Research Fellow, Christ Church, Oxford 1993; Visiting Scholar, Wolfson Coll. Oxford 1996; Founder/Conductor Univ. Collegium Musicum, 1976–83; Founder/Chair. York Winter Music Festival, 1982–; Founder/Dir The Terrace Proms, Perth; Nat. Pres. Musicological Soc. of Australia 1980–81; Chair. Music Bd, Australia Council 1984–85; Fellow, Australian Acad. of the Humanities 1980. *Compositions include:* Two Preludes for Piano 1962, Concerto for Clarinet and Strings 1966 (revised 2000), A Wedding Masque 1970, Two Carols (words by Gerard Manley Hopkins) 1995, Immortal Fire 1999. *Publications:* The 18th-Century French Cantata 1974, Couperin 1982, Harmony in Action 1984, The French Cantata in Facsimile, 17 Vols 1990, Romantic French Song in Facsimile (6 Vols) 1994, The Bel Canto Violin: the life and times of Alfredo Campoli 1906–1991 1999, Salons, Singers and Songs: A Background to Romantic French Song 1830–70 2002, François Couperin and The Perfection of Music 2004, William James and the Beginnings of Modern Musical Australia; contribs to the New Grove Dictionary of Music and Musicians, the New Grove Dictionary of Opera, the New Oxford History of Music, European Music 1520–1640; numerous articles in major musicological journals. *Honours:* Chevalier, Ordre des Palmes académiques; Hon. DMus (Western Australia); Australian Centenary Medal. *Address:* School of Music, University of Western Australia, (M413), 35 Stirling Highway, Crawley, WA 6009 (office); 100 Dalkeith Road, Nedlands, WA 6009, Australia (home). *Telephone:* (8) 9386-1934 (home). *E-mail:* david.tunley@uwa.edu.au (office). *Website:* www.music.uwa.edu.au (office).

TUNNELL, Jonathon; British cellist; b. 1955, England. *Career:* debut at Wigmore Hall 1984, with Peter Pears; mem., Tunnell Trio; co-founder, Brindisi String Quartet at Aldeburgh 1984; concerts in a wide repertory throughout the UK, France, Germany, Spain, Italy and Switzerland; festival engagements at Aldeburgh (residency 1990), Arundel, Bath, Brighton, Huddersfield, Norwich and Warwick; first London performance of Colin Matthews's 2nd Quartet 1990, premiere of David Matthews's 6th Quartet 1991; Quartet by Mark Anthony Turnage 1992; many BBC recitals and resident artist with the Univ. of Ulster. *Recordings include:* quartets by Britten, Bridge and Imogen Holst, works by Pierné and Lekeu. *Honours:* prizewinner (with Brindisi Quartet) Third Banff Int. String Quartet Competition, Canada 1989.

TUOMELA, Tapio Juhani, DipMus, MMus; Finnish composer and conductor; *Composer-in-Residence, Joensuu City Orchestra;* b. 11 Oct. 1958, Kuusamo; m. Helena Tuovinen 1985; three d. *Education:* Sibelius Acad., Helsinki, Eastman School of Music, Rochester, NY, USA, Hochschule der Künste, Berlin. *Career:* profile concerts of own compositions, Helsinki Festival 1991, Antwerp 2000, Paris 2003, Aboa Nova 2008, Sibelius Acad. 2008; Featured Composer, Nordic Music Days, St Petersburg 2006, Festivals des musiques démesurées, Clermont-Ferrand, France 2006; performances of works at UNM Festivals (Young Scandinavian Composers) 1985–89, Scandinavian Music Days 1990–, Time of Music Festival, Finland 1993–, Tampere Biennale 1994–, Musica Nova Helsinki 1997–; performances in the USA, Japan, Germany, Russia, Portugal, Spain, Hungary, Yugoslavia, Netherlands, Belgium, all Scandinavian countries; also active as a conductor, including numerous first performances in Scandinavia, Portugal and Germany; Artistic Dir, Time of Music Festival 2000–08; Composer-in Residence, Joensuu City Orchestra 2008–; Chair., Soc. of Finnish Composers 2010–. *Exhibition:* UNESCO Rostrum (twice placed among Selected Works). *Compositions include:* stage works: The Ear's Tale (chamber opera) 1993, Mothers and Daughters (based on the Kalevala) 1999 (both commissioned by the Finnish Nat. Opera), Melodrama Antti Puuhaara 2008; works for orchestra: 2 Symphonies 1991, 2005, Jokk, Lemminkäinen, Nordan, Lappic, Vuohenki Luohti, Piano Concerto 2008, Two Quintets, Spurt I and II, Pilke I and II, Escape Ladder, Lamentation (chamber orchestra); numerous works for choir, solo instruments. *Music for film:* The Sorcerer's Curse (1927), performed by the Finnish RSO on YLE Teema channel and live with the film. *Radio:* recordings for the Finnish, Spanish, Portuguese Radio and NRD3 Germany. *Recordings:* Composer Profile Jokk 2000, Lullabies and Spells: Choral Music of T. Tuomela 1993–2008, Choral Works (Helsinki Chamber Choir) 2010, Antti Puuhaara (Ensemble Musicatreize) 2010, Escape Ladder (AVnati!) 1995; solo works on CDs of Matti Rantanen (acc.), Elisa Kerola (kantele), Jouko Tötterström (piano). *Honours:* composition contests: Finnish Independence 1987, 1992, Lahti Choir Competition Contest, Uussävel etc., Kalevala Prize 2006, prizewinner, Washington Square Contemporary Music Craig Hultgren Cello Competition. *Address:* Temppelikatu 14 A 12, 00100 Helsinki, Finland (home).

Telephone: (9) 490586 (home). *Fax:* (9) 490586 (home). *E-mail:* ttuomela@siba.fi (home). *Website:* webusers.siba.fi/~ttuomela/koti.htm.

TURBAN, Ingolf; German violinist and academic; *Professor of Music, Munich Musikhochschule;* b. 17 March 1964, Munich; m. Barbara Meier 1994; two s. *Education:* Munich Musikhochschule with Gerhart Hetzel, Aspen, Colorado with Dorothy DeLay and Jens Ellerman. *Career:* debut with Munich Philharmonic, Munich 1986; Nat. Symphony Orchestra, Washington, DC 1991; Leader, Munich Philharmonic 1985–88; solo career world-wide 1988–; debut with New York Philharmonic, Avery Fisher Hall 2006; Prof., Stuttgart Musikhochschule 1995–2007, Munich Musikhochschule 2006–; Founder I Virtuosi di Paganini 2005. *Compositions:* cadenzas to numerous violin concertos, A Niccolò for five violins 1998. *Recordings include:* Paganini Caprices with piano accompaniment by Schumann, Hartmann Solo Sonatas and Suites, Ernst Pieces, Respighi with English Chamber Orchestra, Marek with the Philharmonia, London. *Address:* Künstlersekretariat Andreas Liebrandt, Holzbergstr. 11, 82541 Münsing, Germany (office). *Telephone:* (89) 72649660 (office). *Fax:* (89) 74879448 (office). *E-mail:* ingolf.turban@t-online.de (home); info@liebrandt.com (office). *Website:* www.ingolfturban.de; www.liebrandt.com (office).

TURBET, Richard Beaumont, BA, MLitt; British librarian; b. 5 Feb. 1948, Ilford, Essex, England; m.; two s. *Education:* Bancroft's School, Woodford, Essex, Univ. Coll., London, Leeds Polytechnic, Univ. of Aberdeen. *Career:* trainee asst librarian, Univ. of Dundee 1969–70; grad. teaching asst, Univ. of Calgary, Canada 1971–72; Asst Librarian, Nat. Cen. Library 1972–74; Librarian, Prison Service Coll., Wakefield 1974–77; Asst Librarian, Univ. of Aberdeen 1977–90, Sub-Librarian 1990–2003, Special Collections Cataloguer and Music Librarian 2003–09 (retd); Lay Clerk, Wakefield Cathedral 1976–77, Aberdeen Cathedral 1977–92; mem. Royal Musical Asscn, Int. Asscn of Music Libraries, British Music Soc., Viola da Gamba Soc., Elgar Soc., Armstrong Gibbs Soc., Nat. Early Music Asscn, Friends of Cathedral Music. *Publications:* William Byrd: A Guide to Research 1987 (third edn 2012), Tudor Music: A Research and Information Guide 1994, William Byrd: Lincoln's Greatest Composer 1993, Byrd Studies (co-ed. with Alan Brown) 1992, Music Librarianship in the United Kingdom (ed.) 2003, Annual Byrd Newsletter (ed.) 1995–2004 cumulative edn 2005, A Byrd Celebration (ed.) 2008; contrib. to Sundry Sorts of Music Books (Festschrift for O.W. Neighbour 1993), Aspects of British Song 1992, Branches of Literature and Music 2000, New Grove Dictionary of Music and Musicians (second edn), Oxford Dictionary of National Biography, British Union Catalogue of Music Periodicals; more than 100 articles in journals. *Honours:* Hon. Research Fellow, Univ. of Aberdeen; C.B. Oldman Prize 1994, 2013. *Address:* 24 Cley Road, Holt, Norfolk, NR25 6JG, England (home). *Telephone:* (1263) 711123 (home). *E-mail:* r.turbet@abdn.ac.uk (office).

TURCO, Enrico; Italian singer (bass); b. 1962, Genoa. *Education:* Accademia di Santa Cecilia, Rome. *Career:* sang at first in concert and made stage debut in 1987, as King Philip in Don Carlos; Macerata Festival 1991, as Leporello, and Frankfurt Alte Oper in a concert of Franchetti's Cristoforo Colombo; guest appearances at La Scala, Turin, Parma and the Scottish Opera; sang Capello in Bellini's Capuleti at Reggio Emilia 1998; sang role of Capulet in Roméo et Juliette by Gounod 2011. *Recordings include:* Don Giovanni, Cristoforo Colombo, La fanciulla del West, Iphigénie en Tauride, Don Carlo, Le convenienze e inconvenienze teatrali, Giulietta e Romeo by Nicola Vaccaj, La sonnambula. *Honours:* Giacomo Lauri Volpi (Opera Voices Competition) 1987, Sperimentale di Spoleto (Young Opera Singers Competition of EU) 1988, Winner of scholarship and finalist, Third Int. Competition Maria Callas new voices for opera 1988. *Current Management:* c/o A.C Artists. S.r.l. via Tracia 2, 00183 Roma, Italy. *Telephone:* (06) 77202447. *E-mail:* alecatteruccia@tiscali.it. *Website:* www.ac-artists.com.

TURETZKY, Bertram Jay, MM; American double bassist and composer; b. 14 Feb. 1933, Norwich, CT. *Education:* Hartt School of Music, New York Univ. with Curt Sachs, Univ. of Hartford, studied with David Walter. *Career:* played double bass in various orchestras and ensembles; solo debut at Judson Hall, New York 1964, with works by Donald Erb and Barney Childs; novel performing techniques have been exploited by such composers as Donald Martino, Richard Felciano, Paul Chihara, Kenneth Gaburro, George Perle and Ben Johnston. *Compositions:* Collages I–IV 1976–81, Reflections on Ives and Whittier for double bass and tape 1979–81, In memoriam Charles Mingus 1979, Baku for tape 1980. *Publications include:* The Contemporary Contrabass 1974, Editions of double bass studies for the American String Teachers Association, Editor of series published by the University of California Press on contemporary performance techniques.

TURKOVIC, Milan; Austrian bassoonist; b. 14 Sept. 1939, Zagreb, Yugoslavia. *Education:* studied in Vienna. *Career:* performed with the Philharmonia Hungarica, then soloist with the Bamber Symphony and member of the Bamberg Wind Quintet; soloist with the Vienna Symphony from 1967, with freelance concert performances from 1984; further concerts at the Salzburg Mozarteum and with Concentus Musicus at Vienna, under Harnoncourt; Created Helmut Eder's concerto in 1968 and with Helmut and Wolfgang Schulz formed the Vienna Trio.

TURNAGE, Mark-Anthony, CBE; British composer; b. 10 June 1960, Corringham, Essex; s. of Roy Turnage and Patricia Knowles; m. 1st Susan Shaw 1989 (divorced 1990); m. 2nd Helen Reed 1992; two s. *Education:* Hassenbrook Comprehensive School, Palmers Sixth Form, Grays, Royal Coll.

of Music with Oliver Knussen and John Lambert and Tanglewood, USA with Hans Werner Henze and Gunther Schuller. *Career:* first opera, Greek, premiered at first Munich Biennale 1988; Composer-in-Asscn with City of Birmingham Symphony Orchestra, composing three major works 1989–93; Composer-in-Asscn with ENO 1995–99; Assoc. Composer in Asscn with BBC Symphony Orchestra 2000–03; Momentum, BBC 3 composer weekend dedicated to his music, Barbican Hall, London 2003; Composer-in-Residence, London Philharmonic Orchestra 2005–, Chicago Symphony Orchestra 2006–08; one of 20 composers commissioned to write a piece of music for the 2012 Cultural Olympiad. *Compositions include:* Night Dances for orchestra 1980, Lament for a Hanging Man for soprano and ensemble 1983, Sarabande for soprano saxophone and piano 1985, On All Fours for chamber ensemble 1985, Greek (opera) 1987, Three Screaming Popes for orchestra 1988, Greek Suite for mezzo soprano, baritone and ensemble 1989, Kai for solo cello and ensemble 1989, Some Days 1989, Killing Time (television scena) 1991, Drowned Out 1992, Your Rockaby saxophone concerto 1992, Blood on the Floor for large ensemble 1994, Dispelling the Fears 1994, Twice Through the Heart for mezzo and 16 players 1997, Country of the Blind 1997, The Silver Tassie (opera) 1997, Silent Cities for orchestra 1998, About Time for two orchestras 1999, Evening Songs for orchestra 2000, Another Set To for trombone and orchestra 2000, Scorched for jazz trio and orchestra (with John Scofield) 2000, On Opened Ground concerto for viola and orchestra 2000, Bass Inventions for double bass and ensemble 2001, The Torn Fields for orchestra 2001, Dark Crossing 2001, A Quick Blast 2001, The Game is Over for orchestra 2002, Scherzoid for orchestra 2003–04, From the Wreckage for trumpet and orchestra 2004, Riffs and Refrains 2005, Ceres for orchestra 2005, Lullaby for Hans for orchestra 2005, From all Sides for orchestra 2005–06, Chicago Remains for orchestra 2007, Milo 2009, Texan Tenebrae for orchestra 2010, Hammered Out 2010, Anna Nicole (opera) 2011, Beyond This 2012, Frieze (commissioned for bicentenary of Royal Philharmonic Soc.) 2013, Duetti d'Amore (2015), for violin and cello 2015. *Honours:* Guinness Prize for Composition 1982, Benjamin Britten Young Composers Prize 1983, BMW Music Theatre Prize 1988, Laurence Olivier Award 2001. *Address:* c/o Boosey and Hawkes Music Publishers, Aldwych House, 71–91 Aldwych, London, WC2B 4HN, England. *Telephone:* (20) 7054-7200. *E-mail:* composers@boosey .com. *Website:* www.boosey.com.

TURNER, Bruno; British choral director; b. 7 Feb. 1931, London. *Education:* studied Gregorian chant and renaissance choral music. *Career:* many performances of medieval and renaissance music, notably as Dir of Pro Musica Sacra 1956–64, Pro Cantione Antiqua 1968–2002, Coro Cappella 1977–84; liturgical reconstruction of the Missa Tecum Principium by Robert Fayrfax, 1962; Iberian, English and Franco-Flemish choral music of the 15th and 16th centuries; regular contributor to BBC Radio Broadcasts 1959–80; co-f. Mapa Mundi with Martyn Imrie 1977. *Recordings include:* albums of early choral music. *Publications:* Ylario/Illario (ed), Hispaniæ Cantica Sacra (ed). *Address:* Mapa Mundi Renaissance Performing Scores, 15 Marvig, Lochs, Isle of Lewis, HS2 9QP, Scotland. *Telephone:* (1851) 880216. *E-mail:* mapamundi@ madasafish.com; bruno.t@freedom255.com.

TURNER, Jane; British singer (mezzo-soprano); b. 1960, County Durham, England. *Education:* Guildhall School of Music, Opera Studio, London. *Career:* German debut as Wellgunde and Siegrune in The Ring at Bayreuth 1984, as a Flower Maiden and Flosshilde; British opera debut 1985 as Carmen with the Glyndebourne Tour; Flora in Peter Hall's production of Traviata at the Festival 1987; Covent Garden debut 1987, as Ann Who Strips in the Hytner production of The King Goes Forth to France; returned as a Flower Maiden in Parsifal and as Flosshilde in Das Rheingold; ENO as Maddalena in Rigoletto and as Lola in Cavalleria Rusticana; sang Siebel in Faust at Dublin 1995.

TURNER, Margarita; singer (soprano); b. 11 March 1943, Perth, Australia. *Education:* studied in London and West Germany. *Career:* debut, Krefeld 1969, as Micaela; appearances in opera at Cologne, Saarbrucken, Wiesbaden and Wuppertal; 15-year career at the Essen Opera as Fiordiligi, Pamina, Marguerite, Martha, Marenka, Violetta, Marzelline (Fidelio), Mélisande, Eva, Concepcion and Nedda; Sophie in Der Rosenkavalier, Mimi, Liu, Rosalinde and Luise in Der Junge Lord by Henze; frequent concert engagements; teacher, Essen Musikhochschule; season 2000–01 at Essen, in Elektra, Faust and Jenůfa.

TURNER, Paul, BMus, MMus; Australian composer; b. 16 April 1948, Morwell, Vic. *Education:* Univ. of Melbourne, studied with Barry Conyngham. *Career:* Composer-in-the-Community, Hamilton, Vic. 1981; faculty mem., Univ. of Adelaide 1987–92. *Compositions include:* Panels II for violin, clarinet and piano 1974, Grand Pocket Sonata in B Minor for piano 1986, Herbivores for piano 1987, Sonata for tape 1994, A Spangled Pandemonium Escapes from the Zoo for ensemble, Chronic Interludes I–III for saxophone and piano, Geraniums or Nasturtiums for saxophone and piano, Instrumental Rationality for various combinations, Icarus Flying for guitar or tape, Machines I–III for harp and tape, Phrygian Misery for saxophone and piano.

TURNOVSKÝ, Martin; Austrian conductor; b. 29 Sept. 1928, Prague, Czechoslovakia. *Education:* Music Acad., Prague; studied conducting with Dedecek and Ančerl, Prague Acad. of Music; pvt studies in conducting with Szell. *Career:* Conductor, Czech Army Symphony Orchestra 1955–60, State Philharmonic Orchestra, Brno 1960–63; Music Dir, Plzeň Radio Orchestra 1963–66, Dresden State Opera and State Orchestra 1966–68; guest conductor

with numerous orchestras, including Radio Orchestra, Berlin, Cleveland Orchestra, New York Philharmonic Orchestra, Detroit Symphony Orchestra, Toronto Symphony, Stockholm Philharmonic Orchestra, BBC Northern Orchestra, Manchester 1968, Norwegian Opera, Oslo 1975–80, Bonn Opera 1979–83, Prague Symphony Orchestra 1992; opera engagements with Deutsche Oper Berlin, Welsh Nat. Opera (British opera debut, Eugene Onegin 1988), Staatsoper Stuttgart, Royal Opera Stockholm and Savonlinna Festival, Finland; season 1992–93 conducted Otello and Un Ballo in Maschera at Prague State Opera; American opera debut with Jenůfa at Cincinnati 1998; Dvořák's Rusalka with Seattle Opera 1998; currently Prin. Guest Conductor, Gunma Symphony Orchestra, Japan. *Recordings:* numerous recordings for Supraphon, including 4th Symphony of Bohuslav Martinů (Grand Prix du Disque 1968). *Honours:* Österreichisches Ehrenkreuz für Wissenschaft und Kunst 1. Klasse; first prize Int. Competition for Conductors, Besancon, France 1958. *Current Management:* Baron & Weingartner KEG, International Artists Management, Bösendorferstrasse 4/12, 1010 Vienna, Austria. *Telephone:* (1) 489-61-54 (office). *Fax:* (1) 489-61-54-44 (office). *E-mail:* schwemle@ baronartists.com. *Website:* www.baronartists.com. *Telephone:* 272769879 (home). *Fax:* 272769879 (home).

TURPIN, Kathryn; British singer (mezzo-soprano); b. 1968, England. *Education:* New Hall, Cambridge, Royal College of Music, Samling Foundation. *Career:* Lady de Hautdesert in Birtwistle's Gawain at the Royal Opera House; Margaretha in Schumann's Genoveva at Garsington; Bizet's Djamileh at Cap Ferrat; Lucretia in The Rape of Lucretia for Music Theatre Wales; Carmen at the Festival de la Vezère; Cherubino at Neuchâtel; Ulisse in Deidamia, London Handel Society; Madame Popova in The Bear at Cambridge; Conductors worked for include Simon Rattle, Neville Marriner, David Willcocks, Elgar Howarth, Matthew Best and Martyn Brabbins; Orchestras include CBSO, Orchestra of the Age of Enlightenment, London Sinfonietta, Bournemouth Sinfonietta, London Mozart Players, Hanover Band, Orchestre National de Lille, Orchestre de Besançon, National Youth Orchestra of Wales, Academy of St Martin in the Fields. *Recordings:* In The Beginning, Copland, with the Choir of St John's College, Cambridge; Duruflé Requiem; Broadcasts for BBC Radio 3 and Classic FM. *Honours:* Welsh Arts Council Scholar. *Current Management:* c/o Foxroe Artist Management, 103 Nottingham Road, New Basford, Nottingham NG7 7AJ, England. *Telephone:* (115) 847-8719. *Fax:* (115) 847-8719. *E-mail:* info@foxroe.com. *Website:* www.foxroe.com.

TURSKA, Joanna Lucja, MMus; flautist; b. 16 Oct. 1958, Warsaw, Poland; m. Roman Siczek 1986, one d. *Education:* Warsaw Academy of Music, Royal Conservatory, The Netherlands, Conservatories in Creteil and Paris, France, studied with E. Gajewska, F. Vester, A. Marion, S. T. Preston, P. Sechet. *Career:* appearances at recitals, chamber music concerts and as soloist with orchestras in Europe and America, Germany, France, Italy, Switzerland, Austria, The Netherlands, Belgium, Luxembourg, Poland, Cuba, USA; performances at festivals, including Paris, Youth Music Festival (Bayreuth, Germany), Warsaw Autumn, New Music Festival and Early Music Festival (Chicago, USA). *Recordings:* solo, chamber music and orchestral performances recorded by Polish radio and television, Belgian radio, French radio, and US radio, television classical and ethnic channels; album for winners of Premio Ancona competitions.

TUSA, Andrew; British singer (tenor); b. 1966, England. *Education:* New College, Oxford, Pears-Britten School. *Career:* sang in the Play of Daniel at the Queen Elizabeth Hall 1989, followed by Asterion in Rameau's Nais for the English Bach Festival; Concert engagements include Messiah with the Leicester Bach Choir, St John Passion in Krefeld, soloist with Gothic Voices in Milan and Second Shepherd in Monteverdi's Orfeo at the 1990 Salzburg Festival; Appearances with the Gabrieli and Taverner Consorts, Christmas Oratorio under Andrew Parrott in Oslo, Masses by Mozart in Barbican Hall, 1991, St Matthew Passion with Birmingham Bach Society and Messiah with the Stavanger Symphony in Norway. *Recordings include:* Mozart's Salzburg Masses with the Winchester College Choir and Monteverdi Madrigals with I Fagiolini.

TUTINO, Marco; Italian composer; *Artistic Director, Teatro Comunale, Bologna;* b. 30 May 1954, Milan. *Education:* Giuseppe Verdi Conservatory, Milan. *Career:* works performed at the 1976 Gaudeamus Festival in Amsterdam; operas produced in Genoa, Alessandria, Livorno and Modena; Sovrintendente, Artistic Dir Teatro Comunale, Bologna 2006–. *Compositions:* a synthesis between 19th century procedures and more modern methods; opera: Pinnochio 1985, Cirano (commedia lirica) 1987, La lupa 1990, Le vite immaginarie (chamber opera) 1990.

TUVÅS, Linda; Swedish singer (soprano); b. 1972, Stockholm. *Education:* Stockholm University, Birkagarden School of Music and the Guildhall School, London. *Career:* engagements as Mozart's Donna Anna and Fatima in Grétry's Zémire et Azor at Drottningholm and the Théâtre Champs-Elysées, Paris; Kate Pinkerton, Jano in Jenůfa and Micaela (Carmen) for Gothenburg Opera; further roles as Musetta for WNO, Tatiana for British Youth Opera and the title role in Il Segretto di Susanna for Newbury Opera; also sings Massenet's Grisélidis, Arminda in La Finta Giardiniera by Mozart, and Offenbach's Giulietta; sang Barbarina in Le nozze de Figaro at the 1997 Glyndebourne Festival; season 1998 as Amor in Poppea for WNO, Varvara (Katya Kabanova) for the Glyndebourne Opera. *Current Management:* c/o Neil Dalrymple, Music International, 13 Ardilaun Road, London, N5 2QR, England.

TWARDOWSKI, Romuald, (Adam Lass), DipMus; Polish composer and academic; *Professor, Warsaw Academy of Music*; b. 17 June 1930, Wilno; m. Alice Stradczuk 1981; one s. *Education:* Wilno Conservatory, Higher School of Music, Warsaw, studied with Nadia Boulanger in Paris. *Career:* Prof., Warsaw Acad. of Music. *Compositions include:* opera: Cyrano de Bergerac 1963, Tragedy 1969, Lord Jim 1976, Maria Stuart 1979, Story of St Catherine 1985; works for orchestra, choirs, theatre, cinema: Old Polish Concerto for strings 1988, Little Concerto for vocal orchestra 1988, Michelangelo Sonnets for baritone and piano 1988, Lithuanian Variations for winds/quartet 1988, Niggunim for violin and orchestra 1991. *Recordings include:* Gershwin Variations for symphony orchestra (Polish Radio, Kraków) 1980, Spanish Fantasy for cello and orchestra (Polish Radio, Warsaw), Alleluia for mixed choir 1990, Espressioni for violin and piano 1990, Orthodox Liturgy of St John Chrysostom 2005, Niggunim, chassidim tunes for violin and piano or orchestra, numerous recordings of own compositions. *Publication:* It Has Been, It Has Not Passed (biog.) 2000. *Honours:* Order of Polonia Restituta; Second Prize, Tribune Internationale des Compositeurs, UNESCO, Paris 1963, Grand Prix, Monaco 1965, 1973, First Prize, Prague Spring Competition 1966, Paderewski Award 2006. *Address:* ul Miaczynska 54 m 61, 02-637 Warsaw, Poland (home). *Telephone:* (22) 8483862 (home). *E-mail:* alicja .twardowska@wp.pl (home).

TYLER, Marilyn; American singer (soprano); b. 6 Dec. 1928, New York, NY. *Education:* studied with Friedrich Schorr in New York and with Toti dal Monte in Venice. *Career:* sang first in operetta; Basle Opera 1948; Netherlands Opera 1955, as Violetta; sang title role in Die Entführung; Bayreuth; Bayreuth 1961, Brünnhilde in Die Walküre; appearances in Italy, Germany, North America and Israel. *Recordings include:* Die Zauberflote, Die Entführung, Serse by Handel, Stravinsky's Pulcinella.

TYNAN, Kathleen; Irish singer (soprano); b. 1960. *Education:* Royal Irish Acad. of Music, Dublin and Guildhall School of Music and Drama, London. *Career:* selected by RTE, representative Ireland, Cardiff Singer of the World Competition 1987; sang for Opera Theatre Co., Expo '98, Lisbon; Cork Opera House; performed songs with pianist Dearbhla Collins and Irish Piano Trio in recitals, Theatre Royal, Wexford, Belfast Waterfront Hall, RHA Gallery, Dublin, Boyle Arts Festival, St James's, Picadilly; new work for voice and electronics by Fergus Johnston 2000; Opera Ireland; Wexford Festival Opera; RTE television production Riders to the Sea; Opera South, Cork; Olympia Theatre, Dublin; Opera Theatre Co., Dublin; QEH, London; toured France; Bermuda Festival for MidSummer Opera; sang Marzelline for new adaptation in English, Zulu and Afrikaans, Broomhill Opera/Opera Africa, with Northern Sinfonia; toured the UK extensively; extensive concert and song recital; London Festival orchestra; St John's Smith Square; Liverpool Cathedral Festival; National Symphony Orchestra, Ireland; concerts with RTE Concert Orchestra; presented recitals for music network, Ireland; broadcasts for BBC Radio Ulster. *Recordings include:* album: Romancing Rebellion.

TYNES, Margaret; American singer (soprano); b. 11 Sept. 1929, Saluda, VA. *Education:* studied with Emil Cooper in New York and with Tullio Serafin in Italy. *Career:* debut with New York City Opera 1952, as Fata Morgana in The Love for Three Oranges; Montréal 1959, as Lady Macbeth; has sung in Spoleto (as Salome), Vienna, Budapest, Toronto, Milan, Prague, Naples and Bologna; Metropolitan Opera debut 1973, as Jenůfa; other roles have included Norma, Aida, Desdemona, Dido and Marie in Wozzeck; many concert appearances.

TYRRELL, John, BMus, DPhil, FRCM; British musicologist and academic; *Honorary Professor, Cardiff University*; b. 17 Aug. 1942, Salisbury, Southern Rhodesia. *Education:* Univ. of Cape Town, S Africa, Univ. of Oxford. *Career:* fmr Assoc. Ed. Musical Times; mem. editorial staff, New Grove Dictionary of Music –1976; apptd Lecturer, Univ. of Nottingham 1976, Reader in Opera Studies 1989, Prof. 1995; Exec. Ed. The New Grove Dictionary of Music and Musicians Second Edn 1996–2001; Professorial Research Fellow, Cardiff Univ. 2000–03, Prof., School of Music 2003–08, Hon. Prof. 2008–. *Publications include:* Leoš Janáček: Kát'a Kabanová 1982, Czech Opera 1988, Janáček's Operas: A Documentary Account 1992, Intimate Letters: Leoš Janáček to Kamila Stösslová (ed. and trans.) 1994, Leoš Janáček: Jenůfa (co-ed.) 1996, Janáček's Works: A Catalogue of the Music and Writings of Leoš Janáček (co-author) 1997, My Life with Janáček: The Memoirs of Zdenka Janáčková (ed. and trans.) 1998, Janáček: Years of a Life Vol. 1: The Lonely Blackbird (1854–1914) 2006, Vol. 2: Tsar of the Forests (1914–1928) 2007. *Honours:* Dr hc (Masaryk Univ. of Brno) 2002, (Janáček Acad. of Performing Arts, Brno) 2011. *Address:* School of Music, Cardiff University, 31 Corbett Road, Cardiff, CF10 3EB, Wales (office). *E-mail:* tyrrellj@cardiff.ac.uk (office). *Website:* www .cardiff.ac.uk/music/contactsandpeople/profiles/tyrrellj.html (office).

TYRRELL, Lisa Jane, AGSMD; British singer (soprano); b. 7 June 1967, Salford. *Education:* Chetham's School of Music, Manchester, Guildhall School of Music, London, Banff Centre of Fine Arts, Canada. *Career:* debut, Pamina in Die Zauberflöte, English Touring Opera 1990; Zerlina in Don Giovanni with the English Touring Opera; Lace Seller in Death in Venice at Glyndebourne Festival Opera; Semire in Les Boreádes, Birmingham Touring Opera; Judith in European Story, Garden Venture (Covent Garden); Naiad in Ariadne auf Naxos, Garsington Opera; Euridice in Orfeo, Scottish Opera-go-Round; debut at the WNO in The Doctor of Myddfai; as the Child, a new opera written by Peter Maxwell Davies; debut at the Royal Opera, Covent Garden as Barbarina in The Marriage of Figaro; concerts include St John Passion in Salzburg, Handel's Messiah in St John's Smith Square; concerts with Fretwork at St John's; Monteverdi Vespers; Ariadne auf Naxos at Endellion Festival, with Richard Hickox; Vivaldi's Gloria at St Paul's Cathedral and Brazil; Brahms' Requiem; The Fairy Queen, ENO Bayliss Programme; new commission by Peter Maxwell Davies, with Scottish Chamber Orchestra 1997; Janáček's Vixen with City of Birmingham Touring Opera 1998. *Honours:* Wyburd Trust Award (for advanced lieder study) 1990, Wingate Scholar 1996.

TZINCOCA, Remus; conductor and composer; b. 1920, Iassy, Romania; m. Anisia Campos. *Education:* Iassy Conservatory of Music, Conservatoire National Superieur de Musique de Paris, studied with George Enescu. *Career:* debut, led Colonne Orchestra with George Enescu as soloist, Paris; conducted major orchestras in Europe and North America, including London Philharmonic, Zürich Tonhalle, Lamoureux, Pasdeloup and Colonne in Paris, Radiotelevision Française, New York Philharmonic, Cleveland Orchestra, CBC Orchestra, Bucharest Philharmonic; Radio Television and Bucharest Opera; founder and Musical Dir, Newport Music Festival, Rhode Island, USA; founder and Musical Dir, New York Orchestra da Camera, with concerts at Metropolitan Museum, Carnegie Hall and Town Hall; discovered with Anisia Campos, original version, in Romanian, of Bartók's Cantata Profana, in New York Bartók Archives and gave premiere in Bucharest with the Philharmonic Orchestra 1984. *Compositions:* oratorios, symphonies, lieder and a Byzantine Mass. *Address:* 632 Avenue Herve-Beaudry, Laval, QC H7E 2X6, Canada.

U

UCHIDA, Dame Mitsuko; Japanese/British pianist; b. 20 Dec. 1948, Tokyo; d. of Fujio Uchida and Yasuko Uchida; partner Sir Robert Cooper. *Education:* Vienna Acad. of Music, Austria with Prof. R. Hauser. *Career:* debut Vienna 1963; recitals and concerto performances with major London orchestras, Chicago Symphony, Boston Symphony, Cleveland Orchestra, Berlin Philharmonic, Vienna Philharmonic, New York Philharmonic, Los Angeles Philharmonic and others; played and directed the cycle of 21 Mozart piano concertos with the English Chamber Orchestra, London 1985–86; gave US premiere of piano concerto Antiphonies by Harrison Birtwistle 1996; Co-Artistic Dir (with Richard Goode) Marlboro Music Festival 1999–2013, Artistic Dir 2013–; Perspectives recital series at Carnegie Hall 2003; Artist-in-Residence, Cleveland Orchestra 2002–07, Berlin Philharmonic Orchestra 2008–09, Vienna Konzerthaus 2008–09; Trustee, Borletti-Buitoni Trust. *Recordings include:* Mozart Complete Piano Sonatas and 24 Piano Concertos (English Chamber Orchestra and Jeffrey Tate), Mozart Piano Concertos (Cleveland Orchestra), Chopin Piano Sonatas, Debussy 12 Etudes, Schubert Piano Sonatas, Beethoven Piano Concertos, Schoenberg Piano Concerto, Beethoven Piano Sonatas Op. 109, 110 and 111, Beethoven: Sonatas Op. 101 and 106, Schumann: Kreisleriana Carnaval Davidsbündlertänze Fantasie, Berg: Chamber Concerto, Mozart Piano Concertos Nos 23 & 24 (Grammy Award for Best Instrumental Soloist Performance) 2011. *Honours:* Hon. CBE 2001; Hon. DBE 2009; First Prize, Beethoven Competition Vienna 1969, Second Prize, Chopin Competition Warsaw 1970, Second Prize, Leeds Competition 1975, Gramophone Award (Mozart Piano Sonatas) 1989, Gramophone Award (Schoenberg Piano Concerto) 2001, Royal Philharmonic Soc.'s Instrumentalist Award 2004, Royal Philharmonic Soc. Gold Medal 2012. *Current Management:* c/o Victoria Rowsell Artist Management Ltd, 34 Addington Square, London, SE5 7LB, England. *Telephone:* (20) 7701-3219. *Fax:* (20) 7701-3219. *E-mail:* management@victoriarowsell.co.uk. *Website:* www.victoriarowsell.co.uk; www.marlboromusic.org; www.mitsukouchida.com.

UDAGAWA, Hideko; Japanese violinist; b. 1960. *Education:* Tokyo Univ. of Arts, Juilliard School of Music, New York, studied with Nathan Milstein in London. *Career:* orchestral debut with London Symphony Orchestra under Sir Charles Mackerras, playing Bruch's G minor concerto, Barbican Hall, London; TV appearances and radio broadcasts, concerts in USA and Europe; recitals at Queen Elizabeth Hall, Lincoln Center; concerto performances with London Symphony Orchestra, Philharmonia, Royal, London and Liverpool Philharmonics, City of Birmingham Symphony, English Chamber and Polish Chamber Orchestras, Berlin Symphony and Bucharest Philharmonic Orchestra. *Recordings:* virtuoso violin pieces, Heifetz Transcriptions, Brahms and Bruch Concertos with Charles Mackerras and London Symphony, Aram Khachaturian Sonata and Dances 2005, Rachmaninov's Sonata in G Minor. *Current Management:* c/o Genroh Hara, Pro Arte Musicae Co. Ltd, Otowa 1-20-14-5F, Bunkyo-ku, Tokyo 112-0013, Japan. *Telephone:* (3) 3943-6677. *Fax:* (3) 3943-6659. *E-mail:* pam@proarte.co.jp. *Website:* www.proarte.co.jp; www.hidekoudagawa.com.

UDALOVA, Irina; Russian singer (soprano); b. 1957, Nikolaevsk na, Amur. *Education:* Kishinev Conservatory. *Career:* sang in opera at Aschchabad, Turkmenistan, notably as Tatiana, Iolanta, Amelia (Ballo in Maschera) and Nedda; Bolshoi Opera, Moscow, from 1985, as Militrissa in The Tale of Tsar Sultan, and Tchaikovsky's Lisa and Maid of Orleans; guest with the Bolshoi at Glasgow 1990 and elsewhere as Voyslada in Rimsky's Mlada. *Recordings include:* Judith by Serov.

UEHARA, Ayako; Japanese pianist; b. 1980, Takamatsu. *Education:* Yamaha Music School, Yamaha masterclass, studied with Fumiko Eguchi, Shinji Urakabe, Vera Gornostaeva. *Career:* concert debut with Nat. Symphony Orchestra, Tokyo 1994; concert performances with orchestras, including Japan PO, Moscow SO, Moscow Radio SO, Russian Nat. SO, Washington Nat. SO, Prague SO, Bamberg SO, LSO, Dresden Philharmonic, Toscanini Philharmonic; toured Australia with Sydney SO and Paavo Jarvi, Japan with Berlin Radio Orchestra and Marek Janowski; recitals at Wigmore Hall, London, Fondo per l'Ambiente Italiano, Ruhrgebiet Piano Festival, Int. Chopin Festival, Poland, Dubrovnik Festival, Croatia, Tokyo Opera City Recital Hall. *Recording:* Tchaikovsky Grand Sonata 2003. *Honours:* first prize Int. Competition for Young Pianists, Ettlingen, Germany, second prize Sydney Int. Piano Competition 2000, second prize Hamamatsu Int. Piano Competition 2000, first prize Int. Tchaikovsky Competition, Moscow 2002.

UGORSKI, Anatol; Russian pianist; b. 28 Sept. 1942, Leningrad. *Education:* Leningrad Conservatoire. *Career:* from 1962 has given many concerts and recitals, including works by Boulez, Messiaen, Berg and Schoenberg; teacher, Leningrad Conservatoire from 1982; resident in Germany 1992–; taught at Hochschule für Musik, Detmold –2007. *Recordings include:* Beethoven's Sonata Op 111, Scriabin's Piano Sonata Nos 1–10. *Address:* Humboldtstrasse 8, 32756 Detmold, Germany (home). *Telephone:* (5231) 18241 (home).

UHLIK, Tomislav; Croatian composer, conductor and academic; *Professor, Zagreb Music Academy;* b. 24 Oct. 1956, Zagreb; m. Lidija; one s. one d. *Education:* Zagreb Music Acad. *Career:* Music Dir Lado Folklore Ensemble 1983–85; Conductor, Komedija Theatre, Zagreb 1992–; Prof., Zagreb Music Acad.; regular guest conductor of symphonic wind orchestra of Croatian army;

mem. Croatian Composers' Asscn. *Compositions:* Six Episodes for wind quintet 1986, The Body of Our Lord (liturgical cantata for folk choir and tambouras) 1990, Divertimento for strings 1991, Melancholy Variations for harp solo 1991, Don Quixote and Dulcinea for cello and double bass, Concerto for horn and wind orchestra 1997, Quartetto Concertante for guitars 1998, First String Quartet 2000, Centurion for orchestra 2000, Elegy and Dance for flute, viola and harp 2001, Tov lehodos for mixed choir 2002, Sonata for flute and piano 2003, Paraphrases of Croatian Folk Songs for piano 2003–05, Something Nice for harp and string orchestra 2004, Second String Quartet 2006, Mediterranean Dance for guitar 2012. *Honours:* First Prize for the Nocturne, for mixed choir a cappella, Matetic Days Festival in Ronjgi 1988, Croatian Ministry of Culture Award for Hymne for Soprano and Orchestra. *Address:* 10010 Zagreb, V. Varicakova 4, Croatia (home). *E-mail:* tomislav.uhlik@zg.t-com.hr (office).

UHRMACHER, Hildegard; German singer (soprano); b. 15 Dec. 1939, Mönchen Gladbach. *Education:* studied in Waldniel and Düsseldorf. *Career:* debut at Deutsche Oper am Rhein 1964, as Vespina in Haydn's L'Infedeltà delusa; sang at Kassel Opera, 1967–73, Hamburg from 1974, Munich, 1970–78; further appearances at Vienna, Amsterdam, Florence and Cardiff; Staatsoper Stuttgart, 1981–89; roles have included Salome, The Queen of Night, Constanze, Zerbinetta, Gilda, Traviata, Musetta and Flotow's Martha; Düsseldorf, 1995, as Hanna Glawari and Mannheim, 1996 in Amandas Traum by Harold Weiss; modern repertoire also includes Zimmermann's Die Soldaten (Hanover, 1989) and works by Dessau and Britten.

ULBRICH, Andrea Edina; Hungarian-Italian singer (mezzo-soprano); b. Budapest, Hungary; d. of József Ulbrich and Eva Mészáros; one s. *Education:* Budapest Music Acad. *Career:* has sung with Hungarian Nat. Opera, Budapest from 1988, notably as Nicklausse in Les Contes d'Hoffmann, Sextus in Clemenza di Tito, Mercédès in Carmen and as Flotow's Nancy; Frankfurt 1991, in a concert of Franchetti's Cristoforo Colombo; guest at Ludwigshafen 1992, as Cherubino, Dorabella in Così fan tutte, Olga in Onegin, Judith in Bluebeard's Castle, Octavian in Der Rosenkavalier, Rosina in Barber of Seville, Dryad in Ariadne auf Naxos, Priestess in Aida, Mirinda in Cavalli's Ormindo, Angelina in La Cenerentola, Lolette in La Rondine-Puccini and others; guest at Deutsche Oper Berlin, Oper Frankfurt, Brussels, Klagenfurt, Wiener Konzerthaus, appearing as Amneris in Verdi's Aida, Eboli in Verdi's Don Carlos, Cuniza in Verdi's Oberto and Melibea in Rossini's Il Viaggio a Reims, La Principessa in Puccini's Suor Angelica, Düsseldorf, Sara in Donizetti's Roberto Devereux, Bratislava, Ameris in Verdi's Aida, Torino, Adalgisa in Bellini's Norma, Fenena in Verdi's Nabucco, Basel, Azucena in Verdi's Trovatore, Semper Oper, Dresden, Azucena in Budapest, Toulouse, Cologne, Trieste, Tokyo, Arena di Verona, Roma-Vatican 2011. *Recordings include:* La Canterina, Haydn; Donizetti and Rossini songs and duets; Opera Gala, Berlin; Die Hochzeit des Camacho, Mendelssohn; Serenata, Scarlatti, Verdi's Requiem; opera film: Così fan tutte (Mozart). *Honours:* prizewinner, Dvořák Competition, Prague and Paris competition, Belvedere Competition, Vienna, Mandi Prize Foundation from Hungarian State Opera 1989, Grand Prix Brussels Bel Canto competition 1990, Béla Bartók-Pasztory Ditta Prix 1992, Mihaly Szekely Prize 1994. *Address:* c/o Hungarian National Opera, Népöztársaság utja 22, 1061 Budapest, Hungary (office). *Telephone:* (1) 3848658 (home). *Fax:* (1) 3848658 (home). *E-mail:* andreaedina@andreaulbrich.com (home). *Website:* www.andreaulbrich.com (home); www.opera.hu.

ULFUNG, Ragnar; Norwegian singer (tenor) and opera producer; b. 28 Feb. 1927, Oslo. *Education:* Oslo Conservatory and studied in Milan. *Career:* debut in concert from 1949; first stage role in Menotti's The Consul, Oslo, 1952; mem., Royal Opera Stockholm from 1958; sang Renato in Un Ballo in Maschera at Covent Garden 1960; sang Don Carlos at Covent Garden for two seasons, 1963–64; returned in the premiere of Maxwell Davies's Taverner, 1972 and as Mime in the Götz Friedrich production of the Ring, 1974–6; Metropolitan Opera debut 1972, as Mime; later sang Strauss's Herod, Wagner's Loge, Berg's Captain and Weill's Fatty in New York; other appearances include Strauss's Liebe der Danaë and Penderecki's Die schwarze Maske in Santa Fe, as Kent in Reimann's Lear in San Francisco and Tom Rakewell in The Rake's Progress; concert performances of Messiaen's St Francois d'Assise in London and Lyon; sang Herod in Salome at San Francisco 1986; Paris Opéra and Geneva 1988, as Shuisky (Boris Godunov) and in The Fiery Angel; Alfred in Die Fledermaus as Oslo, 1988; Festival Hall London 1989, Aegisthus in Elektra; Herod at Los Angeles; Valzacchi in Der Rosenkavalier at Santa Fe 1989; sang Goro in Butterfly at Lyon, 1990; season 1992 as the Witch in Hansel and Gretel at Los Angeles, Fatty in Mahagonny at Geneva and Valzacchi in Rosenkavalier at the Santa Fe Festival; debut as stage dir at Santa Fe 1973, with La Bohème; other stagings include Lulu for Santa Fe, Otello in Stockholm and Der Ring des Nibelungen in Seattle; sang Hauk in The Makropulos Case, Chicago, 1995; Bill Poster in US premiere of A Dream Play by Lindberg, Santa Fe, 1998; sang Aegisthus in Elektra at Santa Fe, 2000. *Recordings include:* Monostatos in Ingmar Bergman's version of Die Zauberflöte.

ULIVIERI, Nicola; Italian singer (bass); b. 7 Sept. 1967, Arco di Trento. *Education:* Claudio Monteverdi Conservatory. *Career:* debut in Wolf-Ferrari's

I Quattro Rusteghi 1993; appearances from 1995 at La Scala of Milan, Rossini Opera Festival, Teatro Regio, Turin, Salzburg Festival, Aix en Provence Festival (Don Giovanni, conducted by Claudio Abbado) Liceu, Barcelona, Teatro Real, Madrid, Naples, Palermo, Genoa, Santa Cecilia, Bologna, Florence, Edinburgh Festival, Venice, Cagliari, Dresden, Welsh National Opera, Wexford, Montpellier, Tel-Aviv, Lyon, Bruxelles, Royal Philharmonic Orchestra, Teatro Colón, Buenos Aires. *Recordings include:* Dottor Mangiacarta in Spontini's Li puntigli delle donne, Guido in Elena da Feltre, Sulpice in La Fille du Régiment, Don Profondo in Viaggio a Reims. *Honours:* winner Belli Competition at Spoleto 1995, winner Riccardo Zandonai Competition at Rovereto 1995. *Current Management:* c/o Ernesto Palacio Artists Management, Via Donizetti 11, Lurano (BG), Italy. *Telephone:* (035) 800645. *Fax:* (035) 4877767. *E-mail:* ernestopalacio@ernestopalacio.com. *Website:* www.ernestopalacio.com; www.nicolaulivieri.it.

ULLMANN, Elisabeth; Austrian organist and academic; *Professor, Mozarteum, Salzburg;* b. 20 April 1952, Zwettl; m. Prof. Bigenzahn 1981; one s. *Education:* music studies in Vienna, Salzburg and London, UK. *Career:* debut winning first prize, Bach Competition, Leipzig 1976; has given numerous recitals and performed on radio and TV; Artistic Dir 25th Anniversary Int. Stift Zwettl Organ Festival, Austria; Prof., Mozarteum, Salzburg 1988–; mem. European Acad. of Sciences and Arts 2009. *Recordings:* Muffat: Apparatus Complete (Diapason Award), Hindemith Organ Sonatas, Mozart: Complete Church Sonatas, Haydn: Great Organ Mass, Wagenseil: Concerti per organo, Gottlieb Muffat: Selected keyboard music, Kerll: Selected keyboard music, Bach: Selected keyboard music, Stumm organ Meisenheim, Great Hall Mozarteum Salzburg Eule organ portrait. *Honours:* First Prize, Int. Bach Competition, Leipzig 1976, First Prize, Bruckner Competition 1978, Diapason Award, Deutscher Schallplattenpreis, Organist of the Year ('organ' journal) 2006. *Address:* Bennoplace 8/28, 1080 Vienna, Austria. *E-mail:* elisabeth.bigenzahn-ullmann@moz.ac.at (office). *Website:* www.elisabeth-ullmann.com.

ULLMANN, Jakob, PhD; German composer, organist and philosopher; b. 12 July 1958, Freiberg. *Education:* studied in Naumburg School of Sacred Music, Dresden. *Compositions include:* Komposition for string quartet 1985, Ensemblekomposition, theatre music 1986–, Symmetries on Aleph Zero, 1–3, for ensemble 1987, Alakata, for ensemble 1989, Due Frammenti, for orchestra 1990, Komposition I–III for orchestra 1991, 1993, 1994, Meeting John Cage under the Tropic of the late Eighties, graphic score 1990, Disappearing Musics 1990, Pianissimo, for viola and electronics 1990, Echoing A Distant Sound, for ensemble 1991–93, A Catalogue of Sounds for 13 solo strings 1996, voice, books and Fire I 1991–2004, voice, books and Fire II (1–5), graphic score 1991–2005, Solo (flute), Solo (trombone), Solo (organ) 1992–93, composition for string quarter 2 1997–99, kol 1 for ensemble 2000, kol 2 for ensemble 2001. *Address:* c/o GEMA, Rosenheimstr. 11, 8166 Munich, Germany (office). *Telephone:* (89) 4800300 (office); (30) 2858767 (home). *Fax:* (89) 48003495 (office); (30) 2858767 (home). *E-mail:* tloen_uqbar@gmx.de (home).

ULLMANN, Marcus; German singer (tenor); b. 1970, Olbernhau. *Education:* Dresden Kreuzchor and Musikhochschule, lieder classes with Dietrich Fischer-Dieskau. *Career:* concerts and opera with Helmuth Rilling (Bach B minor Mass), Sylvain Cambreling, Leopold Hager and Peter Schreier; orchestras include Bamberg SO, Staatskapelle Berlin and Dresden, Gewandhaus Orchestra, Munich PO and Salzburg Mozarteum; sang in Schoenberg's Moses und Aron, under Kent Nagano, at the Vienna Konzerthaus, 2001; festival appearances at Milan, Savonlinna, Philadelphia, Madrid, Utrecht and Salzburg. *Current Management:* Ariën Arts & Music Management, De Boeystraat 6, 2018 Antwerp, Belgium. *Telephone:* (3) 285-96-80. *Fax:* (3) 230-35-23. *E-mail:* arien@pandora.be.

UNDERWOOD, John; British violist; b. 11 Oct. 1932, Luton, Bedfordshire, England. *Education:* Royal Coll. of Music with Frederick Riddle. *Career:* co-principal viola, RPO under Beecham 1962–62; co-founder, Delmé Quartet 1962; many performances in the UK and Europe in the classical and modern repertory; concerts at the Salzburg Festival and the Brahms Saal of the Musikverein Vienna; season 1990 included Haydn's Seven Last Words in Italy and elsewhere, three Brahms programmes at St John's Smith Square with Iain Burnside, piano; concerts at St David's Hall Cardiff with quartets by Tchaikovsky and Robert Simpson (premiere of 13th quartet); appearances in Bremen, Hamburg and Trieste, followed by festival engagements 1991; other repertory includes works by Paul Patterson, Daniel Jones, Wilfred Josephs, Iain Hamilton and Bernard Stevens. *Recordings include:* Haydn Seven Last Words, Vaughan Williams On Wenlock Edge and Gurney's Ludlow and Teme, Simpson Quartets 1–9 and String Trio, Daniel Jones's Three Quartets and Bridge No. 2, Bliss Nos 1 and 2, Josef Holbrooke Piano Quartet and Clarinet Quintet, Brahms Clarinet Quintet and Dvořák F major, Verdi Quartet and Strauss A major Op 2.

UNG, Chinary; American composer; *Professor of Composition, University of California at San Diego;* b. 24 Nov. 1942, Prey Lovea, Cambodia. *Education:* studied clarinet at the Manhattan School of Music; studied composition with Chou Wen-Chung at Columbia Univ. DMA, 1974. *Career:* Regents Prof. at Arizona State Univ., Tempe 1987–95; Prof. of Composition, Univ. of California at San Diego 1995–. *Compositions include:* Tall Wind for soprano and ensemble, after e. e. cummings 1969, Anicca for chamber orchestra 1970, Mohori for mezzo and ensemble 1974, Khse Buon for cello 1979, Child Song I–

VII for various instrumental ensembles 1979–89, Inner Voices for chamber orchestra (Grawemeyer Award 1989) 1986, Grand Spiral 'Desert Flowers Bloom' for orchestra 1990, Spiral VI for clarinet, violin, cello and piano 1992, Water Rings for chamber orchestra 1993, Antiphonal Spirals for orchestra 1995, '...Still Life after Death' for high voice and ensemble 1995, Seven Mirrors for solo piano 1997, Spiral XII: Space between Heaven and Earth 2008. *Honours:* Kennedy Center Friedheim Award 1991, Koussevitzsky Foundation Commission 1992. *Address:* Department of Music, University of California at San Diego, CPMC 352, 9500 Gilman Drive, MC 0099, La Jolla, CA 92093-0099, USA (office). *Telephone:* (858) 822-0269 (office). *E-mail:* clung123@aol.com (office). *Website:* musicweb.ucsd.edu (office).

UNGVARY, Tamas; Swedish/Hungarian composer, conductor, double bass player, teacher and academic; b. 12 Nov. 1936, Kalocsa; one d. *Education:* Mozarteum, Salzburg, Béla Bartók Conservatory, Budapest, Univ. of California at San Diego, Qigong Akademien, Swedish School of Manual Kinesiology, Silva Mind Control. *Career:* Solo Double Bass, Camerata Academica, Salzburg 1967–69; Composer at four ISCM Festivals; has broadcast on all major European radio stations; lecturer on computer music; Artistic Man. EMS, Stockholm, Sweden and Dir of Kineto-auditory Communication Research, Royal Inst. of Tech., Stockholm; Leader, EA-Music Courses, Vienna Univ. of Music and Performing Art 1992–2002. *Compositions include:* Seul, Traum des Einsamen, Akonel No. 2 for Flute and Tape, Interaction No. 2 for Organ and Tape, Ite missa est, Dis-Tanz for Ensemble and Tape, Istenem Uram! for Tape, Sentograffito, live computer music 1993, Grattis for Tape 1994, Sinus-Coitus for piano and tape, Recollection No. 1 1996, No. 2 2007, No. 3 2007. *Film:* EMS-TU 1. *Publications:* articles and book chapters on the design of musical cyberinstruments published in scientific journals. *Honours:* Hon. Prof., Austrian Govt 1996–. *Address:* Hagalundsgatan 31, 16966 Solna, Sweden (home). *Telephone:* (8) 828991 (home). *Fax:* (8) 828991 (home). *E-mail:* ungvary@mdw.ac.at (home).

UNRUH, Stan; American singer (tenor); b. 20 Nov. 1938, Beaver, OK. *Education:* Juilliard School, New York. *Career:* debut in Geneva 1970, as Melot in Tristan; appearances at Paris, Orange, Rouen, Bordeaux (Lohengrin 1979 and Aeneas 1980) and Toulouse; mem., Krefeld Opera 1977–85, notably in Der Ring des Nibelungen; New York City Opera 1976, as Erik in Der fliegende Holländer, Strasbourg 1977, as Parsifal; further guest appearances at Barcelona 1978, Brunswick and Innsbruck 1983, Buenos Aires 1985 (Siegfried in Götterdämmerung) and Freiburg 1986, in the premiere of Hunger und Durst by Violeta Dinescu; sang at the Staatstheater Kassel 1989–90; other roles include Wagner's Tristan, Siegmund, Loge and Walther von Stolzing, Florestan, Shuratov in From the House of the Dead, Max, Don José, Samson, Stravinsky's Oedipus and Bacchus.

UNWIN, Nicholas, ARCM, DipRCM, LGSM; British pianist; b. 1962, Cambridge, England. *Education:* Royal Coll. of Music and studied with Philip Fowke. *Career:* played Bartók, Lambert and McCabe at the Purcell Room, London 1986; Bartók's 2nd Concerto at St John's Smith Square (also on BBC Radio 3); Wigmore Hall recital 1987; BBC recital 1989, followed by Univ. of Birmingham and Leeds Town Hall; Artist-in-Residence, King's Lynn Festival 1989, 1991, with Nights in the Gardens of Spain and Ravel's G major Concerto then Barber Piano Concerto with Bournemouth Symphony Orchestra; BBC documentary on Michael Tippett 1990; specialized in Spanish music, culminating in Images of Iberia at Blackheath Concert Halls; performed Tippett in Madrid and Radio France, also at Barbican's Tippett Festival 1994; first work written for him by Luis De Pablo 1997; moved to Tokyo 1999, returned to UK 2004, decided to develop his jazz skills, now promoting and playing jazz and popular styles with his trio. *Recordings:* Tippett Sonata 4, with Robert Saxton and Colin Matthews 1995, Tippett Sonatas 1–3 1995, Joaquín Nin: Piano Works 1998, Albeniz: Iberia 1999, Jean-Michel Damase: Piano Works 2003. *Honours:* Chappell Gold Medal and Cyril Smith Recital Prize, Royal Coll. of Music, Winner, Lambeth Music Award, Hastings Concerto Festival and Brant Piano Competition, Schott Award 1990, Roussel Prize, Epinal International. *Address:* Mendham Mill, Mendham, Harleston, Norfolk, IP20 0NN, England. *Website:* www.nicholasunwin.com.

UPSHAW, Dawn, MA; American singer (soprano) and academic; *Charles Franklin Kellogg and Grace E. Ramsey Kellogg Professor of the Arts and Humanities, Bard College Conservatory of Music;* b. 17 July 1960, Nashville, Tenn.; m. Michael Nott 1986 (divorced); two c. *Education:* Illinois Wesleyan Univ. and Manhattan School of Music, Metropolitan Opera School. *Career:* sang in the US premiere of Hindemith's Sancta Susanna 1983; joined young artists devt program at the Metropolitan Opera, New York after winning int. auditions sponsored by Young Concert Artists 1984; sang at the Met, appearing as Countess Ceprano, Echo (Ariadne), Adina, Despina, Susanna, Sophie (Werther), the Woodbird and Zerlina 1985–; has performed with major orchestras, opera cos and chamber groups in the USA and Europe, including the Netherlands Opera Co., Vienna Opera, Hamburg Opera, Berlin Philharmonic, Los Angeles Philharmonic, Rotterdam Philharmonic and Chicago Symphony Orchestras; festival appearances include Salzburg Festival as Barbarina 1987, as L'Ange in St François at Salzburg 1992, 1998, Clémence in Saariaho's L'Amour de loin 2000, Aix-en-Provence as Despina and Pamina 1988–89, Anne Trulove 1992, sang Pamina at the London Proms 1990, Judith Weir's Natural History 1999, sang Theodora at Glyndebourne 1996; appearances include at Barbican and Covent Garden, London, at Paris Châtelet; other roles include Marzelline (Fidelio), Constance in Les Dialogues des Carmélites, Mozart's Cherubino, Daisy in Harbison's The Great Gatsby,

Janáček's Vixen; Charles Franklin Kellogg and Grace E. Ramsey Kellogg Prof. of the Arts and Humanities, Bard Coll. Conservatory of Music 2004–, also Artistic Dir, Graduate Program in Vocal Arts; Music Dir Ojai Music Festival 2011; Head of the Vocal Arts Program, Tanglewood Music Center; Fellow, MacArthur Foundation 2007, American Acad. of Arts and Sciences 2008. *Operas include:* Rigoletto, Simon Boccanegra, Khovanshchina, Carmen, La Clemenza di Tito, Dialogues of the Carmelites, The Magic Flute 1985, Death in the Family 1986, Alice in Wonderland, The Marriage of Figaro (also on TV), L'elisir d'amore 1988, Così fan Tutte 1988, Idomeneo 1988–89, Werther 1988–89, Don Giovanni 1989–90. *Recordings include:* Ariadne auf Naxos, songs by Rachmaninov, Hugo Wolf, Richard Strauss, Charles Ives and Kurt Weill, songs and pieces by Samuel Barber, John Harbison, Stravinsky and Gian-Carlo Menotti (Grammy Award for Best Classical Vocal Soloist 1990), Bach's Magnificat and Vivaldi's Gloria 1989, Lucio Silla, L'elisir d'amore, Henryk Górecki Symphony No 3: Symphony of Sorrowful Songs (Symfonia pieśni żałosnych) 1993, Voices of Light 2005, Dawn Upshaw Sings Rodgers and Hart 2007, Dawn Upshaw – The Girl with Orange Lips 2008, Mozart: Le Nozze di Figaro - Highlights (with Thomas Hampson 2014, Winter Morning Walks (with Maria Schneider) (Grammy Award for Best Classical Vocal Soloist 2014). *Honours:* Dr hc (Yale Univ., Manhattan School of Music, Illinois Wesleyan Univ., Allegheny Coll., Juilliard School); jt first prize, Naumburg Competition 1985, Opera News Award for invaluable contribution to opera 2012. *Current Management:* Colbert Artists Management, 307 Seventh Avenue, Suite 2006, New York, NY 10001, USA. *Address:* Bard College, 30 Campus Road, Annandale-on-Hudson, NY 12504-5000, USA (office). *Telephone:* (845) 758-7196 (office). *E-mail:* conservatory@bard.edu (office).

URBAIN, Mady; Belgian singer (mezzo-soprano); b. 27 April 1946, Montegnée. *Education:* Liège Conservatoire, studied in Vienna and Salzburg. *Career:* sang at the Liège Opera from 1967, and made many guest appearances elsewhere in Belgium and throughout France; roles have included Amneris, Preziosilla, Mistress Quickly, Carmen, Marcellina, Charlotte, Puccini's Princess (Suor Angelica) and Suzuki, Strauss's Adelaide and Mère Marie in The Carmélites; concerts include Messiah, Bach's B Minor Mass, the Verdi Requiem and Beethoven's Ninth; Professor at the Grétry Academy, Liège, from 1970.

URBANNER, Erich; Austrian composer and conductor; b. 26 March 1936, Innsbruck. *Education:* Vienna Music Acad. with Hans Swarowsky, Darmstadt courses with Bruno Maderna and Karl-Heinz Stockhausen. *Career:* Prof., Vienna Music Acad. 1969–; Dir, Institut für Electroakustik und Experimentelle Musik 1986–89. *Compositions include:* String quartets Nos 2 and 3 1957, 1972, Piano Concerto 1958, Flute Concertino 1959, Der Gluckreich (comic opera) 1963, Oboe Concerto 1966, Violin Concerto 1971, Concerto 'Wolfgang Amadeus' 1972, Sinfonietta '79 1979, Cello Concerto 1981, Requiem 1983, Ninive, oder Das Leben geht weiter (opera) 1987, Concerto for saxophone quartet and orchestra 1989, Quasi una fantasia for 15 instruments 1993, Zyklus for organ 1993, Begegnung for 12 instruments 1996, Formen in Wandel for piano 1996.

URBANOVÁ, Eva; Czech singer (soprano); b. 20 April 1961, Slaný. *Education:* Acad. of Musical Arts. *Career:* opera debut at Plzeň Josef Kajetan Tyl Theatre 1987; soloist, Plzeň Opera 1988–90; Chief of Opera Singer section, Conservatory Plzeň 1989; soloist, Nat. Theatre Opera, Prague 1990–, Metropolitan Opera, New York 1996–; charity concert tours with Karel Gott, Czech Repub. 1998; concert tours and opera performances in Canada, France, Italy, USA (Dvořák operas), Hong Kong (Janáček operas) and Germany (Verdi opera); charity concerts after floods in Czech Repub. 2002. *Recordings include:* Celeste Aida: Famous Opera Arias (Grammy Award) 1998, Duets (with Karel Gott) 1998, Czech Opera Airs 1998, Czech Christmas Carols 2000. *Honours:* Chevalier, Ordre des Arts et des Lettres 2003–; Classic Prize for propagation of Czech music in the world 1999, Ceny Thálie (for her portrayal of Kostelnička) 1997, Dora Mavor Moore Award for Outstanding Performance in an Opera (for her portrayal of Kostelnička) 2003. *Website:* www.evaurbanova.com/en.

URBAŃSKI, Krzysztof; Polish conductor; *Music Director, Indianapolis Symphony Orchestra;* b. 1982, Pabianice; m. Joanna Urbański. *Education:* Chopin Music Acad., Warsaw. *Career:* Asst Conductor, Warsaw Philharmonic Orchestra 2007–09; Chief Conductor, Trondheim Symphony Orchestra 2010–; Music Dir Indianapolis Symphony Orchestra 2011–; Prin. Guest Conductor, Tokyo Symphony Orchestra 2013–; fmr Guest Conductor with WDR Sinfonieorchester, Oslo Philharmonic Orchestra, Wiener Symphoniker, Finnish Radio Symphony Orchestra, Deutsche Kammerphilharmonie Bremen, Nat. Symphony Orchestra Washington, Los Angeles Philharmonic, Tokyo Symphony Orchestra; Adjunct Prof. of Music (Orchestral Conducting), Jacobs School of Music, Indiana Univ. 2010–. *Honours:* First Prize, Prague Spring Int. Conducting Competition 2007. *Current Management:* Harrison-Parrott Ltd, 5-6 Albion Court, Albion Place, London, W6 0QT, England. *Telephone:* (20) 7313-3531 (office). *E-mail:* jennifer.spencer@harrisonparrott.co.uk (office). *Website:* krzysztofurbanski.com.

URBANYI-KRASNODĘBSKA, Zofia Jadwiga, MA; Polish conductor; *Professor, Karol Lipinski Academy of Music;* b. 18 March 1934, Bydgoszcz; d. of the late F. Z. Urbanyi and Jadwiga Urbanyi; m. Ryszard Krasnodębska 1975; one s. *Education:* Frederick Chopin Acad. of Music, Warsaw. *Career:* Conductor, Choirmaster, then Man. Great Theatre Choir, Warsaw 1957–72; Conductor State Opera House, Wrocław 1972–80; Founder Warsaw Madrigal Ensemble y Musici Cantanti 1966; Founder and Chief Conductor, Frassino Stormente Choir in Wrocław 1986; Founder, organizer and promoter Int. Tournament of Choir Conducting, Wrocław 1991, 1999, 2005; Lecturer, Frederick Chopin Acad. of Music; Lecturer then Prof. Karol Lipinski Univ. of Music, Wrocław 1980–; Man. Feichtinum Academic Choir; Prin. Conducting Inst.; has performed in Yugoslavia, Czechoslovakia, Germany, Italy, Belgium, the Netherlands, France, Belarus, Spain and Russia; has composed music for choirs, and made radio recordings; expert for Gen. Council of Higher Educ. *Honours:* prizes from Ministry of Culture and Fine Arts 1989, 1991, 2001, 2004; Medal of Nat. Educ. Cttee 2000. *Address:* Karol Lipinski Univ. of Music, pl. Jana Pawla II 2, 50-043 Wrocław (office); nl. M. Kasprzaka 4/1, 51-676 Wrocław, Poland (home). *Telephone:* (71) 3555543 (office); (71) 3478318 (home). *Fax:* (71) 3552849 (office). *E-mail:* info@amuz.wroc.pl (office). *Website:* www.amuz.wroc.pl (office).

URIA-MONZON, Beatrice; French singer (mezzo-soprano); b. 28 Dec. 1963, Agen; d. of Antonio Uria-Monzon and Anne-Marie Uria-Monzon (née Biar); one c. *Education:* Univ. of Bordeaux, Conservatoire Nat. de musique de Bordeaux, Opéra Nat. de Paris. *Career:* debut at Nancy, 1989, as Cherubino in The Marriage of Figaro by Mozart; Lyon and Aix, 1989, as Smeraldine in The Love for Three Oranges by Prokofiev; Sang Mignon at Avignon 1990, Charlotte in Werther by Massenet at Opéra de Rouen 1990, Opéra de Lille 1993, Teatro di Bologna 1993, Opéra comique de Paris 1994, Théâtre du Capitole 1997; Béatrice in Béatrice and Bénédict by Berlioz at Théâtre du Capitole, Opéra de Nantes, Opéra de Lyon 1991, Baden Baden 1992, Opéra de Nancy 2000; Marguerite in La Damnation de Faust at The Royal Opera of Wallonia 1992, Avignon 1993, Opéra de Paris 1995, 1997; Carmen at the Opéra Bastille, 1993, 1994, 1997, 1998, 1999, Buenos Aires 1994, Grand théâtre de Bordeaux 1994, Royal Opera of Wallonia 1995, Teatro Massimo, Palermo 1996, Teatro di Torino 1996, Théâtre du Capitole 1997, Chorégies d'Orange, Vienna Staatsoper, Metropolitan Opera, New York 1998. *Recordings include:* Beethoven's Ninth; The Love for Three Oranges; Carmen. *Honours:* Chevalier des Arts et des Lettres. *Current Management:* c/o Agence Artistique Thérèse Cédelle, Boulevard Malesherbes 78, 75008 Paris, France. *Telephone:* 1-49-53-00-02. *Fax:* 1-45-63-70-23. *E-mail:* Agence.Cedelle@wanadoo.fr. *E-mail:* beatrice.uriamonzon@free.fr. *Website:* beatrice.uriamonzon.free.fr.

URMANA, Violeta; Lithuanian singer (soprano); b. 1961. *Education:* Vilnius and Munich High Schools for Music. *Career:* fmr mezzo-soprano, now soprano; sang at the Munich Opera from 1992; State Opera of Stuttgart 1994; Lucerne Opera as Princess Eboli, and Bayreuth as Waltraute 1994; Opéra Bastille and Ravenna Festival 1995, as Fenena in Nabucco; season 1996 at La Scala as Wagner's Fricka and La Haine in Gluck's Armide; Azucena at the Deutsche Oper Berlin; further roles include Santuzza, Preziosilla and Eboli in Don Carlos (Vienna Staatsoper); concerts include Das Lied von der Erde in Bologna and Bach's B minor Mass at Wuppertal 1996; season 1998 as Kundry at the Deutsche Oper Berlin, Eboli with the Royal Opera at Edinburgh, Bartók's Judith at Aix; Act II of Parsifal with Placido Domingo at St Petersburg; season 2000–01 as Azucena at La Scala, Adalgisa in Seville, Santuzza at Florence, Amneris in Geneva, Waltraute for the Bayreuth Festival and Kundry at the Met (debut role); sang Kundry at Covent Garden 2002; Les Troyens in Florence and Iphigénie en Aulide in Milan 2002; Tosca in Florence and Los Angeles 2005, Ariadne auf Naxos, Metropolitan Opera, New York 2005; Aida at La Scala, Milan 2006; Ighigénie en Tauridde in Valencia 2008. *Honours:* Royal Philharmonic Soc. Award for Singers 2002, Premio della Critica Musicale 'Franco Abbiati' 2003. *Current Management:* Caecilia Lyric Department, Rennweg 15, 8001 Zürich, Switzerland. *Telephone:* 442213388. *Fax:* 442117182. *E-mail:* caecilia@caecilia-lyric.ch. *Website:* www.caecilia.ch.

URRILA, Irma; Finnish singer (soprano); b. 29 Jan. 1943, Helsinki. *Education:* studied in Helsinki, Milan and Essen. *Career:* debut in Helsinki 1964, as Mimi in La Bohème; sang with the Finnish Nat. Opera, notably as Pamina, and in the 1975 premiere of The Last Temptations by Jonas Kokkonen; premiere of Antonio Bilbalo's Macbeth, Oslo 1990; sang throughout Scandinavia in concert and opera; many broadcasts and appearances; Pamina in the film version of Die Zauberflöte, directed by Ingmar Bergman. *Recordings include:* Die Zauberflöte, The Last Temptations. *Honours:* prizewinner Lonigo Competition 1965, Parma Competition 1996.

URROWS, David Francis, AB, MMus, DMA; American composer and music historian; *Associate Professor and Director of Research, Hong Kong Baptist University;* b. 25 Oct. 1957, Honolulu, HI. *Education:* Brandeis Univ., Univ. of Edinburgh, UK, Boston Univ. *Career:* compositions performed, commissioned and broadcast in N America, Asia and Europe; taught at Boston Univ., Univ. of Massachusetts, Hong Kong Acad. for Performing Arts, Eastern Mediterranean Univ.; Conductor, Hong Kong Bach Choir 1989–91, Cecilian Singers 1997–2000; Dean, Peninsula/Palo Alto Chapter, American Guild of Organists 1995–97; Assoc. Prof., Hong Kong Baptist Univ. 2001–, also Dir of Research; Dir The Pipe Organ in China Project 1989–; Fellow, Virginia Center for the Creative Arts 1986. *Compositions:* String Quartet 1978, Piano Sonata 1979, A Midsummer Night's Dream (opera) 1980, Quintet for winds 1981, Three Vailima Episodes for soprano and string orchestra 1984, A New England Almanack for baritone and piano 1985, Duo for oboe and harp 1985, Partita: Nun Komm, der Heiden Heiland for organ 1985, Sonata San Angelo for two violas 1986, Ricordanza dell'Umbria for piano 1987, Lycidas (oratorio) 1987, Winterreise for soprano and chamber orchestra 1988, Sonata for violin and piano 1991, Epiphany Cantata 1993, Nova Gaudia for mixed voices and organ

1997, Exaltabo te for soloists, choir and orchestra 2005, Prelude and A Psalm of Francis Thompson for mixed voices, organ, timpani, and strings 2007, La Castrata (opera) 2009, Paroles pour musique (peut-être), for mezzo, baritone and piano 2012; numerous shorter choral works and art songs. *Publications include:* The Choral Music of Christopher le Fleming 1986, Randall Thompson: A Bio-Bibliography 1991, Otto Dresel: Collected Vocal Music (ed.) 2002, Word and Music Studies, Vol. 7 (ed.) 2005, Vol. 9 (ed.) 2008, Otto Dresel: Chamber Music (ed.) 2009; numerous journal articles and reviews in The American Organist, American Music, Journal of the Society for American Music, Journal of Musicological Research, The Tracker, American Choral Review. *Honours:* Reiner Prize in Composition, Brandeis Univ. 1978, Julius Adams Stratton Preis-Stipendium 1980, ASCAP Foundation Grant to Young Composers Award 1981, Malloy Miller Composition Prize, Boston Univ. 1985, ASCAP Special Awards 1987–, Winner, Nat. Asscn of Teachers of Singing Art Song Composition Contest 1987, Outstanding Teaching Award, Hong Kong Baptist Univ. 1990. *Address:* Department of Music, Hong Kong Baptist University, Kowloon Tong, Hong Kong Special Administrative Region, People's Republic of China (office). *Telephone:* 3411-7596 (office). *Fax:* 3411-7870 (office). *E-mail:* urrows@hkbu.edu.hk (office). *Website:* mus.hkbu.edu.hk/urrows.html (office).

URTEAGA, Irma Graciela; Argentine composer and pianist; b. 7 March 1929, San Nicolás, Buenos Aires; widow. *Education:* Nat. Conservatory and Instituto del Teatro Colón, Buenos Aires. *Career:* Prof., Instituto del Teatro Colón 1964–84 (Coach 1974–78, Prof. Summer Courses 1985–93), Nat. Conservatory 1974–88; Coach, Opera from Ecuador 1986, 1987, 1988. *Compositions:* Piano Sonata 1968, String Quartet 1969, Ambitos for orchestra 1970, Existenciales for voice and piano 1974, Designios for flute, clarinet, viola, and piano 1976, Expectación for soprano and mixed choir 1977, Turbulencias for violin and piano 1979, Sueños de Yerma for mezzo and ensemble 1986, La maldolida (chamber opera) 1987, El mundo del ser for mezzo and orchestra 1990, Luz de mundos for choir 1990, Los alumbramientos for children's choir or female choir and string orchestra 1992, Escalénicas for piano 1992, Cánticos para soñar for voice and piano 1993, Marimba Concerto 1994, Tiempo de memorias for clarinet, violin and piano 1996, Variaciones sobre un tema de Beatriz Sosnik for piano 1997, Aquellos villancicos for choir

1999, Todavía Buenos Aires for saxophone quartet 2000, Ayer del Buen Ayre for piano 2001 (two-piano version 2004), Tangoforte for violin, French horn and piano 2003 (violin, cello and piano version 2004), Mar verde, verde… for baritone, soprano and percussion 2004, La mariposa en el pozo for cello and mezzo-soprano 2005, Cordamentes for viola d'amore and violin 2006, Silencio de alas, amor y sombras, four-song cycle for baritone and piano based on poems by Héctor Daniel Dei 2007. *Honours:* City Hall Award 1974, 1976, 1977, Nat. Fund for the Arts 1976, 1980, 1988, Lifetime Achievement Award, Nat. Fund for the Arts 2009, Life Achievement Award, Argentine Music Critics Asscn . *Address:* Rio Bamba 944, 6-C, 1116 Buenos Aires, Argentina (home). *Telephone:* (11) 48130435 (home). *Fax:* (11) 48130435 (home). *E-mail:* irmaurteaga2015@gmail.com. *Website:* www.irmaurteaga.com.ar.

USHAKOVA, Natalia; Russian singer (soprano); b. 1969, Tashkent. *Education:* Munich Conservatoire, Germany. *Career:* appearances with the Kirov Opera, St Petersburg, from 1998, as Maria in Mazeppa, Lyubka in Prokofiev's Semyon Kotko, Tatiana (Eugene Onegin) and Mozart's Countess and Donna Elvira; sang with the Kirov Opera in Summer season at Covent Garden, 2000. *Honours:* prizewinner Wroclaw International Competition 1993, Pechkovsky St Petersburg Competition 1994, Volkswagen Competition 1997.

USPENSKAYA, Maria; Russian musician (harpsichord, piano); b. 1982, Moscow. *Education:* Gnessin Special School of Music, Moscow Tchaikovsky Conservatory, Sweelinck Conservatory, Amsterdam. *Career:* concert tours in Germany and South Korea; int. festivals include Utrecht, Netherlands 2003, Sopron, Hungary 2005, Helsinki, Finland 2006, St Petersburg, Russia 2006–10, Bach Festival, Dordrecht, Germany 2010; appeared with Alexey Shevchenko (piano duet), Dmitry Sinkovsky (baroque violin) and Paolo Pandolfo (viola da gamba); performed with The Piccola Accademia di Montisi, London 2007; Chair, Keyboard Instruments, Historical and Contemporary Performance Dept, Moscow Conservatory 2007–. *Honours:* winner, Int. Johann Sebastian Bach Competition, harpsichord 2010. *Address:* Moscow P. I. Tchaikovsky Conservatory, 125009 Moscow, Bolshaya Nikitskaya Street 13/6, Russia (office). *Telephone:* (495) 629-94-01 (office). *E-mail:* maalusp@yahoo .com (home).

V

VACCHI, Fabio; Italian composer; b. 19 Feb. 1949, Bologna; m. Lidia Bramani; three c. *Education:* Bologna Conservatory, Accad. Chigiana, Siena and Tanglewood, USA. *Career:* has written for Berlin Philharmonic Orchestra, Teatro alla Scala, Opera Nat. de Lyon, Radio France, Opéra Comique and Théâtre du Châtelet, Paris, Nat. Symphony Orchestra, Washington, DC, Pittsburgh Orchestra, Wien Modern, Wiener Philharmoniker, Hilliard Ensemble, Tokyo String Quartet, Accad. Chigiana; compositions have been conducted and commissioned by Claudio Abbado, Riccardo Chailly, Riccardo Muti, Zubin Mehta, MyungWun Chung, Daniel Harding, Sir Neville Marriner, Luciano Berio, Antonio Pappano, Giuseppe Sinopoli; fmr Prof. of Composition, Conservatorio Giuseppe Verdi, Milan; currently Prof. of Composition, Scuola di Musica, Fiesole; mem. Accad. Nazionale di Santa Cecilia; Composer-in-Residence, Bari's Teatro Petruzzelli and Milan's Orchestra Verdi. *Compositions include:* Il Viaggio (opera) 1990, 1989, Luoghi immaginari, for ensemble 1987–92, La station thermale (opera) 1993, Dai Calanchi di Sabbiuno (by Claudio Abbado), for orchestra 1997, Les Oiseaux de passage (opera) 1998, Quartet No. 3 (by Tokyo Quartet, Lully Award for the Best New Piece of the Year, USA 2002), Tre Veglie (Salzburger Festspiele) 2000, Diario dello sdegno (Scala, Riccardo Muti) 2002, Terra Comune, for the opening of the new Rome Auditorium (for orchestra and choir, Myung-Whun Chung) 2002, Il Letto della storia (opera) (Abbiati Prize, Associazione Nazionale Critici Musicali) 2003, La giusta Armonia (Riccardo Muti, Salzburger Festspiele) for orchestra 2006, Teneke, Scala (opera) 2007, Prospero, o dell'Armonia (Scala, Riccardo Chailly) 2009, D'un tratto nel folto del bosco (melologue, Milan) 2010, Lo stesso mare (opera, Bari) 2011, Notte italiana (Milan, Turin, London Sinfonietta, D. Atherton) 2011, Il piacere di leggere (melologue, L'Aquila) 2012, Triplo concerto (Bari) 2013, Veronica Franco (Milan) 2014, Il bordo vertiginoso delle cose (melologue, Bari) 2014, Der Walddämon, (conductor R. Chailly, Lipsia, Gewandhaus Orchestra) 2015, Sull'acqua- Sotto di noi il diluvio (melologue, Milano) 2015, Lo specchio magico (opera, Florence) 2016; contribs to film scores: Ermanno Olmi's Il Mestiere delle Armi (David di Donatello Prize, for the Best Incidental Music 2002), Cantando dietro i Paraventi and I Cento Chiodi 2007, Patrice Chéreau's Gabrielle (Colonna Sonora Prize, RDC Award) 2005. *Honours:* Hon. mem. Accad. Filarmonica di Bologna; Koussevitsky Prize for Composition, Tanglewood 1974, First Prize, Gaudeamus Competition 1976, Lully Award (USA) 2003, Premio Abbiati della Critica Musicale Italiana 2004; Koussevitzky Prize in Composition, Tanglewood 1974, First Prize, Gaudeamus Competition 1976. *Address:* via Montegani 4–1, 20141 Milan, Italy. *Telephone:* (02) 8436798 (home). *E-mail:* fabio.vacchi@fastwebnet.it (office).

VĂDUVA, Leontina; French singer (soprano); b. 1 Dec. 1960, Rosiile, Romania; d. of Maria Ciobanu; m. Gheorghe Codre. *Education:* Bucharest Conservatoire. *Career:* gained political asylum in France; debut in Massenet's Manon, Toulouse 1987; appeared as Ninetta in La Gazza Ladra at the Théâtre des Champs Elysées, Paris 1988; Covent Garden debut as Manon 1988; appeared at Covent Garden as Gilda in Rigoletto 1989; sang Drusilla at Théâtre du Châtelet, Paris, and at the Grand Théâtre, Geneva; other roles included appearances in Les Pêcheurs de Perles and L'Elisir d'amore at Toulouse, Manon at Montpellier, Bordeaux, Avignon, Paris (Opéra Comique) and Vienna, Rigoletto at Bonn, Donizetti's Il Campanello di Notte at Monte Carlo, Les Contes d'Hoffmann in Paris (Théâtre du Châtelet) and London (Covent Garden), Ismene in Mitridate by Mozart at the Châtelet, Micaela in Carmen at Covent Garden (returned 1996 as Mimi); sang Juliet in Romeo and Juliet at Covent Garden, Adina at Barcelona, Marguerite and Mimi at Los Angeles, Poulenc's Blanche at La Scala, Offenbach's Antonia for Festival d'Orange and Adina at Savonlinna 2000; season 2003–04 as Euridice at Barcelona, as Marguérite in Turin, Alice Ford for Bordeaux Opéra and Mimi on tour of Japan for Catania Opera. *Recordings include:* Mitridate, Le nozze di Figaro 1993. *Honours:* Chevalier, Ordre des Arts et des Lettres 1998, Grand Officer Order of Merit (Romania); winner Concours de Chant, Toulouse 1986, Hertogenbosch Competition, Netherlands 1987, Olivier Award for Outstanding Achievement in Opera 1988, Medal of the City of Toulouse. *Current Management:* Stafford Law, Candleway, Broad Street, Sutton Valence, Kent ME17 3AT, England. *Website:* www.stafford-law.com.

VAGGIONE, Horacio; Argentine composer; b. 21 Jan. 1943, Cordoba. *Education:* Nat. Univ. of Cordoba. *Career:* co-founder, Experimental Music Centre, Univ. of Cordoba 1964–69; Alea Electronic Music Group, Madrid, Spain 1969–74; Computer Music Project, Univ. of Madrid 1970–73; guest composer, IRCAM/Centre Georges Pompidou 1981–85, Groupe de Musique Experimentale de Bourges, France 1983, Technische Universität, West Berlin 1987–88; Dir Electro-acoustic Music Studio, Univ. of Paris VIII 1985–; performances of works at Festivals of Warsaw, Stockholm, Berlin, Kassel, Frankfurt, Amsterdam, Helsinki, Oslo, Paris, Venice, La Rochelle, Bourges, Geneva, Lausanne, Milan, Turin, Rome, Madrid, Athens and at UNESCO's Rostrum of Composers, World Music Days, Los Angeles Olympic Arts Festival, ICMC (Rochester, Illinois, The Hague, Venice, Paris, Cologne), British Arts of London, Berlin Kulturstadt Europas 88, Darmstadt Ferienkurse für Neue Musik. *Compositions include:* Myr-S for cello and electronics 1996, Frauyage for violin, cello and tape 1997, Nodal for tape.

VAJDA, Janos; Hungarian composer; b. 8 Oct. 1949, Miskolc. *Education:* Franz Liszt Acad., Budapest, Amsterdam Conservatory. *Career:* Prof., Budapest Acad. 1981–. *Compositions:* De Angelis, wind quintet, 1978, Stabat Mater 1978, Barabbas, opera 1978, Farewell, for orchestra 1980, Mario and the Magician, opera 1980–85, The Moment of Truth, ballet 1981, Don Juan, ballet 1981, Via Crucis, for chorus 1983, The Circus is Coming, ballet 1984, Duo, for violin and cello 1989–91, Sinfonia Retrograde, 1990, Missa in A 1990, Magnificat 1991, Double Concerto, violin and cello 1993, Leonce and Lena, opera 1990–95, Violin Concerto 1995, Two String Quartets 1995, 1997, Piano Sonata 1996, O Magnum Mysterium, for chorus 1999, Titanic 2000, Missa in H 2000, Missa in D 2001, Trio for violin, cello and piano 2001, String Quarter No. 3 2001, Sinfonietta 2001, Így volt, Így se (oratorio) 2002. *Honours:* Erkel Prize 1981, Bartók-Pasztory Prize 1990, Kossuth Prize 2003. *Current Management:* c/o ARTISJUS, Mészáros u. 15–17, PO Box 593, 1539 Budapest 114, Hungary. *Telephone:* (1) 212-1553. *Fax:* (1) 212-1544. *Address:* Pomázi str. 9, 2000 Szenteudre, Hungary (home). *Telephone:* (626) 316222 (home). *E-mail:* vajdanet@t-online.hu (home). *Website:* kincsestar.radio.hu/ktz (office).

VAJNAR, Frantisek; Czech conductor; b. 15 Sept. 1930, Strasice u Rokycan. *Education:* Prague Conservatoire. *Career:* mem. orchestra of the Prague Nat. Theatre 1950–53; conducted the ensemble of Czech Army 1953–55; conducted at the State Theatre of Karlina 1955–60, Ostrava 1960–62; Dir, Nejedly Theatre Usti nad Labem 1962–73, with operas by Smetana (complete), Dvořák, Janáček, Wagner, Verdi, Puccini, Strauss, Prokofiev, Henze and Hartmann; Conductor, Nat. Theatre Prague 1973–79, Artistic Dir from 1985; Chief Conductor, Czech Radio Symphony Orchestra 1979–85; guest conductor of the Czech Philharmonic; Dir of the Collegium Musicum Pragense; guest conductor in Australia, Brazil, Germany, France, Greece, Italy, Japan, Poland, Scandinavia, Russia and Switzerland; festival appearances at Salzburg, Vienna, Prague; conducted Prokofiev's Betrothal in a Monastery at the 1979 Wexford Festival; Teacher, Prague Acad. of Arts. *Recordings include:* Smetana The Kiss; Shostakovich 10th and 15th Symphonies (Czech Philharmonic); Beethoven Overtures; Brixi Organ Concertos; Mozart arranged Wendt Le nozze di Figaro; Dvořák's The Cunning Peasant.

VAKARELIS, Janis; Greek pianist; b. 1950, Thessaloniki. *Education:* Vienna Music Acad. with Nikita Magaloff and Bruno Leonardo Gelber. *Career:* engagements from 1979 with the Gewandhaus Orchestra, Mozarteum Orchestra of Salzburg, Zürich Chamber, Monte Carlo Philharmonic, Berlin Symphony, Stuttgart Philharmonic, Staatskapelle Dresden and BBC Symphony; recitals at the Concertgebouw in Amsterdam and the Teatro Real Madrid; festival appearances at Spoleto and Athens, BBC Prom Concerts 1986; currently Artistic Dir Nafplion International Music Festival, Greece. *Recordings include:* Prokofiev's 3rd Concerto and works by Brahms and Liszt. *Honours:* Order of the Golden Phoenix; Winner, Queen Sofia Competition, Madrid 1979, Pan-Hellenic Piano Competition and the Prix d'Academie d'Athenes. *Current Management:* Office of the Artistic Director, Nafplion International Music Festival, Trion Navarhon Square, 21 100 Nafplion, Greece. *Website:* www.nafplionfestival.gr/en; vakarelis.com.

VALADE, Pierre-André; French conductor; b. 14 Oct. 1959, Brive, France; s. of Jean Valade and Marie Valade; m. 2004. *Education:* studied flute with Michel Debost in Paris, and with Marcel Moyse, Maxence Larrieu and Alain Marion. *Career:* flautist 1979–95; numerous stage appearances, including ensemble, chamber music and soloist appearances in repertoire from Mozart 1982–95; as a soloist, numerous world premieres including Eolia by Philippe Hurel, Paris, Radio-France 1983, Jupiter by Philippe Manoury on Flute-4x, IRCAM, Paris 1987, …explosante-fixe… for flute, computer and ensemble by Pierre Boulez, Paris 1991; concerts with ensembles, including Ensemble Musique Oblique 1983–93, Ensemble Intercontemporain 1985–90, London Proms 1985, US tour with Pierre Boulez 1986; …explosante-fixe… in New York, Carnegie Hall with P. Boulez 1993; Dir Collection Pierre-André Valade, Editions Henry Lemoine, Paris 1985–95; as a conductor, Co-founder and Musical Dir Ensemble Court-Circuit, Paris 1991–2008; Chief Conductor, Athelas Sinfonietta Copenhagen 2009–14; Guest Conductor, West Australian Symphony Orchestra 1995, 1996, 1998, Melbourne Symphony Orchestra 1998, London Sinfonietta 1999–2014, Ensemble Intercontemporain 2000–06, Ensemble Modern 2001–04, Bodø Sinfonietta 2007–10, Musikfabrik Ensemble 2009, Philharmonia Orchestra 2003–04, 2013–14, BBC Symphony Orchestra 2001–05, 2010, Tonhalle Orchester, Zurich 2003, 2005, 2007, 2012, 2014, Orchestre Symphonique de Montréal 2003, 2005, Tokyo Philharmonic 2007–08, Polish Nat. Radio Symphony Orchestra 2012–13, New Zealand Symphony Orchestra 2008, Auckland Philharmonia 2012, Milano Filarmonica della Scala 2014, BBC Scottish Symphony, BBC Nat. Orchestra of Wales, Philharmonia, Ulster Orchestra, RTE Nat. Symphony Orchestra, Luxembourg Philharmonic, Oslo Philharmonic, Göteborgs Symfoniker, Orchestre Philharmonique de Radio France, Orchestre de Paris, Saarbrucken Radio Symphony, Montreal Symphony, Northern Sinfonia, Orchestra della RAI Torino, Accad. Nazionale di Santa Cecilia Rome, Teatro Carlo Felice Genova, Birmingham Contemporary Music Group; Prin. Guest Conductor, Ensemble Orchestral Contemporain, Lyon, France 2013–; festivals include Festival of Perth, Australia 1996, 1998, Ultima Festival, Oslo, Norway 1998–2006,

Festival de Strasbourg 1995–2005, Festival of Bath, UK 1999, Aldeburgh, UK 2002, Festival Présence de Radio-France, Paris 1998, 1999, 2005, Festival Manca, Nice 2001, 2003, 2007, 2011, Festival Agora, IRCAM, Paris 1998–2006, BBC Proms 2002, 2004, Festival Le Printemps des Arts de Monte Carlo 2004, 2006, 2009, 2011, Athelas New Music Festival 2010, 2011, Lucerne Festival 2002, 2004, Salzburg Easter Festival 2002, Montréal Nouvelles Musiques Festival 2003–05, Sydney Festival, Australia 2003, Milano Musica Festival, Italy 2014, Festival Manifeste Ircam 2015, 2016, Tage für neue Musik Zürich, Switzerland 2014, 2016; mem. Int. Contemporary Music Soc. *Recordings include:* A. Schoenberg: Pierrot Lunaire 1992, A. Jolivet: The Complete Works for Flute 1993, T. Murail, Portrait 1998, G. Grisey, Portrait 1998, J. Fineberg, Portrait 2002, H. Birtwistle: Theseus Game 2004, Ph. Leroux, Portrait 2004, G. Verrando, Portrait 2007, H. Dufourt, Portrait Vol. 1 2007, M. Monnet, Portrait 2010, H. Dufourt, Portrait Vol. 2 2012, T. Murail, Portrait 2015. *Publications include:* La Flûte dans le Répertoire du XXe Siècle pour Ensemble Instrumental 1987, Flûte et Créations 1991. *Honours:* Chevalier des Arts et des Lettres 2001; Grand Prix de la Nouvelle Acad. du Disque Français, Grand Prix Charles Cros 2008. *Current Management:* c/o Ralph Blackbourne, Rayfield Allied, Southbank House, Black Prince Road, London, SE1 7SJ, England. *Telephone:* (20) 3176-5503. *Fax:* 700-602-4143. *E-mail:* ralph.blackbourn@rayfieldallied.com. *Website:* www.rayfieldallied.com. *E-mail:* artisticmanagement@pierreandrevalade.com; www.pierreandrevalade.com.

VALAYRE, Sylvie; French singer (soprano); b. 10 Oct., Paris. *Education:* Conservatoire de Paris. *Career:* first performance as Lady Macbeth (now signature role), Netherlands 1995; debut at Royal Opera, Covent Garden in Nabucco 1996, Metropolitan Opera New York in Madame Butterfly 2000; has also appeared at Rome Opera, La Fenice, Venice, La Scala, Milan, Dresden Staatsoper, Leipzig Oper, Roman Arena, Verona, San Francisco Opera, Carnegie Hall, New York, Graz Opera, Opera Pacific, Madrid Opera and many others; roles include: Countess in Le nozze di Figaro, Donna Elvira in Don Giovanni, Fiordiligi in Così fan Tutte, Pamina in Die Zauberflöte, Leonora in Fidelio, Mimi in La Bohème, Magda in La Rondine, Violetta in La Traviata, Adina in L'Elisir d'Amore, Liú in Turandot, the Infante in The Dwarf, Elisabetta in Don Carlo, the Empress in Die Frau Ohne Schatten, Minnie in La Fanciulla Del West, Amelia in Ballo in Maschera, title roles in Turandot, Tosca, Norma, Manon Lescaut, Thaïs, Salome. *Current Management:* Zemsky/Green Artists Management, 104 West 73rd Street, Suite #1, New York, NY 10023, USA. *Telephone:* (212) 579-6700. *Fax:* (212) 579-4723. *E-mail:* agreen@zemskygreen.com. *Website:* www.zemskygreen.com. *E-mail:* info@sylvievalayre.com (office). *Website:* www.sylvievalayre.com.

VALČUHA, Juraj; Slovak conductor; *Chief Conductor, Orchestra Sinfonica Nazionale della Radiotelevisione Italiana (RAI);* b. 1976, Bratislava. *Education:* Bratislava Conservatory, St Petersburg Conservatory, Russia, Conservatoire National Supérieur, Paris. *Career:* Asst Dir Orchestre et Opéra Nat. de Montpellier 2003–05; Chief Conductor, Orchestra Sinfonica Naz. della RAI 2009–; guest conductor, Orchestre Nat. de France, Orchestre Philharmonique de Radio-France, Rotterdam Philharmonic, Philharmonia Orchestra, Deutsche Symphonie Orchester, Filarmonica Toscanini, Orchestre Philharmonique de Monte Carlo, Oslo Philharmonic, Gewandhaus Leipzig, Staatskapelle Dresden, Filarmonica della Scala, Orchestre Naz. dell'Accad. di Santa Cecilia, Orchestra del Maggio Musicale Florence, Wiener Symphoniker, Konzerthausorchester Berlin, NDR Symphony Orchestra Hamburg, WDR Symphony Orchestra Cologne, Munich Philharmonic, Concertgebouw Orkest Amsterdam, Danish Nat. Orhcestra, Swedish Radio Orchestra, Orchestre Philharmonique de Luxembourg, Berlin Philharmonic, Bamberg Symphony Orchestra, New York Philharmonic, Boston Symphony, Pittsburgh Symphony, Nat. Symphony Washington DC, Cincinnati Symphony, Los Angeles Philharmonic, San Francisco Symphony, Houston Symphony, Ottawa Centre Orchestra, Orchestre Symphonique Montréal, NHK Tokyo, Seoul Philharmonic; opera conducting includes Staatsoper Munich, Teatro la Fenice, Teatro Comunale Florence, Teatro Comunale Bologna, Deutsche Oper Berlin. *Honours:* Ludovít Rajter Prize 2006. *Current Management:* c/o Anne Petkov, Vermont Classics GmbH, Reinhardstrasse 47, 10117 Berlin, Germany. *Telephone:* (30) 20648078; 1721878701. *Fax:* (30) 20453480. *E-mail:* ap@vermont-classics.com. *Website:* www.vermont-classics.com.

VALDES, Maximiano; Chilean conductor; b. 17 June 1949, Santiago. *Education:* studied in Santiago, at the Santa Cecilia Rome and with Franco Ferrara. *Career:* Asst Conductor, Teatro la Fenice, Venice 1976–80; Principal Guest, Spanish Nat. Orchestra from 1984; Music Dir, Buffalo Philharmonic, USA 1989–99; Music Dir Orquesta Sinfonica del Principado de Asturias, Spain 1992–2008, Conductor Laureate 2008–; Music Dir and Principal Conductor, Puerto Rico Symphony 2008–; Artistic Dir Festival Casals, San Juan. 2010–; guest appearances with Indianapolis, Vancouver, Phoenix, Edmonton, Syracuse and San Diego symphonies, Buffalo and Louisiana Philharmonics, National Arts Centre Orchestra, Ottawa, Dresden Philharmonie, Russian State Symphony Orchestra, Warsaw, Krakow and Katowice Philharmonics, Nice Opera Orchestra, Lisbon Philharmonic and others in Spain and Europe, Malaysian Philharmonic, Orquesta de Sao Paolo, Brazil, Mexico City Philharmonic, Orquesta Sinfonica del Principado de Asturias. *Honours:* First Prize, Vittorio Gui Competition, Florence, Second Prize, Rupert Foundation Conducting Competition 1978, First Prize, Nikolai Malko Competition, Copenhagen 1980. *Address:* CM Artists, 127 West 96th Street,

#13B, New York, NY 10025, USA. *Website:* www.sinfonicapr.gobierno.pr; www.cmartists.com/artists/maximiano-valdes.htm.

VÁLEK, Vladimír; Czech conductor; b. 2 Sept. 1935, Nový Jičín; m. 1st Jana Adamová; m. 2nd Hana Patočková 1986; two s. one d. *Education:* Acad. of Musical Arts, Bratislava, Acad. of Performing Arts, Prague. *Career:* conductor with several Czech orchestras 1962–75; Conductor FOK Prague Symphony Orchestra 1975–87; Chief Conductor Prague Radio Symphony Orchestra 1985–2011; Conductor Czech Philharmonic 1996–2006; Prin. Guest Conductor Orchestra Osaka Symphoniker 2003–; Chief Conductor, Slovakian Philharmonic Orchestra 2004–07; Chief Conductor.Guest Conductor with many orchestras world-wide including The Big Radio Orchestra Leipzig, Tonkuenstler and ORF (Vienna), Israeli and Japan Philharmonics. *Performances include:* concert tours include Japan, France, Spain, USA and Singapore; has appeared as guest conductor with numerous symphony orchestras in many countries. *Recordings include:* more than 100 classical music recordings and more than 1,000 recordings for radio. *Honours:* Music Critics' Award, MIDEM Classic Cannes (for recording of piano concertos by Ervin Schulhoff) 1996, Medal of Merit 2010. *Address:* Nad údolím 24, 140 00 Prague 4, Czech Republic (home). *Telephone:* (2) 4177-1463 (home).

VALENTE, Benita; American singer (lyric soprano); b. 19 Oct. 1934, Delano, Calif.; d. of Lorenzo Giuseppe Valente and the late Severina Antonia Valente (née Masonati); m. Anthony Checchia 1959; one s. *Education:* Delano High School, Music Acad. of the West, Curtis Inst. of Music. *Career:* concert debut in New York 1960; singer with Freiburg Opera, then Nuremberg Opera, Germany 1966; US opera debut in The Magic Flute at the Metropolitan Opera, New York 1973; has performed with major nat. and int. orchestras; nat. and int. opera performances and concert recitals include Carnegie Hall, Tully Hall, Mostly Mozart Festival, Rome 1968, Paris Opera, Boston Opera, Washington Opera, Aspen Music Festival, Zürich, Switzerland, Columbus Opera 1999, Strasbourg, France, Frankfurt, Germany, Netherlands etc.; teacher, Aspen Music Festival; winner Metropolitan Opera, New York auditions 1960. *Operas include:* The Magic Flute, Turn of the Screw, Falstaff, Orfeo, Vanqui, Rigoletto, Marriage of Figaro, Rinaldo, Abduction, Ariodante, Idomeneo, Ariadne, Arabella. *Recordings include:* Schubert and Brahms songs on Marlboro Festival album 1960, David del Tredici's Night Conjure-Verse 1966. *Address:* c/o Anthony Checchia, 1616 Walnut Street, Philadelphia, PA 19103, USA (office). *Telephone:* (215) 569-4690 (office). *Fax:* (215) 569-9497 (office); (215) 732-7735 (home). *E-mail:* achecchia@marlboromusic.org.

VALENTI, James; American tenor; b. New Jersey. *Education:* Acad. of Vocal Arts, Philadelphia. *Career:* roles include Puccini's Rodolfo in La Bohème and Pinkerton in Madama Butterfly, Verdi's Duke of Mantua and Alfredo, Gounod's Roméo and Faust, Nemorino in L'Elisir d'amore and Edgardo in Lucia di Lammermoor; has appeared with Opera Nat. de Lyon, Deutsche Oper Berlin, Washington Concert Opera, Teatro alla Scala, Milan, Teatro Verdi in Trieste, Dresden's Semperoper, New York City Opera, Florida Grand Opera, Teatro dell'Opera, Rome, San Francisco Opera, Teatro Carlo Felice in Genoa, New York City Opera, Chicago Symphony at Ravinia Festival, Opéra de Marseille, Michigan Opera Theater and Palm Beach Opera; worked with conductors including Leonard Slatkin, Yves Abel, Gustavo Dudamel, Daniel Oren, James Conlon, Carlo Rizzi, Daniele Gatti; debut as Alfredo at Metropolitan Opera and Royal Opera House, Covent Garden 2010. *Honours:* awards at voice competitions include Licia Albanese-Puccini 2002, Opera Index 2003, Mario Lanza 2003, Violetta Du Pont/Opera Florham 2004, George London Foundation 2004, Loren Zachary 2004, Caruso Int., Dallas Opera's Maria Callas Debut Artist of the Year 2009, winner, Richard Tucker Award 2010. *Current Management:* c/o Jack Mastroianni, IMG Artists, 152 West 57th Street, 5th Floor, New York, NY 10019, USA. *Telephone:* (212) 994-3500. *E-mail:* jmastroianni@imgartists.com. *Website:* www.imgartists.com. *E-mail:* james@jamesvalenti.com. *Website:* www.jamesvalenti.com.

VALERA, Roberto; Cuban composer; b. 21 Dec. 1938, Havana. *Education:* Havana Conservatory, Warsaw School of Music. *Career:* Prof. of Composition, Instituto Superior de Arte, Havana 1976–. *Compositions include:* Toccata for piano 1965, Conjuro for soprano and orchestra 1967, Devenir for orchestra 1969, Iré a Santiago for mixed chorus 1969, Tres Impertinencias for 12 instruments 1971, Quisiera for mixed chorus 1971, Es rojo for baritone, flute and piano 1979, Violin Concerto 1982, Concierto por la paz for saxophone and orchestra 1985, Ajiaco for tape 1989, Nadie oye for female chorus 1990, Palmas for tape 1991, Tierra de sol, cielo y tierra for ensemble 1992, Periodo espacial for tape 1993, Yugo y estrella for soprano, baritone, chorus and orchestra 1995, Hic et Nunc for tape 1996, Concierto de Cojimer for guitar and orchestra 1998. *E-mail:* rvalera@cubarte.cult.cu.

VALERA CHAMIZO, Roberto, MM; Cuban composer and teacher; *Professor of Composition and Contemporary Techniques, Instituto Superior de Arte;* b. 21 Dec. 1938, Havana. *Education:* Havana Municipal Conservatory, Havana Pedagogical School, Havana Univ., Warsaw Conservatory, Poland. *Career:* teacher at elementary and high schools, Havana 1957–64; began composing 1961; Musical Adviser, Cuban Inst. of Cinematographic Arts and Industry 1961–64, 1967–68; taught harmony, counterpoint, composition and contemporary techniques, Alejandro García Caturla School of Music 1967–76, Asst Dir 1967–68; taught classes in harmony, counterpoint, composition and contemporary technique, Nat. School of the Arts 1967–76, Asst Dir 1972, Dir 1973–76; Prof. of Composition and Contemporary Techniques, Music Faculty,

Instituto Superior de Arte, Havana 1976–, Asst Dean 1976–79, 1987–90; mem. Asscn of Musicians (pres. 1989–92). *Compositions for film:* Revolución en el mar 1961, Minerva traduce el mar 1964, Pueblo de estrellas bajas 1964, Era Nickel Co. 1964, Escena de los mueles 1967, Páginas del diario de José Marti 1967, El mar 1967, La salación 1967, Sigma 33 1967, Tránsito 1967, Angola victoria de la esperanza 1967, Che, hoy y siempre 1967, El cero 1967. *Compositions:* Mi niña 1960, Soy como un niño distraido 1960, Es por ti 1960–63, Las cebollas mágicas 1961, Estudio ritmico (ballet) 1962, Siete piezas para piano 1962, Ensayo (ballet) 1963, Chachachá 1963, Música para cuerdas 1964, Toccata 1965, Cuarteto de cuerdas 1966, Cinco mínimas 1966, Conjuro 1967, Culturosamente 1968, Iré a Santiago 1969, Devenir 1969, Claustros de mármol 1970, Tres impertinencias 1971, Quisiera (or Guaguancaglia, quasi una passacaglia) 1971, Retrato de Camilo 1972, Qué yo pueda tocar 1973, Así cantaba que yo la ví 1975, Extraplan 1975, Compañero Presidente 1975, Dos líneas 1976, Diálogos para uno solo 1978, Vocalizo 1978, Es rojo 1979, Capitán Camilo 1979, La pequeñas balada de Plovdiv 1980, Solo de guitarra 1980, Tiempo para un tiempo 1980, Movimiento concertante 1980, Tiempo para un tiempo 1980, Responde tú 1980, Concierto para violín y orquesta 1982, Rondo cubana 1984, Concierto por la paz 1985, Cuba, tu cielo y tu bandera 1985, Cubana 1986, Lágrimas barrocas 1988, Madrigal 1988, Ajiaco 1989, La barbacoa 1989, Si a mí me hubieran dicho 1989, Yo soy el que te canta 1989, La vida empieza a correr 1989, Nadie oye 1990, Palmas 1991, Tierra de sol, cielo y tierra 1992, Aquí en Varadero 1992, Período espacial 1993, Yugo y estrella 1995, Hic et Nunc 1996, Concierto de Cojímar 1998. *Honours:* Premio Alcaldia 1960, Highest Nat. Cultural Award 1982, winner Cuban Nat. Compositional Contest, Ministry of Cultural Affairs 1985; Order Alejo Carpentier 1988. *Address:* Instituto Superior de Arte, Calle 120, No. 1110 entre 9na y 13, Cubanacán Playa, Havana, 12100, Cuba (office). *Telephone:* (7) 208-0017 (office). *E-mail:* isa@isa.cult.cu (office). *Website:* www.isa.cult.cu (office).

VALJAKKA, Taru Aura Helena; Finnish singer (mezzo-soprano); b. 16 Sept. 1938, Helsinki; d. of Oiva Kumpunen and Aili Kumpunen (née Kivirinta); m. Risto Valjakka 1960; one s. one d. *Education:* Sibelius Acad., Mozarteum Salzburg, Austria, Santiago de Compostela, Spain. *Career:* Guest Prof., Estonian Music Acad. 1966–; singer with Finnish Nat. Opera 1969–89; Guest Singer, Int. Soc. for Contemporary Music 1968–90; Singing Prof., Tallinn Music Acad. 1995–; performances include Bolshoi Theatre (Moscow, USSR, now Russian Fed.) 1982, 1984, Metropolitan, New York, USA 1984, Teatro Colón, Buenos Aires 1987, and appearances in Europe, N and S America, Canada, fmr USSR, Japan and People's Repub. of China. *Recordings:* Reittersman (also film), Red Line, Lady Macbeth of Mtsensk, Peer Gynt, The Damask Drum (also film). *Honours:* Second Prize, Rio de Janeiro singing competition 1966, Sibelius Prize 1978, Pro Finlandia Medal 1989.

VALLE, José Nilo, BA, BMus, MMus, DMA; Brazilian conductor, composer and teacher; *Music Director and Conductor, Orquestra Sinfônica de Santa Catarina*; , ; b. 20 Feb. 1946, Santa Catarina State. *Education:* Paraná Music Coll., Nat. School of Music, Federal Univ. of Rio de Janeiro, Univ. of Washington School of Music, USA. *Career:* debut with Federal Univ. of Rio de Janeiro Symphony Orchestra 1983; teacher of Music Theory, Parana Music Coll.; Asst Conductor, Federal Univ. of Rio de Janeiro 1981–83; Conductor, Florianópolis Choral Asscn 1985–86; Asst Conductor, Univ. of Washington 1989–91; Founder and Conductor, Proconart Ensemble for Contemporary Music, Univ. of Washington 1989–91; Founder and Conductor, Camerata Simfonica, Seattle, WA 1989–91; founder and Music Dir and Conductor, Orquestra Sinfônica de Santa Catarina, Florianópolis 1993–; Pres. and Dir, Santa Catarina Cultural Asscn. *Address:* c/o Fundação Catarinense da Cultura, Rua Eduardo Gonçalves D'Avila 303, Santa Mônica, 88035-490 Florianópolis, Santa Catarina, Brazil (office).

VALLER, Rachel, AM, BA, DipEd; Australian pianist; b. 14 Sept. 1929, Sydney; m. Walter Travers 1965. *Education:* Conservatorium of Music, Sydney, Univ. of Sydney, studied with Ignaz Friedman. *Career:* debut in Sydney 1940; soloist, Asscn Artist of chamber ensembles, ABC radio and television; appearances with Sydney, Melbourne and Queensland Symphony Orchestras; toured with cellist André Navarra, with violinists Wanda Wilkomirska, Stoika Milanova, Zvi Zeitlin, Erick Friedman, Erich Gruenberg, Thomas Zehetmair, and bassoonist George Zukerman. *Recordings include:* lesser-known piano works of Beethoven issued to mark Beethoven bicentenary 1970, Schubert's Sonatinas with violinist Susanne Lautenbacher to commemorate 150th anniversary of his death 1978. *Honours:* Harriet Cohen Commonwealth Medal 1956. *Address:* 22 Allen's Parade, Bondi Junction, NSW 2022, Australia. *E-mail:* waltrav@bigpond.com.

VAMOS, Brandon, BMus, MMus; American cellist; s. Roland Vamos and Almita Vamos. *Education:* Eastman School of Music, studied with Paul Katz, Yale Univ., studied with Aldo Parisot. *Career:* founder mem. Pacifica Quartet 1994–, Faculty Quartet-in-Residence, Univ. of Illinois at Champagn/Urbana 2003–, Quartet-in-Residence, Metropolitan Museum of Art 2009–; faculty mem., Univ. of Illinois at Champagn/Urbana 2003–, Univ. of Chicago. *Recordings:* with The Pacifica Quartet: String Quartets by Easley Blackwood 1999, Dvorak: String Quartet No. 13 in G Major and String Quintet in E-flat Major 2001, Mendelssohn: The Complete String Quartets 2005, Declarations: Music Between the Wars 2006, Elliott Carter: String Quartets Nos 1 and 5 (Grammy Award for Best Chamber Music Performance 2009) 2008. *Honours:* Grand Prize, Coleman Chamber Music Competition 1996, Walter F. Naumburg Chamber Music Award 1998, Chamber Music America's Cleveland Quartet Award 2002, Avery Fisher Career Grant 2006, Musical America Award for Ensemble of the Year 2009. *Current Management:* Melvin Kaplan Inc., 115 College Street, Burlington, VT 05401, USA. *Telephone:* (802) 658-2592. *Fax:* (802) 658-6089. *E-mail:* music@melkap.com. *Website:* www.melkap.com. *E-mail:* pacificaquartet@yahoo.com (office); bvamos@ameritech.net (home). *Website:* www.pacificaquartet.com.

VAN ALTENA, Marius; Dutch singer (countertenor); b. 10 Oct. 1938, Amsterdam; m. Marianne Syses; two s. *Education:* Conservatory of Music, Amsterdam. *Career:* debut, Germany 1970; concerts throughout Europe and the US with early music groups; further tours to Japan and Australia, Holland Festival 1974, in Eumelio by Agazzari and in Seelewig by Staden; returned 1980, for Gluck's L'Isle de Merlin; performed with Vienna-based group Spectaculum 1980–84, in stage works by Fux, Leopold I and Conti; later turned to conducting. *Recordings include:* Leopold I's Il figliuol prodigo, Madrigals by Monteverdi, Bach Concertos with Harnoncourt and Gustav Leonhardt 1985, Hodges Ensemble with Paul V Nevel 1990–97, Camerata Trajectina 1988–97.

VAN ASPEREN, Bob; Dutch harpsichordist, clavichordist, organist and conductor; *Professor of Harpsichord, Sweelinck Conservatory, Amsterdam*; b. 8 Oct. 1947, Amsterdam. *Education:* Amsterdam Conservatory, studied with Gustav Leonhardt and Albert de Klerk. *Career:* debut in Haarlem 1968; early music specialist; from 1971 many concerts as soloist and in concert worldwide; mem., La Petite Bande, Quadro Hotteterre 1968–84; founder mem., Melante Amsterdam ensemble; teacher, Royal Conservatory, The Hague 1973–88, Berlin Hochschule from 1987; Prof. of Harpsichord, Sweelinck Conservatory, Amsterdam; holds masterclasses at summer acads in Europe and Canada. *Recordings include:* complete works of Antonio Soler (12 vols), complete printed keyboard works of C.P.E. Bach, keyboard works of Jan Pieterszoon Sweelinck, J.S. Bach's The Well Tempered Clavier Book I and II, The Toccatas, Goldberg Variations, Harpsichord Concerti Volumes I and II (with Melante Amsterdam ensemble), French Suites, English Suites, Inventions and Little Preludes. *Publications:* Complete Works of Froberger and Louis Couperin, Harpsichord Music in The Netherlands, 17th Century Keyboard Music in the Low Countries, Complete Organ Concertos by Handel, Handel Harpsichord Works, War and Peace (the Peace of Westfalia), F. Couperin Harpsichord Works, John Bull Harpsichord Works, Frescobaldi Harpsichord Works, Scarlatti Harpsichord Works, J. S. Bach Italian Coverto and Fantasia and Fugue in A minor, Transcriptions by BvA of Violin Works by J. S. Bach; articles on Froberger, Couperin, C.P.E. Bach, Cembalo Cromatico, Sweelinck. *Honours:* Edison Award, Preis der Deutschen Schallplattenkritik, Cecilia Prize, Belgium, Timbre d'Argent, Diapason d'Or, Ondas de Musica. *Current Management:* Andrea Hampl Konzertdirektion, Karl-Schrader Str. 6, 10781 Berlin, Germany. *Telephone:* (30) 4782699. *Fax:* (30) 4783792. *E-mail:* hampl@konzertdirektion.de. *Address:* Reek 3, 2121 GT, Bennebroek, The Netherlands (office). *Telephone:* (23) 5840707 (office). *E-mail:* bobvanasperen@hetnet.nl (office). *Website:* bobvanasperen.canbefoundhere.eu (office).

VAN AST, Jochem; Dutch singer (baritone); b. 1970, Amsterdam. *Education:* studied in Jerusalem; Guildhall School of Music and Drama. *Career:* appearances with The Opera Company, Kent Opera; British Youth Opera and in Hong Kong; roles have included Mozart's Count and Guglielmo, Dandini in Cenerentola, Aeneas in Dido and Aeneas, roles in The Fairy Queen, Marullo in Rigoletto, roles in Le Bourgeois Gentilhomme, Dr Falke in Die Fledermaus, Gershwin's Of Thee I Sing (debut with Opera North 1998), Figaro in Il Barbiere di Siviglia, Papageno in Die Zauberflote, Leporello in Don Giovanni, Guglielmo in Cosi fan Tutte, Dancairo in Carmen; concerts include Bach's Passions and Magnificat, Messiah, Judas Maccabaeus, Haydn's Creation and Seasons, Mozart's Requiem. *Address:* c/o Quietroom, 40 Bowling Green Lane, London EC1R 0NE, England (office). *E-mail:* info@quietroom.co.uk (office). *Website:* www.quietroom.co.uk (office).

VAN BARTHOLD, Kenneth, LRAM; British pianist and teacher; b. 10 Dec. 1927, Surabaya, Java, Indonesia; m. 1st Prudence van Barthold; m. 2nd Sarianne van Barthold; m. 3rd Gillian van Barthold; two s. two d. *Education:* Bryanston School, Paris Nat. Conservatoire of Music (class of Yves Nat), France. *Career:* debut, Bournemouth Municipal Orchestra 1944, Wigmore Hall 1956; frequent recitals in London Piano Series, Queen Elizabeth Hall and throughout UK; concerts in Canada, France, Israel and Ireland, including broadcasts; concerto appearances with numerous orchestras, including London Symphony Orchestra, English Chamber Orchestra, London Classical Players and Polyphonia under Sir Adrian Boult, Raymond Leppard, Sir Roger Norrington and Bryan Fairfax; Dir of Studies, Victoria Coll. of Music 1953–1959; Prof. of Piano, Trinity Coll. of Music 1959–65; Head of Music, City Literary Inst. 1960–1983; Univ. of Edinburgh annual master-classes during Int. Festival 1968–; Sr Piano Tutor, Inner London Educ. Authority 1983–90; Lecturer on 19th- and 20th-century Opera, Wimbledon Coll. of Art 1983–94; master-classes in Israel, Canada and throughout UK; int. juror in France, Canada and Hong Kong. *Recordings include:* Decca/Argo: Mozart Recital, Sonatas K284 and K332, Chopin Recital, Ballade No. 4, Mazurkas, Etudes etc., Schumann Recital; Decca: Couronne Compilation; Darmo: Liszt Sonata, 4 Chopin Ballades, Hommage à Pierre Max Dubois. *Television includes:* has written and presented 21 hour-long documentaries, including first ever full-length studio documentary (BBC) 1964; further frequent appearances interviewing, linking, profiling and performing on both BBC and ITV. *Publications include:* The Story of the Piano (co-author) 1976; reviewer for BBC Music Magazine and various articles. *Honours:* Critics Award (TV) 1972, Laureat du Conservatoire Nat. Supérieur de Musique de

Paris. *Address:* Arvensis, Stour Lane, Stour Row, Shaftesbury, Dorset, SP7 0QJ, England (home). *E-mail:* kvanbarthold@aol.com. *Website:* www.kennethvanbarthold.com.

VAN BOER, Bertil Herman, Jr, PhD; American musicologist, conductor and academic; *Professor of Music History and Theory, Western Washington University*; b. 2 Oct. 1952, Florida; s. of Alf Bertil Herman van Boer and Helen Shirley Bush; m. Margaret Fast 1977. *Education:* Univ. of California, Berkeley, Univ. of Oregon, Uppsala Univ., Sweden. *Career:* Musical Dir Opera Kansas 1989–95; Asst Prof., later Assoc. Prof., later Full Prof., Wichita State Univ. 1987–96; Asst Prof. of Music, Brigham Young Univ. 1983–87; Instructor, Shasta Coll. 1981–83; currently Prof. of Music History and Theory, Western Washington Univ., Dean of Coll. of Fine and Performing Arts 1996–2002. *Publications include:* The Symphony: Richter, Sweden I and II 1983–86, Joseph Martin Kraus Der Tod Jesu 1987, Joseph Martin Kraus: Systematisch-thematisches Werkverzeichnis 1988, Dramatic Cohesion in the Works of Joseph Martin Kraus 1989, Gustav III and the Swedish Stage 1993, Historical Dictionary of Music in the Classical Period 2012, The Letters of Joseph Martin Kraus 2014; contrib. of articles to Fontes, Svensk tidskrift for Musikforskning, Journal of Musicology, Journal of Musicological Research, Scandinavian Studies; numerous conf. reports. *Address:* Department of Music, Western Washington University, 516 High Street, Bellingham, WA 98225-9107, USA (office). *Telephone:* (360) 650-2282 (office). *Fax:* (360) 650-7538 (office). *E-mail:* bertil.vanboer@wwu.edu (office). *Website:* www.wwu.edu/music (office).

VAN BUREN, John Hidden, DipMus; American composer; b. 21 Sept. 1952, Portland, Ore.; m. Margret Ulrike Schaal 1988. *Education:* Reed Coll., Portland, Oregon State Univ., Staatliche Hochschule für Musik, Stuttgart, Germany, studied with Milko Kelemen, Edgar Trauer, Erhard Karkoschka. *Career:* performances of his works include ZDF national television 1979, Städtisch Bühne Mainz Ballet 1981, American Composers' Orchestra, Carnegie Hall 1987, Deutsche Sinfonie Orchester, Berlin 1994; organizer new music concerts, Stuttgart, notably as Artistic Dir and Man., Musica Nova Soc.; has taught music at Ludwigsburg Univ., John-Cranko Ballet School of Stuttgart State Opera, City School of Music, Stuttgart; teaches at Hochschule für Music Nürnberg-Augsburg, Augsburg 1991–; taught int. masterclass in Verulà, Spain. *Compositions include:* String Quartet No. 1 1981, Fünf Gesänge nach Catull 1985, Les Nuages de Magritte for violin, cello and piano 1989, Symphony No. 1: Mementos 1990, Aufbruch for orchestra 1992, String Quartet No. 2 1996, Night Scenes for orchestra 1996, Flute Concerto 1998, Luxe, Calme et Volupté for violoncello and piano 1998.

VAN DAM, José; Belgian singer (bass-baritone); b. (Joseph van Damme), 25 Aug. 1940, Brussels, Belgium; m. *Education:* Acad. de Musique, Belgium, Conservatoire Royal, Belgium. *Career:* operatic debut as Don Basilio in The Barber of Seville, Liège; debut in Paris in Carmen (Escamillo) 1961, with Grand Théâtre, Geneva 1965–67, Deutsche Oper, Berlin 1967–, Salzburg Festival, opera and concerts 1966–, Festival d'Aix en Provence 1966–, operatic repertoire includes title roles in St-François d'Assise, Wozzeck, Simon Boccanegra, Elijah, Boris Gudunov, Falstaff, Don Giovanni, The Flying Dutchman, Gianni Schicchi, the Speaker in Die Zauberflöte, Fra Melitone in La Forza del Destino, Germont in La Traviata, the Father in Louise, Claudius in Hamlet, Sachs in Die Meistersinger von Nürnberg, Amfortas in Parsifal, Jochanaan in Salome, Mephisto in Faust, Scarpia in Tosca; recital repertoire includes Verdi's Requiem, La Damnation de Faust. *Films:* Don Giovanni, 1976, The Music Teacher 1988. *Honours:* given title Kammersänger by City of Berlin 1974; named Baron by His Majesty Prince Albert II of Belgium 1998; winner, Bel Canto Competition, Liège, Concours Ecole des Vedettes, Paris, Concours de la Chanson, Toulouse, Int. Music Competition, Geneva; Gold Medal of the Belgian Press 1976, Grand Prix de l'Academie Française du Disque 1979, Orphée d'Or de l'Academie Lyrique Française 1980, European Critics' Prize 1985, Diapason d'Or, 1993, Prix de la Nouvelle Academie du Disque 1993, Orphée d'Or de l'Academie du Disque Lyrique 1994. *Current Management:* Colbert Artists Management, 307 Seventh Avenue, Suite 2006, New York, NY 10001, USA. *Telephone:* (212) 757-0782. *Fax:* (212) 541-5179. *Website:* www.colbertartists.com.

VAN DE SANT, Cécile; Dutch singer (mezzo-soprano); b. 1970, Arnhem; m.; one s. *Education:* Sweelinck Conservatory, Amsterdam, studied in New York and with Regine Crespin, Charlotte Margiono and Robert Holl. *Career:* appearances at the Göttingen Festival in cantatas by Handel and Vivaldi, and as Tauride in Handel's Arianna in Creta; sang Gualtiero in Bononcini's Griselda at Utrecht and Handel's Tamerlano in Amsterdam; other roles include Messagiera and Proserpina in Monteverdi's Orfeo, Amastre in Xerxes, Monteverdi's Nerone, Jezibaba in Rusalka, Orfeo in Gluck's Orfeo ed Euridice, Third Lady in Mozart's Die Zauberflöte, Sesto in Mozart's La Clemenza di Tito, Tauride in Handel's Arianna in Creta, Unulfo in Handel's Rodelinda, Goffredo in Handel's Rinaldo, Second Harlot and Queen of Sheba in Handel's Solomon, Cornelia in Giulio Cesare, Irene in Atalanta, Medea in Teseo, title role in Tamerlano, title role in Rossini's La Cenerentola, Rosina in Rossini's Il barbiere di Siviglia, Olga in Eugene Onegin, Geneviève, Pelléas et Mélisande, Suzuki in Puccin's Madama Butterfly, Tamiri in Il Rè pastore, Kate in Britten's Owen Wingrave; concerts include Mahler's Lieder eines fahrenden Gesellen and Knaben Wunderhorn, Elijah, Les Nuits d'été, the Alto Rhapsody and sacred music by Bach, Haydn's Seven Last Words (at the Concertgebouw, Amsterdam); season 2000–01 with Cenerentola at Kaiserslautern, Unulfo in Rodelinda at Göttingen and Messenger in Monteverdi's Orfeo at Munich, Olga in Eugene Onegin for Opera North, and Rosina for Opera Holland Park, London; 2006 roles included Cyrus in Belshazzar, San Francisco, Cornelia in Giulio Cesare, Göttingen, Cornelius' Stabat Mater, Handel's Messiah, Mozart's Requiem. *Recordings:* Mitridate, La Clemenza di Tito, Matteus Passie. *Current Management:* c/o Athole Still Opera Ltd, Foresters Hall, 25–27 Westow Street, London, SE19 3RY, England. *Telephone:* (20) 8771-5271. *Fax:* (20) 8771-8172. *E-mail:* enquiries@atholestill.co.uk. *Website:* www.atholestill.co.uk.

VAN DE VATE, Nancy Hayes, AB, MM, DrMus; American/Austrian composer, record producer and music publisher; *President and Artistic Director, Vienna Modern Masters*; b. (Nancy Jean Hayes), 30 Dec. 1930, Plainfield, New Jersey; d. of John Fleming Hayes and Anna T. Hayes; m. 1st Dwight Van de Vate, Jr 1952 (died 2012); one s. two d.; m. 2nd Clyde Arnold Smith 1979 (died 1999). *Education:* Eastman School of Music, Univ. of Rochester, Wellesley Coll., Univ. of Mississippi, Florida State Univ., postdoctoral study in electronic music at Dartmouth Coll. and Univ. of New Hampshire. *Career:* opera premieres: In the Shadow of the Glen, Cambridge, Massachusetts, USA 1999, All Quiet on the Western Front (Acts II and III), New York City Opera 2003, Im Westen nichts Neues, Osnabrück, Germany 2003, Where the Cross is Made, Illinois State Univ. 2005; orchestral premieres: Distant Worlds, Concerto for Percussion and Orchestra, Concertpiece for Cello and Small Orchestra, all premiered by Polish Radio Symphony Orchestra of Kraków, Szymon Kawalla conductor 1987–89; premieres, Musica Viva Festival, Munich, Aspekte, Salzburg, Poznań Spring Festival, Poland, Chernobyl for orchestra, Vienna 1994, Dark Nebulae, Vienna Musikverein 2000; Pres. and Artistic Dir Vienna Modern Masters 2000–; Vice-Pres. Österreichische Frauenkammerorchester, Vienna 2004–09; mem. Int. Honour Cttee of Fondazione Donne in Musica, Rome 2003–; Composer-in-Residence, Festival of Women in Music, Eastman School of Music, Univ. of Rochester 2008, Inst. for European Studies, Vienna 2010–12; composer portrait concert, Austrian Nat. Library 2009; Opera Extraganza (five Van de Vate chamber operas and music theatre works), Longy School of Music 2010; Adagio Expressivo for string orchestra, Mürzzuschlag and Vienna, Austria 2010, 2011; frequent radio broadcasts of recorded works in Africa, Asia, Australia, Europe, N and S America. *Compositions include:* Cocaine Lil, 5 singers, percussion; Teufelstanz, percussion ensemble, A Night in the Royal Ontario Museum, soprano, CD, Pura Besakih for large orchestra, Nine Preludes for Piano, Twelve Pieces for Piano (vols 1, 2, 3), Trio for Violin, Violoncello and Piano, many choral, vocal, brass and solo string works, Viola Concerto, Four Sombre Songs, for mezzo and orchestra; premieres: Katyn 1989, Polish Radio Symphony Orchestra and Chorus, S. Kawalla, Conductor; Concerto for Violin and Orchestra 1992, Vienna Konzerthaus, Vienna Musiksommer; operas: Nemo: Jenseits von Vulkania, In the Shadow of the Glen, All Quiet on the Western Front, Where the Cross is Made, Mozart Year for String Quartet No. 2 2006. *Recordings include:* Operas Nemo: Jenseits von Vulkania, Im Westen Nichts Neues (All Quiet on the Western Front), In the Shadow of the Glen, Where the Cross is Made, and Hamlet; orchestral works with Polish Radio Symphony Orchestra of Kraków, Chautauqua Symphony, Portland Symphony, Yale Symphony Orchestra; Niederösterreichischer Tonkünstler Orchester, Staatskapelle Halle; numerous solo and chamber works also commercially recorded, Violin Concerto No. 2, 1996, Suite from Nemo for Orchestra 1996, A Peacock Southeast Flew: Concerto for Pipa and Orchestra 1997, Western Front 1997. *Publications include:* Journeys Through the Life and Music of Nancy Van de Vate 2003, Nancy Van de Vate: Biographie und Analyse eines Stückes 2010, Die Remarque-Oper der austro-amerikanischen Komponistin Dr. Nancy Van de Vate: All Quiet on the Western Front. Im Westen nichts Neues 2013, The Theatrical Vocal Music of Nancy Van de Vate: Volume I 1958-2000 2014. *Honours:* Lifetime Hon. mem., Club der Wiener Musikerinnen 2011; Faculty Citation for Distinguished Achievement in Composition, Florida State Univ. 1999, Wellesley Coll. Alumnae Achievement Award 2001, elected to Hall of Fame, North Plainfield High School, NJ 2004, Alumni Hall of Fame, Univ. of Mississippi 2007. *Address:* Khleslplatz 6, #3008, 1120 Vienna, Austria (office). *Telephone:* (1) 545-17-78 (office). *E-mail:* nancy.vandevate@aon.at; vmm@aon.at (office). *Website:* www.viennamodernmasters.at (office); www.nancy-vandevate.at; nancyvandevate.musicaneo.com.

VAN DELDEN, Alex (Lex); Dutch actor and singer (tenor); b. 21 June 1947, Amsterdam; s. of Lex van Delden and Jetty van Dijk. *Education:* Drama School, Amsterdam, studied singing with Jan Keizer, Marianne Blok and Andrew Field. *Career:* debut 1967; opera includes Gianni Schicchi (G. Puccini), Turandot (F. Busoni), Die Fledermaus (Johann Strauss), Il Ritorno d'Ulisse (Claudio Monteverdi), Ariadne auf Naxos (Richard Strauss), and others; also extensive stage, film and TV work. *Compositions include:* Romeo and Juliet (after Shakespeare), Dance of Death (after Strindberg), The Spanish Brabantine (after Bredero). *E-mail:* lexvandelden@onetel.net.uk.

VAN DEN HOEK, Martijn; Dutch pianist; b. 1955, Rotterdam. *Education:* Rotterdam Conservatory, studied in Moscow with Valeri Kastelskii, in Budapest with Pal Kadosa, in Weimar with Ludwig Hofmann, in New York with Joseff Raieff and Eugene Liszt, in Vienna with Paul Angerer. *Career:* has performed as soloist with the Amsterdam Concertgebouw Orchestra, the Wiener String Quartet and the Nat. Hungarian Post Orchestra; performances in Belgium, France, Germany, Austria, Portugal, USA, Japan and Hong Kong; recital with the BBC, London; repertoire includes concertos by Bach, Bartók, Beethoven, Chopin, Haydn, Hummel, Mozart and Schumann; sonatas by Beethoven, Berg, Brahms, Chopin, Haydn, Mozart, Scarlatti, Schubert,

Impromptus and Moments Musicaux, Schoenberg's Op 23; Schumann's Kreisleriana and Faschingsschwank aus Wien; Liszt Consolations, Sonata, Spanish Rhapsody, Valses oubliées and opera transcriptions. *Honours:* Prix d'Excellence and Goethe Prize 1978, Public Prize of the City of Amsterdam 1981, first prize Int. Liszt Competition, Utrecht 1986.

VAN DER AA, Michel; Dutch composer and film and stage director; b. 10 March 1970, Oss. *Education:* Royal Conservatory, The Hague, New York Film Acad., Lincoln Center Theater Dir's Lab. *Career:* trained as recording engineer; works performed by ensembles and orchestras worldwide, including the ASKO/Schoenberg Ensemble, Freiburg Baroque Orchestra, Melbourne Symphony Orchestra, Ensemble Modern, BBC Scottish Symphony Orchestra, De Nederlandse Opera, Mozarteum Orchestra Salzburg, Seattle Chamber Players, New Nat. Theatre Tokyo, musikFabrik, Continuum Ensemble Toronto, SWR Orchestras of Baden-Baden & Freiburg, Netherlands Radio Orchestras, Norrköping Symphony Orchestra, Sweden, Helsinki Avanti Ensemble and at festivals. *Compositions include:* for ensemble: Here [in circles] for soprano and ensemble 2002, Imprint for baroque orchestra 2005, Mask for ensemble and soundtrack 2006; for orchestra: See-through 2000, Here [to be found] for soprano, chamber orchestra and soundtrack 2001, Here [enclosed] for chamber orchestra and soundtrack 2003, Second Self for orchestra and soundtrack 2004; chamber music: Caprice for solo violin 1999, Just Before for piano and soundtrack 2000, Memo for violin and portable cassette recorder 2003, Up-close (Grawemeyer Award for Music Composition 2013) 2011; opera (scores and stage direction): One (Matthijs Vermeulen Prize 2004) 2002, After Life 2005–06; film soundtrack: The New Math(s) 2000, Passage (also Dir) 2002, One (for TV); Up-close for solo cello, string ensemble and film 2010. *Honours:* Int. Gaudeamus Prize 1999, Charlotte Köhler Prize 2005, Siemens Composers' Grant 2005, Paul Hindemith Prize 2006. *Current Management:* c/o Boosey and Hawkes, Aldwych House, 71–91 Aldwych, London, WC2B 4HN, England. *Telephone:* (20) 7054-7200. *E-mail:* hannah.waddell@boosey.com. *Website:* www.boosey.com/aa; www.vanderaa.net.

VAN DER GIESSEN, Simone; Dutch viola player; b. 1984, Amsterdam. *Education:* Royal Northern Coll. of Music, Guildhall School of Music and Drama, London, pvt. study with Predrag Katanic. *Career:* started to play violin aged five; performed Walton's concerto for viola with RNCM Symphony Orchestra 2007; plays viola with Navarra String Quartet 2002–; has attended various festivals including Calif. Summer Music Festival, Bowdoin Int. Music Festival, Maine, USA, Int. Musicians Seminar, Prussia Cove, Cornwall. *Honours:* RNCM Cecil Aronowitz Prize 2006, award-winner Martin Musical Scholarship Fund. *Current Management:* c/o Sue Hudson and Rosemary Pickering, Young Concert Artists Trust, 23 Garrick Street, London WC2E 9BN, England. *Telephone:* (20) 7379-8477. *Fax:* (20) 7379-8467. *E-mail:* info@ycat.co.uk. *Website:* www.ycat.co.uk. *E-mail:* svdg@navarra.co.uk (office). *Website:* www.navarra.co.uk.

VAN DER KAMP, Harry; Dutch singer (bass); *Artistic Director, Gesualdo Consort Amsterdam;* b. (Harm van der Kamp), 7 Feb. 1947, Kampen; m. Marijke van der Harst. *Education:* Sweelinck Conservatory, Amsterdam, studied with Alfred Deller, Pierre Bernac, Max van Egmond and Herman Woltman. *Career:* Founding mem. Cappella Amsterdam ensemble under Jan Boeke 1970–74; mem. Netherlands Chamber Choir 1974–94, Artistic Adviser 1980–87; Founder and Artistic Dir, Gesualdo Consort Amsterdam (vocal ensemble) 1984–; Prof. of Singing (Alte Musik), Hochschule für Künste, Bremen; Guest Teacher at the Early Music Acad. in Bremen; appearances in solo recitals and in oratorios; appeared with conductors including Nikolaus Harnoncourt, Gustav Leonhardt and Ton Koopman; leading parts in operas by Monteverdi, Handel, Mozart, Pergolesi and Rossini in Milan, Venice and elsewhere in Europe; engagements at the Berlin, Carinthian, Flanders, Spoleto and Holland Festivals. *Recordings:* more than 120 recordings. *Publication:* The Complete Vocal Works by Jan Pieterszoon Sweelinck. *Honours:* Kt, Order of the Netherlands Lion; Edison Prize, for Ezra Pound Recording, Echo Klassik Prize (for J.S. Bach recording) 2006, Edison Prize (for 'De Wereldlijke Werken' Part I of the Complete Vocal Works by Jan Pieterszoon Sweelinck) 2010, VSCD Classical Music Prize (for the Gesualdo Consort Amsterdam) 2010. *Current Management:* c/o Uithof 22, 1353 Almere, Netherlands. *Telephone:* (65) 570-26-75 (mobile). *Address:* Gesualdo Consort Amsterdam, Uithof 22, 1353 Almere-Haven, Netherlands (office). *Telephone:* (36) 529-78-73 (office). *E-mail:* info@gesualdoconsort.nl (office). *Website:* www.gesualdoconsort.nl (office).

VAN DER LINDE, Clint; singer (countertenor); b. 1976, South Africa. *Education:* University of Pretoria, Eton College, Choral College of Music with Ashley Stafford, studied with Peter Schreier. *Career:* boy soprano in Drakenberg Boys' Choir School, S Africa 1988; appearances with the Orchestra of the Age of Enlightenment in Bach's B minor Mass; title roles in Lotario, Ottone and Flavio for the London Handel Festival (1999, 2000, 2001); St Matthew Passion at St George's Hanover Square, 2001. *Honours:* Queen Elizabeth, the Queen Mother Scholarship, RCM; Kathleen Ferrier Bursary for Young Singers. *Current Management:* c/o Alferink Artists Management, Herengracht 340, 1016 CG Amsterdam, The Netherlands. *Telephone:* (20) 6643151. *Fax:* (20) 6752426. *E-mail:* info@alferink.org. *Website:* www.alferink.org.

VAN DER MEER, Ruud; Dutch singer (baritone) (retd); b. (Rudolf Cornelis Adrianus van der Meer), 23 June 1936, The Hague; m. Annetje Schonk 1979; one s. two d. *Education:* Royal Conservatory, The Hague, Mozarteum,

Salzburg, studied with Pierre Bernac in Paris, also studied with Gerald Moore and Paul von Schilhavsky. *Career:* debut, Concertgebouw, Amsterdam 1967; concerts, recitals and oratorio in USA, Western and Eastern Europe; regular BBC radio recitals, Dutch and German radio stations; Co-founder and Man. Special Projects and Int. Relations, Princess Christina Concours, Netherlands 1967–2001; jury mem. Int. Vocal Competition, 's-Hertogenbosch. *Recordings include:* Bach Cantatas with Harnoncourt, Vienna, Bach St Matthew Passion with Royal Concertgebouw Orchestra, Duparc, Schumann and Brahms Lieder, Bach's St John Passion (Grand Prix du Disque) 1970. *Honours:* Hon. Medal, City of The Hague 1984; Kt, Order of Orange Nassau 1990, Order of the Dutch Lion 2001; Prizewinner, int. competitions in Barcelona, Toulouse, 's-Hertogenbosch. *Address:* Palisiumpark 75, 6691 KW Eerbeek, The Netherlands. *Telephone:* (313) 659490. *E-mail:* ruud.vandermeer@planet.nl.

VAN DER PUTTEN, Thea; Dutch singer (soprano); b. 1950, Eindhoven. *Education:* Hague Conservatory. *Career:* soloist, Nederlandse Opera 1975–88, Komische Oper Berlin 1986–96; repertoire includes Papagena in Die Zauberflöte, Despina in Così fan tutte, Susanna in Le Nozze di Figaro, Donna Elvira in Don Giovanni, Gabrielle in La Vie Parisienne, Tatiana in Eugene Onegin, Nedda in I Pagliacci, Mimi in La Bohème, Nele in TomVeal, Max in Where the Wild Things Are; singing tutor, Royal Conservatory, The Hague 1995–2004; currently teaches privately. *Recordings include:* Die Zauberflöte. *Address:* Liendenhof 259, Amsterdam, Netherlands (home). *E-mail:* tputten@xs4all.nl (home). *Website:* www.xs4all.nl/~wrvh/tputten.

VAN DER ROOST, Jan Frans Joseph; Belgian composer and conductor; b. 1 March 1956, Duffel; m. Bernadette Johnson 1980, two s. two d. *Education:* Lemmens Inst., Leuven, Royal Acad. of Music, Antwerp and Ghent. *Career:* Prof., Lemmensinstituut in Leuven; Guest Prof., Senzoku Univ., Kawasaki, and Nagoya Univ. of Arts. *Compositions:* Divertimento for piano 1982, Canzona Gothica for trombone and piano 1982, Melopee e Danza for two guitars 1982, Per Archi for string orchestra 1983, three Bagatels for flute and piano 1984, Rikudim for band, orchestra or string orchestra 1985, Van Maan en Aarde (Of the Moon and the Earth) for mixed choir 1985, Mozaieken (Mosaics) for orchestra 1986, Concerto Grosso for cornet, trombone and brass band 1986, Jaargang (Turning of the Year) for choir and piano 1986–87, Puszta for band 1987, Excalibur for brass band 1987, Elckerlyc (Everyman) oratorio for soloists, choir and orchestra 1987, Obsessions for brass instrument and piano 1987–88, Arghulesques for clarinet quartet 1988, Spartacus for band 1988, Symphony for orchestra 1988–89, Chemical Suite for trombone quartet 1990, Amazonia for band 1990, Met Annie in Toverland for children's choir and ensemble 1990, Olympica for band 1992, Stonehenge for brass band 1992, A Year has Four Lives for female choir and guitar 1993, Exodus Oratorio for soloists, choir, organ and brass band 1994, Concierto de Homenaje for guitar and orchestra 1995, Rhapsody for horn, winds and percussion 1995, Poème Montagnard for band 1996, canTUBAllada for solo tuba 1997, Contrasto Grosso for recorder quartet and string quartet 1997, Et in Terra Pax for band 1998, Credentium for band 1998, Canti d'Amore for baritone and chamber orchestra 1999, Concerto Doppio for two clarinets and string orchestra 1999, Sinfonia Hungarica for band 2000, Albion for brass band 2001, Concerto per Tromba for trumpet, cembalo and string orchestra 2001, I Continenti for recorder quartet 2001, Partita for guitar quartet 2002, Sirius for orchestra 2002, Sinfonietta for band 2003, Contemplations for choir and organ 2003, Carmen Amoris for soloists, choir and chamber orchestra 2003, Tre Sentimenti for bass clarinet and wind orchestra 2004, Scaldis for symphony orchestra 2005. *Recordings include:* Per Archi, Canti D'Amore, Contrasto Grosso and Concerto Doppio. *Address:* Albrecht Rodenbachlaan 13, 2550 Kontich, Belgium (home). *Telephone:* (34) 572289 (home). *E-mail:* vanderroost@telnet.be (home). *Website:* www.janvanderroost.be.

VAN EETVELT, Francois; Belgian singer (bass-baritone); b. 23 May 1946, Bornem. *Education:* Brussels and Antwerp Conservatories and in Italy and Germany. *Career:* sang Amfortas in Parsifal at Antwerp in 1976, has sung in Brussels, Prague, Leipzig, Bratislava, Dresden and Helsinki as Don Giovanni, Wagner's Donner, Gunther, Wolfran and Kurwenal; Sang Apollo in Monteverdi's Orfeo, Jochanaan and Tarquinius in The Rape of Lucretia; sang in the premiere of Das Schloss by André Laporte, Brussels 1986; festival engagements at Flanders and Aldeburgh; television appearances include Monteverdi's Orfeo. *Honours:* winner, Belcanto Competition, Ostend 1978.

VAN EGMOND, Max Rudolf; Dutch singer (baritone) and teacher; b. 1 Feb. 1936, Semarang, Indonesia; s. of Jacobus van Egmond; pnr Jean-François Boucher. *Education:* Univ. of Utrecht, studied in The Netherlands with Tine van Willigen-de Lorme. *Career:* radio announcer at Dutch Radio 1956–60; mem. Dutch Bach Choir, Naarden 1955, Netherlands Chamber Choir 1959; also soloist 1959–99; after winning prizes in Netherlands, Brussels and Munich made numerous appearances as concert soloist (baritone) from 1960, notably in Baroque music, concerts, oratorios and operas in The Netherlands, UK, Brazil, Germany, Austria, Italy, Poland, Belgium, USA and Canada; engagements at most leading music festivals and centres; numerous radio and TV appearances as speaker and singer; master classes in many countries, especially USA 1970–; teacher of singing, Amsterdam Sweelinck Conservatory 1973–98; mem. Choir of the Westerkerk, Amsterdam 1999–; mem. numerous juries in singing competitions and examinations; speaker and writer about musical subjects. *Recordings:* St Matthew and St John Passions by Bach, Bach Cantatas conducted by Gustav Leonhardt and Nikolaus Harnoncourt, Der Tag des Gerichts by Telemann, Reger's Requiem, Il Ritorno d'Ulisse, Orfeo and Il Combattimento by Monteverdi, St Luke Passion by Schütz, Schubert's Schwanengesang and Winterreise, Lully's Alceste, etc. *Publication:* Max van Egmond (online biog.). *Honours:* Hon. DMus (McGill Univ.) 2012; Kt, Order of Orange-Nassau 1980; winner, 's-Hertogenbosch Competition 1959, Edison Awards for Gramophone Recordings 1969, 1971. *E-mail:* info@maxvanegmond.com (office). *Website:* www.maxvanegmond .com.

VAN GEMERT, Theo; Dutch singer (baritone); b. 20 Oct. 1940, Kerkrade. *Education:* Maastricht Conservatory. *Career:* fmr professional footballer, including Dutch national team, before career as a singer; sang at Aachen 1970–71 as Germont and Jochanaan, and at Wuppertal from 1973 as Wotan and Gunther in The Ring, Creonte in Médée, Rigoletto, Iago, Nabucco, Count Luna, Simon Boccanegra, Telramund, Amfortas, Orestes, Grand Inquisitor in Don Carlos; guest appearances in Germany, France, Netherlands and Barcelona.

VAN GOETHEM, Patrick; Belgian singer (countertenor); b. 1969. *Education:* studied with Paul Esswood, Julia Hamari, Andreas Scholl. *Career:* fmr mem., Flemish Schola Cantorum Cantate Domingo; founder mem. and Artistic Adviser, The Flander Baroque Consort; appearances with Laudantes Consort; permanent soloists' ensemble; performed with Ricercar Consort, Les Rumeurs Souterraines and Akademia; appearances at festivals all over Europe including Passau Mozart Festival, Festival van Vlaanderen, Bruges, Ensemble Vocal Regional de Champagne-Ardenne, Dresden State Theatre, Bach weekends of the European Music Festival, Musica Antiqua Köln, Concentus Musicus Wien, Freiburger Barokorchestra and Hasse, Dresden Chamber Choir, Baroque Orchestra; has sung with Orquesta Ciudad de Malaga, Netherlands Bach Society, Netherlands Handel Society, Concerto Köln, Baroque cantatas, Bach cantatas in Leipzig, as part of the Bach 250 celebrations, American Bach Soloists, Washington Bach Consort, Les Idées Heureuses. *Recordings:* three Bach cantatas; Monteverdi 1610 Vespers; Zelenka Te Deum; Heinichen Mass Opus 9; Scheidt Magnificat. *Current Management:* c/o Hester Zevenhuizen, Zevenhuizen Artists Agency, Agamemnonstraat 59-1, 1076 Amsterdam, Netherlands. *Telephone:* (21) 254520. *Fax:* (20) 6751680. *E-mail:* hester.zevenhuizen@planet.nl. *Website:* www .patrickvangoethem.com.

VAN HOVE, Luc; Belgian composer; b. 3 Feb. 1957, Wilrijk. *Education:* Antwerp Conservatory with Wiilem Kersters. *Career:* Lecturer, Antwerp Conservatory, Lemmens Inst., Leuven from 1984. *Compositions:* Wood-Wind Quintet 1982, Trois poèmes (Verlaine) for soprano, chorus and chamber orchestra 1984, two symphonies 1989, 1997, Septet 1989, Cello Sonata 1991, Aria for cello 1992, Triptych oboe concerto 1993, String Quartet 1994, Piano Concerto 1995, Nonet 1995, Strings 1997.

VAN IMMERSEEL, Jos; Belgian harpsichordist, fortepianist and conductor; *Artistic Director and Conductor, Anima Eterna;* b. 1945, Antwerp. *Education:* Antwerp Conservatoire with Flor Peeters and Kenneth Gilbert. *Career:* Prof., Anvers Conservatoire from 1972; Artistic Dir, Sweelinck Conservatoire, Amsterdam 1981–85; founder, Artistic Dir and Conductor, Baroque orchestra, Anima Eterna 1987–, leading it in Handel's Serse for Flanders Opera 1996, became Orchestra-in-Residence, Concertgebouw Brugge 2010; Prof. of Piano, Paris Conservatoire 1992–; many recitals and concerts throughout France. *Honours:* winner, Forum International de Clavecin, Paris 1973, named Cultural Amb. of the Flemish Community, ECHO Klassik Award for Concerto Recording of the Year/Piano – 20th/21st Century (for Poulenc Concerto for Two Clarinets) 2012. *Address:* Anima Eterna, Koolmijnenkaai 30, Quai des Charbonnages, 1080 Brussels, Belgium (office). *Telephone:* (2) 201-08-74 (office). *Fax:* (2) 201-54-18 (office). *E-mail:* jos@animaeterna.be (office). *Website:* www.animaeterna.be (office).

VAN KAMPEN, Bernhardt Anthony; British artist, musician (double bass, violone, viol), composer and teacher; b. 4 March 1943, Bushey, Herts., England; s. of Hans Bernhardt Albert van Kampen and Dorothy Frances van Kampen (née Smithers); m. Julia Henriette Margarete Bockhacker 1991; one d. *Education:* Hornsey Coll. of Art, Guildhall School of Music and Drama, studied with Josef Rač, and with Prof. František Pošta, Solo Bassist of the Czech Philharmonic Orchestra, viola da gamba with Alison Crum and Mark Caudle. *Career:* Art Ed. Aldus Books 1964–66; Founder-mem. New BBC Orchestra (later Acad. of the BBC) 1966; Prin. Bass, New BBC Orchestra 1967–68; freelance in London with London Symphony Orchestra, Royal Philharmonic Orchestra and others; BBC Symphony Orchestra 1972–78; freelance musician and artist, composer, arranger and conductor, viols, violone and baroque and classical double-bass with various early music groups; teacher, pianist and harpsichordist; Founder and Dir Harmonie Universelle; Life mem. Nat. Trust 1981–. *Exhibitions:* London, North Cornwall (St Endellion), Goch, Nivelles, Friedersdorf, Waldbröl, Berlin, Reichshof-Hespert, Gummersbach, Bonn, etc. *Recordings:* with BBC Symphony Orchestra, Acad. of Ancient Music, London Classical Players, City of London Sinfonia, Hanover Band, London Sinfonietta and many others. *Address:* Harmonie Universelle, Heinrich-Krapoth-Str. 4, 51647 Gummersbach/Hülsenbusch, Germany (office). *Telephone:* (2261) 28067 (office). *E-mail:* juliavankampen@web.de (office).

VAN KEULEN, Isabelle; Dutch violinist and violist; *Artistic Director, Norwegian Chamber Orchestra;* b. 16 Dec. 1966, Mijdrecht. *Education:* Sweelinck Conservatory, Amsterdam, Salzburg Mozarteum with Sándor Végh, masterclasses with Max Rostal and Vladimir Spivakov. *Career:* debut as violist 1992; has appeared with Berlin Philharmonic, Royal Concertgebouw Orchestra, Bayerischer Rundfunk, NDR Sinfonieorchester Hamburg, Gewandhausorchester Leipzig, Vienna Radio Symphony, Tonhalle Zürich, NHK Symphony Tokyo, London Philharmonic, The Philharmonia, the Hallé Orchestra, Netherlands, Royal Stockholm and Helsinki Philharmonic Orchestras, the Minnesota Orchestra and Cincinnati Symphony Orchestra, Toronto Symphony Orchestra 1983–; conductors have included Thomas Dausgaard, Mark Elder, Valery Gergiev, Philippe Herreweghe, Neeme and Paavo Järvi, Sir Neville Marriner, Andris Nelsons, Sir Roger Norrington, Joseph Swensen, Osmo Vänskä, Hugh Wolff, David Zinman; appearances at the Salzburg Festival and tours with the Bamberg Symphony and Gidon Kremer's Lockenhaus Soloists; BBC Proms debut 1990, in Mozart with the Rotterdam Philharmonic; Strauss's Concerto with the BBC Philharmonic and the Dutilleux Concerto with the Concertgebouw; other repertoire includes concertos by Bach, Haydn, Henkemans, Schnittke, Spohr and Stravinsky; Messiaen's Quartet for the End of Time; as violist has collaborated with the Hagen, Orlando and Borodin Quartets; mem., Leopold String Trio 1991–; Dir-Soloist, London Mozart Players 2006–; Artistic Dir, Norwegian Chamber Orchestra 2009–. *Recordings include:* Saint-Saëns and Vieuxtemps Concertos, Schubert's Octet, Shostakovich Sonatas for Violin and Viola, Berg Violin Concerto, Sergei Prokofiev: Works for Violin and Piano (with Ronald Brautigam), 2012, Tango! Music by Astor Piazzolla 2013. *Honours:* Silver Medal, Int. Yehudi Menuhin Violin Competition 1983, winner, Eurovision Young Musician of the Year Competition 1984. *Current Management:* c/o Astrid Schoerke, Kuenstlersekretariat Schoerke, Grazerstrasse 30, 30519 Hanover, Germany. *Telephone:* (511) 401048. *Fax:* (511) 407435. *E-mail:* a.schoerke@ks-schoerke.de. *Website:* www.ks-schoerke.de; www .isabellevankeulen.com.

VAN KOOTEN, Katie; American singer (soprano). *Education:* Biola Univ., CA with Jeanne Robinson, and GSMD with Rudolf Piernay, masterclasses with Sir Colin Davis, Graham Johnson, Martin Katz, Eugene Asti, Ian Burnside, Robin Bowman, Earl Patriarco. *Career:* fmr mem. Jette Parker Young Artists Programme, ROH; professional debut as Magda in La Rondine at ROH, Covent Garden 2004; debut at Metropolitan Opera as Magda in La Rondine; roles include Pamina in Die Zauberflöte, Aminta in Il Re Pastore, Kate Pinkerton in Madama Butterfly, Eurydice in Orphée, Arbate in Mitridate, Helena in A Midsummer Night's Dream, Antonia in Les Contes d'Hoffmann, Mimi in La Bohème, Marguerite in Faust; concert appearances include Mozart's Requiem, Strauss' Four Last Songs;. *Current Management:* c/o Peter Wiggins, IMG Artists, 31–33 rue du Temple, 75004 Paris, France. *Telephone:* 1-44-31-00-10. *Fax:* 1-44-31-44-40. *E-mail:* pwiggins@imgartists .com. *Website:* www.imgartists.com. *E-mail:* katievankooten@gmail.com (office). *Website:* www.katievankooten.com.

VAN MECHELEN, Werner; Belgian singer (bass-baritone); b. 16 Dec. 1961, Turnhout; s. of Leo Van Mechelen and Lydie Van Mechelen; m. Sabine Van Mechelen; four c. *Education:* Lemmens Inst., Leuven, studied under Roland Bufkens, masterclasses with Dietrich Fischer-Dieskau, Elisabeth Schwarzkopf, Robert Holl, Mitsuko Shirai, Hartmut Höll, Malcolm King. *Career:* repertoire includes the Count and Figaro in Le Nozze di Figaro, Guglielmo and Don Alfonso in Così fan tutte, Don Giovanni and Leporello in Don Giovanni, Papageno in Die Zauberflöte, Pizarro in Fidelio, Schaunard and Marcello in La Bohème, Sonora in La Fanciulla del West, Dandini in La Cenerentola, Wolfram in Tannhäuser, Kothner in Die Meistersinger von Nürnberg, Wotan in Das Rheingold, Alberich in Der Ring des Nibelungen, Count Eberbach in Der Wildschütz, Karnac in Le Roi d'Ys, Gamekeeper in The Cunning Little Vixen, Tamer and Athlete in Lulu, Wozzeck, Mandryka in Arabella, Gyges in Der König Kandaules, Rigoletto, Amonasro in Aida, Thoas in Iphigénie en Tauride, Ford in Falstaff, Varlaam in Boris Godunov, Jochanaan in Salome, Music Master in Ariadne auf Naxos, Nekrotzar in Le Grand Macabre; has sung in Antwerp/Ghent, Brussels, Liège, Amsterdam, Cologne, Dortmund, Paris, Lyon, Nancy, Avignon, Geneva, Venice, Barcelona, Santiago de Compostela, Göteborg, Seoul and Tel-Aviv. *Recordings include:* Richard Strauss's Lieder, Poulenc Songs, Don Giovanni, Nozze di Figaro, Rheingold, Meistersinger von Nürnberg. *Television:* Yvonne (Boesmans), Don Quichotte (Massenet), Les Mamelles de Tirésias (Poulenc). *Honours:* prizewinner, Queen Elisabeth Competition Brussels, 's-Hertogenbosch, Concours Int., Toulouse, Concurs Viñas, Barcelona. *Current Management:* c/o Konstantin Unger Artists Management, Scheffelstrasse 11, 65187 Wiesbaden, Germany. *Telephone:* (611) 51009976. *E-mail:* unger@ungerartists.com. *Website:* www .ungerartists.com. *Address:* Thonetlaan 110/3F, 2050 Antwerp, Belgium (home). *E-mail:* info@wernervanmechelen.eu (office). *Website:* www .wernervanmechelen.eu.

VAN NES, Jard; Dutch singer (mezzo-soprano); b. 15 June 1948, Zwolle. *Career:* debut in Mahler's Second Symphony under Bernard Haitink at Concertgebouw 1983; appearances in Bach's St Matthew Passion under Nikolaus Harnoncourt and in Mahler's 8th Symphony; further concerts in USA, Paris, London, Oslo, Montreal and Ludwigsburg; stage debut as Bertarido in Rodelinda, Netherlands Opera 1983; repertoire includes Orlando, Naima; gave last professional performance 2000; currently vocal tutor. *Recordings:* Mozart Requiem, Brahms Alto Rhapsody, Mahler 2nd Symphony and Zemlinsky Lieder; Messiah; Beethoven's Ninth; Handel's Theodora and Das Lied von der Erde. *Honours:* Ridder, Orde van de Nederlandse Leeuw 2002.

VAN NESS, Patricia Catheline; American composer, violinist and poet; *Staff Composer, First Church in Cambridge, Congregational, Massachusetts;* b. 25 June 1951, Seattle, Wash.; d. of C. Charles Van Ness and Marjorie Van Ness (née Dexter); m. Peter C. Marks 2000. *Education:* Wheaton and Gordon Colls. *Career:* Founder-mem. Private Lightning 1975–82; composer of numerous ballet and dance scores 1985–; Staff Composer, First Church in Cambridge, Congregational, Mass 1996–; Composer-in-Residence, Coro Allegro 1998, Boston Landmarks Orchestra 2003; mem. Advisory Bd, Cappella Clausura; mem. American Composers' Forum, Int. Alliance for Women in Music, American Soc. of Composers, Authors and Publrs, American Composers' Forum, The Harry Fox Agency; fmr mem. Bd Cambridge Soc. for Early Music. *Compositions include:* Michael, Arcane, Ego sum Custos Angela, Cor mei cordis, The Nine Orders of the Angels, The Voice of the Tenth Muse, Cor meum est templum sacrum (My Heart is a Holy Place), Into Winter's Glimm'ring Night, The Phoenix, 250 works 1995–. *Recordings:* compositions featured on: Angeli 1995, In the Clearing 1997, The Fourth River 1999, Somewhere I Have Never Traveled 2002, Advent and Other Anthems of the Liturgical Year 2003, Sapphire Night 2005, Sound in Spirit 2005, Passionately Unconventional 2007, Sing the Glory 2007, My Heart is a Holy Place 2010, In Paradisum 2012, The Best of the King's Singers 2012, A Marvelous Love 2012, Glorious the Song 2012, Quietus Caritas 2013. *Honours:* numerous awards and grants including Echo Klassik Prize 2005, Daniel Pinkham Award 2011. *E-mail:* patriciavanness@patriciavanness.com. *Website:* www.PatriciaVanNess.com.

VAN RAAT, Ralph; Dutch pianist; b. 1978. *Education:* Amsterdam Conservatory, Univ. of Amsterdam, and with Claude Helffer in Paris, Ursula Oppens at Northwestern Univ., Chicago and Pierre-Laurent Aimard at Musikhochschule, Cologne. *Career:* recitalist and soloist with orchestras worldwide including Nieuw Ensemble, Radio Symphony Orchestra, Frankfurt, Dutch Radio Symphony Orchestra, London Sinfonietta, Nizhny Novgorod Philharmonic Orchestra; festivals include Holland Festival, Time of Music Festival, Viitasaari, Finland, Tanglewood Festival; debut at BBC Proms with BBC Symphony Orchestra 2007; contemporary music series presenter Dutch national radio (NPS Radio 4) 2006; teaches contemporary piano music at Utrecht and Amsterdam Conservatories. *Recordings include:* Discovering Dutch Ensembles, Bart Spaan – Silencios, Louis Andriessen: Complete Piano Works 2005, Fingerprints 2005, John Adams: Complete Piano Works 2007, John Taverner: Complete Piano Works 2007. *Honours:* First Prize Int. Gaudeamus Interpreters Competition 1999, Philip Morris Arts Award 2003, Elisabeth Everts Prize 2005, VSCD Classical Music Prize 2005, Borletti-Buitoni Trust Fellowship 2005, Fortis MeesPierson Award, Concertgebouw, Amsterdam 2006. *Current Management:* Connaught Artists Management, 2 Molasses Row, Plantation Wharf, London SW11 3UX, England. *Telephone:* (20) 7738-0017. *Fax:* (20) 7738-0909. *E-mail:* classicalmusic@connaughtartists.com. *E-mail:* ralph@ralphvanraat.com (office). *Website:* www.ralphvanraat.com.

VAN REE, Jean; Dutch singer (tenor); b. 7 March 1943, Kerkrade. *Education:* studied with Else Bischof-Bornes in Aachen and Franziska Martienssen-Lohmann in Düsseldorf. *Career:* debut in Zar und Zimmermann, Mainz, 1963; sang in Basle, Augsburg and Cologne; guest appearances in Paris, Amsterdam, Barcelona, Cologne, New York, Brussels, Buenos Aires, Hamburg, Madrid, Vienna, Munich; has performed in the premiere of Rafael Kubelik's opera on the life of Titian, as Alwa in Lulu, Matteo in Arabella, Jim in Aufstieg und Fall der Stadt Mahgonny, Hoffmann in Hoffmanns Erzählungen, Don Ottavio in Don Giovanni, Count Almaviva, Alfredo, Mephistopheles in Doktor Faust, Nicias in Thaïs, Hauptmann und Andres in Wozzeck. Hans in Die verkaufte Braut, Kavalier in Cardillac, Faust in Faust et Helene, Sinowi in Lady Macbeth of Mtsensk, Stewa in Jenufa, Kudrajas in Katja Kabanova, Grigory in Boris Gudunov. *Recordings include:* Freunde, vernehmet die Geschichte. *E-mail:* info@jeanvanree.de (office). *Website:* www.jeanvanree.com.

VAN SAMBEEK, Bram; Dutch bassoonist; *Bassoon Teacher, Rotterdam Conservatory;* b. 20 Aug. 1980, Groningen. *Education:* Royal Conservatory of The Hague with Joep Terwey and Johan Steinmann, private lessons with Gustavo Núñez, masterclasses with Klaus Thunemann and Sergio Azzolini. *Career:* began learning bassoon aged ten; Prin. Bassoonist with Rotterdam Philharmonic Orchestra 2002–11; teaches at Rotterdam Conservatory, Codarts Univ. for the Arts; has played with Royal Concertgebouw Orchestra, Mahler Chamber Orchestra, Orchestre de la Suisse Romande, London Symphony Orchestra, Dutch Wind Ensemble, Asko Ensemble, the Ebony Band; regular guest at int. festivals including the Delft Chamber Music Festival, Orlando Festival, West Cork Chamber Music Festival, Oxford Chamber Music Festival; mem. CMS 2, Chamber Music Soc. of Lincoln Center, New York. *Recordings:* The Art of the Bassoon (bassoon concertos) 2009, Bassoon Kaleidoscope (chamber music works for bassoon) 2012. *Honours:* Winner, Dutch Ministry of Cultural Affairs State Music Award (first bassoonist) 2009, Borletti-Buitoni Trust Award 2011. *Address:* c/o Brinks Artist Management, Herengracht 453, 1017 BS Amsterdam, Netherlands. *Telephone:* 65-3220618 (mobile). *E-mail:* marianne@brinksartists.nl. *Website:* www.bramvansambeek.com.

VAN SPAENDONCK, Ronald; Belgian clarinettist and teacher; *Clarinet Teacher, Brussels and Mons Royal Academies;* b. 31 March 1970, Namur. *Education:* studied with Léon Jacot, Walter Boeykens, Anthony Pay in London, Karl Leister in Berlin. *Career:* has performed with Orchestre Philharmonique de Liège, Orquestra Classica de Porto, Oulu Orchestra, Orchestre Symphonique de Zürich, Orchestre Philharmonique de Luxembourg, Het Brabants Orkest, Orchestre de la Radio Belge, Orchestre Nat. de Belgique, BBC Scottish Symphony, BBC Philharmonic Orchestra, BBC Nat. Orchestra of Wales; has appeared at Wigmore Hall, London, Suntory Hall, Tokyo, BBC Proms, and at festivals in Edinburgh, Chester, Brighton, Buxton, City of London, Epau, Stavelot, Juventus in Cambrai, Arpae in Brussels; concerts in Russia and China 2005; performs chamber music with Alexandre Tharaud, Jérôme Ducros, Muhiddin D. Demiriz, Gidon Kremer, Catherine Leonard, Lawrence Power, Marie Hallynck, and with the Skampa Quartet, Serenata Forlana; Clarinet Teacher, Brussels and Mons Royal Acads; Artistic Adviser, Buffet Crampon Co. *Recordings:* Michel Lysight, Labyrinthes, Michel Lysight, Oréades, XXth Century Belgian Works for Clarinet and Piano, Musique française pour clarinette et piano (with Alexandre Tharaud, piano), Poulenc, Complete Chamber Music (five vols), Gershwin/Mortier/Pelckmans/Rodgers/Bernstein (with the Belgian Nat. Orchestra clarinet quartet), Saint-Saëns, Le Carnaval des Animaux, Beethoven et Mozart (with Skampa Quartet), Mozart/Brahms, Clarinet Quintets (Radio 3 New Generation Artists), American music for clarinet and piano, Concert pour Vous (with Orchestre de Chambre de Waterloo), Von Weber, Grand duo concertant op.48, Michel Lysight/Glenn Gould (with Bruxellensis Quartet) 2006; with Serenata Forlana: Mozart 2002, Serenata for 2000, Mozart, Gran Partita 2002, Michel Lysight, Enigma 2006. *Honours:* First Prize, Int. TROMP Competition, First Prize, Dos Hermanas Int. Competition, First Prize, A. Gi. Mus Wind Instruments Int. Competition, Rome. *E-mail:* r.vanspaendonck@skynet.be. *Website:* www.vanspaendonck.be.

VAN STEEN, Jac; Dutch conductor; *Music Director, Dortmunder Philharmoniker;* b. 1956, Eindhoven. *Education:* Brabants Conservatory, Tilburg. *Career:* conducted Univ. of Leiden Student Orchestra and Nat. Youth Orchestra; participant in BBC European Conductors' Seminar, London 1986; Music Dir Nijmegen Bach Choir 1986–90, Amsterdam Nat. Ballet – 1994; Chief Conductor Nuremberg Symphony 1989–1994; Permanent Guest Conductor Bochum Symphony, Germany 1992–94; Music Dir, Neues Berliner Kammerorchester 1999–02; Music Dir Deutsches Nationaltheater Weimar 2002–05; Chief Conductor Staatskapelle Weimar 2002–05, Orkester Musikkollegium Winterhur 2002–08; Prin. Guest Conductor, BBC Nat. Orchestra of Wales 2005–; Music Dir, Dortmund Philharmoniker 2008–; appearances as guest conductor in Holland, Germany and the UK include Rotterdam Philharmonic, Netherlands Philharmonic, Residentie Orkest Den Haag, Hamburg Symphonic Orchestra, Saarbrücken Orchestra, Mannheim Nat. Theatre Orchestra, BBC SO, BBC Philharmonic, Hallé Orchestra, London Sinfonietta; world premieres include Jonathan Harvey's Concerto for Percussion and Orchestra, with BBC SO, London, Christian Jost's Lux Aeterna, with Residentie Orkest Den Haag 2003; Prof., Royal Conservatory of Music, The Hague and Fontys Music Acad., Tilburg. *Recordings:* David Bedford, Symphony No. 1 1998, Elgar/Lutoslawski, Cello Concertos 2001, Themes and Variations 2001, David Matthews, In the Dark Time 2001, Thea Musgrave, Memento Vitae 2003, Purcell/Handel/Mozart, Arias 2003, Love from a Stranger (film scores) 2004, Bruch, Das Lied von der Glocke 2005. *Honours:* Preis der Deutschen Schallplattenkritik. *Address:* Theater Dortmund, Kukstrasse 12, 44137 Dortmund, Germany (office). *Telephone:* (231) 5025547 (office). *Fax:* (231) 5029773 (office). *E-mail:* webmaster-theater@theaterdo.de (office). *Website:* www.theaterdo.de/philharmoniker (office).

VAN VLIET, Xander; Dutch violinist. *Education:* Enschede Conservatory, Amsterdam Conservatory, Royal Northern Coll. of Music. *Career:* started to play violin aged seven; plays violin with Navarra String Quartet 2002–; Asst to Jan Repko (violin) and Christopher Rowland (chamber music) 2007; currently Tutor of Violin, Royal Coll. of Music, London, Royal Northern Coll. of Music Junior School and Chetham's School of Music, Manchester. *Honours:* Rodger Raphael Prize, Royal Nat. Coll. of Music 2004. *Current Management:* c/o Sue Hudson and Rosemary Pickering, Young Concert Artists Trust, 23 Garrick Street, London WC2E 9BN, England. *Telephone:* (20) 7379-8477. *Fax:* (20) 7379-8467. *E-mail:* info@ycat.co.uk. *Website:* www.ycat.co.uk. *E-mail:* xvv@navarra.co.uk (office). *Website:* www.navarra.co.uk.

VAN VROOMAN, Richard; American singer (tenor); b. 29 July 1936, Kansas City, MO. *Education:* Kansas City Conservatory, Salzburg Mozarteum with Max Lorenz. *Career:* debut, as Lorenzo in Fra Diavalo, Bregenz Festival 1962; many appearances in West Germany, Austria and Switzerland, notably at the Zürich Opera 1964–78; guest engagements at Salzburg 1964–65, Aix-en-Provence, with the Deutsche Oper am Rhein and the Paris Opéra and in Lisbon, Geneva, Frankfurt, Hamburg, Rome, Bordeaux and Marseille; Glyndebourne Festival 1968, as Belmonte in Die Entführung; best known in operas by Mozart, Rossini and Donizetti and in the Baroque repertoire; many concert appearances. *Recordings:* Wozzeck, Mozart's Davidde Penitente, Handel's Acis and Galatea, Dittersdorf's Doktor und Apotheker, Cimarosa Requiem, Haydn Salve Regina.

VAN ZWEDEN, Jaap; Dutch conductor; *Music Director, Hong Kong Philharmonic Orchestra;* b. 12 Dec. 1960, Amsterdam. *Education:* Amsterdam Conservatory and with Dorothy DeLay at Juilliard, New York. *Career:* as violinist, Leader Royal Concertgebouw Orchestra 1979–; solo performances under conductors Haitink, Giulini, Solti and Bernstein; Conductor from 1995 including tours with Berlin Symphony Orchestra, Salzburg Mozarteum, Israel Concert Orchestra and Japanese Concert Orchestra; Music Dir Netherlands Symphony Orchestra 1997–2003; Buenos Aires Philharmonic

Orchestra in Argentina and on tour to Europe; US debut with St Louis Symphony Orchestra 1997; Prin. Guest Conductor, Brabants Orchestra 1997; Season 1999–2000 with Netherlands Symphony Orchestra on tour to USA and debut with London Philharmonic; Prin. Conductor Residentie Orchestra, The Hague 2000–05, Hon. Guest Conductor 2005–09; Chief Conductor and Artistic Dir Netherlands Radio Philharmonic Orchestra and Radio Kamer Filharmonie 2005–11, Hon. Chief Conductor; Music Dir Dallas Symphony Orchestra 2008–12; Prin. Conductor Royal Flemish Philharmonic Orchestra 2008–12; Chief Conductor Hong Kong Philharmonic Orchestra 2012–; Guest Conductor, Chicago Symphony, Philadelphia Orchestra, Gothenburg Symphony, WDR Symphony Orchestra Cologne, Orchestre National de France, Munich Philharmonic, Oslo Philharmonic, Cleveland Orchestra, Philadelphia Orchestra, London Philharmonic, Royal Concertgebouw Orchestra, New York Philharmonic, Boston Symphony; has appeared at BBC Proms, Carnegie Hall and Tanglewood and Aspen Festivals; Music Dir-Desig., New York Philharmonic 2017–18, Music Dir 2018–. *Recordings include:* Beethoven, Brahms and Bruckner complete symphonies, Shostakovich's Symphony No. 5, Mahler's Symphony No. 5, Stravinsky Ballets, Haydn Symphonies, Tchaikovsky Symphonies Nos 4 and 5. *Honours:* First Prize, Dutch Nat. Violin Competition 1977, Musical America's Conductor of the Year 2012. *Current Management:* c/o IMG Artists, The Light Box, 111 Power Road, London, W4 5PY, England. *Telephone:* (20) 7957-5800. *Fax:* (20) 7957-5801. *E-mail:* nmathias@imgartists.com. *Website:* www.imgartists.com.

VANAUD, Marcel; Belgian singer (baritone); b. 1952, Brussels. *Education:* Brussels Conservatoire and at Liège. *Career:* sang at the Liège Opera 1975–83, notably as Papageno, Escamillo, Alfonso in La Favorita, Renato and Ourrais in Mireille; guest appearances at Pittsburgh and New Orleans 1984; New York City Opera 1985 as Zurga in Les Pêcheurs de Perles; Théâtre de la Monnaie Brussels as Raimund in Comte Ory and Mozart's Figaro; season 1987–88 as Lescaut at Montreal, Posa in Don Carlos at Tulsa, Figaro at Santa Fe and Rimbaud at Toulouse; La Scala Milan 1989 in the premiere of Doktor Faustus by Manzoni; returned to Liège 1992 as Mephistopheles in La Damnation de Faust and sang Germont at Los Angeles; Festival de Radio France at Montpellier 1992, as Sacchini's Oedipus and in Château des Carpathes by Philippe Hersant; season 2000–01 as Count Luna at Montpellier, Amonasro in Geneva, and the Dutchman at Liège; appearances with Opera Ireland in Falstaff and Madam Butterfly 2008 and Romeo and Juliet 2010; LaNavarraise and L'Enfant et les Sortilèges with Opera Monte Carlo 2012; title role in Rigoletto, Maribor 2012, Germont in La Traviata, Rouen 2013. *Recordings include:* Les Contes d'Hoffmann and Franck's Les Béatitudes; Karnac in Le Roi d'Ys. *Current Management:* c/o Monique Baudouin Opéra, 44 rue des Gravilliers, 75003 Paris, France. *Telephone:* 1-42-71-20-08. *Fax:* 1-42-71-10-50. *E-mail:* marcel.vanaud@gmail.com. *Website:* www.marcelvanaud.be.

VANDERSTEENE, Zeger; Belgian singer (tenor); b. 5 June 1940, Ghent. *Career:* sang at first in concert and appeared in opera from 1980; Théâtre de la Monnaie at Brussels 1981–84, as Evandre in Alceste and Steuermann in Fliegende Holländer; Théâtre du Châtelet, Paris 1983, in Rameau's Les Indes Galantes; Bologna 1987, in Gluck's La Danza; sang Aegisthus in Elektra at Antwerp 1990; song recitals in works by Schubert, Schumann and Fauré. *Recordings include:* Castor et Pollux by Rameau, Armide by Lully.

VANDERVELDE, Janika, PhD; American composer; b. 1955, Ripon, Wis.; m. Lawrence Fuchsberg. *Education:* Univ. of Wisconsin, Univ. of Minnesota with Dominick Argento, Eric Stokes. *Career:* comms from Minnesota Orchestra, St Paul Chamber Orchestra, Dale Warland Singers, Chanticleer; mem. Faculty, Perpich Center for Arts Educ. 1990–; Composer-in-Residence, Minnesota Chorale 1999–2002. *Compositions include:* Genesis I (for oboe and piano) 1983, II (for piano and trio) 1983, III (for flute, viola and harp) 1984, IV (for violin, clarinet and piano) 1987, V (for four guitars 1987), VI (for string trio) 1988, VII (for saxophone, piano and percussion) 1989, Clockwork Concerto (for viola and orchestra) 1987, Hildegard (video opera) 1989, O viridissima virga (for chorus and percussion) 1992, Polyhymnia (for chorus and orchestra) 1992, Seven Sevens (opera) 1993, Echoes across the Stara Planina (for female chorus and orchestra) 1995, The Dreamweaver (for speaker and orchestra) 1996, Cafés of Melbourne (for accordion and orchestra) 1997, Beijing Cai Hong (for chorus and pipa) 1997, Wataridori (for chorus and oboe) 1997, Pacific Transit (for pipa and orchestra) 1998, Cosmos (for speaker and orchestra) 1999, Tutti for Earth and Heaven (for chorus and organ) 1999, Cançao de Embalar (for chorus) 2000, Dance Ablaze! (for chorus and percussion) 2001, Adventures of the Black Dot (for speaker, four instruments and chorus) 2001, O factura dei (for chorus, percussion and electric bass) 2002, Birds of Oz (for chorus) 2003, Monapacataca (String Quartet No. 1) 2004, Villancico (for chorus and percussion) 2004, Candoncilla del primer deseo (for chorus and percussion) 2004, Petric's Web (for accordion) 2005, Mar (for chorus) 2005, We Are All Chosen People (for chorus and piano) 2006, Medicine Woman (for chorus and native American flutes) 2006, Slip Away (for children's chorus and Orff instruments) 2006, All Things Resounding (for chorus) 2007, Sing Me a Home (for chorus and percussion) 2007, HaChZaRH (for organ and violin) 2007, Labyrinth (for organ) 2009, Water Dance (for two choruses and four instrumentalists) 2009, Water of Life (for chorus and chamber orchestra or piano four-hands) 2010, Max Found Two Sticks (for speaker and eight instrumentalists) 2010, The Bee and the Soul (for three sopranos and six instrumentalists) 2011, Diana Takes a Swim (electronic) 2011, Wisdom 2:23 (for chorus) 2013, Bdote (for women's choir) 2014. *Honours:* Lili Boulanger

Award 1994, American Composers Forum/Jerome Foundation Commissioning Awards 1980, 1985, 1990, 1992, 1995, Bush Foundation Fellowships 1986, 1995, McKnight Foundation Fellowships 1984, 1994, 2003, 2009, Meet The Composer New Residencies Award 1999, Minnesota State Arts Board Fellowships 1985, 2003. *Address:* c/o Hothouse Press, 1631 Highland Parkway, Saint Paul, MN 55116, USA (office). *Telephone:* (651) 690-3000 (office). *E-mail:* janikav@visi.com. *Website:* www.janikavandervelde.com.

VANDOR, Ivan, DipMus, MA; composer; b. 13 Oct. 1932, Pecs, Hungary. *Education:* S Cecilia, UCLA. *Career:* mem., Musica Elettronica Viva 1966–68; mem., Nuova Consonanza Improvis Group 1967–68; research in Tibetan Buddhist music 1970–71; Dir, Int. Inst. for Comparative Music Studies, Berlin 1977–83; founder, Dir, Scuola Interculturale di Musica 1979–; Prof. of Composition, Conservatory of Music, Bologna 1979–; Prof. of Music, Conservatory of Music S Cecilia. *Compositions:* Quartetto Per Archi 1962, Moti 1963, Serenata 1964, Dance Music 1969, Esercizi 1966, Winds 1970, Cronache 1981, Cronache II 1989, Concerto for violoncello and orchestra 1991, Fantasie for piano and orchestra 1992, Offrande II 1993, some short pieces for harpsichord. *Publications:* La Musique du Bouddhisme Tibetain 1976, The World of Music (ed.) 1975–85.

VANEEV, Vladimir; Russian singer (bass); b. 1961. *Education:* Gorky Conservatoire. *Career:* sang with the Mussorgsky Opera, St Petersburg, 1986–97; Kirov Opera from 1997, as Verdi's Philip II and Grand Inquisitor Boris and Pimen in Boris Godunov and Prince Gremin in Eugene Onegin; Further appearances as Dosifei in Khovanshchina, Ruslan, Wagner's Wotan and Dutchman and Boris in Katerina Izmailova; Sang Ivan Khovansky in Khovanshchina with the Kirov at Covent Garden, 2000; Other roles include Prince Galitsky and Khan Konchak in Prince Igor, Monterone (Rigoletto), Remeniuk in Prokofiev's Semyon Kotko and Kochubei in Mazeppa; sang Klingsor in Parsifal, with the Kirov at the Royal Albert Hall, 1999. *Honours:* Honoured Artist of Russia; Prize Winner Voce Verdiani, All-Russian Chaliapin and Russian State Competitions.

VANELLI, Adriana; American singer (soprano); b. 1957, Detroit. *Education:* Cleveland Inst. of Music. *Career:* sang at New York Grand Opera as Butterfly, Mimi and Aida, Liu in Turandot and Nedda in Pagliacci for Stamford State Opera, Mozart's Countess in Nevada and Tosca for New Jersey Opera; Violetta for Connecticut Grand Opera 1985 and Desdemona at Providence, 1986; European debut as Liu, at Hamburg; Tatiana in Eugene Onegin for Netherlands Opera, Manon Lescaut at Wiesbaden 1985 and Tosca at Nice 1986; Deutsche Oper Berlin 1986–89; sang Annina in Menotti's The Saint of Bleecker Street 1989; concert engagements in Europe and North America.

VANESS, Carol; American singer (soprano); b. 27 July 1952, San Diego, CA. *Education:* studied in California with David Scott. *Career:* San Francisco 1977, as Vitellia in La Clemenza di Tito; New York City Opera from 1979, as Alcina, Antonia in Les Contes d'Hoffmann, Vitellia, Flotow's Frau Fluth, Mimi, and Leila in Les pêcheurs de Perles, Rigoleto (Gilda), Traviata (Violetta); Donna Anna; Glyndebourne Opera from 1982, as Donna Anna, Electra in Idomeneo, Fiordiligi and Amelia Boccanegra (1986); Covent Garden debut 1982, as Mimi: returned for Vitellia and Dalila in Handel's Samson; Countess Almaviva, 1989; Rosalinda in Der Fledermaus; Metropolitan Opera from 1984, as Armida in Rinaldo, Fiordiligi, Electra and the Countess in Figaro, Manon; Australian Opera 1985, Amelia in Un Ballo in Maschera; Seattle Opera 1986, as Massenet's Manon; Desdemona, 1986; Violetta, 1988; Leonora in Trovatore, 1989; concert appearances in the Choral Symphony in Paris, the Verdi Requiem in Philadelphia and at the Lincoln Center New York with Pavarotti; sang in Beethoven Missa solemnis at the Barbican Hall, London, 1989; Royal Opera, Vitellia in La Clemenza di Tito 1989; Trovatore 1990 at the Metropolitan Opera and Faust (Marguerite); Don Giovanni (Anna) at Covent Garden, 1992; season 1992–93 as Iphigénie en Tauride at La Scala, Mathilde in Guillaume Tell at San Francisco and Olympia at the Met; sang Desdemona at the Metropolitan, 1994; Norma at Seattle, 1994, (Amelia, Ballo in Maschera, 1995); Fiordiligi at the Met, 1997; Elisabeth de Valois at the Opéra Bastille, 1998; season 2000–01 as Donna Elvira for San Francisco Opera, the Trovatore Leonora in Washington and Mathilde in Guillaume Tell for the Vienna Staatsoper; sang Tosca at Covent Garden, 2002. *Recordings include:* Donna Anna in the Glyndebourne production of Don Giovanni conducted by Bernard Haitink; Masses by Haydn; Glyndebourne, Haitink, Così fan tutte; Beethoven's Ninth with Dohnányi and Cleveland Orchestra; Missa Solemnis with Tate and the ECO; Don Giovanni (Elvira), conducted by Muti; Tosca; Rossini, Stabat Mater. *Honours:* winner San Francisco Opera Auditions 1976. *Current Management:* Zemsky/Green Artists Management, 730 Fifth Avenue, Suite 1802, New York, NY 10019, USA. *Telephone:* (212) 300-8003. *Fax:* (212) 300-8001. *E-mail:* zgartists@aol.com. *Website:* www.zemskygreen.com.

VÄNSKÄ, Osmo; Finnish conductor; b. 28 Feb. 1953, Sääminki. *Education:* Sibelius Acad., Helsinki with Jorma Panula. *Career:* co-principal clarinet, Helsinki PO 1977–82; Principal Guest Conductor, Lahti SO 1985, Music Dir 1988–03, Chief Conductor 2003–08, Conductor Laureate 2008–; Music Dir, Iceland SO 1993–96, Tapiola Sinfonietta 1990–92; Chief Conductor BBC Scottish SO –2002; Music Dir, Minnesota Orchestra 2003–(11); guest conductor with New York Philharmonic, Chicago Symphony, Cleveland Orchestra, Boston Symphony, San Francisco Symphony, Detroit, Houston and Saint Louis Symphonies, Yomiuri Nippon Symphony, Berlin Philharmonic, Munich Philharmonic, Leipzig Gewandhaus Orchestra, Oslo Philharmonic, Concertgebouw Orchestra, BBC Symphony, Czech Philharmonic, London Philharmonic, Orchestre Nat. de Paris, Royal Concertgebouw Orchestra; symphonic cycles of Beethoven, Sibelius and Nielsen with BBC Scottish SO; Tapiola by Sibelius and Nielsen's 4th at the London Proms 2002. *Recordings include:* complete Beethoven symphonies, Sibelius Edition (with Lahti SO), albums of Kalevi Aho, Sofia Gubaidulina, Kokkonen and Rautavaara, Nielsen Symphonies. *Honours:* Hon. DHumLitt (Univ. of Minnesota) 2008; Royal Philharmonic Soc. Award 2002, Musical America Conductor of the Year 2005. *Current Management:* Harrison Parrott Ltd, 5–6 Albion Court, London, W6 0QT, England. *Telephone:* (20) 7229-9166. *Fax:* (20) 7221-5042. *E-mail:* info@harrisonparrott.co.uk. *Website:* www .harrisonparrott.com. *Address:* c/o Minnesota Orchestra, Orchestra Hall, 1111 Nicollet Mall, Minneapolis, MN 55403, USA (office). *Website:* www .minnesotaorchestra.org (office).

VARCOE, Stephen, MA, PhD; British singer (baritone) and singing teacher; *Professor of Singing, Royal College of Music;* b. 19 May 1949, Lostwithiel, Cornwall, England; m. Melinda Davies 1972; three s. (one deceased) two d. *Education:* Cathedral Choir School and King's School, Canterbury, King's Coll., Cambridge, Guildhall School of Music, Univ. of York. *Career:* concerts in most major British and European festivals; specialist in Lieder, French Mélodies and English song; numerous appearances on British, French and German radio stations; sang Sarastro in Die Zauberflöte at the Mozart Experience, London 1989, Haydn's L'Infedeltà Delusa, Antwerp 1990; cr. Zossima in premiere of Tavener's Mary of Egypt, Aldeburgh 1992, Peri's Eurydice in Drottningholm 1997; sang Bartley in Riders to the Sea, Vaughan Williams Festival, London 1997; currently Prof. of Singing, Royal Coll. of Music, London; also teaches at Clare Coll., Cambridge. *Recordings include:* more than 150 albums, including: Purcell's Indian Queen, Fairy Queen, King Arthur and The Tempest, Handel's Partenope, L'Allegro, Triumph of Time and Truth, Alessandro and Israel in Egypt, Bach's B Minor Mass, Masses, Cantatas and Matthew and John Passions, Fauré's Requiem, Finzi's Songs of Thomas Hardy, Rameau's Motets, French Mélodies, Britten's Cantata Misericordium and Tavener's Mary of Egypt, Schubert's Lieder. *Publications include:* Sing English Song 2000; contrib. to Cambridge Companion to Singing 2000, New Percy Grainger Companion 2010. *Honours:* Gulbenkian Foundation Fellowship 1977. *E-mail:* stephen@varcoe.com. *Website:* www .stephenvarcoe.co.uk.

VARGA, Balint Andras; Hungarian music publisher; b. 3 Nov. 1941, Budapest; s. of the late Pál Varga and Piroska Nasser; m. Katalin Zsoldos 1977; two d. *Education:* Univ. of Budapest, Hungarian Journalism School. *Career:* regular radio and TV broadcasts; Head of Promotion, Editio Musica Budapest 1971–90; Deputy Dir, Hungarian Cultural Inst., Berlin 1991–92; Head of Promotion, Universal Edition, Vienna 1992–2007; retd 2008. *Publications include:* Conversations with Lutosławski 1974, Conversations with Iannis Xenakis 1980, 1989, Conversations with Luciano Berio 1981, four anthologies of musical interviews 1972, 1974, 1979, 1986, Aaron Copland's The New Music (trans. into Hungarian) 1973, Conversations with György Kurtág 2009, Three Questions for Sixty-Five Composers 2011, From Boulanger to Stockhausen: Interviews and a Memoir 2013, Drei Fragen an 73 Komponisten 2014; contrib. of regular articles to Muzsika. *Address:* Kolschitzkygasse 23/22, 1040 Vienna, Austria (home). *Telephone:* (1) 505-5163 (home); 650-4177161 (mobile) (home). *E-mail:* varga_balint@yahoo.com.

VARGA, Gilbert; British conductor; *Principal Conductor, Taipei Symphony Orchestra;* b. 17 Jan. 1952, London, England; m.; two c. *Education:* studied with Franco Ferrara, Sergiu Celibidache and Charles Bruck. *Career:* originally concentrated on work with chamber orchestras, particularly the Tibor Varga Chamber Orchestra, before developing a reputation as a symphonic conductor; Chief Conductor, Hofer Symphoniker 1980–85; Chief Conductor, Philharmonia Hungarica, Marl 1985–90, conducted their debut tour to Hungary with Yehudi Menuhin; Perm. Guest Conductor, Stuttgart Chamber Orchestra 1991–95; Prin. Guest Conductor, Malmö Symphony 1997–2000; Music Dir Basque Nat. Symphony Orchestra 1997–2008, tours to UK, Germany, Spain and South America; currently Prin. Conductor, Taipei Symphony Orchestra; season 2012–13 returned to conducting symphony orchestras of Baltimore, Houston, Atlanta, St Louis, Milwaukee, Colorado and Utah, among others, and to Minnesota Orchestra which he conducts every season; regularly conducts the major European orchestras in Berlin, Leipzig, Frankfurt, Cologne, Budapest, Lisbon, Brussels and Glasgow, with soloists including Mørk, Ehnes, Vinnitskaya, Hamelin and Gerstein; programmes frequently feature the ballet suites, tone poems and symphonies of the late 19th and early 20th centuries; recent performance of Kodály's Dances of Galánta, the Leipziger-Volkszeitung; Jury Chair., Int. Violin Competition Henri Marteau, Lichtenberg and Hof, Germany. *Recordings include:* Symphony No. 6 of Anton Rubinstein and solo cello concertos with BBC Philharmonic and Rolland; Ravel recording with Orquestre Sinfonica de Euskadi and recordings with Munich Chamber Orchestra and Bamberg Symphony; Concertos by Ravel and Prokofiev with Deutsches Symphonie-Orchester Berlin and Anna Vinnitskaya (Five Stars, BBC Music Magazine) 2011. *Current Management:* c/o Intermusica Artists' Management Ltd, 36 Graham Street, Crystal Wharf, London, N1 8GJ, England. *Telephone:* (20) 7608-9900. *Fax:* (20) 7490-3263. *E-mail:* lgunes@intermusica.co.uk. *Website:* www.intermusica.co.uk; english.tso.gov.taipei.

VARGAS, Milagro; singer (mezzo-soprano); b. 1958, USA. *Education:* Oberlin Coll., Eastman School of Music with Jan DeGaetani. *Career:* mem.,

Stuttgart Staatsoper 1983–88, notably in the premiere of Akhnaten by Philip Glass 1984 and as Cherubino, Nancy in Albert Herring, Orlofsky, and Lybia in Jommelli's Fetonte; Komische Oper Berlin as Cherubino, Heidelberg Festival as Ramiro in La Finta Giardiniera; sang Charlotte in Zimmermann's Die Soldaten at Strasbourg and Stuttgart 1988; sang Ravel's Shéhérazade at the Cabrillo Festival 1986 and has appeared elsewhere in concert at the Aspen and Marlboro Festivals, with the Philadelphia Orchestra and the Rochester Philharmonic; season 2000–01 as Nemorino at Houston, Lensky in Florence, Donizetti's Roberto Devereux for the Vienna Staatsoper and Don Carlos for Washington Opera; Duke of Mantua at Covent Garden 2002. *Recordings include:* Akhnaten, Die Soldaten.

VARGAS, Ramón; Mexican singer (tenor); b. 1959, Mexico City. *Career:* has sung in opera at Mexico City as Fenton in Falstaff, Nemorino, Don Ottavio and Count Almaviva; sang Gelsomino in Il Viaggio a Reims at the Vienna Staatsoper 1987; Pesaro and Salzburg Festivals 1987, Mexico City 1988 as Tamino; further appearances at Lucerne 1989, Zürich 1990 as Lorenzo in Fra Diavalo and Enschede Holland, as Fenton; season 1991–92 as Leicester in Rossini's Elisabetta at Naples, Almaviva at Rome, Rodrigo in a concert performance of La Donna del Lago at Amsterdam and Paolina in Il Matriomonio Segreto at Martina Franca; sang Rossini's Almaviva, Verona Arena 1996; Alfredo Germont, Opéra Bastille 1998–99; Rodolfo in La Bohème, Covent Garden 1999 and at New York Met 2002; London Proms 2002; title role in Don Carlos, New York Met and Wiener Staatsoper 2013; Münchner Opernfestspiele 2015; Rodolfo in La Bohème, La Scala 2016 and New York Met 2016. *Recordings include:* Rossini's Il Turco in Italia; Massenet's Werther, Donizetti/Rossini Tenor Arias 1999, Mexico Lindo 2000, Ramon Vargas Opera Arias 2013. *Honours:* Kammersänger (Austria) 2008. *Current Management:* Iberkonzert, Calle Rodríguez Arias 23 - 6° - Dt.10, 48011 Bilbao, Spain. *Telephone:* (94) 4104-746. *Fax:* (94) 4218-582. *E-mail:* agencia@iberkonzert .com. *Website:* www.iberkonzert.com/artistas.html; www.ramonvargas.com.

VARONA, Luciano; Argentine stage designer and costume designer; b. 14 Aug. 1930, Mendoza. *Education:* Escuela Superior de Bellas Artes, Buenos Aires. *Career:* debut at Teatro Colón, Buenos Aires 1959, Prokofiev's The Love for Three Oranges; collaborated with Tito Capobianco at the New York City 1966–73, with Giulio Cesare, The Golden Cockerel, Manon, Lucia di Lammermoor and Donzetti's Tudor trilogy; Handel's Ariodante for the opening of the Kennedy Center at Washington, DC 1971; San Francisco and Vancouver Opera 1972–73, with Norma and Lucrezia Borgia; further association with Capobianco at the Deutsche Oper Berlin and the Netherlands Opera 1971–74, Attila, Aida, Rodelinda and La Traviata; returned to the Teatro Colón 1981–88, with designs for Romeo et Juliette, Die Zauberflöte, Carmen and Die Entführung; Norma, San Francisco Opera 1998.

VARPIO, Marja-Leena; Finnish singer (soprano); b. 1956, Helsinki. *Education:* Munich Musikhochschule and Salzburg Mozarteum. *Career:* Vienna Kammeroper 1985–87, as Paisiello's Rosina, Susanna, and Blondchen in Die Entführung; Vienna Volksoper 1987–90, as Mozart's Despina and Papagena; festival appearances as Schwetzingen, Vienna and Savonlinna (Telemann's Pimpinone, 1990); premiere of Adriana Hölszky's Bremer Freiheit, Munich 1998; season 1993–94 as Axiniain in Katerina Izmailova at Stuttgart and Musetta for Finnish National Opera; other roles include Mozart's Countess, and Lucia in Hindemith's The Long Christmas Dinner; frequent engagements in operetta; concerts include Mozart's Requiem, Beethoven's Ninth, Masses by Haydn, and Carmina Burana.

VÁSÁRY, Tamás; Hungarian concert pianist and conductor; b. 11 Aug. 1933, Debrecen; s. of Jozsef Vasary and Elizabeth Vasary (née Baltazàr); m. Henriette Tunyogi 2000. *Education:* Ferenc Liszt Acad. of Music, Budapest under Lajos Hernádi, József Gát and Zoltán Kodály, also studied with Ernő Dohnányi. *Career:* first solo performance aged eight; studied with Ernst von Dohnányi at Ferenc Liszt Acad. of Music –1954; remained at Ferenc Liszt Acad. as Asst Prof. to Zoltán Kodály; recitals in Leningrad (now St Petersburg), Moscow and Warsaw; settled in Switzerland 1958; London debut 1961, New York 1962; debut as conductor in Menton Festival of Music 1971; has since appeared in Europe, S Africa, S America, USA, Canada, India, Thailand, Hong Kong, Australia, Japan and Mexico; Jt Music Dir Northern Sinfonia, Newcastle, UK 1979–82; Musical Dir Bournemouth Sinfonietta 1988–96; Chief Musical Dir and Prin. Conductor Budapest Symphony Orchestra (Symphony Orchestra of the Hungarian Radio and Television) 1993–2004, Lifetime Hon. Chief Musical Dir 2004–; f. Zoltán Kodály World Youth Orchestra 2006–; Guest Conductor, London Philharmonic, Royal Philharmonic, Philharmonia, New York Philharmonic, Dallas and Houston Symphonies, Detroit Symphony; performances at Salzburg, Edin. and Merano Music Festivals. *Principal recordings:* three records of works of Liszt; eight of works of Chopin and various recordings of works of Rachmaninoff, Dohnányi, Debussy and Mozart; all symphonies and overtures of Beethoven, Schubert and Schumann 1997–98; further records for Hungaroton. *Publications:* A zenén túl 2003. *Honours:* Hon. Chair. and Conductor Savaria Symphonic Orchestra 2009–10; Chevalier des arts et lettres, Middle Cross of the Hungarian Order of Merit; winner, Marguerite Longue Competition 1955; Int. Competition, Warsaw 1955, Queen Elisabeth Competition, Belgium 1956, Int. Competition, Brazil 1957; Bach and Paderewski Medals (London), Kossuth Prize, Presidential Gold Medal 1998, Hungarian Heritage Prize. *Address:* c/o Zoltán Kodály World Youth Orchestra, 6000 Kecskemét, Kápolna Street 24. PO Box 312, Hungary (office). *E-mail:* csipero@t-online.hu (office).

VASILYEVA, Alla; Russian cellist; b. 1933, Moscow. *Education:* Central Music School, Moscow State Conservatoire with Rostropovich. *Career:* joined the Moscow Chamber Orchestra under Rudolf Barshai 1958, later principal cellist; many tours with the Moscow Chamber Orchestra and as solo recitalist, notably in modern Russian works; plays her own arrangements of works by Respighi and Vivaldi. *Recordings:* works by Bach, Geminiani, Vivaldi, Moshei Wainberg, Boris Tchaikovsky, Khrennikov and Shostakovich.

VASILYEVA, Marianna; Russian violinist; b. 25 Nov. 1986, St Petersburg. *Education:* studied at Special Music Lyceum, St Petersburg Conservatory with Prof. V. Y. Ovcharek and at Vienna Music Univ. with Prof. Dora Schwartzberg. *Career:* began playing violin at age five; awarded scholarships from Herbert von Karajan Foundation, Int. Vladimir Spivakov Foundation, Russian Ministry of Culture and Mass Communications; often performs in concert in St Petersburg, Germany, Austria, Switzerland, USA, Canada, France, Croatia and Finland; invited by conductor Valery Gergiev to participate in Music Festival of the Mariinsky Theatre on tour in Finland 1996. *Honours:* winner, Lipinski and Wieniawski Int. Competition for Young Violinists 2009, Prague Spring Int. Music Competition 2010, First Prize at Sion-Valais Int. Violin Competition 2011. *Address:* c/o The Paganini Moscow International Violin Competition, 107045 Moscow, Daev pereulok 20, office 204, Russia.

VASKS, Peteris; Latvian composer and double bassist; b. 16 April 1946, Aizpute. *Education:* Lithuanian Conservatory, Vilnius, Latvian Conservatory, Rīga. *Career:* double bassist in orchestras throughout Latvia and Lithuania 1963–74; Lecturer, Rīga Music School 1989–. *Compositions:* Music for Fleeting Birds for wind quintet 1977, three string quartets 1997, 1984, 1995, In Memoriam for two pianos 1997, Cantabile for strings 1979, Book for cello 1979, In Memory of a Friend for wind quintet 1982, Message for orchestra 1982, Piano Trio 1985, Double Bass Sonata 1986, Latvija chamber cantata 1987, English Horn Concerto 1989, Symphony: Voices for strings 1991, Litene for 12 voices 1992, Cello Concerto 1994, Violin Concerto 1997, Dona nobis pacem for chorus and seven instruments 1997, Symphony No. 2 1998.

VASSALLO, Marie Thérèse, DipLCM, LLCM; Maltese singer (mezzo-soprano), singing teacher and choir mistress; *Director, Marie Thérèse Vassallo Voice Studio, Malta Cultural Institute*; b. 4 March 1949, St Julian's; d. of the late Francis X. Vassallo and of Theresa Vassallo (née Theuma); m. Charles Axiak 1969; two s. *Education:* St Catherine's High School, Maria Regina Grammar School and Acad. Int. de Formation Musicale, France. *Career:* performances include Stabat Mater (Dvořák), Paulus (Mendelssohn), Missa Requiem and Coronation Mass (Mozart), Messiah and Judas Maccabaeus (Handel), Oratorio For Our Time (Lisiecki), Stabat Mater (Pergolesi), Te Deum (Bruckner), Dido and Aeneas (Purcell), Symphony No. 9 (Beethoven), Stabat Mater (Rossini), Missa Sancti Nicolai and Paukenmesse (Hadyn), Carmen (Bizet), Cavalleria Rusticana and L'Amico Fritz (Mascagni), Ipogeana and Caterina Desguanez (Pace), Il-Weghda (Camilleri), Madam Butterfly (Puccini), Le Nozze di Figaro (Mozart), Cenerentola and Il Barbiere di Siviglia (Rossini), Otello (Verdi); has premiered several works by Maltese composers; Head of Del. to Democratic People's Repub. of Korea 1986, 1987; mem. Bd of Dirs, Marie Thérèse Vassallo Voice Studio 2004–, Malta Cultural Inst., U3E Univ. Choir 2012–; Pres. Asscn of Maltese Lyrical Singers; organiser of annual Melita-Rossiya Competition for lyrical singers and of concerts for Foundation for Int. Studies, Univ. of Malta and Malta Cultural Inst.; Assoc. mem. Performing Rights Soc., London; Cultural Amb., LM100, Le Meridien St Julian's Hotel & Spa for Starwood Hotels International. *Publications include:* Songs: Bit-Tlikki Tlikki 1967, Stejjer Ghal Qabel Jidlam 1979, ITTRA ITTRA (for children's TV series). *Honours:* Diploma London Coll. of Music (Singing) 2002, Licenciate 2004; Mem. of Merit, Order of St Lazarus of Jerusalem (MMLJ) 2007, Commdr, Order of St Lazarus of Jerusalem (CLJ) 2009, Pilgrim's Decoration of Order (PSLJ) 2010, Dame, Order of St Lazarus of Jerusalem (DLJ) 2012, Dame Commdr (DCLJ) 2015; twice winner of Festival del Vulcano d'Oro, winner of Festival del Grappolo d'Oro and Festival della Canzone Mediterranea, Premio Città di Valletta 1994, Award for the Promotion of Cultural Relations between Malta and Russia 1995. *Address:* Malta Cultural Institute, La Paloma, 16 St Henry Street, Sliema SLM 1321, Malta (office). *Telephone:* 21333831 (office); 21338923 (home). *E-mail:* maltacultinst@gmail.com (office); marietvassallo@yahoo.com; marietheresevassallo@gmail.com. *Website:* maltaculturalinstitute.yolasite .com (office).

VASSILEV, Vasko; Bulgarian/British violinist and concertmaster; *Concertmaster, Royal Opera House, London*; b. 1970, Sofia, Bulgaria. *Education:* studied in Moscow. *Career:* after early competition success, joined Orchestra of Royal Opera House, 1991, as youngest ever leader and Concertmaster; solo career in Europe, North America and the Far East; European tour with the Royal Opera Orchestra 1998, with Mendelssohn and Tchaikovsky Concertos; Artistic Director of the Soloists of the Royal Opera House Orchestra 1998; Laureate of the String Ensemble. *Recordings include:* Solo and chamber music including Brahms Sonatas and Concerto by John Adams (Harmonia Mundi; Trittico Classics and Erato); Tartini Devil's Trill Sonata and The Original Four Seasons, with the Royal Opera String Ensemble and Vanessa Mae. *Honours:* prizewinner at Jacques Thibaud, Carl Flesch and Paganini Competitions. *Address:* Royal Opera House (Contracts), Covent Garden, London, WC2E 9DD, England (office). *Telephone:* (20) 7930-0330 (office). *Fax:* (20) 7930-0440 (office). *E-mail:* inbox@trittico.org (office). *Website:* www .vaskovassilev.com (office).

VASSILIEV, Alexander; German singer (bass); b. 20 March 1971, St Petersburg, Russia. *Education:* Tchaikovsky Conservatory, Moscow with Evgeny Nesterenko, master classes with Ernst Haefliger in Moscow, Hanna Ludwig in Salzburg and Astrid Varnay in Munich. *Career:* engagements at the Bavarian State Opera, Munich 1994–95, Freiburg Opera 1995–97, Cologne Opera 1997–2000; Co-founder and Artistic Dir Klassikfest Kaiserstuhl Int. Chamber Music Festival, Ihringen, Germany 2008–; roles have included Bottom in Britten's Midsummer Night's Dream, Alidoro in Rossini's Cenerentola, Don Basilio in Rossini's Il Barbiere di Seviglia, Figaro in Mozart's Le Nozze di Figaro, Leporello in Mozart's Don Giovanni, Kaspar in Der Freischütz, Bluebeard in Bartok's Bluebeard's Castle, Méphistophélès in Gounod's Faust, Méphistophélès in Berlioz's La Damnation de Faust, Forester in Janáček's The Cunning Little Vixen, Filippo II in Verdi's Don Carlo, Oedipe in Enescu's Oedipe, Don Pasquale in Donizetti's Don Pasquale, Gurnemanz in Wagner's Parsifal, Gremin in Tchaikovsky's Eugene Onegin and many others; appearances at prin. opera houses of Paris, Milan, Munich, Bologna, Brussels, Rome, Geneva, Amsterdam, Singapore, London, Glyndebourne, Madrid, Buenos Aires and St Petersburg; concerts and recitals at Cologne Philharmonie, Concertgebouw in Amsterdam, Palau de la Musica Catalana in Barcelona, as well as in Strasbourg, Freiburg, Munich, Cagliari, Bielefeld, Palma de Mallorca, Stuttgart, Bremen, Paris, Ithaca, Lockenhaus, Davos, Boswil and Città di Castello. *Films include:* DVDs: Shostakovich, Lady Macbeth of Mtsensk, Prokofiev, The Love for Three Oranges, Tchaikovsky, Cherevichki (all at Opus Arte). *Radio includes:* recital of Shostakovich songs (WDR 2, Germany), Shostakovich's 14th Symphony (Deutschlandfunk). *Recordings include:* Bizet – Ivan IV, Reznicek – Tragische Geschichte, 'Memento vivere' – Rudi Stephan, Complete Songs. *Honours:* Lemeshev Scholarship, First Prize, Int. Singing Competition 'Opera de Tenerife' 2013. *Current Management:* c/o Haydn Rawstron Ltd, 55 Langley Street, West Wickham, Kent, BR4 0DH, England. *Telephone:* (20) 8777-9214. *E-mail:* enquiries@haydn-rawstron.com. *Website:* www.haydnrawstron.com. *E-mail:* agentur@vassiliev.eu. *Website:* www.vassiliev.de.

VASSILIEVA, Elena; singer (soprano); b. 1956, France. *Education:* Paris Conservatoire. *Career:* won various awards in the early 1980s and sang in Henze's Boulevard Solitude at Paris 1984; has sung in operas by Puccini, Massenet, Verdi, Strauss and Mozart and notably as Tatiana in Eugene Onegin; Saffi in Der Zigeunerbaron at Liège; many concert appearances, including modern repertory and songs by Russian composers.

VATER, Wolfgang; German singer (bass-baritone); b. 1949, Bremerhaven. *Education:* Hanover Musikhochschule. *Career:* sang at Bielefeld from 1975, notably as Leporello; Bremen Opera from 1986; Gelsenkirchen 1987, as Faber in Tippett's The Knot Garden; season 1991 at Bielefeld in the premiere of Katharina Blum by Tilo Medek; Kothner in Die Meistersinger at Wiesbaden and Wiedehopf in Die Vögel by Braunfels; other roles include Mephistopheles in Faust, Don Alfonso in Così fan tutte and Gessler in Guillaume Tell; many concert and oratorio appearances. *Recordings include:* Werther, Strauss's Daphne.

VAUGHAN, Denis Edward, BMus; Australian conductor and organist; b. 6 June 1926, Melbourne. *Education:* University of Melbourne, Royal College of Music, London, England. *Career:* debut as conductor, Royal Festival Hall, London, 1953; annual harpsichord concerts, Royal Festival Hall, 1948–58; concert to honour Toscanini, with Bernstein, Klemperer, Celibidache and Maazel, Parma, 1959; adviser to UNESCO and Berne Union on musical aspects of copyright matters, 1962–67; Music Director, Australian Elizabethan Theatre Trust, 1966; orchestral concerts, operas in Europe, Australia, USA, Canada, 1970–2002; Munich State Opera House, 1972–80; Musical Director, State Opera of South Australia, 1981–84; operas conducted include Così fan tutte, Faust, Fidelio, Falstaff, Boris Godunov, The Rake's Progress, Giulio Cesare; concert in Vienna to celebrate the Austrian Millennium, 1996. *Recordings include:* 23 with Orchestra of Naples, including complete Schubert symphonies, 12 Haydn, 11 Mozart, Re Pastore. *Publications:* Le Discrepanze Nei Manoscritti Verdiani, La Scala, 1959; Preface on organ articulation and phrasing, Stanley Voluntaries, 1959; Puccini's Orchestration, Royal Musical Association, 1961; The Evaluation of Errors and Omissions in Dvořák's Manuscripts, Prague, 1999. *Current Management:* Hazard Chase Ltd, Norman House, Cambridge Place, Cambridge, CB2 1NS, England. *Telephone:* (1223) 312400. *Fax:* (1223) 460827. *Website:* www.hazardchase.co.uk. *Address:* 41 Floral Street, London WC2E 9DG, England (home). *Telephone:* (20) 7836-7399 (home). *Fax:* (20) 7836-2289 (home). *E-mail:* denisvaughan2001@yahoo.co.uk (home).

VAUGHAN, Elizabeth, FRAM; British singer (mezzo-soprano); b. 12 March 1937, Llanfyllin, Montgomeryshire, Wales. *Education:* Royal Acad. of Music. *Career:* debut, WNO 1960, as Abigaille in Nabucco; Covent Garden from 1961, as Mimi, Liu (Turandot), Teresa (Benvenuto Cellini), Gayle (The Ice Break, world premiere), Andromache and Hecuba (King Priam), Mozart's Elvira and Electra, Madama Butterfly, and Verdi's Amelia (Boccanegra), Abigaille, Alice (Falstaff), Leonore (Trovatore), Gilda and Violetta; Opera North as Tosca, Lady Macbeth and Abigaille; WNO as Tosca, Leonora (La Forza del Destino) and Maddalena in Andrea Chénier; ENO as Aida, Penelope Rich (Gloriana) and Beethoven's Leonore; Metropolitan Opera debut 1972, as Donna Elvira; guest engagements in Vienna, Berlin, Paris, Hamburg, Munich and Prague; appearances in Australia, Canada, South America, Japan; toured USA with ENO 1984; other roles include Herodias, Kabanicha (Katya Kabanova), and the Witch in Hansel and Gretel; sang the Overseer in Elektra at Covent

Garden 1997; La Frugola in Il Tabarro for ENO 1998; season 1999 Princess in Suor Angelica and Old Prioress in Carmélites; sang Herodias in Salome for Scottish Opera 2000. *Honours:* Hon. DMus (Univ. of Wales).

VAVILOV, Gennadi Alekseevich; Russian composer and academic; b. 7 May 1932; m. Natalia Romanenko 1971; one s. *Education:* Moscow Musical High School, Leningrad Conservatory, Moscow Conservatory, Petrozavodsk Univ. *Career:* debut performing Cantata for Choir and Symphony Orchestra, Moscow 1959; composer 1958–; teacher of theory of music and composition 1958; Prof. of Theory of Music, Instruments and Scores of Symphony Orchestra 1989–; Lecturer in Music 1982, in Music Accompaniment 1982; involved in Int. Open Young Pianist Competition, Barents Region, Karelia 2002–. *Compositions include:* Symphony No. 1, Voroneh 1982, Philadelphia, USA 1992, Symphony No. 4, Finland 1990, Sochi, Russia 1996, Symphony No. 3, Moscow 1973, Sonata No. 2 for piano, Paris, France 1996, Piano music: Allegro Barbaro, Dreams… Bushnell, USA 1998, Concert for piano and big symphony orchestra 2006, Symphony No. 5, Waterloo Bridge 2007; various original musical themes, traditions of Russian classical music, intonations for Karelian and Finnish Folk Tunes. *Recordings:* albums: Symphonietta for full symphony orchestra, Sonata for piano, Karelia tunes for symphony orchestra; Songs About Karelia 1985. *Publications:* contrib. Typical Features of Opera Orchestra by Mussorgsky 1984, Some Problems in the Usage of Folk in Composing 1985, Polifonia forms in Symphony Music 1985; scores: Symphony No. 1 for big symphony orchestra 2005, Concerto for violin and symphony orchestra 2008, Whirlwind of Waltz, album for piano 2009. *Honours:* Order of Friendship, Moscow 2002; second place in the competitions of Young Composers, Moscow, 1958; Television Competition of the USSR, Moscow, 1959. *Address:* Lenin Street 13-3, 185035 Petrozavodsk, Russia (office). *Telephone:* (814) 2781265 (office). *Fax:* (814) 2782578 (office). *E-mail:* galptz@karelia.ru (office).

VEASEY, Josephine, CBE; British singer (mezzo-soprano) (retd) and vocal consultant; b. 10 July 1930, Peckham, London, England; m. Ande Anderson 1951 (divorced 1969); one s. one d. *Education:* studied with Audrey Langford. *Career:* mem. chorus, Covent Garden Opera Company 1948–50, returned as soloist 1955; prin. mezzo-soprano, Royal Opera House, Covent Garden; has sung every major mezzo-soprano role in repertory; numerous foreign engagements have included Salzburg Festival, La Scala, Milan, Metropolitan Opera House, New York and Paris Opera; Prof., RAM 1982–83; vocal consultant, ENO 1985–94. *Recordings include:* recordings with Karajan, Solti, Bernstein and Colin Davis. *Honours:* Hon. RAM . *Address:* 99 Micheldever Road, Whitchurch, Hants., RG28 7JH, England (home). *Telephone:* (1256) 892930 (home).

VECCIA, Angelo; Italian singer (baritone); b. 1963, Rome. *Education:* Santa Cecilia Academy, Rome, Juilliard School, New York. *Career:* debut in Mozart's Figaro at Juilliard; gave concerts at the Lincoln Center, New York, and elsewhere in America, and appeared in Tosca with Placido Domingo; Appearances throughout Italy as Rossini's Figaro, Belcore, Marcello (at Verona, Venice and Florence) and Silvio; Further roles in Gluck's Iphigénie en Tauride at La Scala, Rimsky's Golden Cockerel at Rome and Schoenberg's Moses und Aron in Florence; Zürich Opera as Sharpless (Madama Butterfly), Gianni Schicchi and Marcello; Season 1997 in Bohème and Turandot at Tel-Aviv, Il Barbiere di Siviglia at Zürich and Lucia di Lammermoor at La Scala; Sang as guest in Aida at Berlin and in the 1996 Christmas Concert under Riccardo Chailly at the Amsterdam Concertgebouw. *Current Management:* c/o Ouverture, Via Braccianese Claudia 44, 00062 Bracciano (Roma), Italy. *Telephone:* (6) 9986602. *Fax:* (6) 9986603. *E-mail:* info@ouverture.net. *Website:* www.ouverture.net.

VEDERNIKOV, Alexander Aleksandrovich; Russian conductor; *Chief Conductor and Artistic Adviser, Odense Symphony Orchestra;* b. 11 Jan. 1964, Moscow; s. of Aleksander F. Vedernikov and Natalya Guryeva; m. Olga Aleksandrovna Vedernikova. *Education:* Moscow P. I. Tchaikovsky State Conservatory. *Career:* Music Dir Stanislavsky Music Theatre, Moscow 1988–90; Asst, then Conductor Prin. Symphony Orchestra of Russian TV and Radio 1989–95; Founder and Chief Conductor Russian Philharmonia Symphony Orchestra 1995–98, 2000–04; Musical Dir and Chief Conductor Bolshoi Theatre of Russia 2001–09; mem. conductor's collegium, Russian Nat. Orchestra 2003–; Chief Conductor and Artistic Adviser, Odense Symphony Orchestra 2009–; conducted opera and ballet productions in European theatres including Covent Garden, London, La Scala, Milan and symphony orchestras in Russia; debuts at Carnegie Hall and Kennedy Center, Washington, DC 2004. *Current Management:* c/o Bridget Canniere, IMG Artists, The Light Box, 111 Power Road, London, W4 5PY, England. *Telephone:* (20) 7957-5800. *Fax:* (20) 7957-5801. *E-mail:* bcanniere@imgartists.com. *Website:* www.imgartists.com. *Address:* Pyryeva str. 4, korp. 1, apt. 24, 119285 Moscow, Russia (home). *Telephone:* (495) 147-52-17 (home).

VEDERNIKOV, Alexander Filoppovich; Russian singer (bass); b. 23 Dec. 1927, Mokino, nr Kirov. *Education:* studied in Moscow with Alpert-Khasina. *Career:* debut, Bolshoi Theatre Moscow 1957, as Ivan Susanin in Glinka's A Life for the Tsar; Appearances in Moscow, Leningrad, Tbilisi and Kiev as Boris and Varlaam in Boris Godunov, Dosifey (Khovanshchina) and Konchak in Prince Igor; Engagements with the company of the Bolshoi at Paris, New York and Milan as Philip II and the Grand Inquisitor in Don Carlos and Massimilione in Verdi's I Masnadieri; Toured West Germany with the Bolshoi 1987; Other roles include Daland in Der fliegende Holländer, Prince Gremin

(Eugene Onegin), Kutuzov in War and Peace and Mephistopheles (Faust). *Recordings include:* The Stone Guest by Dargomyzhsky; Rimsky-Korsakov's The Snow Maiden, Pimen in a video of Boris Godunov from the Bolshoi (National Video Corporation). *Address:* c/o Bolshoi Theatre, Pr Marxa 8/2, 103009 Moscow, Russia.

VEIRA, Jonathan; singer (bass-baritone); b. 1960, England. *Education:* Trinity College of Music, London and the National Opera Studio. *Career:* debut as soloist, Wexford, 1986; at Glyndebourne appeared as Lemokh in the premiere of The Electrification of the Soviet Union; Die Entführung and Capriccio; other engagements include a tour with Opera 80; Antonio, in Le nozze di Figaro at the Prom concerts and Tippett's New Year for the Glyndebourne Tour; Broadcasts of Mahagonny and Rossini's Tancredi for the BBC; Television appearances in La Traviata, The Electrification of the Soviet Union and Death in Venice; Engagements with Opera Factory, London; As a concert artist has performed at many major London venues; Has broadcast Leoncavallo's La Bohème and Königskinder for RTE Dublin; Television appearances include The Marriage of Figaro, La Traviata and Death in Venice; In 1993 he sang his first Papageno in a new production of The Magic Flute conducted by Jane Glover at the Covent Garden Festival; Sang Bartolo in Barber of Seville for Opera Northern Ireland and at Garsington Festival in 1994; Other performances include a premiere of a new opera by Stuart Copeland in the Barbados Festival, Bottom in A Midsummer Night's Dream, for Covent Garden Festival and Scarpia in a concert performance of Tosca for the opening of the 1994 Bournemouth International Festival; In 1995 he sang Dulcamara in L'Elisir d'amore for Opera Northern Ireland, Dr Bartolo in The Marriage of Figaro, Melitone in La Forza del Destino and Calchas in La Belle Hélène for Scottish Opera; Engagements in 1996 included Leporello in Don Giovanni for Auckland Opera with Kiri Te Kanawa, Melitone with the Royal Danish Opera, Dr Bartolo for Opéra de Nice; Banker in Lulu and roles for Glyndebourne Festival Opera; 1997 with Bartolo for Welsh National Opera; Sharpless in Madama Butterfly, Dr Bartolo in Le Nozze di Figaro for Opera Ireland; Dr Kolonaty in The Makropulos Case for Glyndebourne at the Proms, Royal Albert Hall; Engagements in 1998 included Baron Zeta, The Merry Widow, for Royal Opera; Dr Bartolo, The Marriage of Figaro, Zürich Opera; Vaarlam, Boris Gedonov, Welsh National Opera; Tonio, Pagliacci, Opera Ireland; Jake, Porgy and Bess, BBC Proms; Engagements in 1999–2000 included Talum Hadjo in Delius's Godunov, The Magic Fountain at Scottish Opera; Title role in Falstaff, Royal Danish Opera, Copenhagen, Mustafà, The Italian Girl in Algiers, Garsington Festival; Kecal, The Bartered Bride, Glyndebourne Festival and tour; Season 2000–01 as Leporello with GTO, Bunoafede in Haydn's Il mondo della luna at Garsington and Janáček's Kolenaty at the Academy of Music, New York. *Recordings:* two solo albums; featured soloist on recording of operatic excerpts for Opera Rara; Elgar's The Spanish Lady. *Honours:* Winner, Peter Pears Singing Competition; Anna Instone Memorial Award. *Address:* 4 Lincoln Road, Guildford, Surrey GU2 6JT, England.

VELA, Andrea, MMus; Ecuadorean conductor and violinist; *Artistic Director, Orquesta Sinfónica Nacional de Ecuador;* b. Quito. *Education:* Conservatorio Nacional de Música, Peabody Conservatory of Music, Univ. of Louisville, Hartford Univ., USA, Shanghai Conservatory of Music, China. *Career:* has served as Asst Dir to Orchestra of Shanghai Conservatory, Louisville Univ. Opera, Jewish Orchestra of Louisville, Tel-Aviv Philharmonic Orchestra; Asst Dir Orquesta Sinfónica Nacional de Ecuador 2008–10, Music Dir 2010–. *Honours:* winner, Concurso de Dirección de Orquesta, Quito 1998. *Address:* Orquesta Sinfónica Nacional de Ecuador, Leonidas Plaza 19–34, entre Patria y 18 de Septiembre, Quito, Ecuador (office). *Telephone:* (2) 2502814 (office). *Website:* www.sinfonicanacional.gov.ec (office).

VELIS, Andrea; American singer (tenor); b. 7 June 1932, New Kensington, PA. *Education:* studied with Louise Taylor in Pittsburgh, Royal Coll. of Music, London, Accademia di Santa Cecilia, Rome. *Career:* debut in Pittsburgh 1954, as Goro in Madama Butterfly; appearances in Chicago, Cincinnati, Philadelphia and San Francisco; Metropolitan Opera from 1961 in performances of 50 operas, including La Fanciulla del West, Death in Venice, Hansel and Gretel, Eugene Onegin, The Ring (Mime), Les Contes d'Hoffmann, Otello, Der Rosenkavalier, Tosca and Boris Godunov; sang Mardian in the premiere of Barber's Antony and Cleopatra 1966. *Recordings include:* Tosca.

VELLA, Joseph, BMus; Maltese composer and conductor; *Associate Professor of Composition, University of Malta;* b. 9 Jan. 1942, Gozo; m. Nathalie Portelli; two c. *Education:* Accademia Musicale, Siena with Franco Donatoni and Franco Ferrara, University of Durham. *Career:* guest appearances as conductor in Europe, USA, Asia; Musical Dir, Astra Opera House, Gozo 1970–; Associate Professor of Composition, Univ. of Malta 1994–; Composer-in-Residence, Malta Philharmonic Orchestra. *Compositions include:* Trio for violin, horn and piano 1968, Sinfonia De profundis 1969, Clarinet Quintet 1973, The Seasons, Madrigal cycle 1980, String Quartet 1981, Piano concerto 1984, Sinfonietta, for strings 1984, A Canticle Cantata 1985, Sinfonia No. 2 1989, Blood on the Verna, oratorio 1989, Brass Quintet 1992, Love Textures, for baritone and orchestra 1993, Violin Concerto 1993, Cello Concerto 1995, Flute Concerto 1996, Concerto Barocco for bassoon and orchestra 1998, Concerto for two pianos solo 2000, Sinfonietta for 13 woodwind players 2001, Symphony No. 3 (The Apocalypse Verses) 2003, Riflessioni for wind quintet 2005, Sonata for alto sax and piano 2006, Concerto for piccolo 2008, Fun Fair for three trumpets and timpani 2009. *Honours:* Gieh ir-Republika. *Address:* Music Department, University of Malta, Sliema, Malta (office). *Telephone:*

79618470 (home). *Fax:* 21454133 (office). *E-mail:* joseph.vella@um.edu.mt (office).

VELLA, Richard, BA, MA; Australian composer and academic; b. 1 Dec. 1954, Melbourne, Vic. *Education:* La Trobe Univ. *Career:* Gen. Ed., Music Currency Press, 1989–; Prof., La Trobe Univ. 1996–97, Advisory Prof. 1998–99; Artistic Dir, Calculated Risks Opera Productions 1990–. *Compositions include:* Tales of Love, opera, 1990; A Piano Reminisces, 1991; Remember, Unending Love, for chorus, 1992; The Last Supper, opera, 1993; Concerto for Trombone, 1995; Commissions from Astra Choir, One Extra Dance Company, The Elizabethan Theatre Trust, and others. *Publication:* Musical Environments 2000. *Honours:* Commonwealth Postgraduate Research Award 1979. *Address:* c/o Red House Editions, PO Box 2123, Footscray, Vic. 3011, Australia.

VENGEROV, Maxim; Israeli (b. Russian) violinist and conductor; *Menuhin Professor, Royal Academy of Music*; b. 1974, Novosibirsk, Western Siberia, USSR; s. of Alexander Vengerov and Larissa Vengerov; m. Olga Gringolts 2011; two d. *Education:* studied with Vag Papian in St Petersburg and with Yuri Simonov. *Career:* began career as a solo violinist aged five; made first recording aged ten; turned his attention to conducting 2007, Carnegie Hall conducting debut during Verbier Festival Orchestra's tour 2007; has since conducted major orchestras, including the Toronto and Montreal Symphony orchestras, Enescu, Israel, London and Russian Nat. Philharmonic orchestras, as well as the English and Paris Chamber orchestras; first Chief Conductor, Gstaad Festival Orchestra 2010; returned to the violin in 2011, now divides his time equally between violin performance, conducting and teaching; annual Vengerov Festival in Tokyo launched 2013; Prof. of Violin, RAM, London 2005–, Menuhin Prof. 2012–; Amb. and Visiting Prof. of Menuhin Acad., Switzerland; Artist-in-Residence, Oxford Philomusica 2013–; regularly serves on competition juries, including the Yehudi Menuhin Int. Violin Competition, Donatella Flick Conducting Competition, appeared at Montreal Int. Violin Competition as conductor of the competition finals 2013; Chair. Wieniawski Violin Competition 2011, re-elected to return as Chair. in 2016; UNICEF Goodwill Amb. (first classical musician) 1997–; fellowships and honours from several insts, including RAM. *Recordings include:* Sonatas by Beethoven and Brahms and Paganini 1st Concerto 1992, Sonatas by Mozart, Beethoven and Mendelssohn 1992, Virtuoso Violin Pieces, Bruch and Mendelssohn Violin Concertos, Britten Violin Concerto and Walton Viola Concerto with Mstislav Rostropovich and London Symphony Orchestra (Grammy Award 2004, Classical BRIT Critics' Award 2004) 2002, Best of Maxim Vengerov 2006, Phenomenal Vengerov 2011, Khrennikov Violin & Piano Concertos 2013, The Complete Recordings 1991-2007 2014. *Honours:* won Wieniawski and Carl Flesch int. competitions aged ten 10 and 15, respectively; First Prize, Jr Wieniawski Competition, Poland 1984, Winner Carl Flesch Int. Violin Competition 1990, Gramophone Young Artist of the Year 1994, Ritmo Artist of the Year 1994, Gramophone Record of the Year 1996, Edison Award 1997, Gramophone Artist of the Year 2002. *Current Management:* c/o Nicola-Fee Bahl, NFBM Ltd, 3rd Floor Offices, 24 Endell Street, London, WC2H 9HQ, England. *Telephone:* (20) 7359-4771. *Fax:* (20) 3292-1913. *E-mail:* nicola-fee@nfbm.com. *Website:* www.nfbm.com.

VENN, Edward John, BA, MA, PhD, LRSM; British academic; b. 31 Oct. 1974, Watford, England. *Education:* Univ. of Birmingham. *Career:* Lecturer in Dept of Music, Lancaster Univ. 2001–; cttee mem. Soc. for Music Analysis 2004–. *Publications:* 'Idealism and Ideology in Tippett's writings', in Michael Tippett: Music and Literature (ed. Suzanne Robinson), The Music of Hugh Wood. *Address:* Department of Music, Lancaster University, Lancaster, LA1 4YW, England (office). *Telephone:* (1524) 593105 (office). *E-mail:* e.venn@lancaster.ac.uk (office). *Website:* www.lanc.ac.uk/staff/venn (office).

VENTRE, Carlo; Italian/Uruguayan singer (tenor); b. 23 Feb. 1969, Montevideo, Uruguay. *Education:* studied in Uruguay, in New York with Armen Boiayan and in Italy with Gino Bechi, Magda Olivero and Vittorio Terranova. *Career:* debut at La Scala Milan under Riccardo Muti as the Duke of Mantua, and Ismaele in Nabucco; roles include Radames in Aida, Don José in Carmen, Attila, Calaf in Turandot, Gabriele Adorno in Simon Boccanegra, Manrico in Il Trovatore, Riccardo in Un Ballo in Maschera, Turiddu in Cavalleria Rusticana, Arrigo in I Vespri Siciliani, Rodolfo in La Bohème, Pinkerton in Madame Butterfly, Luigi in Il Tabarro, Macbeth, Carlo in I Masnadieri, Alzira, Cavaradossi in Tosca, Andrea Chénier, Federico in Germania, Roberto in Le Villi; future appearances include Des Grieux in Manon Lescaut, Don Carlos, Otello, Dick Johnson in La Fanciulla del West and Maurizio in Adriana Lecouvreur; has sung in La Scala Milan, Teatro Regio Turin, Teatro Lirico Cagliari, Teatro Carlo Felice Genoa, Teatro Massimo Palermo, Teatro dell'Opera and Terme di Caracalla Rome, Teatro Verdi Trieste, Arena and Teatro Filarmonico Verona, Teatro Regio Parma, Sferisterio Macerata, Maggio Musicale Fiorentino, Bayerische Staatsoper München, Deutsche Oper and Staatsoper unter den Linden Berlin, Oper Frankfurt, Hamburgische Staatsoper, Dresden Semperoper, Oper Leipzig, Opernhaus Zürich, Wiener Staatsoper, Teatro Colón Buenos Aires, Dallas Opera, Chicago Opera, San Francisco Opera, Kennedy Center, Welsh Nat. Opera, Liceu Barcelona, Opéra de Nice, La Monnaie Bruxelles, Grand Théâtre de Genève, Opéra de Lausanne, New Nat. Theatre, Tokyo; future engagements at San Diego Opera, Royal Opera House, London, Opéra Bastille, Paris and Chorégies d'Orange. *Honours:* Gino Bechi Prize at Francisco Viñas Competition 1990, winner Luciano Pavarotti Competition, Philadelphia 1995, Gigli d'oro 2009, Premio Lugo 2010, Premio Matassa d'oro Carpi 2011. *Current Management:* c/o Punto Opera, Piazza IV Novembre 16/b, 37064 Povegliano, Verona, Italy. *Telephone:* (045) 7364601. *Fax:* (045) 6359172. *E-mail:* info@puntoopera.net. *Website:* www.puntoopera.net; www.carloventre.com.

VENTRIS, Christopher, ARAM; British singer (tenor); b. 5 May 1965, London, England. *Education:* Royal Acad. of Music, London. *Career:* joined Glyndebourne Festival Chorus; touring opera debut as Vanya in Katya Kabanova; later appearances as Tom Rakewell with Glyndebourne Festival Opera and The Porter in Death in Venice, Jacquino in Fidelio, and Števa in Jenůfa with Glyndebourne Touring Opera; opera work with Opera North, ENO and Royal Opera; performed in Magic Flute in Geneva 1993, King Priam and Eugene Onegin at Antwerp 1994 and Flying Dutchman 1992 and Salome 1994 at Leipzig; further engagements include Steuermann at Amsterdam 1995, Midsummer Marriage with Royal Opera, title role in Parsifal at Antwerp; debut at La Scala as Max in Der Freischütz 1998; engaged as Parsifal at San Francisco 2000, and Siegmund in Die Walküre at Cologne 2001; more recent engagements include Peter Grimes, Barcelona, Washington Opera and Zurich Opera, Parsifal at Royal Opera, Seattle, Bayreuth 2008–10; Laca with Zurich Opera 2012, Grimes with Deutsche Oper Berlin and Lohengrin Madrid Opera (2014). *Recordings include:* Parsifal, Zurich Opera, Baden Baden Festival, Lady Macbeth of Mtsensk, Amsterdam Opera, Peter Grimes, Zurich Opera, Parsifal, Zurich Opera. *Honours:* Esso GTFO Singer's Award 1988–89, Glyndebourne John Christie Award, Dallas Opera's Maria Callas Debut Artist of the Year Award 2007. *Current Management:* c/o Artists Management Zürich, Rütistrasse 52, 8044 Zürich-Gockhausen, Switzerland. *E-mail:* schuetz@artistsman.com. *Website:* www.artistsman.com.

VENUTI, Maria; American singer (soprano); b. 1953, New York. *Education:* Eastman School, Rochester, Detmold Musikhochschules with Helmut Kretzschmar and Gunter Weissenborn. *Career:* sang at the Vienna Staatsoper from 1976, Lyric Opera Chicago from 1978; appearances throughout Europe in operas by Mozart, Amor in Orfeo ed Euridice, Oscar in Un ballo in Maschera, Sophie in Der Rosenkavalier and Bizet's Micaela; engagements at Augsburg, Kassel (Mozart's Ilia, 1984), Salzburg and Brussels; concert repertoire has included Schubert's Lazarus, Utrecht Te Deum by Handel, and the Mozart Requiem. *Recordings include:* Inez, in Il Trovatore, under Karajan. *Current Management:* Hannagret Bueker Agentur für Musiktheater und Konzert, Fuhsestrasse 2, 30419 Hannover, Germany. *Telephone:* (511) 2716910. *Fax:* (511) 2717873. *E-mail:* mail@buekervoice.de. *Website:* www.buekervoice.de.

VENZAGO, Mario; Swiss conductor; *Chief Conductor, Bern Symphony Orchestra*; b. 1 July 1948, Zurich. *Education:* Univ. of Zurich, Zurich Conservatory, conducting studies with Hans Swarowsky, Vienna Conservatory. *Career:* began playing the piano aged five; travelled extensively for10 years following graduation; official pianist of Swiss Italian Broadcasting Television Co. and Orchestra (RTSI); began conducting career as Prin. Conductor, Winterthur Symphony Orchestra 1978; later led Lucerne Opera House and served as Prin. Conductor for broadcast recordings of Orchestre de la Suisse Romande, Geneva; Music Dir Heidelberg Philharmonic Orchestra and Opera House 1986–89; later served as Chief Conductor of German Kammerphilharmonie Bremen, Graz Opera, Basque Nat. Orchestra, Basel Symphony Orchestra, Swedish Nat. Orchestra, Gothenburg; fmr Artistic Dir Baltimore Summer Music Fest; Music Dir Indianapolis Symphony Orchestra 2002–09; apptd Prin. Conductor Northern Sinfonia, Newcastle upon Tyne, UK 2010; Chief Conductor Bern Symphony Orchestra 2010–; Artist in Asscn with Tapiola Sinfonietta 2010–; Schumann Guest Conductor, Düsseldorfer Symphoniker; career has included engagements with Berlin Philharmonic, Leipzig Gewandhaus Orchestra, Munich Philharmonic, London Philharmonic, BBC Symphony Orchestra, City of Birmingham Symphony Orchestra, Vienna Symphony, La Scala di Milano, Melbourne Symphony Orchestra, NHK Symphony, Tokyo, and symphony orchestras of Copenhagen, Helsinki and Paris; has also conducted at Salzburg and Lucerne Festivals, amongst others; US debut at invitation of Leonard Bernstein at the Hollywood Bowl with Los Angeles Philharmonic Inst. Orchestra 1988; has appeared with Boston Symphony, Philadelphia Orchestra, Toronto Symphony, New Jersey Symphony and Nat. Arts Center Orchestra of Ottawa; conducted Baltimore Symphony on short notice 1995, since then has conducted annual subscription concerts and was Artistic Dir of the summer festivals 2000–03; has collaborated with stage dirs including Ruth Berghaus, Peter Konwitschny and Hans Neuenfels; performs with concert artists including Argerich, Bell, Freire, Josefowicz, Kremer, Lang Lang, Levin, Lupu, Maisky, Mutter, Nicolet, Ohlsson, Pletnev, Shaham, Steuerman, Tetzlaff, Vengerow, Zehetmair, K. Zimerman, F. P. Zimmermann, and with singers including Araiza, Banse, Baltsa, Häfliger, Heppner, Kalisch, Naef, Moser, Popp and Ziesak. *Recordings include:* complete symphonic works of Schumann, Ravel and Nono with the Basel Symphony, complete choral works of Othmar Schoeck with the choir and orchestra of the MDR Leipzig, complete orchestral works of Alban Berg with the Gothenburg Symphony Orchestra. *Honours:* Diapason d'Or, two Grand Prix du Disque, Edison Prize. *Current Management:* c/o Felix Freitag, Concerto Winderstein, Brunnstraβe 1, 80331 Munich, Germany. *Telephone:* (89) 38384631. *Fax:* (89) 38384633. *E-mail:* freitag@winderstein.de. *Website:* www.concerto.de. *E-mail:* contact@mariovenzago.com. *Website:* www.mariovenzago.com.

VERA-RIVERA, Santiago Oscar, DMus; Chilean academic and composer; b. 2 Nov. 1950, Santiago; m. Maria Angelica Bustamante 1974, two s. one d. *Education:* Univ. of Chile, Univ. of Oviedo, Spain. *Career:* Prof., Univ. of Chile 1974–81, Univ. of Tarapaca 1984, Acad. Pedag. Santiago 1981–85, Univ.

Metropolitana 1986, Escuela Moderna de Música 1976–87; Intern/OAS 1984. *Compositions include:* Tres Temporarias 1987, Cirrus 1987, Apocaliptika II 1988, Tres Acuareskas 1989, Chiloé, Tierra de Agua 1989, Silogistika I for flute and guitar 1989, Silogistika II for voice, clarinet, violin, violoncello and piano 1989, Silogistika III for voice and orchestra, Harmony for two voices 1990.

VERBITSKY, Vladimir, PhD; Russian conductor; *Music Director and Chief Conductor, Voronezh State Symphony Orchestra;* b. 24 Oct. 1943, Leningrad, USSR; m. Ninel; one s. one d. *Education:* studied piano, choral, operatic and symphony conducting, Leningrad Conservatoire, graduated in piano 1966. *Career:* various orchestral appointments, including Music Dir and Chief Conductor Voronezh State Philharmonic 1972–; Guest Conductor, State Orchestra of the USSR, Moscow 1976–89; Chief Conductor, Slovak Philharmonic Orchestra, Bratislava, Czechoslovakia 1982–84; Music Dir State Orchestra of Victoria, Melbourne, Australia 1987–88; Guest Conductor, West Australian Symphony Orchestra 1987–91; Guest Conductor 1992–97, Conductor Laureate 1997–; Prof., Voronezh State Inst. of Art; publs and recordings of classical music with major orchestras world-wide. *Recordings:* classical music with major orchestras worldwide, Best Ever Russian Orchestral Music Collection (three-CD set) 2006. *Honours:* Order of Honour 1980, Order for Services to the Fatherland 2004; Herbert von Karajan Int. Young Conductors' Competition diploma, Berlin 1973, Laureate Villa Lobos Int. Young Conductors' Competition, Rio de Janeiro 1975, Laureate Hungarian Radio and Television Int. Conductors' Competition, Budapest 1976, People's Artist of Russian Fed. 1993. *Current Management:* c/o Kenneth Wentworth, Jonathan Wentworth Associates Ltd, 10 Fiske Place, Suite 530, Mount Vernon, NY 10550-3205, USA. *Telephone:* (914) 667-0707. *Fax:* (914) 667-0784. *E-mail:* kenneth@jwentworth.com. *Address:* PO Box 34, 70 Malyj Prospekt, St Petersburg, 199406 Russian Federation (office). *Telephone:* (812) 355-24-11 (office). *E-mail:* vnverbitsky@yandex.ru (home).

VERBRUGGEN, Marion, DipMus, BA; Dutch recorder player and teacher; b. 2 Aug. 1950, Amsterdam. *Education:* Amsterdam Conservatory with Kees Otten, Muziek Lyceum, Amsterdam with Frans Brüggen, Royal Conservatory, The Hague. *Career:* performances with various ensembles and solo concerts in The Netherlands, USA, Canada, Japan, most European countries; regular guest, Gustav Leonhardt, Amsterdam Baroque Orchestra, Musica Antiqua, Cologne, Tafelmusik Toronto, many others; plays at Holland Festival of Early Music; Teacher, Royal Conservatory, The Hague, Utrecht Conservatory; guest teacher, Malmö Conservatory, Sweden; masterclasses and workshops, Stanford Univ., Toronto, Montréal, New York, Philadelphia, Malmö, Trondheim, Copenhagen, Jerusalem.

VERBY, Theo; Dutch composer; b. 5 July 1959, Delft. *Education:* Royal Conservatory, The Hague. *Career:* Lecturer in Composition, Amsterdam Sweelinck Conservatory 1997–; commissions from London Sinfonietta, Residentie-Orkest and Royal Concertgebouw Orchestra. *Compositions:* Caprice Symphonique 1976, Triplum for wind instruments 1982, Random Symphonies (electronic) 1985, Contrary Motion for orchestra 1986, Inversie for ensemble 1987, Expulsie for ensemble 1990, De Peryton for seven wind instruments 1990, Triade for orchestra 1991, revised 1994, Whitman for soprano and orchestra 1992, Notturno for oboe, two horns and strings 1995, Conciso for ensemble 1996, Alliage for orchestra 1996, Six Rilke Lieder for baritone and small orchestra 1998. *Honours:* Amsterdam Art Fund award 1987.

VERCO, Wendy; singer (mezzo-soprano); b. 1945, Melbourne, Australia. *Education:* Sydney Conservatory and Opera Studio, London. *Career:* debut at Opera 80 1982, as Orlofsky in Die Fledermaus; appearances with Opera 80 as Dorabella and with WNO as Maddalena in Rigoletto and Meg Page in Falstaff; Glyndebourne Festival from 1981, in Poppea, Idomeneo and Arabella; Opera North 1985, as Irene in Tamerlano, Covent Garden 1986, as Rossweise in Die Walküre; WNO on tour to Japan 1990; sang Clytemnestra in Gluck's Iphigénie operas at the Théâtre des Champs Elysées, Paris 1991; concerts with the City of Birmingham Symphony Orchestra and the London Mozart Players. *Recordings:* Poppea, Arabella and Idomeneo from Glyndebourne.

VERCOE, Elizabeth, BA, MMus, DMA; American composer and academic; *Adjunct Professor, Regis College;* b. (Elizabeth Hendry), 23 April 1941, Washington, DC; one s. one d. *Education:* Wellesley Coll., Univ. of Michigan, Boston Univ. *Career:* Instructor of Musical Theory, Westminster Choir Coll. 1969–71; Asst Prof. of Music, Framingham State Coll., Mass 1973–74; Composer, Cité Internationale des Arts, Paris, France 1983–85, Charles Ives Center for American Music 1984, 1992; Co-Dir Women's Music Festival, Boston 1985, MacDowell Colony 1992, St Petersburg, Russia, Spring Music Festival 1993; Dir Soc. of Composers Festivals 1995–96; Lecturer, Regis Coll., Weston, Mass 1997, now Adjunct Prof.; residencies at Civitella Ranieri Foundation, Italy 1998, Virginia Center for the Arts, MacDowell Colony, Charles Ives Center for American Music, Cité Internationale des Arts, Paris; Guest Composer, Goethe Inst., Bangkok 2009, Illinois Coll., Goucher Coll. 2012, Longwood Univ. 2013. *Compositions include:* Fantasy for piano, Balance for violin and cello, Sonario for cello, Three Studies for piano, Irreveries from Sappho for SSA and piano or soprano and piano, Herstory I & II for soprano, piano and percussion, Herstory III, Persona for piano, Rhapsody for violin and orchestra, Despite our Differences No. 1 for piano trio, No. 2 for piano and orchestra, A la Fin tout seul for mandolin and optional piano, A Dangerous Man for baritone and piano, Changes for chamber orchestra, Four Humors for

clarinet and piano, Herstory IV for soprano and mandolin or marimba, Umbrian Suite for piano 4-hands, Kleemation for flute and piano, To Music for solo flute, Five Inventions for horn and piano, Butterfly Effects for flute and harp (also arranged for oboe and harp), Corollaries for horn, Zwei Klavierstucke. *Dance:* Persona choreographed by Beth Soll for the Beth Soll Dance Co.. *Publications include:* Where are the Great Women Conductors? (International Choral Bulletin), The Lady Vanishes? (Perspectives of New Music) 1982, A Composer's View (Journal of Early Music America) 1990, Interview with Vivian Fine (Journal of the International League of Women Composers), A Composer's View (Historical Performance: The Journal of Early Music America). *Honours:* Acuff Chair of Excellence, Austin Peay State Univ., Tenn. 2003; Meet the Composer grants 1981, 1987, 1994, 1999, Massachusetts Artist Fellowship 1985, Artists' Foundation project grant 1983, First Prize in Music Theory and Composition, Boston Univ., Hubert Weldon Lamb Prize in Composition, Wellesley Coll. *Address:* Music Department, Regis College Fine Arts Center 209A, PO Box 1015, 235 Wellesley Street, Weston, MA 02493 (office); c/o Arsis Press, Empire Publishing Service, PO Box 1344, Studio City, CA 91614, USA. *Telephone:* (781) 768-8331 (office). *E-mail:* elizvercoe@yahoo.com. *Website:* elizabethvercoe.com.

VERGARA, Victoria; singer (mezzo-soprano); b. 1948, Santiago, Chile. *Education:* studied in Santiago, in New York with Nicola Moscona and Anton Guadagno, Juilliard School with Daniel Ferro and Rose Bampton. *Career:* sang minor roles in the USA, before New York City Opera debut 1977; sang at Detroit from 1977, Santiago 1978, Houston Grand Opera from 1980; has sung Carmen at San Francisco, Cincinnati, Zürich, Lisbon, Vancouver, Philadelphia, Seattle, New Orleans and Berlin; Chicago Lyric Opera 1982, Vienna Staatsoper 1984, as Amneris; Washington Opera 1987, as the Duchess of Alba in the premiere of Menotti's Goya, opposite Placido Domingo; Metropolitan Opera debut 1988, as Carmen; Teatro Liceo Barcelona 1989, in the premiere of Cristóbal Colón by Leonardo Balada, with Caballé and Carreras; season 1990 sang Herodias (Salome) at Santiago and at the Zarzuela Theatre Madrid in El viajero indiscreto, as Dona; other roles include Donna Elvira, Cherubino, Federica in Luisa Miller, Maddalena, Rosina, Dalila, Nicklausse, Charlotte and Massenet's Dulcinée. *Recordings include:* Maddalena in Rigoletto.

VERMEERSCH, Jef; singer (baritone); b. 7 Feb. 1928, Bruges, Belgium. *Education:* studied in Bruges, Ghent and Antwerp. *Career:* Wotan in Das Rheingold 1960; sang at Gelsenkirchen from 1966; mem., Deutsche Oper Berlin from 1973; guest appearances in Germany and Brussels, Amsterdam, Lyon, Venice, Lisbon, Prague, Geneva, San Francisco, Barcelona and Stockholm; Salzburg Easter Festival 1973, as Kurwenal in Tristan and Isolde, conducted by Karajan; Bayreuth Festival 1981–83, Kothner in Die Meistersinger; other roles include Hans Sachs, Amfortas, the Dutchman, Boris Godunov, Golaud, Pizarro, Kaspar, the title role in Giulio Cesare by Handel, Leporello, Jochanaan, Kepler in Hindemith's Die Harmonie der Welt, Falstaff, Amonasro and St Just in Von Einem's Dantons Tod; sang Kothner at Bayreuth 1988; Kurwenal at Wuppertal 1989.

VERMILLION, Iris; German singer (soprano); b. 1960, Bielefeld. *Education:* studied with Mechthild Bohme and Judith Beckmann. *Career:* debut at Brunswick 1986 as Zulma in L'Italiana in Algeri and as Barbara in Eine Nacht in Venedig; sang Dorabella and Octavian in Brunswick; Deutsche Oper Berlin from 1988 as a Rhinemaiden, Hansel and Cherubino; Darmstadt 1988 as Judith in Duke Bluebeard's Castle; sang Dorabella with Netherlands Opera in Amsterdam 1990; Salzburg Festival 1990 as Clairon in Capriccio; other roles include Werther, Charlotte and Mozart's Sextus; also sings in the St Matthew Passion and Mozart's Davidde Penitente; sang Bianca in Zemlinsky's Florentinische Tragödie at Florence 1995; season 2000 as Strauss's Composer at La Scala, Waltraute for the Vienna Staatsoper, premiere of Rihm's St Luke Passion at Stuttgart and Adriano in Wagner's Rienzi at Dresden (concert). *Recordings include:* Second Lady in Die Zauberflöte under Neville Marriner. *Honours:* prizewinner Cardiff Singer of World Competition.

VERNEROVA-NOVAKOVA, Ludmila; Czech singer (soprano); b. 6 Dec. 1962, Prague; m. Pravomil Novák; one d. *Education:* Acad. of Musical Arts, Prague. *Career:* debut at Nat. Theatre, Prague 1987; Bach Acad. at Stuttgart, Germany three times, Handel Messiah; Bach Mass in B Minor; Mozart Festival at Citta del Castello, Italy 1991; Mozart's Missa C Major; Sommerfestspiele at Stuttgart 1993; Festival at Marbella, Spain 1994, with Beethoven's Missa Solemnis; Festival Prague Spring 1995, with Mozart's Concert Arias; Festival in Ludwigsburg, Germany 1995, with Mozart's Requiem; Music Festival Bratislava, Slovakia 1997, with Mozart's Missa C Minor; Festival Prague Autumn 1997; other repertory includes Myslivecek's Isaac, Purcell's Dido and Aeneas (Dido, Belinda), Britten's Beggar's Opera, Mozart's Nozze di Figaro (Countess), Don Giovanni (Donna Anna), Bizet's Carmen (Micaela), Handel's Samson, Judas Maccabaeus, Rodelinda, Alcina, Jephtha, several cantatas; Beethoven's 9th Symphony and Songs; Bach's St John Passion, St Mark Passion, Mass in B minor, Magnificat, numerous cantatas; Haydn's Die Schöpfung, Stabat Mater, Vier Jahreszeiten and Masses; Schubert's Stabat Mater, Masses, Salve Regina, Erstes Offertorium (Op 45); Brahms' Ein Deutsches Requiem, songs; Dvořák's Stabat Mater, Mass in D, songs; also music by Mendelssohn, Schumann, Rameau, Pergolesi, Carissimi, Vivaldi, Zelenka, Buxtehude and others. *Recordings include:* albums: Dvořák's Stabat Mater, Haydn's Nelson Mass, Stabat Mater, Schubert's Mass No. 3 B Flat, Pergolesi's Stabat Mater, J. S. Bach's St John Passion, Mozart's Coronation Mass, Vesperae Solemnes.

909

VERNET, Isabelle; French singer (soprano); b. 1966, Paris. *Education:* studied with Regine Crespin in Paris. *Career:* sang in Der Rosenkavalier at Paris 1989; season 1991 as Fauré's Pénélope at Nancy and in La Vie Parisienne at Geneva; Opéra de Lyon 1993–95, as Offenbach's Giulietta and Donna Elvira; Frankfurt 1994, as Gluck's Iphigénie en Tauride; season 1996 as Alceste at Scottish Opera and Nice, Phèdre in Hippolyte et Aricie at the Palais Garnier, Paris; season 1998 as Vitellia in La Clemenza di Tito for WNO; engaged as Iphigénie at Bordeaux 2000; sang the Trovatore Leonora at Montpellier and Mozart's Elettra in Toronto 2000. *Recordings include:* Oedipe by Enescu, Le Domino Noir by Auber.

VERNHES, Alain; French singer (baritone); b. 1944. *Career:* sang at the Opéra de Lyon, 1969–72, and made many appearances throughout France; Opéra d'Avignon, 1982–85, with such singers as Caballé, Aragall and Bruson; Orange Festival, 1987, as Vitellius in Massenet's Herodiade, and Opéra du Rhin, Strasbourg, as Zuniga in Carmen; Avignon, 1992, as Ourrais in Gounod's Mireille; Has also sung Puccini's Marcello and Scarpia in concert performances; Sang Melitone in La Forza del Destino at Orange, 1996; Marquis in The Carmélites at Amsterdam, 1998; Season 2000–01 as Massenet's Des Grieux at Monte Carlo, in Chausson's Le Roi Arthus at Edinburgh and Ramon in Gounod's Mireille for Opéra de Nice; Massenet's Sancho Panza for Washington Opera and Lothario in Mignon at Toulouse. *Current Management:* c/o François Rousseau, Le Bureau, 26 rue Duperré, 75009 Paris, France. *Telephone:* 1-45-26-79-36. *E-mail:* frousseau@fr -lebureau.com.

VERNON, Richard; American singer (bass); b. 1950, Memphis, TN. *Education:* Memphis State Univ. *Career:* debut in Memphis 1972, as Pimen in Boris Godunov; has sung with Houston Opera Studio from 1977, in operas by Verdi; appearances with Washington Opera and Pittsburgh Opera; Metropolitan Opera from 1981, in L'Enfant et les Sortilèges, and as Titurel (Parsifal) and the Commendatore (Don Giovanni); sang Foltz in a new production of Die Meistersinger at the Metropolitan 1993.

VERNON, Timothy, OC; Canadian conductor; *Artistic Director, Pacific Opera Victoria;* b. 3 July 1948, Vancouver. *Education:* Victoria School (now Conservatory) of Music, Vienna Acad. of Music and Mozarteum, Salzburg. *Career:* studied voice, cello, piano and conducting; treble soloist, Christ Church Cathedral; held appointments from age 14 as organist and choirmaster in Anglican churches in Victoria area; Conductor and Music Dir, Regina Symphony Orchestra 1975–77; Music Dir, COC touring co. 1977–80; Founder and Artistic Dir, Pacific Opera Victoria 1980–; Artistic Dir, Courtenay Youth Music Centre 1985; teacher, Faculty of Music, McGill Univ., Conductor, McGill Symphony Orchestra, Assoc. Dir, Opera McGill 1986–; Music Dir and Principal Conductor Orchestra London 2000–; Guest Conductor, Calgary Philharmonic, Vancouver Symphony, Edmonton Symphony, L'Orchestre Symphonique de Montréal, Winnipeg and Toronto Symphonies, Ottawa's Thirteen Strings; jurist, Canada Council, S.C. Eckhardt-Gramatté Competition, GPA Dublin Int. Piano Competition. *Recordings include:* Korngold's Symphony in F Sharp 1991, Mahler: Symphony No. 5 in C-Sharp Minor 1997. *Honours:* Opera Canada Awards Ruby Award 2005. *Current Management:* Dean Artists Management, 204 George Street, Toronto, Ontario M5R 2N5, Canada. *Telephone:* (416) 969-7300. *Fax:* (416) 969-7969. *E-mail:* admin@ deanartists.com. *Website:* www.deanartists.com.

VERONELLI, Ernesto; Italian singer (tenor); b. 1948, Milan. *Education:* Giuseppe Verdi Conservatory, Milan. *Career:* has sung in operas by Verdi, Puccini, Massenet and Giordano at Paris, Zürich, Berlin, Barcelona, Vienna and Verona; debut with the Royal Opera Covent Garden at Manchester as Cavaradossi 1983, later singing Chevalier Roland in Esclarmonde, opposite Joan Sutherland; season 1985–86 sang Canio at the Metropolitan, Cavaradossi in Pretoria and Pinkerton at the Cologne Opera; Calaf in Detroit and Radames at Toronto; other roles have been Verdi's Macduff, Carlo (Giovanna d'Arco), Don Carlos and Manrico.

VERONESI, Alberto; Italian conductor; *Artistic and Music Director, Puccini Festival Foundation;* b. 1967, Milan. *Education:* Giuseppe Verdi Conservatory, Milan. *Career:* f. Guido Cantelli Orchestra 1992, Artistic Dir 1992–2000; opera debut at Brooklyn Acad. of Music Spring Festival conducting Salieri's Falstaff, New York 1998; debut at Teatro alla Scala, Milan 1999; Artistic and Music Dir, Puccini Festival Foundation, Torre del Lago 1999–; Artistic and Music Dir, Orchestra Sinfonica Siciliana, Palermo 2001; Music Dir, Opera Orchestra of New York (2011–); has conducted many leading orchestras including Florence Maggio Musicale Orchestra, Orchestra of the Nat. Acad. of Santa Cecilia, Orchestra of the Festival dei Due Mondi, Spoleto, Philharmonic Orchestra of La Fenice Theatre, Venice, Philharmonic Orchestra of St Petersburg, Orchestra of the Colón Theatre, Buenos Aires, Orchestra of the Metropolitan Theatre, New York, Tokyo Philharmonic Orchestra of the Japan Broadcasting Corpn. *Recordings:* Salieri's Falstaff 1998, Edgar (with Orchestra and Chorus of the National Academy of Santa Cecilia) 2006. *Honours:* Accademia Internazionale Medicea of Florence Lorenzo il Magnifico Prize 2006. *Current Management:* Atelier Musicale, Via Caselle 76, 40068 San Lazzaro di Savena, Italy. *Telephone:* (51) 19-98-44-44. *Fax:* (51) 19-98-44-20. *E-mail:* info@ateliermusicale.com. *Website:* www.ateliermusicale.it. *Address:* Puccini Festival Foundation, Piazzale Belvedere Puccini 4, 55048 Torre del Lago, Italy (office). *Telephone:* (584) 350567 (office). *Fax:* (584) 341657 (office). *E-mail:* affarigenerali@puccinifestival.it (office). *Website:* www.puccinifestival .it (office).

VERROT, Pascal; French conductor; b. 9 Jan. 1959, Lyon. *Education:* studied at the Sorbonne and Conservatoire, Paris. *Career:* debut as asst to Seiji Ozawa at Boston Symphony Orchestra 1986–90, giving concerts at Symphony Hall Boston, Tanglewood and with Boston Chamber Players; Music Dir Québec Symphony Orchestra 1991–97; Prin. Conductor Sendai Philharmonic, Japan 2006–; Musical Dir Picardie Orchestra, France 2003–10; Artistic Dir Théâtre Impérial de Compiègne 2009–10; Music Dir Orchestre Dijon-Bourgogne 2010–. *Honours:* Prizewinner, Tokyo Int. Competition 1985. *Address:* 154 avenue Maréchal Foch, 69110 Ste-Foy Les Lyon, France (office). *E-mail:* verrot@free.fr (office). *Website:* verrot.free.fr.

VERROUST, Denis, DEUG, DE, CA; French flautist and musicologist; b. 21 Feb. 1958, Vincennes. *Education:* Saint-Maur CNR. *Career:* flute teacher; Prof. of Flute, Palaiseau Conservatory 1979–; appearances, St Malo Festival, Brittany, 1980–90; several tours in France, Germany, Netherlands as soloist with Cologne Chamber Ensemble; solo and chamber music concerts in France and abroad; participation in flute conventions in USA and UK; Dir of Collection for Billaudot Edn, Paris 2004–; Chief Ed. French Flute Asscn 1990–2000, Pres. 1991–2004; Organizer, French Flute Conventions 1992, 1996, 2000, 2008; Founder and Pres. Jean-Pierre Rampal Asscn (AJPR) 2005–; co-founder and Artistic Dir Au temps de Mozart Music Festival, Palaiseau 2003–; recording producer for Traversières label and Premiers Horizons (recordings of the Jean-Pierre Rampal Asscn; researcher and leading authority on the late classical and romantic flute repertoire. *Radio:* programmes for Radio-France and Radio Classique, Paris. *Recordings:* A. Stamitz, Sinfonia concertante in D for 2 flutes (with C. Arimany, Wrocław Chamber Orchestra, Dir J.L. Moraleda) 1996. *Publications:* several titles ed for Billaudot Edn, Paris 1980–, J.S. Bach: Sinfonia from Cantata BWV 209, four characteristic XIXth century pieces by W. Popp, F. Doppler and A. Fürstenberg, C.L. Dieter's Concerto for two flutes, I. Pleyel's Sinfonia Concertante for two flutes, F. Devienne's Trios for two flutes and bassoon, P.Ph. Bauzin's Flute concerto, two titles edited for Stravaganza Edn, Paris: Mozart, Haydn, Kreussn (Overtures for two flutes) and A. Hugot (Trios for two flutes and bass) 1987, Jean-Pierre Rampal, A Half-Century of Recordings (ed. La Flute Traversière, S. Faulisi) 1991; numerous contribs to professional journals; numerous CD sleeve notes. *Address:* 16 avenue Aubert, 94300 Vincennes, France (home). *E-mail:* denis.verroust@wanadoo.fr (home). *Website:* www.jprampal.com (office).

VERSCHRAEGEN, Herman, DipMus; Belgian organist, director of music and organ master; b. 4 April 1936, Ghent; m. Genevieve Van Hove 1963, one s. one d. *Education:* Royal Conservatory of Music, Ghent. *Career:* debut in Ghent 1957; Organist, St Josef Church, Antwerp 1962; Master of Music Theory and History, Music Acad. of Wilrijk 1963–73; Organ Master, Music Acad. of Aalst 1965–73, Music Acad. of Geel 1966–73; Dir, Music Acad. of Wilrijk-Antwerp 1974–; Organ Master, Royal Conservatory of Music, Brussels 1976–; more than 700 organ concerts and recitals worldwide; several seminars about C. Franck and the Flemish Organ School and also masterclasses in Japan; mem. of jury, int. organ contests, Nuremberg 1970, Lokeren 1972; recitals broadcast worldwide. *Compositions include:* Fantasy for Organ. *Recordings:* Handel, Bach, Couperin, Van den Gheyn.

VEZNIK, Vaclav; Czech stage director; b. 1 Aug. 1930, Brno, Moravia; m. Helena Rozsypalova 1957, one s. one d. *Education:* Masaryk State University, Janáček Academy of Music. *Career:* debut with Donizetti's Don Pasquale, State Theater Brno 1955; Stage Dir, State Theater, Brno 1954; guest dir at all theatres in Czech Republic and Slovakia 1955–97; also at theatres in Norway, Germany, Switzerland, Italy, Spain, Belgium, Austria, Greece; operatic productions include: Janáček's Fate (world premiere) 1958, Martinů's The Marriage (Czech premiere) 1960, Fischer's Rome, Julia and the Darkness (world premiere) 1962, Martinů's The Voice of the Forest 1964, Martinů's Alexander bis (Czech premiere) 1964, Von Einem's Dantons Tod (Czech premiere) 1966, Gershwin's Porgy and Bess (Czech premiere) 1968, Szokolay's The Blood Wedding (Czech premiere) 1971; television productions include Prokofiev's Duenna, Prague 1972, Janáček's Jenůfa, Brno 1972, Rimsky-Korsakov's The Golden Cockerel, Prague 1973, Janáček's The Excursions of Mr Brouček, Brno 1978, Janáček's The Cunning Little Vixen, Brno 1979, Verdi's Simon Boccanegra, Brno 1984, Verdi's Nabucco, Brno 1989; Prof., Janáček Academy of Music, Brno 1990–. *Publications:* contrib. many articles about opera productions in Program (journal of the Janáček Opera, Brno). *Honours:* Bedrich Smetana Medal 1974, Leoš Janáček Medal 1978–79, Czech Ministry of Culture. *Address:* Kolákova 676/19, 621 00 Brno, Czech Republic (home). *Telephone:* 545577190 (home).

VIALA, Jean-Luc; French singer (tenor); b. 5 Sept. 1957, Paris. *Education:* studied in Paris with Michel Sénéchal. *Career:* debut at Paris Opéra-Comique 1983 in Pomme d'Apis by Offenbach; sang at the Opéra-Comique in César Franck's Stradella and has made many appearances at provincial French opera houses; Glydebourne Festival 1986, as the Italian Singer in Capriccio, Dublin 1987, Aix-en-Provence Festival 1989, as the Prince in the Love of Three Oranges; engagements at the Opéra de Lyon including Rodolfo 1990; sang in Sacchini's Oedipe à Colone for the Festival de Radio France at Montpellier, 1992; other roles include Paolino in Il Matrimonio Segreto, Giannetto (La Gazza Ladra), Fenton, George Brown in La Dame Blanche and Iopas in Les Troyens; Guercoeur by Magnard and Les Brigands by Offenbach; Narraboth in the French version of Salome, Osmin in Gluck's La Rencontre Imprévue and Bénédict in Béatrice et Bénédict, all with the Lyon Opéra; The Love for Three Oranges; engaged as George Brown in La Dame Blanche at St

Etienne 1996–97; Rossini's Otello at the Theater an der Wien, Vienna 1998; sang Belfiore in Il Viaggio a Reims at Liège, 2000.

VICAR, Jan, PhDr, CSc; Czech musicologist and composer; *Professor of Theory and History of Music, Academy of Music and Performing Arts*; b. 5 May 1949, Olomouc, Czechoslovakia; m. 1st Anna Betkova 1979; two s.; m. 2nd Eva Slavickova 2001; one s. one d. *Education:* Conservatory in Ostrava, Palacky Univ., Olomouc, Acad. of Music and Performing Arts, Prague 1981. *Career:* Lecturer, Dept of Music, Palacky Univ. 1973–85, Prof. and Head, Dept of Musicology 1990–98, 2000–03; Sr Lecturer, Acad. of Music and Performing Arts, Prague 1985–, Prof. of Theory and History of Music 1998–; Ed.-in-Chief Hudebni Rozhledy 1986–89; Prof. of Composition, Birmingham-Southern Coll., Ala, USA 2005; mem. Czechoslovak Soc. of Arts and Sciences. *Compositions:* String Quartet 1978, Nones 1979, Music For Strings and Timpani 1980, The Cry 1981, Japanese Year (prizes 1980) 1979, Night Prayer 1996, Instructions of Surruppak 1996, Choruses and Songs For Children 1997, Three Marches for Dr Kabyl for brass band 1999, Vivat universitas! 2000, Preludes/Phantasms 2000, Musica profunda 2003, Toward the Mountain 2004. *Publications:* Akordeon a Jeho Hudebni Uplatneni (The Accordion and Its Music Use) 1981, Vaclav Trojan 1989, Hudebni Kritika A Popularizace Hudby (Musical Criticism and Popularization of Music) 1997, Music Aesthetics (with Roman Dykast) 1998, Imprints: Essays on Czech Music and Aesthetics 2005. *Honours:* Mickly's Dissies 1995, Fulbright Scholar-in-Residence 1998–99. *Address:* Malostranske Namesti 13, 118 00 Prague 1, Mala Strana, Czech Republic. *E-mail:* janvicar@seznam.cz (office).

VICK, Graham, CBE, FRNCM; British opera producer; *Artistic Director, Birmingham Opera Company*; b. 30 Dec. 1953, Liverpool. *Career:* Dir of Productions, Scottish Opera 1984–87; Dir of Productions, Glyndebourne 1994–2000; Founder and Artistic Dir, Birmingham Opera Co. 1987–; productions for ENO include Ariadne auf Naxos, The Rape of Lucretia, Madama Butterfly, Eugene Onegin, Timon of Athens by Stephen Oliver (world premiere 1991), and The Marriage of Figaro; for Opera North, Così fan tutte, Die Zauberflöte and Katya Kabanova; for Glyndebourne Festival, Queen of Spades, Lulu, Eugene Onegin and Manon Lescaut; productions for Birmingham Opera Co. include Ariadne, Fidelio 2002, La traviata 2007, Othello 2009, A Man of Feeling 2010, Life is a Dream 2012; European engagements in Brussels, Bonn, Venice, Netherlands, Berlin, Paris, Italy and St Petersburg; Covent Garden debut in 1989 with British premiere of Un Re in Ascolto by Berio, returning for Mozart's Mitridate 1991 and Die Meistersinger 1993, The Midsummer Marriage at Royal Opera House 1996; Parsifal for Opéra Bastille, Paris 1997; season 1998–99 with Don Carlos at Opéra Bastille, Così fan tutte at Glyndebourne, Ernani in Vienna and Moses and Aron at the Met in New York; Il Trovatore at the Met 2001; The Ring in Lisbon 2006–08; Orfeo in Ravenna 2007; Tannhäuser in San Francisco 2007; Werther in Lisbon 2014; Don Giovanni in Como, Pavia, and Cremina 2014; The Ice Break, Birmingham Opera Co. 2015; Morgen und Abend, Royal Opera House, Covent Garden 2015, Deutsche Oper Berlin 2016. *Television includes:* Il Segreto di Susanna for Scottish TV, The Rape of Lucretia for Channel Four, a live BBC TV broadcast of War and Peace from St Petersburg, and The Queen of Spades from Glyndebourne. *Honours:* Hon. Prof. of Music, Univ. of Birmingham; Hon. Dr (Birmingham City Univ.) 2012; Chevalier, Ordre des Arts et Lettres; Premi Abbiati Award as Best Dir for Mahagonny at the Teatro Communale in Florence and a Soc. of West End Theatres (SWET) Olivier Award for Mitridate at the Royal Opera, Covent Garden. *Current Management:* c/o Ingpen & Williams, 7 St George's Court, 131 Putney Bridge Road, London, SW15 2PA, England. *Telephone:* (20) 8874-3222. *Fax:* (20) 8877-3113. *E-mail:* info@ingpen.co.uk. *Website:* www.ingpen.co.uk.

VICKERS, Catherine Myrle; Canadian pianist; b. 24 July 1952, Regina, Sask.; d. of John Wesley Vickers and Anne Nelson Vickers (née MacColl). *Education:* Albert and Connaught Schools, Regina, Univ. of Alberta, Staatliche Hochschule für Musik und Theater, Hannover, Germany. *Career:* first public performance as pianist aged five, first concerto performance aged eight; teacher of music, Folkwang Hochschule, Essen, Germany 1981–2002, Prof. 2002–; Prof., Hochschule für Musik und Darstellende Kunst, Frankfurt am Main 2002–. *Recordings include:* The Listening Hand. *Honours:* Busoni Prize and Gold Medal 1979, Prize at Sydney Int. Piano Competition 1981, award winner Canada Council. *Address:* Waldsaum 72, 45134 Essen, Germany (home). *Telephone:* (201) 440491 (home). *Fax:* (201) 444341 (home).

VIDAL, Elizabeth; French singer (soprano); b. 1961, Nice. *Education:* studied in Paris with Elisabeth Grümmer and Eric Tappy. *Career:* sang at Opéra de Lyon from 1985, as Nannetta, Mozart's Blondchen, Charpentier's Glauce (Médée) and Paisiello's Rosina; Aix-en-Provence, 1987, in Lully's Psyché, Spoleto, 1989, as Offenbach's Olympia; season 1991 as Auber's Manon Lescaut at the Paris Opéra Comique and Strauss's Sophie at Montpellier; Queen of Night at Avignon and Olympia at Covent Garden; sang Oscar in Un Ballo in Maschera at Santiago, 1996; Sophie in Massenet's Werther at Venice, 1998; concerts include Mozart's Requiem and Haydn's Creation. *Recordings include:* Scylla et Glaucus by Leclair. *Current Management:* Musicaglotz, 11 rue le Verrier, 75006 Paris, France. *Telephone:* 1-42-34-53-40. *Fax:* 1-40-46-93-77. *E-mail:* general@musicaglotz.com. *Website:* www.musicaglotz.com.

VIDOVSZKY, László; Hungarian composer; *Professor of Composition, Franz Liszt Academy*; b. 25 Feb. 1944, Békéscsaba. *Education:* Franz Liszt Acad., Budapest, 1962–67; further study with Messiaen in Paris, 1970–71. *Career:* Co-f. Budapest New Music Studio 1970; Lecturer, Pécs Univ. 1984–93; Prof. of Composition, Pécs Univ. 1993–, Franz Liszt Acad., Budapest 1999–. *Compositions include:* Music for Györ for orchestra 1971, Double for two prepared pianos 1968–72, Autokoncert 1972, Circus, electronic music 1975, Schroeder's Death for Piano 1975, Encounter, Melodrama 1980, Narcissus and Echo, opera 1981, Motetta, for chorus and horn 1981, Une Semaine de beauté, synthesizer 1983–89, Romantic Readings for Ensemble or Orchestra 1985, Twelve Duos for violin and viola 1989, Danses Allemandes for string quartet 1989, Etudes for MIDI-piano 1989–93, Lear, ballet 1988, German Dances, for orchestra 1990, Soft Errors, for ensemble 1990, Black Quartet for percussion 1993–97, Cinema for ensemble and tape 1993, Nine Little Greeting Chorales to Kurtág for piano 1996, Ady: the Black Piano for orchestra 1997, Flute Sonata 1997, Silly Old Muzak, electronic 1997, Zwölf Streichquartette, for string quartet 2000, Commentaries on Machaut for solo voice and instrument 2000, Hoquetus 2000, Sonata for Violin and Radio 2001, Closing Time 2001, Notturno 2002, Doubles 2003, Souvenir d'Asch 2006. *Current Management:* c/o ARTISJUS, Mészáros u. 15–17, PO Box 593, 1539 Budapest 114, Hungary. *E-mail:* vid@art.pte.hu. *Address:* Mogyorós köz 7, 7635 Pécs, Hungary (home).

VIEAUX, Jason; American guitarist. *Education:* studied with Jeremy Sparks and John Holmquist. *Career:* solo recitals at guitar series in N America and at guitar festivals in Asia, Australia, Europe and Mexico; appearances for Chamber Music Soc. of Lincoln Center, Music@Menlo, Strings Music Festival, Grand Teton; recitals with Escher Quartet, harpist Yolanda Kondonassis and accordion/bandoneón virtuoso Julien Labro; has premiered new works by Dan Visconti, David Ludwig, Jerod Tate, Eric Sessler, José Luis Merlin and Gary Schocker; concerto soloist with numerous orchestras, including Cleveland, Houston, Toronto, San Diego, Fort Worth, Santa Fe, Charlotte, Buffalo, Grand Rapids, Kitchener-Waterloo, Richmond, Edmonton, IRIS Chamber, Chamber Orchestra of Philadelphia, Chautauqua Festival and New Hampshire Music Festival; has worked with numerous conductors including David Robertson, Miguel Harth-Bedoya, Jahja Ling, Stefan Sanderling, Michael Stern, David Lockington, Steven Smith and Edwin Outwater; co-f. Guitar Dept, Curtis Inst. of Music 2011; teacher, Cleveland Inst. of Music 1997–, Head, Guitar Dept 2001–; mem. Advisory Bd Guitar Foundation of America. *Recordings include:* solo: Sevilla: The Music of Isaac Albeniz 2003, Images of Metheny 2005, Bach: Works for Lute, Vol. 1 2009, Play (Grammy Award for Best Classical Instrumenetal Solo 2015) 2014; other: Astor Piazzolla works, with Julien Labro and A Far Cry Chamber Orchestra 2011, Together, with harpist Yolanda Kondonassis 2015. *Honours:* First Prize, GFA International Guitar Competition 1992. *Current Management:* Jonathan Wentworth Associates, 5 Lockwood Road, Scarsdale, NY 10583, USA. *Telephone:* (914) 667-0707. *E-mail:* mjws@jwentworth.com. *Website:* www.jwentworth.com. *E-mail:* jvieaux@gmail.com. *Website:* www.jasonvieaux.com.

VIER, Michael; German singer (bass-baritone); b. 27 Aug. 1963, Hamburg. *Education:* studied in Hamburg and Paris. *Career:* sang Mozart's Count at Pforzheim, then at Bielefeld from 1986, as Nelusko in L'Africaine, as Spohr's Faust and in Gerhard's Duenna; Bernstein's Songfest, with the composer, in London and Moscow; season 1993–94 as the Herald in Lohengrin at Kiel and Papageno at Zürich; Cologne Opera from 1995, as Papageno, Sharpless and Elviro in Handel's Xerxes; Melot in Tristan und Isolde 1998; season 1999–2000 at Cologne in Der König Kandaules by Zemlinsky, Die Vogel by Braunfels, and as Guglielmo and Marcello. *Recordings include:* Spohr's Faust and Lortzing's Ali Pascha von Janina.

VIGNOLES, Roger Hutton, BA, BMus, ARCM; British pianist and conductor; b. 12 July 1945, England; m. 1st Teresa Ann Elizabeth Henderson 1972 (divorced 1982); m. 2nd Jessica Virginia Ford 1982. *Education:* Canterbury Cathedral Choir School, Sedbergh School, Magdalene Coll., Cambridge, Royal Coll. of Music, London. *Career:* accompanist of nat. and int. reputation, regularly appearing with distinguished singers and instrumentalists, in London and provinces and at major music festivals, including Aldeburgh, Cheltenham, Edinburgh, Brighton, Bath, Salzburg, Prague; broadcasts for BBC Radio 3 and television; int. tours include USA, Canada, Australia, New Zealand, Hong Kong, Scandinavia; recitals at Opera Houses of Cologne 1982, Brussels 1983, Frankfurt 1984, Lincoln Center, New York 1985, San Francisco 1986, Tokyo 1985, 1987; Repetiteur, Royal Opera House, Covent Garden 1969–71, English Opera Group 1968–74, Australian Opera Co. 1976; Prof. of Accompaniment, Royal Coll. of Music 1974–81; conducted Handel's Agrippina at the 1992 Buxton Festival; accompanist to Inger Dam-Jensen in Strauss, Poulenc and Nielsen at the V&A Museum, London 1999; London Proms Chamber Music 2002. *Recordings include:* English song, various, with Graham Trew, Baritone; Lieder by Schumann and Brahms/Dvořák; Cabaret Songs by Britten, Gershwin and Dankworth with Sarah Walker, Mezzo; Premiere recording of The Voice of Love (Nicholas Maw); Franck and Grieg cello sonatas with Robert Cohen, Cello; The Sea, songs and duets with Sarah Walker and Thomas Allen, Baritone; Parry Violin Sonatas with Erich Gruenberg, Violin. *Honours:* Hon. RAM 1984. *Current Management:* c/o Ingpen & Williams, 7 St George's Court, 131 Putney Bridge Road, London, SW15 2PA, England. *Telephone:* (20) 8874-3222. *Fax:* (20) 8877-3113. *E-mail:* info@ingpen.co.uk.

VIGNON, Lucille; French singer (mezzo-soprano); b. 1963, Paris. *Education:* studied in Paris and Venice and with Isabel Garcisanz. *Career:* debut at Treviso, 1988, as Tisbe in Cenerentola; appearances throughout France and Italy as Cenerentola, Rosina, and Pippo in La Gazza Ladra; Sara in Donizetti's Roberto Devereux at Montpellier and Bologna; season 1991 as Fenena at Caracalla and Anne Boleyn in Henry VIII by Saint-Saëns at Compiègne; other roles include Maddalena in Rigoletto, Nicklausse in Les Contes d'Hoffmann and Léonor in La Favorite, at Nantes; Oreste in La Belle Hélène at Montpellier and at Zürich, 1994–95; concerts include works by Berio, and the Verdi Requiem. *Current Management:* c/o Agence Artistique Mi-Fa, 70 Boulevard de Picpus, 75012 Paris, France. *Telephone:* 1-43-40-02-10. *Fax:* 1-43-40-02-12. *E-mail:* info@mi-fa.com. *Website:* www.mi-fa.com.

VIHAVAINEN, Ilkka; Finnish singer (bass-baritone); b. 18 Oct. 1960. *Education:* Sibelius Acad., Helsinki, studied in Berlin and Zürich. *Career:* soloist with Finnish Nat. Opera 1988, guest soloist 1993–96, 2005–08; sang with Zürich Opera as Lord Walton in I Puritani, Belcore, Garibaldo in Rodelinda and Nick Shadow in The Rake's Progress; Royal Opera Stockholm 1988, as the Commendatore in Don Giovanni, and the Savonlinna Festival in Sallinen's The King goes forth to France; soloist with Deutsche Oper am Rhein, Düsseldorf 1996–2005; sang Bartolo in Le nozze de Figaro, Düsseldorf and Duisberg 2009; concert appearances in Bach, Mozart's Requiem and Haydn's Creation. *Current Management:* Alste Artists' Management, Tiirinniementie 28, 73320 Nilsiä, Finland. *Website:* www.alsteartists.com.

VIHAVAINEN, Satu; Finnish singer (soprano); b. 1958. *Education:* Sibelius Acad., Helsinki. *Career:* sang in concert from 1981, Finnish Nat. Opera from 1982; roles have included Micaela, Nedda, Donna Elvira, Susanna, Mimi and Marguerite; Savonlinna Festival from 1981, as First Lady and Pamina in Zauberflöte, Priestess in Aida and Marzelline in Fidelio; guested at Los Angeles 1992, in premiere of Sallinen's Kullervo; sang Freia in Das Rheingold at Helsinki 1996; sang Wagner's Gutrune at Helsinki 1999; Tatyana in Eugene Onegin, Helsinki 2008; many concert engagements. *Website:* personal .inet.fi/koti/satu.vihavainen/Etusivu.html.

VILÉGIER, Jean Marie; French stage director; b. 1940. *Education:* Ecole Normale Supérieure Paris. *Career:* Lecturer at the Theatre Studies department, University of Nancy; Director of Théâtre National de Strasbourg, 1990–93; founder and Director of L'Illustré Théâtre; opera productions have included La Cenerentola 1983, Lully's Atys 1986, La fée Urgèle by Duni and Favart 1991, Charpentier's Médée 1993, Rameau's Hippolyte et Aricie 1996; tours of Atys, Médée and Hippolyte to the Brooklyn Academy, New York; further collaborations, with William Christie include Handel's Rodelinda at Glyndebourne 1998. *Recordings include:* Rodelinda (video).

VILJAKAINEN, Raili; Finnish singer (soprano); b. 1954, Helsinki. *Education:* Sibelius Acad., studied with Luigi Ricci in Rome. *Career:* sang in Stuttgart from 1978 as Aennchen in Der Freischütz, Sophie, Pamina, Ilia, Micaela, Mimi, Liu, Eva, Freia in Das Rheingold and Countess in Figaro; guest appearances at the Savonlinna Festival, Salzburg and the Saratoga Springs Festival; concert appearances in works by Bach, Mozart, Beethoven, Handel and Mahler; has sung at Carnegie Hall, New York and in Finland, throughout Germany, Austria, USA, Australia, France and Spain; sang Pamina at the Savonlinna Festival 1981–90, Tatiana in Eugene Onegin and Desdemona in Otello at Helsinki; contemporary music in Paris, Biennale Helsinki, Opera in Bonn, and in Sciarrino's Lohengrin; sang Ellen Orford in Helsinki and Berlin 1999. *Recordings include:* Aennchen in Der Freischütz. *Honours:* first prize Timo Callio Competition at Savonlinna Festival 1976, first prize 's-Hertogenbosch Competition, The Netherlands 1977.

VILLA, Edoardo; American singer (tenor); b. 19 Oct. 1953, Los Angeles. *Education:* University of Southern California, studied with Martial Singher, Horst Gunter and Margaret Harshaw. *Career:* many appearances in opera throughout the USA and abroad; Paris Opéra 1986, as Don Carlos, Houston 1988, as Don José; sang at the Munich Staatsoper, 1989, and has appeared widely in Canada; sang Jacopo Foscari in I Due Foscari with the Opera Orchestra of New York, 1992; other roles include Corrado in Il Corsaro, Ruggero in La Rondine, Hoffmann, the Italian Singer in Rosenkavalier and Albert Herring; season 1999–2000 as Enzo in La Gioconda for Miami Opera and Radames at Heidenheim. *Recordings include:* Le Roi d'Ys by Lalo. *Current Management:* Pinnacle Arts: Miller Division, 889 Ninth Avenue, Second Floor, New York, NY 10019, USA. *Telephone:* (212) 397-7911. *Fax:* (212) 397-7920. *E-mail:* jmiller@pinnaclearts.com. *Website:* www.pinnaclearts .com.

VILLAROEL, Veronica; Chilean singer (soprano); b. 1962. *Education:* studied in Chile and the USA. *Career:* debut in Santiago, 1988, as Marguerite in Faust; sang Antonia at the 1989 Spoleto Festival, Fiordiligi at Barcelona, 1990 (returned for Violetta 1992); season 1991 as Nedda at Miami, Traviata at Milwaukee and Mimi at Opéra de Lyon; Los Angeles and Théâtre du Châtelet, Paris, as Violetta; sang Nedda in Pagliacci at Los Angeles; season 2000 as Desdemona for Washington Opera, Nedda and Boito's Margherita at the Met, Hélène in Verdi's Jérusalem at Genoa and the Trovatore Leonora for the Teatro Colón, Buenos Aires; London Proms, 2002; many concert engagements. *Current Management:* Zemsky/Green Artists Management, 730 Fifth Avenue, Suite 1802, New York, NY 10019, USA. *Telephone:* (212) 300-8003. *Fax:* (212) 300-8001. *E-mail:* zgartists@aol.com. *Website:* www.zemskygreen.com.

VILLARS, John; American singer (tenor); b. 1965, Panama City, FL. *Education:* Juilliard Opera School, New York. *Career:* sang Midir in Boughton's The Immortal Hour at Juilliard 1994; season 1997–98 as the Drum Major in Wozzeck at Salzburg and Bacchus in Ariadne auf Naxos at Florence; season 1998–99 as Calaf for Canadian Opera, Apollo in Strauss's Daphne at the Deutsche Oper Berlin and the Drum Major in Gurlitt's Wozzeck, Enée in Les Troyens at Salzburg 2000; other roles include Strauss's Emperor, Werther,

Stravinsky's Oedipus Rex, Cavaradossi and Don José; concerts include Mahler's 8th Symphony at the London Proms 2002. *Recordings include:* Video of Ariadne auf Naxos 1999. *Honours:* winner Nat. Competition for Young Opera Singers, New York 1994.

VILLAUME, Emmanuel; French conductor; *Artistic Director and Chief Conductor, Slovenian Philharmonic Orchestra;* b. 1964, Strasbourg. *Education:* Strasbourg Conservatory, and in Paris. *Career:* Dramaturg, Opéra du Rhin, Strasbourg, aged 21; US debut with Mozart's Le Nozze di Figaro, Spoleto Festival USA 1990; has led opera performances at all main opera houses and concert halls in USA, Europe and Japan, and concerts with symphony orchestras world-wide; has worked with Anna Netrebko, Rolando Villazón, Natalie Dessay, Plácido Domingo and Renée Fleming; Music Dir for Opera and Orchestra, Spoleto USA Festival 2000–10; Artistic Dir and Chief Conductor, Slovenian Philharmonic Orchestra 2008–; Chief Conductor, Slovakian Philharmonic Orchestra 2009–. *Honours:* Dr hc (Indianapolis). *Current Management:* c/o Jeffrey Vanderveen, Opus 3 Artists, 470 Park Avenue South, Ninth Floor North, New York, NY 10016, USA. *Telephone:* (212) 584-7532. *E-mail:* jvanderveen@opus3artists.com. *E-mail:* emmanuel@ emmanuelvillaume.com (office). *Website:* www.emmanuelvillaume.com (home).

VILLAZÓN, Rolando; Mexican singer (tenor); b. 1972, Mexico City; m.; two s. *Education:* Espacios Acad., Nat. Conservatory of Music, studied with Arturo Nieto, Enrique Jaso, Gabriel Mijares, San Francisco Opera Merola Program, Pittsburgh Opera Young Artists Program, masterclasses with Joan Sutherland. *Career:* Mexican debut as Parpignol in La Bohème 1995; European debut as Des Grieux in Manon, Genoa 1999; Met, New York debut as Alfredo in La Traviata 2004; has performed with many leading opera companies including Hamburg State Opera, Lyon Opera, Rome Opera, Bregenz Festival, Bellas Artes Mexican Opera, Antibes Festival, Munich State Opera, Berlin Deutsche Oper and Staatsoper, Glyndebourne Festival, Paris Bastille Opera, Oviedo, Trieste, Brussels La Monnaie, Los Angeles Opera, Pittsburgh Opera, Macerata Festival, Orange Festival, New York City Opera, Vienna Staatsoper, Covent Garden, London, La Scala, Milan; operatic roles include Tebaldo in I Capuleti e i Montecchi, Don José in Carmen, Nemorino in L'Elisir d'Amore, Rodolfo in La Bohème, Edgardo di Ravenswood in Lucia di Lammermoor, Roberto Conte di Leicester in Maria Stuarda, Roméo in Roméo et Juliette, Manon in Des Grieux, The Duke in Rigoletto, Macduff in Macbeth, Alfredo Germont in La Traviata, Lensky in Eugene Onegin, title roles in Les Contes d'Hoffmann, Don Carlo and Faust; directed Massenet's Werther at Opéra de Lyon 2011; European concert tour with Cecilia Bartoli 2015. *Recordings include:* Romeo y Julieta 2002, Wagner, Der Fliegende Holländer 2002, Italian Opera Arias 2004, Berlioz: La Révolution Grecque 2004, Gounod and Massenet Arias (Gramophone Award) 2005, Tristan and Isolde 2005, Opera Recital 2006, Combattimento 2006, Gitano 2007, Duets (with Anna Netrebko) 2007, Cielo e Mar 2008, Handel 2009, La Traviata (with Anna Netrebko) (also DVD) 2009, Tenor 2010, La Strada – Songs From The Movies 2011, Don Giovanni 2012, Villazón Verdi 2012, Rolando Villazón Sings Verdi 2013, Viva Verdi! 2013, Treasures of Belcanto 2015, Die Entführung aus dem Serail (with Chamber Orchestra of Europe) 2015. *Honours:* Chevalier des Arts et des Lettres; Zarzuela Prize 1999, Prize of the Public and second prize Plácido Domingo's Operalia 1999, Victoires de la Musique 2003. *Current Management:* c/o Judith Neuhoff, Universal Music Group, Stralauer Allee 1, 10245 Berlin, Germany. *Telephone:* (30) 52007 1762. *E-mail:* judith.neuhoff@ umusic.com. *Website:* www.centrestagemanagement.com; www .rolandovillazon.com.

VILMA, Michele; French singer (mezzo-soprano); b. 23 Feb. 1932, Rouen. *Education:* Studied at the Rouen Conservatoire. *Career:* debut as Léonor in La Favorite at Verviers; appearances at the Rouen Opera, notably as Dalila, and elsewhere in France as Charlotte, Carmen, Herodiade, Azucena and Dulcinée in Don Quichotte by Massenet; Paris Opéra from 1970 as Eboli, Fricka and the Kostelnicka in Jenůfa; Marseille Opéra as Laura in La Gioconda, Fricka at Bayreuth and Brangaene at the Metropolitan; sang Clytemnestra in Elektra at the Opéra de Toulouse.

VINE, Carl; Australian composer, pianist and conductor; b. 8 Oct. 1954, Perth, WA. *Education:* studied with Stephen Dornan and John Exton at the Univ. of Western Australia. *Career:* co-founder of contemporary music ensemble Flederman 1979; appearances as conductor and pianist in the UK, Europe and the USA; resident composer with the Sydney Dance Co 1979, London Contemporary Dance Theatre 1979, Australian Chamber Orchestra 1987 and Univ. of Western Australia 1989; Lecturer in Electronic Music at the Queensland Conservatorium 1980–82; Artistic Dir of Musica Viva Australia 2000–. *Compositions include:* Cafe Concertino 1984, Canzona 1985, Love Song for trombone and tape 1986, Six Symphonies (No. 6 Choral Symphony) 1986–96, Defying Gravity for four percussion 1987, Percussion Concerto 1987, Piano Sonata 1990, The Tempest, ballet 1991, String Quartet No. 3 1993, Esperance for chamber orchestra 1994, Five Bagatelles for piano 1994, Inner World for cello and tape 1994, Gaijin for koto, strings and electronics 1994, Oboe Concerto 1996, Flag Handover Music (for Atlanta Olympic Games) 1996, Metropolis, for Melbourne Symphony Orchestra 1997, Piano Concerto, for Sydney Symphony Orchestra 1997, Piano Sonata No. 2 1998, Pipe Dreams (flute concerto) 2002, V (an orchestral fanfare) 2002. *Honours:* Australian Commonwealth Govt Centenary Medal for Contrib. to Australian Society 2000; John Bishop Memorial Award 1990, Don Banks Award for Outstanding Contrib. to Australian Music, Australia Council for the Arts 2005, Sir Bernard

Heinze Memorial Award for outstanding contrib. to music in Australia 2012. *Address:* c/o Faber Music Ltd, 74–77 Great Russell Street, London, WC1B 3DA, England. *E-mail:* carlvine2@gmail.com (office). *Website:* www.carlvine .com.

VINE, David Charles, BMus (Hons), ARCM; British/New Zealand conductor, harpsichordist, pianist, composer and teacher; *Editor, David Vine Music (Publications);* b. 30 May 1943, London, England, UK; s. of Cyril Charles Vine and Lorna Marian Clarke. *Education:* Royal Coll. of Music, London, Univ. of Canterbury, NZ, studied with Cornelius Fischer, Bernard Roberts, Eric Harrison, Joan Trimble, Millicent Silver, Hubert Dawkes, Adrian Boult. *Career:* tutored in Baroque music, Guildhall School of Music and City Literary Inst.; Founder London Telemann Ensemble; settled in NZ 1974; Conductor NZ Nat. Youth Orchestra, Wellington Polytechnic Orchestra, Dunedin Sinfonia and Schola Cantorum, Amici Chamber Orchestra, Christchurch Symphony Orchestra, Orpheus Choir, Phoenix Choir of Wellington, and Cantoris; Musical Dir Gisborne Choral Soc., Christchurch Operatic Soc., Jubilate Singers, Perkel Opera, Acad. Chamber Orchestra and Ensemble Divertimento, Wellington Gilbert and Sullivan Light Opera Co.; orchestral keyboard, New Zealand Symphony Orchestra; recitalist, presenter and announcer with Radio NZ 's Concert FM; Musical Dir Phoenix Choir; Founder-Dir Academy Opera 1982, conducting seven NZ premieres of Handel, Mozart and Puccini operas; apptd Musical Dir Queen's Singers, Queen Margaret Coll., Wellington 2009; has lectured at Univs of Canterbury, Auckland, Waikato and Massey Univ. of Wellington; Asst Ed., Massey Univ. Music; currently Ed. David Vine Music (Publications) (DVM). *Recording:* Serenata, Recital of songs by Italian operatic composers. *Radio:* ed. and pianist, world premiere recording of 16 songs by Arturo Toscanini, Radio NZ 2007; ed. and arranger, Verdi, Terzetto (I Lombardi), Benjamin Morrison (violins), David Vine (piano), Radio NZ 2012. *Publications:* Handel: Suite in C minor, reconstruction for two keyboards 1992, A. Caldara, 16 Sonatas for cello and continuo 1996–, Fandango Ardiente for two harpsichords 2005, Samuel Arnold: Hear, O Thou Shepherd, The Tuneful Lark, William Shield: Search All The Wide Creation Round, Omai (opera), Thomas Attwood: Piano Trio in C, Op. 1 No. 2, Thomas Arne: Love in a Village (opera), Samuel Arnold: Hymn to Adam and Eve 2008, Arturo Toscanini: Complete Songs 2010, Complete Compositions of David Vine 2013. *Honours:* First Prize, Northampton Eisteddfod Piano Section 1958, 1959, 1960, Alabaster Knowles Prize in Music, Univ. of Canterbury 1983, 1984. *Address:* 1, Clos Maes Mawr, Energlyn, Caerphilly, CF83 2UY, Wales. *Telephone:* (2921) 157574. *E-mail:* davidCvine@gmail.com. *Website:* davidvinemusic.com (office).

VINIKOUR, Jory, BA, MA; French/American harpsichordist; b. 12 May 1963, Chicago, Ill. *Education:* Peabody Conservatory, Mannes Coll. of Music, Rutgers Univ., Conservatoire National Supérieur de Musique de Paris, France. *Career:* recitals at festivals in Deauville, Paris, Monaco, Prague, London, Latin America, USA; soloist with Rotterdam and Netherlands Philharmonics, Orchestre de la Suisse Romande, Orchestre Philharmonique de Radio France, Flanders Opera Orchestra, Orchestre de Chambre de Grenoble, Moscow Chamber Orchestra; contemporary music concerts in France, Germany and Netherlands; performances of contemporary works including Amsterdam Festival of Contemporary Harpsichord Music, Festival Présences, Radio France; numerous performances of Michael Nyman's harpsichord concerto, Poulenc's Concert Champêtre, etc. *Recordings include:* J.S. Bach: Toccatas for Harpsichord 1998, Goldberg Variations 2001, Music for a While (with Anne Sofie von Otter) 2001, Handel: The Eight Great Suites 2008, Complete Harpsichord Works of Rameau 2012, American Contemporary Works 2013, Bach: Six Partitas 2015. *Honours:* Fulbright Award 1990, Médaille d'Or and Prix d'Excellence, Conservatoire National de Musique de Rueil-Malmaison 1991, Prix de Virtuosité, Conservatoire National de Musique de Rueil-Malmaison 1992, Nadia et Lily Boulanger Foundation 1994, First Prize, Int. Harpsichord Competition of Warsaw 1993, First Prize, Int. Harpsichord Competition, Prague 1994. *Address:* 1225 North Wells Street, Apt 1305, Chicago, IL 60610, USA (home); 1 boulevard de la République, 71100 Chalon-sur-Saône, France. *Telephone:* (312) 405-7702 (Chicago). *E-mail:* jvinikour@mac.com. *Website:* www.joryvinikour.com.

VINK, Elena; Dutch singer (soprano); b. 1962. *Education:* The Hague Conservatory. *Career:* broadcast performances with conductors Jean Fournet, Kenneth Montgomery and Hans Vonk; Netherlands Opera as Lucia di Lammermoor, Constanze, Gilda, Poppea and Oscar; Mozart's Queen of Night at Lausanne, Brussels, the Berlin Staatsoper and the Opéra Bastille, Paris 1994; sang in Mozart's Sogno di Scipione at Aix, 1991; Bath Festival, 1992, as Musetta; Amsterdam from 1994, as Aminta in Il Re Pastore, in The Nose by Shostakovich and as the Dove in Heppener's A Soul of Wood, 1998. *Recordings include:* Donna Anna in Don Giovanni. *Current Management:* Opernagentur Inge Tennigkeit, Kempener Strasse 4, 40474 Düsseldorf, Germany. *Telephone:* (211) 5160060. *Fax:* (211) 51600616. *E-mail:* opera@tennigkeit-ag.de. *Website:* www.tennigkeit-ag.de.

VINZING, Ute; German singer (soprano); b. 9 Sept. 1936, Wuppertal. *Education:* studied with Martha Mödl. *Career:* sang at Lubeck 1967–70, notably as Marenka in The Bartered Bride and Senta in Der fliegende Holländer; Wuppertal Opera 1971–76, sang Brünnhilde in Der Ring des Nibelungen; has sung in Hamburg, Munich, Vienna, Buenos Aires, Geneva and Seattle (as Brünnhilde); Paris Opéra 1977, 1985, as Brünnhilde and Isolde; Teatro Liceo 1983; Metropolitan Opera from 1984, debut as Elektra; other roles include Ortrud, Kundry, Leonore and the Dyer's Wife in Die Frau

ohne Schatten; Teatro Colón, Buenos Aires 1987, as Elektra; sang Isolde at Florence 1988; Elektra at Marseilles 1989; sang Ortrud at Buenos Aires 1991. *Recordings include:* Elektra, Die Frau ohne Schatten.

VIR, Param; British composer; b. 6 Feb. 1952, Delhi, India. *Education:* Delhi Univ., Dartington Summer School with Peter Maxwell Davies, Guildhall School, London with Oliver Knussen. *Career:* Composition Fellow at Tanglewood 1986; Broken Strings and Snatched by the Gods commissioned by Hans Werner Henze for the Munich Biennale 1992; Ion premiered at Aldeburgh 2000. *Compositions:* The Demons of Bara Tooti (music theatre) 1980, Besura Desh (theatre) 1982, Fall Out (musical) 1984, Contra-pulse for ensemble 1985, Pragati concertante 1986, Antiphons and Elegies for chamber orchestra 1986, Before Krishna for strings 1987, Krishna (children's opera) 1988, Brahma, Vishnu Sita for six solo voices 1988, Snatched by the Gods (chamber opera) 1990, Broken Strings (chamber opera) 1992, Horse Tooth White Rock for orchestra 1994, The Comfort of Angels for two pianos 1995, Tender Light for viola da gamba 1996, Ultimate Words: Infinite Song for baritone, six percussion and piano 1997, Ion (opera after Euripides) 2000. *Honours:* Tippett Composition Award, Britten Prize 1987.

VIRAGH, Endre; Hungarian academic and conductor; b. 23 March 1928, Vasvár; m. Margit Piláth 1958. *Education:* Liszt Ferenc Academy of Music, Budapest, studied with J. Reinberger in Prague, M. Dupré in Paris, Germani in Rome and Siena. *Career:* debut at Bartók Conservatoire, Miskolc 1955; Principal Parish Church, Budapest 1961; regular appearances as soloist at concert on Hungarian radio and television; organ recitals in Brune and Siena; permanent interpreter at prestigious organ concerts; extensive repertoire includes all organ works of J. S. Bach, Liszt, and César Franck, sonatas of Mendelssohn and Hindemith, organ works by modern composers such as Dupré, Messiaen, Janáček and Kodály, and organ concertos including Vivaldi's 2nd; Prof. of Organ, Miskolc from 1955, Belá Bartók Conservatoire, Budapest from 1969; mem. Saint Cecilia OMCE, Ferenc Liszt Soc., Zoltán Kodály Soc., Lajos Bardos Soc. *Honours:* Diploma of Honour, Siena 1967, Pro-Arte Prize 1980, Eminent Pedagogue of Organ 1991, Rectorate Honourable Mention 1992.

VIRKHAUS, Taavo, BM, MM, DMA; American (b. Estonian) conductor; *Conductor Emeritus, Huntsville Symphony Orchestra;* b. 29 June 1934, Tartu, Estonia; m. Nancy Ellen Herman 1969. *Education:* Univ. of Miami, Eastman School of Music, Pierre Monteux master-classes. *Career:* emigrated to USA 1949; debut conducting Miami Ballet Guild Orchestra 1956; Dir of Music, Univ. of Rochester 1966–77; Music Dir and Conductor, Duluth-Superior Symphony Orchestra, Duluth, Minn. 1977–94; Music Dir and Conductor, Huntsville (Ala) Symphony Orchestra 1990–2003, Conductor Emer. 2003–; guest conductor with Rochester Philharmonic, Baltimore Symphony, Estonian SSR State Symphony, Minnesota Orchestra, Vancouver Symphony, Volgagrad Symphony, Russia, Kuopio Symphony, Finland and others. *Compositions include:* six symphonies, two violin concerti. *Honours:* Fulbright grant to Cologne, Germany 1963–64, Howard Hanson Prize 1966. *Address:* 111 Lake Shore Drive, Madison, AL 35758, USA (home). *Telephone:* (256) 461-7667 (home). *E-mail:* taavo@knology.net.

VIRSALADZE, Elisso Konstantinovna; Georgian pianist; b. 14 Sept. 1942, Tbilisi. *Education:* studied under grandmother, Prof. Anastasia Virsaladze, then at Tbilisi Conservatory. *Career:* began piano lessons aged eight; teacher, Moscow Conservatory 1962, apptd Full Prof. 1994; Prof., Musikhochschule, Munich; regular tours as piano soloist across Europe, USA, South America, Japan and Australia; f. Telavi Music Festival, Georgia; regularly serves as juror at int. piano competitions including Queen Elisabeth Competition, Brussels 2010. *Recordings include:* Schumann Second Sonata 1973, Schumann First Sonata 1980, Brahms: String Quartet No. 2; Piano Quintet 1995, Elisso plays Mozart & Prokoviev 1996, Schubert: Wanderer-Fantasie/Impromptus 1997, Chopin: Etudes 1998, Schumann: Piano Sonata 1 & 2; Waldszenen 2000, Mozart: Chamber Music, Vol. 1 2003, Mozart: Concertos for 2 & 3 Pianos 2005, Elisso Virsaladze Live 2011. *Honours:* First Prize, All-Union Competition of Performing Musicians, Moscow 1961, Bronze Medal, Tchaikovsky Competition 1962, Prize at Schumann Competition, Georgian State Prize 1983, People's Artist of the USSR 1989, Order of Merit 2007, Order of Honour 2013. *Telephone:* (89) 26024335 (home). *Fax:* (89) 26024344 (home). *E-mail:* hahn@augstein.info. *Website:* www.augstein.info.

VISCONTI, Piero; singer (tenor); b. 1947, Valenze, Piedmont, Italy. *Education:* studied in Rome. *Career:* debut in Naples 1975, as Rodolfo in La Bohème; sang at Miami 1979, Rome Opera from 1978 (debut as Ernani); Vienna Staatsoper 1980, as Edgardo, the Duke of Mantua at the 1981 Verona Arena, Barcelona and Mannheim from 1982; US appearances at Houston and Philadelphia, Verdi Requiem in London 1985, and Sydney Opera 1986; other roles include Almaviva, Arturo in La Straniera, Pollione in Norma, Nemorino, Foresto, Gabriele Adorno, Pinkerton, Calaf, Enzo and Andrea Chénier.

VISSE, Dominique; French singer (countertenor); *Director, Ensemble Clément Janequin;* b. 30 Aug. 1955, Lisieux, Calvados, Basse-Normandie; m. Agnès Mellon; one s. one d. *Education:* chorister at Notre Dame in Paris, studied organ and flute at Versailles Conservatory, studied with Alfred Deller, Nigel Rogers, René Jacobs and William Christie. *Career:* f. Ensemble Clément Janequin 1978, made series of recordings of French polyphonic chansons of 16th century; Co-founding mem. Les Arts Florissants 1979, edited much of ensemble's repertoire; popular lyric artists in Baroque opera, working with René Jacobs, Jean-Claude Malgoire, Philippe Herreweghe, Ton Koopman,

William Christie, Alan Curtis, Nicholas McGegan, Christophe Rousset, Ivor Bolton and Robert King, in opera houses of Paris, Berlin, Cologne, Amsterdam, Lausanne, Tel-Aviv, Montpellier, Houston, Barcelona, Munich, Versailles, at the Monnaie in Brussels, at the Châtelet and the Théâtre des Champs Elysées in Paris, on tour in Japan and N America and at Festivals of Aix-en-Provence, Innsbruck and Edinburgh; also frequently performs contemporary music; participated in Luciano Berio's opera Outis at La Scala, Milan and at Théâtre du Châtelet, Paris; played role of Oreste in Offenbach's La Belle Hélène, Festival of Aix-en-Provence 1999, revived in Salzburg 2001; performed in another production of La Belle Hélène in Israel 2002, Rinaldo in Berlin 2003, Perela, l'Homme de Fumée by Pascal Dusapin at Opéra de Paris in February 2003, Florian Gassmann's Opera seria at the Théâtre des Champs Elysées in March 2003, revivals of Il ritorno d'Ulisse and Rinaldo in Munich in July 2003, revivals of Agrippina at La Monnaie and the Théâtre des Champs Elysées 2003, revival of La Calisto in Vienna 2003, Luxemburg 2003; La Frontière by Philippe Manoury, Carré St Vincent, Orléans, Bouffes du Nord, Paris and on tour in France late 2003; played Nerone in L'incoronazione di Poppea, Théâtre des Champs Elysées 2004, Opéra de Paris 2005, Handel's Agrippina with Jean-Claude Malgoire 2005, Cavalli's La Calisto in Munich 2005, Sartori's Don Quichotte, Innsbruck 2005 and revivals of Monteverdi's operas in Munich 2005, 2006; other appearances include Kagel's Mare Nostrum and Il ritorno d'Ulisse with Jean-Claude Malgoire and Atelier Lyrique de Tourcoing 2007, further revivals of La Calisto and Monteverdi operas in Munich, Giulio Cesare, La Monnaie, Brussels, L'incoronazione di Poppea, Glyndebourne 2008, new Poppea production, Barcelona 2009, revival of the Munich Calisto production 2009, Mare Nostrum in Tourcoing 2009; Narciso in Agrippina, Berlin 2010, Berlin and Barcelona 2013; Tolomeo in Giulio Cesare, Reims and Versailles 2011; La Pythonisse in David and Jonathas, Edinburgh Festival 2012, Opéra Comique, Paris and Caen 2013; performs recital programmes of music ranging from Machaut to Berio, via Dowland, Schubert, Offenbach, Massenet, Satie, Poulenc and Takemitsu. *Recordings:* more than 50 recordings, including L'Incoronazione di Dario by Vivaldi, Charpentier's Actéon, Les Arts Florissants and David et Jonathan, Cavalli's Xerxes and Giasone, Octavia's Nurse in L'Incoronazione di Poppea, Rameau's Anacréon and Hasse's Cleofide, Comic French Baroque Cantatas (with Café Zimmermann) 2008; Ensemble Clément Janequin: programme of French 'Cries' ranging from the Renaissance to the present day 2009. *Current Management:* c/o Ian Malkin, Satirino, 59 rue Orfila, 75020 Paris, France. *Telephone:* (9) 77-19-80-77. *Fax:* 1-53-01-33-46. *E-mail:* ianmalkin@satirino .fr. *Website:* www.satirino.fr; www.dominique-visse.com.

VITALI, Marisa; singer (soprano); b. 1964, South Africa. *Education:* studied in Cape Town and New York. *Career:* sang at Bonn Opera from 1989, as Rosina, Strauss's Composer, Wellgunde and Donna Elvira; guest appearances elsewhere in Germany as Traviata, Liu in Turandot, Suor Angelica, Micaela, Mélisande and Offenbach's Antonia; Fiora in Montemezzi's L'Amore dei tre Ré at Hanover 1993, and Despina at Catania; season 1995–96 as Nedda in Pagliacci at Verona, Maria in Guglielmo Ratcliff by Mascagni at Livorno, and Donna Elvira at the Deutsche Oper Berlin. *Honours:* winner Francisco Viñas Competition, Barcelona 1989.

VITMAN, Yelena; Russian singer (mezzo-soprano); b. 1969. *Education:* St Petersburg Conservatoire. *Career:* appearances at the Mariinsky Theatre, Kirov Opera, from 1996; roles have included Lyubava in Sadko and Lyubasha in The Tsar's Bride, both by Rimsky-Korsakov; Olga in Eugene Onegin, Puccini's Suzuki, Konchakovna in Prince Igor and Siebel in Faust; sang with the Kirov Opera in summer season at Covent Garden, 2000; other roles include Clarice in The Love for Three Oranges, and Maria Bolkonskaya in War and Peace. *Honours:* Prizewinner at Wroclaw (1992) and St Petersburg (1994) Vocal Competitions.

VIZZUTTI, Allen, MMus; American musician (trumpet), composer and teacher; b. 13 Sept. 1952, Missoula, Mont. *Education:* Eastman School of Music. *Career:* classical and jazz artist, has performed recitals and concerts world-wide and worked with artists and ensembles including Chick Corea, 'Doc' Severinsen, Airmen Of Note, Army Blues and Army Symphony Orchestra, Chuck Mangione, Woody Herman, NHK Orchestra Japan and New Tokyo Philharmonic, Budapest Radio Orchestra, St Paul Chamber Orchestra, Leipzig Wind Symphony and Kosie Wind Orchestra; has appeared as guest soloist with numerous symphony orchestras; solo performances at Hollywood Bowl, Carnegie Hall, Newport Jazz Festival, Banff Center for the Performing Arts, Montreux Jazz Festival, Teton, Vail, Aspen and Brechenridge Music Festivals, Charles Ives Center and Lincoln Center in New York; as Artist-in-Residence, taught at Eastman School of Music, Banff Center for the Performing Arts, Kansas State Univ., Ohio State Univ., West Texas State Univ., Univ. of S Carolina, Skidmore Jazz Inst. and Trompeten Akademie Bremen, Germany. *Recordings include:* The Emerald Concerto and Other Gems (with Budapest Radio Orchestra), Vizzutti Plays Vizzutti, Vizzutti and Soli On Tour, Baroque and Beyond, The Carnival of Venus, A Trumpeter's Dream; also recordings with such artists as Frank Sinatra, Barbra Streisand, Neil Diamond, Chick Corea, the Commodores and Prince. *Compositions include:* works include solo pieces for flute, clarinet, saxophone, trombone, tuba, harp, chamber groups, wind ensemble, jazz ensemble and symphony orchestra; compositions premiered by Los Angeles Philharmonic, Budapest Radio Orchestra, Royal Philharmonic London, Nuremberg Symphony, Rochester Philharmonic, Syracuse Symphony, London Symphony, Summit Brass and others. *Films:* performed on more than 100 film soundtracks,

including Back To The Future, Star Trek and Scary Movie Four. *Publications include:* The Allen Vizzutti Trumpet Method, New Concepts for Trumpet. *E-mail:* alviz4@comcast.net. *Website:* www.vizzutti.com.

VLAD, Alessio; Italian conductor, composer and artistic director; *Artistic Director, Teatro dell'Opera, Rome*; b. 15 May 1955, Rome; s. of Roman Vlad. *Education:* Conservatorio Nazionale di Santa Cecilia, Rome; also studied with Franco Ferrara, Sergiu Celibidache, Bruno Campanella and Leonard Bernstein. *Career:* began career as Asst Conductor, Spoleto Festival and Teatro dell'Opera, Rome; Artistic Dir Ravello Festival 1991–; Artistic Dir Teatro Donizetti, Bergamo 1999; Artistic Dir Teatro Carlo Felice, Genoa 1999–2002; Artistic Dir Teatro delle Muse, Ancona 2004–; Artistic Dir Teatro dell'Opera, Rome 2010–; guest conductor with Schleswig-Holstein Philharmonic, Philharmonie der Nationen, Dresden Philharmonic, Nürnberg Philharmonic, Weimar Staatskapelle, Orchestre du Capitole de Toulouse, Filharmonica Enescu, Bucharest, Symphony Orchestra of Israel, Toronto Philharmonic, Orchestra Sinfonica Nazionale della RAI, Orchestra Sinfonica Siciliana. *Films:* as composer: La Bocca 1990, La fine è nota 1993, Sparrow 1993, La Storia che seque 1994, Croce e Delizia 1995, Va dove ti porta il cuore 1996, Necista krv 1996, Cervellini fritti impanati 1996, Jane Eyre 1996, Besieged (Golden Globe for Best Soundtrack 1999) 1998, Tea with Mussolini 1999, Liberate i Pesci 2000, Il Piacere di Piacere 2002, Callas Forever 2002, Omaggio a Roma 2009. *Honours:* three Franco Abbiato prizes. *Address:* Teatro dell'Opera, Piazza Beniamino Gigli 7, Rome, Italy (office). *E-mail:* ufficio.stampa@operaroma.it (office). *Website:* www.operaroma.it (office).

VLAD, Marta Marina; Romanian composer; b. 8 March 1949, Bucharest; m. Ulpiu Vlad 1973; one s. *Education:* Music High School, Bucharest, High School I. L. Caragiale, Nat. Univ. of Music, Bucharest. *Career:* Univ. Asst, Nat. Univ. of Music 1973–91, Prof. 1991–2002; mem. Union of Composers and Musicologists of Romania. *Compositions include:* Sonata for violin and piano 1978, Rondo for piano 1978, Symphony Movement 1979, Images for string orchestra 1980, Sonata for piano 1981, String Quartet No. 1 1981, String Quartet No. 2 1982, Legend and In Search of the Game for piano 1983, String Trio No. 1: Inscriptions for Peace 1984, In the Forest for piano 1984, String Trio No. 2: Dream of Peace 1985, String Trio No. 3 1986, This Country's Land cantata for solo voice, choir and orchestra (a verse by Jon Brad) 1987, Light Rays trio for flute, oboe and clarinet 1988, Thoughts for the Future quartet for flute, violin, viola and cello 1989, In Search of the Game No. 2 for piano 1994, Still Life I for oboe solo 1996, Still Life II for clarinet solo 1997, Still Life III for piano solo 1997, Still Life IV for violin solo 1998, Still Life V for viola solo 1999, Still Life VI for cello solo 2000, Still Life VII for flute solo 2000, Still Life VIII for bassoon solo 2002, Two Contrastive Pieces for orchestra 2004. *Honours:* Prize (for The Cantata Resonance), Nat. Univ. of Music 1972. *Address:* 011724 Bucharest, Str. Andrei Popovici 18, Bl 8A, Sc c et IV, Apt 39, Romania (home). *Telephone:* (21) 2306712 (home).

VLAD, Ulpiu, DMus; Romanian composer and academic; *President, Romanian Section, International Society for Contemporary Music*; b. 27 Jan. 1945, Zărnești, jud. Brasov; m. Marta-Marina Vlad 1973; one s. *Education:* Music High School, Bucharest, Nat. Univ. of Music, Bucharest, Santa Cecilia Conservatory, Italy, Int. Composers' Workshop, Borovetz, Int. Composers' Workshop – Gaudeamus, Netherlands. *Career:* debut with Septet for winds and piano 1970, Conservatory of Music C. Porumbescu; Researcher in Romanian folk music, Nat. Univ. of Music (fmrly Acad. of Music), Bucharest 1971–77, Prof. 1993–2012, mem. Senate 2004–12; Researcher in Romanian folk music, Institutul de Cercetari Etnologice si Dialectologice, Bucharest, 1977–80; Ed., Romanian Musical Publishing Co. 1980–84, Man. 1984–92; Music Dept Dir, Ministry of Culture 1992–93; Vice-Pres. Union of Composers and Musicologists of Romania 2006–, Romanian Community of Electronic and Computer Assisted Music 2004–; Pres. Romanian Section, Int. Soc. for Contemporary Music 2013–; TV and radio broadcasts; mem. Union of Composers and Musicologists 1973, Bd Nat. Alliance of Creators Union 2006–, Bd Romanian Cultural Inst. 2009–2013. *Compositions include:* orchestral: As Hardly from Depths (sinfonia concertante) for cello, piano, orchestra 1971, revised 1981, Dreams I for string orchestra 1972, The Time of Mirrors for small orchestra 1974, Inscriptions in Hearts – Simfonia Brevis 1978, Symphony I, Roads in the Light 1979, Dreams II (concerto) for string orchestra 1982, The Scales of Light for small orchestra 1982 (variation of Mosaic), Symphony II, From Our Hearts 1984, Lights in the Sunset 1991, The Game of Dreams I (concerto) for small orchestra 1992, Suddenly, Dreams (concerto) for small orchestra 1994, The Light of Dreams 1995, Interlocking Dreams II for small orchestra (13 players) 1997, Light for Future for flute, harp and flute orchestra 2006, From the Sound of Earth for cello and chamber orchestra 2007, Inscriptions in Hearts II for orchestra 2012, Wild flowers for string orchestra 2013, Sonorities and Anemone II (concerto) for cello and string orchestra 2015, Sonorities and Anemone III (concerto) for violin, cello and string orchestra 2016; chamber music: Thoughts, for flute and harp 1971, Mosaic, for violin, viola and cello 1978, The Spring (String Trio No. 1) for violin, viola and cello 1984, Codex Caioni for flute, oboe, clarinet, French horn and bassoon 1984, Voices of Peace for flute, oboe, clarinet, French horn, bassoon and tape 1986, The Joy of Dreams I for flute, violin, viola, cello and percussion 1990, The Joy of the Passage (String Trio No. 4) for violin, viola and cello 1991, The Secret of Dreams I for flute, oboe, clarinet, French horn and bassoon 1992, From the Light of Dreams II for flute, violin, viola and cello 1996, Resonances on a Light Blue Background for flute and cello 2000, Flowers and Resonances – Trio for saxophones, viola and piano 2005, On this

Sunny Land II (string quartet) 2006, Light for Future II for flute and harp 2006, Light for Future III for flute solo 2008, Echos I for violin and piano 2012, Echos II, trio for violin, cello and piano 2013, Resonances on a Yellow Background I for violin and cello 2014, Sonorities and Anemone I string quartet 2014; choral: Lead (text by George Bacovia) for 4 mixed voices, flute, clarinet, 2 trombones and tuba (any player + gong) 1970, This is the Earth (cantata, text by Eugen Frunză) for mixed chorus and orchestra 1970, The Tears (text by Lucian Blaga) for soprano, English horn and piano 1970, Mosaic, symphonic-chamber-cycle for any combination of the 24 solo pieces from a symphony orchestra and vocal quartet (text by the composer) 1974–78 (also three variations: Quintet, Winter Landscape, The Scales of Light); vocal: Interlocking Dreams III (text by the composer) for soprano and small orchestra (13 players) 1999; electroacoustic: Resonances on a Red Background I (music for tape) 2004, White and Resonances for viola and tape 2005, Beyond Dreams VI for winds, percussion, strings and tape 2006, Gray and Resonances for harp and tape 2006, Thoughts and Resonances for string trio and tape 2007, The Sparkle of the Mosaic for cello and tape 2007, Red and Resonances for flute, harp, cello, piano and tape 2007, From the Sounds of Sight I for basso and tape 2007, From the Sounds of Sight II for cello and tape 2007, From the Sounds of Sight III for flute and tape 2007, From the Sounds of Sight IV for violin and tape 2007, Through the Sounds of Sight I for cello and tape 2008, Through the Sounds of Sight I, piece 2 for cello and tape 2009, Through the Sounds of Sight II for violin and tape 2008, In the Light of Evocation – Dan Constantinescu, for oboe and tape 2009, In the Light of Evocation – Anatol Vieru, for cello and tape 2010, Ad Libitum fusion for corno and tape 2014. *Recordings include:* Dreams I, Paul Staicu/Orchestra Camerata, Winter Landscape, The Scales of Light, Beyond Dreams III, Partita Radicale, Beyond Dreams V, Partita Radicale, The Joy of Achievement – Wedding Songs, Marin Constantin/Madrigal Chorus, The Joy of Achievement – Wedding Songs, Dorel Paşcu Rădulescu/Madrigal Chorus, Suddenly, Dreams, Dorel Paşcu Rădulescu/Concerto Orchestra, The Legend of Dreams, Archaeus Ensemble, Pro Contemporania 2005, Flowers and Resonances 2007, For You 2011, Thoughts and Resonances for String Trio and Tape 2013, Wild Flowers 2014, Sonorities and Anemone II 2015. *Publications include:* Mosaic, symphonic-chamber-cycle 1982, 1st Symphony, Roads in The Light 1985, Second Symphony, From Our Hearts 1988, Inscriptions in Hearts 1989, Dreams II 1992, Concerto for String Orchestra 1992, The Spring, String Trio No. 1 1994, The Legend of Dreams 1999, Selective Determination in the Poetry of Dreams 2005, Nuptial Repertory – The Bride's Song 2009, The Light of Dreams 2012, Inscriptions in Hearts II 2013. *Honours:* Hon. mem. Nat. Union of Music Performers of Romania 2013; Officer, Order of Cultural Merit 2004; Oboe Prize, Festival of Young Performers of Romania 1964, Special Prize of Univ. of Music, Bucharest 1971, Medal for Distinction in Culture (2nd Class) 1983, George Enescu Prize of the Acad. of Romania 1985, First Prize, Union of Composers and Musicologists, Nat. Festival of Song, Romania 1987, Prize, Union of Romanian Composers and Musicologists 1991, 1995, 2000, 2003, 2006, 2009, Honour Medal, Nat. Univ. of Music 2011. *Current Management:* c/o Calea Victoriei nr. 141, sector 1, Bucharest, Romania. *Telephone:* (21) 3177966 (home). *Fax:* (21) 3057997 (home). *Address:* Str. Andrei Popovici 18, Bl 8A, Sc c et IV, Apt 39, 011724 Bucharest, Romania (home). *Telephone:* (21) 2306712 (home). *E-mail:* ulpiuvlad@yahoo.com (home). *Website:* composers21.com/compdocs/vladu.htm; www.ucmr.org.ro.

VLADAR, Stefan; Austrian pianist and conductor; *Chief Conductor, Wiener KammerOrchester*; b. 1965, Vienna. *Education:* Univ. für Musik und darstellende Kunst, Vienna. *Career:* performed as piano soloist in Europe, USA and Far East with orchestras including Vienna Philharmonic, Acad. of St Martin in the Fields, Chicago Symphony Orchestra, Bavarian State Orchestra and Royal Concertgebouw Orchestra, under dirs including Claudio Abbado, Sir Yehudi Menuhin, Seiji Ozawa, Riccardo Chailly and Christoph von Donhnányi; Artistic Dir, Neuberg Festival 1988, Upper Austrian Monastery Concerts 1999; Principal Dir, Recreation – Grosses Orchester Graz 2002–06; Chief Conductor and Artistic Dir, Wiener KammerOrchester 2008–; Prof. of Piano, Univ. für Musik und darstellende Kunst, Vienna 1999–. *Recordings include:* Brahms Piano Sonata No. 1 and Four Ballades 1991, Mozart Piano Concertos 25 & 20 1996, Beethoven Piano Sonatas 2002, Chopin Preludes 2004, Mozart Piano Concertos 21 & 24 (with Camerata Salzburg) 2006, Dvorak Piano Quintet (with Jerusalem Quartet) 2006, Beethoven Diabelli Variations 2006, Brahms 2006, Schumann: Carnaval, Papillons & Carnival of Venice 2006, Haydn, Prokofieff and J.S. Bach 2009. *Honours:* Grosses Goldenes Ehrenzeichen für Verdienste um die Republik Österreich 2009; winner, Int. Beethoven Piano Competition, Vienna 1985. *Address:* Wiener KammerOrchester, Schachnerstrasse 27, A-1220, Vienna, Austria (office). *Telephone:* (1) 2036357 (office). *Fax:* (1) 2043750 (office). *E-mail:* wiener@kammerorchester.com (office). *Website:* www.kammerorchester.com (office); www.stefanvladar.com.

VLATKOVIC, Radovan; horn player; b. 1962, Zagreb, Croatia. *Education:* Zagreb Acad. of Music, Northwest German Music Acad., Detmold. *Career:* Principal, Berlin Radio Symphony Orchestra 1982–90; solo engagements from 1979, notably at Salzburg 1984, the Vienna Konzerthaus, the Barbican, the Théâtre de la Ville in Paris, Pushkin Museum Moscow, Metropolitan Museum New York, Orchestra Hall Chicago and Suntory Hall, Tokyo; soloist with leading orchestras; chamber music performer with Gidon Kremer, Heinz Holliger, András Schiff and Aurèle Nicolet; Prof. of Horn, Stuttgart Hochschule für Musik 1992–. *Recordings include:* Mozart's four concertos, R. Strauss Concertos (with the English Chamber Orchestra conducted by Jeffrey Tate). *Honours:* prizewinner Wind Instruments Competition in Ancona 1979, Horn Competition in Liège 1981, first prize Int. ARD Competition in Munich 1983, German Music Critics' Prize three times (for recordings of solo Mozart and chamber music Gubaidulina and Hindemith repertoire).

VODICKA, Leo Marian; Czech singer (tenor); b. 1950, Brno. *Education:* Janáček Acad. of Arts with Josef Valek. *Career:* has sung in most Czech opera houses, notably the Janáček Opera Brno and the Prague Nat. Theatre; guest engagements in Bologna, Rome, Milan, Geneva, Zürich, Berne, Graz, Salzburg, Cologne, Paris, Nice, Tokyo, Osaka and in Bulgaria, Hungary, the fmr Soviet Union and East Germany; major roles have included Verdi's Rigoletto, Don Carlos, Manrico and Otello; Puccini's Cavaradossi, Des Grieux, Pinkerton and Rodolfo; Janáček's Laca and Boris, the Prince in Rusalka and Smetana's Jenik and Dalibor; Don José and Stravinsky's Oedipus; concert repertoire includes Verdi Requiem; Dvořák Stabat Mater and Requiem; Janáček Amarus, Glagolitic Mass, Diary of One Who Disappeared and Everlasting Gospel; Martinů's Field Mass and Bartók's Cantata Profana; Staatsoper Vienna for role of Prince in Rusalka by Dvořák 1990; Vienna, L. Janáček-Glagolitic Mass and Osud (Fate) 1990; solo tour in Japan/Tokyo, Koriyama, Kumamoto, Matsuyama with airs from Carmen, Andrea Chénier, La Forza del Destino, Otello, Tosca, Traviata, conducted by Shigeo Genda 1992; season 2000 as Don José, Max in Der Freischütz and Cavaradossi, at the Prague State Opera. *Recordings:* Smetana The Kiss, The Secret and Libuše; Dvořák The Cunning Peasant; Foerster Eva; Janáček Amarus conducted by Charles Mackerras; Antonin Dvořák–Dimitrij, title role, conducted by Gerd Albrecht 1989; London BBC, Diary of One Who Disappeared, with Radoslav Kvapil-piano, 1993. *Address:* Zlichovska 6, Prague, Czech Republic.

VOGEL, Harald; German organist, organologist and author; b. 21 June 1941, Ottersburg. *Education:* Musikhochschule Hamburg. *Career:* expert on Gothic, Renaissance and Baroque organ music; recorded and documented historic organs in N Germany and Dutch province of Groningen; f. Organeum, to produce recordings of organ music from late Gothic era to the present, played on new and antique organs on every continent 1997–; Superintendent of Church Music and Organ Advisor, Protestant Reformed Church, with responsibility for historical organs in NW Germany 1983–2006; oversaw restoration of many historic organs and designed new ones in Stanford Univ. Memorial Church (USA), St Paul's, Tokyo (Japan) and Örgryte Kyrkan, Göteborg (Sweden); f. Dollart Festival for early music 1981; f. North German Organ Acad. 1972, teacher 1978–2002; Prof. of Organ, Westminster Choir Coll., Princeton NJ, USA 1976–; Prof. of Organ, Hochschule für Künste Bremen 1994–. *Radio:* as organist: recordings of historic organs of NW Germany (Radio Bremen) 1961–75. *Recordings include:* The Golden Age of the North German Organ Music 1985, Dietrich Buxtehude: Organ Works, 7 Vols 1987–93, Arp Schnitger in Groningen 1989, Bach Organ Works 1992, Organs in East Frisia 1996/97, Jacob Praetorius: Motets & Organ Works 1996, The Young Bach 1999, Sweelinck: Organ Works Vol. 1 (ECHO Klassik Award for Instrumentalist of the Year/Organ 2012) 2011, Bach Early Organ Works 2012. *Publications include:* co-author: Hamburg's Role in North European Organ Building 1995, Orgellandschaft Ostfriesland 1996, Orgeln in Niedersachsen 1997, Arp Schnitger und sein Werke 2009; editor of several historic scores; numerous articles in professional journals. *Honours:* Dr hc (Tech. Univ. of Luleå) 2008; Bremen Music Festival Prize 2012. *Address:* c/o Fachbereich Musik, Hochschule für Künste, Dechanatstraße 13-15, 28195 Bremen, Germany (office). *Telephone:* (421) 95951517 (office). *E-mail:* h.vogel@hfk-bremen.de (office). *Website:* www.hfk-bremen.de (office).

VOGEL, Siegfried; German singer (bass); b. 6 March 1937, Chemnitz. *Education:* studied in Dresden with H. Winkler and J. Kemter. *Career:* debut at Dresden Staatsoper 1959, as Zizell in Si j'etais roi by Adam; sang Mozart roles in Dresden; Sarastro, Osmin and the Commendatore; Berlin Staatsoper from 1965 as Leporello, Alfonso, Hunding, Basilio, Count Almaviva, Escamillo, Kecal and Ochs; guest appearances in Moscow, Paris, Lausanne (Hans Sachs and Baron Ochs 1983), Brussels and Vienna; further engagements at La Scala and in Venice, Stockholm, Helsinki, Amsterdam and Cairo; Bayreuth Festival 1985–86, as Biterolf in Tannhäuser; sang Kaspar, Rocco and the King Henry in Lohengrin 1986 at the Berlin Staatsoper; Metropolitan debut 1986, as Hunding, sang Morosus in Die schweigsame Frau at Palermo 1988; Bayreuth 1989, as Fasolt, Biterolf and Titurel; Toronto Opera 1990, as the Doctor in Wozzeck; sang the Athlete in Lulu at the Semper Oper Dresden 1992; concert repertoire includes sacred music by Bach and Handel; sang Rocco in Fidelio at the 1996 Edinburgh Festival; sang Saul in the premiere of Weill's The Eternal Road, Chemnitz 1999; Fafner in The Ring at the Berlin Staatsoper 2001. *Recordings:* Der Freischütz; Ariadne auf Naxos, Die Meistersinger, Zar und Zimmermann, Genoveva, Rienzi; St Matthew Passion; Karl V by Krenek.

VOGEL, Volker; German singer (tenor); b. 13 Oct. 1950, Karlsruhe. *Education:* Hanover Musikhochschule. *Career:* sang at the Dortmund Opera, then at Freiburg, 1984–85, and the Vienna Volksoper, 1984–90; Zürich Opera from 1991; guest appearances in Barcelona, Berlin, Bregenz and Verona; Vienna, 1990, in the premiere of Einem's Tuliphant; Salzburg and London, 1992, in Weill's Sieben Todsünden; other roles include Mozart's Pedrillo and Beethoven's Jacquino; season 1999–2000 as Herod in Salome and Shuisky in Boris Godunov, at Dublin; Wagner's Melot and Mime for Zürich Opera. *Recordings include:* Zemlinsky's Kleider machen Leute; Monostatos in Die Zauberflöte. *Current Management:* Artists Management Zürich, Rütistrasse

52, 8044 Zürich-Gockhausen, Switzerland. *Telephone:* (44) 8218957. *Fax:* (44) 8210127. *E-mail:* schuetz@artistsman.com. *Website:* www.artistsman.com.

VOGLER, Jan; German cellist; b. 18 Feb. 1964, Berlin. *Education:* Hanns Eisler Hochschule für Musik, Berlin, Basle Music Academy, Switzerland, studied with Josef Schwab, Heinrich Schiff. *Career:* Concertmaster, cello, Staatskapelle Dresden 1985–; concerts as soloist with orchestras, including Berlin Radio Orchestra 1986, 1987, 1989, Staatskapelle Dresden, Berlin Chamber Orchestra, Dresden Chamber Orchestra, Virtuosi Saxoniae; US debut, Chicago 1987; Marlboro Festival, USA 1988, 1989; numerous radio broadcasts, live recordings; recitals in many countries. *Honours:* Echo Klassik Instrumentalist of the Year – Cello (for J. S. Bach: Suiten für Cello 1-6) 2014. *Address:* Bahnhofstrasse 47, 1123 Berlin, Germany.

VOGT, Lars; German concert pianist; b. 8 Sept. 1970, Düren; m. Tatiana Komarova. *Education:* Hanover Conservatoire with Prof. Kämmerling. *Career:* numerous concerto and recital performances throughout Europe, Asia and North America; London debut, Royal Albert Hall 1990; work with numerous British orchestras, including Philharmonia, London Symphony, Royal Scottish Nat. and all BBC Orchestras; Berlin concerto debut with Deutsches Symphonie-Orchester under Leonard Slatkin; performed with LA Philharmonic, including Hollywood Bowl under Simon Rattle; played 16-concert tour of Australia 1997; Far East tour, including performances with NHK Symphony, Tokyo 1998; season 1998–99 included engagements with Salzburg Mozarteum Orchestra, Leipzig Gewandhaus, City of Birmingham Symphony; played Mostly Mozart Festival, New York; debut with Atlanta and Montreal Symphony Orchestras; recitals in London, Salzburg, Berlin, Rome, Amsterdam and Bilbao; played Brahms with Skampa Quartet, Wigmore Hall, London; Beethoven concerto cycle with Gurzenich Orchestra under James Conlon; founder, chamber music festival in Heimbach, Germany 1998; season 1999–2000 included engagements with the Komische Oper Berlin, Dresden Philharmonic, BBC Nat. Orchestra of Wales; Lutoslawski's Piano Concerto in Zürich, Dresden, Stuttgart, Bremen and Vienna; recitals in London, Los Angeles and Montreaux and chamber concerts in London, Vienna, Salzburg, Lucerne and Frankfurt; premiere of a new concerto by Tatiana Komarova 2001; Schumann's concerto in A minor at the London Proms 2002. *Recordings:* Schumann Concerto, Grieg Concerto with City of Birmingham Symphony and Simon Rattle, first two Beethoven concertos with Simon Rattle, 19th and 20th century Russian works, Haydn sonatas and Schumann's Kreisleriana and Bunte Blätter, Beethoven Sonatas op 10 No. 1 and Op 111, Prokofiev and Shostakovich cello sonatas with Truls Mork, Hindemith piano concerto No. 1 with Berlin Philharmonic and Claudio Abbado. *Honours:* Diapason d'Or for Prokofiev and Shostakovich cello sonatas. *Current Management:* Opus 3 Artists, 470 Park Avenue South, 9th Floor North, New York, NY 10016, USA. *Telephone:* (212) 584-7500. *Fax:* (646) 300-8200. *E-mail:* info@opus3artists .com. *Website:* www.opus3artists.com. *E-mail:* lars@larsvogt.com. *Website:* www.larsvogt.com.

VOICULESCU, Dan, DipMus, DMus; Romanian composer, musicologist and academic; *Professor of Counterpoint and Composition, National University of Music, Bucharest*; b. 20 July 1940, Transylvania. *Education:* Acad. of Music Gh. Dima, Cluj, studied with V. Mortari in Venice, Italy, K. Stockhausen in Cologne, Germany. *Career:* Prof. of Counterpoint and Composition, Acad. of Music, Cluj 1963–2000, Nat. Univ. of Music, Bucharest 2000–; Ed., Lucrari de Muzicologie (Musicological Works), Cluj 1979–91; mem. Union of Romanian Composers. *Compositions:* Sinfonia Ostinato 1963, Visions Cosmiques 1968, Music for strings 1971, Pieces for orchestra 1973, Suite from Codex Caioni for strings 1996, Inflorescences for strings 2001, Fables, Dialogues, Sonata, Croquis, Sonantes, Spirals (four toccatas for piano solo), Canonica (24 canons for piano solo), Sonata brava for harpsichord, nine Sonatas for flute solo, Sonata for clarinet solo, Sketches and Sonata for oboe solo, Fioriturі for violin and piano, Dilemmas for seven, Trilemmas for seven, Concertant Diptych for Baroque ensemble, Cantata for baritone, choir and orchestra 1977, Homage to Blaga for mixed choir, Mass for children's choir, four vols choral music for children, Book Without End (three vols of piano pieces for children), 60 lieder for voice and piano, The Bald Chanteuse chamber comic opera 1993. *Publications:* Polyphony of Baroque in the Works of J. S. Bach 1975, Bachian Fugue 1986, Polyphony of the 20th Century 2005. *Honours:* Union of Romanian Composers Prizes 1972–1978, 1995, 2000, 2005, G. Enescu Prize from the Romanian Acad. 1984. *E-mail:* dan.voiculescu@clicknet.ro (home).

VOIGT, Deborah; American singer (soprano); b. 4 Aug. 1960, Chicago. *Education:* San Francisco Opera's Merola Program. *Career:* debut, Shostakovich's 14th Symphony, San Francisco Chamber Symphony; European engagements include Schubert's Fierrabras at Brussels, Electra in Idomeneo for Finnish Nat. Opera, 1991, and Elvira in Ernani for Chelsea Opera Group, 1990; other opera performances in concert include Das Rheingold with the Minnesota Orchestra, Weber's Agathe in New York, Die Walküre, La Wally and Il Piccolo Marat for Dutch Radio; season 1990–91, with Amelia, Ballo in Maschera, at San Francisco and Strauss's Ariadne with the Boston Lyric Opera; Metropolitan Opera debut 1991, as Amelia; season 1992–93 included Leonora in Il Trovatore with the Metropolitan Opera and as Amelia in Un ballo in maschera with the Lyric Opera of Chicago; highlights of the 1993–94 season included debut with the Berlin Philharmonic in Zemlinsky's Lyrische Symphonie, performances of the Verdi Requiem and debut with the Philadelphia Orchestra in a series of Wagner concerts in Philadelphia and Carnegie Hall; first concert appearance with Luciano Pavarotti in Lincoln Center's Pavarotti Plus! gala, 1994; European engagements in 1995–96 included Senta in Wagner's Der fliegende Holländer with the Vienna Staatsoper and a gala concert in Tel-Aviv under Daniel Oren, and as Amelia, Covent Garden (debut) 1995; Amelia at the Met 1997; season 1998 with Sieglinde in Die Walküre at St Petersburg and Strauss's Aegyptische Helena for the Royal Opera, London, in concert; season 2002 as Danae in Die Liebe der Danae at the Salzburg Festival, Ariadne in Ariadne auf Naxos at San Francisco Opera, in Elektra at the New York Met, and in Tosca at Vienna State Opera; Salome at Chicago's Lyric Opera 2006; 2009 appearances included Isolde in Tristan und Isolde, Chicago and Amelia in Un ballo in maschera, Paris; Senta in Der fliegende Hollander, Met 2010, title role in Salome, Washington 2010, Dallas Opera 2014; Met appearances included Minnie in La fanciulla del West 2010–11, Brünnhilde 2011–13, Marie in Wozzeck 2014. *Recordings include:* Strauss's Die Frau ohne Schatten 1999, Strauss's Ariadne auf Naxos 2009, La Forza del Destino, Wagner: Tristan und Isolde 2010, Berlioz: Les Troyens 2011, Wagner: Der Ring des Nibelungen (with Met Opera, Grammy Award for Best Opera Recording 2013) 2012, Let The Season In (with Mormon Tabernacle Choir) 2014. *Publication:* Call Me Debbie: True Confessions of a Down-to-Earth Diva (autobiography) 2015. *Honours:* Prizewinner, Metropolitan Opera Auditions and the Pavarotti Int. Competition at Philadelphia; Winner, 1989 Bussetto Verdi Competition and Tchaikovsky Int., Moscow 1990; Opera Debut of the Year, New York Times, 1991; Title role in Strauss's Die Liebe der Danaë, Salzburg Festival 2002, Metropolitan Opera Guild Opera News Award 2006. *Current Management:* c/o Jesslyn Cleary, Ariadne Productions, LLC, 163 Amsterdam Avenue, Box 150, New York, NY 10023, USA. *E-mail:* AriadneLLC@aol.com. *Website:* www .deborahvoigt.com.

VOKETAITIS, Arnold; American singer (bass); b. 11 May 1931, New Haven, CT. *Education:* studied in New York. *Career:* debut at New York City Opera 1958, as Vanuzzi in Die schweigsame Frau; sang in New York as Britten's Theseus, Creon in Oedipus Rex and the Father in the local premiere of Douglas Moore's Carrie Nation 1968; guest engagements at Houston, Miami, Pittsburgh, Mexico City, San Antonio, Montréal and Vancouver; Chicago 1968–73 in Le Rossignol, Madama Butterfly, Carmen, I Due Foscari, Werther and Billy Budd; other roles have included Don Magnifico (Metropolitan Opera Nat. Touring Co.), Don Pasquale, Dulcamara, Basilio and John Hale in The Crucible by Robert Ward, Milwaukee 1976. *Recordings include:* Le Cid by Massenet.

VOLANS, Kevin; Irish composer; b. 26 July 1949, Pietermaritzburg, South Africa. *Education:* Univs of Witwatersrand and Aberdeen, Hochschüle für musik, Cologne with Karl-Heinz Stockhausen, Mauricio Kagel and Alois Kontarsky. *Career:* Lecturer in Composition, Univ. of Natal 1981–85; composer-in-residence, Queen's Univ., Belfast 1986–89, Princeton Univ. 1992. *Compositions include:* White Man Sleeps for two harpsichords, bass viol and percussion 1982 (arranged as String Quartet No. 1 1986), Walking Song for ensemble 1984, She Who Sleeps with a Small Blanket for percussion 1985, Kneeling Dance for two pianos 1985, Into the Darkness for ensemble 1987, Hunting, Gathering String Quartet No. 2 1987, The Songlines String Quartet No. 3 1988, revised 1993, Chevron (dance) 1990, The Ramanujan Notebooks String Quartet No. 4 1990, Kneeling Dance for six pianos 1992, The Man with Footsoles of Wind (chamber opera) 1993, Plane-song (film music) 1993, Concerto for piano and wind 1995, Blue, Yellow (dance) 1995, Dancers on a Plane for string quartet 1995, Slow for piano and wind 1996, Asanga for percussion 1997, Violin Concerto 1997, Double Violin Concerto 1999, Piano Trio 2001, Concerto for double orchestra 2002, Strip Weave for orchestra 2002, Trumpet and String Quartet No. 1 and No. 2 2002, String Quartet No. 7: Similarity 1 2002, Confessions of Zeno 2002, String Quartet No. 8: Black Woman Rising 2004, String Quartet No. 9: Shiva Dances 2004, Trio Concerto 2005, String Quartet No. 10 2006, Atlantic Crossing Concerto for piano 2006, Partenheimer 2008, 100 notes 2009, No Translation 2009, Trumpet Vibe Cello Piano 2009, violin:piano 2009, viola:piano (Royal Philharmonic Soc. Award for Chamber-Scale Composition 2010) 2009. *Address:* c/o Promotion Department, Chester Music, 14–15 Berners Street, London W1T 3LJ, England (office). *Telephone:* (20) 7612-7400 (office). *E-mail:* promotion@musicsales.co.uk (office). *Website:* www.chesternovello.com (office).

VOLKERT, Gudrun; singer (soprano); b. 1942, Brno, Czeckoslovakia. *Education:* Linz Conservatory. *Career:* sang dramatic roles at Klagenfurt 1966–67, Kiel 1967–74, Bielefield 1974–83; guest appearances at Brunswick 1983–88, Kassel from 1984, Hamburg 1986 and Turin 1987; performances as Brünnhilde in Der Ring des Nibelungen at Rotterdam 1988, Warsaw 1988–89, and Seattle 1991; sang Cherubini's Médée at Wuppertal 1988, followed by Isolde 1989; Metropolitan Opera 1990, as Brünnhilde; Scottish Opera 1991, as Leonore in a new production of Fidelio; other roles include Senta, Ortrud, Salome, the Marschallin, Gioconda, Tosca, Turandot and the Countess in Die Soldaten.

VOLKOV, Ilan; Israeli conductor; *Music Director and Chief Conductor, Iceland Symphony Orchestra*; b. 1976, Tel Aviv; m.; one d. *Education:* Rubin Acad. of Music, Jerusalem, Royal Acad. of Music, London. *Career:* apptd Young Conductor in Asscn, Northern Sinfonia 1995; Principal Conductor, London Philharmonic Youth Orchestra 1997–99; Asst Conductor (to Seiji Ozawa), Boston Symphony Orchestra 1999; Chief Conductor, BBC Scottish Symphony Orchestra 2003–09, Prin. Guest Conductor 2009–; Music Dir and Chief Conductor, Iceland Symphony Orchestra 2011–; guest appearances worldwide include Nat. Symphony Orchestra, Washington, Orchestre de Paris, Czech Philharmonic, City of Birmingham Symphony Orchestra; has conducted Eugene Onegin with Glyndebourne Touring Opera 2002, and at San Francisco Opera 2004, A Midsummer Night's Dream with London Philharmonic Orchestra at Glyndebourne Festival Opera 2006. *Recordings include:* works by Stravinsky and Britten, music of Jonathan Harvey (Gramophone Award for Contemporary Music 2008). *Honours:* Royal Philharmonic Soc. Young Musician of the Year 2004. *Current Management:* Van Walsum Management, The Tower Building, 11 York Road, London SE1 7NX, England. *Telephone:* (20) 7902-0520. *Fax:* (20) 7902-0530. *E-mail:* info@vanwalsum.com. *Website:* www.vanwalsum.com.

VOLKOV, Solomon; American musicologist; b. 17 April 1944, Ura-Tyube, Tajikistan. *Education:* Leningrad Conservatory. *Career:* Artistic Dir, Leningrad Experimental Studio of Chamber Opera 1965–70; staging of Fleischmann's Rothschild's Violin, completed by Shostakovich; conducted research at Russian Inst., Columbia Univ. 1976. *Publications:* Young Composers of Leningrad 1971, Remembrance of the 'Leningrad Spring' 1974, Testimony: The Memoirs of Dmitri Shostakovich (ed.) 1979, Scissors and Music: Music Censorship in the Soviet Union 1983, Balanchine's Tchaikovsky 1985, Yevgeny Mravinsky, Leningrad's Master Builder 1988, From Russia to the West: the Musical Memoirs of Nathan Milstein (with N. Milstein) 1990, St Petersburg: A Cultural History 1995, Conversations with Joseph Brodsky 1998, Shostakovich and Stalin 2004, The Magical Chorus 2008; contrib. articles in journals and newspapers 1959–. *Address:* c/o Knopf Publishing/Author Mail, 1745 Broadway, New York, NY 10019, USA (office).

VOLKOVA, Olga; Russian musician (violin); b. 1991, Vladivostock. *Education:* Sergei Prokofiev Music School, Vladivostock, Moscow Central Music School, Hochschule für Musik, Köln, studied with Felix Kalman, Irina Botschkova and Zakhar Bron. *Career:* debut aged nine, playing Bruck's Violin Concerto; numerous int. appearances as soloist and chamber musician; has worked with conductors including Mstislav Rostropovich, Vladimir Ziva, Joshua Weilerstein, Maxim Vengerov, Vadim Repin, Vladimir Fedoseyev, Boris Berezovsky and Seiji Ozawa and performed in halls including Wigmore Hall, London, Théâtre des Champs Elysées, Paris, Lincoln Hall, Washington DC, Kyoto Concert Hall, Seoul Arts Center and Moscow Hall of Music. *Honours:* scholarships from Mstislav Rostropovich Foundation, Vladimir Spivakov Foundation, Russian Artists Foundation and Doms Stiftung Basel, First Prize, Paganini Int. Violin Competition 2007, Lipizer Int. Violin Competition 2011, Carl Nielsen Int. Violin Competition 2012. *Current Management:* Blackmore International Artists, Hannah-Arendt-strasse 3, 10117 Berlin, Germany. *Telephone:* (30) 20689159. *Fax:* (30) 91683804. *E-mail:* office@blackmore-artists.com. *Website:* www.blackmore-artists.com.

VOLKOVA, Svetlana; Russian singer (soprano); b. 1950. *Career:* many appearances throughout Russia in concerts and opera; Kirov Opera, St Petersburg, from 1990, as Pauline in The Gambler by Prokofiev, Sonya in War and Peace, the Hostess in The Fiery Angel and Fata Morgana in The Love for Three Oranges; sang with the Kirov Opera in summer season at Covent Garden, 2000; other roles include Tisbe in Cenerentola, Susanna (Khovanshchina), Herodias in Salome, Mozart's Marcellina, Fricka in Das Rheingold, Larina (Eugene Onegin) and Skomoroshina in Sadko by Rimsky-Korsakov.

VOLLE, Michael; German singer (baritone); b. 1959. *Education:* studied in Stuttgart and Trossingen with Joseph Metternich and Rudolf Piernay. *Career:* sang first at Mannheim, then three seasons at Bonn as Mozart's Guglielmo, Count, Don Giovanni and Papageno, Marcello in La Bohème and Rossini's Figaro; Further engagements at Hanover, Wiesbaden, Dresden, Düsseldorf, Leipzig and Paris; Season 1997–98 with Covent Garden and La Scala debuts, as the Herald in Lohengrin and the Speaker in Die Zauberflöte; Other roles include Silvio, Don Fernando (Fidelio) and Ottokar in Der Freischütz; Don Giovanni at the 1998 Schwetzingen Festival; Season 2000–01 as Billy Budd, Eugene Onegin and Mozart's Count at Cologne, Don Giovanni at the Berlin Staatsoper and Ford in Falstaff at Brussels; Bach's St Mathew Passion at the London Proms, 2002; Many concert appearances. *Recordings include:* Britten's War Requiem; Schubert's Mass in A-flat and Bach's Christmas Oratorio. *Honours:* winner of numerous competitions. *Current Management:* IMG Artists, 31–33 rue du Temple, 75004 Paris, France. *Telephone:* 1-44-31-10-01. *Fax:* 1-44-31-44-40. *E-mail:* pwiggins@imgartists.com. *Website:* www.imgartists.com.

VOLMER, Arvo; Estonian conductor; *Music Director and Chief Conductor, Estonian National Opera;* b. 4 Nov. 1962. *Education:* Estonian Acad. of Music, St Petersburg State Conservatory, Russia. *Career:* made debut with Estonian Nat. Opera 1985; Assoc. Conductor, Estonian Nat. Symphony Orchestra 1989–93, Music Dir 1993–2001; Artistic Dir and Chief Conductor, Oulu Symphony Orchestra, Finland 1994–2005; Music Dir, Adelaide Symphony Orchestra 2003–; Music Dir and Chief Conductor, Estonian Nat. Opera 2003–; guest conductor, Bolshoi Theatre, Moscow Philharmonic, City of Birmingham Orchestra, Melbourne Symphony, Queensland Symphony, West Australian Symphony, Tasmanian Symphony, Orchestre de Bretagne, Orchestre National de France, Iceland Symphony, Staatsphilharmnnie Dortmund, Finnish Radio Symphony, Helsinki Philharmonic, Royal Philharmonic, Stockholm, Copenhagen Philharmonic. *Honours:* winner, Malko Competition for Young Conductors. *Address:* Estonian National Opera, Estonia pst. 4, 10148 Tallinn, Estonia (office). *Telephone:* 683-1201 (office). *Fax:* 631-3080 (office). *E-mail:* info@opera.ee (office). *Website:* www.arvolmer.com.

VOLODOS, Arcadi; Russian pianist; b. 24 Sept. 1972, St Petersburg. *Education:* St Petersburg and Moscow Conservatories, Paris Conservatoire

with Jacques Rouvier, Madrid Conservatory with Dmitri Bashkirov. *Career:* frequent recital and concerto engagements in Russia and Europe; Carnegie Hall, New York debut 1998; Salzburg Festival debut 2002; has played with Berlin Philharmonic, New York Philharmonic, London Philharmonic, Israel Philharmonic, Chicago Philharmonic, Boston Philharmonic and Concertgebouw Orchestra; repertoire includes Bach, Mozart, Schumann and Russian Masters. *Recordings include:* Piano Transcriptions (Preis der Deutschen Schallplattenkritik) 1997, Live at Carnegie Hall (Preis der Deutschen Schallplattenkritik, Echo Klassik Award, Gramophone Award) 1999, Rachmaninov's Piano Concerto No. 3 2000, Schubert's Solo Piano Works 2002, Tchaikovsky's Piano Concerto No. 1 2003, Volodos Plays Liszt (Diapason d'Or) 2007, Live from the Musikverein Wien (Gramophone Award for Best Instrumental Recording 2010) 2009. *Current Management:* c/o Till Janczukowicz, Vermont Classics GmbH, Reinhardtstrasse 47, 10117 Berlin, Germany. *Telephone:* (30) 20648078. *Fax:* (30) 20453480. *E-mail:* info@vermont-classics.com. *Website:* www.vermont-classics.com; klassik.sonymusic.de/Arcadi-Volodos.

VOLPE, Joseph; American music administrator; *Director of Strategic Development, Theatre Projects Consultants;* b. 2 July 1940, Brooklyn, NY; m. Jean Anderson. *Career:* joined the Metropolitan Opera as apprentice carpenter, New York 1964, apptd Master Carpenter 1966, Tech. Dir 1978–81, Asst Man. 1981–90, Gen. Man. 1990–2006; Dir of Strategic Devt, Theatre Projects Consultants, Connecticut 2008–; guest lecturer Columbia Univ., New York Univ. Stern School of Business, Wharton School of Business. *Publication:* The Toughest Show on Earth: My Rise and Reign at the Metropolitan Opera (memoir) 2006. *Address:* Theatre Projects Consultants, Inc., 25 Elizabeth Street, South Norwalk, NY 06854, USA (office). *Telephone:* (203) 299-0830 (office). *Fax:* (203) 299-0835 (office). *E-mail:* josephv@tpcworld.com (office). *Website:* www.theatreprojects.com (office).

VOLZ, Manfred; German singer (bass-baritone); b. 1949, Darmstadt. *Career:* sang in concert from 1972; stage debut as Mozart's Figaro at Trier, 1980; further appearances as Melitone in La Forza del Destino and Papageno; Engaged at Aachen 1981–83, Kassel from 1985, as Alberich, Ford, Amonasro, Mozart's Count, and Faninal; Bad Gandersheim 1986, as the King in Der Kluge by Orff; sang Alberich in Ring cycles at Rotterdam 1988 and Dortmund 1991; season 2000–01 at Kassel as Banquo, Faninal in Der Rosenkavalier, Berg's Dr Schön and Rangoni in Boris Godunov; concert repertoire includes Verdi's Requiem. *Current Management:* c/o Konzertdirektion Fritz Dietrich, Sigmund-Freud-Strasse 1, 60435 Frankfurt am Main, Germany. *Telephone:* (69) 544504. *Fax:* (69) 5484107. *E-mail:* info@konzertdirektion-dietrich.de. *Website:* www.konzertdirektion-dietrich.de.

VON ALPENHEIM, Ilse; Swiss (b. Austrian) pianist; b. (Helff-Hibler von Alpenheim), 11 Feb. 1927, Innsbruck; d. of Rüdiger von Alpenheim and Hermine von Alpenheim; m. Antal Dorati 1969 (died 1988); m. Claudio Veress. *Education:* Salzburg Mozarteum with Franz Ledwinka and Winfried Wolf. *Career:* soloist with major European and USA orchestras; numerous engagements as recitalist and chamber music player. *Recordings include:* complete Haydn piano music, Schubert complete chamber music with piano, Mendelssohn songs without words, complete Mendelssohn, all Mozart piano trios (with the Arion Trio), Dorati solo works and piano concerto. *Address:* Worbstrasse 346, 3073 Gümligen, Switzerland (home). *Telephone:* 319525606 (home). *E-mail:* ilse.dorati@gmx.ch.

VON BAHR, Robert; Swedish recording executive, producer and sound engineer; b. 27 Aug. 1943, Solna; s. of Lars von Bahr and Margaretha von Bahr; m. 1st Gunilla von Bahr 1970–77 (divorced); m. 2nd Sharon Bezaly 2002–10 (divorced). *Education:* Swedish Royal Coll. of Music. *Career:* Founder and CEO, BIS Records 1973–. *Honours:* Int. Classical Music Awards Special Achievement Award 2013. *Address:* BIS Records, Stationsvägen 20, 18450 Åkersberga, Sweden (office). *Telephone:* 854410230 (office). *Fax:* 854410240 (office). *E-mail:* info@bis.se (office). *Website:* www.bis.se (office).

VON BINZER, Kim; Danish singer (tenor); b. 2 March 1952. *Career:* sang with the Choir of Danish Radio in Copenhagen; Soloist with Jutland Opera, Århus, 1979–87; Roles include Tamino in Zauberflöte, Ramiro in La Cenerentola, Alfred in Fledermaus, Piquillo in Offenbach's La Périchole, Goro in Madama Butterfly; Aix-en-Provence Festival, 1985, in Monteverdi's Orfeo; Royal Opera Copenhagen from 1987 as Count Almaviva in Il Barbiere, Tamino in Zauberflöte, Ferrando in Così fan tutte, Don Ottavio in Don Giovanni and Cassio in Otello; Opera productions for Danish Radio and Television; Frequent concert engagements; Stage Director, Royal Opera Copenhagen, 1994–; Head, Opera Academy, 1999–. *Recordings:* Fynsk Foraar by Nielsen; Kuhlau's Lulu. *Address:* c/o The Royal Opera, PO Box 2185, 1017 Copenhagen, Denmark.

VON BOSE, Hans-Jurgen; German composer; b. 24 Dec. 1953, Munich. *Education:* Hoch Conservatory, Frankfurt am Main, 1969–72; Pupil in composition of Hans Ulrich Engelmann; In piano of Klaus Billing, Hochschule für Musik Frankfurt am Main, 1972–75; Opera 63; Dream Palace performed at Munich, 1990; Slaughterhouse Five premiered at the 1996 Munich Festival. *Compositions:* Stage: Blutbund, chamber opera, 1974; Das Diplom, chamber opera, 1975; Die Nacht aus Blei, kinetic action, 1980–81; Die Leiden des jungen Werthers, lyrical scenes, 1986; 63: Dream Place, 1990; Slaughterhouse Five, 1995; Orchestra: Morphogenesis, 1975; Symphony No. 1, 1976; Musik für ein Haus voll Zeit, 1977; Songs for Tenor and Chamber Orchestra, 1977; Travesties in a Sad Landscape for Chamber Orchestra, 1978; Symphonic

Fragment for Tenor, Baritone, Bass, Chorus; Orchestra, 1980; Variations for 15 strings, 1980; Idyllen, 1983; Sappho-Gesänge for Mezzo-Soprano and Chamber Orchestra, 1982–83; Labyrinth I, 1987; Oboe Concerto, 1986–87; 5 Children's Rhymes for Alto and 5 Instrumentalists, 1974; Threnos-Hommage à Bernd Alois Zimmermann for Viola and Cello, 1975; Solo Violin Sonata, 1977; Variations for Cello, 1978–79; Vom Wege abkommen for viola, 1982; Guarda el Canto for Soprano and String Quartet, 1982; Studie I for Violin and Piano, 1986; Lorca-Gesänge for Baritone and 10 instruments, 1986; Wind Sextet, 1986. *Address:* c/o GEMA, Herzog-Wilhelm Strasse 38, 8000 Munich 2, Germany.

VON DER GOLTZ, Gottfried; German/Norwegian violinist and conductor; *Joint Artistic Director, Freiburg Baroque Orchestra;* b. 1964, Würzburg; s. of Konrad von der Goltz and Kirsti Hjort. *Education:* Juilliard School, New York, and with Rainer Kussmaul in Freiburg. *Career:* violinist at Norddeutscher Rundfunk, Hamburg 1975–77; soloist and chamber musician 1977–; mem. Apponyi Quartett 1986–; Baroque Violinist, Freiburg Baroque Orchestra 1987–, Jt Artistic Dir 1990–; Artistic Dir, Norwegian Baroque Orchestra 2007–; Prof. of Baroque Violin, Würzburg Musikhochschule 1997–2004; Prof. of Violin, Hochschule für Musik Freiburg 2004–. *Recordings include:* with Freiburg Baroque Orchestra: Vivaldi: The Four Seasons 1997, Vivaldi: I Concerto de Dresda 2002, Mozart Concerto pour Flute et Harpe 2006, Telemann Musique de Table 2010, Mendelssohn Double Concerto and Piano Concerto 2011, Bach Orchestral Suites (Gramophone Award for Best Baroque Instrumental Recording 2012). *Address:* c/o Caroline Hassler, Freiburger Barockorchester, Freiburg, Germany (office). *E-mail:* hassler@barockorchester.de (office). *Website:* www.barockorchester.de.

VON DER WETH, Alexandra; German singer (soprano); b. 1972, Coburg. *Education:* studied in Munich. *Career:* debut in Leipzig 1993, in Grétry's Zémire et Azor; appearances with the Deutsche Oper am Rhein, Düsseldorf, from 1996 as Mozart's Pamina and Sandrina, Manon, Lucia di Lammermoor and Alcina; season 1999–2000 as Micaela at Cologne, Fiordiligi at the Glyndebourne Festival and Musetta for the Vienna Staatsoper; Lulu and Violetta at Düsseldorf; season 2000–01 with Lucia at Santa Fe, Musetta at the New York Met and Violetta in Chicago; Covent Garden debut 2001, as Manon Lescaut in Henze's Boulevard Solitude; engaged as Strauss's Daphne at Covent Garden (concert) 2002. *Recordings include:* concert arias by Mozart and Beethoven, lieder by Clara Schumann.

VON DOHNÁNYI, Christoph; German conductor; b. 8 Sept. 1929, Berlin; s. of Hans von Dohnányi and Christine von Dohnányi (née Bonhoeffer); brother of Klaus von Dohnányi; m. 1st Renate Zillessen; one s. one d.; m. 2nd Anja Silja 1979; one s. two d.; m. 3rd Barbara Koller. *Education:* Munich Musikhochschule. *Career:* abandoned legal training to study music 1948; studied in USA under grandfather, Ernst von Dohnányi 1951; répétiteur and conductor under Georg Solti, Frankfurt Oper 1952–56; Gen. Music Dir Lübeck 1957–63, Kassel 1963–66; London debut with London Philharmonic Orchestra 1965; Chief Conductor of Cologne Radio Symphony Orchestra 1964–69; Gen. Music Dir and Opera Dir, Frankfurt 1968–77; Chief Conductor and Intendant, Hamburg State Opera 1977–84; Music Dir (desig.) Cleveland Orchestra 1982–84, Music Dir 1984–2002, Music Dir Laureate 2002–; Prin. Guest Conductor Philharmonia Orchestra 1994, Prin. Conductor 1997–08, Hon. Conductor for Life 2008–; Chief Conductor, NDR Sinfonieorchester Hamburg 2004–11; numerous guest appearances; numerous recordings of symphonies with Cleveland Orchestra and opera recordings. *Honours:* Commdr des Arts et des Lettres, Commdr's Cross, Order of Merit, Commdr's Cross (Austria); Dr hc (Kent State Univ.), (Case Western Univ.), (Oberlin Coll.), (Eastman School of Music), (Cleveland Inst. of Music), (RAM) 2013; Richard Strauss Prize, Bartok Prize, Goethe Medal, Frankfurt, Arts and Science Prize, City of Hamburg, Abraham Lincoln Award. *Current Management:* c/o Harrison Parrott, 5–6 Albion Court, London, W6 0QT, England. *Telephone:* (20) 7229-9166. *Fax:* (20) 7221-5042. *E-mail:* info@harrisonparrott.co.uk. *Website:* www.harrisonparrott.com/artist/profile/christoph-von-dohnanyi.

VON DOHNÁNYI, Oliver; Czech conductor; b. 2 March 1955, Trencin; m. Natalia Melnik 1996; one d. *Education:* Konzervatorium in Bratislava (violin, conducting and composition), Academy of Music Prague, Hochschüle für Musik, Vienna (both conducting). *Career:* Conductor of the Radio Symphony Orchestra, Bratislava, 1979–86; Principal Conductor of the Slovak National Opera House in Bratislava, conducted new productions of Borodin's Prince Igor, Puccini's Tosca, Rossini's Il Barbiere di Siviglia, Smetana's The Bartered Bride, Verdi's Rigoletto, Gounod's Faust; Conductor, Slovak Philharmonic Orchestra; Istropolitana Chamber Orchestra); Music Director of the National Theatre in Prague, 1993–96; Conducted Smetana's Libuše, Gounod's Romeo and Juliet, Puccini's La Bohème, Verdi's Rigoletto, Prokofiev's Cinderella, and two Mozart operas; Don Giovanni and The Marriage of Figaro, which toured Japan, 1995, 1997; Regular guest conductor Czech National Symphony Orchestra, Prague, Yomiuri Nippon Symphony Orchestra in Tokyo, Hungarian State Philharmonic, Portugal State Symphony Orchestra, Northern Philharmonic in Leeds, Kosice State Philharmonic, Brno State Philharmonic and Slovak Sinfonietta, Zilina; Also conducts at the Danish Royal Opera House, Copenhagen, National Theatre, Brno, Teatro San Carlo, Naples, the Royal Liverpool Philharmonic, English National Opera, English Chamber Orchestra, London Mozart Players, Northern Philharmonic in Leeds, BBC Belfast and Irish National Symphony Orchestra; Conducted Verdi's Falstaff and a new production of Boito's Mephistopheles for English National Opera, 1999. *Recordings:* Smetana's Libuše and My Country (with National Theatre

of Prague); Famous Russian Masterpieces; Bach's St John Passion; Works by F Mendelssohn-Bartholdy. *Current Management:* c/o Neil Dalrymple, Music International, 13 Ardilaun Road, London, N5 2QR, England. *Telephone:* (20) 7359-5183. *Fax:* (20) 7226-9792. *E-mail:* music@musicint.co.uk. *Address:* Renoirova 2A, 152 00 Prague 5, Czech Republic. *E-mail:* o.v.dohnanyi@volny.cz.

VON GYLDENFELDT, Graciela; German singer (soprano); b. 22 June 1958, Buenos Aires, Argentina. *Education:* Conservatorio Nacional de Música Carlos López Buchardo, Buenos Aires. *Career:* debut as Norina in Don Pasquale at Buenos Aires in 1979; sang at Bern Opera 1980, debut as Gilda, then as Zerlina, Martha, Pamina, Echo in Ariadne auf Naxos and Corilla in Donizetti's Convenzione Teatrali; sang at Vienna Staatsoper 1982–86, Salzburg Festival 1984–86, Enschede Netherlands 1988, Kiel Opera 1989–94, debut as Elvira in Don Giovanni, Teatro Colón, Buenos Aires; repertoire includes Elsa in Lohengrin, Elisabeth in Tannhäuser, Senta in Der Fliegende Holländer, Sieglinde in Die Walküre, Leonore in Fidelio, Chrysothemis in Elektra, Salome, Kaiserin in Die Frau ohne Schatten, Marietta in Die Tote Stadt, Amelia in Simon Boccanegra, Desdemona in Otello, Elisabetta in Don Carlo, Aida Amelia in La Forza del Destino, Manon Lescaut, Madama Butterfly, Tosca, Suor Angelica, Marghertia in Mefistofele, Katja Kabanova, Tatjana in Eugene Onegin, Lisa in Pique Dame, Liù in Turandot, Salud in La Vida Breve; concert engagements in Beethoven's 9th and Janáček's Glagolitic Mass, Salud in La Vida Breve of Manuel de Falla. *Current Management:* c/o Wolfgang Hoyer, H&H Kuenstleragentur, Brandvorwerkstrasse 78, 04275 Leipzig, Germany. *Telephone:* (341) 3018318. *Fax:* (341) 3918611. *E-mail:* hoyer@hh-kuenstleragentur.de. *Website:* www.hh-kuenstleragentur.de; www.gracieladegyldenfeldt.de.

VON HALEM, Victor; German singer (bass); b. 26 March 1940, Berlin. *Education:* Musikhochschule Munich, studied with Else Domberger. *Career:* has sung at the Deutsche Oper Berlin 1966–; guest appearances in Hamburg, Munich, Stuttgart, Cologne, Frankfurt, Dresden, Rome, Geneva, Montreal, Lisbon, Tokyo, Vienna, Athens and London; roles include Wagner's Daland, Pogner, King Henry, Fafner, Fasolt and Hans Sachs, Verdi's Padre Guardiano, The Grand Inquisitor, Mozart's Sarastro and Osmin, Puccini's Colline, Mephistopheles, St Bris in Les Huguenots, Gurnemanz in Parsifal, King Heinrich in Lohengrin, Hans Sachs in Die Meistersinger, Hunding in Die Walküre; debut. La Scala 1994. *Current Management:* c/o Brian Jauhiainen, Bel Canto Global Arts, 17 Auburn Avenue, Bay Shore, NY 11706, USA. *Telephone:* (631) 206-0260. *Fax:* (631) 206-0260. *E-mail:* brian@belcantoglobal.com. *Website:* www.belcantoglobalarts.com.

VON JORDIS, Eelco; Austrian singer (bass); b. 11 May 1943, Graz. *Education:* studied in Graz, Zürich and Milan. *Career:* debut, Graz 1967, as the Monk in Don Carlos; sang at Regensburg Opera 1969–72, Saarbrucken and Kassel 1972–79; Bielefeld Opera from 1979, notably as Mephisto in Faust by Spohr 1993; further engagements throughout Germany and in Milan, Brussels and Zagreb; other roles include Mozart's Alfonso, Don Giovanni and Sarastro, Verdi's King Philip and Ramphis, Scarpia in Tosca, Boris Godunov, Prince Igor, Daland and Wagner's Landgrave; guest appearances in Russia and North America; Dresden Semperoper, 1999–2001, Gianni Schichi, Music Master in Ariadne; Opera Leipzig 1998, Gustav in Abraum, Herchet; Opera Hamburg 1984–1991, Ferrando in Trovatore, Grandinquisitore in Don Carlo; Munich Nat. Opera 1984–1988, Monterone in Rigoletto; Felsensteinoper in Dessau 1997–2002, Die Kluge (Orff), Don Alfonso in Così fan tutte, Reich in Lustige Weiber; Prof. of Solo Singing; performances for Deutschland Radio, Cologne, including Karl Löwe's Hiob. Oratorium. *Recordings:* Ludwig Spohr, Faust, Mephistofeles, CPO; Catott-Romanzia Mario Ruffini, E. Pentirario-Editoria Ellectronica; Charles Gounod, Margarethe. *Publication:* Gedichte 2003. *Honours:* Second Prize, Schubertwettbewerb, Vienna 1967, Third Prize, Staatlicher Preis (Udssr) Paliaschwilli Tiflis Georgien 1976. *Address:* Bremerstrasse 28, 33613 Bielefeld, Germany (office); Via Santa Lucia 8, 09045 Quartu SE, Italy (home). *Telephone:* (521) 130730 (office); (070) 3355661843 (home). *Fax:* (521) 130730 (office).

VON KANNEN, Günter; singer (bass-baritone); b. 22 March 1940, Rheydt, Germany. *Education:* studied with Paul Lohmann and Franziska Martienssen. *Career:* sang first at the Pfalztheater Kaiserslautern; subsequently member of the troupe in Bonn and Karlsruhe, and from 1979–90 Principal Bass at the Zürich Opera; since 1992, at the Staatsoper in Berlin; Guest appearances in Cologne, Hamburg, Deutsche Oper Berlin, Washington DC, Vienna, Brussels, Dresden, Amsterdam, Paris Châtelet, with NHK Symphony Tokyo (Pizarro under Ferdinand Leitner), Israel Philharmonic (Doktor in Wozzeck under Daniel Barenboim), Chicago Symphony Orchestra (Klingsor in Parsifal); Sang at the Festivals of Santa Fe, Salzburg, Drottningholm, Schwetzingen, Aix-en-Provence, Lucerne; From 1988–92, Alberich in the Bayreuth Festival's Ring cycle, conducted by Daniel Barenboim and produced by Harry Kupfer; Sang also Klingsor at Bayreuth, (conductor James Levine); Alberich at both Berlin Opera Houses and at Hamburg State Opera; Alberich in the Bayreuth Millennium Cycle 2000, conductor Giuseppe Sinopoli, producer Jürgen Flimm; Other important roles are Hans Sachs in Meistersinger; Ochs Von Lerchenau in Rosenkavalier, La Roche in Capriccio; Cardillac; Sang Alberich in Harry Kupfer's production of The Ring at the Berlin Staatsoper, 1996; Sang Morosus in Die schweigsame Frau by Strauss, Dresden, 1998; Season 2000–01 as the Doctor in Wozzeck at La Scala and Falstaff in Dresden, Alberich at Bayreuth and the Berlin Staatsoper. *Recordings include:* Lebendig Begraben by Schoeck (Atlantis); Bartolo in

Nozze di Figaro (Barenboim); Klingsor in Parsifal (Barenboim/Berlin Philharmonic); Osmin in Entführung aus dem Serail; Tiresias in Oedipus Rex by Stravinsky (Neeme Järvi); Manasse in Brautwahl by Busoni (Barenboim); Commendatore in Gazzaniga's Don Giovanni; Alberich in the Bayreuth Ring (Barenboim); Doktor in Wozzeck and Pizarro in Fidelio (Colin Davis); Capriccio/La Roche, conductor Georges Prêtre. *Current Management:* Balmer & Dixon Management AG, Kreuzstrasse 82, 8032 Zürich, Switzerland. *Telephone:* (43) 244-8644. *Fax:* (43) 244-8649. *Website:* www.badix.ch.

VON MAGNUS, Elisabeth; Austrian singer (mezzo-soprano); b. Vienna. *Education:* drama school, Salzburg, studied with Hertha Töpper in Munich, S. Schouten in The Netherlands. *Career:* own programme on Austrian radio; soloist in nearly all European countries, Japan and the USA; venues include the Alte Oper, Frankfurt, the Barbican Centre, London, the Vienna Musikverein, the Concertgebouw, Amsterdam, the Berlin Philharmonic and the Cologne Philharmonic; US debut 1991 with St Matthew Passion with the Los Angeles Philharmonic under Peter Schreier; Salzburg Festival debut in Mozart's C Minor Mass, Monteverdi's L'Incoronazione di Poppea and Vespers of 1610 1993; has appeared in many and varied roles at several leading opera houses and music festivals, with recitals of songs ranging from Haydn to Berg and Weill; has featured on numerous radio and television broadcasts, including Mozart's Le nozze di Figaro from Zürich Opera House; sang Piramus in Hasse's Piramo e Tisbe, Wiener Schauspielhaus 2001. *Recordings include:* Zigeunerbaron; Stabat mater; Bach's Christmas Oratorio and Magnificat; Shostakovich, Sieben Romanzen with Stononi Trio; Arianna and Canzonettes by Haydn. *Address:* Künstleragentur Dr Raab and Dr Böhm, Plankeng 7, 1010 Vienna, Austria.

VON OSTEN, Sigune; German singer (soprano); b. 8 March 1950, Dresden. *Education:* studied in Hamburg and Karlsruhe and with Elisabeth Grümmer and Eugen Rabine. *Career:* debut singing John Cage's Aria at Hanover 1973; noted interpreter of 20th century repertoire at the Dresden and Salzburg Festivals, the Bonn and Vienna Festivals at Venice, Berlin, Donaueschingen, Madrid, Strasbourg, St Petersburg, Moscow, Tokyo, Stuttgart, Wiesbaden, Paris, Venice and Lisbon; repertoire includes Berg's Marie and Lulu, the Woman in Schoenberg's Erwartung, Lady Macbeth, Fusako in Des verratene Meer, the Mother in Turnage's Greek; worked with composers such as Halffter, Penderecki, Denisov, Messiaen, Cage, Scelsi and Nono; founding mem. and Artistic Dir, Musica Temporale ensemble 1995–2003; f. Neue Ho(e)rizonte (arts project) 1996–. *Recordings:* Penderecki's Luke Passion, Messiaen's Harawi, Halffter's Noche pasiva, Dittrich's Engführung; songs by Ives, Satie, Cage. *Address:* Artpoint, Trombacher Hof, 55583, Bad Münster am Stein, Germany (office). *Telephone:* (6708) 2616 (office). *E-mail:* info@artpoint-th.com (office). *Website:* www.artpoint-th.com.

VON OTTER, Anne-Sofie; Swedish singer (mezzo-soprano); b. 9 May 1955, Stockholm. *Education:* Stockholm Conservatory, Guildhall School of Music and Drama, UK, studied interpretation with Erik Werba in Vienna and Geoffrey Parsons in London, vocal studies with Vera Rozsa. *Career:* mem. Basel Opera, Switzerland 1982–85; French debut at Opéra de Marseille (Nozze di Figaro—Cherubino) and Aix-en-Provence Festival (La Finta Giardiniera) 1984, Rome, Accad. di Santa Cecilia 1984, Geneva (Così fan tutte—Dorabella) 1985, Berlin (Così fan tutte) 1985, USA in Chicago (Mozart's C minor Mass) and Philadelphia (Bach's B minor Mass) 1985, London at Royal Opera, Covent Garden (Le Nozze di Figaro) 1985, Lyon (La Finta Giardiniera) 1986, La Scala, Milan (Alceste) 1987, Munich (Le Nozze di Figaro) 1987, Stockholm (Der Rosenkavalier) 1988, The Metropolitan Opera, New York (Le Nozze di Figaro) 1988, The Royal Albert Hall, London (Faust) 1989, Handel's Ariodante 1997, Glyndebourne (Carmen) 2002, Théâtre des Champs Elysées (Handel's Serse) 2003, Metropolitan Opera, New York (Mélisande) 2005, Santa Fe (Carmen) 2006; Waltraute in Götterdammerung for Aix-en-Provence Festival 2009 and Salzburg Easter Festival 2010; appeared in Lulu at the Met 2010; Irene in Tamerlano, Liceu Barcelona 2011; Marcellina in Le nozze di Figaro, Badeb Baden 2015; repertoire extends from baroque music, German lieder through opera to 20th century music; has given recitals in New York, Paris, Brussels, Geneva, Stockholm, Vienna, London, Verbier, Toulouse and numerous other cities. *Recordings include:* Speak Low (Songs by Kurt Weill) & The Seven Deadly Sins [Die Sieben Todsunden] 1995, Home for Christmas 1999, For the Stars (with Elvis Costello) 2001, Terezín/Theresienstadt 2008, Love Songs (with jazz pianist Brad Mehldau) 2010, Mahler - Des Knaben Wunderhorn 2010, Berlioz: Les Nuits d'été; Harold en Italie 2011, Sogno Barocco 2012, Swedish Romantic Songs (with Bengt Forsberg) 2012, Douce France 2013. *Honours:* Hon. DSc (Bath) 1992. *Current Management:* c/o Shirley Thomson, Harrison Parrott Ltd, 5-6 Albion Court, Albion Place, London, W6 0QT, England. *E-mail:* shirley.thomson@harrisonparrott.co.uk. *Website:* www.annesofievonotter.com.

VON SCHWEINITZ, Wolfgang; German composer; *Professor in Composition, California Institute of the Arts;* b. 7 Feb. 1953, Hamburg. *Education:* American Univ., Washington, DC, Hamburg Hochschule für Musik with Ernst G. Klussmann and György Ligeti. *Career:* Center for Computer Research in Music and Acoustics, Stanford Univ., Calif., USA 1975–76; Resident Composer, German Acad., Rome, Italy 1978–79; Patmos, azione musicale (opera) premiered at Munich 1990; Guest Prof. in Composition, Weimar 1994–96; Prof. in Composition (Roy E. Disney Family Chair in Musical Composition), Calif. Inst. of the Arts 2007–. *Compositions include:* Two Symphonies 1973, 1974, Mozart Variations, for orchestra 1976, Die Brücke, for tenor, baritone and chamber orchestra 1978, Piano Concerto 1979,

Papiersterne Song Cycle, for mezzo and piano 1981, Englische Serenade, for six wind instruments 1984, Mass, for soloists, chorus and orchestra 1984, Patmos, azione musicale 1990, Morgenlied, for flute 1990, . . . Wir aber singen, symphonic cycle in three parts, for cello and orchestra 1992, 1995, 1996, Franz and Morton for piano trio 1993–94, O-Ton Automne, Linguistikherbst, song on a poem by Oskar Pastior for soprano and piano 1996, Helmholtz-Funk for eight computer-controlled sine generators and two ringmodulated pianos with natural tuning 1997, Klang auf Schön Berg La Monte Young for string trio and live-electronic ring modulation 1999, JUZ (a Yodel Cry) for trombone and pre-recorded sounds 1999, Naturgesang mit Fröschen und Rotbauchunken (live electronic sound performance) 2000, des Himmel Höhe glänzet, song in just intonation for soprano and 2 violins 2002, Die Kantate oder, Gottes Augenstern bist du 2003, Radio Play by and with Friederike Mayröcker, Plainsound-Litanei for cello solo 2004, Plainsound Symphony, for clarinet, ensemble and orchestra 2004–05, Plainsound Glissando Modulation for violin and double bass 2007, Plainsound Brass Trio 2008. *Publications:* Kursbuch 122 'Die Zukunft der Moderne' 1995, Alef Bet/Kometendeutsch, Psalm 119 in Sinn-Silben- und akzentgetreur Übersetzung des Althebräischen Wortlauts (a radically literal German trans. of Psalm 119) 1999; several articles in music journals and magazines including Neue Zeitschrift für Musik, Neue Musik, Positionen, MusikTexte. *Honours:* Scholarship Studienstiftung des deutschen Volkes 1973–78, Scholarship Deutsche Akademie Villa Massiomo, Rome, Schneider-Schott Prize for Young Composers 1986, Plöner-Hindemith Preis 1988, Scholarship Schloss Wiepersdorf 2000. *Address:* 33628 Lancaster Road, Hwy 138, Lancaster, CA 93536, USA (home). *Telephone:* (661) 248-6989 (home). *E-mail:* schweinitz@plainsound.org (home). *Website:* plainsound.org (home).

VON STADE, Frederica; American mezzo-soprano; b. 1 June 1945, Somerville, NJ; m. 1st Peter Elkus 1973 (divorced); two d.; m. 2nd Michael G. Gorman 1991. *Education:* Mannes Coll. of Music. *Career:* opera début with Metropolitan Opera, New York (in Le Nozze di Figaro) 1970; has also sung with Paris Opera, San Francisco Opera, Lyric Opera of Chicago, LA Opera, Salzburg Festival, Covent Garden, London, Spoleto Festival, Boston Opera Co., Santa Fe Opera, Houston Grand Opera, La Scala, Milan, Vienna State Opera; appearances with Lyric Opera of Chicago in 2010 included Madeline in Three Decembers and Despina in Cose fan tutte; sang role of Myrtle Bledsoe (created for her by the composer Ricky Ian Gordon) in A Coffin in Egypt, Chicago Opera Theater 2015; mem. American Acad. of Arts and Sciences 2012. *Recordings include:* over 70 recordings, including Frederica von Stade Sings Mozart and Rossini Opera Arias, French Opera Arias 1998, Songs of the Cat (with Garrison Keillor) 2010, Fauré: Mélodies 2011, A Portrait On Record 2014, Complete RCA and Columbia Recital Albums (box set) 2016. *Honours:* Officier, Ordre des Arts et des Lettres 1998; Dr hc (Yale Univ.), (Boston Univ.), (Georgetown Univ. School of Medicine), (Mannes School of Music), (San Francisco Conservatory of Music), (Cleveland Inst. of Music); two Grand Prix du Disc awards, Deutsche Schallplattenpreis, Premio della Critica Discografica and numerous other awards and prizes. *Current Management:* c/o Matthew A. Horner, IMG Artists, Carnegie Hall Tower, 152 West 57th Street, 5th Floor, New York,, NY 10019, USA. *E-mail:* mhorner@imgartists.com. *Website:* www.fredericavonstade.com.

VONDRÁCEK, Lukás; Czech pianist; b. 1986, Ostrava. *Education:* Acad. of Music, Latowice, Vienna Musikhochschule and Ostrava Univ. *Career:* first public recital aged four; performed in various piano festivals in USA, including Gilmore Festival, Ravinia Rising Stars Series and New York Int. Piano series; UK recital performances include appearances at Buxton, Ryedale, Music at Oxford and Harrogate Festivals; recital debut in Paris La Cite, Brussels Palais des Beaux Arts and Madrid Auditorio Nacional; has performed with Helsinki Philharmonic, BBC Orchestra, Deutsches Symphonie-Orchester Berlin, Cincinnati Symphony Orchestra, Czech Philharmonic, St Petersburg Philharmonic, Hong Kong Philharmonic, Lake Forest Symphony, Cape Town Philharmonic, Flemish Radio Orchestra, Orquesta Filarmonica de Galicia, Iceland and Dallas Symphony Orchestras and has toured with NHK Symphony in Japan; projects in 2004–05 included debuts with Helsinki Philharmonic, BBC Orchestra, Deutsches Symphonie-Orchester, Berlin and Cincinnati Symphony Orchestra; projects in 2008–09 include debuts with El Paso, Colorado and Baltimore Symphony orchestras, return visit to Bournemouth Symphony Orchestra, a concert with Kassel State Orchestra with Estonian conductor Anu Tali, recital at the Belfast Festival and a performance at Lille Piano(s) Festival. *Recordings:* albums: Prodigy – Lukas Vondracek, repertoire including Mendelssohn, Liszt, Janacek and Dohnanyi. *Current Management:* Harrison Parrott GmbH, Lucile-Grahn-Strasse 37, 81675 Munich, Germany. *Telephone:* (89) 45726154. *Fax:* (89) 45726150. *E-mail:* info@harrisonparrott.de. *Website:* www .harrisonparrott.com.

VOROPAEV, Dmitri; Russian singer (tenor); b. 1980, Baku, Azerbaijan. *Education:* M. I. Glinka Choral Coll., St Petersburg Conservatory. *Career:* joined Mariinsky Young Singers' Acad., Moscow 2000; Mariinsky Theatre debut as Don Ottavio in Don Giovanni 2002, currently soloist with Mariinsky Theatre; roles include Chevalier Belfiore in Il Viaggio a Reims, Mariinsky Theatre and in Paris 2005, Maese Pedro in El Retablo de Maese Pedro, Vienna 2004, Un laquais in La Guerre et la Paix, Opera Bastille 2005, L'innocent in Boris Godunov, La Monnaie, Brussels, Kennedy Center's Opera House, Washington; appeared in Ten Tenors concert, Royal Festival Hall, London 2004. *Address:* c/o Mariinsky Theatre, 1 Theatre Square, St Petersburg

190000, Russia (office). *Telephone:* (812) 3264141 (office). *Website:* www .mariinsky.ru/en (office).

VOSCHEZANG, Hans; Dutch singer (baritone); b. 1970. *Education:* Utrecht School of Arts, Guildhall School of Music and Drama, London, UK. *Career:* appearances in Netherlands and London as Masetto in Don Giovanni, Purcell's Aeneas, Nick Shadow, Silvio (Pagliacci), Argante in Rinaldo, Ctésippe in Faure's Pénélope, Gianni Schicchi, and Esteban Montejo in Henze's El Cimarrón; concerts in Wuppertal, with the Brabants Orchestra, Orchestre Symphonique de la Monnaie under Marc Soustrot, Acad. of Ancient Music with Paul Goodwin, Hanover Band, London Philharmonic Orchestra, Netherlands Radio Philharmonic Orchestra; engagements include Conte Almaviva with European Camerata in Amsterdam and Brussels, Robert in Les Vêpres Siciliennes for The Saturday Matinee in the Concertgebouw and Junius in The Rape of Lucretia in UK its Hungarian premiere; debut at the Liceu, Barcelona in Saint-Saens Henry VIII 2002, Glyndebourne Festival in new production of Carmen 2002. *Recording:* Carmen, Glyndebourne Festival 2002. *Honours:* Prizewinner, Hertogenbosch Int. Singing Competition, Netherlands 2000. *Website:* www.hansvoschezang.com.

VOSS, Elverta Lynn (Ealynn), BS; American singer (soprano); b. 10 March 1949, Pittsburgh, Pa. *Education:* Oberlin Conservatory of Music. *Career:* operatic appearances at various US venues, in Canada, Australia, Spain, Japan, The Netherlands and Denmark; frequent appearances in Turandot title role include Arizona Opera 1988, Opera Carolina 1990, Miami Opera 1990, the Australian Opera 1991, 1994, New York City Opera 1991, 1992, Arena di Verona in Japan 1991, Baltimore Opera 1992, San Francisco 1993, Michigan Opera 1994, Houston Grand Opera 1994, Copenhagen Opera, Denmark 1996; sang the Foreign Princess in Rusalka at the Spoleto Festival, USA 1988, and again at Seattle Opera 1990; Ariadne (Ariadne auf Naxos) at Victoria State Opera, Australia 1988, and Los Angeles Music Center Opera 1992, where she also sang Chrysothemis in Elektra 1991, 1994, Amelia (Un Ballo in Maschera) 1991, 1994, and Senta (Der fliegende Holländer) 1995; Manitoba Opera, Canada 1989, as Lady Macbeth, returning as Amelia 1992; other appearances include Elvira (Ernani) at the Oviedo Festival, Spain 1991, Tove in Gurre-Lieder at the Concertgebouw Amsterdam 1995, and Brünnhilde in Götterdämmerung at the Aspen Festival; concerts include Beethoven's 9th with Santa Barbara Symphony and Verdi's Requiem with Pasadena Symphony; debut with the Rome Opera singing Turandot 1996. *Recordings* include: Turandot (video, with Australian Opera) 1991.

VOSS, Friedrich; German composer; b. 12 Dec. 1930, Halberstadt; m. Erna Lewann 1965; one s. *Education:* Gymnasium Halberstadt, Hochschule für Musik, Berlin. *Career:* performances with Berlin Philharmonic Orchestra, under Karajan, Radio Symphony Orchestra, Berlin, under Maazel, Japan Philharmonic Orchestra, under James Loughran; in Germany, Western Europe, USA, Australia, Asia, South Africa, Latin America; television performances in Madrid, Johannesburg, Adelaide (Australia). *Compositions include:* five symphonies, two violin concertos, one cello concerto, one cello concertino, five string quartets, one saxophone quartet, Concertino for organ, strings and timpani, two works for choir, Hamlet overture, Dithyrambus for orchestra, Metamorphosis for orchestra, Die Nachtigall und die Rose (ballet), Leonce und Lena (opera), Cantata of Psalms for soloists, choir and orchestra, Missa MM (Versöhnungsmesse) for soloists, chorus and orchestra (Composers' Prize, Catholic and Evangelical Churches in Baden-Württemberg 2001). *Recordings:* some 100 broadcast recordings in Germany and Western Europe. *Honours:* first place Composers' Competition, Munich Chamber Orchestra 1955, Stuttgart Music Prize 1960, Berlin Art Prize (Young Generation) 1961, Düsseldorf Robert Schumann Prize 1962, Villa Massimo Award 1964, 1977, Johann Wenzel Stamitz Prize, Mannheim 1985. *Address:* Hoppenstedts Weg 5, 29308 Winsen an der Aller, Germany (home). *Telephone:* (5143) 911752 (office).

VOSS, Hermann; violist; b. 9 July 1934, Brunen, Germany. *Education:* studied in Düsseldorf with Maier and in Freiburg with Végh. *Career:* fmr mem., Karl Munchinger's Stuttgart Chamber Orchestra in Heibronn; co-founder, Melos Quartet of Stuttgart 1965; first concert tours sponsored by the Deutsches Musikleben Foundation and represented West Germany at the Jeunesse Musicales in Paris 1966; int. concert tours from 1967; bicentenary concerts in the Beethoven House at Bonn 1970, and toured the USSR, Eastern Europe, Africa, N and S America, the Far East and Australia; British concerts and festival appearances from 1974; cycle of Beethoven quartets at Edinburgh Festival 1987; Wigmore Hall, St John's Smith Square and Bath Festival 1990; associations with Rostropovich in the Schubert Quintet and the Cleveland Quartet in works by Spohr and Mendelssohn; Teacher, Stuttgart Musikhochschule. *Recordings:* complete quartets of Beethoven, Schubert, Mozart and Brahms, quintets by Boccherini with Narciso Ypes and by Mozart with Franz Beyer. *Honours:* Grand Prix du Disque (with Melos Quartet), Academie du Disque, Brussels Prix Caecilia (with Melos Quartet).

VOSTRIAKOV, Alexander; Russian singer (tenor); b. 1948, Kurgan Region. *Education:* studied in Kursk and at the Kharkov Inst. of the Arts. *Career:* mem., Kharkov Opera from 1973, then Dnepropetrovsk Opera Theatre –1983; Principal, Kiev Nat. Opera from 1983, notably as Lohengrin and Ismaele in Nabucco; tour of the UK 1996 with the Perm State Opera as Lensky in Eugene Onegin.

VOYTIK, Viktor Antonovich; composer; b. 3 Oct. 1947, Grodno, Belarus. *Education:* Conservatories of Belarus and Moscow. *Career:* Lecturer, Conservatory of Belarus from 1980. *Compositions:* Two Symphonies. 1972, 1974; How the Gnat went Wooing, Cantata, 1972; Remembering Khatin, oratorio, 1973; Suite in the Olden Style for orchestra, 1973; Cossack songs, cantata, 1974; Paraphrases, Suite for orchestra, 1975; Day of the Homeland, oratorio, 1977; Sonata for two cimbaloms, 1979; String Quartet, 1979; Clarinet Concerto, 1984; Cimbalom Concerto, 1988; Suite, for male voices, 1990; Patriotic Chant for chorus and orchestra, 1991; The Last Autumn of the Poet for soprano, baritone and ensemble, 1992; Spring Song, opera, 1995; Journey to the Alphabet Castle, 1996. *Address:* c/o RAO, 6a B. Bronnya, Moscow 103670, Russia. *Telephone:* (495) 203 3777. *Fax:* (495) 200 1263.

VRIEND, Jan; Dutch composer, conductor and pianist; b. (Johannes Nicolaas Maria Vriend), 10 Nov. 1938, Benningbroek; s. of Jacob Vriend and Elisabeth Ursem; m. Josie Price; two d. *Education:* Amsterdam Conservatory, Inst. of Sonology, Utrecht. *Career:* Founder and first Conductor, ASKO-Amsterdam 1964; conductor of choirs, orchestras and ensembles 1961–70; Conductor, Stroud Symphony Orchestra 1989–94; lecturer on composition, the use of mathematics in composition and the philosophy of music. *Compositions include:* Paroesie for 10 Instruments 1963–67, Huantan for organ and four groups of wind instruments 1968, Ensembles for mixed choir 1971, Elements of Logic for wind orchestra 1972, Heterostase for piano, flute and bass clarinet 1980, Gravity's Dance for piano 1983, Jets d'Orgue for large organ 1984–90, Hallelujah I for large orchestra 1986–97, Hallelujah II for 26 instruments 1987, Three Songs for Soprano and Orchestra 1991, De Origen Volcánico for orchestra 1992, Symbiosis for nine instruments 1992, Khepera for alto flute and alto clarinet 1997, Du-Dich-Dir for mixed choir 1998, Piano Quintet 1999, Choirbook part 1 for male choir 1999, In Paradisum for large ensemble 2000, Grosse Fuge for six percussion and organ 2001, Hymn to Ra for choir, soloists and orchestra 2002, Entre el Olivo y el Hombre for mixed choir 2003, Pas Crever for soprano and small ensemble 2003, Anatomy of Passion for cello and piano 2004, Voice of the Planet for cello and orchestra 2005, Echo 13.7 for piano and orchestra 2006, Meden Agan for solo piano 2006, Phagocitosis for orchestra 2007, Imagine the Mountain for violin and pianoforte 2007, Lune Plaine Ciel et Mort for mixed choir 2007, Bachanalia for organ 2007, Manitou for string quartet 2008, Critical Mass for string quartet 2008, Liebesträume for piano solo 2009, Metamorphoses for orchestra 2010, Poldergezangen for choir a cappella 2010, Koyopa for choir and percussion 2011, Joy for cello and piano 2011, The Shining for string orchestra 2012. *Publications include:* Essays on the music of Xenakis and Varèse and various other topics concerning new music and the philosophy of music. *Honours:* Schnittger Organ Prize for Herfst 1966, Prize for Composition, Amsterdam Conservatory 1967, Int. Gaudeamus Prize 1970. *Address:* 5 Silver Street, Tetbury, Glos., GL8 8DH, England. *Telephone:* (1666) 503807. *E-mail:* jan@janvriend.co.uk. *Website:* www.janvriend.co.uk.

VRONSKY, Petr; Czech conductor; b. 4 March 1946, Prague; one d. *Education:* Conservatoire Plzeň, Acad. of Music Arts, Prague. *Career:* debut in Prague 1971; Opera, Plzeň 1971; Opera, Usti Nad Labem, Aussig 1974; State Philharmonic Orchestra, Brno 1979–91; Sr Lecturer, Prague 1990; Kammeroper Wien 1991; Dance Theatre, Haag 1995; guest conductor, Czech Philharmonic Orchestra, Prague, Symphony Orchestra, Prague, Nat. Theatre, Prague, State Opera, Prague, Metropolitan Orchestra, Tokyo, Radio Symphony Orchestra, Munchen, Philharmonic Orchestra, Dortmund; mem. Asscn of Music Scientists and Musicians, Prague. *Honours:* Conducting Competition Prizes, Olomouc 1970, Besancon 1971, Berlin 1973. *Address:* Majerskeho 2049, PO Box 29, 14900 Prague 4, Czech Republic.

VUORI, Harri; Finnish composer; b. 10 Jan. 1957, Lahti. *Education:* Sibelius Academy with Eino Rautavaara. *Career:* Dept of Musicology, Helsinki Univ. 1993–; Composer-in-Residence, Hyvinkää Orchestra 1997. *Compositions:* Piano Sonata 1976, In Natural State for ensemble 1978, String Quartet 1979, The Seasons in Natura Naturally for four female voices and ensemble 1982, Like a Bird's footprints in the Sky (chamber opera) 1983, Mystical metamorphoses nocturnae for two sopranos and ensemble 1985, Kri for orchestra 1988, Songs of Dreaming and Death for soprano and cello 1990, Interrupted Movements for chamber orchestra 1991, Above and Below for wind and percussion 1995, Violin Sonata 1996, The Mandelbrot Echoes for orchestra 1996, Sky Line (electro-acoustic) 1997, Invitation to a Nocturnal Dance for two viols and harpsichord 1997, Awakenings for chorus 1997.

WAAGE, Lars; Danish singer (bass-baritone); b. 1948, Århus. *Education:* Århus Conservatory. *Career:* sang with the Lubeck Opera 1975–80, as King Henry in Lohengrin and Wagner's Gurnemanz; Jyske Opera at Århus from 1980, notably as Wotan and Gunther in The Ring; guest appearances as Sharpless, Iago, Pizarro, Mephistopheles and Kurwenal; concert singer in France, Germany and Italy.

WACHNER, Julian, DMA; American conductor, composer and musician (piano, organ); *Director of Music and the Arts, Trinity Wall Street;* b. 1970, Hollywood, Calif. *Education:* Boston Univ. School for the Arts, studied with David Hoose and Lukas Foss. *Career:* currently Dir of Music and the Arts, Trinity Wall Street, New York, Principal Conductor, NOVUS NY and Trinity Baroque Orchestra & Choir of Trinity Wall Street; Music Dir Washington Chorus; guest appearances with Philadelphia Orchestra, Montreal and Pittsburgh Symphonies, Spoleto Festival USA, Handel and Haydn Soc., Glimmerglass Opera, Hawaii Opera Theater, New City Opera, Boston Pops, Lincoln Center Festival, Rolling Stones (50th anniversary tour), New York City Opera, Hong Kong Philharmonic, Portland Baroque and at Carnegie Hall; Founder and fmrly Music Dir, Boston Bach Ensemble and Bach Acad. de Montréal; fmrly Artistic Dir, Int. Bach Festivals in Boston and Montréal; f. The Twelfth Night Festival of Early Music; conductor and composer, New York City Opera VOX Festival of contemporary opera 2010, sole conductor 2012; performances as organist and pianist have included solo recital at Spoleto Festival USA and Rachmaninov at Kennedy Center; Fellow, American Guild of Organists. *Compositions include:* orchestral works: Rondo for Piano and Orchestra 1993, Incantations 1999, Symphony No. 1 for choir and orchestra 2001, Concerto for Clarinet 2002, Apollo's Fire 2003, The Midnight Ride of Paul Revere 2004, Triptych for organ/large orchestra 2006, Come, My Dark-Eyed One 2009, Lifting the Curse 2011, Un Flambeau for unison chorus, brass sextet and organ 2011; chamber works: Canticles for chamber orchestra and choir 1991, Dances and Apparitions for violin, marimba, double bass and piano 1991, Psalm Cycle for soprano, violin, viola, cello, double bass and organ 1991, Landscapes for flute, alto saxophone, marimba, piano and cello 1992, Cycles for clarinet and piano 1997, Enchantment for flute, bassoon and piano 1998, War Songs for solo baritone and chamber orchestra 1998, Soliloquies and Transformations for flute, bass clarinet, trumpet, trombone, violin and cello 2000, Concerning Passion for horn and piano 2001, Toccata, Adagio and Fugue for solo organ 2011; sacred vocal works: Missa Brevis 1987, A Festive Gloria 1991, Aaronic Benediction 1992, All Creatures of our God & King 1992, Hear My Cry, O Lord 1992, Introit for All Saints 1993, By the Waters of Babylon 1995, Alleluias, Intercessions & Remembrances 1995, Arise My Love 1998, At the Lighting of the Lamps 1999, Behold the Tabernacle of God 2003, Ave, Dulcissima Maria 2011; operas: Mobster Lobster 2003, Evangeline Revisited 2005; secular vocal works: Mirrorlight Blue for voice and piano 1991, Sometimes I Feel Alive 1998, Rilke Songs for choir a cappella 2001, Planet X for women's choir 2003, Four Scenes from The Rubayyat for men's choir and piano 2006. *Recordings include:* as composer: Chamber Music 2000, Sacred Music 2000, The Midnight Ride of Paul Revere 2002, Julian Wachner: Complete Works for Chorus, Vol. 1 2010, Triptych 2012; other: J. S. Bach: Weinachts-Oratorium 2000, The Company of Heaven: Works by Benjamin Britten 2001, Lukas Foss: Griffelkin 2003, Christmas and The Washington Chorus 2010, Bach: Complete Motets 2011, Elena Ruehr: Averno 2012, Israel in Egypt 2012. *Honours:* ASCAP's Alice Parker Award for Adventurous Programming (with Washington Chorus) 2011. *Current Management:* c/o Thomas Leslie, 606 Cathcart, #335, Montreal, PQ H3B 1K9, Canada; Opus 3 Artists, 470 Park Avenue South, 9th Floor North, New York, NY 10016, USA. *Telephone:* (514) 293-7333 (Montreal); (212) 584-7576 (Opus 3). *Fax:* (646) 300–8276 (Opus 3). *E-mail:* moberstein@opus3artists.com. *E-mail:* thomas@julianwachner.com (office); julian@thewashingtonchorus.org (office); julian@julianwachner.com. *Website:* www.julianwachner.com.

WÄCHTER, Erich; German conductor; b. 3 July 1945, Bielefeld. *Education:* Hochschule für Musik, Berlin. *Career:* Repetiteur, Kaiserslautern 1969–71, Kapellmeister der Oper 1971–74; Kapellmeister, Saarbrucken State Opera 1974–77; Musical Dir, Saarbrucken City Choir; Musical Asst, Bayreuth 1975 (and conducted Der fliegende Holländer and Die Zauberflöte at Tbilisi); Conductor, Baden State Opera in Karlsruhe 1977–85; guest conductor, Wiesbaden (with Der Rosenkavalier, Carmen and La Forza del Destino); Lecturer in Music, State Music Acad., Karlsruhe 1980; Kapellmeister, Darmstadt 1985–87; Nat. Theatre at Mannheim 1987–90; Gen.l Music Dir, Lübeck Opera 1987–; also engaged by the Stuttgart Opera, Vienna Volksoper, Oslo, Munich State Opera, Hamburg, Leipzig, Dresden, Stockholm, Antwerp, Zürich Opera; Leiter des Hochschulorchesters und Leiter der Dirigierabteilung Musikhochschule Lübeck 1993.

WADDINGTON, Henry; British singer (bass); b. 1968, Kent, England. *Education:* Royal Northern College of Music with Barbara Robotham. *Career:* debut as Bottom in A Midsummer Night's Dream, at the RNCM; Glyndebourne Touring Opera from 1992, in The Rake's Progress, and in the premiere of Birtwistle's The Second Mrs Kong 1994; appearances in Le Comte Ory and Tchaikovsky's The Enchantress for New Sussex Opera, as Colline for GTO, Farlaf in Ruslan and Lyudmila for Dorset Opera, as Falstaff for Opera North and Fiorello in Il Barbiere di Siviglia for Royal Opera House; Count Lamoral in Arabella and Mozart's Antonio at the Glyndebourne Festival, 1996–97; season 1998 with Major Domo in Capriccio at Glyndebourne, Verdi's Ribbing for WNO, Don Magnifico in Cenerentola for English Touring Opera, Count Horn in Ballo in Maschera for WNO and Oroe in Semiramide for Chelsea Opera Group; 1999, Banquo in Macbeth for ETO; Concerts include: Mozart's Requiem with the English CO at the Barbican Hall, Sir John in Love for British Youth Opera, the Verdi Requiem, and The Rake's Progress with the BBC Symphony Orchestra at the Festival Hall 1997.

WADE, Simon, BMus, MA; Australian composer; b. 28 Aug. 1958, Devonport, Tasmania. *Education:* Tasmanian Conservatory. *Career:* Tasmanian Conservatory 1980; Univ. of Sydney 1988; Rare Birds Productions Co. 1993; commissions from Tasmanian Opera Co., New England String Quartet and others. *Compositions include:* Saxophone Quartet 1984, Extracts for saxophone and piano 1984, Songs from Shakespeare for chorus and orchestra 1984, Introduction to the String Quartet 1985, The Other Meaning song cycle for tenor and piano 1985, Sequences for clarinet and piano 1985, The Watching Clock (chamber opera) 1992, The Herald Angel for alto trombone and piano 1993, computer-generated music for film and theatre 1993–.

WADSWORTH, Matthew; British lutenist. *Education:* Chetham School of Music, RAM, Royal Conservatory, The Hague. *Career:* founder mem., Ricordo Ensemble 1997–; Wigmore Hall solo debut 2003; US concert tour 2005; continuo player and chamber musician with leading early music ensembles; lute song recitals with Faye Newton; workshops with Live Music Now! for visually-impaired children; guest tutor, Royal Northern Coll. of Music. *Recordings:* Away Delights (lute solos and songs from Shakespeare's England), 14 Silver Strings (music by Kapsberger and Piccinini). *Honours:* London Student of the Year Award for development of Braille lute tablature 1997. *Current Management:* Chameleon Arts Management, 32 St Michael's Road, Sandhurst, GU47 8HE, England. *Telephone:* (20) 8521-4959. *E-mail:* concerts@matthewwadsworth.com. *Website:* www.matthewwadsworth.com.

WADSWORTH, Stephen; American stage director, translator and librettist; b. 3 April 1953, Mount Kisco, NY. *Career:* Artistic Dir and Stage Dir, Skylight Opera, Milwaukee; productions of Monteverdi's three principal operas from 1982; wrote libretto for Bernstein's A Quiet Place 1983 and has directed productions of it at La Scala, Milan and in Vienna; for Seattle Opera has directed Jenůfa, Fliegende Holländer, and Gluck's Orphée; Handel's Xerxes at Milwaukee 1985 and Partenope at Omaha 1988; Fidelio and La Clemenza di Tito for Scottish Opera 1991, Die Entführung at San Francisco 1990, other productions include Le nozze di Figaro and Alcina (St Louis) and Simon Boccanegra (Netherlands Opera); Head of the Opera Program, Manhattan School of Music 1991; translations of Monteverdi's Orfeo and Handel's Xerxes, Alcina and Partenope; Covent Garden debut 1992, Handel's Alcina; staging of Xerxes seen at Santa Fe, Los Angeles and Boston 1996. *Honours:* Chevalier, Ordre des Arts et des Lettres. *Address:* c/o Boston Lyric Opera, 114 State Street, Boston, MA 02109, USA.

WADSWORTH, Tony, CBE; British music industry executive; b. 1957. *Education:* Newcastle Univ. *Career:* mem. Archie Brown & The Young Bucks 1975–87; fmrly worked for Logo Records, RCA Records; joined EMI Records 1982, Strategic Marketing Div. –1987; Marketing Dir, Parlophone Records 1987–93, Man. Dir 1993–98; Pres., EMI Records Group UK and Ireland 1998–2002, Chair. and CEO EMI Recorded Music UK and Ireland 2002–08; Chair., Brit Awards Cttee 2000–03; apptd Visiting Fellow in Popular Music, Univ. of Gloucester 2005; Visiting Prof., Music and Business Schools, Newcastle Univ.; Chair. British Phonographic Industry (BPI) 2007–14; mem. Bd Brits Trust; Trustee, Music Sound Foundation, EMI Archive Trust. *Recording:* album: Bring Me the Head of Jerry Garcia (with Archie Brown & The Young Bucks) 1987. *Honours:* Strat Award, Music Week Awards 2008. *Address:* BPI, Riverside Building, County Hall, Westminster Bridge Road, London, SE1 7JA, England (office). *Telephone:* (20) 7803-1300 (office). *Fax:* (20) 7803-1310 (office). *E-mail:* general@bpi.co.uk (office). *Website:* www.bpi.co.uk (office).

WAGEMANS, Peter-Jan; Dutch composer; b. 7 Sept. 1952, The Hague. *Education:* The Hague Conservatory, studied with Klaus Huber in Freiburg. *Career:* Lecturer, Hague Conservatory 1978–84, Rotterdam Conservatory 1982–; promoter of modern music concerts at Rotterdam from 1990. *Compositions include:* Symphony 1972, Wind Quintet 1973, Musiek I–IV 1974, 1977, 1985, 1988, Cantata 1979, Octet 1980, Trio for clarinet, violin and piano 1985, Klang for orchestra 1986, Wie for alto, two clarinets and two horns 1987, Walk on Water for trumpet and ensemble 1988, Rosebud for orchestra and female chorus 1988, Requiem for strings and percussion 1992, Panthalassa for wind 1994, Wind Quintet No. 2 1994, Concerto for two pianos 1994, revised 1997, Nachtvlucht for soprano and orchestra 1997, String Quartet 1998. *Honours:* Matthijs Vermeulen Prize 1990.

WAGENAAR, Diderik; Dutch composer; b. 10 May 1946, Utrecht. *Education:* Royal Conservatory, The Hague. *Career:* Lecturer, Royal Conservatory 1969–. *Compositions include:* Canzonas for 15 brass instruments, double bass and two pianos 1976, Tam Tam for ensemble 1978, Canapé for clarinet, violin, cello and piano 1980, Metrum for four saxophones and orchestra 1984, Limiet for string quartet 1985, Triforium for wind ensemble and percussion 1988,

Tessituur for orchestra 1990, Solenne for six percussion 1992, Cat Music for two violins 1994, Trios Poèmes en prose for soprano and orchestra 1995, Rookery Hill for ensemble 1998, Galilei for chamber orchestra 1999, Arrangement of Berg's Altenberglieder for medium voice and ensemble 1985. *Honours:* Matthijs Vermeulen Prize 1996.

WAGENFUHRER, Roland; German singer (tenor); b. 1964, Hof/Saale. *Education:* Nuremberg Conservatory. *Career:* mem., Bavarian State Opera Studio 1987–89, as Ferrando and as Chlestakov in Der Revisor; Landestheater Coburg 1989–95, as Jenik in The Bartered Bride, Lensky, Don José and Wagner's Erik; Dresden Semper Oper from 1995, as Max, Laca (Jenůfa), Desportes in Zimmermann's Soldaten and Dionysos in The Bassarids by Henze; Guest appearances as Florestan at the Bregenz Festival (1995–96), Tamino in Cologne, Walther von Stolzing in Lubeck and Erik at the Vienna Staatsoper; season 1997–98 as Florestan at the Komische Oper Berlin and Hoffmann at Cologne; engagements for 1998 in The Bartered Bride in Munich, Fliegender Holländer at the Bayreuth Festival and New York Met, and Freischütz/Max in Vienna; Lohengrin at Bayreuth, 1999; further engagements include Elijah in Zürich, Beethoven's 9th in Brussels and Duisburg, Bruch's Moses-Oratorium in Berlin and Munich, and Berlioz's Faust Studies in Paris; season 2000–01 as Florestan at Munich and Dresden, Lohengrin for the Bayreuth Festival and Wagner's Erik at the Met. *Current Management:* Hilbert Artists Management, Maximilianstrasse 22, 80539 Munich, Germany. *Telephone:* (89) 2907470. *Fax:* (89) 29074790. *E-mail:* agentur@hilbert.de. *Website:* www.hilbert.de.

WAGNER, Jacquelyn, MMus; American soprano. *Education:* Oakland Univ., Mich., Manhattan School of Music, Int. Inst. of Vocal Arts. *Career:* roles have included Contessa in Le nozze di Figaro and Nuri in Tiefland, Fiordiligi in Così fan tutte, Donna Anna in Don Giovanni; appeared at Deutsche Oper Berlin, Theater Basel, Opéra National du Rhin, Opéra de Lyon, Grand Théâtre de Genève, Vlaamse Oper, Staatstheater Stuttgart, Opéra de Marseille, Orquestra de l'Acadèmia del Gran Teatre del Liceu; concert performances with Deutsche Symphonie-Orchester Berlin, St Gallen Symphony Orchestra, Detroit Symphony Orchestra, Deutsches Kammerorchester Berlin, Berlin Philharmonie, Grosse Pointe Symphony Orchestra and Ann Arbor Symphony Orchestra. *Honours:* Fulbright Study Grant, two Jenny Lind Soc. Scholarships, winner, Panasonic Voice Competition at Alice Tully Hall, New York, winner, Ann Arbor Symphony Orchestra Mozart Competition. *Current Management:* c/o Kristin Cowdin, Guy Barzilay Artists, International Artists Management, 420 West 25th Street, Suite 4F, New York, NY 10001, USA. *Telephone:* (212) 741-6118. *Fax:* (212) 741-2558. *E-mail:* kristin@guybarzilayartists.com. *Website:* www.guybarzilayartists.com.

WAGNER, James; singer (tenor); b. 1949, New Orleans, Louisiana, USA. *Education:* Rochester Univ., studied in Vienna. *Career:* sang at the Frankfurt Opera 1975–76, Kassel 1976–80, New York City Opera 1981–82, Vienna Volksoper 1983–84; Theater am Gärtnerplatz, Munich 1985–88, and elsewhere, as Almaviva, Xerxes, Belmonte, Giasone in Cherubini's Médée, Florestan, Edgardo, and Dionysos in Henze's Bassarids; guest appearances in Berne, Bologne 1987, Venice 1990, Greece; season 2000–01 in the Verdi Requiem in Vienna and as Rossini's Otello (concert) at Halle. *Recordings include:* Amadis de Gaule by J. C. Bach.

WAGNER, Katharina; German opera director; *Co-Director, Bayreuther Festspiele;* b. 21 May 1978, Bayreuth, Bavaria; d. of Wolfgang Wagner and Gudrun Wagner; great-grand-d. of Richard Wagner. *Education:* Freie Universität Berlin. *Career:* Production Asst, Bayreuther Festspiele 1996–2006, becoming Stage Dir 2007–, also Co-Dir (with half-sister Eva Wagner-Pasquier) 2008–. *Productions include:* Der Fliegende Holländer, Würzburg 2002, Lohengrin, Budapest 2004, Der Waffenschmied, Munich 2005, Il trittico, Berlin 2006, Die Meistersinger von Nürnberg, Bayreuth 2007, Rienzi, Bremen 2008, Tannhäuser, Las Palmas de Gran Canaria 2009, Madama Butterfly, Mainz 2010, Tiefland, Mainz 2011. *Publication:* Bayreuth Backstage, Innenansichten vom Grünen Hügel 2009. *Honours:* Hon. Prof. (Stage Direction), Hanns Eisler Acad. of Music, Berlin 2010–; Grand Decoration of the Land Burgenland 2013; Berlin Bear (BZ Cultural Award) (jtly with half-sister) 2010, Bavarian Cultural Award (jtly with half-sister) 2012. *Address:* Bayreuther Festspiele, Festspielhügel 1–2, 95445 Bayreuth, Germany (office). *Telephone:* (921) 78780 (office). *Fax:* (921) 83312 (office). *Website:* www.bayreuther-festspiele.de (office).

WAGNER-PASQUIER, Eva; German opera director; *Co-Director, Bayreuther Festspiele;* b. 14 April 1945, Oberwarmensteinach; d. of Wolfgang Wagner and Ellen Wagner (née Drexel); great grand-daughter of Richard Wagner; m. Yves Pasquer 1977; one s. *Education:* Musical High School, Bayreuth. *Career:* Artistic Agent, Robert Schulz Agency, Munich 1967; Asst to Dir Bayreuth Festival, then Production Asst and Asst Dir working on various musical productions 1967–76; mem. New Philharmonia Chorus, London 1970–72; Production Asst Wiener Staatsoper, Vienna 1972; Artistic Dir Unitel Film and TV Productions, Munich 1973–84; Dir Royal Opera, Covent Garden, London 1984–87; Dir of Programming Opéra-Bastille, Paris 1988–93; Artistic Adviser Théâtre du Châtelet 1994; Founder-mem. Fondation Orcofi pour l'Opéra et la Musique 1986; currently Artistic Consultant Aix-en-Provence Opera Festival, France; co-Dir (with half-sister Katharina Wagner) Bayreuther Festspiele 2008–; fmr Artistic Consultant, Metropolitan Opera, NY; mem. Film and Opera Comm., Cannes Film Festival 1987. *Honours:* Nin-On Art Award, Japan 1986; Berlin Bear (BZ Cultural Award) (jtly with half-

sister) 2010. *Address:* Bayreuther Festspiele, Festspielhügel 1–2, 95445 Bayreuth, Germany (office). *Telephone:* (921) 78780 (office). *Website:* www.bayreuther-festspiele.de (office).

WAHLGREN, Per-Arne; Swedish singer (baritone); b. 1953. *Education:* Opera School of the Royal Opera Stockholm. *Career:* debut with Norrland Opera 1978, as Don Giovanni; sang at the Stora Teater Gothenburg from 1979 as Germont and Belcore; Guest appearances at the Theater an der Wien, Vienna 1980, in the premiere of Jesu Hochzeit by Gottfried von Einem; Royal Opera Stockholm from 1981, as Mozart's Count and Guglielmo, Marcello, Sharpless and Wolfram; Humbert Humbert in the premiere of Rodion Shchedrin's Lolita under the direction of M Rostropovich, 1994; Further engagements at Nice in Tannhäuser and The Queen of Spades, at Lausanne in Dido and Aeneas and in Madrid in Mendelssohn's Elijah; Stockholm 1986 in the premiere of Christina by Hans Gefors; Drottningholm Court Theatre 1991, as Orestes in a revival of Electra by J C F Haeffner; Sang Frank in Korngold's Die tote Stadt, Stockholm, 1995. Concert repertory includes Bach's Passions, Christmas Oratorio and Cantatas, the Brahms Requiem, Messiah, Utrecht Te Deum by Handel, the Fauré Requiem, Lieder eines fahrenden Gesellen and Carmina Burana. *Recordings include:* Dido and Aeneas.

WAKEFIELD, John, FRAM; British academic and singer (tenor); b. 21 June 1936, Yorkshire, England; m. Rilla Welborn; two s. one d. *Education:* Royal Acad. of Music. *Career:* debut with WNO 1960; Macduff at Glyndebourne 1964; Rinuccio at Royal Opera House 1965; other roles include Fenton, Tamino, Paris, Don Ottavio, Ferrando, Belmonte, Idamante, Rodolfo, Orfeo, Cavalli's Ormindo, Essex in Britten's Gloriana and Saul; currently Sr Lecturer, Trinity Coll. of Music, London; mem. Equity, NATFHE. *Recordings:* La Traviata, Ormindo, The Mikado, Messiah. *Honours:* Kathleen Ferrier Scholarship 1958, 's-hertogenbosch Tenor Prize 1959, Hon. FTCL. *Address:* 5 Longford, 181 Uxbridge Road, Hampton Hill, Middlesex TW12 1BH, England (home).

WALACINSKI, Adam; Polish composer; b. 18 Sept. 1928, Kraków. *Education:* Kraków Conservatory, studied with Stefan Kisielewski. *Career:* violinist in the Kraków Radio Orchestra 1948–56; Teacher, Kraków Conservatory 1972–92, Prof. 1993–96, Prorector; Music Critic, Dziennik Polski 1962–; collaborations with PWM Music Cyclopedia as Area Editor of 20th Century composers; mem., Grupa Krakowska, for promotion of New Music; Chair. Kraków section, Polish Composers' Union 1971–87. *Compositions include:* Alfa for orchestra 1958, String Quartet 1959, Intrada for seven players 1962, Canto Tricolore for flute, violin and vibraphone 1962, Horizons for chamber orchestra 1962, A Lyric Before Falling Asleep for soprano, flute and two pianos 1963, Concerto de Camera for violin and strings 1964, Fogli volanti for string trio 1985, Canzona for cello, piano and tape 1966, Epigrams for chamber ensemble 1967, Refrains and Reflections for orchestra 1969, Notturno 70 for 24 strings, three flutes and percussion, Concerto in Festa 1971, Divertimento interrotto for 13 players 1974, Mirophonies for soprano and ensemble 1974, Ballada for flute and piano 1986, Little Autumn Music for flute and string trio 1986, Drama e Burla for orchestra 1988, Pastorale for flute, oboe, violin 1992, La Vida es Sueño (reminiscences from Calderón) for flute, guitar and viola 1998, Aria for orchestra 1998, Spirale of Time for 15 players 2000, also music for theatre, cinema and television. *Honours:* State Award 1966, Prize of the City of Kraków 1976.

WALDIN, Lucas, BMus; Canadian conductor; *Endbridge Resident Conductor, Edmonton Symphony Orchestra;* b. 1983, Toronto. *Education:* Cleveland Inst. of Music, Int. Music Acad., Leipzig, Bayreuth Youth Orchestra, Acanthes New Music Festival, France; master classes with Michael Tilson Thomas and Bernard Haitink. *Career:* began studying flute before switching to conducting; fmr Asst Conductor of RED (contemporary orchestra), Cleveland; fmr Dir Cleveland Bach Consort; fmr Discovery Series Conductor, Oregon Bach Festival; Endbridge Resident Conductor, Edmonton Symphony Orchestra 2009–; has performed with several int. orchestras including L'Orchestre du Festival Beaulieu-Sur-Mer, Monaco, Staatstheater Cottbus, Brandenburg, Bachakademie Stuttgart, Scottish Chamber Orchestra, BBC Scottish Symphony. *Address:* Edmonton Symphony Orchestra, 102 Avenue NW, Edmonton, AB T5J 4B2, Canada (office). *Telephone:* (780) 428-1108 (office). *Fax:* (780) 425-0167 (office). *E-mail:* lucas.waldin@gmail.com (office). *Website:* www.edmontonsymphony.com (office).

WALENDOWSKI, Dario; singer (tenor); b. 1 Aug. 1955, Łódź, Poland. *Career:* debut, Łódź 1980, as Alfredo in La Traviata; Nat. Opera Warsaw from 1982, as Donizetti's Edgardo, Nadir in Les Pêcheurs de Perles, Tamino, Captain, Tebaldo in Capuleti ed i Montecchi and Shuisky in Boris Godunov; engagements in Austria from 1985 and Germany 1989; Oberhausen and Giessen Operas as Count Almaviva, the Duke of Mantua, Rodolfo, Jontek in Halka, Edgardo, Des Grieux, Macduff, Romeo, Jenik in Bartered Bride, Don José, Hoffmann and Pinkerton; Staatstheater Schwerin from 1993, as Cavaradossi, Pedro (Tiefland), Sly, Radames, Faust, Nemorino, and Manrico; guest appearances at the Bolshoi (Moscow), Mannheim, Berlin, Madrid, Hamburg, Barcelona and Paris; guest appearances at Lübeck and Rostock as Alva in Lulu, Don Alvaro in La Forza del Destino from 1996; modern repertory includes Jedidia in Penderecki's The Black Mask; Der schöne Herr Herrmann in Hindemith's Neues vom Tage, Sandy in The Lighthouse, Pierrot/Soldât.

WALKER, Adam; British flautist; *Principal Flute, London Symphony Orchestra;* b. 1987, Retford, Notts. *Education:* Chetham's School of Music with Gitte Sorensen, Royal Acad. of Music with Michael Cox. *Career:*

youngest-ever winner of British Flute Soc. Competition 2002; appeared as soloist with Vienna Chamber Orchestra at the Konzerthaus, the Solistes Européens at the Philharmonie in Luxembourg, BBC Nat. Orchestra of Wales, Northern Sinfonia, Hallé Orchestra at Bridgewater Hall, Royal Philharmonic Orchestra at Cadogan Hall, and with City of Birmingham and Bournemouth Symphony Orchestras; concert appearances have included Wigmore Hall, LSO St Lukes (broadcast by BBC Radio 3), City of London Festival, Varese (Italy), Salle des Variétés, Monaco, and Festspiele Mecklenburg Vorpommern, Germany; gave world premiere of new work by Huw Watkins at Gregynog Festival and toured China with guitarist Morgan Szymanski; Proms debut with BBC Nat. Orchestra of Wales and with Acad. of St Martin-in-the-Fields at the Barbican; recitals at Wigmore Hall, Berlin Konzerthaus, Spitalfields and Isle of Man Festivals; Prin. Flute, London Symphony Orchestra 2009–. *Honours:* Outstanding Young Artist Award, MIDEM Classique Awards, Borletti-Buitoni Trust Fellowship Award 2010. *Current Management:* c/o Young Concert Artists Trust, 23 Garrick Street, London, WC2E 9BN, England. *E-mail:* info@ycat.co.uk. *Address:* London Symphony Orchestra, 6th Floor Barbican Centre, Silk Street, London, EC2Y 8DS, England (office). *Telephone:* (20) 7588-1116 (office). *Fax:* (20) 7374-0127 (office). *E-mail:* admin@lso.co.uk (office). *Website:* lso.co.uk (office).

WALKER, Antony, BMus; Australian conductor; *Music Director, Pittsburgh Orchestra;* b. 1967, Sydney. *Education:* Univ. of Sydney. *Career:* Musical Dir, The Contemporary Singers 1987–2000; Musical Dir, Sydney Philharmonia Choirs 1993–97; Musical Dir, Sydney Philharmonia Orchestra 1992–97; Chorus Master and Staff Conductor Welsh Nat. Opera 1998–2002; Founder and Music Dir, Cantillation, Orchestra of the Antipodes & Sinfonia Australis 2001–; Co-Artistic Dir, Pinchgut Opera 2002–; Music Dir, Washington Concert Opera 2002–; Music Dir, Pittsburgh Orchestra 2006–; conducted over 50 operas, 47 choral and orchestral works and numerous symphonic and chamber works with companies in Europe, USA and Australia including Minnesota Opera, Pittsburgh Opera, Hawaii Opera, New York City Opera, Musica Viva Australia, Chautauqua Opera, Melbourne Symphony Orchestra, Arizona Opera, Opera Australia, Glimmerglass. *Recordings include:* Missa Solemnis 1992, An Australian Christmas 1995, Sydney Dreaming 1996, Strange Attractions 1997, Ode to Joy 2000, Lotus Moon 2001, Fauré Requiem and La Naissance de Venus 2001, Willow Spirit Song 2002, Carmina Burana 2002, Prayer for Peace 2002, Handel Messiah 2002, Allegri Miserere 2003, Bach Arias and Duets 2003, Beethoven Piano Concertos 2003, Handel Semele 2003, Silent Night 2004, Purcell: The Fairy Queen 2004, Baroque Duets 2005, Monteverdi: L'Orfeo 2005, Magnificat 2006, Ye Banks and Braes 2006, Rameau and Dardanus 2006, A Celebration of Baroque Choruses 2007. *Honours:* Queen's Trust Award 1995, Churchill Fellowship 1995, British Council Travel Grant 1996, Australia Council Development Award 1996, British Council and the Australia Britain Soc. Sir Charles Mackerras Conducting Award 1997, Richard F. Gold debut award, New York City Opera 2005. *Current Management:* Virgina Braden Arts Management, Level 1, 405 Elizabeth Street, Surry Hills, NSW 2010, Australia. *Telephone:* (2) 9211-9422. *Fax:* (2) 9211-9466. *E-mail:* enquiries@artsmanagement.com.au. *Website:* www.artsmanagement.com.au. *E-mail:* antony@antonywalker.com (office). *Website:* www.antonywalker.com.

WALKER, Diana; American singer (soprano); b. 1958, Salt Lake City, UT. *Career:* has sung at the New York City Opera 1983–, as Leila (Les Pêcheurs de Perles), Gilda, Adele, Micaela, Barbara (Argento's Casanova) and Ninetta (The Love of Three Oranges); Seattle Opera in the title roles of The Ballad of Baby Doe and Lucia di Lammermoor; Utah Opera as the Queen of Night; European debut as Blondchen in Die Entführung with Nice Opera; modern repertory includes Laetitia in The Old Maid and the Thief with St Louis Opera, Abigail in The Crucible by Robert Ward and Ariel in Lee Hoiby's The Tempest (Kansas City); performances of the ballet Alice, after Del Tredici's in Memory of a Summer Day, in Toronto, Chicago, Washington, DC, Florida, California, New York (Metropolitan Opera) and London; sang Lakmé for Chicago Opera Theatre 1990; premieres of Victoria Bond's Travels in Virginia 1995; concert repertory includes, Messiah, Handel's Joshua and Rinaldo (at Kennedy Center) and Mahler's 4th Symphony; further roles include Donizetti's Norina, Adina and Marie; Gluck's Iphigénie; Mozart's Mme Silberklang, Blondchen and Susanna; Strauss's Sophie and Zerbinetta; Verdi's Nannetta and Ophelia in Hamlet by Thomas; guest artist with Miami Chamber Symphony, Brooklyn Symphony, New York, Utah Symphony, Kansas City Philharmonic, Roanoke, Virginia Symphony, Aspen Symphony.

WALKER, George Theophilus, BMus, Artist Dipl, DMA; American composer, pianist and educator; *Professor Emeritus of Music, Rutgers University;* b. 27 June 1922, Washington, DC; two s. *Education:* Oberlin Coll., Curtis Inst. of Music, American School, Fontainebleau, France, Univ. of Rochester, New York. *Career:* first professional concert, Shiloh Baptist Church, Washington, DC 1939; organist, Oberlin Theological Seminary 1939–41; debut as pianist at Town Hall, New York 1945; numerous recitals world-wide; teacher, Dillard Univ., New Orleans 1953–54, Dalcroze School of Music, New York 1960–61, New School for Social Research, New York 1960–61, Smith Coll., Northampton, Mass 1961–68, Peabody Inst. Conservatory at Johns Hopkins Univ., Baltimore, Md 1975–78; Visiting Prof. of Piano and Piano Literature, Univ. of Colorado at Boulder 1968–69; Distinguished Prof. of Music, Univ. of Delaware, Newark, New Jersey 1975–76; teacher of piano, theory, music history and composition, Rutgers Univ., Newark 1969–92, Chair. Music Dept 1975–77, Prof. Emer. 1992–. *Compositions include:* Lyric for Strings 1946, 18

songs for voice and piano 1941–94, arrangements of spirituals for voice and piano 1947–62, five piano sonatas, two string quartets, two sonatas for violin and piano, concertos for cello, trombone, violin and piano, Concerto for piano and orchestra, Concerto for trombone and orchestra, Cantata for soprano, tenor boys' choir and chamber orchestra, Mass for chorus and orchestra, Address for orchestra, three Sinfonias for orchestra, Serenata for chamber orchestra, Poem for soprano and chamber ensemble, Variations for orchestra, Antifonys for chamber orchestra, Orpheus for chamber orchestra 1994, Lilacs for soprano or tenor and orchestra (Pulitzer Prize 1996) 1995, Pageant and Proclamation for orchestra 1997, Wind Set for woodwind quintet 1999, Modus for two guitars, winds and strings 1999, Abu for narrator and chamber ensemble 2004, Icarus in Orbit for orchestra 2004, Hoopla (A Touch of Glee) for orchestra 2005, Foils (Homage à Saint George) for orchestra 2005, Concerto for violin and orchestra 2008, Da Camera for piano trio, percussion and strings 2009, Bleu for Violin Unaccompanied 2010, Sinfonia No. 4 2011, Movements for Cello and Orchestra 2013. *Recordings include:* George Walker in Recital 1994, George Walker A Portrait 1994, George Walker (Chamber Works) 1995, George Walker plays Bach, Schumann, Chopin and Poulenc 1997, The Music of George Walker 1997, George Walker: Works for Chamber Orchestra, George Walker: 60th Anniversary Retrospective, George Walker: American Virtuoso 2001, George Walker, Composer 2005, George Walker: Great American Orchestral Works Vol. 1 2008, Vol. II 2010, Vol. IV 2013, George Walker: Great American Chamber Music 2009, George Walker Chamber Music and Songs 2010, George Walker: Great Orchestral Music Vol. 3 2012, George Walker, Great American Concert Music 2012, George Walker, Composer and Pianist 2013. *Publications include:* Make Room for Black Classical Music (in New York Times) 1992, The Lot of the Black Composer 1992, Recordings of Solo Piano Works: George Walker in Recital, George Walker Plays Bach, Schumann, Chopin and Poulenc, Lilacs: The Music of George Walker 2000, George Walker: American Virtuoso 2001, George Walker in Concert 2002, George Walker: Composer-Pianist 2005, George Walker: Reminiscences of an American Composer and Pianist (autobiog.) 2009. *Honours:* Dr hc (Lafayette Coll., Easton) 1982, (Oberlin Coll.) 1983, (Curtis Inst.) 1997, (Montclair State Univ.) 1997, (Bloomfield Coll.) 1997, (Spelman Coll.) 2001, (Eastman School of Music) 2013; John Hay Whitney Fellowship 1958, Religious Arts Festival Award 1961, Carnegie Mellon Inst. Harvey Gaul Prize 1963, Bok Foundation grant for European concerts 1963, Bennington Composers Conf. Fellowships 1967, 1968, Guggenheim Fellowships 1969, 1988, MacDowell Colony Fellowships 1966–69, Yaddo Fellowship 1969, Rutgers Univ. Research Council grant 1969, Rockefeller Fellowships 1971, 1974, Nat. Endowment for the Arts grants 1971, 1975, 1978, 1984, Koussevitzky Award 1988, Pulitzer Prize 1996, Univ. of Rochester Distinguished Scholar Medal 1996, American Acad. of Arts and Letters Award 1999, American Classical Music Hall of Fame 2000, Nat. Opera Asscn Legacy Award 2007, ASCAP Aaron Copland Award 2012. *Address:* 323 Grove Street, Montclair, NJ 07042, USA (home). *E-mail:* gtwalker@verizon .net. *Website:* georgetwalker.com.

WALKER, Helen; British singer (soprano); b. 1952, Tunbridge Wells, England. *Education:* Guildhall School, London with Noelle Barker. *Career:* sang Verdi's Giovanna d'Arco 1977; Glyndebourne Festival as Fiordiligi, Monteverdi's Poppea 1984, and Helena in A Midsummer Night's Dream; Glyndebourne Touring Opera as Pamina, Ann Trulove in The Rake's Progress, and Ninetta in The Love of Three Oranges; Opera North as Pamina, and Fenena in Nabucco; Helena at Aldeburgh and Covent Garden; Handel roles include Polissena in Radamisto (Handel Opera Soc.) and Teseo, for the English Bach Festival at Sadler's Wells Theatre; foreign engagements in Hong Kong and Nancy (with Glyndebourne Touring Opera), Montpellier and La Fenice, Venice (as Anne Trulove); sang a Maid in Elektra at Covent Garden 1990; Freia, Sieglinde and Gutrune in the City of Birmingham Touring Opera version of the Ring; premiered Leaving by Turnage, Symphony Hall and Radio 3 1992. *Recordings include:* Dido and Aeneas (1st Witch). *Honours:* winner Susan Longfield Competition 1977, Ricordi Prize for Opera, Mozart Memorial Prize 1978, South East Arts Young Musicians Platform, Glyndebourne Touring Award, Christie Award, Glyndebourne.

WALKER, John Edward; American singer (tenor); b. 19 Aug. 1933, Bushnell, IN. *Education:* Univs of Denver, Urbana and Bloomington. *Career:* debut in Berne 1963, as Tamino; appearances in Europe at Zürich, Cologne, Frankfurt, Stuttgart and Brussels; US engagements at San Francisco, Dallas, Santa Fe, Chicago, Seattle, San Diego, Omaha and Portland; other roles have included Mozart's Belmonte, Don Ottavio and Ferrando, Nadir, Almaviva, Alfredo, Fenton, Ernesto, Nemorino, Werther, Lensky and Britten's Lysander; has also sung Jenik in The Bartered Bride, Nureddin in the Barber of Baghdad, Albert Herring, and David in Die Meistersinger; many concert and oratorio engagements.

WALKER, Malcolm; American singer (baritone); b. 1958. *Career:* sang Pelléas at the Opéra du Rhin, Strasbourg, and Monteverdi's Orfeo at Milan; Glyndebourne 1985, as Morales in Carmen and 1987–88 in L'Enfant et les Sortilèges; Don Giovanni on tour to Hong Kong; Lille Opéra in The Rake's progress and Geneva Opera in Manon; Pelléas at the Vienna Staatsoper, La Scala, Florence, Seattle 1993 and Venice 1995; other roles include Varbel in Cherubini's Lodoiska, at Montpellier, Fürst in Guillaume Tell at Théâtre des Champs Elysées, and Massenet's Lescaut at Opéra-Comique 1999. *Recordings include:* Gluck's Les Pèlerins de la Mecque, Chabrier's Le Roi malgré Lui.

WALKER, Nina, LRAM, ARMCM, FRMCM; British pianist, opera coach and chorus master; b. 30 May 1926, Hyde, Cheshire, England; m. Francis Barnes; two s. one d. *Education:* Royal Manchester Coll. of Music, studied with Alfred Cortot in Lausanne, Bridget Wild. *Career:* accompanist and solo pianist, Arts Council Recitals, Germany, Italy, Sweden, Greece; solo pianist, Marquis de Cuevas Ballet, Paris 1957; accompanist for Caballé, La Scala, Milan, Spain, Japan, Germany, Royal Opera House 1975–90; masterclasses, Pavarotti, etc.; Chorus Master, Royal Choral Soc. 1970–75, Huddersfield Choral Soc. 1980–83; music staff, Royal Opera House 1974–83; Chorus Master 1981–83; founder and Dir, Nimbus Records 1973. *Recordings:* Schubert Song Cycles, Shura Gehrman; Argentinian Songs, Raul Gimenez; Rossini, Soirées Musicales, June Anderson; Complete Schubert Piano Duets, Adrian Farmer; Fauré and Duparc Songs, Shura Gehrman; Mussorgsky (Songs and Dances of Death) Songs I Love, Jenny Drivala, Soprano. *Honours:* Open Scholarship to RMCM 1946, Hilary Haworth Memorial Prize 1949, Edward Hecht Prize 1949.

WALKER, Penelope; British singer (mezzo-soprano); b. 12 Oct. 1956, Manchester, England; m. Phillip Joll, two c. *Education:* GSMD, 1974–78 (AGSM and advanced studies); National Opera Studio, 1979–80. *Career:* debut, Royal Albert Hall, 1976; Prom Debut, Grimgerde in Die Walküre with Gwyneth Jones and the National Youth Orchestra, 1989; Canada with Regina Symphony Orchestra, 1993, singing Wesendonck Lieder, and Chausson's Poème de l'amour et de la mer; Royal Opera House, Covent Garden, Die Walküre, 1994; BBC television and radio, including Elgar documentary with Simon Rattle and CBSO, Operatic debut in Paris, 1982 with Opéra-Comique; London debut at Camden Festival, Maria Tudor (Pacini) Opera Rara; ENO, Siegrune in Die Walküre, Kate Pinkerton in Madama Butterfly and Madame Sosostris in Midsummer Marriage; Opera North, Madame Sosostris; Welsh National Opera, Fricka in Das Rheingold and Die Walküre, Anna in The Trojans, Madame Larina in Eugene Onegin, Tornrak-Main Protagonist in Metcalf Opera; Geneviève, Pelléas; Zürich Opera, 1991, 3rd Lady; Hedwig in William Tell; Mozart Requiem; Grimgerde in Die Walküre, Chatelêt Ring, 1994; Debut at La Scala, 1994; Rossweisse, Covent Garden 1994; Sang Handel's Riccardo Primo at the 1996 Göttingen Festival. *Recordings:* London Opera, Hippolyta (Midsummer Night's Dream), Virgin, Hickox; Schwertleite (Die Walküre) C. Dohnányi, Cleveland Symphony, Decca; Flosshilde and Fricka, Das Rheingold, Operavox Animated Opera, television; Geneviève, (Pelléas et Mélisande) WNO Video, Peter Stein production, Pierre Boulez; New Israeli Opera, Mamma Lucia (Cavalleria Rusticana).

WALKER, Robert Ernest; British composer; b. 18 March 1946, Northampton, England. *Education:* chorister St Matthew's Church, Northampton, choral scholar and organ scholar Jesus Coll., Cambridge. *Career:* organist and schoolmaster in Lincolnshire; freelance composer from 1975; featured composer at 1982 Greenwich Festival; living composer, Eastern Orchestral Board 1990–91; works performed by Royal Philharmonic Orchestra at Chichester and Exeter Festivals; regular broadcasts on BBC Radio 3. *Compositions:* orchestral: Pavan for violin and strings 1975, At Bignor Hill 1979, Chamber Symphony No. 1 1981, Variations on a Theme of Elgar 1982, Charms and Exultations of trumpets 1985, Symphony No. 1 1987; vocal: The Sun on the Celandines 1973, Psalm 150 1974, Requiem 1976, The Norwich Service 1977, Canticle of the Rose 1980, The Sun Used to Shine for tenor, harp and strings 1983, Magnificat and Nunc Dimittis in D 1985, Missa Brevis 1985, Singer by the Yellow River for soprano, flute and harp 1985, Five Summer Madrigals 1985, Jubilate 1987, English Parody Mass for choir and organ 1988; instrumental: String Quartet No. 1 1982, Five Capriccios 1 and 2 1982–85, Piano Quintet 1984, Passacaglia for two pianos, Serenade for flute, harp, violin and cello, Journey into Light, A Choral Symphony 1992, Melelivida (after Catullus) for chorus, percussion, piano and strings 1997, also music for BBC1, BBC2 and Channel 4.

WALKER, Sandra; American singer (mezzo-soprano); b. 1 Oct. 1948, Richmond, VA. *Education:* Univ. of North Carolina and the Manhattan School of Music, New York. *Career:* debut in San Francisco 1972, as Flosshilde in Das Rheingold; sang in opera at Philadelphia, Chicago and the New York City Opera; European engagements at Gelsenkirchen 1985 and Wiesbaden 1987; sang the Nurse in Ariane et Barbe-bleue at Amsterdam 1989; San Francisco Opera 1989, 1992, as Bradamante in Vivaldi's Orlando Furioso and Hedwige in Guillaume Tell; Lyric Opera Chicago 1990–91, as Olga in Eugene Onegin and Marta in Mefistofele; other roles include Carmen, Suzuki, Lola, the Marquise in La Fille du Régiment and Frugola in Il Tabarro; Hostess in Boris Godunov at the New York Met 1998.

WALKER, Sarah Elizabeth Royle, CBE, FRCM, FGS, LRAM; British singer (mezzo-soprano); b. 11 March 1943, Cheltenham, Glos., England; d. of Alan Royle Walker and Elizabeth Brownrigg; m. Graham Allum 1972. *Education:* Pate's Grammar School for Girls, Cheltenham and Royal Coll. of Music, studied violin and cello and then voice with Ruth Packer and Cuthbert Smith. *Career:* Martin Musical Trust Scholarship to begin vocal studies with Vera Rozsa 1967; operatic debuts: Kent Opera, Ottavia in Coronation of Poppea 1969, Glyndebourne Festival, Diana/Giove in La Calisto 1970, Scottish Opera, Didon in Les Troyens 1971, ENO, Wellgunde in The Ring 1971; Prin. Singer with ENO 1972–76; debut at Royal Opera House, Covent Garden as Charlotte in Werther 1979; debut at Metropolitan Opera, New York, as Micha in Handel's Samson 1986; also at opera houses worldwide including La Scala Milan, Théâtre du Châtelet Paris, Lyric Opera of Chicago, San Francisco, Geneva, Vienna and Brussels; concert repertoire includes, in addition to

standard works, contemporary and avant-garde works by Berio, Boulez, Cage, Ligeti, Xenakis and others; sang Rule Britannia at last night of 1985 and 1989 BBC Promenade Concerts, London; recital début, Wigmore Hall, London 1979; recital tours Australia, N America, Europe; numerous recordings including Handel's Hercules and Julius Caesar and Stravinsky's Rake's Progress; video recordings of Gloriana (title role), Julius Caesar (Cornelia) and King Priam (Andromache); Prince Consort Prof. of Singing, Royal Coll. of Music 1993–; vocal performance consultant, Guildhall School of Music and Drama 1999–; Prof., Vocal Dept, RAM 2009–; Pres. Cheltenham Bach Choir 1986–; Liveryman, Worshipful Co. of Musicians. *E-mail:* megamezzo@ sarahwalker.com. *Website:* www.sarahwalker.com.

WALKER, Thomas, AB; American music historian; b. 5 Nov. 1936, Malden, MA; m. Barbara Bland 1965; one d. *Education:* Harvard Univ., Univ. of California, Berkeley. *Career:* Asst Prof., State Univ. of New York, Buffalo 1968–73; Lecturer, King's Coll. London 1973–80; Prof. Ordinario di Storia della Musica, Universita della Calabria 1980–81, Universita di Ferrara 1981–; mem. Consiglio Direttivo, Societa Italiana di Musicologia; responsible for Rivista Italiana di Musicologia. *Publications:* Drammaturgia Musicale Veneta (co-ed. eight vols) 1983–; contrib. to Musica Disciplina, Journal of the A.M.S. Musica/Realta, Rivista Italiana di Musicologia, concert criticism for The Times and other newspapers 1973–77.

WALKER, Timothy Alexander, AM, BA (Hons), DipEd, AMusA, DipFinMgt; Australian arts administrator; *Chief Executive and Artistic Director, London Philharmonic Orchestra;* b. 23 Nov. 1954, Hobart, Tasmania; s. of Keith James Walker and Elaine Walker (née Edwards). *Education:* Univ. of Tasmania at Hobart, Univ. of New England at Armidale. *Career:* Concert Man., Canberra School of Music 1981–87; Marketing and Development Man., Australian Chamber Orchestra 1987–89, Gen. Man. 1989–99; Chief Exec. World Orchestras 1999–2003; Chief Exec. and Artistic Dir London Philharmonic Orchestra 2003– (also Dir and Trustee); Chair. Asscn of British Orchestras 2008–10; Visiting Fellow (Commoner), Corpus Christi Coll., Cambridge; Dir London Music Masters, Rachmaninoff Foundation; mem. Int. Soc. for Performing Arts, Royal Philharmonic Soc.; Trustee, Henry Wood Hall. *Honours:* Sidney Myer Performing Arts Awards 1999, Australian Inst. of Arts Man. Nugget Award 2000. *Address:* London Philharmonic Orchestra, Level 4, 89 Albert Embankment, London, SE1 7TP, England (office). *Telephone:* (20) 7840-4218 (office). *Fax:* (20) 7840-4201 (office). *E-mail:* timothy.walker@lpo.org.uk (office). *Website:* www.lpo.org.uk (office).

WALLACE, Stephen; British singer (countertenor); b. 1970. *Education:* Royal Northern Coll. of Music. *Career:* appearances as Athamas in Handel's Semele for ENO and the Staatsoper Berlin; Gluck's Orpheus for English Touring Opera, Orlofsky in Die Fledermaus for Dublin Lyric Opera and Anfinomus in Monteverdi's Ulysses for Opera North; Athamas, and Hasse's Solimano at the Innsbruck Early Music Festival; Madam Bubble in The Pilgrim's Progress by Vaughan Williams at Manchester and Bach's Magnificat for Israel Camerata; season 2001 with James the Less in Birtwistle's The Last Supper, at Glyndebourne, Monteverdi's Orfeo in Brussels, Gassmann's L'Opera Seria in Paris and Death in Venice for Opera Zuid; concerts with Les Arts Florissants and Akademie für Alte Musik Berlin. *Current Management:* c/o John McHugh, Hazard Chase Limited, 25 City Road, Cambridge, CB1 1DP, England. *Telephone:* (12) 2331-2400. *Fax:* (12) 2346-0827. *E-mail:* john.mchugh@hazardchase.co.uk. *Website:* www.hazardchase.co.uk.

WALLACE, Stewart; American composer; b. 1960, Philadelphia; m. Dianne Festa; one s. *Education:* Univ. of Texas, Austin. *Career:* played in a rock band and sang as a cantor in a synagogue; has received commissions from Houston Grand Opera, New York City Opera, San Francisco Opera, Nat. Symphony Orchestra, American Composers Orchestra, Bochum Symphony, Germany, ASCAP Foundation; Artist-in-Residence, Princeton Univ. 2000; Music Alive Composer-in-Residence, Nat. Symphony 2001–02. *Compositions:* opera includes: Where's Dick (with librettist Michael Korie) (Houston Grand Opera 1978), Kabbalah 1989, Harvey Milk (with librettist Michael Korie) (Houston Grand Opera 1995), Hopper's Wife (Long Beach Opera 1997), The Bonesetter's Daughter, Yiddisher Teddy Bears, Supermax; chamber works: trilogy (for percussionist Evelyn Glennie): Gorilla in a Cage for percussion and orchestra (Kennedy Center 1999, Paris 2000), The Cheese and the Worms 1999, Irving in Indonesia (Wigmore Hall, London 2001), Hat Trunk, Sh'ma, Sweet Nightmares, Slap Your Neighbor's Face, Three Complaints; concert works: Skvera for Electric Guitar and Orchestra (Kennedy Center 2004), Book of Five for Icebreaker and Orchestra (Carnegie Hall, New York 2002), Peter Pan Suite and Overture (Fort Worth Dallas Ballet 2000). *Film scores:* Book of Love, Persons of Interest (documentary), Afraid of Everything 1999, Seven Days, Where's Dick – The Cartoon. *E-mail:* mail@stewartwallace.com (office). *Website:* www.stewart-wallace.com.

WALLACE, William, BMus, PhD; Canadian/American composer and educator (retd); b. (Henry Wallace), 25 Nov. 1933, Salt Lake City, UT; s. of Henry Ashley Wallace and Dorothy Robinson; m. Harriette Kippley 1957; two s. *Education:* Univ. of Utah, Univ. of Oxford. *Career:* educator, Rutgers, McMaster and Utah Univs; commissioned concerti 1995, 1996, 1998, 1999; mem. Canadian League of Composers, Canadian Music Centre, Soc. of Composers, Authors and Music Publrs of Canada. *Compositions:* Concerto Variations for orchestra, Concerto for piano and orchestra, Concerto for clarinet, violin and orchestra, Concerto for clarinet, violin, piano and orchestra, Concerto for piano and orchestra, several chamber works. *Record-*

ings: Dances and Variations (with London Symphony), Luminations, Epilogue (with Warsaw Chamber Orchestra), Concerto for clarinet, violin, piano and orchestra (with Janáček Symphony Orchestra), Concerto for clarinet, violin and orchestra (with Martinu Symphony Orchestra), Concerto for piano and orchestra (with Slovak Radio Symphony Orchestra), Concertino for viola and orchestra (with Slovak Radio Symphony Orchestra). *Publications:* Concerto Variations 1990, Symphonic Variations 1990, Dance Suite 1990, Introduction and Passacaglia 1990. *Address:* PO Box 203, Wilson, WY 83014-0203, USA (home). *Telephone:* (307) 733-3570 (home). *E-mail:* wwallcomp@aol.com (home).

WALLEN, Errollyn, BMus, MMus, Mphil, MBE; British composer and musician (keyboard); *Visiting Composer-in-Residence, Birmingham Conservatoire*; b. 10 April 1968, Belize City, Belize. *Education:* Dance Theatre of Harlem, New York, USA, Goldsmiths' Coll., London, King's Coll., London, King's Coll., Cambridge. *Career:* joined alternative cabaret band, Pulse as composer, singer and keyboardist 1983–85; freelance keyboard player 1985; opened Wallen Parr recording studio and music-production co., London 1986; composer for corporate video, film and TV 1986–; featured composer for Huddersfield Contemporary Music Festival; mem. and composer, Nanquidno 1987; composer-in-residence, Newcastle Electric Music 3 Festival 1988; founder mem. Women in Music 1987, Ensemble X 1990; part-time lecturer, Nottingham Trent Univ. 1991; guest performer and lecturer, Ga State Univ., Atlanta 1991, Lincoln Centre, New York 2003; external examiner, Brighton Univ.; leader of composition workshops in various schools, and in asscn with London Sinfonietta and Hayward Gallery 1998; founder mem. Women in Music 1987–; mem. Performing Rights Soc., British Asscn of Songwriters, Composers and Authors; Research Assoc., Middlesex Univ.; commission to compose Community Opera for Oldham 2002; Composer in Residence, Trinity Coll. of Music, Birmingham Conservatoire; mem. Bd of Trustees, Children's Music Workshop 2005–. *Compositions:* It's a Quarter to Nine 1968, Song Cycle 1976, Deaths and Entrances 1979, Concert 1980, Three Piano Pieces 1980, Three Elizabethan Songs 1980, Violin 1981, We Four Kings 1981, Quartet for wind instruments and cello 1982, Trio for two flutes and vibraphone 1982, Lines 1982, Music for small orchestra 1983, Still Lives 1983, Variations for string quartet 1983, Pulse Songs 1983–85, Psalm 150 1986, Second String Quartet 1988, Big Business 1988, Take 1988, Mythologies 1988, Memorias de un corazón en un pueblo pequeño 1989, It All Depends on You 1989, Jelly Dub Mix 1990, The Girl in My Alphabet 1990, Favourite Things 1990, In Our Lifetime 1990, The Singing Ringing Tree 1991, Dark Heart 1991, Until You Do 1991, Having Gathered his Cohorts 1991, I Hate Waiting 1991, Mondrian 1992, Heart 1992, E.D.R. 1993, Four Figures with Harlequin (opera) 1993, 1-2-3-4 (ballet) 1993, Waiting (ballet) 1993, Concerto for percussion and orchestra 1993–94, My Lazy Goodheart 1994, Are You Worried about the Rising Cost of Funerals?: Five Simple Songs 1994, Gastarbeiter 1994, Teeth 1994, Dogness 1994, Phonecalls from Besieged Cities 1994, Chorale 1995, Jig 1995, Look! No Hands! (opera) 1995, The Constant Nymph (for radio) 1996, Prelude 1996, Hunger 1996, Music for Alien Tribes 1996, Earth Stood Hard as Iron 1996, The Devil and the Doctor 1997, One Week Short of a Valentine 1997, Shit in her Eyes 1997, Chrome 1997, Never Ending 1997, Horseplay (ballet) 1997, Oil 1997–98, Peace on Earth (voice and piano) 2007. *Television:* Documentary on composer Samuel Coleridge-Taylor (BBC) 2001. *Recordings:* The Girl In My Alphabet 1990, Meet Me At Harold Moore's 1998, Errollyn 2004, Spirit Symphony – Speed-Dating for Two Orchestras (BBC Radio 3 Listeners Award British Composer Awards British Acad. of Composers and Songwriters 2005). *Publications:* Art Not Chance (contrib.), Private Views (contrib. *Honours:* Arts Council Bursary 1987, Holst Award 1991, Cosmopolitan Achievement Award 1993, Peter Whittingham Award 1995. *Address:* c/o Volker Schirp, Peters Edition, 10–12 Baches Street, London, N1 6DN, England (office). *E-mail:* errollyn@errollynwallen.com (office). *Website:* www.errollynwallen.com.

WALLÉN, Martti; Finnish singer (bass); b. 20 Nov. 1948, Helsinki. *Education:* Sibelius Acad., Helsinki. *Career:* debut, Helsinki; Finnish Nat. Opera 1973–75; Principal Bass, Royal Opera, Stockholm 1975–; roles include Colline in La Bohème, Ferrando, Philip II in Don Carlos, Sparafucile in Rigoletto, Spirit Messenger in Die Frau ohne Schatten, Dikoy in Katya Kabanova, Baron Ochs, Marke, Landgraf, Daland, Orestes, Pimen, Falstaff; roles in Finnish modern operas, such as The Last Temptations (Paavo), The Horseman (Judge); sang Fasolt in Das Rheingold at Helsinki 1996.

WALLER, Adalbert; German singer (baritone); b. 1932, Danzig. *Education:* studied in Frankfurt. *Career:* opera appearances at Bielefeld, 1958–59; Passau, 1962–65; Aachen, 1968–74, as Rigoletto, Scarpia, Alfio; Sang Telramund in Lohengrin, 1976–77; Sang Wozzeck in the Brazilian premiere of Berg's opera, São Paulo, Cologne, 1981, as the Dutchman; Member of Frankfurt Opera Company, from 1981; Brunswick, 1985 as Reimann's Lear and Antwerp 1982, as Dr Schön in Lulu; Further engagements as Alberich in Der Ring des Nibelungen at Buenos Aires, 1982; Kurwenal at Bologna, 1984; Season 2000–01 in Reimann's Gespenstersonate, at Berlin, and Schigolch in Lulu at the Vienna Staatsoper; Other centres as Hans Sachs, Wotan, Falstaff, Count Luna.

WALLEZ, Jean-Pierre; French/Swiss violinist and conductor; *Musical Director, Orchestre Régional de Basse-Normandie*; b. 18 March 1939, Lille, France; m. Sophie Lemonnier; four s. *Education:* Conservatoire de Lille, Conservatoire Nat. Supérieur de Musique, Paris. *Career:* Founder and Leader Ensemble Instrumental de France 1968–83; Leader Orchestre de Paris 1975–77; Founder and Dir Ensemble Orchestral de Paris 1978–87; first Guest Conductor Sonderjyllands Symfoniorkester, Denmark; Musical Dir Orchestre Royal de Chambre de Wallonie, Örebro Orchestra, Sweden, Orchestre Régional de Basse-Normandie; Prin. Guest Conductor Orchestra Ensemble Kanazawa, Japan 1994–2000, Orchestre Pasdeloup, Paris 1996–2002; Artistic Dir Albi Music Festival 1974–91; premiered works by Landowski, Bondon, Martinů, Jolivet, Florentz, Finzi, Sciortino, Loussier, Hersant, Capdenat, Bon, Bacri; Prof. of Violin, Geneva Conservatory 1987–2011. *Honours:* Commdr, Ordre nat. du Mérite; Chevalier, Légion d'honneur; Officier, Ordre des Arts et des Lettres; promoted Living Patrimony (Japan); Médaille de vermeil de la Ville de Paris. *Address:* 15 route de Florissant, 1206 Geneva, Switzerland (home). *Telephone:* (22) 3462263 (office). *E-mail:* jp.wallez@gmail.com (home).

WALLFISCH, Benjamin, BMus (Hons), MMus, PPRNCM, GRNCM; British composer, conductor and pianist; *Associate Composer, Orchestra of St John's*; b. 7 Aug. 1979, London; s. of Raphael Wallfisch and Elizabeth Wallfisch. *Education:* Royal Northern Coll. of Music, Univ. of Manchester, Royal Acad. of Music, studied conducting in London with Sir Charles Mackerras and Vernon Handley and in Germany with Bruno Weil. *Career:* began composing aged ten; has received more than 50 comms for the concert hall, cinema, ballet and theatre since 1996; debut as film composer aged 24, scoring Lars von Trier and Thomas Vinterberg's Dear Wendy; orchestrated and conducted Dario Marianelli's Academy Award- and Golden Globe-winning score for Atonement and his Academy Award-nominated score for Pride and Prejudice; BBC Proms debut conducting world première of Escape Velocity 2006; Assoc. Conductor, English Chamber Orchestra 2001–07; Asst Conductor, Netherlands Radio Philharmonic 2003–05, assisted Vladimir Ashkenazy, Valery Gergiev, Edo de Waart and Leonard Slatkin and frequently conducted orchestra in venues including the Concertgebouw, De Doelen Rotterdam and the Muziekcentrum Vredenburg, Utrecht and in numerous studio recordings; Assoc. Composer, Orchestra of St John's 2004–; has also written for the BBC Singers, Bath Int. Festival of Music, Belcea Quartet, Goldberg Ensemble, Hallé Orchestra, Hamburg Symphony Orchestra, Netherlands Radio Philharmonic and the Manchester Camerata; music has been performed at venues including the Barbican, Berlin Philharmonie, Sadler's Wells, Bridgewater Hall, Cadogan Hall, Royal Opera House Linbury Theatre, and broadcast on BBC Radio 3 and Radio 4 and Classic FM; commissioned by Rambert Dance Co. to compose electro-acoustic ballet score for choreographer Rafael Bonachela 2003, work premiered at Sadler's Wells, featured in their UK tour 2003–04; has conducted the London Symphony Orchestra, Philharmonia and City of London Sinfonia and has performed in venues including the Barbican, Cadogan Hall, Royal Festival Hall and St . George's Bristol; Australian debut conducting the Sydney Symphony Orchestra in series of live broadcast Gala performances at Sydney Opera House 2005; other guest conducting highlights have included the Bavarian Radio Philharmonic, Orchestre de Bretagne, Tivoli Symphony Orchestra, Ulster Orchestra, Weimar Staatskapelle; debut conducting Los Angeles Philharmonic at Hollywood Bowl 2009; recent conducting appearances have included Hamburg Symphony, Zagreb Philharmonic, Netherlands Symphony, RTÉ Concert Orchestra, Philharmonia Orchestra, SWR Stuttgart Radio Symphony Orchestra, Bournemouth Symphony; future performances with Los Angeles Chamber and Helsingborg Symphony Orchestras; has performed concerti with soloists including Evelyn Glennie, Pekka Kuusisto, Freddy Kempf, Dame Felicity Lott, Branford Marsalis, Igor Oistrakh, Jean-Yves Thibaudet and John Williams. *Dance:* '21' (commissioned by Rambert Dance Co.) 2003. *Film scores include:* Chasing Liberty 2004, Les Fils du Vent 2004, Beyond the Gates 2005, Dear Wendy 2005, V for Vendetta 2005, Pride and Prejudice 2005, The Brothers Grimm 2005, Copying Beethoven 2005, Nanny McPhee 2005, Opal Dream 2005, Goodbye Bafana 2006, The Return 2006, Eragon 2006, The Brave One 2007, Miss Potter 2007, Shrooms 2007, Nutcracker 2007, The Soloist 2008, The Escapist 2008, The Mutant Chronicles 2008, Atonement 2008, Doghouse 2009, Agora 2009, Everybody's Fine 2009, Robin Hood 2010, The Rite 2011, Life in a Day 2011, Summer in February 2013. *Compositions include:* orchestral: Rhapsody 1998, Sudden Light 2000; ensemble: Suite 2002, Speaking Silence 2001, Quatre Petites Images 2005, Concertino 2005, Speed 2005, Escape Velocity 2006, Child 2006, The Torrent Leaves 2008, Anillo 2009; vocal: Nightingale 1999, Sappho 2000, Mirage 2001, Agnus Dei 2001, Two Haiku 2002, Witness 2003, A Winter's Tale 2004, Ein Traum 2005, . . .But One Equal Eternity 2007; chamber: Pulse 1999, Æternam 2000, Trio 2001, Prelude 2001, Three Haiku 2001, String Quartet No. 1 2001, Prism 2001, Recitative 2001, Quintet 2002, Impulse 2002, String Quartet No. 2 2003, Four Etudes 2003, Rhapsody 2003, Requiem 2005, Spectra 2006, Radical Light 2008, Syzygy 2008; other: Echo Tense for flute, quadraphonic sound and video 2002, Nocturne for harp and tape 2006, Apex for percussion and tape 2006, Peter Pan (incidental music for theatre) 2009. *Recordings include:* debut recording 2006, Shostakovich's First Violin Concerto with Ruth Palmer and the Philharmonia Orchestra 2006, disc of bassoon concerti with Orchestra of Opera North. *Television soundtracks:* Breaking the Mould: The Story of Penicillin 2009, When We Left Earth: The NASA Missions 2008. *Honours:* Hon. Dip RAM; Theodore Holland Intercollegiate Prize, Performing Right Soc. Foundation Scholarship, First Prize, British Reserve Insurance Conducting Competition 2001, multiple int. awards. *Current Management:* c/o IMG Artists, The Light Box, 111 Power Road, London, W4 5PY, England. *Telephone:* (20) 7957-5800. *Fax:* (20) 7957-5801. *E-mail:* twalton@imgartists.com. *Website:* www.imgartists.com. *E-mail:* contact@benjaminwallfisch.com (office). *Website:* www.benjaminwallfisch.com.

WALLFISCH, Elizabeth Tamara, ARAM, LRAM, FRAM; Australian violinist; *Professor of Baroque Violin, Royal Academy of Music, London*; b. (Elizabeth Hunt), 28 Jan. 1952, Melbourne, Vic.; d. of Kenneth Hunt and Tamara Coates; m. Raphael Wallfisch. *Education:* Royal Acad. of Music, London. *Career:* has taught the violin nearly all her life; Baroque Violin Prof., RAM, London 1990–, specializing in the art and craft of playing historical instruments; Baroque Violin Prof., Royal Conservatory of Music, The Hague, the Netherlands 1990–2005; String Teacher, Meisterkurs Klang und Raum, Klang und Raum, Kloster Irsee for seven years; has taught masterclasses world-wide, including at Curtis Inst., Boston, Berkeley School of Music, Calif., Oberlin Coll., Ohio, Univ. of Boulder, Colo, Eastman School of Music, Rochester, NY, Cornell Univ., NY, Denver Univ., California Summer Music, Monterey, Banff Centre, Canada, McGill Univ., Montreal, Edmonton Univ. Music Dept, Alberta, Canada, Australian Nat. Acad. of Music, Melbourne, Sydney Conservatorium of Music, Univ. of Melbourne Music Dept, Prize Winners Bach Week, Hannover, Zürich Hochschule fur Musik, Shanghai Conservatorium students at Expo 2010, ANU, Canberra; Music Dir Nat. Music Camp Australia, under the Australian Youth Orchestra 2007, 2013, has worked with the latter in Style Workshop, Young Symphonists; leading interpreter of music on the baroque and classical violins, prominent interpreter of 17th and 18th century violin music, also leader and director; Guest Dir/Leader on the violin with many of the world's period instrument orchestras, including Orchestra of the Age of Enlightenment, Netherlands Bach Soc., Tafelmusik-Canada, Apollo's Fire, Hanover Band, L'Orfeo Barockorchester, Australian Brandenburg Orchestra and Philharmonia Baroque, Carmel Bach Festival Orchestra, Concerto d'Amsterdam, Brandywine Baroque, Raglan Baroque, Musica Angelica, Pacific Baroque Orchestra; guest conductor with modern chamber orchestras including Saint Paul Chamber Orchestra, Israel Chamber Orchestra, Vancouver Symphony (twice), NWDR-Herford Symphony Orchestra, Leipzig Chamber Orchestra, Stuttgart Chamber Orchestra, Västerås Sinfonietta, Australian Chamber Orchestra; formed the Wallfisch Band, debut at Lufthansa Festival of Baroque Music 2008, has performed in UK, Germany, NZ and Australia; other orchestras she has performed with include Queensland Symphony Orchestra, West Australian Symphony Orchestra, Melbourne Chamber Orchestra, Israeli Camerata, Les Violons du Roy, Quebec, Calgary Symphony Orchestra, European Union Chamber Orchestra, La Scintilla, Zürich, London Philharmonic Orchestra (leading for Frans Brüggen), Haydn Victoria Symphony Orchestra, Canada, Concerto of Mendelssohn, Viotti Musica Angelica, Los Angeles, Music of the Baroque, Chicago, Les Musiciens du Louvre, Grenoble, Berkeley Arion Ensemble, Montreal; has explored the music of Paganini and Viotti and has recorded much of the music of the great Baroque tradition, from the earliest Italian violin music of Cima, to Biber, Telemann, Bach and the music of the French Baroque. *Recordings include:* music of the High Baroque Italian violinist-composers such as Vivaldi, Corelli, Veracini, Tartini, Geminiani and of the Classical and Romantic perios from Mozart to Mendelssohn; Complete Violin Concerti by Bach (including those reconstructed from Bach's Harpsichord Concertos in D minor and G minor); Haydn, including the Sinfonia Concertante; recorded a series of early Italian Violin Sonatas with the Locatelli Trio, Locatelli, Tartini and Corelli with Albinoni and Veracini; Trio has also recorded Handel Sonatas Op. 1, Locatelli Violin Concertos Op. 3, L'Arte del Violino performed by Elizabeth Wallfisch with Raglan Baroque Players under Nicholas Kraemer; Locatelli Concerti Grossi (also with Raglan Baroque Players); Locatelli Op. 8 Sonatas with the Locatelli Trio; solo recording of Bach Solo Sonatas and Partitas; Telemann Concertos; Vivaldi's L'estro armonico concertos; Biber Rosary Sonatas; Kreutzer Etudes. *Publications:* The Art of Playing 'Chin-Off' for the Brave and the Curious 2003. *E-mail:* elizabethwallfisch@mac.com (home). *Website:* www.elizabethwallfisch.com; www.wallfischband.com.

WALLFISCH, Raphael; British cellist; b. 15 June 1953, London, England; s. of Peter Wallfisch. *Education:* Royal Acad. with Derek Simpson, studied with Amaryllis Fleming, Amadeo Baldavino in Rome, Gregory Piatigorsky in Calif. *Career:* since winning the 1977 Gaspar Cassado Int. Cello Competition in Florence, has appeared widely in Europe, Australia, USA, with Auckland Philharmonia, BBC Nat. Orchestra of Wales, Vancouver Symphony, Västerås Sinfonietta; has performed with most major British orchestras including BBC Philharmonic, London Symphony, London Philharmonic and at the BBC Proms; regularly invited to play at major festivals including the BBC Proms, Edinburgh, Aldeburgh, Spoleto, Prades, Oslo and Schleswig-Holstein; gives masterclasses world-wide; Prof. of Cello, Zürich Winterthur Konservatorium, Switzerland, Royal Northern Coll. of Music, Manchester; composers who have written for him include Sir Peter Maxwell Davies, Kenneth Leighton, James MacMillan, John Metcalf, Paul Patterson, John Joubert, Robert Simpson, Robert Saxton, Roger Smalley, Giles Swayne, Sir John Tavener and Adrian Williams. *Recordings include:* has recorded nearly every major work for his instrument, including the mainstream concerto repertoire and numerous lesser-known works by Dohnányi, Respighi, Barber, Hindemith and Martinů, as well as Richard Strauss, Dvořák, Kabalevsky and Khachaturian; has recorded a wide range of British cello concertos, including works by MacMillan, Finzi, Delius, Bax, Bliss, Britten, Moeran and Kenneth Leighton; recorded Walton's Cello Concerto for Chandos Walton Edition. *Current Management:* c/o Pippa Patterson, Ikon Arts Management, Suite 114 Business Design Centre, 52 Upper Street, London, N1 0QH, England. *E-mail:* pippa@ikonarts.com. *Website:* www.raphaelwallfisch.com.

WALLSTRÖM, Tord; Swedish singer (baritone); b. 1952. *Education:* Stockholm Music Acad. *Career:* engagements at the Royal Opera, Stockholm, the Drottningholm Theatre, and at Gothenburg; appearances in Soliman II by J. M. Kraus and as Masetto in Don Giovanni; Essen Opera and Stockholm from 1985, as Telramund in Lohengrin, Don Giovanni, Cecil in Roberto Devereux, Tonio in Pagliacci and Klingsor in Parsifal 1995; guest appearances in Scandinavia and Germany as Handel's Giulio Cesare and Arsamenes (Xerxes), Mandryka in Arabella and Fra Melitone in La Forza del Destino; frequent concert engagements. *Recordings include:* Soliman II by Kraus, and Don Giovanni.

WALMSLEY-CLARK, Penelope; British singer (soprano); b. 19 Feb. 1949, London, England. *Career:* sang the Queen of Night in Die Zauberflöte at Covent Garden; returned for British premiere of Berio's Un Re in Ascolto, 1989; Glyndebourne Festival in The Electrification of the Soviet Union by Nigel Osborne; has sung the Queen of Night for Geneva Opera, and ENO 1989; Ligeti's Le Grand Macabre in Vienna; concert engagements include the Brahms Requiem at the City of London Festival; Carmina Burana with the London Symphony Orchestra; Elijah in Liverpool with Marek Janowski; Shostakovich Symphony No. 14, with City of London Sinfonia; title roles in Maria Stuarda and Norma, Leonora in La Forza del Destino and Il Trovatore, all with Scottish Opera; concert performances of the operas Moses und Aron at the Festival Hall and Elegy for Young Lovers at La Fenice, Venice; further appearances in Vienna, Berlin, Salzburg, Frankfurt, Czechoslovakia and Russia; sang as Guinevere in the world premiere of Birtwistle's Gawain at Covent Garden, 1991; Donna Anna for ENO 1995; Hecuba in King Priam for Flanders Opera, 1996. *Recordings:* Ligeti: Le Grand Macabre 1991, Gawain (complete opera) under Elgar Howarth 1996, Jonathan Harvey: Song Offerings (with London Sinfonietta) 1999, George Benjamin: A Mind of Winter (with London Sinfonietta) 2000, Prokofiev: Peter & the Wolf 2004.

WALSH, Diane, MusM; American pianist; b. 16 Aug. 1950, Washington, DC; d. of William Walsh and Estelle Walsh (née Stokes); m. 1st Henry Forbes 1969 (divorced 1979); m. 2nd Richard Pollak 1982. *Education:* Juilliard School of Music and Mannes Coll. *Career:* made professional debut in Young Concert Artists series 1974; piano teacher, The New School for Music, Mannes Coll. 1982–; Founder and performer, Mannes Trio 1983–94; performances include Kennedy Center for Performing Arts, Washington, DC 1976, Concertgebouw 1976, Wigmore Hall, London 1980, Library of Congress 1987, Philharmonia Hall, St. Petersburg 1990, Miller Theatre 1994, Dvorak Hall, Prague 1999; appearances with major orchestras including San Francisco Symphony, Bavarian Radio Symphony of Munich, Berlin Radio Symphony; tours of USA, South America, Russia and Europe; Artistic Dir Skaneateles Festival, NY 1999–2004. *Honours:* Otto Storm Prize, Juilliard School of Music 1971, First Prize, Munich Int. Piano Competition 1975, Performance Prize, Mannes Coll. 1982, Naumburg Chamber Music Award 1986, Second Prize, Salzburg Int. Mozart Competition 1975, First Prize, Concert Artists Guild and Young Concert Artists auditions, Second Prize, J.S. Bach Int. Competition, Washington, DC, Second Prize, William Kapell Int. Competition, Third Prize, Busoni Int. Competition, Van Cliburn Competition Medallist, Van Cliburn Chamber Music Prize, John Anson Kittredge Foundation grant, Nat. Endowment for the Arts grant. *Current Management:* c/o Jonathan Wentworth Associates Ltd, 10 Fiske Place, Suite 530, Mt Vernon, NY 10550, USA. *Telephone:* (914) 667-0707. *Fax:* (914) 667-0784. *E-mail:* kenneth@jwentworth.com. *Website:* www.jwentworth.com; www.dianewalsh.com.

WALSH, Louise; Irish singer (soprano); b. 16 March 1966, Dublin. *Education:* Trinity College and College of Music, Dublin, Royal Northern College of Music, National Opera Studio, London. *Career:* opera engagements as Susanna, and La Fée in Cendrillon, for RNCM; Britten's Tytania for the Broomhill Trust, Janáček's Vixen for Opera Northern Ireland and in Handel's Tamerlano for the Covent Garden Festival; Stuttgart Opera (contract 1995–97) in Hansel and Gretel, as Serpina in La Serva Padrona, Servilia in La Clemenza di Tito, Pauline in La Vie Parisienne for Stuttgart Opera, Xenia in Boris Godunov and Musetta in La Bohème; Ilia in Idomeneo for Opera Northern Ireland, 1997; Adele in Die Fledermaus, for Opera Ireland, 1998, and Carl Rosa opera company, 1999; Rosina in Sarlatan by P. Hass, for Wexford Festival Opera, 1998; Anne Trulove in The Rake's Progress for Opera Theatre, 1999; concerts include Bach's St John Passion and Mass in B Minor, Elijah, Carmina Burana, Messiah and Mozart's Mass in C Minor; engaged as a Flowermaiden at Brussels, 1998 (production of Parsifal). *Honours:* prizewinner Vienna Belvedere International Singing Competition 1994, RNCM Elizabeth Harwood Memorial Scholarship, RNCM Curtis Gold Medal for Singing, RNCM Ricordi Prize for Opera. *E-mail:* louise@louisewalsh.com (office). *Website:* www.louisewalsh.com.

WALSHE, Jennifer, PhD; Irish composer, performer and visual artist; b. 1974, Dublin. *Education:* Royal Scottish Acad. of Music and Drama, Northwestern Univ., USA. *Career:* commissions from Radio Telefís Éireann (RTÉ), Westdeutscher Rundfunk (WDR), Sudwest Rundfunk (SWR), Internationale Ferienkurse für Neue Musik, Darmstadt, Maerzmusik, Musik der Jahrhunderte, Huddersfield Contemporary Music Festival, Dresdener Tage der zeitgenössischen Musik, Wien Modern, Dresden Semperoper, Center for Art and Media Karlsruhe, Irish Chamber Orchestra, Crash Ensemble, Project Arts Centre and Nat. Concert Hall, Ireland; works performed and broadcast worldwide by ensembles including Alter Ego, ensemble recherche, Nat. Symphony Orchestra of Ireland, Orchestra Sinfonica del Teatro La Fenice, Solistenensemble Kaleidoskop, Ensemble Resonanz, Apartment House, ensemble Intégrales, Neue Vocalsolisten Stuttgart, Stuttgarter Kammerorchester, Schlagquartett Köln, Crash Ensemble, Con Tempo Quartet, ensemble ascolta, Champ d'Action, ensemble laboratorium, ensemble surplus, trio nexus, Rilke Ensemble, Irish Chamber Orchestra, Irish Youth Wind Ensemble, Bozzini Quartet, Callino Quartet, Ensemble 2000, Concorde, Black Hair, Continuum, Ensemble Musica Nova, ensemble chronophonie, Scottish Chamber Orchestra Wind Quintet, Hebrides Ensemble, Psappha and Q-02; vocal works performed by her and others at festivals across Europe and in North America including RTÉ Living Music (Dublin), Båstad Kammarmusik Festival (Sweden), Ultraschall (Berlin), Transit (Leuven), Ars Musica (Brussels), Ultima and Borealis (Norway), Steirischer Herbst, Wien Modern, Wittener Tage für neue Kammermusik, Donaueschinger Musiktagen, Huddersfield Contemporary Music Festival, Late Music Festival (York), Hamburger Klangwerktage, Gaida (Lithuania), BMIC Cutting Edge, Composer's Choice (Dublin), Internationale Ferienkurse für Neue Musik Darmstadt, Stockholm New Music, BELEF (Belgrade), Traiettorie (Parma), Cut & Splice (London), Lucerne Festival (Switzerland), SPOR (Denmark), Frau Musica Nova (Cologne), Reihe 0 (Austria), SoundField (Chicago), Performa (New York), Electric Eclectics (Canada) and Experimental Intermedia and Music at the Anthology (New York); also improviser in duo Ma La Pert with Tony Conrad; lecturer in composition, Darmstadt summer course for new music 2002; Reader in Music, Brunel Univ. *Exhibition:* No Irish Need Apply, Chelsea Art Museum, New York. *Compositions include:* opera: XXX_LIVE_NUDE_-GIRLS, The Geometry; other: Your Name Here 1998, Here We are Now 2002, The Loneliness of the Long Distance Conductor 2004, Physics for the Girl in the Street 2007, Grúpat (as nine alter egos, members of an art collective, compositions, installations, films, photography, sculptures and fashion, performed and exhibited worldwide) 2007–09, The White Noisery 2012. *Recordings include:* XXX_LIVE_NUDE_GIRLS 2003, Nature Data 2010; Grúpat And Jennifer Walshe – The Wasistas Of Thereswhere 2009. *Honours:* grants and fellowships from Akademie Schloss Solitude, Stuttgart, DAAD Berliner Künstlerprogramm, Foundation for Contemporary Arts, New York, Fondazione Claudio Buziol, Venice, Arts Council of Ireland, Scottish Arts Council; winner Kranichstein Music Prize, Internationale Ferienkurse für Neue Musik Darmstadt, Praetorius Music Prize for Composition, Niedersächsisches Ministerium für Wissenschaft und Kultur 2008. *Address:* Room GB108, Brunel University, Uxbridge, UB8 3PH, England (office). *Telephone:* (1895) 267868 (office). *E-mail:* jennifer.walshe@brunel.ac.uk (office). *Website:* www.milker.org (office).

WALTER, Bertrand; French violinist; b. 17 March 1962, Metz. *Education:* Metz and Paris Conservatories, Univ. of Indiana, USA with Franco Gulli. *Career:* Co-leader Orchestre Philharmonique de France; with violist Laurent Verney and cellist Dominique de Williencourt f. string trio BWV and has given many recital concerts throughout France. *Honours:* Prizes at Paris Conservatoire and Paganini Int. Competition 1980. *Address:* Orchestre Philharmonique de France, 116 avenue du Président Kennedy, 75786 Paris Cedex 16, France.

WALTER, Horst, DPh; German musicologist; b. 5 March 1931, Hannover; m. Liesel Roth 1959; two s. *Education:* Univ. of Cologne. *Career:* Scientific Cooperator, Joseph Haydn Inst., Cologne 1962–92, Dir of the Inst. 1992–96. *Publications include:* Complete Haydn Edition Symphonies i/4, i/17 (ed.) 1964, 1966, Music History of Lüneburg from the End of 16th Century to Early 18th Century 1967, G. van Swieten's Manuscript Notebooks of The Creation and The Seasons (Haydn Studies i/4) 1967, Baryton trios xiv/5 1968, Haydn's Pianos (Haydn Studies ii/4) 1970, The Biographical Relationship Between Haydn and Beethoven (Report of Bonn Conference 1970) 1973, An Unknown Schütz Autograph in Wolfenbüttel (Festschrift K. G. Fellerer) 1973, La Vera Costanza xxv/8 1976, The Posthorn Signal in the Works of Haydn and Other 18th Century Composers (Haydn Studies iv/1) 1976, Haydn's Pupils at the Esterhazy Court (Festschrift H. Hüschen) 1980, Keyboard Concertos xv/2 1983, Haydn Bibliography 1973–83 (Haydn Studies v/4) 1985, String Quartets Dedicated to Haydn, Tradition and Reception (Report of the Gesellschaft für Musikforschung Köln 1982) 1985, Accompanied Keyboard Divertimenti and Concertini xvi 1987, Wind-band Divertimenti and Scherzandi viii/2 1991, Haydn Bibliography 1984–90 (Haydn Studies vi/3) 1992, Hanky-Panky Around Haydn (Haydn Studies vi/4) 1994, The Viennese String Quartet from 1780 to 1800 (Haydn Studies vii/3–4) 1998, On Haydn's 'Characteristic' Symphonies (Internationales Musikwissen schaftliches Symposium Eisenstadt) 1995, 2000, String Quartets op.76, op.77 and op.103, xii/6 2003, Mozart's Hairdresser and the Pianos of Stein (Festschrift O. Biba) 2006; contrib. to Music Past and Present, New Grove Dictionary, Proceedings of the International Haydn Conference, Washington, DC 1975, 1981, International Haydn Congress, Vienna 1982, 1986, The Haydn Lexikon, Laaber 2010. *Address:* Herkenfelder Weg 146, 51467 Bergisch Gladbach, Germany (home). *Telephone:* 220284389 (home).

WALTHER, Ute; German singer (mezzo-soprano); b. 23 June 1945, Jena. *Education:* Musikhochschule, Berlin. *Career:* debut, Schwerin 1968, as Octavian in Der Rosenkavalier; sang at Rostock 1974–80, Dresden Staatsoper from 1980 and Deutsche Oper Berlin 1986; tours of Japan with the Vienna Staatsoper and Deutsche Oper companies, as Fricka and Waltraute in The Ring; guest appearances at Warsaw, Cologne (Brangaene in Tristan) 1990, the Moscow Bolshoi, Edinburgh Festival and Madrid; season 1995–96 at Berlin as Brangaene, Dorabella, Cherubino, Carmen, Eboli in Don Carlos, Amneris, and the Hostess in Boris Godunov; sang the Witch in Hansel and Gretel season 1997–98; season 2000 at the Deutsche Oper as Brangaene, Wagner's Mary,

Nicolai's Frau Fluth and Meg Page in Falstaff; many concert appearances, notably in music by Bach.

WALZ, Melanie; German singer (soprano); b. 1965, Stuttgart. *Career:* many appearances in concert and opera throughout Europe, notably in contemporary music; sang in Einstein on the Beach and The Fall of the House of Usher by Philip Glass, at Stuttgart; Hamburg, Staatsoper 1997, in the premiere of Helmut Lachenmann's Mädchen mit den Schwefelhölzern; engagements at the Vienna Konzerthaus in Luigi Nono's La fabbrica illuminata and Intolleranza, Noti by Heinz Holliger, and Schoenberg's Moses und Aron 2001; Basle Theatre from 1998, as Mozart's Blondchen and Sophie in Der Rosenkavalier.

WANAMI, Takayoshi; Japanese violinist; b. 1945, Tokyo; m. Mineko Tsuchiya. *Education:* studied with Kichinouska Tsuji, Saburo Sumi and Toshiya Eto. *Career:* debut playing the Glazunov Concerto with the Japan Philharmonic 1963; performed with orchestras including the Leipzig Gewandhaus, City of Birmingham Symphony, Bournemouth Symphony, BBC Philharmonic, BBC Nat. Orchestra of Wales, Acad. of St Martin in the Fields, London Mozart Players, Zürich Chamber, Festival Strings Lucerne, Vienna Chamber, Slovak Chamber and Boston Pops; collaborated with conductors including Kurt Masur, Sir Neville Marriner, Tadaaki Otaka and Seiji Ozawa; performed with pianists, including S. Lorenzi, B. Canino, E. Lush, G. Pratley and H. Barth; duo partnership with the pianist Mineko Tsuchiya since 1980; festivals include Lucerne Int. Music Festival 1980, 1988, Festival Estivalde, Paris 1981, Schaffhausen Bach Festival 1982, Seon Bach Festival 1984, Japan Week in Cairo 1986, Meiningen Summer Festival 1991; tours of USA, fmr Soviet Union, Egypt and Morocco; numerous recitals at QEH, Purcell Room and Wigmore Hall, London, including three solo recitals performing all solo works by Bach and Ysaye 1998; in Tokyo, directing Izumigoh Festival Orchestra 1991; annual recital Christmas Bach Series since 1991; three recitals performing complete Beethoven Sonatas with Mineko Tsuchiya 2003; 60th Birthday Concert 2005; recital at Wigmore Hall, London 2003; recital tour in Germany and Switzerland 2003–04. *Recordings include:* Tchaikovsky, Bruch and Mendelssohn Concertos with the Philharmonia; Bach Concertos with the London Mozart Players; Brahms and Schumann Concertos with London Philharmonic; Bach Solo Sonatas and Partitas (complete) Ysaÿe Six Solo Sonatas; Brahms Violin Sonatas with Mineko Tsuchiya. *Publication:* The Gift of Music (autobiog.) 1994. *Honours:* Suntory Music Award 1995, prizewinner Long-Thibaud Competition 1965, Carl Flesch Int., London 1970, Ysaÿe Medal 1970, Mobil Music Award 1993. *Current Management:* c/o Manygate Management, Trees, Ockham Road South, East Horsley, Surrey KT24 6QE, England. *Telephone:* (1483) 281300. *Fax:* (1483) 281811. *E-mail:* manygate@easynet.co.uk.

WANG, Jian; Chinese cellist; b. 1968, Shanghai. *Education:* Shanghai Conservatoire, Yale School of Music, studied with Aldo Parisot. *Career:* debut with Brahms Double Concerto with Maxim Vengerov and the Mahler Youth Orchestra under Claudio Abbado 1995; appeared with Royal Concertgebouw Orchestra and Riccardo Chailly in Amsterdam and on tour in China 1996; has performed with many of the world's leading orchestras, including Philadelphia, Cleveland, Minnesota and Chicago Symphony Orchestras, NHK Symphony, Berlin Philharmonic, Hong Kong Philharmonic, Zurich Tonhalle, Stockholm Philharmonic, Santa Cecilia, Halle, Mahler Chamber and the Orchestre Nat. de France; played with many conductors, including Dutoit, Krivine, Sawallisch, Bergland, Eschenbach, Chung, Hickox, Neeme Jarvi, Ashkenazy, Wigglesworth and Harding. *Recordings include:* Brahms Double Concerto (with Berlin Philharmonic Orchestra, Claudio Abbado and Gil Shaham), Haydn Concerti (with the Gulbenkian Orchestra under Muhai Tang), Messaieen's Quartet for the End of Time (with Myung-Whun Chung, Gil Shaham and Paul Meyer), Brahms, Mozart and Schumann chamber music (with Pires and Dumay), Baroque album (with the Camerata Salzburg), Bach solo cello suites, Reverie. *Address:* c/o Deutsche Grammophon GmbH, Baumwall 3, 20459 Hamburg, Germany (office). *Telephone:* (40) 441810 (office). *Fax:* (40) 44181188 (office). *E-mail:* deutschegrammophon@umusic.com (office). *Website:* www.deutschegrammophon.com (office).

WANG, Jin; Chinese conductor, composer and music teacher; b. 9 July 1960, Beijing; s. of Wang Fu Zeng and Xu Huan; m.; four s. *Education:* Vienna Acad. of Music, studied with Karl Österreicher, Leopold Hager, Zubin Mehta, Leonard Bernstein. *Career:* has conducted over 100 orchestras, including Göteborg Symphony, Oslo Philharmonic, Helsinki Philharmonic, Finnish Nat. Radio Symphony, Berlin Radio-Symphony, Royal Liverpool Philharmonic, Toscanini Symphony, Yomiuri Nippon Symphony, Tokyo, Seoul Philharmonic, Singapore Symphony, Taiwan Nat. Symphony; fmr Chief Conductor Moravian Philharmonic Orchestra, Prin. Guest Conductor Janácek Philharmonie, Prin. Guest Conductor Romanian Radio Symphony; Conductor and Dir of Music, Komische Oper Berlin 2003–07, performances there included Carmen, Don Giovanni, Der Freischütz, La Bohème, Rigoletto, The Rider with the Wind in his Hair, Albert Herring; Guest Prof. of Conducting, Swedish Royal Acad. of Music, Göteborg Music Acad.; Gen. Music Dir, Mainfranken Theatre 2007–08; Prin. Conductor, Würzburg Philharmonic Orchestra 2006–08; Chief Conductor Vaasa City Orchestra; Chief Conductor Eurasia Sinfonietta; Guest Conductor Romanian Nat. Radio Orchestra (permanent guest 1993–); Deputy Dir Xiamen Opera Centre. *Compositions include:* Tibet Impressions Suites I-V, Hymnus To all my friends, Würzburg Nachtwächter Stories I, Nokia Variations - A journey through music styles with the famous ring-tone, Romanian Dances For the young Romanian friends. *Recordings* *include:* Organ concertos by Haydn and Poulenc, Eurasia Sinfonietta, Malpopitá Komische Oper Berlin, Opera Rin po che - reborn Buddha (excerpts). *Honours:* winner of eight int. conducting competitions including Prague Spring Conducting Competition 1991, Nicolai Malko Competition, Arturo Toscanini Competition. *Address:* Wagramer Straße 4, Top 1802, Berlin 1220 Vienna, Austria (office). *Telephone:* (650) 27 00 761 (office). *E-mail:* wangjin@live.at (office); wangmichaela@hotmail.com (office).

WANG, Jue; Chinese pianist; b. 5 March 1984, Shanghai. *Education:* Shanghai Conservatory with Prof. Li Minduo. *Career:* first public performance at age 10; invited to many musical festivals, including solo appearance at Kremlin Musical Festival, Moscow 2008. *Concert repertoire includes:* Prokofiev Suggestion Diabolique, Liszt Transcendental Etude in F minor, Beethoven 7 Bagatelles, op. 33, Stevenson Peter Grimes, Liszt Sonata in B minor, Liszt Hungarian Rhapsody No. 15, Mozart Piano Concerto No. 27 in B flat major, Prokofiev Piano Concerto No. 2 in G minor. *Honours:* Gold Medal, First Chinese Young Artists Competition 2001, First Prize, Maria Canals Int. Piano Competition, Barcelona 2005, winner, Paloma O'Shea Int. Piano Contest, Santander 2008. *Address:* c/o Shanghai Conservatory of Music, 20 Fenyang Road, Xuhui District, Shanghai 200031, People's Republic of China (office). *Website:* www.shcmusic.edu.cn (office).

WANG, Yuja; Chinese pianist; b. 10 Feb. 1987, Beijing. *Education:* studied at Central Conservatory of Music, Beijing with Ling Yuan and Zhou Guangren, at Mount Royal Coll., Calgary with Hung Kuan Chen and Tema Blackstone and at Curtis Inst. of Music, Philadelphia with Gary Graffman. *Career:* began studying piano at age six; European debut with Tonhalle Orchestra, Zurich, Switzerland 2003; debut with Nat. Arts Center Orchestra, Ottawa 2005; Carnegie Hall (Stern Hall) debut 2011; toured Asia with San Francisco Symphony 2012; recital tour of Japan 2013; has performed with numerous int. orchestras including Baltimore Symphony, Boston Symphony, Chicago Symphony, Dallas Symphony, Detroit Symphony, Houston Symphony, Los Angeles Philharmonic, Nat. Symphony, New World Symphony, Philadelphia Orchestra, Pittsburgh Orchestra, San Francisco Symphony, Tonhalle Orchestra, China Philharmonic, Filarmonica della Scala, Gulbenkian Orchestra, London Philharmonic, Nagoya Philharmonic, NHK Symphony, Tokyo, Orchestra Mozart, among others; has worked with many conductors including Claudio Abbado, Daniel Barenboim, Charles Dutoit, Daniele Gatti, Manfred Honeck, Pietari Inkinen, Lorin Maazel, Kurt Masur, Sir Roger Norrington, Antonio Pappano, Yuri Temirkanov, Michael Tilson-Thomas, Pinchas Zukerman. *Recordings:* Sonatas & Etudes 2009, Transformation 2010, Rachmaninoff's Rhapsody on a Theme of Paganini 2011, Fantasia 2012. *Honours:* winner, Aspen Music Festival concerto competition 2002, Gilmore Young Artist Award 2006, Classic FM Gramophone Awards Young Artist of the Year 2009, Echo Klassik Young Artist of the Year 2011. *Current Management:* Opus 3 Artists, 470 Park Avenue South, 9th Floor, New York, NY 10016, USA. *Telephone:* (212) 584-7514 (office). *E-mail:* eblackburn@opus3artists.com (office). *Website:* www.yujawang.com.

WANGEMANN, Hendrikje; German singer (soprano); b. 1961, Kropstädt. *Education:* Leipzig Musikhochschule. *Career:* debut as Armida in Handel's Rinaldo at Halle; sang at Halle 1987–91, as Asteria in Handel's Tamerlano, Gilda, Susanna, Marzelline in Fidelio, Nannetta in Falstaff and Micaela in Carmen; Leipzig Opera from 1991, as Musetta, Zerlina 1994, Amanda in Ligeti's Le Grand Macabre; guest appearances in Austria, Switzerland, Hungary and Germany; other roles include Mozart's Pamina and Servilia, Baroness in Lortzing's Der Wildschütz and Jenny in Weill's Mahagonny; season 1996 in Greek by Marc Anthony Turnage, at Leipzig. *Recordings include:* Deutsche Sinfonia by Hanns Eisler.

WARD, David W. B.; British pianist, conductor and academic; b. 28 Dec. 1942, Sheffield, Yorks.; m. Elizabeth Gladstone 1963; one s. one d. *Education:* Bryanston School, Dorset, Caius Coll., Cambridge, Royal Coll. of Music, London, studied with Nadia Boulanger in Paris. *Career:* debut in Purcell Room, London 1972; numerous concerts as soloist in UK, the Netherlands, France, Germany, South Africa, USA, Australia and NZ; Conductor, La Spiritata Chamber Orchestra and others; Prof., Royal Coll. of Music 1969–; well known for interpretation of Mozart on piano and fortepiano; teacher of fortepiano, Birmingham Conservatoire. *Recordings:* Mozart Piano Music (three vols), duets with Susan Rennie and solo works, radio recordings with BBC, RTÉ and ORTF, Mozart piano and violin sonatas (with Yossi Zivoni), Haydn Trios and Piano Solos (with Badinage, on fortepiano and original instruments), duets and solos by J.C. Bach and C.P.E. Bach and Haydn, first recording of a new piece by David Stoll for two fortepianos (with Marejka Smit-Sibinga, Amsterdam), Mozart Keyboard Music on fortepiano, David Stoll Chamber Music (including Piano Sonata and Two-Piano Sonata with Noel Skinner), From Two to Six, works by Rossini, Haydn, Mozart, Wesley. *Address:* 4 Patten Road, London, SW18 3RH, England (home). *Telephone:* (20) 8874-4938 (home). *Fax:* (20) 8874-4938 (home). *E-mail:* davidwb.ward@virgin.net (home).

WARD, Joseph, OBE, FRNCM; British singer (tenor); b. 22 May 1942, Preston, Lancashire, England. *Education:* Royal Manchester Coll. of Music. *Career:* debut, Royal Opera House, Covent Garden 1962; many appearances in opera in the USA, Germany, Portugal, France and Austria; formerly Head of Vocal Studies, Royal Northern Coll. of Music; formerly Principal Tenor, Royal Opera House, Covent Garden; consultant in opera and vocal studies, Hong Kong Acad. for Performing Arts; freelance opera director; course director, European

Opera Centre, Manchester from 1998 (Tosca and Mozart's Lucio Silla); many BBC broadcasts. *Recordings include:* Norma, Beatrice di Tenda, Montezuma, Wuthering Heights, Pilgrim's Progress and Albert Herring.

WARD, Nicholas; British violinist; b. 1954, England. *Education:* Royal Northern Coll. of Music and in Brussels. *Career:* joined the Royal Philharmonic 1977 and is co-leader of the City of London Sinfonia and Dir of the Northern Chamber Orchestra, Manchester; mem. of the Instrumental Quintet of London, with repertoire including works by Jongen, Mozart, Debussy and Villa-Lobos; mem. of the Melos and Radcliffe Ensembles. *Current Management:* Upbeat Classical Management, PO Box 479, Uxbridge, UB8 2ZH, England. *Telephone:* (1895) 259441. *Fax:* (1895) 259341. *E-mail:* info@upbeatclassical.co.uk. *Website:* www.upbeatclassical.co.uk.

WARD JONES, Peter Arthur, MA, FRCO; British music librarian (retd), musicologist, organist and harpsichordist; b. 30 March 1944, Chester, England; m. Shirley Bailey 1978 (died 2001); one s. one d. *Education:* Balliol Coll., Oxford. *Career:* part-time Prof., Royal Coll. of Music 1967–69; Music Librarian, Bodleian Library, Oxford 1969–2009; harpsichordist, City of Oxford Orchestra 1968–99; Conductor, Oxford Harmonic Soc. 1971–80; Organist, St Giles' Church, Oxford 1971–2000; mem. Editorial Bd Leipzig Mendelssohn edn 1993; mem. Royal Coll. of Organists, Royal Musical Asscn, Mendelssohn-Gesellschaft; Fellow, St Cross Coll. Oxford 2007–09. *Publications include:* Catalogue of the Mendelssohn Papers in the Bodleian Library Oxford Vol. 3 1989, Revision of P. Radcliffe's Mendelssohn 1990, The Mendelssohns on Honeymoon 1997, Mendelssohn: An Exhibition 1997, George Butterworth's Orchestral Works (Musica Britannica) (ed.) 2012; contrib. to Music and Letters, Brio, Mendelssohn-Studien, RMA Research Chronicle, New Grove Dictionary of Music and Musicians 1980, 2000, Die Musik in Geschichte und Gegenwart (second edn), Festschrift Rudolf Elvers, The Encyclopaedia of Oxford. *Honours:* F.J. Read Prize, Royal Coll. of Organists 1962, Festschrift 'Felix Mendelssohn Bartholdy: Essays in Honor of Peter Ward Jones' (Special Issue of Journal of Musicologial Research) 2010. *Address:* 25 Harbord Road, Oxford, OX2 8LH, England (home).

WARING, Kate, BMus, MMus; American composer; b. 22 April 1953, Alexandria, La; m. 1981; one s. one d. *Education:* Louisiana State Univ., Sorbonne Univ. of Paris, France. *Career:* solo flute recitals in Italy, France, Germany, USA; original compositions performed in USA, Italy, France, Switzerland and Germany; radio performances of compositions on Swiss, German and US radio; Founder American Music Week (concert series in Germany). *Compositions include:* Variations for flute and harpsichord 1984, Assemblages for soprano, flute, trombone, percussion and piano 1977, three-act ballet, Acteon for large orchestra 1983, Rapunzel (chamber opera) 1988, Remember the Earth Whose Skin You Are (oratorio) 1994.

WARLAND, Dale, DMA; American composer and conductor; b. 14 April 1932, Fort Dodge, Ia. *Education:* St Olaf Coll., Northfield, Minn., Univ. of Minnesota, Univ. of Southern California. *Career:* fmrly Dir of choral music, Humboldt State Coll., Arcata, Calif. and Keuka Coll., New York; Prof. of Music and Dir of Choral Activities, Macalester Coll., St Paul, Minn. 1967–85; f. The Dale Warland Singers 1972, commissioned 270 choral works and presented over 400 concerts –2004; collaborated with conductors and composers including Robert Shaw, Edo de Waart, Leonard Slatkin, Stanislaw Skrowaczewski, Sir Neville Marriner, Kryzstof Penderecki, Roger Norrington, James Conlon, Hugh Wolff and Bobby McFerrin; guest conductor with Swedish Radio Choir, Danish Radio Choir, Mormon Tabernacle Choir, Estonian Philharmonic Chamber Choir, Opus 7 Vocal Ensemble, Utah Chamber Artists, Vocal Arts Ensemble, Choral Arts Soc. of Philadelphia, Rochester Choral Arts and Israel's Cameran Singers; fmr Co-chair, choral and recording panels of Nat. Endowment for the Arts. *Compositions:* Never Seek to Tell Thy Love for TBB soli, SATB, Boyo Balu for SATB, There Will Be Rest for SATB, harp, flute, Simple Gifts for SATB, guitar/harp, flute, So Thin a Veil for SATB, piano, Pied Beauty for SATB, A Somerset Carol for SATB, harp/guitar, Wexford Carol for SATB, flute, Coventry Carol for SATB, Catalonian Carol for SATB, oboe, O Little Town of Bethlehem for SATB, Huran Carol for SATB, oboe, What Child is This? for SATB, flute, harp, What is This Fragrance? for SATB, oboe, Of the Father's Love Begotten for SATB. *Recordings include:* with Dale Warland Singers: Lux Aurumque, Reincarnations, Harvest Home, Cathedral Classics, A Rose In Winter, Argento: Walden Pond, Blue Wheat, Rachmaninoff Vespers, Bernstein & Britten, December Stillness. *Honours:* Hon. doctorates from Macalester Coll., Univ. of Minnesota 2004; Michael Korn Founder's Award 1995, special award from Chorus America and ASCAP for pioneering vision, leadership and commitment to commissioning and performing new choral works 2002, Sally Irvine Ordway Award for Vision 2003, ASCAP Victor Herbert Award 2003, Univ. of S Florida Distinguished Master Artist Award 2004, American Composers Forum Champion of New Music Award from the 2005, Choral Arts Society of Philadelphia Individual Leadership in Choral Music Award 2006. *E-mail:* dharrer@dalewarland.com (office). *Website:* www.dalewarland.com (office).

WARNER, Deborah, CBE; British theatre and opera director; b. 12 May 1959, Oxford; d. of Ruth Warner and Roger Warner. *Education:* Sidcot School, Avon, St Clare's, Oxford, Cen. School of Speech and Drama. *Career:* Founder and Artistic Dir Kick Theatre Co 1980–86; Resident Dir RSC 1987–89; Assoc. Dir Royal Nat. Theatre 1989–98; Assoc. Dir Abbey Theatre, Dublin 2000; has also staged productions at ENO Glyndebourne Festival Opera, Royal Opera House, Opera North, London Proms, La Scala, and has staged productions for

Fitzroy Productions, Odeon Theatre, Chaillot and Bobigny Theatre, Paris, Salzburg Festival, LIFT and Perth Int. Arts Festival, Lincoln Center Festival, New York, Venice Festival, Bavarian State Opera; Dir Fitzroy Productions. *Productions include:* Titus Andronicus (RSC), King John (RSC), Electra (RSC), Hedda Gabler (Abbey Theatre, Dublin/West End), The Good Person of Sichuan (Royal Nat. Theatre), King Lear (Royal Nat. Theatre), Richard II (Royal Nat. Theatre), The Powerbook (Royal Nat. Theatre), The Waste Land (Fitzroy Productions), Medea (Abbey Theatre/West End/Broadway), The St Pancras Project (LIFT), The Tower Project (LIFT) The Angel Project (Perth Int. Arts Festival and Lincoln Center Festival), Readings (Fitzroy Productions); Tchaikovsky's Eugene Onegin, Metropolitan Opera, New York 2013–14, Fidelio, La Scala, Milan 2015, Between Worlds (ENO, Barbican) 2015. *Films:* The Waste Land 1996, The Last September 1999. *Television includes:* Richard II (BBC), Hedda Gabler (BBC), Don Giovanni (Channel 4). *Honours:* Chevalier, Ordre des Arts et des Lettres 2000; Evening Standard Award 1988, 1998, 2002, Laurence Olivier Award 1989, 1992, New York Drama Desk Award 1997, South Bank Arts Award 1998, OBIE Award 2003. *Website:* www.askonasholt.co.uk/artists/directors/deborah-warner.

WARNER, Keith; British stage director; b. 6 Dec. 1956, London. *Education:* Univ. of Bristol, studied in London and at Bayreuth. *Career:* early work in fringe theatre; staff producer, ENO 1981–, Assoc. Dir 1984–89, staging Rossini's Moïse, Dargomizhsky's Stone Guest, Pacific Overtures, Werther; Co-producer (with David Pountney) A Midsummer Marriage, The Flying Dutchman and The Queen of Spades; Assoc. Dir Scottish Opera, with Carmen, Tosca, Werther, Die Zauberflöte and Iolanthe; Handel's Flavio at Florence and Batignano; further productions of Trovatore at Dortmund, Norma in Bielefeld and Un Ballo in Maschera with the Canadian Opera Co.; Madama Butterfly and Casken's Golem at Omaha, The Queen of Spades in Madrid, Tannhäuser for the Brighton Festival, My Fair Lady for Houston; production of Janáček's The Makropulos Case in Oslo 1992; Dir and Designer Der fliegende Holländer in Minneapolis, transferring to Omaha and Portland, Weill's Lost in the Stars for the Brighton Festival; Head of Productions, Omaha Fall Opera and the Omaha festival from 1992 (Eugene Onegin and Weisgall's Gardens of Adonis 1992); Dir Tosca for ENO 1994, Pagliacci and Cavalleria Rusticana at Berlin Staatsoper, From the House of the Dead for Opéra du Rhin and Carmen at Turin 1996, Carmen for Minnesota Opera and La Finta Giardiniera for Opera Zuid 1997, The Turn of the Screw at La Monnaie, Brussels 1998, Der fliegende Holländer for Opera Pacific, Il Trittico for Spoleto Festival, USA and Lohengrin for Bayreuth Festival 1999; season 2000 with Der fliegende Holländer for de Vlaamse Opera, The Cunning Little Vixen for Portland Opera, Manon Lescaut for ENO, Lohengrin for Bayreuth Festival and God's Liar for La Monnaie, Brussels (for which he also wrote the libretto), Wagner's Ring at Covent Garden 2005, Don Giovanni for Royal Danish Theatre 2006, Wozzeck, Royal Danish Theatre 2008; Artistic Dir, Royal Danish Opera July 2010–Jan. 2011. *Address:* The Royal Danish Theatre, Postbox 2185, 1017 Copenhagen, Denmark (office). *Telephone:* 33-69-69-33 (office). *E-mail:* admin@kglteater.dk (office). *Website:* www.kglteater.dk.

WARRACK, John, MA, DLitt, ARCM; British musicologist; b. 9 Feb. 1928, London; s. of Guy Warrack; m. Lucy Beckett 1970; four s. *Education:* Winchester Coll., Royal Coll. of Music, London. *Career:* freelance oboist 1951–54; Asst Music Critic, Daily Telegraph 1954–61; Chief Music Critic, Sunday Telegraph 1961–72; Dir Leeds Musical Festival 1977–83; Univ. Lecturer in Music and Fellow, St Hugh's Coll. Oxford 1984–93; mem. Royal Musical Asscn. *Publications include:* Concise Oxford Dictionary of Opera 1964, Carl Maria von Weber 1968, Tchaikovsky Symphonies and Concertos 1969, Tchaikovsky 1973, Tchaikovsky Ballet Music 1979, Carl Maria von Weber: Writings on Music (ed.) 1981, Oxford Dictionary of Opera 1992 (concise version 1996), Richard Wagner: Die Meistersinger von Nürnberg 1994; contrib. to Musical Times, Music and Letters, Opera, Gramophone, International Record Review, opera trans, articles in the New Grove Dictionary of Music and Musicians 1980. *Honours:* Royal Coll. of Music Colles Prize 1951. *Address:* Beck House, Rievaulx, Helmsley, York, YO62 5LB, England (home). *Telephone:* (1439) 798322 (home). *E-mail:* warrack@aelred.demon.co.uk.

WARREN, Raymond Henry Charles, MA, MusD (Cantab.); British composer and academic; b. 7 Nov. 1928, Weston-super-Mare; m. Roberta Smith 1953; three s. one d. *Education:* Corpus Christi Coll., Cambridge with Robin Orr, studied with Michael Tippett and Lennox Berkeley. *Career:* teacher, Queen's Univ. of Belfast 1955–66, Prof. of Composition 1966–72; Prof. of Music, Univ. of Bristol 1972–94; mem. ISM, BASCA. *Compositions:* incidental music for 11 plays by W. B. Yeats: The Lady of Ephesus (chamber opera) 1959, Finn and the Black Hag (children's opera) 1959, Graduation Ode (three-act opera) 1963; church operas: Let my People Go 1972, St Patrick 1979, In the Beginning 1982; The Passion (oratorio) 1962, Violin Concerto 1966, Three Symphonies 1965, 1969, 1996, Three String Quartets 1965, 1975, 1977, Oratorio Continuing Cities 1989, Violin Sonata 1993; song cycles: The Pity of Love (Yeats) 1965, Songs of Old Age (Yeats) 1968, In My Childhood (MacNeice) 1998, Ballet shoes (ballet) 2001, Two Wind Quintets 2003, The Death of Orpheus (cantata) 2006, The Coming (R.Williams) 2009, Variations for Orchestra on a Gloucester Chime 2012, At the Hawk's Well (Yeats) (cantata) 2012, Gwent Carnival: Overture for Orchestra 2013, Dancing in the Wind (cantata) 2013. *Publication:* Opera Workshop 1995. *Address:* 4 Contemporis Court, Merchants Road, Bristol, BS8 4HB, England (home).

WARREN-GREEN, Christopher; British violinist and educator; b. 30 July 1955, Cheltenham, England. *Education:* Royal Acad. of Music. *Career:* debut

solo in Berlin; London 1984; Leader, BBC National Orchestra of Wales 1977, Philharmonia Orchestra 1980, Academy of St Martin-in-the-Fields 1985; Music Dir and Principal Conductor, London Chamber Orchestra 1988–2010; Chief Conductor, Joenkoeping Sinfonietta 1998–2001, Nordic Chamber Orchestra 1998–2005; Principal Conductor, Camerata Orchestra of the Megaron, Athens 2004–; Music Dir, Charlotte Symphony Orchestra, USA 2010–; Prof., Royal Acad. of Music 1985; television presenter, BBC Music and Arts. *Recordings:* Mozart Violin concerti, Vivaldi Four Seasons, Haydn Concerti (with Philharmonia), Mendelssohn Concerto, Tchaikovsky. *Honours:* Hon. ARAM 1983. *Current Management:* Harrison Parrott, 5–6 Albion Court, Albion Place, :London W6 0QT, England. *Telephone:* (20) 7229-9166. *E-mail:* info@harrisonparrott.co.uk. *Website:* www.harrisonparrott.com.

WASCHINSKI, Jörg; German singer (countertenor); b. 1966, Berlin. *Education:* Berlin Music College, masterclasses with Barbara Schlick and Peter Schreier. *Career:* many appearances in Germany and elsewhere in Europe in the baroque music repertory; operas by Jommelli at Stuttgart. *Recordings include:* title role in Jommelli's Il Vologeso. *Honours:* Second Prize, International J H Schmetzer Competition for Baroque Music, Melk, 1996; Prize of the German State Association at the State Singing Competition, Berlin. *Current Management:* Agentur Sigrid Rostock, Eugen-Schönhaar-Strasse 1, 10407 Berlin, Germany. *Telephone:* (30) 4257514. *Fax:* (30) 4239136. *E-mail:* sigridrostock@web.de.

WASFI, Karim; Iraqi cellist and conductor; *Director, Iraqi National Symphony Orchestra*; b. 1972, Cairo, Egypt; m. Nivan Saada (divorced). *Education:* Music and Ballet School, Baghdad, Indiana Univ., Cairo Univ., Boston Univ. *Career:* began learning cello aged six; joined Iraqi Nat. Symphony Orchestra (INSO) 1986, becoming Prin. Cellist, also Dir 2004–; several posts as Asst Prin. Cellist in USA including Bangor and Portland, Me, Columbus, OH and Evansville, Ind.; Prin. Cellist with several ensembles, including Cairo Symphony Orchestra and Egyptian Chamber Group 1993–96; fmr Instructor, Cairo Acad. of Arts, Music and Ballet School of Baghdad, Indiana Univ. School of Music; Head, British Council in Baghdad 2003–04; mem. Musicians for Harmony; f. Bridges Quartet. *Address:* c/o Musicians for Harmony, 345 E. 93rd Street, Suite 12B, New York, NY 10128, USA (office); c/o Attitudes Society of Art & Culture, Al-Wazeereia, Baghdad, Iraq (office). *Telephone:* (7901) 789622 (office). *E-mail:* info@artiniraq.org (office); karimwasfi@yahoo.com (office).

WASS, Ashley, ARAM; British pianist; b. Skegness. *Education:* Chetham's Music School, Royal Acad. of Music. *Career:* recitals at major UK concert halls and in Amsterdam, Lisbon, Istanbul, Chicago, Mexico City; concerto performances include Beethoven and Brahms with the Philharmonia, Mendelssohn with Orchestre Nat. de Lille, Mozart with Vienna Chamber Orchestra at Vienna Konzerthaus and Brucknerhaus, Linz; has worked with conductors including Sir Simon Rattle, Osmo Vänskä, Ilan Volkov, Vassily Sinaisky, Martyn Brabbins and orchestras such as CBSO, BBC Symphony Orchestra, London Mozart Players, BBC Scottish Symphony Orchestra, BBC Philharmonic, BBC Concert Orchestra, and at several festivals; debuts in Germany, France, Finland, Sweden, Portugal, Israel, Germany, Switzerland, USA and Cuba; also chamber music; founder mem. Denali Trio 2004–; Artistic Dir Lincolnshire Int. Chamber Music Festival. *Recordings include:* César Franck, Beethoven 3rd Piano Concerto, Poulenc Piano Concerto, In Tune With The Piano: Chopin, piano music of Arnold Bax, piano works of Elgar and Bridge, Bax violin sonatas (with Laurence Jackson). *Honours:* First Prize, World Piano Competition 1997. *Current Management:* Upbeat Classical Management, PO Box 479, Uxbridge, UB8 2ZH, England. *Telephone:* (1895) 259441. *Fax:* (1895) 259341. *E-mail:* enquiry@upbeatclassical.co.uk. *Website:* www .upbeatclassical.co.uk; www.ashleywass.com.

WASSILJEV, Nikolai; Russian singer (tenor); b. 1957, Leningrad. *Education:* studied in Leningrad. *Career:* sang with the Bolshoi Opera from 1982, with guest appearances at La Scala Milan and the Metropolitan Opera, New York; roles have included Alfredo, Cavaradossi, Turiddu, Lensky, Prince Gvidon in Rimsky's Tale of Tsar Saltan, Vladimir in Prince Igor and Dimitri in Boris Godunov; sang in Mlada at New York, 1991. *Honours:* prizewinner Glinka Competition 1984, Voci Verdiane at Busseto 1986.

WATERMAN, David Allen Woodrow, MA, PhD; British cellist, teacher and writer; *Cellist, Endellion Quartet*; b. 24 March 1950, Leeds, Yorks. *Education:* Trinity Coll., Cambridge (Research Scholar), studied cello/music with Martin Lovett, William Pleeth, Jane Cowan and Sándor Végh. *Career:* cellist and Founding mem. Endellion Quartet 1979–; resident at Univ. of Cambridge 1992–, Royal Northern Coll. of Music 2001–10, Guildhall School of Music and Drama 2011–; has coached cello, quartet and chamber music at Int. Musicians' Seminar, Prussia Cove, Cornwall 1991–, for Chamber Studio at Kings Place London; Co-Dir Rathbone-Dickson Course, Westonbirt, Glos. 1995–2004; has also taught at Menuhin School, RAM, Guildhall School of Music and Drama, Bloomington, Ind. and MIT, USA and in Portugal, Belgium, Switzerland, Spain, Canada, Mexico, Hong Kong, China and Korea; appearances at Kennedy Center, Washington, DC, Ambassadors Auditorium, Los Angeles, Carnegie Hall, Metropolitan Museum of Art, Frick Gallery and The Y in New York, many times at London, Bath Festival, Concertgebouw, Amsterdam, Zurich Tonhalle and Lucerne and Gstaad Festivals, Switzerland, Spoleto and Fiesole Festivals, South Bank Festival, City of London Festival, Aldeburgh Festival; tours of USA, Australia, New Zealand, India and most major European centres and radio stations, S Africa, S America and Western

Europe, with Endellion Quartet; has also performed chamber music with numerous other musicians, including Sir Thomas Allen, fmr mems of Amadeus Quartet, Joshua Bell, William Bennett, Michael Collins, the Chilingirian, Elias and Belcea Quartets, Imogen Cooper, Jeremy Denk, Isabelle Faust, Julia Fischer, Peter Frankl, Ivry Gitlis, Philippe Graffin, Lukacs Hagen, Marc-Andre Hamelin, Erich Hobarth, Steven Isserlis, Stephen Kovacevich, Pekka Kuusisto, Gabor Takacs-Nagy, Mitsuko Uchida, Sándor Végh and Tabea Zimmerman. *Films:* interviewed about Beethoven in Phil Grabsky's In Search of Beethoven and In Search of Haydn. *Recordings include:* with the Endellion Quartet: John Foulds' Quartetto Intimo, complete Britten Chamber Music, Haydn, Mozart, Dvořák, Smetana, Bartók, Martinů, Walton, Schubert, Barber, Amy Beach, Tchaikovsky, Frank Bridge, and Thomas Adès's Arcadia, complete Beethoven quartets and quintets and rare fragments released to mark the Endellion's 30th Anniversary. *Publications include:* contrib. to European String Teachers' Association Magazine, American Record Guide, chapter on playing quartets for the Cambridge Companion to the String Quartet and articles in the Guardian, Strad Magazine, Philosophy in Cambridge, Quodlibet and other publs. *Honours:* (with Endellion Quartet) Royal Philharmonic Soc. Medal for Chamber Music 1996. *Current Management:* c/o Hazard Chase Ltd, 25 City Road, Cambridge, CB1 1DP, England. *Telephone:* (1223) 312400. *Fax:* (1223) 460827. *E-mail:* info@hazardchase.co.uk. *Website:* www.hazardchase.co.uk. *Address:* 27 Lancaster Grove, London, NW3 4EX, England (office). *E-mail:* info@ endellionquartet.com (office). *Website:* www.endellionquartet.com (office).

WATERMAN, Dame Fanny, DBE, DMus, FRCM; British pianist and piano teacher; b. 22 March 1920, Leeds, England; d. of Myer Waterman and Mary Waterman (née Behrmann); m. Geoffrey de Keyser 1944; two s. *Education:* Allerton High School, Leeds, Royal Coll. of Music with Tobias Matthay and Cyril Smith. *Career:* Co-founder (with Marion Harewood) Leeds Int. Pianoforte Competition 1961, Chair. and Artistic Dir 1963–2015 (retd); Vice-Pres. European Piano Teachers Asscn 1975; Trustee Edward Boyle Memorial Trust 1981; Gov. Harrogate Festival 1983; mem. Int. Juries, Vienna 1977, 1993, Terni (Italy) 1978, Munich 1979, 1986 and Leipzig (Germany) 1980, 1984, Calgary (Canada) 1982, Salt Lake City (USA) 1982, 1984, Viña del Mar (Chile) 1982, 1987, 1992, Maryland (USA) 1983, Cologne (Germany) 1983, 1986, Pretoria (S Africa) 1984, 1992, Santander (Spain) 1984, Rubinstein 1986, 1989, Moscow 1986, Vladigerov (Bulgaria) 1986, Lisbon 1987, 1991, CBC Toronto (Canada) 1989; Patron Shanghai Pudong Int. Conservatory of Music. *Television:* Piano Progress (series on ITV, Channel 4). *Publications:* Piano Tutors (series, with Marion Harewood) 1967–, Fanny Waterman on Piano Playing and Performing 1983, Young Violinists Repertoire (series, with Paul de Keyser) 1984, Music Lovers' Diary 1984–86, Merry Christmas Carols 1986, Christmas Carol Time 1986, Nursery Rhyme Time 1987, Piano for Pleasure (books 1–2) 1988, Me and My Piano: Repertoire and Duets (books 1–2) 1988, Animal Magic 1989, Piano Competition: the story of Leeds (jtly) 1990. *Honours:* Hon. Vice-Pres. Harrogate Royal Hall Restoration, Freeman of the City of Leeds 2004; Hon. MA (Leeds) 1966, Hon. MusDoc (Leeds) 1992, (Leeds Metropolitan) 2006, Hon. DUniv (York) 1995. *Address:* c/o Leeds International Pianoforte Competition, Piano Competition Office, University of Leeds, Leeds, LS2 9JT, England. *Website:* www.leedspiano.com.

WATERMAN, Ruth Anna; British violinist; b. 14 Feb. 1947, Harrogate, Yorkshire, England. *Education:* Juilliard School, New York and Royal Manchester Coll. of Music. *Career:* recitals and concerts throughout Europe and USA, radio and television, lecture-recitals, lecturing, coaching; concerts include Bath Festival with Yehudi Menuhin as Conductor 1966; televised Prom 1966; New York recital debut, Int. Artists series, Carnegie Hall 1974; concertos with London Symphony, BBC Symphony, BBC Scottish, English Chamber, Orpheus Chamber Orchestra and others; festivals include Aldeburgh, Montreux; BBC Radio 3, complete Bach Sonatas 1992; lecture-recitals at Wigmore Hall, South Bank, Great Performers at Lincoln Center, New York 2000, Avery Fisher Hall, New York 1997; recital at Hermitage Museum, St Petersburg 2001; Prof., Queens Coll., CUNY 1975–92; faculty mem., New York Univ., Royal Acad. of Music; masterclasses and lectures at Univ. of Oxford 1994, Juilliard School 2000, Royal Northern Coll. of Music, New England Conservatory, Menuhin School, St Petersburg Conservatoire; mem. ISM. *Recordings:* Bach Brandenburg Concertos, 1985; Bach Sonatas with Keyboard, 1997. *Publications:* contrib. articles on interpretation and reviews to The Strad, BBC Music Magazine. *Honours:* Gramophone Critic's Choice 1997; Fellow, George Bell Inst. *E-mail:* amanda.smith@ruthwaterman.com. *Website:* www.ruthwaterman.com.

WATERS, Rosalind; British singer (soprano); b. 1965, Somerset. *Education:* Welsh College of Music and Drama, Cardiff and Royal College of Music. *Career:* appearances with Musicians of the Globe, under Philip Pickett, the Gabrieli Consort, Corydon Singers and the Monteverdi Choir (tours of Europe); Handel's Saul in France, Mozart's Requiem in Madrid and Gubaidulina's The Canticle of the Sun in London, with Mstislav Rostropovich; further engagements at the Purcell Room and QEH, London, and at the Strasbourg Festival; Elizabethan Lute Songs in Tel-Aviv; tour of Spain, France and Turkey with Florilegium. *Recordings:* albums with the New London Consort and the Philharmonia Orchestra. *E-mail:* ros_waters@ hotmail.com.

WATERS, Susannah; British writer, director and fmr singer (soprano); b. 1965, Kent, England. *Education:* Bennington College, USA, Guildhall School of Music and Drama, London. *Career:* debut as Belinda, in Dido and Aeneas at

Symphony Place, New York 1986; The Princess in L'Enfant et les Sortilèges at 1989 Aldeburgh Festival and Louise in German production of Henze's The English Cat; season 1990–91 as Nannetta in Falstaff, Scottish Opera, Papagena at Glyndebourne, Philine in Thomas' Mignon at the Vienna Volksoper and Cherubino for Opera Factory, London; many recital and oratorio appearances; season 1991–92 as Despina in Così fan tutte, Zerlina in Don Giovanni for Opera Factory, London; Martha, Sarasota Opera, USA; 1st Niece, in Peter Grimes for Glyndebourne Festival Opera; Dorlinda, in Orlando for Musica nel Chiostro, Italy; season 1992–93 as Gilda in Rigoletto for Opera Northern Ireland, Pamina in The Magic Flute, Scottish Opera, Susanna in The Marriage of Figaro for Opera Factory, Cunégonde in Candide at Musica nel Chiostro; season 1993–94 as Fairy Godmother, in Cendrillon and Dalinda, in Ariodante, WNO, Blonde, in Abduction from the Seraglio, for Sante Fe Opera; season 1994–95 as Atlanta, in Xerxes, Los Angeles Music Center Opera, Cupidon and Nereid, in King Arthur at Théâtre du Châtelet, Paris and Covent Garden; Despina, WNO; Belinda for Royal Opera of Stockholm at Drottningholm; Elizabeth, in Elegy for Young Lovers at Lausanne and on South Bank, London 1997; sang Salome in Stradella's San Giovanni Battista, Batignano 1996; New York City Opera and Los Angeles 1997, as Atlanta in Serse and Countess in Fedora; retired from singing 2002; directed opera The Finnish Prisoner 2007, Imago 2013, Down by the Greenwood Side 2014; f. The Paddock (production co.) 2004, currently Artistic Dir; Assoc. Tutor in Creative Writing, Univ. of Sussex 2005–12; runs an Advanced Writing Workshop. *Recordings include:* as Evato in King Arthur (with William Christie and Les Arts Florissants). *Publications include:* Long Gone Anybody 2004, Cold Comfort 2006. *Website:* www.susannahwaters.com.

WATERS, Willie Anthony; American conductor; b. 1952, Miami, FL. *Education:* Univ. of Miami. *Career:* Asst Conductor, Memphis Opera 1973–75; Music Asst to Kurt Herbert Adler at San Francisco Opera 1975–79; Music Dir, San Antonio Festival 1983–84; Artistic Dir, Greater Miami Opera, conducting La Gioconda, L'Italiana in Algeri, Madama Butterfly, Ernani 1984–85, Of Mice and Men by Floyd, Rigoletto, Cav and Pag 1985–86, Salome, La Traviata, Hamlet, Aida 1986–87, Bellini's Bianca e Falliero, Tosca, Otello 1987–88, Le nozze di Figaro, Die Walküre, La Forza del Destino 1988–89, I Vespri Siciliani, Idomeneo, Elektra 1989–90, Così fan tutte and Falstaff 1990–91; has also worked with the Detroit Symphony Orchestra, Fort Worth Opera, Miami City Ballet, Florida Symphony Orchestra, Cincinnati, Chautaqua and Connecticut Opera Cos, Australian Opera Sydney, Cologne Opera, Sudwestfunk Orchestra and Essen Philharmonic debuts 1990–91; season 1991–93 conducting Aida with Connecticut Opera, Greater Miami Opera, SWF Sinfonieorchester, Baden-Baden, Florida Philharmonic Orchestra, and Macbeth with Charlotte Opera; led an all-black Bohème at Cape Town 1997–98.

WATKIN, David Evan, BA; British cellist and conductor; *Principal Cello, Scottish Chamber Orchestra*; b. 8 May 1965, Crowthorne, Berks., England; s. of Kenneth and Christine Watkin; m. Sara nee Burton; two s. *Education:* studied with Sharon McKinley, Wells Cathedral School with Margaret Moncrieff and Amaryllis Fleming, St Catharine's Coll., Cambridge with William Pleeth and Kenneth Bowen, conducting with Jorma Panula and Joseph Swensen. *Career:* St John's Smith Square debut recital 1989; Lincoln Centre, New York debut 1999; Prin. Cello, Orchestre Révolutionnaire et Romantique, English Baroque Soloists, Orchestra of the Age of the Enlightenment, Academy of Ancient Music, Philharmonia Orchestra 2002–06, Scottish Chamber Orchestra 2006–; revived realization of figured bass on the cello; conducted Royal Scottish Nat. Orchestra, Scottish Chamber Orchestra, Orchestra of the Royal Conservatoire of Scotland, RAM, Guildhall School, Meadows Chamber Orchestra; mem. Eroica Quartet 1999–; has taught at Royal Northern Coll. of Music, Guildhall School of Music and Drama, Royal Acad. of Music, Trinity Coll. of Music, Welsh Coll. of Music and Drama, Royal Scottish Acad. of Music and Drama; Visiting Prof., Royal Conservatoire of Scotland; Asst Conductor, Glyndebourne Festival Opera 2014. *Recordings include:* Farewell to Hirta (cello sonata by Francis Pott), Vivaldi's Cello Sonatas (with King's Consort), Beethoven's Cello Sonatas, Geminiani Sonata, Mozart Clemenza di Tito, Cosí fan tutte, Corelli's Op. 5 Violin Sonatas (with Trio Veracini, Andrew Manze), Handel's Concerti Grossi, Schubert Quintet (with Tokyo Quartet), JS Bach Cello Suites (Gramophone Award for Best Baroque Instrumental Recording 2015) 2014. *Publications:* article on the Beethoven Cello Sonatas, in Performing Beethoven, Corelli's Op. 5 in Early Music 1996, articles and book reviews in The Strad. *Honours:* Bulgin Medal, Nat. Youth Orchestra, Great Britain 1982. *Current Management:* c/o Logan Arts Management, 15 Crawford Road, Milngavie, Glasgow, G62 7LE, Scotland. *Telephone:* (141) 404-7444. *E-mail:* andrewlogan@ loganartsmanagement.com. *Website:* www.loganartsmanagement.com/david -watkin.html; www.eroicaquartet.net; www.davidwatkin.com.

WATKINS, Glenn, BA, DipMus, MMus, PhD; American musicologist; b. 30 May 1927, McPherson, KS. *Education:* Univ. of Michigan, Univ. of Rochester, American Conservatory, Fontainebleau. *Publications:* Gesualdo Complete Works (co-ed.) 1959–66, Gesualdo: The Man and his Music 1973, S. D'India Complete Works (co-ed.) 1980–, Soundings Music in the 20th Century 1988, Pyramids at the Louvre 1994, Proof Through the Night: Music and the Great War 2003, The Gesualdo Hex: Music, Myth and Memory 2010. *Honours:* Fulbright, England 1953–54, Sr Fellow Nat. Endowment for the Humanities 1976–77; Premio Internazionale Carlo Gesualdo 2005; hon. mem. American

Musicological Soc. 2005. *Address:* 1336 Glendaloch Circle, Ann Arbor, MI 48104, USA (home).

WATKINS, Huw, MA, MMus; British composer, pianist and academic; *Professor of Composition, Royal Academy of Music;* b. 13 July 1976, Pontypool, Wales. *Education:* Chetham's School of Music, studied piano with Peter Lawson, composition with Robin Holloway, Alexander Goehr and Julian Anderson at Univ. of Cambridge and Royal Coll. of Music. *Career:* commissions/works performed by ensembles including LSO (to mark centenary), Nat. Orchestra of Wales, Cincinnati Chamber Orchestra, Nash Ensemble, Mark Padmore, Petersen Quartet, Florestan Trio; performed at festivals including Cheltenham, Presteigne (featured composer) and Gstaad, also at Wigmore Hall and Purcell Room Southbank Centre, London, La Monnaie, Brussels; Double Concerto for viola, cello and orchestra premiered at BBC Proms 2005, Violin Concerto performed by Alina Ibragimova BBC Proms 2010; as pianist, performed concertos with BBC Symphony Orchestra, London Sinfonietta and Orchestra of the Swan; premieres of works by Alexander Goehr, Peter Maxwell Davies, John Woolrich and Mark-Anthony Turnage; regular radio broadcasts as soloist and with artists such as Alina Ibragimova, Daniel Hope, Nicholas Daniel and Alexandra Wood; pianist, Britten Sinfonia; Prof. of Composition, RAM 2003–; Jerwood Assoc. Composer, Music Theatre Wales 2005; Composer-in-Residence, Heimbach and Nurnberg Festivals 2011; Composer-in-the-House, Orchestra of the Swan 2012–14; Composer-in-Residence, Leicester Festival 2013. *Compositions include:* orchestral: Sonata for Cello and 8 Instruments 1999, Sinfonietta 2000, Nocturne for horn and chamber orchestra 2001, Piano Concerto 2002, London Concerto, Anthem for orchestra 2005, Double Concerto for viola, cello and orchestra 2005, Three Welsh Songs for strings 2008–09, Concertino for violin and string orchestra 2010–11,Violin Concerto, Little Symphony for Strings 2013, Flute Concerto 2014; chamber: Cello Sonata 2000, Four Spencer Pieces for piano 2001, Gig for ensemble 2004, Rondo for ensemble, Pièce d'orgue 2005, Partita for violin 2006, Suite for harp 2006, Fantasy for viola, Horn Trio 2008, Piano Trio, Four Inventions for piano, Miniatures for viola and piano 2009, Capriccio for flute and piano 2010, Speak Seven Seas for clarinet, viola and piano 2011, Blue Shadows Fall for cello and piano 2012–13, Toccata for organ, Out of the Stillness for cor anglais and strings 2012, Callisto for solo oboe, String Quartet 2013; vocal: Psalms 11 & 22, In my craft or sullen art for tenor and string quartet 2007, Three Auden Songs for tenor and piano 2008, Five Larkin Songs for soprano and piano (British Composer Award vocal category 2011) 2009, Crime Fiction, chamber opera 2008, In the Locked Room, chamber opera 2011, The Phoenix and the Turtle for choir 2014, Remember for soprano and string orchestra 2014. *Address:* Royal Academy of Music, Marylebone Road, London, NW1 5HT, England (office). *Telephone:* (20) 7873-7373 (office). *Fax:* (20) 7873-7374 (office). *Website:* www.ram.ac.uk (office).

WATKINS, Michael Blake; British composer; b. 4 May 1948, Ilford, Essex; m. Tessa Marion Fryer 1975; two d. *Education:* studied guitar and lute with Michael Jessett, composition with Elisabeth Lutyens and Richard Rodney Bennett. *Career:* Fellow in TV Composition, LWT 1981–83. *Compositions include:* orchestral works: Clouds and Eclipses for guitar and strings 1973, Aubade for brass band 1973, Horn Concerto 1974, Violin Concerto 1977, Etalage for symphony orchestra 1979, Trumpet Concerto 1988, Cello Concerto 1992, Viola Concerto 1998; chamber works: Solus for guitar solo 1975, The Wings of Night for solo violin 1975, All That We Read in Their Smiles for tenor, horn and piano 1977, The Spirit of the Universe for soprano and ensemble 1978, The Spirit of the Earth for guitar solo 1978, String Quartet 1979, The Magic Shadow Show for cello and ensemble 1980, Sinfonietta for 12 instruments 1982, Clarinet Quintet 1984, Somnial for guitar solo 1988, La Mort de l'aigle for solo trumpet 1993, Piano Quintet 1995, The River of Time for guitar trio 1996, Viola Concerto 1998. *Recordings include:* Trumpet Concerto (with Håkan Hardenberger and the BBC Philharmonic Orchestra conducted by Elgar Howarth), La Mort de l'aigle (with trumpet played by Håkan Hardenberger), The River of Time (with Zagreb Guitar Trio). *Honours:* Menuhin Prize 1975, Carl Flesch Composition Prize 1976, Guinness Prize 1978. *Current Management:* c/o Novello Publishing Ltd, 8–9 Frith Street, London, W1D 3JB, England. *Telephone:* (20) 7434-0066. *Fax:* (20) 7287-6329. *E-mail:* michaelblakewatkins@yahoo.co.uk (office).

WATKINS, Paul; British cellist and conductor; *Artistic Director, Great Lakes Chamber Music Festival;* b. 4 Jan. 1970, South Wales. *Education:* Yehudi Menuhin School, St Catharine's Coll., Cambridge. *Career:* Prin. Cellist, BBC Symphony Orchestra 1990–97; mem. Nash Ensemble 1997–2013; Assoc. Conductor, English Chamber Orchestra 2007–09, Prin. Guest Conductor and Music Dir 2009–14; Prin. Guest Conductor, Ulster Orchestra 2009–12; Artistic Dir Great Lakes Chamber Music Festival 2014–; performs cello regularly with major UK orchestras; six solo performances at BBC Proms, including Elgar's Cello Concerto at First Night of the Proms 2007; solo and duo recitals at Wigmore Hall, City of London Festival, South Bank Centre, Bridgewater Hall, Manchester and Queens Hall, Edinburgh; has conducted all leading British orchestras including London Symphony, London Philharmonic and Philharmonia orchestras, and works regularly with orchestras abroad, including Royal Flemish Philharmonic, Ensemble Orchestral de Paris, Norwegian Radio Orchestra, Queensland Orchestra and Tokyo Metropolitan Symphony Orchestra; mem. Emerson String Quartet 2013–. *Honours:* winner, Strings Section, BBC Young Musician of the Year 1988, winner, Leeds Conductors' Competition 2002. *Current Management:* c/o Thomas Walton, IMG Artists London, The Light Box, 111 Power Road, London, W4 5PY,

England. *Telephone:* (20) 7957-5800. *E-mail:* twalton@imgartists.com. *Address:* Great Lakes Chamber Music Festival, 24901 Northwestern Highway, Suite 312, Southfield, MI 48075, USA (office). *Telephone:* (248) 559-2097 (office). *Website:* greatlakeschambermusic.org (office).

WATKINS, Richard, FRAM; British horn player; *Dennis Brain Chair of Horn Playing, Royal Academy of Music. Career:* Principal Horn, Philharmonia Orchestra 1985–1996; as soloist and chamber musician has performed at major venues in UK, Europe and USA; has premiered concertos by Maxwell Davies, Osborne, Lindberg, Muldowney, Lefanu, and Colin and David Matthews; mem. Nash Ensemble; Founder mem. London Winds; holds Dennis Brain Chair of Horn Playing, Royal Acad. of Music; Visiting Prof. Royal Coll. of Music. *Recordings include:* Horn Concerts by Mozart, Malcolm Arnold, Glière and Ethel Smyth, Mozart's Sinfonia Concertante, Poulenc's Chamber Music for Horn. *Current Management:* Christa Phelps Artist Management, 7 Merchant House, 184–186 Sutherland Avenue, London, W9 1HR, England. *Telephone:* (20) 7286-7134. *Fax:* (20) 7286-8499. *E-mail:* info@christaphelps.com. *Website:* freespace.virgin.net/christa.phelps/watkins.htm. *Address:* Department of Brass, Royal Academy of Music, Marylebone Road, London, NW1 5HT, England (office). *Telephone:* (20) 7873-7320 (office). *E-mail:* brass@ram.ac.uk (office). *Website:* www.ram.ac.uk (office).

WATKINS, Sara Van Horn, BMus; American oboist and conductor; b. 12 Oct. 1945, Chicago, IL; m. John Shirley Quirk 1981, one s. two d. *Education:* Oberlin Conservatory of Music, studied with Ray Still, Marc Lifschey, Marcel Moyse, fellowship student at Tanglewood Music Festival. *Career:* Principal Oboist, American Nat. Opera Co. 1967, Honolulu Symphony Orchestra 1969–73, Nat. Symphony Orchestra 1973–81; Prof. of Oboe, Univ. of Hawaii 1969–73, Catholic Univ. 1973–81, Oberlin Conservatory 1984; residency, Scottish Acad. of Music 1985; oboe soloist and conductor 1981–; oboe soloist at Aldeburgh, Sofia, Spoleto Festivals, Vienna, The Hague, Moscow, Leningrad, London, São Paulo, New York and other major US cities; conducting appearances in Glasgow, Cambridge, London QEH, Britten-Pears School, Snape Maltings, Paris, New York Glimmerglass Opera; mem. Musicians' Union of Chicago and London, Conductors' Guild USA. *Recordings:* albums: Britten Chamber Music with John Shirley-Quirk, Osian Ellis, Philip Ledger; Handel Cantatas, Arias and Sonatas with Yvonne Kenny, John Shirley-Quirk, Martin Isepp.

WATKINSON, Andrew; British violinist; b. 1955, England. *Career:* founder mem. and leader, Endellion String Quartet from 1979; many concerts in Amsterdam, Frankfurt, Paris, Munich, Rome and Salzburg; appeared at South Bank Haydn Festival 1990, the Wigmore Hall Beethoven Series and the Quartet Plus Series 1994; Quartet-in-Residence, Univ. of Cambridge from 1992; Residency at MIT, USA 1995. *Recordings include:* works by Haydn, Bartók, Dvořák, Walton, Smetana, Beethoven, Tchaikovsky, Schubert, Britten, Vaughan Williams, Barber. *Current Management:* Hazard Chase Ltd, 25 City Road, Cambridge, CB1 1DP, England. *Telephone:* (1223) 312400. *Fax:* (1223) 460827. *E-mail:* info@hazardchase.co.uk. *Website:* www.hazardchase.co.uk. *E-mail:* info@endellionquartet.com (office). *Website:* www.endellionquartet.com.

WATKINSON, Carolyn; British singer (mezzo-soprano); b. 19 March 1949, Preston, Lancashire, England. *Education:* Royal Manchester Coll. of Music, Muzieklyceum, The Hague, Netherlands. *Career:* early specialisation in Baroque music, and sang with Syntagma Musicum, Grande Ecurie de la Chambre du Roi, with Jean-Claude Malgoire and Gächinger Kantorei, under Helmuth Rilling; Sang Phèdre in Hippolyte et Aricie at Covent Garden and Versailles 1978, English Bach Festival; Nero in L'Incoronazione di Poppea with Netherlands Opera 1979; guest in Stuttgart as Rossini's Rosina and at Ludwigsburg as Mozart's Cherubino 1980; 1981 as Handel's Ariodante at La Scala, Milan; 1982 Edinburgh Festival, Ariodante; Glyndebourne Festival debut 1984, as Cherubino, returned as Cenerentola; Aix-en-Provence debut 1985, as the Messenger in Monteverdi's Orfeo; concerts include Mahler's 3rd and 8th Symphonies, conducted by Haitink, Das Lied von der Erde, and appearances with the Royal Liverpool Philharmonic, BBC Symphony, Scottish Chamber and Nat. Orchestras and the Philharmonia; sang with Boston Symphony at Tanglewood 1985; engagements in Paris, Vienna, San Francisco, Washington, DC, Madrid, Barcelona; toured Australia 1987, and appeared at Sydney Opera; sang in Gloucester Cathedral performance of St John Passion, shown by BBC television 1989; sang Nero in L'Incoronazione di Poppea at Montpellier 1989; Purcell's Dido conducted by John Eliot Gardiner at Salerno Cathedral 1990; Nero at the 1990 Innsbruck Festival. *Recordings:* Handel Messiah (Hogwood), Rinaldo and Xerxes; Solomon (Gardiner); Mozart Requiem and Bach B Minor Mass (Schreier) and St Matthew Passion; solo album recorded live at her debut, Wigmore Hall recital, London.

WATSON, Janice; British singer (soprano); b. 1964. *Education:* Guildhall School, studied with Johanna Peters. *Career:* concert repertory has included the Four Last Songs of Strauss, Stravinsky's Pulcinella, Les Nuits d'Eté by Berlioz, Mahler's 4th Symphony and Berio's Sinfonia (Barbican Hall, London); has sung the Brahms Requiem with Dulwich Choral Soc., Haydn's Nelson Mass and Seasons at the Usher Hall, Edinburgh; Bach's Magnificat, Christmas Oratorio and St Mark Passion on South Bank, Britten's Les Illuminations at Salisbury Cathedral; Elgar's The Spirit of England with the Hallé Orchestra; Messiah in St Alban's Cathedral and Beethoven's Missa Solemnis with the Chichester Singers; Hummel's E flat Mass and Schubert's Stabat Mater at the Queen Elizabeth Hall; Mendelssohn's Elijah with the

Bristol Bach Choir; further repertory includes Handel's Saul, Mendelssohn's Hymn of Praise (2nd Symphony), Vaughan Williams's Pastoral Symphony and Beethoven's Mass in C (Barcelona Palace of Music); recitals with the Songmakers' Almanac and in the crush bar at Covent Garden; opera engagements at Glyndebourne, in Monteverdi's L'Incoronazione di Poppea at the City of London Festival and Musetta in La Bohème at Covent Garden 1990; with WNO has sung Musetta, Fiordiligi, Micaela, Adèle in Le Comte Ory, Pamina and Rosalinde (Die Fledermaus); US and Canadian debuts in Messiah, conducted by Trevor Pinnock, 1990; Eugene Onegin for WNO and Lucia di Lammermoor, Daphne for San Francisco Opera and at Santa Fe 1996, Les Illuminations by Benjamin Britten at the Proms, Messiah at the Barbican with Richard Hickox; engaged as Pamina at Berlin Staatsoper and Arabella at San Francisco 1998; Beethoven's Choral Symphony with the London Symphony Orchestra, London Proms 1999; season 1999–2000 as Mozart's Elettra at Santa Fe, Micaela for Chicago Lyric Opera, Governess in The Turn of the Screw for ENO and Ellen Orford (in Peter Grimes) at Amsterdam; Mendelssohn's Elijah, London Proms 2002; Ellen Orford in Naples 2009; title role in Katya Kabanova, Orvieto 2010; Sylvia in Zanetto, Opera Holland Park 2012. *Recordings:* Poulenc, Gloria/Stabat Mater 1995, Britten, Peter Grimes 1996, Lehmann, Bird Songs 2004, Weill, Royal Palace 2004, Janacek, Jenufa 2004, Orff, Carmina Burana 2005, Vaughan Williams, Hodie 2007, Mozart, Cosi fan tutte 2008, Britten, Owen Wingrave 2008, Verdi, Don Carlos 2009, Sullivan, Ivanhoe 2010. *Address:* Chandos Records Ltd, Chandos House, 1 Commerce Park, Commerce Way, Colchester, Essex, CO2 8HX, England (office). *Telephone:* (1206) 225200 (office). *Fax:* (1206) 225201 (office). *E-mail:* enquiries@chandos.net (office). *Website:* www.chandos.net (office).

WATSON, Lillian; British singer (soprano); b. 4 Dec. 1947, London, England. *Education:* Guildhall School of Music and London Opera Centre. *Career:* sang first at the Wexford Festival, then with the WNO; Glyndebourne from 1976, as Susanna, Despina, Sophie, Tytania in A Midsummer Night's Dream and Blondchen 1988; Covent Garden debut, 1971, as Barbarina in Le nozze di Figaro; appearances in die Entführung, Der Rosenkavalier and Arabella; guest engagements with ENO and Scottish Opera and in Munich, Paris, Rouen, Marseilles and Bordeaux; Salzburg Festival, 1982, as Marzelline in Fidelio; Vienna Staatsoper in Le nozze di Figaro; sang Strauss's Sophie at the Théâtre des Champs-Elysées, 1989; Norina in Don Pasquale at Amsterdam; title role in The Cunning Little Vixen at Covent Garden, 1990; Sadler's Wells Theatre, 1990, as Britten's Tytania; television engagements in Don Pasquale and Orpheus in the Underworld; sang Fairy Godmother in Massenet's Cendrillon for WNO 1993 and at Ghent, 1998; Bella in The Midsummer Marriage at Covent Garden, 1996; Despina, 1997; sang Britten's Tytania at Rome 1999 and Naples 2001. *Recordings:* Carmen; Le nozze di Figaro; Monteverdi Madrigals and Handel's Israel in Egypt; Die Entführung aus dem Serail; The Cunning Little Vixen; Così fan tutte; Britten's A Midsummer Night's Dream. *Current Management:* IMG Artists, The Light Box, 111 Power Road, London, W4 5PY, England. *Telephone:* (20) 7957-5800. *Fax:* (20) 7957-5801. *E-mail:* salmansi@imgartists.com. *Website:* www.imgartists.com.

WATSON, Linda; American opera singer (dramatic soprano); b. 18 Nov. 1959, Oakland, Calif.; d. of Mr and Mrs Franklin H. Watson, III. *Education:* New England Conservatory, Boston, Conservatory of Music, Vienna, Austria, pvt. studies with Prof. Carol Mayo. *Career:* began career in Aachen Opera 1992–95; sang in Essen and Leipzig 1995–97, Deutsche Oper am Rhein 1997–2005, Bayreuth Festival 1997–2010; guest appearances at Vienna Staatsoper, Metropolitan Opera, New York, La Scala, Milan, Bavarian State Opera, Munich, Los Angeles Opera, Washington Nat. Opera, Deutsche Oper, Berlin, Hamburg, Prague, Seattle Opera, Madrid, Châtelet, Paris, Barcelona, Dusseldorf, Maggio Musicale, Florence, Bologna, Toulouse, London, Moscow, Tokyo, Taipei, Boston, Copenhagen and Amsterdam; repertoire includes Leonore in Fidelio, Marie in Wozzeck, Jezibaba in Rusalka, Santuzza in Cavalleria Rusticana, Ariadne in Ariadne auf Naxos, Elektra in Elektra, Färberin in Die Frau ohne Schatten, Marschallin in Der Rosenkavalier, Lady Macbeth in Verdi's Macbeth, Ortrud in Lohengrin, Elizabeth and Venus in Tannhäuser, Isolde and Brangäne in Tristan und Isolde, Kundry in Parsifal, Sieglinde in Die Walküre, Brünnhilde in The Ring cycle; Artist in Residence, Chapman Univ. *Recordings include:* DVD: Elektra, Thielemann; Walküre, Barcelona; Kundry, Bayreuth 98; Ring: Teatro Colon; CD: Bayreuther Ring, Thielemann; Ring: Vienna Staatsoper/Thielemann, Ring: Prague/Fiore, Ring: Teatro Colon/Paternostro; Tristan and Isolde – Highlights; Ring-Amsterdam, Haenchen. Siegfried, J. Levine, Munich. *Honours:* Kammersängerin (German Govt). *Current Management:* Askonas Holt Limited, Lincoln House, 300 High, Holborn, London, WC1V 7JH, England. *Telephone:* (20) 7400-1700. *Fax:* (20) 7400-1799. *E-mail:* info@askonasholt.co.uk. *Website:* www.askonasholt.co.uk; www.lindawatson.net.

WATSON, Russell; British singer (tenor); b. 1974, Salford. *Career:* professional singer 1996–; numerous TV and radio broadcasts; concert performances include Wembley Arena, Royal Albert Hall, Carnegie Hall, Sydney Opera House, opening ceremony of the Commonwealth Games, Manchester 2002. *For film and television* sang Pelagia's Song (from film, Captain Corelli's Mandolin) 2001; sang theme tune to Star Trek Enterprise (TV series) 2002. *Recordings include:* albums: The Voice 2000, Encore 2001, Reprise 2002, Amore Musica 2004, The Ultimate Collection 2006, That's Life 2007, Outside In 2007, People Get Ready 2008, La Voce 2010, The Platinum Collection 2012. *Current Management:* Merlin Elite Ltd, Hammersmith Studios, 55 Yeldham Road, London, W6 8JF, England. *Telephone:* (20) 8834-8900. *Fax:* (20) 8834-

8901. *E-mail:* info@merlinelite.co.uk. *Website:* www.merlin-elite.com; www.russell-watson.com.

WATT, Alan; British singer (baritone); b. 1947, Aberdeen, Scotland. *Education:* Scottish Acad. of Music, Glasgow. *Career:* debut with Scottish Opera, Glasgow 1970; sang as Háry János by Kodály at the Buxton Festival 1971; Glyndebourne Festival and Touring Opera from 1973, as Marcello, Guglielmo and Figaro; appearances in The Cunning Little Vixen, Strauss's Intermezzo and The Visit of the Old Lady by Einem; Covent Garden 1976, in the premiere of Henze's We Come to the River; Wexford Festival 1978, as Ernesto in Haydn's Il mondo della luna; sang Guglielmo at Venice 1983, and Strasbourg 1989, Figaro at Vienna 1986, and for WNO 1987; Papageno at Tel-Aviv 1991; Festival Hall, London 1998, as Pish-Tush in The Mikado; many concert and oratorio engagements.

WATTS, André; pianist; b. 20 June 1946, Nuremberg, Germany. *Education:* Philadelphia Musical Acad. with Genia Robiner, Doris Bawden and Clement Petrillo, Peabody Conservatory of Music, Baltimore, studied with Leon Fleisher. *Career:* debut as soloist, Haydn's Concerto in D Major, Philadelphia Orchestra Children's Concert 1955; soloist, Franck's Symphonic Variations, Philadelphia Orchestra 1960; soloist, Liszt's Concerto No. 1, with Bernstein and New York Philharmonic Orchestra 1963; European debut, London Symphony Orchestra 1966; New York recital debut 1966; world tour 1967; first pianist to play a recital on live network television in USA, New York 1976; celebrated 25th anniversary of debut as soloist with New York Philharmonic Orchestra, Liszt Concerto No. 1, the Beethoven Concerto No. 2 and Rachmaninov Concerto No. 2 1988; Rachmaninov's concerto No. 2 in C minor at the London Proms 2002. *Honours:* Dr hc (Yale Univ.) 1973, (Albright Coll.) 1975.

WATTS, Andrew; British singer (countertenor); b. 1967, Middlesex. *Education:* Royal Acad. of Music. *Career:* appearances at the Almeida and Montepulciano Festivals in works by Smirnov, McQueen and Henze; opera roles include Tolomeo in Giulio Cesare, Lidio in Cavalli's L'Egisto, Handel's Sosarme, Scarlatti's Tigrane and Britten's Oberon, Arsamenes in Xerxes, and Monteverdi's Orfeo (1999–2000) for ENO; double bill of Dido and Aeneas and Venus and Adonis for De Vlaamse Opera; season 1998–99 as Gluck's Orpheus at Sydney and for ENO, and in Cesti's Il Pomo d'Oro at Batignano; season 2000 in Birtwistle's Gawain at Covent Garden and premiere of Guarnieri's Passione Secondo Matteo at La Scala; appearances with ENO in Le grand macabre 2009, A Dog's Heart 2010; Das Schicksal in Miss Fortune, Bregenz Festival 2011; concerts include Bach's Passions and Magnificat, Charpentier's Te Deum (at Lourdes), Purcell's Indian Queen in France, Messiah at Oxford, Handel's Jephtha on tour to Italy and Judas Maccabaeus in France.

WATTS, Elizabeth; British singer (soprano); b. 1979, Norfolk; d. of Rosemary Watts. *Education:* Sheffield Univ., Royal Coll. of Music. *Career:* fmr chorister, Norwich Cathedral; joined ENO as company artist 2005, mem. Young Singers' Programme 2005–07, performing Papagena in the Magic Flute and roles in Orfeo and King Arthur; has performed in King Arthur in Berkeley, Calif., Barbarina in Marriage of Figaro, Susanna in Marriage of Figaro for Santa Fe Opera, Flora in The Knot Garden, Handel's Semele, and Arthébuze in Charpentier's Actéon at Aldeburgh Festival; has worked with City of Birmingham Symphony Orchestra, Royal Liverpool Philharmonic Orchestra, London Philharmonic Orchestra, BBC Symphony Orchestra and The English Concert; has appeared at London's Purcell Room, Bridgewater, Wigmore and Queen Elizabeth Halls and at Aldeburgh and Chelthenham Festivals; one of BBC Radio 3's New Generation Artists. *Honours:* Philip and Dorothy Green Award for Young Concert Artists 2003, Kathleen Ferrier Prize 2006, Outstanding Young Artist Award MIDEM Classical Awards 2007, BBC Cardiff Singer of the World Rosenblatt Recital Song Prize 2007. *Current Management:* c/o Ingpen & Williams, 7 St George's Court, 131 Putney Bridge Road, London, SW15 2PA, England. *Telephone:* (20) 8874-3222. *Fax:* (20) 8877-3113. *E-mail:* info@ingpen.co.uk. *Website:* www.ingpen.co.uk; www.elizabethwattssoprano.com.

WAYENBERG, Daniel Ernest Joseph Carel; Dutch pianist and composer; b. 11 Oct. 1929, Paris, France. *Education:* studied with his mother and with Marguerite Long. *Career:* played in private houses 1939–46; public debut, Paris 1949; opening recital of the Chopin Centenary Festival, Florence 1949; Besançon Festival 1951; US debut, Carnegie Hall 1953, conducted by Mitropoulos; numerous concert appearances throughout the world (tours of USA and Indonesia 1955); repertoire centres on 19th-century classics, but also plays Haydn and Stockhausen; teacher, Conservatory of Rotterdam –1994; concert performances in duo with Yana Boukoff 2005–. *Compositions:* Ballet Solstice 1955, Sonata for violin and piano, Concerto for five wind instruments and piano, Capella Symphony, Concerto for three pianos and orchestra 1975. *Recordings include:* concertos by Brahms, Tchaikovsky, Beethoven, Gershwin and Rachmaninov. *Address:* 17 rue Thibault, 94520 Mandres-Les Roses, France (home). *Telephone:* 1-45-98-94-41 (home).

WAYNE-WRIGHT, Timothy; Briitsh singer (countertenor); b. Chelmsford. *Education:* Goldsmiths Coll., London, Trinity Coll. of Music. *Career:* chorister, Chelmsford Cathedral; Choral Scholar, Royal Naval Coll. Chapel, Greenwich; Lay Clerk, St George's Chapel, Windsor Castle 2006–08; mem., The King's Singers 2009–; has performed at venues including Concertgebouw, Amsterdam, Carnegie Hall, New York, Royal Albert Hall, London, Kennedy Center, Washington, DC, and Suntory Hall, Tokyo. *Recordings:* with The King's Singers: Romance du Soir 2009, Swimming over London 2010; with Eric

Whitacre, the Eric Whitacre Singers, Christopher Glynn, Laudibus and the Pavão Quartet: Light and Gold (Grammy Award for Best Choral Performance 2012) 2010. *E-mail:* timothy@kingssingers.com (office). *Current Management:* c/o Alec C. Treuhaft, IMG Artists, Carnegie Hall Tower, 152 West 57th Street, 5th Floor, New York 10019, USA. *Telephone:* (212) 994-3500. *Fax:* (212) 994-3550. *E-mail:* atreuhaft@imgartists.com. *Website:* www.imgartists.com. *Address:* c/o Claire Long, The King's Singers, Music Productions Ltd, Unit 14, 21 Wadsworth Road, Perivale, Middlesex, UB6 7JD, England (office). *Telephone:* (1753) 646100 (office). *E-mail:* timothy@kingssingers.com (office). *Website:* www.kingssingers.com (office).

WEAVER, James Merle, BA, MM; American harpsichordist and pianist; b. 25 Sept. 1937, Champaign, IL. *Education:* Univ. of Illinois, Urbana-Champaign, Sweelinck Conservatory, Amsterdam with Gustav Leonhardt. *Career:* many appearances as keyboard artist; curator of historic instruments at the Smithsonian Institution, Washington, DC 1967; co-founder, Smithsonian Chamber Players 1976; Teacher, Cornell Univ. and American Univ.; various masterclasses in 18th-century performance practice. *Recordings include:* Smithsonian Collection.

WEBB, Jonathan; British conductor; b. 1963, England. *Education:* Univ. of Manchester. *Career:* appearances with New Israel Opera with Jenůfa, Così fan tutte, Midsummer Night's Dream, Faust, Carmen, Don Pasquale, Butterfly, Der Freischütz, Hoffmann, Samson et Dalila, Cavalleria Rusticana, Pagliacci, Traviata, L'Elisir d'amore, Cenerentola and Lucia di Lammermoor; Head of Music, Opera Ireland; Resident Conductor, New Israeli Opera; festival appearances in Turin and Rome; Don Pasquale, Der Zigeunerbaron and Die Zauberflöte at the Vienna Volksoper; Peter Grimes in Genoa and Balfe's The Rose of Castile at Wexford; Figaro, The Rape of Lucretia, Falstaff and L'Histoire du Soldât in Ireland; co-production between Kirov Opera and New Israel Opera of Lady Macbeth of Mtsensk; season 1999–2000 with L'Italiana in Algeri, Tosca, La Juive, Macbeth and Eugene Onegin in Tel-Aviv; Mahagonny for the Deutsche Oper Berlin, La Traviata in Cologne and Turandot for the Caesarea Festival; season 2000–01 with Tancredi in Venice and Carmen at the Deutsche Oper, Berlin. *Current Management:* Robert Gilder and Co., 91 Great Russell Street, London, WC1B 3PS, England. *Telephone:* (20) 7580-7758. *Fax:* (20) 7580-7739. *E-mail:* rgilder@robert-gilder.com. *Website:* www.robert-gilder.com.

WEBB, Peter, BA; Australian composer and conductor; b. 29 Feb. 1948, Melbourne, Vic. *Education:* Univ. of Melbourne. *Career:* oboe and cor anglais in the Adelaide Symphony Orchestra 1975–95; conductor and teacher; commissions from ABC, Adelaide Harmony Choir, Unley Chamber Orchestra and others. *Compositions include:* Songs of the Wind (song cycle) for soprano and orchestra 1978, Quintet for brass 1980, Sonata for clarinet and piano 1981, Songs of the Shadows (song cycle) for mezzo-soprano and orchestra 1985, The Christmas Kangaroo for narrator and orchestra 1986, Sextet for pairs of horns, clarinets and bassoons 1987, Sonata for bassoon and piano 1987, Five Blake Songs for chorus and orchestra 1988, Trio for clarinet, bassoon and piano 1989, Sinfonietta for orchestra 1990, Trio for two oboes and piano 1992, Trio for flute, oboe and piano 1992, Sonata for cor anglais and piano 1995, Sonata for cello and piano 1998, Retrospection for eight cellos 1999, Sonata for flute and piano 2001. *E-mail:* pjwebb@senet.com.au.

WEBBER, Oliver; British violinist; b. 1969, Essex, England. *Education:* studied at Wells Cathedral, Cambridge and The Hague, Netherlands. *Career:* appearances from 1995 with the Charivari Agréable Sinfonie, Gabrieli Consort and Florilegium; violin and viola with the Revolutionary String Quartet, Red Priest and the Consort of Musicke; soloist with Florilegium, the Avison Baroque Ensemble, La Serenissima and London Musical Arts; exponent of early and Baroque music performance practice, including ornamentation and the use of gut strings; European tour with the London Handel Festival 2001.

WEBER, Peter, DipMus; Austrian singer (baritone); b. 1955, Vienna. *Education:* Hochschule für Musik, Vienna. *Career:* engaged by the Studio of the Vienna Staatsoper 1976; mem. ensemble of the Vienna Staatsoper 1978; engaged at the Nuremberg Opera 1980, Hanover Staatsoper 1982; regular appearances at the Salzburg Festival and the Vienna Festwochen from 1977; appeared at Glyndebourne Festival 1985–89 as Mandryka in Arabella and Olivier in Capriccio; debut at the Teatro Colón in Buenos Aires 1986 as Mozart's Count; debuts at the Teatro Liceo Barcelona and the Teatro dell'Opera Rome 1988; guest engagements in Hamburg, Düsseldorf, Geneva, Paris and Milan; sang Mandryka at Covent Garden 1990; US debut as Amonasro at Dallas Opera 1991; contracted to Vienna State Opera 1992; other roles include Silvio, Sharpless, Malatesta, Falke and the Secretary in Der Junge Lord by Henze, Don Giovanni, Don Alfonso, Telramund, Pizarro, Amfortas, Eisenstein, Onegin; debuts as Wagner's Gunther and Strauss's Barak at Hanover 1993; concerts and recitals in Europe and the USA; radio and television broadcasts; engaged as the Count in Capriccio, Vienna 1996–97; season 2000–01 as Wozzeck at La Scala, the Speaker in Die Zauberflöte, Kurwenal and the Chosen One in Schoenberg's Die Jakobsleiter, at the Vienna Staatsoper; Hindemith's Mathis at Hannover. *Recordings:* Ariadne auf Naxos, Un Ballo in Maschera, Die Frau ohne Schatten, Die Zauberflöte, Schoeck Penthesilea, Schubert Alfonso und Estrella, Haydn's Die Feuerbrunst. *Honours:* prizewinner Hugo Wolf Competition, Salzburg 1976, Mozartgemeinde Vienna Interpretation Prize 1976, Int. Schubert-Wolf Competition, Vienna 1978. *Current Management:* Aria's di Novella Partacini & Alexandra Plaickner, Rappresentanza Artisti, Via Josef Weingartner, 4, 39022 Lagundo, Italy. *Telephone:* (0473) 200200. *Fax:* (0473) 222424. *E-mail:* info@arias.it. *Website:* www.arias.it.

WEBSTER, Gillian; British singer (soprano); b. 2 May 1964, Scotland; m. Brian Kay. *Education:* studied at Royal Northern Coll. of Music and Nat. Opera Studio. *Career:* began her career with Royal Opera, Covent Garden in roles of Pamina and First Lady in Die Zauberflöte, La Contessa in Le nozze di Figaro, Ilia in Idomeneo, Servilia in La clemenza di Tito, First and Second Nieces in Peter Grimes, Micaela in Carmen, Mimi, Euridice, Marzelline in Fidelio, Woglinde and Wellgunde in Der Ring des Nibelungen, Le Coq d'Or, Kátya Kabanova, Rigoletto, Médée, Elektra and Prince Igor 1988; appearances with the English Bach festival, Scottish Opera, Glyndebourne Festival and ENO; roles have included Micaela, Pamina and Leila in Les Pêcheurs de Perles, Agilea Handel's Teseo and Ilia in Idomeneo; sang Klim (debut) in The Making of the Representative from Planet 8 by Philip Glass for ENO; sang Micaela with WNO 1990; TV appearances include Gluck's Euridice at Covent Garden; sang Mozart's Countess with Royal Opera at Shaftesbury Theatre 1998; int. opera appearances have included Pamina in Stuttgart, Euridice at the Komische Oper Berlin, La Contessa for Vlaamse Opera, Servilia for L'Opéra de Nancy, Micaela in Tours, Mimi in Las Palmas, Comtesse de la Roche in Die Soldaten and Elsa in Lohengrin in Nantes, Elsa in Dijon, First Lady in Bordeaux, Geneva, Aix-en-Provence, Chorégies d'Orange, Amsterdam, and at Bastille and Ginevra with Les Musiciens du Louvre; noted exponent of Baroque music and later vocal works of Mahler, Strauss, Mozart and Beethoven; has performed with conductors, including Bernard Haitink, Jeffrey Tate, John Eliot Gardiner, Sir Georg Solti, Marc Minkowski, Paul McCreesh, Sir Yehudi Menuhin and Sir Colin Davis; concert engagements have included Mahler Symphony No. 4 with New York Philharmonic, Four Last Songs with L'Orchestre de l'Opéra de Nancy, Beethoven Missa Solemnis with Madrid Nat. Orchestra, Pallas Athene in Gluck's Paride ed Elena and Galatea with Les Musiciens du Louvre; other engagements have included First Lady in Die Zauberflöte for Royal Opera, Galatea in Acis and Galatea with Les Musiciens du Louvre under Marc Minkowski, Messiah with City of Birmingham Symphony Orchestra and with Gabrieli Consort, Haydn and Mozart Masses with Birmingham Festival Choral Soc., Mendelssohn Second Symphony at Three Choirs Festival and performances with L'Orchestre de l'Opéra de Nancy; chamber music recitals with Alice Ader Ensemble, Arpeggione quartet, Talich quartet and Wanderer Trio in works by Shostakovich, Chausson, Schubert and Schoenberg. *Recordings:* role of Juno in Offenbach's Orpheus in the Underworld with Chorus and Orchestra of the D'Oyly Carte Opera Co. under John Owen Edwards 1994, Beethoven Choral Symphony, Second Niece in Peter Grimes, Pallas in Athene Paride ed Elena, Covent Garden DVDs of Orfeo and Die Zauberflöte. *Honours:* John Noble Award, Scottish Opera 1986. *Current Management:* Helen Sykes Artists' Management, 100 Felsham Road, Putney, London, SW15 1DQ, England. *Telephone:* (20) 8780-0060. *Fax:* (20) 8780-8772. *E-mail:* info@helensykesartists.com. *Website:* www.helensykesartists.com.

WEDD, Peter; British singer (tenor); b. 1970, England. *Education:* Guildhall School, National Opera Studio. *Career:* season 1998–99 in Die Lustige Witwe and Paul Bunyan for the Royal Opera, Pavel Haas's Sarlatan and Zandonai's I Cavalieri di Ekebù at Wexford; Don José for WNO, Britten's Lysander at Singapore, Tamino for European Chamber Opera and Federico in L'Arlesiana for Opera Holland Park; Covent Garden season 1999–2000 in Gawain, Der Rosenkavalier, The Greek Passion, Die Meistersinger and La Battaglia di Legnano; concerts include Mozart's Requiem, Haydn's Mass in Time of War, Messiah, the Glagolitic Mass, St John Passion and The Dream of Gerontius; Britten's Serenade at Neuchâtel. *Current Management:* Ingpen & Williams, 7 St George's Court, 131 Putney Bridge Road, London, SW15 2PA, England. *Telephone:* (20) 8874-3222. *Fax:* (20) 8877-3113. *E-mail:* info@ingpen.co.uk.

WEGMAN, Rob Cornelis, MPhil, PhD; Dutch musicologist; *Associate Professor of Music, Princeton University;* b. 26 Jan. 1961, Emmen; m. Helene van Rossum; one s. one d. *Education:* Univ. of Manchester, Univ. of Amsterdam. *Career:* Asst Lecturer, Univ. of Amsterdam 1983–85; Researcher, Univ. of Amsterdam 1987–91; Weston Jr Research Fellow, Univ. of Oxford 1991–93, British Acad. Post-Doctoral Research Fellow 1993–95, concentrating on 15th-century polyphony; Asst Prof. of Music, Princeton Univ. 1995–2000, Assoc. Prof. 2000–. *Publications include:* Born for the Muses: The Life and Masses of Jacob Obrecht 1994, The Crisis of Music in Early Modern Europe 1470–1530 2005, The War of Love in the Late-Medieval Courtly Song. *Honours:* Westrup Prize 1990, Music and Letters Award 1992, American Musicological Soc. Alfred Einstein Award 1996, Royal Musical Asscn Edward J. Dent Medal 1998, Nat. Endowment for the Humanities grant 1999. *Address:* Department of Music, Princeton University, Princeton, NJ 08544, USA (office). *Telephone:* (609) 258-4248 (office). *Fax:* (609) 258-6793 (office). *E-mail:* rwegman@princeton.edu (office). *Website:* www.princeton.edu/~rwegman (office).

WEGNER, John; singer (bass-baritone); b. 1950, Germany. *Education:* Victorian College of the Arts, Australia. *Career:* Australian Opera, 1981–92, as Britten's Theseus, Collatinus and Swallow, Mozart's Commendatore and Leporello, Escamillo, Baron Ochs, Banquo and Boris Godunov; Falstaff for Queensland Opera; 1992–95 with Karlsruhe Opera as Orestes, Wotan, Cardillac (Hindemith), Prince Igor and Iago; Wagner's Dutchman at Berne and Leipzig, Scarpia at Sydney and Copenhagen; Wotan and the Wanderer in The Ring, at Adelaide, 1999; Bayreuth debut, 1997, as Donner in Das Rheingold; Season 1999–2000 as Escamillo and Scarpia for Opera Australia,

Wotan at Toulouse and Alberich in Götterdämmerung at Stuttgart; Season 2000–01 as the Dutchman, Boris and Wotan at Düsseldorf, Scarpia in Brussels, Kurwenal for Opera North in Leeds and on tour to Germany; Jochanaan in Salome at the Berlin Staatsoper and Telramund at Sydney. *Recordings:* Wotan/Wanderer in The Ring, from Stuttgart (Bella Music). *Honours:* Mo Award as Operatic Performer of the Year 1998–89 from the Australian Entertainment Industry. *Current Management:* c/o Opernagentur Inge Tennigkeit, Kempener Strasse 4, 40474 Düsseldorf, Germany; c/o Jennifer Eddy Artists' Management, Suite 11, 596 St Kilda Road, Melbourne, VIC 3004, Australia. *Telephone:* (211) 5160060 (Germany); (3) 9525-2700 (Australia). *Fax:* (211) 51600616 (Germany); (3) 9529-5410 (Australia). *E-mail:* opera@tennigkeit-ag.de; info@jeam.com.au. *Website:* www .tennigkeit-ag.de.

WEHOFSCHITZ, Kurt; Austrian singer (tenor); b. 3 May 1923, Vienna. *Education:* Vienna Music Acad. *Career:* debut in Linz 1948 as Wilhelm Meister; sang at Kiel 1953–54, notably as Ulrich Greiner-Mars in the premiere of Hindemith's Harmonie der Welt 1957; sang at Düsseldorf 1959–64, Frankfurt 1964–66, notably in The Photo of the Colonel by Humphrey Searle, Düsseldorf 1960, as Creon in the German premiere of Oedipe Re by Enescu; guest appearances at Zürich, Lisbon, Rio de Janeiro and the Vienna Staatsoper; sang at the Vienna Volksoper until 1980; other roles have included Mozart's Belmont and Basilio, Leandro in Haydn's Mondo della Luna, Strauss's Leukippos and Flamand, Alfredo, Germont, Don Carlos, Riccardo and Tom Rakewell.

WEIDENAAR, Reynold Henry, BMus, MA, PhD; American composer and video artist; b. 25 Sept. 1945, East Grand Rapids, MI. *Education:* Cleveland Inst. of Music, New York Univ., studied with Donald Erb and Brian Fennelly. *Compositions include:* Between the Motion and the Act Falls the Shadow 1981, Love of Line, of Light and Shadow: The Brooklyn Bridge 1982, Night Flame Ritual 1983, The Stillness 1985, The Thundering Scream of the Seraphim's Delight 1987, Long River 1993, Long into the Night, Heavenly Music Flowed Out of the Street 1995, Swing Bridge 1997. *Recordings:* The Tinsel Chicken Coop 1978, 1982, Twilight Flight 1986, Harmony 1986, Imprint; Footfalls to Return 1986, Night Flame Ritual 1986, Bass Bars for video tape 1988, Long River for piano and tape 1993, Magic Music from the Telharmonium 1997, Swing Bridge for clarinet and tape 1997. *Publications:* Magic Music from the Telharmonium 1995; contrib. to New Music America: A Moveable Fest (in The Independent) 1984, Down Memory Lane: Forerunners of Music and the Moving Image and So You Want to Compose for the Moving Image (in Ear Magazine) 1985, Live Music and Moving Images: Composing and Producing the Concert Video (in Perspectives of New Music) 1986, The Alternators of the Telharmonium (in Proceedings of the International Computer Music Conference) 1991.

WEIDINGER, Christine, BA; American singer (soprano); b. 31 March 1946, Springville, NY; m. Kenneth Smith 1976. *Education:* Grand Canyon Coll., studied singing with Marlene Delavan in Phoenix, Adrian de Peyer in Wuppertal, Germany and Dean Verhines in Los Angeles. *Career:* debut as Musetta in La Bohème at Metropolitan Opera 1972, sang at Metropolitan Opera 1972–76, at Stuttgart and Bielefeld Operas, Germany 1979–; roles include Malvina in Heinrich Marschner's Der Vampyr, Anina in Bellini's La Sonnambula, Berthe in Meyerbeer's Le Prophète, Elizabeth I in Donizetti's Roberto Devereux, Inez in L'Africaine, Lucia and Juliet in I Capuleti e i Montecchi, Pamira in Rossini's Siege of Corinth, Eupaforice in Heinrich Graun's Spanish Conquest, Constanze in Abduction from the Seraglio, Electra in Idomeneo, Leonora in Trovatore, Adèle in Le Comte Ory, Vitellia in La Clemenza di Tito, Tancredi, Violetta, Gilda, Donna Anna, Mimi, Liu, and the title roles in Thea Musgrave's Mary, Queen of Scots, Donizetti's Lucia di Lammermoor, Bellini's Norma, Bellini's Beatrice di Tenda. *Recordings include:* Handel's Rinaldo with Marilyn Horne, L'Africaine with Caballé and Domingo, Die Freunde von Salamanka by Schubert, Médée with Caballé and Lima, Mitridate by Mozart. *Honours:* Nat. First Prize, Metropolitan Opera Auditions 1972.

WEIGLE, Jorg-Peter; German conductor; b. 1953, Greifswald. *Education:* Thomasschule, Leipzig, Hochschule für Musik, Berlin. *Career:* first kapellmeister at the State Symphony Orchestra of Neubrandenburg 1978–80; Conductor, Leipzig Radio Chorus 1980; Chief Conductor, Dresden Philharmonic Orchestra; repertoire has included Bach's Christmas Oratorio, St John Passion and B Minor Mass, symphonies by Beethoven, Haydn, Mozart, Shostakovich and Schubert, and Janáček's Sinfonietta; visited Wales and the West Country, UK with the Dresden Philharmonic 1989, with works by Beethoven, Brahms, Weber and Tchaikovsky, Hamburg and Spain 1989 and Czechoslovakia 1990; season 1990–91 included Mahler's Das Klagende Lied, Haydn's Symphony No. 92, Mozart's Requiem and Concertante K364, Sibelius's Symphonies 2, 3 and 7, Brahms' 2nd Symphony and D Minor Concerto, Berg's Violin Concerto; concert performance of Meyerbeer's Il Crociato in Egitto, to celebrate the bicentenary of the composer's birth. *Recordings:* Albeniz' Iberia Suite, Falla's Three-Cornered Hat, Mozart's Horn Concertos, Arias and Duets, Ravel's Rhapsodie Espagnole, Reger's Böcklin Tone Pictures, Mozart Variations.

WEIKERT, Ralf; Austrian conductor; b. 10 Nov. 1940, St Florian, nr Linz; s. of Fritz Weikert and Sigrid Weikert; m. Heidemarie Weikert; two s. *Education:* Bruckner Conservatory, Linz, State Acad., Vienna with Hans Swarowsky. *Career:* coach, conductor, Landestheater Salzburg 1963; concerts

in Austria, Scandinavia from 1965; conductor, Bonn Opera 1966, Music Dir 1968; Salzburg Festival (concert) 1971; guest conductor, Royal Opera Copenhagen with works by Mozart, Verdi, Stravinsky 1972; Hamburg Staatsoper from 1975, with Don Quichotte, works by Mozart, Puccini and Donizetti; Vienna Staatsoper debut with Il Trovatore 1974; Zurich Opera with Le nozze di Figaro, Arabella, Fidelio, La Cenerentola and Il Barbiere di Siviglia 1976–80; Deutsche Oper Berlin with Figaro and Don Pasquale 1978–80; US debut 1980, with the City Opera's Giulio Cesare in New York and Los Angeles; Teatro La Fenice, Venice with Tancredi by Rossini 1981; further engagements in Barcelona, Munich, Vienna 1968–88, Rosenkavalier, Carmen, Die Entführung and L'Elisir d'amore; Metropolitan Opera 1987–90, Elisir, Barbiere and Bohème; Finnish Nat. Opera 2001–04, with La Fanciulla del West, Die Entführung aus dem Serail, Arabella, Der Ring des Nibelungen, Salome Arena di Verona 1987, La Traviata; concert engagements with leading orchestras in Berlin, Vienna, Scandinavia, Paris, Japan, Hungary, West Germany, UK (English Chamber Orchestra, Welsh Nat. Opera, Academy of St Martin-in-the-Fields); festival appearances at Salzburg (Mozart Matinées, Serenades and Cenerentola), Aix-en-Provence, Orange, Bregenz and Lucerne; Perm. Guest Conductor, Zurich Opera, Rushton 2008–10; conducted Offenbach's Barbe Bleue at Stuttgart 1996, Fidelio at Catania 1998; Verdi's I Vespri Siciliani at Palermo 2004, Manon at Seville, Parsifal and Holländer at Wagner-Festival Wels 2005–11; Ariadne at Tokyo, Maria Stuarda, Fledermaus (Zurich Opera), Lohengrin, Fliegender Holländer, Parsifal, Tristan und Isolde (Wagner-Festival Wels), Walküre and Elektra (Royal Opera House Stockholm), Salome (Maggio Musicale), Salome (Teatro Petruzzelli Bari), Mozart concerts (Napoli), Salome (New Nat. Theatre, Tokyo) 2011, Zauberflöte, NNT, Tokyo 2013, Tannhäuser (Royal Opera Stockholm) 2014, Concerttournée with NHK Orchestra, Tokyo and Don Giovanni, NNT, Tokyo 2014, Lohengrin, Fliegender Holländer (Wagner-Festival Wels) 2014; Prof. of Master Conducting, Univ. of Lucerne, Arabella (Teatro Liceu Barcelona) 2014, Concerts (New Japan Philharmonic, Tokyo) 2015, Tannhäuser, Tristan & Isolde, (Wagner-Festival Wels) 2015, Fliegender Holländer (Korean National Opera), Teatro San Carlo Napoli. *Radio:* Don Giovanni (NHK Tokyo) 2014. *Television includes:* Barber of Seville (MET), Flying Dutchman (Budapest). *Recordings include:* Rossini's Tancredi, Schoeck's Lebendig begraben, James Morris Recital, Love Duets Araiza-Lind, Barbiere di Siviglia (Metropolitan Opera, video), Alexander von Zemlinsky: Kleider Machen Leute (opera), Eugen d'Albert: Die tote Stadt (opera), Rossini's Barbiere di Siviglia, L'Italiana in Algeri (DVD), Recital of Michael Volle (CD), Beethoven 9th Symphony(CD). *Honours:* Hon. mem. AMG Zürich; Großes Goldenes Ehrenzeichen der Republik; Nicolai Malko Prize 1965, Mozart Prize 1966, Dr Karl Böhm Prize 1975, Platine d'Or 2005, ECHO Klassik Award 2005. *Current Management:* c/o Künstleragentur Dr Raab & Dr Böhm Gesellschaft, Plankengasse, 18-20, 1040 Vienna, Austria; c/o Künstleragentur Dr G. Hilbert, Maximilianstrasse 22, Munich, Germany. *Telephone:* (1) 5120501. *Fax:* (1) 5127743. *E-mail:* zeugswetter@rbartists.at. *Website:* www.rbartists .at. *Address:* Neubruchstrasse 5, 8127 Forch, Switzerland (home). *Telephone:* (44) 9803473 (home). *Fax:* (44) 9803473 (home). *E-mail:* ralf.weikert@bluewin .ch.

WEIKL, Bernd; Austrian singer (baritone); b. 29 July 1942, Vienna. *Education:* Mainz Conservatoire and Hochschule für Musik, Hanover. *Career:* operatic debut as Ottakar in Der Freischütz 1968; mem. Düsseldorf Opera 1970–73, Hamburg State Opera 1973–, Deutsche Oper Berlin 1974–; debut at Salzburg Festival as Melot in Tristan und Isolde 1971, at Bayreuth Festival as Wolfram in Tannhäuser 1972 (guest artist 1973–75), at Covent Garden as Rossini's Figaro in The Barber of Seville 1975, at Metropolitan Opera as Wolfram 1977, at La Scala, Milan as Ford in Falstaff 1980; numerous guest engagements including Bavarian State Opera, Salzburg Festival; has sung over 120 roles during his career, especially as Hans Sachs in Die Meistersinger von Nürnberg; other roles include title roles in Don Giovanni, Rigoletto, Eugene Onegin and The Flying Dutchman, Count Almaviva in The Marriage of Figaro, Amfortas in Parsifal, Belcore in L'elisir d'amore, di Luna in Il trovatore, Eisenstein in Die Fledermaus, Ford in Falstaff, Golaud in Pelléas et Mélisande, Guglielmo in Così fan tutte, Jokanaan in Salome, Mandryka in Arabella, Cardinal Morone in Palestrina, Rodrigo in Don Carlos, Tomsky in The Queen of Spades, Zurga in Les pêcheurs de perles, Wolfram in Tannhäuser. *Recordings include:* Der Freischütz (Carl Maria von Weber): Carlos Kleiber conducting the Staatskapelle Dresden 1973, Die Fledermaus (Johann Strauss II): Carlos Kleiber conducting the Orchestra of the Bavarian State Opera 1975, Il segreto di Susanna (Ermanno Wolf-Ferrari): Lamberto Gardelli, conducting the Orchestra of the Royal Opera House Covent Garden 1977, Parsifal (Richard Wagner): Rafael Kubelík conducting the Bavarian Radio Symphony Orchestra 1980, Lohengrin (Richard Wagner): Woldemar Nelsson conducting the Bayreuth Festival 1982, Tiefland (Eugen d'Albert): Marek Janowski, conducting the Münchner Rundfunkorchester 1983, Rigoletto (Giuseppe Verdi): Lamberto Gardelli, conducting the Münchner Rundfunkorchester 1984, Carmina Burana (Orff): James Levine conducting the Chicago Symphony Orchestra and Chorus 1984, Die Meistersinger von Nürnberg (Richard Wagner): Horst Stein conducting the Orchester der Bayreuther Festspiele 1984, The Flying Dutchman (Richard Wagner): Giuseppe Sinopoli conducting the Berlin State Opera Orchestra 1991, Götterdämmerung (Richard Wagner): James Levine conducting the Metropolitan Opera Orchestra (Grammy Award for Best Opera Recording 1992) 1991. *Publication:* Warum Richard Wagner in Deutschland verboten werden muss 2014. *Current Management:* c/o Hilbert Artists Management, Maximilianstrasse 22, 80539 Munich, Germany. *E-mail:* agentur@hilbert.de.

WEIL, Bruno; German conductor; b. 24 Nov. 1949, Hahnstatten. *Education:* studied with Franco Ferrara in Italy and with Hans Swarowsky in Vienna. *Career:* conducted at the opera houses of Wiesbaden and Brunswick; debut with the Berlin Radio Symphony Orchestra 1977; concerts with the Berlin Philharmonic from 1979; Gen. Music Dir, City of Augsburg 1981–89, City of Duisberg 1989–2002; debut at the Deutsche Oper Berlin 1980 with Weill's Die Sieben Todsünden; Salzburg Festival from 1982; initiated series of Mozart operas in joint production with the Vienna Volksoper and Austrian television 1987; US debut with Schubertiade in New York 1988; Music Dir and Conductor, Carmel Bach Festival 1992–(2011); Prof. of Conducting, Hochschule für Musik, Munich 2001–; guest conductor, Yomiuri Nippon Symphony Orchestra, Vienna Staatsoper, Orchestre National de France, the Montréal Symphony Orchestra, Vienna Philharmonic Orchestra, Dresden Staatskapelle, Boston Symphony Orchestra, Sydney Symphony Orchestra, Tafelmusik; concerts in Netherlands with the Residentie Orchestra, Rotterdam Philharmonic, the Los Angeles Philharmonic, BBC Scottish Symphony, English Chamber Orchestra, Orchestra of the Age of Enlightenment. *Honours:* second prize Herbert von Karajan Conductors' Competition 1979, Echo Klassik Conductor of the Year Award 1997. *Current Management:* Ingpen & Williams, 7 St George's Court, 131 Putney Bridge Road, London, SW15 2PA, England. *Telephone:* (20) 8874-3222. *Fax:* (20) 8877-3113. *E-mail:* info@ingpen.co.uk. *Website:* www.ingpen.co.uk.

WEIL, Tibor V., MA; singer (baritone), pianist, cellist and economist; b. 16 May 1942, Hungary. *Education:* Mackenzie University, São Paulo, Brazil, New York University, USA, Budapest Music High School, Salvador Music High School, Pro Arte Music High School. *Career:* debut with piano and cello 1960; concerts, television appearances in São Paulo, Rio de Janeiro, and Salvador, 1958–; regular chamber music performances; frequent concerts as lieder and light opera singer, sacred music and requiems, 1989–; mem, Pro Arte, São Paulo; Managing Adviser, Centro de Musica Brasileira. *Honours:* Viscua Konservatoire Scholarship, 1956; Pro Arte Scholarship, 1959. *Address:* TAW Promotions SP, Rua Angatuba 80, Bairro, Pacaembu, CEP 01247 São Paulo SP, Brazil.

WEILERSTEIN, Alisa, BA; American cellist; b. 14 April 1982, Rochester, New York; d. of Donald Weilerstein and Vivian Hornik Weilerstein; partner Rafael Payare. *Education:* Cleveland Inst. of Music, Columbia Univ. *Career:* began playing cello aged four, first public recital aged five; debut with Weilerstein Trio (family ensemble), Top Festival, Tex. aged six; debut as soloist aged 13 1995; Artist-in-Residence, Cleveland Inst. of Music 2009; has worked with numerous conductors, including Marin Alsop, Daniel Barenboim, Sir Andrew Davis, Gustavo Dudamel, Sir Mark Elder, Christoph Eschenbach, Manfred Honeck, Marek Janowski, Paavo Järvi, Jeffrey Kahane, Lorin Maazel, Zubin Mehta, Ludovic Morlot, Peter Oundjian, Matthias Pintscher, Yuri Temirkanov, Osmo Vänskä, Simone Young, David Zinman; has visited Venezuela several times to work with the Simon Bolívar Youth Orchestra and El Sistema music educ. system. *Recordings include:* Weilerstein Recital 2000, Shostakovich: Cello Concerto No. 1 2007, Various: Europakonzert 10 (Elgar: Cello Concerto/Brahms: Symphony 1/Wagner: Meistersinger) 2010, Elgar and Carter Concerti with Staatskapelle Berlin and Daniel Barenboim (BBC Music Magazine Award for Recording of the Year 2014) 2012. *Honours:* Avery Fisher Career Grant 2000, Schleswig-Holstein Music Festival Leonard Bernstein Prize 2006, Lincoln Center Martin E. Segal Prize 2008, MacArthur Foundation 'genius grant' 2011. *Current Management:* c/o Opus 3 Artists (New York), 470 Park Avenue South, 9th Floor North, New York, NY 10016, USA. *Telephone:* (212) 584-7500. *E-mail:* info@opus3artists.com. *Website:* www.opus3artists.com.

WEILERSTEIN, Donald, BS, MS; American violinist; b. 14 March 1940, Washington, DC. *Education:* Juilliard School of Music. *Career:* debut, New York 1963; founding First Violinist, Cleveland Quartet 1969–89; Prof. of Violin and Chamber Music, Cleveland Inst. of Music 1967–71, 1989–, SUNY at Buffalo 1971–76, Eastman School of Music, NY 1976–89; mem. American String Teachers' Asscn. *Recordings:* Complete Brahms Quartets; Complete Beethoven Quartets; Schubert 2 cello Quintet; Schubert Trout Quintet; Mendelssohn and Schubert Octets; Complete Violin and Piano and Solo Violin Works of Ernest Bloch; Sonatas of Dohnányi and Janáček; The Complete Sonatas of Robert Schumann with pianist Ulvian Hornik Weilerstein, 1995; The Complete Sonatas and Partitas of J. S. Bach, 2000. *Publication:* contrib. chapter on violin technique in Medical Problems of Instrumental Musicians, 2000. *Honours:* NEA grant, prizewinner Munich Competition for Violin and Piano Duo. *Address:* 2645 Fairmount Blvd, Cleveland Heights, OH 44106, USA.

WEINGARTNER, Elisabeth; Swiss singer (mezzo-soprano); b. 23 Jan. 1938, Sissach. *Education:* studied in Basle and with Res Fischer in Stuttgart. *Career:* sang at the Basle Opera, 1973–81 and made guest appearances at Nantes, Paris, Trier and Cannes; roles have included Dorabella in Così fan tutte by Mozart, Carmen by Bizet, Isabella in L'Italiana in Algeri, Idamantes in Idomeneo, Geneviève in Pelléas, Annina, and the Hostess in Boris Godunov; sang at Strasbourg in 1984 in the premiere of H.H. Ulysse by Prodromidés; concert and lieder engagements in France and Switzerland and at Liège, Stuttgart and Vienna; sang in Verdi's Requiem in Paris with Orchestra

Lamoureux and Dvořák's Requiem at San Sebastian in Spain. *Recordings include:* H. H. Ulysse.

WEINSCHENK, Hans-Jorg; German singer (tenor); b. 14 Nov. 1955, Stuttgart. *Career:* sang in Opera at Heidelberg, 1974–76, and Wuppertal, 1976–80; mem., Zürich Opera, 1981–85, and Theater am Gärtnerplatz Munich from 1984; guest appearances at Lausanne in 1985, and the Grand Opera Paris in 1986; sang in the premiere of Der Meister und Margarita by Kunad, Karlsruhe, 1986; roles have included such buffo and character repertory as Pedrillo, the Witch in Hansel and Gretel, Monostatos, David in Die Meistersinger and the Steuermann in Fliegende Holländer; frequent concert engagements; sang in The Cunning Little Vixen at Karlsruhe, 1996 and in Hindemith/Milhaud/Weill/Toch programme, 1998; season 2000–01 as Flaminio in A. Scarlatti's Il trionfo dell'onore, at Halle, Victorin in Die tote Stadt, Mozart's Basilio and Finn in Ruslan and Lyudmila, at Karlsruhe.

WEINSTEIN, Mark J., MBA; American opera administrator; *Executive Director, Washington National Opera;* s. of Lawrence Weinstein; m. Susanne Marsee 1987. *Education:* Carleton Coll., Harvard Graduate School of Business Admin. *Career:* joined New York City Opera 1984, becoming Dir of Finance, later Exec. Dir 1994–96; Vice-Pres. of Operations, Nat. Artists Man. Co. 1996–97; Gen. Dir and Vice-Pres., Pittsburgh Opera 1997–2008; Exec. Dir, Washington Nat. Opera 2008–; Founding Chair., Pittsburgh Arts Council; fmr Vice-Chair., OPERA America. *Address:* Washington National Opera, 2600 Virginia Avenue, NW, Suite 301, Washington, DC 20037, USA (office). *Telephone:* (202) 295-2420 (office). *Fax:* (202) 295-2479 (office). *Website:* www.dc-opera.org (office).

WEIR, Dame Gillian Constance, DBE, LRAM, LTCL, FRCM; British concert organist, harpsichordist, broadcaster and lecturer; *Prince Consort Professor of Organ, Royal College of Music;* b. 17 Jan. 1941, Martinborough, New Zealand; d. of Cecil Alexander Weir and Clarice Mildred Foy Weir (née Bignell); m. 1st Clive Rowland Webster 1967 (divorced 1971); m. 2nd Lawrence Irving Phelps 1972 (died 1999). *Education:* Wanganui Girls Coll., NZ and Royal Coll. of Music, with Cyril Smith (piano) and Ralph Downes (organ), pvt. studies in London and Paris with Anton Heiller, Marie-Claire Alain and Nadia Boulanger. *Career:* debuts at Royal Festival Hall and Royal Albert Hall, London 1965; worldwide career since 1965 as concert organist, comprising some 2,000 appearances in major concert halls etc., including 50 at South Bank Centre, London; has appeared with all leading British orchestras and many abroad, including Vienna Symphony, Boston Symphony, San Francisco Symphony, ORF, under leading conductors; many radio and TV appearances; adjudicator in int. competitions and artist-in-residence at major univs including Yale; gives lectures and master classes in many countries; organ consultant, Birmingham Symphony Hall; Visiting Prof. of Organ, RAM, London 1997–98; Prince Consort Prof. of Organ, Royal Coll. of Music, London 1999–; Int. Chair. in Organ, Royal Northern Coll. of Music, Manchester 2006–07; Distinguished Visiting Artist, Peabody Conservatory of Music, Baltimore, USA 2006–12; Visiting Tutor, Curtis Inst., Philadelphia 2006–09; numerous premières including first British performance of Messiaen's Meditations of 1972; numerous works written for her including concertos by William Mathias and Peter Racine Fricker; numerous recordings including complete organ works of Olivier Messiaen 1995 and complete works of César Franck 1997; recognized world-wide as authority on and pre-eminent performer of Messiaen; Concerto soloist First Night of the Proms 1967 and Last Night of the Proms 1999, numerous other Proms appearances; Pres. Inc. Asscn of Organists (first woman Pres.) 1981–83, Inc. Soc. of Musicians 1992–93, Soloists' Ensemble 1998–2000; mem. Exec. Council, Royal Coll. of Organists (first woman mem.) 1981–85, Council (first woman mem.) 1977–, Pres. (first woman Pres.) 1994–96; mem. Council of Royal Philharmonic Soc. 1995–2001; mem. Royal Soc. of Musicians of GB 1996–; Trustee, Eric Thompson Charitable Trust 1993–; Patron Friends of Young Artists' Platform 1991–, Oundle Int. Festival 1998–, Cirencester Early Music Festival 1999, Northern Ireland Int. Organ Competition 2011–, various organ socs in UK and abroad. *Television:* presenter and performer, The King of Instruments (six-part series, BBC) 2000, A Year in the Life of Gillian Weir (NZTV), appearances on Omnibus (BBC), South Bank Show (ITV) 2000, and numerous other programmes. *Publications include:* contrib. to Grove's Dictionary of Music and Musicians 1980, Faber's The Messiaen Companion 1995; articles in professional journals. *Honours:* Hon. FRCO 1975; Hon. Fellow, Royal Canadian Coll. of Organists 1983; Hon. RAM 1989; Hon. Bencher of the Middle Temple, London 2012; Hon. DMus (Victoria Univ. of Wellington, NZ) 1983, (Hull) 1996, (Exeter) 2001, (Leicester) 2003, (Aberdeen) 2004, (London) 2008, (Durham) 2012; Hon. DLitt (Huddersfield) 1997; Hon. DUniv (Univ. of Central England) 2001; Winner, St Albans Int. Organ Festival Competition 1964, Countess of Munster Award 1965, Int. Performer of the Year Award, American Guild of Organists 1981, Musician of the Year, Int. Music Guide 1982, Turnovsky Foundation Award for Outstanding Contrib. to the Arts (first musician) 1985, Silver Medal, Albert Schweitzer Asscn (Sweden) 1998, Evening Standard Award for Outstanding Solo Performance 1999, Lifetime Achievement Award, The Link Foundation 2005. *E-mail:* gillianweir@onetel.com (home). *Website:* gillianweir.com.

WEIR, Judith, CBE, MA; British composer; *Master of the Queen's Music;* b. 11 May 1954, Cambridge, England. *Education:* North London Collegiate School, King's Coll., Cambridge. *Career:* Composer-in-Residence, Southern Arts Asscn 1976–79; Fellow in Composition, Univ. of Glasgow 1979–82, Creative Arts Fellowship, Trinity Coll. Cambridge 1983–85, Composer-in-Residence,

Royal Scottish Acad. of Music and Drama (RSAMD) 1988–91; Fairbairn Composer in Asscn with City of Birmingham Symphony Orchestra 1995–98; Artistic Dir Spitalfields Festival 1995–2000; Hambro Visiting Prof. in Opera Studies, Univ. of Oxford 1999–2000; Visiting Prof., Princeton Univ., USA 2001; Fromm Foundation Visiting Prof., Harvard Univ. 2004; Distinguished Visiting Research Prof. in Composition, School of Music, Cardiff Univ. 2006–13; Master of the Queen's Music 2014–; Assoc. Composer, BBC Singers 2015–; Trustee, Royal Opera House 2002–11. *Compositions include:* King Harald's Saga 1979, The Consolations of Scholarship 1985, The Black Spider 1985, A Night At The Chinese Opera 1987, Missa Del Cid 1988, Heaven Ablaze In His Breast 1989, The Vanishing Bridegroom 1990, Music Untangled 1991–92, Heroic Strokes of the Bow 1992, Blond Eckbert 1993, Musicians Wrestle Everywhere 1994, Moon and Star 1995, Forest 1995, Storm 1997, Piano Concerto 1997, Piano Trio 1998, Natural History 1999, We Are Shadows (South Bank Show Award 2001) 2000, Piano Quartet 2000, The Welcome Arrival of Rain 2001, Tiger under the Table 2002, The Voice of Desire 2004, Piano Trio No. 2 2004, Armida 2005, Blond Eckbert Pocket Version 2006, Winter Song 2007, Concrete 2008, Miss Fortune 2009–11, I give you the end of a golden string 2011–13. *Honours:* Hon. Fellow, St Hilda's Coll. Oxford 2000, King's Coll. Cambridge 2003; Hon. RAM 1997; Hon. FRCM 2006; Dr hc (Aberdeen) 1995, (Univ. of Central England) 1999, (RSAMD) 2001, (Queen's Univ. Belfast) 2001, (Glasgow) 2005, (King's Coll. London) 2007, (Glasgow Caledonian) 2008; Critics' Circle Award 1994, Elise L Stoeger Prize 1997, South Bank Award 2000, Queen's Medal for Music 2007, Distinguished Musician Award, Incorporated Soc. of Musicians 2010. *Current Management:* c/o Promotion Department, Chester Music, 14–15 Berners Street, London, W1T 3LJ, England. *Telephone:* (20) 7612-7400. *Fax:* (20) 7612-7549. *E-mail:* promotion@musicsales.co.uk. *Website:* www.judithweir.com; www.royal.gov .uk/TheRoyalHousehold/OfficialRoyalposts/MasterofTheQueensMusic.aspx.

WEIR, Scot; singer (tenor); b. 1954, New Mexico, USA. *Education:* Colorado Univ. and studied in Graz. *Career:* sang at the Gelsenkirchen Opera 1981–85, notably as Don Ottavio, Lenski and Xerxes; Wiesbaden Opera 1985–89, as Almaviva, Medoro in Haydn's Orlando Paladino, Belfiore in La finta giardiniera, and Veit in Lortzing's Undine; sang Hylas in Les Troyens at Brussels 1992; has appeared as guest in Canada, Israel, Japan and the USA; sang Monteverdi's Ulisse at Vienna 1998. *Recordings include:* Franck's Les Béatitudes, Mozart C minor Mass. *Current Management:* c/o Colwell Arts Management, 1580 Line 37, New Hamburg, ON N3A 4B7, Canada. *Telephone:* (519) 662-3499. *Fax:* (519) 662-2777. *E-mail:* jcolwell@golden.net. *Website:* www.colwellarts.com.

WEISBROD, Annette, DipEd, DipMus; Swiss pianist; b. 9 Dec. 1937, Blackburn, Lancashire, England; m. Charles Kirmess 1967 (died 1979). *Education:* Zürich Conservatory, Basle Conservatoire. *Career:* debut at Wigmore Hall, London 1960; concert appearances worldwide; radio and television broadcasts in Switzerland, Germany, England, France, the fmr Yugoslavia and People's Republic of China; Prof., Berne Conservatoire; mem. Swiss Tonkünstler Verein, Swiss Musikpädagogischer Verein, Int. Piano Teachers' Asscn, Soroptimist Int. (Zürich), Business and Professional Women Zürich, Lyceum Club. *Recordings include:* albums: Haydn Trios (with the Swiss Festival Trio), Complete Works for Piano and Cello by Beethoven, several piano concertos and many piano works. *Address:* Heuelstr 33, 8032 Zürich, Switzerland (home). *Telephone:* 442519430 (home). *E-mail:* a.weisbrod-k@bluewin.ch (home).

WEISE, Klaus; conductor; b. 30 Jan. 1936, Kolpin, Poland. *Education:* studied in Berlin, Dresden and Leipzig. *Career:* conducted first at Wuppertal, then principal conductor of the Essen Opera; Musical Dir, Fribourg Opera 1978–81, Kiel 1981–85, Dortmund 1985–90; Dir, Nice Opera and Philharmonic Orchestra from 1990.

WEISEL-CAPSOUTO, Robin; singer (soprano); b. 1952, USA. *Education:* Oberlin Coll., Univ. of Illinois, studied with Jennie Tourel in Jerusalem and with Heather Harper in London. *Career:* debut, sang Vivaldi's Gloria with the Jerusalem Symphony Orchestra 1974; sang in Mahler's 4th with Israel Philharmonic 1976; opera engagements in USA and Israel as Gluck's Amor, Lucy in The Beggar's Opera, and in La Voix Humaine, Le Roi David, Bacchus and Ariadne by Thomas Arne and Rameau's Les Fêtes d'Hébé; sang Zerlina with New England Opera Company 1984, and The Governess in The Turn of The Screw for New Israeli Opera 1992; concert repertoire includes Bach's B minor Mass, Carissimi's Jephté, Solomon and other oratorios by Handel.

WEISS, Ferdinand, DipMus, MA; Austrian composer, conductor and educator; b. 6 June 1933, Vienna; s. of Ferdinand Weiss and Antonia Weiss; m. Ingeborg Scheibenreiter 1967; two s. *Education:* Viennese Acad. of Music. *Career:* debut as composer, Eisenstadt 1957; freelance composer, private teacher of music theory, conductor and orchestra musician 1960–; Music Master, Vienna Conservatory and Baden Pädagogische Akad.; Man., Concert Chamber Ensemble, Lower Austria Composer's Soc.; Pres. Inoek; performances, concerts and radio broadcasts world-wide. *Compositions include:* over 250 works, including three symphonies, concertos for flute, oboe, clarinet, violin, trumpet and trombone, chamber music, guitar quartet, Lieder, Quattrofonia for saxophone quartet, 5 Scènes pour quatuor de guitares, à sa fin for orchestra 1994, Avec un Souffle de Tristesse for flute and string orchestra 1997, Quartetto Egiziano 2002, Quartet for flute, violin, violoncello, piano 2004, six string quartets, Relazioni veriabili for orchestra, 10 Chansons, Bruchstück for 12 saxophones, Petit concert pour four guitars and chamber

orchestra, Quartetto Novo per antico, Orgelsuite, Trio Concertante, Quartetto Disparato, Verwandlungen for string quartet (Transformation), Concertino per orchestra (1st performance in Shanghai), Bruchstück II for big band. *Honours:* 16 awards, including Award of Vienna 1960, Award of the Austrian State 1972, Award of Lower Austria 1970, 1984. *Address:* Christalnigg-Gasse 11, 2500 Baden, Austria (home). *Telephone:* (2252) 22632 (home). *Fax:* (2252) 22632 (home). *E-mail:* ferdinandweiss@gmx.at (home).

WEISS, Howard A., BM, MM; American violinist, conductor, concertmaster and educator; b. 1935, Chicago, IL. *Education:* Chicago Musical Coll., Roosevelt Univ. *Career:* founder, Music Dir, Conductor, Rochester Philharmonic Youth Orchestra 1970–89, with 12 tours including England, Scotland 1984, Germany, Austria, Switzerland 1986, Dominican Republic 1987, Alaska 1988, Jamaica 1989, also on Voice of America; Concertmaster, Rochester Chamber Orchestra 1981–89; Prof. of Violin, Eastman School of Music, Rochester 1981–, Nazareth Coll., Rochester 1983–85; Concertmaster, Chicago Chamber Orchestra 1962–70, San Francisco Ballet Orchestra 1962, Virginia Symphony 1964, Rochester Philharmonic 1967–87 (Concertmaster Emeritus 1987–), Eastern Music Festival, Greensboro, North Carolina 1976–80, Grand Teton Music Festival Seminar, Jackson Hole, Wyoming 1983–86, Rochester Oratorio Society 1987–, Bear Lake Music Festival, Utah 1992–93; Music Dir, Conductor String Orchestra, Siena Festival, Italy 1998–; First Violinist, Cleveland Orchestra 1965–67; as soloist, performed over 45 concerti with Cleveland Orchestra, Rochester and New Orleans Philharmonics, Chicago Grant Park Symphony, Cincinnati, Chicago and Rochester Chamber Orchestras, Siena Festival, Italy, with conductors including James Levine, David Zinman, Alexander Schneider, Walter Hendl and Gerard Schwarz; soloist in US premiere of the Carl Nielsen Violin Concerto 1967; soloist in the Rochester, New York premieres of the violin concertos of Berg, Nielsen and Vaughan Williams; violinist, Brockport Piano Trio 1971–74; Leader, Hartwell String Quartet 1975–78; performed chamber music with Misha Dichter, Leonard Rose, Lynn Harrell, Yo-Yo Ma, Elly Ameling, Jaime Laredo, Walter Trampler, Lillian Fuchs, James Buswell, Gary Karr, Alan Civil, Lukas Foss; mem. Advisory Bd, Young Audiences of Rochester 1975–;. *Honours:* Outstanding Graduate of 1966, Roosevelt Univ. 1973, Monroe County (New York) Medallion 1986. *Address:* 228 Castlebar Road, Rochester, NY 14610-2914, USA (home). *Telephone:* (585) 473-6894 (home).

WEITHAAS, Antje; German concert violinist; *Professor of Violin, Hochschule für Musik Hanns Eisler*; b. 21 Nov. 1966, Guben. *Education:* Hochschule für Musik Hanns Eisler, Berlin with Werner Scholz. *Career:* frequent concerts with Deutsches Symphony Orchestra and Vladimir Ashkenazy, Leipzig Gewandhaus Orchestra, Suisse Romande and Academy of St Martin-in-the-Fields; Los Angeles Philharmonic Orchestra, Boston Symphony Orchestra and Minneapolis Orchestra; Philharmonia, BBC Symphony Orchestra, Dresdner Staatskapelle and Scottish Chamber Orchestra; season 1995–96 with recitals at the Bath Festival and Wigmore Hall, London, San Francisco Symphony Orchestra Debut Series and in Toronto; season 1996–97 with Orchestre de Paris, Zürich Tonhalle, Gothenburg Symphony Orchestra, BBC Symphony Orchestra, and tour of Germany with Bournemouth Symphony Orchestra; season 1998–99 with Scottish Chamber Orchestra, English Northern Philharmonic and BBC Symphony Orchestra; other engagements with Royal Liverpool Philharmonic Orchestra and Hallé Orchestra; season 1999–2000 with Royal Liverpool Philharmonic, Brabant and Residentie Orchestras, Orchestra Sinfonica Palermo and Malaysian Philharmonic; season 2001–02 with Tokyo Metropolitan, Copenhagen Philharmonic, Ulster, Capetown Philharmonic and Swedish Chamber Orchestras; season 2002–03 with Gothenburg Symphony, BBC Philharmonic, Scottish Chamber and Lisbon Gulbenkian Orchestras; season 2003–04 with Orchestre de Chambre de Lausanne, BBC Nat. Orchestra of Wales; season 2004–05 with Bournemouth Symphony Orchestra, Gothenburg Symphony; soloist in concerts with Orchestra of Teatro La Fenice, Venice under Antonello Manacorda and with Dresden Philharmonic under Dmitrij Kitajenko 2015–16; regularly performs chamber music with Ex Aequo Trio, Vancouver Festival resident 1998–99; festivals include Kuhmo, Bath, Vancouver, Heimbach, Mondsee, Risör and Delft; numerous other concerts and tours; playsa 2001 Peter Greiner violin; Artistic Dir Camerata Bern 2009–; Prof. of Violin, Hochschule für Musik Hanns Eisler, Berlin 2004–. *Honours:* Winner, Wieniawski, Kreisler, Bach and Joseph Joachim Competitions. *Current Management:* c/o Karsten Witt Musik Management, Leuschnerdamm 13, 10999 Berlin, Germany. *Telephone:* (30) 214594220. *Fax:* (30) 214594101. *E-mail:* info@ karstenwitt.com (office). *Website:* www.karstenwitt.com.

WELBORN, Tracey; American singer (tenor); b. 1967, Stoneville, NC. *Education:* Curtis Institute of Music, Philadelphia. *Career:* school teacher until 1989; opera engagements with Lausanne Opera, Boston Lyric Opera, Spoleto USA, Opera Co of Philadelphia and Portland Opera; Season 1993–94 with Rossini's Lindoro for Utah Opera, Ernesto and Tamino for Canadian Opera and Gluck's Pylade at Strasbourg; season 1994–95 with Paris in La Belle Hélène for Scottish Opera, Ferrando at Pittsburgh and Jupiter in Semele at Spoleto, Italy; concerts include Candide with the San Francisco Symphony Orchestra, Messiah with the Baltimore Symphony Orchestra, Honegger's King David, and Mozart's Requiem; Phoenix Symphony Orchestra in Bach's St Matthew Passion; season 1997 with Mozart's Belmonte at Edmonton, Don Ottavio at Costa Mesa and in Prokoviev's The Duenna at Geneva; title role in Rossini's Le Comte Ory, at Glyndebourne; season 1998 with Bernstein's Candide at Turin and in Prokofiev's Duenna at Geneva.

Recordings include: Paolo in Il Matrimonio Segreto. *Honours:* winner Washington Int. Competition and Mario Lanza Competition. *Current Management:* Matthew Laifer Artists Management, 410 West 24th Street, Suite 2i, New York, NY 10011, USA. *Telephone:* (212) 929-7429. *Fax:* (212) 633-2628. *E-mail:* laiferart@aol.com. *Website:* www.laiferart.com.

WELCHER, Dan Edward, BMus, MM; American composer and conductor; *Lee Hage Jamail Regents Professor of Composition, University of Texas School of Music;* b. 2 March 1948, Rochester, NY; s. of Jack Welcher and Carol Welcher; m. Linda Howard. *Education:* Eastman School at Rochester with Samuel Adler, Manhattan School of Music, Aspen Music School. *Career:* bassoonist, Rochester Philharmonic Orchestra 1968–69, US Mil. Band, West Point 1969–72, Louisville Orchestra 1972–78; Asst Conductor, Austin, Texas Symphony Orchestra 1980–90; Founder/Conductor Univ. of Texas New Music Ensemble 1979–; Faculty mem. Butler School of Music, Univ. of Texas 1978, tenured 1982, Full Prof. 1989–, Lee Hage Jamail Regents Prof. of Composition 1998–; Faculty of Aspen Music Festival 1976–93; Composer-in-Residence, Honolulu Symphony Orchestra 1990–93; composer of more than 100 works, commissioned by Aspen Music Festival, Boston Symphony, Handel and Haydn Soc., Dallas Symphony, Cleveland Quartet, Nat. Endowment for the Arts (NEA), many other agencies and soloists; Lotte Lehmann Foundation Artistic Advisory Bd mem. 2001–09. *Compositions include:* Flute Concerto 1974, four Wind Quintets 1972, 1977, 1986, 2008, Concerto da Camera for bassoon and chamber orchestra 1975, Trio for violin, cello and piano 1976, The Visions of Merlin for orchestra 1980, Partita for horn, violin and piano 1980, Vox Femina for soprano and ensemble 1984, Quintet for clarinet and strings 1984, Prairie Light for orchestra 1985, Arches: An Impression for concert band 1985, Evening Scenes: Three Poems of James Agee 1985, Della's Gift (opera) 1986, The Yellowstone Fires for wind ensemble 1988, Clarinet Concerto 1989, Bridges five pieces for strings 1989, three string quartets 1987, 1992, 2007, five symphonies 1992, 1994, 1998, 2005, 2009, Violin Concerto 1993, Shiva's Drum Piano Concerto 1994, Zion for wind ensemble 1994, Bright Wings for orchestra 1996, Brass Quintet 1983, Symphony No. 3: Shaker Life for wind ensemble 1998, JFK: The Voice of Peace (oratorio) 1999, Oboe Concerto Venti di Mare 1999, Beyond Sight for orchestra 1999, Zion for orchestra 2000, Perpetual Song for wind ensemble 2000, Songs without Words 2001, Minstrels of the Kells 2002, Glacier 2003, Holy Night (opera) 2004, Timpani Concerto 2004, Symphony No. 4 (wind ensemble) 2005, Symphony No. 5 (large orchestra) 2009; various songs, chamber music. *Honours:* MacDowell Colony residencies 1989, 2001, 2002, 2009, Bellagio residency (Italy) 1997, Guggenheim Fellowship 1997, Atlantic Center for Arts residency 1999, Yaddo residencies 2000, 2007, 2008, three NEA awards, Bogliasco Foundation, Genoa, Italy 2003, Camargo Foundation Residency, Cassis, France 2010. *Address:* Butler School of Music, University of Texas, 1 University Station E3100, Austin, TX 78712, USA (office). *Telephone:* (512) 471-0943 (office). *E-mail:* dwelcher@mail.utexas.edu (office). *Website:* www.danwelcher.com.

WELKER, Hartmut; German singer (bass-baritone); b. 27 Oct. 1941, Velbert, Rhineland; m. Edeltraut 1982; one s. one d. *Education:* studied for tech. career. *Career:* took up singing 1972; debut, Opera, Aachen 1974; British debut, Edinburgh Festival with London Symphony Orchestra/Abbado 1983; Aachen Opera 1974–80; since then has had three-year contract with Karlsruhe Opera; sang at La Scala (Lohengrin with Abbado), Geneva, Paris (Khovanshchina); sang Don Pizarro (Fidelio), Madrid and at Maggio Musicale, Florence, Italy and for Scottish Opera 1984; appeared in Hamburg, Munich and Stuttgart, Boris Godunov in North America with Chicago Symphony Orchestra/Abbado, Vienna State Opera, Berlin and Hamburg in productions of Fidelio, Flying Dutchman, Salome, Lohengrin; Covent Garden debut in Fidelio 1986; sang also with Philharmonia Orchestra/Muti, also at Turin, Vienna, Madrid, Bologna, Naples, Tokyo, Chicago; season 1988 included appearances in San Francisco, Berlin, Geneva, with further visits to La Scala, Covent Garden and Salzburg; sang in London as Pizarro and Kaspar 1986–89, Theater an der Wien and Turin in Schubert's Fierrabras and as Wozzeck 1989, Telramund in Lohengrin at Vienna Staatsoper and Deutsche Oper Berlin 1990; other roles include Kurwenal, Klingsor, Macbeth, Carlos in La Forza del Destino, Amonasro, Barnaba and Scarpia; sang Pizarro in Fidelio at the Metropolitan, New York 1991, Wozzeck at Catania 1996, Pizarro in Beethoven's Leonore at Théâtre de Champs Elysées, Paris 1998; season 1997–98, Semperoper, Dresden as Kurwenal, Holländer, Pizarro; further roles as Amfortas in Parsifal, and Wotan and Alberich in Wagner's Ring, Bayreuth 2000–; season 2000 as Alberich at Cologne and Scarpia at Essen, Kurwenal, Amonasro and Wotan for Karlsruhe Opera, Kurwenal in Tristan und Isolde at Bayreuth Festival 2006. *Recordings include:* Schönberg Gurrelieder/Bauer, Zemlinksy's Der Traumgörge as Kaspar/Hans, Notre Dame by F. Schmidt as Archidiakonus, Fierrabras, Brutamonte 1992, Fidelio (Pizarro), Lohengrin (Telramund), Das Wunder der Heliane, Korngold 1992, Arcesius in Die toten Augen, d'Albert 1997. *Honours:* Kammersänger. *Address:* Frühlingstrasse 10, 76327 Pfintzal/Wöschbach, Germany (home). *Telephone:* (7240) 942548 (home). *Fax:* (7240) 942549 (home). *E-mail:* hartmut.welker@web.de (home).

WELLER, Dieter; singer (bass-baritone); b. 25 May 1937, Essen, Germany; m. Dorte Fischer. *Education:* studied with Erwin Rottgen in Essen, further studies in Cologne. *Career:* debut at Bremerhaven, 1963–66 as Padre Guardiano in La Forza del Destino; Member of the Frankfurt Opera from 1966; Appeared in San Francisco in 1974 as Wurm in Luisa Miller; Further appearances in Berlin, Düsseldorf, Hamburg, Brussels and Edinburgh; Sang at Teatro Regio Turin in 1983 in Berg's Lulu, at Metropolitan Opera in 1985 as

the Music Master in Ariadne auf Naxos; Season 2000 as Joe in Mahagonny at Hamburg and Reimann's Lear for the Dresden Staatsoper; Many appearances in operas by Rossini, Lortzing, Weber, Smetana, Wagner and Wolf-Ferrari; frequent concert engagements. *Recordings:* Der Freischütz and Martha; Der Zwerg by Zemlinsky.

WELLINGTON, Christopher Ramsay, MA, ARCM; British violist and viola d'amore player; b. 5 Feb. 1930, London, England; m. 1st Joanna Donat 1954; one s. one d.; m. 2nd Eileen Darlow 1988. *Education:* Univ. of Oxford, Royal Coll. of Music, London. *Career:* Sadler's Wells Opera Orchestra 1954–58; Philharmonia Orchestra 1958–65; Prin. Viola, London Bach Orchestra, Philomusica of London, Tilford Bach Orchestra, Southern Pro Musica; viola player, Zorian String Quartet, Amici String Quartet, Nemet Piano Quartet, Music Group of London, Rasumovsky String Quartet; frequent soloist at Queen Elizabeth Hall; Prof. of Viola, Univ. Coll., Chichester; warden, solo performers section, Inc. Soc. of Musicians 1986–87; Prof., Royal Coll. of Music 1972–96, Trinity Coll. of Music 1996–2001. *Recordings:* Elegiac Meditation by Robin Milford, works by Haydn, Rubbra, Charles Ives, Shostakovich with Amici Quartet, works by Elgar, Vaughan Williams, Frank Bridge, Schubert with Music Group of London, works by Jadin, Vachon, Boughton, Holbrooke, Padre Soler with Rasumovsky String Quartet. *Publications:* Concerto for viola and orchestra by William Walton (Vol. 12, ed.) 2002. *Address:* 7 Fraser Gardens, Emsworth, Hants., PO10 8PY, England (home). *Telephone:* (1243) 378300 (home). *Fax:* (1243) 378300 (home). *Website:* www.rasumovsky.com.

WELLS, Jeffrey; American singer (bass-baritone); b. 1957. *Career:* sang Donizetti's Raimondo at New Orleans in 1985; season 1986–87 as Assur in Semiramide and Ferrando in Il Trovatore at Washington; Sang Stravinsky's Nick Shadow at Glyndebourne 1989, and Rossini's Basilio at Toronto; Metropolitan Opera from 1990, in Semiramide, Billy Budd, Carmen (as Zuniga), and A Midsummer Night's Dream 1996; guest appearances at Washington as Enrico in Anna Bolena 1993, at Bonn as Escamillo 1994, Detroit as Don Giovanni 1995, and San Francisco 1996–98, as Glinka's Ruslan, and Escamillo; sang the Rheingold Wotan at San Francisco 1999; Britten's Claggart in Seattle and Toronto 2001. *Recordings include:* Il Trovatore. *Address:* Jeffrey Wells Music, PO Box 24473, Knoxville, TN 37933, USA (office). *E-mail:* operajeff@aol.com (office). *Website:* www .jeffreywellsmusic.com.

WELSBY, Norman; British singer (baritone); b. 7 Feb. 1939, Warrington, Cheshire, England. *Education:* Royal Coll. of Music in Manchester, studied with Gwilym Jones and Otakar Kraus in London. *Career:* debut at Sadler's Wells Opera, London 1968 as Masetto; many appearances at Covent Garden and with ENO in the standard repertoire and in modern works; sang Gunther in The Ring, under Reginald Goodall 1973–74; sang in the premiere concert of The Magic Fountain by Delius, BBC 1977; sang Pentheus in the British premiere of The Bassarids for ENO 1974, The General in the premiere of We Come to the River, at Covent Garden 1976; many concert appearances. *Recordings include:* The Ring of the Nibelung conducted by Reginald Goodall, The Magic Fountain.

WELSER-MÖST, Franz; Austrian conductor; *Music Director, Cleveland Orchestra;* b. 16 Aug. 1960, Linz; m. *Education:* Musikgymnasium, Linz and Staatliche Musikhochschule, Munich. *Career:* Chief Conductor, Jeunesse Orchestra, Linz 1982–85, Norrköping Symphony Orchestra 1985, Musikkollegium Winterthur, Switzerland 1986; Music Dir London Philharmonic Orchestra 1990–96; Music Dir Zürich Opera 1995–2002, Principal Conductor 2002–05, Music Dir 2005–08; Music Dir Cleveland Orchestra 2002–; Gen. Music Dir Vienna Staatsoper 2010–14; has appeared at Deutsche Oper Berlin, Glyndebourne Festival, Salzburg Festival; regularly works with Berlin Philharmonic, Vienna Philharmonic, Royal Concertgebouw Orchestra, Gewandhausorchester Leipzig, Staatskapelle Dresden, Bavarian Radio Symphony and Gustav Mahler Youth Orchestra; has conducted all major US orchestras; Academician, European Acad. of Yuste. *Recordings include:* Mendelssohn Symphonies Nos 3 and 4, Schumann Symphonies Nos 2 and 3, Bruckner Symphony No. 7, Strauss Waltzes, Carl Orff's Carmina Burana, Stravinsky's Oedipus Rex, Bartók's Miraculous Mandarin, Kodaly's Peacock Variations, Kancheli's Symphony No. 3, Pärt's Symphony No. 3, Fratres, Schmidt's Symphony No. 4 (Gramophone Award 1996) (all with LPO), world premiere recording of Johann Straus Jr's Simplicius with Zurich Opera Orchestra, Beethoven's Symphony No. 9 (with The Cleveland Orchestra), The Welser-Möst Edition, New Year's Day Concert (Vienna Musikverein) on CD and DVD 2011, 2013. *Publication:* Kadenzen: Notizen und Gespräche 2007. *Honours:* Hon. mem. Gesellschaft der Musikfreunde Wien and Wiener Singverein; Decoration of Honour; Outstanding Achievement Award, Western Law Centre, LA, for work for people with disabilities, Musical America's Conductor of the Year 2003, Diapason d'Or, Japanese Record Acad. Award, Gold Medal of Upper Austria, Kilenyi Medal of Honour, Bruckner Soc. of America. *Current Management:* c/o IMG Artists, The Light Box, 111 Power Road, London, W4 5PY, England. *Telephone:* (20) 7957-5800; (20) 7957-5801. *E-mail:* jchadwick@imgartists.com; jchadwick@enticottmusicmanagement .com. *Website:* www.imgartists.com. *Address:* The Cleveland Orchestra, Severance Hall, 11001 Euclid Avenue, Cleveland, OH 44106-1796, USA (office). *Telephone:* (216) 231-7300 (office). *E-mail:* info@clevelandorchestra .com (office). *Website:* www.clevelandorchestra.com (office).

WELSH, Moray Meston, BA, GradDip, LRAM, ARCM; British cellist, teacher and painter; b. 1 March 1947, Haddington, East Lothian, Scotland; s. of D. A.

Welsh and C. Welsh (née Meston); partner Jonathan Papp. *Education:* York Univ. and Moscow Conservatoire, Russia. *Career:* debut, Wigmore Hall 1972; cello solo appearances in UK, USA, USSR, Europe and Scandinavia; principal cellist, London Symphony Orchestra 1992–2007; appeared with major UK orchestras, including Royal Philharmonic Orchestra, BBC Symphony; festivals at Bath, Edinburgh, Aldeburgh, Bergen and Helsinki; appeared as soloist internationally under Colin Davis, André Previn, Rafael Frühbeck de Burgos, Bernard Haitink; chamber music performances with Previn, Bashmet, Midori, Galway and Chung; Prin. Cellist, London Symphony Orchestra 1992–2005; mem. Cropper-Welsh-Roscoe Trio 2005–15; recitals with Jonathan Papp, Martin Roscoe and Caroline Palmer; teaches privately and in master-classes. *Recordings include:* concertos by Boccherini, Vivaldi, Alexander Goehr, Hoddinott, Hugh Wood (Sunday Times record of the year); recorded with James Galway, Kyung-Wha Chung, Allegri Quartet, Alberni Quartet; cello and orchestra music by Herbert Howells with LSO; Rachmaninov Complete Works for Cello and Piano. *Art exhibition:* Kingsgate Studios 2013, 2014. *Film:* Barry Lyndon (soundtrack). *Radio includes:* frequent broadcasts on BBC Radio 3. *Publications:* articles in The Strad Magazine and nat. newspapers. *Honours:* British Council Scholarship 1969, Gulbenkian Fellowship 1970. *Address:* 32 Dartmouth Road, London, NW2 4EX, England (home). *Telephone:* (20) 8933-3032 (home). *E-mail:* moraywelsh@thecello.net. *Website:* www.moraywelsh.com.

WEN, De-Qing; Chinese composer; b. 10 July 1958, Jian Yang, Fujian. *Education:* Fujian Normal University, China Conservatory of Music, Beijing, Conservatoire de Musique de Genève, Switzerland, Conservatoire National Supérieur de Musique de Lyon, France. *Career:* debut as composer, Ningxia Ensemble, China, 1984; Concert Portrait performed by Ningxia Ensemble, Xining, 1986; Music for Fan Jun's film My Childhood in Ruijing, 1990; Concert Portrait performed by Ensemble Contrechamps and Ensemble CIP, Geneva, 1995; Concert Portrait performed by Quatuor du Temps, La Chaux-de-Fonds, 1998; Concert Portrait tour in China, 1999. *Compositions:* Ji I and Ji II for piano, 1992–93; Complainte for 1 speaker of Beijing Opera and 3 percussionists, 1994; Le souffle for 6 instruments, 1994; String Quartet No. 1, 1995; Spring, River, Flowers, Moon, Night for 12 women's voices, 1995; Traces II for 9 instruments, 1996; Divination for 6 instrumentalists, 1997; Petit Chou variation for erhu and string quartet, 1997; String Quartet No. 2, 1997; Ballade, for pipa and string quartet, 1998; Kung-fu, for percussion solo, 1998; Quatre Poésies for chamber orchestra, 1999. *Recordings:* De-qing Wen, Ensemble Contrechamps and CIP, Quatuor du Temps, recorded for Radio Suisse Romande, Espace 2, 1996. *Address:* 36 avenue de la Roseraie, 1205 Geneva, Switzerland.

WENKEL, Ortrun; German singer (mezzo-soprano, alto); b. 25 Oct. 1942, Buttstadt, Thuringia; m. Peter Rothe 1966. *Education:* Franz Liszt Hochschule Weimar, Hochschule für Musik, Frankfurt, Lohmann masterclass and operatic studies with Cavelti. *Career:* debut concert, as student, in London 1964; opera debut in Heidelberg 1971; performed at opera houses throughout Europe including La Scala, Milan, Covent Garden, Bayerische Staatsoper, Hamburg, with appearances at the Salzburg Festival, Munich Opera Festival and festivals of Schwetzingen, Edinburgh, Berlin, Spoleto and Vienna, notably as Penelope in the Zürich production of the Monteverdi Cycle; has given numerous lieder recitals and made guest appearances with symphony orchestras in New York, San Francisco, Washington, London, Berlin, Vienna, Paris, Bayreuth, Amsterdam, Buenos Aires and Rio de Janeiro among others; alto part of Erda in Wagner's Rheingold and Siegfried; debuts in new mezzo-soprano roles as Adriano in Wagner's Rienzi, Staatsoper Prague, Fricka in Wagner's Rheingold and Walküre, Herodias in Salome and Klytämnestra in Elektra by Richard Strauss, Spring Festival, Budapest 1999, Magda Schneider in Kühr/Turrini's Tod und Teufel, world premiere, Graz, Steirischer Herbst 1999, Beroe in Henze's The Bassarids at New York and Moscow, Bernarda in Reimann's Bernarda Albas Haus, Swiss premiere, Bern 2002; numerous concert engagements. *Recordings include:* Boulez's Bayreuth Centenary Ring, The Ring with Dresdner Staatskapelle, Mahler's 3rd Symphony and 8th Symphony; Mozart's Requiem, The Magic Flute, Schoenberg's Jacob's Ladder, Dvořák's Stabat Mater, Handel's Xerxes, Strauss's Daphne (Gaea); solo recitals of Italian Baroque music, St Matthew Passion by Bach and several of his cantatas, Zemlinsky Lieder, Schreker and Shostakovich Lieder, Henze's The Bassarids, Wagner's Ring with Badische Staatskapelle 1995, Lieder Recital (Bayreuth). *Honours:* Grammy Award for Wagner's Ring des Nibelungen 1982, Deutscher Schallplattenpreis for Mozart's Requiem 1983. *Address:* Eichendorffstrasse 25, 69493 Hirschberg-Leutershausen, Germany (home). *Telephone:* (6201) 55356 (also fax) (home).

WENNBERG, Siv Anna Margareta; Swedish singer (soprano); b. 18 Sept. 1944, Timrå. *Education:* Ingesunds Musikskola, Musikaliska Akademien, Stockholm. *Career:* debut at Royal Opera House, Stockholm 1972; opera performances from 1972 throughout Europe; extensive concert engagements, with roles including Brünnhilde in Siegfried and Die Walküre, Empress in Die Frau ohne Schatten (television), Amelia in Ballo in Maschera (television), Alice in Falstaff, Puccini's Tosca, Leonora in Fidelio, Mozart's Donna Elvira, Daisy Doody in Aniara, Euridice in Orpheus in the Underworld and Beatrice in von Suppé's Boccaccio; TV and radio broadcasts in Sweden, throughout Europe and the USA; permanent mem., Royal Opera Stockholm; sang Verdi title role, Aida and Lady Macbeth; Wagner: Senta, Elisabeth, Elsa and Sieglinde; Strauss: Elektra, Salome, Ariadne. *Recordings:* Scandinavian Songs with Geoffrey Parsons; Wagner's Rienzi, Irene, with Dresden

Staatskapelle; Royal Opera Stockholm Gala excerpt from Aida, 1995; Schubert and Strauss songs with Jan Eyron, 1997. *Honours:* first prize Jussi Björling Competition, Scandinavian Singing Contest 1971, Swedish Opera Prize for Wagner's Isolde 1988, Apptd Court Singer by King Carl Gustaf XVI of Sweden 1994. *Address:* Odengatan 32, 11351 Stockholm, Sweden.

WERBA, Markus; Austrian singer (baritone); b. 14 Nov. 1973, Villach. *Career:* debut at La Scala, Milan as Harlequin in Ariadne auf Naxos 2005, Royal Opera House debut as Harlequin in 2008; US debut as Papageno with Los Angeles Opera 2009; has appeared with leading int. opera cos including Vienna Volksoper, Zurich Opera, Komische Oper Berlin, Opéra Bastille Paris, Theatre du Capitole Toulouse, Teatro Comunale Bologna, Teatro Massimo Palermo, La Fenice, Venice, Opéra de Lyon, Bayerische Staatsoper München; has performed at many leading festivals including Mozart Festival, Vienna, Salzburg Festival, Aix en Provence Festival; extensive recital and concert career, including performances at Wigmore Hall, London for BBC, Musikverein Vienna; roles include: Figaro in The Barber of Seville, Harlequin in Ariadne auf Naxos, Guglielmo in Così fan Tutte, Nardo in La Finta Giardiniera, Mercurio in La Calisto, Il Conte in The Marriage of Figaro, Marianus in Faust, Papageno in The Magic Flute, Olivier in Capriccio, Don Giovanni, Hans Heiling. *Recordings include:* Schubert, Alfonso und Estrella 2004, Haydn, The Creation 2007.

WERRES, Elisabeth; German singer (soprano); b. 1954, Bonn; m. Anthony Bramall (conductor). *Education:* Cologne Conservatory with D. Jacob. *Career:* debut aged 22, Cologne Opera in small roles for one season; resident soprano, Staatstheater Karlsruhe, 1978–80, roles included Rosina, Marguerite in Gounod's Faust, Adele, Eurydice, Frau Fluth; Resident soprano, Dortmund Opera, 1980–82: roles included Nedda, Susanna, Musetta, Gilda, Aminta, Adina; resident soprano, Staatsoper Hannover, 1989–97, roles included Tatjana, Rosalinde, Musetta, Freia, Merry Widow, Marschallin, Mazenka, Helmwige; guest engagements in theatres across Europe including Staatsoper Hamburg, Staatsoper Munich, Deutsche Oper Berlin, Cologne Opera, Komische Oper Berlin, Essen, Leipzig, Zürich, Mannheim, Strasbourg, Wiesbaden, Weimar, Dortmund, Karlsruhe, Amsterdam, Vienna Volksoper; roles included Rosalinde, Marie in Wozzeck, Turandot by Busoni, The Merry Widow, Milada in Dalibor, Chrysothemis in Elektra, Arabella, Countess in Figaro, Elena in I Vespri Siciliani and especially Feldmarschallin in Der Rosenkavalier; Concerts in Barcelona, Chicago, Tokyo, Hamburg, Essen, Stuttgart, Karlsruhe, Strasbourg, Luxembourg, Vienna, Munich, Cologne, Zürich, Luzern, Berlin: Beethoven's 9th, Strauss' 4 Last Songs, Weill's Seven Deadly Sins, Wozzeck Fragments, opera and operetta galas; Prof. of Voice, Univ. of the Arts, Berlin 2003–. *Recordings:* Laura in Hindemith's opera Neues Vom Tage, conductor Jan Latham-Koenig; Offenbachiade: Gala for opening of Cologne Philharmonic, conductor Pinchas Steinberg. *Honours:* Special Award, Mozart Competition Würzburg, 1977. *Address:* Wehrastr. 11, 76199 Karlsruhe, Germany.

WERTHEN, Rudolf; violinist and conductor; b. 16 July 1946, Malines, Belgium. *Education:* Ghent and Brussels Conservatories with André Gertler. *Career:* soloist with the NDR Symphony Orchestra at Hamburg; Prof., Robert Schumann Inst., Detmold; Flanders Chamber Orchestra from 1977; Musical Dir, Flanders Opera at Antwerp from 1992; rediscovered and premiered the 7th Concerto of Vieuxtemps and the Russian Concerto of Lalo. *Honours:* prizewinner competitions at Vienna, Amsterdam and Brussels.

WEST, Ewan Donald, BA, MA, MBA, DPhil; British writer on music; b. 9 Aug. 1960, Cheltenham, Gloucestershire. *Education:* Exeter Coll., Oxford, Cranfield School of Management. *Career:* Lecturer on History of Music, Worcester Coll., Oxford 1986–94; Jr Research Fellow, Mansfield Coll., Oxford 1988–92; Dir of Studies in Music, Somerville Coll., Oxford 1989–94; Univ. of Oxford James Ingham Halstead Scholar 1985–87; mem. American Musicological Soc., Royal Musical Asscn. *Publications:* The Hamlyn Dictionary of Music 1982, The Oxford Dictionary of Opera (with John Warrack) 1992, The Concise Oxford Dictionary of Opera (third edn, with John Warrack) 1996; contrib. to Music and Letters, Austrian Studies. *Address:* 14 Moorhouse Road, London, W2 5DJ, England (office). *Telephone:* (20) 7221-6001 (home). *E-mail:* ewan_west@hotmail.com (home).

WEST, John; American singer (bass); b. 25 Oct. 1938, Cleveland, OH. *Education:* Curtis Inst. of Music, with Martial Singher, in New York with Beverley Johnson. *Career:* debut in San Francisco in 1963 as Sarastro; many appearances at US opera centres including Houston, Philadelphia, Seattle, Santa Fe, Portland, San Francisco, Washington and Fort Worth; guest engagements at Vancouver, Mexico City, Hanover and Spoleto; roles include Don Alfonso, Oroveso in Norma, Basilio, Mephistopheles of Gounod and Berlioz, Boris Godunov, Ramphis, Arkel, Ochs, La Roche in Capriccio, Hunding and Tiresias; frequent concert engagements.

WEST, John Frederic; American singer (tenor); b. 4 March 1952, Dayton, OH. *Education:* Manhattan School of Music and American Opera Center at Juilliard, New York. *Career:* sang Tamino and Stravinsky's Tom Rakewell at Glens Falls, 1975; Scottish Opera, 1980, as Gabriele Adorno; Season 1982–83 as Manrico at Frankfurt and Calaf at the New York City Opera; Waldemar in Schoenberg's Gurrelieder at the Edinburgh Festival; Toronto, 1986, as Apollo in Strauss's Daphne, Bacchus in Ariadne auf Naxos at Washington and the Metropolitan Opera, 1993; Wagner's Tristan at the reopening of the Prinzregententheater, Munich, 1996; Season 1997–98 as Tannhäuser at the Metropolitan and Tristan at the Nationaltheater, Munich; Tristan at Covent

Garden, 2001; Engaged as Siegfried in The Ring at the Deutsche Oper, Berlin, 2003. *Recordings include:* DVD of Tristan, from Munich.

WEST, Kevin; British singer (tenor); b. 1960, England. *Education:* Guildhall School with Walter Gruner. *Career:* sang first with the D'Oyly Carte Opera Company; appearances with Opera 80 as Sellem in The Rake's Progress and Don Ottavio, and Britten's Peter Quint for Music Theatre Wales; engagements with Opera Restor'd in English Baroque Music and throughout the UK; sang Monteverdi's Orfeo at the Prom Concerts in London; ENO debut, 1989 as David in The Mastersingers; has also sung with English National Contemporary Opera Studio, Opera Factory as Trimalchio in Maderna's Satyricon in 1990 and the Montepulciano Festival in Henze's The English Cat in 1990; appeared with Opera Northern Ireland in 1991 as Mozart's Don Basilio (repeated for Opera North, 1996); sang in Bernstein's Candide at Turin, 1997; concert repertoire includes Bach's St John Passion and Easter Oratorio, works by Handel, Mozart and Schubert and Tippett's A Child Of Our Time at South Bank in London.

WEST, Stephen; American singer (bass-baritone); b. 1950, New York. *Education:* Curtis Inst., Philadelphia, studied with Jerome Hines in New Jersey. *Career:* debut, Bonze in Butterfly at Philadelphia 1973; sang with the Metropolitan Opera, Chicago, Washington, Seattle and many others; New York City Opera from 1995, as Boito's Mefistofele and Verdi's Attila; Deutsche Staatsoper, Berlin as Weber's Kaspar and Paris Bastille as Berg's Dr Schön; concert appearances with the Philadelphia Orchestra at Carnegie Hall, and with the Denver and Montréal Symphony Orchestras; season 1997–98 as Adams in the premiere of Amistad by Anthony Davis at Chicago, and Kolenaty in The Makropulos Case by Janáček at the New York Metropolitan; further engagements as King Henry in Lohengrin at Bayreuth, Dr Schön at the Met, Gounod's Mephistopheles at Baltimore and Massenet's Comte des Grieux for Dallas Opera; season 2000–01 as Mars in Henze's Venus and Adonis, at Santa Fe and Acrobat in Lulu at the Met. *Honours:* prizewinner Met Audition and Tchaikovsky Competition. *Current Management:* Herbert Barrett Management, 266 W 37th Street, 20th Floor, New York, NY 10018, USA. *Telephone:* (212) 245-3530. *Fax:* (212) 397-5860. *Website:* www.herbertbarrett.com.

WESTENRA, Hayley Dee; New Zealand singer; b. 10 April 1987, Christchurch; d. of Gerald and Jill Westenra; m. Arnaud Sabard 2013. *Career:* performer in classical, pop and traditional Maori choral styles; fmr Amb. to Save The Children, Hong Kong; Amb. for UNICEF. *Recordings include:* albums: Hayley Westenra 2001, Pure 2003, My Gift To You 2004, Odyssey 2005, Treasures 2007, River of Dreams 2008, Winter Magic 2009, Paradiso 2011, Hushabye 2013, Hayley Westenra- The Best 2014. *Publication:* In Her Own Voice (auto-biog.) 2007. *Current Management:* c/o Giselle Allier, Bedlam Management Ltd, PO Box 34449, London, W6 0XU, England. *E-mail:* hayleyw@bedlammanagement.com. *Website:* www.hayleywestenra.com.

WESTERGAARD, Peter, AB, MFA; American composer and academic; b. 28 May 1931, Champaign, IL. *Education:* Harvard Coll., Princeton Univ., studied with Walter Piston, Darius Milhaud, Roger Sessions and Wolfgang Fortner. *Career:* Asst Prof., Columbia Coll. 1963–66; Visiting Lecturer (Assoc. Prof.), Princeton Univ. 1966–67; Assoc. Prof., Amherst Coll. 1967–68; Princeton Univ. 1968–71; Prof., Princeton Univ. 1971–; Chair Dept of Music, Princeton Univ. 1974–78, 1983–86; Dir, Princeton Univ. Orchestra 1968–73; Bd of Dirs, American Music Centre 1969–72; Int. Soc. for Contemporary Music 1970–74; Dir, Princeton Univ. Opera Theatre 1970–; Visiting Prof., Univ. of British Columbia 1987; Lecturer Int. Music Seminar, Univ. of Bahia, Brazil 1992; Interdepartmental Cttee for the Program in Musical Performance, Princeton Univ. 1992–93; William Shubael Conant Prof. of Music, Princeton Univ. 1995–, Acting Chair Dept of Music 1995. *Compositions include:* five Movements for small orchestra 1959, Cantata II 1959, III 1966, Quartet for violin, vibraphone, clarinet and violoncello 1961, Variations for six players 1967, Mr and Mrs Discobbolos 1967, Divertimento on Discobbolic Fragments 1967, Noises, Sounds and Sweet Airs 1968, Tuckets and Sennets 1969, Cantata I 1956, Two Rhymes for soprano and violin 1979, 1997, Ariel Music 1987, Ode 1989, The Tempest (opera in three acts after William Shakespeare) 1990, Ringing Changes 1996, All 4s 1996, anyone lived in a pretty how town 1996, Byzantium for baritone and percussion quartet on poems by Yeats 1997, Chicken Little (opera for children) 1997, Cantata VI To The Dark Lady 1998, Chaconne 1999, Epithalamium 2000; also singing translations of The Magic Flute, Don Giovanni, Der Freischütz, Fidelio (original version of 1805), Così fan tutte, The Marriage of Figaro, Cinderella and The Coronation of Poppea.

WESTERN, Hilary; British singer (soprano); b. 1948, Cardiff, Wales. *Education:* Royal Acad. of Music, London Opera Centre. *Career:* sang at the Wexford and Glyndebourne Festivals and in Angers as Mimi and Toulouse as Frasquita; appearances as Fiordiligi in Grenoble, Anchorage and Britain; sang Mimi, Papagena and Diana for Opera North; Ariadne, Louise, Micaela, Christine in Blake's Toussaint, Musetta and Diana; sang at Almeida Festival 1990 in the world premiere of Europeras III and IV by John Cage; performances of Birtwistle's Punch and Judy, The Beggar's Opera and Orfeo with Opera Factory; Schoenberg's Pierrot Lunaire for Ballet Rambert; has sung in the musicals, Chess and A Little Night Music, in the West End and at the Chichester Festival in Born Again. *Honours:* Arts Council Award to study with Martin Isepp in New York.

WESTLAKE, Nigel; Australian composer and clarinettist; b. 6 Sept. 1958, Perth, WA. *Education:* studied with Don Westlake, Harry Sparnay. *Career:* freelance clarinettist from 1975; Principal, Australia Ensemble 1987–92, with

tours throughout Australia and abroad; tour of Australia and England 1992, with John Williams' group, Attaca; composer of film and television music. *Compositions include:* Onomatopoeia for bass clarinet and digital delay 1984, Omphalo Centric Lecture for four percussion 1984, Entomology for chamber ensemble and tape 1988, Refractions at Summercloud Bay for bass clarinet, flute and string trio 1989, Malachite Glass for bass clarinet and percussion quartet 1990, Antarctica Suite for guitar and orchestra (from the film score) 1992, Tall Tales But True for two guitars and ensemble 1992, Songs from the Forest for guitar duo 1994, High Tension Wires for string quartet 1994, Invocations concerto for bass clarinet and orchestra 1995, Babe: orchestral excerpts from the film 1996, Piano Sonata 1997, Miss Potter 2006. *Honours:* gold medal New York radio festival 1987, APRA Award for Best Film Score (for Babe) 1996.

WETHERELL, Eric David, BA, BMus, MA; British composer and conductor; b. 30 Dec. 1925, Tynemouth, Northumberland, England; m. 1st Jean Bettany 1949; one s. one d.; m. 2nd Elizabeth Major 1976; two d. *Education:* Queen's Coll., Oxford, Royal Coll. of Music. *Career:* horn player 1949–59; Repetiteur, Royal Opera House, Covent Garden 1960–63; Asst Music Dir, WNO 1963–69; Music Dir, HTV 1969–76; Chief Conductor, BBC Northern Ireland Orchestra 1976–81; Sr Music Producer, BBC Bristol 1981–85. *Compositions:* choral, solo songs, orchestral, including Airs and Graces and Welsh Dresser for orchestra, Bristol Quay for string orchestra, Your Gift to Man for chorus, music for TV plays and films, Alto Saxophone Concerto, Flute Concerto. *Publications:* Life of Gordon Jacob 1995, Arnold Cooke 1996, Patrick Hadley 1997, Albert Sammons 1998. *Address:* c/o British Music Information Centre, 11 Stratford Place, London, W1, England.

WETHERILL, Linda; flautist; b. 1950, USA. *Career:* recital and concerto soloist in major cities of Europe, Canada, USA; principal flautist with the orchestras of Hessischer Rundfunk Frankfurt and of Pierre Boulez's IRCAM at Pompidou Centre, Paris, France; repertoire includes Baroque, Classic, Romantic and Impressionist works; performed and premiered the flute music of Luciano Berio, Pierre Boulez, Elliott Carter, Olivier Messiaen, Goffredo Petrassi and Karl-Heinz Stockhausen; taught masterclasses in English, French, German, Spanish and American Conservatories. *Honours:* winner New York Young Artists debut 1979.

WEWEL, Gunter; singer (bass); b. 29 Nov. 1934, Arnsberg, Sauerland, Germany. *Education:* studied with Johannes Kobeck in Vienna, Rudolf Watzke in Dortmund, Emmi Muller in Krefeld. *Career:* mem., Dortmund Opera from 1963; guest appearances in Düsseldorf, Cologne, Karlsruhe, Hanover, Budapest, Paris, Zürich, Salzburg, Munich; radio and television engagements in Germany, France; roles include Wagner's Daland, Titurel, Fafner, King Mark, Landgrave and King Heinrich; Philip II in Don Carlos, Gremin in Eugene Onegin and Beethoven's Rocco; Mozart's Sarastro, Osmin and Commendatore; Nicolai's Falstaff and Rossini's Bartolo. *Recordings include:* Die Zauberflöte conducted by Sawallisch; Schumann's Paradies und die Peri under Henryk Czyz; Suppé's Boccaccio with Willi Boskovsky; Die Königskinder, Mendelssohn's Die Beiden Pädagogen, Les Contes d'Hoffmann and Millöcker's Gasparone, conducted by Heinz Wallberg; La Vie Parisienne, with Willy Mattes.

WHATELY, (Catherine) Kitty; British singer (mezzo soprano); b. 1983, London; d. of Kevin Whately and Madelaine Newton; one d. *Education:* Chetham's School of Music, Guildhall School of Music and Drama with Jane Highfield and Robert Dean, Royal Coll. of Music Int. Opera School with Tim Evans-Jones. *Career:* two years as mem. Glyndebourne chorus; has performed with Buxton Festival Opera, Glyndebourne Festival Opera, English Touring Opera. *Operatic repertoire includes:* Dorabella in Così fan tutte, Eduige in Rodelinda, Kate in Owen Wingrave, Idamante in Idomeneo, Cherubino in Le Nozze di Figaro, Nancy in Albert Herring, Juno in Semele, Second Lady in Die Zauberflöte, Johanna in Sweeney Todd, Teodata in Flavio, Rosina in Il barbiere di Siviglia. *Honours:* First Prize, Kathleen Ferrier Award 2011, Royal Over-Seas League Annual Music Competition Award for Singers 2011. *Current Management:* Intermusica Artists' Management Ltd, 36 Graham Street, Crystal Wharf, London, N1 8GJ, England. *Telephone:* (20) 7608-9900 (office). *E-mail:* mail@intermusica.co.uk (office). *Website:* www.intermusica.co.uk/whately (office).

WHEATLEY, Patrick; British singer (baritone); b. 1950, Hinckley, Leicestershire, England. *Education:* London Opera Centre. *Career:* appeared with ENO 1974–80, as Germont, Amonasro, Marcello, Sharpless, Donner, Gunther, De Bretigny in Manon, Albert in Werther, Schelkalov in Boris Godunov and the King in Dalibor; guest appearances as Escamillo, Kothner, Hans Sachs and Talbot and Cecil in Maria Stuarda; other roles include Renato (Northern Ireland Opera Trust), Ezio in Attila (Univ. Coll. Opera), Falstaff and Papageno (City of Birmingham Touring Opera), Zurga in Les Pêcheurs de Perles (Scottish Opera), Jochanaan, and Yeletsky in The Queen of Spades (Chelsea Opera Group), Nabucco (Opera West), Mercutio in Roméo et Juliette (Las Palmas), Don Pasquale (Neath Opera), Rigoletto (WNO); sang Wotan and the Wanderer in a version of Wagner's Ring for the City of Birmingham Touring Opera 1990–91; concert engagements in Italy, Belgium and Spain and at the Promenade Concerts, London.

WHEELER, Antony, BMus, MPhil; Australian composer, clarinettist and saxophonist; b. 9 Aug. 1958, Dunedin, New Zealand. *Education:* Queensland Conservatory, Shanghai Conservatory, Hong Kong Univ., studied with Ann Boyd. *Career:* clarinettist with Queensland Symphony Orchestra and Philharmonic Orchestra 1980–82, ABC Sinfonia 1983–85, Sydney Symphony Orchestra 1983–85; Freelance Teacher and Performer 1987–95, Lane Cove Public School 1992–99, Trinity Grammar School 1996–99, Australian Inst. of Music 1992–99; active in wide range of performance styles, including traditional Chinese music, contemporary, improvisation, using clarinet, saxophone, qin, ruan; mem. APRA, Musicians' Union of Australia, Australian Music Centre. *Compositions include:* many for Chinese instruments, Piano Variations 1982, Incidental Music for Ubu the King for ensemble 1983, Sarabande and Fugue for brass quintet 1984, Winter 1986, Bodhisattva of the Silk Road 1986, Cold Moon Shines South of the River 1987, Approach to Peace for Chinese orchestra 1988, Snake 1988, Wind Quintet in Five Movements 1988, Love Songs of the Grasslands for chorus and string orchestra 1989, Rising for Chinese orchestra 1990, Hearing Thunder on the Fishing Boat for Chinese percussion ensemble 1990, Back to the Bush for clarinet, saxophone and piano 1990, Birthday Variations for wind quintet 1991, Now Close the Windows for tenor and piano 1991, Jin Beng Bong for Chinese ensemble 1998.

WHELAN, Paul; New Zealand singer (bass-baritone); b. 29 Sept. 1966, Christchurch; s. of Don Whelan and Beris Whelan; one s. *Education:* Wellington Conservatoire and the Royal Northern College of Music. *Career:* pursues concert and recital career; recent highlights have included Bluebeard in Bluebeard's castle with New Zealand Opera, Escamillo with Welsh Nat. Opera, Christus in St Matthew Passion with London Bach choir, concerts in Sydney with Sir Charles Mackerras, Gerontius in Berlin and Beethoven Missa Solemnis with Sydney Symphony Orchestra conducted by Gelmetti in the presence of the Pope; with ENO has sung Shaklovity in Khovanshchina, Christ in St John Passion (also for BBC TV) and Schaunard in La Bohème by Leoncavallo; roles of Schaunard in Puccini's La Bohème with Royal Opera House, Covent Garden, Metropolitan Opera, Netherlands Opera and Stuttgart Opera, Flint in Billy Budd with Paris and Geneva Opera, Figaro at Scottish Opera, The Villains in Les Contes d'Hoffmann in NZ and Amfortas in Parsifal at New Zealand Int. Festival, Don Giovanni in Sydney, Japan, NZ and Lithuania, and Mephistopheles in Damnation de Faust at the Brighton and Leeds Festivals; future engagements include Alidoro in La Cenerentola with Glyndebourne tour, and rejoins Metropolitan Opera roster for the Magic Flute as well as concerts in Perth, WA, at Grant Park Festival in Chicago, in Eugene, Ore. and with San Francisco Symphony; other forthcoming engagements include a return to Glyndebourne as Schwartz in new production of Die Meistersinger, and Seneca in new production of L'Incoronazione di Poppea in France. *Honours:* Brigitte Fassbaender Award for Lieder Wolfson Trust Award, Marianne Mathy Award, Webster Booth-Esso Award, Cardiff Singer of the World Lieder Prize. *Current Management:* c/o Ken Benson & Rob Scott, Columbia Artists Management LLC, 1790 Broadway, New York, NY 10019-1412, USA. *Telephone:* (212) 841-9545. *Fax:* (212) 841-9687. *E-mail:* info@cami.com. *Website:* www.cami.com; www.paulwhelan.co.uk.

WHITACRE, Eric, MM; American composer and conductor; b. 2 Jan. 1970, Reno, Nev.; m. Hila Plitmann; one s. *Education:* Univ. of Nevada, Las Vegas with David Weiller, Juilliard School, with John Corigliano and David Diamond. *Career:* commissions include music for BBC Proms, London Symphony Orchestra and Chorus, Chanticleer, Julian Lloyd Webber and Philharmonia Orchestra, Berlin Rundfunkchor and The King's Singers; f. The Eric Whitacre Singers 2010, BBC Proms debut 2012, debut US tour 2013; cr. Virtual Choir projects 1–4; Composer-in-Residence, Sidney Sussex Coll., Cambridge; Guest Presenter, The Choir (BBC Radio 3) March 2013. *Film music:* co-writer: Mermaid Theme for Pirates of the Caribbean: On Stranger Tides. *Compositions include:* choral: A Boy and a Girl, Alleluia, Animal Crackers, Cloudburst, Five Hebrew Love Songs, Little Birds, Lux Aurumque, Nox Aurumque, Sleep, The Chelsea Carol, The Seal Lullaby, Three Flower Songs, Water Night, Sainte-Chapelle; for wind symphony: Equus, Ghost Train, Libertas Imperio, Noisy Wheels of Joy, October; other: Paradise Lost: Shadows and Wings, musical theatre (ASCAP Harold Arlen Award, Richard Rodgers Award). *Recordings include:* as composer: Cloudburst 2006, Choral Music 2010, Music of Eric Whitacre 2012; as composer/conductor, with The Eric Whitacre Singers: Light & Gold (Grammy Award for Best Choral Performance 2012) 2010, Water Night 2012. *Honours:* awards from Barlow Int. Composition Competition and American Composers' Forum, American Choral Directors Assn Raymond C. Brock Commission 2001. *Current Management:* c/o Claire Long, Music Productions Ltd, Pinewood Studios, Pinewood Road, Iver Heath, Bucks., SLO ONH, England. *Telephone:* (1753) 783739. *E-mail:* claire@musicprods.co.uk. *Website:* www.musicprods.co.uk; ericwhitacre.com.

WHITBOURN, James, BA, MA, DMus; British composer and conductor; b. 17 Aug. 1963. *Education:* Magdalen Coll., Oxford. *Career:* began career as BBC producer; concert-length choral work, Annelies, setting words from The Diary of Anne Frank, premiered by Leonard Slatkin at Cadogan Hall, London 2005; choral works have been performed world-wide, especially Son of God Mass and Annelies; choral music has been recorded by Choir of Clare Coll. Cambridge, Commotio and Westminster Williamson Voices; film and TV work includes orchestral score for BBC series Son of God, together with music for 9/11, Cenotaph and Queen Mother's funeral; works have been performed and broadcast by Daniel Hope, Arianna Zukerman, BBC Philharmonic Orchestra and choirs of King's Coll. Cambridge, Westminster Abbey and numerous other cathedral choirs; Research Fellow, St Stephen's House, Oxford; Co-Dir, Westminster Choir Coll., Choral Inst., Oxford. *Compositions include:* for chorus: Of One That Is So Fair and Bright 1992, The Song of Hannah 1994, Glory to Thee, O Lord 1995, Blessings on You from the Lord 1996, This Is My Commandment 1997, Come to the Wedding 1999, Crown My Heart 1999, Hodie 1999, Venite 2000, Living Voices 2001, A Celtic Prayer 2001, Son of God Mass 2001, The Mystery of Love 2001, Eternal Rest 2002, Give Us the Wings of Faith 2002, A Prayer of Desmond Tutu 2003, A Ring of White Gold 2004, Annelies 2004, Annelies Chamber version 2004–09, Missa Carolae 2004–09, There is No Speech or Language 2004, Magnificat and Nunc Dimittis (Collegium regale) 2005, Luminosity 2007, Alleluia Jubilate 2008–10, Pure River of Water of Life 2008, All Shall Be Amen and Alleluia 2009, He Carried Me Away in the Spirit 2009, A Little Night Music 2010, A Prayer from South Africa 2010, Requiem Canticorum 2010, Among the Angels 2011, Festival Alleluia 2011, The Magi's Dream 2011, Magnificat and Nunc Dimittis (Eboracum) 2011, A Prayer of Cardinal Newman 2011, The Canticles of Mary and Simeon 2011, Silent Night 2013, The Twenty-Eight Times 2013, Were You There? 2013, The Voices Stilled (Agnus Dei) 2013, The Seven Heavens 2014, Video caelos apertos 2014, Ada 2015, Gratias agimus tibi 2015, Veni et illumina 2015, Pater Noster 2016, for soprano and orchestra: Iqhude we Ma 2014; for orchestra: Bridge over Tay (also Eternal Rest for wind band), Adagio for strings and horn. *Music for film and TV:* Miracle of Tears (BBC film) 1998, Cherub Song (BBC series titles) 1999, Burma Journey (BBC Everyman film) 2001, Living Voices (BBC 9/11 titles) 2001, Son of God (BBC/Discovery landmark series, complete film scores) 2001, Bridge over Tay (BBC broadcast of Queen Mother's funeral) 2002, Ancient Evidence, aka Bible Mysteries 2004, D-Day 60 (BBC coverage titles and extras) 2004, A Passion for Churches (BBC series titles), Poppy Fields (BBC Cenotaph coverage) 2007–11, Opus Odyssey (cinema titles for Royal Opera House films) 2008. *Honours:* Royal Television Soc. Award, Sony Gold Award, Sandford St Martin Premier Award, two Diapason D'or awards, two Gramophone Awards. *Current Management:* c/o Meg Monteith, Chester Music Ltd and Novello Publishing Ltd, 14–15 Berners Street, London, W1T 3LJ, England. *Telephone:* (20) 7612-7400. *E-mail:* meg.monteith@musicsales.co.uk. *Website:* www.chesternovello.com. *E-mail:* info@jameswhitbourn.com (office). *Website:* www.jameswhitbourn.com.

WHITE, Andrew Nathaniel, III, BMus; American musician (saxophone, oboe, English horn, bass), composer, arranger, conductor and musicologist; b. 6 Sept. 1942, Washington, DC; m. Jocelyne H. J. Uhl. *Education:* Howard Univ., Washington, DC. *Career:* jazz saxophonist, JFK Quintet 1960–64, New Jazz Trio 1965–66; oboist and English horn player, Center of Creative and Performing Arts 1965–67; Principal Oboe and English Horn, American Ballet Theater 1968–70; electric bassist, Stevie Wonder and Motown Records 1968–70, Fifth Dimension 1970–76, Weather Report (recordings) 1970–73, The Jupiter Hair Company 1971–; solo debut at Carnegie Hall 1974; jazz saxophonist with Elvin Jones 1980–81, Beaver Harris 1983–; staff writer, Saxophone Journal; mem. Int. Double Reed Soc., Soc. for American Music, Pi Kappa Lambda. *Compositions include:* Concerto 1963, Concertina 1963, Shepherd Song 1963, Andrew with Strings 1987, A Jazz Concerto (five versions) 1988, 20 Jazz Caprices for string quartet 2007. *Recordings:* 48 self-produced recordings, collaborations include JFK Quintet, McCoy Tyner. *Publications include:* Saxophone Transcriptions – The Works of John Coltrane (15 vols), The Eric Dolphy Series Limited, The Charlie Parker Collection (four vols), The Andrew White Transcription Series (10 vols), Andy's Song Book, Chamber Music Series, Saxophone Recital Series, Saxophone Etudes, Saxophone Trios, Quartets, Quintets, Two Symphonies for Eight Saxophones, Four Jazz Duets, 12 Jazz Miniatures; books on improvisation, practice, transcription, jazz education, self-production, Coltrane's music, five comedy books; Everybody Loves The Sugar – The Book (autobiog.) 2001; contrib. of numerous articles to trade journals. *Honours:* numerous study grants; Dean Dixon Memorial Award for oboe playing 1984, Washington Area Music Asscn Award 1985, Soc. of Arts, Sciences and Letters Gold Medal, Paris, France 2006. *Address:* Andrew's Musical Enterprises Inc., 4830 South Dakota Avenue, NE, Washington, DC 20017, USA (office). *Telephone:* (202) 526-3666 (office). *Fax:* (202) 526-4013 (office).

WHITE, (Edwin) Chappell, BA, BMus, MFA, PhD; American educator and musicologist; b. 16 Sept. 1920, Georgia; m. Barbara Tyler 1959; one s. two d. *Education:* Emory Univ., Westminster Choir Coll., Princeton Univ. *Career:* Instructor, Agnes Scott Coll. 1950–52; Instructor and Assoc. Prof., Emory Univ. 1952–74; Prof., Kansas State Univ. 1974–91 (retd); Violist with Atlanta Symphony, 1950–57; music critic, Atlanta Journal, 1959–72; Visiting Prof., Univ. of Georgia 1970–71, Indiana Univ. 1972–73, Univ. of the South 1993–2002; Brown Foundation Fellow, Univ. of the South 1993; mem. College Music Soc. (pres. 1979–80), American Musicological Soc. *Publications:* G. B. Viotti: A Thematic Catalogue of his Works 1985, Intro to Life and Works of R. Wagner 1969, Four Concertos by G. B. Viotti (ed.) 1976, Three Concertos by J. Myslivecek (ed.) 1994, From Vivaldi to Viotti: A History of the Classical Violin Concerto 1992; contrib. 15 articles to New Grove Dictionary 1980, Journal of American Musicological Society, Fontes Artis Musiche, Musical Quarterly. *Honours:* NEH Research Grant 1982–83. *Address:* 150 Bobtown Circle, Sewanee, TN 37375, USA.

WHITE, Frances, BMus, MA; American composer; b. 30 Aug. 1960, Philadelphia. *Education:* University of Maryland, Princeton University. *Career:* technical asst to John Cage 1985–87, collaborating on works for computer-generated tape; freelance composer. *Compositions include:* Ogni pensiero vola, for tape, 1985; Chiaroscura, for percussion and tape, 1986; Design for an Invisible City for tape, 1987; Valdrada, 1988; Still Life with

Piano, for piano and tape, 1989; Resonant Landscape, interactive computer-music, 1990; Trees for 2 violins, viola and tape, 1992; Nocturne, 1992; Walks Through Resonant Landscapes 1–5 for tape, 1992; Winter Aconites (commission from ASCAP in memory of John Cage) for clarinet and ensemble, 1993. *Honours:* First Prize, programme music category, 18th Bourges International Electro-Acoustic Music Competition, 1990; ASCAP Awards, 1990, 1993, 1994.

WHITE, Harry, DMus, PhD, MA, MRIA, FRIAM; Irish university professor and musicologist; *Professor and Chair of Music, University College Dublin*; b. 4 July 1958, Dublin; m. 1st Eithne Graham 1980 (divorced 2005); two s.; m. 2nd Qu Xiao Mei 2006. *Education:* Univ. Coll. Dublin, Univ. of Toronto, Canada, Univ. of Dublin (Trinity Coll.). *Career:* Jr Fellow, Massey Coll., Univ. of Toronto 1983–84; part-time Lecturer, St Patrick's Coll., Maynooth 1984–85; Asst Lecturer in Music, Univ. Coll. Dublin 1985–88, Coll. Lecturer 1988–93, Prof. of Music 1993–, also Chair., School of Music; Visiting Prof. of Music, Univ. of Western Ontario 1996; Visiting Prof. of Musicology, Ludwig-Maximilians-Universität, Munich 1999, Zagreb Univ. 2006; Visiting Prof., King's Coll. Cambridge 2005; Pres. Soc. for Musicology in Ireland 2003–06; Sr Research Fellow, Irish Research Council for the Humanities and Social Sciences 2005–06; Gen. Ed. Irish Musical Studies, Dublin 1990–, Encyclopaedia of Music in Ireland 2005–; Foreign Corresp. Ed., Current Musicology, New York 1996–; DAAD Research Fellowship 1999; mem. Editorial Bd International Review of the Aesthetics and Sociology of Music, Zagreb 2001–, Journal of the Society for Musicology in Ireland 2005–; Advisory Ed., Int. Panel, Journal of the Royal Musical Association 2010–, Canadian Journal of Irish Studies 2011, Dictionary of Irish Biography 2014–; mem. Academia Europaea 2015. *Publications include:* Johann Joseph Fux, Il Trionfo della Fede (ed.) 1988, Musicology in Ireland (co-ed.) 1990, Johann Joseph Fux and the Music of the Austro-Italian Baroque (ed.) 1992, Music and the Church (co-ed.) 1993, Music and Irish Cultural History (co-ed.) 1995, The Keeper's Recital: Music and Cultural History in Ireland 1770–1970 1998, Musical Constructions of Nationalism (co-ed.) 2001, The Progress of Music in Ireland 2005, Music and the Irish Literary Imagination 2008, Musicology without Frontiers (co-ed.) 2010, Musical Theatre as High Culture? (co-ed.), Polite Forms 2012, The Encyclopaedia of Music in Ireland (co-ed.) 2013; contrib. to numerous publs including Acta Musicologica, Bach, Fontes Artis Musicae, International Review of the Aesthetics and Sociology of Music, Irish University Review, Eighteenth Century Ireland, Irish Review, Journal of American Studies, Kirchenmusikalisches Jahrbuch, Canadian Journal of Irish Studies, Journal of Musicology, Atti del Antiquae Musicae Italicae Studiosi, Music and Letters, The New Grove Dictionary of Music and Musicians (revised edn 2001), Oxford Bach Companion, Oxford Companion to Irish History, Musica e Storia, Irish Music in the Twentieth Century, Current Musicology, The Life and Music of Brian Boydell, Samuel Beckett and Music, Die Musik in Geschichte und Gegenwart, Music and Literature in German Romanticism, Journal of the Society for Musicology in Ireland, Music in Nineteenth-Century Ireland, Dictionary of Irish Biography, New Hibernia Review, Eighteenth-Century Music, Enzyklopaedie der Kirchenmusik, Synge and Edwardian Ireland, The Musicology Review. *Honours:* Hon. Fellow, Acad. of St Cecilia 2006, Royal Irish Acad. of Music 2007; Hon. mem. Croatian Musicological Soc. 2012, Hon. Life Mem., Soc. for Musicology in Ireland 2015; Hon. DMus (Nat. Univ. of Ireland) 2007; Univ. of Toronto E.J. Pratt Medal for Poetry 1984, Michael J. Durkan Prize, American Conference for Irish Studies 2009, Premio Istranza, Associazione Amistade, Olbia 2011, Soc. for Musicology in Ireland Harrison Medal 2014. *Address:* School of Music, Room J310, Newman Building, University College Dublin, Belfield, Dublin 4, Ireland (office). *E-mail:* harry.white@ucd.ie (office). *Website:* www.ucd.ie/music/staff/academic/professorharrywhite (office).

WHITE, Ian David, ARCM; British violist, teacher and stringed instrument restorer; b. 16 Sept. 1941, Battersea, London; s. of A. J. White and Lilly Elsie White; m. Annelise White 1987; four s. *Education:* Royal Coll. of Music (RCM) with Arthur Councell and Carl Dolmetsch, Southwark Cathedral with Dr Campbell, viola with Frederick Riddle and Cecil Aronowitz. *Career:* debut with Royal Philharmonic Orchestra 1960; first appearance in Wigmore Hall 1966, Purcell Room 1967, Smith Square 1969; Music for A Man for All Seasons; chamber music on BBC TV; performances with English Chamber Orchestra, with Benjamin Britten; Hold the Front Page; Haslemere Festival with Carl Dolmetsch 1967–95; teacher of violin and viola, Jr Dept, RCM 1961–66; Lecturer, Univ. of Guildford; Prin. Viola, BBC London Studio Strings 1970–87, L'Estro Armonico 1976–90; Leader Misbourne Orchestra 1982–94; Dir Viola d'Amore Soc. of GB 1967–; violinist, Chorleywood Chamber Orchestra 1981–; mem. London Harpsichard Ensemble 1967–72, London Early Music Consort 1968–73, American Viola d'Amore Soc. *Arrangements:* Trio in E flat for viola, cello and bass (by Michael Haydn), Concertos for Viola d'Amore (by Vivaldi, Böhm, Carl Stamitz and W. F. Rust), Pfeiffer Trio, Quantz Trios; as editor: Concerto in G major for two violas (Böhm). *Recordings:* Brandenberg Concertos with English Chamber Orchestra and Benjamin Britten, Nisi Dominus by A. Vivaldi, Christmas Story, Heinrich Schütz, Bach St John Passion, at King's College, Cambridge—Instruments with Sympathetic Strings, 64 Haydn symphonies. *Publication:* The Chamber Music Compositions of Alexander Tinlin 1979. *Honours:* RCM Alfred Gibson Viola Prize, RCM Percy Carter Buck Prize 1958–60. *Address:* Viola d'Amore Society, 4 Constable Road, Felixstowe, Suffolk, IP11 7HH, England (office). *Telephone:* (7799) 263837 (mobile).

WHITE, Jeremy; British singer (bass-baritone); b. 1953, Liverpool, England. *Education:* Queen's College and Christ Church, Oxford, studied with David Johnston, Elisabeth Fleming. *Career:* many performances with early music ensembles in the UK and Europe; Acis and Galatea for Swiss Television, debut at the Amsterdam Concertgebouw in Bach cantatas under Ton Koopman; Performances in Vienna, Budapest and Turku (Finland); Bach's St John Passion in England and Spain with The Sixteen; CPE Bach's Oratorio Auferstehung und Himmelfahrt Jesu, in Munich; Bach's Magnificat and Christmas Oratorio in Oxford and London with King's College Choir and English Chamber Orchestra; Handel/Mozart Messiah in Paris and Lucerne; Bach's Passions in English Cathedrals; Modern concert repertoire includes Abraham and Isaac by Stravinsky, and music by Berio and Taverner; Has sung in The Lighthouse by Maxwell Davies, Walton's The Bear (title role), Pfitzner's Palestrina (Cardinal Morone), Les Troyens and Der Rosenkavalier (the Notary, Aix-en-Provence Festival); Roles in operas by Mozart and Rossini; engagements 1993: Tour of Verdi's Requiem, including Paris and the Flanders Festival; Series of performances of Arvo Pärt's Passio in Jerusalem, Seville and throughout Poland and Finland, Berio in Helsinki conducted by the composer and Beethoven's Ninth Symphony for Swiss Radio; sang Don Prudenzio in Rossini's Il Viaggio a Reims, Covent Garden, 1992; sang Webern's Second Cantata with Pierre Boulez in a broadcast from Birmingham Symphony Hall; season 1993–94: Contemporary Music Network tour as Peter in Jonathan Harvey's Passion and Resurrection, followed by a return to the Royal Opera to sing Benoit in La Bohème; Visit to Brazil with the Scottish Chamber Orchestra; Return to Swiss Radio in Lugano; Concert appearances with The Sixteen and The Taverner Players in Beethoven and Schütz in Germany, Norway and Switzerland, and Handel's La Resurrezione in Paris and Bourges; Concerts in London and the provinces; Sang in Pfitzner's Palestrina at Covent Garden, 1997; Season 1998 with Talbot in Verdi's Giovanna d'Arco in London and Leeds; Sang Colonna in Wagner's Rienzi for Chelsea Opera Group, 1999; season 2000–01 as Rossini's Selim for ENO and Mesner in Tosca at Covent Garden. *Recordings include:* John Tavener's Great Canon of St Andrews; Monteverdi's Vespers, with The Sixteen; Handel Israel in Egypt conducted by Andrew Parrott. *Current Management:* Musicmakers International Artists Representation, Tailor House, 63–65 High Street, Whitwell, Hertfordshire SG4 8AH, England. *Telephone:* (1438) 871708. *Fax:* (1438) 871777. *E-mail:* musicmakers@compuserve.com. *Website:* www.operauk.com.

WHITE, John; composer; b. 5 April 1936, Berlin, Germany. *Education:* Royal Coll. of Music with Elisabeth Lutyens. *Career:* Music Dir, Western Theatre Ballet 1959–60; Teacher of Composition, Royal Coll. of Music 1961–66; tuba player with the London Gabrieli Brass Ensemble 1971–72. *Compositions include:* 136 Piano Sonatas 1957–96, 26 Symphonies 1965–90, 35 Ballets 1957–93, music for film and TV, Stanley (opera), Monkey King (opera) 1975, The Trial (opera), Orpheus: Eurydice 1976, music theatre Man-Machine Interface.

WHITE, John David, BA, MA, PhD; American composer and cellist; b. 28 Nov. 1931, Rochester, Minn.; m. Marjorie Manuel 1952, two s. one d. *Education:* Univ. of Minnesota, Eastman School of Music, Univ. of Rochester, studied composition with Howard Hanson and Bernard Rogers, also studied with Nadia Boulanger and Ross Lee Finney. *Career:* fmr mem. Faculty, Music Dept, Univ. of Wisconsin, Kent State Univ., Univ. of Michigan; Chair. Music Dept, Whitman Coll. 1978–80; Dean School of Music, Ithaca Coll. 1973–75; Prof. and Head of Composition and Theory, Univ. of Florida 1980, now Prof. Emer.; fmr Visiting Prof., Univ. of Innsbruck; Distinguished Chair., Fulbright-Univ. of Vienna 2003–04; soloist with Atlanta, Rochester, Madison and Akron Orchestras; composer, with performances by Cleveland, Atlanta, Rochester, Madison and Akron Orchestras. *Compositions include:* Symphony No. 2 1960; Symphony No. 3; Legend of Sleepy Hollow 1962; 3 Choruses from Goethe's Faust; 3 Madrigals for Chorus and Orchestra; Numerous choral works 1960–87; Variations for Clarinet and Piano; Zodiac, Chorus and Piano; Music for Oriana 1979 (for Violin, Cello and Piano); Pied Beauty, Chorus and Piano; Eiseleic Madrigals; Sonata for Cello and Piano 1982; Music for Violin and Piano 1983; Concerto for Flute and Wind Ensemble 1984; Symphony for Wind Band 1985; Dialogues for Trombone and Piano 1984; Symphony for A Saint 1987; Songs of the Shulamite 1988; Mirrors for Piano and Orchestra 1990, The Divine Image 2007. *Recordings:* Variations for Clarinet and Piano, Advent 5005. *Publications include:* Understanding and Enjoying Music 1968, Music in Western Culture 1972, Guidelines for College Teaching of Music Theory 1981, The Analysis of Music (second edn) 1984; contrib. to Journal of Music Theory, Journal for Musicological Research, Music and Man.

WHITE, Wendy; American singer (mezzo-soprano); b. 1959. *Career:* sang Valencienne in The Merry Widow at Washington 1984, Carmen at Cincinnati 1985; New York City Opera 1986, as Charlotte in Werther (also at Nice 1990); Chicago Lyric Opera from 1987, as Siebel in Faust, Charmian in Barber's Antony and Cleopatra, and Suzuki in Butterfly 1998; Metropolitan Opera from 1990, in La Traviata, Rusalka, Les Troyens (as Anna), Otello and Andrea Chénier 1996; Magdalena in Die Meistersinger 1998; sang Cherubino in Corigliano's The Ghosts of Versailles, Metropolitan and Chicago 1995; sang Mascagni's Lola, Annina in Der Rosenkavalier and Fenena (Nabucco) at the Met 1999–2001. *Recordings include:* Parsifal, Bernstein's A Quiet Place.

WHITE, Sir Willard Wentworth, Kt, OM, CBE, BA; Jamaican/British singer (bass); *President, Royal Northern College of Music*; b. 10 Oct. 1946, Ewarton, St Catherine, Jamaica; s. of Egbert White and Gertrude White; m. Gillian

Jackson 1972; three s. one d. *Education:* Excelsior School, Kingston and Juilliard School of Music, USA. *Career:* early mem. Jamaica Amateur Operatic Soc.; Founding mem. Jamaican Folk Singers; .debut with New York City Opera as Colline in La Bohème 1974–75; European debut as Osmin with Welsh Nat. Opera 1976; has performed in most int. opera houses, including Royal Opera House, La Scala, Glyndebourne; roles include Porgy, Orestes, Banquo, King Henry (Lohengrin), Pizarro, Wotan, Mephistopheles, Boris Godunov, Golau, Leporello, Prince Kovansky, Napoleon; extensive concert appearances; appeared as Othello, RSC, Stratford-upon-Avon; Falstaff at Aix Festival 2001, Klingsor in Parsifal, Covent Garden 2001, Bartok's Bluebeard 2002, Messiaen's St Francis, San Francisco 2002, Wotan in the Ring, Aix and Salzburg 2005; Méphistophélès in La Damnation de Faust, Geneva 2008; appeared in Janáček's From the House of the Dead at the Met, New York 2009, La Scala 2010 and Unter den Linden, Berlin 2011; Bottom in A Midsummer Night's Dream for ENO 2011; Pres. Royal Northern Coll. of Music 2008–; Patron, London Southbank Scheme for Young Singers. *Recordings include:* Porgy and Bess 1991, Mozart Requiem, Orfeo, Die Aegyptische Helena, Acis and Galatea, Willard White Sings: Copland; American Spirituals; Folk Songs 1999, Willard White in Concert 2004, The Paul Robeson Legacy 2007, Dvořák: Rusalka 2014, Ol' Man River/I Got Plenty O' Nuttin' 2015. *Honours:* Order of Merit 2000; Prime Minister of Jamaica's Medal of Appreciation 1987, Gold Musgrave Medal, Inst. of Jamaica 2000, Golden Mask Award for Best Male Artist (for his role of Bottom in Midsummer Night's Dream at Mariinsky Theatre), Theatre Union of Russia 2012. *Current Management:* IMG Artists, The Light Box, 111 Power Road, London, W4 5PY, England. *Telephone:* (20) 7957-5100. *Fax:* (20) 7957-5801. *E-mail:* bsegal@imgartists.com. *Website:* www.imgartists.com. *Address:* Royal Northern College of Music, 124 Oxford Road, Manchester, M13 9RD, England. *Telephone:* (161) 907-5200. *Website:* www.rncm.ac.uk.

WHITEHEAD, Dame Gillian Karawe, DNZM, DCNZM, BMus, MMus; New Zealand composer; b. 23 April 1941, Whangarei. *Education:* Univ. of Auckland, Univ. of Wellington, Univ. of Sydney, Australia, studied with Peter Maxwell Davies in Adelaide, then in UK. *Career:* worked in London composing and copying music 1967–68, then in Portugal and Italy 1969–70, then freelance composer in UK 1971–78; Composer-in-Residence, Northern Arts, Newcastle upon Tyne, England 1978–80; Lecturer in Composition, Sydney Conservatorium of Music, Australia 1981–96; Mozart Fellow, Otago Univ. 1992; Composer-in-Residence, Auckland Philharmonia 2000–01; Lilburn Residence, Wellington 2005–06; Artist-in-Residence, Henderson House 2009; James Wallace Arts Trust Residency, Pah Homestead 2013; f. ensemble Tuhonohono 2004; various commissions funded by Music Bd of Australia Council, Arts Council of Great Britain, New Zealand Arts Council; Pres. Composers' Asscn of New Zealand 1998–2003. *Compositions include:* Missa Brevis 1963, Qui Natus Est, Carol 1966, Fantasia on Three Notes for piano solo 1966, Whakatau-Ki (chamber music with voice) 1970, La Cadenza Sia Corta for piano solo 1974, Tristan and Iseult for four singers, mimes and puppets, instrumental ensemble 1975, Voices of Tane for piano solo 1976, At Night the Garden Was Full of Flowers for four recorders 1977, The Tinker's Curse (children's opera) 1979, Requiem for male soprano and organ (dance score) 1981, The King of the Other Cowboy (chamber opera) 1984, The Pirate Moon (chamber opera) 1986, Resurgences for orchestra 1989, Angels Born at the Speed of Light for string quartet 1990, Moments for chorus 1993, The Art of Pizza (chamber opera) 1995, Outrageous Fortune (opera) 1998, Alice 2002, Karohirohi 2006, Puhake ki te rangi 2007. *Honours:* Hon. DMus (Victoria Univ. of Wellington) 2003; numerous grants, including New Zealand Queen Elizabeth II Arts Council and Vaughan Williams Trust; SOUNZ Contemporary Award 1999 (for opera Outrageous Fortune), 2001 (for the improbable ordered dance), 2003 (for Alice), Artist Laureate, NZ Arts Foundation 2001, KBB Citation for outstanding services to New Zealand music, CANZ 2007. *Current Management:* Australian Music Centre Ltd, 16 Mountain Street, APRA|AMCOS Building, Sydney, NSW 2007, Australia. *E-mail:* info@australianmusiccentre.com.au. *Website:* www.australianmusiccentre.com.au/artist/whitehead-gillian.

WHITFIELD, John Peter; British conductor, music director and bassoonist; *Musical Director, Sinfonia Ariella;* b. 21 March 1957, Darlington, County Durham. *Education:* Chetham's School of Music, Keble Coll., Oxford, Nat. Youth Orchestra, European Community Youth Orchestra, Int. Youth Orchestra; studied with Charles Cracknell, Martin Gatt, and Mordechai Rechtmann in Tel-Aviv. *Career:* South Bank conducting debut 1983; has worked with Israel Chamber Orchestra, City of London Sinfonia, English Baroque Orchestra, London Sinfonietta and London Symphony Orchestra, among others; founder and Musical Dir, Endymion Ensemble; many concerts in London and UK festivals as bassoonist, conductor, and with soloists; commissioned and conducted premieres of works by David Bedford, Dominic Muldowney, Nigel Osborne, Michael Nyman, Giles Swayne, Anthony Payne; Asst Conductor, Spitalfields Festival Production and on EMI recording of Armide (Gluck) with Felicity Palmer in title role; fmr Asst to Richard Hickox; stage debut as conductor of Birtwistle's Down by the Greenwood Side at the Bath Festival, also broadcast by BBC Radio 3; Musical Dir, Sinfonia Ariella 2009–. *Recordings:* Stravinsky records including Symphonies of Wind and Dumbarton Oaks, Britten: Phaedra, Les Illuminatons (with Felicity Palmer and Jill Gomez) 1996. *Website:* www.sinfonia-ariella.co.uk.

WHITICKER, Michael, BMus; Australian composer; b. 1954, Gundagai, NSW. *Education:* New South Wales Conservatorium of Music, studied with

Richard Troop, and with Isang Yun and Witold Szalonek in Germany. *Compositions:* orchestral works: Ad Marginem 1986, Tartengk 1985, Tya 1984; works for the stage: The Bamboo Flute 1982, Gesualdo 1987; ensemble works: Hunufcu 1979, Korokon 1983, Quidong 1983, Kwa 1986, Winamin 1986, Orpheus and Persephone 1987, Plangge 1987, Venus Asleep 1987, Minamé 1988, Ad Parnassum 1989, Redror 1989; solo instrumental works: Vibitqi 1980, Tulku 1982, If Buifs 1981, Kiah 1986, The Hands, The Dream 1987, In Prison Air 1988, On Slanting Ground 1988; vocal works: A Voice Alone 1982, Night Swimming 1984, Sheaf Tosser 1984, As Water Bears Salt 1989; works for students: Boinko the Billio 1979, Homage to Alban Berg 1980, Liexliu 1980, Introduction for Concert Band 1985, Karobaan 1985, Taldree 1985, The Bankstown Pageant 1985, The Hollow Crown 1985, The Serpent Beguiles 1985, Three Episodes 1985; works for tape alone: Cement Mounted Inlays 1981, Model Sequence II 1981, Slid PC 1982; ballets: Factor X 1980, Passion 1989; film scores: Atlantis 1981, Conferenceville 1982, The Bus Trip 1982, Jellingroo for didjeridoo, flute and cello 1990, Man, The Skin Cancer of the Earth for three voices, saxophone, percussion and tape 1991, Encircled by Lillies for soprano, tenor and piano 1991.

WHITTALL, Arnold, MA, PhD; British musicologist; b. 11 Nov. 1935, Shrewsbury, Shropshire. *Education:* Emmanuel Coll., Cambridge. *Career:* Lecturer, Univ. of Nottingham 1964–69; Sr Lecturer, Univ. Coll., Cardiff 1969–75; Reader, King's Coll., London 1976–81, Prof. of Musical Theory and Analysis 1981–96; Visiting Prof., Yale Univ. 1985. *Publications include:* Post-Twelve Note Analysis 1968, Stravinsky and Music Drama 1969, Schoenberg Chamber Music 1972, Music Since the First World War 1977, The Music of Britten and Tippett 1982, Romantic Music 1987, Wagner's Later Stage Works 1990, The Emancipation of Dissonance: Schoenberg and Stravinsky 1993, Musical Composition in the Twentieth Century 1999, Jonathon Harvey (biog.) 1999, Exploring Twentieth Century Music 2003, Introduction to Serialism 2008.

WHITTLESEY, Christine; singer (soprano); b. 12 Jan. 1950, New York, NY, USA. *Education:* studied in Boston. *Career:* sang with opera companies in Boston, Washington and Santa Fe; concerts with the New York Pro Musica Antique and other chamber ensembles; resident in Europe from 1981; concert engagements with the Sudwestfunk and Austrian Radio, conducted by Boulez and Michael Gielen; tours of Russia and South America with Ensemble Modern; Ensemble Intercontemporain in Paris and Ensemble Kontrapunkte in Vienna; debut with the BBC Symphony 1988, in Pli selon Pli under Boulez; sang in Dallapiccola's Ulisse with the BBC Symphony Orchestra under Andrew Davis and appeared at the Henze Festival at the Barbican Centre, London 1991, with the BBC Philharmonic and the Scottish Chamber Orchestra; further concerts in Berlin, Salzburg, Strasbourg and Warsaw; season 1992–93 with Debussy's Damoiselle Elue in The Netherlands and Russian songs in Paris; performs at all major music festivals. *Recordings include:* Homage to T. S. Eliot by Gubaidulina; Schoenberg: String Quartet No. 2; Harrison Birtwistle: Three Celan Settings; Benedict Mason: Self-Referential Songs and Realistic Virelais; Mahler Symphony No. 4; Dieter Schnebel: Dahlemer Messe.

WHITWORTH-JONES, Anthony, CA; British arts administrator; b. 1 Sept. 1945, Bucks., England; s. of Henry Whitworth-Jones and Patience Martin; m. Camilla Barlow 1974; one d. *Education:* Wellington Coll. *Career:* Admin. Dir London Sinfonietta 1972–81; Admin. Glyndebourne Touring Opera 1981–89, Opera Man. Glyndebourne Festival Opera 1981–89, Gen. Dir Glyndebourne 1989–98; Chair. Michael Tippett Musical Foundation 1998–; Gen. Dir The Dallas Opera 2000–02; Artistic Dir Casa da Musica, Oporto, Portugal 2004–05, Artistic Consultant 2007–08; Gen. Dir Garsington Opera 2005–12; mem. Bd Spitalfields Festival 2003–06 (Hon. Adviser 2006–), Young Classical Artists Trust 2006–14, ENO 2012–; Trustee, Leonard Ingrams Foundation 2006–. *Address:* 81 St Augustine's Road, London, NW1 9RR, England (home). *Telephone:* (20) 7267-3154 (home). *E-mail:* antwjones@gmail.com.

WIBAUT, Frank, ARCM; British pianist; b. 10 Nov. 1945, London, England; m. Kay Alexander. *Education:* Royal Coll. of Music. *Career:* debut at Wigmore Hall, London 1969; concert performances in Netherlands, Belgium, Denmark, Germany, Ireland, Spain and Malta; frequent broadcaster on radio and television; mem., Camirilla Ensemble; mem. Musicians' Union, Incorporated Soc. of Musicians. *Recordings:* The Romantic Chopin; Favourite Piano Classics; Elgar's From the Bavarian Highlands (in original form); Piano Quintets by Elgar, Suk and others. *Honours:* Royal Coll. of Music Sr Foundation Scholarship, Royal Coll. of Music Leverhulme Scholarship, Royal Coll. of Music Countess of Munster Award, first prize Chopin Competition, London, Chappell Gold Medal, BBC Piano Competition 1968.

WICH, Gunther; German conductor; b. 23 May 1928, Bamberg. *Education:* studied in Freiburg. *Career:* conducted at the Freiburg Town Theatre 1952–59; Opera Dir, Graz 1959–61; Gen. Music Dir, Hanover 1961–65; conducted the first production of Schoenburg's three one-act operas as a triple bill 1963; Gen. Music Dir, Deutsche Oper am Rhein, Düsseldorf/Duisburg 1965–87; took the co. to Edinburgh 1972, for the British premiere of Zimmermann's Die Soldaten; Covent Garden debut 1968, Die Zauberflöte; Prof. of Conducting, Musikhochschule, Würzburg 1982–94; guest conductor with major orchestras in Europe, Japan and the USA; has led the Capella Coloniensis on tours to North and South America. *Recordings include:* Handel's Concerti Grossi Op 3 and Alexander's Feast; Haydn's Symphonies Nos 82 and 85; Serenades by Dvořák, Mozart and Tchaikovsky; Early Mozart

Piano Concertos with Martin Galling; Pfitzner's Violin Concerto with Susanne Lautenbacher, 21.

WICKS, Camilla; American violinist and academic; b. 1925; m.; five c. *Education:* Fellowship to Juilliard School. *Career:* debut in New York Town Hall aged 13; solo appearances with the Hollywood Bowl Orchestra, the Los Angeles and New York Philharmonic Orchestras and the Chicago Symphony; many concerts with European Orchestras from age 18; played the Sibelius Concerto before the composer in Helsinki and has also featured the Bloch Concerto in addition to the standard repertory; frequent engagements in Norway and elsewhere in Scandinavia; teaching appointments from 1960s, notably faculties of North Texas State Univ., California State Coll. at Fullerton, San Francisco Conservatory of Music, Banff Centre for the Performing Arts, Univ. of Washington and Univ. of Southern California; Prof. and Head of the String Dept, Royal Acad. of Music, Oslo; Prof. of Violin, Univ. of Michigan School of Music 1984, Shepherd School of Music at Rice Univ., Houston, TX from 1988; performances in recital and as orchestral soloist and in chamber music concerts. *Recordings include:* the Sibelius Concerto.

WIDDICOMBE, Gillian, ARCM, ARAM; British music critic and journalist; b. 11 June 1943, Aldham, Suffolk, England; m. Sir Jeremy Isaacs 1988. *Education:* Royal Acad. of Music, Gloucester Cathedral. *Career:* with music division, BBC 1966; Glyndebourne Festival Opera 1969; critic and journalist for various publs, including Financial Times 1970–76, The Observer 1977–93; Opera Consultant, Channel Four 1983–88; Arts Ed., The Observer 1988–93; Features Writer, The Independent 1993–95; Dir, Jeremy Isaacs Productions 1995–; Production Exec., Cold War 1998; Assoc. Producer, Millennium 1999; Producer, Artsworld TV Programmes, including Star Recitals with Paco Peña, Amanda Roocroft and Simon Preston 2000–; Poulenc, A Human Voice (for BBC 2); has created subtitles for TV opera productions. *Honours:* Prix Italia 1982, BP Award for Arts Journalism 1986. *Address:* Chapel Cottage, Church Road, Market Weston, nr Diss, IP22 2NX, England.

WIDMANN, Carolin; German musician (violin); b. 1976, Munich; sister of Jörg Widmann. *Education:* studied with Igor Ozim in Cologne, Michèle Auclair in Boston, USA and David Takeno in London, UK. *Career:* has appeared as soloist with Gewandhaus Orchestra Leipzig, Orchestre Nat. de France, Orchestra dell' Accad. Nazionale di Santa Cecilia, Tonhalle Orchestra Zürich, RSO Vienna, BBC Symphony Orchestra, London Philharmonic Orchestra, Royal Danish Orchestra, Czech Philharmonic Orchestra and China Philharmonic, Beijing; has worked with conductors including Riccardo Chailly, Sir Roger Norrington, Silvain Cambreling, Vladimir Jurowski, Emanuel Krivine, Peter Eötvös and Heinz Holliger, Sir Simon Rattle and Ingo Metzmacher; performed regularly at festivals of Lucerne, Schleswig-Holstein and Salzburg and at Enescu Festival Bucharest, Festival d'Automne Paris and chamber music festivals in Lockenhaus, Heimbach and Jerusalem; Artistic Dir Sommerliche Musiktage Hitzacker (chamber music festival); teacher, Hoschschule für Musik und Theater F. Mendelssohn Bartholdy, Leipzig 2006–. *Recordings:* Reflections I 2006, Robert Schumann: The Violin Sonatas 2008, Erkki-Sven Tüür: Strata 2009, Phantasy of Spring: Feldman/Zimmermann/Schoenberg/Xenakis 2009, Schubert: Fantasie C-Dur 2012. *Honours:* Int. Classical Music Awards Artist of the Year 2013. *Current Management:* Askonas Holt, Lincoln House, 296–302 High Holborn, London, WC1V 7JH, England. *Telephone:* (20) 7400-1700. *Website:* www.askonasholt.co.uk. *E-mail:* mail@carolinwidmann.com (office). *Website:* www.carolinwidmann.com (office).

WIDMANN, Jörg; German composer and clarinettist; b. 19 June 1973, Munich. *Education:* Hochschule für Musik with Prof. Gerd Starke, Juilliard School, New York with Charles Neidich, studied with Hans Werner Henze, Wilfried Hiller and Wolfgang Rihm. *Career:* debut as soloist in Mozart's Clarinet Concerto with members of Munich Philharmonic on a tour of Japan (aged 12); soloist with orchestras including Münchener Rundfunkorchester, Sinfonia Varsovia, Capella Istropolitana; collaborations with Tabea Zimmermann, Heinz Holliger, András Schiff, Kim Kashkashian, and Hélène Grimaud. *Compositions include:* Absences 1990, La Verrière Lilas 1991, Jardin du Luxembourg 1992, Carillon 1992–93, Kreisleriana 1993, 180 Beats per minute 1993, Tränen der Musen 1993, Stimmbruch 1994, Nickel List 1994, Badinerie 1994, Wunder Verwirklichen 1995, Knastgesänge 1995, Trauergesang und Frühlingsmusik 1995–96, Three Rilke Fragments 1996, Beitrage, Lea and Rachel, Lilith 1996, Fleurs du Mal 1996–97, Fünf Bruchstücke 1997, Mullewapp 1997, Sieben Abesänge Auf Eine Tote Linde 1997, Insel der Sirenen (premiere with Isabelle Faust on violin in Warsaw) 1997, Kleine Morgenstern-Szene for soprano, cymbalon and schlagzeug 1997, Werk für klarinette, streichquartett und klavier 1997, Sieben Miniaturen, Pas de deux, Ritual für zwei flöten und orchester 1997. *Honours:* Kulturfördpreis of city of Munich 1996, first prize Wettbewerb Deutscher Musikhochschulen, Berlin 1996, first prize Carl Maria Von Weber Competition, Munich 1996, Bavarian State Prize for Young Artists 1997, Belmont-Preis für Zeitgenössische Musik der Forberg-Schneider-Stiftung 1998, Schneider-Schott-Musikpreis Mainz 2002, Hindemith-Preis des Landes Schleswig-Holstein 2002, Förderpreis der Ernst-von-Siemens-Musikstiftung 2003, Arnold-Schönberg-Preis des Schönberg-Centers Wien und des Deutschen Symphonie Orchesters Berlin 2004, Kompositionspreis des SWR-Sinfonieorchesters Baden-Baden und Freiburg für Zweites Labyrinth (Donaueschinger Musiktage) 2006, Claudio-Abbado-Preis der Orchesterakademie der Berliner Philharmoniker 2006, Musikpreis der Christoph und Stephan Kaske-

Stiftung 2007. *Current Management:* c/o Harrison Parrott, GmbH, Lucile-Grahn-Strasse 37, 81674 Munich, , Germany. *Telephone:* (89) 45726154. *Fax:* (89) 45726150. *E-mail:* info@harrisonparrott.de. *Website:* www.harrisonparrott.com; www.schott-musik.de; www.joergwidmann.com.

WIDMER, Oliver; Swiss singer (baritone); b. 1965, Zürich; m. Cecilia Bartoli. *Education:* Basle Music Acad. with Kurt Widmer, studied with Fischer-Dieskau in Berlin. *Career:* concert appearances at the Salzburg Festival, Festival de Musique de Strasbourg, the Vienna Musikverein, the San Francisco Symphony Hall and the Leipzig Gewandhaus; Recitals at the Schubertiade in Hohenems, the Wigmore Hall, London, the Residenz in Munich, Alte Oper Frankfurt, Fêtes Musicales de Touraine, Louvre de Paris, the Vienna Konzerthaus and the 1992 Aldeburgh Festival; Zürich Opera from 1991 as Mozart's Papageno and Guglielmo, Olivier in Capriccio and Harlequin in Ariadne auf Naxos; Salzburg Festival 1993, conducted by Harnoncourt; Season 2000–01 as Guglielmo for Zürich Opera, Rocco in Paër's Leonora at Wintherthur and Christus in the St Matthew Passion at La Scala; mem. Opera House Zürich ensemble 1991–. *Recordings include:* Die Zauberflöte and Schreker's Die Gezeichneten. *Honours:* prizewinner at ARD Competition Munich, Hugo Wolf International Competitions Stuttgart and the Othmar Schoeck Competition in Lucerne. *Address:* Opera House Zürich, Falkenstrasse 1, 8008 Zürich, Switzerland. *Website:* www.opernhaus.ch.

WIEDER-ATHERTON, Sonia; French/American cellist; b. 1961, San Francisco. *Education:* Conservatoire Nat. Supérieur de Musique, Paris, Tchaikovsky Conservatory, Moscow; studied with Mstislav Rostropovitch and Natalia Shakhovskaia. *Career:* solo performances with orchestras including Orchestre de Paris, Orchestre Nat. de France, Israel Philharmonic, Gulbenkian Orchestra, Lisbon, Chamber Orchestra of Lausanne, Orchestre Philarmonique du Luxembourg and at int. festivals; also recitals and chamber music with pianists Imogen Cooper and Laurent Cabasso and violinist Raphael Oleg among others. *Recordings include:* Au Commencement Monteverdi, En concerto, En sonate, Schubert Trios, Chants Juifs, L'Ecclésiaste, Dusapin Concertos, Brahms – Bach, Après un Rêve, Shostakovitch Concertos, Duos pour violon et violoncelle. *Honours:* Grand Prix Del Duca Acad. des Beaux-Arts 1999. *Current Management:* c/o Caroline Maby, Instant Pluriel, 10 rue Bleue, 75009 Paris, France. *Telephone:* 1-48-00-81-01. *Fax:* 1-48-00-81-11. *E-mail:* caroline.maby@instantpluriel.com. *Website:* www.instantpluriel.com. *E-mail:* swa@soniawiederatherton.com (office). *Website:* www.soniawiederatherton.com.

WIEDSTRUCK, Yvonne; German singer (soprano); b. 1960, Potsdam. *Education:* studied in Germany. *Career:* sang first at Altenburg, in Rusalka, Hänsel und Gretel, La Bohème and Faust; Komische Oper Berlin as Despina, Zerlina, Euridice, Susanna, Micaela, the Daughter in Hindemith's Cardillac and Stella in Goldschmidt's Der Gewaltige Hahnrei; Schwetzingen Festival, 1992, in the premiere of Desdemona und ihre Schwestern, by Siegfried Matthus; Appearances as Octavian in Der Rosenkavalier at the Deutsche Oper Berlin and Covent Garden (1995); La Scala debut 1996, in Das Rheingold under Riccardo Muti, and debut as Beethoven's Leonore at Essen Opera, 1997; Engaged as the Composer in Ariadne auf Naxos, Bayerische Staatsoper Munich, 1998; Resident artist at the Deutsche Oper Berlin from 1996; Concert repertory includes Bach's St Matthew Passion (under Kurt Masur), Schubert's E-flat Mass, Pergolesi's Stabat Mater and Les Illuminations by Britten; Pfitzner's choral fanatasia Das Dunkle Reich under Rolf Reuter; Season 2000–01 at the Deutsche Oper as Rossini's Zulma, Octavian and Gertrude in Hans Heiling; Waltraute at Bayreuth (2002) and Brangaene at Glyndebourne, 2003. *Recordings include:* Songs by Shostakovich.

WIEGOLD, Peter John, BMus, MMus, PhD; British composer, conductor and teacher; b. 29 Aug. 1949, Ilford, Essex, England. *Education:* Univ. Coll. of Wales, Aberystwyth, Univ. of Durham. *Career:* Dir, Gemini, regular tours of the UK, including many broadcasts; many residencies involving local participance in shared concerts; Artistic Dir Performance and Communication Skills Project, Guildhall School of Music; has directed many workshops in music and music theatre, including with London Sinfonietta, Royal Opera House, ENO, Scottish Chamber Orchestra and City of London Sinfonia; Junge Deutsche Philharmonie in Greece, Canada, Spain and Sweden; London Symphony Orchestra. *Compositions include:* Gemini, Sing Lullaby, The Flowers Appear on the Earth, Preludes I–V, The Dancing Day, Songs from Grimm (half-hour opera, commissioned by the Royal Opera House) 1989, The Seventh Wave for cello and tape 1997, Earth Receive/an Honoured Guest for cor anglais and string trio 1998, Kalachakrá for 18 players 2000, Farewells Take Place in Silence (octet) 2001. *Honours:* several Arts Council awards.

WIEN, Erika; singer (mezzo-soprano); b. 2 Sept. 1928, Vienna, Austria. *Education:* Vienna Music Acad. with Erik Werba. *Career:* sang at the Vienna Volksoper 1952–53, Bremen 1953–59, and Düsseldorf 1959–64; engagements at the Zürich Opera 1964–80, notably in the premieres of Sutermeister's Madame Bovary 1967, and Kelterborn's Ein Engel Kommt nach Babylon 1977; guest appearances in Berlin, the State Operas of Munich, Hamburg, Stuttgart, Frankfurt and Cologne, at the Holland Festival, Florence, Lyon, Buenos Aires, Paris, San Francisco and Turin; roles included Carmen, Azucena, Amneris, Eboli, Ulrica, Ortud, Fricka, Brangane, Venus, Orpheus, Marina in Boris Godunov, Clytemnestra and Berg's Marie; concert showings in works by Bach, Beethoven and Brahms; lieder recitals and concerts in Germany, Switzerland, Spain and Austria. *Recordings include:* highlights from Rigoletto and Nabucco.

WIENS, Edith, OC; Canadian singer (soprano); b. 1950. *Career:* concert engagements with orchestras in Berlin, London, Israel, Munich, New York (Philharmonic), and with Cleveland, Philadelphia, San Francisco, Montréal and London Symphony Orchestras; broadcasts on Bavarian Radio, Dresden Staatskapelle, Leipzig Gewandhaus Orchestra; conductors include Barenboim, Georg Solti, Colin Davis, Haitink, Kurt Masur, Marriner, Sawallisch and Tennstedt; Salzburg debut 1984, with the Boston Symphony under Ozawa, with whom she has also sung Mozart's Ilia in Japan; other operatic roles include Donna Anna (at Glyndebourne under Haitink, in Paris and at Amsterdam under Harnoncourt) and Mozart's Countess (Buenos Aires); St Matthew Passion in Paris and Salzburg under Masur, with whom she also appeared in Mendelssohn's Elijah in New York; L'Enfant et les Sortilèges at Carnegie Hall; Mahler's 4th Symphony in Munich; recitals in Paris, Vienna, Florence, Buenos Aires, New York and Montréal; Concertgebouw, Amsterdam, and the Pushkin Museum, Moscow; jury mem. of int. competitions; Rotarian 2001; Prof. of Voice, Hochschule für Musik, Augsburg, and Hochschule für Musik und Theater München 2000. *Recordings include:* Schubert, Schumann, Strauss and Zemlinsky Lieder, the title role in Schumann's Das Paradies und die Peri (Grammy Award 1990, Maurice Fleuret (Paris) Prize 1991), Flowermaiden in Parsifal, conducted by Barenboim, Mahler's 8th Symphony, conducted by Tennstedt, Haydn's Creation conducted by Neville Marriner, Brahms Lieder, Zemlinsky's Lyrical Symphony with the Swiss Romande Orchestra. *Honours:* Hon. DMus (Oberlin Coll., USA) 1997. *Address:* Georg-Schuster-Str. 10, 82152 Krailling, Germany (home). *Website:* www.edithwiens.com (home).

WIESE, Henrik; flautist; b. 22 July 1971, Vienna, Austria. *Education:* studied with Ingrid Koch, Roswitha Staege and Paul Meisen at Musikhochschule Hamburg and Musikhochschule Munich. *Career:* engaged as first Principal Flautist, Bavarian State Opera, Munich 1995–; solo concerts with various orchestras, including Berlin Radio Symphony Orchestra, Orchestra of the Beethovenhalle in Bonn, Polish Chamber Philharmonic; solo concerts with Berlin Radio Symphony Orchestra, Hanover Radio-Philharmonie of NDR, Lower Saxonian State Orchestra. *Recordings:* chamber music works including Mozart, flute quartets and overtures arranged for flute and string quartet, Bach flute sonatas with Anikó Soltész. *Honours:* prizewinner German Music Competition 1995, Elise Meyer Competition 1996, Kobe Int. FLute Competition 1997, Markneukirchen and Munich Int. Music Competition 2000. *E-mail:* zauberfloete@henrikwiese.de. *Website:* www.henrikwiese.de.

WIGGLESWORTH, Mark; British music director and conductor; *Music Director, English National Opera;* b. 19 July 1964, Ardingly, Sussex. *Education:* Bryanston School, Univ. of Manchester, Royal Acad. of Music, London. *Career:* Assoc. Conductor, BBC Symphony Orchestra 1991–93; Music Dir Opera Factory 1991–94, Premiere Ensemble 1989–, BBC Nat. Orchestra of Wales 1996–2000; Music Dir English Nat. Opera 2015–; Prin. Guest Conductor, Swedish Radio Orchestra 1998–2001; worked in UK with BBC Symphony, BBC Scottish Symphony, London Philharmonic, London Symphony, Bournemouth Symphony, English and Scottish Chamber Orchestras, Royal Scottish Nat. Orchestra, European Community Youth Orchestra; conducted Premiere Ensemble and BBC Nat. Orchestra of Wales in Centenary Season of BBC Proms; guest conductor in Europe, including Berlin Philharmonic and Deutsches-Symphonie Orchester Berlin, Bavarian State Opera Orchestra, Royal Concertgebouw Orchestra, Rotterdam Philharmonic, Residentie Orchestra, Netherlands Radio Philharmonic and Netherlands Wind Ensemble, Stockholm Philharmonic, Gothenburg Symphony, Oslo Philharmonic, Finnish Radio Symphony Orchestra, Salzburg Camerata, Mozarteum Orchester at Salzburg Festival, Orchestra of La Scala Milan, Santa Cecilia Orchestra of Rome, Israel Philharmonic, in Australia with Melbourne and Sydney Symphony Orchestras, in USA with Boston Symphony, Chicago Symphony, Cleveland Orchestra, New York Philharmonic, Boston Symphony, Philadelphia Orchestra, San Francisco Symphony, Minnesota Orchestra, Detroit Symphony, Los Angeles Philharmonic Orchestra at the Hollywood Bowl, Aspen Music Festival, New World Symphony Orchestra, in Canada with Montreal and Toronto Symphony Orchestras; opera work includes ENO (Lady Macbeth of Mtsensk, Così fan tutte, Falstaff, Katya Kabanova, Parsifal), Glyndebourne (Peter Grimes, La Bohème, Le Nozze di Figaro), Netherlands Opera (Peter Grimes), Welsh Nat. Opera (Rake's Progress, Elektra, Tristan), Covent Garden debut with Die Meistersinger 2002; Met debut with Le Nozze di Figaro 2006; Opera Australia debut with Peter Grimes 2009, Bavarian State Opera debut with Così fan tutte 2011. *Television:* Everything to Play For (BBC). *Honours:* First Prize, Int. Kondrashin Competition, Netherlands 1989. *Current Management:* c/o CM Artists, 127 W 96th Street, No. 13B, New York, NY 10025, USA. *Telephone:* (212) 864-1005. *Fax:* (212) 864-1066. *E-mail:* lymarder@aol.com. *Website:* www.cmartists.com. *E-mail:* info@markwigglesworth.com. *Website:* www.markwigglesworth.com.

WIGGLESWORTH, Ryan; British composer, conductor and pianist; *Artist in Association, Netherlands Radio Chamber Orchestra;* b. 31 Aug. 1979, Yorks. *Education:* New Coll., Oxford, Guildhall School of Music and Drama. *Career:* Lecturer, Univ. of Cambridge and Fellow, Corpus Christi Coll. 2007–09; Artist in Asscn with Netherlands Radio Chamber Orchestra 2010–; Composer-in-Residence with Netherlands Philharmonic Orchestra 2011–; ENO 2012–; regularly conducts BBC Symphony Orchestra; has also conducted Philharmonia Orchestra, Hallé Orchestra, Royal Liverpool Philharmonic, Britten Sinfonia, Scottish Chamber Orchestra, London Sinfonietta, Birmingham Contemporary Music Group, Ensemble Intercontemporain,

Avanti!, Ensemble Modern, English Touring Opera; debut Royal Opera House, Covent Garden conducting Birtwistle's The Minotaur 2013; also regularly performs as concert pianist. *Compositions include:* Sternenfall 2008, The Genesis of Secrecy 2009, Augenlieder (British Composer Awards Vocal Prize 2010) 2009, Tenebrae 2009, A First Book of Inventions 2010. *Recordings include:* Birtwistle's Night's Black Bird (with Hallé Orchestra) (Gramophone Award for Best Contemporary Recording) 2011, Echo and Narcissus 2015. *Current Management:* Konzertdirektion Schmid, Postfach 34 09, 30034 Hannover, Germany. *Telephone:* (511) 366 07-60 (office). *E-mail:* mail@kdschmid.de (office). *Website:* www.kdschmid.de (office).

WILBY, Philip; British composer and academic; *Professor Emeritus, School of Music, University of Leeds;* b. 18 July 1949, Pontefract, Yorks. *Education:* Leeds Grammar School, with Herbert Howells and at Keble Coll., Oxford. *Career:* violinist with Covent Garden Orchestra and City of Birmingham Symphony Orchestra; Sr Lecturer, Univ. of Leeds 1972, now Prof. Emer. *Compositions include:* orchestral: Sunstudy, The Wings of Morning 1988, Vocal: Et Surrexit Christus for 3 Sopranos and Ensemble 1979, Ten Songs of Paul Verlaine for Baritone and Piano 1983, The Temptations of Christ for Soprano and Ensemble 1983, Winter Portrait in Grey and Gold for Voice and Ensemble 1977–85, Cantiones Sacrae: In Darkness Shine 1987, Magnificat and Nunc Dimittis 1988, Easter Wings for Soprano and Ensemble 1989, A Passion of our Times 1997; chamber: Little Symphony for Brass 1985, The Night and All The Stars, Horn Quintet 1985, And I Move Around The Cross for Double Wind Quintet 1985, Sonata Sacra: In Darkness Shine for Clarinet, Viola and Piano 1986, Two Concert Studies for Violin and Piano 1986, Capricorn Suite for 4 Trombones 1987, Parables for Cello and Piano 1988, Classic Images, Partita for Brass Quintet 1988, Concert music for Winds 1988, Green Man Dancing, Wind Quintet 1988, Breakdance for Recorder and Tape 1988; for wind band: Firestar 1983, Symphonia Sacra: In Darkness Shine 1986, Catcher of Shadows 1988, Laudibus in sanctis 1994; for keyboard: Roses for the Queen of Heaven 1982, Two Preludes on English Tunes 1987, Lifescape-Mountains 1987, . . .Aunque es de Noche 1989; Mozart Reconstructions include Concerto for Violin and Piano K315f and Concerto for Violin, Viola, Cello and Orchestra K320e, for the Philips Mozart Edition; comms include Symphony for the BBC Philharmonic. *Address:* School of Music, University of Leeds, Leeds, LS2 9JT, England (office). *E-mail:* P.Wilby@leeds .ac.uk (office). *Website:* www.music.leeds.ac.uk (office).

WILDE, David Clark; British pianist, composer, conductor and academic; b. 25 Feb. 1935, Manchester; m. 1st Jeanne Lukey 1956; one s. one d.; m. 2nd Jane Heller 1984. *Education:* studied with Solomon and Reizenstein, Royal Manchester Coll. of Music with Elinson, Hall and Cohen, studied with Nadia Boulanger, American Conservatoire, Fontainebleau. *Career:* concerts in the USA, Canada, Australia, New Zealand, India, Brazil, France, Belgium, Netherlands, Spain, Germany, Hungary, Russia; international recording and concert artist for BBC, 1961–; Henry Wood Proms from 1961; soloist, royal concert in HM the Queen's presence, Royal Festival Hall, and at BBC television inaugural concert, Manchester (Hallé Orchestra, Barbirolli) 1962; Edinburgh, Cheltenham, Three Choirs, Perth (Australia) festivals; Conductor, Worthing Symphony season 1967–68; writer, narrator, pianist, BBC television Liszt and Bartók documentary programmes 1972–73; Guest Conductor, Royal Philharmonic 1975; Liszt in Weimar, film, Granada television 1986; soloist, Tippett's Concerto, BBC Philharmonic, conducted Tippett (Manchester), Edward Downes (London Proms) 1988. *Compositions include:* Love, song for baritone and cello 1981; Jens, Heidi and die Schneekönigin 1984; Vocalise, mezzo soprano, guitar; Die Jahreszeiten, song cycle 1986; Mandala, solo viola 1986; Piano trio 1987–88; String quartet 1991; The Cellist of Sarajevo, solo cello 1992; Suite, Cry Bosnia-Herzogovina, violin, piano 1993. *Recordings include:* Schumann Fantasie; Liszt Sonata; Complete Beethoven Sonatas with Gruenberg, violin. *Publications include:* Transcriptions for piano, chapter in Franz Liszt, The Man and His Music 1970, Liszt's Consolations, complete (ed.) 1978. *Current Management:* c/o J. Audrey Ellison International Artists' Management, 135 Stevenage Road, Fulham, London, SW6 6PB, England. *Telephone:* (20) 7381-9751. *Fax:* (20) 7381-2406. *E-mail:* Audrey@ellison-intl.freeserve.co.uk. *Website:* www.ellison -intl.freeserve.co.uk.

WILDE, Mark; British singer (tenor); b. 1960, Dundee, Scotland. *Education:* Univ. of East Anglia, choral scholar Norwich Cathedral Choir, Royal Coll. of Music. *Career:* lay clerk, Queen's Free Chapel of St George, Windsor Castle; performs regularly throughout the UK and abroad in oratorio and recital; Bach's St Matthew Passion, Helsinki; Britten's War Requiem, Westminster Cathedral, Norwich Cathedral; Berlioz Te Deum, Orleans Cathedral; Mozart's Requiem, Israel; Monteverdi Vespers, Norway; Handel's Arminio, RCM; Maxwell Davies' The Lighthouse and Vivaldi's Ottone in Villa and Giustino for BBC Radio 3; Ferrando, Royal Acad. of Music and Pimlico Opera tour; many recitals and oratorio appearances, including appearances with Osmo Vanska, Liège Philharmonic Orchestra, Southend Festival Choir, The Aldeburgh Music Club, Birmingham Festival Choral Soc.; solo recitals in London and Aberdeen; title role in Albert Herring, Perth Festival 1998; Buxton Festival and appearances in recital and oratorio 1999. *Recordings:* Requiem with the National Youth Choir of Great Britain and music by Wren Baroque Ensemble. *Current Management:* Hazard Chase, 25 City Road, Cambridge CB1 1DP, England. *Telephone:* (1223) 312400. *Fax:* (1223) 460827. *E-mail:* info@hazardchase.co.uk. *Website:* www.hazardchase.co.uk.

WILDING, Simon, BMus; British singer (bass); b. 10 May 1970, Leigh, Lancashire, England. *Education:* Royal Northern Coll. of Music with Robert Alderson, and with Patrick McGuigan. *Career:* at Royal Northern Coll. of Music, sang Quince and Snug in separate productions of Britten's Midsummer Night's Dream; Geronimo in Il Matrimonio Segreto; and Walter Raleigh in Donizetti's Roberto Devereux; Luka in Walton's The Bear at Manchester and UK/Los Angeles Festival at Los Angeles; sang Count Ceprano in Rigoletto for English National Opera; and Foltz in Die Meistersinger (ROH debut), ein Brabantische Edle in Lohengrin, and the Cappadocian in Salome at Covent Garden; also covered and performed roles including Theseus in A Midsummer Night's Dream; The Drunken Poet in The Fairy Queen; The Speaker in The Magic Flute; Kotwitz in The Prince of Homburg; General in Die Soldaten; 5th Jew in Salome; Angelotti in Tosca; other roles include Jove in La Calisto and roles in Il Pomo d'Oro for the Batignano Festival; sang Fasolt in Das Rheingold and Hagen in Götterdämmerung for the Mastersingers and Wagner Soc. *Recordings include:* Cappadocian in Salome (ROH); Lt Ratcliffe in Billy Budd (Hallé); Dick Deadeye in HMS Pinafore (D'Oyle Carte). *Honours:* Wagner Bursary Award for most promising singer of Wagner 1991. *Current Management:* c/o Samuel Krum, Robert Gilder & Co., N102, Westminster Business Square, 1–45 Durham Street, London, SE11 5JH, England. *Telephone:* (20) 7580-7758. *Fax:* (20) 7580-7739. *E-mail:* sam@robert-gilder.com. *Website:* www.robertgilder.com. *E-mail:* simoncwilding@mac.com. *Website:* www.simonwilding.org.

WILDNER, Johannes; Austrian conductor and musicologist; *Principal Guest Conductor, BBC Concert Orchestra*; b. 1956, Mürzzuschlag, Styria. *Education:* Vienna Musikhochschule. *Career:* fmr violinist, Vienna Philharmonic Orchestra; Chief Conductor, State Philharmonic Orchestra of Košice, Slovakia 1990–93; Chief Conductor, Prague State Opera, Czech Repub. 1994–95; First Perm. Conductor, Leipzig Opera, Germany 1996–98; Gen. Music Dir New Philharmonic Orchestra of Westphalia 1997–2007; as guest conductor has conducted major orchestras world-wide including Royal Philharmonic Orchestra, London, St Petersburg Philharmonic, Russian State Symphony Orchestra, Symphony Orchestra of Bavarian Radio, Tokyo Philharmonic Orchestra, Danish Nat. Symphony Orchestra Copenhagen, Zagreb Philharmonic Orchestra, New Zealand Symphony Orchestra, China and Hong Kong Philharmonic, Guangzhou and Shanghai Symphonies; also worked with MDR-Symphony-Orchestra, Dresden Philharmonic, State Philharmonic of Rhineland-Palatinate, Radio Symphony Orchestra and State Orchestra of Saarbruecken, Vienna Symphony, Tonkuenstler Orchester Niederoesterreich, Mozarteum-Orchestra Salzburg; opera appearances include Prague State Opera, Leipzig Opera (Così fan tutte and Le nozze di Figaro), Wiener Volksoper (Ein Nacht in Venedig), Vienna Summer Festival (Don Giovanni, Die Zauberflöte), Carinthian Summer (The Martyrdom of St Magnus), Arena di Verona (Carmen) and New Nat. Theatre Tokyo (Die Fledermaus); Principal Guest Conductor, BBC Concert Orchestra, London 2010–. *Recordings include:* works of Strauss, Tchaikovsky, Schubert, Mozart, Bruckner's 3rd and 9th symphonies, music by Erich Zeisl, Josef Marx and Johann Nepomuk David, Schumann's complete works for piano and orchestra. *Current Management:* c/o James Black Management, The Old Grammar School, High Street, Rye, East Sussex, TN31 7JF, England. *Telephone:* 1797 224668. *E-mail:* james@jamesblackmanagement.com. *Website:* www.jamesblackmanagement.com/artists/category/conductors/johannes-wildner.

WILKE, Elisabeth; German singer (mezzo-soprano); b. 19 May 1952, Dresden. *Education:* Musikhochschule Dresden. *Career:* debut in Dresden 1974, as Hansel; appearances with the Dresden Staatsoper-Semper Oper in Germany and on tour as Dorabella, Amastris in Handel's Serse, Olga (Eugene Onegin) and Tisbe in Cenerentola 1992; sang Veronika in the premiere of Der Goldene Topf by E. Mayer 1989; Zulma in L'Italiana in Algeri at Dresden 1997; soloist in the St Matthew Passion at Magdeburg 2000. *Recordings include:* Symphoniae Sacrae by Schütz (Capriccio), Saint-Saëns Christmas Oratorio, Missa Brevis by C. P. E. Bach, J. S. Bach's St Matthew Passion.

WILKENS, Anne; British singer (mezzo-soprano); b. 1 July 1947, Romford, Essex, England. *Education:* Guildhall School of Music, London Opera Centre, study with Eva Turner. *Career:* sang in Verdi's Ernani at the Festival Hall, 1972; The Nose by Shostakovich for the New Opera Company, 1973; Sang with English Opera Group in operas by Britten, in Aldeburgh, Venice and Brussels; Sang in world premieres of Death in Venice, 1973, and Musgrave's The Voice of Ariadne, 1974; Member of the Royal Opera Company, Covent Garden, 1974–78, as Olga in Eugene Onegin, Maddalena in Rigoletto, and in the world premiere of Henze's We Come to the River, 1976; Appearances with Handel Opera Society: Handel roles include Julius Caesar, Dejanaira (Hercules) and Ezio; Welsh National Opera 1979, as Brangaene in Tristan und Isolde; Guest appearances in Frankfurt (Azucena), Marseille and Stuttgart (Brangaene); Bayreuth 1983, in the Solti/Hall production of The Ring; Karlsruhe from 1983, as Eboli in Don Carlos and as Wagner's Venus, Fricka, Ortrud and Waltraute; Sang in the premiere of Der Meister und Margarita by Kunaud, Karlsruhe, 1986; Sang Neris in Cherubini's Médée for Opera North, 1996; Mme Larina in Eugene Onegin for ENO, 1997; Season 2000–01 as Wagner's Mary at Covent Garden and in Dublin; Concert engagements with the London Symphony Orchestra, Hallé Orchestra, Bournemouth Symphony and in Netherlands, Spain, Brussels and Stockholm. *Recordings include:* Tristan und Isolde, conducted by Reginald Goodall.

WILKINS, Caroline, BMus; composer; b. 31 July 1953, Somerset, England. *Education:* Royal Coll. of Music, London, Cologne Music Acad. with Mauricio Kagel. *Career:* composer and performer with new music projects in Australia 1984–86; freelance composer in Germany 1989–; commissions from Ensemble Köln 1991, the Hilliard Ensemble 1994 and others; festival participation at Darmstadt, Rheinland, Zürich and Witten 1990–94. *Compositions include:* piece for accordion and phonograph 1988, piece for accordion with screens 1988, Arias for phonograph and singers 1988, piece for 17 tones, two pianos 1990, piece for piano player and piano 1990, Loquela for one to eight female voices 1991, Automatophone for ensemble 1991, The Bird Organ is Made of Wood for percussion 1991, Camera Aeolia for organ 1992, Auroram Lucifer for chorus 1993, For These My Friends and Yours for four male voices 1994, With Circle and Axis for string quartet 1998. *Honours:* first prize Frauenmusik-Forum, Berne 1992. *Website:* www.tremediamusicedition.de.

WILKINS, Margaret Lucy, BMus, AMusD, LRAM; British composer and music educator (retd) and writer; b. (Margaret Lucy Moore), 13 Nov. 1939, Kingston upon Thames, Surrey, England; d. of Harold Herbert Moore and Clarice Annie Lydia Moore (née Schofield); m. Nigel E. Wilkins 1962 (divorced 1977); two d. *Education:* Trinity Coll. of Music, London, Univ. of Nottingham. *Career:* debut on BBC; music teacher, Mansfield Grammar School, Nottingham 1961–62; pvt. teacher of piano and theory, St Andrews, Scotland 1964–1976; Founder-mem. and performer, Scottish Early Music Consort 1970–76; Sr Lecturer, Huddersfield Polytechnic/Univ. of Huddersfield 1976–99, Prin. Lecturer in Music 1999–2003, CALMA Fellowship 2000; Artistic Dir Polyphonia 1989–95; Maude Clarke Visiting Prof., Queen's Univ., Belfast 1995; External Assessor for BA in Performing Arts, Anglia Polytechnic Univ. 1997–2001; Doctoral Comm., Univ. of Music, Bucharest, Romania 2001; works performed world-wide, South Bank and Wigmore Hall, London, and elsewhere in UK, USA, Canada, Germany, Italy, Switzerland, Bulgaria, Austria, Netherlands, Spain, Romania, Poland, China, Russia, Ukraine, Slovenia, Brazil; comms include for BBC Scottish Symphony Orchestra, Univ. of St Andrews, New Music Group of Scotland, William Byrd Singers, John Turner, Julie Wilson, Goldberg Ensemble, Kirklees Cultural Services, Philip Mead; festivals include Durham, Edinburgh, Huddersfield Contemporary Music, Nottingham, Llangollen Eistedfodd, Donne in Musica (Italy), ISCM World Music Days (Poland and Slovenia), Middelburg (Netherlands), New Music Bucharest, Europa–Asia Festival, Kazan Russia, "Two Days and Two Nights of New Music", Odessa Ukraine, London New Wind Festival. *Compositions include:* Witch Music 1971, Struwwelpeter 1973, Hymn to Creation 1973, Orpheus 1973, Burnt Sienna 1974, Circus 1975, Music of the Spheres 1975, The Tree of Life 1979, A Dance to the Music of Time 1980, Three Skelmanthorpe Carols 1980, Gitanjali 1981, Deus ex Machina 1982, Study in Black and White No. 1 1983, Playtime 1985, 366" for solo trombone 1986, Epistola da San Marco 1987, A Joyful Noise! 1988, Rêve, Réveil, Révélations, Réverbérations 1988, Revelations of the Seven Angels 1988, The Cello in My Life 1989, Kanal 1990, Musica Angelorum 1991, Stringsing 1992, Study in Black and White No. 2 1992, L'Attente 1994, A Baker's Dozen 1994, Study in Black and White No. 3 1995, Fearful Apathy 1997, Ring Out, Wild Bells 1998, Ballymo 1998, Rituelle 1999, Trompettes de Mort 2003, Lullaby for Jesus 2010, Fanfare for Colchester 2011. *Recordings include:* Deus ex Machina (Keith Jarvis, solo organ) 1988, Study in Black & White Nos 1 and 2 for solo piano (Ananda Sukarlan, solo piano), The Pentatonic Connection 1996, Musica Angelorum, Struwwelpeter, Burnt Sienna, 366" for solo trombone, Symphony, Free Spirit 2003, Vienna Modern Masters CD 2003, Revelations of the Seven Angels (Orchestra e Coro Simfonica Timisoara, conductor Barrie Webb) (DVD) 2004, Vienna Modern Masters DVD 2004. *Art exhibition:* Essex Art Trail 2011. *Publications include:* Pirouette for solo oboe, and Pas de Quatre for 4 oboes, in Modern Wind Music, Vol. 2 (ed. John Turner) 1985, Aries for descant recorder, in Pieces for Solo Recorder, Vol. 1 (ed. John Turner) 1986, Circuit for bassoon & piano, in Modern Wind Music, Vol. 4 (ed. John Turner) 1986, 366" for solo trombone 1988, Struwwelpeter for soprano, 3 clarinets, percussion, piano, in Music File (ed. Michael Burnett, Stanley Thornes) 1997, Study in Black & White No. 3 for solo piano, in British Contemporary Music Anthology 1996–97 1997, Study in Black & White Nos 1, 2 and 3 for solo piano 1998, Creative Music Composition: The Young Composer's Voice 2006. *Honours:* Scottish Arts Council Bursary for Composers 1970, Winner, The New Cantata Orchestra of London's Competition for Young British Composers (Concerto Grosso) 1970, Winner, Cappiani Prize for Women Composers (The Silver Casket), Soc. for Women Musicians (UK) 1971, First Prize, Halifax (Canada) Int. Competition for Teaching Music (Instrumental Interludes) 1973, Hinrichsen Foundation Award for Composers (UK) 1979, Arts Council of GB Bursary for Composers 1981–82, First Prize, Miriam Gideon Int. Prize for Composers (Struwwelpeter), Int. Alliance for Women Musicians 2000, LTSN Palatine Devt Award (UK) 2002. *Telephone:* (1277) 625593. *E-mail:* margaretlucywilkins@btinternet.com. *Website:* composers21.com/compdocs/wilkinsm.htm; margaretlucywilkins.musicaneo.com.

WILKINSON, Katie; British violist; b. 1960, England. *Career:* debut at Wigmore Hall 1984, with Peter Pears; co-founder, Brindisi String Quartet at Aldeburgh 1984; concerts in a wide repertory throughout the UK and in France, Germany, Spain, Italy and Switzerland; festival engagements at Aldeburgh (residency 1990), Arundel, Bath, Brighton, Huddersfield, Norwich and Warwick; first London performance of Colin Matthews's 2nd Quartet 1990, premiere of David Matthews's 6th Quartet 1991; Quartet by Mark Anthony Turnage 1992; many BBC recitals; Resident Artist, Univ. of Ulster. *Recordings include:* Quartets by Britten, Bridge and Imogen Holst; Works by Pierné and Lekeu. *Honours:* prizewinner Banff Int. String Quartet Competition, Canada (with Brindisi Quartet) 1989.

WIŁKOMIRSKA, Wanda, MMus; Polish violinist; b. 11 Jan. 1929, Warsaw; d. of Alfred Wiłkomirski and Dorota Temkin; divorced since 1976; two s. *Education:* Higher State of Music, Łódź, Franz Liszt Acad. of Music, and pvt. studies with Henryk Szeryng, France. *Career:* public debut playing a Mozart Sonata aged seven; first appearance with orchestra aged 15, in Kraków; numerous recordings; concerts in 50 countries with most major orchestras worldwide; toured as soloist with, amongst others, Nat. Philharmonic, Warsaw and Minnesota Symphony; has given world premiere performances of numerous contemporary works including works by Baird and Penderecki; has toured with her sister and brother as the Wiłkomirska Trio and has performed with Martha Argerich, Gidon Kremer, Daniel Barenboim, Misha Maisky and others; defected whilst on tour of FRG March 1982; Prof., Hochschule für Musik, Heidelberg-Mannheim 1983–98; Guest Prof. then part-time staff mem., Sydney Conservatorium of Music, Australia 1999–; has also worked with Australian Nat. Acad. of Music, Melbourne 2001–; master-classes in Melbourne and Sydney; adjudicator, Hannover Int. Violin Competition 1997, 2000, Kendall Nat. Violin Competition (Australia). *Honours:* Officer's Cross Order of Polonia Restituta 1953, Commdr's Cross with Star 2001, Order of Banner of Labour 2nd Class 1959, (1st Class) 1964; Dr hc (Music Acad., Łódź) 2006; Polish State Prize 1952, 1964; several foreign prizes, including Second Prize, Leipzig 1950, Bach Competition Award of Democratic German Radio, Culture and Arts Prize (1st Class) 1975, Orpheus Prize, Polish Musicians' Asscn 1979, Karol Szymanowski Foundation Prize 1997. *Website:* www.wandawilkomirska.com.

WIŁKOMIRSKI, Józef, MA; Polish conductor, composer, broadcaster, lecturer and journalist and writer; b. 15 May 1926, Kalisz; m. Margaret Zasinska 1980; one d. *Education:* State High School of Music, Warsaw and Łódz Univ. *Career:* debut, Warsaw Philharmonic 1950; Asst Conductor, Kraków Philharmonic 1950–51; Conductor, Poznań Philharmonic 1954–57; Dir and Chief Conductor, State Philharmonic M. Karlowicz in Szczecin 1957–71; Founder, Chief Man. and Artistic Dir, Sudettic Philharmonic, Walbrzych 1978–2005, later renamed the Sudettic Philharmonia; guest conductor in numerous countries in Europe, Asia and America; composer from 1968; numerous radio and television programme appearances, including over 300 lectures. *Compositions:* two sinfoniettas, Symphonic Poems, Symphonic Suite (Royal Castle in Warsaw), sonatas for violin, cello and double bass, Harp Concerto, Concerto for violin and cello, trio, songs. *Publications:* 1926–2006: Memoirs 2009; contrib. over 400 articles and pieces of journalism. *Honours:* Cross of Warsaw Insurrection 1985, Order of the Banner of Labour (First Class) 1986, Cross of the Home Army 1995, Medal of the Veteran of the War for Independence 1995, Commander's Cross with Star of the Order of Polonia Restituta 1998; Gold Medal of Pomeranian Gryphon 1960, Musical Prize of the City of Szczecin 1961, Medal for Merit in Culture 1967, Prize for Public Cultivation of Music 1970, Prize of the City of Walbrzych 1979, Prize of Lower Silesia Press 1982, Prize of the Province of Walbrzych 1983, Medal of National Education 1984, Cultural Award of the City of Walbrzych 1999, Key of Success Prize 2003, Prize of the Province of Lower Silesia 2003, Hon. Citizen of Walbrzych region 2005, Hon. Citizen of Walbrzych city 2006, Gloria Artis Medal 2008, Honorary Citizen of Kalisz 2015. *Address:* ul. Kasztelańska 88 m 5, 58-316 Walbrzych, Poland (home). *Telephone:* (74) 8413111 (home). *E-mail:* jotwu3@wp.pl (home).

WILL, Jacob; singer (bass); b. 8 June 1957, Hartsville, SC, USA. *Education:* Cincinnati Conservatory, San Francisco Opera Studio. *Career:* sang Masetto at San Francisco, followed by appearances with Long Beach and Anchorage Operas, as Basilio in Il Barbiere di Siviglia; Carmel Beach Festival as Mozart's Figaro; appearances throughout the USA as Don Giovanni, Frank in Die Fledermaus, and Dulcamara; sang in Europe from 1986, Zürich Opera from 1988 as Basilio and Melcthal in Guillaume Tell; St Gallen as Sparafucile and Raimondo in Lucia di Lammermoor, Barnaba in Andrea Chénier 1989; Vancouver 1990, as Oroveso, Bregenz Festival 1992, as Zuniga in Carmen; concert engagements include Rossini's Petite Messe Solennelle, Lincoln Center 1989; sang the Speaker in Die Zauberflöte at Zürich and Giachino in Paër's Leonora at Winterthur 2000. *Recordings include:* Zemlinsky's Kleider Machen Leute.

WILLCOCK, Christopher John, BMus, DTheol; Australian composer; b. 8 Feb. 1947, Sydney, NSW. *Education:* Univ. of Sydney. *Compositions include:* Trinity Mass for cantor, chorus, congregation and organ 1977, Psalms for Feasts and Seasons 1977, Convict and the Lady for chorus and chamber ensemble 1977, Lines from Little Gidding for chorus and organ 1978, Friday 3.30 for chorus and string orchestra 1986, Easter Moon for chorus and brass instruments 1988, Two Pastorals for voice and harpsichord 1990, Duo for oboe and harpsichord 1992, Plaint Over Dili for oboe and harpsichord 1992, The Frilled Lizard for viola and harp 1993, Here be Dragons for harpsichord 1994. *Honours:* Dr Percy Jones Award for Outstanding Services to Liturgical Music 1993.

WILLEN, Niklas Olov; Swedish conductor; b. 30 March 1961, Stockholm; m. Anna Schulze 1997; three s. one d. *Education:* Royal Coll. of Music, Stockholm. *Career:* Principal Conductor, The Sundsvall Chamber Orchestra 1993–97; Principal Guest Conductor, Royal Stockholm Philharmonic Orchestra 1993–96; Principal Conductor, South Jutland Symphony Orchestra 2002–06; guest appearances in Europe and USA; mem. Swedish Soc. of Musical Artists. *Compositions:* Lux Aeterna for Choir 1983, Bassoon Concerto 1988, Wind Quintet 1993. *Recordings include:* symphonies by Hugo Alfrein with Royal Scottish Nat. Orchestra. *Honours:* second prize Nordic Competi-

tion 1990. *Current Management:* Patrick Garvey Management, Cedar House, 40 North Parade, York YO30 7AB, England. *Telephone:* (1904) 621222. *Fax:* (1723) 330050. *E-mail:* patrick@patrickgarvey.com. *Website:* www .patrickgarvey.com.

WILLI, Herbert, MPhil, MA; composer; b. 7 Jan. 1956. *Education:* Univ. of Innsbruck, Mozarteum, Salzburg, studied with Helmut Eder and Boguslav Schaeffer. *Career:* performances of his works New York (Carnegie Hall), London (Royal Albert Hall), Vienna (Konzerthaus/Musikverein), Salzburg Festival (Grosses Festspielhaus), Berlin Philharmonic Hall, performed by international orchestras Vienna Philharmonic, Berlin Philharmonic, Cleveland Orchestra, conducted by Claudio Abbado and Christoph von Dohnányi. *Compositions:* Opera Schlafes Bruder (libretto by Robert Schneider); orchestral works: Der Froschmäusekrieg–for sprechgesang for three orchestral groups and tape 1989, Räume für orchester 1991, Konzert für orchester 1991–92, Flötenkonzert 1993; chamber music: Stück für flöte solo 1985, 1986, Streichquartett 1986, Trio für violine, horn und klavier 1992, Concerto for orchestra 1992, Flute Concerto 1993, Begegnung for orchestra 1999. *Honours:* Prize of the Republic of Austria 1986, Rome Prize 1987, 1988, Rolf Liebermann Scholarship 1990, Ernst-von-Siemens Prize 1991, Composer-in-Residence, Salzburg Festival 1992.

WILLIAM, Louis Hagen; American singer (bass-baritone); b. 1950, New Orleans. *Education:* University of Los Angeles opera workshop, Paris Conservatoire. *Career:* With Lyon Opéra sang Sarastro, Daland and the Landgrave in Tannhäuser, Paris Opéra Company in Turandot and L'Heure Espagnole; Other roles include Mephistopheles, Nilakanta in Lakmé, Rossini's Bartolo and the villians in Les Contes d'Hoffmann; has sung in various versions of Porgy and Bess with the Royal Liverpool Philharmonic, the Scottish Chamber Orchestra under Carl Davis, the Ulster Orchestra under Yan Pascal Tortelier, and the Hallé and Royal Philharmonic Orchestras; Has also sung in Handel's Judas Maccabaeus and on French Radio and Television. *Recordings include:* Negro Spitituals, Mozart Concert Arias. *Honours:* First Prizes for Opera and Concert Singing at the Paris Conservatoire.

WILLIAMS, Adrian; British composer and pianist; b. 30 April 1956, Watford, Hertfordshire, England. *Education:* Royal Coll. of Music, London. *Career:* Composer-in-Residence, Charterhouse 1980–82; founder Dir, Presteigne Int. Festival 1983–92. *Compositions:* Sonata for solo cello 1977, String Quartet No. 2 1981, Tess (orchestral poem) 1982, Cantata: September Sky 1985, Mass 1986, Chaconne for guitar 1986, Images of a Mind for cello and piano 1986, Cantata: Not Yet Born 1986, Leaves from the Lost Book 1987, Dies Irae 1988, music for the film Gernika 1987, Cantata: The Ways of Going 1990, String Quartet No. 3 1991, The King of Britain's Daughter 1993. *Honours:* Menuhin Prize 1978, Guinness Prize 1986.

WILLIAMS, Bradley; American singer (tenor); b. 1965, Texas. *Education:* University of Texas, Cincinnati Conservatory of Music. *Career:* debut as Ernesto in Don Pasquale with the Metropolitan Opera Guild 1991; performances include Korngold's Die Tote Stadt with New York City Opera and Zimmermann's Die Soldaten; Opera Orchestra of New York as Georges in Boieldieu's La Dame Blanche; Don Ramiro in La Cenerentola and Giannetto in La Gazza Ladra at Gran Teatro del Liceu in Barcelona; Italian debut as Salvini in world premiere of Bellini's Adelson e Salvini at Teatro Massimo Bellini 1992; Beppe in Pagliacci for New York City Opera; Canadian debut as Ernesto in Don Pasquale in Edmonton; Arturo in I Puritani in Malaga; Carmina Burana at Teatro Regio Torino under Hubert Soudant; Alphonse in Hérold's Zampa at the Wexford Festival; created role of Scott for Houston Grand Opera's world premiere of Wallace 1995 and Korie's Harvey Milk; Count Almaviva in Il Barbiere di Siviglia; performances of Handel's Judas Maccabaeus and Messiah with Collegiate Chorale for Carnegie Hall debut; Australian debut as Tonio in Fille du Régiment with Opera Australia 1997; Connecticut Opera debut as Ernesto; Ernesto for Opéra de Québec and Ferrando in Cosí fan tutte for Dayton Opera; Lindoro in l'Italiana in Algeri for Garsington Opera Festival, Oxford; Duke in Rigoletto in Anchorage, Alaska, debut at Strasbourg's Opéra du Rhin as Tonio in Fille du Régiment and Edgardo in Lucia di Lammermoor in Anchorage. *Recordings:* Salvini in Adelson e Salvi; Harvey Milk with San Francisco Opera. *Current Management:* Pinnacle Arts, Miller Division, 889 Ninth Avenue, 2nd Floor, New York, NY 10019, USA. *Telephone:* (212) 397-7911. *Fax:* (212) 397-7920. *E-mail:* jmiller@pinnaclearts.com. *Website:* www.pinnaclearts.com.

WILLIAMS, Daniel Lewis; American singer (bass); b. 1960. *Education:* Univ. of Utah, Salt Lake City, Musikhochschule, Munich, Germany, studied with Kurt Böhme and Kurt Moll. *Career:* first operatic engagement as serious bass at City Opera House of Trier, Germany, followed by engagements as serious bass of opera houses of Kiel and Krefeld, German Opera on the Rhein, Düsseldorf 1989; numerous prestigious debuts internationally as Gremin, Sarastro, Sparafucile, Daland, Pater Barre, Rocco, Landgraf, Kezal, Basilio, Dossifej, Hunding, Fafner, Eeremit, Osmin, Fillippo, King Marke, Commendatore, Sir Morosus and Ochs von Lerchenau, which role he has now sung in 22 new productions internationally of Strauss opera Der Rosenkavalier; has sung at world's major opera houses and festivals, including, John F. Kennedy Center for the Performing Arts, Semper-Oper, Dresden, Teatro Carlo Felice, Genoa, Italy, Opera de Nice, France, Opera de Marseilles, France, Opera Cologne, Staatstheater Hamburg, Staatstheater Hannover, Saito Kinen Festival, Matsumoto, Japan, Spoleto Festival, USA, Opera Costa Mesa, Calif., Prinzregenten-Theater, Munich, Oper Frankfurt, Oper Leipzig, Deutsche

Oper, Berlin, Teatro Massimo, Palermo, Italy, Opera di Roma, Italy, Opera Trieste, Italy, Teatro la Fenice di Venezia, Italy, among others; also much in demand as a concert artist singing the bass solos of the concert repertoire of Beethoven, Verdi, Mozart, Dvorak, Schostakowitsch, Schubert, Schumann, Löwe and Stravinsky. *Current Management:* c/o Athole Still Opera Ltd, Foresters Hall, 25–27 Westow Street, London, SE19 3RY, England. *Telephone:* (20) 8771-5271. *Fax:* (20) 8771-8172. *E-mail:* enquiries@atholestill.co .uk. *Website:* www.atholestill.co.uk; www.daniel-lewis-williams.de.

WILLIAMS, Edgar Warren, BA, MA, MFA, PhD; American composer, conductor and academic; b. 12 June 1949, Orlando, FL; m. Christine Anderson 1971; one s. one d. *Education:* Duke Univ., Columbia Univ., Princeton Univ. *Career:* Teaching Asst, Columbia Univ. 1972–73; Asst in Instruction, Princeton Univ. 1977–78; Visiting Lecturer in Music, Univ. of California, Davis 1978–79; Asst Prof., Coll. of William and Mary, Williamsburg, VA 1979–82, Assoc. Prof. 1982; guest conductor with orchestras, including Bennington Composers Conference Ensemble 1969–70, Columbia Composers Ensemble 1973; Conductor, William and Mary Orchestra 1979–82. *Compositions include:* Three Songs 1977, Across a Bridge of Dreams 1979–80, Amoretti 1980, Some Music for Merry Wives 1982, Landscapes with Figure 1983, Now Showing for wind and percussion 1993, Pentimenti for chamber orchestra 1993, String Quartet II 1996, String Quartet III 1997, Nosferata: A Symphony of Horror for large orchestra 1998, Lone for solo saxophone 1998. *Publications:* Harmony and Voice Leading (with Taylor and Miller) 1993, Introduction to Music 1993; contrib. to In Theory Only, 19th-Century Music.

WILLIAMS, Harriet Eliza Jean, DipDrama; British singer (mezzo-soprano); b. London, England; d. of Gordon Williams and Claerwen Williams; m.; one s. one d. *Education:* Arts Educational School, Guildhall School with Johanna Peters, studies with Hazel Wood. *Career:* with Welsh Nat. Opera (WNO) from 1993 in operas by Mozart, Strauss, Berlioz, Verdi and Janáček; Purcell's Dido at Bath, Suzuki in Butterfly at the Mananan Festival and Cenerentola for Clonter Opera; other roles include Mozart's Cherubino and Dorabella; concerts include the Mozart and Verdi Requiems, St Matthew Passion, Haydn's Nelson and St Theresa Masses and Mahler's Rückert Lieder; season 1998–99: Poppea for WNO and The Dream of Gerontius with the Liverpool Philharmonic; season 2003: Carmen for English Pocket Opera; Storge in Handel's Jephtha with Konzertchor Darmstadt with performances in Babenhausen, Frankfurt, Amorbach and Darmstadt; season 2004: Cherubino for WNO, Old Sister 1 in Babette's Feast for Royal Opera in Linbury Studio, Nenila in The Enchantress for Grange Park Opera; season 2005: Marcellina for Opera 2005 in Cork, Hannah Kennedy in Maria Stuarda for Grange Park Opera; season 2006: Smeaton in Anna Bolena for Tower of London Festival, Fenena in Nabucco for Dorset Opera, Mistress Quickly in Falstaff for English Touring Opera, Mozart Requiem with English Chamber Orchestra; season 2007: Ersteknappe in Parsifal, Royal Opera House 2007, Beethoven's Ninth Symphony with Royal Philharmonic Orchestra, Bizet's La Jolie Fille de Perth for Chelsea Opera Group, Cadogan Hall, Polinesso in Ariodante for ENO, Albine in Thaïs for Grange Park Opera; season 2008: Mrs Olsen in Street Scene for The Opera Group, L'Invitation au Voyage for The Royal Ballet, Dorothée in Cendrillon for Chelsea Opera Group, Handel's Messiah with Royal Choral Soc. at Royal Albert Hall, Bach Cantata No. 21 with the City of Birmingham Symphony Orchestra; season 2009: Haydn's Harmoniemesse, Beethoven's Ninth Symphony and Ravel's Chansons Madécasses with The Northern Sinfonia at The Sage, Gateshead and Hong Kong Arts Centre, Arnalta for Early Opera Co., Iford, Handel's Messiah with Royal Choral Soc. at Royal Albert Hall; season 2010: Maria, For You for Accademia Filarmonica Romana at Teatro Olimpico, Rome, Mrs Olsen in Street Scene for Opéra de Toulon, Waltraute in Die Walküre for Longborough Festival Opera, Handel's Messiah with Royal Choral Soc. at Royal Albert Hall; season 2011: Mrs Rogers in The Doctor's Tale for Royal Opera in Linbury Studio, Mrs Olsen in Street Scene for The Opera Group; season 2012: Rosina in The Barber of Seville and Madame Larina in Eugene Onegin for English Touring Opera, Flosshilde in Der Ring des Nibelungen, Royal Opera House; season 2013: Mrs Olsen in Street Scene for The Opera Group, Théâtre du Châtelet, Paris and Gran Teatre del Liceu, Waltraute in Die Walküre for Longborough Festival Opera; season 2014: Lea and Madame in world premier of An Eye for an Eye at the Bath Festival and St Magnus Int. Festival: season 2015: Flosshilde in scenes from Das Rheingold with the London Philharmonic at Royal Festival Hall, Brangäne in Tristan und Isolde at Longborough Festival Opera. *Television includes:* Katerina in The Applicant, Harriet in Drinking in Nottingham, for Kombat Opera (BBC TV) 2007. *Honours:* Countess of Munster Scholarship 1991, Sir James Caird Travelling Scholarship 1991, Ian Fleming Award 1991, Sybil Tutton Award 1992. *Current Management:* c/o Helen Sykes Artists Management, 100 Felsham Road, Putney, London, SW15 1DQ, England. *Telephone:* (20) 8780-0060. *Fax:* (20) 8780-8772. *E-mail:* info@ helensykesartists.com. *Website:* www.helensykesartists.co.uk.

WILLIAMS, Helen; British singer (soprano); b. 16 Jan. 1963, Merseyside; m. John Graham Hall; two d. *Education:* Royal Northern Coll. of Music. *Career:* appearances with Glyndebourne Festival and tour 1980s, including Sashka in Osborne's The Electrification of the Soviet Union, and Emme in Albert Herring on tour to Italy; peformances include Handel's Rodelinda in Dublin, in Jephtha with The Sixteen in Rome and London, Dalinda in Ariodante and Amor in Gluck's Orfeo, ENO, Britten's Helena, Opera North, Flaminia in Haydn's Mondo della luna, Netherlands Opera, Naiad in Ariadne auf Naxos, Mozart's First Lady, Scottish Opera, Polinesso in Handel's Radamisto, Opera

North, Rodelinda, Aldeburgh and New York; concerts include The Poisoned Kiss by Vaughan Williams (London and Birmingham), Messiah at the Albert Hall and Handel's Israel in Egypt at St John's Smith Square 2000. *Recordings include:* Gianetta in L'Elisir d'amore and Frasquita in Carmen. *Current Management:* Musichall Ltd, Vicarage Way, Ringmer, East Sussex, BN8 5LA, England. *Telephone:* (1273) 814240. *Fax:* (1273) 813637. *E-mail:* info@ musichall.uk.com. *Website:* www.musichall.uk.com. *E-mail:* Helwilliam@ btinternet.com (home).

WILLIAMS, Howard, BMus, MA; British conductor; *Permanent Guest Conductor, Pannon Philharmonic;* b. 25 April 1947, Hemel Hempstead, Herts., England; m. Juliet Solomon 1977; one s. one d. *Education:* King's School, Canterbury, New Coll., Oxford, Univ. of Liverpool, Guildhall School of Music and Drama, London. *Career:* Asst Conductor BBC Philharmonic 1969–70; Music Dir Queen Mary Coll., London 1972–75; Music Dir Renaissance Singers, London 1971–76; Répétiteur/Conductor ENO 1975–79, Chorus Master 1979–81; Prin. Conductor Ernest Read Symphony Orchestra, London 1981–89; Chief Guest Conductor Royal Ballet, London 1983–85; Prin. Conductor and Artistic Dir Pécs Symphony Orchestra, Hungary 1989–93, 1996–2000; Prin. Conductor Oxford Orchestra da Camera 2000–04; Head of Conducting, Royal Welsh Coll. of Music and Drama, Cardiff 2000–06; Musical Dir Choir of the 21st Century, London 2000–; currently Perm. Guest Conductor Pannon Philharmonic, Hungary; operatic repertoire consists of more than 70 works, including several premieres as well as his own completion of Bizet's largest opera, Ivan IV; has conducted most of the major UK orchestras and at BBC Proms and Edinburgh, Leeds, Bath and Brighton Festivals, as well as at festivals in Budapest, Hong Kong, and throughout France, Spain and Hungary; European orchestras with whom he has worked have included Vienna Radio Symphony, Bavarian Radio Symphony, Swedish Radio Orchestra, Belgian Radio Orchestra, Netherlands Radio Philharmonic, Symphony and Chamber Orchestras, Slovak Philharmonic, Orchestre Nationale de Lyon, Orchestre de Strasbourg and Portuguese Nat. Symphony Orchestra. *Compositions:* Shadowdance 1991. *Recordings include:* three vols of music by Frank Bridge, including his opera The Christmas Rose; Bizet's Ivan The Terrible. *Honours:* Artisjus Award for his services to Hungarian music, Bartók Medal for services to Hungarian music abroad 1997, Pro Civitate Award, City of Pécs, Bartók/Pásztory Prize. *Current Management:* c/o Connaught Artists Management Ltd, 2 Molasses Row, Plantation Wharf, London, SW11 3UX, England. *Telephone:* (20) 7738 0017. *Fax:* (20) 7738 0909. *E-mail:* classicalmusic@connaughtartists.com. *Website:* www .connaughtartists.com; www.wHowardWilliams.com.

WILLIAMS, Huw, BMus, FRCO, ARAM; British organist; b. 2 June 1971, Swansea, Wales. *Education:* organ scholar Christ's Coll., Cambridge, RAM, organ scholar St Paul's Cathedral, London. *Career:* Asst Organist, Hereford Cathedral, Three Choirs Festival; Sub-Organist, St Paul's Cathedral; BBC broadcasts with both cathedral choirs; mem. ISM. *Recordings:* 10 recordings with cathedral choirs of Hereford and St Paul's. *Honours:* Limpus Prize 1991, RAM Countess of Munster Music Scholar 1993–95, Ian Fleming Musical Trust Scholar 1994–95.

WILLIAMS, Janet; American singer (soprano); b. 1965, Detroit. *Career:* debut, San Francisco Opera 1989, as Despina in Così fan tutte; roles at San Francisco included Adele in Die Fledermaus, Nannetta, Musetta, and Elvira in L'Italiana in Algeri; guest at Los Angeles as Mozart's Blondchen and at Wexford as Rezia in Gluck's La Rencontre imprévue 1991; season 1992–93 as Zerlina in Lyon and Rosina at Washington; Berlin Staatsoper from 1992, as Pamina, Graun's Cleopatra, and Oresia in Telemann's Orfeo; Deutsche Oper Berlin 1996, as Handel's Semele; Verdi's Oscar at the Paris Opéra Bastille and Elisa in Mozart's Il Re Pastore at Nice 1994; Adele in Die Fledermaus at the New York Met 1996; season 1997–98 in Opera Gala at San Francisco, and as Manon in Henze's Boulevard Solitude at Frankfurt; sang Poppea in Handel's Agrippina at Graz 2000; concerts include Tippett's A Child of Our Time at Berlin and Mozart's Requiem at New York. *Recordings include:* Messiah and Graun's Cesare e Cleopatra. *E-mail:* info@janetwilliams.de. *Website:* www .janetwilliams.de.

WILLIAMS, Jeremy Huw; British singer (baritone); b. 1965, England. *Education:* St John's Coll., Cambridge, Nat. Opera Studio, studied with April Cantelo. *Career:* debut, Guglielmo in Così fan tutte with WNO; appearances with L'Opéra de Nantes as Papageno, Olivier in Capriccio and title role in Karetnikov's Till Eulenspiegel; Escamillo, Germont and Marcello in La Bohème for WNO; further engagements for Music Theatre Wales, Opera Ireland and the City of Birmingham SO; Buxton Festival, Holland Park Opera and Ulm, Germany; sang M. Gaye in the Lully/Molière Bourgeois Gentilhomme, for the English Bach Festival at the Linbury Theatre, Covent Garden 2001. *Honours:* Hon. DMus (Univ. of Aberdeen) 2011; Welsh Music Guild Sir Geraint Evans Award 2005, winner, Classical Music category, Creative Wales Awards 2008. *Current Management:* c/o Samuel Krum, Robert Gikder & Co., N102, Westminster Business Square, 1–45 Durham Street, London, SE11 5JH, England. *Telephone:* (20) 7580-7758. *Fax:* (20) 7580-7739. *E-mail:* sam@ robert-gilder.com. *Website:* www.robertgilder.co. *E-mail:* jhw@ jeremyhuwwilliams.com. *Website:* www.jeremyhuwwilliams.com.

WILLIAMS, John, AO, OBE; Australian classical guitarist; b. 24 April 1941, Melbourne; s. of Len Williams and Melaan Ket; m. 1st Linda Susan Kendall 1964 (divorced); one d.; m. 2nd Sue Cook 1981 (divorced); one s.; m. 3rd Kathleen Panama 2000. *Education:* Friern Barnet Grammar School and

Royal Coll. of Music, UK, studied guitar with father, Segovia and at Accad. Chigiana, Siena, Italy. *Career:* has toured widely and appears frequently on TV and radio; numerous transcriptions and gramophone recordings as solo guitarist and with leading orchestras; f. The Height Below (ensemble) with Brian Gascoigne, John Williams and Friends (ensemble) and Founder-mem. groups, SKY and John Williams' Attacca; current ensembles include John Williams and Richard Harvey's World Tour and 'Together and Solo' with John Etheridge, as well as solo recitals worldwide; other collaborations with Julian Bream, Itzhak Perlman, Andre Previn, Cleo Lane and John Dankworth, Nat. Youth Jazz Orchestra, Paco Pena and Inti Illimani; Artistic Dir South Bank Summer Music Festival 1984–85, Melbourne Arts Festival 1987. *Films:* composed and played music for film Emma's War. *Recordings include:* include Takemitsu Played by John Williams (music by Toru Takemitsu, with the London Sinfonietta) 1991, several of Rodrigo's Conciertos de Aranjuez, Vivaldi Concertos 1991, The Seville Concert/The Film Profile of John Williams (also on laserdisc and VHS) 1993, From Australia (featuring music by Peter Sculthorpe and Nigel Westlake) 1994, The Great Paraguayan 1995, concerti by Richard Harvey and Steve Gray 1996, John Williams Plays the Movies 1997, The Black Decameron (music by Leo Brouwer) 1997, The Guitarist 1998, Schubert and Giuliani 1999, The Magic Box 2002, El Diablo Suelto 2003, The Ultimate Guitar Collection 2004, Places Between (with John Etheridge) 2006, From a Bird 2008, The Guitarist (3 CD set) 2011, Stepping Stones 2014, The Great Movie Soundtracks 2015. *Honours:* Hon. FRCM, FRAM, FRNCM; Dr hc (Melbourne); Edison Award for Lifetime Achievement 2007. *Website:* www .JohnWilliamsGuitarNotes.com.

WILLIAMS, John Towner; American composer, conductor and pianist; b. 8 Feb. 1932, Flushing, NY. *Education:* Juilliard School, New York, Univ. of California, Los Angeles, studied composition with Mario Castelnuovo-Tedesco. *Career:* pianist, Columbia Pictures; jazz pianist working with Henry Mancini on television scores; Conductor, Boston Pops Orchestra 1980–98. *Film scores:* The Secret Ways 1961, Diamond Head 1962, None But the Brave 1965, How to Steal a Million 1966, Valley of the Dolls 1967, The Cowboys 1972, The Poseidon Adventure 1972, Tom Sawyer 1973, Earthquake 1974, The Towering Inferno 1974, Jaws (Acad. Award) 1975, The Eiger Sanction 1975, Family Plot 1976, Midway 1976, The Missouri Breaks 1976, Raggedy Ann and Andy 1977, Black Sunday 1977, Star Wars (Acad. Award) 1977, Close Encounters of the Third Kind 1977, The Fury 1978, Jaws II 1978, Superman 1978, Dracula 1979, 1941 1979, The Empire Strikes Back 1980, Raiders of the Lost Ark 1981, E.T.: The Extra Terrestrial (Acad. Award) 1982, Return of the Jedi 1983, Indiana Jones and the Temple of Doom 1984, The River 1985, Space Camp 1986, The Witches of Eastwick 1987, Empire of the Sun (BAFTA Award for Best Score) 1988, Always 1989, Born on the Fourth of July 1989, Indiana Jones and the Last Crusade 1989, Stanley and Iris 1990, Presumed Innocent 1990, Home Alone 1990, Hook 1991, JFK 1993, Far and Away 1993, Home Alone 2: Lost in New York 1993, Jurassic Park 1993, Schindler's List (Acad. Award) 1993, Sabrina 1995, The Reivers 1995, Nixon 1995, Sleepers 1996, Rosewood 1996, Land of the Giants 1997, Seven Years in Tibet 1997, The Lost World: Jurassic Park 1997, Amistad 1997, Lost in Space 1997, Time Tunnel 1997, Saving Private Ryan 1998, Star Wars: Episode I – The Phantom Menace 1999, Angela's Ashes 1999, Harry Potter and the Sorcerer's Stone 2001, Star Wars: Episode II – Attack of the Clones 2001, Minority Report 2002, Harry Potter and the Chamber of Secrets 2002, Catch Me if You Can 2002, Harry Potter and the Prisoner of Azkaban 2004, The Terminal 2004, Star Wars: Episode III – Revenge of the Sith 2005, War of the Worlds 2005, Harry Potter and the Goblet of Fire 2005, Memoirs of a Geisha (Golden Globe for Best Original Score in a Motion Picture 2006, BAFTA Anthony Asquith Award for Achievement in Film Music 2006, Grammy Award for Best Score Soundtrack Album for Motion Picture 2007) 2005, Munich 2005, Superman Returns 2006, Harry Potter and the Order of the Phoenix 2007, Indiana Jones and the Kingdom of the Crystal Skull 2008, Harry Potter and the Half-Blood Prince 2009, Lincoln (Critics Choice Award 2013) 2012, The Book Thief 2013. *Recordings include:* John Williams Plays The Movies 1996, Music From The Star Wars Saga 1999, Jane Eyre 1999, Themes From Academy Award Winners, Over The Rainbow: Songs From The Movies 1992, John Williams Conducting The Boston Pops 1996, The Hollywood Sound 1997, From Sousa To Spielberg, Best Of John Williams 1998, Treesong 2001, Call Of The Champions (official theme of 2002 Winter Olympics, Salt Lake City) 2001, John Williams Trumpet Concerto 2002, American Journey 2002; recordings of film scores. *Honours:* numerous hon. degrees; five Academy Awards, seven BAFTA Awards, three Emmy Awards, four Golden Globes, 21 Grammy Awards, recipient of Kennedy Center Honors 2004, Classical BRIT Award for Soundtrack Composer of the Year 2005, Grammy Awards for Best Instrumental Composition (for A Prayer for Peace, from Munich) 2007, (for The Adventures of Mutt, from Indiana Jones and the Kingdom of the Crystal Skull) 2009, Nat. Medal of Arts 2009, Ken Burns Lifetime Achievement Award 2013. *Current Management:* c/o Michael Gorfaine, Gorfaine/Schwartz Agency, 4111 West Alameda Avenue, Suite 509, Burbank, CA 91505, USA. *Website:* www.johnwilliams.org.

WILLIAMS, Julius Penson, BS, MM; American composer and conductor; b. 22 June 1954, Bronx, NY; m. Lenora B. Williams 1977; one s. one d. *Education:* Andrew Jackson High School, Herbert H. Lehman Coll., CUNY, Hartt School of Music, Aspen Music School. *Career:* debut with premiere of A Norman Overture, New York Philharmonic and Zubin Mehta 1985; Music Dir, CPTV 1984–85; Arts Award Guest Conductor, Connecticut Opera 1983, Dallas Symphony 1986, Savannah Symphony 1987; Asst Conductor, Aspen Music

Festival 1985; Conductor, Composer-in-Residence, Nutmeg Ballet, CT 1986–88; Guest Conductor, New Haven Symphony 1987, Amor Artist Chamber Orchestra 1987; Artistic Dir, New York State Summer School of the Arts (Choral Studies) 1988–; Principal Guest, School of Orchestral Studies; Assoc. Prof., Univ. of Vermont; Artist-in-Residence, Saratoga Arts Festival 1988. *Compositions:* A Norman Overture, Toccatina for strings, Incommendation of Music, The Spring, Rise Up Shepherd and Follow, Vermont's Escape, Alison's Dream, The Fall, Summers Good Ecelin. *Publications:* contrib. to American Choral Directors' Journal Choral Review 1982. *Address:* Henderson, Seventh Avenue, Apt 4K, New York, NY 10026-2231, USA.

WILLIAMS, Laverne, MA; American singer (tenor); b. 1935, San Francisco, CA. *Education:* Univ. of California, Alfred Hertz Memorial Scholarship and Rockefeller Foundation Scholarship for studies in Europe. *Career:* concerts and opera appearances ranging from baroque to contemporary; L'Incoronazione di Poppea, Salome, Idomeneo and Porgy and Bess, Switzerland; appeared with Jessye Norman in Great Day in the Morning, Paris; Porgy and Bess, Glagolitic Mass and Jenůfa under Simon Rattle, UK; appearances with most major orchestras in London and the UK including London Symphony, Royal Philharmonic and the Royal Liverpool Philharmonic Orchestra; directed and sang in an experimental evening of spirituals, Almeida Theatre; performed Virgil Thomson's Four Saints in Three Acts, Almeida Theatre; European Opera appearances include Zürich, Lyon and Brussels operas; television and radio broadcasts include Gershwin's Blue Monday in Switzerland, Hermann Prey Show for German television, Here Come the Classics and excerpts from Carmen Jones for BBC television, Club Mix for Channel 4; leading role, European premiere of Carmen Jones; Weber's Oberon, Edinburgh Festival, Tanglewood and Frankfurt 1986. *Recordings:* Great Day in the Morning, with Jessye Norman. *Honours:* competition successes in 'S-Hertogenbosch, Rio de Janeiro and Barcelona.

WILLIAMS, Llŷr, BMus, DipRAM; British pianist; b. 1976, Pentrebychan, Wrexham, Wales. *Education:* Queen's Coll., Oxford, Royal Acad. of Music, London. *Career:* selected by Young Concert Artists Trust 2002; selected as a BBC New Generation Artist; recital debut Edinburgh Festival 2002, performs there regularly; has performed with all the BBC orchestras, London Mozart Players, London Philharmonic Orchestra, Hallé Orchestra, Sinfonia Cymru and Minnesota Orchestra; has worked with conductors including Carlo Rizzi, Jiri Bělohlávek, Jukka-Pekka Saraste, Osmo Vanska and Thierry Fisher; performed at BBC Proms 2005, Bath Int. Music Festival 2005, Barbican Centre 2006, Edinburgh Festival 2010; official accompanist, Cardiff Singer of the World Competition 2007. *Recordings:* Frederic Chopin: Complete Preludes 2006, Mussorgsky: Pictures at an Exhibition 2010, Liszt: Excerpts from Années de pèlerinage: DeuxiemeAnnée: Italie and other works 2012, Wagner Without Words 2014. *Honours:* Borletti-Buitoni Trust Award 2004, MIDEM Classique/IAMA Outstanding Young Artist Award 2005, South Bank Sky Arts Award, Classical 2012. *Current Management:* c/o Victoria Rowsell Artist Management, 34 Addington Square, London, SE5 7LB, London. *E-mail:* management@victoriarowsell.co.uk. *Website:* www.victoriarowsell.co.uk.

WILLIAMS, Louise, ARAM; British violist and violinist; b. 23 Sept. 1955, England; d. of P. M. de C. Williams and Moza Williams; m. Lionel de Rothschild; two s. one d. *Education:* Royal Acad. of Music, London, Juilliard School of Music, New York, USA. *Career:* Co-founder and Second Violinist, Endellion Quartet 1979–83; Violist, Chilingirian Quartet 1987–92; mem. Raphael Ensemble 1996–2003; Quintet Partner, Lindsay Quartet 1995–; Founder-mem. Merel Quartet 2002–05; mem. Frith Piano Quartet and Arpege, Cappella Andrea Barca; freelance chamber musician and soloist. *Recordings:* Complete Quartets of Bartók and Dvořák, Bartók Piano Quintet, Dvorak Quintets, Mozart Flute Quartets, Beethoven Serenade, Haydn Quartets, Prokofiev Quartets, Mendelssohn Viola Quintets, Bridge Sextet, Quintet and Viola Duo, Bridge Music for Viola and Piano, Walton, Bridge and Lekeu Piano Quartets, Bax, McEwen Viola Sonatas, Maconchy, Rawsthorne and pieces by Gordon Jacob, Kenneth Leighton and Robin Milford for viola and piano with David Owen Norris. *Address:* 52 Masbro Road, London, W14 0LT, England. *Telephone:* 7767-685058 (mobile). *E-mail:* louise@louiseviola.co .uk. *Website:* www.louiseviola.co.uk.

WILLIAMS, Peter Fredric, BA, MusB, MA, PhD, LittD; British musicologist, organist and harpsichordist; b. 14 May 1937, Wolverhampton, Staffordshire; m. Rosemary Seymour 1982; three s. one d. *Education:* Birmingham Inst., St John's Coll., Cambridge. *Career:* Lecturer, Univ. of Edinburgh 1962–72, Reader 1972–82, Prof. 1982–85, Dean 1984; Dir Russell Coll. of Harpsichords, Edinburgh 1969; Founder-Ed., The Organ Yearbook (Regensburg) 1969–; Arts and Sciences Distinguished Prof., Duke Univ., USA 1985–95, Dir Graduate Center for Performance Practice Studies 1990–96; John Bird Prof., Univ. of Wales, Cardiff 1996–2002; Vice-Pres. Royal Coll. of Organists 2005; mem. British Inst. of Organ Studies (chair.). *Publications include:* The European Organ 1450–1850 1966, Figured Bass Accompaniment (two vols) 1970, Vente/Peeters' The Organ and its Music in the Netherlands (trans.) 1971, A New History of the Organ From the Greeks to the Present Day 1980, The Organ Music of J. S. Bach (three vols) 1980–84, Bach, Handel and Scarlatti: Tercentenary Essays (ed.) 1985, Playing the Works of Bach 1986, Playing the Organ Music of Bach 1988, Mozart: Perspectives in Performance (ed. with L. Todd) 1991, The Organ in Western Culture 750–1250 1992, The King of Instruments: How Do Churches Come to Have Organs? 1993, The Chromatic Fourth During Four Centuries of Music 1995, Cambridge Studies in

Performance Practice (series ed., six vols) 1995, Music to Hear, or Fears for Higher Music Study 2001, The Life of Bach 2005 (expanded as J.S. Bach: A Life in Music 2007); several vols of keyboard music by Bach and Handel; contrib. to scholarly books and journals. *Honours:* Research Fellow, Cornell Univ., New York 1982, Hon. Fellow, Royal Coll. of Organists 1982, Royal Scottish Acad. of Art 1990; Hon. Prof. (Edinburgh) 1992; Curt Sachs Award, American Musical Instrument Soc. 1996. *Address:* c/o Department of Music, Corbett Road, University of Wales, Cardiff, CF10 3EB, Wales. *Telephone:* (1452) 831195 (home).

WILLIAMS, Sioned, DipMus; British harpist; b. 1 July 1953, Mancot, Clwyd, North Wales; m. Kim A. L. Sargeant 1977. *Education:* Welsh Coll. of Music and Drama, Royal Acad. of Music. *Career:* debut in Purcell Room, Park Lane Group Young Artists/20th Century Music 1977; Carnegie Hall, New York, USA (Concert Artists Guild Award) 1980; appearances worldwide with London Symphony Orchestra, Philharmonia, London Philharmonic Orchestra, RPO, BBC Symphony Orchestra, BBC Philharmonic, CBSO, Royal Ballet, London Sinfonietta, Royal Opera House, ENO, WNO, SNO; solo and concerto performances, premiering over 80 works; chamber music with Uroboros, Gemini, Spectrum, Endymion, Divertimenti, Koenig, Grosvenor, Circle; theatre, radio, television and festival appearances; Prof. of Harp, Royal Coll. of Music Jr Dept 1976–85, Royal Acad. of Music 1983–84, London Coll. of Music 1985–86, Trinity Coll. of Music 1986–; adjudicator at major Welsh Eisteddfods 1981–. *Compositions:* Cyfres i'r Delyn (special prize, 17th International Harp Week) 1973, Serenata e Danza 1983. *Recordings:* Harp Music, John Thomas; Harp Music, John Parry; Spun Gold for Flute and Harp; Ceremony of Carols, Britten; Nielsen with James Galway. *Publications:* John Parry: Four Sonatas (ed.) 1982, Four Sonatas (ed.) 1982, J. S. Bach: Suite BMV1006a (ed.) 1986. *Honours:* bursary Arts Council Advanced Training Scheme 1982. *E-mail:* sionedwilliams@email.com. *Website:* www.sionedwilliams.com.

WILLIAMS, Wayne; American singer (tenor); b. 1960, Cleveland, OH. *Education:* Cleveland Music Settlement, studied with Gerard Souzay in Geneva. *Career:* concert appearances with the Suisse Romande, Chamber Orchestra of Lausanne, Berne Symphony, Tonhalle Zürich, YMSO (London), Orchestra Haydn (Italy) and the Shanghai Symphony (China); recitals throughout the USA and Europe with Dalton Baldwin; appearances in Paris in Dvořák's Requiem and Stabat Mater, Switzerland in The Creation and St Matthew Passion; opera repertoire includes Schubert's Fierrabras, L'Elisir d'amore, La Traviata and A Midsummer Night's Dream. *Recordings include:* Poulenc Gloria; Great Day in the Morning, with Jessye Norman; Dvořák Stabat Mater.

WILLIAMS-KING, Anne; singer (soprano); b. 1960, Wrexham, Wales. *Education:* Royal Northern College of Music, National Opera Studio, London. *Career:* sang with the Welsh National Opera as Lenio in The Greek Passion by Martinů, Mimi, Gilda, Fiordiligi, Marzelline in Fidelio and Micaela; Covent Garden debut in 1988 as Freia in Das Rheingold; Appearances with Opera North as Mimi and in Rebecca by Josephs and A Village Romeo and Juliet by Delius; Scottish Opera as Freia and Violetta, invited to return as Jenůfa, Madama Butterfly and Mimi; Foreign engagements include Anne Trulove in The Rake's Progress at Berne; Frequent concert appearances with leading British orchestras and on television; Sang Butterfly with Scottish Opera at Edinburgh, 1990; Suor Angelica for ENO, 1998; Season 1999–2000 as Lisa in The Queen of Spades, at Antwerp, and Janáček's Emilia Marty at Osnabrück.

WILLIS, Helen, DipMus; British singer (mezzo-soprano); b. 25 July 1959, Newport, Gwent, Wales; m. Robert Venn 1983. *Education:* Royal Acad. of Music. *Career:* debut, Wigmore Hall, London 1983; mem., Glyndebourne Festival Chorus 1983–85; solo operatic debut with WNO as Siegrune in Die Walküre 1984; concerts and recitals throughout the UK and abroad; broadcasts include Sea Pictures and Wesendonck Lieder with BBC Nat. Orchestra of Wales. *Honours:* Triennial Young Welsh Singer of the Year 1982.

WILLIS, Nuala; British singer (mezzo-soprano); b. 1950, England. *Career:* worked as designer and costumier and as actress in England in N America, appeared in Medea on Broadway 1994; sang with Opera Studio in Brussels and small roles with Glyndebourne Tour; Aldeburgh Festival in Eugene Onegin and A Midsummer Night's Dream; guest appearances at Nancy, Metz, Marseilles (Herodias in Salome), Geneva (Larina in Eugene Onegin), Marseilles (Jezibab in Rusalka) and Zürich (The Hostess in Boris Godunov); appeared in A Midsummer Night's Dream, Eugene Onegin and Faust as Martha at Covent Garden; in Ireland has sung Widow Bebick (Mahagonny) at Wexford and Clytemnestra in Elektra conducted by Janos Fürst in Dublin; Season 1989–90 included Herodias in Swedish Folkopera's Salome at Edinburgh Festival, Ulrica in Un Ballo in Maschera for Canadian Opera in Toronto, Royal Nat. Theatre in Sondheim's Sunday in the Park with George; engagements with D'Oyly Carte Opera; sang the Elephant in Paran Vir's Broken Strings at Almeida Theatre 1996, Older Woman in premiere of Dove's Flight, Glyndebourne 1998; Season 1999–2000 as Stravinsky's Mother Goose at Lausanne and Glyndebourne and premiere of Ion by Param Vir at Aldeburgh; season 2005–06 Mistress Quickly in Falstaff with Stanley Hall Opera, Older Woman in Flight, Glyndebourne 2005, Adelaide Festival and Opera 2006, Holland Park Opera 2007. *Films include:* Warm in the Bud 1970, The Death of Klinghoffer 2003. *Television includes:* The Rake's Progress 1975, The Sorcerer 1982, When She Died... Death of a Princess 2002.

WILLS, Arthur, OBE, DMus, ADCM, FRSCM, FRCO; British composer and cathedral organist; b. 19 Sept. 1926, Coventry, Warwicks.; m. Mary Elizabeth Titterton 1953; one s. one d. *Education:* St John's School, Coventry, St Nicholas Coll., Canterbury. *Career:* organist, Ely Cathedral 1958–90; Prof., RAM 1964–92; organ recitals in Europe, USA, Australia and NZ. *Compositions:* Organ Concerto 1970, An English Requiem 1971, Guitar Sonata 1974, Three Poems of E.E. Cummings for tenor, oboe and piano 1974, Love's Torment (Four Elizabethan Love Songs) for alto and piano 1975, The Fenlands (Symphonic Suite for brass band and organ) 1981, Overture: A Muse of Fire for brass band 1983, Concerto Lirico for guitar quartet 1987, When the Spirit Comes (Four Poems of Emily Brontë for mezzo-soprano and piano) 1985, Piano Sonata '1984', The Dark Lady (Eight Sonnets of Shakespeare for baritone and piano) 1986, Sacrae Symphonia: Veni Creator Spiritus 1987, Choral Concerto: The Gods of Music 1992, Eternity's Sunrise, Three Poems by William Blake 1992, A Toccata of Galuppi's, Scena for countertenor and string quartet 1993, Missa Sancti Stephani 2001, Missa Incarnationis 2002, Crossing the Bar 2004. *Recordings include:* Music for Organ and Brass, The Praises of the Trinity, Full Stops, Music of Six Centuries, Wondrous Machine!: Organ Music of Arthur Wills. *Publications:* Organ (Menuhin Music Guide Series) 1984; contrib. to Musical Times. *Honours:* Hon. mem. RAM 1974. *Address:* Paradise House, 26 New Barns Road, Ely, Cambs, CB7 4PN, England (home). *Telephone:* (1353) 662084 (home). *Fax:* (1353) 662084 (home). *E-mail:* artwill@argonet.co.uk (home). *Website:* www.impulse-music.co.uk/arthurwills.htm (home).

WILSON, Catherine, FRNCM; British singer (soprano) and performance coach; b. 1936, Glasgow, Scotland; m. Leonard Hancock (died 1999). *Education:* Royal Manchester Coll. of Music with Elsie Thurston; further study with Ruth Packer in London and Maria Carpi in Geneva. *Career:* debut, Sadler's Wells, London in 1960 as Angelina in La Cenerentola; Glyndebourne in 1960 in Die Zauberflöte; Sadler's Wells in 1965 in the premiere of Bennett's The Mines of Sulphur; Scottish Opera in the 1977 Edinburgh Festival, title role in Thea Musgrave's Mary Queen of Scots; Scottish Opera in 1974 in the premiere of Hamilton's The Catiline Conspiracy; guest appearances in Aldeburgh, Cologne, Geneva, Boston, Houston, Louisville and ENO in London, and Santa Fe; often heard in operas by Mozart, Rossini, Puccini, Strauss and Britten and as a concert singer; teacher at Royal Northern Coll. of Music 1980–91; performance coach, William Walton Trust 1990–95, Guildhall School of Music and Drama 1994–2004. *Films:* appeared in: Quartet 2012. *Recordings include:* Albert Herring by Britten, The Merry Widow, Dido and Aeneas, Richard Rodney Bennett's The Mines of Sulphur 1964, Thea Musgrave: Mary Queen of Scots, Edinburgh Festival 1977. *Address:* 18 St Mary's Grove, London, N1 2NT, England. *Telephone:* (20) 7226-0724.

WILSON, Charles Mills, MusBac, MusDoc; Canadian composer (retd); b. 8 May 1931, Toronto, Ont.; m. 1st Jennifer Wilson (deceased); two s. one d.; m. 2nd Elizabeth Wilson; one d. *Education:* Toronto Conservatory with Godfrey Ridout, Toronto Univ., Berkshire Music Center with Lukas Foss and Carlos Chavez. *Career:* Head of Music Dept, Guelph Collegiate Inst. 1962–70; Composer-in-Residence, Canadian Opera Co. 1972–, Univ. of Guelph, Ont.; Chorus Master Canadian Opera Co.; Assoc. Composer Canadian Music Centre; Choral Conductor Bach-Elgar Choir of Hamilton, Ont. 1992–; mem. Canadian League of Composers. *Compositions include:* four string quartets 1950, 1968, 1975, 1983, The Strolling Clerk from Paradise (chamber opera) 1952, Symphony in A 1954, Sonata de Chiesa for oboe and strings 1960, The Angels of the Earth (oratorio) 1966, En Guise for baritone and strings 1968, Concert 5x4x3 for string quintet, woodwind quartet and brass trio 1970, Johnny Fibber (operetta) 1970, Phrases from Orpheus (multimedia opera) 1971, Dona Nobis Pacem for choir and brass sextet 1972, The Summoning of Everyman (church opera) 1973, Heloise and Abelard (opera in three acts) 1973, The Selfish Giant (children's opera) 1973, Image Out of Season for chorus and brass quintet 1973, Christo Paremus Canticum for chorus and orchestra 1973, Symphonic Perspectives: Kingsmere for orchestra 1974, Missa Brevis for chorus and organ 1975, Psycho Red (opera in two acts) 1980, Kamouraska (opera in two acts) 1979 (revised 2007–08), Revelations to John: A Festival Cantata for three choirs and organ, Seasons of Life song cycle for contralto and piano 1998, Cantata for Palm Sunday for choir, soli, strings and piano 1998, Images for contralto and flute 1999, Cantata for Tenebrae 1999, The Cave song cycle for contralto and piano 2000, Dream Telescope song cycle for contralto and chamber orchestra 2001, She, to Him song cycle for contralto, oboe and piano 2002, Cantata for the Resurrection for choir, soli and strings and harpsichord or piano 2004. *Address:* 536 Flannery Drive, Fergus, Ont. N1M 3P4, Canada (home). *Telephone:* (519) 843-7581 (home). *E-mail:* charlesmillswilson@gmail.com (home).

WILSON, Christopher; British lutenist and vihuela player; b. 1951. *Education:* Royal Coll. of Music with Diana Poulton. *Career:* specialises in the performance of Renaissance music throughout the United Kingdom; concert tours of Europe, Scandinavia, USA, the Baltic States, Russia and the Far East; as well as working with his own group Kithara, interest in the lute song repertoire has led him to work with such song recitalists as countertenor Michael Chance and the tenor Rufus Müller; performs with Fretwork, Gothic Voices, the Consort of Musicke and the English Baroque Soloists. *Recordings include:* appeared on over 50 recordings and on solo recordings.

WILSON, Christopher R., BA, MA, DPhil, FSA; British academic; *Professor of Music, University of Hull;* b. 1 Oct. 1952, Hull, Humberside; s. of Canon J. C. H. Wilson; m. Christine Wilson; three c. *Education:* Univ. of Oxford. *Career:*

temporary Lecturer, Univ. of St Andrews 1978; Lecturer, Univ. of Reading 1979; Sr Lecturer and Head of Music Dept, Univ. of Reading 2001–05; Prof. of Music, Univ. of Hull 2006–, Assoc. Dean, Faculty of Arts and Social Sciences 2013–; mem. Royal Musical Assen (Council 1989–92, 2001–03), Finzi Trust Friends. *Publications include:* Campion, A Critical Study 1989, Campion and Coprario Treatises 2003, Music in Shakespeare 2005, Shakespeare's Musical Imagery 2011; contrib. to Music and Letters 1979–, Review of English Studies 1981–, Early Music 1981–, A Shakespeare Music Catalogue 1991, Grove Opera 1992, Modern Language Review 1993–, Grove Dictionary of Music 2001, Comparative Literature 2001, New Oxford Companion to Music 2002, John Donne Journal 2006, Tempo 2010, Comparatio 2014. *Honours:* Louise Dyer Award 1978, Leverhulme Trust research project grant 2001–04. *Address:* Music Department, University of Hull, Cottingham Road, Hull, HU6 7RX, England (office). *Telephone:* (1482) 465609 (office). *E-mail:* christopher.wilson@hull.ac.uk (office). *Website:* www.hull.ac.uk/music (office).

WILSON, Elisa, AMusA; Australian singer (soprano); b. 22 Oct. 1965, Perth, Western Australia; d. of Cyril William Wilson and Gloria Elwyn Stitfold; m.; three s. *Education:* Western Australia Conservatorium, Perth, Univ. of Western Australia. *Career:* debut as Despina in Così fan tutte, Western Australia Opera, and Adele in Die Fledermaus; other engagements throughout Australia for Western Australia Opera Co. include Nanetta in Falstaff, the Sandman and Dew Fairy in Hansel & Gretel, Micaela in Carmen, Pamina in The Magic Flute, Gilda in Rigoletto, Susanna in The Marriage of Figaro, Norina in Don Pasquale, Adina in The Elixir of Love, Musetta in La Bohème, Leila in The Pearl Fishers, Alice Ford in Falstaff and world premieres, Nanette in The Eureka Stockade and Heloise in Heloise and Abelard; also performed Greta in Brian Howard's Metamorphosis and Mrs Green in Harrison Birtwistle's Down by the Greenwood Side for other cos in WA; Donna Elvira in Don Giovanni and The Girl in The Emperor of Atlantis for Victoria State Opera; Echo in Ariadne auf Naxos, Spoleto Festival, Melbourne; debut with Opera Australia as Helena in A Midsummer Night's Dream at Edinburgh Festival 1994; Handel's Alcina in Sydney and Melbourne; Rosalinda in Die Fledermaus and Musetta in La Bohème at Sydney Opera House; Blanche Dubois in A Streetcar Named Desire; Cio-Cio-San in Madama Butterfly; Marschallin in Der Rosenkavalier; Countess in Capriccio; First Lady and Pamina in The Magic Flute; Marcellina in The Marriage of Figaro (Opera Australia); concert appearances as soloist with Australian Symphony Orchestra and other Australian orchestras, with Vienna Male Voice Choir and Opera Australia; live broadcasts of operas Rita and Susanna's Secret for ABC. *Recording:* Bruckner's Mass in D Minor (soprano soloist). *Leisure interests:* martial arts, genealogy. *Honours:* Creative Development Fellowship, Arts WA 1994, Armstrong-Martin Opera Award 1992, Dame Mabel Brookes Award 1992, ABC Prize 1992. *Current Management:* c/o Patrick Togher Artists Management, Suite 25, 450 Elizabeth Street, Surry Hills, NSW 2010, Australia. *Telephone:* (2) 9319-6255. *Fax:* (2) 9319-7611. *E-mail:* pjtogher@ozemail.com.au. *Website:* www.patricktogher.com.

WILSON, Fredric Woodbridge, BA, MA; American musicologist; b. 8 Sept. 1947, Point Pleasant, NJ. *Education:* Lehigh Univ., Bethlehem, PA, New York Univ. *Career:* Dir, The Wall Choirs, NJ 1969–81; Ed., Allaire Music Publications 1980–; Curator, The Pierpont Morgan Library, New York 1981; Prof. of Museum Studies, Graduate School of Arts and Science, New York Univ. 1994–; musical and textual consultant to opera cos; organized conferences in English Opera, New York 1985, Gilbert and Sullivan, New York 1989, Purchase Coll. 1994; organized exhibitions at Pierpont Morgan Library 1985, 1989, Kentucky Center for the Arts 1987, 1988, Purchase Coll. 1994. *Compositions:* more than 50 musical editions published, including motets by Gallus, Charpentier, mass by Lotti. *Publications:* Introduction to the Gilbert and Sullivan Operas 1989, index to the Opus Musicum of Jacob Handl 1992, The W. S. Gilbert Edition (gen. ed.) 1986–, Complete Savoy Opera Libretti (Folio Soc.) 1994; contrib. to New Grove Dictionary of Opera, many papers and articles to various publications.

WILSON, Gordon; British singer (tenor); b. 1968, Scotland. *Education:* Royal Scottish Academy. *Career:* appearances at Covent Garden, Glyndebourne, Scottish Opera, Opera North and the Buxton Festival; Sang Philidor's Tom Jones at Drottningholm and in Massenet's Chérubin at Covent Garden; roles have included Nathaniel in Hoffmann, Alfredo, the Duke of Mantua, Riccardo in Oberto, Jenik in The Bartered Bride and Walton's Troilus; concerts with the Ulster Orchestra, Northern Sinfonia and Manchester Camerata.

WILSON, Ian, BMus, DPhil; Northern Irish composer; b. 26 Dec. 1964, Belfast. *Education:* Univ. of Ulster. *Career:* AHRB Research Fellow in Creative and Performing Arts, Univ. of Ulster 2000–03; featured composer at Presteigne Festival 2005. *Compositions include:* Prime 1987, Running, Thinking, Finding 1989, nine(birds)there 1990, BIG 1991, Drive 1992, Winter's Edge (String Quartet No. 1) 1992, Rise 1993, The Capsizing Man and other stories 1994, Rich Harbour 1994–95, I Sleep at Waking 1995, The Seven Last Words (Piano Trio No. 2) 1995, Six Days at Jericho 1995, For Eileen, after rain 1995, Catalan Tales (Piano Trio No. 3) 1996, Towards the Far Country 1996, From the Book of Longing 1996, A Haunted Heart 1996, Between the Moon and the Deep Blue Sea 1997, Who's Afraid of Red, Yellow, and Blue? 1998, Limena 1998, Messenger 1998–99, Spilliaert's Beach 1999, What we Can See of the Sky has Fallen 1999, An Angel Serves a Small Breakfast 1999, bluebrighteyes 1999, Under the Lark Full Cloud 1999, Limbo 1999, In Blue Sea or Sky 2000, Hamelin 2001–02, Verschwindend 2001, Inquieto 2001, Man 'o War 2001, Arbres d'alignment 2003, Games 2003, Hunpty Dumpty 2003, Currach 2003, Nine Hours of Moonlight 2003, Licht/ung 2004, Winter Finding 2004–05, Minsk 2005, Sullen Earth 2005, Pieces of Elsewhere 2005, Seascape with High Cliffs 2006, Miranda, Ariel, Umbriel 2006, Little Red Fish 2006, An tOilean 2006, Ohne Dich 2006, White Guardians of the Universe of Sleep 2006, Harbouring 2007, The Handsomest Drowned Man in the World 2007, Cast 2007, Tundra 2008, sKiPpY 2008, Eyeless Upon a Dark River 2008, Double Trio 2008, Bealach Conglais 2009, Come to me Here 2009, Across a Clear Blue Sky 2009, 1927 2009, Heaven Lay Close 2009. *Honours:* Ultima Festival, Oslo composition prize 1991, Macaulay Fellowship 1992, elected to Aosdána 1998. *E-mail:* mail@ianwilson.org.uk (office). *Website:* www.ianwilson.org.uk.

WILSON, Keri-Lynn, BMus, MMus; Canadian conductor and flautist; b. 17 May 1947, Milwaukee; m. Peter Gelb 2003. *Education:* Juilliard School. *Career:* fmr mem., Musique Mobile, Continuum ensembles; as flautist performed with Calgary Philharmonic, Winnipeg Symphony, Manitoba Chamber Orchestra; as conductor, made debut with Nat. Arts Centre Orchestra; Asst to Seiji Ozawa, Tanglewood Festival 1994; Assoc. Conductor, Dallas Symphony Orchestra 1994–98; guest conductor, Juilliard Orchestra, Cosmopolitan Symphony, Opera Français, New York, Rome Opera Orchestra, Hong Kong Orchestra, Toronto Symphony, Edmonton Symphony, Montreal Symphony, Kirov Orchestra, Israeli Opera, Vienna Staatsoper, Los Angeles Philharmonic, St Louis Symphony, Palermo Opera. *Honours:* winner, Artists Int. Competition 1989. *Current Management:* DM Artist Management, Alte Landstrasse 40, 8702 Zollikon, Switzerland. *Telephone:* 434994363. *Fax:* 434994364. *E-mail:* office@dmartist.com. *Website:* www.dmartist.com.

WILSON, Olly W., Jr, BMus, MMus, PhD; American composer, professor and scholar; *Professor of Music Emeritus, University of California at Berkeley*; b. 7 Sept. 1937, St Louis, MO. *Education:* Washington Univ., St Louis, Univ. of Ill. at Urbana-Champaign, Univ. of Iowa, Univ. of Ill. Studio for Experimental Music, studied African music in Ghana. *Career:* played jazz piano with local groups in St Louis; played double bass in several orchestras including St Louis Philharmonic, St Louis Summer Chamber Players, Cedar Rapids Symphony; studied electronic music at Studio for Experimental Music, Univ. of Illinois 1967; faculty positions at Florida A & M Univ. 1960–62, 1964–65, Oberlin Conservatory of Music 1965–70; with faculty, Univ. of California, Berkeley 1970–, Asst Chancellor for Int. Affairs 1986–90, Chair. Dept Music 1993–97, Jerry and Evelyn Hemmings Chambers Distinguished Chair. in Music 1995–98, currently Prof. Emer. of Music; compositions include chamber works, orchestral works and works for electronic media; works have been performed by numerous orchestras including Boston, Chicago, New York Philharmonic, Cleveland, Moscow Philharmonic, St Louis, San Francisco, Baltimore, Houston, Atlanta, Louisville, Oakland, Detroit, Minneapolis, Dallas, All Netherlands Symphony orchestras; Resident Fellow, Rockefeller Foundation Center, Bellagio, Italy 1991; Lila Wallace Meet the Composer commission for Youth Symphony Consortium 1991; Visiting Artist, American Acad. in Rome 1978, Fromm Composer in Residence 2008; elected to American Acad. of Arts and Letters 1995. *Compositions:* Trio for flute, cello and piano 1957–58, Prelude and Line Study 1959, String Quartet 1960, Structure for orchestra 1960, Two Dutch Songs 1960, Wry Fragments 1961, Gloria 1961, Violin Sonata 1961, Soliloquy 1962, Dance Suite 1962, And Death Shall Have No Dominion 1963, Sextet 1963, Dance Music No. 1 1963, Three Movements for orchestra 1964, Chanson Innocent 1964, Dance Music No. 2 1965, Piece for Four 1966, Biography 1966, Cetus 1967 (Dartmouth Arts Council Prize for electronic compositions 1968), In Memoriam Martin Luther King Jr 1968, Piano Piece 1969, Voices 1970, The Eighteen Hands of Jerome Harris (ballet) 1971, Black Mass (incidental music) 1971, Black Martyrs 1972, Akwan 1972, Spirit Song 1973, Echoes 1974, Sometimes 1976, Trio for piano, violin and cello 1977, Reflections 1979, Expansions 1979, Trilogy for orchestra 1979–80, Lumina 1981, Sinfonia 1983–84, No More 1985, Houston Fanfare 1986, Expansions II 1987, Moe Fragmenti 1987, A City Called Heaven 1988, Viola Concerto 1990, Of Visions and Truth 1990–91, I Shall Not Be Moved 1991–92, Expansions III 1993, Soweto's Children 1994–95, Shango Memory 1995, Fanfare for the Millennium for brass quintet and electronic sound 1996, Hold On 1997–98. *Recordings include:* Sinfonia (Boston Symphony), Akwan (Baltimore Symphony), Cetus (electronic sound), Sometimes (William Brown, tenor and electronic sound), Trio (Francesco Trio), A City Called Heaven (Boston Musica Viva, Thamyris Ensemble). *Publications:* several scholarly articles on African and African American music; contrib. numerous articles to Black Perspective in Music, Black Music Research Journal, American Organist, New Perspectives on Jazz and others. *Honours:* Guggenheim Fellowship 1971–72, 1977–78, American Acad. of Arts and Letters and Nat. Inst. of Arts and Letters Achievement in Music Composition Award 1974, Washington Univ. Distinguished Alumni Award 1991, Missouri Historical Soc. Award 1991, Lincoln Center Chamber Music Soc. Elise Stoeger Prize 1992. *Address:* Department of Music, University of California at Berkeley, 104 Morrison Hall, Room 1200, Berkeley, CA 94720-1200, USA (office). *E-mail:* ollywil@berkeley.edu (office).

WILSON, Paul, MA, ARCM; British singer (tenor, baritone); *Director of Music and the Performing Arts, Whitgift School, Croydon*; b. 1952, Gloucester. *Education:* Jesus Coll., Oxford and Royal Coll. of Music. *Career:* appearances with ENO, WNO and Scottish Opera, Kent Opera, Glyndebourne Festival, Chelsea Opera and Opera North; engagements abroad with the Opera Factory Zürich, Pocket Opera Nürnberg and Nairobi Opera; roles include Tom Rakewell, Andrea Chénier, Bacchus, Mark in The Wreckers, and Don José;

Royal Opera Covent Garden in Handel's Samson, Ariadne auf Naxos, King Priam and Der Rosenkavalier; WNO debut in 1987 as Florestan, and ENO debut in 1988 as Monostatos; sang in the world premieres of Golem by John Casken and Cage's Europeras III and IV (Almeida Festival 1989–90) and Oliver's Timon of Athens (ENO 1991); Opera North from 1990 in Gianni Schicchi and L'Heure Espagnole; sang Siegmund and Siegfried in Birmingham Touring Opera's truncated Ring performances in the UK 1990–91; concert repertory includes The Dream of Gerontius, the Glagolitic Mass, Verdi's Requiem and Beethoven's 9th Symphony, conducted by Roger Norrington; performance of Stravinsky's Les Noces with the Nat. Youth Orchestra of Spain; Aldeburgh Festival in 1990 in Goehr's Triptych; Garsington Manor Opera in Ariadne auf Naxos 1993; Kong in Harrison Birtwistle's The Second Mrs Kong, Glyndebourne 1995; retired from full-time performing 1996; Dir of Drama, Whitgift School, Croydon 1998–2007, Dir of Music and the Performing Arts 2007–. *Recordings:* Golem, John Gasken 1991, Caritas, Robert Saxton 1992, Four Seafarers' Songs, Alan Bush 1999. *Honours:* First Wagner Soc. Bayreuth Bursary 1983, Arts Council Bursary. *Address:* Whitgift School, South Croydon, CR2 6YT (office); 76 Avondale Road, South Croydon, CR2 6JA, England (home). *Telephone:* (20) 8688-9222 (office); (20) 8681-2938 (home). *E-mail:* psw@whitgift.co.uk (office); paulstuartwilson@sky.com (office).

WILSON, Richard Edward, AB, MA; American composer, pianist and academic; *Mary Conover Mellon Chair in Music, Vassar College*; b. 15 May 1941, Cleveland, Ohio; s. of James Franklin Wilson and Edith Zingler Wilson; m. Adene Stevenson Green 1971; one s. one d. *Education:* Harvard Univ., Rutgers Univ., studied with Ernst Silberstein, Leonard Shure, Randall Thompson and Robert Moevs. *Career:* composed over 100 works, which have been performed in New York, London, Tokyo, St Petersburg, Jerusalem, San Francisco, Los Angeles, Bogotá, Stockholm, The Hague, Vienna, Aspen, Boston, Chicago; Asst Prof., Vassar Coll., New York 1966, Assoc. Prof. 1970, Prof. 1976–, Mary Conover Mellon Chair in Music 1988–; Composer in Residence, American Symphony 1992–; comms from The Library of Congress, Naumburg, Koussevitzky and Fromm Foundations, Chamber Music America, The Chicago Chamber Musicians, Concert Artists Guild; mem. ASCAP 1970–. *Compositions include:* String Quartets 1–5, Symphonies 1–3; opera: Aethelred the Unready; Concertos for violin, bassoon, piano and Triple Concerto for horn, bass clarinet and marimba; Eclogue, Fixations, Intercalations, Sour Flowers, Mnemonics for solo piano; The Ballad of Longwood Glen for tenor and harp; Visits to St Elizabeth's, Five Love Songs, Eight Comic Songs for voice and piano; Persuasions for voice and instruments, Affirmations for flute, clarinet, cello and piano, Timeshare for clarinet and cello, Gravitas for solo bass, Chamisha Mizmorey for soprano, baritone and orchestra, Senza Furore for flute, clarinet, viola and piano, Brash Attacks for trumpet and trombone, The Cello Has Many Secrets for cello, mezzo-soprano and orchestra, Soundcheck for string orchestra, Mixed Signals for violin and piano, Speculation for chamber ensemble of 15 players, Distractions for six players, Limericks, Reed Action, Add Hocket for percussion ensemble. *Recordings include:* Bassoon Concerto, Piano Concerto, Symphony No. 1, Aethelred the Unready, complete choral works, String Quartets 3 & 4 and Canzona, Affirmations for chamber ensemble, Viola Sonata, Transfigured Goat for 2 singers and instruments; Eclogue, Fixations, Intercalations; Sour Flowers, Timeshare, Senza Furore, Gravitas. *Honours:* Guggenheim Fellowship 1992, Elise L. Stoeger Prize for Chamber Music Composition 1994, Acad. Award for Music, American Acad. of Arts and Letters 2004, Roger Sessions Memorial Bogliasco Fellowship in Music 2006. *Address:* 27 Vassar Lake Drive, Poughkeepsie, NY 12603, USA (home). *E-mail:* riwilson@vassar.edu (office). *Website:* www.richardwilson.org.

WILSON, Robert M.; American theatre and opera director and artist; b. 4 Oct. 1941, Waco, Tex.; s. of D. M. Wilson and Velma Loree Wilson (née Hamilton). *Education:* Univ. of Texas, Pratt Inst. *Career:* began creating theatre in New York in the 1960s; worked mainly in Europe in 1980s and 1990s, directed original works as well as traditional opera and theatre; Guggenheim Fellow 1971, 1980; Trustee Nat. Inst. of Music Theatre; mem. Dramatists Guild, Soc. des Auteurs et Compositeurs Dramatiques, Soc. of Stage Dirs and Choreographers, PEN American Center, American Acad. of Arts and Letters. *Solo exhibitions of drawings and sculpture:* Iolas Gallery, NY, Palazzi Gallery, Milan, Galerie Fred Lanzenberg, Brussels, Musée Galliera, Paris 1972, 1974, Contemporary Art Center, Cincinatti 1980, Galerie der Stadt, Stuttgart, Galerie Herald Behm, Hamburg 1988, Anne Marie Verna Galerie, Zurich 1989, Museum of Fine Arts, Boston 1991, Centre Georges Pompidou, Paris 1991, Galerie Fred Jahn, Munich 1991, IVAM, Valencia 1992, Museum Boymans-Van Beuningen Rotterdam 1993, Galeria Luis Serpa, Lisbon 1995, Thaddeus Ropac Gallery Salzburg and Paris 1996, Clink Street Vaults, London 1996, Art Cologne, Cologne 1996, Villa Stuck Museum, Munich 1997, Palazzina dei Giardini, Modena 1998–99, Harvard Grad. School of Design Cambridge Mass. 1999 Rotunda della Besana, Milan 2000, Oberammergau Passion Theater 2000, Guggenheim Museum, New York and Bilbao 2000–01, Kunstindustrimuseet, Copenhagen 2001. *Dance created and choreographed:* Snow on the Mesa (for Martha Graham Dance Co.) 1995. *Stage appearances include:* Deafman Glance 1970, The Life and Times of Joseph Stalin (Dir) 1974, A Letter for Queen Victoria 1974, Einstein on the Beach 1976, 1984, Death, Destruction and Detroit 1979, The Golden Windows 1982, 1985, The Civil Wars 1983–85, Hamletmachine 1986, Doktor Faustus 1989, The Black Rider 1990, King Lear 1990, The Magic Flute 1991, Alice 1993, Der Mond in Gras 1994, The Death of Molière 1994, Hamlet: A Monologue 1995, Prometeo 1997, Saints and Singing 1997, Monsters of Grace 1998, Dream Play 1998, Scourge of Hyacinths 1999, The Days Before 1999, Hot Waters 2000, Relative Light 2000. *Plays directed and designed include:* Deafman Glance 1970, Einstein on the Beach 1976, Death, Destruction and Detroit 1979, The Golden Windows 1982, the CIVIL warS 1983–85, Hamletmachine 1986, Doktor Faustus 1989, The Black Rider 1990, The Magic Flute 1991, Doktor Faustus Lights the Lights 1992, Alice 1992, Madame Butterfly 1993, Hanjo 1994, Hamlet: A Monologue 1995, Time Rocker 1996, Lady from the Sea 1998, Das Rheingold 2000, POEtry 2000, Woyzeck 2001, Three Penny Opera, Spoleto Festival, Italy 2008. *Films include:* Overture for a Deafman, Monsters of Grace 1998. *Videos include:* The Spaceman 1976, 1984, Video 50 1978, Stations 1982, La Femme à la Cafétière 1989, Mr. Bojangles' Memory 1991, La Mort de Molière 1994. *Publications include:* The King of Spain 1970, Einstein on the Beach: An Opera in Four Acts (with Philip Glass) 1976, A Letter for Queen Victoria 1977, Death, Destruction and Detroit 1979, the CIVIL warS 1985, Mr. Bojangles' Memory 1991, RW Notebook 1999. *Honours:* Hon. Dir American Repertory Theatre; Commdr des Arts et des Lettres, Goethe-Medaille (Germany) 2014; Dr hc (Calif. Coll. of Arts and Letters), (Pratt Inst.); Maharam Award for Best Set Design 1975, Lumen Award 1977, First Prize, San Sebastian Film and Video Festival 1984, Picasso Award 1986, Inst. Skowhegan Medal for drawing 1987, Grand Prix Biennale, Barcelona Festival of Cinema Art 1989, Germna Theatre Critics Award 1990, Brandeis Univ. Poses Creative Arts Award 1991, Venice Biennale Golden Lion Award for Sculpture 1993, Dorothy and Lillian Gish Prize Prize for Lifetime Achievement 1996, Tadeusz Kantor Prize 1997, Harvard Excellence in Design Award 1998, Pushkin Prize 1999; Most Outstanding Theater Designer of the Seventies, US Inst. of Theater Tech. 1977. *Address:* RW Work Ltd, 155 Wooster Street, Suite 4F, New York, NY 10012, USA. *Telephone:* (212) 253-7484. *Fax:* (212) 253-7485 (office). *Website:* www.robertwilson.com (office).

WILSON, Terrence; American pianist; b. Bronx, New York. *Education:* Juilliard School with Yoheved Kaplinsky. *Career:* has appeared with numerous ensembles, including the symphony orchestras of Atlanta, Baltimore, Cincinnati, Dallas, Detroit, Houston, San Francisco, St Louis and St Paul Chamber Orchestra, Nat. Symphony, as well as with orchestras of Cleveland, Minnesota and Philadelphia, Lausanne Chamber Orchestra, Switzerland, Malaysian Philharmonic, Orquestra Sinfonica do Estado de Minas Gerais, Belo Horizonte, Brazil, Scottish Nat. Orchestra; also active as recitalist; has worked with conductors including Christoph Eschenbach, Alan Gilbert, Hans Graf, Neeme Järvi, Jesús López-Cobos, Kenneth Schermerhorn, Stanisław Skrowaczewski, Robert Spano, Yuri Temirkanov. *Recording:* Michael Daugherty Metropolis Symphony (Grammy Award for Best Orchestral Performance 2011) 2009. *Current Management:* Bill Capone Arts Management Group, 37 West 26th Street, Suite 403, New York, NY 11010-1006, USA. *Telephone:* (212) 337-0839 (office). *E-mail:* TW@TerrenceWilsonPiano.com (office). *Website:* www.terrencewilsonpiano.com (office).

WILSON, Timothy, ARAM; British singer (countertenor); b. 18 July 1961, England. *Education:* Royal Acad. of Music. *Career:* fmr mem., Chapel Royal and St George's Chapel Choir, Windsor Castle; opera debut in Orlando, Scottish Opera 1985; founder mem., Gabrieli Consort, The Queen's Six 2008–; operatic engagements include Handel's Orlando and Britten's Death in Venice for Scottish Opera, Dido and Aeneas in Frankfurt, Gluck's Orfeo in Kassel, L'Incoronazione di Poppea in Gelsenkirchen, The Fairy Queen in Florence, Oberon in A Midsummer Night's Dream, the modern premiere of Cesti's Il Pomo d'Oro in Vienna, world premieres of Maxwell Davies's Resurrection in Darmstadt, Luis de Pablo's El Viajero Indiscreto in Madrid, Handel's Xerxes, Agrippina Alcina, Giulio Cesare; further concert appearances with Mackerras, Hickox, Pinnock, Herreweghe, Leonhardt, Norrington and Parrott; venues include Netherlands, France, Germany, Austria, Spain, Italy and the United Kingdom including the Promenade Concerts. *Recordings include:* Gassir, Hail Bright Cecilia, Venetian Vespers, Akathist of Thanksgiving, Come Ye Sons of Art, Israel in Egypt. *Honours:* winner, Young Concert Artists Competition 1984, John Scott Prize 1985. *E-mail:* thequeenssix@gmail.com (office). *Website:* thequeenssix.com.

WILSON-JOHNSON, David Robert, BA, FRAM; British baritone; b. 16 Nov. 1950, Northampton; s. of Harry K. Johnson and Sylvia C. Wilson. *Education:* Wellingborough School, Northants., British Inst. of Florence, St Catharine's Coll., Cambridge and Royal Acad. of Music. *Career:* debut at Royal Opera House, Covent Garden in We Come to the River 1976; regular appearances for over 20 years including in Billy Budd, L'Enfant et les Sortilèges, Le Rossignol, Les Noces, Boris Godunov, Die Zauberflöte, Turandot, Werther, Madame Butterfly, Così fan tutte; Wigmore Hall recital debut 1977; BBC Promenade Concert debut 1981; debut at Edin. Festival 1976, Glyndebourne Festival 1980 and at festivals in Bath, Bergen, Berlin, Geneva, Graz, Netherlands, Hong Kong, Jerusalem, Orange, Paris, Salzburg, Tanglewood and Vienna; Paris Opera debut in Die Meistersinger 1989; American debut in Paulus (title role) 1990; ENO debut (in Billy Budd) 1991; Netherlands Opera debut in Birtwistle's Punch and Judy 1993; Founder Dir Ferrandou Summer Singing School 1985–; numerous concert tours with David Owen Norris (voice and piano duo for 40 years), Pierre Boulez/ Ensemble Intercontemporain, Gennadi Rozhdestvensky /BBCSO, David Atherton/London Sinfonietta/Hong Kong Symphony, Charles Dutoit Philadelphia Orchestra/Tonhalle Orchestra/ NHK Symphony, Frans Bruggen/Orchestra of the 18th Century, Robert King/The King's Consort; Prof. of Voice, Amsterdam Conservatorium 2005–10;

Gulbenkian Fellowship 1978–81. *Films include:* Give my Regards to Broad Street (The Beatles), A Midsummer Marriage (Michael Tippett) 1988, Or Shall We Die? (Michael Berkeley/Ian McEwan). *Television:* BBC Handel 250th Anniversary Celebrations from Westminster Abbey 1985, BBC TV Purcell Tercentenary Celebration from Westminster Abbey 1995, Olivier Messiaen's 80 birthday Concert from Royal Festival Hall (title role in St François d'Assise) 1988. *Recordings include:* Schubert's Winterreise with David Owen Norris, Mozart Masses from King's Coll., Cambridge, Haydn's Nelson Mass (English Concert/Trevor Pinnock), Schoenberg's Ode to Napoleon (Ensemble Intercontemporain), King Priam, Punch and Judy, The Ice Break (London Sinfonietta/ David Atherton), La Traviata, Lucrezia Borgia (Joan Sutherland, Luciano Pavarotti/Richard Bonynge), Michael Berkeley's Or Shall We Die?, Belshazzar's Feast, The Kingdom, Caractacus (LSO/ Richard Hickox), Odes (Purcell), Black Pentecost (BBCPO/Maxwell Davies), Mass in B Minor (Bavarian Radio Symphony Orchestra/Carlo Maria Giulini, Peter Grimes (ROH /Bernard Haitink), Roméo et Juliette, Damnation of Faust, Oedipus Rex (Philadelphia Orchestra/Charles Dutoit). *Honours:* Nat. Fed. of Music Soc. Award 1977, Evening Standard Award for Opera 1989. *Current Management:* c/o Ben Rayfield, Rayfield Artists, Southbank House, Black Prince Road, London, SE1 7SJ, England. *Telephone:* (20) 7193-1531. *E-mail:* ben@rayfieldartists.com. *Website:* www.rayfieldartists.com. *Address:* Prinsengracht 455, 1016 HN Amsterdam, Netherlands (home); 28 Englefield Road, London, N1 4ET, England (home). *Telephone:* (20) 7254-0941 (London); 5-65-10-94-11 (France); (20) 7728104 (home). *E-mail:* info@ferrandou.org (office). *Website:* www.ferrandou.org (office); www.davidwilsonjohnson.com.

WIMBERGER, Peter; Austrian singer (bass-baritone); b. 14 May 1940, Vienna. *Education:* Vienna Music Acad. with Paul Schöffler and Adolf Vogel. *Career:* debut in Dortmund 1963, as Pietro in Simon Boccanegra; appearances in the opera houses of Frankfurt, Karlsruhe, Kassel, Düsseldorf, Munich, Warsaw and Copenhagen; Barcelona 1985, as the Wanderer in Siegfried; festivals of Bregenz and Florence; repertoire includes principal roles in operas by Mussorgsky, Mozart, Wagner, Rossini, Verdi and Strauss; sang at Palermo and Naples 1988, as Amfortas; Rangoni at the Vienna Staatsoper 1988; Kuno in Der Freischütz 1996; mem., Vienna Staatsoper from 1968. *Recordings:* Haydn's Harmoniemesse; Spirit Messenger in Die Frau ohne Schatten by Strauss.

WINBECK, Heinz; German composer and teacher; b. 11 Feb. 1946, Piflas, Landshut. *Education:* Munich Richard Strauss Conservatory, Munich Hochschule with Harald Genzmer and Gunter Bialas. *Career:* conductor and composer at Ingolstadt and Wunsiedel 1974–78; Teacher, Munich Hochschule 1980–88; Prof. of Composition, Würzburg Hochschule from 1988; Composer-in-Residence, Cabrillo, CA music festival 1985. *Compositions include:* In Memorian Paul Celan for soprano, flute, piano and percussion 1970, Sie Tanzt for baritone and ensemble 1971, Sonosillent for cello and strings 1971, Musik for wind quintet 1971, Espaces for four percussionists, piano and flute 1972, Nocturne I for chamber ensemble 1972, Lenau-Fantasien for cello and chamber orchestra 1979, three String Quartets 1979, 1980, 1984, Chansons a Temps for women's voices and 13 instruments 1979, four Symphonies 1983, 1987, 1988, 1993, Blick in den Strom for string quintet 1993. *Honours:* music prize Akademie der Schonen Kunste, Berlin 1985.

WINDMULLER, Yaron; singer (baritone); b. 1956, Israel. *Education:* studied in Tel-Aviv, Munich with Ernst Haefliger, Vicenza with Malcolm King, at the Opera Studio of the Bayerische Staatsoper. *Career:* debut at City of London Festival in 1982, in Gluck's Armide; Sang as soloist with the Israel Philharmonic, and as member of Theater am Gärtnerplatz, Munich, from 1986, as Purcell's Aeneas, Mozart's Count, Guglielmo, Don Giovanni and Papageno, Wolfram, Marcello, Hans Jürgen von Bose's Werther and Kaspar in Der Zaubergeige by Werner Egk; Sang Trinity Moses in Weill's Mahagonny at Frankfurt in 1990; Sang Paolo in Simon Boccanegra at Wellington, 2000; many concert appearances and lieder recitals. *Current Management:* c/o Ariën Arts & Music Management, De Boeystraat 6, 2018 Antwerp, Belgium. *Telephone:* (3) 285-96-80. *Fax:* (3) 230-35-23. *E-mail:* arien@pandora.be.

WINKLER, Peter, BA, MFA; American composer, pianist and musicologist; *Professor of Music, State University of New York at Stony Brook*; b. 26 Jan. 1943, Los Angeles, Calif.; s. of David P. Winkler and Elizabeth Babcock Winkler; m. Dorothea Cook; one s. one d. *Education:* Univ. of California at Berkeley with Andrew Imbrie and Seymour Shifrin, Princeton Univ. with Milton Babbitt and Earl Kim. *Career:* Music Faculty, State Univ. of NY (SUNY), Stony Brook from 1971, Prof. of Music 1999–, mem. Stony Brook Acad. of Scholar-Teachers 1999–2000; Ed. Journal of Popular Music Studies 1992–95. *Compositions include:* String Quartet 1967, Humoresque for piano (Finalist, League/ISCM Int. Piano Music Competition) 1977) 1970, Symphony 1978, Clarinet Bouquet: Four Concert Rags 1976–80, Recitativo e Terzetto for woodwind trio (First Prize, New England Reed Trio Competition) 1980, Professionally Speaking (satirical review, with Frederic Block and Ernst Muller) 1986, Yaa Amponsah: Fantasy on a Ghanaian Popular Song for violin and piano 1988, No Condition is Permanent, for Pierrot ensemble 1989, Solitaire, for solo clarinet 1989, Waterborne, for violin and tape 1991, Saboreando el Gusto Cubano, for violin, piano and percussion 1994, Tingle-Tangle: A Wedekind Cabaret, collaboration with Eric Bentley, William Bolcom and Arnold Black 1994, Nine Waltzes for piano trio 1997, Serenade for String Orchestra 1998, Out! The Musical (book and lyrics: Winston Clark) for male chorus, piano, bass and drums 1997–98, Returning to the Root, for horn and piano (Hon. Mention, Int. Horn Soc. Composition Contest 2003) 2000, Requiem Aeternam, for chorus 2001, Partita for Baroque Ensemble 2001, A Midsummer Overture for orchestra 2002, Gili's Music for bassoon and cello 2003, Gathering Reel/Departing Reel for chamber orchestra 2004, Walnut Hill for violin and piano 2005, The Darkling Spring, Fantasia a5 for Low Consort 2006, Cabo Maio for violin and piano 2006, Fantasy for Cello Solo and Cello Ensemble 2007, Sarabande-Tombeau for violin, gamba and harpsichord 2001–08, Fox Fables (opera, libretto by Rhoda Levine) (Winner, Americana Music Competition, Boston Metro Opera 2011) 2008–10. *Honours:* Jr Fellow, Harvard Univ. Soc. of Fellows 1968–71, MacDowell Colony Fellowship 1971, SUNY Faculty Research Fellowships 1975, 1979, SUNY Chancellor's Award for Excellence in Teaching 1977, SUNY Foundation Travel Grant (travel to Accra, Ghana) 1987, Residency, Hambidge Center for the Creative Arts and Sciences 2001, 2003, 2005, Residency, Virginia Center for the Creative Arts, 2001, Composer Fellow, John Duffy Composers Inst., Virginia Festival of the Arts 2009, 2010. *Address:* Department of Music, Stony Brook University, Stony Brook, NY 11733-5475 (office); 15 Bayview Avenue, East Setauket, New York, NY 11733, USA (home). *Telephone:* (631) 632-7330 (office); (631) 751-7672 (home). *Fax:* (631) 632-7404 (office). *E-mail:* peter.winkler@sunysb.edu (office). *Website:* peterwinklermusic.com.

WINKLER, Wolfgang; Austrian musicologist; *Artistic Director and CEO, LIVA*; b. (Wolfgang Peter Hendler), 12 June 1945, Graz; m. Elisabeth Winkler; one d. *Education:* Univ. of Graz, Musikhochschule Graz. *Career:* Brucknerkonservatorium Linz, Bibliothek und musikwissenschaftliches Referat 1978; Referent für U. Musik im ORF Landesstudio 1979; Head of Music, ORF 1985; Artistic Dir and CEO, LIVA (Linzer Veranstaltungsgesellschaft mbH) 1998–; Chair. Bd of Trustees Diakoniewerk 2013–. *Publications:* contrib. to Musik in Österreich (Gottfried Kraus Verlag), Musicolociga austriaca 11, Umkunst (publ. of the Hochschule für künstlerisches und industrielle Gestaltung, Linz), 20 Jahre Bruckenhaus, Gedanken zu Balduin Sulzer (Musikarchiv der Österreichisch Nationalbibliothek), Musikgeschichte Österreichs, Neue Musik und Medien, echt falsch Will die Welt betrogen werden?. *Address:* Untere Donaulände 7, Linz 4020, Austria (office). *Telephone:* (732) 7612 2025 (office). *Fax:* (732) 7612 2030 (office). *E-mail:* wolwin@a1.net; w.winkler@liva .co.at (office). *Website:* www.wolfgang-winkler.at (office).

WINLAND, Ida Falk; Swedish singer (soprano); b. 1982. *Education:* Royal Coll. of Music, pvt. study with Lillian Watson at Benjamin Britten Int. Opera School. *Career:* began studying cello and piano at age 10; performed with Royal Philharmonic Orchestra of Stockholm at Nobel Prize Award Ceremony 2007; Artist-in-Residence, Swedish Classical Radio 2007–09; operatic roles with Drottningholm Opera Co., Stockholm, Gothenburg Opera; recitals with Helsinki Philharmonic Orchestra, Swedish Radio Symphony Orchestra, Asian Youth Orchestra, Lahti Symphony Orchestra, Gothenburg Symphony Orchestra, English Chamber Orchestra, Finnish Chamber Orchestra, Swedish Radio Symphony Orchestra, Helsingborg Symphony Orchestra; roles include: Euridice in L'Orfeo, Cleopatra, Anne Truelove in The Rake's Progress, Fox in The Cunning Little Vixen. *Honours:* finalist, BBC Singer of the World Competition 2007, Song Prize, Ferrier Awards 2008. *Telephone:* (7884) 255782 (office). *E-mail:* contact@idasings.com (office). *Website:* www.idasings.com.

WINSCHERMANN, Helmut; German oboist and conductor; b. 22 March 1920, Munich. *Education:* studied in Essen and Paris. *Career:* principal with the Frankfurt Radio Symphony Orchestra 1945–51; co-founder, Collegium Instrumental Detmold 1954, later Prof. Detmold Acad. 1956; appearances with the Capella Coloniensis and Stuttgart Chamber Orchestra; founded the Deutsche Bachsolisten, giving many performances throughout Europe and elsewhere; premiered La tomba di Igor Stravinsky by Giselher Klebe 1979.

WINSLADE, Glenn; singer (tenor); b. 1958, Australia. *Education:* New South Wales Conservatorium, Vienna Conservatory. *Career:* has sung with ENO as Ferrando, Victoria State Opera as Belmonte, Walter von der Vogelweide and Don Ottavio, Scottish Opera as Mozart's Titus and Australian Opera as Oronte in Alcina; Covent Garden debut 1990 as Vogelgesang in Die Meistersinger; further appearances with Glyndebourne Festival and Touring Opera, New Sadler's Wells Opera in Merry Widow, Freiburg Opera, Semper Oper Dresden as Belmonte, Stuttgart Opera and the Netherlands Opera in Idomeneo; other roles include Tamino, The Prince in The Love of Three Oranges, Stroh (Intermezzo), Elemer in Arabella, Amenophis in Mosè, Ernesto and Nemorino, Fracasso in La Finta Semplice, Lindoro and Alfredo, Jacquino in Fidelio, Steuermann in Der fliegende Holländer and Jason in Cherubini's Médée; Mozart's Titus for Welsh National Opera; engaged as Wagner's Rienzi at the Vienna Staatsoper 1998; Strauss's Emperor at Covent Garden 2001; sang in Mahler's 8th at Vienna 2002; concert engagements with the Musica Antiqua Vienna, Duke Univ., NC, RAI Milan and the BBC. *Recordings include:* Messiah with the Scottish Chamber Orchestra, Merry Widow. *Honours:* winner Australian Opera Auditions, Esso/Glyndebourne Touring and John Christie Glyndebourne Awards.

WINSTIN, Robert; American composer, conductor and pianist; b. 6 June 1959, Chicago, IL. *Education:* Chicago Musical Coll., Roosevelt Univ., Univ. of Colorado. *Career:* debut as pianist, Carnegie Hall 1986; first American composer to have worked and performed in mainland China 1995; Shanghai and Beijing, piano concerto No. 2; Music Dir and Principal Conductor, Metropolis Youth Symphony; Music Dir and Principal Conductor, Derriere Guard Festival Orchestra; Musical Dir and Principal Conductor, Millennium Symphony; Exec. Dir, Foundation for Music; Music Ed., Nit and Wit magazine 1985–88; radio producer and writer, Nuovo Voce 1990–; mem. ASCAP,

NARAS, Derriere Guard Soc. *Compositions include:* Dedo (opera), Scherzo Burlesque 1988, Symphony No. 2 1989, Etudes 1993, Piano Concerto No. 2 1994, Piano Art 1995, Symphony No. 5 1996, Cello Concerto 1997, Millennium Symphony. *Honours:* Joseph Jefferson Citations Wing Recommendation for Oedipus Requiem 1989, Concours Caveat Prim Palm D'Or 1992, Barrettson Prize in American Music (for Piano Concerto No. 1) 1998.

WINTER, Louise; British singer (mezzo-soprano); *Vocal Tutor, Royal Northern College of Music;* b. 29 Nov. 1959, Preston, Lancs., England. *Education:* Chetham's School of Music and Royal Northern Coll. of Music, Manchester with Frederick Cox. *Career:* with Glyndebourne Touring Opera from 1982, has sung Tisbe in La Cenerentola, Dorabella in Così fan tutte and Mercédès in Carmen; sang Zerlina on Glyndebourne's tour to Hong Kong, Nancy in Albert Herring at the 1986 summer festival and in the Ravel double bill in 1987–88; Covent Garden debut as a Flower maiden in Parsifal 1988; has sung Janáček's Varvara and Ravel's Concepcion for Opera North; Netherlands Opera as Rosina in Il Barbiere di Siviglia and Second Lady in Die Zauberflöte; Glyndebourne Festival in Katya Kabanova, Il Barbiere di Siviglia and the Ravel double bill 1988–90; appearances with Canadian Opera Co. in Eugene Onegin and as Dorabella in Così fan tutte 1991; concert engagements with the König Ensemble and in the Choral Symphony conducted by Simon Rattle; season 1997 with Carmen and the Berlioz Marguerite for ENO and Jocasta in Oedipus Rex at the Festival Hall; season 1998 with Eduige in Rodelinda at Glyndebourne and Marina in Boris Godunov for New Sussex Opera, Berlioz's Damnation of Faust in Sydney and Mahler's Des Knaben Wunderhorn in Kuala Lumpur with Malaysian Philharmonic Orchestra; Britten's Phaedre, London Proms 1999; sang Carmen for ENO 2001; appeared as Wife in Turnage's opera Greek at Buxton Festival Opera and Cardiff (Music Theatre Wales) 2011; returned to sing at Linbury Theatre, Royal Opera House, Covent Garden 2013; Vocal Tutor, Royal Northern Coll. of Music 2010–. *Recordings include:* Songs of Frank Bridge 1997, Lucia di Lammermoor with Hanover Band, conducted by Charles Mackerras. *Current Management:* c/o Owen White Management, 139 Brookwood Road, London, SW18 5BD, England. *Telephone:* (20) 8480-1152. *Fax:* (20) 3397-1354. *E-mail:* info@ owenwhitemanagement.com. *Website:* www.owenwhitemanagement.com.

WINTER, Nils Tomas; Swedish composer; b. 1 March 1954, Arboga. *Education:* university studies, studied composition with Werner Wolf Glaser, Daniel Börtz, Miklós Maros. *Career:* debut, Swedish Nat. Radio programme, Monologue No. 10 for bassoon and Monologue No. 2 for guitar 1982; FST 1998–; mem. Soc. of Swedish Composers. *Compositions:* Sargasso for saxophone quartet 1995–96, Istros for string quartet 1996–97, Symphony No. 1 1998–99, Piano Trio 2000. *Honours:* three scholarships 1997–2001.

WINTER, Quade; American composer and singer (tenor); b. 1950, Oregon. *Career:* debut as Max in Der Freischütz at San Francisco; has sung the Duke of Mantua for Eugene Opera, Canio at Anchorage, Don Ottavio at the Carmel Bach Festival and Ishmael in Nabucco for San Francisco Opera; appeared in US premiere of The Excursions of Mr Brouček, with the Berkeley Symphony; concerts have included Beethoven's Ninth with the Stockton Symphony and the Verdi Requiem at the San Francisco Festival of Masses, conducted by Robert Shaw; European debut as Hermann in The Queen of Spades with Graz Opera 1982; La Scala Milan 1982 as Cherubini's Anacréon; roles with the Stadtheater Würzburg have included Don Carlos, Lensky, Herod, Rodolfo and Canio; has sung Parsifal at Graz and Herod in Heidelberg and Seattle; Scottish Opera debut as Mark in The Midsummer Marriage 1989; music for Gilbert and Sullivan's Thespis performed by Ohio Light Opera, 1996. *Current Management:* Dorothy Cone Artists Representatives, 150 West 55 Street, New York, NY 10019, USA. *Telephone:* (212) 765-7412. *Fax:* (212) 765-7443. *E-mail:* dcone@ix.netcom.com. *Website:* www.dorothyconeartistsrep.com.

WINTER, Sidonie, BA, LRAM, DipRAM; British singer (soprano); b. (Sidonie Bond), 18 Feb. 1965, England; m. Nigel Stevens. *Education:* Univ. of East Anglia, Royal Acad. of Music, Nat. Opera Studio. *Career:* frequent concerts throughout UK, including Wigmore Hall, St John's Smith Square and South Bank; Proms debut as Lady Angela in Patience; other concerts include Messiah and Handel's Dixit Dominus, Mass in D Minor by Haydn, Beethoven's Mass in C and Elgar's Apostles; opera debut as Leila in Iolanthe for D'Oyly Carte Opera; other roles include Siebel in Faust, Elena (Aroldo), Sofia (Lombardi) and Priestess (Aida, Covent Garden 1996); Fiordiligi at Ischia for the Walton Trust, Geisha in Mascagni's Iris for Chelsea Opera Group, Mozart's Countess and Donna Elvira at Aldeburgh; Lady Billows in Rheinsberg Sieglinde for Wagner Soc. *Address:* 21 Flower Farm Close, Henfield, West Sussex, BN5 9QA, England (home). *Telephone:* (1273) 493723 (home); 7973-315413 (mobile) (office). *E-mail:* sidonie@sidonie.freeserve.co.uk (office).

WIRKKALA, Merja; Finnish singer (soprano); b. 7 Oct. 1954, Kaustinen. *Education:* Sibelius Acad., Helsinki. *Career:* sang with the Helsinki Opera from 1976, notably as Nannetta, Zerlina, Despina, Susanna, Kaisa in Merikanto's Juha, and Siebel; sang Marzelline in Fidelio at the Vienna Staatsoper 1980, Zerlina at Covent Garden 1981, and the title role in the premiere of Elina by Liukolas at Helsinki 1992; guest in Juha at the Edinburgh Festival 1987.

WIRTZ, Dorothea; singer (soprano); b. 13 March 1953, Tuttlingen, Germany. *Education:* studied with Hugo Diez in Berlin, Hanno Blaschke in Munich. *Career:* sang at the Munich Staatsoper 1979–80, Kassel 1980–84; mem., Zürich Opera from 1984; guest appearances in Düsseldorf, Venice,

Naples, Lisbon, Bologna, Berlin, Cologne, Wiesbaden, Florence and Strasbourg; roles include Olympia in Les Contes d'Hoffmann, Blondchen, the Queen of Night, Zerlina, Despina, Ilia in Idomeneo, Rosina, Sophie in Der Rosenkavalier, Zerbinetta, Norina, Adina, Marzelline and the Woodbird in Siegfried; sang Blondchen at Buenos Aires 1987; Prof., Freiburg Musikhochschule from 2000; concert repertoire includes works by Handel, Mozart, Bach and Schumann including Paradies und die Peri. *Recordings include:* Strauss's Daphne.

WIRTZ, Tiny Katharina; German pianist. *Education:* student of Prof. Hans Anwander, Univ. of Cologne, and of Marguerite Long, Paris. *Career:* has performed with major orchestras and conductors and given concerts in Europe, America and Asia; solo recitals and chamber music; world premiere of B. A. Zimmermann's piano works and those of other composers; numerous radio and TV broadcasts; master-classes in many countries in Europe and Asia; Prof., Concert Pianist and Head, Piano Master Class, Cologne Univ. of Music 1963–94, Prof. Emer. 1994–. *Recordings:* numerous records and CDs, including A. Reicha, 36 Fugues; B.A. Zimmermann: The Works for Piano Solo; R. Schumann: Fantasy of 17, Sonata; W.A. Mozart: The Fantasies; Esquisses de Jazz: Hindemith, Stravinsky, Copland, Debussy; Piano Concertos by Mendelssohn and E. Künneke; O. Messiaen: Trois petites Liturgies for piano, chorus and orchestra conducted by Günter Wand; Tiny Wirtz plays Hermann Schroeder Sonata and Trio Opus 43; Joachim Blüme chamber music. *Publications:* Chorus in Dialogue 1972, Memories of B.A. Zimmermann (in Musica, Vol. 39 (4) 1995), Memories, Cogitations, Experiences (in Festschrift: 75 Years The Cologne University of Music, Cologne) 2000. *Honours:* Bundesverdienstkreuz (First Class) 2000; Tiny-Wirtz-Archives opened at Acad. of Fine Arts, Berlin 1998, entered in Golden Book of the City of Cologne 1999. *Address:* Belvederestr. 34, 50933 Cologne, Germany (home). *Telephone:* (221) 4971826 (home). *Fax:* (221) 4971826 (home).

WISE, Patricia; singer (soprano); b. 31 July 1944, Wichita, KS, USA. *Education:* Kansas Univ., Santa Fe, studied in New York with Margaret Harshaw. *Career:* debut as Susanna in The Marriage of Figaro, Kansas City 1966; appearances at Houston Opera, New York City Opera, New Orleans, Philadelphia, Chicago, San Francisco, Washington, Miami, Baltimore, San Antonio and Pittsburgh; Carnegie Hall, New York 1971 in Handel's Ariodante, Covent Garden, London 1971 as Rosina in Rossini's Barber of Seville with New York City Opera; Glyndebourne 1972 as Zerbinetta in Ariadne auf Naxos; Vienna Staatsoper 1983 as Pamina, Nannetta and Sophie; sang at the 1984 Salzburg Festival in the premiere of Un Re in Ascolto by Berio; first appearance in Geneva 1985 as Lulu; repertoire includes roles in operas by Donizetti, Gounod, Gluck, and Verdi's Gilda; sang with the Vienna Staatsoper 1976–91, in 300 performances, many of which were Strauss or Mozart operas; from 1985 appeared in five other productions of Berg's three-act Lulu, from Berlin to Paris; sang Lulu at Madrid 1987, Sophie in Der Rosenkavalier at Budapest 1989, Gilda in Rigoletto at Madrid 1989, Fiordiligi in Mozart's Così fan tutte, and Violetta in Verdi's Traviata 1990; guest appearances in European opera houses including La Scala, Munich, Berlin, Hamburg, Barcelona, Geneva, Glyndebourne and at Salzburg Festival. *Honours:* Kammersängerin, Vienna Staatsoper 1996.

WISEMAN, Debra (Debbie), MBE, FGSM, FTCL; British composer and conductor; b. 10 May 1963, London; d. of Paul Wiseman and Barbara Wiseman; m. Tony Wharmby 1987. *Education:* Trinity Coll. of Music, Kingsway Princeton/Morley Coll., Guildhall School of Music and Drama. *Career:* composer and conductor of music for film and TV productions 1989–; Visiting Prof. of Film Composition, Royal Coll. of Music 1995–; mem. Performing Right Soc., BAFTA, Musicians' Union, British Acad. of Composers and Songwriters. *Compositions include:* Inside Looking Out 1989, Squares and Roundabouts 1989, Echoes of Istria 1989, The Guilty, Lighthouse, Female Perversions, The Dying of the Light, Shrinks (Silents to Satellite Award for Best Original TV Theme Music 1991), The Good Guys (Television and Radio Industries Club Award for TV Theme Music of the Year 1993), Tom and Viv 1994, The Project, Judge John Deed, P.O.W., Wilde Stories, The Upper Hand, The Churchills, Serious and Organised, The Second Russian Revolution, Little Napoleons, Children's Hospital, Death of Yugoslavia, Haunted 1995, Wilde 1997, The Fairy Tale of the Nightingale and the Rose 1999, The Fairy Tale of the Selfish Giant 1999, It Might be You, A Week in Politics, People's Century, What Did You Do In The War, Auntie?, The Cuban Missile Crisis, Vet's School, The Missing Postman, Tom's Midnight Garden, Absolute Truth, Warriors (Royal TV Soc. Award) 2000, My Uncle Silas 2001, Othello 2001, Oscar Wilde Fairy Stories 2002, Freeze Frame 2004, He Knew He Was Right 2004, The Andrew Marr Show, The Truth About Love 2004, Arsène Lupin 2004, Johnny and the Bomb 2005, Middletown 2005, Feather Boy: The Musical 2005, Middletown (film music) 2006, Jekyll 2007, Walter's War 2008, Stephen Fry in America 2008, The Passion 2008, Lesbian Vampire Killers 2009, The Hide 2009, Land Girls 2009, 2010, 2011, Joanna Lumley's Nile 2010, Martin Clunes: Horsepower 2010, The Promise 2011, Joanna Lumley's Greek Odyssey 2011, Fry's Planet Word 2011, Lost Christmas 2011, The Whale 2013, Father Brown 2013–16, WPC 56 2013–14, A Poet in New York 2014, Wolf Hall 2015, The Coroner, Dickensian 2015–16. *Honours:* Hon. Fellow, Trinity Coll. of Music, London 2006, Guildhall School of Music and Drama 2007; Hon. DMus (Univ. of Sussex) 2015. *Current Management:* c/o Roz Colls, Music Matters International, Crest House, 102–104 Church Road, Teddington, Middx, TW11 8PY, England; c/o Rich Jacobellis, First Artists Management, 4764 Park Granada, Suite 210, Calabasas, CA 91302, USA.

Telephone: (20) 8979-4580 (Teddington). *E-mail:* dwiseman10@aol.com (office). *Website:* www.debbiewiseman.co.uk.

WISHART, Trevor, BA, MA, DPhil; British composer; *Composer in Residence, Durham University;* b. 11 Oct. 1946, Leeds, Yorks., England; m. Jacqueline Joan Everett; two d. *Education:* Univs of Oxford, Nottingham and York. *Career:* tours of Scandinavia, Australia, Japan, USA, the Netherlands, Spain, Germany, Mexico; IRCAM comm., Vox-5 1986; sound designer, Jorvik Viking Centre Museum, York; Special Prof. of Music, Univ. of Nottingham 1990–92; Visiting Fellow, Bretton Hall Coll., Univ. of Leeds 1994; Research Fellow, Univ. of Birmingham; Chair. Sonic Arts Network 1990–92; Founder Composers Desktop Project; Arts Council Composer Fellow, Durham Univ. 2006–11, Composer in Residence 2012–; Artist in Residence, Univ. of Oxford 2010–11. *Compositions include:* Red Bird, Anticredos, The Vox Cycle, Pastorale–Walden 2, Beach Singularity, Tongues of Fire 1994, Fabulous Paris 1997, Two Women (for DAAD, Berlin) 1998, The Division of Labout 1999, American Triptych (for French Ministry of Culture) 2000, Imago 2002, Globalalia 2004, Memories of Madrid 2005, Angel 2007, Encounters in the Republic of Heaven 2006–10. *Publications:* Sounds Fun (educational music games) 1974, On Sonic Art 1985, Audible Design 1994, Sun, Creativity and Environment, Sun-2: A Creative Philosophy, Whose Music: A Sociology of Musical Language, Encounters in the Republic of Heaven (booklet) 2010, Studies in Composition 2012; contrib. to Contact, Musics, Ear Magazine (New York), Interface (Utrecht), Computer Music Journal (USA), Musica Realta (Milan), Les Cahiers d'Ircam (Paris), etc. *Honours:* Hon. Visiting Prof., Univ. of York 2002–; Prizewinner, Bourges Int. Electro-Accoustic Music Festival 1978, Gaudeamus Int. Festival, the Netherlands 1979, Golden Nica Linz Ars Electronica 1995, Euphonie d'Or Bourges 1997, Giga-Hertz Grand Prize Electronic Music Award 2008. *Address:* Department of Music, Durham University, Palace Green, Durham, DH1 3RL, England (office). *Telephone:* (191) 334-3156 (office). *E-mail:* trevor.wishart@durham.ac.uk (office). *Website:* www.dur.ac.uk/music (office); www.trevorwishart.co.uk.

WISŁOCKI, Leszek; Polish composer and pianist; *Professor, Academy of Music, Wrocław;* b. 15 Dec. 1931, Chorzow; m. Renata Krumpholz 1968; two s. *Education:* Acad. of Music, Wrocław. *Career:* concerts as pianist and composer for Polish radio and television; Prof., Acad. of Music, Wrocław. *Compositions:* Andante and Presto for xylophone and piano, Two Miniatures for violin and cello, Sonata for oboe and cello, Ostinato and Toccatina for piano solo, Polonaise for piano solo, Suita Lubuska for wind orchestra, Songs for choir a cappella (male and female), four symphonies, Rhapsody for the great symphonic orchestra 1996, four concerti for instruments (piano, oboe, bassoon, trombone) and orchestra, VIth Piano Trio 1997, Dilectissimo Papae Ioanni Paulo Secundo ad honorem maximum for ten brass instruments and four kettle drums (for 46th Int. Eucharistic Congress, Wrocław) 1997, The Shepherd Goes, cantata for choir and symphonic orchestra (for 46th Int. Eucharistic Congress, Wrocław) 1997, XIth String Quartet 2002, Two Sonnets for baritone and piano (text by John Gracen-Brown) 2002, Concerto for orchestra 2003, XII String Quartet 2005, Sinfonietta for chamber orchestra 2006, Saxophone Quartet 2006, XIII String Quartet 2007, Sonata for guitar 2009, XIV String Quartet 2010, String Trio for two violins and viola 2011, Two Impressions for coloratura soprano and viola 2012, XV String Quartet 2013, Caprice for violin solo 2013, Podhalean meditation for organ solo 2014. *Recording:* Andante and Presto for xylophone and piano (for Radio-Wrocław). *Address:* ul Komandorska 48-8, 53-343 Wrocław, Poland. *Telephone:* (71) 367-61-38.

WISPELWEY, Pieter; Dutch cellist; b. 1965. *Career:* appearances with the Rotterdam Philharmonic, under Kent Nagano, L'Orchestre des Champs Elysées (Philippe Herreweghe), BBC SO, Netherlands Radio SO (Frans Brüggen), and the Camerata Academica Salzburg (Roger Norrington); further engagements in Argentina, Japan, S Africa and Australia; Bach-Marathon concerts with the six solo suites throughout Europe 2000, including the Wigmore Hall; tours with Nat. Orchestra of Lille and Baseler Kammerorchester 2001; with piano pnr, Dejan Lazic, performed complete Beethoven cello sonatas, Edinburgh Festival 2001; repertoire also includes works by Kagel, Carter and Schnittke. *Recordings include:* Suites by Bach, Britten and Reger, Sonatas by Schubert, Brahms and Beethoven, Concertos by Haydn, Vivaldi, Elgar, Dvořák and Schumann. *Honours:* Netherlands Music Prize, Diapason d'Or. *Current Management:* c/o Mark Doorn, DaPonte Artist Management, Prinsengracht 17, 1015 DK, Amsterdam, The Netherlands. *Telephone:* (6) 15149001. *E-mail:* mark@dapontesolutions.nl. *Website:* www.dapontesolutions.nl; www.pieterwispelwey.com.

WIT, Antoni; Polish conductor and academic; *Artistic Director, Orquesta Sinfónica de Navarra;* b. 7 Feb. 1944, Kraków; m. Zofia Ćwikilewicz. *Education:* State Higher School of Music, Kraków, Jagiellonian Univ., studied with Nadia Boulanger, Paris. *Career:* Asst Conductor Nat. Philharmonic Orchestra of Poland, 1967–70, Man. Dir and Artistic Dir 2002–13; Conductor, Poznań Nat. Philharmonic 1970–72; Artistic Dir Pomeranian Philharmonic, Bydgoszcz 1974–77; Man. and Artistic Dir, Polish Radio Symphony Orchestra and Choir, Kraków 1977–83; Dir Polish Nat. Radio Symphony Orchestra, Katowice 1983–2000; Artistic Dir Orquesta Filarmonica de Gran Canaria, Las Palmas 1987–91; First Guest Conductor, Orquesta Sinfónica de Navarra, Pamplona 2010–, Artistic Dir 2013–; Prof., Fryderyk Chopin Acad. of Music, Warsaw 1997–; has conducted LPO, RPO, BBC Symphony Orchestra, Berliner Philharmoniker, Orchestre National de Belgique, Tokyo Symphony Orchestra, Montreal Symphony Orchestra, Orquesta Nacional de España,

Staatskapelle Dresden, Accad. di Santa Cecilia, Rome, Tonhalle-Orchester. *Compositions include:* soundtracks: Kronika wypadków miłosnych (The Chronicle of Love Affairs) 1986, Korczak 1990, Pan Tadeusz (Last Foray in Lithuania) 1999. *Recordings include:* more than 90 recordings, albums include symphonies by Tchaikovsky, Górecki, Schumann, Penderecki, Lutosławski (all), Olivier Messiaen (Turangalila Symphony) (Cannes Classical Award—Midem Classique 2002), Penderecki: Fonogrammi; Horn Concerto; Partita; The Awakening Of Jacob; Anaklasis (Grammy Award for Best Classical Compendium 2013). *Honours:* numerous prizes include Second Prize, Herbert von Karajan Conducting Competition, Berlin 1971, Orpheus (Warsaw Autumn Festival Critics' Award) 1984, 1996, Diapason d'Or, Grand Prix de Disque de la Nouvelle Académie du Disque 1992, Diamond Baton Award of Polish Public Radio 1998, Cannes Classical Award, Midem Classique 2002, Classical Internet Award 2004, Record Acad. Award of Japanese music magazine Record Geijutsu (for Penderecki's Polish Requiem) 2005, Karol Szymanowski Foundation Award 2010, four Fryderyk Awards, Polish Phonographic Acad. *Address:* Orquesta Sinfónica de Navarra, Calle Sandoval, 6, 1 Izq., 31002 Pamplona, Navarra, Spain (office). *Website:* www.orquesta-pablo-sarasate.com (office).

WITT, Kerstin; German singer (mezzo-soprano); b. 1960, Altentreptow, Brandenburg. *Education:* Hanns Eisler Conservatory, Berlin. *Career:* appearances at the Dresden Staatsoper from 1988, as Donna Elvira, Strauss's Clairon (Capriccio), Octavian and Composer (Ariadne), Medea in Handel's Teseo, Leonore in Fidelio and Offenbach's Nicklauss; modern repertory includes the Mother in Janáček's Osud, Countess Geschwitz in Lulu and Bartók's Judith; guest appearances at Montpellier, Venice and elsewhere; Wagner roles include Brangaene in Tristan, and Magdalena in Die Meistersinger; concerts include the Wesendoncklieder and Kindertotenlieder and Dvořák's Gypsy Songs; sang Brangaene at Enschede 1999 and Herodias in Salome for the Dresden Staatsoper 2001. *Recordings include:* Herodias in Salome.

WITZENMANN, Wolfgang, DipMus, DPhil; German composer; b. 26 Nov. 1937, Munich; m. Renata Di Salvo 1977; one s. one d. *Education:* Musikhochschule, Stuttgart, Univ. of Tübingen. *Career:* as composer: Gaudeamus-Festival, Netherlands 1967, 1968, 1970, 1971, Internationale Ferienkurse für Neue Musik, Darmstadt, Germany 1969, Autunno Musicale, Como, Italy 1975, Festival Internazionale Nuova Consonanza, Rome 1985, Festival Internazionale Terenzio Gargiulo, Naples 1986; f. Wolfgang Witzenmann Musikverlag 2003. *Compositions:* Choirs, Oden I–V for voice and piano, six cycles of Lieder, Operas Nivasio, Mary and Sappho, Oratorio Christus and Gilgamesh, Orchestra Eigenklänge Natur Deutschland-Lieder, Sinfonia 1 and 2 for orchestra, Violin Concerto, Antiphonales Konzert for trumpet and orchestra, piano and organ music, chamber music, and music for early instruments; arrangements from original works by Macque, Gesualdo, Bellini. *Recordings:* Monographic 1989. *Publications:* Domenico Mazzocchi (1592–1665), Dokumente und Interpretationen 1970; contrib. to Analecta Musicologica, Acta Musicologica, Die Musikforschung, Recercare, Rivista Italiana di Musicologica, Studi Musicali. *Honours:* Festschrift: 'Vanitatis fuga, aeternitatis amor' Wolfgang Witzenmann zum 65. Geburtstag 2005. *Address:* Via Mario Fascetti 67, 00136 Rome, Italy (home). *Telephone:* (06) 35498447 (home). *Fax:* (06) 660492-75 (office). *E-mail:* wo_witzenmann@msn.com (home). *Website:* www.literadur.de (home).

WLASCHIHA, Ekkerhard; singer (baritone); b. 28 May 1938, Pirna, Germany. *Education:* Franz Liszt Musikhochschule in Leipzig and with Helene Jung. *Career:* debut, Gera 1961 as Don Fernando in Fidelio; sang in Dresden and Weimar 1964–70; Leipzig Opera from 1970 as Scarpia, Pizarro, Alfio, Tonio, Dr Coppelius, and Jochanaan in Salome; sang in the premieres of Greek Wedding by Hannell 1969 and The Shadow by Fritz Geissler 1975; Lausanne Opera and Staatsoper Berlin 1983 as Kurwenal and Telramund; sang Kaspar in Der Freischütz at the reopening of the Semper Opera House in Dresden 1985; Bayreuth Festival 1986 as Kurwenal; appeared on Russian television in Fidelio by Beethoven; sang Telramund at the Berlin Staatsoper 1990, and Alberich in a new production of Siegfried at Covent Garden 1990; returned to London 1997, as Bishop Ercole in Pfitzner's Palestrina and 1998 as Alberich at the Albert Hall; season 2000–01 as Alberich and Klingsor at the Met, Pizarro in Dresden and Biterolf in Tannhäuser for the Munich Staatsoper.

WOHLER, Rudiger; singer (tenor); b. 4 May 1943, Hamburg, Germany. *Education:* Hamburg Musikhochschule. *Career:* sang at Darmstadt 1968–71; sang at Zürich 1971–74 as Mozart's Belmonte, Ferrando, Tamino and Don Ottavio; sang at Stuttgart from 1974 and has made guest appearances in Hamburg, Munich, Vienna and Frankfurt; Schwetzingen Festival 1975 as Belmonte; Deutsche Oper Berlin from 1977; sang Tamino at the 1981 Salzburg Festival; La Scala Milan 1983 as Ferrando in Così fan tutte; sang in Cavalli's L'Ormindo at the Hamburg Staatsoper 1984 and toured with the company to Japan; Stuttgart in 1984 as Don Ottavio in the newly restored opera house; other roles include Fenton in Die Lustigen Weiber von Windsor, Lionel in Martha, Nemorino, Lensky and Almaviva in Il Barbiere di Siviglia; many concert engagements and lieder recitals; sang Idomeneo with the English Bach Festival at Covent Garden 1990. *Recordings:* Jacquino in Fidelio; Cantatas by Bach, Fux and Scarlatti; Die Schöpfung by Haydn.

WOHLHAUSER, René Claude; Swiss composer, pianist, singer and conductor; b. 24 March 1954, Zürich; two s. two d. *Education:* Basel

Conservatory, Staatliche Musikhochschule Freiburg, studied with Klaus Huber and Brian Ferneyhough, courses with Kazimierz Serocki, Mauricio Kagel, Herbert Brün, Heinz Holliger. *Career:* works played by Arditti String Quartet, Basel, Biel and Luzern Symphony Orchestras, also at Schweizer Tonkünstlerfeste and Int. Darmstädter Ferienkurse für Neue Musik, Notre Dame de Paris, Toronto, Newcastle, Baku, Klangforum Wien and Schauspielhaus Berlin; portraits and works on radio programmes; lectures on musical and philosophical aspects of his works at Darmstadt, Winterthur and Basel; Founder Komponistenforum Basel and Co-founder Adesso, contemporary music of independently published composers; currently teacher of composition and music theory, Musik-Akad. Basel; Conductor, tours with Ensemble Polysono and Duo Simolka-Wohlhauser. *Compositions include:* Souvenirs de l'Occitanie for solo clarinet 1978, Stilstudien for piano, four guitars and two percussionists 1981, Fragmente for orchestra 1984, Adagio assai for string quartet 1982–88, Duometrie for flute and bass clarinet 1985–86, Orgelstück 1987, Adagio assai for string quartet 1988, Klarinettentrio Metamusik 1990, In statu mutandi for orchestra 1991–93, Vocis Imago for flute, clarinet, percussion, piano, violin and cello 1993–95, Gantenbein (opera) 2002–04. *Radio includes:* Swiss Radio Portraits 1982, 1991, 1993, 1995, 2000. *Recordings include:* In Statu Mutandi 1996, René Wohlhauser 2009. *Honours:* bursaries from Luzern Dept of Educ. 1991, Basel-Landschaft Dept of Educ. 1998; Valentino Bucchi Composition Prize, Rome 1978, Asscn of German Music Schools' Composition Prize, Bonn 1981, VJMZ Composition Prize, Zürich 1983, City and Canton Fribourg Composition Prize 1984, Salzburg Cathedral Chapter Composition Prize 1987, Kranichsteiner Stipendienpreis, Internationale Ferienkurse für Neue Musik Darmstadt 1988, Eastern Swiss Foundation for Music and Theatre Composition Prize, St Gallen 1990, Commendation Prize of Swiss Soc. for Furtherance of Musical Educ., Zürich 1992, Selection Prize from Swiss Radio Int. 1996. *Address:* Schillerstrasse 5, 4053 Basel, Switzerland. *Website:* www.renewohlhauser.com.

WOLF, Gerd; German singer (bass); b. 18 April 1940, Floha, Saxony. *Education:* Berlin Musikhochschule. *Career:* debut at Dresden Radesbeul 1970 as the Hermit in Der Freischütz; sang at Dresden and elsewhere in East Germany until 1982, Berlin Staatsoper from then as Mozart's Osmin, Leporello and Bartolo, Nicolai's Falstaff, Bett in Zar und Zimmerman, Geronimo in Il Matrimonio Segreto and the Doctor in Wozzeck; Guest appearances in Leipzig, Karlsruhe and with the Berlin Staatsoper company at Naples, Messina, Prague, Bratislava, Japan and Netherlands; season 2000–01 in Berlin as Mozart's Bartolo and Kuno in Der Freischütz. *Recordings include:* Pfitzner's Palestrina; Graf Mirabeau by Siegfried Matthus; Ariadne auf Naxos. *Current Management:* c/o Agentur Sigrid Rostock, Eugen-Schönhaar-Strasse 1, 10407 Berlin, Germany. *Telephone:* (30) 4257514. *Fax:* (30) 4239136. *E-mail:* sigridrostock@web.de.

WOLF, Markus, DipMus; Austrian violinist, violist, violin teacher, chamber musician and concertmaster; *Principal Concertmaster, Bavarian State Opera, Munich, and Professor of Violin and Chamber Music, Musikhochschule Munich;* b. 28 May 1962, Vienna; two s. *Education:* Wiener Musikhochschule with Edith Bertschinger and Guenter Pichler, studied with Max Rostal in Klagenfurt and Bern, masterclasses with Nathan Milstein, Oscar Shumsky and Sándor Végh. *Career:* debut, Wiener Musikverein 1976, Wigmore Hall, London 1987, Suntory Hall, Tokyo 1990, Carnegie Hall (Weill Hall), New York 1996; violist, string trio with brothers Reinhold and Peter Wolf 1973–81; appearances with the Alban Berg Quartet 1986; violinist, asst to Guenter Pichler, Wiener Musikhochschule 1983–89; Prin. Concertmaster, Wiener Symphoniker 1987–88, Bavarian State Opera in Munich 1989–; guest leader, London Symphony Orchestra 1997–2002; founder, Beethoven Trio Wien 1981; founder, Münchner Horntrio with Johannes Dengler (horn) and Julian Riem (piano) 1999; mem. and teacher, Junge Münchner Philharmonie 1999–2002; teacher, Richard Strauss Conservatory, Munich 2000–08, Musikhochschule Augsburg 2005–08, Musikhochschule Munich 2008–, Prof. 2012–. *Recordings:* Mozart with Alban Berg Quartet, Tchaikovsky, Beethoven, Mendelssohn, Mozart, Schubert, Dvořák, Smetana, Suk, Mahler, Schoenberg and Korngold with Beethoven Trio Wien, Webern with Jérôme Granjon, Wagner with Wolfgang Sawallisch, Schoenberg with Zubin Mehta, Mendelssohn with Munich Youth Orchestra, Brahms, Franck, Grieg, Strauss and Pfitzner with Julian Riem, Strauss with Kent Nagano, Brahms, Ligeti and Köchlin with Münchner Horntrio, Reger with Michael Hartmann. *Honours:* Bayerischer Kammervirtuose 2000, ORF Pasticcioprize 2004, Echo Klassik Prize 2012. *Address:* Bayerisches Staatsorchester München, Max Joseph Platz 2, 80539 Munich, Germany (office). *Telephone:* (89) 89891553 (home).

WOLF, R. Peter, AB, MPhil, PhD; American musicologist and harpsichordist; b. 5 Dec. 1942, Washington, DC. *Education:* Harvard Univ., Yale Univ., Amsterdam Conservatorium with Gustav Leonhardt, Yale School of Music with Ralph Kirkpatrick. *Career:* debut at Carnegie Recital Hall, New York, 1975; numerous concerts as harpsichord soloist and continuo player; Musician-in-Residence, North Carolina State Univ., Raleigh; two television shows, NC Educational Network, 1972; Instructor in Music, SUNY, Stony Brook 1972–78; Asst Prof. of Music, Univ. of Utah, 1978–80, and at Rutgers Univ. 1980–85; Ed., Brouda Brothers Ltd, 1985–89; Dir of Development, Hoboken Chamber Orchestra, 1989–; mem., Bowers-Wolf Duo, Salt Lake Chamber Ensemble, Apollo's Banquet, New York Baroque. *Recordings:* Telemann's Instrumental Chamber Music with Concertmasters Ensemble; works by Rameau, J.S. Bach, C.P.E. Bach; Violin Sonatas by Biber 1681 (with Sonya Monosoff and Judith Davidoff). *Publications include:* ms Bauyn (co-ed.),

Rameau, Les Paladins (ed.), facsimile edn of Rameau, Les Paladins (ed.) 1986; contrib. to The Scriblerian; Actes; Colloque International Rameau, Dijon, 1983; The Musical Quarterly; Journal of The American Musical Instrument Society; Recherches; Early Music; Journal of The American Musicological Society. *Address:* 37A Phelps Avenue, New Brunswick, NJ 08901, USA.

WOLF, Reinhold Michael; Austrian violinist; b. 23 May 1956, Vienna. *Education:* Wiener Musikakademie, studied with Alban Berg Quartet, Amadeus Quartet, Kuenstlerische Diplompruefung mit Auszeichnung, studied with G. Poulet in Paris, Max Rostal in Cologne, Konzert-Examen mit Auszeichnung Cologne. *Career:* established the Wolf Trio (with brothers Markus on viola and Peter on violoncello); Concertmaster, World Youth Orchestra (with L. Bernstein) at Tanglewood, USA aged 18; Concertmaster, Orchestra of the Deutsche Oper Berlin 1982–; soloist with various European orchestras; appeared as double concerto pnr of H. Szeryng with Vienna Symphony Orchestra; established ensemble, Contraste in Berlin 1989. *Honours:* special prize Jeunesse Musicales, Austria (with Wolf Trio) 1973, first prize as soloist Jugend Musiziert Competition, Austria 1975.

WOLF, Sally; American singer (soprano); b. 1957. *Career:* Santa Fe Opera from 1982, as the Queen of Night, in the premiere of Eaton's The Tempest (1985) and in Sallinen's The King goes forth to France; has sung the Queen of Night throughout North America, at Covent Garden (1986) and with Opera North at Leeds (1987); Seattle Opera, 1992, as Lucia di Lammermoor, Netherlands Opera, 1990, as Constanze, and San Francisco, 1991, as Giunia in Mozart's Lucio Silla; other roles include Eternita in La Calisto (at Santa Fe), Gilda, Violetta and Oscar; sang Donna Anna at the 1996 Munich Festival and Mozart's Queen of Night at Los Angeles, 1998; season 1999–2000 as Donna Elvira in Los Angeles, Amalia in Verdi's Masnadieri at Carnegie Hall and Mme Cortese in Il Viaggio a Reims at the New York City Opera. *Current Management:* Columbia Artists Management, 1790 Broadway, New York, NY 10019-1412, USA. *Telephone:* (212) 841-9500. *Fax:* (212) 841 9744. *E-mail:* info@cami.com. *Website:* www.cami.com.

WOLFE, Duain; American conductor; *Music Director and Conductor, Chicago Symphony Chorus. Career:* 20 years as Conductor, Central City Opera Festival, Colo; Founder and Conductor, Colorado Children's Chorale 1974–99; Founder and Dir Colorado Symphony Chorus; Music Dir and Conductor, Chicago Symphony Chorus 1994–; fmr Chair. Chorus America; regular work with Pinchas Zuckerman and Canadian Nat. Arts Centre Orchestra, Ottawa. *Recordings include:* with Chicago Symphony Orchestra: Bartok: The Miraculous Mandarin 1997, Verdi Messa da Requiem (Grammy Awards for Best Choral Performance and Best Classical Album 2011) 2010. *Honours:* Hon. DMus (Univ. of Denver); Bonfils Stanton Award in Arts and Humanities, Colo Gov.'s Award for Excellence, Mayor of Denver Award for Excellence in an Artistic Discipline. *Address:* Chicago Symphony Chorus, 220 South Michigan Avenue, Chicago, IL 60604-2559, USA (office). *Telephone:* (312) 294-300 (office). *Website:* cso.org (office).

WOLFE, Julia; American composer and teacher. *Career:* commissions for Munich Chamber Orchestra, Kronos Quartet, Orchestre National de France, American Composers Orchestra conducted by Dennis Russell Davies, Trio Mediaeval and the Bang on a Can All-Stars, Colin Currie and BBC Symphony Orchestra; works premiered at Spoleto Festival, Cabrillo Festival under Marin Alsop, and by San Francisco Symphony; multimedia works with composers Michael Gordon and David Lang, including Lost Objects (Concerto Köln, directed by François Girard), Shelter (Musikfabrik and Ridge Theater), The Carbon Copy Building (with comic-book artist Ben Katchor); cr. Traveling Music with architects Diller Scofidio+Renfro in Bordeaux, France; works performed at Brooklyn Acad. of Music, LG Arts Center, South Korea, Sydney Olympic Arts Festival, Settembre Musica, Théâtre de la Ville, Lincoln Center and Carnegie Hall, New York, New York Phil Biennial; mem. Composition Faculty, Steinhardt School, New York Univ. 2009; Co-founder and Co-Artistic Dir Bang on a Can music collective, New York. *Compositions include:* The Vermeer Room for orchestra 1989, Girlfriend for mixed chamber ensemble and recorded sound, Window of Vulnerability 1991, Lick 1994, Believing 1997, Dark Full Ride for drums 2002, My Beautiful Scream, string quartet concerto 2003, Cruel Sister for string orchestra 2004, Lad for nine bagpipes 2007, Fuel 2007, Steel Hammer, cantata 2009, riSE and fLY, body concerto 2012, Anthracite Fields, oratorio (Pulitzer Prize in Music 2015) 2014. *Music for theatre:* Deveare Smith's House Arrest, Ridge Theater's Jennie Richie (Obie Award). *Music for film:* Fuel (for Hamburg-based Ensemble Resonanz and filmmaker Bill Morrison), Impatience and Combat de Boxe (for Asko-Schoenberg Ensemble and 1920s film experimentalist Charles De Keukeleire). *Recordings include:* Julia Wolfe – The String Quartets 2003, Arsenal of Democracy 2003, Dark Full Ride 2009, Cruel Sister 2011, Steel Hammer 2014. *Address:* c/o Mike McCurdy, Red Poppy Music, 80 Hanson Place, #701, Brooklyn, NY 11217, USA. *E-mail:* info@juliawolfemusic.com. *Website:* juliawolfemusic.com.

WOLFF, Christian, BA, MA, PhD; American composer; *Jacob H. Strauss 1922 Professor Emeritus of Music, Dartmouth College;* b. 8 March 1934, Nice, France; s. of Kurt Wolff and Helen Wolff; m. Holly Nash 1965; three s. one d. *Education:* Harvard Univ., influenced by John Cage, Morton Feldman and Earle Brown. *Career:* moved to USA 1941; taught at Harvard Univ. 1962–70; teacher of Classics and Music, Dartmouth Coll. 1971–99, now Jacob H. Strauss 1922 Prof. Emer. of Music; mem. Akademie der Künste, Berlin, American Acad. of Arts and Sciences 2005. *Compositions include:* Nine for ensemble 1951, Suite for prepared piano 1954, Duo for pianists I and II 1957–58, Music for Merce Cunningham 1959, Duo for violin and piano 1961, Summer for string quartet 1961, In Between Pieces for three players 1963, Septet 1964, Quartet for four horns 1966, Elec Spring I–III 1966–67, Toss for eight or more players 1968, Snowdrop for harpsichord 1970, Burdocks for one or more orchestras or five or more players 1971, Accompaniments 1972, Lines for string quartet 1972, Changing the System 1973, Exercises 1–28 1973–2000, Wobbly Music for mixed chorus and instruments 1976, Bread and Roses for piano and for violin 1976, Dark as a Dungeon for clarinet 1977, for trombone and double bass 1977, The Death of Mother Jones for violin 1977, Stardust Pieces for cello and piano 1979, Isn't This a Time for saxophone 1981, Eisler Ensemble Pieces 1983, Piano Song – I am a Dangerous Woman 1983, Peace March 1–3 1983–84, I Like to Think of Harriet Tubman for female voice, treble and alto 1984, Piano Trio 1985, Bowery Preludes 1986, Long Peace March for chamber ensemble 1987, From Leaning Forward (songs) 1988, Rosas for piano and percussion 1990, Ruth for piano and trombone 1991, Merce for percussion ensemble 1993, Two Pianists 1994, Memory for octet 1994, Percussionist Songs 1995, John, David for orchestra 1998, Pebbles for violin and piano 1999, Cello Suite Variation 2000, Ordinary Matter for three orchestras 2001, Fragment for two pianos 2001, Apartment House Exercises for chamber ensemble 2002, Peace March 8 for orchestra 2002, John Heartfield for four or more players and voice, 37 Haiku (songs) 2005, Long Piano 2005, Orchestra: Pieces 2005, Microexercises 2006. *Recordings:* For Ruth Crawford, Stones, Bread and Roses, I Like to Think of Harriet Tubman, Look She Said, Works for Trombone, Complete Works for Violin and Piano, Percussionist Songs, Early Piano Music, Burdocks, For Two Pianists... and Three, Exercise 15, Making Music – Works 1962–99. *Publications:* Cues: Writing and Conversations 1998, Compositions (ca. 210 titles) (with C.F. Peters). *Honours:* Dr hc (Calif. Inst. of Arts) 2004, (Huddersfield Univ.) 2009; John Cage Award for Music 1996, Fromm Foundation Commissioning grant 1998, Mellon Foundation grant 2003. *Address:* 104 South Main Street, Hanover, NH 03755, USA (home).

WOLFF, Christoph Johannes, PhD; German academic, writer and editor; *Adams University Professor, Harvard University*; b. 24 May 1940, Solingen; m. Barbara Mahrenholz 1964; three d. *Education:* Univ. of Berlin, Univ. of Freiburg im Breisgau, Univ. of Erlangen. *Career:* Lecturer, Univ. of Erlangen 1966–69; Asst Prof., Univ. of Toronto 1968–70; Assoc. Prof., Columbia Univ. 1970–73; Prof. of Musicology 1973–76; Visiting Prof. Princeton Univ. 1973, 1975; Ed. Bach-Jahrbuch 1974–; Prof. of Musicology, Harvard Univ. 1976–, Dept Chair. 1980–88, 1990–91, William Powell Mason Prof. 1985–, Acting Dir University Library 1991–92, Dean Graduate School of Arts and Sciences 1992–2000, Adams Univ. Prof. 2002–; Dir Bach Archive, Leipzig 2000–; mem. American Musicological Soc., Gesellschaft für Musikforschung, International Musicological Soc., American Philosophical Soc. *Publications:* Der stile antico in der Musik Johann Sebastian Bachs 1968, The String Quartets of Haydn, Mozart, and Beethoven: Studies of the Autograph Manuscripts (ed.) 1980, Bach Compendium: Analytisch-bibliographisches Repertorium der Werke Johann Sebastian Bachs (ed. with H.-J. Schulze), seven vols 1986–89, Bach: Essays on His Life and Music 1991, Mozart's Requiem: Historical and Analytical Studies, Documents, Score 1993, Wereld van de Bach-cantatas: The World of the Bach Canatatas 1997, The New Bach Reader (ed.) 1998, Driven Into Paradise: The Musical Migration from Nazi Germany to the United States (ed. with R. Brinkmann) 1999, Johann Sebastian Bach: The Learned Musician (Otto Kinkeldey Award) 2000; other: critical edns of works by Scheidt, Buxtehude, Bach, Mozart and Hindemith; contrib. to scholarly books and journals. *Honours:* Hon. Prof. University of Freiburg im Breisgau 1990–, Fellow American Acad. of Arts and Sciences 1982–; Dent Medal Royal Musical Asscn, London 1978, Humboldt Research Prize 1996, Bach Prize, Royal Acad. of Music 2006. *Address:* Department of Music, Harvard University, Music Building 204S, North Yard, Cambridge, MA 02138, USA (office). *Telephone:* (617) 495-2791 (office). *Fax:* (617) 496-8081 (office). *E-mail:* cwolff@fas.harvard.edu (office). *Website:* www.music.fas.harvard.edu (office).

WOLFF, Hugh; American conductor; *Stanford and Norma Jean Calderwood Director of Orchestras, New England Conservatory of Music*; b. 21 Oct. 1953, Paris, France; m. Judith Kogan; three s. *Education:* Harvard Univ. *Career:* began career as Asst Conductor, Nat. Symphony Orchestra, with the late Mstislav Rostropovich; Musical Dir New Jersey Symphony 1985–92; Prin. Conductor, Saint Paul Chamber Orchestra 1988–92, Musical Dir 1992–2000; Prin. Conductor, Frankfurt Radio Symphony Orchestra 1997–2006; Stanford and Norma Jean Calderwood Dir of Orchestras, New England Conservatory of Music 2008–; regularly guest-conducts the major orchestras in N America and Europe. *Honours:* Seavor/Nat. Endowment for the Arts Conducting Prize 1985, Cannes Classical Award 2001. *E-mail:* lsam@icartists.co.uk. *Website:* www.icartists.co.uk. *Address:* New England Conservatory of Music, 290 Huntingdon Avenue, Boston, MA 02115, USA (office). *Telephone:* (617) 585-1100 (office). *Website:* www.newenglandconservatory.edu (office); www.hughwolff.com.

WOLFF, Jean-Claude; French composer; b. 1946, Paris. *Education:* Ecole Normale de Musique de Paris, Conservatoire Nat. Supérieur de Musique de Paris with Henri Dutilleux, Jean-Pierre Guezec, Michel Philippot, Ivo Malec, Centre Int. de Recherches Musicales with Jean-Etienne Marie, Accademia Chigiana, Siena, Italy with Franco Donatoni, Académie de France, Rome (Villa Medici). *Career:* works performed at various festivals and concerts of contemporary music in France (Radio-France, Int. Musical Weeks in Orleans,

Angers Music Festival, Contemporary Music Meetings at Metz) and abroad in Italy, Switzerland, Denmark, Spain, The Netherlands; for several years concentrated mainly on chamber music. *Compositions include:* Symphony for voices and large orchestra. *Honours:* first prize Vienna Modern Masters 1991. *Address:* 39 rue Bouret, 75019 Paris, France (home). *E-mail:* jeanclaude.wolff@free.fr (home).

WOLLENBERG, Susan L. F., BA, MA, DPhil; British composer and academic; *Reader in Music, University of Oxford*; b. 28 April 1949, Lancs., England; m. Dr L. Wollenberg; one s. one d. *Education:* Withington Girls' School, Manchester, Royal Northern Coll. of Music, Lady Margaret Hall, Oxford. *Career:* Clara Sophie Deneke Music Scholar, Lady Margaret Hall 1966–69, Halstead Postgraduate Scholar, Faculty of Music, Univ. of Oxford 1969–72, Univ. Lecturer in Music, Faculty of Music 1972–2002, Fellow and Tutor in Music, Lady Margaret Hall 1972–, Reader in Music 2002–, Lecturer in Music, Brasenose Coll. Oxford 1987–; mem. Royal Musical Asscn (Vice-Pres.), Oxford Architectural and Historical Soc. *Compositions include:* The Survivor (song cycle), Alles auf der Welt ist Wandel (song cycle), Für Fanny Hensel (piano variations), Forgotten Voices (string quartet and reader). *Publications:* Music at Oxford in the 18th and 19th Centuries, Concert Life in 18th-Century Britain (co-ed. with S. McVeigh), The Piano in Nineteenth-Century British Culture (co-ed. with T. Ellsworth); contrib. to New Grove Dictionary of Music and Musicians, Oxford Dictionary of National Biography, various musical journals and symposia. *Address:* 131 Eynsham Road, Botley, Oxford, OX2 9BY, England (home). *Telephone:* (1865) 276125 (office). *Fax:* (1865) 276128 (office). *E-mail:* office@music.ox.ac.uk (office).

WOLOVSKY, Leonardo; American singer (bass-baritone); b. 1922, York, PA. *Education:* Oberlin Coll., OH. *Career:* sang at first in concert then appeared with Maria Callas in Norma at Catania 1952; engaged at Wiesbaden Opera 1953–57, Nuremberg 1957–73; guest appearances at Frankfurt 1959–73, Bayerische Staatsoper Munich 1961–69, Hanover 1961–73, Hamburg 1956–60; sang also at Graz, Essen, Amsterdam, Zürich, Paris, Barcelona and Athens; Bielefeld 1988, as Simon Mago in Nerone by Boito; other roles have included Enrico (Lucia di Lammermoor), Oroveso, King Philip, Nabucco, the Dutchman, Hans Sachs, the Wanderer in Siegfried and Boris Godunov; concert repertoire included Beethoven's Ninth, the Verdi Requiem and Bach's Christmas Oratorio.

WOLPE, Michael, MA; Israeli composer; b. 4 March 1960, Tel-Aviv. *Education:* Rubin Acad., Jerusalem, Univ. of Cambridge. *Career:* founder regional music school, Sdeh Boker kibbutz; teacher, High School of Sciences and the Arts 1991–96, Rumin Acad., Jerusalem 1996–99; Head of Music Dept, Jerusalem Acad. of Music and Dance 1999–; founder and Artistic Dir, Music in the Desert festival, Caprisma (chamber music ensemble); Jewish Music Inst. Visiting Prof. from Israel, School of Oriental and African Sciences, London 2008–09. *Compositions include:* Capella Kolot 1988, Stabat Mater 1994, Concerto for flutes and orchestra 1995, Trio 1996, Songs of Memory 1998, The Return of the Jackals 2000, Hatarat Nedarim 2002, Songs of the Land (cycle of symphonic poems), Kaprisma Nos 1–9. *Recordings:* Kaprisma No. 8. *Address:* Jerusalem Academy of Music and Dance, Givat Ram Campus, 91904 Jerusalem, Israel (office). *Telephone:* (2) 6759911 (office). *Fax:* (2) 6512824 (office). *E-mail:* schul@jamd.ac.il (office). *Website:* www.jamd.ac.il (office).

WOLVERTON, Joseph; American singer (tenor); b. 9 Sept. 1959, Chicago, Ill. *Education:* Juilliard School, New York and American Conservatory of Music, Chicago. *Career:* first came to int. attention by winning the Opera Company of Philadelphia's Pavarotti Competition; debut as Alfredo in La Traviata with Minnesota Opera and Opera Colorado; subsequently sang Paul in Krasa's Verlobung im Traum with Washington Opera, and Pinkerton (Madama Butterfly) with New York City Opera; numerous performances world-wide; European highlights have included Edgardo at Gran Teatro del Liceo, Barcelona, Nemorino (L'Elisir d'amore) with Hamburgische Staatsoper, title role in Werther in Malaga, Cavaradossi at Théatre Royal de la Monnaie, and Roberto (Le Villi) and Turiddu for Opera Bergen; concert repertoire includes Beethoven's Missa Solemnis and Ninth Symphony, Berlioz's Requiem, Mahler's Eighth Symphony and Verdi's Requiem, performed with orchestras including Chicago Symphony Orchestra, Detroit Symphony, Buffalo Philharmonic and Indianapolis Symphony; recent successes include Nemorino for L'Opéra de Montréal, Pinkerton for New Orleans Opera and Opera Grand Rapids, Cavaradossi for Dallas Opera, Duca for Tulsa Opera, Pollione for Fort Worth Opera, Cavaradossi and Romeo, both in Umeå, Sweden, Faust for Utah Opera and Malmö, Sweden, Rodolfo (La Bohème) for Phoenix Opera, Edgardo at Opera Carolina and Cavaradossi at the Royal Albert Hall, London; recently invited by The Amici di Verdi Soc. to perform a recital at the Salone di Barezzi in Busseto, Italy. *Recordings include:* Mascagni's Silvano. *Current Management:* c/o Athole Still Opera Ltd, Foresters Hall, 25–27 Westow Street, London, SE19 3RY, England. *Telephone:* (20) 8771-5271. *Fax:* (20) 8771-8172. *E-mail:* enquiries@atholestill.co.uk. *Website:* www.atholestill.com; www.josephwolverton.com.

WONG, Randall Kevin, BMus, MMus, DMusA; American singer (male soprano, countertenor) and composer; b. 10 April 1955, Oakland, CA. *Education:* Stanford Univ., San Francisco State Univ. *Career:* opera debut, Bernabei's Ascanio, Teatro Olimpico, Vicenza, Italy; San Francisco Opera; NY City Opera; appeared in premieres of Stewart Wallace's Where's Dick and Harvey Milk, Meredith Monk's Atlas, at Houston Grand Opera; mem., Meredith Monk Vocal Ensemble 1990–; opera repertoire includes Handel's Teseo, Hasse's

Olimpiade, Artemisia, Attilio Regolo, Jomelli's Vologeso, Demofoonte, Bach's Endimione, Mozart's Il Re Pastore; mem, AGMA, NARAS. *Recordings:* Hasse's Cleofide, Atlas, Harvey Milk; Wallace, Korie's Kabbalah; solo soprano cantatas of Vivaldi. *Honours:* California Arts Council Touring Grant 1986, NY Dance and Performance Award 1997. *E-mail:* rkw@neptune.net (office). *Website:* www.randall-wong.com.

WOOD, Hugh; British composer; b. 27 June 1932, Parbold, Lancashire, England. *Education:* Univ. of Oxford, studied in London with W. S. Lloyd Webber, and with Anthony Milner, Iain Hamilton and Matyas Seiber. *Career:* Prof. of Harmony, Royal Acad. of Music 1962–65; Teacher, Morley Coll. 1958–67; Research Fellow in Composition, Glasgow Univ. 1966–70; Lecturer in Music, Liverpool Univ. 1971–73, Univ. of Cambridge from 1976; talks on BBC Radio 3; Piano Concerto premiered at the 1991 Promenade Concerts. *Compositions:* Songs for Springtime for chorus and piano 1954, Suite for piano 1956, String Quartet 1957, Variations for viola and piano 1958, Laurie Lee Songs 1959, Songs to Poems by Christopher Logue 1961, Trio for flute, viola and piano 1961, String Quartet No. 1 1962, Scenes from Comus for soprano, tenor and chorus 1965, Three Choruses 1966, Songs to Poems by D. H. Lawrence 1966, Capriccio for organ 1967, Quintet for clarinet, horn and piano trio 1967, The Horses song cycle 1967, The Rider Victory song cycle 1968, Cello Concerto 1969, String Quartet No. 2 1970, Chamber Concerto 1971, Violin Concerto 1972, Two Choruses 1973, Songs to Poems by Robert Graves 1973, Songs to Poems by Pablo Neruda for high voice and chamber orchestra 1973, String Quartet No. 4 1978, Symphony 1979–82, Piano Trio 1984, Comus Quadrilles 1988, Horn Trio 1987–89, Cantata for chorus and orchestra 1989, Marina for high voice and ensemble 1989, Piano Concerto 1990, Funeral Music for brass quintet 1992, String Quartet No. 3 1993, Poem for violin and piano 1993, The Kingdom of God (anthem) 1994, Variations for orchestra 1997, Clarinet Trio 1997, Greek Songs 1998, Serenade and Elegy for string quartet and orchestra 1999, String Quartet No. 5 2001.

WOOD, James Peter, BA (Hons), FRCO, FRAM; British composer and conductor; b. 27 May 1953, Barton-on-Sea, Hants., England; s. of Peter Ley Wood and Elizabeth Gillian Wood; m. Penny Irish 1977 (divorced); one s. one d. *Education:* Radley Coll., Sidney Sussex Coll., Cambridge, Royal Acad. of Music, London, studied with Nadia Boulanger in Paris. *Career:* Conductor, Schola Cantorum of Oxford 1977–81; Founder and Conductor, New London Chamber Choir 1981; Prof. of Percussion, Internationale Ferienkurse, Darmstadt 1982–94; Founder and Dir Centre for Microtonal Music and Ensemble Critical Band 1990–98; freelance conductor, regular work with Netherlands Radio Choir, Berlin Radio Choir, RIAS Kammerchor, Collegium Vocale, Vocal Consort Berlin, Latvian Radio Choir, Cappella Amsterdam, MDR Chor, Champ d'Action, MusikFabrik. *Compositions include:* Phaedrus, Oreion (BBC Symphony Orchestra comm., premiered at Promenade Concerts 1989), Stoicheia (Darmstadt comm.), Ho Shang Yao, T'ien Chung Yao, Choroi Kai Thaliai, Spirit Festival with Lamentations, Village Burial with Fire, Incantamenta, The Parliament of Angels for 18 instruments 1995, Children at a Funeral for prepared piano 1996, The Parliament of Angels 1996, Séance 1996, Mountain Language 1998, Jodo 1999, Journey of the Magi 2000, Hildegard 2002–05, De telarum mechanicae 2007, Le Petit Bossu 2009, Cloud-Polyphonies 2010, Sea Dances 2012. *Recordings include:* Stoicheia, Two Men Meet, Venancio Mbande Talking with the Trees, Phainomena, Music for Voices and Percussion, Crying Bird, Echoing Star, Village Burial with Fire, Spirit Festival with Lamentations, Reconstruction of Missing Voices of Gesualdo Sacrae Cantiones, Book II; numerous CDs with New London Chamber Choir. *Publications:* contrib. to A New System for Quarter-Tone Percussion (in Musical Times and Percussive Notes). *Honours:* Lili Boulanger Prize 1975, Lili Boulanger Memorial Award 1980, Holst Foundation Award 1995, Gemini Fellowship 1995, Arts Foundation Fellowship for electro-acoustic music 1996, ECHO Klassik Award (Choir Recording of the Year) 2013. *Address:* Dorfstrasse 32, 14913 Schlenzer, Germany. *Telephone:* (33) 74680508. *E-mail:* james.wood@gmx.net. *Website:* www.choroi.net.

WOOD, Jeffrey Neal, BMus, MMus, MA, PhD; American composer and academic; b. 3 Oct. 1954, Allentown, PA; one s. *Education:* Oberlin Coll. Conservatory of Music, State Univ. of New York, Stony Brook. *Career:* Visiting Lecturer, Univ. of New Mexico, Albuquerque, New Mexico Inst. of Mining and Technology 1983–84, Austin Peay State Univ., Clarksville, TN 1984–. *Compositions:* Duo for cello and piano 1982, In Memoriam Magistri for brass quintet 1982, Sonata for cello and piano 1984, String Quartet No. 2 1985, MCMXIV for tenor and piano 1985, Now the Most High is Born 1985, Trio-Sonata for cello, piano and percussion 1986, The Dream of the Rood for tenor solo, chorus and organ 1986, Swifts for violin and cello 1986, First Essay for orchestra 1986, Music for concert band 1987, Comedies for woodwind quintet 1988, Quartet for flute, violin, cello and piano 1988, Lay Your Sleeping Head My Love for soprano, tenor and piano 1987, Kreigeslieder for mezzo-soprano and piano 1988, Time Let Me Hail and Climb for chorus, brass quintet and piano 1990, The Killing for tenor and piano 1989, Four Deadly Serious Songs for baritone and piano 1990, Ballads for the Goodly Fere for voice and piano 1991, Dances for two pianos 1992, Preludes for piano solo 1992, Ghosts for clarinet, viola and piano 1993. *Address:* c/o Department of Music, Austin Peay State University, Clarksville, TN 37044, USA.

WOODROW, Alan; Canadian singer (tenor); b. 1952, Toronto, Ont.; m. Vivien Tierney. *Education:* Royal Conservatory, Toronto and London Opera Centre. *Career:* has sung Herodes at San Diego Opera, Tannhäuser at Teatro San Carlo, Naples and Teatro Massimo di Palermo, Hüon (Oberon) with City of London Sinfonia, Florestan with San Antonio Symphony, Tambourmajor with Philharmonia Orchestra, Der Schäbige (Lady Macbeth of Mtsensk) at Teatro Comunale di Firenze, Strauss's Guntram at the Richard Strauss Festspiele, Garmisch and Don José for ENO; other int. projects have included Der Kaiser at Bayerische Staatsoper, Deutsche Oper Berlin and Gran Teatre del Liceu, Barcelona, Bacchus at Teatro San Carlo, Naples, Aegisth at Bayerische Staatsoper, Herodes for Scottish Opera and Siegfried at the Tiroler Festspiele; repeated role of Siegfried in the Seattle Opera Ring cycle (also The Prince, Rusalka) and made role debuts at Liceu Barcelona as Rienzi, Canadian Opera Co. as Clemente (Venus and Adonis) and New Nat. Theatre, Tokyo as Siegfried (Die Walküre); French debut as Siegfried in new Ring cycle at Théâtre du Capitole, Toulouse, repeated role for Perth Int. Arts Festival, Liceu, Barcelona, Opéra Royal de Wallonie Liège, Festival Amazonas in Manaus and Teatro Real, Madrid. *Recordings include:* Siegfried and Götterdämmerung (from the Tyrol Festival). *Current Management:* c/o Athole Still Opera Ltd, Foresters Hall, 25–27 Westow Street, London, SE19 3RY, England. *Telephone:* (20) 8771-5271. *Fax:* (20) 8771-8172. *E-mail:* enquiries@atholestill.co.uk. *Website:* www.atholestill.co.uk. *E-mail:* woodrowalan@hotmail.com (home).

WOODS, Elaine; British singer (soprano); b. 1958, Lancashire. *Education:* Univ. of Oxford, Royal Manchester Coll. of Music with Elsie Thurston, studied with Marjorie Thomas. *Career:* debut with Kent Opera as Violetta 1979, at the Edinburgh Festival; sang in Handel's Tolomeo at the Batigniano Festival in Italy 1980; German debut 1981 as Mimi in Mannheim; Bremen Opera from 1982 as Fiordigili, Tatiana, Eva, Liu and the Countess in Capriccio; sang in J.C. Bach's Lucio Silla in Frankfurt and Acis and Galatea at Karlsruhe 1983; appeared as Pamina at the 1986 Bregenz Festival and sang Belinda in a new production of Dido and Aeneas at Frankfurt; with WNO has sung Donna Elvira, Fiordigili and Mozart's Countess; concert repertoire includes the Verdi and Mozart Requiems, Haydn's Creation and Seasons, Messiah and Beethoven's Missa Solemnis and Ninth Symphony. *Honours:* prizewinner, Hertogenbosch Competition 1978.

WOODS, Robert; American record company executive and record producer; *President, Chief Operating Officer and Senior Producer, Telarc International Corporation.* *Career:* classically trained musician and fmr music teacher; co-founder, Telarc Int. Corpn (with Jack L. Renner) 1977, pioneered use of digital recording in classical and jazz music, currently Pres., COO and Sr Producer. *Honours:* Grammy Award for Classical Producer of the Year 1980, 1982, 1985, 1987, 1988, 1989, 2003. *Address:* Telarc International Corporation, 23307 Commerce Park Road, Cleveland, OH 44122, USA (office). *Website:* www.telarc.com (office).

WOODS, Thomas; Australian conductor; *Artistic Director and Principal Conductor, Christchurch Symphony Orchestra*; b. 1969, Tanzania. *Education:* Western Australian Conservatorium, Perth and with Vladimir Ponkin at the Gnessin Institute, Moscow. *Career:* Asst Conductor with West Australian Opera Company for productions of Don Pasquale and Madama Butterfly, 1982–93; Asst Chorus Master and Conductor, Opera Australia 1993–97, leading over 60 operas including Il Barbiere di Siviglia, A Midsummer Night's Dream, La Traviata and The Gondoliers, Un Ballo in Maschera, Les Dialogues des Carmélites, The Cunning Little Vixen, Gianni Schicchi, La Fille du Régiment, Patience, The Gondoliers, The Mikado, Die Fledermaus; Artistic Dir, Sydney Youth Orchestra –2005; currently Man. of Artistic Planning, Queensland Orchestra; also Artistic Dir and Principal Conductor, Christchurch Symphony Orchestra; guest conductor, Opera Queensland, Sydney Symphony Sinfonia, Queensland Symphony, Queensland Philharmonic, State Orchestra of Victoria, Sydney Opera House Orchestra, Bangkok Symphony Orchestra, London Festival Orchestra. *Honours:* Cultural Exchange Scholarship 1989. *Current Management:* Patrick Togher Artists' Management, Suite 25, 450 Elizabeth Street, Surry Hills, NSW 2010, Australia. *Telephone:* (2) 9319-6255. *Fax:* (2) 9319-7611. *E-mail:* pjtogher@ozemail.com.au. *Website:* www.christchurchsymphony.co.nz.

WOODWARD, Roger Robert, AC, OBE; Australian pianist, conductor, composer and academic; *Professor, School of Music and Dance, San Francisco State University*; b. 20 Dec. 1942, Sydney; s. of Francis W. Woodward and Gladys A. Woodward; one s. one d. *Education:* Univ. of Sydney, Conservatorium of Music, Sydney, Pomorska Wyzsza Szkola Humanistyczna (PWSH), Poland. *Career:* debut with Orkiestra Filharmonii Narodowej w Warszawie (Warsaw National Philharmonic Orchestra), then at Royal Festival Hall, London 1970; has performed throughout Eastern and Western Europe, Japan and USA; has appeared at int. festivals and with major orchestras world-wide; extensive repertoire and is noted for interpretation of Chopin, Beethoven, Bach and Twentieth Century Music; Artistic Dir Nat. Chamber Orchestra for Contemporary Music in Australia 'Alpha Centaure' 1989 and festivals in London; Fellow, Chopin Inst., Warsaw 1976; apptd Dir School of Music and Dance, San Francisco State Univ. 2002, now Prof. *Honours:* Commdr, Order of Merit (Poland) 1993, Chevalier, Ordre des Arts et des Lettres 2004, Order of Solidarność (Poland) 2008; Preis der Deutschen Schallplattenkritik (for his Celestial Harmonies recording of Bach C-minor and E-minor Partitas), Goethe Prize, Diapaison d'or, Medal for Merit to Culture Gloria Artis (Zasłużony Kulturze- Gloria Artis) (Poland) 2011. *Address:* Creative Arts Building, Room 145, School of Music and Dance, San Francisco State University, 1756 Holloway Avenue, San Francisco, CA 94132, USA. *E-mail:* roger@rogerwoodward.com; woodward@sfsu.edu (office). *Website:* musicdance.sfsu.edu (office); www.rogerwoodward.com.

WOODWARD-STADTMUELLER, Donna Lynn, AA, BMus; American singer and voice teacher; b. 2 June 1946, Baltimore, Md; d. of Hubert Woodward and June K. Woodward; m. Juergen Stadtmueller 1983. *Education:* Virginia Intermont Coll., Coll. Conservatory of Music, Univ. of Cincinnati, Univ. of Hamburg, Germany. *Career:* coloratura and lyric soubrette, Stadttheater Lucerne 1970, Staatstheater Darmstadt 1971–73, Stadttheater Heidelberg 1973–75, Nationaltheater Mannheim 1975–86; frequent guest at Nationaltheater Munich, Cologne, Karlsruhe and Stuttgart; freelance from 1986; appearances in Germany, Switzerland, France and Belgium; roles have included Blonde, Despina, Oscar, Gretel, Aennchen, Rosina, Sophie, Adele, Fiakermilli, Musetta, Waldvogel, Najade; Voice Teacher, Voice Dept, Univ. of Mainz, Germany 1991–2001, Hochschule für Musik, Heidelberg/Mannheim 1992–97; private voice studios in Frankfurt-am-Main and Limburg, Germany; Musica Viva music vacation courses in Italy and Germany 2003–, IGP Dept, Voice Majors, Hochschule für Musik und Darstellende Kunst, Frankfurt 2006–12; voice trainer for prizewinning Harmonie Männerchor, Lindenholzhausen 2004–; mem. Nat. Asscn of Teachers of Singing. *Recording:* Rosalia in Karl von Dittersdorf's Doktor und Apotheker. *Honours:* Giorno Memorial Prize 1969, Corbett Foundation stipend for study in Europe 1969. *Address:* Auf der Weide 4a, 65550 Limburg, Germany (home); 2244 Ashley Crossing Drive, Charleston, SC 29414, USA (home). *Telephone:* 171-955-3034 (mobile) (home). *E-mail:* woodstadt@aol.com. *Website:* www.musica-viva.de/dozenten.

WOOF, Barbara, BMus; Australian composer; b. 2 Sept. 1958, Sydney, NSW, Australia. *Education:* Univ. of Sydney, Royal Conservatory, The Hague, studied with Peter Sculthorpe and Jan van Vlijman. *Career:* faculty mem., Utrecht School of Arts, The Netherlands 1988–; Resident Composer, Sydney Symphony Orchestra 1992. *Compositions include:* Maldoror for violin 1983, Caoine for alto saxophone 1985, Hymns and Melodies for saxophone quartet 1989, Soundings for gamelan 1990, Banshee's Dance for orchestra 1992, Night Crossing for orchestra 1993, Táragató-Ray for chamber ensemble 1998, Alchimien du verbe for voice and chamber orchestra 1999, Naxos Revisited for soprano and four-channel tape 2003, Traumland for soprano and chamber orchestra 2003. *Honours:* winner Martin Codex Composition Competition, Spain 1985. *Address:* c/o DONEMUS, Paulus Potterstraat 16, 1016-CZ Amsterdam, The Netherlands.

WOOLFENDEN, Guy Anthony, OBE, MA, LGSM, FBSM; British composer and conductor; b. 12 July 1937, Ipswich, England; m. Jane Aldrick 1962; three s. *Education:* Westminster Abbey Choir School, Whitgift School, Christ's Coll., Cambridge. *Career:* Head of Music, Royal Shakespeare Co., Stratford-upon-Avon and London, composed more than 150 scores for the co. 1963–98; composed scores for Burgtheater (Vienna), Comédie Française (Paris), Teatro di Stabile (Genoa) and National Theatre (Norway); compositions for films, radio, television; conducted concerts with most British symphony orchestras; conducted concerts and ballet in Canada, Germany, Japan, USA, Hong Kong, and France; conducted opera for BBC radio, television and productions with Scottish Opera; Conductor, Birmingham Conservatoire Wind Orchestra; arranged and composed music for four full-length ballets by choreographer André Prokovsky: Anna Karenina, The Three Musketeers, La Traviata and The Queen of Spades, all in the repertory of the world's major cos; conducted Russian premiere of Anna Karenina with Kirov Ballet in St Petersburg 1993; Artistic Dir Cambridge Festival 1986–91. *Compositions include:* three musicals, Comedy of Errors (for RSC), A Children's Opera, The Last Wild Wood Sector 88 with Adrian Mitchell; works for the concert hall include concertos, chamber music and several works for symphonic band. *Recordings:* Music for Royal Shakespeare Company, Music for The Winter's Tale, Songs of Ariel, Gallimaufry featuring the wind music of Guy Woolfenden, Sweet Swan of Avon. *Honours:* Hon. LCM; Ivor Novello Award for Best British Musical 1976, Soc. of West End Theatre Award for Best British Musical 1977. *Telephone:* (1295) 780679. *Fax:* (1295) 788630. *E-mail:* guy@arielmusic.co.uk. *Website:* www.arielmusic.co.uk.

WOOLLAM, Kenneth Geoffrey; British singer (tenor); b. 16 Jan. 1937, Chester; m. Phoebe Elizabeth Scrivenor; four d. *Education:* Chester Cathedral Choir School, Royal Coll. of Music, London. *Career:* debut, Sadler's Wells, London 1972; appearances with Royal Opera Copenhagen, Saul and David, David; Florestan in Frankfurt; ENO roles include Rienzi, Radames, Aida, Tristan; sang with Scottish Opera, Royal Opera, Ghent, Opéra du Nord, Warsaw Philharmonic Orchestra in various roles, including Walther in Die Meistersinger, Siegfried in The Ring, Laca in Jenůfa; sang Husband in world premiere of John Tavener's Gentle Spirit at Bath; three film appearances as Canio, Alfredo and Hoffmann; concerts and oratorios with leading socs; sang in the premieres of Hamilton's Royal Hunt of The Sun and Blake's Toussaint L'Ouverture 1977; Covent Garden debut 1988, as Aegisthus; Prof. of Singing, Royal Coll. of Music; vocal consultant to David Puttnam's film, Meeting Venus 1990; appointed vocal consultant to DeVlaamse Opera in Antwerp and Ghent, Belgium 1995; Pierre in War and Peace (Prokofiev), ENO 1972; BBC Proms 1981; mem. Incorporated Soc. of Musicians, Savage Club, Glass Circle. *Recordings include:* Delius's Margot-La-Rouge, Berlioz's La Mort d'Orphée (conductor Jean Fournet) 1987, Songfest by Bernstein (TV), Elgar's Gerontius (BBC, conducted by Vernon Handley) 1987, Gurre-Lieder (televised Bergen Int. Festival), Herod in Salome (Edinburgh Festival) 1989. *Honours:* Hon. mem. Royal Coll. of Music 1992. *Address:* 33 Marlborough Crescent, Bedford Park, Chiswick, London, W4 1HE, England.

WOOLLETT, Elizabeth; British singer (soprano); b. 13 March 1959, Hillingdon, Middlesex, England. *Education:* Royal Academy of Music. *Career:* sang Magda in La Rondine and Irene in Donizetti's Belisario at the RAM; Opera North from 1984, as the Owl in The Cunning Little Vixen, Papagena, Kate Pinkerton, Mermaid in Oberon at Le Fenice, Venice, Anna in Intermezzo and Second Maid in the British premiere of Strauss's Daphne; Scottish Opera debut 1989, as Mozart's Susanna; Buxton festival, 1990, as Amenaide in Tancredi; Debut, Royal Opera House, Covent Garden, 1991, as Clorinda in La Cenerentola; other roles include Adina (L'Elisir d'amore), Cherubino, Micaela, Bella (The Midsummer Marriage) and Despina; Isabella in L'Assedio di Calais by Donizetti for the Wexford Festival, 1991; Sang Weber's Agathe for Chelsea Opera Group, South Bank, 1997; season 1998 as Musetta for ENO and Violetta for Castleward Opera; Has also sung for the BBC Radio 3 and has recorded works by Gilbert and Sullivan for TER records. *Honours:* Alec Redshaw Memorial Award, Grimsby 1986. *Current Management:* Music-makers International Artists Representation, Tailor House, 63–65 High Street, Whitwell, Hertfordshire SG4 8AH, England. *Telephone:* (1438) 871708. *Fax:* (1438) 871777. *E-mail:* musicmakers@compuserve.com. *Website:* www.operauk.com.

WOOLLEY, Robert; British harpsichordist and organist; b. 8 Jan. 1954, London, England. *Education:* Royal Coll. of Music with Ruth Dyson. *Career:* mem., Purcell Quartet, debut concert at St John's Smith Square, London 1984; Prof., Royal Coll. of Music; extensive tours and broadcasts in France, Belgium, The Netherlands, Germany, Austria, Switzerland, Italy and Spain; British appearances include four Purcell concerts at the Wigmore Hall 1987, later broadcast on Radio 3; tours of USA and Japan 1991–92; repertoire includes music on the La Folia theme by Vivaldi, Corelli, C.P.E. Bach, Marais, Scarlatti, Vitali and Geminiani, instrumental music by Purcell, music by Matthew Locke, John Blow and fantasias and airs by William Lawes, 17th-century virtuoso Italian music by Marini, Buonamente, Gabrieli, Fontana, Stradella and Lonati, J. S. Bach and his forerunners Biber, Scheidt, Schenk, Reinken and Buxtehude; many concerts with other ensembles and as soloist. *Recordings include:* Complete Keyboard works of Henry Purcell, solo recordings of Bach, Scarlatti, Frescobaldi, Couperin and Gibbons. *Telephone:* (20) 8398-6085. *E-mail:* robert@woolleys.org.uk. *Website:* www.robertwoolley.net.

WOOLRICH, John; British composer; *Concerts Director, Almeida Theatre;* b. 3 Jan. 1954, Cirencester, England. *Education:* Univ. of Manchester, Univ. of Lancaster with Edward Cowie. *Career:* Northern Arts Fellow in Composition at Durham Univ. 1982–85; composer-in-residence, Nat. Centre for Orchestral Studies 1985–86; animateur of various educational and music-theatre projects; Visiting Lecturer and composer-in-residence, Goldsmiths Coll., London 1987–88; Artistic Dir, Composers' Ensemble 1989–; Tutor, Guildhall School of Music 1990–91; composition teacher, Dartington Summer School 1991–93; Prof., Stage Internacional de Musica de Cambra 1992; Visiting Lecturer, Reading Univ. 1993; Lecturer, Royal Holloway Univ. of London 1994–98; Concerts Dir Almeida Theatre, London 1999–; Visiting Fellow, Clare Hall, Cambridge 1999–2001; Guest Artistic Dir Aldeburgh Festival 2004, Assoc. Artistic Dir 2005–. *Compositions include:* Four Songs after Hoffmann for soprano and clarinet 1981, Spalanzani's Daughter for instrumental ensemble 1983, Black Riddle for soprano and chamber orchestra 1984, The Barber's Timepiece for orchestra 1986, Dartington Doubles for chamber ensemble 1988, Night Machines for instrumental ensemble 1988, The Turkish Mouse for soprano and ensemble 1988, Barcarolle for six players 1989, Lending Wings 1989, The Ghost in the Machine 1990, Berceuse 1990, Quicksteps 1990, The Death of King Renaud 1991, The Theatre Represents a Garden: Night 1991, It is Midnight, Dr Schweitzer 1992, A Farewell 1992, String Quartet 1995, In the House of Crossed Desires (opera) 1996, Oboe Concerto 1996, String Trio 1996, Cello Concerto 1998, Little Walserings for chorus 1999, Accord for mixed orchestra 1999, Wind Sextet 1999, A Shadowed Lesson for piano and strings 1999, Bitter Fruit for 16 players 2000, Fanfarronda for chamber orchestra 2002, Watermark for violin and bass clarinet 2002, Good Morning-Midnight five songs for soprano and piano 2002, Arcangelo Homage to Corelli 2003. *Recordings:* Lending Wings, Ulysses Awakes, The Ghost in the Machine. *Honours:* Hon. Fellow Trinity Coll., London 1996. *Address:* c/o Almeida Theatre, Almeida Street, Islington, London, N1 1TA, England.

WORDSWORTH, Barry; British conductor; *Principal Guest Conductor, The Royal Ballet;* b. 20 Feb. 1948, Surrey. *Education:* Royal Coll. of Music, London, studied with Adrian Boult in London and Gustav Leonhardt in Amsterdam. *Career:* debut as soloist in Frank Martin's Harpsichord Concerto at the Royal Opera House, for Kenneth Macmillan's ballet, Las Hermanas; freelance conductor with the Royal Ballet, the Australian Ballet and the Nat. Ballet of Canada (including performances at the Metropolitan, New York); Prin. Conductor, Brighton Philharmonic Orchestra 1989–; Music Dir BBC Concert Orchestra 1989–2006, Conductor Laureate 2006–; Music Dir, Royal Ballet 1991–95, 2007–15, Prin. Guest Conductor 2015–; Music Dir Birmingham Royal Ballet 2005–08; debut with Royal Opera at Covent Garden with Carmen 1991; conducted the BBC Concert Orchestra, London Proms 1991; Piano Concerto by Bliss, Malcolm Arnold's Guitar Concerto, Vaughan Williams' 8th Symphony, and Act 3 of Sleeping Beauty; conducted Last Night of The Proms, with the BBC Symphony Orchestra 1993; conducted New Queen's Hall Orchestra at 1995 Proms; Raymond Gubbay's Carmen at the Albert Hall 1997; Poulenc's Les Biches and Roussel's 3rd Symphony, London Proms 1999; conducted the BBC Concert Orchestra, London Proms 2002. *Recordings* *include:* series of British music with BBC Concert Orchestra 1990–91. *Current Management:* IMG Artists, The Light Box, 111 Power Road, London, W4 5PY, England. *Telephone:* (20) 7957-5800. *Fax:* (20) 7957-5801. *E-mail:* amonsey@ imgartists.com. *Website:* www.imgartists.com.

WORKMAN, Charles; American singer (tenor); b. 1965, Arkansas; m. Alexandra Harwood. *Education:* Juilliard School, New York. *Career:* appearances in operas by Mozart and Rossini at the New York Met, ENO, Geneva, Nice, Amsterdam and the Spoleto Festival; further roles as Henn Smith in Bizet's Jolie Fille de Perth, Jupiter in Semele and Fenton in Falstaff; season 1998 in Semele for Flanders Opera, as Giocondo in La Pietra del paragone at Garsington and Iago in Rossini's Otello at Pesaro; season 1999–2000 as Alamar in Donizetti's Alahor in Granata, Ferrando at Ferrara and Monteverdi's Orfeo for the Munich Staatsoper; Don Ottavio at Salzburg, Cherubini's Anacréon in Venice and Belfiore in Il Viaggio a Reims, at La Coruña. *Recordings include:* Renaud in Gluck's Armide. *Current Management:* c/o Hilbert Artists Management, Maximilianstrasse 22, 80539 Munich, Germany. *Telephone:* (89) 2907470. *Fax:* (89) 29074790. *E-mail:* agentur@ hilbert.de. *Website:* www.hilbert.de; www.charlesworkmantenor.moonfruit .com.

WOSNITZA, Cornelia; German singer (soprano); b. 28 Nov. 1960, Dresden. *Education:* Dresden Musikhochschule. *Career:* sang Yniold in Pelléas and the Shepherd Boy in Tannhäuser at Dresden 1979; has appeared throughout Germany and in Russia, Amsterdam and elsewhere as Aennchen, Gretel, Blondchen, Norina, Susanna, Zerlina, Papagena and Musetta; concert appearances in works by Bach, Handel, Mozart, Schumann, Strauss and Orff (Carmina Burana). *Honours:* prizewinner Robert Schumann Competition at Zwickau 1981, Mozart Competition at Salzburg 1985.

WOTTRICH, Endrik; German singer (tenor); b. 1964, Celle. *Education:* studied in Würzburg with Ingeborg Hallstein, Juilliard School, New York. *Career:* debut at Wiesbaden, 1992, as Cassio in Otello; Berlin Staatsoper from 1993, as Tamino in Die Zauberflöte, Alfredo in La Traviata, Sänger in Rosenkavalier and Capriccio and Gernando in Haydn's L'isola disabitatà; Vienna Staatsoper, 1994, as Wagner's Steuermann and Théâtre du Châtelet, Paris, as Andres (Wozzeck) and in Fidelio, 1995–97; Bayreuth from 1996, as David in Die Meistersinger; concerts include Verdi Requiem with Zubin Metha in Berlin; Das Lied von der Erde by Mahler, Matthäus Passion by Bach, Faustszenen by Schumann with Abbado and Harnoncourt; season 1999–2000 as David at Bayreuth, Jacquino in Fidelio at La Scala and Don Carlos for Bonn Opera; Steuermann in Der fliegende Holländer at Chicago and Konrad in Hans Heiling for the Deutsche Oper, Berlin, 2001. *Recordings include:* Braunfels's Die Vögel, Der Freischütz with Berlin Philharmonic, Korngold, Ring des Polykrates, Kalman's Herzogin von Chicago, Beethoven's 9th Symphony. *Current Management:* Theateragentur Heidi Steinhaus, Auerfeldstrasse 26, 81541 Munich, Germany. *Telephone:* 89 93 93 01 10. *Fax:* 89 93 93 01 11. *E-mail:* steinhaus@heidi-steinhaus.de. *Website:* www.heidi -steinhaus.de.

WOYKE, Andreas; pianist; b. 28 April 1966, Siegen, Germany; m. Beate, one s. one d. *Education:* Jugendmusikschule Siegen with Pál Molnar, Aldo Antognazzi, Julio Largacha, Siegfried Fiedler, Musikhochschule Cologne with Pavel Gililov, Musikhochschule Vienna with Rudolf Kehrer. *Career:* concerts in Germany at Philharmonie Cologne, Gasteig Munich, Tonhalle Düsseldorf; concerts in Austria at Konzerthaus Vienna, Musikverein Vienna, Schloá Eggenberg Graz; concerts throughout Europe and in USA, Canada, South Africa, Russia and Chile; radio appearances in Germany, Austria, USA, Canada, South Africa; television appearances in Germany, Switzerland and South Africa; mem. Studienstiftung des Deutschen Volkes 1988–92. *Recordings:* Bach Concertos for two, three and four pianos, Bremen Competition: Ginastera, Danzas Argentinas. *Honours:* first prize Bremen Piano Competition 1987, first prize Int. Brahms Competition, Hamburg, Germany 1992, second prize UNISA-Transnet Int. Piano Competition, Pretoria, South Africa 1996, first prize Knezkova-Hussey Int. Piano Competition, Bathurst, Canada 1996.

WRAY, Steven Donald, MA (Oxon.), LRAM; British pianist and piano teacher; *Piano Teacher and Music Examiner, Westminster School and Associated Board of the Royal Schools of Music;* b. 10 June 1959, Bolton, Lancs. *Education:* Balshaw's Grammar School, Leyland, Blackpool Collegiate Grammar School, The Queen's Coll., Oxford, Universität für Musik und darstellende Kunst, Vienna. *Career:* studied privately with Dorothea Law and Ruth Nye whilst gaining recital experience through various young artists' platforms; invited to join Yehudi Menuhin's Live Music Now!, including foyer recital Barbican Centre, London; obtained bursaries through Austrian Cultural Inst., London to participate in masterclasses of Prof. Hans Graf at Int. Summer Acad. at Salzburg Mozarteum; later moved to Vienna and enrolled in advanced chamber music class at Hochschule; as soloist, worked with Carmen Graf-Adnet and Hans Graf and played to Prof. Paul Badura-Skoda; keen interest in 20th century and contemporary music; solo debut at Purcell Room, South Bank Centre, London in Park Lane Group Young Artists Series 1988; performed new music in Vienna with ENSEMBLE 9 and conductor Yuki Morimoto; worked closely with Andrew Keeling and premiered several of his works at St John's Smith Square and other concert halls; other premieres include works by Czech composer Petr Pokorny and by Wilfred Josephs for his 70th birthday celebrations at the Purcell Room; orchestral repertoire includes concertos by Mozart, Beethoven, Liszt, Brahms,

Grieg and Saint-Saens; has performed with several orchestras in Europe and UK; appeared in series of subscription concerts in Czech Repub. playing Beethoven concertos with South Bohemian Chamber Philharmonic Orchestra 1990s; has worked with chamber music instrumentalists including violinists Tomas Tulacek, Maria Ingolfsdottir, Marina Marsden, violist Cathy Stevens, and cellists Jaroslav Ondracek, Nitzan Laster, Jonathan Ayling and Janet Coles; formed duo with violinist Tomas Tulacek for concert tour in Middle East, with further appearances during 1990s in Vienna, Prague, Ljubljana, Paris, Jerusalem, London and throughout UK; collaborated with baritone Petr Matuszek in concert tour for Schubert Soc. of Czech Repub. for Schubert bicentenary; participated in 'rediscovery' of several composers silenced during oppression of 1938–45 and following World War II; invited by festival dir and composer, Petr Pokorny, to perform in Prague's Musica Iudaica festival 1993, performed and recorded works by Viktor Ullmann and Ervin Schulhoff; series of London recitals at The Warehouse, Waterloo (under the title Romantic Generations) 2004–05; invited by composer Andrew Keeling to record his solo piano music and the cycle Blue Dawn. *Radio:* Czech Radio recording of Ullmann's Fourth Sonata featured in Gaby Flatow's historical documentary Nicht bloß klagend an Babylons Flüßen for German radio (Sender Freies Berlin) along with an interview. *Recordings:* Blue Dawn, Quickening the Dead 2005, Crucifixus 2012, Resonances: Classical, Romantic and Modern in Central Europe, Imanaka. *Address:* 17 Adamsrill Road, London, SE26 4AL, England (home). *Telephone:* (20) 8291-4456 (home). *E-mail:* enquiries@ stevenwray.com (home). *Website:* www.stevenwray.com (home).

WRIGHT, Brian James, AGSM, FGSM; British conductor; b. 4 Aug. 1946, Tonbridge, Kent, England. *Education:* Guildhall School of Music, studied with George Hurst and Jascha Horenstein, Munich Music Acad., Germany. *Career:* fmr Asst Conductor to André Previn and London Symphony Orchestra, Assoc. Conductor, BBC Symphony Orchestra; has conducted major British orchestras, including performances of Berlioz and Liszt at BBC Proms; regular guest conductor in Britain and Europe, also conducted the Hong Kong Philharmonic and Singapore Symphony Orchestras; currently Music Dir, Maidstone Symphony Orchestra, Goldsmiths Choral Union, London; tour of China with Royal Philharmonic Orchestra 2000–01; season 2005/6 conducted the opening concert of BBC Radio 3's Beethoven Experience and Britten's War Requiem at Royal Albert Hall and Cadogan Hall; season 2006/7 conducted performance of Berlioz's Grande Messe des Morts with Royal Philharmonic Orchestra, also guest conductor in Norway, Slovenia, and Romania; season 2008/9 includes programme of Fauré and Berlioz at Royal Albert Hall and conducting the George Enescu Philharmonic, Bucharest; concerts include programmes of Mahler's 6th Symphony, Elgar 2 & Sibelius and Brahms & Bruckner 6. *Honours:* Gulbenkian Scholarship, second prize, LSO/Rupert Foundation Competition 1974, Guido Cantelli Competition, Milan 1975. *Current Management:* c/o Connaught Artists Management Ltd, 2 Molasses Row, Plantation Wharf, London, SW11 3UX, England. *Telephone:* (20) 7738-0017. *Fax:* (20) 7738-0909. *E-mail:* classicalmusic@connaughtartists.com.

WRIGHT, Mary Jean, (Gee Karlshonn); Panamanian musician, composer and conductor; b. 12 Oct. 1945. *Education:* Instituto Nacional de Música de Panamá, Univ. of Chile, Palacio de Bellas Artes, Dominican Repub., Acad. de Santa Cecilia, Rome, Univ. de Rosario, Argentina, Fla State Univ., USA). *Career:* teacher of Musical Educ., Panamá 1962–66; founder, Dir children's choir of Panama 1962–66; Prof. of Harmony, History and Musical Form, Conservatorio Nacional de Música de El Salvador 1975; writer of musical arrangements; Man. Artistic Dept and Production Chief of DECESA (subsidiary of RCA in Cen. America and Panama), El Salvador 1975–76; Dir of El Salvador Orchestra at Int. song festival, Caracas (Venezuela) 1979; Pres., Dir-Gen. Tukan Productions (jingles), Tukan Record and Tapes and Tukan-Alba Productions, Panamá 1981–; Nat. Supervisor of Music, Instituto Nacional de Cultura, Panamá, then Dir Instituto Nacional de Música 1991; has written jingles for Cen. and S American countries; composer of many works for orchestra and choirs. *Publications:* The Jingle as Substantial Element in Modern Advertising 1988, Compendio de Armonía Funcional 1989, Canciones para Lectura a Primera Vista 1991; Music: Elegía a Victoriano Lorenzo 1968, Rondo Espacial 1982, Fantasía Burlesque 1984. *Honours:* prize-winner at Festival of Children's Song, San Salvador 1979, Panama Rep. (composer, music arranger and conductor) to OTI Int. Song Festival, Brazil 1973, Acapulco, Mexico 1974, El Salvador Rep. to OTI Int. Song Festival, Madrid (fourth prize) 1977, First Prize First Belmont Song Fes. *Address:* Tukan-Alba Productions, Panamá, Panama.

WRIGHT, Peter, MA, FRCO, FRSCM, FGCM; British organist and conductor; *Organist and Director of Music, Southwark Cathedral;* b. 6 March 1954, Herts., England. *Education:* Royal Coll. of Music, London with Richard Popplewell and Angus Morrison, Emmanuel Coll., Cambridge with Dame Gillian Weir, studied with Flor Peeters in Belgium. *Career:* mem. Royal Coll. of Organists 1970–, Council mem. 1990–, Hon. Sec. 1997–2002, Chief Examiner 1997–2005, Vice-Pres. 2003–05, 2008–, Pres. 2005–08; apptd Sub-Organist, Guildford Cathedral 1977; Prin. Conductor Guildford Chamber Choir 1984–1994, Surrey Festival Choir 1987–2001; Organist and Dir of Music, Southwark Cathedral 1989–; numerous int. concerts and tours with Southwark Cathedral Choir, including performances at St Alban's Int. Organ Festival 2001, BBC Proms 2002, City of London Festival 2011; Fellow, Royal School of Church Music, Guild of Church Musicians. *Recordings:* Augustin Barié, Organ Works; French and Belgian Organ Music. *Address:* Southwark Cathedral, London Bridge, London, SE1 9DA, England (office). *Telephone:*

(20) 7367-6703 (office). *Fax:* (20) 7367-6725 (office). *E-mail:* peter.wright@southwark.anglican.org (office). *Website:* www.southwark.anglican.org (office).

WRIGHT, Peter Anthony, BA, BMus, MA, PhD; British musicologist; b. 14 April 1953, Vienna, Austria. *Education:* Pembroke Coll., Oxford, Univ. of Nottingham. *Career:* freelance teacher and writer 1975–77, 1981–85; Lecturer, Univ. of Exeter 1987–88; Lecturer, Univ. of Nottingham 1988, Reader 2000–06, Prof. of Music 2007–14; British Acad. Sr Research Fellowship 2012; Visiting Fellowship, All Souls Coll., Oxford 2012; mem. Royal Musical Asscn (Council mem. 2001–04), Cttee for Early English Church Music 2002– (Chair. 2012–), American Musicological Soc., Plainsong and Mediaeval Music Soc. *Publications include:* The Related Parts of Trent, Museo Provinciale d'Arte, MSS 87 (1374) and 92 (1379) 1989, I codici musicali trentini 2 (ed.) 1996, Der Mensuralcodex St Emmeram (co-author) 2006, Fifteenth-Century Liturgical Music V (ed.) 2006, Hermann Pötzlinger's Music Book (co-author) 2009, Fifteenth-Century Liturgical Music VIII (ed.) 2013; contrib. to Early Music, Early Music History, Journal of Musicology, Leading Notes, Music & Letters, Music & Musicians, Plainsong and Medieval Music, Revised New Grove Dictionary of Music and Musicians, Die Musik in Geschichte und Gegenwart. *Honours:* John Lowell Osgood Memorial Prize for Musical Composition, Oxford 1973, Westrup Prize 1995, C.B. Oldman Prize (with Ian Rumbold), Int. Asscn of Music Libraries, Archives and Documentation Centres 2011.

WRIGHT, Roger, CBE, BMus; British radio executive and arts administrator; *Chief Executive, Aldeburgh Music;* b. 15 Aug. 1956, Manchester, England; m. Rosie Wright; one s. one d. *Education:* Chetham's School of Music, Royal Holloway Coll., London. *Career:* librarian and Man., later Dir, British Music Information Centre 1978–87; Sr Producer, BBC Symphony Orchestra 1987–89; Artistic Admin., Cleveland Orchestra 1989–92; Exec. Producer, later Vice-Pres. Artists & Repertoire, Deutsche Grammophon 1992–97; Head of BBC Classical Music 1997–98, Controller, BBC Radio 3 (with responsibility for BBC Concert Orchestra, BBC Philharmonic, BBC Symphony Orchestra and BBC Singers) 1998–2014, Dir, BBC Proms 2007–14; Chief Exec. Aldeburgh Music 2014–; mem. Music Advisory Panel and Recordings Panel, Arts Council of GB and Music Panel, Greater London Arts Asscn; Chair. Soc. for the Promotion of New Music, Contemporary Concerts Co-ordination; Fellow, Radio Acad. *Publications:* New Music (co-author) 1989; ed books on new music for Oxford University Press. *Honours:* Hon. FRCM; Hon. Fellow, Royal Holloway Coll. 2002; Asscn of British Orchestras Award for outstanding contrib. to orchestral life in the UK 2005. *Address:* Aldeburgh Music, Snape Maltings Concert Hall, Snape, IP17 1SP, Suffolk, England (office). *Telephone:* (1728) 687100 (office). *Fax:* (1728) 687120 (office). *E-mail:* jalexander@aldeburgh.co.uk (office). *Website:* www.aldeburgh.co.uk (office).

WRIGHT, Rosemarie, ARAM, LRAM, Dip(Hons); British pianist; b. 12 Dec. 1931, Chorley, Lancs.; m. Michel Brandt 1961; two s. *Education:* Royal Acad. of Music, London, Staatsakademie, Vienna, masterclasses with Edwin Fischer, Pablo Casals and Wilhelm Kempff. *Career:* debut at Grosser Musikvereinssaal, Vienna 1960; concerts throughout Europe, USA, Far East, Australasia; broadcasts worldwide; concertos with London Philharmonic, Philharmonia, English Chamber Orchestra, London Mozart Players, BBC Orchestras, Vienna Symphony Orchestra and Danish and French Radio; Prof. of Piano, Royal Northern Coll. of Music, Manchester 1973–78, RAM, London 1978–97; Pianist-in-Residence, Univ. of Southampton 1972–80; Examiner, Associated Bd of the Royal Schools of Music 1972–2004; mem. British Fed. of Festivals for Music, Dance and Speech, Adjudicator. *Recordings:* Piano Music by Edward Macdowell, Vols 1, 2 and 3, double album of Haydn Sonatas on 1799 Broadwood Fortepiano. *Honours:* Chappell Silver Medal 1953, Tobias Matthay Fellowship 1954, Haydn Prize, Vienna 1959, Bösendorfer Prize 1960. *Address:* 84 Filsham Road, Hastings, East Sussex, TN38 0PG, England (home). *Telephone:* (1424) 423260 (home).

WRIGHT, William George C.; British pianist; b. 14 Dec. 1936, Airdrie, Scotland; m. Janette Montgomery Rose 1961; two s. one d. *Education:* Royal Scottish Acad. of Music and Drama. *Career:* Liszt scholar; gives lectures and recitals in Belgium, Canada, France, Hungary and the USA; numerous radio and TV appearances; mem. Liszt Soc., London, American Liszt Soc. *Recordings:* BBC Scotland world premiere recording of Liszt's Piano Piece in A flat S189 1987, first modern performance (BBC recording) of Liszt/de Swert Consolations I and IV and Liszt's Enchaînement D11 for cello and piano (with Mark Bailey) 1991, first modern performance (BBC recording) of Liszt's Die Vätergruft, 1886 version for baritone and piano (with Christopher Underwood) 1998, first modern performance of Hérold/Herz/Liszt Cavatine de Zampa 2004. *Publications include:* More Light on Young Liszt: Liszt 2000, Liszt's Chamber Compositions and Transcriptions: The Liszt Companion 2002; numerous essays on Franz Liszt in journals and publs including Journal of the American Liszt Society (Vols 29, 31, 33, 35, 54, 55, 56), Letters from the Royal Library, Copenhagen: Liszt Saeculum Nr 54 1995, The Hungarian Quarterly (Vol. 44, No. 170), Hérold/Herz/Liszt Cavatine de Zampa 2004, Studia Musicologica (Vol. 48, Nos 3 and 4) 2007, Liszt Society Journal (Vols 32, 34), Les Élèves de Liszt, Figures connues et inconnues, dir M. Haine (S. Dufetel and C. Reynaud, Numéro spécial de Liszt, Quaderni (contrib.) 2011, Liszt et la France, Musique, Culture et Société dans l'Europe du XIX Siècle (contrib.) 2012, Journal of the American Liszt Society (Vol. 64) 2003, Liszt's "Rather Long Excursion in Asia" 2013, Liszt Society Journal (Vol. 39) 2014, Liszt and England, Liszt Studies Series (Vol. 16) 2016. *Address:* 24 Ayr Road,

Giffnock, Glasgow, G46 6RY, Scotland (home). *E-mail:* wright24@ntlworld.com (home).

WROBLEWSKI, Patryk; American singer (baritone); b. 4 Dec. 1956, Mishawaka, IN. *Career:* debut singing Malatesta at the 1980 Blossom Festival; appearances as Fernando in La Gazza Ladra at Philadelphia, Silvio, Valentin and Monteverdi's Orfeo at Dallas; Lyric Opera of Chicago as Germont and Marcello and in Satyagraha by Glass; Opera Grand Rapids as Don Giovanni; season 1991–92 with debut at New York City Opera as Zurga in Les pêcheurs de perles and as Silvio; Puccini's Lescaut with Greater Miami Opera and Silvio at the Munich Staatsoper (European stage debut); season 1992–93 as Zurga in Holland, Taddeo in L'Italiana in Algeri at Dublin, and Marcello and Rossini's Figaro for the New Israel Opera; concert appearances with the Chicago Symphony under Leppard and the Grant Park Concerts under Leonard Slatkin; Santa Fe Opera in Henze's Young Lord; Weill, The Protagonist; Dublin Grand Opera, Marcello in La Bohème; Manitoba Opera, Zurga, Carmen. *Honours:* Grand Prize Rosa Ponselle Int. Competition 1984, winner Luciano Pavarotti Competition 1985.

WU, Man; Chinese musician (pipa) and composer; b. 1963, Hangzhou, Zhejiang; m.; one s. *Education:* studied with Lin Shicheng, Kuang Yuzhong, Chen Zemin, and Liu Dehai, Cen. Conservatory of Music, Beijing. *Career:* an exponent of the Pudong School of pipa playing (Chinese lute); moved to USA 1990; fmr Bunting Fellow, Radcliffe Inst. of Advanced Study, Harvard Univ.; performs regularly with Yo-Yo Ma's Silk Road Project and the Kronos Quartet; collaborations with musicians and conductors including David Zinman, Yuri Bashmet, Cho-liang Lin, Dennis Russell Davies, Christoph Eschenbach, Gunther Herbig, Esa-Pekka Salonen, Michael Stern, David Robertson; first Chinese musician to perform at the White House; has performed numerous world premieres including Chen Yi's Ning! with Yo-Yo Ma, Bright Sheng's Nanking! Nanking! with NDR Radio Symphony Orchestra, Bright Sheng's Songs for Cello and Pipa with Yo Yo Ma, Ye Xiaogang's Pipa Concerto with RSO Radio Symphony Orchestra, Tan Dun's Ghost Opera with Kronos Quartet, Terry Riley's Cusp Of Magic with Kronos Quartet 2005, Chen Yi and Wu Man's Ancient Dances multimedia work 2005, Philip Glass' Sound of a Voice 2005; collaborated with Philip Glass and five other world musicians to create Orion, Cultural Olympiad, Athens 2004; has performed with leading orchestras including Austrian ORF Radio Symphony Orchestra, Boston Symphony Orchestra, Los Angeles Philharmonic New Music Group, Moscow Soloists, Nashville Symphony, German NDR and RSO Radio Symphony Orchestras, New York Philharmonic, Seattle Symphony Orchestra, Stuttgart Chamber Orchestra; concerts at venues including Carnegie Hall, New York, Amsterdam's Concertgebouw, Moscow Great Hall, Kennedy Center, Washington, DC, Lincoln Center, New York, Opera Bastille, Paris, Royal Albert Hall and Royal Festival Hall, London, Theatre de la Ville, Paris; festival appearances include Bang on a Can Festival, Festival d'Automne, Paris, BBC Proms, Hong Kong Arts Festival, La Jolla Summerfest, Le Festival de Radio France, Lincoln Center Festival, NextWave!/BAM, Ravinia Festival, Silk Road Festival, Tanglewood, Wien Modern, Yatsugatake Kogen Festival, Japan. *Honours:* first prize, First Nat. Music Performance Competition, China 1989, City of Toronto Glenn Gould Protégé Prize 1999. *Current Management:* Opus 3 Artists, 470 Park Avenue South, 9th Floor North, New York, NY 10016, USA. *Telephone:* (212) 584-7500. *Fax:* (646) 300-8200. *E-mail:* info@opus3artists.com. *Website:* www.opus3artists.com; www.wumanpipa.org.

WU, Mary Mei-Loc, MMus, DMA; Chinese pianist; b. 22 Dec. 1964, Hong Kong; m. James Wong, 4 July 1992. *Education:* Yehudi Menuhin School, Royal College of Music, London, Banff Center of Fine Arts (winter school) Canada, State University of New York at Stony Brook, USA. *Career:* debut at Queen Elizabeth Hall, London, 1979; Beethoven Sonata with Yehudi Menuhin in Germany, 1985; Bach Double Concerto with Vlado Perlemuter, London South Bank, 1986; solo recital, Wigmore Hall, London, 1994; artist-in-residence, Chinese University, Hong Kong, 1997. *Recordings:* Fantasias; Chinese Contemporary Piano Music; Piano Classico. *Address:* 135 Stevenage Road, Fulham, London, SW6 6PB, England.

WU, Zuqiang; Chinese musician, composer and academic; *Vice-Chairman, China Federation of Literary and Art Circles;* b. 24 July 1927, Beijing; s. of Wu Jingzhou and Wu Qinqi (née Zhou); m. Li-qin Zheng 1953; one s. one d. *Career:* Vice-Pres. Cen. Conservatory of Music 1978–82, Pres. 1982–88, now Prof. and Hon. Pres.; Vice-Pres. Chinese Musicians' Asscn 1985, now Hon. Chair.; Vice-Exec. Chair. China Fed. of Literary and Art Circles 1988–92, Vice-Chair. 1992–; Adviser to China Nat. Symphony Orchestra 1996; Alt. mem. 12th CCP Cen. Cttee 1982–87; Perm. mem. Nat. Cttee 7th, 8th and 9th CPPCC 1988–2003; Artistic Adviser, Yong Siew Toh Conservatory of Music; Artistic Adviser for opening and closing ceremonies, Beijing Summer Olympic Games 2008. *Compositions include:* Sunrise at the Tu Mountains – Fighting against the Floods, Little Sisters at the Grasslands, The Moon's Reflection On ErQuan, Listening to the Pines, A Lovely Night, Revival. *Publications:* Musical Form, Analysis of Music Works 1962. *Address:* Central Conservatory of Music, 43 Baojiajie Street, Xicheng District, Beijing 100031, People's Republic of China (office). *Telephone:* (10) 66414887 (office). *Fax:* (10) 66417211 (office). *E-mail:* fao@ccom.edu.cn (office). *Website:* en.ccom.edu.cn (office).

WULKOPF, Cornelia; German singer (contralto); b. 1952, Braunschweig. *Education:* Detmold Music Academy with Gunther Weissenborn,. *Career:* debut as Sieglinde and Flosshilde at the 1977 Bayreuth Festival, in The Ring conducted by Pierre Boulez; sang at the Bavarian State Opera from 1977, notably as Erda and Waltraute in The Ring, 1978; Lieder and Oratorio concerts from 1981, at Munich and elsewhere; Schmidt's Das Buch mit Sieben Siegeln, Salzburg, 1981; Cornelia in Giulio Cesare at the 1993 Schwetzingen Festival; Brangaene in Tristan at Hamburg, 1996; sang Erda in Das Rheingold for Cologne Opera, and Amelfa in The Golden Cockerel at Bregenz, 2000; Wagner's Mary at Trieste 2001; further concerts include Schubert's Lazarus, Vier Ernste Gesänge by Brahms and the Verdi Requiem. *Recordings include:* Mozart's Apollo et Hyacinthus. *Current Management:* c/o Peter Seyfferth Artists Management, Avenue de la Concorde 385, 06190 Roquebrune, Cap Martin, France; c/o Opera Vladarski, Döblinger Hauptstrasse 57/18, 1190 Vienna, Austria. *Telephone:* 4-93-35-01-05 (Seyfferth); (1) 368-6960/6961 (Vladarski). *Fax:* 4-93-35-02-17 (Seyfferth); (1) 368-6962 (Vladarski). *E-mail:* peter@seyfferth.de; opera.vladarski@utanet.at. *Website:* www.seyfferth.de.

WULSTAN, David, BSc, MA, ARCM; British academic; *Research Professor, Department of European Languages, University of Wales, Aberystwyth*; b. 18 Jan. 1937, Birmingham, England; s. of the Rev. Norman Jones and Margaret Jones; m. Susan Nelson Graham 1967; one s. *Education:* Coll. of Technology, Birmingham, Magdalen Coll., Oxford. *Career:* Founder and Dir, The Clerkes of Oxenford 1961–; numerous appearances on BBC TV and Radio 3, Thames TV, NWDR, BRT and at Cheltenham, York, Bologna, Holland and Flanders Festivals, Proms and in various films; Visiting Prof., Univ. of California, Berkeley 1977; Prof. of Music, Univ. Coll., Cork 1980; Prof. of Music, Univ. of Wales, Aberystwyth 1983–90, Research Prof. 1991–; Consulting Ed., Spanish Academic Press; mem. of Council, Plainsong and Medieval Music Soc.; mem. Royal Soc. of Musicians, Soc. for OT Studies. *Compositions:* various Christmas carols, hymns, chants and film music. *Recordings include:* Tallis, Sheppard, Gibbons: Church Music, Play of Daniel, Robert White. *Publications include:* Early English Church Music, vol. 3 1964, vol. 27 1979, Anthology of Carols 1968, Anthology of English Church Music 1971, Play of Daniel 1976, Coverdale Chant Book 1978, Sheppard: Complete Works 1979–, Tudor Music 1984, The Emperor's Old Clothes 2001, The Poetic and Musical Legacy of Heloise and Abelard 2003, Music from the Paraclete 2004, The Canterbury Dictionary of Hymnology 2005, Three Haworth Hymns 2005, St Peter's Chantbook 2012, St Bernard and the Cistercian Antiphoner 2012, Listen Again: A New History of Music 2015; contrib. to Journal of Theological Studies, Journal of the American Oriental Society, Music and Letters, Galpin Society Journal, Musical Times Iraq, Early Music, English Historical Review, Plainsong and Medieval Music, Cantigueiros, Al-Masāq, Faith & Worship, Mapping the Medieval Mediterranean, Liber Amicorum Gerardo Huseby, Journal of Strategic Studies. *Honours:* Hon. Fellow, St Peter's Coll., Oxford 2006. *Address:* Hillview Croft, Lon Tyllwyd, Llanfarian, Aberystwyth, Cardiganshire, SY23 4UH, Wales (home).

WUORINEN, Charles, BA, MA; American composer and academic; b. 9 June 1938, New York, NY; m. Howard Stokar. *Education:* Columbia Univ., New York. *Career:* co-f. Group for Contemporary Music 1962; teacher, Columbia Univ. 1964–71; Prof. of Music, Rutgers Univ. 1984–; Visiting Prof., New York Univ. 1990, State Univ. of NY at Buffalo 1989–94; Composer-in-Residence, San Francisco Symphony 1985–89, also New Music Advisor to Music Dir Herbert Blomstedt; mem. American Acad. of Arts and Letters, American Acad. of Arts and Sciences, American Acad. in Rome 1990. *Compositions include:* stage: The Politics of Harmony 1968, The W. of Babylon; opera: Haroun and the Sea of Stories 2001, Brokeback Mountain 2012; orchestral: Music for orchestra 1956, Orchestral and Electronic Exchanges 1965, four Piano Concertos 1966, 1975, 1984, 2003, Contrafactum 1969, Grand Bamboula 1971, Concerto for Amplified Violin and Orchestra 1972, A Reliquary for Igor Stravinsky 1975, Tashi 1976, Percussion Symphony 1976, Two-Part Symphony 1978, Crossfire 1984, Bamboula Squared 1984, Movers and Shakers 1984, Rhapsody for violin and orchestra 1984, The Golden Dance 1986, Bamboula Beach 1986, Five (concerto) for Amplified Cello and Orchestra 1987, The Mission of Virgil 1993, Concerto for Saxophone Quartet and Orchestra 1993, The River of Light 1995–96, The Great Procession 1995, Symphony Seven 1997, Theologoumenon 2005, Eighth Symphony (Theologoumena) 2006, Synaxis 2007, Time Regained 2008; chamber music: four String Quartets 1971, 1979, 1987, 2000, Chamber Concerto for Cello 1963, Chamber Concerto for Flute 1964, Janissary Music 1966, Duo for violin and piano 1967, String Trio 1968, Ringing Changes 1970, three sets of Cello Variations 1970, 1975, 1997, On Alligators 1972, Speculum Speculi 1972, Arabia Felix 1973, Hyperion 1975, Fortune 1975, Fast Fantasy 1977, The Winds 1977, Archaeopteryx 1978, New York Notes 1981, Horn Trios 1981, 1985, Spinoff 1983, Piano Trio 1983, Trombone Trio 1985, Sonata for violin and piano 1988, String Sextet 1989, Percussion Quartet 1994, two Piano Quintets 1994, 2008, Sonata for guitar and piano 1995, Cyclops 2000, Duo Sonata 2004, Spin 5 2006, Iridule 2006, Viola Variations 2008, Trio for flute, bass clarinet and piano 2008, Metagong 2008; vocal music: Genesis 1989, The Celestial Sphere (oratorio) 1980, Mass 1982, A Winter's Tale 1991, Fenton Songs 1997, 2002, Ashberyana 2004, It Happens Like This 2010, 2010 Alphabetical Ashbery 2013; piano and organ music; keyboard works: four Sonatas 1969, 1976, 1986, 2007, The Blue Bamboula 1980, Scherzo 2007, Oros 2009, Adagio 2011; electronic: Time's Encomium 1970. *Honours:* Joseph Bearns Prize 1958 and Letters Award 1967, Guggenheim Fellowship 1968–72, Pulitzer Prize (for Time's Encomium) 1970, Rockefeller Foundation Fellowship 1979, 1981, 1982, American Acad. of Arts and Letters Prize 1985, American Acad. of Arts and Sciences Prize, MacArthur Foundation Fellowship 1986–91. *Current Management:* c/o Howard Stokar Management, 870 West End Avenue, New York, NY 10025, USA. *Telephone:* (212) 866-5798. *E-mail:* hstokar@stokar.com. *Website:* www.stokar.com; www.charleswuorinen.com.

WÜTHRICH, Hans; Swiss composer; b. 3 Aug. 1937, Aeschi; m. Beatrice Mathez 1977, one d. *Education:* Conservatory of Music, Berne, Acad. of Music with Klaus Huber, Univ. of Zürich. *Career:* Lecturer in Linguistics, Zürich Univ. 1971–85; Teacher, Winterhur Conservatory 1985–; performances of compositions in Donaueschingen 1978, 1985, at ISCM World Music Festival, Bonn 1977 and at Athens 1979. *Compositions:* Kommunikationsspiele 1973, Das Glashaus 1974–75, Netz-Werke I, II 1983–85, Annäherungen an Gegenwart 1986–87, Procuste Deux Etoiles 1980–81, Supplement: Netz-Werk III 1987–89, Chopin im TGV Basel-Paris 1989, Wörter Bilder Dinge 1990–91, Leve 1992, Ah! Vous voila! 1994, Happy Hour 1995–97.

WUYTS, Christiane J. J.; Belgian harpsichordist; b. 16 July 1938, Antwerp; d. of Jacques Crèvecoeur and Irene Crèvecoeur; m. Alfons H. Wuyts 1960; one s. one d. *Education:* music studies with Ahlgrim. *Career:* began with piano recitals aged ten; began playing concertos with orchestras aged 12; recitals and concerts on organ and harpsichord in Europe 1965–81; various solo recordings 1970–; currently Prof. in Harpsichord, specialising in Baroque music. *Recordings:* Works of J. H. Fiocco 1988, 22 Works of J. S. Bach 1989, Baroque Music of the Low Countries 1990, J.S. Bach: Complete Sonatas for Flute 2003. *Honours:* Croix de Chevalier, Ordre Léopold II 1989. *Address:* Irisstreet 14, 2850 Boom, Belgium. *Telephone:* (3) 888-22-99; 47-8494276 (mobile). *E-mail:* alfons.wuyts@telenet.be (home).

WYN-DAVIES, Catrin; British singer (soprano); b. 1969, England. *Education:* Guildhall School of Music. *Career:* roles with Welsh National Opera (1994–96) have included Mozart's Ilia, Zerlina and Susanna, and Anne Trulove in The Rake's Progress; Season 1996–97 with Gilda for WNO, First Flower Maiden in Parsifal at the Paris Châtelet and Handel's Acis and Galatea with the English Concert; Concerts have included Soprano Solo in Schoenberg's Moses und Aron with the Philharmonia (1996), Handel's Orlando, Elijah with David Willcocks and Bach's Christmas Oratorio with René Jacobs on tour to Europe; Wigmore Hall debut recital 1994; Further opera roles include Kristine in The Makropulos Case and Monteverdi's Poppea (for WNO), 1998; Leader of the Flower Maidens in Parsifal at the Festival Hall, 1998; Engaged for the Beggar's Opera at Strasbourg; Sang Ginevra in Ariodante for ENO, London, 2002; Engaged as Jenůfa for WNO, 2003. *Recordings include:* Sacred music by Vivaldi with the King's Consort; Weill's Der Silbersee under Marcus Stenz; Beethoven Folk Songs, with Malcolm Martineau. *Honours:* Kathleen Ferrier Decca Award 1994.

WYN-ROGERS, Catherine; British singer (contralto); b. 1958. *Education:* Royal Coll. of Music with Meriel St Clair, studied later with Ellis Keeler and Diane Forlano. *Career:* regular concerts with the Bach Choir under David Willcocks in London and abroad; frequent appearances with the UK's major orchestras; tours with English Concert and Trevor Pinnock including Messiah in Germany and Vivaldi's Gloria in Rome for TV/Deutsche Grammophon recording; appearances at the Proms with The Sixteen, Nat. Youth Orchestra and English Concert Opera including Il Ritorno d'Ulisse for ENO and Stuttgart, Maddalena in Rigoletto in Nantes, La Gioconda for Opera North, Die Zauberflöte for ROH and Salzburg Festival; sang First Norn in Götterdämmerung at Covent Garden 1995; sang in Palestrina and Pfitzner recital at Covent Garden 1997; Mary Magdalene in The Kingdom by Elgar, London Prom Concerts 1999; Bach's Magnificat with The Sixteen 2000; season 2000–01 in the St John Passion and as La Cieca in La Gioconda for ENO, Adelaide in Arabella at Munich and Hero in Béatrice et Bénédict for WNO; Dvořák's Stabat mater, London Proms 2002; title role in Phèdre, Bordeaux 2008; Waltraute in Götterdämmerung, Valencia and Florence 2009; 2011 appearances included Auntie in Peter Grimes for Royal Opera House (also La Scala 2012) and Filipyevna in Eugene Onegin for ENO. *Recordings include:* Vaughan Williams's Serenade To Music and Magnificat with Matthew Best; Teixera Te Deum and Bach's Christmas Oratorio with the Sixteen; Elgar's Dream of Gerontius with Vernon Handley and the Royal Liverpool Philharmonic, Handel's Messiah and Christians Awake 2011, Britten: Peter Grimes (BBC Music Magazine Opera Award 2014). *Honours:* Coll. Song Recital Prize, Dame Clara Butt Award, Countess of Munster Trust grant, RCM.

WYNER, Susan Davenny; American singer (soprano); b. 17 Oct. 1945, New Haven, CT. *Education:* Cornell Univ., studied with Herta Glaz. *Career:* debut Carnegie Hall recital 1972; Alice Tully Hall recital 1973; orchestral debut with the Boston Symphony 1974; engagements with all leading orchestras in USA and Canada and with Israel Philharmonic and London Symphony; repertoire includes baroque and contemporary works; operatic debut as Monteverdi's Poppea, New York City Opera 1977; Metropolitan Opera 1982 as Woglinde in Das Rheingold; has sung in the premieres of Del Tredici's Adventures Underground 1975 and Carter's A Mirror On Which To Dwell 1965, and in the premieres of Memorial Music and Fragments from Antiquity by Yehudi Wyner; also sings works by Rochberg (Quartet No. 2) and Reimann (Inane).

WYNER, Yehudi, BMus, MA, MMus; American composer, pianist and conductor; *Professor Emeritus of Composition, Brandeis University*; b. 1 June 1929, Calgary, Alberta, Canada; m. 1st Nancy Joan Braverman 1951 (divorced 1967); two s. one d.; m. 2nd Susan Davenny Wyner 1967. *Education:* Juilliard School, Yale Univ. with Paul Hindemith, Harvard Univ. with Walter Piston. *Career:* American Acad. in Rome 1953–56; performed and recorded contemporary music in New York; directed the Turnau Opera; Prof., Yale School of Music from 1963, Chair. of Composition 1969–73; Music Dir, New Haven Opera Soc.; keyboard player with the Bach Aria Group 1968–; Tanglewood Music Center 1975–; Prof. of Music, State Univ. of New York, Purchase 1978, Dean of Music 1978–82; Visiting Prof., Brandeis Univ. 1988, Cornell Univ. 1989, Harvard Univ. 1991–93, 1996–98, 2003–04, 2008–09; Prof. of Composition, Brandeis Univ. 1990–2005, Prof. Emer. 2005–; mem. American Composers' Alliance, American Music Center, American Acad. of Arts and Letters, American Acad. of Arts and Sciences. *Compositions include:* Partita for piano 1952, Piano Sonata 1954, Concert Duo for violin and piano 1955–57, Serenade for seven instruments 1958, Passover Offering for mixed ensemble 1959, Three Informal Pieces for violin and piano 1961, Friday Evening Service 1963, Torah Service 1966, Cadenza for clarinet and harpsichord 1969, Memorial Music for soprano and three flutes 1971–73, Intermedio for soprano and strings 1974, Dances of Atonement for violin and piano 1976, Fragments from Antiquity for soprano and orchestra 1978–81, Romances for piano quartet 1980, On This Most Voluptuous Night for soprano and seven instruments 1982, String Quartet 1985, Toward the Center for piano 1988, Il Cane Minore for two clarinets and bassoon 1992, Concerto for cello and orchestra 1994, Lyric Harmony for orchestra 1995, Epilogue for orchestra 1996, A Mad Tea Party for soprano, two baritones and ensemble 1996, Horn Trio 1997, The Second Madrigal for soprano, string quartet, wind quintet and percussion 1999, Oboe Quartet 1999, Tuscan Triptych for string orchestra 2002, Commedia for clarinet and piano 2002, Piano Concerto 2004, Piano Concerto 'Chiavi in Mano' (Pulitzer Prize in Music 2006) 2005, TRIO 2009 for clarinet, cello and piano, Fantasy on B.A.C.H. for piano 2010, Give Thanks for All Things for chorus, orchestra and soloists 2010. *Honours:* Rome Prize fellow 1953–56, Univ. of Calif. Alfred E. Hertz fellow 1953–54, Guggenheim fellow 1960, 1977, Inst. of Arts and Letters grant 1961, NEA grantee 1976, Rockefeller Foundation fellow, Bellagio 1998, Lincoln Center Elise Stoeger Prize 1998;Atlantic Center for the Arts Master Composer 2005. *Address:* c/o Associated Music Publishers, 257 Park Avenue S, New York, NY 10023 (office); 49 Brooks Street, Medford, MA 02155, USA (home). *Telephone:* (781) 396-3385. *Website:* www.schirmer.com/composers/wyner/.

WYSOCKI, Zdzislaw, MA; Austrian (b. Polish) composer; b. 18 July 1944, Poznań, Poland; m.; one s. one d. *Education:* Music School, Poznań, Music High School Poznań, Univ. of Music, Poznań, Univ. of Music, Vienna, Austria. *Career:* debut, Poznań 1963; performances in Austria, Poland, Germany, France, the UK, Italy, Denmark, Spain, Portugal, Hungary, Romania, Ukraine, Slovakia, fmr Yugoslavia, Soviet Union and Russia, USA, Canada, Brazil, China, Japan; festivals in Germany, Brazil, Slovakia, Austria, Hungary, Italy, Portugal, Poland; world premieres include Double Concerto with Berkeley Symphony Orchestra under Kent Nagano 2002, Concerto

Doppio with Ensemble Wiener Collage/René Staar, Salzburg Festival 2003; radio broadcasts in Poland, Austria, Germany, Japan, USA, France, Denmark, and television appearances in Poland. *Compositions include:* Missa in honorem Ioannis Pauli secundi op.30, Fantasia op. 33, Quasi concerto grosso op. 36, Quartetto op. 46 1990, Movimento Saxophonquartet op. 47 1991, Quasi Divertimento op. 49 1993, Trio op. 51, De finibus temporum op. 52 1994, Etudes for chamber ensemble op. 54, 56, 60 1995–2001, Gespräch mit einem guten Menschen (opera) 1992, Musica de la passione for strings 1999, Etudes op. 65 2001–06, Double Concerto op. 63 2002, In Memoriam op. 66 2002, Concerto Doppio op. 67 2003, Etudes op. 69 2007– (work in progress), Violoncello Concerto op. 71 2010, 2 Bagatellen op. 73 for brass orchestra and percussion (world premiere Sommerakademie der Wiener Philharmoniker, Salzburg) 2011. *Recordings:* Austrian contemporary music, works of Z. Wysocki op. 46, 49, 51, 52, Ensemble Wiener Collage, Klang debuts Ensemble Graz, St Petersburg, Etudes op. 54/7,9, guitar recital performed by Leo Witoszynskyj, Due Caratteri op. 29, Violoncellomusik des 20 Jahrhunderts performances by Adalbert Skocic, Walter Delahunt, Fantasia op. 33. *Publications:* Quartetto op. 46, Quasi Divertimento op. 49, Movimento Saxophonquartet op. 47, Etudes op. 54 (nos. 1–12), op. 56 (nos. 1, 3, 5, 6, 9, 10, 17), op. 60 (nos. 1, 2, 8–14, 20–23), op. 65 (no. 1), Double Concerto op. 63, In Memoriam op. 66, Concerto Doppio op. 67 (eds: Edition Contemp Art (Verlagsgruppe Hermann), Ensemble Wiener Collage, Apoll-Edition), 2 Bagatellen op. 73 for brass orchestra and percussion 2011. *Honours:* Ordre du Merite en Faveur de la Culture Polonaise 1984; Award of Distinction, Competition for Piano Composition, Poland 1968, Theodor Körner Prize 1977, City of Vienna Recognition Prize 1977, Adolf Schärf Fund Z Prize for Artistic Merit 1984, first prize Int. Competition for Choir Composition, Vienna 1988. *Address:* Pfarrgasse 34-44/16/7, 1230 Vienna, Austria (home). *Telephone:* (1) 6153024 (home). *Fax:* (1) 6153024 (home). *E-mail:* office@hermann.co.at (editor) (office); zdzislaw.wysocki@aon.at (home).

WYZNER, Franz; singer (bass); b. 1932, Vienna, Austria. *Education:* studied in Vienna. *Career:* sang at the Landestheater in Salzburg 1958–59, Gelsenkirchen 1959–64, Wuppertal 1964–85, notably in the German premiere of Crime and Punishment by Petrovic 1971, and the first performance of The Gamblers by Shostakovich in the arrangement by K. Meyer 1986; guest appearances at the Schwetzingen Festival 1970, Vienna Volksoper in the Austrian premiere of The Burning Fiery Furnace by Britten 1977, Salzburg Festival in Dantons Tod 1983, Buenos Aires as Alberich 1983, and Cologne 1985; other roles have included Mozart's Leporello, Figaro, Papageno and Alfonso, Kaspar in Der Freischütz, Don Magnifico, Mephistopheles, the Doctor in Wozzeck, and Kecal in The Bartered Bride. *Recordings include:* Dantons Tod, Orfeo.

X

XANTHOUDAKIS, Elena, BMus (Hons), Grad Dip Opera, Master of Music Performance, MMus; Greek/Australian singer (soprano); b. 4 Dec. . *Education:* Victorian Coll. of Arts, Australia, Univ. of Melbourne, Guildhall School of Music, London. *Career:* operatic roles include Lucia di Lammermoor (Opera de Québec), Adina L'elisir d'amore (Scottish Opera and Victorian Opera, Melbourne), Blonde in Abduction from the Seraglio (Opera North), Pamina in The Magic Flute (ENO), both Euridice & Genio in L'anima del Filosofo (Pinchgut Opera, Sydney), Krista in The Makropulos Case (ENO Opera), La Contessa di Folleville in Il viaggio a Rheims (Maggio Musicale, Florence), Jemmy in Guillaume Tell (Accad. di Santa Cecilia, BBC Proms), Clorinda in La Cenerentola (Royal Opera House—ROH, Covent Garden, Glyndebourne), Frasquita in Carmen (ROH 2005–06, 2007–08, 2009–10 and ENO), Miss Schlesen in Satyagraha (ENO) 2007, 2010, Xenia Boris in Godunoff (Opera Nat. du Rhin), Lady Ella in Patience (BBC Proms), Pamina (ENO et al.), Gilda (Opera Queensland) and Leila in The Pearl Fishers, Anne Truelove in The Rake's Progress in Australia; other roles: Amor in Orfeo ed Euridice (Gluck/J.C. Bach), Matilde in Matilde di Shabran, Dido in Dido & Aeneas, Iris in Semele, Ismene in Mitridate, Constance in Carmelites and Dalinda in Ariodante, Micaela in Carmen, Comtesse Adele in Comte Ory; concert engagements include Beethoven's 9th Symphony, Rossini's Petite Messe Solennelle (Montreal) and Stabat Mater, Bach's Missa Brevis, B Minor Mass, St John Passion, St Matthew Passion, Christmas Oratorio and several cantatas, Fauré Requiem, Handel Messiah and Jeptha, Mozart Requiem and Vivaldi and Poulenc's Gloria, a touring programme of Mozart arias with Melbourne Symphony Orchestra, Mozart's Exsultate Jubilate with St Petersburg Camerata and performing Mozart concert arias at Salzburg's Mozart Woche; has performed with orchestras including Scottish Chamber Orchestra, Royal Scottish Nat. Orchestra, Melbourne Symphony Orchestra, Orchestra Victoria, Sydney Symphony Orchestra, Tasmanian Symphony Orchestra, Montreal Symphonic, Orchestra de Quebec, Oxford Philomusica, Philharmonia Orchesta, London, Krakow and Poznań Filharmonia Orchestras, Mozarteum Orchestra, BBC Concert Orchestra, Orchestra of the Age of the Enlightenment and Accad. di Santa Cecilia, Rome; concert and recital performances in Japan, Hong-Kong, St Petersburg, Montreal, and Quebec City, in Germany, USA and throughout Australia, UK Ireland and Italy. *Film:* Frasquita Carmen (Royal Opera House) (DVD, 3D and Real D cinema). *Recordings include:* Krista The Makropulos Case (ENO), Mendelssohn's Lobgesang (Tasmanian Symphony Orchestra), Jemmy Guillaume Tell (Accademia di Santa Cecilia), Euridice & Genio, L'anima del filosofo, Trio KROMA – The Shepherd and the Mermaid, German Romantic Music for Piano, Voice and Clarinet, Jewels of the Bel Canto 2014. *Honours:* more than 80 first prizes in competitions and Eisteddfodau in Australia and internationally; has won the Maria Callas Int. Grand Prix (Oratorio – Lied), Athens 2003, Int. Mozart Competition, Salzburg 2006, female First Prize and Overall Grand Prize, Int. Adam Didur Opera Singers Competition; other major prizes include Winner, Australian Nat. Liederfest 2004, Third Prize and Best Interpretation of the set composition, Montreal Jeunesse Musicales (Voice) 2005, Tait Vocal Prize, Performing Australian Music Competition, London 2008, Third Prize, Operalia 2008, Solti Foundation Award 2008, Borletti-Buitoni Trust Grant. *Current Management:* c/o Deborah Sanders, Rayfield Allied, Southbank House, Black Prince Road, London, SE1 7S, England; c/o John Miller, Pinnacle Arts Management, 889 Ninth Avenue, 2nd Floor, New York, NY 10019, USA. *Telephone:* (212) 397-7915 (London); (20) 3176-5500 (New York). *Fax:* (700) 602-4143 (London); (212) 397-7920 (New York). *E-mail:* deborah.sanders@rayfieldallied.com. *Website:* www.rayfieldallied.com; www.pinnaclearts.com. *E-mail:* elenaxan@gmail.com (office). *Website:* www.elenaxan.com; www.triokroma.com.

XIA, Liping; Chinese composer and music educator; b. Feb. 1935, China; m. 1963; three s. *Education:* Music Inst. of China. *Career:* Music Ed., radio station of Hainan, China; leader, music group at radio station, Guangdong, China for 21 years; Music Prof., Hainan Normal Inst. and Guangdong Univ. of Foreign Studies for 20 years; MA Adviser in Music Education, Jiao Tong Univ. of Shanghai 1993–2004. *Compositions:* Song of Spring Ploughing 1965, Song of Rubber Forest 1981, Joy Over a Bumper Harvest 1989, Having Classes 1993, Dance Music in Praise of Youth 1993. *Recordings:* The Pass to South Guangdong (third part of the music programme series, Along Today's Long March) 1986. *Publications:* Appreciation of Chinese Classical Music 1993, Appreciation and Analysis of Ancient Chinese Melodies 1993, A Music Course for College Students 1999. *Address:* 388-5 Dong-Hua Doag Road, Rm# 703, Guangzhou (office); Room 19D, No. 3 Yong Sheng Shang Sha, Donghu Road, Guangzhou, Guangdong Province, 510100, People's Republic of China (home).

XIONG, Jihua; Chinese academic; b. 24 Feb. 1932, Beijing; m. Cai Rengi 1953; two d. *Education:* Chengdu Arts School, studied conducting with Russian and German teachers. *Career:* debut conducting Shanghai Symphony Orchestra, 1958; debuted several new works including Recollection of the past on the Grassland (Gao Weijie, Tang Qingshi) and Symphonic Suite (Zou Lu) and Symphonic Poem, Chant of the River (Li Zhongyong); conducted various master works, including Bruch, Violin Concerto No. 1 in G minor; Chopin, Piano Concerto No. 1 in E Minor; Rachmaninov, Piano Concerto No. 2 in C minor, Beethoven, Symphony No. 3 (Eroica) and Symphony No. 5 (Fate); Dvořák, Symphony No. 9 New World; Tchaikovsky Symphony Pathétique; Rimsky-Korsakoff, Symphony Suite Scheherezade; conducted orchestras for numerous films and plays; conducted 200 dance theatres; conducted several broadcast symphony concerts; invited participant, 20th Century Classical Music Works Chinese Composers; conducted all the major Chinese orchestras. *Compositions:* Wan Xi Sha (symphony) 1962, Die Lian Hua (orchestra piece) 1964, A Stormy October (film music) 1979, Mystic Giant Buddha (film music) 1981, The Soul of Hua Xia (series of TV plays) 1984, Welcoming the New Year (solo works for pipa), Morning Song (solo for violin), Pour Out One's Heart (piano solo). *Recordings:* Recollections of the Past on Grassland. *Publications:* How to Read the Orchestra Score (article). *Address:* c/o Sichuan Conservatory of Music, 6 Xinsheng Road, Chengdu, Sichuan 610021, People's Republic of China.

Y

YAHR, Carol; American singer (mezzo-soprano); b. 1959. *Career:* sang at the Cologne Opera 1987, as Venus in Tannhäuser, Théâtre des Champs-Elysées 1988, as Fricka in The Ring; Nice Opéra 1988–89, as Geneviéve in Pelléas and Dido in Les Troyens; Seattle 1989, as Wagner's Eva, Leonore at Innsbruck 1990, and with Glyndebourne Tour; Scottish Opera and Innsbruck 1991, as Sieglinde and Elisabeth; sang the Walküre Brünnhilde at Wiesbaden 1993; sang Brünnhilde in The Ring for Norwegian Opera 1996; sang Isolde for Hawaiian Opera 2000. *Current Management:* c/o Zemsky/Green Artists Management, 730 Fifth Avenue, Suite 1802, New York, NY 10019, USA. *Telephone:* (212) 300-8003. *Fax:* (212) 300-8001. *E-mail:* zgartists@aol.com. *Website:* www.zemskygreen.com.

YAKAR, Rachel; French singer (soprano); b. 3 March 1938, Lyon. *Education:* Paris Conservatoire, studied with Germaine Lubin. *Career:* sang with Deutsche Oper am Rhein, Düsseldorf from 1964 in roles, including Antonia in Les Contes d'Hoffmann; sang at Aix-en-Provence 1966 in Ariadne auf Naxos, Strasbourg Opera 1967 in a new production of Der Junge Lord by Henze, Amsterdam 1968–69 as Cleopatra in Giulio Cesare and as Marguerite, at Düsseldorf 1969, and Paris Opéra 1970 as Gilda and Micaela; baroque repertoire from 1971 includes Deidamia by Handel; Munich Festival in 1974 as Donna Elvira, Bayreuth Festival 1976 as Freia and Gerhilde in Patrice Chéreau's centenary production of Der Ring des Nibelungen, Glyndebourne Festival, 1977, 1980 as Donna Elvira and the Marschallin, Strasbourg and Düsseldorf 1978 as Mélisande; sang Cycle of operas by Monteverdi at Zürich 1978; Geneva Opera 1981 as Janáček's Jenůfa; guest appearances in San Francisco, East Berlin, Edinburgh, Lausanne, Monte Carlo and Santiago; other roles include Mozart's Ilia and Fiordigili; sang Madame Lidoine in Dialogues des Carmélites at Lyon, 1990; Climène in Lully's Phaëton at Lyon, 1993. *Recordings include:* Rameau's Les Indes Galantes, and Pygmalion; Idomeneo; Monteverdi's Orfeo; Dido and Aeneas; Bach B minor Mass; Lully's Armide; Schütz's Christmas Story and Magnificat; Fux's and Scarlatti's Baroque Cantatas; Die Zauberflöte, from the Salzburg Festival conducted by James Levine.

YAMADA, Kazuki; Japanese conductor; *Residential Conductor, Tokyo Philharmonic Chorus*; b. 1979, Kanagawa. *Education:* Tokyo Nat. Univ. of Fine Arts and Music, with Ken-ichiro Kobayashi and Yoko Matsuo. *Career:* formed Yokohama Sinfonietta at college, conducted all nine Beethoven symphonies at age 22, music director 2000–; Residential Conductor, Tokyo Philharmonic Chorus; London debut with BBC Symphony Orchestra, Barbican Hall 2011, also Paris and Berlin debuts with Orchestre de Paris and Rundfunk Sinfonieorchester; guest conducting appearances include Japan Philharmonic Orchestra, Tokyo Symphony Orchestra, Kanagawa Philharmonic Orchestra, Nagoya Philharmonic Orchestra, Orchestra Ensemble Kanazawa, Hiroshima Symphony Orchestra and Sendai Philharmonic Orchestra, Saito-Kinen Orchestra, Ensemble Orchestral Kanazawa, Orchestre de la Suisse Romande; worked with conductors Seiji Ozawa and Charles Dutoit, and soloists including Nicolas Altstaedt, Isabelle Faust, Francesco Piemontesi, Vadim Repin, Jean-Yves Thibaudet and Tamas Varga. *Honours:* Grand Prize and Audience Award, Besançon Int. Young Conductors Competition 2009. *Current Management:* c/o Konzertdirektion Schmid, Postfach 34 09, 30034 Hannover, Germany; KDS UK Ltd, 40 St Martin's Lane, London, WC2N 4ER, England. *Telephone:* (511) 366076027 (Germany); (20) 7395-0910. *Fax:* (511) 3660734 (Germany); (20) 7395-0911. *E-mail:* mail@kdschmid.de; mail@kdschmid.co.uk. *Website:* www.kdschmid.de/en/Kuenstler/Yamada .php.

YAMASHITA, Kazuhito; Japanese guitarist; b. 25 March 1961, Nagasaki; s. of Toru Yamashita. *Education:* Nagasaki Guitar Acad., studied with Kojiro Kobune, J. Thomas, Narciso Yepes, Andres Segovia, Toru Takemitsu. *Career:* debut recitals in Tokyo 1978, Paris 1979; concert at the Toronto Guitar Festival with his guitar transcription of Mussorgsky's Pictures at an Exhibition 1984; transcribed and performed Stravinsky's Firebird Suite, Dvořák's 'New World' Symphony for solo guitar, and Beethoven's Violin Concerto for guitar and orchestra; duo tour of USA with James Galway 1987; mem., Nagasaki Guitar Ensemble; 'The World of Kazuhito Yamashita' recital series, Casals Theatre, Tokyo 1989, 1994, 1999. *Compositions include:* Imaginary Forest for solo guitar 1982. *Recordings:* transcriptions of Mussorgsky's Pictures at an Exhibition, Stravinsky's Firebird Suite, Dvořák's 'New World' Symphony, J. S. Bach's Sonatas, Partitas and Suites for unaccompanied flute, violin, cello and lute, the complete works of Fernando Sor, Giuliani and Ponce. *Honours:* winner Kyushu Guitar Competition 1972, All-Japan Guitar Competition 1976, Ramirez competition, Spain 1977, Alessandria competition, Italy 1977, Concours International de Guitare, Paris 1977, Nat. Arts Festival Grand Prize 1999.

YANAGIDA, Takayoshi; Japanese composer; *Professor of Music, Bunkyo University;* b. 27 March 1948, Sapporo, Hokkaido; m. Keiko Tsuhako 1973; one s. one d. *Education:* Musashino Music Coll. and Grad. School, Hochschule für Musik und Theater, Munich, Germany. *Career:* debut at Iino Hall, Tokyo 1969; Prof. of Music, Bunkyo Univ.; composer of music for NHK educational programme; Pres. Japan Soc. of Electronic Keyboard Music; mem. Japan Soc. for Contemporary Music, Japan Fed. of Composers. *Exhibitions include:* Orchestra Project '93, Orchestra Project 2010, Orchestra Project 2014.

Compositions include: Mixed Chorus Suite, Kitano-kawa, MCS Pony of Stars, Seen in the Twilight for flute, violin and piano, Memory of Time for orchestra, Lydian Portrait for violin and orchestra, From beyond the Aurora Borealis for orchestra, Viola concerto a grace of Harmonia. *Radio:* English conversation on NHK. *Recordings:* Concert Tableau for wind orchestra, Johi-haku-un, Portrait of the West Wind. *Publication:* Works Vol. 1 (orchestral works), Lydian Portrait (orchestra works). *Honours:* First Prize, 38th Japan Music Competition, Composition Div., Third Prize, F. Ticheli Composition Contest, New York. *Address:* 7-23-13, Higashi-urawa, Midori-ku, Saitama-shi 336-0926, Japan (home). *Telephone:* (48) 873-3014 (home). *Fax:* (48) 873-3048 (home). *E-mail:* yanagida-t@jcom.home.ne.jp.

YANAGITA, Masako, DipArt; Japanese violinist; b. 30 March 1944, Tokyo; m. Abba Bogin. *Education:* Mannes Coll. of Music, New York, USA, studied with Eijin Tanaka, Louis Graeler, William Kroll. *Career:* debut in Tokyo 1966; concert appearances throughout USA, Europe, Near and Far East; soloist, orchestras in Japan, the UK, Germany, Philippines, USA; First Violinist, toured with Vieuxtemps String Quartet; faculty mem., Mannes Coll. of Music. *Recordings include:* complete Schubert violin and piano repertoire (with Abba Bogin, pianist). *Honours:* Berkshire Music Center Silverstein Prize, USA 1966, Carl Flesch Competition, London, England 1968, Paganini Competition, Genoa, Italy 1968, Munich Int. Competition 1969.

YANG, Guang; Chinese singer (mezzo-soprano); b. 1970, Peking. *Education:* Central Conservatory, Peking. *Career:* concerts at Carnegie Hall, New York, Bournemouth, London, Newcastle and Stockholm; Verdi Requiem at the Wales National Eisteddfod; Philharmonic Orchestra at Symphony Hall, Birmingham, 1999; opera roles include Rossini's Rosina (WNO 1999) and Mozart's Dorabella; celebrity recital at the 1999 International Eisteddfod. *Honours:* winner, 1997 Cardiff Singer of the World Competition. *Current Management:* Harlequin Agency Ltd, 203 Fidlas Road, Cardiff CF4 5NA, Wales.

YANG, Liqing, BA, MA, DipMus; Chinese composer; b. 30 April 1942, Sichuan; m. (divorced); one d. *Education:* Shenyang Conservatory, Shanghai Conservatory, Musikhochschule, Hannover, Germany. *Career:* debut with violin concerto, White Hair Girls, Shenyang Conservatory of Music, 1970; 24th Tage der Neuen Musik Hannover, poems from Tang Dynasty, Germany, 1982; Musique en Scene, France, 1997; Glocke Musikhall, Bremen, Germany, 1998; 17th Asian Art Festival, Hong Kong, 1997. *Compositions:* Grievances at Wujiang 1986, Festive Overture 1987, Prelude, Interlude and Postlude 1991, Elegy 1991, 1998. *Recordings include:* Yang Liqing's Orchestral Works. *Publications:* The Composition Techniques of Olivier Messiaen 1989, Style Evolution in Orchestration 1986–87, On Postmodernism in Contemporary Western Music 1994, Contemporary Instrumentation Techniques 2001. *Address:* 1855 Tianshan Road, Apt. 1710#, Shanghai 200051, People's Republic of China.

YANG, Simon; South Korean singer (bass); b. 1960, Seoul. *Education:* Cologne Musikhochschule with Kurt Moll. *Career:* debut in Düsseldorf 1992, as Giorgio in I Puritani; sang at Karlsruhe Opera 1993–95, then with the Hamburg Staatsoper; roles include Mozart's Sarastro and Commendatore, King Philip in Don Carlos and Padre Guardiano in La Forza del Destino; Fasolt and Fafner in The Ring at Karlsruhe; concerts include Beethoven's Ninth, the Verdi Requiem and Schumann's Paradies und der Peri; sang Osmin in Die Entführung at Vienna Schönbrunn 1998; season 2000–01 at Hamburg as Mozart's Bartolo, Varlaam in Boris Godunov and in Donizetti's Roberto Devereux (concert). *Recordings include:* Wagner's Ring. *Honours:* winner Vienna Belvedere Competition.

YANG, Sinn; South Korean violinist; *Concertmaster, Nuremberg Philharmonic Orchestra;* b. 1982, Würzburg. *Education:* Hochschule für Musik, Wurzburg, Hochschule für Musik Lubeck. *Career:* Concertmaster, Meiningen Symphony Orchestra 2005–06; Concertmaster, Nuremberg Philharmonic Orchestra 2009–. *Recording:* Sinn Yang 2008. *Honours:* winner, Purcell Concour, first prize, Bundesverband der Deutschen Industrie (BDI) Competition. *Address:* Nuremberg Philharmonic Orchestra, Staatstheater Nürnberg, Richard-Wagner-Platz 2-10, 90443 Nürnberg, Germany (office). *Telephone:* (911) 2313524 (office). *Fax:* (911) 2313769 (office). *Website:* www .staatstheater.nuernberg.de (office).

YANG, Sung-won; South Korean cellist and academic; *Professor of Cello, Yonsei University School of Music;* b. Seoul. *Education:* Conservatoire Nat. de Musique, Paris, Indiana Univ., USA. *Career:* performed worldwide as soloist and chamber musician; solo recitals and performances in concert halls including Alice Tully Hall, Lincoln Center, New York, Salle Pleyel, Paris, Concertgebouw, Amsterdam, Opera City Hall, Tokyo, Symphony Hall, Osaka, Nat. Center for Performing Arts, Beijing and in London, Rome, Frankfurt, Madrid, Prague, Helsinki, Boston, Seattle, Tel Aviv, Shanghai and Sydney; collaborated with artists including Christoph Eschenbach, Myung Whun Chung, Yuri Bashmet, Dong-Suk Kang and Pascal Devoyon; currently Prof. of Cello, Yonsei Univ. School of Music; Artistic Dir, LG Chamber Music School; Prof.-in-Residence, RAM, London 2011–12; mem. jury, Banff Int. Chamber Music Competition, Canada, André Navarra Int. Cello Competition, France, and Cassado Int. Cello Competition, Japan. *Recordings include:* Kodály

(Gramophone Critics Choice Award 2003) 2000, Rachmaninoff/Chopin 2002, Bach Solo Cello Suites 2005, Complete Beethoven Sonatas and Variations for Piano and Cello 2007, Schubert Sonata for Arpeggione and Piano in A minor 2009, Dvořák Cello Concerto 2010, Sung-won Yang & Les Bon Becs 2011. *E-mail:* swyang@chol.com (office). *Website:* www.sungwonyang.com.

YANG, Sungsic; South Korean violinist; b. 1966. *Education:* Paris Conservatoire, studied with Yfrah Neaman at the Guildhall School of Music. *Career:* debut recital in Seoul 1977; solo appearances throughout Europe including tour with the Seoul Philharmonic; Tchaikovsky and Mendelssohn Concertos with the Moscow Philharmonic at Seoul for the Olympic Festival in 1988; Paris concerto debut with Orchestre National de France, conducted by Lorin Maazel, 1988; appearances with National Symphony Orchestra, RTE, Dublin, and Gävleborgs Symfoniorkester, Sweden, 1991; plays a Joseph Guarneri del Gesu of 1720; repertoire also includes concertos by Bach, Brahms, Bruch, Beethoven, Mozart, Prokofiev, Saint-Saëns, Sibelius and Wieniawski; solo works by Bach, sonatas by Brahms, Beethoven, Debussy, Fauré, Franck, Tartini and Ysaÿe, and Stravinsky's Suite Italienne. *Honours:* Prizewinner in Paganini Competition, Genoa, Long-Thibaud Paris, and Indianapolis, USA; 1st Prize, Carl Flesch Competition, London, 1988.

YANG, Tianjie; Chinese composer; b. 5 Sept. 1952, Changsha City, Hunan Province; m. Shuyun He 1979, one d. *Education:* Shanghai Conservatory of Music, Beijing Broadcasting College. *Career:* debut with The Legend of Mountains, orchestral music played at Beijing Music Hall, 1979; started professional composing, 1972; created more than 1,000 pieces of music, many of which have been performed in the USA, Russia, Austria, Poland, Hong Kong and elsewhere; mem. Chinese Musicians' Institute, 1990–; Manager of China International Famous Association, 1999. *Compositions:* Orchestral Music: The Carnival of the Miaos; Spring of the Yao Shan; Symphony: Linhai Cuts Firewood; Erhu Concerto: Yearning; Dance Drama: Border Town; Opera: The Remote Days. *Television music:* for the serial, Nuo Yao. *Recordings:* Border Town, 1990; The Carnival of the Miaos, 1993; Spring of Yao Shan, 1994; Children Sing Ancient Poetries, 1994. *Publications:* On Opera Music's Reforming, 1991; Chinese Theatre: A Talk on the Music Creation of Dance Drama, Border Town, 1996. *Honours:* Title of National First Degree Composer; Wenhua Award (the most prestigious art award in China), 1996; World Cultural Celebrities' Achievement Award, 1998. *Address:* The Song and Dance Theatre of Hunan, 9 Ren Min Road, Changsha City, Hunan Province 410011, People's Republic of China.

YANG, Tianwa; Chinese musician (violin) and academic; *Professor of Violin University of the Arts, Bern*; b. Beijing. *Education:* Central Conservatory of Music, Beijing as student of Lin Yaoji. *Career:* began studying violin aged four, accepted at Beijing Conservatory aged 10; moved to study in Karlsruhe; has performed with numerous orchestras including the Detroit, Seattle, Baltimore, Winnipeg, Pacific Symphonies, BBC Philharmonic, Royal Liverpool Philharmonic, Royal Philharmonic Orchestra and Slovak Philharmonic Bratislava, MDR Radio Symphony Leipzig, SWR Symphony Baden-Baden and Freiburg, German Radio Philharmonic, Bavarian State Opera Orchestra, Warsaw Philharmonic, Orchestre Philharmonique de Strasbourg, Hong Kong Philharmonic, Malaysia Philharmonic and New Zealand Symphony, with conductors including Marc Albrecht, JoAnn Falletta, Günther Herbig, Yoel Levi, Carlos Miguel Prieto, Gerard Schwarz and Vassily Sinaisky; has appeared in concert halls and festivals across Europe, Australasia and North America including Ravinia Festival, Virginia Arts Festival, Schwetzinger SWR Festival, Montpellier Festival, Lincoln Center New York, Wigmore Hall London, Salle Pleyel Paris, Philharmonic Hall Berlin and Gewandhaus Leipzig; currently Prof. of Violin, Univ. of the Arts, Bern. *Recordings include:* Paganini 24 Caprices 2004, Vivaldi/Piazzolla Eight Seasons, Sarasate complete works for violin (4 vols) 2006–14, Wolfgang Rihm complete works for violin and piano 2012, Mendelssohn violin concertos (Echo Klassik Award for Best Newcomer 2014) 2013, Ysaÿe 6 sonatas for solo violin (Echo Klassik Award for Instrumentalist of the Year/Violin 2015) 2014, Castelnuovo-Tedesco violin concertos 2015. *Honours:* several competition prizes as a child, DAAD (German Academic Exchange Service) scholarship 2003, Volkswagen Foundation prize "Star of Tomorrow" awarded by Seiji Ozawa, Prix Montblanc 2006. *Current Management:* AOR Management, 6910 Roosevelt Way NE, PMB 221, Seattle, WA 98115, USA; c/o Markus Bröhl, Artists and Concerts, Schröderstr. 11/II, 10115 Berlin, Germany. *Telephone:* (206) 729-6160 (USA); (30) 2821111. *Fax:* (206) 985-8499 (USA); (30) 246 286 57. *E-mail:* aormanagement@gmail.com; info@artistsandconcerts.de. *Website:* www.aormanagement.com; www.artistsandconcerts.de. *Address:* Department of Music, University of the Arts, Fellerstrasse 11, 3027 Bern, Switzerland (office). *E-mail:* contact@tianwayang.com. *Website:* www.tianwayang.com.

YANG, Xuefei (Fei), DipRAM, FRAM; Chinese classical guitarist; b. Beijing. *Education:* Royal Acad. of Music, UK. *Career:* first public appearance aged 10 at China Int. Guitar Festival; debut concert at age 14 in Madrid attended by composer Rodrigo; has performed concerts world-wide at concert halls including Wigmore Hall, London, Philharmonie Berlin, Concertgebouw Amsterdam, Konzerthaus Vienna, Laeiszhalle Hamburg, Nat. Auditorium Madrid, Dvořák Hall Prague, Carnegie Hall and Lincoln Center New York and venues across Asia; first solo guitar and first guitar concerto recitals ever in Beijing's Nat. Centre for Performing Arts; chamber music with numerous artists including Elias String Quartet, cellist Jian Wang, tenor Ian Bostridge and Sir James Galway (Beijing Music Festival); close collaboration with British composer Stephen Goss. *Recordings include:* Classical Guitar 1999, Si Ji 2005, Romance de Amor 2006, 40 Degrees North (Canton Radio's Best Instrumental CD) 2008, Rodrigo: Concierto de Aranjuez (with Barcelona Symphony Orchestra) 2010, Bach Concertos 2012, Soujourn 2013. *Honours:* ARAM 1985; RAM full scholarship. *Website:* www.askonasholt.co.uk; www.xuefeiyang.com.

YANG, Youqing, BA, MA, DMA; Chinese conductor and pianist; b. 10 Dec. 1952, Shanghai. *Education:* Shanghai Conservatory of Music, Michigan State University, USA, studied with Prof. Leon Gregorian. *Career:* debut with Brahms Symphony No. 4, Mozart Piano Concerto No. 20 and Berlioz Overture to Benvenuto Cellini, with Guangzhou Symphony Orchestra, 1984; Conductor, Symphony Orchestra of China National Opera Theatre 1984–, appearances including world premiere of opera Savage Land at 1st China Arts Festival in Beijing 1987; appeared from 1986 as Guest Conductor for Shanghai Philharmonic Orchestra, Shangdong Symphony Orchestra, Central Philharmonic Orchestra of China, China Broadcasting Symphony Orchestra, China Film Philharmonic Orchestra and at Zhou Xiaoyan Opera Centre, Shanghai; Music Dir, Chinese Musicians' Delegation Concert Tour in Europe 1995; Guest Conductor, Das Saarlandisches Staatsorchester Saarbrucken, with concerts at Kunst und Ausstellungshalle der Bundesrepublik Deutschland and Saarlandisches Staatstheater, Germany, at the Classic Open-Air in Solothurn, Switzerland, and the Municipal Theatre, Luxembourg; Prof. of Music and Dir of Orchestras, Central Conservatory of Music, Beijing 2005–; mem. Chinese Musicians' Association. *Honours:* Shanghai Conservatory of Music Merit Fellowship and Scholarship 1982–84. *Address:* c/o Central Conservatory of Music, Baojia Street W, City District, Beijing 100031, People's Republic of China (office).

YANKO, Yuriy; Russian/Ukrainian conductor; *Music Director and Chief Conductor, Kharkov State Philharmonic*; b. Kharkiv. *Education:* Univ. of Art, Kharkiv State Acad. of Culture, Ukrainian Nat. Acad. of Music. *Career:* Conductor, Philharmonic Orchestra of Zaporizhya 1991–94, Acad. Theatre of Opera and Ballet by N. Lusenko 1994–2001; Chief Conductor and Artistic Dir Symphony Orchestra of Kharkov regional philharmonic Soc., Conductor, Academic Theatre of Opera and Ballet by N. Lusenko 1997–2001; Artist Dir, Chamber Orchestra, Kharkov boarding school 2000–03; Resident Conductor, Music Dir and Conductor, Kharkiv Acad. of Music Chamber Orchestra 1999–2004; Music Dir and Chief Conductor, Kharkov State Philharmonic, Ukraine 2001–, Kharkov regional Philharmonic 2004–; Gen. Man. Kharkiv Philharmonic Soc. 2004–; currently Prof., Nat. Univ. of Art by I.P. Kotlyarevskiy, also Rector, Univ. of Culture, Univ. of Internal Affairs, Kharkov; Guest Conductor, Hradec Kralove Philharmonic Orchestra Prague, Budapest Symphony MAV, Hainburg, Austria, Teatro Massimo, Palermo, Italy, Palau de la Musica, Barcelona, Spain, Dallas Symphony Orchestra, Academic Symphonic Orchestra Kharkov; Stage Dir for opera and ballet performances of Othello, Aida, Rigoletto, Tosca, Madama Butterfly, Carmen, Aleko, Francesca da Rimini, The Tsar's Bride, P.Tchaikovsky's works, Schedrin's, K.Hachaturyan's, operas of Ukrainian authors. *Honours:* Honoured Worker of Arts of Ukraine 2004; numerous awards from Kharkiv regional govt . *Address:* Kharkov Regional Philharmonic, Rumarskaya Street, 21, 61057 Kharkov, Ukraine (office). *Telephone:* (57) 705-08-61 (office); (57) 705-08-54 (office). *E-mail:* inter@filarmonia.kharkov.ua (office). *Website:* www.filarmonia.kharkov.ua (office).

YANNAY, Yehuda, MFA, DMA; American/Israeli composer; b. 26 May 1937, Timisoara, Romania. *Education:* Rubin Acad. of Music, Tel-Aviv, Brandeis Univ., USA with Berger, Shapero and Krenek, Univ. of Illinois at Urbana. *Career:* resident in Israel from 1951–68, in USA 1968–; Prof. of Composition, Univ. of Wisconsin, Milwaukee 1970–2004; music from Almost Yesterday concert series 1971–. *Compositions include:* Spheres for soprano and ten instruments 1963, Two Fragments for violin and piano 1966, Wraphap (theatre music) 1969, Coloring Book from the Harpist 1969, Concert for audience and orchestra 1971, The Hidden Melody for cello and horn 1977, Concertino for violin and chamber orchestra 1980, Celan Ensembles: Augentanz and Galgenlied for tenor and instruments 1986–, In Madness There is Order for voice, projections and synthesizers 1988–92, The Oranur Experiment (music video) Part 1: Journey to Orgonon for actor, projections and synthesizer 1991, Five Pieces for Three Players for soprano saxophone, clarinet and marimba 1994, Exit Music at Century's End for orchestra 1995, Geometry of Aloneness for low voice, glass harmonica and slide projections 1996, Marrakesh Bop for flute and guitar 1999.

YANOV-YANOVSKY, Dmitri Feliksovich; Uzbekistani composer; b. 24 April 1963, Tashkent; s. of Felix Yanov-Yanovsky. *Education:* Tashkent State Conservatory. *Career:* founder and Artistic Dir, Int. Festival of Contemporary Music ILKHOM-XX, Tashkent. *Compositions include:* Bagatelles 1982, Piano Concerto 1983, Anno Domini 1985, Chang-Music I–V 1990–94, Lacrymosa 1991, Awakening 1993, Ritual 1994, Conjunctions 1995, Takyr 1995, Come and Go (for theatre) 1995, Hommage à Gustav Mahler 1996, The Little Match-Girl (ballet) 1996–97, Lux aeterna 1997, Music of Dreams 1999, Night Music: Voices in the Leaves 2000, Eh Joe (chamber opera) 2001, Twilight Music 2002, scores for over 40 films. *Recordings:* Night Prayers 1993, Chang-Music V (with Kronos Quartet), Lacrymosa, Dawn Upshaw (with Kronos Quartet), Music of Dreams (with Elisabeth Chojnacka), Opus 111. *Honours:* second prize Int. Competition de Musique Sacrée, Fribourg 1991, ALEA III Int. Prize, Boston 1992, Cannes Int. Film Festival Special Award of Nantes 1992. *Address:* C-1 47-ap. 42, 100000 Tashkent, Uzbekistan. *Telephone:* (71) 136-13-82. *Fax:* (71) 256-02-96. *E-mail:* yanovsky@mail.tps.uz.

YARON, Gilah; Israeli singer (soprano); b. 1941, Tel-Aviv. *Education:* studied in Tel-Aviv with Hede Tuerk-Bernstein and with Gunter Reich, George London and Elisabeth Schwarzkopf. *Career:* sang with the Israel Philharmonic and other orchestras from 1970; Israel Festival 1972 in Bach's Magnificat; sang in Switzerland and other European centres from 1975, including concert at Berlin Festival with works by Hindemith and Webern; guest appearances in Austria, Belgium, Netherlands, Italy, Denmark and England; sang Psaumes Hebraiques by Markevitch and Poèmes pour Mi by Messiaen; other repertoire includes Penderecki's St Luke Passion, Mahler's 2nd Symphony and Mendelssohn's music for A Midsummer Night's Dream; singing teacher, Rubin Acad. of Music and Dance, Jerusalem 1982–. *Honours:* Ministry of Educ. and Culture Prize for Outstanding Performance of Israeli Music. *Current Management:* Monica Fallon, 10 Hatchiya Street, Apartment 19, Holon 58401, Israel. *Telephone:* 3-5509597. *Fax:* 3-5594161. *E-mail:* info@ monica-fallon.com. *Website:* www.monica-fallon.com.

YASSA, Ramzi, DipMus, FTCL; Egyptian pianist; b. 15 March 1948, Cairo; m. Brigitte Chevrot 1978, one s. one d. *Education:* Lycee of Heliopolis, Cairo Conservatory, Tchaikovsky Conservatory, Moscow, Ecole Normale, Paris. *Career:* appearances at the Barbican, London with Royal Philharmonic Orchestra, conductor Charles Groves, Kennedy Center, Mann Auditorium with IPO, conductor Zubin Mehta, Musikverein, Palau, Barcelona, Théâtre des Champs Elysées and South Bank, London; television broadcast with Zubin Mehta 1987; inaugural concert, Cairo Opera House 1988; BBC recordings and live broadcasts; adjudicator for int. piano competitions; appearances with Yehudi Menuhin as conductor; Dir, Cairo Opera House 1998–; special adviser for music to the Egyptian Minister of Culture 1999–. *Recordings:* Tchaikovsky's The Seasons, Ades, France; Prokofiev's Cinderella, 2nd Sonata, Belgium; Chopin's Ballades and Opus 22, Belgium; Beethoven Appassionata/Waldstein/ Lieder von Goethe; Beethoven 5 Piano Concertos and Choral Fantasy Op 80. *Address:* c/o Cairo Opera House, El Borg Gezira, Cairo, Egypt. *Website:* www .cairooperahouse.org.

YASUNAGA, Toru; Japanese violinist; b. 14 Nov. 1951, Fukuoka. *Education:* Toho Music Acad., Tokyo, studied with Michael Schwalbe in Berlin. *Career:* many appearances in Europe and the Far East as recitalist and in concert; joined Berlin Philharmonic Orchestra 1977, and became leader. *Honours:* winner All-Japan Music Competition Leu Cadia Prize 1971.

YAUGER, Margaret, BM, MM; American singer (mezzo-soprano); b. 1947, Birmingham, AL; m. Malcolm Smith 1975. *Education:* Converse Coll., New England Conservatory of Music, American Opera Centre, Juilliard School of Music, New York and Goldovsky Opera Studio. *Career:* debut with American Nat. Opera Co.; performances with New York City Opera 1973–74, Lake George Opera Festival 1972–74, Central City Opera Festival 1973–76, Boris Goldovsky Opera Tour 1973–74, Mexico City Opera, Teatro Regio Turin, Italy; sang at Knoxville with Tennessee Opera, Birmingham Alabama Civic Opera, Fort Worth, Texas Opera; Deutsche Oper am Rhein, Düsseldorf, Germany 1977–86; sang at Krefeld, Hanover, Karlsruhe, Freiburg, Wiesbaden and Gelsenkirchen Opera Houses and with Solingen, Duisburg, Münchengladbach-Krefeld and Trier Symphonies; appearances on East Berlin Radio and with Dresden Philharmonic; sang Fricka in Das Rheingold, Washington Nat. Symphony, Margret in Wozzeck, with Boston Symphony Orchestra, 3rd Magd, Elektra with London Symphony Orchestra; Heidelberg Schloss, Festspiele 1992; sang in Verdi Requiem, Delaware Symphony Orchestra 1993; Mahler Symphony No. 2, Roanoke Symphony 1994; Choral Arts Soc. of Washington tour of France 1996; Youngstown Symphony 1996; Cincinnati Opera 1996; Portland Maine Symphony, Cesky Krumlov Summer Festival, Czech Republic; voice teacher, Univ. of Southern Maine 1999–; mem. AGMA. *Recordings:* Beethoven Symphony No. 9, alto part, with Mexico City Symphony; live recording of Rigoletto, New York City Opera. *Honours:* Miss Alabama Competition Scholarship, three William Mathis Sullivan Foundation scholarships. *Current Management:* c/o Thea Dispeker Inc, 59 East 54th Street, Suite 81, New York NY 10022, USA. *Telephone:* (212) 421-7676. *Fax:* (212) 935-3279. *E-mail:* info@dispeker.com. *Website:* www.dispeker.com.

YE, Shaolan, (Ye Qiang); Chinese singer, actor and playwright; b. Sept. 1943, Beijing; s. of Ye Shenglan. *Education:* China Acad. of Traditional Operas, Cen. Acad. of Drama. *Career:* started studying at Peking Opera at age of 9; Art Dir Zhanyou Peking Opera Troupe, PLA Beijing Mil. Command; mem. Exec. Council of Chinese Dramatists Asscn. *Peking operas include:* Lu Bu and Diao Chan, Luo Cheng, Story of the Willow Tree, A Meeting of Heroes, Butterfly Lovers. *Recordings include:* Selected Arias of Ye Shaolan 1995. *Honours:* won 1st Nat. Theatre Plum Blossom Award 1984; Fulbright Int. Scholar; New York Lincoln Center Life Achievement Award.

YEN, Wen-hsiung, BA, MA, PhD; American (b. Taiwanese) musician (piano, erhu, guzheng), composer and conductor; *Music Director and Conductor, Chinese Music Orchestra of Southern California;* b. 26 June 1934, Tainan, Taiwan; m. Yuan Yuan 1961; three s. *Education:* Nat. Taiwan Normal Univ., Chinese Culture Univ., Univ. of California, Los Angeles, World Univ., studied piano with Qing-Yan Zhou, Fu-Mei Lee, composition with Paul Chihara Hsu, Chang-Houei and Mike Mitacek, ethnomusicology with Mantle Hood, Nazir Jarazbhoy, Timothy Rice and Ali Jihad Racy. *Career:* instructor, Taiwan Provincial Taichung Teacher Coll. 1961–62; Prof., Chinese Culture Univ. 1964–69; Founder, Music Dir and Conductor Chinese Music Orchestra of Southern California 1974–, The Yue You Chorus; Founder, Chinese Culture School, Los Angeles 1976–; Lecturer, West Los Angeles Coll. 1978–82;

Faculty, Dept of Music, Univ. of Maryland 1982–83; Instructor, Los Angeles City Coll., California State Univ., Los Angeles 1984–, California State Univ., Northridge and Santa Monica City Coll. 1986–; Founder and Pres. Chinese Musicians' Asscn of Southern California 1990–; conducted orchestra for Dragon Boat Festival at Chinese Cultural Center, Chinatown, Los Angeles 1993 and for opening ceremony of annual Chinese Writers' Asscn of Southern California Conf. 1993; Prof. of Music, American Purlinton Univ. 2009–; Pres. Chinese Writers Asscn of Southern California 2008–; mem. Soc. for Ethnomusicology, Int. Council for Traditional Music, Soc. for Asian Music; Fellow, UCLA. *Compositions:* Drinking Alone in the Moonlight (words by L. Bai), Song of 911, Pure Even Tune (words by L. Bai), Roc Flies Ten Thousand Miles, Mother Earth – Four Seasons, The Phoenix Hair Pin (words by Lu You), Piano Suite for A Happy Reunion, Elements. *Recording:* East-West Music Concert (DVD) 2004. *Publications:* Taiwan Folk Songs Vol. I 1967, Vol. II 1969, A Dictionary of Chinese Music (co-author) 1967, A Collection of Wenhsiung Yen's Songs Vol. I 1968, Vol. II 1987, Vol. III 2002, Chinese Musical Culture and Folk Songs 1989, A Study of Si Xiang Qi (article) 1989, Silk and Bamboo Expresses Emotion of Meaning 2000, Wen-hsiung's Composition Vol. 3 2000, Ethnomusicology Series. *Honours:* Confucius Commemorative Day Ceremony Outstanding Teacher Award, Los Angeles 1984, UCLA Assocs of Ethnic Artists Award, Fed. of Overseas Chinese Asscns Award 2000, 2002, Outstanding Teacher Award, Jt Teacher Coll. and Normal Univ. of Taiwan Alumni Asscn 2005, 16th World Chinese Cultural and Artistic Heritage Award 2010, Outstanding Chinese Purlinton Cerebrity Award 2013. *Address:* Chinese Culture School of Los Angeles, 615 Las Tunas Drive, Suite B, Arcadia, CA 91007 (office); 9458 Pentland Street, Temple City, CA 91780, USA (home). *Telephone:* (626) 447-3823 (office); (626) 318-7210 (home). *Fax:* (626) 447-3823 (office); (626) 447-3823 (home). *E-mail:* wenhyen2000@yahoo.com (office). *Website:* www.chinesecultureschool.net (office).

YENDE, Pretty; South African soprano; b. 1985, Piet Retief, Mpumalanga. *Education:* Univ. of Cape Town. *Career:* appeared as Clara in Porgy and Bess in Malmö, Sweden and at Deutche Oper in Berlin 2008; sang at opening ceremony of UN Ass. (WHO), Geneva and performed with Andrea Bocelli in FIFA 2010 World Cup Closing Concert; mem. Young Artists Programme at La Scala, Milan, debut as Elvira in L'Italiana in Algeri 2010. *Honours:* winner, Hans Gabor Belvedere Singing Competition, Austria 2009, Savonnlina Int. Singing Competition, Finland 2010, Montserrat Caballé Int. Singing Competition, Zaragoza, Spain 2010, Leyla Gencer Voice Competition 2010. *Address:* c/o Accademia Teatro alla Scala, Via Santa Marta 18, 20123 Milan, Italy (office). *Telephone:* (2) 8545111 (office). *Fax:* (2) 86460020 (office). *Website:* www.accademialascala.it (office).

YERNA, Alexise; Belgian singer (mezzo-soprano); b. 1959. *Education:* Brussels Conservatoire with Jules Bastin. *Career:* sang in operas by Handel, Chabrier and Puccini at the Brussels opera studio; Opéra Wallonie at Liège from 1982, as Orlofsky and in operettas by Offenbach; has appeared throughout Belgium and France at Lola, Pepa in Goyescas, Fenena (Nabucco) and the Priestess in Aida; many concert engagements.

YEROFEEVA, Yelena; Russian cellist; b. 1960, Moscow. *Education:* Moscow Conservatoire with Alexei Shislov. *Career:* co-founder, Glazunov Quartet 1985; many concerts in the former Soviet Union and appearances in Greece, Poland, Belgium, Germany and Italy; works by Beethoven and Schumann at the Beethoven Haus in Bonn; further engagements in Canada and The Netherlands; teacher, Moscow State Conservatoire; resident cellist, Tchaikovsky Conservatoire; repertoire includes works by Borodin, Shostakovich and Tchaikovsky, in addition to the standard works. *Recordings include:* The six quartets of Glazunov. *Honours:* (with the Glazunov Quartet) prizewinner Borodin Quartet and Shostakovich Chamber Music Competitions.

YIM, Jay Alan, BA, MMus; American composer; b. 24 April 1958, St Louis, MO. *Education:* University of California, Royal College of Music, London, England, studied at Dartington, England and Tanglewood. *Career:* Lecturer, Director of Electronic Music Studio, University of California, Santa Barbara, 1978–80; Composer-in-Residence, Cummington School of the Arts, 1984; Major festival performances at Huddersfield, 1982, International Computer Music Conference 1985, Tanglewood 1986, 1987, and Gaudeamus 1987. *Compositions:* orchestral: Askesis, 1980–81, Eastern Windows, 1981, Karénas, 1986; Chamber: Palimpsest, 1979, Piak, 1981, Autumn Rhythm, 1984–85, Moments Of Rising Mist, 1986, Mille Graces, 1986, Geometry And Delirium, 1987; Solo instrument: Timescreen for Pianoforte No. 1, 1984, No. 2, 1983, Furiosamente for Piccolo, 1985, Más Furiosamente for Flute, 1985; Electronic: Kinkakuji, 1984, Shiosai, 1984.

YING, Shi Zhen, BMus, MMus; Chinese pianist and academic; b. 29 Nov. 1937; m. Pan Yi Ming 1960, two s. *Education:* Central Conservatory of Music, Beijing. *Career:* debut at seven years of age; piano teacher, Department of Central Conservatory of Music, Beijing, 1962–91; performed numerous piano recitals and concerts in China and around the world; recitals, the Tchaikovsky Conservatory of Moscow and other cities in Russia; Lecturer, many Chinese conservatories including Hong Kong University, 1984; Music Adviser, Singapore Yamaha Music Academy, Singapore, 1991–; examiner, Guildhall School of Music and Drama, England. *Compositions:* many piano examination pieces. *Publications:* The Methods of Piano Teaching and Performance, 1990; articles in magazines in China; text books. *Honours:* first prize, Conservatory Piano Competition, 1961. *Address:* Blk 38, 14-2406 Upper Boon, Kent Road, 5380038, Singapore.

YOES, Janice, BMus, MMus; American singer (soprano); b. 1947, Fayetteville, Arkansas. *Education:* Drake Univ., Tulsa Univ. *Career:* debut with New York City Opera 1973 as Santuzza; sang at the Augsburg Opera 1975–77, Saarbrucken 1976–77, Karlsruhe 1977–78; engaged at Nuremberg 1978–84, with guest appearances at Graz 1980–83; sang Strauss's Elektra at the Vienna Staatsoper, Marseilles, Madrid, the Deutsche Oper Berlin, Seattle and Santiago 1984; Bregenz Festival 1977 as Reiza in Oberon; appearances as Brünnhilde in Der Ring de Nibelungen at Naples, Lisbon and Seattle 1982–86; further engagements at Basle, Trieste, Brunswick and Pretoria 1987–88; other roles have included Isolde, Salome and Lady Macbeth; mem. music faculty, Univ. of Arkansas, Fayetteville 1985–. *Address:* Department of Music, University of Arkansas, Room 201, Fayetteville, AR 72701, USA (office). *Telephone:* (479) 575-4199 (office). *E-mail:* jyoes@iuark.edu (office). *Website:* comp.uark.edu/~jyoes/title-frame.htm (office).

YONCHEVA, Sonia; Bulgarian soprano; b. 25 Dec. 1981, Plovdiv. *Education:* Conservatoire de Genève, Switzerland. *Career:* debut with Les Arts Florissants under William Christie at venues including Lincoln Center, New York, Barbican Centre, London, Alte Oper Frankfurt, Palais de Beaux-Arts, Brussels, Auditorio Nacional de Madrid, Cité de la Musique, Paris and Gulbenkian Foundation, Lisbon; roles have included Norina in Don Pasquale at Opéra de Caen, Le Coq and La Chouette in Janáček's La Petite Renarde Rusée at Grand Théâtre de Genève 2005–06, also Junon in L'Incoronazione di Poppea with Emmanuelle Haim at Glyndebourne Festival 2010, Agata in Il Flaminio at Pergolesi Spring Festival 2010, Leila in Bizet's Les Pêcheurs de Perles at Opéra Comique in Paris and Nice Opéra, Dido in Purcell's Dido and Aeneas at the Brooklyn Acad. of Music, and in Moscow, St Petersburg and Valladolid with Les Arts Florissants, Rossini's Stabat Mater, Cleopatra in Handel's Giulio Cesare, and title role in L'incoronazione di Poppea conducted by Emmanuelle Haïm in Lille, Dijon, Nice and Amsterdam; debut with New York Philharmonic (under Placido Domingo) 2011. *Honours:* winner, Operalia Placido Domingo World Opera Competition 2010. *Current Management:* c/o Allegorica Opera Management, 36 Rue de la Roquette, 75011 Paris, France. *Telephone:* 1-43-73-09-32. *Fax:* 1-43-73-09-61. *E-mail:* info@allegorica.it. *Website:* www.allegorica.it.

YORK, Deborah; British singer (soprano); b. 9 Nov. 1964, Sheffield, Yorkshire, England. *Education:* Manchester University, Guildhall School of Music with Laura Sarti, studied with Janice Chapman. *Career:* opera engagements with Glyndebourne Touring Opera as Servilia in La Clemenza di Tito, Mirror in Birtwistle's The Second Mrs Kong; Emilia in Handel's Flavio for Dublin Touring Opera; Mozart's Barbarina at Covent Garden and Fortuna in Monteverdi's Poppea for Netherlands Opera (1995–96); Concerts include Pergolesi's Stabat Mater under Marc Minkowski, Purcell's Tempest with Ivor Bolton, Handel's Israel in Egypt with the Brandenburg Consort and Dixit Dominus with the Hallé Orchestra; Purcell's King Arthur with the King's Singers in Italy and with the English Concert at the 1995 London Proms; Further concerts with the Collegium Vocale, Ghent, under Phillipe Herreweghe; Other broadcasts include music by Purcell with the King's Consort for the BBC, and with the Gabrieli Players in France; Music for the Mona Lisa on Radio 3; Season 1997–98 with Gianetta in L'Elisir d'amore at Covent Garden, Semele at Berlin, Anne Trulove in concert with the London Symphony Orchestra and Handel's Jephtha at the 1997 London Proms; Acis and Galatea in Spain and the St John Passion at Montpellier; sang Alceste in Handel's Admeto at Beaune, 1998; season 2000–01 with Almirena in Handel's Rinaldo at Munich and Anne Trulove at Teatro Colón, Buenos Aires.

YORK, John, AGSM, ARCM; British pianist and academic (retd); b. 20 March 1949, Eastbourne, Sussex, England; m. Fiona Osborne 1981; one s. one d. *Education:* Guildhall School of Music and Drama, London, studied in Paris with Jacques Février, Vienna Hochschule with Dieter Weber. *Career:* debut at Wigmore Hall 1974; recitals and concerts in UK, Ireland, France and throughout Europe, USA, Canada, Brazil, Bermuda, Oman, Singapore, Malaysia, Australia; partner to Raphael Wallfisch on cello; mem. York 2 Piano Duo; various performances for radio and TV; fmr Prof. and Sr Music Head, St Paul's Girls' School, London. *Recordings include:* three albums of York Trio, 14 on Nimbus with cellist Raphael Wallfisch, three on Nimbus and Black Box with York 2. *Publications include:* selector and asst in issue of Mikrokosmos (Bartók), Fingers and Thumbs 1993, 20th Century Collections 1998; contrib. as reviewer for Piano Magazine, The Strad, The Pianist. *Honours:* Debussy Prize, Paris 1973. *Address:* 38 Caterham Road, Lewisham, London, SE13 5AR, England (home). *Telephone:* (20) 8318-1824 (office). *E-mail:* john@yorkpiano.co.uk (home). *Website:* yorkpiano.co.uk.

YORK, Richard, BEd; British musician and music historian; b. 15 May 1953, Northampton, England; m. Elizabeth York; two d. *Education:* Culham Coll., Abingdon and Northampton Coll. *Career:* freelance education workshop leader in schools and museums; music historian and interpreter at museums and heritage sites, including Victoria & Albert museum, Tower of London, Greenwich Foundation, English Heritage and Nat. Trust properties, Beamish et al.;; plays a large collection of instruments from medieval clarsach to Victorian concertina and hammer dulcimer; mem. Inc. Soc. of Musicians, Tabulae Ltd. *Address:* 1 Exmoor Close, Northampton, NN3 3AU, England (home). *Telephone:* (1604) 639581 (home). *E-mail:* richard@richard-york.co.uk (office). *Website:* www.richard-york.co.uk (office).

YOSHINO, Naoko; Japanese harpist; b. 1967, London, England. *Education:* Indiana Univ. with Susan McDonald, Int. Christian Univ., Tokyo. *Career:* soloist with leading orchestras from 1977, notably the Israel Philharmonic under Mehta 1985, the Philadelphia Orchestra under Frühbeck de Burgos 1987, and in Japan with Seiji Ozawa and Wolfgang Sawallisch; New York recital debut at Merkin Hall 1987 and chamber concert with mems of the Berlin Philharmonic; soloist with the Berlin Philharmonic under Ozawa 1988; Classic Aid concerts with Lorin Maazel in Paris 1988, and Yehudi Menuhin at Gstaad Festival 1988; London debut with James Galway in Mozart's Concerto K299 1990; London recital debuts 1990; English Chamber Orchestra at the Barbican under Menuhin 1990; played at the World Harp Festival, Cardiff 1991. *Recordings:* album with the English Chamber Orchestra under Menuhin, five other albums recorded (three as solo artist, one with flute and one concerto album). *Honours:* second prize Int. Harp Contest, Santa Cecilia Acad., Rome 1981, first prize Int. Harp Contest, Israel 1985. *Current Management:* Kajimoto Concert Management Ltd, Kahoku Building 8-6-25 Ginza, Chuo-Ku, Tokyo, Japan. *Telephone:* (3) 2574-0969. *Fax:* (3) 3574-0980. *E-mail:* yuji.arai@kajimotomusic.com. *Website:* www.kajimotomusic.com; www.naokoyoshino.com.

YOST, Ricardo; Chilean singer (bass-baritone); b. 1943. *Education:* studied in Santiago. *Career:* sang at the Teatro Colón Buenos Aires from 1973, notably as Guglielmo, Rigoletto, Amonasro, Iago, Renato, Malatesta, Escamillo and Napoleon in Prokofiev's War and Peace; has appeared throughout South America and in bass roles such as Mephistopheles and Rossini's Basilio; sang Amonasro at Buenos Aires 1996; sang in Francesca da Rimini at Buenos Aires 2000.

YOUN, Kwangchul; South Korean singer (bass); b. 1970. *Education:* Chong-Ju Univ., Sofia Music School, Berlin Hochschule der Künste with Herbert Brauer. *Career:* sang in concert at Seoul from 1998; South Korean State Opera 1988–90; engaged at the Deutsche Oper Berlin 1993; mem. Staatsoper Unter den Linden, Berlin 1994–2004; made Bayreuth Festival debut as Ein Nachtwächter in Die Meistersinger von Nürnberg 1996; debut at Royal Opera House as King Heinrich der Vogler in Lohengrin 2009; repertoire includes the Priest in Schoenberg's Moses und Aron, Bartolo, the High Priest in Idomeneo, Méphistophéles in Faust, Veit Pogner in Die Meistersinger von Nürnberg, Titurel and Gurnemanz in Parsifal, Landgraf Hermann in Tannhäuser, König Marke in Tristan und Isolde, Hunding in Die Walküre, Fasolt in Das Rheingold, Commendatore in Don Giovanni, Ferrando in Il Trovatore, King of Egyot in Aida, Colline in La Bohème, Philip II in Don Carlo, Leporello in Don Giovanni, Don Fernando in Fidelio, Figaro in Le Nozze di Figaro. *Current Management:* c/o Suzana Djordjevic, Opern-Agentur, Maassenstrasse 14, 10777 Berlin, Germany. *Telephone:* (30) 2168214. *Fax:* (30) 2159776. *E-mail:* kursidem@opern-agentur; Tschaidse@opern-agentur.com. *Website:* www .opern-agentur.com. *E-mail:* mail@kwangchulyoun.info (office). *Website:* kwangchulyoun.info.

YOUNG, Douglas, ATCL, BMus; British composer, pianist, conductor, writer and broadcaster; b. 18 June 1947, London, England; m. Susan Anne Devlin 1980, one d. *Education:* Trinity Coll. of Music, Royal Coll. of Music, London. *Career:* debut as pianist, Royal Festival Hall, London 1970; works with Ronald Hynd, choreographer for Royal Ballet and München Staatsoper Ballet 1970–; Fellow, Commoner in the Creative Arts, Trinity Coll., Cambridge 1973–75; Composer-in-Residence, Leicester Education Authority 1975–77; founder, Dreamtiger ensemble 1975; trustee LAMA; mem. SPNM, BMIC. *Compositions include:* Virages–Region One for cello and large orchestra, Night Journeys Under the Sea (series of concerti), Trajet, Inter Lignes 1980, Third Night Journey Under the Sea 1980–82, The Hunting of the Snark (after Lewis Carroll) 1982, Rain, Steam and Speed 1982, Dreamlandscapes, Portrait of Apollinaire 1983, Dreamlandscapes Book II 1986, Ludwig–Fragments Eines Rätsels (ballet in two acts) 1986, Mr Klee Visits the Botanical Gardens for string quartet 1993, Herr Schoenberg Plays Ping-Pong for piano 1992–99, The Excursions of M. Jannequin for piano 1997, The Eternal Waterfall for cello and piano 1998, The Lost Puzzle of Gondwana (stage) 1999. *Honours:* Cobbett Prize for Chamber Music 1968, Karl Rankl Prize for Orchestral Composition, Musica Nova 1970–71.

YOUNG, Josephine; New Zealand cellist; b. 1960, Auckland. *Education:* New England Conservatory, studied in London with Christopher Bunting. *Career:* debut concert in Wellington 1988; chamber musician and soloist in New Zealand; co-founder of the New Zealand String Quartet 1987, under the auspices of the Music Federation of New Zealand; concerts at the Tanglewood School in USA, Banff Int. Competition in Canada and performances with the Lindsay Quartet at the 1990 Int. Festival of the Arts, Wellington; soloist with the New Zealand Symphony Orchestra; Artist-in-Residence, Victoria Univ., Wellington; tour to Australia 1990, for Musica Viva Australia; tours of New Zealand 1992; concerts in New York 1993.

YOUNG, Julianne; South African singer (mezzo-soprano); b. 1973, Cape Town. *Education:* Royal Coll. of Music with Lillian Watson. *Career:* concert engagements include Mozart's Requiem at King's Coll. Chapel, Bach's Passions at St John's Smith Square, St John Passion, Rossini's Petite Messe in Glasgow; opera roles include Adalberto in Ottone and Vitige in Flavio, Baba the Turk in The Rake's Progress; further concerts include Linbury Theatre, Covent Garden recital 2000, masterclass with Barbara Bonney, concert tour of Japan with the BBC Concert Orchestra and engagement with the Cape Town Symphony

Orchestra 2000. *Honours:* winner RCM Lady Maud Warrender and Cuthbert Smith Prizes, John McCormack Golden Voice Competition, Ireland.

YOUNG, La Monte Thornton; American composer and performer; b. 14 Oct. 1935, Bern, ID; m. Marian Zazeela 1963. *Education:* Los Angeles City Coll., Los Angeles State Coll., UCLA with Robert Stevenson, New School for Social Research, New York, studied with Andrew Imbrie at the Stockhausen masterclasses at Darmstadt. *Career:* performed and taught Kirana style of North Indian classical vocal music, with Pran Nath; collaborations with Marian Zazeela; associations with the fluxus and minimalist movements of artistic endeavour; Music Dir, Ann Halprin Dance Co. 1959–60; with Marian Zazeela made tours of USA and Europe with the Theatre of Eternal Music 1969–75; Dir, Kirana Center for Indian Classical Music 1971; Dream House maintained by the Dia Art Foundation's programme at Harrison Street, New York 1979–85. *Compositions include:* pieces for electronic and mixed-media forces 1959–67, Trio for strings 1958, Studies I–III 1959, Arabic Numeral 1960, Death Chant for male voices and carillon 1961, The Well-Tuned Piano (series of pieces for prepared piano), Orchestral Dreams 1985, The Subsequent Dreams of China 1993, The Empty Base, Sound Environments 1991–. *Publications include:* An Anthology 1963, Selected Writings 1969. *Honours:* Woodrow Wilson Fellowship 1959, Guggenheim Fellowship 1966, Creative Arts Public Service Grants, Commission from the Dia Art Foundation 1975–85.

YOUNG, Richard; American violist; b. 1945. *Education:* Indiana Univ., Catholic Univ., studied with Josef Gingold, Aaron Rosand and William Primrose. *Career:* performed at Queen Elisabeth of Belgium Competition aged 13; faculty mem., Oberlin Conservatory of Music 1972–84; performances with the Rogeri Trio and the New Hungarian Quartet, USA, Europe, South America, Africa and Australia; mem., Vermeer Quartet from 1985; performances at all major US centres and in Europe, Israel and Australia; festival engagements at Tanglewood, Aspen, Spoleto, Edinburgh, Mostly Mozart in New York, Aldeburgh, South Bank, Santa Fe, Chamber Music West and the Casals Festival; resident quartet for Chamber Music Chicago; annual masterclasses at the Royal Northern Coll. of Music, Manchester; mem. resident artists faculty, Northern Illinois Univ.; Prod. of the Vermeer Quartet's album of Haydn's the Seven Last Words of Christ; Mozart K421 and Beethoven op 95 with the Vermeer Quartet at the 2001 Bath Festival. *Recordings include:* Quartets by Beethoven, Dvořák, Verdi and Schubert; Brahms Clarinet Quintet with Karl Leister.

YOUNG, Simone Margaret, AM; Australian conductor; *Music Director and General Manager, Staatsoper Hamburg;* b. 2 March 1961; m. Greg Condon; two d. *Education:* Sydney Conservatorium of Music. *Career:* Conductor, Vienna Staatsoper, Bastille (Paris), Berlin Staatsoper, Cologne Opera, Royal Opera House (London), Metropolitan Opera (New York), Houston Grand Opera, Los Angeles Opera, New York Philharmonic Orchestra, Oslo Philharmonic Orchestra, Munich Philharmonic Orchestra, Maggio Musicale (Florence), ORF Radio Orchestra Vienna, NDR Hanover, NHK Symphony Orchestra (Japan), Hamburg Philharmonic Orchestra Sydney, Melbourne and West Australian Symphony Orchestras; Chief Conductor, Bergen Philharmonic Orchestra 1999–2002; Music Dir, Opera Australia 2001–05; Music Dir and Gen. Man. Hamburg State Opera 2005–, Prin. Musical Dir Hamburg Philharmonic State Orchestra 2005–; Prof. of Music and Theatre, Hamburg Univ. 2006–; First Guest Conductor Gulbenkian Orchestra, Lisbon 2007–. *Repertoire includes:* opera: Rigoletto, Tosca, La Traviata, Oberto, Der fliegende Holländer, Der Rosenkavalier, Macbeth, Elektra, La Bohème, Cavalleria rusticana, Pagliacci, Tales of Hoffmann, Il Trovatore, Lohengrin, Eugène Onegin, Salomé, Fidelio, Peter Grimes, Wozzeck, La Juive, Der Ring des Nibelungen, Die Meistersinger von Nürnberg, Die Fledermaus, Die Frau ohne Schatten, Faust, Ariadne auf Naxos, Simon Boccanegra, Tannhäuser, Falstaff, Don Carlos, Andrea Chenier, Tristan und Isolde, The Marriage of Figaro, Don Giovanni, Lulu, Otello; extensive symphonic repertoire, including works of Mahler, Strauss, Wagner, Brahms, Beethoven, Bruckner and Bartók. *Honours:* Chevalier, Ordre des Arts et des Lettres; Hon. DMus (Monash Univ.) 1998, (Univ. of New South Wales) 2001; Dr hc (Sydney) (Melbourne); Young Australian of the Year 1987, Goethe Medal, Goethe Inst. 2005, Conductor of the Year, Opernwelt magazine 2006, Schleswig-Holstein Brahms Prize 2009. *Current Management:* Michael Lewin International Artists' Management, Euroartists Künstlermanagement GmbH, Gluckgasse 1/1, 1010, Vienna, Austria. *Address:* c/o Hamburgische Staatsoper, Große Theaterstraße 34, 20354 Hamburg, Germany. *Website:* www.simoneyoung.com; www.hamburgische-staatsoper.de.

YOUNG, Thomas; American singer (tenor); b. 1962. *Career:* debut singing the Inspector in the premiere of Under the Double Moon by Anthony Davis, St Louis 1989; New York City Opera from 1990, as Schoenberg's Aron, Molqi in The Death of Klinghoffer by John Adams (also in Brussels and San Francisco) and in Zimmermann's Die Soldaten; season 1992 as Frère Elie in Messiaen's St François d'Assise, at Salzburg, and in Birtwistle's Punch and Judy at Amsterdam; Florence Maggio Musicale 1994, as Aron; Chicago Lyric Opera 1997, as the Trickster God in the premiere of Amistad, by Anthony Davis; concerts include Mendelssohn's Elijah, and modern repertory. *Recordings include:* The Death of Klinghoffer.

YTTREHUS, Rolv Berger, BS, MM Diploma; American composer and academic; *Professor Emeritus, Rutgers University;* b. 12 March 1926, Duluth, Minn.; s. of Christopher Yttrehus and Petra Andal Yttrehus. *Education:* Univ. of Minnesota, Duluth, Univ. of Michigan with Ross Lee Finney, Accad. di

Santa Cecilia, Rome, studied with Brustad in Oslo, Boulanger in Paris, Sessions at Princeton, Copland in Tanglewood and Petrassi in Rome. *Career:* teacher, Lawrenceville School 1957–60; Instructor in Music, Univ. of Missouri 1963–67; Asst Prof. of Music, Purdue Univ. 1968–69; Assoc. Prof. of Music, Univ. of Wisconsin, Oshkosh 1969–77; Prof. of Music, Rutgers Univ., NJ 1977–96, Prof. Emer. 1996–; Guest Composer, Paterson State Univ., NJ 2001; Guest Lecturer, New York State Univ. at Stony Brook 2007, Queens Coll., New York 2008. *Compositions include:* Cosmophography for four clarinets 1948, Prelude for concert band 1950, Sonata for violin and piano 1951, Overture for orchestra 1951, Fantasy for orchestra 1953, Duo for violin and viola 1954, Quartet for flute and strings 1955, Six Pieces for piano 1957, Six Haiku for flute, cello, harp and soprano 1959, Two Movements for string quartet 1960, Music for winds, percussion and viola 1961, Espressioni per orchestra 1962, Sextet for horn, trumpet, violin, double bass, piano and percussion 1964–70 (revised 1974), Music for winds, percussion, cello and voices (voices part on tape) 1969, Angstwagen for soprano and percussion 1971 (revised 1981), Quintet for flute, violin, clarinet, cello and piano 1973, Gradus ad Parnassum for soprano, chamber orchestra and tape (after Nietzsche and Fux) 1974–79, Sonata for percussion and piano 1983 (revised 1988), Explorations for piano 1985, Sonata for violoncello and piano 1988, Raritan Variation for piano 1989, Symphony No. 1 1995 (revised 1998), Plectrum Spectrum for two guitars, flute, oboe, violin and violoncello 2000, Sextet II for flute, clarinet, violin, cello, piano and percussion 2004–06 (revised 2008), Laudate Milton Babbitt for violin and clarinet 2006. *Recordings:* works recorded on CRI CD843, MMC-Modern American Classics Vol. VI, Centaur, CRC 2291 and Bridge Records-9195. *Publications:* musical works published by ACA, APNM and C.F. Peters. *Honours:* Martha Baird Rockefeller Recording Award 1974, Nat. Endowment for Arts Fellowship grant 1976, American Composers Alliance Recording Award 1985, NJ State Council on Arts grant 1989. *Address:* c/o BMI, 320 West 57th Street, New York, NY 10019 (office); 1 Wood Circle, East Brunswick, NJ 08816, USA (home). *Telephone:* (732) 249-1776 (home). *E-mail:* yttrehus@rci.rutgers.edu (office).

YU, Chun Yee; Chinese pianist; b. 12 July 1936, Shanghai; m. 1st Isabella Miao 1963, two s.; m. 2nd Jung Chang 1982. *Education:* Royal College of Music, UK with Kendall Taylor, studied in Italy and France. *Career:* examiner for the Associated Board of Royal School of Music; Professor of Piano, Royal College of Music; represented Singapore at the First Asian Music Festival in Hong Kong; first appeared at the Royal Festival Hall in 1963 as soloist with London Philharmonic Orchestra; has played extensively in the Far East and throughout the UK; toured Taiwan and People's Republic of China. *Honours:* Recordi Prize for Conducting; Prizewinner, International Piano Competition; Scholarship to study in Siena under Agosti.

YU, Guanqun; Chinese singer (soprano); b. 1983. *Education:* Shandong Inst. of Arts, Shanghai Conservatory of Music (SHCM), studied with Prof. Zhou Xiaoyan. *Career:* masterclasses with Renée Fleming and Carlo Bergonzi; has appeared in several operas including The Magic Flute and Rigoletto. *Honours:* winner, opera category, 27th Int. Hans Gabor Belvedere Singing Competition, Vienna 2008. *Address:* c/o Shanghai Conservatory of Music, 20 Fenyang Road, Xuhui District, Shanghai 200031, People's Republic of China (office). *Website:* www.shcmusic.edu.cn (office).

YU, Hyunah, MMus; American singer (soprano); b. 1969, Republic of Korea. *Education:* Peabody Conservatory, Johns Hopkins Univ. *Career:* moved with family to USA aged 13; fmr microbiologist; recital debut Carnegie Hall, New York 2004; other concerts have included Mahler Symphony No. 8 with Rotterdam Philharmonic conducted by Valery Gergiev, Bach Mass in B minor under Semyon Bychkov with Orchestra of West Deutsche Rundfunk in Cologne, Beethoven 9th Symphony with David Zinman at Aspen Music Festival, and with Seoul Philharmonic under Myung Whun Chu in Seoul; operatic debut in title role of Zaide, conducted by Louis Langrée, in Vienna, London and New York 2006. *Recording:* Bach and Mozart Arias. *Honours:* Borlett-Buitoni Trust Fellowship 2003, Borletti-Buitoni Trust Award 2006. *Current Management:* Connaught Artists Management, 2 Molasses Row, Plantation Wharf, London SW11 3UX, England. *Telephone:* (20) 7738-0017. *Fax:* (20) 7738-0909. *E-mail:* classicalmusic@connaughtartists.com. *Website:* www.connaughtartists.com.

YU, Julian Jing-Jun, DipMus, MA, DMus; Australian/Chinese composer; *Teacher of Composition, University of Melbourne;* b. (Yu Jing-Jun), 2 Sept. 1957, Beijing, China; s. of Yu Li-Min and Zhu Shu-Lan; m. Marion Hazel Gray 1984. *Education:* Central Conservatory of Music, Beijing, Tokyo Coll. of Music, Queensland Conservatorium of Music, Brisbane, La Trobe Univ., Melbourne, Univ. of Melbourne. *Career:* teacher, Cen. Conservatory of Music, Beijing 1977–85; emigrated to Australia 1985; Tanglewood Fellow 1988; Victorian Ministry for the Arts Music Advisory Panel 1991–93, 1995–96; teacher of composition, Univ. of Melbourne 1992–, Victorian Coll. of the Arts 1993–2000; work commissioned by ABC, Ensemble Intercontemporain, IRCAM, Tokyo Philharmonic Orchestra, Chamber Made Opera, Australia Ensemble, Synergy Percussion, The City of Munich, BBC Proms, 2008 Olympic Games; jury mem. BMW Music Theatre Prize at Munich Biennale 1992, for ACL Young Composer's Competition 2003, 2007; works performed at Huddersfield Contemporary Music Festival 1990, ISCM World Music Days, Zürich 1991, New Mexico 1993, Luxembourg 2000, Lausanne 2004, Hong Kong 2007, Suntory Foundation Int. Programme 2009. *Compositions:* music for film, TV and stage productions –1986; Impromptu for piano 1987, Wu-Yu for orchestra 1987, Scintillation I, II and III 1987, Great Ornamented Fuga Canonica for orchestra

1988, Medium Ornamented Fuga Canonica for woodwind quintet 1988, Reclaimed Prefu I for two pianos 1989, The White Snake (music theatre) 1989, First Australian Suite for chamber orchestra 1990, Reclaimed Prefu II for SATB choir and two pianos 1990, In the Sunshine of Bach for a capella choir 1990, Hsiang-Wen (Filigree Clouds) for orchestra 1991, Philopentatonia for chamber orchestra 1994, Three Symphonic Poems 1994, Sinfonia Passacaglissima 1995, Marimba Concerto 1996, Lyrical Concerto for flute and orchestra 1996, Fresh Ghosts (opera) 1997, Concerto for zheng and orchestra 1999, Not a Stream but an Ocean for orchestra 1999, The Future of Water for choir and orchestra 2001, Pictures at an Exhibition modern chamber rendition 2001, The Possessed (opera) 2002, Clarinet Concerto on Chinese Themes 2002, Willow and Wattle for erhu and orchestra 2002, Chaconnissima for four percussionists and piano 2004, New Upbeat 2005, Symphonic Variations on a Theme of Paganini 2006, Sinfonia Chaconnissima 2006, Passacaglia after Biber for solo violin 2006, Oriental Rain 2007, Sonata for piano 2007, Mozartiana for strings 2007, orchestral section for Saint-Saen's Violin Concert No. 3 2007, That Eye the Sky (opera) 2008. *Recordings include:* Classical Allusion: Selected Works by Julian Yu, Dovetailing, Impromtu, In the Sunshine of Bach, Pictures at an Exhibition: Modern Version, Scintillation II, Scintillation III, Six Pieces for Young Pianists, Ten Chinese Folk and Art Songs, The Future of Water, Trio for Violin, Cello and Piano, Wu-Yu, Yellow Beanleaves, Arrangements of Russian Classics: Gliere Coloratura Concerto, Tchaikovsky Seasons, Glinka Nightingale, Sinfonia Chaconnissima 2007, Young Person's Guide to Composition 2009, Composer's Parade 2009, Mozartiana 2009. *Publications:* Modest Mussorgsky Pictures at an Exhibition: a moderately modern rendition by immodest Julian Yu for sixteen players or chamber orchestra, Zen-On Sinfonietta Series, Tokyo 2006; articles: Transfiguring Bach: Chinese ornamentation in Reclaimed Prefu, in Studien zur Wertungsforschung 48 2007, Analysis of Julian Yu's modern rendition of Pictures at an Exhibition, in Journal of the Central Conservatory of Music, Beijing Vol 110 no.1 2008. *Honours:* Hon. Fellow, Faculty of Music, Univ. of Melbourne 2005–10; prize winner, Int. New Music Composers' Competition 1987, 1988, 1989, 1990, Albert H. Maggs Composition Award 1988, Koussevitzky Tanglewood Composition Prize 1988, Premio Musicale Citta di Trieste 1988, Paul Lowin Orchestral Prize 1991, 1994, 2009, Vienna Modern Masters Composition Award 1992, Adolf Spivakovsky Composition Prize 1993, Australia Council Composer Fellowship 1995, 56th Japan Music Concours 1987, Piano 2000 Int. Composition Competition 2000, APRA Award 2008. *Address:* c/o Australian Music Centre, PO Box N690, Grosvenor Place, NSW 1220, Australia (office). *Telephone:* (2) 9247-4677 (office). *Fax:* (2) 9241-2873 (office). *E-mail:* info@australianmusiccentre.com.au (office). *Website:* www.australianmusiccentre.com.au (office).

YU, Long; Chinese conductor; *Artistic Director, China Philharmonic Orchestra;* b. 1964, Shanghai; grandson of Ding Shande. *Education:* Shanghai Music Conservatory, Hochschule der Kunst, Berlin. *Career:* many appearances with leading orchestras in Europe and the Far East; Principal Conductor, Central Opera Theatre, Beijing 1992; Conductor, Beijing New Year's Concert 1992–95; founder and Artistic Dir, Beijing Int. Music Festival 1998–; co-founder and Artistic Dir, China Philharmonic Orchestra 2000–; Music Dir, Guangzhou Symhpony Orchestra 2003–; Music Dir, Shanghai Symphony Orchestra 2009–; regularly appears in Germany, France, the Northlands, Switzerland, Poland, Hungary, Portugal, Slovakia, Australia, Singapore, Thailand, Hong Kong, Macao; Pres., Artistic Cttee, Shanghai Oriental Centre. *Recordings include:* albums with the China Philharmonic Orchestra. *Honours:* Chevalier, Ordre des Arts et des Lettres 2003, L'onorificenza di commendatore, Italy 2005; Montblanc Arts Patronage Award 2002. *Current Management:* c/o Jean-Jacques Cesbron, CAMI Music, 1790 Broadway, 16th Floor, New York, NY 10019, USA. *E-mail:* jmehr@cami.com. *Website:* www.camimusic.com; www.chinaphilharmonic.org; www.sh-symphony.com.

YU, Xiang (Angelo); Chinese violinist; b. 27 Oct. 1988, Hohhot, Inner Mongolia; s. of the late Yuan Ding. *Education:* Shanghai Conservatory with Qing Zheng and Shisheng Zheng, New England Conservatory, Boston with Donald Weilerstein. *Career:* began playing violin at age five; First Violin and Asst Concertmaster, Atlantic Symphony Orchestra; has performed as solo violinist in numerous venues including Konzerthaus Berlin, Germany, Shanghai Grand Theatre, China, Wieniawski Hall, Poland, Grand Theatre of Calgary, Canada, Victoria Concert Hall, Singapore, Oslo Opera House and Troldsalen Bergen, Norway, Auckland Town Hall, New Zealand, Bennett-Gordon Hall, Boston Jordan Hall, USA; has appeared as soloist with int. orchestras including Nat. Theatre Symphony Orchestra, Calgary Philharmonic Orchestra, Norwegian Broadcasting Orchestra, Shanghai Symphony Orchestra, Young Euro Classic Orchestra, Auckland Symphony Orchestra, Oslo Philharmonic Orchestra; also active as chamber musician in addition to solo career. *Honours:* First, Bach and Audience Prizes, Yehudi Menuhin Int. Violin Competition 2010. *Address:* Atlantic Symphony Orchestra, 408 Washington Street, Weymouth, MA 02188, USA (office). *Telephone:* (781) 331-3600 (office). *E-mail:* info@atlanticsymphony.org (office). *Website:* www.atlanticsymphony.org (office).

YUASA, Takuo, BMus, Diplom; Japanese conductor; *Associate Professor, Tokyo University of the Arts, Performing Art Centre;* b. 27 July 1949, Osaka; m. Shigeko Yuasa; one d. *Education:* Univ. of Cincinnati, USA, in France with Igor Markevich, Hochschule, Vienna with Hans Swarowsky, in Siena with Franco Ferrara. *Career:* fmr Asst to Lovro von Matacic in Monte Carlo, Milan and Vienna; fmrly Prin. Conductor Gumma Symphony Orchestra, Japan, Prin. Guest Conductor BBC Scottish Symphony Orchestra; Prin. Guest

Conductor Ulster Orchestra, Northern Ireland –2005; currently Assoc. Prof. Tokyo Univ. of the Arts, Performing Art Centre; regularly performs throughout Europe and the Far East; has played with numerous orchestras, including Adelaide Symphony, BBC Scottish Symphony Orchestra, Berliner Symphoniker, Bournemouth Symphony Orchestra, Brabants Orkest, Gelders Orkest, Hallé Orchestra, Hong Kong Philharmonic, London Philharmonic, Luxembourg Philharmonic, Nat. Symphony Orchestra of Ireland, New Zealand Symphony Orchestra, North Netherlands Orchestra, Norwegian Radio Orchestra, Oslo Philharmonic, Polish Radio Nat. Symphony Orchestra, Queensland Orchestra, Royal Liverpool Philharmonic Orchestra, Royal Scottish Nat. Orchestra, Sonderjyllands Symphony Orchestra, Sydney Symphony Orchestra, Trondheim Symphony, Ulster Orchestra, Warsaw Nat. Philharmonic, Royal Flanders Philharmony Orchestra, Orchestre Nat. de l'Ile de France, Porto Nat. Symphony. *Honours:* Fitelberg Int. Conducting Competition special award, Katowice, Poland, Iue Cultural Prize. Int. Soroptimist Kobe Prize. *Current Management:* Patrick Garvey Management, Cedar House, 40 North Parade, York YO30 7AB, England. *Telephone:* (1904) 621222. *Fax:* (1723) 330050. *E-mail:* patrick@patrickgarvey.com. *Website:* www.patrickgarvey.com.

YUEN, Nancy; Singaporean singer (soprano); b. 1965, Hong Kong. *Education:* Royal Acad. of Music, London, studied lieder in Germany. *Career:* extensive concert repertoire; has performed with WNO, ENO, Mid-Wales Opera, Los Angeles Music Centre Opera, West Australian Opera, New Zealand Int. Festival of the Arts, Singapore Lyric Opera, Barbados Festival 1995, Hong Kong Arts Festival, Singapore Lyric Opera, Opera Northern Ireland and Kentish Opera; extensive tour of Middle East and Far East; regularly performs at Royal Festival Hall, QEH and the Purcell Room, London; concerts in France and around the UK; touring production in the Middle East and Far East; Festival of the Asian Performing Arts, Singapore; Singapore Lyric Theatre; Lyric Opera productions, National Concert Hall, Dublin; toured France with London City Opera; sang for Opera Queensland; currently Head of Vocal Studies, Nanyang Acad. of Fine Arts. *Recordings:* recorded for BBC radio, Television Hong Kong, Radio FM, New Zealand. *Address:* Department of Music, Nanyang Academy of Fine Arts, 80 Bencoolen Street, Singapore 189655, Singapore (office). *Telephone:* 65124165 (office). *Fax:* 63368021 (office). *E-mail:* music@nafa.edu.sg (office). *Website:* www.nafa.edu.sg (office).

YUNUS, Dilber, MA; Finnish (b. Chinese) singer (lyric coloratura soprano); b. 1958, Kashgar, Xinjiang Uyghur Autonomous Region, China. *Education:* Music Acad., Beijing. *Career:* performed with major Chinese ensembles while at school and at the music acad.; debut as Gilda in Rigoletto with Finnish Nat. Opera 1987; numerous engagements throughout Europe and the rest of the world; repertoire includes Adina, Amina, Angelica, Annchen, Haydn's Orlando Paladino, Blondchen, Lucia, Marie, Königin der Nacht, Despina, Elvira, Gilda, Lakmé, Nannetta, Olympia, Oscar, Rosina, Sophie in Werther and Der Rosenkavalier, Zerbinetta and Zerlina; performances with major orchestras including the Symphony Orchestra of Beethovenhalle, Bonn, Orchestra Sinfonica di Milano della RAI, Singapore Symphony Orchestra, Taiwan Nat. Symphony Orchestra, Israel Sinfonietta, Radio Orchestras of Denmark, China, Finland, Frankfurt; Mitteldeutschen Rundfunk, Århus, Malmö, Helsinki; has performed in major opera venues worldwide; subject of documentaries with Swedish, Finnish and Chinese tv; Prof. China Music Acad., Beijing. *Recordings:* five albums in China; Coloratura arias; Folk Songs; Lieder with piano; Nannetta in Falstaff; Lisa in La Sonnambula; The Art of Coloratura with Malmö Opera Orchestra. *Honours:* Hon. Prof. Xinjiang Arts Coll. 2000–; Second Prize, Int. Mirjam Helin Singing Competition, Helsinki, 1984; Birgit Nilsson Prize 1997, 1998, Golden Record and Best Performer Awards, China 2003. *Current Management:* Walter Beloch Artists Management S.R.L, Via Melzi d'Eril 26, Milan 20 154, Italy; Vocalmusic D.Y.AB, Bågängsvägen 53, Malmö 216 20, Sweden. *Telephone:* (70) 3277728 (Vocalmusic). *E-mail:* lirica@walterbeloch.com. *Website:* www.walterbeloch.com. *Address:* Bågängsvägen 53, 21620 Malmö, Sweden (home). *E-mail:* dilber@telia.com (home). *Website:* www.dilber.se.

YURISICH, Gregory; Australian singer (baritone); b. 13 Oct. 1951, Mount Lawley, WA. *Education:* studied in Perth. *Career:* debut as Paolo in Simon Boccanegra for Australian Opera at Sydney 1978; roles in Australia have included Mozart's Masetto and Don Alfonso, Verdi's Germont and Melitone, Alberich in The Ring, Varlaam in Boris Godunov, Beethoven's Pizarro and Wagner's Dutchman; European debut, Frankfurt 1989, as Bottom in A Midsummer Night's Dream; Covent Garden debut 1990, as William Tell, returning as Dr Bartolo, the villains in Les Contes d'Hoffmann, Don Profondo in a new production of Il Viaggio a Reims 1992; Pizarro in Fidelio and Scarpia in Tosca; for ENO has sung in two world premieres: Alcibiades in Timon of Athens by Stephen Oliver 1991 and Cadmus in Bakxai by John Buller 1992; sang Stankar in a new production of Verdi's Stiffelio at Covent Garden 1993; other roles include Escamillo, Leporello (at Glyndebourne 1991), King Henry in Anna Bolena, and Verdi's Iago, Simon Boccanegra, Rigoletto and Nabucco; further engagements include San Francisco and Geneva (Germont Père in La Traviata), Covent Garden (title role in Nabucco), Australia (title role in Falstaff), Vienna (Balstrode in Peter Grimes and title role in Rigoletto), Munich (title role in Nabucco); sang in opening gala concert of Belfast Concert Hall 1997; Tonio in Pagliacci at Washington; sang the High Priest in Samson et Dalila at Los Angeles 1999. *Recordings:* Leporello with Roger Norrington.

ZABARA, Maksim; Belarusian bassoonist; b. 12 April 1957, Minsk, Byelorussian SSR, USSR. *Education:* Belarus Lyceum of Music, Kiev Special Music School Lisenko, Nat. Acad. of Music, Ukraine. *Career:* many recital and concert appearances in Belarus, Ukraine, Germany, The Netherlands and Canada; repertory includes C.P. Bach Sonatas, concertos by Devienne, Françaix, Hummel, Mozart, Vivaldi and Weber, sonatas by Glinka, Saint-Saëns and Schubert (arrangement of Arpeggione Sonata), Beethoven's Trio Op. 11 (arranged), Kreutzer's Trio Op. 43 and the Trio Pathétique by Glinka. *Honours:* Second Prize, Belarus Youth Woodwind Competition 1991, diploma, Int. Woodwind Competition, Minsk 1994. *E-mail:* mazabara@mail.ru (home).

ZABILIASTA, Lydia; Ukrainian singer (soprano); b. 1959, Oleno-Koshorivka, Kirovohrad. *Education:* Kiev State Conservatoire, studied in Kirovgrad and with Giulietta Simionato at La Scala, Italy. *Career:* Principal, Nat. Opera in Kiev from 1982, with such roles as Elsa, Tatiana, Nedda, Xenia in Boris Godunov and Mimi; tours to North and South America, Japan, Australia and the UK (with Perm Opera 1996), adding roles of Abigaille in Nabucco and Madama Butterfly. *Honours:* gold medal Tchaikovsky Singing Competition, Moscow 1982.

ZACHARIAS, Christian; German pianist and conductor; *Artistic Partner, Saint Paul Chamber Orchestra;* b. 27 April 1950, Jamshedpur, India. *Education:* studied with Irene Slavin in Karlsruhe, Germany, with Vlado Perlemuter in Paris, France. *Career:* appeared in USA with San Francisco and Boston Symphony, Cleveland Orchestra and New York Philharmonic, in Canada with Montreal Symphony; regular appearances in Europe and Japan; engagements at major European and US festivals, including Salzburg, Tanglewood, Mostly Mozart, Schleswig-Holstein, Edinburgh, La Roque d'Anthéron; chamber concerts with violinist Frank Peter Zimmermann and Leipziger Streichquartett; Carnegie Hall recital debut 2011; long-term relationships with Gothenburg Symphony and Orchestre de Chambre de Lausanne whose principal conductor he was for many years; Artistic Partner, Saint Paul Chamber Orchestra. *Recordings include:* Mozart Piano Concertos (several ECHO Klassik Awards), Schumann Symphonies and C.P.E. Bach Berlin Symphonies with the Orchestre de Chambre de Lausanne 2008, Schubert, Scarlatti and Mozart Sonatas, Concertos by Beethoven. *Honours:* Officier, Ordre des Arts et des Lettres; prizewinner in Geneva 1969, Van Cliburn Competition 1969, European Broadcasting Union Ravel Prize 1975, Artist of the Year, Midem Classical Awards 2007, awarded prize for his contributions to culture in Romania 2009, several Echo Klassik Awards. *Current Management:* c/o Künstlersekretariat A. Schoerke, Grazer Strasse 30, 30519 Hannover, Germany. *Telephone:* (511) 401048. *Fax:* (511) 407435. *E-mail:* info@ks-schoerke.de; www.ks-schoerke.de. *Website:* www.christian -zacharias.com.

ZACHARIASSEN, Mathias; Swedish singer (tenor); b. 1968, Stockholm. *Education:* Stockholm College of Opera with Nicolai Gedda. *Career:* debut as Eurimedes in Telemann's Orfeo, at the Staatsoper Berlin and Innsbruck Festival of Early Music, 1994; opera engagements as the Singer in Der Rosenkavalier at Stockholm and Oslo, Mozart's Ferrando and Idamante at Brussels, Lenski and Elemer in Arabella at the 1996 Glyndebourne Festival; season 1996–97 with Ferrando and Tamino at Graz, Don Ottavio in Oslo; season 1998 with Jacquino in Leonore and Fidelio, Théâtre des Champs Elysées, Paris; concerts have included Mozart's C Minor Mass in Oslo and Gothenburg, the Requiem with the Danish Radio Symphony Orchestra and Schubert's A-flat Mass; Verdi Requiem at Norrkoping; further concerts in Helsinki, Trondheim, Bad Kissingen and Amsterdam. *Current Management:* Ann Braathen Artist Management, Folkskolegatan 5, 11735 Stockholm, Sweden. *Telephone:* (8) 55690850. *Fax:* (8) 55690851. *E-mail:* info@braathenmanagement.com. *Website:* www.braathenmanagement.com.

ZADEK, Hildegard (Hilde); Austrian singing teacher and fmr singer; *President, Hildegard Zadek Foundation;* b. 15 Dec. 1917, Bromberg, Germany; d. of Alex Zadek and Elisabeth Zadek. *Education:* Conservatories of Jerusalem (Israel) and Zurich (Switzerland). *Career:* with Austrian State Opera, Vienna 1947–71; has performed at Royal Opera House, Covent Garden, London, Metropolitan Opera, New York, in Berlin, Düsseldorf and Zurich, and at Glyndebourne, UK, Salzburg, and Amsterdam (Netherlands) Festivals; Head of Vocal Dept, Vienna Municipal Conservatory 1964–78; has given masterclasses worldwide since 1978; Pres. Hildegard Zadek Foundation; numerous recordings. *Operas include:* Aida, Tosca, Ariadne, Salome, Don Giovanni (Donna Anna), Lohengrin (Elsa). *Publication:* Hilde Zadek: Mein Leben. *Honours:* Kammersängerin; Hon. mem. Vienna State Opera; Austrian Ehrenkreuz for Arts and Sciences (First Class). *Address:* Gustav-Tschermak-Gasse 34, 1190 Vienna, Austria.

ZAGORZANKA, Barbara; Polish singer (soprano); b. 31 July 1938, Kazimierzow. *Career:* sang at the Bydgoszcz Opera as Madama Butterfly, Gilda, Tosca and Tatiana 1960–67; in Poznań as Halka, Micaela, Elisabeth de Valois, Marguerite, Odabella in Attila, Mozart's Countess and Fiordiligi, and Lucia 1967, with Warsaw Opera as Aida, Liu, Leonore, Norma, Abigaille, Sieglinde and Roxana in Szymanowski's King Roger 1967; has sung Halka on tour to the USA and Roxana in Vienna in 1989; concert of Penderecki's

Utrenja at Frankfurt in 1992; further guest appearances in Paris including Lisa in The Queen of Spades.

ZAGROSEK, Lothar; German conductor and composer; b. 13 Nov. 1942, Waging. *Education:* studied in Vienna with Hans Swarowsky, and with Karajan and Bruno Maderna. *Career:* appointments at opera houses in Salzburg, Kiel and Darmstadt 1967–73; frequent appearances with the London Sinfonietta from 1978, conducting music by Weill, Ligeti, Messiaen and Stravinsky; engagements in USA, notably San Diego and Seattle from 1984; guest conductor for BBC Symphony Orchestra; Musical Dir, Paris Opéra 1986–88; Glyndebourne debut 1987 with Così fan tutte; conducted the premiere of Krenek's oratorio, Symeon Stylites at the 1988 Salzburg Festival; conducted the Paris Opéra Orchestra in York Höller's Der Meister und Margarita 1989 (the last new production at the Paris Opéra, Palais Garnier, before the opening of the Opéra de la Bastille); conducted the BBC Symphony Orchestra at the 1989 Promenade Concerts, in music by Markevitch, Mozart, Mendelssohn, Kodály and Brahms' Ein Deutsches Requiem; conducted Peter Sellars' production of Die Zauberflöte at Glyndebourne 1990; Promenade Concerts 1991; Music Dir, Stuttgart State Opera 1996; Chief Conductor, Städtische Theater, Leipzig; led the premiere of Das Mädchen by Lachenmann, Hamburg 1997; season 1997–98 with King Roger, Die Entführung and Tosca at Stuttgart; double bill of Bluebeard's Castle and Erwartung at Covent Garden 2002. *Recordings include:* Jonny spielt auf (Krenek), Goldschmidt's Der gewaltige Hahnrei and Die Vögel by Braunfels, Gruber's Cello Concerto, Schnittke's Piano Concerto, Haydn's 47th Symphony, Brahms No. 1 and Mendelssohn's Violin Concerto.

ZAHORTSEV, Volodymr Mykolayovych; Ukrainian composer; b. 27 Oct. 1944, Kiev. *Education:* Tchaikovsky Conservatory, Kiev. *Career:* joined avant-garde group of post-Stalinist composers in Kiev; mem. Composers' Union of the Ukraine. *Compositions include:* Priskaski, song cycle 1963, Violin Sonata 1964, String Quartet 1964, Sizes for five instruments 1965, Graduations for chamber group 1966, Games for chamber orchestra 1968, Symphony No. 1 1968, Music for four strings 1968, Sonata for strings, piano and percussion 1969, Rhythms for Piano 1970, Symphony No. 2 for soprano, tenor and orchestra 1978, Oboe Sonata 1978, Music for four strings, No. 2 1978, A Day In Pereyaslavl for soloists, chorus and orchestra 1979, In The Children's Room, cantata 1979, Chamber Concertos Nos 1–4 1981, Maty (Mother), Lvov, opera 1985, Chamber Concerto No. 5 1997, Epitaph No. 1, No. 2, No. 3 1998, Sonata for piano No. 3 1999, Chamber Concerto No. 7 2002, Chamber Concerto No. 8: Gaugrewailer 2003, Road of Dreams 2004, Chamber Concerto No. 9 2004, Symphony for Wandering 2005, Concerto for Violin and Orchestra 2006, Trio for Violin, Cello and Piano 2007, Transcendental 2009. *Honours:* Zyatoshinsky Prize 1997. *Address:* 03150 Kyiv, 15/4 Shchrsa str. Apt. 7 (home); c/o Composers' Union of the Ukraine, 252001 Kyiv, Ul Sofiuska 16/16, Ukraine (office). *Telephone:* (44) 528-12-10 (home).

ZAIDEL, Nahum; Russian flautist and conductor; b. 20 Sept. 1933, Russia; m. 1976. *Education:* P. I. Tchaikovsky State Conservatoire, Moscow, studied with Igor Markevitch and Genady Rozhdestvensky. *Career:* solo flautist, Moscow Chamber Orchestra under Rudolf Barschai 1957–58, Moscow Radio Symphony Orchestra under Rozhdestvensky 1959–72, Jerusalem Symphony Orchestra, Israel 1972–; Prof., Rubin Music Acad., Jerusalem 1972–; master-classes for flute and appearances as guest conductor. *Recordings:* works by Handel, Bach, Beethoven, Gluck, Hindemith, Prokofiev, Doppler, Vivaldi, Stamitz, Cimarosa, Salieri, Chaminade, Bloch, Dvořák, Stravinsky and Kurt Weill. *Honours:* first prize for flute Int. Competition in Moscow 1957.

ZAJICK, Dolora; American singer (mezzo-soprano); b. 24 March 1952, Salem, Ore. *Education:* Univ. of Nevada with Ted Puffer, Manhattan School of Music with Helen Vanni and Lou Galtiero, studied with Donald Hall. *Career:* debut at San Francisco Opera as Azucena 1986; Metropolitan Opera debut as Azucena 1988; season 1988–89 with further debuts at Lyric Opera of Chicago, Vienna Staatsoper, Rome's Caracalla Festival and Verona Arena; sang Rossini's Stabat Mater at Cincinnati May Festival and Mahler's 8th Symphony at Washington, DC under Rostropovich, Verdi's Requiem at Carnegie Hall and in Paris and London, Mahler's 2nd Symphony in Paris under Lorin Maazel; season 1989–90 as Amneris and Azucena at the Metropolitan, Tchaikovsky's Maid of Orleans at Carnegie Hall, Il Trovatore in Toulouse and Florence, Aïda in Reno, Verona Arena and at Caracalla Festival, as Marfa in Khovanshchina at San Francisco Opera 1990, Eboli in Don Carlo at the Metropolitan, La Scala and in Reno, 1990; sang Principessa in Adriana Lecouvreur at San Carlo, Naples 1992, and Jezibaba in Rusalka at the Metropolitan 1993; other opera house performances include Barcelona, Houston, Florence, Orange Festival and Covent Garden with debut 1994; sang Amneris at Verona Arena 1996; sang in Cav and Pag double bill, Met 1997; Paris Opéra Bastille debut as Eboli 1998; season 2000–01 as Azucena at the Met; Ortrud in Los Angeles 2010; Countess in Pique Dame at Metropolitan Opera 2011. *Films:* Aïda (various productions), Il Trovatore (various productions), Verdi Requiem 2009, Don Carlo 2010. *Recordings include:* La Forza del Destino and Verdi Requiem under Muti; Aida; Il Trovatore 1991; Don Carlo, under Levine; Alexander Nevsky, under Rostropovich; Herodiade 1995; Dolora Zajick – The Art of the Dramatic Mezzo-Soprano 2000. *Honours:* Bronze Medal, Tchaikovsky Int. Competition, Moscow 1982, Opera News

Award 2005, honoured by the Giulio Gari Foundation in recognition of her operatic career 2009. *Current Management:* c/o Columbia Artists Management, 1790 Broadway, New York, NY 10019-1412, USA. *Telephone:* (212) 841-9500. *Fax:* (212) 841 9744. *E-mail:* info@cami.com. *Website:* www.cami.com; www.dolorazajick.com.

ŻAK, Jerzy, MA, ARCM; Polish musician and musicologist; *Senior Lecturer, Academy of Music, Kraków*; b. 31 March 1954, Łódź. *Education:* Higher School of Music, Łódź, Conservatorio Superior de Musica, Alicante, Early Music Centre, London. *Career:* chamber musician and basso continuo player on lute, theorbo and guitar; chamber concerts, recitals and participation or directing opera performances in Poland, several European countries and in Canada; several broadcasts on Polish radio, and television appearances 1980–; Asst, Acad. of Music, Łódź 1983–94; Sr Lecturer, Acad. of Music, Kraków 1993–; taught at int. summer courses in Wilanów, Poland (Early Music) 1993–94, and in Szczawno Zdrój, Poland (guitar) 1992–99; Artistic Dir, Days of Guitar Music, Int. Festival, Łódź 1984, 1986; Consultant, Akademie Weiss-Inst. for Lute Studies, Parc de Schoppenwihr, France 1992–; founder and Dir of the Kleine Cammer-Musique ensemble 1993–; researcher, chamber music with plucked instruments; specialist in historical plucked instruments, lute and guitar. *Recordings include:* A. Scarlatti, 'San Casimiro', 'Re di Polonia', oratorio (Direction), A. Cesti, 'Secular Chamber Cantatas' (Continuo and direction), Silvius Leopold Weiss, 'Lute Music from Grüssau manuscript'. *Publications:* contrib. articles to musicological journals. *Address:* Pustola 32A m 6, 01-107 Warsaw, Poland (home). *E-mail:* jurekzak@gazeta.pl (home).

ZAKAI, Mira, BA, BMus, MMus; Israeli singer (contralto) and voice teacher; *Professor Emerita, Buchman-Mehta School of Music, Tel-Aviv University*; b. (Mira Vivian Koigen), 21 Sept. 1942, Jerusalem; d. of George Koigen and Eva Koigen (née Patai); m. Jacob Zakai; two d. *Education:* college for teachers of visual arts, Tel-Aviv, Rubin Acad. of Music and Lahav School of Man. at Tel-Aviv Univ., studied in Tel-Aviv with Gross-Levin, Jennie Tourel, in London with Yvonne Rodd-Marling and Hans Hotter, in New York with Chloe Owen and Marlena Malas. *Career:* debut in Vienna with Mahler's Rückert Lieder 1976; further concerts with the Philharmonia Orchestra, Berlin Philharmonic (debut: Mahler No. 2 under Abbado and Solti), in New York (debut: Bach B Minor Mass under Leinsdorf), and throughout Germany (Das Lied von der Erde and Mahler No. 3 1987); sang with Israel Nat. Opera in The Medium and Hansel and Gretel from 1990; sang at Bonn in Beethoven's Ninth 1992; opera roles include Gluck's Orpheus with Scottish Opera, Anne in Les Troyens with Opéra de Lyon; collaborations with pianists Mikael Eliasen, Graham Johnson, Cristian Ivaldi, Andras Schiff; Sr Teacher, Rubin Acad. of Music 1978–85, Sr Lecturer and Faculty mem. 1991–97, Adjunct Assoc. Prof. 1997–99, tenure 1999–, Adjunct Full Prof. of Vocal Arts, Lied and Oratorio, Buchman-Mehta School of Music, Tel-Aviv Univ. 2001–11, Prof. Emer. 2011–, fmr Head of Dept; Visiting Prof. of Voice, Theater Dept, Tel-Aviv Univ. 1997–, Eastman School of Music, New York, Curtis Inst., Philadelphia; Chair. Sal Tarbut (Special Cttee for Music Educ. in Schools), Ministry of Educ. 2001–11, Ben Haim Competition of Performing Israeli Music 2002, 2004, 2006, 2008, 2010, 2012; mem. Music Cttee, Israel Arts Council 2002–08; mem. jury for The Israel Prize 2006; mem. jury for Gary Bertini Scholarship. *Recordings include:* Mahler 2nd Symphony with the Chicago Symphony Orchestra and George Solti (Grammy Award). *Publication:* Whereto do the Salmons swim? – Mira Zakai and André Haydu: A Dialogue 1999; articles: Time and Space in Vocal Music, The Journey in Vocal Music, Objects – Tangible and Virtual in Vocal Music, The Dialogue with Death and Solitude in Vocal Music, The Mother's Voice in Vocal Music, Life and Death are in the Power of the Tongue, Between Hearing and Listening, Text and Music's Journey from Score to Stage. *Honours:* Composers and Playwrights Assen Award 1988, Arts and Culture Council Prize for best performance of Israeli compositions 1990, Ministry of Educ. Prize for Contrib. to Israeli Music 1998. *Address:* 6 Patai Street, 53203 Givatayim (home); Buchman-Mehta School of Music, Faculty of the Arts, Tel-Aviv University, Ramat Aviv, 69978 Tel-Aviv, Israel (office). *Telephone:* (3) 5714934 (home); (3) 6408415 (office). *Fax:* (3) 7324207 (home). *E-mail:* mzakai@post.tau.ac.il (office). *Website:* www.tau.ac.il/~mzakai (office).

ZALEWSKI, Wlodzimerz; Polish singer (bass-baritone); b. 1949. *Career:* sang at Łódź Opera 1975–82, Gelsenkirchen from 1982; Bregenz Festival 1978 as the Dutchman, and Philadelphia 1988 as Don Alfonso in Così fan tutte; Prof., Łódź Music Acad. from 1981; sang in the 1989 premiere of Michael Kohlhaas by Karl Kogler at the Landestheater, Linz; appearances at Łódź and elsewhere as Boris Godunov; other roles have included Hindemith's Cardillac, Kaspar in Der Freischütz, Basilio, Mustafà, Wotan and Scarpia; frequent concert appearances.

ZAMBELLI, Marco; Italian conductor; b. 1965, Genoa. *Education:* Geneva Conservatoire. *Career:* Chorus Master at the Grasse Boys Choir, 1988–89, Opéra de Lyon 1989–92 (including the premiere of Debussy's Rodrigue et Chimène); other repertory includes all major operas of Mozart, L'Elisir d'amore, La Bohème, Butterfly, Poppea, Orfeo and Il Trovatore; asst with such conductors as John Eliot Gardiner (Manon Lescaut at Glyndebourne and other repertory with Monteverdi/EBS), Luciano Berio and Woldemar Nelsson; season 1996–97 with Pergolesi/Cimarosa double bill at Messina, La Cenerentola at Ascoli and Don Giovanni for Opera Zuid; Haydn's Creation in Cogliou, 1996; Madama Butterfly, 1996, and Don Pasquale and Rigoletto, 1997, at the Tenerife Opera Festival; Luisa Miller and Madama Butterfly for Opera North and Manon Lescaut at the 1997 Glyndebourne Festival; Così fan tutte.

ZAMBELLO, Francesca, BA; American opera and theatre director; *Artistic Director, Washington National Opera*; b. 24 Aug. 1956, New York; d. of Charles Carmine Zambello and Jean Sincere Zambello. *Education:* American School of Paris, Moscow Univ., Colgate Univ. *Career:* Asst Dir, Lyric Opera of Chicago 1981–82, San Francisco Opera 1983–84, later Artistic Advisor; Artistic Dir, Skylight Music Theatre 1984–91; Gen. and Artistic Dir, Glimmerglass Opera, New York 2010–; fmr Artistic Advisor, Washington Nat. Opera, Artistic Dir 2013–; guest producer, Met, Chicago Lyric Opera, La Scala, ROH, Paris Opera, San Francisco Opera, Teatro La Fenice, Savonlinna Festival, Houston Grand Opera, Nat. Opera of Iceland, Seattle Opera, San Diego Opera, Opera Theatre of St Louis, Rome Opera, Théâtre Municipal de Lausanne, Teatro Regio, Greater Miami Opera, Pesaro Festival, Parma and Wexford Festival; has worked on theatre productions in London's West End and New York's Broadway; fmr Visiting Prof., Harvard Univ., Univ. of Calif., Berkeley. *Works directed include:* The Makropolous Case (Skylight Opera Theater) 1984, Albert Herring (Savonlinna Opera Festival, Finland) 1984, Fidelio (Houston Grand Opera) 1984, (Washington Opera) 2003, The Mikado (Nat. Opera of Iceland) 1985, Tosca (Nat. Opera of Puerto Rico) 1985, 1986, (Earl's Court Arena, London) 1991, Carmen (Texas Opera Theater) 1986, (Skylight Opera Theater) 1988, (ROH) 2006, 2009, 2010, 2013, The Barber of Seville (Nat. Opera of Iceland) 1986, (Santa Fe Opera) 1994, Faust (Houston Grand Opera) 1986, (San Francisco Opera) 1987, (Seattle Opera and San Diego Opera) 1988, Beatrice di Tenda (Teatro La Fenice, Venice) 1987, L'Elisir d'Amore (Teatro Regio, Parma) 1988, 1992, The Devil and Kate (Wexford Festival) 1988, Salome (Houston Grand Opera) 1988, (Lyric Opera of Chicago) 2006, Don Giovanni (New Israeli Opera, Tel-Aviv) 1988, (ROH) 2002, 2003, 2012, La Bohème (San Francisco Opera) 1988, (Teatro Regio, Parma) 1991, (Royal Albert Hall) 2004, 2006, Idomeneo (Chicago Early Music Opera) 1989, Rigoletto (San Francisco Opera) 1989, War and Peace (Seattle Goodwill Festival) 1990, (Opéra Nat. de Paris) 2000, 2005, La Traviata (Skylight Opera Theater) 1990, (Roman Arena of the Orange Festival, France) 1993, (Bordeaux Opera) 1997, Les Troyens (Los Angeles Music Center Opera) 1991, (Met) 2003,2012–13, Lucia di Lammermoor (Dublin Grand Opera) 1991, (Met) 1992, The Sorrows of Young Werther (Santa Fe Opera) 1992, Il Pirata (Zurich Opera) 1992, (Théâtre Municipal de Lausanne) 1993, Romulus Hunt (Met) 1993, Jenůfa (San Francisco Opera) 2001, (Dallas Opera) 1993, 2004, Khovanshchina (ENO) 1994, 2003, Blond Eckbert (Santa Fe Opera) 1994, Billy Budd (Grand Théâtre de Genève) 1994, (ROH) 1995, (Opéra Nat. de Paris) 1996, 2001, (Washington Opera and Teatro Regio, Parma) 2004, Street Scene (Houston Grand Opera) 1994, (Theater des Westens) 1995, Arianna (ROH) 1995, Tannhäuser (Royal Danish Opera, Copenhagen) 1995, Die Meistersinger von Nürnberg (Royal Danish Opera, Copenhagen) 1996, The Tales of Hoffmann (Staat Theater, Aalto) 1996, Emmeline (Santa Fe Opera) 1996, (New York City Opera) 1998, Paul Bunyan (Aldeburgh Festival) 1997, (ROH) 1999, Turandot (Opéra Nat. de Paris) 1997, 1999, Iphigénie en Tauride (Glimmerglass Opera) 1997, The Bartered Bride (ROH) 1998, 2001, Boris Godunov (ENO) 1998, (Canadian Opera Co.) 2002, (Paris Opera) 2005, Dialogues des Carmélites (Saito Kinen Festival, Japan) 1998, (Santa Fe Opera and Opéra Nat. de Paris) 1999, (Opéra Nat. de Paris) 2004, Tristan and Isolde (Seattle Opera) 1998, The Flying Dutchman (Bordeaux Opera) 1998, 2002, Madama Butterfly (Grand Théâtre de Genève) 1998, (Pittsburgh Opera) 2002, (San Diego Opera) 2003, (Houston Grand Opera) 2004, Aida (Grand Théâtre de Genève) 1999, Otello (Bayerisches Staatsoper) 1999, 2012, Peter Grimes (Netherlands Opera, Amsterdam) 2000, 2004, Luisa Miller (San Francisco Opera) 2000, (Dallas Opera) 2005, Thérèse Raquin (Dallas Opera) 2001, (L'Opéra de Montréal) 2002, (San Diego Opera) 2003, Of Mice and Men (Bregenz Festival and Washington Opera) 2001, (Houston Grand Opera) 2002, Florencia en el Amazons (Houston Grand Opera) 2001, (Seattle Opera) 2005, Die Walküre (Washington Opera) 2003, San Francisco) 2011, Alcina (New York City Opera) 2003, West Side Story (Bregenz Festival) 2003, 2004, The Little Prince (Houston Grand Opera) 2003, (Skylight Music Theater) 2004, (Boston Lyric Opera and New York City Opera) 2005, Queen of Spades (Grand Théâtre de Genève) 2003, (ROH) 2006, Guillaume Tell (Opéra Nat. de Paris) 2003, Fiery Angel (Bolshoi Theater) 2004, Der fliegende Holländer (Lithuanian Opera, Vilnius) 2004, Tibet Through the Red Box (Seattle Children's Theater) 2004, An American Tragedy (Met) 2005, Porgy and Bess (Washington Opera) 2005, Cyrano de Bergerac (Met) 2005, (ROH and Met) 2006, The Love for Three Oranges (Opera Australia) 2005, Das Rheingold (Washington Opera) 2006, The Little Mermaid (Broadway), Little House on the Prairie (Guthrie), First Wives Club (Old Globe), Cyrano (La Scala), Show Boat (Washington) 2013. *Honours:* Dr hc (Colgate Univ.); Chevalier des Arts et des Lettres; Medal for Service to Culture, Russian Fed.; three Olivier Awards from London Soc. of Theatres and two Evening Standard Awards for Best Musical and Best Opera. *Current Management:* c/o Caroline Woodfield, Opus Artists Ltd, 470 Park Avenue South, 9th Floor North, New York, NY 10016, USA. *Telephone:* (212) 584-7580. *Fax:* (646) 300-8280. *E-mail:* cwoodfield@opus3artists.com. *Website:* www.opus3artists.com. *Address:* 257 West 52nd Street, 4th Floor, New York, NY 10019, USA (office). *Telephone:* (646) 736-2900 (office). *E-mail:* francesca@francescazambello.com (office); fzambello@mac.com (home); Jtantleff@paradigmagency.com (office). *Website:* www.francescazambello.com.

ZAMBORSKY, Stanislav, PhD; Slovak pianist; b. 12 April 1946, Košice; m. Zlata Olachova 1972, two d. *Education:* Konservatorium Košice, Acad. of Music and Dramatic Arts, Bratislava, Franz Liszt Acad., Budapest. *Career:* debut at Bratislava Music Festival; many concerts with orchestras and recitals worldwide. *Recordings:* Mozart, Haydn Concertos; Schumann, Sonata G minor; Liszt, Liebesträume, Au bord d'une source, Death of Isolde; Hummel Works for four hands piano; Sixta Piano Sonata; Bokes Piano concerto; Parik Dropping Foliage Songs, Hrusovsky Sonata No. 2; Mozart Piano Sonatas; Grieg Piano Concerto. *Honours:* second prize Prague 1968, fourth prize Utrecht 1969, Frico Kafenda Prize for Interpretation, Slovak Music, Bratislava 1995, Complete Musical Critic Prize, Bratislava 1996.

ZAMIR, Yaakov; American singer (high tenor); b. 1953. *Education:* Univ. of Massachusetts at Amherst, Univ. of Maine at Portland-Gorham, Chicago and San Francisco Conservatories of Music. *Career:* has appeared since 1985 in major cities of Israel, USA, Iceland, Germany, England and Cyprus in wide range of concert and operatic music; Conductors include Marc Minkowski, Christopher Hogwood, Nicholas McGegan, and Richard Westenberg; has performed as male soprano, countertenor and baritone as well as tenor, specializing as high tenor, Tenore di Grazia; has sung in Die Fledermaus, Cendrillon, A Midsummer Night's Dream, La Bohème, Lucia di Lammermoor, Mefistofele, Attila, Platée and Cavalleria Rusticana, La Clemenza di Tito, Alcina, Riccardo Primo.

ZAMPARINO, Cesare; Italian singer (tenor); b. 1969, Italy. *Career:* sang Alfredo in Traviata at Rieti (1992) followed by the Duke of Mantua at Buenos Aires; Teatro San Carlo Naples from 1993, as Alfredo and as Alfred in Fledermaus; other repertory includes Rodolfo, Nemorino, Elvino (La Sonnambula), Edgardo, Ernesto and Cavaradossi.

ZAMPIERI, Maria; Italian singer (soprano); b. 24 May 1941, Padua. *Education:* Padua Conservatory. *Career:* debut in Pavia 1972; La Scala Milan from 1977 as Amalia in I Masnadieri, Leonora in Il Trovatore and Elisabeth de Valois; Trieste as Elvira in Ernani; Lisbon as Amelia Boccanegra; Vienna Staatsoper from 1979 in Il Giuramento, Attila and Macbeth; Deutsche Oper Berlin and Verona Arena as Aida; Covent Garden debut 1984 as Tosca; other engagements in Munich, Buenos Aires, San Francisco, Bregenz, Bonn and Frankfurt; sang Francesca da Rimini at Karlsruhe in 1986; season 1987–88 as Norma at Nîmes and Lady Macbeth at Spoleto; Stuttgart Staatsoper 1990 as Tosca, Bregenz Festival 1990 in the title role of La Wally; debut as Salome at Vienna 1991; sang Suor Angelica at Zürich, 1996; Verdi's Elena and Lady Macbeth at the Vienna Staatsoper, 1999. *Recordings include:* Il Giuramento; Attila; Belisario by Donizetti; Macbeth. *Current Management:* Baron & Weingartner International Artists Management, Bösendorferstrasse 4/12, 1010 Vienna, Austria. *Telephone:* (1) 4896154. *Fax:* (1) 4856711. *E-mail:* office@baronartists.com. *Website:* www.baronartists.com.

ZAMUSZKO, Slawomir; Polish composer, violist and teacher of music theory; b. 30 Dec. 1973, Łódź; m. Weronika Ratusińska-Zamuszko; two d. *Education:* H. Wieniawski State Music Lyceum, Łódź, G. & K. Bacewicz Acad. of Music, Łódź, F. Chopin Acad. of Music, Warsaw with Prof. Marian Borkowski, Computer Eng Dept, Tech. Univ. of Łódź. *Career:* debut as composer, Stage Music for David Mercer's Flint for flute, French Horn, trombone, strings and synthesizer, 'Pole' (Słup) Theatre Studio, Łódź 1993; viola player with Strings of Łódź Chamber Orchestra 1990–93, Polish Camerata Orchestra 1993–94; First and Solo Violist, Young Austrian Philharmony 1996–99; contrib. to Justus Frantz's Philharmony of Nations 1998; numerous concerts performing own work in Poland, Germany, Netherlands, Slovenia, Russia, USA, NZ, 47th Warsaw Autumn Festival of Contemporary Music, Warsaw 2004, 11th, 13th, 17th Lab. of Contemporary Music, Warsaw 2004, 2006, Białystok 2010; 25th Musica Polonica Nova Festival, Wrocław 2006, 10th Festival of New Music, Bytom 2011; participant in Young Composers' tribute to Frédéric Chopin programme, European Krzysztof Penderecki Music Centre 2007–10; mem. Polish Composers' Union, Łódź's Soc. for Ancient Music. *Compositions include:* instrumental and vocal instrumental: Suite for viola solo 1995, Controversies an instrumental theatre for two flutes 1996, Portal 1 for horn and piano 1996, Concerto for clarinet and string orchestra 1998, An die unsterbliche Geliebte (cantata, after Beethoven) for baritone and orchestra 1998, Portal 2 for viola, cello and orchestra 1999, Preludes for piano 1999–2000, Requiem (text by Anna Akhmatova) for alto and string quartet 2000, Permeatings for string orchestra 2001, Repercussions for two trumpets and two percussion groups 2001, Preludes for organ 2001, Psalm 15 for lyric soprano and chamber orchestra 2001–02, The Mask (after S. Lem) monodrama for female speaking voice and chamber orchestra 2004, An European in Mexico for flute or clarinet and string quartet or string orchestra 2004, Six Persons for cello and piano 2004, Events for small orchestra 2005, Cantata Seriosa and Cantata Serena (text by Johann Heermann) for soprano, mixed choir and harpsichord or organ 2005, Divertimento in memoriam W.A.M. for string orchestra 2005–06, Nasha Shkhapa (Nash's Hag) (text by Ogden Nash & Hilaire Belloc) for mezzosoprano and piano or symphony orchestra 2007, 89 Degrees North for symphony orchestra 2007–08, Five Bulgarian Tunes for symphony orchestra 2008, Dissociations for string quartet 2008, Concerto for viola and symphony orchestra 2009, Polish Flowers (text by Julian Tuwim) for speaking voice and symphony orchestra 2010, Pia-No Concerto for prepared piano (seven non-musical performers) and symphony orchestra 2010, The Silesian Concerto for 23 string instruments 2013, From the Definitive Stories for three flutes, viola and tape 2013; vocal: A Heart Grows Up song for four-voiced male choir a cappella (text by Jan Kochanowski) 1999, Lingvariations on theme of John Cage for speaking voice 2001; electronic: Babel FM for tape 1997, Play-tin for tape 1997, Ampliviola 1 for tape 2001–02, Ampliviola 2 for tape 2003; music for the spectacles of 'Pole', Theatre Studio in Łódź and motion pictures by

students of Film/Television Directing and Cinematography Depts of L. Schiller State Film, Television and Theatre School in Łódź, also for audiobooks for children by the 'Festina lente' Foundation. *Recordings:* Portal 1 for horn and piano 2000, Preludes for organ 2003, Events for small orchestra 2005, Nasha Shkhapa for mezzo-soprano and piano 2007, A Glowing Stained Glass for vibraphone 2007, Concerto for clarinet and string orchestra 2010, Divertimento in memoriam W.A.M. for string orchestra 2010, Nasha Shkhapa for mezzo-soprano and symphony orchestra 2010, A European in Mexico for flute and string orchestra 2010, Concerto for viola and symphony orchestra 2010, Pia-No Concerto for prepared piano and symphony orchestra 2011. *Publications:* contrib. to Muzyka 21 2000–02, Koneser 2001–02, Musical Education in School 2002–03, Dobre Radio Broadcasting Corpn 2003–04, Arthur Rubinstein Łódź Philharmonic programme notes 2008–12. *Honours:* Ministry of Culture and Arts scholarship 1997–98, First Prize, Int. Composers' Competition, Cottbus, Germany 2000, 2003. *Address:* Gdanska 32, 90-716 Łódź, Poland (office). *E-mail:* zamek@amuz.lodz.pl (office); zamuszko@gmail.com (home). *Website:* www.zamuszko.com.

ZANAZZO, Alfredo; Italian singer (bass); b. 14 Oct. 1946, Imperia. *Education:* studied with Tancredi Pasero. *Career:* debut at Verona Arena 1981 as the King in Aida; Verona Arena 1982–89, as Ramphis and Timur; sang Wagner's Dutchman at Treviso 1981, La Scala Milan 1982 as Narbal in Les Troyens, and the King of Scotland in Ariodante; season 1986–87 as Colline in La Bohème at the Paris Opéra, Padre Guardiano at Rome, Zaccaria and Masetto at Turin and Ramphis at the Metropolitan; appearances at Luxor and the Vienna Staatsoper as Ramphis, Macerata Festival as Raimondo in Lucia di Lammermoor; Zürich Opera 1988 as Banquo and Walter Furst in Guillaume Tell; further engagements at the Geneva Opera as Pluto in Monteverdi's Orfeo, at Frankfurt as Raimondo, in Toronto as Procida in Les Vêpres Siciliennes and at Las Palmas as Alvise in La Gioconda; Teatro Margherita Genoa 1991 as Roucher in La Gioconda; sang Pagano in I Lombardi at Piacenza 1995.

ZANCANARO, Giorgio; Italian singer (baritone); b. 9 May 1939, Verona. *Career:* debut in I Puritani, Teatro Nuovo Milan 1971; sang widely in Italy 1971–; int. career from 1977, notably in London, Frankfurt, Rome, Hamburg, Paris; resident artist, Zurich Opernhaus 1977–; debut at La Scala, Milan as Ford in Falstaff 1981; Metropolitan Opera debut as Renato in Un Ballo in Maschera 1982; other roles include Posa in Don Carlos, Germont, Gerard in Andrea Chénier, Rigoletto, Luna and Ezio in Attila, Escamillo, Tonio in Pagliacci and Albert in Werther, Count Luna, Guillaume Tell, Donizetti's Parisina d'Este, Michele in Il Tabarro, Nabucco, the High Priest in Samson et Dalila. *Recordings include:* Il Trovatore, conducted by Giulini, Andrea Chenier, La Traviata, La Forza del Destino, Rigoletto, Guillaume Tell, Attila, I Vespri Siciliani and Tosca. *Honours:* Busetto Int. Singing Competition 1970. *Current Management:* Stafford Law, Candleway, Broad Street, Sutton Valence, Kent ME17 3AT, England. *Telephone:* (1622) 840038. *E-mail:* staffordlaw@btinternet.com. *Website:* www.stafford-law.com.

ZANDER, Benjamin, BA; American (b. British) conductor; b. 9 March 1939, Gerrard's Cross, Bucks, England; s. of Dr Walter Zander; m. 1st Patricia Zander 1966; one d.; m. 2nd Rosamund Stone Zander 1981. *Education:* Univ. Coll. London, Brandeis Univ., Harvard Univ., USA; studied with Benjamin Britten and Imogen Holst at Aldeburgh, in Florence with cellist Gaspar Cassado, at the Academica Chigiana in Siena, the State Conservatory Cologne and London Univ.; graduate work at Harvard and in New York. *Career:* became youngest mem. of Nat. Youth Orchestra of Great Britain, aged 12; faculty mem., New England Conservatory 1967–, conducting the Youth Philharmonic Orchestra and the Conservatory's Symphony Orchestra; ten int. tours with the Youth Philharmonic Orchestra, including South America; Music Dir and Conductor, Boston Philharmonic Orchestra 1979–; Guest Conductor, Israel Philharmonic Orchestra, Bournemouth Symphony Orchestra, Scottish Nat. Orchestra, Irish Nat. Orchestra, St Petersburg Philharmonic Orchestra, Malaysian Symphony Orchestra, St Louis Symphony Orchestra, Indianapolis Symphony Orchestra, Youth Orchestra of the Americas; debut with the London Philharmonic Orchestra 1995, with Mahler's Sixth, returning for the Ninth Symphony. *Recordings include:* Mahler's Symphony No. 6, Beethoven's Ninth and The Rite of Spring, Bruckner's Symphony No. 5. *Address:* Boston Philharmonic Orchestra, 295 Huntingdon Avenue, Suite 210, Boston, MA 02115–4433, USA (office). *E-mail:* info@benjaminzander.com (office). *Website:* www.benjaminzander.com.

ZANETTOVICH, Renato, DipMus; Italian violinist; b. 28 July 1921, Trieste; m. Bianca Negri 1947; three s. *Education:* Trieste Conservatory. *Career:* debut with the Trio Di Trieste 1933; concerts and recordings with Trio Di Trieste worldwide; violin teacher at Conservatories of Bolzano 1950–55, Trieste 1955–70, Venice 1970–86; fmr teacher, Accad. Musicale Chigiana in Siena, Scuola di Musica di Fiesole; currently teacher, Scuola Superiore Internazionale di Musica da Camera del Trio di Trieste in Duino; mem. Rotary Club, Trieste. *Publications:* Revision of Etudes by Kayser Op. 20 1965, Scale and Arpeggio Exercises 1973, Scale and Arpeggio Exercises for Violin Students 1974, Mazas Op. 36 1979, Sitt Op. 32 1986, Dont Op. 37 1993, Double-Stopping Scale Exercises 2005. *Honours:* Accademico di S Cecilia, Grande Ufficiale dell'Ordine al Merito della Repubblica Italiana. *Address:* Via Cataro 9, Trieste, Italy (home). *Telephone:* (040) 305159 (home). *Fax:* (040) 307212 (home). *Website:* www.trioditrieste.com (home).

ZANNINI, Laura; Italian singer (mezzo-soprano); b. 4 April 1937, Trieste. *Education:* Conservatorio Benedetto Marcello, Venice with Gilda dalla Rizza, studied with Bruno Maderna. *Career:* debut in Spoleto 1955 as Isabella in L'Italiana in Algeri; sang leading roles at La Scala Milan, Genoa, Palermo, Naples, Parma, Venice, Turin and Trieste; sang at Verona Arena 1957, 1967, 1979–80, 1986, and Piccola Scala 1966 in the premiere of Flavio Testi's Albergi dei Poveri; further appearances at the Maggio Musicale Fiorentino, the State Operas of Vienna and Munich, the Paris Opéra, Brussels, Bordeaux, Wiesbaden, Copenhagen, London, Edinburgh, Moscow and Budapest; sang Alisa in Lucia di Lammermoor at Bari and Tisbe in La Cenerentola at Glyndebourne 1983; also sang in operas by Henze, Britten, Menotti, Poulenc, Stravinsky, Schoenberg and Zandonai; sang Caterina in L'Amico Fritz at Livorno 1996. *Recordings:* Tisbe in La Cenerentola; Flora in La Traviata with Callas; Mascagni's Isabeau.

ZANOLLI, Silvana; Italian singer (soprano); b. 14 Oct. 1928, Fiume; m. Otello Borgonova. *Education:* Milan Opera School, studied with Luciano Tomerilli and Tomaso Japelli. *Career:* debut at La Scala Milan 1951 in La Buona Figliuola, by Piccinni; appearances in leading roles at Rome, Palermo, Bologna, Parma, Turin, Trieste, Naples and Venice; festival engagements at Florence and Rome with guest showings at Buenos Aires, the State Operas of Vienna, Stuttgart and Munich, at Brussels, Cologne, Rio de Janeiro, Geneva, Barcelona, Lisbon and London Covent Garden; Verona Arena 1957–58 and Glyndebourne 1959–60 as Clorinda in La Cenerentola; also sang in Mexico City, Monte Carlo and New York at Metropolitan Opera. *Recordings:* Amelia al Ballo by Menotti; Cimarosa's Il Matrimonio Segreto; Il Campiello by Wolf-Ferrari.

ZANON, Fabio, MMus, ARAM; Brazilian guitarist and academic; *Visiting Professor of Guitar, Royal Academy of Music;* b. 1966; m.; two c. *Education:* Univ. of São Paulo, Royal Acad. of Music, London, masterclasses with Julian Bream. *Career:* London concert debut, Wigmore Hall 1995; debut with London Philharmonic Orchestra 1998; played at Royal Festival Hall, London, Carnegie Hall in New York, Sala Verdi in Milan, KKR in Lucerne, Tchaikovsky Hall in Moscow, Philharmonie in St Petersburg and São Paulo Hall and Rio Opera House in Brazil; tours of USA and Canada, performances in S America, Australia, Middle East and throughout Europe; premiered/recorded new guitar concertos by Crowl, Dwyer, Faria, Hime, Kenyon and van der Roost; Visiting Prof. of Guitar, RAM, London 2008–; masterclasses at Royal Coll. of Music, London, Gnessin School, Moscow, Univ. of Vienna and music colls in USA. *Radio:* produced 26-programme radio series, The Art of the Guitar for Rádio Cultura Brazil. *Recordings include:* Tarrega/Bach/de Faria/Mertz/Ponce recital CD 1998, Scarlatti Sonatas Arranged for Guitar 1999, Yanomami: Music for Choir and Guitar 2009, Villa-Lobos: The Complete Solo Guitar Works 2010, Mountain Songs: Music for Flute & Guitar 2012. *Honours:* Francisco Tarrega Prize, Spain 1996, Guitar Foundation of America Guitar Competition 1996, Moinho Santista Prize for contrib. to development of Brazilian music 1997, Carlos Gomes Prize for Best Solo Performer (Brazil) 2005. *Address:* Royal Academy of Music, Marylebone Road, London, NW1 5HT, England (office). *Telephone:* (20) 7873 7373 (office). *E-mail:* guitar@ram .ac.uk (office). *Website:* www.ram.ac.uk (office).

ZAROU, Jeannette; Canadian singer (soprano); b. 1942, Ramallah, Palestine. *Education:* Royal Conservatory of Music, Toronto, Canada with Irene Jessner, Halina Wyszkowski and Herman Geiger-Torel. *Career:* debut as Priestess in Aida with Canadian Opera at Toronto 1964; sang Liu in Turandot for Canadian Opera 1965; mem., Deutsche Oper am Rhein, Düsseldorf 1967–74; guest appearances in Toronto, Deutsche Oper Berlin, Hamburg and Munich State Opera, Cologne, Frankfurt, Karlsruhe, Nuremberg, Bordeaux and Rouen; other roles have included Liù in Turandot, Micaela in Carmen, Mimi in La Bohème, Marguerite in Faust, Ilia in Idomeneo, Pamina, Sophie in Rosenkavalier; modern repertoire has included Miss Wordsworth in Albert Herring and Blanche in Dialogues des Carmélites; concert appearances include Mahler's Fourth Symphony; currently voice tutor, Anton Rubinstein Akademie, Düsseldorf. *Recordings include:* Requiem by Draeske. *Address:* c/o Anton Rubinstein Akademie, im Steinway-Haus Heinersdorff, Kronprinzenstrasse 97, 40217 Düsseldorf, Germany (office). *E-mail:* blatow@rubinstein -akademie.de (office). *Website:* www.rubinstein-akademie.de (office).

ZARTNER, Rose Marie; German pianist; b. 14 Sept. 1939, Nuremberg; m. Wolfgang Schwabe; one s. one d. *Education:* studied in Nuremberg with Ernst Gröschel, Frankfurt am Main with Brauka Musulin, Cologne with Bruno Seidlhofer. *Career:* many solo concert engagements and tours in Germany and abroad; numerous appearances as lieder accompanist in chamber engagements; performed at recitals at Beethoven and Reger festivals, Bonn, Palais Schaumburg, German Federal Chancellery, Minsk and Bucharest; concerts with Berlin Philharmonie, in Vienna, Salzburg, Nuremberg, Mannheim; Schwetzingen Musik Festival and Haydn Festival in Burgenland; concerts with numerous orchestras, including Bamberg and Nuremberg Symphonies, Symphony Orchestra of Romania, Orchester of Beethovenhalle and Classical Philharmonie, Bonn; extensive classic repertory, including works of Haydn and Mozart, also modern and lesser-known works; numerous radio performances at home and in Europe; many works dedicated to her; as mem. of Bonn Ensemble, appearances at International Music Days in Bonn and at Royal Danish Opera, Copenhagen, and in Seoul, Republic of Korea; Docent, Music School, Bonn and private tuition. *Recordings include:* works of Schumann, Haydn, Schubert, Dittersdorf, Reger. *Honours:* cultural prize Sudetendeutsche Landsmannschaft 1975, Grand Cultural Prize 1997.

ZARZO, José; Spanish French horn player; *Principal Horn, Gran Canaria Philharmonic Orchestra;* b. 6 Aug. 1966, Mexico City, Mexico; m. Mari Carmen Lobeira 1992 (divorced 2001); one s. one d. *Education:* studied music from age seven, with father; Royal Conservatory of the Hague, Netherlands with Prof. Vicente Zarzo, master-classes with Profs Radovan Vlatkovic and Dale Clevenger. *Career:* debut at Orlando Festival with Orlando String Quartet, Heinz Holliger 1983; appeared on Dutch TV with Punto's Horn Concerto No. 5; has performed with almost all Dutch symphony orchestras 1989–; Prin. Horn, Gran Canaria Philharmonic Orchestra, performing solo and recording major symphony repertoire 1989–; tours of major cities in Austria, Switzerland, Germany; Founding mem. chamber music group, Ensemble Isola, with principals from Gran Canaria Philharmonic Orchestra and pianist Juan Francisco Parra; Guest Artist, Int. Horn Soc. Symposium, Valencia 2004; soloist with Sinfonia Concertante for winds and orchestra by Peter Josef von Lindpaintner 2005; tour of Japan with Gran Canaria Philharmonic 2006; mem. Sojara Brass Quintet; mem. Int. Horn Soc. *Recordings:* Virtuoso Bläsermusik, Gustav Mahler's Symphony No. 5, Gustav Mahler's Symphony No. 4 (with Gran Canaria Philharmonic Orchestra, Adrian Leaper conductor), Choros of Villa Lobos, Horn in Trios, Isola Romantica. *Address:* Avenue Santiago de Cuba 22, 35330 Teror, Gran Canaria, Spain (home). *Telephone:* (92) 8631246 (home).

ZAWADZKA, Barbara, MA; Polish composer; b. 21 Sept. 1951, Warsaw. *Education:* Acad. of Music, Kraków, studied with Krzysztof Penderecki, Conservatoire de Paris, with Guy Riebel, IRCAM, Paris. *Career:* mem., LOBO contemporary music concert team 1972–76; participated in music festivals in Poland, France, Germany, Norway, Switzerland and Hong Kong 1988–; Lecturer, Krakow Conservatory. *Compositions:* Motif of Space for strings 1977, Quartetto d'Archi 1981, 4+1 quintet for oboe, cor anglais, clarinet, bass clarinet and piano 1981, Stabat Mater for choir 1981, Esperanza for tape 1984, Medytacje 1984, Locus Solus for piano 1984, Divertimento 1984, Sources for tape, 80 projectors and percussion 1986–87, Greya for tape 1987, Horizontal and Vertical Games 1993–94, Tutti 1994, Eolomea 1995, Aube...Soleil 1996, Monodrama for violin 1996. *Publications:* Ruch Muzyczny 1988, Ars Electronica 1988, Boswil 1988. *Address:* Academy of Music, 31-027 Krakow, 43, Sw. Tomasza Street, Poland (office). *E-mail:* zbzawadz@cyf-kr.edu.pl (office). *Website:* www.amuz.krakow.pl (office).

ZAWADZKA-GOLOSZ, Anna, DipMus; Polish composer; b. 1 Dec. 1955, Kraków; m. Jerzy Golosz 1986. *Education:* Acad. of Music, Kraków with Krystyna Moszumanska-Nazar, Hochschule für Musik, Theater und Tanz, Essen with Wolfgang Hufschmidt. *Career:* Teacher of Theory of Music 1981–; Asst. Acad. of Music, Kraków; performances in Poland and abroad, including Warsaw Autumn–Int. Festival of Contemporary Music 1986; mem. Polish Section of ISCM. *Compositions:* A Duo for double bass and tape 1980, Esoterikos for soprano and oboe quartet 1984, Senza for double bass 1984, Girare for percussion and tape 1986, Obraz w Pieciu Ujeciach 1987, Vitrail II for clarinet, cello, accordion and vibraphone 1988.

ZAZOFSKY, Peter; American violinist; b. 1955, Boston. *Education:* Curtis Inst. of Music with Joseph Silverstein, Dorothy DeLay and Ivan Galamian. *Career:* frequent appearances from 1977 with orchestras including the Berlin and Rotterdam Philharmonics, the Vienna Symphony and the Amsterdam Concertgebouw Orchestra; North American engagements at Atlanta, Baltimore, Boston, Minnesota, Montréal, Philadelphia, San Francisco, Toronto and Vancouver; tour of the USA with the Danish Radio Orchestra and recitals at the Kennedy Center and New York's Carnegie Hall; further concerts in Israel and throughout Europe; 1978 recital tour of South America; season 1995–96 with concertos by Bartók and Mendelssohn in Germany and Belgium; also plays Nielsen and Bernstein (Serenade). *Honours:* prizewinner Wieniawski Competition 1977, Montréal Int. 1978, Queen Elisabeth of the Belgians Competition, Brussels 1980, Avery Fisher career grant 1985.

ZAZZO, Lawrence; American singer (countertenor); b. 1970, Phila. *Education:* King's Coll., Cambridge, Royal Coll. of Music with David Lowe. *Career:* concerts include Bach Cantatas at the 1997 Lufthansa Festival, London, Vivaldi Nisi Dominus and Handel's Messiah with the Israel Camerata; season 1996–97; opera debut as Oberon in A Midsummer Night's Dream at the RAM, London 1996; title role in Handel's Arminio and Alessandro Severo for the London Handel Festival, Bacco in Goehr's Arianna at Cambridge 1996, Athamas in Semele at Santa Fe Opera; 1998 season included Unulfo in Rodelinda at the Karlsruhe Handel Festival and with the Glyndebourne Touring Opera, title role in Cavalli's Giasone at the Spoleto Festival in Charleston, South Carolina. *Recordings include:* Purcell's Jubilate, Britten's Rejoice in the Lamb, Bernstein's Chichester Psalms and Pergolesi's Stabat Mater, Handel's Messiah 2006, Byrdland (with the Paragon Saxophone Quartet) 2007, Fernando 2007, Duetti amorosi (with Nuria Rial) 2008, Riccardo Primo 2008, Athalia 2010, Alessandro 2012, Apollo et Hyacinthus 2012, Mozart In-Between 2012. *Current Management:* c/o Shirley Thomson, Harrison/Parrott Ltd., 5-6 Albion Court, Albion Place, London, W6 0QT, England. *Telephone:* (20) 7229-9166. *Fax:* (20) 7221-5042. *E-mail:* shirley .thomson@harrisonparrott.co.uk. *Website:* www.harrisonparrott.com. *E-mail:* larry@lawrencezazzo.com. *Website:* www.lawrencezazzo.com.

ZEANI, Virginia; Romanian singer (soprano); *Professor Emerita, School of Music, Indiana University;* b. 21 Oct. 1925, Solovastru; m. Nicola Rossi-Lemeni 1957 (died 1991). *Education:* studied in Bucharest with Lucia Angel and Lydia Lipkovska, with Aureliano Pertile in Milan. *Career:* debut as

Violetta, Bologna 1948; London debut, as Violetta, Stoll Theatre 1953; as Cleopatra in Giulio Cesare, La Scala 1956; sang Blanche in premiere of Dialogues des Carmélites 1957; Vienna and Paris debuts 1957; at Verona Arena 1956–63; took part in revivals of Donizetti's Maria di Rohan, Naples 1965, Rossini's Otello, Rome 1968, Verdi's Alzira, Rome 1970; further appearances at Covent Garden 1959, Metropolitan 1966, and Budapest, Bucharest, Mexico City, Rio de Janeiro, Zürich, Amsterdam, Belgrade, Moscow, Madrid; other roles included Aida, Desdemona, Tosca, Manon and Manon Lescaut, Lucia di Lammermoor, Elvira (I Puritani), Magda Sorel in The Consul (Menotti); further engagements, Barcelona, Lisbon, Leningrad, Houston, Philadelphia, Berlin and New Orleans 1966; sang Giordano's Fedora, Barcelona 1977–78; sang 67 roles, sang La Traviata 648 times around the world; Prof. of Voice, School of Music, Indiana Univ., USA 1980–2004, Distinguished Prof. 1994–2004, Prof. Emerita 2004–; mem. Accademia Tiberina-Roma, Soroptimist Club of Rome. *Recordings:* La Traviata; Rossini's Otello; Elisa e Claudio by Mercadante; Rossini's Zelmira; Alzira; La Serva Padrona. *Honours:* Commendatore of Italian Republic, Gold Medal, Egypt 1951, Gold Medal, Barcelona 1963, Maschera d'Argento 1965–70, Arena d'Oro 1966, Diapason d'Oro 1968, Viotti D'Oro 1999, Una Vita per la Lirica, San Remo 1999. *Address:* 9188 Lakeview Drive, West Palm Beach, FL 33412, USA (home). *Telephone:* (561) 656-0901 (home).

ZEAVIN, Carol; American violinist; b. 2 May 1948, San Bernardino, CA. *Education:* studied in New York. *Career:* co-founder, Columbia String Quartet 1977, initially called Schoenberg String Quartet; many performances in the standard and modern repertory, including the premieres of Wuorinen's Archangel and Second Quartet 1978, 1980, Roussaki's Ephemeris 1979, and quartets by Morton Feldman 1980, Wayne Peterson 1984, and Larry Bell 1985; Abraham Goodman House, New York, played in the premiere of Berg's Lyric Suite with recently discovered vocal finale 1979. *Recordings include:* String Quartet No. 3 by Lukas Foss and Ned Rorem's Mourning Song.

ZEBELJAN, Isidora; Serbian composer, pianist and conductor; b. 27 Sept. 1967, Belgrade. *Education:* Belgrade Music Acad. *Career:* began composing in 1985; works performed at festivals and halls across Europe, including Zagreb Music Biennale, Belgrade Music Festival, Crossing Borders Festival, Bregenzer Festspiel, Festival Nous Sons, Barcelona, Galway Arts Festival, WDR Musikfest and Settembre Musica; commissions include Genesis Foundation, Venice Biennale, Brodsky Quartet, Jeunesses Musicales, Int. Horn Players Soc. and Univ. of Kent at Canterbury; works performed by Amsterdam and Vienna Chamber Operas, Acad. of St Martin in the Fields at Wigmore Hall, London, Symphony Orchestra of RAI Torino, Janáček Philharmonic Orchestra, Belgrade Philharmonic, Neue Filharmonie Westfalen, Brodsky Quartet, Nieuw Ensemble, Zagros Ensemble Helsinki, Ensemble Sentieri Selvaggi Milan, London Brass; opera Zora D. premiered in Amsterdam 2003, 22 performances in five European countries in four years; Prof. of Composition, Belgrade Music Acad. 2002–; mem. Serbian Acad. of Sciences and Arts. *Compositions include:* Hero's Miseries for mixed choir 1985, Suite for Piano 1985, Glory for 42 female voices 1987, Deserted Village, elegy for string orchestra 1987, Il Circo, sketch for piano 1993, Three Pieces for solo guitar 1998, Four Old Serbian Songs for soprano and string orchestra 1999, Sarabande for flute, soprano and piano 2001, The Miracle in Shargan, song for solo oboe 2002, Song of a Traveller in the Night for clarinet and string quartet 2003, The Horses of St Mark for symphony orchestra 2004, Minstrel's Dance for chamber orchestra 2005, The Ghost from the Pumpkin for brass quintet 2006, Dark Velvet for piano 2006, Dance of Wooden Sticks for horn and string orchestra 2008, Latum lalo for 12 singers 2008, Polomka Quartet for strings 2009. *Music for stage:* incidental music for over 40 theatre productions in Serbia, Croatia and Montenegro; opera: Zora D. 2002, The Marathon Family 2008, Two Heads and a Girl 2011. *Music for film:* numerous scores; orchestrated music for The Time of the Gypsies, Arizona Dream, Underground, Queen Margot and The Serpent's Kiss. *Honours:* Stevan Mokranjać Nat. Music Award 2004, Civitella Ranieri Foundation fellowship 2005, 2006, Sterbija Prize for Theatre (three times), Best Composer of Music for Theatre, Yustate Biennale of Theatre Design (four times). *Current Management:* c/o Sorek Artists Management, Burgemeester Patijnlaan 450, 2585 BW The Hague, Netherlands. *Telephone:* (70) 3317902. *E-mail:* info@sorekartists.com. *Website:* www.sorekartists.com. *Current Management:* c/o Casa Ricordi, Via Benigno Crespi 19, 20159 Milan, Italy. *Website:* www.ricordi.it.

ZEBINGER, Franz, PhD; Austrian composer, harpsichordist and organist; b. 29 April 1946, Styria; m.; two s. one d. *Education:* Musikhochschule Graz, Karl-Franzens-Univ. of Graz. *Career:* harpsichord and organist with Gamerith Consort, Ljubljana Barocni Trio, Ramovs Consort, Concilium Musicum, Trumpet and Strings Vienna; concerts as a soloist, organ and forte piano; Vice-Pres. Steirischer Tonkünstlerbund; Vice-Pres. Verein zur Erhaltung musikalischer Kostbarkeiten der Steiermark. *Compositions include:* Carmen Miserabile 1988, Drachenkampf 1995, Markuspassion 1996, Heller als die Sonn 1998, Dies Illa 1999, Bruder Sonne, Schwester Mond 2002, Geschichte von Adam und Eva 2003, Feuer von Himmel 2004, Burgenland Kammermusic 2005, Oratorium Mein Kosmos 2006, Klezmeriade for trumpet and strings 2007, Butterblumenglück for choir 2008, Oratorium Die Abschaffung der Zeit, Concerto Pagano for trumpet and strings 2009, Todestöter: Die Abschaffung der Zeit Oratorium 2010, Oratorium Abrahams Opfer 2013. *Recordings include:* Gamerith Consort 1989, Dedications for Sax 1993, Stay a Weill 1994, Haydn Keyboard Trios 1994, Spectaculars 1997, Barré en Bloc 1999, Franz Zebinger compositions 2000, Haydn music for Forte Piano on original instruments 2002, Der Weisse Wolf 2007, Steirisch aufg'spielt: Violarra 2011, Őrvidéki Karácsony – Weihnachten in der Wart 2013. *Publication:* Ikonographie zum Musikleben der Etrusker (dissertation) 1982. *Honours:* Hon. Pres. Komponisten und Interpreten Burgenlands 2008; Kulturpreis Burgenland 2004, Staatliches Ehrenzeichen für Besondere Verdienste um die Kulturarbeit 2007, Theodor Kery Preis 2009. *Address:* Kroisegg Nr. 25, 7423 Pinkafeld, Austria (home). *Telephone:* (664) 505-4805 (home).

ZECHBERGER, Gunther; Austrian composer and conductor; b. 24 April 1951, Zams, Tyrol. *Education:* Innsbruck Conservatory, Univ. of Innsbruck with Witold Rowicki and Boguslaw Schaeffer. *Career:* founder and Conductor, Tyroler Ensemble für Neue Musik 1984. *Compositions include:* Trio for clarinet, horn and bassoon 1973, Trio for violins 1975, Das Neue Preislied for women's chorus and speaker 1975, Schlus Stuck for mixed chorus and orchestra 1979, Mass for mixed chorus and orchestra 1979, Trombone Quartet 1980, Stabat Mater for mixed chorus 1981, Im Nebel for mezzo and orchestra 1982, Study for 12 strings 1983, Hendekegon for 26 instruments 1984, Tieferschuttert for mezzo, trombone and guitar 1984, String Quartet 1985, Chorus for five musicians 1985, Stabat Mater II for mezzo and ensemble 1985–88, Kammermusik for conductor and five musicians 1986, Dear Mr J 1987, Interview for tape 1987, Guitar Concerto 1988, Duet for guitars 1988.

ZEDDA, Alberto; Italian conductor; *Artistic Director, Rossini Opera Festival (Pesaro Festival)*; b. 2 Jan. 1928, Milan. *Education:* Univ. of Urbino, studied in Milan with Antonino Votto and Carlo Maria Giulini. *Career:* debut as conductor, Milan 1956; teacher, Cincinnati Coll. of Music 1957–59; conductor with Deutsche Oper, Berlin 1961–63, with New York City Opera 1967–69; Covent Garden debut 1975; fmr Music Dir Festival della Valle d'Itria; Artistic Dir Teatro alla Scala, Milan 1992–93; currently Artistic Dir Rossini Opera Festival, Pesaro; guest conductor with numerous opera cos including La Scala, Milan, Vienna State Opera, La Fenice, Venice, San Francisco Opera, Royal Opera House, London, Mariinsky Theatre, St Petersburg; mem. Cttee Rossini Foundation, Pesaro. *Recordings include:* Bellini: Beatrice di Tenda 1986, Rossini: Tancredi 1994. *Honours:* Hon. Pres. Deutsche Rossini Gesellschaft 2000. *Address:* Rossini Opera Festival, Via Rossini, 24, 61121 Pesaro, Italy (office). *Telephone:* (0721) 3800213 (office). *E-mail:* rof@rossinioperafestival.it (office). *Website:* www.rossinioperafestival.it (office).

ZEDNIK, Heinz; Austrian singer (tenor); b. 21 Feb. 1940, Vienna. *Education:* Vienna Conservatory with Marga Wissmann. *Career:* debut in La Forza del Destino, Graz 1964; with Wiener Staatsoper 1964–, notably in the 1976 premiere of Von Einem's Kabale und Liebe; other roles include Mozart's Pedrillo and Monostatos, Beethoven's Jacquino and Peter the Great in Zar und Zimmermann, Penderecki's Die schwarze Maske, Baron Laur in Weill's Silbersee, Bob Boles in Peter Grimes, the Villians in Les Contes d' Hoffmann, the Captain in Wozzeck, the Monk in Schoenberg's Die Jakobsleiter; guest appearances at Metropolitan Opera, New York, La Scala, Milan, Maggio Musicale, Florence, Teatro San Carlo, Naples, Opera de Paris, Zurich Opera, Frankfurt Opera, Berlin Staatsoper, Stuttgart Staatsoper, Bavarian State Opera in Munich; annual performances at the Bayreuth Festival as David, the Steersman, Mime and Loge 1970–80; Visiting Prof. Universität für Musik und Darstellende Kunst, Vienna 1996–. *Recordings:* Parsifal, Lustige Weiber Von Windsor, Le Nozze di Figaro, Wozzeck, Salome, Wiener Blut, Die Zauberflöte, Das Rheingold, Siegfried from Bayreuth. *Publication:* Mein Opernleben 2008. *Honours:* Hon. mem., Wiener Staatsoper 1994; Hon. Cross for Science and Art 1996, Fidelio Medal 1997. *Current Management:* c/o Markus Bendl, Künstleragentur Dr. Raab & Dr. Böhm, Plankengasse 7, 1010 Vienna, Austria. *Telephone:* (1) 512-05-01. *Fax:* (1) 512-7-43. *E-mail:* bendl@rbartists.at. *Website:* www.rbartists.at.

ZEFFIRELLI, Franco (Gian Franco Corsi); Italian theatre, opera and film director and set designer; b. 12 Feb. 1923, Florence. *Education:* Liceo Artistico, Florence and Univ. of Florence School of Architecture. *Career:* moved to Rome to debut as an actor in cinema and theatre 1946; met Luchino Visconti which proved crucial for his film and theatre training, hired as asst and later as set designer for productions of William Shakespeare's Troilus and Cressida 1949 and Tennessee Williams' A Streetcar Named Desire; worked as asst dir in various theatre productions and in films The Earth Trembles 1947, Bellissima 1951, Senso 1954; produced set designs for Romeo and Juliet, staged at the Old Vic Company, London 1960; staged, amongst others, productions of La Cenerentola by Gioachino Rossini 1953, La Traviata by Giuseppe Verdi with Maria Callas 1958; release of film The Taming of the Shrew 1967, Romeo and Juliet 1968; commissioned by leading opera houses world-wide, including Teatro alla Scala of Milan, The Met, New York, Covent Garden, London and Staatsoper, Vienna, to stage performances; numerous opera productions with artists including Maria Callas, Plácido Domingo, Luciano Pavarotti, Herbert Von Karajan, Leonard Bernstein, Carlos Kleiber; productions include Il Turco in Italia with Maria Callas, Aïda and La Bohéme at Teatro alla Scala, Milan, Carmen at the Staatsoper, Vienna, Tosca, Turandot, Falstaff and La Traviata at the Metropolitan, New York, Aïda, Il Trovatore, Carmen and Madama Butterfly in Verona, and two experiments in Busseto with small productions of Aïda and La Traviata; Aïda of Busseto brought to Moscow 2004, La Traviata of Busseto staged in Moscow and Tel-Aviv 2005 (also I Pagliacci); Teatro dell'Opera, Rome presented Don Giovanni 2006, followed by Aïda 2006; returned to Teatro dell'Opera, Rome for a new comeback of La Traviata 2007, Tosca 2008, I Pagliacci 2009, Falstaff 2010; production of Carmen at Arena of Verona 2009, Turandot 2010, also Aïda, Madama Butterfly, Carmen and Il Trovatore; new Turandot celebrated the opening of Royal Opera House of Muscat, Sultanate of Oman 2011; presented Mozart's Don Giovanni at Arena di Verona 2012; made film-opera of Cavalleria Rusticana by Pietro Mascagni and I Pagliacci by Ruggero Leoncavallo 1980; cr. film version of Verdi's La Traviata; also successful in prose theatre, both in Italy and abroad, with works by Shakespeare: Hamlet with Giorgio Albertazzi, also performed in London, and Romeo and Juliet; other works include La Lupa by Verga, starring Anna Magnani, and pieces by contemporary authors: Who's Afraid of Virginia Woolf by Edward Albee, After the Fall by Arthur Miller, Due più due non fa più quattro by Lina Wertmüller, Sabato, Domenica e Lunedì by Eduardo, at the Old Vic, London and featuring Sir Laurence Olivier. *Exhibition:* Zeffirelli – The Art of Spectacle (Tokyo, Athens, Florence, Milan). *Theatre:* Romeo and Juliet (Old Vic, London) 1960, Othello (Stratford) 1961, Hamlet (Nat. Theatre, London) 1964, After the Fall (Rome) 1964, Who's Afraid of Virginia Woolf (Paris) 1964, (Milan) 1965, La Lupa (Rome) 1965, Much Ado About Nothing (Nat. Theatre, London) 1966, Black Comedy (Rome) 1967, A Delicate Balance (Rome) 1967, Saturday, Sunday, Monday (Nat. Theatre, London) 1973, Filumena (Lyric, London) 1977, Six Characters in Search of an Author (London) 1992, Absolutely Perhaps! (London) 2003, Pagliacci (Teatro Carlo Felice, Genoa) 2011. *Operas include:* Lucia di Lammermoor, Cavalleria Rusticana, Pagliacci (Covent Garden) 1959, 1973, Falstaff (Covent Garden) 1961, L'Elisir d'amore (Glyndebourne) 1961, Don Giovanni, Alcina (Covent Garden) 1962, Tosca, Rigoletto (Covent Garden) 1964, 1966, 1973, (Metropolitan, New York) 1985, Don Giovanni (Staatsoper Wien) 1972, (Metropolitan, New York) 1990, Otello (Metropolitan, New York) 1972, Antony and Cleopatra (Metropolitan, New York) 1973, Otello (La Scala) 1976, La Bohème (Metropolitan, New York) 1981, Turandot (La Scala) 1983, 1985, (Metropolitan, New York) 1987, Don Carlos 1992, Carmen 1996, Aïda (New Theatre, Tokyo) 1997, (Busseto) 2000, La Traviata (Metropolitan, New York) 1998, Tosca (Rome) 2000, Il Trovatore (Arena di Verona) 2001, Aïda (Arena di Verona) 2002, La Bohème (La Scala) 2003, (Rome) 2003, Carmen (Arena di Verona) 2003, I Pagliacci (Covent Garden, London) 2003, (Tel-Aviv, Israel) 2005, Madama Butterfly (Arena Di Verona) 2004, Aïda (La Scala, Milan) 2006, La Traviata (Rome) 2007, I Pagliacci (Taormina) 2008, La Bohème (Tel-Aviv) 2008, Aïda (Tel-Aviv) 2009, I Pagliacci (Rome) 2009, Falstaff (Rome) 2010, Carmen (Arena di Verona) 2009, Turandot (Arena di Verona) 2010, Aïda (Arena di Verona) 2010, Madama Butterfly (Arena di Verona) 2010, Il Trovatore (Arena di Verona) 2010, Turandot (Royal Opera House of Muscat, Sultanate of Oman) 2011, Don Giovanni and Pagliacci (Arena di Verona) 2012. *Ballet:* Swan Lake 1985; produced Beethoven's Missa Solemnis, San Pietro, Rome 1971. *Films:* The Taming of the Shrew 1966, Romeo and Juliet (five Nastri d'argento Awards, Italian cinematographic journalists) 1967, Brother Sun and Sister Moon 1973, The Champ 1979, Endless Love 1981, La Traviata 1983, Cavalleria Rusticana 1983, Otello 1986, The Young Toscanini 1987, Hamlet 1990, Storia di una capinera (Sparrow) 1993, Jane Eyre 1995, Tea with Mussolini 1998, Callas Forever 2002, Omaggio a Roma (short) 2009. *Television includes:* Florence, Days of Destruction (film) 1966, Jesus of Nazareth (mini-series) 1977, celebrative concert of the second century of the birth of Ludwig van Beethoven (RAI) held in St Peter's Basilica in the presence of Pope Paul VI. *Publication:* Zeffirelli by Zeffirelli (autobiog.) 1986 (second edn 2006). *Honours:* Hon. KBE 2005; Prix des Nations 1976, Premio Colosseo, City of Rome 2009 and numerous others. *Address:* Via Lucio Volumnio 45, 00178 Rome, Italy. *Fax:* (06) 7184213. *E-mail:* fzeffirelli@tin.it.

ZEHETMAIR, Thomas; Austrian violinist; *Principal Conductor and Music Director, Orchestre de Chambre de Paris;* b. 23 Nov. 1961, Salzburg; s. of Helmut Zehetmair and Erika Lösch; m. Ruth Killius. *Education:* Salzburg Mozarteum, masterclasses with Max Rostal and Nathan Milstein. *Career:* concert appearances with the Boston, Chicago, Cleveland, Minnesota and San Francisco Orchestras, Philharmonia, English and Scottish Chamber, BBC Symphony, City of Birmingham, Rotterdam Philharmonic and Concertgebouw, Stockholm Philharmonic, Berlin Philharmonic and Leipzig Gewandhaus; guest engagements at int. music festivals; chamber music with Gidon Kremer at Lockenhaus; London recital debut at Wigmore Hall 1993; concerto engagements with the BBC Philharmonic, Bournemouth Symphony, Northern Sinfonia and Scottish Chamber Orchestra 1993; Edinburgh Festival with Bach's works for solo violin 1995; Berlioz' Harold in Italy, London Proms 1997; repertoire includes concertos by Szymanowski, Bach, Bartók, Henze, Berg and Prokofiev, in addition to the standard works; founder, Zehetmair Quartet; Music Dir, Northern Sinfonia 2002–13, Artistic Partner, St Paul Chamber Orchestra 2010–; Prin. Conductor and Music Dir Orchestre de Chambre de Paris 2012–. *Recordings:* Beethoven's Kreutzer and Spring Sonatas, Concertos by Brahms, Joseph and Michael Haydn, Mendelssohn, Mozart, Schumann and Sibelius, Berg's Chamber Concerto and Schoenberg's Violin Concerto under Heinz Hoffiger, Szymanowski Concertos Nos 1 and 2 with Simon Rattle, Bartók Concertos Nos 1 and 2 with Ivan Fischer, Paganini's 24 Capricci, Elgar Violin Concerto (Gramophone Award for Best Concerto Recording 2010), Brahms' Violin concerto and Schumann's Symphony No. 4 (soloist and conductor), Sibelius' Symphonies 3 and 6, Stravinsky's Violin Concerto in D Major, Schubert's Symphony Nos 6 and 9 Gál's Symphony Nos 1, and 2, Unknown Britten with Northern Sinfonia and Sandrine Piau, Zehetmair Quartet: Hartmann String quartet no. 1, Bartók String quartet no. 4 Sz 91, Schumann String quartet Nos 1 & 3, Bartók String quartet no. 5 Sz 102, Hindemith String quartet no. 4 op. 22, Zehetmair Duo: Manto and Madrigals. *Honours:* Dr hc (Music Acad. Franz Liszt, Weimar, Newcastle Univ., UK).

Address: Orchestre de Chambre de Paris, 218 avenue Jean Jaurès, 75019 Paris, France (office). *Website:* www.orchestredechambredeparis.com (office).

ZEHNDER, Kaspar; Swiss flautist and conductor; *Artistic Director, Murten Classics Festival;* b. 27 Aug. 1970, Riggisberg. *Education:* musical studies at the Univ. of the Arts in Bern with Heidi Péter-Indermühle (flute), Agathe Rytz-Jaggi (piano), Peter Streiff, Arthur Furer (musical theory) and Dr Ewald Körner (conducting) 1986–92; masterclasses with Ralf Weikert and Horst Stein, flute studies with Aurèle Nicolet in Basel and Siena 1993, conducting studies with Charles Dutoit at the Orchestre Nat. de France 1994. *Career:* Artistic Dir and Conductor, Chamber Orchestra Neufeld, Bern Symphony 1991–2001, Chamber Orchestra Burgdorf 1996–; mem. European Mozart Acad. 1995–96; Assoc. Prof. and Conductor, Orchestra of Bern Acad. of Arts 1997–2006; conducted Tchaikovsky Symphony Orchestra, Moscow 1999; Artistic Dir Murten Classics Festival 1999–; Music Dir Zentrum Paul Klee 2003–; Dir Ensemble Paul Klee 2003–; Chief Conductor, Sibiu Philharmonic Orchestra 2002–05, Prague Philharmonic Orchestra 2005–08, Biel Solothurn Symphony Orchestra 2012–; concerts throughout Europe with orchestras including Capella Istropolitana, Bratislava 2000, Prague Philharmonia 2001, Bucharest Symphony Orchestra 2001, Slovak Philharmonic Orchestra 2014, Sinfonia Varsovia 2014, Nat. Radio Orchestra, Bucharest 2015; appeared at festivals, including Mecklenberg-Vorpommern, Germany and Le Stelle del futuro, Venice 1996; Pres. Swiss Brahms Soc. 2000–; mem. Swiss Musicians' Soc. *Recordings include:* French Music for flute and piano, Sonatas for flute and piano by Franck, Martinů, Prokofiev. *Honours:* Hon. Diploma (Accademia Chigiana, Siena) 1994, 1998; winner, Swiss Youth Competition 1984, 1986, Kiwanis Award 1990, Migros Foundation Scholarship 1994. *E-mail:* info@kasparzehnder.com. *Website:* www.kasparzehnder.com.

ZEIGLER, Jeffrey, MMus; American cellist and teacher. *Education:* Eastman School of Music, Rice Univ. *Career:* mem. Corigliano Quartet 1998–2004; mem. (cello) Kronos Quartet 2005–13; mem. faculty Mannes Coll. The New School for Music 2013–. *Recordings include:* with Kronos: Górecki: String Quartet No. 3 (Songs are Sung) 2007, The Fountain (soundtrack) 2008, Jerry Riley: The Cusp of Magic 2008, Floodplain 2009. *Honours:* with Kronos: Musical America Musicians of the Year 2003. *Address:* c/o Kronos Quartet, 1242 Ninth Avenue, San Francisco, CA 94122, USA (office). *Telephone:* (415) 731-3533 (office). *Fax:* (415) 664-7590 (office). *E-mail:* janet@kronosarts.com (office). *Website:* kronosquartet.org (office).

ZEITOUNI, Jean-Marie; Canadian conductor; *Music Director, Columbus Symphony Orchestra;* b. 1974, Montr.; s. of Nicolas Zeitouni and Marguerite Zeitouni. *Education:* studied conducting, percussion and theory at Montréal Conservatory with Raffi Armenian. *Career:* Dir, Orchestra and Opera Workshop, Laval Univ. Faculty of Music 1999–2002; Choir Dir, Québec Symphony Orchestra 2001–03; Assoc. Conductor and Chorus Master, Opéra de Montréal 2002–06, also Music Dir, Young Artist Program; Chorus Master, Opéra de Québec 2003–05; Asst Conductor, Mostly Music Festival, New York City 2004; Music Dir, Banff Centre Opera as Theatre program 2005–06; fmr Conductor-in-Residence, Les Violons du Roy, Québec, later Assoc. Conductor, Prin. Guest Conductor 2008–; Music Dir, Columbus Symphony Orchestra 2010–; Prin. Conductor and Artistic Dir, I Musici de Montréal 2012–; has guest conducted orchestras and opera cos throughout N America. *Recordings include:* with Les Violons du Roy: Piazzolla (JUNO Award for Solo or Chamber Ensemble Classical Album of the Year 2007) 2006, Bartók Divertimento, Danses Populaires Roumaines 2008, Britten Les Illuminations 2010. *Honours:* Jean-Marie Beaudet Award in Orchestra Conducting, Canada Council for the Arts 2005. *Address:* Columbus Symphony Orchestra, 55 East State Street, Columbus, OH 43215, USA (office). *Telephone:* (614) 228-9600 (office). *Fax:* (614) 224-7273 (office). *Website:* www.columbussymphony.com (office).

ZELENSKAYA, Elena Emilyevna; Russian singer (soprano); b. 1 June 1961, Baku, Azerbaijan. *Education:* Baku State Conservatory. *Career:* soloist, Moscow Municipal Theatre New Opera 1991–96, Bolshoi Theatre 1996–; tours abroad 1992–; guest singer, Wiener Kammeroper 1992–; debut as Lady Macbeth in Lucerne, as Donna Elvira in Savonlinna Opera Festival (Finland), as Aida in Deutsche Oper Düsseldorf 1997, as Lisa in Queen of Spades in Berlin Oper, as Tosca in Norway; leading parts include Tatyana in Eugene Onegin, Yaroslavna in Prince Igor, Lady Macbeth in Macbeth, Amelia in Ballo in Maschera, Leonora in La Forza del Destino, Countess in Le Nozze di Figaro, Donna Elvira in Don Giovanni. *Current Management:* APA Artists Management, Studio 1, 79 Bedford Gardens, London, W8 7EG, England.

ZELTSER, Mark, DMus; American pianist; b. 3 April 1947, Kischiniev, Russia; m.; one d. *Education:* Moscow Conservatory. *Career:* resident in USA from 1976; played at the 1977 Salzburg Festival under Karajan and performed in Berlin with the Philharmonic 1979; debut with the New York Philharmonic 1980; further appearances with leading orchestras in Europe and USA; fmr Prof. of Music, Centenary Coll., Louisiana. *Recordings:* works by Prokofiev, Rachmaninov and Beethoven. *Honours:* winner, Marguerite Long-Jacques Competition, France, Busoni Competition, Italy. *E-mail:* mzmus@aol.com (office). *Website:* www.markzeltser.com.

ZELTZER, Sandra; French singer (soprano); b. 1972, Paris. *Education:* Paris Conservatoire with Christiane Eda-Pierre, Guildhall School, London. *Career:* Covent Garden recital 1995, with appearances in Così fan tutte and Elektra 1997; further engagements at Tatiana at the Paris Conservatoire, Linda di Chamounix at the Guildhall, Micaela in Carmen for Mid-Wales Opera, Bizet's Leila in The Pearls Fishers, for English Touring Opera, Arminda in La Finta

Giardiniera for Opera Zuid, The Netherlands, Melia in Mozart's Apollo et Hyacinthus, Britten Theatre, London, Despina in Cosi fan Tutte, Fifth Maid in Elektra, Marzelline in Fidelio, Jenny in La Dame Blanche, Donna Elvira in Don Giovanni for Opéra Comique, Paris, l'Amour in Anacréon, Lauretta in Gianni Schicchi, Natasha in War and Peace; concerts include Gounod's Requiem, Scmitt's La Tragédie à la Vierge. *Recordings:* recital recording of songs 2001. *Honours:* James Gulliver Prize 1994, Bourse Lavoisier Scholarship, prizewinner Maggie Teyte Competition 1995.

ZEMTSOVSKY, Izaly Iosifovich, DipMus, MA, PhD; Russian ethnomusicologist; b. 22 Feb. 1936, St Petersburg; m. Alma Kunanbay 1982. *Education:* Univ. of Leningrad, Leningrad Conservatoire. *Career:* debut in 1958; Sr Research Fellow and Head of Folklore Dept, Leningrad State Inst. of Theatre, Music and Cinema (later Russian Inst. of History of the Arts 1990–) 1960–95; Head Dept of Traditional Culture, Russian Pedagogic Univ. 1989–93; Vice-Pres., Jewish Musical Soc. of St Petersburg 1992–96; Vice-Pres., Int. Delphic Council 1994–96; Pres., Delphic Movement in Russia 1995–97; Fellow Inst. for Research in the Humanities, Univ. of Wisconsin-Madison 1995–97; Visiting Prof. in Slavic and E. Bloch Prof. in Music, Univ. of California at Berkeley 1997–99; Visiting Prof., Stanford Univ.; currently Bd Sec., Silk Road House (non-profit org.). *Publications include:* Russian Folk Song 1964, The Russian Drawn-Out Song 1967, Songs of Toropets: Songs of the Homeland of Moussorgsky 1967, Song Hunters 1967, The Poetry of Peasant Holidays 1970, The Melodics of Calendar Songs 1975, Folklore and the Composer 1978, Tracing the Melody Vesnianka from P. Tchaikovsky's Piano Concerto: The Historical Morphology of Folk Songs 1987, 'Russian Folk Music' (in Grove Dictionary of Music and Musicians) 1980, Boris Asaf'yev on Folk Music 1987, Jewish Folk Songs: An Anthology 1994, An Attempt at a Synthetic Paradigm 1997. *Address:* c/o Silk Road House, 1944 University Avenue, Room 107, Berkeley, CA 94704, USA (office).

ZENATY, Ivan; Czech violinist; b. 1960. *Education:* Prague Conservatoire, Acad. of Arts, Weimar with André Gertler, studied in Zürich with Nathan Milstein. *Career:* soloist, Berliner Symphoniker 1990; permanent soloist, Prague Symphony Orchestra, Czech Radio Symphony Orchestra; solo appearances with leading orchestras in Austria, Bulgaria, England, Finland, The Netherlands, Italy, Poland, Spain, Russia, Switzerland and Yugoslavia; festival engagements in Prague, Dubrovnik, Moscow, Sofia, Berlin and Havana; repertoire includes concertos by Bach, Haydn, Mozart, Vivaldi, Myslivicek, Sibelius, Dvořák, Vieuxtemps and Kalabis, Bach solo sonatas and Telemann solo fantasies, sonatas by Mozart, Beethoven, Vanhal, Schubert, Schumann, Brahms, Prokofiev, Dvořák, Janáček and Martinů; Prof. of Music, Hochschule für Musik, Dresden 1996–. *Honours:* first prize Prague Spring Festival Competition 1987, Laureate, Int. Tribune of Young Performers, UNESCO 1989, first prize, Ruggiero Ricci Int. Competition 1990. *Current Management:* c/o Ingrid Hellmann, Konzertagentur Hellmann, Bimenweg 12, 06112 Halle an der Saale, Germany. *Telephone:* (345) 5603041. *Fax:* (345) 5603654. *E-mail:* kahellmann@aol.com. *Address:* Wolfhügelstrasse 1, 01324 Dresden, Germany (office). *Telephone:* (351) 265-6464 (office). *Fax:* (351) 265-4338 (office). *E-mail:* katarinazenata@hotmail.com (office). *Website:* www.ivanzenaty.de.

ZENDER, J(ohannes) W(olfgang) Hans; German composer and conductor; b. 22 Nov. 1936, Wiesbaden; s. of Dr Franz Zender and Marianne Zender (née Fromm); m. Gertrud-Maria Achenbach 1962. *Education:* Acad. of Music, Freiburg. *Career:* studied composition and piano; Conductor, Freiburg im Breisgau 1959–63; Chief Conductor, Bonn City Theatre 1964–68; Gen. Dir of Music, Kiel 1969–72; Chief Conductor, Radio Symphony and Chamber Orchestras, Saarbrücken 1972–82; Gen. Dir of Music (Philharmonia and City Opera), Hamburg 1984–87; Chief Conductor Radio Chamber Orchestra, Netherlands Broadcasting Corpn; Prin. Guest Conductor, Opéra Nat., Brussels 1987–90; Prof. of Composition, Frankfurt Musikhochschule 1988–; Permanent Guest Conductor SWF Symphony Orchestra 1999–; Composer-in-Residence, Deutsches Symphonie-Orchester Berlin 2005–06; mem. Freie Akad. der Künste, Hamburg, Akad. der Künste, Berlin, Bayerische Akad. der Künste. *Compositions include:* Canto I–VIII 1965–96, Zeitströme 1974, Mujinokyo 1975, Litanei 1976, Lo-Shu I–VI 1977–89, Hölderlin Lesen (string quartet) 1979–91, Dialog mit Haydn 1982, Stephen Climax (opera) 1979–84, Don Quixote (opera) 1989–91, Schubert's Winterreise (for soloists, choir, large orchestra and live electronics) 1993–97, Chief Joseph (opera) 2003. *Publications include:* Happy New Ears (essays) 1991, Wir steigen niemals in den selben Fluss (essays) 1996. *Honours:* Goethe Prize, City of Frankfurt 1997. *Current Management:* Künstlersekretariat Astrid Schoerke, Grazer Str. 30, 30519 Hannover, Germany. *E-mail:* info@ks-schoerke.de. *Website:* ks-schoerke.de.

ZENKER, Silvia; German pianist; b. Kiel; d. of Erich Zenker and Gerda Zenker (née Rohwer). *Education:* London, Lübeck and Hamburg. *Career:* piano duettist with Ulrike Bachmann-Arnold (q.v.) 1984–89, with Evelinde Trenkner 1989–; nat. and int. concert tours 1985–, toured fmr USSR 1991–92; has performed on radio and TV; first album made 1986. *Honours:* First Prize in Music, Possehlstiftung, Lübeck 1984, Hanse-Kulturpreis, Stadt Lübeck 1987, First Prize Carlo Soliva Music Competition, Italy 1988.

ZENTAI, Csilea; Hungarian singer (soprano); b. 23 May 1940, Mako. *Education:* studied in Budapest and in Stuttgart. *Career:* debut at Stuttgart Opera School 1969, in Ibert's Angelique; sang at Ulm Opera 1969–1972, Bremen 1973–79, Deutsche Oper am Rhein from 1979; guest appearances at

the state operas of Stuttgart, Hamburg and Munich, Vienna Staatsoper as Mozart's Countess and Fiordigili, Luise (Junge Lord), Zürich as the Marschallin, Deutsche Oper Berlin as Elvira and Blumenmädchen 1, and Cologne Opera as Fiordigili, Agathe, Butterfly, Rosalinde, Countess and Marenka; further engagements at Bordeaux, Brussels, Salzburg as Donna Anna in concert performance of Don Giovanni, and Moscow; other roles have included Violetta, Composer, Jenůfa, Pamina, Rosalinde, Marguerite and Amaranta in La Fedeltà Premiata by Haydn, Konstanze, Susanna, Jlica, Donna, Elviva, Marzelline; Leonore (Fidelio and Troubadour), Tosca, Traviata, Lucia, Mimi, Nedde, Euydice, Antonia, Martha, Michaela; concert appearances in Germany, The Netherlands, Belgium, Italy, Spain, Mexico and Hungary; Kammersängerin, Deutsche Oper am Rhein 1990–2005; Prof., Folkwang Musikhochschule 1991–. *Honours:* first prize s'Hertogeubosch 1968, silver medal Toulouse 1968, first prize Francisco Viñas Vocal Competition, Barcelona 1969.

ZENZIPER, Arkadi, MMus; Russian pianist; b. 10 April 1958, Leningrad; m. Tatjana Zenzipér 1990; three s. two d. *Education:* Leningrad Conservatory with T. Orlovsky, studied with N. Perlmann and G. Sokolov. *Career:* debut in television piano recital in Vilnius, Lithuania 1982; concerts with orchestras, including Berlin Symphonic Orchestra 1990, Munich Klaviersommer 1994, Ljubljana Festival 1994, Stuttgart Chamber Orchestra 2002, Krakauer Philharmonic Orchestra 2001, 2002, 2004; chamber music concerts include Schleswig-Holstein Music Festival 1989, 1990, Lucerne Festival 1989, Concertgebouw, Amsterdam 1990, 1991, Berlin Philharmonic Hall 1992, and frequently at Berlin Konzerthaus; radio performance of Prokofiev 4th and 5th Piano Concertos with Berlin Radio Orchestra, 1992; television portrait and recording of Rachmaninov with Staatskapelle Dresden; La Chaise Dieu Music Festival with Orchestre Nat. de Lyon 1998, 1999, 2000; chamber music: Rheingau Festival 1996, Dresdner Musikfestspiele 1996, Tibor Varga Festival Sion 1997, Beethovenhaus Bonn 1997, Hitzacker-Festival 1997, Prague Spring Festival 2003, Rostica Music Festival London 2003; concerts with soloists of the Israeli Philharmonic Orchestra 2003; Art Dir, Dreiklang Music Festival 2001–; Professor, Dresden Musikhochschule 1993–. *Recordings:* radio recordings of chamber music with RIAS-Berlin, Hessischer Rundfunk, South German Radio, Deutschland Radio; nine albums. *Address:* Hochschule für Musik Carl Maria von Weber Dresden, Wettiner Platz 13, 01067 Dresden, Germany (office). *Telephone:* (351) 4923600 (office). *Website:* www.hfmdd.de (office).

ZHADKO, Victoria; Ukrainian conductor; b. 23 Aug. 1967, Kyiv; two c. *Education:* Lugansk State Music Coll., Kiev Conservatory. *Career:* Conductor, Nat. Radio Symphony Orchestra of Ukraine 1993–94, 2000–; Lecturer, Kyiv State Inst. of Culture 1995–97; Chief Conductor, Kharkiv Symphony Orchestra 1997–2000; founder and Chair., Eastern Europe Cathedra for Ancient and Chamber Music 1997–2000; Prof., Kyiv Nat. Univ. for Culture and Arts 1997–; Artistic Dir and Jury Chair., M. Sokolowski Int. Classical Guitar Competition 2005–; performances of Ukrainian music with the St Petersburg Philharmonic and guest engagements with the Moscow State Symphony Orchestra, Warsaw Radio Symphony, Philharmonia Sląska, London Schubert Players, Helsinki Philharmonic, Wroclaw Philharmonic, Danish Radio Symphony Orchestra, Odense Symphony, Tivoli Symphony, Nat. Symphony Orchestra of Ukraine, Symphony Orchestra of Nat. Opera of Ukraine, Rotterdam Philharmonic; repertoire includes the Viennese classics, Strauss, Tchaikovsky, Brahms, Liszt and Ravel; teacher at the Kiev School of Arts and Odessa Conservatoire. *Honours:* Honoured Artist of Ukraine 1994; winner, Nat. Performers Competition, Ukraine 1988, Sergei Prokofiev Int. Conducting Competition 1993, Stefan Turchak Conducting Competition 1994, Grzegorz Fitelberg Conducting Competition, Poland 1995.

ZHANG, Haochen; Chinese pianist; b. 3 June 1990, Shanghai. *Education:* Shanghai Conservatory of Music, Shenzhen Arts School, Curtis Inst. of Music, USA. *Career:* debut recital at Shanghai Concert Hall age five, performing the complete Bach Two-Part Inventions and sonatas by Haydn and Mozart; orchestral debut age six; moved to USA to study in 2005; engagements included Philadelphia Orchestra debut performing Rachmaninov's Second Piano Concerto 2006, Carnegie Hall debut aged 18 with the New York Youth Symphony 2008; world-wide tour 2009–2010 with appearances at Carnegie Hall Neighbourhood Concert Series, Beijing Music Festival, Wolf Trap Discovery Series, San Francisco Symphony, Rochester Philharmonic, Aspen Festival, Krannert Center for the Performing Arts, Hannover Prize Winners Series and recitals in Krakow and Lodz (Poland). *Honours:* winner, Shanghai Piano Competition at ages seven and nine, Int. Tchaikovsky Competition for Young Musicians 2002, China Int. Piano Competition 2007, co-winner, Van Cliburn Piano Competition 2009. *Current Management:* c/o Kajjimoto Concert Management, 5 rue Barbette, 75003 Paris, France. *E-mail:* paris@kajimotomusic.comm. *Website:* www.kajimotomusic.com/en.

ZHANG, Jian-Yi; American singer (tenor); b. 3 Aug. 1959, Shanghai, China; s. of Yang-Guang Zhang and Pei-Qin Cai; m. Wei-Ping Yang; one d. *Education:* Shanghai Conservatory of Music, Opera Center of the Juilliard School. *Career:* debut as the Lover in Amelia al Ballo 1987; appeared as the Duke of Mantua in Rigoletto at Teatro Comunale di Firenze 1989; as Rodolfo in La Bohème at New York City Opera and Werther at Opera de Nice 1990–91; performed Nadir in the Pearl Fishers at Washington Opera and Opera Pacific 1991–92; Roldolfo at Opéra de Lyon and Opera Nice and Des Grieux in Manon at Opéra Comique Paris 1992–93; season 1993–94 as Don José in Carmen at the Nat. Opéra de Paris Bastille; Faust in Paris, Washington, Michigan Opera

Theatre and Miami Grand Opera 1994–95; as Alfredo in La Traviata at Staatsoper Hamburg and Rodolfo at Stattsoper Stuttgart 1995–96; season 1996–97 as Faust at the Metropolitan Opera and The Duke of Mantua in Rigoletto at the Montréal Opera and as Nemorino in L'Elisir D'Amore at the New Israeli Opera; sang Rodolfo and Alfredo at New York City Opera and as Des Grieux at the Metropolitan Opera 1997–98; appearances as Rodolfo at Dallas Opera and Alfredo at Vancouver Opera and Tamino in The Magic Flute at Florentine Opera, Faust at Savonlinna Opera Festival at the Seattle Opera 1998–99; sang Meyerbeer's Robert for Deutsche Staatsoper, Berlin, Gerald in Lakmé at Montréal, Massenet's Des Grieux in Madrid and Cavaradossi at Hong Kong 1999–2001; Calos in Linda di Chamounix at Vienna State Opera, Faust at Bavaria State Opera, Munich 2001–02; Leopold in La Juive at Vienna State Opera, Edgardo in Lucia di Lammermour at Metropolitan Opera and Palm Beach Opera, Nemorino in L'Elisir D'Amore at Frankfurt Opera 2002–03; Rodolfo in La Bohème at Metropolitan Opera, Ismaele in Nabucco at Metropolitan Opera, Cellini in Benvenuto Cellini at Metropolitan Opera 2003–04; Roméo in Roméo and Julliette at Beijing Int. Music Festival 2004–05; Alfredo in La Traviata at Opera Carolina, Edgardo in Lucia di Lammermoor at Lyric Opera Kansas City Opera, Leopold in La Juive at Vienna State Opera 2005–06; Macduff in Macbeth at Arizona Opera, Alfredo in La Travita in Beijing Central Conservatory of Music, Don Jose in Carmen at China Philharmonic 2006–07; Nadir in the Pearl Fishers, the Duke of Mantua in Rigoletto, Don Jose in Carmen at Shanghai Opera Company 2007–08; Cavaradossi in Tosca, Guang Zhou Opera Company, concerts with Shanghai Symphony Orchestra, Beijing Symphony Orchestra, China Philharmonic, Hang Zhou Philharmonic, Macao Philharmonic, Guang Zhou Philharmonic 2008–09. *Recordings:* albums: solo: Jianyi Zhang: Tenor (solo album), Great Opera Arias, Italian Songs, Chinese Songs; Leopold in La Juive (DVD). *Honours:* first prize Belvedere Int. Opera Singer Competition, Vienna 1984, Grand Winner Luciano Pavarotti Int. Voice Competition, Philadelphia 1988, first prize EMF, New York 1989, first prize Opera Index of New York 1989, winner Metropolitan Opera Audition 1989. *Address:* c/o 62-54 97th Place, Apt PH-1, Rego Park, NY 11374, USA (home). *E-mail:* tenorzhang@gmail.com (office); BCCMGMT@yahoo.com (office). *Website:* www.jianyizhang.com.

ZHANG, Liping; Chinese/Canadian singer (soprano); b. Hubei, China. *Education:* Beijing Conservatoire. *Career:* began professional career in Canada, with int. debut as Liu in Turandot, ROH 2002; operatic roles include Mimi in La Bohème (Canada, Hong Kong, New York, Baltimore, Detroit, Oslo), Leila in Les Pêcheurs de Perles (Canada), Liu in Turandot (Canada, ROH London, New York), Marguerite in Faust (Canada), Lucia in Lucia di Lammermoor (Canada, ROH, Deutsche Oper, Berlin), Cio-Cio-San in Madama Butterfly (ROH, New York, Michigan, Deutsche Oper Berlin, Oslo, Opéra de Paris, Teatro del Liceu Barcelona), Violetta in La Traviata (Shanghai Int. Festival), Gilda in Rigoletto (Oslo, Parma), Micaela in Carmen (ROH). *Current Management:* Stafford Law, Candleway, Broad Street, Sutton Valence, Kent ME17 3AT, England. *Telephone:* (1622) 840-038 (office). *Fax:* (1622) 840-039 (office). *E-mail:* staffordlaw@btinternet.com (office). *Website:* www.stafford-law.com.

ZHANG, Peiyu; Taiwanese conductor; *Chief Conductor, Luzern Opera House;* b. 1959. *Education:* Taichung Normal Univ., conductor training, Vienna Conservatory, Austria. *Career:* went to Vienna, Austria to pursue conducting career 1985; returned to Taiwan, given opportunity to conduct Taipei Philharmonic; went to Italy and became Asst Conductor to Zubin Mehta 1994; hired as tenured Prof. of Xi'an Conservatory of Music, Beijing 2005; currently Chief Conductor, Luzern Opera House, Switzerland. *Address:* Xi'an Conservatory of Music, 18 Chang'anzhong Road, Central Xiaozhai, South Suburbs, Xi'an 710061, Shaanxi, People's Republic of China (office). *Telephone:* (29) 5239738 (office).

ZHANG, Xian; Chinese conductor; *Music Director, Orchestra Sinfonica di Milano Giuseppe Verdi;* b. Dandong; one c. *Education:* Beijing Central Conservatory. *Career:* professional debut with Le Nozze di Figaro at Central Opera House, Beijing; Conductor-in-Residence, China Opera House 1995–96; fmr conductor, Jin Fan Symphony Orchestra; one year teaching at Beijing Central Conservatory; moved to USA 1998; Asst Prof. of Orchestra Conducting and Music Dir of the Concert Orchestra, Univ. of Cincinnati Conservatory of Music 2000; Music Dir Lucca Festival Orchestra 2000; Asst Conductor New York Philharmonic Orchestra 2004, Assoc. Conductor 2005–07, Arturo Toscanini Assoc. Conductor 2007–09, collaborating with Lorin Maazel and conducting family and young people's concerts; Music Dir Sioux City Symphony Orchestra 2005–07; Music Dir Orchestra Sinfonica di Milano Giuseppe Verdi 2009–; Artistic Dir Dutch Orchestra and Ensemble Academy (NJO) 2011–; has conducted Cincinnati Opera in La Traviata 2003, Don Giovanni 2004, La Bohème 2005; guest conductor with Cincinnati Symphony Orchestra, Colorado Symphony, Louisiana Philharmonic, Omaha Symphony, Charlotte Symphony, Orchestra of St Luke's, China Philharmonic, Auckland Philharmonia, LSO, Sinfonica Arturo Toscanini. *Honours:* winner Maazel/Vilar Int. Conductors' Competition 2002. *Current Management:* Harrison Parrott, 5–6 Albion Court, London, W6 0QT, England. *Telephone:* (20) 7229-9166. *Fax:* (20) 7221-5042. *E-mail:* info@harrisonparrott.co.uk. *Website:* www.harrisonparrott.com. *Address:* Fondazione Orchestra Sinfonica di Milano Giuseppe Verdi, Corso San Gottardo 39, 20136 Milan, Italy (office). *Website:* www.laverdi.org (office); www.njo.nl (office).

ZHAO, Pingguo; Chinese pianist and academic; b. 1934; m. Ling Yuan 1956; one s. one d. *Education:* Central Conservatory of Music, Central Conservatory of St Petersburg with Aram Taturan and Tachiana Kravchenko. *Career:* joined piano faculty, Central Conservatory of Music 1951, currently Professor of Piano; took part in International Tchaikovsky Piano Competition 1962; performance tour of Japan with promising pupils 1996; numerous piano concert performances; repertoire includes Beethoven Sonatas, Chopin, Mozart Concertos, Tchaikovsky Concertos; numerous lectures in cities worldwide including Russia, Ukraine, Los Angeles, Japan; Judge, several piano competitions; Grader, National Examinational Piano Playing. *Address:* Central Conservatory of Music, 43 Baojia Street, Beijing 100031, People's Republic of China (office). *E-mail:* contactus@ccom.edu.cn (office). *Website:* www.ccom.edu.cn (office).

ZHAO, Xiaosheng, BA, MA; Chinese composer, pianist, musicologist and academic; b. 27 July 1945, Shanghai. *Education:* Shanghai Conservatory of Music, Columbia Univ., Missouri State Univ. *Career:* Visiting Scholar, Visiting Professor, UMC, USA 1981–84; over 100 piano recitals in 20 main cities of China, in USA and Hong Kong; created Taiji Composition 1987, Tonesets Motion Theory 1991; guest host, Radio Shanghai, Oriental Radio Shanghai, STV and OTV, Shanghai; Editor-in-Chief, Shanghai Piano Guild 1994, 1995; Vice Editor-in-Chief, Piano Artistry magazine. *Compositions include:* Six Concert Etudes for piano 1976, Two String Quartets 1980, 1981, The Goddess of Hope, Piano Concerto 1985, Four Movements of Jian 1986, Taiji, piano solo 1987, Three Movements of Yin-Yang for 16 players 1987, Bi Xiao Pai Yun for flute 1988, Double Concerto for Gaohu and Erhu and Chinese Orchestra 1988, LuYao, pipa solo 1989, Ting Qin for Erhu and Piano 1989, Huan Feng, sheng solo 1989, Hui Liu, quartet 1989, Three Symphonic Suites 1990, Sound of Man 1990, The Song of Earth 1990–91, Sacrifice to Heaven 1990–91, Liao Yin, piano concerto 1991, The Sun over the Wasteland, ballet 1992, Shi Lou for Chinese Chamber Orchestra 1994, Stephen Hawking's View of Cosmos, Filter, Eight Scenes of West Lake, Qin Yun, Xiao Xue, A-Bing Sui Xiang (Capriccio from Blind Abing), Blake and White, Drum and Bell, 62343314, Echoes from Empty Valley, Ancient Sound of Mt Yu 1999; more than 30 improvisations. *Recordings:* Music from His Heart–Zhao Plays His 14 Own Piano Pieces 1999, How to Play The 'Music Note Book for Anna Magdalena Bach' 1999. *Address:* Composition Department, Shanghai Conservatory of Music, 20 Fenyang Lu, Shanghai 200031, People's Republic of China (office). *E-mail:* smph2010@yahoo.com.cn (office). *Website:* www.zhaoxiaosheng.com.

ZHEN, Su, LRAM; Chinese violist and academic; *Professor of Viola, Central Conservatory of Music, Beijing.* *Education:* Central Conservatory of Music, Beijing, Royal Acad. of Arts, UK, studied with John White. *Career:* apptd Asst Prin. Viola, China Nat. Symphony Orchestra at age 23; Asst Prin. Viola, BBC Philharmonic Orchestra 2000–04; solo violist, Det Jyske Ensemble (Denmark); concerts worldwide as soloist and chamber musician, including festivals in Edinburgh and Geneva, Int. Arts Festival in Tokyo and Viola Arts Festival in UK; Prof. of Viola, Central Conservatory of Music, Beijing 2004–; taught int. masterclasses at festivals including Great Mountains Int. Music Festival, South Korea, Great Wall Int. Music Festival and Austria Acad. of Music; Visiting Prof. of Viola, RAM, London 2011–; mem. jury, Lionel Tertis Int. Viola Competition 2010 and Beijing Int. Music Competition (strings category) 2011. *Honours:* Huo Yingdong Outstanding Youth Teacher Award, Ministry of Educ. 2006. *Address:* Central Conservatory of Music, 43 Baojia Street, Xicheng District, Beijing 100031, People's Republic of China (office); Royal Academy of Music, Marylebone Road, London, NW1 5HT, England (office). *E-mail:* fao@ccom.edu.cn (office).

ZHIDKOVA, Elena; Russian singer (mezzo-soprano); b. 1972. *Education:* St Petersburg Conservatory and Opera Studio of Hamburg State Opera. *Career:* mem. Berlin Deutsche Opera 1997–99; roles include Maddalena in Rigoletto, Olga in Eugene Onegin, Hansel in Handel und Gretel, Siebel in Faust, Fides in Le Prophète, Fricka in Die Walküre, Fricka in Das Rheingold, Waltraute in Götterdämmerung, King Lear, Carmen, Judith in Blaubarts Burg, Varvara in Katja Kabanova, Lola in Cavalleria Rusticana, Sesto in La Clemenza di Tito, Dorabella in Cosi fan Tutte, Marina and Fjodor in Boris Gudunov, Dido in Dido and Aeneas, Komponist in Ariadne auf Naxos, Octavian in Der Rosenkavalier, Orlofsky in Die Fledermaus, Adriana in Rienzi, Kundry in Parsifal, Venus in Tannhäuser, Brangane in Tristan und Isolde; appearances at Théâtre du Châtelet, Paris, Nederlandse Opera, Amsterdam, Lincoln Center, New York, Teatro Real, Madrid and Barbican Hall, London, Bayreuth Festival, Salzburg Easter Festival; concerts include Mahler's 8th Symphony in Rome, under Myung-Whun Chung. *Honours:* prizewinner Dvořák Competition, Prague. *Current Management:* c/o Hilbert Artists Management, Maximilianstrasse 22, 80539 Munich, Germany; c/o Opéra et Concert, 37 rue de la Chaussée d'Antin, 75009 Paris, France. *Telephone:* (89) 2907470 (Germany); 1-42-96-18-18 (France). *Fax:* (89) 29074790 (Germany); 1-42-96-18-00 (France). *E-mail:* agentur@hilbert.de; agence@opera-concert.com. *Website:* www.hilbert.de; www.opera-concert.com.

ZHIKALOV, Yuri; Russian singer (tenor); b. 1948. *Education:* St Petersburg Conservatoire. *Career:* many engagements in concerts and opera throughout Russia; performing with Kirov Opera, St Petersburg 1977–, roles include Lensky in Eugene Onegin, Mozart's Monostatos, Andrei in Mazeppa and Khovanshchina, Finn in Ruslan, Lyudmila; sang with the Kirov in summer season at Covent Garden 2000; other roles include Prince Guidon in Rimsky-

Korsakov's The Tale of Tsar Saltan, Norman in Lucia di Lammermoor, Mikhail and Nikita in The Maid of Pskov, Platon in War and Peace.

ZHISLIN, Grigory Yefimovich; Russian/British violinist and violist; *Professor, Hochschule für Musik, Würzburg;* b. 14 May 1945, Leningrad (now St Petersburg); s. of Yefim Zhislin and Sarra Zhislin; m. Valentina Murashova 1980; one s. *Education:* Moscow State Conservatory, studied with Yuny Yankelevich. *Career:* concerts in USSR and abroad 1966–; participated in major music festivals, including Maggio Musicale Fiorentino, Warsaw Autumn, Prague Spring, Kuhmi Chamber Music, Berliner Biennale, Pablo Casals in Puerto Rico, Paganini in Genoa and others; teacher, Kharkov Inst. of Arts 1971–73, Moscow Gnessin Pedagogical Inst. 1973–90, Prof. 1978–90; Royal Coll. of Music, London 1990–2004; Prof., Hochschule für Musik, Würzburg 1993–; Visiting Prof., Oslo Conservatory, Kraków Musik Akad., Warsaw Conservatory; master-classes in USA, Italy, France, Finland, Sweden. *Recordings include:* Penderecki Viola Concerto/Cello Concerto No. 2 (Int. Classical Music Award for Best Contemporary Music Recording 2012) 2011. *Honours:* Ordre du Mérite Culturel, Gloria Artist (Poland); winner, Int. Competitions of Paganini in Genoa 1967 and Queen Elizabeth in Brussels 1976. *Address:* Friedenstrasse 6A, 97072 Würzburg, Germany (home). *Telephone:* (931) 54772. *E-mail:* grig.zhislin@freenet.de. *Website:* www.hfm -wuerzburg.de; www.grigori-zhislin.info.

ZHIVOPISTEV, Vladimir; singer (baritone); b. 1960, Dobrush, Belarus. *Education:* Odessa State Conservatoire. *Career:* appearances at the Maly Opera Theatre, St Petersburg; Kirov Opera, Mariinsky Theatre, from 1996; roles have included Giorgio Germont, Yeletsky in The Queen of Spades, Eugene Onegin, Rossini's Figaro, Goro in Madama Butterfly, War and Peace, Khovanshchina and Semyon Kotko (British premiere) with the Kirov at Covent Garden 2000; other roles include Robert in Tchaikovsky's Iolanta, the Indian Guest in Rimsky's Sadko, Spoletta in Tosca and Bayan in Ruslan and Lyudmila. *Honours:* prizewinner Lysenko International Vocal Competition.

ZHOU, Long, DMA; Chinese/American composer and academic; b. 8 July 1953, Beijing; m. Chen Yi. *Education:* Central Conservatory of Music, Beijing, Columbia Univ., USA. *Career:* sent to rural state farm during Cultural Revolution; Composer-in-Residence, Nat. Broadcasting Symphony Orchestra of China 1983; moved to USA in 1985; Music Dir, Music from China, New York 1988–99; Music Alive! Composer-in-Residence, Seattle Symphony's Silk Road Project Festival with Yo-Yo Ma May 2002; commissions from Koussevitsky and Fromm Music Foundations, Chamber Music America and New York State Council on the Arts, and from ensembles including Bavarian Radio Symphony Orchestra, Tokyo and Brooklyn Philharmonics, New Music Consort, Pittsburgh New Music Ensemble, Peabody Trio and Kronos, Shanghai, Ciompi and Chester String Quartets and vocal ensemble Chanticleer; currently Distinguished Prof. of Music Composition, Univ. of Missouri-Kansas City Conservatory of Music and Dance. *Compositions include:* Poems from Tang, The Future of Fire, The Ineffable, Soul, Tian Ling, Spirit of Chimes, Dhyana, Ding, Madame White Snake (Pulitzer Prize for Music 2011), University Festival Overture 2012, Beijing Rhyme—A Symphonic Suite 2012, Nine Odes 2013, Tales from the Nine Bells 2014. *Honours:* fellowships from American Acad. of Arts and Letters, Nat. Endowment for the Arts and Guggenheim and Rockefeller Foundations, ASCAP Adventurous Programming Award 1999, Lifetime Achievement Award, American Acad. of Arts and Letters 2003, CalArts/Alpert Award in the Arts 2009, Barlow Int. Composition Competition, Fifth Int. Composition Competition, d'Avray (France), Ensemblia Competition, Mönchengladbach (Germany). *Address:* UMKC Conservatory of Music and Dance, Grant Hall, 5227 Holmes Street, Kansas City, MO 64110-2229, USA (office). *E-mail:* zhoul@umkc.edu (office). *Website:* conservatory.umkc .edu (office).

ZHOU, Xiaoyan; Chinese singer (coloratura soprano); b. 1918, Wuhan City, Hubei Prov.; d. of Zhou Changguo. *Education:* Shanghai Guoli Professional Training School, Paris Russia Conservatory of Music, France. *Career:* teacher, Shanghai Conservatory of Music 1949, Dir of Vocal Dept 1987–, f. Zhou Xiaoyan Opera Centre 1988; performed in Luxembourg 1946, later performances include London, Paris, Geneva, Berlin, Prague and Warsaw; a Vice-Chair. Chinese Musicians' Asscn 1979–. *Address:* Shanghai Conservatory of Music, No. 20 Fenyang Road, Xuhui District, Shanghai 200031, People's Republic of China (office).

ZHU, Ai-Lan; Chinese singer (soprano); b. 1957, Nanking. *Education:* Central Conservatory of Music, Beijing, Hartt School of Music. *Career:* sang first with the Central Opera Theater, Beijing, notably as Cio-Cio-San i Madama Butterfly and Mimi in La Bohéme; made American debut with Texas Opera Theater; roles include Marguerite in Faust, Micaela in Carmen, Liu in Turandot, Maddalena in Andrea Chenier, Leila in Les Pêcheurs des Perles, Violetta in La Traviata, Gilda in Rigoletto, the Countess in Le Nozze de Figaro, Pamina in Die Zauberflöte, Mélisande in Impressions de Pelléas, Zerlina in Don Giovanni, Marzelline in Fidelio, Xola in Under the Double Moon; has performed with National Reisopera, Netherlands, Opera de Montréal, Opéra de Quebec, Vancouver Opera, Arizona Opera, Connecticut Opera, Orlando Opera, Opera Carolina, Austin Lyric Opera, Kentucky Opera, Tulsa Opera, San Antonio Symphony, Atlanta Opera, Chautauqua Opera, Connecticut Opera, Virginia Opera, Vancouver Opera, Austin Lyric Opera, Opera Pacific, Michigan Opera Theater, Connecticut Opera, Orlando Opera, San Diego Opera. *Honours:* winner, SAI Competition, Liederkranz Competition, New York. *Current Management:* Pinnacle Arts Management, 889 Ninth

Avenue, 2nd Floor, New York, NY 10019, USA. *Telephone:* (212) 397-7915. *Fax:* (212) 397-7920. *E-mail:* vuzan@pinnaclearts.com. *Website:* www .pinnaclearts.com.

ZHU, Jian-Er; Chinese composer and academic; b. 18 Oct. 1922, Tianjin; m. Qun Shu 1949; two s. one d. *Education:* Moscow State Conservatory, studied with Prof. Sergey Balasanian. *Career:* composer, Art Troupe, New 4th Army 1945–49; Conductor, Brass Band 1946–49; composer, Shanghai and Peking Film Studios 1949–63; Shanghai Opera House 1963–75; Shanghai Symphony Orchestra 1975–; Professor of Composition, Shanghai Conservatory of Music. *Compositions include:* orchestral: Festival Overture 1958, In Memorian for Strings 1978, Symphonic Fantasia 1980, Sketches in Mountains of Guizhou 1982, The Butterfly Fountain for Er-hu and Orchestra 1983, A Wonder of Naxi 1984, Symphonies No. 1 1986, No. 2 1987, No. 3 Tibet 1988, No. 4 1990, No. 5 1991, No. 6 1994, No. 7 1994, No. 8 1994, No. 9 1999, No. 10 1998, Sinfonietta 1994, Concerto for Sona and Orchestra 1989, Hundred Year Vicissitudes 1996, Silk Road Reverie 2000; choral: Salute 1946 1945, Gada-meilin 1958, Symphony-Cantata Heroic Poems 1960, A Cappella Cycle The Green, Green Water Village 1981; for piano: Preludes 1955, Theme and Var 1956, Ballade 1958, Five Yunnan Folk Songs 1962, Quintet 1992, Folk Instrumental Ensemble Day of Liberation 1953, Song of the Spring for oboe and piano 1956. *Address:* 105 Hu Nan Road, Shanghai Symphony Orchestra, Shanghai 200031, People's Republic of China (office).

ZHU, Kunqiang; Chinese French horn player; b. 10 April 1963, Bengbu, Anhui Province. *Education:* Army Art Academy of China. *Career:* Principal French Horn, Symphony Orchestra of the Chinese Army, 1983; toured Russia, Hungary, Poland, Romania and Germany, 1988; performed at the Hong Kong Arts Festival with the China Youth Symphony Orchestra, 1991; Macao Music Festival with the China Chamber Music Orchestra, 1995; Principal French Horn with the China National Symphony Orchestra, 1996–; has toured China, and abroad, including Hong Kong Arts Festival, 1997, 1998 and 2000, Germany, the UK and Austria, 1998, Japan and the Osaka International Music Festival, 1999, Mexico, 2000, and Hong Kong and Macao, 2001; co-founded and performs with the Wuxing Brass Quintet; mem. International Horn Society, Chinese Musician's Association. *Recordings include:* numerous works for television and film with the China Radio Symphony Orchestra and the China Film Orchestra; Chinese Folk Song Collection with the Wuxing Brass Quintet; Many Chinese and Western symphonic works with the China National Symphony Orchestra. *Honours:* First Prize at the Second Chinese Horn Competition, 1991. *Address:* c/o The China National Symphony Orchestra, 11-1 Hepingjie, Chaoyang District, Beijing 100013, People's Republic of China.

ZHUKOV, Sergey; Russian composer; b. 30 Aug. 1951, Zhitomir, Ukraine; s. of the late Victor Zhukov and Aurora Zhukova; m. Natalia Zhukova 1982; two d. *Education:* Music Coll., Zhitomir, Moscow State Conservatory. *Career:* debut chamber music concert, Maliy Hall, Moscow Conservatory 1973; participated in All-Union and int. concerts, festivals, symposia, including Moscow Autumn Musical Festival 1981–2007, Warsaw Autumn 1988, Int. Musical Festival, Leningrad 1989, Charles Ives Festival, USA 1990, Week Van de Hedendaagse Musiek, Belgium 1991; teacher, Dept of Theory and Composition, Moscow State Conservatory 1991; mem. Bd Union of Composers of Russia, also mem. Selection Cttee; mem. Union of Theatre Workers of Russia; mem. of Org. Cttee, Moscow Autumn Festival. *Television and radio broadcasts:* Symphony No. 1 (All-Union Radio) 1987, Moments, Running in Successions (oratorio, All-Union TV) 1987, Partita for violin solo (Donderdag, Dutch Radio) 1990, Landscape for clarinet solo (BRT-3, Belgium Radio), Solaris (ballet, Ukrainian TV) 1991. *Compositions include:* Lullaby (to verses by M. Lermontov) for chorus a cappella 1973, Black Keys for voice and ensemble 1973, Listen (four poems by V. Mayakovsky) for vocal quartet 1974, Spivanochcki chamber cantata to traditional words 1975, On the Shore (soundtrack to verses by A. Tarkovsky) 1976, Echo (three poems by A. Pushkin) for soprano and piano trio 1979, Sonata-Capriccio for solo cello 1980, Lyrical Scenes for soprano and string orchestra (to verses by T. Shevchenko) 1981, Choreographic Pictures for symphony orchestra (based on N. Gogol's short novel Viy) 1982, Refracted Sounds wind quintet 1984, Symphony No. 1 1985, Moments, Running in Successions (verses by I. Bunin) for narrator, soloists, women and children's chorus, and symphony orchestra 1987, Sonata-Bussanda for piano 1988, Landscape for solo clarinet 1988, Solaris (ballet) 1990, Image and Transfiguration for organ 1991, Concerto-Partes for string orchestra 1992, Bless the Lord, O My Soul for chorus a cappella 1992, Lot of Nemesida choreographic composition for clarinettist, dancer, magnetic tape 1992, Songs of Farewell (verses by J. H. Leopold) for soprano, flute, cello and piano 1992, De Tuinman en de Dood (verses by P. N. van Eyck) for contralto and cello 1993, Concerto-Mystery for piano, violin, violoncello and orchestra 1994, Repented Prayer of Saint S. Sarovsky for chorus a cappella 1994, Revelation to John, chapters 21 and 22, for chorus a cappella 1995, Transforms of the Limited Space, scene for flute solo 1995, Concerto Grosso (Concerto Sacra) for piano, violin, cello and orchestra 1997, The Soul of the Night (based on texts by Maeterlinck) 1999, Insomnia (ballet after Pushkin) 1999, Palindromeo (to verses by V. Sofronitsky) for chorus a cappella 2000, In Search of the Missing Score for clarinet, harpsichord and soundtrack 2000, Book of Transformations for prepared piano 2000, Fatum (ballet based on M. Lermontov's poem, Demon) 2001, Silentium concerto for piano and orchestra 2001, Belgorod's Variations for symphony orchestra 2002, Hommage Holland for three organs 2002, Gethsemanian Night concerto for electric cello, mixed chorus, horns, percussion and prepared piano 2003, Angel's Day concerto for violin and orchestra 2004, Alleluja for violin and string orchestra 2006, Wedding veil of Pierette (pantomime based on a drama by A. Shnitzler) 2007, Scarlet Floret, ballet in two acts (based on a fairy tale by S. Aksakov) 2007, The King Matiush I, musical performance (based on play by Janush Korchak) 2008, Symphony No. 2: Navna 2009, Star Maps for solo piano 2010, Life of Insects, or Deceit and Love (musical based on the story of K. Chukovsky 'Muha-tsokotuha') 2010, Stihomania (solo performance based on poems by Lena Eltang) 2010, Symphony No.3 2012, Litania (voices, chamber orchestra and soundtrack) 2012, Ave Maria (stage composition for female voice, piano and soundtrack) 2013. *Recordings:* Spivanochcki 1982, Sonata-Capriccio 1983, Concerto Mystery 1998, Concerto Grosso 1998, Image and Transfiguration 2000, Landscape 2005, Concerto Partes 2006. *Radio:* Partita for violin solo (Donderdag, Dutch Radio) 1990, Landscape for clarinet solo (BRT-3, Belgium Radio). *Television:* Symphony No. 1 (All-Union Radio) 1987, Moments, Running in Successions (oratorio, All-Union TV) 1987, Solaris (ballet, Ukrainian TV) 1991. *Publications:* contrib. of numerous articles, including Some Aspects of Creation of Musical Compositions 1980, series of articles for The Musical Encyclopedia 1991, Spivanochki for two sopranos, clarinet, violin, temple-blocks and piano (in collection Works for voice and chamber ensemble) 1983, Partita for solo violin (in Selected works of Soviet composers for violin solo) 1986, Landscape, for solo clarinet 1997, Sempre Sonare for two pianos and percussion (in Book of transformations for prepared piano), The Secret Story of the Old Music Box 2008. *Honours:* Honoured Art Worker of the Russian Fed. *Address:* Studencheskaja Street 44/28, Apartment 128, 121165 Moscow, Russia (home). *Telephone:* (495) 249-5515 (home). *Fax:* (495) 249-5515 (home). *E-mail:* zhukov.sergei@gmail.com (home); sergzhukov@umail.ru (home). *Website:* zhukovsergey.ru.

ZIEGLER, Delores; American singer (mezzo-soprano); *Associate Professor of Voice, University of Maryland*; b. 4 Sept. 1951, Atlanta, GA. *Education:* Univ. of Tennessee. *Career:* sang at first in concert then made stage debut as Flora in La Traviata, Knoxville, Tennessee 1978; sang Maddalena in Rigoletto at St Louis 1979; with Bonn Opera 1981, with performances as Emilia in Otello, Dorabella and Octavian; mem., Cologne Opera 1982, notably as Cherubino, Orlofsky and Octavian; at La Scala Milan, notably in Bellini's Romeo 1984–87; as Siebel and Octavian, Metropolitan Opera 1989–91; in Der Rosenkavalier, Canadian Opera Co. at Toronto 1990; sang Dorabella at Washington, DC 1996; Mozart's Marcellina at the Met 1999, in Rameau's Hippolyte et Aricie at Saint Louis 2001; guest engagements in Munich, Oslo, San Diego, Toronto, Hamburg; festivals performances include Dorabella, Glyndebourne Fesival 1984, as Mozart's Sextus, Salzburg Festival 1988, as Idamantes, Maggio Musicale, Florence 1989; many concert engagements; currently Assoc. Prof. of Voice, Univ. of Maryland. *Recordings include:* Bach's B minor Mass, Così fan Tutte, Mozart's Mass in C, Second Lady in Die Zauberflöte, Le Roi d'Ys by Lalo. *Address:* School of Music, University of Maryland, 2110 Clarice Smith Performing Arts Center, College Park, MD 20742-1620, USA (office). *Telephone:* (301) 405-5511 (office). *E-mail:* dziegler@umd.edu (office). *Website:* www.music.umd.edu (office).

ZIELIŃSKA, Lidia, Dr Hab.; Polish composer and academic; *Professor of Composition and Electroacoustics and Director, SMEAMuz Poznan Electroacoustic Music Studio, Akademia Muzyczna, Poznań*; b. 9 Oct. 1953, Poznań; m. Zygmunt Zielinski 1974; one d. *Education:* State Higher School of Music, Poznań, studied composition with Andrzej Koszewski. *Career:* worked in Electronics Music Studio Kraków 1978–, Polish Radio Experimental Studio 1980–81, 1986–, Studio IPEM Ghent, ENS Stockholm, ZKM Karlsruhe, IMEB Bourges; composers' workshops in Poland, the Netherlands, France and Switzerland 1979–87; collaborated with Polish Centre of Art for Children, Artistic Group Artificial Cult; concerts and performances in Europe, Asia, Australia and NZ, N and S America; Asst Prof., later Prof. of Composition, Multimedia and Electroacoustics, Akademia Muzyczna, Poznań 1983–, Dir SMEAMuz Poznań Electroacoustic Music Studio; Co-founder Brevis Publrs, Child and Sound Foundation, music quarterly Monochord, Friends of Warsaw Autumn Foundation, Zachęta Fine Arts Soc. Poznań, Polish Soc. for Electroacoustic Music; Vice-Pres. Polish Composers' Union, Polish Asscn for Electroacoustic Music; mem. Programme Cttee, Warsaw Autumn Festival 1989–92, 1996–2005, ISCM World Music Days, Warsaw, Polish-German Radio Copernicus; Artistic Dir Musical Spring Contemporary Music Festival, Poznań 1989–92, Child and Sound int. festival, Poznań. *Compositions include:* Violin Concerto 1979, Farewell Mr Toorop for orchestra 1981, Lullaby Gagaku for double bass 1984, Sonnet on the Tatras for four musicians 1985, Music for Stanislaw Wyspianski for tape 1985, Glossa for viola or violin 1986, Polish Dances for tape after (Father Baka) 1986, Pleonasmus for oboe, violin and string orchestra 1986, Kaleidoscope, Passacaglia for percussion, slides and clapping hands for children 1987, Concrete Music for choir and orchestra 1987, The Same 1988, Little Atrophic Symphony 1988, Musica Humana or How Symphonies are Born (radio piece) 1989, Jacquard Loom for 14 musicians 1991, Fago for bassoon, double bass and accordion or electronic keyboard 1992, Venture Unknown (ballet) 1995, The Plot Theory of Sound (installation) 1996, Expandata for percussion and tape 1996, Soaked Ground Music with children audience participation, narrator, conductor and tape 1993, Zeitschlingen, sound spectacle 1994, Venture Unknown, ballet 1995, Section Togo for male choir and prepared piano 1995, Schon wieder diese weissen Mäuse for tape 1996, Expandata for snare drum and tape 1997, Motetus universalis, installation 1997, Ballad about a Ballata for tape 1997, Percussionata for 40–60 percussionists 1998, Zoom for violin and orchestra 2000, Just Too Many Words for tape 2001, Grain to Grain for 13 instruments 2002, A Sketch Drawn from Nature, multimedia performance 2002, From a Sketchbook II, multimedia show 2003, dumchrzquii for tape 2004, Rapsodia for violin and electronic sounds 2004, Nobody is Perfect for electronic sounds and 17 instruments 2004, Przypadki pana von K./Die Fälle des Herrn von K., ballet, electroacoustic music 2005, Lunches in Rejowiec 1965–1665, text-sound-composition 2006, Wszystko juz bylo/Alles gab's schon mal/Everything Has Already Happened, audiovisual installation 2006, From the Garden of Sciences for choir and electronic sounds to words from Ecclesiastes 2006, Conrad's Seven Islands for tape and 10 amplified instruments 2007, The Eighth Island for stereo tape 2008, The Eighth Island for 8 loudspeakers 2011, Rust for 5 or 6 instruments and CD 2010, Canción triste for violin and CD 2010, Backstage Pass for computer (ambisonics) or multi-channel diffusion 2010, Melodramat for orchestra 2011, X3 for 14 instruments 2011, Lata for orchestra 2011, Muzyczne pejzaże wczoraj, dziś, jutro, multimedia concert for children 2011, Aphasia for tenor saxophone and CD 2012, Ukiyo for 19 instruments 2012, 53 Oddechy for glissando flute, live electronics and 8-channel tape 2013, Polish Sonorities, sound installation 2013, Lutosławski DIY, sound installation and flash mob 2013, Slices of Music, interactive installation for children 2013. *Publications:* 75 scores and CDs. *Honours:* 17 awards at composers' competitions, including first prizes: Jeunesses Musicales, Belgrade 1979, Internationale Wettbewerb für Komponistinnen, Mannheim 1981, ZAIKS, Warszawa 1982, The Max Deutsch Contest, Paris 1984, Künstlerhaus, Boswil 1986, L'Opera autrement, Avignon 1988; Polish Composers' Union Award 2007.

ZIESAK, Ruth; German singer (soprano); b. 9 Feb. 1963, Hofheim, Taunus. *Education:* studied with Christoph Pregardien, Frankfurt Musikhochschule with Elsa Cavelti, Frankfurt Opera School. *Career:* debut in Heidelberg as Valencienne in Die Lustige Witwe; sang at Heidelberg as Pamina, Gilda, Sesto in Giulio Cesare and Despina; Deutsche Oper am Rhein as Marzelline; tour of Tokyo, Osaka and Kyoto with the Ludwigsburg Festival Ensemble, singing in Messiah and Mozart's Requiem, 1989; sang Susanna at the Opéra Bastille, Paris, and Pamina, 1991, and at the Salzburg Festival, 1993; season 1993–94 as Sophie in Rosenkavalier at the Deutsche Oper Berlin, 1993; sang Ighino in Pfitzner's Palestrina at Covent Garden, 1997; Aennchen in Der Freischütz at La Scala, 1998; season 2000–01 as Marzelline in Fidelio at Munich, and Aennchen in Der Freischütz; Mozart's Countess at Glyndebourne, 2003 and at Opera Stuttgart 2010. *Recordings include:* Servilia in La Clemenza di Tito. *Current Management:* KünstlerSekretariat am Gasteig, Rosenheimer Strasse 52, 81669 Munich, Germany. *Telephone:* (89) 44488790. *Fax:* (89) 4489522. *E-mail:* team@ks-gasteig.de. *Website:* www.ks-gasteig.de.

ZIFFRIN, Marilyn, BM, MA; American composer and writer; *Professor Emerita, New England College, Henniker*; b. 7 Aug. 1926, Moline, IL; d. of Harry B. Ziffrin and Betty S. Ziffrin. *Education:* Univ. of Wisconsin, Columbia Univ., Univ. of Chicago. *Career:* teacher, Chicago Public Schools 1952–56; Asst Prof. of Music Northeastern Ill. Univ. 1956–66; Assoc. Prof. of Music New England Coll., Henniker, NH 1957–83, Prof. Emer. 1983–; MacDowell Colony Fellowships 1961, 1963, 1971, 1977, 1980, 1989. *Compositions include:* solo: Theme and Variations for piano 1949, Suite for piano 1955, Toccata and Fugue for organ 1956, Three Songs for woman's voice 1957, Rhapsody for solo guitar 1958, Four Pieces for tuba 1973, Three Movements for guitar 1989, Themes and Variations for organ 1990, Three Songs of the Trobairitz 1991, Recurrences piano solo 1998, Moods piano solo 2003, Three Songs for D'Anna 2003, Piano Sonata 2005–06; chamber music: The Little Prince for clarinet and bassoon 1953, Make a Joyful Noise quintet for recorder 1966, In the Beginning for percussion ensemble 1968, XIII for chamber ensemble 1969, String Quartet 1970, Haiku for soprano, viola and harpsichord 1971, Movements for clarinet and percussion 1972, Sonata for organ and cello 1973, Trio for xylophone, soprano and tuba 1974, Trio for violin, cello and piano 1975, Quintet for oboe and string quartet 1976, Concerto for viola and woodwind quintet 1978, SONO for cello and piano 1980, White Lies (film score) 1983, Yankee Hooray piano duet 1984, Duo for alto recorders 1985, Conversations for double bass and harpsichord 1986, Tributum for clarinet, viola and double bass 1992, Flute Fun for two flutes 1995, Fantasy for two pianos 1995, Lines and Spaces for brass quintet 1996, For Love of Cynthia for baritone and classical accordion, or violin, horn and piano 1997, Two Songs for soprano, viola and piano 1998, String Quartet No. 2 1999, Two Movements for woodwind quintet 2000, Abbot's Duo for alto sax and violin 2001, Sonatina for trumpet and piano 2001, Trio for flute, clarinet and piano 2004, A Little Music for handbells 2006; choral: Jewish Prayer 1950, Death of Moses 1954, Prayer 1966, Drinking Song and Dance, from Captain Kidd 1971, Chorus from Alcestis 1990, Choruses from the Greeks 1992, New England Epitaphs 1994, Cantata for Freedom 2000, Almanack 1688 2002, Two Holiday Songs for chorus 2005; orchestral: Strings 1966, Soundscape 2000, Soundscape II 2002, Trio for flute, clarinet and piano 2004, Soundscape III 2005, Duo for Flute and Piano 2006, Lament for flute and string quartet 2009, Ten for woodwind quintet and string quartet 2009–10, Sonata for viola and piano 2011, Piano Sonata No. 2 2012, Sept Caprices for Early Piano 2013, String II 2014. *Publications:* Carl Ruggles: Composer, Painter and Storyteller 1994; contrib. to The New Grove Dictionary of Music and Musicians 1980, The New Grove Dictionary of American Music 1986. *Honours:* Special Mention Delius Composition Competition 1971, first prize Delius Composition Competition 1972, ASCAP Awards 1981–2007, Virginia Center for the Creative Arts Residency 1987, Music Fix Prize 1996, New Hampshire MTA Composer of the Year 1997, Laureate mem. 2006, Lotte Jacobi Living Treasure Award, New

Hampshire Council on the Arts 2007. *Address:* PO Box 179, Bradford, NH 03221, USA (home).

ZIKMUNDOVÁ, Eva, MgA; Czech singer (soprano); b. (Eva Františka Barbora), 4 May 1932, Kroměří; m. (divorced); one s. *Education:* State Conservatory, Brno and Music Acad., Prague. *Career:* debut at Opera House, Ostrava; mem. Opera Co. of Nat. Theatre, Prague 1958–92; Asst Producer, State Opera, Prague 1992–95; guest appearances at State Opera, Berlin, Hannover, Mannheim (Germany), Venice, Genoa, Naples (Italy), Lausanne (Switzerland), Vienna (Austria), Edinburgh (Scotland), Amsterdam (The Netherlands), Warsaw (Poland), Budapest (Hungary), Sofia (Bulgaria) and Brussels (Belgium); recitals for Czech radio and television; Prof. of Singing, Prague Conservatory, Teplice Conservatory, Int. Conservatory, Prague. *Recordings:* Dvořák's St Ludmila and Moravian duets, Janáček's The Cunning Little Vixen (Supraphon Annual Award 1974), numerous recordings of arias and duets. *Publications:* translations into Czech of Martienssen-Lohmann, Der wissende Sänger and Das bewusste Singen 1994, Bedingungen des gesanglichen Unterrichts 2011; Rodolfo Celletti: Storia del belcanto 1988. *Honours:* Merited mem. Nat. Theatre, Ministry of Culture, Gold Medal for Interpretation of Janáček's Music Abroad, Janáček Acad., Brno. *Address:* Mánesova 23, 12000 Prague 2, Czech Republic. *Telephone:* (2) 22250818. *E-mail:* santuzza@seznam.cz.

ZILBERSTEIN, Lilya; Russian pianist; b. 19 April 1965, Moscow; m. Alexander Gerzenberg 1988; two s. *Education:* Moscow Gnessin Special Music School with Ada Traub, Gnessin Music Pedagogical Institute with Alexander Satz. *Career:* began playing piano, aged five; made European debut at Maggio Musicale Festival, Florence and Piano Festival, Bergamo 1988; has also played with St Louis Symphony, Chicago Symphony, Berlin Philharmonic, London Symphony, Royal Philharmonic, Dresden Staatskapelle, Moscow Philharmonic, Montréal Symphony Orchestra, Teatro alla Scala, Concertgebouw Amsterdam. *Recordings include:* albums: Rachmaninov's Concertos Nos 2 and 3, Grieg Concerto, works by Shostakovich, Brahms, Liszt, Schubert, Mussorgsky, Taneyev, Medtner. *Honours:* first prize Busoni International Piano Competition 1987, International Prize of Academia Musicals Chigiana in Siena, Italy. *Current Management:* c/o Transart UK, Cedar House, 10 Rutland Street, Filey, N Yorks. YO14 9JB, England. *Telephone:* (1723) 515819. *Fax:* (1723) 514678. *E-mail:* transartuk@transartuk.com. *Website:* www.transartuk.com.

ZILIO, Elena; Italian singer (soprano); b. 1941, Bolzano; m. Stillo Burchiellaro. *Education:* Conservatorio Monteverdi, Bolzano, Accademia Chigiana, Siena and Accademia di Santa Cecilia, Rome. *Career:* debut as Sofia in Rossini's Il Signor Bruschin at Spoleto 1963; has sung at La Scala Milan, Rome, Genoa, Palermo, Naples, Turin, Trieste, Venice and Verona Arena in 1970, 1973, 1978; festivals at Caracalla and Florence; sang Lisa in La Sonnambula at Geneva 1982; Suzuki in Madama Butterfly, Chicago Opera 1983, Amore in Cherubini's Anacréon and Dardane in La Rencontre Imprévue by Gluck, La Scala, Milan and Piccola Scala 1983; sang Smeaton in Anna Bolena, Bergamo 1983, returning as the Page in Donizetti's Gianni di Parigi 1988; with San Carlo Naples sang Giustinio in Pergolesi's Flaminio at Versailles and Spoleto, USA 1983, Wiesbaden 1985; Pippo in La Gazza Ladra, Cologne Opera 1984; sang in a revival of Orfeo, La Scala 1985; further appearances in Brussels, at Paris Opéra, in Boston, San Antonio, Montreal, Bregenz and Dubrovnik; sang Elena in La Gazza Ladra, Palermo 1996; Marquise in La Fille du Régiment, Rome 1998; sang Mistress Quickly in Falstaff at Lyon and Frankfurt 1999–2000; Zita in Gianni Schicchi, Royal Opera House, London 2007. *Recordings:* La Buona Figliuola by Piccinni, La Straniera by Bellini, Un Giorno di Regno by Verdi.

ZIMANSKY, Robert; American violinist; b. 20 April 1948, Iowa City; m. Lucia Borsatti 1979. *Education:* Univ. of Iowa, Juilliard School of Music, studied with John Ferrell, Sally Thomas, Ivan Galamian. *Career:* debut at Orchestra Hall, Chicago with Civic Symphony Orchestra; resident in Europe from 1972; leader, Symphonie-Orchester Graunke 1972–73, Suddeutsche Rundfunk 1974, Orchestre de la Suisse Romande 1975–99, Symphonische Orchester Zürich 2000–; Prof. of Advanced Classes, Geneva Conservatory 1980–; mem. Zurich String Quartet; soloist with Wolfgang Sawallisch, Horst Stein, Charles Dutoit, Leif Segerstam, David Zinman, George Cleve and Herbert Blomstedt; mem. bd of dirs, Asscn des Musiciens Suisses. *Recordings:* X. and P. Scharwenka Violin Sonatas, Bach 5th Brandenberg, Albéric Magnard Sonata, Schumann three Sonatas, Reger: Sonatas op 72 and 84, Schubert: Octet and Janáček complete violin works. *Honours:* Grand Prix du Disque, Academie Charles Cros 1986. *Address:* Dorfstrasse 10, 8902 Urdorf, Switzerland (home). *Telephone:* 447343444 (home). *E-mail:* robertzimansky@zuercherstreichquartett.com (office). *Website:* zuercherstreichquartett.com (office).

ZIMERMAN, Krystian; Polish pianist and conductor; b. 5 Dec. 1956, Zabrze; m. Maria Drygajło; one s. one d. *Education:* State Higher Inst. of Music, Katowice, student of Prof. Andrzej Jasiński. *Career:* Lecturer, Acad. of Music, Basel, Switzerland 1996–; Founder and Conductor Polish Festival Orchestra 1999–; collaborated with conductors Abbado, Bernstein, von Karajan, Ozawa, Muti, Maazel, Previn, Boulez, Mehta, Haitink, Skrowaczewski, Rattle and others; has performed in numerous European countries and USA. *Recordings include:* works for piano and chamber music by Schumann, Grieg (with H. von Karajan), Mozart (with K. Danczowska), Schubert, Brahms, Chopin Piano Concertos (with Polish Festival Orchestra), Liszt, Debussy and others, Bartók

Piano Concertos (with Andsnes and Grimaud) (Midem Classical Music Award for Concertos 2006). *Honours:* numerous prizes in prin. pianist competitions in Poland and abroad including First Prize, Beethoven Competition, Hradec Kralové 1973, Grand Prix IX Chopin Int. Pianist Competition, Warsaw 1975, Chigiana's Acad. Award for Best Young Pianist of the Year, Siena 1985, Orfeusz (Critics' Award), Polish Artists of Music Asscn 1988, Grand Prix de Disque, French Acad. 1989, Int. Critics' Award 1989, Edison Classical Music Award for Best Concert 2007. *Current Management:* Harrison/Parrott Ltd, 5-6 Albion Court, Albion Place, London, W6 0QT, England. *E-mail:* jasper .parrott@harrisonparrott.co.uk. *Website:* www.harrisonparrott.com/artist/ profile/krystian-zimerman. *Address:* Kernmatterstrasse 8B, 4102 Binningen, Switzerland.

ZIMMER, Hans Florian; German film score composer; b. 12 Sept. 1957, Frankfurt am Main; m. Vicki Carolyn (separated); one d. *Education:* in England. *Career:* mem. The Buggles (produced hit song Video Killed the Radio Star); pioneered use of digital synthesizers with computer tech. and traditional orchestras; mem. BMI. *Film scores include:* Moonlighting 1982, Histoire d'O: Chapitre 2 1984, Success is the Best Revenge 1984, Insignificance 1985, Separate Vacations 1986, The Wind 1987, Terminal Exposure 1987, Rain Man 1988, Twister 1988, Taffin 1988, Spies Inc 1988, The Fruit Machine 1988, Burning Secret 1988, A World Apart (with Stanley Myers) 1988, Wiezien Rio 1989, Paperhouse 1989, Dark Obsession 1989, Black Rain 1989, Driving Miss Daisy 1989, Green Card 1990, Pacific Heights 1990, Nightmare at Noon 1990, Fools of Fortune 1990, Chicago Joe and the Showgirl 1990, Bird on a Wire 1990, Days of Thunder 1990, K2 (European version) 1991, Backdraft 1991, Regarding Henry 1991, Thelma & Louise 1991, Where Sleeping Dogs Lie 1992, The Power of One 1992, A League of Their Own 1992, Radio Flyer 1992, Toys 1992, Cool Runnings 1993, Calendar Girl 1993, Point of No Return 1993, True Romance 1993, Younger and Younger 1993, The House of the Spirits 1993, The Lion King (Acad. Award, Golden Globe) 1994, Africa: The Serengeti 1994, I'll Do Anything 1994, Renaissance Man 1994, Drop Zone 1994, Two Deaths 1995, Crimson Tide (Grammy Award) 1995, Nine Months 1995, Something to Talk About 1995, Beyond Rangoon 1995, Muppet Treasure Island 1996, Broken Arrow 1996, The Preacher's Wife 1996, The Whole Wide World, 1996, The Fan 1996, The Peacemaker 1997, As Good As It Gets 1997, The Last Days 1998, The Thin Red Line 1998, The Prince of Egypt 1998, Chill Factor 1999, Gladiator (Golden Globe) 2000, The Road to El Dorado 2000, Mission: Impossible II 2000, An Everlasting Piece 2000, Hannibal 2001, Pearl Harbor 2001, Riding in Cars with Boys 2001, Invincible 2001, Black Hawk Down 2001, Spirit 2002, The Ring 2002, Tears of the Sun 2003, Matchstick Men 2003, The Last Samurai 2003, Something's Gotta Give 2003, King Arthur 2004, Thunderbirds 2004, Shark Tale 2004, Lauras Stern 2004, Spanglish 2004, The Ring Two 2005, Madagascar 2005, Batman Begins 2005, The Weather Man 2005, The Little Polar Bear: The Mysterious Island (with Nick Glennie-Smith) 2005, Pirates of the Caribbean: Dead Man's Chest 2006, The Holiday 2006, Pirates of the Caribbean: At World's End 2007, The Simpsons Movie 2007, Casi divas 2008, Kung Fu Panda 2008, The Dark Knight (Grammy Award for Best Score Soundtrack Album for Motion Picture 2009, Classical BRIT Award for Soundtrack of the Year 2009) 2008, The Burning Plain 2008, Frost/Nixon 2008, Madagascar: Escape 2 Africa 2008, The Dark Knight Rises 2012, Man of Steel 2013, 12 Years a Slave 2013, The Amazing Spider-Man 2 2014, Interstellar 2014. *Television scores:* Wild Horses 1985, First Born 1989, Millennium 1992, Space Rangers 1993, The Critic (theme) 1994, High Incident (theme) 1996, Die Motorrad-Cops: Hart am Limit 1999, El Candidato 1999, Carnivàle (series) 2003, Threat Matrix (series title theme) 2003, The Contender (series) 2005, The Pacific (mini-series) 2010, Through the Wormhole 2011–14. *Recordings:* Wings of Film 2001, numerous soundtrack recordings. *Honours:* Lifetime Achievement Award in Film Composition, Nat. Board of Review' Frederick Loewe Award, Palm Springs Int. Film Festival 2003, ASCAP Henry Mancini Award for Lifetime Achievement. *Current Management:* William Morris Endeavor Entertainment, LLC, 9601 Wilshire Blvd, Beverly Hills, CA 90210, USA. *Website:* www.hans -zimmer.com.

ZIMMERMAN, Christopher, BA, MM; British conductor; *Music Director, Fairfax Symphony Orchestra;* b. 12 Aug. 1957, Sutton, Surrey, England; s. of Philip Russell Zimmerman and Adeline Thoms Zimmerman; m. Stephanie Zimmerman; four c. *Education:* Yale Univ., Univ. of Michigan, Pierre Monteux School of Conducting, Diploma from Fontainebleau American Conservatory. *Career:* Music Dir Yale Bach Soc. 1980; conducted Michigan Univ. Symphony Orchestra in USA and Europe; worked with Toronto Symphony, Czech Philharmonic 1983–85; London 1985, leading concerts with Royal Philharmonic and London Symphony Orchestras; appearances with Royal Liverpool Philharmonic and at Concertgebouw, Amsterdam; Prague 1987, with Prague Symphony Orchestra; conducted Seoul Philharmonic in Repub. of Korea 1989; Guest Music Dir Mexico City Opera; Music Dir City of London Chamber Orchestra 1989–93, Cincinnati Concert Orchestra 1993–99, Bangor Symphony Orchestra 1999, Symphony of Southeast Texas 2001–; Primrose Fuller Prof. of Orchestral Studies and Music Dir Hartt Symphony, Hartt School of Music 1999–; Music Dir Fairfax Symphony Orchestra 2009–. *Honours:* First Prize, Nat. Opera Asscn 1993. *Address:* 2329 Senseney Lane, Falls Church, VA 22043, USA (home). *Telephone:* (703) 204-0208 (home). *E-mail:* chris@christopherzimmerman.net. *Website:* christopherzimmerman.net.

ZIMMERMAN, Franklin B., BLitt, PhD, FACLS; American musician, conductor and musicologist; b. 20 June 1923, Wanneta, Kan.; m. 1988; one s. five d. *Education:* Univ. of Southern California, Univ. of Oxford, UK, studied French Horn with Aubrey Brain, conducting with Ernest Read, orchestration with Leon Kirchner and Ingolf Dahl. *Career:* created Music SoundScapes, a three-dimensional, animated and colour-coded graphic musical notation; debut, London 1957; Founder and Dir, Pennsylvania Pro Musica playing over 5,200 concerts; mem. AMS, IMS. *Recordings include:* Handel L'Allegro ed Il Penseroso 1981. *Publications include:* Henry Purcell: Analytical Catalog 1963, Henry Purcell: Life and Times 1967, Henry Purcell: Thematic Index 1973, Words to Music 1965, Facsimile Editions: An Introduction to the Skill of Musick by John Playford (12th edn, corrected and amended by Henry Purcell, with index, introduction and glossary) 1972, Henry Purcell: a Guide to Research 1989, Henry Purcell (1659–1695): Analytical Essays on his Music 2001, Visible Music Sound-Scapes: A New Approach to Musical Notation and Understanding, Purcellian Melodies Indexed: A Thematic Index to the Complete Work of Henry Purcell; contrib. numerous articles and monographs. *Honours:* Arnold Bax Medal for Musicology 1958. *Address:* Visible Music SoundScapes Inc., Suite 1A, 225 S 42nd Street, Philadelphia, PA 19104, USA. *E-mail:* musica@dca.net. *Website:* www.visiblemusics.com/new.

ZIMMERMAN, Willi; Swiss violinist; b. 1955. *Education:* studied with the Alban Berg Quartet, Vienna, Amadeus and Bartók Quartets, and with Walter Levin. *Career:* leader, Amati String Quartet 1981–; many performances in Switzerland, USA and elsewhere in the classical repertoire, and in works by Szymanowski, Tailleferre, Cui, Steuermann, Vladimir Vogel, Kelterborn and Robert Suter; recitals at Basle 1986 and tours of the UK 1990–91; Menuhin Festival at Gstaad 1991; recitals with Bruno Canino, Malcolm Frager, Bruno Giuranna, Karl Leister and others. *Honours:* Grand Prix, Concours Int., Evian (with Amati Quartet) 1982, Lions Club Art Prize (with Amati Quartet) 1985, first prize Karl Klinger Competition in Munich (with Amati Quartet) 1986.

ZIMMERMANN, Frank Peter; German violinist; b. 27 Feb. 1965, Duisburg; m. Young Joo Zimmermann; two s. *Education:* Folkwang Musikhochschule, Essen, Staatliche Hochschule der Künste, Berlin and with Herman Krebbers in Amsterdam. *Career:* made debut aged 10 playing Mozart's violin concerto in G major, K216 in Duisburg; now performs with all major orchestras in world and has undertaken extensive tours in Europe, USA, Japan and Australia; also gives worldwide recitals, with pianists Alexander Lonquich –1994 and Enrico Pace 1998– and with Heinrich Schiff (q.v.), Christian Zacharias, Piotr Anderszewski and Emanuel Ax; Founder, Trio Zimmerman with Antoine Tamestit and Christian Poltera; appeared with English Chamber Orchestra conducted by Sir Colin Davis at Buckingham Palace by special invitation of HRH The Prince of Wales 1991; soloist at Europa Concert given by Berlin Philharmonic under Bernard Haitink at Royal Albert Hall, London and televised live world-wide 1993. *Recordings include:* concertos of Tchaikovsky, Brahms, Beethoven, Mozart, Prokofiev, Sibelius, Mendelssohn, Dvořák, Glazunov, Berg, Britten, Hindemith, Dean, Bruch, Busoni, Saint-Saëns, Szymanowski, Weill, Ligeti and Stravinsky; with pianist Alexander Lonquich recorded all Mozart and Prokofiev sonatas and works by Ravel, Debussy, Janáček etc.; with pianist Enrico Pace, 6 Sonatas by J.S. Bach; with Heinrich Schiff, duo works for violin and cello by Honegger, Martinů, J.S. Bach, Ravel and Pintscher; with Trio Zimmermann, string trios by Beethoven, Mozart and Schubert, Hindemith: Violin Sonatas & Concerto (Echo Klassik Instrumentalist of the Year – Violin 2014) 2013. *Honours:* Bundesverdienstkreuz 1 Klasse; Premio Accad. Musicale Chigiana, Siena 1990, Rheinischer Kulturpreis 1994, Musikpreis, City of Duisburg 2002; numerous awards and prizes for recordings. *Current Management:* Nymus Artists, 34 Avenue du Beau Sejour, 1180 Brussels, Belgium. *Telephone:* (2) 372-30-05 (home). *Fax:* (2) 372-30-06 (home). *E-mail:* jt@nymusartists.com. *Website:* www.nymusartists.com.

ZIMMERMANN, Margarita; Argentine singer (mezzo-soprano); b. Aug. 1942, Buenos Aires. *Education:* studied in Buenos Aires. *Career:* debut as Orpheus in the opera by Gluck, Teatro Colón Buenos Aires 1977; European debut as Carmen and Ulrica in Un Ballo in Maschera at the Landestheater, Salzburg; Covent Garden debut as Cherubino 1980; US appearances as Dalila, Miami 1979 and as Rosina, San Francisco 1982; further engagements at Naples, Bologna, Venice, Rome, Lyon, Geneva and Paris; further roles include Mozart's Sextus, Idamante and Zerlina, Handel's Giulio Cesare and Agrippina, Juno in Cavalli's Ercole Amante, Wagner's Fricka, Massenet's Charlotte, Andromache in Rossini's Ermione, Astor Piazzolla's María de Buenos Aires. *Recordings include:* Maometto Secondo, Gloria. *Honours:* Premio Konex 1989.

ZIMMERMANN, Margrit, DipMus; Swiss composer; b. 7 Aug. 1927, Bern. *Education:* Ecole Normale de Musique de Paris with Arthur Honegger, Giuseppe Verdi Conservatorium, Milan, studied with Jeanne Bovet and Walter Furrer in Bern, Denise Bidal in Lausanne, masterclasses with Alfred Cortot, Igor Markevitch in Monte Carlo and Hans Swarowsky in Ossiach, Municipal Theatre of Bern with Ewald Korner. *Career:* music teacher, Bern. *Compositions include:* Panta Rhei (op 39) 1987, Cloccachordia (op 40) 1987, Die Gestundete Zeit (op 52) 1987, Piano Time (op 46) 1987, Quadriga (op 51) 1987, Murooji for guitar solo (op 57), Trptychon (op 58), Pianorama (op 59), In Urbis Honorem symphony for orchestra and choir, Jubilation concerto for orchestra, Pensieri, Orphische Taenze, Quartetto d'Archi.

ZIMMERMANN, Tabea; German violist and academic; *Professor of Viola, Hanns Eisler Hochschule für Musik*; b. 8 Oct. 1966, Lahr. *Education:* studied with Ulrich Koch and Sándor Végh. *Career:* as a soloist, regularly works with leading orchestras world-wide, including the Berlin Philharmonic, Orchestre de Paris, London Symphony Orchestra, Israel Philharmonic Orchestra, Czech Philharmonic; residencies in Weimar, Luxembourg, Hamburg and with Bamberg Symphony; Artist-in-Residence with Ensemble Resonanz 2013–15, performing concerts in Hamburg at the Laeiszhalle, at Concertgebouw Amsterdam and in Wiesloch; performances as soloist in Bartók's Viola Concerto with the Orchestre de Paris under Christoph Eschenbach 2014; solo works by Hindemith at the Wigmore Hall, London and in Tokyo; chamber music collaborations with the Arcanto Quartet, with violinists Antje Weithaas and Daniel Sepec and cellist Jean-Guihen Queyras, quartet performed at Carnegie Hall, New York, Gulbenkian Foundation, Lisbon, Palau de la Música Barcelona, Théâtre du Châtelet and Cité de la Musique, Paris, Philharmonie, Berlin and Konzerthaus, Vienna and toured Israel, Japan and N America; Prof., Conservatoire in Frankfurt 1994–2002; Prof. of Viola, Hanns Eisler Hochschule für Musik, Berlin 2002–; Foundation Bd mem. Hindemith Foundation, Blonay, Switzerland; Amb. of the Bundesstiftung Kinderhospiz (German Foundation for Children's Hospices); Chair. Beethoven-Haus, Bonn 2013–. *Recordings include:* Mozart's Concertante K364, Bach Trio Sonatas, Gubaidulina Hommage, Chamber works by Bruch, Mozart and Schumann, The Concerto in Europe, Double Concertos and works by Penderecki, Berlioz's Harold in Italy with London Symphony Orchestra and Colin Davis, Reger/Bach Suites for Viola, Paul Hindemith's complete works for the viola, Vol. 1 (Echo Klassik Instrumentalist of the Year – Viola 2014) 2013. *Honours:* first prize competitions in Geneva and Budapest, awarded Vatelot Viola, Paris, Frankfurter Musikpreis 1995, Hessischer Kulturpreis, Rheingau Musikpreis, Accad. Musicale Chigiana, Sienna 1997, Paul Hindemith Prize, City of Hanau. *Current Management:* c/o Karsten Witt Musik Management GmbH, Leuschnerdamm 13, 10999 Berlin, Germany. *Telephone:* (30) 214594-0. *Fax:* (30) 214594-101. *E-mail:* info@karstenwitt.com. *Website:* www.karstenwitt.com.

ZIMMERMANN, Udo; German composer and conductor; b. 6 Oct. 1943, Dresden. *Education:* Dresden Musikhochschule with J. P. Thilman, masterclasses at the Akademie der Kunste, Berlin. *Career:* Composer and Prod., Dresden State Opera 1970; founder, Studio Neue Musik, Dresden (later renamed Zentrum für Zeitgenössische Musik) 1974; Prof. of Composition, Dresden Hochshule für Musik 1976–79, Prof. of Experimental Music Theatre 1979; conducted the Bavarian Radio Symphony Orchestra in the premiere of Hartmann's Sinfonia Tragica, Munich 1989; premiere of Bernhard Jesl's Opera Der König Stirbt at Bonn 1990; Music Dir, Leipzig State Opera 1990–2001; Artistic Dir, Viva series, Bayerischer Rundfunk 1997; Music Dir, Deutsche Oper 2001–03; Dir, Europäischen Zentrums der Künste Hellerau (European Centre for the Arts), Dresden 2003–08; Pres., Saxony Acad. of the Arts 2008–. *Compositions include:* opera: Die Weisse Rose 1967, Die zweite Entscheidung 1970, Levins Muhle 1973, Der Schuhu und die fliegende Prinzessin 1976, Die Wundersame Schusterfrau 1982, Die Sündflut 1988; instrumental: Five songs for baritone and orchestra 1964, Musik für Streicher 1967, String Quartet 1967, Sieh, Meine Augen for chamber orchestra 1970, Mutazioni for Orchestra 1972, Choreographien Nach Edgar Degas for 21 instruments 1974, Hymnus An Die Sonne, after Kleist for soprano, flute and harpsichord 1976, Pax Questuosa for five soloists, three choirs and orchestra 1980, Ich bin eine rufende Stimme 1997. *Honours:* German Critics; Prize 1991. *Address:* Sächsische Akademie der Künste, Neustädter Markt 19, 01097 Dresden, Germany (office). *Telephone:* (351) 81416766 (office). *Fax:* (351) 81416777 (office). *E-mail:* info@sadk.de (office). *Website:* www.sadk.de (office).

ZIMMERMANN, Walter; German composer and academic; *Professor of Composition, Universität der Künste, Berlin*; b. 15 April 1949, Schwabach, Franconia. *Education:* composition studies with Werner Heider in Nuremberg, briefly attended Mauricio Kagel's New Music Courses in Cologne, studied simultaneously at Inst. for Sonology, Utrecht and Jaap-Kunst Ethnology Centre, Amsterdam, computer studies in Hamilton, USA. *Career:* early studies of oboe, violin, piano; first compositions aged 12; pianist, Ars-Nova Ensemble of Nuremberg 1968–70; ethnological research, gathering folk music, especially from Native American Indian reservations 1975–76; f. Beginner Studio, Cologne 1977, organized concert series 1977–84; Composition teacher at Liège Conservatoire from 1982; taught at Darmstadt Summer Courses 1982–84; teaching post at Royal Conservatoire, The Hague 1988; Composition teacher in Karlsruhe from 1990; Visiting Prof., Folkwang-shochschule 1992–93; Prof. of Composition, Universität der Künste, Berlin 1993–; Dozent, 'June in Buffalo', USA 1996; Guest Prof., Escola Superior de Música de Catalunya, Barcelona 2003; Lecturer, Julliard School, Columbia Univ., New York, USA 2005; Dozent, Universidad de Alcalà de Henares, Spain 2005; Lecturer, Shanghai Conservatory 2006, Beijing Cen. Conservatory, People's Repub. of China 2006; Composer-in-Residence, New England Conservatory, Boston, USA 2007; mem. Akad. der Künste, Berlin 2006. *Compositions include:* Frühe Stücke 1965–1970, Parabel for string quarter 1965, Nothing But for piano, celesta, harpsichord, electronic organ 1969, As a Wife Has a Cow for piano four hands (after Gertrude Stein) 1970, Einer ist Keiner for seven instruments and Live-Elektronics 1972, In Understanding Music the Sound Dies for 21 instrumentalists 1974, Ländler Topographien for orchestra, Fränkische Tänze sublimiert for string quartet, Kärwa-Melodien substituiert for two clarinets, Figuren-Tänze transformiert for six instruments, accordion, clarinet and double bass 1994, 3 Stille Tänze, Erd-Wasser-Luft-Töne for trumpet, piano and string glass game, Riuti (Rodungen und

Wüstungen) for drums, Seiltänze for cello and orchestra 2002–04, Freunde 1979–84, Sternwanderung 1982–84, Gaze – Bedouin Song for oboe and tape, Mandingo – Koroharfe for mandolin, Prolog: Gelassenheit for alto and two guitars, In der Welt Sein for solo horn, Abgeschiedenheit for piano, Epilog: Selbstvergessen for speaking voice (Version for Merce Cunningham Dance Company 'Change of Address'), Die Blinden statisches Drama (after Maurice Maeterlinck) for 12 singers and nine instruments 1984, Anhang: Singbarer Rest 1993 (text by Edmond Jabès from his 'Buch der Fragen'), Über die Dörfer, dramatic song based on Peter Handke for soloist, three choirs and large orchestra 1985–86, As I was walking along I came upon chance for tenor saxophone, drums and piano 2008, Fragmente der Liebe based on Roland Barthes for saxophone and string quartet 1987, Emanatio/Conversio/Remeatio Marginalie: The Paradoxes of Love for soprano and saxophone (Text: Hadewijch), The Echoing Green for violin and piano 1989, Briefoper after Hölderlin (Libretto D. E. Sattler) for writers, singers and instrumentalists 1989–90, Ueber die Zeit 1990–92, Schatten der Ideen 1992–2001, Schatten der Ideen 1 (after Giordano Bruno's 'Umbrae Idearum') for octet 1992, Schatten der Ideen 2 (with essay 'Unisono' by Hannes Böhringer) for piano quartet 1993, Schatten der Ideen 4 'Wandernde Wege' for piano quintet 2000–08, Schatten der Ideen 6 'Blaupause' for piano 2003, Aimide for solo piano 1987/ 2001/2002, Prolog: Daimon I Cura II Fuga III Svara Epilog: Synastria, Ritornell 1989–2007, Kindheitsblock for viola and celesta 1994, Irrgarten (Choka für Junko) for zither 1997/2008, Ritornelle 1989–2007, When I'm 84 for piano 1989, Romanska Bågar for left hand piano 2004, The missing nail at the river for piano and toy piano 2003–04, Shadows of Cold Mountain 1 for 3 tenor recorders 1993, The Edge for (mezzo-)soprano, clarinet, cello, piano and tape 1994, Streifzüge for pianist and speaking voice 1995, Monade/Nomade 1 Dit for cello and tape 1999, Taula & Novo Ben (text by Roman Llull & Biagio Marin) for viola and vocals 2003, Verdrehtes Lied - Interieur (text by Michael Donhauser/Gottfried Benn) for violin and vocals 2004, Aus der Bibliothek des Meeres – Die Litanei des Auges (text by Tomas Tranströmer and Cees Nooteboom) for cello and vocals 2005–06, Das irakische Alphabet (text by Joachim Sartorius) for bass flute and vocals with drones 2005, Himmeln (text by Felix Philipp Ingold) for soprano 2007, Voces Abandonadas (text by Antonio Porchia) for piano first series 2005, second series 2006. *Publications:* Desert Plants 1975, Insel Musik 1980, Morton Feldman: Essays 1985, Anarchic Harmony: John Cage 1992. *Honours:* Hon. Prof., Cen. Conservatory of Music, Beijing 2009; City of Cologne Förderpreis 1980, Ensemblia First Prize 1981, Villa Massimo stipendium, Rome 1987, Schneider-Schott Prize 1989, Prix Italia for Die Blinden 1990. *Address:* Universität der Künste, Fakultät Musik, Pf 120544, 10595 Berlin, Germany (office). *Website:* www.home.snafu.de/walterz (home).

ZIMMERMANN, Wolfram; German singer (bass-baritone); b. 17 April 1920, Stuttgart. *Education:* Stuttgart Acad., Vienna Acad., studied with Anna Bahr-Mildenburg. *Career:* debut at Stuttgart 1947 as Rossini's Basilio; radio broadcasts in Germany and Austria; sang Beckmesser in Die Meistersinger, under Furtwängler at La Scala 1952; created title role in Titus Feuerfuchs by Heinrich Sutermeister for television in Austria 1959; Vienna Staatsoper 1958–63, notably as Leporello, Mozart's Papageno and the Doctor in Wozzeck by Berg; Rome Opera 1956, Graz 1958, Barcelona 1958–63, and Mexico City 1966 as Beckmesser; other roles include the title roles in Mozart's Figaro, Gounod's Mephistopheles and Donizetti's Don Pasquale. *Recordings:* Zar und Zimmermann by Lortzing, Tannhäuser by Wagner. *Honours:* Hon. Cavalier, Deutscherrn-Ritterbund Norimberga; Diploma in Int. Song, Geneva 1949, Bach Prize, Leipzig 1950, gold medal Accademia Italia 1980.

ZINKLER, Christianne; German singer (mezzo-soprano); b. 23 Nov. 1947, Coburg. *Education:* studied with Willi Domgraf-Fassbaender in Nuremberg, with Clemens Kaiser-Breme in Essen. *Career:* debut as Messenger in Dallapiccola's Job at Deutsche Oper am Rhein, Düsseldorf 1968; mem., Dortmund Opera notably as Gluck's Orpheus, Erda and Fricka in Der Ring des Nibelungen, Ulrica, Hansel, Monteverdi's Poppea, Anina in Der Rosenkavalier, Cherubino and Dorabella; guest appearances in Hamburg, Essen, Copenhagen, Wiesbaden and Florence; many concert appearances.

ZINMAN, David Joel; American conductor; b. 9 July 1936, New York; s. of Samuel Zinman and Rachel Ilo Zinman (née Samuels); m. 1st Leslie Heyman (deceased); one s. one d.; m. 2nd Mary Ingham 1974; one s. *Education:* Oberlin Coll. Conservatory of Music, Univ. of Minnesota, Tanglewood Music Center. *Career:* studied conducting at Berkshire Music Center, Tanglewood and with Pierre Monteux; Asst to Monteux 1961–64; Music Dir, Nederlands Kamerorkest 1964–77, Rochester Philharmonic Orchestra, New York 1974–85, Baltimore Symphony Orchestra 1985–98; Prin. Guest Conductor, Rotterdam Philharmonic Orchestra 1977–79, Chief Conductor 1979–82; Music Dir Minnesota Orchestra's Viennese Sommerfest 1994–96, Tonhalle Orchester Zürich 1995–2014; Music Dir, Aspen Music Festival and School 1997–2010; numerous recordings. *Honours:* Chevalier, Ordre des Arts et des Lettres 2000; three Grammy Awards, two Grand Prix du Disques, two Edison Awards, Gramophone Best Selling Record (for Górecki) 1993, Gramophone Award (for Jungle Book) 1994, Peabody Medal 1996, Ditson Award, Columbia Univ. 1997, Deutschen Schallplatten Prize 1999, Art Prize of the City of Zurich 2002, Theodore Thomas Award, Conductors Guild 2006, MIDEM Classical Artist of the Year Award 2008. *Current Management:* Harrison Parrott, 5–6 Albion Court, London, W6 0QT, England. *Telephone:* (20) 7229-9166. *Fax:* (20) 7221-5042. *E-mail:* info@harrisonparrott.co.uk. *Website:* www.harrisonparrott .com; www.davidzinman.org.

ZINOVENKO, Yuri; Ukrainian singer (bass); b. 1955, Simferopol. *Education:* studied in Tashkent. *Career:* sang first at the Kirov Opera, St Petersburg; Croatian Nat. Opera, Zagreb 1981–87; further engagements at the Frankfurt Opera and the Staatstheater, Darmstadt; guest appearances in Italy, Israel, Austria, Russia and the USA; roles have included the Hermit in Der Freischütz, Water Sprite in Rusalka, Prince Gremin in Eugene Onegin, Kochubey in Tchaikovsky's Mazeppa; Verdi roles include Zaccaria and Lodovico; sang The Prophet in Zemlinsky's first opera, Sarema (Trier Opera 1996); concerts include Mozart's Requiem and Shostakovich's 13th Symphony, Babi-Yar. *Recordings include:* Sarema.

ZINSSTAG, Gérard; Swiss composer; b. 9 May 1941, Geneva; m. 1984; one s. one d. *Education:* Conservatory, Geneva, Conservatoire nat. supérieur de musique, Paris, Accademia Chigiana, Siena, Musikhochschule Zürich, studied with H. U. Lehmann in Zurich, Helmut Lachenmann in Stuttgart and Hannover. *Career:* orchestral musician touring Europe 1964–67; flautist, Tonhalle Orchestra, Zürich 1967–75; participant in summer courses, Darmstadt 1976, 1978; lecture at Univ. of California, Berkeley 1979 and several stays in New York; composer-in-residence, Berlin (DAAD) 1981; founder of Festival of Zürich, Tage für neue Musik Zürich 1986–92; tour of Russia, Moscow and Baku 1990; several confs and lectures in Moscow, Taipei, Paris (Sorbonne and IRCAM), Salzburg, Geneva, Zürich, Bamberg etc.; mem. Suisa, Swiss Soc. of Authors. *Compositions include:* Déliements for flute and organ 1975, Wenn zum Beispiel for four speakers and five instruments 1975, Tatastenfelder for three typewriters, piano and tape 1976, Suono Reale for piano solo 1976, Innanzi for double bass and orchestra 1978, Foris for two orchestras 1979, Altération for chamber orchestra 1991, Trauma for double choir a cappella 1980, Stimuli for bass string trio 1984, Tempi Inquieti for piano, two percussion and orchestra 1984–86, Cut Sounds for organ 1991, Incalzando for two pianos 1981, Artifices for ensemble and electronics 1982–83, String Quartet No. 1 1982, Eden Jeden for mezzo and ensemble 1987, Artifices II for ensemble and electronics 1988, Tempor for sextet 1992, String Quartet No. 2 1995, Ergo for piano and ensemble 1996, Anaphores for Piano and Orchestra 1989, Espressivo for cymbalum and ensemble 1990, Hommage à Charles Racine for mezzo soprano and ensemble 1997, Trois Etudes for bass marimba 1998, Ubu Cocu (opéra bouffe in one act) 2000, Passage for orchestra 2002, String Quartet No. 3 2003, Kinêsis for oboe and piano 2003, Empreintes for voice and orchestra 2004, Ubuphonie for three soloist voices and orchestra 2005, Quatre mouvements for ensemble 2005, Rémanences for voice ensemble and live electronics 2006, Gilgamesh for speaker, ensemble and CD electronics 2007, Mozaic for cello and piano 2008, Cinq petites études for piano solo 2008, Bing (Samuel Beckett) for voice and ensemble 2009, Lasciar vibrar for ensemble 2010, Réitération for piano solo 2010, Anaphores for piano and ensemble 2011, Seul, l'écho for voice and ensemble 2012, Tahir for viola solo string quartet and small percussion 2012, Eskatos for 12 solo voices, brass and percussion 2012–13, Ricercari for accordion (bayan) and ensemble 2014, Rilke-Lieder (voice and ensemble). *Publications include:* contrib. to Pro Musica 1988, Revue Musicale Suisse 1979–80, Die Musik des 20 Jahrhunderts 1993, New Grove 2000, Präsenz in Literatur und Kunst 2008; numerous articles in journals, texts accompanying album recordings. *Current Management:* c/o G. Ricordi & Co., Bühnen- und Musikverlag GmbH, Stralauer Allee 1, 10245 Berlin, Germany. *Telephone:* (52) 0071322 (home). *E-mail:* info@ricordi.de. *Website:* www.ricordi.de/zinsstag-gerard.0.html. *Address:* Seefeldstrasse 191, 8008 Zürich, Switzerland (home); 4 place Victor Basch, 30400 Villeneuve-lés-Avignon, France (home). *E-mail:* gerard.zinsstag@wanadoo.fr. *Website:* www.gerardzinsstag .com.

ZIVA, Vladimir P.; Russian conductor; *Artistic Director and Principal Conductor, Moscow Symphony Orchestra;* b. 7 March 1957, Arkhangelsk; m. Anna Ziva; two s. *Education:* Leningrad State Conservatory, Moscow State Conservatory. *Career:* asst to Prin. Conductor, Symphony Orchestra of Moscow Philharmonics 1984–87; teacher, Moscow State Conservatory 1988–89; Artistic Dir and Chief Conductor Nizhne-Novgorod Philharmonic Orchestra 1988–2000; Prin. Conductor St Petersburg Mussorgsky Theatre of Opera and Ballet 1990–92; Prin. Conductor Moscow Symphony Orchestra 1997–, Artistic Dir 2000–; Co-founder Krasnodar Opera Co. 2003–; also currently Artistic Dir and Chief Conductor, South Jutland Symphony Orchestra; opera stage productions, in collaboration with B. Pokrovsky, include The Turn of the Screw, Albert Herring by B. Britten, Snow Maiden by P. Tchaikovsky. *Honours:* Honoured Artist of Russia 1994, State Prize of the Russian Federation 1995, Conductor of the Year 1996, 1997, Music Review; State Prize of Russian Federation 1995. *Address:* Moscow Symphony Orchestra, 191285 Moscow, Mosfilmovskaya 1, Russia (office). *Telephone:* (499) 143-97-13 (office). *E-mail:* info@moscowsymphony.ru (office). *Website:* www .moscowsymphony.ru (office).

ZIVKOVIC, Djuro; Serbian composer and musician (violin); b. 15 Dec. 1975, Belgrade. *Education:* studied composition with Vlastimir Trajković at Music Acad. Belgrade, Royal Coll. of Music, Sweden. *Career:* works commissioned, performed, recorded and broadcast across Europe and North America, by ensembles including the Sonanza Ensemble (Sweden), pre-art (Switzerland), Klangforum Wien (Austria), Malmö Symphony Orchestra (Sweden), Trio Fibonacci (Canada/Belgium), Musica Vitae Chamber Orchestra (Sweden), Stockholm's Wind Orchestra (Sweden), Tokyo Int. Ensemble (Japan), New European Ensemble (Netherlands), Musica Vitae (Sweden), BIT20 (Norway), Zeitfluss (Austria), L'Itinéraire (France); taught at Royal Coll. of Music,

Stockholm; appears as violinist and recently as violist. *Compositions include:* Le Cimetière Marin for mezzo-soprano and ensemble (Swedish Grammi Award 2010), Ascetic Discourse, cantata for mezzo-soprano and ensemble (Mokranjac Award for best Serbian composition premiered in the year 2012), On the Guarding of the Heart (Univ. of Louisville Grawemeyer Award 2014). *Website:* www.zivkovic.eu.

ZIVONI, Yossi, FRNCM, FRCM; British violinist; *Professor of Violin, Royal College of Music*; b. 1939, Tel-Aviv, Israel; m. Jeanne 1962; one d. *Education:* Israel Acad. of Music, Tel-Aviv, Conservatoire Royal de Musique de Bruxelles, Belgium. *Career:* debut, Amsterdam, Netherlands 1964; concert tours in Europe, Israel, Australia, Canada, Far East and South America; Principal Tutor, Royal Northern Coll. of Music, Manchester 1968–2005; Prof. of Violin, Royal Coll. of Music, London 1997–; Leader Gabrieli String Quartet 1995–2000; mem. Royal Soc. of Musicians of Great Britain. *Recordings:* Mozart Sonatas, Bach Sonatas and Partitas, Mendelssohn Sonatas, Bartók Sonata for solo violin and violin duos, Schumann Quartets, Mozart Early Quartets (with Gabrieli Quartet). *Honours:* Hon. Fellow Royal Northern Coll. of Music; Paganini Int. Competition 1960, Bavarian Radio Int. Competition, Munich 1961, Queen Elisabeth Int. Competition, Brussels, Belgium 1963. *E-mail:* yossi.zivoni@btinternet.com (home). *Website:* www.yossizivoni.com.

ZLATKOVA, Sonia; Austrian singer (soprano); b. 11 Sept. 1963, Dobritsch, Bulgaria. *Education:* studied in Varna and Sofia. *Career:* made stage debut as Gilda in Rigoletto 1989; mem. Bulgarian Nat. Opera at Sofia as Gilda, Lucia, the Queen of Night and Rosina 1989–92; mem. Dortmund Theatre as Rosina in Il Barbiere di Siviglia, Despina in Cosi fan Tutte, Pamina in Die Zauberflote, Susanna in Le Nozze di Figaro, Musetta in La Bohème, Violetta in La Traviata, Gilda in Rigoletto and Sophie in Der Rosenkavalier 1992–95; mem. Oper Graz 1995–, roles includes Gretel in Hansel und Gretel, Nanetta in Falstaff, Adina in L'Elisir D'Amore; guest appearances as Frasquita in Carmen, Bregenz Festival 1991, as Oscar in Il Ballo in Maschera 1991, as Pamina at Schönbrunn, Vienna 1996. *Honours:* Gold Medal, Maria Callas Grand Prix 1989, winner, Bertelsmann-Stiftung Competition 1991. *Address:* c/o Opera House Graz GmbH, Kaiser-Josef-Platz 10, 8010 Graz, Austria. *Telephone:* 316-8008. *Fax:* 316- 8008 1565. *Website:* www.oper-graz.com/oper.

ZLOKOVIĆ, Vera, BMus; Serbian composer, conductor and singer; b. 30 Nov. 1950, Belgrade; d. of Bozidar Zloković and Marianne Elisabeth Zloković (née Puschner); m. Stefaan de Meester 1992. *Education:* Acad. of Arts, Novi Sad. *Career:* specialised in early music performing in Florence, Vienna, Basel, Thessalonika and Athens; Founder and Artistic Dir Musica Antiqua early music ensemble, Belgrade 1977–, Musica Antiqua Serbiana vocal ensemble, specialising in early prayer music of Orthodox people 1987–; ensembles have performed at more than 2,000 concerts, festivals, radio and TV appearances in Yugoslavia and abroad (Bruges, Berlin, Leipzig, Rostock, Munich, Trieste, Venice, Zadar, Dubrovnik, Ohrid, Kastoria, Athens, Moldavia and Czech Repub.); est. Acad. of Early Music to train professional musicians in early music interpretation; mem. Asscn of Serbian Music Artists. *Television includes:* Music of the Elizabethan Epoch 1980, A Musical Feast 1983, Musica Adriatica 1986, Viva Musica Antiqua 1988–91, The East Empire Light 1985, The Istrian Legends 1990, The Presence of Prayer in Music and Music in Prayer 1996, The Gifts to the Home of Holy Warriors 2000, The Prayer and Love of Knights, Ave Regina Coelorum, The Return of the Shakespearean Time, Music of Old Serbia. *Recordings:* The Feast of Music, The East Empire Light, The Music of Kings, The Feast of Music 2. *Honours:* numerous festival awards, including St Donates Evenings, Zadar 1983–84, Van Vlaanderen, Belgium 1984, Summer Festivals in Berlin, Dresden, Potsdam and Frankfurt 1985, Dubrovnik Festival of Chamber Music 1986, BEMUS Award, Belgrade Music Festival 1987, Kastoria, Greece 1995, Byzantine Festival, Jashi Romania 1997; radio and TV awards include TV Festival, Portoroz 1981, TV Festival, Montréal, Canada 1983, Radio Berlin, Leipzig, Dresden 1985, Golden Rose of Montreuil, Switzerland 1988, Radio Paris 1989, Venice TV Festival 1992, Radio Tokyo 1996, Golden Prague TV Festival, Czech Repub. 1997. *Address:* Kosovska 32, 11000 Belgrade, Serbia (home). *Telephone:* 64-2710483 (mobile) (office). *E-mail:* iv_vivy@yahoo.co.uk.

ZNAIDER, Nikolaj; violinist; *Artistic Director, Nordic Music Academy*; b. 1975, Denmark. *Education:* Royal Danish Acad., Juilliard School of Music, Vienna Conservatory with Boris Kuschnir. *Career:* Founder and Artistic Dir, Nordic Music Acad.; Prin. Guest Conductor, Swedish Chamber Orchestra 2009–, Mariinsky Theatre, Russia 2010–; appearances with the Cleveland, Leipzig Gewandhaus and St Petersburg Philharmonic Orchestras; season 1999–2000 with the Berlin Philharmonic Orchestra under Daniel Barenboim, London Symphony under Rostropovich at the Barbican and on tour to Japan and London Philharmonic with Kurt Masur at the Royal Festival Hall; Los Angeles Philharmonic, Czech, Oslo and Munich Philharmonics, BBC Symphony and Budapest Festival Orchestra; Yehudi Menuhin Memorial Concert at the Albert Hall; tour of Australia 2000; Nielsen's concerto at the London Proms 2002; recitals in New York, Paris, Amsterdam and Lucerne; frequent guest with the Chicago Symphony Orchestra, Cleveland Orchestra, Detroit Symphony, Nat. Symphony, New York Philharmonic Orchestra and the Philadelphia Orchestra; he has collaborated with Daniel Barenboim, Herbert Blomstedt, Myung Whun Chung, Sir Colin Davis, Charles Dutiut, Valery Gergiev, Mariss Jansons, Neeme Järvi, Lorin Maazel, Kurt Masur, Zubin Mehta, Mstislav Rostropovich, Leonard Slatkin and Yuri Temirkanov. *Recordings:* Bruch No. 1 and Nielsen Concertos with the London Philharmonic and Lawrence Foster, Elgar Violin Concerto. *Honours:* winner Queen

Elisabeth Violin Competition, Brussels 1997, first prize Carl Nielson Int. Violin Competition 1992. *Current Management:* IMG Artists, The Light Box, 111 Power Road, London W4 5PY, England. *Telephone:* (20) 7957-5800. *Fax:* (20) 7957-5801. *E-mail:* shunt@imgartists.com. *Website:* www.imgartists.com; www.znaider.com.

ZOBEL, Ingeborg; German singer (soprano); b. 31 July 1928, Gorlitz, Schlesien. *Education:* Dresden State Music Acad. with Eduard Plate. *Career:* debut as Amelia in Un Ballo in Maschera 1952; sang in Schwerin 1955–57, Rostock 1957–66, and Weimar 1966–72; Dresden Staatsoper from 1972, notably as Wagner's Brünnhilde, Isolde and Ortrud, the Marschallin, Tosca, Santuzza, Lady Macbeth and Leonore in Fidelio; guest appearances in Leningrad, Barcelona, Budapest, Wiesbaden, Prague, Belgrade and Sofia; teacher, Franz Liszt Musikhochschule, Weimar.

ZOGHBY, Linda, BMus, MMus, FSU; American singer (soprano) and teacher; *Professor of Voice, University of South Alabama*; b. 17 Aug. 1949, Mobile, AL; m.; three c. *Education:* Florida State Univ., studied with Elena Nikolaidi, two years at Juilliard's American Opera Center. *Career:* sang at first in concert; stage debut at Houston 1974 as Donna Elvira in Don Giovanni; Dallas Opera 1976 as Giulietta in I Capuleti e i Montecchi; Glyndebourne Festival from 1978 as Mimi in La Bohème and in Haydn's La Fedeltà Premiata; Metropolitan Opera 1982, 1986 as Mimi and as Ilia in Idomeneo; other roles include Mozart's Fiordigili and Pamina; currently Prof. of Voice, Univ. of South Alabama. *Recordings:* Haydn's L'Isola Disabitata, L'Incontro Improvviso, Christmas with Linda Zoghby. *Address:* Department of Music, University of South Alabama, LPAC 1123, Mobile, AL 36688, USA (office). *Telephone:* (251) 460-6292 (office). *E-mail:* lzoghby@usouthal.edu (office). *Website:* www .southalabama.edu/music (office).

ZOLLMAN, Ronald, DipMus; Belgian conductor; *Director of Orchestral Studies, School of Music, Carnegie Mellon University*; b. 8 April 1950, Antwerp; m. Dominique G. Mols. *Education:* Brussels Conservatoire, Academy Chigiana. *Career:* Music Dir Orchestre National de Belgique 1989–93; Music Dir Philharmonic Orchestra of UNAM, Mexico 1993–2002; Music Dir and Principal Conductor, Northern Israel Symphony Orchestra 2002–05; Dir of Orchestral Studies, School of Music, Carnegie Mellon Univ. 2009–; has conducted throughout Europe, North and South America, and in Australia. *Recordings:* Belgian Music for Ministry of Culture, Brussels; various recordings with the National Orchestra of Belgium, the World Orchestra, the London Sinfonietta; Basle Symphony Orchestra, Northern Sinfonia, Barcelona Orchestra and Northern Sinfonia. *Honours:* Premio Firenze for Conductors 1972. *Current Management:* Music Inter Alia, 12 Eastcourt Road, Worthing, BN14 7DA, England. *Telephone:* (1903) 531668. *Fax:* (7798) 531819. *E-mail:* info@musicinteralia.com. *Website:* www.musicinteralia.com. *Address:* School of Music, Carnegie Mellon University, 5000 Forbes Avenue, Pittsburgh, PA 15213-3815, USA (office). *E-mail:* rzollman@andrew.cmu.edu (office). *Website:* music.cmu.edu (office).

ZOMER, Johannette; Dutch singer (soprano). *Education:* Conservatorium Amsterdam. *Career:* originally worked as a microbiology analyst, before beginning music studies; opera debut as Tebaldo in Don Carlo with Nationale Reisopera 1996; recital repertoire ranges from medieval music to baroque and classical, including opera, Lieder, French Romanticism and contemporary music; regularly gives recitals with pianist Arthur Schoonderwoerd or theorbe player Fred Jacobs; debut with Royal Concertgebouw Orchestra in St Matthew Passion 2008. *Recordings:* numerous recordings including L'Esprit Galant 2007, Bach Hohe Messe 2007, Bach Cantatas (with Ensemble Florilegium) (Edison Award 2008) 2007, German Baroque Cantatas 2008. *Current Management:* Impulse Art Management, Oudezijds Voorburgwal 74, PO Box 15401, 1001 Amsterdam, Netherlands. *Telephone:* (20) 626-6944. *Fax:* (20) 622-7118. *E-mail:* info@impulseartmanagement.nl. *Website:* www .impulseartmanagement.nl; www.johannettezomer.com.

ZON, Bennett, BMus, MMus, DPhil; American musicologist and composer; b. 10 Aug. 1961, New York, NY; m. Clare; two s. *Education:* Univ. of Michigan, Univs of Edinburgh and Oxford, UK. *Career:* Prof. of Music, Univ. of Durham 2000–; Sr Lecturer in Music, Univ. of Hull 1994–2000; Tutor in Music, Univ. of Oxford 1990–94; Gen. Ed. Nineteenth-Century Music Review 2002–, Music in Nineteenth-Century Britain (book series) 1997–; mem. American Musicological Soc., Coll. Music Soc., Royal Musical Asscn; Fellow, Inst. of Advanced Study 2007. *Compositions:* Litany of the Sea for Orchestra 2000, Gothic Fragment 2000, Military Fanfare 1998, Communion Service 1995, Matins Responsary for Woman's Choir 1994. *Recordings:* The Gentlemen of St John's College Choir 1990. *Publications:* The English Plainchant Revival 1992, Music and Metaphor in Nineteenth-Century British Musicology 2000; contrib. to numerous publs and journals from 1989, including Nineteenth-Century British Music Studies, Music & Letters, Music & Liturgy, The Hymn Tune Index (ed. Nicholas Temperley), The Shorter Oxford Book of Carols, Early Music, New Dictionary of National Biography, The New Grove Dictionary of Music (second edn), Irish Musical Studies. *Honours:* Arts and Humanities Research Bd research leave grant 2003, Musica Britannica Trust Louise Dyer Award 1992, CVCP Overseas Research Student Awards 1990, 1991, Univ. of Hull Research Leave Award 1999. *Address:* University of Durham School of Music, Palace Green, Durham, DH1 3RL, England (office). *Telephone:* (191) 3343156 (office). *E-mail:* bennett.zon@durham.ac.uk (office). *Website:* www .dur.ac.uk/music (office).

ZOUHAR, Vit, MA, DMus, PhD; Czech composer and musicologist; *Associate Professor, Department of Music Education, Palacký University, Olomouc*; b. 13 March 1966, Brno; m. Karla Zemanová 1997; one s. one d. *Education:* Janáček Univ. of Music and Dramatic Arts, Brno, Univ. of Music and Dramatic Arts, Graz, Accad. Chigiana, Siena, Masaryk Univ., Brno. *Career:* teacher of musical theory, State Conservatory, Brno 1989; apptd Asst, Palacky Univ., Olomouc 1992, Vice-Dean, Pedagogical Faculty 2003–06, Vice-Rector 2010–, Co-founder programme Slyset jinak (Different Hearing) composing in the classroom 2001, Assoc. Prof., Dept of Music Educ. 2006–; teacher, Inst. of Electronic Music, Graz, Austria 1992–2004, Guest Composer 1993; Guest Composer, Werkstadt Graz 1994; Co-founder and teacher, computer music study room, Ostrava Univ. 1996, habilitation 2005; works performed by Philharmonic Orchestra, Brno, Moravian Symphony Orchestra, DAMA DAMA percussion ensemble, Ensemble Damian, Malle Symen Quartet, Sonata a Tre, also many concerts, festivals, radio broadcasts, TV appearances, including Hörgänge Wien, Poesiefestival Berlin, Experimental Music Festival, Prague, Ostrava Days, Ist alles (ballet, Czech TV) 1992, The Garden, Forfest Music Festival 1995, Like Water Is (ballet, Janáček Theatre, Brno and Nat. Theatre, Prague) 1996, Wide Crossing (ballet, Graz Opernhaus) 1997, Coronide, Torso (operas, Nat. Theatre, Prague), 2004, Noci Dnem (The Days of Nights, opera, Nat. Theatre, Brno) 2005, Radúz and Mahulena (Nat. Theatre, Prague) 2009, La Dafne (opera, Nat. Theatre, Brno) 2011, Monsieur de Pourceaugnac (comédie-ballet, Nat. Theatre, Prague) 2012, Prague Spring, Schleswig Holstein Music Festival, Melos-Etos Bratislava, Golden Prague, Music of our Age Budapest, Exposition of New Music Brno, Europalia Brussels, EXPO. *Art exhibitions:* Sternchen, Werkstadt Graz 1994, Sound and files, Künstlerhaus Wien 2000. *Compositions include:* Le Vedute di Bruna for string quartet 1985, Agastia for large orchestra 1988, The Sun Gate for four percussionists and large orchestra 1989, Es scheint mir aber immer for violin, clarinet and piano 1992, Ist alles for two guitarists 1992, Close Encounters of Those Wild at Heart for stereo-orchestra 1993, Like Water Is for clarinet, bassoon and piano 1994, Wide Crossing 1994, Il Pendolo for chamber ensemble 1998, Coronide (chamber opera) 2000, Petite sirène for four percussionists 2001, Rings of Levels for a recorder quartet 2003, Torso (chamber opera, together with Tomáš Hanzlík) 2003, Scary Dreaming for four hands piano 2004, Multiple Gestures 2004, Noci Dnem (The Days of the Nights, opera) 2005, Multiple Gesture 2005, Ariosi per canto e pianoforte 2006, Ritorni pera archi e cembalo 2006, Hark for voice and percussion 2007, M-Line-M 2007, Mente 2008, Gardens of Haven's Delight 2009, Radúz and Madulena 2009, Pinnas Columbae for countertenor, cimbalon and orchestra 2010, La Dafne (chambre opera, together with Tomáš Hanzlík) 2011, Knots for four-hand piano 2011, Days for chamber ensemble 2012. *Films:* Amerika 1994, OMO 2007, S.S. Palo Alto 2011 Project. *Radio:* Tartuffe 2006. *Television:* Kouzlo jedné flétny 2006. *Publications:* Texte 1994, Postmoderní hudba? Německá debata na sklonku 20. století (Postmodern Music? German Debate at the End of 20th Century) 2004, Dear Friend. Bohuslav Martinů's Letters to Zdeněk Zouhar (co-author) 2008; several book chapters and numerous articles in professional journals. *Honours:* Generace Award 1992–99, Musica Nova Award 1994, Palacký Univ. Award 2005, 2009, Jan Amos Komenský Medal 2006, Radok Award 2009, Nuberg 2010. *Address:* Dobratice 339, 73952 Czech Republic (home). *E-mail:* vit.zouhar@upol.cz (office). *Website:* khv.upol.cz/staff/Vit-Zouhar (office).

ZSCHAU, Marilyn; American singer (soprano); b. 9 Feb. 1944, Chicago, IL. *Education:* Juilliard School of Music, studied with John Lester in Montana. *Career:* toured with Metropolitan Nat. Co. 1965–66; debut at Vienna Volksoper as Marietta in Die Tote Stadt 1967; Vienna Staatsoper 1971 as the Composer in Ariadne auf Naxos; New York City Opera from 1978, as Puccini's Minnie and Butterfly, Odabella in Attila, and Maddalena in Andrea Chénier; Metropolitan Opera debut 1985 as Musetta in La Bohème; La Scala debut 1986 as the Dyer's Wife in Die Frau ohne Schatten; appearances worldwide in operatic roles including Aida, Leonora, Desdemona, Butterfly, Brünnhilde in Die Walküre and Götterdämmerung, Salome, Elektra, Prokofiev's Renata in The Fiery Angel, Shostakovich's Katerina in Lady Macbeth of Mtsensk, Santuzza and Manon Lescaut; sang Puccini's Minnie at Reggio Emilia and Chicago 1990, and The Fiery Angel at the 1990 Holland Festival; other roles include Janáček's Vixen and Kostelnicka in Jenůfa, the Marschallin and Octavian in Der Rosenkavalier, Mozart's Fiordigili, Countess and Pamina, Lucille in Dantons Tod, and Tatiana in Eugene Onegin; sang Elektra at Buenos Aires 1996; season 1998 as Kostelnicka in Jenůfa at Santiago; sang Elektra with New Israeli Opera at Savonlinna 2000; currently therapist in Calif. *Recordings include:* La Bohème (at Covent Garden, video). *Honours:* Martha Baird Rockefeller Foundation scholarships 1962, 1963. *Address:* 4246 Wilshire Boulevard, Oakland, CA 94602-3549, USA (home). *E-mail:* marilynandfransbaars@yahoo.com (office). *Website:* www.marilynandfransbaars.com.

ZUKERMAN, Eugenia; American flautist; b. (Eugenia Rich), 25 Sept. 1944, Cambridge, MA; m. 1st Pinchas Zukerman (divorced); m. 2nd David Seltzer 1988. *Education:* Juilliard School with Julius Baker. *Career:* debut, New York Town Hall 1971; has played with most major orchestras in the USA and Canada; tour of USA with English Chamber Orchestra; European performances with the Royal Philharmonic, Israel Chamber Orchestra and the Hamburg Bach Solisten; participation in Festival of Two Worlds at Spoleto, London's South Bank Festival and the Edinburgh Festival; collaborations with Jean-Pierre Rampal at Carnegie Hall 1976, and James Galway; music commentator on CBS News 'Sunday Morning' programme; Artistic Dir, Vail Valley Music Festival 1998–. *Recordings include:* C.P.E. Bach,Stamitz,Vivaldi: Flute Concertos, Mozart: Flute Concertos Nos. 1 & 2, C.P.E. Bach: Trios for Flute, Violin and Continuo, Bach Family Trios and Quartets, Music for Flute and Violin/Viola, Beethoven: Serenade for Flute, Viola and Violin, For the Friends of Alec Wilder, Vive Ibert, Mozart: Seven Sonatas for Flute and Keyboard, Time Pieces, The Best of Peter Pan, An Awfully Big Adventure, Biddidi! Bobbidi! Bach, Heigh-ho! Mozart, Incantation, Music for a Sunday Morning, Lowell Liebermann, Symphony No. 2, Favorite Arias from Opera. *Publications:* Deceptive Cadence, Taking the Heat, Coping with Prednisone, In My Mother's Closet. *Current Management:* Opus 3 Artists, 470 Park Avenue South, 9th Floor North, New York, NY 10016, USA. *Telephone:* (212) 584-7500. *Fax:* (646) 300-8200. *E-mail:* info@opus3artists.com. *Website:* www.opus3artists.com. *Address:* c/o M.L. Falcone, 155 West 68th Street, Suite 1114, New York, NY 10023-6817, USA (office). *Telephone:* (212) 580-4302 (office). *Fax:* (212) 787-9638 (office). *Website:* www.eugeniazukerman.com.

ZUKERMAN, Pinchas; Israeli violinist, violist and conductor; b. 16 July 1948, Tel-Aviv; s. of Yehuda Zukerman and Miriam Zukerman; m. 1st Eugenia Rich 1968 (divorced); two d.; m. 2nd Tuesday Weld 1985 (divorced); m. 3rd Amanda Forsyth 2004. *Education:* Israel Conservatory, Acad. of Music, Tel-Aviv, Juilliard School of Music, New York with Ivan Galamian. *Career:* debut in New York with New York Philharmonic 1969, in UK at Brighton Festival 1969; concert and recital performances throughout USA and Europe; debut as conductor, London 1970; appearances as conductor with orchestras worldwide; has performed at Spoleto, Pablo Casals and Edinburgh Festivals; Dir S Bank Summer Music 1978–80; Musical Dir St Paul Chamber Orchestra 1980–87; Prin. Conductor Dallas Symphony Orch. 1993–95 (Prin. Guest Conductor Int. Summer Music Festival 1990–95); Music Dir Baltimore Symphony Orchestra Summer MusicFest 1997–99; Music Dir Nat. Arts Centre Orchestra, Canada 1998–2015; Prin. Guest Conductor, Royal Philharmonic Orchestra, London 2009–; Chair. Pinchas Zukerman Performance Program, Manhattan School of Music. *Film soundtracks:* Prince of Tides, Critical Care. *Honours:* Hon. DMus (Brown Univ.) 1989; winner, Leventritt Competition 1967, Isaac Stern Award for Artistic Excellence (Nat. Arts Awards) 2002, Grammy Award for Best Chamber Music Performance 1980, Grammy Award for Best Classical Performance, Instrumental Soloist without Orchestra 1981. *Current Management:* Kirshbaum Demler & Associates, Inc., 711 West End Avenue, Suite 5KN, New York, NY 10025, USA. *E-mail:* info@kirshdem.com. *Website:* www.kirshdem.com.

ZUKOFSKY, Paul, BM, MS; American violinist and conductor; b. 22 Oct. 1943, Brooklyn, NY. *Education:* Juilliard School of Music. *Career:* Creative Assoc., SUNY at Buffalo 1964–65; various positions as violinist and violin teacher 1965–75; Pres., Musical Observations Inc. 1975–; principal investigator and project dir, Limits 1976–82; conductor with various orchestras 1977–79; programme co-ordinator, American Portraits concert series at John F. Kennedy Center 1980–; Conductor, Contemporary Chamber Ensemble at Juilliard School of Music 1984–; founder and Prin. Conductor, Sinfoniuhljomsveit Aeskunnar 1985–; Dir of Chamber Music Activities, Juilliard School 1987–89; Artistic Dir, Summer Garden Concert Series, Museum of Modern Art, New York 1987–; Pres. Musical Observations Inc. *Recordings include:* 60 recordings including as conductor: Various Icelandic Orchestral Works 1987, Sixteen Dances by Cage 1984; as violinist: Penderecki's Capriccio for violin and orchestra 1968, Babbitt and Milton Sextets 1972, Glass's Strung Out 1977, Cage's Cheap Imitation 1981, Sonata for solo violin 1983, For John Cage, Feldman, Morton 1984. *Publications:* contrib. articles to professional journals, including The Psychology of Music, with Sternberg and Knoll. *Honours:* ASCAP Community Orchestra Award 1979, ASCAP Citation 1979, Guggenheim Fellowship 1983–84, NEA Fellowship 1983, Knight's Cross, Icelandic Order of the Falcon. *E-mail:* info@musicalobservations.com (office). *Website:* www.musicalobservations.com.

ZUPKO, Ramon, BS, MS; American composer; *Professor Emeritus of Music, Western Michigan University*; b. 14 Nov. 1932, Pittsburgh, Pa; s. of Michael Zupko and Frances Zupko; m. Vonette Zupko; one s. *Education:* Juilliard School with Vincent Persichetti, Vienna Acad. of Music with Karl Schiske, Columbia Univ., Univ. of Utrecht with Michael Koenig, Tanglewood with Aaron Copland. *Career:* Teacher of Theory and Dir of Electronic Music, Chicago Musical Coll. of Roosevelt Univ. 1967–71; Prof. of Composition and Dir of Electronic Music, Western Michigan Univ., Kalamazoo 1971–97, Prof. Emer. 1997–; Gilmore Foundation Comm. 1990. *Compositions include:* Night Music 1955, Songs of Childhood 1955, The City in the Sea 1955, Fantasia for orchestra 1956, Pastorale 1956, Adagio and Scherzo 1956, Two Canzonas 1956, Interlude 1956, Spring Pastorale 1956, Aria and Toccata 1956, Elegy for string orchestra 1957, Ballade for orchestra 1957, Epitaph for string quintet 1957, Introduction and Bagatelle 1957, Six Preludes for piano 1957, Cradle Song 1957, Song and Dance 1957, Images: 15 Pieces for Children 1960–64, Variations for orchestra 1961, Violin Concerto 1962, Translucents for strings 1967, Tangents for 18 bass instruments 1967, Radiants for orchestra 1971, Proud Music of the Storm (multimedia theatre) 1976, Wind Song piano concerto 1979, Life Dances for orchestra 1981, Where the Mountain Crosses song cycle for mezzo and piano 1982, Canti Terrae for orchestra 1982, two symphonies 1984, 1986, Fluxus for various instrumental combinations (series of 12 chamber pieces) 1977–94, Vox Naturae Concerto for brass quintet and orchestra 1992, Chaconne for piano 1995, The Nightingale (opera) 1995–97, Fantasia for Piano 2004. *Honours:* three NEA grants, Koussevitzky Foundation Comm., Guggenheim Fellowship 1981–82, Fulbright Fellowship 1958, works selected twice by Int. Soc. for Contemporary Music for performance at Int. Festival, Distinguished Faculty Scholar, Western Michigan Univ. 1983, various other comms and music awards. *Address:* 1633 West Estes, 1E, Chicago, IL 60626, USA (home). *Telephone:* (773) 465-8553 (home). *E-mail:* zupko@wmich.edu (office).

ZUR, Menachem, DipEd, BMus, MFA; Israeli/American composer, teacher and academic; *Professor Emeritus of Theory and Composition, Jerusalem Academy of Music and Dance;* b. 6 March 1942, Tel-Aviv, Israel; m. Lila Zur; two d. *Education:* Coll. for Teachers of Music, Jerusalem, Jerusalem Acad. of Music and Dance, Mannes Coll. of Music, Sarah Lawrence Coll., Columbia Univ., New York, USA. *Career:* Musical Adviser to the Israel Museum, Jerusalem; Chair. and Dean of Music Theory Dept, Jerusalem Acad. of Music and Dance 1991–2011, Prof. Emer. 2011–; Chair. Israeli Composers' League 1992–94, 2000–03. *Compositions include:* Fantasy for piano 1992, Sonata for cello and piano 1973, Clarinet Quintet 1978, Violin Concerto 1978, Centers for piano 1979, Quartet for flute and strings 1979, Four for four 1980, Short Symphony 1981, Clarinet Trio 1981, Lamentations Cantata for alto and chamber orchestra 1982, Sim Shalom for choir and organ 1983, Piano Concerto 1983, A Tale of Two Sandals for choir 1983, Hallelujah for choir 1984, Sonata for violin and piano 1984, String Quartet 1985, Prelude for band 1986, Neighbors (opera) 1986, Shiluvium for choir 1986, Piano Trio 1987, Sonata for French horn and piano 1988, Fantasy for brass quintet 1988, Sonata for oboe and piano 1988, The Golem for 11 instruments and baritone solo 1988, Akedat Ytzchak 1989, Circles of Time for piano solo 1990, Prelude for violin solo 1991, Sonata No. 2 for piano and cello 1991, Concerto Grosso 1992, Concerto for tuba and orchestra 1992, Discussions #3 for flute and piano 1994, Discussions #4 for trumpet and piano 1994, Discussions #4a for trombone and piano 1994, Gesang Eines Hundes for soprano and piano 1994, Sonata for two pianos 1994, Symphony #2, #3 1994, Syncopa for wind octet 1995, Discussions #5 for clarinet and piano 1996, On the Wings of an Echo for piano 1997, Cadenza for violin 1997, Concert da Camera for viola and ensemble 1997, Concerto for piano four-hands and orchestra 1997, String Sextet 1998, Discussions #6 for saxophone quartet and magnetic tape 1999, Alleluia for vocal sextet and magnetic tape 1999, Mittersil Quintet for clarinet, French horn, guitar, cello and vibraphone 1999, A Note for a Neighbor for clarinet, violin, cello and piano 1999, Kedusha Prayer for choir 1999, Prisma for piano duet 1999, Sovev for horn, violin and piano 2000, And a Whisper Will be Heard for violin 2001, Concerto for orchestra 2001, Discussions #7 for flute and harpsichord 2002, Threads of the Heart for large ensemble 2003, Translations for percussion and electronics 2003, Psalm 23 for choir and marimba 2003, Discussions Quartet #8 for guitar and strings 2004, Discussions Quartet #9 for piano and strings 2004, Threads of The Heart 2006, Cartoons 2008, The Fig Tree 2010, At an Ancient Garden 2012, Concerto for Violin 2013, There Dwell the Wolf with the Sheep 2014, Concerto da Camera 2014, Arrow concertino for Mandolin 2015. *Publications include:* Keyboard Harmony (co-author) 1980, The Theory of Composition: Music in Time 2005; contrib. to Musical Quarterly. *Honours:* Guggenheim Fellowship 1981–82, Acum Prize for Lifetime Achievement 2001, Prime Minister's Prize for Composition 2001, 2010. *Telephone:* 9-9505816 (Israel). *Fax:* 9-9505817 (Israel). *Website:* www.artpro.co.il/menachemzur. *Address:* Publishing House of the Israeli Composers' League, Israel Music Center, 36 Zahal Street, POB 10039, Tel-Aviv 69351-58, Israel (office). *Telephone:* 2-621282. *E-mail:* music.imc@gmail.com; icl@zahav.net.il (office). *Website:* www.imi.org.il.

ZVETANOV, Boiko; Bulgarian singer (tenor); b. 14 June 1955, Sofia; two c. *Education:* Sofia Conservatory. *Career:* sang with the Bulgarian National Opera from 1982 as the Duke of Mantua, Foresto in Attila, Fernando in La Favorita, Pollione and Radames; concerts in Russia, Czechoslovakia and France (Verdi's Requiem at Paris), and the Italian Singer in Der Rosenkavalier at the Vienna Staatsoper; sang at St Gallen 1991 as Riccardo in Un Ballo in Maschera, Opernhaus Zürich as Lensky, Alvaro in Forza del Destino, Arnold in Guillaume Tell and Rodolfo; 1992 included Capriccio, Wiener Staatsoper, La Forza del Destino in Zürich, Guillaume Tell, La Bohème and Il Pirata in Zürich; 1993 included Hérodiade in Zürich, Cavalleria rusticana in Wiesbaden and Capriccio in Dresden; La Forza del Destino in Karlsruhe 1993–94; season 1994–95 included Rosenkavalier and Ballo in Maschera with Deutsche Oper Berlin; Lucia di Lammermoor at Teatro Principal in Valencia with L. Alberti 1995; Rosenkavalier, Oper der Stadt Bonn, director Spiros Argiris 1995; season 1999–2000 as Arvino in I Lombardi for Opernhaus Zürich and Manrico at the Prague State Opera; Don Carlos in Mainz 2002; currently with Opernhaus Zürich. *Recordings:* albums of arias and duets from Verdi's operas. *Current Management:* c/o Artists Management Verena Keller, Lohwisstrasse 52, 8123 Ebmatingen, Switzerland; c/o Opera Vladarski, Döblinger Hauptstrasse 57/18, 1190 Vienna, Austria. *Telephone:* (44) 9801513 (Keller); (1) 368-6960/6961 (Vladarski). *Fax:* (44) 9803686 (Keller); (1) 368-6962 (Vladarski). *E-mail:* keller.verena@bluewin.ch; opera.vladarski@ utanet.at.

ZWIAUER, Florian; Austrian violinist; b. 1954, Vienna. *Education:* Vienna Conservatory, Vienna Acad. of Music. *Career:* co-founder, Franz Schubert Quartet 1974; appearances at Amsterdam Concertgebouw, Vienna Musikverein and Konzerthaus, the Salle Gaveau, Paris, and Sydney Opera House; visits to Zürich, Geneva, Basle, Berlin, Hamburg, Rome, Rotterdam, Madrid, Copenhagen, Stockholm, Dublin, Manchester, Munich, Lisbon and elsewhere; festival engagements include Salzburg, Wiener Festwochen, Prague Spring, Bregenz Festival, Schubertiade at Hohenems, the Schubert Festival at

Washington, DC and the Belfast and Istanbul festivals; tours of Australasia, fmr USSR and USA; British debut at the QEH 1979; frequent appearances at Wigmore Hall and Cheltenham Festival; Concertmaster, Vienna Symphony Orchestra 1989–; regular guest concertmaster, Nederlands Philharmonisch Orkest, Orquestra Gulbenkian; teacher, Vienna Conservatory 1983–, Scuola di Musica di Fiesole, Italy; masterclasses at the Royal Northern Coll. of Music, the Lake District Summer Music. *Recordings include:* Schubert's Quartet in G, D887, Complete Quartets of Dittersdorf, Haydn's Three Last String Quartets, The 10 Late Mozart String Quartets, Complete Tchaikovsky String Chamber Music, Complete String Quartets of Franz Schmidt, Complete String Quartets of Hans Pfitzner, works by Joseph Haydn, Erich Wolfgang Korngold, Emil Nikolaus von Reznicek. *Honours:* Österreichisches Ehrenkreuz für Wissenschaft und Kunst 2000; winner European Broadcasting Union Int. String Quartet Competition, Stockholm 1974, second prize W. A. Mozart Int. Violin Competition, Salzburg (as soloist) 1978. *E-mail:* florian@zwiauer .com (office). *Website:* www.florianzwiauer.com.

ZWIEBEL, Marek; Slovak violinist; b. Bratislava. *Education:* Kosice Conservatory, Univ. of Music, Vienna, Musikhochschule Lucerne, master-classes with Amadeus, Alban Berg, Bartòk, Hagen, Mosaique and Smetana quartets. *Career:* early career as concert performer in Germany, Poland, Hungary, Czech Repub., Italy, Japan and Switzerland; joined Pavel Haas Quartet as second violinist 2012, performed world-wide in concert halls including London's Wigmore Hall, Concertgebouw Amsterdam, Palais des Beaux-Arts Brussels, Auditorio Nacional Madrid, Zurich Tonhalle, Munich Herkulessaal and Luxembourg Philharmonie and at Aldeburgh, Edinburgh, Verbier and Zeist festivals. *Recordings include:* with Pavel Haas Quartet: Franz Schubert works (Gramophone Award for Best Chamber Recording 2014) 2013, Smetana string quartets (Gramophone Award for Best Chamber Recording 2015). *Current Management:* Intermusica Artists' Management, 36 Graham Street, Crystal Wharf, London, N1 8GJ, England. *Telephone:* (20) 7608-9918. *E-mail:* nfriemel@intermusica.co.uk. *Website:* www.intermusica.co.uk; www .pavelhaasquartet.com.

ZWILICH, Ellen Taaffe, DMus; American composer and academic; *Francis Eppes Distinguished Professor, College of Music, Florida State University;* b. 30 April 1939, Miami, Fla; d. of Edward Taaffe and Ruth Taaffe (née Howard); m. Joseph Zwilich 1969 (died 1979). *Education:* Florida State Univ. and Juilliard School, New York. *Career:* violinist, American Symphony, New York 1965–73; Composer-in-Residence, Santa Fe Chamber Music Festival 1990, American Acad., Rome 1990; Carnegie Hall Composer's Chair. 1995–99; currently Francis Eppes Distinguished Prof., Coll. of Music, Florida State Univ.; Guggenheim Fellow 1981; mem. American Acad. of Arts and Letters 1992, American Acad. of Arts and Sciences 2004. *Compositions include:* Einsame Nacht 1971, Im Nebel 1972, Sonata in Three Movements 1973, String Quartet 1974, Clarino Quartet 1977, Chamber Symphony 1979, Passages 1981, String Trio 1982, Symphony No 1: Three Movements for Orchestra 1982, Fantasy for Harpsichord 1983, Double Quartet for Strings 1984, Concerto Grosso 1985, Concerto for Piano and Orchestra 1986, Tanzspiel 1987, Symphony No 2 1985, Piano Trio 1987, Concerto for Trombone and Orchestra 1988, Symbolon 1988, Concerto for Bass Trombone, Strings, Timpani and Cymbals 1989, Concerto for Flute and Orchestra 1989, Concerto for Oboe and Orchestra 1990, Quintet for Clarinet and Strings 1990, Concerto for Violin, Cello and Orchestra 1991, Concerto for Bassoon and Orchestra 1992, Symphony No 3 1992, Concerto for Horn and String Orchestra 1993, Fantasy for Orchestra 1993, American Concerto for Trumpet and Orchestra 1994, A Simple Magnificat 1994, Triple Concerto 1995, Jubilation 1995, Peanuts Gallery 1996, Violin Concerto 1997, String Quartet No 2 1998, Lament for Piano 1999, Upbeat! 1999, Symphony No 4 1999, Lament for Cello and Piano 2000, Millennium Fantasy for Piano and Orchestra 2000, Partita for Violin and String Orchestra 2000, Clarinet Concerto 2002, 'Rituals' for 5 Percussionists and Orchestra 2003, Episodes for violin and piano 2003, Quartet for oboe and strings 2004, LUVN BLM for mixed ensemble 2005, Quintet for Alto Saxophone and String Quartet 2006, Episodes for Soprano Saxophone and Piano 2006, Symphony No. 5 2008, Septet for Piano Trio and String Quartet 2009. *Honours:* Lifetime Hon. mem. American Fed. of Musicians; Hon. DMus (Oberlin Coll.) 1987, (Manhattanville Coll.) 1990, (Marymount Manhattan Coll., Converse Coll.) 1994, (New School, Mannes Coll.) 1995; Elizabeth Sprague Coolidge Chamber Music Prize 1974, Gold Medal G.B. Viotti, Vercelli, Italy 1975, Ernst Von Dohnanyi Citation 1981, Pulitzer Prize for Music (first woman) 1983, Acad. Award, American Acad. of Arts and Letters 1984, Arturo Toscanini Music Critics Award 1987, Florida Artists Hall of Fame 1993, Musical America Composer of the Year 1999. *Address:* 600 West 246th Street, Riverdale, NY 10471 (home); Florida State University College of Music, Tallahassee, FL 32306-1180, USA (office). *Telephone:* (850) 644-3424 (office). *Fax:* (850) 644-2033 (office). *Website:* www .music.fsu.edu (office).

ŻYLIS-GARA, Teresa; Polish singer (soprano); b. 23 Jan. 1930, Landwarow, nr Wilno (now Vilnius, Lithuania); m.; one c. *Education:* State Higher School of Music, Łódź with Prof. Olga Olgina. *Career:* operatic debut in titles roles in Halka (Moniuszko), Madame Butterfly (Puccini) and as Giuletta in Les contes d'Hoffmann (Offenbach); soloist, Kraków Philharmonic 1954–58 and Kraków Opera 1958–59; foreign contracts in operas: Oberhausen 1961–63, Städtische Bühnen, Dortmund 1963–65, Deutsche Oper am Rhein, Düsseldorf 1965–70; regular performances at Metropolitan Opera, New York, Berlin, Hamburg, Munich, La Scala, Milan, Staatsoper, Vienna and several times at Mozart

Salzburg Festival under Herbert von Karajan; repertoire includes prin. roles in operas by Mozart, Verdi, Puccini, R. Strauss, Chausson, Tchaikovsky and others; has sung with artists such as Franco Corelli, Placido Domingo, Luciano Pavarotti and José Cameras; has worked with directors including Franco Zeffirelli and conductors such as Herbert von Karajan, Karl Böhm, Carl-Maria Giulini and many others; song recitals have included Richard Strauss's Four Last Songs, Mercadante's Il Giuramento, Airs d'Opéras slaves, Rossini's Mose in Egitto; master-classes in interpretation and vocal technique in Poland, France, Monaco and USA; Prof. of Lyric Art, State Higher School of Music, Łódź 1999–. *Recordings include:* Mozart's Don Giovanni, Chausson's Le Roi Arthus, Richard Strauss' Ariadne auf Naxos, Bach's St Matthew Passion, Dvořak's Requiem, Verdi's Messa da Requiem, Mahler's Das Klagende Lied, and songs by Canteloube, Chopin, Duparc, Fauré, Karlowicz, Lalo, Moniuszko, Paderewski and Szymanowski. *Honours:* Kt's Cross, Order of Polonia Restituta 1975, Commdr's Cross, Order of Polonia Restituta 2000; Dr hc (Karol Lipinski Music Acad., Wrocław) 2003; Gold Medal for roles of Mimi in Puccini's La Bohème and Fiordiligi in Mozart's Così fan tutte, Opera Bellas Artes, Mexico City 1967, Nat. Prize, Ministry of the Arts and Culture 1975, Winner, All-Polish Competition of Young Vocalists, Warsaw, Prime Minister's Prize (First Class) 1979, Prix de la Saison de 1'Opera for "an extraordinary interpretation of Desdemona in Otello", Associación Verdiana Teatro Colon Buenos Aires 1981, Max Reinhardt Medal, Salzburg Opera Festival, Prix d'honneur de la Ville de Pont St Esprit (France) for musical educ. of the young, Medal of the Music Acad. of Łódź on its 50th anniversary 1999, Nat. Prize 'Gloria Artis', Ministry of the Arts and Culture 2006.

ZYSSET, Martin; Swiss singer (tenor); b. 1965, Solothurn. *Education:* Berne Conservatory, studied with Ernst Haefliger, Edith Mathis and Roland Hermann. *Career:* debut at Selzach Summer Festival 1992, as Pedrillo in Die Entführung; appearances at the Zürich Opera 1992–, as Scaramuccio in Ariadne auf Naxos, Monostatos in Die Zauberflöte, Count Hohenzollern (Henze's Der Prinz von Homburg), Cassio, Jacquino and Tamino; performed in premiere of Ein Narrenparadies by Ofer Ben-Amots, Vienna Festival 1994; further engagements with the Radio della Svizzera Italiana, in Antwerp and in Luxembourg (concert performance of Fidelio, under Leopold Hager); other roles include Don Ottavio, Goro in Butterfly and Spoletta in Tosca, Strauss's Simplicius Simplicissimus, in Tosca, The Queen of Spades, Lulu and Carmen. *Honours:* prizewinner Pro Arte Lyrica Competition, Lausanne 1990. *Address:* c/o Opernhaus Zürich, Falkenstrasse 1, 8008 Zürich, Switzerland (office). *E-mail:* info@opernhaus.ch (office).

Directory

APPENDIX A: ORCHESTRAS

Argentina

Orquesta Filarmónica de Buenos Aires: Teatro Colón, Cerrito 618, 1010 Buenos Aires. *Telephone:* (11) 4378-7344. *Fax:* (11) 4378-7305. *E-mail:* info@ofba.com.ar. *Website:* www.ofba.org.ar. f. 1946 as the Orquesta Sinfónica del Teatro Municipal; changed name to Orquesta Sinfónica de la Ciudad de Buenos Aires 1948, and to current name in 1958; permanently based at the Teatro Colón from 1958.

Orquesta Sinfónica Nacional: Avda Córdoba 1155, CP 1055 Buenos Aires. *Telephone:* (11) 4815-8883. f. 1948 as Orquesta Sinfónica del Estado.

Armenia

Armenian Philharmonic Orchestra: Aram Khachaturian Concert Hall, 0002 Yerevan, 46 Mashtots Avenue. *Telephone:* (10) 56-06-45. *Fax:* (10) 56-49-65. *E-mail:* philharmonic@apo.am. *Website:* www.apo.am.

Australia

Adelaide Symphony Orchestra: PO Box 2121, Adelaide, SA 5001. *Telephone:* (8) 8233-6233. *Fax:* (8) 8233-6222. *E-mail:* aso@aso.com.au. *Website:* www.aso.com.au.

Australian Chamber Orchestra: PO Box R21, Royal Exchange, Sydney, NSW 1225. *Telephone:* (2) 8274-3800. *Fax:* (2) 8274-3801. *E-mail:* headoffice@aco.com.au. *Website:* www.aco.com.au. f. 1975; based in Opera Quays, Sydney.

Canberra Symphony Orchestra: PO Box 1919, Canberra, ACT 2601. *Telephone:* (2) 6247-9191. *Fax:* (2) 6247-9026. *E-mail:* contact@cso.org.au. *Website:* www.cso.org.au.

Melbourne Symphony Orchestra: PO Box 9994, Melbourne, Vic. 3001. *Telephone:* (3) 9626-1111. *Fax:* (3) 9626-1101. *E-mail:* mso@mso.com.au. *Website:* www.mso.com.au.

Orchestra Victoria: PO Box 836, S Melbourne, Vic. 3205. *Telephone:* (3) 9694-3600. *Fax:* (3) 9694-3611. *E-mail:* info@orchestravictoria.com.au. *Website:* www.orchestravictoria.com.au.

The Queensland Orchestra: GPO Box 9994, Brisbane, Qld 4001. *Telephone:* (7) 3833-5000. *Fax:* (7) 3833-5001. *E-mail:* info@thequeenslandorchestra.com.au. *Website:* www.thequeenslandorchestra.com.au.

Sydney Symphony Orchestra: GPO Box 4338, Sydney, NSW 2001. *Telephone:* (2) 8215-4644. *Fax:* (2) 8215-4646. *E-mail:* info@sydneysymphony.com. *Website:* www.sydneysymphony.com.

Tasmanian Symphony Orchestra: PO Box 1450, Hobart, TAS 7001. *Fax:* (3) 6232-4455. *E-mail:* boxoffice@tso.com.au. *Website:* www.tso.com.au.

West Australian Symphony Orchestra: PO Box 3041, Perth, WA 6832. *Telephone:* (8) 9326-0000. *Fax:* (8) 9326-0099. *E-mail:* waso@waso.com.au. *Website:* www.waso.com.au.

Austria

Grazer Philharmonische Orchester: Theaterkasse am Kaiser-Josef-Platz 10, 8010 Graz. *Telephone:* (316) 80-00. *E-mail:* (316) 80-08. *Website:* www.theater-graz.com.

Mozarteum Orchester: Erzbischof-Gebhardstrasse 10, 5020, Salzburg. *Telephone:* (662) 84-35-71. *Fax:* (662) 84-35-71-23. *E-mail:* office@mozarteumorchester.at. *Website:* www.mozarteumorchester.at.

Radio-Symphonieorchester Wien: Argentinierstrasse 30a, 1040 Vienna. *Telephone:* (1) 501-01 / 18420. *Fax:* (1) 501-01 / 18358. *E-mail:* rso-wien@orf.at. *Website:* www.rso-wien.orf.at. Formerly the Österreichisches Rundfunk (ORF), later changing its name to the Radio-Symphonieorchester Wien (Vienna Radio Symphony Orchestra).

Wiener Kammerorchester: Schachnerstrasse 27, 1220 Vienna. *Telephone:* (1) 203-63-57. *Fax:* (1) 204-37-50. *E-mail:* wiener@kammerorchester.com. *Website:* www.kammerorchester.com.

Wiener Philharmoniker: Bösendorferstrasse 12, 1010 Vienna. *Telephone:* (1) 505-65-25. *Fax:* (1) 505-42-99. *Website:* www.wienerphilharmoniker.at.

Wiener Symphoniker: Lehárgasse II, 1060 Vienna. *Telephone:* (1) 589-79-0. *Fax:* (1) 589-79-54. *E-mail:* office@wiener-symphoniker.at. *Website:* www.wiener-symphoniker.at.

Azerbaijan

Azerbaijan State Symphony Orchestra: c/o Ministry of Culture and Tourism, 1000 Baku, Azadliq meydani 1, House of Government, 3rd Floor. *Telephone:* (12) 493-43-98. *Fax:* (12) 493-56-05. *E-mail:* info@mct.gov.az. *Website:* www.mct.gov.az.

Belarus

Orchestra of the National Academic Opera and Ballet: 220029 Minsk, 1 Parizhskaya Kommuna pl. 1. *Telephone:* (17) 334-10-41. *Fax:* (17) 334-07-72. *E-mail:* belarus_opera@tut.by. *Website:* www.belarusopera.com.

Belarusian State Philharmonic Society: 220005 Minsk, pr. Nezavisimosti 50. *Telephone:* (17) 284-77-66. *Fax:* (17) 231-90-50. *E-mail:* bkzf@mail.ru. *Website:* www.philharmonic.by.

Belgium

Koninklijke Filharmonie van Vlaanderen: Filharmonisch Huis, Brazilliëstraat 15, 2000 Antwerp. *Telephone:* (3) 213-54-20. *Fax:* (3) 213-54-00. *E-mail:* info@defilharmonie.be. *Website:* www.defilharmonie.be.

Orchestre National de Belgique: Galerie Ravenstein 28/6, 1000 Brussels. *Telephone:* (2) 552-04-60. *Fax:* (2) 552-04-68. *E-mail:* info@nob-onb.be. *Website:* www.nob-onb.be.

Orchestre Philharmonique de Liège: Salle Philharmonique, Blvd Piercot 25-27, 4000 Liège. *Telephone:* (4) 220-00-00. *Fax:* (4) 220-00-01. *E-mail:* opl@opl.be. *Website:* www.opl.be.

Orchestre Symphonique du Théâtre Royal de la Monnaie: 4 rue Léopold, 1000 Brussels. *Telephone:* (2) 229-12-00. *Fax:* (2) 229-13-30. *E-mail:* info@lamonnaie.be. *Website:* www.lamonnaie.be.

Vlaams Radio Orkest: Eugène Flageyplein 18, 1050 Brussels. *Telephone:* (2) 627-11-60. *Fax:* (2) 627-11-61. *E-mail:* info@brusselsphilharmonic.be. *Website:* www.vro-vrk.be.

Bolivia

Orquesta Sinfónica Nacional: Centro Sinfónico Nacional, Ayacucho No. 366, Casilla 6690, La Paz. *Telephone:* (2) 220-3063. *Fax:* (2) 220-3063. *E-mail:* sinfobolivia@acelerate.com. *Website:* www.sinfonicabolivia.org.

Bosnia and Herzegovina

Sarajevo Philharmonic Orchestra: 71000 Sarajevo, Obala Kulina Bana 9. *Telephone:* (33) 666519. *Fax:* (33) 666521. *E-mail:* info@saph.ba. *Website:* www.saph.ba.

Brazil

Orquestra Filarmônica do Rio de Janeiro: Rua das Marrecas 25, Sala 501, Centro, 20013-120 Rio de Janeiro, RJ. *Telephone:* (21) 2240-7354. *E-mail:* orquestra@filarmonica-rio.com.br. *Website:* www.filarmonica-rio.com.br.

Orquestra Sinfônica Brasileira: Avda Rio Branco 135, Salas 915–920, 20040-006 Rio de Janeiro, RJ. *Telephone:* (21) 2142-5800. *Fax:* (21) 2142-5844. *Website:* www.osb.com.br.

Orquestra Sinfônica do Estado de São Paulo (OSESP): Praça Júlio Prestes 16, 01218-020 São Paulo, SP. *Telephone:* (11) 3367-9500. *Fax:* (11) 3367-9501. *E-mail:* orquestra@osesp.art.br. *Website:* www.osesp.art.br. f. 1954.

Bulgaria

Bulgarian Symphony Orchestra: *E-mail:* office@sif309.com. *Website:* www.sif309.com.

Sofia Philharmonic Orchestra: 1000 Sofia, Benkovski str 1. *Telephone:* (2) 88-31-97. *Fax:* (2) 87-40-72. *E-mail:* sofiaphil@ibn.bg. *Website:* www.sofiaphilharmonie.bg.

Canada

Calgary Philharmonic Orchestra: 205 Eighth Avenue SE, Calgary, AB T2G 0K9. *Telephone:* (403) 571-0270. *Fax:* (403) 294-7424. *E-mail:* info@cpo-live.com. *Website:* www.cpo-live.com.

Edmonton Symphony Orchestra: 9720-102 Avenue NW, Edmonton, AB T5J 4B2. *Telephone:* (780) 428-1108. *Fax:* (780) 425-0167. *E-mail:* info@winspearcentre.com. *Website:* www.edmontonsymphony.com.

Hamilton Philharmonic Orchestra: 105 Main Street E, Suite 1002, Hamilton, ON L8N 1G6. *Telephone:* (905) 526-1677. *Fax:* (905) 526-0616. *E-mail:* office@hpo.org. *Website:* www.hpo.org.

National Arts Centre Orchestra: PO Box 1534, Station B, Ottawa, ON K1P 5W1. *Telephone:* (613) 947-7000. *E-mail:* info@nac-cna.ca. *Website:* www.nac-cna.ca.

Orchestre Symphonique de Montréal: 260 Boulevard de Maisonneuve W, Second Floor, Montréal, QC H2X 1Y9. *Telephone:* (514) 842-3402. *Fax:* (514) 842-0728. *Website:* www.osm.ca.

Orchestre Symphonique de Québec: 130 Grande Alleé E, Québec, QC G1R 2G7. *Telephone:* (418) 643-8486. *Fax:* (418) 646-9665. *E-mail:* info@osq.org. *Website:* www.osq.org.

Toronto Symphony Orchestra: 212 King Street W, Sixth Floor, Toronto, ON M5H 1K5. *Telephone:* (416) 593-7769. *Fax:* (416) 977-2912. *Website:* www.tso.on.ca.

Vancouver Symphony Orchestra: 601 Smithe Street, Vancouver, BC V6B 5G1. *Telephone:* (604) 684-9100. *Fax:* (604) 684-9264. *E-mail:* customerservice@vancouversymphony.ca. *Website:* www.vancouversymphony.ca.

Victoria Symphony Orchestra: 620 View Street, Suite 610, Victoria, BC V8W 1J6. *Telephone:* (250) 385-9771. *Fax:* (250) 385-7767. *E-mail:* administration@victoriasymphony.bc.ca. *Website:* www.victoriasymphony.bc.ca.

Winnipeg Symphony Orchestra: 555 Main Street, Suite 1020, Winnipeg, MB R3B 1C3. *Telephone:* (204) 949-3999. *Fax:* (204) 956-4271. *E-mail:* wso@wso.mb.ca. *Website:* www.wso.mb.ca.

Chile

Orquesta Filarmónica de Santiago: Teatro Municipal, Agustinas 794, Santiago. *Telephone:* (2) 639-9735. *Fax:* (2) 633-7214. *E-mail:* contacto@municipalsantiago.cl.. *Website:* www.municipal.cl. Based at the Teatro Municipal, Santiago.

The People's Republic of China

Beijing Symphony Orchestra: 1 Ba Keyang Shu, Shuangjing, Chaoyang District, Beijing 100022. *Website:* www.bjso.cn. f. 1977.

China National Symphony Orchestra: *E-mail:* cnso@cnso.com.cn. *Website:* www.cnso.com.cn. f. 1956 as the Central Philharmonic Orchestra of China, changed to current name 1996.

Shanghai Symphony Orchestra: 105 Hunan Lu, Shanghai 200031. *Telephone:* (21) 64333574. *Fax:* (21) 64333752. *E-mail:* shso105@sh163.net. *Website:* www.sh-symphony.com. f. 1879 as the Shanghai Public Band; expanded to full-size orchestra 1919.

Colombia

Orquesta Filarmónica de Bogotá: Calle 39A, No. 14-57, PO Box 16034, Bogotá. *Telephone:* (1) 288-3466. *Fax:* (1) 320-8813. *E-mail:* info@ofb.gov.co. *Website:* www.filarmonicabogota.gov.co.

Orquesta Sinfónica Nacional de Colombia: Calle 11, No. 5-51, Bogotá DC. *Telephone:* (1) 350-5325. *Fax:* (1) 350-5324. *E-mail:* jmosquera@mincultura.gov.co. *Website:* www.asociacion-sinfonica.org.

Costa Rica

Orquesta Sinfónica Nacional: Apdo Postal 1035, 1000 San José. *Telephone:* 2240-0333. *E-mail:* info@osn.go.cr. *Website:* www.osn.go.cr.

Croatia

Zagreb Philharmonic Orchestra: 10000 Zagreb, Trg Stjepana Radića 4 p.p. 909. *Telephone:* (1) 6060103. *Fax:* (1) 6111577. *E-mail:* zgfilhar@zgf.hr. *Website:* www.zgf.hr.

Czech Republic

Brno State Philharmonic Orchestra: Komenského námestí 534/8, 602 00 Brno. *Telephone:* 539092801. *E-mail:* info@filharmonie-brno.cz. *Website:* www.filharmonie-brno.cz.

Česká filharmonie (Czech Philharmonic Orchestra): Alšovo nábřeži 12, 110 00 Prague 1. *Telephone:* 227059227. *Fax:* 227059327. *E-mail:* info@cfmail.cz. *Website:* www.ceskafilharmonie.cz.

Czech National Symphony Orchestra: Weilova 2/114, 102 00 Prague 10. *Telephone:* 267215576. *Fax:* 267215361. *E-mail:* cnso@cnso.cz. *Website:* www.cnso.cz.

Prague Radio Symphony Orchestra: Vinohradská 12, 120 99 Prague 2. *Telephone:* 221551401. *Fax:* 221551413. *E-mail:* info@rozhlas.cz. *Website:* www.rozhlas.cz/socr.

Symfonického orchestru hl.m. Prahy (Prague Symphony Orchestra): nám Republiky 5, 110 21 Prague 1. *Telephone:* 222310784. *Website:* www.fok.cz.

Denmark

Ålborg Symfoniorkester: Kjellerupsgade 14, 9000 Ålborg. *Telephone:* 98-13-19-55. *Fax:* 98-13-03-78. *E-mail:* info@aalborgsymf.dk. *Website:* www.aalborgsymfoniorkester.dk.

Århus Symfoniorkester: Musikhuset Århus, Skovgaardsgade 2c, 8000 Århus. *Telephone:* 89-40-90-90. *Fax:* 89-40-91-00. *E-mail:* symfoni@aarhus.dk. *Website:* www.aarhussymfoni.dk.

Danish National Symphony Orchestra: DR Byen, Emil Holms Kanal 20, 0999 Copenhagen. *Telephone:* 35-20-30-40. *Fax:* 35-20-61-21. *E-mail:* drso@dr.dk. *Website:* www.dr.dk/rso.

Det Kongelige Kapel (Royal Danish Orchestra): PO Box 2185, 1017 Copenhagen. *Telephone:* 33-69-69-33. *Fax:* 33-69-65-19. *E-mail:* admin@kglteater.dk. *Website:* www.kglteater.dk.

Odense Symphony Orchestra: Claus Bergs Gade 9, 5000 Odense C. *Telephone:* 63-75-00-50. *Fax:* 65-91-00-47. *E-mail:* orchestra@odensesymfoni.dk. *Website:* www.odensesymfoni.dk.

Dominican Republic

Orquesta Sinfónica Nacional: Sinfonia Foundation, Eduardo Vicisoso No.1, Santo Domingo, DN. *Telephone:* 532-6600. *Fax:* 533-1941. *E-mail:* f.sinfonia@codetel.net.do. *Website:* www.sinfonia.org.do.

Ecuador

Orquesta Sinfónica Nacional: Manabí N8-131, entre Guayaquil y Flores, Quito. *Telephone:* (2) 257-2823. *E-mail:* informes@teatrosucre.com. *Website:* www.teatrosucre.com. f. 1956; productions at the Teatro Nacional Sucre.

Egypt

Cairo Symphony Orchestra: Cairo Opera House, PO Box 11567 El Borg Gezira, Cairo 11211. *Telephone:* (2) 7398144. *Fax:* (2) 7370599. *E-mail:* info@cairoopera.org. *Website:* www.cairoopera.org.

National Arab Music Ensemble: Cairo Opera House, PO Box 11567 El Borg Gezira, Cairo 11211. *Telephone:* (2) 7398144. *Fax:* (2) 7370599. *E-mail:* info@cairoopera.org. *Website:* www.cairoopera.org.

El Salvador

Orquesta Sinfónica de El Salvador: 8a Avda Norte #228, una cuadra al norte del mercado Ex-Cuartel, San Salvador. *Telephone:* 2221-2373. *Fax:* 2221-2373. *E-mail:* orquestasinfonicaes@yahoo.com. *Website:* www.clic.org.sv/Orquesta_Sinfonica_Nacional.html.

Estonia

Eesti Riikliku Sümfooniaorkestri (Estonian National Symphony Orchestra): Estonia PO Box 4, Tallinn 10148. *Telephone:* 614-7787. *Fax:* 631-3133. *E-mail:* erso@erso.ee. *Website:* www.erso.ee.

Finland

Finnish Radio Symphony Orchestra: PO Box 97, 00024 Yleisradio, Helsinki. *Telephone:* (9) 14801. *Fax:* (9) 14803551. *E-mail:* radion.sinfoniaorksteri@yle.fi. *Website:* www.yle.fi/rso.

Helsinki Philharmonic Orchestra: Finlandia Hall, PO Box 4400, 00099 Helsinki. *Telephone:* (9) 40241. *Fax:* (9) 406484. *E-mail:* helsinki.philharmonic@hel.fi. *Website:* www.hel.fi/filharmonia.

Tampere Philharmonic Orchestra: PO Box 487, 31101 Tampere. *Telephone:* (3) 565611. *Fax:* (3) 56566710. *E-mail:* tiedotus@tampere.fi. *Website:* www.tampere.fi.

France

Les Arts Florissants: 46 rue Fortuny, 75017 Paris. *Telephone:* 1-43-87-98-88. *Fax:* 1-43-87-37-31. *E-mail:* contact@arts-florissants.com. *Website:* www.arts-florissants.com. Group performs early music.

Orchestre de Paris: Salle Pleyel, 252 rue du Faubourg Saint-Honoré, 75008 Paris. *Telephone:* 1-42-56-13-13. *E-mail:* contact@orchestredeparis.com. *Website:* www.orchestredeparis.com.

Orchestre National de France: c/o Radio France, 116 avenue du Président Kennedy, 75786 Paris cedex 16. *Telephone:* 1-56-40-29-07. *Fax:* 1-42-30-14-88. *Website:* radiofrance.fr/chaines/orchestres/national.

Orchestre National de Lyon: 84 rue de Bonnel, 69003 Lyon cedex 3. *Telephone:* 4-78-95-95-00. *Fax:* 4-78-60-13-08. *Website:* www.orchestrelyon.com.

Orchestre Philharmonique de Nice: 4-6 rue St François de Paule, 06300 Nice. *Telephone:* 4-92-17-40-00. *Fax:* 4-93-80-34-83. *Website:* www.philharmonique-nice.org.

Orchestre Philharmonique de Radio France: 116 avenue du Président Kennedy, 75786, Paris cedex 16. *Telephone:* 1-56-40-29-07. *Fax:* 1-42-30-14-88. *E-mail:* philhar@radiofrance.com. *Website:* www.radiofrance.fr.

Orchestre Philharmonique de Strasbourg: Palais de la Musique et des Congrès, place de Bordeaux, 67000 Strasbourg cedex. *Telephone:* 3-69-06-37-00. *Fax:* 3-69-06-27-01. *Website:* www.philharmonique-strasbourg.com.

Germany

Berliner Philharmoniker: Stiftung Berlin Philharmoniker, Herbert-von-Karajan-Str. 1, 10785 Berlin. *Telephone:* (30) 25488999. *Fax:* (30) 25488323.

E-mail: kartenbuero@berliner-philharmoniker.de. *Website:* www.berliner
-philharmoniker.de.

Berliner Symphoniker: Wangenheimstr. 37–39, 14193 Berlin. *Telephone:* (30) 3211017. *Fax:* (30) 3255326. *E-mail:* kontakt@berlin-symphoniker.de. *Website:* www.berliner-symphoniker.de.

Deutsches Symphonie Orchester Berlin: Charlottenstrasse 56, 10117 Berlin. *Telephone:* (30) 20298711. *Fax:* (30) 20298729. *E-mail:* tickets@dso
-berlin.de. *Website:* www.dso-berlin.de.

Gewandhausorchester Leipzig: Augustusplatz 8, 04109 Leipzig. *Telephone:* (341) 1270280. *E-mail:* presse@gewandhaus.de. *Website:* www
.gewandhaus.de.

Hamburger Symphoniker: Dammtorwall 46, 20355 Hamburg. *Telephone:* (40) 344851. *Fax:* (40) 353788. *E-mail:* info@hamburgersymphoniker.de. *Website:* www.hamburgersymphoniker.de.

Münchner Philharmoniker: Kellerstrasse 4, 81667 Munich. *Telephone:* (89) 480985500. *Fax:* (89) 480985400. *E-mail:* presse.philharmoniker@
muenchen.de. *Website:* www.mphil.de.

Münchner Symphoniker: Drächslstrasse 14, 81541 Munich. *Telephone:* (89) 4411960. *Fax:* (89) 44119615. *E-mail:* info@muenchner-symphoniker.de. *Website:* www.muenchner-symphoniker.de.

Philharmoniker Hamburg: Grosse Theaterstrasse 25, Postfach 20308, 20354 Hamburg. *Telephone:* (40) 35680. *Fax:* (40) 3568464. *E-mail:* info@
philharmoniker-hamburg.de. *Website:* www.philharmoniker-hamburg.de.

Rundfunk Sinfonieorchester Berlin: Charlottenstrasse 56, 10117 Berlin. *E-mail:* info@rsb-online.de. *Website:* www.rsb-online.de.

Sächsische Staatskapelle Dresden: Theaterplatz 2, 01067 Dresden. *Telephone:* (351) 49110. *E-mail:* intoffice@semperoper.de. *Website:* www
.semperoper.de/de/staatskapelle.

Symphonieorchester des Bayerischen Rundfunks: Rundfunkplatz 1, 80335 Munich. *Telephone:* (89) 590001. *E-mail:* info@br-online.de. *Website:* www.br-online.de.

Greece

Athens State Orchestra: 17–19 Vas. Georgious B'Str, 106 75 Athens. *Telephone:* (210) 7257601. *Fax:* (210) 7257600. *Website:* www.koa.gr.

Thessaloniki State Symphony Orchestra: 21 Kolokotroni Str., Moni Lazariston Building, 564 30 Thessaloniki. *Telephone:* (2310) 589163. *Fax:* (2310) 604854. *E-mail:* info@tsso.gr. *Website:* www.tsso.gr.

Guatemala

Orquesta Sinfónica de Guatemala: 3a Avenida 4-61, Zona 1, Guatemala City. *Telephone:* 2232-2167. *Fax:* 2253-9023. *E-mail:* orsinagua@hotmail.com.

Honduras

Orquesta Sinfónica Nacional: Apdo Postal 4087, Tegucigalpa. *Telephone:* 2232-2167.

Hong Kong

Hong Kong Philharmonic Orchestra: Level 8, Administration Building, Hong Kong Cultural Centre, Tsim Sha Tsui, Kowloon. *Telephone:* 27212030. *Fax:* 23116229. *E-mail:* webmaster@hkpo.com. *Website:* www.hkpo.com.

Hungary

Budapest Festival Orchestra: Budapest, Lajos utca 48/66, C Building, Floor 5. *Telephone:* (1) 489-4330. *Fax:* (1) 355-4049. *E-mail:* bfofound@mail
.datanet.hu. *Website:* www.bfz.hu.

Budapest Philharmonic Orchestra: 1065 Budapest, Hajós utca 8–10. *Telephone:* (1) 331-9478. *Fax:* (1) 331-9478. *E-mail:* info@bpo.hu. *Website:* www.bpo.hu.

Hungarian National Philharmonic Orchestra: 1095 Budapest, Komor Marcell utca 1. *Telephone:* (1) 411-6600. *Fax:* (1) 411-6699. *E-mail:* info@
filharmonikusok.hu. *Website:* www.filharmonikusok.hu.

Hungarian Radio Symphony Orchestra: 1800 Budapest, Bródy Śndor utca 5–7. *Telephone:* (1) 328-7000. *Fax:* (1) 328-7332. *E-mail:* gonczzo@bartok
.radio.hu. *Website:* www.radio.hu. Also known as the Budapest Symphony Orchestra.

Iceland

Iceland Symphony Orchestra: Háskólabió v/Hagatorg, PO Box 7052, 127 Reykjavík. *Telephone:* 5452500. *Fax:* 5624475. *E-mail:* sinfonia@sinfonia.is. *Website:* www.sinfonia.is.

India

Symphony Orchestra of India: National Centre for the Performing Arts, NCPA Marg, Nariman Point, Mumbai 400 021. *Telephone:* (22) 66223729. *Fax:* (22) 22845350. *E-mail:* info@soimumbai.in. *Website:* www.soimumbai.in.

Indonesia

Jakarta Symphony Orchestra: Komplek Jatipadang Baru, Blok F No 1, Jakarta 12540. *Telephone:* (21) 7804910. *Fax:* (21) 78842848. *E-mail:* info@
thejakartasymphony.com. *Website:* www.thejakartasymphony.com.

Iran

Tehran Symphony Orchestra: c/o Vahdat Hall, Shahriar Street, Hafez Avenue, Tehran.

Ireland

Irish Chamber Orchestra: Foundation Building, University of Limerick, Castletroy, Limerick. *Telephone:* (61) 202620. *Fax:* (61) 202617. *E-mail:* ico@ul
.ie. *Website:* www.irishchamberorchestra.info.

Radio Telefis Éireann (RTÉ) Concert Orchestra: Radio Telefis Éireann, Administrative Building, Donnybrook, Dublin 4. *Telephone:* (1) 2082617. *Fax:* (1) 2082511. *Website:* www.rte.ie/music.

Radio Telefis Éireann (RTÉ) National Symphony Orchestra: National Concert Hall, Earlsfort Terrace, Dublin 2. *Telephone:* (1) 2082530. *Fax:* (1) 2082160. *E-mail:* info@nch.ie. *Website:* www.nch.ie.

Israel

Israel Chamber Orchestra: Jaffa Music Center, 10 She'erit Israel Street, Jaffa 68164. *Telephone:* 3-5188845. *Fax:* 3-5188846. *E-mail:* ico2000@
netvision.net.il. *Website:* www.ico.co.il.

Israel Philharmonic Orchestra: PO Box 23500, 1 Huberman Street, Tel-Aviv 61231. *Telephone:* 3-6293345. *Fax:* 3-6290097. *E-mail:* eli@ipo.co.il. *Website:* www.ipo.co.il. f. 1936.

Jerusalem Symphony Orchestra: PO Box 4640, Jerusalem 91040. *Telephone:* 2-5660211. *Fax:* 2-5671043. *E-mail:* info@jso.co.il. *Website:* www
.jso.co.il.

New Haifa Symphony Orchestra: *Telephone:* 4-8599499. *Fax:* 4-8330626. *E-mail:* info@haifasymphony.co.il. *Website:* www.haifasymphony.co.il.

Italy

I Solisti Veneti: Piazzale Pontecorvo 4/A, 35121 Padua. *Telephone:* (049) 666128. *Fax:* (49) 8752598. *E-mail:* info@solistiveneti.it. *Website:* www
.solistiveneti.it. f. 1959.

Orchestra della Toscana: Via Verdi 5, 50122 Florence. *Telephone:* (055) 2340710. *Fax:* (055) 2008035. *E-mail:* info@orchestradellatoscana.it. *Website:* www.orchestradellatoscana.it.

Orchestra dell'Accademia Nazionale di Santa Cecilia: Auditorium Parco della Musica, l.go Luciano Berio 3, 00196 Rome. *E-mail:* info@
santacecilia.it. *Website:* www.santacecilia.it.

Orchestra Sinfonica di Milano Giuseppe Verdi: Corso San Gottardo 39, 20136 Milan. *Telephone:* (011) 024950153. *Fax:* (011) 9590152. *E-mail:* amministrazione@laverdi.org. *Website:* www.laverdi.org. f. 1993.

Orchestra Sinfonica Nazionale della Radiotelevisione Italiana (RAI): Piazza Rossaro, 10124 Turin. *Telephone:* (011) 8104653. *Fax:* (011) 8104961. *E-mail:* info.osn@rai.it. *Website:* www.orchestrasinfonica.rai.it. f. 1994.

Japan

Japan Philharmonic Orchestra: 1-6-1 Umezato, Suginami-ku, Tokyo 166-0011. *Telephone:* (3) 5378-6311. *Fax:* (3) 5378-6161. *E-mail:* office@japanphil
.or.jp. *Website:* www.japanphil.or.jp.

Kanagawa Philharmonic Orchestra: Hanami-dai 4-2, Hodogaya-ku, Yokohama 240. *Telephone:* (45) 331-4001. *Fax:* (45) 331-4022. *Website:* www
.kanaphil.com.

Kyoto Symphony Orchestra: 1-26 Shimogamo Hangi-cho, Sakyo-ku, Kyoto 606-0823. *Telephone:* (75) 711-3110. *Fax:* (75) 711-2955. *Website:* www.city
.kyoto.jp/bunshi/symphony. f. 1956.

Nagoya Philharmonic Orchestra: Nagoya City Music Plaza 4F, 1-4-10 Kanayama, Naka-ku, Nagoya 460-0022. *Telephone:* (52) 322-2774. *Fax:* (52) 322-3066. *E-mail:* meiphil@nagoya-phil.or.jp. *Website:* www.nagoya-phil.or
.jp.

New Japan Philharmonic Orchestra: Sumida Triphony Hall, 1-2-3 Kinshi, Sumida-ku, Tokyo 130-0013. *Telephone:* (3) 5610-3820. *Fax:* (3) 5610-3825. *E-mail:* info@njp.or.jp. *Website:* www.njp.or.jp.

NHK Symphony Orchestra: 2-16-49 Takanawa, Minato-ku, Tokyo 108. *Telephone:* (3) 5793-8111. *Fax:* (3) 3443-0278. *Website:* www.nhkso.or.jp.

Formerly the Japan Symphony Orchestra; funded by the Japan Broadcasting Corporation (NHK).

Osaka Philharmonic Orchestra: 1-1-44 Kishinosato, Nishinari-ku, Osaka 557-0041. *Telephone:* (6) 6656-7701. *Fax:* (6) 6656-7714. *E-mail:* info@osaka -phil.com. *Website:* www.osaka-phil.com.

Saito Kinen Orchestra: 5F 3-8-13 Ohte, Matsumoto 390-0874. *Fax:* (2) 6334-3290. *Website:* www.saito-kinen.com.

Tokyo Metropolitan Symphony Orchestra: Tokyo Bunka Kaikan, 5-45 Ueno Park, Taito-ku, Tokyo 110-0007. *Telephone:* (3) 3822-0727. *Fax:* (3) 3822-0729. *E-mail:* tmsoinfo@tmso.or.jp. *Website:* www.tmso.or.jp.

Tokyo Philharmonic Orchestra: Tokyo Opera City Tower 8F, 3-20-2 Nishi Shinjuku, Shinjuku-ku, Tokyo 163-1408. *Telephone:* (3) 5353-9521. *Fax:* (3) 5353-9523. *E-mail:* info@tpo.or.jp. *Website:* www.tpo.or.jp.

Tokyo Symphony Orchestra: Muza Kawasaki Central Towe, Fifth Floor, 1310 Omiya-cho, Saiwai-ku, Kawasaki City, Kanagawa 212-8554. *Telephone:* (4) 4520-1518. *Fax:* (3) 3360-8249. *E-mail:* tokyosymphony@musicinfo.com. *Website:* www.tokyosymphony.com.

Yomiuri Nippon Symphony Orchestra: 7F Daiichi Nurihiko Bldg, 2-9-2 Kyobashi Chuo-ku, Tokyo 104-0031. *Telephone:* (3) 3562-1550. *Fax:* (3) 3562-1544. *Website:* yomikyo.or.jp.

Jordan

Orchestra of the National Music Conservatory: National Music Conservatory, Yarmouk University, POB 566, Irbid.

Republic of Korea

Korean Broadcasting System (KBS) Symphony Orchestra: 18 Yoido-dong, Youngdungpo-gu, Seoul 150-790. *Telephone:* (2)781-2241. *Fax:* (2)781-2249. *E-mail:* kbssymphony@kbs.co.kr. *Website:* kbsso.kbs.co.kr.

Seoul Philharmonic Orchestra: 81-3 Sejong-Ro, Chong Ro-Gu, Seoul 110-050. *Telephone:* (2) 6002-6290. *Fax:* (2) 6002-6292. *Website:* www .seoulphilharmonic.org.

Latvia

Latvian National Symphony Orchestra: 6 Amatu Street, Rīga 1664. *Telephone:* 6722-4850. *Fax:* 6722-4997. *E-mail:* secretary@lnso.lv. *Website:* www.music.lv/Orchestra.

Liepaja Symphony Orchestra: Graudu iela 50, Liepaja 3401. *Telephone:* 6342-5588. *Fax:* 6348-9269. *E-mail:* info@lso.lv. *Website:* www.orkestris -liepaja.lv.

New Chamber Orchestra of Rīga: *Telephone:* 7211-297. *Fax:* 7281-737. *E-mail:* chamberorchestra@music.lv. *Website:* www.music.lv/ chamberorchestra. f. 2000.

Liechtenstein

Symphonisches Orchester Liechtenstein: Zollstr. 9 / Dr Ernst Walch, 9490 Vaduz. *Telephone:* 2372000. *Fax:* 2372100.

Lithuania

Lietuvos Nacionalinis Simfoninis (Lithuanian National Symphony Orchestra): 5 Ausros Vartu g., Vilnius 01304. *Telephone:* (5) 266-5210. *Fax:* (5) 266-5266. *E-mail:* info@filharmonija.lt. *Website:* www.filharmonija.lt.

Lithuanian State Symphony Orchestra: Vilniausstr. 6/16, Vilnius 01102. *Telephone:* (5) 262-8825. *Fax:* (5) 212-0966. *E-mail:* akvile@lvso.lt. *Website:* www.lvso.lt.

Luxembourg

Orchestre Philharmonique du Luxembourg: PO Box 2243, 1022 Luxembourg. *Telephone:* 52-22-99-01. *Fax:* 52-22-99-98. *E-mail:* info@opl.lu. *Website:* www.opl.lu.

Macedonia

Makedonska Filharmonija (Macedonian Philharmonic Orchestra): 1000 Skopje, Bul. Makedonija b.b, p.f. 507. *Telephone:* (2) 3118450. *Fax:* (2) 3165753. *E-mail:* makfil@t-home.mk. *Website:* www.filharmonija.org.mk.

Malaysia

Malaysian Philharmonic Orchestra: Ground Floor, Tower 2, Petronas Twin Towers, 50088 Kuala Lumpur. *Telephone:* (3) 20517008. *Fax:* (3) 20517007. *E-mail:* dfp_contactus@petronas.com.my. *Website:* www.mpo.com .my.

Malta

Orkestra Nazzjonali (National Orchestra of Malta): 88 Old Mint Street, Valletta VLT 12. *Telephone:* 21244473. *Fax:* 21244473. *E-mail:* info@ maltaorchestra.com. *Website:* www.maltaorchestra.com.

Mexico

Orquesta Filarmónica de Jalisco (Jalisco Philharmonic Orchestra): Altos del Teatro Degollado, Colonia Centro, 44100 Guadalajara, Jalisco. *Telephone:* (33) 3030-9772. *Fax:* (33) 3030-9772. *E-mail:* info@ofj.com.mx. *Website:* www.ofj.com.mx.

Orquesta Filarmónica de la Ciudad de México (Mexico City Philharmonic Orchestra): Sala Silvestre Revueltas del Centro Cultural Ollin Yolitzli, Periferico Sur 5141, Col. Isidro Fabela, 14030 Mé, DF. *Telephone:* (55) 5606-4583. *Fax:* (55) 5606-4583. *E-mail:* filarmex@prodigy.net.mx. *Website:* www.cultura.df.gob.mx.

Orquesta Sinfónica del Estado de México (Mexico Symphony Orchestra): Villada 406, primer piso, Colonia Centro Toluca, México, DF. *Telephone:* (72) 2214-4684. *Fax:* (72) 2214-5219. *E-mail:* osem@edomex.gob.mx. *Website:* www.edomex.gob.mx.

Orquesta Sinfónica Nacional de México (Mexico National Symphonic Orchestra): Regina 52, segundo piso, Colonia Centro, 06080 Mé, DF. *Telephone:* (55) 5709-8118. *Fax:* (55) 5709-3533. *E-mail:* osn@correo.inba.gob .mx. *Website:* www.osn.bellasartes.gob.mx.

Moldova

National Philharmonic Orchestra of Moldova: 2012 Chişinău, str. Metropolit Varlaam 78. *Telephone:* (22) 22-61-91. *Fax:* (22) 22-82-93. *E-mail:* simphony@moldovacc.md.

Monaco

Orchestre Philharmonique de Monte Carlo: Auditorium Rainier III, Boulevardd Louis II, BP 197, Monte Carlo 98004. *Telephone:* 93-10-85-00. *Fax:* 93-15-08-71. *E-mail:* info@opmc.mc. *Website:* www.opmc.mc.

Morocco

Orchestre Philharmonique du Maroc: Théâtre Royal, Guéliz, 40000 Marrakesh. *Website:* www.opm.ma. f. 1996.

The Netherlands

Koninklijk Concertgebouworkest: PO Box 78098, 1070 LP Amsterdam. *Telephone:* (20) 3051010. *Fax:* (20) 3051001. *E-mail:* info@ concertgebouworkest.nl. *Website:* www.concertgebouworkest.nl.

Nederlands Philharmonisch Orkest: Beurs van Berlage, Damrak 213, 1012 ZH Amsterdam. *Telephone:* (20) 5217500. *Fax:* (20) 5217501. *E-mail:* info@nedpho.nl. *Website:* www.orkest.nl.

Residentie Orkest (Hague Philharmonic): PO Box 11543, 2502 AM The Hague. *Telephone:* (70) 8800200. *E-mail:* info@residentieorkest.nl. *Website:* www.residentieorkest.nl.

Rotterdams Philharmonisch Orkest: PO Box 962, 3000 AZ Rotterdam. *Telephone:* (10) 2171717. *Fax:* (10) 4116215. *E-mail:* info@rpho.nl. *Website:* www.rpho.nl.

New Zealand

Auckland Philharmonia Orchestra: PO Box 56-024, Dominion Road, Auckland 1446. *Telephone:* (9) 623-1052. *Fax:* (9) 630-9687. *E-mail:* ap@ aucklandphil.co.nz. *Website:* www.apo.co.nz.

Christchurch Symphony Orchestra: 47 Hereford Street, PO Box 3260, Christchurch. *Telephone:* (3) 379-3886. *Fax:* (3) 379-3861. *E-mail:* office@ christchurchsymphony.co.nz. *Website:* www.christchurchsymphony.co.nz.

New Zealand Symphony Orchestra: Level 2, 101 Wakefield Street, PO Box 6640, Wellington 6001. *Telephone:* (4) 801-3890. *Fax:* (4) 801-3891. *E-mail:* info@nzso.co.nz. *Website:* www.nzso.co.nz.

Wellington Orchestra: PO Box 11-977, Wellington 6142. *Telephone:* (4) 801-3882. *Fax:* (4) 801-3888. *E-mail:* admin@wellingtonorchestra.co.nz. *Website:* www.wellingtonsinfonia.co.nz.

Norway

Bergen Filharmoniske Orkester: Stiftelsen Harmonien, Edvard Griegs-plass 1, 5015 Bergen. *Telephone:* 55-21-61-00. *Fax:* 55-31-85-34. *E-mail:* post@ harmonien.no. *Website:* www.filharmonien.no. f. 1765; international and national tours.

Det Norsk Kammerorkester (Norwegian Chamber Orchestra): Kongensgate 4, 0153 Oslo. *Telephone:* 24-05-55-50. *Fax:* 24-05-55-51. *E-mail:* adm@kammerorkesteret.no. *Website:* www.detnorskekammerorkester.no. f. 1975.

Filharmonien Oslo: Postboks 1607, Vika, 0119 Oslo. *Telephone:* 22-01-49-00. *Fax:* 22-01-49-01. *E-mail:* administrasjon@oslofilharmonien.no. *Website:* www.oslophil.com.

Stavanger Symfoniorkester: Sandvigå 27, Bjergsted, 4007 Stavanger. *Telephone:* 51-50-88-30. *Fax:* 51-50-88-39. *E-mail:* post@sso.no. *Website:* www .sso.no.

Trondheim Symfoniorkester: Postboks 774 Sentrum, 7408 Trondheim. *Telephone:* 73-53-98-00. *Fax:* 73-53-98-01. *E-mail:* post@tso.no. *Website:* www.tso.no.

Oman

Royal Oman Symphony Orchestra: c/o Oman Auditorium, al-Bustan Palace InterContinental Muscat, PO Box 1998, Postal Code 114, Muscat. *Telephone:* (24) 799 666. *E-mail:* boxoffice@albustanpalace.com. f. 1985.

Panama

Orquesta Sinfónica Nacional: Apto 9190, Panama City 6.

Paraguay

Orquesta Sinfónica de la Ciudad de Asunción: Estación Ferrocarril Pdte. Carlos A. López, Eligio Ayala 571 con Mexico, Asunción. *Telephone:* (21) 49-2416. *E-mail:* sfa@pol.com.py. *Website:* www.sfa.org.py.

Peru

Orquesta Sinfónica Nacional: Avenida Javier Prado Este 2465, San Borja, Lima 41. *Telephone:* (1) 2258882. *Fax:* (1) 2258882. *E-mail:* sinfonicaperu@inc.gob.pe.

The Philippines

Manila Symphony Orchestra: c/o St Scholastica's College, 1560 Leon Guinto Street, Malate, Manila. *Telephone:* (2) 889 1900. *Fax:* (2) 793 2162. *E-mail:* manilasymphonyorchestra@gmail.com.

Philippine Philharmonic Orchestra: Lower Basement, Cultural Centre of The Philippines, Roxas Boulevard, Pasay City, Manila. *Telephone:* (2) 8321125. *Fax:* (2) 8323683. *E-mail:* ppo@culturalcenter.gov.ph. *Website:* www.culturalcenter.gov.ph. f. 1973.

Poland

Filharmonia im. Karola Szymanowskiego w Krakowie (Karola Szymanowskiego Kraków Philharmonic Orchestra): 31-103 Kraków, Ul. Zwierzyniecka 1. *Telephone:* (12) 4229477. *Fax:* (12) 4291438. *E-mail:* sekretariat@filharmonia.krakow.pl. *Website:* www.filharmonia.krakow.pl.

Filharmonia Narodowa (National Philharmonic Orchestra): 00-950 Warsaw, ul. Jasna 5. *Telephone:* (22) 5517111. *Fax:* (22) 5517200. *E-mail:* filharmonia@filharmonia.pl. *Website:* www.filharmonia.pl.

Filharmonia Poznańska im. Tadeusza Szeligosdkiego (Tadeusz Szeligowski Poznań Philharmonic Orchestra): 61-808 Poznań, ul. Św. Marcin 81. *Telephone:* (61) 8524708. *Fax:* (61) 8523451. *E-mail:* sekretariat@filharmoniapoznanska.pl. *Website:* www.filharmoniapoznanska.pl.

Filharmonia Wrocławska (Wrocław Philharmonic Orchestra): 50-044 Wrocław, Ul. Marszalka Józefa Pilsudskiego 19. *Telephone:* (71) 3422001. *Fax:* (71) 3422002. *E-mail:* office@filharmonia.wroclaw.pl. *Website:* www.filharmonia.wroclaw.pl.

Narodowa Orkiestra Symfoniczna Polskiego Radia w Katowicach (National Polish Radio Symphony Orchestra): 40-032 Katowice, Plac Sejmu Ślajskiego 2. *Telephone:* (32) 2518903. *Fax:* (32) 2571384. *E-mail:* nospr@nospr.org.pl. *Website:* www.nospr.org.pl.

Portugal

Orquestra Gulbenkian: Fundação Calouste Gulbenkian, Serviço de Música, Avda de Berna 45a, 1067-001 Lisbon. *Telephone:* (21) 7823000. *Fax:* (21) 7823021. *E-mail:* musica@gulbenkian.pt. *Website:* www.gulbenkian.pt.

Orquestra Nacional do Porto: Casa da Música, Avenida Boavista 604-610, 4149-071, Porto. *Telephone:* (22) 0120200. *E-mail:* info@casadamusica.com. *Website:* www.casadamusica.com. f. 1997.

Orquestra Sinfónica Portuguesa: c/o Teatro Nacional de São Carlos, Rua de Serpa Pinto 9, 1200-442 Lisbon. *Telephone:* (21) 3253000. *Fax:* (21) 3253083. *E-mail:* geral@saocarlos.pt. *Website:* www.saocarlos.pt. f. 1993.

Romania

Radio Romania National Orchestra: Bucharest 1, str. General Berthelot nr. 60-64. *Telephone:* (21) 3190512. *Fax:* (21) 3190563. *E-mail:* fmuzicale@radio.rornet.ro. *Website:* rchestre.srr.ro.

Bucharest State Philharmonic Orchestra George Enescu: Bucharest 1, Ateneul Roman, Franklin Str 1-3. *Telephone:* (21) 3152567. *Fax:* (21) 3122983. *E-mail:* info@fge.org.ro. *Website:* www.fge.org.ro.

Iaşi State Philharmonic Orchestra: 700037 Iaşi, Str Cuza Voda 29. *Telephone:* (232) 314601. *Fax:* (232) 214160. *E-mail:* secretary@filarmonicais.ro. *Website:* www.filarmonicais.ro.

Russia

Bolshoi Orchestra: 103009 Moscow, Teatralnaya pl. 1. *Telephone:* (495) 292-08-18. *Fax:* (495) 292-33-67. *E-mail:* pr@bolshoi.ru. *Website:* www.bolshoi.ru.

Mariinsky Theatre Orchestra: 190000 St Petersburg, Teatralnaya pl. 1. *Telephone:* (812) 326-41-41. *Fax:* (812) 314-17-44. *E-mail:* post@mariinsky.ru. *Website:* www.mariinsky.ru.

Radio and Television Symphony Orchestra: 12812 Moscow, 24 Malaya Nikitskaya. *Telephone:* (495) 290-05-01. *Fax:* (495) 573-61-75. *E-mail:* letter@rtvsymphony.ru. *Website:* www.rtvsymphony.ru.

Russian Symphony Orchestra: 105264 Moscow, 9 Parkovaia, 37/51. *Telephone:* (495) 179-01-70. *Fax:* (495) 179-01-70. *E-mail:* symor_orch@mail.ru. *Website:* www.symor.ru.

Russian State Philharmonic Orchestra: 129075 Moscow, 18 Murmansky Proezd, App 77. *Telephone:* (495) 233-89-96.

Saint Petersburg Philharmonic Orchestra: 219011 Saint Petersburg, Grand Hall, Mikhailovskaya str. 2. *Telephone:* (812) 312-98-71. *Fax:* (812) 571-21-26. *E-mail:* mail@philharmonia.spb.ru. *Website:* www.philharmonia.spb.ru.

Serbia

Belgrade Philharmonic Orchestra: 11000 Belgrade, Studentski trg 11. *Telephone:* (11) 3282977. *Fax:* (11) 2187533. *E-mail:* office@bgf.co.rs. *Website:* www.bgf.co.rs. f. 1923.

Singapore

Singapore Symphony Orchestra: 11 Empress Place, Second Floor, Victoria Memorial Hall, Singapore 179558. *Telephone:* 63381230. *Fax:* 63366382. *E-mail:* ssonet@singnet.com.sg. *Website:* www.sso.org.sg.

Slovakia

Slovak Radio Symphony Orchestra: Mýtna 1, PO Box 55, 817 55 Bratislava 15. *Telephone:* (7) 5727-3475. *Fax:* (7) 5727-3386. *Website:* www.slovakradio.sk/sosr.

Slovenská Filharmónia (Slovakian Philharmonic Orchestra): 816 01 Bratislava. *E-mail:* schoeferova@filharmonia.sk. *Website:* www.filharm.sk.

Slovenia

Slovenska filharmonija (Slovenian Philharmonic Orchestra): 1000 Ljubljana, Kongresni trg 10. *Telephone:* (1) 2410800. *Fax:* (1) 2410900. *E-mail:* info@filharmonija.si. *Website:* www.filharmonija.si.

South Africa

Cape Philharmonic Orchestra: PO Box 4040, Cape Town 8000. *Telephone:* (21) 4109809. *Fax:* (21) 4251009. *E-mail:* ivan@cpo.org.za. *Website:* www.cpo.org.za.

Johannesburg Philharmonic Orchestra: SAMET House, 18 Evelyn Street, Bordeaux, Randburg, Johannesburg. *Telephone:* (11) 7892733. *Fax:* (11) 7897256. *E-mail:* info@jpo.co.za. *Website:* www.jpo.co.za.

KwaZulu-Natal (KZN) Philharmonic Orchestra: PO Box 5353, Durban 4000. *Telephone:* (31) 3699438. *Fax:* (31) 3699403. *E-mail:* kznpo@kznpo.co.za. *Website:* www.kznpo.co.za.

Spain

Orquesta Nacional de España: Príncipe de Vergara 146, 28002 Madrid. *Telephone:* (91) 3370140. *Fax:* (91) 5632907. *Website:* ocne.mcu.es.

Orquesta Sinfónica de Barcelona i Nacional de Catalunya (OBC): Lepant 150, 08013 Barcelona. *Telephone:* (93) 2479300. *Fax:* (93) 2479301. *E-mail:* informacio.obc@auditori.cat. *Website:* www.obc.es.

Orquesta Sinfónica de Euskadi (Basque National Symphony Orchestra): Miramon Pasealekua 124, 20014 San Sebastián. *Telephone:* (943) 013232. *Fax:* (943) 308324. *E-mail:* medios@orquestadeeuskadi.es. *Website:* www.orquestadeeuskadi.es.

Orquesta Sinfónica de Radiotelevisión Española (RTVE): Avenida Radio Televisión 4, Edificio Prado del Rey, Planta 2a Despacho 2/072, 28223 Pozuelo de Alarcón, Madrid. *Telephone:* (91) 5817211. *Website:* www.rtve.es/oficial/orquesta-coro.

Sri Lanka

Symphony Orchestra of Sri Lanka: c/o Administrative Officer SOSL, 83 Dickman's Road, Colombo 5. *Telephone:* (11) 2501209. *E-mail:* soslnet@yahoo.com. *Website:* www.symphonyorchestraofsrilanka.org.

Sweden

Göteborgs Symfoniker: Götaplatsen, 412 56 Göteborg. *Telephone:* (3) 172-653-00. *Fax:* (3) 172-653-70. *E-mail:* info@gso.se. *Website:* www.gso.se. The national orchestra of Sweden.

Kungliga Filharmonikerna: Stockholms Konserthus, Hötorget 8, Box 7083, 103 87 Stockholm. *Telephone:* (8) 786-02-00. *E-mail:* info@konserthuset.se. *Website:* www.konserthuset.se.

Malmö SymfoniOrkester: Konserthuset, 205 80 Malmö. *Telephone:* (40) 630-45-00. *Fax:* (40) 611-75-05. *E-mail:* info@mso.se. *Website:* www.mso.se.

Sveriges Radio Symfoniorkester: Berwaldhallen, Dag Hammarskjölds väg 3, 105 10 Stockholm. *Telephone:* (8) 784-50-00. *Fax:* (8) 662-58-45. *E-mail:* michael.tyden@sr.se. *Website:* www.sr.se/berwaldhallen.

Switzerland

Berner Symphonie Orchester: Münzgraben 2 (4 Stock), 3000 Bern. *Telephone:* 313282424. *Fax:* 313282425. *E-mail:* info@bernorchester.ch. *Website:* www.bernorchester.ch.

Orchestre de la Suisse Romande: Place du Cirque 2, 1205 Geneva. *Telephone:* 228070000. *Fax:* 228070018. *E-mail:* music@osr.ch. *Website:* www.osr.ch.

Sinfonieorchester Basel: Steinenberg 14, 4051 Basel. *Telephone:* 612050095. *Fax:* 612050099. *E-mail:* info@sinfonieorchesterbasel.ch. *Website:* www.sinfonieorchesterbasel.ch.

Symphonisches Orchester Zürich: Hallwylstr. 78, 8004 Zürich. *Telephone:* 444624440. *Fax:* 444624442. *E-mail:* info@s-o-z.ch. *Website:* www.s-o-z.ch.

Syria

Syrian National Symphony Orchestra: PO Box 6645, Damascus. *Telephone:* (11) 2230447. *Fax:* (11) 2245054. *E-mail:* info@syriansymphony.org. *Website:* www.syriansymphony.org. f. 1994.

Taiwan

National Taiwan Symphony Orchestra: 738-2 Zhongzheng Road, Wu-Feng, Taichung 413. *Telephone:* (4) 23391141. *Fax:* (4) 23399072. *E-mail:* chief@ntso.gov.tw. *Website:* www.ntso.gov.tw. f. 1945.

Thailand

Bangkok Symphony Orchestra: Nai Lert Tower 48, 3rd Floor, 2/4 Wireless Road, Lumpini, Pathumwan, Bangkok 10330. *Telephone:* (2) 255-6617. *Fax:* (2) 255-6619. *E-mail:* wbsof@bangkoksymphony.org. *Website:* www.bangkoksymphony.org.

Siam Philharmonic Orchestra: c/o Bangkok Opera, Fenix Tower, 10th Floor, 571 Sukhumvit Road, Bangkok 10110. *Telephone:* (2) 259-7183. *Fax:* (2) 662-3416. *E-mail:* somtow@mindspring.com. *Website:* www.siamphilharmonic.com. f. 2002 as the Mifa Sinfonietta; renamed Bangkok Sinfonietta 2003, then as above 2004; resident orchestra of Bangkok Opera.

Turkey

İstanbul State Symphony Orchestra: Haci Hesna Hatun Mah, Eski Tekel Binasi 66, Paşalimani-Üsküdar, İstanbul. *Telephone:* (216) 4958200. *Fax:* (216) 4958200. *E-mail:* info@idso.gov.tr. *Website:* www.idso.gov.tr.

Presidential Symphony Orchestra: Talatpasa Bulvari 38A, 06330 Ankara. *Telephone:* (312) 3091343. *Fax:* (312) 3117548. *E-mail:* 1826cso@gmail.com. *Website:* www.cso.gov.tr.

Ukraine

Kharkiv Philharmonic Orchestra: 61057 Kharkiv, Rimskaja 21. *Telephone:* (57) 705-08-57. *E-mail:* dir@filarmonia.kharkov.ua. *Website:* www.filarmonia.kharkov.ua.

National Symphony Orchestra of Ukraine: 252001 Kyiv, Volodymyrskiy Uzviz 2. *Telephone:* (44) 229-68-42. *Fax:* (44) 229-68-42. f. 1937 as the Ukrainian State Symphony Orchestra.

National Philharmonia of Ukraine: 01001 Kyiv, 2 Volodymyrskyi uzviz. *Telephone:* (44) 279-62-51. *Fax:* (44) 278-03-30. *E-mail:* philarmonia@ukrpost.ua. *Website:* www.filarmonia.com.ua.

Odesa Philharmonic Orchestra: 65026 Odesa, 15 R. Vul. I. Bunina. *Telephone:* (48) 222-63-49. *Fax:* (48) 222-63-49. *E-mail:* info@odessaphilharmonic.org. *Website:* www.odessaphilharmonic.org.

United Kingdom

BBC Orchestras: *Website:* www.bbc.co.uk/orchestras. These include the BBC Philharmonic Orchestra, BBC Symphony Orchestra and Chorus, BBC National Orchestra and Chorus of Wales, BBC Concert Orchestra, and BBC Scottish Symphony Orchestra.

Hallé Orchestra: The Bridgewater Hall, Manchester, M1 5HA, England. *Telephone:* (161) 237-7000. *E-mail:* info@halle.co.uk. *Website:* www.halle.co.uk.

London Philharmonic Orchestra: 89 Albert Embankment, London, SE1 7TP, England. *Telephone:* (20) 7840-4200. *Fax:* (20) 7840-4201. *E-mail:* admin@lpo.org.uk. *Website:* www.lpo.co.uk.

London Symphony Orchestra: Barbican Centre, Sixth Floor, Silk Street, London, EC2Y 8DS, England. *Telephone:* (20) 7588-1116. *Fax:* (20) 7374-0127. *E-mail:* admin@lso.co.uk. *Website:* www.lso.co.uk.

Northern Sinfonia: The Sage Gateshead, St Mary's Square, Gateshead Quays, Gateshead, NE8 2JR, England. *Telephone:* (191) 443-4661. *Fax:* (191) 443-4551. *E-mail:* exploremusic@gateshead.gov.uk. *Website:* www.thesagegateshead.org/sinfonia.

Royal Liverpool Philharmonic: Philharmonic Hall, Hope Street, Liverpool, L1 9BP, England. *Telephone:* (151) 210-2895. *Fax:* (151) 210-2902. *E-mail:* info@liverpoolphil.com. *Website:* www.liverpoolphil.com.

Royal Philharmonic Orchestra: 16 Clerkenwell Green, London, EC1R 0QT, England. *Telephone:* (20) 7608-8800. *Fax:* (20) 7608-8801. *E-mail:* info@rpo.co.uk. *Website:* www.rpo.co.uk. Resident at Cadogan Hall, London SW1.

Royal Scottish National Orchestra: 73 Claremont Street, Glasgow, G3 7JB, Scotland. *Telephone:* (141) 226-3868. *Fax:* (141) 221-4317. *E-mail:* info@rsno.org.uk. *Website:* www.rsno.org.uk.

Ulster Orchestra: Elmwood Hall at Queen's University, 89 University Road, Belfast, BT7 7FF, Northern Ireland. *Telephone:* (28) 9023-9900. *Fax:* (28) 9026-0483. *E-mail:* info@ulsterorchestra.com. *Website:* www.ulster-orchestra.org.uk.

United States of America

Boston Symphony Orchestra: Symphony Hall, 301 Massachusetts Avenue, Boston, MA 02115. *Telephone:* (617) 266-1492. *Fax:* (617) 638-9367. *Website:* www.bso.org. Also the Boston Pops Orchestra.

Chicago Symphony Orchestra: Symphony Center, 220 South Michigan Avenue, Chicago, IL 60604. *Telephone:* (312) 294-3000. *Fax:* (312) 294-3035. *Website:* www.cso.org.

The Cleveland Orchestra: Severance Hall, 11001 Euclid Avenue, Cleveland, OH 44106-1796. *Telephone:* (216) 231-7300. *Fax:* (216) 231-0202. *E-mail:* info@clevelandorchestra.com. *Website:* www.clevelandorchestra.com.

Dallas Symphony Orchestra: 2301 Flora Street, Dallas, TX 75201. *Telephone:* (214) 871-4000. *E-mail:* customerservice@dalsym.com. *Website:* www.dallassymphony.com.

Houston Symphony: 615 Louisiana Street, Suite 102, Houston, TX 77002. *Telephone:* (713) 224-4240. *Fax:* (713) 222-7024. *E-mail:* office@houstonsymphony.org. *Website:* www.houstonsymphony.org.

Los Angeles Philharmonic Orchestra: 111 South Grand Avenue, Los Angeles, CA 90012. *Telephone:* (323) 850-2000. *Website:* www.laphil.org. Resident at the Walt Disney Concert Hall.

Metropolitan Opera Orchestra: Lincoln Center, New York, NY 10023. *Telephone:* (212) 799-3100. *Website:* www.metoperafamily.org.

National Symphony Orchestra: John F. Kennedy Center for the Performing Arts, 2700 F Street NW, Washington, DC 20566. *Telephone:* (202) 416-8000. *Fax:* (202) 416-8105. *Website:* www.kennedy-center.org/nso.

New York Philharmonic: Avery Fisher Hall, 10 Lincoln Center Plaza, New York, NY 10023-6970. *Telephone:* (212) 875-5900. *Fax:* (212) 875-5717. *E-mail:* customerservice@nyphil.org. *Website:* www.newyorkphilharmonic.org.

The Philadelphia Orchestra: 260 South Broad Street, Suite 1600, Philadelphia, PA 19102. *Telephone:* (215) 893-1900. *Fax:* (215) 893-7649. *E-mail:* philadelphia_orchestra@philadelphiaorchestra.org. *Website:* www.philorch.org.

Saint Louis Symphony Orchestra: Powell Symphony Hall, 718 North Grand Boulevard, Saint Louis, MO 63103. *Telephone:* (314) 533-2500. *Fax:* (314) 286-4111. *E-mail:* pr@slso.org. *Website:* www.slso.org.

San Francisco Symphony: Davies Symphony Hall, 201 Van Ness Avenue, San Francisco, CA 94102. *Telephone:* (415) 552-8000. *Fax:* (415) 431-6857. *E-mail:* publicrelations@sfsymphony.org. *Website:* www.sfsymphony.org.

Uruguay

Orquesta Filarmónica de Montevideo: Bacacay 1325, CP 11000, Montevideo. *Telephone:* (2) 9154167. *E-mail:* filarmonica@filarmonica.org.uy. *Website:* www.filarmonica.org.uy.

Venezuela

Orquesta Sinfónica Municipal de Caracas: Avda Guaicaipuro, Edif. YMCA, PB, San Bernardino, Caracas 1010. *Telephone:* (212) 550-0522. *Fax:* (212) 550-0767. *E-mail:* sinfonicamunicipal@sinfonicamunicipal.org.ve. *Website:* www.sinfonicamunicipal.org.ve.

Viet Nam

Hanoi Philharmonic Orchestra: c/o Hanoi Opera House, 1 Pho Trang Thi, Hanoi. *Telephone:* (4) 8515799. *Fax:* (4) 8513545. *E-mail:* nhacvienhn@netnam.vn.

Viet Nam National Symphony Orchestra: 226 Cau Giay, Hanoi. *Telephone:* (4) 38331448. *Fax:* (4) 38334968. *E-mail:* dnghvn@hn.vnn.vn. *Website:* www.vnso.org.vn.

APPENDIX B: OPERA COMPANIES

Argentina

Buenos Aires Lírica: Talcuahuano 833, 6° E, C1013AAQ Buenos Aires. *Telephone:* (11) 4812-6369. *Fax:* (11) 4813-0651. *E-mail:* recepcion@balirica .org.ar. *Website:* www.balirica.org.ar.

Teatro Colón: Cerrito 618, 1010 Buenos Aires. *Telephone:* (11) 4378-7344. *Fax:* (11) 4378-7305. *E-mail:* informaciones@teatrocolon.org.ar. *Website:* www .teatrocolon.org.ar.

Armenia

Spendiaryan State Academic Opera and Ballet Theatre: Yerevan, 54 Toumanian Str. *Telephone:* (10) 52-02-41. *Fax:* (10) 52-02-41. *E-mail:* info@ opera.am. *Website:* www.opera.am. Opened 1933.

Australia

Melbourne Opera Company Ltd: PO Box 174, Collins Street West, Melbourne, Vic. 8007. *Telephone:* (3) 9614-4188. *Fax:* (3) 9620-3831. *E-mail:* info@melbourneopera.com. *Website:* www.melbourneopera.com. f. 2002; tours Victoria.

Opera Australia: The Opera Centre Sydney, 480 Elizabeth Street, Surry Hills NSW 2010. *Telephone:* (2) 9699-1099. *Fax:* (2) 9699-3184. *E-mail:* enquiries@opera-australia.org.au. *Website:* www.opera-australia.org.au. Performances at Sydney Opera House and Melbourne Arts Theatre.

Opera Queensland: PO Box 3677, South Brisbane, Qld 4101. *Telephone:* (7) 3735-3030. *Fax:* (7) 3844-5352. *E-mail:* info@operaqueensland.com.au. *Website:* www.operaqld.org.au.

State Opera of South Australia: Adelaide Festival Centre, PO Box 211, Marleston, SA 5033. *Telephone:* (8) 8226-4790. *Fax:* (8) 8226-4791. *E-mail:* info@saopera.sa.gov.au. *Website:* www.saopera.sa.gov.au.

Stopera: GPO Box 2481, Canberra, ACT 2601. *Telephone:* (2) 6232-4082. *Fax:* (2) 6282-0674. *E-mail:* info@stopera.org.au. *Website:* www.stopera.org.au. Chamber opera company; performs at Street Theatre, Canberra and elsewhere.

West Australian Opera: His Majesty's Theatre, 825 Hay Street, Perth, WA 6850. *Telephone:* (8) 9278-8999. *Fax:* (8) 9324-1134. *E-mail:* administration@ waopera.asn.au. *Website:* www.waopera.asn.au.

Austria

Grazer Oper: Theaterkasse am Kaiser-Josef-Platz 10, 8010 Graz. *Telephone:* (316) 80-00. *Fax:* (316) 80-08. *E-mail:* oper@oper-graz.com. *Website:* www .theater-graz.com.

Volksoper Wien: Währingerstrasse 78, 1090 Vienna. *Telephone:* (1) 514-44-36-70. *E-mail:* office@volksoper.at. *Website:* www.volksoper.at.

Wiener Kammeroper (Vienna Chamber Opera): Fleischmarkt 24, 1010 Vienna. *Telephone:* (1) 512-01-00-77. *Fax:* (1) 512-01-00-70. *E-mail:* information@wienerkammeroper.at. *Website:* www.wienerkammeroper.at.

Wiener Staatsoper (Vienna State Opera): Opernring 2, 1010 Vienna. *Telephone:* (1) 514-44-22-50. *E-mail:* information@wiener-staatsoper.at. *Website:* www.wiener-staatsoper.at.

Azerbaijan

Azerbaijan State Theatre of Opera and Ballet: c/o Ministry of Culture and Tourism, 1000 Baku, Azadliq meydani 1, House of Government, 3rd Floor. *Telephone:* (12) 493-43-98. *Fax:* (12) 493-56-05. *E-mail:* info@mct.gov.az. *Website:* www.mct.gov.az.

Belarus

National Academic Opera and Ballet: 220029 Minsk, 1 Parizhskaya Kommuna Square. *Telephone:* (17) 334-10-41. *Fax:* (17) 334-07-72. *E-mail:* belarus_opera@tut.by. *Website:* www.belarusopera.com.

Belgium

Opéra Royal de Wallonie: 1 rue des Dominicains, 4000 Liège. *Telephone:* (4) 221-47-22. *Fax:* (4) 221-02-01. *E-mail:* accueil@orwbe. *Website:* www.orw.be.

Théâtre Royal de la Monnaie: 4 rue Léopold, 1000 Brussels. *Telephone:* (2) 229-12-00. *Fax:* (2) 229-13-30. *E-mail:* info@lamonnaie.be. *Website:* www .lamonnaie.be.

Vlaamse Opera: Van Ertbornstraat 8, 2018 Antwerp. *Telephone:* (3) 202-10-11. *Fax:* (3) 231-07-85. *E-mail:* info@vlaamseopera.be. *Website:* www .vlaamseopera.be.

Bosnia and Herzegovina

National Theater Opera: 71000 Sarajevo, Obala Kulina Bana 9. *Telephone:* (33) 663647. *Fax:* (33) 445138.

Brazil

Theatro Municipal: Praça Floriano s/n, Centro, 20031-050 Rio de Janeiro, RJ. *Telephone:* (21) 2299-1711. *E-mail:* contato@theatromunicipal.rj.gov.br. *Website:* www.theatromunicipal.rj.gov.br.

Bulgaria

National Opera: 1000 Sofia, 30 Dondoukov Blvd. *Telephone:* (2) 98-77-01-1. *Fax:* (2) 98-77-99-8. *E-mail:* office@operasofia.bg. *Website:* www.operasofia.bg.

Canada

Calgary Opera Association: Arrata Opera Centre, 1315-7 Street SW, Calgary, AB T2R 1A5. *Telephone:* (403) 262-7286. *Fax:* (403) 263-5428. *E-mail:* info@calgaryopera.com. *Website:* www.calgaryopera.com.

Canadian Opera Company: 227 Front Street East, Toronto, ON M5A 1E8. *Telephone:* (416) 363-6671. *Fax:* (416) 363-5584. *E-mail:* info@coc.ca. *Website:* www.coc.ca.

Edmonton Opera Association: Francis Winspear Centre for Music, 9720-102 Avenue NW, Edmonton, AB T5J 4B2. *Telephone:* (780) 424-4040. *Fax:* (780) 429-0600. *E-mail:* edmopera@edmontonopera.com. *Website:* www .edmontonopera.com.

Manitoba Opera: Room 1060, 555 Main Street, Winnipeg, MB R3B 1C3. *Telephone:* (204) 942-7479. *Fax:* (204) 949-0377. *E-mail:* mbopera@ manitobaopera.mb.ca. *Website:* www.manitobaopera.mb.ca.

L'Opéra de Montréal: 260 boulevard de Maisonneuve Ouest, Montréal, QC H2X 1Y9. *Telephone:* (514) 985-2222. *Fax:* (514) 985-2219. *E-mail:* info@ operademontreal.com. *Website:* www.operademontreal.com.

Opéra de Québec: 1220 Avenue Taché, Québec, QC G1R 3B4. *Telephone:* (418) 529-4142. *Fax:* (418) 529-3735. *E-mail:* operaqc@mediom.qc.ca. *Website:* www.operadequebec.qc.ca.

Opera Ontario Inc.: Opera Hamilton, 69 Hughson Street North, Hamilton, ON L8R 1G5. *Telephone:* (905) 527-7627. *Fax:* (905) 527-0014. *E-mail:* info@ operaontario.com. *Website:* www.operaontario.com.

Pacific Opera Victoria: 1815 Blanshard Street, Suite 500, Victoria, BC V8T 5A4. *Telephone:* (250) 382-1641. *Fax:* (250) 382-4944. *Website:* www.pov.bc.ca.

Royal Opera Canada: 43 Cheltenham Avenue, Toronto, ON M4N 1P6. *Telephone:* (416) 322-0456. *Fax:* (416) 482-7044. *E-mail:* info@ royaloperacanada.com. *Website:* www.royaloperacanada.com.

Vancouver Opera: 835 Cambie Street, Vancouver, BC V6B 2P4. *Telephone:* (604) 682-2871. *Fax:* (604) 682-3981. *E-mail:* tickets@vancouveropera.ca. *Website:* www.vancouveropera.ca.

Chile

Opera del Teatro Municipal: Agustinas 794, Casilla 18, Santiago 6500771. *Telephone:* (2) 463-1000. *Fax:* (2) 463-1008. *E-mail:* contacto@ municipalsantiago.cl. *Website:* www.municipal.cl.

The People's Republic of China

Beijing Opera: Haihu West Lane No. 30, Fengtai District, Beijing 100077. *Telephone:* (10) 67227775. *Fax:* (10) 67541215. *E-mail:* huangye@public.bta .net.cn. Also known as Peking Opera.

Shanghai Opera Theatre: No. 10 Lane 100, Changshu Road, Shanghai 200040. *Telephone:* (21) 62485359. *Fax:* (21) 62498127. f. 1956.

Colombia

Opera de Colombia: Teatro de Cristóbal Colón, Calle 10 No. 5-32, Bogotá. *Telephone:* (1) 2847420. *Fax:* (1) 2846245. *E-mail:* operadecolombia@cable.net .co.

Costa Rica

Compañía Lírica Nacional: Teatro Popular Melico Salazar, 3er Piso, Avenida Segunda, Calles Central y Dos, San José 1035-1000. *Telephone:* 2233-5424. *Fax:* 2233-5387. *E-mail:* proartes@teatromelico.go.cr. *Website:* www .teatromelico.go.cr.

Croatia

Hrvatsko Narodno Kazalište u Zagrebu (Croatian National Theatre in Zagreb): Trg Maršala Tita 15, 10000 Zagreb. *Telephone:* (1) 4888418. *Fax:* (1) 4888417. *E-mail:* infocentar@hnk.hr. *Website:* www.hnk.hr.

Cuba

Gran Teatro de la Habana: Paseo de Martí 458 esquina a San Rafael, Centro Habana, 10600, Havana.

Teatro Lírico Nacional: Calle Zulueta No. 253, entre Ánimas y Neptuno, La Habana Vieja, Havana. *Telephone:* (8) 66-5430. *Fax:* (8) 60-2660. *E-mail:* lirico@cubarte.cult.cu. *Website:* www.liricocuba.cult.cu.

Czech Republic

Národní divadlo Moravskoslezské (National Moravian-Silesian Theatre): Příspěvková organizace ul. Cs. legií 148/14, 701 04 Ostrava. *Telephone:* 596276203. *E-mail:* info@ndm.cz. *Website:* www.ndm.cz.

Národní divadlo v Brně (National Theatre Brno): Dvořákova 11, 657 70 Brno. *Telephone:* 542158111. *Fax:* 542127045. *E-mail:* info@ndbrno.cz. *Website:* www.ndbrno.cz.

Státní Opera Praha (Prague State Opera): Wilsonova 4, 110 00 Prague 1. *Telephone:* 224229437. *Fax:* 224229898. *Website:* www.state-opera.com.

Denmark

Den Jyske Opera (Danish National Opera): Musikhuset Århus, Skovgaardsgade 2C, 8000 Århus. *Telephone:* 89-40-91-10. *Fax:* 86-13-37-10. *E-mail:* info@jyske-opera.dk. *Website:* www.jyske-opera.dk.

Det Kongelige Teater (Royal Danish Opera): Ekvipagemestervej 10, 1438 Copenhagen K. *Telephone:* 33-69-69-33. *Fax:* 33-69-65-19. *E-mail:* admin@kglteater.dk. *Website:* www.kgl-teater.dk. Performs at the Copenhagen Opera House.

Egypt

Cairo Opera Company: Cairo Opera House, PO Box 11567 El Borg Gezira, Cairo 11211. *Telephone:* (2) 7398144. *Fax:* (2) 7370599. *E-mail:* info@cairoopera.org. *Website:* www.cairoopera.org.

Estonia

Rahvusooper (Estonian National Opera): Estonia pst 4, 10148 Tallinn. *Telephone:* 683-1201. *Fax:* 631-3080. *E-mail:* info@opera.ee. *Website:* www.opera.ee.

Finland

Suomen Kansallisooppera (Finnish National Opera): Helsinginkatu 58, PO Box 176, 00251 Helsinki. *Telephone:* (9) 40302211. *Fax:* (9) 40302305. *E-mail:* liput@operafin.fi. *Website:* www.operafin.fi.

France

Châtelet Théâtre Musical: 2 rue Edouard Colonne, 75001 Paris. *Telephone:* 1-40-28-28-00. *Fax:* 1-42-28-29-01. *E-mail:* relations-publiques@chatelet-theatre.com. *Website:* www.chatelet-theatre.com.

L'Opéra Comique: 5 rue Favart, 75002 Paris. *Telephone:* 1-42-44-45-40. *Fax:* 1-49-26-05-93. *E-mail:* info@opera-comique.com. *Website:* www.opera-comique.com.

Opéra de La Bastille: 120 rue de Lyon, 75012 Paris. *Telephone:* 1-40-01-17-89. *Fax:* 1-44-73-13-00. *Website:* www.opera-de-paris.fr.

Georgia

Tbilisi Z. Paliashvili Opera and Ballet State Theatre: 0108 Tbilisi, 25 Rustaveli. *Telephone:* (32) 98-32-50. *E-mail:* info@opera.ge. *Website:* www.opera.ge.

Germany

Bayerische Staatsoper: Max-Joseph-Platz 2, 80539 Munich. *Telephone:* (89) 218501. *Fax:* (89) 21851133. *E-mail:* presse@st-oper.bayern.de. *Website:* www.staatstheater.bayern.de.

Deutsche Oper Berlin: Bismarckstrasse 35, 10627 Berlin. *Telephone:* (30) 3438401. *Fax:* (30) 34384232. *E-mail:* info@deutscheoperberlin.de. *Website:* www.deutscheoperberlin.de.

Deutsche Staatsoper Berlin: Unter den Linden 7, 10117 Berlin. *Telephone:* (30) 203540. *Fax:* (30) 20354480. *E-mail:* tickets@staatsoper-berlin.de. *Website:* www.staatsoper-berlin.org.

Greece

Greek National Opera: Charilaou Trikoupi 18, 106 79 Athens. *Telephone:* (210) 3600180. *Fax:* (210) 3648309. *E-mail:* info@nationalopera.gr. *Website:* www.nationalopera.gr.

Hungary

Budapesti Operettszinház (Budapest Operetta Theatre): 1065 Budapest, Nagymező utca 17. *Telephone:* (1) 472-2030. *E-mail:* marketing@operett.hu. *Website:* www.operettszinhaz.hu.

Magyar Állami Operaház (Hungarian State Opera House): 1061 Budapest, Andrássy utca 22. *Telephone:* (1) 331-2550. *Fax:* (1) 472-0449. *E-mail:* info@opera.hu. *Website:* www.opera.hu.

Iceland

Íslenska Óperan (Icelandic Opera): Ingólfsstraeti, PO Box 1416, 121 Reykjavík. *Telephone:* 5116400. *Fax:* 5527384. *E-mail:* opera@opera.is. *Website:* www.opera.is.

Ireland

Opera Ireland: West Wing 3, Adelaide Chambers, Peter Street, Dublin 8. *Telephone:* (1) 4786041. *Fax:* (1) 4786046. *E-mail:* info@operaireland.ie. *Website:* www.operaireland.com. f. 1941 as the Dublin Grand Opera Society; changed its name in 1996.

Opera Theatre Company: Temple Bar Music Centre, Curved Street, Dublin 2. *Telephone:* (1) 6794962. *Fax:* (1) 6794963. *E-mail:* info@opera.ie. *Website:* www.opera.ie. National touring company, f. 1986.

Israel

New Israeli Opera: 19 Shaul Hamelech Street, Tel-Aviv 61332. *Telephone:* 3-6927804. *Fax:* 3-6954886. *E-mail:* opera@mail.israel-opera.co.il. *Website:* www.israel-opera.co.il.

Italy

Gran Teatro La Fenice: Campo San Fantin 1965, 30124 Venice. *Telephone:* (041) 786-511. *E-mail:* info@teatrolafenice.org. *Website:* www.teatrolafenice.it.

Teatro alla Scala: Via Filodrammatici 2, 20121 Milan. *Telephone:* (02) 88791. *Fax:* (02) 88792331. *E-mail:* biglietteria@teatroallascala.org. *Website:* www.teatroallascala.org.

Teatro dell'Opera di Roma: Piazza B. Gigli 8, 00184 Rome. *Telephone:* (06) 481601. *E-mail:* ufficiostampa@operaroma.it. *Website:* www.operaroma.it.

Japan

New National Theatre Foundation: 1-1-1 Hon-machi, Shibuya-ku, Tokyo 151-0071. *Telephone:* (3) 5351-3011. *Website:* www.nntt.jac.go.jp. f. 1997.

Nihon Opera Shinkokai (The Japan Opera Foundation): Nishiazabu 28, Mori Building, Eighth Floor, 4-16-13 Nishiazabu, Minato-ku, Tokyo 106-8625. *Telephone:* (3) 5466-3185. *Fax:* (3) 5466-3186. *E-mail:* jof@jof.or.jp. *Website:* www.jof.or.jp.

Tokyo Opera Nomori: Committee Office, Jimbo-cho Mitsui Building 17F, Kanda Jimbo-cho 1-105, Chiyoda-ku, Tokyo 101-0051. *Telephone:* (3) 5205-6401. *Fax:* (3) 5205-6403. *E-mail:* info@tokyo-opera-nomori.com. *Website:* www.tokyo-opera-nomori.com.

Kazakhstan

Astana Opera: K. Baiseitova National Opera and Ballet Theatre, 010000 Astana, Akzhaik 10. *Telephone:* (7172) 39-27-60. *Fax:* (7172) 39-00-86. Based in the 1,500-seat opera house, built 2006.

Republic of Korea

The National Opera of Korea: Fourth Floor, Opera House, Seoul Arts Center, 700 Seocho-dong, Seocho-gu, Seoul. *Telephone:* (2) 586-5282. *Fax:* (2) 586-5286. *E-mail:* webmaster@nationalopera.org. *Website:* www.nationalopera.org.

Seoul Metropolitan Opera: Sejong Center, 81-3 Sejong-no,Jongno-gu, Seoul 110-821. *Telephone:* (2) 399-1111. *Fax:* (2) 399-1787. *E-mail:* webmaster@sejongpac.or.kr. *Website:* www.sejongpac.or.kr.

Latvia

Latvijas Nacionâlajâ operâ (Latvian National Opera): Aspazijas Blvd 3, Rīga 1050. *Telephone:* 707-3777. *Fax:* 722-8930. *E-mail:* info@opera.lv. *Website:* www.opera.lv.

Liechtenstein

Opernverein Vaduz: Langgasse 2, 9495 Triesen. *Telephone:* 3922835. *E-mail:* info@opernvereinvaduz.li. *Website:* www.opernvereinvaduz.li.

Lithuania

Kauno Valstybinis Muzikinis Teatras (Kaunas State Musical Theatre): Laisves al. 91, Kaunas 44297. *Telephone:* (37) 200633. *Fax:* (37) 227787. *E-mail:* ofisas@muzikinisteatras.lt. *Website:* www.muzikinisteatras.lt.

Lietuvos Nacionalinis Operos ir Baleto Teatras (Lithuanian State Opera and Ballet Theatre): A. Vienuolio 1, Vilnius 01104. *Telephone:* (5) 262-0727. *Fax:* (5) 262-3503. *E-mail:* info@opera.lt. *Website:* www.opera.lt.

Luxembourg

Grand Théâtre: 1 rond-point Schuman, 2525 Luxembourg. *Telephone:* 96-39-00. *Fax:* 46-57-77. *E-mail:* grandtheatre@vdl.lu. *Website:* www.theater-vdl.lu.

Macedonia

Opera of the Macedonian National Theatre: 1000 Skopje, MNT - Theater Center, Kliment Ohridski bb. *Telephone:* (2) 3164667. *Fax:* (2) 3216366. *E-mail:* contact@mnt.com.mk. *Website:* www.mnt.com.mk.

Malaysia

Lyric Opera Malaysia: Kuala Lumpur.

Malta

Teatru Manoel: 115 Old Theatre Street, Valetta VLT 12. *Telephone:* 21222618. *E-mail:* info@teatrumanoel.com.mt. *Website:* www.teatrumanoel.com.mt.

Mexico

Opera Nacional: Palacio de Bellas Artes, Paseo de la Reforma y Campo Marte, Col. Polanco Chapultepec, Del. Miguel Hidalgo, 11560 México, DF. *Telephone:* (55) 5280-8771. *E-mail:* dsi@correo.inba.gob.mx. *Website:* www.bellasartes.gob.mx.

Moldova

Chișinău Opera and Ballet Theatre: 2012 Chișinău, bd. Ștefan cel Mare 152. *Telephone:* (22) 24-51-04. *E-mail:* info@nationalopera.md. *Website:* www.nationalopera.md.

Monaco

Opéra de Monte-Carlo: Place du Casino, BP 139, Monaco 98007. *Telephone:* 98-06-28-28. *Fax:* 98-06-28-29. *E-mail:* contact@opera.mc. *Website:* www.opera.mc.

The Netherlands

De Nederlandse Opera: Waterlooplein 22, 1011 PG Amsterdam. *Telephone:* (20) 5518922. *Fax:* (20) 5518311. *E-mail:* info@dno.nl. *Website:* www.dno.nl.

New Zealand

National Opera: State Opera House, PO Box 9132, Wellington 6141. *Telephone:* (4) 802-4060. *Fax:* (4) 802-4030. *Website:* www.stjames.co.nz.

New Zealand Opera: PO Box 6478, Wellesley Street, Auckland 1141. *Telephone:* (9) 379-4020. *Fax:* (9) 379-4066. *E-mail:* info@nzopera.co.nz. *Website:* www.nzopera.com.

Norway

Den Norske Opera: Postboks 785, Sentrum, 0106 Oslo. *Telephone:* 21-42-21-00. *E-mail:* post@operaen.no. *Website:* www.operaen.no.

Opera Bergen: Komediebakken 9, 5807 Bergen. *Telephone:* 55-90-75-20. *Fax:* 55-54-43-41. *E-mail:* post@operabergen.no. *Website:* www.operabergen.no.

Peru

Prolírica: Teatro Segura, Avenida Reducto 976, Oficina 102, Miraflores, Lima 18. *Telephone:* (1) 2418851. *Fax:* (1) 2418924. *E-mail:* lirica@prolirica.com. *Website:* www.prolirica.com. f. 1980 as the Fundación Pro Arte Lírico, changing its name in 1989.

Poland

Opera Bałtycka (Baltic Opera): 80-219 Gdańsk, Al Zwyciêstwa 15. *Telephone:* (58) 7634912. *Fax:* (58) 7634914. *E-mail:* opera@operabaltycka.pl. *Website:* www.operabaltycka.pl.

Opera Narodowa (National Opera): 00-950 Warsaw, Teatr Wielki, Plac Teatralny 1, PO Box 59. *Telephone:* (22) 6920200. *Fax:* (22) 8260423. *E-mail:* office@teatrwielki.pl. *Website:* www.teatrwielki.pl. Performs at the Teatr Wielki, Warsaw.

Opera Wrocławska: 50-066 Wrocław, ul. Świdnicka 35. *Telephone:* (71) 3708800. *Fax:* (71) 3708852. *E-mail:* opera@opera.wroclaw.pl. *Website:* www.opera.wroclaw.pl.

Teatr Wielki w Poznaniu (Grand Theatre Poznań): 60-967 Poznań, ul. Fredry 9. *Telephone:* (61) 6590200. *Fax:* (61) 8527464. *Website:* www.opera.poznan.pl. Opera company at the theatre.

Warszawska Opera Kameralna (Warsaw Chamber Opera): 00-695 Warsaw, ul. Nowogrodzka 49. *Telephone:* (22) 6283006. *Fax:* (22) 6293233. *E-mail:* publicrelations@wok.pol.pl. *Website:* www.operakameralna.pl. Repertoire spans wide range of musical styles and genres; holds annual festivals and numerous concerts.

Portugal

Teatro Nacional de São Carlos: Rua Serpa Pinto 9, 1200-442 Lisbon. *Telephone:* (21) 3253000. *Fax:* (21) 3253083. *E-mail:* geral@saocarlos.pt. *Website:* www.saocarlos.pt.

Romania

Opera Nationala din București (National Opera): 706091 Bucharest, Bd Mihail Kogălniceanu 70–72. *Telephone:* (21) 3157939. *Fax:* (21) 3157849. *E-mail:* office@operanb.ro. *Website:* www.operanb.ro.

Russia

Bolshoi Opera: 103009 Moscow, Teatralnaya pl. 1. *Telephone:* (495) 292-08-18. *Fax:* (495) 292-33-67. *E-mail:* pr@bolshoi.ru. *Website:* www.bolshoi.ru.

Mariinsky Opera Company: 190000 St Petersburg, Teatralnaya pl. 1. *Telephone:* (812) 114-12-11. *Fax:* (812) 314-17-44. *E-mail:* post@mariinsky.ru. *Website:* www.mariinsky.ru.

Serbia

Orkestar Beogradske Opere (Belgrade Opera Orchestra): 11000 Belgrade, Francuska 3. *Telephone:* (11) 2624565. *Fax:* (11) 2633376. *E-mail:* opera@narodnopozoriste.co.rs. *Website:* www.narodnopozoriste.co.rs.

Singapore

Singapore Lyric Opera: The Singapore Lyric Opera Ltd, 155 Waterloo Street #03-06, Stamford Arts Centre, Singapore 187962. *Telephone:* 63361929. *Fax:* 63371706. *E-mail:* gm@singaporeopera.com.sg. *Website:* www.singaporeopera.com.sg.

Slovakia

Slovenské Národné Divadlo Opera (Slovak National Theatre Opera): Pribinova 17, 819 01 Bratislava. *Telephone:* (2) 5778-2201. *Fax:* (2) 5778-2376. *E-mail:* operasnd@nextra.sk. *Website:* www.snd.sk.

Štátne Divadlo Košice Opera (Košice State Theatre Opera): Hlavná 58, 042 77 Košice. *Telephone:* (55) 622-1231. *Fax:* (55) 622-8235. *E-mail:* sdke@sdke.sk. *Website:* www.sdke.sk.

Slovenia

Slovensko Narodno Gledališč Opera in Balet Ljubljana (Slovenian National Theatre Opera): 1000 Ljubljana, Cankarjeva 1. *Telephone:* (1) 2411700. *Fax:* (1) 4262249. *E-mail:* info@opera.si. *Website:* www.opera.si.

South Africa

Cape Town Opera: PO Box 4107, Cape Town 8000. *Telephone:* (21) 4109807. *Fax:* (21) 4283623. *Website:* www.capetownopera.co.za.

Spain

Gran Teatre del Liceu: La Rambla 51–59, 08002 Barcelona. *Telephone:* (93) 4859900. *Fax:* (93) 4859918. *E-mail:* informacio@liceubarcelona.com. *Website:* www.liceubarcelona.com.

Madrid Opera: Teatro Real, Plaza Isabel II, 28013 Madrid. *Telephone:* (91) 5160600. *Fax:* (91) 5160651. *E-mail:* info@teatro-real.com. *Website:* www.teatro-real.com.

Palau de les Arts Reina Sofía: Autopista del Saler 1, 46013 Valencia. *Telephone:* (96) 1975800. *Fax:* (96) 3952201. *E-mail:* info@lesarts.com. *Website:* www.lesarts.com. Opened 2006.

Teatro de la Zarzuela: Jovellanos 4, 28014 Madrid. *Telephone:* (91) 5245410. *Fax:* (91) 5233059. *Website:* www.teatrodelazarzuela.mcu.es.

Sweden

Folkoperan: Hornsgatan 72, 118 21 Stockholm. *Telephone:* (8) 616-07-50. *Fax:* (8) 84-41-46. *E-mail:* info@folkoperan.se. *Website:* www.folkoperan.se.

Göteborgs Operan: Christina Nilssons Gata, 411 04 Göteborg. *Telephone:* (31) 10-80-00. *Fax:* (31) 10-80-30. *E-mail:* info@opera.se. *Website:* www.opera.se.

Kungliga Operan (Royal Swedish Opera): PO Box 16094, 103 22 Stockholm. *Telephone:* (8) 791-43-00. *Fax:* (8) 791-44-44. *E-mail:* reception@operan.se. *Website:* www.operan.se.

Malmö Opera: Ö. Rönneholmsv 20, 200 10 Malmö. *Telephone:* (40) 20-84-00. *Fax:* (40) 20-84-27. *E-mail:* info@malmoopera.se. *Website:* www.malmoopera.se.

Switzerland

Grand Théâtre de Genève: 11 boulevard du Théâtre, 1211 Geneva 11. *Telephone:* 224183000. *Fax:* 224183001. *Website:* www.geneveopera.ch.

Opéra de Lausanne: 12 avenue du Théâtre, CP 7543, 1002 Lausanne. *Telephone:* 213101600. *Fax:* 213101620. *E-mail:* opera@lausanne.ch. *Website:* www.opera-lausanne.ch.

Opernhaus Zürich: Falkenstrasse 1, 8008 Zürich. *Telephone:* 442686400. *Fax:* 442686401. *E-mail:* info@opernhaus.ch. *Website:* www.opernhaus.ch.

Stadttheater Bern: Postfach, 3000 Bern 7. *Telephone:* 313295111. *Fax:* (31) 3295122. *E-mail:* info@stadttheaterbern.ch. *Website:* www.stadttheaterbern .ch.

Thailand

Bangkok Opera: 232/14-16 Sukhumvit Soi 22, Bangkok 10110. *Telephone:* (2) 663-3236. *Fax:* (2) 663-3237. *E-mail:* info@bangkokopera.com. *Website:* www.bangkokopera.com.

Turkey

İstanbul State Opera: Paşalimani Cad., Eski Tekel, Üsküdar, İstanbul. *Telephone:* (216)3347380. *E-mail:* idobale@idobale.com. *Website:* www.idobale .com.

Turkish State Opera: Opera Sahnesi, Resim ve Heykel, Müzesi Talatpasa, Bulvan Sihhiye, Ankara. *Telephone:* (312) 3244519. *E-mail:* dobgm@dobgm .gov.tr. *Website:* www.dobgm.gov.tr.

Ukraine

Lviv Opera: 79000 Lviv, pr. Svobody 28. *Telephone:* (32) 272-85-62. *Website:* www.lvivopera.org. f. 1900.

National Opera of Ukraine: 01034 Kyiv, vul. Volodymrska 50. *Telephone:* (44) 279-11-69. *Fax:* (44) 234-71-65. *E-mail:* info@opera.kiev.ua. *Website:* www .opera.com.ua.

Odesa State Academic Opera: 65026 Odesa, prov. Chchaikovskoho 1. *E-mail:* opera-ballet@tm.odessa.ua. *Website:* www.opera-ballet.tm.odessa.ua.

United Kingdom

D'Oyly Carte Opera Company: 295 Kennington Road, London, SE11 4QE, England. *Telephone:* (844) 606-0007. *Fax:* (20) 7820-0240. *Website:* www .doylycarte.org.uk. f. 1870s.

English National Opera (ENO): London Coliseum, St Martin's Lane, London, WC2N 4ES, England. *Telephone:* (20) 7836-0111. *Fax:* (20) 7845-9296. *E-mail:* mediaenquiries@eno.org. *Website:* www.eno.org.

Glyndebourne Festival Opera: Glyndebourne Productions Ltd, Glyndebourne, Lewes, East Sussex BN8 5UU, England. *Telephone:* (1273) 812321. *Fax:* (1273) 812783. *E-mail:* info@glyndebourne.com. *Website:* www .glyndebourne.com. Also the Glyndebourne On Tour company.

Opera North: Grand Theatre, 46 New Briggate, Leeds, Yorkshire LS1 6NU, England. *Telephone:* (113) 243-9999. *Fax:* (113) 244-0418. *E-mail:* info@ operanorth.co.uk. *Website:* www.operanorth.co.uk.

The Royal Opera: Royal Opera House, Bow Street, Covent Garden, London, WC2E 9DD, England. *Telephone:* (20) 7240-1200. *Fax:* (20) 7212-9502. *E-mail:* webmaster@roh.org.uk. *Website:* www.royalopera.org.

Scottish Opera: 39 Elmbank Crescent, Glasgow, G2 4PT, Scotland. *Telephone:* (141) 248-4567. *Fax:* (141) 221-8812. *E-mail:* info@scottishopera .org.uk. *Website:* www.scottishopera.org.uk. Performs main opera events at venues in Glasgow, Edinburgh, Aberdeen and Stoke-on-Trent, and smaller-scale performances at venues across Scotland.

Welsh National Opera (WNO): Wales Millennium Centre, Bute Place, Cardiff, CF10 5AL, Wales. *Telephone:* (29) 2063-5000. *Fax:* (29) 2063-5099. *E-mail:* enquiries@wno.org.uk. *Website:* www.wno.org.uk.

United States of America

Boston Lyric Opera Company: 45 Franklin Street, Fourth Floor, Boston, MA 02110-1316. *Telephone:* (617) 542-4912. *Fax:* (617) 542-4913. *E-mail:* boxoffice@blo.org. *Website:* www.blo.org.

Glimmerglass Opera: PO Box 191, 7300 State Highway 80, Cooperstown, NY 13326. *Telephone:* (607) 547-5704. *Fax:* (607) 547-6030. *E-mail:* info@ glimmerglass.org. *Website:* www.glimmerglass.org.

Houston Grand Opera Association: 510 Preston Street, Houston, TX 77002. *Telephone:* (713) 546-0200. *Fax:* (713) 225-2574. *Website:* www .houstongrandopera.org.

Lyric Opera of Chicago: 20 North Wacker Drive, Suite 860, Chicago, IL 60606-2801. *Telephone:* (312) 332-2244. *Fax:* (312) 419-8345. *Website:* www .lyricopera.org.

The Metropolitan Opera: 30 Lincoln Center, New York, NY 10023. *Telephone:* (212) 799-3100. *Fax:* (212) 874-2659. *Website:* www .metoperafamily.org.

San Francisco Opera: War Memorial Opera House, 301 Van Ness Avenue, San Francisco, CA 94102-4509. *Telephone:* (415) 861-4008. *Fax:* (415) 621-7508. *E-mail:* webmaster@sfopera.com. *Website:* www.sfopera.com.

Washington National Opera: 2600 Virginia Avenue NW, Suite 301, Washington, DC 20037. *Telephone:* (202) 295-2420. *Fax:* (202) 295-2479. *E-mail:* info@dc-opera.org. *Website:* www.dc-opera.org.

Venezuela

Opera de Caracas: Museo del Teclado, Parque Central, Edif. Tacaqua, Mezzanina, Caracas 1010. *Telephone:* (212) 572-0713. *Fax:* (212) 572-9024.

Viet Nam

Hanoi Opera: Hanoi Opera House, 1 Pho Trang Tien, Hanoi. *Telephone:* (4) 9330114. *Fax:* (4) 9330116. *E-mail:* haseco@hn.vnn.vn. *Website:* www.cinet .gov.vn.

APPENDIX C: MUSIC FESTIVALS

Australia

Australian Festival of Chamber Music: PO Box 5871, Townsville, Qld 4810. *Telephone:* (7) 4771-4144. *Fax:* (7) 4771-4122. *E-mail:* info@afcm.com .au. *Website:* www.afcm.com.au. Held in July–August.

Austria

Bregenz Festival: Platz der Wiener Symphoniker 1, 6900 Bregenz. *Telephone:* (5574) 407-0. *Fax:* (5574) 407-400. *E-mail:* info@ bregenzerfestspiele.com. *Website:* www.bregenzerfestspiele.com. Held in July–August.

Carinthian Summer Music Festival: Stuft Ossiach, 9570 Ossiach 1. *Telephone:* 4243-2510. *Fax:* 4243-2353. *E-mail:* office@carinthischersommer .at. *Website:* www.carinthischersommer.at. Held in June–August.

Eisenstadt Haydn Festival: Schloss Esterhazy, 7000 Eisenstadt. *Telephone:* (2682) 618-66. *Fax:* (2682) 618-05. *E-mail:* office@haydnfestival.at. *Website:* www.haydnfestival.at. Held in September.

Innsbruck Festival of Early Music: Burggraben 3, 6020 Innsbruck. *Telephone:* (512) 56-15-61. *E-mail:* festwochen@altemusik.at. *Website:* www .altemusik.at. Held in July–August.

Lehár Festival Bad Ischl: Kurhausstrasse 8, 4820 Bad Ischl. *Telephone:* (6132) 238-39. *Fax:* (6132) 238-39-39. *E-mail:* info@leharfestival.at. *Website:* www.leharfestival.at. Held in July–August.

Salzburg Festival: Herbert-von-Karajan-Platz 11, Postfach 140, 5010 Salzburg. *Telephone:* (662) 80-45-50-0. *Fax:* (662) 80-45-55-5. *E-mail:* info@ salzburgfestival.at. *Website:* www.salzburgfestival.at. Held in July–August at various locations.

Schubertiade: Villa Rosenthal, Schweizer Strasse 1, Postfach 100, 6845 Hohenems. *Telephone:* (5576) 72091. *Fax:* (5576) 75-54. *E-mail:* info@ schubertiade.at. *Website:* www.schubertiade.at. f. 1976; festival of Schubert, held annually in Schwarzenberg and Hohenems, in June–July.

Seefestspiele Mörbisch: Joseph Haydngasse 40/1, 7000 Eisenstadt. *Telephone:* (2682) 662-100. *Fax:* (2682) 662-10-14. *E-mail:* tickets@seefestspiele -moerbisch.at. *Website:* www.seefestspiele-moerbisch.at. Operetta festival, held in June–August.

Styriarte Festival: c/o Steirische Kulturveranstaltungen GmbH, Sackstrasse 17, 8010 Graz. *Telephone:* (316) 81-29-41-0. *Fax:* (316) 82-50-00-15. *E-mail:* info@styriarte.com. *Website:* www.styriarte.com. f. 1985; held in June–July.

Wien Modern: PO Box 140, Lothringerstrasse 20, 1037 Vienna. *Telephone:* (1) 24200. *E-mail:* office@wienmodern.at. *Website:* www.wienmodern.at. Contemporary music festival, held in October–November.

Wiener Festwochen (Vienna Music Festival): Lehárgasse 11, 1060 Vienna. *Telephone:* (1) 589-220. *Fax:* (1) 589-2249. *E-mail:* festwochen@ festwochen.at. *Website:* www.festwochen.at. Held in May–June.

Belgium

Ars Musica: Galerie Louise, 203/1, 1050 Brussels. *Telephone:* (2) 219-26-60. *Fax:* (2) 219-88-14. *E-mail:* info@arsmusica.be. *Website:* www.arsmusica.be. Held in March–April.

Festival de Wallonie: Rue de l'Armée Grouchy 20, 5000 Namur. *Telephone:* (81) 73-37-81. *E-mail:* info@festivaldewallonie.be. *Website:* www .festivaldewallonie.be. Held in June–November.

Festival Van Vlaanderen: Vlasmarkt 4, 3700 Tongeren. *Telephone:* (12) 23-57-19. *Fax:* (12) 26-41-26. *E-mail:* coordinatieSV@festival.be. *Website:* www .festival.be. Multiple festivals all over Belgium.

Brazil

Bienal de Música Brasileira Contemporânea: *E-mail:* bienalmt@gmail .com. *Website:* www.bienalmt.com.br. Held in October.

Festival Amazonas de Ópera (Amazonas Opera Festival): Praça São Sebastião s/n, Manaus. *Telephone:* (92) 3622-1880. *E-mail:* teatroamazonas@ culturamazonas.am.gov.br. f. 1997; held April–May at the Teatro Amazonas.

Festival Música Nova: Centro Universitário, Rua Maria Antonia 294, 01222-010 São Paulo SP. *Telephone:* (11) 3255-7182. *E-mail:* musicanova@usp .br. *Website:* www.festivalmusicanova.com.br.

Petrópolis Festivals: *E-mail:* festival@dellarte.com.br. *Website:* www .dellarte.com.br/festival. Summer Music Festival held in January–February; Winter Music Festival held in June–August.

Bulgaria

Apollonia Spring Music Festival: 1125 Sofia, Slaveikov Sq. 11. *Telephone:* (2) 98-07-83-3. *Fax:* (2) 98-05-64-2. *E-mail:* fest@apollonia.bg. *Website:* www .apollonia.bg. Organized by the Apollonia Arts Foundation; held in April.

March Music Days: 7000 Rousse, 3 Tzaribrod Street. *Telephone:* (82) 50-65-07. *Fax:* (82) 82-50-73. *E-mail:* chavdarova@mlnk.net. *Website:* rousefestival .mlnk.net. Part of the Sofia Music Weeks Festival, held in May–June.

Varna Summer International Music Festival: 9000 Varna, Varna Municipality, Culture Department, 43 Osmi Primorski Polk Blvd. *Telephone:* (52) 65-92-36. *Fax:* (52) 65-91-23. *E-mail:* mincheva@varnasummerfest.org. *Website:* www.varnasummerfest.org. f. 1926; arts festival held annually in June–July.

Canada

Le Festival de Lanaudière: 1500 boulevard Base-de-Roc, Joliette, QC J6E 3Z1. *Telephone:* (450) 759-7636. *Fax:* (450) 759-3082. *Website:* www .lanaudiere.org. Held in June–August.

Festival of the Sound: PO Box 750, Parry Sound, ON P2A 2Z1. *Telephone:* (705) 746-2410. *Fax:* (705) 746-5639. *E-mail:* info@festivalofthesound.ca. *Website:* www.festivalofthesound.ca. Held in July–August.

Guelph Spring Festival: PO Box 1718, Guelph, ON N1H 6Z9. *Telephone:* (519) 821-3210. *E-mail:* information@guelphspringfestival.org. *Website:* www .guelphspringfestival.org. Held in April–May.

Scotia Festival of Music: 6181 Lady Hammond Road, Halifax, NS B3K 2R9. *Telephone:* (902) 429-9467. *Fax:* (902) 425-6785. *E-mail:* admin@scotiafestival .ns.ca. *Website:* www.scotiafestival.ns.ca. Held in May–June.

Vancouver Early Music Summer Festival: 1254 W Seventh Avenue, Vancouver, BC V6H 1B6. *Telephone:* (604) 732-1610. *Fax:* (604) 732-1602. *E-mail:* workshops@earlymusic.bc.ca. *Website:* www.earlymusic.bc.ca. Held in July–August.

Croatia

Biennale Zagreb: 10000 Zagreb, Berislavićeva 9. *Telephone:* (1) 4872369. *Fax:* (1) 4872372. *E-mail:* info@mbz.hr. *Website:* www.mbz.hr. Festival of contemporary music.

Czech Republic

International Music Festival Brno: c/o Ars Koncert, Hybešova 29, 602 00 Brno. *Telephone:* 543420951. *Fax:* 543420950. *E-mail:* ars@arskoncert.cz. *Website:* www.mhf-brno.cz. f. 1966; main festival held in September–October; other festivals throughout the year.

Prague Spring International Music Festival: Hellichova 18, 118 00 Prague 1. *Telephone:* 257312547. *Fax:* 257313725. *E-mail:* info@festival.cz. *Website:* www.festival.cz. Held in May–June.

Denmark

Fanø Music Festival: Toftestein 21, Sønderho, 6720 Fanø. Held in June–August.

Estonia

Tallinn International Organ Festival: c/o Eesti Kontsert, Estonia blvd 4, Tallinn 10148. *Telephone:* 6147700. *Fax:* 6147709. *E-mail:* info@concert.ee. *Website:* www.concert.ee. Held in July–August.

Finland

Korsholm Music Festival: Frilundsvägen 2, 65270 Vasa. *Telephone:* (6) 3222390. *Fax:* (6) 3222393. *E-mail:* info@korsholmmusicfestival.fi. *Website:* www.korsholmmusicfestival.fi. Held in June–July.

Kuhmo Chamber Music Festival: Torikatu 39, 88900 Kuhmo. *Telephone:* (8) 6520936. *Fax:* (8) 6521961. *E-mail:* kuhmo.festival@kuhmofestival.fi. *Website:* www.kuhmofestival.fi. Held in July–August.

Lahti Organ Festival: Kirkkokatu 5, 15110 Lahti. *Telephone:* (3) 877230. *Fax:* (3) 8772320. *E-mail:* urkuviikko@lahtiorgan.fi. *Website:* www.lahtiorgan .fi. f. 1973; held in August.

Naantali Music Festival: PO Box 46, 21101 Naantali. *Telephone:* (2) 4345363. *Fax:* (2) 4345425. *E-mail:* info@naantalimusikkijuhlat.fi. *Website:* www.naantalimusic.com. Held in June.

Savonlinna Opera Festival: Olavinkatu 27, 57130 Savonlinna. *Telephone:* (15) 476750. *Fax:* (15) 4767540. *E-mail:* info@operafestival.fi. *Website:* www .operafestival.fi. Held in June–July.

Suvisoitto-Porvoo Summer Sounds: Erottajankatu 19 D 21, 00130 Helsinki. Held in June–July.

Tampere Biennale: Tullikamarinaukio 2, 33100 Tampere. *Telephone:* (3) 56566172. *Fax:* (3) 2230121. *E-mail:* music@tampere.fi. *Website:* www .tampere.fi/musicfestivals. Held in April.

Turun Musiikkijuhlat (Turku Music Festival): Aninkaistenkatu 9, 20100 Turku. *Telephone:* (2) 2620814. *Fax:* (2) 2620830. *E-mail:* info@tmj.fi. *Website:* www.tmj.fi. Held in August.

France

Aix-en-Provence: La Boutique du Festival, 11 rue Gaston de Saporta, 13100 Aix-en-Provence. *Telephone:* 4-42-17-34-34. *Fax:* 4-42-63-13-74. *E-mail:* billetterie@festival-aix.com. *Website:* www.festival-aix.com. Held in June–July.

Beaune International Baroque Opera Festival: BP 71, 21202 Beaune cedex. *Telephone:* 3-80-22-97-20. *Fax:* 3-80-24-90-09. *E-mail:* festival.beaune@ wanadoo.fr. *Website:* www.festivalbeaune.com. Held in July–August.

Les Chorégies d'Orange: BP 205, 84107 Orange cedex. *Telephone:* 4-90-34-24-24. *Fax:* 4-90-11-04-04. *E-mail:* billetterie@choregies.com. *Website:* www .choregies.asso.fr. Held in July–August.

Colmar International Festival: 8 rue Kléber, 68000 Colmar. *Telephone:* 3-89-20-68-97. *Fax:* 3-89-41-34-13. *E-mail:* infofestival@ot-colmar.fr. *Website:* www.festival-colmar.com. Held in July.

Festival du Comminges: Academie Internationale, 31260 Mazeres-sur-Salat. *E-mail:* info@festival-du-comminges.com. *Website:* www.festival-du -comminges.com. Held in July–August.

Festival International de Chant Choral de Nancy: PO Box 13335, 54000 Nancy. *Telephone:* 3-83-27-56-56. *Fax:* 3-83-27-55-66. *E-mail:* festival-choral@ orange.fr. *Website:* www.chantchoral.org. Held in May.

Festival International de Musique Besançon et Franche-Comté: 3 bis rue Léonel de Moustier, Square Saint-Amour, 25000 Besançon. *Telephone:* 3-81-25-05-85. *Fax:* 3-81-81-52-15. *E-mail:* contact@festival-besancon.com. *Website:* www.festival-besancon.com. Held in September.

Festival International de Musique de Toulon: 117 avenue Lazare Carnot, 83000 Toulon. *Telephone:* 4-94-93-55-45. *Fax:* 4-94-24-16-10. *E-mail:* musiquetoulon@wanadoo.fr. *Website:* www.festival-musique-toulon.com. Held in June–July.

Festival Pablo Casals de Prades: BP 24-33, rue de l'Hospice, 66502 Prades cedex. *Telephone:* 4-68-96-33-07. *Fax:* 4-68-96-50-95. *E-mail:* contact@prades -festival-casals.com. *Website:* www.prades-festival-casals.com. Chamber music festival, held in July–August.

Lyrique-en-mer Festival: BP 80, 56360 Le Palais. *Telephone:* 2-97-31-59-59. *E-mail:* lyrique.en.mer@orange.fr. *Website:* www.belle-ile.net. Held in July–August.

Germany

Bachwoche Ansbach: Karlsplatz 7, 91522 Ansbach. *Telephone:* (981) 15037. *Fax:* (981) 15501. *E-mail:* info@bachwoche.de. *Website:* www.bachwoche.de. Biennial festival held in July–August.

Bayreuth Festival: Festspielhügel 1-2, 95445 Bayreuth. *Telephone:* (921) 78780. *Website:* www.bayreuther-festspiele.de. f. 1976; held in July–August.

Beethovenfest Bonn: Kurt-Schumacherstrasse 3, 53113 Bonn. *Telephone:* (228) 2010345. *Fax:* (228) 2010333. *E-mail:* info@beethovenfest.de. *Website:* www.beethovenfest.de. Triennial festival, held in August–October.

Corveyer Musikwochen: Schloss Corvey, 37671 Höxter. *Telephone:* (5271) 694401. *Fax:* (5271) 694400. *E-mail:* empfang@schloss-corvey.de. *Website:* www.schloss-corvey.de. Held in May–June.

Dresdner Musikfestspiele: PO Box 100453, 01074 Dresden. *Telephone:* (351) 478560. *Fax:* (351) 4785623. *Website:* www.musikfestspiele.com. Held in May–June.

Europäisches Musikfest Stuttgart: Internationale Bachakademie Stuttgart, Johann-Sebastian-Bach-Platz, 70178 Stuttgart. *Telephone:* (711) 619210. *Fax:* (711) 6192123. *E-mail:* office@bachakademie.de. *Website:* www .bachakademie.de. Annual festival held in September.

Göttingen Handel Festival: Hainholzweg 3–5, 37085 Göttingen. *Telephone:* (551) 3848130. *Fax:* (551) 38481310. *E-mail:* info@haendel-festspiele.de. *Website:* www.haendel-festspiele.de. Held in May.

Händel Festspiele in Halle an der Saale: Händel-Haus Halle, Grosse Nikolaistrasse 5, 06108 Halle. *Telephone:* (345) 50090221. *Fax:* (345) 50090416. *E-mail:* stiftung@haendelhaus.de. *Website:* www.haendelhaus.de. Held in May–June.

Moritzburg Festival: Maxstrasse 8, 01067 Dresden. *Telephone:* (351) 8105495. *Fax:* (351) 8105496. *E-mail:* buero@moritzburgfestival.de. *Website:* www.moritzburgfestival.de. Chamber music festival, held in August.

Mozart Festival Würzburg: Oeggstrasse 2, 97070 Würzburg. *Telephone:* (931) 372336. *Fax:* (931) 3908300. *E-mail:* info@mozartfest-wuerzburg.de. *Website:* www.mozartfest-wuerzburg.de. Held in June.

Munich Opera Festival: Bayerische Staatsoper, Max Jospeh Platz 2, 80539 Munich. *Telephone:* (89) 218501. *Fax:* (89) 21851133. *Website:* www .bayerische.staatsoper.de. Held in June–July.

Rheingau Musik Festival: Rheinallee 1, 65375 Oestrich-Winkel. *Telephone:* (1805) 743464. *E-mail:* info@rheingau-musik-festival.de. *Website:* www .rheingau-musik-festival.de. Held in June–September.

Schleswig-Holstein Music Festival: Palais Rantzau, Parade 1, 23552 Lübeck. *Telephone:* (451) 3895752. *Fax:* (451) 3895726. *E-mail:* info@shmf.de. *Website:* www.shmf.de. Held in July–September.

Greece

Athens and Epidaurus Festival: Hadjichristou 23, 117 42 Athens. *Telephone:* (210) 9282900. *Fax:* (210)9282941. *E-mail:* info@greekfestival.gr. *Website:* www.greekfestival.gr. Held in June–July.

Patras International Festival: Papadiamantopoulou 17a, 262 25 Patras. *Telephone:* (2610) 270512. *Fax:* (2610) 222157. *E-mail:* depap@otenet.gr. *Website:* www.depap.gr. Held in June–August.

Hungary

Miskolci Nemzetközi Operafesztivál (Miskolc International Opera Festival): 3525 Miskolc, Déryné u. 1. *Telephone:* (46) 509-407. *Fax:* (46) 509-408. *E-mail:* operami@t-online.hu. *Website:* www.operafesztival.hu. Held in June.

Iceland

Dark Music Days: Laufásvegur 40, 101 Reykjavík. *E-mail:* hallivs@hive.is. *Website:* www.listir.is/myrkir. Held in January–February.

Ireland

Cork International Choral Festival: Civic Trust House, 50 Pope's Quay, Cork. *Telephone:* (21) 4215125. *Fax:* (21) 4215192. *E-mail:* info@corkchoral.ie. *Website:* www.corkchoral.ie. Held in April–May.

Waterford International Festival of Light Opera: 60 Morrissons Avenue, Waterford. *Telephone:* (86) 8196618. *Website:* www.waterfordfestival.com. Held in September–October.

Wexford Festival Opera: Wexford Opera House, High Street, Wexford. *Telephone:* (53) 9122400. *Fax:* (53) 9122144. *E-mail:* info@wexfordopera.com. *Website:* www.wexfordopera.com. Held in October–November.

Israel

Ein Gev Music Festival: Ein Gev, 14940 Kibbutz Ein Gev.

Italy

Autunno Musicale: Via Cantoni 1, 22100 Como. *Telephone:* (31) 571150. *Fax:* (31) 570540. *E-mail:* autunnomusicale@camtam.it. *Website:* www .camtam.it. Held in September–October.

Festival Barocco: *E-mail:* turismo@provincia.vt.it. *Website:* www.provincia .vt.it/barocco. Held in August–October.

Festival dei Due Mondi (Festival of Two Worlds): Associazione Festival dei Due Mondi, Piazza del Duomo 8, 06049 Spoleto (PG). *Telephone:* (743) 45028. *Fax:* (743) 220321. *E-mail:* info@spoletofestival.it. *Website:* www .spoletofestival.it.

Festival Internazionale di Musica Contemporanea: Palazzo Giustinian Lolin, San Vidal, San Marco 2893, 30124 Venice. *Telephone:* (041) 5218898. *Fax:* (041) 5218843. *E-mail:* dmtsegreteria@labiennale.org. *Website:* www .labiennale.org. Part of the Venice Biennale; held September–October.

Festival Spaziomusica: Via Liguria 60, 09127 Cagliari. *Telephone:* (070) 400844. *Fax:* (070) 400844. *E-mail:* info@festivalspaziomusica.it. *Website:* www.festivalspaziomusica.it. Held in October–November.

Festival Toscano di Musica Antica: c/o Teatro Verdi, via Palestro 40, 56127 Pisa. *Telephone:* (050) 941144. *Fax:* (050) 941198. *E-mail:* info@ tesorimusicalitoscani.org. *Website:* www.tesorimusicalitoscani.org. Held in June–July, in the province of Pisa.

Gubbio Festival: Piazza Oderisi 5–6, 06024 Gubbio (PG). *Telephone:* (075) 9220693. *Fax:* (075) 9273409. *E-mail:* info@iat.gubbio.pg.it.

Maggio Musicale Fiorentino: Via Solferino 15, 50123 Florence. *Telephone:* (055) 27791. *Fax:* (055) 2396954. *E-mail:* protocollo@maggiofiorentino.com. *Website:* www.maggiofiorentino.com. Held in April–June.

Nuovi Spazi Musicali: Via Divisione Torino 139, 00143 Rome. *Telephone:* (06) 5021208. *Fax:* (06) 5021208. *E-mail:* ada.gentile@tin.it. *Website:* web .tiscalinet.it/nuovispazimusicali. Annual festival of contemporary music, held in the autumn.

Opera Barga Festival: Piazza Angelio 8, 55051 Barga Lucca. *Telephone:* (583) 723250. *Website:* www.barganews.com/festival. Held in July–August.

Puccini Festival: Viale Giacomo Puccini 273, 55048 Torre del Lago Puccini, Lucca. *Telephone:* (584) 350567. *Fax:* (584) 341657. *E-mail:* info@puccinifestival.it. *Website:* www.puccinifestival.it. Held in July–August.

Rassegna di Nuova Musica: Arena Sferisterio, Via Santa Maria della Porta 65, 62100 Macerata. *Telephone:* (733) 261335. *Fax:* (733) 261499. *E-mail:* info@rassegnadinuovamusica.it. *Website:* www.rassegnadinuovamusica.it. Held in February–March.

Ravenna Festival: Via Dante Alighieri 1, 48100 Ravenna. *Telephone:* (544) 249211. *Fax:* (544) 36303. *E-mail:* info@ravennafestival.org. *Website:* www.ravennafestival.org. Festival of Mozart, held in June–July.

Rossini Opera Festival: Via Rossini 37, 61100 Pesaro. *Telephone:* (721) 3800291. *Fax:* (721) 3800220. *E-mail:* rof@rossinioperafestival.it. *Website:* www.rossinioperafestival.it. Held in August.

Sagra Musicale Umbra: Fondazione Perugia Musica Classica, Via Danzetta 7 (1o piano), Perugia. *Telephone:* (075) 5722271. *Fax:* (075) 5725264. *E-mail:* info@perugiamusicaclassica.com. Held in September.

Settembre Musica: via San Francesco de Paola 3, 10123 Turin. *Telephone:* (011) 4424703. *Fax:* (011) 4434468. *E-mail:* settembre.musica@comune.torino.it. *Website:* www.comune.torino.it/settembremusica. Held in August–September.

Settimane Musicali di Stresa e del Lago Maggiore: Via Carducci 38, 28838 Stresa. *Telephone:* (323) 31095. *Fax:* (323) 33006. *E-mail:* info@stresafestival.eu. *Website:* www.stresafestival.eu. Held in August–September.

Verona Opera Festival: Servizio Biglietteria, Via Dietro Anfiteatro 6/b, 37121 Verona. *Telephone:* (045) 8005151. *E-mail:* info@arena.it. *Website:* www.arena.it. f. 1913; held in June–September.

Japan

Kusatsu International Summer Festival: Wako Bldg 2f, 14-3 Motoyoyogi-cho, Shibuya-ku, Tokyo 151-0062. *Telephone:* (3) 5790-5561. *Fax:* (3) 5790-5562. *E-mail:* info@kusa2.jp. *Website:* www.kusa2.jp. Held annually in the last two weeks of August.

Pacific Music Festival: Sumitomo Seimei Sapporo Chuo Bldg 1F, 1-14 Minami 2 jo, Higashi 1 chome, Chuo-ku, Sapporo 060-0052. *Telephone:* (11) 242-2211. *Fax:* (11) 242-1687. *E-mail:* webmaster@pmf.jp. *Website:* www.pmf.or.jp. Held in July–August.

Republic of Korea

Autumn Music Festival in Seoul: Dong-Hwa Building, Suite 210, 43-1, Pil-Dong 1-Ga, Choong-gu, Seoul 100-271. Held in October–November.

Seoul International Music Festival: Korean Broadcasting System, 18 Yoido-dong, Youngdungpo-gu, Seoul 150-790. *E-mail:* music@mak.or.kr. *Website:* www.mak.or.kr/e_simf. Organized by the Music Association of Korea; held in October–November.

Latvia

Rīga Opera Festival: Latvian National Opera, Aspazijas bulvaris 3, Rīga 1050. *Telephone:* 7073-845. *Fax:* 7073-782. *E-mail:* info@opera.lv. *Website:* www.opera.lv. Held in June.

Lithuania

Festival Gaida: Vilnius Festivaliai, Klaipedos 6, Vilnius 01117. *Telephone:* (5) 212-7364. *Fax:* (5) 212-7364. *E-mail:* info@vilniusfestivals.lt. *Website:* www.vilniusfestivals.lt. Formerly the Baltic Music Festival; contemporary music festival held in October.

Luxembourg

Festival International Echternach: PO Box 30, 6401 Echternach. *Telephone:* 72-83-47. *Fax:* 72-71-12. *E-mail:* musique@internet.lu. *Website:* www.echternachfestival.lu. Held in May–July.

Macao (China)

Macao International Music Festival: c/o Cultural Affairs Bureau, Praça do Tap Seac, Edif. do Instituto Cultural, Macao (China). *Telephone:* 83996699. *E-mail:* webmaster@icm.gov.mo. *Website:* www.icm.gov.mo. Held in October.

Mexico

Festival de Música de Cámara de San Miguel de Allende: Calle Hernández Macías 75, San Miguel de Allende, 37700 Guanajuato, Gto. *Telephone:* (415) 154-8722. *Fax:* (415) 550-1395. *E-mail:* info@festivalsanmiguel.com. *Website:* www.chambermusicfestival.com. Held in July–August.

The Netherlands

Festival Nieuwe Muziek: PO Box 15, 4330 AA Middleburg. *Telephone:* (118) 623650. *Fax:* (118) 624754. *E-mail:* cnmzld@aeelandnet.nl. Held in June–July.

Gaudeamus Music Week: Contemporary Music Centre, Piet Heinkade 5, 1019 BR Amsterdam. *Telephone:* (20) 5191800. *Fax:* (20) 5191801. *E-mail:* info@gaudeamus.nl. *Website:* www.gaudeamus.nl. Held in September.

Holland Festival Early Music Utrecht: PO Box 19267, 3501 AS Utrecht. *Telephone:* (30) 2329000. *Fax:* (30) 2329001. *E-mail:* info@oudemuziek.nl. *Website:* www.oudemuziek.nl. Held in August–September.

International Organ Festival Haarlem: Postbus 1091, 1000 BB Amsterdam. *Telephone:* (20) 4880479. *Fax:* (20) 4880478. *E-mail:* office@organfestival.nl. *Website:* www.organfestival.nl. Held in July.

Norway

Bergen International Festival: PO Box 183, Sentrum, 5804 Bergen. *Telephone:* 55-21-06-30. *Fax:* 55-21-06-40. *E-mail:* info@fib.no. *Website:* www.fib.no. Held in May–June.

Elverum Festival: Storgata 24, postboks 313, 2403 Elverum. *Telephone:* 62-41-94-34. *Fax:* 62-41-00-20. *E-mail:* festspill@fie.no. *Website:* www.fie.no. Held in August.

Lofoten Internasjonale Kammermusikkfest: Våganveien 30, 8310 Kabelvåg. *Fax:* (760) 74912. *E-mail:* knut@lofotenfestival.com. *Website:* www.lofotenfestival.no. Held in July.

Poland

Festival of Early Music of Central and Eastern Europe: 85-080 Bydgoszcz, Libelta 16. Held in September.

Mozart Festival: 00-695 Warsaw, Nowogrodzka 49. *Telephone:* (22) 6283096. *Fax:* (22) 6293233. *E-mail:* tickets@operakameralna.pl. *Website:* www.operakameralna.pl. Held in June–July.

Music in Old Kraków: 31-103 Kraków, ul. Zwierzyniecka 1. *Telephone:* (12) 4214566. *Fax:* (12) 4294328. *E-mail:* biuro@capellacracoviensis.pl. *Website:* www.capellacracoviensis.pl. Held in August.

Warsaw Autumn International Festival of Contemporary Music: 00-272 Warsaw, Rynek Starego Miasta 27. *Telephone:* (22) 8310607. *Fax:* (22) 8310607. *E-mail:* festival@warsaw-autumn.art.pl. *Website:* www.warsaw-autumn.art.pl. Held in September.

Romania

Cluj-Napoca Musical Autumn: 3400 Cluj-Napoca, Str E. de Martonne 1. Held in October.

George Enescu International Festival: Artexim, 010073 Bucharest 1, Calea Victoriei 155, Bl D1, Sc 8 et 2. *Telephone:* (21) 3178081. *Fax:* (21) 3110200. *E-mail:* info@festivalenescu.ro. *Website:* www.festivalenescu.ro. Held in September.

Târgu Mureş Musical Days: c/o Filarmonica de Stat Târgu Mureş, 540052 Tîrgu Mureş, Str Enescu nr. 2. *Telephone:* (265) 262548. *Fax:* (265) 262548. *E-mail:* office@filarmonicams.ro. *Website:* www.filarmonicams.ro. Held in May.

Russia

St Petersburg Palaces International Music Festival: c/o Committee for Culture of St Petersburg Local Administration, 191060 St Petersburg, Smolny. *Telephone:* (812) 572-22-26. f. 1990; concerts held at palaces and halls across St Petersburg, during June–July.

White Nights in Moscow International Music Festival: Mariinskii Theatre, 190000 St Petersburg, Teatralnaya pl. 1. *Telephone:* (812) 114-12-11. *Fax:* (812) 314-17-44. *E-mail:* post@mariinsky.ru. *Website:* www.mariinsky.ru. Held in May.

Serbia

Belgrade Music Festival: c/o Jugokoncert, 11000 Belgrade, Terazije 41/I. *Telephone:* 3241-303. *Fax:* 3240-478. *E-mail:* bemus@jugokoncert.rs. *Website:* www.bemus.org. Held in October.

Slovakia

Evenings of New Music: Medená 29, 811 02 Bratislava. *Telephone:* (9) 0872-8970. *Fax:* (1) 5443-3569. *E-mail:* evenings@nextra.sk. *Website:* home.nextra.sk/evenings. Held in October–November.

Slovenia

Festival Ljubljana: 1000 Ljubljana, Trg francoske revolucije 1. *Telephone:* (1) 2416026. *Fax:* (1) 2416037. *E-mail:* info@ljubljanafestival.si. *Website:* www.ljubljanafestival.si. Held in July–September.

Spain

Festival de Música de Canarias: Avenida de Canarias, 8 (Trasera) Edificio Tucán, 35002 Las Palmas de Gran Canaria. *Telephone:* (928) 247442. *Fax:* (928) 276042. *E-mail:* info.festival@canariasculturaenred.com. *Website:* www.festivaldecanarias.com. Held in January–February.

Festival Internacional de Música Castell de Peralada: Calle Pere II de Montcada 1, 08034 Barcelona. *Telephone:* (93) 5038646. *Fax:* (93) 2038700. *E-mail:* info@festivalperalada.com. *Website:* www.festivalperalada.com. Held in July–August.

Festival Internacional de Música Contemporánea de Alicante: Centro de Arte Reina Sofía, Calle Santa Isabel, No 52 E, 28012 Madrid. *Telephone:* (914) 7741072. *Fax:* (91) 7741075. *Website:* cdmc.mcu.es.

Granada Festival: Taquilla del Festival, Corral del Carbón, Calle Mariana Pineda s/n, 18009 Granada. *Telephone:* (958) 221844. *Fax:* (958) 220691. *E-mail:* info@granadafestival.org. *Website:* www.granadafestival.org. Held in June–July.

Sweden

Dalhalla: Box 1, Stationshuset, 795 21 Rättvik. *Telephone:* (248) 79-79-50. *Fax:* (248) 79-79-60. *E-mail:* info@dalhalla.se. *Website:* www.dalhalla.se. Held in August.

Drottningholms Slottsteater: Föreställningar, Box 15417, 104 65 Stockholm. *Telephone:* (8) 556-931-00. *Fax:* (8) 556-931-01. *E-mail:* dst@dtm.se. *Website:* www.dtm.se. 18th-century opera festival, held in May–August.

Royal Palace Music Festival: The Royal Palace, 111 30 Stockholm. *E-mail:* info@royalfestivals.se. *Website:* www.royalfestivals.se. Held in July–August.

Stockholm New Music: PO Box 1225, 111 82 Stockholm. *Telephone:* (8) 407-16-00. *E-mail:* info@stockholmnewmusic.se. *Website:* www.stockholmnewmusic.se. Held in March.

Umeå International Chamber Music Festival: c/o BotniaMusik, Operaplan 5, Box 360, 901 08 Umeå. *Telephone:* (90) 15-43-31. *Fax:* (90) 12-68-45. *E-mail:* info@botniamusik.se. *Website:* www.botniamusik.se. Held in June.

Switzerland

Festival International de Musiques Sacrées: Rue des Alpes 7, Case postale 540, 1701 Fribourg. *Telephone:* 263224800. *Fax:* 263228331. *E-mail:* office@fims-fribourg.ch. *Website:* www.fims-fribourg.ch. Held in July.

International Music Festival Tibor Varga Sion: Académie de Musique Tibor Varga, Rue de Vieux Collège 13, 1950 Sion. *Telephone:* 273226652. *Fax:* 273226652. *E-mail:* info@amsion.ch. *Website:* www.amsion.ch. Held in July–September.

Lucerne Festival: Hirschmattstrasse 13, PO Box, 6002 Lucerne. *Telephone:* 412264400. *Fax:* 412264460. *E-mail:* info@lucernefestival.ch. *Website:* www.lucernefestival.ch. Held in August–September.

Montreux Choral Festival: CP 1526, 1820 Montreux. *Telephone:* 219665550. *Fax:* 219665569. *E-mail:* montreuxchoralfestival@bluewin.ch. *Website:* www.choralfestival.ch. Held in April; choirs from around the world sing classical, popular and folk repertoires.

Settimane Musicali d'Ascona: c/o Ente Turistico Lago Maggiore, Viale B. Papio 5, 6612 Ascona. *Telephone:* (91) 7851965. *Fax:* (91) 7851969. *E-mail:* booking@settimane-musicali.ch. *Website:* www.settimane-musicali.ch. Held in August–October.

Verbier Festival: Verbier Festival & Academy, 4 rue Jean-Jacques Rousseau, 1800 Vevey. *Telephone:* (21) 9259060. *Fax:* (21) 9259068. *E-mail:* info@verbierfestival.com. *Website:* www.verbierfestival.com. Held in July–August.

Zürich Festival: Ticket Office, c/o Opernhaus Zürich, Falkenstrasse 1, 8008 Zürich. *Telephone:* 442699090. *Fax:* 442607025. *E-mail:* info-office@zuercher-festspiele.ch. *Website:* www.zuercher-festspiele.ch. Held in June–July.

Taiwan

Taipei Music Festival: c/o Taipei Symphony Orchestra, 7F 25 Bade Road, Sec. 3, Taipei 10554. *Telephone:* (2) 25786731. *Fax:* (2) 25778244. *E-mail:* tso_service@tso.gov.tw. *Website:* www.tso.gov.tw. Held in September–October.

Turkey

International İstanbul Music Festival: Istiklal Caddesi 146, Beyoglu 34435, İstanbul. *Telephone:* (212) 3340734. *Fax:* (212) 3340705. *E-mail:* music.fest@iksv.org. *Website:* www.iksv.org/muzik. Held in June–July.

United Kingdom

Aldeburgh Festival: Aldeburgh Productions, Snape Maltings Concert Hall, Snape, Suffolk IP17 1SP, England. *Telephone:* (1728) 687100. *Fax:* (1728) 687120. *E-mail:* enquiries@aldeburgh.co.uk. *Website:* www.aldeburgh.co.uk. Held in June.

Almeida Festival: Almeida Theatre, Almeida Street, Islington, London, N1 1TA, England. *Telephone:* (20) 7288-4900. *E-mail:* info@almeida.co.uk. *Website:* www.almeida.co.uk. Opera festival, held in July.

Arundel Festival: Arundel Castle, Arundel, West Sussex BN18 9AB, England. *Telephone:* (1903) 882173. *E-mail:* info@arundelcastle.org. *Website:* www.arundelfestival.co.uk. Held at Arundel Castle, in August.

Bath International Music Festival: Bath Festivals Trust, Abbey Chambers, Kingston Buildings, Bath, BA1 1NT, England. *Telephone:* (1225) 462231. *Fax:* (1225) 445551. *E-mail:* info@bathfestivals.org.uk. *Website:* www.bathmusicfest.org.uk. Held in May–June.

Bath Mozartfest: Bath Festivals Trust, Abbey Chambers, Kingston Buildings, Bath, BA1 1NT, England. *Telephone:* (1225) 462231. *Fax:* (1225) 445551. *E-mail:* info@bathfestivals.org.uk. *Website:* www.bathmusicfest.org.uk. Ten-day festival, held in November.

BBC Promenade Concerts (Proms): 16 Langham Street, Room 425, London, W1A 1AA, England. *E-mail:* proms@bbc.co.uk. *Website:* www.bbc.co.uk/proms. Held in July–September, principally at the Royal Albert Hall.

Birmingham Early Music Festival: PO Box 9442, Birmingham, B15 3QA, England. *E-mail:* info@bemf.net. *Website:* www.bemf.net. Held in October–November.

Buxton Festival: 3 The Square, Buxton, Derbyshire SK17 6AZ, England. *Telephone:* (1298) 70395. *Fax:* (1298) 72289. *E-mail:* info@buxtonfestival.co.uk. *Website:* www.buxtonfestival.co.uk. Festival of opera and music, held in July.

Castleward Opera: Unit A, 280 Comber Road, Lisburn, BT27 6TA, Northern Ireland. *Telephone:* (28) 9263-9545. *Fax:* (28) 9263-9588. *E-mail:* info@castlewardopera.com. *Website:* www.castlewardopera.com. Held in June.

Cheltenham Music Festival: 109 Bath Road, Cheltenham, Gloucestershire GL53 7LS, England. *Telephone:* (1242) 774400. *E-mail:* music@chelthenhamfestivals.com. *Website:* www.cheltenhamfestivals.org.uk. Held in July.

Chester Summer Music Festival: Festival Box Office, Chester Gateway Theatre, Hamilton Place, Chester, England. *Telephone:* (1244) 304618. *Website:* www.chesterfestivals.co.uk. Held in July.

City of London Festival: Fitz Eylwin House, 25 Holborn Viaduct, London, EC1A 2BP, England. *Telephone:* (20) 7583-3505. *Fax:* (20) 7353-0455. *E-mail:* admin@colf.org. *Website:* www.colf.org. Held in June–July.

Edinburgh Festival: The Hub, Castlehill, Edinburgh, EH1 2NE, Scotland. *Telephone:* (131) 473-2000. *Website:* www.eif.co.uk. Held in August–September.

Fishguard International Music Festival: Festival Box Office, Theatr Gwaun, West Street, Fishguard, Pembrokeshire SA65 9AD, Wales. *Telephone:* (1348) 875538. *Fax:* (1348) 873612. *E-mail:* info@fishguardmusicfestival.co.uk. *Website:* www.fishguardmusicfestival.co.uk. Held in July.

Garsington Opera Festival: Garsington Opera, Garsington, Oxfordshire OX44 9DH, England. *Telephone:* (1865) 361636. *E-mail:* office@garsingtonopera.org. *Website:* www.garsingtonopera.org. Held in June–July.

Glyndebourne Festival: Glyndebourne, PO Box 2624, Lewes, East Sussex BN8 5UW, England. *Telephone:* (1273) 812321. *Fax:* (1273) 812783. *E-mail:* info@glyndebourne.com. *Website:* www.glyndebourne.com. Held June–August.

Grange Park Opera: 24 Broad Street, Alresford, SO24 9AQ, England. *Telephone:* (1962) 737366. *E-mail:* info@grangeparkopera.co.uk. *Website:* www.grangeparkopera.co.uk. Held in June–July.

Huddersfield Contemporary Music Festival: University of Huddersfield, Room TC/09, Huddersfield, HD1 3DH, England. *Telephone:* (1484) 472900. *E-mail:* hcmfinfo@hud.ac.uk. *Website:* www.hcmf.co.uk. Held in November.

Iford Arts: The Gatehouse, Iford, Wiltshire BA15 2BA, England. *Telephone:* (1225) 868124. *Fax:* (1225) 867471. *E-mail:* info@ifordarts.co.uk. *Website:* www.ifordarts.co.uk. Opera festival, held in June–August.

International Organ Festival at St Albans: International Organ Festival Society, PO Box 80, St Albans, Hertfordshire AL3 4HR, England. *Telephone:* (1727) 844765. *Fax:* (1727) 844765. *E-mail:* info@organfestival.com. *Website:* www.organfestival.com. Held in July.

King's Lynn Festival: 5 Thoresby College, Queen Street, King's Lynn, Norfolk PE30 1HX, England. *Telephone:* (1553) 767557. *Fax:* (1553) 767688. *Website:* www.kingslynnfestival.org.uk. Held in July.

Lake District Summer Music: Stricklandgate House, 92 Stricklandgate, Kendal, Cumbria LA9 4PU, England. *Telephone:* (8456) 442144. *Fax:* (8456) 442506. *E-mail:* info@ldsm.org.uk. *Website:* www.ldsm.org.uk. Annual festival and summer school, held in August.

Longborough Festival Opera: Longborough, Moreton-in-Marsh, Gloucestershire GL56 0QE, England. *Telephone:* (1451) 830292. *Fax:* (1451) 830605. *E-mail:* admin@lfo.org.uk. *Website:* www.lfo.org.uk. Held in June–July.

Lufthansa Festival of Baroque Music: c/o Lucy Bending Management, 70 Overstone Road, Harpenden, Hertfordshire AL5 5PJ, England. *E-mail:* info@lufthansafestival.org.uk. *Website:* www.lufthansafestival.org.uk. Held in May.

Mostly Mozart: Barbican Centre, Silk Street, London, EC2Y 8DS, England. *Telephone:* (20) 7638-4141. *E-mail:* info@barbican.org.uk. *Website:* www.barbican.org.uk/mostlymozart. Held in July.

Musicfest Aberystwyth: Aberystwyth Arts Centre, University of Wales, Aberystwyth, Ceredigion SY23 3DE, Wales. *Telephone:* (1970) 622338. *E-mail:* musicfest@aber.ac.uk. *Website:* www.abermusicfest.org. Held in July.

Newbury Spring Festival: 1 Bridge Street, Newbury, Berkshire RG14 5BE, England. *Telephone:* (1635) 32421. *Fax:* (1635) 528690. *E-mail:* info@newburyspringfestival.org.uk. *Website:* www.newburyspringfestival.org.uk. Held in May.

North Wales International Music Festival: Irish Square, Upper Denbigh Road, St Asaph, Denbighshire LL17 0RL, Wales. *Telephone:* (1745) 584508. *E-mail:* admin@northwalesmusicfestival.co.uk. *Website:* www.northwalesmusicfestival.co.uk. Held in September.

Opera Holland Park: Central Library, Phillimore Walk, London, W8 7RX, England. *Telephone:* (20) 7361-3570. *E-mail:* info@operahollandpark.com. *Website:* www.operahollandpark.com. Held in Holland Park, London; season runs from June–August.

Presteigne Festival of Music and the Arts: PO Box 30, Presteigne, Powys LD8 2WF, Wales. *Telephone:* (1544) 267800. *Website:* www.presteignefestival.com. Held in August.

Sheffield Music in the Round Festival: 4th Floor, Sheffield Central Library, Surrey Street, Sheffield, S1 1XZ, England. *Telephone:* (114) 281-4660. *Fax:* (114) 281-4661. *E-mail:* info@musicintheround.co.uk. *Website:* www.musicintheround.co.uk. Held in May–July.

Spitalfields Festival: 61 Brushfield Street, London, E1 6AA, England. *Telephone:* (20) 7377-0287. *Fax:* (20) 7247-0494. *E-mail:* info@spitalfieldsfestival.org.uk. *Website:* www.spitalfieldsfestival.org.uk. Held in June and December.

Three Choirs Festival: 7c College Green, Gloucester, GL1 2LX, England. *Telephone:* (1452) 529819. *Fax:* (1905) 610559. *E-mail:* info.gloucester@3choirs.org. *Website:* www.3choirs.org. Held in August.

Vale of Glamorgan Festival of Music: St Donat's Castle, Llantwit Major, CF6 9WF, Wales. *E-mail:* administration@valeofglamorganfestival.org. *Website:* valeofglamorganfestival.org. Festival of living composers' work, held in August.

Warwick International Festival: Pageant House, 2 Jury Street, Warwick, CV34 4EW, England. *Telephone:* (1926) 410018. *Fax:* (1926) 409050. *E-mail:* wmladmin@armonico.org.uk. *Website:* www.warwickintfestival.org. Held in July; includes chamber music concerts, New Music Day, world music.

York Early Music Festival: National Centre for Early Music, St Margaret's Church, Walmgate, York, YO1 9TL, England. *Telephone:* (1904) 632220. *Fax:* (1904) 612631. *E-mail:* info@ncem.co.uk. *Website:* www.ncem.co.uk. Held in July.

United States of America

Aspen Music Festival: 2 Music School Road, Aspen, CO 81611. *Telephone:* (970) 925-3254. *Fax:* (970) 925-3802. *E-mail:* festival@aspenmusic.org. *Website:* www.aspenmusicfestival.com. Held in June–August.

Bard Music Festival: PO Box 5000, Bard College, Annandale-on-Hudson, NY 12504. *Telephone:* (845) 758-7900. *E-mail:* fishercenter@bard.edu. *Website:* www.bard.edu/bmf. Held in August and October.

Berkshire Choral Festival: 245 North Undermountain Road, Sheffield, MA 01257. *Telephone:* (413) 229-8526. *Fax:* (413) 229-0109. *E-mail:* bcf@choralfest.org. *Website:* www.chorus.org. Held in July–August.

Boston Early Music Festival: 161 First Street, Suite 202, Cambridge, MA 02412. *Telephone:* (617) 661-1812. *Fax:* (617) 661-1816. *E-mail:* bemf@bemf.org. *Website:* www.bemf.org. Held in June.

Cabrillo Festival of Contemporary Music: 104 Walnut Avenue, Suite 206, Santa Cruz, CA 95060. *Telephone:* (831) 426-6966. *Fax:* (831) 426-6968. *E-mail:* info@cabrillomusic.org. *Website:* www.cabrillomusic.org. Held in July–August.

Carmel Bach Festival: PO Box 575, Carmel-by-the-Sea, CA 93921. *Telephone:* (831) 624-1521. *Fax:* (831) 624-2788. *E-mail:* info@bachfestival.org. *Website:* www.bachfestival.org. 23 days of concerts and recitals held in July–August; baroque and classical repertoire.

Central City Opera: Central City Opera House Association, Village of Glendale, 400 South Colorado Boulevard, Suite 530, Denver, CO 80246. *Telephone:* (303) 292-6500. *Fax:* (303) 292-4958. *E-mail:* admin@centralcityopera.org. *Website:* www.centralcityopera.org. Held in June–August.

Chamber Music Northwest: 522 Fifth Avenue SW, Suite 920, Portland, OR 97204. *Telephone:* (503) 223-3202. *Fax:* (503) 294-1690. *E-mail:* info@cmnw.org. *Website:* www.cmnw.org. Held in June–July.

Chautauqua Opera: Chautauqua Institution, PO Box 28, Chautauqua, NY 14722. *Telephone:* (716) 357-6286. *E-mail:* chautoperanyc@aol.com. *Website:* opera.ciweb.org. f. 1929; held in July–August.

Cincinnati May Festival: Music Hall, 1241 Elm Street, Cincinnati, OH 45202. *Telephone:* (513) 621-1919. *Fax:* (513) 744-3535. *E-mail:* information@mayfestival.com. *Website:* www.mayfestival.com. Choral festival, held in May–June.

Cincinnati Opera Summer Festival: Music Hall, 1241 Elm Street, Cincinnati, OH 45202. *Telephone:* (513) 768-5500. *Fax:* (513) 768-5552. *E-mail:* info@cincinnatiopera.org. *Website:* www.cincinnatiopera.org. Held in June–July.

Cleveland Blossom Music Festival: Cleveland Orchestra, Severance Hall, 11001 Euclid Avenue, Cleveland, OH 44106-1796. *Telephone:* (216) 231-7300. *E-mail:* info@clevelandorchestra.com. *Website:* www.clevelandorch.org. Held in July–September.

Colorado Music Festival: 900 Baseline Road, Cottage 100, Boulder, CO 80302. *Telephone:* (303) 449-1397. *Fax:* (303) 449-0071. *E-mail:* cmf@coloradomusicfest.org. *Website:* www.coloradomusicfest.org. Held in June–August.

Daytona Beach International Festival: PO Box 1310, Daytona Beach, FL 32115-1310. *Telephone:* (386) 681-2410. *Fax:* (386) 238-1663. *Website:* www.dbif.com. Biennial festival, held in July.

Festival Casals: PO Box 41227, San Juan, Puerto Rico 00940-1227. *Telephone:* (787) 721-7727. *Fax:* (787) 723-7442. *E-mail:* festcasals@cam.gobierno.pr. *Website:* www.festcasalspr.gobierno.pr. Held in February–March.

Irving S. Gilmore International Keyboard Festival: 359 South Kalamazoo Mall, Suite 101, Kalamazoo, MI 49007-4843. *Telephone:* (269) 342-1166. *Fax:* (269) 342-0968. *Website:* www.gilmore.org. Biennial festival, held in April–May.

Glimmerglass Opera Festival: PO Box 191, Cooperstown, NY 13326. *Telephone:* (607) 547-2255. *Website:* www.glimmerglass.org. Held in June–August; held at the Alice Busch Opera Theater.

Grand Canyon Music Festival: PO Box 1332, Grand Canyon, AZ 86023. *Telephone:* (928) 638-9215. *E-mail:* gcmf@infomagic.net. *Website:* www.grandcanyonmusicfest.org. Held in September.

Grand Teton Music Festival: 4015 West Lake Creek Drive, Suite 1, Wilson, WY 83014. *Telephone:* (307) 733-3050. *Fax:* (307) 739-9043. *E-mail:* gtmf@gtmf.org. *Website:* www.gtmf.org. Held in June–August.

Grant Park Music Festival: 205 East Randolph Drive, Chicago, IL 60601. *Telephone:* (312) 742-7638. *Fax:* (312) 742-7662. *E-mail:* info@grantparkmusicfestival.com. *Website:* www.grantparkmusicfestival.com. Outdoor festival, held in June–August.

Lake George Opera Festival: 480 Broadway, Suite 336, Saratoga Springs, NY 12866. *Telephone:* (518) 584-6018. *Fax:* (518) 584-6775. *E-mail:* info@lakegeorgeopera.org. *Website:* www.lakegeorgeopera.org. Held in July–August.

Lincoln Center Festival: 70 Lincoln Center Plaza, Ninth Floor, New York, NY 10023. *Telephone:* (212) 875-5000. *Website:* www.lincolncenter.org. Held in July.

Manchester Music Festival: 42 Dillingham Avenue, PO Box 33, Manchester, VT 05254. *Telephone:* (802) 362-1956. *Fax:* (802) 362-0711. *E-mail:* info@manchestermusicfestival.org. *Website:* www.mmfvt.org. Held in July–August.

Midsummer Mozart Festival: 760 Market Street, Suite 749, San Francisco CA 94102. *Telephone:* (415) 627-9141. *Fax:* (415) 627-9142. *Website:* www.midsummermozart.org. f. 1974, held in July–August.

Mostly Mozart Festival: Lincoln Center for the Performing Arts, 70 Lincoln Center Plaza, New York, NY 10023. *Telephone:* (212) 875-5000. *Website:* www.lincolncenter.org. Held in July–August.

Oregon Bach Festival: 1257 University of Oregon, Eugene, OR 97403-1257. *Telephone:* (541) 346-5666. *Fax:* (541) 346-5669. *E-mail:* bachfest@darkwing.uoregon.edu. *Website:* www.oregonbachfestival.com. Held in June–July.

Ravinia Festival: 418 Sheridan Road, Highland Park, IL 60035. *Fax:* (845) 433-7983. *E-mail:* ravinia@ravinia.org. *Website:* www.ravinia.org. Outdoor music festival held in June–September.

Santa Fe Chamber Music Festival: PO Box 2227, Santa Fe, NM 87504-2227. *Telephone:* (505) 983-2075. *Fax:* (505) 986-0251. *E-mail:* info@sfcmf.org. *Website:* www.sfcmf.org. Held over six weeks in July–August.

Santa Fe Opera Festival: PO Box 2408, Santa Fe, NM 87504-2408. *Telephone:* (505) 986-5900. *E-mail:* press@santafeopera.org. *Website:* www.santafeopera.org. Held in July–August.

Spoleto Festival USA: PO Box 157, Charleston, SC 29402-0157. *Telephone:* (843) 579-3100. *Fax:* (843) 723-6383. *E-mail:* info@spoletousa.org. *Website:* www.spoletousa.org. Formerly linked to Spoleto Festival, Italy; held in May–June.

Tanglewood Festival: Symphony Hall, 301 Massachusetts Avenue, Boston, MA 02115. *Telephone:* (617) 266-1492. *Fax:* (617) 638-9367. *Website:* www.tanglewood.org. Festival of the Boston Symphony Orchestra, held in June–August.

Winter Park Bach Festival: Bach Festival Society, Rollins College, 1000 Holt Avenue, Suite 2763, Winter Park, FL 32789. *Telephone:* (407) 646-2182. *E-mail:* info@bachfestivalflorida.org. *Website:* www.bachfestivalflorida.org. Held in February–March.

APPENDIX D: MUSIC ORGANIZATIONS

It would be impossible to list all the music organizations that exist worldwide. Therefore, we include the large international music organizations (listed once only, under the head office) and the principal national music or arts organizations of each country. Many of these organizations have websites with information on, or links to smaller or more specific groups, covering all aspects of the musical community.

Albania

Albanian National Music Committee: Pallatet 9 kate, Shkalla 2, Ap. 4, Tirana. *Telephone:* (4) 374127. *Fax:* (4) 222857. *E-mail:* vasitole@hotmail.com.

Argentina

Fondo Nacional de las Artes: Alsina 673 (1087), Buenos Aires. *Telephone:* (11) 4343-1590. *Fax:* (11) 4343-1590. *E-mail:* fnartes@fnartes.gov.ar. *Website:* www.fnartes.gov.ar.

Sindicato Argentino de Músicos (SADEM): Avenida Belgrano 3655, 2007 Buenos Aires. *Telephone:* (11) 4957-3522. *E-mail:* internacionales@sadem.com .ar. *Website:* www.sadem.org.ar.

Sociedad Argentina de Autores y Compositores de Música (SADAIC): Lavalle 1547, 1048 Buenos Aires. *Telephone:* (11) 4379-8600. *Fax:* (11) 4379-8633. *E-mail:* consultas@sadaic.org.ar. *Website:* www.sadaic.org.ar.

Australia

APRA/AMCOS: Locked Bag 5000, Strawberry Hills, NSW 2012. *Telephone:* (2) 9935-7900. *Fax:* (2) 9935-7999. *E-mail:* apra@apra.com.au. *Website:* www .apra-amcos.com.au. The Australasian Performing Right Association (APRA) is a non-profit organization that collects royalties on behalf of its members; since 1997, it has been associated with the Australasian Mechanical Copyright Owners Society (AMCOS).

Australia Council for the Arts: PO Box 788, Strawberry Hills, NSW 2012. *Telephone:* (2) 9215-9000. *Fax:* (2) 9215-9111. *E-mail:* mail@australiacouncil .gov.au. *Website:* www.australiacouncil.gov.au. Government arts funding and advisory body.

Australian Recording Industry Association (ARIA): PO Box Q20, Queen Victoria Building, NSW 1230. *Telephone:* (2) 8569-1144. *Fax:* (2) 8569-1183. *E-mail:* aria.mail@aria.com.au. *Website:* www.aria.com.au. Organization aiming to advance the interests of the Australian record industry.

International Council for Traditional Music (ICTM): ICTM Secretariat, School of Music, Australian National University, Building 100, Canberra, ACT 0200. *Telephone:* (2) 6125-5700. *Fax:* (2) 6125-9775. *E-mail:* secretariat@ ictmusic.org. *Website:* www.ictmusic.org/ICTM. Organization aiming to increase the study, preservation and dissemination of the traditional music of all countries.

International Society for Music Education (ISME): International Office, PO Box 909, Nedlands, WA 6909. *Telephone:* (8) 9386-2654. *Fax:* (8) 9386-2658. *E-mail:* isme@isme.org. *Website:* www.isme.org. Worldwide network for music educators.

Musicians' Union of Australia: c/o Federal Secretary, 150 Bell Street, Coburg, VIC 3058. *Telephone:* (3) 9355-7620. *Fax:* (3) 9355-7621. *E-mail:* federal.secretary@musicians.asn.au. *Website:* www.musicians.asn.au.

TasMusic: PO Box 435, Level 2, 54 Brisbane Street, Launceston, TAS 7250. *Telephone:* (3) 6331-4470. *E-mail:* info@tasmusic.com.au. *Website:* www .tasmusic.com.au. Independent, not-for-profit organization, supporting the Tasmanian music industry.

Austria

Gesellschaft der Autoren, Komponisten und Musikverleger (AKM): Baumannstrasse 10, 1030 Vienna. *Telephone:* (1) 050-71-70. *E-mail:* direktion@akm.co.at. *Website:* www.akm.co.at. Performing rights organization.

International Music and Media Centre (IMZ): Stiftgasse 29, 1070 Vienna. *Telephone:* (1) 889-03-15. *Fax:* (1) 889-03-15-77. *E-mail:* office@imz .at. *Website:* www.imz.at.

Musiker-Komponisten-Autoren Gilde: Gartengasse 22, 1050 Vienna. *Telephone:* (1) 54-55-99. *Fax:* (1) 545-65-10. *E-mail:* text@musikergilde.at. *Website:* www.musikergilde.at. f. 1989; musicians' union.

Musikverleger Union Österreich (MUO): Baumannstrasse 8–10, Postfach 3, 1030 Vienna. *Telephone:* (1) 337-23-0. *Fax:* (1) 337-23-40-0. Musicians' union.

Belgium

European Forum of Worldwide Music Festivals (EFWMF): Jan Frans Willemsstraat 10a, 2530 Boechout. *Telephone:* (3) 455-69-44. *Fax:* (3) 454-11-62. *E-mail:* info@efwmf.org. *Website:* www.efwmf.org. f. 1991.

European Music Office (EMO): Rue du Trône 51, 1050 Brussels. *Telephone:* (2) 213-14-00. *Fax:* (2) 213-14-01. *E-mail:* info@emo.org. *Website:* www .musicineurope.org. International non-profit organization linking the national professional organizations, associations and federations of Europe.

The Global Entertainment Retail Association-Europe (GERA-Europe): Chaussée de Wavre 214d, 1050 Brussels. *Telephone:* (2) 626-19-91. *Fax:* (2) 626-95-01. *E-mail:* info@gera-europe.org. *Website:* www.gera-europe.org. f. 2000; trade association of entertainment retailers in Europe.

Independent Music Companies Association (IMPALA): Coudenberg 70, 1000 Brussels. *Telephone:* (2) 503-31-38. *Fax:* (2) 503-23-91. *E-mail:* info@ impalamusic.com. *Website:* www.impalasite.org. f. 2000 to represent European independent music companies and promote the competitiveness and development of the sector.

International Association of Music Information Centres (IAMIC): Steenstraat 25, 1000 Brussels. *Telephone:* (2) 504-90-99. *Fax:* (2) 502-81-03. *E-mail:* iamic@iamic.net. *Website:* www.iamic.net. Worldwide network of organizations that document and promote contemporary music.

International Organisation of Performing Artists (GIART): GIART Permanent Representation, La Maison des Auteurs, Rue Prince Royal 87, 1050 Brussels. *Telephone:* (2) 290-44-38. *Fax:* (2) 551-08-92. *E-mail:* giart@ chello.be. *Website:* www.giart.org. f. 2003; a group of management societies of performing artists' rights, aiming to defend and promote intellectual property rights of performing artists.

Jeunesses Musicales International: Palais des Beaux Arts, 13 rue Baron Horta, 1000 Brussels. *Telephone:* (2) 513-97-74. *Fax:* (2) 514-47-55. *E-mail:* mail@jmi.net. *Website:* www.jmi.net. Youth and music network with members and contact organizations worldwide.

La Société Belge des Auteurs, Compositeurs et Editeurs (SABAM): Rue d'Arlon 75/77, Arlenstraat, 1040 Brussels. *Telephone:* (2) 286-82-11. *Fax:* (2) 230-05-89. *E-mail:* info@sabam.be. *Website:* www.sabam.be.

Benin

Organisation des Musiciens du Bénin (OMB): 04 BP 0066, Cotonou. *Telephone:* 95-96-01-59. *Fax:* 91-30-95-35. *E-mail:* omuzbenin@yahoo.fr. Musicians' union.

Bolivia

Sociedad Boliviana de Autores y Compositores de Música (SOBODAYCOM): PO Box 5107, La Paz. *Telephone:* (2) 248-9888. *Fax:* (2) 248-9882. *E-mail:* informaciones@sobodaycom.org. *Website:* www.sobodaycom.org. Society of writers and composers of music.

Brazil

Fundação Nacional de Arte (Funarte): Centro da Música, Rua da Imprensa 16, 5° andar Centro, 20030-120 Rio de Janeiro, RJ. *Telephone:* (21) 2279-8003. *Fax:* (21) 2232-3431. *E-mail:* faleconosco@funarte.gov.br. *Website:* www.funarte.gov.br.

Ordem dos Músicos do Brasil (OMB): SCS QD. 04, Edifício Israel Pinheiro 3°, Brasília DF 70300-500. *Telephone:* (61) 226-0311. *E-mail:* ombcf@ombcf .com.br. National organization, with chapters in various areas of the country, defending the rights of musicians.

Sociedade Brasileira de Música Contemporânea: SQS 105, Bloco B, Apt 506, 70344-020 Brasília, DF. *Telephone:* (11) 3672-3115. *Fax:* (11) 3673-0321.

Bulgaria

Musicautor: 1000 Sofia, ul. Budapest 17, Floor 4. *Telephone:* (2) 9801035. *Fax:* (2) 9800253. *E-mail:* musicautor_bg@musicautor.org. *Website:* www .musicautor.org. Society of authors and composers for performing and mechanical rights.

Burkina Faso

Syndicat National des Artistes Musiciens (SYNAM): 01 BP 2091, Ouagadougou 01. *Telephone:* 50-31-15-91. *Fax:* 50-30-06-82. *E-mail:* studio .des@fasonet.bf. Musicians' union.

Cameroon

Syndicat Camerounais des Artistes et Compositeurs de Musique (SCACOM): BP 3978, Yaoundé. *Telephone:* 7765-687. *Fax:* 2205-152. *E-mail:* sycamu@yahoo.fr. Musicians' union.

Canada

American Federation of Musicians: 75 The Donway West, Suite 1010, Don Mills, ON M3C 2E9. *Telephone:* (416) 391-5161. *Fax:* (416) 391-5165. *E-mail:*

afmcan@afm.org. *Website:* www.afm.org. Organization representing the interests of professional musicians in the USA and Canada.

Canada Council for the Arts—Conseil des Arts du Canada: PO Box 1047, 350 Albert Street, Ottawa, ON K1P 5V8. *Telephone:* (613) 566-4414. *Fax:* (613) 566-4390. *Website:* www.canadacouncil.ca.

Canadian Academy of Recording Arts and Sciences (CARAS): 345 Adelaide Street West, 2nd Floor, Toronto, ON M5V 1R5. *Telephone:* (416) 485-3135. *Fax:* (416) 485-4978. *E-mail:* info@carasonline.ca. *Website:* www.carasonline.ca.

Canadian Music Centre—Centre de Musique Canadienne (CMC): Chalmers House, 20 St Joseph Street, Toronto, ON M4Y 1J9. *Telephone:* (416) 961-6601. *Fax:* (416) 961-7198. *E-mail:* info@musiccentre.ca. *Website:* www.musiccentre.ca. Promotes the work of its members worldwide; extensive library and archive.

Canadian Musical Reproduction Rights Agency (CMRRA): 56 Wellesley Street W, Suite 320, Toronto, ON M5S 2S3. *Telephone:* (416) 926-1966. *Fax:* (416) 926-7521. *E-mail:* inquiries@cmrra.ca. *Website:* www.cmrra.ca. Non-profit music licensing agency.

The Canadian Recording Industry Association—L'Association de l'industrie canadienne de l'enregistrement (CRIA): 85 Mowat Avenue, Toronto, ON M6K 3E3. *Telephone:* (416) 967-7272. *Fax:* (416) 967-9415. *E-mail:* info@cria.ca. *Website:* www.cria.ca. f. 1964; non-profit trade organization representing the interests of Canadian companies that create, manufacture and market recordings.

Société du droit de reproduction des auteurs, compositeurs et éditeurs au Canada (SODRAC): 759 Victoria Square, Suite 420, Montréal, QC H2Y 2J7. *Telephone:* (514) 845-3268. *Fax:* (514) 845-3401. *E-mail:* sodrac@sodrac.ca. *Website:* www.sodrac.com. Organization promoting copyright of its members.

The Society of Composers, Authors and Music Publishers of Canada—La Société canadienne des auteurs, compositeurs et éditeurs de musique (SOCAN): 41 Valleybrook Drive, Toronto, ON M3B 2S6. *Telephone:* (416) 445-8700. *Fax:* (416) 445-7108. *E-mail:* socan@socan.ca. *Website:* www.socan.ca. Organization administering the communication and performing rights of copyright-protected music, when used in Canada.

Chile

Asociación Nacional de Compositores (ANC): Almirante Moritt 453, Santiago. *Website:* www.anc.scd.cl.

Sociedad Chilena del Derecho de Autor (SCD): Bernarda Morin 440, Providencia, Santiago. *Telephone:* (2) 370-8731. *Fax:* (2) 370-8030. *E-mail:* comunicaciones@scd.cl. *Website:* www.musica.cl.

People's Republic of China

Chinese Musicians' Association: No.10, Nanli, Nong Zhanguan, Beijing 100026. *Telephone:* (71) 88852485. *Fax:* (71) 88852485. *Website:* www.musician.org.cn.

Colombia

La Asociación Colombiana de Músicos Profesionales: Calles 17, 10–16, Oficina 607, Santafé de Bogotá, DC.

La Asociación de Artistas de Colombia: Calle 13, 9-63, Interior 104, PO Box 24627, Bogotá, DC.

La Sociedad de Autores y Compositores de Colombia (SAYCO): Calle 95, 11-31, Santafé de Bogotá, DC. *E-mail:* soniap@sayco.org. *Website:* www.sayco.org.

The Democratic Republic of the Congo

Syndicat National des Artistes et Musiciens du Congo (SYNAMCO): BP 16668, Kinshasa 1. *Telephone:* 89 21 550. *Fax:* (12) 7278619. *E-mail:* samc_aug@yahoo.fr. Musicians' union.

The Republic of the Congo

Centrale Syndicale Congolaise des Artistes: BP 5340, Brazzaville. *Telephone:* 81-16-12. *Fax:* 81-03-30. Musicians' union.

Croatia

Hrvatska Glazbena Unija: 10000 Zagreb, Ivana Broza 8a. *Telephone:* (1) 3668227. *Fax:* (1) 3668216. *E-mail:* hgu@hgu.hr. *Website:* www.hgu.hr. Musicians' union.

Hrvatsko Društvo Skladatelja: 10000 Zagreb, Berislavićeva 9. *Telephone:* (1) 4872370. *Fax:* (1) 4872372. *E-mail:* info@hds.hr. *Website:* www.hds.hr. Composers' society.

Cuba

Centro Nacional de Derecho de Autor (CENDA): Calle 15 #604, entre B y C, Vedado, Havana. *Telephone:* (8) 32-3571. *E-mail:* cenda@cenda.cu. *Website:*

www.cenda.cu. f. 1978; oversees numerous other organizations, including La Agencia Cubana de Derecho de Autor Musical.

Centro Nacional de Música Popular: Avenida 1a, esq. 10 y 12, Playa, Havana.

Unión Nacional de Escritores y Artistas de Cuba (UNEAC): Calle 17 No. 354, esquina G y H, Vedado, CP 10400, Havana. *Telephone:* (7) 83-24551. *Fax:* (7) 33-3158. *E-mail:* uneac@cubarte.cult.cu. *Website:* www.uneac.org.cu. f. 1961.

Czech Republic

Český hudební fond: Besední 487, 110 00 Prague 1. *Telephone:* 257320008. *Fax:* 257312834. *E-mail:* info@hudebnifond.cz. *Website:* www.hudebnifond.cz. Czech music fund.

Ochranný svaz autorský pro práva k dílům hudebním (OSA): Čs. armády 20, 160 56 Prague 6. *Telephone:* 220315111. *Fax:* 233343073. *E-mail:* osa@osa.cz. *Website:* www.osa.cz. Performing and mechanical rights society for composers, authors and publishers.

Denmark

Dansk Musiker Forbund (DMF): Sankt Hans Torv 26, 2200 Copenhagen N. *Telephone:* 35-24-02-40. *Fax:* 35-24-02-50. *E-mail:* dmf@dmf.dk. *Website:* www.dmf.dk. Musicians' union.

Nordisk Copyright Bureau (NCB): Hammerichsgade 14, 1611 Copenhagen V. *Telephone:* 33-36-87-00. *Fax:* 33-36-46-90. *E-mail:* ncb@ncb.dk. *Website:* www.ncb.dk.

Ecuador

Sociedad de Autores y Compositores Ecuatorianos (SAYCE): Avenida Diez de Agosto 43147 y Río Coca, Quito. *Telephone:* (2) 224-3083. *Fax:* (2) 246-2638. *Website:* www.sayce.com.ec. f. 1973; performing rights society.

El Salvador

Centro Nacional de Artes (CENAR): Calle Valero Lecha, Colonia San Mateo, San Salvador. *Telephone:* 2298-1839. *Fax:* 2298-1843.

Estonia

Eesti Autorite Ühing (EAU): Lille 13, Tallinn 10614. *Telephone:* 668-4360. *Fax:* 668-4361. *E-mail:* eau@eau.org. *Website:* www.eauthors.ee. Represents authors' rights (principally works music and drama) and gives legal advice concerning copyright.

Fiji

Fiji Performing Right Association Ltd: GPO Box 15061, Suva. *Telephone:* 3312494. *Fax:* 3303340. *E-mail:* fpra@connect.com.fj. *Website:* www.fpra.com.fj.

Finland

Suomen Muusikkojen Liitto ry: Pieni Roobertinkatu 16, 00120 Helsinki. *Telephone:* (9) 68034070. *Fax:* (9) 68034087. *E-mail:* sml@muusikkojenliitto.fi. *Website:* www.musicfinland.com/sml/. Musicians' union.

TEOSTO: Säveltäjäin Tekijänoikeustoimisto Teosto ry, Lauttasaarentie 1, 00200 Helsinki. *Telephone:* (9) 681011. *Fax:* (9) 677134. *E-mail:* teosto@teosto.fi. *Website:* www.teosto.fi. f. 1928; organization protecting the copyright of Finnish composers and songwriters.

France

ADAMI: 14–16 rue Ballu, 75311 Paris cedex 09. *Telephone:* 1-44-63-10-00. *Fax:* 1-44-63-10-10. *Website:* www.adami.fr. Formed an alliance with SPEDIDAM in 2004, to manage common activities, called the Société des Artistes-Interprètes.

Confédération Internationale des Sociétés d'Auteurs et Compositeurs (CISAC): CISAC Secretariat, 20–26 Boulevard du Parc, 92200 Neuilly-sur-Seine. *Telephone:* 1-55-62-08-50. *Fax:* 1-55-62-08-60. *E-mail:* cisac@cisac.org. *Website:* www.cisac.org. f. 1926; a non-governmental, non-profit organization working for increased recognition and protection of creators' rights.

Fédération Internationale des Musiciens (FIM): 21 bis, rue Victor Massé, 75009 Paris. *Telephone:* 1-45-26-31-23. *Fax:* 1-45-26-31-57. *E-mail:* office@fim-musicians.com. *Website:* www.fim-musicians.com. f. 1948; international organization representing musicians of all genres of music.

International Federation for Choral Music (IFCM): International Office, Z.A. Le Mesnil, Chemin des Carreaux, 14111 Louvigny. *Telephone:* 2-31-73-38-81. *Fax:* 2-31-73-54-15. *E-mail:* info@ifcm.net. *Website:* www.ifcm.net. f. 1982 to facilitate communication between choral musicians worldwide.

International Music Council: 1 rue Miollis, 75732 Paris cedex 15. *Telephone:* 1-45-68-48-50. *Fax:* 1-43-06-87-98. *E-mail:* imc@unesco.org. *Website:* www.unesco.org/imc. f. 1949 by UNESCO; worldwide network of organizations and individuals in the field of music, promoting musical diversity and supporting cultural rights for all.

MIDEM Organization: 11 rue du Colonel Pierre Avia, BP 572, 75726 Paris cedex 15. *Telephone:* 1-41-90-44-60. *Fax:* 1-41-90-44-50. *E-mail:* info.midem@reedmidem.com. *Website:* www.midem.com.

Société des Auteurs, Compositeurs et Editeurs de Musique (SACEM): 225 avenue Charles de Gaulle, 92528 Neuilly-sur-Seine Cedex. *Telephone:* 1-47-15-47-15. *Website:* www.sacem.fr. Represents French performers.

SPEDIDAM: 16 rue Amélie, 75007 Paris cedex 07. *Telephone:* 1-44-18-58-58. *Website:* www.spedidam.fr. Monitors artist remuneration and artistic property rights; formed an alliance with ADAMI in 2004, to manage common activities, called the Société des Artistes-Interprètes.

Union Nationale des Syndicats d'Artistes Musiciens de France (SNAM): 14–16 rue des Lilas, 75019 Paris. *Telephone:* 1-42-02-30-80. *Fax:* 1-42-02-34-01. *E-mail:* snam-cgt@wanadoo.fr. *Website:* www.snam-cgt.org.

Gabon

Syndicat National des Artistes Musiciens (SYNAM): c/o Mme Véronique Eboa, BP 2206, Libreville. *Telephone:* 26-06-71. *Fax:* 73-39-09. Musicians' union.

Germany

Deutscher Musikverleger-Verband eV (DMV): Friedrich-Wilhelm-Strasse 31, 53113 Bonn. *Telephone:* (228) 539700. *Fax:* (228) 5397070. *E-mail:* info@dmv-online.com. *Website:* www.dmv-online.com. Represents the interests of music publishers throughout Germany.

Gesellschaft für Musikalische Aufführungs und Mechanische Vervielfältigungsrechte (GEMA): Postfach 30 12 40, 10722 Berlin. *Telephone:* (30) 2124500. *Fax:* (30) 21245950. *E-mail:* gema@gema.de. *Website:* www.gema.de. Performing rights organization.

Internationaler Arbeitskreis für Musik eV (IAM): Am Kloster 1a, 49565 Bramsche-Malgarten. *Telephone:* (5461) 99630. *Fax:* (5461) 996310. *E-mail:* iamev@t-online.de. *Website:* www.iam-ev.de.

Ghana

Musicians' Union of Ghana (MUSIGA): PO Box CT 2240, Cantonments, Accra. *Telephone:* (21) 775128. *Fax:* (21) 775128. *E-mail:* sidiku@dslghana.com. *Website:* www.musiga.com.gh.

Greece

Panhellenic Musicians' Union: 10 Sapfous str, 10553 Athens. *Website:* www.pmu.gr.

Société Hellenique pour la Protection de la Propriété Intellectuelle (AEPI): Fragoklisias 51, Samou Str, Amarousio, 15125 Athens. *Telephone:* (211) 11029000. *Fax:* (210) 6851576. *E-mail:* info@aepi.gr. *Website:* www.aepi.gr. Intellectual property organization.

Guatemala

Asociación Guatemalteca de Autores y Compositores (AGAYC): 14 Calle 11-42, Zona 1, 01001 Guatemala City. *Telephone:* 2384-921. *Fax:* 2513-057. *E-mail:* agayc@intelnet.net.gt.

Guinea

Association des Musiciens Interprètes de Guinée (AMIG): Centre Culturel de la Paillote, BP 53 Conakry. *Telephone:* 45-49-48. *Fax:* 45-49-48. *E-mail:* barrysko@yahoo.fr. Musicians' union.

Hong Kong

Asian Composers' League: c/o Dr Joshua Chan, Department of Music, University of Hong Kong, Pokfulam Road, Hong Kong. *Telephone:* 28597045. *Fax:* 28584933. *Website:* www.asiancomposersleague.com. f. 1973; member countries and regions: Australia, Azerbaijan, People's Republic of China, Hong Kong, Indonesia, Israel, Japan, Republic of Korea, New Zealand, The Philippines, Taiwan, Thailand and Viet Nam; holds annual conference and festival.

Composers' and Authors' Society of Hong Kong Ltd (CASH): 18/F Universal Trade Centre, 3 Arbuthnot Road, Central, Hong Kong. *Telephone:* 28463268. *Fax:* 28463261. *E-mail:* general@cash.org.hk. *Website:* www.cash.org.hk.

Music Office: Wanchai Tower 25/F, 12 Harbour Road, Wanchai. *Telephone:* 2582-5314. *Fax:* 2802-8440. *E-mail:* cmooffice@lcsd.gov.hk. *Website:* www.lcsd.gov.hk. Government organization to promote music.

Hungary

Hungarian Musicians' and Dancers' Union: 1068 Budapest, Vàrosligeti Fasor 38. *Telephone:* (1) 342-8927. *Fax:* (1) 322-5446. *E-mail:* mztszgyimesi@axelero.hu.

Magyar Zenei Tanács: 1537 Budapest, PO Box 401. *Telephone:* (1) 318-4243. *Fax:* (1) 317-4243. *E-mail:* info@hunmusic.hu. *Website:* www.hunmusic.hu. Music council, f. 1990.

Iceland

Samband tónskálda og eigenda flutningsréttar (STEF): Laufásvegi 40, 101 Reykjavík. *Telephone:* 5616173. *Fax:* 5626273. *E-mail:* info@stef.is. *Website:* www.stef.is.

India

Musicians' Federation of India: Redwood A-103, Evershine Green, New Link Road, Oshivara, Andheri (W) Mumbai 400053. *Telephone:* (22) 26399009. *E-mail:* kishorjawade@rediffmail.com.

Indonesia

Karya Cipta Indonesia: Golden Plaza Fatmawati C-12, Jl. RS. Fatmawati 15, Jakarta 12420. *Telephone:* (21) 75905884. *Fax:* (21) 7656051. *E-mail:* kci@kci.or.id. *Website:* www.kci.or.id. Copyright protection agency.

Ireland

An Chomhairle Ealaíon (The Arts Council): 70 Merrion Square, Dublin 2. *Telephone:* (1) 6180200. *Fax:* (1) 6761302. *Website:* www.artscouncil.ie. f. 1951 to promote the knowledge, appreciation and practice of the arts.

Irish Music Rights Organisation (IMRO): Regus House, 30 Upper Pembroke Street, Dublin 2. *Telephone:* (1) 6614844. *Fax:* (1) 6763125. *E-mail:* info@imro.ie. *Website:* www.imro.ie. Non-profit organization, administering performing rights and copyright of music in Ireland.

Israel

Israeli Musicians' Union: 6 Malkay Israel Square, 64951 Tel-Aviv. *Telephone:* 3-6959355. *Fax:* 3-6963528. *E-mail:* eilam@netvision.net.il. *Website:* www.eilam.org.il.

Society of Authors, Composers and Music Publishers in Israel (ACUM): Tuval 9st. (Hilazon Corner), PO Box 1704, Ramat-Gan 52117. *Telephone:* 3-6113400. *Fax:* 3-6122629. *E-mail:* info@acum.org.il. *Website:* www.acum.org.il. f. 1936.

Italy

Associazione di Informatica Musicale Italiana (AIMI): c/o Davide Rocchesso, Giudecca 494, 30133 Venice. *E-mail:* info@aimi-musica.org. *Website:* www.aimi-musica.org.

Sindacato Nazionale Musicisti (SNM): 22 via Domodossola, 00183 Rome. *E-mail:* snm@snm.it. *Website:* www.snm.it.

Società Italiana degli Autori ed Editori (SIAE): Viale della Letteratura 30, 00144 Rome. *Telephone:* (06) 59901. *Fax:* (06) 59647050. *E-mail:* urp@siae.it.. *Website:* www.siae.it. Performing rights and copyright society.

Japan

Japanese Society for Rights of Authors, Composers and Publishers (JASRAC): 3-6-12 Uehara, Shibuya-ku, Tokyo 151-8540. *Telephone:* (3) 3481-2121. *Website:* www.jasrac.or.jp.

Recording Industry Association of Japan (RIAJ): 11F Kita-Aoyama Yoshikawa Building, 2-12-16 Kita-Aoyama, Minato-ku, Tokyo 107-0061. *Telephone:* (3) 6406-0510. *Fax:* (3) 6406-0520. *E-mail:* info@riaj.or.jp. *Website:* www.riaj.or.jp.

Kenya

Kenya Union of Entertainment and Music Industry Employees (KUEMIE): Off Shimo la Tewa Road, Industrial Area, PO Box 4622, 00506 Nairobi. *Telephone:* (20) 545317. *Fax:* (20) 251938. *E-mail:* kuemie@hotmail.com.

Republic of Korea

Korea Music Copyright Association (KOMCA): KOMCA Building, Naebalsan-dong 649, Kangseo-gu, Seoul 57-824. *Telephone:* (2) 2660-0400. *Fax:* (2) 2660-0429. *E-mail:* webmaster@komca.or.kr. *Website:* komca.or.kr.

Music Association of Korea: 1-117 Tong-Sung Dong, Chongro-ku, Seoul 110-765. *Telephone:* (2) 744-8060. *Fax:* (2) 741-2378. *Website:* www.mak.or.kr.

Macao (China)

Cultural Affairs Bureau: Praça do Tap Seac, Edif. do Instituto Cultural, Macao (China). *Telephone:* 83996699. *Fax:* 28366899. *E-mail:* webmaster@icm.gov.mo. *Website:* www.icm.gov.mo. Government organization to promote the arts.

Malawi

Musicians' Association of Malawi (MAM): Private Bag 127, Blantyre. *Telephone:* 5633012. *Fax:* 5624186. *E-mail:* goodson@accessmalawi.com.

Mali

Association Nationale des Artistes du Mali (ANAM): BP E 4005, Bamako. *Telephone:* 223-52-60. *Fax:* 222-36-70. *E-mail:* nicole .sounfountera@delmli.cec.eu.int. Musicians' union.

Mexico

Sociedad de Autores y Compositores de Música (SACM): Mayorazgo 129, 03330 México, DF. *Telephone:* (56) 0477-33. *Fax:* (56) 0479-23. *E-mail:* sacm@sacm.org.mx. *Website:* www.sacm.org.mx.

Mozambique

Associaçao dos Musicos Moçambicanos: Avenida Magiguana, N° 710 R/C, Predio Macau, 6°, Maputo. *Telephone:* 1428706. *Fax:* 1301604. *E-mail:* h_langa1@hotmail.com. Musicians' union.

Namibia

Namibian Artists' Union: PO Box 22287, Windhoek. *Telephone:* (61) 240535. *Fax:* (61) 248097. *E-mail:* artistna@iway.na.

The Netherlands

BUMA/STEMRA: Siriusdreef 22–28, 2132 WT Hoofddorp. *Telephone:* (23) 7997999. *Fax:* (23) 7997777. *E-mail:* info@bumastemra.nl. *Website:* www .bumastemra.nl. Performing rights organization.

International Society for Contemporary Music (ISCM): ISCM Secretariat, c/o Muziek Centrum Nederland, ROKIN 111, 1012 KN Amsterdam. *Telephone:* (20) 3446060. *E-mail:* info@iscm.org. *Website:* www.iscm.org. f. 1922; an international network devoted to the promotion and presentation of contemporary music.

SENA: Catharina van Renneslaan 8, 1217 CX Hilversum. *Telephone:* (35) 6251700. *E-mail:* sena@sena.nl. *Website:* www.sena.nl. Promotes the rights of both performers and producers of music.

New Zealand

Creative New Zealand: National Office, Old Public Trust Building, 131–135 Lambton Quay, PO Box 3806, Wellington. *Telephone:* (4) 473-0880. *Fax:* (4) 471-2865. *E-mail:* info@creativenz.govt.nz. *Website:* www.creativenz.govt.nz. Government arts council.

Recording Industry Association of New Zealand (RAINZ): Private Bag 78 850, Grey Lynn, Auckland 1245. *Telephone:* (9) 360-5085. *Fax:* (9) 360-5086. *E-mail:* music@rianz.org.nz. *Website:* www.rianz.org.nz.

Niger

Association Nationale des Auteurs, Compositeurs et Interprètes de Musique Moderne (ANACIMM): BP 11 203, Niamey. *Telephone:* 740895. *Fax:* 743123. *E-mail:* zibo_ali@yahoo.fr.

Norway

Musikernes Fellesorganisasjon (MFO): Postboks 8806, Youngstorget, 0028 Oslo. *Telephone:* 23-06-21-50. *Fax:* 23-06-21-51. *E-mail:* mfo@musikerorg .no. *Website:* www.musikerorg.no. Musicians' union.

TONO: Galleriet, Tøyenbekken 21, Postboks 9171, Grønland, 0134 Oslo. *Telephone:* 22-05-72-00. *Fax:* 22-05-72-50. *E-mail:* tono@tono.no. *Website:* www.tono.no. Represents artists in Norway.

Paraguay

Asociación de Músicos del Paraguay: Calle 15 de agosto 1365, Asunción. *Telephone:* (21) 44-3276. *Fax:* (21) 44-3276. *E-mail:* cesar_burian@hotmail .com.

Peru

Asociación Peruana de Autores y Compositores (APDAYC): Avenida Petit Thouars 5038, Miraflores, Lima 18. *Telephone:* (1) 7158122. *Fax:* (1) 2423248. *E-mail:* dirgen@apdayc.org.pe. *Website:* www.apdayc.org.pe.

The Philippines

Filipino Society of Composers, Authors and Publishers Inc. (FILSCAP): 140 Scout Rallos St., Brgy. Sacred Heart, Quezon City, Metro Manila. *Telephone:* (2) 4156277. *Fax:* (2) 9289852. *E-mail:* info@filscap.com.ph. *Website:* www.filscap.com.ph. f. 1965; non-profit organization administering public performance and mechanical reproduction rights.

Philippine Association of the Record Industry (PARI): Suite 207 Greenhills Mansion, 37 Annapolis Street, Greenhills, San Juan, Metro Manila. *Telephone:* (2) 7250770. *Fax:* (2) 7250786. *E-mail:* writeus@pari.com .ph. *Website:* www.pari.com.ph.

Poland

Stowarzyszenie Muzykow Rozrywkowych w Polsce (STOMUR): 00-660 Warsaw, Ul. Lwowska 13. *Telephone:* (22) 6214709. *Fax:* (22) 6292854. *E-mail:* stomur@stoart.org.pl. *Website:* stomur.stoart.org.pl. Association of musicians.

Zwiazek Polskich Autorów i Kompozytorów (ZAKR): 00-093 Warsaw, Daniłowiczowska 18/5A. *Telephone:* (22) 8283735. *Fax:* (22) 8283735. *E-mail:* zakr@zakr.pl. *Website:* www.zakr.pl. f. 1946; association of authors, lyricists and composers.

Zwiazek Producentów Audio Video (ZPAV): 00-380 Warsaw, Ul. Kruczkowskiego 12 m 2. *Telephone:* (22) 6229219. *Fax:* (22) 6251661. *E-mail:* biuro@zpav.pl. *Website:* www.zpav.pl. Polish society of the recording industry.

Portugal

Associação Fonográfica Portuguesa (AFP): Rua Augusto dos Santos No. 2, 4°, 1050-028 Lisbon. *Telephone:* (21) 3529189. *Fax:* (21) 3147325. *E-mail:* contactar@afp.org.pt. *Website:* www.afp.org.pt.

Romania

Union des Musiciens Professionnels: 70149 Bucharest, Str Franklin nr 1, sect. 1. *Telephone:* (21) 6504118. *Fax:* (21) 01788. Musicians' union.

Union of Composers and Musicologists: 70149 Bucharest, Calea Victoriei 141, Sector 1. *Telephone:* (21) 2127966. *Fax:* (21) 2107211. *E-mail:* ucmr@ itcnet.ro.

Russia

Russian Authors' Society: *Telephone:* (495) 697-37-77. *Fax:* (495) 609-93-63. *E-mail:* rao@rao.ru. *Website:* www.rao.ru. Legal support for musicians.

Russian Phonographic Association: 125047 Moscow, 1 Miusskaya Str., Bld. 24/22, Office 62A. *Telephone:* (495) 626-44-47. *Fax:* (495) 626-44-47. *E-mail:* international@fonogram.ru. *Website:* www.rpa-society.com.

Senegal

Association des Métiers de la Musique du Sénégal (AMS): 758 Sicap Baobab, BP 166 12, Dakar-Fann. *Telephone:* 21-633-0672. *Fax:* 21-822-2459. *E-mail:* malickmusic@yahoo.fr. Musicians' union.

Singapore

Composers' and Authors' Society of Singapore Ltd (COMPASS): 37 Craig Road, Singapore 089675. *Telephone:* 63236630. *Fax:* 63236639. *Website:* www.compass.org.sg.

National Arts Council: 140 Hill Street, # 03-01 MICA Building, Singapore 179369. *Telephone:* 67464622. *Fax:* 68373010. *Website:* www.nac.gov.sg. Government organization for the promotion of the arts.

Recording Industry Association (Singapore) (RIAS): 4 Leng Kee Road, 03-07 SiS Building, Singapore 159088. *Telephone:* 62204166. *Fax:* 62209452. *E-mail:* oinfo@rias.org.sg. *Website:* www.rias.org.sg. f. 1976 as Singapore Phonogram & Videogram Association; fosters and maintains fair business practices within the industry.

Slovakia

Hudobné Centrum: Michalská 10, 815 36 Bratislava 1. *Telephone:* (2) 5920-4811. *Fax:* (2) 5443-0379. *E-mail:* hc@hc.sk. *Website:* www.hc.sk. Music centre.

Odborovczvaz profesionalnych orchestralnych hudobnikov Slovenska: Jakubovo nam 15, 811 09 Bratislava. *Telephone:* (2) 5296-4555. *Fax:* (2) 5296-4555. *E-mail:* karol@petocz.sk. Union of orchestral musicians.

South Africa

Musicians' Union of South Africa (MUSA): PO Box 35, Newtown, Johannesburg 2113. *Telephone:* (11) 3391676. *Fax:* (11) 3391677. *E-mail:* musa2@absamail.co.za.

Recording Industry of South Africa (RiSA): PO Box 367, Randburg 2125. *Telephone:* (11) 8861342. *Fax:* (11) 8864169. *Website:* www.risa.org.za.

South African Music Rights Organisation (SAMRO): PO Box 31609, Braamfontein, Johannesburg 2017. *Telephone:* (11) 7128000. *Fax:* (11) 4031934. *E-mail:* webmaster@samro.org.za. *Website:* www.samro.org.za.

South African Recording Rights Association Ltd (SARRAL): PO Box 31091, Braamfontein, Johannesburg 2017. *Telephone:* (11) 3391333. *Fax:* (11) 3391403. *E-mail:* info@sarral.org.za. *Website:* www.sarral.org.za.

Spain

Sindicato Profesional de Músicos Españoles (SPME): Calle de Alcalá 182, 1° Izquierda, 28028 Madrid. *Telephone:* (91) 3554870. *Fax:* (91) 3554870. *E-mail:* forma-spme@teleline.es.

Sociedad General de Autores y Editores (SGAE): Fernando VI 4, 28004 Madrid. *Telephone:* (91) 3499550. *Fax:* (91) 3499500. *Website:* www.sgae.es. Organization for performing rights.

Swaziland

Swaziland Arts and Music Association (SWAMA): PO Box 5836, Manzini. *Telephone:* 5058785. *Fax:* 5058785. *E-mail:* artsandculture@africaonline.co.sz.

Sweden

International Association of Music Libraries, Archives and Documentation Centres (IAML): c/o Statens musikbibliotek, Box 16 326, 103 26 Stockholm. *E-mail:* secretary@iaml.info. *Website:* www.iaml.info. f. 1951 to promote international co-operation and to support the interests of the profession; has individual and institutional members worldwide.

Nordic Music Committee (NOMUS): Nybrokajen 11, 111 48 Stockholm. *Telephone:* (8) 407-16-00. *Fax:* (8) 407-17-21. *E-mail:* nomus@nomus.org. *Website:* www.nomus.org. The Nordic Council expert group in matters regarding Nordic music collaboration.

Svenska Artisters och Musikers Intresseorganisation (SAMI): Döbelnsgatan 3, 111 40 Stockholm. *Telephone:* (8) 453-34-00. *Fax:* (8) 453-34-40. *Website:* www.sami.se. Swedish artists' and musicians' organization.

Svenska Tonsättares Internationella Musikbyrå (STIM): PO Box 27327, 102 54 Stockholm. *Telephone:* (8) 783-88-00. *Fax:* (8) 662-62-75. *E-mail:* info@stim.se. *Website:* www.stim.se. Performing right society.

Switzerland

Fédération Mondiale des Concours Internationaux de Musique (FMCIM): Headquarters, 104 rue de Carouge, 1205 Geneva. *Telephone:* 223213620. *Fax:* 227811418. *E-mail:* info@wfimc.org. *Website:* www.fmcim.org. f. 1957; world federation of international music competitions.

International Confederation of Music Publishers—Confédération Internationale des Editeurs de Musique (ICMP/CIEM): 6 rue de Bourg, 1002 Lausanne. *E-mail:* 101374.25@compuserve.com. *Website:* www.icmp-ciem.org. International trade association representing the interests of the music-publishing industry worldwide.

International Musicological Society (IMS): POB 1561, 4001 Basel. *E-mail:* imsba@swissonline.ch. *Website:* www.ims-online.ch. f. 1927 to advance musicological research through international co-operation.

SUISA: Bellariastrasse 82, Postfach 782, 8038 Zürich. *Telephone:* 444856666. *Fax:* 444824333. *E-mail:* suisa@suisa.ch. *Website:* www.suisa.ch; www.fondation-suisa.ch. Performing rights society; includes the Fondation SUISA pour la Musique.

World Intellectual Property Organization: Information Centre, 34 chemin des Colombettes, Geneva. *Telephone:* 223389111. *Fax:* 227335428. *E-mail:* information.center@wipo.int. *Website:* www.wipo.int. International organization promoting respect for intellectual property throughout the world.

Tanzania

Tanzania Musicians' Network: PO Box 32429, Dar es Salaam. *Telephone:* (741) 274747. *E-mail:* musicnettz@yahoo.com.

Thailand

Thai Composers' Association: 107–108 Siripong Road, Sao Chingcha, Samranrat, Bangkok 10200.

Turkey

Muzik Yapimcilari Dernegi (MUYAP): IMC 6, Blok 6437, 34470 Unkapani, İstanbul.

United Kingdom

Arts Council England: 14 Great Peter Street, London, SW1P 3NQ, England. *Telephone:* (845) 300-6200. *Fax:* (20) 7973-6590. *E-mail:* enquiries@artscouncil.org.uk. *Website:* www.artscouncil.org.uk. National development agency for the arts in England, distributing public money from the Government and the National Lottery.

British Academy of Composers and Songwriters (BAC&S): British Music House, 26 Berners Street, London, W1T 3LR, England. *Telephone:* (20) 7636-2929. *Fax:* (20) 7636-2212. *E-mail:* info@britishacademy.com. *Website:* www.britishacademy.com. Formerly the Association of Professional Composers (APC), the British Academy of Songwriters, Composers & Authors (BASCA), and the Composers' Guild of Great Britain; changed name as above

1999; activities include lobbying for music writers, providing membership services, honouring achievements through award ceremonies (Ivor Novello and British Composer Awards).

British Phonographic Industry (BPI): Riverside Building, County Hall, Westminster Bridge Road, London, SE1 7JA, England. *Telephone:* (20) 7803-1300. *Fax:* (20) 7803-1310. *E-mail:* general@bpi.co.uk. *Website:* www.bpi.co.uk.

Celfyddydau Cymru—Arts Council of Wales: 9 Museum Place, Cardiff, CF10 3NX, Wales. *Telephone:* (29) 2037-6500. *Fax:* (29) 2022-1447. *Website:* www.artswales.org. f. 1994 to fund and develop the arts in Wales.

Incorporated Society of Musicians: 10 Stratford Place, London, W1C 1AA, England. *Telephone:* (20) 7629-4413. *Fax:* (20) 7408-1538. *E-mail:* membership@ism.org. *Website:* www.ism.org. Professional body for all musicians: performers, composers, teachers, conductors, organists, etc.; represents musicians' interests, raises professional standards, and provides services (insurance, legal advice, etc.) to members.

International Artist Managers' Association (IAMA): Headquarters, 23 Garrick Street, Covent Garden, London, WC2E 9BN, England. *Telephone:* (20) 7379-7336. *Fax:* (20) 7379-7338. *E-mail:* info@iamaworld.com. *Website:* www.iamaworld.com. Worldwide association for classical music artist managers and concert agents.

International Federation of the Phonographic Industry (IFPI): Secretariat, 10 Piccadilly, London, W1J 0DD, England. *Telephone:* (20) 7878-7900. *Fax:* (20) 7878-7950. *E-mail:* info@ifpi.org. *Website:* www.ifpi.org. Promotes the interests of the recording industry worldwide.

International Music Managers' Forum (IMMF): IMMF Headquarters, British Music House, 26 Berners Street, London, W1T 3LR, England. *Telephone:* (870) 8507-800. *Fax:* (870) 8507-801. *E-mail:* info@musicmanagersforum.co.uk. *Website:* www.musicmanagersforum.co.uk. Non-governmental organization representing the interests of music managers worldwide, through national-level Music Managers Forums.

MCPS-PRS: Copyright House, 29–33 Berners Street, London, W1T 3AB, England. *Telephone:* (20) 7580-5544. *Fax:* (20) 7306-4455. *Website:* www.prs.co.uk. Collects and distributes licence fees for the public performance and broadcast of musical works; formed as alliance between two royalty collection societies, MCPS and PRS, in 1997, to manage common activities.

Musicians' Union (MU): National Office, 60–62 Clapham Road, London, SW9 0JJ, England. *Telephone:* (20) 7582-5566. *Fax:* (20) 7582-9805. *E-mail:* info@musiciansunion.org.uk. *Website:* www.musiciansunion.org.uk. UK trade union for musicians of all genres.

PPL: 1 Upper James Street, London, W1F 9DE, England. *Telephone:* (20) 7534-1000. *Fax:* (20) 7534-1111. *E-mail:* info@ppluk.com. *Website:* www.ppluk.com. Established in 2007 following merger between Performing Artists' Media Rights Association (PAMRA) and The Association of United Recording Artists (AURA). Licenses recorded music and music videos for public performance, broadcast and new media use.

Pro-Music: c/o IFPI Secretariat, 10 Piccadilly, London, W1J 0DD, England. *Telephone:* (20) 7878-7900. *Fax:* (20) 7878-7950. *E-mail:* info@ifpi.org. *Website:* www.pro-music.org. f. 2003; international website promoting legitimate online music services and answering questions about copyright law for online music.

Scottish Arts Council: 12 Manor Place, Edinburgh, EH3 7DD, Scotland. *Telephone:* (131) 226-6051. *Fax:* (131) 225-9833. *E-mail:* help.desk@scottisharts.org.uk. *Website:* www.scottisharts.org.uk. Funds and develops the arts in Scotland.

UK Music: British Music House, 26 Berners Street, London, W1T 3LR, England. *Telephone:* (20) 7306-4446. *Fax:* (20) 7306-4449. *E-mail:* contact@ukmusic.org. *Website:* www.ukmusic.org. Formerly known as British Music Rights. Established in 1996 by the British Academy of Composers & Songwriters, the Music Publishers Association, the Mechanical-Copyright Protection Society and the Performing Right Society, to represent the interests of composers, songwriters and music publishers.

United States of America

American Academy of Arts and Letters: 633 West 155th Street, New York, NY 10032-1799. *Telephone:* (212) 368-5900. *Fax:* (212) 491-4615. *E-mail:* academy@artsandletters.org. *Website:* www.artsandletters.org.

American Federation of Musicians: 1501 Broadway, Suite 600, New York, NY 10036. *Telephone:* (212) 869-1330. *Fax:* (212) 764-6134. *Website:* www.afm.org. Organization representing the interests of professional musicians in the USA and Canada.

American Mechanical Rights Agency Inc. (AMRA): 149 S Barrington Avenue, Suite 810, Los Angeles, CA 90049. *Telephone:* (310) 440-8778. *Fax:* (310) 440-0059. *E-mail:* info@amermechrights.com. *Website:* www.amermechrights.com.

American Society of Composers, Authors and Publishers (ASCAP): ASCAP Building, 1 Lincoln Plaza, New York, NY 10023. *Telephone:* (212) 621-

6000. *Fax:* (212) 724-9064. *E-mail:* info@ascap.com. *Website:* www.ascap.com. f. 1914; performing rights organization.

Broadcast Music Inc. (BMI): 320 West 57th Street, New York, NY 10019-3790. *Telephone:* (212) 586-2000. *Website:* www.bmi.com. Performing rights organization, representing songwriters, composers and music publishers.

National Academy of Recording Arts and Sciences (NARAS): 3402 Pico Boulevard, Santa Monica, CA 90405. *Telephone:* (310) 392-3777. *Fax:* (310) 399-3090. *Website:* www.naras.org. Incorporates the Grammy Foundation and the MusiCares charity.

National Endowment for the Arts (NEA): 1100 Pennsylvania Avenue NW, Washington, DC 20506-0001. *Telephone:* (202) 682-5400. *E-mail:* webmgr@arts.endow.gov. *Website:* www.nea.gov.

National Music Council: c/o Dr David Sanders, Director, 425 Park Street, Montclair, NJ 07043. *E-mail:* sandersd@mail.montclair.edu. *Website:* www.musiccouncil.org. f. 1940 to strengthen the importance of music in US life and culture.

Recording Industry Association of America (RIAA): 1025 F Street N.W., 10th Floor, Washington, DC 20004. *Telephone:* (202) 775-0101. *Fax:* (202) 775-7253. *Website:* www.riaa.com. f. 1972 as the National Association of Independent Record Distributors & Manufacturers (NAIRD).

SESAC: 55 Music Square East, Nashville, TN 37203. *Telephone:* (615) 320-0055. *Fax:* (615) 329-9627. *Website:* www.sesac.com. f. 1930 as the Society of European Stage Authors & Composers (now simply known as SESAC); performing rights organization; also SESAC Latina (Spanish-language section).

Uruguay

Asociación Uruguaya de Músicos (AUDEM): Calle Maldonado 983, CP 11 100 Montevideo. *Telephone:* (2) 9087370. *Fax:* (2) 9080477. *E-mail:* audem@adinet.com.uy. *Website:* www.audem-uy.org.

Federación Uruguaya de Músicos (FUDEM): Gutemberg 6334, Montevideo. *Telephone:* (2) 6984376. *Fax:* (2) 3228477. *E-mail:* fudemuru@yahoo.com.

Venezuela

Sociedad de Autores y Compositores de Venezuela (SACVEN): Avenida Andrés Bello, Edificio VAM, Torre Oeste, Pisos 9 y 10, Caracas DC 1050. *Telephone:* (212) 507-7211. *Fax:* (212) 507-7287. *Website:* www.sacven.org.

APPENDIX E: COMPETITIONS AND AWARDS

Details may vary from year to year and interested readers are advised to contact the sponsoring organizations directly for complete information.

Armenia

Aram Khachaturian International Competition: 5001 Yerevan, Yerevan State Conservatory, Room 211, Sayat-Nova. *Telephone:* (10) 56-27-50. *Fax:* (10) 56-27-50. *E-mail:* akhic@akhic.am. *Website:* www.akhic.am. Awards open to musicians of all nationalities. Entrants must be between the ages of 16 and 32.

Australia

Australian Singing Competition: The Australian Singing Competition, Level 4, 67 Castlereagh Street, Sydney, NSW 2000. *Telephone:* (2) 9231-4293. *Fax:* (2) 9221-8201. *E-mail:* asc@mostlyopera.org.au. *Website:* www.aussing .com.au. Annual awards for operatic and classical singers. Entrants must be an Australian or New Zealand citizen, and classical singers must be under the age of 26.

Sydney International Piano Competition of Australia: PO Box 420, Double Bay, Sydney, NSW 1360. *Telephone:* (2) 9326-2405. *Fax:* (2) 9326-2604. *E-mail:* sipca@bigpond.com. *Website:* www.sipca.com.au. Quadrennial competition open to pianists of all nationalities between the ages of 17 and 30.

Symphony Australia Young Performer of the Year: Artist Development, Symphony Services Australia, GPO Box 1145, Darlinghurst NSW 1300. *Telephone:* (2) 8333-1651. *Fax:* (2) 8333-1678. *E-mail:* artists@symphony.net .au. *Website:* www.symphony.net.au. Annual competition held in three categories: strings, keyboards and other instruments. Performers must be under the age of 30 and have been in continuous residence in Australia for one year. Must compete in state of residence.

Austria

International Beethoven Piano Competition: c/o Elga Ponzer, Universi- tär für Musik und darstellende Kunst, Lothringerstrasse 18, 1030 Vienna. *Telephone:* (1) 711-55-60-50. *Fax:* (1) 711-55-60-59. *E-mail:* ponzer@mdw.ac .at. *Website:* www.beethoven-comp.at. Quadrennial competition open to pianists of all nationalities between the ages of 16 and 31.

International Choir Competition: Spittal an der Drau, Postfach 90, 9800 Spittal/Drau. *Telephone:* (650) 2708780. *Fax:* (4246) 71767. *E-mail:* singkreis .porcia@aon.at. *Website:* www.singkreis-porcia.at. Annual competition for mixed choirs, in two categories: folksong and choral works, and classical and modern.

International Fritz Kreisler Competition: Postfach 76, 1030 Vienna. *Telephone:* (1) 225-24-10-03. *Fax:* (1) 225-221-993. *E-mail:* frischenschlager@ fritzkreisler.com. *Website:* www.fritz-kreisler.music.com. Quadrennial com- petition for violin and viola. Entrants must be under the age of 30.

International Hans Gabor Belvedere Singing Competition: Wiener Kammeroper, Fleischmarkt 24, 1010 Vienna. *Telephone:* (1) 512-01-00-0. *Fax:* (1) 512-01-00-30. *E-mail:* belvedere@wienerkammeroper.at. *Website:* www .wienerkammeroper.at. Annual competition for singers to the age of 35.

International Mozart Competition: Universität Mozarteum Salzburg, Mirabellplatz 1, 5020 Salzburg. *Telephone:* (662) 61-98-22-00. *Fax:* (662) 61- 98-30-33. *E-mail:* ulrike.godler@moz.ac.at. *Website:* www.moz.ac.at. Quad- rennial competition open to musicians of all nationalities. Prizes include the Mozart Prize from the Austrian Ministry of Science and Research, as well as other prizes and concert engagements.

Nancy Van de Vate International Composition Prize for Opera: c/o Vienna Masterworks, Khleslplatz 6, No. 2309, 1120 Vienna. *Website:* www .xs4all.nl/~gdv/vmm. Annual competition open to all female composers of opera and music theatre.

Belgium

Musica Antiqua Early Music Festival: 't Zand 34 (Concertgebouw), 8000 Bruges. *Telephone:* (50) 33-22-83. *Fax:* (50) 34-52-04. *E-mail:* info@mafestival .be. *Website:* www.mafestival.be. Annual competition, instrumentalist cate- gories rotating annually on a triennial schedule.

Printemps de la Guitare – Concours International de Guitare: Place du Chef Lieu 9, 6040 Charleroi. *Telephone:* (71) 35-53-20. *E-mail:* info@printemps -guitare.be. *Website:* www.printemps-guitare.be. Biennial competition open to solo classical guitarists of all nationalities to the age of 32.

Queen Elisabeth International Music Competition of Belgium: 20 rue Aux Laines, 1000 Brussels. *Telephone:* (2) 213-40-50. *Fax:* (2) 514-32-97. *E-mail:* info@qeimc.be. *Website:* www.cmireb.be. Open to musicians who have completed their training, the competition rotates annually between piano, voice, violin and composition.

Bulgaria

Boris Christoff International Competition for Young Opera Singers: 1612 Sofia, 41 Tzar Boris III Blvd. *Telephone:* (2) 951-59-03. *Fax:* (2) 952-15- 58. *E-mail:* borischristoff@abv.bg. *Website:* www.borischristoff.dir.bg. Quad- rennial competition open to singers of all nationalities, up to the age of 33.

Canada

Banff International String Quartet Competition: 107 Tunnel Mountain Drive, Box 1020, Station 23, Banff, AB T1L 1H5. *Telephone:* (403) 762-6231. *E-mail:* bisqc@banffcentre.ca. *Website:* www.banffcentre.ca/bisqc. Triennial competition open to quartets whose members are under 35 years of age at the time of the competition.

Canada Council for the Arts/Conseil des Arts du Canada Grants and Awards: PO Box 1047, 350 Albert Street, Ottawa, ON K1P 5V8. *Telephone:* (613) 566-4414. *Fax:* (613) 566-4390. *Website:* www.canadacouncil.ca. Grants and awards to artists of Canadian citizenship and to non-profit arts organizations.

Canadian Music Competition/Concours de Musique du Canada: 1450 City Councillors Street, Suite 220, Montréal, QC H3A 2E6. *Telephone:* (514) 284-5398. *Fax:* (514) 284-6828. *E-mail:* info@cmcnational.com. *Website:* www .cmcnational.com. Annual competition for pianists, string players, wind players and singers. Open to Canadian citizens or those holding a Landed Immigrant Certificate or those studying with a Canadian teacher for the last three years, aged between 7 and 31.

Concours Orchestre Symphonique de Montréal: 260 boulevard de Maisonneuve Ouest, 2e étage, Montréal, QC H2X 1Y9. *Telephone:* (514) 842- 3402. *Fax:* (514) 842-0728. *Website:* www.osm.ca. Annual competition open to Canadian citizens or those holding a Landed Immigrant Certificate, featuring piano and voice one year and strings and wind the following year, with various age categories.

Eckhardt-Gramatté National Music Competition: Queen Elizabeth II Music Building, Brandon University, 270 18th Street, Brandon, MB R7A 6A9. *Telephone:* (204) 728-8212. *Fax:* (204) 729-9085. *E-mail:* eckhardt@brandonu .ca. *Website:* www.brandonu.ca/egre. Annual competition open to Canadian citizens or Canadian residents, alternating annually between voice, strings and piano.

Glenn Gould Prize: The Glenn Gould Foundation, 69 Yonge Street, Suite 1401, Toronto, ON M5E 1K3. *Telephone:* (416) 962-6200. *Fax:* (416) 962-0135. *E-mail:* info@glenngould.ca. *Website:* www.glenngould.ca. Triennial honour to an individual of any nationality who has made an exceptional contribution to music and its communication through the use of any communication technology.

Montréal International Musical Competition: 305 Mount-Royal Avenue East, Montréal, QC H2T 1P8. *Telephone:* (514) 845-4108. *Fax:* (514) 845-8241. *E-mail:* info@concoursmontreal.ca. *Website:* www.concoursmontreal.ca. Annual competition, rotating between voice, violin and piano, for entrants of any nationality under the age of 33.

Czech Republic

Prague Spring International Music Competition: Hellichova 18, 118 00 Prague 1. *Telephone:* 257312547. *Fax:* 257313725. *E-mail:* info@festival.cz. *Website:* www.festival.cz. Annual competition open to performers under the age of 30, of all nationalities with categories rotating annually in five-year cycles. Prizes include an appearance at the Prague Spring International Music Festival.

Denmark

Malko Competition for Young Conductors: c/o Copenhagen Artists, Postbox 2693, 2100 Copenhagen. *Telephone:* 44-49-29-00. *E-mail:* info@ malkocompetition.com. *Website:* www.malkocompetition.com. Triennial com- petition open to conductors between the ages of 20 and 35.

Carl Nielsen International Music Competitions: Claus Bergs Gade 9, 5000 Odense C. *Telephone:* 63-75-00-55. *Fax:* 65-91-00-47. *E-mail:* cncomp@ odensesymfoni.dk. *Website:* www.odensesymfoni.dk/cncomp. Quadrennial competitions open to instrumentalists of all nationalities to the age of 30, in the categories of violin, flute and clarinet.

Finland

Mirjam Helin International Singing Competition: c/o Finnish Cultural Foundation, PO Box 203, Bulevardi 5A, 00121 Helsinki. *Telephone:* (9) 61281248. *Fax:* (9) 640474. *E-mail:* info@mirjamhelin.fi. *Website:* www .mirjamhelin.fi. Quinquennial competition open to singers of all nationalities, women under the age of 31 and men under the age of 33.

International Paulo Cello Competition: PO Box 1105, 00101 Helsinki. *Telephone:* (40) 5467079. *E-mail:* cello@paulo.fi. *Website:* www

.cellocompetitionpaulo.org. Quinquennial competition for young cellists of all nationalities.

Sibelius International Conductors' Competition: Finlandia Hall, 00100 Helsinki. *Telephone:* (40) 5030997. *Fax:* (9) 497597. *E-mail:* info@sibeliusconductorscompetition.org. *Website:* www .sibeliusconductorscompetition.org. Quinquennial competition for conductors under the age of 35.

Jean Sibelius International Violin Competition: Sibelius Academy, PO Box 86, 00251 Helsinki. *Telephone:* (20) 7539645. *Fax:* (20) 7539600. *E-mail:* anna.krohn@siba.fi. *Website:* www.siba.fi/sibeliuscompetition. Quinquennial competition for violinists under the age of 30.

France

Concours de Jeunes Chefs d'Orchestre: 3 bis rue Léonel de Moustier, Square Saint Amour, 25000 Besançon. *Telephone:* 3-81-25-05-85. *Fax:* 3-81-81-52-15. *E-mail:* contact@festival-besancon.com. *Website:* www.festival -besancon.com. Annual competition as part of the Festival international de musique de Besançon Franche-Comté, open to conductors under the age of 35 of any nationality. Prizes include Emile Vuillermoz Prize.

Concours International de Chant de la ville de Toulouse: c/o Théâtre du Capitole, BP 41408, 31014 Toulouse cedex 6. *E-mail:* chant.toulouse@mairie -toulouse.fr. *Website:* www.toulouse.fr. Annual competition open to singers between the ages of 18 and 33.

Concours International de Chant-Piano Nadia et Lili Boulanger: Fondation International Nadia et Lili Boulanger, 25 avenue des Gobelins, 75013 Paris. *Telephone:* 1-45-35-09-43. *Fax:* 1-45-35-09-43. *E-mail:* contact@ fondation-boulanger.com. *Website:* www.fondation-boulanger.com. Biennial competition open to singers and their piano accompanists.

Concours International d'Orgue Grand Prix de Chartres: Association des Grandes Orgues de Chartres, 22 Cloitre Notre Dame, 28000 Chartres. *Telephone:* 2-37-36-67-48. *E-mail:* orgues.chartres@yahoo.fr. *Website:* orgues .chartres.free.fr. Biennial competition open to all organists under the age of 35. Prizes for interpretation and for improvisation.

Concours International Marguerite Long–Jacques Thibaud: 32 avenue Matignon, 75008 Paris. *Telephone:* 1-42-66-66-80. *Fax:* 1-42-66-06-43. *Website:* www.concours-long-thibaud.org. Triennial competition open to pianists and violinists between the ages of 16 and 30.

Concours Internationaux de la Ville de Paris: Association pour la Création et la Diffusion Artistique, 3 rue des Couronnes, 75020 Paris. *Telephone:* 1-40-33-45-35. *E-mail:* info@civp.com. *Website:* www.civp.com. A series of competitions, including Concours de Flûte Jean-Pierre Rampal, Concours de Trompette Maurice André, Concours de Violoncelle Rostropovitch, Concours Olivier Messiaen de Piano Contemporain.

Florilège Vocal de Tours: c/o Mairie de Tours, 1-3 rue des Minimes, 37926 Tours cedex 9. *Telephone:* 2-47-21-65-26. *Fax:* 2-47-21-67-71. *E-mail:* florilege .vocal@free.fr. *Website:* www.florilegevocal.com. Annual competition open to choral and vocal performers and composers.

Operalia Plácido Domingo World Opera Competition: 230 rue de Faubourg Saint-Honoré, 75008 Paris. *Telephone:* 1-53-75-00-82. *Fax:* 1-53-76-00-92. *E-mail:* operalia.paris@wanadoo.fr. *Website:* www.operalia.org. Annual competition open to singers of all nationalities between the ages of 18 and 30.

Germany

Hannover International Violin Competition: Stiftung Niedersachsen, Sophienstrasse 2, Kuenstlerhaus, 30159 Hannover. *Telephone:* (511) 9905413. *Fax:* (511) 9905419. *E-mail:* info@violin-competition.de. *Website:* www.violin -competition.de. Triennial competition open to violinists of all nationalities between the ages of 18 and 30. Prizes include a recording and concert engagements.

Internationaler Johann-Sebastian-Bach-Wettbewerb (International Johann Sebastian Bach Competition): Postfach 101349, 04013 Leipzig. *Telephone:* (341) 9137300. *Fax:* (341) 9137305. *E-mail:* wettbewerb@bach -leipzig.de. *Website:* www.bach-leipzig.de. Biennial competition open to instrumentalists (aged 16–32) and singers (aged 16–34) of all nationalities.

Internationaler Kuhlau Wettbewerb für Flötisten: Herzogenplatz 2, Postfach 2061, 29525 Uelzen. *Telephone:* (581) 800-6247. *Fax:* (581) 800-76247. *E-mail:* ute.lange-brachmann@stadt.uelzen.de. *Website:* www .kulturkreis-uelzen.de. Triennial competition for solo flute and flute with piano, two flutes or two flutes with piano, or three or four flutes. For instrumentalists up to the age of 32.

Internationaler Musikwettbewerb der ARD München (ARD International Music Competition): c/o Bayerischer Rundfunk, Rundfunkplatz 1, 80300 Munich. *Telephone:* (89) 59002471. *Fax:* (89) 59003573. *E-mail:* ard -musikwettbewerb@br-online.de. *Website:* www.ard-musikwettbewerb.de. Annual competition, with categories rotating between solo instrumentalists, string quartets and singers.

Internationaler Wettbewerb für Junge Pianisten Ettlingen: Pforzhei- merstrasse 25a, 76275 Ettlingen. *Telephone:* (7243) 1013-11. *Fax:* (7243) 1014-

---

36. *E-mail:* info@pianocompetition.org. *Website:* www.pianocompetition.org. Biennial competition open to pianists of all nationalities, in two age categories.

Greece

Dmitris Mitropoulos International Competition: 4, Kriezotou Str., 106 71 Athens. *Telephone:* (210) 3605129. *E-mail:* info@mitropouloscompetition .gr. *Website:* www.mitropouloscompetition.gr. Annual competition for conducting.

Hungary

Béla Bartók International Choir Competition: 4026 Debrecen, Hunyadi utca 1-3. *E-mail:* bartokcomp@bbcc.hu. *Website:* www.bbcc.hu. Competition open to both amateur and professional choirs.

Ireland

Dublin International Piano Competition: PO Box 71, Bray, County Wicklow. *Telephone:* (1) 2721523. *Fax:* (1) 2721508. *E-mail:* dublinpianocomp@gmail.com. *Website:* www.axadipc.com. Triennial competition open to pianists between the ages of 17 and 30.

Israel

International Harp Contest in Israel: 34, Yecheskel Street, 62595 Tel- Aviv. *Telephone:* 3-6041808. *Fax:* 3-6041688. *E-mail:* harzimco@netvision.net .il. *Website:* www.harpcontest-israel.org.il. Triennial competition open to harpists of all nationalities up to the age of 35. Prizes include first prize of a Lyon & Healy concert harp.

Arthur Rubinstein International Piano Master Competition: 12 Huberman Str., Tel-Aviv 64075. *Telephone:* 3-6856684. *Website:* www.arims .org.il. Triennial competition open to pianists of all nationalities between the ages of 18 and 32. Prizes include the Arthur Rubinstein Gold, Silver and Bronze Medals.

Italy

Concorsi della Fondazione Guido d'Arezzo: Corso Italia 102, 52100 Arezzo. *Telephone:* (575) 356203. *Fax:* (575) 324735. *E-mail:* fondguid@ polifonico.org. *Website:* www.polifonico.org. Three annual competitions: Concorso Polifonico Nazionale, Concorso Polifonico Internazionale and Concorso Internazionale di Composizione.

Concorso Internazionale di Chitarra Classica Michele Pittaluga: Piazza Garibaldi 16, 15100 Alessandria. *Telephone:* (131) 235507. *Fax:* (131) 251207. *E-mail:* concorso@pittaluga.org. *Website:* www.pittaluga.org. Annual competition open to solo classical guitarists of all nationalities.

Concorso Internazionale di Composizione 2 Agosto: Via Oberdan 24, 40126 Bologna. *E-mail:* info@concorso2agosto.it. *Website:* www .concorso2agosto.it.

Concorso Internazionale di Composizione Camillo Togni: Dèdalo Ensemble, Villaggio Prealpino, trav.X No. 25, 25136 Brescia. *E-mail:* info@ dedaloensemble.it. *Website:* www.dedaloensemble.it. Biennial competition open to composers of all nationalities, of any age. Prizes include publication and performance of winning composition.

Concorso Internazionale di Composizione Musicale Goffredo Pet- rassi: Associazione Ars Latina, Viale Pier Luigi Nervi 164, 04100 Latina. *Telephone:* (773) 629098. *Fax:* (773) 602266. *E-mail:* musastudio@libero.it. *Website:* www.premiopetrassi.it. Biennial competition open to composers of all nationalities born after 6 Nov. 1964 for an unpublished symphonic composition not exceeding 30 minutes in length.

Concorso Internazionale di Musica da Camera Vittorio Gui: Teatro del Maggio Musicale Fiorentino, Via Solferino 15, 50123 Florence. *Telephone:* (055) 2779446. *Fax:* (055) 2779446. *E-mail:* info@premiogui.it. *Website:* www .premiogui.it.

Concorso Internazionale di Musica Gian Battista Viotti: Segreteria del Concorso Viotti, Via Monte di Pietà 39, 13100 Vercelli. *Telephone:* (161) 252667. *Fax:* (161) 255575. *E-mail:* info@concorsoviotti.it. *Website:* www .concorsoviotti.it. Annual competition, rotating between singers, pianists and composers, open to people of any nationality.

Concorso Internazionale di Violino Alberto Curci: Fondazione Alberto Curci, Via Santa Brigida 68, 80132 Naples. *Telephone:* (81) 5513030. *Fax:* (81) 7649370. *E-mail:* info@fondazionecurci.it. *Website:* www.fondazionecurci.it. Competition open to violinists to the age of 32.

Concorso Internazionale di Violino Rodolfo Lipizer: Associazione Culturale Mo Rodolfo Lipizer, Via don Giovanni Bosco 91, 34170 Gorizia GO. *Telephone:* (481) 547863. *Fax:* (481) 536710. *E-mail:* lipizer@lipizer.it. *Website:* www.lipizer.it. Annual competition open to violinists of all nationalities, under the age of 35. Prizes include concert appearances.

Concorso Internazionale per Quartetto d'Archi Premio Paolo Borciani: Teatro Municipale Valli, Piazza Martiri del 7 luglio, 42100 Reggio Emilia. *Telephone:* (522) 458811. *Fax:* (522) 458822. *E-mail:* premioborciani@ iteatri.re.it. *Website:* premioborciani.iteatri.re.it. Triennial competition open to string quartets of all nations whose members' total age does not exceed 128 years on 12 June of the competition year.

Concorso Internazionale Voci Verdiane: Segreteria del Concorso Voci Verdiane, Piazza G. Verdi 10, 43011 Parma. *Telephone:* (524) 931706. *Fax:* (524) 92360. *E-mail:* segreteria.concorsovociverdiane@comune.busseto.pr.it.

Concorso Pianistico Internazionale Alessandro Casagrande: Fondazione Alessandro e Adriana Casagrande, Via I Maggio 65, 05100 Terni. *Telephone:* (744) 549713. *Fax:* (744) 449877. *E-mail:* fondazionecasagrande@gmail.com. *Website:* www.concorsocasagrande.org. Biennial competition open to pianists born after 1 January 1970.

Concorso Pianistico Internazionale Ettore Pozzoli: Piazza Libertà 1, 20038 Seregno. *Telephone:* (362) 222914. *Fax:* (362) 222914. *E-mail:* info@concorsopozzoli.it. *Website:* www.concorsopozzoli.it. Biennial competition open to pianists of all nationalities, under the age of 30. Prizes include the recording and release of a CD.

Concorso Pianistico Internazionale Ferruccio Busoni: Segreteria della Fondazione, c/o Conservatorio statale di musica C. Monteverdi, Piazza Domenicani 25, PO Box 368, 39100 Bolzano. *Telephone:* (471) 976568. *Fax:* (471) 326127. *E-mail:* info@concorsobusoni.it. *Website:* www.concorsobusoni.it. Biennial competition open to pianists of all nationalities between the ages of 15 and 28. Prizes include concert engagements.

Nicolò Paganini Premio Internazionale di Violino (Nicolò Paganini International Violin Competition): Comune di Genova – Settore Promozione della Città Turismo e Spettacolo, Via Sottoripa 5, 16124 Genoa. *Telephone:* (10) 5574215. *Fax:* (10) 5574326. *E-mail:* violinopaganini@comune.genova.it. *Website:* www.paganini.comune.genova.it. Biennial competition open to violinists of all nationalities between the ages of 16 and 33.

Premio Valentino Bucchi Parole e Musica: Fondazione Valentino Bucchi, Via Ubaldino Peruzzi 20, 00139 Rome. *Telephone:* (687) 200121. *Fax:* (687) 131527. *E-mail:* bucchi@premiobucchi.it. *Website:* www.premiobucchi.it. Annual competition open to performers and composers.

Japan

Gaspar Cassado International Violoncello Competition: Secretariat of The Gaspar Cassado International Violoncello Organizing Committee, 1-29-3 Motoyokoyama-cha, Hachioji, Tokyo 192-0063. *Telephone:* (42) 631-1466. *Fax:* (42) 631-1205. *E-mail:* info@cassado-cello.jp. *Website:* www.cassado-cello.jp. f. 2006 to replace an earlier competition held in Florence, Italy.

The Irino Prize: 5-22-2 Matsubara, Setagaya-ku, Tokyo 156-0043. *Telephone:* (3) 3323-0646. *Fax:* (3) 3325-5468. *E-mail:* info@jml-irino.jp. *Website:* www.jml-irino.jp/IrinoPrize. Annual prize open to composers of all nationalities under the age of 40, rotating annually between an orchestral and a chamber music composition.

Sendai International Music Competition: Secretariat, 3-27-5 Asahigaoka, Aoba-ku, Sendai City 981-0904. *Telephone:* (22) 727-1872. *Fax:* (22) 727-1873. *E-mail:* info@simc.jp. *Website:* www.simc.jp. f. 2001; triennial competition in two categories: violin and piano, for musicians under 28 years old.

Monaco

Fondation Prince Pierre de Monaco Prix de Composition Musicale: Fondation Prince Pierre, 4 boulevard des Moulins, 98000 Monaco. *Telephone:* 98-15-85-15. *Fax:* 93-50-66-94. *E-mail:* communication@fondationprincepierre.mc. *Website:* www.fondationprincepierre.mc. Annual prize awarded to the best musical composition of the year.

The Netherlands

Gaudeamus Competitions: Contemporary Music Center, Piet Heinkade 5, 1019 BR Amsterdam. *Telephone:* (20) 5191800. *Fax:* (20) 5191801. Annual competitions in two categories: Gaudeamus Prize, open to composers up to the age of 30; the International Gaudeamus Interpreters Competition, open to instrumentalists and singers of contemporary music.

Internationaal Vocalisten Concours 's-Hertogenbosch: PO Box 1225, 5200 BG 's-Hertogenbosch. *Telephone:* (73) 6900999. *Fax:* (73) 6901166. *E-mail:* info@ivc.nu. *Website:* www.ivc.nu. Annual competition open to singers.

The International César Franck Organ Competition: Leidsevaart 146, 2014 Haarlem. *E-mail:* info@cesarfranckcompetition.org. *Website:* www.cesarfranckconcours.nl.

International Franz Liszt Piano Competition: Muziekcentrum Vredenburg, PO Box 550, 3500 AN Utrecht. *Telephone:* (30) 2862258. *Fax:* (30) 2316522. *E-mail:* info@liszt.nl. *Website:* www.liszt.nl. Biennial competition open to pianists of all nationalities between the ages of 16 and 30.

International Organ Improvisation Competition: PO Box 1091, 1000 BB Amsterdam. *Telephone:* (20) 4880479. *Fax:* (20) 4880478. *E-mail:* office@organfestival.nl. *Website:* www.organfestival.nl. Annual competition open to concert organists experienced in improvisation, up to the age of 40.

Norway

The Queen Sonja International Music Competition: Universitetsgaten 14, 0164 Oslo. *Telephone:* 22-99-21-05. *Fax:* 22-99-21-01. *E-mail:* post@qsimc.no. *Website:* www.qsimc.no. Triennial competition open to instrumentalists or singers. Prizes include concert engagements.

Poland

Grzegorz Fitelberg International Competition for Conductors: 40-084 Katowice, Sokolska 2. *Telephone:* (32) 3511709. *E-mail:* konkurs@filharmoniaslaska.art.pl. *Website:* www.konkursfitelberg.art.pl. Quadrennial competition open to conductors of all nationalities up to the age of 35.

International Frederick Chopin Piano Competition: The Frederick Chopin Society, 00-078 Warsaw, Pl. Pilsudskiego 9. *Telephone:* (22) 8275471. *Fax:* (22) 8279599. *E-mail:* konkurs@nifc.pl. *Website:* www.konkurs.chopin.pl. Quinquennial competition open to pianists of all nationalities, aged between 17 and 30. Prizes include gold, silver and bronze medals.

International Henryk Wieniawski Competitions: 61-840 Poznań, ul. Świętosławska 7. *Telephone:* (61) 8522642. *Fax:* (61) 8528991. *E-mail:* violinmaker@wieniawski.pl. *Website:* www.wieniawski.pl. Quinquennial competition in two categories: Violin Competition open to violinists of all nationalities to the age of 30; Violin Maker Competition open to all nationalities, with no age limit.

Kazimierz Serocki International Composers' Competition: ISCM Polish Section, 00-052 Warsaw, ul. Mazowiecka 11. *Telephone:* (22) 8276981. *Fax:* (22) 8277804. *E-mail:* ptmw@epistola.pl. *Website:* www.ptmw.art.pl. Triennial competition open to composers of all nationalities.

Portugal

Porto International Music Competition: Avda da Boavista 1681, 2o Sala 2.10, 4100-132 Porto. *Telephone:* (22) 6067258. *Fax:* (22) 6067471. *E-mail:* concurso.porto@clix.pt. *Website:* www.concursomusicaporto.com. Annual competition.

Romania

George Enescu International Competition: 010073 Bucharest 1, Calea Victoriei 155, bl. D1, Sc.8, et.2. *Telephone:* (21) 3178081. *Fax:* (21) 3110200. *E-mail:* info@festivalenescu.ro. *Website:* www.festivalenescu.ro. Annual competition, rotating between piano, violin and composition, open to participants of all nationalities up to the age of 33.

Russia

International Tchaikovsky Competition: 125009 Moscow, Bolshaya Nikitskaya 13/6. *Telephone:* (495) 629-49-03. *E-mail:* olegskor@inbox.ru. Quadrennial competition open to pianists, violinists, cellists and singers of any nationality.

San Marino

Concorso Internazionale di Canto Renata Tebaldi: Fondazione Renata Tebaldi, Via O. Scarito 84, 47893 Borgo Maggiore. *Telephone:* 0549 886344. *Fax:* 0549 886345. *E-mail:* info@renatatebaldi.info. *Website:* www.renatatebaldi.info. Open to singers of any nationality, aged between 18 and 35.

Spain

Concurso Internacional de Canto Francisco Viñas: Secretaría del Concurso, Calle Bruc 125, 08037 Barcelona. *E-mail:* info@francisco-vinas.com. *Website:* www.francisco-vinas.com. Annual competition open to singers (women aged between 18 and 32, men aged between 20 and 35).

Concurso Internacional de Canto Julián Gayarre: Calle Navarrería, 39, 31001 Pamplona. *Telephone:* (848) 424683. *Fax:* (848) 424629. *E-mail:* canto@cfnavarra.es. *Website:* www.cfnavarra.es/gayarre. Biennial competition open to singers of all nationalities between the ages of 18 and 30.

Concurso Internacional de Musica Maria Canals de Barcelona: Calle Palau de la Música 4–6, 08003 Barcelona. *Telephone:* (93) 2957251. *Fax:* (93) 2957209. *E-mail:* info@mariacanals.org. *Website:* www.mariacanals.org. Annual competitions open to participants of any nationalty. Pianists must be between the ages of 18 and 30; trio entrants between the ages of 18 and 35.

Concurso Internacional de Piano de Santander Paloma O'Shea: Calle Hernán Cortés 3, 39003 Santander. *Telephone:* (942) 311451. *Fax:* (942) 314816. *E-mail:* concurso@albeniz.com. *Website:* www.santanderpianocompetition.com. Triennial competition open to pianists of any nationality between the ages of 17 and 30. Prizes include recordings, concerts and travel grants.

Concurso Internacional de Piano José Iturbi: Plaza de Manises 4, 46003 Valencia. *Telephone:* (63) 882500. *Fax:* (63) 882775. *E-mail:* pianoiturbi@dival.es. *Website:* www.pianoiturbi.com. Biennial competition open to pianists of any nationality, under the age of 31 on the date of the competition. Prizes include recitals.

Concurso Internacional de Piano Premio Jaén: Plaza de San Francisco, 23071 Jaén. *E-mail:* cdcult@promojaen.es. *Website:* www.dipujaen.com/premiopiano. Annual competition open to pianists of any nationality who have not previously won the Jaén Prize. Prizes include money and concert engagements, and the Rose Sabater Prize for the best interpreter of Spanish music.

Concursos de la Fundación Jacinto e Inocencio Guerrero: Gran Vía 78, 1°, 28013 Madrid. *Telephone:* (91) 5476618. *Fax:* (91) 5476618. *E-mail:* fguerrero@fundacionguerrero.com. *Website:* www.fundacionguerrero.com. Song competition, guitar competition, piano competition and Premio de Música.

Pablo Sarasate International Violin Competition: Calle Navarrería 39, 31001 Pamplona. *Telephone:* (848) 424683. *Fax:* (848) 424629. *E-mail:* violin@cfnavarra.es. *Website:* www.cfnavarra.es/sarasate. Biennial competition open to violinists of any nationality, aged between 15 and 28.

Sweden

Rolf Schock-prisen de musikaliska konsterna (Rolf Schock Prize in Musical Arts): Kungl. Musikaliska Akademien, Blasieholmstorg 8, 111 48, Stockholm. *Telephone:* (8) 407-18-00. *Fax:* (8) 611-87-18. *E-mail:* adm@musakad.se. *Website:* www.musakad.se. f. 1993; biennial award for a musician, with the recipient chosen by the Kungl. Musikaliska Akademien (Royal Swedish Academy of Music).

Switzerland

Concours de Genève: 8 rue Bovy Lysberg, 1204 Geneva. *Telephone:* 223286208. *Fax:* 223284366. *E-mail:* music@concoursgeneve.ch. *Website:* www.concoursgeneve.ch. Annual competition open to performers of all nationalities with categories changing annually.

Concours Géza Anda: Bleicherweg 18, 8002 Zürich. *Telephone:* 442051423. *Fax:* 442051205. *E-mail:* info@gezaanda.ch. *Website:* www.gezaanda.ch. Triennial competition open to pianists to the age of 32. Prizes include concert engagements.

Concours International de Piano Clara Haskil: 31 rue de Conseil, Case Postale 234, 1800 Vevey. *Telephone:* 219226704. *Fax:* 219226734. *E-mail:* info@clara-haskil.ch. *Website:* www.regart.ch/clara-haskil. Biennial competition open to pianists under the age of 27.

Concours International de Violon Sion-Valais: PO Box 1429, 1950 Sion. *Telephone:* 273234317. *Fax:* 273234662. *E-mail:* info@sion-festival.ch. *Website:* www.sion-festival.ch. Annual competition open to violinists of any nationality between the ages of 15 and 32.

Concours International de Violon Tibor Varga: c/o Bersy Consulting, Route de Monteiller, 1965 Savièse. *Telephone:* 273955333. *Fax:* 273955334. *E-mail:* info@concours-violon.ch. *Website:* www.concours-violon.ch. Biennial competition open to violinists of any nationality between the ages of 15 and 32.

United Kingdom

BBC Cardiff Singer of the World: c/o BBC Wales, Music Department, Broadcasting House, Llandaff, Cardiff, CF5 2YQ, Wales. *Website:* www.bbc.co.uk/cardiffsinger. Biennial competition open to singers 18 years of age or older. Prizes include concert engagements.

BBC Young Musician of the Year: c/o BBC TV, Kensington House, Richmond Way, London, W14 0AX, England. *Website:* www.bbc.co.uk/youngmusician. Biennial televised competition open to British resident performers and composers to age 18.

Kathleen Ferrier Awards: PO Box 667, Dunsford, Devon EX6 7WW, England. *Telephone:* (845) 070-4969. *Fax:* (845) 070-4969. *E-mail:* info@ferrierawards.org.uk. *Website:* www.ferrierawards.org.uk. Annual competition open to singers of any nationality under the age of 29, who have studied for at least one year in the UK or Republic of Ireland. Public auditions at the Wigmore Hall, London.

Donatella Flick Conducting Competition: PO Box 34227, London, NW5 1XP, England. *Fax:* (20) 7267-0068. *Website:* www.conducting.org. Biennial competition open to European Community nationals under the age of 35.

Gramophone Awards: Teddington Studios, Broom Road, Teddington, Middlesex TW11 9BE, England. *Telephone:* (20) 8267-5050. *Fax:* (20) 8267-5844. *E-mail:* gramophone@haymarket.com. *Website:* www.gramophone.co.uk. Annual awards from Gramophone magazine, in numerous categories.

The Leeds Conductors' Competition: Music Department, Leeds Leisure Service, Town Hall, The Headrow, Leeds, LS1 3AD, England. *Telephone:* (113) 395-1246. *Fax:* (113) 247-8334. *E-mail:* music@leeds.gov.uk. *Website:* www.leedsconductors.com. Triennial competition open to British-born conductors under the age of 35.

Leeds International Pianoforte Competition: Piano Competition Office, The University of Leeds, Leeds, LS2 9JT, England. *Telephone:* (113) 244-6586. *Fax:* (113) 234-6106. *E-mail:* pianocompetition@leeds.ac.uk. *Website:* www.leedspiano.com. Triennial competition open to professional pianists under the age of 30. Prizes include concert engagements worldwide.

London International Piano Competition: 28 Wallace Road, London, N1 2PG, England. *Telephone:* (20) 7354-1087. *E-mail:* lipc@lipc.org.uk. *Website:* www.lipc.org.uk. Triennial competition open to pianists of all nationalities up to the age of 29. Prizes include concert engagements and scholarships.

London International String Quartet Competition: London String Quartet Foundation, 8 Woodlands Road, Romford, RM1 4HD, England. *Telephone:* (1708) 761423. *Fax:* (1708) 761423. *E-mail:* info@playquartet.com. *Website:* www.lsqf.com. Triennial competition open to string quartets whose aggregate ages do not exceed 120 years. Prizes include the Amadeus Trophy.

The Queen's Medal for Music: c/o Public Information Office, Buckingham Palace, London, SW1A 1AA, England. *Website:* www.royal.gov.uk. Annual award, f. 2005, to raise the profile of music within the UK; winners may be of any nationality but they must have had a major influence on the musical life of the UK; decisions on eligibility for the Medal are made by the Music Committee, chaired by the current Master of The Queen's Music; the winner is announced on 22 November, the day of the patron saint of music, St Cecilia.

Royal Over-Seas League Annual Music Competition: Over-Seas House, Park Place, St James's Street, London, SW1A 1LR, England. *Telephone:* (20) 7408-0214. *Fax:* (20) 7499-6738. *E-mail:* culture@rosl.org.uk. *Website:* www.roslarts.co.uk. f. 1952; annual competition open to Commonwealth and former Commonwealth citizens, for instrumentalists (keyboard, strings, wind) and singers up to the age of 30; winners in each category compete for the Gold Medal.

Scottish International Piano Competition: c/o Royal Scottish Academy of Music and Dance, 100 Renfrew Street, Glasgow, G2 3DB, Scotland. *Telephone:* (141) 270-8322. *Fax:* (141) 332-8901. *E-mail:* sipc@rsamd.ac.uk. *Website:* www.scottishinternationalpianocompetition.com. Triennial competition open to pianists of all nationalities to the age of 32.

Wigmore Hall/Kohn Foundation International Song Competition: Room 616a, Langham House, 308 Regent Street, London, W1B 3AT, England. *Telephone:* (20) 7258-8200. *Fax:* (20) 7258-8201. *E-mail:* comp@wigmore-hall.org.uk. *Website:* www.wigmore-hall.org.uk. Biennial competition for singers and pianists of any nationality up to the age of 32. Awards for singers, for pianists, and for a duo of singer and pianist.

United States of America

Academy Awards: Academy Foundation, 8949 Wilshire Boulevard, Beverly Hills, CA 90211. *Telephone:* (310) 247-3000. *Fax:* (310) 859-9619. *Website:* www.oscars.org. Annual awards from the Academy of Motion Picture Arts and Sciences; categories include achievement in music written for motion pictures (original score), achievement in music written for motion pictures (original song).

Marian Anderson Award: The John F. Kennedy Center for the Performing Arts, 2700 F Street NW, Washington, DC 20566. *Telephone:* (202) 416-8081. *Website:* www.kennedy-center.org. f. 2002; biennial award to a mid-career American vocalist.

ASCAP Foundation Awards: 1 Lincoln Plaza, New York, NY 10023. *Fax:* (212) 595-3276. *Website:* www.ascap.com. Gives numerous awards and grants to musicians, composers and associated individuals.

American Academy of Arts and Letters Awards: 633 West 155th Street, New York, NY 10032-1799. *Telephone:* (212) 368-5900. *Fax:* (212) 491-4615. *E-mail:* academy@artsandletters.org. *Website:* www.artsandletters.org. Gives various awards in the field of music.

Gina Bachauer International Artists Piano Competition: 138 West Broadway, Suite 220, Salt Lake City, UT 84101. *Telephone:* (801) 297-4250. *Fax:* (801) 521-9202. *E-mail:* gina@bachauer.com. *Website:* www.bachauer.com. Annual competition, rotating between four age groups (11–13, 14–18, 19–32 and 33–100).

Cleveland International Piano Competition: 1988 Ford Drive, Cleveland, OH 44106. *Telephone:* (216) 707-5397. *Fax:* (216) 707-0224. *E-mail:* info@clevelandpiano.org. *Website:* clevelandpiano.org. Biennial competition open to pianists between the ages of 17 and 32. Prizes include concert engagements.

The Corporation of Yaddo: PO Box 395, Union Avenue, Saratoga Springs, NY 12866-0395. *Telephone:* (518) 584-0746. *Fax:* (518) 584-1312. *E-mail:* webmaster@yaddo.org. *Website:* www.yaddo.org. Offers residencies for up to two months, for professional composers of any nationality.

Kenneth Davenport National Competition for Orchestral Works: c/o School of Fine and Performing Arts, State University of New York at New Paltz, 1 Hawk Drive, New Paltz, NY 12561-2443. *Telephone:* (845) 257-3860. *Fax:* (845) 257-3859. *E-mail:* arts@lan.newpaltz.edu. *Website:* www.newpaltz.edu/davenport. Biennial competition open to composers who are American citizens or permanent residents.

Murray Dranoff International Two Piano Competition: The Murray Dranoff Foundation, 3550 Biscayne Blvd, Suite 702, Miami, FL 33137. *Telephone:* (305) 572-9900. *Fax:* (305) 572-9922. *E-mail:* mail@dranoff2piano.org. *Website:* www.dranoff2piano.org. Biennial competition open to duo pianists between the ages of 18 and 35. Prizes include concert engagements.

John Simon Guggenheim Memorial Foundation: 90 Park Avenue, New York, NY 10016. *Telephone:* (212) 687-4470. *Fax:* (212) 697-3248. *E-mail:* fellowships@jsgmf.org. *Website:* www.gf.org. Offers annual fellowships in music open to composers and scholars who have demonstrated previous outstanding ability.

Holtkamp/American Guild of Organists Award in Organ Composition: 475 Riverside Drive, Suite 1260, New York, NY 10115. *Telephone:* (212) 870-2310. *Fax:* (212) 870-2163. *E-mail:* info@agohq.org. *Website:* www.agohq.org. Biennial competition open to composers of organ music.

International Violin Competition of Indianapolis: 32 East Washington Street, Suite 1320, Indianapolis, IN 46204. *Telephone:* (317) 637-4574. *Fax:* (317) 637-1302. *E-mail:* ivci@violin.org. *Website:* www.violin.org. Quadrennial competition open to violinists of any nationality, between the ages of 18 and 30. Prizes include concert engagements and recordings.

The MacDowell Colony: 100 High Street, Peterborough, NH 03458. *Telephone:* (603) 924-3886. *Fax:* (603) 924-9142. *E-mail:* info@ macdowellcolony.org. *Website:* www.macdowellcolony.org. Awards residency fellowships to composers.

National Medal of Arts: National Endowment for the Arts, 1100 Pennsylvania Avenue NW, Washington, DC 20506. *Telephone:* (202) 682-5400. *E-mail:* webmgr@arts.endow.gov. *Website:* www.nea.gov. Awarded by the US Government in recognition of contribution to visual, performing and literary arts.

National Young Artists/American Guild of Organists Competition in Organ Performance: 475 Riverside Drive, Suite 1260, New York, NY 10115. *Telephone:* (212) 870-2310. *Fax:* (212) 870-2163. *E-mail:* info@agohq.org. *Website:* www.agohq.org. Biennial competition open to organists between the ages of 22 and 32.

Oratorio Society of New York Solo Competition: 1440 Broadway, 23rd Floor, New York, NY 10018. *Telephone:* (212) 400-7255. *E-mail:* solocompetition@oratoriosocietyofny.org. *Website:* www.oratoriosocietyofny

.org. Annual competition, held in March–April, open to solo oratorio singers under the age of 40.

Pro Musicis International Award: 140 West 79th Street, Suite 9F, New York, NY 10024. *Telephone:* (212) 787-0993. *Fax:* (212) 362-0352. *Website:* www.promusicis.org. Annual career development award. Prizes include recitals in New York, Boston and Paris.

The Pulitzer Prize in Music: The Pulitzer Prizes, Columbia University, 709 Journalism Building, 2950 Broadway, New York, NY 10027. *Telephone:* (212) 854-3841. *Fax:* (212) 854-3342. *E-mail:* pulitzer@pulitzer.org. *Website:* www .pulitzer.org. Annual prize to an American composer for a major composition premiered in the USA during the previous year.

University of Maryland International Competitions: Clarice Smith Performing Arts Centre, Suite 3800, University of Maryland, College Park, MD 20742-1625. *Telephone:* (301) 405-8174. *Fax:* (301) 405-5977. *Website:* www.claricesmithcenter.umd.edu. Competitions open to instrumentalists and singers of any nationality; competitions include the Leonard Rose International Cello Competition and the William Kapell International Piano Competition.

USA International Harp Competition: PO Box 5008, Bloomington, IN 47407-5008. *Telephone:* (812) 856-5715. *Fax:* (812) 856-5715. *E-mail:* harpcomp@indiana.edu. *Website:* usaihc.org. Triennial competition open to harpists of all nationalities, aged between 16 and 32.

Van Cliburn International Piano Competition: The Van Cliburn Foundation, 2525 Ridgmar Blvd, Suite 307, Fort Worth, TX 76116. *Telephone:* (817) 738-6536. *Fax:* (817) 738-6534. *Website:* www.cliburn.org. Quadrennial piano competition open to pianists between the ages 18 and 30. Prizes include a Carnegie Hall recital and various orchestral tours.

Uruguay

Concurso Internacional de Piano Ciudad de Montevideo: Santiago Vásquez 1178, Montevideo. Triennial competition open to pianists up to the age of 32.